D0010340

The Norton Anthology
of American Literature

FOURTH EDITION

VOLUME 1

Nina Baym
UNIVERSITY OF ILLINOIS
Wayne Franklin
UNIVERSITY OF IOWA
Ronald Gottesman
UNIVERSITY OF SOUTHERN CALIFORNIA
Laurence B. Holland
LATE OF THE JOHNS HOPKINS UNIVERSITY
David Kalstone
LATE OF RUTGERS, THE STATE UNIVERSITY OF NEW JERSEY
Arnold Krupat
SARAH LAWRENCE COLLEGE
Francis Murphy
SMITH COLLEGE
Hershel Parker
UNIVERSITY OF DELAWARE
William H. Pritchard
AMHERST COLLEGE
Patricia B. Wallace
VASSAR COLLEGE

The Norton Anthology
of American Literature

FOURTH EDITION
VOLUME 1

W • W • NORTON & COMPANY • *New York* • *London*

Copyright © 1994, 1989, 1985, 1979 by W. W. Norton & Company, Inc.
All rights reserved
Printed in the United States of America
Fourth Edition

The text of this book is composed in Electra with the display set in Bernhard Modern
Composition by Maple-Vail Composition. Manufacturing by R. R. Donnelley
Book design by Antonina Krass

Library of Congress Cataloging-in-Publication Data
The Norton anthology of American literature / [edited by] Nina Baym
. . . [et al.]. — 4th ed.
2 v.   cm.
Includes bibliographical references (p.) and index.
1. American literature.   I. Baym, Nina.
PS507.N65   1994
810′.8—dc20   93-45720

Cover painting is a detail from "Kindred Spirits," 1849, by Asher Durand. Oil on canvas.
Reproduced by courtesy of the collection of The New York Public Library, Astor, Lenox and
Tilden Foundations.

Since this page cannot legibly accommodate all the copyright notices, pages 2529-2530
constitute an extension of the copyright page.

ISBN 0-393-96461-2

W. W. Norton & Company, Inc., 500 Fifth Avenue, New York, N.Y. 10110
W. W. Norton & Company Ltd., 10 Coptic Street, London WC1A 1PU

2 3 4 5 6 7 8 9 0

Contents

American Literature 1820–1865 879

Preface to
the Fourth Edition

From its inception, a guiding principle of *The Norton Anthology of American Literature* has been to provide a balanced combination of traditional and emergent works. Like all Norton anthologies, the Fourth Edition reflects an ongoing collaboration among the teachers who assign the book, the students who read it, and the editors; the major changes in its contents have been made in response to detailed suggestions from nearly 150 reviewers of the preceding edition.

In response to significant changes in critical interest, the Fourth Edition introduces two major innovations. An entirely new section, Literature to 1620, gathers the writings of encounter—the journals and letters of the first European explorers. Texts such as Columbus's *Letter to Luis de Santangel* and Arthur Barlowe's *First Voyage Made to the Coast of America* bear witness to the natural wonders of the New World, a tradition that has remained strong in American writing ever since. At the same time, the literature of encounter tells of violence and devastation; texts such as Bernal Díaz del Castillo's *True History of the Conquest of New Spain* detail with grim force the brutality of the Spanish conquest of Mexico; and the writings of the soldier-entrepreneur John Smith (moved to this section with other chroniclers of exploration) and the aristocrat George Percy describe the harsh conditions of life in the early settlement of Jamestown.

Literature to 1620 also introduces the second major innovation in the Fourth Edition—the greatly increased attention to Native American oral and written traditions. The first of three new sections of oral materials, Stories of the Beginning of the World, includes creation stories from the Iroquois and the Pima. Headnotes here give special attention to the political, cultural, and linguistic complexities of transcription and translation.

Changes in critical and classroom interest have also led to innovations in every period of the anthology.

Early American Literature 1620–1820. Notable additions are the Quaker John Woolman's *Some Considerations on the Keeping of Negroes,* and five letters by Phillis Wheatley that reveal the strength of her opposition to slavery. Countering the myth of the pastoral New World, a selection from Crèvecoeur's *Letter X, On Snakes; and on the Humming Bird,* shows a view of Nature as distinctly "red in tooth and claw." Newly anthologized is the Mohegan missionary Samson Occom, whose fervent *Sermon at the Execution of Moses Paul,* exhorting Indians to temperance, appeared in no fewer than nineteen editions after its publication.

American Literature 1820–1865. The additions to this great period enlarge instructors' options by expanding the kinds of texts offered. A powerful defense of the sovereignty of the Cherokee Nation, the *Memorials of the Cherokees* link the Native American oratorical tradition to the Euro-American tradition of political protest writing. A chapter from William Apess's biographical work, *The Experiences of Five Christian Indians of the Pequot Tribe*, asserts that those who profess Christianity must also uphold racial equality, an argument from faith that resounds in Frederick Douglass's brilliant speech *The Meaning of July Fourth for the Negro*, newly anthologized. Six chapters from Harriet Jacobs's *Incidents in the Life of a Slave Girl* convey the drama of Linda Brent's bondage and escape, as well as Jacobs's skillful use of melodrama in the cause of abolition. The period 1820–1865 also includes notable additions to two major authors. Freshly collated from manuscript is Walt Whitman's poem-sequence *Live Oak, with Moss*, celebrating sexual "adhesiveness" of man for man. These poems are here restored to Whitman's first and most personal ordering. The headnote to Emily Dickinson has been entirely rewritten and appropriately expanded; her poetry has been enriched with twenty-seven new poems that reveal both her growing self-awareness as a poet and her sense of connection to other poets and writers—Shakespeare, the Brownings, the Brontës.

American Literature 1865–1914. The additions to this section strengthen the offerings by a number of women writers. Charlotte Perkins Gilman's brief *Why I Wrote "The Yellow Wallpaper"* provides a companion piece for that haunting work. Kate Chopin's evocative short stories *At the 'Cadian Ball* and *The Storm* are now included along with the complete *Awakening*. Mary Austin, an original and fiercely independent writer who has recently come into her own, is newly anthologized with *The Walking Woman*. Building on the Native American works in Volume 1, this section includes two new Native American writers: the Dartmouth-educated Sioux physician Charles Alexander Eastman, represented by selections from his autobiography *From the Deep Woods to Civilization*, and John M. Oskison, whose short story *The Problem of Old Harjo* captures the irony of the Christian campaign to "uplift" Native Americans. The attention to the Native American oral tradition is also carried forward in Volume 2, where two new sections—Native American Oratory and Native American Chants and Songs—provide a rich introduction to several complex forms. While the selections from *The Night Chant* and the Chippewa and Ghost Dance songs may be read simply as poems in translation, to underscore their essential role as *performances* we accompany the texts with music notation and a period drawing illustrating the dance.

American Literature between the Wars 1914–1945. The outpouring between the wars of political poetry by women and African-American poets, eclipsed in the academy by High Modernism, is now significantly recovered with the inclusion of Muriel Rukeyser, Angelina Weld Grimké, Genevieve Taggard, and Sterling Brown. The prominent imagist Amy Lowell is newly anthologized, as is Anzia Yezierska, represented by her sharply observed story of immigrant life on the Lower East Side, *The Lost "Beautifulness."* Poems by Marianne Moore, Edna St. Vincent Millay, and Langston Hughes have been reselected to better show these poets' range and variety.

American Prose since 1945. A major figure in the Native American Renaissance, N. Scott Momaday is newly represented with selections chosen to show the "arc" of *The Way to Rainy Mountain*. Strengthening our offering of modern American drama, already unsurpassed, we now add to Eugene O'Neill, Tennessee Williams, and Arthur Miller two major playwrights: August Wilson, with his powerful family drama *Fences*, and David Mamet, whose hard-edged *House of Games* introduces to the anthology an increasingly important literary form: the screenplay.

American Poetry since 1945. As the introduction to this section observes, "What best characterizes the world of contemporary American poetry is its pluralism and the power of its best poets to absorb a variety of influences." This widely praised section has been updated with new poems by Gwendolyn Brooks, Philip Levine, Adrienne Rich, Lorna Dee Cervantes, and Rita Dove. Two new poets have been added: the influential early experimentalist George Oppen, and the vibrant and contemporary Li-Young Lee.

Teaching with The Norton Anthology of American Literature: A *Guide for Instructors*, by Marjorie Pryse, makes available to instructors teaching notes and suggested essay topics and exam questions for works in the anthology, as well as class plans for a variety of approaches to the survey course. Also available, for instructors who teach Whitman and Dickinson in the second part of a two-semester survey, are student copies of a supplemental pamphlet, *Selections from Walt Whitman and Emily Dickinson*. Information for ordering the pamphlet or the *Guide for Instructors* (in either print or disk versions) may be obtained from the publisher.

It will be clear from the foregoing that, in compiling the Fourth Edition, we have also held fast to two other important principles. First, teachers are offered more authors and more selections than they will have time to teach. Such copiousness is designed to allow flexibility within any course and variety from year to year. Second, on the principle of making the anthology self-sufficient—thereby minimizing the frustration of having to teach excerpts, and eliminating the need for costly supplements—we include many long works in their entirety, all of them notable achievements in American literature. In the Third Edition these ranged from Rowlandson's captivity narrative to Miller's *Death of a Salesman*; added to these in the Fourth Edition are Wilson's full-length drama and Mamet's screenplay.

Readers already familiar with the anthology will have noticed that the present edition retains the larger trim size of its predecessor, which allows the volume, even in its middle section, to open out and stay flat. It retains, too, the page design and line-length that allow maximum ease of reading. The format is that of a book to be read for pleasure; the text is inviting to the eye, and the special paper makes it possible to keep each volume to a size and weight that allow it to be easily carried to a classroom.

Similarly, this edition continues to incorporate the editorial features that have established a standard in the classroom. The introductions, headnotes, and footnotes are concise but full and are designed to give the student the information needed, without preempting the interpretive function of the student or of the instructor. The Selected Bibliographies at the end of each volume provide guides to further readings and research and complete the self-sufficiency of the anthology, which permits each of its selections to be read, understood, and placed in historical context without dependence on reference books.

The editors have taken scrupulous care to represent the most accurate available version of each work. Indeed, several of the major texts—Franklin's *Auto-biography*, some of the materials by Clemens, and Howells's *Novel-Writing and Novel-Reading*—were edited from manuscript. Among the standard editions used in the Fourth Edition are those of Philip Barbour for John Smith, John Bierhorst for *The Night Chant*, Louis Martz for H. D., Marc Simon for Hart Crane, and Francis E. Skipp for Thomas Wolfe.

Our policy has been to reprint each text in the form that accords, as far as it is possible to determine, to the intention of its author. There is one exception: we have modernized most spellings and (very sparingly) the punctuation in the sections Literature to 1620 and Early American Literature 1620–1820, on the principle that nonfunctional features such as archaic spellings and typography pose unnecessary problems for beginning students. We have, however, since it is a new edition from the manuscript, left Franklin's *Autobiography* unchanged. For the convenience of the student, we have used square brackets to indicate titles supplied by the editors and have, whenever a portion of a text has been omitted, indicated that omission with three asterisks. To ensure the accuracy of all texts, the Fourth Edition has been proofread in its entirety against copy text.

The editors of this anthology were selected on the basis of their expertness in their individual areas. They combine respect for the best that has been thought and said about literature with alertness (as participants, as well as observers) to the altering interests of contemporary scholarship and criticism. Each editor was given ultimate responsibility for his or her period, but all collaborated in the final enterprise. New contributors to the Fourth Edition, Wayne Franklin edited Literature to 1620, and Arnold Krupat edited Native American Literatures, in Volume One and the oratory, songs and chants, Eastman, and Oskison selections in Volume Two. In the 1820–1865 section, Ronald Gottesman prepared the texts and introductions for Lincoln, Stowe, and Douglass; and Nina Baym prepared the text and introduction for Harriet Jacobs.

In preparing these volumes, we have incurred obligations to hundreds of teachers throughout the country who have answered our questions; we take this opportunity to thank them warmly for their invaluable assistance. Those teachers who prepared detailed critiques, or who offered special help in selecting or preparing texts, are listed under Acknowledgments, on a separate page. The editors would like to express appreciation for their assistance to Kevin Affonso, Olivia Banner, Mark Canner, Daniel Chiasson, Joseph Coulombe, Sarah Hurley, Sharon Lee, Ted Loos, Thomas Osmond, Rilla Park, Heddy Richter, Danny Rose, Beth Shube, and Stellene Vollandes.

The publisher's editor, in turn, would like to express her thanks to her coworkers on the Fourth Edition: Susan Brekka, Virginia Creeden, Anna Karvellas, Antonina Krass, Candace Levy, Polly Mancini, Mike McIver, Hugh O'Neil, Nancy Palmquist, and Peter Simon. Special thanks are in order to Marian Johnson and Diane O'Connor for their tireless and multiple contributions to this edition. We also wish to acknowledge our debt to George P. Brockway, former president and chairman at Norton, who invented this anthology; to M. H. Abrams (Cornell), Norton's advisor on English texts, and to the late John G. Benedict and the late Barry K. Wade, anthology editors and teachers whose contribution is and will be ongoing. All have helped us to create an anthology that has been called "the standard of comparison for all American-literature survey texts."

Acknowledgments

Among our many critics, advisors, and friends, the following were of especial help toward the preparation of the Fourth Edition either with advice or by providing critiques of particular periods of the anthology as a whole: M. H. Abrams (Cornell University); Donald Bahr (Arizona State University); Betty Louise Bell (University of Michigan); John Bierhorst; John Blassingame (Yale University); Joseph Boissé (University of California at Santa Barbara); William Dowling (Rutgers University); Michael Elliott (Columbia University); Larry Evers (University of Arizona); William Fenton; Robert Foulke (Skidmore College); Chris Lohman (Indiana University); Marianne Mithun (University of California at Santa Barbara); Mark Niemeyer (University of Reims); David Nordloh (Indiana University); Barry O'Connell (Amherst College); Robert Parker (University of Illinois); Joel Porte (Cornell University); Marjorie Pryse (State University of New York, College at Plattsburgh); Jarold Ramsey (University of Rochester); Mark W. Rocha (California State University at Northridge); Blair Rudes; A. LaVonne Brown Ruoff (University of Illinois at Chicago); Jack Stillinger (University of Illinois); Tom Wolfe (California State University at Northridge); Hertha D. Wong (University of California at Berkeley); Paul G. Zolbrod (Allegheny College).

We take pleasure in thanking, once again, those who advised us on the first three editions: Bruce Adams (Tuskegee University); Frederick Anderson (late General Editor of The Mark Twain Papers, University of California at Berkeley); Liahna Babener (Montana State University); John Bassett (Wayne State University); Peter J. Bellis (University of Miami); Alfred Bendixen (California State University); Ronald A. Bosco (State University of New York at Albany); Panthea Reid Broughton (Louisiana State University); Lawrence Buell (Harvard University); Sargent Bush, Jr. (University of Wisconsin); Edwin H. Cady (Duke University); D. Dean Cantrell (Berry College); Evan B. Carton (University of Texas); William Bedford Clark (Texas A & M University); Sarah Blacher Cohen (State University of New York at Albany); Thomas W. Cooley (The Ohio State University); James M. Cox (Dartmouth College); Donald H. Craver (Towson State University); Robert Creeley (State University of New York at Buffalo); Hugh J. Dawson (University of San Francisco); Sterling F. Delano (Villanova University); Joanne Feit Diehl (Bowdoin College); Doris I. Eder (University of New Haven); Thomas R. Edwards (Rutgers University); Allison Ensor (University of Tennessee); Jim Ewing (Mississippi College); Suzanne Ferguson (Case Western Reserve University); Judith Fetterley (State University of New York at Albany); Noel Riley Fitch (University of Southern California); Rosemary F. Franklin (University of Georgia); Vincent Freimarck (State University of New York at Binghamton); Lucy M. Friebert (University of Louisville); Albert Gelpi (Stanford University);

of Louisville); Albert Gelpi (Stanford University); Barbara Charlesworth Gelpi (Stanford University); Donna Gerstenberger (University of Washington); William M. Gibson (late of the University of Wisconsin); Marshall Gilliland (University of Saskatchewan); Seymour Gross (University of Detroit); Harrison Hayford (Northwestern University); Carolyn Heilbrun (Columbia University); Anthony C. Hilfer (University of Texas at Austin); Faith Mackey Holland; C. Hugh Holman (late of University of North Carolina); Glen M. Johnson (The Catholic University of America); Myrl G. Jones (Radford University); Elaine H. Kim (University of California at Berkeley); Charles Klingler (Manchester College); Jerome F. Klinkowitz (University of Northern Iowa); Paul Lauter (Trinity College); J. A. Leo Lemay (University of Delaware); Perry Lentz (Kenyon College); Kenneth Lincoln (University of California at Los Angeles); Ilse Lind (New York University); Jay Martin (University of Southern California); Wendy Martin (Claremont Graduate School); Charlotte S. McClure (Georgia State University); Joseph R. McElrath, Jr. (Florida State University); Diane Middlebrook (Stanford University); Teresa McKenna (University of Southern California); Molly Francis Moore (University of Vermont); Adalaide K. Morris (University of Iowa); Thomas Moser (Stanford University); Frederick Newberry (Duquesne University); Robert O'Clair (late of Manhattanville College); Cheryl Z. Oreovicz (Purdue University); Nancy Packer (Stanford University); Raymund A. Paredes (University of California at Los Angeles); Thornton H. Parsons (Syracuse University); Alan Perlis (University of Alabama at Birmingham); Marjorie Perloff (Stanford University); William L. Phillips (University of Washington); Donald Pizer (Tulane University); Sidney Poger (University of Vermont); Carol H. Poston; William Powers (Michigan Technical University); Dorothy Redden (Douglass College); Jerome H. Rosenberg (Miami University of Ohio); M. L. Rosenthal (New York University); Nicholas Ruddick (University of Regina); Constantine Santas (Flagler College); Joan Schulz (State University of New York at Albany); George Sebouhian (State University of New York at Fredonia); Ann Semel; Judith L. Sensibar (Arizona State University); Daniel B. Shea (Washington University); Alan Shucard (University of Wisconsin at Parkside); Frank Shuffleton (University of Rochester); Merrill Skaggs (Drew University); Robert Spiegel (Central Connecticut State University); Catharine R. Stimpson (Rutgers University); Ely Stock (The College of Staten Island); J. Maurice Thomas (Wingate College); Eleanor M. Tilton (Barnard College); Darwin T. Turner (late of the University of Iowa); Linda C. Wagner-Martin (University of North Carolina); Laurence Wharton (University of Alabama); Sidney Howard White (University of Rhode Island); Kathleen Woodward (University of Wisconsin at Milwaukee).

The Norton Anthology of American Literature

FOURTH EDITION

VOLUME 1

Literature to 1620

THE MARVELS OF SPAIN—AND AMERICA

In 1494 a man who had crossed the Atlantic in a large ship returned home to amaze those whom he had left behind with tales of a new world full of "marvels." None of those who listened to him had accomplished anything remotely like this. None had heard of this other world, let alone seen it, and none could begin to comprehend what its discovery might mean for their own familiar universe. As they listened with rapt attention, the voyager told of things undreamed of, plants and animals and most of all strange peoples whose uncanny customs, costumes, and beliefs astonished all who heard him.

The man in question might have been Christopher Columbus or any of the dozens of Europeans who accompanied him on his first voyage, but he was not. In fact, this teller of tales did join in that voyage, but he had not sailed from Palos, Spain, with the other men on August 6, 1492, and had not been with them when, at two in the morning of October 12, they sighted the Bahamian island they named San Salvador. Twice he crossed the Atlantic with Columbus, but in reverse: first to Spain from the Indies and then back again. We do not know his original name, but we know that he was a Taino Indian from the Bahamas, one of seven natives whom Columbus seized and took to Spain. There he was baptized and renamed Diego Colón, after the son of Columbus himself. (Colón was the Spanish version of the family's name.) Of the other natives, all of whom were similarly rechristened, one remained in Spain, where he died within a few years. Four others died of sickness on the passage back to America with Columbus and Colón. Colón and the sixth man escaped the same fate only "by a hair's breadth," as the fleet's physician, Diego Alvarez Chanca, wrote in his important letter on the second voyage. Returned to the Caribbean, the two served as translators for the much larger party of Spaniards, perhaps fifteen hundred strong, who arrived in seventeen ships early in November 1493. Colón himself already had seen service as an intermediary during the first voyage.

Of the two men, only Colón is reported by the historian Andrés Bernáldez, who knew Columbus and used the mariner's own lost account of the second voyage, to have regaled the other natives with tales of "the things which he had seen in Castile and the marvels of Spain, . . . the great cities and fortresses and churches, . . . the people and horses and animals, . . . the great nobility and wealth of the sovereigns and great lords, . . . the kinds of food, . . . the festivals and tournaments [and] bull-fighting." Perhaps the other man had died by this point in the second voyage. Perhaps Columbus singled out Colón for special mention because Colón had learned Castilian well enough to speak it and had shown himself to be an intelligent man and a good guide. He was to accompany Columbus on the whole of this voyage, which lasted three years.

The story of Colón catches in miniature the extraordinary changes that were to occur as natives of the Old World encountered natives of the New for the first time in recorded history. His story reminds us first that discovery was mutual rather than one sided. To be sure, far more Europeans voyaged to America than Americans to Europe, and they sent home thousands of reports and letters detailing what they saw and did in the New World. Because many of these European travelers came

1

to America to stay, however, the Indians soon had a colonial imitation of Europe developing before their eyes, complete with fortresses, churches, horses, new foods (on the second voyage, Columbus brought wheat, melons, onions, radishes, salad greens, grapevines, sugar cane, and various fruit trees) and much else that Colón in 1493 could have only found in Europe. Over time the natives of America could discover Europe encroaching on their villages and fields as the imported European landscape vied with their own. Europe was present in the textiles on the colonists' bodies, in the tools in their hands, for both of which the American Indians traded, and in the institutions of the church and state (slavery being the most obvious example) that had begun to reshape the identities and reorganize the lives of Native American peoples. In such concrete terms a new world was being created in the West Indies. It was not the new world Columbus himself was speaking of near the end of his life when he wrote in 1500 to the Spanish sovereigns Ferdinand and Isabella that he had "brought under [their] dominion . . . another world, whereby Spain, which was called poor, is now most rich." The new world that mattered was not just an expanse of space previously unknown to Europeans; it was a genuinely new set of social relationships that would evolve over the next centuries as Europe and the Americas continued to interact. With the European introduction of African slaves early in the sixteenth century, the terms of this new world became much more complex. The cultural and social relations of Americans took their origin in a great mixing of peoples from the whole Atlantic basin during the first century and a half after 1492.

Discovery began with wonder—that of Colón's listeners on his return in 1494 and that of Columbus as he descanted on the green beauty of the islands—evoking a mood that has remained strong in American writing ever since: he saw "trees of a thousand kinds" on San Salvador in November 1492, trees that seemed to "touch the sky . . . as green and as lovely as they are in Spain in May." But beyond that transcendent moment, discovery entailed a many-sided process of influence and exchange that ultimately produced the hybrid cultural universe of the Atlantic world, of which the English colonies were one small part. Much of this universe came through struggle rather than cooperation. Each people used its own traditions or elements recently borrowed from others to endure or conquer or outwit its opposite numbers, and violence often swallowed up the primal wonder glimpsed in the earliest documents. With gunpowder and steel, Europeans had the technological edge in warfare, and it would seem that—despite centuries of propaganda to the contrary—they took violence more seriously than the American Indians. The natives at first found the scale of European warfare appalling. In New England, the colonists' native allies against the Pequot tribe in 1637 complained that the English manner of fighting, as soldier John Underhill noted in his Newes from America (1638), "[was] too furious, and slay[ed] too many men." The natives were quick to adopt European weapons and tactics, however, applying them to their own disputes and to their disputes with the Europeans. The ferocity of what Europeans have called the "Indian wars" was the violent recoil in the face of violence from interlopers who threatened the very life of the native peoples.

Almost literally from 1492, the natives began to die in large numbers, if not from war then from enslavement, brutal mistreatment, despair, or disease. One of the more insidious forms of "exchange" involved the transfer to the American Indians of the microbes to which Europeans had become inured but to which the Indians had virtually no resistance. Nothing better displays the isolation of the continents and the drama of encounter that began in 1492 than the epidemic disasters that smallpox, measles, typhus, and other Old World maladies unleashed on the American natives. Whole populations plummeted as such diseases, combined with the other severe stresses placed on the natives, spread throughout the Caribbean and then on the mainland of Central and South America. The institutional disease of slavery further decimated the native peoples. It is widely agreed that the original population of the island of Hispaniola (estimated at anywhere from one hundred thousand to eight million in 1492) plunged once the Spanish took over the island, partly through disease and partly through the abuses of the *encomienda* system of virtual enslavement. In the face of this sudden decline in available native labor, Spain introduced African slavery into Hispaniola as early as 1501. By the middle of the sixteenth century the native population had been so completely displaced by African slaves that the Spanish historian Antonio de Herrera called the island "an effigy or an image of Ethiopia itself." Thus the destruction of one people was accompanied by the displacement and enslavement of another. By that point, the naive "wonder" of discovery was all but unrecoverable.

It would be inaccurate to picture the Indians, however, as merely victims, suffering decline. The natives made shrewd use of the European presence in America to forward their own aims, as Colón reminds us. In 1519 the disaffected natives in the Aztec empire clearly threw their lot in with Cortés because they saw in him a chance to settle the score with their overlord Montezuma, which they assuredly did. In New England, the Pequot War of 1637 saw a similar alignment on the English side of tribes such as the Narragansetts and the Mohegans, who had grievances with the fierce Pequots, interlopers in the region. Under ordinary circumstances, as among the Iroquois in the Northeast, European technology and the European market were seized on as a means of consolidating advantages gained before the arrival of the colonists. The Iroquois had begun to organize their famous League of the Five Nations before European settlement, but they solidified their earlier victories over other native peoples by forging canny alliances with the Dutch and then the English in New York. In the Southeast, remnant peoples banded together in the early eighteenth century to create the Catawba, a new political group that constructed what one recent historian has called a "new world" for itself. No longer known by a bewildering diversity of names, the former Nassaw and Suttirie and Charra and Succa peoples banded together with several others in an attempt to deal more effectively with the encroaching Euro-Americans of Charleston and the Low Country. This hardly was a case of diminishment or reduction. It suggests the important truth that Indians were not ahistorical before 1492, just as they were not monolithic culturally or politically then or afterward. Even as fewer and fewer of the original millions remained, they showed themselves resourceful in resisting, transforming, and exploiting the exotic cultures the Europeans were imposing on their original landscape.

VOYAGES OF DISCOVERY

Columbus was still making voyages to America (1492–93; 1493–96; 1498; 1502–04) as other Europeans, following his example, found their way to the West Indies. Giovanni Caboto (known as John Cabot to the English for whom he sailed) and his fellow Italian Amerigo Vespucci both crossed the ocean before 1500, as did the Portuguese native Pedro Cabral. After that date the voyagers became too many to track. Unlike the Viking invasion of five hundred years before, which had established modest coastal settlements in North America that the natives soon wiped out, this second European wave quickly gathered momentum and extended itself far to the north and south of the Caribbean basin that Columbus explored. Cabot was near the mouth of the St. Lawrence in Canada the year before Vespucci found that of the Amazon, nearly five thousand miles away in South America. Soon the Europeans were leaving colonies everywhere. The first colonists lingered on the Caribbean island of Hispaniola following the departure of Columbus in 1493. Although that small settlement of La Navidad was soon destroyed in a clash with Taino natives under the cacique Caonabo of Maguana, the massive second voyage in 1493 came equipped to stay, and from that point on Spain and Europe generally maintained an aggressive presence in the West Indies. The constant battles along vague frontiers with Native Americans added fuel to the dissension and political in-fighting among the settlers themselves, whose riots and mutinies nearly ruined settlement after settlement. John Smith's experience during the first Jamestown voyage of 1607 provides probably the most famous example from Anglo-America. Arrested and nearly executed (probably for offending his "betters," something he had the habit of doing) en route to America in 1607, Smith was released in Virginia when the colony's sealed instructions were opened, revealing that this apparently modest soldier had been named to the prestigious governing council even before the ships had left England. Columbus himself became the focus of fierce competitions among greedy settlers and officials in Hispaniola by the time of his third voyage and, stripped of his property and powers by a royal official maddened by the uproar, went back to Spain in chains in 1500.

Europe continued to expand in the New World amid the disorder within settlement walls and the great violence outside. Columbus found the mainland of South America in 1498 and Central America in 1502, by which time John Cabot and the Portuguese Corte-Real brothers, Gaspar and Miguel, had been down the coast of North America from Labrador to the Chesapeake, and Cabral and Vespucci had covered the east coast of South America from the Orinoco River in present-day Venezuela to well south of the Río de la Plata on the border of present-day Uruguay and Argentina. Between 1515 and the 1520s, Spain, under the reign of Charles V, aggressively reached out over the Gulf of Mexico, toward the Yucatan peninsula and Mexico and Florida and the Isthmus of Panama, then sent expeditions into the heart of North America from the 1520s to the 1540s, covering a vast region stretching from Florida to the Gulf of California and north as far as Kansas and the Tennessee River. At the same time, other Spanish explorers and conquistadors spread out over South America, especially its west coast, where in imitation of Cortés' Conquest of Mexico a decade earlier Juan Pizarro overcame the Incan empire, recently beset with violent civil war. In that same period, the Portuguese established their first permanent settlements in Brazil, and the French explorer Jacques Cartier sailed into the Gulf of St. Lawrence, then up its chief river as far as the site of the future Montreal. Within fifty years of 1492, then, the east coasts of much of both continents had been explored, and many of their major regions had been traversed; the most spectacular of their peoples, the Aztecs and the Incas, had been conquered; and Europe had settled in for a long stay.

Spain under Ferdinand and Isabella and their grandson Charles V took the most aggressively expansive role in America. Other European nations, most conspicuously France and England, were more self-absorbed, awakening slowly to what was happening across the sea. Their first explorers enjoyed bad luck and inconsistent support. John and Sebastian Cabot had sailed for English merchants and the monarchs Henry VII and Henry VIII, but the first Cabot was lost on his voyage in 1498, and the second kept his interest in America alive only by entering the service of the Spanish Crown after 1512. A return to his adopted homeland of England and a royal pension from Edward VI came to him only in the 1540s, by which point he had committed himself to the search for an eastward route to China via the seas north of Russia. In France, Cartier enjoyed early support from Francis I, but his failure to find gold and other riches in the St. Lawrence valley and his dispute with the nobleman Roberval, whom the king appointed to command Cartier's third voyage in 1541, led to profound disenchantment in France. Fishermen from both nations continued to harvest the fabulous riches of the shoals off North America and summered on the shore, drying their catch. But not until the 1570s for England and the beginning of the next century for France, as a new generation of adventurers arose and a period of commercial expansion set in, did broad public support and governmental sanction combine to stir lasting curiosity and investment. A series of luckless North American voyages by the English under Martin Frobisher, Humphrey Gilbert, and then Walter Ralegh ended in the tragedy of the "Lost Colony" of Roanoke Island in the 1580s. For another twenty years few

English explorers made serious new efforts, although the press bubbled with publications regarding the New World, particularly the works of Richard Hakluyt the younger, whose great collections gathered the fugitive records of English, and indeed European, expansion overseas. Hakluyt's masterwork, *The Principall Navigations* (1598–1600), brought the literary productions of countless European mariners to the attention of a public newly stirred by what Shakespeare soon was to call this "brave new world" of Euro-America. Hakluyt notwithstanding, only in 1606 did a second Virginia colony set forth, and this one faltered grievously at the start with a shipwreck on Bermuda (which was to inspire Shakespeare's *The Tempest*), riots at Jamestown, near starvation, and violent encounters. By 1603 French interest had revived under the direction of a group of explorers and expansionists, Samuel de Champlain most significantly, who hoped for profit from the New World and, even more, a route through it to the fabled riches of Asia. Seasoned from his voyages to Spanish America, Champlain picked up where Cartier had left off sixty years earlier, founded permanent settlements in the St. Lawrence valley, and through his agents and followers pushed French exploration as far west as Lake Superior at a time when the English were still struggling in Virginia and New England settlement had just begun at Plymouth.

LITERARY CONSEQUENCES OF 1492

The period of European exploration in the New World produced a surprisingly large and intriguing body of literature. While many manuscripts were archived and out of reach until the nineteenth century, a number of texts found their way into print and were widely dispersed, thanks to the establishment of printing in the half century before 1492. Shortly after Columbus's return to Spain in early 1493, there appeared in print his letter to the court official Luis de Santangel, narrating the voyage and lushly describing the perpetual spring Columbus had found in the West Indies the previous autumn. From the appearance of that letter on, the printing press and the European expansion into America were reciprocal parts of a single engine. Without the ready dispersal of texts rich with imagery that stirred individual imagination and national ambition in regard to the West Indies, Europe's movement westward would have been blunted and perhaps thwarted. The sword of conquest found in the pen, and in the printing press, an indispensable ally.

The great mass of early American writings came from the hands of Europeans rather than the native peoples of the New World. Important exceptions happily exist. The natives had a lively oral culture that valued memory over mechanics as a means of preserving texts, although among some groups such as the Aztecs written traditions existed (in North America these records included shellwork belts and painted animal hides, tepees, and shields) and many more groups used visual records in subtle and sophisticated ways. Such cataclysms as the Conquest of Mexico produced not only the Spanish narratives of Cortés, Bernal Díaz del Castillo, and others but also native responses, many of which perished with those who knew them. Those that survived in original native characters or in transliterated form have inestimable ethnographic and literary value. For instance, anonymous native writers working in the Nahuatl language of the Aztecs in 1528—significantly, they used the Roman alphabet introduced by the Spanish—lamented the fall of their capital to Cortés in the following lines:

> Broken spears lie in the roads;
> we have torn our hair in our grief.
> The houses are roofless now, and their walls
> are red with blood.

No one reading these four lines will easily glorify the Conquest of Mexico or of the Americas more generally. The story of the transoceanic encounter, however, ceases to be a matter of easy contrasts once one reads widely in the texts on either side. Although Europeans committed atrocities in the New World, often they did so as a result of blundering and miscommunication rather than cool, deliberate policy. In fact, the split between policy and action goes to the heart of the infant Atlantic world of the sixteenth century and is mirrored in and influenced by the character of the writing that survives from the period. The great distance separating the hemispheres made the coordination of intention and performance extremely difficult. The authorities at home lacked the knowledge to form prudent or practical policy; as a result many texts written by explorers or colonists were intended as "briefs" meant to inform or influence policy decisions made at a distance. To cite a simple example, Columbus himself wrote a point-by-point description of his second voyage in 1495, addressed to Ferdinand and Isabella in a series of "items" to which the specific responses of the sovereigns were added by a court scribe. More complexly, Cortés sought to justify his patently illegal invasion of Mexico in 1519 by sending several long letters to Charles V defending his actions and promising lavish returns if his Conquest could proceed.

Most documents sent from America to the European powers reveal such generally political intentions. Europe responded by issuing directives aimed at controlling events across the sea. Even when good policies were articulated in Europe, however, applying them in the New World entailed further problems. By the time instructions arrived in Hispaniola or Mexico or Jamestown or Quebec, new events in the colony might have rendered them pointless. Distance made control both crucial and difficult. Whereas formal authority typically resided in Europe, power as an informal fact of life and experience and circumstance belonged to America, to those who could seize and use it or who acquired it by virtue of what they did rather than the official investitures they bore. Mutiny became so pervasive a fact or fear in America precisely because individuals and groups had, morally and geographically, great latitude in the thinly populated colonial enclaves. If writing served in this fluid, ambiguous universe as a means to influence official policy at home, it also emerged as a means of justifying actions (as with Cortés) that violated or ignored European directives.

Early American writing had, though, a third and more compelling purpose as a literature of witness. That we know so much about the European devastation of the West Indies comes from the fact that some Europeans responded powerfully to that devastation in writing. Although no one typifies this mood better than Bartolomé de las Casas, who assailed Spain's ruthless destruction of whole peoples in America, it is the rare European document that does not reveal the bloody truths of Europe's colonial dreams. Starting on the Columbian voyages themselves and flowering in the Spanish West Indies, especially in the 1540s and 1550s when debates about the mistreatment of the natives earnestly moved the clerics and government officials at home, the New World inspired an outpouring of written expression. Not all the literature of witness speaks to specific issues of policy, or particular public debates, but in many of the texts one senses a critical eye, a point of view not likely to be swayed by the slogans of empire or faith or even wealth. Writers such as Diaz del Castillo, the chronicler of Cortés, and England's John Smith came from the underclass of their native countries, where but for the opportunities represented by America they might well have spent their days in silence. As a result, their writing could be subversive, even mutinous, achieving its greatest depth when it captured a vision of America as more than a dependent province of the Old World, rather as a place where much that was genuinely new might be learned.

NATIVE AMERICAN ORAL LITERATURE

When Columbus sailed from Europe in 1492, he left behind him a number of relatively centralized nation-states with largely agricultural economies. Europeans spoke some two or three dozen languages, most of them closely related; and they were generally Christian in religious belief and worldview, although many groups had had contact—and conflict—with adherents of Judaism and Islam. A written alphabet had been used by Europeans to preserve and communicate information for many centuries and Gutenberg's invention of moveable type in the mid-1400s had shown the way to a mechanical means of "writing"; by 1492, Europe was on its way to becoming a print culture.

By contrast, in 1492 in North America, native people spoke hundreds of languages, belonging to entirely different linguistic families (e.g., Athapascan, Uto-Aztecan, Chinookan, Siouan, and Algonquian) and structured their cultures in extraordinarily diverse economic and political forms. In the Great Basin of the West, small, loosely organized bands of Utes eked out a bare subsistence by hunting and gathering, while the sedentary Pueblo peoples of the Southwest and the Iroquoians of the Northeast had both highly developed agricultural economies and complex modes of political organization. In spite of some common features, religious and mythological beliefs were also diverse. Among North American peoples alone, eight different types of creation stories have been documented, with wide variations among them. All of these differ substantially from the creation stories of Judaism, Christianity, and Islam.

Also unlike European cultures, North American peoples did not use a written alphabet. Theirs were oral cultures, relying on the spoken word—whether chanted, sung, or presented in lengthy narratives—and the memory of those words to preserve important cultural information. The term *literature* comes from the Latin *littera*, "letter." Native American literatures were not, until long after the arrival of the Europeans, written "littera-tures." Indeed, as the phrase *oral literature* might appear to be a contradiction in terms, some have chosen to call the expressions of the oral tradition *orature*.

These expressions were, like the languages, political economies, and religious beliefs of Native American peoples, extremely various. Europeans in 1492 could name the tragedy, the comedy, the epic, the ode, and a variety of lyric forms as types of literature. In Native America there were probably (*probably*, because we have no actual records that predate 1492) such things as Kwakiutl winter ceremonies, Winnebago trickster tale cycles, Apache jokes, Hopi personal naming and grievance chants, Yaqui deer songs, Yuman dream songs, Piman shamanic chants, Iroquois condolence rituals, Navajo curing and blessing chants, and Chippewa songs of the Great Medicine Society, to name only some of the types of Native American verbal expression.

That there are many such types is unquestionable, but are these literary types? This question would not make sense to traditional native peoples, who do not have a category of language use corresponding to our category of literature. From a Western perspective, however, the types of native verbal expression could only be considered as literature after that late-eighteenth- and early-nineteenth-century revolution in European consciousness known as Romanticism. In that period the concept of literature shifted away from being defined by the *medium* of expression (all language preserved in *letters*) to the *kind* of expression (those texts that emphasized the imaginative and emotional possibilities of language). With this shift in the meaning of *literature*, many Native American verbal types could quite comfortably be considered literary.

We shall read these forms on the page, but it bears repeating that traditional Native American literatures originate as *oral* performances. They are offered to audiences as dramatic events in time, language for the ear, rather than objects in space for the eye. And in performance, a pause, a quickening of pace or a sudden retardation, a gesture, or a lowering of the voice affects meaning. Not surprisingly, scholars differ about the best way to transfer performance to the page. Some have opted for a stylized typography where type size and arrangement seek to convey something of the feeling of what an actual performance might have been like. Others, acknowledging that black marks on a white page cannot reproduce a living voice, have tried to translate the words as effectively as possible, leaving it to the reader to imagine these words in performance.

This matter of translating the words effectively is also controversial. When we know that the original performance used archaic and unfamiliar terms, should we use archaic and unfamiliar terms in the translation, even though they may appear stiff and old-fashioned on the page? What would the contemporary reader think of the following excerpt from J. N. B. Hewitt's rendition of the Iroquois creation story: "Through the crafty machinations of the Fire Dragon of the White Body, the consuming jealousy of the aged presiding chief was kindled against his young spouse." Should we instead opt for the nonstandard English, the Red English, or Reservation English as it has been called, of native collaborators in the translation process—even if it may strike some readers not as lively and colloquial but illiterate? Here are a few lines from a contemporary translation in Red English of a folktale from the Northwest: "He told the chief: 'Yes, I remember, I thought of it, I have a worker[,] a boy, and I asked him [to come] but no, he didn't want to leave his work and his eatings.' " Of course, if we translate these texts into standard, or "literary," English, we may have substantially misrepresented verbal expression that, in the original, would surely strike us as strange. Consider the following translation:

> You
> have been
> falling
> falling
> Have you
> fallen
> from the top
> of the salmon-
> berry bushes
> falling
> falling

This is attractive by contemporary standards, but for the sake of aesthetics, it gives up a good deal of fidelity to the original, which never appeared on the page.

While the question of how best to translate Native American verbal expression must remain open, reading the words of native oral literature conveys some sense of indigenous literary expression as it may have been before the coming of the Europeans.

CHRISTOPHER COLUMBUS
1451–1506

Born into a family of wool workers near the once supreme Mediterranean port of Genoa, Christopher Columbus followed that rather sedentary trade for a time, but by his early adulthood he had left wool, Genoa, and land itself behind, venturing onto the broad Atlantic, north to England and perhaps beyond, and south along the African shore as far as the Gold Coast. During this time he began to develop a plan to find a new, commercially viable route to Asia by sailing west across the ocean. For eight years he sought support for such a journey. Then, in 1492, the Spanish monarchs Ferdinand and Isabella, having just defeated the last of Spain's Moorish rulers at Granada, finally agreed to back Columbus's "enterprise of the Indies."

He made a quick passage across the sea, anxiously watching for signs of land, until at two in the morning of October 12 the sailor Juan Rodríguez Bermejo saw the outline of one of the Bahama Islands, and the three ships shortened sail and waited for daylight. After sunrise, "some naked people" appeared on the beach as Columbus and the others came ashore, carrying the royal standard and his own ship's banners. On this island of Guanahaní and others, including Juana and Española (Cuba and Hispaniola), he marveled at the natural scene ("my eyes never weary of looking on this fine vegetation") and found the Taino Indians to be "of a very acute intelligence," a people "so guileless and so generous" that although naturally timid they approached the strangers and gave them anything they had. Carried away on a flood of superlatives, Columbus even thought he heard European nightingales singing in the warm Caribbean autumn. Although the newness of everything in this green paradise left him unable to identify few actual commodities, he kept a sharp eye out for anything he might take home, and by the time he returned to Spain in early January 1493 he took many specimens with him—including several of the Taino Indians. The flagship *Santa Maria* having been lost in a wreck off Hispaniola on Christmas day, he left the forty-man crew of the unlucky vessel as a colony there, confident that even if the peaceable Tainos should turn against La Navidad ("the Nativity," named for the day of the shipwreck), the well-armed Europeans could easily defend themselves. All seemed peaceful as the two remaining vessels took their leave of Guacanagarí, the friendly Taino chieftain, in the vicinity of La Navidad, on January 2, 1493.

When Columbus returned to Hispaniola on his second voyage in November 1493, at the head of a fleet of seventeen ships crammed with twelve to fifteen hundred men, La Navidad was in ruins, and all the settlers were dead. Although the greed of La Navidad's settlers for gold and women was revealed as the motive for their annihilation by the Tainos, this bloody prelude to Spain's New World empire accurately forecast much that was to follow. By the time Columbus left his new Hispaniola settlement of Isabella in April 1494 to explore Cuba and Jamaica, signs of disorder had appeared, and by the time he returned that August, wholesale disorder was the norm. Columbus sought to restore some control, but he made the strange mistake of punishing the Tainos who had resisted abuse by renegade Spaniards, seizing them and enslaving them as rebels, and then subjugating the island's whole population. With some irony, he was forced to leave for Spain again in March 1496 to answer charges made against him by some of the Spanish renegades.

Having cleared his name of the worst slanders in Spain, Columbus mounted a third voyage in 1498, sailing south until he encountered the mainland of South America near the Orinoco delta in modern Venezuela. Here, increasingly absorbed in religious speculations and afflicted with arthritis and severe eye trouble, Columbus took the vast outflow of fresh water as proof that he was near the site of the Terrestrial Paradise, from which four great rivers were said to flow, and he proclaimed that God had made him "the messenger" of "the new heaven and . . . earth" of the Book of Revelation. Meanwhile, the new earth of Hispaniola fell ever deeper into a hellish state marked by outright rebellion among the Spaniards and uprisings among the Tainos. Columbus returned from the Orinoco to the new Hispaniola capital of Santo Domingo at the end of August 1498 to find one of his appointees, Chief Justice Francisco Roldán, in open rebellion against Columbus's own brother, Bartholomew. Many of the ordinary Spaniards on the island sympathized with or openly supported Roldán, and he won some converts among the Tainos as well by promising better treatment than they had so far received. The promise was empty; when Columbus eventually reached a truce with Roldán and his confederates, one of the rebels' key points, to which Columbus reluctantly assented, was that they be granted whole Taino communities to labor for them. Not even this sad agreement could end the disorder in the Spanish colony. When the newly appointed chief justice of the island, Francisco de Bobadilla, arrived from Spain in August 1500, he found seven Spanish rebels hanging from a gallows in Santo Domingo, and five more slated for execution the next day, for with the help of Roldán, Columbus was suppressing a rebellion led by an old lieutenant of Roldán. Bobadilla, charged by Ferdinand and Isabella to investigate (among other reported problems) the rumored abuse of ordinary Spanish colonists by the Italian Columbus, saw the corpses as proof that the rumors were correct. Overreacting, he seized the house and belongings of Columbus and by the end of a month seized Columbus himself, whom he sent back to Spain in chains.

Despite this turn of events, in Spain Columbus won the sympathy of the Crown and permission to undertake a fourth voyage in 1502, although he was to avoid visiting Hispaniola, which had been put under the rule of a royal governor, Nicolás de Ovando. After a passage of only twenty-one days across the Atlantic to the island of Martinique, this "High Voyage," as Columbus himself called it, turned disastrous. First came a hurricane off the south coast of Hispaniola and then, as he turned south following the long, thin shores of Central America, came the worst weather Columbus had ever encountered in his long experience at sea. In a place called Veragua (in modern Panama) he was led to expect great deposits of gold but instead found torrential rains. He took refuge in a shallow bay where his four ships, made leaky as sieves by worms, became landlocked for several months. One day as Columbus, sick with malaria, lay alone on one of the vessels, the stress and distress of this High Voyage overcame him. Climbing up the mast by a superhuman effort, he tried to shout to the men on shore for help, but the surf drowned out his voice. Still on the mast, he fell asleep and experienced a vision—or a delusion: "I heard a very compassionate voice, saying, 'O fool and slow to believe and serve thy God, the God of all!' " In this "trance" the voice assured Columbus that he had as much support from above as did David or Moses and that he should keep his faith.

At last he departed "on Easter night, with ships rotten, worm-eaten, all full of holes." By the end of June, the hulls in worse shape yet and more bad weather and contrary winds behind them, the ships arrived at Jamaica, unable to go farther. Columbus sent one of his company, Diego Mendez, in a Caribbean Indian canoe to Hispaniola for help. It was a desperate measure, but Mendez made it across the sea in five days.

Mendez carried with him a letter written in Jamaica in July 1503 by Columbus, a letter into which Columbus poured the accumulating despair of this final voyage and the life of frustration and sorrow it seemed to summarize. As he contemplated Hispaniola, now removed from his control, he thought of its "exhausted state," so different from what he had hoped for it. Rescued from Jamaica later that year, he never was rescued from the sadness that had overtaken him. And fate had reserved for him a last indignity: when he died in 1506, the hemisphere he had stumbled across in his search for Asia was about to be named for another Italian, Amerigo Vespucci, who had little to do with Europe's presence there.

Several documents regarding the four voyages survive from Columbus's hand. The supposed "Journal" of his first voyage is actually a summary prepared by the cleric and reformer Bartolomé de las Casas. A letter sent by Columbus to Luis de Santangel, a royal official and an early supporter of his venture, provides a more authentic account and served as the basis for the first printed description of America, issued in 1493 in Spain and widely translated and reprinted across Europe. A memorandum regarding the second voyage, intended by Columbus for the Spanish monarchs (whose responses to each point also survive), offers useful insights into the emerging ambiguities and problems of the colony on Hispaniola. For the third and fourth voyages, three letters from Columbus, two sent to the

Crown and one to a woman of the Spanish court, detail his deepening worldly and spiritual troubles.

From Letter to Luis de Santangel Regarding the First Voyage[1]

[At sea, February 15, 1493]

Sir,

As I know that you will be pleased at the great victory with which Our Lord has crowned my voyage, I write this to you, from which you will learn how in thirty-three days, I passed from the Canary Islands to the Indies with the fleet which the most illustrious king and queen our sovereigns gave to me. And there I found very many islands filled with people innumerable, and of them all I have taken possession for their highnesses, by proclamation made and with the royal standard unfurled, and no opposition was offered to me. To the first island which I found I gave the name *San Salvador*,[2] in remembrance of the Divine Majesty, Who has marvelously bestowed all this; the Indians call it "Guanahani." To the second I gave the name *Isla de Santa María de Concepción*; to the third, *Fernandina*; to the fourth, *Isabella*; to the fifth, *Isla Juana*, and so to each one I gave a new name.[3]

When I reached Juana I followed its coast to the westward, and I found it to be so extensive that I thought that it must be the mainland, the province of Catayo.[4] And since there were neither towns nor villages on the seashore, but only small hamlets, with the people of which I could not have speech because they all fled immediately, I went forward on the same course, thinking that I should not fail to find great cities and towns. And at the end of many leagues, seeing that there was no change and that the coast was bearing me northwards, which I wished to avoid since winter was already beginning and I proposed to make from it to the south, and as moreover the wind was carrying me forward, I determined not to wait for a change in the weather and retraced my path as far as a certain harbor known to me. And from that point I sent two men inland to learn if there were a king or great cities. They traveled three days' journey and found an infinity of small hamlets and people without number, but nothing of importance. For this reason they returned.

I understood sufficiently from other Indians, whom I had already taken, that this land was nothing but an island. And therefore I followed its coast eastwards for one hundred and seven leagues to the point where it ended. And from that cape I saw another island distant eighteen leagues from the former, to the east, to which I at once gave the name "Española."[5] And I went there and followed its northern coast, as I had in the case of Juana, to the eastward for one hundred and eighty-eight great leagues in a straight line. This island and all the others are very fertile to a limitless degree, and this island is extremely so. In it there are many harbors on the coast of the sea, beyond comparison with others which I know in Christendom, and many rivers, good

1. The text is from *Select Documents Illustrating the Four Voyages of Columbus*, translated and edited by Cecil Jane (1930–33). Luis de Santangel, a former merchant and a court official since 1478, had supported Columbus's proposal to the Spanish Crown and had helped secure financing for the first voyage.
2. The precise identity of the Bahamian island Co-

lumbus named San Salvador is not known today, although many theories have been put forward.
3. Of these four islands, only the identity of Juana (Cuba) is today certain.
4. I.e., China (or "Cathay").
5. I.e., Hispaniola, where the countries of Haiti and the Dominican Republic are located.

and large, which is marvelous. Its lands are high, and there are in it very many sierras and very lofty mountains, beyond comparison with the island of Tenerife.[6] All are most beautiful, of a thousand shapes, and all are accessible and filled with trees of a thousand kinds and tall, and they seem to touch the sky. And I am told that they never lose their foliage, as I can understand, for I saw them as green and as lovely as they are in Spain in May, and some of them were flowering, some bearing fruit, and some in another stage, according to their nature. And the nightingale was singing and other birds of a thousand kinds in the month of November there where I went. There are six or eight kinds of palm, which are a wonder to behold on account of their beautiful variety, but so are the other trees and fruits and plants. In it are marvelous pine groves, and there are very large tracts of cultivatable lands, and there is honey,[7] and there are birds of many kinds and fruits in great diversity. In the interior are mines of metals, and the population is without number. Española is a marvel.

1493

From Letter to Ferdinand and Isabella Regarding the Fourth Voyage[1]

[Jamaica, July 7, 1503]

*   *   *

Of Española, Paria,[2] and the other lands, I never think without weeping. I believed that their example would have been to the profit of others; on the contrary, they are in an exhausted state; although they are not dead, the infirmity is incurable or very extensive; let him who brought them to this state come now with the remedy if he can or if he knows it; in destruction, everyone is an adept. It was always the custom to give thanks and promotion to him who imperiled his person. It is not just that he who has been so hostile to this undertaking should enjoy its fruits or that his children should. Those who left the Indies, flying from toils and speaking evil of the matter and of me, have returned with official employment.[3] So it has now been ordained in the case of Veragua.[4] It is an ill example and without profit for the business and for justice in the world.

The fear of this, with other sufficient reasons, which I saw clearly, led me to pray your highnesses before I went to discover these islands and Terra Firma, that you would leave them to me to govern in your royal name. It pleased you; it was a privilege and agreement, and under seal and oath, and you granted me the title of viceroy and admiral and governor general of all. And you fixed the boundary, a hundred leagues beyond the Azores and the

---

6. The largest of the Canary Islands.
7. The honeybee, presumably the source of the honey found on the island, is not native to the Western Hemisphere. Nor is the nightingale, mentioned above.
1. The text is from *Select Documents Illustrating the Four Voyages of Columbus*, translated and edited by Cecil Jane (1930–33). Written on Jamaica in 1503, this letter was hand carried from there to Hispaniola by Diego Mendez.

2. Paria was the mainland region of what is now Venezuela, near the island of Trinidad. Columbus, who had first landed in South America ("Terra Firma," as he terms it later) in 1498, argued that the terrestrial paradise lay nearby.
3. Although it appears that Columbus has specific personal enemies in mind, it is not clear whom he means.
4. I.e., Panama, where Columbus was shipwrecked earlier in this voyage.

Cape Verde Islands, by a line passing from pole to pole, and you gave me wide power over this and over all that I might further discover. The document states this very fully.

The other most important matter, which calls aloud for redress, remains inexplicable to this moment. Seven years I was at your royal court, where all to whom this undertaking was mentioned, unanimously declared it to be a delusion. Now all, down to the very tailors, seek permission to make discoveries. It can be believed that they go forth to plunder, and it is granted to them to do so, so that they greatly prejudice my honor and do very great damage to the enterprise. It is well to give to God that which is His due and to Caesar that which belongs to him. This is a just sentiment and based on justice.

The lands which here obey Your Highnesses are more extensive and richer than all other Christian lands. After I, by the divine will, had placed them under your royal and exalted lordship, and was on the point of securing a very great revenue, suddenly, while I was waiting for ships to come to your high presence with victory and with great news of gold, being very secure and joyful, I was made a prisoner and with my two brothers was thrown into a ship, laden with fetters, stripped to the skin, very ill-treated, and without being tried or condemned. Who will believe that a poor foreigner could in such a place rise against Your Highnesses, without cause, and without the support of some other prince, and being alone among your vassals and natural subjects, and having all my children at your royal court?

I came to serve at the age of twenty-eight years, and now I have not a hair on my body that is not gray, and my body is infirm, and whatever remained to me from those years of service has been spent and taken away from me and sold, and from my brothers, down to my very coat, without my being heard or seen, to my great dishonor. It must be believed that this was not done by your royal command. The restitution of my honor, the reparation of my losses, and the punishment of him who did this, will spread abroad the fame of your royal nobility. The same punishment is due to him who robbed me of the pearls, and to him who infringed my rights as admiral.[5] Very great will be your merit, fame without parallel will be yours, if you do this, and there will remain in Spain a glorious memory of Your Highnesses, as grateful and just princes.

The pure devotion which I have ever borne to the service of Your Highnesses, and the unmerited wrong that I have suffered, will not permit me to remain silent, although I would fain do so; I pray Your Highnesses to pardon me. I am so ruined as I have said; hitherto I have wept for others; now, Heaven have mercy upon me, and may the earth weep for me. Of worldly goods, I have not even a blanca[6] for an offering in spiritual things. Here in the Indies I have become careless of the prescribed forms of religion. Alone in my trouble, sick, in daily expectation of death, and encompassed about by a million savages, full of cruelty and our foes, and so separated from the holy Sacraments of Holy Church, my soul will be forgotten if it here leaves my body. Weep for me, whoever has charity, truth, and justice.

I did not sail upon this voyage to gain honor or wealth; this is certain, for already all hope of that was dead. I came to Your Highnesses with true devotion and with ready zeal, and I do not lie. I humbly pray Your Highnesses that

5. The reference is to Alonso de Ojeda (c. 1468–c. 1516), who had taken pearls (part of what was reserved to Columbus under his agreement with the Spanish Crown) from Paria to Española.
6. A small Spanish coin.

if it please God to bring me forth from this place, that you will be pleased to permit me to go to Rome and to other places of pilgrimage. May the Holy Trinity preserve your life and high estate, and grant you increase of prosperity.

Done in the Indies in the island of Jamaica, on the seventh of July, in the year one thousand five hundred and three.

1505

BARTOLOMÉ DE LAS CASAS
1474–1566

Early modern Europe's most eloquent apologist for Native American rights, Bartolomé de las Casas first heard of the new "discoveries" as a student in Seville in 1493, when Columbus triumphantly entered that Spanish city. All his life, Casas recalled how Columbus brought with him "seven Indians who had survived the voyage," and "beautiful green parrots, . . . masks made of precious stones and fishbone, . . . sizable samples of very fine gold, and many other things never before seen in Spain." Although Casas later called the seizure of those seven Taino Indians on the island of Guanahaní "the first injustice committed in the Indies," in the Spain of 1493, neither Casas nor anyone else had time to reflect on the moral implications of the pageant taking place before their eyes.

Spain's enthusiastic reception of Columbus in 1493 helped recruit the large party of soldiers, settlers, clergy, and adventurers who joined his second voyage later that year, among whom was Casas's father, an impoverished merchant lured to the West Indies by the hope of new wealth. Nine years later, when Casas himself sailed to the Caribbean, his father (having returned home in the interim) sailed back with him. Both went in the company of Nicolás de Ovando, newly appointed to succeed Columbus as royal governor of the now-chaotic island of Hispaniola. Casas was not immediately alarmed by conditions on Hispaniola, which resulted partly from rivalries among the Spanish (Columbus was a good commander, but a bad administrator, and the rumored riches of the West Indies attracted many opportunists) and partly from profound conflicts between the Europeans and the Native Americans. The island, roughly the size of South Carolina, had a population of perhaps one million Taino Indians in 1492 (estimates range from about a tenth of this figure up to eight million). These inhabitants lived in culturally interrelated subgroups in various regions of the island and had complex dealings with each other, both friendly and otherwise, before the arrival of Columbus. Relations between the Tainos and the Spaniards soured as early as the winter of 1493, when a party of sailors left in a small settlement named La Navidad ("the Nativity") stole many women from a village, rousing the jealousy of the men there, who brutally murdered the settlers of La Navidad. From that point on, Spanish policy in regard to the island's inhabitants was a matter of force, direct or implied, and the population soon plummeted under the effects of war, enslavement, and disease.

Casas came to lament all three means of the natives' decline, on Hispaniola and elsewhere in the West Indies, but was particularly concerned with the legality and morality of enslavement. Slavery hardly was invented in the Americas, although once imported from the Old World it gradually lost its quasi-feudal trappings and became a more absolute, crudely economic institution. The Spanish-American institution first called the *repartimiento* and later the *encomienda* thus had deep roots on the other side of the ocean but evolved in the West under the pressure of political and economic circumstances. *Repartimiento* applied first (in 1497, as part of an outline of Columbus's powers by the Crown) to the distribution of land grants to settlers in the West Indies as a means of encouraging emigration. But as Columbus was forced to negotiate for peace with the Spanish rebel Francisco Roldán on Hispaniola in the late 1490s, he applied this term to a new distribution of whole Taino Indian communities—as a source of labor—to Roldán's allies, who would lay down their arms only if such awards were made to them. The land that the Spanish claimed through conquest would now be worked by the peoples who had been deprived of it in the first place.

Casas knew this history well because in his early years in America he had supported and benefited from these very institutions. The year after arriving on Hispaniola, he joined in a brutal attack on the Taino inhabitants of the province of Higuey, on the island's eastern end, an attack the Spaniards claimed was in response to a Taino rebellion. As a member of this expedition, Casas saw cruelties on every hand: "It was a general rule among Spaniards to be cruel, not just cruel, but extraordinarily cruel so that harsh and bitter treatment would prevent Indians from daring to think of themselves as human beings." But Casas himself received an *encomienda* of Native Americans for helping to hunt down the "rebels" during the Higuey campaign. Later (even after he had joined the priesthood), he received other grants for his part in the conquest of Cuba. In his *History of the Indies*, he wrote of his moral blindness during this period, noting that he "went about his concerns like the others, sending his share of Indians to work fields and gold mines, taking advantage of them as much as he could."

Only in 1514 did Casas enter on his long, gradually intensifying crusade for the dignity and rights of the native peoples. In June of that year, as he prepared to preach during Pentecost to a Spanish congregation in a town near his estate, one biblical text, from the apochryphal book of Ecclesiasticus, gripped his imagination.

> Bread is life to the destitute,
> and it is murder to deprive them of it.
> To rob your neighbor of his livelihood is to kill him,
> and the man who cheats a worker of his wages sheds blood.

Contemplating this text, Casas knew he could not keep on owning his fellow human beings. He relinquished his slaves secretly to Governor Velázquez, then on the Feast of Assumption (August 15), announced from the pulpit that he had done so and that all masters should do so, because holding Native Americans as slaves was a sin.

In 1515 Casas took the case to Spain, where the government appointed him "protector of the Indians" and gave him permission to undertake a peaceful, exemplary colonization on the Venezuelan coast. That venture failed, however, when Spaniards already residing there refused to give up their lucrative slave-hunting raids; their refusal in turn brought the wrath of the Cumaná Indians down on the colonists. Casas himself escaped but, abashed, withdrew into Dominican monasteries on Hispaniola between 1522 and 1529. During those years, brutal new conquests in Guatemala, Nicaragua, and Peru buried the promise of his Venezuelan project ever deeper. Only in the 1530s, as Casas returned to political activity, traveling throughout Spain's American possessions fighting new enslavements of the American Indians and voyaging to Europe to lobby for change, did his arguments have widespread effect. In 1537 Pope Paul III forbade all further enslavements; in 1542 Emperor Charles V followed suit in the New Laws of the Indies, which gave Native Americans full protection of the courts, forbidding their enslavement on any grounds and threatening confiscation for any *encomendero* who violated the new code. "We order and command that henceforth," ran one clause, "for no cause whatever, whether of war, rebellion, ransom, or in any other manner, can any Indian be made a slave."

Such victories were bittersweet. As bishop of Chiapas, Mexico, from 1544 to 1547, Casas sought to enforce the new laws, but riots there and broad resistance throughout the Spanish colonies made it clear that his goals would not be easily achieved. Disillusioned by Charles V's revocation, in the face of pressure from the settlers, of key features of the 1542 code, Casas returned in 1547 to Spain, where he spent the last twenty years of his life writing about his long crusade in the West Indies.

Angered and saddened by what he had witnessed of the Spanish Conquest of America, Casas urged change by his own example, by public and private discourse, by influence at court and in the church, and by his writings. Of the latter, the most important in his own era was *The Very Brief Relation of the Devastation of the Indies*, first published in 1552 but based on oral arguments used by Casas a decade earlier to persuade a special royal commission to frame the new code of 1542. The *Relation* details with chilling effect the destruction visited on Native Americans by conquistadors and colonizers in pursuit of wealth beyond the reach of the authorities in Spain. In his own day, Casas was widely accused of treason and even endured charges of heresy, partly because the quick translation of his *Relation* into several other languages provided Spain's enemies with ample evidence of his country's sins in America—a point the Protestant nations such as the Netherlands and England especially wished to make. Ironically, the Protestant "Black Legend" of Spain's devastation of the West Indies roots itself in the polemical exposé of the Catholic priest Bartolomé de las Casas, an exposé he intended as a call to Spain's future reform rather than as a denunciation of its past.

From The Very Brief Relation of the Devastation of the Indies[1]

From *Hispaniola*

This was the first land in the New World to be destroyed and depopulated by the Christians, and here they began their subjection of the women and children, taking them away from the Indians to use them and ill use them, eating the food they provided with their sweat and toil. The Spaniards did not content themselves with what the Indians gave them of their own free will, according to their ability, which was always too little to satisfy enormous appetites, for a Christian eats and consumes in one day an amount of food that would suffice to feed three houses inhabited by ten Indians for one month. And they committed other acts of force and violence and oppression which made the Indians realize that these men had not come from Heaven.[2] And some of the Indians concealed their foods while others concealed their wives and children and still others fled to the mountains to avoid the terrible transactions of the Christians.

And the Christians attacked them with buffets and beatings, until finally they laid hands on the nobles of the villages. Then they behaved with such temerity and shamelessness that the most powerful ruler of the islands had to see his own wife raped by a Christian officer.

From that time onward the Indians began to seek ways to throw the Christians out of their lands. They took up arms, but their weapons were very weak and of little service in offense and still less in defense. (Because of this, the

---

1. The text comes from *The Devastation of the Indies: A Brief Account*, translated by Herma Briffault (1974).
2. Columbus and other early European voyagers

reported that the natives took them to be gods who had come from the heavens. See Thomas Harriot's *A Brief and True Report* (p. 77) for a good example.

wars of the Indians against each other are little more than games played by children.) And the Christians, with their horses and swords and pikes began to carry out massacres and strange cruelties against them. They attacked the towns and spared neither the children nor the aged nor pregnant women nor women in childbed, not only stabbing them and dismembering them but cutting them to pieces as if dealing with sheep in the slaughter house. They laid bets as to who, with one stroke of the sword, could split a man in two or could cut off his head or spill out his entrails with a single stroke of the pike. They took infants from their mothers' breasts, snatching them by the legs and pitching them headfirst against the crags or snatched them by the arms and threw them into the rivers, roaring with laughter and saying as the babies fell into the water, "Boil there, you offspring of the devil!" Other infants they put to the sword along with their mothers and anyone else who happened to be nearby. They made some low wide gallows on which the hanged victim's feet almost touched the ground, stringing up their victims in lots of thirteen, in memory of Our Redeemer and His twelve Apostles, then set burning wood at their feet and thus burned them alive. To others they attached straw or wrapped their whole bodies in straw and set them afire. With still others, all those they wanted to capture alive, they cut off their hands and hung them round the victim's neck, saying "Go now, carry the message," meaning, Take the news to the Indians who have fled to the mountains. They usually dealt with the chieftains and nobles in the following way: they made a grid of rods which they placed on forked sticks, then lashed the victims to the grid and lighted a smoldering fire underneath, so that little by little, as those captives screamed in despair and torment, their souls would leave them.

I once saw this, when there were four or five nobles lashed on grids and burning; I seem even to recall that there were two or three pairs of grids where others were burning, and because they uttered such loud screams that they disturbed the captain's sleep, he ordered them to be strangled. And the constable, who was worse than an executioner, did not want to obey that order (and I know the name of that constable and know his relatives in Seville), but instead put a stick over the victim's tongues, so they could not make a sound, and he stirred up the fire, but not too much, so that they roasted slowly, as he liked. I saw all these things I have described, and countless others.

And because all the people who could do so fled to the mountains to escape these inhuman, ruthless, and ferocious acts, the Spanish captains, enemies of the human race, pursued them with the fierce dogs they kept which attacked the Indians, tearing them to pieces and devouring them. And because on few and far between occasions, the Indians justifiably killed some Christians, the Spaniards made a rule among themselves that for every Christian slain by the Indians, they would slay a hundred Indians.

From *The Coast of Pearls, Paria, and the Island of Trinidad*

[The Spaniards] have brought to the island of Hispaniola and the island of San Juan[3] more than two million souls taken captive, and have sent them to do hard labor in the mines, labors that caused many of them to die. And it is a great sorrow and heartbreak to see this coastal land which was so flourishing, now a depopulated desert.

---

3. I.e., Puerto Rico.

This is truth that can be verified, for no more do they bring ships loaded with Indians that have been thus attacked and captured as I have related. No more do they cast overboard into the sea the third part of the numerous Indians they stow on their vessels, these dead being added to those they have killed in their native lands, the captives crowded into the holds of their ships, without food or water, or with very little, so as not to deprive the Spanish tyrants who call themselves ship owners and who carry enough food for themselves on their voyages of attack. And for the pitiful Indians who died of hunger and thirst, there is no remedy but to cast them into the sea. And verily, as a Spaniard told me, their ships in these regions could voyage without compass or chart, merely by following for the distance between the Lucayos Islands[4] and Hispaniola, which is sixty or seventy leagues, the trace of those Indian corpses floating in the sea, corpses that had been cast overboard by earlier ships.

Afterward, when they disembark on the island of Hispaniola, it is heartbreaking to see those naked Indians, heartbreaking for anyone with a vestige of piety, the famished state they are in, fainting and falling down, weak from hunger, men, women, old people, and children.

Then, like sheep, they are sorted out into flocks of ten or twenty persons, separating fathers from sons, wives from husbands, and the Spaniards draw lots, the ship owners carrying off their share, the best flock, to compensate them for the moneys they have invested in their fleet of two or three ships, the ruffian tyrants getting their share of captives who will be house slaves, and when in this "*repartimiento*"[5] a tyrant gets an old person or an invalid, he says, "Why do you give me this one? To bury him? And this sick one, do you give him to me to make him well?" See by such remarks in what esteem the Spaniards hold the Indians and judge if they are accomplishing the divine concepts of love for our fellow man, as laid down by the prophets.

The tyranny exercised by the Spaniards against the Indians in the work of pearl fishing is one of the most cruel that can be imagined. There is no life as infernal and desperate in this century that can be compared with it, although the mining of gold is a dangerous and burdensome way of life. The pearl fishers dive into the sea at a depth of five fathoms, and do this from sunrise to sunset, and remain for many minutes without breathing, tearing the oysters out of their rocky beds where the pearls are formed. They come to the surface with a netted bag of these oysters where a Spanish torturer is waiting in a canoe or skiff, and if the pearl diver shows signs of wanting to rest, he is showered with blows, his hair is pulled, and he is thrown back into the water, obliged to continue the hard work of tearing out the oysters and bringing them again to the surface.

The food given the pearl divers is codfish, not very nourishing, and the bread made of maize, the bread of the Indies. At night the pearl divers are chained so they cannot escape.

Often a pearl diver does not return to the surface, for these waters are infested with man-eating sharks of two kinds, both vicious marine animals that can kill, eat, and swallow a whole man.

In this harvesting of pearls let us again consider whether the Spaniards pre-

4. I.e., the Bahamas.
5. Distribution (Spanish). Attempts were made, by royal decree in 1503, to require that the masters of the American Indians convert them to Christianity and serve as trustees for their property, but the *repartimiento* ceased to be anything more than a slave-holding system.

serve the divine concepts of love for their fellow men, when they place the
bodies of the Indians in such mortal danger, and their souls, too, for these
pearl divers perish without the holy sacraments. And it is solely because of the
Spaniards' greed for gold that they force the Indians to lead such a life, often a
brief life, for it is impossible to continue for long diving into the cold water
and holding the breath for minutes at a time, repeating this hour after hour,
day after day; the continual cold penetrates them, constricts the chest, and
they die spitting blood, or weakened by diarrhea.

The hair of these pearl divers, naturally black, is as if burnished by the
saltpeter in the water, and hangs down their backs making them look like sea
dogs or monsters of another species. And in this extraordinary labor, or, better
put, in this infernal labor, the Lucayan Indians are finally consumed, as are
captive Indians from other provinces. And all of them were publicly sold for
one hundred and fifty castellanos,[6] these Indians who had lived happily on
their islands until the Spaniards came, although such a thing was against the
law. But the unjust judges did nothing to stop it. For all the Indians of these
islands are known to be great swimmers.[7]

1542–46   1552

6. A Spanish gold coin bearing the arms of Castile.   as pearl divers were so extraordinary that the Spanish
7. I.e., the physical abilities of the Caribbean natives   judges overlooked their mistreatment.

HERNÁN CORTÉS
1485–1547

Hernán Cortés, a native of the Spanish province of Estremadura, left in 1504 for
Hispaniola, where he was to serve as notary of the town of Azúa. He joined Diego
Velázquez in the conquest of Cuba in 1511, became his secretary, then settled
down—eventually joined by his wife, Catalina Xuarez—in the town of Santiago
de Baracoa. There he used the Caribbean Indian laborers granted to him as an
encomienda to mine gold and raise sheep, cattle, and horses. Although he apparently showed no interest in the two expeditions sent west from Cuba in 1517 and
1518 to the Yucatan peninsula of Mexico (his future chronicler Bernal Díaz del
Castillo was a member of both), Cortés was chosen by Velázquez to lead a third,
more ambitious expedition planned for 1518.

Velázquez later changed his mind and tried to prevent the expedition from leaving Cuba, but Cortés anticipated this reversal and hastily left for the mainland anyway. Without Velázquez's official sanction, Cortés sailed past Yucatan and headed
west along the Mexican coast to locate a suitable site for a settlement. Near the
natural harbor of San Juan de Ullua, due east of Mexico City, he founded Vera
Cruz, whose "citizens" (under the medieval legal code of the Spanish region of
Castile) could proclaim him their rightful governor. This jury-rigged authority gave
all Cortés's subsequent acts in the Conquest of the Aztec empire their basis—
however tenuous—in Spanish law.

Sinking his ships so that there would be no retreat, Cortés set his army marching
west from Vera Cruz in the middle of August 1519 and arrived in the Aztec capital
of Tenochtitlán (Mexico City) at the beginning of November. Here the ruler,
Montezuma, about whom the Spaniards had heard much, greeted them warmly

but warily. Cortés, stupefied by the splendor and scope of the city, with its grand public spaces, temples, markets, palaces, and substantial houses, confessed in a letter to the Emperor Charles V that there was much he could not describe. Even the grandeurs of Spain could provide only weak comparisons. Tenochtitlán was "as big as Seville or Córdoba," he wrote; the tower of its great temple was "higher than that of the cathedral of Seville"; the great square was "twice as big as that of Salamanca"; and the main palace of Montezuma there was so splendid "that in Spain there is nothing to compare it with."

Initial diplomacy between the Spaniards and the grand city's rulers soon gave way to a struggle for control. Montezuma sat uneasily at the pinnacle of the so-called Triple Alliance of three Aztec city-states (Texcoco, Tlacopán, and Tenochtitlán—occupied, respectively, by the Acolhua, Tepaneca, and Mexica ethnic groups) that exerted broad control over other native groups in the Basin of Mexico, but that was also the object of resentment and resistance. Not surprisingly, at Cortés's urging, disaffected natives joined the Spanish effort against Montezuma, while Montezuma's officials and priests likewise exploited internal conflicts among the Spaniards. Cortés was forced to fight on two fronts when, in April 1520, Pánfilo de Narváez landed an army on the coast with orders from the ruling Council of the Indies to arrest him for treason. Although Cortés outmaneuvered the unfortunate Narváez, persuading his army by promises and bribes to join in the Conquest of Mexico, his rush to meet this threat on the coast allowed Montezuma to reclaim power in Tenochtitlán. In a bloody two-and-a-half-month siege Cortés retook the city, this time with the aid of many natives from semi-independent states located between Mexico City and the coast who joined forces with the Spanish army as it moved back. The siege left the city in ruins.

From the time of his arrival in Mexico, Cortés had been aware that he had another war to fight, this one in words. Beyond the opponents arrayed around him was the figure of Charles V, grandson of the monarchs who had sent Columbus west to the Indies a generation earlier, who at nineteen was not merely king of Spain but the Holy Roman emperor as well. If Cortés was to solidify his victory and enjoy the fame and wealth it might bring him, he had to convince Charles V that what he had undertaken would benefit Spain profoundly. Across the vast distance separating the Aztecs' empire from Charles V's, Cortés wrote between 1519 and 1526 a series of letters that aimed to secure the Crown's retrospective permission for his daring disobedience. Even before he had made his way to the heart of the Aztec empire, Cortés addressed to Charles V the first of these long letters, detailing his early impressions of the Mexican coast and ending with a catalog of gifts presented to Cortés by Montezuma's subjects (although the original is lost, a contemporary letter evidently copied from his dictation and sent to the Crown by the new municipality of Vera Cruz is usually substituted for it). A second letter, dated October 1520, describes the first march inland, the city of Tenochtitlán and its initial conquest, and the counteroffensive against Narváez; while a third, written in May 1522, tells of the long and bloody reconquest completed in 1521. By portraying himself in all three of these documents as the unwavering servant of the emperor, to whom he boldly made a direct appeal, Cortés secured what he wanted: in 1522, Charles V appointed him governor and captain general of New Spain, although he appointed a four-member council to assist (and restrain) him as well. Two subsequent letters Cortés sent to Charles V, one in 1524 and the other in 1526, report the tightening control the Spaniards were exerting over the fallen empire of Montezuma.

From First Letter from Mexico to the Spanish Crown[1]

[*Gifts of the Aztecs to Cortés*]

First a large gold wheel with a design of monsters on it and worked all over with foliage. This weighed 3,800 *pesos de oro*.[2] From this wheel, because it was the best that has been found here and of the finest gold, a fifth was taken for Their Highnesses; this amounted to two thousand *castellanos* which belonged to Them of Their fifth and Royal privilege according to the stipulation that the captain Fernando Cortés brought from the Hieronymite Fathers[3] who reside on the island of Hispaniola and on the other islands. The eighteen hundred *pesos* that remained and all the rest that goes to make up twelve hundred *pesos*, the council of this town bequeath to Their Highnesses, together with everything else mentioned in this list, which belonged to the people of the aforementioned town.

Item: Two necklaces of gold and stone mosaic, one of which has eight strings of 232 red jewels and 163 green jewels. Hanging from the border of this necklace are twenty-seven small gold bells; and in the center of them are four figures in large stones inlaid with gold. From each of the two in the center hang single pendants, while from each of the ends hang four double pendants. The other necklace has four strings of 102 red jewels and 172 which appear to be green in color; around these stones there are twenty-six small gold bells. In this necklace there are ten large stones inlaid with gold from which hang 142 pendants.

Item: Four pairs of screens, two pairs being of fine gold leaf with trimmings of yellow deerskin, and the other two (pairs) of fine silver leaf with trimmings in white deerskin. The remainder are of plumes of various colors, and very well made. From each of these hang sixteen small gold bells, all with red deerskin.

Another item: One hundred *pesos de oro* for melting, so that Their Highnesses may see how the gold is taken from the mines here.

Another item: In a box, a large piece of featherwork, lined with animal skin which, in color, seems like that of a marten. Fastened to this piece, and in the center of it, is a large disk of gold which weighed sixty *pesos de oro*, and a piece of blue and red stone mosaic in the shape of a wheel, and another piece of stone mosaic, of a reddish color; and at the end of the piece there is another piece of colored featherwork that hangs from it.

Item: A fan of colored featherwork with thirty-seven small rods cased in gold.

Another item: A large piece of colored featherwork to be worn on the head and encircled by sixty-eight small pieces of gold, each of which is as large as a half *cuarto*.[4] Beneath them are twenty little gold towers.

Item: A miter[5] of blue stone mosaic with a design of monsters in the center of it. It is lined with an animal skin which by its color appears to be that of a marten, and has a small piece of featherwork which, together with the one mentioned above, is of the same miter.

1. The text, the final section of this document, is from *Letters from Mexico*, translated and edited by A. R. Pagden (1971).
2. Spanish gold coins.
3. A holy order whose members had been sent to the Indies in 1516, as a result of pressure from Casas and other reformers on the Crown, to investigate alleged mistreatment of the natives by the Spaniards. As the Crown's direct representatives in the Indies, they had broad powers to which Cortés and others submitted.
4. A small copper coin (Spanish).
5. A headcovering.

Item: Four harpoons of featherwork with their stone heads fastened by a gold thread, and a jeweled scepter with rings of gold and the rest of featherwork.

Item: A bracelet of blue jewels and, in addition, a small piece of black featherwork and with other colors.

Item: A large pair of sandals of leather whose color resembles that of a marten. The soles are white and sewn with gold thread.

Furthermore, a mirror set in a piece of blue and red jewelry, with a piece of featherwork and two strips of red leather attached to it, together with a skin which seems to be from those same martens.

Item: Three pieces of colored featherwork that belong to a large gold head which seems to be that of an alligator.

Item: Some screens of blue stone mosaic, lined with a skin which by its color seems to come from a marten; and from each one of them hang fifteen small gold bells.

Another item: A maniple[6] of wolfskin with four strips of leather that look like martenskin.

Another item: Some fibers placed in some colored feathers; the which fibers are white and look like locks of hair.

Another item: Two pieces of colored featherwork that are for two helmets of stone mosaic which are mentioned below.

Furthermore, two pieces of colored featherwork which are for two pieces of gold, made like large shells and worn on the head.

Furthermore, two birds with green plumage and their feet, beaks and eyes made of gold. These are put on one of those pieces of gold that resemble shells.

Furthermore, two large ear ornaments of blue stone mosaic which are for the large alligator head.

In another square box, a large alligator head in gold, which is the one mentioned above where the aforementioned pieces are to be put.

Also, a helmet of blue stone mosaic with twenty small gold bells hanging round the outside of it with two strings of beads above each bell: and two ear ornaments of wood with gold plates.

Also, a bird with green plumage and with feet, beak and eyes of gold.

Another item: Another helmet of blue stone mosaic with twenty-five little gold bells and two beads of gold above each bell, which hang round it, with some wooden ear ornaments with gold plates; and a bird with green plumage and feet, beak and eyes of gold.

Another item: A reed container with two large pieces of gold to be worn on the head; they are made like gold shells with ear ornaments of wood with gold plates. Also two birds with green plumage and feet, beaks and eyes of gold.

Also, sixteen bucklers of stone mosaic with pieces of colored featherwork hanging round the outside of them, and with a wide-angled board of stone mosaic with its pieces of colored featherwork. In the center of this board is a cross inside a wheel made of the same stone mosaic, and lined with leather the color of martenskin.

Furthermore, a scepter of a red stone mosaic, made to resemble a snake with head, teeth and eyes in what seems to be mother-of-pearl. The hilt is adorned with the skin of a spotted animal, and beneath this hilt there hang six small pieces of featherwork.

Another item: A fan of featherwork in a reed adorned with the skin of a

6. In Christian practice, a small cloth vestment worn on the left forearm.

spotted animal, in the manner of a weathercock. Above it has a crown of featherwork and finally many long green feathers.

Item: Two birds made of thread and featherwork. The quills of their wings and tails, the claws of their feet, their eyes and the tips of their beaks are of gold, each placed in its respective gold-covered reed. And below some feather down, one white and the other yellow, with some gold embroidery between the feathers; and from each of these hang seven strands of feathers.

Item: Four pieces made after the manner of skates,[7] placed in their respective gold-covered canes. Their tails, gills, eyes and mouths are of gold; below, on their tails, are some pieces of green featherwork, while toward their mouths each has a crown of colored featherwork, and in some of the white feathers there is some gold embroidery, and beneath the handle of each one hang six strands of colored featherwork.

Item: A small copper rod lined with a skin in which is placed a piece of gold in the manner of a piece of featherwork, which has some pieces of colored featherwork above and below it.

Another item: Five fans of colored featherwork, four of which have ten small quills covered with gold while the fifth has thirteen.

Item: Four harpoons of white flint, fastened to four rods of featherwork.

Item: A large buckler[8] of featherwork trimmed on the back with the skin of a spotted animal. In the center of the field of this buckler is a gold plate with a design such as the Indians make, with four other half plates of gold round the edge, which together form a cross.

Another item: A piece of featherwork of various colors made in the manner of a half chasuble,[9] lined with the skin of a spotted animal. This, the lords of these parts, which we have seen up to now, hang from about their necks. On the front it has thirteen pieces of gold very well fitted together.

Item: A piece of colored featherwork, made in the manner of a jousting helmet, which the lords of this land wear on their heads. From it hang two ear ornaments of stone mosaic with two small bells and two beads of gold; and above there is a piece of featherwork of broad green feathers, while below hang some white hairs.

Furthermore, four animal heads, two of which seem to be wolves, the other two tigers, with some spotted skins: from these heads hang some small bronze bells.

Item: Two animal skins of spotted animals, lined with some cotton mantles: these skins appear to be those of a mountain cat.

Item: The red and gray skin of another animal, which seems to be a lion, and two deerskins.

Item: Four skins of small deer from which here they make small tanned gloves.

And, moreover, two books which the Indians have: also half a dozen fans of colored featherwork and a perfume container of colored featherwork.

Furthermore, a large silver wheel which weighed forty-eight silver marks, and also some bracelets, some beaten [silver] leaves; and one mark five ounces and forty *adarmes*[1] of silver; and a large buckler and another small one of

---

7. Flat fish resembling rays.
8. A round shield.
9. A sleeveless cloak worn by Christian priests during the eucharist service.

1. About two and a half ounces. The mark, roughly equivalent to eight ounces, was a much larger measure of weight.

silver, which weighed four marks and two ounces; and another two bucklers which appear to be silver and which weighed six marks and two ounces; and another buckler, which likewise appears to be of silver, which weighed one mark and seven ounces, which is in all sixty-two marks of silver.

Another item: Two large pieces of cotton richly woven in white, black and tawny.

Item: Two pieces woven with feathers and another piece woven in various colors; another piece woven in patterns of red, black and white, and on the back these patterns do not show.

Item: Another piece woven with patterns and in the center a black wheel of feathers.

Item: Two white cotton cloths woven with some pieces of featherwork.

Another cotton cloth with some white cords attached. A peasant smock.

A white piece with a large wheel of white feathers in the middle.

Two pieces of gray cord with some wheels of feathers, and another two of tawny cord.

Six painted pieces; another red piece with some wheels and another two pieces painted blue; and two women's shirts.

Item: Six bucklers, each one with a gold plate covering the whole buckler.

Another item: A half miter of gold.[2]

1519   1842

2. The chronicler Bernal Díaz del Castillo helps explain this last item. A soldier's helmet was sent to Montezuma, who had seen a painting of one and was curious about it. Cortés asked that it be returned filled with gold for Emperor Charles V.

BERNAL DÍAZ DEL CASTILLO
1492–1584

Bernal Díaz del Castillo, born in the town of Medina del Campo in the Spanish province of Castile in the momentous year 1492, went to the West Indies as a young man and remained there, except for two brief returns to Spain, for the rest of his long life. His first American voyage came in 1514, in the company of the future explorer Hernando de Soto and under the command of Pedrárias Dávila, who was sent to replace his son-in-law Vasco Nuñez del Balboa as governor of Darien, a colony in what is now Panama. Eventually, the political turmoil of Darien (where Dávila was later to arrest Balboa on flimsy charges of treason and execute him) disillusioned young Díaz, who along with several companions sailed to Cuba, then under the rule of his own kinsman Diego Velázquez. From there, in 1517 and 1518, Díaz went out with two brief expeditions to Yucatan and Florida before joining Hernán Cortés in the conquest of Mexico (1591–21).

Because he marched as a mere footsoldier when the army moved inland from Vera Cruz to conquer and later reconquer Tenochtitlán (Mexico City), Díaz knew the grim story in vivid detail. Many years later, the lone survivor of all the conquistadors, living in modest circumstances on a small land grant in Guatemala, he at last undertook to put on paper what he could recall. The tale was the only thing, he said, that he had to leave his children and grandchildren: "I am now an old man, over eighty-four years of age, and have lost both sight and hearing; and unfortunately I have gained no wealth to leave to my children and descendants, except this true story, which is a most remarkable one, as my readers will presently see."

Among the remarkable features of *The True History of the Conquest of New Spain* is the fact that Díaz seems never to have regretted the violence that flooded Mexico with Aztec blood or the subsequent enslavement of the natives there. He had the ordinary soldier's gift, however, for telling what he had seen without dwelling on the official justifications for all the violence and suffering he was party to. As a consequence, his prose catches with rough power this extraordinary meeting of two civilizations as they vied for control of Mexico. During the last siege of the city, for several days he watched across the battle lines as the Aztecs executed captive Spaniards—"their chests struck open and their palpitating hearts drawn out"—and he found his own courage weakened. "I came to fear death more than ever in the past. Before I went into battle, a sort of horror and gloom would seize my heart and I would [urinate] once or twice and commend myself to God, and His blessed Mother."

Such experiences changed Díaz profoundly. Late in his account of the fall of the city, he confessed that even now, more than sixty years later, he could never sleep through the night: "Some may ask when we slept [during the Conquest], and what our beds are like. They were nothing but a little straw and a mat, and anyone who had a curtain put it underneath him. We slept in our armour and sandals with our weapons close beside us. . . . I grew so accustomed to sleeping [this way] that after the conquest of New Spain I kept the habit of sleeping in my clothes and without a bed. . . . Even [now] when I go to the villages of my *encomienda* I do not take a bed, or if I sometimes do, it is not because I want it, but because some gentlemen are travelling with me, and I do not want them to think I do not possess a good bed. But I always lie down fully dressed. What is more, I can only sleep for a short time at night. I have to get up and look at the sky and stars and walk about for a bit in the dew." The passage is especially suggestive, but in some ways it is typical of the artless power of the whole long narrative. Few writers of the age of Conquest told such concrete tales, full of sights and sounds, beauties and horrors, all of it amounting to an ironic commentary on the Christian culture of Europe.

From The True History of the Conquest of New Spain[1]

[*Gifts Presented to Cortés*]

About this time[2] many Indians came from the towns of which these two great servants of Montezuma were governors, some of them bringing gold and jewels of little value, or fowls, to exchange with us for green beads, clear glass beads, and other articles. In this way we kept ourselves fed, for almost all the soldiers had brought goods for barter, and we had learnt in Grijalva's[3] time that beads were a good thing to bring.

Six or seven days passed in this way. Then one morning Tendile[4] returned with more than a hundred Indian porters, and accompanied by a great Mexican chief, who in face, features, and body was very like our Captain. The great Montezuma had chosen him on purpose. For it is said when Tendile showed him the portrait of Cortés all the princes present exclaimed that one

---

1. The text is from *The Conquest of New Spain*, translated by J. M. Cohen (1963).
2. I.e., April 1519, when Cortés had arrived in the vicinity of the future Vera Cruz and the port of San Juan de Ulua on the Gulf coast of Mexico but had not yet ventured far inland.
3. Juan de Grijalva (1489?–1527) had led an expedi-

tion along the coast of Yucatan in 1518, of which Díaz had been a member.
4. Tendile (or Teuhtlilli) was a Mexican leader—or cacique, as the Spanish called such a leader—who conveyed messages and gifts from Cortés to Montezuma. He first approached the Spaniards at their camp on Easter Sunday 1519, three days after their landing.

of their number, Quintalbor, looked exactly like him; and it was Quintalbor who now accompanied Tendile. On account of this resemblance we in the camp called them "our Cortés" and "the other Cortés."

To return to my story, when these people arrived before our Captain they kissed the earth and perfumed him and all the soldiers near him with incense that they had brought in earthenware braziers. Cortés received them kindly and seated them beside him. The prince Quintalbor, who bore the presents and had been appointed joint spokesman with Tendile, welcomed us to the country and after a long speech ordered them to be brought forward. The various objects were placed on mats, which they call *petates*, on which were spread other cotton cloths. The first was a disk in the shape of the sun, as big as a cartwheel and made of very fine gold. It was a marvelous thing engraved with many sorts of figures and, as those who afterward weighed it reported, was worth more than ten thousand pesos. There was another larger disk of brightly shining silver in the shape of the moon, with other figures on it, and this was worth a great deal for it was very heavy. Quintalbor also brought back the helmet[5] full of small grains of gold, just as they come from the mines and worth three thousand pesos.

The gold in the helmet was worth more than twenty thousand pesos to us, because it proved to us that there were good mines in the country. Next came twenty golden ducks, of fine workmanship and very realistic, some ornaments in the shape of their native dogs, many others in the shapes of tigers, lions, and monkeys, ten necklaces of very fine workmanship, some pendants, twelve arrows and a strung bow, and two rods like staffs of justice twenty inches long, all modeled in fine gold. Next they brought crests of gold, plumes of rich green feathers, silver crests, some fans of the same material, models of deer in hollow gold, and many other things that I cannot remember, since all this was very long ago; and after this came thirty loads of beautiful cotton cloth of various patterns, decorated with feathers of many colors, and so many other things that I cannot attempt to describe them.

When the presents had been displayed these great *Caciques* Quintalbor and Tendile asked Cortés to accept them with the same grace as Montezuma had shown in sending them, and to divide them among the *Teules*[6] and men who accompanied him. Cortés accepted the gifts with delight, whereupon the ambassadors told him that they wished to repeat the message with which Montezuma had charged them. First, that he was pleased such valiant men as he had heard we were should come to his country—for he knew what we had done at Tabasco[7]—and that he would much like to see our great Emperor, who was such a mighty prince that his fame had reached him even from the distant lands whence we came. Second, that he would send the Emperor a present of precious stones, and serve us in any way he could during our stay in that port. But as for a meeting, he told us not to think of it, for it was not necessary; and he put forward many objections.

Cortés thanked them with a good countenance, and with many flattering

---

5. Cortés sent Tendile to Mexico City with this helmet, requesting that it be sent back filled with gold. Díaz reports that the gilded helmet, which belonged to an ordinary soldier, was rusty.
6. Gods (Nahuatl); i.e., the Mexicans apparently assumed that at least some of the Cortés party were of divine origin.

7. Cortés had arrived at the mouth of the Tabasco River, south of the future Vera Cruz on the Gulf coast of Mexico, in late March. The year before, Grijalva had found the Mayans there friendly, but Díaz reports that in 1519 they attacked Cortés, who lost a shoe in the mud; Díaz received an arrow wound in the thigh.

protestations gave each governor two holland[8] shirts, some blue glass beads, and other things, and begged them to go back as his ambassadors to Mexico and inform their lord, the great Montezuma, that since we had crossed so many seas and journeyed from such distant lands solely to see and speak with him in person, our great King and lord would got give us a good reception if we were to return without doing so. Wherever their king might be, said Cortés, we should like to go and visit him and carry out his commands.

✳ ✳ ✳

[The Approach to Tenochtitlán]

Next morning,[9] we came to a broad causeway and continued our march toward Iztapalapa.[1] And when we saw all those cities and villages built in the water, and other great towns on dry land, and that straight and level causeway leading to Mexico, we were astounded. These great towns and *cues*[2] and buildings rising from the water, all made of stone, seemed like an unchanged vision from the tale of Amadis.[3] Indeed, some of our soldiers asked whether it was not all a dream. It is not surprising therefore that I should write in this vein. It was all so wonderful that I do not know how to describe this first glimpse of things never heard of, seen or dreamed of before.

When we arrived near Iztapalapa we beheld the splendor of the other *Caciques* who came out to meet us, the lord of that city whose name was Cuitlahuac, and the lord of Culuacan,[4] both of them close relations of Montezuma. And when we entered the city of Iztapalapa, the sight of the palaces in which they lodged us! They were very spacious and well built, of magnificent stone, cedar wood, and the wood of other sweet-smelling trees, with great rooms and courts, which were a wonderful sight, and all covered with awnings of woven cotton.

When we had taken a good look at all this, we went to the orchard and garden, which was a marvelous place both to see and walk in. I was never tired of noticing the diversity of trees and the various scents given off by each, and the paths choked with roses and other flowers, and the many local fruit-trees and rose-bushes, and the pond of fresh water. Another remarkable thing was that large canoes could come into the garden from the lake, through a channel they had cut, and their crews did not have to disembark. Everything was shining with lime[5] and decorated with different kinds of stonework and paintings which were a marvel to gaze on. Then there were birds of many breeds and varieties which came to the pond. I say again that I stood looking at it, and thought that no land like it would ever be discovered in the whole world, because at that time Peru was neither known nor thought of. But today all that I then saw is overthrown and destroyed; nothing is left standing.

The *Caciques* of that town and of Coyoacan[6] brought us a present of gold worth more than two thousand pesos; and Cortés thanked them heartily for it,

---

8. Linen.
9. According to Díaz, this was November 7, 1519.
1. An Aztec town located on a peninsula jutting into Lake Texcoco south of the island capital of Tenochtitlán. The causeway led north across two smaller lakes to the peninsula; other causeways led from Iztapalapa to the capital on Lake Texcoco.
2. Temples (Nahuatl).
3. The medieval romance of the warrior Amadis,

based on French originals, survives in the 15th-century version by Garcia de Montalvo.
4. Cuitlahuac and Culuacan were cities to the south of Tenochtitlán.
5. I.e., whitewash.
6. A city west of Iztapalapa and due south of Tenochtitlán selected by Cortés as his headquarters during the second siege of the capital in 1520.

and he showed them great kindness, telling them through our interpreters something about our holy faith, and declaring to them the great power of our lord the Emperor. But there were too many conversations for me to describe them all.

Early next day we left Iztapalapa with a large escort of these great *Caciques*, and followed the causeway, which is eight yards wide and goes so straight to the city of Mexico that I do not think it curves at all. Wide though it was, it was so crowded with people that there was hardly room for them all. Some were going to Mexico and others coming away, besides those who had come out to see us, and we could hardly get through the crowds that were there. For the towers and the *cues* were full, and they came in canoes from all parts of the lake. No wonder, since they had never seen horses or men like us before!

With such wonderful sights to gaze on we did not know what to say, or if this was real that we saw before our eyes. On the land side there were great cities, and on the lake many more. The lake was crowded with canoes. At intervals along the causeway there were many bridges, and before us was the great city of Mexico. As for us, we were scarcely four hundred strong, and we well remembered the words and warnings of the people of Huexotzinco and Tlascala and Tlamanalco,[7] and the many other warnings we had received to beware of entering the city of Mexico, since they would kill us as soon as they had us inside. Let the interested reader consider whether there is not much to ponder in this narrative of mine. What men in all the world have shown such daring? But let us go on.

We marched along our causeway to a point where another small causeway branches off to another city called Coyoacan, and there, beside some towerlike buildings, which were their shrines, we were met by many more *Caciques* and dignitaries in very rich cloaks. The different chieftains wore different brilliant liveries, and the causeways were full of them. Montezuma had sent these great *Caciques* in advance to receive us, and as soon as they came before Cortés they told him in their language that we were welcome, and as a sign of peace they touched the ground with their hands and kissed it.

There we halted for some time while Cacamatzin, the lord of Texcoco, and the lords of Iztapalapa, Tacuba,[8] and Coyoacan went ahead to meet the great Montezuma, who approached in a rich litter, accompanied by other great lords and feudal *Caciques* who owned vassals. When we came near to Mexico, at a place where there were some other small towers, the great Montezuma descended from his litter, and these other great *Caciques* supported him beneath a marvelously rich canopy of green feathers, decorated with gold work, silver, pearls, and *chalchihuites*,[9] which hung from a sort of border. It was a marvelous sight. The great Montezuma was magnificently clad, in their fashion, and wore sandals of a kind for which their name is *cotaras*, the soles of which are of gold and the upper parts ornamented with precious stones. And the four lords who supported him were richly clad also in garments that seem to have been kept ready for them on the road so that they could accom-

7. The peoples in question all had differences with Montezuma. Tlascala (or Tlaxcala), for instance, was an independent state east of Mexico City and supplied much support for Cortés in his battles with the Aztecs. The Aztecs told Cortés they could conquer Tlaxcala anytime they wished, but left it free to use Tlaxcala as a nearby training ground for Aztec warriors and a handy source of sacrificial victims.

8. A city west of Tenochtitlán. Texcoco is a city on the lake of that name, east of Tenochtitlán.

9. Chalchihuites was the Aztec goddess of fresh water bodies; because her name translates as "She Who Wears a Jade Skirt," Díaz seems to be using it here as a term for jade stones.

pany their master. For they had not worn clothes like this when they came out to receive us. There were four other great *Caciques* who carried the canopy above their heads, and many more lords who walked before the great Montezuma, sweeping the ground on which he was to tread, and laying down cloaks so that his feet should not touch the earth. Not one of these chieftains dared to look him in the face. All kept their eyes lowered most reverently except those four lords, his nephews, who were supporting him.

When Cortés saw, heard, and was told that the great Montezuma was approaching, he dismounted from his horse, and when he came near to Montezuma each bowed deeply to the other. Montezuma welcomed our Captain, and Cortés, speaking through Doña Marina,[1] answered by wishing him very good health. Cortés, I think, offered Montezuma his right hand, but Montezuma refused it and extended his own. Then Cortés brought out a necklace which he had been holding. It was made of those elaborately worked and colored glass beads called *margaritas*, of which I have spoken, and was strung on a gold cord and dipped in musk to give it a good odor. This he hung round the great Montezuma's neck, and as he did so attempted to embrace him. But the great princes who stood round Montezuma grasped Cortés' arm to prevent him, for they considered this an indignity.

Then Cortés told Montezuma that it rejoiced his heart to have seen such a great prince, and that he took his coming in person to receive him and the repeated favors he had done him as a high honor. After this Montezuma made him another complimentary speech, and ordered two of his nephews who were supporting him, the lords of Texcoco and Coyoacan, to go with us and show us our quarters. Montezuma returned to the city with the other two kinsmen of his escort, the lords of Cuitlahuac and Tacuba; and all those grand companies of *Caciques* and dignitaries who had come with him returned also in his train. And as they accompanied their lord we observed them marching with their eyes downcast so that they should not see him, and keeping close to the wall as they followed him with great reverence. Thus space was made for us to enter the streets of Mexico without being pressed by the crowd.

Who could now count the multitude of men, women, and boys in the streets, on the roof-tops and in canoes on the waterways, who had come out to see us? It was a wonderful sight and, as I write, it all comes before my eyes as if it had happened only yesterday.

They led us to our quarters, which were in some large houses capable of accommodating us all and had formerly belonged to the great Montezuma's father, who was called Axayacatl. Here Montezuma now kept the great shrines of his gods, and a secret chamber containing gold bars and jewels. This was the treasure he had inherited from his father, which he never touched. Perhaps their reason for lodging us here was that, since they called us *Teules* and considered us as such, they wished to have us near their idols. In any case they took us to this place, where there were many great halls, and a dais hung with the cloth of their country for our Captain, and matting beds with canopies over them for each of us.

On our arrival we entered the large court, where the great Montezuma was awaiting our Captain. Taking him by the hand, the prince led him to his apartment in the hall where he was to lodge, which was very richly furnished

1. A native woman of high caste who was disowned by her mother and stepfather in favor of Marina's half-brother. Cortés made crucial use of her as an interpreter and a negotiator.

in their manner. Montezuma had ready for him a very rich necklace, made of golden crabs, a marvelous piece of work, which he hung round Cortés's neck. His captains were greatly astonished at this sign of honor.

After this ceremony, for which Cortés thanked him through our interpreters, Montezuma said: "Malinche, you and your brothers are in your own house. Rest awhile." He then returned to his palace, which was not far off.

We divided our lodgings by companies, and placed our artillery in a convenient spot. Then the order we were to keep was clearly explained to us, and we were warned to be very much on the alert, both the horsemen and the rest of us soldiers. We then ate a sumptuous dinner which they had prepared for us in their native style.

So, with luck on our side, we boldly entered the city of Tenochtitlan or Mexico on 8 November in the year of our Lord 1519.

* * *

[Cortés in Difficulties]

There was never a time when we were not subject to surprises so dangerous that but for God's help they would have cost us our lives.[2] No sooner had we set up the image of Our Lady on the altar, and said mass, than Huichilobos and Tezcatlipoca seem to have spoken to their *papas*,[3] telling them that they intended to leave their country, since they were so ill-treated by the *Teules*. They said that they did not wish to stay where these figures and the cross had been placed, nor would they stay unless we were killed. This, they said, was their answer, and the *papas* need expect no other, but must convey to it Montezuma and all his captains, so that they might at once attack us and kill us. Their gods also observed that they had seen us break up the gold that was once kept in their honor and forge it into ingots, and warned the Mexicans that not only had we imprisoned five great *Caciques* but were now making ourselves masters of their country. They recited many more of our misdeeds in order to incite their people to war.

Wishing us to hear what his gods had said, Montezuma sent Orteguilla[4] to our Captain with the message that he wished to speak to him on very serious business. The page said that Montezuma was very sad and agitated, and that on the previous night and during much of the day many *papas* and important captains had been with him, holding secret discussions which he could not overhear.

On receiving this message Cortés hurried to the palace where Montezuma was, taking with him Cristóbal de Olid, the captain of the guard, and four other captains, also Doña Marina and Jerónimo de Aguilar.[5] All paid great respect to the great Montezuma, who addressed them in these words: "My lord Malinche and captains, I am indeed distressed at the answer which our *Teules*

2. Díaz is writing here of a complex period in the history of the Cortés invasion. In the winter that followed his entrance into Tenochtitlán, Cortés had taken Montezuma hostage under the pretense of protecting him and thus had effective control of the city and much surrounding territory. Cortés began a search for gold mines, built a flotilla to sail on the city's lakes, and ordered the removal of the native idols from the temples. His control of the country was far from complete, however, and as troubles emerged among the Aztec ruling class and the priests by the following spring, a party of Spanish soldiers under Pánfilo de Narváez landed near Villa Rica (Vera Cruz) with the intent of arresting Cortés on orders from Diego Velázquez.
3. Priests. Huichilobos is the Aztec god of war and Tezcatlipoca, the god of creation.
4. A young Aztec who served as page for Cortés.
5. Aguilar, shipwrecked on the Yucatan coast in 1511, had been ransomed from the Mayans by Cortés. His expertise in the Mayan language made him of vital assistance during the invasion.

have given to our *papas*, to me, and to all my captains. They have commanded us to make war on you and kill you and drive you back across the sea. I have reflected on this command, and think it would be best that you should at once leave this city before you are attacked, and leave no one behind. This, my lord Malinche, you must certainly do, for it is in your own interest. Otherwise you will be killed. Remember that your lives are at stake."

Cortés and our captains were distressed and even somewhat alarmed; which was not surprising, for the news was so sudden and Montezuma was so insistent that our lives were in the greatest and immediate danger. The matter was clearly urgent. Cortés replied by thanking him for the warning, and saying that at the moment he was troubled by two things: that he had no ships in which to depart, since he had ordered those in which we came to be broken up, and that Montezuma would have to accompany us so that our great emperor might see him. He begged him as a favor therefore to restrain his *papas* and captains until three ships could be built in the sand-dunes. This course, he argued, would be to their advantage, for if they began a war they would all be killed. And to show that he really meant to build these ships without delay, he asked Montezuma to tell his carpenters to go with two of our soldiers who were expert shipbuilders, and cut wood near the coast.

On hearing Cortés say that he would have to come with us and visit the Emperor, Montezuma was even sadder than before. He said he would let us have the carpenters, and urged Cortés to hurry up and not waste time in talk but get to work. In the meantime he promised to tell his *papas* and captains not to foment disturbances in the city, and to see that Huichilobos was appeased with sacrifices, though not of human lives. After this excited conversation Cortés and our captain took their leave of Montezuma and we were all left in great anxiety wondering when the fighting would begin.

Cortés immediately sent for Martin López, the ship's carpenter, and Andrés Nuñez,[6] and the Indian carpenters whom Montezuma had lent us, and after some discussion about the size of the three vessels to be built, he ordered López to start work at once and get them ready. For all that was necessary in the way of iron and blacksmith's tackle, tow, caulkers, and tar was to be found at Villa Rica. So they set out and cut the wood near the coast, and after making calculations and templates hastily began to build the ships.

Meanwhile we in Mexico went about in great depression, fearing that at any moment we might be attacked. Our Tlascalan auxiliaries and Doña Marina told Cortés that this was imminent, and the page Orteguilla was always in tears. We all kept on the alert and placed a strong guard on Montezuma. I say that we were on the alert, but I do not have to repeat this so often, since we never took off our armor, gorgets, or leggings by night or day. Some may ask when we slept, and what our beds were like. They were nothing but a little straw and a mat, and anyone who had a curtain put it underneath him. We slept in our armor and sandals with our weapons close beside us. The horses stood saddled and bridled all day, and everything was so fully prepared that at a call to arms we were already at our posts, and waiting. We posted sentinels every night, and every soldier did his guard-duty. There is something else I would say, though I do not like to boast: I grew so accustomed to going about armed and sleeping in the way I have described that after the conquest of New

6. Nuñez was an expert shipbuilder often put to work on such projects during the Conquest.

Spain I kept the habit of sleeping in my clothes and without a bed. I slept better that way than on a mattress.

Even when I go to the villages of my *encomienda*[7] I do not take a bed or, if I sometimes do, it is not because I want it, but because some gentlemen are traveling with me, and I do not wish them to think I do not possess a good bed. But I always lie down fully dressed. What is more, I can only sleep for a short time at night. I have to get up and look at the sky and stars and walk about for a bit in the dew; and this without putting a cap or a handkerchief on my head. I am so used to it that, thank God, it does me no harm. I have said all this so that my readers shall know how we, the true conquistadors, lived, and how accustomed we became to our arms and to keeping watch.

*   *   *

One day when our Captain went to make his usual state visit on Montezuma, he noticed, after the usual civilities, that Montezuma appeared more cheerful and happy. He asked him how it was, and Montezuma replied that his health was better. But when Cortés paid him a second visit on the same day the prince was afraid that he had learnt about Narváez' ships. So to get the advantage of our Captain and to avoid suspicion, he said: "Lord Malinche, just a moment ago some messengers came to tell me that eighteen or more ships with a great many men and horses have arrived at the port where you disembarked. They brought me a picture of it all painted on cloths; and seeing you visiting me for a second time today I thought you had come to bring me the same news, for now you will not need to build ships. But you have told me nothing about it. So I have been annoyed with you, on the one hand, for keeping me in ignorance, and delighted, on the other hand, at the arrival of your brothers. For now you can all return to Spain without more discussion."

When Cortés heard about the ships and saw the painting on the cloth, he rejoiced greatly. "Thank God, who provides for us at the right time," he said. And we soldiers were so pleased that we could not keep quiet. The horsemen rode skirmishing round, and musket shots were fired. But Cortés grew very thoughtful, for he knew quite well that the fleet had been sent against him and us by the Governor Diego Velázquez. Being a wise man, he told us soldiers and captains what he felt, and by great gifts of gold and promises to make us rich persuaded us to stand by him. He did not yet know who was in command of the fleet, but we were highly delighted with the news, and with the gold he had given us by way of gratuity, since it came from his own property and not from what should have fallen to our share. Our Lord Jesus Christ was indeed sending us help and assistance.

*   *   *

[The Destruction of Tenochtitlán]

*   *   *

Just then many companies of Mexicans came down the causeway, wounding us all, including the horsemen. Sandoval[8] too received a stone full

---

7. A grant of Native Americans (with their lands) supposedly to encourage their conversion to Christianity. In practice, the *encomienda* system degenerated into slavery. Díaz's *encomienda* was located in Guatemala.
8. A cavalry officer and close associate of Cortés'. Cortés returned to the coast to meet Narváez in the spring

in the face. But Pedro de Alvarado and some other horsemen went to his assistance. As so many bands were coming on, and only I and twenty soldiers were opposing them, Sandoval ordered us to retire gradually in order to save the horses; and because we did not retire as quickly as he wished he turned on us furiously and said: "Do you want me and all my horsemen to be killed because of you? For my sake, Bernal Díaz, my friend, please fall back!" Then Sandoval received another wound, and so did his horse. By this time we had got our allies off the causeway; and facing the enemy and never turning our backs, we gradually retired, forming a kind of dam to hold up their advance. Some of our crossbowmen and musketeers shot while others were loading, the horsemen made charges, and Pedro Moreno[9] loaded and fired his cannon. Yet despite the number of Mexicans that were swept away by his shot we could not keep them at bay. On the contrary, they continued to pursue us, in the belief that they would carry us off that night to be sacrificed.

When we had retired almost to our quarters, across a great opening full of water, their arrows, darts, and stones could no longer reach us. Sandoval, Francisco de Lugo, and Andrés de Tápia[1] were standing with Pedro de Alvarado, each one telling his story and discussing Cortés' orders, when the dismal drum of Huichilobos sounded again, accompanied by conches, horns, and trumpet-like instruments. It was a terrifying sound, and when we looked at the tall *cue* from which it came we saw our comrades who had been captured in Cortés' defeat being dragged up the steps to be sacrificed. When they had hauled them up to a small platform in front of the shrine where they kept their accursed idols we saw them put plumes on the heads of many of them; and then they made them dance with a sort of fan in front of Huichilobos. Then after they had danced the *papas* laid them down on their backs on some narrow stones of sacrifice and, cutting open their chests, drew out their palpitating hearts which they offered to the idols before them. Then they kicked the bodies down the steps, and the Indian butchers who were waiting below cut off their arms and legs and flayed their faces, which they afterward prepared like glove leather, with their beards on, and kept for their drunken festivals. Then they ate their flesh with a sauce of peppers and tomatoes. They sacrificed all our men in this way, eating their legs and arms, offering their hearts and blood to their idols as I have said, and throwing their trunks and entrails to the lions and tigers and serpents and snakes that they kept in the wild-beast houses I have described in an earlier chapter.

On seeing these atrocities, all of us in our camp said to one another: "Thank God they did not carry me off to be sacrificed!" My readers must remember that though we were not far off we could do nothing to help, and could only pray God to guard us from such a death. Then at the very moment of the

---

of 1520, leaving half his men under the command of Pedro de Alvarado in the Aztec capital. After decisively defeating Narváez and convincing his army to join his cause, Cortés hurried back to Tenochtitlán, enlisting many native allies en route. Badly managed by Alvarado, affairs were in deep confusion when Cortés arrived late in June. Montezuma, now a captive of the invaders set up as a figurehead, was forced to plead for calm, only to be struck down by stones hurled by his people. He soon died, either from the resulting injuries or from stab wounds of uncertain but probably Spanish origin. Cortés was forced to flee the city shortly thereafter, in a long bloody retreat during what became

known as *la noche triste*, or the night of sorrow. He was able to regroup again and eventually attacked the following winter. This account of the slow but finally devastating Spanish victory, which was secured in August 1521, begins here with the chilling tale of how some five dozen Spanish captives were sacrificed earlier that summer as their companions, barely escaping over a causeway, looked back in horror at the temple of the war god.

9. An artillery officer.
1. A soldier who also wrote an account of the Conquest.

sacrifice, great bands of Mexicans suddenly fell upon us and kept us busy on all sides. We could find no way of holding them. "Look!" they shouted, "that is the way you will all die, as our gods have many times promised us," and the threats they shouted at our Tlascalan allies were so cruel and so frightening that they lost their spirit. The Mexicans threw them roasted legs of Indians and the arms of our soldiers with cries of: "Eat the flesh of these *Teules* and of your brothers, for we are glutted with it. You can stuff yourselves on our leavings. Now see these houses you have pulled down. We shall make you build them again, much finer, with white stone and fine masonry. So go on helping the *Teules*. You will see them all sacrificed."

Guatemoc[2] did something more after his victory. He sent the hands and feet of our soldiers, and the skin of their faces, and the heads of the horses that had been killed, to all the towns of our allies and friends and their relations, with the message that as more than half of us were dead and he would soon finish off the rest, they had better break their alliance with us and come to Mexico, because if they did not desert us quickly he would come and destroy them.

The Mexicans went on attacking us by day and night; and we all kept guard together, Gonzalo de Sandoval, Pedro de Alvarado, and all the other captains included. So although great bands of warriors came by night, we were able to repel them. Both by day and night half the horsemen remained in Tacuba[3] and the other half on the causeway. But this was not all the harm we suffered. The enemy returned and reopened all the channels that we had blocked since we had first advanced along the causeway, and built even stronger barricades than before. Then our friends from the cities on the lake who had recently allied themselves to us and were coming to help us with their canoes decided that they had "come for wool but gone away shorn." For many of them lost their lives and many went home wounded, and more than half their canoes were destroyed. But even so they did not help the Mexicans any more, for they loathed them. They stood aside, however, and watched events.

*   *   *

Guatemoc and his captains thanked Cortés for this assurance.[4] Then Cortés asked after his wife and the other great ladies, wives of other captains, whom he knew to have come with the prince; and Guatemoc himself answered that he had begged Gonzalo de Sandoval and García Holguin[5] to leave them in their canoes while he came to learn Malinche's orders. Cortés at once sent for them, and ordered that they should be given of the best we had in the camp to eat. Then, as it was late and it was beginning to rain, he arranged for them to be sent to Coyoacan and, taking Guatemoc, his family, and household, and many other chieftains with him, he ordered Pedro de Alvarado, Gonzalo de Sandoval, and the other captains each to go to his own camp and quarters. We went to Tacuba, Sandoval to Tepeaquilla,[6] and Cortés himself to Coyoacan. Guatemoc and his captains were captured on the evening of 13 August 1521. Thanks be to our Lord Jesus Christ and Our Lady the Virgin Mary, His Blessed Mother.

2. A young Aztec chieftain who had led the repulse of Cortés the year before; he had become the Lord of Mexico and now was making heroic efforts to defeat Cortés for good. Cortés executed him in 1524.
3. A city west of Tenochtitlán.
4. Díaz has just told how, with Tenochtitlán in the

hands of the Spanish, Cortés assured the captured Guatemoc that the latter would continue to rule over Mexico.
5. A Spanish sea captain responsible for the capture of Guatemoc.
6. A city north of Tenochtitlán.

It rained and thundered that evening, and the lightning flashed, and up to midnight heavier rain fell than usual. After Guatemoc's capture all we soldiers became as deaf as if all the bells in a belfry had been ringing and had then suddenly stopped. I say this because during the whole ninety-three days[7] of our siege of the capital, Mexican captains were yelling and shouting night and day, mustering the bands of warriors who were to fight on the causeway, and calling to the men in the canoes who were to attack the launches and struggle with us on the bridges and build barricades, or to those who were driving in piles, and deepening and widening the channels and bridges, and building breastworks, or to those who were making javelins and arrows, or to the women shaping rounded stones for their slings. Then there was the unceasing sound of their accursed drums and trumpets, and their melancholy kettledrums in the shrines and on their temple towers. Both day and night the din was so great that we could hardly hear one another speak. But after Guatemoc's capture, all the shouting and the other noises ceased, which is why I have made the comparison with a belfry.

Guatemoc was very delicate, both in body and features. His face was long but cheerful, and when his eyes dwelt on you they seemed more grave than gentle, and did not waver. He was twenty-six, and his complexion was rather lighter than the brown of most Indians. They said he was a nephew of Montezuma, the son of one of his sisters; and he was married to one of Montezuma's daughters, a young and beautiful woman.

*   *   *

Now to speak of the dead bodies and heads that were in the houses where Guatemoc had taken refuge. I solemnly swear that all the houses and stockades in the lake were full of heads and corpses. I do not know how to describe it but it was the same in the streets and courts of Tlatelolco. We could not walk without treading on the bodies and heads of dead Indians. I have read about the destruction of Jerusalem, but I do not think the mortality was greater there than here in Mexico, where most of the warriors who had crowded in from all the provinces and subject towns had died. As I have said, the dry land and the stockades were piled with corpses. Indeed, the stench was so bad that no one could endure it, and for that reason each of us captains returned to his camp after Guatemoc's capture; even Cortés was ill from the odors which assailed his nostrils and from headache during those days in Tlatelolco.

The soldiers in the launches came off best and gained most spoil, because they were able to go to the houses in certain quarters of the lake where they knew there was cloth, gold, and treasure. They also searched the reed-beds in which the Mexicans had hidden their property when we were assaulting some quarter or group of houses. Under cover of chasing the canoes that were bringing in food and water, they would sometimes capture some chieftains fleeing to the mainland to take refuge in the towns of their neighbors the Otomis,[8] and would rob them of everything they had. We soldiers, on the other hand, who were fighting on the causeways and on land, gained no profit, but plenty of arrows and lance-thrusts and wounds from darts and stones. For when we captured houses, the inhabitants had already carried off any property they possessed, since we could not go through the water without first blocking the gaps and bridges. Therefore, as I said when speaking of Cortés' search for sailors to

---

7. An exaggerated figure.
8. One of the constituent peoples of Tlaxcala, neighbors, but not allies, of the Aztecs.

go in the launches, they were better off than we who fought on land. This was clearly proved when Cortés demanded Montezuma's treasure from Guatemoc and his captains. They told him that the men in the launches had stolen most of it.

As there was such a stench in the city, Guatemoc asked Cortés' permission for all the Mexican forces who remained there to go out to the neighboring towns, and they were promptly told to do so. For three whole days and nights they never ceased streaming out, and all three causeways were crowded with men, women, and children so thin, sallow, dirty, and stinking that it was pitiful to see them. Once the city was free from them Cortés went out to inspect it. We found the houses full of corpses, and some poor Mexicans still in them who could not move away. Their excretions were the sort of filth that thin swine pass which have been fed on nothing but grass. The city looked as if it had been plowed up. The roots of any edible greenery had been dug out, boiled, and eaten, and they had even cooked the bark of some of the trees. There was no fresh water to be found; all of it was brackish. I must also remark that the Mexicans did not eat the flesh of their own people, only that of our men and our Tlascalan allies whom they had captured. There had been no live births for a long time, because they had suffered so much from hunger and thirst and continual fighting.

Cortés ordered a banquet to be held in Coyoacan to celebrate the capture of the city, and got plenty of wine for the purpose from a ship that had just come from Spain to Villa Rica, also some pigs that had been brought to him from Cuba. He invited all of us captains and soldiers whom he thought worthy of consideration, from all three camps. But when we came to the banquet there were not enough seats or tables for even a third of the invited guests. Consequently there was much disorder. So many discreditable things occurred, indeed, that it would have been better if the banquet had never been held.

Now that our daily and nightly battles with the Mexicans are far away in the past, for which I give great thanks to God who delivered me from them, there is one thing that I wish to relate, which happened to me after seeing the death by sacrifice of the sixty-two soldiers who were carried off alive. What I am going to say may seem to some to arise from my lack of any great inclination for battle. But, on the contrary, anyone will see on reflection that it was due rather to the excessive daring with which I had to risk my life in the thickest of the fighting. For great courage was at that time required of a soldier. I must say that when I saw my comrades dragged up each day to the altar, and their chests struck open and their palpitating hearts drawn out, and when I saw the arms and legs of these sixty-two men cut off and eaten, I feared that one day or another they would do the same to me. Twice already they had laid hands on me to drag me off, but it pleased God that I should escape from their clutches. When I remembered their hideous deaths, and the proverb that the little pitcher goes many times to the fountain, and so on, I came to fear death more than ever in the past. Before I went into battle, a sort of horror and gloom would seize my heart, and I would make water once or twice and commend myself to God and His blessed Mother. It was always like this before battle, but my fear quickly left me.

It must seem very strange to my readers that I should have suffered from this unaccustomed terror. For I had taken part in many battles, from the time when I made the voyage of discovery with Francisco Hernández de Córdoba till the defeat of our army on the causeway under Alvarado. But up to that time when I saw the cruel deaths inflicted on our comrades before our very eyes, I had never felt such fear as I did in these last battles. Let those experienced in soldiering, who have been at times in great peril of death, say whether my fear is to be attributed to faint-heartedness or to excessive valor. For, as I have said, my own opinion is that having to thrust myself when fighting into such dangerous positions, I was bound to fear death more at that time than at others. Besides, I was not always in good health. I was many times severely wounded, and for this reason was not able to go on all the expeditions. Still, the hardships and risks of death to which I was personally exposed were not insignificant, either before the capture of Mexico or afterward.

The first orders Cortés gave to Guatemoc were that the conduits from Chapultepec[9] should be repaired and restored to their former condition, so that the water could flow again into the city; that the streets should be cleared of the bodies and heads of the dead, which should be buried, so that the city should be left clean and free from any stench; that all bridges and causeways should be thoroughly restored to their former condition, and the palaces and houses rebuilt so as to be fit for habitation within two months. He marked out the parts in which the Indians were to settle, and those which were to be left clear for us.

Guatemoc and his captains complained to Cortés that many of our men had carried off the daughters and wives of chieftains, and begged him as a favor that they should be sent back. Cortés answered that it would be difficult to take them from their present masters, but they might seek them out and bring them before him, and he would see whether they had become Christians or preferred to go home with their fathers and husbands, in which case he would order them to be given up. So he gave the Mexicans permission to search in all three camps, and issued an order that any soldier who had an Indian woman should surrender her at once if she of her own free will wished to return home. Many chieftains searched from house to house and persevered until they found them. But there were many women who did not wish to go with their fathers or mothers or husbands, but preferred to remain with the soldiers with whom they were living. Some hid themselves, others said they did not wish to return to idolatry, and yet others were already pregnant. So they did not bring back more than three, who by Cortés' express command were handed over to them.

Everyone was agreed that all the gold and silver and jewels in Mexico should be collected together. But this seems to have amounted to very little. For there was a report that Guatemoc had thrown all the rest into the lake four days before we captured him, and that the Tlascalans and the people of Huexotzingo and Cholula[1] and all the rest of our allies who had taken part in the war, also the *Teules* themselves who went about in the launches, had stolen their share. The officers of the Royal Treasury publicly proclaimed therefore that Guatemoc had hidden the treasure, and that Cortés was delighted since he would not have to give it up but could keep it all for himself. For this reason these officers decided to torture Guatemoc and his cousin the lord of Tacuba, who was his great favorite. Cortés and some of the rest of us were very much

9. A town on the site of a fine spring southwest of Mexico City. Water flowed from it via an aqueduct to the capital.

1. Independent states to the east of Mexico City, near Tlaxcala.

distressed that they should torture a prince like Guatemoc for greed of gold. Thorough inquiries about the treasure had been made, and all Guatemoc's stewards had said that there was no more than the king's officials already had, which amounted to three hundred and eighty thousand gold pesos, and had been melted and cast into bars, and mulcted of the royal fifth and another fifth for Cortés. On finding that the sum was so little, Cortés' enemies among the Conquistadors, and Narváez' men who distrusted him, told the treasurer Julián de Alderete that they suspected him of opposing the arrest and torture of Guatemoc and his captains only because he wanted to keep the gold for himself. So, to avoid making any accusations against Cortés, who could not prevent their action, they tortured Guatemoc and the lord of Tacuba by burning their feet with oil, and extorted the confession that four days before they had thrown the gold into the lake, together with the cannon and muskets they had captured from us when they drove us out of Mexico. The place Guatemoc indicated was the palace in which he had lived, where there was a large pond, from which we fished up a great golden sun like the one that Montezuma had given us, and many jewels and articles of small value which belonged to Guatemoc himself. The lord of Tacuba said that in his house at Tacuba, about twelve miles away, he had some gold objects, and that if we would take him there he would tell us where they were buried and give them to us. Pedro de Alvarado and six soldiers, myself among them, took him there. But when we arrived he said he had only told us this story in the hopes of dying on the road, and invited us to kill him, for he possessed neither gold nor jewels. So we returned empty-handed. The truth is that Montezuma's treasure-chamber, of which Guatemoc took possession at his death, did not contain many jewels or golden ornaments, because all the best had been extracted to form the magnificent offering that we had sent to His Majesty, which was worth twice as much as the fifth deducted for him and Cortés' own fifth as well. This we sent to the Emperor by Alonso de Avila, who had just returned from the island of Santo Domingo.

We captains and soldiers were all somewhat sad when we saw how little gold there was and how poor and mean our shares would be. The Mercedarian friar,[2] Pedro de Alvarado, Cristóbal de Olid, and other captains told Cortés that since there was so little gold, the entire share that would fall to us ought to be divided among those who were maimed and lame and blind, or had lost an eye or their hearing, and others who were crippled or had pains in their stomachs, or had been burnt by the powder, or were suffering from pains in their sides. They said that it was only right that it should all be given to them, and that the rest of us who were more or less sound ought to approve. After due consideration they repeated this to Cortés, believing that he would increase our shares, for there was a strong suspicion that he had hidden all the gold away and ordered Guatemoc to say he had none.

Cortés replied that he would see we came out all right, and would take measures to that effect. As we were all anxious to see what our share would be, we were in a hurry for the accounts to be issued. After making the calculation, they told us a horseman would receive eighty pesos, and a crossbowman, musketeer, or shield-bearer fifty or sixty—I do not remember which—and when we heard this figure not a single soldier was willing to accept his share.

While Cortés was at Coyoacan, he lodged in a palace with whitewashed

2. The Mercedarian order, or the Order of Our Lady of Mercies, was founded in Barcelona early in the 13th century.

walls on which it was easy to write with charcoal and ink; and every morning malicious remarks appeared, some in verse and some in prose, in the manner of lampoons. One said the sun, moon, and stars, and earth and sea followed their courses, and if they ever deviated from the plane for which they were created, soon reverted to their original place. So it would be with Cortés' ambition for command. He would soon return to his original condition. Another said that he had dealt us a worse defeat than he had given to Mexico, and that we ought to call ourselves not the victors of New Spain but the victims of Hernán Cortés. Another said he had not been content with a general's share but had taken a king's, not counting other profits; and yet another: "My soul is very sad and will be till that day when Cortés gives us back the gold he's hidden away." It was also remarked that Diego Velázquez had spent his whole fortune and discovered all the northern coast as far as Panuco, and then Cortés had come to enjoy the benefit and rebelliously taken both the land and the treasure. And other words were written up too, unfit to record in this story.

When Cortés came out of his quarters of a morning he would read these lampoons. Their style was elegant, the verses well rhymed, and each couplet not only had point but ended with a sharp reproof that was not so naive as I may have suggested. As Cortés himself was something of a poet, he prided himself on composing answers, which tended to praise his own great deeds and belittle those of Diego Velázquez, Grijalva, and Francisco Hernández de Córdoba. In fact, he too wrote some good verses which were much to the point. But the couplets and sentences they scrawled up became every day more scurrilous, until in the end Cortes wrote: "A blank wall is a fool's writing paper." And next morning someone added: "A wise man's too, who knows the truth, as His Majesty will do very soon!" Knowing who was responsible for this (a certain Tirado, a friend of Diego Velázquez and some others who wished to make their defiance clear) Cortés flew into a rage and publicly proclaimed that they must write up no more libels or he would punish the shameless villains.

Many of us were in debt to one another. Some owed fifty or sixty pesos for crossbows, and others fifty for a sword. Everything we had bought was equally dear. A certain surgeon called Maestre Juan, who tended some bad wounds, charged excessive prices for his cures, and so did a sort of quack by the name of Murcia, who was an apothecary and barber and also treated wounds, and there were thirty other tricks and swindles for which payment was demanded out of our shares. The remedy that Cortés provided was to appoint two trust-worthy persons who knew the prices of goods and could value anything that we had bought on credit. An order went out that whatever price was placed on our purchases or the surgeons' cures must be accepted, and that if we had no money, our creditors must wait two years for payment. And I must say that in the end, in compensation for slaves sold by auction, the remaining gold all fell to the King's officials.

When Cortés found that many of the soldiers were still insolently demanding larger shares, and saying that he had stolen everything for himself, and begging him to lend them money, he decided to free himself from their clutches and send them to settle in any province that seemed to him suitable.

* * *

When the news spread through all these distant provinces that Mexico was destroyed their *Caciques* and lords could not believe it. However, they sent chieftains to congratulate Cortés on his victories and yield themselves as vassals to His Majesty, and to see if the city of Mexico, which they had so dreaded, was really razed to the ground. They all carried great presents of gold to Cortés, and even brought their small children to show them Mexico, pointing it out to them in much the same way that we would say: "Here stood Troy."

But let us leave this topic for another that richly deserves explanation. Many interested readers have asked me why the true Conquistadors who won New Spain and the great and strong city of Mexico did not stay to settle, but went on to other provinces. I think this question is justified, and I will give them an answer. Learning from Montezuma's account-books the names of the places which sent him tributes of gold, and where the mines and chocolate and cotton-cloths were to be found, we decided to go to these places; and our resolve was strengthened when we saw so eminent a captain and so close a friend of Cortés as Gonzalo de Sandoval leaving Mexico, and when we realized that there were no gold or mines or cotton in the towns around Mexico, only a lot of maize and the *maguey*[3] plantations from which they obtained their wine. For this reason we thought of it as a poor land, and went off to colonize other provinces. But we were thoroughly deceived.

I remember that when I went to ask Cortés for leave to go with Sandoval he said to me: "On my conscience, Señor Bernal Díaz del Castillo, you are making a mistake. I wish you would stay here with me. But as you want to go with your friend Sandoval, go and good luck to you. I shall always consider your wishes, but I know very well that you will be sorry you left."

1568?   1632

3. An agave plant used by the Aztecs as the source of *pulque*, a fermented drink that in turn is the source of mescal.

ÁLVAR NÚÑEZ CABEZA DE VACA
c. 1490–1558

Among those who may have witnessed the disgrace of Columbus as he passed in chains through Cádiz in 1498 was a boy from the nearby village of Jerez de la Frontera. Álvar Núñez Cabeza de Vaca was the son of the village alderman, grandson of the conqueror of the Guanche people of Grand Canary Island, and a descendent on his mother's side from a hero of the wars against the Moors who was given the family name "Cabeza de Vaca" (or "cow's head") when he used a cow's skull to mark a strategic route through an unguarded mountain pass. Mindful of this family heritage, as a young man Cabeza de Vaca went off to the wars in Italy (he later was to say that the American Indians of Texas were as shrewd in battle "as if they had been reared in Italy in continual feuds") before coming home to serve as a steward to the duke of Medina Sidonia in campaigns against Spain's *communero* rebels and a French invasion force in the Spanish province of Navarre. His next exploit took him farther afield. In 1527, a few years after the Conquest of Mexico by Hernán Cortés set all Spain dreaming of golden realms in the New World, Cabeza de Vaca sailed on Pánfilo de Narváez's Florida expedition as *aquacil mayor* (provost marshal) and treasurer—an important royal appointee charged with ensuring that the Crown received its share of any riches gathered by Narváez.

The expedition endured many disasters. The first problem was Narváez himself, an impetuous, self-centered man and a bad leader. In 1520 Narváez had led an army from Cuba to the coast of Mexico with orders to arrest Cortés; instead Cortés convinced the army to switch sides, defeated Narváez, and jailed him for three years. Narvaéz, who lost an eye in the fray, finally had a chance to see the glories and the gold of Mexico's central valley shortly before Cortés released him in 1523, whereupon he returned to Spain to complain of Cortés and seek approval for a great conquest of his own. Once he had royal permission to sail for Florida in 1527, he led his six hundred men to Hispaniola, where a quarter of them deserted, and then to Cuba, where two of the six ships were lost in a hurricane. Ten months after leaving Spain the expedition landed in the vicinity of Sarasota Bay, on Florida's west coast. Against Cabeza de Vaca's advice, Narváez sent the ships farther along the shore in search of a rumored port where his army might rejoin them, but the ships were never seen again.

Now began a series of mistakes and follies on Narváez's part that resulted in the loss of all but four of his company. In a formal ceremony, Narváez took possession of Florida while the inhabitants of Sarasota Bay (probably Calusa Indians) made "many signs and threats [that] left little doubt that they were bidding us to go." Soon the signs changed to arrows, and dwarfed by the great expanse of Florida, the expedition was reduced to eating its horses and trying to escape many groups of Florida natives, from the Timucuan of the Suwannee River area to the Apalachees of the Panhandle. Building clumsy "barges" out of any material at hand, the Spaniards retreated to the sea, hoping to go west to Panuco (modern Tampico, Mexico), which they took to be close, but which in fact was almost two thousand miles away. Narváez took the best oarsmen in his own barge and left the other barges behind him as they neared Mobile Bay; when he pulled away from the others he told them, with false magnanimity, that "it was no longer a time when one should command another"—that is, every man for himself! With that, Narváez and his crew disappeared, apparently lost at sea. It was a fitting last act for this commander of the ill-fated undertaking.

The other rafts passed the mouth of what must have been the Mississippi, and finally wrecked on Galveston Island, now Texas, in November 1528. Here began a further whittling away of the survivors and a time of extraordinary struggles for Cabeza de Vaca and the three men who survived with him: the Spaniards Andrés Dorantes and Alonso del Castillo Maldonado, and Dorantes's black slave, Estevánico, a native of the Moroccan town of Azemmor. The itinerary of Cabeza de Vaca's North American odyssey was long and involved. Alone or with drifting groups of other survivors, he spent his first two years on the Texas coast as a prisoner and slave of the Han and Capoque clans of the Karankawa Indians and then gradually progressed north and west, gaining status and power among the Caddos, Atakapas, Coahuiltecans, and other natives from his activities as a merchant and especially his skill as a healer. By 1535, he reached present-day New Mexico, where he encountered the Jumanos and Conchos, then headed southwest into Mexico as the leader of a vast crowd of Pimas and Opatas who, revering him, followed him from village to village.

The heady mood of the journey dissipated the following March, however, when he and the other survivors came across a party of Spaniards under the slave-hunter Diego de Alcaraz in western Mexico. Seeing the terror of his American Indian escorts at these Spaniards, Cabeza de Vaca felt genuine sympathy for the people of the region, who were being hunted down by what he acerbically called "Christian slavers." His closeness to the Pimas and Opatas and his obvious criticism of Alcaraz led to a falling-out with his countrymen, who arrested him, sent him south, and seized as slaves the six hundred natives in his company. From Mexico City, where he agitated against the cruel (and strictly illegal) activities of the likes of Alcaraz, Cabeza de Vaca went to Spain in 1537, intent on making similar representations to Emperor Charles V himself and hopeful that he would be allowed to lead an expedition back to the New World—one that would treat the Native Americans with justice and humanity.

In 1540 he secured appointment as governor of the South American region of Río de la Plata, but his attempt to enact an enlightened American Indian policy there met stiff resistance from those who benefited from more brutal ones; they removed him from office and sent him in chains back to Spain in 1545. After long delays in settling the dispute, in 1551 he was exiled to modern Algeria and forbidden to return to America.

During the three years he spent in Spain before his departure for Río de la Plata in 1540, Cabeza de Vaca completed his first narrative of the Narváez expedition. It was published in Spain in 1542; a corrected and expanded version that includes the story of his South American experience appeared in 1555. Addressed to Charles V, the 1542 account sought to justify his conclusions regarding Spanish policy and behavior in America as well as to argue for renewed explorations and settlement in the regions he had traversed (several later Spanish expeditions, including those of Coronado and De Soto, clearly drew on Cabeza de Vaca's arguments and knowledge). More important, however, *The Relation of Álvar Núñez Cabeza de Vaca* sought to recount (with remarkable understatement) his sufferings and many brushes with death and to explore his complex feelings regarding the Native Americans and his own countrymen's dealings with them.

From The Relation of Álvar Núñez Cabeza de Vaca[1]

[Dedication]

Sacred Caesarian Catholic Majesty:

Among all the princes who have reigned, I know of none who has enjoyed the universal esteem of Your Majesty[2] at this day, when strangers vie in approbation with those motivated by religion and loyalty.

Although everyone wants what advantage may be gained from ambition and action, we see everywhere great inequalities of fortune, brought about not by conduct but by accident, and not through anybody's fault but as the will of God. Thus the deeds of one far exceed his expectation, while another can show no higher proof of purpose than his fruitless effort, and even the effort may go unnoticed.

I can say for myself that I undertook the march abroad, on royal authorization, with a firm trust that my service would be as evident and distinguished as my ancestors', and that I would not need to speak to be counted among those Your Majesty honors for diligence and fidelity in affairs of state. But my counsel and constancy availed nothing toward those objectives we set out to gain, in your interests, for our sins. In fact, no other of the many armed expeditions into those parts has found itself in such dire straits as ours, or come to so futile and fatal a conclusion.

My only remaining duty is to transmit what I saw and heard in the nine years I wandered lost and miserable over many remote lands. I hope in some measure to convey to Your Majesty not merely a report of positions and distances, flora and fauna, but of the customs of the numerous, barbarous people

---

1. The text is based on *Adventures in the Unknown Interior of America*, edited and translated by Cyclone Covey (1961).

2. Emperor Charles V (1500–1558), grandson and successor of Ferdinand and Isabella.

I talked with and dwelt among, as well as any other matters I could hear of or observe. My hope of going out from among those nations was always small; nevertheless, I made a point of remembering all the particulars, so that should God our Lord eventually please to bring me where I am now, I might testify to my exertion in the royal behalf.

Since this narrative, in my opinion, is of no trivial value for those who go in your name to subdue those countries and bring them to a knowledge of the true faith and true Lord and bring them under the imperial dominion, I have written very exactly. Novel or, for some persons, difficult to believe though the things narrated may be, I assure you they can be accepted without hesitation as strictly factual. Better than to exaggerate, I have minimized all things; it is enough to say that the relation is offered Your Majesty for truth.

I beg that it may be received as homage, since it is the most one could bring who returned thence naked.

* * *

[The Malhado Way of Life]

The people[3] we came to know there are tall and well-built. Their only weapons are bows and arrows, which they use with great dexterity. The men bore through one of their nipples, some both, and insert a joint of cane two and a half palms long by two fingers thick. They also bore their lower lip and wear a piece of cane in it half a finger in diameter.

Their women toil incessantly.

From October to the end of February every year, which is the season these Indians live on the island, they subsist on the roots I have mentioned,[4] which the women get from under water in November and December. Only in these two months, too, do they take fish in their cane weirs. When the fish is consumed, the roots furnish the one staple. At the end of February the islanders go into other parts to seek sustenance, for then the root is beginning to grow and is not edible.

These people love their offspring more than any in the world and treat them very mildly.

If a son dies, the whole village joins the parents and kindred in weeping. The parents set off the wails each day before dawn, again at noon, and at sunset, for one year. The funeral rites occur when the year of mourning is up. Following these rites, the survivors wash off the smoke stain of the ceremony in a symbolic purgation. All the dead are lamented this way except the aged, who merit no regrets. The dead are buried, except medicine-men, who are cremated. Everybody in the village dances and makes merry while the pyre of a medicine-man kindles, and until his bones become powder. A year later, when his rites are celebrated, the entire village again participating, this powder is presented in water for the relatives to drink.

Each man has an acknowledged wife, except the medicine-men, who may have two or three wives apiece. The several wives live together in perfect amity.

When a daughter marries, she must take everything her husband kills in

3. The Capoques and Hans of coastal Texas, near today's Galveston Island, which Cabeza de Vaca calls *Malhado*, or the Island of Doom.

4. I.e., "certain roots which taste like nuts, mostly grubbed from [under] the water with great labor."

hunting or catches in fishing to the house of her father, without daring to eat or to withhold any part of it, and the husband gets provided by female carrier from his father-in-law's house. Neither the bride's father nor mother may enter the son-in-law's house after the marriage, nor he theirs; and this holds for the children of the respective couples. If a man and his in-laws should chance to be walking so they would meet, they turn silently aside from each other and go a crossbow-shot out of their way, averting their glance to the ground. The woman, however, is free to fraternize with the parents and relatives of her husband. These marriage customs prevail for more than fifty leagues inland from the island.

At a house where a son or brother may die, no one goes out for food for three months, the neighbors and other relatives providing what is eaten. Because of this custom, which the Indians literally would not break to save their lives, great hunger reigned in most houses while we resided there, it being a time of repeated deaths. Those who sought food worked hard, but they could get little in that severe season. That is why Indians who kept me left the island by canoe for oyster bays on the main.

Three months out of every year they eat nothing but oysters and drink very bad water. Wood is scarce; mosquitoes, plentiful. The houses are made of mats; their floors consist of masses of oyster shells. The natives sleep on these shells—in animal skins, those who happen to own such.

Many a time I would have to go three days without eating, as would the natives. I thought it impossible that life could be so prolonged in such protracted hunger; though afterwards I found myself in yet greater want, as shall be seen.

The Indians who had Alonso del Castillo, Andrés Dorantes, and the others of their barge who remained alive, spoke a different dialect and claimed a different descent from these I lived among. They frequented the opposite shore of the main to eat oysters, staying till the first of April, then returning.

The distance to the main is two leagues at the widest part of the channel. The island itself, which supports the two tribes commodiously, is half a league wide by five long.

The inhabitants of all these parts go naked, except that the women cover some part of their persons with a wool that grows on trees,[5] and damsels dress in deerskin.

The people are generous to each other with what little they have. There is no chief. All belonging to the same lineage keep together. They speak two languages: Capoque and Han.

They have a strange custom when acquaintances meet or occasionally visit, of weeping for half an hour before they speak. This over, the one who is visited rises and gives his visitor all he has. The latter accepts it and, after a while, carries it away, often without a word. They have other strange customs, but I have told the principal and most remarkable of them.

In April [1529] we went to the seashore and ate blackberries all month, a time of [dance ceremonies] and *fiestas* among the Indians.

---

5. I.e., Spanish moss.

* * *

[Our Life among the Avavares and Arbadaos]

All the Indians of this region[6] are ignorant of time, either by the sun or moon; nor do they reckon by the month or year. They understand the seasons in terms of the ripening of fruits, the dying of fish, and the position of stars, in which dating they are adept.

The Avavares always treated us well. We lived as free agents, dug our own food, and lugged our loads of wood and water. The houses and our diet were like those of the nation we had just come from, but the Avavares suffer yet greater want, having no corn, acorns, or pecans. We always went naked like them and covered ourselves at night with deerskins.

Six of the eight months we dwelled with these people we endured acute hunger; for fish are not found where they are either. At the end of the eight months, when the prickly pears were just beginning to ripen again [mid-June 1535], I traveled with the Negro[7]—unknown to our hosts—to others a day's journey farther on: the Maliacones.[8] When three days had passed, I sent Estevánico to fetch Castillo and Dorantes.

When they got there, the four of us set out with the Maliacones, who were going to find the small fruit of certain trees which they subsist on for ten or twelve days while the prickly pears are maturing. They joined another tribe, the Arbadaos, who astonished us by their weak, emaciated, swollen condition.

We told the Maliacones with whom we had come that we wanted to stop with these Arbadaos. The Maliacones despondently returned the way they came, leaving us alone in the brushland near the Arbadao houses. The observing Arbadaos talked among themselves and came up to us in a body. Four of them took each of us by the hand and led us to their dwellings.

Among them we underwent fiercer hunger than among the Avavares. We ate not more than two handfuls of prickly pears a day, and they were still so green and milky they burned our mouths. In our lack of water, eating brought great thirst. At nearly the end of our endurance we bought two dogs for some nets, with other things, and a skin I used for cover.

I have already said that we went naked through all this country; not being accustomed to going so, we shed our skins twice a year like snakes. The sun and air raised great, painful sores on our chests and shoulders, and our heavy loads caused the cords to cut our arms. The region is so broken and so overgrown that often, when we gathered wood, blood flowed from us in many places where the thorns and shrubs tore our flesh. At times, when my turn came to get wood and I had collected it at heavy cost in blood, I could neither drag nor bear it out. My only solace in these labors was to think of the sufferings of our Redeemer, Jesus Christ, and the blood He shed for me. How much worse must have been his torment from the thorns than mine here!

I bartered with these Indians in combs I made for them and in bows, arrows, and nets. We made mats, which are what their houses consist of and for which they feel a keen necessity. Although they know how to make them, they prefer to devote their full time to finding food; when they do not, they get too pinched with hunger.

6. At this point in his story, having escaped from his captivity among the Capoques and Hans, Cabeza de Vaca is among the Avavares and Arbadaos in inland Texas.

7. Estevánico, a Moorish slave from the west coast of Morocco.

8. Neighbors of the Avavares and Arbadaos.

Some days the Indians would set me to scraping and softening skins. These were my days of greatest prosperity in that place. I would scrape thoroughly enough to sustain myself two or three days on the scraps. When it happened that these or any people we had left behind gave us a piece of meat, we ate it raw. Had we put it to roast, the first native who came along would have filched it. Not only did we think it better not to risk this, we were in such a condition that roasted meat would have given us pain. We could digest it more easily raw.

Such was our life there, where we earned our meager subsistence by trade in items which were the work of our own hands.

[Pushing On]

Eating the dogs seemed to give us strength enough to go forward; so commending ourselves to the guidance of God our Lord, we took leave of our hosts, who pointed out the way to others nearby who spoke their language.

Rain caught us. We traveled the day in the wet and got lost. At last, we made for an extensive scrub wood stretch, where we stopped and pulled prickly pear pads, which we cooked overnight in a hot oven we made. By morning they were ready.

After eating, we put ourselves again in the hands of God and set forth. We located the path we had lost and, after passing another scrub wood stretch, saw houses. Two women who were walking in the "forest" with some boys fled deep into it in fright to call their men, when they noticed us heading for the houses. The men arrived and hid behind trees to look at us. We called to them, and they came up very timidly. After some conversation, they told us their food was very scarce and that many houses of their people stood close by, to which they would conduct us.

At nightfall we came to a village of fifty dwellings. The residents looked at us in astonishment and fear. When they grew somewhat accustomed to our appearance, they felt our faces and bodies and then their own, comparing.

We stayed in that place overnight. In the morning the Indians brought us their sick, beseeching our blessing. They shared with us what they had to eat— prickly pear pads and the green fruit roasted. Because they did this with kindness and good will, gladly foregoing food to give us some, we tarried here several days.

Other Indians came from beyond in that interval and, when they were about to depart, we told our hosts we wanted to go with them. Our hosts felt quite uneasy at this and pressed us warmly to stay. In the midst of their weeping we left them.

[Customs of That Region]

From the Island of Doom to this land, all the Indians we saw have the custom of not sleeping with their wives from the time they are discovered pregnant to two years after giving birth. Children are suckled until they are twelve, when they are old enough to find their own support. We asked why they thus prolonged the nursing period, and they said that the poverty of the land frequently meant—as we witnessed—going two or three days without eating, sometimes four; if children were not allowed to suckle in seasons of scarcity, those who did not famish would be weaklings.

Anyone who chances to fall sick on a foraging trip and cannot keep up with the rest is left to die, unless he be a son or brother; him they will help, even to carrying on their back.

It is common among them all to leave their wives when there is disagreement, and directly reconnect with whomever they please. This is the course of men who are childless. Those who have children never abandon their wives.

When Indian men get into an argument in their villages, they fist-fight until exhausted, then separate. Sometimes the women will go between and part them, but men never interfere. No matter what the disaffection, they do not resort to bows and arrows. After a fight, the disputants take their houses (and families) and go live apart from each other in the scrub wood until they have cooled off; then they return and from that moment are friends as if nothing had happened. No intermediary is needed to mend their friendship.

In case the quarrelers are single men, they repair to some neighboring people (instead of the scrub wood), who, even if enemies, welcome them warmly and give so largely of what they have that when the quarrelers' animosity subsides, they return to their home village rich.

*   *   *

[The Long Swing-Around]

After the two days of indecision,[9] we concluded that our destiny lay toward the sunset and so took the trail north only as far as we had to in order to reach the westward one, and then swung down until eventually we came out at the South Sea. The seventeen *jornadas*[1] of hunger the Cow People warned us of, and which proved to be just as bad as they said, could not deter us.

During this desert ascent by the river, the Indians gave us many cowhides, but we passed up their *chacan*[2] in favor of about a handful of deep tallow a day, which we had long since learned to save for such times of famine.

After seventeen *jornadas* we forded the very wide, chest-deep, southern flowing river and traveled another seventeen.

One day as the sun went down out on the plains between massive mountains, we came upon people who for a third of the year eat nothing but powdered straw and, that being the season we passed through, we had to eat it ourselves until at last, at the end of the seventeen *jornadas*, we got to the people of permanent houses who had plenty of corn.[3]

They gave us a great quantity of corn, cornmeal, calabashes, beans, and cotton blankets, all of which we loaded onto the guides who had led us here, and they went back the happiest people on earth. We gave many thanks to God our Lord for bringing us to this land of abundance.

Some of the houses here are made of earth, the rest of cane mats. We marched more than a hundred leagues through continuously inhabited country of such domiciles, where corn and beans remained plentiful. The people gave us innumerable deerhide and cotton blankets, the latter better than those

9. Tarrying in the Río Grande valley among the Cow People (so-called by the Spaniards because they hunted buffalo), Cabeza de Vaca's party was reluctant to leave the hospitality and easy living experienced there.
1. Roughly the distance covered in a day's journey, or between stops on a longer trip. The "seventeen *jorna-*

das of hunger" may refer to the infamous "Journey of Death," the ninety-mile stretch separating the Cow People from the Pueblo Indians of New Mexico.
2. Juniper berries, much used by Suma Indians.
3. These house-dwelling Opata Indians lived in the region of Sonora, in northwestern Mexico.

of New Spain, beads made of coral from the South Sea, fine turquoises from the north—in fact, everything they had, including a special gift to me of five emerald arrowheads such as they use in their singing and dancing. These looked quite valuable. I asked where they came from. They said from lofty mountains to the north, where there were towns of great population and great houses, and that the arrowheads had been purchased with feather bushes and parrot plumes.

Among this people, women are better treated than in any part of the Indies we had come through. They wear knee-length cotton shirts and, over them, half-sleeved skirts of scraped deerskin that reach to the ground and that are laced together in front with leather strips. The women soap this outer garment with a certain root which cleanses well and keeps the deerskin becoming. And they wear shoes.

All the people, sick and well, came to us in an attitude of urgency to be touched and blessed; only with great labor did we get through them all. Speaking of labor, there were many times that women accompanying us gave birth to babies and, as soon as they were born, the mothers would bring them to us for our touch and blessing.

These Indians ever stayed with us until they safely delivered us to others. They were all convinced that we came from Heaven. (Anything that is new to them or beyond their comprehension is explained as coming from Heaven.) We Christians traveled all day without food, eating only at night—and then so little as to astonish our escort. We never felt tired, being so inured to hardship, which increased our enormous influence over them. To maintain this authority the better, we seldom talked with them directly, but made the Negro [Estevánico] our intermediary. He was constantly in conversation, finding out about routes, towns, and other matters we wished to know.

We passed from one strange tongue to another, but God our Lord always enabled each new people to understand us and we them. You would have thought, from the questions and answers in signs, that they spoke our language and we theirs. We did know six Indian languages, but could not always avail ourselves of them; there are a thousand dialectical differences.

Through all these nations, the people who were at war quickly made up so they could come meet us with everything they possessed. Thus we left all the land in peace. And we taught all the people by signs, which they understood, that in Heaven was a Man we called God, who had created the heavens and the earth; that all good came from Him and that we worshiped and obeyed Him and called him our Lord; and that if they would do the same, all would be well with them. They apprehended so readily that, if we had had enough command of their language to make ourselves perfectly understood, we would have left them all Christians.

We told them what we could and, from then on, at sunrise, they would raise their arms to the sky with a glad cry, then run their hands down the length of their bodies. They repeated this ritual at sunset.

They are a substantial people with a capacity for unlimited development.

[The Town of Hearts]

In the town where the emeralds were presented us, the people gave Dorantes over 600 opened deer hearts, which they always kept in great supply for food.

So we called this place the Town of Hearts. It is the gateway to many provinces on the South Sea, and whoever seeks them without entering here will surely be lost.

The timid, surly Indians of the coast grow no corn; they eat powdered rushes, straw, and fish, which they catch from rafts, having no canoes. The women cover themselves somewhat, with grass and straw.

We think that near the coast, along the line of those permanent towns we came through, must be more than a thousand leagues of settled, productive land, where three crops a year of corn and beans are sown.

Deer in that belt are of three kinds, one of which are as big as yearling steers in Castile.

The houses are of the kind called *bahíos* in the West Indies.

These people get poison from a certain tree which is about the size of our apple trees. All they have to do is pick the fruit and wet the arrow with it or, if there be no fruit, break a twig and the milk will do as well. The tree is so deadly that, if deer or other animals drink where its bruised leaves have been steeped, they will burst.

We stayed in the Town of Hearts three days.

[The Buckle and the Horseshoe Nail]

A few days farther on we came to another town where rain was falling so heavily that we could not cross the swollen river and had to wait fifteen days.

In this time Castillo happened to see an Indian wearing around his neck a little sword-belt buckle with a horseshoe nail stitched to it.

He took the amulet, and we asked the Indian what it was. He said it came from Heaven. But who had brought it? He and the Indians with him said that some bearded men like us had come to that river from Heaven, with horses, lances, and swords, and had lanced two natives.

Casually we inquired what had become of those men. They had gone to sea, said the Indians. They had put their lances into the water, got into the water themselves, and finally were seen moving on top of the water into the sunset.

We gave many thanks to God our Lord. Having almost despaired of finding Christians again, we could hardly restrain our excitement. Yet we anxiously suspected that these men were explorers who had merely made a flying visit on their voyage of discovery. But having at last some exact information to go on, we quickened our pace and, as we went, heard more and more of Christians. We told the natives we were going after those men to order them to stop killing, enslaving, and dispossessing the Indians; which made our friends very glad.

We hastened through a vast territory, which we found vacant, the inhabitants having fled to the mountains in fear of Christians. With heavy hearts we looked out over the lavishly watered, fertile, and beautiful land, now abandoned and burned and the people thin and weak, scattering or hiding in fright. Not having planted, they were reduced to eating roots and bark; and we shared their famine the whole way. Those who did receive us could provide hardly anything. They themselves looked as if they would willingly die. They brought us blankets they had concealed from the other Christians and told us how the latter had come through razing the towns and carrying off half the men and all the women and boys; those who had escaped were wandering about as fugitives. We found the survivors too alarmed to stay anywhere very long, unable or unwilling to till, preferring death to a repetition of their recent horror. While they seemed delighted with our company, we grew apprehensive that the Indians resisting farther on at the frontier would avenge themselves on us.

When we got there, however, they received us with the same awe and respect the others had—even more, which amazed us. Clearly, to bring all these people to Christianity and subjection to Your Imperial Majesty, they must be won by kindness, the only certain way.

They took us to a village on the crest of a range of mountains; it was a difficult ascent. The many people who had taken refuge there from the Christians received us well, giving us all they had: over 2,000 backloads of corn, which we distributed to the distressed, pathetic beings who had guided us to that place.

Next day, we despatched four heralds through the country, according to our custom, to call together all the rest of the Indians at a town three *jornadas* distant. We set out, ourselves, the day after that, with all who had congregated on the mountain top.

All along the way we could see the tracks of the Christians and traces of their camps. We met our messengers at noon. They had been unable to contact any Indians, who roved the woods out of sight, eluding the Christians. The night before, our heralds had spied on the Christians from behind trees and seen them marching many Indians in chains.

This intelligence terrified our escort, some of whom ran to spread the news that the Christians were coming, and many more would have followed if we had not managed to forbid them and to palliate their fright. We had with us Indians from a hundred leagues back whom we could not at this time discharge with the recompense due them.

For further reassurance to our escort, we held up where we were for the night. The following day we slept on the trail at the end of the *jornada*. The day after that, our heralds guided us to the place they had watched the Christians. We got there that afternoon and saw at once they had told the truth. We noted by the stakes the horses had been tied to that the men were mounted.

*　　*　　*

[The First Confrontation]

When we saw for certain that we were drawing near the Christians, we gave thanks to God our Lord for choosing to bring us out of such a melancholy and wretched captivity. The joy we felt can only be conjectured in terms of the time, the suffering, and the peril we had endured in that land.

The evening of the day we reached the recent campsite, I tried hard to get Castillo or Dorantes to hurry on three days, unencumbered, after the Christians who were now circling back into the area we had assured protection. They both reacted negatively, excusing themselves for weariness, though younger and more athletic than I; but they being unwilling, I took the Negro and eleven Indians next morning to track the Christians. We went ten leagues, past three villages where they had slept.

The day after that, I overtook four of them on their horses. They were dumbfounded at the sight of me, strangely undressed and in company with Indians. They just stood staring for a long time, not thinking to hail me or come closer to ask questions.

"Take me to your captain," I at last requested; and we went together half a league to a place where we found their captain, Diego de Alcaraz.

When we had talked awhile, he confessed to me that he was completely undone, having been unable to catch any Indians in a long time; he did not know which way to turn; his men were getting too hungry and exhausted. I told him of Castillo and Dorantes ten leagues away with an escorting multitude. He immediately dispatched three of his horsemen to them, along with fifty of his Indian allies. The Negro went, too, as a guide; I stayed behind.

I asked the Christians to furnish me a certificate of the year, month, and day I arrived here, and the manner of my coming; which they did.[4] From this river to the Christian town, Sant Miguel[5] within the government of the recently created province of New Galicia, is a distance of thirty leagues.

[The Falling-Out with Our Countrymen]

After five days, Andrés Dorantes and Alonso del Castillo arrived with those who had gone for them; and they brought more than 600 natives of the vicinity whom the Indians who had been escorting us drew out of the woods and took to the mounted Christians, who thereupon dismissed their own escort.

When they arrived, Alcaraz begged us to order the villagers of this river out of the woods in the same way to get us food. It would be unnecessary to command them to bring food, if they came at all; for the Indians were always diligent to bring us all they could.

We sent our heralds to call them, and presently there came 600 Indians with all the corn they possessed. They brought it in clay-sealed earthen pots which had been buried. They also brought whatever else they had; but we wished only a meal, so gave the rest to the Christians to divide among themselves.

After this we had a hot argument with them, for they meant to make slaves of the Indians in our train. We got so angry that we went off forgetting the many Turkish-shaped bows, the many pouches, and the five emerald arrowheads, etc., which we thus lost. And to think we had given these Christians a supply of cowhides and other things that our retainers had carried a long distance!

It proved difficult to persuade our escorting Indians to go back to their homes, to feel apprehensive no longer, and to plant their corn. But they did not want to do anything until they had first delivered us into the hands of other Indians, as custom bound them. They feared they would die if they returned without fulfiling this obligation whereas, with us, they said they feared neither Christians nor lances.

This sentiment roused our countrymen's jealousy. Alcaraz bade his interpreter tell the Indians that we were members of his race who had been long lost; that his group were the lords of the land who must be obeyed and served, while we were inconsequential. The Indians paid no attention to this. Conferring among themselves, they replied that the Christians lied: We had come

4. It was probably March 1536.
5. I.e., Culiacán, the northernmost Spanish settle-
ment in Mexico at that time, located in Sinaloa near the mouth of the Gulf of California.

from the sunrise, they from the sunset; we healed the sick, they killed the sound; we came naked and barefoot, they clothed, horsed, and lanced; we coveted nothing but gave whatever we were given, while they robbed whomever they found and bestowed nothing on anyone.

* * *

To the last I could not convince the Indians that we were of the same people as the Christian slavers. Only with the greatest effort were we able to induce them to go back home. We ordered them to fear no more, reestablish their towns, and farm.

Already the countryside had grown rank from neglect. This is, no doubt, the most prolific land in all these Indies. It produces three crops a year; the trees bear a great variety of fruit; and beautiful rivers and brimming springs abound throughout. There are gold- and silver-bearing ores. The people are well disposed, serving such Christians as are their friends with great good will. They are comely, much more so than the Mexicans. This land, in short, lacks nothing to be regarded as blest.

When the Indians took their leave of us they said they would do as we commanded and rebuild their towns, if the Christians let them. And I solemnly swear that if they have not done so it is the fault of the Christians.

After we had dismissed the Indians in peace and thanked them for their toil in our behalf, the Christians subtly sent us on our way in the charge of an *alcalde* named Cebreros, attended by two horsemen.[6] They took us through forests and wastes so we would not communicate with the natives and would neither see nor learn of their crafty scheme afoot. Thus we often misjudge the motives of men; we thought we had effected the Indians' liberty, when the Christians were but poising to pounce.

* * *

ca. 1536–40   1542

6. I.e., they were, in effect, under arrest.

STORIES OF THE BEGINNING OF THE WORLD

Stories about the creation of the world tell people who they are by telling them where they come from. Native American creation stories, although never written down or gathered into a Bible, serve for native cultures in much the same way as the Book of Genesis serves for the Judeo-Christian world: they posit a general cultural outlook and offer perspectives on what life is and how to understand it. All native peoples have stories of the earliest times; anthologized here are three, one from the Iroquois of the Northeast and two from the Pima of the Southwest. These peoples encountered European explorers, missionaries, and colonists very early in the period of contact, and information and conjecture about the Iroquois and the Pima appear in European texts that go back almost four hundred years. But these early records offer only bare sketches of what native people said, sang, chanted, and narrated, and of course, North American Indians did not themselves write down their stories.

It was not until the mid to late nineteenth century that Euro-Americans developed the linguistic skills and cultural understanding necessary to translate and transcribe Native American creation stories in a manner that begins to do justice to them. It was also not until this time that native people collaborated extensively in recording the myths and legends of their people. In the Southwest, the army doctor Washington Matthews began to work on the Navajo Night Chant and Mountain Chant in the 1880s, while Frank Hamilton Cushing, employed by the Bureau of American Ethnology, had installed himself among the Zuni and begun to record their legends in 1879. J. W. Fewkes, after the turn of the century, and J. W. Lloyd, somewhat later, both worked with the Pima Indian known as Thin Leather to record stories of the earliest times. Among the Iroquois, David Cusick, a Tuscarora (the Tuscarora joined the Iroquois Confederacy early in the eighteenth century), had begun to document the legends of his people as early as 1825. He was followed by the distinguished Tuscarora anthropologist J. N. B. Hewitt shortly after the turn of the century.

For all the admirable labors of these Native American and Euro-American people, it is impossible to say with assurance whether one or another of the stories they recorded is more ancient or more authentic, more true to indigenous narrative practice before the arrival of Europeans. And while the stories do change with time and circumstance, because the oral tradition favors continuity, it seems reasonable to turn to later accounts for a window on what came before.

THE IROQUOIS CREATION STORY

The people known as the Iroquois were made up of the Mohawk, Seneca, Oneida, Onondaga, and Cayuga nations. Joined in the early eighteenth century by the Tuscarora of North Carolina, the Five Nations became the Six Nations. The original Five Nations occupied lands that ranged from the area northeast of lakes Ontario and Erie around the St. Lawrence and Ottawa rivers, then south of the lakes, and eastward almost to the Hudson River. These inhabitants of the eastern woodlands spoke Algonquian languages, and it was an unidentified Algonquian word that early French explorers seized on to coin the term *Iroquois*. (Dutch and English settlers called all of these peoples Mohawk, Maqua, or Seneca.) The Iroquois, whose towns contained as many as two thousand people, called themselves People of the Longhouse (*Haudenosaunee* in Seneca, *Kanosoni* in Mohawk), in reference to their primary type of dwelling. Iroquois longhouses were some twenty feet wide and from forty to two hundred feet long, accommodating several families who shared cooking fires.

Warfare was an important element of Iroquois life. Late in the fifteenth century, in response to the terrible consequences of ongoing wars, a man named Hiawatha founded the League, or Confederacy, of the Five Nations. According to Iroquois legend, having lost all of his daughters in war, Hiawatha, in a rage of grief and despair, went by himself into the forest. There he encountered a supernatural being named Deganawidah, the Peacemaker, perhaps a reincarnation of the Good Twin of the Iroquois creation story. Deganawidah comforted Hiawatha and taught him Rituals of Condolence that were to be the core of a new creed, the Good News of Peace and Power. Thus the cultural ideal of peace was established. While war continued as a central reality of Iroquois life, there were now ritual means of comforting the bereaved—and an ongoing hope for more lasting peace.

Of special note is the importance of women in Iroquois life. Women owned the property and took responsibility for major decisions of social life (indeed, society is referred to as "she"), attending to agricultural duties in the clearings while the men hunted in the woods or warred against traditional enemies such as the fierce Huron to the north. The principal male figure in an Iroquois child's life was not the father but the mother's brother, and the image of mother-dominated families is established strongly in the creation legend. In the version printed here males are entirely absent at the beginning of the tale, appearing neither as husbands nor as fathers. Indeed, stories of fatherless boys who become heroes are common in Iroquois folk history.

The Iroquois creation myth exists in some twenty-five versions, the earliest of which was taken down by the Frenchman Gabriel Sagard in 1623 from the Huron, near neighbors and enemies of the Five Nations. Other early accounts derive from the Mohawk and the Seneca. There is, however, no actual transcription and translation of an Iroquois cosmogonic myth—a narrative of the establishment of the world—until that of David Cusick, a Tuscarora, in the nineteenth century.

Little is known about Cusick. He was born in Madison County, New York, before 1800, when his family moved to the lands granted the Tuscarora by the Seneca and Oneida in Niagara County, New York. Most likely, he attended a mission school where he learned to read and write English. He died in 1840. Cusick's Tuscarora version shares many elements with the creation stories of other members of the Iroquois League; indeed, it has surely been influenced by them. But it also omits much material that other versions include.

Other accounts begin with a man and a woman who live together in the sky world on opposite sides of a fire. Although these two do not sleep together, the woman finds herself pregnant and eventually gives birth to a daughter. The man falls ill and dies, and the daughter grieves intensely for him. When the young woman is grown, her father's spirit instructs her to make a difficult journey to a place where she will meet the man destined to become her husband. When at last she finds this man, he too is ill, but the young woman cures him. The two marry but do not sleep together; nonetheless, as had happened to her mother, she becomes pregnant. It is at this point that Cusick picks up the story of the woman who "would have the twin born." Other versions continue past the point where Cusick's terminates. Some tell, for example, of a toad that hoards water long enough for a flood to burst from its belly or armpit, an indigenous account of a flood uninfluenced by the Judeo-Christian account.

Cusick's English, as the phrase quoted above makes clear, is not standard. Aware of that, he noted in the preface to his work that he found himself "so small educated that it was impossible for me to compose the work without much difficulty." His style is a curious combination of an Indian-inflected English and what the Euro-American culture of the period would have defined as polite literary style. We have selected Cusick's version of the Iroquois creation story because it is early, because it is by a native person (Cusick was the first Native American to record on his own the founding myths of his own people), and because it is fairly accessible to the contemporary reader.

The Iroquois Creation Story[1]

A Tale of the Foundation of the Great Island, Now North America;— the Two Infants Born, and the Creation of the Universe

Among the ancients there were two worlds in existence. The lower world was in great darkness;—the possession of the great monster; but the upper

---

1. From *Sketches of the Ancient History of the Six Nations* (1827).

world was inhabited by mankind; and there was a woman conceived[2] and would have the twin born. When her travail drew near, and her situation seemed to produce a great distress on her mind, and she was induced by some of her relations to lay herself on a mattrass which was prepared, so as to gain refreshments to her wearied body; but while she was asleep the very place sunk down towards the dark would.[3] The monsters[4] of the great water were alarmed at her appearance of descending to the lower world; in consequence all the species of the creatures were immediately collected into where it was expected she would fall. When the monsters were assembled, and they made consultation, one of them was appointed in haste to search the great deep, in order to procure some earth, if it could be obtained; accordingly the monster descends, which succeeds, and returns to the place. Another requisition was presented, who would be capable to secure the woman from the terrors of the great water, but none was able to comply except a large turtle came forward and made proposal to them to endure her lasting weight, which was accepted. The woman was yet descending from a great distance. The turtle executes upon the spot, and a small quantity of earth was varnished on the back part of the turtle. The woman alights on the seat prepared, and she receives a satisfaction.[5] While holding her, the turtle increased every moment and became a considerable island of earth, and apparently covered with small bushes. The woman remained in a state of unlimited darkness, and she was overtaken by her travail to which she was subject. While she was in the limits of distress one of the infants in her womb was moved by an evil opinion and he was determined to pass out under the side of the parent's arm, and the other infant in vain endeavoured to prevent his design.[6] The woman was in a painful condition during the time of their disputes, and the infants entered the dark world by compulsion, and their parent expired in a few moments. They had the power of sustenance without a nurse, and remained in the dark regions. After a time the turtle increased to a great Island and the infants were grown up, and one of them possessed with a gentle disposition, and named ENIGORIO, i.e. the good mind. The other youth possessed an insolence of character, and was named ENIGONHAHETGEA, i.e. the bad mind.[7] The good mind was not contented to remain in a dark situation, and he was anxious to create a great light in the dark world; but the bad mind was desirous that the world should remain in a natural state. The good mind determines to prosecute his designs, and therefore commences the work of creation. At first he took the parent's

2. The woman who conceives is, in most Iroquois accounts of the creation, the second generation of sky women to become pregnant without sexual activity. "Mankind": i.e., humans rather than "monsters"—undefined creatures of a time before the world as we know it was established—although these humans have powers quite different from those humans usually possess.
3. Other versions have Sky Woman either being pushed out of the upper world or accidentally falling.
4. In other versions the monsters are a variety of familiar animals. Cusick's sense of them as monsters conveys the mysterious and dangerous state of affairs in the as-yet-unformed universe.
5. I.e., she lands safely, without harm.
6. Other versions of the story have Sky Woman give birth to a daughter, who again becomes supernaturally pregnant (perhaps by the spirit of the turtle), and it is *she* who conceives the twins. The twins argue even in

the womb, the Evil Twin deciding not to be born in the normal way but to burst through his mother's side, which leads to her death. The theme of rival twins is widespread in the Americas.
7. More commonly, the Good Twin is called Tharonhiawagon (Sky-Grasper, Creator or Upholder of the Heavens), and the Evil Twin is named Tawiscaron (Evil-Minded, Flint, Ice, Patron of Winter, and other disasters). Cusick's Enigorio is a rough translation of the Tuscarora word for "good minded" into Mohawk, while his Enigonhahetgea is an equally rough translation into Seneca, Onondaga, or Cayuga of the Tuscarora word for "bad minded." Cusick has probably changed the Tuscarora words best known to him into these other Iroquois languages, because they were considered to be more prestigious than Tuscarora, the Tuscaroras only recently having joined the Iroquois Confederacy.

head, (the deceased) of which he created an orb, and established it in the centre of the firmament, and it became of a very superior nature to bestow light to the new world, (now the sun) and again he took the remnant of the body and formed another orb, which was inferior to the light (now moon). In the orb a cloud of legs appeared to prove it was the body of the good mind, (parent). The former was to give light to the day and the latter to the night; and he also created numerous spots of light, (now stars): these were to regulate the days, nights, seasons, years, etc. Whenever the light extended to the dark world the monsters were displeased and immediately concealed themselves in the deep places, lest they should be discovered by some human beings. The good mind continued the works of creation, and he formed numerous creeks and rivers on the Great Island, and then created numerous species of animals of the smallest and the greatest, to inhabit the forests, and fishes of all kinds to inhabit the waters. When he had made the universe he was in doubt respecting some being to possess the Great Island; and he formed two images of the dust of the ground in his own likeness, male and female, and by his breathing into their nostrils he gave them the living souls, and named them EA-GWE-HOWE, i.e., a real people;[8] and he gave the Great Island all the animals of game for their maintenance and he appointed thunder to water the earth by frequent rains, agreeable of the nature of the system; after this the Island became fruitful and vegetation afforded the animals subsistance. The bad mind, while his brother was making the universe, went throughout the Island and made numerous high mountains and falls of water, and great steeps, and also creates various reptiles which would be injurious to mankind; but the good mind restored the Island to its former condition. The bad mind proceeded further in his motives and he made two images of clay in the form of mankind; but while he was giving them existence they became apes;[9] and when he had not the power to create mankind he was envious against his brother; and again he made two of clay. The good mind discovered his brothers contrivances, and aided in giving them living souls, (it is said these had the most knowledge of good and evil). The good mind now accomplishes the works of creation, notwithstanding the imaginations of the bad mind were continually evil; and he attempted to enclose all the animals of game in the earth, so as to deprive them from mankind; but the good mind released them from confinement, (the animals were dispersed, and traces of them were made on the rocks near the cave where it was closed). The good mind experiences that his brother was at variance with the works of creation, and feels not disposed to favor any of his proceedings, but gives admonitions of his future state. Afterwards the good mind requested his brother to accompany him, as he was proposed to inspect the game, etc., but when a short distance from their monina[1] [sic] residence, the bad mind became so unmanly that he could not conduct his brother any more.[2] The bad mind offered a challenge to his brother and resolved that who gains the victory should govern the universe; and appointed a day to meet the contest. The good mind was willing to submit to the offer, and he enters the

8. Humans. Ea-gwe-howe is a Tuscarora term used by speakers of all the languages of the Six Nations and, today, simply means Indian, or Indians.
9. Cusick may have seen an ape or a depiction of apes (there are no apes native to the New World) and decided to name them as the creatures made by the Evil Twin in contrast to the humans made by the Good Twin. John Buck and Chief John Gibson, in their later renditions of the Iroquois creation narrative also refer to apes at this point in the narrative.
1. Cusick perhaps means nominal, their named or designated residence.
2. I.e., the Evil Twin became so rude and obnoxious that the Good Twin could not lead ("conduct") his brother to the appointed place any longer.

reconciliation with his brother; which he falsely mentions that by whipping with flags would destroy his temporal life;[3] and he earnestly solicits his brother also to notice the instrument of death, which he manifestly relates by the use of deer horns, beating his body he would expire. On the day appointed the engagement commenced, which lasted for two days: after pulling up the trees and mountains as the track of a terrible whirlwind, at last the good mind gained the victory by using the horns, as mentioned the instrument of death, which he succeeded in deceiving his brother and he crushed him in the earth; and the last words uttered from the bad mind were, that he would have equal power over the souls of mankind after death; and he sinks down to eternal doom, and became the Evil Spirit.[4] After this tumult the good mind repaired to the battle ground, and then visited the people and retires from the earth.[5]

1827

3. The Good Twin tells his brother that he can be killed by being beaten with corn stalks, rushes, reeds, or cattails. Cusick calls this a deception; other accounts treat it as a confession of weakness. Below, the Evil Twin admits that he would die if beaten with the antlers of deer.

4. This may reflect an awareness of the Christian belief in the devil as the evil spirit, ruler over the lower depths.

5. Other versions go on to say that the Good Twin teaches the people how to grow corn and how to keep from harm by means of prayer and ritual.

PIMA STORIES OF THE BEGINNING OF THE WORLD

The Pima live along the Gila and Salt rivers in the desert of central Arizona and are close relations of the Tohono O'odham (formerly known as the Papago), who occupy lands in the mostly riverless desert to the south of them. Farming close to the rivers, the Pima grew corn and beans, gathered wild plants, and hunted small game. Late in the fifteenth century, they encountered the Spanish, who named them "Pima" sometime around 1600. Because of their remoteness from Spanish and Mexican centers of power, the Pima were not immediately subjected to strong European influence. In 1694 Spanish missionaries were sent out to convert them. Today, like many native people, most Pima are Christian, although their Christianity both includes and exists alongside traditional beliefs and practices.

The first Pima mythological narrative to be recorded dates from a 1694 journal account written by the Spaniard Juan Manje; Pedro Font, another Spaniard, also recorded a Pima story in 1775. These stories concern the ancestors of the Pima, the Hohokam (meaning, roughly, the "finished ones" or "those who are gone"). Of great importance to the Pima, the narratives offer an account of how the cultural practices of everyday Pima life came to be established. But these earliest stories do not tell of the creation of the world, of the origins of things, or the actions of the most distant ancestors. Such tales were not recorded until the turn of the twentieth century.

At the Pan-American Fair in Buffalo, New York, in July of 1901, J. W. Lloyd met a man named Edward H. Wood, a full-blood Pima, who told him that his greatest dream was to preserve the ancient legends and tales of his people. Wood's grand-uncle, Thin Leather, was a *see-nee-yaw-kum*, a recognized master who knew all the ancient stories. Thin Leather, as Wood told Lloyd, had no successor and feared that with his death the stories would be lost to his people and to the world.

Wood persuaded Lloyd to go to the Southwest and work with him and his uncle to record the stories in English. In 1903 Lloyd traveled to Sacaton, Arizona, where he met Thin Leather and, with Wood acting as interpreter, recorded a number of his tales. Lloyd published the results of his work with Wood and Thin Leather privately in 1911, as *Aw-aw-tam, Indian Nights, Being the Myths and Legends of the Pimas of Arizona*. The title refers to the fact that these stories were traditionally told over a period of four nights.

Although the *Story of the Creation* was not narrated until the twentieth century, it is little influenced by the origin story in Genesis, which, however, Thin Leather probably knew. The important animals and vegetation, the chief protagonists, and their personalities and actions are all specific to Pima culture.

Thin Leather's story of the great flood here follows the creation story. Flood stories are among the fifteen pre-Columbian tale types cataloged in Mexico, Central America, and the American Southwest. Although Thin Leather may have heard the stories of Genesis, his Pima version shows no particular European influence. The flood story is important as a foundational narrative in that it tells not of creation but of re-creation, of the reestablishment or rebirth of the divine, natural, and social orders. In addition, the Pima flood story tells or, rather, *specifies* the location of the "middle of the earth," the navel of the universe, the center of all the world—where the Pima, like all Southwestern peoples, believe themselves to dwell.

The Story of the Creation[1]

In the beginning there was no earth, no water—nothing. There was only a Person, *Juh-wert-a-Mah-kai* (The Doctor of the Earth).[2]

He just floated, for there was no place for him to stand upon. There was no sun, no light, and he just floated about in the darkness, which was Darkness itself.

He wandered around in the nowhere till he thought he had wandered enough. Then he rubbed on his breast and rubbed out *moah-haht-tack*, that is perspiration, or greasy earth. This he rubbed out on the palm of his hand and held out. It tipped over three times, but the fourth time[3] it staid straight in the middle of the air and there it remains now as the world.

The first bush he created was the greasewood bush.[4]

And he made ants, little tiny ants, to live on that bush, on its gum which comes out of its stem.

But these little ants did not do any good, so he created white ants, and these worked and enlarged the earth; and they kept on increasing it, larger and larger, until at last it was big enough for himself to rest on.

Then he created a Person. He made him out of his eye, out of the shadow of his eyes, to assist him, to be like him, and to help him in creating trees and human beings and everything that was to be on the earth.

---

1. From *Aw-aw-tam, Indian Nights, Being the Myths and Legends of the Pimas of Arizona* (1911). The editor is indebted to Donald Bahr for his help with the annotation of the Pima selections.
2. This title is equivalent to respectfully calling Juh-wertamahkai a medicine person, or shaman, with great powers, although his powers seem, in a Western sense, to be godlike.
3. This is the first of several actions that must be

attempted four times before it is achieved [adapted from Lloyd's note]. Four is the pattern number of the Pima, as it is of a great many native peoples; it corresponds to the importance of three and seven as pattern numbers in Western cultures.
4. "The local touch in making the greasewood bush the first vegetation is very strong" [Lloyd's note]. Greasewood bushes are abundant in the Pima homelands.

The name of this being was *Noo-ee* (the Buzzard).[5]
Nooee was given all power, but he did not do the work he was created for.
He did not care to help Juhwertamahkai, but let him go by himself.

And so the Doctor of the Earth himself created the mountains and everything that has seed and is good to eat. For if he had created human beings first
they would have had nothing to live on.

But after making Nooee and before making the mountains and seed for
food, Juhwertamahkai made the sun.

In order to make the sun he first made water, and this he placed in a hollow
vessel, like an earthen dish *(hwas-hah-ah)* to harden into something like ice.
And this hardened ball he placed in the sky. First he placed it in the North,
but it did not work; then he placed it in the West, but it did not work; then he
placed it in the South, but it did not work; then he placed it in the East and
there it worked as he wanted it to.

And the moon he made in the same way and tried in the same places, with
the same results.

But when he made the stars he took the water in his mouth and spurted it
up into the sky. But the first night his stars did not give light enough. So he
took the Doctor-stone[6] (diamond), the *tone-dum-haw-teh*, and smashed it up,
and took the pieces and threw them into the sky to mix with the water in the
stars, and then there was light enough.

Juhwertamahkai's Song of Creation

Juhwerta mahkai made the world—
Come and see it and make it useful!
He made it round—
Come and see it and make it useful!

And now Juhwertamahkai, rubbed again on his breast, and from the substance
he obtained there made two little dolls, and these he laid on the earth. And
they were human beings, man and woman.

And now for a time the people increased till they filled the earth. For the
first parents were perfect, and there was no sickness and no death. But when
the earth was full, then there was nothing to eat, so they killed and ate each
other.

But Juhwertamahkai did not like the way his people acted, to kill and eat
each other, and so he let the sky fall to kill them. But when the sky dropped
he, himself, took a staff and broke a hole thru, thru which he and Nooee
emerged and escaped, leaving behind them all the people dead.

And Juhwertamahkai, being now on the top of this fallen sky, again made a
man and a woman, in the same way as before. But this man and woman
became grey when old, and their children became grey still younger, and their
children became grey younger still, and so on till the babies were gray in
their cradles.

And Juhwertamahkai, who had made a new earth and sky, just as there had
been before, did not like his people becoming grey in their cradles, so he let
the sky fall on them again, and again made a hole and escaped, with Nooee,
as before.

5. He is a person and also a buzzard, which, in the earliest times, is not a contradiction or paradox to the Pima.
6. I.e., it is a particularly powerful stone. Lloyd's interpreter called it a diamond, but as diamonds are uncommon in North America, this is probably a quartz crystal.

And Juhwertamahkai, on top of this second sky, again made a new heaven and a new earth, just as he had done before, and new people.

But these new people made a vice of smoking. Before human beings had never smoked till they were old, but now they smoked younger, and each generation still younger, till the infants wanted to smoke in their cradles.

And Juhwertamahkai did not like this, and let the sky fall again, and created everything new again in the same way, and this time he created the earth as it is now.

But at first the whole slope of the world was westward,[7] and tho there were peaks rising from this slope there were no true valleys, and all the water that fell ran away and there was no water for the people to drink. So Juhwertamahkai sent Nooee to fly around among the mountains, and over the earth, to cut valleys with his wings, so that the water could be caught and distributed and there might be enough for the people to drink.

Now the sun was male and the moon was female and they met once a month. And the moon became a mother and went to a mountain called *Tahs-my-et-tahn Toe-ahk* (sun striking mountain) and there was born her baby. But she had duties to attend to, to turn around and give light, so she made a place for the child by tramping down the weedy bushes and there left it. And the child, having no milk, was nourished on the earth.

And this child was the coyote,[8] and as he grew, he went out to walk and in his walk came to the house of Juhwertamahkai and Nooee, where they lived.

And when he came there Juhwertamahkai knew him and called him *Toe-hahvs*,[9] because he was laid on the weedy bushes of that name.

But now out of the North came another powerful personage, who has two names, *See-ur-huh* and *Ee-ee-toy*.[1]

Now Seeurhuh means older brother, and when this personage came to Juhwertamahkai, Nooee and Toehahvs he called them his younger brothers. But they claimed to have been here first, and to be older than he, and there was a dispute between them. But finally, because he insisted so strongly, and just to please him, they let him be called older brother.

1911

The Story of the Flood[1]

Now Seeurhuh was very powerful, like Juhwerta Mahkai,[2] and as he took up his residence with them, as one of them, he did many wonderful things which pleased Juhwerta Mahkai, who liked to watch him.

And after doing many marvelous things he, too, made a man.

7. A specifically local element of the Pima story, as both the Gila and the Salt rivers, important to the Pima, flow westward [adapted from Lloyd's note].

8. It is appropriate that the night-prowling coyote is born of the moon, and there is a symmetry in having the buzzard serve as Juhwertamahkai's agent of the sky and the coyote as his agent of the earth [adapted from Lloyd's note].

9. Toehahvs, or Tohawes, means "brittlebush," a common plant in Pima country.

1. The name either means "drink it all up" or, according to present-day Pimas, just sounds like the word that means "drink it all up," i.e., it is not translatable. This character is "the most active and mysterious

personality in Piman mythology. Out of the North, apparently self-existent, but little inferior in power to Juhwertamahkai, and claiming greater age, he appears, by pure 'bluff,' and persistent push and wheedling, to have induced the really more powerful, but good-natured and rather lazy Juhwertakmahkai to give over most of the real work and government of the world to him" [Lloyd's note].

1. From *Aw-aw-tam, Indian Nights, Being the Myths and Legends of the Pimas of Arizona* (1911).

2. The Doctor of the Earth, the creator. Seeurhuh means "Elder Brother" (see *The Story of the Creation*, p. 58).

And to this man whom he had made, Seeurhuh (whose other name was Ee-ee-toy) gave a bow & arrows, and guarded his arm against the bow string by a piece of wild-cat skin, and pierced his ears & made ear-rings for him, like turquoises to look at, from the leaves of the weed called *quah-wool*.[3] And this man was the most beautiful man yet made.

And Ee-ee-toy told this young man, who was just of marriageable age, to look around and see if he could find any young girl in the villages that would suit him and, if he found her, to see her relatives and see if they were willing he should marry her.

And the beautiful young man did this, and found a girl that pleased him, and told her family of his wish, and they accepted him, and he married her.

And the names of both these are now forgotten and unknown.

And when they were married Ee-ee-toy, foreseeing what would happen, went & gathered the gum of the greasewood tree.[4]

✳   ✳   ✳

Now there was a doctor who lived down toward the sunset whose name was Vahk-lohv Mahkai, or South Doctor, who had a beautiful daughter. And when his daughter heard of this young man and what had happened to his wives she was afraid and cried every day. And when her father saw her crying he asked her what was the matter? was she sick? And when she had told him what she was afraid of, for every one knew and was talking of this thing, he said yes, he knew it was true, but she ought not to be afraid, for there was happiness for a woman in marriage and the mothering of children.

And it took many years for the young man to marry all these wives, and have all these children, and all this time Ee-ee-toy was busy making a great vessel of the gum he had gathered from the grease bushes, a sort of olla[5] which could be closed up, which would keep back water. And while he was making this he talked over the reasons for it with Juhwerta Mahkai, Nooee, and Toe-hahvs,[6] that it was because there was a great flood coming.

And several birds heard them talking thus—the woodpecker, *Hick-o-vick*; the humming-bird, *Vee-pis-mahl*; a little bird named *Gee-ee-sop*, and another called *Quota-veech*.[7]

Eeeetoy said he would escape the flood by getting into the vessel he was making from the gum of the grease bushes or *ser-quoy*.

And Juhwerta Mahkai said he would get into his staff, or walking stick, and float about.

And Toehahvs said he would get into a canetube.

And the little birds said the water would not reach the sky, so they would fly up there and hang on by their bills till it was over.

And Nooee, the buzzard, the powerful, said he did not care if the flood did reach the sky, for he could find a way to break thru.

Now Ee-ee-toy was envious, and anxious to get ahead of Juhwerta Mahkai

3. This is actually a shrub that produces edible fruit, known today as the squawberry.

4. A plant that is common in central Arizona. Here, Lloyd has omitted the details of the young man's "marrying" many women in succession and their delivery of a great many children in a very short time as well as Juhwertamahkai and Ee-ee-toy's sense that these unnatural proceedings will lead to "convulsions" in nature and a flood that will "cover the world." Lloyd

does not translate this part of the story because it contains "far too much plainness of circumstantial detail for popular reading."

5. A large earthenware jar (Spanish).

6. The coyote. Nooee is the buzzard (see *The Story of Creation*, p. 58).

7. A black phoebe. "Gee-ee-sop": a thrasher [adapted from Lloyd's note].

and get more fame for his wonderful deeds, but Juhwerta Mahkai, though really the strongest, was generous and from kindness and for relationship sake let Ee-ee-toy have the best of it.

And the young girl, the doctor's daughter, kept on crying, fearing the young man, feeling him ever coming nearer, and her father kept on reassuring her, telling her it would be all right, but at last, out of pity for her fears & tears, he told her to go and get him the little tuft of the finest thorns on the top of the white cactus, the *haht-sahn-kahm*,[8] and bring to him.

And her father took the cactus-tuft which she had brought him, and took hair from her head and wound about one end of it, and told her if she would wear this it would protect her. And she consented and wore the cactus-tuft.

And he told her to treat the young man right, when he came, & make him broth of corn. And if the young man should eat all the broth, then their plan would fail, but if he left any broth she was to eat that up and then their plan would succeed.

And he told her to be sure and have a bow and arrows above the door of the *kee*,[9] so that he could take care of the young man.

And after her father had told her this, on that very evening the young man came, and the girl received him kindly, and took his bows & arrows, and put them over the door of the kee, as her father had told her, and made the young man broth of corn and gave it to him to eat.

And he ate only part of it and what was left she ate herself.

And before this her father had told her: "If the young man is wounded by the thorns you wear, in that moment he will become a woman and a mother and you will become a young man."

And in the night all this came to be, even so, and by day-break the child was crying.

And the old woman ran in and said: "*Mossay!*" which means an old woman's grandchild from a daughter.

And the daughter, that had been, said: "It is not your *moss*, it is your *cah-um-maht*," that is an old woman's grandchild from a son.

And then the old man ran in and said: "*Bah-ahm-ah-dah!*" that is an old man's grandchild from a daughter, but his daughter said: "It is not your *bah-ahm-maht*, but it is your *voss-ahm-maht*," which is an old man's grandchild from a son.[1]

And early in the morning this young man (that had been, but who was now a woman & a mother) made a *wawl-kote*, a carrier, or cradle, for the baby and took the trail back home.

And Juhwerta Mahkai told his neighbors of what was coming, this young man who had changed into a woman and a mother and was bringing a baby born from himself, and that when he arrived wonderful things would happen & springs would gush forth from under every tree and on every mountain.

And the young man-woman came back and by the time of his return Ee-

---

8. The cholla or "jumping" cactus, which has particularly sharp and stiff needles.
9. House or dwelling.
1. There is a good deal of wordplay here as various kinship terms are tried out to determine just where this child belongs in the structure of the extended family. The young man's turning into a woman and giving birth to a child continues the theme of aberrations in

marriage and childbearing summarized by Lloyd earlier (see n. 4, p. 61). Social interactions and responsibilities are determined by kinship ties, and the story tells of a time when important matters such as these were unsettled and strange. Thus the flood will be necessary to wipe away this earlier, chaotic world and allow a new and more appropriate order to be established.

ee-toy had finished his vessel and had placed therein seeds & everything that is in the world.

And the young man-woman, when he came to his old home, placed his baby in the bushes and left it, going in without it, but Ee-ee-toy turned around and looked at him and knew him, for he did not wear a woman's dress, and said to him: "Where is my Bahahmmaht? Bring it to me. I want to see it. It is a joy for an old man to see his grandchild.

I have sat here in my house and watched your going, and all that has happened you, and foreseen some one would send you back in shame, although I did not like to think there was anyone more powerful than I. But never mind, he who has beaten us will see what will happen."

And when the young man-woman went to get his baby, Ee-ee-toy got into his vessel, and built a fire on the hearth he had placed therein; and sealed it up.

And the young man-woman found his baby crying, and the tears from it were all over the ground, around. And when he stooped over to pick up his child he turned into a sand-snipe, and the baby turned into a little teeter-snipe.[2]

Juhwertamahkai's Song before the Flood

My poor people,
Who will see,
Who will see
This water which will moisten the earth!

And then that came true which Juhwerta Mahkai had said, that water would gush out from under every tree & on every mountain; and the people when they saw it, and knew that a flood was coming, ran to Juhwerta Mahkai; and he took his staff and made a hole in the earth and let all those thru who had come to him, but the rest were drowned.

Then Juhwerta Mahkai got into his walking stick & floated, and Toehahvs got into his tube of cane and floated, but Ee-ee-toy's vessel was heavy & big and remained until the flood was much deeper before it could float.

And the people who were left out fled to the mountains; to the mountains called *Gah-kote-kih* (Superstition Mts.)[3] for they were living in the plains between Gahkotekih and Cheoffskawmack (Tall Gray Mountain.)

And there was a powerful man among these people, a doctor (mahkai), who set a mark on the mountain side and said the water would not rise above it.

And the people believed him and camped just beyond the mark; but the water came on and they had to go higher. And this happened four times.[4]

And the mahkai did this to help his people, and also used power to raise the mountain, but at last he saw all was to be a failure. And he called the people and asked them all to come close together, and he took his doctor-stone[5] (*mah-kai-haw-teh*) which is called Tonedumhawteh or Stone-of-Light, and held it in the palm of his hand and struck it hard with his other hand, and it thun-

---

2. The snipe is a small bird. This is perhaps their only chance to escape destruction in the flood.
3. In central Arizona, just east of Phoenix; the mountains derive their name from this story.
4. Four is the pattern number of the Pima (see n. 3,

p. 58). The terraces of cliffs in the Superstition Mountains are said to mark the successive pausing places of the people, and the clusters of rocks on the top to represent their petrified forms [adapted from Lloyd's note].
5. I.e., a particularly powerful stone (see n. 6, p. 59).

dered so loud that all the people were frightened and they were all turned into stone.

The Song of Superstition Mountains

We are destroyed!
By my stone we are destroyed!
We are rightly turned into stone.

And the little birds, the woodpecker, Hickovick; the humming-bird, Veepis-mahl; the little bird named Ge-ee-sop, and the other called Quotaveech, all flew up to the sky and hung on by their bills, but Nooee still floated in the air and intended to keep on the wing unless the floods reached the heavens.

But Juhwerta Mahkai, Ee-ee-toy and Toehahvs floated around on the water and drifted to the west and did not know where they were.

And the flood rose higher until it reached the woodpecker's tail, and you can see the marks to this day.

And Quotaveech was cold and cried so loud that the other birds pulled off their feathers and built him a nest up there so he could keep warm. And when Quotaveech was warm he quit crying.

And then the little birds sang, for they had power to make the water go down by singing, and as they sang the waters gradually receded.

But the others still floated around.

When the land began to appear Juhwerta Mahkai and Toehahvs got out, but Ee-ee-toy had to wait for his house to warm up, for he had built a fire to warm his vessel enough for him to unseal it.

When it was warm enough he unsealed it, but when he looked out he saw the water still running & he got back and sealed himself in again.

And after waiting a while he unsealed his vessel again, and seeing dry land enough he got out.

And Juhwerta Mahkai went south and Toehahvs went west, and Ee-ee-toy went northward. And as they did not know where they were they missed each other, and passed each other unseen, but afterward saw each other's tracks, and then turned back and shouted, but wandered from the track, and again passed unseen. And this happened four times.

And the fourth time Juhwerta Mahkai and Ee-ee-toy met, but Toehahvs had passed already.

And when they met, Ee-ee-toy said to Juhwerta Mahkai "My younger brother!" but Juhwerta Mahkai greeted him as younger brother & claimed to have come out first. Then Ee-ee-toy said again: "I came out first and you can see the water marks on my body." But Juhwerta Mahkai replied: "I came out first and also have the water marks on my person to prove it."

But Ee-ee-toy so insisted that he was the eldest that Juhwerta Mahkai, just to please him, gave him his way and let him be considered the elder.

And then they turned westward and yelled to find Toehahvs, for they remembered to have seen his tracks, and they kept on yelling till he heard them. And when Toehahvs saw them he called them his younger brothers, and they called him younger brother. And this dispute continued till Ee-ee-toy again got the best of it and, although really the younger brother[,] was admitted by the others to be Seeurhuh, or the elder.

And the birds came down from the sky and again there was a dispute about the relationship, but Ee-ee-toy again got the best of them all.[6]

But Quotaveech staid up in the sky because he had a comfortable nest there, and they called him *Vee-ick-koss-kum Mahkai*, the Feather-Nest Doctor.

And they wanted to find the middle, the navel[7] of the earth, and they sent Veeppismahl, the humming bird, to the west, and Hickovick, the woodpecker, to the east, and all the others stood and waited for them at the starting place. And Veepismahl & Hickovick were to go as far as they could, to the edge of the world, and then return to find the middle of the earth by their meeting. But Hickovick flew a little faster and got there first, and so when they met they found it was not the middle, and they parted & started again, but this time they changed places and Hickovick went westward and Veepismahl went east.

And this time Veepismahl was the faster, and Hickovick was late, and the judges thought their place of meeting was a little east of the center so they all went a little way west. Ee-ee-toy, Juhwerta Mahkai and Toehahvs stood there and sent the birds out once again, and this time Hickovick went eastward again, and Veepismahl went west. And Hickovick flew faster and arrived there first. And they said: "This is not the middle. It is a little way west yet."

And so they moved a little way, and again the birds were sent forth, and this time Hickovick went west and Veepismahl went east. And when the birds returned they met where the others stood and all cried "This is the *Hick*, the Navel of the World!"

And they stood there because there was no dry place yet for them to sit down upon; and Ee-ee-toy rubbed upon his breast and took from his bosom the smallest ants, the *O-auf-taw-ton*, and threw them upon the ground, and they worked there and threw up little hills; and this earth was dry. And so they sat down.

Ee-ee-toy's Song
When He Made the World Serpents

> I know what to do;
> I am going to move the water
> both ways.

But the water was still running in the valleys, and Ee-ee-toy took a hair from his head & made it into a snake—*Vuck-vahmuht*.[8] And with this snake he pushed the waters south, but the head of the snake was left lying to the west and his tail to the east.

But there was more water, and Ee-ee-toy took another hair from his head and made another snake, and with this snake pushed the rest of the water north. And the head of this snake was left to the east and his tail to the west. So the head of each snake was left lying with the tail of the other.

And the snake that has his tail to the east, in the morning will shake up his tail to start the morning wind to wake the people and tell them to think of their dreams.

---

6. These disputes among the gods and then the birds are probably meant to be comic and amusing, although they contribute to the serious business of the reorganization of the world based on proper kinship ties.
7. The Pima, like all Southwestern peoples, believe they live in "the middle, the navel," of the world. In this narration, the middle of the world is not specified at the time of creation but only at the time of re-creation, here, after the flood.
8. I.e., red snake.

And the snake that has his tail to the west, in the evening will shake up his tail to start the cool wind to tell the people it is time to go in and make the fires & be comfortable.

And they said: "We will make dolls, but we will not let each other see them until they are finished."

And Ee-ee-toy sat facing the west, and Toehahvs facing the south, and Juhwerta Mahkai facing the east.

And the earth was still damp and they took clay and began to make dolls. And Ee-ee-toy made the best. But Juhwerta Mahkai did not make good ones, because he remembered some of his people had escaped the flood thru a hole in the earth, and he intended to visit them and he did not want to make anything better than they were to take the place of them. And Toehahvs made the poorest of all.

Then Ee-ee-toy asked them if they were ready, and they all said yes, and then they turned about and showed each other the dolls they had made.

And Ee-ee-toy asked Juhwerta Mahkai why he had made such queer dolls. "This one," he said, "is not right, for you have made him without any sitting-down parts, and how can he get rid of the waste of what he eats?"

But Juhwerta Mahkai said: "He will not need to eat, he can just smell the smell of what is cooked."

Then Ee-ee-toy asked again: "Why did you make this doll with only one leg—how can he run?" But Juhwerta Mahkai replied: "He will not need to run; he can just hop around."

Then Ee-ee-toy asked Toehahvs why he had made a doll with webs between his fingers and toes—"How can he point directions?" But Toehahvs said he had made these dolls so for good purpose, for if anybody gave them small seeds they would not slip between their fingers, and they could use the webs for dippers to drink with.

And Ee-ee-toy held up his dolls and said: "These are the best of all, and I want you to make more like them." And he took Toehahv's dolls and threw them into the water and they became ducks & beavers. And he took Juhwerta Mahkai's dolls and threw them away and they all broke to pieces and were nothing.

And Juhwerta Mahkai was angry at this and began to sink into the ground; and took his stick and hooked it into the sky and pulled the sky down while he was sinking. But Ee-ee-toy spread his hand over his dolls, and held up the sky, and seeing that Juhwerta Mahkai was sinking into the earth he sprang and tried to hold him & cried, "Man, what are you doing! Are you going to leave me and my people here alone?"

But Juhwerta Mahkai slipped through his hands, leaving in them only the waste & excretion of his skin. And that is how there is sickness & death among us.[9]

And Ee-ee-toy, when Juhwerta Mahkai escaped him, went around swinging his hands & saying: "I never thought all this impurity would come upon my people!" and the swinging of his hands scattered disease over all the earth. And he washed himself in a pool or pond and the impurities remaining in the water are the source of the malarias and all the diseases of dampness.

And Ee-ee-toy and Toehahvs built a house for their dolls a little way off,

9. In *The Story of Creation* (p. 58) Juhwertamahkai's bodily products (e.g., perspiration) were used for creating, not destroying.

and Ee-ee-toy sent Toehahvs to listen if they were yet talking. And the *Aw-up*, (the Apaches) were the first ones that talked. And Ee-ee-toy said: "I never meant to have those Apaches talk first, I would rather have had the *Aw-aw-tam*,[1] the Good People, speak first."

But he said: "It is all right. I will give them strength, that they stand the cold & all hardships."

And all the different people that they had made talked, one after the other, but the Awawtam talked last.

And they all took to playing together, and in their play they kicked each other as the Maricopas[2] do in sport to this day; but the Apaches got angry and said: "We will leave you and go into the mountains and eat what we can get, but we will dream good dreams and be just as happy as you with all your good things to eat."

And some of the people took up their residence on the Gila, and some went west to the Rio Colorado. And those who builded vahahkkees, or houses out of adobe and stones, lived in the valley of the Gila, between the mountains which are there now.

1911

1. The Pima term for themselves (currently spelled "O'odham"). A more accurate translation is simply "people" or "us," as distinct from animals and from other groups of people. The Pima and Apache were traditional enemies.

2. Traditional allies of the Pima.

ARTHUR BARLOWE
fl. 1584–85

The English explorer Arthur Barlowe is known almost exclusively from his voyage, in 1584–85, to the area surrounding the island of Roanoke, in Albemarle and Pamlico Sounds in what is now North Carolina (a region soon named "Virginia" by Sir Walter Ralegh in honor of his "Virgin Queen," Elizabeth). Both Barlowe and the commander of the expedition, Philip Amadas, seem to have been associated before that time with Ralegh, sponsor of the 1584–85 voyage and of the whole Roanoke venture. Barlowe saw military service under Ralegh in the war in Ireland in 1580–81 and at some point sailed as far as the eastern Mediterranean. For the Roanoke voyage Barlowe commanded the smaller of two vessels, on which it is possible that the artist-explorer John White and the naturalist Thomas Harriot (associated together in the second Roanoke voyage of 1585) were present.

Aside from that sketchy history, we know only that Barlowe wrote the surviving account of the voyage, with its glowing depiction of the Virginia landscape and the Native Americans who inhabited it and welcomed the English ashore. The text anthologized here begins with the expedition's departure from a port in the west of England, probably Plymouth, in April 1584. After stops at the Canary Islands and in the West Indies, early in July the two vessels arrived at the Carolina coast off Cape Hatteras. The party spent about six weeks exploring the vicinity of nearby Roanoke Island, the lush home of Wingina and the Roanoke people, then made a quick passage home.

The narrative as it survives actually bears traces of having been rewritten, perhaps by Ralegh (to whom it is addressed) or Harriot, a not uncommon practice at a time when such texts were often used to encourage further financial and political support for overseas ventures. Be that as it may, Barlowe's own accent is clear in this narrative. His openness to the American Indians and their world is more lively than the intellectual Harriot's, and his evanescent apprehension of a wondrous New World, capturing the moment of England's first real contact with North America, lacks Ralegh's political and imperial calculations. It seems oddly right that this idyllic glimpse of the New World should have no more certain source than the obscure Barlowe, who witnessed something that must have moved him deeply—who even before he could see the American coast, "smelled so sweet and so strong a smell, as if [he] had been in the midst of some delicate garden." Only in John White's later writings, and especially his paintings, does anything like it recur, and then as briefly too. It is a moment that haunts the American imagination.

From The First Voyage Made to the Coasts of America[1]

The 27th day of April in the year of our redemption 1584, we departed [from] the West of England, with two barks[2] well furnished with men and victuals, having received our last and perfect[3] directions by your letters, confirming the former instructions and commandments delivered by yourself at our leaving the river of Thames. And I think it a matter both unnecessary for the manifest discovery of the country, as also for tediousness sake, to remember unto you the diurnal[4] of our course, sailing thither and returning: [except] I have presumed to present unto you this brief discourse, by which you may judge how profitable this land is likely to succeed,[5] as well to yourself (by whose direction and charge and by whose servants this our discovery hath been performed) as also to her Highness, and the Commonwealth, in which we hope your wisdom will be satisfied, considering that as much by us hath been brought to light as by those small means and [the small] number of men we had, could any way have been expected or hoped for.

The tenth of May we arrived at the Canaries, and the tenth of June in this present year we were fallen with the islands of the West Indies, keeping a more southeasternly course than was needfull, because we doubted that the current of the Bay of Mexico, disbogging between the Cape of Florida and Havana, had been of greater force than afterwards we found it to be.[6] At which islands we found the air very unwholesome, and our men grew for the most part ill-disposed, so that having refreshed ourselves with sweet water and fresh victual we departed the twelfth day [after] our arrival there. These islands, with the rest adjoining, are so well known to yourself and to many others [that] I will not trouble you with the remembrance of them.

The second of July we found shoal water, where we smelled so sweet and so strong a smell, as if we had been in the midst of some delicate garden abounding with all kind of odoriferous flowers, by which we were assured that the land could not be far distant. And keeping good watch and bearing but slack sail, the fourth of the same month we arrived upon the coast, which we sup-

---

1. The text is based on Richard Hakluyt, *The Principall Navigations, Voyages, Traffiques, & Discoveries of the English Nation*, vol. 8 (1904).
2. Ships.
3. Complete, mature.

4. I.e., to recite the daily record for Ralegh.
5. Prove.
6. I.e., they thought the Gulf Stream would be stronger and so sailed south to avoid its effect. "Doubted": suspected. "Disbogging": discharging.

posed to be the continent and firm land, and we sailed along the same a hundred-and-twenty English miles before we could find any entrance or river issuing into the sea. The first that appeared unto us we entered, though not without some difficulty, and cast anchor about three arquebus-shot[7] within the haven's mouth, on the left hand of the same, and after thanks given to God for our safe arrival thither, we manned our boats and went to view the land next adjoining, and "to take possession of the same, in the right of the Queen's most excellent Majesty, as rightful Queen and Princess of the same," and after delivered the same over to your use,[8] according to her Majesty's grant and letters patent, under her Highness's great seal. Which [actions] being performed according to the ceremonies used in such enterprises, we viewed the land about us, being where we first landed very sandy and low towards the waterside, but so full of grapes as the very beating and surge of the sea overflowed them, of which we found such plenty as well there as in all places else, both on the sand and on the green soil on the hills, [and] in the plains as well [as] on every little shrub, as also climbing towards the top of the high cedars, [so] that I think in all the world the like abundance is not to be found, and myself having seen those parts of Europe that most abound, find such difference [here] as were incredible to be written.[9]

We passed from the seaside towards the tops of those hills next adjoining, being but of mean height, and from thence we beheld the sea of both sides, to the north and to the south, finding no end any of both ways.[1] This land lay stretching itself to the west, which afterwards we found to be but an island twenty miles long and not above six miles broad. Under the bank or hill whereon we stood, we beheld the valleys replenished with goodly cedar trees, and having discharged our arquebus-shot, such a flock of cranes (for the most part white) arose under us, with such a cry redoubled by many echoes, as if an army of men had shouted all together.

This island had many goodly woods full of deer, coneys,[2] hares, and fowl, even in the midst of summer in incredible abundance. The woods are not such as you find in Bohemia, Moscovia, or Hercynia,[3] barren and fruitless, but the highest and reddest cedars of the world, far bettering the cedars of the Azores, of the Indies, or Lebanon, [and] pines, cypress, sassafras, the lentisk, or the tree that bears the rind of black cinnamon, of which Master Winter brought [some] from the straits of Magellan,[4] and many other [trees] of excellent smell and quality. We remained by the side of this island two whole days before we espied one small boat rowing towards us, having in it three persons. This boat came to the island side, four arquebus-shot from our ships, and there two of the people remaining, the third came along the shore towards us, and we being then all [on board], he walked up and down upon the point of land next to us. Then the master and pilot of the admiral, Simon Ferdinando,

7. Three times the distance that a shot from an arquebus, a heavy gun, could cover.
8. I.e., Ralegh's (as the patentee authorized by Elizabeth to undertake the Roanoke venture).
9. I.e., there were so many more in Virginia that it would be hard to describe them—or to believe the description.
1. I.e., in either direction.
2. Rabbits.
3. Central European regions named here because of their extensive forests.
4. John Winter (fl. 1577–79) accompanied Sir Francis Drake (1540–1596) on his voyage around the world in 1577, although his ship was separated from Drake in October 1578 and he returned to England by himself via the strait near Cape Horn first passed by Ferdinand Magellan (c. 1480–1521) in 1520. The bark samples he brought with him became known as "Winter's Bark," the subject of much interest for its supposed medicinal properties. "Lentisk": the mastic tree, a European native from which varnish was made. As this was not native to the New World, Barlowe is probably referring to the American sweet gum tree. "Black cinnamon": perhaps the American dogwood is meant.

and the captain Philip Amadas,[5] myself, and others rowed to the land, whose coming this fellow attended [to], never making any show of fear or doubt. And after he had spoken of many things not understood by us, we brought him, [to] his own good liking, aboard the ships, and gave him a shirt, a hat, and some other things, and made him taste of our wine, and our meat, which he liked very well. And after having viewed both barks, he departed, and went to his own boat again, which he had left in a little cove or creek adjoining. As soon as he was two bow-shots into the water, he fell to fishing, and in less than half an hour he had loaded his boat as deep as it could swim,[6] [after] which he came again to the point of the land, and there he divided his fish into two parts, pointing one part to the ship and the other to the pinnace. [With] which, after he had (as much as he might) requited the former benefits received [from us], he departed out of our sight.

The next day there came unto us divers[7] boats, and in one of them the King's brother, accompanied with forty or fifty men, very handsome and goodly people, and in their behavior as mannerly and civil as any of Europe. His name was Granganimeo, and the King is called Wingina, the country Wingandacoa, and now by her Majesty, "Virginia." The manner of his coming was in this sort: he left his boats altogether as the first man did, a little from the ships by the shore, and came along to the place over against the ships, followed [by] forty men. When he came to the place, his servants spread a long mat upon the ground, on which he sat down, and at the other end of the mat four others of his company did the like, the rest of his men stood round about him, somewhat far off. When we came to the shore to him with our weapons, he never moved from his place, nor [did] any of the other four, nor ever mistrusted any harm to be offered from us, but sitting still he beckoned us to come and sit by him, which we performed. And being set, he made all signs of joy and welcome, striking on his head and his breast and afterwards on ours, to show we were all one, smiling and making show the best he could of all love,[8] and familiarity. After he had made a long speech unto us, we presented him with divers things, which he received very joyfully, and thankfully. None of the company dared to speak one word all the time, [except that] the four who were at the other end spoke one in the other's ear very softly.

The King is greatly obeyed, and his brothers and children reverenced. The King himself in person was, at our being there, sore wounded in a fight which he had with the King of the next country. [He is] called Wingina, and was shot in two places in the body, and once clean through the thigh, but he recovered. By reason [of these wounds] and [because] he lay at the chief town of the country, being six days journey off, we saw him not at all.

After we had presented this his brother with such things as we thought he liked, we likewise gave somewhat to the others that sat with him on the mat, but presently he arose and took all from them and put it into his own basket, making signs and tokens, that all things ought to be delivered unto him, and the rest were but his servants, and followers. A day or two after this, we fell to

5. An "admiral"is the chief ship of a fleet, here the larger of two vessels sent to Virginia in 1584 (the name of neither survives), which was commanded by Amadas (1565–1586?) and piloted by Fernandes (c. 1538–1590), a Portuguese native but sometime resident of England who was much employed in English voyages. Barlowe commanded the second ship, a small sailing vessel called a pinnace.

6. I.e., with as many fish as it could hold without sinking.

7. Several.

8. I.e., he expressed his love for the English in the best way he could.

trading with them, exchanging some things that we had for chamois, buff,[9] and deer skins. When we showed him all our packets of merchandise, of all [the] things that he saw, a bright tin dish most pleased him, which he presently took up and clapped it before his breast, and after made a hole in the brim thereof and hung it about his neck, making signs that it would defend him against his enemies' arrows, for those people maintain a deadly and terrible war with the people and King adjoining. We exchanged our tin dish for twenty skins, worth twenty crowns, or twenty nobles[1] and a copper kettle for fifty skins worth fifty crowns. They offered us good exchange for our hatchets, and axes, and for knives, and would have given anything for swords, but we would not part with any. After two or three days the King's brother came aboard the ships, and drank wine, and ate of our meat and of our bread, and liked exceedingly [these things], and after a few days passed he brought his wife with him to the ships, his daughter and two or three children. His wife was very well favored,[2] of mean stature, and very bashful. She had on her back a long cloak of leather, with the fur side next to her body, and before her a piece of the same. About her forehead she had a band of white coral, and so had her husband many times.[3] In her ears she had bracelets of pearls, hanging down to her middle (whereof we delivered your Worship a little bracelet[4]) and those were of the bigness of good peas. The rest of her women of the better sort had pendants of copper hanging in either ear, and some of the children of the King's brother and other noblemen have five or six in either ear. He himself had upon his head a broad plate of gold, or copper, for being unpolished we knew not what metal it should be, neither would he by any means suffer us to take it off his head, but feeling it, it would bow[5] very easily. His apparel was [like] his wife's, only the women wear their hair long on both sides, and the men but on one. They are of color yellowish, and their hair black for the most part, and yet we saw children that had very fine auburn and chestnut colored hair.

After these women had been there, there came down from all parts great store of people, bringing with them leather, coral, divers kinds of dyes (very excellent), and exchanged with us. But when Granganimeo the King's brother was present, none dared to trade but himself, except such as wear red pieces of copper on their heads like himself, for that is the difference between the noblemen and the governors of countries and the meaner sort. And we both noted here, and you have understood since by these men whom we brought home,[6] that no people in the world carry more respect to their King, Nobility, and Governors, than these do. The King's brother's wife, when she came to us (as she did many times) was followed [by] forty or fifty women always, and when she came into the ship, she left them all on land, saving her two daughters, her nurse, and one or two more. The King's brother always kept this order:[7] as many boats as he would come with to the ships, so many fires would he make on the shore afar off, to the end [that] we might understand with what strength and company he approached. Their boats are made of one tree, either

9. Buffalo skins. "Chamois": probably dressed deerskin.
1. Crowns and nobles were English coins worth then about five and six shillings, respectively.
2. Pleasant looking.
3. Barlowe means that her husband either often wore such decoration or wore several such bands, compared with her single one.

4. Used here in the older sense of jewelry in general. "Your Worship": Ralegh.
5. Bend.
6. Amadas and Barlowe brought to England two Native Americans, Manteo, a Croatoan, and Wanchese, a Roanoke, with whom Ralegh was by this time familiar.
7. Practice or custom.

of pine or of pitch trees, a wood not commonly known to our people, nor found growing in England. They have no edge tools to make them with, [or] if they have any they are very few, and those it seems they had [acquired] twenty years since, which, as [Wanchese and Manteo] declared, were out of a wreck which happened upon their coast, of some Christian ship being beaten that way by some storm and outrageous weather, whereof none of the people was saved, but only the ship, or some part of her, being cast upon the sand, out of whose sides they drew the nails and the spikes and with those they made their best instruments. The manner of making their boats is thus: they burn down some great tree, or take such as are wind-fallen, and putting gum and rosin upon one side thereof they set fire into it, and when [the fire] hath burnt it hollow, they cut out the coals with their shells, and wherever they would burn it deeper or wider they lay on gums, which burn away the timber, and by this means they fashion very fine boats and such as will transport twenty men. Their oars are like scoops, and many times they set with long poles, as the depth serves.[8]

The King's brother had great liking of our armor, a sword, and divers other things which we had, and offered to lay a great box of pearl in gage for them,[9] but we refused it for this time, because we would not make them know, that we esteemed thereof until we had understood in what places of the country the pearl grew, which now your Worship doth very well understand.

He was very just of his promise,[1] for many times we delivered [to] him merchandise upon his word, but ever he came within the day and performed his promise. He sent us every day a brace or two or fat bucks, coneys, hares, fish, the best of the world. He sent us divers roots, and fruits very excellent good, and of their country corn, which is very white, fair and well-tasted, and grows three times in five months: in May they sow, in July they reap; in June they sow, in August they reap; in July they sow, in September they reap. Only they[2] cast the corn into the ground, breaking a little of the soft turf with a wooden mattock or pickaxe. [We] ourselves proved[3] the soil, and put some of our peas in the ground, and in ten days they were of fourteen inches [height]. They have also beans very fair, of divers colors and wonderful plenty, some growing naturally and some in their gardens, and so have they both wheat and oats.[4]

The soil is the most plentiful, sweet, fruitful and wholesome of all the world. There are above fourteen several sweet-smelling timber trees, and the most part of their underwoods are bays[5] and such like. They have those oaks that we have, but far greater and better. After they had been divers times aboard our ships, myself with seven more went twenty miles into the river, that runs toward the city of Skicoak, which river they call Occam, and the evening following we came to an island which they call Roanoke, distant from the harbor by which we entered, seven leagues, and at the north end thereof was a village of nine houses, built of cedar, and fortified round about with sharp trees, to keep out their enemies, and the entrance into it made like a turn pike, very artificially.[6] When we came towards it, standing near unto the

---

8. I.e., as the varying depth of the water determines.
9. I.e., he promised to exchange a box of pearls for these items.
1. I.e., he was very fair in keeping his promises.
2. I.e., all they do is.
3. Tested.
4. Barlowe is technically wrong here, as wheat and oats were both Old World crops not then known in North America.
5. Sweet bay or magnolia. "Several": different.
6. I.e., it was artfully constructed. "Turn pike": a medieval military device designed to limit access, made of a revolving frame to which spikes were fixed.

waterside, the wife of Granganimeo the King's brother came running out to meet us very cheerfully and friendly. Her husband was not then in the village. Some of her people she commanded to draw our boat on shore [because of] the beating of the billows; others she appointed to carry us on their backs to the dry ground, and others to bring our oars into the house for fear of stealing. When we were come into the utter[7] room, [there being] five rooms in her house, she caused us to sit down by a great fire, and afterward took off our clothes and washed them, and dried them again. Some of the women plucked off our stockings and washed them, some washed our feet in warm water, and she herself took great pains to see all things ordered in the best manner she could, making great haste to dress some meat for us to eat.

After we had thus dried ourselves, she brought us into the inner room, where she set on the board standing [all] along the house some wheat-like frumenty; sodden venison, and roasted; fish sodden, boiled, and roasted; melons[8] raw, and sodden; roots of divers kinds, and divers fruits. Their drink is commonly water, but while the grape lasts they drink wine, and for want of casks to keep it, all the year after they drink water, but it is sodden with ginger in it, and black cinnamon, and sometimes sassafras, and divers other wholesome and medicinal herbs and trees.[9] We were entertained[1] with all love and kindness, and with as much bounty (after their manner) as they could possibly devise. We found the people most gentle, loving, and faithful, void of all guile and treason, and such as live after the manner of the golden age. The people only care how to defend themselves from the cold in their short winter, and to feed themselves with such meat[2] as the soil affords. Their meat is very well sodden and they make broth very sweet and savory. Their vessels are earthen pots, very large, white, and sweet,[3] [and] their dishes are wooden platters of sweet timber. Within the place where they feed was their lodging,[4] and within that, their Idol, which they worship, of whom they speak incredible things. While we were at meat, there came in at the gates two or three men with their bows and arrows from hunting, whom when we espied, we began to look one towards another, and offered to reach[5] our weapons, but as soon as she espied our mistrust she was very much moved, and caused some of her men to run out and take away their bows and arrows and break them, and withall[6] beat the poor fellows out of the gate again. When we departed in the evening and would not tarry all night, she was very sorry, and gave us into our boat[7] our supper half dressed, pots and all, and brought us to our boat's side, [on board] which we lay all night, removing the same a pretty distance from the shore. She, perceiving our jealousy,[8] was much grieved, and sent divers men and thirty women to sit all night on the bank side by us, and sent us into our boats five mats to cover us from the rain, using very many words to entreat us to rest in their houses, but because we were very few men and if we had miscarried the voyage had been in very great danger, we dared not to adventure anything, though there was no cause for doubt, for a more kind and

---

7. Outer.
8. Probably pumpkins. "Frumenty": an English dish consisting of wheat boiled in milk, with seasoning; the Roanoke dish was probably made of boiled corn (maize) and herbs. The "sodden" foods were probably soaked or stewed.
9. I.e., both green plants and woody ones. Barlowe is mistaken here, North American Indians generally did not ferment grapes or any other food stuff.
1. Fed.

2. I.e., food.
3. By "white and sweet," Barlowe probably means clean, although the coastal clays did produce light-colored pots.
4. I.e., their sleeping quarters were farther inside or within the dwellings.
5. Made a move toward. "Espied": saw.
6. In addition.
7. Sent on board with us.
8. Suspicion. "Pretty": considerable.

loving people there cannot be found in the world, as far as we have hitherto
had trial.[9]

Beyond this island there is the mainland,[1] and over against this island falls
into this spacious water the great river called Occam by the inhabitants, on
which stands a town called Pomeiock, and six days' journey from the same is
situated their greatest city, called Skicoak, which this people affirm to be very
great, [although] the savages were never at it, [they only] speak of it by the
report of their fathers and other men, whom they have heard affirm it to be
above one hour's journey about.[2]

Into this river falls another great river, called Cipo, in which there is found
great store of mussels in which there are pearls. Likewise there descends into
this Occam another river, called Nomopana, on the one side whereof stands
a great town called Chawanoak, and the Lord of that town and country is
called Pooneno. This Pooneno is not subject to the King of Wingandacoa, but
is a free Lord. Beyond this country there [is] another King, whom they call
Menatonon, and these three Kings are in league with each other. Towards the
southwest, four days' journey, is situated a town called Secotan, which is the
southernmost town of Wingandacoa, near unto which six and twenty years
past there was a ship cast away, whereof some of the people were saved, and
those were white people, whom the country people preserved.

And after ten days remaining [on] an outer island [which was] uninhabited,
called Wococon, they with the help of some of the dwellers of Secotan fastened two boats of the country together and made masts [for] them and sails
[from] their shirts. And having taken into them such victuals as the country
yielded, they departed after they had remained [on] this outer island three
weeks, but shortly after, it seems, they were cast away, for the boats were found
upon the coast, cast [ashore on] another island adjoining. Other than these,
there were never any people apparelled, or white of color, either seen or heard
of amongst these people, and these aforesaid were seen only [by] the inhabitants of Secotan, which appeared to be very true, for they wondered marvelously when we were amongst them at the whiteness of our skins, ever coveting
to touch our breasts, and to view the same. Besides, they had our ships in
marvelous admiration,[3] and all things else were so strange unto them [that] it
appeared that none of them had ever seen the like. When we discharged any
piece, were it but an arquebus, they would tremble thereat for very fear, and
for the strangeness of the same, for the weapons which [they] themselves use
are bows and arrows, [and] the arrows are but [made from] small canes, headed
with a sharp shell or tooth of a fish, [though] sufficient enough to kill a naked
man. Their swords [are] of wood, hardened; likewise they use wooden breast-

9. D. B. Quinn calls this passage, "The most precise
example in Renaissance English of the myth of the
gentle savage." "Miscarried": perished. "To adventure": to risk.
1. Barlowe's geographical comments throughout this
section sketch in the map of the mainland that lies
adjacent to Roanoke and the barrier islands. He was
largely basing his information on hearsay, however,
and the 1584 voyagers did not verify much of it. Hence
not all of his place names have been positively identified by modern scholars, and some names have been
proved wrong. Occam, which Barlowe took to be the
local word for Albemarle Sound (his "great river"),
has been identified as an Algonquian word for the land
that lay beyond it, on the mainland proper. Cipo was a

general Algonquian term for "river," not apparently a
specific place name. On the other hand, Pomeiock was
a village located near Albemarle Sound roughly southwest of Roanoke, and Secotan was a village located
near the Pamlico River west of Pomeiock. John White
has left a detailed and very revealing rendering of
Secotan.
2. In circumference.
3. "Marvelous admiration" and "wondered marvelously" have a more powerful force than is commonly
true in modern English. These words suggest a shock
of primal amazement at something completely
unknown, and unsuspected, beforehand. "Coveting":
desiring.

plates for their defense. They have besides a kind of club, on the end whereof they fasten the sharp horns of a stag or other beast. When they go to wars they carry about with them their Idol, of whom they ask counsel, as the Romans were wont [to do] of the Oracle of Apollo.[4] They sing songs as they march towards the battle instead of [using] drums and trumpets; their wars are very cruel and bloody, by reason whereof [as well as the] civil dissensions which have happened of late years amongst them, the people are marvelously wasted, and in some places the country left desolate.[5]

Adjoining to this country aforesaid called Secotan begins a country called Pomovik, belonging to another King whom they call Piemacum, and this King is in league with the next King adjoining towards the setting of the sun, and the country Newsiok, situated upon the goodly river called Neuse. These Kings have mortal war with Wingina, King of Wingandacoa, but about two years past there was a peace made between the King Piemacum, and the Lord of Secotan, as these men whom we have brought with us to England, have given us to understand. But there remains a mortal malice in the Secotans, for many injuries and slaughters done upon them by this Piemacum. They invited divers men and thirty women of the best of his country to their town to a feast, and when they were altogether merry and praying before their Idol (which is nothing else but a mere illusion[6] of the devil) the captain or Lord of the town suddenly came upon them, and slew them every one, reserving the women and children. And [Manteo and Wanchese] have oftentimes since persuaded us[7] to surprise [Piemacum's] town, having promised and assured us, that there will be found in it great store of commodities, but whether their persuasion be to the end [that] they may be revenged [on] their enemies, or for the love they bear to us, we leave that to the trial hereafter.[8]

Beyond this island called Roanoke are many islands very plentiful of fruits and other natural increases,[9] together with many towns and villages along the side of the continent, some bounding upon the islands and some stretching into the land.

When we first had sight of this country, some thought the first land we saw to be the continent, but after we entered into the haven, we saw before us another mighty long sea, for there lie along the coast a trace of islands, two hundred miles in length, adjoining to the Ocean sea, and between the islands, two or three entrances. When you are entered between them (these islands being very narrow for the most part, [that is,] in most places six miles broad, in some places less, in [a] few more), then there appears another great sea, containing in breadth in some places forty, and in some fifty, in some twenty miles over, before you come unto the continent. And in this enclosed sea there are above a hundred islands of divers bignesses, whereof one is sixteen miles long, at which we were, finding it a most pleasant and fertile ground replenished with goodly cedars and divers other sweet woods, full of currants,

4. The originally Greek deity Apollo became important in matters of prophecy for the Romans, especially after Emperor Augustus (63 B.C.–A.D. 14) erected the Palatine temple for him in Rome during the 1st century B.C.
5. The source of Barlowe's comments about eastern American Indian warfare must have been Native Americans who told him of past encounters, so that his evaluation of the whole question cannot have rested on firsthand observation. This fact does not mean that the

points he makes are thus exaggerated or wrong; note, however, that the people with whom he actually dealt treated the English with utmost courtesy, suggesting that any such warfare resulted from a complex local political context.
6. Image.
7. I.e., argued that we should.
8. I.e., to a later attempt.
9. Produce.

of flax, and many other notable commodities, which we at that time had no leisure to view. Besides this island there are many, as I have said, some of two or three, of four, or five miles, some more, some less, most beautiful and pleasant to behold, replenished with deer, coneys, hares, and divers beasts, and about them the goodliest and best fish in the world, and in great abundance.

Thus, Sir, we have acquainted you with the particulars of our discovery, made this present voyage, as far forth as[1] the shortness of the time we there continued would afford us [to] take view thereof. And so, contenting ourselves with this service at this time, which we hope hereafter to enlarge as occasion and assistance shall be given, we resolved to leave the country and to apply ourselves to return for England, which we did accordingly, and arrived safely in the West of England about the [middle] of September [1584]. * * *

We brought home also two of the savages, being lusty[2] men, whose names were Wanchese and Manteo.

ca. 1585   1589

---

1. As far as.   2. Healthy, handsome.

THOMAS HARRIOT
1560–1621

An Oxford graduate who had entered Sir Walter Ralegh's employment in the early 1580s, Thomas Harriot probably trained Ralegh and the members of the first Roanoke expedition in navigational skills, and he may have accompanied Arthur Barlowe when the expedition left England in the spring of 1584. It is certain, in any case, that he went on the second voyage, in 1585, as a naturalist who was to collaborate with the painter John White. Having landed in America in April 1585, Harriot and White passed much of the time between then and July of the following year studying and collecting (the two spent that fall and winter, for instance, with an exploring party farther north, in the Chesapeake). In the process, Harriot must have compiled substantial notebooks. These do not survive, but we have a glimpse of them in his descriptive work, A *Brief and True Report of the New Found Land of Virginia* (1588). A *Brief and True Report* gives much information about the flora and fauna the two men found as well as about the American Indians from whom Harriot, having been taught their language (perhaps by Wanchese, a Roanoke Indian who returned with Barlowe to England in 1584), learned a great deal.

While Harriot and White were surveying the landscape, the infant colony—planted on Roanoke, an island off the coast of what is now the North Carolina mainland, at the suggestion of Granganimeo, brother of the Roanoke Indian chief Wingina—was struggling with political unrest. Ralegh's commander-in-chief, the hot-headed Sir Richard Grenville, exerted his authority by bullying the Native Americans and alienating and threatening his own people. When Grenville left for England in August 1585, one of his opponents, Governor Ralph Lane, expressed a relief many must have felt. But Lane himself dealt poorly with the Roanoke Indians and other nearby native groups, so that relations deteriorated, despite the fact that Wingina's people gave much aid to the colonists. Exasperated, the chief began to withhold crucial food supplies from the English, who were told by other Native Americans that he was plotting their annihilation. After nightfall on June 1, 1586, Lane led a preemptive attack on Dasemunkepeuc, Wingina's mainland village. Wounded while asleep, Wingina escaped but was chased down in the woods, killed, and beheaded.

Few of these increasingly serious events are mentioned by Harriot in his *Brief and True Report*. Harriot does glance at Lane's "fierce" dealings with Wingina's people, and he does give ample evidence that diseases imported by the English had already begun to decimate the Native Americans. Had Harriot's own purpose as a writer been less descriptive and propagandistic (apparently he wrote at Ralegh's direction as a new colony was being readied under John White's command), this history of England's first Virginia colony might have been more candid. Harriot's narrative does not acknowledge the disorderly end of the first colony, most of whose survivors were rescued from Roanoke Island by Sir Francis Drake during a severe storm in June 1586. When Grenville returned with reinforcements and supplies later that summer, he found the compound abandoned. Grenville left behind a handful of men (some of whom perished there, some of whom went off in a boat but were never seen again) when he departed on what was to prove a long, circuitous return to England via the Azores, Newfoundland, and then the Azores once again.

Harriot did not see his optimistic text through the press until 1588. By that point, a new group of colonists under his collaborator White's command had left England and sailed for Roanoke, and White had hastily returned to England for more supplies. The great naval encounter between England and the Spanish Armada in 1588 disrupted almost all English shipping, leaving White unable to return to America as quickly as he wished; he was forced to abandon his colonists, whose disappearance from Roanoke Island has never been adequately explained. Ironically, Harriot's propaganda came forth after the fate of the "Lost Colony" had been all but sealed.

From A Brief and True Report of the New Found Land of Virginia

From *Of the Nature and Manners of the People*[1]

[In] respect of troubling our inhabiting and planting [the natives] are not to be feared,[2] but * * * shall have cause both to fear and love us, that shall inhabit with them.

They are a people clothed with loose mantles made of deerskins, and aprons of the same round about their middles, all else naked, of such a difference of statures only as we in England,[3] having no edge tools or weapons of iron or steel to offend us with (neither know they how to make any). Those weapons that they have are only bows made of witch hazel, and arrows of reeds, [and] flat-edged truncheons[4] also of wood, about a yard long. Neither have they anything to defend themselves [with] but targets made of bark, and some armor made of sticks wickered[5] together with thread.

Their towns are but small, and near the seacoast but few, some containing but ten or twelve houses, some twenty. The greatest that we have seen has

1. The text is from Richard Hakluyt, *The Principall Navigations, Voyages, Traffiques & Discoveries of the English Nation*, vol. 8 (1904). "Manners": customs, practices.

2. I.e., they will not resist English settlement.
3. Varying in height much as the English do.
4. Heavy clubs.
5. Woven. "Targets": small shields.

been out of thirty houses. If they be walled, it is only done with bark of trees made fast to stakes, or else with poles only fixed upright, and close, one by another.[6]

Their houses are made of small poles, made fast at the tops in round form, after the manner as is used in many arbors[7] in our gardens in England. In most towns [they are] covered with bark, and in some with artificial mats made of long rushes,[8] from the tops of the houses down to the ground. The length of them is commonly double to the breadth. In some places they are but twelve and sixteen yards long, and in other some[9] we have seen [them] of four and twenty.

In some places of the country, one only[1] town belongs to the government of a Wiroans or chief Lord, in other some two or three, in some six, eight, and more. The greatest Wiroans that yet we had been dealing with, had but eighteen towns in his government, and [was] able to make[2] not above seven or eight hundred fighting men at the most. The language of every government is different from any other, and the further they are distant, the greater is the difference.

Their manner of wars amongst themselves is either by sudden surprising one another, most commonly about the dawning of the day, or moonlight, or else by ambushes, or some subtle devices. Set battles are very rare, except it falls out[3] where there are many trees, where either part may have some hope of defence, after the delivery of every arrow, in leaping behind some [tree] or other.

If there fall out any wars between us and them, what their fight[ing] is likely to be (we having advantages against them so many manner of ways, as by our discipline, our strange weapons and [other devices], especially ordinance great and small), it may easily be imagined. By the experience we have had in some places, the turning up of their heels against us in running away was their best defense.[4]

In respect of us, they are a poor people, and for want of skill and judgment in the knowledge and use of our things,[5] do esteem our trifles before things of greater value. Notwithstanding [this,] in their proper manner[6] (considering the want of such means as we have), they seem very ingenious, for although they have no such tools, nor any such crafts, sciences, and arts as we, yet in those things they do, they show excellence of wit. And by how much they upon due consideration shall find our manner of knowledges and crafts to exceed theirs in perfection, and speed for doing or execution, by so much the more is it probable that they should desire our friendship and love, and have the greater respect for pleasing and obeying us. Whereby may be hoped, if means of good government be used, that they may in short time be brought to civility, and the embracing of true religion.

Some religion they have already, which although it is far from the truth, yet being as it is, there is hope it may be easier and sooner reformed.

They believe that there are many gods, which they call Mantoac, but of

---

6. I.e., with palisade fences.
7. Small, open shelters.
8. Artfully made from reeds.
9. I.e., in other places.
1. Single, solitary.
2. Recruit, call on.
3. Happens.
4. Perhaps an obscure reference to Roanoke governor

Ralph Lane's (1530–1603) surprise attack on Chief Wingina. After he was attacked in his village, Wingina indeed ran away; he was tracked down, shot in the back, and then beheaded.
5. I.e., European weapons, tools, and so forth. "In respect of": by comparison with. "Want": lack.
6. I.e., within the limits of their own culture and technology.

different sorts and degrees, one only chief and great God, who has been from all eternity. Who (as they affirm) when he purposed to make the world, made first other gods of a principal order to be as means and instruments to be used in the creation and government to follow, and afterwards [made] the sun, moon, and stars as petty gods. * * * First (they say) were made waters, out of which by the gods was made all diversity of creatures that are visible or invisible.

For mankind they say a woman was made first, who by the working of one of the gods, conceived and brought forth children. And in such sort they say they had their beginning. But how many years or ages have passed since, they say they can make no relation,[7] having no letters or other such means as we to keep records of the particularities of times past, but only tradition from father to son.

They think that all the gods are of human shape, and therefore they represent them by images in the forms of men, which they call Kewasowok (one alone is called Kewas).[8] Them they place in houses appropriate, or temples, which they call Machicomuck, where they worship, pray, sing, and make many times [an] offering unto them. In some Machicomuck we have seen but one Kewas, in some two, and in other some three. The common sort think them to be also gods.[9]

They believe also [in] the immortality of the soul, that after this life as soon as the soul is departed from the body, according to the works it hath done, it is either carried to heaven the habitacle[1] of gods, there to enjoy perpetual bliss and happiness, or else to a great pit or hole, which they think to be in the furthest parts of their part of the world toward the sunset, there to burn continually—[that] place they call Popogusso.

For the confirmation of this opinion, they told me two stories, of two men that had been lately dead and revived again. The one [incident] happened but [a] few years before our coming into the country [to] a wicked man, who having [died and been] buried, the next day the earth of the grave being seen to move, [he] was taken up again. [He] made declaration where his soul had been, that is to say, very near entering into Popogusso, had not one of the gods saved him, and [given] him leave to return again, and teach his friends what they should do to avoid that terrible place of torment. The other [incident] happened in the same year we were there, but in a town that was sixty miles from us, and it was told [to] me for strange news, that one being dead, buried, and taken up again [like] the first, showed that although his body had lain dead in the grave, yet his soul was alive and had traveled far in a long broad way, on both sides whereof grew most delicate and pleasant trees, bearing more rare and excellent fruits than ever he had seen before, or was able to express. And at length [he] came to most brave and fair[2] houses, near which he met his father, [who] had been dead before, who gave him great charge to go back

7. Narration.
8. In the 1590 edition of Harriot's text, which was published on the Continent and contained engravings taken from the watercolors of John White (c. 1545–93), one such idol is shown. The accompanying text explains, in part: "The people of this country have an Idol, which they call Kiwasa (it is carved of wood; in length, four foot), whose head is like the heads of the people of Florida. The face is of flesh color, the breast white, the rest is all black, the thighs are also spotted with white. He hath a chain around his neck of white beads, between which are other round beads of copper which they esteem more than gold or silver."
9. This comment about the commoner's confusion of the image or icon with the god it represented would be of particular importance to a Protestant English audience, because there was a strong iconoclastic element in English religious thought.
1. Dwelling place.
2. Splendid, well-built.

again, and show his friends what good they were to do to enjoy the pleasures of that place, which when he had done he should afterwards come again.

What subtlety soever [there may] be in the Wiroances and priests, this opinion works so much [effect] in many of the common and simple sort of people, that it makes them have great respect to their Governors, and also great care what they do, to avoid torment after death, and to enjoy bliss, although notwithstanding [this fact], there is punishment ordained for malefactors, [such] as stealers, whoremongers, and other sorts of wicked doers, some punished with death, some with forfeitures, some with beating, according to the greatness[3] of the facts.

And this is the sum of their religion, which I learned by having special familiarity with some of their priests, wherein they were not so sure grounded,[4] nor gave such credit to their traditions and stories, but through conversing with us they were brought into great doubts of their own [faith], and no small admiration of ours, [so that there was] earnest desire in many, to learn more than we had means, for want of perfect utterance in their language, to express.

Most things they saw with us—[such] as mathematical instruments; sea compasses; the virtue of the load-stone in drawing iron; a perspective glass[5] whereby were shown many strange sights; burning glasses; wild fireworks; guns; hooks; writing and reading; spring-clocks that seem to go of themselves; and many other things that we had—were so strange unto them, and so far exceeded their capacities to comprehend the reason and means how they should be made and done, that they thought they were rather the works of gods than of men, or at the [least] they had been given and taught [to] us [by] the gods. Which made many of them to have such [an] opinion of us, that if they knew not the truth of God and Religion already, it was rather to be had from us whom God so specially loved, than from a people that were so simple, as they found themselves to be in comparison [with] us. Whereupon greater credit was given unto that [which] we spoke of, concerning such matters.

Many times and in every town where I came, according as I was able, I made declaration of the contents of the Bible, [namely,] that therein was set forth the true and only God, and his mighty works, that therein was contained the true doctrine of salvation through Christ, with many particularities of Miracles and chief points of Religion, as I was able then to utter, and thought fit for the time. And although I told them the book materially and of itself was not of any such virtue, as I thought they did conceive, but only the doctrine therein contained; yet would many be glad to touch it, to embrace it, to kiss it, to hold it to their breasts and heads, and stroke over all their body with it, to show their hungry desire of that knowledge which was spoken of.

The Wiroans with whom we dwelled, called Wingina, and many of his people would be glad many times to be with us at our Prayers, and many times would call upon us both in his own town [and] in others whither he sometimes accompanied us, to pray and sing Psalms, hoping thereby to be partaker of the same effects which we by that means also expected.

Twice this Wiroans was so grievously sick that he was like to die, and as he lay languishing (doubting of any help [from] his own priests and thinking he was in such danger for offending us and thereby our God), sent for some of us to pray and be a means to our God, [so] that it would please Him either that

---

3. I.e., seriousness.
4. I.e., secure.

5. A device that produced distorted views of the world. "Load-stone": magnet.

he might live, or after death dwell with Him in bliss, [and] so likewise were the requests of many others in the like case.

[At] a time also when their corn began to wither by reason of a drought which happened extraordinarily,[6] fearing that it had come to pass [because] in something they had displeased us, many would come to us and desire us to pray to our God of England, that he would preserve their corn, promising that when it was ripe we also should be partakers of the fruit.

There could at no time happen any strange sickness, losses, hurts, or any other cross[7] unto them, but that they would impute to us the cause or means thereof, for offending or not pleasing us. One other rare and strange accident, leaving others, will I mention before I end, which moved the whole country that either knew or heard of us, to [hold] us in wonderful admiration.[8]

There was no town where we had any subtle device practiced against us (we leaving it unpunished or not revenged because we sought by all means possible to win them by gentleness) but that within a few days after our departure from every such town, the people began to die very fast, and many in short space, in some towns about twenty, in some forty, and in one six score, which in truth was very many in respect of their numbers. This happened in no place that we could learn, but where we had been, where they used some practice against us, and after such time.[9] The disease also was so strange, that they neither knew what it was, nor how to cure it, [for] the like by report of the oldest men in the country never [had] happened before, time out of mind (a thing especially observed by us, as also by the natural inhabitants themselves). Insomuch that when some of the inhabitants which were our friends, and especially the Wiroans Wingina, had observed such effects in four or five towns [following] their wicked practices, they were persuaded that it was the work of God through our means, and that we by him might kill and slay whom we would without weapons, and not [have to] come near them. And thereupon when it had happened that they had understanding that any of their enemies had abused us in our journeys (hearing that we had wrought no revenge with our weapons, and fearing upon some cause the matter should so rest), [they] did come and entreat us that we would be a means to our God that they as others that had dealt ill with us might in like sort die, alleging how much it would be for our credit and profit (as also theirs) and hoping furthermore that we would do so much at their request [out] of the friendship we professed them.[1]

[We, however, argued that these requests] were ungodly, affirming that our God would not subject himself to any such prayers and requests of men; that indeed all things have been and were to be done according to his good pleasure as he had ordained; and that we, to show ourselves his true servants, ought rather to make petition for the contrary, [namely], that they with them[2] might

---

6. I.e., the drought was extraordinarily severe.
7. Accident.
8. I.e., in awe. "Leaving": passing over.
9. I.e., it happened after the English had left.
1. Neither Harriot nor the Native Americans understood the accidental exchange of disease that was beginning to devastate the local population with European pathogens. That the ill effects were thought to be limited to villages in which some dispute had arisen between the two groups gave the American Indians the impression that the English were taking revenge. This pattern in the outbreaks has, however, a simpler explanation: the greater intimacy that may well have preceded and even produced the disagreements was one precondition for the spread of infection. Despite their confusion, Wingina's people seized on the usefulness of "English" sickness for their own political disputes with other Indian groups.
2. I.e., both Wingina's people and their enemies.

live together with us, be made partakers of His truth, and serve Him in righteousness.

But, notwithstanding [our disavowals], * * * because the effect fell out so
suddenly and shortly afterwards according to their desires,[3] they thought nevertheless [that] it came to pass by our means, and that we in using such speeches
[with] them, did but dissemble the matter; and therefore [they] came unto us
to give us thanks in their manner, [because] although we satisfied them not in
promise,[4] yet in deeds and effect we had fulfilled their desires.

This marvelous accident[5] [produced] in all the country [such] strange opinions of us, that some people could not tell whether to think us gods or men,
and the rather because that all the space of their sickness, there was no man of
ours known to die, or [be] especially sick. They noted also that we had no
women amongst us, [and] that we did [not] care for any of theirs.

Some therefore were of [the] opinion that we were not born of women, and
therefore not mortal, but that we were men of an old generation many years
past, then risen again to immortality.

Some would likewise seem to prophecy that there were more of our generation yet to come [to this land] to kill theirs and take their places, as some
thought the purpose was, [judging] by that which was already done. Those
that were immediately to come after us they imagined to be in the air, yet
invisible and without bodies, and [imagined] that they by our entreaty and for
the love of us, did make the people to die in [the way] they did, by shooting
invisible bullets into them.

To confirm this opinion, their physicians (to excuse their ignorance in curing the disease)[6] would not be ashamed to * * * make the simple people
believe that the strings of blood they sucked out of the sick bodies, were the
strings wherewith the invisible bullets were tied and cast.[7] Some also thought
that we shot them ourselves out of our pieces, from the place where we
dwelled, and killed the people in any [such] town that had offended us, as we
listed,[8] how far distant from us soever it was. And [others] said that it was the
special work of God for our sakes, as we ourselves have cause in some sort to
think no less. * * * Their opinions I have set down the more at large, that it
may appear unto you that there is good hope they may be brought through
discreet dealing and government[9] to the embracing of the truth, and consequently to honor, obey, fear, and love us.

And although some of our company towards the end of the year showed
themselves too fierce in slaying some of the people in some towns, upon causes
that on our part might easily enough have been borne * * * by carefulness of
ourselves [there is] nothing at all to be feared.[1]

1588

---

3. I.e., the enemies for whose suffering they petitioned the English soon were visited with illness.
4. I.e., the English had not vowed to punish Wingina's enemies.
5. Occurrence, incident.
6. I.e., to find an excuse for their own failure to cure
the illness.
7. Shot, thrown. The "strings" of blood may have
been partly coagulated strands produced by the
unknown illness.

8. Wished.
9. I.e., direction, control. "At large": at such length.
1. Here Harriot hints at the brutal behavior of Ralph
Lane, who as governor of the infant colony reacted to
rumors of a Roanoke Indian plot against the English by
attacking the village of Dasemunkepeuc. By the time
Harriot published his Relation in 1588, Wingina (one
of "some of the people in some towns" whom Lane
had killed) had been dead for two years.

JOHN WHITE

c. 1545–1593

According to the Elizabethan herbalist John Gerard, John White was "an excellent painter who carried very many people into Virginia . . . there to inhabite." White captured the sights of the Roanoke region and the Chesapeake with brush and pen in 1585 and 1586, collaborating with Thomas Harriot, who described the region in writing. In 1587 White was chosen governor of the tragic second colony sent to Roanoke. Although this man of modest background played a central role in the whole Ralegh enterprise, we know little of his life before 1585 or after 1590. His many excellent maps suggest that he was trained as a land surveyor, and his skills as an ethnographic artist may well have been honed during Sir Martin Frobisher's second voyage (1577) to Baffin Island, in the Canadian Arctic, located due west of Greenland. How many voyages White made to America is uncertain. The one he undertook in 1590 was described as his "fifth," so clearly he had been to the New World before the Roanoke voyage of 1585 and (like Harriot) may have been on one of the vessels that went there in 1584 as well.

White's last voyage, in 1590, was a desperate attempt to locate the survivors of the second Roanoke contingent, whom he last saw in 1587 before he sailed to England for fresh supplies. Unable to return quickly to America because of shipping disruptions caused by the great sea battle between England and the Spanish Armada, White at last arrived there in 1590, only to find that the settlers, including his daughter and her family, had vanished. At Roanoke, the capital "City of Ralegh" yielded only a clutter of broken objects and ruined houses, perhaps a testimony to Governor Ralph Lane's vicious attack in 1586 on Chief Wingina and his people. Further searching might have turned up clues, or perhaps even the colonists themselves, but White was not able to linger in Virginia. He had come as a passenger in a loosely allied group of privateers (private vessels licensed to disrupt enemy shipping) more interested in raiding Spanish ships in the Caribbean than in adding their own names to the death toll of Ralegh's Roanoke Colony. Though White found hints of the settlers' relocation to nearby Croatoan, the deaths of one of the privateer captains and several other men, together with fierce weather, forced him to abandon the search.

Anthologized here is White's account of what he found on the island in 1590, along with part of his record of the voyage home to England, prepared three years later for inclusion in the great collection of voyage narratives edited by Richard Hakluyt, *The Principall Navigations . . . of the English Nation* (1599–1600). In a letter to Hakluyt that accompanied his narrative, White summed up the course of his American career: "Thus may you plainly perceive the success [i.e., outcome] of my fifth and last voyage to Virginia, which was no less unfortunately ended than [adversely] begun, and [was] as luckless to many, as [it was] sinister to myself. But I would to God it had been as prosperous to all, as [it was troublesome] to the planters; and as joyfull to me, as discomfortable to them."

From The Fifth Voyage of Mr. John White[1]

On the first of August the wind scanted, and from thence forward we had very foul weather with much rain, thundering, and great [water]spouts, which fell round about us nigh unto our ships.

1. The text is derived from Richard Hakluyt, *The Principall Navigations, Voyages, Traffiques, & Discoveries of the English Nation*, vol. 8 (1904).

The third we stood again in for the shore, and at midday we took the height[2] of the same. The height of that place we found to be 34° of latitude. Towards night we were within three leagues of the low sandy islands west of Wococon.[3] But the weather continued so exceedingly foul, that we could not come to an anchor nigh the coast, wherefore we stood off again to sea until Monday, the ninth of August.

On Monday the storm ceased, and we had very great likelihood of fair weather. Therefore, we stood in again for the shore, and came to an anchor at eleven fathoms in 35° of latitude, within a mile of the shore, where we went on land on the narrow sandy island, being one of the islands west of Wococon. In this island we took in some fresh water and caught great store of fish in the shallow water. Between the main[land] (as we supposed) and that island it was but a mile over, and three or four foot deep in most places.

On the twelfth in the morning we departed from thence and toward night we came to an anchor at the northeast end of the island of Croatoan, by reason of a breach which we perceived to lie out two or three leagues into the sea.[4] Here we rode all night.

The thirteenth in the morning, before we weighed our anchors, our boats were sent to sound[5] over this breach, our ships riding on the side thereof at five fathom, and a ship's length from us we found but four and a quarter, and then deepening and shallowing for the space of two miles; so that sometimes we found five fathom, and by and by seven, and within two casts with the lead nine, and then eight, next cast five, and then six, and then four, and then nine again, and deeper. [A mere] three fathoms was the last, two leagues off from the shore. This breach is in 35°30', and lies at the very northeast point of Croatoan, where [there is] a fret[6] out of the main sea into the inner waters, which part the islands and the mainland.

The fifteenth of August towards evening we came to an anchor at Hatorask, in 36°20', in five fathoms [of] water, three leagues from the shore. At our first coming to anchor on this shore we saw a great smoke rise on the isle [of] Roanoke, near the place where I left our colony in the year 1587, which smoke put us in good hope that some of the colony were there expecting my return out of England.

The sixteenth, [the] next morning, our two boats went ashore, and Captain Cocke and Captain Spicer and their company with me, with [the] intention to pass to the place at Roanoke where our countrymen were left. At our putting [off] from the ship, we commanded our master gunner to make ready two minions and a falcon,[7] well loaded, and to shoot them off with reasonable space between every shot, to the end that their reports might be heard to the place where we hoped to find some of our people. This was accordingly per-

---

2. They determined the latitude of this stretch of the coast by measuring the height of the sun above the horizon at noon, using a quadrant, or a cross-staff.
3. On the maps he drew of the Carolina coast, White identified Wococon as the southernmost of the four major islands of the Outer Banks, with Croatoan, Paquiwoc, and Hatorask ranging northward from it. Together, the four islands defined Pamlico Sound, within which (near Hatorask at the north end) lay Roanoke Island. The configuration of the barrier islands has changed much over the intervening centuries. Although the general features of the area remain roughly similar, White's "Hatorask" is not the same as

the modern Hatteras Island, "Croatoan" was roughly equivalent to the south end of modern Hatteras plus the north part of modern Ocracoke Island, and Wococon probably encompassed parts of modern Ocracoke and Portsmouth islands.
4. White means that they came to anchor for the night because, as they sailed by Croatoan on their way north, they could see dangerous shoals offshore. These would be the 16th-century predecessors of Diamond and Outer Shoals, located off modern Cape Hatteras.
5. I.e., check the depth of water over the shallows.
6. An opening or passage.
7. Kinds of light artillery.

formed, and our two boats put off unto the shore. In the admiral's boat[8] we sounded all the way and found from our ship until we came within a mile of the shore, nine, eight, and seven fathom; but before we were halfway between our ships and the shore we saw another great smoke to the southwest of Kenrick's Mounts.[9] We therefore thought [it] good to go to that second smoke first, but it was much farther from the harbor where we [had] landed [on Roanoke] than we supposed it to be, so that we were very sorely tired before we came to the smoke. But that which grieved us more was that when we came to the smoke we found no man nor [any] sign that any had been there lately, nor yet any fresh water in all this way to drink. Being thus wearied with this journey, we returned to the harbor where we [had] left our boats, [whose crews] in our absence had brought their casks ashore for fresh water, so we deferred our going to Roanoke until the next morning, and caused some of those sailors to dig in those sandy hills for fresh water, whereof we found sufficient [supply]. That night we returned aboard with our boats and our whole company in safety.

The next morning, being the seventeenth of August, our boats and company were prepared again to go up to Roanoke, but Captain Spicer had then sent his boat ashore for fresh water, by means whereof it was ten of the clock aforenoon before we put [off] from our ships, which were then come to an anchor within two miles of the shore. The admiral's boat was halfway toward the shore when Captain Spicer put off from his ship. The admiral's boat first passed the breach,[1] but not without some danger of sinking, for we had a sea break into our boat which filled us half full of water, but by the will of God and [the] careful steerage of Captain Cocke, we came safely ashore, saving only that our furniture, victuals, match,[2] and powder were much wet and spoiled. For at this time the wind blew at northeast and direct into the harbor, so great a gale that the sea broke extremely[3] on the bar and the tide went very forcibly at the entrance. By [the] time our admiral's boat was hauled ashore, and most of our things taken out to dry, Captain Spicer came to the entrance of the breach with his mast standing up, and was half passed over, but by the rash and indiscreet steerage of Ralph Skinner, his master's mate, a very dangerous sea broke into their boat and overset them quite. The men kept [to] the boat, some in it and some hanging on it, but the next sea set the boat on ground,[4] where it beat so that some of them were forced to let go their hold, hoping to wade ashore. But the sea still beat them down, so that they could neither stand nor swim, and the boat twice or thrice was turned the keel upward, whereon Captain Spicer and Skinner hung until they sunk, and were seen no more. But four that could swim a little kept themselves in deeper water and were saved by Captain Cocke's means, who so soon as he saw their oversetting, stripped himself, [as did] four others that could swim very well, and with all haste possible [they] rowed unto them, and saved [those] four.

8. I.e., the one from the largest ship, in this case the *Hopewell*.

9. High sand dunes on Cape Kenrick, then the outermost point of land on the Outer Banks, located between White's Hatorask and Paquiwoc. This cape disappeared toward the end of the following century. The boats of which White writes had headed roughly west (or perhaps northwest) to reach Roanoke and would have had to swing around to the south to seek out the place where this second fire had been lighted.

1. One of the channels separating the ends of the Outer Banks islands from each other. Because the water is typically shallow in such places, however, the word still carries the meaning it had in his earlier usage (see n. 4, p. 84).

2. Wick used in firing matchlock guns or cannons. "Steerage": steering. "Furniture": gear.

3. I.e., with extreme force.

4. I.e., forced it down against the sea bottom.

They were eleven in all, and seven of the chief were drowned, whose names were Edward Spicer, Ralph Skinner, Edward Kelley, Thomas Bevis, Hance the Surgeon, Edward Kelborne, [and] Robert Coleman. This mischance did so much discomfort the sailors, that they were all of one mind, [namely,] not to go any further to seek the planters. But in the end by the commandment and persuasion of me and Captain Cocke, they prepared the boats, and seeing the Captain and me so resolute, they seemed much more willing. Our boats and all things fitted again, we put off from Hatorask, being the number of nineteen persons in both boats, but before we could get to the place where our planters were left, it was so exceedingly dark that we overshot the place [by] a quarter of a mile. There we espied towards the north end of the island the light of a great fire through the woods, [toward] which we presently rowed. When we came right over against it, we let fall our grapnel[5] near the shore, and sounded with a trumpet a call, and afterwards many familiar English tunes of songs, and called to them friendly, but we had no answer. We therefore landed at daybreak, and coming to the fire, we found the grass and sundry rotten trees burning about the place. From hence we went through the woods to that part of the island directly over against Dasemunkepeuc,[6] and from thence we returned by the waterside, round about the north point of the island, until we came to the place where I left our colony in the year [1587]. In all this way we saw in the sand the print of the savages' feet, of two or three sorts, trodden [that] night, and as we entered up the sandy bank [we saw that], upon a tree in the very brow thereof,[7] were curiously carved these fair Roman letters,[8] C R O: which letters presently we knew to signify the place where I should find the planters seated, according to a secret token agreed upon between them and me at my last departure from them, which was that in any ways[9] they should not fail to write or carve on the trees or posts of the doors the name of the place where they should be seated, for at my coming away they were prepared to remove from Roanoke fifty miles into the main[land]. Therefore at my departure from them in Anno 1587, I willed them that if they should happen to be distressed in any of those places that then they should carve over the letters or name a cross ✚ in this form, but we found no such sign of distress. And having well considered of this, we passed toward the place where they were left in sundry houses, but we found the houses taken down, and the place very strongly enclosed with a high palisade of great [posts], with curtains and flankers,[1] very fort-like, and one of the chief trees or posts at the right side of the entrance had the bark taken off, and five feet from the ground in fair capital letters was graven CROATOAN, without any cross or sign of distress. This done, we entered into the palisade, where we found many bars of iron, two pigs of lead, four iron fowlers, iron saker-shot,[2] and such like heavy things, thrown here and there, almost overgrown with grass and weeds. From thence we went along by the waterside, towards the point of the creek to see if we could find any of their boats or [the] pinnace,[3] but we could perceive no sign of them, nor any of the last falcons and other small ordnance[4] which were left

5. Grappling hook, used as an anchor. "Over against it": directly opposite it.
6. Chief Wingina's principal village, located on the mainland across a narrow channel west of Roanoke Island.
7. I.e., at the very top ("brow") of the sandy bank.
8. I.e., in the style of inscriptions found on Roman buildings, consisting of simple large capitals.
9. I.e., by all means. "To Ken": sign.
1. Defensive walls on the front and sides.
2. Shot for a small cannon used in sieges and on shipboard. "Pigs": crude ingots.
3. A small sailing vessel.
4. Artillery. "Falcons": light artillery pieces.

with them, at my departure from them. At our return from the creek, some of our sailors, meeting us, told us that they had found where divers[5] chests had been hidden, and long [since] dug up again and broken up, and much of the goods in them spoiled and scattered about, but nothing left (of such things as the savages knew any use of) undefaced. Presently Captain Cocke and I went to the place, which was in the end of an old trench, made two years past by Captain Amadas,[6] where we found five chests that had been carefully hidden [by] the planters, and of the same chests three were my own, and about the place many of my things [lay] spoiled and broken, and my books torn from the covers, the frames of some of my pictures and maps rotten and spoiled with rain, and my armor almost eaten through with rust.[7] This could be [nothing] but the deed of the savages our enemies[8] at Dasemunkepeuc, who [must have] watched the departure of our men to Croatoan, and as soon as they were departed dug up every place where they suspected anything [was] buried. But although it much grieved me to see such spoil of my goods, yet on the other side I greatly joyed that I had safely found a certain token of their being safe at Croatoan, which is the place where Manteo[9] was born, and the savages of the island [were] our friends.

When we had seen in this place so much as we could, we returned to our boats and departed from the shore towards our ships with as much speed as we could, for the weather began to [be] overcast, and [it seemed] very likely that a foul and stormy night would ensure. Therefore, the same evening, with much danger and labor, we got ourselves aboard, by which time the wind and seas were so greatly risen that we doubted our cables and anchors would scarcely hold until morning. Wherefore the captain caused the boat to be manned with five lusty[1] men who could [all] swim well, and sent them to the little island on the righthand of the harbor, to bring aboard six of our men who had filled our casks with fresh water. The boat the same night returned aboard with our men, but all our casks, ready-filled, they left behind, impossible to be had aboard without danger of casting away both men and boats, for this night proved very stormy and foul.

The next morning it was agreed by the captain and myself, with the master and others, to weigh anchor and go for the place at Croatoan where our plant-ers were, for that[2] then the wind was good for that place, and [we agreed] also to leave [those] casks with fresh water on shore [on] the island until our return. So then they brought the cable to the captain, but when the anchor was almost apeak[3] the cable broke, by means whereof we lost another anchor, wherewith we drove so fast [onto] the shore, that we were forced to let fall a third anchor, which came so fast home that the ship was almost aground by Kenrick's Mounts, so that we were forced to let slip [this] cable, end for end.[4] And if it had not chanced that we had fallen into a channel of deeper water, closer by the shore than we accounted of, we could never have gone clear of the point that lies to the southwards of Kenrick's Mounts. Being thus clear of some

---

5. Several.
6. Captain Philip Amadas (c. 1565–1586?), Arthur Barlowe's commander on the 1584 voyage, and "admi-ral of Virginia" in 1585–86.
7. The ruined objects suggest that considerable time had passed since the looting of the settlement.
8. Unlike Harriot, White acknowledges the antago-nism between Wingina's people and the English.
9. One of the two natives who had been taken back to

England by Amadas and Barlowe in 1584, Manteo had come home with the 1585–86 expedition.
1. Strong.
2. Because.
3. Raised to the ship's railing.
4. Run out the cable rope so as to free the ship from the hold of the anchor, in this instance to gain maneu-verability.

dangers, and gotten into deeper waters (but not without some loss: for we had but one cable and anchor left us of the four, and the weather grew to be fouler and fouler; our victuals [were] scarce, and our casks and fresh water lost), it was therefore determined that we should go for St. John[5] or some other island to the southward for fresh water. And it was further proposed that if we could anyway supply our wants of victuals and other necessaries either at Hispaniola, St. John, or Trinidad, that then we should continue in the [West] Indies all the winter following, with [the] hope to make two rich voyages of one,[6] and at our return to visit our countrymen [in] Virginia. The captain and the whole company in the admiral (with my earnest petitions) thereunto agreed, so that it rested only to know what the master of the *Moonlight*, our consort,[7] would do herein. But when we demanded [of] them if they would accompany us in that new determination, they alleged that their weak and leaky ship was not able to continue it; wherefore the same night we parted, leaving the *Moonlight* to go directly for England, and the admiral set [its] course for Trinidad, which course we kept two days.

On the twenty-eighth the wind changed, and it was set on foul weather every way. But this storm brought the wind west and northwest, and blew so forcibly that we were able to bear no sail, [except] our fore-course half mast high,[8] wherewith we ran upon the wind perforce, the due course for England, [so] that we were driven to change our first determination [of] Trinidad, and stood for the Islands of [the] Azores, where we purposed to take in fresh water, and also there hoped to meet with some English men of war about those islands, at whose hands we might obtain some supply of our wants. And thus continuing our course for the Azores, sometimes with calms, and sometimes with very scarce winds, on the fifteenth of September the wind came south-southeast and blew so exceedingly, that we were forced to lie atry[9] all that day. At this time by account we judged ourselves to be about twenty leagues to the west of Corvo and Flores,[1] but about night the storm ceased, and fair weather ensued.

*   *   *

1593   1600

5. San Juan, i.e., Puerto Rico.
6. The small fleet had already taken a Spanish ship as a prize before going to Roanoke, so a successful return to the West Indies would make "two rich voyages [out] of one."

7. Companion ship. "Rested": remained.
8. I.e., they shortened their foresail.
9. I.e., with the bow of the ship held to the weather by the counteraction of fore and aft sails.
1. Islands in the Azores.

SAMUEL DE CHAMPLAIN

c. 1570–1635

Born around 1570 in Brouage, an important seaport and center of the salt industry near La Rochelle on the Atlantic coast of France, Samuel de Champlain served more than any other Frenchman of his time to deepen his country's interest in America and to plant that interest solidly in American soil. Champlain served in the French army as a quartermaster during the 1590s (he fought in the battle in which the English explorer and French ally Sir Martin Frobisher was killed), but soon this merchant captain's son turned to the sea. In 1598 he sailed for Spain on a vessel commanded by an uncle, and the next year he crossed the Atlantic. He crossed it five more times in the next few years—in what capacity or for what purposes we do not know—traveled widely in the Spanish West Indies and Mexico, and then, after 1603, turned his attention toward what was to become France's main base of operations in the West, the northeastern part of North America.

The 1603 voyage to Canada, for which Champlain was recruited as "geographer royal" (perhaps at King Henri IV's urging), was under the command of François Pont-Gravé, who was sent out by a merchant holding the royal fur trade monopoly. Pont-Gravé followed Jacques Cartier's 1530 route up the St. Lawrence River as far as the future site of Montreal, where the expedition took on valuable furs before returning to the French port of Havre de Grace that fall. Early in 1604 Champlain published his official report, *Des Sauvages*, illustrated with his own maps, and in April returned to America along with Pont-Gravé under the command of the Sieur de Monts, the current holder of the royal monopoly and a Protestant merchant from Champlain's home region. Temporarily settled on an island in the St. Croix River between Maine and New Brunswick and then at Port-Royal in Nova Scotia, the Frenchmen spent much of their time exploring the coasts of what would become Maritime Canada and New England, reaching as far south as Cape Cod. Their first two winters in North America, especially that of 1604–05 on St. Croix Island, sorely tested their resolve, and although the third was milder, Champlain concluded, as he convinced the Sieur de Monts once back in France in 1607, that this northeastern coastal zone was not the ideal place for the permanent colony that they hoped to establish. Far better, argued Champlain, would be the valley of the St. Lawrence, first explored for France by Cartier seventy years earlier. On the next voyage, begun in 1608, Champlain returned up that river, on whose shores in that summer he founded Quebec City.

Although Champlain spent much of the rest of his life shuttling back and forth across the Atlantic, crossing it eighteen times between 1610 and 1633, he committed himself fully to the success of the new settlement of Quebec, and thereby ensured the survival of New France. Under his guidance, the French made bold claims to much of North America at a time when the English, with the exception of their small and frail coastal settlement in Virginia, had barely arrived. Champlain himself explored as far inland as Georgian Bay on Lake Huron. And Etienne Brulé, under the direction of Champlain, traveled as far as Lake Superior in the very year that the Pilgrims set out from England and, losing their route on the way to the Hudson River, settled at Plymouth, an area explored and mapped by Champlain fifteen years before.

As well as claiming new territory, Champlain did not neglect relations with the Native Americans. He established strong ties with the Montagnais Indians in the vicinity of his settlement, with the Algonkians farther upriver, and ultimately with the Hurons, who dwelled in what the French came to call Huronia, the large peninsula between lakes Erie and Huron. But in acquiring their friendship (such as it was: he long complained that no American Indian would lead him farther into the country), Champlain encountered and fought with a group of Mohawk, members of the Iroquois Confederacy, with whose expanding empire the French were to be long in conflict.

Like his English contemporary John Smith, Champlain assiduously recorded his experiences, leaving a large body of works that were mostly published in his own day, from *Des Sauvages* (1603) to *Les Voyages* (1613), *Voyages et Descouvertures* (1619), and the last and largest of his books, *Les Voyages de la Nouvelle France* (1632). Because he kept detailed journals of his explorations and of affairs in the French settlements where he lived, Champlain's narratives offer a great deal of information about colonial experience but also about Native American culture and life, particularly in the case of the Hurons, to whom a good part of *Voyages et*

Descouvertures is devoted. Champlain's accounts also offer a valuable perspective on the cultural and economic life of the Massachusetts and Cape Cod Indians before the coming of permanent European settlement (and disease). He describes an agricultural region, thickly settled, rather than the vacant "wilderness" (awaiting the impress of European order) that the English settlers in this region tended to find, especially as they later sought to justify their presence on the land. The different basis of French and English colonial economies, which were sustained by fur trading and agriculture, respectively, helps account for this difference of view. For the French the fur trade would flourish only if the American Indians themselves did, because the Indians with whom the French dealt hunted the fur-bearing animals and transported the pelts and trade goods over long distances. By contrast, the English, although also engaged in the fur trade, were more in competition with agricultural groups of Native Americans for the scarce farmland of New England and other regions to the south.

Part personal history, part propaganda, part communal record, Champlain's works were widely read and consulted during his lifetime. They accorded him a place in the history of New France that he has never lost.

From The Voyages of Sieur de Champlain[1]

From *Chapter VIII*

CONTINUATION OF THE EXPLORATION OF THE COAST OF THE ALMOUCHIQUOIS, AND WHAT OF NOTE WE THERE OBSERVED.

The next day we doubled cape St. Louis,[2] so named by the Sieur de Monts, a moderately low shore in latitude 42° 45'. That day we made two leagues along a sandy coast, and saw as we passed a number of wigwams and gardens. The wind coming ahead, we entered a little bay to await suitable weather for continuing our route. Two or three canoes approached us on their way back from fishing for cod and other fish, which are plentiful thereabouts. These they catch with hooks made of a piece of wood, to which they attach a bone shaped like a harpoon, which they fasten very securely for fear lest it come out. The whole thing has the form of a little crook. The line which is attached to it is made of tree-bark. They gave me one of them, which I took as a curiosity. In this the bone was attached with hemp, which in my opinion is like that of France. They informed me that they gathered this plant in their country without cultivating it, indicating its height as about four to five feet. The said canoe returned to shore to notify the people in the settlement, who made signal-smokes for us; and we perceived eighteen or twenty Indians who came down to the beach and began to dance. Our canoe went ashore to give them some trifles, with which they were much pleased. Some of them came out to beg us to enter their river. We raised anchor to do so, but were unable to get in because the tide was out and the water too shallow; and were obliged to anchor at the entrance. I went on shore, where I saw many more Indians, who received us very kindly. I went to explore the river, but saw only an arm of the sea which extends some little distance into the country, which is par-

1. The text is derived from *The Works of Samuel de Champlain*, edited by Henry P. Biggar, vol. 1 (1922). Champlain recorded these observations of the landscape and peoples of the Massachusetts coast from Gloucester to the southern shore of Cape Cod, during two leisurely voyages in 1605 and 1606.
2. Champlain's party rounded Cape St. Louis (modern Brant Point), just north of what became Plymouth harbor, Massachusetts, on July 18, 1605. The Almouchiquois were inhabitants of this region.

tially cleared. Here it becomes only a brook, which cannot float boats except at high tide. The bay is about a league in circumference. On one side of the entrance is a kind of island covered with trees, especially pines, and it adjoins some sand-dunes which are fairly extensive: on the other side the land is rather high. Within the said bay are two islets, which cannot be seen unless one is inside, and round about them the sea recedes almost completely at low tide. This place is very conspicuous from the sea, inasmuch as the coast is very low except the cape at the entrance to this bay, which we named Cape St. Louis harbor.[3] It is distant from the said cape two leagues, and from Island Cape ten. It lies in approximately the same latitude as cape St. Louis.

On the nineteenth of the month we set out from this place. Coasting toward the south we made four to five leagues, and passed close to a rock which lies on a level with the surface of the water. Continuing our route, we caught sight of some land which we took to be islands, but when nearer perceived that it was mainland, which continued to the north-north-west of us, and that it was the cape of a large bay more than eighteen to nineteen leagues in circumference.[4] We had run so far into this bay that we had to stand on the other tack to double the cape we had seen, which we named the White Cape, because there were sands and dunes which presented this appearance. The favorable wind was of great service here; for otherwise we should have been in danger of being driven upon the coast. This bay is very clear, provided one does not approach the shore nearer than a good league, there being no islands or rocks except the one I have mentioned, which is near a river that extends some distance inland and which we named Ste. Suzanne of the White Cape. From here to cape St. Louis the distance is ten leagues. The White Cape is a point of sand which bends southward some six leagues. This coast has fairly high sand-banks which are very conspicuous from the sea, where soundings are found of thirty, forty and fifty fathoms nearly fifteen or eighteen leagues from land, until one comes to ten fathoms in approaching the shore, which is very clear. There is a great extent of open country along the shore before one enters the woods, which are very delightful and pleasant to the eye. We cast anchor off shore and saw some Indians, toward whom four of our party advanced. Making their way along the sandy beach, they perceived as it were a bay with wigwams bordering it all around. When they were about a league and a half from us an Indian came toward them dancing all over (as they reported to us). He had come down from the high shore, but returned shortly after to give notice of our arrival to those in his settlement.

The next day, the twentieth of the month, we went to the place which our men had discovered, and found it to be a very dangerous port on account of the shoals and sand-banks, where we saw breakers on every side. It was almost low tide when we entered, and there were only four feet of water in the north passage; at high tide there are two fathoms. When we were inside, we saw that this place was rather large, being about three to four leagues in circumference, with all around it little houses about which each owner had as much land as was necessary for his support. A little river enters it which is very pretty; at low tide it has some three and a half feet of water. There are also two or three brooks bordered with meadows. The place would be very fine if only the harbor were good. I took an observation, and found the latitude 42°; and the

3. Plymouth harbor.   4. Cape Cod and Cape Cod Bay.

magnetic variation 18° 40'. There came to us from all sides, dancing, a number of Indians, both men and women. We named this place Malle-barre harbor.[5]

On the next day, the twenty-first of the month, the Sieur de Monts resolved to go and inspect their settlement, and nine or ten of us accompanied him with our arms; the remainder stayed behind to guard the pinnace. We went about a league along shore. Before reaching their wigwams we entered a field planted with Indian corn in the manner I have already described. The corn was in flower, and some five and a half feet in height. There was some less advanced, which they sow later. We saw an abundance of Brazilian beans, many edible squashes of various sizes, tobacco, and roots which they cultivate, the latter having the taste of artichoke. The woods are full of oaks, nut-trees, and very fine cypresses, which are of reddish color and have a very pleasant smell. There were also several fields not cultivated, for the reason that the Indians let them lie fallow. When they wish to plant them they set fire to the weeds and then dig up the field with their wooden spades. Their wigwams are round, and covered with heavy thatch made of reeds. In the middle of the roof is an opening, about a foot and a half wide, through which issues the smoke of their fire. We asked them if they had their permanent residence in this place, and whether there was much snow; but we could not find this out very well since we did not understand their language, although they attempted to explain by signs, taking up sand in their hand, then spreading it on the ground, and indicating that the snow was the same color as our collars and fell to the depth of a foot. Others indicated that it was less, giving us also to understand that the harbor never froze over; but we were unable to ascertain whether the snow lasted a long time. I consider, however, that this country is temperate and the winter not severe.[6] During the time we were there it blew a gale from the north-east which lasted four days, with the sky so overcast that the sun was hardly visible at all. It was very cold, so that we were obliged to put on our greatcoats which we had entirely laid aside. However, I believe this was exceptional, just as often happens in other localities out of season.

On the twenty-third of the said month of July, four or five sailors having gone ashore with some large kettles to fetch fresh water from among the sand-hills at a distance from our pinnace, certain Indians, being desirous to possess some of these kettles,[7] watched for the time when our men went there, and snatched one by force out of the hands of a sailor who had filled his the first and who had no weapons. One of his companions, starting to run after the Indian, quickly returned, being unable to catch him, inasmuch as the latter was a swifter runner than himself. The other Indians, when they saw our sailors running toward our pinnace and shouting to us to discharge some musket-shots at the Indians who were in considerable numbers, took to flight. At that time there were a few Indians on board our pinnace who threw themselves into the sea, and we were able to seize only one of them. Those on shore who had taken to flight, seeing the others swimming, turned back straight to the

---

5. Modern Nauset Harbor, on the Atlantic side of Cape Cod.
6. Because this part of North America lay far south of the latitude of France and England, many early voyagers assumed it would have a mild climate. After visiting this landscape, however, William Bradford wrote, "They that know the winters of that country know them

to be sharp and violent and subject to cruel and fierce storms, dangerous to travel to known places, much more to search an unknown coast."
7. Kettles made of iron and other metals were to be much sought after by Northeast Indian groups who traded their furs for European goods. "Pinnace": a small sailing vessel.

sailor from whom they had taken the kettle and shot several arrows at him from behind and brought him down. Perceiving his condition, they at once rushed upon him and despatched him with their knives. Meantime we made haste to go on shore, and fired muskets from our pinnace. Mine exploded in my hands and nearly killed me. The Indians, hearing this fusillade, again took to flight, and redoubled their speed when they saw that we had landed, being frightened on seeing us run after them. There was no likelihood of catching them; for they are as swift-footed as horses. The dead man[8] was brought in, and some hours later was buried. Meanwhile we kept our prisoner bound hand and foot on board our pinnace, fearing lest he should escape. The Sieur de Monts determined to let him go, feeling persuaded he was not to blame and knew nothing of what had occurred, as was the case also with those who were at the time on board and alongside our pinnace. A few hours later some Indians came toward us, making excuses by signs and outward show that it was not they who had done this evil deed but others farther off in the interior. We were unwilling to do them harm, although it was in our power to avenge ourselves.

* * *

From *Chapter XIII*

THE SIEUR DE POUTRINCOURT SETS OUT FROM PORT ROYAL TO MAKE DISCOVERIES. EVERYTHING WE SAW AND THAT HAPPENED AS FAR AS MALLEBARRE.

* * *

Continuing our route we went to Island Cape,[9] where we were delayed a little by bad weather and fog, and where we did not see much probability of spending the night, inasmuch as the place was not suitable for this purpose. Whilst we were in this predicament I remembered that when following this coast with the Sieur de Monts, I had noted on my map at a league's distance a place which appeared suitable for vessels, into which we had not entered because, at the time we were passing, the wind was favorable for holding on our course. This place lay behind us, on which account I said to the Sieur de Poutrincourt that we must stand in for a point which was then visible, where was situated the place in question which seemed to me suitable for passing the night. We proceeded to anchor at the entrance, and the next day went inside.[1]

The Sieur de Poutrincourt landed with eight or ten of our company. We saw some very fine grapes which were ripe, Brazilian peas, pumpkins, squashes, and some good roots with a flavor like that of chards, which the Indians cultivate. They presented us with a number of these in exchange for other little trifles which we gave them. They had already completed their harvest. We saw two hundred Indians in this place, which is pleasant enough; and here are many nut-trees, cypresses, sassafras, oaks, ashes, and beeches, which are very fine. The chief of this place, who is called Quiouhamenec, came to see us with another chief, a neighbor of his named Cohouepech, whom we entertained. Onemechin, chief of Saco,[2] also came to see us there, and we gave him a coat, which he did not keep long, but presented to another

8. A carpenter from the town of St. Malo.
9. Cape Ann, north of Boston. Champlain writes in this chapter of a voyage undertaken in the fall of 1606, under the Sieur de Poutrincourt, head of the French settlement of Port-Royal, Nova Scotia.
1. Gloucester Harbor, in the south shore of Cape Ann.
2. A river in Maine.

because, being uncomfortable in it, he could not adapt himself to it. At this place we also saw an Indian who wounded himself so badly in the foot, and lost so much blood, that he fainted. A number of other Indians gathered about him, and sang for some time before touching him. Afterward they made certain motions with their feet and hands, and shook his head; then while they breathed upon him, he came to. Our surgeon dressed his injuries, and afterward he was able to go off in good spirits.

The next day, as we were caulking our shallop,[3] the Sieur de Poutrincourt caught sight in the woods of a great many Indians, who with the intention of doing us some injury were on their way toward a little brook in the strait at the causeway leading to the mainland, where some of our men were washing their clothes. As I was walking along the causeway these Indians caught sight of me, and in order to put a good face upon the matter, since they saw clearly that I at the same time had discovered them, they began to shout and to dance; then they came toward me with their bows, arrows, quivers, and other arms. And inasmuch as there was a meadow between them and me, I made a sign to them to dance again, which they did in a circle, putting all their arms in the center. They had hardly begun when they espied in the woods the Sieur de Poutrincourt with eight musketeers, which astonished them. Nevertheless they did not fail to complete their dance, but when it was finished, they withdrew in all directions, being apprehensive lest some bad turn should be done to them. However, we said nothing to them, and showed them only evidences of good will. Then we returned to our shallop to launch it and to take our departure. They begged us to remain a day longer, saying that more than two thousand men would come to see us; but as we could not afford to lose time we were unwilling to delay any longer. I believe that their plan was to surprise us. Some of the land is cleared, and they were constantly clearing more, in the following fashion. They cut down the trees at a height of three feet from the ground; then they burn the branches upon the trunk, and sow their corn between the fallen timber; and in course of time they take out the roots. There are also fine meadows for supporting numbers of cattle. This port is very beautiful and a good one, with water enough for vessels, and shelter behind the islands. It lies in latitude 43°, and we have named it the Beautiful Port.

On the last day of September we departed from the Beautiful Port, and passed cape St. Louis; and we sailed all night to reach the White Cape. The next morning, an hour before daylight, we found ourselves in the White Bay to leeward of White Cape, in eight feet of water, at a distance of a league from the land. Here we cast anchor in order not to approach closer before daylight, and in order to see how we stood regarding the tide. Meanwhile we sent our shallop to make soundings, and they did not find more than eight feet of water, so that it was necessary to determine, while awaiting daylight, what we should do. The water fell to five feet, and our pinnace sometimes touched upon the sand, without, however, being injured or doing herself any damage; for the sea was calm; and we had not more than three feet of water under us, when the tide began to come in, which gave us great encouragement.

When day dawned we descried to leeward a very low sandy coast off which we lay. We sent the boat to make soundings in the direction of a tract of upland which is somewhat elevated, and where we judged there was much

3. A small vessel useful in coastal explorations.

water; and in fact we found there seven fathoms. We went there and cast anchor, and at once prepared the shallop with nine or ten men to go on shore and examine a place where we judged there was a good, safe harbor, in which we might find safety should the wind become stronger. Having explored it, we entered with two, three, and four fathoms of water. When we were inside, we found five and six. There were plenty of oysters, of very good quality, which we had not hitherto seen; and we named the port Oyster Harbor.[4] It is in latitude 42°. There came to us three canoes of Indians. That day the wind was favorable, and for this reason we weighed anchor to go to White Cape, distant from this place five leagues north a quarter north-east, and we doubled it.

The following day, the second of October, we arrived off Mallebarre, where we remained some time on account of the bad weather we experienced. During this time the Sieur de Poutrincourt, accompanied by twelve to fifteen men, paid a visit to the port in the shallop. There came to meet him some 150 Indians, singing and dancing, in accordance with their custom. After having viewed this place we returned to our vessel, and, the wind coming fair, made sail along the coast, steering south.

Chapter XIV

CONTINUATION OF THE ABOVE-MENTIONED DISCOVERIES; AND WHAT OF NOTE WAS OBSERVED DURING THESE.

When we were some six leagues from Mallebarre, we cast anchor near the shore because the wind was not favorable. Along this coast we observed smoke which the Indians were making; and this made us decide to go and visit them. For this purpose the shallop was got ready; but when we were near the shore, which is sandy, we were unable to land, as the swell was too great. The Indians, seeing this, launched a canoe; and eight or nine of them came out to us, singing and indicating by signs the joy it gave them to see us; and they showed us that lower down was a port where we could place our pinnace in safety.

Being unable to land, the shallop came back to the pinnace, and the Indians, who had been kindly treated, returned to the shore.

The next day, the wind being fair, we continued our course to the [south] five leagues, and we had no sooner gone this far than we found three and four fathoms of water at a distance of a league and a half from the shore. And going a little farther, the depth suddenly lessened to a fathom and a half and two fathoms, which made us apprehensive, since the sea was breaking everywhere, and we could perceive no passage along which we could return upon our course; for the wind was altogether against us.

So it came about that, being caught among the breakers and sand-banks, we had to run at haphazard where one judged there was water enough for our pinnace, which drew but at the most four feet. We kept on among these breakers until we found four feet and a half. Finally by God's favor we succeeded in passing over a sandy point which projects about three leagues into the sea to the south-south-east, making a very dangerous place. Doubling this cape, which we named Reef Cape,[5] and which is twelve or thirteen leagues from Mallebarre, we anchored in two and a half fathoms of water, inasmuch as we

4. Either Barnstable Harbor or Wellfleet Harbor, the major inlets on the inner shore of Cape Cod.
5. Some part of the group of dangerous shoals and reefs lying off Monomoy Point, Cape Cod's "elbow."

It was here, in 1620, that the *Mayflower* was forced to turn back from its intended route to the Hudson River, ultimately leaving William Bradford and the other Pilgrims at Plymouth.

found ourselves surrounded on all sides by breakers and shoals, save only in certain places where the sea was not breaking very much. We sent the shallop to seek out a channel in order that we might go to a place which we concluded was the one indicated to us by the Indians. We also believed there was a river there where we could lie in safety.

When our shallop reached the place, our men landed and inspected the locality, after which they came back with an Indian whom they brought with them. They informed us that at high tide we could enter, and it was resolved to do so. We at once weighed anchor and, under the guidance of the Indian, who acted as our pilot, proceeded to anchor in a roadstead[6] in front of the port, in six fathoms of water and good bottom; for we could not go inside because night had overtaken us.

The next day men were sent to place buoys upon the extremity of a sand-bank which lies at the harbor's mouth; then at high tide we entered the place with two fathoms of water. Once inside we gave praise to God for bringing us to a place of safety. Our rudder had broken and been mended with ropes, and we feared lest in the midst of these shallows and strong tides it should break again, which would have resulted in our destruction. Inside this harbor there is but one fathom of water, and at high tide two fathoms. Toward the east lies a bay which doubles to the north some three leagues, and therein is an island and two other little coves, which give beauty to the landscape. Here there is much cleared land and many little hills, whereon the Indians cultivate corn and other grains on which they live. Here are likewise very fine vines, plenty of nut-trees, oaks, cypresses, and a few pines. All the inhabitants of this place are much given to agriculture, and lay up a store of Indian corn for the winter, which they preserve in the following manner.

In the sand on the slope of the hills they dig holes some five to six feet deep more or less, and place their corn and other grains in large grass sacks, which they throw into the said holes, and cover them with sand to a depth of three or four feet above the surface of the ground. They take away this grain according to their needs, and it is preserved as well as it would be in our granaries.[7]

At this place we saw some five to six hundred Indians who were all naked except for their privy parts, which they cover with a little piece of deer or sealskin. The women are the same, and, like the men, cover their parts with skins or leaves. Both men and women wear their hair neatly combed and braided in various ways, after the fashion of the Indians at Saco, and are well-proportioned in body, with olive-colored skins. They adorn themselves with feathers, wampum beads, and other knick-knacks, which they arrange very neatly after the manner of embroidery. Their arms consist of bows, arrows, and clubs. They are not so much great hunters as good fishermen and tillers of the soil.

Regarding their polity, government, and religious belief, we were unable to form a judgment, and I believe that in this they do not differ from our Souriquois[8] and Canadians, who worship neither moon nor sun nor any other thing, and pray no more than the beasts. They have indeed among them certain persons who, they say, have communication with the devil, and in

6. An exposed anchoring place; the party evidently had rounded Monomoy Point and was about to enter modern Stage Harbor, which Champlain later names "Misfortune Harbor."

7. William Bradford notes that the Pilgrims dug up some of these caches during their exploration of Cape Cod fifteen years later.

8. The Micmac, who then inhabited Nova Scotia.

these they have great faith. These persons tell them all that is to happen, in which for the most part they lie. Sometimes they succeed in hitting it right, and in telling them things similar to what actually happens. This is why they have faith in these persons, as if they were prophets, although they are naught but scamps who inveigle them, as the Egyptians and gypsies do the simple village folk. They have chiefs whom they obey in regard to matters of warfare but not in anything else. These chiefs work, and assume no higher rank than their companions. Each possesses only sufficient land for his own support.

Their lodges are separated from one another according to the extent of land that each is able to occupy. They are lofty, circular, and covered with matting made of grass or husks of Indian corn. Their only furniture consists of a bed or two raised one foot from the floor, and made of a number of saplings laid one against the other, whereon they place a reed-mat, in the Spanish manner (which is a kind of thick mattress two or three fingers in depth), and upon this they sleep. They have a great many fleas in summer, even in the fields. One day when we were out walking, we attracted such a number of them that we were obliged to change our clothes.

All the harbors, bays, and coasts from Saco onward are filled with every kind of fish like those we have near our settlements, and in such abundance that I can guarantee there was never a day or a night during which we did not see and hear more than a thousand porpoises passing alongside our pinnace and chasing the smaller fry. Here are likewise plenty of shellfish of several kinds, and especially oysters. Game birds are very plentiful.

This would prove a very good site for laying and constructing the foundations of a state, if the harbor were a little deeper and the entrance safer than it is.

Before leaving port our rudder was repaired, and we made bread from flour we had brought for our subsistence when our biscuit gave out. Meanwhile we sent the shallop with five or six men and an Indian to see whether they could find a passage more suitable for leaving than that by which we had entered.

When they had gone five or six leagues, and we were close inshore, the Indian took to flight. He gave those in the shallop to understand that he was afraid lest he should be carried off to other Indians farther south who are enemies of his tribe. Upon their return they reported that as far as they had gone, there were at least three fathoms of water, and that farther on there were neither shoals nor reefs.

We accordingly made haste to repair our pinnace and to provide bread for fifteen days. Meanwhile the Sieur de Poutrincourt, accompanied by ten or twelve musketeers, visited all the surrounding country, which is very fine, as I have already stated. Here and there we saw a good number of small lodges.

Some eight or nine days later, on the Sieur de Poutrincourt's going out walking as he had done before, we observed that the Indians were taking down their wigwams and were sending into the woods their wives, children and provisions, and other necessaries of life. This made us suspect some evil design, and that they wished to attack our people who were working on shore, where they remained every night to guard whatever could not be taken on board in the evening except with much labor. This proved to be quite true; for they had resolved among themselves that, when all their goods were in safety, they would surprise the men on shore as best they could, and would carry off everything these men had there. But if perchance they found them on their guard, they would come with signs of friendship, as they were accustomed to do, laying aside their bows and arrows.

Now in view of what the Sieur de Poutrincourt had seen, and of the mode of procedure he had been told they observed when they wished to do a bad turn, we passed among their wigwams where were a number of women, to whom we gave bracelets and rings, in order to keep them quiet and from becoming afraid of us, while to the majority of the prominent and older men we gave axes, knives, and other articles of which they stood in need. This pleased them much, repaying for all by dances, gambols, and speeches, which latter we did not in the least understand. We went about everywhere without their having the boldness to say anything to us. It amused us greatly to see them look so innocent as they made themselves appear.

We came back very quietly to our pinnace, accompanied by a few Indians. On the way we met with several small troops who were gradually collecting together, fully armed, and were much surprised to see us so far inland, little thinking that we had just made a tour of from four to five leagues through their country. When passing near us they trembled for fear lest we should harm them, which it was in our power to do; but we did nothing, although we were aware of their evil intentions. On reaching the spot where our men were at work, the Sieur de Poutrincourt asked if all things were in readiness to oppose the designs of these rascals.

He gave orders for every one on shore to be taken on board: which was done, except that the man who was making the bread remained behind to finish a baking, and two other men with him. They were told that the Indians had some evil design, and that they should make haste in order to come on board in the evening, as it was known that the Indians only put their plans into execution at night or at daybreak, which is the hour for making surprises in most of their schemes.

The evening having come, the Sieur de Poutrincourt ordered the shallop to be sent ashore to fetch the men who were left. This was done as soon as the tide would permit, and those on shore were told that they must embark for the reason already given them. This they refused to do despite the remonstrances made to them on the risks they were running and the disobedience they were showing to their chief. To these they paid no attention, except a servant of the Sieur de Poutrincourt, who came aboard; but two others disembarked from the boat and went off to the three on shore, who remained to eat some biscuits made at the same time as the bread. Since these were unwilling to do what they were told, the shallop returned alongside, but without informing the Sieur de Poutrincourt, who was asleep, and who believed they were all on board the vessel.

The next morning, the fifteenth of October, the Indians did not fail to come and see in what state were our men, whom they found asleep, except one who was before the fire. Seeing them in this condition, the Indians, to the number of four hundred, came quietly over a little hill, and shot such a salvo of arrows at them as to give them no chance of recovery before they were struck dead. Fleeing as fast as they could toward our pinnace, and crying out, "Help, help, they are killing us," some of them fell dead in the water, while the rest were all pierced with arrows, of whom one died a short time afterward.[9] These

9. Of the five Frenchmen ashore, the single one who escaped death, Jean Du Val, was executed in Quebec in 1608 for conspiring against Champlain. Marc Lescarbot (c. 1570–c. 1603), a lawyer and writer who

Indians made a desperate row, with war-whoops which it was terrible to hear.

At this noise, and that of our men, the sentinel on our vessel cried out, "To arms; they are killing our men." Thereupon each quickly seized his weapons, and at the same time some fifteen or sixteen of us embarked in the shallop to go ashore. But being unable to land on account of a sand-bank which lay between us and the shore, we jumped into the water and waded from this bank to the mainland, a distance of a musket-shot. As soon as we reached it, the Indians, seeing us within bowshot, fled inland. To pursue them was useless, for they are wonderfully swift. All we could do was to carry off the dead bodies and bury them near a cross which had been set up the day before, and then to look about to see whether we could catch sight of any Indians; but in this we wasted our time. Realising this we returned. Three hours later they reappeared on the shore. We discharged several shots at them from our little brass cannon; and whenever they heard the report, they threw themselves flat on the ground to avoid the charge. In derision of us they pulled down the cross, and dug up the bodies, which displeased us greatly, and made us go after them a second time;[1] but they fled as they had done before. We again set up the cross, and reinterred the bodies, which they had scattered here and there among the heaths, where they had kindled a fire to burn them. We returned without having accomplished more than before, seeing clearly that there was hardly any chance of taking vengeance for this blow, and that we must postpone the matter until it should please God.

On the sixteenth of the month we set out from Misfortune harbor, so named by us on account of the misfortune which happened to us there. This place is in latitude 41° 20', and distant some twelve or thirteen leagues from Malle-barre.

1613

accompanied this expedition, wrote that the mutinous shore party was led by a young braggart (probably of noble background) who resented the fact that he had been denied alcohol on the ship. He was found dead on shore, Lescarbot wrote, "his face on the ground, having a little dog upon his back, both of them shot together, and pierced through with one and the selfsame arrow."

1. Lescarbot added that these Nauset Indians turned their backs to those on the ship and "cast sand with their two hands together betwixt their buttocks in derision, howling like wolves."

GEORGE PERCY
1580–1632

Educated at Oxford and trained in the law in London, George Percy traveled in Ireland and fought against the Spanish army in the Netherlands with his brother, the ninth earl of Northumberland, before he set sail with the first Jamestown colonists in 1606. Percy, who was to serve twice as the colony's head, faithfully kept a diary during the voyage and for the five years he lived in Virginia. From this source he prepared in 1607 the most detailed account of the first months of the undertaking, A *Discourse of the Plantation of the Southern Colony of Virginia*. The whole text does not survive, only an abridgement published in 1625.

Percy's paradoxical personality—he was proud of his social position but insecure—made him ill-suited to the world of Jamestown, where decisiveness was crucial and a concern for physical survival more important than a regard for hierarchy. Captain John Smith, president of the colony's ruling council, who disliked many of the Virginia aristocrats because they lacked survivor's instincts, did think well of Percy. Percy, on the other hand, thought Smith was always trying to deprive his "betters" of their authority. While Smith's writings show his firm grasp of the limits imposed by the colony's weaknesses and the obstacles it faced, Percy seemed oddly out of touch. In 1611 he wrote to his brother the earl complaining about the meager food doled out from the common supply. Despite the high expense of keeping "a continual and daily table for gentlemen of fashion" in Jamestown, Percy believed his "reputation" demanded it. Thus he blithely borrowed large sums from his brother to support the family name in this way, at least until 1612, when he left Virginia forever. Though this concern bespeaks a mind detached from its surroundings, by a final paradox it is from Percy's pen that we have the chilling account of the 1607 time of sickness, anthologized here, which unflinchingly catalogs the dead.

From Observations Gathered out of a Discourse of . . . Virginia[1]

Monday the two and twentieth of June [1607], in the morning, Captain Newport in the admiral[2] departed from James Port for England.

Captain Newport being gone for England, [left] us (one hundred and four persons) very bare and scanty of victuals, furthermore in wars and in danger [from] the savages. We hoped [for] a supply which Captain Newport promised within twenty weeks.[3] But if the beginners of this action do carefully further us, the country being so fruitful, it would be as great a profit to the realm of England as the Indies [are] to the King of Spain; if this river which we have found had been discovered in the time of war with Spain, it would have been a commodity to our realm and a great annoyance to our enemies.[4] The seven and twentieth of July the King of Rapahanna[5] demanded [the return of] a canoe, which was restored; after which he lifted up his hand to the sun, which they worship as their God, [and] he laid his hand on his heart, [vowing] that he would be our special friend. It is a general rule of these people when they swear by their God, which is the sun, [to carry out what they swear]: no Christian will keep their oath better upon this promise. These people have a great reverence to the sun above all other things. At the rising and setting of the same, they sit down, lifting up their hands and eyes to the sun, making a round circle on the ground with dried tobacco, then they begin to pray, making many devilish gestures with a hellish noise, foaming at the mouth, staring with their eyes, wagging their heads and hands in such a fashion and deformity[6] as it was monstrous to behold.

1. The text is derived from Samuel Purchas, *Hakluytus Posthumus; or Purchas His Pilgrimes*, vol. 18 (1906).
2. Captain Christopher Newport (d. 1617) had served as a privateer in the West Indies in the 1590s. Employed by the Virginia Company in 1606, he directed the voyages sent forth under its auspices. His ship, the *Susan Constant*, was called the "admiral" because of Newport's official status.
3. Newport arrived in Plymouth, England, on July 29, 1607, five weeks after leaving Virginia. He left England again in October but did not arrive in the colony until January of 1608; his second ship did not arrive until

April. Hence the time of sickness that Percy goes on to describe.
4. During the conflict with Spain, which reached its climax in the English defeat of the Spanish Armada in 1588, a base of operations in America would have enabled the English to impede Spanish shipping in the Caribbean. "This river": the James. "Commodity": benefit.
5. A region on the south bank of the James River, upstream from Jamestown.
6. I.e., in a contorted manner. "Devilish": i.e., satanic.

The sixth of August there died John Asbie of the bloody flux.[7] The ninth day died George Flower of the swelling. The tenth day [died] William Brewster, Gentleman, of a wound given by the savages, and was buried the eleventh day.

The fourteenth day, Jeremy Alicock, ensign, died of a wound; the same day, Francis Midwinter [and] Edward Morris, corporal, died suddenly.

The fifteenth day, there died Edward Browne and Stephen Galthorpe. The sixteenth day, there died Thomas Gore, gentleman. The seventeenth day, there died Thomas Mounslic. The eighteenth day, there died Robert Pennington and John Martin, gentleman. The nineteenth day, died Drew Pickhouse, gentleman. The two and twentieth day of August, there died Captain Bartholomew Gosnold,[8] one of our Council; he was honorably buried, having all the ordnance in the fort shot off with many volleys of small shot.

After Captain Gosnold's death, the Council could hardly agree [due to] the dissension of Captain Kendall, [who] afterward was committed [on] heinous matters which were proved against him.[9]

The four and twentieth day, died Edward Harrington and George Walker, and [they] were buried the same day. The six and twentieth day, died Kellam Throgmorton. The seven and twentieth day died William Roods. The eight and twentieth day died Thomas Studley, cape merchant.[1]

The fourth day of September, there died Thomas Jacob, sergeant. The fifth day, there died Benjamin Beast. Our men were destroyed with cruel diseases, [such] as swellings, fluxes, burning fevers, and by wars, and some departed suddenly, but for the most part they died of mere famine.[2] There were never Englishmen left in a foreign country in such misery as we were in this new-discovered Virginia. We watched every three nights, lying on the cold ground, [and] what weather soever came [we] warded all the next day,[3] which brought our men to be most feeble wretches. Our food was but a small can of barley sodden in water to five men a day, our drink cold water taken out of the river, which was at a flood[4] very salt, at a low tide full of slime and filth, which was the destruction of many men. Thus we lived for the space of five months in this miserable distress, not having five able men to man our bulwarks upon any occasion. If it had not pleased God to have put a terror in the savages' hearts, we had all perished by those vile and cruel pagans, being in that weak state [that] we were. Our men night and day groaning in every corner of the fort most pitiful to hear; if there were any conscience in men, it would make their hearts to bleed to hear the pitiful murmurings and outcries of our sick men without relief every night and day for the space of six weeks, some departing out of the world, many times three or four in a night, in the morning their bodies [being] trailed out of their cabins like dogs to be buried. In this sort did I see the mortality of divers[5] of our people.

It pleased God, after awhile, to send those people which were our mortal enemies to relieve us with victuals, [such] as bread, corn, fish, and flesh in

7. Severe diarrhea.
8. Gosnold (c. 1572–1607) had explored New England (where he named Cape Cod in 1602) before being taken on as Newport's vice admiral for the Jamestown voyage of 1607. He probably was responsible for recruiting John Smith as a colonist, and the two men shared membership in Virginia's ruling council.
9. Captain George Kendall (fl. 1600–7) was executed for mutiny late in 1607.

1. Head merchant in a trading post or, in this case, supervisor of the colony's supplies. The position was later filled by John Smith.
2. Starvation alone.
3. Percy apparently means that individuals held the night watch every third night, then had to stand guard the following day regardless of bad weather.
4. I.e., at high tide. "Sodden": soaked.
5. Several. "Cabins": bunks. "Sort": way.

great plenty, which was the setting up[6] of our feeble men. Otherwise we had all perished. Also we were frequented by divers Kings in the country, bringing us store of provision to our great comfort.

The eleventh day [of September, 1607], there were certain articles laid against Master Wingfield, who was then President; thereupon he was not only displaced out of his Presidentship, but also from being [on] the Council. Afterwards, Captain John Ratcliffe was chosen President.[7]

That eighteenth day, died one Ellis Kingston, who was starved to death with cold. The same day, at night, died one Richard Simons. The nineteenth day, there died one Thomas Mouton.

1607   1625

6. Salvation.
7. Edward Maria Wingfield (c. 1560–1613) was deeply involved in the affairs of the colony, and was elected the first president of the council. He proved a poor administrator, however, and in 1608 he left Virginia, never to return. He was the author of a *Discourse*

of Virginia, based on his journal, eventually published in 1860. Ratcliffe, who was no great improvement over Wingfield, was actually one John Sicklemore, captain of the small ship *Discovery* on the voyage over in 1607. He remains neither satisfactorily identified nor explained.

JOHN SMITH
1580–1631

Under the patent granted to Sir Walter Ralegh by Queen Elizabeth I in 1584, the English undertook their first serious effort at colonization in Virginia. By 1590 this attempt, in the vicinity of Roanoke, had ended in disaster. When the English renewed their involvement in America in the 1600s, they replaced the older heroic model of exploration and colonization with a more corporate one. Under this new model, the single controlling figure of Ralegh's era was replaced by larger companies of investors (often merchants), who had more capital to support costly expansion overseas. In fact, King James I split the vaguely defined region of Virginia, which ran from Florida to Canada, into two more manageable parts, giving the direction of each to separate but related groups of investors who together composed the Virginia Company. The southern part (including the area now known as the state of Virginia) came under the care of the company's members from London, while the northern part (from which New England was to be developed) fell to members in the West Country towns of Bristol, Plymouth, and Exeter. Although the so-called First Charter was succeeded by new ones in 1609 and 1612, its broad base of formalized support set the standard for English colonial practice over the next hundred years. As a compromise between large-scale governmental action and isolated individual effort, the format of the colonial "company" proved both useful and enduring.

The push toward corporate structures did not mean that interesting individuals disappeared. Indeed, one of the most colorful of all the Englishmen ever involved in America, the legendary Captain John Smith, proved by his crucial role in the establishment and continuance of the new colony at Jamestown that success in such ventures still required individual initiative and commitment. Few people had more pertinent preparation to reteach the English this old lesson. When named by the London partners to the ruling council (that is, the local governing committee) for the Virginia colony sent out in late December 1606, John Smith brought rich experience to his charge. His early life was deceptively sedate: born into a farmer's family in Lincolnshire, he was apprenticed at fifteen to a shopkeeper near his home. But tales of exploration, piracy, and military adventure already had stirred his imagination. In 1593 he may have tried to join a punitive expedition Sir Francis Drake was thought to be readying against England's enemy Spain, although his father apparently intervened. Shortly after his father's death in 1596, the fiery sixteen-year-old managed to have his indenture to the shopkeeper canceled and went to the Netherlands as a volunteer soldier to fight for the Dutch in their long war of independence from Philip II.

Following his tour of duty in the Netherlands, he saw action in the Mediterranean on a privateer, winning a good share of the prize money when a Venetian galley was captured. Smith next joined the Austrian army in its continuing war (1593–1606) against the Turks, and while in the Austrian service, he fought valiantly in Hungary and was promoted to a captaincy. Eventually, after defeating and beheading a succession of three Turkish officers in single combat in Rumania (his coat of arms, awarded later, showed the three severed heads), Smith was wounded in battle, taken prisoner, and sold into slavery to a Turk. Smith was passed from place to place until, held prisoner on the Black Sea, he murdered his master and fled back to Rumania via Russia and Poland, returning to England in the winter of 1604–5.

Many of these details come to us only through Smith's own at times garbled narratives, most of them penned long after the events. But when the Jamestown backers encountered him as they readied their expedition, he must have had the air of someone deeply experienced in the skills that the quasi-military venture would require. Smith's military background (and temperament), however, also carried liabilities in that age when warfare was brutal and soldiers were far from professional: he sometimes used force unnecessarily, and his hard-to-control temper and stubborn self-reliance made him an often troublesome companion. Already on the voyage over, Smith ran afoul of those in charge, was placed under arrest while the fleet was near the Canary Islands in February 1607, and was threatened with execution in the West Indies the following month. By June 10, some weeks after the arrival in Virginia and the opening of the heretofore secret list of the council members (not revealed sooner so as to prevent difficulties on shipboard!), Smith had been given a reprieve and was sworn in to his seat on the council. From then until his final departure for England in October 1609, he was in the middle of the tumultuous colony's affairs. Smith survived the grim period of sickness in 1607 and missed the bleaker "starving time" that came shortly after his departure, but during his years there, he was always at the epicenter of the various political earthquakes that rocked early Virginia.

Placed in charge of its supplies in the fall of 1607, he was elected president of the council—in effect, the colony's governor—the following year, after a series of wide-ranging explorations that made him the most knowledgeable of the settlers regarding the new land. The explorations also led to his imprisonment at the hands of Powhatan, overlord of the Chesapeake Bay Indians, from whom he claimed (much later) that the king's young daughter Pocahontas rescued him. Whatever the role Pocahontas played, what Smith took to be his impending execution may have been nothing more than a harmless adoption ceremony inducting him into Powhatan's tribe. In this episode as in others, Smith's volatile and unpredictable relations with the Native Americans were characteristic. Also characteristic was the fact that as a writer Smith milked the story of his rescue by Pocahontas. Although he failed to have the lasting influence on Virginia's affairs that he sought, in recasting that story fifteen years after the fact he found the immortality that otherwise eluded him. How easily we forget that on his return to Jamestown from Powhatan's village he was charged with the loss of two soldiers and would have been hanged had a fleet with much-needed supplies not arrived from England. Or that when he left Virginia in 1609 (never to return), it was because he had been

severely injured when his gunpowder bag mysteriously exploded in his lap while
he napped on the deck of an exploring vessel.

Smith and his works form an important bridge between the first two permanent
English colonies in North America. The first of his publications, *A True Relation
of Such Occurrences and Accidents of Note as Hath Happened in Virginia* (1608),
was a badly edited version of a letter he had sent back from the colony without
intending that it be published. It was followed by a work to which many colonists
including Smith contributed, *A Map of Virginia, with a Description of the Country
. . .* [and] *The Proceedings of those Colonies* [sic] (1612). Some years later, Smith
enlarged this book by adding more texts by other hands, expanding his own prose,
and extending its geographical range and chronological coverage. More its editor
than its author, Smith published the resulting *General History of Virginia, New
England, and the Summer Isles* [i.e., Bermuda] in 1624. This book demonstrated
the later reach of Smith's American ambitions beyond Virginia proper, for his
knowledge of New England was based on a voyage he made there in 1614 and on
his continuing involvement with the region—which in fact he, not the Puritans,
named. During his life, Smith published more works on New England than on
Virginia (*A Description of New England*, 1616; *New England's Trials*, 1620 and
1622; and *Advertisements for the Inexperienced Planters of New England, or Anywhere*, 1631). But for some unfortunate setbacks (bad weather several times forced
him to abandon other voyages for New England), he might well have become
more famous for this second aspect of his American career than for the first. An
energetic promoter of the potential of this new region for English settlers, Smith
offered the Pilgrims his services as guide for their voyage in 1620, but they chose
instead to put Smith's helpful books in the hands of the more temperate Myles
Standish. From that point on Smith's America was not the geographical realm
about which he had entertained such bright hopes at the century's start but rather
the verbal domain he continued to explore in his later writings. When he closed
the Virginia part of his *General History* by writing "Thus far have I travelled in this
Wilderness of Virginia," he was revealing how much like a country of his mind
Virginia had become. Long gone from that still-struggling colony by then, he had
internalized it so well that he helped to make it a permanent part of the English—
and the Anglo-American—imagination.

From The General History of Virginia, New England, and the Summer Isles[1]

From *The Third Book.* From *Chapter 2. What Happened till the First Supply*

Being thus left to our fortunes, it fortuned that within ten days,[2] scarce ten
amongst us could either go or well stand, such extreme weakness and sickness

---

1. The text used here is taken from *The Complete
Works of Captain John Smith*, edited by Philip L. Barbour (1986). The Summer Isles are the Bermuda
Islands. The *Third Book* is titled "The Proceedings and
Accidents of the English Colony in Virginia," and is
derived from Smith's Virginia book of 1612. The bulk
of this chapter, which opens with an account of the
sickness whose dire results were chronicled by George
Percy, may have been written by John Smith himself,
although at its publication in 1612 it was credited solely
to Thomas Studley, chief storekeeper of the colony. In
1624, Smith added to Studley's signature at the end of
this section of the text not only his own initials but also
the names of Robert Fenton and Edward Harrington as
part authors. According to George Percy (See *Observations Gathered*, p. 100), Thomas Studley died early in
the first year, on August 28, 1607, four days after Harrington, so neither could have written much of what is
in part attributed to them. Of Robert Fenton nothing
is known.
2. By the end of June 1607, after Captain Christopher
Newport (d. 1617) left to fetch new supplies from
England. "Fortuned": happened.

oppressed us. And thereat none need marvel if they consider the cause and reason which was this: While the ships stayed, our allowance was somewhat bettered by a daily proportion of biscuit which the sailors would pilfer to sell, give, or exchange with us for money, sassafras,[3] furs, or love. But when they departed, there remained neither tavern, beer-house, nor place of relief but the common kettle.[4] Had we been as free from all sins as [we were free from] gluttony and drunkenness we might have been canonized for saints, but our President would never have been admitted for engrossing to his private, oat-meal, sack, oil, aqua vitae, beef, eggs, or what not but the kettle;[5] that indeed he allowed equally to be distributed, and that was half a pint of wheat and as much barley boiled with water for a man a day, and this, having fried some twenty-six weeks in the ship's hold, contained as many worms as grains so that we might truly call it rather so much bran than corn; our drink was water,[6] our lodgings castles in the air.

With this lodging and diet, our extreme toil in bearing and planting pali-sades so strained and bruised us and our continual labor in the extremity of the heat had so weakened us, as were cause sufficient to have made us as miserable in our native country or any other place in the world.

From May to September, those that escaped lived upon sturgeon and sea crabs. Fifty in this time we buried; the rest seeing the President's[7] projects to escape these miseries in our pinnace by flight (who all this time had neither felt want nor sickness) so moved our dead spirits as we deposed him and established Ratcliffe in his place (Gosnold being dead), Kendall deposed. Smith newly recovered, Martin[8] and Ratcliffe were by his care preserved and relieved, and the most of the soldiers recovered with the skillful diligence of Master Thomas Wotton our surgeon general.

But now was all our provision spent, the sturgeon gone, all helps aban-doned, each hour expecting the fury of the savages, when God, the patron of all good endeavors, in that desperate extremity so changed the hearts of the savages that they brought such plenty of their fruits and provision as no man wanted.[9]

And now where some affirmed it was ill done of the Council to send forth men so badly provided, this incontradictable reason will show them plainly they are too ill advised to nourish such ill conceits: First, the fault of our going was our own; what could be thought fitting or necessary we had, but what we should find, or want, or where we should be, we were all ignorant and suppos-ing to make our passage in two months, with victual to live and the advantage of the spring to work; we were at sea five months where we both spent our victual and lost the opportunity of the time and season to plant, by the unskill-

---

3. The bark of the sassafras tree, sold for its supposed medicinal qualities, was a valuable commodity in London.
4. The communal resources.
5. I.e., President Edward Maria Wingfield (c. 1560–1613), a man of high connections in England, would not have been canonized as a saint because he diverted many supplies (everything except the contents of the common kettle) for his own use, including sack (wine) and aqua vitae (brandy).
6. It was more customary to drink wine or beer. "Corn": grain.
7. I.e., Wingfield.
8. Captain John Martin (c. 1567–1632?) was a colo-

nist best known for his contentiousness. "Captain John Ratcliffe" was an alias of John Sicklemore (dates uncer-tain), master of one of the vessels on the voyage over and a member of the local council. The most enig-matic figure in Jamestown, he was elected president of the council in September 1607, but later fell out with Smith. Captain Bartholomew Gosnold (c. 1572–1607), who had explored New England before the first Jamestown voyage, probably had been responsible for Smith's recruitment to the venture. Captain George Kendall (d. 1607) was executed for mutiny later in the year.
9. I.e., was in want.

ful presumption of our ignorant transporters that understood not at all what they undertook.

Such actions have ever since the world's beginning been subject to such accidents, and everything of worth is found full of difficulties, but nothing [is] so difficult as to establish a commonwealth so far remote from men and means and where men's minds are so untoward[1] as neither do well themselves nor suffer others. But to proceed.

The new President and Martin, being little beloved, of weak judgment in dangers, and less industry in peace, committed the managing of all things abroad[2] to Captain Smith, who, by his own example, good words, and fair promises, set some to mow, others to bind thatch, some to build houses, others to thatch them, himself always bearing the greatest task for his own share, so that in short time he provided most of them lodgings, neglecting any for himself.

This done, seeing the savages' superfluity begin to decrease, [Smith] (with some of his workmen) shipped himself in the shallop to search the country for trade. The want of[3] the language, knowledge to manage his boat without sails, the want of a sufficient power (knowing the multitude of the savages), apparel for his men, and other necessaries, were infinite impediments yet no discouragement.

Being but six or seven in company he went down the river to Kecoughtan[4] where at first they scorned him as a famished man and would in derision offer him a handful of corn, a piece of bread for their swords and muskets, and such like proportions also for their apparel. But seeing by trade and courtesy there was nothing to be had, he made bold to try such conclusions as necessity enforced; though contrary to his commission, [he] let fly[5] his muskets, ran his boat on shore; whereat they all fled into the woods.

So marching towards their houses, they might see great heaps of corn; much ado he had to restrain his hungry soldiers from present taking of it, expecting as it happened that the savages would assault them, as not long after they did with a most hideous noise. Sixty or seventy of them, some black, some red, some white, some particolored, came in a square order,[6] singing and dancing out of the woods with their Okee (which was an idol made of skins, stuffed with moss, all painted and hung with chains and copper) borne before them, and in this manner, being well armed with clubs, targets, bows, and arrows, they charged the English that so kindly[7] received them with their muskets loaded with pistol shot that down fell their god, and divers lay sprawling on the ground; the rest fled again to the woods and ere long sent one of their Quiyoughkasoucks[8] to offer peace and redeem their Okee.

Smith told them if only six of them would come unarmed and load his boat, he would not only be their friend but restore them their Okee and give them beads, copper, and hatchets besides, which on both sides was to their contents[9] performed, and then they brought him venison, turkeys, wild fowl, bread,

1. Intractable.
2. I.e., outside the palisade.
3. Inability to speak. "Shallop": an open boat.
4. A village near the mouth of the James River whose inhabitants, the Kecoughtans, were members of the Powhatan Confederacy.
5. Fired.

6. Formation. "Particolored": i.e., painted for the battle.
7. In such a way. "Targets": small shields.
8. Smith elsewhere defines this term as referring to the "petty gods" of the Algonquian-speaking peoples, but here it may be used to mean priests. "Divers": several.
9. I.e., in mutual contentment.

and what they had, singing and dancing in sign of friendship till they departed.

In his return he discovered the town and country of Warraskoyack.[1]

> Thus God unboundless by His power,
> Made them thus kind, would us devour.

Smith, perceiving (notwithstanding their late misery) not any regarded but from hand to mouth,[2] (the company being well recovered) caused the pinnace to be provided with things fitting to get provision for the year following, but in the interim he made three or four journeys and discovered the people of Chickahominy,[3] yet what he carefully provided the rest carelessly spent.

Wingfield and Kendall, living in disgrace * * * strengthened themselves with the sailors and other confederates to regain their former credit and authority, or at least such means aboard the pinnace (being fitted to sail as Smith had appointed for trade), to alter her course and to go for England.

Smith, unexpectedly returning, had the plot discovered to him, much trouble he had to prevent it, till with store of saker[4] and musket shot he forced them [to] stay or sink in the river: which action cost the life of Captain Kendall.

These brawls are so disgustful, as some will say they were better forgotten, yet all men of good judgment will conclude it were better their baseness should be manifest to the world, than the business bear the scorn and shame of their excused disorders.[5]

The President and Captain Archer[6] not long after intended also to have abandoned the country, which project also was curbed and suppressed by Smith.

The Spaniard never more greedily desired gold than he victual, nor his soldiers more to abandon the country than he to keep it. But [he found] plenty of corn in the river of Chickahominy, where hundreds of savages in divers places stood with baskets expecting his coming.

And now the winter approaching, the rivers became so covered with swans, geese, ducks, and cranes that we daily feasted with good bread, Virginia peas, pumpkins, and putchamins, fish, fowl, and divers sort of wild beasts as fast as we could eat them, so that none of our tuftaffety humorists[7] desired to go for England.

But our comedies never endured long without a tragedy, some idle exceptions[8] being muttered against Captain Smith for not discovering the head of Chickahominy river and [he being] taxed by the Council to be too slow in so worthy an attempt. The next voyage he proceeded so far that with much labor by cutting of trees asunder he made his passage, but when his barge could pass no farther, he left her in a broad bay out of danger of shot, commanding none

1. A village on the south side of the James River near the mouth of the modern Pagan River, approximately opposite Smithfield.
2. I.e., none of the settlers, despite their recent sufferings, gave any thought to gathering a store of provision for the future.
3. The region along the Chickahominy River, which empties into the James River a short distance west of Jamestown.
4. Shot for a small cannon used in sieges and on shipboard. "Discovered": revealed.
5. I.e., it is necessary to rehearse the troubles to lay the blame on the responsible individuals (Wingfield and Kendall), rather than let the whole "business" of the colony suffer ill repute.
6. Captain Gabriel Archer (c. 1575–1609?) had been an associate of Bartholomew Gosnold before the Jamestown voyage. Having gone back to England in 1608 as a confirmed opponent of Smith, he showed up in Virginia again the following year to head an anti-Smith faction but died during the starving time the next winter. Ratcliffe / Sicklemore was still president.
7. Self-indulgent persons who might be given to wearing lace. "Putchamins": persimmons.
8. Objections.

should go ashore till his return; himself with two English and two savages went up higher in a canoe, but he was not long absent but his men went ashore, whose want of government gave both occasion and opportunity to the savages to surprise one George Cassen whom they slew and much failed not to have cut off the boat and all the rest.[9]

Smith little dreaming of that accident, being got to the marshes at the river's head twenty miles in the desert,[1] had his two men slain (as is supposed) sleeping by the canoe, while himself by fowling sought them victual, who finding he was beset with 200 savages, two of them he slew, still defending himself with the aid of a savage his guide, whom he bound to his arm with his garters and used him as a buckler,[2] yet he was shot in his thigh a little, and had many arrows that stuck in his clothes but no great hurt, till at last they took him prisoner.

When this news came to Jamestown, much was their sorrow for his loss, few expecting what ensued.

Six or seven weeks those barbarians kept him prisoner, many strange triumphs and conjurations they made of him, yet he so demeaned[3] himself amongst them, as he not only diverted them from surprising the fort, but procured his own liberty, and got himself and his company such estimation amongst them, that those savages admired him more than their own Quiyoughkasoucks.

The manner how they used and delivered him is as followeth:

The savages having drawn from George Cassen whither Captain Smith was gone, prosecuting that opportunity they followed him with 300 bowmen, conducted by the King of Pamunkey, who in divisions searching the turnings of the river found Robinson and Emry[4] by the fireside; those they shot full of arrows and slew. Then finding the Captain, as is said, that used the savage that was his guide as his shield (three of them being slain and divers others so galled[5]), all the rest would not come near him. Thinking thus to have returned to his boat, regarding them, as he marched, more than his way, [he] slipped up to the middle in an oozy creek and his savage with him, yet dared they not come to him till being near dead with cold he threw away his arms. Then according to their composition[6] they drew him forth and led him to the fire where his men were slain. Diligently they chafed his benumbed limbs.

He demanding for their captain, they showed him Opechancanough,[7] King of Pamunkey, to whom he gave a round ivory double compass dial. Much they marveled at the playing of the fly[8] and needle, which they could see so plainly and yet not touch it because of the glass that covered them. But when he demonstrated by that globe-like jewel the roundness of the earth and skies, the sphere of the sun, moon, and stars, and how the sun did chase the night round about the world continually, the greatness of the land and sea, the diversity of nations, variety of complexions, and how we were to them anti-

---

9. I.e., only through fault of their own did they fail to wipe out Cassen's whole party. "Government": discipline.
1. Wilderness.
2. Shield. "Garters": laces used for tying clothing.
3. Behaved.
4. The two men mentioned above as having been killed while they slept. Thomas Emry was a carpenter. John Robinson was a "gentleman."

5. Wounded.
6. Agreement for surrender.
7. Powhatan's younger half-brother and Smith's captor, Opechancanough (d. 1644) was to lead the Indian Confederacy's attack on the colonists in 1622 and as late as 1644 attempted one last time to expel them from the country.
8. Compass card.

podes[9] and many other such like matters, they all stood as amazed with admiration.

Notwithstanding, within an hour after, they tied him to a tree, and as many as could stand about him prepared to shoot him, but the King holding up the compass in his hand, they all laid down their bows and arrows and in a triumphant manner led him to Orapaks[1] where he was after their manner kindly feasted and well used.

Their order in conducting him was thus: Drawing themselves all in file, the King in the midst had all their pieces and swords borne before him. Captain Smith was led after him by three great savages holding him fast by each arm, and on each side six went in file with their arrows nocked.[2] But arriving at the town (which was but only thirty or forty hunting houses made of mats, which they remove as they please, as we our tents), all the women and children staring to behold him, the soldiers first all in file performed the form of a bissom[3] so well as could be, and on each flank, officers as sergeants to see them keep their orders. A good time they continued this exercise and then cast themselves in a ring, dancing in such several postures and singing and yelling out such hellish notes and screeches; being strangely painted, every one [had] his quiver of arrows and at his back a club, on his arm a fox or an otter's skin or some such matter for his vambrace, their heads and shoulders painted red with oil and pocones mingled together, which scarlet-like color made an exceeding handsome show, his bow in his hand and the skin of a bird with her wings abroad,[4] dried, tied on his head, a piece of copper, a white shell, a long feather with a small rattle growing at the tails of their snakes tied to it, or some such like toy. All this while, Smith and the King stood in the midst, guarded as before is said, and after three dances they all departed. Smith they conducted to a long house where thirty or forty tall fellows did guard him, and ere long more bread and venison was brought him than would have served twenty men. I think his stomach at that time was not very good; what he left they put in baskets and tied over his head. About midnight they set the meat again before him; all this time not one of them would eat a bit with him, till the next morning they brought him as much more, and then did they eat all the old and reserved the new as they had done the other, which made him think they would fat him to eat him. Yet in this desperate estate, to defend him from the cold, one Maocassater brought him his gown in requital[5] of some beads and toys Smith had given him at his first arrival in Virginia.

Two days after, a man would have slain him (but that the guard prevented it) for the death of his son, to whom they conducted him to recover the poor man then breathing his last. Smith told them that at Jamestown he had a water would do it, if they would let him fetch it, but they would not permit that, but made all the preparations they could to assault Jamestown, craving his advice, and for recompence he should have life, liberty, land, and women. In part of a table book[6] he wrote his mind to them at the fort, what was intended, how they should follow that direction to affright the messengers, and without fail send him such things as he wrote for. And an inventory with them. The diffi-

9. On the opposite side of the globe.
1. A village located farther inland, later the residence of Powhatan.
2. Notched; i.e., with their arrows fitted on the bowstring ready to use.
3. From an Italian term denoting a snakelike for-

mation.
4. Outspread. "Vambrace": forearm protection. "Pocones": a dye of vegetative origin.
5. Payment.
6. A notebook.

culty and danger, he told the savages, of the mines, great guns, and other engines[7] exceedingly affrighted them, yet according to his request they went to Jamestown in as bitter weather as could be of frost and snow, and within three days returned with an answer.

But when they came to Jamestown, seeing men sally out as he had told them they would, they fled, yet in the night they came again to the same place where he had told them they should receive an answer and such things as he had promised them, which they found accordingly, and with which they returned with no small expedition to the wonder of them all that heard it, that he could either divine[8] or the paper could speak.

Then they led him to the Youghtanunds, the Mattapanients, the Pianka-tanks, the Nantaughtacunds, and Onawmanients[9] upon the rivers of Rappa-hannock and Potomac, over all those rivers and back again by divers other several nations[1] to the King's habitation at Pamunkey where they entertained him with most strange and fearful conjurations:[2]

> As if near led to hell
> Amongst the devils to dwell.

Not long after, early in a morning, a great fire was made in a long-house and a mat spread on the one side as on the other; on the one they caused him to sit, and all the guard went out of the house, and presently came skipping in a great grim fellow all painted over with coal[3] mingled with oil, and many snakes' and weasels' skins stuffed with moss, and all their tails tied together so as they met on the crown of his head in a tassel, and round about the tassel was as a coronet of feathers, the skins hanging round about his head, back, and shoulders and in a manner covered his face, with a hellish voice, and a rattle in his hand. With most strange gestures and passions be began his invo-cation and environed[4] the fire with a circle of meal; which done, three more such like devils came rushing in with the like antic tricks, painted half black, half red, but all their eyes were painted white and some red strokes like mus-taches along their cheeks. Round about him those fiends danced a pretty while, and then came in three more as ugly as the rest, with red eyes and white strokes over their black faces. At last they all sat down right against him, three of them on the one hand of the chief priest and three on the other. Then all with their rattles began a song; which ended, the chief priest laid down five wheat corns;[5] then straining his arms and hands with such violence that he sweat and his veins swelled, he began a short oration;[6] at the conclusion they all gave a short groan and then laid down three grains more. After that, began their song again, and then another oration, ever laying down so many corns as before till they had twice encircled the fire; that done, they took a bunch of little sticks prepared for that purpose, continuing still their devotion, and at the end of every song and oration they laid down a stick betwixt the divisions of corn. Till night, neither he nor they did either eat or drink, and then they feasted merrily with the best provisions they could make. Three days they used this ceremony; the meaning whereof, they told him, was to know if he

7. Weaponry.
8. Perform magic. "Expedition": speed.
9. These groups were part of the confederacy that was under the rule of Powhatan.
1. Other Algonquian-speaking groups.
2. Incantations; but the following couplet Smith

derived from a translation of Seneca published by Bishop Martin Fotherby in his *Atheomastix* (1622).
3. I.e., charcoal.
4. Encircled.
5. I.e., five kernels of Indian corn.
6. Prayer.

intended them well or no. The circle of meal signified their country, the circles of corn the bounds of the sea, and the sticks his country. They imagined the world to be flat and round, like a trencher,[7] and they in the midst.

After this they brought him a bag of gunpowder, which they carefully preserved till the next spring, to plant as they did their corn, because they would be acquainted with the nature of that seed.

Opitchapam, the King's brother,[8] invited him to his house, where, with as many platters of bread, fowl, and wild beasts as did environ him, he bid him welcome, but not any of them would eat a bit with him but put up all the remainder in baskets.

At his return to Opechancanough's, all the King's women and their children flocked about him for their parts,[9] as a due by custom, to be merry with such fragments:

> But his waking mind in hideous dreams did
>   oft see wondrous shapes,
> Of bodies strange, and huge in growth, and
>   of stupendous makes.[1]

At last they brought him to Werowocomoco,[2] where was Powhatan, their Emperor. Here more than two hundred of those grim courtiers stood wondering at him, as [if] he had been a monster, till Powhatan and his train had put themselves in their greatest braveries.[3] Before a fire upon a seat like a bedstead, he sat covered with a great robe made of raccoon skins and all the tails hanging by. On either hand did sit a young wench of sixteen or eighteen years and along on each side [of] the house, two rows of men and behind them as many women, with all their heads and shoulders painted red, many of their heads bedecked with the white down of birds, but every one with something, and a great chain of white beads about their necks.

At his entrance before the King, all the people gave a great shout. The Queen of Appomattoc[4] was appointed to bring him water to wash his hands, and another brought him a bunch of feathers, instead of a towel, to dry them; having feasted him after their best barbarous manner they could, a long consultation was held, but the conclusion was, two great stones were brought before Powhatan; then as many as could, laid hands on him, dragged him to them, and thereon laid his head and being ready with their clubs to beat out his brains, Pocahontas,[5] the King's dearest daughter, when no entreaty could prevail, got his head in her arms and laid her own upon his to save him from death, whereat the Emperor was contented he should live to make him hatchets, and her bells, beads, and copper, for they thought him as well of all occupations as themselves.[6] For the King himself will make his own robes, shoes, bows, arrows, pots; plant, hunt, or do anything so well as the rest.

---

7. A flat wood dish.
8. Actually the chief's half-brother; he succeeded Powhatan in 1618.
9. Gifts.
1. From a translation of Lucretius by Fotherby.
2. Powhatan's village on the north shore of the York River, almost due north of Jamestown.
3. Finery; i.e., costumes.
4. Opossunoquonuske was the weroansqua, or leader, of a small village (Appamatuck) near the future site of

Petersburg, Virginia. In 1610, she was killed by the English in retaliation for the deaths of fourteen settlers.
5. Daughter of Powhatan (c. 1591–1617), she was mentioned in Smith's earlier versions of his captivity narrative, but first emerged as its heroine only in the History, which was published seven years after her death in England.
6. I.e., they thought him as variously skilled as themselves.

> They say he bore a pleasant show,
> But sure his heart was sad.
> For who can pleasant be, and rest,
> That lives in fear and dread:
> And having life suspected, doth
> It still suspected lead.[7]

Two days after, Powhatan, having disguised himself in the most fearfulest manner he could, caused Captain Smith to be brought forth to a great house in the woods and there upon a mat by the fire to be left alone. Not long after, from behind a mat that divided the house, was made the most dolefulest noise he ever heard; then Powhatan more like a devil than a man, with some two hundred more as black as himself, came unto him and told him now they were friends, and presently he should go to Jamestown to send him two great guns and a grindstone for which he would give him the country of Capahowasic and forever esteem him as his son Nantaquoud.[8]

So to Jamestown with twelve guides Powhatan sent him. That night they quartered in the woods, he still expecting (as he had done all this long time of his imprisonment) every hour to be put to one death or other, for all their feasting. But almighty God (by His divine providence) had mollified the hearts of those stern barbarians with compassion. The next morning betimes they came to the fort, where Smith having used the savages with what kindness he could, he showed Rawhunt, Powhatan's trusty servant, two demi-culverins[9] and a millstone to carry [to] Powhatan; they found them somewhat too heavy, but when they did see him discharge them, being loaded with stones, among the boughs of a great tree loaded with icicles, the ice and branches came so tumbling down that the poor savages ran away half dead with fear. But at last we regained some conference with them and gave them such toys and sent to Powhatan, his women, and children such presents as gave them in general full content.

Now in Jamestown they were all in combustion, the strongest preparing once more to run away with the pinnace; which, with the hazard of his life, with saker falcon[1] and musket shot, Smith forced now the third time to stay or sink.

Some, no better than they should be, had plotted with the President the next day to have him put to death by the Levitical law,[2] for the lives of Robinson and Emry; pretending the fault was his that had led them to their ends; but he quickly took such order with such lawyers that he laid them by the heels till he sent some of them prisoners for England.

Now every once in four or five days, Pocahontas with her attendants brought him so much provision that saved many of their lives, that else for all this had starved with hunger.

> Thus from numb death our good God sent relief,
> The sweet assuager of all other grief.[3]

7. Derived from a translation of Euripides by Fotherby.
8. I.e., Powhatan would esteem him as highly as his own son Nantaquoud. Capahowasic was along the York River near where Smith was held prisoner.
9. Large cannons.
1. Small falcon.

2. "And he that killeth any man shall surely be put to death" (Leviticus 24.17).
3. Apparently the first line is Smith's own, based on Fotherby, but the second is borrowed directly from Fotherby's translation from a quotation of Euripides found in Plutarch.

His relation of the plenty he had seen, especially at Werowocomoco, and of the state and bounty of Powhatan (which till that time was unknown), so revived their dead spirits (especially the love of Pocahontas)[4] as all men's fear was abandoned.

Thus you may see what difficulties still crossed any good endeavor; and the good success of the business being thus oft brought to the very period of destruction; yet you see by what strange means God hath still delivered it.

* * *

From *The Fourth Book*

[SMITH'S FAREWELL TO VIRGINIA]

Thus far I have traveled in this Wilderness of Virginia, not being ignorant for all my pains this discourse will be wrested, tossed and turned as many ways as there is leaves;[5] that I have written too much of some, too little of others, and many such like objections. To such I must answer, in the Company's name I was requested to do it,[6] if any have concealed their approved experiences from my knowledge, they must excuse me: as for every fatherless or stolen relation,[7] or whole volumes of sophisticated rehearsals, I leave them to the charge of them that desire them. I thank God I never undertook anything yet [for which] any could tax me of carelessness or dishonesty, and what[8] is he to whom I am indebted or troublesome? Ah! were these my accusers but to change cases and places with me [for] but two years, or till they had done but so much as I, it may be they would judge more charitably of my imperfections. But here I must leave all to the trial of time, both myself, Virginia's preparations, proceedings and good events, praying to that great God the protector of all goodness to send them as good success as the goodness of the action[9] and country deserveth, and my heart desireth.

1624

From A Description of New England[1]

Who can desire more content, that hath small means; or but only his merit to advance his fortune, than to tread, and plant that ground he hath purchased by the hazard of his life? If he have but the taste of virtue, and magnanimity,[2] what to such a mind can be more pleasant, than planting and building a foundation for his posterity, got from the rude earth, by God's blessing and his own industry, without prejudice[3] to any? If he have any grain of faith or zeal

4. I.e., the evident affection of Pocahontas for Smith and the English was instrumental in reviving the colonists' spirits.
5. Pages.
6. Smith was not requested to write the whole *General History* by the Virginia Company, so it is not clear what his reference is here. Possibly the discourse to which he refers is the brief summary of recommendations for the "reformation" of Virginia that ends the *Fourth Book* and that he drew up at the request of the royal commissioners charged with effecting that refor-

mation.
7. I.e., anonymous or "fugitive" narratives. "Approved": proven.
8. Who; i.e., he has been a burden to nobody.
9. Venture. "Events": results.
1. The text is derived from *The Complete Works of Captain John Smith*, edited by Philip L. Barbour (1986).
2. Greatness of spirit.
3. Harm.

in religion, what can he do less hurtful to any; or more agreeable to God, than
to seek to convert those poor savages to know Christ, and humanity, whose
labors with discretion will triple requite thy charge and pains? What so truly
suits with honor and honesty, as the discovering things unknown? erecting
townes, peopling countries, informing the ignorant, reforming things unjust,
teaching virtue; and gain[ing] to our native mother country a kingdom to
attend her; find[ing] employment for those that are idle, because they know
not what to do: so far from wronging any, as to cause posterity to remember
thee; and remembering thee, ever honor that remembrance with praise?

*   *   *

Then, who would live at home idly (or think in himself any worth to live)
only to eat, drink, and sleep, and so die? Or by consuming that carelessly,
[which] his friends got worthily? Or by using that miserably, [which] maintained virtue honestly? Or, for being descended nobly, pine with the vain
vaunt of great kindred, in penury?[4] Or (to maintain a silly show of bravery) toil
out thy heart, soul, and time, basely, by shifts, tricks, cards, and dice? Or by
relating news of others' actions, shark[5] here or there for a dinner, or supper;
deceive thy friends, by fair promises, and dissimulation, in borrowing where
thou never intendest to pay; offend the laws, surfeit with excess, burden thy
country, abuse thyself, despair in want, and then cozen[6] thy kindred, yea even
thine own brother, and wish thy parents' death (I will not say damnation) to
have their estates? though thou seest what honors, and rewards, the world yet
hath for them will seek them and worthily deserve them.

*   *   *

Let this move you to embrace employment, for those whose educations,
spirits, and judgments, want but your purses; not only to prevent such accustomed dangers, but also to gain more thereby than you have. And you fathers
that are either so foolishly fond, or so miserably covetous, or so wilfully ignorant, or so negligently careless, as that you will rather maintain your children
in idle wantonness, till they grow your masters; or become so basely unkind,
as they wish nothing but your deaths; so that both sorts grow dissolute: and
although you would wish them anywhere to escape the gallows, and ease your
cares; though they spend you here one, two, or three hundred pound a year;
you would grudge to give half so much in adventure with them, to obtain an
estate, which in a small time but with a little assistance of your providence,[7]
might be better than your own. But if an angel should tell you, that any place
yet unknown can afford such fortunes; you would not believe him, no more
than Columbus was believed there was any such land as is now the well-known
abounding America; much less such large regions as are yet unknown, as well
in America, as in Africa, and Asia, and Terra Incognita; where were courses
for gentlemen (and them that would be so reputed) more suiting their qualities,
than begging from their Prince's generous disposition, the labors of his subjects, and the very marrow of his maintenance.

I have not been so ill bred, but I have tasted of plenty and pleasure, as well
as want and misery: nor doth necessity yet, or occasion of discontent, force me

---

4. I.e., live in poverty while claiming great ancestors.   6. Deceive. "Excess": overindulge.
5. Sponge. "Bravery": fine appearances. "Shifts":   7. Provision.
expedients.

to these endeavors: nor am I ignorant what small thank I shall have for my pains; or that many would have the world imagine them to be of great judgment, that can but blemish these my designs, by their witty objections and detractions: yet (I hope) my reasons with my deeds, will so prevail with some, that I shall not want[8] employment in these affairs, to make the most blind see his own senselesness, and incredulity; hoping that gain will make them affect that, which religion, charity, and the common good cannot. It were but a poor device in me, to deceive myself; much more the king, and state, my friends, and country, with these inducements: which, seeing his Majesty hath given permission, I wish all sorts of worthy, honest, industrious spirits, would understand: and if they desire any further satisfaction, I will do my best to give it: Not to persuade them to go only;[9] but go with them: Not leave them there; but live with them there. I will not say, but by ill providing and undue managing, such courses may be taken, may make us miserable enough:[1] But if I may have the execution of what I have projected; if they want to eat, let them eat or never digest me.[2] If I perform what I say, I desire but that reward out of the gains may suit my pains, quality, and condition. And if I abuse you with my tongue, take my head for satisfaction. If any dislike at the year's end, defraying their charge,[3] by my consent they should freely return. I fear not want of company sufficient, were it but known what I know of those countries; and by the proof of that wealth I hope yearly to return, if God please to bless me from such accidents, as are beyond my power in reason to prevent: For, I am not so simple, to think, that ever any other motive than wealth, will ever erect there a Commonwealth; or draw company from their ease and humors at home, to stay in New England to effect my purposes. And lest any should think the toil might be insupportable, though these things may be had by labor, and diligence: I assure myself there are who delight extremely in vain pleasure, that take much more pains in England, to enjoy it, than I should do here to gain wealth sufficient: and yet I think they should not have half such sweet content: for, our pleasure here is still gains; in England, charges and loss. Here nature and liberty afford us that freely, which in England we want, or it costs us dearly. What pleasure can be more, than (being tired with any occasion ashore)[4] in planting vines, fruits, or herbs, in contriving their own grounds, to the pleasure of their own minds, their fields, gardens, orchards, buildings, ships, and other works, etc., to recreate themselves before their own doors, in their own boats upon the sea, where man, woman and child, with a small hook and line, by angling, may take diverse sorts of excellent fish, at their pleasures? And is it not pretty sport, to pull up two pence, six pence, and twelve pence, as fast as you can haul and veer[5] a line? He is a very bad fisher [who] cannot kill in one day with his hook and line, one, two, or three hundred cods: which dressed and dried, if they be sold there for ten shillings the hundred (though in England they will give more then twenty); may not both the servant, the master, and merchant, be well content with this gain? If a man work but three days in seven, he may get more than he can spend, unless he will be excessive. Now that carpenter, mason, gardener, tailor, smith, sailor, forgers,[6] or what other, may they not make this a pretty recreation

---

8. Lack.
9. Alone.
1. I.e., he won't promise that even with bad management they'll succeed.
2. I.e., or never read Smith's works.

3. I.e., once they have paid the cost of their support for the year.
4. Some casual occurrence.
5. I.e., fish.
6. I.e., ironworkers.

though they fish but an hour in a day, to take more than they eat in a week: or if they will not eat it, because there is so much better choice; yet sell it, or change it, with the fishermen, or merchants, for anything they want. And what sport doth yield a more pleasing content, and less hurt or charge than angling with a hook, and crossing the sweet air from isle to isle, over the silent streams of a calm sea, wherein the most curious may find pleasure, profit, and content. Thus, though all men be not fishers: yet all men, whatsoever, may in other matters do as well. For necessity doth in these cases so rule a Commonwealth, and each in their several functions, as their labors in their qualities may be as profitable, because there is a necessary mutual use of all.

For Gentlemen, what exercise should more delight them, than ranging daily those unknown parts, using fowling and fishing, for hunting and hawking? and yet you shall see the wild hawks give you some pleasure, in seeing them stoop[7] (six or seven after one another) an hour or two together, at the schools of fish in the fair harbors, as those ashore at a fowl; and never trouble nor torment yourselves, with watching, mewing, feeding, and attending them: nor kill horse and man with running and crying, See you not a hawk?[8] For hunting also: the woods, lakes, and rivers, afford not only chase sufficient, for any that delights in that kind of toil, or pleasure; but such beasts to hunt, that besides the delicacy of their bodies for food, their skins are so rich, as may well recompence thy daily labor, with a captain's pay.

For laborers, if those that sow hemp, rape,[9] turnips, parsnips, carrots, cabbage, and such like; give twenty, thirty, forty, fifty shillings yearly for an acre of ground, and meat, drink, and wages to use it, and yet grow rich: when better, or at least as good ground, may be had and cost nothing but labor; it seems strange to me, any such should there grow poor.

My purpose is not to persuade children [to go] from their parents; men from their wives; nor servants from their masters: only, such as with free consent may be spared: But that each parish, or village, in city, or country, that will but apparel their fatherless children, of thirteen or fourteen years of age, or young married people, that have small wealth to live on; here by their labor may live exceedingly well: provided always that first there be a sufficient power to command them, houses to receive them, means to defend them, and meet provisions for them; for, any place may be overlain:[1] and it is most necessary to have a fortress (ere this grow to practice) and sufficient masters (as, carpenters, masons, fishers, fowlers, gardeners, husbandmen, sawyers, smiths, spinsters, tailors, weavers, and such like) to take ten, twelve, or twenty, or as there is occasion, for apprentices. The masters by this may quickly grow rich; these may learn their trades themselves, to do the like; to a general and an incredible benefit, for king, and country, master, and servant.

1616

---

7. Swoop down.
8. Smith contrasts the delight of watching wild hawks hunt their prey in America with the tedious care that keepers of trained hawks in England must give their birds—as when such birds fly away and must be hunted for all over the countryside.
9. I.e., the rape plant.
1. Overcome.

From New England's Trials[1]

Here I must entreate a little your favors to digress. They did not kill the English because they were Christians,[2] but for their weapons and commodities, that were rare novelties; but now they fear we may beat them out of their dens, which lions and tigers would not admit but by force. But must this be an argument for an Englishman,[3] or discourage any either in Virginia or New England? No: for I have tried them both. For Virginia, I kept that country with thirty-eight, and had not[4] to eat but what we had from the savages. When I had ten men able to go abroad, our commonwealth was very strong: with such a number I ranged that unknown country fourteen weeks; I had but eighteen to subdue them all, with which great army I stayed six weeks before their greatest king's habitations, till they had gathered together all the power they could; and yet the Dutchmen sent at a needless excessive charge did help Powhatan how to betray me.[5]

* * *

For wronging a soldier but the value of a penny, I have caused Powhatan [to] send his own men to Jamestown to receive their punishment at my discretion. It is true in our greatest extremity they shot me, slew three of my men, and by the folly of them that fled took me prisoner; yet God made Pocahontas the king's daughter the means to deliver me: and thereby taught me to know their treacheries to preserve the rest. It was also my chance in single combat to take the king of Paspahegh[6] prisoner, and by keeping him, [I] forced his subjects to work in chains, till I made all the country pay contribution, having little else whereon to live.

Twice in this time I was their president,[7] and none can say in all that time I had a man slain: but for keeping them in that fear I was much blamed both there and here: yet I left 500 behind me that through their confidence in six months came most to confusion, as you may read at large in the description of Virginia.[8] When I went first to those desperate designs, it cost me many a forgotten pound to hire men to go; and procrastination caused more [to] run away than went. But after the ice was broken, came many brave voluntaries: notwithstanding since I came from thence, the honorable Company have been humble suitors to his Majesty to get vagabonds and condemned men to go thither; nay so much scorned was the name of Virginia, some did choose to

1. The text is derived from *The Complete Works of Captain John Smith*, edited by Philip L. Barbour (1986). By "trials" Smith means tests or experiments, not sufferings.
2. Smith here is speaking of the massacre of settlers in Virginia in March 1622, news of which reached New England sometime in May of that year. In mustering support for settlement in New England, he obviously had to take into account the damping effect of events in Virginia.
3. I.e., such events are not strong enough to dissuade an Englishman. "Admit": allow.
4. Nothing. "With thirty-eight": i.e., he protected or secured Virginia by means of a very modest force.
5. Several "Dutch" (probably German) skilled workers had been shipped to Virginia in 1608. Sent to build a house for Powhatan, they hinted to him that they would take his side against the English, and soon were plotting against Smith and the colony. Arrested by the English and brought back to Jamestown for execution, they were saved when a new ship arrived from England, bringing fresh supplies and important new instructions for President Smith and Virginia's governing council.
6. Paspahegh was the Algonquian name for the region around Jamestown. Smith took its chief, Wowinchopunck, prisoner in 1609. An engraving in the 1st edition of the *General History* shows this episode.
7. Smith was president of the Virginia council for only a single term; editors generally assume that he here means "twice during the time I was their president these things happened," although the passage may have been garbled.
8. I.e., Smith's first book, which contains a section so titled. "Confidence": i.e., overconfidence.

be hanged ere they would go thither, and were: yet for all the worst of spite, detraction and discouragement, and this lamentable massacre, there is more honest men now suitors to go, than ever hath been constrained knaves; and it is not unknown to most men of understanding, how happy many of those calumniators do think themselves, that they might be admitted, and yet pay for their passage to go now to Virginia: and had I but means to transport as many as would go, I might have choice of 10,000 that would gladly be in any of those new places, which were so basely condemned by ungrateful base minds.

To range this country of New England in like manner I had but eight, as is said, and amongst their brute[9] conditions I met many of their silly encounters, and without any hurt, God be thanked; when your West country men were many of them wounded and much tormented with the savages that assaulted their ship, as they did say themselves, in the first year I was there 1614, and though Master Hunt then master with me did most basely in stealing some savages from that coast to sell, when he was directed to have gone for Spain.[1] * * * I speak not this out of vainglory, as it may be some gleaners,[2] or some was never there may censure me, but to let all men be assured by those examples, what those savages are that thus strangely do murder and betray our countrymen. But to the purpose.

What is already written of the healthfulness of the air, the richness of the soil, the goodness of the woods, the abundance of fruits, fish, and fowl in their season, they still affirm that have been there now near two years, and at one draught[3] they have taken 1000 basses, and in one night twelve hogsheads of herring. They are building a strong fort, they hope shortly to finish, in the interim they are well provided: their number is about a hundred persons, all in health, and well near sixty acres of ground well planted with corn, besides their gardens well replenished with useful fruits; and if their adventurers would but furnish them with necessaries for fishing, their wants would quickly be supplied.[4] To supply them this sixteen of October is going the *Paragon* with sixty-seven persons, and all this is done by private men's purses. And to conclude in their own words, should they write of all plenties they have found, they think they should not be believed.

* * *

Thus you may see plainly the yearly success from New England (by Virginia)[5] which hath been so costly to this kingdom and so dear to me, which either to see perish or but bleed, pardon me though it passionate me beyond the bounds of modesty, to have been sufficiently able to foresee it, and had neither power nor means how to prevent it. By that acquaintance I have with them, I may call them my children, for they have been my wife, my hawks, my hounds, my cards, my dice, and in total my best content, as indifferent to

9. Tough.

1. Smith here refers to the tough going among earlier English voyagers to New England, especially Sir Ferdinando Gorges (1568–1647), a backer of Smith, and Thomas Hunt (dates unknown), who had been with Smith on the latter's 1614 voyage to the region. Hunt had stirred up much trouble with the local American Indians by kidnapping more than twenty of them, including the Native American Tisquantum (called "Squanto" by the Pilgrims) to sell into slavery in Spain.

2. Those who pick through events in search of bits of scandal.

3. A single haul of the fish net.

4. Here Smith speaks of the Plymouth settlers. "Adventurers": the investors who backed the Pilgrim venture.

5. I.e., by Virginia's example; Plymouth had barely been settled, but the longer experience of the English in Virginia (with all its faults) could be used to suggest the probable course of events in New England.

my heart as my left hand to my right;[6] and notwithstanding all those miracles of disasters have crossed both them and me, yet were there not one Englishman remaining (as God be thanked there is some thousands) I would yet begin again with as small means as I did at the first; not for that I have any secret encouragement from any I protest, more than lamentable experiences: for all their discoveries I can yet hear of, are but pigs of my own sow;[7] nor more strange to me than to hear one tell me he hath gone from Billingsgate and discovered Greenwich, Gravesend, Tilbury, Queenborough, Leigh and Margate, which to those did never hear of them, though they dwell in England, might be made seem some rare secrets and great countries unknown, except the relations of Master Dirmer.[8]

* * *

What here I have written by relation, if it be not right, I humbly entreat your pardons, but I have not spared any diligence to learn the truth of them that have been actors or sharers in those voyages: in some particulars they might deceive me, but in the substances they could not, for few could tell me anything, except where they fished: but seeing all those [that] have lived there, do confirm more than I have written, I doubt not but all those testimonies with these new-begun examples of plantation, will move both city and country freely to adventure with me and my partners more than promises, seeing I have from his Majesty letters pattent, such honest, free and large conditions assured me from his commissioners, as I hope will satisfy any honest understanding.

1622

---

6. I.e., as equally dear to me as one hand or the other.
7. The offspring of Smith's deeds; i.e., the accomplishments of others would not have been possible had he not gone before.
8. These are all well-known places in England. Smith's point is that once he had led the way into America, the English who followed him had accomplished nothing truly bold. The exception was Master Thomas Dermer (d. 1621), who had accompanied Smith to New England in 1614, had spent two years in Newfoundland (1616–18), and had returned to New England in 1619—in the process acquiring more knowledge about the region than Smith.

Early American Literature 1620-1820

Long before Captain John Smith established Jamestown in 1607, the European imagination had been entranced by rumors of the New World's plenty. But it was probably Smith, rather than any other, who convinced English readers that there was an earthly paradise not far from their shores. In his *Description of New England* (1616) he wrote, "Here nature and liberty afford us that freely which in England we want [i.e., lack], or it costs us dearly." What greater satisfaction is there, he asked, than hauling in one's supper by dropping a hook and line into any plentiful river or stream; is it not "pretty sport" to "pull up two pence, six pence, and twelve pence" as fast as you can let out a line? One hundred twenty-five years later another Virginia planter, William Byrd, would add to the fabled accounts of the place in his *History of the Dividing Line*, and it is significant that Thomas Jefferson's one book, *Notes on the State of Virginia* (1785, 1787), was written in response to inquiries made by a French naturalist concerning the geography and resources of his state. In replying, however, Jefferson the scientist is quickly supplanted by Jefferson the artist: no country, he writes, has more sublime mountains, rivers, and waterfalls, all objects of such "stupendous" power that they are "worth crossing the Atlantic" to witness. European readers for three centuries were anxious to sort American fable from fact, but as American writers convinced them, the facts themselves were fabulous.

THE PURITAN EXPERIMENT: PLYMOUTH PLANTATION

Although those Separatists from the Church of England whom we call Pilgrims were familiar with Smith's *Description* and followed his map of the Atlantic coast, they were not sympathetic to his proposal that he join their emigration to the New World; for Smith was primarily an adventurer, explorer, and trader, and while this group was not composed entirely of "reborn" Christians (only about twenty-seven of the one hundred persons aboard the *Mayflower* were Puritans), and even those were not indifferent to the material well-being of their venture, their leaders had more in mind than mercantile success. These pilgrims thought of themselves as soldiers in a war against Satan—the Arch-Enemy—who planned to ruin the kingdom of God on earth by sowing discord among those who professed to be Christians. This small band of believers saw no hope of reforming a national church and its Anglican hierarchy from within. In 1608, five years after the death of Queen Elizabeth and with an enemy of Puritanism, James Stuart, on the throne, they left England and settled in Holland, where, William Bradford tells us, they saw "fair and beautiful cities" and the "grisly face of poverty" confronting them. Isolated by their language, and unable to farm, they turned to mastering trades (Bradford himself became a weaver). Later, fearing that they would eventually lose their identity as a religious community living as strangers in a foreign land, they applied for a charter to settle in the Virginia Plantation—a vast tract of land that included what is now New England. Sponsored by merchants who were anxious to receive repayment in goods from the New World, they sailed from Southampton, England, in September 1620. Sixty-six days later, taken by strong winds much farther north than they had anticipated, they dropped anchor at Cape Cod and established their colony at Plymouth.

In spite of the fact that their separatism does not make them representative of the large number of emigrants who came to these shores in the seventeenth century (Plymouth was eventually absorbed into the Massachusetts Bay Colony in 1691 when a new charter was negotiated), their story has become an integral part of our literature. Bradford's account of a chosen people, exiles in a "howling wilderness," who struggled against all adversity to bring into being the City of God on earth, is ingrained in our national consciousness. Both in the nineteenth century and in the twentieth, Americans have seen themselves as a "redeemer nation," without, of course, possessing Bradford's Christian ideals. What gives Bradford's book its great strength, in spite of his obvious prejudices, is his ability to keep the ideals of the Pilgrims before us as he describes the harsh reality of their struggle against not only the external forces of nature but the even more damaging corruption of worldliness within the community.

THE PURITAN EXPERIMENT: THE MASSACHUSETTS BAY COLONY

Far more representative in attitude toward the Church of England were the Puritans who joined the Massachusetts Bay Colony under the leadership of John Winthrop. They were dissenting but nonseparating—although it might be argued that geographical distance from London and a charter that located the seat of their colony in Boston left them nonseparating in theory rather than practice. Whatever their difference with respect to the Church of England, however, the basic beliefs of both groups were identical: both held with Martin Luther that no pope or bishop had a right to impose any law on a Christian soul without consent and, following John Calvin, that God chose freely those He would save and those He would damn eternally.

Too much can be made of this doctrine of election; those who have not read the actual Puritan sermons often come away from secondary sources with the mistaken notion that Puritans talked about nothing but damnation. Puritans did indeed hold that God had chosen, before their birth, those whom He wished to save; but it does not follow that the Puritans considered most of us to be born damned. While Puritans argued that Adam broke the "Covenant of Works" (the promise God made to Adam that he was immortal and could live in Paradise forever as long as he obeyed God's commandments) when he disobeyed and ate of the tree of knowledge of good and evil, thereby bringing sin and death into the world, their central doctrine was the new "Covenant of Grace," a binding agreement Christ made with all men who believed in Him, and which He sealed with His Crucifixion, promising them eternal life. Puritans thus addressed themselves not to the hopelessly unregenerate but to the indifferent, and they addressed the heart more often than the mind, always distinguishing between "historical" or rational understanding and heartfelt "saving faith." There is more joy in Puritan life and thought than we often credit, and this joy is the direct result of meditation on the doctrine of Christ's redeeming power. Edward Taylor is not alone in making his rapturous litany of Christ's attributes: "He is altogether lovely in everything, lovely in His person, lovely in His natures, lovely in His properties, lovely in His offices, lovely in His titles, lovely in His practice, lovely in His purchases and lovely in His relations." All of Taylor's art is a meditation on the miraculous gift of the Incarnation, and, in this respect, his sensibility is typically Puritan. Anne Bradstreet, who is remarkably frank about confessing her religious doubts, told her children that it was "upon this rock Christ Jesus" that she built her faith.

Their lives, however, were hard. Anne Bradstreet's father told people in England to come over and join them if their lives were "endued with grace," but that others were "not fitted for this business"; that there was not a house where one had not died, and that if they survived the terrible winter they had to face the devastating infections that were the result of summer heat. Bradford's account of what he called "the starving time" is among the most moving in his history, and nothing in Smith's *Discovery* had hinted at how oppressive daily life might be. Sarah Kemble Knight of Boston provides a number of healthy antidotes to any sentimental notion we might have that life in the hinterland was invigorating. Puritan letters, diaries, histories, and poetry all attest to their faith in a larger plan, however, a "noble design" as Cotton Mather put it, which made daily life bearable.

In this Christocentric world it is not surprising that Puritans held to the strictest requirements regarding communion, or as they preferred to call it, the Lord's Supper. It was the most important of the two sacraments they recognized (baptism being the other), and they guarded it with a zeal that set them apart from all other dissenting churches. In the beginning, communion was taken only by church members—those who had stood before their minister and elders and given an account (or "relation") of their conversion—and was regarded as a sign of election. This insistence on challenging their members made these New England churches more rigorous than any others and confirmed the feeling that they were a special few. Thus, when John Winthrop addressed the immigrants to the Bay Colony aboard the flagship *Arbella* in 1630, he told them that the eyes of the world were on them and that they would be an example for all, a "city upon a hill."

PURITAN HISTORIOGRAPHY

Puritans held the writing of history in high regard, for as heirs of Renaissance thought, they believed that lasting truths were to be gained by studying the lives of noble individuals. Cotton Mather urged students of the ministry to read not only early church historians but the classical historians Xenophon, Livy, Tacitus, and Plutarch as well. Puritans saw all of human time as a progression toward the fulfillment of God's design on earth. Therefore, pre-Christian history could be read as a preparation for Christ's entry into the world. They learned this lesson from medieval biblical scholars, who interpreted figures in the Old Testament as foreshadowings of Christ. This method of comparison, called typology, was an ingrained habit of Puritan thinking, and it made them compare themselves, as a chosen people, to the Israelites of old, who had been given the promise of a new land. Cotton Mather said that John Winthrop was the Puritan Moses whose education had prepared him to fulfill the "noble design of carrying a colony of chosen people into an American wilderness."

Puritans believed that God's hand was present in every human event and that He rewarded good and punished bad. History, therefore, revealed what God approved of or condemned, and if God looked favorably on a nation, His approval could be evidenced in its success. Puritans had enough confidence in God's design to believe that no facts were too small or insignificant to be included in that design; everything could emblemize something. In writing about Anne Bradstreet, Adrienne Rich observes that seventeenth-century Puritan life was perhaps "the most self-conscious ever lived"; that "faith underwent its hourly testing, the domestic mundanities were episodes in the drama; the piecemeal thoughts of a woman stirring a pot, clues to her 'justification' in Christ." John Winthrop in his diary records a struggle between a snake and a mouse and is surprised to see the seemingly weaker emerge the victor. His Boston friend, Mr. Wilson, however, saw the event as a battle between Satan and a "poor contemptible people, which God hath brought hither, which should overcome Satan here and disposses him of his kingdom." When a young sailor on board the *Mayflower* mocked those Puritans who were sick, Bradford found it fitting that the sailor should himself succumb to a "grievous disease." This sense of the universal significance of all things meant that drama was present in every believer's life and that individual lives could be as symbolic as the life of a nation. Mary Rowlandson, who had been captured by American Indians, saw her captivity as a lesson in the life of a representative soul who once wished to experience affliction and later experienced it only too well. Her captors were, to her, more than uncivilized savages; they were devils incarnate. In 1833, William Apess, a Pequot and a Christian, wondered if it might not be possible to "penetrate the conduct" of those who profess to follow Christ and "see if they came anywhere near Him and His ancient disciples" in compassion and understanding.

The greatest of all the Puritan historians was Cotton Mather, and in his *Magnalia Christi Americana* (1702) the myth of a chosen people took on its fullest resonance of meaning. By the time Mather undertook his history, the original Puritan community had vanished, leaving behind heirs to its lands and fortunes but not to its spirituality. Mather saw himself as one of the last defenders of the "old New England way," and all the churches as under attack from new forces of secularism. As a historian, Mather solved his problem by not focusing on the dissolution of the Puritan community but writing "saints' lives" instead, each of which (like those of Eliot, Bradford, and Winthrop) would serve as an example of the progress of the individual Christian soul and an allegory of the potential American hero. Under Mather's artistry, Winthrop's vision of a community of saints living in mutual concern and sympathy became an ideal rather than a historical reality. The words *New England* would symbolize the effort to realize the City of God on earth, and "whether New England may live anywhere else or no," he said, "it must live in our history."

AN EXPANDING UNIVERSE

It should come as no surprise to learn that Mather was defensively retrospective in his ecclesiastical history of New England; for the enormous changes—economic, social, philosophical, and scientific—that occurred between Mather's birth in 1663 and the publication of the *Magnalia* in 1702 inevitably affected the influence and authority of Congregational churches. In 1686 Mather himself joined with Boston merchants in jailing their colonial governor, Sir Edmund Andros, and was successful in getting him sent back to England. It was a rare occasion when church and trade saw eye to eye; the Puritan clergy disliked Andros's Anglicanism as much as the merchants hated his taxes. It was an act celebrated annually in Boston until it was replaced by celebrations honoring American independence.

The increase in population alone would account for a greater diversity of opinion in the matter of churches. In 1670, for example, the population of the colonies numbered approximately 111,000. Thirty years later the colonies contained more than 250,000 persons; by 1760, if one included Georgia, they numbered 1,600,000, and the settled area had tripled. The demand for and price of colonial goods increased in England, and vast fortunes were to be made in New England with any business connected with shipbuilding: especially timber, tar, and pitch. Virginia planters became rich in tobacco, and rice and indigo from the Carolinas were in constant demand. New England Indians, on the other hand, estimated to number 25,000 in 1600, were reduced by one-third during the plague of 1616–18 and declined steadily thereafter; many communities disappeared entirely during this period of expansion.

New England towns were full of acrimonious debate between first settlers and newcomers. Town histories are full of accounts of splinter groups and the establishment of the "Second" church. In the beginning land was apportioned to settlers and allotted free, but by 1713 speculators in land were hard at work, buying as much as possible for as little as possible and selling high. The idea of a "community" of mutually helpful souls was fast disappearing. Life in the colonies was not easy, but the hardships and dangers the first settlers faced were mostly overcome, and compared with crowded cities like London, it was healthier, cheaper, and more hopeful. Those who could arrange their passage came in great numbers. Boston almost doubled in size from 1700 to 1720. It is also important to note that the great emigration to America that occurred in the first half of the eighteenth century was not primarily English. Dutch and Germans came in large numbers and so did French Protestants. Jewish merchants and craftsmen were well known in New York and Philadelphia.

By 1750 Philadelphia had become the unofficial capital of the colonies and was second only to London as a city of commerce. In 1681 the Quaker William Penn exchanged a large claim against the Crown for land in the New World. He was named proprietor (rather than governor, because he actually owned the territory) of Pennsylvania and immediately opened the land to settlement by people of all faiths. Penn had the genius to bestow the privilege of self-government on the people of Pennsylvania and in his "Frame of Government" told them that "Liberty without obedience is confusion, and obedience without liberty is slavery." These thousands of emigrants did not think of themselves as displaced British citizens; they thought of themselves as Americans. In 1702 no one would have dreamed of an independent union of colonies, but by 1752, fifty years later, it was a distinct possibility.

THE ENLIGHTENMENT

Great challenges to seventeenth-century beliefs were posed by scientists and philosophers, and it has sometimes been suggested that the "modern" period dates from 1662 and the founding of the British scientific academy known, because of the patronage of King Charles II, as the Royal Society. The greatest scientists of the age like Sir Isaac Newton (1642–1727) and philosophers like John Locke (1632–1704) saw no conflict between their discoveries and traditionally held Christian truths. They saw nothing heretical in arguing that the universe was an orderly system and that by the application of reason humanity would comprehend its laws. But the inevitable result of their inquiries was to make the universe seem more rational and benevolent than it had been represented by Puritan doctrine. Because the world seemed more comprehensible, people paid less attention to revealed religion, and a number of seventeenth-century modes of thought—Bradford Winthrop's penchant for the allegorical and emblematic, seeing every natural and human event as a message from God, for instance—seemed almost medieval and decidedly quaint. These new scientists and philosophers were called Deists; they deduced the existence of a supreme being from the construction of the universe itself rather than from the Bible. "A creation," as one distinguished historian has put it, "presupposes a creator." People were less interested in the metaphysical wit of introspective divines than in the progress of ordinary individuals as they made their way in the world. They assumed that humankind was naturally good and dwelt on neither the Fall nor the Incarnation. A harmonious universe proclaimed the beneficence of God, and Deists argued that humans should be as generous. They were not interested in theology but in humankind's own nature. American as well as English citizens knew Alexander Pope's famous couplet:

> Know then thyself, presume not God to scan,
> The proper study of mankind is man.

Locke said that "our business" here on earth "is not to know all things, but those which concern our conduct." In suggesting that we are not born with a set of innate ideas of good or evil and that the mind is rather like a blank wax tablet on which experiences are inscribed (a *tabula rasa*), Locke qualified traditional belief.

THE GREAT AWAKENING

A conservative reaction against the worldview of the new science was bound to follow, and the first half of the eighteenth century witnessed a number of religious revivals in both England and America. They were sometimes desperate efforts to reassert the old values in the face of the new and, oddly enough, were themselves the direct product of the new cult of feeling, a philosophy that argued that our greatest pleasure was derived from the good we did for others and that our sympathetic emotions (our joy as well as our tears) should not be contained. Phillis Wheatley, whose poem on the death of the Methodist George Whitefield (1714–1770) made her famous, said that Whitefield prayed that "grace in every heart might dwell" and longed to see "America excell." Whitefield's revival meetings along the Atlantic seaboard were a great personal triumph, but they were no more famous than the "extraordinary circumstances" that occurred in Northampton, Massachusetts, under the leadership of Jonathan Edwards in the 1730s and that have come to be synonymous with the "Great Awakening."

Edwards also read his Locke, but he wished to liberate human beings from their senses, not define them by those senses. Edwards was fond of pointing out that the five senses are what we share with beasts, and that if our ultimate goal were merely a heightened sensibility, feverish sickness is the condition in which the senses are most acute. Edwards was interested in *supernatural* concerns, but he was himself influenced by Locke in arguing that true belief is something that we feel and do not merely comprehend intellectually. Edwards took the one doctrine most difficult for eighteenth-century minds to accept—election—and persuaded his congregation that God's sovereignty was not only the most reasonable doctrine but was the most "delightful" and appeared to him (using adjectives that suggest that the best analogy is to what can be apprehended sensually) "exceeding pleasant, bright, and sweet." In carefully reasoned, calmly argued prose, as harmonious and as ordered as anything the age produced, Edwards brought his great intellect to bear on doctrines that had been current the century before. Most people, when they think about the Puritans, remember Edwards's sermon Sinners in the Hands of an Angry God, forgetting that one hundred years had lapsed between that sermon and Winthrop's Model of Christian Charity. When Edwards tried to reassert "the old New England way" and demanded accounts of conversion before admission to church membership, he was accused of being a reactionary who thrived on hysteria, was removed from his pulpit, and was effectively silenced. He spent his last years as a missionary to the American Indians in Stockbridge, Massachusetts, a town forty miles to the west of Northampton, imitating the call of the Reverend David Brainard, a young man who, had he lived, would have married Edwards's daughter Jerusha. There he remained until invited to become president of the College of New Jersey. His death in Princeton was the direct result of his willingness to be vaccinated against smallpox and so to set an example for his frightened and superstitious students; it serves as a vivid reminder of how complicated in any one individual the response to the "new science" could become.

THE AMERICAN CRISIS

On June 7, 1776, at the second Continental Congress, Richard Henry Lee of Virginia moved that "these united colonies are, and of a right ought to be, free and independent states." A committee was duly appointed to prepare a declaration of independence, and it was approved on July 4. Although these motions and their swiftness took some delegates by surprise—the purpose of the congress had, after all, not been to declare independence but to protest the usurpation of rights by king and Parliament and to effect a compromise with the homeland—others saw them as the inevitable consequence of the events of the decade preceding. The

Stamp Act of 1764, taxing all newspapers, legal documents, and licenses, had infuriated Bostonians and resulted in the burning of the governor's palace; in Virginia, Patrick Henry had taken the occasion to speak impassionedly against taxation without representation. In 1770 a Boston mob had been fired on by British soldiers, and three years later the famous "Tea Party" occurred, an act that drew hard lines in the matter of acceptable limits of British rule. In adopting the dress of Native Americans, these protesters declared themselves antithetical to everything British. The news of the April confrontation with the British in Concord and Lexington, Massachusetts, was still on everyone's tongue in Philadelphia when the second Continental Congress convened in May of 1775.

Although the drama of these events cannot be underestimated, most historians agree that it was Thomas Paine's *Common Sense*, published in January 1776, that gave the needed push for revolution. In the course of two months it was read by almost every American. In arguing that separation from England was the only reasonable course and that "the Almighty" had planted these feelings in us "for good and wise purposes," Paine was appealing to basic tenets of the Enlightenment. His clarion call to those that "love mankind," those "that dare oppose not only the tyranny but the tyrant, stand forth!" did not got unheeded. Americans needed an apologist for the Revolution, and in December of 1776, when Washington's troops were at their most demoralized, it was, again, Paine's first *Crisis* paper—popularly called *The American Crisis*—that was read to all the regiments and was said to have inspired their future success.

Paine first came to America in 1774 with a note from Benjamin Franklin recommending him to publishers and editors. He was only one of a number of young writers who were able to take advantage of the times. This was, in fact, the great age of the newspaper and the moral essay; Franklin tells us that he modeled his own style on the clarity, good sense, and simplicity of the English essayists Joseph Addison and Richard Steele. The first newspaper in the colonies appeared in 1704, but by the time of the Revolution there were almost fifty papers and forty magazines. The great cry was for a "national literature" (meaning anti-British), and the political events of the 1770s were advantageous for a career. Philip Freneau made his first success as a writer as a satirist of the British, and after the publication of his *Poems Written Chiefly during the Late War* (1786) he turned to newspaper work, editing the *New York Daily Advertiser* and writing anti-Federalist party essays, making himself an enemy of Alexander Hamilton in the process. The most distinguished political writings of the period are, in fact, the essays Hamilton, John Jay, and James Madison wrote for New York newspapers in 1787 and 1788 and collectively known as *The Federalist Papers*. In attempting to get New Yorkers to support the new Constitution they provided an eloquent defense of the framework of the Republic. Joel Barlow also published anti-British satires in the *New Haven Gazette and Connecticut Magazine* and envisioned an American literature that would extol our government, our educational institutions, and the arts. He spent most of his life revising a long hymn to the Republic called *The Columbiad*. But Barlow never settled down to the life of the artist; he was too much the entrepreneur and world traveler for that. His best poems are not his philosophical epics but poems, like *The Hasty Pudding*, in praise of the simple life. Freneau's career was also marked by restlessness and indecision, although in his case financial necessity came between his life and his art. The first American writer able to live exclusively by his craft was Washington Irving.

The crisis in American life caused by the Revolution made artists self-conscious about American subjects. It would be another fifty years before writers discovered ways of being American without compromising their integrity. One of the ironies of our history is that the Revolution itself has rarely proved to be a usable subject for American literature and art.

THE PURSUIT OF HAPPINESS

When John Winthrop described his "model" for a Christian community, he envisioned a group of men and women working together for the common good, each one of whom knew his or her place in the social structure and accepted God's disposition of goods. At all times, he said, "some must be rich, some poor, some high and eminent in power and dignity," others low and "in subjection." Ideally, it was to be a community of love, all made equal by their fallen nature and their concern for the salvation of their souls, but it was to be a stable community, and Winthrop would not have imagined very much social change. One hundred forty years later John Adams, our second president, envisioned a model community, decreed by higher laws, when he said that the American colonies were a part of a "grand scheme and design in Providence for the illumination of the ignorant and the emancipation of the slavish part of mankind all over the earth." Adams witnessed social mobility of a kind and an extent, however, that no European before him would have dreamed possible. As historians have observed, European critics of America in the eighteenth and nineteenth centuries never understood that great social change was possible without social upheaval primarily because there was no feudal hierarchy to overthrow. When Crèvecoeur wanted to distinguish America from Europe, it was the medievalism of the latter that he wished to stress. The visitor to America, he said, "views not the hostile castle, and the haughty mansion, contrasted with the clay-built hut and miserable cabin, where cattle and men help to keep each other warm, and dwell in meanness, smoke and indigence."

Of course, not everyone was free, and for indentured servants and Native Americans, being "free" was relative. Some of our founding fathers, like Thomas Jefferson, were large slaveowners, and it was still not possible to vote without owning property. Women had hardly any rights at all: they could not vote and young women were educated at home, excluded by their studies from anything other than domestic employment. Nevertheless, the same forces that were undermining church authority in New England (in New York and Philadelphia no such hierarchy existed) were effecting social change. The two assumptions held to be true by most eighteenth-century Americans were, as Russel Nye once put it, "the perfectability of man, and the prospect of his future progress." Much of the imaginative energy of the second half of the eighteenth century was expanded in correcting institutional injustices: the tyranny of monarchy, the tolerance of slavery, the misuse of prisons. Few doubted that with the application of intelligence the human lot could be improved, and writers like Freneau, Franklin, and Crèvecoeur argued that, if it were not too late, the transplanted European might learn something about fellowship and manners from "the noble savages" rather than from rude white settlers, slaveowners, and backwoods pioneers.

In many ways it is Franklin who best represents the spirit of the Enlightenment in America: self-educated, social, assured, a man of the world, ambitious and public-spirited, speculative about the nature of the universe, but in matters of religion content to observe the actual conduct of humanity rather than to debate supernatural matters that are unprovable. When Ezra Stiles asked him about his religion, he said he believed in the "creator of the universe" but he doubted the "divinity of Jesus." He would never dogmatize about it, however, because he expected soon "an opportunity of knowing the truth with less trouble." Franklin always presents himself as a man depending on firsthand experience, too worldly wise to be caught off guard. His posture, however, belies one side of the eighteenth century that can be accounted for neither by the inheritance of Calvin nor by the empiricism of Locke: those idealistic assumptions that underlie the great public documents of the American Revolution, especially the Declaration of Independence. These are truths that, Joel Barlow once said, were "as perceptible when first presented to the mind as age or world of experience could make them." Given the representative nature of Franklin's character, it seems right that of the documents most closely associated with the formation of the American republic—the Declaration of Independence, the treaty of alliance with France, the Treaty of Paris, and the Constitution—only he should have signed all four.

The fact that Americans in the last quarter of the eighteenth century would hold that "certain truths are self-evident, that all men are created equal, that they are endowed by their Creator with certain unalienable Rights, that among these are Life, Liberty and the pursuit of Happiness" is the result, as both Leon Howard and Gary Wills have argued, of their reading the Scottish philosophers, particularly Francis Hutcheson and Lord Kames (Henry Home), who argued that all people in all places possess a sense common to all—a moral sense—that contradicted the notion of the mind as an empty vessel awaiting experience. This idealism paved the way for writers like Bryant, Emerson, Thoreau, and Whitman, but in the 1770s its presence is found chiefly in politics and ethics. The assurance of a universal sense of right and wrong made possible both the overthrow of tyrants and the restoration of order, and it allowed humankind to make new earthly covenants, not, as was the case with Bradford and Winthrop, for the glory of God, but, as Thomas Jefferson argued, for an individual's right to happiness on earth.

WILLIAM BRADFORD
1590–1657

William Bradford epitomizes the spirit of determination and self-sacrifice that seems to us characteristic of our first "Pilgrims," a word Bradford himself used to describe the community of believers who sailed from Southampton, England, on the *Mayflower* and settled in Plymouth, Massachusetts, in 1620. For Bradford, as well as for the other members of this community, the decision to settle at Plymouth was the last step in a long march of exile from England, and the hardships they suffered in the new land were tempered with the knowledge that they were in a place they had chosen for themselves, where they were safe from persecution. Shortly after their arrival Bradford was elected governor. His duties involved more than that title might imply today: he was chief judge and jury, superintended agriculture and trade, and made allotments of land. It would be hard to imagine a historian better prepared to write the history of this colony.

Bradford's own life provides a model of the life of the community as a whole. He was born in Yorkshire, in the town of Austerfield, of parents who were modestly well off. Bradford's father died when he was an infant. His mother remarried in 1593, and he was brought up by his paternal grandparents and uncles. He did not receive a university education; instead, he was taught the arts of farming. When he was only twelve or thirteen, he heard the sermons of the Nonconformist minister Richard Clyfton, who preached in a neighboring parish; these sermons changed Bradford's life. For Clyfton was the religious guide of a small community of believers who met at the house of William Brewster in Scrooby, Nottinghamshire, and it was with this group, in 1606, that Bradford wished to be identified. Much against the opposition of uncles and grandparents, he left home and joined them. They were known as "Separatists," because unlike the majority of Puritans, they saw no hope of reforming the Church of England from within. They wished to follow Calvin's model and to set up "particular" churches, each one founded on a formal covenant, entered into by those who professed their faith and swore to the covenant. Their model was the Old Testament covenant God made with Adam and that Christ renewed. In their covenanted churches God offered himself as a contractual partner to each believer; it was a contract freely initiated but perpetually binding. They were not sympathetic to the idea of a national church. Separating was, however, by English law an act of treason, and many believers paid a high price for their dreams of purity. Sick of the hidden life that the Church of England forced on them, the Scrooby community took up residence in Holland. Bradford joined them in 1609 and there learned to be a weaver. When he came into his inheritance he went into business for himself.

Living in a foreign land was not easy, and eventually the Scrooby community petitioned for a grant of land in the New World. Their original grant was for land in the Virginia territory, but high seas prevented them from reaching those shores and they settled at Plymouth, Massachusetts, instead. In the second book of Bradford's history he describes the signing of the "Mayflower Compact," a civil covenant designed to allow the temporal state to serve the godly citizen. It was the first of a number of plantation covenants designed to protect the rights of citizens beyond the reach of established governments.

Bradford was a self-educated man, deeply committed to the Puritan cause. In his ecclesiastical history of New England, Cotton Mather describes him as "a person for study as well as action; and hence notwithstanding the difficulties which he passed in his youth, he attained unto a notable skill in languages. . . . but the Hebrew he most of all studied, because, he said, he would see with his own eyes the ancient oracles of God in their native beauty. . . . The crown of all his life was his holy, prayerful, watchful and fruitful walk with God, wherein he was exemplary." Bradford served as governor for all but five of the remaining years of his life.

The manuscript of Bradford's *History*, although known to early historians, disappeared from Boston after the revolution. The first book (through chapter IX) had been copied into the Plymouth church records and was thus preserved, but the second book was assumed lost. The manuscript was found in the residence of the bishop of London and published for the first time in 1856. In 1897 it was returned to this country by ecclesiastical decree and was deposited in the State House in Boston.

From Of Plymouth Plantation[1]

From Book I, Chapter I. [The Separatist Interpretation of the Reformation in England, 1550–1607]

* * * When as by the travail and diligence of some godly and zealous preachers, and God's blessing on their labors, as in other places of the land, so in the North parts,[2] many became enlightened by the Word of God and had their ignorance and sins discovered[3] unto them, and began by His grace to reform their lives and make conscience of their ways; the work of God was no sooner manifest in them but presently they were both scoffed and scorned by the profane[4] multitude; and the ministers urged with the yoke of subscription,[5] or else must be silenced. And the poor people were so vexed with apparitors and pursuivants and the commissary courts,[6] as truly their affliction was not small. Which, notwithstanding, they bore sundry years with much patience, till they were occasioned by the continuance and increase of these

---

1. The text is from *Of Plymouth Plantation*, edited by Samuel Eliot Morison (1953).
2. I.e., of England and Scotland.
3. Revealed.
4. Unholy.

5. I.e., to subscribe to the tenets of the Church of England. "Urged": threatened.
6. I.e., vexed with officers and summoners of the Church of England and the court of a bishop's jurisdiction.

troubles, and other means which the Lord raised up in those days, to see further into things by the light of the Word of God. How not only these base and beggarly ceremonies were unlawful, but also that the lordly and tyrannous power of the prelates ought not to be submitted unto; which thus, contrary to the freedom of the gospel, would load and burden men's consciences and by their compulsive power make a profane mixture of persons and things in the worship of God. And that their offices and callings, courts and canons, etc. were unlawful and antichristian; being such as have no warrant in the Word of God, but the same that were used in popery and still retained. Of which a famous author thus writeth in his Dutch commentaries, at the coming of King James into England:

> The new king (saith he) found there established the reformed religion according to the reformed religion of King Edward VI, retaining or keeping still the spiritual state of the bishops, etc. after the old manner, much varying and differing from the reformed churches in Scotland, France and the Netherlands, Emden, Geneva, etc., whose reformation is cut, or shapen much nearer the first Christian churches, as it was used in the Apostles' times.[7]

So many, therefore, of these professors as saw the evil of these things in these parts, and whose hearts the Lord had touched with heavenly zeal for His truth, they shook off this yoke of antichristian bondage, and as the Lord's free people joined themselves (by a covenant[8] of the Lord) into a church estate, in the fellowship of the gospel, to walk in all His ways made known, or to be made known unto them, according to their best endeavors, whatsoever it should cost them, the Lord assisting them. And that it cost them something this ensuing history will declare.

These people became two distinct bodies or churches, and in regard of distance of place did congregate severally; for they were of sundry towns and villages, some in Nottinghamshire, some of Lincolnshire, and some of Yorkshire where they border nearest together. In one of these churches (besides others of note) was Mr. John Smith, a man of able gifts and a good preacher, who afterwards was chosen their pastor. But these afterwards falling into some errors in the Low Countries,[9] there (for the most part) buried themselves and their names.

But in this other church (which must be the subject of our discourse) besides other worthy men, was Mr. Richard Clyfton, a grave and reverend preacher, who by his pains and diligence had done much good, and under God had been a means of the conversion of many. And also that famous and worthy man Mr. John Robinson, who afterwards was their pastor for many years, till the Lord took him away by death. Also Mr. William Brewster[1] a reverend man, who afterwards was chosen an elder of the church and lived with them till old age.

7. From Emanuel van Meteren's *General History of the Netherlands* (1608). King James (1566–1625) ascended the throne in 1603. Most Puritans preferred the model of the Calvinist system in Geneva or the Church of Scotland, which replaced a hierarchy of archbishops, bishops, and priests with a national assembly and a parish presbytery consisting of ministers and elders.
8. A solemn agreement between the members of a church to act together in harmony with the precepts of the Gospel.
9. Holland.
1. A church leader of the Pilgrims in both Leyden and Plymouth (1576–1644). John Smith was a Cambridge University graduate who seceded from the Church of England in 1605. Richard Clyfton and John Robinson were also Cambridge University graduates who were Separatists.

But after these things they could not long continue in any peaceable condition, but were hunted and persecuted on every side, so as their former afflictions were but as flea-bitings in comparison of these which now came upon them. For some were taken and clapped up in prison, others had their houses beset and watched night and day, and hardly escaped their hands; and the most were fain to flee and leave their houses and habitations, and the means of their livelihood.

Yet these and many other sharper things which afterward befell them, were no other than they looked for, and therefore were the better prepared to bear them by the assistance of God's grace and Spirit.

Yet seeing themselves thus molested, and that there was no hope of their continuance there, by a joint consent they resolved to go into the Low Countries, where they heard was freedom of religion for all men; as also how sundry from London and other parts of the land had been exiled and persecuted for the same cause, and were gone thither, and lived at Amsterdam and in other places of the land. So after they had continued together about a year, and kept their meetings every Sabbath in one place or other, exercising the worship of God amongst themselves, notwithstanding all the diligence and malice of their adversaries, they seeing they could no longer continue in that condition, they resolved to get over into Holland as they could. Which was in the year 1607 and 1608; of which more at large in the next chapter.

Book I, Chapter IV. Showing the Reasons and Causes of Their Removal

After they had lived in this city about some eleven or twelve years (which is the more observable being the whole time of that famous truce between that state and the Spaniards)[2] and sundry of them were taken away by death and many others began to be well stricken in years (the grave mistress of Experience having taught them many things), those prudent governors with sundry of the sagest members began both deeply to apprehend their present dangers and wisely to foresee the future and think of timely remedy. In the agitation of their thoughts, and much discourse of things hereabout, at length they began to incline to this conclusion: of removal to some other place. Not out of any newfangledness or other such like giddy humor by which men are oftentimes transported to their great hurt and danger, but for sundry weighty and solid reasons, some of the chief of which I will here briefly touch.

And first, they saw and found by experience the hardness of the place and country to be such as few in comparison would come to them, and fewer that would bide it out and continue with them. For many that came to them, and many more that desired to be with them, could not endure that great labor and hard fare, with other inconveniences which they underwent and were contented with. But though they loved their persons, approved their cause and honored their sufferings, yet they left them as it were weeping, as Orpah did her mother-in-law Naomi, or as those Romans did Cato[3] in Utica who desired to be excused and borne with, though they could not all be Catos. For many,

2. The struggle for independence by provinces of the Netherlands against Spain was interrupted by a twelve-year truce on March 30, 1609; that truce was now coming to a close. "This city": Leyden.
3. Roman statesman of unbending integrity, who committed suicide in 46 B.C. when Julius Caesar's cause triumphed. Orpah was the sister-in-law of Ruth: "And they lifted up their voice, and wept again: and Orpah kissed her mother-in-law; but Ruth clave unto her" (Ruth 1.14).

though they desired to enjoy the ordinances of God in their purity and the liberty of the gospel with them, yet (alas) they admitted of bondage with danger of conscience, rather than to endure these hardships. Yea, some preferred and chose the prisons in England rather than this liberty in Holland with these afflictions. But it was thought that if a better and easier place of living could be had, it would draw many and take away these discouragements. Yea, their pastor would often say that many of those who both wrote and preached now against them, if they were in a place where they might have liberty and live comfortably, they would then practice as they did.

Secondly. They saw that though the people generally bore all these difficulties very cheerfully and with a resolute courage, being in the best and strength of their years; yet old age began to steal on many of them; and their great and continual labors, with other crosses and sorrows, hastened in before the time. So as it was not only probably thought, but apparently seen, that within a few years more they would be in danger to scatter, by necessities pressing them, or sink under their burdens, or both. And therefore according to the divine proverb, that a wise man seeth the plague when it cometh, and hideth himself, Proverbs xxii.3, so they like skillful and beaten soldiers were fearful either to be entrapped or surrounded by their enemies so as they should neither be able to fight nor fly. And therefore thought it better to dislodge betimes to some place of better advantage and less danger, if any such could be found.

Thirdly. As necessity was a taskmaster over them so they were forced to be such, not only to their servants but in a sort to their dearest children, the which as it did not a little wound the tender hearts of many a loving father and mother, so it produced likewise sundry sad and sorrowful effects. For many of their children that were of best dispositions and gracious inclinations, having learned to bear the yoke in their youth[4] and willing to bear part of their parents' burden, were oftentimes so oppressed with their heavy labors that though their minds were free and willing, yet their bodies bowed under the weight of the same, and became decrepit in their early youth, the vigor of nature being consumed in the very bud as it were. But that which was more lamentable, and of all sorrows most heavy to be borne, was that many of their children, by these occasions and the great licentiousness of youth in that country,[5] and the manifold temptations of the place, were drawn away by evil examples into extravagant and dangerous courses, getting the reins off their necks and departing from their parents. Some became soldiers, others took upon them far voyages by sea, and others some worse courses tending to dissoluteness and the danger of their souls, to the great grief of their parents and dishonor of God. So that they saw their posterity would be in danger to degenerate and be corrupted.

Lastly (and which was not least), a great hope and inward zeal they had of laying some good foundation, or at least to make some way thereunto, for the propagating and advancing the gospel of the kingdom of Christ in those remote parts of the world; yea, though they should be but even as stepping-stones unto others for the performing of so great a work.

These and some other like reasons moved them to undertake this resolution

4. "It is good for a man that he bear the yoke in his youth" (Lamentations 3.27).
5. Morison notes that the Dutch did not keep the Sabbath Day in the strict sense that the English Puritans did.

of their removal; the which they afterward prosecuted with so great difficulties, as by the sequel will appear.

The place they had thoughts on was some of those vast and unpeopled countries of America, which are fruitful and fit for habitation, being devoid of all civil inhabitants, where there are only savage and brutish men which range up and down, little otherwise than the wild beasts of the same. This proposition being made public and coming to the scanning of all, it raised many variable opinions amongst men and caused many fears and doubts amongst themselves. Some, from their reasons and hopes conceived, labored to stir up and encourage the rest to undertake and prosecute the same; others again, out of their fears, objected against it and sought to divert from it; alleging many things, and those neither unreasonable nor unprobable; as that it was a great design and subject to many unconceivable perils and dangers; as, besides the casualties of the sea (which none can be freed from), the length of the voyage was such as the weak bodies of women and other persons worn out with age and travail (as many of them were) could never be able to endure. And yet if they should, the miseries of the land which they should be exposed unto, would be too hard to be borne and likely, some or all of them together, to consume and utterly to ruinate them. For there they should be liable to famine and nakedness and the want, in a manner, of all things. The change of air, diet and drinking of water would infect their bodies with sore sicknesses and grievous diseases. And also those which should escape or overcome these difficulties should yet be in continual danger of the savage people, who are cruel, barbarous and most treacherous, being most furious in their rage and merciless where they overcome; not being content only to kill and take away life, but delight to torment men in the most bloody manner that may be; flaying some alive with the shells of fishes, cutting off the members and joints of others by piecemeal and broiling on the coals, eat the collops[6] of their flesh in their sight whilst they live, with other cruelties horrible to be related.

And surely it could not be thought but the very hearing of these things could not but move the very bowels of men to grate within them and make the weak to quake and tremble. It was further objected that it would require greater sums of money to furnish such a voyage and to fit them with necessaries, than their consumed estates would amount to; and yet they must as well look to be seconded with supplies as presently to be transported. Also many precedents of ill success and lamentable miseries befallen others in the like designs were easy to be found, and not forgotten to be alleged; besides their own experience, in their former troubles and hardships in their removal into Holland, and how hard a thing it was for them to live in that strange place, though it was a neighbor country and a civil and rich commonwealth.

It was answered, that all great and honorable actions are accompanied with great difficulties and must be both enterprised and overcome with answerable courages. It was granted the dangers were great, but not desperate. The difficulties were many, but not invincible. For though there were many of them likely, yet they were not certain. It might be sundry of the things feared might never befall; others by provident care and the use of good means might in a great measure be prevented; and all of them, through the help of God, by fortitude and patience, might either be borne or overcome. True it was that

6. Slices, portions.

such attempts were not to be made and undertaken without good ground and reason, not rashly or lightly as many have done for curiosity or hope of gain, etc. But their condition was not ordinary, their ends were good and honorable, their calling lawful and urgent; and therefore they might expect the blessing of God in their proceeding. Yea, though they should lose their lives in this action, yet might they have comfort in the same and their endeavors would be honorable. They lived here but as men in exile and in a poor condition, and as great miseries might possibly befall them in this place; for the twelve years of truce were now out and there was nothing but beating of drums and preparing for war, the events whereof are always uncertain. The Spaniard might prove as cruel as the savages of America, and the famine and pestilence as sore here as there, and their liberty less to look out for remedy.

After many other particular things answered and alleged on both sides, it was fully concluded by the major part to put this design in execution and to prosecute it by the best means they could.

From Book I, Chapter VII. Of Their Departure from Leyden, and Other Things Thereabout; with Their Arrival at Southampton, Where They All Met Together and Took in Their Provisions

[MR. ROBINSON'S LETTER]

At length, after much travel and these debates, all things were got ready and provided. A small ship[7] was bought and fitted in Holland, which was intended as to serve to help to transport them, so to stay in the country and attend upon fishing and such other affairs as might be for the good and benefit of the colony when they came there. Another was hired at London, of burthen about 9 score,[8] and all other things got in readiness. So being ready to depart, they had a day of solemn humiliation, their pastor taking his text from Ezra viii.21: "And there at the river, by Ahava, I proclaimed a fast, that we might humble ourselves before our God, and seek of him a right way for us, and for our children, and for all our substance." Upon which he spent a good part of the day very profitably and suitable to their present occasion; the rest of the time was spent in pouring out prayers to the Lord with great fervency, mixed with abundance of tears. And the time being come that they must depart, they were accompanied with most of their brethren out of the city, unto a town sundry miles off called Delftshaven, where the ship lay ready to receive them. So they left that goodly and pleasant city which had been their resting place near twelve years; but they knew they were pilgrims,[9] and looked not much on those things, but lift up their eyes to the heavens, their dearest country, and quieted their spirits.

When they came to the place they found the ship and all things ready, and such of their friends could not come with them followed after them, and sundry also came from Amsterdam to see them shipped and to take their leave of

---

7. "Of some 60 tun" [Bradford's note]. The Pilgrims left Amsterdam for Leyden because of disagreements "with the church that was there before them." They decided to leave Holland for reasons Bradford cites in the fourth chapter of book 1: economic hardship, the availability of inexpensive land for farming, the fear that their children were becoming Hollanders rather than English, and the advancement of the Gospel.

8. The Mayflower, a ship weighing 180 tons.
9. "Hebrews xi.31–16" [Bradford's note]. "These all died in faith, not having received the promises, but having seen them afar off, and were persuaded of them and embraced them, and confessed that they were strangers and pilgrims on the earth." It was this passage that caused the Mayflower company to be known as Pilgrims.

them. That night was spent with little sleep by the most, but with friendly entertainment and Christian discourse and other real expressions of true Christian love. The next day (the wind being fair) they went aboard and their friends with them, where truly doleful was the sight of that sad and mournful parting, to see what sighs and sobs and prayers did sound amongst them, what tears did gush from every eye, and pithy speeches pierced each heart; that sundry of the Dutch strangers that stood on the quay as spectators could not refrain from tears. Yet comfortable and sweet it was to see such lively and true expressions of dear and unfeigned love. But the tide, which stays for no man, calling them away that were thus loath to depart, their reverend pastor falling down on his knees (and they all with him) with watery cheeks commended them with most fervent prayers to the Lord and His blessing. And then with mutual embraces and many tears they took their leaves of one another, which proved to be the last leave to many of them.

✿　✿　✿

At their parting Mr. Robinson writ a letter to the whole company; which though it hath already been printed;[1] yet I thought good here likewise to insert it. As also a brief letter writ at the same time to Mr. Carver,[2] in which the tender love and godly care of a true pastor appears.

MY DEAR BROTHER, I received enclosed in your last letter the note of information, which I shall carefully keep and make use of as there shall be occasion. I have a true feeling of your perplexity of mind and toil of body, but I hope that you who have always been able so plentifully to administer comfort unto others in their trials, are so well furnished for yourself, as that far greater difficulties than you have yet undergone (though I conceive them to have been great enough) cannot oppress you; though they press you, as the Apostle speaks.[3] The spirit of a man (sustained by the Spirit of God) will sustain his infirmity; I doubt not so will yours.[4] And the better much when you shall enjoy the presence and help of so many godly and wise brethren, for the bearing of the part of your burthen, who also will not admit into their hearts the least thought of suspicion of any the least negligence, at last presumption, to have been in you, whatsoever they think in others.

Now what shall I say or write unto you and your good wife my loving sister?[5] Even only this: I desire, and always shall unto you from the Lord, as unto my own soul. And assure yourself that my heart is with you, and that I will not forslow[6] my bodily coming at the first opportunity. I have written a large letter to the whole, and am sorry I shall not rather speak than write to them; and the more, considering the want of a preacher, which I shall also make some spur

---

1. In *Mourt's Relation* (1622), an account of the first year of the plantation at Plymouth taken from the journals of Edward Winslow and William Bradford and brought to London for publication by Bradford's brother-in-law, George Mourt. Morison places the letters that follow in his appendix; we have restored them to their original position in the manuscript.
2. John Carver (d. 1621) was the first governor of the colony.
3. "For we would not, brethren, have you ignorant of

our trouble which came to us in Asia, that we were pressed out of measure, above strength, insomuch that we despaired even of life" (2 Corinthians 1.8); "And when Silas and Timotheus were come from Macedonia, Paul was pressed in the spirit and testified to the Jews that Jesus was Christ" (Acts 18.5).
4. "Counsel is mine, and sound wisdom: I am understanding; I have strength" (Proverbs 8.14).
5. Mrs. Carver (d. 1621) was John Robinson's sister.
6. Delay.

to my hastening after you. I do ever commend my best affection unto you, which if I thought you made any doubt of, I would express in more and the same more ample and full words.

And the Lord in whom you trust and whom you serve ever in this business and journey, guide you with His hand, protect you with His wing, and show you and us His salvation in the end, and bring us in the meanwhile together in this place desired, if such be His good will, for His Christ's sake. Amen.

Yours, etc.

July 27, 1620   JOHN ROBINSON

This was the last letter that Mr. Carver lived to see from him. The other follows:

LOVING AND CHRISTIAN FRIENDS, I do heartily and in the Lord salute you all as being they with whom I am present in my best affection, and most earnest longings after you. Though I be constrained for a while to be bodily absent from you. I say constrained, God knowing how willingly and much rather than otherwise, I would have borne my part with you in this first brunt, were I not by strong necessity held back for the present. Make account of me in the meanwhile as of a man divided in myself with great pain, and as (natural bonds set aside) having my better part with you. And though I doubt not but in your godly wisdoms you both foresee and resolve upon that which concernth your present state and condition, both severally and jointly, yet have I thought it but my duty to add some further spur of provocation unto them who run already; if not because you need it, yet because I owe it in love and duty. And first, as we are daily to renew our repentance with our God, especially for our sins known, and generally for our unknown trespasses; so doth the Lord call us in a singular manner upon occasions of such difficulty and danger as lieth upon you, to a both more narrow search and careful reformation of your ways in His sight; lest He, calling to rememberance our sins forgotten by us or unrepented of, take advantage against us, and in judgment leave us for the same to be swallowed up in one danger or other. Whereas, on the contrary, sin being taken away by earnest repentance and the pardon thereof from the Lord, sealed up unto a man's conscience by His Spirit, great shall be his security and peace in all dangers, sweet his comforts in all distresses, with happy deliverance from all evil, whether in life or in death.

Now, next after this heavenly peace with God and our own consciences, we are carefully to provide for peace with all men what in us lieth, especially with our associates. And for that, watchfulness must be had that we neither at all in ourselves do give, no, nor easily take offense being given by others. Woe be unto the world for offenses, for though it be necessary (considering the malice of Satan and man's corruption) that offenses come, yet woe unto the man, or woman either, by whom the offense cometh, saith Christ, Matthew xviii.7. And if offenses in the unseasonable use of things, in themselves indifferent, be more to be feared than death itself (as the Apostle teacheth, I Corinthians ix.15) how much more in things simply evil, in which neither honor of God nor love of man is thought worthy to be regarded. Neither yet is it sufficient that we keep ourselves by the grace of God from giving offense, except withal we be armed against the taking of them when they be given by others. For how unperfect and lame is the work of grace in that person who wants charity to cover a multitude of offenses, as the Scriptures speak![7]

Neither are you to be exhorted to this grace only upon the common grounds of Christianity, which are, that persons ready to take offense either want[8] charity to cover offenses, or wisdom duly to weigh human frailty; or lastly, are gross, though close hypocrites as Christ our Lord teacheth (Matthew vii.1, 2, 3), as indeed in my own experience few or none have been found which sooner give offense than such as easily take it. Neither have they ever proved sound and profitable members in societies, which have nourished this touchy humor.

But besides these, there are divers motives provoking you above others to great care and conscience this way: As first, you are many of you strangers, as to the persons so to the infirmities one of another, and so stand in need of more watchfulness this way, lest when such things fall out in men and women as you suspected not, you be inordinately affected with them; which doth require at your hands much wisdom and charity for the covering and preventing of incident offenses that way. And, lastly, your intended course of civil community will minister continual occasion of offense, and will be as fuel for that fire, except you diligently quench it with brotherly forebearance. And if taking of offense causelessly or easily at men's doings be so carefully to be avoided, how much more heed is to be taken that we take not offense at God Himself, which yet we certainly do so for as we do murmur at His providence in our crosses, or bear impatiently such afflictions as wherewith He pleaseth to visit us. Store up, therefore, patience against that evil day, without which we take offense at the Lord Himself in His holy and just works.

A fourth thing there is carefully to be provided for, to wit, that with your common employments you join common affections truly bent upon the general good, avoiding as a deadly plague of your both common and special comfort all retiredness of mind for proper advantage, and all singularly affected any manner of way. Let every man repress in himself and the whole body in each person, as so many rebels against the common good, all private respects of men's selves, not sorting with the general coveniency. And as men are careful not to have a new house shaken with any violence before it be well settled and the parts firmly knit, so be you, I beseech you, brethren, much more careful that the house of God, which you are and are to be, be not shaken with unnecessary novelties or other oppositions at the first settling thereof.

Lastly, whereas you are become a body politic, using amongst yourselves civil government, and are not furnished with any persons of special eminency above the rest, to be chosen by you into office of government; let your wisdom and godliness appear, not only in choosing such persons as do entirely love and will promote the common good, but also in yielding unto them all due honor and obedience in their lawful administrations, not beholding in them the ordinariness of their persons, but God's ordinance for your good; not being like the foolish multitude who more honor the gay coat than either the virtuous mind of the man, or glorious ordinance of the Lord. But you know better things, and that the image of the Lord's power and authority which the magistrate beareth,[9] is honorable, in how mean persons soever. And this duty you

---

7. "And above all things have fervent charity among yourselves: for charity shall cover the multitude of sins" (1 Peter 4.8).

8. Lack.

9. "For he is the minister of God to thee for good. But if thou do that which is evil, be afraid; for he beareth

both may the more willingly and ought the more conscionably to perform, because you are at least for the present to have only them for your ordinary governors, which yourselves shall make choice of for that work.

Sundry other things of importance I could put you in mind of, and of those before mentioned in more words, but I will not so far wrong your godly minds as to think you heedless of these things, there being also divers among you so well able to admonish both themselves and others of what concerneth them. These few things, therefore, and the same in few words, I do earnestly commend unto your care and conscience, joining therewith my daily incessant prayers unto the Lord, that He who hath made the heavens and the earth, the sea and all rivers of waters, and whose providence is over all His works, especially over all His dear children for good, would so guide and guard you in your ways, as inwardly by His Spirit, so outwardly by the hand of His power, as that both you and we also, for and with you, may have after matter of praising His name all the days of your and our lives. Fare you well in Him whom you trust, and in whom I rest.

An unfeigned wellwiller of your happy success in this hopeful voyage,

JOHN ROBINSON

This letter, though large, yet being so fruitful in itself and suitable to their occasion, I thought meet to insert in this place.

All things being now ready, and every business dispatched, the company was called together and this letter read amongst them, which had good acceptation with all, and after fruit with many. Then they ordered and distributed their company for either ship, as they conceived for the best; and chose a Governor and two or three assistants for each ship, to order the people by the way, and see to the disposing of their provisions and such like affairs. All which was not only with the liking of the masters of the ships but according to their desires. Which being done, they set sail from thence about the 5th of August. But what befell them further upon the coast of England will appear in the next chapter.

Book I, Chapter IX. Of Their Voyage and How They Passed the Sea; and of Their Safe Arrival at Cape Cod

September 6. These troubles[1] being blown over, and now all being compact together in one ship, they put to sea again with a prosperous wind, which continued divers days together, which was some encouragement unto them; yet, according to the usual manner, many were afflicted with seasickness. And I may not omit here a special work of God's providence. There was a proud and very profane young man, one of the seamen, of a lusty,[2] able body, which made him the more haughty; he would always be condemning the poor people in their sickness and cursing them daily with grievous exercations; and did not let[3] to tell them that he hoped to help to cast half of them overboard before they came to their journey's end, and to make merry with what they had; and

not the sword in vain: for he is the minister of God, a revenger to execute wrath upon him that doeth evil" (Romans 13.4). Morison notes that this passage "is sometimes said to have inspired the drafting of the Mayflower Compact."

1. Some of the Scrooby community originally sailed from Delftshaven about August 1, 1620, on board the *Speedwell*, but it proved unseaworthy and it was necessary to transfer everything to the *Mayflower*.
2. Strong, energetic.
3. Hesitate.

if he were by any gently reproved, he would curse and swear most bitterly. But it pleased God before they came half seas over, to smite this young man with a grievous disease, of which he died in a desperate manner, and so was himself the first that was thrown overboard. Thus his curses light on his own head, and it was an astonishment to all his fellows for they noted it to be the just hand of God upon him.

After they had enjoyed fair winds and weather for a season, they were encountered many times with cross winds and met with many fierce storms with which the ship was shroudly[4] shaken, and her upper works made very leaky; and one of the main beams in the midships was bowed and cracked, which put them in some fear that the ship could not be able to perform the voyage. So some of the chief of the company, perceiving the mariners to fear the sufficiency of the ship as appeared by their mutterings, they entered into serious consultation with the master and other officers of the ship, to consider in time of the danger, and rather to return than to cast themselves into a desperate and inevitable peril. And truly there was great distraction and differ-ence of opinion amongst the mariners themselves; fain would they do what could be done for their wages' sake (being now near half the seas over) and on the other hand they were loath to hazard their lives too desperately. But in examining of all opinions, the master and others affirmed they knew the ship to be strong and firm under water; and for the buckling of the main beam, there was a great iron screw the passengers brought out of Holland, which would raise the beam into his place; the which being done, the carpenter and master affirmed that with a post put under it, set firm in the lower deck and otherways bound, he would make it sufficient. And as for the decks and upper works, they would caulk them as well as they could, and though with the working of the ship they would not long keep staunch,[5] yet there would other-wise be no great danger, if they did not overpress her with sails. So they com-mitted themselves to the will of God and resolved to proceed.

In sundry of these storms the winds were so fierce and the seas so high, as they could not bear a knot of sail, but were forced to hull[6] for divers days together. And in one of them, as they thus lay at hull in a mighty storm, a lusty young man called John Howland, coming upon some occasion above the gratings was, with a seele[7] of the ship, thrown into sea; but it pleased God that he caught hold of the topsail halyards which hung overboard and ran out at length. Yet he held his hold (though he was sundry fathoms under water) till he was hauled up by the same rope to the brim of the water, and then with a boat hook and other means got into the ship again and his life saved. And though he was something ill with it, yet he lived many years after and became a profitable member both in church and commonwealth. In all this voyage there died but one of the passengers, which was William Butten, a youth, servant to Samuel Fuller, when they drew near the coast.

But to omit other things (that I may be brief) after long beating at sea they fell with that land which is called Cape Cod; the which being made and cer-tainly known to be it, they were not a little joyful. After some deliberation had amongst themselves and with the master of the ship, they tacked about and resolved to stand for the southward (the wind and weather being fair) to find

4. Shrewdly, in its original sense of wickedly.
5. Watertight.
6. Drift with the wind under short sail.
7. Roll.

some place about Hudson's River for their habitation. But after they had sailed that course about half the day, they fell amongst dangerous shoals and roaring breakers, and they were so far entangled therewith as they conceived themselves in great danger; and the wind shrinking upon them withal, they resolved to bear up again for the Cape and thought themselves happy to get out of those dangers before night overtook them, as by God's good providence they did. And the next day they got into the Cape Harbor[8] where they rid in safety.

A word or two by the way of this cape. It was thus first named by Captain Gosnold and his company, Anno 1602, and after by Captain Smith was called Cape James; but it retains the former name amongst seamen. Also, that point which first showed those dangerous shoals unto them they called Point Care, and Tucker's Terror; but the French and Dutch to this day call it Malabar[9] by reason of those perilous shoals and the losses they have suffered there.

Being thus arrived in a good harbor, and brought safe to land, they fell upon their knees and blessed the God of Heaven who had brought them over the vast and furious ocean, and delivered them from all the perils and miseries thereof, again to set their feet on the firm and stable earth, their proper element. And no marvel if they were thus joyful, seeing wise Seneca was so affected with sailing a few miles on the coast of his own Italy, as he affirmed, that he had rather remain twenty years on his way by land than pass by sea to any place in a short time, so tedious and dreadful was the same unto him.[1]

But here I cannot but stay and make a pause, and stand half amazed at this poor people's present condition; and so I think will the reader, too, when he well considers the same. Being thus passed the vast ocean, and a sea of troubles before in their preparation (as may be remembered by that which went before), they had now no friends to welcome them nor inns to entertain or refresh their weatherbeaten bodies; no houses or much less towns to repair to, to seek for succor. It is recorded in Scripture as a mercy to the Apostle and his shipwrecked company, that the barbarians showed them no small kindness in refreshing them,[2] but these savage barbarians, when they met with them (as after will appear) were readier to fill their sides full of arrows than otherwise. And for the season it was winter, and they that know the winters of that country know them to be sharp and violent, and subject to cruel and fierce storms, dangerous to travel to known places, much more to search an unknown coast. Besides, what could they see but a hideous and desolate wilderness, full of wild beasts and wild men—and what multitudes there might be of them they knew not. Neither could they, as it were, go up to the top of Pisgah[3] to view from this wilderness a more goodly country to feed their hopes; for which way soever they turned their eyes (saved upward to the heavens) they could have little solace or content in respect of any outward objects. For summer being done, all things stand upon them with a weatherbeaten face, and the whole country, full of woods and thickets, represented a wild and savage hue. If they

8. Cape Harbor is now Provincetown harbor; they arrived on November 11, 1620, the journey from England having taken sixty-five days.
9. The prefix *mal* means "bad"; the reference here is to the dangerous sandbars.
1. Bradford notes that this remark may be found in the *Moral Epistles to Lucilius*, line 5, of the Roman Stoic philosopher (4? B.C.–A.D. 65).

2. "And when they were escaped, then they knew that the island was called Melita. And the barbarous people showed us no little kindness: for they kindled a fire, and received us every one, because of the present rain, and because of the cold" (Acts 28.1–2).
3. Mountain from which Moses saw the Promised Land (Deuteronomy 34.1–4).

looked behind them, there was the mighty ocean which they had passed and was now as a main bar and gulf to separate them from all the civil parts of the world. If it be said they had a ship to succor them, it is true; but what heard they daily from the master and company? But that with speed they should look out a place (with their shallop[4]) where they would be, at some near distance; for the season was such as he would not stir from thence till a safe harbor was discovered by them, where they would be, and he might go without danger; and that victuals consumed apace but he must and would keep sufficient for themselves and their return. Yea, it was muttered by some that if they got not a place in time, they would turn them and their goods ashore and leave them. Let it also be considered what weak hopes of supply and succor they left behind them, that might bear up their minds in this sad condition and trials they were under; and they could not but be very small. It is true, indeed, the affections and love of their brethren at Leyden[5] was cordial and entire toward them, but they had little power to help them or themselves; and how the case stood between them and the merchants at their coming away hath already been declared.

What could now sustain them but the Spirit of God and His grace? May not and ought not the children of these fathers rightly say "Our fathers were Englishmen which came over this great ocean, and were ready to perish in this wilderness; but they cried unto the Lord, and He heard their voice and looked on their adversity,"[6] etc. "Let them therefore praise the Lord, because He is good: and His mercies endure forever." "Yea, let them which have been redeemed of the Lord, show how He hath delivered them from the hand of the oppressor. When they wandered in the desert wilderness out of the way, and found no city to dwell in, both hungry and thirsty, their soul was over- whelmed in them. Let them confess before the Lord His loving kindness and His wonderful works before the sons of men."[7]

From Book I, Chapter X. Showing How They Sought Out a Place of Habitation; and What Befell Them Thereabout

Being thus arrived at Cape Cod the 11th of November, and necessity calling them to look out a place for habitation (as well as the master's and mariners' importunity); they having brought a large shallop with them out of England, stowed in quarters in the ship, they now got her out and set their carpenters to work to trim her up; but being much bruised and shattered in the ship with foul weather, they saw she would be long in mending. Whereupon a few of them tendered themselves to go by land and discover those nearest places, whilst the shallop was in mending; and the rather because as they went into that harbor there seemed to be an opening some two or three leagues off, which the master judged to be a river.[8] It was conceived there might be some

4. Small boat fitted with one or more masts.
5. In Holland. A substantial number of Separatists re- mained in the Netherlands.
6. "And the Egyptians evil entreated us, and afflicted us, and laid upon us hard bondage: And when we cried unto the Lord God of our fathers, the Lord heard our voice, and looked on our affliction, and our labor and our oppression: And the Lord brought us forth out of Egypt with a mighty hand" (Deuteronomy 26.6–8).
7. "O give thanks unto the Lord, for he is good: for his

mercy endureth for ever. Let the redeemed of the Lord say so, whom he hath redeemed from the hand of the enemy; And gathered them out of the lands, from the east, and from the west, from the north and from the south" (Psalm 107.1–5).
8. Morison observes that "Looking south from Prov- incetown Harbor where the Pilgrims were, the high land near Plymouth looks like an island on clear days, suggesting that there is a river or arm of the sea between it and Cape Cod."

danger in the attempt, yet seeing them resolute, they were permitted to go, being sixteen of them well armed under the conduct of Captain Standish,[9] having such instructions given them as was thought meet.

They set forth the 15th of November; and when they had marched about the space of a mile by the seaside, they espied five or six persons with a dog coming towards them, who were savages; but they fled from them and ran up into the woods, and the English followed them, partly to see if they could speak with them, and partly to discover if there might not be more of them lying in ambush. But the Indians seeing themselves thus followed, they again forsook the woods and ran away on the sands as hard[1] as they could, so as they could not come near them but followed them by the track of their feet sundry miles and saw that they had come the same way. So, night coming on, they made their rendezvous and set out their sentinels, and rested in quiet that night; and the next morning followed their track till they had headed a great creek and so left the sands, and turned another way into the woods. But they still followed them by guess, hoping to find their dwellings; but they soon lost both them and themselves, falling into such thickets as were ready to tear their clothes and armor in pieces; but were most distressed for want of drink. But at length they found water and refreshed themselves, being the first New England water they drunk of, and was now in great thirst as pleasant unto them as wine or beer had been in foretimes.

Afterwards they directed their course to come to the other shore, for they knew it was a neck of land they were to cross over, and so at length got to the seaside and marched to this supposed river, and by the way found a pond[2] of clear fresh water, and shortly after a good quantity of clear ground where the Indians had formerly set corn, and some of their graves. And proceeding further they saw new stubble where corn had been set the same year; also they found where lately a house had been, where some planks and a great kettle was remaining, and heaps of sand newly paddled with their hands. Which, they digging up, found in them divers fair Indian baskets filled with corn, and some in ears, fair and good, of divers colors, which seemed to them a very goodly sight (having never seen any such before). This was near the place of that supposed river they came to seek, unto which they went and found it to open itself into two arms with a high cliff of sand in the entrance[3] but more like to be creeks of salt water than any fresh, for aught they saw; and that there was good harborage for their shallop, leaving it further to be discovered by their shallop, when she was ready. So, their time limited them being expired, they returned to the ship lest they should be in fear of their safety; and took with them part of the corn and buried up the rest. And so, like the men from Eshcol, carried with them of the fruits of the land and showed their brethren;[4] of which, and their return, they were marvelously glad and their hearts encouraged.

After this, the shallop being got ready, they set out again for the better discovery of this place, and the master of the ship desired to go himself. So there went some thirty men but found it to be no harbor for ships but only for

---

9. Myles Standish (1584?–1656) was a professional soldier who had fought in the Netherlands; he was not a Pilgrim.
1. Fast.
2. The pond from which Pond Village, Truro, Massachusetts, gets its name.

3. A salt creek known as Pamet River.
4. In the Numbers 13.23–26, Moses' scouts, after searching the wilderness for forty days, brought back clusters of grapes, which they found near the brook that they called "Eshcol."

boats. There was also found two of their houses covered with mats, and sundry of their implements in them, but the people were run away and could not be seen.[5] Also there was found more of their corn and of their beans of various colors; the corn and beans they brought away, purposing to give them full satisfaction when they should meet with any of them as, about some six months afterward they did, to their good content.

And here is to be noted a special providence of God, and a great mercy to this poor people, that here they got seed to plant them corn the next year, or else they might have starved, for they had none nor any likelihood to get any till the season had been past, as the sequel did manifest. Neither is it likely they had had this, if the first voyage had not been made, for the ground was now all covered with snow and hard frozen; but the Lord is never wanting unto His in their greatest needs; let His holy name have all the praise.

The month of November being spent in these affairs, and much foul weather falling in, the 6th of December they sent out their shallop again with ten of their principal men and some seamen, upon further discovery, intending to circulate that deep bay of Cape Cod. The weather was very cold and it froze so hard as the spray of the sea lighting on their coats, they were as if they had been glazed. Yet that night betimes they got down into the bottom of the bay, and as they drew near the shore[6] they saw some ten or twelve Indians very busy about something. They landed about a league or two from them, and had much ado to put ashore anywhere—it lay so full of flats. Being landed, it grew late and they made themselves a barricado with logs and boughs as well as they could in the time, and set out their sentinel and betook them to rest, and saw the smoke of the fire the savages made that night. When morning was come they divided their company, some to coast along the shore in the boat, and the rest marched through the woods to see the land, if any fit place might be for their dwelling. They came also to the place where they saw the Indians the night before, and found they had been cutting up a great fish like a grampus,[7] being some two inches thick of fat like a hog, some pieces whereof they had left by the way. And the shallop found two more of these fishes dead on the sands, a thing usual after storms in that place, by reason of the great flats of sand that lie off.

So they ranged up and down all that day, but found no people, nor any place they liked. When the sun grew low, they hasted out of the woods to meet with their shallop, to whom they made signs to come to them into a creek[8] hard by, the which they did at high water; of which they were very glad, for they had not seen each other all that day since the morning. So they made them a barricado as usually they did every night, with logs, stakes and thick pine boughs, the height of a man, leaving it open to leeward, partly to shelter them from the cold and wind (making their fire in the middle and lying round about it) and partly to defend them from any sudden assaults of the savages, if they should surround them; so being very weary, they betook them to rest. But about midnight they heard a hideous and great cry, and their sentinel called "Arm! arm!" So they bestirred them and stood to their arms and shot off a couple of muskets, and then the noise ceased. They concluded it was a com-

5. Descendants of these Nauset Indians may still be found today at Mashpee on Cape Cod.
6. Somewhere near Eastham, Massachusetts.

7. Probably a blackfish (*Globicephala melæna*).
8. The mouth of Herring River in Eastham.

pany of wolves or such like wild beasts, for one of the seamen told them he had often heard such a noise in Newfoundland.

So they rested till about five of the clock in the morning; for the tide, and their purpose to go from thence, made them be stirring betimes. So after prayer they prepared for breakfast, and it being day dawning it was thought best to be carrying things down to the boat. But some said it was not best to carry the arms down, others said they would be the readier, for they had lapped them up in their coats from the dew; but some three or four would not carry theirs till they went themselves. Yet as it fell out, the water being not high enough, they laid them down on the bank side and came up to breakfast.

But presently, all on the sudden, they heard a great and strange cry, which they knew to be the same voices they heard in the night, though they varied their notes; and one of their company being abroad came running in and cried, "Men, Indians! Indians!" And withal, their arrows came flying amongst them. Their men ran with all speed to recover their arms, as by the good providence of God they did. In the meantime, of those that were there ready, two muskets were discharged at them, and two more stood ready in the entrance of their rendezvous but were commanded not to shoot till they could take full aim at them. And the other two charged again with all speed, for there were only four had arms there, and defended the barricado, which was first assaulted. The cry of the Indians was dreadful, especially when they saw the men run out of the rendezvous toward the shallop to recover their arms, the Indians wheeling about upon them. But some running out with coats of mail on, and cutlasses in their hands, they soon got their arms and let fly amongst them and quickly stopped their violence. Yet there was a lusty man, and no less valiant, stood behind a tree within half a musket shot, and let his arrows fly at them; he was seen [to] shoot three arrows, which were all avoided. He stood three shots of a musket, till one taking full aim at him and made the bark or splinters of the tree fly about his ears, after which he gave an extraordinary shriek and away they went, all of them. They[9] left some to keep the shallop and followed them about a quarter of a mile and shouted once or twice, and shot off two or three pieces, and so returned. This they did that they might conceive that they were not afraid of them or any way discouraged.

Thus it pleased God to vanquish their enemies and give them deliverance; and by His special providence so to dispose that not any one of them were either hurt or hit, though their arrows came close by them and on every side [of] them; and sundry of their coats, which hung up in the barricado, were shot through and through. Afterwards they gave God solemn thanks and praise for their deliverance, and gathered up a bundle of their arrows and sent them into England afterward by the master of the ship, and called that place the First Encounter.

From hence they departed and coasted all along but discerned no place likely for harbor; and therefore hasted to a place that their pilot (one Mr. Coppin who had been in the country before) did assure them was a good harbor, which he had been in, and they might fetch it before night; of which they were glad for it began to be foul weather.

9. I.e., the English.

After some hours' sailing it began to snow and rain, and about the middle of the afternoon the wind increased and the sea became very rough, and they broke their rudder, and it was as much as two men could do to steer her with a couple of oars. But their pilot bade them be of good cheer for he saw the harbor; but the storm increasing, and night drawing on, they bore what sail they could to get in, while they could see. But herewith they broke their mast in three pieces and their sail fell overboard in a very grown sea, so as they had like to have been cast away. Yet by God's mercy they recovered themselves, and having the flood[1] with them, struck into the harbor. But when it came to, the pilot was deceived in the place, and said the Lord be merciful unto them for his eyes never saw that place before; and he and the master's mate would have run her ashore in a cove full of breakers before the wind. But a lusty seaman which steered bade those which rowed, if they were men, about with her or else they were all cast away; the which they did with speed. So he bid them be of good cheer and row lustily, for there was a fair sound before them, and he doubted not but they should find one place or other where they might ride in safety. And though it was very dark and rained sore, yet in the end they got under the lee of a small island and remained there all that night in safety. But they knew not this to be an island till morning, but were divided in their minds; some would keep the boat for fear they might be amongst the Indians, others were so wet and cold they could not endure but got ashore, and with much ado got fire (all things being so wet); and the rest were glad to come to them, for after midnight, the wind shifted to the northwest and it froze hard.

But though this had been a day and night of much trouble and danger unto them, yet God gave them a morning of comfort and refreshing (as usually He doth to His children) for the next day was a fair, sunshining day, and they found themselves to be on an island secure from the Indians, where they might dry their stuff, fix their pieces[2] and rest themselves; and gave God thanks for His mercies in their manifold deliverances. And this being the last day of the week, they prepared there to keep the Sabbath.

On Monday they sounded[3] the harbor and found it fit for shipping, and marched into the land and found divers cornfields and little running brooks, a place (as they supposed) fit for situation.[4] At least it was the best they could find, and the season and their present necessity made them glad to accept of it. So they returned to their ship again with this news to the rest of their people, which did much comfort their hearts.

On the 15th of December they weighed anchor to go to the place they had discovered, and came within two leagues of it, but were fain to bear up again; but the 16th day, the wind came fair, and they arrived safe in this harbor. And afterwards took better view of the place, and resolved where to pitch their dwelling; and the 25th day began to erect the first house for common use to receive them and their goods.

---

1. I.e., the flood tide.
2. Armaments.
3. Measured the depth of.
4. Morison notes that this is "the only contemporary

authority for the 'Landing of the Pilgrims at Plymouth Rock' on December 21, 1620" (or December 11 Old Style, since the Julian calendar differs from the present Gregorian calendar by ten days).

From *Book II, Chapter XI.*[5] *The Remainder of Anno 1620*

[THE MAYFLOWER COMPACT]

I shall a little return back, and begin with a combination[6] made by them before they came ashore; being the first foundation of their government in this place. Occasioned partly by the discontented and mutinous speeches that some of the strangers[7] amongst them had let fall from them in the ship: That when they came ashore they would use their own liberty, for none had power to command them, the patent they had being for Virginia and not for New England, which belonged to another government, with which the Virginia Company had nothing to do. And partly that such an act by them done, this their condition considered, might be as firm as any patent,[8] and in some respects more sure.

The form was as followeth:
IN THE NAME OF GOD, AMEN.

We whose names are underwritten, the loyal subjects of our dread Sovereign Lord King James, by the Grace of God of Great Britain, France, and Ireland King, Defender of the Faith, etc.

Having undertaken, for the Glory of God and advancement of the Christian Faith and Honor of our King and Country, a Voyage to plant the First Colony in the Northern Parts of Virginia, do by these presents solemnly and mutually in the presence of God and one of another, Covenant and Combine ourselves together into a Civil Body Politic, for our better ordering and preservation and furtherance of the ends aforesaid; and by virtue hereof to enact, constitute and frame such just and equal Laws, Ordinances, Acts, Constitutions and Offices, from time to time, as shall be thought most meet and convenient for the general good of the Colony, unto which we promise all due submission and obedience. In witness whereof we have hereunder subscribed our names at Cape Cod, the 11th of November, in the year of the reign of our Sovereign Lord King James, of England, France and Ireland the eighteenth, and of Scotland the fifty-fourth. Anno Domini 1620.

After this they chose, or rather confirmed, Mr. John Carver[9] (a man godly and well approved amongst them) their Governor for that year. And after they had provided a place for their goods, or common store (which were long in unlading[1] for want of boats, foulness of the winter weather and sickness of divers) and begun some small cottages for their habitation; as time would admit, they met and consulted of laws and orders, both for their civil and military government as the necessity of their condition did require, still adding thereunto as urgent occasion in several times, and as cases did require.

In these hard and difficult beginnings they found some discontents and mur-

---

5. Bradford numbered only the first ten chapters of his manuscript.
6. A form of union, a joining together.
7. Puritans called themselves "saints" and those outside their church "strangers." Many of those who came to Plymouth with them were not church members but adventurers looking forward to business success and making new lives in the New World.

8. A document signed by a sovereign granting privileges to those named in it.
9. Carver (c. 1576–1621), like Bradford, was an original member of the group who went to Holland and, like Bradford, a tradesman. Bradford was elected governor after Carver's death.
1. Unloading.

murings arise amongst some, and mutinous speeches and carriages in other;
but they were soon quelled and overcome by the wisdom, patience, and just
and equal carriage of things, by the Governor and better part, which clave[2]
faithfully together in the main.

[THE STARVING TIME]

But that which was most sad and lamentable was, that in two or three
months' time half of their company died, especially in January and February,
being the depth of winter, and wanting houses and other comforts; being
infected with the scurvy and other diseases which this long voyage and their
inaccommodate condition had brought upon them. So as there died some
times two or three of a day in the foresaid time, that of 100 and odd persons,
scarce fifty remained. And of these, in the time of most distress, there was but
six or seven persons who to their great commendations, be it spoken, spared
no pains night nor day, but with abundance of toil and hazard of their own
health, fetched them wood, made them fires, dressed them meat, made their
beds, washed their loathsome clothes, clothed and unclothed them. In a word,
did all the homely[3] and necessary offices for them which dainty and queasy
stomachs cannot endure to hear named; and all this willingly and cheerfully,
without any grudging in the least, showing herein their true love unto their
friends and brethren; a rare example and worthy to be remembered. Two of
these seven were Mr. William Brewster, their reverend Elder, and Myles
Standish, their Captain and military commander, unto whom myself and
many others were much beholden in our low and sick condition. And yet the
Lord so upheld these persons as in this general calamity they were not at all
infected either with sickness or lameness. And what I have said of these I may
say of many others who died in this general visitation, and others yet living;
that whilst they had health, yea, or any strength continuing, they were not
wanting[4] to any that had need of them. And I doubt not but their recompense
is with the Lord.

But I may not here pass by another remarkable passage not to be forgotten.
As this calamity fell among the passengers that were to be left here to plant,
and were hasted ashore and made to drink water that the seamen might have
the more beer, and one[5] in his sickness desiring but a small can of beer, it was
answered that if he were their own father he should have none. The disease
began to fall amongst them also, so as almost half of their company died before
they went away, and many of their officers and lustiest men, as the boatswain,
gunner, three quartermasters, the cook and others. At which the Master was
something strucken and sent to the sick ashore and told the Governor he
should send for beer for them that had need of it, though he drunk water
homeward bound.

But now amongst his company there was far another kind of carriage in
this misery than amongst the passengers. For they that before had been boon
companions in drinking and jollity in the time of their health and welfare,
began now to desert one another in this calamity, saying they would not hazard
their lives for them, they should be infected by coming to help them in their

---

2. Past tense of *cleave*.
3. Intimate.
4. Lacking in attention.
5. "Which was this author himself" [Bradford's note].

cabins; and so, after they came to lie by it, would do little or nothing for them but, "if they died, let them die." But such of the passengers as were yet aboard showed them what mercy they could, which made some of their hearts relent, as the boatswain (and some others) who was a proud young man and would often curse and scoff at the passengers. But when he grew weak, they had compassion on him and helped him; then he confessed he did not deserve it at their hands, he had abused them in word and deed. "Oh!" (saith he) "you, I now see, show your love like Christians indeed one to another, but we let one another lie and die like dogs." Another lay cursing his wife, saying if it had not been for her he had never come this unlucky voyage, and anon cursing his fellows, saying he had done this and that for some of them; he had spent so much and so much amongst them, and they were now weary of him and did not help him, having need. Another gave his companion all he had, if he died, to help him in his weakness; he went and got a little spice and made him a mess of meat once or twice. And because he died not so soon as he expected, he went amongst his fellows and swore the rogue would cozen[6] him, he would see him choked before he made him any more meat; and yet the poor fellow died before morning.

From Book II, Chapter XII. Anno 1621

* * *

[FIRST THANKSGIVING]

They began now to gather in the small harvest they had, and to fit up their houses and dwellings against winter, being all well recovered in health and strength and had all things in good plenty. For as some were thus employed in affairs abroad, others were exercised in fishing, about cod and bass and other fish, of which they took good store, of which every family had their portion. All the summer there was no want;[7] and now began to come in store of fowl, as winter approached, of which this place did abound when they came first (but afterward decreased by degrees). And besides waterfowl there was great store of wild turkeys, of which they took many, besides venison, etc. Besides they had about a peck a meal a week to a person, or now since harvest, Indian corn to that proportion. Which made many afterwards write so largely of their plenty here to their friends in England, which were not feigned but true reports.

From Book II, Chapter XIX. Anno Dom: 1628

* * *

[THOMAS MORTON OF MERRYMOUNT][8]

About some three or four years before this time, there came over one Captain Wollaston (a man of pretty parts)[9] and with him three or four more of

6. Cheat.
7. Lack.
8. Almost nothing is known of either Thomas Morton or Captain Wollaston other than what Bradford tells us. By all accounts Morton left England with a bad reputation and a history of unrests behind him. Unlike the Puritans, however, Morton relished the sensuality of the wild and took great pleasure in the American landscape. Bradford tells us that Morton did not think that "in all the world it could be paralleled" for its plenitude and beauty.
9. I.e., of a clever nature.

some eminency, who brought with them a great many servants, with provisions and other implements for to begin a plantation. And pitched themselves in a place within the Massachusetts which they called after their Captain's name, Mount Wollaston. Amongst whom was one Mr. Morton, who it should seem had some small adventure of his own or other men's amongst them, but had little respect amongst them, and was slighted by the meanest servants. Having continued there some time, and not finding things to answer their expectations nor profit to arise as they looked for, Captain Wollaston takes a great part of the servants[1] and transports them to Virginia, where he puts them off at good rates, selling their time to other men; and writes back to one Mr. Rasdall (one of his chief partners and accounted their merchant) to bring another part of them to Virginia likewise, intending to put them off there as he had done the rest. And he, with the consent of the said Rasdall, appointed one Fitcher to be his Lieutenant and govern the remains of the Plantation till he or Rasdell returned to take further order thereabout. But this Morton abovesaid, having more craft than honesty (who had been a kind of pettifogger of Furnival's Inn[2]) in the others' absence watches an opportunity (commons being but hard amongst them)[3] and got some strong drink and other junkets[4] and made them a feast; and after they were merry, he began to tell them he would give them good counsel. "You see," saith he, "that many of your fellows are carried to Virginia, and if you stay till this Rasdall return, you will also be carried away and sold for slaves with the rest. Therefore I would advise you to thrust out this Lieutenant Fitcher, and I, having a part in the Plantation, will receive you as my partners and consociates; so may you be free from service, and we will converse, plant, trade, and live together as equals and support and protect one another," or to like effect. This counsel was easily received, so they took opportunity and thrust Lieutenant Fitcher out o' doors, and would suffer him to come no more amongst them, but forced him to seek bread to eat and other relief from his neighbors till he could get passage for England.

After this they fell to great licentiousness and led a dissolute life, pouring out themselves into all profaneness. And Morton became Lord of Misrule,[5] and maintained (as it were) a School of Atheism. And after they had got some goods into their hands, and got much by trading with the Indians, they spent it as vainly in quaffing and drinking, both wine and strong waters in great excess (and, as some reported) £10 worth in a morning. They also set up a maypole, drinking and dancing about it many days together, inviting the Indian women for their consorts, dancing and frisking together like so many fairies, or furies, rather; and worse practices. As if they had anew revived and celebrated the feasts of the Roman goddess Flora, or the beastly practices of the mad Bacchanalians.[6] Morton likewise, to show his poetry composed sundry rhymes and verses, some tending to lasciviousness, and others to the detraction and scandal of some persons, which he affixed to this idle or idol maypole. They changed also the name of their place, and instead of calling it

1. A servant was anyone who worked for another in agriculture or domestic economy. An indentured servant was one who agreed to work for another for seven years to pay for transportation to the New World.
2. A ward in the city of London. "Pettifogger": a shifty lawyer.
3. I.e., there were few responsible citizens among them.

4. Delicacies; food for banqueting.
5. One who presides over games and revels, usually at Christmastime in a great person's house; here one who presides over revelry and licentiousness.
6. The Maenads or Bacchantes were women drunk with wine who worshiped Bacchus and tore anyone they met to pieces. "Flora": Roman goddess of flowers and vegetation.

Mount Wollaston they call it Merry-mount, as if this jollity would have lasted ever. But this continued not long, for after Morton was sent for England (as follows to be declared) shortly after came over that worthy gentleman Mr. John Endicott, who brought over a patent under the broad seal for the government of the Massachusetts. Who, visiting those parts, caused that maypole to be cut down and rebuked them for the profaneness and admonished them to look there should be better walking. So they or others now changed the name of their place again and called it Mount Dagon.[7]

Now to maintain this riotous prodigality and profuse excess, Morton, thinking himself lawless, and hearing what gain the French and fishermen made by trading of pieces,[8] powder and shot to the Indians, he as the head of this consortship began the practice of the same in these parts. And first he taught them how to use them, to charge and discharge, and what proportion of powder to give the piece, according to the size or bigness of the same; and what shot to use for fowl and what for deer. And having thus instructed them, he employed some of them to hunt and fowl for him, so as they became far more active in that employment than any of the English, by reason of their swiftness of foot and nimbleness of body, being also quick-sighted and by continual exercise well knowing the haunts of all sorts of game. So as when they saw the execution that a piece would do, and the benefit that might come by the same, they became mad (as it were) after them and would not stick to give any price they could attain to for them; accounting their bows and arrows but baubles in comparison of them.

*　*　*

This Morton having thus taught them the use of pieces, he sold them all he could spare, and he and his consorts determined to send for many out of England and had by some of the ships sent for above a score. The which being known, and his neighbors meeting the Indians in the woods armed with guns in this sort, it was a terror unto them who lived stragglingly[9] and were of no strength in any place. And other places (though more remote) saw this mischief would quickly spread over all, if not prevented. Besides, they saw they should keep no servants, for Morton would entertain any, how vile soever, and all the scum of the country or any discontents would flock to him from all places, if this nest was not broken. And they should stand in more fear of their lives and goods in short time from this wicked and debased crew than from the savages themselves.

So sundry of the chief of the straggling plantations, meeting together, agreed by mutual consent to solicit those of Plymouth (who were then of more strength than them all) to join with them to prevent the further growth of this mischief, and suppress Morton and his consorts before they grew to further head and strength. Those that joined in this action, and after contributed to the charge of sending him for England, were from Piscataqua, Naumkeag, Winnisimmet, Wessagusset, Nantasket and other places where any English were seated. Those of Plymouth being thus sought to by their messengers and

---

7. Named after the god of the Philistines: "Then the lords of the Philistines gathered them together for to offer a great sacrifice unto Dagon their god, and to rejoice: for they said, Our god hath delivered Samson our enemy into our hand" (Judges 16.23).
8. Guns.
9. Spread out in a scattered fashion; far apart.

letters, and weighing both their reasons and the common danger, were willing to afford them their help though themselves had least cause of fear or hurt. So, to be short, they first resolved jointly to write to him, and in a friendly and neighborly way to admonish him to forbear those courses, and sent a messenger with their letters to bring his answer.

But he was so high as he scorned all advice, and asked who had to do with him, he had and would trade pieces with the Indians, in despite of all, with many other scurrilous terms full of disdain. They sent to him a second time and bade him be better advised and more temperate in his terms, for the country could not bear the injury he did. It was against their common safety and against the King's proclamation. He answered in high terms as before; and that the King's proclamation was no law, demanding what penalty was upon it. It was answered, more than he could bear—His Majesty's displeasure. But insolently he persisted and said the King was dead and his displeasure with him, and many the like things. And threatened withal that if any came to molest him, let them look to themselves for he would prepare for them.

Upon which they saw there was no way but to take him by force; and having so far proceeded, now to give over would make him far more haughty and insolent. So they mutually resolved to proceed, and obtained of the Governor of Plymouth to send Captain Standish and some other aid with him, to take Morton by force. The which accordingly was done. But they found him to stand stiffly in his defense, having made fast his doors, armed his consorts, set divers dishes of powder and bullets ready on the table; and if they had not been over-armed with drink, more hurt might have been done. They summoned him to yield, but he kept his house and they could get nothing but scoffs and scorns from him. But at length, fearing they would do some violence to the house, he and some of his crew came out, but not to yield but to shoot; but they were so steeled[1] with drink as their pieces were too heavy for them. Himself with a carbine, overcharged and almost half filled with powder and shot, as was after found, had thought to have shot Captain Standish; but he stepped to him and put by his piece and took them. Neither was there any hurt done to any of either side, save that one was so drunk that he ran his own nose upon the point of a sword that one held before him, as he entered the house; but he lost but a little of his hot blood.[2]

Morton they brought away to Plymouth, where he was kept till a ship went from the Isle of Shoals for England, with which he was sent to the Council of New England, and letters written to give them information of his course and carriage. And also one was sent at their common charge to inform their Honors more particularly and to prosecute against him. But he fooled of the messenger, after he was gone from hence, and though he went for England yet nothing was done to him, not so much as rebuked, for aught was heard, but returned the next year. Some of the worst of the company were dispersed and some of the more modest kept the house till he should be heard from. But I have been too long about so unworthy a person, and bad a cause.

---

1. Insensible.
2. Morton refers to Captain Standish in his *New English Canaan* (1637) as "Captain Shrimp," and tells us that it would have been easy for him to destroy these nine "worthies" like a "flock of wild geese" but that he loathed violence and asked for his freedom to leave. He suggests that he was treated brutally because the Puritans wished to shame him before the Nausets.

From *Book II, Chapter XXIII. Anno Dom: 1632*

*   *   *

[PROSPERITY BRINGS DISPERSAL OF POPULATION]

Also the people of the Plantation began to grow in their outward estates, by reason of the flowing of many people into the country, especially into the Bay of the Massachusetts. By which means corn and cattle rose to a great price, by which many were much enriched and commodities grew plentiful. And yet in other regards this benefit turned to their hurt, and this accession of strength to their weakness. For now as their stocks increased and the increase vendible,[3] there was no longer any holding them together, but now they must of necessity go to their great lots. They could not otherwise keep their cattle, and having oxen grown they must have land for plowing and tillage. And no man now thought he could live except he had cattle and a great deal of ground to keep them, all striving to increase their stocks. By which means they were scattered all over the Bay quickly and the town in which they lived compactly till now was left very thin and in a short time almost desolate.

And if this had been all, it had been less, though too much; but the church must also be divided, and those that had lived so long together in Christian and comfortable fellowship must now part and suffer many divisions. First, those that lived on their lots on the other side of the Bay, called Duxbury, they could not long bring their wives and children to the public worship and church meetings here, but with such burthen as, growing to some competent number, they sued to be dismissed and become a body of themselves. And so they were dismissed about this time, though very unwillingly. But to touch this sad matter, and handle things together that fell out afterward; to prevent any further scattering from this place and weakening of the same, it was thought best to give out some good farms to special persons that would promise to live at Plymouth, and likely to be helped to the church or commonwealth, and so tie the lands to Plymouth as farms for the same; and there they might keep their cattle and tillage by some servants and retain their dwellings here. And so some special lands were granted at a place general called Green's Harbor, where no allotments had been in the former division, a place very well meadowed and fit to keep and rear cattle good store. But alas, this remedy proved worse than the disease; for within a few years those that had thus got footing there rent themselves away, partly by force and partly wearing the rest with importunity and pleas of necessity, so as they must either suffer them to go or live in continual opposition and contention. And other still, as they conceived themselves straitened[4] or to want accommodation, broke away under one pretence or other, thinking their own conceived necessity and the example of others a warrant sufficient for them. And this I fear will be the ruin of New England, at least of the churches of God there, and will provoke the Lord's displeasure against them.

*   *   *

---

3. Salable.   4. Financially restricted.

From *Book II, Chapter XXXII. Anno Dom: 1642*

* * *

[A HORRIBLE CASE OF BESTIALITY]

And after the time of the writing of these things befell a very sad accident of the like foul nature in this government, this very year, which I shall now relate. There was a youth whose name was Thomas Granger. He was servant to an honest man of Duxbury, being about 16 or 17 years of age. (His father and mother lived at the same time at Scituate.) He was this year detected of buggery, and indicted for the same, with a mare, a cow, two goats, five sheep, two calves and a turkey. Horrible it is to mention, but the truth of the history requires it. He was first discovered by one that accidentally saw his lewd practice towards the mare. (I forbear particulars.) Being upon it examined and committed, in the end he not only confessed the fact with that beast at that time, but sundry times before and at several times with all the rest of the forenamed in his indictment. And this his free confession was not only in private to the magistrates (though at first he strived to deny it) but to sundry, both ministers and others; and afterwards, upon his indictment, to the whole Court and jury; and confirmed it at his execution. And whereas some of the sheep could not so well be known by his description of them, others with them were brought before him and he declared which were they and which were not. And accordingly he was cast by the jury and condemned, and after executed about the 8th of September, 1642. A very sad spectacle it was. For first the mare and then the cow and the rest of the lesser cattle were killed before his face, according to the law, Leviticus xx.15,[5] and then he himself was executed. The cattle were all cast into a great and large pit that was digged of purpose for them, and no use made of any part of them.

Upon the examination of this person and also of a former that had made some sodomitical attempts upon another, it being demanded of them how they came first to the knowledge and practice of such wickedness, the one confessed he had long used it in old England; and this youth last spoken of said he was taught it by another that had heard of such things from some in England when he was there, and they kept cattle together. By which it appears how one wicked person may infect many, and what care all ought to have what servants they bring into their families.

But it may be demanded how came it to pass that so many wicked persons and profane people should so quickly come over into this land and mix themselves amongst them? Seeing it was religious men that began the work and they came for religion's sake? I confess this may be marveled at, at least in time to come, when the reasons thereof should not be known; and the more because here was so many hardships and wants met withal. I shall therefore endeavor to give some answer hereunto.

1. And first, according to that in the gospel, it is ever to be remembered that where the Lord begins to sow good seed, there the envious man will endeavour to sow tares.[6]

2. Men being to come over into a wilderness, in which much labor and

---

5. "And if a man lie with a beast, he shall surely be put to death: and ye shall slay the beast."
6. Weedy plants that grow in grainfields. "But while men slept, his enemy came and sowed tares among the wheat, and went his way" (Matthew 13.25).

service was to be done about building and planting, etc., such as wanted help in that respect, when they could not have such as they would, were glad to take such as they could; and so, many untoward servants, sundry of them proved, that were thus brought over, both men and womenkind who, when their times were expired, became families of themselves, which gave increase hereunto.

3. Another and a main reason hereof was that men, finding so many godly disposed persons willing to come into these parts, some began to make a trade of it, to transport passengers and their goods, and hired ships for that end. And then, to make up their freight and advance their profit, cared not who the persons were, so they had money to pay them. And by this means the country became pestered with many unworthy persons who, being come over, crept into one place or other.

4. Again, the Lord's blessing usually following His people as well in outward as spiritual things (though afflictions be mixed withal) do make many to adhere to the People of God, as many followed Christ for the loaves' sake (John vi. 26)[7] and a "mixed multitude" came into the wilderness with the People of God out of Egypt of old (Exodus xii. 38).[8] So also there were sent by their friends, some under hope that they would be made better; others that they might be eased of such burthens, and they kept from shame at home, that would necessarily follow their dissolute courses. And thus, by one means or other, in 20 years' time it is a question whether the greater part be not grown the worser?

From *Book II, Chapter XXXIII*. *Anno Dom:* 1643

[THE LIFE AND DEATH OF ELDER BREWSTER]

I am to begin this year with that which was a matter of great sadness and mourning unto them all. About the 18th of April died their Reverend Elder and my dear and loving friend Mr. William Brewster, a man that had done and suffered much for the Lord Jesus and the gospel's sake, and had borne his part in weal and woe with this poor persecuted church above 36 years in England, Holland and in this wilderness, and done the Lord and them faithful service in his place and calling. And notwithstanding the many troubles and sorrows he passed through, the Lord upheld him to a great age. He was near fourscore years of age[9] (if not all out) when he died. He had this blessing added by the Lord to all the rest; to die in his bed, in peace, amongst the midst of his friends, who mourned and wept over him and ministered what help and comfort they could unto him, and he again recomforted them whilst he could. His sickness was not long, and till the last day thereof he did not wholly keep his bed. His speech continued till somewhat more than half a day, and then failed him, and about nine or ten a clock that evening he died without any pangs at all. A few hours before, he drew his breath short, and some few minutes before his last, he drew his breath long as a man fallen into a sound sleep without any pangs or gaspings, and so sweetly departed this life unto a better.

I would now demand of any, what he was the worse for any former suffer-

---

7. "Jesus answered them and said, 'Verily, verily, I say unto you, Ye seek me, not because ye saw the miracles, but because ye did eat of the loaves' " that Christ had miraculously multiplied to feed five thousand.

8. "And a mixed multitude went up also with them; and flocks, and herds, even very much cattle."

9. Brewster was born in England in 1567.

ings? What do I say, worse? Nay, sure he was the better, and they now added to his honor. "It is a manifest token," saith the Apostle, 2 Thessalonians i.5, 6, 7, "of the righteous judgment of God that ye may be counted worthy of the kingdom of God, for which ye also suffer; seeing it is a righteous thing with God to recompense tribulation to them that trouble you; and to you who are troubled, rest with us, when the Lord Jesus shall be revealed from heaven, with his mighty angels." 1 Peter iv.14: "If you be reproached for the name of Christ, happy are ye, for the spirit of glory and a God resteth upon you."

What though he wanted[1] the riches and pleasure of the world in his life, and pompous monuments at his funeral? Yet "the memorial of the just shall be blessed, when the name of the wicked shall rot" (with their marble monuments). Proverbs x.7.

I should say something of his life, if to say a little were not worse than to be silent. But I cannot wholly forbear, though happily more may be done hereafter. After he had attained some learning, viz. the knowledge of the Latin tongue and some insight in the Greek, and spent some small time at Cambridge, and then being first seasoned with the seeds of grace and virtue, he went to the Court and served that religious and godly gentleman Mr. Davison, divers[2] years when he was Secretary of State. Who found him so discreet and faithful as he trusted him above all other that were about him, and only employed him in all matters of greatest trust and secrecy; he esteemed him rather as a son than a servant, and for his wisdom and godliness, in private he would converse with him more like a friend and familiar than a master. He attended his master when he was sent in ambassage by the Queen into the Low Countries, in the Earl of Leicester's time, as for other weighty affairs of state; so to receive possession of the cautionary towns,[3] and in token and sign thereof the keys of Flushing being delivered to him in Her Majesty's name, he kept them some time and committed them to this his servant who kept them under his pillow, on which he slept the first night. And at his return the States[4] honored him with a gold chain and his master committed it to him and commanded him to wear it when they arrived in England, as they rid through the country, till they came to the Court. He afterwards remained with him till his troubles, that he was put from his place about the death of the Queen of Scots;[5] and some good time after doing him many faithful offices of service in the time of his troubles. Afterwards he went and lived in the country, in good esteem amongst his friends and the gentlemen of those parts, especially the godly and religious.

He did much good in the country where he lived in promoting and furthering religion, not only by his practice and example, and provoking and encouraging of others, but by procuring of good preachers to the places thereabout and drawing on of others to assist and help forward in such a work. He himself most commonly deepest in the charge, and sometimes above his ability. And in this state he continued many years, doing the best good he could and walking according to the light he saw, till the Lord revealed further unto him. And in the end, by the tyranny of the bishops against godly preachers and people in silencing the one and persecuting the other, he and many more of those times began to look further into things and to see into the unlawfulness of their

---

1. Lacked.
2. Several.
3. Towns pledged as security by treaty.

4. The States General, the two-chamber legislative body of Holland.
5. In 1587.

callings, and the burthen of many antichristian corruptions, which both he and they endeavored to cast off; as they also did as in the beginning of this treatise is to be seen.

After they were joined together in communion, he was a special stay and help unto them. They ordinarily met at his house on the Lord's Day (which was a manor of the bishop's) and with great love he entertained them when they came, making provision for them to his great charge, and continued so to do whilst they could stay in England. And when they were to remove out of the country he was one of the first in all adventures, and forwardest in any charge. He was the chief of those that were taken at Boston,[6] and suffered the greatest loss, and of the seven that were kept longest in prison and after bound over to the assizes.[7] After he came into Holland he suffered much hardship after he had spent the most of his means, having a great charge and many children; and in regard of his former breeding and course of life, not so fit for many employments as others were, especially such as were toilsome and laborious. But yet he ever bore his condition with much cheerfulness and contentation.

Towards the latter part of those twelve years spent in Holland, his outward condition was mended, and he lived well and plentifully; for he fell into a way (by reason he had the Latin tongue) to teach many students who had a desire to learn the English tongue, to teach them English; and by his method they quickly attained it with great facility, for he drew rules to learn it by after the Latin manner. And many gentlemen, both Danes and German, resorted to him as they had time from other studies, some of them being great men's sons. He also had means to set up printing by the help of some friends, and so had employment enough, and by reason of many books which would not be allowed to be printed in England, they might have had more than they could do.

But now removing into this country all these things were laid aside again, and a new course of living must be framed unto, in which he was no way unwilling to take his part, and to bear his burthen with the rest, living many times without bread or corn many months together, having many times nothing but fish and often wanting that also; and drunk nothing but water for many years together, yea till within five or six years of his death. And yet he lived by the blessing of God in health till very old age. And besides that, he would labor with his hands in the fields as long as he was able. Yet when the church had no other minister, he taught twice every Sabbath, and that both powerfully and profitably, to the great contentment of the hearers and their comfortable edification; yea, many were brought to God by his ministry. He did more in this behalf in a year than many that have their hundreds a year do in all their lives.

For his personal abilities, he was qualified above many. He was wise and discreet and well spoken, having a grave and deliberate utterance, of a very cheerful spirit, very sociable and pleasant amongst his friends, of an humble and modest mind, of a peaceable disposition, undervaluing himself and his own abilities and sometime overvaluing others. Inoffensive and innocent in his life and conversation, which gained him the love of those without as well as those within; yet he would tell them plainly of their faults and evils, both

6. Boston, England.   7. I.e., made to await trial.

publicly and privately, but in such a manner as usually was well taken from him. He was tenderhearted and compassionate of such as were in misery, but especially of such as had been of good estate and rank and were fallen unto want and poverty either for goodness and religion's sake or by the injury and oppression of others; he would say of all men these deserved to be pitied most. And none did more offend and displease him than such as would haughtily and proudly carry and lift up themselves, being risen from nothing and having little else in them to commend them but a few fine clothes or a little riches more than others.

In teaching, he was very moving and stirring of affections,[8] also very plain and distinct in what he taught; by which means he became the more profitable to the hearers. He had a singular good gift in prayer, both public and private, in ripping up the heart and conscience before God in the humble confession of sin, and begging the mercies of God in Christ for the pardon of the same. He always thought it were better for ministers to pray oftener and divide their prayers, than be long and tedious in the same, except upon solemn and special occasions as in days of humiliation and the like. His reason was that the heart and spirits of all, especially the weak, could hardly continue and stand bent as it were so long towards God as they ought to do in that duty, without flagging and falling off.

For the government of the church, which was most proper to his office, he was careful to preserve good order in the same, and to preserve purity both in the doctrine and communion of the same, and to suppress any error or contention that might begin to rise up amongst them. And accordingly God gave good success to his endeavors herein all his days, and he saw the fruit of his labors in that behalf. But I must break off, having only thus touched a few, as it were, heads of things.

[LONGEVITY OF THE PILGRIM FATHERS]

I cannot but here take occasion not only to mention but greatly to admire the marvelous providence of God! That notwithstanding the many changes and hardships that these people went through, and the many enemies they had and difficulties they met withal, that so many of them should live to very old age! It was not only this reverend man's condition (for one swallow makes no summer as they say) but many more of them did the like, some dying about and before this time and many still living, who attained to sixty years of age, and to sixty-five, divers to seventy and above, and some near eighty as he did. It must needs be more than ordinary and above natural reason, that so it should be. For it is found in experience that change of air, famine or unwholesome food, much drinking of water, sorrows and troubles, etc., all of them are enemies to health, causes of many diseases, consumers of natural vigor and the bodies of men, and shorteners of life. And yet of all these things they had a large part and suffered deeply in the same. They went from England to Holland, where they found both worse air and diet than that they came from; from thence, enduring a long imprisonment as it were in the ships at sea, into New England; and how it hath been with them here hath already been shown, and what crosses, troubles, fears, wants and sorrows they had been liable unto

---

8. Religious feelings.

is easy to conjecture. So as in some sort they may say with the Apostle, 2 Corinthians xi.26, 27, they were "in journeyings often, in perils of waters, in perils of robbers, in perils of their own nation, in perils among the heathen, in perils in the wilderness, in perils in the sea, in perils among false brethren; in weariness and painfulness, in watching often, in hunger and thirst, in fasting often, in cold and nakedness."

What was it then that upheld them? It was God's visitation that preserved their spirits. Job x.12: "Thou hast given me life and grace and thy visitation hath preserved my spirit." He that upheld the Apostle upheld them. "They were persecuted, but not forsaken, cast down, but perished not." "As unknown, and yet known; as dying, and behold we live; as chastened, and yet not killed"; 2 Corinthians vi.9.

God, it seems, would have all men to behold and observe such mercies and works of His providence as these are towards His people, that they in like cases might be encouraged to depend upon God in their trials, and also to bless His name when they see His goodness towards others. Man lives not by bread only, Deuteronomy viii.3. It is not by good and dainty fare, by peace and rest and heart's ease in enjoying the contentments and good things of this world only that preserves health and prolongs life; God in such examples would have the world see and behold that He can do it without them; and if the world will shut their eyes and take no notice thereof, yet He would have His people to see and consider it. Daniel could be better liking with pulse than others were with the king's dainties. Jacob,[9] though he went from one nation to another people and passed through famine, fears and many afflictions, yet he lived till old age and died sweetly and rested in the Lord, as infinite others of God's servants have done and still shall do, through God's goodness, notwithstanding all the malice of their enemies, "when the branch of the wicked shall be cut off before his day" (Job xv.32) "and the bloody and deceitful men shall not live [out] half their days"; Psalm lv.23

From *Book II, Chapter XXXIV. Anno Dom: 1644*

[PROPOSAL TO REMOVE TO NAUSET]

Mr. Edward Winslow was chosen Governor this year.

Many having left this place[1] (as is before noted) by reason of the straitness and barrenness of the same and their finding of better accommodations elsewhere more suitable to their ends and minds; and sundry others still upon every occasion desiring their dismissions, the church began seriously to think whether it were not better jointly to remove to some other place than to be thus weakened and as it were insensibly dissolved. Many meetings and much consultation was held hereabout, and divers[2] were men's minds and opinions. Some were still for staying together in this place, alleging men might here live if they would be content with their condition, and that it was not for want or necessity so much that they removed as for the enriching of themselves. Others were resolute upon removal and so signified that here they could not stay; but if the church did not remove, they must. Insomuch as many were swayed

---

9. The father of the Chosen People (Genesis 26–50). Pulses are peas and beans. In Daniel 1 the prophet Daniel refuses to eat the "king's dainties" provided by Nebuchadnezzar, preferring "pulse to eat, and water to drink."

1. I.e., Plymouth.
2. Unlike, divided.

rather than there should be a dissolution, to condescend to a removal if a fit place could be found that might more conveniently and comfortably receive the whole, with such accession of others as might come to them for their better strength and subsistence; and some such-like cautions and limitations.

So as, with the aforesaid provisos, the greater part consented to a removal to a place called Nauset, which had been superficially viewed and the good will of the purchasers to whom it belonged obtained, with some addition thereto from the Court. But now they began to see their error, that they had given away already the best and most commodious places to others, and now wanted themselves. For this place was about 50 miles from hence, and at an outside of the country remote from all society; also that it would prove so strait as it would not be competent to receive the whole body, much less be capable of any addition or increase; so as, at least in a short time, they should be worse there than they are now here. The which with sundry other like considerations and inconveniences made them change their resolutions. But such as were before resolved upon removal took advantage of this agreement and went on, notwithstanding; neither could the rest hinder them, they having made some beginning.

And thus was this poor church left, like an ancient mother grown old and forsaken of her children, though not in their affections yet in regard of their bodily presence and personal helpfulness; her ancient members being most of them worn away by death, and these of later time being like children translated into other families, and she like a widow left only to trust in God. Thus, she that had made many rich became herself poor.[3]

1630–50   1856

3. "Now she that is a widow indeed, and desolate, trusteth in God, and continueth in supplications and prayers night and day" (1 Timothy 5.5). "As sorrowful, yet always rejoicing; as poor, yet making many rich; as having nothing and yet possessing all things" (2 Corinthians 6.10).

THOMAS MORTON
c. 1579–1647

Little is known of Thomas Morton's life before he came to New England for the first time in 1622, but we do know that he was a capable attorney for the London-based Council for New England and a friend of many highly placed persons at the court of King Charles I; all were strong supporters of the Church of England and unsympathetic to the Puritans. He had the advantages of a traditional education provided for a young man of means and was fond of falconry and other gentlemanly sports. But the shadow of a scandal hangs over Morton's name—the murder of a business partner and the abuse of his wife were two rumors widely circulated—and persists even in the absence of particulars. His behavior in Massachusetts, however, makes it seem likely that he did something nefarious. When he was in his forties he had his eye on the fur trade in New England, and he must have decided that if he could wreak havoc on the Puritans and enrich himself at the same time, so much the better.

Morton's first visit to New England lasted only three months, but in 1625 he returned with a group led by one Captain Wollaston (nothing more is known of him) and they settled too close to Plymouth for comfort. After only one winter Wollaston decided that Virginia was a better place to spend his time. Morton never mentions him. He renamed the Wollaston settlement Merry Mount (or, as he preferred, Ma-re Mount) and began to exchange rum and guns for furs. "Mine host," as Morton liked to refer to himself, saw himself as the only civilized person in a world of spoilsports, an assimilator of foreign culture and a man of tolerance and wit. But for Bradford and Winthrop he was Lord of Misrule, a man who entertained a flock of anarchists and "discontents" under his "licentious" roof and who posed a serious threat to the general welfare. When Morton set up a Maypole in the spring of 1627 to celebrate the death of winter and to honor—"after the old English custom"—Saints Philip and James, the community at Plymouth determined to act. It has been argued that if Morton had merely danced his time away at Merry Mount the Separatists would never have descended on him, but the combination of arming the Nausets Indians and this open display of "Bacchanalian" rites was enough for them to determine to rout him out.

Morton was arrested and returned to England in 1628 and the charges brought against him were dropped. The Pilgrims could not believe their eyes when, in the company of their own London representative, he returned a year later. In 1630 they brought the same charges of arming the Nausets against him and when they deported him four months after his arrest they burned his house down for extra measure. Morton's only published work, New English Canaan, was written after his ignominious return to England and in the years that followed he tried to persuade people close to Archbishop Laud and Charles I that the Puritans in New England had betrayed church and Crown and that all title to their property should be reassigned. Morton was unsuccessful, but he spent long hours devising complicated legal maneuvers from which the Puritans had a difficult time extricating themselves. It was only with Oliver Cromwell's rise to power that Morton's schemes were put to an end.

In 1643 he had the audacity to return to Massachusetts one last time, but he was powerless and without financial backing. He seemed a pitiable figure even to his enemies, but they arrested him, nevertheless, one last time in 1644. He was released in 1645 and, in John Winthrop's words, "old and crazy," "poor and despised," he was last heard of in Maine where, Winthrop notes, he died "within two years" after his release.

From New English Canaan[1]

From *The Second Book*.

From CHAPTER I. THE GENERAL SURVEY OF THE COUNTRY

In the month of June, *Anno Salutis*[2] 1622, it was my chance to arrive in the parts of New England with 30 servants and provision of all sorts fit for a plantation; and while our houses were building, I did endeavor to take a survey of the country. The more I looked, the more I liked it. And when I had more seriously considered of the beauty of the place, with all her fair endowments, I did not think that in all the known world it could be paralleled for so many goodly groves of trees, dainty fine round rising hillocks, delicate fair large

1. Canaan was, for the Israelites, the Promised Land. The text used here is that edited by Charles Francis Adams, Jr., for the Prince Society (1883). Morton's book is in three parts; the first provides a description of "the natives, their manners and customs, with their tractable nature and love towards the English." The second book is titled "Containing a Description of the Beauty of the Country with Her Natural Endowments, Both in the Land and Sea; with the Great Lake of Iroquois" (Lake Champlain, New York).
2. In the year of our prosperity.

plains, sweet crystal fountains, and clear running streams that twine in fine meanders through the meads,[3] making so sweet a murmuring noise to hear as would even lull the senses with delight asleep, so pleasantly do they glide upon the pebble stones, jetting most jocundly where they do meet, and hand in hand run down to Neptune's[4] court, to pay the yearly tribute which they owe to him as sovereign lord of all the springs. Contained within the volume of the land, [are] fowls in abundance, [and] fish in multitude. And [I] discovered, besides, millions of turtledoves on the green boughs, which sat pecking of the full ripe pleasant grapes that were supported by the lusty[5] trees, whose fruitful load did cause the arms to bend: [among] which here and there dispersed, you might see lillies and of [sic] the Daphnean-tree,[6] which made the land to me seem paradise. For in mine eye t'was Nature's masterpiece, her chiefest magazine[7] of all where lives her store. If this land be not rich, then is the whole world poor.

* * *

From The Third Book. [The Incident at Merry Mount]

CHAPTER XIV. OF THE REVELS OF NEW CANAAN

The inhabitants of Passonagessit[8] (having translated the name of their habitation from that ancient savage name to Ma-re Mount, and being resolved to have the new name confirmed for a memorial to after ages) did devise amongst themselves to have it performed in a solemn manner, with revels and merriment after the old English custom; [they] prepared to set up a Maypole upon the festival day of Philip and Jacob,[9] and therefore brewed a barrel of excellent beer and provided a case of bottles to be spent, with other good cheer, for all comers of that day. And because they would have it in a complete form, they had prepared a song fitting to the time and present occasion. And upon May Day they brought the Maypole to the place appointed, with drums, guns, pistols, and other fitting instruments for that purpose, and there erected it with the help of savages that came thither of purpose to see the manner of our revels. A goodly pine tree of 80 foot long was reared up, with a pair of buckhorns nailed on somewhat near unto the top of it, where it stood as a fair seamark for directions how to find out the way to mine host[1] of Ma-re Mount.

And because it should more fully appear to what end it was placed there, they had a poem in readiness made, which was fixed to the Maypole, to show the new name confirmed upon that plantation, which, although it were made according to the occurrence of the time, it being enigmatically composed, puzzled the Separatists[2] most pitifully to expound it, which (for the better information of the reader) I have here inserted.

3. Meadows.
4. In Roman mythology the god of the sea.
5. Fertile, healthy.
6. The goddess Daphne was changed into a laurel tree.
7. Warehouse.
8. At [a place] near the little point (Algonquian, literal trans.). It was first known as Mount Wollaston and, after the departure of Captain Wollaston for Virginia, came to be called "Merry Mount." Only Morton ever refers to it as "Ma-re Mount" (that is, "a place by the sea"), because he enjoyed the pun. It is a part of present-day Quincy, Massachusetts, a few miles south of Boston. The third book is titled "Containing a Description of the People That Are Planted There, What Re-

markable Accidents Have Happened There Since They Were Settled, What Tenents [religious doctrines] They Hold, Together with the Practice of Their Church."
9. May 1 is the feast day of Saints Philip and James (Jacob being the Latin form of James), and why they are joined together on this day is not known. The raising of a Maypole was a secular holiday harking back to the Roman festivals in honor of the renewal of vegetative life.
1. I.e., Morton himself.
2. The colonists at Plymouth, who distinguished themselves from other Puritans by separating from the Church of England, having no hope of internal reform.

THE POEM

Rise Oedipus,[3] and, if thou canst, unfold
What means Charybdis underneath the mold,
When Scylla solitary on the ground[4]
(Sitting in form of Niobe[5]) was found,
Till Amphitrite's darling did acquaint
Grim Neptune with the tenor of her plaint,[6]
And caused him send forth Triton[7] with the sound
Of trumpet loud, at which the seas were found
So full of protean[8] forms that the bold shore
Presented Scylla a new paramour
So strong as Samson and so patient
As Job[9] himself, directed thus, by fate,
To comfort Scylla so unfortunate.
I do profess, by Cupid's beauteous mother,[1]
Here's Scogan's choice[2] for Scylla, and none other;
Though Scylla's sick with grief, because no sign
Can there be found of virtue masculine.
Asclepius[3] come; I know right well
His labor's lost when you may ring her knell.
The fatal sisters'[4] doom none can withstand,
Nor Cytherea's[5] power, who points to land
With proclamation that the first of May
At Ma-re Mount shall be kept holiday.

The setting up of this Maypole was a lamentable spectacle to the precise[6] Separatists that lived at New Plymouth. They termed it an idol; yea, they called it the Calf of Horeb[7] and stood at defiance with the place, naming it Mount Dagon, threatening to make it a woeful mount and not a merry mount.

The riddle, for want of Oedipus,[8] they could not expound, only they made some explication of part of it and said it was meant by Samson Job, the carpenter of the ship that brought over a woman to her husband that had been there long before and thrived so well that he sent for her and her children to come to him, where shortly after he died; having no reason but because of the sound of those two words, when as (the truth is) the man they applied it to was altogether unknown to the author.

3. In Greek mythology Oedipus solved the riddle of the Sphinx.
4. In Greek mythology the monster Scylla lived in a cave opposite the whirlpool Charybdis and devoured sailors.
5. Niobe's fourteen children were slain by the gods, and in Greek mythology she is usually depicted weeping for her children.
6. Complaint, lament. Venus, the daughter of Neptune (in Greek mythology Poseidon, god of the sea) and Amphitrite, tells her father that Scylla is alone and needs a mate.
7. The son of Poseidon, Triton is usually depicted with a conch shell as his horn.
8. Changing.
9. The long-suffering Old Testament patriarch. Samson was the Israelite who brought down with his own hands the temple of the Philistines as they honored their god Dagon.
1. Venus.
2. When John Scogan (1442–1483), jester to Edward IV, was condemned to be hung, he was given an opportunity to choose the tree and escaped hanging because he could find none to suit him. "Scogan's choice" became a popular expression in Morton's time and suggested that choice, even between two unfortunate alternatives, is better than no choice at all.
3. The Greek god of healing.
4. In Greek and Roman mythology the three women who determine human destiny.
5. Also called Aphrodite, goddess of love and beauty.
6. Strict, inflexible.
7. The idol that the Israelites falsely worshiped as their deliverer from Egypt (Exodus 32; Deuteronomy 9.16).
8. I.e., lacking Oedipus's insight.

There was likewise a merry song made which (to make their revels more fashionable) was sung with a chorus, every man bearing his part, which they performed in a dance, hand in hand about the Maypole, while one of the company sang and filled out the good liquor, like Ganymede and Jupiter.[9]

THE SONG

Chorus.
>Drink and be merry, merry, merry boys;
>Let all your delight be in the Hymen's[1] joys;
>Io[2] to Hymen, now the day is come,
>About the merry Maypole take a room.
>>Make green garlands, bring bottles out
>>And fill sweet nectar freely about.
>>Uncover thy head and fear no harm,
>>For here's good liquor to keep it warm.
>Then drink and be merry, &c.
>*Io* to Hymen, &c.
>>Nectar is a thing assigned
>>By the Deity's own mind
>>To cure the heart oppressed with grief,
>>And of good liquors is the chief.
>Then drink, &c.
>*Io* to Hymen, &c.
>>Give to the melancholy man
>>A cup or two of't now and then;
>>This physic will soon revive his blood,
>>And make him be of a merrier mood.
>Then drink, &c.
>*Io* to Hymen, &c.
>>Give to the nymph that's free from scorn
>>No Irish stuff nor Scotch over worn.[3]
>>Lasses in beaver coats[4] come away,
>>Ye shall be welcome to us night and day.
>To drink and be merry, &c.
>*Io* to Hymen, &c.

This harmless mirth made by young men (that lived in hope to have wives brought over to them, that would save them a labor to make a voyage to fetch any over) was much distasted of the precise Separatists that keep much ado about the tithe of mint and cummin,[5] troubling their brains more than reason would require about things that are indifferent,[6] and from that time [they] sought occasion against my honest host of Ma-re Mount, to overthrow his undertakings and to destroy his plantation quite and clean. But because they presumed [that] with their imaginary gifts (which they have out of Phaon's

---

9. Just as the cupbearer Ganymede brought wine to the most powerful of the Roman gods.
1. In Roman mythology the god of marriage.
2. Hail.
3. No wornout Irish or Scottish cloth.
4. Native American women.

5. "Woe unto you, scribes and Pharisees, hypocrites! for ye pay tithe of mint, anise, and cummin, and have omitted the weightier matters of the law, judgment, mercy, and faith" (Matthew 23.23).
6. Insignificant.

box[7]) they could expound hidden mysteries, to convince them of blindness as well in this as in other matters of more consequence, I will illustrate the poem according to the true intent of the authors of these revels, so much distasted by those moles.

Oedipus is generally received[8] for the absolute reader of riddles, who is invoked; Scylla and Charybdis are two dangerous places for seamen to encounter, near unto Venice, and have been by poets formerly resembled to man and wife. The like license the author challenged for a pair of his nomination, the one lamenting for the loss of the other as Niobe for her children. Amphitrite is an arm of the sea, by which the news was carried up and down of a rich widow, now to be taken up or laid down. By Triton is the fame spread that caused the suitors to muster (as it had been to Penelope[9] of Greece), and, the coast lying circular, all our passage to and fro is made more convenient by sea than land. Many aimed at this mark, but he that played Proteus[1] best and could comply with her humor must be the man that would carry her; and he had need have Samson's strength to deal with a Delilah,[2] and as much patience as Job that should come there, for a thing that I did observe in the lifetime of the former.

But marriage and hanging (they say) come by destiny, and Scogan's choice is better [than] none at all. He that played Proteus (with the help of Priapus[3]) put their noses out of joint, as the proverb is.

And this the whole company of the revelers at Ma-re Mount knew to be the true sense and exposition of the riddle that was fixed to the Maypole which the Separatists were at defiance with. Some of them affirmed that the first institution thereof was in memory of a whore, not knowing that it was a trophy erected at first in honor of Maia.[4] The Lady of Learning which [sic] they despise, vilifying the two universities[5] with uncivil terms, accounting what is there obtained by study is but unnecessary learning, not considering that learning does enable men's minds to converse with elements of a higher nature than is to be found within the habitation of the mole.

CHAPTER XV. OF A GREAT MONSTER SUPPOSED TO BE AT MA-RE MOUNT; AND THE PREPARATION MADE TO DESTROY IT

The Separatists, envying the prosperity and hope of the plantation at Ma-re Mount (which they perceived began to come forward and to be in a good way for gain in the beaver trade), conspired together against mine host especially (who was the owner of that plantation) and made up a party against him and mustered up what aid they could, accounting of him as of a great monster.

Many threatening speeches were given out both against his person and his habitation, which they divulged should be consumed with fire. And taking

7. Aphrodite rewarded the aged boatman Phaon with a chest that contained an elixir that made him young.
8. Taken as.
9. The wife of Odysseus, who refused many suitors in his absence.
1. In Greek mythology the sea god who assumed many shapes.
2. The woman who betrayed Samson (Judges 16).
3. In Greek and Roman mythology the god of procreation.

4. Morton argues that the Separatists accused the revelers at Merry Mount of honoring the licentious Roman goddess Flora rather than Maia, the goddess of the spring.
5. I.e., in the Separatist confusion of Flora and Maia they reveal their contempt for the wisdom of Athena or Minerva, and in their hatred for the classical studies at Oxford and Cambridge they reveal their, for Morton, unsophisticated minds.

advantage of the time when his company (which seemed little to regard their threats) were gone up unto the inlands to trade with the savages for beaver, they set upon my honest host at a place called Wessaguscus,[6] where, by accident, they found him. The inhabitants there were in good hope of the subversion of the plantation at Ma-re Mount (which they principally aimed at) and the rather because mine host was a man that endeavored to advance the dignity of the Church of England, which they (on the contrary part) would labor to vilify with uncivil terms, inveighing against the sacred Book of Common Prayer[7] and mine host that used it in a laudable manner amongst his family as a practice of piety.

There he would be a means to bring sacks to their mill (such is the thirst after beaver) and [it] helped the conspirators to surprise mine host (who was there all alone), and they charged him (because they would [want to] seem to have some reasonable cause against him, to set a gloss upon[8] their malice) with criminal things, which indeed had been done by such a person, but was of their conspiracy. Mine host demanded of the conspirators who it was that was author of that information that seemed to be their ground for what they now intended. And because they answered they would not tell him, he as peremptorily replied that he would not say whether he had or he had not done as they had been informed.

The answer made no matter (as it seemed) whether it had been negatively or affirmatively made, for they had resolved what he would suffer because (as they boasted) they were now become the greater number; they had shaken off their shackles of servitude and were become masters and masterless people.

It appears they were like bears' whelps in former time when mine host's plantation was of as much strength as theirs, but now (theirs being stronger) they (like overgrown bears) seemed monstrous. In brief, mine host must endure to be their prisoner until they could contrive it so that they might send him for England (as they said), there to suffer according to the merit of the fact which they intended to father upon him, supposing (belike) it would prove a heinous crime.

Much rejoicing was made that they had gotten their capital enemy (as they concluded him) whom they purposed to hamper in such sort that he should not be able to uphold his plantation at Ma-re Mount.

The conspirators sported themselves at my honest host, that meant them no hurt, and were so jocund that they feasted their bodies and fell to tippling as if they had obtained a great prize, like the Trojans when they had the custody of Epeios' pinetree horse.[9]

Mine host feigned grief and could not be persuaded either to eat or drink, because he knew emptiness would be a means to make him as watchful as the geese kept in the Roman Capital,[1] whereon, the contrary part, the conspirators would be so drowsy that he might have an opportunity to give them a slip instead of a tester.[2]

Six persons of the conspiracy were set to watch him at Wessaguscus. But he kept waking, and in the dead of the night (one lying on the bed for further

---

6. Now Weymouth, Massachusetts.
7. Containing the prayers adopted for use by the national Church of England and rejected by the Separatists.
8. Explain, rationalize.
9. The wooden horse used to conquer Troy was built

by Epeios.
1. When the Gauls attempted to invade Rome in 390 B.C. the geese on the Capitoline Hill spoiled the surprise attack by hissing.
2. A counterfeit coin rather than a true sixpence.

surety), up gets mine host and got to the second door that he was to pass, which, notwithstanding the lock, he got open and shut it after him with such violence that it affrighted some of the conspirators.

The word which was given with an alarm was, "O he's gone, he's gone, what shall we do, he's gone!" The rest (half asleep) start up in amaze[3] and like rams, ran their heads one at another full butt in the dark.

Their grand leader, Captain Shrimp,[4] took on most furiously and tore his clothes for anger, to see the empty nest and their bird gone.

The rest were eager to have torn their hair from their heads, but it was so short that it would give them no hold.[5] Now Captain Shrimp thought in the loss of this prize (which he accounted his masterpiece) all his honor would be lost forever.

In the meantime mine host was got home to Ma-re Mount through the woods, eight miles round about the head of the river Monatoquit that parted the two plantations, finding his way by the help of the lightning (for it thundered as he went terribly), and there he prepared powder, three pounds dried, for his present employment, and four good guns for him and the two assistants left at his house, with bullets of several sizes, three hundred or thereabouts, to be used if the conspirators should pursue him thither; and these two persons promised their aids in the quarrel and confirmed that promise with health in good *rosa solis*.[6]

Now Captain Shrimp, the first captain in the land (as he supposed) must do some new act to repair this loss and to vindicate his reputation, who had sustained blemish by this oversight, begins now to study how to repair or survive his honor; in this manner, calling of council, they conclude.

He takes eight persons more to him, and (like the nine worthies[7] of New Canaan) they embark with preparation against Ma-re Mount where this monster of a man, as their phrase was, had his den; the whole number, had the rest not been from home, being but seven, would have given Captain Shrimp (a *quondam* drummer)[8] such a welcome as would have made him wish for a drum as big as Diogenes' tub,[9] that he might have crept into it out of sight.

Now the nine worthies are approached, and mine host prepared, having intelligence by a savage that hastened in love from Wessaguscus to give him notice of their intent.

One of mine host's men proved a craven; the other had proved his wits to purchase a little valor, before mine host had observed his posture.

The nine worthies coming before the den of this supposed monster (this seven-headed hydra,[1] as they termed him) and began, like Don Quixote[2] against the windmill, to beat a parley and to offer quarter[3] if mine host would yield, for they resolved to send him to England and bade him lay by[4] his arms.

But he (who was the son of a soldier), having taken up arms in his just defense, replied that he would not lay by those arms because they were so needful at sea, if he should be sent over. Yet, to save the effusion of so much worthy blood as would have issued out of the veins of these nine worthies of

---

3. I.e., in astonishment.
4. Morton's favorite epithet for Captain Myles Standish, who had a ruddy complexion and was short.
5. Puritans objected to fashionable long hair.
6. A cordial red like the sun.
7. A group of heroes and kings who, to the medieval mind, represented an ideal of human conduct.

8. A one-time drummer and thus a man of low rank.
9. The Greek philosopher Diogenes (c. 412–323 B.C.) was indifferent to status and lived in a tub.
1. Monster of Greek myth.
2. The hero of the novel by Cervantes (1547–1616).
3. Clemency. "Beat a parley": to suggest a conference.
4. Put down.

New Canaan if mine host should have played upon them out at his portholes (for they came within danger like a flock of wild geese, as if they had been tailed[5] one to another, as colts to be sold at a fair), mine host was content to yield upon quarter and did capitulate with them in what manner it should be for more certainty, because he knew what Captain Shrimp was.

He expressed that no violence should be offered to his person, none to his goods, nor any of his household but that he should have his arms and what else was requisite for the voyage, which their herald returns;[6] it was agreed upon and should be performed.

But mine host no sooner had set open the door and issued out, but instantly Captain Shrimp and the rest of the worthies stepped to him, laid hold of his arms, and had him down; and so eagerly was every man bent against him (not regarding any agreement made with such a carnal man), that they fell upon him as if they would have eaten him; some of them were so violent that they would have a slice with scabbard, and all for haste, until an old soldier (of the Queen's, as the proverb is) that was there by accident, clapped his gun under the weapons and sharply rebuked these worthies for their unworthy practices. So the matter was taken into more deliberate consideration.

Captain Shrimp and the rest of the nine worthies made themselves (by this outrageous riot) masters of mine host of Ma-re Mount and disposed of what he had at his plantation.

This they knew (in the eye of the savages) would add to their glory and diminish the reputation of mine honest host, whom they practiced to be rid of upon any terms, as willingly as if he had been the very hydra of the time.

CHAPTER XVI. HOW THE NINE WORTHIES PUT MINE HOST OF MA-RE MOUNT INTO THE ENCHANTED CASTLE AT PLYMOUTH AND TERRIFIED HIM WITH THE MONSTER BRIAREUS[7]

The nine worthies of New Canaan having now the law in their own hands (there being no general governor in the land, nor none of the separation that regarded the duty they owe their sovereign, whose natural born subjects they were, though translated out of[8] Holland from whence they had learned to work all to their own ends and make a great show of religion but no humanity), for [sic] they were now to sit in council on the cause.

And much it stood mine honest host upon to be very circumspect and to take Eacus[9] to task for that his voice was more allowed of than both the other; and had not mine host confounded all the arguments that Eacus could make in their defense and confuted him that swayed the rest, they would have made him unable to drink in such manner of merriment any more. So that following this private counsel, given him by one that knew who ruled the roost, the hurrican ceased that else would split his pinnace.[1]

A conclusion was made and sentence given that mine host should be sent to England a prisoner. But when he was brought to the ships for that purpose, no man dared be so foolhardy as to undertake to carry him. So these worthies

---

5. Tied.
6. Reports.
7. In Greek mythology a giant who fought the gods. Morton does not identify his tormentor.
8. Removed from.

9. In Greek mythology a judge in the infernal regions. Morton later identifies him as Samuel Fuller of Plymouth and names William Bradford and Myles Standish as his other two judges.
1. A small sailboat.

set mine host upon an island, without gun, powder, or shot, or dog, or so much as a knife to get anything to feed upon, or any other clothes to shelter him with at winter than a thin suit which he had on at that time. Home he could not get to Ma-re Mount. Upon this island he stayed a month at least and was relieved by savages that took notice that mine host was a sachem[2] of Passonagessit, and would bring bottles of strong liquor to him and unite themselves into a league of brotherhood with mine host, so full of humanity are these infidels before those Christians.

From this place for England sailed mine host in a Plymouth ship (that came into the land to fish upon the coast) that landed him safe in England at Plymouth; and he stayed in England until the ordinary time for shipping to set forth for these parts, and then returned, no man being able to tax[3] him of anything.

But the worthies (in the meantime) hoped they had been rid of him.

*　　*　　*

c. 1635   1637

2. Ruling chief.
3. Charge. Morton was successful more than once in

having charges made against him by the Puritans dismissed.

JOHN WINTHROP
1588–1649

John Winthrop, the son of Adam Winthrop, a lawyer, and Anne Browne, the daughter of a tradesman, was born in Groton, England, on an estate that his father purchased from Henry VIII. It was a prosperous farm, and Winthrop had all the advantages that his father's social and economic position would allow. He went to Cambridge University for two years and married at the age of seventeen. It was probably at Cambridge University that Winthrop was exposed to Puritan ideas. Unlike Bradford and the Pilgrims, however, Winthrop was not a Separatist; that is, he wished to reform the national church from within, purging it of everything that harked back to Rome, especially the hierarchy of the clergy and all the traditional Catholic rituals. For a time Winthrop thought of becoming a clergyman himself, but instead he turned to the practice of law.

In the 1620s severe economic depression in England made Winthrop realize that he could not depend on the support of his father's estate. The ascension of Charles I to the throne—who was known to be sympathetic to Roman Catholicism and impatient with Puritan reformers—was also taken as an ominous sign for Puritans, and Winthrop was not alone in predicting that "God will bring some heavy affliction upon the land, and that speedily." Winthrop came to realize that he could not antagonize the king by expressing openly the Puritan cause without losing all that he possessed. The only recourse seemed to be to obtain the king's permission to emigrate. In March of 1629 a group of enterprising merchants, all sympathetic believers, were able to get a charter from the Council for New England for land in the New World. They called themselves "The Company of Massachusetts Bay in New England."

From four candidates, Winthrop was chosen governor in October 1629; for the next twenty years most of the responsibility for the colony rested in his hands. On

April 8, 1630, an initial group of some seven hundred emigrants sailed from England. The ship carrying Winthrop was called the *Arbella*. Somewhere in the middle of the Atlantic Ocean Winthrop delivered his sermon *A Model of Christian Charity*. It set out clearly and eloquently the ideals of a harmonious Christian community and reminded all those on board that they would stand as an example to the world either of the triumph or else the failure of this Christian enterprise. When Cotton Mather wrote his history of New England some fifty years after Winthrop's death, he chose Winthrop as his model of the perfect earthly ruler. Although the actual history of the colony showed that Winthrop's ideal of a perfectly selfless community was impossible to realize in fact, Winthrop emerges from the story as a man of unquestioned integrity and deep humanity.

A Model of Christian Charity[1]

1

A MODEL HEREOF

God Almighty in His most holy and wise providence, hath so disposed of the condition of mankind, as in all times some must be rich, some poor, some high and eminent in power and dignity; others mean and in subjection.

THE REASON HEREOF

First, to hold conformity with the rest of His works, being delighted to show forth the glory of His wisdom in the variety and difference of the creatures; and the glory of His power, in ordering all these differences for the preservation and good of the whole; and the glory of His greatness, that as it is the glory of princes to have many officers, so this great King will have many stewards, counting Himself more honored in dispensing His gifts to man by man, than if He did it by His own immediate hands.

Secondly, that He might have the more occasion to manifest the work of His Spirit: first upon the wicked in moderating and restraining them, so that the rich and mighty should not eat up the poor, nor the poor and despised rise up against their superiors and shake off their yoke; secondly in the regenerate, in exercising His graces, in them, as in the great ones, their love, mercy, gentleness, temperance, etc., in the poor and inferior sort, their faith, patience, obedience, etc.

Thirdly, that every man might have need of other, and from hence they might be all knit more nearly together in the bonds of brotherly affection. From hence it appears plainly that no man is made more honorable than another or more wealthy, etc., out of any particular and singular respect to himself, but for the glory of his Creator and the common good of the creature, man. Therefore God still reserves the property of these gifts to Himself as [in] Ezekiel: 16.17. He there calls wealth His gold and His silver.[2] [In] Proverbs: 3.9, he claims their service as His due: honor the Lord with thy riches, etc.[3]

---

1. The text is from Old South Leaflets, Old South Association, Old South Meetinghouse, Boston, Massachusetts, No. 207, edited by Samuel Eliot Morison. The original manuscript for Winthrop's sermon is lost, but a copy made during Winthrop's lifetime was published by the Massachusetts Historical Society in 1838.
2. "Thou hast also taken thy fair jewels of my gold and my silver, which I had given thee, and madest to thyself images of men, and didst commit whoredom with them."
3. "Honor the Lord with thy substance, and with the first fruits of all thine increase: so shall thy barns be filled with plenty, and thy presses burst out with new wine" (Proverbs 3.9–10).

All men being thus (by divine providence) ranked into two sorts, rich and poor; under the first are comprehended all such as are able to live comfortably by their own means duly improved; and all others are poor according to the former distribution.

There are two rules whereby we are to walk one towards another: justice and mercy. These are always distinguished in their act and in their object, yet may they both concur in the same subject in each respect; as sometimes there may be an occasion of showing mercy to a rich man in some sudden danger of distress, and also doing of mere justice to a poor man in regard of some particular contract, etc.

There is likewise a double law by which we are regulated in our conversation one towards another in both the former respects: the law of nature and the law of grace, or the moral law or the law of the Gospel, to omit the rule of justice as not properly belonging to this purpose otherwise than it may fall into consideration in some particular cases. By the first of these laws man as he was enabled so withal [is] commanded to love his neighbor as himself.[4] Upon this ground stands all the precepts of the moral law, which concerns our dealings with men. To apply this to the works of mercy, this law requires two things: first, that every man afford his help to another in every want or distress; secondly, that he performed this out of the same affection which makes him careful of his own goods, according to that of our Savior. Matthew: "Whatsoever ye would that men should do to you."[5] This was practiced by Abraham and Lot in entertaining the Angels and the old man of Gibeah.[6]

The law of grace or the Gospel hath some difference from the former, as in these respects: First, the law of nature was given to man in the estate of innocency; this of the Gospel in the estate of regeneracy.[7] Secondly, the former propounds one man to another, as the same flesh and image of God; this as a brother in Christ also, and in the communion of the same spirit and so teacheth us to put a difference between Christians and others. *Do good to all, especially to the household of faith:* Upon this ground the Israelites were to put a difference between the brethren of such as were strangers though not of Canaanites.[8] Thirdly, the law of nature could give no rules for dealing with enemies, for all are to be considered as friends in the state of innocency, but the Gospel commands love to an enemy. Proof. If thine Enemy hunger, feed him; Love your Enemies, do good to them that hate you. Matthew: 5.44.

This law of the Gospel propounds likewise a difference of seasons and occasions. There is a time when a Christian must sell all and give to the poor, as they did in the Apostles' times.[9] There is a time also when a Christian (though they give not all yet) must give beyond their ability, as they of Macedonia,

---

4. Matthew 5.43; 19.19.
5. "Therefore all things whatsoever ye would that men should do to you, do ye even so to them: for this is the law of the prophets" (Matthew 7.12).
6. Abraham entertains the angels in Genesis 18: "And the Lord appeared unto him in the plains of Mamre: and he sat in the tent door in the heat of the day; And he lifted up his eyes and looked, and, lo, three men stood by him: and when he saw them, he ran to meet them" (Genesis 18.1–2). Lot was Abraham's nephew, and he escaped the destruction of the city of Sodom because he defended two angels who were his guests from a mob (Genesis 19.1–14). In Judges 19.16–21, an old citizen of Gibeah offered shelter to a traveling priest or Levite and defended him from enemies from a neighboring city.
7. Humanity lost its natural innocence when Adam and Eve fell; that state is called unregenerate. When Christ came to ransom humankind for Adam and Eve's sin, He offered salvation for those who believed in Him and became regenerate, or saved.
8. One who lived in Canaan, the Land of Promise for the Israelites.
9. In Luke, Jesus tells a ruler who asks him what he must do to gain eternal life: "sell all that thou hast, and distribute unto the poor, and thou shalt have treasure in heaven: and come, follow me" (Luke 18.22).

they give not all yet) must give beyond their ability, as they of Macedonia, Corinthians: 2.8.[1] Likewise community of perils calls for extraordinary liberality, and so doth community in some special service for the Church. Lastly, when there is no other means whereby our Christian brother may be relieved in his distress, we must help him beyond our ability, rather than tempt God in putting him upon help by miraculous or extraordinary means.

This duty of mercy is exercised in the kinds, *giving, lending* and *forgiving.*—

Quest. What rule shall a man observe in giving in respect of the measure?

Ans. If the time and occasion be ordinary, he is to give out of his abundance. Let him lay aside as God hath blessed him. If the time and occasion be extraordinary, he must be ruled by them; taking this withal, that then a man cannot likely do too much, especially if he may leave himself and his family under probable means of comfortable subsistence.

Objection. A man must lay up for posterity, the fathers lay up for posterity and children and he "is worse than an infidel" that "provideth not for his own."

Ans. For the first, it is plain that it being spoken by way of comparison, it must be meant of the ordinary and usual course of fathers and cannot extend to times and occasions extraordinary. For the other place, the Apostle speaks against such as walked inordinately, and it is without question, that he is worse than an infidel who through his own sloth and voluptuousness shall neglect to provide for his family.

Objection. "The wise man's eyes are in his head" saith Solomon, "and foreseeth the plague,"[2] therefore we must forecast and lay up against evil times when he or his may stand in need of all he can gather.

Ans. This very argument Solomon useth to persuade to liberality, Ecclesiastes: "Cast thy bread upon the waters," and "for thou knowest not what evil may come upon the land."[3] Luke: 16.9. "Make you friends of the riches of iniquity."[4] You will ask how this shall be? very well. For first he that gives to the poor, lends to the Lord and He will repay him even in this life an hundred fold to him or his—The righteous is ever merciful and lendeth and his seed enjoyeth the blessing; and besides we know what advantage it will be to us in the day of account when many such witnesses shall stand forth for us to witness the improvement of our talent.[5] And I would know of those who plead so much for laying up for time to come, whether they hold that to be Gospel, Matthew: 6.19: "Lay not up for yourselves treasures upon earth,"[6] etc. If they acknowledge it, what extent will they allow it? if only to those primitive times, let them consider the reason whereupon our Savior grounds it. The first is that they are subject to the moth, the rust, the thief. Secondly, they will steal away

---

1. "Moreover, brethren, we do you to wit of the grace of God bestowed on the churches of Macedonia; How that in a great trial of affliction, the abundance of their joy and their deep poverty abounded unto the riches of their liberality. For to their power, I bear record, yea, and beyond their power they were willing of themselves; Praying us with much entreaty that we would receive the gift, and take upon us the fellowship of the ministering to the saints" (2 Corinthians 8.1–4).
2. Ecclesiastes 2.14. Solomon was the son of David and successor to David as king of all Israel.
3. "Cast thy bread upon the waters: for thou shalt find it after many days. Give a portion to seven, and also to eight; for thou knowest not what evil shall be upon the earth" (Ecclesiastes 11.1–2). Winthrop either makes

his own translations from the Bible or uses the King James or Geneva versions; his quotations, therefore, differ occasionally from the King James version used in these notes.
4. The passage in Luke refers to the servant who, removed from his stewardship, resolves to be received in the houses of his master's debtors and cuts their bills in half. "And I say unto you, Make to yourselves friends of the mammon of unrighteousness; that, when ye fail, they may receive you into everlasting habitations" (Luke 16.9).
5. Originally a measure of money.
6. "Lay not up for yourselves treasures upon earth, where moth and rust doth corrupt, and where thieves break through and steal: But lay up for yourselves trea-

the heart; where the treasure is there will the heart be also. The reasons are of like force at all times. Therefore the exhortation must be general and perpetual, with always in respect of the love and affection to riches and in regard of the things themselves when any special service for the church or particular distress of our brother do call for the use of them; otherwise it is not only lawful but necessary to lay up as Joseph[7] did to have ready upon such occasions, as the Lord (whose stewards we are of them) shall call for them from us. Christ gives us an instance of the first, when he sent his disciples for the ass, and bids them answer the owner thus, the Lord hath need of him.[8] So when the tabernacle was to be built he sends to His people to call for their silver and gold, etc.; and yields them no other reason but that it was for His work. When Elisha comes to the widow of Sareptah and finds her preparing to make ready her pittance for herself and family, He bids her first provide for Him; he challengeth first God's part which she must first give before she must serve her own family.[9] All these teach us that the Lord looks that when He is pleased to call for His right in anything we have, our own interest we have must stand aside till His turn be served. For the other, we need look no further than to that of John: 1: "He who hath this world's goods and seeth his brother to need and shuts up his compassion from him, how dwelleth the love of God in him," which comes punctually to this conclusion: if thy brother be in want and thou canst help him, thou needst not make doubt, what thou shouldst do, if thou lovest God thou must help him.

Quest. What rule must we observe in lending?

Ans. Thou must observe whether thy brother hath present or probable, or possible means of repaying thee, if there be none of these, thou must give him according to his necessity, rather than lend him as he requires. If he hath present means of repaying thee, thou art to look at him not as an act of mercy, but by way of commerce, wherein thou art to walk by the rule of justice; but if his means of repaying thee be only probable or possible, then is he an object of thy mercy, thou must lend him, though there be danger of losing it, Deuteronomy: 15.7: "If any of thy brethren be poor," etc., "thou shalt lend him sufficient."[1] That men might not shift off this duty by the apparent hazard, He tells them that though the year of Jubilee[2] were at hand (when he must remit it, if he were not able to repay it before) yet he must lend him and that cheerfully: "It may not grieve thee to give him" saith He; and because some might object; "why so I should soon impoverish myself and my family," he adds "with all thy work,"[3] etc; for our Savior, Matthew: 5.42: "From him that would borrow of thee turn not away."

Quest. What rule must we observe in forgiving?

---

sures in heaven, where neither moth nor rust doth corrupt, and where thieves do not break through nor steal" (Matthew 6.19–20).

7. Joseph, the son of Jacob and Rachel, stored up the harvest in the seven good years before the famine (Genesis 41).

8. Matthew 21.5–7.

9. 1 Kings 17.8–24.

1. "If there be among you a poor man of one of thy brethren within any of thy gates in thy land which the Lord thy God giveth thee, thou shalt not harden thine heart, nor shut thine hand from thy poor brother: But thou shalt open thine hand wide unto him, and shalt surely lend him sufficient for his need, in that which

he wanteth" (Deuteronomy 15.7–8).

2. According to Mosaic law, every seventh year the lands would lie fallow, all work would cease, and all debts would be canceled. The Jubilee year concluded a cycle of seven sabbatical years.

3. "The seventh year, the year of release, is at hand; and thine eye be evil against thy poor brother, and thou givest him nought; and he cry unto the Lord against thee, and it be sin unto thee. Thou shalt surely give him, and thine heart shall not be grieved when thou givest unto him: because that for this thing the Lord thy God shall bless thee in all thy works, and in all that thou puttest thine hand unto" (Deuteronomy 15.9–10).

Ans. Whether thou didst lend by way of commerce or in mercy, if he have nothing to pay thee, [you] must forgive, (except in cause where thou hast a surety or a lawful pledge) Deuteronomy: 15.2. Every seventh year the creditor was to quit that which he lent to his brother if he were poor as appears—verse 8: "Save when there shall be no poor with thee." In all these and like cases, Christ was a general rule, Matthew: 7.22: "Whatsoever ye would that men should do to you, do ye the same to them also."

Quest. What rule must we observe and walk by in cause of community of peril?

Ans. The same as before, but with more enlargement towards others and less respect towards ourselves and our own right. Hence it was that in the primitive church they sold all, had all things in common, neither did any man say that which he possessed was his own. Likewise in their return out of the captivity, because the work was great for the restoring of the church and the danger of enemies was common to all, Nehemiah exhorts the Jews to liberality and readiness in remitting their debts to their brethren, and disposing liberally of his own to such as wanted, and stand not upon his own due, which he might have demanded of them.[4] Thus did some of our forefathers in times of persecution in England, and so did many of the faithful of other churches, whereof we keep an honorable remembrance of them; and it is to be observed that both in Scriptures and later stories of the churches that such as have been most bountiful to the poor saints, especially in these extraordinary times and occasions, God hath left them highly commended to posterity, as Zacheus, Cornelius, Dorcas, Bishop Hooper, the Cuttler of Brussells[5] and divers others. Observe again that the Scripture gives no caution to restrain any from being over liberal this way; but all men to the liberal and cheerful practice hereof by the sweetest promises; as to instance one for many, Isaiah: 58.6: "Is not this the fast I have chosen to loose the bonds of wickedness, to take off the heavy burdens, to let the oppressed go free and to break every yoke, to deal thy bread to the hungry and to bring the poor that wander into thy house, when thou seest the naked to cover them. And then shall thy light break forth as the morning, and thy health shall grow speedily, thy righteousness shall go before God, and the glory of the Lord shall embrace thee; then thou shalt call and the Lord shall answer thee" etc. [Verse] 10: "If thou pour out thy soul to the hungry, then shall thy light spring out in darkness, and the Lord shall guide thee continually, and satisfy thy soul in drought, and make fat thy bones; thou shalt be like a watered garden, and they shalt be of thee that shall build the old waste places" etc. On the contrary, most heavy curses are laid upon such as are straightened towards the Lord and His people, Judges: 5.[23]: "Curse ye Meroshe because ye came not to help the Lord," etc. Proverbs: [21.13]: "He who shutteth his ears from hearing the cry of the poor, he shall cry and shall not be heard." Matthew: 25: "Go ye cursed into everlasting fire" etc. "I was hungry and ye fed me not." 2 Corinthians: 9.6: "He that soweth sparingly shall reap sparingly."

Having already set forth the practice of mercy according to the rule of God's law, it will be useful to lay open the grounds of it also, being the other part of the commandment, and that is the affection from which this exercise of mercy

4. Nehemiah was sent by King Artaxerxes to repair the walls of the city of Jerusalem; he saved the city as governor when he persuaded those lending money to charge no interest, and to think first of the common good (see Nehemiah 3).
5. Christian martyrs.

must arise. The apostle[6] tells us that this love is the fulfilling of the law, not that it is enough to love our brother and so no further; but in regard of the excellency of his parts giving any motion to the other as the soul to the body and the power it hath to set all the faculties on work in the outward exercise of this duty. As when we bid one make the clock strike, he doth not lay hand on the hammer, which is the immediate instrument of the sound, but sets on work the first mover or main wheel, knowing that will certainly produce the sound which he intends. So the way to draw men to works of mercy, is not by force of argument from the goodness or necessity of the work; for though this course may enforce a rational mind to some present act of mercy, as is frequent in experience, yet it cannot work such a habit in a soul, as shall make it prompt upon all occasions to produce the same effect, but by framing these affections of love in the heart which will as natively bring forth the other, as any cause doth produce effect.

The definition which the Scripture gives us of love is this: "Love is the bond of perfection." First, it is a bond or ligament. Secondly it makes the work perfect. There is no body but consists of parts and that which knits these parts together gives the body its perfection, because it makes each part so contiguous to others as thereby they do mutually participate with each other, both in strength and infirmity, in pleasure and pain. To instance in the most perfect of all bodies: Christ and His church make one body. The several parts of this body, considered apart before they were united, were as disproportionate and as much disordering as so many contrary qualities or elements, but when Christ comes and by His spirit and love knits all these parts to Himself and each to other, it is become the most perfect and best proportioned body in the world. Ephesians: 4.16: "Christ, by whom all the body being knit together by every joint for the furniture thereof, according to the effectual power which is the measure of every perfection of parts," "a glorious body without spot or wrinkle," the ligaments hereof being Christ, or His love, for Christ is love (1 John: 4.8). So this definition is right: "Love is the bond of perfection."

From hence we may frame these conclusions. 1. First of all, true Christians are of one body in Christ, 1 Corinthians: 12.12, 27: "Ye are the body of Christ and members of their part." Secondly: The ligaments of this body which knit together are love. Thirdly: No body can be perfect which wants its proper ligament. Fourthly. All the parts of this body being thus united are made so contiguous in a special relation as they must needs partake of each other's strength and infirmity; joy and sorrow, weal and woe. 1 Corinthians: 12.26: "If one member suffers, all suffer with it, if one be in honor, all rejoice with it." Fifthly. This sensibleness and sympathy of each other's conditions will necessarily infuse into each part a native desire and endeavor to strengthen, defend, preserve and comfort the other.

To insist a little on this conclusion being the product of all the former, the truth hereof will appear both by precept and pattern. 1 John: 3.10: "Ye ought to lay down your lives for the brethren." Galatians: 6.2: "bear ye one another's burthens and so fulfill the law of Christ." For patterns we have that first of our Savior who out of His good will in obedience to His father, becoming a part of this body, and being knit with it in the bond of love, found such a native sensibleness of our infirmities and sorrows as He willingly yielded Himself to

6. St. Paul in his Epistle to the Romans 9.31.

death to ease the infirmities of the rest of His body, and so healed their sorrows. From the like sympathy of parts did the apostles and many thousands of the saints lay down their lives for Christ. Again, the like we may see in the members of this body among themselves. Romans: 9. Paul could have been contented to have been separated from Christ, that the Jews might not be cut off from the body. It is very observable what he professeth of his affectionate partaking with every member: "who is weak" saith he "and I am not weak? who is offended and I burn not;"[7] and again, 2 Corinthians: 7.13. "therefore we are comforted because ye were comforted." Of Epaphroditus[8] he speaketh, Philippians: 2.30. that he regarded not his own life to do him service. So Phoebe[9] and others are called the servants of the church. Now it is apparent that they served not for wages, or by constraint, but out of love. The like we shall find in the histories of the church in all ages, the sweet sympathy of affections which was in the members of this body one towards another, their cheerfulness in serving and suffering together, how liberal they were without repining, harborers without grudging and helpful without reproaching; and all from hence, because they had fervent love amongst them, which only make the practice of mercy constant and easy.

The next consideration is how this love comes to be wrought. Adam in his first estate[1] was a perfect model of mankind in all their generations, and in him this love was perfected in regard of the habit. But Adam rent himself from his creator, rent all his posterity also one from another; whence it comes that every man is born with this principle in him, to love and seek himself only, and thus a man continueth till Christ comes and takes possession of the soul and infuseth another principle, love to God and our brother. And this latter having continual supply from Christ, as the head and root by which he is united, gets the predomining in the soul, so by little and little expels the former. 1 John: 4.7. "love cometh of God and every one that loveth is borne of God," so that this love is the fruit of the new birth, and none can have it but the new creature. Now when this quality is thus formed in the souls of men, it works like the spirit upon the dry bones. Ezekiel: 37: "bone came to bone." It gathers together the scattered bones, of perfect old man Adam, and knits them into one body again in Christ, whereby a man is become again a living soul.

The third consideration is concerning the exercise of this love which is twofold, inward or outward. The outward hath been handled in the former preface of this discourse. For unfolding the other we must take in our way that maxim of philosophy *simile simili gaudet*, or like will to like; for as it is things which are turned with disaffection to each other, the ground of it is from a dissimilitude arising from the contrary or different nature of the things themselves; for the ground of love is an apprehension of some resemblance in things loved to that which affects it. This is the cause why the Lord loves the creature, so far as it hath any of His image in it; He loves His elect because they are like Himself, He beholds them in His beloved son. So a mother loves her child, because she thoroughly conceives a resemblance of herself in it. Thus it is

---

7. 2 Corinthians 11.29.
8. St. Paul tells the Philippians that he will send to them as a spiritual guide "Epaphroditus, my brother and companion in labor, and fellow soldier, but your messenger, and he that ministered to my wants" (Phil-

ippians 2.25).
9. A Christian woman praised by St. Paul in Romans 16.1.
1. I.e., in his innocence.

between the members of Christ. Each discerns, by the work of the spirit, his own image and resemblance in another, and therefore cannot but love him as he loves himself. Now when the soul, which is of a sociable nature, finds anything like to itself, it is like Adam when Eve was brought to him. She must have it one with herself. This is flesh of my flesh (saith the soul) and bone of my bone. She conceives a great delight in it, therefore she desires nearness and familiarity with it. She hath a great propensity to do it good and receives such content in it, as fearing the miscarriage of her beloved she bestows it in the inmost closet of her heart. She will not endure that it shall want any good which she can give it. If by occasion she be withdrawn from the company of it, she is still looking towards the place where she left her beloved. If she heard it groan, she is with it presently. If she find it sad and disconsolate, she sighs and moans with it. She hath no such joy as to see her beloved merry and thriving. If she see it wronged, she cannot hear it without passion. She sets no bounds to her affections, nor hath any thought of reward. She finds recompense enough in the exercise of her love towards it. We may see this acted to life in Jonathan and David.[2] Jonathan a valiant man endowed with the spirit of Christ, so soon as he discovers the same spirit in David had presently his heart knit to him by this lineament of love so that it is said he loved him as his own soul. He takes so great pleasure in him, that he strips himself to adorn his beloved. His father's kingdom was not so precious to him as his beloved David. David shall have it with all his heart, himself desires no more but that he may be near to him to rejoice in his good. He chooseth to converse with him in the wilderness even to the hazard of his own life, rather than with the great courtiers in his father's palace. When he sees danger towards him, he spares neither rare pains nor peril to direct it. When injury was offered his beloved David, he would not bear it, though from his own father; and when they must part for a season only, they thought their hearts would have broke for sorrow, had not their affections found vent by abundance of tears. Other instances might be brought to show the nature of this affection, as of Ruth and Naomi,[3] and many others; but this truth is cleared enough.

If any shall object that it is not possible that love should be bred or upheld without hope of requital, it is granted; but that is not our cause; for this love is always under reward. It never gives, but it always receives with advantage; first, in regard that among the members of the same body, love and affection are reciprocal in a most equal and sweet kind of commerce. Secondly, in regard of the pleasure and content that the exercise of love carries with it, as we may see in the natural body. The mouth is at all the pains to receive and mince the food which serves for the nourishment of all the other parts of the body, yet it hath no cause to complain; for first the other parts send back by several passages a due proportion of the same nourishment, in a better form for the strengthening and comforting the mouth. Secondly, the labor of the mouth is accompanied with such pleasure and content as far exceeds the pains it takes. So is it in all the labor of love among Christians. The party loving, reaps love again, as was showed before, which the soul covets more than all the wealth in the world. Thirdly: Nothing yields more pleasure and content to the soul than when it finds that which it may love fervently, for to love and live beloved

---

2. The story of David and Jonathan is told in 1 Samuel 19ff.
3. Naomi was the mother-in-law of Ruth, whom Ruth refused to leave when her husband died, telling her, "For whither thou goest, I will go; and where thou lodgest, I will lodge" (Ruth 1.16).

is the soul's paradise, both here and in heaven. In the state of wedlock there be many comforts to bear out the troubles of that condition; but let such as have tried the most, say if there be any sweetness in that condition comparable to the exercise of mutual love.

From former considerations arise these conclusions.

First: This love among Christians is a real thing, not imaginary.

Secondly: This love is as absolutely necessary to the being of the body of Christ, as the sinews and other ligaments of a natural body are to the being of that body.

Thirdly: This love is a divine, spiritual nature free, active, strong, courageous, permanent; undervaluing all things beneath its proper object; and of all the graces, this makes us nearer to resemble the virtues of our Heavenly Father.

Fourthly: It rests in the love and welfare of its beloved. For the full and certain knowledge of these truths concerning the nature, use, and excellency of this grace, that which the Holy Ghost hath left recorded, 1 Corinthians: 13, may give full satisfaction, which is needful for every true member of this lovely body of the Lord Jesus, to work upon their hearts by prayer, meditation, continual exercise at least of the special [influence] of His grace, till Christ be formed in them and they in Him, all in each other, knit together by this bond of love.

II

It rests now to make some application of this discourse by the present design, which gave the occasion of writing of it. Herein are four things to be propounded: first the persons, secondly the work, thirdly the end, fourthly the means.

First, For the persons. We are a company professing ourselves fellow members of Christ, in which respect only though we were absent from each other many miles, and had our employments as far distant, yet we ought to account ourselves knit together by this bond of love, and live in the exercise of it, if we would have comfort of our being in Christ. This was notorious in the practice of the Christians in former times; as is testified of the Waldenses,[4] from the mouth of one of the adversaries *Æneas Sylvius*[5] "mutuo [ament] penè antequam norunt," they used to love any of their own religion even before they were acquainted with them.

Secondly, for the work we have in hand. It is by a mutual consent, through a special overvaluing providence and a more than an ordinary approbation of the Churches of Christ, to seek out a place of cohabitation and consortship under a due form of government both civil and ecclesiastical. In such cases as this, the care of the public must oversway all private respects, by which, not only conscience, but mere civil policy, doth bind us. For it is a true rule that particular estates cannot subsist in the ruin of the public.

Thirdly. The end is to improve our lives to do more service to the Lord; the comfort and increase of the body of Christ whereof we are members; that

4. The Waldenses took their name from Pater Valdes, an early French reformer of the church. They still survive as a religious community.
5. Aeneas Sylvius Piccolomini (1405–1464), Pope

Pius II, was a historian and scholar. *Solent amare* is a closer approximation of the Latin than Morison's suggestion of *ament*.

ourselves and posterity may be the better preserved from the common corruptions of this evil world, to serve the Lord and work out our salvation under the power and purity of His holy ordinances.

Fourthly, for the means whereby this must be effected. They are twofold, a conformity with the work and end we aim at. These we see are extraordinary, therefore we must not content ourselves with usual ordinary means. Whatsoever we did or ought to have done when we lived in England, the same must we do, and more also, where we go. That which the most in their churches maintain as a truth in profession only, we must bring into familiar and constant practice, as in this duty of love. We must love brotherly without dissimulation; we must love one another with a pure heart fervently. We must bear one another's burthens. We must not look only on our own things, but also on the things of our brethren, neither must we think that the Lord will bear with such failings at our hands as he doth from those among whom we have lived; and that for three reasons.

First, In regard of the more near bond of marriage between Him and us, where-in He hath taken us to be His after a most strict and peculiar manner, which will make Him the more jealous of our love and obedience. So He tells the people of Israel, you only have I known of all the families of the earth, therefore will I punish you for your transgressions. Secondly, because the Lord will be sanctified in them that come near Him. We know that there were many that corrupted the service of the Lord, some setting up altars before His own, others offering both strange fire and strange sacrifices also; yet there came no fire from heaven or other sudden judgment upon them, as did upon Nadab and Abihu,[6] who yet we may think did not sin presumptuously. Thirdly. When God gives a special commission He looks to have it strictly observed in every article. When He gave Saul a commission to destroy Amaleck, He indented with him upon certain articles,[7] and because he failed in one of the least, and that upon a fair pretense, it lost him the kingdom which should have been his reward if he had observed his commission.

Thus stands the cause between God and us. We are entered into covenant[8] with Him for this work. We have taken out a commission, the Lord hath given us leave to draw our own articles. We have professed to enterprise these actions, upon these and those ends, we have hereupon besought Him of favor and blessing. Now if the Lord shall please to hear us, and bring us in peace to the place we desire, then hath He ratified this covenant and sealed our commission, [and] will expect a strict performance of the articles contained in it; but if we shall neglect the observation of these articles which are the ends we have propounded, and, dissembling with our God, shall fall to embrace this present world and prosecute our carnal intentions, seeking great things for ourselves and our posterity, the Lord will surely break out in wrath against us; be revenged of such a perjured people and make us know the price of the breach of such a covenant.

6. "And Nadab and Abihu, the sons of Aaron, took either of them his censer, and put fire therein, and put incense thereon, and offered strange fire before the Lord, which he commanded them not. And there went out fire from the Lord, and devoured them, and they died before the Lord" (Leviticus 10.1–2). Winthrop's point is that the chosen people are often punished more severly than unbelievers.

7. I.e., made an agreement with him on parts of a contract or agreement. Saul was instructed to destroy the Amalekites and all that they possessed, but he spared their sheep and oxen, and in doing so disobeyed the Lord's commandment and was rejected as king (1 Samuel 15.1–34).

8. A legal contract; the Israelites entered into a covenant with God in which He promised to protect them if they kept His word and were faithful to Him.

Now the only way to avoid this shipwreck, and to provide for our posterity, is to follow the counsel of Micah,[9] to do justly, to love mercy, to walk humbly with our God. For this end, we must be knit together in this work as one man. We must entertain each other in brotherly affection, we must be willing to abridge ourselves of our superfluities, for the supply of other's necessities. We must uphold a familiar commerce together in all meekness, gentleness, patience and liberality. We must delight in each other, make other's conditions our own, rejoice together, mourn together, labor and suffer together, always having before our eyes our commission and community in the work, our community as members of the same body. So shall we keep the unity of the spirit in the bond of peace. The Lord will be our God, and delight to dwell among us as His own people, and will command a blessing upon us in all our ways, so that we shall see much more of His wisdom, power, goodness and truth, than formerly we have been acquainted with. We shall find that the God of Israel is among us, when ten of us shall be able to resist a thousand of our enemies; when He shall make us a praise and glory that men shall say of succeeding plantations, "the Lord make it like that of NEW ENGLAND." For we must consider that we shall be as a city upon a hill.[1] The eyes of all people are upon us, so that if we shall deal falsely with our God in this work we have undertaken, and so cause Him to withdraw His present help from us, we shall be made a story and a by-word through the world. We shall open the mouths of enemies to speak evil of the ways of God, and all professors for God's sake. We shall shame the faces of many of God's worthy servants, and cause their prayers to be turned into curses upon us till we be consumed out of the good land whither we are agoing.

And to shut up this discourse with that exhortation of Moses, that faithful servant of the Lord, in his last farewell to Israel, Deuteronomy 30.[2] Beloved, there is now set before us life and good, death and evil, in that we are commanded this day to love the Lord our God, and to love one another, to walk in His ways and to keep His commandments and His ordinance and His laws, and the articles of our covenant with Him, that we may live and be multiplied, and that our Lord our God may bless us in the land whither we go to possess it. But if our hearts shall turn away, so that we will not obey, but shall be seduced, and worship other gods, our pleasures and profits, and serve them; it is propounded unto us this day, we shall surely perish out of the good land whither we pass over this vast sea to possess it.

> Therefore let us choose life,
> that we and our seed
> may live by obeying His
> voice and cleaving to Him,
> for He is our life and
> our prosperity.

1630   1838

9. The Book of Micah preserves the words of this 8th-century-B.C. prophet. Micah speaks continually of the judgment of God on His people and the necessity for hope for salvation: "I will bear the indignation of the Lord, because I have sinned against him, until he plead my cause, and execute judgment for me: he will bring me forth to the light, and I shall behold his righteousness" (Micah 7.9).

1. "Ye are the light of the world. A city that is set on a hill cannot be hid. Neither do men light a candle, and put it under a bushel, but on a candlestick; and it giveth light unto all that are in the house" (Matthew 5.14–15).
2. "And it shall come to pass, when all these things are come upon thee, the blessing and the curse, which I have set before thee, and thou shalt call them to mind

From The Journal of John Winthrop[1]

[June 8, 1630] The wind still W. and by S., fair weather, but close and cold. We stood N. N. W. with a stiff gale, and, about three in the afternoon, we had sight of land to the N. W. about ten leagues, which we supposed was the Isles of Monhegan, but it proved Mount Mansell.[2] Then we tacked and stood W. S. W. We had now fair sunshine weather, and so pleasant a sweet air as did much refresh us, and there came a smell off the shore like the smell of a garden.

There came a wild pigeon into our ship, and another small land bird.

[July 5, 1632] At Watertown there was (in view of divers witnesses) a great combat between a mouse and a snake; and, after a long fight, the mouse prevailed and killed the snake. The pastor of Boston, Mr. Wilson, a very sincere, holy man, hearing of it, gave this interpretation: That the snake was the devil; the mouse was a poor contemptible people, which God had brought hither, which should overcome Satan here, and dispossess him of his kingdom. Upon the same occasion, he told the governor,[3] that, before he was resolved to come into this country, he dreamed he was here, and that he saw a church arise out of the earth, which grew up and became a marvelous goodly church.

[December 27, 1633] The governor and assistants met at Boston, and took into consideration a treatise, which Mr. Williams[4] (then of Salem) had sent to them, and which he had formerly written to the governor and council of Plymouth, wherein, among other things, he disputes their right to the lands they possessed here, and concluded that, claiming by the king's grant, they could have no title, nor otherwise, except they compounded[5] with the natives. For this, taking advice with some of the most judicious ministers, (who much condemned Mr. Williams's error and presumption,) they gave order, that he should be convented[6] at the next court, to be censured, etc. There were three passages chiefly whereat they were much offended: 1, for that he chargeth King James to have told a solemn public lie, because in his patent he blessed God that he was the first Christian prince that had discovered this land; 2, for that he chargeth him and others with blasphemy for calling Europe Christendom, or the Christian world; 3, for that he did personally apply to our present king, Charles, these three places in the Revelations,[7] viz., [*blank*].

Mr. Endicott being absent, the governor wrote to him and let him know what was done, and withal added divers arguments to confute the said errors, wishing him to deal with Mr. Williams to retract the same, etc. Whereto he returned a very modest and discreet answer. Mr. Williams also wrote to the governor,[8] and also to him and the rest of the council, very submissively, professing his intent to have been only to have written for the private satisfac-

---

among all the nations, whither the Lord thy God hath driven thee, And shalt return unto the Lord thy God, and shalt obey his voice according to all that I command thee this day, thou and thy children, with all thine heart, and with all thy soul; That then the Lord thy God will turn thy captivity, and have compassion upon thee, and will return and gather thee from all the nations, whither the Lord thy God hath scattered thee" (Deuteronomy 30.1–3).

1. The text used here is from *Winthrop's Journal: History of New England 1630–1649*, edited by James Kendall Hosmer (1908).

2. What Winthrop saw was Mount Desert, Maine, named by the French explorer Champlain in 1604.
3. I.e., Winthrop himself.
4. Roger Williams (c.1603–1683), who had emigrated to New England in 1630 and refused a call to the First Church of Boston because he would not preach to "an unseparated people."
5. Arranged to purchase.
6. Summoned to appear.
7. I.e., the Book of Revelation. Winthrop never added the citations.
8. In 1633 Edward Winslow was governor.

tion of the governor, etc., of Plymouth, without any purpose to have stirred any further in it, if the governor here had not required a copy of him; withal offering his book, or any part of it, to be burnt.

At the next court he appeared penitently, and gave satisfaction of his intention and loyalty. So it was left, and nothing done in it.

[January 20, 1634] Hall and the two others,[9] who went to Connecticut November 3, came now home, having lost themselves and endured much misery. They informed us that the small pox was gone as far as any Indian plantation was known to the west, and much people dead of it, by reason whereof they could have no trade.

At Naragansett, by the Indians' report, there died seven hundred; but, beyond Pascataquack, none to the eastward.

[January 24, 1634] The governor and council met again at Boston, to consider of Mr. Williams's letter, etc., when, with the advice of Mr. Cotton[1] and Mr. Wilson, and weighing his letter, and further considering of the aforesaid offensive passages in his book,[2] (which, being written in very obscure and implicative phrases, might well admit of doubtful interpretation,) they found the matters not to be so evil as at first they seemed. Whereupon they agreed, that, upon his retractation, etc., or taking an oath of allegiance to the king, etc., it should be passed over.

[January 11, 1636] The governor[3] and assistants met at Boston to consider about Mr. Williams, for that they were credibly informed, that, notwithstanding the injunction laid upon him (upon the liberty granted him to stay till the spring) not to go about to draw others to his opinions, he did use to entertain company in his house, and to preach to them, even of such points as he had been censured for; and it was agreed to send him into England by a ship then ready to depart. The reason was, because he had drawn above twenty persons to his opinion, and they were intended to erect a plantation about the Naragansett Bay,[4] from whence the infection would easily spread into these churches, (the people being, many of them, much taken with the apprehension of his godliness). Whereupon a warrant was sent to him to come presently to Boston, to be shipped,[5] etc. He returned answer, (and divers of Salem came with it,) that he could not come without hazard of his life, etc. Whereupon a pinnace[6] was sent with commission to Capt. Underhill, etc., to apprehend him, and carry him aboard the ship, (which then rode at Natascutt;) but, when they came at his house, they found he had been gone three days before; but whither they could not learn.

He had so far prevailed at Salem, as many there (especially of devout women) did embrace his opinions, and separated from the churches, for this cause, that some of their members, going into England, did hear the ministers there, and when they came home the churches here held [to be in] communion with them.

[October 21, 1636] One Mrs. Hutchinson,[7] a member of the church of

---

9. Not further identified.

1. John Cotton (1584–1652) emigrated to Boston in 1633 and from that time until his death was a major figure in the hierarchy of the town. He was pastor of the First Church of Boston.

2. Winthrop is referring to a now-lost Williams manuscript or treatise, mentioned in the entry for December 27, 1633, rather than a published book.

3. John Hays (1594–1654). Winthrop was reelected

governor in 1637.

4. Providence Plantation in Rhode Island received its patent in 1644.

5. I.e., returned to Boston by ship.

6. A small, light vessel, usually with two masts.

7. Anne Hutchinson (1591–1643), originally a follower of John Cotton, soon pursued an extreme position in which she argued that the elect were joined in personal union with God and superior to those lacking

Boston, a woman of a ready wit and bold spirit, brought over with her two dangerous errors: 1. That the person of the Holy Ghost dwells in a justified[8] person. 2. That no sanctification can help to evidence to us our justification.[9]—From these two grew many branches; as, 1. Our union with the Holy Ghost, so as a Christian remains dead to every spiritual action, and hath no gifts nor graces, other than such as are in hypocrites, nor any other sanctification but the Holy Ghost himself.

There joined with her in these opinions a brother of hers, one Mr. Wheelwright, a silenced[1] minister sometimes in England.

[October 25, 1636] The other ministers in the bay, hearing of these things, came to Boston at the time of a general court, and entered conference in private with them, to the end they might know the certainty of these things; that if need were, they might write to the church of Boston about them, to prevent (if it were possible) the dangers, which seemed hereby to hang over that and the rest of the churches. At this conference, Mr. Cotton was present, and gave satisfaction to them, so as he agreed with them all in the point of sanctification, and so did Mr. Wheelwright; so as they all did hold, that sanctification did help to evidence justification. The same he had delivered plainly in public, divers times; but, for the indwelling of the person of the Holy Ghost, he held that still, as some others of the ministers did, but not union with the person of the Holy Ghost, (as Mrs. Hutchinson and others did,) so as to amount to a personal union.

[November 1, 1637] There was great hope that the late general assembly would have had some good effect in pacifying the troubles and dissensions about matters of religion; but it fell out otherwise. For though Mr. Wheelwright and those of his party had been clearly confuted and confounded in the assembly, yet they persisted in their opinions, and were as busy in nourishing contentions (the principal of them) as before. * * *

The court also sent Mrs. Hutchinson, and charged her with divers matters, as her keeping two public lectures every week in her house, whereto sixty or eighty persons did usually resort, and for reproaching most of the ministers (viz., all except Mr. Cotton) for not preaching a covenant of free grace, and that they had not the seal of the spirit, nor were able ministers of the New Testament; which were clearly proved against her, though she sought to shift it off.[2] And, after many speeches to and fro, at last she was so full as she could not contain, but vented her revelations; amongst which this was one, that she had it revealed to her, that she should come into New England, and should here be persecuted, and that God would ruin us and our posterity, and the whole state, for the same. So the court proceeded and banished her; but, because it was winter, they committed her to a private house, where she was well provided, and her own friends and the elders permitted to go to her, but none else.

The court called also Capt. Underhill, and some five or six more of the principal, whose hands were to the said petition; and because they stood to justify it, they were disfranchised, and such as had public places were put from them.

Inner Light. She also denied that good works were in any way a sign of God's favor, arguing that justification was by faith alone and had nothing to do with either piety or worldly success.

8. I.e., one elected or chosen for salvation by God.

9. I.e., that proper moral conduct is no sign of justification.

1. Mr. Wheelwright had probably refused to take an oath of loyalty to the Church of England.

2. I.e., to qualify her statements.

The court also ordered, that the rest, who had subscribed the petition, (and would not acknowledge their fault, and which near twenty of them did,) and some others, who had been chief stirrers in these contentions, etc., should be disarmed. This troubled some of them very much, especially because they were to bring them in themselves; but at last, when they saw no remedy, they obeyed.[3]

All the proceedings of this court against these persons were set down at large, with the reasons and other observations, and were sent into England to be published there, to the end that all our godly friends might not be discouraged from coming to us, etc.

[March 1638] While Mrs. Hutchinson continued at Roxbury,[4] divers of the elders and others resorted to her, and finding her to persist in maintaining those gross errors beforementioned, and many others, to the number of thirty or thereabout, some of them wrote to the church at Boston, offering to make proof of the same before the church, etc., 15; whereupon she was called, (the magistrates being desired to give her license to come,) and the lecture was appointed to begin at ten. (The general court being then at Newtown, the governor[5] and the treasurer, being members of Boston, were permitted to come down, but the rest of the court continued at Newtown.) When she appeared, the errors were read to her. The first was, that the souls of men are mortal by generation,[6] but, after, made immortal by Christ's purchase. This she maintained a long time; but at length she was so clearly convinced by reason and scripture, and the whole church agreeing that sufficient had been delivered for her conviction, that she yielded she had been in an error. Then they proceeded to three other errors: 1. That there was no resurrection of these bodies, and that these bodies were not united to Christ, but every person united hath a new body, etc. These were also clearly confuted, but yet she held her own; so as the church (all but two of her sons) agreed she should be admonished, and because her sons would not agree to it, they were admonished also.

Mr. Cotton pronounced the sentence of admonition with great solemnity, and with much zeal and detestation of her errors and pride of spirit. The assembly continued till eight at night, and all did acknowledge the special presence of God's spirit therein; and she was appointed to appear again the next lecture day.

[March 22, 1638] Mrs. Hutchinson appeared again; (she had been licensed by the court, in regard she had given hope of her repentance, to be at Mr. Cotton's house, that both he and Mr. Davenport[7] might have the more opportunity to deal with her;) and the articles being again read to her, and her answer required, she delivered it in writing wherein she made a retractation of near all, but with such explanations and circumstances as gave no satisfaction to the church; so as she was required to speak further to them. Then she declared, that it was just with God to leave her to herself, as He had done, for her slighting His ordinances, both magistracy and ministry;[8] and confessed that what she had spoken against the magistrates at the court (by way of revela-

3. They were also forbidden to borrow to buy guns until "the court shall take further order therein."
4. Near Boston.
5. Winthrop himself.
6. I.e., from the beginning. Orthodox believers hold the soul immortal.
7. John Davenport (1597–1670), a Puritan minister.
8. Because her unorthodox beliefs threatened both civil and ecclesiastical law.

tion) was rash and ungrounded; and desired the church to pray for her. This gave the church good hope of her repentance; but when she was examined about some particulars, as that she had denied inherent righteousness, etc., she affirmed that it was never her judgment; and though it was proved by many testimonies, that she had been of that judgment, and so had persisted, and maintained it by argument against divers, yet she impudently persisted in her affirmation, to the astonishment of all the assembly. So that, after much time and many arguments had been spent to bring her to see her sin, but all in vain, the church, with one consent, cast her out. Some moved to have her admonished[9] once more; but, it being for manifest evil in matter of conversation, it was agreed otherwise; and for that reason also the sentence was denounced[1] by the pastor, matter of manners belonging properly to his place.

After she was excommunicated,[2] her spirits, which seemed before to be somewhat dejected, revived again, and she gloried in her sufferings, saying, that it was the greatest happiness, next to Christ, that ever befell her. Indeed, it was a happy day to the churches of Christ here, and to many poor souls, who had been seduced by her, who, by what they heard and saw that day, were (through the grace of God) brought off quite from her errors, and settled again in the truth.

* * *

After two or three days, the governor sent a warrant to Mrs. Hutchinson to depart this jurisdiction before the last of this month, according to the order of court, and for that end set her at liberty from her former constraint, so as she was not to go forth of her own house till her departure; and upon the 28th she went by water to her farm at the Mount, where she was to take water, with Mr. Wheelwright's wife and family, to go to Pascataquack; but she changed her mind, and went by land to Providence, and so to the island in the Narragansett Bay, which her husband and the rest of that sect had purchased of the Indians. * * *

[September 1638] . . . Mrs. Hutchinson, being removed to the Isle of Aquiday, in the Naragansett Bay, after her time was fulfilled, that she expected deliverance of a child, was delivered of a monstrous birth, which, being diversely related in the country, (and, in the open assembly at Boston, upon a lecture day, [was] declared by Mr. Cotton to be twenty-seven several lumps of man's seed, without any alteration or mixture of anything from the woman, and thereupon gathered that it might signify her error in denying inherent righteousness, but that all was Christ in us, and nothing of ours in our faith, love, etc.). Hereupon the governor wrote to Mr. Clarke, a physician and a preacher to those of the island, to know the certainty thereof.

* * *

[July 3, 1645] * * * Then was the deputy governor[3] desired by the court to go up and take his place again upon the bench, which he did accordingly, and the court being about to arise, he desired leave for a little speech, which was to this effect.

9. Warned.
1. Publicly condemned.
2. Excluded, banished; not to be confused with the rite of excommunication performed by the Roman Catholic Church.
3. Winthrop. The governor in 1645 was Thomas Dudley (1576–1654).

I suppose something may be expected from me, upon this charge that is befallen me, which moves me to speak now to you; yet I intend not to intermeddle in the proceedings of the court, or with any of the persons concerned therein. Only I bless God, that I see an issue of this troublesome business. I also acknowledge the justice of the court, and, for mine own part, I am well satisfied, I was publicly charged, and I am publicly and legally acquitted, which is all I did expect or desire. And though this be sufficient for my justification before men, yet not so before the God, who hath seen so much amiss in my dispensations (and even in this affair) as calls me to be humble. For to be publicly and criminally charged in this court, is matter of humiliation, (and I desire to make a right use of it,) notwithstanding I be thus acquitted. If her father had spit in her face, (saith the Lord concerning Miriam,) should she not have been ashamed seven days?[4] Shame had lien upon her, whatever the occasion had been. I am unwilling to stay you from your urgent affairs, yet give me leave (upon this special occasion) to speak a little more to this assembly. It may be of some good use, to inform and rectify the judgments of some of the people, and may prevent such distempers as have arisen amongst us. The great questions that have troubled the country, are about the authority of the magistrates and the liberty of the people. It is yourselves who have called us to this office, and being called by you, we have our authority from God, in way of an ordinance, such as hath the image of God eminently stamped upon it, the contempt and violation whereof hath been vindicated with examples of divine vengeance. I entreat you to consider, that when you choose magistrates, you take them from among yourselves, men subject to like passions as you are. Therefore when you see infirmities in us, you should reflect upon your own, and that would make you bear the more with us, and not be severe censurers of the failings of your magistrates, when you have continual experience of the like infirmities in yourselves and others. We account him a good servant, who breaks not his covenant. The covenant between you and us is the oath you have taken of us, which is to this purpose, that we shall govern you and judge your causes by the rules of God's laws and our own, according to our best skill. When you agree with a workman to build you a ship or house, etc., he undertakes as well for his skill as for his faithfulness, for it is his profession, and you pay him for both. But when you call one to be a magistrate, he doth not profess nor undertake to have sufficient skill for that office, nor can you furnish him with gifts, etc., therefore you must run the hazard of his skill and ability. But if he fail in faithfulness, which by his oath he is bound unto, that he must answer for. If it fall out that the case be clear to common apprehension, and the rule clear also, if he transgress here, the error is not in the skill, but in the evil of the will: it must be required of him. But if the case be doubtful, or the rule doubtful, to men of such understanding and parts as your magistrates are, if your magistrates should err here, yourselves must bear it.

For the other point concerning liberty, I observe a great mistake in the country about that. There is a twofold liberty, natural (I mean as our nature is now corrupt)[5] and civil or federal. The first is common to man with beasts and other creatures. By this, man, as he stands in relation to

---

4. The sister of Moses and Aaron. "And the Lord said unto Moses, If her father had but spit in her face, should she not be ashamed seven days? let her be shut out from the camp seven days, and after that let her be received in again" (Numbers 12.14).

5. I.e., because we are fallen and subject to death.

man simply, hath liberty to do what he lists; it is a liberty to evil as well as to good. This liberty is incompatible and inconsistent with authority, and cannot endure the least restraint of the most just authority. The exercise and maintaining of this liberty makes men grow more evil, and in time to be worse than brute beasts: *omnes sumus licentia deteriores.*[6] This is that great enemy of truth and peace, that wild beast, which all the ordinances of God are bent against, to restrain and subdue it. The other kind of liberty I call civil or federal, it may also be termed moral, in reference to the covenant between God and man, in the moral law, and the politic covenants and constitutions, amongst men themselves. This liberty is the proper end and object of authority, and cannot subsist without it; and it is a liberty to that only which is good, just, and honest. This liberty you are to stand for, with the hazard (not only of your goods, but) of your lives, if need be. Whatsoever crosseth this, is not authority, but a distemper thereof. This liberty is maintained and exercised in a way of subjection to authority; it is of the same kind of liberty wherewith Christ hath made us free. The woman's own choice makes such a man her husband; yet being so chosen, he is her lord, and she is to be subject to him, yet in a way of liberty, not of bondage; and a true wife accounts her subjection her honor and freedom, and would not think her condition safe and free, but in her subjection to her husband's authority. Such is the liberty of the church under the authority of Christ, her king and husband; his yoke is so easy and sweet to her as a bride's ornaments; and if through forwardness or wantonness, etc., she shake it off, at any time, she is at no rest in her spirit, until she take it up again; and whether her lord smiles upon her, and embraceth her in his arms, or whether he frowns, or rebukes, or smites her, she apprehends the sweetness of his love in all, and is refreshed, supported, and instructed by every such dispensation of his authority over her. On the other side, ye know who they are that complain of this yoke and say, let us break their bands, etc., we will not have this man to rule over us. Even so, brethren, it will be between you and your magistrates. If you stand for your natural corrupt liberties, and will do what is good in your own eyes, you will not endure the least weight of authority, but will murmur, and oppose, and be always striving to shake off that yoke; but if you will be satisfied to enjoy such civil and lawful liberties, such as Christ allows you, then will you quietly and cheerfully submit unto that authority which is set over you, in all the administrations of it, for your good. Wherein, if we fail at any time, we hope we shall be willing (by God's assistance) to hearken to good advice from any of you, or in any other way of God; so shall your liberties be preserved, in upholding the honor and power of authority amongst you.

The deputy governor having ended his speech, the court arose, and the magistrates and deputies retired to attend their other affairs. * * *

6. We are all the worse for license (Latin).

ROGER WILLIAMS
c. 1603–1683

In his journal for January 1636, John Winthrop tells us that when the governor of Massachusetts and his assistants met to redetermine the charge of divisiveness that had been brought against Roger Williams, they agreed that they could not wait until spring to banish him from the commonwealth. They must move against him immediately, they argued, and ship him back to England. His opinions were dangerous and spreading. When they went to Salem to seize him and "carry him aboard the ship," however they found he "had been gone three days before; but whither they could not learn." Williams had, of course fled Massachusetts for Rhode Island. He found shelter there with the Narragansett Indians and, from that time until his death almost fifty years later, Williams and Providence Plantation were synonymous with the spirit of religious liberty. Rhode Island became a sanctuary for those who found the strictures of the Massachusetts Bay insufferable: Separatists, Baptists, Seekers, Antinomians, Jews, and Quakers were all to find a home there. In 1663 Rhode Island received a royal charter from Charles II in which freedom of conscience was guaranteed. It was something of which not even Englishmen were ensured, and it became so indelibly "American" an idea that provision was made for it in our 1791 Bill of Rights.

Williams had infuriated and threatened the leaders of Massachusetts by taking four rather extreme positions, any one of which seriously undermined the theocracy that was at the heart of the Bay Colony government. He denied, first, that Massachusetts had a proper title to its land, arguing that King Charles I could not bestow a title to something that belonged to the natives. Second, he argued that no unregenerate person could be required either to pray in churches or to swear in a court of law on oath; third, that Massachusetts Bay Colony ministers, who had persuaded the king of England when they left their native country that they wished to remain a part of the national church, should not only separate from the Church of England but repent that they had ever served it; last, that civil authority was limited to civil matters and that magistrates had no jurisdiction over the soul. Williams, as the historian Perry Miller has put it, wanted to "build a wall of separation between state and church not to prevent the state from becoming an instrument of 'priestcraft,' but in order to keep the holy and pure religion of Jesus Christ from contamination by the slightest taint of earthly support." It was a disturbing position for Separatist and non-Separatist alike, and Williams has the distinction of having made himself unwelcome in both Plymouth and Boston.

In 1631 Williams and his wife, Mary, arrived in Boston aboard the ship *Lyon*. He had graduated from Cambridge University in 1627 and sometime before 1629 took holy orders and served as a chaplain to Sir William Masham at Otis in Essex County. It was there that Williams's interest in church reform developed. Years later he said that it was Archbishop Laud (who required an oath of loyalty to the Church of England from all ministers) who "pursued" him "out of this land." When he refused a call to the prestigious First Church of Boston because he "durst not officiate to an unseparated people," Massachusetts authorities must have had their first inkling of just how assured Williams was in matters of belief. It was in October 1635 that he was first accused of holding "new and dangerous opinions against the authority of magistrates."

The Massachusetts authorities did not cite Williams's attitude toward the American Indians in their charges against him, but like most of his postures, his attitude was antithetical to their own. From the beginning, he wrote, his "soul's desire was to do the natives good, and to that end to have their language." Although he was not interested in assimilating their culture, Williams nevertheless saw that the American Indians were no better or worse than the "rogues" who dealt with them, and that in fact they possessed a marked degree of civility. Williams must have known that when he prepared his *Key into the Language of America* (1634) his book would benefit those who wished to convert Native Americans to Christianity, but Williams was not primarily interested in the conversion of others. *Anyone* not regenerate was, Williams argued, outside the people of God, and to refer to the American Indians as "heathen" was "improperly sinful" and "unchristianly." Williams himself remained a Seeker and detached from the community of any church for the greater part of his life. His great disappointment, however, was that in spite of his efforts to befriend the Narragansetts, they joined their brothers in King Philip's War and burned the settlements at both Warwick and Providence. By the time Williams died, sometime between January and March of 1683, the question of Native Americans became moot. The great Narragansett tribe would never recover from the toll taken during that war.

From A Key into the Language of America[1]

To My Dear and Well-Beloved Friends and Countrymen, in Old and New England

I present you with a key; I have not heard of the like, yet framed, since it pleased God to bring that mighty continent of America to light. Others of my countrymen have often, and excellently, and lately written of the country (and none that I know beyond the goodness and worth of it).

This key, respects the native language of it, and happily may unlock some rarities concerning the natives themselves, not yet discovered.

I drew the materials in a rude lump at sea, as a private help to my own memory, that I might not, by my present absence, lightly lose what I had so dearly bought in some few years hardship, and charges among the barbarians. Yet being reminded by some, what pity it were to bury those materials in my grave at land or sea; and withal, remembering how oft I have been importuned by worthy friends of all sorts, to afford them some helps this way. I resolved (by the assistance of The Most High) to cast those materials into this key, pleasant and profitable for all, but especially for my friends residing in those parts.

A little key may open a box, where lies a bunch of keys.

With this I have entered into the secrets of those countries, wherever English dwell about two hundred miles, between the French and Dutch plantations; for want of this, I know what gross mistakes myself and others have run into.

There is a mixture of this language north and south, from the place of my abode, about six hundred miles; yet within the two hundred miles (aforementioned) their dialects do exceedingly differ; yet not so, but (within that compass) a man may, by this help, converse with thousands of natives all over the country: and by such converse it may please the Father of Mercies to spread civility, (and in His own most holy season) Christianity. For one candle will light ten

---

1. The text used here is a reprint of the 1st edition (1643), reprinted by the Rhode Island and Providence Tercentenary Committee (1936).

thousand, and it may please God to bless a little leaven to season the mighty lump of those peoples and territories.

It is expected, that having had so much converse with these natives, I should write some little of them.

Concerning them (a little to gratify expectation) I shall touch upon four heads:

First, by what names they are distinguished.

Secondly, their original[2] and descent.

Thirdly, their religion, manners, customs, etc.

Fourthly, that great point of their conversion.

To the first, their names are of two sorts:

First, those of the English giving: as natives, savages, Indians, wildmen, (so the Dutch call them *wilden*) Abergeny[3] men, pagans, barbarians, heathen.

Secondly, their names which they give themselves.

I cannot observe that they ever had (before the coming of the English, French or Dutch amongst them) any names to difference themselves from strangers, for they knew none; but two sorts of names they had, and have amongst themselves:

First, general, belonging to all natives, as Nínnuock, Ninnimissinnûwock, Eniskeetompaũwog, which signifies Men, Folk, or People.

Secondly, particular names, peculiar to several nations, of them amongst themselves, as Nanhiggenêuck, Massachusêuck, Cawasumsêuck, Cowwesêuck, Quintikóock, Qunnipiēuck, Pequttóog, etc.

They have often asked me, why we call them Indians, natives, etc. And understanding the reason, they will call themselves Indians, in opposition to English, etc.

For the second head proposed, their original and descent:

From Adam and Noah[4] that they spring, it is granted on all hands.

But for their later descent, and whence they came into those parts, it seems as hard to find, as to find the wellhead of some fresh stream, which running many miles out of the country to the salt ocean, hath met with many mixing streams by the way. They say themselves, that they have sprung and grown up in that very place, like the very trees of the wilderness.

They say that their great god Kautántowwìt created those parts, as I observed in the chapter of their religion. They have no clothes, books, nor letters, and conceive their fathers never had; and therefore they are easily persuaded that the God that made Englishmen is a greater God, because He hath so richly endowed the English above themselves. But when they hear that about sixteen hundred years ago, England and the inhabitants thereof were like unto themselves, and since have received from God, clothes, books, etc. they are greatly affected with a secret hope concerning themselves.

Wise and judicious men, with whom I have discoursed, maintain their original to be northward from Tartaria:[5] and at my now taking ship, at the Dutch plantation, it pleased the Dutch Governor, (in some discourse with me about the natives), to draw their line from Iceland, because the name Sackmakan (the name for an Indian prince, about the Dutch) is the name for a prince in Iceland.

---

2. Place of origin.

3. Aboriginal.

4. After the great flood described in the Bible only

Noah and his family remain.

5. Mongolia.

Other opinions I could number up: under favor I shall present (not mine opinion, but) my observations to the judgment of the wise.

First, others (and myself) have conceived some of their words to hold affinity with the Hebrew.

Secondly, they constantly anoint their heads as the Jews did.

Thirdly, they give dowries for their wives, as the Jews did.

Fourthly (and which I have not so observed amongst other nations as amongst the Jews, and these:) they constantly separate their women (during the time of their monthly sickness) in a little house alone by themselves four or five days, and hold it an irreligious thing for either father or husband or any male to come near them.

They have often asked me if it be so with women of other nations, and whether they are so separated: and for their practice they plead nature and tradition. Yet again I have found a greater affinity of their language with the Greek tongue.

2. As the Greeks and other nations, and ourselves call the seven stars (or Charles' Wain, the Bear,)[6] so do they Mosk or Paukunnawaw, the Bear.

3. They have many strange relations of one Wétucks, a man that wrought great miracles amongst them, and walking upon the waters, etc., with some kind of broken resemblance to the Son of God.

Lastly, it is famous that the Sowwest (Sowaniu) is the great subject of their discourse. From thence their traditions. There they say (at the southwest) is the court of their great god Kautántowwìt: at the southwest are their forefathers' souls: to the southwest they go themselves when they die; from the southwest came their corn, and beans out of their great god Kautántowwìt's field: and indeed the further northward and westward from us their corn will not grow, but to the southward better and better. I dare not conjecture in these uncertainties. I believe they are lost, and yet hope (in the Lord's holy season) some of the wildest of them shall be found to share in the blood of the Son of God. To the third head, concerning their religion, customs, manners etc. I shall here say nothing, because in those 32 chapters of the whole book,[7] I have briefly touched those of all sorts, from their birth to their burials, and have endeavored (as the nature of the work would give way) to bring some short observations and applications home to Europe from America.

Therefore fourthly, to that great point of their conversion, so much to be longed for, and by all New-English so much pretended,[8] and I hope in truth.

For myself I have uprightly labored to suit my endeavors to my pretenses: and of later times (out of desire to attain their language) I have run through varieties of intercourses[9] with them day and night, summer and winter, by land and sea, particular passages tending to this, I have related divers, in the chapter of their religion.

Many solemn discourses I have had with all sorts of nations of them, from one end of the country to another (so far as opportunity, and the little language I have could reach).

I know there is no small preparation in the hearts of multitudes of them. I know their many solemn confessions to myself, and one to another of their lost wandering conditions.

6. I.e., the constellation known as Ursa Major (Great Bear), the Big Dipper, or Charlemagne's wagon ("wain").

7. I.e., the thirty-two chapters of Williams's A Key.

8. Asserted, proffered (with none of the modern connotations of deceit).

9. Conversations.

I know strong convictions upon the consciences of many of them, and their desires uttered that way.

I know not with how little knowledge and grace of Christ the Lord may save, and therefore, neither will despair, nor report much.

But since it hath pleased some of my worthy countrymen to mention (of late in print) Wequash, the Péquot captain, I shall be bold so far to second their relations, as to relate mine own hopes of him (though I dare not be so confident as others).

Two days before his death, as I passed up to Qunníhticut[1] River, it pleased my worthy friend Mr. Fenwick, (whom I visited at his house in Saybrook Fort at the mouth of that river,) to tell me that my old friend Wequash lay very sick. I desired to see him, and himself was pleased to be my guide two miles where Wequash lay.

Amongst other discourse concerning his sickness and death (in which he freely bequeathed his son to Mr. Fenwick) I closed[2] with him concerning his soul: he told me that some two or three years before he had lodged at my house, where I acquainted him with the condition of all mankind, & his own in particular; how God created man and all things; how man fell from God, and of his present enmity against God, and the wrath of God against him until repentance. Said he, "your words were never out of my heart to this present;" and said he "me much pray to Jesus Christ." I told him so did many English, French, and Dutch, who had never turned to God, nor loved Him. He replied in broken English: "Me so big naughty heart, me heart all one stone!" Savory expressions using to breathe from compunct and broken hearts, and a sense of inward hardness and unbrokenness. I had many discourses with him in his life, but this was the sum of our last parting until our General Meeting.[3]

Now, because this is the great inquiry of all men: what Indians have been converted? what have the English done in those parts? what hopes of the Indians receiving the knowledge of Christ?

And because to this question, some put an edge from the boast of the Jesuits in Canada and Maryland, and especially from the wonderful conversions made by the Spaniards and Portugals in the West-Indies, besides what I have here written, as also, beside what I have observed in the chapter of their religion, I shall further present you with a brief additional discourse concerning this great point, being comfortably persuaded that that Father of Spirits, who was graciously pleased to persuade Japhet[4] (the Gentiles) to dwell in the tents of Shem[5] (the Jews), will, in His holy season (I hope approaching), persuade these Gentiles of America to partake of the mercies of Europe, and then shall be fulfilled what is written by the prophet Malachi,[6] from the rising of the sun (in Europe) to the going down of the same (in America), My name shall be great among the Gentiles. So I desire to hope and pray,

Your unworthy countryman,

ROGER WILLIAMS

---

1. Connecticut.
2. Came to the end of his talk.
3. I.e., Judgment Day.
4. The third son of Noah and, in some traditions, the progenitor of the Indo-European race (see Genesis 9.18).
5. The eldest son of Noah.
6. "For from the rising of the sun even unto the going down of the same my name shall be great among the Gentiles" (Malachi 1.11).

Directions for the Use of the Language

1. A dictionary or grammar way I had consideration of, but purposely avoided, as not so accommodate to the benefit of all, as I hope this form is.

2. A dialogue also I had thoughts of, but avoided for brevity's sake, and yet (with no small pains) I have so framed every chapter and the matter of it, as I may call it an implicit dialogue.

3. It is framed chiefly after the *Narragansett* dialect, because most spoken in the country, and yet (with attending to the variation of peoples and dialects) it will be of great use in all parts of the country.

4. Whatever your occasion be, either of travel, discourse, trading etc. turn to the table which will direct you to the proper chapter.

5. Because the life of all language is in the pronunciation, I have been at the pains and charges to cause the accents, tones or sounds to be affixed, (which some understand, according to the Greek language, acutes, graves, circumflexes) for example, in the second leaf[7] in the word *Ewò He*: the sound or tone must not be put on *E*, but *wò* where the grave accent is.

In the same leaf, in the word *Ascowequássin*, the sound must not be on any of the syllables, but on *quáss*, where the acute or sharp sound is.

In the same leaf in the word *Anspaumpmaûntam*, the sound must not be on any other syllable but *maûn*, where the circumflex or long sounding accent is.

6. The English for every Indian word or phrase stands in a straight line directly against the Indian: yet sometimes there are two words for the same thing (for their language is exceeding copious, and they have five or six words sometimes for one thing) and then the English stands against them both: for example in the second leaf:

Cowáunckamish & Cuckquénamish | I pray your favor.

An Help to the Native Language of that Part of America Called New England

From CHAPTER XXI. OF RELIGION, THE SOUL, ETC.

Manìt-manittó, wock. | God, Gods.

Obs. He that questions whether God made the world, the Indians will teach him. I must acknowledge I have received in my converse[8] with them many confirmations of those two great points, Hebrews II. 6. viz:

1. That God is.

2. That He is a rewarder of all them that diligently seek Him.

They will generally confess that God made all, but them in special, although they deny not that Englishman's God made Englishmen, and the heavens and earth there! yet their Gods made them and the heaven, and earth where they dwell.

Nummusquauna-múckqun manìt. | God is angry with me?

Obs. I have heard a poor Indian lamenting the loss of a child at break of day, call up his wife and children, and all about him to lamentation, and with abundance of tears cry out! "O God thou hast taken away my child! thou art

---

7. Page.   8. Conversation.

angry with me: O turn Thine anger from me, and spare the rest of my children."

If they receive any good in hunting, fishing, harvest etc. they acknowledge God in it.

Yea, if it be but an ordinary accident, a fall, etc. they will say God was angry and did it, *musquàntum manit* God is angry. But herein is their misery:

First, they branch their God-head into many gods.

Secondly, attribute it to creatures.

First, many gods: they have given me the names of thirty seven which I have, all which in their solemn worships they invocate, as:

Kautántowwìt the great Southwest God, to whose house all souls go, and from whom came their corn, beans, as they say.

Wompanand.	The Eastern God.
Chekesuwànd.	The Western God.
Wunnanaméanit.	The Northern God.
Sowwanànd.	The Southern God.
Wetuómanit.	The House God.

Even as the papists have their he and she saint protectors as St. George, St. Patrick, St. Denis, Virgin Mary, etc.

Squáuanit.	The Woman's God.
Muckquachuckquànd.	The Children's God.

Obs. I was once with a native dying of a wound, given him by some murderous English who robbed him and ran him through with a rapier, from whom in the heat of his wound, he at present escaped from them, but dying of his wound, they suffered death at New Plymouth, in New England, this native dying called much upon *Muckquachuckquànd*, which of other natives I understood (as they believed) had appeared to the dying young man, many years before, and bid him whenever he was in distress call upon him.

Secondly, as they have many of these fained deities; so worship they the creatures in whom they conceive doth rest some deity:

Keesuckquànd.	The Sun God.
Nanepaûshat.	The Moon God.
Paumpágussit.	The Sea.
Yotáanit.	The Fire God.

Supposing that deities be in these, etc.

* * *

They have a modest religious persuasion not to disturb any man, either themselves English, Dutch, or any in their conscience, and worship, and therefore say:

Aquiewopwaūwash.	Peace, hold your peace.
Aquiewopwaūwock.	
Peeyàuntam.	He is at prayer.
Peeyaúntamwock	They are praying.
Cowwéwonck.	The soul.

Derived from *cowwene* to sleep, because say they, it works and operates when the body sleeps. *Míchachunck*, the soul, in a higher notion which is of affinity, with a word signifying a looking glass, or clear resemblance, so that it hath its name from a clear sight or discerning, which indeed seems very well to suit with the nature of it.

Wuhóck.	The body
Nohòck: cohòck	My body, your body
Awaunkeesitteoúwincohòck:	
Tunna-awwa commítchichunck-	Whether goes your soul when you
kitonckquèan?	die?
An. *Sowánakitaúwaw.*	It goes to the southwest.

Obs. They believe that the souls of men and women go to the southwest, their great and good men and women to Kautántowwìt, his house, where they have hopes (as the Turks have of carnal joys). Murderers, thieves and liars, their souls (say they) wander restless abroad.

Now because this book (by God's good providence) may come into the hand of many fearing God, who may also have many an opportunity of occasional discourse with some of these, their wild brethren and sisters, and may speak a word for their and our glorious Maker, which may also prove some preparatory mercy to their souls: I shall propose some proper expressions concerning the creation of the world, and man's estate, and in particular theirs also, which from myself many hundreds of times, great numbers of them have heard with great delight, and great convictions; which, who knows (in God's holy season), may rise to the exalting of the Lord Jesus Christ in their conversion, and salvation?

Nétop Kunnatótemous.	Friend, I will ask you a question.
Natótema:	Speak on.
Tocketunnântum?	What think you?
Awaun Keesiteoûwin Kéesuck?	Who made the heavens?
Aûke Wechêkom?	The earth, the sea?
Míttauke.	The world.

Some will answer *Tattá*, I cannot tell, some will answer *Manittôwock*, the gods.

Tà suóg Maníttôwock	How many gods be there?
Maunaŭog Mishaúnawock.	Many, great many.
Nétop machàge.	Friend, not so.
Paŭsuck naŭnt manìt.	There is only one God.
Cuppíssittone.	You are mistaken.
Cowauwaúnemun.	You are out of the way.

A phrase which much pleaseth them, being proper for their wandering in the woods, and similitudes greatly please them.

Kukkakótemous, wâchit-quáshouwe.	I will tell you, presently.
Kuttaunchemókous.	I will tell you news.
Paûsuck naŭnt manit kéesittin	One only God made the heavens etc.
keesuck, etc.	
Napannetashèmittan	Five thousand years ago and
naugecautúmmonab nshque.	upwards.
Naŭgom naŭnt wukkesittínnes wâme	He alone made all things.
teâgun.	
Wuche mateâg.	Out of nothing.
Quttatashuchuckqún-nacaus-	In six days He made all things.
keesitínnes wâme.	
Nquittaqúnne.	The first day He made the light.
Wuckéesitin wequâi.	

Néesqunne.	The second day He made the firmament.
Wuckéesitin Keésuck.	
Shúckqunnewuckéesitin Aūke kà wechêkom.	The third day He made the earth and sea.
Yóqunne wuckkéesitin Nippaūus kà Nanepaūshat.	The fourth day He made the sun and the moon.
Neenash-mamockíuwash wêquanantíganash.	Two great lights.
Kà wáme anócksuck.	And all the stars.
Napannetashúckqunne Wuckéesittin pussuckseésuck wâme.	The fifth day He made all the fowl.
Keesuckquíuke	In the air, or heavens.
Ka wáme namaūsuck.	And all the fish in the sea.
Wechekommíuke.	
Quttatashúkqunne wuckkeésittin penashímwock wamè.	The sixth day He made all the beasts of the field.
Wuttàke wuchè wuckeesittin pausuck Enìn, or, Eneskéetomp.	Last of all he made one man.
Wuche mishquòck.	Of red earth,
Ka wesuonckgonnakaûnes Adam, túppautea mishquòck.	And called him Adam, or red earth.
Wuttàke wuchè, Câwit míshquock,	Then afterward, while Adam, or red earth, slept,
Wuckaudnúmmenes manìt peetaūgon wuche Adam.	God took a rib from Adam, or red earth.
Kà wuchè peteaúgon. Wukkeesitínnes pausuck squàw.	And of that rib he made one woman.
Kà pawtouwúnnes Adâmuck	And brought her to Adam.
Nawônt Adam wuttúnnawaun nuppeteâgon ewò.	When Adam saw her, he said, "This is my bone."
Enadatashúckqunne, aquêi,	The seventh day He rested,
Nagaû wuchè quttatashúckqune anacaûsuock Englishmánuck.	And, therefore, Englishmen work six days
Enadatashuckqunnóckat taubataūmwock.	On the seventh day they praise God.

Obs. At this relation they are much satisfied, with a reason why (as they observe) the English and Dutch, etc, labor six days, and rest and worship the seventh.

Besides, they will say, we never heard of this before: and then will relate how they have it from their fathers, that Kautántowwìt made one man and woman of a stone, which disliking, he broke them in pieces, and made another man and woman of a tree, which were the fountains of all mankind.

*   *   *

From The Bloody Tenet of Persecution, for Cause of Conscience, in a Conference between Truth and Peace[1]

To every Courteous Reader.

While I plead the cause of *truth* and *innocency* against the bloody *doctrine* of *persecution* for cause of *conscience*, I judge it not unfit to give *alarm* to myself, and all men to prepare to be *persecuted* or hunted for cause of *conscience*.

Whether thou standest charged with ten or but two talents,[2] if thou huntest any for cause of *conscience*, how canst thou say thou followest the *Lamb of God* who so abhorred that practice?

If Paul, if Jesus Christ, were present here at London, and the question were proposed what religion would they approve of: the Papists, Prelatists,[3] Presbyterians, Independents, etc. would each say, "Of mine, of mine."

But put the second question, if one of the several sorts should by major vote attain the sword of steel: what weapons doth Christ Jesus authorize them to fight with in His cause? Do not all men hate the persecutor, and every conscience true or false complain of cruelty, tyranny? etc.

Two mountains of crying guilt lie heavy upon the backs of all that name the name of Christ in the eyes of Jews, Turks and Pagans.

First, the blasphemies of their idolatrous inventions, superstitions, and most unchristian conversations.

Secondly, the bloody, irreligious and inhumane oppressions and destructions under the mask or veil of the name of Christ, etc.

O how like is the jealous Jehovah, the consuming fire to end these present slaughters in a greater slaughter of the holy witnesses? Revelation 11.

Six years preaching of so much truth of Christ (as that time afforded in King Edward's days) kindles the flames of Queen Mary's bloody persecutions.[4]

Who can now but expect that after so many scores of years preaching and professing of more truth, and amongst so many great contentions amongst the very best of Protestants, a fiery furnace should be heat, and who sees not now the fires kindling?

I confess I have little hopes till those flames are over, that this discourse against the doctrine of persecution for cause of conscience should pass current (I say not amongst the wolves and lions, but even amongst the sheep of Christ themselves) yet *liberavi animam meam*,[5] I have not hid within my breast my soul's belief; and although sleeping on the bed either of the pleasures or profits of sin thou thinkest thy conscience bound to smite at him that dares to waken thee? Yet in the midst of all these civil and spiritual wars[6] I hope we shall agree in these particulars.

First, however, the proud (upon the advantage of an higher earth or ground) overlook the poor and cry out schismatics, heretics, etc. shall blasphemers and seducers escape unpunished, etc. Yet there is a sorer punishment in the Gos-

---

1. The text used here is from *The Writings of Roger Williams*, vol. 3 (1866–74). Williams wrote this tract while in London attempting to get a patent for Providence Plantation. It is one of a series of tracts in which Williams debated John Cotton on the question of freedom of conscience. Neither the author's name or the publisher appeared on the title page and copies were burned by order of Parliament because of its democratic implications.
2. Here meaning simply "individuals."
3. Episcopalians.
4. Edward VI (r. 1547–53) and Queen Mary (r. 1553–58). Many Protestants were burned at the stake during the reign of Queen Mary.
5. I have freed my soul (Latin).
6. Civil war had broken out in England in 1642.

pel for despising of Christ than Moses, even when the despiser of Moses was put to death without mercy, Hebrews 10.28–29. "He that believeth not shall be damned," Mark 16.16.

Secondly, whatever worship, ministry, ministration, the best and purest are practiced without faith and true persuasion that they are the true institutions of God, they are sin, sinful worships, ministries, etc. And however in civil things we may be servants unto men, yet in divine and spiritual things the poorest peasant must disdain the service of the highest prince: "Be ye not the servants of men," I Corinthians 14.

Thirdly, without search and trial no man attains this faith and right persuasion, I Thessalonians 5. "Try all things."

In vain have English Parliaments permitted English Bibles in the poorest English houses, and the simplest man or woman to search the Scriptures, if yet against their soul's persuasion from the Scripture, they should be forced (as if they lived in Spain or Rome itself without the sight of a Bible) to believe as the Church believes.

Fourthly, having tried, we must hold fast, I Thessalonians 5. upon the loss of a crown, Revelation 13. we must not let go for all the flea bitings of the present afflictions, etc. having bought truth dear, we must not sell it cheap, not the least grain of it for the whole world, no not for the saving of souls, though our own most precious; least of all for the bitter sweetening of a little vanishing pleasure.

For a little puff of credit and reputation from the changeable breath of uncertain sons of men.

For the broken bags of riches on eagles' wings: For a dream of these, any or all of these which on our deathbed vanish and leave tormenting stings behind them: Oh, how much better is it from the love of truth, from the love of the Father of Lights, from whence it comes, from the love of the Son of God, who is the way and the truth, to say as He, John 18.37: "For this end was I born, and for this end came I into the world that I might bear witness to the truth."

1643–44   1644

A Letter to the Town of Providence[1]

That ever I should speak or write a tittle,[2] that tends to such an infinite liberty of conscience, is a mistake, and which I have ever disclaimed and abhorred. To prevent such mistakes, I shall at present only propose this case: There goes many a ship to sea, with many hundred souls in one ship, whose weal and woe is common, and is a true picture of a commonwealth, or a human combination or society. It hath fallen out sometimes, that both Papists and Protestants, Jews and Turks, may be embarked in one ship; upon which supposal I affirm, that all the liberty of conscience, that ever I pleaded for, turns upon these two hinges—that none of the Papists, Protestants, Jews, or Turks be forced to come to the ship's prayers or worship, nor compelled from

1. The text used here is from *The Writings of Roger Williams*, vol. 6 (1866–74). Williams wrote this letter after his return to Providence from England in 1654 in hopes of settling a controversy that divided the town over the question of religious autonomy and civil restraint.
2. I.e., write as much as a dot, the smallest part.

their own particular prayers or worship, if they practice any. I further add, that I never denied, that notwithstanding this liberty, the commander of this ship ought to command the ship's course, yea, and also command that justice, peace, and sobriety be kept and practiced, both among the seamen and all the passengers. If any of the seamen refuse to perform their services, or passengers to pay their freight; if any refuse to help, in person or purse, towards the common charges or defence; if any refuse to obey the common laws and orders of the ship, concerning their common peace or preservation; if any shall mutiny and rise up against their commanders and officers; if any should preach or write that there ought to be no commanders or officers, because all are equal in Christ, therefore no masters nor officers, no laws nor orders, nor corrections nor punishments; I say, I never denied, but in such cases, whatever is pretended, the commander or commanders may judge, resist, compel, and punish such transgressors, according to their deserts and merits. This if seriously and honestly minded, may, if it so please the Father of Lights, let in some light to such as willingly shut not their eyes.

I remain studious of your common peace and liberty.

ROGER WILLIAMS

1655   1874

ANNE BRADSTREET
c. 1612–1672

Anne Bradstreet's father, Thomas Dudley, was the manager of the country estate of the Puritan earl of Lincoln, and his daughter was very much the apple of his eye. He took great care to see that she received an education superior to that of most young women of the time. When she was only sixteen she married a young man, Simon Bradstreet, a recent graduate of Cambridge University, who was associated with her father in conducting the affairs of the earl of Lincoln's estate. He also shared her father's Puritan beliefs. A year after the marriage her husband was appointed to assist in the preparations of the Massachusetts Bay Company, and the following year the Bradstreets and the Dudleys sailed with Winthrop's fleet. Bradstreet tells us that when she first "came into this country" she "found a new world and new manners," at which her "heart rose" in resistance. "But after I was convinced it was the way of God, I submitted to it and joined the church at Boston."

We know very little of Bradstreet's daily life, except that it was a hard existence. The wilderness, Samuel Eliot Morison once observed, "made men stern and silent, children unruly, servants insolent." William Bradford's wife, Dorothy, staring at the barren dunes of Cape Cod is said to have preferred the surety of drowning to the unknown life ashore. Added to the hardship of daily living was the fact that Bradstreet was never very strong. She had rheumatic fever as a child and as a result suffered recurrent periods of severe fatigue; nevertheless, she risked death by childbirth eight times. Her husband was secretary to the company and later governor of the Bay Colony; he was always involved in the colony's diplomatic missions; and in 1661 he went to England to renegotiate the Bay Company charter with Charles II. All of Simon's tasks must have added to her responsibilities at home. And like any good Puritan she added to the care of daily life the examination of her conscience. She tells us in one of the "Meditations" written for her children that she was troubled many times about the truth of the Scriptures, that she never saw any convincing miracles, and that she always wondered if those of which she read "were feigned." What proved to her finally that God exists was not her reading but the evidence of her own eyes. She is the first in a long line of American poets who took their consolation not from theology but from the "wondrous works," as she wrote, "that I see, the vast frame of the heaven and the earth, the order of all things, night and day, summer and winter, spring and autumn, the daily providing for this great household upon the earth, the preserving and directing of all to its proper end."

When Bradstreet was a young girl she had written poems to please her father, and he made much of their reading them together. After her marriage she continued writing. Quite unknown to her, her brother-in-law, John Woodbridge, pastor of the Andover church, brought with him to London a manuscript collection of her poetry and had it printed there in 1650. It was the first published volume of poems written by a resident in the New World and was widely read. Reverend Edward Taylor, also a poet, and living in the frontier community of Westfield, Massachusetts, had a copy of the second edition of Bradstreet's poems (1678) in his library. Although she herself probably took greatest pride in her long meditative poems on the ages of humankind and on the seasons, the poems that have attracted present-day readers are the more intimate ones, which reflect her concern for her family and home and the pleasures she took in everyday life rather than in the life to come.

The text used is the *Works of Anne Bradstreet*, edited by Jeannine Hensley (1967).

The Prologue

1

To sing of wars, of captains, and of kings,
Of cities founded, commonwealths begun,
For my mean[1] pen are too superior things:
Or how they all, or each their dates have run
Let poets and historians set these forth,   5
My obscure lines shall not so dim their worth.

2

But when my wond'ring eyes and envious heart
Great Bartas'[2] sugared lines do but read o'er,
Fool[3] I do grudge the Muses[4] did not part
'Twixt him and me that overfluent store;   10
A Bartas can do what a Bartas will
But simple I according to my skill.

3

From schoolboy's tongue no rhet'ric we expect,
Nor yet a sweet consort[5] from broken strings,
Nor perfect beauty where's a main defect: 15
My foolish, broken, blemished Muse so sings,

1. Humble.
2. Guillaume du Bartas (1544–1590) was a French writer much admired by the Puritans. He was most famous as the author of *The Divine Weeks*, an epic poem translated by Joshua Sylvester and intended to recount the great moments in Christian history.
3. I.e., like a fool.
4. In Greek mythology, the nine goddesses of the arts and sciences.
5. Accord, harmony of sound.

And this to mend, alas, no art is able,
'Cause nature made it so irreparable.

4

Nor can I, like that fluent sweet tongued Greek,
Who lisped at first, in future times speak plain.[6]   20
By art he gladly found what he did seek,
A full requital of his striving pain.
Art can do much, but this maxim's most sure:
A weak or wounded brain admits no cure.

5

I am obnoxious to each carping tongue   25
Who says my hand a needle better fits,
A poet's pen all scorn I should thus wrong,
For such despite they cast on female wits:
If what I do prove well, it won't advance,
They'll say it's stol'n, or else it was by chance.   30

6

But sure the antique Greeks were far more mild
Else of our sex, why feigned they those nine
And poesy made Calliope's[7] own child;
So 'mongst the rest they placed the arts divine:
But this weak knot they will full soon untie.   35
The Greeks did nought, but play the fools and lie.

7

Let Greeks be Greeks, and women what they are;
Men have precedency and still excel,
It is but vain unjustly to wage war,
Men can do best, and women know it well   40
Preeminence in all and each is yours;
Yet grant some small acknowledgment of ours.

8

And oh ye high flown quills[8] that soar the skies,
And ever with your prey still catch your praise,
If e'er you deign these lowly lines your eyes   45
Give thyme or parsley wreath, I ask no bays;[9]
This mean and unrefined ore of mine
Will make your glist'ring gold but more to shine.

1650

To the Memory of My Dear and Ever Honored Father Thomas Dudley Esq. Who Deceased, July 31, 1653, and of His Age 77

By duty bound and not by custom led
To celebrate the praises of the dead,
My mournful mind, sore pressed, in trembling verse
Presents my lamentations at his hearse,

6. The Greek orator Demosthenes (c. 383–322 B.C.) conquered a speech defect.
7. The muse of epic poetry.

8. Pens.
9. Garlands of laurel, used to crown the head of a poet.

Who was my father, guide, instructor too, 5
To whom I ought whatever I could do.
Nor is't relation near my hand shall tie;
For who more cause to boast his worth than I?
Who heard or saw, observed or knew him better?
Or who alive than I a greater debtor? 10
Let malice bite and envy gnaw its fill,
He was my father, and I'll praise him still.
Nor was his name or life lead so obscure
That pity might some trumpeters procure
Who after death might make him falsely seem 15
Such as in life no man could justly deem.
Well known and loved, where e'er he lived, by most
Both in his native and in foreign coast,
These to the world his merits could make known,
So needs no testimonial from his own; 20
But now or never I must pay my sum;
While others tell his worth, I'll not be dumb.
One of thy Founders,[1] him New England know,
Who stayed thy feeble sides when thou wast low,
Who spent his state,[2] his strength and years with care 25
That after-comers in them might have share.
True patriot of this little commonweal,
Who is't can tax thee ought, but for thy zeal?
Truth's friend thou wert, to errors still a foe,
Which caused apostates to malign so. 30
Thy love to true religion e'er shall shine;
My father's God, be God of me and mine.
Upon the earth he did not build his nest,
But as a pilgrim, what he had, possessed.
High thoughts he gave no harbor in his heart, 35
Nor honors puffed him up when he had part;
Those titles loathed, which some too much do love,
For truly his ambition lay above.
His humble mind so loved humility,
He left it to his race for legacy; 40
And oft and oft with speeches mild and wise
Gave his in charge that jewel rich to prize.
No ostentation seen in all his ways,
An in the mean ones of our foolish days,
Which all they have and more still set to view, 45
Their greatness may be judged by what they shew.
His thoughts were more sublime, his actions wise,
Such vanities he justly did despise.
Nor wonder 'twas, low things ne'er much did move
For he a mansion had, prepared above, 50
For which he sighed and prayed and longed full sore
He might be clothed upon for evermore.
Oft spake of death, and with a smiling cheer
He did exult his end was drawing near;

1. Thomas Dudley came to Massachusetts in 1630.   2. Short for "estate," position in life.

Now fully ripe, as shock of wheat that's grown,   55
Death as a sickle hath him timely mown,
And in celestial barn hath housed him high,
Where storms, nor show'rs, nor ought can damnify.
His generation served, his labors cease;
And to his fathers gathered is in peace.   60
Ah happy soul, 'mongst saints and angels blesst,
Who after all his toil is now at rest.
His hoary[3] head in righteousness was found;
As joy in heaven, on earth let praise resound.
Forgotten never be his memory,   65
His blessing rest on his posterity;
His pious footsteps, followed by his race,
At last will bring us to that happy place
Where we with joy each other's face shall see,
And parted more by death shall never be.   70

His Epitaph

Within this tomb a patriot lies
That was both pious, just, and wise,
To truth a shield, to right a wall,
To sectaries a whip and maul,[4]
A magazine[5] of history,   75
A prizer of good company,
In manners pleasant and severe;
The good him loved, the bad did fear,
And when his time with years was spent,
If some rejoiced, more did lament.   80

1678

To Her Father with Some Verses

Most truly honored, and as truly dear,
If worth in me or ought[1] I do appear,
Who can of right better demand the same
Than may your worthy self from whom it came?
The principal[2] might yield a greater sum,   5
Yet handled ill, amounts but to this crumb;
My stock's so small I know not how to pay,
My bond[3] remains in force unto this day;
Yet for part payment take this simple mite,[4]
Where nothing's to be had, kings loose their right.   10
Such is my debt I may not say forgive,
But as I can, I'll pay it while I live;

---

3. Gray-haired.
4. Hammer or club. "Sectaries": opposing believers.
5. Storehouse.
1. Anything at all.

2. The capital that yields interest.
3. I.e., contract.
4. The smallest possible denomination.

Such is my bond, none can discharge but I,
Yet paying is not paid until I die.

1678

Contemplations

1

Some time now past in the autumnal tide,
When Phoebus[1] wanted but one hour to bed,
The trees all richly clad, yet void of pride,
Were gilded o'er by his rich golden head.
Their leaves and fruits seemed painted, but was true,   5
Of green, of red, of yellow, mixed hue;
Rapt were my senses at this delectable view.

2

I wist not what to wish, yet sure thought I,
If so much excellence abide below,
How excellent is He that dwells on high,   10
Whose power and beauty by His works we know?
Sure He is goodness, wisdom, glory, light,
That hath this under world so richly dight;[2]
More heaven than earth was here, no winter and no night.

3

Then on a stately oak I cast mine eye,   15
Whose ruffling top the clouds seemed to aspire;
How long since thou wast in thine infancy?
Thy strength, and stature, more thy years admire,
Hath hundred winters past since thou wast born?
Or thousand since thou brakest thy shell of horn?   20
If so, all these as nought, eternity doth scorn.

4

Then higher on the glistering Sun I gazed.
Whose beams was shaded by the leafy tree;
The more I looked, the more I grew amazed,
And softly said, "What glory's like to thee?"   25
Soul of this world, this universe's eye,
No wonder some made thee a deity;
Had I not better known, alas, the same had I.

5

Thou as a bridegroom from thy chamber rushes,
And as a strong man, joys to run a race;[3]   30
The morn doth usher thee with smiles and blushes;
The Earth reflects her glances in thy face.
Birds, insects, animals with vegative,
Thy heat from death and dullness doth revive,
And in the darksome womb of fruitful nature dive.   35

---

1. Apollo, the sun god.
2. Furnished, adorned.
3. The sun "is as a bridegroom coming out of his

chamber, and rejoiceth as a strong man to run a race"
(Psalm 19.5).

6

Thy swift annual and diurnal course,
Thy daily straight and yearly oblique path,
Thy pleasing fervor and thy scorching force,
All mortals here the feeling knowledge hath.
Thy presence makes it day, thy absence night,   40
Quaternal seasons caused by thy might:
Hail creature, full of sweetness, beauty, and delight.

7

Art thou so full of glory that no eye
Hath strength thy shining rays once to behold?
And is thy splendid throne erect so high,   45
As to approach it, can no earthly mold?
How full of glory then must thy Creator be,
Who gave this bright light luster unto thee?
Admired, adored for ever, be that Majesty.

8

Silent alone, where none or saw, or heard,   50
In pathless paths I lead my wand'ring feet,
My humble eyes to lofty skies I reared
To sing some song, my mazéd[4] Muse thought meet.
My great Creator I would magnify,
That nature had thus decked liberally;   55
But Ah, and Ah, again, my imbecility!

9

I heard the merry grasshopper then sing.
The black-clad cricket bear a second part;
They kept one tune and played on the same string,
Seeming to glory in their little art.   60
Shall creatures abject thus their voices raise
And in their kind resound their Maker's praise
Whilst I, as mute, can warble forth no higher lays?

10

When present times look back to ages past,
And men in being fancy those are dead,   65
It makes things gone perpetually to last,
And calls back months and years that long since fled.
It makes a man more aged in conceit
Than was Methuselah,[5] or's grandsire great,
While of their persons and their acts his mind doth treat.   70

11

Sometimes in Eden fair he seems to be,
Sees glorious Adam there made lord of all,
Fancies the apple, dangle on the tree,
That turned his sovereign to a naked thrall.[6]
Who like a miscreant's driven from that place,   75
To get his bread with pain and sweat of face,
A penalty imposed on his backsliding race.

4. Amazed.   of thought.
5. Methuselah was thought to have lived 969 years   6. Slave.
(Genesis 5.27). "Conceit": apprehension, the processes

12

Here sits our grandame in retired place,
And in her lap her bloody Cain new-born;
The weeping imp oft looks her in the face,   80
Bewails his unknown hap[7] and fate forlorn;
His mother sighs to think of Paradise,
And how she lost her bliss to be more wise,
Believing him that was, and is, father of lies.[8]

13

Here Cain and Abel come to sacrifice,   85
Fruits of the earth and fatlings[9] each do bring.
On Abel's gift the fire descends from skies,
But no such sign on false Cain's offering;
With sullen hateful looks he goes his ways,
Hath thousand thoughts to end his brother's days,   90
Upon whose blood his future good he hopes to raise.

14

There Abel keeps his sheep, no ill he thinks;
His brother comes, then acts his fratricide:
The virgin Earth of blood her first draught drinks,
But since that time she often hath been cloyed.   95
The wretch with ghastly face and dreadful mind
Thinks each he sees will serve him in his kind,
Though none on earth but kindred near then could he find.

15

Who fancies not his looks now at the bar,
His face like death, his heart with horror fraught,   100
Nor malefactor ever felt like war,
When deep despair with wish of life hath fought,
Branded with guilt and crushed with treble woes,
A vagabond to Land of Nod[1] he goes.
A city builds, that walls might him secure from foes.   105

16

Who thinks not oft upon the father's ages,
Their long descent, how nephew's sons they saw,
The starry observations of those sages,
And how their precepts to their sons were law,
How Adam sighed to see his progeny,   110
Clothed all in his black sinful livery,
Who neither guilt nor yet the punishment could fly.

17

Our life compare we with their length of days
Who to the tenth of theirs doth now arrive?
And though thus short, we shorten many ways,   115
Living so little while we are alive;
In eating, drinking, sleeping, vain delight
So unawares comes on perpetual night,
And puts all pleasures vain unto eternal flight.

---

7. Fortune, circumstances.
8. By believing in the "father of lies," Eve lost Paradise
(Genesis 3); her elder son, Cain, slew his brother, Abel
(Genesis 4.8).

9. Animals for slaughter.
1. An unidentified region east of Eden where Cain
dwelled after slaying Abel (Genesis 4.16).

18

When I behold the heavens as in their prime,   120
And then the earth (though old) still clad in green,
The stones and trees, insensible of time,
Nor age nor wrinkle on their front are seen;
If winter come and greenness then do fade,
A spring returns, and they more youthful made;   125
But man grows old, lies down, remains where once he's laid.

19

By birth more noble than those creatures all,
Yet seems by nature and by custom cursed,
No sooner born, but grief and care makes fall
That state obliterate he had at first;   130
Nor youth, nor strength, nor wisdom spring again,
Nor habitations long their names retain,
But in oblivion to the final day remain.

20

Shall I then praise the heavens, the trees, the earth
Because their beauty and their strength last longer?   135
Shall I wish there, or never to had birth,
Because they're bigger, and their bodies stronger?
Nay, they shall darken, perish, fade and die,
And when unmade, so ever shall they lie,
But man was made for endless immortality.   140

21

Under the cooling shadow of a stately elm
Close sat I by a goodly river's side,
Where gliding streams the rocks did overwhelm,
A lonely place, with pleasures dignified.
I once that loved the shady woods so well,   145
Now thought the rivers did the trees excel,
And if the sun would ever shine, there would I dwell.

22

While on the stealing stream I fixt mine eye,
Which to the longed-for ocean held its course,
I marked, nor crooks, nor rubs,[2] that there did lie   150
Could hinder aught,[3] but still augment its force.
"O happy flood," quoth I, "that holds thy race
Till thou arrive at thy beloved place,
Nor is it rocks or shoals that can obstruct thy pace,

23

Nor is't enough, that thou alone mayst slide   155
But hundred brooks in thy clear waves do meet,
So hand in hand along with thee they glide
To Thetis' house,[4] where all embrace and greet.
Thou emblem true of what I count the best,
O could I lead my rivulets to rest,   160
So may we press to that vast mansion, ever blest."

2. Difficult ties.   4. I.e., the sea; Thetis was Achilles' mother and a sea
3. Anything.   nymph.

24

Ye fish, which in this liquid region 'bide,
That for each season have your habitation,
Now salt, now fresh where you think best to glide
To unknown coasts to give a visitation,   165
In lakes and ponds you leave your numerous fry;
So nature taught, and yet you know not why,
You wat'ry folk that know not your felicity.

25

Look how the wantons frisk to taste the air,
Then to the colder bottom straight they dive;   170
Eftsoon to Neptune's[5] glassy hall repair
To see what trade they great ones there do drive,
Who forage o'er the spacious sea-green field,
And take the trembling prey before it yield,
Whose armor is their scales, their spreading fins their shield. 175

26

While musing thus with contemplation fed,
And thousand fancies buzzing in my brain,
The sweet-tongued Philomel[6] perched o'er my head
And chanted forth a most melodious strain
Which rapt me so with wonder and delight,   180
I judged my hearing better than my sight,
And wished me wings with her a while to take my flight.

27

"O merry Bird," said I, "that fears no snares,
That neither toils nor hoards up in thy barn,
Feels no sad thoughts nor cruciating[7] cares   185
To gain more good or shun what might thee harm.
Thy clothes ne'er wear, thy meat is everywhere,
Thy bed a bough, thy drink the water clear,
Reminds not what is past, nor what's to come dost fear."

28

"The dawning morn with songs thou dost prevent,[8]   190
Sets hundred notes unto thy feathered crew,
So each one tunes his pretty instrument,
And warbling out the old, begin anew,
And thus they pass their youth in summer season,
Then follow thee into a better region,   195
Where winter's never felt by that sweet airy legion."

29

Man at the best a creature frail and vain,
In knowledge ignorant, in strength but weak,
Subject to sorrows, losses, sickness, pain,
Each storm his state, his mind, his body break,   200
From some of these he never finds cessation,
But day or night, within, without, vexation,
Troubles from foes, from friends, from dearest, near'st relation.

---

5. Roman god of the ocean. "Eftsoon": soon afterward.
6. I.e., the nightingale. Philomela, the daughter of
King Attica, was transformed into a nightingale after
her brother-in-law raped her and tore out her tongue.
7. I.e., excruciating, painful.
8. Anticipate.

30

And yet this sinful creature, frail and vain,
This lump of wretchedness, of sin and sorrow,   205
This weatherbeaten vessel wracked with pain,
Joys not in hope of an eternal morrow;
Nor all his losses, crosses, and vexation,
In weight, in frequency and long duration
Can make him deeply groan for that divine translation.[9]   210

31

The mariner that on smooth waves doth glide
Sings merrily and steers his bark with ease,
As if he had command of wind and tide,
And now become great master of the seas:
But suddenly a storm spoils all the sport,   215
And makes him long for a more quiet port,
Which 'gainst all adverse winds may serve for fort.

32

So he that saileth in this world of pleasure,
Feeding on sweets, that never bit of th' sour,
That's full of friends, of honor, and of treasure,   220
Fond fool, he takes this earth ev'n for heav'n's bower.
But sad affliction comes and makes him see
Here's neither honor, wealth, nor safety;
Only above is found all with security.

33

O Time the fatal wrack[1] of mortal things,   225
That draws oblivion's curtains over kings;
Their sumptuous monuments, men know them not,
Their names without a record are forgot,
Their parts, their ports, their pomp's[2] all laid in th' dust
Nor wit nor gold, nor buildings scape times rust;   230
But he whose name is graved in the white stone[3]
Shall last and shine when all of these are gone.

1678

The Flesh and the Spirit

In secret place where once I stood
Close by the banks of Lacrim[1] flood,
I heard two sisters reason on
Things that are past and things to come;
One Flesh was called, who had her eye   5
On worldly wealth and vanity;
The other Spirit, who did rear
Her thoughts unto a higher sphere:
Sister, quoth Flesh, what liv'st thou on,
Nothing but meditation?   10

9. Transformation.
1. Destroyer.
2. Vanity. "Parts": features. "Ports": places of refuge.
3. "To him that overcometh will I give to eat of the

hidden manna and will give him a white stone, and in
the stone a new name written, which no man knoweth
saving he that receiveth it" (Revelation 2.17).
1. In Latin *lacrima* means "tear."

Doth contemplation feed thee so
Regardlessly to let earth go?
Can speculation satisfy
Notion[2] without reality?
Dost dream of things beyond the moon,   15
And dost thou hope to dwell there soon?
Hast treasures there laid up in store
That all in th' world thou count'st but poor?
Art fancy sick, or turned a sot[3]
To catch at shadows which are not?   20
Come, come, I'll show unto thy sense,
Industry hath its recompense.
What canst desire, but thou may'st see
True substance in variety?
Dost honor like? Acquire the same,   25
As some to their immortal fame,
And trophies[4] to thy name erect
Which wearing time shall ne'er deject.
For riches doth thou long full sore?
Behold enough of precious store.   30
Earth hath more silver, pearls, and gold,
Than eyes can see or hands can hold.
Affect's thou pleasure? Take thy fill,
Earth hath enough of what you will.
Then let not go, what thou may'st find   35
For things unknown, only in mind.

Spirit: Be still thou unregenerate[5] part,
Disturb no more my settled heart,
For I have vowed (and so will do)
Thee as a foe still to pursue.   40
And combat with thee will and must,
Until I see thee laid in th' dust.
Sisters we are, yea, twins we be,
Yet deadly feud 'twixt thee and me;
For from one father are we not,   45
Thou by old Adam wast begot.
But my arise is from above,
Whence my dear Father I do love.
Thou speak'st me fair, but hat'st me sore,
Thy flatt'ring shows[6] I'll trust no more.   50
How oft thy slave, hast thou me made,
When I believed what thou hast said,
And never had more cause of woe
Than when I did what thou bad'st do.
I'll stop mine ears at these thy charms,   55
And count them for my deadly harms.
Thy sinful pleasures I do hate,
Thy riches are to me no bait,

---

2. Thought.
3. Fool. "Art fancy sick": i.e., do you have hallucina-
tions?
4. Monuments.
5. Unrepentant.
6. Exhibitions, displays.

Thine honors do, nor will I love;
For my ambition lies above.   60
My greatest honor it shall be
When I am victor over thee,
And triumph shall with laurel head,[7]
When thou my captive shalt be led,
How I do live, thou need'st not scoff,   65
For I have meat thou know'st not of;
The hidden manna[8] I do eat,
The word of life it is my meat.
My thoughts do yield me more content
Than can thy hours in pleasure spent.   70
Nor are they shadows which I catch,
Nor fancies vain at which I snatch,
But reach at things that are so high,
Beyond thy dull capacity:
Eternal substance I do see,   75
With which enrichéd I would be.
Mine eye doth pierce the heavens and see
What is invisible to thee.
My garments are not silk nor gold,
Nor such like trash which earth doth hold,   80
But royal robes I shall have on,
More glorious than the glist'ring sun;
My crown not diamonds, pearls, and gold,
But such as angels' heads enfold.
The city[9] where I hope to dwell,   85
There's none on earth can parallel;
The stately walls both high and strong,
Are made of precious jasper stone;
The gates of pearl, both rich and clear,
And angels are for porters there;   90
The streets thereof transparent gold,
Such as no eye did e'er behold;
A crystal river there doth run,
Which doth proceed from the Lamb's throne.
Of life, there are the waters sure,   95
Which shall remain forever pure,
Nor sun, nor moon, they have no need,
For glory doth from God proceed.
No candle there, nor yet torchlight,
For there shall be no darksome night.   100
From sickness and infirmity
For evermore they shall be free;
Nor withering age shall e'er come there,
But beauty shall be bright and clear;
This city pure is not for thee,   105
For things unclean there shall not be.

7. In Roman times a crown of laurel was a sign of victory for poets, heroes, and athletes.
8. The food sent by God to the Israelites in the wilderness (Exodus 16.15).

9. Lines 85 to 106 follow the description of the heavenly city of the New Jerusalem in Revelation 21 and 22.

If I of heaven may have my fill,
Take thou the world and all that will.

1678

The Author to Her Book[1]

Thou ill-formed offspring of my feeble brain,
Who after birth didst by my side remain,
Till snatched from thence by friends, less wise than true,
Who thee abroad, exposed to public view,
Made thee in rags, halting to th' press to trudge,   5
Where errors were not lessened (all may judge).
At thy return my blushing was not small,
My rambling brat (in print) should mother call,
I cast thee by as one unfit for light,
Thy visage was so irksome in my sight;   10
Yet being mine own, at length affection would
Thy blemishes amend, if so I could:
I washed thy face, but more defects I saw,
And rubbing off a spot still made a flaw.
I stretched thy joints to make thee even feet,[2]   15
Yet still thou run'st more hobbling than is meet;
In better dress to trim thee was my mind,
But nought save homespun cloth i' th' house I find.
In this array 'mongst vulgars[3] may'st thou roam.
In critic's hands beware thou dost not come,   20
And take thy way where yet thou art not known;
If for thy father asked, say thou hadst none;
And for thy mother, she alas is poor,
Which caused her thus to send thee out of door.

1678

Before the Birth of One of Her Children

All things within this fading world hath end,
Adversity doth still our joys attend;
No ties so strong, no friends so dear and sweet,
But with death's parting blow is sure to meet.
The sentence past is most irrevocable,   5
A common thing, yet oh, inevitable.
How soon, my Dear, death may my steps attend,
How soon't may be thy lot to lose thy friend,
We both are ignorant, yet love bids me
These farewell lines to recommend to thee,   10
That when that knot's untied that made us one,

---

1. *The Tenth Muse* was published in 1650 without
Bradstreet's knowledge. She is thought to have written
this poem in 1666 when a 2nd edition was contemplated.
2. I.e., metrical feet; to smooth out the lines.
3. The common people.

I may seem thine, who in effect am none.
And if I see not half my days that's due,
What nature would, God grant to yours and you;
The many faults that well you know I have   15
Let be interred in my oblivious grave;
If any worth or virtue were in me,
Let that live freshly in thy memory
And when thou feel'st no grief, as I no harms,
Yet love thy dead, who long lay in thine arms,   20
And when thy loss shall be repaid with gains
Look to my little babes, my dear remains.
And if thou love thyself, or loved'st me,
These O protect from stepdame's[1] injury.
And if chance to thine eyes shall bring this verse,   25
With some sad sighs honor my absent hearse;
And kiss this paper for thy love's dear sake,
Who with salt tears this last farewell did take.

1678

To My Dear and Loving Husband

If ever two were one, then surely we.
If ever man were loved by wife, then thee;
If ever wife was happy in a man,
Compare with me, ye women, if you can.
I prize thy love more than whole mines of gold   5
Or all the riches that the East doth hold.
My love is such that rivers cannot quench,
Nor ought but love from thee, give recompense.
Thy love is such I can no way repay,
The heavens reward thee manifold, I pray.   10
Then while we live, in love let's so persevere
That when we live no more, we may live ever.

1678

A Letter to Her Husband,
Absent upon Public Employment

My head, my heart, mine eyes, my life, nay, more,
My joy, my magazine[1] of earthly store,
If two be one, as surely thou and I,
How stayest thou there, whilst I at Ipswich[2] lie?
So many steps, head from the heart to sever,   5
If but a neck, soon should we be together.
I, like the Earth this season, mourn in black,
My Sun is gone so far in's zodiac,

1. I.e., stepmother's.   2. Ipswich, Massachusetts, is north of Boston.
1. Warehouse, storehouse.

Whom whilst I 'joyed, nor storms, nor frost I felt,
His warmth such frigid colds did cause to melt.   10
My chilled limbs now numbed lie forlorn;
Return, return, sweet Sol, from Capricorn;[3]
In this dead time, alas, what can I more
Than view those fruits which through thy heat I bore?
Which sweet contentment yield me for a space,   15
True living pictures of their father's face.
O strange effect! now thou art southward gone,
I weary grow the tedious day so long;
But when thou northward to me shalt return,
I wish my Sun may never set, but burn   20
Within the Cancer[4] of my glowing breast,
The welcome house of him my dearest guest.
Where ever, ever stay, and go not thence,
Till nature's sad decree shall call thee hence;
Flesh of thy flesh, bone of thy bone,   25
I here, thou there, yet both but one.

                                                                      1678

Another [Letter to Her Husband, Absent upon Public Employment]

As loving hind that (hartless) wants[1] her deer,
Scuds through the woods and fern with hark'ning ear,
Perplext, in every bush and nook doth pry,
Her dearest deer, might answer ear or eye;
So doth my anxious soul, which now doth miss   5
A dearer dear (far dearer heart) than this,
Still wait with doubts, and hopes, and failing eye,
His voice to hear or person to descry.
Or as the pensive dove doth all alone
(On withered bough) most uncouthly bemoan   10
The absence of her love and loving mate,
Whose loss hath made her so unfortunate,
Ev'n thus do I, with many a deep sad groan,
Bewail my turtle[2] true, who now is gone,
His presence and his safe return still woos,   15
With thousand doleful sighs and mournful coos.
Or as the loving mullet,[3] that true fish,
Her fellow lost, nor joy nor life do wish,
But launches on that shore, there for to die,
Where she her captive husband doth espy.   20
Mine being gone, I lead a joyless life,
I have a loving peer, yet seem no wife;
But worst of all, to him can't steer my course,

---

3. Capricorn, the tenth sign of the zodiac, represents winter. "Sol": sun.
4. Cancer, the fourth sign of the zodiac, represents summer.

1. Lacks. "Hind": female deer. "Hartless" puns on *hart* (male deer) and *heart*.
2. I.e., turtle dove.
3. A common species of fish.

I here, he there, alas, both kept by force.
Return my dear, my joy, my only love,   25
Unto thy hind, thy mullet, and thy dove,
Who neither joys in pasture, house, nor streams,
The substance gone, O me, these are but dreams.
Together at one tree, oh let us browse,
And like two turtles roost within one house,   30
And like the mullets in one river glide,
Let's still remain but one, till death divide.
    Thy loving love and dearest dear,
    At home, abroad, and everywhere.

                        1678

In Reference to Her Children, 23 June, 1659

I had eight birds hatched in one nest,
Four cocks there were, and hens the rest.
I nursed them up with pain and care,
Nor cost, nor labor did I spare,
Till at the last they felt their wing,   5
Mounted the trees, and learned to sing;
Chief of the brood then took his flight
To regions far and left me quite.
My mournful chirps I after send,
Till he return, or I do end: 10
Leave not thy nest, thy dam and sire,
Fly back and sing amidst this choir.
My second bird did take her flight,
And with her mate flew out of sight;
Southward they both their course did bend,   15
And seasons twain they there did spend,
Till after blown by southern gales,
They norward steered with filled sails.
A prettier bird was no where seen,
Along the beach among the treen.[1]   20
I have a third of color white,
On whom I placed no small delight;
Coupled with mate loving and true,
Hath also bid her dam adieu;
And where Aurora[2] first appears,   25
She now hath perched to spend her years.
One to the academy flew
To chat among that learned crew;
Ambition moves still in his breast
That he might chant above the rest,   30
Striving for more than to do well,
That nightingales he might excel.
My fifth, whose down is yet scarce gone,
Is 'mongst the shrubs and bushes flown,

---

1. Trees.
                            2. In Roman mythology the goddess of the dawn.

And as his wings increase in strength,   35
On higher boughs he'll perch at length.
My other three still with me nest,
Until they're grown, then as the rest,
Or[3] here or there they'll take their flight,
As is ordained, so shall they light.   40
If birds could weep, then would my tears
Let others know what are my fears
Lest this my brood some harm should catch,
And be surprised for want of watch,
Whilst pecking corn and void of care,   45
They fall un'wares in fowler's[4] snare,
Or whilst on trees they sit and sing,
Some untoward[5] boy at them do fling,
Or whilst allured with bell and glass,
The net be spread, and caught, alas.   50
Or lest by lime-twigs they be foiled,[6]
Or by some greedy hawks be spoiled.
O would my young, ye saw my breast,
And knew what thoughts there sadly rest,
Great was my pain when I you bred,   55
Great was my care when I you fed,
Long did I keep you soft and warm,
And with my wings kept off all harm,
My cares are more and fears than ever,
My throbs such now as 'fore were never.   60
Alas, my birds, you wisdom want,
Of perils you are ignorant;
Oft times in grass, on trees, in flight,
Sore accidents on you may light.
O to your safety have an eye,   65
So happy may you live and die.
Meanwhile my days in tunes I'll spend,
Till my weak lays[7] with me shall end.
In shady woods I'll sit and sing,
And things that past to mind I'll bring.   70
Once young and pleasant, as are you,
But former toys (no joys) adieu.
My age I will not once lament,
But sing, my time so near is spent.
And from the top bough take my flight   75
Into a country beyond sight,
Where old ones instantly grow young,
And there with seraphims[8] set song;
No seasons cold, nor storms they see;
But spring lasts to eternity.   80
When each of you shall in your nest
Among your young ones take your rest,

3. Either.
4. Bird catcher's.
5. Unruly, fractious.
6. I.e., caught by means of birdlime (a sticky sub- stance) spread on twigs.
7. Ballads, poems.
8. Winged angels.

In chirping language, oft them tell,
You had a dam that loved you well,
That did what could be done for young,   85
And nursed you up till you were strong,
And 'fore she once would let you fly,
She showed you joy and misery;
Taught what was good, and what was ill,
What would save life, and what would kill.   90
Thus gone, amongst you I may live,
And dead, yet speak, and counsel give:
Farewell, my birds, farewell adieu,
I happy am, if well with you.

1678

In Memory of My Dear Grandchild Elizabeth Bradstreet, Who Deceased August, 1665, Being a Year and Half Old

1

Farewell dear babe, my heart's too much content,
Farewell sweet babe, the pleasure of mine eye,
Farewell fair flower that for a space was lent,
Then ta'en away unto eternity.
Blest babe, why should I once bewail thy fate,   5
Or sigh thy days so soon were terminate,
Sith[1] thou art settled in an everlasting state.

2

By nature trees do rot when they are grown,
And plums and apples thoroughly ripe do fall,
And corn and grass are in their season mown,   10
And time brings down what is both strong and tall.
But plants new set to be eradicate,
And buds new blown to have so short a date,
Is by His hand alone that guides nature and fate.

1678

In Memory of My Dear Grandchild Anne Bradstreet, Who Deceased June 20, 1669, Being Three Years and Seven Months Old

With troubled heart and trembling hand I write,
The heavens have changed to sorrow my delight.
How oft with disappointment have I met,
When I on fading things my hopes have set.
Experience might 'fore this have made me wise,   5
To value things according to their price.
Was ever stable joy yet found below?

---

1. Since.

Or perfect bliss without mixture of woe?
I knew she was but as a withering flower,
That's here today, perhaps gone in an hour;   10
Like as a bubble, or the brittle glass,
Or like a shadow turning as it was.
More fool then I to look on that was lent
As if mine own, when thus impermanent.
Farewell dear child, thou ne'er shall come to me,   15
But yet a while, and I shall go to thee;
Mean time my throbbing heart's cheered up with this:
Thou with thy Savior art in endless bliss.

1678

On My Dear Grandchild Simon Bradstreet, Who Died on 16 November, 1669, Being But a Month, and One Day Old

No sooner came, but gone, and fall'n asleep.
Acquaintance short, yet parting caused us weep;
Three flowers, two scarcely blown, the last i' th' bud,
Cropped by th' Almighty's hand; yet is He good.
With dreadful awe before Him let's be mute,   5
Such was His will, but why, let's not dispute,
With humble hearts and mouths put in the dust,
Let's say He's merciful as well as just.
He will return and make up all our losses,
And smile again after our bitter crosses   10
Go pretty babe, go rest with sisters twain;
Among the blest in endless joys remain.

1678

For Deliverance from a Fever

When sorrows had begirt me round,
And pains within and out,
When in my flesh no part was found,[1]
Then didst Thou rid[2] me out.
My burning flesh in sweat did boil,   5
My aching head did break,
From side to side for ease I toil,
So faint I could not speak.
Beclouded was my soul with fear
Of Thy displeasure sore,   10
Nor could I read my evidence
Which oft I read before.
"Hide not Thy face from me!" I cried,

---

1. I.e., when nothing was spared.   2. Cleanse. "Thou": God.

"From burnings keep my soul.
Thou know'st my heart, and hast me tried;   15
I on Thy mercies roll."
"O heal my soul," Thou know'st I said,
"Though flesh consume to nought,
What though in dust it shall be laid,
To glory t' shall be brought."   20
Thou heard'st, Thy rod Thou didst remove
And spared my body frail,
Thou show'st to me Thy tender love,
My heart no more might quail.
O, praises to my mighty God,   25
Praise to my Lord, I say,
Who hath redeemed my soul from pit,[3]
Praises to Him for aye.[4]

1867

Here Follows Some Verses upon the Burning of Our House
July 10th, 1666

Copied Out of a Loose Paper

In silent night when rest I took
For sorrow near I did not look
I wakened was with thund'ring noise
And piteous shrieks of dreadful voice.
That fearful sound of "Fire!" and "Fire!"   5
Let no man know is my desire.
I, starting up, the light did spy,
And to my God my heart did cry
To strengthen me in my distress
And not to leave me succorless.   10
Then, coming out, beheld a space
The flame consume my dwelling place.
And when I could no longer look,
I blest His name that gave and took,[1]
That laid my goods now in the dust.   15
Yea, so it was, and so 'twas just.
It was His own, it was not mine,
Far be it that I should repine;
He might of all justly bereft
But yet sufficient for us left.   20
When by the ruins oft I past
My sorrowing eyes aside did cast,
And here and there the places spy
Where oft I sat and long did lie:
Here stood that trunk, and there that chest,   25

---

3. Hell.
4. Ever.

1. "The Lord gave, and the Lord hath taken away;
blessed be the name of the Lord" (Job 1.21).

There lay that store I counted best.
My pleasant things in ashes lie,
And them behold no more shall I.
Under thy roof no guest shall sit,
Nor at thy table eat a bit.   30
No pleasant tale shall e'er be told,
Nor things recounted done of old.
No candle e'er shall shine in thee,
Nor bridegroom's voice e'er heard shall be.
In silence ever shall thou lie,   35
Adieu, Adieu, all's vanity.
Then straight I 'gin my heart to chide,
And did thy wealth on earth abide?
Didst fix thy hope on mold'ring dust?
The arm of flesh didst make thy trust?   40
Raise up thy thoughts above the sky
That dunghill mists away may fly.
Thou hast an house on high erect,
Framed by that mighty Architect,
With glory richly furnished,   45
Stands permanent though this be fled.
It's purchaséd and paid for too
By Him who hath enough to do.
A price so vast as is unknown
Yet by His gift is made thine own;   50
There's wealth enough, I need no more,
Farewell, my pelf,[2] farewell my store.
The world no longer let me love,
My hope and treasure lies above.

                                                          1867

As Weary Pilgrim

As weary pilgrim, now at rest,
    Hugs with delight his silent nest,
His wasted limbs now lie full soft
    That mirey steps have trodden oft,
Blesses himself to think upon   5
    His dangers past, and travails done.
The burning sun no more shall heat,
    Nor stormy rains on him shall beat.
The briars and thorns no more shall scratch.
    Nor hungry wolves at him shall catch.   10
He erring paths no more shall tread,
    Nor wild fruits eat instead of bread.
For waters cold he doth not long
    For thirst no more shall parch his tongue.
No rugged stones his feet shall gall,   15
    Nor stumps nor rocks cause him to fall.

---

2. Possessions, usually in the sense of being falsely gained.

All cares and fears he bids farewell
   And means in safety now to dwell.
A pilgrim I, on earth perplexed
   With sins, with cares and sorrows vext,   20
By age and pains brought to decay,
   And my clay house[1] mold'ring away.
Oh, how I long to be at rest
   And soar on high among the blest.
This body shall in silence sleep,   25
   Mine eyes no more shall ever weep,
No fainting fits shall me assail,
   Nor grinding pains my body frail,
With cares and fears ne'er cumb'red be
   Nor losses know, nor sorrows see.   30
What though my flesh shall there consume,
   It is the bed Christ did perfume,
And when a few years shall be gone,
   This mortal shall be clothed upon.
A corrupt carcass down it lies,   35
   A glorious body it shall rise.
In weakness and dishonor sown,
   In power 'tis raised by Christ alone.
Then soul and body shall unite
   And of their Maker have the sight.   40
Such lasting joys shall there behold
   As ear ne'er heard nor tongue e'er told.
Lord make me ready for that day,
   Then come, dear Bridegroom,[2] come away.

Aug. 31, 1669   1867

From Meditations Divine and Moral[1]

1

There is no object that we see, no action that we do, no good that we enjoy, no evil that we feel or fear, but we may make some spiritual advantage of all; and he that makes such improvement is wise as well as pious.

5

It is reported of the peacock that, priding himself in his gay feathers, he ruffles them up, but spying his black feet, he soon lets fall his plumes; so he that

1. I.e., the body.
2. Christ is the bridegroom and the soul is married to him. "And Jesus said unto them, Can the children of the bridechamber fast, while the bridegroom is with them? as long as they have the bridegroom with them, they cannot fast" (Mark 2.19).
1. These meditations are addressed to Bradstreet's son Simon. In the dedicatory letter, dated March 20, 1664, she writes: "Parents perpetuate their lives in their posterity and their manners; in their imitation children do

naturally rather follow the failings than the virtues of their predecessors, but I am persuaded better things of you. You once desired me to leave something for you in writing that you might look upon, when you should see me no more; I could think of nothing more fit for you nor of more ease to myself than these short meditations following. Such as they are, I bequeath to you; small legacies are accepted by true friends, much more by dutiful children. I have avoided encroaching upon others' conceptions because I would leave you nothing glories in his gifts and adornings should look upon his corruptions, and that will damp his high thoughts.

13

The reason why Christians are so loath to exchange this world for a better is because they have more sense[2] than faith: they see what they enjoy; they do but hope for that which is to come.

38

Some children are hardly weaned; although the teat be rubbed with worm-wood or mustard,[3] they will either wipe it off, or else suck down sweet and bitter together. So is it with some Christians: let God embitter all the sweets of this life, that so they might feed upon more substantial food, yet they are so childishly sottish that they are still hugging and sucking these empty breasts that God is forced to hedge up their way with thorns or lay affliction on their loins that so they might shake hands with the world, before it bid them farewell.

40

The spring is a lively emblem of the Resurrection: after a long winter we see the leafless trees and dry stocks (at the approach of the sun) to resume their former vigor and beauty in a more ample manner than what they lost in the autumn; so shall it be at that great day after a long vacation, when the Sun of Righteousness[4] shall appear; those dry bones shall arise in far more glory than that which they lost at their creation, and in this transcends the spring that their leaf shall never fail nor their sap decline.

48

There is nothing admits of more admiration than God's various dispensation of His gifts among the sons of men, betwixt whom He hath put so vast a disproportion that they scarcely seem made of the same lump or sprung out of the loins of one Adam, some set in the highest dignity that mortality is capable of, and some again so base that they are viler than the earth, some so wise and learned that they seem like angels among men, and some again so ignorant and sottish that they are more like beasts than men, some pious saints, some incarnate devils, some exceeding beautiful, and some extremely deformed, some so strong and healthful that their bones are full of marrow and their breasts of milk, and some again so weak and feeble that while they live they are accounted among the dead; and no other reason can be given of all this but so it pleased Him whose will is the perfect rule of righteousness.

---

but mine own, though in value they fall short of all in this kind; yet I presume they will be better prized by you for the author's sake. The Lord bless you with grace here and crown you with glory hereafter, that I may meet you with rejoicing at that great day of appearing, which is the continual prayer of *your affectionate mother, A. B."*
2. I.e., they are more concerned with physical sensa-

tion and the things of this world than with faith.
3. A common way of weaning children, making the mother's breast bitter.
4. "But unto you that fear my name shall the Sun of righteousness arise with healing in his wings; and ye shall go forth, and grow up as calves of the stall" (Malachi 4.2). "Long vacation": i.e., the sleep of the dead, awaiting the Second Coming of Christ.

51

The eyes and the ears are the inlets or doors of the soul, through which innumerable objects enter; yet is not that spacious room filled, neither doth it ever say it is enough, but like the daughters of the horseleach, cries, "Give, give";[5] and, which is most strange, the more it receives, the more empty it finds itself and sees an impossibility ever to be filled but by Him in whom all fullness dwells.

62

As a man is called the little world, so his heart may be called the little commonwealth; his more fixed and resolved thoughts are like to inhabitants, his slight and flitting thoughts are like passengers that travel to and fro continually; here is also the great court of justice erected, which is always kept by conscience, who is both accuser, excuser, witness, and judge, whom no bribes can pervert nor flattery cause to favor, but as he finds the evidence, so he absolves or condemns; yea, so absolute is this court of judicature that there is no appeal from it, no not to the court of heaven itself, for if our conscience condemn us, He also who is greater than our conscience will do it much more, but he that would have boldness to go to the throne of grace to be accepted there must be sure to carry a certificate from the court of conscience that he stands right there.

67

All the works and doings of God are wonderful, but none more awful than His great work of election and reprobation;[6] when we consider how many good parents have had bad children, and again how many bad parents have had pious children, it should make us adore the sovereignty of God, who will not be tied to time nor place, nor yet to persons, but takes and chooses, when and where and whom He pleases; it should also teach the children of godly parents to walk with fear and trembling, lest they through unbelief fall short of a promise; it may also be a support to such as have or had wicked parents, that if they abide not in unbelief, God is able to gaff[7] them in. The upshot of all should make us with the apostle to admire the justice and mercy of God and say how unsearchable are His ways and His footsteps past finding out.[8]

71

All weak and diseased bodies have hourly mementos of their mortality, but the soundest of men, have likewise their nightly monitor by the emblem of death, which is their sleep (for so is death often called), and not only their death, but their grave is lively represented before their eyes by beholding their bed, the morning may mind them of the Resurrection, and the sun approaching of the

---

5. "The horseleach [veterinarian] hath two daughters, crying, Give, give. There are three things that are never satisfied, yea, four things say not, It is enough: The grave, and the barren womb; the earth that is not filled with water; and the fire that saith not, It is enough" (Proverbs 30.15–16).
6. God's decision upon those who are to be rejected and damned. "Election": God's choice of those who

are to be eternally saved.
7. Hook; to bring to shore a large fish by means of a long pole with a hook.
8. "O the depth of the riches both of the wisdom and knowledge of God! how unsearchable are his judgments, and his ways past finding out!" (Romans 11.33).

appearing of the Sun of Righteousness, at Whose coming they shall all rise out of their beds, the long night shall fly away, and the day of eternity shall never end. Seeing these things must be, what manner of persons ought we to be, in all good conversation?

1664(?)   1867

To My Dear Children

This book by any yet unread,
I leave for you when I am dead,
That being gone, here you may find
What was your living mother's mind.
Make use of what I leave in love,   5
And God shall bless you from above.
                            A. B.

My dear children,

I, knowing by experience that the exhortations of parents take most effect when the speakers leave to speak,[1] and those especially sink deepest which are spoke latest, and being ignorant whether on my death bed I shall have opportunity to speak to any of you, much less to all, thought it the best, whilst I was able, to compose some short matters (for what else to call them I know not) and bequeath to you, that when I am no more with you, yet I may be daily in your remembrance (although that is the least in my aim in what I now do), but that you may gain some spiritual advantage by my experience. I have not studied in this you read to show my skill, but to declare the truth, not to set forth myself, but the glory of God. If I had minded the former, it had been perhaps better pleasing to you, but seeing the last is the best, let it be best pleasing to you.

The method I will observe shall be this: I will begin with God's dealing with me from my childhood to this day.

In my young years, about 6 or 7 as I take it, I began to make conscience of my ways, and what I knew was sinful, as lying, disobedience to parents, etc., I avoided it. If at any time I was overtaken with the like evils, it was as a great trouble, and I could not be at rest till by prayer I had confessed it unto God. I was also troubled at the neglect of private duties though too often tardy that way. I also found much comfort in reading the Scriptures, especially those places I thought most concerned my condition, and as I grew to have more understanding, so the more solace I took in them.

In a long fit of sickness which I had on my bed I often communed with my heart and made my supplication to the most High who set me free from that affliction.

But as I grew up to be about 14 or 15, I found my heart more carnal,[2] and sitting loose from God, vanity and the follies of youth take hold of me.

About 16, the Lord laid His hand sore upon me and smote me with the smallpox. When I was in my affliction, I besought the Lord and confessed my

---

1. I.e., stop speaking.   2. I.e., worldly.

pride and vanity, and He was entreated of me and again restored me. But I rendered not to Him according to the benefit received.

After a short time I changed my condition and was married, and came into this country, where I found a new world and new manners, at which my heart rose. But after I was convinced it was the way of God, I submitted to it and joined to the church at Boston.

After some time I fell into a lingering sickness like a consumption together with a lameness, which correction I saw the Lord sent to humble and try me and do me good, and it was not altogether ineffectual.

It pleased God to keep me a long time without a child, which was a great grief to me and cost me many prayers and tears before I obtained one, and after him gave me many more of whom I now take the care, that as I have brought you into the world, and with great pains, weakness, cares, and fears brought you to this, I now travail[3] in birth again of you till Christ be formed in you.

Among all my experiences of God's gracious dealings with me, I have constantly observed this, that He hath never suffered me long to sit loose from Him, but by one affliction or other hath made me look home, and search what was amiss; so usually thus it hath been with me that I have no sooner felt my heart out of order, but I have expected correction for it, which most commonly hath been upon my own person in sickness, weakness, pains, sometimes on my soul, in doubts and fears of God's displeasure and my sincerity towards Him; sometimes He hath smote a child with a sickness, sometimes chastened by losses in estate,[4] and these times (through His great mercy) have been the times of my greatest getting and advantage; yea, I have found them the times when the Lord hath manifested the most love to me. Then have I gone to searching and have said with David, "Lord, search me and try me, see what ways of wickedness are in me, and lead me in the way everlasting,"[5] and seldom or never but I have found either some sin I lay under which God would have reformed, or some duty neglected which He would have performed, and by His help I have laid vows and bonds upon my soul to perform His righteous commands.

If at any time you are chastened of God, take it as thankfully and joyfully as in greatest mercies, for if ye be His, ye shall reap the greatest benefit by it. It hath been no small support to me in times of darkness when the Almighty hath hid His face from me that yet I have had abundance of sweetness and refreshment after affliction and more circumspection[6] in my walking after I have been afflicted. I have been with God like an untoward child, that no longer than the rod has been on my back (or at least in sight) but I have been apt to forget Him and myself, too. Before I was afflicted, I went astray, but now I keep Thy statutes.[7]

I have had great experience of God's hearing my prayers and returning comfortable answers to me, either in granting the thing I prayed for, or else in satisfying my mind without it, and I have been confident it hath been from Him, because I have found my heart through His goodness enlarged in thankfulness to Him.

I have often been perplexed that I have not found that constant joy in my

---

3. Toil, labor.
4. Financial losses.
5. Psalm 139.23–24.

6. Prudence.
7. Psalm 119.8.

pilgrimage and refreshing which I supposed most of the servants of God have, although He hath not left me altogether without the witness of His holy spirit, who hath oft given me His word and set to His seal that it shall be well with me. I have sometimes tasted of that hidden manna that the world knows not, and have set up my Ebenezer,[8] and have resolved with myself that against such a promise, such tastes of sweetness, the gates of hell shall never prevail; yet have I many times sinkings and droopings, and not enjoyed that felicity that sometimes I have done. But when I have been in darkness and seen no light, yet have I desired to stay myself upon the Lord, and when I have been in sickness and pain, I have thought if the Lord would but lift up the light of His countenance upon me, although He ground me to powder, it would be but light to me; yea, oft have I thought were I in hell itself and could there find the love of God toward me, it would be a heaven. And could I have been in heaven without the love of God, it would have been a hell to me, for in truth it is the absence and presence of God that makes heaven or hell.

Many times hath Satan troubled me concerning the verity of the Scriptures, many times by atheism how I could know whether there was a God; I never saw any miracles to confirm me, and those which I read of, how did I know but they were feigned? That there is a God my reason would soon tell me by the wondrous works that I see, the vast frame of the heaven and the earth, the order of all things, night and day, summer and winter, spring and autumn, the daily providing for this great household upon the earth, the preserving and directing of all to its proper end. The consideration of these things would with amazement certainly resolve me that there is an Eternal Being. But how should I know He is such a God as I worship in Trinity, and such a Savior as I rely upon? Though this hath thousands of times been suggested to me, yet God hath helped me over. I have argued thus with myself. That there is a God, I see. If ever this God hath revealed himself, it must be in His word, and this must be it or none. Have I not found that operation by it that no human invention can work upon the soul, hath not judgments befallen divers who have scorned and contemned it, hath it not been preserved through all ages maugre[9] all the heathen tyrants and all of the enemies who have opposed it? Is there any story but that which shows the beginnings of times, and how the world came to be as we see? Do we not know the prophecies in it fulfilled which could not have been so long foretold by any but God Himself?

When I have got over this block, then have I another put in my way, that admit this be the true God whom we worship, and that be his word, yet why may not the Popish religion be the right? They have the same God, the same Christ, the same word. They only interpret it one way, we another.

This hath sometimes stuck with me, and more it would, but the vain fooleries that are in their religion together with their lying miracles and cruel persecutions of the saints, which admit were they as they term them, yet not so to be dealt withal.

The consideration of these things and many the like would soon turn me to my own religion again.

But some new troubles I have had since the world has been filled with blasphemy and sectaries,[1] and some who have been accounted sincere Chris-

8. In 1 Samuel 7.12, a stone monument to commemorate a victory over the Philistines. "Manna": the "bread from heaven" (Exodus 16.4) that fed the Israelites in the wilderness.
9. In spite of.
1. Unbelievers, heretics.

tians have been carried away with them, that sometimes I have said, "Is there faith upon the earth?" and I have not known what to think; but then I have remembered the works of Christ that so it must be, and if it were possible, the very elect should be deceived. "Behold," saith our Savior, "I have told you before." That hath stayed my heart, and I can now say, "Return, O my Soul, to thy rest, upon this rock Christ Jesus will I build my faith, and if I perish, I perish"; but I know all the Powers of Hell shall never prevail against it. I know whom I have trusted, and whom I have believed, and that He is able to keep that I have committed to His charge.

Now to the King, immortal, eternal and invisible, the only wise God, be honor, and glory for ever and ever, Amen.

This was written in much sickness and weakness, and is very weakly and imperfectly done, but if you can pick any benefit out of it, it is the mark which I aimed at.

1867

MICHAEL WIGGLESWORTH
1631–1705

It is clear from the diary that Michael Wigglesworth kept in his early twenties that the Judgment Day was never very far from his mind. When he learned, for example, that eight houses in Boston had burned, he immediately thought about how destruction "seals" God's word in his "dreadful works," and shortly after the news of his father's death was brought to him (and he had to acknowledge to himself that in his heart he was "secretly glad"), he "dreamed of the approach of the great and dreadful Day of Judgment." Wigglesworth wept, he writes, when he awoke, and determined to "follow God with tears and cries until He gave me some hopes of His gracious good will toward me." Like any sensitive believer, he was bound to have moments of doubt and joy, but ambiguity about his feelings toward his father's death never seems to have been resolved. Two months later he despaired of his "senselessness" toward this loss and bewailed his "secure, hard heart." "The death of the righteous unlamented," he notes, "is a forerunner of evil to come."

Nine years later Wigglesworth turned his dream of Judgment Day into one of the most popular poems ever written in America. Its 224 eight-line stanzas captivated the Puritan imagination, and many pious souls learned its verses by heart. Edward Taylor said that one of the reasons he loved his wife was that "the Doomsday verses much perfumed her breath." Committing it to memory would be a formidable task for anyone, but Puritans were helped by the fact that Wigglesworth used common hymn meter (alternating rhymed lines of eight and six syllables) and that the subject of his poem was familiar to them from sermons. In the first year of its publication, 1662, it sold eighteen hundred copies and it was frequently reprinted thereafter. Although Wigglesworth published other poems, nothing he wrote ever achieved the popularity of these "Doomsday verses." About one out of every twenty persons in New England bought it, and there are no complete copies of the first edition extant, for it was literally read to pieces. Its great appeal to this generation of Puritans is sometimes attributed to its "sulferousness," and it does indeed portray a vivid picture of hell fire; but its appeal can equally be laid to the fact that it assured the reader that a final order prevailed in all things, and that the regenerate would reign with Christ eternally. The poem is, finally, as comforting as it is frightening.

Wigglesworth must have been as surprised as anyone to find himself the author of a best-selling work, for nothing in his earlier career hinted at popularity. He was a neurotic young man, sometimes almost paralyzed with anxiety and self-doubt. As he was never physically strong, some of his illnesses (syphilis was one) were clearly imagined, but others were not. He came to Harvard College at sixteen, traveling from New Haven, Connecticut, where his father, recently injured, had had to give up farming. It is clear from his diary that the family expected him to do well. Wigglesworth intended to become a physician, but his introspective, bookish, and didactic nature impelled him to the ministry. In 1655 he accepted a call to the church in Malden, Massachusetts, and remained there for the next fifty years. He was not, however, a favorite of the townspeople, and he turned to writing as an alternative to his lack of success in the pulpit. Only when he jeopardized his reputation by marrying someone much younger did the attitude of his parishioners toward him soften. Nothing he ever did or did not do, however, detracted from his reputation as chief poet of the age. Samuel Sewall notes in his diary for June 10, 1705, that Mr. Michael Wigglesworth died that day in Malden: "He was the author of the poem entitled The Day of Doom, which has been so often printed; and was very useful as a physician."

From The Day of Doom[1]

1

The security of the world before Christ's coming to judgment.
Luk. 12.19

Still was the night, serene and bright,
   when all men sleeping lay;
Calm was the season, and carnal reason[2]
   thought so 'twould last for ay.[3]
Soul, take thine ease, let sorrow cease,   5
   much good thou hast in store:
This was their song, their cups among,
   the evening before.   ·

2

Wallowing in all kind of sin,
   vile wretches lay secure: 10
The best of men had scarcely then
   their lamps kept in good ure.[4]

Mat. 25.5

Virgins unwise, who through disguise
   amongst the best were numberéd,
Had closed their eyes: yea, and the wise   15
   through sloth and frailty slumberéd.

3

Like as of old, when men grow bold
   God's threat'nings to contemn,[5]

Mat. 24.37–38

Who stopped their ear, and would not hear,
   when Mercy warned them: 20
But took their course, without remorse,
   till God began to pour

---

1. The text used here is from *The Day of Doom or a Poetical Description of the Great and Last Judgment with Other Poems*, edited by Kenneth B. Murdock (1929), which reprints the only complete American edition (1701).

2. The rationalizations of the flesh as opposed to spiritual "right reason."
3. Ever.
4. Use, condition.
5. Despise.

Destruction the world upon
   in a tempestuous shower.

4

They put away the evil day,   25
   and drowned their care and fears,
Till drowned were they, and swept away
   by vengeance unawares:

1 Thes. 5.3

So at the last, whilst men sleep fast
   in their security,   30
Surprised they are in such a snare
   as cometh suddenly.

5

The suddenness,
majesty, &
terror of Christ's
appearing.
Mat. 25.6
2 Pet. 3.10

For at midnight brake forth a light,
   which turned the night to day,
And speedily an hideous cry   35
   did all the world dismay.
Sinners awake, their hearts do ache,
   trembling their loins surpriseth;
Amazed with fear, by what they hear,
   each one of them ariseth.   40

6

They rush from beds with giddy heads,
   and to their windows run,
Viewing this light, which shines more bright
   then doth the noon-day sun.

Mat. 24.29–30

Straightway appears (they see't with tears)   45
   the Son of God most dread;
Who with His train comes on amain
   to judge both quick[6] and dead.

7

Before his face the Heav'ns gave place,
   and skies are rent asunder,   50

2 Pet. 3.10

With mighty voice, and hideous noise,
   more terrible than thunder.
His brightness damps Heav'n's glorious lamps
   and makes them hide their heads,
As if afraid and quite dismayed,   55
   they quit their wonted steads.[7]

8

Ye sons of men that durst contemn
   the threat'nings of God's word,
How cheer you now? your hearts, I trow,
   are thrilled[8] as with a sword.   60
Now atheist blind, whose brutish mind
   a God could never see,
Dost thou perceive, dost now believe,
   that Christ thy Judge shall be?

9

Stout courages,[9] (whose hardiness   65
   could death and hell out-face)

---

6. Living. "Train": retinue. "Amain": in full force.   8. Pierced. "Trow": trust, believe.
7. Accustomed places.   9. Haughty and defiant souls.

Are you as bold now you behold
   your Judge draw near apace?
They cry, no, no: alas! and woe!
   our courage all is gone: 70
Our hardiness (fool hardiness)
   hath us undone, undone.

10

No heart so bold, but now grows cold
   and almost dead with fear:

Rev. 6.16

No eye so dry, but now can cry,   75
   and pour out many a tear.
Earth's potentates and powerful states,
   captains and men of might
Are quite abashed, their courage dashed
   at this most dreadful sight.   80

11

Mean[1] men lament, great men do rent
   their robes, and tear their hair:

Mat. 24.30

They do not spare their flesh to tear
   through horrible despair.
All kindreds wail: all hearts do fail: 85
   horror the world doth fill
With weeping eyes, and loud out-cries,
   yet knows not how to kill.

12

Rev. 6.15–16

Some hide themselves in caves and delves,
   in places under ground: 90
Some rashly leap into the deep,
   to scape by being drowned:
Some to the rocks (O senseless blocks!)
   and woody mountains run,
That there they might this fearful sight,   95
   and dreaded presence shun.

13

In vain do they to mountains say,
   "Fall on us, and us hide
From Judge's ire, more hot than fire,
   for who may it abide?"   100
No hiding place can from His face,
   sinners at all conceal,
Whose flaming eyes hid things doth 'spy,
   and darkest things reveal.

14

The Judge draws nigh, exalted high   105

Mat. 25.31

   upon a lofty throne,
Amidst the throng of angels strong,
   lo, Israel's Holy One!
The excellence of Whose presence
   and awful Majesty,   110
Amazeth Nature, and every creature,
   doth more than terrify.

1. Ordinary.

15

Rev. 6.14

The mountains smoke, the hills are shook,
   the earth is rent and torn,
As if she should be clean dissolved,   115
   or from the center born.
The sea doth roar, forsakes the shore,
   and shrinks away for fear;
The wild beasts flee into the sea,
   so soon as He draws near.   120

16

Whose glory bright, whose wondrous might,
   whose power imperial,
So far surpass whatever was
   in realms terrestrial;
That tongues of men (nor Angel's pen)   125
   cannot the same express,
And therefore I must pass it by,
   lest speaking should transgress.

17

1 Thes. 4.16
*Resurrection
of the dead.*
Joh. 5.28–29

Before His throne a trump is blown,
   proclaiming the Day of Doom: 130
Forthwith He cries, *"Ye dead arise,
   and unto Judgment come."*
No sooner said, but 'tis obeyed;
   sepulchers opened are:
Dead bodies all rise at His call,   135
   and's mighty power declare.

18

Both sea and land, at His command,
   their dead at once surrender:
The fire and air constrained are
   also their dead to tender.   140
The mighty word of this great Lord
   links body and soul together
Both of the just, and the unjust,
   to part no more forever.

*   *   *

21

2 Cor. 5.10
*The sheep
separated from
the goats.*
Mat. 25

Thus everyone before the throne
   of Christ the Judge is brought,
Both righteous and impious
   that good or ill had wrought.
A separation, and differing station[2]   165
   by Christ appointed is
(To sinners sad) 'twixt good and bad,
   'twixt heirs of woe and bliss.

22

*Who are
Christ's sheep.*
Mat. 5.10–11

At Christ's right hand the sheep do stand,
   His holy martyrs, who   170
For His dear name suffering shame,

2. Standing, place.

calamity and woe,
Like champions stood, and with their blood
    their testimony sealed;
Whose innocence without offense,   175
    to Christ their Judge appealed.

23

Heb. 12.5–7

Next unto whom there find a room
    all Christ's afflicted ones,
Who being chastised, neither despised
    nor sank amidst their groans: 180
Who by the rod were turned to God,
    and lovéd Him the more,
Not murmuring nor quarreling
    when they were chastened sore.

24

Luk. 7.41,47

Moreover, such as lovéd much,   185
    that had not such a trial,
As might constrain to so great pain,
    and such deep self-denial:
Yet ready were the cross to bear,
    when Christ them called thereto,   190
And did rejoice to hear His voice,
    they're counted sheep also.

25

Joh. 21.15
Mat. 19.14
Joh. 3.3

Christ's flock of lambs there also stands,
    whose faith was weak, yet true;
All sound believers (Gospel receivers)   195
    whose grace was small, but grew:
And them among an infant throng
    of babes, for whom Christ died;
Whom for His own, by ways unknown
    to men, He sanctified.   200

26

Rev. 6.11
Phil. 3.21

All stand before their Savior
    in long white robes yclad,[3]
Their countenance full of pleasance,
    appearing wondrous glad.
O glorious sight! Behold how bright   205
    dust heaps are made to shine,
Conforméd so their Lord unto,
    whose glory is divine.

27

The goats
described or the
several sorts of
reprobates on
the left hand.
Mat. 24.51

At Christ's left hand the goats do stand,
    all whining hypocrites,   210
Who for self-ends did seem Christ's friends,
    but fostered guileful sprites;[4]
Who sheep resembled, but they dissembled
    (their hearts were not sincere);
Who once did throng Christ's lambs among,   215
    but now must not come near.

3. Dressed.   4. Spirits.

28

Luk. 11.24,26
Heb. 6.4–6
Heb. 10.29

Apostates[5] and run-aways,
    such as have Christ forsaken,
Of whom the devil, with seven more evil,[6]
    hath fresh possession taken: 220
Sinners ingrain,[7] reserved to pain
    and torments most severe:
Because 'gainst light they sinned with spite,
    are also placéd there.

29

There also stand a num'rous band,   225

Luk. 12.47
Prov. 1.24,26
Joh. 3.19

    that no profession made
Of godliness, nor to redress
    their ways at all essayed:
Who better knew, but (sinful crew)
    Gospel and law despised;   230
Who all Christ's knocks[8] withstood like blocks
    and would not be advised.

30

Moreover, there with them appear
    a number, numberless

Gal. 3.10
1 Cor. 6.9
Rev. 21.8

Of great and small, vile wretches all,   235
    that did God's Law transgress;
Idolaters, false worshipers,
    profaners of God's name,
Who not at all thereon did call,
    or took in vain the same.   240

*   *   *

38

All silence keep, both goats and sheep,
    before the Judge's throne;

The saints
cleared &
justified.

With mild aspect to His elect[9]
    then spake the Holy One: 300
"My sheep draw near, your sentence hear,
    which is to you no dread,
Who clearly now discern, and know
    your sins are pardonéd.

39

2 Cor. 5.10
Eccles. 3.17
Joh. 3.18

" 'Twas meet that ye should judgéd be,   305
    that so the world may spy
No cause of grudge, when as I judge
    and deal impartially.
Know therefore all, both great and small,
    the ground and reason why   310
These men do stand at My right hand,
    and look so cheerfully.

40

Joh. 17.6
Eph. 1.4

"These men be those My Father chose
    before the world's foundation,

---

5. Turncoats.
6. I.e., with seven accomplices more evil than he.
7. Inveterate.

8. Attempts to gain admittance to their souls. "Behold, I stand at the door and knock" (Revelation 3.20).
9. Those chosen by God for eternal life.

And to Me gave, that I should save   315
    from death and condemnation.
For whose dear sake I flesh did take,
    was of a woman born,
And did inure[1] Myself t'endure,
    unjust reproach and scorn.   320

41

"For them it was that I did pass
    through sorrows many one:
That I drank up that bitter cup,
Rev. 1.5   which made Me sigh and groan.
The cross his pain I did sustain;   325
    yea more, My Father's ire
I underwent, My blood I spent
    to save them from hell fire.

*   *   *

48

Luk. 22.29–30   "Come, blessed ones, and sit on thrones,
Mat. 19.28   judging the world with Me:
Come, and possess your happiness,
    and bought felicity.   380
Henceforth no fears, no care, no tears,
    no sin shall you annoy,
Nor anything that grief doth bring:
    eternal rest enjoy.

49

Mat. 25.34   "You bore the cross, you suffered loss   385
They are placed on   of all for My name's sake:
thrones to join   Receive the crown that's now your own;
with Christ in   come, and a kingdom take."
judging the wicked.
Thus spake the Judge; the wicked grudge,
    and grind their teeth in vain;   390
They see with groans these placed on thrones
    which addeth to their pain:

50

That those whom they did wrong and slay,
    must now their judgment see!
Such whom they slighted, and once despited,[2]   395
    must now their judges be!
Thus 'tis decreed, such is their meed,
1 Cor. 6.2   and guerdon[3] glorious!
With Christ they sit, judging is fit[4]
    to plague the impious.   400

51

The wicked   The wicked are brought to the bar,[5]
brought to the bar.   like guilty malefactors,
Rom. 2.3,6,11
That oftentimes of bloody crimes
    and treasons have been actors.

---

1. Accustom.   4. Appropriate.
2. Held in contempt.   5. The wood rail separating the accused from the
3. Recompense. "Meed": reward.   judge and where they are sentenced.

Of wicked men, none are so mean 405
    as there to be neglected:
Not none so high in dignity,
    as there to be respected.

52

Rev. 6.15–16
Isa. 30.33

The glorious Judge will privilege
    nor[6] emperor, nor king: 410
But every one that hath mis-done
    doth into judgment bring.
And every one that hath mis-done,
    the Judge impartially
Condemneth to eternal woe, 415
    and endless misery.

53

Thus one and all, thus great and small,
    the rich as well as poor,
And those of place as the most base,
    do stand the Judge before. 420
They are arraigned, and there detained,
    before Christ's judgment-seat
With trembling fear, their doom to hear,
    and feel His anger's heat.

54

Eccles. 11.9 &
12.14

There Christ demands at all their hands 425
    a strict and strait account
Of all things done under the sun,
    whose number far surmount
Man's wit and thought: yet all are brought
    unto this solemn trial; 430
And each offense with evidence,
    so that there's no denial.

* * *

58

Eccles. 12.14

All filthy facts, and secret acts,
    however closely done,
And long concealed, are there revealed
    before the mid-day sun. 460
Deeds of the night shunning the light,
    which darkest corners sought,
To fearful blame, and endless shame,
    are there most justly brought.

* * *

60

*An account
demanded of all
their actions.
Joh. 5.40
& 3.19
Mat. 25.19,27*

At this sad season, Christ asks a reason
    (with just austerity)
Of grace refused, of light abused 475
    so oft, so willfully:
Of talents lent by them misspent,

6. Neither. "Privilege": grant immunity to.

and on their lust bestown;
Which if improved, as it behoved,
    heav'n might have been their own!   480

                        61

Of times neglected, of means rejected,
    of God's long-suffering,

Rom. 2.4–5
And patience, to penitence
    that sought hard hearts to bring.
Why cords of love did nothing move   485
    to shame or to remorse?
Why warnings grave, and counsels,[7] have
    nought changed their sinful course?

                        62

Why chastenings, and evil things,
    why judgments so severe   490
Isa. 1.5
Prevailed not with them a jot,
    nor wrought an awful fear?
Jer. 2.20
Why promises of holiness,
    and new obedience,
They oft did make, but always brake[8]   495
    the same, to God's offense?

                    *   *   *

                        66

Thus He doth find of all mankind,
Rom. 3.10,12
    that stand at His left hand,
No mother's son, but hath mis-done,
    and broken God's command.
All have transgressed, even the best,   525
    and merited God's wrath
Unto their own perdition,
    and everlasting scath.

                    *   *   *

                        107

*Those that
pretend want of
opportunity
to repent.
Prov. 27.1
Jam. 4.13*
A wond'rous crowd then 'gan aloud,
    thus for themselves to say,   850
"We did intend, Lord to amend,
    and to reform our way:
Our true intent was to repent,
    and make our peace with Thee;
But sudden death stopping our breath,   855
    left us no liberty.

                        108

"Short was our time, for in his prime
    our youthful flower was cropped:
We died in youth, before full growth,
    so was our purpose stopped.   860
Let our good will to turn from ill,
    and sin to have forsaken,

---

7. Advice.   8. I.e., broke.

Accepted be, O Lord, by Thee,
and in good part be taken."

109

*Are confuted
and convinced.
Eccles. 12.1
Rev. 2.21*

To whom the Judge: "Where you allege   865
the shortness of the space,
That from your birth you lived on earth,
to compass saving grace:
It was free grace that any space
was given you at all   870
To turn from evil, defy the devil,
and upon God to call.

110

*Luk. 13.24
2 Cor. 6.2
Heb. 3.7–9*

"One day, one week, wherein to seek
God's face with all your hearts,
A favor was that far did pass   875
the best of your deserts. [9]
You had a season, what was your reason
such precious hours to waste?
What could you find, what could you mind
that was of greater haste?   880

*   *   *

113

*Luk. 13.24–25
etc.
Phil. 2.12*

"Had your intent been to repent,
and had you it desired,   900
There would have been endeavors seen,
before your time expired
God makes no treasure, nor hath he pleasure,
in idle purposes:
Such fair pretenses are foul offenses,   905
and cloaks for wickedness."

*   *   *

130

*Others plead for
pardon both from
God's mercy and
justice.
Psal. 78.38*

Others argue, and not a few,
"Is not God gracious?
His equity and clemency   1035
are they not marvelous?
Thus we believed; are we deceived?
cannot His mercy great,
(As hath been told to us of old)
assuage His anger's heat?   1040

*   *   *

132

"Can God delight in such a sight
as sinners' misery?   1050
Or what great good can this our blood
bring unto The Most High?

---

9. Good deeds, merits.

Psal. 30.9
Mic. 7.18
Oh, Thou that dost Thy glory most
   in pard'ning sin display!
Lord, might it please Thee to release,   1055
   and pardon us this day?"

                              *   *   *

                              134
But all too late, grief's out of date,   1065
   when life is at an end.
The glorious King thus answering,
   all to His voice attend:
They answered.   "God gracious is," quoth He, "like His
   no mercy can be found;   1070
His equity and clemency
   to sinners do abound.

                              135
Mercy that now   "As may appear by those that here
shines forth in the   are placed at My right hand;   1075
vessels of mercy.   Whose stripes I bore, and cleared the score,
Mic. 7.18   that they might quitted stand.
Rom. 9.23   For surely none, but God alone,
   whose grace transcends men's thought,
For such as those that were His foes
   like wonders would have wrought.   1080

                              *   *   *

                              137
Luk. 13.34   "With cords of love God often strove
The day of grace   your stubborn hearts to tame: 1090
now past.   Nevertheless your wickedness,
   did still resist the same.
If now at last mercy be past
   from you forevermore,
And justice come in mercy's room,   1095
   yet grudge you not therefore.

                              138
"If into wrath God turnéd hath
   His long long suffering,
Luk. 19.42–43   And now for love you vengeance prove,
Jud. 4   it is an equal thing.   1100
Your waxing[1] worse, hath stopped the course
   of wonted[2] clemency:
Mercy refused, and grace misused,
   call for severity."

                              *   *   *

                              156
These words appall and daunt them all;
   dismayed, and all amort,

1. Growing.   2. Familiar, usual.

Like stocks[3] they stand at Christ's left hand,
   and dare no more retort.

*   *   *

182

Behold the
formidable estate
of all the ungodly,
as they stand
hopeless &
helpless before an
impartial Judge,
expecting their
final sentence.
Rev. 6.16–17

Thus all men's pleas the Judge with ease
   doth answer and confute,   1450
Until that all, both great and small,
   are silencéd and mute.
Vain hopes are cropped, all mouths are stopped,
   sinners have naught to say,
But that 'tis just, and equal most   1455
   they should be damned for ay.

183

Now what remains, but that to pains
   and everlasting smart,[4]
Christ should condemn the sons of men,
   which is their just desert;   1460
Oh, rueful plights of sinful wights![5]
   oh wretches all forlorn:
'T had happy been they ne're had seen
   the sun, or not been born.

184

Yea, now it would be good they could   1465
   themselves annihilate,
And cease to be, themselves to free
   from such a fearful state.
Oh happy dogs, and swine, and frogs:
   yea serpent's generation,   1470
Who do not fear this doom to hear,
   and sentence of damnation!

185

Psal. 139.2–4
Eccles. 12.14

This is their state so desperate:
   their sins are fully known;
Their vanities and villanies   1475
   before the world are shown.
As they are gross and impious,
   so are their numbers more
Than motes i'th' air, or than their hair,
   or sands upon the shore.   1480

186

Divine justice offended is
   and satisfaction claimeth:
God's wrathful ire kindled like fire,
   against them fiercely flameth.
Their Judge severe doth quite cashier[6]   1485

Mat. 25.45

   and all their pleas off take,
That never a man, or dare, or can
   a further answer make.

---

3. Blocks of wood, speechless persons. "Amort": spiritless, inanimate.
4. Hurt.

5. Souls, persons.
6. Dismiss from fellowship.

187

Mat. 22.12
Rom. 2.5–6
Luk. 19.42

Their mouths are shut, each man is put
   to silence and to shame: 1490
Nor have they ought within their thought,
   Christ's justice for to blame.
The Judge is just, and plague[7] them must,
   nor will He mercy show
(For mercy's day is past away)   1495
   to any of this crew.

*   *   *

195

Unto the saints[8] with sad complaints
   should they themselves apply?

Rev. 21.4

They're not dejected, nor ought affected   1555
   with all their misery.
Friends stand aloof, and make no proof
   what prayers or tears can do:

Psal. 58.10

Your godly friends are now more friends
   to Christ than unto you.   1560

196

Where tender love men's hearts did move
   unto a sympathy,
And bearing part of other's smart
   in their anxiety;

1 Cor. 6.2

Now such compassion is out of fashion   1565
   and wholly laid aside:
No friends so near, but saints to hear
   their sentence can abide.

197

One natural brother beholds another
   in this astonied[9] fit,   1570

Compare
Prov. 1.26 with
1 Joh. 3.2 &
2 Cor. 5.16

Yet sorrows not thereat a jot,
   nor pities him a whit.
The godly wife conceives no grief,
   nor can she shed a tear
For the sad state of her dear mate,   1575
   When she his doom doth hear.

198

He that was erst[1] a husband pierced
   with sense of wife's distress,
Whose tender heart did bear a part
   of all her grievances,   1580
Shall mourn no more as heretofore
   because of her ill plight;
Although he see her now to be
   a damned forsaken wight.

199

The tender mother will own no other   1585
   of all her num'rus brood,

---

7. Punish.
8. Those who experienced saving grace and in this life
felt assurance of salvation; not to be confused with the

canonized saints of the Catholic Church.
9. Dazed.
1. At one time.

But such as stand at Christ's right hand
  acquitted through His blood.

Luk. 16.25

The pious father had now much rather
  his graceless son should lie   1590
In hell with devils, for all his evils
  burning eternally,

200

Than God most high should injury,

Psal. 58.10

  by sparing him sustain;
And doth rejoice to hear Christ's voice   1595
  adjudging him to pain;
Who having all, both great and small,
  convinced and silencéd,
Did then proceed their doom to read,
  and thus it utteréd: 1600

201

The Judge
pronounceth the
sentence of
condemnation.
Mat. 25.41

"Ye sinful wights, and cursed sprights,[2]
  that work iniquity,
Depart together from me forever
  to endless misery;
Your portion take in yonder lake,   1605
  where fire and brimstone flameth:
Suffer the smart, which your desert
  as its due wages claimeth."

*   *   *

205

Luk. 13.28

They wring their hands, their caitiff[3]-hands
  and gnash their teeth for terror;
They cry, they roar for anguish sore,   1635
  and gnaw their tongues for horror.
But get away without delay,
  Christ pities not your cry:
Depart to hell, there may you yell,

Prov. 1.26

  and roar eternally.   1640

206

It is put in
execution.

That word, *Depart*, maugre their heart,[4]
  drives every wicked one,
With mighty power, the self-same hour,
  far from the Judge's throne.

Mat. 25.46

Away they're chased by the strong blast   1645
  of His death-threat'ning mouth:
They flee full fast, as if in haste,
  although they be full loath.[5]

207

As chaff that's dry, and dust doth fly
  before the northern wind: 1650
Right so are they chaséd away,
  and can no refuge find.
They hasten to the pit of woe,

---

2. Spirits.
3. Wretched.

4. Despite their wishes.
5. Reluctant to do so.

Mat. 13.41–42
guarded by angels stout;[6]
Who to fulfill Christ's holy will,   1655
    attend this wicked rout.[7]

208

HELL.
Mat. 25.30
Mar. 9.43
Isa. 30.33
Rev. 21.8
Whom having brought, as they are taught,
    unto the brink of hell
(That dismal place far from Christ's face,
    where death and darkness dwell: 1660
Where God's fierce ire kindleth the fire,
    and vengeance feeds the flame
With piles of wood, and brimstone flood,
    that none can quench the same),

209

Wicked men
and devils cast into
it forever.
Mat. 22.13 &
25.46
With iron bands they bind their hands,   1665
    and curséd feet together,
And cast them all, both great and small,
    into that lake forever.
Where day and night, without respite,
    they wail, and cry, and howl   1670
For tort'ring pain, which they sustain
    in body and in soul.

210

Rev. 14.10–11
For day and night, in their despite,
    their torment's smoke ascendeth.
Their pain and grief have no relief,   1675
    their anguish never endeth.
There must they lie, and never die,
    though dying every day:
There must they dying ever lie,
    and not consume away.   1680

*   *   *

218

Mar. 9.44
Rom. 2.15
Thus shall they lie, and wail, and cry,
    tormented, and tormenting
Their galléd hearts with poisoned darts
    but now too late repenting.   1740
There let them dwell i'th' flames of hell;
    there leave we them to burn,
And back again unto the men
    whom Christ acquits, return.

219

The saints rejoice
to see judgment
executed upon the
wicked world.
Psal. 58.10
Rev. 19.1–3
The saints behold with courage bold,   1745
    and thankful wonderment,
To see all those that were their foes
    thus sent to punishment:
Then do they sing unto their King
    a song of endless praise: 1750
They praise His name, and do proclaim
    that just are all His ways.

6. Resolute, brave.   7. Fleeing mob.

220

They ascend with Christ into heaven triumphing.
Mat. 25.46
I Joh. 3.2
1 Cor. 13.12

Thus with great joy and melody
    to heav'n they all ascend,
Him there to praise with sweetest lays,[8]   1755
    and hymns that never end,
Where with long rest they shall be blest,
    and nought shall them annoy:
Where they shall see as seen they be,
    and whom they love enjoy.   1760

221

Their eternal happiness and incomparable glory there.

O glorious place! where face to face
    Jehovah may be seen,
By such as were sinners whilere[9]
    and no dark veil between.
Where the sun shine, and light divine,   1765
    of God's bright countenance,
Doth rest upon them every one,
    with sweetest influence.

222

O blessed state of the renate![1]
    O wondrous happiness,   1770
To which they're brought, beyond what thought
    can reach, or words express!

Rev. 21.4

Grief's water-course,[2] and sorrow's source,
    are turned to joyful streams.
Their old distress and heaviness   1775
    are vanishéd like dreams.

223

For God above in arms of love
    doth dearly them embrace,

Psal. 16.11

And fills their sprights with such delights,
    and pleasures in His grace;   1780
As shall not fail, nor yet grow stale
    through frequency of use:
Nor do they fear God's favor there,
    to forfeit by abuse.

224

Heb. 12.23

For there the saints are perfect saints,   1785
    and holy ones indeed,
From all the sin that dwelt within
    their mortal bodies freed:
Made kings and priests to God through Christ's

Rev. 1.6
& 22.5

    dear love's transcendency,   1790
There to remain, and there to reign
    with Him eternally.

1662

8. Songs.
9. Once, earlier.

1. Reborn.
2. Channel bed.

MARY ROWLANDSON
c. 1636–1711

On June 20, 1675, Metacomet, who was called Philip by the colonists, led the first of a series of attacks on colonial settlements that lasted for more than a year. Before they were over, more than twelve hundred houses had been burned, about six hundred English colonials were dead, and three thousand American Indians killed. These attacks have become known as "King Philip's War." It was the direct result of the execution in Plymouth, Massachusetts, of three of Philip's Wampanoag tribesmen, but the indirect causes were many; not the least was the fact that the Native Americans were starving and desperate to retain their lands. In a sense, the war may be seen as a last-ditch effort by the Wampanoags and their allies against further expansion by the colonists. By the time the war was over, in August of 1676, with Philip slain and his wife and children sold into slavery in the West Indies, the independent power of the New England American Indians had ended.

Probably the most famous victim of these attacks is the author of *A Narrative of the Captivity and Restoration of Mrs. Mary Rowlandson*, the wife of the minister of the town of Lancaster. With the exception of the eleven weeks she spent as a captive among the Wampanoags, however, almost everything about Mrs. Rowlandson's life remains conjectural. She was probably born in England and brought to this country at an early age. Her father, John White, was a wealthy landholder in the Massachusetts Bay Colony who settled in Lancaster. About 1656 she married Joseph Rowlandson and for the next twenty years led a busy life of mother and minister's wife. The attack on Lancaster occurred on February 10, 1676, and she was not released until the second of May, having been ransomed for twenty pounds. The following year she went with her husband to Wethersfield, Connecticut; Mr. Rowlandson died there in 1678. The town voted to pay her an annuity "so long as she remains a widow among us." For lack of any further information, most biographical entries conclude here. Recently, David Greene has verified that Mary Rowlandson married Captain Samuel Talcott in Wethersfield on August 6, 1679, and that she died in that Connecticut Valley town on January 5, 1711, thirty-five years after her famous ordeal.

Shortly after her return to Lancaster, Mrs. Rowlandson began to make a record of her life in captivity. Her *Narrative* (published in 1682) is the only evidence we have of her skill as a writer. The account of her captivity became one of the most popular prose works of the seventeenth century, both in this country and in England. It combined high adventure, heroism, and exemplary piety and is the first and, in its narrative skill and delineation of character, the best of what have become popularly known as "Indian captivities." As transformed into fictional form by writers like James Fenimore Cooper (in *The Last of the Mohicans*) and William Faulkner (in *Sanctuary*), it is a genre that has proven to be an integral part of our American literary consciousness.

A Narrative of the Captivity and Restoration of Mrs. Mary Rowlandson[1]

On the tenth of February 1675,[2] came the Indians with great numbers upon Lancaster:[3] their first coming was about sunrising; hearing the noise of some guns, we looked out; several houses were burning, and the smoke ascending to heaven. There were five persons taken in one house; the father, and the mother and a sucking child, they knocked on the head; the other two they took and carried away alive. There were two others, who being out of their garrison[4] upon some occasion were set upon; one was knocked on the head, the other escaped; another there was who running along was shot and wounded, and fell down; he begged of them his life, promising them money (as they told me) but they would not hearken to him but knocked him in head, and stripped him naked, and split open his bowels.[5] Another, seeing many of the Indians about his barn, ventured and went out, but was quickly shot down. There were three others belonging to the same garrison who were killed; the Indians getting up upon the roof of the barn, had advantage to shoot down upon them over their fortification. Thus these murderous wretches went on, burning, and destroying before them.

At length they came and beset our own house, and quickly it was the dolefulest day that ever mine eyes saw. The house stood upon the edge of a hill; some of the Indians got behind the hill, others into the barn, and others behind anything that could shelter them; from all which places they shot against the house, so that the bullets seemed to fly like hail; and quickly they wounded one man among us, then another, and then a third. About two hours (according to my observation, in that amazing time) they had been about the house before they prevailed to fire it (which they did with flax and hemp, which they brought out of the barn, and there being no defense about the house, only two flankers[6] at two opposite corners and one of them not finished); they fired it once and one ventured out and quenched it, but they quickly fired it again, and that took. Now is the dreadful hour come, that I have often heard of (in time of war, as it was the case of others), but now mine eyes see it. Some in our house were fighting for their lives, others wallowing in their blood, the house on fire over our heads, and the bloody heathen ready to knock us on the head, if we stirred out. Now might we hear mothers and children crying out for themselves, and one another, "Lord, what shall we do?" Then I took my children (and one of my sisters', hers) to go forth and leave the house: but as soon as we came to the door and appeared, the Indians shot so thick that the bullets rattled against the house, as if one had taken an handful of stones and threw them, so that we were fain to give back. We had six stout dogs belonging to our garrison, but none of them would stir, though

---

1. The text used is *Original Narratives of Early American History, Narratives of Indian Wars 1675–1699*, Vol. 14, edited by C. H. Lincoln (1952). The full title is *The sovereignty and goodness of GOD, together with the faithfulness of his promises displayed; being a narrative of the captivity and restoration of Mrs. Mary Rowlandson, commended by her, to all that desires to know the Lord's doings to, and dealings with her. Especially to her dear children and relations. The second Addition Corrected and amended. Written by her own hand for her private use, and now made public at the earnest desire of some friends, and for the benefit of the afflicted.*

Deut. 32.39. *See now that I, even I am he, and there is no god with me; I kill and I make alive, I wound and I heal, neither is there any can deliver out of my hand.*
2. A Thursday, Using the present Gregorian calendar, adopted in 1752, February 20, 1676.
3. Lancaster, Massachusetts, was a frontier town of approximately fifty families, about thirty miles west of Boston.
4. I.e., houses in the town where people gathered for defense.
5. Belly.
6. Projecting fortifications.

another time, if any Indian had come to the door, they were ready to fly upon him and tear him down. The Lord hereby would make us the more acknowledge His hand, and to see that our help is always in Him. But out we must go, the fire increasing, and coming along behind us, roaring, and the Indians gaping before us with their guns, spears, and hatchets to devour us. No sooner were we out of the house, but my brother-in-law (being before wounded, in defending the house, in or near the throat) fell down dead, whereat the Indians scornfully shouted, and hallowed, and were presently upon him, stripping off his clothes, the bullets flying thick, one went through my side, and the same (as would seem) through the bowels and hand of my dear child in my arms. One of my elder sisters' children, named William, had then his leg broken, which the Indians perceiving, they knocked him on [his] head. Thus were we butchered by those merciless heathen, standing amazed, with the blood running down to our heels. My eldest sister being yet in the house, and seeing those woeful sights, the infidels hauling mothers one way, and children another, and some wallowing in their blood: and her elder son telling her that her son William was dead, and myself was wounded, she said, "And Lord, let me die with them," which was no sooner said, but she was struck with a bullet, and fell down dead over the threshold. I hope she is reaping the fruit of her good labors, being faithful to the service of God in her place. In her younger years she lay under much trouble upon spiritual accounts, till it pleased God to make that precious scripture take hold of her heart, "And he said unto me, my Grace is sufficient for thee" (2 Corinthians 12.9). More than twenty years after, I have heard her tell how sweet and comfortable that place was to her. But to return: the Indians laid hold of us, pulling me one way, and the children another, and said, "Come go along with us"; I told them they would kill me: they answered, if I were willing to go along with them, they would not hurt me.

Oh the doleful sight that now was to behold at this house! "Come, behold the works of the Lord, what desolations he has made in the earth."[7] Of thirty-seven persons who were in this one house, none escaped either present death, or a bitter captivity, save only one, who might say as he, "And I only am escaped alone to tell the News" (Job 1.15). There were twelve killed, some shot, some stabbed with their spears, some knocked down with their hatchets. When we are in prosperity, Oh the little that we think of such dreadful sights, and to see our dear friends, and relations lie bleeding out their heart-blood upon the ground. There was one who was chopped into the head with a hatchet, and stripped naked, and yet was crawling up and down. It is a solemn sight to see so many Christians lying in their blood, some here, and some there, like a company of sheep torn by wolves, all of them stripped naked by a company of hell-hounds, roaring, singing, ranting, and insulting, as if they would have torn our very hearts out; yet the Lord by His almighty power preserved a number of us from death, for there were twenty-four of us taken alive and carried captive.

I had often before this said that if the Indians should come, I should choose rather to be killed by them than taken alive, but when it came to the trial my mind changed; their glittering weapons so daunted my spirit, that I chose rather to go along with those (as I may say) ravenous beasts, than that moment to end my days; and that I may the better declare what happened to me during

7. Psalm 46.8.

that grievous captivity, I shall particularly speak of the several removes[8] we had up and down the wilderness.

The First Remove

Now away we must go with those barbarous creatures, with our bodies wounded and bleeding, and our hearts no less than our bodies. About a mile we went that night, up upon a hill within sight of the town, where they intended to lodge. There was hard by a vacant house (deserted by the English before, for fear of the Indians). I asked them whether I might not lodge in the house that night, to which they answered, "What, will you love English men still?" This was the dolefulest night that ever my eyes saw. Oh the roaring, and singing and dancing, and yelling of those black creatures in the night, which made the place a lively resemblance of hell. And as miserable was the waste that was there made of horses, cattle, sheep, swine, calves, lambs, roasting pigs, and fowl (which they had plundered in the town), some roasting, some lying and burning, and some boiling to feed our merciless enemies; who were joyful enough, though we were disconsolate. To add to the dolefulness of the former day, and the dismalness of the present night, my thoughts ran upon my losses and sad bereaved condition. All was gone, my husband gone (at least separated from me, he being in the Bay;[9] and to add to my grief, the Indians told me they would kill him as he came homeward), my children gone, my relations and friends gone, our house and home and all our comforts—within door and without—all was gone (except my life), and I knew not but the next moment that might go too. There remained nothing to me but one poor wounded babe, and it seemed at present worse than death that it was in such a pitiful condition, bespeaking compassion, and I had no refreshing for it, nor suitable things to revive it. Little do many think what is the savageness and brutishness of this barbarous enemy, Ay, even those that seem to profess more than others among them, when the English have fallen into their hands.

Those seven that were killed at Lancaster the summer before upon a Sabbath day, and the one that was afterward killed upon a weekday, were slain and mangled in a barbarous manner, by one-eyed John, and Marlborough's Praying Indians, which Capt. Mosely brought to Boston, as the Indians told me.[1]

The Second Remove[2]

But now, the next morning, I must turn my back upon the town, and travel with them into the vast and desolate wilderness, I knew not whither. It is not my tongue, or pen, can express the sorrows of my heart, and bitterness of my spirit that I had at this departure: but God was with me in a wonderful manner, carrying me along, and bearing up my spirit, that it did not quite fail. One of the Indians carried my poor wounded babe upon a horse; it went moaning all along, "I shall die, I shall die." I went on foot after it, with sorrow that cannot be expressed. At length I took it off the horse, and carried it in my arms till my strength failed, and I fell down with it. Then they set me upon a horse

---

8. I.e., departures; movings from place to place.
9. I.e., Boston, or Massachusetts Bay.
1. On August 30, 1675, Captain Samuel Mosely, encouraged by a number of people who were skeptical of converted American Indians, brought to Boston by force fifteen Christianized American Indians who lived on their own lands in Marlborough, Massachusetts, and accused them of an attack on the town of Lancaster on August 22.
2. To Princeton, Massachusetts, near Mount Wachusett.

with my wounded child in my lap, and there being no furniture upon the horse's back, as we were going down a steep hill we both fell over the horse's head, at which they, like inhumane creatures, laughed, and rejoiced to see it, though I thought we should there have ended our days, as overcome with so many difficulties. But the Lord renewed my strength still, and carried me along, that I might see more of His power; yea, so much that I could never have thought of, had I not experienced it.

After this it quickly began to snow, and when night came on, they stopped, and now down I must sit in the snow, by a little fire, and a few boughs behind me, with my sick child in my lap; and calling much for water, being now (through the wound) fallen into a violent fever. My own wound also growing so stiff that I could scarce sit down or rise up; yet so it must be, that I must sit all this cold winter night upon the cold snowy ground, with my sick child in my arms, looking that every hour would be the last of its life; and having no Christian friend near me, either to comfort or help me. Oh, I may see the wonderful power of God, that my Spirit did not utterly sink under my afflic-tion: still the Lord upheld me with His gracious and merciful spirit, and we were both alive to see the light of the next morning.

The Third Remove[3]

The morning being come, they prepared to go on their way. One of the Indians got up upon a horse, and they set me up behind him, with my poor sick babe in my lap. A very wearisome and tedious day I had of it; what with my own wound, and my child's being so exceeding sick, and in a lamentable condition with her wound. It may be easily judged what a poor feeble condi-tion we were in, there being not the least crumb of refreshing that came within either of our mouths from Wednesday night to Saturday night, except only a little cold water. This day in the afternoon, about an hour by sun, we came to the place where they intended, *viz.* an Indian town, called Wenimesset, northward of Quabaug. When we were come, Oh the number of pagans (now merciless enemies) that there came about me, that I may say as David, "I had fainted, unless I had believed, etc" (Psalm 27.13). The next day was the Sab-bath. I then remembered how careless I had been of God's holy time; how many Sabbaths I had lost and misspent, and how evilly I had walked in God's sight; which lay so close unto my spirit, that it was easy for me to see how righteous it was with God to cut off the thread of my life and cast me out of His presence forever. Yet the Lord still showed mercy to me, and upheld me; and as He wounded me with one hand, so he healed me with the other. This day there came to me one Robert Pepper (a man belonging to Roxbury) who was taken in Captain Beers's fight, and had been now a considerable time with the Indians; and up with them almost as far as Albany, to see King Philip, as he told me, and was now very lately come into these parts.[4] Hearing, I say, that I was in this Indian town, he obtained leave to come and see me. He told me he himself was wounded in the leg at Captain Beer's fight; and was not able some time to go, but as they carried him, and as he took oaken leaves and laid to his wound, and through the blessing of God he was able to travel again. Then I took oaken leaves and laid to my side, and with the blessing of God it

3. February 12–27; they stopped at a Native American village on the Ware River near New Braintree.

4. Captain Beers had attempted to save the garrison of Northfield, Massachusetts, on September 4, 1675.

cured me also; yet before the cure was wrought, I may say, as it is in Psalm 38.5–6 "My wounds stink and are corrupt, I am troubled, I am bowed down greatly, I go mourning all the day long." I sat much alone with a poor wounded child in my lap, which moaned night and day, having nothing to revive the body, or cheer the spirits of her, but instead of that, sometimes one Indian would come and tell me one hour that "your master will knock your child in the head," and then a second, and then a third, "your master will quickly knock your child in the head."

This was the comfort I had from them, miserable comforters are ye all, as he[5] said. Thus nine days I sat upon my knees, with my babe in my lap, till my flesh was raw again; my child being even ready to depart this sorrowful world, they bade me carry it out to another wigwam (I suppose because they would not be troubled with such spectacles) whither I went with a very heavy heart, and down I sat with the picture of death in my lap. About two hours in the night, my sweet babe like a lamb departed this life on Feb. 18, 1675. It being about six years, and five months old. It was nine days from the first wounding, in this miserable condition, without any refreshing of one nature or other, except a little cold water. I cannot but take notice how at another time I could not bear to be in the room where any dead person was, but now the case is changed; I must and could lie down by my dead babe, side by side all the night after. I have thought since of the wonderful goodness of God to me in preserving me in the use of my reason and senses in that distressed time, that I did not use wicked and violent means to end my own miserable life. In the morning, when they understood that my child was dead they sent for me home to my master's wigwam (by my master in this writing, must be understood Quinnapin, who was a Sagamore,[6] and married King Philip's wife's sister; not that he first took me, but I was sold to him by another Narragansett Indian, who took me when first I came out of the garrison). I went to take up my dead child in my arms to carry it with me, but they bid me let it alone; there was no resisting, but go I must and leave it. When I had been at my master's wigwam, I took the first opportunity I could get to go look after my dead child. When I came I asked them what they had done with it; then they told me it was upon the hill. Then they went and showed me where it was, where I saw the ground was newly digged, and there they told me they had buried it. There I left that child in the wilderness, and must commit it, and myself also in this wilderness condition, to Him who is above all. God having taken away this dear child, I went to see my daughter Mary, who was at this same Indian town, at a wigwam not very far off, though we had little liberty or opportunity to see one another. She was about ten years old, and taken from the door at first by a Praying Ind. and afterward sold for a gun. When I came in sight, she would fall aweeping; at which they were provoked, and would not let me come near her, but bade me be gone; which was a heart-cutting word to me. I had one child dead, another in the wilderness, I knew not where, the third they would not let me come near to: "Me (as he said) have ye bereaved of my Children, Joseph is not, and Simeon is not, and ye will take Benjamin also, all these things are against me."[7] I could not sit still in this condition, but kept walking from one place to another. And as I was going along, my heart was even overwhelmed with the thoughts of my condition, and that I should have children, and a

---

5. I.e., as Job said. "I have heard many such things: miserable comforters are ye all" (Job 16.2).
6. A subordinate chief among the Algonquin Indians.

Quinnapin was the husband of Weetamoo, and Rowlandson became her servant.
7. Jacob's lamentation in Genesis 42.36.

nation which I knew not, ruled over them. Whereupon I earnestly entreated the Lord, that He would consider my low estate, and show me a token for good, and if it were His blessed will, some sign and hope of some relief. And indeed quickly the Lord answered, in some measure, my poor prayers; for as I was going up and down mourning and lamenting my condition, my son came to me, and asked me how I did. I had not seen him before, since the destruction of the town, and I knew not where he was, till I was informed by himself, that he was amongst a smaller parcel of Indians, whose place was about six miles off. With tears in his eyes, he asked me whether his sister Sarah was dead; and told me he had seen his sister Mary; and prayed me, that I would not be troubled in reference to himself. The occasion of his coming to see me at this time, was this: there was, as I said, about six miles from us, a small plantation of Indians, where it seems he had been during his captivity; and at this time, there were some forces of the Ind. gathered out of our company, and some also from them (among whom was my son's master) to go to assault and burn Medfield.[8] In this time of the absence of his master, his dame brought him to see me. I took this to be some gracious answer to my earnest and unfeigned desire. The next day, *viz.* to this, the Indians returned from Medfield, all the company, for those that belonged to the other small company, came through the town that now we were at. But before they came to us, Oh! the outrageous roaring and hooping that there was. They began their din about a mile before they came to us. By their noise and hooping they signified how many they had destroyed (which was at that time twenty-three). Those that were with us at home were gathered together as soon as they heard the hooping, and every time that the other went over their number, these at home gave a shout, that the very earth rung again. And thus they continued till those that had been upon the expedition were come up to the Sagamore's wigwam; and then, Oh, the hideous insulting and triumphing that there was over some Englishmen's scalps that they had taken (as their manner is) and brought with them. I cannot but take notice of the wonderful mercy of God to me in those afflictions, in sending me a Bible. One of the Indians that came from Medfield fight, had brought some plunder, came to me, and asked me, if I would have a Bible, he had got one in his basket. I was glad of it, and asked him, whether he thought the Indians would let me read? He answered, yes. So I took the Bible, and in that melancholy time, it came into my mind to read first the 28th chapter of Deuteronomy,[9] which I did, and when I had read it, my dark heart wrought on this manner: that there was no mercy for me, that the blessings were gone, and the curses come in their room, and that I had lost my opportunity. But the Lord helped me still to go on reading till I came to Chap. 30, the seven first verses, where I found, there was mercy promised again, if we would return to Him by repentance;[1] and though we were scattered from one end of the earth to the other, yet the Lord would gather us together, and turn all those curses upon our enemies. I do not desire to live to forget this Scripture, and what comfort it was to me.

Now the Ind. began to talk of removing from this place, some one way, and some another. There were now besides myself nine English captives in this place (all of them children, except one woman). I got an opportunity to go

8. The attack on Medfield, Massachusetts, occurred on February 21.
9. This chapter of Deuteronomy is concerned with blessings for obedience to God and curses for disobedience.
1. "That then the Lord thy God will turn thy captivity, and have compassion upon thee, and will return and gather thee from all the nations." (Deuteronomy 30.3).

and take my leave of them. They being to go one way, and I another, I asked them whether they were earnest with God for deliverance. They told me they did as they were able, and it was some comfort to me, that the Lord stirred up children to look to Him. The woman, *viz.* goodwife[2] Joslin, told me she should never see me again, and that she could find in her heart to run away. I wished her not to run away by any means, for we were near thirty miles from any English town, and she very big with child, and had but one week to reckon, and another child in her arms, two years old, and bad rivers there were to go over, and we were feeble, with our poor and coarse entertainment. I had my Bible with me, I pulled it out, and asked her whether she would read. We opened the Bible and lighted on Psalm 27, in which Psalm we especially took notice of that, *ver. ult.*, "Wait on the Lord, Be of good courage, and he shall strengthen thine Heart, wait I say on the Lord."[3]

The Fourth Remove[4]

And now I must part with that little company I had. Here I parted from my daughter Mary (whom I never saw again till I saw her in Dorchester, returned from captivity), and from four little cousins and neighbors, some of which I never saw afterward: the Lord only knows the end of them. Amongst them also was that poor woman before mentioned, who came to a sad end, as some of the company told me in my travel: she having much grief upon her spirit about her miserable condition, being so near her time, she would be often asking the Indians to let her go home; they not being willing to that, and yet vexed with her importunity, gathered a great company together about her and stripped her naked, and set her in the midst of them, and when they had sung and danced about her (in their hellish manner) as long as they pleased they knocked her on head, and the child in her arms with her. When they had done that they made a fire and put them both into it, and told the other children that were with them that if they attempted to go home, they would serve them in like manner. The children said she did not shed one tear, but prayed all the while. But to return to my own journey, we traveled about half a day or little more, and came to a desolate place in the wilderness, where there were no wigwams or inhabitants before; we came about the middle of the afternoon to this place, cold and wet, and snowy, and hungry, and weary, and no refreshing for man but the cold ground to sit on, and our poor Indian cheer.

Heart-aching thoughts here I had about my poor children, who were scattered up and down among the wild beasts of the forest. My head was light and dizzy (either through hunger or hard lodging, or trouble or all together), my knees feeble, my body raw by sitting double night and day, that I cannot express to man the affliction that lay upon my spirit, but the Lord helped me at that time to express it to Himself. I opened my Bible to read, and the Lord brought that precious Scripture to me. "Thus saith the Lord, refrain thy voice from weeping, and thine eyes from tears, for thy work shall be rewarded, and they shall come again from the land of the enemy" (Jeremiah 31.16). This was a sweet cordial to me when I was ready to faint; many and many a time have I sat down and wept sweetly over this Scripture. At this place we continued about four days.

2. I.e., the mistress of a house.
3. Verse 14.
4. February 28 to March 3. The camp was between

Ware River and Miller's River in present-day Petersham, Massachussetts.

The Fifth Remove[5]

The occasion (as I thought) of their moving at this time was the English army, it being near and following them. For they went as if they had gone for their lives, for some considerable way, and then they made a stop, and chose some of their stoutest men, and sent them back to hold the English army in play whilst the rest escaped. And then, like Jehu,[6] they marched on furiously, with their old and with their young: some carried their old decrepit mothers, some carried one, and some another. Four of them carried a great Indian upon a bier; but going through a thick wood with him, they were hindered, and could make no haste, whereupon they took him upon their backs, and carried him, one at a time, till they came to Banquaug river. Upon a Friday, a little after noon, we came to this river. When all the company was come up, and were gathered together, I thought to count the number of them, but they were so many, and being somewhat in motion, it was beyond my skill. In this travel, because of my wound, I was somewhat favored in my load; I carried only my knitting work and two quarts of parched meal. Being very faint I asked my mistress to give me one spoonful of the meal, but she would not give me a taste. They quickly fell to cutting dry trees, to make rafts to carry them over the river: and soon my turn came to go over. By the advantage of some brush which they had laid upon the raft to sit upon, I did not wet my foot (which many of themselves at the other end were mid-leg deep) which cannot but be acknowledged as a favor of God to my weakened body, it being a very cold time. I was not before acquainted with such kind of doings or dangers. "When thou passeth through the waters I will be with thee, and through the rivers they shall not overflow thee" (Isaiah 43.2). A certain number of us got over the river that night, but it was the night after the Sabbath before all the company was got over. On the Saturday they boiled an old horse's leg which they had got, and so we drank of the broth, as soon as they thought it was ready, and when it was almost all gone, they filled it up again.

The first week of my being among them I hardly ate any thing; the second week I found my stomach grow very faint for want of something; and yet it was very hard to get down their filthy trash; but the third week, though I could think how formerly my stomach would turn against this or that, and I could starve and die before I could eat such things, yet they were sweet and savory to my taste. I was at this time knitting a pair of white cotton stockings for my mistress; and had not yet wrought upon a Sabbath day. When the Sabbath came they bade me go to work. I told them it was the Sabbath day, and desired them to let me rest, and told them I would do as much more tomorrow; to which they answered me they would break my face. And here I cannot but take notice of the strange providence of God in preserving the heathen. They were many hundreds, old and young, some sick, and some lame; many had papooses at their backs. The greatest number at this time with us were squaws, and they traveled with all they had, bag and baggage, and yet they got over this river aforesaid; and on Monday they set their wigwams on fire, and away they went. On that very day came the English army after them to this river,

5. March 3 to March 5. They crossed the Banquaug or present-day Miller's River in Orange, Massachusetts. The "English army" Rowlandson refers to consisted of Massachusetts and Connecticut forces under the command of Captain Thomas Savage.
6. King of Israel (c. 843–816 B.C.) who killed kings Jehoram and Ahaziah (cf. 2 Kings 9.20).

and saw the smoke of their wigwams, and yet this river put a stop to them. God did not give them courage or activity to go over after us. We were not ready for so great a mercy as victory and deliverance. If we had been God would have found out a way for the English to have passed this river, as well as for the Indians with their squaws and children, and all their luggage. "Oh that my people had hearkened to me, and Israel had walked in my ways, I should soon have subdued their enemies, and turned my hand against their adversaries" (Psalm 81.13–14).

The Sixth Remove[7]

On Monday (as I said) they set their wigwams on fire and went away. It was a cold morning, and before us there was a great brook with ice on it; some waded through it, up to the knees and higher, but others went till they came to a beaver dam, and I amongst them, where through the good providence of God, I did not wet my foot. I went along that day mourning and lamenting, leaving farther my own country, and traveling into a vast and howling wilderness, and I understood something of Lot's wife's temptation, when she looked back.[8] We came that day to a great swamp, by the side of which we took up our lodging that night. When I came to the brow of the hill, that looked toward the swamp, I thought we had been come to a great Indian town (though there were none but our own company). The Indians were as thick as the trees: it seemed as if there had been a thousand hatchets going at once. If one looked before one there was nothing but Indians, and behind one, nothing but Indians, and so on either hand, I myself in the midst, and no Christian soul near me, and yet how hath the Lord preserved me in safety? Oh the experience that I have had of the goodness of God, to me and mine!

The Seventh Remove[9]

After a restless and hungry night there, we had a wearisome time of it the next day. The swamp by which we lay was, as it were, a deep dungeon, and an exceeding high and steep hill before it. Before I got to the top of the hill, I thought my heart and legs, and all would have broken, and failed me. What, through faintness and soreness of body, it was a grievous day of travel to me. As we went along, I saw a place where English cattle had been. That was comfort to me, such as it was. Quickly after that we came to an English path, which so took with me, that I thought I could have freely lyen down and died. That day, a little after noon, we came to Squakeag, where the Indians quickly spread themselves over the deserted English fields, gleaning what they could find. Some picked up ears of wheat that were crickled down; some found ears of Indian corn; some found ground nuts, and others sheaves of wheat that were frozen together in the shock, and went to threshing of them out. Myself got two ears of Indian corn, and whilst I did but turn my back, one of them was stolen from me, which much troubled me. There came an Indian to them at that time with a basket of horse liver. I asked him to give me a piece. "What,"

7. Monday, March 6, ending near Northfield, Massachusetts.
8. Lot's wife looked back upon the wicked city of Sodom and was turned into a pillar of salt (cf. Genesis 19.24).
9. To Squakeag, near Beer's Plain, in Northfield, Massachusetts.

says he, "can you eat horse liver?" I told him, I would try, if he would give a piece, which he did, and I laid it on the coals to roast. But before it was half ready they got half of it away from me, so that I was fain to take the rest and eat it as it was, with the blood about my mouth, and yet a savory bit it was to me: "For to the hungry soul every bitter thing is sweet."[1] A solemn sight methought it was, to see fields of wheat and Indian corn forsaken and spoiled and the remainders of them to be food for our merciless enemies. That night we had a mess of wheat for our supper.

The Eighth Remove[2]

On the morrow morning we must go over the river, *i.e.* Connecticut, to meet with King Philip. Two canoes full they had carried over; the next turn I myself was to go. But as my foot was upon the canoe to step in there was a sudden outcry among them, and I must step back, and instead of going over the river, I must go four or five miles up the river farther northward. Some of the Indians ran one way, and some another. The cause of this rout was, as I thought, their espying some English scouts, who were thereabout. In this travel up the river about noon the company made a stop, and sat down; some to eat, and others to rest them. As I sat amongst them, musing of things past, my son Joseph unexpectedly came to me. We asked of each other's welfare, bemoaning our doleful condition, and the change that had come upon us. We had husband and father, and children, and sisters, and friends, and relations, and house, and home, and many comforts of this life: but now we may say, as Job, "Naked came I out of my mother's womb, and naked shall I return: the Lord gave, the Lord hath taken away, blessed be the name of the Lord."[3] I asked him whether he would read. He told me he earnestly desired it, I gave him my Bible, and he lighted upon that comfortable Scripture "I shall not die but live, and declare the works of the Lord: the Lord hath chastened me sore, yet he hath not given me over to death" (Psalm 118.17–18). "Look here, mother," says he, "did you read this?" And here I may take occasion to mention one principal ground of my setting forth these lines: even as the psalmist says, to declare the works of the Lord, and His wonderful power in carrying us along, preserving us in the wilderness, while under the enemy's hand, and returning of us in safety again. And His goodness in bringing to my hand so many comfortable and suitable scriptures in my distress.[4] But to return, we traveled on till night; and in the morning, we must go over the river to Philip's crew. When I was in the canoe I could not but be amazed at the numerous crew of pagans that were on the bank on the other side. When I came ashore, they gathered all about me, I sitting alone in the midst. I observed they asked one another questions, and laughed, and rejoiced over their gains and victories. Then my heart began to fail: and I fell aweeping, which was the first time to my remembrance, that I wept before them. Although I had met with so much affliction, and my heart was many times ready to break, yet could I not shed one tear in their sight; but rather had been all this while in a maze, and like one astonished. But now I may say as Psalm 137.1, "By the Rivers of

---

1. Proverbs 27.7.
2. To Coasset in South Vernon, Vermont.
3. Job 1.21.

4. Rowlandson probably has in mind Psalm 145.4: "One generation shall praise thy works to another, and shall declare thy mighty acts."

Babylon, there we sate down: yea, we wept when we remembered Zion." There one of them asked me why I wept. I could hardly tell what to say: Yet I answered, they would kill me. "No," said he, "none will hurt you." Then came one of them and gave me two spoonfuls of meal to comfort me, and another gave me half a pint of peas; which was more worth than many bushels at another time. Then I went to see King Philip. He bade me come in and sit down, and asked me whether I would smoke it (a usual compliment nowadays amongst saints and sinners[5]) but this no way suited me. For though I had formerly used tobacco, yet I had left it ever since I was first taken. It seems to be a bait the devil lays to make men lose their precious time. I remember with shame how formerly, when I had taken two or three pipes, I was presently ready for another, such a bewitching thing it is. But I thank God, He has now given me power over it; surely there are many who may be better employed than to lie sucking a stinking tobacco-pipe.

Now the Indians gather their forces to go against Northampton. Over night one went about yelling and hooting to give notice of the design. Whereupon they fell to boiling of ground nuts, and parching of corn (as many as had it) for their provision; and in the morning away they went. During my abode in this place, Philip spake to me to make a shirt for his boy, which I did, for which he gave me a shilling. I offered the money to my master, but he bade me keep it; and with it I bought a piece of horse flesh. Afterwards he asked me to make a cap for his boy, for which he invited me to dinner. I went, and he gave me a pancake, about as big as two fingers. It was made of parched wheat, beaten, and fried in bear's grease, but I thought I never tasted pleasanter meat in my life. There was a squaw who spake to me to make a shirt for her *sannup*,[6] for which she gave me a piece of bear. Another asked me to knit a pair of stockings, for which she gave me a quart of peas. I boiled my peas and bear together, and invited my master and mistress to dinner; but the proud gossip,[7] because I served them both in one dish, would eat nothing, except one bit that he gave her upon the point of his knife. Hearing that my son was come to this place, I went to see him, and found him lying flat upon the ground. I asked him how he could sleep so? He answered me that he was not asleep, but at prayer; and lay so, that they might not observe what he was doing. I pray God he may remember these things now he is returned in safety. At this place (the sun now getting higher) what with the beams and heat of the sun, and the smoke of the wigwams, I thought I should have been blind. I could scarce discern one wigwam from another. There was here one Mary Thurston of Medfield, who seeing how it was with me, lent me a hat to wear; but as soon as I was gone, the squaw (who owned that Mary Thurston) came running after me, and got it away again. Here was the squaw that gave me one spoonful of meal. I put it in my pocket to keep it safe. Yet notwithstanding, somebody stole it, but put five Indian corns in the room of it;[8] which corns were the greatest provisions I had in my travel for one day.

The Indians returning from Northampton, brought with them some horses, and sheep, and other things which they had taken; I desired them that they would carry me to Albany upon one of those horses, and sell me for powder:

5. I.e., among believers ("saints") as well as the unregenerate.
6. Husband.

7. Relation, i.e., wife.
8. I.e., five kernels of corn in place of it.

for so they had sometimes discoursed. I was utterly hopeless of getting home on foot, the way that I came. I could hardly bear to think of the many weary steps I had taken, to come to this place.

The Ninth Remove[9]

But instead of going either to Albany or homeward, we must go five miles up the river, and then go over it. Here we abode a while. Here lived a sorry Indian, who spoke to me to make him a shirt. When I had done it, he would pay me nothing. But he living by the riverside, where I often went to fetch water, I would often be putting of him in mind, and calling for my pay: At last he told me if I would make another shirt, for a papoose not yet born, he would give me a knife, which he did when I had done it. I carried the knife in, and my master asked me to give it him, and I was not a little glad that I had anything that they would accept of, and be pleased with. When we were at this place, my master's maid came home; she had been gone three weeks into the Narragansett country to fetch corn, where they had stored up some in the ground. She brought home about a peck and half of corn. This was about the time that their great captain, Naananto, was killed in the Narragansett country. My son being now about a mile from me, I asked liberty to go and see him; they bade me go, and away I went; but quickly lost myself, traveling over hills and through swamps, and could not find the way to him. And I cannot but admire at the wonderful power and goodness of God to me, in that, though I was gone from home, and met with all sorts of Indians, and those I had no knowledge of, and there being no Christian soul near me; yet not one of them offered the least imaginable miscarriage to me. I turned homeward again, and met with my master. He showed me the way to my son. When I came to him I found him not well: and withall he had a boil on his side, which much troubled him. We bemoaned one another a while, as the Lord helped us, and then I returned again. When I was returned, I found myself as unsatisfied as I was before. I went up and down mourning and lamenting; and my spirit was ready to sink with the thoughts of my poor children. My son was ill, and I could but not think of his mournful looks, and no Christian friend was near him, to do any office of love for him, either for soul or body. And my poor girl, I knew not where she was, nor whether she was sick, or well, or alive, or dead. I repaired under these thoughts to my Bible (my great comfort in that time) and that Scripture came to my hand, "Cast thy burden upon the Lord, and He shall sustain thee" (Psalm 55.22).

But I was fain to go and look after something to satisfy my hunger, and going among the wigwams, I went into one and there found a squaw who showed herself very kind to me, and gave me a piece of bear. I put it into my pocket, and came home, but could not find an opportunity to broil it, for fear they would get it from me, and there it lay all that day and night in my stinking pocket. In the morning I went to the same squaw, who had a kettle of ground nuts boiling. I asked her to let me boil my piece of bear in her kettle, which she did, and gave me some ground nuts to eat with it: and I cannot but think how pleasant it was to me. I have sometime seen bear baked very handsomely among the English, and some like it, but the thought that it was bear made

9. To the Ashuelot valley in New Hampshire.

me tremble. But now that was savory to me that one would think was enough to turn the stomach of a brute creature.

One bitter cold day I could find no room to sit down before the fire. I went out, and could not tell what to do, but I went in to another wigwam, where they were also sitting round the fire, but the squaw laid a skin for me, and bid me sit down, and gave me some ground nuts, and bade me come again; and told me they would buy me, if they were able, and yet these were strangers to me that I never saw before.

The Tenth Remove[1]

That day a small part of the company removed about three-quarters of a mile, intending further the next day. When they came to the place where they intended to lodge, and had pitched their wigwams, being hungry, I went again back to the place we were before at, to get something to eat, being encouraged by the squaw's kindness, who bade me come again. When I was there, there came an Indian to look after me, who when he had found me, kicked me all along. I went home and found venison roasting that night, but they would not give me one bit of it. Sometimes I met with favor, and sometimes with nothing but frowns.

The Eleventh Remove[2]

The next day in the morning they took their travel, intending a day's journey up the river. I took my load at my back, and quickly we came to wade over the river; and passed over tiresome and wearisome hills. One hill was so steep that I was fain to creep up upon my knees, and to hold by the twigs and bushes to keep myself from falling backward. My head also was so light that I usually reeled as I went; but I hope all these wearisome steps that I have taken, are but a forewarning to me of the heavenly rest: "I know, O Lord, that thy judgments are right, and that thou in faithfulness hast afflicted me" (Psalm 119.75).

The Twelfth Remove[3]

It was upon a Sabbath-day-morning, that they prepared for their travel. This morning I asked my master whether he would sell me to my husband. He answered me "Nux,"[4] which did much rejoice my spirit. My mistress, before we went, was gone to the burial of a papoose, and returning, she found me sitting and reading in my Bible; she snatched it hastily out of my hand, and threw it out of doors. I ran out and catched it up, and put it into my pocket, and never let her see it afterward. Then they packed up their things to be gone, and gave me my load. I complained it was too heavy, whereupon she gave me a slap in the face, and bade me go; I lifted up my heart to God, hoping the redemption was not far off; and the rather because their insolency grew worse and worse.

But the thoughts of my going homeward (for so we bent our course) much

---

1. To another location in the Ashuelot valley.
2. April 1676, near Chesterfield, New Hampshire. This is as far north as Rowlandson was taken.
3. Sunday, April 9.
4. Yes.

cheered my spirit, and made my burden seem light, and almost nothing at all.
But (to my amazement and great perplexity) the scale was soon turned; for
when we had gone a little way, on a sudden my mistress gives out; she would
go no further, but turn back again, and said I must go back again with her,
and she called her *sannup*, and would have had him gone back also, but he
would not, but said he would go on, and come to us again in three days. My
spirit was, upon this, I confess, very impatient, and almost outrageous. I
thought I could as well have died as went back; I cannot declare the trouble
that I was in about it; but yet back again I must go. As soon as I had the
opportunity, I took my Bible to read, and that quieting Scripture came to my
hand, "Be still, and know that I am God" (Psalm 46.10). Which stilled my
spirit for the present. But a sore time of trial, I concluded, I had to go through,
my master being gone, who seemed to me the best friend that I had of an
Indian, both in cold and hunger, and quickly so it proved. Down I sat, with
my heart as full as it could hold, and yet so hungry that I could not sit neither;
but going out to see what I could find, and walking among the trees, I found
six acorns, and two chestnuts, which were some refreshment to me. Towards
night I gathered some sticks for my own comfort, that I might not lie a-cold;
but when we came to lie down they bade me to go out, and lie somewhere
else, for they had company (they said) come in more than their own. I told
them, I could not tell where to go, they bade me go look; I told them, if I went
to another wigwam they would be angry, and send me home again. Then one
of the company drew his sword, and told me he would run me through if I did
not go presently. Then was I fain to stoop to this rude fellow, and to go out in
the night, I knew not whither. Mine eyes have seen that fellow afterwards
walking up and down Boston, under the appearance of a Friend Indian, and
several others of the like cut. I went to one wigwam, and they told me they
had no room. Then I went to another, and they said the same; at last an old
Indian bade me to come to him, and his squaw gave me some ground nuts;
she gave me also something to lay under my head, and a good fire we had;
and through the good providence of God, I had a comfortable lodging that
night. In the morning, another Indian bade me come at night, and he would
give me six ground nuts, which I did. We were at this place and time about
two miles from [the] Connecticut river. We went in the morning to gather
ground nuts, to the river, and went back again that night. I went with a good
load at my back (for they when they went, though but a little way, would carry
all their trumpery with them). I told them the skin was off my back, but I had
no other comforting answer from them than this: that it would be no matter if
my head were off too.

The Thirteenth Remove[5]

Instead of going toward the Bay, which was that I desired, I must go with
them five or six miles down the river into a mighty thicket of brush; where we
abode almost a fortnight. Here one asked me to make a shirt for her papoose,
for which she gave me a mess of broth, which was thickened with meal made
of the bark of a tree, and to make it the better, she had put into it about a

5. To Hinsdale, New Hampshire, near the Connecticut River.

handful of peas, and a few roasted ground nuts. I had not seen my son a pretty while, and here was an Indian of whom I made inquiry after him, and asked him when he saw him. He answered me that such a time his master roasted him, and that himself did eat a piece of him, as big as his two fingers, and that he was very good meat. But the Lord upheld my Spirit, under this discouragement; and I considered their horrible addictedness to lying, and that there is not one of them that makes the least conscience of speaking of truth. In this place, on a cold night, as I lay by the fire, I removed a stick that kept the heat from me. A squaw moved it down again, at which I looked up, and she threw a handful of ashes in mine eyes. I thought I should have been quite blinded, and have never seen more, but lying down, the water run out of my eyes, and carried the dirt with it, that by the morning I recovered my sight again. Yet upon this, and the like occasions, I hope it is not too much to say with Job, "Have pity upon me, O ye my Friends, for the Hand of the Lord has touched me."[6] And here I cannot but remember how many times sitting in their wigwams, and musing on things past, I should suddenly leap up and run out, as if I had been at home, forgetting where I was, and what my condition was; but when I was without, and saw nothing but wilderness, and woods, and a company of barbarous heathens, my mind quickly returned to me, which made me think of that, spoken concerning Sampson, who said, "I will go out and shake myself as at other times, but he wist not that the Lord was departed from him."[7] About this time I began to think that all my hopes of restoration would come to nothing. I thought of the English army, and hoped for their coming, and being taken by them, but that failed. I hoped to be carried to Albany, as the Indians had discoursed before, but that failed also. I thought of being sold to my husband, as my master spake, but instead of that, my master himself was gone, and I left behind, so that my spirit was now quite ready to sink. I asked them to let me go out and pick up some sticks, that I might get alone, and pour out my heart unto the Lord. Then also I took my Bible to read, but I found no comfort here neither, which many times I was wont to find. So easy a thing it is with God to dry up the streams of Scripture comfort from us. Yet I can say, that in all my sorrows and afflictions, God did not leave me to have my impatience work towards Himself, as if His ways were unrighteous. But I knew that He laid upon me less than I deserved. Afterward, before this doleful time ended with me, I was turning the leaves of my Bible, and the Lord brought to me some Scriptures, which did a little revive me, as that [in] Isaiah 55.8: "For my thoughts are not your thoughts, neither are your ways my ways, saith the Lord." And also that [in] Psalm 37.5: "Commit thy way unto the Lord; trust also in him; and he shall bring it to pass." About this time they came yelping from Hadley, where they had killed three Englishmen, and brought one captive with them, viz. Thomas Read. They all gathered about the poor man, asking him many questions. I desired also to go and see him; and when I came, he was crying bitterly, supposing they would quickly kill him. Whereupon I asked one of them, whether they intended to kill him; he answered me, they would not. He being a little cheered with that, I asked him about the welfare of my husband. He told me he saw him such a time in the Bay, and he was well, but very melancholy. By which I certainly understood (though I suspected it before) that whatsoever the Indians told me respecting

6. Job 19.21.   7. Judges 16.20.

him was vanity and lies. Some of them told me he was dead, and they had killed him; some said he was married again, and that the Governor wished him to marry; and told him he should have his choice, and that all persuaded I was dead. So like were these barbarous creatures to him who was a liar from the beginning.[8]

As I was sitting once in the wigwam here, Philip's maid came in with the child in her arms, and asked me to give her a piece of my apron, to make a flap for it. I told her I would not. Then my mistress bade me give it, but still I said no. The maid told me if I would not give her a piece, she would tear a piece off it. I told her I would tear her coat then. With that my mistress rises up, and take up a stick big enough to have killed me, and struck at me with it. But I stepped out, and she struck the stick into the mat of the wigwam. But while she was pulling of it out I ran to the maid and gave her all my apron, and so that storm went over.

Hearing that my son was come to this place, I went to see him, and told him his father was well, but melancholy. He told me he was as much grieved for his father as for himself. I wondered at his speech, for I thought I had enough upon my spirit in reference to myself, to make me mindless of my husband and everyone else; they being safe among their friends. He told me also, that awhile before, his master (together with other Indians) were going to the French for powder; but by the way the Mohawks met with them, and killed four of their company, which made the rest turn back again, for it might have been worse with him, had he been sold to the French, than it proved to be in his remaining with the Indians.

I went to see an English youth in this place, one John Gilbert of Springfield. I found him lying without doors, upon the ground. I asked him how he did? He told me he was very sick of a flux,[9] with eating so much blood. They had turned him out of the wigwam, and with him an Indian papoose, almost dead (whose parents had been killed), in a bitter cold day, without fire or clothes. The young man himself had nothing on but his shirt and waistcoat. This sight was enough to melt a heart of flint. There they lay quivering in the cold, the youth round like a dog, the papoose stretched out with his eyes and nose and mouth full of dirt, and yet alive, and groaning. I advised John to go and get to some fire. He told me he could not stand, but I persuaded him still, lest he should lie there and die. And with much ado I got him to a fire, and went myself home. As soon as I was got home his master's daughter came after me, to know what I had done with the Englishman. I told her I had got him to a fire in such a place. Now had I need to pray Paul's Prayer "That we may be delivered from unreasonable and wicked men" (2 Thessalonians 3.2). For her satisfaction I went along with her, and brought her to him; but before I got home again it was noised about that I was running away and getting the English youth, along with me; that as soon as I came in they began to rant and domineer, asking me where I had been, and what I had been doing? and saying they would knock him on the head. I told them I had been seeing the English youth, and that I would not run away. They told me I lied, and taking up a hatchet, they came to me, and said they would knock me down if I stirred out again, and so confined me to the wigwam. Now may I say with David, "I am in a great strait" (2 Samuel 24.14). If I keep in, I must die with hunger,

8. I.e., Satan.   9. Dysentery.

and if I go out, I must be knocked in head. This distressed condition held that day, and half the next. And then the Lord remembered me, whose mercies are great. Then came an Indian to me with a pair of stockings that were too big for him, and he would have me ravel them out, and knit them fit for him. I showed myself willing, and bid him ask my mistress if I might go along with him a little way; she said yes, I might, but I was not a little refreshed with that news, that I had my liberty again. Then I went along with him, and he gave me some roasted ground nuts, which did again revive my feeble stomach.

Being got out of her sight, I had time and liberty again to look into my Bible; which was my guide by day, and my pillow by night. Now that comfortable Scripture presented itself to me, "For a small moment have I forsaken thee, but with great mercies will I gather thee" (Isaiah 54.7). Thus the Lord carried me along from one time to another, and made good to me this precious promise, and many others. Then my son came to see me, and I asked his master to let him stay awhile with me, that I might comb his head, and look over him, for he was almost overcome with lice. He told me, when I had done, that he was very hungry, but I had nothing to relieve him, but bid him go into the wigwams as he went along, and see if he could get any thing among them. Which he did, and it seems tarried a little too long; for his master was angry with him, and beat him, and then sold him. Then he came running to tell me he had a new master, and that he had given him some ground nuts already. Then I went along with him to his new master who told me he loved him, and he should not want. So his master carried him away, and I never saw him afterward, till I saw him at Piscataqua in Portsmouth.

That night they bade me go out of the wigwam again. My mistress's papoose was sick, and it died that night, and there was one benefit in it—that there was more room. I went to a wigwam, and they bade me come in, and gave me a skin to lie upon, and a mess of venison and ground nuts, which was a choice dish among them. On the morrow they buried the papoose, and afterward, both morning and evening, there came a company to mourn and howl with her; though I confess I could not much condole with them. Many sorrowful days I had in this place, often getting alone. "Like a crane, or a swallow, so did I chatter; I did mourn as a dove, mine eyes ail with looking upward. Oh, Lord, I am oppressed; undertake for me" (Isaiah 38.14). I could tell the Lord, as Hezekiah, "Remember now O Lord, I beseech thee, how I have walked before thee in truth."[1] Now had I time to examine all my ways: my conscience did not accuse me of unrighteousness toward one or other; yet I saw how in my walk with God, I had been a careless creature. As David said, "Against thee, thee only have I sinned":[2] and I might say with the poor publican, "God be merciful unto me a sinner."[3] On the Sabbath days, I could look upon the sun and think how people were going to the house of God, to have their souls refreshed; and then home, and their bodies also; but I was destitute of both; and might say as the poor prodigal, "He would fain have filled his belly with the husks that the swine did eat, and no man gave unto him" (Luke 15.16). For I must say with him, "Father, I have sinned against Heaven and in thy sight."[4] I remembered how on the night before and after the Sabbath, when my family was about me, and relations and neighbors with us, we could pray

1. Isaiah 38.3.   3. Luke 18.13.
2. Psalm 51.4.   4. Luke 15.21.

and sing, and then refresh our bodies with the good creatures of God; and then have a comfortable bed to lie down on; but instead of all this, I had only a little swill for the body and then, like a swine, must lie down on the ground. I cannot express to man the sorrow that lay upon my spirit; the Lord knows it. Yet that comfortable Scripture would often come to mind, "For a small moment have I forsaken thee, but with great mercies will I gather thee."[5]

The Fourteenth Remove[6]

Now must we pack up and be gone from this thicket, bending our course toward the Baytowns; I having nothing to eat by the way this day, but a few crumbs of cake, that an Indian gave my girl the same day we were taken. She gave it me, and I put it in my pocket; there it lay, till it was so moldy (for want of good baking) that one could not tell what it was made of; it fell all to crumbs, and grew so dry and hard, that it was like little flints; and this refreshed me many times, when I was ready to faint. It was in my thoughts when I put it into my mouth, that if ever I returned, I would tell the world what a blessing the Lord gave to such mean food. As we went along they killed a deer, with a young one in her, they gave me a piece of the fawn, and it was so young and tender, that one might eat the bones as well as the flesh, and yet I thought it very good. When night came on we sat down; it rained, but they quickly got up a bark wigwam, where I lay dry that night. I looked out in the morning, and many of them had lain in the rain all night, I saw by their reeking.[7] Thus the Lord dealt mercifully with me many times, and I fared better than many of them. In the morning they took the blood of the deer, and put it into the paunch, and so boiled it. I could eat nothing of that, though they ate it sweetly. And yet they were so nice[8] in other things, that when I had fetched water, and had put the dish I dipped the water with into the kettle of water which I brought, they would say they would knock me down; for they said, it was a sluttish trick.

The Fifteenth Remove

We went on our travel. I having got one handful of ground nuts, for my support that day, they gave me my load, and I went on cheerfully (with the thoughts of going homeward), having my burden more on my back than my spirit. We came to Banquang river again that day, near which we abode a few days. Sometimes one of them would give me a pipe, another a little tobacco, another a little salt: which I would change for a little victuals. I cannot but think what a wolvish appetite persons have in a starving condition; for many times when they gave me that which was hot, I was so greedy, that I should burn my mouth, that it would trouble me hours after, and yet I should quickly do the same again. And after I was thoroughly hungry, I was never again satisfied. For though sometimes it fell out, that I got enough, and did eat till I could eat no more, yet I was as unsatisfied as I was when I began. And now could I see that Scripture verified (there being many Scriptures which we do not take notice of, or understand till we are afflicted) "Thou shalt eat and not

---

5. Isaiah 54.7.
6. The fourteenth to nineteenth removes (April 20 to April 28) retrace the path taken earlier. The "Baytowns" are the towns near Boston.
7. Steaming.
8. Fastidious.

be satisfied" (Micah 6.14). Now might I see more than ever before, the miseries that sin hath brought upon us. Many times I should be ready to run against the heathen, but the Scripture would quiet me again, "Shall there be evil in a City and the Lord hath not done it?" (Amos 3.6). The Lord help me to make a right improvement of His word, and that I might learn that great lesson: "He hath showed thee (Oh Man) what is good, and what doth the Lord require of thee, but to do justly, and love mercy, and walk humbly with thy God? Hear ye the rod, and who hath appointed it" (Micah 6.8-9).

The Sixteenth Removal

We began this remove with wading over Banquang river: the water was up to the knees, and the stream very swift, and so cold that I thought it would have cut me in sunder. I was so weak and feeble, that I reeled as I went along, and thought there I must end my days at last, after my bearing and getting through so many difficulties. The Indians stood laughing to see me staggering along; but in my distress the Lord gave me experience of the truth, and goodness of that promise, "When thou passest through the waters, I will be with thee; and through the rivers, they shall not overflow thee" (Isaiah 43.2). Then I sat down to put on my stockings and shoes, with the tears running down mine eyes, and sorrowful thoughts in my heart, but I got up to go along with them. Quickly there came up to us an Indian, who informed them that I must go to Wachusett to my master, for there was a letter come from the council to the Sagamores, about redeeming the captives, and that there would be another in fourteen days, and that I must be there ready. My heart was so heavy before that I could scarce speak or go in the path; and yet now so light, that I could run. My strength seemed to come again, and recruit my feeble knees, and aching heart. Yet it pleased them to go but one mile that night, and there we stayed two days. In that time came a company of Indians to us, near thirty, all on horseback. My heart skipped within me, thinking they had been Englishmen at the first sight of them, for they were dressed in English apparel, with hats, white neckcloths, and sashes about their waists; and ribbons upon their shoulders; but when they came near, there was a vast difference between the lovely faces of Christians, and foul looks of those heathens, which much damped my spirit again.

The Seventeenth Remove

A comfortable remove it was to me, because of my hopes. They gave me a pack, and along we went cheerfully; but quickly my will proved more than my strength; having little or no refreshing, my strength failed me, and my spirits were almost quite gone. Now may I say with David "I am poor and needy, and my heart is wounded within me. I am gone like the shadow when it declineth: I am tossed up and down like the locust; my knees are weak through fasting, and my flesh faileth of fatness" (Psalm 119.22-24). At night we came to an Indian town, and the Indians sat down by a wigwam discoursing, but I was almost spent, and could scarce speak. I laid down my load, and went into the wigwam, and there sat an Indian boiling of horses feet (they being wont to eat the flesh first, and when the feet were old and dried, and they had nothing else, they would cut off the feet and use them). I asked him to give me a little of his broth, or water they were boiling in; he took a dish, and gave me one spoonful of samp,[9] and bid me take as much of the broth as I would. Then I put some of the hot water to the samp, and drank it up, and my spirit came again. He gave me also a piece of the ruff or ridding[1] of the small guts, and I broiled it on the coals; and now may I say with Jonathan, "See, I pray you, how mine eyes have been enlightened, because I tasted a little of this honey" (1 Samuel 14.29). Now is my spirit revived again; though means be never so inconsiderable, yet if the Lord bestow His blessing upon them, they shall refresh both soul and body.

The Eighteenth Remove

We took up our packs and along we went, but a wearisome day I had of it. As we went along I saw an Englishman stripped naked, and lying dead upon the ground, but knew not who it was. Then we came to another Indian town, where we stayed all night. In this town there were four English children, captives; and one of them my own sister's. I went to see how she did, and she was well, considering her captive condition. I would have tarried that night with her, but they that owned her would not suffer it. Then I went into another wigwam, where they were boiling corn and beans, which was a lovely sight to see, but I could not get a taste thereof. Then I went to another wigwam, where there were two of the English children; the squaw was boiling horses feet; then she cut me off a little piece, and gave one of the English children a piece also. Being very hungry I had quickly eat up mine, but the child could not bite it, it was so tough and sinewy, but lay sucking, gnawing, chewing and slabbering of it in the mouth and hand. Then I took it of the child, and eat it myself, and savory it was to my taste. Then I may say as Job 6.7, "The things that my soul refused to touch are as my sorrowful meat." Thus the Lord made that pleasant refreshing, which another time would have been an abomination. Then I went home to my mistress's wigwam; and they told me I disgraced my master with begging, and if I did so any more, they would knock me in the head. I told them, they had as good knock me in head as starve me to death.

The Nineteenth Remove

They said, when we went out, that we must travel to Wachusett this day. But a bitter weary day I had of it, traveling now three days together, without resting any day between. At last, after many weary steps, I saw Wachusett hills, but many miles off. Then we came to a great swamp, through which we traveled, up to the knees in mud and water, which was heavy going to one tired before. Being almost spent, I thought I should have sunk down at last, and never got out; but I may say, as in Psalm 94.18, "When my foot slipped, thy mercy, O Lord, held me up." Going along, having indeed my life, but little spirit, Philip, who was in the company, came up and took me by the hand, and said, two weeks more and you shall be mistress again. I asked him, if he spake true? He answered, "Yes, and quickly you shall come to your master again; who had been gone from us three weeks." After many weary steps we came to Wachusett, where he was: and glad I was to see him. He

---

9. A porridge made of Indian corn.   1. I.e., the refuse, that which he was casting away.

asked me, when I washed me? I told him not this month. Then he fetched me some water himself, and bid me wash, and gave me the glass to see how I looked; and bid his squaw give me something to eat. So she gave me a mess of beans and meat, and a little ground nut cake. I was wonderfully revived with this favor showed me: "He made them also to be pitied of all those that carried them captives" (Psalm 106.46).

My master had three squaws, living sometimes with one, and sometimes with another one, this old squaw, at whose wigwam I was, and with whom my master had been those three weeks. Another was Weetamoo[2] with whom I had lived and served all this while. A severe and proud dame she was, bestowing every day in dressing herself neat as much time as any of the gentry of the land: powdering her hair, and painting her face, going with necklaces, with jewels in her ears, and bracelets upon her hands. When she had dressed herself, her work was to make girdles of wampum and beads. The third squaw was a younger one, by whom he had two papooses. By the time I was refreshed by the old squaw, with whom my master was, Weetamoo's maid came to call me home, at which I fell aweeping. Then the old squaw told me, to encourage me, that if I wanted victuals, I should come to her, and that I should lie there in her wigwam. Then I went with the maid, and quickly came again and lodged there. The squaw laid a mat under me, and a good rug over me; the first time I had any such kindness showed me. I understood that Weetamoo thought that if she should let me go and serve with the old squaw, she would be in danger to lose not only my service, but the redemption pay also. And I was not a little glad to hear this; being by it raised in my hopes, that in God's due time there would be an end of this sorrowful hour. Then came an Indian, and asked me to knit him three pair of stockings, for which I had a hat, and a silk handkerchief. Then another asked me to make her a shift, for which she gave me an apron.

Then came Tom and Peter,[3] with the second letter from the council, about the captives. Though they were Indians, I got them by the hand, and burst out into tears. My heart was so full that I could not speak to them; but recovering myself, I asked them how my husband did, and all my friends and acquaintance? They said, "They are all very well but melancholy." They brought me two biscuits, and a pound of tobacco. The tobacco I quickly gave away. When it was all gone, one asked me to give him a pipe of tobacco. I told him it was all gone. Then began he to rant and threaten. I told him when my husband came I would give him some. Hang him rogue (says he) I will knock out his brains, if he comes here. And then again, in the same breath they would say that if there should come an hundred without guns, they would do them no hurt. So unstable and like madmen they were. So that fearing the worst, I durst not send to my husband, though there were some thoughts of his coming to redeem and fetch me, not knowing what might follow. For there was little more trust to them than to the master they served. When the letter was come, the Sagamores met to consult about the captives, and called me to them to inquire how much my husband would give to redeem me. When I came I sat down among them, as I was wont to do, as their manner is. Then they bade me stand up, and said they were the General Court.[4] They bid me

---

2. Rowlandson spells the name "Wattimore" here.
3. Christian Indians.

4. In imitation of the colonial assembly of Massachusetts.

speak what I thought he would give. Now knowing that all we had was destroyed by the Indians, I was in a great strait. I thought if I should speak of but a little it would be slighted, and hinder the matter; if of a great sum, I knew not where it would be procured. Yet at a venture I said "Twenty pounds," yet desired them to take less. But they would not hear of that, but sent that message to Boston, that for twenty pounds I should be redeemed. It was a Praying Indian that wrote their letter for them. There was another Praying Indian, who told me, that he had a brother, that would not eat horse; his conscience was so tender and scrupulous (though as large as hell, for the destruction of poor Christians). Then he said, he read that Scripture to him, "There was a famine in Samaria, and behold they besieged it, until an ass's head was sold for four-score pieces of silver, and the fourth part of a cab of dove's dung for five pieces of silver" (2 Kings 6.25). He expounded this place to his brother, and showed him that it was lawful to eat that in a famine which is not at another time. And now, says he, he will eat horse with any Indian of them all. There was another Praying Indian, who when he had done all the mischief that he could, betrayed his own father into the English hands, thereby to purchase his own life. Another Praying Indian was at Sudbury fight,[5] though, as he deserved, he was afterward hanged for it. There was another Praying Indian, so wicked and cruel, as to wear a string about his neck, strung with Christians' fingers. Another Praying Indian, when they went to Sudbury fight, went with them, and his squaw also with him, with her papoose at her back. Before they went to that fight they got a company together to pow-wow.[6] The manner was as followeth: there was one that kneeled upon a deerskin, with the company round him in a ring who kneeled, and striking upon the ground with their hands, and with sticks, and muttering or humming with their mouths. Besides him who kneeled in the ring, there also stood one with a gun in his hand. Then he on the deerskin made a speech, and all manifested assent to it; and so they did many times together. Then they bade him with the gun go out of the ring, which he did. But when he was out, they called him in again; but he seemed to make a stand; then they called the more earnestly, till he returned again. Then they all sang. Then they gave him two guns, in either hand one. And so he on the deerskin began again; and at the end of every sentence in his speaking, they all assented, humming or muttering with their mouths, and striking upon the ground with their hands. Then they bade him with the two guns go out of the ring again; which he did, a little way. Then they called him in again, but he made a stand. So they called him with greater earnestness; but he stood reeling and wavering as if he knew not whither he should stand or fall, or which way to go. Then they called him with exceeding great vehemency, all of them, one and another. After a little while he turned in, staggering as he went, with his arms stretched out, in either hand a gun. As soon as he came in they all sang and rejoiced exceedingly a while. And then he upon the deerskin, made another speech unto which they all assented in a rejoicing manner. And so they ended their business, and forthwith went to Sudbury fight. To my thinking they went without any scruple, but that they should prosper, and gain the victory. And they went out not so rejoicing, but they came home with as great a victory. For they said they had killed two captains and almost an hundred men. One Englishman they brought along

5. An attack on Sudbury, Massachusetts, April 18.   6. Confer.

with them: and he said, it was too true, for they had made sad work at Sudbury, as indeed it proved. Yet they came home without that rejoicing and
triumphing over their victory which they were wont to show at other times;
but rather like dogs (as they say) which have lost their ears. Yet I could not
perceive that it was for their own loss of men. They said they had not lost
above five or six; and I missed none, except in one wigwam. When they went,
they acted as if the devil had told them that they should gain the victory; and
now they acted as if the devil had told them they should have a fall. Whither
it were so or no, I cannot tell, but so it proved, for quickly they began to fall,
and so held on that summer, till they came to utter ruin. They came home
on a Sabbath day, and the *Powaw* that kneeled upon the deer-skin came home
(I may say, without abuse) as black as the devil. When my master came home,
he came to me and bid me make a shirt for his papoose, of a holland-laced
pillowbere.[7] About that time there came an Indian to me and bid me come to
his wigwam at night, and he would give me some pork and ground nuts.
Which I did, and as I was eating, another Indian said to me, he seems to be
your good friend, but he killed two Englishmen at Sudbury, and there lie their
clothes behind you: I looked behind me, and there I saw bloody clothes, with
bullet-holes in them. Yet the Lord suffered not this wretch to do me any hurt.
Yea, instead of that, he many times refreshed me; five or six times did he and
his squaw refresh my feeble carcass. If I went to their wigwam at any time,
they would always give me something, and yet they were strangers that I never
saw before. Another squaw gave me a piece of fresh pork, and a little salt with
it, and lent me her pan to fry it in; and I cannot but remember what a sweet,
pleasant and delightful relish that bit had to me, to this day. So little do we
prize common mercies when we have them to the full.

The Twentieth Remove[8]

It was their usual manner to remove, when they had done any mischief,
lest they should be found out; and so they did at this time. We went about
three or four miles, and there they built a great wigwam, big enough to hold
an hundred Indians, which they did in preparation to a great day of dancing.
They would say now amongst themselves, that the governor would be so angry
for his loss at Sudbury, that he would send no more about the captives, which
made me grieve and tremble. My sister being not far from the place where we
now were, and hearing that I was here, desired her master to let her come and
see me, and he was willing to it, and would go with her; but she being ready
before him, told him she would go before, and was come within a mile or two
of the place. Then he overtook her, and began to rant as if he had been mad,
and made her go back again in the rain; so that I never saw her till I saw her
in Charlestown. But the Lord requited many of their ill doings, for this Indian
her master, was hanged afterward at Boston. The Indians now began to come
from all quarters, against their merry dancing day. Among some of them came
one goodwife Kettle. I told her my heart was so heavy that it was ready to
break. "So is mine too," said she, but yet said, "I hope we shall hear some

7. Pillowcase.
8. April 28 to May 2, to an encampment at the southern end of Wachusett Lake, Princeton, Massachusetts.

good news shortly." I could hear how earnestly my sister desired to see me, and I as earnestly desired to see her; and yet neither of us could get an opportunity. My daughter was also now about a mile off, and I had not seen her in nine or ten weeks, as I had not seen my sister since our first taking. I earnestly desired them to let me go and see them: yea, I entreated, begged, and persuaded them, but to let me see my daughter; and yet so hard-hearted were they, that they would not suffer it. They made use of their tyrannical power whilst they had it; but through the Lord's wonderful mercy, their time was now but short.

On a Sabbath day, the sun being about an hour high in the afternoon, came Mr. John Hoar[9] (the council permitting him, and his own foreward spirit inclining him), together with the two forementioned Indians, Tom and Peter, with their third letter from the council. When they came near, I was abroad. Though I saw them not, they presently called me in, and bade me sit down and not stir. Then they catched up their guns, and away they ran, as if an enemy had been at hand, and the guns went off apace. I manifested some great trouble, and they asked me what was the matter? I told them I thought they had killed the Englishman (for they had in the meantime informed me that an Englishman was come). They said, no. They shot over his horse and under and before his horse, and they pushed him this way and that way, at their pleasure, showing what they could do. Then they let them come to their wigwams. I begged of them to let me see the Englishman, but they would not. But there was I fain to sit their pleasure. When they had talked their fill with him, they suffered me to go to him. We asked each other of our welfare, and how my husband did, and all my friends? He told me they were all well, and would be glad to see me. Amongst other things which my husband sent me, there came a pound of tobacco, which I sold for nine shillings in money; for many of the Indians for want of tobacco, smoked hemlock, and ground ivy. It was a great mistake in any, who thought I sent for tobacco; for through the favor of God, that desire was overcome. I now asked them whether I should go home with Mr. Hoar? They answered no, one and another of them, and it being night, we lay down with that answer. In the morning Mr. Hoar invited the Sagamores to dinner; but when we went to get it ready we found that they had stolen the greatest part of the provision Mr. Hoar had brought, out of his bags, in the night. And we may see the wonderful power of God, in that one passage, in that when there was such a great number of the Indians together, and so greedy of a little good food, and no English there but Mr. Hoar and myself, that there they did not knock us in the head, and take what we had, there being not only some provision, but also trading-cloth,[1] a part of the twenty pounds agreed upon. But instead of doing us any mischief, they seemed to be ashamed of the fact, and said, it were some matchit[2] Indian that did it. Oh, that we could believe that there is nothing too hard for God! God showed His power over the heathen in this, as He did over the hungry lions when Daniel was cast into the den.[3] Mr. Hoar called them betime to dinner, but they ate very little, they being so busy in dressing themselves, and getting ready for their dance, which was carried on by eight of them, four men and four

---

9. John Hoar was from Concord, Massachusetts. He had been delegated by Rowlandson's husband to represent him at the council for the Sagamore Indians, and to bargain for Rowlandson's redemption.

1. Cloth used for barter.
2. Bad.
3. The prophet Daniel was cast into a den of lions, but they did not harm him (see Daniel 6.1–29).

squaws. My master and mistress being two. He was dressed in his holland[4] shirt, with great laces sewed at the tail of it; he had his silver buttons, his white stockings, his garters were hung round with shillings, and he had girdles of wampum[5] upon his head and shoulders. She had a kersey[6] coat, and covered with girdles of wampum from the loins upward. Her arms from her elbows to her hands were covered with bracelets; there were handfuls of necklaces about her neck, and several sorts of jewels in her ears. She had fine red stockings, and white shoes, her hair powdered and face painted red, that was always before black. And all the dancers were after the same manner. There were two others singing and knocking on a kettle for their music. They kept hopping up and down one after another, with a kettle of water in the midst, standing warm upon some embers, to drink of when they were dry. They held on till it was almost night, throwing out wampum to the standers by. At night I asked them again, if I should go home? They all as one said no, except[7] my husband would come for me. When we were lain down, my master went out of the wigwam, and by and by sent in an Indian called James the Printer,[8] who told Mr. Hoar, that my master would let me go home tomorrow, if he would let him have one pint of liquors. Then Mr. Hoar called his own Indians, Tom and Peter, and bid them go and see whether he would promise it before them three; and if he would, he should have it; which he did, and he had it. Then Philip[9] smelling the business called me to him, and asked me what I would give him, to tell me some good news, and speak a good word for me. I told him I could not tell what to give him. I would [give him] anything I had, and asked him what he would have? He said two coats and twenty shillings in money, and half a bushel of seed corn, and some tobacco. I thanked him for his love; but I knew the good news as well as the crafty fox. My master after he had had his drink, quickly came ranting into the wigwam again, and called for Mr. Hoar, drinking to him, and saying, he was a good man, and then again he would say, "hang him rogue." Being almost drunk, he would drink to him, and yet presently say he should be hanged. Then he called for me. I trembled to hear him, yet I was fain to go to him, and he drank to me, showing no incivility. He was the first Indian I saw drunk all the while that I was amongst them. At last his squaw ran out, and he after her, round the wigwam, with his money jingling at his knees. But she escaped him. But having an old squaw he ran to her; and so through the Lord's mercy, we were no more troubled that night. Yet I had not a comfortable night's rest; for I think I can say, I did not sleep for three nights together. The night before the letter came from the council, I could not rest, I was so full of fears and troubles, God many times leaving us most in the dark, when deliverance is nearest. Yea, at this time I could not rest night nor day. The next night I was overjoyed, Mr. Hoar being come, and that with such good tidings. The third night I was even swallowed up with the thoughts of things, *viz.* that ever I should go home again; and that I must go, leaving my children behind me in the wilderness; so that sleep was now almost departed from mine eyes.

On Tuesday morning they called their general court (as they call it) to con-

---

4. Linen.
5. Beads of polished shells used by some American Indians as currency.
6. Coarse cloth woven from long wool and usually ribbed.

7. Unless.
8. An American Indian who assisted the Rev. John Eliot in his printing of the Bible.
9. An American Indian who aided Rowlandson earlier on the journey.

sult and determine, whether I should go home or no. And they all as one man did seemingly consent to it, that I should go home; except Philip, who would not come among them.

But before I go any further, I would take leave to mention a few remarkable passages of providence, which I took special notice of in my afflicted time.

1. Of the fair opportunity lost in the long march, a little after the fort fight, when our English army was so numerous, and in pursuit of the enemy, and so near as to take several and destroy them, and the enemy in such distress for food that our men might track them by their rooting in the earth for ground nuts, whilst they were flying for their lives. I say, that then our army should want provision, and be forced to leave their pursuit and return homeward; and the very next week the enemy came upon our town, like bears bereft of their whelps, or so many ravenous wolves, rending us and our lambs to death. But what shall I say? God seemed to leave his People to themselves, and order all things for His own holy ends. Shall there be evil in the City and the Lord hath not done it?[1] They are not grieved for the affliction of Joseph, therefore shall they go captive, with the first that go captive.[2] It is the Lord's doing, and it should be marvelous in our eyes.

2. I cannot but remember how the Indians derided the slowness, and dullness of the English army, in its setting out. For after the desolations at Lancaster and Medfield, as I went along with them, they asked me when I thought the English army would come after them? I told them I could not tell. "It may be they will come in May," said they. Thus did they scoff at us, as if the English would be a quarter of a year getting ready.

3. Which also I have hinted before, when the English army with new supplies were sent forth to pursue after the enemy, and they understanding it, fled before them till they came to Banquaug river, where they forthwith went over safely; that that river should be impassable to the English. I can but admire to see the wonderful providence of God in preserving the heathen for further affliction to our poor country. They could go in great numbers over, but the English must stop. God had an over-ruling hand in all those things.

4. It was thought, if their corn were cut down, they would starve and die with hunger, and all their corn that could be found, was destroyed, and they driven from that little they had in store, into the woods in the midst of winter; and yet how to admiration did the Lord preserve them for His holy ends, and the destruction of many still amongst the English! strangely did the Lord provide for them; that I did not see (all the time I was among them) one man, woman, or child, die with hunger.

Though many times they would eat that, that a hog or a dog would hardly touch; yet by that God strengthened them to be a scourge to His people.

The chief and commonest food was ground nuts. They eat also nuts and acorns, artichokes, lilly roots, ground beans, and several other weeds and roots, that I know not.

They would pick up old bones, and cut them to pieces at the joints, and if they were full of worms and maggots, they would scald them over the fire to make the vermine come out, and then boil them, and drink up the liquor, and then beat the great ends of them in a mortar, and so eat them. They would eat horse's guts, and ears, and all sorts of wild birds which they could catch;

1. Amos 3.6.   2. Amos 6.6–7.

also bear, venison, beaver, tortoise, frogs, squirrels, dogs, skunks, rattlesnakes; yea, the very bark of trees; besides all sorts of creatures, and provision which they plundered from the English. I can but stand in admiration to see the wonderful power of God in providing for such a vast number of our enemies in the wilderness, where there was nothing to be seen, but from hand to mouth. Many times in a morning, the generality of them would eat up all they had, and yet have some further supply against they wanted. It is said, "Oh, that my People had hearkened to me, and Israel had walked in my ways, I should soon have subdued their Enemies, and turned my hand against their Adversaries" (Psalm 81.13–14). But now our perverse and evil carriages in the sight of the Lord, have so offended Him, that instead of turning His hand against them, the Lord feeds and nourishes them up to be a scourge to the whole land.

5. Another thing that I would observe is the strange providence of God, in turning things about when the Indians was at the highest, and the English at the lowest. I was with the enemy eleven weeks and five days, and not one week passed without the fury of the enemy, and some desolation by fire and sword upon one place or other. They mourned (with their black faces) for their own losses, yet triumphed and rejoiced in their inhumane, and many times devilish cruelty to the English. They would boast much of their victories; saying that in two hours time they had destroyed such a captain and his company at such a place; and boast how many towns they had destroyed, and then scoff, and say they had done them a good turn to send them to Heaven so soon. Again, they would say this summer that they would knock all the rogues in the head, or drive them into the sea, or make them fly the country; thinking surely, Agag-like, "The bitterness of Death is past."[3] Now the heathen begins to think all is their own, and the poor Christians' hopes to fail (as to man) and now their eyes are more to God, and their hearts sigh heaven-ward; and to say in good earnest, "Help Lord, or we perish." When the Lord had brought His people to this, that they saw no help in anything but Himself; then He takes the quarrel into His own hand; and though they had made a pit, in their own imaginations, as deep as hell for the Christians that summer, yet the Lord hurled themselves into it. And the Lord had not so many ways before to preserve them, but now He hath as many to destroy them.

But to return again to my going home, where we may see a remarkable change of providence. At first they were all against it, except my husband would come for me, but afterwards they assented to it, and seemed much to rejoice in it; some asked me to send them some bread, others some tobacco, others shaking me by the hand, offering me a hood and scarfe to ride in; not one moving hand or tongue against it. Thus hath the Lord answered my poor desire, and the many earnest requests of others put up unto God for me. In my travels an Indian came to me and told me, if I were willing, he and his squaw would run away, and go home along with me. I told him no: I was not willing to run away, but desired to wait God's time, that I might go home quietly, and without fear. And now God hath granted me my desire. O the wonderful power of God that I have seen, and the experience that I have had. I have been in the midst of those roaring lions, and savage bears, that feared

3. 1 Samuel 15.32. Agag was the king of Amalek; he was defeated by Saul and thought himself spared, but was slain by Samuel (see 1 Samuel 15).

neither God, nor man, nor the devil, by night and day, alone and in company, sleeping all sorts together, and yet not one of them ever offered me the least abuse of unchastity to me, in word or action. Though some are ready to say I speak it for my own credit; but I speak it in the presence of God, and to His Glory. God's power is as great now, and as sufficient to save, as when He preserved Daniel in the lion's den; or the three children in the fiery furnace.[4] I may well say as his Psalm 107.12 "Oh give thanks unto the Lord for he is good, for his mercy endureth for ever." Let the redeemed of the Lord say so, whom He hath redeemed from the hand of the enemy, especially that I should come away in the midst of so many hundreds of enemies quietly and peaceably, and not a dog moving his tongue. So I took my leave of them, and in coming along my heart melted into tears, more than all the while I was with them, and I was almost swallowed up with the thoughts that ever I should go home again. About the sun going down, Mr. Hoar, and myself, and the two Indians came to Lancaster, and a solemn sight it was to me. There had I lived many comfortable years amongst my relations and neighbors, and now not one Christian to be seen, nor one house left standing. We went on to a farmhouse that was yet standing, where we lay all night, and a comfortable lodging we had, though nothing but straw to lie on. The Lord preserved us in safety that night, and raised us up again in the morning, and carried us along, that before noon, we came to Concord. Now was I full of joy, and yet not without sorrow; joy to see such a lovely sight, so many Christians together, and some of them my neighbors. There I met with my brother, and my brother-in-law, who asked me, if I knew where his wife was? Poor heart! he had helped to bury her, and knew it not. She being shot down by the house was partly burnt, so that those who were at Boston at the desolation of the town, and came back afterward, and buried the dead, did not know her. Yet I was not without sorrow, to think how many were looking and longing, and my own children amongst the rest, to enjoy that deliverance that I had now received, and I did not know whether ever I should see them again. Being recruited[5] with food and raiment we went to Boston that day, where I met with my dear husband, but the thoughts of our dear children, one being dead, and the other we could not tell where, abated our comfort each to other. I was not before so much hemmed in with the merciless and cruel heathen, but now as much with pitiful, tender-hearted and compassionate Christians. In that poor, and distressed, and beggarly condition I was received in; I was kindly entertained in several houses. So much love I received from several (some of whom I knew, and others I knew not) that I am not capable to declare it. But the Lord knows them all by name. The Lord reward them sevenfold into their bosoms of His spirituals, for their temporals.[6] The twenty pounds, the price of my redemption, was raised by some Boston gentlemen, and Mrs. Usher, whose bounty and religious charity, I would not forget to make mention of. Then Mr. Thomas Shepard of Charlestown received us into his house, where we continued eleven weeks; and a father and mother they were to us. And many more tender-hearted friends we met with in that place. We were now in the midst of love, yet not without much and frequent heaviness of heart for our poor children, and other relations, who were still in affliction. The week following,

---

4. Shadrach, Meshach, and Abednego refused to worship false gods and were cast into a fiery furnace but saved from death by an angel (see Daniel 3.13–30).

5. Refreshed.

6. Worldly goods and gifts.

after my coming in, the governor and council sent forth to the Indians again; and that not without success; for they brought in my sister, and goodwife Kettle. Their not knowing where our children were was a sore trial to us still, and yet we were not without secret hopes that we should see them again. That which was dead lay heavier upon my spirit, than those which were alive and amongst the heathen: thinking how it suffered with its wounds, and I was no way able to relieve it; and how it was buried by the heathen in the wilderness from among all Christians. We were hurried up and down in our thoughts, sometime we should hear a report that they were gone this way, and sometimes that; and that they were come in, in this place or that. We kept inquiring and listening to hear concerning them, but no certain news as yet. About this time the council had ordered a day of public thanksgiving. Though I thought I had still cause of mourning, and being unsettled in our minds, we thought we would ride toward the eastward, to see if we could hear anything concerning our children. And as we were riding along (God is the wise disposer of all things) between Ipswich and Rowley we met with Mr. William Hubbard, who told us that our son Joseph was come in to Major Waldron's, and another with him, which was my sister's son. I asked him how he knew it? He said the major himself told him so. So along we went till we came to Newbury; and their minister being absent, they desired my husband to preach the thanksgiving for them; but he was not willing to stay there that night, but would go over to Salisbury, to hear further, and come again in the morning, which he did, and preached there that day. At night, when he had done, one came and told him that his daughter was come in at Providence. Here was mercy on both hands. Now hath God fulfilled that precious Scripture which was such a comfort to me in my distressed condition. When my heart was ready to sink into the earth (my children being gone, I could not tell whither) and my knees trembling under me, and I was walking through the valley of the shadow of death; then the Lord brought, and now has fulfilled that reviving word unto me: "Thus saith the Lord, Refrain thy voice from weeping, and thine eyes from tears, for thy Work shall be rewarded, saith the Lord, and they shall come again from the Land of the Enemy."[7] Now we were between them, the one on the east, and the other on the west. Our son being nearest, we went to him first, to Portsmouth, where we met with him, and with the Major also, who told us he had done what he could, but could not redeem him under seven pounds, which the good people thereabouts were pleased to pay. The Lord reward the major, and all the rest, though unknown to me, for their labor of Love. My sister's son was redeemed for four pounds, which the council gave order for the payment of. Having now received one of our children, we hastened toward the other. Going back through Newbury my husband preached there on the Sabbath day; for which they rewarded him many fold.

On Monday we came to Charlestown, where we heard that the governor of Rhode Island had sent over for our daughter, to take care of her, being now within his jurisdiction; which should not pass without our acknowledgments. But she being nearer Rehoboth than Rhode Island, Mr. Newman went over, and took care of her and brought her to his own house. And the goodness of God was admirable to us in our low estate, in that He raised up passionate[8] friends on every side to us, when we had nothing to recompense any for their

___

7. Jeremiah 31.16.   8. Compassionate.

love. The Indians were now gone that way, that it was apprehended dangerous to go to her. But the carts which carried provision to the English army, being guarded, brought her with them to Dorchester, where we received her safe. Blessed be the Lord for it, for great is His power, and He can do whatsoever seemeth Him good. Her coming in was after this manner: she was traveling one day with the Indians, with her basket at her back; the company of Indians were got before her, and gone out of sight, all except one squaw; she followed the squaw till night, and then both of them lay down, having nothing over them but the heavens and under them but the earth. Thus she traveled three days together, not knowing whither she was going; having nothing to eat or drink but water, and green hirtle-berries. At last they came into Providence, where she was kindly entertained by several of that town. The Indians often said that I should never have her under twenty pounds. But now the Lord hath brought her in upon free-cost, and given her to me the second time. The Lord make us a blessing indeed, each to others. Now have I seen that Scripture also fulfilled, "If any of thine be driven out to the outmost parts of heaven, from thence will the Lord thy God gather thee, and from thence will he fetch thee. And the Lord thy God will put all these curses upon thine enemies, and on them which hate thee, which persecuted thee" (Deuteronomy 30.4–7). Thus hath the Lord brought me and mine out of that horrible pit, and hath set us in the midst of tender-hearted and compassionate Christians. It is the desire of my soul that we may walk worthy of the mercies received, and which we are receiving.

Our family being now gathered together (those of us that were living), the South Church in Boston hired an house for us. Then we removed from Mr. Shephard's, those cordial friends, and went to Boston, where we continued about three-quarters of a year. Still the Lord went along with us, and provided graciously for us. I thought it somewhat strange to set up house-keeping with bare walls; but as Solomon says, "Money answers all things"[9] and that we had through the benevolence of Christian friends, some in this town, and some in that, and others; and some from England; that in a little time we might look, and see the house furnished with love. The Lord hath been exceeding good to us in our low estate, in that when we had neither house nor home, nor other necessaries, the Lord so moved the hearts of these and those towards us, that we wanted neither food, nor raiment for ourselves or ours: "There is a Friend which sticketh closer than a Brother" (Proverbs 18.24). And how many such friends have we found, and now living amongst? And truly such a friend have we found him to be unto us, in whose house we lived, viz. Mr. James Whitcomb, a friend unto us near hand, and afar off.

I can remember the time when I used to sleep quietly without workings in my thoughts, whole nights together, but now it is other ways with me. When all are fast about me, and no eye open, but His who ever waketh, my thoughts are upon things past, upon the awful dispensation of the Lord towards us, upon His wonderful power and might, in carrying of us through so many difficulties, in returning us in safety, and suffering none to hurt us. I remember in the night season, how the other day I was in the midst of thousands of enemies, and nothing but death before me. It is then hard work to persuade myself, that ever I should be satisfied with bread again. But now we are fed

9. Ecclesiastes 10.19.

with the finest of the wheat, and, as I may say, with honey out of the rock.[1] Instead of the husk, we have the fatted calf.[2] The thoughts of these things in the particulars of them, and of the love and goodness of God towards us, make it true of me, what David said of himself, "I watered my Couch with my tears" (Psalm 6.6). Oh! the wonderful power of God that mine eyes have seen, affording matter enough for my thoughts to run in, that when others are sleeping mine eyes are weeping.

I have seen the extreme vanity of this world: One hour I have been in health, and wealthy, wanting nothing. But the next hour in sickness and wounds, and death, having nothing but sorrow and affliction.

Before I knew what affliction meant, I was ready sometimes to wish for it. When I lived in prosperity, having the comforts of the world about me, my relations by me, my heart cheerful, and taking little care for anything, and yet seeing many, whom I preferred before myself, under many trials and afflictions, in sickness, weakness, poverty, losses, crosses, and cares of the world, I should be sometimes jealous least I should have my portion in this life, and that Scripture would come to my mind, "For whom the Lord loveth he chasteneth, and scourgeth every Son whom he receiveth" (Hebrews 12.6). But now I see the Lord had His time to scourge and chasten me. The portion of some is to have their afflictions by drops, now one drop and then another; but the dregs of the cup, the wine of astonishment, like a sweeping rain that leaveth no food, did the Lord prepare to be my portion. Affliction I wanted, and affliction I had, full measure (I thought), pressed down and running over. Yet I see, when God calls a person to anything, and through never so many difficulties, yet He is fully able to carry them through and make them see, and say they have been gainers thereby. And I hope I can say in some measure, as David did, "It is good for me that I have been afflicted."[3] The Lord hath showed me the vanity of these outward things. That they are the vanity of vanities, and vexation of spirit, that they are but a shadow, a blast, a bubble, and things of no continuance. That we must rely on God Himself, and our whole dependance must be upon Him. If trouble from smaller matters begin to arise in me, I have something at hand to check myself with, and say, why am I troubled? It was but the other day that if I had had the world, I would have given it for my freedom, or to have been a servant to a Christian. I have learned to look beyond present and smaller troubles, and to be quieted under them. As Moses said, "Stand still and see the salvation of the Lord" (Exodus 14.13).

Finis.

1682

1. "He should have fed them also with the finest of the wheat: and with honey out of the rock should I have satisfied thee" (Psalm 81.16).

2. "And bring hither the fatted calf, and kill it; and let us eat, and be merry" (Luke 15.23).
3. Psalm 119.71.

EDWARD TAYLOR

c. 1642–1729

Given the importance of Edward Taylor's role in the town in which he lived for fifty-eight years, it is curious that we should know so little about his life. Taylor was probably born in Sketchly, Leicestershire County, England; his father was a "yeoman farmer"—that is, he was not a "gentleman" with large estates, but an independent landholder with title to his farm. Although his poetry contains no images that reflect his boyhood in Leicestershire, the dialect of that farming country is ever-present and gives his verse an air of provincial charm but also, it must be admitted, makes it difficult and complex for the modern reader. Taylor did not enter Harvard until he was twenty-nine years old and stayed only three years. It is assumed, therefore, that he had some university education in England, but it is not known where. We do know that he taught school and that he left his family and sailed to New England in 1668 because he would not sign an oath of loyalty to the Church of England. Rather than compromise his religious principles as a Puritan, he preferred exile in what he once called a "howling wilderness." It was at Harvard that he must have decided to leave teaching and prepare himself for the ministry.

In 1671 a delegation from the frontier town of Westfield, Massachusetts, asked Taylor to join them as their minister, and after a good deal of soul-searching he journeyed with them the hundred miles west to Westfield, where he remained the rest of his life. As by far the most educated member of that community, he served as minister, physician, and public servant. Taylor married twice and had fourteen children, many of whom died in infancy. A rigorous observer of all churchly functions, Taylor did not shy away from the religious controversies of the period. He was a strict observer of the "old" New England way, demanding a public account of conversion before admission to church membership and the right to partake of the sacrament of communion.

Taylor was a learned man as well as a pious one. Like most Harvard ministers, he knew Latin, Hebrew, and Greek. He had a passion for books and copied out in his own hand volumes that he borrowed from his college roommate, Samuel Sewall. He was known to Sewall and others as a good preacher, and on occasion he sent poems and letters to Boston friends, some parts of which were published during his lifetime. But Taylor's work as a poet was generally unknown until, in the 1930s, Thomas H. Johnson discovered that most of Taylor's poems had been deposited in the Yale University Library by Taylor's grandson, Ezra Stiles, a former president of Yale. It was one of the major literary discoveries of the twentieth century and revealed a body of work by a Puritan divine that was remarkable both in its quantity and quality.

Taylor's interest in poetry was lifelong, and he tried his hand at a variety of poetic genres: elegies on the death of public figures; lyrics in the manner of Elizabethan songs; a long poem, *God's Determinations*, in the tradition of the medieval debate; and an almost unreadable five-hundred-page *Metrical History of Christianity*, primarily a book of martyrs. But Taylor's best verse is to be found in a series called *Preparatory Meditations*. These poems, written for his own pleasure and never a part of any religious service, followed chiefly upon his preparation for a sermon to be delivered at monthly communion. They gave the poet an occasion to summarize the emotional and intellectual content of his sermon and to speak directly and fervently to God. Sometimes these poems are gnarled and difficult to follow, but they also reveal a unique voice, unmistakably Taylor's. They are written in an idiom that harks back to the verse Taylor must have known as a child in

England—the Metaphysical lyrics of John Donne and George Herbert—and so delight in puns and paradoxes and a rich profusion of metaphors and images. Nothing previously discovered about Puritan literature had suggested that there was a writer in New England who had sustained such a long-term love affair with poetry.

Psalm Two[1]

(First Version)

Why do the Heathen rage? & folk
   A vain thing meditate?
Kings of the earth do set themselves
   & Rulers Counsel take
Against the Lord, & 'gainst His Christ   5
   Anointed, saying thus,
Let us asunder break Their bands,
   & cast Their Cords[2] from us.

He that doth in the heavens sit
   Shall laugh deridingly;   10
The Lord Himself shall have them in
   derision mightily.
T[h]en shall He speak in's wra[th]
   I[n] fury vex them will.
[Ye]t have I set my King un[to]   15
   Zion my Holy hill.[3]

I will declare out the dec[re]e
   The Lord hath said to me:
Thou art Mine only Son, I ha[ve]
   this day begotten Thee.   20
Ask of Me, & the heathen for
   Thine 'heritance I'll give
And th' utmost parts of th' earth f[or]
   Possession will bequeath.

Thou shalt them into pieces [wi]th   25
   A rod of iron break;
Thou shalt them dash in pieces, li[ke]
   A Potter's vessel weak.
Be wise ye Kings, instructed
   Ye Judges of the earth.   30
Serve ye the Lord with fear th[en]
   Rejoice with trembling mirth.

1. Taylor made two attempts at paraphrasing the Psalms, putting them into the common meter (i.e., alternating lines of eight and six syllables) used for singing hymns, but never completed paraphrasing all 150. A comparison with the King James version is useful: "Why do the heathen rage, and the people imagine a vain thing? The kings of the earth set themselves, and the rulers take counsel together, against the Lord, and against his anointed, saying, Let us break their bands asunder, and cast away their cords from us." The text used here is from *Edward Taylor's Minor Poetry*, edited by Thomas M. and Virginia L. Davis (1981).
2. Ropes.
3. The hill in Jerusalem on which Solomon's temple was built.

Kiss th' Son lest He be wroth, &
The way ye perish must,
When His wrath but a little bu[rn].   35
Blesst all that in Him trust.

c. 1674–75   1981

FROM PREPARATORY MEDITATIONS[1]

Prologue

Lord, Can a Crumb of Dust the Earth outweigh,
        Outmatch all mountains, nay, the Crystal sky?
Embosom in't designs that shall Display
        And trace into the Boundless Deity?
        Yea, hand a Pen whose moisture doth guide o'er   5
        Eternal Glory with a glorious glore.[2]

*If it its Pen had of an Angel's Quill,
        And sharpened on a Precious Stone ground tight,
And dipped in liquid Gold, and moved by Skill
        In Crystal leaves should golden Letters write,   10
        It would but blot and blur, yea, jag, and jar
        Unless Thou mak'st the Pen, and Scrivener.*

*I am this Crumb of Dust which is designed
        To make my Pen unto Thy Praise alone,
And my dull Fancy[3] I would gladly grind   15
        Unto an Edge on Zion's[4] Precious Stone.
        And Write in Liquid Gold upon Thy Name
        My Letters till Thy glory forth doth flame.*

*Let not th' attempts break down my Dust, I pray,
        Nor laugh Thou them to scorn but pardon give.*   20
*Inspire this crumb of Dust till it display
        Thy Glory through't: and then Thy dust shall live.
        Its failings then Thou'lt overlook, I trust,
        They being Slips slipped from Thy Crumb of Dust.*

Thy Crumb of Dust breathes two words from its breast,   25
        That Thou wilt guide its pen to write aright
To Prove Thou art, and that Thou art the best
        And show Thy Properties to shine most bright.

1. The full title is *Preparatory Meditations before my Approach to the Lord's Supper. Chiefly upon the Doctrine preached upon the Day of Administration [of Communion]*. Taylor administered communion once a month to those members of his congregation who had made a declaration of their faith. He wrote these meditations in private; they are primarily the result of his contemplation of the biblical texts that served as the basis for the communion sermon. A total of 217 meditations survive, dating from 1682 to 1725. The text used here is from *Poems of Edward Taylor*, edited by Donald E. Stanford (1960).
2. Glory (Scottish).
3. I.e., imagination.
4. The hill in Jerusalem on which Solomon built his temple; the city of God on earth.

> *And then Thy Works will shine as flowers on Stems*
> *Or as in Jewelry Shops, do gems.*   30

c. 1682   1939

Meditation 8 (First Series)

John 6.51. I am the Living Bread.[1]

I kenning through Astronomy Divine
   The World's bright Battlement,[2] wherein I spy
A Golden Path my Pencil cannot line,
    From that bright Throne unto my Threshold lie.
    And while my puzzled thoughts about it pour,   5
    I find the Bread of Life in't at my door.

When that this Bird of Paradise[3] put in
   This Wicker Cage (my Corpse) to tweedle praise
Had pecked the Fruit forbade: and so did fling
    Away its Food; and lost its golden days;   10
    It fell into Celestial Famine sore:
    And never could attain a morsel more.

Alas! alas! Poor Bird, what wilt thou do?
   The Ceatures' field no food for Souls e'er gave.
And if thou knock at Angels' doors they show   15
    An Empty Barrel: they no soul bread have.
    Alas! Poor Bird, the World's White Loaf is done.
    And cannot yield thee here the smallest Crumb.

In this sad state, God's Tender Bowels[4] run
   Out streams of Grace: and He to end all strife   20
The Purest Wheat in Heaven His dear-dear son
    Grinds, and kneads up into this Bread of Life.
    Which Bread of Life from Heaven down came and stands
    Dished on Thy Table up by Angels' Hands.

Did God mold up this Bread in Heaven, and bake,   25
   Which from His Table came, and to thine goeth?
Doth He bespeak thee thus, This Soul Bread take.
    Come Eat thy fill of this thy God's White Loaf?
    It's Food too fine for Angels, yet come, take
    And Eat thy fill. It's Heaven's Sugar Cake.   30

---

1. "The Jews then murmured at him, because he said, I am the bread which came down from heaven. And they said, Is not this Jesus, the son of Joseph, whose father and mother we know? how is it then that he saith, I came down from heaven? Jesus therefore answered . . . Verily, verily, I say unto you, He that believeth on me hath everlasting life. I am that bread of life" (John 6.41–51). Christ offers a "New Covenant of Faith" in place of the "Old Covenant of Works," which Adam broke when he disobeyed God's commandment.

2. I.e., discerning, by means of "divine astronomy," the towers of heaven. Taylor goes on to suggest that there is an invisible golden path from this world to the Gates of Heaven.

3. I.e., the soul, which is like a bird kept in the body's cage.

4. Here used in the sense of the interior of the body, the "seat of the tender and sympathetic emotions," the heart.

What Grace is this knead in this Loaf? This thing
    Souls are but petty things it to admire.
Ye Angels, help: This fill would to the brim
    Heav'ns whelmed-down[5] Crystal meal Bowl, yea and higher.
      This Bread of Life dropped in thy mouth, doth Cry: 35
      Eat, Eat me, Soul, and thou shalt never die.

June 8, 1684   1939

Meditation 16 (First Series)

Luke 7.16. A Great Prophet is risen up.[1]

Leaf Gold, Lord of Thy Golden wedge[2] o'erlaid
    My Soul at first, Thy Grace in every part
Whose pert,[3] fierce Eye Thou such a Sight hadst made
    Whose brightsome beams could break into Thy heart
      Till Thy Cursed Foe had with my Fist mine Eye   5
      Dashed out, and did my Soul Unglorify.

I cannot see, nor Will Thy will aright.
    Nor see to wail my Woe, my loss and hue
Nor all the Shine in all the Sun can light
    My Candle, nor its heat my Heart renew.   10
      See, wail, and Will Thy Will, I must, or must
      From Heaven's sweet Shine to Hell's hot flame be thrust.

Grace then Concealed in God Himself, did roll
    Even Snowball like into a Sunball Shine
And nestles all Its beams bunched in Thy soul   15
    My Lord, that sparkle in Prophetic Lines.
      Oh! Wonder more than Wonderful! this Will
      Lighten the Eye which Sight Divine did spill.

What art Thou, Lord, this Ball of Glory bright?
    A Bundle of Celestial Beams up bound   20
In Grace's band fixed in Heaven's topmost height
    Pouring Thy golden beams thence, Circling round
      Which show Thy Glory, and Thy Glory's Way
      And Everywhere will make Celestial Day.

Lord, let Thy Golden Beams pierce through mine Eye   25
    And leave therein an Heavenly Light to glaze

---

5. Turned over. The *Oxford English Dictionary* quotes a passage from Dryden that is relevant: "That the earth is like a trencher and the Heavens a dish whelmed over it."

1. Taylor refers to the passage in the New Testament in which Jesus raised from the dead the only son of a widow. When the dead man spoke, fear took hold of all the witnesses to this miracle and they said: "That a great prophet is risen up among us; and, that God hath visited his people. And this rumor of him went forth throughout all Judea, and throughout all the region round about" (Luke 7.16–17).

2. In gilding it is customary to apply small squares of gold leaf to a surface; here the shape would seem to be triangular.

3. Sharp, quick to see.

My Soul with glorious Grace all o'er, whereby
    I may have Sight, and Grace in me may blaze.
My Lord ting[4] my Candle at Thy Burning rays,
    To give a gracious Glory to Thy Praise   30

Thou Lightning Eye, let some bright Beams of Thine
    Stick in my Soul, to light and liven it:
Light, Life, and Glory, things that are Divine;
    I shall be graced withall for glory fit.
    My heart then stuffed with Grace, Light, Life, and Glee   35
    I'll sacrifice in Flames of Love to Thee.

March 6, 1686   1960

Meditation 22 (First Series)

Philippians 2.9. God hath highly exalted Him.[1]

When Thy Bright Beams, my Lord, do strike mine Eye,
    Methinks I then could truly Chide outright
My Hide-bound Soul that stands so niggardly
    That scarce a thought gets glorified by't.
    My Quaintest[2] metaphors are ragged Stuff,   5
    Making the Sun seem like a Mullipuff.[3]

It's my desire, Thou shouldst be glorified:
    But when Thy Glory shines before mine eye,
I pardon Crave, lest my desire be Pride,
    Or bed Thy Glory in a Cloudy Sky.   10
    The Sun grows wan; and Angels palefaced shrink,
    Before Thy Shine, which I besmear with Ink.

But shall the Bird sing forth Thy Praise, and shall
    The little Bee present her thankful Hum?
But I who see Thy shining Glory fall   15
    Before mine Eyes, stand Blockish, Dull, and Dumb?
    Whether I speak, or speechless stand, I spy,
    I fail Thy Glory: therefore pardon Cry.

But this I find; My Rhymes do better suit
    Mine own Dispraise than tune forth praise to Thee.   20
Yet being Chid, whether Consonant,[4] or Mute,
    I force my Tongue to tattle, as You see.

4. Perhaps to "ring" with light.
1. "Let this mind be in you, which was also in Christ Jesus: Who, being in the form of God, thought it not robbery to be equal with God: But made himself no reputation, and took upon him the form of a servant, and was made in the likeness of men: And being found in fashion as a man, he humbled himself, and became obedient unto death, even the death of the cross. Wherefore God also hath highly exalted him, and given him a name which is above every name: That at the name of Jesus every knee should bow, of things in heaven, and things in earth, and things under the earth; And that every tongue should confess that Jesus Christ is Lord, to the glory of God the Father" (Philippians 2.5–11).
2. Most skilled, wise.
3. Fuzz ball.
4. Talkative, making sounds.

That I Thy glorious Praise may Trumpet right,
  Be Thou my Song, and make, Lord, me Thy pipe.

This shining Sky will fly away apace,   25
  When Thy bright Glory splits the same to make
Thy Majesty a Pass, whose Fairest Face
  Too foul a Path is for Thy Feet to take.
  What Glory then, shall tend Thee through the Sky
  Draining the Heaven much of Angels dry?   30

What Light then flame will in Thy Judgment Seat,
  'Fore which all men and Angels shall appear?
How shall Thy Glorious Righteousness them treat,
  Rend'ring to each after his Works done here?
  Then Saints with Angels Thou wilt glorify: 35
  And burn Lewd[5] Men, and Devils Gloriously.

One glimpse, my Lord, of Thy bright Judgment Day,
  And Glory piercing through, like fiery Darts,
All Devils, doth me make for Grace to pray,
  For filling Grace had I ten thousand Hearts.   40
  I'd through ten Hells to see Thy Judgment Day
  Wouldst Thou but gild my Soul with Thy bright Ray.

June 12, 1687   1960

Meditation 38 (First Series)

1 John 2.1. An Advocate with the Father.[1]

Oh! What a thing is Man? Lord, Who am I?
  That Thou shouldst give him Law (Oh! golden line)[2]
To regulate his Thoughts, Words, Life thereby.
  And judge him Wilt thereby too in Thy time.
  A Court of Justice Thou in Heaven holdst   5
  To try his Case while he's here housed on mold.[3]

How do Thy Angels lay before Thine eye
  My Deeds both White and Black I daily do?
How doth Thy Court Thou Panelist[4] there them try?
  But flesh complains. What right for this? let's know.   10
  For right, or wrong I can't appear unto't.
  And shall a sentence Pass on such a suit?

Soft; blemish not this golden Bench, or place.
  Here is no Bribe, nor Colorings[5] to hide,

---

5. Worthless, fallen.
1. "And if any man sin, we have an advocate with the Father, Jesus Christ the righteous: And he is the propitiation for our sins: and not for our's only, but also for the sins of the whole world" (1 John 2.1–2).
2. "Law": i.e., the Ten Commandments set forth in the Old Testament prescribing our behavior. This inheritance is our "golden line," or lineage.
3. I.e., the body will decay; only the soul is immortal.
4. I.e., impanel, as a jury.
5. Deceitful appearances.

Nor Pettifogger[6] to befog the Case,   15
    But Justice hath Her Glory here well tried.
Her spotless Law all spotted Cases tends.
Without Respect or Disrespect them ends.

God's Judge Himself: and Christ Attorney is,
    The Holy Ghost Registerer[7] is found.   20
Angels the Sergeants[8] are, all Creatures kiss
    The Book, and do as Evidences[9] abound.
All Cases pass according to pure Law
And in the sentence is no Fret,[1] nor flaw.

What sayst, my Soul? Here all thy Deeds are tried.   25
    Is Christ thy Advocate to plead thy Cause?
Art thou His Client? Such shall never slide.
    He never lost His Case: He pleads such Laws
As Carry do the same, nor doth refuse
The Vilest sinner's Case that doth Him Choose.   30

This is His honor, not Dishonor: nay,
    No Habeas-Corpus[2] against His Clients came.
For all their Fines His Purse doth make down pay.
    He Non-Suits Satan's Suit or Casts[3] the Same.
He'll plead thy Case, and not accept a Fee.   35
He'll plead Sub Forma Pauperis[4] for thee.

My Case is bad. Lord, be my Advocate.
    My sin is red: I'm under God's Arrest.
Thou hast the Hint of Pleading; plead my State.
    Although it's bad Thy Plea will make it best.   40
If Thou wilt plead my Case before the King:
I'll Wagonloads of Love and Glory bring.

July 6, 1690   1939

Meditation 42 (First Series)

Revelation 3.21. I will give Him to sit with Me in my Throne.[1]

Apples of gold, in silver pictures shrined[2]
Enchant the appetite, make mouths to water.

---

6. Lawyer who handles trivial cases and is given to professional tricks and quibblings.
7. I.e., registrar, court recorder and keeper of records.
8. Attendants at court who maintain order.
9. Witnesses.
1. Malice, ill will.
2. Thou shall have the body (Latin, literal trans.), i.e., no person may be kept in jail without the charge against him or her being quickly brought before a judge. Christ's clients are brought to trial immediately; He has Himself paid for humanity's sins with His Crucifixion and covered their fines with His own blood.

3. Dismisses. He stops a suit because of insufficient evidence.
4. According to form of poverty (Latin, literal trans.), a procedure in which an impoverished person is able to sue another without threat of costs in the event that the case should be lost.
1. "To him that overcometh will I grant to sit with me in my throne, even as I also overcame, and am set down with my Father in his throne. He that hath an ear, let him hear what the Spirit saith unto the churches" (Revelation 3.21–22).
2. Enshrined, enclosed.

And Loveliness in Lumps, tunn'd, and enrined[3]
    In Jasper[4] Cask, when tapped, doth briskly vapor:
    Bring forth a birth of Keys t'unlock Love's Chest,   5
    That Love, like Birds, may fly to't from its nest.

Such is my Lord, and more. But what strange thing
    Am I become? Sin rusts my Lock all o'er.
Though He ten thousand Keys all on a string
    Takes out, scarce one is found unlocks the Door.   10
    Which ope, my Love crinched[5] in a Corner lies
    Like some shrunk Crickling[6] and scarce can rise.

Lord, ope the Door: rub off my Rust, Remove
    My sin, and Oil my Lock. (Dust there doth shelf).
My Wards will trig[7] before Thy Key: my Love   15
    Then, as enlivened, leap will on Thyself.
    It needs must be, that giving hands receive
    Again Receivers Hearts furled in Love Wreath.

Unkey my Heart; unlock Thy Wardrobe: bring
    Out royal Robes: adorn my Soul, Lord: so,   20
My Love in rich attire shall on my King
    Attend, and honor on Him well bestow.
    In Glory He prepares for His a place
    Whom He doth all beglory here with Grace.

He takes them to the shining threshold clear   25
    Of His bright Palace, clothed in Grace's flame.
Then takes them in thereto, not only there
    To have a Prospect,[8] but possess the same.
    The Crown of Life, the throne of Glory's Place,
    The Father's House blanched o'er with orient Grace.   30

Canaan[9] in gold print enwalled with gems:
    A Kingdom rimmed with Glory round: in fine[1]
A glorious Crown paled[2] thick with all the stems
    Of Grace, and of all Properties Divine.
    How happy wilt Thou make me when these shall   35
    As a blest Heritage unto me fall?

Adorn me, Lord, with Holy Huswifry.[3]
    All blanch my Robes with Clusters of Thy Graces:
Thus lead me to Thy threshold: give mine Eye
    A Peephole there to see Bright Glory's Chases.[4]   40

---

3. Rendered, melted down. "Tunn'd": placed in a casket.
4. A precious stone, usually green in color.
5. Shrunken, gnarled up.
6. Properly "crinkling," a small, withered apple.
7. Open. "Wards": the protective ridges of a lock that prevent any but the proper key to open it.
8. View, range of vision.
9. The land promised by God to Abraham; the biblical name of Jerusalem (cf. Genesis 12.5–8).
1. In essence.
2. Striped.
3. Cloth woven in the home, and the traditional task of the housewife.
4. The settings of precious stones.

Then take me in: I'll pay, when I possess
Thy Throne, to Thee the Rent in Happiness.

August 2, 1691   1939

Meditation 26 (Second Series)

Hebrews 9.13–14. How much more shall the blood of Christ, etc.[1]

Unclean, Unclean: My Lord, Undone, all vile,
    Yea, all Defiled: What shall Thy Servant do?
Unfit for Thee: not fit for holy Soil,
    Nor for Communion of Saints[2] below.
    A bag of botches, Lump of Loathsomeness: 5
    Defiled by Touch, by Issue: Leproused flesh.

Thou wilt have all that enter to Thy fold
    Pure, Clean, and bright, Whiter than whitest Snow
Better refined than most refined Gold:
    I am not so: but foul: What shall I do?   10
    Shall Thy Church Doors be shut, and shut out me?
    Shall not Church Fellowship my portion be?

How can it be? Thy Churches do require
    Pure Holiness: I am all filth, alas!
Shall I defile them, tumbled thus in mire?   15
    Or they me cleanse before I current pass?[3]
    If thus they do, Where is the Nitre[4] bright
    And Soap they offer me to wash me White?

The brisk Red heifer's Ashes, when calcined,[5]
    Mixed all in running Water, is too Weak   20
To wash away my Filth: The Doves assigned
    Burnt and Sin Offerings ne'er do the feat
    But[6] as they Emblemize the Fountain Spring
    Thy Blood, my Lord, set ope to wash off Sin.

Oh! richest Grace! Are Thy Rich Veins then tapped   25
    To ope this Holy Fountain (boundless sea)
For Sinners here to laver[7] off (all sapped
    With Sin) their Sins and Sinfulness away?
    In this bright Crystal Crimson Fountain flows
    What washeth whiter than the Swan or Rose.   30

---

1. "For if the blood of bulls and of goats, and the ashes of an heifer sprinkling the unclean, sanctifieth to the purifying of the flesh: How much more shall the blood of Christ, who through the eternal Spirit offered himself without spot to God, purge your conscience from dead works to serve the living God?" (Hebrews 9.13–14).
2. "Visible saints," i.e., living church members.
3. I.e., pass accepted.
4. Potassium nitrate, used in whitening.
5. Burned.
6. Except, i.e., the sacrificial doves cannot cleanse his soul, but their blood serves as a symbol of ("emblemizes") the power of Christ's blood to wash us clean.
7. Wash.

Oh! wash me, Lord, in this Choice Fountain, White
        That I may enter, and not sully here
Thy Church, whose floor is paved with Graces bright
        And hold Church Fellowship with Saints most clear.
        My Voice all sweet, with their melodious lays   35
        Shall make sweet Music blossomed with Thy praise.

June 26, 1698   1960

FROM GOD'S DETERMINATIONS[1]

The Preface

        Infinity, when all things it beheld
In Nothing, and of Nothing all did build,
        Upon what Base was fixed the Lath wherein
He turned this Globe, and riggalled[2] it so trim?
Who blew the Bellows of His Furnace Vast?   5
Or held the Mold wherein the world was Cast?
Who laid its Corner Stone?[3] Or whose Command?
Where stand the Pillars upon which it stands?
Who Laced and Filleted[4] the earth so fine,
With Rivers like green Ribbons Smaragdine?[5]   10
Who made the Sea's its Selvage,[6] and its locks
Like a Quilt Ball[7] within a Silver Box?
Who Spread its Canopy? Or Curtains Spun?
Who in this Bowling Alley bowled the Sun?
Who made it always when it rises set   15
To go at once both down, and up to get?
Who th' Curtain rods made for this Tapestry?
Who hung the twinkling Lanthorns in the Sky?
Who? who did this? or who is He? Why, know
It's Only Might Almighty this did do.   20
His hand hath made this noble work which Stands
His Glorious Handiwork not made by hands.
Who spake all things from Nothing; and with ease
Can speak all things to Nothing, if He please.
Whose Little finger at His pleasure Can   25

1. The subject of this "debate" poem is made clear in the full title: *God's determinations touching His Elect: and the Elect's combat in their conversion, and coming up to God in Christ, together with the comfortable effects thereof.* In this group of poems Taylor explores the progress of the human soul from the creation of the world and the fall from Grace to the redemption of the Christian soul through Christ's Crucifixion: Christ's mercy triumphs over justice—the punishment that humanity deserves for disobedience—and the soul is finally carried to heaven to share in the joys of the Resurrection. The text used here is from *Poems of Edward Taylor,* edited by Donald E. Stanford (1960).
2. Grooved.
3. "Where wast thou when I laid the foundations of the earth? declare, if thou hast understanding. Who hath laid the measures thereof, it thou knowest? or who hath stretched the line upon it? Whereupon are the foundations thereof fastened? or who laid the corner stone thereof; When the morning stars sang together, and all the sons of God shouted for joy? Or who shut up the sea with doors, when it brake forth, as if it had issued out of the womb?" (Job 38.4–8).
4. Encircled, bound around.
5. Emerald green.
6. The border of woven material that prevents unraveling.
7. A ball of wool that would unravel if it were not kept in a box.

Out mete[8] ten thousand worlds with half a Span:
Whose Might Almighty can by half a looks
Root up the rocks and rock the hills by the'roots.
Can take this mighty World up in His hand,
And shake it like a Squitchen[9] or a Wand.   30
Whose single Frown will make the Heavens shake
Like as an aspen leaf the Wind makes quake.
Oh! what a might is this Whose single frown
Doth shake the world as it would shake it down?
Which All from Nothing fet,[1] from Nothing, All: 35
Hath All on Nothing set, lets Nothing fall.
Gave All to Nothing Man indeed, whereby
Through Nothing man all might Him Glorify.
In Nothing then embossed the brightest Gem
More precious than all preciousness in them.   40
But Nothing man did throw down all by Sin:
And darkened that lightsome Gem in him.
    That now his Brightest Diamond is grown
    Darker by far than any Coalpit Stone.

c. 1685   1939

The Soul's Groan to Christ for Succor

Good Lord, behold this Dreadful Enemy
    Who makes me tremble with his fierce assaults;
I dare not trust, yet fear to give the lie,
    For in my soul, my soul finds many faults
    And though I justify myself to's face: 5
    I do Condemn myself before Thy Grace.

He strives to mount my sins, and them advance
    Above Thy Merits, Pardons, or Good Will
Thy Grace to lessen, and Thy Wrath t'enhance
    As if Thou couldst not pay the sinner's bill.   10
    He Chiefly injures Thy rich Grace, I find,
    Though I confess my heart to sin inclined.

Those Graces which Thy Grace enwrought in me,
    He makes as nothing but a pack of Sins.
He maketh Grace no grace, but Cruelty;   15
    Is Grace's Honeycomb a Comb of Stings?
    This makes me ready leave Thy Grace and run.
    Which if I do, I find I am undone.

I know he is Thy Cur, therefore I be
    Perplexed lest I from Thy Pasture stray.   20
He bays, and barks so veh'mently at me.
    Come rate[1] this Cur, Lord, break his teeth, I pray.

8. Outmeasure.
9. Switch.

1. Made.
1. Give reproof, specifically, to a dog.

Remember me, I humbly pray Thee first.
Then halter up this Cur that is so Cursed.

c. 1685   1939

Christ's Reply

Peace, Peace, my Honey, do not Cry,
My Little Darling, wipe thine eye,
     Oh Cheer, Cheer up, come see.
Is anything too dear,[1] my Dove,
Is anything too good, my Love,   5
     To get or give for thee?

If in the several[2] thou art,
This Yelper fierce will at thee bark:
     That thou art Mine this shows.
As Spot barks back the sheep again   10
Before they to the Pound are ta'en,
     So he and hence 'way goes.

But yet this Cur that bays so sore
Is broken-toothed, and muzzled sure,
     Fear not, my Pretty Heart.   15
His barking is to make thee Cling
Close underneath thy Savior's Wing.
     Why did my sweeten[3] start?

And if he run an inch too far,
I'll Check his Chain, and rate[4] the Cur.
     My Chick, keep close to me.   20
The Poles shall sooner kiss, and greet
And Parallels shall sooner meet
     Than thou shalt harmed be.

He seeks to aggravate thy sin   25
And screw them to the highest pin,
     To make thy faith to quail.
Yet mountain Sins like mites should show
And then these mites for naught should go
     Could he but once prevail.   30

I smote thy sins upon the Head.
They Deadened are, though not quite dead:
     And shall not rise again.
I'll put away the Guilt thereof,
And purge its Filthiness clear off: 35
     My Blood doth out the stain.

---

1. Difficult to get; expensive.   3. Beloved.
2. Divided, in the sense that the soul is torn between   4. Give reproof; specifically, to a dog.
Christ and the Devil.

And though thy judgment was remiss
Thy Headstrong Will too willful is.
    I will Renew the same.
And though thou do too frequently   40
Offend as heretofore hereby,
    I'll not severely blame.

And though thy senses do inveigle
Thy Noble Soul to tend the Beagle,
    That t'hunt her games forth go,   45
I'll Lure her back to me, and Change
Those fond Affections that do range
    As yelping beagles do.

Although thy sins increase their race,
And though when thou hast sought for Grace,   50
    Thou fallst more than before,
If thou by true Repentence Rise,
And Faith makes Me Thy Sacrifice,
    I'll pardon all, though more.

Though Satan strive to block thy way   55
By all his Stratagems he may:
    Come, come though through the fire.
For Hell that Gulf of fire for sins,
Is not so hot as t'burn thy Shins.
    Then Credit not the Liar.   60

Those Cursed Vermin Sins that Crawl
All o'er thy Soul, both Great and small,
    Are only Satan's own:
Which he in his Malignity
Unto thy Soul's true Sanctity   65
    In at the doors hath thrown.

And though they be Rebellion high,
Ath'ism or Apostasy;
    Though blasphemy it be:
Unto what Quality, or Size   70
Excepting one, so e'er it rise.
    Repent, I'll pardon thee.

Although thy Soul was once a Stall[5]
Rich hung with Satan's nicknacks all;
    If thou Repent thy sin,   75
A Tabernacle in't I'll place
Filled with God's Spirit, and His Grace.
    Oh, Comfortable thing!

I dare the World therefore to show
A God like Me, to anger slow: 80
    Whose wrath is full of Grace.

5. A small booth in which things are sold.

Doth hate all Sins both Great and small:
Yet when Repented, pardons all.
  Frowns with a Smiling Face.

As for thy outward Postures each,   85
Thy Gestures, Actions, and thy Speech,
  I Eye and Eying spare,
If thou repent. My Grace is more
Ten thousand times still trebled o'er
  Than thou canst want, or wear.   90

As for the Wicked Charge he makes,
That he of Every Dish first takes
  Of all thy holy things,
It's false, deny the same, and say,
That which he had he stole away   95
  Out of thy Offerings.[6]

Though to thy Grief, poor Heart, thou find
In Prayer too oft a wandering mind,
  In Sermons Spirits dull,
Though faith in fiery furnace flags,   100
And Zeal in Chilly Seasons lags,
  Temptation's powerful.

These faults are his, and none of thine
So far as thou dost them decline.
  Come, then receive My Grace.   105
And when he buffets thee therefore,
If thou My aid and Grace implore,
  I'll show a pleasant face.

But still look for Temptations Deep,
Whilst that thy Noble Spark doth keep   110
  Within a Mudwalled Cote.[7]
These White Frosts and the Showers that fall
Are but to whiten thee withall,
  Not rot the Web they smote.

If in the fire where Gold is tried   115
Thy Soul is put, and purified,
  Wilt thou lament thy loss?
If silver-like this fire refine
Thy Soul and make it brighter shine:
  Wilt thou bewail the Dross?   120

Oh! fight My Field: no Colors fear:
I'll be thy Front, I'll be thy rear.
  Fail not: My Battles fight.

---

6. Satan argues that humanity does nothing in a disinterested way for the love of God but only from the fear
of hell. Christ argues that the soul should affirm its
generous impulses and put Satan in his place.
7. Cottage.

> Defy the Tempter, and his Mock.
> Anchor thy heart on Me thy Rock.   125
> I do in thee Delight.

c. 1685   1939

The Joy of Church Fellowship Rightly Attended[1]

> In Heaven soaring up, I dropped an Ear
>   On Earth: and oh! sweet Melody!
> And listening, found it was the Saints[2] who were
>   Encoached for Heaven that sang for Joy.
>   For in Christ's Coach they sweetly sing;   5
>   As they to Glory ride therein.
>
> Oh! joyous hearts! Enfired with holy Flame!
>   Is speech thus tasseléd[3] with praise?
> Will not your inward fire of Joy contain:
>   That it in open flames doth blaze?   10
>   For in Christ's Coach Saints sweetly sing,
>   As they to Glory ride therein.
>
> And if a string do slip, by Chance, they soon
>   Do screw it up again; whereby
> They set it in a more melodious Tune   15
>   And a Diviner Harmony.
>   For in Christ's Coach they sweetly sing
>   As they to Glory ride therein.
>
> In all their Acts, public, and private, nay
>   And secret, too, they praise impart.   20
> But in their Acts Divine and Worship, they
>   With Hymns do offer up their Heart.
>   Thus in Christ's Coach they sweetly sing
>   As they to Glory ride therein.
>
> Some few not in;[4] and some whose Time and Place   25
>   Block up this Coach's way do go
> As Travelers afoot, and so do trace
>   The Road that gives them right thereto;
>   While in this Coach these sweetly sing
>   As they to Glory ride therein.   30

c. 1685   1939

---

1. The final poem in *God's Determinations*.
2. I.e., "visible saints," those who were church members when alive.
3. Ornamented. in the sense in which tassels might be applied to a piece of fabric.
4. I.e., those who are saved but are outside the church.

Upon Wedlock, and Death of Children[1]

A Curious Knot[2] God made in Paradise,
    And drew it out enameled[3] neatly Fresh.
It was the True-Love Knot, more sweet than spice,
    And set with all the flowers of Grace's dress.
      It's Wedden's[4] Knot, that ne're can be untied: 5
      No Alexander's Sword[5] can it divide.

The slips[6] here planted, gay and glorious grow:
    Unless an Hellish breath do singe their Plumes.
Here Primrose, Cowslips, Roses, Lilies blow[7]
    With Violets and Pinks that void[8] perfumes: 10
      Whose beauteous leaves o'erlaid with Honey Dew,
      And Chanting birds Chirp out sweet Music true.

When in this Knot I planted was, my Stock[9]
    Soon knotted, and a manly flower out brake.[1]
And after it, my branch again did knot,   15
    Brought out another Flower, its sweet-breathed mate.
      One knot gave one tother[2] the tother's place.
      Whence Chuckling smiles fought in each other's face.

But Oh! a glorious hand from glory came
    Guarded with Angels, soon did crop this flower[3]   20
Which almost tore the root up of the same,
    At that unlooked for, Dolesome, darksome hour.
      In Prayer to Christ perfumed it did ascend,
      And Angels bright did it to heaven 'tend.

But pausing on't, this sweet perfumed my thought: 25
    Christ would in Glory have a Flower, Choice, Prime,
And having Choice, chose this my branch forth brought.
    Lord take't. I thank Thee, Thou tak'st ought of mine:
      It is my pledge in glory, part of me
      Is now in it, Lord, glorified with Thee.   30

But praying o're my branch, my branch did sprout,
    And bore another manly flower, and gay,[4]
And after that another, sweet brake[5] out,
    The which the former hand soon got away.
      But Oh! the tortures, Vomit, screechings, groans,   35
      and six week's Fever would pierce hearts like stones.[6]

---

1. The text used here is from *Poems of Edward Taylor*, edited by Donald E. Stanford (1960).
2. Flower bed.
3. Polished, shining.
4. I.e., wedding's.
5. Alexander the Great cut the Gordian knot devised by the king of Phyrgia when he learned that anyone who could undo it would rule Asia.
6. Cuttings.
7. Bloom.
8. Emit.

9. Stem.
1. Samuel Taylor was born on August 27, 1675, and lived to maturity.
2. To the other.
3. Elizabeth Taylor was born on December 27, 1676, and died on December 25, 1677.
4. James Taylor was born on October 12, 1678, and lived to maturity.
5. I.e., broke out.
6. Abigail Taylor was born on August 6, 1681, and died on August 22, 1682.

Grief o're doth flow: and nature fault would find
    Were not Thy Will, my Spell, Charm, Joy, and Gem:
That as I said, I say, take, Lord, they're Thine.
    I piecemeal pass to Glory bright in them.   40
    In joy, may I sweet flowers for glory breed,
    Whether thou get'st them green, or lets them seed.

c. 1682   1939

[When] Let by Rain[1]

Ye Flippering[2] Soul,
    Why dost between the Nippers[3] dwell?
Not stay, Nor go. Not yea, nor yet Control.
    Doth This do well?
        Rise journey'ng when the skies fall weeping Showers.   5
        Not o'er nor under th'Clouds and Cloudy Powers.

Not yea, nor no:
    On tiptoes thus? Why sit on thorns?
Resolve the matter: Stay thyself or go.
    Be n't both ways borne.   10
        Wager thyself against thy surplice,[4] see,
        And win thy Coat: or let thy Coat Win thee.

Is this th'Effect,
    To leaven[5] thus my Spirits all?
To make my heart a Crabtree Cask direct?   15
    A Verjuiced[6] Hall?
        As Bottle Ale, whose Spirits prisoned nursed[7]
        When jogged, the bung[8] with Violence doth burst?

Shall I be made
    A sparkling Wildfire Shop   20
Where my dull Spirits at the Fireball trade[9]
    Do frisk and hop?
        And while the Hammer doth the Anvil pay,
        The fireball matter sparkles ev'ry way.

One sorry fret,[1]   25
    An anvil Spark, rose higher,
And in Thy Temple falling almost set
    The house on fire.

---

1. The text used here is from *Poems of Edward Taylor*, edited by Donald E. Stanford (1960). "Let": prevented, hindered.
2. Hesitant, indecisive.
3. Iron forcepslike instrument.
4. Outer garment.
5. Ferment.
6. Soured. Verjuice is the acid juice of green or unripe grapes.
7. Cultured, brought up.
8. Cork, stopper.
9. I.e., the blacksmith's trade. Taylor goes on to suggest that the soul is like hot metal, and when struck by the blacksmith's hammer it sends sparks flying and is thus like a "wildfire shop."
1. Irritation of mind, vexation; compared here to a spark from the blacksmith's anvil.

Such fireballs dropping in the Temple Flame
Burns up the building: Lord forbid the same.   30

1939

Upon a Wasp Chilled with Cold[1]

The Bear that breathes the Northern blast[2]
Did numb, Torpedo-like,[3] a Wasp
Whose stiffened limbs encramped, lay bathing
In Sol's[4] warm breath and shine as saving,
Which with her hands she chafes and stands   5
Rubbing her Legs, Shanks, Thighs, and hands.
Her petty toes, and fingers' ends
Nipped with this breath, she out extends
Unto the Sun, in great desire
To warm her digits at that fire.   10
Doth hold her Temples in this state
Where pulse doth beat, and head doth ache.
Doth turn, and stretch her body small,
Doth Comb her velvet Capital.[5]
As if her little brain pan were   15
A Volume of Choice precepts clear.
As if her satin jacket hot
Contained Apothecary's Shop
Of Nature's receipts,[6] that prevails
To remedy all her sad ails,   20
As if her velvet helmet high
Did turret[7] rationality.
She fans her wing up to the Wind
As if her Pettycoat were lined,
With reason's fleece, and hoists sails   25
And humming flies in thankful gales
Unto her dun Curled[8] palace Hall
Her warm thanks offering for all.

Lord, clear my misted sight that I
May hence view Thy Divinity,   30
Some sparks whereof Thou up dost hasp[9]
Within this little downy Wasp
In whose small Corporation[1] we
A school and a schoolmaster see,
Where we may learn, and easily find   35

1. The text used here is from *Poems of Edward Taylor*, edited by Donald E. Stanford (1960).
2. The northern constellation the Big Dipper, also called Ursa Major, or the Great Bear.
3. The torpedo is a fish, like a stingray, and discharges a shock to one who touches it, causing numbness. Sir Thomas Browne writes: "Torpedoes deliver their opium at a distance and stupify beyond themselves" (1646).
4. The sun personified.
5. Head.
6. Remedies, prescriptions. "Apothecary's Shop": what we would now call a drugstore or pharmacy.
7. Contain, encompass.
8. Dark curved.
9. Enclose, confine.
1. Body.

A nimble Spirit bravely mind
Her work in every limb: and lace
It up neat with a vital grace,
Acting each part though ne'er so small
Here of this Fustian[2] animal,   40
Till I enravished Climb into
The Godhead on this Ladder do,
Where all my pipes inspired upraise
An Heavenly music furred[3] with praise.

                                        1960

Huswifery[1]

Make me, O Lord, Thy Spinning Wheel complete.
Thy Holy Word my Distaff make for me.
Make mine Affections Thy Swift Flyers neat
    And make my Soul Thy holy Spool to be.
    My conversation make to be Thy Reel   5
    And reel the yarn thereon spun of Thy Wheel.[2]

Make me Thy Loom then, knit therein this Twine:
    And make Thy Holy Spirit, Lord, wind quills:[3]
Then weave the Web Thyself. The yarn is fine.
    Thine Ordinances make my Fulling Mills.[4]   10
    Then dye the same in Heavenly Colors Choice,
    All pinked with Varnished[5] Flowers of Paradise.

Then clothe therewith mine Understanding, Will,
    Affections, Judgment, Conscience, Memory,
My Words, and Actions, that their shine may fill   15
    My ways with glory and Thee glorify.
    Then mine apparel shall display before Ye
    That I am Clothed in Holy robes for glory.

                                        1939

A Fig for Thee, Oh! Death[1]

Thou King of Terrors with thy Ghastly eyes,
With Butter[2] teeth, bare bones, Grim looks likewise,

---

2. Coarse-clothed.
3. Trimmed or embellished, as with fur.
1. Housekeeping: used here to mean weaving. In Taylor's *Treatise Concerning the Lord's Supper* (see the following selection) he considers the significance of the sacrament of communion and takes as his text a passage from the New Testament: "And he saith unto him, Friend, how camest thou in hither not having a wedding garment? And he was speechless" (Matthew 22.12). Taylor argues that the wedding garment is the proper sign of the regenerate Christian. The text used here is from *Poems of Edward Taylor*, edited by Donald E. Stanford (1960).

2. In the lines above Taylor refers to the working parts of a spinning wheel: the "distaff" holds the raw wool or flax; the "flyers" regulate the spinning; the "spool" twists the yarn; and the "reel" takes up the finished thread.
3. I.e., be like a spool or bobbin.
4. Where cloth is beaten and cleansed with fuller's earth, or soap.
5. Glossy, sparkling. "Pinked": adorned.
1. A fig is anything that is valueless, small, and contemptible. The text used here is from *Poems of Edward Taylor*, edited by Donald E. Stanford (1960).
2. Yellow.

And Grizzly hide, and clawing Talons fell,[3]
Op'ning to Sinners Vile, Trap Door of Hell,
That on in Sin impenitently trip,   5
The Downfall[4] art of the infernal Pit,
Thou struck'st thy teeth deep in my Lord's bless'd side:
Who dashed it out, and all its venom 'stroyed[5]
That now thy Pounderall[6] shall only dash
My Flesh and bones to bits, and Cask shall clash.[7]   10
Thou'rt not so frightful now to me, thy knocks
Do crack my shell. Its Heavenly kernel's box
Abides most safe. Thy blows do break its shell,
Thy Teeth its Nut. Cracks are that on it fell.
Thence out its kernel fair and nut, by worms   15
Once Vitiated out, new formed forth turns
And on the wings of some bright Angel flies
Out to bright glory of God's blissful joys.
Hence thou to me with all thy Ghastly face
Art not so dreadful unto me through Grace.   20
I am resolved to fight thee, and ne'er yield,
Blood up to th'Ears; and in the battlefield
Chasing thee hence. But not for this, my flesh;
My Body, my vile harlot, it's thy Mess,[8]
Laboring to drown me into Sin's disguise   25
By Eating and by drinking, such evil joys—
Though Grace preserved me that I ne'er have
Surpriséd been nor tumbled in such grave.[9]
Hence for my strumpet I'll ne'er draw my Sword,
Nor thee restrain at all by Iron curb,   30
Nor for her safety will I 'gainst thee strive,
But let thy frozen grips take her Captive
And her imprison in thy dungeon Cave
And grind to powder in thy Mill the grave,
Which powder in thy Van[1] thou'st safely keep   35
Till she hath slept out quite her fatal Sleep.
When the last Cock shall Crow the Last Day[2] in,
And the Archangel's Trumpet's sound shall ring,
Then th'Eye Omniscient seek shall all there round,
Each dust death's mill had very finely ground,   40
Which in death's smoky furnace well refined
And Each to 'ts fellow hath exactly joined,
Is raised up anew and made all bright
And Crystallized; all topfull of delight,
And entertains its Soul again in bliss,   45
And Holy Angels waiting all on this,
The Soul and Body now, as two true lovers,
E'ry night how do they hug and kiss each other.

3. Deadly.
4. Descending precipice.
5. Destroyed.
6. Pestle.
7. I.e., his body will feel the resounding blow.
8. Dinner.
9. Taylor made two versions of this poem. In the first version these difficult lines (24–28) are made clearer:

"My harlot body, make thou it thy mess, / That oft ensnared me with its strumpet's guise / Of meat's and drink's dainty sensualities. / Yet grace ne'er suffer[ed] me to turn aside / As sinners oft fall in and do abide."
1. Winnowing basket, used to separate chaff from the grain.
2. I.e., when Judgment Day comes.

And going hand in hand thus through the skies
Up to Eternal glory glorious rise.   50
Is this the Worst thy terrors then canst, why
Then should this grimace at me terrify?
Why cam'st thou then so slowly? Mend thy pace.
Thy Slowness me detains from Christ's bright face.
Although thy terrors rise to th'highst degree,   55
I still am where I was. A Fig for thee.

1960

From Treatise Concerning the Lord's Supper[1]

From *Sermon VI*

Doctrine: *There is no reason of approaching to the wedden feast, without the wedden garment.*

Touching these positive helps, they are such as tend to put the soul into a due state to be informed, and to receive information in its trying itself, and therefore:

You are to shrive your will and affections of all their own conclusions made beforehand of things. You stand not in a receptive frame unto the truth to be discovered, while you are prepossessed with your own persuasions. Oftentimes persons rivet their affections to raw notions picked up out of some cursory expressions let fall by such as never well concocted the same: and being thus received, they prejudice the truth and forestall the soul, that such discoveries as strike against such espoused notions will in no wise gain acceptance. For such notions frequently are with them as true as gospel; nay, and are made the standards of the market to measure all things by. And such things as will not receive countenance therefrom must be chased away, as faulty. Hence in your trying of yourselves you must shake off all such things prejudicial to truth from your wills and affections, or it is to be feared your search will be in vain. It is a snare to a man after vows to make inquiry (Proverbs 20.25). Therefore in thy search put thyself into a receptive capacity unto truth to be discovered.

You are to clear up the light of your eyes. Get clear glasses. Use good spectacles. Avoid raw notions that, like ill-concocted matter, send gross vapors into the ventricles of the brain, and so cloud the head. But get a clear head: be well insighted into the nature of the matter before you. Remove the beam,[2] mote, or gravel out of thine eye (Matthew 7.5).[3] Anoint thine eyes with Christ's eye salve (Revelation 3.18),[4] and this lies in getting a clear sight in:

The rule: and this is the holy scriptures. The thing to be tried must be

---

1. Edited by Norman S. Grabo (1966). Taylor prepared eight untitled sermons on the subject of the sacrament of communion and completed them in 1694. He took as his text the parable of the wedding feast in Matthew: "And he saith unto him, Friend, how camest thou in hither not having a wedding garment? And he was speechless" (Matthew 22.12). Taylor argues that the garment referred to is the sign of the garment of righteousness, the garment worn by the regenerate Christian.

2. An irritating particle in the eye.
3. "Thou hypocrite, first cast out the beam out of thine own eye; and then shalt thou see clearly to cast out the mote out of thy brother's eye."
4. "I counsel thee to buy of me gold tried in the fire, that thou mayest be rich; and white raiment, that thou mayest be clothed, and that the shame of thy nakedness do not appear; and anoint thine eyes with eyesalve, that thou mayest see."

brought to the rule. The trial itself lieth in two things: viz., the laying the thing to be tried unto the rule, according to which it ought to be squared; and the determination made by the conformity it hath unto the rule. Hence get good insight into the rule. Study the scriptures.

The wedden garment. For your judgment being to be made whether this is yours, you must have a clear insight into the nature of it, that wherever you see it you may be able to say, this is it, whether in yourselves or in others. Therefore endeavor to be well insighted in the nature of this wedden garment, and that in these things:

As to the matter it is made on. And this you have heard to be the grace of God as saving, and therefore both inherent, as the sanctifying grace of God's Spirit, as you have had it evidenced unto you, and the adherent grace of God, viz., imputed righteousness of Christ. Hence you must get a true knowledge of the nature of every grace, that so you may discern them in the web. You must know what faith is, what humility is, what hope is, what patience is, what repentance is, etc. For these are some of the fine twine of the Spirit that are woven into this web.

* * *

* * * Where the wedden garment is, there there is an exercise of these two properties incessantly as that of invincible hatred and love.

Invincible hatred. Now hatred is a virtue, its object hateful, viz., whatever is contrary to this wedden garment. It is so choice of it, that whatever tends to defile it hath the irreconcilable enmity of the soul rising up against it: all the enchantments of hell cannot charm this enmity. It is the property of all to be offended at what defiles his best apparel. So it is here: it's the property of the soul in the wedden garment to be utterly wroth with all array contrary to it, and all things, whatever do defile it. There is nothing can defile it but sin: there is nothing contrary to it but sin. Hence the soul that hath it hates sin. He is called to it, Psalm 97.10. Hate the very garment spotted with the flesh (Jude 23). Such as have this garment reply to this call: I hate every false way; I hate vain thoughts; I hate and abhor lying. Well then here lies the trial of the case. Dost thou hate sin? Dost thou hate sin as it is defiling thy garments? Dost thou hate sin as sin? Because it makes unclean, and unlike God? This is a casting note. But if thou hatest it, thou watchest against it, keepest far from it, repentest of it, and loathest thyself as defiled by it. But if sin be not in truth hateful unto thee, thou hast not this property, and so the wedden garment is none of thine, and this is a sad word to be spoken to thee, yet it is a true word. But here is this ease to be administered to the doubting soul. You are not to conclude that you do not hate sin in that you find in you a principle of love to sin. For so long as sanctification is but in part, there will be a party holding in thee with sin. But then if thou art sanctified in part, thou wilt be grieved that thou hast no more hatred of sin, or that thou hast anything in thee that doth hinder thee that thou canst not hate sin as thou wouldst. Well then try by this; and accordingly thou mayst draw up the conclusion.

Invincible love: as it is the property of the person that hath the wedden garment to bear invincible hatred to whatever is against the wedden garment any way, so it is his property to have invincible love to it in all its respects. And therefore consider it as laid out on the wedden garment.

Invincible love runs upon the wedden garment simply and relatively.

Simply: take this wedden garment in its simple and absolute consideration and it's the object of insuperable love to everyone that hath it. The Spirit of God saith that love is strong as death. Many waters cannot quench it; neither can the floods drown it; and this love is fixed upon these wedden robes, for they are the richest robes that ever were worn. They are the best robes; they are royal robes. Joseph must be arrayed in vesture of fine linen, or rather in silk or satin[5] (Genesis 41.42). These are festival clothes, wedden clothes. The church in them is said to stand in gold of Ophir,[6] and to be all glorious within, and to be arrayed in wrought gold (Psalms 45.9, 13). Nay, the Lord Christ highly esteems this, and knows that the soul doth that hath it on, that He lays it down as a promise (Revelation 3.5). Hence it must needs be prized by such as have it. For Christ Himself saith of it, "the smell of thy garments is as Lebanon"[7] (Canticles 4.11). Now then, here is thy trial: what is thy respect to this garment? Is it low? If below what is laid out on others, if not above what goes to others, it is not thine. Everyone doth love his own above another's; if this which is in its own nature above another's is not esteemed by thee above all others, it is none of thine. And this is an hard word. But if thy love to it excels, then it is thine.

Relatively: take this wedden garment in its relative consideration, as it is related to thee, and thy love to it excels and comes upon it invincibly. And as it stands under this consideration, we are to note it in its aspect to our wear and ways.

Our wear. We love to wear it. We are never well but when we are in it. A child of God in this is like to the little children of men, ever best when he is in best clothes. Nay, he is loathsome to himself if he find himself in any respect out of this wedden garment. This is his joy and rejoicing, to be wearing this apparel. He hath the shame of his nakedness appear, if he find his wear is not this white raiment, and this is that that his glory lieth in. Here his garments are always white and shining, as a robe of solid metal, whether silver or of gold, by wearing made more shining. So it is here: the more it is worn, the more it shines. It is not worn out by wearing, but worn more bright and shining, and hence he ever lives to be wearing of it.

* * *

As to the celebration of the wedden feast, in which, what height is the love advanced unto in the soul that is invested in this wedden attire? We are not able to take an observation of love's elevation in order to the solemnizing this feast. For consider and you shall find all the beams of gospel grace communicated unto the soul through the dispensation of the Word concentrating in the preparation adorning the soul for it, as they in this wedden garment. Now this is the highest preparation under heaven that mortals arrive at, and yet this is not a preparation above this feast: nay, the highest preparation under heaven below this is a preparation below the welcome to this feast. Consider the nature of the feast, and you shall find it is the marriage feast of the King's Son. The King of Glory, King of Kings, the King Immortal and Invisible and Eternal herein celebrates the espousals made between His own and only begotten Son,

5. The son of Jacob and Rachel, Joseph was made the ruler of Egypt by Pharaoh: "See, I have set thee over all the land of Egypt. And Pharaoh took off his ring from his hand, and put it upon Joseph's hand, and arrayed him in vestures of fine linen, and put a gold chain about his neck" (Genesis 41.41–42).

6. Ophir is mentioned in the Old Testament (1 Kings 10.11) as a place where fine gold was found.

7. Mountainous land noted for its fragrant cedars.

and heir of all things, and the souls of His elect drawn up in an holy contract at the time of their particular conversions. Wherein He entertains them with the royalest dainties, and the richest provision that heaven itself affords: with that miraculous water out of the rock, and Manna,[8] the breads of heaven, angels' bread. Not that these were properly types of the festival provision in the elemental signs. For as Ames[9] saith, "there are no figures of figures, or sacraments that God hath instituted, or the scripture teacheth." But this rock notes[1] Christ, and the water the graces of the Holy Ghost communicated by Christ, and the Manna, angels' bread, some think, because the angels in their judgment were the makers of it. But now God provides the true Manna, or Bread of Life here to feast His with, not such as the angels made, but the which the God of angels Himself made. Oh! the provision here, the flesh and the blood, the precious blood of His own Son, most richly dressed, is the provision God makes now to entertain His guests with all the benefits thereof. Here is a feast, a soul feast "of fat things, a feast of wines on the lees,[2] a feast of fat things full of marrow, of wines on the lees well refined" (Isaiah 25.6). It is the richest and royalest feast that ever was made. George Neville's[3] feast at York was nothing to this for costliness. Nor was King Ahasuerus his feast (Esther 1) to be mentioned with this. This feast for the provision of it in signs, and things signified, is an epitome of all gospel grace, or all the grace of the gospel. Now then think of it. Hence how can it be that the soul dressed up in the wedden garment should not have an high esteem and an unspeakable love unto it? If thou hast not such a love, thou hast not this wedden garment. If the wedden garment is thine, thou hast lapt upon it[4] this love. Try therefore by thy love unto the wedden.

As to the celebrators of this feast. Thy love runs out to these with all its might, if thou are arrayed in this rich robe. And these that celebrate it are authors and guests.

The authors of it, the King the Father, and the Prince the Son. The Father makes the wedden for the Son and the Son acts with the Father. Now these have all loveliness in them. The Father, He is the foundation of loveliness, being the fountain of love. "Oh!" saith the soul, "whom have I in heaven but thee, and in all the earth I desire nothing in comparison of thee" (Psalm 74.25). Oh! God is all to the soul in this royal array. So the Son. Now it is the Father's design to set out the Son as most lovely, and therefore He celebrates the feast for this end. He is the lovely rose of Sharon,[5] and glorious lily of the valley. He is altogether lovely in everything, lovely in His person, lovely in His natures, lovely in His properties, lovely in His offices,[6] lovely in His titles, lovely in His practice, lovely in His purchases and lovely in His relations. And in all these, and all other things, He is altogether lovely. Now this is the Bridegroom, and His love doth mostly show itself in this feast, wherein He feasts the souls of His upon His own flesh and blood most royally served up, as the viands of their peace offering. Oh! how should the soul choose but love

8. The substance miraculously offered as food for the Children of Israel in their journey through the wilderness.
9. William Ames (1576–1633), an English theologian well known among Puritan divines.
1. Denotes.
2. Dregs; i.e., wine drunk to the last drop.
3. George Neville (1433?–1476) was made archbishop of York in 1464, and the occasion was followed by a celebrated feast. Taylor was interested enough to keep a list of the dishes served.
4. Wrapped around it.
5. Sharon is the name of a fertile land along the coast of Israel. The phrase "rose of Sharon" comes from the Song of Solomon 2.1: "I am the rose of Sharon and the lily of the valleys."
6. Duties; things undertaken.

Him that hath received this wedden attire of Him. If now thou hast no love to Him, or if thy love to other things shuffles Him into a corner, thou hast not His wedden garment. But if thy love now runs out to Him above all things, so that nothing can separate thee from loving Him above all things, nay above life itself, then this robe is thine.

⁂　⁂　⁂

c. 1694   1966

SAMUEL SEWALL
1652–1730

Samuel Sewall's pursuit of the hand of the widow Katherine Winthrop has provided most readers of American literature with needed comic relief in the drama of Puritan salvation. There is something very satisfying in looking over the shoulder of the distinguished jurist subjecting his pride and reputation to the whims of courtship and adopting the role of a petitioner that, after a happy marriage of forty-two years, he probably never thought he would have to assume again. But Sewall is a more complicated figure than this small episode in his career would suggest. He became a part of the public life of Massachusetts in his late twenties and rose to a position of great authority. In the late 1870s, when the Massachusetts Historical Society began to publish his diary, his private life intrigued colonial historians, but before that Sewall was best known as the hanging judge of the Salem witch trials, a man who presided over one of the saddest episodes in our history and was a symbol of misguided authority and self-satisfied complacency.

Sewall's self-confidence was derived, in part, from having had every material advantage. Although his father had served briefly as a Puritan minister, his chief interest was business, and when the vast land-holdings in New England held by Samuel Sewall's grandfather, Henry Sewall, Sr., passed to him, he determined to stay in Massachusetts rather than try to manage his estates while living abroad. Sewall and his mother joined him in Boston on July 6, 1661. Samuel was only nine.

It was said of young Samuel that he was "born to be educated," and upon arrival at the house in Newbury that his father had prepared for them, he was placed under the care of the minister of the town and instructed in those subjects that would make him eligible for admission to Harvard in the class of 1671. He loved books and debated matters of theology with a passion. It seems fitting that Edward Taylor became his "chum and bedfellow" their senior year. Both were a little old before their time, very conservative in matters of church doctrine and apprehensive about the secularization of the age. Sewall stayed on as a resident tutor and teaching fellow and after completing his master's degree (his thesis concerned the nature of Original Sin) he was given an appointment as Keeper of the College Library. He maintained close ties with Harvard and his classmates, eventually outliving them all.

Seven out of the eleven members of Sewall's class became ministers, and all of Sewall's education was directed toward that end. He remained bookish and familiar with new theological subtleties all his life, and because he traveled extensively in Massachusetts regularly, few people were more informed than he about the activities of local churches. But it must have become clear to him in his last years at Harvard that his true bent was in another direction; he refused a call to a pulpit in

Woodbridge, New Jersey. One reason must have been that the town of Boston was attractive to him; for in spite of an introspective side, Sewall's temperament was basically outgoing and social. His marriage in 1676 to Hannah Hull, the daughter of the affluent merchant John Hull, determined Sewall's career. He learned how to manage his father-in-law's interests and after John Hull's death in 1684 became a central figure in the great mercantile life of the town. He learned when to borrow and when to lend, filled his ships with goods Londoners were eager to buy (timber, molasses, pitch), and learned to anticipate public demand in New England for English goods (metalwares, fabrics, tiles), which his agent in London purchased for him and loaded in his ships for their return.

Sewall's ability to manage his fortune left him with the time to indulge his passion for civic duties. His diary, which he began in 1673 and continued for fifty-six years, reveals just how much the public and private life for Sewall were one. In 1679 he was elected a "constable" and represented the king in military affairs, and from then until 1729 he worked to become identified more as a public servant than as an importer. He represented Edward Taylor's town of Westfield in the General Court (or legislature) of Massachusetts, he moderated public meetings, he served as magistrate, he performed marriages and executed wills, and he became a judge of the Superior Court in 1692 and chief justice in 1717. He delighted in the ceremonies of his office and preferred the old forms to the new. His respect for tradition makes him seem at times inflexible and pompous, but for Sewall appearances mattered. He was not, however, ignorant of his own sins or the sins of the Commonwealth. On January 14, 1697, a fast day, Sewall placed in the hand of his minister, Samuel Willard, a statement acknowledging his wrong in the trials at Salem. He was the only witchcraft judge to do so. It was read aloud from the pulpit and posted for all to read. Three years later he published the first antislavery tract in America, *The Selling of Joseph*, and tells us that he received "frowns and hard words" for his pains. In matters of church discipline he was as strict as his friend Taylor, but in the matter of slavery he welcomed change. "Perfect servitude," he wrote, "can have no place by right . . . because our liberty in the natural account, is the very next thing to life itself, yea by many is preferred before it."

From The Diary of Samuel Sewall[1]

Saturday Even. Aug. 12, 1676. just as prayer ended Tim. Dwight sank down in a Swoun, and for a good space was as if he perceived not what was done to him: after, kicked and sprawled, knocking his hands and feet upon the floor like a distracted man. Was carried pickpack to bed by John Alcock, there his cloaths pulled off. In the night it seems he talked of ships, his master, father, and unckle Eliot.[2] The Sabbath following Father[3] went to him, spake to him to know what ailed him, asked if he would be prayed for, and for what he would desire his friends to pray. He answered, for more sight of sin, and God's healing grace. I asked him, being alone with him, whether his troubles were from some outward cause or spiritual. He answered, spiritual. I asked him why then he could not tell it his master, as well as any other, since it is the honor of any man to see sin and be sorry for it. He gave no answer, as I remember. Asked him if he would goe to meeting. He said, 'twas in vain for

1. The first entry of Sewall's diary is dated December 3, 1673, and the last entry December 25, 1728. The text used here is from *The Diary of Samuel Sewall*, edited by M. Halsey Thomas (1973). To preserve the special flavor of Sewall's style, the text has been only slightly modernized. The dates, however, have been changed to conform to the modern calendar.
2. Timothy Dwight (1654–1692) was the nephew of Jacob Eliot (1632–1693), dean of Old South Church, Boston; Timothy apprenticed to Sewall's father-in-law, John Hull, the silversmith.
3. Sewall always refers to Hull as "father."

him; his day was out. I asked, what day: he answered, of Grace. I told him 'twas sin for any one to conclude themselves Reprobate,[4] that this was all one. He said he would speak more, but could not, &c. Notwithstanding all this semblance (and much more than is written) of compunction for Sin, 'tis to be feared that his trouble arose from a maid whom he passionately loved: for that when Mr. Dwight[5] and his master had agreed to let him goe to her, he eftsoons[6] grew well.

Friday, Aug. 25[, 1676.] I spake to Tim of this, asked him whether his convictions were off. He answered, no. I told him how dangerous it was to make the convictions wrought by God's spirit a stalking horse to any other thing. Broke off, he being called away by Sam.

Even. Mar. 15, [1677.] Was holp affectionately to argue in prayer the promise of being heard because asking in Christ's name.

March 16, [1677.] Dr. [Samuel] Alcock[7] dyes about midnight. *Note,* Mrs. Williams told us presently after Dutyes[8] how dangerously ill he was, and to get John to go for his Grandmother. I was glad of that Information, and resolved to goe and pray earnestly for him; but going into the Kitchin, fell into discourse with Tim about Mettals, and so took up the time. The Lord forgive me and help me not to be so slack for time to come, and so easy to disregard and let dye so good a Resolution. Dr. Alcock was 39 yeers old.

March 19, 1677. Dr. Alcock was buried, at whoes Funeral I was. After it, went to Mr. Thachers.[9] He not within, so walkt with Capt. Scottow on the Change[1] till about 5, then went again, yet he not come. At last came Elder Rainsford, after, Mr. Thacher, who took us up into his Chamber; went to prayer, then told me I had liberty to tell what God had done for my soul. After I had spoken, prayed again. Before I came away told him my Temptations to him alone, and bad him acquaint me if he knew any thing by me that might hinder justly my coming into Church. He said he thought I ought to be encouraged, and that my stirring up to it was of God.

March 21, 1677. Father and self rode to Dorchester to the Fast, which is the first time that ever I was in that [new] Meeting-House. So was absent from the private Meetings.

Mane.[2] March 21[, 1677.] God help me affectionately to pray for a communication of his Spirit in attending on him at Dorchester, and the night before I read the 9th and 10th of Nehemiah, out of which Mr. [Increase] Mather happened to take his Text, which he handled to good purpose, and more taking it was with me because I had perused those chapters for my fitting to attend on that exercise. Mr. [Josiah] Flint prayed admirably in the morn, & pressed much our inability to keep Covenant with God, and therefore begged God's Spirit. Mr. Thacher began the afternoon: then Mr. Flint preached and so concluded.

Note. I have been of a long time loth to enter into strict Bonds with God, the sinfullness and hypochrisy of which God hath showed me by reading of a Sermon that Mr. [Cornelius] Burgess preached before the House of Commons, Nov. 17, 1640, and by the forementioned Sermons and prayers. *Omnia*

---

4. One who is rejected by God.
5. Here Captain Dwight, Timothy's father. "Mr." usually refers to a minister.
6. Again.
7. Dr. Samuel Alcock graduated from Harvard College in 1659.

8. Attendance at church.
9. Thomas Thacher was pastor of the Old South Church and was succeeded by Samuel Willard.
1. I.e., until the changing of the night watch.
2. In the morning (Latin).

in bonum mihi vertas, O Deus[3] I found the Sermon accidentally in Mr. [John] Norton's Study.

Remember, since I had thoughts of joining to the Church, I have been exceedingly tormented in my mind, sometimes lest the Third church [*the South*] should not be in God's way in breaking off from the old. (I resolved to speak with Mr. Torrey about that, but he passed home when I was called to business at the Warehouse. Another time I got Mr. Japheth Hobart to promise me a Meeting at our House after Lecture,—but she that is now his wife, being in town, prevented him.) Sometimes with my own unfitness and want of Grace: yet through importunity of friends, and hope that God might communicate himself to me in the ordinance, and because of my child (then hoped for) its being baptised, I offered myself, and was not refused. Besides what I had written, when I was speaking [*about admission to the church*] I resolved to confess what a great Sinner I had been, but going on in the method of the Paper, it came not to my mind. And now that Scruple of the Church vanished, and I began to be more afraid of myself. And on Saturday Goodman [Robert] Walker[4] came in, who used to be very familiar with me. But he said nothing of my coming into the Church, nor wished God to show me grace therein, at which I was almost overwhelmed, as thinking that he deemed me unfit for it. And I could hardly sit down to the Lord's Table. But I feared that if I went away I might be less fit next time, and thought that it would be strange for me who was just then joined to the Church, to withdraw, wherefore I stayed. But I never experienced more unbelief. I feared at least that I did not believe there was such an one as Jesus Xt.,[5] and yet was afraid that because I came to the ordinance without belief, that for the abuse of Xt. I should be stricken dead; yet I had some earnest desires that Xt. would, before the ordinance were done, though it were when he was just going away, give me some glimpse of himself; but I perceived none. Yet I seemed then to desire the coming of the next Sacrament day, that I might do better, and was stirred up hereby dreadfully to seek God who many times before had touched my heart by Mr. Thacher's praying and preaching more than now. The Lord pardon my former grieving of his Spirit, and circumcise my heart to love him with all my heart and soul.

March 30, 1677. I, together with Gilbert Cole, was admitted into Mr. Thacher's Church, making a Solemn covenant to take the L. Jehovah for our God, and to walk in Brotherly Love and watchfulness to Edification. Goodm. Cole first spake, then I, then the Relations of the Women were read: as we spake so were we admitted; then alltogether covenanted.[6] Prayed before, and after.

Mar. 31[, 1677.] Old Mr. [Edward] Oakes[7] came hether, so I wrote a Letter to his Son, after this tenor:

SIR, I have been, and am, under great exercise of mind with regard to my Spiritual Estate. Wherefore I do earnestly desire that you would bear me on your heart tomorrow in Prayer, that God would give me a true Godly Sorrow for Sin, as such: Love to himself and Christ, that I may admire his goodness, grace, kindness in that way of saving man, which I greatly want. I think I shall

3. Turn all to good to me, O Lord (Latin).

4. "Goodman" was the appropriate title for the head of a household. Robert Walker was one of the founders of the Old South Church in 1669.

5. Christ.

6. Admitted to church membership. Statements of conversion for women were usually read from testimony recorded in conversations with the pastor.

7. Edward Oakes was the father of Urian Oakes, president of Harvard College.

sit down tomorrow to the Lords Table, and I fear I shall be an unworthy partaker. Those words, *If your own hearts condemn you, God is greater, and knoweth all things,* have often affrighted me.

SAMUEL SEWALL

Satterday, Jany 2^d[, 1686.] Last night had a very unusual Dream; *viz.* That our Savior in the dayes of his Flesh when upon Earth, came to Boston and abode here sometime, and moreover that He Lodged in that time at Father Hull's; upon which in my Dream had two Reflections, One was how much more Boston had to say than Rome boasting of Peter's being there. The other a sense of great Respect that I ought to have shewed Father Hull since Christ chose when in town, to take up His Quarters at his House. Admired the goodness and Wisdom of Christ in coming hither and spending some part of His short Life here. The Chronological absurdity never came into my mind, as I remember. Jany 1, 1688, finished reading the Godly Learned ingenious Pareus[8] on the Revelation.

Sabbath, Augt. 10th[, 1690.] Went to see Cous. [Daniel] Quinsey; read the 102. Psal. and begin 103. pray'd, and so went home. Put up a Bill[9] at his request. Just after Contribution in the Afternoon, was call'd out, Cousin being very bad, so far as I could perceive. He desired me to pray, which I did: Afterward sent for Mr. Willard, and He pray'd, then Cousin pull'd his hand out of the Bed, and gave it to Mr. Willard. Seem'd to pray himself; but I could hear little except Jesus Christ; breath'd quick and hard, till at last abated and He quietly expired about Seven aclock. Mother Hull and I being there. I have parted with a cordial fast Friend, such an one as I shall hardly find. The Lord fit me for my Change and help me to wait till it come. Cousin was concern'd what he should doe for Patience, but God graciously furnish'd him, and has how translated Him to that State and place wherein He has no occasion for any.

Tuesday, Augt. 12[, 1690.] About 7. P.M. we lay the Body of Cous. Daniel Quinsey in my Father's Tomb. Mr. Serjeant, Dummer, H. Usher, Davis, Williams, Conney, Bearers. I led the Widow, then the Children, next, Mr. T. Brattle, Mis. Shepard, H. Newman, Mistress Margaret, Mr. Willard, Mother Hull, Mr. Parson, my wife and so on. *Note.* My wife[1] was so ill could hardly get home, taking some harm in going in Pattens[2] or some wrench, so had a great flux of Blood, which amaz'd us both, at last my wife bade me call Mrs. Ellis, then Mother Hull, then the Midwife, and throw the Goodness of God was brought to Bed of a Daughter between 3. and four aclock, Aug. 13th, 1690. *mane* Mrs. Elisabeth Weeden, Midwife. Had not Women nor other preparations as usually, being wholly surpris'd, my wife expecting to have gone a Moneth longer.

*   *   *

Augt. 17[, 1690.] Mr. Willard keeps his Sabbath at Roxbury, and so the Baptism of my little Daughter is deferred to the next Lord's Day.

Sabbath-day, August the four and twentieth, 1690. I publish my little

---

8. David Pareus (1548–1622) was a theologian and biblical commentator and one of Sewall's favorite authors.

9. A legal petition.

1. Sewall married Hannah Hull (1658–1717) in February 1676.

2. Wearing high-heeled shoes.

Daughter's name to be Judith, held her up for Mr. Willard to baptize her. She cried not at all, though a pretty deal of water was poured on her by Mr. Willard when He baptized her: Six others were baptized at the same time; Capt. Davis's Son James, and a grown person, Margaret Clifford, two of them. I named my Daughter Judith for the sake of her Grandmother and great Grandmother, who both wore that Name, and the Signification of it very good: The Lord grant that we may have great cause to praise Him on her account and help her to speak the Jews Language and to forget that of Ashdod,[3] Nehemiah 13.24. And that she may follow her Grandmother Hull, as she follows Christ, being not slothfull in Business, fervent in Spirit, serving the Lord. Her Prayers and Painstaking for all my Children are incessant, voluntary, with condescension to the meanest Services night and day: that I judg'd I could in justice doe no less than endeavor her remembrance by putting her Name on one of her Grand-Daughters. I have now had my health and opportunity to offer up Nine Children to God in Baptisme. Mr. Tho. Thacher baptized the two eldest; John and Samuel; Mr. Samuel Willard baptized the Seven younger. Lord grant that I who have thus solemnly and frequently named the name of the Lord Jesus, may depart from Iniquity; and that mine may be more His than Mine, or their own.

Sept. 20[, 1690.] * * * My little Judith languishes and moans, ready to die.

Sabbath, Sept. 21[, 1690.] About 2 mane, I rise, read some Psalms and pray with my dear Daughter. Between 7. and 8. (Mr. Moodey preaches in the Forenoon,) I call Mr. Willard, and he prays. Told Mr. Walter of her condition * * * desiring him to give her a Lift towards heaven. Mr. Baily sat with me in the Afternoon. I acquainted Him. Between 7. and 8. in the evening the child died, and I hope sleeps in Jesus.

Sept. 22[, 1690.] In the even, Mr. Moodey, Allen, Mather come from Mrs. Clark's Funeral to see us. Mr. Moodey and I went before the other came, to neighbor Hord, who lay dying; where also Mr. Allen came in. Nurse Hord told her Husband who was there, and what he had to say; whether he desir'd them to pray with him: He said with some earnestness, Hold your tongue, which was repeated three times to his wive's repeated intreaties; once he said, Let me alone, or, be quiet, (whether that made a fourth or was one of the three do not remember) and, My Spirits are gon. At last Mr. Moodey took him up pretty roundly and told him he might with the same labor have given a pertinent answer. When were ready to come away Mr. Moodey bid him put forth a little Breath to ask prayer, and said twas the last time had to speak to him; At last ask'd him, doe you desire prayer, shall I pray with you, He answer'd, Ay for the Lord's sake, and thank'd Mr. Moodey when had done. His former carriage was very startling and amazing to us. About One at night he died. About 11. aclock I supposed to hear neighbor Mason at prayer with him, just as I and my wife were going to bed. Mr. Allen prayed with us when came from said Hord's.

Sept. 23[, 1690.] Tuesday, between 5. and 6. Sir[4] Moodey carries the Body of my dear Judith to the Tomb, Solomon Rainsford receives it on the Stairs and sets it in. On the Coffin is the year 1690. made with little nails. Govr Bradstreet and Lady,[5] Mrs. Moodey, Mather the Mother, Mr. Winthrop,

---

3. I.e., be true believers and speak the language of Judah. Children of Jews who married Ashdod women were unable to speak the language of their fathers.

4. Here meaning minister.
5. Simon Bradstreet's second wife.

Richards here, with many others; Ministers, Willard, Moodey, Mather.

June 2[d], *1691.* Mr. Edward Taylor[6] puts his Son James to Mr. Steward, Shopkeeper of Ipswich, for Seven years, to serve him as an Apprentice, Term to begin the first of July next. Mr. Taylor desires me to represent himself in making the Indenture, if Mr. Steward desire the accomplishment of it befor He comes down again.

Monday, Dec. 7th, *[1691.]* I ride to New-Cambridge to see Sam.[7] He could hardly speak to me, his affections were so mov'd, having not seen me for above a fortnight; his Cough is still very bad, much increas'd by his going to Cambridge on foot in the night. * * *

April 11th, *1692.* Went to Salem, where, in the Meeting-house, the persons accused of Witchcraft were examined; was a very great Assembly; 'twas awfull to see how the afflicted persons were agitated. Mr. Noyes pray'd at the beginning, and Mr. Higginson concluded. [*In the margin*], Væ, Væ, Væ, Witchcraft.[8]

July 30, 1692. Mrs. Cary makes her escape out of Cambridge-Prison, who was Committed for Witchcraft.[9]

Thorsday, Augt. 4, *[1692.]* At Salem, Mr. Waterhouse brings the news of the desolation at Jamaica, June 7th. 1700 persons kill'd, besides the Loss of Houses and Goods by the Earthquake.

Augt. 19th, *1692.* * * * This day [*in the margin*, Dolefull Witchcraft] George Burrough, John Willard, Jn[o] Procter, Martha Carrier and George Jacobs were executed at Salem, a very great number of Spectators being present. Mr. Cotton Mather was there, Mr. Sims, Hale, Noyes, Chiever, &c. All of them said they were innocent, Carrier and all. Mr. Mather says they all died by a Righteous Sentence. Mr. Burrough by his Speech, Prayer, protestation of his Innocence, did much move unthinking persons, which occasions their speaking hardly[1] concerning his being executed.

Augt. 25, *[1692.]* Fast at the old [*First*] Church, respecting the Witchcraft, Drought, &c.

Monday, Sept. 19, *1692.* About noon, at Salem, Giles Corey was press'd to death[2] for standing Mute; much pains was used with him two days, one after another, by the Court and Capt. Gardner of Nantucket who had been of his acquaintance: but all in vain.

Sept. 20, *[1692.]* Now I hear from Salem that about 18 years agoe, he was suspected to have stamped and press'd a man to death, but was cleared. Twas not remembred till Anne Putnam was told of it by said Corey's Spectre the Sabbath-day night before Execution.[3]

Sept. 20, *1692.* The Swan[4] brings in a rich French Prize of about 300 Tuns, laden with Claret, White Wine, Brandy, Salt, Linnen Paper, &c.

Sept. 21, *[1692.]* A petition is sent to Town in behalf of Dorcas Hoar, who now confesses: Accordingly an order is sent to the Sheriff to forbear her

6. The poet from Westfield (c. 1642–1729) and Sewall's Harvard College roommate. Sewall represented the town of Westfield in the General Court of Massachusetts.
7. Sewall's thirteen-year-old son, boarding at school.
8. Woe, woe, woe, witchcraft (Latin). Governor William Phips (1651–1695) appointed Sewall one of seven councillors of a court of Oyer and Terminer (i.e., to hear and determine) to judge those accused of witchcraft in Salem on May 24, 1692. The court met in Salem on June 2 and Bridget Bishop was hanged on

June 10. On June 30 they met again and five more accused were executed on July 19. Unfortunately for us, Sewall kept his entries regarding the trials at Salem to a minimum.
9. Cary was given protection in New York.
1. Vigorously.
2. Corey was eighty years old at the time. Heavy stones were placed on him until he died.
3. Putnam was only twelve when she made, along with her mother, accusations against "witches."
4. A ship.

Execution, notwithstanding her being in the Warrant to die to morrow. This
is the first condemned person who has confess'd.[5]

Nov. 6[, 1692.] Joseph threw a knop of Brass and hit his Sister Betty on the
forhead so as to make it bleed and swell; upon which, and for his playing at
Prayer-time, and eating when Return Thanks, I whipd him pretty smartly.
When I first went in (call'd by his Grandmother) he sought to shadow and
hide himself from me behind the head of the Cradle: which gave me the
sorrowfull remembrance of Adam's carriage.

Apr. 16, 1695. My Appletree which I nourish from a kernel, has the growth
of 1694 and is now scarce Ten inches high; removd it this Spring into the
room of a young Appletree that dyed.

*   *   *

Monday, April 29, 1695. The morning is very warm and Sunshiny; in the
Afternoon there is Thunder and Lightening, and about 2 P.M. a very extraordinary Storm of Hail, so that the ground was made white with it, as with the
blossoms when fallen; 'twas as bigg as pistoll and Musquet Bullets; It broke of
the Glass of the new House about 480 Quarrels [squares] of the Front; of Mr.
Sergeant's about as much; Col. Shrimpton, Major General, Gov[r] Bradstreet,
New Meetinghouse, Mr. Willard, &c. Mr. Cotton Mather dined with us, and
was with me in the new Kitchen when this was; He had just been mentioning
that more Minister Houses than others proportionably had been smitten with
Lightening; enquiring what the meaning of God should be in it. Many Hail-
Stones broke throw the Glass and flew to the middle of the Room, or farther:
People afterward Gazed upon the House to see its Ruins. I got Mr. Mather to
pray with us after this awfull Providence; He told God He had broken the
brittle part of our house, and prayd that we might be ready for the time when
our Clay-Tabernacles should be broken. Twas a sorrowfull thing to me to see
the house so far undon again before twas finish'd. It seems at Milton[6] on the
one hand, and at Lewis's [the tavern at Lynn] on the other, there was no Hail.

Jan[y] 15, [1697.] * * * Copy of the Bill I put up on the Fast day [January
14]; giving it to Mr. Willard as he pass'd by, and standing up at the reading of
it, and bowing when finished; in the Afternoon.

Samuel Sewall, sensible of the reiterated strokes of God upon himself and
family;[7] and being sensible, that as to the Guilt contracted, upon the opening
of the late Commission of Oyer and Terminer at Salem (to which the order
for this Day relates) he is, upon many accounts, more concerned than any
that he knows of, Desires to take the Blame and Shame of it, Asking pardon
of Men, And especially desiring prayers that God, who has an Unlimited
Authority, would pardon that Sin and all other his Sins; personal and Relative:
And according to his infinite Benignity, and Soveraignty, Not Visit the Sin of
him, or of any other, upon himself or any of his, nor upon the Land: But that
He would powerfully defend him against all Temptations to Sin, for the future;
and vouchsafe him the Efficacious, Saving Conduct of his Word and Spirit.

July 15, 1698. Mr. Edward Taylor comes to our house from Westfield.
Monday, July 18, [1698.] I walk'd with Mr. Edward Taylor upon Cotton Hill,

5. Confession of witchcraft automatically set the accused free.
6. Milton is south of Boston.
7. On May 22, 1696, Sewall buried a premature son
born dead and on December 23 his daughter Sarah

died. When his son Samuel read from Matthew 12.7
("But if ye had known what this meaneth, I will have
mercy, and not sacrifice, ye would not have condemned the guiltless.") it did "awfully bring to mind,"
Sewall noted, "the Salem tragedy."

thence to Becon Hill, the Pasture, along the Stone-wall: As came back, we sat down on the great Rock, and Mr. Taylor told me his courting his first wife,[8] and Mr. Fitch his story of Mr. Dod's prayer to God to bring his Affection to close with a person pious, but hard-favored. Has God answered me in finding out one Godly and fit for me, and shall I part for fancy? When came home, my wife gave me Mr. Tappan's Letter concerning Eliza,[9] which caus'd me to reflect on Mr. Taylor's Discourse. And his Prayer was for pardon of error in our ways—which made me think whether it were not best to overlook all, and go on. This day John Ive, fishing in great Spiepond, is arrested with mortal sickness which renders him in a manner speechless and senseless; dies next day; buried at Charlestown on the Wednesday. Was a very debauched, atheistical man. I was not at his Funeral. Had Gloves sent me, but the knowledge of his notoriously wicked life made me sick of going; and Mr. Mather, the president, came in just as I was ready to step out, and so I staid at home, and by that means lost a Ring:[1] but hope had no loss. Follow thou Me, was I suppose more complied with, than if had left Mr. Mather's company to go to such a Funeral.

Fourth-day, June 19, 1700. * * * Having been long and much dissatisfied with the Trade of fetching Negros from Guinea; at last I had a strong Inclination to Write something about it; but it wore off. At last reading Bayne, Ephes.[2] about servants, who mentions Blackamoors; I began to be uneasy that I had so long neglected doing any thing. When I was thus thinking, in came Bro[r] Belknap to shew me a Petition he intended to present to the Gen[l] Court for the freeing a Negro and his wife, who were unjustly held in Bondage. And there is a Motion by a Boston Committee to get a Law that all Importers of Negros shall pay 40[s] *per* head, to discourage the bringing of them. And Mr. C. Mather resolves to publish a sheet to exhort Masters to labor their Conversion. Which makes me hope that I was call'd of God to Write this Apology[3] for them; Let his Blessing accompany the same.

Tuesday, June 10[th][*, 1701.*] Having last night heard that Josiah Willard had cut off his hair (a very full head of hair) and put on a Wigg, I went to him this morning. Told his Mother what I came about, and she call'd him. I enquired of him what Extremity had forced him to put off his own hair, and put on a Wigg? He answered, none at all. But said that his Hair was streight, and that it parted behinde. Seem'd to argue that men might as well shave their hair off their head, as off their face. I answered men were men before they had hair on their faces, (half of mankind have never any). God seems to have ordain'd our Hair as a Test, to see whether we can bring our minds to be content to be at his finding: or whether we would be our own Carvers, Lords, and come no more at Him. If disliked our Skin, or Nails; 'tis no Thanks to us, that for all that, we cut them not off: Pain and danger restrain us. Your Calling is to teach men self Denial. Twill be displeasing and burdensom to good men: And they that care not what men think of them care not what God thinks of them. Father, Bro[r] Simon, Mr. Pemberton, Mr. Wigglesworth, Oakes, Noyes (Oliver), Brattle of Cambridge their example. Allow me to be so far a *Censor Morum*[4] for this end of the Town. Pray'd him to read the Tenth Chapter of

---

8. Elizabeth Fitch died on July 7, 1689.
9. Elizabeth Tappan (or Toppan) was Sewall's niece.
1. A memorial gift. Gloves were sent as an invitation to a funeral.
2. Paul Baynes, A *Commentary upon the First Chap-*

ter *of the Epistle of Saint Paul. Written to the Ephesians* (1618).
3. *The Selling of Joseph* was published on June 24, 1700.
4. Judge of morals (Latin).

the Third book of Calvins Institutions. I read it this morning in course, not of choice. Told him that it was condemn'd by a Meeting of Ministers at North-ampton in Mr. [Solomon] Stoddards house, when the said Josiah was there. Told him of the Solemnity of the Covenant which he and I had lately entered into, which put me upon discoursing to him. He seem'd to say would leave off his Wigg when his hair was grown. I spake to his Father of it a day or two after: He thank'd me that had discoursed his Son, and told me that when his hair was grown to cover his ears, he promis'd to leave off his Wigg. If he had known of it, would have forbidden him. His Mother heard him talk of it; but was afraid positively to forbid him; lest he should do it, and so be more faulty.

Sabbath, Novr 30, [1701.] * * * I spent this Sabbath at Mr. Colman's, partly out of dislike to Mr. Josiah Willard's cutting off his Hair, and wearing a Wigg: He preach'd for Mr. Pemberton in the morning; He that contemns the Law of Nature, is not fit to be a publisher of the Law of Grace. * * *

Lord's Day, June 10, 1705. The Learned and pious Mr. Michael Wig-glesworth dies at Malden about 9. m. Had been sick about 10. days of a Fever; 73 years and 8 moneths old. He was the Author of the Poem entituled The Day of Doom, which has been so often printed: and was very useful as a Phy-sician.

Febr. 6, [1718.] This morning wandering in my mind whether to live a Single or a Married Life;[5] I had a sweet and very affectionat Meditation Con-cerning the Lord Jesus; Nothing was to be objected against his Person, Parent-age, Relations, Estate, House, Home! Why did I not resolutely, presently close with Him! And I cry'd mightily to God that He would help me so to doe! * * *

March, 14, [1718.] Deacon Marion comes to me, sits with me a great while in the evening; after a great deal of Discourse about his Courtship—He told [me] the Olivers said they wish'd I would Court their Aunt.[6] I said little, but said twas not five Moneths since I buried my dear Wife. Had said before 'twas hard to know whether best to marry again or no; whom to marry. * * *

Septr 5, [1720.] Mary Hirst goes to Board with Madam Oliver and her Mother Loyd. Going to Son Sewall's I there meet with Madam Winthrop, told her I was glad to meet her there, had not seen her a great while; gave her Mr. Homes's Sermon.

Sept. 30, [1720.] Mr. Colman's Lecture: Daughter Sewall acquaints Madam Winthrop that if she pleas'd to be within at 3. P.M. I would wait on her. She answer'd she would be at home.

Satterday, October 1, [1720.] I dine at Mr. Stoddard's: from thence I went to Madam Winthrop's just at 3. Spake to her, saying, my loving wife[7] died so soon and suddenly, 'twas hardly convenient for me to think of Marrying again; however I came to this Resolution, that I would not make my Court to any person without first Consulting with her. Had a pleasant discourse about 7 Single persons sitting in the Fore-seat [September] 29th, viz. Mad^m Rebekah Dudley, Catharine Winthrop, Bridget Usher, Deliverance Legg, Rebekah

5. Hannah Hull Sewall had died on October 19, 1717; they had been married almost forty-two years. Sewall married Abigail Tilley on October 29, 1719, and she died suddenly in May of 1720. Sewall's courtship of Madame Winthrop began seriously in the fall of 1720. On March 29, 1722, Sewall married a widow, Mary Gibbs, and she survived him.

6. Katherine Brattle Winthrop was the widow of Chief Justice Wait Still Winthrop, Sewall's friend. Instead, he married Tilley.

7. I.e., Abigail.

Loyd, Lydia Colman, Elizabeth Bellingham.[8] She propounded one and another for me; but none would do, said Mrs. Loyd was about her Age.

Octob[r] 3, 2, [1720.] Waited on Madam Winthrop again; 'twas a little while before she came in. Her daughter Noyes[9] being there alone with me, I said, I hoped my Waiting on her Mother would not be disagreeable to her. She answer'd she should not be against that that might be for her Comfort. I Saluted her, and told her I perceiv'd I must shortly wish her a good Time; (her mother had told me, she was with Child, and within a Moneth or two of her Time). By and by in came Mr. Airs, Chaplain of the Castle,[1] and hang'd up his Hat, which I was a little startled at, it seeming as if he was to lodge there. At last Madam Winthrop came in. After a considerable time, I went up to her and said, if it might not be inconvenient I desired to speak with her. She assented, and spake of going into another Room; but Mr. Airs and Mrs. Noyes presently rose up, and went out, leaving us there alone. Then I usher'd in Discourse from the names in the Fore-seat; at last I pray'd that Katharine [Mrs. Winthrop] might be the person assign'd for me. She instantly took it up in way of Denyal, as if she had catch'd at an Opportunity to do it, saying she could not do it before she was asked. Said that was her mind unless she should Change it, which she believed she should not; could not leave her Children. I express'd my Sorrow that she should do it so Speedily, pray'd her Consideration, and ask'd her when I should wait upon her agen. She setting no time, I mention'd that day Sennight.[2] Gave her Mr. Willard's Fountain[3] open'd with the little print and verses; saying I hop'd if we did well read that book, we should meet together hereafter, if we did not now. She took the Book, and put it in her Pocket. Took Leave.

Midweek, Oct. 5, [1720.] I din'd with the Court; from thence went and visited Cousin Jonathan's wife, Lying in with her little Betty. Gave the Nurse 2[s4] Although I had appointed to wait upon her, M[m] Winthrop, next Monday, yet I went from my Cousin Sewall's thither about 3. P.M. The Nurse told me Madam dined abroad at her daughter Noyes's, they were to go out together. * * *

[Oct.] 6[th][, 1720.] A little after 6 P.M. I went to Madam Winthrop's. She was not within. I gave Sarah Chickering the Maid 2[s], Juno, who brought in wood, 1[s] Afterward the Nurse came in, I gave her 18[d], having no other small Bill. After awhile Dr. Noyes came in with his Mother; and quickly after his wife came in: They sat talking, I think, till eight aclock. I said I fear'd I might be some Interruption to their Business: Dr. Noyes reply'd pleasantly: He fear'd they might be an Interruption to me, and went away. Madam seem'd to harp upon the same string. Must take care of her Children; could not leave that House and Neighborhood where she had dwelt so long. I told her she might doe her children as much or more good by bestowing what she laid out in Hous-keeping, upon them. Said her Son would be of Age the 7th of August. I said it might be inconvenient for her to dwell with her Daughter-in-Law, who must be Mistress of the House. I gave her a piece of Mr. Belcher's Cake and Ginger-Bread wrapped up in a clean sheet of Paper; told her of her Father's

---

8. Widows usually sat in a front pew reserved for them.
9. The wife of Dr. Oliver Noyes.
1. I.e., Castle Island in Boston Harbor. "Saluted": kissed.

2. A week hence.
3. Samuel Willard, *The Fountain Opened, or the Great Gospel Privilege of Having Christ Exhibited to Sinful Men* (1700).
4. Eight shillings.

kindness to me when Treasurer, and I Constable. My Daughter Judith was gon from me and I was more lonesom—might help to forward one another in our Journey to Canaan.[5] * * *

[Oct.] 10th[, 1720.] * * * In the Evening I visited Madam Winthrop, who treated me with a great deal of Curtesy; Wine, Marmalade. I gave her the News-Letter[6] about the Thanksgiving Proposals, for sake of the verses for David Jeffries. She tells me Dr. Increase Mather visited her this day, in Mr. Hutchinson's Coach. * * *

[Oct.] 12[, 1720.] At Madm Winthrop's Steps I took leave of Capt Hill, &c.

Mrs. Anne Cotton came to door (twas before 8.) said Madam Winthrop was within, directed me into the little Room, where she was full of work[7] behind a Stand; Mrs. Cotton came in and stood. Madam Winthrop pointed to her to set me a Chair. Madam Winthrop's Countenance was much changed from what 'twas on Monday, look'd dark and lowering. At last, the work, (black stuff or Silk) was taken away, I got my Chair in place, had some Converse, but very Cold and indifferent to what 'twas before. Ask'd her to acquit me of Rudeness if I drew off her Glove. Enquiring the reason, I told her twas great odds between handling a dead Goat, and a living Lady. Got it off. I told her I had one Petition to ask of her, that was, that she would take off the Negative she laid on me the third of October; She readily answer'd she could not, and enlarg'd upon it; She told me of it so soon as she could; could not leave her house, children, neighbors, business. I told her she might do som Good to help and support me. * * * Sarah fill'd a Glass of Wine, she drank to me, I to her, She sent Juno home with me with a good Lantern, I gave her 6d and bid her thank her Mistress. In some of our Discourse, I told her I had rather go to the Stone-House[8] adjoining to her, than to come to her against her mind. Told her the reason why I came every other night was lest I should drink too deep draughts of Pleasure. She had talk'd of Canary,[9] her Kisses were to me better than the best Canary. * * *

Oct. 13, [1720.] I tell my Son and daughter Sewall, that the Weather was not so fair as I apprehended. * * *

Monday, [Oct.] 17, [1720.] Give Mr. Dan Willard, and Mr. Pelatiah Whittemore their Oaths to their Accounts; and Mr. John Briggs to his, as they are Attornys to Dr. Cotton Mather, Administrator to the estate of Nathan Howell deceased. In the Evening I visited Madam Winthrop, who Treated me Courteously, but not in Clean Linen as somtimes. She said, she did not know whether I would come again, or no. I ask'd her how she could so impute inconstancy to me. (I had not visited her since Wednesday night being unable to get over the Indisposition received by the Treatment received that night, and I *must* in it seem'd to sound like a made piece of Formality.) Gave her this day's Gazett. Heard David Jeffries say the Lord's Prayer, and some other portions of the Scriptures. He came to the door, and ask'd me to go into Chamber, where his Grandmother was tending Little Katee, to whom she had given Physick; but I chose to sit below. Dr. Noyes and his wife came in, and sat a Considerable time; had been visiting Son and dâter Cooper. Juno came home with me.

[Oct.] 18, [1720.] Visited Madam Mico, who came to me in a splendid

---

5. I.e., to paradise.
6. *The Boston News-Letter* published the governor's proclamation for Thanksgiving Day 1720.

7. I.e., her needlework.
8. A prison.
9. A sweet wine from the Canary Isles.

Dress. I said, It may be you have heard of my Visiting Madam Winthrop, her Sister. She answered, Her Sister had told her of it. I ask'd her good Will in the Affair. She answer'd, If her Sister were for it, she should not hinder it. I gave her Mr. Homes's Sermon. She gave me a Glass of Canary, entertain'd me with good Discourse, and a Respectfull Remembrance of my first Wife. I took Leave.

Midweek, [*Oct.*] *19*, [*1720.*] Visited Madam Winthrop; Sarah told me she was at Mr. Walley's, would not come home till late. I gave her Hannah's 3 oranges with her Duty, not knowing whether I should find her or no. Was ready to go home: but said if I knew she was there, I would go thither. Sarah seemd to speak with pretty good Courage, She would be there. I went and found her there, with Mr. Walley and his wife in the little Room below. At 7 aclock I mentioned going home; at 8. I put on my Coat, and quickly waited on her home. She found occasion to speak loud to the servant, as if she had a mind to be known. Was Courteous to me; but took occasion to speak pretty earnestly about my keeping a Coach: I said 'twould cost £100. per annum: she said 'twould cost but £40. Spake much against John Winthrop, his false-heartedness. Mr. Eyre came in and sat awhile; I offer'd him Dr. Incr. Mather's Sermons, whereof Mr. Appleton's Ordination-Sermon was one; said he had them already. I said I would give him another. Exit. Came away somewhat late.

Oct. 20, [*1720.*] Mr. Colman preaches from Luke 15.10. Joy among the Angels: made an Excellent Discourse.

At Council, Col. Townsend spake to me of my Hood: Should get a Wigg.[1] I said twas my chief[2] Ornament: I wore it for sake of the Day. Bro^r Odlin, and Sam, Mary, and Jane Hirst dine with us. Promis'd to wait on the Govr about 7. Madam Winthrop not being at Lecture, I went thither first; found her very Serene with her dâter Noyes, Mrs. Dering, and the widow Shipreev sitting at a little Table, she in her arm'd Chair. She drank to me, and I to Mrs. Noyes. After awhile pray'd the favor to speak with her. She took one of the Candles, and went into the best Room, clos'd the shutters, sat down upon the Couch. She told me Madam Usher had been there, and said the Coach must be set on Wheels, and not by Rusting. She spake something of my needing a Wigg. Ask'd me what her Sister said to me. I told her, She said, If her Sister were for it, She would not hinder it. But I told her, she did not say she would be glad to have me for her Brother. Said, I shall keep you in the Cold, and ask her if she would be within tomorrow night, for we had had but a running Feast. She said she could not tell whether she should, or no. I took Leave. As were drinking at the Governor's, he said: In England the Ladies minded little more than that they might have Money, and Coaches to ride in. I said, And New-England brooks its Name.[3] At which Mr. Dudley smiled. Govr said they were not quite so bad here.

Friday, Oct. 21, [*1720.*] My Son, the Minister, came to me p. m. by appointment and we pray one for another in the Old Chamber; more especially respecting my Courtship. About 6. aclock I go to Madam Winthrop's; Sarah told me her Mistress was gon out, but did not tell me whither she went.

---

1. I.e., in addition to Sewall's judicial hood, he should acquire a wig such as English judges wear today, and to be distinguished from the periwig that Madame Winthrop wanted Sewall to wear to disguise his baldness. Sewall chose to wear a velvet cap instead.
2. Principal.
3. I.e., it is the same in New England.

She presently order'd me a Fire; so I went in, having Dr. Sibb's Bowels[4] with me to read. I read the two first Sermons, still no body came in: at last about 9. aclock Mr. Jn° Eyre came in; I took the opportunity to say to him as I had done to Mrs. Noyes before, that I hoped my Visiting his Mother would not be disagreeable to him; He answered me with much Respect. When twas after 9. aclock He of himself said he would go and call her, she was but at one of his Brothers: A while after I heard Madam Winthrop's voice, enquiring somthing about John. After a good while and Clapping the Garden door twice or thrice, she came in. I mention'd somthing of the lateness; she banter'd me, and said I was later. She receiv'd me Courteously. I ask'd when our proceedings should be made publick: She said They were like to be no more publick than they were already. Offer'd me no Wine that I remember. I rose up at 11 aclock to come away, saying I would put on my Coat, She offer'd not to help me. I pray'd her that Juno might light me home, she open'd the Shutter, and said twas pretty light abroad; Juno was weary and gon to bed. So I came hôm by Star-light as well as I could. At my first coming in, I gave Sarah five Shillings. I writ Mr. Eyre his Name in his book with the date Octob[r] 21, 1720. It cost me 8[s]. Jehovah jireh![5] Madam told me she had visited M. Mico, Wendell, and Wm Clark of the South [Church].

Octob[r] 22, [1720.] Dâter Cooper visited me before my going out of Town, staid till about Sun set. I brought her going near as far as the Orange Tree.[6] Coming back, near Leg's Corner, Little David Jeffries saw me, and looking upon me very lovingly, ask'd me if I was going to see his Grandmother? I said, Not to-night. Gave him a penny, and bid him present my Service to his Grandmother.

Octob[r] 24, [1720.] I went in the Hackny Coach through the Common, stop't at Madam Winthrop's (had told her I would take my departure from thence). Sarah came to the door with Katee in her Arms: but I did not think to take notice of the Child. Call'd her Mistress. I told her, being encourag'd by David Jeffries loving eyes, and sweet Words, I was come to enquire whether she could find in her heart to leave that House and Neighborhood, and go and dwell with me at the South-end; I think she said softly, Not yet. I told her It did not ly in my hands to keep a Coach. If I should, I should be in danger to be brought to keep company with her Neighbor Brooker, (he was a little before sent to prison for Debt). Told her I had an Antipathy against those who would pretend to give themselves; but nothing of their Estate. I would a proportion of my Estate with my self. And I suppos'd she would do so. As to a Perriwig, My best and greatest Friend, I could not possibly have a greater, began to find me with Hair before I was born, and had continued to do so ever since; and I could not find in my heart to go to another. She commended the book I gave her, Dr. Preston, the Church's Marriage; quoted him saying 'twas inconvenient keeping out of a Fashion commonly used. I said the Time and Tide did circumscribe my Visit. She gave me a Dram of Black-Cherry Brandy, and gave me a lump of the Sugar that was in it. She wish'd me a good Journy. I pray'd God to keep her, and came away. Had a very pleasant Journy to Salem.

[October] 31, [1720.] * * * At night I visited Madam Winthrop about 6.

---

4. Heart. Dr. Richard Sibbes was the author of *Bowels Opened; or a Discovery of the Neere and Deere Love, Union, and Communion between Christ and the Church* (1641).

5. The Lord will provide (Hebrew), from Genesis 22.14.

6. An inn.

P.M. They told me she was gone to Madam Mico's. I went thither and found she was gone; so return'd to her house, read the Epistles to the Galatians, Ephesians in Mr Eyre's Latin Bible. After the Clock struck 8. I began to read the 103. Psalm. Mr. Wendell came in from his Warehouse. Ask'd me if I were alone? Spake very kindly to me, offer'd me to call Madam Winthrop. I told him, She would be angry, had been at M. Mico's; he help'd me on with my Coat and I came home: left the Gazett in the Bible, which told Sarah of, bid her present my Service to M. Winthrop, and tell her I had been to wait on her if she had been at home.

Novr 1, [1720.] I was so taken up that I could not go if I would.

Midweek, Novr 2, [1720.] went again, and found Mrs. Alden there, who quickly went out. Gave her [Madam Winthrop] about ½ pound of Sugar Almonds, cost 3^s per £. Carried them on Monday. She seem'd pleas'd with them, ask'd what they cost. Spake of giving her a Hundred pounds per annum if I dy'd before her. Ask'd her what sum she would give me, if she should dy first? Said I would give her time to Consider of it. She said she heard as if I had given all to my Children by Deeds of Gift. I told her 'twas a mistake, Point-Judith was mine &c. That in England, I own'd, my Father's desire was that it should go to my eldest Son; 'twas 20£ per annum; she thought 'twas forty. I think when I seem'd to excuse pressing this, she seem'd to think 'twas best to speak of it; a long winter was coming on. Gave me a Glass or two of Canary.

Friday, Novr 4th[, 1720.] Went again about 7. aclock; found there Mr. John Walley and his wife: sat discoursing pleasantly. I shew'd them Isaac Moses's [an Indian] Writing. Madam W. serv'd Comfeits[7] to us. After awhile a Table was spread, and Supper was set. I urg'd Mr. Walley to Crave a Blessing; but he put it upon me. About 9. they went away. I ask'd Madam what fashioned Neck-lace I should present her with, She said, None at all. I ask'd her Where-about we left off last time; mention'd what I had offer'd to give her; Ask'd her what she would give me; She said she could not Change her Condition: She had said so from the beginning; could not be so far from her Children, the Lecture. Quoted the Apostle Paul affirming that a single Life was better than Married. I answer'd That was for the present Distress. Said she had not plea-sure in things of that nature as formerly: I said, you are the fitter to make me a Wife. If she held in that mind, I must go home and bewail my Rashness in making more haste than good Speed. However, considering the Supper, I desired her to be within next Monday night, if we liv'd so long. Assented. She charg'd me with saying, that she must put away Juno, if she came to me: I utterly deny'd it, it never came in my heart; yet she insisted upon it; saying it came in upon discourse about the Indian woman that obtained her Freedom this Court. About 10. I said I would not disturb the good orders of her House, and came away. She not seeming pleas'd with my Coming away. Spake to her about David Jeffries, had not seen him.

Monday, Novr 7th[, 1720.] My son pray'd in the Old Chamber. Our time had been taken up by Son and Daughter Cooper's Visit; so that I only read the 130th and 143. Psalm. Twas on the Account of my Courtship. I went to Mad. Winthrop; found her rocking her little Katee in the Cradle. I excus'd my Com-ing so late (near Eight). She set me an arm'd Chair and Cusheon; and so the

7. Sweetmeats; fruits preserved in sugar.

Cradle was between her arm'd Chair and mine. Gave her the remnant of my Almonds; She did not eat of them as before; but laid them away; I said I came to enquire whether she had alter'd her mind since Friday, or remained of the same mind still. She said, Thereabouts. I told her I loved her, and was so fond[8] as to think that she loved me: She said had a great respect for me. I told her, I had made her an offer, without asking any advice; she had so many to advise with, that twas a hindrance. The Fire was come to one short Brand besides the Block, which Brand was set up in end; at last it fell to pieces, and no Recruit was made:[9] She gave me a Glass of Wine. I think I repeated again that I would go home and bewail my Rashness in making more haste than good Speed. I would endeavor to contain myself, and not go on to sollicit her to do that which she could not Consent to. Took leave of her. As came down the steps she bid me have a Care. Treated me Courteously. Told her she had enter'd the 4th year of her Widowhood. I had given her the News-Letter before: I did not bid her draw off her Glove as sometime I had done. Her Dress was not so clean as sometime it had been. Jehovah jireh!

Midweek, [*Nov.*] 9[th][, *1720.*] Dine at Bro[r] Stoddard's: were so kind as to enquire of me if they should invite M[m] Winthrop; I answer'd No. Thank'd my Sister Stoddard for her Courtesie; sat down at the Table Simeon Stoddard esqr, Mad. Stoddard, Samuel Sewall, Mr. Colman, M[m] Colman, Mr. Cooper, Mrs. Cooper, Mrs. Hannah Cooper, Mr. Samuel Sewall of Brooklin, Mrs. Sewall, Mr. Joseph Sewall, Mrs. Lydia Walley, Mr. William Stoddard. Had a noble Treat. At night our Meeting was at the Widow Belknap's. Gave each one of the Meeting one of Mr. Homes's Sermons, 12 in all; She sent her servant home with me with a Lantern. Madam Winthrop's Shutters were open as I pass'd by.

Nov[r] 11, [*1720.*] Went not to M[m] Winthrop's. This is the 2[d] Withdraw.[1]

Nov[r] 14, [*1720.*] Madam Winthrop visits my daughter Sewall with her [*granddaughter*] Katee [*Walley*].

March, 29th, [*1722.*] Samuel Sewall, and Mrs. Mary Gibbs were joined together in Marriage by the Rev[d] Mr. William Cooper; Mr. Sewall pray'd once. Mr. Jn[o] Cotton was at Sandwich, sent for by Madam Cotton after her Husband's death.

Lord's day, April 1, [*1722.*] Sat with my wife in her Pue.

April, 2, [*1722.*] Brought her home to my House.

April, 8, [*1722.*] introduc'd her into my Pue, and sat with her there.

June 15, [*1725.*] I accompanied my Son to Mad. Winthrop's. She was a-bed about 10. *mane.* I told her I found my Son coming to her and took the Opportunity to come with him. She thank'd me kindly, enquired how Madam Sewall did. Ask'd my Son to go to Prayer. Present Mr. John Eyre, Mrs. Noyes, Mrs. Walley and David Jeffries. At coming I said, I kiss your hand Madame (her hand felt very dry). She desired me to pray that God would lift up upon her the Light of his Countenance.

Monday, Augt 2, [*1725.*] Mrs. Katherine Winthrop, Relict[2] of the hon[ble] Waitstill Winthrop esqr., died, Ætatis 61. She was born in September 1664. The Escutcheons on the Hearse bore the Arms of Winthrop and Brattle, The Lion Sable.[3] *Augt 5, 1725.* Bearers, His Hon[r] Lt Govr Dummer, Saml Sewall;

---

8. Foolish.
9. Added logs would indicate that Sewall was expected to stay longer.

1. I.e., the second time he decided not to visit.
2. Widow.
3. Black. "Escutcheons"; heraldic shields.

Col. Byfield, Edw. Bromfield esqr; Simeon Stoddard esqr., Adam Winthrop esqr. Was buried in the South-burying place, in a Tomb near the North-east Corner. Will be much miss'd. After the Funeral, Many of the Council, went and wish'd Col. Fitch Joy of his daughter Martha's Marriage with Mr. James Allen. Had good Bride-Cake, good Wine, Burgundy and Canary, good Beer, Oranges, Pears.

Friday, April 28, 1727. The first half sheet of the Phenomena is wrought off.[4]

Lords day, Decr 17, [1727.] I was surprised to hear Mr. Thacher of Milton, my old Friend, pray'd for as dangerously Sick. Next day. *Decr 18, 1727.* I am inform'd by Mr. Gerrish, that my dear friend died last night; which I doubt bodes ill to Milton and the Province, his dying at this Time, though in the 77th year of his Age. *Deus avertat Omen!*[5]

Friday, Decr 22, [1727.] the day after the Fast, was inter'd. Bearers Rev^d Mr. Nehemiah Walter, Mr. Joseph Baxter; Mr. John Swift, Mr. Saml Hunt; Mr. Joseph Sewall, Mr. Thomas Prince. I was inclin'd before, and having a pair of Gloves sent me, I determined to go to the Funeral, if the Weather prov'd favorable, which it did, and I hired Blake's Coach with four Horses; my Son, Mr. Cooper and Mr. Prince went with me. Refresh'd there with Meat and Drink; got thither about half an hour past one. It was sad to see triumphed over my dear Friend! I rode in my Coach to the Burying place; not being able to get nearer by reason of the many Horses. From thence went directly up the Hill where the Smith's Shop, and so home very comfortably and easily, the ground being mollified. But when I came to my own Gate, going in, I fell down, a board slipping under my Left foot, my right Legg raised off the skin, and put me to a great deal of pain, especially when 'twas washed with Rum. It was good for me that I was thus Afflicted that my spirit might be brought into a frame more suitable to the Solemnity, which is apt to be too light; and by the loss of some of my Skin, and blood I might be awakened to prepare for my own Dissolution. Mr. Walter prayed before the Corps was carried out. I had a pair of Gloves sent me before I went, and a Ring given me there. Mr. Millar, the Church of England Minister, was there. At this Funeral I heard of the death of my good old Tenant Capt Nathan^l Niles, that very Friday morn. I have now been at the Interment of 4 of my Class-mates. First, the Rev'd Mr.

---

4. Set in type. The 2nd edition of Sewall's first book, published in 1697. The full title is *Phaenomena quaedam Apocalyptica ad Aspectum Novi Orbis configurate. Or, some few lines towards a description of the New Heaven as it makes to those who stand upon the New Earth.* Although it is now hardly ever read, it contains a passage describing Plum Island, Massachusetts, which remains one of the best 17th-century American hymns to the New World:

As long as Plum Island shall faithfully keep the commanded post; notwithstanding all the hectoring words, and hard blows of the proud and boisterous ocean; as long as any salmon, or sturgeon shall swim in the streams of Merrimack; or any perch or pickrel in Crane Pond; as long as the sea-fowl shall know the time of their coming, and not neglect seasonably to visit the places of their acquaintance; as long as any cattle shall be fed with the grass growing in the meadows, which do humbly bow down themselves before Turkey Hill; as long as any sheep shall walk upon Old Town Hills, and shall from thence pleas-

antly look down upon the river Parker, and the fruitful marshes lying beneath; as long as any free and harmless doves shall find a white oak or other tree within the township to perch, or feed, or build a careless nest upon; and shall voluntarily present themselves to perform the office of gleaners after barley-harvest; as long as Nature shall not grow old and date, but shall constantly remember to give the rows of Indian corn their education by pairs: so long shall Christians be born there; and being first made meet, shall from thence be translated to be made partakers of the inheritance of the saints in light. Now seeing the inhabitants of Newbury, and of New England, upon the observance of their tenure, we may expect that their rich and gracious Lord will continue and confirm them in the possession of these invaluable privileges. *Let us have grace, whereby we may serve God acceptably with reverence and godly fear, for our God is a consuming fire.* Hebrews 12.28–29.

5. May God turn aside all bad tidings (Latin).

William Adams at Dedham, Midweek, Augt. 19, 1685. Second, Mr. John
Bowles, at Roxbury, March 31, 1691. Was one of his Bearers. Third, Capt.
Samuel Phips at Charlestown. He was laid in his Son-in-Law Lemmon's
Tomb. Had a good pair of Gloves, and a gold Ring. He was Clerk of the Court
and Register many years. Clerk to his death, and his Son succeeded him. Was
Præcentor[6] many years to the congregation. Inter'd Augt. 9, 1725. Fourth, the
Rev'd Mr. Thachar at Milton. Now I can go to no more Funerals of my
Classmates; nor none be at mine; for the survivers, the Rev'd Mr. Samuel
Mather at Windsor, and the Rev[d] Mr. Taylor at Westfield, [are] one Hundred
Miles off, and are extremly enfeebled. I humbly pray that CHRIST may be
graciously present with us all Three both in Life, and in Death, and then we
shall safely and Comfortably walk through the shady valley that leads to Glory.

   Lords-day, Dec[r] 24[th][, 1727.] am kept from the solemn Assembly by my
bruised Shin.

   October 19, 1728. Seeing this to be the same day of the week and Moneth
that the Wife of my youth expired Eleven years agoe, it much affected me. I
writ to my dear Son Mr. Joseph Sewall of it, desiring him to come and dine
with me: or however that he would call some time to join my Condolence.
He came about Noon and made an excellent Prayer in the East Chamber.
Laus Deo.[7] I told him of the death of the Widow Wheeler yesterday morning,
which he had not heard of. When Sam came to read, I wrap'd up a Silver
Cup with one ear,[8] weighing about 3 ounces and 12 Grains, to give his
Mother, which I had promis'd her. A Minister's Wife, I told her, ought not to
be without such a one. I went to looke [for] silver to make such a one, and
unexpectedly met with one ready made.

   Ditto, die, feria Septima.[9] I gave my dear Wife a Book of 7 Sermons, which
had been my Daughter Hannah's, for whom she had labored beyond measure.

1673–1729   1878–82

---

6. One who leads the congregation in singing.   8. Handle.
7. Praise God (Latin).   9. Same place, the day, Sunday (Latin).

COTTON MATHER
1663–1728

Cotton Mather, as the eldest son of Increase Mather and the grandson of Richard
Mather and John Cotton, was the heir apparent to the Congregational hierarchy
that had dominated the churches of New England for almost fifty years. Like his
father before him, Cotton Mather attended Harvard College. He was admitted at
the age of twelve, and when he graduated in 1678, President Urian Oakes told the
commencement audience that his hope was great that "in this youth, Cotton and
Mather shall, in fact as well as name, joint together and once more appear in life."
He was expected by his family to excel and did not disappoint them, but there is
no doubt he had to pay a price for his ambition: he stammered badly when young,
so much so that it was assumed he could never be a preacher, and he was subject
all his life to nervous disorders that drove him alternatively to ecstasy and despair.
His enemies often complained that he was vain and aggressive. But he was also a
genius of sorts, competent in the natural sciences and gifted in the study of ancient

languages. He possessed a strong mind, and by the time he had stopped writing he could boast that he had published more than four hundred separate works. A worthy successor to his father's position as pastor of the Second Church of Boston, he remained connected with that church from 1685, when he was ordained, until his death.

Like Benjamin Franklin, Mather found great satisfaction in doing good works, and organized societies for building churches, supported schools for the children of slaves, and worked to establish funds for indigent clergy. But for all his worldly success, Mather's life was darkened by disappointment and tragedy. He lost two wives and saw his third wife go insane, and of his fifteen children, only two lived until his death. More than one of his contemporaries observed that he never overcame his bitterness at being rejected for the presidency of Harvard. It was the one thing his father had achieved that he could not succeed in doing.

Although he was a skillful preacher and an eminent theologian, it is his work as a historian that has earned Mather a significant place in American literature. No one has described more movingly the hopes of the first generation of Puritans, and what gives Mather's best writing its urgency is the sense that the Puritan community as he knew it was fading away. By the time that Mather was writing his history of New England, the issues that seemed most pressing to his parishioners were political and social rather than theological. In his diary of 1700 he noted that "there was hardly any but my father and myself to appear in defense of our invaded churches." Everything that Mather wrote can be seen as a call to defend the old order of church authority against the encroachment of an increasingly secular world. As an apologist for the "old New England way" there is no doubt that Mather left himself open to attack, and by the end of the seventeenth century he had become a scapegoat for the worst in Puritan culture. He is often blamed for the Salem witch trials, for example, but he never actually attended one of them; his greatest crime was in not speaking out against those who he knew had exceeded the limits of authority. Mather saw the devil's presence in Salem as a final effort to undermine and destroy religious community.

In spite of its rambling and sometimes self-indulgent nature, the *Magnalia Christi Americana* (the title may be translated as "A history of the wonderful works of Christ in America") remains Mather's most impressive work. It is described on the title page as an "ecclesiastical history of New England," and in the course of its seven books, Mather attempts to record for future readers not only a history of the New England churches and the college (Harvard) where its ministers were trained but representative biographies of "saint's" lives. Although it is true that Mather was so caught up in his vision of a glorious past that he was sometimes quite blind to the suffocating realities of the world in which he lived, no one has set forth more clearly the history of a people who transformed a wilderness into a garden and the ideal of a harmonious community that has been characterized time and again as the "American dream." It is, however, in Mather's biographical sketches—his lives of Bradford, Winthrop, Eliot, and Phips—that the *Magnalia* is most arresting, for it is in his account of a particular saint's reconciliation with God on earth that New England's story is most eloquently realized.

Much has been said about Mather's style, mostly by those who hate his pedantry. But Mather did not favor any one manner of writing. He is fond of paradoxes and repetition, and he sometimes displays his learning shamelessly, but his prose can be quite straightforward when the occasion demands it. Mather also tolerated a variety of prose styles, but clearly liked the allusive style best. He tells us in his guide to young ministers (*Manuductio ad Ministerium*, 1726) that the prose he likes best is that in which "there is not only a vigor sensible in every sentence, but the paragraph is embellished with profitable references, even to something beyond what is directly spoken. Formal and painful quotations are not studied; yet all that could be learnt from them is insinuated. The writer pretends not unto reading, yet he could not have written as he does if he had not read very much in his time; and his composures are not only a cloth of gold, but also stuck with as many jewels as the gown of a Russian ambassador."

From The Wonders of the Invisible World[1]

[A *People of God in the Devil's Territories*]

The New Englanders are a people of God settled in those, which were once the devil's territories; and it may easily be supposed that the devil was exceedingly disturbed, when he perceived such a people here accomplishing the promise of old made unto our blessed Jesus, that He should have the utmost parts of the earth for His possession.[2] There was not a greater uproar among the Ephesians,[3] when the Gospel was first brought among them, than there was among the powers of the air (after whom those Ephesians walked) when first the silver trumpets of the Gospel here made the joyful sound. The devil thus irritated, immediately tried all sorts of methods to overturn this poor plantation: and so much of the church, as was fled into this wilderness, immediately found the serpent cast out of his mouth a flood for the carrying of it away. I believe that never were more satanical devices used for the unsettling of any people under the sun, than what have been employed for the extirpation of the vine which God has here planted, casting out the heathen, and preparing a room before it, and causing it to take deep root, and fill the land, so that it sent its boughs unto the Atlantic Sea eastward, and its branches unto the Connecticut River westward, and the hills were covered with a shadow thereof. But all those attempts of hell have hitherto been abortive, many an Ebenezer[4] has been erected unto the praise of God, by his poor people here; and having obtained help from God, we continue to this day. Wherefore the devil is now making one attempt more upon us; an attempt more difficult, more surprising, more snarled with unintelligible circumstances than any that we have hitherto encountered; an attempt so critical, that if we get well through, we shall soon enjoy halcyon days with all the vultures of hell trodden under our feet. He has wanted his incarnate legions to persecute us, as the people of God have in the other hemisphere been persecuted: he has therefore drawn forth his more spiritual ones to make an attack upon us. We have been advised by some credible Christians yet alive, that a malefactor, accused of witchcraft as well as murder, and executed in this place more than forty years ago, did then give notice of an horrible plot against the country by witchcraft, and a foundation of witchcraft then laid, which if it were not seasonably discovered, would probably blow up, and pull down all the churches in the country. And we have now

1. In May 1692, Governor William Phips of Massachusetts appointed a court to "hear and determine" the cases against some nineteen persons in Salem, Massachusetts, accused of witchcraft. Mather had long been interested in the subject of witchcraft, and in this work, written at the request of the judges, he describes the case against the accused. Mather, like many others, saw the evidence of witchcraft as the devil's work, a last-ditch effort to undermine the Puritan ideal. Mather was himself skeptical of much of the evidence used against the accused, especially as the trials proceeded in the summer of 1692, but like a number of prominent individuals in the community, he made no public protest. First published in 1693, the text used here is taken from the reprint by John Russell Smith (1862).

2. After Jesus was baptized he went into the desert to fast for forty days; it was there that the devil tempted him and offered him the world (see Luke 4).

3. Ephesus was an ancient city of Ionia in west Asia Minor and famous for its temples to the goddess Diana. When St. Paul preached there he received hostile treatment and riots followed the sermons of missionaries who attempted to convert the Ephesians.

4. Stone of help (Hebrew, literal trans.); a commemorative monument like the one Samuel erected to commemorate victory over the Philistines (1 Samuel 7.12).

with horror seen the discovery of such a witchcraft! An army of devils is horribly broke in upon the place which is the center, and after a sort, the first-born of our English settlements: and the houses of the good people there are filled with the doleful shrieks of their children and servants, tormented by invisible hands, with tortures altogether preternatural. After the mischiefs there endeavored, and since in part conquered, the terrible plague of evil angels hath made its progress into some other places, where other persons have been in like manner diabolically handled. These our poor afflicted neighbors, quickly after they become infected and infested with these demons, arrive to a capacity of discerning those which they conceive the shapes of their troublers; and notwithstanding the great and just suspicion that the demons might impose the shapes of innocent persons in their spectral exhibitions upon the sufferers (which may perhaps prove no small part of the witch-plot in the issue), yet many of the persons thus represented, being examined, several of them have been convicted of a very damnable witchcraft: yea, more than one [and] twenty have confessed, that they have signed unto a book, which the devil showed them, and engaged in his hellish design of bewitching and ruining our land. We know not, at least I know not, how far the delusions of Satan may be interwoven into some circumstances of the confessions; but one would think all the rules of understanding human affairs are at an end, if after so many most voluntary harmonious confessions, made by intelligent persons of all ages, in sundry towns, at several times, we must not believe the main strokes wherein those confessions all agree: especially when we have a thousand preternatural things every day before our eyes, wherein the confessors do acknowledge their concernment, and give demonstration of their being so concerned. If the devils now can strike the minds of men with any poisons of so fine a composition and operation, that scores of innocent people shall unite, in confessions of a crime, which we see actually committed, it is a thing prodigious, beyond the wonders of the former ages, and it threatens no less than a sort of a dissolution upon the world. Now, by these confessions 'tis agreed that the devil has made a dreadful knot of witches in the country, and by the help of witches has dreadfully increased that knot: that these witches have driven a trade of commissioning their confederate spirits to do all sorts of mischiefs to the neighbors, whereupon there have ensued such mischievous consequences upon the bodies and estates of the neighborhood, as could not otherwise be accounted for: yea, that at prodigious witch-meetings, the wretches have proceeded so far as to concert and consult the methods of rooting out the Christian religion from this country, and setting up instead of it perhaps a more gross diabolism than ever the world saw before. And yet it will be a thing little short of miracle, if in so spread a business as this, the devil should not get in some of his juggles,[5] to confound the discovery of all the rest.

*   *   *

But I shall no longer detain my reader from his expected entertainment, in a brief account of the trials which have passed upon some of the malefactors lately executed at Salem, for the witchcrafts whereof they stood convicted. For my own part, I was not present at any of them; nor ever had I any personal prejudice at the persons thus brought upon the stage; much less at the surviving relations of those persons, with and for whom I would be as hearty a mourner

5. Tricks.

as any man living in the world: The Lord comfort them! But having received a command[6] so to do, I can do no other than shortly relate the chief matters of fact, which occurred in the trials of some that were executed, in an abridgment collected out of the court papers on this occasion put into my hands. You are to take the truth, just as it was; and the truth will hurt no good man. There might have been more of these, if my book would not thereby have swollen too big; and if some other worthy hands did not perhaps intend something further in these collections; for which cause I have only singled out four or five, which may serve to illustrate the way of dealing, wherein witchcrafts use to be concerned; and I report matters not as an advocate, but as an historian.

* * *

The Trial of Martha Carrier

AT THE COURT OF OYER AND TERMINER,[7] HELD BY ADJOURNMENT AT SALEM, AUGUST 2, 1692.

I. Martha Carrier was indicted for the bewitching certain persons, according to the form usual in such cases, pleading not guilty to her indictment; there were first brought in a considerable number of the bewitched persons who not only made the court sensible[8] of an horrid witchcraft committed upon them, but also deposed that it was Martha Carrier, or her shape, that grievously tormented them, by biting, pricking, pinching and choking of them. It was further deposed that while this Carrier was on her examination before the magistrates, the poor people were so tortured that every one expected their death upon the very spot, but that upon the binding of Carrier they were eased. Moreover the look of Carrier then laid the afflicted people for dead; and her touch, if her eye at the same time were off them, raised them again: which things were also now seen upon her trial. And it was testified that upon the mention of some having their necks twisted almost round, by the shape of this Carrier, she replied, "It's no matter though their necks had been twisted quite off."

II. Before the trial of this prisoner, several of her own children had frankly and fully confessed not only that they were witches themselves, but that this their mother had made them so. This confession they made with great shows of repentance, and with much demonstration of truth. They related place, time, occasion; they gave an account of journeys, meetings and mischiefs by them performed, and were very credible in what they said. Nevertheless, this evidence was not produced against the prisoner at the bar,[9] inasmuch as there was other evidence enough to proceed upon.

III. Benjamin Abbot gave his testimony that last March was a twelvemonth, this Carrier was very angry with him, upon laying out some land near her husband's: her expressions in this anger were that she would stick as close to Abbot as the bark stuck to the tree; and that he should repent of it afore seven years came to an end, so as Doctor Prescot should never cure him. These words were heard by others besides Abbot himself; who also heard her say, she would hold his nose as close to the grindstone as ever it was held since his name was Abbot. Presently after this, he was taken with a swelling in his foot, and then with a pain in his side, and exceedingly tormented. It bred into a

6. I.e., the request by the judges of the Salem trials to explain the sentencing of people accused of witchcraft.
7. To hear and determine.
8. Aware.
9. Court.

sore, which was lanced[1] by Doctor Prescot, and several gallons of corruption[2] ran out of it. For six weeks it continued very bad, and then another sore bred in the groin, which was also lanced by Doctor Prescot. Another sore than bred in his groin, which was likewise cut, and put him to very great misery: he was brought unto death's door, and so remained until Carrier was taken, and carried away by the constable, from which very day he began to mend, and so grew better every day, and is well ever since.

Sarah Abbot also, his wife, testified that her husband was not only all this while afflicted in his body, but also that strange, extraordinary and unaccountable calamities befell his cattle; their death being such as they could guess at no natural reason for.

IV. Allin Toothaker testified that Richard, the son of Martha Carrier, having some difference with him, pulled him down by the hair of the head. When he rose again he was going to strike at Richard Carrier but fell down flat on his back to the ground, and had not power to stir hand or foot, until he told Carrier he yielded; and then he saw the shape of Martha Carrier go off his breast.

This Toothaker had received a wound in the wars; and he now testified that Martha Carrier told him he should never be cured. Just afore the apprehending of Carrier, he could thrust a knitting needle into his wound four inches deep; but presently after her being seized, he was thoroughly healed.

He further testified that when Carrier and he some times were at variance, she would clap her hands at him, and say he should get nothing by it; whereupon he several times lost his cattle, by strange deaths, whereof no natural causes could be given.

V. John Rogger also testified that upon the threatening words of this malicious Carrier, his cattle would be strangely bewitched; as was more particularly then described.

VI. Samuel Preston testified that about two years ago, having some difference with Martha Carrier, he lost a cow in a strange, preternatural, unusual manner; and about a month after this, the said Carrier, having again some difference with him, she told him he had lately lost a cow, and it should not be long before he lost another; which accordingly came to pass; for he had a thriving and well-kept cow, which without any known cause quickly fell down and died.

VII. Phebe Chandler testified that about a fortnight before the apprehension of Martha Carrier, on a Lordsday, while the Psalm was singing in the Church, this Carrier then took her by the shoulder and shaking her, asked her, where she lived: she made her no answer, although as Carrier, who lived next door to her father's house, could not in reason but know who she was. Quickly after this, as she was at several times crossing the fields, she heard a voice, that she took to be Martha Carrier's, and it seemed as if it was over her head. The voice told her she should within two or three days be poisoned. Accordingly, within such a little time, one half of her right hand became greatly swollen and very painful; as also part of her face: whereof she can give no account how it came. It continued very bad for some days; and several times since she has had a great pain in her breast; and been so seized on her legs that she has hardly been able to go. She added that lately, going well to the house of God, Richard, the son of Martha Carrier, looked very earnestly upon her, and immediately her

---

1. Cut open.   2. Pus; infected matter.

hand, which had formerly been poisoned, as is abovesaid, began to pain her greatly, and she had a strange burning at her stomach; but was then struck deaf, so that she could not hear any of the prayer, or singing, till the two or three last words of the Psalm.

VIII. One Foster, who confessed her own share in the witchcraft for which the prisoner stood indicted, affirmed that she had seen the prisoner at some of their witch-meetings, and that it was this Carrier, who persuaded her to be a witch. She confessed that the devil carried them on a pole to a witch-meeting; but the pole broke, and she hanging about Carrier's neck, they both fell down, and she then received an hurt by the fall, whereof she was not at this very time recovered.

IX. One Lacy, who likewise confessed her share in this witchcraft, now testified, that she and the prisoner were once bodily present at a witch-meeting in Salem Village; and that she knew the prisoner to be a witch, and to have been at a diabolical sacrament, and that the prisoner was the undoing of her and her children by enticing them into the snare of the devil.

X. Another Lacy, who also confessed her share in this witchcraft, now testified, that the prisoner was at the witch-meeting, in Salem Village, where they had bread and wine administered unto them.

XI. In the time of this prisoner's trial, one Susanna Sheldon in open court had her hands unaccountably tied together with a wheel-band[3] so fast that without cutting, it could not be loosed: it was done by a specter; and the sufferer affirmed it was the prisoner's.

Memorandum. This rampant hag, Martha Carrier, was the person of whom the confessions of the witches, and of her own children among the rest, agreed that the devil had promised her she should be Queen of Hebrews.

1692, 1693

FROM MAGNALIA CHRISTI AMERICANA[1]

Galeacius Secundus:[2] The Life of William Bradford, Esq., Governor of Plymouth Colony

Omnium Somnos illius vigilantia defendit; omnium otium, illius Labor; omnium Delitias, illius Industria; omnium vacationem, illius occupatio.[3]

It has been a matter of some observation, that although Yorkshire be one of the largest shires in England; yet for all the fires of martyrdom which were

3. A band or strap that goes around a wheel.

1. A History of the Wonderful Works of Christ in America (Latin). Mather's book is subtitled *The ecclesiastical History of New England from its first planting, in the year 1620, unto the year of our Lord, 1698.* The *Magnalia* contains seven books. The first book is concerned with the landing of the first Europeans in America and the founding and history of the New England settlements. The second book contains lives of governors of New England, and the lives of Bradford and Winthrop may be found there; the third book contains lives of sixty famous "Divines, by whose ministry the churches of New England have been planted and continued." Other books contain a history of Harvard College, a record of church ordinances passed in synods, and a record of "illustrious" and "wonderous" events that have been witnessed by people in New England. First published in London in 1702, the text used here is taken from that edited by Thomas Robbins (1855).

2. The second Galeazzo (Latin). Galeazzo Caraccoli (1517–1586) was a Neopolitan nobleman who left home and country to follow the example of Calvin in Geneva.

3. His vigilance defends the sleep of all; his labor, their rest; his industry, their pleasures; and his diligence, their leisure (Latin).

kindled in the days of Queen Mary,[4] it afforded no more fuel than one poor leaf; namely, John Leaf, an apprentice, who suffered for the doctrine of the Reformation at the same time and stake with the famous John Bradford.[5] But when the reign of Queen Elizabeth[6] would not admit the reformation of worship to proceed unto those degrees, which were proposed and pursued by no small number of the faithful in those days, Yorkshire was not the least of the shires in England that afforded suffering witnesses thereunto. The churches there gathered were quickly molested with such a raging persecution, that if the spirit of separation in them did carry them unto a further extreme than it should have done, one blamable cause thereof will be found in the extremity of that persecution. Their troubles made that cold country too hot for them, so that they were under a necessity to seek a retreat in the Low Countries;[7] and yet the watchful malice and fury of their adversaries rendered it almost impossible for them to find what they sought. For them to leave their native soil, their lands and their friends, and go into a strange place, where they must hear foreign language, and live meanly[8] and hardly, and in other employments than that of husbandry, wherein they had been educated, these must needs have been such discouragements as could have been conquered by none, save those who sought first the kingdom of God, and the righteousness thereof. But that which would have made these discouragements the more unconquerable unto an ordinary faith, was the terrible zeal of their enemies to guard all ports, and search all ships, that none of them should be carried off. I will not relate the sad things of this kind then seen and felt by this people of God; but only exemplify those trials with one short story. Divers of these people having hired a Dutchman, then lying at Hull, to carry them over to Holland, he promised faithfully to take them in, between Grimsby and Hull; but they coming to the place a day or two too soon, the appearance of such a multitude alarmed the officers of the town adjoining, who came with a great body of soldiers to seize upon them. Now it happened that one boat full of men had been carried aboard, while the women were yet in a bark that lay aground in a creek at low water. The Dutchman perceiving the storm that was thus beginning ashore, swore by the sacrament that he would stay no longer for any of them; and so taking the advantage of a fair wind then blowing, he put out to sea for Zeeland[9] The women thus left near Grimsby-common, bereaved of their husbands, who had been hurried from them, and forsaken of their neighbors, of whom none durst in this fright stay with them, were a very rueful spectacle; some crying for fear, some shaking for cold, all dragged by troops of armed and angry men from one Justice to another, till not knowing what to do with them, they even dismissed them to shift as well as they could for themselves. But by their singular afflictions, and by their Christian behaviors, the cause for which they exposed themselves did gain considerably. In the meantime, the men at sea found reason to be glad that their families were not with them, for they were surprised with an horrible tempest, which held them for fourteen days together, in seven whereof they saw not sun, moon or star, but were driven upon the coast of Norway. The mariners often despaired of life, and once with

4. During the reign of Mary Tudor (1553–58) an effort was made to restore Roman Catholicism to the position of a national church, and a number of Protestants were executed.
5. John Bradford (1510?–1555) was burned at the stake with Leaf on July 1, 1555. Their story was well known from John Foxe's *Book of Martyrs*.
6. Elizabeth followed Mary Tudor to the throne (1558–1603) and by virtue of the Act of Uniformity prescribed traditional church ritual.
7. A number of English Puritans went to Holland to form their own churches without being accused of treason.
8. In poverty.
9. I.e., the Netherlands.

doleful shrieks gave over all, as thinking the vessel was foundered: but the vessel rose again, and when the mariners with sunk hearts often cried out, "We sink! we sink!" the passengers, without such distraction of mind, even while the water was running into their mouths and ears, would cheerfully shout, "Yet, Lord, thou canst save! Yet, Lord, thou canst save!" And the Lord accordingly brought them at last safe unto their desired haven: and not long after helped their distressed relations thither after them, where indeed they found upon almost all accounts a new world, but a world in which they found that they must live like strangers and pilgrims.

Among these devout people was our William Bradford, who was born *Anno* 1588, in an obscure village called Austerfield, where the people were as unacquainted with the Bible, as the Jews do seem to have been with part of it in the days of Josiah;[1] a most ignorant and licentious people, and like unto their priest. Here, and in some other places, he had a comfortable inheritance left him of his honest parents, who died while he was yet a child, and cast him on the education,[2] first of his grandparents, and then of his uncles, who devoted him, like his ancestors, unto the affairs of husbandry. Soon a long sickness kept him, as he would afterwards thankfully say, from the vanities of youth, and made him the fitter for what he was afterwards to undergo. When he was about a dozen years old, the reading of the Scriptures began to cause great impressions upon him; and those impressions were much assisted and improved, when he came to enjoy Mr. Richard Clifton's[3] illuminating ministry, not far from his abode; he was then also further befriended, by being brought into the company and fellowship of such as were then called professors;[4] though the young man that brought him into it did after become a profane and wicked apostate.[5] Nor could the wrath of his uncles, nor the scoff of his neighbors, now turned upon him, as one of the Puritans, divert him from his pious inclinations.

At last, beholding how fearfully the evangelical and apostolical church-form, whereinto the churches of the primitive times were cast by the good spirit of God, had been deformed by the apostasy of the succeeding times; and what little progress the Reformation had yet made in many parts of Christendom towards its recovery, he set himself by reading, by discourse, by prayer, to learn whether it was not his duty to withdraw from the communion of the parish-assemblies, and engage with some society of the faithful, that should keep close unto the written Word of God, as the rule of their worship. And after many distresses of mind concerning it, he took up a very deliberate and understanding resolution, of doing so; which resolution he cheerfully prosecuted, although the provoked rage of his friends tried all the ways imaginable to reclaim him from it, unto all whom his answer was:

> Were I like to endanger my life, or consume my estate by any ungodly courses, your counsels to me were very seasonable; but you know that I have been diligent and provident in my calling, and not only desirous to augment what I have, but also to enjoy it in your company; to part from which will be as great a cross as can befall me. Nevertheless, to keep a

1. King of Judah (638?–608? B.C.). Josiah was ignorant of the book of the law of the God of Israel and worshiped false gods (see 2 Kings 22ff).
2. I.e., made his education dependent on.
3. A Puritan minister in the town of Scrooby, who also settled in Amsterdam with the Scrooby Separatists. He died in 1616.
4. I.e., those who declared their faith.
5. One who denies what he formerly professed.

good conscience, and walk in such a way as God has prescribed in His Word; is a thing which I must prefer before you all, and above life itself. Wherefore, since 'tis for a good cause that I am like to suffer the disasters which you lay before me, you have no cause to be either angry with me, or sorry for me; yea, I am not only willing to part with every thing that is dear to me in this world for this cause, but I am also thankful that God has given me an heart so to do, and will accept me so to suffer for Him.

Some lamented him, some derided him, all dissuaded him: nevertheless, the more they did it, the more fixed he was in his purpose to seek the ordinances of the Gospel, where they should be dispensed with most of the commanded purity; and the sudden deaths of the chief relations which thus lay at him,[6] quickly after convinced him what a folly it had been to have quitted his profession, in expectation of any satisfaction from them. So to Holland he attempted a removal.

Having with a great company of Christians hired a ship to transport them for Holland, the master perfidiously betrayed them into the hands of those persecutors, who rifled and ransacked their goods, and clapped their persons into prison at Boston,[7] where they lay for a month together. But Mr. Bradford being a young man of about eighteen, was dismissed sooner than the rest, so that within a while he had opportunity with some others to get over to Zeeland, through perils, both by land and sea not inconsiderable; where he was not long ashore ere a viper seized on his hand—that is, an officer—who carried him unto the magistrates, unto whom an envious passenger had accused him as having fled out of England. When the magistrates understood the true cause of his coming thither, they were well satisfied with him; and so he repaired joyfully unto his brethren at Amsterdam, where the difficulties to which he afterwards stooped in learning and serving of a Frenchman at the working of silks, were abundantly compensated by the delight wherewith he sat under the shadow of our Lord, in His purely dispensed ordinances. At the end of two years, he did, being of age to do it, convert his estate in England into money; but setting up for himself, he found some of his designs by the Providence of God frowned upon, which he judged a correction bestowed by God upon him for certain decays of internal piety, whereinto he had fallen; the consumption of his estate he thought came to prevent a consumption in his virtue. But after he had resided in Holland about half a score years, he was one of those who bore a part in that hazardous and generous enterprise of removing into New England, with part of the English church at Leyden, where, at their first landing, his dearest consort[8] accidently falling overboard, was drowned in the harbor; and the rest of his days were spent in the services, and the temptations, of that American wilderness.

Here was Mr. Bradford, in the year 1621, unanimously chosen the governor of the plantation; the difficulties whereof were such, that if he had not been a person of more than ordinary piety, wisdom and courage, he must have sunk under them. He had, with a laudable industry, been laying up a treasure of experiences, and he had now occasion to use it; indeed, nothing but an experienced man could have been suitable to the necessities of the people. The potent nations of the Indians, into whose country they were come, would have

6. I.e., struck out at him and tried to make him change his beliefs.

7. Boston, England.

8. Wife.

cut them off, if the blessing of God upon his conduct had not quelled them; and if his prudence, justice and moderation had not overruled them, they had been ruined by their own distempers. One specimen of his demeanor is to this day particularly spoken of. A company of young fellows that were newly arrived were very unwilling to comply with the governor's order for working abroad on the public account; and therefore on Christmas Day, when he had called upon them, they excused themselves, with a pretense that it was against their conscience to work such a day.[9] The governor gave them no answer, only that he would spare them till they were better informed; but by and by he found them all at play in the street, sporting themselves with various diversions; whereupon commanding the instruments of their games to be taken from them, he effectually gave them to understand that it was against his conscience that they should play whilst others were at work, and that if they had any devotion to the day, they should show it at home in the exercises of religion, and not in the streets with pastime and frolics; and this gentle reproof put a final stop to all such disorders for the future.

For two years together after the beginning of the colony, whereof he was now governor, the poor people had a great experiment of "man's not living by bread alone";[1] for when they were left all together without one morsel of bread for many months, one after another, still the good Providence of God relieved them, and supplied them, and this for the most part out of the sea. In this low condition of affairs, there was no little exercise for the prudence and patience of the governor, who cheerfully bore his part in all; and, that industry might not flag, he quickly set himself to settle propriety[2] among the new planters, foreseeing that while the whole country labored upon a common stock,[3] the husbandry and business of the plantation could not flourish, as Plato[4] and others long since dreamed that it would if a community were established. Certainly, if the spirit which dwelt in the old Puritans, had not inspired these new planters, they had sunk under the burden of these difficulties; but our Bradford had a double portion of that spirit.

The plantation was quickly thrown into a storm that almost overwhelmed it, by the unhappy actions of a minister sent over from England by the adventurers[5] concerned for the plantation; but by the blessing of Heaven on the conduct of the governor, they weathered out that storm. Only the adventurers, hereupon breaking to pieces, threw up all their concernments with the infant colony; whereof they gave this as one reason, that the planters dissembled with his Majesty and their friends in their petition, wherein they declared for a church discipline, agreeing with the French and others of the reforming churches in Europe.[6] Whereas 'twas now urged, that they had admitted into their communion a person who at his admission utterly renounced the churches of England, (which person, by the way, was that very man who had made the complaints against them) and therefore, though they denied the name of Brownists,[7] yet they were the thing. In answer hereunto, the very words written by the governor were these:

---

9. Puritans did not observe Christmas as a holiday.
1. Luke 4.4.
2. I.e., property.
3. Property held in common.
4. Greek philosopher (427?–347 B.C.).
5. English investors.
6. In Europe states were declared as either Protestant

or Catholic; in France the Edict of Nantes (1598) provided liberty of conscience for all without denying the authority of the Crown.
7. Robert Browne (c. 1550–1633) was a Separatist clergyman and identified with Congregationalism, a system whereby each church is independent of any national church.

Whereas you tax us with dissembling about the French discipline, you do us wrong, for we both hold and practice the discipline of the French and other Reformed Churches (as they have published the same in the Harmony of Confessions) according to our means, in effect and substance. But whereas you would tie us up to the French discipline in every circumstance, you derogate from the liberty we have in Christ Jesus. The Apostle Paul would have none to follow him in any thing, but wherein he follows Christ; much less ought any Christian or church in the world to do it. The French may err, we may err, and other churches may err, and doubtless do in many circumstances. That honor therefore belongs only to the infallible Word of God, and pure Testament of Christ, to be propounded and followed as the only rule and pattern for direction herein to all churches and Christians. And it is too great arrogancy for any man or church to think that he or they have so sounded the Word of God unto the bottom, as precisely to set down the church's discipline without error in substance or circumstance, that no other without blame may digress or differ in any thing from the same. And it is not difficult to show that the reformed churches differ in many circumstances among themselves.

By which words it appears how far he was free from that rigid spirit of separation, which broke to pieces the Separatists themselves in the Low Countries, unto the great scandal of the reforming churches.[8] He was indeed a person of a well-tempered spirit, or else it had been scarce possible for him to have kept the affairs of Plymouth in so good a temper for thirty-seven years together; in every one of which he was chosen their governor, except the three years wherein Mr. Winslow,[9] and the two years wherein Mr. Prince,[1] at the choice of the people, took a turn with him.

The leader of a people in a wilderness had need be a Moses;[2] and if a Moses had not led the people of Plymouth Colony, where this worthy person was the governor, the people had never with so much unanimity and importunity still called him to lead them. Among many instances thereof, let this one piece of self-denial be told for a memorial of him, wheresoever this history shall be considered: the patent of the colony was taken in his name, running in these terms: "To William Bradford, his heirs, associates, and assigns," but when the number of the freemen[3] was much increased, and many new townships erected, the General Court there desired of Mr. Bradford that he would make a surrender of the same into their hands, which he willingly and presently assented unto, and confirmed it according to their desire by his hand and seal, reserving no more for himself than was his proportion, with others, by agreement. But as he found the Providence of Heaven many ways recompensing his many acts of self-denial, so he gave this testimony to the faithfulness of the Divine Promises: that he had forsaken friends, houses and lands for the sake of the Gospel, and the Lord gave them him again. Here he prospered in his estate; and besides a worthy son which he had by a former wife, he had also two sons and a daughter by another, whom he married in this land.

8. By the time the movement for reform had come to an end, the movement for separating ended in dissension and mutual recrimination, with particular churches arguing they were more pure than others. Two English Puritans baptized themselves on the grounds that there were no pure churches to baptize them.

9. Edward Winslow (1595–1655).
1. Thomas Prince (1600–1673).
2. The Hebrew lawgiver and prophet who led the Israelites out of Egypt.
3. I.e., those who are not indentured servants and able to work for themselves.

He was a person for study as well as action; and hence, notwithstanding the difficulties through which he passed in his youth, he attained unto a notable skill in languages: the Dutch tongue was become almost as vernacular to him as the English; the French tongue he could also manage; the Latin and the Greek he had mastered; but the Hebrew he most of all studied, because he said he would see with his own eyes the ancient oracles of God in their native beauty. He was also well skilled in history, in antiquity, and in philosophy; and for theology he became so versed in it, that he was an irrefragable disputant against the errors, especially those of Anabaptism,[4] which with trouble he saw rising in his colony; wherefore he wrote some significant things for the confutation of those errors. But the crown of all was his holy, prayerful, watchful, and fruitful walk with God, wherein he was very exemplary.

At length he fell into an indispositon of body, which rendered him unhealthy for a whole winter; and as the spring advanced, his health yet more declined; yet he felt himself not what he counted sick, till one day, in the night after which, the God of Heaven so filled his mind with ineffable consolations, that he seemed little short of Paul, rapt up unto the unutterable entertainments of Paradise.[5] The next morning he told his friends that the good spirit of God had given him a pledge of his happiness in another world, and the first fruits of his eternal glory; and on the day following he died, May 9, 1657, in the 69th year of his age—lamented by all the colonies of New England as a common blessing and father to them all.

O mihi si Similis Contingat Clausula Vitae![6]

Plato's brief description of a governor, is all that I will now leave as his character, in an

EPITAPH.

Νομεν. Τροψο. ἀγελη. ανθρωπινη.[7]

Men are but flocks: Bradford beheld their need,
And long did them at once both rule and feed.

1702

Nehemias Americanus:[1] The Life of John Winthrop, Esq., Governor of the Massachusetts Colony

Quicunque Venti erunt, Ars nostra certe non aberit.
—Cicero[2]

Let Greece boast of her patient Lycurgus,[3] the lawgiver, by whom diligence, temperance, fortitude, and wit were made the fashions of a therefore long-

---

4. Anabaptists opposed the baptism of children and advocated separation of church and state.
5. In 2 Corinthians 12.2–4 Paul describes a man (himself) who experienced a moment in which he "was caught up into paradise, and heard unspeakable words, which it is not lawful for a man to utter."
6. Oh, that such an end of life might come to me (Latin).
7. Shepherd and provider of the human flock (Greek).
1. The American Nehemiah (Latin). As governor of

Judea, Nehemiah rebuilt the walls of Jerusalem (Nehemiah 1.3).
2. Whatever winds may blow, this art of ours can never be lost (Latin). The quotation is from the Roman orator Cicero's (106–43 B.C.) *Epistulae ad Familiares* 12.25.5.
3. Spartan reformer (9th century B.C.) who reshaped the nation's constitution and made it an efficient military state.

lasting and renowned commonwealth: let Rome tell of her devout Numa,[4] the lawgiver, by whom the most famous commonwealth saw peace triumphing over extinguished war and cruel plunders; and murders giving place to the more mollifying exercises of his religion. Our New England shall tell and boast of her Winthrop, a lawgiver as patient as Lycurgus, but not admitting any of his criminal disorders; as devout as Numa, but not liable to any of his heathenish madnesses; a governor in whom the excellencies of Christianity made a most improving addition unto the virtues, wherein even without those he would have made a parallel for the great men of Greece, or of Rome, which the pen of a Plutarch[5] has eternized.

A stock of heroes by right should afford nothing but what is heroical; and nothing but an extreme degeneracy would make anything less to be expected from a stock of Winthrops. Mr. Adam Winthrop,[6] the son of a worthy gentleman wearing the same name, was himself a worthy, a discreet, and a learned gentleman, particularly eminent for skill in the law, nor without remark for[7] love to the gospel, under the reign of King Henry VIII, and brother to a memorable favorer of the Reformed religion in the days of Queen Mary,[8] into whose hands the famous martyr Philpot[9] committed his papers, which afterwards made no inconsiderable part of our martyr-books. This Mr. Adam Winthrop had a son of the same name also, and of the same endowments and employments with his father; and this third Adam Winthrop was the father of that renowned John Winthrop, who was the father of New England, and the founder of a colony, which, upon many accounts, like him that founded it, may challenge the first place among the English glories of America. Our John Winthrop, thus born at the mansion-house of his ancestors, at Groton in Suffolk, on June 12, 1587,[1] enjoyed afterwards an agreeable education. But though he would rather have devoted himself unto the study of Mr. John Calvin, than of Sir Edward Cook;[2] nevertheless, the accomplishments of a lawyer were those wherewith heaven made his chief opportunities to be serviceable.

Being made, at the unusually early age of eighteen, a justice of peace, his virtues began to fall under a more general observation; and he not only so bound himself to the behavior of a Christian, as to become exemplary for a conformity to the laws of Christianity in his own conversation, but also discovered a more than ordinary measure of those qualities which adorn an officer of humane society. His justice was impartial, and used the balance to weigh not the cash, but the case of those who were before him: *prosopolatria* he reckoned as bad as *idolatria*.[3] His wisdom did exquisitely temper things according to the art of governing, which is a business of more contrivance than the seven arts of the schools;[4] *oyer* still went before *terminer* in all his administrations.[5] His courage made him dare to do right, and fitted him to

---

4. Numa Pompilius (715–673 B.C.), second legendary king of Rome.

5. The Greek biographer (A.D. 46?–120?), best known for his lives of Greeks and Romans.

6. Mather refers here to Winthrop's grandfather (1498–1562), father (1548–1623), and uncle William (1529–1582).

7. I.e., notable for. Henry VIII (1491–1547) founded the Church of England and was despised by Puritans.

8. Mary Tudor (1516–1558) reestablished Roman Catholicism in England in 1555.

9. John Philpot (1516–1555) was a Puritan martyr burned at the stake and is included in John Foxe's *Book of Martyrs* (1563).

1. Should read January 12, 1588.

2. I.e., he would have preferred to study for the ministry and read John Calvin's *Institutes* (1536) rather than prepare for the law by reading Lord Chief Justice Edward Coke's *Institutes of English Law* (1628–44).

3. "Prosopolatria," or hero worship (literally "face worship," Latin) he considered no better than the worship of idols or "false gods."

4. The trivium and quadrivium of a classical education consisted of grammar, rhetoric, and logic as well as arithmetic, music, geometry, and astronomy.

5. I.e., in the parlance of English law, "hearing" all the evidence came before "judging."

stand among the lions that have sometimes been the supporters of the throne.[6]
All which virtues he rendered the more illustrious, by emblazoning them with
the constant liberality and hospitality of a gentleman. This made him the
terror of the wicked, and the delight of the sober, the envy of the many, but
the hope of those who had any hopeful design in hand for the common good
of the nation and the interests of religion.

Accordingly, when the noble design of carrying a colony of chosen people
into an American wilderness was by some eminent persons undertaken, this
eminent person was, by the consent of all, chosen for the Moses,[7] who must
be the leader of so great an undertaking: and indeed nothing but a Mosaic
spirit could have carried him through the temptations, to which either his
farewell to his own land, or his travel in a strange land, must needs expose a
gentleman of his education. Wherefore, having sold a fair estate of six or seven
hundred[8] a year, he transported himself with the effects of it into New England
in the year 1630, where he spent it upon the service of a famous plantation,
founded and formed for the seat of the most reformed Christianity: and continued there, conflicting with temptations of all sorts, as many years as the nodes
of the moon take to dispatch a revolution.[9] Those persons were never concerned in a new plantation, who know not that the unavoidable difficulties of
such a thing will call for all the prudence and patience of a mortal man to
encounter therewithal; and they must be very insensible of the influence,
which the just wrath of heaven has permitted the devils to have upon this
world, if they do not think that the difficulties of a new plantation, devoted
unto the evangelical worship of our Lord Jesus Christ, must be yet more than
ordinary. How prudently, how patiently, and with how much resignation to
our Lord Jesus Christ, our brave Winthrop waded through these difficulties,
let posterity consider with admiration. And know, that as the picture of this
their governor was, after his death, hung up with honor in the State House of
his country, so the wisdom, courage, and holy zeal of his life, were an example
well worthy to be copied by all that shall succeed him in government.

Were he now to be considered only as a Christian, we might therein propose
him as greatly imitable. He was a very religious man; and as he strictly kept
his heart, so he kept his house, under the laws of piety;[1] there he was every
day constant in holy duties, both morning and evening, and on the Lord's
days, and lectures,[2] though he wrote not after the preacher,[3] yet such was his
attention, and such his retention in hearing, that he repeated unto his family
the sermons which he had heard in the congregation. But it is chiefly as a
governor that he is now to be considered. Being the governor over the consid-
erablest part of New England, he maintained the figure and honor of his place
with the spirit of a true gentleman; but yet with such obliging condescension
to the circumstances of the colony, that when a certain troublesome and malicious calumniator, well known in those times, printed his libelous nicknames
upon the chief persons here, the worst nickname he could find for the gover-

---

6. Daniel was saved from the Babylonian lions by his
faith (Daniel 6.23). King Solomon's throne had carved
lions on both sides (1 Kings 10.19–20).
7. Moses led the Hebrews out of Egypt into Canaan.
8. I.e., English pounds.
9. Approximately the same number of years that Winthrop lived in Massachusetts: 18.6 years. In astronomy
a "node" is either of two diametrically opposite points

at which the orbit (or revolution) of a planet intersects
the ecliptic.
1. "(For if a man know not how to rule his own house,
how shall he take care of the church of God?)" (1 Timothy 3.5).
2. Days in which less formal sermons were delivered.
3. I.e., although he did not take the sermon down in
shorthand.

nor was John Temperwell;[4] and when the calumnies of that ill man caused the Archbishop to summon one Mr. Cleaves[5] before the King, in hopes to get some accusation from him against the country, Mr. Cleaves gave such an account of the governor's laudable carriage in all respects, and the serious devotion wherewith prayers were both publicly and privately made for his Majesty, that the King expressed himself most highly pleased therewithal, only sorry that so worthy a person should be no better accommodated than with the hardships of America. He was, indeed, a governor, who had most exactly studied that book which, pretending to teach politics, did only contain three leaves, and but one word in each of those leaves, which word was, MODERATION. Hence, though he were a zealous enemy to all vice, yet his practice was according to his judgment thus expressed: "In the infancy of plantations, justice should be administered with more lenity than in a settled state; because people are more apt then to transgress; partly out of ignorance of new laws and orders, partly out of oppression of business, and other straits. [LENTO GRADU][6] was the old rule; and if the strings of a new instrument be wound up unto their height, they will quickly crack." But when some leading and learned men took offense at his conduct in this matter, and upon a conference gave it in as their opinion, "That a stricter discipline was to be used in the beginning of a plantation, than after its being with more age established and confirmed," the governor being readier to see his own errors than other men's, professed his purpose to endeavor their satisfaction with less of lenity in his administrations. At that conference there were drawn up several other articles to be observed between the governor and the rest of the magistrates, which were of this import: That the magistrates, as far as might be, should aforehand ripen their consultations, to produce that unanimity in their public votes, which might make them liker to the voice of God; that if differences fell out among them in their public meetings, they should speak only to the case, without any reflection,[7] with all due modesty, and but by way of question; or desire the deferring of the cause to further time; and after sentence to imitate privately no dislike; that they should be more familiar, friendly and open unto each other, and more frequent in their visitations, and not any way expose each other's infirmities, but seek the honor of each other, and all the court; that one magistrate shall not cross the proceedings of another, without first advising with him; and that they should in all their appearances abroad, be so circumstanced as to prevent all contempt of authority; and that they should support and strengthen all under-officers. All of which articles were observed by no man more than by the governor himself.

But whilst he thus did, as our New English Nehemiah, the part of a ruler in managing the public affairs of our American Jerusalem, when there were Tobijahs and Sanballats enough to vex him,[8] and give him the experiment of Luther's observation, *Omnis qui regit est tanquam signum, in quod omnia jacula, Satan et Mundus dirigunt;*[9] he made himself still an exacter parallel unto that governor of Israel, by doing the part of a neighbor among the dis-

---

4. Thomas Morton (d. 1649) in *New English Canaan* (1637), pt. 4, chap. 23.
5. George Cleaves settled in Maine in 1630 and returned to England in 1636. Archbishop William Laud (1573–1645) was an enemy of the Puritans.
6. By slow degrees (Latin).
7. I.e., without imputing any ill will on the part of another.

8. Both the governor of Samaria, Sanballat, and a Persian officer, Tobijah, opposed the rebuilding of the walls of Jerusalem (Nehemiah 2.10; 4.7).
9. A man in authority is a target at which Satan and the world launch all their darts (Latin), from Martin Luther's (1483–1546) *Loci Communes*.

tressed people of the new plantation. To teach them the frugality necessary for those times, he abridged himself of a thousand comfortable things, which he had allowed himself elsewhere: his habit was not that soft raiment, which would have been disagreeable to a wilderness;[1] his table was not covered with the superfluities that would have invited unto sensualities: water was commonly his own drink, though he gave wine to others. But at the same time his liberality unto the needy was even beyond measure generous; and therein he was continually causing "the blessing of him that was ready to perish to come upon him, and the heart of the widow and the orphan to sing for joy,"[2] but none more than those of deceased ministers, whom he always treated with a very singular compassion; among the instances whereof we still enjoy with us the worthy and now aged son of that Reverend Higginson, whose death left his family in a wide world soon after his arrival here, publicly acknowledging the charitable Winthrop for his foster-father.[3] It was oftentimes no small trial unto his faith, to think how a table for the people should be furnished when they first came into the wilderness![4] and for very many of the people his own good works were needful, and accordingly employed for the answering of his faith. Indeed, for a while the governor was the Joseph, unto whom the whole body of the people repaired when their corn failed them,[5] and he continued relieving of them with his open-handed bounties, as long as he had any stock to do it with; and a lively faith to see the return of the "bread after many days,"[6] and not starve in the days that were to pass till that return should be seen, carried him cheerfully through those expenses.

Once it was observable that, on February 5, 1630,[7] when he was distributing the last handful of the meal in the barrel unto a poor man distressed by the "wolf at the door," at that instant they spied a ship arrived at the harbor's mouth, laden with provisions for them all. Yea, the governor sometimes made his own private purse to be the public: not by sucking into it, but by squeezing out of it; for when the public treasure had nothing in it, he did himself defray the charges of the public. And having learned that lesson of our Lord, "that it is better to give than to receive,"[8] he did, at the General Court, when he was a third time chosen governor, make a speech unto this purpose: That he had received gratuities from divers towns, which he accepted with much comfort and content; and he had likewise received civilities from particular persons, which he could not refuse without incivility in himself: nevertheless, he took them with a trembling heart, in regard of God's word, and the conscience of his own infirmities; and therefore he desired them that they would not hereafter take it ill if he refused such presents for the time to come. 'Twas his custom also to send some of his family upon errands unto the houses of the poor, about their mealtime, on purpose to spy whether they wanted;[9] and if it were

1. "But what went ye out for to see? A man clothed in soft raiment? behold, they that wear soft clothing are in king's houses" (Matthew 11.8).
2. Job 29.13.
3. Francis Higginson (1587–1630) died after only a year's residence in Salem. His "aged son" John (1616–1708) wrote an "Attestation" prefixed to the *Magnalia*.
4. "Yea, they spake against God; they said, Can God furnish a table in the wilderness" (Psalm 78.19).
5. "And the famine was over all the face of the earth: And Joseph opened all the storehouses, and sold unto the Egyptians; and the famine waxed sore in the land

of Egypt" (Genesis 41.56).
6. "Cast thy bread upon the waters: for thou shalt find it after many days" (Ecclesiastes 11.1).
7. Old Style. The present Gregorian calendar designating January 1 as the first day of the year was adopted on March 25, 1752. Earlier, March 21 had served as the first day of the calendar year.
8. "I have shewed you all things, how that so laboring ye ought to support the weak, and to remember the words of the Lord Jesus, how he said, It is more blessed to give than to receive" (Acts 20.35).
9. I.e., lacked anything.

found that they wanted, he would make that the opportunity of sending supplies unto them. And there was one passage of his charity that was perhaps a little unusual: in an hard and long winter, when wood was very scarce at Boston, a man gave him a private information that a needy person in the neighborhood stole wood sometimes from his pile; whereupon the governor in a seeming anger did reply, "Does he so? I'll take a course with him; go, call that man to me; I'll warrant you I'll cure him of stealing." When the man came, the governor considering that if he had stolen, it was more out of necessity than disposition, said unto him, "Friend, it is a severe winter, and I doubt you are but meanly provided for wood; wherefore I would have you supply yourself at my woodpile till this cold season be over." And he then merrily asked his friends whether he had not effectually cured this man of stealing his wood.

One would have imagined that so good a man could have had no enemies, if we had not had a daily and woeful experience to convince us that goodness itself will make enemies. It is a wonderful speech of Plato (in one of his books, *De Republica*), "For the trial of true virtue, 'tis necessary that a good man μηδέν ἀδικῶν, δόξαν ἔχει τὴν μεγίστην ἀδικιας: Though he do no unjust thing, should suffer the infamy of the greatest injustice."[1] The governor had by his unspotted integrity procured himself a great reputation among the people; and then the crime of popularity was laid unto his charge by such, who were willing to deliver him from the danger of having all men speak well of him.[2] Yea, there were persons eminent both for figure and for number, unto whom it was almost essential to dislike everything that came from him; and yet he always maintained an amicable correspondence with them; as believing that they acted according to their judgment and conscience, or that their eyes were held by some temptation in the worst of all their oppositions. Indeed, his right works were so many, that they exposed him unto the envy of his neighbors,[3] and of such power was that envy, that sometimes he could not stand before it; but it was by not standing that he most effectually withstood it all.[4] Great attempts were sometimes made among the freemen to get him left out from his place in the government upon little pretenses, lest by the too frequent choice of one man, the government should cease to be by choice; and with a particular aim at him, sermons were preached at the anniversary Court of Election, to dissuade the freemen from choosing one man twice together. This was the reward of his extraordinary serviceableness! But when these attempts did succeed, as they sometimes did, his profound humility appeared in that equality of mind, wherewith he applied himself cheerfully to serve the country in whatever station their votes had allotted for him. And one year when the votes came to be numbered, there were found six less for Mr. Winthrop than for another gentleman who then stood in competition: but several other persons regularly tendering their votes before the election was published, were, upon a very frivolous objection, refused by some of the magistrates that were afraid lest the election should at last fall upon Mr. Winthrop: which, though it was well perceived, yet such was the self-denial of this patriot, that he would not permit any notice to be taken of the injury. But these trials

1. From *The Republic* of Plato (427?–347 B.C.).
2. "Woe unto you, when all men shall speak well of you! for so did their fathers to the false prophets" (Luke 6.26).
3. "Again, I consider all travail, and every right work,

that for this a man is envied of his neighbor. This is also vanity and vexation of spirit" (Ecclesiastes 4.4).
4. "Wrath is cruel, and anger is outrageous, but who is able to stand before envy" (Proverbs 27.4).

were nothing in comparison of those harsher and harder treats which he sometimes had from the forwardness of not a few in the days of their paroxisms; and from the faction of some against him, not much unlike that of the Piazzi in Florence against the family of the Medicis:[5] all of which he at last conquered by conforming to the famous Judge's motto, *Prudens qui Patiens*.[6] The oracles of God have said, "Envy is rottenness to the bones;"[7] and Gulielmus Parisiensis[8] applies it unto rulers, who are as it were the bones of the societies which they belong unto: "Envy," says he, "is often found among them, and it is rottenness unto them." Our Winthrop encountered this envy from others, but conquered it, by being free from it himself.

Were it not for the sake of introducing the exemplary skill of this wise man, at giving soft answers, one would not choose to relate those instances of wrath which he had sometimes to encounter with; but he was for his gentleness, his forbearance, and longanimity,[9] a pattern so worthy to be written *after*, that something must here be written *of* it. He seemed indeed never to speak any other language than that of Theodosius:[1] "If any man speak evil of the governor, if it be through lightness, 'tis to be contemned;[2] if it be through madness, 'tis to be pitied; if it be through injury, 'tis to be remitted." Behold, reader, the "meekness of wisdom" notably exemplified! There was a time when he received a very sharp letter from a gentleman who was a member of the Court,[3] but he delivered back the letter unto the messengers that brought it, with such a Christian speech as this: "I am not willing to keep such a matter of provocation by me!" Afterwards the same gentleman was compelled by scarcity of provisions to send unto him that he would sell him some of his cattle; whereupon the governor prayed him to accept what he had sent for as a token of his good will; but the gentleman returned him this answer: "Sir, your overcoming of yourself hath overcome me:" and afterwards gave demonstration of it.

The French have a saying that "*Un honesté homme, est un homme mesle!*"—a good man is a mixed man; and there hardly ever was a more sensible mixture of those two things, resolution and condescension, than in this good man. There was a time when the Court of Election being, for fear of tumult, held at Cambridge, May 17, 1637, the sectarian part of the country, who had the year before gotten a governor more unto their mind,[4] had a project now to have confounded the election, by demanding that the court would consider a petition then tendered before their proceeding thereunto. Mr. Winthrop saw that this was only a trick to throw all into confusion, by putting off the choice of the governor and assistants until the day should be over; and therefore he did, with a strenuous resolution, procure a disappointment unto that mischievous and ruinous contrivance. Nevertheless, Mr. Winthrop himself being by the voice of the freemen in this exigency chosen the governor, and all of the other party left out, that ill-affected party discovered the dirt and mire, which remained with them, after the storm was over; particularly the sergeants, whose

---

5. In 1478 an important member of the Medici family was assassinated by one of the Piazzis, and all Italy became involved in the war that followed.

6. He is prudent who is patient (Latin), a maxim attributed to Sir Edward Coke.

7. "A sound heart is the life of the flesh: but envy the rottenness of the bones" (Proverbs 14.30).

8. William of St. Amour (d. 1272), Bishop of Paris, was also known as a satirist.

9. Patience.

1. Theodosius Flavius I (A.D. 346–395) was a Christian Roman emperor.

2. Despised.

3. Thomas Dudley (1574–1653); the messengers were John Haynes and Thomas Hooker.

4. Sir Henry Vane returned to England in 1637; he was sympathetic toward the views expressed by the followers of Anne Hutchinson.

office 'twas to attend the governor, laid down their halberds; but such was the condescension[5] of this governor, as to take no present notice of this anger and contempt, but only order some of his own servants to take the halberds; and when the country manifested their deep resentments of the affront thus offered him, he prayed them to overlook it. But it was not long before a compensation was made for these things by the doubled respects which were from all parts paid unto him. Again, there was a time when the suppression of an *Antinomian* and *Familistical* faction,[6] which extremely threatened the ruin of the country, was generally thought much owing unto this renowned man; and therefore when the friends of that faction could not wreak[7] their displeasure on him with any politic vexations, they set themselves to do it by ecclesiastical ones. Accordingly, when a sentence of banishment was passed on the ringleaders of those disturbances, who

——*Maria et Terras, Cœlumque profundum,*
Quippe ferant Rapidi, secum vertantque per Auras;[8]

many at the church of Boston, who were then that way too much inclined, most earnestly solicited the elders of that church, whereof the governor was a member, to call him forth as an offender, for passing of that sentence. The elders were unwilling to do any such thing; but the governor understanding the ferment among the people took that occasion to make a speech in the congregation to this effect:

> BRETHREN: Understanding that some of you have desired that I should answer for an offense lately taken among you; had I been called upon so to do, I would, first, have advised with the ministers of the country, whether the church had power to call in question the civil court; and I would, secondly, have advised with the rest of the court, whether I might discover their counsels unto the church. But though I know that the reverend Elders of this church, and some others, do very well apprehend that the church cannot inquire into the proceedings of the court; yet, for the satisfaction of the weaker, who do not apprehend it, I will declare my mind concerning it. If the church have any such power, they have it from the Lord Jesus Christ; but the Lord Jesus Christ hath disclaimed it, not only by practice, but also by precept, which we have in his gospel, Matt. xx. 25, 26.[9] It is true, indeed, that magistrates, as they are church-members, are accountable unto the church for their failings; but that is when they are out of their calling. When Uzziah would go offer incense in the temple, the officers of the church called him to an account, and withstood him; but when Asa put the prophet in prison, the officers of the church did not call him to an account for that.[1] If the magistrate shall in a private way wrong any man, the church may call him to an account for

---

5. Humility. "Halberd": a weapon that is a combination spear and battleax.
6. Both Antinomianism and Familism (a word derived from an English religious sect called the Family of Love) hold the regenerate self above ecclesiastical and civil law.
7. Inflict.
8. "Rack sea and land and sky with mingled wrath. / In the wild tumult of their stormy path" (Virgil, *Aeneid* 1.59–60).
9. "But Jesus called them unto him, and said, Ye

know that the princes of the Gentiles exercise dominion over them, and they that are great exercise authority upon them. But it shall not be so among you: but whosoever will be great among you, let him be your minister."
1. Uzziah, king of Judea, was afflicted with leprosy when he tried to burn incense on the altar in spite of the protests of the priests (2 Chronicles 26.18). Asa was the third king of Judea and put the prophet Hanani in prison when he accused him of not relying on the Lord (2 Chronicles 16.7–10).

it; but if he be in pursuance of a course of justice, though the thing that he does be unjust, yet he is not accountable for it before the church. As for myself, I did nothing in the causes of any of the brethren but by the advice of the Elders of the church. Moreover, in the oath which I have taken there is this clause: "In all cases wherein you are to give your vote, you shall do as in your judgment and conscience you shall see to be just, and for the public good." And I am satisfied, it is most for the glory of God, and the public good, that there has been such a sentence passed; yea, those brethren are so divided from the rest of the country in their opinions and practices, that it cannot stand with the public peace for them to continue with us; Abraham saw that Hagar and Ishmael must be sent away.[2]

By such a speech he marvelously convinced, satisfied and mollified the uneasy brethren of the church; *Sic cunctus Pelagi cecidit Fragor*[3]———. And after a little patient waiting, the differences all so wore away, that the church, merely as a token of respect unto the governor when he had newly met with some losses in his estate, sent him a present of several hundreds of pounds.

Once more there was a time when some active spirits among the deputies of the colony, by their endeavors not only to make themselves a Court of Judicature, but also to take away the negative by which the magistrates might check their votes, had like by over-driving to have run the whole government into something too democratical. And if there was a town in Spain undermined by coneys, another town in Thrace destroyed by moles, a third in Greece ranversed[4] by frogs, a fourth in Germany subverted by rats; I must on this occasion add, that there was a country in America like to be confounded by a swine. A certain stray sow being found, was claimed by two several persons with a claim so equally maintained on both sides, that after six or seven years' hunting the business from one court unto another, it was brought at last into the General Court, where the final determination was "that it was impossible to proceed unto any judgment in the case."[5] However, in the debate of this matter, the negative of the upper-house upon the lower in that court was brought upon the stage; and agitated with so hot a zeal, that a little more, and all had been in the fire. In these agitations, the governor was informed that an offense had been taken by some eminent persons at certain passages in a discourse by him written thereabout; whereupon, with his usual condescendency, when he next came into the General Court, he made a speech of this import:

> I understand that some have taken offense at something that I have lately written; which offense I desire to remove now, and begin this year in a reconciled state with you all. As for the matter of my writing, I had the concurrence of my brethren; it is a point of judgment which is not at my own disposing. I have examined it over and over again by such light as God has given me, from the rules of religion, reason and custom; and I see no cause to retract anything of it: wherefore I must enjoy my liberty in that, as you do yourselves. But for the manner, this, and all that was blameworthy in it, was wholly my own; and whatsoever I might allege for my own justification therein before men, I wave it, as now setting myself

---

2. Ishmael was the son of Abraham and his wife's servant Hagar; Abraham sent them into the wilderness at the insistence of his wife, Sarah (Genesis 16.1–16; 21.9–14).
3. "To silence sunk the thunder of the wave" (*Aeneid*

1.154).
4. Overturned. "Coneys": rabbits.
5. Mather refers to a case involving the merchant Robert Keayne (1595–1656) and Goody Sherman, a Boston widow, in 1643.

before another Judgment seat. However, what I wrote was upon great provocation, and to vindicate myself and others from great aspersion; yet that was no sufficient warrant for me to allow any distemper of spirit in myself; and I doubt I have been too prodigal of my brethren's reputation; I might have maintained my cause without casting any blemish upon others, when I made that my conclusion, "And now let religion and sound reason give judgment in the case;" it looked as if I arrogated too much unto myself, and too little to others. And when I made that profession, "That I would maintain what I wrote before all the world," though such words might modestly be spoken, yet I perceive an unbeseeming pride of my own heart breathing in them. For these failings, I ask pardon of God and man.

> Sic ait, et dicto citius Tumida Æquora placat,
> Collectasque fugat Nubes, Solemque reducit.[6]

This acknowledging disposition in the governor made them all acknowledge that he was truly "a man of an excellent spirit."[7] In fine, the victories of an Alexander, an Hannibal, or a Cæsar[8] over other men were not so glorious as the victories of this great man over himself, which also at last proved victories over other men.

But the stormiest of all the trials that ever befell this gentleman was in the year 1645, when he was, in title, no more than deputy governor of the colony. If the famous Cato were forty-four times called into judgment but as often acquitted; let it not be wondered, and if[9] our famous Winthrop were one time so. There happening certain seditious and mutinous practices in the town of Hingham,[1] the deputy governor, as legally as prudently, interposed his authority for the checking of them: whereupon there followed such an enchantment[2] upon the minds of the deputies in the General Court, that upon a scandalous petition of the delinquents unto them, wherein a pretended invasion made upon the liberties of the people was complained of, the deputy governor was most irregularly called forth unto an ignominious hearing before them in a vast assembly; whereto with a sagacious humilitude he consented, although he showed them how he might have refused it. The result of that hearing was, that notwithstanding the touchy jealousy of the people about their liberties lay at the bottom of all this prosecution, yet Mr. Winthrop was publicly acquitted, and the offenders were severally fined and censured. But Mr. Winthrop then resuming the place of deputy governor on the bench, saw cause to speak unto the root of the matter after this manner:[3]

> I shall not now speak anything about the past proceedings of this Court, or the persons therein concerned. Only I bless God that I see an issue[4] of this troublesome affair. I am well satisfied that I was publicly accused,

6. "He speaks—but ere the word is said, / Each mounting billow droops its head, / And brightening clouds one moment stay / To pioneer returning day" (*Aeneid* 1.142–43).
7. "He that hath knowledge spareth his words: and a man of understanding is of an excellent spirit" (Proverbs 17.27).
8. Alexander the Great (356–323 B.C.) king of Macedonia. Hannibal (247–183 B.C.), the Carthaginian general. Julius Caesar (100–44 B.C.), Roman general and statesman. All were pre-Christian warriors.
9. "And if" is the archaic form of *if*. Cato: the Roman

orator (234–149 B.C.).
1. A town about twenty-five miles south of Boston. These challenges to authority were made against the captain of the town militia who was appointed by the state authorities.
2. I.e., a delusion in judgment.
3. "But ye should say, Why persecute we him, seeing the root of the matter is found in me?" (Job 19.28). Mather's version of Winthrop's speech to the General Court differs somewhat from that quoted in Winthrop's *Journal*.
4. End.

and that I am now publicly acquitted. But though I am justified before men, yet it may be the Lord hath seen so much amiss in my administrations, as calls me to be humbled; and indeed for me to have been thus charged by men, is itself a matter of humiliation, whereof I desire to make a right use before the Lord. If Miriam's father spit in her face, she is to be ashamed.[5] But give me leave, before you go, to say something that may rectify the opinions of many people, from whence the distempers have risen that have lately prevailed upon the body of this people. The questions that have troubled the country have been about the authority of the magistracy, and the liberty of the people. It is you who have called us unto this office; but being thus called, we have our authority from God; it is the ordinance of God, and it hath the image of God stamped upon it; and the contempt of it has been vindicated by God with terrible examples of his vengeance. I entreat you to consider, that when you choose magistrates, you take them from among yourselves, "men subject unto like passions with yourselves." If you see our infirmities, reflect on your own, and you will not be so severe censurers of ours. We count him a good servant who breaks not his covenant: the covenant between us and you is the oath you have taken of us, which is to this purpose, "that we shall govern you, and judge your causes, according to God's laws, and our own, according to our best skill." As for our skill, you must run the hazard of it; and if there be an error, not in the will, but only in skill, it becomes you to bear it. Nor would I have you to mistake in the point of your own liberty. There is a liberty of corrupt nature, which is affected both by men and beasts, to do what they list; and this liberty is inconsistent with authority, impatient of all restraint; by this liberty, *Sumus Omnes Deteriores;*[6] 'tis the grand enemy of truth and peace, and all the ordinances of God are bent against it. But there is a civil, a moral, a federal liberty, which is the proper end and object of authority; it is a liberty for that only which is just and good; for this liberty you are to stand with the hazard of your very lives; and whatsoever crosses it is not authority, but a distemper thereof. This liberty is maintained in a way of subjection to authority; and the authority set over you will in all administrations for your good be quietly submitted unto, by all but such as have a disposition to shake off the yoke, and lose their true liberty, by their murmuring at the honor and power of authority.

The spell that was upon the eyes of the people being thus dissolved, their distorted and enraged notions of things all vanished; and the people would not afterwards entrust the helm of the weather-beaten bark in any other hands but Mr. Winthrop's until he died.

Indeed, such was the mixture of distant qualities in him, as to make a most admirable temper; and his having a certain greatness of soul, which rendered him grave, generous, courageous, resolved, well-applied, and every way a gentleman in his demeanor, did not hinder him from taking sometimes the old Roman's way to avoid confusions, namely, *Cedendo;*[7] or from discouraging

---

5. "And the Lord said unto Moses, If her father had but spit in her face, should she not be ashamed seven days? let her be shut out from the camp seven days, and after that let her be received in again" (Numbers 12.14). Miriam was Moses' sister, and was punished

for challenging his choice in a wife.
6. We are all the worse for it (Latin), from Terence, *Heaucton Timorumenos* (3.1).
7. By yielding the point (Latin).

some things which are agreeable enough to most that wear the name of gentle-men. Hereof I will give no instances, but only oppose two passages of his life.

In the year 1632, the governor, with his pastor, Mr. Wilson,[8] and some other gentlemen, to settle a good understanding between the two colonies, traveled as far as Plymouth, more than forty miles, through an howling wilder-ness, no better accommodated in those early days than the princes that in Solomon's time saw "servants on horseback,"[9] or than genus and species in the old epigram, "going on foot."[1] The difficulty of the walk was abundantly compensated by the honorable, first reception, and then dismission, which they found from the rulers of Plymouth, and by the good correspondence thus established between the new colonies, who were like the floating bottles wear-ing this motto: *Si Collidimur Frangimur.*[2] But there were at this time in Ply-mouth two ministers,[3] leavened so far with the humors of the rigid Separation, that they insisted vehemently upon the unlawfulness of calling any unregener-ate man by the name of "Goodman Such-an-One," until by their indiscreet urging of this whimsy, the place began to be disquieted.[4] The wiser people being troubled at these trifles, they took the opportunity of Governor Win-throp's being there, to have the thing publicly propounded in the congregation; who in answer thereunto, distinguished between a theological and a moral goodness; adding, that when juries were first used in England, it was usual for the crier, after the names of persons fit for that service were called over, to bid them all, "Attend, good men and true;" whence it grew to be a civil custom in the English nation, for neighbors living by one another, to call one another "Goodman Such-an-One;" and it was [a] pity now to make a stir about a civil custom, so innocently introduced. And that speech of Mr. Winthrop's put a lasting stop to the little, idle, whimsical conceits, then beginning to grow obstreperous.

Nevertheless, there was one civil custom used in (and in few but) the English nation, which this gentleman did endeavor to abolish in this country; and that was, the usage of drinking to one another. For although by drinking to one another, no more is meant than an act of courtesy, when one going to drink, does invite another to do so too, for the same ends with himself, never-theless the governor (not altogether unlike to Cleomenes, of whom 'tis reported by Plutarch, ἄκοντι οὐδεὶς ποτήριον προσέφερε, *Nolenti poculum nunquam prœbuit,*)[5] considered the impertinency and insignificancy of this usage, as to any of those ends that are usually pretended for it; and that indeed it ordinarily served for no ends at all, but only to provoke persons unto unsea-sonable and perhaps unreasonable drinking, and at last produce that abomina-ble health-drinking, which the Fathers of old[6] so severely rebuked in the pagans, and which the Papists themselves do condemn, when their casuists pronounce it, *Peccatum mortale, provocare ad Æquales Calices, et Nefas Respondere.*[7] Wherefore in his own most hospitable house he left it off; not

---

8. John Wilson (c. 1591–1667).
9. "I have seen servants upon horses, and princes walking as servants upon the earth" (Ecclesiastes 10.7). The Book of Ecclesiastes was mistakenly attributed to Solomon.
1. Better on foot go, than a wicked horse to ride (adage).
2. If we come into collision, we break (Latin).
3. Ralph Smith (1590–1661), Plymouth's first minis-ter (1629–36), and Roger Williams (c. 1604–1683)

were both Separatists.
4. I.e., they used the title "Goodman" to mean only regeneracy and visible sainthood.
5. Never urge the reluctant to drink (Latin). Plutarch (A.D. 46?–120?) writes about the Spartan king Cleomenes III (r. 235–222 B.C.) in his *Parallel Lives.*
6. I.e., church fathers.
7. It is a deadly sin to challenge another to a drinking match, and it is impious to accept such challenges (Latin).

out of any silly or stingy fancy, but merely that by his example a greater temperance, with liberty of drinking, might be recommended, and sundry inconveniences in drinking avoided; and his example accordingly began to be much followed by the sober people in this country, as it now also begins among persons of the highest rank in the English nation itself; until an order of court came to be made against that ceremony in drinking, and then, the old wont violently returned, with a *Nitimur in Vetitum*.[8]

Many were the afflictions of this righteous man![9] He lost much of his estate in a ship, and in an house, quickly after his coming to New England, besides the prodigious expense of it in the difficulties of his first coming hither. Afterwards his assiduous application unto the public affairs, (wherein *Ipse se non habuit, postquam Republica eum Gubernatorem habere cœpit*)[1] made him so much to neglect his own private interests, that an unjust steward[2] ran him £2,500 in debt before he was aware; for the payment whereof he was forced, many years before his decease, to sell the most of what he had left unto him in the country. Albeit, by the observable blessings of God upon the posterity of this liberal man, his children all of them came to fair estates, and lived in good fashion and credit. Moreover, he successively buried three wives; the first of which was the daughter and heiress of Mr. Forth, of Much Stambridge in Essex, by whom he had "wisdom with an inheritance;" and an excellent son. The second was the daughter of Mr. William Clopton, of London, who died with her child, within a very little while. The third was the daughter of the truly worshipful Sir John Tyndal, who made it her whole care to please, first God, and then her husband; and by whom he had four sons, which survived and honored their father.[3] And unto all these, the addition of the distempers, ever now and then raised in the country, procured unto him a very singular share of trouble; yea, so hard was the measure which he found even among pious men, in the temptations of a wilderness, that when the thunder and lightning had smitten a windmill whereof he was owner, some had such things in their heads as publicly to reproach this charitablest of men as if the voice of the Almighty had rebuked, I know not what oppression, which they judged him guilty of; which things I would not have mentioned, but that the instances may fortify the expectations of my best readers for such afflictions.

He that had been for his attainments, as they said of the blessed Macarius,[4] a Παιδαριογερων, (an old man, while a young one,) and that had in his young days met with many of those ill days, whereof he could say, he had "little pleasure in them;" now found old age in its infirmities advancing earlier upon him, than it came upon his much longer-lived progenitors. While he was yet seven years off of that which we call "the grand climacterical,"[5] he felt the approaches of his dissolution; and finding he could say,

> *Non Habitus, non ipse Color, non Gressus Euntis,*
> *Non Species Eadem, quœ fuit ante, manet.*[6]

---

8. "A bias towards the forbidden usage" (Ovid, *Amores* 3.4.17).

9. "Many are the afflictions of the righteous: but the Lord delivereth him of them all" (Psalm 34.19).

1. He no longer belonged to himself, after the Republic had once made him her chief magistrate (Latin).

2. One James Luxford.

3. Winthrop married Mary Forth (1583–1615) in 1606. Much Stambridge is also known as Great Stambridge. They had six children but only one, John (b.

1606), survived his father. Winthrop married Thomasine Clopton (1583–1616) in 1615 and Margaret Tyndal in 1618.

4. Macarius, a 4th-century Egyptian, had a reputation for having accomplished much while still young.

5. I.e., when he was sixty-three; the "grand climacterial" would be age seventy.

6. "I am not what I was in form or face, / In healthful color or in vigorous pace" (Maximianus, *Elegies* 1.210–211).

He then wrote this account of himself: "Age now comes upon me, and infirmities therewithal, which makes me apprehend, that the time of my departure out of this world is not far off.[7] However, our times are all in the Lord's hand, so as we need not trouble our thoughts how long or short they may be, but how we may be found faithful when we are called for." But at last when that year came, he took a cold which turned into a fever, whereof he lay sick about a month, and in that sickness, as it hath been observed, that there was allowed unto the serpent the "bruising of the heel;"[8] and accordingly at the heel or the close of our lives the old serpent will be nibbling more than ever in our lives before; and when the devil sees that we shall shortly be, "where the wicked cease from troubling," that wicked one will trouble us more than ever; so this eminent saint now underwent sharp conflicts with the tempter, whose wrath grew great, as the time to exert it grew short; and he was buffeted with the disconsolate thoughts of black and sore desertions, wherein he could use that sad representation of his own condition:

> Nuper eram Judex; Jam Judicor; Ante Tribunal
> Subsistens paveo; Judicor ipse modo.[9]

But it was not long before those clouds were dispelled, and he enjoyed in his holy soul the great consolations of God! While he thus lay ripening for heaven, he did out of obedience unto the ordinance of our Lord send for the Elders of the church to pray with him; yea, they and the whole church fasted as well as prayed for him; and in that fast the venerable Cotton[1] preached on Psalm 35.13–14: "When they were sick, I humbled myself with fasting; I behaved myself as though he had been my friend or brother; I bowed down heavily, as one that mourned for his mother." From whence I find him raising that observation, "The sickness of one that is to us as a friend, a brother, a mother, is a just occasion of deep humbling our souls with fasting and prayer;" and making this application:

> Upon this occasion we are now to attend this duty for a governor, who has been to us as a friend in his counsel for all things, and help for our bodies by physic, for our estates by law, and of whom there was no fear of his becoming an enemy, like the friends of David:[2] a governor who has been unto us as a brother; not usurping authority over the church; often speaking his advice, and often contradicted, even by young men, and some of low degree; yet not replying, but offering satisfaction also when any supposed offenses have arisen; a governor who had been unto us as a mother, parent-like distributing his goods to brethren and neighbors at his first coming; and gently bearing our infirmities without taking notice of them.

Such a governor, after he had been more than ten several times by the people chosen their governor, was New England now to lose; who having, like Jacob, first left his counsel and blessing with his children gathered about his

---

7. "For I am now ready to be offered, and the time of my departure is at hand" (2 Timothy 4.6).

8. In his anger after the Fall, God tells the devil (in the form of a serpent): "And I will put enmity between thee and the woman, and between thy seed and her seed; it shall bruise thy head, and thou shalt bruise his heel" (Genesis 3.15).

9. I once judged others, but now trembling stand / Before a dread tribunal, to be judged (Latin).

1. John Cotton (1584–1652), Mather's grandfather and namesake.

2. King David's friends and counselors joined Absalom in his revolt against his father (2 Samuel).

bedside;[3] and, like David, "served his generation by the will of God,"[4] he "gave up the ghost," and fell asleep on March 26, 1649. Having like the dying Emperor Valentinian,[5] this above all his other victories for his triumphs, his overcoming of himself. '

The words of Josephus[6] about Nehemiah, the governor of Israel, we will now use upon this governor of New England, as his

EPITAPH

'Ανὴρ εγένετο χρηστὸσ τὴν φύσιν, καὶ δίκαιος,
Καὶ περὶ τοὺς ὁμοευνεῖς φιλοτιμότατος:
Μνημεῖον ἰώνιον ἀυτω καταλιπὼν τὰ τῶν
'Ιεροσολύμων Τείχη:

VIR FUIT INDOLE BONUS, AC JUSTUS:
ET POPULARIUM GLORIÆ AMANTISSIMUS:
QUIBUS ETERNUM RELIQUIT MONUMENTUM,
                    Novanglorum MŒNIA.[7]

1702

From Bonifacius[1]

[Christian Behavior at Home and in the Community]

The useful man may now with a very good grace, extend and enlarge the sphere of his consideration. My next proposal now shall be: Let every man consider the relation, wherein the Sovereign God has placed him, and let him devise what good he may do, that may render his relatives, the better for him. One great way to prove ourselves really good, is to be relatively good. By this, more than be anything in the world, it is, that we adorn the doctrine of God our Savior. It would be an excellent wisdom in a man, to make the interest he has in the good opinion and affection of anyone, an advantage to do good service for God upon them: He that has a friend will show himself indeed friendly, if he thinks, "Such an one loves me, and will hearken to me; what good shall I take advantage hence to persuade him to?"

This will take place more particularly, where the endearing ties of natural relation do give us an interest. Let us call over our several relations, and let us have devices of something that may be called heroical goodness, in our discharging of them. Why should we not, at least once or twice in a week, make this relational goodness, the subject of our inquiries, and our purposes? Particularly, let us begin with our domestic relations, and provide for those of our

3. The aged patriarch Jacob was the second son of Isaac and Rebekah. In Genesis 49 he called his sons about him and told them what would befall them "in the last days" of the world.
4. "For David, after he had served his own generation by the will of God, fell on sleep, and was laid unto his fathers" (Acts 13.36).
5. Christian emperor of Rome (d. 375).
6. Josephus (37–100?) was a Jewish historian and author of *Antiquities of the Jews* where the following quotation appears (book II, chap. 5).
7. He was by nature a man at once benevolent and just: most zealous for the honor of his countrymen and to them he left an imperishable monument—the walls of New England (Latin). The Latin paraphrase of the Greek substitutes *New England* for *Jerusalem*.
1. On Doing Good (Latin). The full title makes clear Mather's intention in writing this book: *Bonifacius. An essay upon the good, that is to be devised and designed, by those who desire to answer the great end of life, and to do good while they live.* The section that follows is from part 11. The text used here is from that edited by David Levin (1966).

own house, lest we deny some glorious rules and hopes of our Christian faith, in our negligence.

First, in the Conjugal Relation, how agreeably may the consorts think on those words: "What knowest thou, O wife, whether thou shalt save thy husband?" Or, "How knowest thou, O man, whether thou shalt save thy wife?"

The Husband will do well to think: "What shall I do, that my wife may have cause forever to bless God, for bringing her unto me?" And, "What shall I do that in my carriage[2] towards my wife, the kindness of the blessed Jesus towards His Church, may be followed and resembled?" That this question may be the more perfectly answered, Sir, sometimes ask her to help you in the answer; ask her to tell you, what she would have you to do.

But then, the Wife also will do well to think: "Wherein may I be to my husband, a wife of that character: she will do him good, and not evil, all the days of his life?"

With my married people, I will particularly leave a good note, which I find in the Memorials of Gervase Disney, Esq.[3] "Family passions cloud faith, disturb duty, darken comfort." You'll do the more good unto one another, the more this note is thought upon. When the husband and wife are always contriving to be blessings unto one another, I will say with Tertullian, *"Unde, sufficiam ad enarrandam faelicitatem ejus matrimonii!"*[4] O happy marriage!

Parents, Oh! how much ought you to be continually devising, and even travailing, for the good of your children. Often devise: how to make them wise children; how to carry on a desirable education for them; an education that shall render them desirable; how to render them lovely, and polite creatures, and serviceable in their generation. Often devise, how to enrich their minds with valuable knowledge; how to instill generous and gracious, and heavenly principles into their mind; how to restrain and rescue them from the paths of the Destroyer, and fortify them against their special temptations. There is a world of good, that you have to do for them. You are without bowels,[5] Oh! be not such monsters! if you are not in a continual agony to do for them all the good that ever you can. It was no mistake of Pacatus Drepanius in his panegyric to Theodosius: *"Instituente natura plus fere filios quam nosmetipsos diligimus."*[6]

I will prosecute this matter, by transcribing a copy of Parental Resolutions, which I have somewhere met withal.[7]

I. "At the birth of my children, I would use all explicit solemnity in the baptismal dedication and consecration of them unto the Lord. I would present them to the Baptism of the Lord, not as a mere formality; but wondering at the grace of the infinite God, who will accept my children, as His, I would resolve to do all I can that they may be His. I would now actually give them up unto God; entreating, that the child may be a child of God the Father, a subject of God the Son, a temple of God the Spirit, and be rescued from the condition of a child of wrath, and be possessed and employed by the Lord as an everlasting instrument of His glory.

---

2. Manner, conduct.
3. A wealthy man whose spiritual autobiography was published in England in 1692.
4. How can I find words to express the happiness of their marriage! (Latin), Tertullian (160?–230?), Carthaginian theologian.
5. Feeling, compassion.

6. Nature teaches us to love our children as ourselves (Latin). Drepanius was a Roman orator who wrote praising Emperor Theodosius in A.D. 389.
7. Mather "met" (i.e., set down) these resolutions in his own autobiography *Paterna*, the complete manuscript of which was not published until 1976.

II. "My children are no sooner grown capable of minding the admonitions, but I would often, often admonish them to be sensible of their baptismal engagements to be the Lord's. Often tell them, of their baptism, and of what it binds 'em to: oftener far, and more times than there were drops of water, that were cast on the infant, upon that occasion!

"Often say to them, 'Child, you have been baptized; you were washed in the name of the great God; now you must not sin against Him; to sin is to do a dirty, a filthy thing.' Say, 'Child, you must every day cry to God that He would be your Father, and your Savior, and your Leader; in your baptism He promised that He would be so, if you sought unto Him.' Say, 'Child, you must renounce the service of Satan, you must not follow the vanities of this world, you must lead a life of serious religion; in your baptism you were bound unto the service of your only Savior.' Tell the child: 'What is your name; you must sooner forget this name, that was given you in your baptism, than forget that you are a servant of a glorious Christ whose name was put upon you in your baptism.'

III. "Let my prayers for my children be daily, with constancy, with fervency, with agony; yea, by name let me mention each one of them, every day before the Lord. I would importunately beg for all suitable blessings to be bestowed upon them: that God would give them grace, and give them glory, and withhold no good thing from them; that God would smile on their education, and give His good angels the charge over them, and keep them from evil, that it may not grieve them; that when their father and mother shall forsake them, the Lord may take them up. With importunity I would plead that promise on their behalf: the Heavenly Father will give the Holy Spirit unto them that ask Him. Oh! happy children, if by asking I may obtain the Holy Spirit for them!

IV. "I would betimes entertain the children, with delightful stories out of the Bible. In the talk of the table, I would go through the Bible, when the olive plants[8] about my table are capable of being so watered. But I would always conclude the stories with some lessons of piety, to be inferred from them.

V. "I would single out some Scriptural sentences, of the greatest importance; and some also that have special antidotes in them against the common errors and vices of children. They shall quickly get those golden sayings by heart, and be rewarded with silver or gold, or some good thing, when they do it. Such as.,

Psalm 111.10.
The fear of the Lord, is the beginning of wisdom.
Matthew 16.26.
What is a man profited, if he gain the whole world,
and lose his own soul.
1 Timothy 1.15.
Jesus Christ came into the world to save
sinners, of whom I am chief.
Matthew 6.6.
Enter into thy closet, and when thou hast shut thy door,
pray to thy Father which is in secret.

---

8. I.e., his children.

Ecclesiastes 12.14.
God shall bring every work into judgment, with every
secret thing.
Ephesians 5.25.
Put away lying, speak everyone the truth.
Psalm 138.6.
The Lord hath respect unto the lowly, but the proud
He knows afar off.
Romans 12.17, 19.
Recompense to no one evil for evil. Dearly beloved,
avenge not yourselves.
Nehemiah 13.18.
They bring wrath upon Israel, by profaning the Sabbath.

"A Jewish treatise quoted by Wagenseil,[9] tells us, that among the Jews, when a child began to speak, the father was bound to teach him that verse: Deuteronomy 33.4, 'Moses commanded us a Law, even the inheritance of the Congregation of Jacob.' Oh! let me betimes make my children acquainted with the Law which our blessed Jesus has commanded us! 'Tis the best inheritance I can derive unto them.

VI. "I would betimes cause my children to learn the Catechism.[1] In catechizing of them, I would break the answer into many lesser and proper questions; and by their answer to them, observe and quicken their understandings. I would bring every truth, into some duty and practice, and expect them to confess it, and consent unto it, and resolve upon it. As we go on in our catechizing, they shall, when they are able, turn to the proofs, and read them, and say to me, what they prove, and how. Then, I will take my times, to put nicer[2] and harder questions to them; and improve the times of conversation with my family (which every man ordinarily has or may have) for conferences on matters of religion.

VII. "Restless would I be, till I may be able to say of my children, 'Behold, they pray!' I would therefore teach them to pray. But after they have learned a form of prayer, I will press them, to proceed unto points which are not in their form. I will show them the state of their own souls; and on every stroke inquire of them, what they think ought now to be their prayer. I will direct them, that every morning they shall take one text or two out of the Sacred Scripture, and shape it into a desire, which they shall add unto their usual prayer. When they have heard a sermon, I will mention to them over again the main subject of it, and ask them thereupon, what they have now to pray for. I will charge them, with all possible cogency, to pray in secret; and often call upon them, 'Child, I hope, you don't forget my charge to you, about secret prayer: your crime is very great, if you do!'

VIII. "I would betimes do what I can, to beget a temper of benignity in my children, both towards one another, and towards all other people. I will instruct them how ready they should be to communicate unto others, a part of what they have; and they shall see, my encouragements, when they discover[3] a loving, a courteous, an helpful disposition. I will give them now and then a piece of money, for them with their own little hands to dispense unto the

---

9. Johann Christoph Wagenseil (1633–1705), German Christian Hebraist.
1. A set of questions and answers concerning the principles of religious faith.
2. More subtle.
3. Disclose.

poor. Yea, if anyone has hurt them, or vexed them, I will not only forbid them all revenge, but also oblige them to do a kindness as soon as may be to the vexatious person. All coarseness of language or carriage in them, I will discountenance it.

IX. "I would be solicitious to have my children expert, not only at reading handsomely, but also at writing a fair hand. I will then assign them such books to read, as I may judge most agreeable and profitable; obliging them to give me some account of what they read; but keep a strict eye upon them, that they don't stumble on the devil's library, and poison themselves with foolish romances, or novels, or plays, or songs, or jests that are not convenient.[4] I will set them also, to write out such things, as may be of the greatest benefit unto them; and they shall have their blank books, neatly kept on purpose, to enter such passages as I advise them to. I will particularly require them now and then, to write a prayer of their own composing, and bring it unto me; that so I may discern, what sense they have of their own everlasting interests.

X. "I wish that my children may as soon as may be, feel the principles of reason and honor, working in them, and that I may carry on their education, very much upon those principles. Therefore, first, I will wholly avoid, that harsh, fierce, crabbed usage of the children, that would make them tremble, and abhor to come unto my presence. I will so use them, that they shall fear to offend me, and yet mightily love to see me, and be glad of my coming home, if I have been abroad at any time. I would have it looked upon as a severe and awful punishment for a crime in the family, to be forbidden for a while to come into my presence. I would raise in them, an high opinion of their father's love to them, and of his being better able to judge what is good for them, than they are for themselves. I would bring them to believe, 'tis best for them to be and do as I would have them. Hereupon I would continually magnify the matter to them, what a brave thing 'tis to know the things that are excellent; and more brave to do the things that are virtuous. I would have them to propose it as a reward of their well-doing at any time, I will now go to my father, and he will teach me something that I was never taught before. I would have them afraid of doing any base thing, from an horror of the baseness in it. My first animadversion on a lesser fault in them shall be a surprise, a wonder, vehemently expressed before them, that ever they should be guilty of doing so foolishly; a vehement belief, that they will never do the like again; a weeping resolution in them, that they will not. I will never dispense a blow, except it be for an atrocious crime, or for a lesser fault obstinately persisted in; either for an enormity, or for an obstinacy. I would ever proportion chastisements unto miscarriages; not smite bitterly for a very small piece of childishness, and only frown a little for some real wickedness. Nor shall my chastisements ever by dispensed in a passion and a fury; but with them, I will first show them the command of God, by transgressing whereof they have displeased me. The slavish, raving, fighting way of education too commonly used, I look upon it, as a considerable article in the wrath and curse of God, upon a miserable world.

XI. "As soon as we can, we'll get up to yet higher principles. I will often tell the children, what cause they have to love a glorious Christ, Who has died for them. And, how much He will be well-pleased with their well-doing. And,

4. Suitable.

what a noble thing 'tis to follow His example; which example I will describe unto them. I will often tell them, that the eye of God is upon them; the great God knows all they do, and hears all they speak. I will often tell them, that there will be a time, when they must appear before the Judgment Seat of the Holy Lord; and they must now do nothing, that may then be a grief and shame unto them. I will set before them, the delights of that Heaven that is prepared for pious children; and the torments of that Hell that is prepared of old, for naughty ones. I will inform them, of the good offices which the good angels do for little ones that have the fear of God, and are afraid of sin. And, how the devils tempt them to do ill things; how they hearken to the devils, and are like them, when they do such things; and what mischiefs the devils may get leave to do them in this world, and what a sad thing 'twill be, to be among the devils in the Place of Dragons.[5] I will cry to God, that He will make them feel the power of these principles.

XII. "When the children are of a fit age for it, I will sometimes closet[6] them; have them with me alone; talk with them about the state of their souls; their experiences, their proficiencies, their temptations; obtain their declared consent unto every stroke in the Covenant of Grace;[7] and then pray with them, and weep unto the Lord for His grace, to be bestowed upon them, and make them witnesses of the agony with which I am travailing to see the image of Christ formed in them. Certainly, they'll never forget such actions!

XIII. "I would be very watchful and cautious, about the companions of my children. I will be very inquisitive, what company they keep; if they are in hazard of being ensnared by any vicious company, I will earnestly pull them out of it, as brands out of the burning. I will find out, and procure, laudable companions for them.

XIV. "As in catechizing the children, so in the repetition of the public sermons, I would use this method. I will put every truth into a question, to be answered still, with Yes, or No. By this method, I hope to awaken their attention as well as enlighten their understanding. And thus I shall have an opportunity to ask, 'Do you desire such or such a grace of God?' and the like. Yea, I may have opportunity to demand, and perhaps to obtain their early, and frequent, and why not sincere?, consent unto the glorious articles of the New Covenant. The Spirit of Grace may fall upon them in this action; and they may be seized by Him, and held as His temples, through eternal ages.

XV. "When a Day of Humiliation[8] arrives, I will make them know the meaning of the day. And after time given them to consider of it, I will order them to tell me: what special afflictions they had met withal? And, what good they hope to get by those afflictions? On a Day of Thanksgiving, they shall also be made to know the intent of the day. And after consideration, they shall tell me, what mercies of God unto them they take special notice of: And, what duties to God, they confess and resolve, under such obligations? Indeed, for something of this importance, to be pursued in my conversation with the children, I would not confine myself unto the solemn days, which may occur too seldom for it. Very particularly, when the birthdays of the children anniversarily arrive to any of them, I would then take them aside, and mind them of the

5. I.e., in hell, with the dragon Satan.
6. I.e., meet with them in the privacy of his study.
7. The original covenant or agreement God made with Adam is referred to as the Covenant of Works; the covenant God made with humanity after the Fall is

called the Covenant of Grace. Puritans also referred to this as the New Covenant as opposed to the Old.
8. I.e, a day in which the child knows he has offended God.

age, which having obtained help from God they are come unto; how thankful they should be for the mercies of God, which they have hitherto lived upon; how fruitful they should be in all goodness, that so they may still enjoy their mercies. And I would inquire of them, whether they have ever yet begun to mind the work which God sent them into the world upon; how far they understand the work; and what good strokes they have struck it; and, how they design to spend the rest of their time, if God still continue them in the world.

XVI. "When the children are in any trouble, as, if they are sick, or pained, I will take advantage therefrom, to set before them the evil of sin, which brings all our trouble; and how fearful a thing it will be to be cast among the damned, who are in easeless and endless trouble. I will set before them the benefit of an interest in a Christ, by which their trouble will be sanctified unto them, and they will be prepared for death, and for fullness of joy in an happy eternity after death.

XVII. "I incline, that among all the points of a polite education which I would endeavor for my children, they may each of them, the daughters as well as the sons, have so much insight into some skill, which lies in the way of gain (the limners, or the scriveners', or the apothecaries', or some other mystery,[9] to which their own inclination may most carry them) that they may be able to subsist themselves, and get something of a livelihood, in case the Providence of God should bring them into necessities. Why not they as well as Paul the Tent-Maker![1] The children of the best fashion may have occasion to bless the parents, that make such a provision for them! The Jews have a saying; 'tis worth my remembering it: *Quicunque filium suum non docet opificium, perinde est ac si eum doceret latrocinium.*[2]

XVIII. "As soon as ever I can, I would make my children apprehensive of the main end, for which they are to live; that so they may as soon as may be, begin to live; and their youth not be nothing but vanity. I would show them, that their main end must be, to acknowledge the great God, and His glorious Christ; and bring others to acknowledge Him: and that they are never wise nor well, but when they are doing so. I would show them, what the acknowledgments are, and how they are to be made. I would make them able to answer the grand question, why they live; and what is the end of the actions that fill their lives? Teach them, how their Creator and Redeemer is to be obeyed in everything; and, how everything is to be done in obedience to Him; teach them, how even their diversions, and their ornaments,[3] and the tasks of their education must all be to fit them for the further service of Him, to whom I have devoted them; and how in these also, His commandments must be the rule of all they do. I would sometimes therefore surprise them with an inquiry, 'Child, what is this for? Give me a good account, why you do it?' How comfortably shall I see them walking in the light, if I may bring them wisely to answer this inquiry; and what children of the light?

XIX. "I would oblige the children, to retire sometimes, and ponder on that question: 'What shall I wish to have done, if I were now a-dying?' And report unto me, their own answer to the question; of which I would then take advantage, to inculcate the lessons of godliness upon them. I would also direct them

---

9. Special skill or craft. "Limners": portrait painters. "Scriveners": those employed to write letters and documents. "Apothecaries": druggists.
1. Acts 18.3. The apostle Paul was a tent maker by trade.
2. He who does not teach his son a craft, teaches him theft (Latin).
3. I.e., attire.

and oblige them, at a proper time for it, seriously to realize, their own appearance before the awful Judgment Seat of the Lord Jesus Christ, and consider what they have to plead, that they may not be sent away into everlasting punishment; what they have to plead, that they may be admitted into the Holy City. I would instruct them, what plea to prepare; first, show them, how to get a part in the righteousness of Him that is to be their Judge; by receiving it with a thankful faith, as the gift of infinite grace unto the distressed and unworthy sinner: then, show them how to prove that their faith is not a counterfeit, by their continual endeavor to please Him in all things, who is to be their Judge, and to serve His Kingdom and interest in the world. And I would charge them, to make this preparation.

XX. "If I live to see the children marriageable, I would, before I consult with Heaven and earth for their best accommodation in the married state, endeavor the espousal of their souls unto their only Savior. I would as plainly, and as fully as I can, propose unto them, the terms on which the glorious Redeemer would espouse them to Himself, in righteousness and judgment, and favor, and mercies forever; and solicit their consent unto His proposals and overtures. Then would I go on, to do what may be expected from a tender parent for them, in their temporal circumstances."

From these parental resolutions, how naturally, how reasonably may we pass on to say:

"Children, the Fifth Commandment[4] confirms all your other numberless and powerful obligations, often to devise, 'Wherein may I be a blessing to my parents?' Ingenuity[5] would make this the very top of your ambition; to be a credit, and a comfort of your parents; to sweeten, and if it may be, to lengthen the lives of those, from whom, under God, you have received your lives. And God the Rewarder usually gives it, even in this life, a most observable recompense. But it is possible, you may be the happy instruments of more than a little good unto the souls of your parents (will you think, how!); yea, though they should be pious parents, you may by some exquisite methods, be the instruments of their growth in piety, and in preparation for the Heavenly world. O thrice and four times happy children! Among the Arabians, a father sometimes takes his name from an eminent son, as well as a son from his reputed father. A man is called with an Abu as well as an Ebn. Verily, a son may be such a blessing to his father that the best surname for the glad father would be, the father of such an one."

Masters, yea, and mistresses too, must have their devices, how to do good unto their servants; how to make them the servants of Christ, and the children of God. God whom you must remember to be your Master in Heaven, has brought them, and put them into your hands. Who can tell what good He has brought them for? How if they should be the Elect of God, fetched from Africa, or the Indies, and brought into your families, on purpose, that by the means of their being there, they may be brought home unto the Shepherd of Souls? Oh! that the souls of our slaves, were of more account with us! that we gave a better demonstration that we despise not our own souls, by doing what we can for the souls of our slaves, and not using them as if they had no souls! that the poor slaves and blacks, which live with us, may by our means be made the candidates of the Heavenly life! How can we pretend unto Christianity,

4. "Honor thy father and thy mother: that thy days may be long upon the land which the Lord thy God giveth thee" (Exodus 20.12).
5. Intelligence, thoughtfulness.

when we do no more to Christianize our slaves! Verily, you must give an account unto God, concerning them. If they be lost, through your negligence, what answer can you make unto God the Judge of all! Methinks, common principles of gratitude should incline you, to study the happiness of those, by whose obsequious labors, your lives are so much accommodated. Certainly, they would be the better servants to you, the more faithful, the more honest, the more industrious, and submissive servants to you, for your bringing them into the service of your Common Lord.

But if any servant of God may be so honored by Him as to be made the successful instrument, of obtaining from a British Parliament, an act for the Christianizing of the slaves in the plantations; then it may be hoped, something more may be done, than has yet been done, that the blood of souls may not be found in the skirts of our nation: a controversy of Heaven with our colonies may be removed, and prosperity may be restored; or, however the honorable instrument, will have unspeakable peace and joy, in the remembrance of his endeavors. In the meantime, the slave trade is a spectacle that shocks humanity.

> The harmless natives basely they trepan.[6]
> And barter baubles for the souls of men.
> The wretches they to Christian climes bring o'er
> To serve worse heathens than they did before.

*   *   *

I will go on to say: Be glad of opportunities to do good in your neighborhood: yea, look out for them, lay hold on them, with a rapturous assiduity. Be sorry for all the bad circumstances of any neighbor, that bespeak you doing of good unto him. Yet, be glad, if any one tell you of them. Thank him who tells you, as having therein done you a very great civility. Let him know, that he could not by anything have more gratified you. Any civility that you can show, by lending, by watching, by—all the methods of courtesy; show it; and be glad you can show it. Show it, and give a pleasant countenance (*cum munere vultum*) in the showing of it. Let your wisdom cause your face always to shine; look, not with a cloudy but a serene and shining face, upon your neighbors; and shed the rays of your courtesy upon them, with such affiability, that they may see they are welcome to all you can do for them. Yea, stay not until you are told of opportunities to do good. Inquire after them; let the inquiry be solicitous, be unwearied. The incomparable pleasure, is worth an inquiry.

There was a generous pagan, who counted a day lost, if he had obliged nobody in the day. *Amici, diem perdidi!*[7] O Christian, let us try whether we can't attain to do something, for some neighbor or other, every day that comes over our head. Some do so; and with a better spirit, than ever Titus Vespasian[8] was acted withal. Thrice in the Scriptures, we find the good angels rejoicing: 'tis always at the good of others. To rejoice in the good of others, and most of all in doing of good unto them, 'tis angelical goodness.

In moving for the devices of good neighborhood, a principal motion which I have to make, is, that you consult the spiritual interests of your neighborhood, as well as the temporal. Be concerned, lest the deceitfulness of sin undo

---

6. Entrap, ensnare.
7. Friends, I have lost the day! (Latin).

8. A popular emperor of Rome (69–79), who built the Baths and the Colosseum and was loved by the people.

any of the neighbors. If there be any idle persons among them, I beseech you, cure them of their idleness; don't nourish 'em and harden 'em in that; but find employment for them. Find 'em work; set 'em to work; keep 'em to work. Then, as much of your other bounty to them, as you please.

If any children in the neighborhood, are under no education, don't allow 'em to continue so. Let care be taken, that they may be better educated; and be taught to read; and be taught their catechism; and the truths and ways of their only Savior.

Once more. If any in the neighborhood, are taking to bad courses, lovingly and faithfully admonish them. If any in the neighborhood are enemies to their own welfare, or their families; prudently dispense your admonitions unto them. If there are any prayerless families, never leave off entreating and exhorting of them, 'til you have persuaded them, to set up the worship of God. If there be any service of God, or of His people, to which any one may need to be excited, give him a tender excitation. Whatever snare you see any one in, be so kind, as to tell him of his danger to be ensnared, and save him from it. By putting of good books into the hands of your neighbors, and gaining of them a promise to read the books, who can tell, what good you may do unto them! It is possible, you may in this way, with ingenuity, and with efficacy, administer those reproofs, which you may owe unto such neighbors, as are to be reproved for their miscarriages. The books will balk nothing, that is to be said, on the subjects, that you would have the neighbors advised upon.

Finally. If there be any base houses, which threaten to debauch, and poison, and confound the neighborhood, let your charity to your neighbors, make you do all you can, for the suppression of them.

That my Proposal to do good in the neighborhood, and as a neighbor, may be more fully formed and followed; I will conclude it, with minding you, that a world of self-denial is to be exercised in the execution of it. You must be armed against selfishness, all selfish and squinting intentions, in your generous resolutions. You shall see how my demands will grow upon you.

First. You must not think of making the good you do, a pouring of water into a pump, to draw out something for yourselves. This might be the meaning of our Savior's direction: Lend, hoping for nothing again.[9] To lend a thing, properly is to hope that we shall receive it again. But this probably refers to the, Ερανισμος, or collation, usual among the ancients, whereof we find many monuments and mentions in antiquity. If any man by burnings, or shipwrecks or other disasters, had lost his estate, his friends did use to lend him considerable sums of money, to be repaid, not at a certain day, but when he should find himself able to repay it, without inconvenience. Now, they were so cunning, that they would rarely lend upon such disasters, unto any but such, as they had hope, would recover out of their present impoverishment, and not only repay them their money, but also Αντερανιζειν requite their kindness, if ever there should be need of it. The thing required by our Savior is, Do good unto such as you are never like to be the better for.[1]

* * *

9. "But love ye your enemies, and do good, and lend, hoping for nothing again; and your reward shall be great" (Luke 6.35).

1. "And if ye lend to them of whom ye hope to receive, what thank have ye?" (Luke 6.34).

In the primitive times of Christianity there was much use made of a saying, which they ascribed unto Matthias the Apostle:[2] Εαν εκλεκτου Τειτων αμαρτηση, ημαρτεν ο εκλεκτος. If the neighbor of an elect, or godly, man sin, the godly man himself has also sinned. The obligations of neighbors watchfully to admonish one another, were what that saying intended. Oh! how much may Christians associated in religious combinations do by watchful and faithful admonitions, to prevent being partakers in other men's sins!

The man, that shall produce, and promote such societies will do an unknown deal of good in the neighborhood.

And so will he, that shall help forward another sort of Societies, namely, those of Young Men Associated.

These duly managed, have been incomparable nurseries to the churches, where the faithful pastors have countenanced them. Young men are hereby preserved from very many temptations, rescued from the paths of the Destroyer, confirmed in the right ways of the Lord, and prepared mightily for such religious exercises as will be expected from them, when they come themselves to be householders.

I will make a tender of some orders, which have been observed in some such Societies.

I. Let there be two hours at a time set apart; and, let there be two prayers made by the members of the Society, in their turns; between which, let a sermon be repeated; and there may be the singing of a Psalm annexed.

II. Let all the members of the Society, resolve to be charitably watchful over one another: never to divulge one another's infirmities; always to inform and advise one another of everything that may appear to call for an admonition, and to take it kindly when they are admonished.

III. Let all who are to be admitted as members of the Society, be accompanied by two or three of the rest, unto the minister of the place, that they may receive his holy counsels, and charges, and that everything may be done with his approbation; and so let their names be added unto the roll.

IV. If any person thus enrolled among them, fall into a scandalous iniquity, let the rebukes of the Society be dispensed unto him; and let them forbid him to come any more among them, until he bring suitable expressions and evidences of repentance with him.

V. Let the list be once a quarter called over; and then, if it be observed, that any of the Society have much absented themselves, let there be some sent unto them, to inquire the reason of the absence; and if no reason be given, but such as intimates an apostasy from good beginnings, let them upon obstinacy, after loving and faithful admonitions, be obliterated.[3]

VI. Once in three months, let there be, if need be, a collection, out of which the necessary charges of the Society shall be defrayed, and the rest be employed upon such pious uses, as may be agreed upon.

VII. Once in two months, let the whole time of the meeting, be devoted unto supplications, for the conversation and salvation of the rising generation in the land; and particularly, for the success of the Gospel, in that congregation, whereto the Society does belong.

VIII. Let the whole Society, be exceedingly careful, that their discourse

---

2. After Judas betrayed Christ, the apostles chose Matthias to replace him (Acts 1.23–26). Mather uses the Greek because his source is the texts of early church founders.

3. I.e., from the roll of members.

while they are together, after the other services of religion are over, have nothing in it, that shall have any taint of backbiting or vanity, or the least relation to the affairs of government, or to things which do not concern them, and do not serve the interests of holiness in their own conversation. But let their discourse be wholly on the matters of religion; and those also, not the disputable and controversial matters, but the points of practical piety. They may propose questions upon this intention, and everyone in an orderly manner, take his liberty to answer them. Or, they may go through the catechism, and one at one time, another at another, hear all the rest recite the answers thereof. Or, they may otherwise be directed by their pastors, to spend their time together profitably.

IX. Let every person in the Society, look upon it, as a special task incumbent on him, to look out, for some other hopeful young man, and use all proper pains, to engage him in the resolutions of godliness, until he also shall be joined unto the Society. And when a Society shall in this way be increased unto a fit number, let it swarm into more; who may hold an useful correspondence with one another.

The man, who shall be the instrument of setting up such a Society in a place, cannot comprehend, unto what a long and rich train of good consequences, he is become instrumental.

And they that shall in such a Society together carry on the duties of Christianity, and the praises of a glorious Christ, will have upon themselves, a blessed symptom, that they shall be together associated in the Heavenly City, and in the blessedness that shall never have an end.

1710

SARAH KEMBLE KNIGHT
1666–1727

Like a number of the classics of early American literature, *The Private Journal* of Mrs. Sarah Kemble Knight was not published until the nineteenth century; it at once found an enthusiastic audience eager to read documents of social history from the American past. Knight's shorthand journal, as transcribed and edited by Theodore Dwight, provided a healthy antidote to the soul-searching journals of Knight's contemporaries, and revealed an earthiness and ready wit, an appetite for living, and a frankness not often found in colonial literature. Knight was a keen observer of provincial America and a woman who did not suffer fools gladly. Something of Knight's tough-mindedness was undoubtedly the result of the fact that she had to make her way in the world with considerable ingenuity and that early on in her life she displayed a gift for managing other people's affairs.

Knight was the daughter of the Boston merchant Thomas Kemble and Elizabeth Trerice of Charlestown, Massachusetts. She married a man much older who was a sometime sea captain and London agent for an American company. After her father died in 1689, Knight assumed full responsibility for being head of the household. While her husband was abroad, she kept a boardinghouse and taught school (hence the title "Madam Knight") and supposedly could number Benjamin Franklin and the Mather children among her pupils. Knight taught penmanship, made copies of court records, and wrote letters for people having business with the courts.

She trained herself in the ways of the law and had a reputation for settling estates with skill. In 1704, while her husband was abroad, Knight took on herself the task of settling her cousin Caleb Trowbridge's estate on behalf of his young widow. Knight set out for New Haven, Connecticut, on Monday, October 2, 1704. From there she went to New York and returned home to Boston in March 1705. It was a hazardous journey, one not undertaken lightly in those years and almost unprecedented for a woman traveling alone.

In 1706 Knight apparently became a widow; at least her husband is not mentioned again after that date. In 1714 she followed her married daughter to Connecticut. Her last years were spent in New London, where she ran an inn and, true to her genius, made shrewd investments in property.

The text used here is from *The Journal of Madame Knight*, edited by George P. Winship (1920; reprinted 1935).

From The Private Journal of a Journey from Boston to New York

* * *

Tuesday, October the Third

About 8 in the morning, I with the post proceeded forward without observing anything remarkable; and about two, afternoon, arrived at the post's second stage,[1] where the western post met him and exchanged letters. Here, having called for something to eat, the woman brought in a twisted thing like a cable, but something[2] whiter; and laying it on the board, tugged for life to bring it into a capacity to spread; which having with great pains accomplished, she served in a dish of pork and cabbage, I suppose the remains of dinner. The sauce was of a deep purple, which I thought was boiled in her dye kettle; the bread was Indian and everything on the table service agreeable to these. I, being hungry, got a little down; but my stomach was soon cloyed, and what cabbage I swallowed served me for a cud the whole day after.

Having here discharged the ordinary[3] for self and guide (as I understood was the custom), about three, afternoon, went on with my third guide, who rode very hard; and having crossed Providence ferry, we come to a river which they generally ride through. But I dare not venture; so the post got a lad and canoe to carry me to t'other side, and he rid through and led my horse. The canoe was very small and shallow, so that when we were in, she seemed ready to take in water, which greatly terrified me, and caused me to be very circumspect, sitting with my hands fast on each side, my eyes steady, not daring so much as to lodge my tongue a hair's breadth more on one side of my mouth than t'other nor so much as think on Lot's wife,[4] for a wry thought would have overset our wherry:[5] but was soon put out of this pain, by feeling the canoe on shore, which I as soon almost saluted with my feet; and rewarding my sculler, again mounted and made the best of our way forwards. The road here was very even and the day pleasant, it being now near sunset. But the post told me we had near 14 miles to ride to the next stage (where we were to lodge). I asked him

---

1. A stopping place where mail was left from the previous stage of a journey and then forwarded to the next. People who traveled "post" accompanied the driver to the next stop.
2. Somewhat.
3. Paid for the meal; an "ordinary" is a meal served at an inn or public house.
4. I.e., not daring to look back. When Sodom was being destroyed, Lot's wife looked back and was turned into a pillar of salt (Genesis 19.26).
5. Small boat.

of the rest of the road, foreseeing we must travail in the night. He told me there was a bad river we were to ride through, which was so very fierce a horse could sometimes hardly stem it: but it was but narrow, and we should soon be over. I cannot express the concern of mind this relation set me in: no thoughts but those of the dangerous river could entertain my imagination, and they were as formidable as various, still tormenting me with blackest ideas of my approaching fate—sometimes seeing myself drowning, otherwhiles drowned, and at the best, like a holy sister just come out of a spiritual bath in dripping garments.

Now was the glorious luminary, with his swift coursers arrived at his stage,[6] leaving poor me with the rest of this part of the lower world in darkness, with which we were soon surrounded. The only glimmering we now had was from the spangled skies, whose imperfect reflections rendered every object formidable. Each lifeless trunk, with its shattered limbs, appeared an armed enemy; and every little stump like a ravenous devourer. Nor could I so much as discern my guide, when at any distance, which added to the terror.

Thus, absolutely lost in thought, and dying with the very thoughts of drowning, I come up with the post, who I did not see till even with his horse: he told me he stopped for me; and we rode on very deliberately a few paces, when we entered a thicket of trees and shrubs, and I perceived by the horse's going, we were on the descent of a hill, which, as we come nearer the bottom, 'twas totally dark with the trees that surrounded it. But I knew by the going of the horse we had entered the water, which my guide told me was the hazardous river he had told me of; and he, riding up close to my side, bid me not fear— we should be over immediately. I now rallied all the courage I was mistress of, knowing that I must either venture my fate of drowning, or be left like the children in the wood.[7] So, as the post bid me, I gave reins to my nag; and sitting as steady as just before in the canoe, in a few minutes got safe to the other side, which he told me was the Narragansett country.

Here we found great difficulty in travailing, the way being very narrow, and on each side the trees and bushes gave us very unpleasant welcomes with their branches and boughs, which we could not avoid, it being so exceeding dark. My guide, as before so now, put on harder than I, with my weary bones, could follow; so left me and the way behind him. Now returned my distressed apprehensions of the place where I was: the dolesome woods, my company next to none, going I knew not whither, and encompassed with terrifying darkness; the least of which was enough to startle a more masculine courage. Added to which the reflections, as in the afternoon of the day that my call[8] was very questionable, which, till then I had not so prudently as I ought considered. Now, coming to the foot of a hill, I found great difficulty in ascending; but being got to the top, was there amply recompensed with the friendly appearance of the kind conductress of the night, just then advancing above the horizontal line. The raptures which the sight of that fair planet produced in me, caused me, for the moment, to forget my present weariness and past toils; and inspired me for most of the remaining way with very diverting thoughts, some of which, with the other occurrences of the day, I reserved to note down

6. I.e., it was night; in Greek mythology the sun god Apollo rides across the sky in a chariot. "Coursers": horses.
7. The phrase "children in the wood" or "babes in the

wood" refers to a ballad in which two children are taken out to be murdered and instead are left in the woods where they die during the night.
8. Mission.

when I should come to my stage. My thoughts on the sight of the moon were
to this purpose:

> Fair Cynthia,[9] all the homage that I may
> Unto a creature, unto thee I pay;
> In lonesome woods to meet so kind a guide,
> To me's more worth than all the world beside.
> Some joy I feel just now, when safe got o'er
> Yon surly river to this rugged shore,
> Deeming rough welcomes from these clownish trees
> Better than lodgings with Nereides.[1]
> Yet swelling fears surprise; all dark appears—
> Nothing but light can dissipate those fears.
> My fainting vitals can't lend strength to say,
> But softly whisper, O I wish 'twere day.
> The murmur hardly warmed the ambient air,
> E're thy bright aspect rescues from despair:
> Makes the old hag[2] her sable mantle loose,
> And a bright joy does through my soul diffuse.
> The boisterous trees now lend a passage free,
> And pleasant prospects thou giv'st light to see.

From hence we kept on, with more ease than before: the way being smooth
and even, the night warm and serene, and the tall and thick trees at a distance,
especially when the moon glared light through the branches, filled my imagination with the pleasant delusion of a sumptuous city, filled with famous
buildings and churches, with their spiring steeples, balconies, galleries and I
know not what: grandeurs which I had heard of, and which the stories of
foreign countries had given me the idea of.

> Here stood a lofty church—there is a steeple,
> And there the grand parade—O see the people!
> That famous castle there, were I but nigh,
> To see the mote and bridge and walls so high—
> They're very fine! says my deluded eye.

Being thus agreeably entertained without a thought of anything but thoughts
themselves, I on a sudden was roused from these pleasing imaginations, by the
post's sounding his horn, which assured me he was arrived at the stage, where
we were to lodge: and that music was then most musical and agreeable to me.

Being come to Mr. Havens', I was very civilly received, and courteously
entertained, in a clean comfortable house; and the good woman was very
active in helping off my riding clothes, and then asked what I would eat. I told
her I had some chocolate, if she would prepare it; which with the help of some
milk, and a little clean brass kettle, she soon effected to my satisfaction. I then
betook me to my apartment, which was a little room parted from the kitchen
by a single board partition; where, after I had noted the occurrences of the past
day, I went to bed, which, though pretty hard, yet neat and handsome. But I
could get no sleep, because of the clamor of some of the town topers in next
room, who were entered into strong debate concerning the signification of the
name of their country (viz.) Narragansett. One said it was named so by the

9. The moon personified.   2. I.e., night.
1. Sea nymphs, daughters of Nereus.

Indians, because there grew a brier there, of a prodigious height and bigness, the like hardly ever known, called by the Indians narragansett; and quotes an Indian of so barbarous a name for his author, that I could not write it. His antagonist replied no—it was from a spring it had its name, which he well knew where it was, which was extreme cold in summer, and as hot as could be imagined in the winter, which was much resorted to by the natives, and by them called Narragansett (hot and cold), and that was the original of their place's name—with a thousand impertinences not worth notice, which he uttered with such a roaring voice and thundering blows with the fist of wickedness on the table, that it pierced my very head. I heartily fretted, and wished 'um tongue-tied; but with as little success as a friend of mine once, who was (as she said) kept a whole night awake, on a journey, by a country left. and a sergeant, insigne[3] and a deacon, contriving how to bring a triangle into a square. They kept calling for t'other gill,[4] which while they were swallowing, was some intermission; but presently, like oil to fire, increased the flame. I set my candle on a chest by the bed side, and setting up, fell to my old way of composing my resentments, in the following manner:

> I ask thy aid, O potent rum!
> To charm these wrangling topers dumb.
> Thou hast their giddy brains possessed—
> The man confounded with the beast—
> And I, poor I, can get no rest.
> Intoxicate them with thy fumes:
> O still their tongues' till morning comes!

And I know not but my wishes took effect; for the dispute soon ended with t'other dram; and so good night! * * *

Friday, October the Sixth

I got up very early, in order to hire somebody to go with me to New Haven, being in great perplexity at the thoughts of proceeding alone; which my most hospitable entertainer observing, himself went, and soon returned with a young gentleman of the town, who he could confide in to go with me; and about eight this morning, with Mr. Joshua Wheeler my new guide, taking leave of this worthy gentleman, we advanced on towards Saybrook. The roads all along this way are very bad, encumbered with rocks and mountainous passages, which were very disagreeable to my tired carcass; but we went on with a moderate pace which made the journey more pleasant. But after about eight miles riding, in going over a bridge under which the river run very swift, my horse stumbled, and very narrowly escaped falling over into the water; which extremely frightened me. But through God's goodness I met with no harm, and mounting again, in about half a mile's riding, come to an ordinary,[5] were well entertained by a woman of about seventy and vantage,[6] but of as sound intellectuals as one of seventeen. She entertained Mr. Wheeler with some passages of a wedding awhile ago at a place hard by, the bride's

---

3. I.e., ensigne, lowest grade of commissioned officer.
"Left": lieutenant.
4. A measure of wine.

5. An inn; a place where meals are served.
6. I.e., about seventy or more.

groom being about her age or something above, saying his children was dreadfully against their father's marrying, which she condemned them extremely
for.

From hence we went pretty briskly forward, and arrived at Saybrook ferry
about two of the clock afternoon; and crossing it, we called at an inn to bait[7]
(foreseeing we should not have such another opportunity till we come to
Killingsworth). Landlady come in, with her hair about her ears, and hands at
full pay[8] scratching. She told us she had some mutton which she would broil,
which I was glad to hear; but I suppose forgot to wash her scratches; in a little
time she brought it in; but it being pickled, and my guide said it smelled strong
of head sauce,[9] we left it, and paid sixpence a piece for our dinners, which
was only smell.

So we put forward with all speed, and about seven at night come to Killingsworth, and were tolerably well with travelers' fare, and lodged there that night.

From *December the Sixth*

※   ※   ※

The city of New York is a pleasant, well-compacted place, situated on a
commodious river which is a fine harbor for shipping. The buildings brick
generally, very stately and high, though not altogether like ours in Boston.
The bricks in some of the houses are of divers colors and laid in checkers,
being glazed look very agreeable. The inside of them are neat to admiration,
the wooden work, for only the walls are plastered, and the sumers and gist[1] are
planed and kept very white scowered as so is all the partitions if made of
boards. The fireplaces have no jambs (as ours have) but the backs run flush
with the walls, and the hearth is of tiles and is as far out into the room at the
ends as before the fire, which is generally five foot in the lower rooms, and the
piece over where the mantle tree should be is made as ours with joiners' work,[2]
and as I suppose is fastened to iron rods inside. The house where the vendue[3]
was, had chimney corners like ours, and they and the hearths were laid with
the finest tile that I ever see, and the staircases laid all with white tile which is
ever clean, and so are the walls of the kitchen which had a brick floor. They
were making great preparations to receive their governor, Lord Cornbury from
the Jerseys,[4] and for that end raised the militia to guard him on shore to the
fort.

They are generally of the Church of England and have a New England
gentleman for their minister, and a very fine church set out with all customary
requisites. There are also a Dutch and divers conventicles as they call them,
viz. Baptist, Quakers, etc. They are not strict in keeping the Sabbath as in
Boston and other places where I had been, but seem to deal with great exactness as far as I see or deal with. They are sociable to one another and courteous
and civil to strangers and fare well in their houses. The English go very fashionable in their dress. But the Dutch, especially the middling sort, differ from
our women, in their habit go loose, wear French muchets which are like a cap
and a headband in one, leaving their ears bare, which are set out with jewels

7. Refresh themselves and rest the horses.
8. I.e., busily.
9. Cheese sauce.
1. Main beams and joists.
2. Joiners were craftsmen who constructed things by
joining pieces of wood together; their work was more
finished than a carpenter's.
3. Auction.
4. Edward Hyde (1661–1723), royal governor of New
York and New Jersey from 1702 to 1708.

of a large size and many in number. And their fingers hooped with rings, some with large stones in them of many colors as were their pendants in their ears, which you should see very old women wear as well as young.

They have vendues very frequently and make their earnings very well by them, for they treat with good liquor liberally, and the customers drink as liberally and generally pay for't as well, by paying for that which they bid up briskly for, after the sack[5] has gone plentifully about, though sometimes good penny worths' are got there. Their diversions in the winter is riding sleighs about three or four miles out of town, where they have houses of entertainment at a place called the Bowery, and some go to friends' houses who handsomely treat them. Mr. Burroughs carried his spouse and daughter and myself out to one Madame Dowes, a gentlewoman that lived at a farm house, who gave us a handsome entertainment of five or six dishes and choice beer and metheglin,[6] cider, etc. all which she said was the produce of her farm. I believe we met 50 or 60 sleighs that day—they fly with great swiftness and some are so furious that they'll turn out of the path for none except a loaden cart. Nor do they spare for any diversion the place affords, and sociable to a degree, their tables being as free to their neighbors as to themselves.

Having here transacted the affair I went upon and some other that fell in the way, after about a fortnight's stay there I left New York with no little regret[.] * * *

January the Sixth

Being now well recruited and fit for business I discoursed the person I was concerned with, that we might finish in order to my return to Boston. They delayed as they had hitherto done hoping to tire my patience. But I was resolute to stay and see an end of the matter let it be never so much to my disadvantage—So January 9th they come again and promise the Wednesday following to go through with the distribution of the estate which they delayed till Thursday and then come with new amusements.[7] But at length by the mediation of that holy good gentleman, the Rev. Mr. James Pierpont, the minister of New Haven, and with the advice and assistance of other our good friends we come to an accommodation and distribution, which having finished though not till February, the man that waited on me to York taking the charge of me I set out for Boston. We went from New Haven upon the ice (the ferry being not passable thereby) and the Rev. Mr. Pierpont with Madam Prout, cousin Trowbridge and divers others were taking leave, we went onward without anything remarkable till we come to New London and lodged again at Mr. Saltonstall's—and here I dismissed my guide, and my generous entertainer provided me Mr. Samuel Rogers of that place to go home with me—I stayed a day here longer than intended by the commands of the honorable Governor Winthrop to stay and take a supper with him whose wonderful civility I may not omit. The next morning I crossed the ferry to Groton, having had the honor of the company, of Madam Livingston (who is the governor's daughter) and Mary Christophers and divers others to the boat—and that night lodged at Stonington and had roast beef and pumpkin sauce for supper. The next night at Haven's and had roast fowl, and the next day we come to a river which by

5. Wine; specifically, white wine imported from Spain or the Canaries.

6. A spiced drink rather like mead.

7. I.e., trifles that caused further delays.

reason of the freshets coming down was swelled so high we feared it impassable and the rapid stream was very terrifying—However we must over and that in a small canoe. Mr. Rogers assuring me of his good conduct,[8] I after a stay of near an hour on the shore for consultation, went into the canoe, and Mr. Rogers paddled about 100 yards up the creek by the shore side, turned into the swift stream and dexterously steering her in a moment we come to the other side as swiftly passing as an arrow shot out of the bow by a strong arm. I stayed on the shore till he returned to fetch our horses, which he caused to swim over, himself bringing the furniture in the canoe. But it is past my skill to express the exceeding fright all their transactions formed in me. We were now in the colony of Massachusetts and taking lodgings at the first inn we come to, had a pretty difficult passage the next day which was the second of March by reason of the sloughy[9] ways then thawed by the sun. Here I met Capt. John Richards of Boston who was going home, so being very glad of his company we rode something harder than hitherto, and missing my way in going up a very steep hill, my horse dropped down under me as dead; this new surprise no little hurt me, meeting it just at the entrance into Dedham from whence we intended to reach home that night. But was now obliged to get another horse there and leave my own, resolving for Boston that night if possible. But in going over the causeway at Dedham the Bridge being overflowed by the high waters coming down, I very narrowly escaped falling over into the river horse and all which 'twas almost a miracle I did not—now it grew late in the afternoon and the people having very much discouraged us about the sloughy way which they said we should find very difficult and hazardous, it so wrought on me being tired and dispirited and disappointed of my desires of going home, that I agreed to lodge there that night which we did at the house of one Draper, and the next day being March 3d we got safe home to Boston, where I found my aged and tender mother and my dear and only child in good health with open arms ready to receive me, and my kind relations and friends flocking in to welcome me and hear the story of my transactions and travails, I having this day been five months from home and now I cannot fully express my joy and satisfaction. But desire sincerely to adore my great Benefactor for thus graciously carrying forth and returning in safety his unworthy handmaid.

1704–5   1825

8. Company for safekeeping   9. Muddy.

WILLIAM BYRD
1674–1744

William Byrd was the son of a wealthy Virginia planter, merchant, and Indian trader. His mother, Mary Horsmanden, came from a family of Royalist refugees. He was educated in England and spent the formative years of his life in London, where he was trained to assume the responsibility of managing his father's estate. Byrd was urbane and witty and traveled in sophisticated London circles. He loved the theater and numbered Wycherley and Congreve among his many friends. The diaries that he kept during his London years tell us little about his private thoughts but a great deal about his social life as a London man-about-town. Byrd recorded his habits of eating and prayer with the same detachment that compelled him to keep track of his whoring and his reading. The London theater, however, did not spoil Byrd's appetite for provincial pleasures. Back home in Virginia he seems to have delighted in the social life of Williamsburg even if the streets were dirty, the servants drunken, and country bumpkins present. He took great pleasure in "walking" his plantation.

More than half of Byrd's life was spent in England, but in 1726, after many years of alternation, he returned to Virginia to stay. In a letter written in that year to his friend Charles Boyle, earl of Orrery, Byrd described the satisfactions to be derived from the role of the Virginia planter:

> Besides the advantage of pure air, we abound in all kinds of provisions without expense (I mean we who have plantations). I have a large family of my own, and my doors are open to everybody, yet I have no bills to pay, and half-a-crown will rest undisturbed in my pockets for many moons altogether. Like one of the patriarchs, I have my flock and herds, my bondmen and bond-women, and every sort of trade amongst my own servants, so that I live in a kind of independence on everyone but Providence. . . . Thus, my Lord, we are very happy in our Canaans if we could but forget the onions and fleshpots of Egypt.

Byrd's "New Canaan," unlike its New England counterpart, and in spite of his nod to Divine Providence, is a self-sufficient, earthly garden, combining the best of civilized and rural life. Byrd's house at Westover epitomized his ideal of the perfect plantation, and he spared no expense to fashion it. The house he rebuilt is still standing, one of the most beautiful examples of eighteenth-century architecture in America. It housed a library of some thirty-six thousand volumes and rivaled Cotton Mather's library in Boston; its gardens were the envy of all who saw them. Byrd had a passion for land, and before he died he escalated the 26,000 acres left to him by his father into a vast holding of 179,000 acres. The cities of Richmond and Petersburg, Virginia, were created from Byrd's landholdings.

Given Byrd's position in the affairs of Virginia, it is not surprising that he was asked to accept a number of public commissions. In 1728 he accepted a commission to survey the much-disputed boundary line between Virginia and North Carolina. The diary that Byrd kept on his trip served as the sourcebook for his *History of the Dividing Line*. Although not published until 1841, Byrd's manuscript was circulated among the London friends, and its existence was known to later naturalists such as Thomas Jefferson. In its wealth of natural detail (some of it—like his description of the possum catching and eating little birds with its claws—quite fantastic) and Indian lore, it helped to satisfy London curiosity for all things American.

From The Secret Diary of William Byrd of Westover
1709–1712[1]

[December] 31. [1710] I rose at 5 o'clock and read a chapter in Hebrew and four leaves in Lucian.[2] I said my prayers and ate boiled milk for breakfast. My daughter was very sick all night and vomited a great deal but was a little better

---

1. The text used here is taken from *The Secret Diary of William Byrd of Westover 1709–1712*, edited by Louis B. Wright and Marion Tinling (1941).

2. I.e., four pages of Lucian, a Greek satirist of the 2nd century A.D.

this morning. All my sick people were better, thank God, and I had another girl come down sick from the quarters.[3] I danced my dance.[4] Then I read a sermon in Dr. Tillotson[5] and after that walked in the garden till dinner. I ate roast venison. In the afternoon I looked over my sick people and then took a walk about the plantation. The weather was very warm still. My wife walked with me and when she came back she was very much indisposed and went to bed. In the evening I read another sermon in Dr. Tillotson. About 8 o'clock the wind came to northwest and it began to be cold. I said my prayers and had good health, good thoughts, and good humor, thank God Almighty.

Some night this month I dreamed that I saw a flaming sword in the sky and called some company to see it but before they could come it was disappeared, and about a week after my wife and I were walking and we discovered in the clouds a shining cloud exactly in the shape of a dart and seemed to be over my plantation but it soon disappeared likewise. Both these appearances seemed to foretell some misfortune to me which afterwards came to pass in the death of several of my negroes after a very unusual manner. My wife about two months since dreamed she saw an angel in the shape of a big woman who told her the time was altered and the seasons were changed and that several calamities would follow that confusion. God avert His judgment from this poor country.

[January] 2. [1711] I rose at 5 o'clock and read a chapter in Hebrew and nothing in Greek because of the company that was here. I said my prayers and ate boiled milk for breakfast. I had six sick negroes come down from the quarters. About 9 o'clock my company went away. My wife was a little better and so was my child, thank God, but C-l-y was extremely ill and so was A-g-y.[6] I tended them as much as I could but God is pleased to afflict me with His judgment for my sins. His holy will be done. I ate some wild turkey. The wind was northeast and it was cold. In the afternoon I read a little English but could not be easy because poor C-l-y was so very ill. I took a melancholy walk. In the evening about 6 o'clock C-l-y died and all the people was [sic] grieved at it. I read a little English and gave the necessary orders about the sick people who were 12 in number. I said my prayers and had good health, good thoughts, and good humor, thank God Almighty.

[January] 6. [1711] I rose at 5 o'clock and read two chapters in Hebrew and six leaves in Lucian. I said my prayers and ate boiled milk for breakfast. Poor old S-r-y died this night to make up the number of the dead. God save the rest. A-g-y seemed to be a little better and so did the rest of the sick, God be praised, except Jenny and she seemed to be worse. The weather threatened rain all day. I removed several things out of the Doctor's closet[7] into mine and was very little with my cousin. I was out of humor with my wife. I ate boiled pork for dinner. In the afternoon Mrs. Dunn[8] went away in the rain. I spent most of my time in looking after my sick. In the evening it rained extremely, and all night. My cousin and I took a walk about the plantation. I said my prayers and had good health, good thoughts, and good humor, thank God Almighty.

[January] 7. [1711] I rose at 5 o'clock and read two chapters in Hebrew and some Greek in Lucian. I said my prayers and ate boiled milk for breakfast. My

3. I.e., slave quarters.
4. I.e., performed my calisthenics.
5. Dr. John Tillotson (1620–1694), archbishop of Canterbury, was one of Byrd's favorite writers.
6. Both were servants.
7. Small private room.
8. A frequent visitor, Mrs. Dunn was the wife of the minister of Hungar's Parish, Northampton County, Virginia.

sick people were some worse and some well enough to go home to the quarters. Jenny and A-g-y were much as they were. The weather held up so that I and my cousin [Guy] went to church, but my wife was afflicted with the headache and stayed at home. People condoled the sickness of my family. Mr. Anderson gave us a sermon. After church I carried him home with me to dinner and to see my sick people. I ate fish for dinner. Mr. Anderson advised me to give my people cordials since other physic failed, which I did. In the afternoon I did nothing but mind them. In the evening my cousin and we talked till 8 o'clock. I said a short prayer and had good health, good thoughts, and good humor, thank God Almighty.

[January] 22. [1711] I rose at 3 o'clock and read a chapter in Hebrew and some Greek in Lucian. I said my prayers and ate boiled milk for breakfast. I danced my dance. I ordered the sloop to be unloaded. Redskin Peter pretended to be sick and I put a [branding-iron] on the place he complained of and put the [bit] upon him.[9] The boy called the Doc was sent from Falling Creek with a swollen thigh. My sick people were better, thank God Almighty. I received a courteous letter from the Governor by Tom, who brought no news. I ate boiled pork for dinner. Mr. Mumford came down after dinner and told me all was well at Appomattox. When he had got some victuals we took a walk to see the people load the sloop and afterwards about the plantation. In the evening G-r-l came and let me know things were well at Falling Creek. He brought me a letter from Tom Turpin in which he agreed to stay with me for £25 a year. I ate some roast beef for supper. I neglected to say my prayers, but had good health, good thoughts, and good humor, thank God.

[January] 23. [1711] I rose at 5 o'clock and read a chapter in Hebrew and some Greek in Lucian. I said my prayers and ate boiled milk for breakfast. I danced my dance. My sick people were better, thank God, and Redskin Peter was particularly well and worked as well as anybody. * * *

[February] 6. [1711] I rose about 9 o'clock but was so bad I thought I should not have been in condition to go to Williamsburg,[1] and my wife was so kind to [say] she would stay with me, but rather than keep her from going I resolved to go if possible. I was shaved with a very dull razor, and ate some boiled milk for breakfast but neglected to say my prayers. About 10 o'clock I went to Williamsburg without the ladies. As soon as I got there it began to rain, which hindered about [sic] the company from coming. I went to the President's[2] where I drank tea and went with him to the Governor's[3] and found him at home. Several gentlemen were there and about 12 o'clock several ladies came. My wife and her sister came about 2. We had a short council but more for form than for business. There was no other appointed in the room of[4] Colonel Digges. My cold was a little better so that I ventured among the ladies, and Colonel Carter's wife and daughter were among them. It was night before we went to supper, which was very fine and in good order. It rained so that several did not come that were expected. About 7 o'clock the company went in coaches from the Governor's house to the capitol where the Governor opened the ball with a French dance with my wife. Then I danced with Mrs. Russell and then several others and among the rest Colonel Smith's son, who made a

9. A device something like a horse's bit and fastened in his mouth.
1. The colonial capital of Virginia, 1699–1779.
2. I.e., the house of the president of the Council of State, to which Byrd had been appointed in 1708.

3. Col. Alexander Spotswood (1676–1740) was the English lieutenant governor of Virginia from 1710 to 1722.
4. I.e., in place of.

sad freak. Then we danced country dances for an hour and the company was carried into another room where was a very fine collation of sweetmeats. The Governor was very gallant to the ladies and very courteous to the gentlemen. About 2 o'clock the company returned in the coaches and because the drive was dirty the Governor carried the ladies into their coaches. My wife and I lay at my lodgings. Colonel Carter's family and Mr. Blair were stopped by the unruliness of the horses and Daniel Wilkinson was so gallant as to lead the horses himself through all the dirt and rain to Mr. Blair's house. My cold continued bad. I neglected to say my prayers and had good thoughts, good humor, but indifferent health, thank God Almighty. It rained all day and all night. The President had the worst clothes of anybody there.

[February] 7. [1711] I rose at 8 o'clock and found my cold continued. I said my prayers and ate boiled milk for breakfast. I went to see Mr. Clayton who lay sick of the gout. About 11 o'clock my wife and I went to wait on the Governor in the President's coach. We went there to take our leave but were forced to stay all day. The Governor had made a bargain with his servants that if they would forbear to drink upon the Queen's birthday, they might be drunk this day. They observed their contract and did their business very well and got very drunk today, in such a manner that Mrs. Russell's maid was forced to lay the cloth, but the cook in that condition made a shift to send in a pretty little dinner. I ate some mutton cutlets. In the afternoon I persuaded my wife to stay all night in town and so it was resolved to spend the evening in cards. My cold was very bad and I lost my money. About 10 o'clock the Governor's coach carried us home to our lodgings where my wife was out of humor and I out of order. I said a short prayer and had good thoughts and good humor, thank God Almighty.

[December] 31. [1711] I rose about 7 o'clock and read a chapter in Hebrew and six leaves in Lucian. I said my prayers and ate boiled milk for breakfast. The weather continued warm and clear. I settled my accounts and wrote several things till dinner. I danced my dance. I ate some turkey and chine[5] for dinner. In the afternoon I weighed some money and then read some Latin in Terence[6] and then Mr. Mumford came and told me my man Tony had been very sick but he was recovered again, thank God. He told me Robin Bolling had been like to die and that he denied that he was the first to mention the imposition[7] on skins which he certainly did. Then he and I took a walk about the plantation. When I returned I was out of humor to find the negroes all at work in our chambers. At night I ate some broiled turkey with Mr. Mumford and we talked and were merry all the evening. I said my prayers and had good health, good thoughts, and good humor, thank God Almighty. My wife and I had a terrible quarrel about whipping Eugene[8] while Mr. Mumford was there but she had a mind to show her authority before company but I would not suffer it, which she took very ill; however for peace sake I made the first advance towards a reconciliation which I obtained with some difficulty and after abundance of crying. However it spoiled the mirth of the evening, but I was not conscious that I was to blame in that quarrel.

[January] 1. [1712] I lay abed till 9 o'clock this morning to bring my wife into temper again and rogered her by way of reconciliation. I read nothing because Mr. Mumford was here, nor did I say my prayers, for the same reason.

---

5. A joint of meat; the ribs or sirloin of beef.
6. Roman playwright (190?–159? B.C..)
7. Taxation.
8. A servant.

However I ate boiled milk for breakfast, and after my wife tempted me to eat some pancakes with her. Mr. Mumford and I went to shoot with our bows and arrows but shot nothing, and afterwards we played at billiards till dinner, and when we came we found Ben Harrison there, who dined with us. I ate some partridge for dinner. In the afternoon we played at billiards again and I won two bits. I had a letter from Colonel Duke by H-l the bricklayer who came to offer his services to work for me. Mr. Mumford went away in the evening and John Bannister with him to see his mother. I took a walk about the plantation and at night we drank some mead of my wife's making which was very good. I gave the people some cider and a dram to the negroes. I read some Latin in Terence and had good health, good thoughts, and good humor, thank God Almighty. I said my prayers.

[January] 15. [1712] I rose about 7 o'clock but read nothing because I wrote some letters and one especially to Will Randolph concerning what I learned the Governor had [been] informed concerning my saying no Governor ought to be trusted with £20,000, and he owned he had told it because I had said it and he thought it no secret, for which I marked him as a very false friend. I said my prayers and ate boiled milk for breakfast. I had a sore throat this morning. The weather was warm and the wind southwest. Mr. G-r-l made an end of putting up the curtain cornice in the library and then went and showed John to plant fruit trees. Drury Stith, Colonel Hill, Mr. Anderson, and Mr. Platt came to see me and put me in mind of the vestry. However we ate our dinner first and I ate some roast mutton. Then we went to the vestry and among other things agreed to make a well in the churchyard. In the evening I was out of humor because my wife broke open Will Randolph's letter. I read some Terence at night and wrote in my journal. Mr. G-r-l went away in the evening. I said my prayers and had good health, good thoughts, and good humor, thank God Almighty.

[January] 16. [1712] I rose about 7 o'clock and read a chapter in Hebrew and some Greek in Lucian. I said my prayers and ate boiled milk for breakfast. I danced my dance. My wife was something better and rode out because it was very fine weather and not cold. We killed a beef this morning that came yesterday from Burkland where they were all well, thank God. I settled some accounts till dinner and than I ate some hash of beef. In the afternoon my wife shaved me and then I walked out to see my people plant trees and I was angry with John for mistaking Mr. G-r-l's directions. Then I showed him again and helped him plant several trees. Then I took a walk till night. When I came in my [wife] persuaded me to eat skim milk for supper. Then I read some Latin in Terence. I said my prayers and had good thoughts, good humor, and good health, thank God Almighty. I dreamed a coffin was brought into my house and thrown into the hall.

[January] 17. [1712] I rose about 7 o'clock and read a chapter in Hebrew and some Greek in Lucian. I said my prayers and ate boiled milk for breakfast. I danced my dance. When I got up I thought to ride to Falling Creek but the weather threatened snow and the wind northeast, which discouraged me from my journey. About 12 o'clock I went to see John and Tom plant the peach orchard where I stayed till dinner was ready. I ate some beefsteak. In the afternoon I looked over some books with pictures for half an hour and then went again to my people to see them plant trees. I stayed there a little time and then went to take a walk about the plantation to examine what the rest had done and was contented with the overseer's management. I also saw all the cattle, which seem to be in good condition. At night I resisted my wife's temptation to eat milk and read some Latin in Terence. I said my prayers and had good health, good thoughts, and good humor, thank God Almighty.

[January] 18. [1712] I rose about 7 o'clock and read a chapter in Hebrew and some Greek in Lucian. I said my prayers and ate boiled milk for breakfast. I danced my dance. The weather was clear and cold but the wind was northeast. I settled several accounts and then read some Latin in Terence till dinner, and then I ate some boiled beef but I was displeased with my wife for giving the child marrow against my opinion. In the afternoon I read a little more Latin and then went to see my people plant peach trees and afterwards took a great walk about the plantation and found everything in order, for which I praised God. I was entertained with seeing a hawk which had taken a small bird pursued by another hawk, so that he was forced to let go his prey. My walk lasted till the evening and at night I read some Latin in Terence. I said my prayers and had good health, good thoughts, and good humor, thank God Almighty.

[May] 22. [1712] I rose about 6 o'clock and read two chapters in Hebrew and some Greek in Lucian. I said my prayers and ate boiled milk for breakfast. I danced my dance. It rained a little this morning. My wife caused Prue to be whipped violently notwithstanding I desired not, which provoked me to have Anaka whipped likewise who had deserved it much more, on which my wife flew into such a passion that she hoped she would be revenged of me. I was moved very much at this but only thanked her for the present lest I should say things foolish in my passion. I wrote more accounts to go to England. My wife was sorry for what she had said and came to ask my pardon and I forgave her in my heart but seemed to resent, that she might be the more sorry for her folly. She ate no dinner nor appeared the whole day. I ate some bacon for dinner. In the afternoon I wrote two more accounts till the evening and then took a walk in the garden. I said my prayers and was reconciled to my wife and gave her a flourish in token of it. I had good health, good thoughts, but was a little out of humor, for which God forgive me.

1941

From History of the Dividing Line[1]

[*The Other British Colonies*]

Before I enter upon the journal of the line between Virginia and North Carolina, it will be necessary to clear the way to it by showing how the other British colonies on the main have, one after another, been carved out of Virginia by grants from His Majesty's royal predecessors. All that part of the northern American continent now under the dominion of the King of Great Britain and stretching quite as far as the Cape of Florida went at first under the general name of Virginia.

The only distinction in those early days was that all the coast to the south-

---

1. The text used here is taken from *The Prose Works of William Byrd of Westover*, edited by Louis B. Wright (1966).

ward of Chesapeake Bay was called South Virginia and all to the northward of it North Virginia.

The first settlement of this fine country was owing to that great ornament of the British nation, Sir Walter Raleigh,[2] who obtained a grant thereof from Queen Elizabeth, of ever-glorious memory, by letters patent[3] dated March 25, 1584.

But whether that gentleman ever made a voyage thither himself is uncertain, because those who have favored the public with an account of his life mention nothing of it. However, thus much may be depended on, that Sir Walter invited sundry persons of distinction to share in his charter and join their purses with his in the laudable project of fitting out a colony to Virginia.

Accordingly, two ships were sent away that very year, under the command of his good friends Amadas and Barlow,[4] to take possession of the country in the name of his royal mistress, the Queen of England.

These worthy commanders, for the advantage of the trade winds, shaped their course first to the Caribbee Islands, thence, stretching away by the Gulf of Florida, dropped anchor not far from Roanoke Inlet. They ventured ashore near that place upon an island now called Colleton Island,[5] where they set up the arms of England and claimed the adjacent country in right of their sovereign lady, the Queen; and this ceremony being duly performed, they kindly invited the neighboring Indians to traffic with them.

These poor people at first approached the English with great caution, having heard much of the treachery of the Spaniards and not knowing but these strangers might be as treacherous as they. But at length, discovering a kind of good nature in their looks, they ventured to draw near and barter their skins and furs for the baubles and trinkets of the English.

These first adventurers made a very profitable voyage, raising at least a thousand percent upon their cargo. Amongst other Indian commodities, they brought over some of that bewitching vegetable, tobacco. And this being the first that ever came to England, Sir Walter thought he could do no less than make a present of some of the brightest of it to his royal mistress for her own smoking. The Queen graciously accepted of it, but finding her stomach sicken after two or three whiffs, 'twas presently whispered by the Earl of Leicester's[6] faction that Sir Walter had certainly poisoned her. But Her Majesty, soon recovering her disorder, obliged the Countess of Nottingham and all her maids to smoke a whole pipe out amongst them.

As it happened some ages before to be the fashion to saunter to the Holy Land and go upon other Quixote adventures,[7] so it was now grown the humor to take a trip to America. The Spaniards had lately discovered rich mines in their part of the West Indies, which made their maritime neighbors eager to do so too. This modish frenzy, being still more inflamed by the charming account given of Virginia by the first adventurers, made many fond of removing to such a Paradise.

Happy was he, and still happier she, that could get themselves transported,

---

2. Sir Walter Raleigh (1552?–1618), author of *The History of the World* (1614), military and naval commander.
3. A public letter, usually signed by a sovereign.
4. Arthur Barlow's account of his voyage with Philip Amadas was printed in Richard Hakluyt's *Principal Navigations* (1589).

5. Now Colington Island.
6. Robert Dudley (1532?–1588), earl of Leicester, was Elizabeth's favorite at court and a man of great political influence.
7. Foolish and impractical ventures, after the character in Cervantes' novel *Don Quixote* (1605–15).

fondly expecting their coarsest utensils in that happy place would be of massy silver.

This made it easy for the Company to procure as many volunteers as they wanted for their new colony, but, like most other undertakers who have no assistance from the public, they starved the design by too much frugality; for, unwilling to launch out at first into too much expense, they shipped off but few people at a time, and those but scantily provided. The adventurers were, besides, idle and extravagant and expected they might live without work in so plentiful a country.

These wretches were set ashore not far from Roanoke Inlet, but by some fatal disagreement or laziness were either starved or cut to pieces by the Indians.

Several repeated misadventures of this kind did for some time allay the itch of sailing to this new world, but the distemper broke out again about the year 1606. Then it happened that the Earl of Southampton[8] and several other persons eminent for their quality and estates were invited into the Company, who applied themselves once more to people the then almost abandoned colony. For this purpose they embarked about an hundred men, most of them reprobates of good families and related to some of the Company who were men of quality and fortune.

The ships that carried them made a shift to find a more direct way to Virginia and ventured through the capes into the Bay of Chesapeake. The same night they came to an anchor at the mouth of Powhatan, the same as James River, where they built a small fort at a place called Point Comfort.

This settlement stood its ground from that time forward, in spite of all the blunders and disagreement of the first adventurers and the many calamities that befell the colony afterwards. The six gentlemen who were first named of the Company by the Crown and who were empowered to choose an annual president from among themselves were always engaged in factions and quarrels, while the rest detested work more than famine. At this rate the colony must have come to nothing had it not been for the vigilance and bravery of Captain Smith,[9] who struck a terror into all the Indians round about. This gentleman took some pains to persuade the men to plant Indian corn, but they looked upon all labor as a curse. They chose rather to depend upon the musty provisions that were sent from England; and when they failed they were forced to take more pains to seek for wild fruits in the woods than they would have taken in tilling the ground. Besides, this exposed them to be knocked in the head by the Indians and gave them fluxes[1] into the bargain, which thinned the plantation very much. To supply this mortality, they were reinforced the year following with a greater number of people, amongst which were fewer gentlemen and more laborers, who, however, took care not to kill themselves with work. These found the first adventurers in a very starving condition but relieved their wants with the fresh supply they brought with them. From Kecoughtan[2] they extended themselves as far as Jamestown, where, like true Englishmen, they built a church that cost no more than fifty pounds and a tavern that cost five hundred.

They had now made peace with the Indians, but there was one thing want-

8. Henry Wriothesley, third earl of Southampton (1573–1624), Shakespeare's patron.
9. Captain John Smith (1580–1631), soldier and colo-

nist, founder of Virginia.
1. Dysentery.
2. Now Hampton, Virginia.

ing to make that peace lasting. The natives could by no means persuade themselves that the English were heartily their friends so long as they disdained to intermarry with them. And, in earnest, had the English consulted their own security and the good of the colony, had they intended either to civilize or convert these gentiles, they would have brought their stomachs to embrace this prudent alliance.

The Indians are generally tall and well proportioned, which may make full amends for the darkness of their complexions. Add to this that they are healthy and strong, with constitutions untainted by lewdness and not enfeebled by luxury. Besides, morals and all considered, I cannot think the Indians were much greater heathens than the first adventurers, who, had they been good Christians, would have had the charity to take this only method of converting the natives to Christianity. For, after all that can be said, a sprightly lover is the most prevailing missionary that can be sent amongst these or any other infidels.

Besides, the poor Indians would have had less reason to complain that the English took away their land if they had received it by way of a portion with their daughters. Had such affinities been contracted in the beginning, how much bloodshed had been prevented and how populous would the country have been, and, consequently, how considerable! Nor would the shade of the skin have been any reproach at this day, for if a Moor may be washed white in three generations, surely an Indian might have been blanched in two.

The French, for their parts, have not been so squeamish in Canada, who upon trial find abundance of attraction in the Indians. Their late grand monarch thought it not below even the dignity of a Frenchman to become one flesh with this people and therefore ordered 100 livres for any of his subjects, man or woman, that would intermarry with a native.

By this piece of policy we find the French interest very much strengthened amongst the savages and their religion, such as it is, propagated just as far as their love. And I heartily wish this well-concerted scheme don't hereafter give the French an advantage over His Majesty's good subjects on the northern continent of America.

About the same time New England was pared off from Virginia by letters patent bearing date April 10, 1608. Several gentlemen of the town and neighborhood of Plymouth obtained this grant, with the Lord Chief Justice Popham at their head.

Their bounds were specified to extend from 38 to 45 degrees of northern latitude, with a breadth of one hundred miles from the seashore. The first fourteen years this company encountered many difficulties and lost many men, though, far from being discouraged, they sent over numerous recruits of Presbyterians every year, who for all that had much ado to stand their ground, with all their fighting and praying.

But about the year 1620 a large swarm of dissenters[3] fled thither from the severities of their stepmother, the church. These saints,[4] conceiving the same aversion to the copper complexion of the natives with that of the first adventurers to Virginia, would on no terms contract alliances with them, afraid, perhaps, like the Jews of old, lest they might be drawn into idolatry by those strange women.

3. English Christians who rejected the authority of the Church of England.

4. Here, Puritan believers.

Whatever disgusted them I can't say, but this false delicacy, creating in the Indians a jealousy that the English were ill affected toward them, was the cause that many of them were cut off and the rest exposed to various distresses.

This reinforcement was landed not far from Cape Cod, where for their greater security they built a fort and near it a small town, which, in honor of the proprietors, was called New Plymouth. But they still had many discouragements to struggle with, though by being well supported from home they by degrees triumphed over them all.

Their brethren, after this, flocked over so fast that in a few years they extended the settlement one hundred miles along the coast, including Rhode Island and Martha's Vineyard.

Thus the colony throve apace and was thronged with large detachments of Independents and Presbyterians who thought themselves persecuted at home.

Though these people may be ridiculed for some pharisaical particularities in their worship and behavior, yet they were very useful subjects, as being frugal and industrious, giving no scandal or bad example, at least by any open and public vices. By which excellent qualities they had much the advantage of the southern colony, who thought their being members of the established church sufficient to sanctify very loose and profligate morals. For this reason New England improved much faster than Virginia, and in seven or eight years New Plymouth, like Switzerland, seemed too narrow a territory for its inhabitants.

* * *

From October[5]

1. There was a white frost this morning on the ground, occasioned by a northwest wind, which stood our friend in dispersing all aguish[6] damps and making the air wholesome at the same time that it made it cold. Encouraged, therefore, by the weather, our surveyors got to work early and, by the benefit of clear woods and level ground, drove the line twelve miles and twelve poles.[7]

At a small distance from our camp we crossed Great Creek and about seven miles farther Nutbush Creek, so called from the many hazel trees growing upon it. By good luck, many branches of these creeks were full of reeds, to the great comfort of our horses. Near five miles from thence we encamped on a branch that runs into Nutbush Creek, where those reeds flourished more than ordinary. The land we marched over was for the most part broken and stony and in some places covered over with thickets almost impenetrable.

At night the surveyors, taking advantage of a very clear sky, made a third trial of the variation and found it still something less than three degrees; so that it did not diminish by advancing toward the west or by approaching the mountains, nor yet by increasing our distance from the sea, but remained much the same we had found it at Currituck Inlet.

One of our Indians killed a large fawn, which was very welcome, though, like Hudibras'[8] horse, it had hardly flesh enough to cover its bones.

In the low grounds the Carolina gentlemen showed us another plant, which they said was used in their country to cure the bite of the rattlesnake. It put

5. The boundary commission began its expedition on March 5, 1728. By October 1, they were close to present-day Bristol, Tennessee.
6. Feverish.

7. A linear measure equal to 5.5 yards.
8. In Samuel Butler's satire Hudibras (1663–78), a Presbyterian minister sets out on a journey upon a starving horse.

forth several leaves in figure like a heart and was clouded so like the common Asarabacca that I conceived it to be of that family.

2. So soon as the horses could be found, we hurried away the surveyors, who advanced the line 9 miles and 254 poles. About three miles from the camp they crossed a large creek, which the Indians called Massamony, signifying in their language "Paint Creek," because of the great quantity of red ocher found in its banks. This in every fresh tinges the water, just as the same mineral did formerly, and to this day continues to tinge, the famous river Adonis in Phoenicia,[9] by which there hangs a celebrated fable.

Three miles beyond that we passed another water with difficulty called Yapatsco or Beaver Creek. Those industrious animals had dammed up the water so high that we had much ado to get over. 'Tis hardly credible how much work of this kind they will do in the space of one night. They bite young saplings into proper lengths with their foreteeth, which are exceeding strong and sharp, and afterwards drag them to the place where they intend to stop the water. Then they know how to join timber and earth together with so much skill that their work is able to resist the most violent flood than can happen. In this they are qualified to instruct their betters, it being certain their dams will stand firm when the strongest that are made by men will be carried down the stream. We observed very broad, low grounds upon this creek, with a growth of large trees and all the other signs of fertility, but seemed subject to be everywhere overflowed in a fresh. The certain way to catch these sagacious animals is this: squeeze all the juice out of the large pride[1] of the beaver and six drops out of the small pride. Powder the inward bark of sassafras and mix it with this juice; then bait therewith a steel trap and they will eagerly come to it and be taken.

About three miles and an half farther we came to the banks of another creek, called in the Saponi language Ohimpamony, signifying "Jumping Creek," from the frequent jumping of fish during the spring season.

Here we encamped, and by the time the horses were hobbled our hunters brought us no less than a brace and an half of deer, which made great plenty and consequently great content in our quarters. Some of our people had shot a great wildcat, which was that fatal moment making a comfortable meal upon a fox squirrel, and an ambitious sportsman of our company claimed the merit of killing this monster after it was dead. The wildcat is as big again as any household cat and much the fiercest inhabitant of the woods. Whenever it is disabled, it will tear its own flesh for madness. Although a panther will run away from a man, a wildcat will only make a surly retreat, now and then facing about if he be too closely pursued, and will even pursue in his turn if he observe the least sign of fear or even of caution in those that pretend to follow him. The flesh of this beast, as well as of the panther, is as white as veal and altogether as sweet and delicious.

3. We got to work early this morning and carried the line 8 miles and 160 poles. We forded several runs of excellent water and afterwards traversed a large level of high land, full of lofty walnut, poplar, and white oak trees, which are certain proofs of a fruitful soil. This level was near two miles in length and of an unknown breadth, quite out of danger of being overflowed, which is a misfortune most of the low grounds are liable to in those parts. As we marched

9. A river that turns red each spring, supposedly with the blood of Adonis, who, a mortal, was beloved of   Aphrodite and wounded while hunting.
1. Testis.

along, we saw many buffalo tracks and abundance of their dung very fresh but could not have the pleasure of seeing them. They either smelt us out, having that sense very quick,[2] or else were alarmed at the noise that so many people must necessarily make in marching along. At the sight of a man they will snort and grunt, cock up their ridiculous short tails, and tear up the ground with a sort of timorous fury. These wild cattle hardly ever range alone but herd together like those that are tame. They are seldom seen so far north as forty degrees of latitude, delighting much in canes and reeds which grow generally more southerly.

We quartered on the banks of a creek that the inhabitants call Tewahominy or Tuskarooda[3] Creek, because one of that nation had been killed thereabouts and his body thrown into the creek.

Our people had the fortune to kill a brace of does, one of which we presented to the Carolina gentlemen, who were glad to partake of the bounty of Providence at the same time that they sneered at us for depending upon it.

4. We hurried away the surveyors about nine this morning, who extended the line 7 miles and 160 poles, notwithstanding the ground was exceedingly uneven. At the distance of five miles we forded a stream to which we gave the name of Bluewing Creek because of the great number of those fowls[4] that then frequented it. About two and a half miles beyond that, we came upon Sugartree Creek, so called from the many trees of that kind[5] that grow upon it. By tapping this tree in the first warm weather in February, one may get from twenty to forty gallons of liquor, very sweet to the taste and agreeable to the stomach. This may be boiled into molasses first and afterwards into very good sugar, allowing about ten gallons of liquor to make a pound. There is no doubt, too, that a very fine spirit may be distilled from the molasses, at least as good as rum. The sugar tree delights only in rich ground, where it grows very tall, and by the softness and sponginess of the wood should be a quick grower. Near this creek we discovered likewise several spice trees, the leaves of which are fragrant and the berries they bear are black when dry and of a hot taste, not much unlike pepper. The low grounds upon the creek are very wide, sometimes on one side, sometimes on the other, though most commonly upon the opposite shore the high land advances close to the bank, only on the north side of the line it spreads itself into a great breadth of rich low ground on both sides the creek for four miles together, as far as this stream runs into Hyco River, whereof I shall presently make mention. One of our men spied three buffaloes, but his piece being loaded only with goose shot, he was able to make no effectual impression on their thick hides; however, this disappointment was made up by a brace of bucks and as many wild turkeys killed by the rest of the company. Thus Providence was very bountiful to our endeavors, never disappointing those that faithfully rely upon it and pray heartily for their daily bread.

5. This day we met with such uneven grounds and thick underwoods that with all our industry we were able to advance the line but 4 miles and 312 poles. In this small distance it intersected a large stream four times, which our Indian at first mistook for the south branch of Roanoke River; but, discovering his error soon after, he assured us 'twas a river called Hycootomony, or Turkey

2. Acutely.
3. Now Tuscarora.

4. I.e., blue-winged teal.
5. I.e., sugar maples.

Buzzard River, from the great number of those unsavory birds that roost on the tall trees growing near its banks.

Early in the afternoon, to our very great surprise, the commissioners of Carolina acquainted us with their resolution to return home. This declaration of theirs seemed the more abrupt because they had not been so kind as to prepare us by the least hint of their intention to desert us. We therefore let them understand they appeared to us to abandon the business they came about with too much precipitation, this being but the fifteenth day since we came out the last time. But although we were to be so unhappy as to lose the assistance of their great abilities, yet we, who were concerned for Virginia, determined, by the grace of God, not to do our work by halves but, all deserted as we were like to be, should think it our duty to push the line quite to the mountains; and if their government should refuse to be bound by so much of the line as was run without their commissioners, yet at least it would bind Virginia and stand as a direction how far His Majesty's lands extend to the southward. In short, these gentlemen were positive, and the most we could agree upon was to subscribe plats[6] of our work as far as we had acted together; though at the same time we insisted these plats should be got ready by Monday noon at farthest, when we on the part of Virginia intended, if we were alive, to move forward without farther loss of time, the season being then too far advanced to admit of any unnecessary or complaisant delays.

6. We lay still this day, being Sunday, on the bank of Hyco River and had only prayers, our chaplain not having spirits enough to preach. The gentlemen of Carolina assisted not at our public devotions, because they were taken up all the morning in making a formidable protest against our proceeding on the line without them. When the divine service was over, the surveyors set about making the plats of so much of the line as we had run this last campaign. Our pious friends of Carolina assisted in this work with some seeming scruple, pretending it was a violation of the Sabbath, which we were the more surprised at because it happened to be the first qualm of conscience they had ever been troubled with during the whole journey. They had made no bones of staying from prayers to hammer out an unnecessary protest, though divine service was no sooner over but an unusual fit of godliness made them fancy that finishing the plats, which was now matter of necessity, was a profanation of the day. However, the expediency of losing no time, for us who thought it our duty to finish what we had undertaken, make such a labor pardonable.

In the afternoon, Mr. Fitzwilliam, one of the commissioners for Virginia, acquainted his colleagues it was his opinion that by His Majesty's order they could not proceed farther on the line but in conjunction with the commissioners of Carolina; for which reason he intended to retire the next morning with those gentlemen. This looked a little odd in our brother commissioner; though, in justice to him as well as to our Carolina friends, they stuck by us as long as our good liquor lasted and were so kind to us as to drink our good journey to the mountains in the last bottle we had left.

7. The duplicates of the plats could not be drawn fair this day before noon, where they were countersigned by the commissioners of each government. Then those of Carolina delivered their protest, which was by this time licked into form and signed by them all. And we have been so just to them as to set

6. Maps.

it down at full length in the Appendix, that their reasons for leaving us may appear in their full strength. After having thus adjusted all our affairs with the Carolina commissioners and kindly supplied them with bread to carry them back, which they hardly deserved at our hands, we took leave both of them and our colleague, Mr. Fitzwilliam. This gentleman had still a stronger reason for hurrying him back to Williamsburg, which was that neither the General Court might lose an able judge nor himself a double salary, not despairing in the least but he should have the whole pay of commissioner into the bargain, though he did not half the work. This, to be sure, was relying more on the interest of his friends than on the justice of his cause; in which, however, he had the misfortune to miscarry when it came to be fairly considered.

It was two o'clock in the afternoon before these arduous affairs could be dispatched, and then, all forsaken as we were, we held on our course toward the west. But it was our misfortune to meet with so many thickets in this afternoon's work that we could advance no further than 2 miles and 260 poles. In this small distance we crossed the Hyco the fifth time and quartered near Buffalo Creek, so named from the frequent tokens we discovered of that American behemoth. Here the bushes were so intolerably thick that we were obliged to cover the bread bags with our deerskins, otherwise the joke of one of the Indians must have happened to us in good earnest: that in a few days we must cut up our house to make bags for the bread and so be forced to expose our backs in compliment to our bellies. We computed we had then biscuit enough left to last us, with good management, seven weeks longer; and this being our chief dependence, it imported us to be very careful both in the carriage and the distribution of it.

We had now no other drink but what Adam drank in Paradise, though to our comfort we found the water excellent, by the help of which we perceived our appetites to mend, our slumbers to sweeten, the stream of life to run cool and peaceably in our veins, and if ever we dreamt of women, they were kind.

Our men killed a very fat buck and several turkeys. These two kinds of meat boiled together, with the addition of a little rice or French barley, made excellent soup, and, what happens rarely in other good things, it never cloyed, no more than an engaging wife would do, by being a constant dish. Our Indian was very superstitious in this matter and told us, with a face full of concern, that if we continued to boil venison and turkey together we should for the future kill nothing, because the spirit that presided over the woods would drive all the game out of our sight. But we had the happiness to find this an idle superstition, and though his argument could not convince us, yet our repeated experience at last, with much ado, convinced him.

We observed abundance of coltsfoot and maidenhair in many places and nowhere a larger quantity than here. They are both excellent pectoral[7] plants and seem to have greater virtues much in this part of the world than in more northern climates; and I believe it may pass for a rule in botanics that where any vegetable is planted by the hand of Nature it has more virtue than in places whereto it is transplanted by the curiosity of man.

* * *

12. We were so cruelly entangled with bushes and grapevines all day that we could advance the line no farther than five miles and twenty-eight poles.

---

7. Good for diseases of the chest.

The vines grew very thick in these woods, twining lovingly round the trees almost everywhere, especially to the saplings. This makes it evident how natural both the soil and climate of this country are to vines, though I believe most to our own vines. The grapes we commonly met with were black, though there be two or three kinds of white grapes that grow wild. The black are very sweet but small, because the strength of the vine spends itself in wood, though without question a proper culture would make the same grapes both larger and sweeter. But, with all these disadvantages, I have drunk tolerable good wine pressed from them, though made without skill. There is then good reason to believe it might admit of great improvement if rightly managed.

Our Indian killed a bear, two years old, that was feasting on these grapes. He was very fat, as they generally are in that season of the year. In the fall the flesh of this animal has a high relish different from that of other creatures, though inclining nearest to that of pork, or rather of wild boar. A true woodsman prefers this sort of meat to that of the fattest venison, not only for the *haut goût*,[8] but also because the fat of it is well tasted and never rises in the stomach. Another proof of the goodness of this meat is that it is less apt to corrupt than any other we are acquainted with.

As agreeable as such rich diet was to the men, yet we who were not accustomed to it tasted it at first with some sort of squeamishness, that animal being of the dog kind, though a little use soon reconciled us to this American venison. And that its being of the dog kind might give us the less disgust, we had the example of that ancient and polite people, the Chinese, who reckon dog's flesh too good for any under the quality of a mandarin. This beast is in truth a very clean feeder, living, while the season lasts, upon acorns, chestnuts, and chinquapins, wild honey and wild grapes. They are naturally not carnivorous, unless hunger constrain them to it after the mast[9] is all gone and the product of the woods quite exhausted. They are not provident enough to lay up any hoard like the squirrels, nor can they, after all, live very long upon licking their paws, as Sir John Mandeville[1] and some travelers tell us, but are forced in the winter months to quit the mountains and visit the inhabitants. Their errand is then to surprise a poor hog at a pinch to keep them from starving. And to show that they are not flesh eaters by trade, they devour their prey very awkwardly. They don't kill it right out and feast upon its blood and entrails, like other ravenous beasts, but, having, after a fair pursuit, seized it with their paws, they begin first upon the rump and so devour one collop after another till they come to the vitals, the poor animal crying all the while for several minutes together. However, in so doing, Bruin acts a little imprudently, because the dismal outcry of the hog alarms the neighborhood, and 'tis odds but he pays the forfeit with his life before he can secure his retreat.

But bears soon grow weary of this unnatural diet, and about January, when there is nothing to be gotten in the woods, they retire into some cave or hollow tree, where they sleep away two or three months very comfortably. But then they quit their holes in March, when the fish begin to run up the rivers, on which they are forced to keep Lent till some fruit or berry comes in season. But bears are fondest of chestnuts, which grow plentifully toward the mountains, upon very large trees, where the soil happens to be rich. We were curious to know how it happened that many of the outward branches of those trees

---

8. Gamy flavor.
9. A collective name for the fruit of the beech, chestnut, oak, and other forest trees.

1. Ostensible author of a mid-14th-century book of travels.

came to be broke off in that solitary place and were informed that the bears are
so discreet as not to trust their unwieldly bodies on the smaller limbs of the
tree that would not bear their weight, but after venturing as far as is safe, which
they can judge to an inch, they bite off the end of the branch, which falling
down, they are content to finish their repast upon the ground. In the same
cautious manner they secure the acorns that grow on the weaker limbs of the
oak. And it must be allowed that in these instances a bear carries instinct a
great way and acts more reasonably than many of his betters, who indiscreetly
venture upon frail projects that won't bear them.

13. This being Sunday, we rested from our fatigue and had leisure to reflect
on the signal mercies of Providence.

The great plenty of meat wherewith Bearskin[2] furnished us in these lonely
woods made us once more shorten the men's allowance of bread from five to
four pounds of biscuit a week. This was the more necessary because we knew
not yet how long our business might require us to be out.

In the afternoon our hunters went forth and returned triumphantly with
three brace of wild turkeys. They told us they could see the mountains distinctly from every eminence, though the atmosphere was so thick with smoke
that they appeared at a greater distance than they really were.

In the evening we examined our friend Bearskin concerning the religion of
his country, and he explained it to us without any of that reserve to which his
nation is subject. He told us he believed there was one supreme god, who had
several subaltern deities under him. And that this master god made the world
a long time ago. That he told the sun, the moon, and stars their business in
the beginning, which they, with good looking-after, have faithfully performed
ever since. That the same power that made all things at first has taken care to
keep them in the same method and motion ever since. He believed that God
had formed many worlds before he formed this, but that those worlds either
grew old and ruinous or were destroyed for the dishonesty of the inhabitants.
That God is very just and very good, ever well pleased with those men who
possess those godlike qualities. That he takes good people into his safe protection, makes them very rich, fills their bellies plentifully, preserves them from
sickness and from being surprised or overcome by their enemies. But all such
as tell lies and cheat those they have dealings with he never fails to punish with
sickness, poverty, and hunger and, after all that, suffers them to be knocked on
the head and scalped by those that fight against them.

He believed that after death both good and bad people are conducted by a
strong guard into a great road, in which departed souls travel together for some
time till at a certain distance this road forks into two paths, the one extremely
level and the other stony and mountainous. Here the good are parted from the
bad by a flash of lightning, the first being hurried away to the right, the other
to the left. The right-hand road leads to a charming, warm country, where the
spring is everlasting and every month is May; and as the year is always in its
youth, so are the people, and particularly the women are bright as stars and
never scold. That in this happy climate there are deer, turkeys, elks, and buffaloes innumerable, perpetually fat and gentle, while the trees are loaded with
delicious fruit quite throughout the four seasons. That the soil brings forth
corn spontaneously, without the curse of labor, and so very wholesome that

2. Their American Indian guide.

none who have the happiness to eat of it are ever sick, grow old, or die. Near the entrance into this blessed land sits a venerable old man on a mat richly woven, who examines strictly all that are brought before him, and if they have behaved well, the guards are ordered to open the crystal gate and let them enter into the land of delight. The left-hand path is very rugged and uneven, leading to a dark and barren country where it is always winter. The ground is the whole year round covered with snow, and nothing is to be seen upon the trees but icicles. All the people are hungry yet have not a morsel of anything to eat except a bitter kind of potato, that gives them the dry gripes[3] and fills their whole body with loathsome ulcers that stink and are insupportably painful. Here all the women are old and ugly, having claws like a panther with which they fly upon the men that slight their passion. For it seems these haggard old furies are intolerably fond and expect a vast deal of cherishing. They talk much and exceedingly shrill, giving exquisite pain to the drum of the ear, which in that place of the torment is so tender that every sharp note wounds it to the quick. At the end of this path sits a dreadful old woman on a monstrous toadstool, whose head is covered with rattlesnakes instead of tresses, with glaring white eyes that strike a terror unspeakable into all that behold her. This hag pronounces sentence of woe upon all the miserable wretches that hold up their hands at her tribunal. After this they are delivered over to huge turkey buzzards, like harpies, that fly away with them to the place above-mentioned. Here, after they have been tormented a certain number of years according to their several degrees of guilt, they are again driven back into this world to try if they will mend their manners and merit a place the next time in the regions of bliss.

This was the substance of Bearskin's religion and was as much to the purpose as could be expected from a mere state of nature, without one glimpse of revelation or philosophy. It contained, however, the three great articles of natural religion: the belief of a god, the moral distinction betwixt good and evil, and the expectation of rewards and punishments in another world. Indeed, the Indian notion of a future happiness is a little gross and sensual, like Mahomet's Paradise. But how can it be otherwise in a people that are contented with Nature as they find her and have no other lights but what they receive from purblind tradition?

*   *   *

1728   1841

3. Dry heaves; vomiting.

JONATHAN EDWARDS
1703–1758

Although it is certainly true that, as Perry Miller once put it, the true life of Jonathan Edwards is the life of a mind, the circumstances surrounding Edwards's career are not without their drama, and his rise to eminence and fall from power remain one of the most moving stories in American literature.

Edwards was born in East Windsor, Connecticut, a town not far from Hartford, the son of the Reverend Timothy Edwards and Esther Stoddard Edwards. There was little doubt from the beginning as to his career. Edwards's mother was the daughter of the Reverend Solomon Stoddard of Northampton, Massachusetts, one of the most influential and independent figures in the religious life of New England. Western Massachusetts clergymen were so anxious for his approval, that he was sometimes called the "Pope of the Connecticut Valley," and his gifted grandson, the only male child in a family of eleven children, was groomed to be his heir.

Edwards was a studious and dutiful child and from an early age showed remarkable gifts of observation and exposition. When he was eleven he wrote an essay on the flying spider, which is still very readable. Most of Edwards's early education he received at home. In 1716, when he was thirteen, Edwards was admitted to Yale College; he stayed on to read theology in New Haven for two years after his graduation in 1720. Like Benjamin Franklin, Edwards determined to perfect himself, and in one of his early notebooks he resolved "never to lose one moment of time, but to improve it in the most profitable way" he could. As a student he always rose at four in the morning, studied thirteen hours a day, and reserved part of each day for walking. It was a routine that Edwards varied little, even when, after spending two years in New York, he came to Northampton to assist his grandfather in his church. He married in 1727. In 1729 Solomon Stoddard died, and Edwards was named to succeed him. In the twenty-four years that Edwards lived in Northampton he managed to tend his duties as pastor of a growing congregation and deliver brilliant sermons, to write some of his most important books—concerned primarily with defining the nature of true religious experience—and watch his five children grow up. Until the mid-1740s his relations with the town seemed enviable.

In spite of the awesome—even imposing—quality of Edwards's mind, all of his work is of a piece and, in essence, readily graspable. What Edwards was trying to do was to restore to his congregation and to his readers that original sense of religious commitment that he felt had been lost since the first days of the Puritan exodus, and he wanted to do this by transforming his congregation from mere believers who understood the logic of Christian doctrine to converted Christians who were genuinely moved by the principles of their belief. Edwards says that he read the work of the English philosopher John Locke (1632–1704) with more pleasure "than the greedy miser finds when gathering up handfuls of silver and gold, from some newly discovered treasure." For Locke confirmed Edwards's conviction that we must do more than comprehend religious ideas; we must be *moved* by them, we must know them experientially: the difference, as he says, is like that between reading the word *fire* and actually being burned. Basic to this newly felt belief is the recognition that nothing that an individual can do warrants his or her salvation—that people are motivated entirely by self-love, and that it is only supernatural grace that alters their natural depravity. In his progress as a Christian, Edwards says that he experienced several steps toward conversion but that his true conversion came only when he had achieved a "full and constant sense of the absolute sovereignty of God, and a delight in that sovereignty." The word *delight* reminds us that Edwards is trying to inculcate and describe a religious feeling that approximates a physical sensation, recognizing always that supernatural feelings and natural ones are actually very different. In his patient and lucid prose Edwards became a master at the art of persuading his congregation that it could—and *must*—possess this intense awareness of humanity's precarious condition. The exaltation that his parishioners felt when they experienced delight in God's sovereignty was the characteristic fervid emotion of religious revivalism.

For fifteen years, beginning in 1734, this spirit of revivalism transformed complacent believers all along the eastern seaboard. This period of new religious fervor has been called the "Great Awakening," and in the early years Edwards could do no wrong. His meetinghouse was filled with newly converted believers, and the details of the spiritual life of Edwards and his congregation were the subject of inquiry by Christian believers everywhere. But in his attempt to restore the church to the position of authority it held in the years of his grandfather's reign, Edwards went too far. When he named backsliders from his pulpit—including the children and parents of the best families in town—and tried to return to the old order of communion, permitting the sacrament to be taken only by those who had publicly declared themselves to be saved, the people of the town turned against him. Residents of the Connecticut Valley everywhere were tired of religious controversy, and the hysterical behavior of a few fanatics turned many against the spirit of revivalism. On June 22, 1750, by a vote of two hundred to twenty, Edwards was dismissed from his church and effectively silenced. Although the congregation had difficulty naming a successor to Edwards, they preferred to have no sermons rather than let Edwards preach. For the next seven years he served as missionary to the Housatonnuck Indians in Stockbridge, Massachusetts, a town thirty-five miles to the west of Northampton. There he wrote his monumental treatises debating the doctrine of the freedom of the will and defining the nature of true virtue: "that consent, propensity and union of heart to Being in general, that is immediately exercised in a general good will." It was in Stockbridge that Edwards received, very reluctantly, a call to become president of the College of New Jersey (later called Princeton). Three months after his arrival in Princeton, Edwards died of smallpox, the result of the inoculation taken to prevent infection.

Personal Narrative[1]

I had a variety of concerns and exercises[2] about my soul from my childhood, but had two more remarkable seasons of awakening[3] before I met with that change by which I was brought to those new dispositions and that new sense of things that I have since had. The first time was when I was a boy, some years before I went to college, at a time of remarkable awakening in my father's congregation. I was then very much affected[4] for many months and concerned about the things of religion and my soul's salvation and was abundant in duties. I used to pray five times a day in secret, and to spend much time in religious talk with other boys and used to meet with them to pray together. I experienced I know not what kind of delight in religion. My mind was much engaged in it, and had much self-righteous pleasure; and it was my delight to abound in religious duties. I, with some of my schoolmates, joined together and built a booth in a swamp, in a very secret and retired place, for a place of prayer. And besides, I had particular secret places of my own in the woods, where I used to retire by myself, and used to be from time to time much affected. My affections seemed to be lively and easily moved, and I seemed to be in my element, when engaged in religious duties. And I am ready to think, many are deceived with such affections and such a kind of delight, as I then had in religion, and mistake it for grace.

But in process of time, my convictions and affections wore off; and I entirely lost all those affections and delights, and left off secret prayer, at least as to any

1. Because of Edwards's reference to an evening in January 1739, this essay must have been written after that date. Edwards's reasons for writing it are not known, and it was not published in his lifetime. After his death his friend Samuel Hopkins had access to his manuscripts and prepared *The Life and Character of the Late Rev. Mr. Jonathan Edwards*, which was published in 1765. In that volume the *Personal Narrative*

appeared in section IV as a chapter titled "An account of his conversion, experiences, and religious exercises, given by himself."
2. Agitations.
3. I.e., spiritual awakenings, renewals.
4. Emotionally aroused, as opposed to merely understanding rationally the arguments for Christian faith.

constant performance of it, and returned like a dog to his vomit, and went on in ways of sin.[5]

Indeed, I was at some times very uneasy, especially towards the latter part of the time of my being at college.[6] Till it pleased God, in my last year at college, at a time when I was in the midst of many uneasy thoughts about the state of my soul, to seize me with a pleurisy;[7] in which he brought me nigh to the grave, and shook me over the pit of hell.

But yet, it was not long after my recovery before I fell again into my old ways of sin. But God would not suffer me to go on with any quietness; but I had great and violent inward struggles: till after many conflicts with wicked inclinations and repeated resolutions and bonds that I laid myself under by a kind of vows to God, I was brought wholly to break off all former wicked ways and all ways of known outward sin, and to apply myself to seek my salvation and practice the duties of religion, but without that kind of affection and delight that I had formerly experienced. My concern now wrought more by inward struggles and conflicts and self-reflections. I made seeking my salvation the main business of my life. But yet it seems to me I sought after a miserable manner, which has made me sometimes since to question whether ever it issued in that which was saving,[8] being ready to doubt, whether such miserable seeking was ever succeeded. But yet I was brought to seek salvation in a manner that I never was before. I felt a spirit to part with all things in the world for an interest in Christ. My concern continued and prevailed, with many exercising thoughts and inward struggles; but yet it never seemed to be proper to express my concern that I had, by the name of terror.

From my childhood up, my mind had been wont to be full of objections against the doctrine of God's sovereignty, in choosing whom He would to eternal life and rejecting whom He pleased, leaving them eternally to perish and be everlastingly tormented in hell. It used to appear like a horrible doctrine to me. But I remember the time very well when I seemed to be convinced, and fully satisfied, as to this sovereignty of God and His justice in thus eternally disposing of men according to His sovereign pleasure. But never could give an account how or by what means I was thus convinced; not in the least imagining, in the time of it nor a long time after, that there was any extraordinary influence of God's spirit in it; but only that now I saw further, and my reason apprehended the justice and reasonableness of it. However, my mind rested in it; and it put an end to all those cavils and objections, that had till then abode with me, all the proceeding part of my life. And there has been a wonderful alteration in my mind, with respect to the doctrine of God's sovereignty, from that day to this; so that I scarce ever have found so much as the rising of an objection against God's sovereignty, in the most absolute sense, in showing mercy to whom He will show mercy and hardening and eternally damning whom He will.[9] God's absolute sovereignty and justice, with respect to salvation and damnation, is what my mind seems to rest assured of, as much as of anything that I see with my eyes; at least it is so at times. But I have oftentimes since that first conviction had quite another kind of sense of God's sovereignty than I had then. I have often since not only had a conviction, but a delightful

---

5. "As a dog returneth to his vomit, so a fool returneth to his folly" (Proverbs 26.11).

6. Edwards was an undergraduate at Yale from 1716 to 1720 and a divinity student from 1720 to 1722.

7. A respiratory disorder.

8. I.e., truly redeeming, capable of making the penitent a "saint."

9. "Therefore hath he mercy on whom he will have mercy, and whom he will be hardeneth" (Romans 9.18).

conviction. The doctrine of God's sovereignty has very often appeared an exceeding pleasant, bright and sweet doctrine to me; and absolute sovereignty is what I love to ascribe to God. But my first conviction was not with this.

The first that I remember that ever I found anything of that sort of inward, sweet delight in God and divine things, that I have lived much in since, was on reading those words, 1 Timothy 1.17, "Now unto the king eternal, immortal, invisible, the only wise God, be honor and glory for ever and ever, Amen." As I read the words, there came into my soul, and was as it were diffused through it, a sense of the glory of the Divine Being, a new sense, quite different from anything I ever experienced before. Never any words of scripture seemed to me as these words did. I thought with myself, how excellent a being that was, and how happy I should be if I might enjoy that God and be rapt[1] up to God in Heaven, and be as it were swallowed up in Him. I kept saying, and as it were singing over these words of scripture to myself; and went to prayer to pray to God that I might enjoy Him; and prayed in a manner quite different from what I used to do, with a new sort of affection. But it never came into my thought that there was anything spiritual or of a saving nature in this.

From about that time I began to have a new kind of apprehensions and ideas of Christ, and the work of redemption, and the glorious way of salvation by Him. I had an inward, sweet sense of these things, that at times came into my heart; and my soul was led away in pleasant views and contemplations of them. And my mind was greatly engaged to spend my time in reading and meditating on Christ, and the beauty and excellency of His person, and the lovely way of salvation, by free grace in Him. I found no books so delightful to me as those that treated of these subjects. Those words Canticles 2.1, used to be abundantly with me: "I am the Rose of Sharon, the lily of the valleys." The words seemed to me, sweetly to represent the loveliness and beauty of Jesus Christ. And the whole book of Canticles[2] used to be pleasant to me; and I used to be much in reading it, about that time. And found, from time to time, an inward sweetness that used, as it were, to carry me away in my con-templations, in what I know not how to express otherwise, than by a calm, sweet abstraction of soul from all the concerns of this world, and a kind of vision, or fixed ideas and imaginations, of being alone in the mountains or some solitary wilderness, far from all mankind, sweetly conversing with Christ, and rapt and swallowed up in God. The sense I had of divine things would often of a sudden as it were, kindle up a sweet burning in my heart, an ardor of my soul, that I know not how to express.

Not long after I first began to experience these things, I gave an account to my father of some things that had passed in my mind. I was pretty much affected by the discourse we had together. And when the discourse was ended, I walked abroad alone, in a solitary place in my father's pasture, for contempla-tion. And as I was walking there, and looked up on the sky and clouds, there came into my mind a sweet sense of the glorious majesty and grace of God that I know not how to express. I seemed to see them both in a sweet conjunc-tion, majesty and meekness joined together. It was a sweet and gentle, and holy majesty; and also a majestic meekness; an awful sweetness; a high, and great, and holy gentleness.

After this my sense of divine things gradually increased, and became more

---

1. Lifted.   2. I.e., Song of Solomon.

and more lively, and had more of that inward sweetness. The appearance of everything was altered: there seemed to be, as it were, a calm, sweet cast, or appearance of divine glory, in almost everything. God's excellency, His wisdom, His purity and love, seemed to appear in everything: in the sun, moon and stars; in the clouds, and blue sky; in the grass, flowers, trees; in the water, and all nature; which used greatly to fix my mind. I often used to sit and view the moon for a long time, and so in the daytime spent much time in viewing the clouds and sky to behold the sweet glory of God in these things, in the meantime, singing forth with a low voice my contemplations of the Creator and Redeemer. And scarce anything, among all the works of nature, was so sweet to me as thunder and lightning. Formerly, nothing had been so terrible to me. I used to be a person uncommonly terrified with thunder, and it used to strike me with terror when I saw a thunderstorm rising. But now, on the contrary, it rejoiced me. I felt God at the first appearance of a thunderstorm. And used to take the opportunity at such times to fix myself to view the clouds, and see the lightnings play, and hear the majestic and awful voice of God's thunder, which often times was exceeding entertaining, leading me to sweet contemplations of my great and glorious God. And while I viewed, used to spend my time, as it always seemed natural to me, to sing or chant forth my meditations, to speak my thoughts in soliloquies, and speak with a singing voice.

I felt then a great satisfaction as to my good estate.[3] But that did not content me. I had vehement longings of soul after God and Christ, and after more holiness, wherewith my heart seemed to be full and ready to break: which often brought to my mind the words of the Psalmist, Psalm 119.28: "My soul breaketh for the longing it hath." I often felt a mourning and lamenting in my heart that I had not turned to God sooner, that I might have had more time to grow in grace. My mind was greatly fixed on divine things; I was almost perpetually in the contemplation of them. Spent most of my time in thinking of divine things, year after year. And used to spend abundance of my time in walking alone in the woods and solitary places for meditation, soliloquy and prayer, and converse with God. And it was always my manner, at such times, to sing forth my contemplations. And was almost constantly in ejaculatory prayer, wherever I was. Prayer seemed to be natural to me, as the breath by which the inward burnings of my heart had vent.

The delights which I now felt in things of religion were of an exceeding different kind from those forementioned, that I had when I was a boy. They were totally of another kind; and what I then had no more notion or idea of, than one born blind has of pleasant and beautiful colors. They were of a more inward, pure, soul-animating and refreshing nature. Those former delights never reached the heart, and did not arise from any sight of the divine excellency of the things of God or any taste of the soul-satisfying and life-giving good there is in them.

My sense of divine things seemed gradually to increase, till I went to preach at New York, which was about a year and a half after they began. While I was there, I felt them, very sensibly,[4] in a much higher degree, than I had done before. My longings after God and holiness, were much increased. Pure and humble, holy and heavenly Christianity appeared exceeding amiable to me. I

---

3. Condition of being.
4. Feelingly. Edwards was in New York from August 1722 to April 1723, assisting at a Presbyterian church.

felt in me a burning desire to be in everything a complete Christian, and conformed to the blessed image of Christ, and that I might live in all things, according to the pure, sweet and blessed rules of the gospel. I had an eager thirsting after progress in these things. My longings after it put me upon pursuing and pressing after them. It was my continual strife day and night, and constant inquiry, how I should be more holy, and live more holily, and more becoming a child of God, and disciple of Christ. I sought an increase of grace and holiness, and that I might live an holy life with vastly more earnestness than ever I sought grace, before I had it. I used to be continually examining myself, and studying and contriving for likely ways and means how I should live holily with far greater diligence and earnestness than ever I pursued anything in my life; but with too great a dependence on my own strength, which afterwards proved a great damage to me. My experience had not then taught me, as it has done since, my extreme feebleness and impotence, every manner of way, and the innumerable and bottomless depths of secret corruption and deceit that there was in my heart. However, I went on with my eager pursuit after more holiness, and sweet conformity to Christ.

The Heaven I desired was a heaven of holiness, to be with God, and to spend my eternity in divine love, and holy communion with Christ. My mind was very much taken up with contemplations on heaven, and the enjoyments of those there, and living there in perfect holiness, humility and love. And it used at that time to appear a great part of the happiness of heaven that there the saints could express their love to Christ. It appeared to me a great clog and hindrance and burden to me that what I felt within I could not express to God and give vent to as I desired. The inward ardor of my soul seemed to be hindered and pent up, and could not freely flame out as it would. I used often to think how in heaven this sweet principle should freely and fully vent and express itself. Heaven appeared to me exceeding delightful as a world of love. It appeared to me that all happiness consisted in living in pure, humble, heavenly, divine love.

I remember the thoughts I used then to have of holiness. I remember I then said sometimes to myself, "I do certainly know that I love holiness such as the gospel prescribes." It appeared to me there was nothing in it but what was ravishingly lovely. It appeared to me to be the highest beauty and amiableness, above all other beauties, that it was a divine beauty, far purer than anything here upon earth; and that everything else, was like mire, filth and defilement in comparison of it.

Holiness, as I then wrote down some of my contemplations on it, appeared to me to be of a sweet, pleasant, charming, serene, calm nature. It seemed to me it brought an inexpressible purity, brightness, peacefulness and ravishment to the soul, and that it made the soul like a field or garden of God, with all manner of pleasant flowers; that is, all pleasant, delightful and undisturbed, enjoying a sweet calm, and the gently vivifying beams of the sun. The soul of a true Christian, as I then wrote my meditations, appeared like such a little white flower as we see in the spring of the year, low and humble on the ground, opening its bosom, to receive the pleasant beams of the sun's glory, rejoicing, as it were, in a calm rapture, diffusing around a sweet fragrancy, standing peacefully and lovingly in the midst of other flowers round about, all in like manner opening their bosoms, to drink in the light of the sun.

There was no part of creature holiness that I then, and at other times, had so great a sense of the loveliness of, as humility, brokenness of heart and poverty of spirit, and there was nothing that I had such a spirit to long for. My heart, as it were, panted after this to lie low before God, and in the dust; that I might be nothing, and that God might be all; that I might become as a little child.[5]

While I was there at New York, I sometimes was much affected with reflections on my past life, considering how late it was, before I began to be truly religious and how wickedly I had lived till then; and once so as to weep abundantly, and for a considerable time together.

On January 12, 1722–3 I made a solemn dedication of myself to God, and wrote it down; giving up myself, and all that I had to God; to be for the future in no respect my own; to act as one that had no right to himself, in any respect. And solemnly vowed to take God for my whole portion and felicity, looking on nothing else as any part of my happiness, nor acting as if it were: and His law for the constant rule of my obedience, engaging to fight with all my might against the world, the flesh and the devil, to the end of my life. But have reason to be infinitely humbled, when I consider, how much I have failed of answering my obligation.

I had then abundance of sweet religious conversation in the family where I lived, with Mr. John Smith, and his pious mother. My heart was knit in affection to those in whom were appearances of true piety, and I could bear the thoughts of no other companions but such as were holy, and the disciples of the blessed Jesus.

I had great longings for the advancement of Christ's kingdom in the world. My secret prayer used to be in great part taken up in praying for it. If I heard the least hint of anything that happened in any part of the world that appeared to me in some respect or other, to have a favorable aspect on the interest of Christ's kingdom, my soul eagerly catched at it; and it would much animate and refresh me. I used to be earnest to read public newsletters, mainly for that end, to see if I could not find some news favorable to the interest of religion in the world.

I very frequently used to retire into a solitary place, on the banks of Hudson's river, at some distance from the city, for contemplation on divine things and secret converse with God, and had many sweet hours there. Sometimes Mr. Smith and I walked there together to converse of the things of God, and our conversation used much to turn on the advancement of Christ's kingdom in the world, and the glorious things that God would accomplish for His church in the latter days.

I had then, and at other times, the greatest delight in the holy Scriptures, of any book whatsoever. Oftentimes in reading it, every word seemed to touch my heart. I felt an harmony between something in my heart, and those sweet and powerful words. I seemed often to see so much light exhibited by every sentence, and such a refreshing ravishing food communicated, that I could not get along in reading. Used oftentimes to dwell long on one sentence, to see the wonders contained in it; and yet almost every sentence seemed to be full of wonders.

I came away from New York in the month of April, 1723, and had a most bitter parting with Madam Smith and her son. My heart seemed to sink within

---

5. "Verily I say unto you, Whosoever shall not receive the kingdom of God as a little child, he shall not enter therein" (Mark 10.15).

me, at leaving the family and city, where I had enjoyed so many sweet and pleasant days. I went from New York to Weathersfield[6] by water. As I sailed away, I kept sight of the city as long as I could; and when I was out of sight of it, it would affect me much to look that way, with a kind of melancholy mixed with sweetness. However, that night after this sorrowful parting. I was greatly comforted in God at Westchester, where we went ashore to lodge, and had a pleasant time of it all the voyage to Saybrook.[7] It was sweet to me to think of meeting dear Christians in heaven, where we should never part more. At Saybrook we went ashore to lodge on Saturday, and there kept sabbath where I had a sweet and refreshing season, walking alone in the fields.

After I came home to Windsor, remained much in a like frame of my mind as I had been in at New York, but only sometimes felt my heart ready to sink with the thoughts of my friends at New York. And my refuge and support was in contemplations on the heavenly state, as I find in my diary of May 1, 1723. It was my comfort to think of that state where there is fulness of joy; where reigns heavenly, sweet, calm and delightful love, without alloy; where there are continually the dearest expressions of this love; where is the enjoyment of the persons loved without ever parting; where these persons that appear so lovely in this world will really be inexpressibly more lovely, and full of love to us. And how sweetly will the mutual lovers join together to sing the praises of God and the Lamb![8] How full will it fill us with joy to think that this enjoyment, these sweet exercises will never cease or come to an end, but will last to all eternity!

Continued much in the same frame in the general that I had been in at New York, till I went to New Haven to live there as tutor of the college, having some special seasons of uncommon sweetness; particularly once at Boston in a journey from Boston, walking out alone in the fields. After I went to New Haven, I sunk in religion, my mind being diverted from my eager and violent pursuits after holiness by some affairs that greatly perplexed and distracted my mind.

In September, 1725, was taken ill at New Haven, and endeavoring to go home to Windsor, was so ill at the North Village that I could go no further, where I lay sick for about a quarter of a year. And in this sickness, God was pleased to visit me again with the sweet influences of His spirit. My mind was greatly engaged there on divine, pleasant contemplations and longings of soul. I observed that those who watched with me would often be looking out for the morning, and seemed to wish for it. Which brought to my mind those words of the psalmist, which my soul with sweetness made its own language: "My soul waitest for the Lord, more than they that watch for the morning, I say, more than they that watch for the morning."[9] And when the light of the morning came, and the beams of the sun came in at the windows, it refreshed my soul from one morning to another. It seemed to me to be some image of the sweet light of God's glory.

I remember, about that time, I used greatly to long for the conversion of some that I was concerned with. It seemed to me I could gladly honor them, and with delight be a servant to them, and lie at their feet, if they were but truly holy.

6. Wethersfield, Connecticut, is very near his father's home in Windsor.
7. Westchester and Saybrook are in New York and Connecticut, respectively.
8. In Revelation the symbol of Christ.
9. Psalm 130.6.

But sometime after this, I was again greatly diverted in my mind with some temporal concerns that exceedingly took up my thoughts, greatly to the wounding of my soul, and went on through various exercises, that it would be tedious to relate, that gave me much more experience of my own heart than ever I had before.

Since I came to this town, I have often had sweet complacency[1] in God, in views of His glorious perfections and the excellency of Jesus Christ. God has appeared to me a glorious and lovely Being, chiefly on the account of His holiness. The holiness of God has always appeared to me the most lovely of all His attributes. The doctrines of God's absolute sovereignty and free grace in showing mercy to whom He would show mercy, and man's absolute dependence on the operations of God's Holy Spirit, have very often appeared to me as sweet and glorious doctrines. These doctrines have been much my delight. God's sovereignty has ever appeared to me as great part of His glory. It has often been sweet to me to go to God and adore Him as a sovereign God, and ask sovereign mercy of Him.

I have loved the doctrines of the gospel; they have been to my soul like green pastures. The gospel has seemed to me to be the richest treasure, the treasure that I have most desired and longed that it might dwell richly in me. The way of salvation by Christ has appeared in a general way glorious and excellent, and most pleasant and beautiful. It has often seemed to me that it would in a great measure spoil heaven to receive it in any other way. That text has often been affecting and delightful to me, Isaiah 32.2: "A man shall be an hiding place from the wind, and a covert from the tempest, etc."

It has often appeared sweet to me to be united to Christ; to have Him for my head, and to be a member of His body; and also to have Christ for my teacher and prophet. I very often think with sweetness and longings and pantings of soul, of being a little child, taking hold of Christ, to be led by Him through the wilderness of this world. That text, Matthew 18.3 at the beginning, has often been sweet to me, "Except ye be converted, and become as little children, etc." I love to think of coming to Christ, to receive salvation of Him, poor in spirit, and quite empty of self; humbly exalting Him alone; cut entirely off from my own root, and to grow into and out of Christ; to have God in Christ to be all in all; and to live by faith in the Son of God, a life of humble, unfeigned confidence in Him. That Scripture has often been sweet to me, Psalm 115.1: "Not unto us, O Lord, not unto us, but unto Thy name give glory, for Thy mercy, and for Thy truth's sake." And those words of Christ, Luke 10.21: "In that hour Jesus rejoiced in spirit, and said, I thank thee, O Father, Lord of heaven and earth, that Thou hast hid these things from the wise and prudent, and hast revealed them unto babes: Even so Father, for so it seemed good in Thy sight." That sovereignty of God that Christ rejoiced in seemed to me to be worthy to be rejoiced in, and that rejoicing of Christ seemed to me to show the excellency of Christ, and the spirit that He was of.

Sometimes only mentioning a single word causes my heart to burn within me, or only seeing the name of Christ or the name of some attribute of God. And God has appeared glorious to me on account of the Trinity. It has made me have exalting thoughts of God, that He subsists in three persons: Father, Son, and Holy Ghost.

1. Contentment. "This town": Northampton, Massachusetts, where, in 1726, Edwards came to help his grandfather in conducting the affairs of his parish.

The sweetest joys and delights I have experienced have not been those that have arisen from a hope of my own good estate,[2] but in a direct view of the glorious things of the Gospel. When I enjoy this sweetness it seems to carry me above the thoughts of my own safe estate. It seems at such times a loss that I cannot bear, to take off my eye from the glorious, pleasant object I behold without me, to turn my eye in upon myself, and my own good estate.

My heart has been much on the advancement of Christ's kingdom in the world. The histories of the past advancement of Christ's kingdom have been sweet to me. When I have read histories of past ages, the pleasantest thing in all my reading has been to read of the kingdom of Christ being promoted. And when I have expected in my reading to come to any such thing, I have lotted[3] upon it all the way as I read. And my mind has been much entertained and delighted with the Scripture promises and prophecies of the future glorious advancement of Christ's kingdom on earth.

I have sometimes had a sense of the excellent fullness of Christ, and His meetness and suitableness as a Savior; whereby He has appeared to me, far above all, the chief of ten thousands.[4] And His blood and atonement has appeared sweet, and His righteousness sweet; which is always accompanied with an ardency of spirit, and inward strugglings and breathings and groanings, that cannot be uttered, to be emptied of myself and swallowed up in Christ.

Once, as I rid out into the woods for my health, Anno[5] 1737, and having lit from my horse in a retired place, as my manner commonly has been, to walk for divine contemplation and prayer, I had a view, that for me was extraordinary, of the glory of the Son of God, as mediator between God and man, and His wonderful, great, full, pure and sweet grace and love, and meek and gentle condescension. This grace, that appeared to me so calm and sweet, appeared great above the heavens. The person of Christ appeared ineffably excellent, with an excellency great enough to swallow up all thought and conception, which continued, as near as I can judge, about an hour, which kept me, the bigger part of the time, in a flood of tears, and weeping aloud. I felt withal an ardency of soul to be, what I know not otherwise how to express, than to be emptied and annihilated; to lie in the dust, and to be full of Christ alone; to love Him with a holy and pure love; to trust in Him; to live upon Him; to serve and follow Him, and to be totally rapt up in the fullness of Christ; and to be perfectly sanctified and made pure with a divine and heavenly purity. I have several other times had views very much of the same nature and that have had the same effects.

I have many times had a sense of the glory of the third person in the Trinity in His office of Sanctifier; in His holy operations communicating divine light and life to the soul. God in the communications of His Holy Spirit has appeared as an infinite fountain of divine glory and sweetness, being full and sufficient to fill and satisfy the soul, pouring forth itself in sweet communications, like the sun in its glory, sweetly and pleasantly diffusing light and life.

I have sometimes had an affecting sense of the excellency of the word of God, as a word of life; as the light of life; a sweet, excellent, life-giving word, accompanied with a thirsting after that word, that it might dwell richly in my heart.

I have often, since I lived in this town, had very affecting views of my own

2. Condition of being.
3. Rejoiced.
4. "My beloved is white and ruddy, the chiefest

among ten thousand" (Song of Solomon 5.10).
5. In the year (Latin).

sinfulness and vileness; very frequently so as to hold me in a kind of loud weeping, sometimes for a considerable time together, so that I have often been forced to shut myself up.[6] I have had a vastly greater sense of my wickedness, and the badness of my heart, since my conversion, than ever I had before. It has often appeared to me, that if God should mark iniquity against me, I should appear the very worst of all mankind, of all that have been since the beginning of the world of this time, and that I should have by far the lowest place in hell. When others that have come to talk with me about their soul concerns have expressed the sense they have had of their own wickedness by saying that it seemed to them that they were as bad as the devil himself, I thought their expressions seemed exceeding faint and feeble to represent my wickedness. I thought I should wonder that they should content themselves with such expressions as these, if I had any reason to imagine that their sin bore any proportion to mine. It seemed to me I should wonder at myself if I should express my wickedness in such feeble terms as they did.

My wickedness, as I am in myself, has long appeared to me perfectly ineffable and infinitely swallowing up all thought and imagination, like an infinite deluge or infinite mountains over my head. I know not how to express better what my sins appear to me to be than by heaping infinite upon infinite, and multiplying infinite by infinite. I go about very often, for this many years, with these expressions in my mind and in my mouth, "Infinite upon infinite. Infinite upon infinite!" When I look into my heart and take a view of my wickedness, it looks like an abyss infinitely deeper than hell. And it appears to me that were it not for free grace, exalted and raised up to the infinite height of all the fullness and glory of the great Jehovah,[7] and the arm of His power and grace stretched forth, in all the majesty of His power and in all the glory of His sovereignty, I should appear sunk down in my sins infinitely below hell itself, far beyond sight of everything but the piercing eye of God's grace, that can pierce even down to such a depth and to the bottom of such an abyss.

And yet I be not in the least inclined to think that I have a greater conviction of sin than ordinary. It seems to me my conviction of sin is exceeding small and faint. It appears to me enough to amaze me that I have no more sense of my sin. I know certainly that I have very little sense of my sinfulness. That my sins appear to me so great don't seem to me to be because I have so much more conviction of sin than other Christians, but because I am so much worse and have so much more wickedness to be convinced of. When I have had these turns of weeping and crying for my sins, I thought I knew in the time of it that my repentance was nothing to my sin.

I have greatly longed of late for a broken heart and to lie low before God. And when I ask for humility of God, I can't bear the thoughts of being no more humble than other Christians. It seems to me that though their degrees of humility may be suitable for them, yet it would be a vile self-exaltation in me not to be the lowest in humility of all mankind. Others speak of their longing to be humbled to the dust. Though that may be a proper expression for them I always think for myself that I ought to be humbled down below hell. 'Tis an expression that it has long been natural for me to use in prayer to God. I ought to lie infinitely low before God.

It is affecting to me to think how ignorant I was, when I was a young Chris-

---

6. I.e., retire to his study.   7. The name used for God in the Old Testament.

tian, of the bottomless, infinite depths of wickedness, pride, hypocrisy and deceit left in my heart.

I have vastly a greater sense of my universal, exceeding dependence on God's grace and strength and mere good pleasure, of late, than I used formerly to have, and have experienced more of an abhorrence of my own righteousness. The thought of any comfort or joy, arising in me, on any consideration or reflection on my own amiableness, or any of my performances or experiences, or any goodness of heart or life is nauseous and detestable to me. And yet I am greatly afflicted with a proud and self-righteous spirit, much more sensibly than I used to be formerly. I see that serpent rising and putting forth its head, continually, everywhere, all around me.

Though it seems to me that in some respects I was a far better Christian for two or three years after my first conversion than I am now, and lived in a more constant delight and pleasure, yet of late years I have had a more full and constant sense of the absolute sovereignty of God and a delight in that sovereignty, and have had more of a sense of the glory of Christ as a mediator as revealed in the Gospel. On one Saturday night in particular, had a particular discovery of the excellency of the Gospel of Christ, above all other doctrines, so that I could not but say to myself, "This is my chosen light, my chosen doctrine," and of Christ, "This is my chosen prophet." It appeared to me to be sweet beyond all expression to follow Christ and to be taught and enlightened and instructed by Him, to learn of Him, and live to Him.

Another Saturday night, January, 1738–9, had such a sense how sweet and blessed a thing it was to walk in the way of duty, to do that which was right and meet to be done and agreeable to the holy mind of God, that it caused me to break forth into a kind of a loud weeping, which held me some time, so that I was forced to shut myself up, and fasten the doors. I could not but as it were cry out, "How happy are they which do that which is right in the sight of God! They are blessed indeed, they are the happy ones!" I had at the same time, a very affecting sense how meet and suitable it was that God should govern the world, and order all things according to His own pleasure, and I rejoiced in it, that God reigned, and that His will was done.

c. 1740   1765

[Sarah Pierrepont][1]

They say there is a young lady in [New Haven] who is beloved of that Great Being, who made and rules the world, and that there are certain seasons in which this Great Being, in some way or other invisible, comes to her and fills her mind with exceeding sweet delight, and that she hardly cares for anything, except to meditate on Him—that she expects after a while to be received up where He is, to be raised up out of the world and caught up into heaven; being assured that He loves her too well to let her remain at a distance from Him always. There she is to dwell with Him, and to be ravished with His love and delight forever. Therefore, if you present all the world before her, with the

1. This tribute to Sarah Pierrepont was written, according to S. E. Dwight, in 1723, when she was thirteen years old and Edwards, twenty. He married her in 1727. The manuscript appeared in a blank leaf in a book, and no holograph exists. It was first published in Sereno E. Dwight's *The Life of President Edwards* (1829).

richest of its treasures, she disregards it and cares not for it, and is unmindful of any pain or affliction. She has a strange sweetness in her mind, and singular purity in her affections; is most just and conscientious in all her conduct; and you could not persuade her to do anything wrong or sinful, if you would give her all the world, lest she should offend this Great Being. She is of a wonderful sweetness, calmness and universal benevolence of mind; especially after this Great God has manifested Himself to her mind. She will sometimes go about from place to place, singing sweetly; and seems to be always full of joy and pleasure; and no one knows for what. She loves to be alone, walking in the fields and groves, and seems to have some one invisible always conversing with her.

1723   1829

A Divine and Supernatural Light[1]

IMMEDIATELY IMPARTED TO THE SOUL BY THE SPIRIT OF GOD, SHOWN
TO BE BOTH A SCRIPTURAL AND RATIONAL DOCTRINE

Matthew 16.17

And Jesus answered and said unto him, Blessed art thou, Simon Barjona;[2] for flesh and blood hath not revealed it unto thee, but my Father which is in heaven.

Christ addresses these words to Peter upon occasion of his professing his faith in Him as the Son of God. Our Lord was inquiring of His disciples, whom men said that He was; not that He needed to be informed, but only to introduce and give occasion to what follows. They answer that some said He was John the Baptist, and some Elias, and others Jeremias, or one of the prophets.[3] When they had thus given an account whom others said that He was, Christ asks them, whom they said that He was? Simon Peter, whom we find always zealous and forward, was the first to answer: he readily replied to the question, Thou art Christ, the Son of the living God.

Upon this occasion, Christ says as He does to him and of him in the text: in which we may observe.

1. That Peter is pronounced blessed on this account.—Blessed art thou— "Thou art an happy man, that thou art not ignorant of this, that I am Christ, the Son of the living God. Thou art distinguishingly happy. Others are blinded, and have dark and deluded apprehensions, as you have now given an account, some thinking that I am Elias, and some that I am Jeremias, and some one thing, and some another: but none of them thinking right, all of them are misled. Happy art thou, that art so distinguished as to know the truth in this matter."

2. The evidence of this his happiness declared, viz., That God, and He only, had revealed it to him. This is an evidence of his being blessed.

First. As it shows how peculiarly favored he was of God above others; q.d.,[4]

1. Edwards delivered this sermon in Northampton, Massachusetts, in 1733; it was published the following year at the request of his congregation. The text used is from *The Works of Jonathan Edwards*, vol. 6, edited by Sereno E. Dwight (1829–30).

2. The apostle Peter (Simon, son of Jona).
3. Matthew 16.14. Elias is the name used in the New Testament for the prophet Elijah.
4. I.e., *quasi dicat*: as if he should say (Latin).

"How highly favored art thou, that others, wise and great men, the scribes, Pharisees,[5] and rulers, and the nation in general, are left in darkness, to follow their own misguided apprehensions; and that thou shouldst be singled out, as it were, by name, that My heavenly Father should thus set His love on thee, Simon Bar-jona.—This argues thee blessed, that thou shouldst thus be the object of God's distinguishing love."

Secondly. It evidences his blessedness also, as it intimates that this knowledge is above any that flesh and blood can reveal. "This is such knowledge as only my Father which is in heaven can give. It is too high and excellent to be communicated by such means as other knowledge is. Thou art blessed, that thou knowest what God alone can teach thee."

The original of this knowledge is here declared, both negatively and positively. Positively, as God is here declared the author of it. Negatively, as it is declared, that flesh and blood had not revealed it. God is the author of all knowledge and understanding whatsoever. He is the author of all moral prudence, and of the skill that men have in their secular business. Thus it is said of all in Israel that were wise-hearted and skilled in embroidering, that God had filled them with the spirit of wisdom. Exodus 28.3.[6]

God is the author of such knowledge; yet so that flesh and blood reveals it. Mortal men are capable of imparting the knowledge of human arts and sciences, and skill in temporal affairs. God is the author of such knowledge by those means: flesh and blood is employed as the mediate or second cause of it; He conveys it by the power and influence of natural means. But this spiritual knowledge, spoken of in the text, is what God is the author of, and none else: He reveals it, and flesh and blood reveals it not. He imparts this knowledge immediately, not making use of any intermediate natural causes, as He does in other knowledge.

What had passed in the preceding discourse naturally occasioned Christ to observe this; because the disciples had been telling how others did not know Him, but were generally mistaken about him, divided and confounded in their opinions of Him: but Peter had declared his assured faith, that He was the Son of God. Now it was natural to observe how it was not flesh and blood that had revealed it to him, but God; for if this knowledge were dependent on natural causes or means, how came it to pass that they, a company of poor fishermen, illiterate men, and persons of low education, attained to the knowledge of the truth, while the Scribes and Pharisees, men of vastly higher advantages, and greater knowledge and sagacity, in other matters, remained in ignorance? This could be owing only to the gracious distinguishing influence and revelation of the Spirit of God. Hence, what I would make the subject of my present discourse from these words, is this:

Doctrine

That there is such a thing as a spiritual and divine light, immediately imparted to the soul by God, of a different nature from any that is obtained by natural means. And on this subject I would,

---

5. A sect hostile to Jesus and known for their arrogance and pride (Matthew 9.9–13). "Scribes": interpreters of the Jewish law.

6. This passage from Exodus refers to God's command to the people of Israel to make proper garments for Aaron's priesthood.

I. Show what this divine light is.

II. How it is given immediately by God, and not obtained by natural means.

III. Show the truth of the doctrine.

And then conclude with a brief improvement.[7]

I. I would show what this spiritual and divine light is. And in order to it would show,

First, In a few things, what it is not. And here,

1. Those convictions that natural men may have of their sin and misery, is not this spiritual and divine light. Men, in a natural condition, may have convictions of the guilt that lies upon them, and of the anger of God, and their danger of divine vengeance. Such convictions are from the light of truth. That some sinners have a greater conviction of their guilt and misery than others is because some have more light, or more of an apprehension of truth than others. And this light and conviction may be from the Spirit of God; the Spirit convinces men of sin; but yet nature is much more concerned in it than in the communication of that spiritual and divine light that is spoken of in the doctrine; it is from the Spirit of God only as assisting natural principles, and not as infusing any new principles. Common grace differs from special in that it influences only by assisting of nature, and not by imparting grace, or bestowing anything above nature. The light that is obtained is wholly natural, or of no superior kind to what mere nature attains to, though more of that kind be obtained than would be obtained if men were left wholly to themselves; or, in other words, common grace only assists the faculties of the soul to do that more fully which they do by nature, as natural conscience or reason will by mere nature make a man sensible of guilt, and will accuse and condemn him when he has done amiss. Conscience is a principle natural to men; and the work that it doth naturally, or of itself, is to give an apprehension of right and wrong, and to suggest to the mind the relation that there is between right and wrong and a retribution. The Spirit of God, in those convictions which unregenerate men sometimes have, assists conscience to do this work in a further degree than it would do if they were left to themselves. He helps it against those things that tend to stupify it, and obstruct its exercise. But in the renewing and sanctifying work of the Holy Ghost, those things are wrought in the soul that are above nature, and of which there is nothing of the like kind in the soul by nature; and they are caused to exist in the soul habitually, and according to such a stated constitution or law, that lays such a foundation for exercises in a continued course, as is called a principle of nature. Not only are remaining principles assisted to do their work more freely and fully, but those principles are restored that were utterly destroyed by the fall; and the mind thenceforward habitually exerts those acts that the dominion of sin had made it as wholly destitute of as a dead body is of vital acts.

The Spirit of God acts in a very different manner in the one case, from what He doth in the other. He may, indeed, act upon the mind of a natural man, but He acts in the mind of a saint[8] as an indwelling vital principle. He acts upon the mind of an unregenerate[9] person as an extrinsic occasional agent;

---

7. Literally, turning something to profit; here used in the sense of the lesson to be learned.

8. Here, a living Christian who has passed from mere understanding of Christ's doctrine to heartfelt commitment; such people were often called "visible saints."

9. One who is not yet saved.

for, in acting upon them, He doth not unite himself to them: for, notwithstanding all His influences that they may possess, they are still sensual, having
not the Spirit. Jude 19.[1] But He unites himself with the mind of a saint, takes
him for His temple, actuates and influences him as a new supernatural principle of life and action. There is this difference, that the Spirit of God, in acting
in the soul of a godly man, exerts and communicates Himself there in His
own proper nature. Holiness is the proper nature of the Spirit of God. The
Holy Spirit operates in the minds of the godly, by uniting Himself to them,
and living in them, and exerting His own nature in the exercise of their faculties. The Spirit of God may act upon a creature, and yet not in acting communicate Himself. The Spirit of God may act upon inanimate creatures, as, the
Spirit moved upon the face of the waters,[2] in the beginning of the creation; so
the Spirit of God may act upon the minds of men many ways, and communicate Himself no more than when He acts upon an inanimate creature. For
instance, He may excite thoughts in them, may assist their natural reason and
understanding, or may assist other natural principles, and this without any
union with the soul, but may act, as it were, upon an external object. But as
He acts in His holy influences and spiritual operations, He acts in a way of
peculiar communication of Himself; so that the subject is thence denominated spiritual.

2. This spiritual and divine light does not consist in any impression made
upon the imagination. It is no impression upon the mind, as though one saw
anything with the bodily eyes. It is no imagination or idea of an outward light
or glory, or any beauty of form or countenance, or a visible luster or brightness
of any object. The imagination may be strongly impressed with such things;
but this is not spiritual light. Indeed when the mind has a lively discovery of
spiritual things, and is greatly affected with the power of divine light, it may,
and probably very commonly doth, much affect the imagination; so that
impressions of an outward beauty or brightness may accompany those spiritual
discoveries. But spiritual light is not that impression upon the imagination,
but an exceedingly different thing. Natural men may have lively impressions
on their imaginations; and we cannot determine but that the devil, who trans-
forms himself into an angel of light, may cause imaginations of an outward
beauty, or visible glory, and of sounds and speeches, and other such things;
but these are things of a vastly inferior nature to spiritual light.

3. This spiritual light is not the suggesting of any new truths or propositions
not contained in the word of God. This suggesting of new truths or doctrines
to the mind, independent of any antecedent revelations of those propositions,
either in word or writing, is inspiration; such as the prophets and apostles had,
and such as some enthusiasts[3] pretend to. But this spiritual light that I am
speaking of, is quite a different thing from inspiration. It reveals no new doctrine, it suggests no new proposition to the mind, it teaches no new thing of
God, or Christ, or another world, not taught in the Bible, but only gives a due
apprehension of those things that are taught in the word of God.

4. It is not every affecting view that men have of religious things that is this
spiritual and divine light. Men by mere principles of nature are capable of
being affected with things that have a special relation to religion as well as

1. "These be they who separate themselves, sensual,
having not the Spirit."
2. Genesis 1.2.

3. People who erroneously claim to be inspired by the
spirit of God.

other things. A person by mere nature, for instance, may be liable to be affected with the story of Jesus Christ, and the sufferings he underwent, as well as by any other tragical story. He may be the more affected with it from the interest he conceives mankind to have in it. Yea, he may be affected with it without believing it; as well as a man may be affected with what he reads in a romance, or sees acted in a stage play. He may be affected with a lively and eloquent description of many pleasant things that attend the state of the blessed in heaven, as well as his imagination be entertained by a romantic[4] description of the pleasantness of fairyland, or the like. And a common belief of the truth of such things, from education or otherwise, may help forward their affection. We read in Scripture of many that were greatly affected with things of a religious nature, who yet are there represented as wholly graceless, and many of them very ill[5] men. A person therefore may have affecting views of the things of religion, and yet be very destitute of spiritual light. Flesh and blood may be the author of this; one man may give another an affecting view of divine things with but common assistance; but God alone can give a spiritual discovery of them.—But I proceed to show.

Secondly, Positively what this spiritual and divine light is.

And it may be thus described: A true sense of the divine excellency of the things revealed in the word of God, and a conviction of the truth and reality of them thence arising. This spiritual light primarily consists in the former of these, viz., a real sense and apprehension of the divine excellency of things revealed in the word of God. A spiritual and saving conviction of the truth and reality of these things, arises from such a sight of their divine excellency and glory; so that this conviction of their truth is an effect and natural consequence of this sight of their divine glory. There is therefore in this spiritual light,

1. A true sense of the divine and superlative excellency of the things of religion; a real sense of the excellency of God and Jesus Christ, and of the work of redemption, and the ways and works of God revealed in the gospel. There is a divine and superlative glory in these things; an excellency that is of a vastly higher kind, and more sublime nature than in other things; a glory greatly distinguishing them from all that is earthly and temporal. He that is spiritually enlightened truly apprehends and sees it, or has a sense of it. He does not merely rationally believe that God is glorious, but he has a sense of the gloriousness of God in his heart. There is not only a rational belief that God is holy, and that holiness is a good thing, but there is a sense of the loveliness of God's holiness. There is not only a speculatively judging that God is gracious, but a sense how amiable God is on account of the beauty of this divine attribute.

There is a twofold knowledge of good of which God has made the mind of man capable. The first, that which is merely notional; as when a person only speculatively judges that anything is, which by the agreement of mankind, is called good or excellent, viz., that which is most to general advantage, and between which and a reward there is a suitableness,—and the like. And the other is, that which consists in the sense of the heart; as when the heart is sensible[6] of pleasure and delight in the presence of the idea of it. In the former is exercised merely the speculative faculty, or the understanding, in distinction from the will or disposition of the soul. In the latter, the will, or inclination, or heart, are mainly concerned.

4. Fanciful, imaginary.   6. Aware.
5. I.e., evil.

Thus there is a difference between having an opinion, that God is holy and gracious, and having a sense of the loveliness and beauty of that holiness and grace. There is a difference between having a rational judgment that honey is sweet, and having a sense of its sweetness. A man may have the former, that knows not how honey tastes; but a man cannot have the latter unless he has an idea of the taste of honey in his mind. So there is a difference between believing that a person is beautiful, and having a sense of his beauty. The former may be obtained by hearsay, but the latter only by seeing the countenance. When the heart is sensible of the beauty and amiableness of a thing, it necessarily feels pleasure in the apprehension. It is implied in a person's being heartily sensible of the loveliness of a thing, that the idea of it is pleasant to his soul; which is a far different thing from having a rational opinion that it is excellent.

2. There arises from this sense of the divine excellency of things contained in the word of God, a conviction of the truth and reality of them; and that, either indirectly or directly.

First, Indirectly, and that two ways:

1. As the prejudices of the heart, against the truth of divine things, are hereby removed; so that the mind becomes susceptive of the due force of rational arguments for their truth. The mind of man is naturally full of prejudices against divine truth. It is full of enmity against the doctrines of the gospel; which is a disadvantage to those arguments that prove their truth, and causes them to lose their force upon the mind. But when a person has discovered to him the divine excellency of Christian doctrines, this destroys the enmity, removes those prejudices, sanctifies the reason, and causes it to lie open to the force of arguments for their truth.

Hence was the different effect that Christ's miracles had to convince the disciples, from what they had to convince the Scribes and Pharisees. Not that they had a stronger reason, or had their reason more improved; but their reason was sanctified, and those blinding prejudices, that the Scribes and Pharisees were under, were removed by the sense they had of the excellency of Christ, and his doctrine.

It not only removes the hindrances of reason, but positively helps reason. It makes even the speculative notions more lively. It engages the attention of the mind, with more fixedness and intenseness to that kind of objects; which causes it to have a clearer view of them, and enables it more clearly to see their mutual relations, and occasions it to take more notice of them. The ideas themselves that otherwise are dim and obscure are by this means impressed with the greater strength, and have a light cast upon them, so that the mind can better judge of them. As he that beholds objects on the face of the earth, when the light of the sun is cast upon them, is under greater advantage to discern them in their true forms and natural relations, than he that sees them in a dim twilight.

The mind, being sensible of the excellency of divine objects, dwells upon them with delight; and the powers of the soul are more awakened and enlivened to employ themselves in the contemplation of them, and exert themselves more fully and much more to the purpose. The beauty of the objects draws on the faculties, and draws forth their exercises; so that reason itself is under far greater advantages for its proper and free exercises, and to attain its proper end, free of darkness and delusion.—But,

Secondly, A true sense of the divine excellency of the things of God's word doth more directly and immediately convince us of their truth; and that because the excellency of these things is so superlative. There is a beauty in them so divine and godlike, that it greatly and evidently distinguishes them from things merely human, or that of which men are the inventors and authors; a glory so high and great, that when clearly seen, commands assent to their divine reality. When there is an actual and lively discovery of this beauty and excellency, it will not allow of any such thought as that it is the fruit of men's invention. This is a kind of intuitive and immediate evidence. They believe the doctrines of God's word to be divine, because they see a divine, and transcendent, and most evidently distinguishing glory in them; such a glory as, if clearly seen, does not leave room to doubt of their being of God, and not of men.

Such a conviction of the truths of religion as this, arising from a sense of their divine excellency, is included in saving faith. And this original of it is that by which it is most essentially distinguished from that common assent, of which unregenerate men are capable.

II. I proceed now to the second thing proposed, viz., to show how this light is immediately given by God, and not obtained by natural means. And here,

1. It is not intended that the natural faculties are not used in it. They are the subject of this light: and in such a manner, that they are not merely passive, but active in it. God, in letting in this light into the soul, deals with man according to his nature, and makes use of his rational faculties. But yet this light is not the less immediately from God for that; the faculties are made use of as the subject, and not as the cause. As the use we make of our eyes in beholding various objects, when the sun arises, is not the cause of the light that discovers those objects to us.

2. It is not intended that outward means have no concern in this affair. It is not in this affair, as in inspiration, where new truths are suggested; for, by this light is given only a due apprehension of the same truths that are revealed in the word of God, and therefore it is not given without the word. The gospel is employed in this affair. This light is the "light of the glorious gospel of Christ" (2 Corinthians 4.3–4).[7] The gospel is as a glass, by which this light is conveyed to us (1 Corinthians 13.12): "Now we see through a glass."[8]—But,

3. When it is said that this light is given immediately by God, and not obtained by natural means, hereby is intended that it is given by God without making use of any means that operate by their own power or natural force. God makes use of means; but it is not as mediate causes to produce this effect. There are not truly any second causes of it; but it is produced by God immediately. The word of God is no proper cause of this effect, but is made use of only to convey to the mind the subject matter of this saving instruction: And this indeed it doth convey to us by natural force or influence. It conveys to our minds these doctrines; it is the cause of a notion of them in our heads, but not of the sense of their divine excellency in our hearts. Indeed a person cannot have spiritual light without the word. But that does not argue, that the word properly causes that light. The mind cannot see the excellency of any doctrine,

7. "But if our gospel be hid, it is hid to them that are lost: In whom the god of this world hath blinded the minds of them which believe not, lest the light of the glorious gospel of Christ, who is the image of God, should shine unto them."

8. "For now we see through a glass, darkly; but then face to face."

unless that doctrine be first in the mind; but seeing the excellency of the doctrine may be immediately from the Spirit of God; though the conveying of the doctrine, or proposition, itself, may be by the word. So that the notions which are the subject matter of this light are conveyed to the mind by the word of God; but that due sense of the heart, wherein this light formally consists, is immediately by the Spirit of God. As, for instance, the notion that there is a Christ, and that Christ is holy and gracious, is conveyed to the mind by the word of God: But the sense of the excellency of Christ, by reason of that holiness and grace, is nevertheless, immediately the work of the Holy Spirit.— I come now,

III. To show the truth of the doctrine; that is, to show that there is such a thing as that spiritual light that has been described, thus immediately let into the mind by God. And here I would show, briefly, that this doctrine is both scriptural and rational.

First, It is scriptural. My text is not only full to the purpose, but it is a doctrine with which the Scripture abounds. We are there abundantly taught, that the saints differ from the ungodly in this; that they have the knowledge of God, and a sight of God, and of Jesus Christ. I shall mention but few texts out of many: 1 John 3.6: "Whosoever sinneth, hath not seen him, nor known him." 3 John 11: "He that doeth good, is of God: but he that doeth evil, hath not seen God." John 14.19: "The world seeth me no more; but ye see me." John 17.3: "And this is eternal life, that they might know thee, the only true God, and Jesus Christ whom thou hast sent." This knowledge, or sight of God and Christ, cannot be a mere speculative knowledge, because it is spoken of as that wherein they differ from the ungodly. And by these scriptures, it must not only be a different knowledge in degree and circumstances, and different in its effects, but it must be entirely different in nature and kind.

And this light and knowledge is always spoken of as immediately given of God; Matthew 11.25–27: "At that time, Jesus answered and said, I thank thee, O Father, Lord of heaven and earth, because thou hast hid these things from the wise and prudent, and hast revealed them unto babes. Even so, Father, for so it seemed good in thy sight. All things are delivered unto me of my Father: and no man knoweth the Father, save the Son, and he to whomsoever the Son will reveal him." Here this effect is ascribed exclusively to the arbitrary operation and gift of God bestowing this knowledge on whom He will, and distinguishing those with it who have the least natural advantage or means for knowledge, even babes, when it is denied to the wise and prudent. And imparting this knowledge is here appropriated to the Son of God, as His sole prerogative. And again, 2 Corinthians 4.6: "For God, who commanded the light to shine out of darkness, hath shined in our hearts, to give the light of the knowledge of the glory of God, in the face of Jesus Christ." This plainly shows, that there is a discovery of the divine superlative glory and excellency of God and Christ, peculiar to the saints: and, also, that it is as immediately from God, as light from the sun, and that it is the immediate effect of His power and will. For it is compared to God's creating the light by his powerful word in the beginning of the creation; and is said to be by the Spirit of the Lord, in the 18th verse of the preceding chapter. God is spoken of as giving the knowledge of Christ in conversion, as of what before was hidden and unseen; Galatians 1.15–16: "But when it pleased God, who separated me from my mother's womb, and called me by his grace, to reveal his son in me." The scripture also speaks plainly of such a knowledge of the word of God, as has been described as the immediate gift of God; Psalm 119.18: "Open thou mine eyes, that I may behold wondrous things out of thy law." What could the Psalmist mean, when he begged of God to open his eyes? Was he ever blind? Might he not have resort to the law, and see every word and sentence in it when he pleased? And what could he mean by those wondrous things? Were they the wonderful stories of the creation, and deluge, and Israel's passing through the Red Sea,[9] and the like? Were not his eyes open to read these strange things when he would? Doubtless, by wondrous things in God's law, he had respect to those distinguishing and wonderful excellencies, and marvelous manifestations of the divine perfections and glory contained in the commands and doctrines of the word, and those works and counsels of God that were there revealed. So the scripture speaks of a knowledge of God's dispensation, and covenant of mercy,[1] and way of grace towards His people, as peculiar to the saints, and given only by God; Psalm 25.14: "The secret of the Lord is with them that fear him; and he will show them his covenant."

And that a true and saving belief of the truth of religion is that which arises from such a discovery is, also, what the scripture teaches. As John 6.40: "And this is the will of him that sent me, that every one who seeth the Son, and believeth on him, may have everlasting life"; where it is plain that a true faith is what arises from a spiritual sight of Christ. And John 17.6–8: "I have manifested thy name unto the men which thou gavest me out of the world. Now, they have known, that all things whatsoever thou hast given me, are of thee. For I have given unto them the words which thou gavest me, and they have received them, and have known surely, that I came out from thee, and they have believed that thou didst send me"; where Christ's manifesting God's name to the disciples, or giving them the knowledge of God, was that whereby they knew that Christ's doctrine was of God, and that Christ Himself proceeded from Him, and was sent by Him. Again, John 12.44–46: "Jesus cried, and said, He that believeth on me, believeth not on me but on him that sent me. And he that seeth me, seeth him that sent me. I am come a light into the world, that whosoever believeth on me, should not abide in darkness." Their believing in Christ, and spiritually seeing Him, are parallel.

Christ condemns the Jews, that they did not know that He was the Messiah, and that His doctrine was true, from an inward distinguishing taste and relish of what was divine, in Luke 12.56–57. He having there blamed the Jews, that, though they could discern the face of the sky and of the earth, and signs of the weather, that yet they could not discern those times—or, as it is expressed in Matthew, the signs of those times—adds, "yea, and why even of your ownselves, judge ye not what is right?" i.e., without extrinsic signs. Why have ye not that sense of true excellency, whereby ye may distinguish that which is holy and divine? Why have ye not that savor of the things of God, by which you may see the distinguishing glory, and evident divinity of me and my doctrine?

The apostle Peter mentions it as what gave him and his companions good and well-grounded assurance of the truth of the gospel, that they had seen the

9. The waters of the Red Sea divided for the Israelites in their exodus from Egypt (Exodus 14.21).
1. The agreement between Christ and those who be-lieve in him that they would be saved; also known as the Covenant of Faith, as distinct from the Covenant of Works, which Adam broke.

divine glory of Christ. 2 Peter 1.16: "For we have not followed cunningly devised fables, when we made known unto you the power and coming of our Lord Jesus Christ, but were eye-witnesses of his majesty." The apostle has respect to that visible glory of Christ which they saw in His transfiguration. That glory was so divine, having such an ineffable appearance and semblance of divine holiness, majesty, and grace, that it evidently denoted Him to be a divine person. But if a sight of Christ's outward glory might give a rational assurance of His divinity, why may not an apprehension of His spiritual glory do so too? Doubtless Christ's spiritual glory is in itself as distinguishing, and as plainly shows His divinity, as His outward glory—nay, a great deal more, for His spiritual glory is that wherein His divinity consists; and the outward glory of His transfiguration showed Him to be divine, only as it was a remarkable image or representation of that spiritual glory. Doubtless, therefore, he that has had a clear sight of the spiritual glory of Christ, may say, "I have not followed cunningly devised fables, but have been an eyewitness of His majesty, upon as good grounds as the apostle, when he had respect to the outward glory of Christ that he had seen." But this brings me to what was proposed next, viz., to show that,

Secondly, This doctrine is rational.[2]

1. It is rational to suppose, that there is really such an excellency in divine things—so transcendent and exceedingly different from what is in other things—that if it were seen, would most evidently distinguish them. We cannot rationally doubt but that things divine, which appertain to the supreme Being, are vastly different from things that are human; that there is a high, glorious, and godlike excellency in them that does most remarkably difference them from the things that are of men, insomuch that if the difference were but seen, it would have a convincing, satisfying influence upon anyone that they are divine. What reason can be offered against it unless we would argue that God is not remarkably distinguished in glory from men.

If Christ should now appear to any one as he did on the mount at His transfiguration,[3] or if He should appear to the world in His heavenly glory, as He will do at the Day of Judgment,[4] without doubt, His glory and majesty would be such as would satisfy everyone that He was a divine person, and that His religion was true; and it would be a most reasonable, and well grounded conviction too. And why may there not be that stamp of divinity or divine glory on the word of God, on the scheme and doctrine of the gospel, that may be in like manner distinguishing and as rationally convincing, provided it be but seen? It is rational to suppose, that when God speaks to the world, there should be something in His word vastly different from men's word. Supposing that God never had spoken to the world, but we had notice that He was about to reveal Himself from heaven and speak to us immediately Himself, or that He should give us a book of His own inditing;[5] after what manner should we expect that He would speak? Would it not be rational to suppose, that His speech would be exceeding different from men's speech, that there should be such an excellency and sublimity in His word, such a stamp of wisdom, holiness, majesty, and other divine perfections, that the word of men, yea of the

---

2. Capable of being grasped by the mind, understandable.
3. In Matthew 17.1–8, Christ appeared to Peter, James, and John shining "as the sun" and his garments "white as the light."
4. See Revelation 4.
5. Composition.

wisest of men, should appear mean and base in comparison of it? Doubtless it would be thought rational to expect this, and unreasonable to think otherwise. When a wise man speaks in the exercise of His wisdom, there is something in everything He says, that is very distinguishable from the talk of a little child. So, without doubt, and much more is the speech of God, to be distinguished from that of the wisest of men; agreeable to Jeremiah 23.28–29. God, having there been reproving the false prophets that prophesied in his name, and pretended that what they spake was His word, when indeed it was their own word, says, "The prophet that hath a dream, let him tell a dream; and he that hath my word let him speak my word faithfully: what is the chaff to the wheat? saith the Lord. Is not my word like as a fire? saith the Lord: and like a hammer that breaketh the rock in pieces?"

2. If there be such a distinguishing excellency in divine things, it is rational to suppose that there may be such a thing as seeing it. What should hinder but that it may be seen? It is no argument that there is no such distinguishing excellency, or that it cannot be seen, because some do not see it, though they may be discerning men in temporal matters. It is not rational to suppose, if there be any such excellency in divine things, that wicked men should see it. It is rational to suppose that those whose minds are full of spiritual pollution, and under the power of filthy lusts, should have any relish or sense of divine beauty or excellency; or that their minds should be susceptive of that light that is in its own nature so pure and heavenly? It need not seem at all strange that sin should so blind the mind, seeing that men's particular natural tempers and dispositions will so much blind them in secular matters; as when men's natural temper is melancholy, jealous, fearful, proud, or the like.

3. It is rational to suppose that this knowledge should be given immediately by God, and not be obtained by natural means. Upon what account should it seem unreasonable that there should be any immediate communication between God and the creature? It is strange, that men should make any matter of difficulty of it. Why should not He that made all things still have something immediately to do with the things that He has made? Where lies the great difficulty, if we own the being of a God, and that He created all things out of nothing, of allowing some immediate influence of God on the creation still? And if it be reasonable to suppose it with respect to any part of the creation, it is especially so with respect to reasonable, intelligent creatures; who are next to God in the gradation of the different orders of beings, and whose business is most immediately with God; and reason teaches that man was made to serve and glorify his Creator. And if it be rational to suppose that God immediately communicates Himself to man in any affair, it is in this. It is rational to suppose that God would reserve that knowledge and wisdom, which is of such a divine and excellent nature, to be bestowed immediately by Himself, and that it should not be left in the power of second causes. Spiritual wisdom and grace is the highest and most excellent gift that ever God bestows on any creature; in this, the highest excellency and perfection of a rational creature consists. It is also immensely the most important of all divine gifts: it is that wherein man's happiness consists, and on which his everlasting welfare depends. How rational is it to suppose that God, however He has left lower gifts to second causes, and in some sort in their power, yet should reserve this most excellent, divine, and important of all divine communications in His own hands to be bestowed immediately by Himself, as a thing too great for

second causes to be concerned in. It is rational to suppose that this blessing should be immediately from God, for there is no gift or benefit that is in itself so nearly related to the divine nature. Nothing which the creature receives is so much a participation of the Deity; it is a kind of emanation of God's beauty, and is related to God as the light is to the sun. It is, therefore, congruous and fit, that when it is given of God, it should be immediately from Himself, and by Himself, according to His own sovereign will.

It is rational to suppose, that it should be beyond man's power to obtain this light by the mere strength of natural reason; for it is not a thing that belongs to reason to see the beauty and loveliness of spiritual things; it is not a speculative thing, but depends on the sense of the heart. Reason, indeed, is necessary, in order to it, as it is by reason only that we are become the subjects of the means of it; which means, I have already shown to be necessary in order to it, though they have no proper causal influence in the affair. It is by reason that we become possessed of a notion of those doctrines that are the subject matter of this divine light or knowledge; and reason may many ways be indirectly and remotely an advantage to it. Reason has also to do in the acts that are immediately consequent on this discovery: for, seeing the truth of religion from hence, is by reason, though it be but by one step, and the inference be immediate. So reason has to do in that accepting of and trusting in Christ that is consequent on it. But if we take reason strictly—not for the faculty of mental perception in general, but for ratiocination, or a power of inferring by arguments— the perceiving of spiritual beauty and excellency no more belongs to reason than it belongs to the sense of feeling to perceive colors, or to the power of seeing to perceive the sweetness of food. It is out of reason's province to perceive the beauty or loveliness of anything; such a perception does not belong to that faculty. Reason's work is to perceive truth and not excellency. It is not ratiocination that gives men the perception of the beauty and amiableness of a countenance, though it may be many ways indirectly an advantage to it; yet it is no more reason that immediately perceives it than it is reason that perceives the sweetness of honey; it depends on the sense of the heart. Reason may determine that a countenance is beautiful to others, it may determine that honey is sweet to others, but it will never give me a perception of its sweetness.

I will conclude with a very brief improvement of what has been said.

First, this doctrine may lead us to reflect on the goodness of God, that has so ordered it, that a saving evidence of the truth of the Gospel is such as is attainable by persons of mean capacities and advantages, as well as those that are of the greatest parts and learning. If the evidence of the Gospel depended only on history and such reasonings as learned men only are capable of, it would be above the reach of far the greatest part of mankind. But persons with an ordinary degree of knowledge are capable, without a long and subtle train of reasoning, to see the divine excellency of the things of religion; they are capable of being taught by the Spirit of God, as well as learned men. The evidence that is this way obtained is vastly better and more satisfying than all that can be obtained by the arguings of those that are most learned and greatest masters of reason. And babes are as capable of knowing these things as the wise and prudent; and they are often hid from these when they are revealed to those. 1 Corinthians 1.26–27: "For ye see your calling, brethren, how that not many wise men, after the flesh, not many mighty, not many noble, are called. But God hath chosen the foolish things of the world."

Secondly, This doctrine may well put us upon examining ourselves, whether we have ever had this divine light let into our souls. If there be such a thing, doubtless it is of great importance whether we have thus been taught by the Spirit of God; whether the light of the glorious gospel of Christ, who is the image of God, hath shined unto us, giving us the light of the knowledge of the glory of God in the face of Jesus Christ; whether we have seen the Son, and believed on Him, or have that faith of gospel doctrines which arises from a spiritual sight of Christ.

Thirdly, All may hence be exhorted earnestly to seek this spiritual light. To influence and move to it, the following things may be considered.

1. This is the most excellent and divine wisdom that any creature is capable of. It is more excellent than any human learning; it is far more excellent than all the knowledge of the greatest philosophers or statesmen. Yea, the least glimpse of the glory of God in the face of Christ doth more exalt and ennoble the soul than all the knowledge of those that have the greatest speculative understanding in divinity without grace. This knowledge has the most noble object that can be, viz., the divine glory and excellency of God and Christ. The knowledge of these objects is that wherein consists the most excellent knowledge of the angels, yea, of God Himself.

2. This knowledge is that which is above all others sweet and joyful. Men have a great deal of pleasure in human knowledge, in studies of natural things; but this is nothing to that joy which arises from this divine light shining into the soul. This light gives a view of those things that are immensely the most exquisitely beautiful and capable of delighting the eye of the understanding. The spiritual light is the dawning of the light of glory in the heart. There is nothing so powerful as this to support persons in affliction, and to give the mind peace and brightness in this stormy and dark world.

3. This light is such as effectually influences the inclination and changes the nature of the soul. It assimilates our nature to the divine nature, and changes the soul into an image of the same glory that is beheld. 2 Corinthians 3.18: "But we all with open face, beholding as in a glass the glory of the Lord, are changed into the same image, from glory to glory, even as by the Spirit of the Lord." This knowledge will wean[6] from the world, and raise the inclination to heavenly things. It will turn the heart to God as the fountain of good, and to choose Him for the only portion. This light, and this only, will bring the soul to a saving close with Christ. It conforms the heart to the gospel, mortifies its enmity and opposition against the scheme of salvation therein revealed; it causes the heart to embrace the joyful tidings, and entirely to adhere to, and acquiesce in, the revelation of Christ as our Savior; it causes the whole soul to accord and symphonize with it, admitting it with entire credit and respect, cleaving to it with full inclination and affection; and it effectually disposes the soul to give up itself entirely to Christ.

4. This light, and this only, has its fruit in an universal holiness of life. No merely notional or speculative understanding of the doctrines of religion will ever bring to this. But this light, as it reaches the bottom of the heart, and changes the nature, so it will effectually dispose to an universal obedience. It shows God as worthy to be obeyed and served. It draws forth the heart in a sincere love to God, which is the only principle of a true, gracious, and univer-

6. Draw us away from.

sal obedience, and it convinces of the reality of those glorious rewards that God has promised to them that obey Him.

1733   1734

Letter to Rev. Dr. Benjamin Colman[1]
(May 30, 1735)
[The Great Awakening]

Dear Sir: In answer to your desire, I here send you a particular account of the present extraordinary circumstances of this town, and the neighboring towns with respect to religion.[2] I have observed that the town for this several years have gradually been reforming; there has appeared less and less of a party spirit, and a contentious disposition, which before had prevailed for many years between two parties in the town.[3] The young people also have been reforming more and more; they by degrees left off their frolicking, and have been observably more decent in their attendance on the public worship. The winter before last there appeared a strange flexibleness in the young people of the town, and an unusual disposition to hearken to counsel, on this occasion. It had been their manner of a long time, and for aught I know, always, to make Sabbath-day nights and lecture days[4] to be especially times of diversion and company keeping. I then preached a sermon on the Sabbath before the lecture, to show them the unsuitableness and inconvenience of the practice, and to persuade them to reform it; and urged it on heads of families that it should be a thing agreed among them to govern their families, and keep them in at those times. And there happened to be at my house the evening after, men that belonged to the several parts of the town, to whom I moved that they should desire the heads of families, in my name, to meet together in their several neighborhoods, that they might know each others' minds, and agree every one to restrain his family; which was done, and my motion complied with throughout the town. But the parents found little or no occasion for the exercise of government in the case; for the young people declared themselves convinced by what they had heard, and willing of themselves to comply with the counsel given them; and I suppose it was almost universally complied with thenceforward.

After this there began to be a remarkable religious concern among some

1. Reverend Colman, pastor of the Brattle Street Church in Boston, had written to Edwards to ask him to explain some of the events concerning the religious revivals in Northampton. Edwards complied and at Colman's request expanded his original letter with a fuller account. Colman published this second letter (abridged) in an appendix to a volume of William Williams's sermons in 1736. Edwards made a copy of his first letter, and the manuscript survives in the Andover Theological Library. It was published for the first time by Clarence H. Faust and Thomas H. Johnson in their 1935 edition of *Jonathan Edwards: Representative Selections*. The text used here is the Yale University edition of *The Works of Jonathan Edwards*, vol. 4. The bracketed emendations are by the editor of that volume, C. C. Goen.

2. Edwards is referring here to the great revival in religious feeling experienced by members of his congregation in 1734. The Northampton revival was the first of a series of such revivals, now known as the "Great Awakening," which spread from Maine to Georgia. By 1750 these revivals seem to have run their course. Edwards's fullest account may be found in *A Faithful Narrative* (1737), an expanded version of his letters to Colman.

3. In a letter to the Reverend Thomas Gillespie of Scotland, July 1, 1751, Edwards refers to these two parties but does not name them. He says that "in one ecclesiastical controversy in Mr. Stoddard's days, wherein the church was divided into two parties, the heat of spirit was raised to such a height, that it came to hard blows; a member of one party met the head of the opposite party, and assaulted him and beat him unmercifully."

4. Days during the week when sermons less formal than the Sabbath sermon were given.

farmhouses at a place called Pascommuck,[5] and five or six that I hoped were savingly wrought upon there. And in April [1734] there was a very sudden and awful death of a young man in town, in the very bloom of his youth, who was violently seized with a pleurisy[6] and taken immediately out of his head, and died in two days; which much affected many young people in the town. This was followed with another death of a young married woman, who was in great distress in the beginning of her illness, but was hopefully converted before her death; so that she died full of comfort, and in a most earnest and moving manner, warning and counseling others, which I believe much contributed to the solemnizing of the spirits of the young people in the town; and there began evidently to appear more of a religious concern upon people's minds. In the fall of the year I moved to the young people that they should set up religious meetings, on evenings after lectures, which they complied with; this was followed with the death of an elderly person in the town, which was attested with very unusual circumstances, which much affected many people. About that time began the great noise that there was in this part of the country about Arminianism,[7] which seemed strangely to be overruled for the promoting of religion. People seemed to be put by it upon inquiring, with concern and engagedness of mind, what was the way of salvation, and what were the terms of our acceptance with God; and what was said publicly on that occasion, however found fault with by many elsewhere, and ridiculed by some, was most evidently attended with a very remarkable blessing of heaven, to the souls of the people in this town, to the giving of them an universal satisfaction and engaging their minds with respect to the thing in question, the more earnestly to seek salvation in the way that had been made evident to them.

And then a concern about the great things of religion began, about the latter end of December and the beginning of January [1735], to prevail abundantly in the town, till in a very little time it became universal throughout the town, among old and young, and from the highest to the lowest. All seemed to be seized with a deep concern about their eternal salvation; all the talk in all companies, and upon occasions was upon the things of religion, and no other talk was anywhere relished; and scarcely a single person in the whole town was left unconcerned about the great things of the eternal world. Those that were wont to be the vainest and loosest persons in town seemed in general to be seized with strong convictions. Those that were most disposed to contemn vital and experimental[8] religion, and those that had the greatest conceit of their own reason, the highest families in the town, and the oldest persons in the town, and many little children were affected remarkably; no one family that I know of, and scarcely a person, has been exempt. And the Spirit of God went on in His saving influences, to the appearance of all human reason and charity, in a truly wonderful and astonishing manner. The news of it filled the neighboring towns with talk, and there were many in them that scoffed and made a ridicule of the religion that appeared in Northampton. But it was observable that it was very frequent and common that those of other towns that came into this town, and observed how it was here, were greatly affected, and went home with wounded spirits, and were never more able to shake off the

---

5. A community three miles from Northampton, Massachusetts, a part of Edwards's congregation.
6. A respiratory disease.
7. Arminians believed that humanity was able to save itself and were, therefore, anathema to the Puritans,

who believed that humanity's salvation was entirely dependent on God.
8. I.e., religious feeling that was tested as to its depth and truth.

impression that it made upon them, till at length there began to appear a general concern in several of the towns in the county.

In the month of March the people in New Hadley[9] seemed to be seized with a deep concern about their salvation, all as it were at once, which has continued in a very great degree ever since. About the same time there began to appear the like concern in the west part of Suffield, which has since spread into all parts of the town. It next began to appear at Sunderland, and soon became universal, and to a very great degree. About the same time it began to appear in part of Deerfield, called Green River, and since has filled the town. It began to appear also at a part of Hatfield, and after that the whole town in the second week in April seemed to be seized at once, and there is a great and general concern there. And there gradually got in a considerable degree of the same concern into Hadley Old Society, and Mr. Hopkins'[1] parish in [West] Springfield, but it is nothing near so great as in many other places. The next place that we heard of was Northfield, where the concern is very great and general. We have heard that there is a considerable degree of it at Longmeadow, and there is something of it in Old Springfield in some parts of the society. About three weeks ago the town of Enfield[2] were struck down as it were at once, the worst persons in the town seemed to be suddenly seized with a great degree of concern about their souls, as I have been informed. And about the same time, Mr. Bull[3] of Westfield [said] that there began to be a great alteration there, and that there had been more done in one week before that time that I spoke with him than had been done in seven years before. The people of Westfield have till now above all other places, made a scoff and derision of this concern at Northampton. There has been a great concern of a like nature at Windsor, on the west side of the [Connecticut] River, which began about the same time that it began to be general here at Northampton; and my father has told me that there is an hopeful beginning on the east side in his society.[4] Mr. Noyes[5] writes me word that there is a considerable revival of religion at New Haven; and I have been credibly informed that there is something of it at Guilford and Lyme, as there also is at Coventry, Bolton, and a society in Lebanon called The Crank. I yesterday saw Mr. White[6] of Bolton, and also last night saw a young man that belongs to [the church at] Coventry, who gave a very remarkable account of that town, of the manner in which the rude debauched young people there were suddenly seized with a concern about their souls.

As to the nature of persons' experiences, and the influences of that spirit that there is amongst us, persons when seized with concern are brought to forsake their vices, and ill practices; the looser sort are brought to forsake and to dread their former extravagances. Persons are soon brought to have done with their old quarrels; contention and intermeddling with other men's matters seems to be dead amongst us. I believe there never was so much done at confessing of faults to each other, and making up differences, as there has

---

9. Later called South Hadley, Massachusetts, about seven miles east of Northampton. Most of the towns mentioned in this paragraph are within a twenty-mile radius of Northampton.
1. Samuel Hopkins (1693–1755) was pastor in West Springfield, Massachusetts.
2. In Connecticut where Edwards gave his sermon *Sinners in the Hands of an Angry God.*
3. Nehemiah Bull (1701–1740) was pastor at West-

field, Massachusetts.
4. Timothy Edwards (1669–1758) was Edward's father, and pastor at East Windsor, Connecticut.
5. Joseph Noyes (1688–1761) was pastor at the First Church in New Haven, Connecticut. Guilford, Lyme, Coventry, and Bolton are all in Connecticut.
6. Thomas White (1701–1763), pastor at Bolton, Connecticut.

lately been. Where this concern comes it immediately puts an end to differences between ministers and people: there was a considerable uneasiness at New Hadley between some of the people and their minister, but when this concern came amongst them it immediately put an end to it, and the people are now universally united to their minister. There was an exceeding alienation at Sunderland, between the minister and many of the people; but when this concern came amongst them it all vanished at once, and the people are universally united in hearty affection to their minister. There were some men at Deerfield, of turbulent spirits, that kept up an uneasiness there with Mr. Ashley;[7] but one of the chief of them has lately been influenced fully and freely to confess his fault to him, and is become his hearty friend.

People are brought off from inordinate engagedness after the world, and have been ready to run into the other extreme of too much neglecting their worldly business and to mind nothing but religion. Those that are under convictions are put upon it earnestly to inquire what they shall do to be saved, and diligently to use appointed means of grace, and apply themselves to all known duty. And those that obtain hope themselves, and the charity of others concerning their good estate, generally seem to be brought to a great sense of their own exceeding misery in a natural condition, and their utter helplessness, and insufficiency for themselves, and their exceeding wickedness and guiltiness in the sight of God; it seldom fails but that each one seems to think himself worse than anybody else, and they are brought to see that they deserve no mercy of God, that all their prayers and pains are exceeding worthless and polluted, and that God, notwithstanding all that they have done, or can do, may justly execute his eternal wrath upon them, and they seem to be brought to a lively sense of the excellency of Jesus Christ and his sufficiency and willingness to save sinners, and to be much weaned in their affections from the world, and to have their hearts filled with love to God and Christ, and a disposition to lie in the dust before Him. They seem to have given [to] them a lively conviction of the truth of the Gospel, and the divine authority of the Holy Scriptures; though they can't have the exercise of this at all times alike, nor indeed of any other grace. They seem to be brought to abhor themselves for the sins of their past life, and to long to be holy, and to live holily, and to God's glory; but at the same time complain that they can do nothing [for] they are poor impotent creatures, utterly insufficient to glorify their Creator and Redeemer. They commonly seem to be much more sensible of their own wickedness after their conversion than before, so that they are often humbled by it; it seems to them that they are really become more wicked, when at the same time they are evidently full of a gracious spirit. Their remaining sin seems to be their very great burden, and many of them seem to long after heaven, that there they may be rid of sin. They generally seem to be united in dear love and affection one to another, and to have a love to all mankind. I never saw the Christian spirit in love to enemies so exemplified in all my life as I have seen it within this half year. They commonly express a great concern for others' salvation; some say that they think they are far more concerned for others' conversion, after they themselves have been converted, than ever they were for their own; several have thought (though perhaps they might be deceived in it) that they could freely die for the salvation of any soul, of the meanest of mankind, of any Indian in the woods.

7. The Reverend Jonathan Ashley (1712–1780).

This town never was so full of love, nor so full of joy, nor so full of distress as it has lately been. Some persons have had those longing desires after Jesus Christ, that have been to that degree as to take away their strength, and very much to weaken them, and make them faint. Many have been even overcome with a sense of the dying love of Christ, so that the home of the body has been ready to fail under it; there was once three pious young persons in this town talking together of the dying love of Christ, till they all fainted away; though 'tis probable the fainting of the two latter was much promoted by the fainting of the first. Many express a sense of the glory of the divine perfections, and of the excellency and fullness of Jesus Christ, and of their own littleness and unworthiness, in a manner truly wonderful and almost unparalleled; and so likewise of the excellency and wonderfulness of the way of salvation by Jesus Christ. Their esteem of the Holy Scriptures is exceedingly increased. Many of them say the Bible seems to be a new book to them, as though they never read it before. There have been some instances of persons that by only an accidental sight of the Bible, have been as much moved, it seemed to me, as a lover by the sight of his sweetheart. The preaching of the Word is greatly prized by them; they say they never heard preaching before: and so are God's Sabbaths, and ordinances,[8] and opportunities of public worship. The Sabbath is longed for before it comes; some by only hearing the bell ring on some occasion in the week time, have been greatly moved, because it has put them in mind of its ringing to call the people together to worship God. But no part of public worship has commonly [had] such an effect on them as singing God's praises. They have a greater respect to ministers than they used to have; there is scarcely a minister preaches here but gets their esteem and affection.

The experiences of some persons lately amongst [us] have been beyond almost all that ever I heard or read of. There is a pious woman in this town that is a very modest bashful person, that was moved by what she heard of the experiences of others earnestly to seek to God to give her more clear manifestations of Himself, and evidences of her own good estate, and God answered her request, and gradually gave her more and more of a sense of His glory and love, which she had with intermissions for several days, till one morning the week before last she had it to a more than ordinary degree, and it prevailed more and more till towards the middle of the day, till her nature began to sink under it, as she was alone in the house; but there came somebody into the house, and found her in an unusual, extraordinary frame. She expressed what she saw and felt to him; it came to that at last that they raised the neighbors, [for] they were afraid she would die; I went up to see her and found her perfectly sober and in the exercise of her reason, but having her nature seemingly overborne and sinking, and when she could speak expressing in a manner that can't be described the sense she had of the glory of God, and particularly of such and such perfections, and her own unworthiness, her longing to lie in the dust, sometimes her longing to go to be with Christ, and crying out of the excellency of Christ, and the wonderfulness of His dying love; and so she continued for hours together, though not always in the same degree. At some times she was able to discourse to those about her; but it seemed to me [that] if God had manifested a little more of Himself to her she would immediately have sunk and her frame dissolved under it. She has since been at my house, and continues as full as she can hold, but looks on herself not as an eminent

8. Church laws and regulations.

saint,[9] but as the worst of all, and unworthy to go to speak with a minister; but yet now beyond any great doubt of her good estate.

There are two persons that belong to other towns that have had such a sense of God's exceeding greatness and majesty, that they were as it were swallowed up; they both of them told me to that purpose that if in the time of it they had had the least fear that they were not at peace with that great God, they should immediately have died. But there is a very vast variety of degrees of spiritual discoveries, that are made to those that we hope are godly, as there is also in the steps, and method of the Spirit's operation in convincing and converting sinners, and the length of time that persons are under conviction before they have comfort.

There is an alteration made in the town in a few months that strangers can scarcely conceive of; our church I believe was the largest in New England before, but persons lately have thronged in, so that there are very few adult persons left out.[1] There have been a great multitude hopefully converted; too many, I find, for me to declare abroad with credit to my judgment. The town seems to be full of the presence of God; our young people when they get together instead of frolicking as they used to do are altogether on pious subjects; 'tis so at weddings and on all occasions. The children in this and the neighboring towns have been greatly affected and influenced by the Spirit of God, and many of them hopefully changed; the youngest in this town is between nine and ten years of age. Some of them seem to be full of love to Christ and have expressed great longings after Him and willingness to die, and leave father and mother and all things in the world to go to him, together with a great sense of their unworthiness and admiration at the free grace of God towards them. And there have been many old people, many above fifty and several near seventy, that seem to be wonderfully changed and hopefully newborn. The good people that have been formerly converted in the town have many of them been wonderfully enlivened and increased.

This work seems to be upon every account an extraordinary dispensation of Providence. 'Tis extraordinary upon the account of [the] universality of it in affecting all sort, high and low, rich and poor, wise and unwise, old and young, vicious and moral; 'tis very extraordinary as to the numbers that are hopefully savingly wrought upon, and particularly the number of aged persons and children and loose livers; and also on the account of the quickness of the work of the Spirit on them, for many seem to have been suddenly taken from a loose way of living, and to be so changed as to become truly holy, spiritual, heavenly persons; 'tis extraordinary as to the degrees of gracious communications, and the abundant measures in which the Spirit of God has been poured out on many persons; 'tis extraordinary as to the extent of it, God's Spirit being so remarkably poured out on so many towns at once, and its making such swift progress from place to place. The extraordinariness of the thing has been, I believe, one principal cause that people abroad have suspected it.

There have been, as I have heard, many odd and strange stories that have been carried about the country of this affair, which it is a wonder some wise men should be so ready to believe. Some indeed under great terrors of conscience have had impressions[2] on their imaginations; and also under the power of spiritual discoveries, they have had livelily impressed ideas of Christ shed-

9. I.e., a "visible saint," one who feels assured of salvation.
1. In November 1736, Edwards counted 620 adult communicants.
2. Strong effects.

ding blood for sinners, His blood running from His veins, and of Christ in His glory in heaven and such like things, but they are always taught, and have been several times taught in public not to lay the weight of their hopes on such things and many have nothing of any such imaginations. There have been several persons that have had their natures overborne under strong convictions, have trembled, and han't been able to stand, they have had such a sense of divine wrath; but there are no new doctrines embraced, but people have been abundantly established in those that we account orthodox; there is no new way of worship affected. There is no oddity of behavior prevails; people are no more superstitious about their clothes, or anything else than they used to be. Indeed, there is a great deal of talk when they are together of one another's experiences, and indeed no other is to be expected in a town where the concern of the soul is so universally the concern, and that to so great a degree. And doubtless some persons under the strength of impressions that are made on their minds and under the power of strong affections[3] are guilty of imprudences; their zeal may need to be regulated by more prudence, and they may need a guide to their assistance; as of old when the church of Corinth had the extraordinary gifts of the Spirit, they needed to be told by the Apostle that the spirit of the prophets were subject to the prophets, and that their gifts were to be exercised with prudence, because God was not the author of confusion but of peace.[4] There is no unlovely oddity in people's temper prevailing with this work, but on the contrary the face of things is much changed as to the appearance of a meek, humble, amiable behavior. Indeed, the Devil has not been idle, but his hand has evidently appeared in several instances endeavoring to mimic the work of the Spirit of God and to cast a slur upon it, and no wonder. And there has hereby appeared the need of the watchful eye of skillful guides, and of wisdom from above to direct them.

There lately came up hither a couple of ministers from Connecticut, viz., Mr. Lord of [North] Preston, and Mr. Owen of Groton,[5] who had heard of the extraordinary circumstances of this and the neighboring towns, who had heard the affair well represented by some, and also had heard many reports greatly to its disadvantage, who came on purpose to see and satisfy themselves; and that they might thoroughly acquaint themselves, went about and spent [the] good part of a day in hearing the accounts of many of our new converts, and examining of them, which was greatly to their satisfaction; and they took particular notice, among other things, of the modesty with which persons gave account of themselves, and said that the one half was not told them, and could not be told them; and that if they renounced these persons' experiences they must renounce Christianity itself. And Mr. Owen said particularly as to their impressions on their imaginations, they were quite different from what had been represented, and that they were no more than might naturally be expected in such cases.

Thus, Sir, I have given you a particular account of this affair which Satan has so much misrepresented in the country.[6] This is a true account of the matter as far as I have opportunity to know, and I suppose I am under greater

---

3. Emotions.
4. "Let the prophets speak two or three, and let the other judge. . . . For ye may all prophesy one by one, that all may learn, and all may be comforted. And the spirits of the prophets are subjects to the prophets. For God is not the author of confusion, but of peace, as in all churches of the saints" (1 Corinthians 14.29–33).

5. Hezekiah Lord (1698–1761), pastor at North Preston, Connecticut, and Joseph Owen (1699–1753), pastor at Groton, Connecticut.
6. There were rumors that the revival produced not truly converted Christians, but a frenzy of uncontrolled emotions.

advantages to know than any person living. Having been thus long in the account, I forbear to make reflections, or to guess what God is about to do; I leave this to you, and shall only say, as I desire always to say from my heart, "To God be all the glory, whose work alone it is." And let him have an interest in your prayers, who so much needs divine help at this day, and is your affectionate brother and humble servant.

Jonathan Edwards

Northampton, June 3, 1735

Since I wrote the foregoing letter, there has happened a thing of a very awful nature in the town. My Uncle Hawley,[7] the last Sabbath-day morning [June 1], laid violent hands on himself, and put an end to his life, by cutting his own throat. He had been for a considerable time greatly concerned about the condition of his soul; till, by the ordering of a sovereign providence he was suffered to fall into deep melancholy, a distemper that the family are very prone to; he was much overpowered by it; the devil took the advantage and drove him into despairing thoughts. He was kept very much awake anights, so that he had but very little sleep for two months, till he seemed not to have his faculties in his own power. He was in a great measure past a capacity of receiving advice, or being reasoned with. The coroner's inquest judged him delirious. Satan seems to be in a great rage, at this extraordinary breaking forth of the work of God. I hope it is because he knows that he has but a short time. Doubtless he had a great reach,[8] in this violent attack of his against the whole affair. We have appointed a day of fasting in the town this week, by reason of this and other appearances of Satan's rage amongst us against poor souls. I yesterday saw a woman that belongs to [the church in] Durham [Connecticut], who says there is a considerable revival of religion there.

I am yours, etc.—
J.E.

1735   1935

Sinners in the Hands of an Angry God[1]

Deuteronomy 32.35

Their foot shall slide in due time.[2]

In this verse is threatened the vengeance of God on the wicked unbelieving Israelites, who were God's visible people, and who lived under the means of

7. Joseph Hawley (1682–1735) married a sister of Edwards's mother. He was one of the "River Gods," as leading businessmen in this rich Connecticut River valley were called. He took his life on June 1, 1735.
8. Power of influence.
1. Edwards delivered this sermon in Enfield, Connecticut, a town about thirty miles south of Northampton, on Sunday, July 8, 1741. In Benjamin Trumbull's A Complete History of Connecticut (1797, 1818) we are told that Edwards read his sermon in a level voice with

his sermon book in his left hand, and in spite of his calm, "there was such a breathing of distress, and weeping, that the preacher was obliged to speak to the people and desire silence, that he might be heard." The text is from The Works of Jonathan Edwards, vol. 7, edited by Sereno E. Dwight (1829–30).
2. "To me belongeth vengeance, and recompense; their foot shall slide in due time: for the day of their calamity is at hand, and the things that shall come upon them make haste."

grace,[3] but who, notwithstanding all God's wonderful works towards them, remained (as in verse 28)[4] void of counsel, having no understanding in them. Under all the cultivations of heaven, they brought forth bitter and poisonous fruit, as in the two verses next preceding the text.[5] The expression I have chosen for my text, "Their foot shall slide in due time," seems to imply the following things, relating to the punishment and destruction to which these wicked Israelites were exposed.

1. That they were always exposed to destruction; as one that stands or walks in slippery places is always exposed to fall. This is implied in the manner of their destruction coming upon them, being represented by their foot sliding. The same is expressed, Psalm 73.18: "Surely thou didst set them in slippery places; thou castedst them down into destruction."

2. It implies that they were always exposed to sudden unexpected destruction. As he that walks in slippery places is every moment liable to fall, he cannot foresee one moment whether he shall stand or fall the next; and when he does fall, he falls at once without warning: which is also expressed in Psalm 73.18–19: "Surely thou didst set them in slippery places; thou castedst them down into destruction: How are they brought into desolation as in a moment!"

3. Another thing implied is, that they are liable to fall of themselves, without being thrown down by the hand of another; as he that stands or walks on slippery ground needs nothing but his own weight to throw him down.

4. That the reason why they are not fallen already, and do not fall now, is only that God's appointed time is not come. For it is said that when that due time, or appointed times comes, their foot shall slide. Then they shall be left to fall, as they are inclined by their own weight. God will not hold them up in these slippery places any longer, but will let them go; and then, at that very instant, they shall fall into destruction; as he that stands on such slippery declining ground, on the edge of a pit, he cannot stand alone, when he is let go he immediately falls and is lost.

The observation from the words that I would now insist upon is this. "There is nothing that keeps wicked men at any one moment out of hell, but the mere pleasure of God." By the mere pleasure of God, I mean His sovereign pleasure, His arbitrary will, restrained by no obligation, hindered by no manner of difficulty, any more than if nothing else but God's mere will had in the least degree, or in any respect whatsoever, any hand in the preservation of wicked men one moment. The truth of this observation may appear by the following considerations.

1. There is no want of power in God to cast wicked men into hell at any moment. Men's hands cannot be strong when God rises up. The strongest have no power to resist Him, nor can any deliver[6] out of His hands. He is not only able to cast wicked men into hell, but He can most easily do it. Sometimes an earthly prince meets with a great deal of difficulty to subdue a rebel, who has found means to fortify himself, and has made himself strong by the numbers of his followers. But it is not so with God. There is no fortress that is

3. I.e., the Ten Commandments. For Protestants following the Westminster Confession (1646), the "means of grace" consist of "preaching of the word and the administration of the sacraments of baptism and the Lord's Supper."
4. "They are a nation void of counsel, neither is there any understanding in them" (Deuteronomy 32.28).
5. "For their vine is of the vine of Sodom, and the

fields of Gomorrah: their grapes are grapes of gall, their clusters are bitter: Their wine is the poison of dragons, and the cruel venom of asps" (Deuteronomy 32.32–33). Sodom and Gomorrah were wicked cities destroyed by a rain of fire and sulfur from heaven (Genesis 19.24).
6. I.e., rescue others.

any defense from the power of God. Though hand join in hand, and vast multitudes of God's enemies combine and associate themselves, they are easily broken in pieces. They are as great heaps of light chaff before the whirlwind; or large quantities of dry stubble before devouring flames. We find it easy to tread on and crush a worm that we see crawling on the earth; so it is easy for us to cut or singe a slender thread that any thing hangs by: thus easy is it for God, when he pleases, to cast His enemies down to hell. What are we, that we should think to stand before Him, at whose rebuke the earth trembles, and before whom the rocks are thrown down?

2. They deserve to be cast into hell; so that divine justice never stands in the way, it makes no objection against God's using His power at any moment to destroy them. Yea, on the contrary, justice calls aloud for an infinite punishment of their sins. Divine justice says of the tree that brings forth such grapes of Sodom, "Cut it down, why cumbereth it the ground? Luke 13.7. The sword of divine justice is every moment brandished over their heads, and it is nothing but the hand of arbitrary mercy, and God's will, that holds it back.

3. They are already under a sentence of condemnation to hell. They do not only justly deserve to be case down thither, but the sentence of the law of God, that eternal and immutable rule of righteousness that God has fixed between Him and mankind, is gone out against them, and stands against them; so that they are bound over already to hell. John 3.18: "He that believeth not is condemned already." So that every unconverted man properly belongs to hell; that is his place; from thence he is, John 8.23: "Ye are from beneath." And thither he is bound; it is the place that justice, and God's word, and the sentence of his unchangeable law assign to him.

4. They are now the objects of that very same anger and wrath of God that is expressed in the torments of hell. And the reason why they do not go down to hell at each moment is not because God, in whose power they are, is not then very angry with them as He is with many miserable creatures now tormented in hell, who there feel and bear the fierceness of His wrath. Yea, God is a great deal more angry with great numbers that are now on earth: yea, doubtless, with many that are now in this congregation, who it may be are at ease, than He is with many of those who are now in the flames of hell.

So that it is not because God is unmindful of their wickedness, and does not resent it, that He does not let loose His hand and cut them off. God is not altogether such an one as themselves, though they may imagine Him to be so. The wrath of God burns against them, their damnation does not slumber; the pit is prepared, the fire is made ready, the furnace is now hot, ready to receive them; the flames do now rage and glow. The glittering sword is whet,[7] and held over them, and the pit hath opened its mouth under them.

5. The devil stands ready to fall upon them, and seize them as his own, at what moment God shall permit him. They belong to him; he has their souls in his possession, and under his dominion. The Scripture represents them as his goods, Luke 11.12.[8] The devils watch them; they are ever by them at their right hand; they stand waiting for them, like greedy hungry lions that see their prey, and expect to have it, but are for the present kept back. If God should withdraw His hand, by which they are restrained, they would in one moment fly upon their poor souls. The old serpent is gaping for them; hell opens its

7. Sharpened.
8. "Or if he shall ask an egg, will he offer him a scorpion?"

mouth wide to receive them; and if God should permit it, they would be hastily swallowed up and lost.

6. There are in the souls of wicked men those hellish principles reigning that would presently kindle and flame out into hell fire, if it were not for God's restraints. There is laid in the very nature of carnal men a foundation for the torments of hell. There are those corrupt principles, in reigning power in them, and in full possession of them, that are seeds of hell fire. These principles are active and powerful, exceeding violent in their nature, and if it were not for the restraining hand of God upon them, they would soon break out, they would flame out after the same manner as the same corruptions, the same enmity does in the hearts of damned souls, and would beget the same torments as they do in them. The souls of the wicked are in Scripture compared to the troubled sea, Isaiah 57.20.[9] For the present, God restrains their wickedness by His mighty power, as He does the raging waves of the troubled sea, saying, "Hitherto shalt thou come, but no further;"[1] but if God should withdraw that restraining power, it would soon carry all before it. Sin is the ruin and misery of the soul; it is destructive in its nature; and if God should leave it without restraint, there would need nothing else to make the soul perfectly miserable. The corruption of the heart of man is immoderate and boundless in its fury; and while wicked men live here, it is like fire pent up by God's restraints, whereas if it were let loose, it would set on fire the course of nature; and as the heart is now a sink of sin, so if sin was not restrained, it would immediately turn the soul into a fiery oven, or a furnace of fire and brimstone.

7. It is no security to wicked men for one moment that there are no visible means of death at hand. It is no security to a natural man that he is now in health and that he does not see which way he should now immediately go out of the world by any accident, and that there is no visible danger in any respect in his circumstances. The manifold and continual experience of the world in all ages, shows this is no evidence that a man is not on the very brink of eternity, and that the next step will not be into another world. The unseen, unthought-of ways and means of persons going suddenly out of the world are innumerable and inconceivable. Unconverted men walk over the pit of hell on a rotten covering, and there are innumerable places in this covering so weak that they will not bear their weight, and these places are not seen. The arrows of death fly unseen at noonday;[2] the sharpest sight cannot discern them. God has so many different unsearchable ways of taking wicked men out of the world and sending them to hell, that there is nothing to make it appear that God had need to be at the expense of a miracle, or go out of the ordinary course of His providence, to destroy any wicked man at any moment. All the means that there are of sinners going out of the world are so in God's hands, and so universally and absolutely subject to His power and determination, that it does not depend at all the less on the mere will of God whether sinners shall at any moment go to hell than if means were never made use of or at all concerned in the case.

8. Natural men's prudence and care to preserve their own lives, or the care of others to preserve them, do not secure them a moment. To this, divine providence and universal experience do also bear testimony. There is this clear

9. "But the wicked are like the troubled sea, when it cannot rest, whose waters cast up mire and dirt."
1. Job 38.11.

2. "Thou shalt not be afraid for the terror by night; nor for the arrow that flieth by day" (Psalm 91.5).

evidence that men's own wisdom is no security to them from death; that if it were otherwise we should see some difference between the wise and politic men of the world, and others, with regard to their liableness to early and unexpected death: but how is it in fact? Ecclesiastes 2.16: "How dieth the wise man? even as the fool."

9. All wicked men's pains and contrivance which they use to escape hell, while they continue to reject Christ, and so remain wicked men, do not secure them from hell one moment. Almost every natural[3] man that hears of hell, flatters himself that he shall escape it; he depends upon himself for his own security; he flatters himself in what he has done, in what he is now doing, or what he intends to do. Every one lays out matters in his own mind how he shall avoid damnation, and flatters himself that he contrives well for himself, and that his schemes will not fail. They hear indeed that there are but few saved, and that the greater part of men that have died heretofore are gone to hell; but each one imagines that he lays out matters better for his own escape than others have done. He does not intend to come to that place of torment; he says within himself that he intends to take effectual care, and to order matters so for himself as not to fail.

But the foolish children of men miserably delude themselves in their own schemes, and in confidence in their own strength and wisdom; they trust to nothing but a shadow. The greater part of those who heretofore have lived under the same means of grace, and are now dead, are undoubtedly gone to hell; and it was not because they were not as wise as those who are now alive: it was not because they did not lay out matters as well for themselves to secure their own escape. If we could speak with them, and inquire of them, one by one, whether they expected when alive, and when they used to hear about hell, ever to be the subjects of that misery, we doubtless, should hear one and another reply, "No, I never intended to come here: I had laid out matters otherwise in my mind; I thought I should contrive well for myself: I thought my scheme good. I intended to take effectual care; but it came upon me unexpected; I did not look for it at that time, and in that manner; it came as a thief: Death outwitted me: God's wrath was too quick for me. Oh, my cursed foolishness! I was flattering myself, and pleasing myself with vain dreams of what I would do hereafter; and when I was saying, peace and safety, then suddenly destruction came upon me."

10. God has laid Himself under no obligation by any promise to keep any natural man out of hell one moment. God certainly has made no promises either of eternal life or of any deliverance or preservation from eternal death but what are contained in the covenant of grace,[4] the promises that are given in Christ, in whom all the promises are yea and amen. But surely they have no interest in the promises of the covenant of grace who are not the children of the covenant, who do not believe in any of the promises, and have no interest in the Mediator of the covenant.[5]

So that, whatever some have imagined and pretended[6] about promises made to natural men's earnest seeking and knocking, it is plain and manifest that whatever pains a natural man takes in religion, whatever prayers he makes, till

3. I.e., unregenerate, unsaved.
4. The original covenant God made with Adam is called the Covenant of Works; the second covenant Christ made with fallen humanity—declaring that if they believed in Him they would be saved—is called the Covenant of Grace.
5. I.e., Christ, who took upon Himself the sins of the world and suffered for them.
6. Claimed.

he believes in Christ, God is under no manner of obligation to keep him a moment from eternal destruction.

So that, thus it is that natural men are held in the hand of God, over the pit of hell; they have deserved the fiery pit, and are already sentenced to it; and God is dreadfully provoked. His anger is as great towards them as to those that are actually suffering the executions of the fierceness of His wrath in hell, and they have done nothing in the least to appease or abate that anger, neither is God in the least bound by any promise to hold them up one moment; the devil is waiting for them, hell is gaping for them, the flames gather and flash about them, and would fain lay hold on them, and swallow them up; the fire pent up in their own hearts is struggling to break out: and they have no interest in any Mediator, there are no means within reach that can be any security to them. In short, they have no refuge, nothing to take hold of; all that preserves them every moment is the mere arbitrary will, and uncovenanted, unobliged forbearance of an incensed God.

Application

The use of this awful[7] subject may be for awakening unconverted persons in this congregation. This that you have heard is the case of every one of you that are out of Christ. That world of misery, that lake of burning brimstone, is extended abroad under you. There is the dreadful pit of the glowing flames of the wrath of God; there is hell's wide gaping mouth open; and you have nothing to stand upon, nor any thing to take hold of; there is nothing between you and hell but the air; it is only the power and mere pleasure of God that holds you up.

You probably are not sensible[8] of this; you find you are kept out of hell, but do not see the hand of God in it; but look at other things, as the good state of your bodily constitution, your care of your own life, and the means you use for your own preservation. But indeed these things are nothing; if God should withdraw His hand, they would avail no more to keep you from falling, than the thin air to hold up a person that is suspended in it.

Your wickedness makes you as it were heavy as lead, and to tend downwards with great weight and pressure towards hell; and if God should let you go, you would immediately sink and swiftly descend and plunge into the bottomless gulf, and your healthy constitution, and your own care and prudence, and best contrivance, and all your righteousness, would have no more influence to uphold you and keep you out of hell, than a spider's web would have to stop a fallen rock. Were it not for the sovereign pleasure of God, the earth would not bear you one moment; for you are a burden to it; the creation groans with you; the creature is made subject to the bondage of your corruption, not willingly; the sun does not willingly shine upon you to give you light to serve sin and Satan; the earth does not willingly yield her increase to satisfy your lusts; nor is it willingly a stage for your wickedness to be acted upon; the air does not willingly serve you for breath to maintain the flame of life in your vitals, while you spend your life in the service of God's enemies. God's creatures are good, and were made for men to serve God with, and do not willingly subserve to any other purpose, and groan when they are abused to purposes so directly

7. Awesome.   8. Aware.

contrary to their nature and end. And the world would spew you out, were it not for the sovereign hand of Him who hath subjected it in hope. There are black clouds of God's wrath now hanging directly over your heads, full of the dreadful storm, and big with thunder; and were it not for the restraining hand of God, it would immediately burst forth upon you. The sovereign pleasure of God, for the present, stays His rough wind; otherwise it would come with fury, and your destruction would come like a whirlwind, and you would be like the chaff of the summer threshing floor.

The wrath of God is like great waters that are dammed for the present; they increase more and more, and rise higher and higher, till an outlet is given; and the longer the stream is stopped, the more rapid and mighty is its course when once it is let loose. It is true that judgment against your evil works has not been executed hitherto; the floods of God's vengeance have been withheld; but your guilt in the meantime is constantly increasing, and you are every day treasuring up more wrath; the waters are constantly rising, and waxing more and more mighty; and there is nothing but the mere pleasure of God that holds the waters back, that are unwilling to be stopped, and press hard to go forward. If God should only withdraw His hand from the floodgate, it would immediately fly open, and the fiery floods of the fierceness and wrath of God, would rush forth with inconceivable fury, and would come upon you with omnipotent power; and if your strength were ten thousand times greater than it is, yea, ten thousand times greater than the strength of the stoutest, sturdiest devil in hell, it would be nothing to withstand or endure it.

The bow of God's wrath is bent, and the arrow made ready on the string, and justice bends the arrow at your heart, and strains the bow, and it is nothing but the mere pleasure of God, and that of an angry God, without any promise or obligation at all, that keeps the arrow one moment from being made drunk with your blood. Thus all you that never passed under a great change of heart, by the mighty power of the Spirit of God upon your souls, all you that were never born again, and made new creatures, and raised from being dead in sin, to a state of new, and before altogether unexperienced light and life, are in the hands of an angry God. However you may have reformed your life in many things, and may have had religious affections,[9] and may keep up a form of religion in your families and closets,[1] and in the house of God, it is nothing but His mere pleasure that keeps you from being this moment swallowed up in everlasting destruction. However unconvinced you may now be of the truth of what you hear, by and by you will be fully convinced of it. Those that are gone from being in the like circumstances with you see that it was so with them; for destruction came suddenly upon most of them; when they expected nothing of it and while they were saying, peace and safety: now they see that those things on which they depended for peace and safety, were nothing but thin air and empty shadows.

The God that holds you over the pit of hell, much as one holds a spider or some loathsome insect over the fire, abhors you, and is dreadfully provoked: His wrath towards you burns like fire; He looks upon you as worthy of nothing else but to be cast into the fire; He is of purer eyes than to bear to have you in His sight; you are ten thousand times more abominable in His eyes than the most hateful venomous serpent is in ours. You have offended Him infinitely

9. Feelings.   1. Studies; rooms for meditation.

more than ever a stubborn rebel did his prince; and yet it is nothing but His hand that holds you from falling into the fire every moment. It is to be ascribed to nothing else, that you did not go to hell the last night; that you was suffered to awake again in this world, after you closed your eyes to sleep. And there is no other reason to be given, why you have not dropped into hell since you arose in the morning, but that God's hand has held you up. There is no other reason to be given why you have not gone to hell, since you have sat here in the house of God, provoking His pure eyes by your sinful wicked manner of attending His solemn worship. Yea, there is nothing else that is to be given as a reason why you do not this very moment drop down into hell.

O sinner! Consider the fearful danger you are in: it is a great furnace of wrath, a wide and bottomless pit, full of the fire of wrath, that you are held over in the hand of that God, whose wrath is provoked and incensed as much against you, as against many of the damned in hell. You hang by a slender thread, with the flames of divine wrath flashing about it, and ready every moment to singe it, and burn it asunder; and you have no interest in any Mediator, and nothing to lay hold of to save yourself, nothing to keep off the flames of wrath, nothing of your own, nothing that you ever have done, nothing that you can do, to induce God to spare you one moment. And consider here more particularly.

1. Whose wrath it is: it is the wrath of the infinite God. If it were only the wrath of man, though it were of the most potent prince, it would be comparatively little to be regarded. The wrath of kings is very much dreaded, especially of absolute monarchs, who have the possessions and lives of their subjects wholly in their power, to be disposed of at their mere will. Proverbs 20.2: "The fear of a king is as the roaring of a lion: Whoso provoketh him to anger, sinneth against his own soul." The subject that very much enrages an arbitrary prince is liable to suffer the most extreme torments that human art can invent, or human power can inflict. But the greatest earthly potentates in their greatest majesty, and strength, and when clothed in their greatest terrors, are but feeble, despicable worms of the dust, in comparison of the great and almighty Creator and King of heaven and earth. It is but little that they can do, when most enraged, and when they have exerted the utmost of their fury. All the kings of the earth, before God, are as grasshoppers; they are nothing, and less than nothing: both their love and their hatred is to be despised. The wrath of the great King of kings, is as much more terrible than theirs, as His majesty is greater. Luke 12.4–5: "And I say unto you, my friends, Be not afraid of them that kill the body, and after that, have no more that they can do. But I will forewarn you whom you shall fear: fear him, which after he hath killed, hath power to cast into hell: yea, I say unto you, Fear him."

2. It is the fierceness of His wrath that you are exposed to. We often read of the fury of God; as in Isaiah 59.18: "According to their deeds, accordingly he will repay fury to his adversaries." So Isaiah 66.15: "For behold, the Lord will come with fire, and with his chariots like a whirlwind, to render his anger with fury, and his rebuke with flames of fire." And in many other places. So, Revelation 19.15: we read of "the wine press of the fierceness and wrath of Almighty God."[2] The words are exceeding terrible. If it had only been said, "the wrath of God," the words would have implied that which is infinitely

---

2. "He treadeth the winepress of the fierceness and wrath of Almighty God."

dreadful: but it is "the fierceness and wrath of God." The fury of God! the fierceness of Jehovah![3] Oh, how dreadful must that be! Who can utter or conceive what such expressions carry in them! But it is also "the fierceness and wrath of Almighty God." As though there would be a very great manifestation of His almighty power in what the fierceness of His wrath should inflict, as though omnipotence should be as it were enraged, and exerted, as men are wont to exert their strength in the fierceness of their wrath. Oh! then, what will be the consequence! What will become of the poor worms that shall suffer it! Whose hands can be strong? And whose heart can endure? To what a dreadful, inexpressible, inconceivable depth of misery must the poor creature be sunk who shall be the subject of this!

Consider this, you that are here present that yet remain in an unregenerate state. That God will execute the fierceness of His anger implies that He will inflict wrath without any pity. When God beholds the ineffable extremity of your case, and sees your torment to be so vastly disproportioned to your strength, and sees how your poor soul is crushed, and sinks down, as it were, into an infinite gloom; He will have no compassion upon you, He will not forbear the executions of His wrath, or in the least lighten His hand; there shall be no moderation or mercy, nor will God then at all stay His rough wind; He will have no regard to your welfare, nor be at all careful lest you should suffer too much in any other sense, than only that you shall not suffer beyond what strict justice requires. Nothing shall be withheld because it is so hard for you to bear. Ezekiel 8.18: "Therefore will I also deal in fury: mine eye shall not spare, neither will I have pity; and though they cry in mine ears with a loud voice, yet I will not hear them." Now God stands ready to pity you; this is a day of mercy; you may cry now with some encouragement of obtaining mercy. But when once the day of mercy is past, your most lamentable and dolorous cries and shrieks will be in vain; you will be wholly lost and thrown away of God as to any regard to your welfare. God will have no other use to put you to, but to suffer misery; you shall be continued in being to no other end; for you will be a vessel of wrath fitted to destruction; and there will be no other use of this vessel, but to be filled full of wrath. God will be so far from pitying you when you cry to Him, that it is said He will only "laugh and mock." Proverbs 1.25–26, etc.[4]

How awful are those words, Isaiah 63.3, which are the words of the great God: "I will tread them in mine anger, and will trample them in my fury, and their blood shall be sprinkled upon my garments, and I will stain all my raiment." It is perhaps impossible to conceive of words that carry in them greater manifestations of these three things, viz., contempt, and hatred, and fierceness of indignation. If you cry to God to pity you, He will be so far from pitying you in your doleful case, or showing you the least regard or favor, that instead of that, He will ony tread you under foot. And though He will know that you cannot bear the weight of omnipotence treading upon you, yet He will not regard that, but He will crush you under His feet without mercy; He will crush out your blood, and make it fly and it shall be sprinkled on His garments, so as to stain all His raiment. He will not only hate you, but He will have you in the utmost contempt: no place shall be thought fit for you, but under His feet to be trodden down as the mire of the streets.

---

3. The name used for God in the Old Testament.
4. "But ye have set at nought all my counsel, and would none of my reproof: I also will laugh at your calamity; I will mock you when your fear cometh."

3. The misery you are exposed to is that which God will inflict to that end, that He might show what that wrath of Jehovah is. God hath had it on His heart to show to angels and men both how excellent His love is, and also how terrible His wrath is. Sometimes earthly kings have a mind to show how terrible their wrath is, by the extreme punishments they would execute on those that would provoke them. Nebuchadnezzar, that mighty and haughty monarch of the Chaldean empire, was willing to show his wrath when enraged with Shadrach, Meshech, and Abednego; and accordingly gave orders that the burning fiery furnace should be heated seven times hotter than it was before; doubtless, it was raised to the utmost degree of fierceness that human art could raise it.[5] But the great God is also willing to show His wrath, and magnify His awful majesty and mighty power in the extreme sufferings of His enemies. Romans 9.22: "What if God, willing to show his wrath, and to make his power known, endure with much long-suffering the vessels of wrath fitted to destruction?" And seeing this is His design, and what He has determined, even to show how terrible the restrained wrath, the fury and fierceness of Jehovah is, He will do it to effect. There will be something accomplished and brought to pass that will be dreadful with a witness. When the great and angry God hath risen up and executed His awful vengeance on the poor sinner, and the wretch is actually suffering the infinite weight and power of His indignation, then will God call upon the whole universe to behold that awful majesty and mighty power that is to be seen in it. Isaiah 33.12–14: "And the people shall be as the burnings of lime, as thorns cut up shall they be burnt in the fire. Hear ye that are far off, what I have done; and ye that are near, acknowledge my might. The sinners in Zion are afraid; fearfulness hath surprised the hypocrites," etc.

Thus it will be with you that are in an unconverted state, if you continue in it; the infinite might, and majesty, and terribleness of the omnipotent God shall be magnified upon you, in the ineffable strength of your torments. You shall be tormented in the presence of the holy angels, and in the presence of the Lamb; and when you shall be in this state of suffering, the glorious inhabitants of heaven shall go forth and look on the awful spectacle, that they may see what the wrath and fierceness of the Almighty is; and when they have seen it, they will fall down and adore that great power and majesty. Isaiah 66.23–24: "And it shall come to pass, that from one new moon to another, and from one sabbath to another, shall all flesh come to worship before me, saith the Lord. And they shall go forth and look upon the carcasses of the men that have transgressed against me; for their worm shall not die, neither shall their fire be quenched, and they shall be an abhorring unto all flesh."

4. It is everlasting wrath. It would be dreadful to suffer this fierceness and wrath of Almighty God one moment; but you must suffer it to all eternity. There will be no end to this exquisite horrible misery. When you look forward, you shall see a long forever, a boundless duration before you, which will swallow up your thoughts, and amaze your soul; and you will absolutely despair of ever having any deliverance, any end, any mitigation, any rest at all. You will know certainly that you must wear out long ages, millions of millions of ages, in wrestling and conflicting with this almighty merciless vengeance; and then when you have so done, when so many ages have actually been spent by you

5. See Daniel 3.1–30.

in this manner, you will know that all is but a point to what remains. So that your punishment will indeed be infinite. Oh, who can express what the state of a soul in such circumstances is! All that we can possibly say about it gives but a very feeble, faint representation of it; it is inexpressible and inconceivable: For "who knows the power of God's anger?"[6]

How dreadful is the state of those that are daily and hourly in the danger of this great wrath and infinite misery! But this is the dismal case of every soul in this congregation that has not been born again, however moral and strict, sober and religious, they may otherwise be. Oh that you would consider it, whether you be young or old! There is reason to think that there are many in this congregation now hearing this discourse that will actually be the subjects of this very misery to all eternity. We know not who they are, or in what seats they sit, or what thoughts they now have. It may be they are now at ease, and hear all these things without much disturbance, and are now flattering themselves that they are not the persons, promising themselves that they shall escape. If they knew that there was one person, and but one, in the whole congregation, that was to be the subject of this misery, what an awful thing would it be to think of! If we knew who it was, what an awful sight would it be to see such a person! How might all the rest of the congregation lift up a lamentable and bitter cry over him! But, alas! instead of one, how many is it likely will remember this discourse in hell? And it would be a wonder, if some that are now present should not be in hell in a very short time, even before this year is out. And it would be no wonder if some persons, that now sit here, in some seats of this meetinghouse, in health, quiet and secure, should be there before tomorrow morning. Those of you that finally continue in a natural condition, that shall keep out of hell longest will be there in a little time! your damnation does not slumber; it will come swiftly, and, in all probability, very suddenly upon many of you. You have reason to wonder that you are not already in hell. It is doubtless the case of some whom you have seen and known, that never deserved hell more than you, and that heretofore appeared as likely to have been now alive as you. Their case is past all hope; they are crying in extreme misery and perfect despair; but here you are in the land of the living and in the house of God, and have an opportunity to obtain salvation. What would not those poor damned hopeless souls give for one day's opportunity such as you now enjoy!

And now you have an extraordinary opportunity, a day wherein Christ has thrown the door of mercy wide open, and stands in calling and crying with a loud voice to poor sinners; a day wherein many are flocking to Him, and pressing into the kingdom of God. Many are daily coming from the east, west, north and south; many that were very lately in the same miserable condition that you are in are now in a happy state, with their hearts filled with love to Him who has loved them, and washed them from their sins in His own blood, and rejoicing in hope of the glory of God. How awful is it to be left behind at such a day! To see so many others feasting, while you are pining and perishing! To see so many rejoicing and singing for joy of heart, while you have cause to mourn for sorrow of heart, and howl for vexation of spirit! How can you rest one moment in such a condition? Are not your souls as precious as the souls of the people at Suffield,[7] where they are flocking from day to day to Christ?

---

6. "Who knoweth the power of thine anger? even according to thy fear, so is thy wrath" (Psalm 90.11).

7. "A town in the neighborhood" [Edwards's note].

Are there not many here who have lived long in the world, and are not to this day born again? and so are aliens from the commonwealth of Israel,[8] and have done nothing ever since they have lived, but treasure up wrath against the day of wrath? Oh, sirs, your case, in an especial manner, is extremely dangerous. Your guilt and hardness of heart is extremely great. Do you not see how generally persons of your years are passed over and left, in the present remarkable and wonderful dispensation of God's mercy? You had need to consider yourselves, and awake thoroughly out of sleep. You cannot bear the fierceness and wrath of the infinite God. And you, young men, and young women, will you neglect this precious season which you now enjoy, when so many others of your age are renouncing all youthful vanities, and flocking to Christ? You especially have now an extraordinary opportunity; but if you neglect it, it will soon be with you as with those persons who spent all the precious days of youth in sin, and are now come to such a dreadful pass in blindness and hardness. And you, children, who are unconverted, do not you know that you are going down to hell, to bear the dreadful wrath of that God, who is now angry with you every day and every night? Will you be content to be the children of the devil, when so many other children in the land are converted, and are become the holy and happy children of the King of kings?

And let every one that is yet of Christ, and hanging over the pit of hell, whether they be old men and women, or middle-aged, or young people, or little children, now hearken to the loud calls of God's word and providence. This acceptable year of the Lord, a day of such great favors to some, will doubtless be a day of as remarkable vengeance to others. Men's hearts harden, and their guilt increases apace at such a day as this, if they neglect their souls; and never was there so great danger of such person being given up to hardness of heart and blindness of mind. God seems now to be hastily gathering in His elect in all parts of the land; and probably the greater part of adult persons that ever shall be saved, will be brought in now in a little time, and that it will be as it was on the great outpouring of the Spirit upon the Jews in the apostles' days;[9] the election will obtain, and the rest will be blinded. If this should be the case with you, you will eternally curse this day, and will curse the day that ever you was born, to see such a season of the pouring out of God's Spirit, and will wish that you had died and gone to hell before you had seen it. Now undoubtedly it is, as it was in the days of John the Baptist, the ax is in an extraordinary manner laid at the root of the trees,[1] that every tree which brings not forth good fruit, may be hewn down and cast into the fire.

Therefore, let everyone that is out of Christ, now awake and fly from the wrath to come. The wrath of Almighty God is now undoubtedly hanging over a great part of this congregation: Let everyone fly out of Sodom: "Haste and escape for your lives, look not behind you, escape to the mountain, lest you be consumed."[2]

1741

---

8. I.e., not among the chosen people and, therefore, saved.

9. In Acts 2 the apostle Peter admonishes a crowd to repent and be converted, saying, "Save yourselves from this untoward generation. Then they that gladly received his word were baptized: and the same day there were added unto them about three thousand souls" (Acts 2.40–41).

1. "And now also the ax is laid unto the root of the trees: therefore every tree which bringeth not forth good fruit is hewn down, and cast into the fire" (Matthew 3.10).

2. Genesis 19.17.

From The Nature of True Virtue[1]

Chapter I. Showing Wherein the Essence of True Virtue Consists

Whatever controversies and variety of opinions there are about the nature of virtue, yet all excepting some sceptics, who deny any real difference between virtue and vice, mean by it something beautiful, or rather some kind of beauty or excellency. It is not all beauty that is called virtue; for instance, not the beauty of a building, of a flower, or of the rainbow; but some beauty belonging to beings that have perception and will. It is not all beauty of mankind that is called virtue; for instance, not the external beauty of the countenance or shape, gracefulness of motion, or harmony of voice: but it is a beauty that has its original seat in the mind. But yet perhaps not every thing that may be called a beauty of mind, is properly called virtue. There is a beauty of understanding and speculation; there is something in the ideas and conceptions of great philosophers and statesmen, that may be called beautiful: which is a different thing from what is most commonly meant by virtue.

But virtue is the beauty of those qualities and acts of the mind that are of a moral nature, i.e. such as are attended with desert or worthiness of praise or blame. Things of this sort it is generally agreed, so far as I know, do not belong merely to speculation: but to the disposition and will, or (to use a general word I suppose commonly well understood) to the heart. Therefore I suppose I shall not depart from the common opinion when I say, that virtue is the beauty of the qualities and exercises of the heart, or those actions which proceed from them. So that when it is inquired, what is the nature of true virtue? This is the same as to inquire what that is, which renders any habit, disposition, or exercise of the heart truly beautiful?

I use the phrase true virtue, and speak of things truly beautiful, because I suppose it will generally be allowed, that there is a distinction to be made between some things which are truly virtuous, and others which only seem to be so, through a partial and imperfect view of things: that some actions and dispositions appear beautiful, if considered partially and superficially, or with regard to some things belonging to them, and in some of their circumstances and tendencies, which would appear otherwise in a more extensive and comprehensive view, wherein they are seen clearly in their whole nature, and the extent of their connections in the universality of things.

There is a general and particular beauty. By a particular beauty, I mean that by which a thing appears beautiful when considered only with regard to its connection with, and tendency to, some particular things within a limited, and as it were a private sphere. And a general beauty is that by which a thing appears beautiful when viewed most perfectly, comprehensively and universally, with regard to all its tendencies, and its connections with every thing to which it stands related. The former may be without and against the latter. As a few notes in a tune, taken only by themselves and in their relation to one another, may be harmonious, which, when considered with respect to all the notes in the tune, or the entire series of sounds they are connected with, may be very discordant, and disagreeable. That only, therefore, is what I mean by true virtue, which, belonging to the heart of an intelligent being, is beautiful by a general beauty, or beautiful in a comprehensive view, as it is in itself, and as related to every thing with which it stands connected. And therefore, when

---

1. The text used here is from *The Works of Jonathan Edwards*, vol. 2, edited by S. Austin (1858).

we are inquiring concerning the nature of true virtue—wherein this true and general beauty of the heart does most essentially consist—this is my answer to the inquiry:

True virtue most essentially consists in *benevolence to being in general.* Or perhaps, to speak more accurately, it is that consent, propensity and union of heart to being in general, which is immediately exercised in a general good will.

The things before observed respecting the nature of true virtue, naturally lead us to such a notion of it. If it has its seat in the heart, and is the general goodness and beauty of the disposition and its exercise, in the most comprehensive view, considered with regard to its universal tendency, and as related to every thing with which it stands connected; what can it consist in, but a consent and good will to being in general? Beauty does not consist in discord and dissent, but in consent and agreement. And if every intelligent being is some way related to being in general, and is a part of the universal system of existence; and so stands in connection with the whole; what can its general and true beauty be, but its union and consent with the great whole?

If any such thing can be supposed as an union of heart to some particular being, or number of beings, disposing it to benevolence to a private circle or system of beings, which are but a small part of the whole; not implying a tendency to an union with the great system, and not at all inconsistent with enmity towards being in general, this I suppose not to be of the nature of true virtue; although it may in some respects be good, and may appear beautiful in a confined and contracted view of things. But of this more afterwards.

It is abundantly plain by the Holy Scriptures, and generally allowed, not only by Christian divines, but by the more considerable Deists,[2] that virtue most essentially consists in love. And I suppose it is owned[3] by the most considerable writers, to consist in general love of benevolence, or kind affection: though it seems to me the meaning of some in this affair is not sufficiently explained; which perhaps occasions some error or confusion in discourses on this subject.

When I say true virtue consists in love to being in general, I shall not be likely to be understood, that no one act of the mind or exercise of love is of the nature of true virtue, but what has being in general, or the great system of universal existence, for its direct and immediate object: so that no exercise of love, or kind affection to any one particular being, that is but a small part of this whole, has any thing of the nature of true virtue. But that the nature of true virtue consists in a disposition to benevolence towards being in general; though from such a disposition may arise exercises of love to particular beings, as objects are presented and occasions arise. No wonder that he who is of a generally benevolent disposition, should be more disposed than another to have his heart moved with benevolent affection to particular persons, with whom he is acquainted and conversant, and from whom arise the greatest and most frequent occasions for exciting his benevolent temper. But my meaning is, that no affections towards particular persons or beings are of the nature of true virtue, but such as arise from a generally benevolent temper, or from that habit or frame of mind, wherein consists a disposition to love being in general.

2. Those who argue that God's existence may be   3. Acknowledged.
proven by reason alone.

And perhaps it is needless for me to give notice to my readers, that when I speak of an intelligent being having a heart united and benevolently disposed to being in general, I thereby mean intelligent being in general. Not inanimate things, or beings that have no perception or will; which are not properly capable objects of benevolence.

Love is commonly distinguished into love of benevolence, and love of complacence. Love of benevolence is that affection[4] or propensity of the heart to any being, which causes it to incline to its well-being, or disposes it to desire and take pleasure in its happiness. And if I mistake not, it is agreeable to the common opinion, that beauty in the object is not always the ground of this propensity; but that there may be a disposition to the welfare of those that are not considered as beautiful, unless mere existence be accounted a beauty. And benevolence or goodness in the divine Being is generally supposed, not only to be prior to the beauty of many of its objects, but to their existence; so as to be the ground both of their existence and their beauty, rather than the foundation of God's benevolence; as it is supposed that it is God's goodness which moved Him to give them both being and beauty. So that if all virtue primarily consists in that affection of heart to being, which is exercised in benevolence, or an inclination to its good, then God's virtue is so extended as to include a propensity not only to being actually existing, and actually beautiful, but to possible being, so as to incline Him to give a being beauty and happiness.

What is commonly called love of complacence, presupposes beauty. For it is no other than delight in beauty; or complacence in the person or being beloved for his beauty. If virtue be the beauty of an intelligent being, and virtue consists in love, then it is a plain inconsistence, to suppose that virtue primarily consists in any love to its object for its beauty; either in a love of complacence, which is delight in a being for his beauty, or in a love of benevolence, that has the beauty of its object for its foundation. For that would be to suppose, that the beauty of intelligent beings primarily consists in love to beauty; or that their virtue first of all consists in their love to virtue. Which is an inconsistence, and going in a circle. Because it makes virtue, or beauty of mind, the foundation or first motive of that love wherein virtue originally consists, or wherein the very first virtue consists; or, it supposes the first virtue to be the consequence and effect of virtue. Which makes the first virtue both the ground and the consequence, both cause and effect of itself. Doubtless virtue primarily consists in something else besides any effect or consequence of virtue. If virtue consists primarily in love to virtue, then virtue, the thing loved, is the love of virtue: so that virtue must consist in the love of the love of virtue—and so on in infinitum. For there is no end of going back in a circle. We never come to any beginning or foundation; it is without beginning, and hangs on nothing. Therefore, if the essence of virtue, or beauty of mind, lies in love, or a disposition to love, it must primarily consist in something different both from complacence, which is a delight in beauty, and also from any benevolence that has the beauty of its object for its foundation. Because it is absurd to say, that virtue is primarily and first of all the consequence of itself; which makes virtue primarily prior to itself.

Nor can virtue primarily consist in gratitude; or one being's benevolence to another for his benevolence to him. Because this implies the same inconsis-

---

4. Partiality. "Complacence": that which pleases.

tence. For it supposes a benevolence prior to gratitude, which is the cause of gratitude. The first benevolence cannot be gratitude. Therefore there is room left for no other conclusion, than that the primary object of virtuous love is being, simply considered; or that true virtue primarily consists, not in love to any particular beings, because of their virtue or beauty, nor in gratitude, because they love us; but in a propensity and union of heart to being simply considered; exciting absolute benevolence, if I may so call it, to being in general. I say true virtue primarily consists in this. For I am far from asserting, that there is no true virtue in any other love than this absolute benevolence. But I would express what appears to me to be the truth on this subject, in the following particulars.

The first object of a virtuous benevolence is being, simply considered; and if being, simply considered, be its object, then being in general is its object; and what it has an ultimate propensity to is the highest good of being in general. And it will seek the good of every individual being unless it be conceived as not consistent with the highest good of being in general. In which case the good of a particular being, or some beings, may be given up for the sake of the highest good of being in general. And particularly, if there be any being statedly and irreclaimably opposite, and an enemy to being in general, then consent and adherence to being in general will induce the truly virtuous heart to forsake that enemy, and to oppose it.

Further, if *being*, simply considered, be the first object of a truly virtuous benevolence, then that object who has most of being, or has the greatest share of existence, other things being equal, so far as such a being is exhibited to our faculties, will have the greatest share of the propensity and benevolent affections of the heart. I say, "other things being equal," especially because there is a secondary object of virtuous benevolence, that I shall take notice of presently, which must be considered as the ground or motive to a purely virtuous benevolence. Pure benevolence in its first exercise is nothing else but being's uniting consent, or propensity to being; and inclining to the general highest good, and to each being, whose welfare is consistent with the highest general good, in proportion to the degree of existence,[5] understand, "other things being equal."

The second object of a virtuous propensity of heart is benevolent being. A secondary ground of pure benevolence is virtuous benevolence itself in its object. When any one under the influence of general benevolence, sees another being possessed of the like general benevolence, this attaches his heart to him, and draws forth greater love to him, than merely his having existence: because so far as the being beloved has love to being in general, so far his own being is, as it were, enlarged; extends to, and in some sort comprehends being in general: and therefore, he that is governed by love to being in general, must of necessity have complacence in him, and the greater degree of benevolence to him, as it were out of gratitude to him for his love to general existence, that his own heart is extended and united to, and so looks on its interest as its own.

---

5. "I say, 'in proportion to the degree of existence,' because one being may have more existence than another, as he may be greater than another. That which is great has more existence, and is further from nothing, than that which is little. One being may have every thing positive belonging to it, or every thing which goes to its positive existence (in opposition to defect) in an higher degree than another; or a greater capacity and power, greater understanding, every faculty and every positive quality in a higher degree. An archangel must be supposed to have more existence, and to be every way further removed from nonentity, than a worm" [Edwards's note].

It is because his heart is thus united to being in general, that he looks on a benevolent propensity to being in general, wherever he sees it, as the beauty of the being in whom it is; an excellency that renders him worthy of esteem, complacence, and the greater good-will. But several things may be noted more particularly concerning this secondary ground of a truly virtuous love.

1. That loving a being on this ground necessarily arises from pure benevolence to being in general, and comes to the same thing. For he that has a simple and pure good will to general existence, must love that temper in others, that agrees and conspires with itself. A spirit of consent to being must agree with consent to being. That which truly and sincerely seeks the good of others, must approve of, and love that which joins with him in seeking the good of others.

2. This secondary ground of virtuous love is the thing wherein true moral or spiritual beauty primarily consists. Yea, spiritual beauty consists wholly in this, and in the various qualities and exercises of mind which proceed from it, and the external actions which proceed from these internal qualities and exercises. And in these things consists all true virtue, viz.,[6] in this love of being, and the qualities and acts which arise from it.

3. As all spiritual beauty lies in these virtuous principles and acts, so it is primarily on this account they are beautiful, viz., that they imply consent and union with being in general. This is the primary and most essential beauty of every thing that can justly be called by the name of virtue, or is any moral excellency in the eye of one who has a perfect view of things. I say, "the primary and most essential beauty," because there is a secondary and inferior sort of beauty; which I shall take notice of afterwards.

4. This spiritual beauty, which is but a secondary ground of virtuous benevolence, is the ground not only of benevolence, but complacence, and is the primary ground of the latter; that is, when the complacence is truly virtuous. Love to us in particular, and kindness received may be a secondary ground: but this is the primary objective foundation of it.

5. It must be noted, that the degree of the amiableness of true virtue primarily consisting in consent, and a benevolent propensity of heart to being in general, is not in the simple proportion of the degree of benevolent affection seen, but in a proportion compounded of the greatness of the benevolent being, or the degree of being and the degree of benevolence. One who loves being in general, will necessarily value good will to being in general, wherever he sees it. But if he sees the same benevolence in two beings, he will value it more in two, than in one only. Because it is a greater thing, more favorable to being in general, to have two beings to favor it, than only one of them. For there is more being that favors being: both together having more being than one alone. So if one being be as great as two, has as much existence as both together, and has the same degree of general benevolence, it is more favorable to being in general, than if there were general benevolence in a being that had but half that share of existence. As a large quantity of gold, with the same quality, is more valuable than a small quantity of the same metal.

6. It is impossible that any one should truly relish this beauty, consisting in general benevolence, who has not that temper himself. I have observed, that if any being is possessed of such a temper, he will unavoidably be pleased with

6. Namely (Latin abbreviation).

the same temper in another. And it may in like manner be demonstrated, that it is such a spirit, and nothing else, which will relish such a spirit. For if a being destitute of benevolence, should love benevolence to being in general, it would prize and seek that for which it had no value. For how should one love and value a disposition to a thing, or a tendency to promote it, and for that very reason, when the thing itself is what he is regardless of, and has no value for, nor desires to have promoted.

Chapter III. Concerning the Secondary and Inferior Kind of Beauty[7]

Though what has been spoken of is alone justly esteemed the true beauty of moral agents, or spiritual beings; this alone being what would appear beautiful in them upon a clear and comprehensive view of things; and therefore alone is the moral amiableness of beings that have understanding and will, in the eyes of him that perfectly sees all things as they are; yet there are other qualities, other sensations, propensities and affections of mind, and principles of action, that often obtain the epithet of virtuous, and by many are supposed to have the nature of true virtue, which are entirely of a distinct nature from this, and have nothing of that kind; and therefore are erroneously confounded with real virtue.

That consent, agreement, or union of being to being, which has been spoken of, viz., the union or propensity of minds to mental or spiritual existence, may be called the highest and primary beauty; being the proper and peculiar beauty of spiritual and moral beings, which are the highest and first part of the universal system, for whose sake all the rest has existence. Yet there is another, inferior, secondary beauty, which is some image of this, and which is not peculiar to spiritual beings, but is found even in inanimate things; which consists in a mutual consent and agreement of different things, in form, manner, quantity, and visible end or design; called by the various names of regularity, order, uniformity, symmetry, proportion, harmony, etc. Such is the mutual agreement of the various sides of a square, or equilateral triangle, or of a regular polygon. Such is, as it were, the mutual consent of the different parts of the periphery of a circle, or surface of a sphere, and of the corresponding parts of an ellipsis. Such is the agreement of the colors, figures, dimensions, and distances of the different spots on a chess board. Such is the beauty of the figures on a piece of chintz or brocade. Such is the beautiful proportion of the various parts of a human body or countenance. And such is the sweet mutual consent and agreement of the various notes of a melodious tune. This is the same that Mr. Hutchinson,[8] in his Treatise on Beauty, expresses by uniformity in the midst of variety. Which is no other than the consent or agreement of different things in form, quantity, etc. He observes, that the greater the variety is in equal uniformity the greater the beauty. Which is no more than to say, the more there are of different mutually agreeing things, the greater is the beauty. And the reason of that is, because it is more considerable to have many things consent one with another, than a few only.

The beauty which consists in the visible fitness of a thing to its use, and unity of design, is not a distinct sort of beauty from this. For it is to be

7. Chapter II, omitted here, is titled "Showing How That Love, Wherein True Virtue Consists, Respects the Divine Being and Created Things."

8. Francis Hutchinson (1694–1796), author of *An Inquiry into the Original of Our Ideas of Beauty and Virtue* (1725).

observed, that one thing which contributes to the beauty of the agreement and proportion of various things, is their relation one to another; which connects them, and introduces them together into view and consideration, and whereby one suggests the other to the mind, and the mind is led to compare them, and so to expect and desire agreement. Thus the uniformity of two or more pillars, as they may happen to be found in different places, is not an equal degree of beauty, as that uniformity in so many pillars in the corresponding parts of the same building. So means and an intended effect are related one to another. The answerableness of a thing to its use is only the proportion and fitness of a cause or means to a visibly designed effect, and so an effect suggested to the mind by the idea of the means. This kind of beauty is not entirely different from that beauty which there is in fitting a mortice to its tenon. Only when the beauty consists in unity of design, or the adaptness of a variety of things to promote one intended effect, in which all conspire, as the various parts of an ingenious complicated machine, there is a double beauty, as there is a twofold agreement and conformity. First, there is the agreement of the various parts to the designed end. Secondly, through this designed end or effect, all the various particulars agree one with another as the general medium of their union, whereby they, being united in this third, are all united one to another.

The reason, or at least one reason, why God has made this kind of mutual agreement of things beautiful and grateful to those intelligent beings that perceive it, probably is, that there is in it some image of the true, spiritual, original beauty which has been spoken of; consisting in being's consent to being, or the union of spiritual beings in a mutual propensity and affection of heart. The other is an image of this, because by that uniformity diverse things become as it were one, as it is in this cordial union. And it pleases God to observe analogy in his works, as is manifest in fact in innumerable instances; and especially to establish inferior things with analogy to superior. Thus, in how many instances has he formed brutes in analogy to the nature of mankind? and plants in analogy to animals, with respect to the manner of their generation, nutrition, etc. And so he has constituted the external world in analogy to the spiritual world in numberless instances; as might be shown, if it were necessary, and here were a proper place for it. Why such analogy in God's works pleased him, it is not needful now to inquire. It is sufficient that he makes an agreement of different things, in their form, manner, measure, etc., to appear beautiful, because here is some image of an higher kind of agreement and consent of spiritual beings. It has pleased him to establish a law of nature, by virtue of which the uniformity and mutual correspondence of a beautiful plant, and the respect which the various parts of a regular building seem to have one to another, and their agreement and union, and the consent or concord of the various notes of a melodious tune, should appear beautiful; because therein is some image of the consent of mind, of the different members of a society or system of intelligent beings, sweetly united in a benevolent agreement of heart.

And here by the way I would further observe, probably it is with regard to this image or resemblance which secondary beauty has of true spiritual beauty, that God has so constituted nature, that the presenting of this inferior beauty, especially in those kinds of it which have the greatest resemblance of the primary beauty, as the harmony of sounds and the beauties of nature, have a tendency to assist those whose hearts are under the influence of a truly virtuous temper to dispose them to the exercises of divine love, and enliven in them a sense of spiritual beauty.

From what has been said we may see that there are two sorts of agreement or consent of one thing to another. (1) There is a cordial[9] agreement; that consists in concord and union of mind and heart: which, if not attended (viewing things in general) with more discord than concord, is true virtue, and the original or primary beauty, which is the only true moral beauty. (2) There is a natural union or agreement; which, though some image of the other, is entirely a distinct thing; the will, disposition, or affection of the heart having no concern in it, but consisting only in uniformity and consent of nature, form, quantity, etc. (as before described), wherein lies an inferior secondary sort of beauty, which may in distinction from the other, be called natural beauty. This may be sufficient to let the reader know how I shall hereafter use the phrase cordial and natural agreement; and moral, spiritual, divine, and primary original beauty, and secondary or natural beauty. Concerning this latter, the inferior kind of beauty, the following things may be observed:

1. The cause why secondary beauty is grateful to men, is only a law of nature which God has fixed, or an instinct he has given to mankind; and not their perception of the same thing which God is pleased to regard as the ground or rule by which he has established such a law of nature. This appears in two things:

(a) That which God respects, as the ground of this law of nature whereby things have a secondary beauty are made grateful to men, is their mutual agreement and proportion, in measure, form, etc. But in many instances, persons who are gratified and affected with this beauty, do not reflect on that particular agreement and proportion which, according to the law of nature, is the ground and rule of beauty in the case, yea, are ignorant of it. Thus a man may be pleased with the harmony of the notes in a tune, and yet know nothing of that proportion or adjustment of the notes, which by the law of nature is the ground of the melody. He knows not, that the vibrations in one note regularly coincide with the vibrations in another; that the vibrations of a note coincide in time with two vibrations of its octave; and that two vibrations of a note coincide with three of its fifth, etc. Yea, he may not know that there are vibrations of the air in the case, or any corresponding motions in the organs of hearing, in the auditory nerve, or animal spirits. So a man may be affected and pleased with a beautiful proportion of the features in a face, and yet not know what that proportion is, or in what measures, quantities, and distances it consists. In this, therefore, a sensation of secondary beauty differs from a sensation of primary and spiritual beauty, consisting in a spiritual union and agreement. What makes the latter grateful, is perceiving the union itself. It is the immediate view of that wherein the beauty fundamentally lies, that is pleasing to the virtuous mind.

(b) God, in establishing such a law—that mutual natural agreement of different things, in form, quantity, etc., should appear beautiful or grateful to men—seems to have had regard to the resemblance there is in such a natural agreement, to that spiritual, cordial agreement, wherein original beauty consists. But it is not any reflection upon, or perception of, such a resemblance, that is the reason why such a form or state of objects appear beautiful to men:

_____

9. Here, vital.

but their sensation of pleasure, on a view of this secondary beauty, is immediately owing to the law God has established, or the instinct he has given.

2. Another thing observable concerning this kind of beauty, is that it affects the mind more (other things being equal), when taken notice of in objects which are of considerable importance, than in little trivial matters. Thus the symmetry of the parts of a human body or countenance, affects the mind more than the beauty of a flower. So the beauty of the solar system, more than as great and as manifold an order and uniformity in a tree. And the proportions of the parts of a church, or a palace, more than the same proportions in some little slight compositions, made to please children.

3. Not only uniformity and proportion, etc., of different things is requisite, in order to this inferior beauty; but also some relation or connection of the things thus agreeing one with another. As the uniformity or likeness of a number of pillars scattered hither and thither, does not constitute beauty, or at least by no means in an equal degree, as uniformity in pillars connected in the same building, in parts that have relation one to another. So if we see things unlike and very disproportioned, in distant places, which have no relation to each other, this excites no such idea of deformity, as disagreement, inequality, or disproportion in things related and connected; and the nearer the relation, and the stricter the connection, so much the greater and more disgustful is the deformity, consisting in their disagreement.

4. This secondary kind of beauty, consisting in uniformity and proportion, not only takes place in material and external things, but also in things immaterial; and is, in very many things, plain and sensible in the latter, as well as the former. And when it is so, there is no reason why it should not be grateful to them that behold it, in these as well as the other, by virtue of the same sense, or the same determination of mind, to be gratified with uniformity and proportion. If uniformity and proportion be the things that affect and appear agreeable to this sense of beauty, then why should not uniformity and proportion affect the same sense in immaterial things as well as material, if there be equal capacity of discerning it in both? and indeed more in spiritual things (*cæteris paribus*)[1] as these are more important than things merely external and material?

This is not only reasonable to be supposed, but is evident in fact, in numberless instances. There is a beauty of order in society, besides what consists in benevolence, or can be referred to it, which is of the secondary kind. As, when the different members of society have all their appointed office, place and station, according to their several capacities and talents, and every one keeps his place, and continues in his proper business. In this there is a beauty, not of a different kind from the regularity of a beautiful building, or piece of skillfull architecture, where the strong pillars are set in their proper place, the pilasters in a place fit for them, the square pieces of marble in the pavement, the panels, partitions, and cornices, etc. in places proper for them. As the agreement of a variety of things in one common design, as of the parts of a building, or complicated machine, is one instance of that regularity which belongs to the secondary kind of beauty, so there is the same kind of beauty in what is called wisdom, consisting in the united tendency of thoughts, ideas and particular volitions, to one general purpose: which is a distinct thing from the goodness of that general purpose, as being useful and benevolent.

---

1. All things being equal (Latin).

There is a beauty in the virtue called justice, which consists in the agreement of different things, that have relation to one another, in nature, manner, and measure; and therefore is the very same sort of beauty with that uniformity and proportion, which is observable in those external and material things that are esteemed beautiful. There is a natural agreement and adaptedness of things that have relation one to another, and a harmonious corresponding of one thing with another. He who from his will does evil to others, should receive evil from the will of him or them whose business it is to take care of the injured, and to act in their behalf, in proportion to the evil of his doings. Things are in natural regularity and mutual agreement, in a literal sense, when he whose heart opposes the general system, should have the hearts of that system, or the heart of the ruler of the system, against him; and, in consequence should receive evil, in proportion to the evil tendency of the opposition of his heart. So there is an agreement in nature and measure, when he that loves has the proper returns of love; when he that from his heart promotes the good of another has his good promoted by the other; for there is a kind of justice in becoming gratitude.

Indeed most of the duties incumbent on us, if well considered, will be found to partake of the nature of justice. There is some natural agreement of one thing to another; some adaptedness of the agent to the object; some answerableness of the act to the occasion; some equality and proportion in things of a similar nature, and of a direct relation one to another. So it is in relative duties; duties of children to parents, and of parents to children; duties of husbands and wives; duties of rulers and subjects; duties of friendship and good neighborhood; and all duties that we owe to God, our Creator, preserver, and benefactor; and all duties whatsoever, considered as required by God, and as what are to be performed with a regard to Christ.

It is the secondary kind of beauty which Mr. Wollaston[2] seems to have had in his eye when he resolved all virtue into an agreement of inclinations, volitions and actions with truth. He evidently has respect to the justice there is in virtues and duties; which consists in one being expressing such affections, and using such a conduct towards another, as hath a natural agreement and proportion to what is in them, and what we receive from them; which is as much a natural conformity of affection and action with its ground, object, and occasion, as that which is between a true proposition and the thing spoken of in it.

But there is another and higher beauty in true virtue, and in all truly virtuous dispositions and exercises, than what consists in any uniformity or similarity of various things; viz., the union of heart to being in general, or to God, the being of beings, which appears in those virtues; and of which those virtues, when true, are the various expressions or effects. Benevolence to being in general, or to being simply considered, is entirely a distinct thing from uniformity in the midst of variety, and is a superior kind of beauty.

It is true, that benevolence to being in general will naturally incline to justice, or proportion in the exercises of it. He who loves being, simply considered, will naturally, other things being equal, love particular beings in a proportion compounded of the degree of being, and the degree of virtue, or benevolence to being, which they have. And that is to love beings in proportion to their dignity. For the dignity of any being consists in those two things. Respect to being, in this proportion, is the first and most general kind of jus-

---

2. William Wollaston (1659–1742), author of *The Religion of Nature Delineated* (1722).

tice: which will produce all the subordinate kinds. So that, after benevolence to being in general exists, the proportion which is observed in objects may be the cause of the proportion of benevolence to those objects; but no proportion is the cause or ground of the existence of such a thing as benevolence to being. The tendency of objects to excite that degree of benevolence which is proportionable to the degree of being, etc., is the consequence of the existence of benevolence, and not the ground of it. Even as a tendency of bodies, one to another, by mutual attraction, in proportion to the quantity of matter, is the consequence of the being of such a thing as mutual attraction; and not attraction the effect of proportion.

By this it appears, that just affections and acts have a beauty in them, distinct from and superior to the uniformity and equality there is in them: for which he that has a truly virtuous temper, relishes and delights in them. And that is the expression and manifestation there is in them of benevolence to being in general. And besides this, there is the agreement of justice to the will and command of God; and also something in the tendency and consequences of justice, agreeable to general benevolence, as the glory of God, and the general good. Which tendency also makes it beautiful to a truly virtuous mind. So that the tendency of general benevolence to produce justice, also the tendency of justice to produce effects agreeable to general benevolence, both render justice pleasing to a virtuous mind. And it is on these accounts chiefly, that justice is grateful to a virtuous taste, or a truly benevolent heart. But though it be true, that the uniformity and proportion there is in justice is grateful to a benevolent heart, as this uniformity and proportion tends to the general good; yet that is no argument that there is no other beauty in it but its agreeing with benevolence. For so the external regularity and order of the natural world gratifies benevolence, as it is profitable, and tends to the general good; but that is no argument that there is no other sort of beauty in external uniformity and proportion, but only its suiting benevolence, by tending to the general good.

5. From all that has been observed concerning this secondary kind of beauty it appears, that the disposition which consists in a determination of mind to approve and be pleased with this beauty, considered simply and by itself, has nothing of the nature of true virtue, and is entirely a different thing from a truly virtuous taste. For it has been shown, that this kind of beauty is entirely diverse from the beauty of true virtue, whether it takes place in material or immaterial things; and therefore it will follow, that a taste of this kind of beauty is entirely a different thing from a taste of true virtue. Who will affirm, that a disposition to approve of the harmony of good music, or the beauty of a square or equilateral triangle, is the same with true holiness, or a truly virtuous disposition of mind? It is a relish of uniformity and proportion that determines the mind to approve these things. And there is no need of any thing higher, or of any thing in any respect diverse, to determine the mind to approve and be pleased with equal uniformity and proportion among spiritual things which are equally discerned. It is virtuous to love true virtue, as that denotes an agreement of the heart with virtue. But it argues no virtue for the heart to be pleased with that which is entirely distinct from it.

Though it be true, that there is some analogy in it to spiritual and virtuous beauty—as far as material things can have analogy to things spiritual, of which they can have no more than a shadow—yet, as has been observed, men do not approve it because of any such analogy perceived. And not only reason but experience plainly shows, that men's approbation of this sort of beauty does not spring from any virtuous temper, and has no connection with virtue. For otherwise their delight in the beauty of squares, and cubes, and regular polygons, in the regularity of buildings, and the beautiful figures in a piece of embroidery, would increase in proportion to men's virtue; and would be raised to a great height in some eminently virtuous or holy men; but would be almost wholly lost in some others that are very vicious and lewd.[3] It is evident in fact, that a relish of these things does not depend on general benevolence, or any benevolence at all to any being whatsoever, any more than a man's loving the taste of honey, or his being pleased with the smell of a rose. A taste of this inferior beauty in things immaterial, is one thing which has been taken by some moralists, for a true virtuous principle, supposed to be implanted naturally in the hearts of all mankind.

c. 1755   1765

[The Beauty of the World][1]

The beauty of the world consists wholly of sweet mutual consents,[2] either within itself or with the Supreme Being. As to the corporeal world, though there are many other sorts of consents, yet the sweetest and most charming beauty of it is its resemblance of spiritual beauties. The reason is that spiritual beauties are infinitely the greatest, and bodies being but the shadows of beings, they must be so much the more charming as they shadow forth spiritual beauties. This beauty is peculiar to natural things, it surpassing the art of man.

Thus there is the resemblance of a decent trust, dependence and acknowledgment in the planets continually moving round the sun, receiving his influences by which they are made happy, bright and beautiful: a decent attendance in the secondary planets, an image of majesty, power, glory, and beneficence in the sun in the midst of all, and so in terrestrial things, as I have shown in another place.

It is very probable that that wonderful suitableness of green for the grass and plants, the blues of the sky, the white of the clouds, the colors of flowers, consists in a complicated proportion that these colors make one with another, either in their magnitude of the rays, the number of vibrations that are caused in the atmosphere, or some other way. So there is a great suitableness between the objects of different senses, as between sounds, colors, and smells; as between colors of the woods and flowers and the smells and the singing of birds, which it is probable consist in a certain proportion of the vibrations that are made in the different organs. So there are innumerable other agreeablenesses of motions, figures, etc. The gentle motions of waves, of [the] lily, etc., as it is agreeable to other things that represent calmness, gentleness, and benevolence, etc., the fields and woods seem to rejoice, and how joyful do the birds seem to be in it. How much a resemblance is there of every grace in the field covered with plants and flowers when the sun shines serenely and undisturbedly upon them, how a resemblance, I say, of every grace and beauti-

---

3. In the old sense: evil.

1. This fragment was found among Edwards's papers and first published, with this title, by Perry Miller in

Images or Shadows of Divine Things (1948). The editorial emendations are by Miller.

2. Agreements.

ful disposition of mind, of an inferior towards a superior cause, preserver, benevolent benefactor, and a fountain of happiness.

How great a resemblance of a holy and virtuous soul is a calm, serene day. What an infinite number of such like beauties is there in that one thing, the light, and how complicated an harmony and proportion is it probable belongs to it.

There are beauties that are more palpable and explicable, and there are hidden and secret beauties. The former pleases, and we can tell why; we can explain the particular point for the agreement that renders the thing pleasing. Such are all artificial regularities; we can tell wherein the regularity lies that affects us. [The] latter sort are those beauties that delight us and we cannot tell why. Thus, we find ourselves pleased in beholding the color of the violets, but we know not what secret regularity or harmony it is that creates that pleasure in our minds. These hidden beauties are commonly by far the greatest, because the more complex a beauty is, the more hidden is it. In this latter fact consists principally the beauty of the world, and very much in light and colors. Thus mere light is pleasing to the mind. If it be to the degree of effulgence, it is very sensible, and mankind have agreed in it: they all represent glory and extraordinary beauty by brightness. The reason of it is either that light or our organ of seeing is so contrived that an harmonious motion is excited in the animal spirits and propogated to the brain. That mixture we call white is a proportionate mixture that is harmonious, as Sir Isaac Newton[3] has shown, to each particular simple color, and contains in it some harmony or other that is delightful. And each sort of rays play a distinct tune to the soul, besides those lovely mixtures that are found in nature. Those beauties, how lovely is the green of the face of the earth in all manner of colors, in flowers, the color of the skies, and lovely tinctures of the morning and evening.

Corollary:[4] Hence the reason why almost all men, and those that seem to be very miserable, love life, because they cannot bear to lose sight of such a beautiful and lovely world. The ideas, that every moment whilst we live have a beauty that we take not distinct notice of, brings a pleasure that, when we come to the trial, we had rather live in much pain and misery than lose.

1948

From Images or Shadows of Divine Things[1]

3 [Roses]

Roses grow upon briars, which is to signify that all temporal sweets are mixed with bitter. But what seems more especially to be meant by it is that

3. Sir Isaac Newton (1642–1727), in his *Opticks* (1704), explained the phenomena of color, proving that differences in color are caused by differing degrees of refrangibility.
4. Something that naturally follows from a proved proposition.
1. Included in Edwards's manuscripts in the Yale University Library is a notebook of some 212 entries to which Edwards had suggested several titles: *The Images of Divine Things, The Shadows of Divine Things, The Book of Nature and Common Providence, The Lan-*

guage and Lessons of Nature. In 1948 Perry Miller published this notebook as *Images or Shadows of Divine Things.* In these notes Edwards continues the medieval tradition of typology, a method of reading the Bible by which Old Testament figures ("types") are fulfilled by Christ in the New Testament ("the anti-type" being that which is foreshadowed by a type). Edwards here extends the idea of typology and suggests that the physical world may be read as a sign or type, revealing ultimate spiritual truth.

pure happiness, the crown of glory, is to be come at in no other way than by bearing Christ's cross, by a life of mortification, self-denial, and labor, and bearing all things for Christ. The rose, that is chief of all flowers, is the last thing that comes out. The briary, prickly, bush grows before that; the end and crown of all is the beautiful and fragrant rose.

64 [Hills and Mountains]

Hills and mountains are types[2] of heaven, and often made use of as such in Scripture. These are with difficulty ascended. To ascend them, one must go against the natural tendency of the flesh; this must be contradicted in all the ascent, in every step of it, and the ascent is attended with labor, sweat and hardship. There are commonly many hideous rocks in the way. It is a great deal easier descending into valleys. This is a representation of the difficulty, labor, and self-denial of the way to heaven, and how agreeable it is, to the inclination of the flesh, to descend into hell. At the bottom of valleys, especially deep valleys, there is water, with a lake or other waters, but water, as has been shown elsewhere in notes on Scripture, commonly signifies misery, especially that which is occasioned by the wrath of God. So in hell is a lake or gulf of misery and wrath.

77 [Rivers]

There is a wonderful analogy between what is seen in rivers, their gathering from innumerable small branches beginning at a great distance one from another in different regions, some on the sides or tops of mountains, others in valleys, and all conspiring to one common issue, all after those very diverse and contrary courses which they held for a while, yet all gathering more and more together the nearer they come to their common end and ultimate issue, and all at length discharging themselves at one mouth into the same ocean. Here is livelily represented how all things tend to one, even to God, the boundless ocean, which they can add nothing to, as mightiest rivers that continually discharge themselves into the ocean add nothing to it sensibly; the waters of the ocean are not raised by it, yea all the rivers together, great and small, together with all the brooks and little streams, can't raise the waters of the ocean in the least degree. The innumerable streams of which great rivers are constituted, running in such infinitely various and contrary courses, livelily represent the various dispensations of divine providence: some of them beginning at the greatest distance from the common mouth, others nearer to it, multitudes of them meeting first to constitute certain main branches of the river before they empty themselves into the main river and so into the ocean; some of the first constituent streams never empty themselves into any of the branches at all, but empty themselves directly into the main river; others first empty themselves into other branches, and those into others, and those still into others, and so on many times before they yield their tribute to the main river; several springs first constitute a brook, and then many of these brooks constitute a small river, and then several of these small rivers meet to constitute a main branch of the main river, and then all together empty into that main

2. Foreshadowings, i.e., things which are fulfilled by the idea of heaven.

river. Some of the constituent branches of the main river have their head or source at the greatest distance from the mouth, others take their source much nearer the mouth, and so all along there are new heads or new sources beginning, from the head to the mouth of the main river. Some of these branches run directly contrary to others, and yet all meet at last. And the same branches don't keep the same course: their course is not continually in a right line, that which appears to us the directest course to the main river, but sometimes they run one way, sometimes another, sometimes their course is directly contrary to what it is at others. Sometimes, instead of going towards the main river they tend to, they run for a considerable space right from it, but yet nothing is lost by this, but something gained; they nevertheless fail not of emptying themselves into the main river in proper time and due place, and bring the greater tribute of waters for their crooked and contrary courses. And so it is with the main river itself: its course is not directly the shortest way towards the ocean to which its waters are due, but tends thither by degrees, with many windings and turnings, sometimes seeming to run from the ocean and not towards it. If a spectator were to judge by the appearances of things before his eyes, he would think the river could [not] reach the ocean. There appears such an innumerable multitude of obstacles in the way, many hills and high mountains, which a person that views at a distance sees no way between; he don't discover those ways through the hideous forests, and the openings between the mountains are not to be seen till we come to them, the winding passages through mountainous country are not to be discovered but by tracing the course of the waters themselves, but yet amidst all these obstacles those rivers find their way, and fail not at last of an arrival at the ocean at last, though they pass through so many vast regions, that all seem to be full of obstacles for so long a course together. And it is observable that those very hills and mountains that appear like the most unsurmountable obstacles, instead of obstructing the course of these rivers, do afford the greatest supplies and additions. Those rivers will at last come to the ocean, and it is impossible to hinder. It is in vain for men to attempt to turn back the stream or put a stay to it. Whatever obstacles are in the way, the waters will either bear them away before them or will find a passage round them, under them, or above them. I need not run the parallel between this and the course of God's providence through all ages from the beginning to the end of the world, when all things shall have their final issue in God, the infinite, inextinguishable fountain whence all things come at first as all the rivers come from the sea and whither they all shall come at last. For of Him and to Him are all things, and He is the alpha and omega, the beginning and the end.[3] God hath provided a water course for the overflowing of the waters, and He turns the rivers of water whithersoever it pleaseth Him.

By what has been spoken of, it is particularly livelily represented and shown after what manner all the dispensations of providence, from the beginning of the world till the coming of Christ, all pointed to Christ, all had respect to his coming and working our redemption and setting up his kingdom in the world, and all finally issued in this great event. From time to time, in the different successive ages of the world, there began new dispensations of providence,

3. "I am Alpha and Omega, the beginning and the ending, saith the Lord, which is, and which was, and which is to come, the Almighty" (Revelation 1.8). Alpha and omega are the first and last letters of the Greek alphabet.

tending to make way and forward this great event, as there are head[s] of new branches all along as we come nearer and nearer to the mouth of the main river. Thus in Noah[4] began a new series of dispensations of providence in addition to what had been begun before, making further preparation for the coming of the Messiah.

* * *

78 [*Trees*]

(See the last.) We see the reverse in trees from what we do in [rivers]. In these, all comes from one common stock and is distributed into innumerable branches, beginning at the root where the trunk is biggest of all and ending in the extremities of the smallest twigs. The water here in the sap of these trees has a contrary course from what it has in rivers, where the course begins in the extremities of the smallest branches and ends in the mouth of the river where the river is largest, and all the waters are collected into one body. What is observable in trees is also a lively emblem of many spiritual things, as particularly of the dispensations of providence since the coming of Christ. Christ is, as it were, the trunk of the tree, and all the church are His branches. I am the vine, ye are the branches, says Christ. Christ rising from the dead is, as it were, the trunk of the tree which appears coming out of the ground, and how do we from this one rising head see the body of Christ multiplied. The Christian church, as distinguished from the Jewish, began in Christ's resurrection, and how many branches shot forth soon after Christ's resurrection: the apostles after that were endowed with power from on high; those were, as it were, main branches, whence all the lesser branches came. The Apostle Paul, who was a branch that shot forth later than the rest,[5] exceeded all in thriftiness and fruitfulness, so that the bigger part of the future tree came from this branch. The tree went on growing, and the further it proceeded in its growth, the more abundantly did its branches multiply, till the tree filled the Roman Empire in a few hundreds of years, and will fill the whole earth at last. Thus the parable of the grain of mustard seed is verified.[6] This tree will appear more and more glorious, till it shall appear in the greatest glory of all at the end of all things, and its full ripe fruits shall be gathered in, and though there have been many winters and may be more, wherein this tree has ceased growing and has been in a great measure stripped of leaves and fruit, and seemed to be dead or dying, yet springs and summers are appointed to follow these winters, wherein the trees shall flourish again and appear higher and larger and more abundantly multiplied in its branches and fruit than ever before. This tree is sometimes represented as first beginning in Abraham,[7] and sometimes in David,[8] and Christ himself as the branch of those roots, but Christ is most properly the trunk or body of the tree. Indeed, the course of the sap of the tree, from its beginning in the extremities of the roots to its end in the extremity of the branches, is an emblem of the whole series and scheme of divine providence,

---

4. "And God spake unto Noah, and to his sons with him, saying, And I, behold, I establish my covenant with you, and with your seed after you" (Genesis 9.8–9).
5. It is generally held that Paul did not come to Jerusalem until after the death of Jesus. His conversion came when Jesus appeared to him on the road to Damascus and, therefore, later than the other apostles (Acts 9).

6. The mustard seed is very small, and the tree which eventuates from it is very large (Matthew 13.31–32).
7. Abraham's descendants would possess Canaan (Genesis 12.7).
8. David succeeded Saul as king of Israel and was the chosen heir favored by God Himself (1 Samuel 16.1–13).

both before and after Christ, from the beginning to the end of the world. The sap in the roots is like the water of a river gathering from small branches into a common body, and this, as was said before, represents the course of divine providence during the times of the Old Testament, when the designs of providence as they related to Christ and the work of redemption, which is as it were the summary comprehension of all God's works of providence, was hid as it were underground. All was under a veil and the scheme of redemption was a mystery kept secret from the foundation of the world; but after this, the mystery was removed, and the scheme of providence was, like a tree above ground, gradually displayed as the branches successively put forth themselves. Hence we may observe that God's calling of Abraham and anointing David was, as it were, the planting the root whence the tree should grow, and Abraham and David were main roots whence the tree grows, but Christ himself is the sprout or branch from these roots which becomes the tree whence all other branches proceed.

156 [The Book of Scripture]

The book of Scripture is the interpreter of the book of nature two ways, viz., by declaring to us those spiritual mysteries that are indeed signified and typified in the constitution of the natural world; and secondly, in actually making application of the signs and types in the book of nature as representations of those spiritual mysteries in many instances.

1948

BENJAMIN FRANKLIN
1706–1790

Benjamin Franklin was born on Milk Street in Boston, the tenth son in a family of fifteen children. His father, Josiah, was a tallow chandler and soap boiler who came to Boston in 1682 from Ecton in Northamptonshire, England, and was proud of his Protestant ancestors. He married Abiah Folger, whose father was a teacher to the Native Americans. Josiah talked of offering his son Benjamin as his "tithe" to the church and enrolled him in Boston Grammar School as a preparation for the study of the ministry, but his plans were too ambitious and Benjamin was forced to leave school and work for his father. He hated his father's occupation and threatened to run away to sea. A compromise was made, and when Benjamin was twelve he was apprenticed to his brother, a printer. He must have been a natural student of the printing trade; he loved books and reading, he learned quickly, and he liked to write. His brother unwittingly published Benjamin's first essay when he printed an editorial left on his desk signed "Silence Dogood." When his brother was imprisoned in 1722 for offending Massachusetts officials, Franklin carried on publication of the paper by himself.

In 1723 Franklin broke with his brother and ran away to Philadelphia. It was a serious act for an apprentice, and his brother was justly indignant and angry. But the break was inevitable; for Franklin was proud and independent by nature and too clever for his brother by far. At seventeen, with little money in his pocket but already an expert printer, he proceeded to make his way in the world, subject to the usual "errata," as he liked to call his mistakes, but confident that he could profit from lessons learned and not repeat them. His most serious error was in trusting a foolish man who wanted to be important to everyone. As a result of Governor Keith's "favors," Benjamin found himself alone and without employment in London in 1724. He returned to the colonies two years later.

Franklin had an uncanny instinct for success. He taught himself French, Spanish, Italian, and Latin yet was shrewd enough to know that people did not like to do business with merchants who were smarter than they. He dressed plainly and sometimes carried his own paper in a wheelbarrow through Philadelphia streets to assure future customers that he was hardworking and not above doing things for himself. By the time he was twenty-four he was the sole owner of a successful printing shop and editor and publisher of the *Pennsylvania Gazette*. He offered his *Poor Richard's Almanac* for sale in 1733 and made it an American institution, filling it with maxims for achieving wealth and preaching hard work and thrift. In 1730 he married Deborah Read, the daughter of his first landlady, and they had two children. Franklin had two illegitimate children, and Deborah took Franklin's son William into the household. He was later to become governor of New Jersey and a Loyalist during the Revolution; Franklin addressed the first part of his *Autobiography* to him. Before he retired from business at the age of forty-two, Franklin had founded a library, invented a stove, established a fire company, subscribed to an academy that was to become the University of Pennsylvania, and served as secretary to the American Philosophical Society. It was his intention when he retired to devote himself to public affairs and his lifelong passion for the natural sciences, especially the phenomena of sound, vapors, earthquakes, and electricity.

Franklin's observations on electricity were published in London in 1751 and, despite his disclaimers in the *Autobiography*, brought him the applause of British scientists. Science was Franklin's great passion, the only thing, the American historian Charles Beard once said, about which Franklin was not ironic. His inquiring mind was challenged most by the mechanics of the ordinary phenomena of the world, and he was convinced that the mind's rational powers would enable him to solve riddles that had puzzled humankind for centuries. Franklin believed that people were naturally innocent, that all the mysteries that charmed the religious mind could be explained to our advantage and that education, properly undertaken, would transform our lives and set us free from the tyrannies of church and monarchy. Franklin had no illusions about the errata of humankind, but his metaphor suggests that we can change and alter our past in a way that the word *sins* does not.

Franklin's remaining years, however, were not spent in a laboratory, but at the diplomatic table in London, Paris, and Philadelphia, where his gift for irony served him well. For he was a born diplomat, detached, adaptable, witty, urbane, charming, and clever and of the slightly more than forty years left to him after his retirement, more than half were spent abroad. In 1757 he went to England to represent the colonies and stayed for five years, returning in 1763. It was in England in 1768 that Franklin first noted his growing sense of alienation and the impossibility of compromise with the homeland. Parliament can make *all* laws for the colonies or *none*, he said, and "I think the arguments for the latter more numerous and weighty, than those for the former." When he returned to Philadelphia in May 1775, he was chosen as a representative to the Second Continental Congress, and he served on the committee to draft the Declaration of Independence. In October 1776, he was appointed minister to France, where he successfully negotiated a treaty of allegiance and became something of a cult hero. In 1781 he was a member of the American delegation to the Paris peace conference, and he signed the Treaty of Paris, which brought the Revolutionary War to an end. Franklin protested his too-long stay in Europe and returned to Philadelphia in 1785, serving as a delegate to the Constitutional Convention. When he died in 1790, he was one of the most beloved Americans. Twenty thousand people attended his funeral.

This hero of the eighteenth century, however, has not universally charmed our own. For a number of readers, Franklin has been identified as a garrulous but insensitive man of the world, too adaptable for a man of integrity and too willing to please. D. H. Lawrence is only one of a number of Franklin's critics who have charged him with insensitivity and indifference to the darker recesses of the soul. There is no question but that Franklin, like Emerson, has been reduced by his admirers—the hero of those who seek only the way to wealth. But such single-mindedness does not do justice to Franklin's complexity. A reading of his letters will serve as a proper antidote; for the voice we find there is fully alert to the best and worst in all of humankind.

All the Franklin texts used here—with the exception of *The Autobiography*—are from *The Writings of Benjamin Franklin*, edited by Albert Henry Smyth (1907).

The Way to Wealth[1]

Preface to Poor Richard Improved

Courteous Reader,

I have heard that nothing gives an author so great pleasure, as to find his works respectfully quoted by other learned authors. This pleasure I have seldom enjoyed; for though I have been, if I may say it without vanity, an eminent author of almanacs annually now a full quarter of a century, my brother authors in the same way, for what reason I know not, have ever been very sparing in their applauses, and no other author has taken the least notice of me, so that did not my writings produce me some solid pudding, the great deficiency of praise would have quite discouraged me.

I concluded at length, that the people were the best judges of my merit; for they buy my works; and besides, in my rambles, where I am not personally known, I have frequently heard one or other of my adages repeated with "as Poor Richard says" at the end on 't; this gave me some satisfaction, as it showed not only that my instructions were regarded, but discovered likewise some respect for my authority; and I own, that to encourage the practice of remembering and repeating those wise sentences, I have sometimes quoted myself with great gravity.

Judge, then, how much I must have been gratified by an incident I am going to relate to you. I stopped my horse lately where a great number of people were collected at a vendue[2] of merchant goods. The hour of sale not being come, they were conversing on the badness of the times and one of the company called to a plain clean old man, with white locks, "Pray, Father Abraham, what think you of the times? Won't these heavy taxes quite ruin the country? How shall we be ever able to pay them? What would you advise us to?" Father Abraham stood up, and replied, "If you'd have my advice, I'll give it you in short, for a *word to the wise is enough, and many words won't fill a*

---

1. Franklin composed this essay for the twenty-fifth anniversary issue of his *Almanac*, the first issue of which, under the fictitious editorship of "Richard Saunders," appeared in 1733. For this essay Franklin brought together the best of his maxims in the guise of a speech by Father Abraham. It is frequently reprinted as *The Way to Wealth*, but is also known by earlier titles: *Poor Richard Improved* and *Father Abraham's Speech*.

2. Auction or sale.

bushel, as Poor Richard says." They joined in desiring him to speak his mind, and gathering round him, he proceeded as follows:

"Friends," says he, "and neighbors, the taxes are indeed very heavy, and if those laid on by the government were the only ones we had to pay, we might more easily discharge them; but we have many others, and much more grievous to some of us. We are taxed twice as much by our idleness, three times as much by our pride, and four times as much by our folly; and from these taxes the commissioners cannot ease or deliver us by allowing an abatement. However, let us hearken to good advice, and something may be done for us; *God helps them that help themselves,* as Poor Richard says, in his Almanac of 1733.

"It would be thought a hard government that should tax its people one-tenth part of their time, to be employed in its service. But idleness taxes many of us much more, if we reckon all that is spent in absolute sloth, or doing of nothing, with that which is spent in idle employments, or amusements, that amount to nothing. Sloth, by bringing on diseases, absolutely shortens life. *Sloth, like rust, consumes faster than labor wears; while the used key is always bright,* as Poor Richard says. *But dost thou love life, then do not squander time, for that's the stuff life is made of,* as Poor Richard says. How much more than is necessary do we spend in sleep, forgetting that *the sleeping fox catches no poultry* and that *there will be sleeping enough in the grave,* as Poor Richard says.

"*If time be of all things the most precious, wasting time must be,* as Poor Richard says, *the greatest prodigality;* since, as he elsewhere tells us, *lost time is never found again; and what we call time enough, always proves little enough:* let us then up and be doing, and doing to the purpose; so by diligence shall we do more with less perplexity. *Sloth makes all things difficult, but industry all easy,* as Poor Richard says; *and he that riseth late must trot all day, and shall scarce overtake his business at night;* while *laziness travels so slowly, that poverty soon overtakes him,* as we read in Poor Richard, who adds, *drive thy business, let not that drive thee,* and *early to bed, and early to rise, makes a man healthy, wealthy, and wise.*

"So what signifies wishing and hoping for better times. We may make these times better, if we bestir ourselves. *Industry need not wish,* as Poor Richard says, *and he that lives upon hope will die fasting. There are no gains without pains; then help hands, for I have no lands,* or if I have, they are smartly taxed. And, as Poor Richard likewise observes, *he that hath a trade hath an estate; and he that hath a calling, hath an office of profit and honor;* but then the trade must be worked at, and the calling well followed, or neither the estate nor the office will enable us to pay our taxes. If we are industrious, we shall never starve; for, as Poor Richard says, *at the workingman's house hunger looks in, but dares not enter.* Nor will the bailiff or the constable enter, for *industry pays debts, while despair increaseth them,* says Poor Richard. What though you have found no treasure, nor has any rich relation left you a legacy, *diligence is the mother of good luck,* as Poor Richard says, and *God gives all things to industry. Then plow deep, while sluggards sleep, and you shall have corn to sell and to keep,* says Poor Dick. Work while it is called today, for you know not how much you may be hindered tomorrow, which makes Poor Richard says, *one today is worth two tomorrows,* and farther, *have you somewhat to do tomorrow, do it today.* If you were a servant, would you not be ashamed that a good master should catch you idle? Are you then your own master, *be ashamed to catch yourself idle*, as Poor Dick says. When there is so much to be done for yourself, your family, your country, and your gracious king, be up by peep of day; *let not the sun look down and say, inglorious here he lies*. Handle your tools without mittens; remember that *the cat in gloves catches no mice*, as Poor Richard says. 'Tis true there is much to be done, and perhaps you are weak-handed, but stick to it steadily; and you will see great effects, for *constant dropping wears away stones*, and *by diligence and patience the mouse ate in two the cable*; and *little strokes fell great oaks*, as Poor Richard says in his Almanac, the year I cannot just now remember.

"Methinks I hear some of you say, 'must a man afford himself no leisure?' I will tell thee, my friend, what Poor Richard says, *employ thy time well, if thou meanest to gain leisure; and, since thou art not sure of a minute, throw not away an hour*. Leisure is time for doing something useful; this leisure the diligent man will obtain, but the lazy man never; so that, as Poor Richard says *a life of leisure and a life of laziness are two things*. Do you imagine that sloth will afford you more comfort than labor? No, for as Poor Richard says, *trouble springs from idleness, and grievous toil from needless ease. Many without labor, would live by their wits only, but they break for want of stock*. Whereas industry gives comfort, and plenty, and respect: *fly pleasures, and they'll follow you. The diligent spinner has a large shift;*[3] *and now I have a sheep and a cow, everybody bids me good morrow*; all of which is well said by Poor Richard.

"But with our industry, we must likewise be steady, settled, and careful, and oversee our own affairs with our own eyes, and not trust too much to others; for, as Poor Richard says

> *I never saw an oft-removed tree,*
> *Nor yet an oft-removed family,*
> *That throve so well as those that settled be.*

And again, *three removes*[4] *is as bad as a fire*; and again, *keep thy shop, and thy shop will keep thee*; and again, *if you would have your business done, go; if not, send*. And again,

> *He that by the plow would thrive,*
> *Himself must either hold or drive.*

And again, *the eye of a master will do more work than both his hands*; and again, *want of care does us more damage than want of knowledge*; and again, *not to oversee workmen is to leave them your purse open*. Trusting too much to others' care is the ruin of many; for, as the Almanac says, *in the affairs of this world, men are saved, not by faith, but by the want of it*; but a man's own care is profitable; for, saith Poor Dick, *learning is to the studious*, and *riches to the careful*, as well as *power to the bold*, and *heaven to the virtuous*, and farther, *if you would have a faithful servant, and one that you like, serve yourself*. And again, he adviseth to circumspection and care, even in the smallest matters, because sometimes *a little neglect may breed great mischief*; adding, *for want of a nail the shoe was lost; for want of a shoe the horse was lost; and for want of a horse the rider was lost, being overtaken and slain by the enemy; all for want of care about a horseshoe nail*.

---

3. Wardrobe.   4. Moves.

"So much for industry, my friends, and attention to one's own business; but to these we must add frugality, if we would make our industry more certainly successful. A man may, if he knows not how to save as he gets, keep his nose all his life to the grindstone, and die not worth a groat[5] at last. *A fat kitchen makes a lean will,* as Poor Richard says; and

> *Many estates are spent in the getting,*
> *Since women for tea forsook spinning and knitting,*
> *And men for punch forsook hewing and splitting.*

If you would be wealthy, says he, in another Almanac, *think of saving as well as of getting: the Indies have not made Spain rich, because her outgoes are greater than her incomes.*

"Away then with your expensive follies, and you will not then have so much cause to complain of hard times, heavy taxes, and chargeable families; for, as Poor Dick says,

> *Women and wine, game and deceit,*
> *Make the wealth small and the wants great.*

And farther, *what maintains one vice would bring up two children.* You may think perhaps, that a little tea, or a little punch now and then, diet a little more costly, clothes a little finer, and a little entertainment now and then, can be no great matter; but remember what Poor Richard says, *many a little makes a mickle;*[6] and farther, *Beware of little expenses; a small leak will sink a great ship*; and again, *who dainties love shall beggars prove*; and moreover, *fools make feasts, and wise men eat them.*

"Here you are all got together at this vendue of fineries and knicknacks. You call them goods; but if you do not take care, they will prove evils to some of you. You expect they will be sold cheap, and perhaps they may for less than they cost; but if you have no occasion for them, they must be dear to you. Remember what Poor Richard says; *buy what thou hast no need of, and ere long thou shalt sell thy necessaries.* And again, *at a great pennyworth pause a while:* he means, that perhaps the cheapness is apparent only, and not real; or the bargain, by straightening thee in thy business, may do thee more harm than good. For in another place he says, *many have been ruined by buying good pennyworths.* Again, Poor Richard says, *'tis foolish to lay out money in a purchase of repentance*; and yet this folly is practiced every day at vendues, for want of minding the Almanac. *Wise men,* as Poor Dick says, *learn by others' harms, fools scarcely by their own*; but *felix quem faciunt aliena pericula cautum.*[7] Many a one, for the sake of finery on the back, have gone with a hungry belly, and half-starved their families. *Silks and satins, scarlet and velvets,* as Poor Richard says, *put out the kitchen fire.*

"These are not the necessaries of life; they can scarcely be called the conveniences; and yet only because they look pretty, how many want to have them! The artificial wants of mankind thus become more numerous than the natural; and, as Poor Dick says, *for one poor person, there are an hundred indigent.* By these, and other extravagancies, the genteel are reduced to poverty, and forced to borrow of those whom they formerly despised, but who through industry and frugality have maintained their standing; in which case it appears plainly,

5. A silver coin worth about four pence.   7. A Latin version of the proverb just quoted.
6. Lot.

that *a plowman on his legs is higher than a gentleman on his knees*, as Poor Richard says. Perhaps they have had a small estate left them, which they knew not the getting of; they think, " 'Tis day, and will never be night"; that a little to be spent out of so much is not worth minding; *a child and a fool*, as Poor Richard says, *imagine twenty shillings and twenty years can never be spent* but, *always taking out of the meal-tub, and never putting in, soon comes to the bottom*; as Poor Dick says, *when the well's dry, they know the worth of water*. But this they might have known before, if they had taken his advice; *if you would know the value of money, go and try to borrow some; for, he that goes a-borrowing goes a-sorrowing*; and indeed so does he that lends to such people, when he goes to get it in again. Poor Dick farther advises, and says,

> Fond pride of dress is sure a very curse;
> E'er fancy you consult, consult your purse.

And again, *pride is as loud a beggar as want, and a great deal more saucy.* When you have bought one fine thing, you must buy ten more, that your appearance may be all of a piece; but Poor Dick says, *'tis easier to suppress the first desire, than to satisfy all that follow it.* And 'tis as truly folly for the poor to ape the rich, as for the frog to swell, in order to equal the ox.

> Great estates may venture more,
> But little boats should keep near shore.

'Tis, however, a folly soon punished; for *pride that dines on vanity sups on contempt*, as Poor Richard says. And in another place, *pride breakfasted with plenty, dined with poverty, and supped with infamy.* And after all, of what use is this pride of appearance, for which so much is risked so much is suffered? It cannot promote health, or ease pain; it makes no increase of merit in the person, it creates envy, it hastens misfortune.

> What is a butterfly? At best
> He's but a caterpillar dressed.
> The gaudy fop's his picture just,

as Poor Richard says.

"But what madness must it be to run in debt for these superfluities! We are offered, by the terms of this vendue, *six months' credit*; and that perhaps has induced some of us to attend it, because we cannot spare the ready money, and hope now to be fine without it. But, ah, think what you do when you run in debt; you give to another power over your liberty. If you cannot pay at the time, you will be ashamed to see your creditor; you will be in fear when you speak to him; you will make poor pitiful sneaking excuses, and by degrees come to lose your veracity, and sink into base downright lying; for, as Poor Richard says, *the second vice is lying, the first is running in debt.* And again, to the same purpose, *lying rides upon debt's back.* Whereas a free-born Englishman ought not to be ashamed or afraid to see or speak to any man living. But poverty often deprives a man of all spirit and virtue: *'tis hard for an empty bag to stand upright*, as Poor Richard truly says.

"What would you think of that prince, or that government, who should issue an edict forbidding you to dress like a gentleman or a gentlewoman, on pain of imprisonment or servitude? Would you not say, that you were free, have a right to dress as you please, and that such an edict would be a breach of your privileges, and such a government tyrannical? And yet you are about to put yourself under that tyranny, when you run in debt for such dress! Your creditor has authority, at his pleasure to deprive you of your liberty, by confining you in gaol[8] for life, or to sell you for a servant, if you should not be able to pay him! When you have got your bargain, you may, perhaps, think little of payment; but *creditors*, Poor Richard tells us, *have better memories than debtors;* and in another place says, *creditors are a superstitious sect, great observers of set days and times.* The day comes round before you are aware, and the demand is made before you are prepared to satisfy it, or if you bear your debt in mind, the term which at first seemed so long will, as it lessens, appear extremely short. Time will seem to have added wings to his heels as well as shoulders. *Those have a short Lent,* saith Poor Richard, *who owe money to be paid at Easter.* Then since, as he says, *The borrower is a slave to the lender, and the debtor to the creditor,* disdain the chain, preserve your freedom; and maintain your independency: be industrious and free; be frugal and free. At present, perhaps, you may think yourself in thriving circumstances, and that you can bear a little extravagance without injury; but,

> For age and want, save while you may;
> No morning sun lasts a whole day,

as Poor Richard says. Gain may be temporary and uncertain, but ever while you live, expense is constant and certain; and *'tis easier to build two chimneys than to keep one in fuel,* as Poor Richard says. So, *rather go to bed supperless than rise in debt.*

> Get what you can, and what you get hold;
> 'Tis the stone that will turn all your lead into gold,

as Poor Richard says. And when you have got the philosopher's stone,[9] sure you will no longer complain of bad times, or the difficulty of paying taxes.

"This doctrine, my friends, is reason and wisdom; but after all, do not depend too much upon your own industry, and frugality, and prudence, though excellent things, for they may all be blasted without the blessing of heaven; and therefore, ask that blessing humbly, and be not uncharitable to those that at present seem to want it, but comfort and help them. Remember, Job[1] suffered, and was afterwards prosperous.

"And now to conclude, *experience keeps a dear[2] school, but fools will learn in no other, and scarce in that;* for it is true, *we may give advice, but we cannot give conduct,* as Poor Richard says: however, remember this, *they that won't be counseled, can't be helped,* as Poor Richard says: and farther, that, *if you will not hear reason, she'll surely rap your knuckles.*"

Thus the old gentleman ended his harangue. The people heard it, and approved the doctrine, and immediately practiced the contrary, just as if it had been a common sermon; for the vendue opened, and they began to buy extravagantly, notwithstanding his cautions and their own fear of taxes. I found the good man had thoroughly studied my almanacs, and digested all I had dropped on these topics during the course of five and twenty years. The frequent mention he made of me must have tired any one else, but my vanity

---

8. Jail.
9. A substance thought to transform base metals into gold, much sought after by alchemists.

1. The Old Testament patriarch whose faith was tested by suffering.
2. Expensive.

was wonderfully delighted with it, though I was conscious that not a tenth part of the wisdom was my own, which he ascribed to me, but rather the gleanings I had made of the sense of all ages and nations. However, I resolved to be the better for the echo of it; and though I had at first determined to buy stuff for a new coat, I went away resolved to wear my old one a little longer. Reader, if thou wilt do the same, thy profit will be as great as mine. I am, as ever, thine to serve thee,

Richard Saunders
July 7, 1757

1757   1758

An Edict by the King of Prussia[1]

Dantzic, Sept. 5, [1773.]

We have long wondered here at the supineness of the English nation, under the Prussian impositions upon its trade entering our port. We did not, till lately, know the claims, ancient and modern, that hang over that nation; and therefore could not suspect that it might submit to those impositions from a sense of duty or from principles of equity. The following Edict, just made public, may, if serious, throw some light upon this matter.

"FREDERICK, by the grace of God, King of Prussia,[2] etc. etc. etc., to all present and to come, (à tous présens et à venir,) Health. The peace now enjoyed throughout our dominions, having afforded us leisure to apply ourselves to the regulation of commerce, the improvement of our finances, and at the same time the easing our domestic subjects in their taxes: For these causes, and other good considerations us thereunto moving, we hereby make known, that, after having deliberated these affairs in our council, present our dear brothers, and other great officers of the state, members of the same, we, of our certain knowledge, full power, and authority royal, have made and issued this present Edict, viz.,

"Whereas it is well known to all the world, that the first German settlements made in the Island of Britain, were by colonies of people, subject to our renowned ducal ancestors, and drawn from their dominions, under the conduct of Hengist, Horsa, Hella, Uff, Cerdicus, Ida, and others; and that the said colonies have flourished under the protection of our august house for ages past; have never been emancipated therefrom; and yet have hitherto yielded little profit to the same: And whereas we ourself have in the last war fought for and defended the said colonies, against the power of France, and thereby enabled them to make conquests from the said power in America, for which we have not yet received adequate compensation: And whereas it is just and expedient that a revenue should be raised from the said colonies in Britain, towards our indemnification; and that those who are descendants of our ancient subjects, and thence still owe us due obedience, should contribute to the replenishing of our royal coffers as they must have done, had their ancestors remained in the territories now to us appertaining: We do therefore hereby

---

1. In this satire Franklin attacks the British taxation of the American colonies by arguing that the immigration of German tribes into Britain in the 5th century gives Germany the right to tax their descendants.

2. Frederick II (the Great), king of Prussia (1740–86), was the ruler of those territories named in the following paragraph.

ordain and command, that, from and after the date of these presents, there shall be levied and paid to our officers of the *customs*, on all goods, wares, and merchandises, and on all grain and other produce of the earth, exported from the said Island of Britain, and on all goods of whatever kind imported into the same, a duty of four and a half per cent *ad valorem*, for the use of us and our successors. And that the said duty may more effectually be collected, we do hereby ordain, that all ships or vessels bound from Great Britain to any other part of the world, or from any other part of the world to Great Britain, shall in their respective voyages touch at our port of Koningsberg, there to be unladen, searched, and charged with the said duties.[3]

"And whereas there hath been from time to time discovered in the said island of Great Britain, by our colonists there, many mines or beds of iron-stone; and sundry subjects, of our ancient dominion, skillful in converting the said stone into metal, have in time past transported themselves thither, carrying with them and communicating that art; and the inhabitants of the said island, presuming that they had a natural right to make the best use they could of the natural productions of their country for their own benefit, have not only built furnaces for smelting the said stone into iron, but have erected plating-forges, slitting-mills, and steel-furnaces, for the more convenient manufacturing of the same; thereby endangering a diminution of the said manufacture in our ancient dominion;—we do therefore hereby farther ordain, that, from and after the date hereof, no mill or other engine for slitting or rolling of iron, or any plating-forge to work with a tilt-hammer, or any furnace for making steel, shall be erected or continued in the said island of Great Britain: And the Lord Lieutenant of every county in the said island is hereby commanded, on information of any such erection within his county, to order and by force to cause the same to be abated and destroyed; as he shall answer the neglect thereof to us at his peril. But we are nevertheless graciously pleased to permit the inhabitants of the said island to transport their iron into Prussia, there to be manufactured, and to them returned; they paying our Prussian subjects for the workmanship, with all the costs of commission, freight, and risk, coming and returning; any thing herein contained to the contrary notwithstanding.

"We do not, however, think fit to extend this our indulgence to the article of wool; but, meaning to encourage, not only the manufacturing of woollen cloth, but also the raising of wool, in our ancient dominions, and to prevent both, as much as may be, in our said island, we do hereby absolutely forbid the transportation of wool from thence, even to the mother country, Prussia; and that those islanders may be farther and more effectually restrained in making any advantage of their own wool in the way of manufacture, we command that none shall be carried out of one county into another; nor shall any worsted, bay, or woollen yarn, cloth, says, bays, kerseys, serges, frizes, druggets, cloth-serges, shalloons, or any other drapery stuffs, or woollen manufactures whatsoever, made up or mixed with wool in any of the said counties, be carried into any other county, or be waterborne even across the smallest river or creek, on penalty of forfeiture of the same, together with the boats, carriages, horses, etc., that shall be employed in removing them. Nevertheless, our loving subjects there are hereby permitted (if they think proper) to use all their wool as manure for the improvement of their lands.

3. Franklin echoes here the demands of the British Navigation Acts that taxed American products and were a cause of the American Revolution.

"And whereas the art and mystery of making hats hath arrived at great perfection in Prussia, and the making of hats by our remoter subjects ought to be as much as possible restrained: And forasmuch as the islanders before mentioned, being in possession of wool, beaver and other furs, have presumptuously conceived they had a right to make some advantage thereof, by manufacturing the same into hats, to the prejudice of our domestic manufacture: We do therefore hereby strictly command and ordain, that no hats or felts whatsoever, dyed or undyed, finished or unfinished, shall be loaded or put into or upon any vessel, cart, carriage, or horse, to be transported or conveyed out of one county in the said island into another county, or to any other place whatsoever, by any person or persons whatsoever; on pain of forfeiting the same, with a penalty of five hundred pounds sterling for every offense. Nor shall any hatmaker, in any of the said counties, employ more than two apprentices, on penalty of five pounds sterling per month; we intending hereby, that such hatmakers, being so restrained, both in the production and sale of their commodity, may find no advantage in continuing their business. But, lest the said islanders should suffer inconveniency by the want of hats, we are farther graciously pleased to permit them to send their beaver furs to Prussia; and we also permit hats made thereof to be exported from Prussia to Britain; the people thus favored to pay all costs and charges of manufacturing, interest, commission to our merchants, insurance and freight going and returning, as in the case of iron.

"And, lastly, being willing farther to favor our said colonies in Britain, we do hereby also ordain and command, that all the thieves, highway and street robbers, housebreakers, forgerers, murderers, s—d—tes,[4] and villains of every denomination, who have forfeited their lives to the law in Prussia; but whom we, in our great clemency, do not think fit here to hang, shall be emptied out of our jails into the said island of Great Britain, for the better peopling of that country.

"We flatter ourselves, that these our royal regulations and commands will be thought just and reasonable by our much-favored colonists in England; the said regulations being copied from their statutes of 10 and 11 William III. c. 10, 5 Geo. II. c. 22, 23, Geo. II. c. 29, 4 Geo. I. c. 11,[5] and from other equitable laws made by their parliaments; or from instructions given by their Princess; or from resolutions of both Houses, entered into for the good government of their *own colonies in Ireland and America*.

"And all persons in the said island are hereby cautioned not to oppose in any wise the execution of this our Edict, or any part thereof, such opposition being high treason; of which all who are suspected shall be transported in fetters from Britain to Prussia, there to be tried and executed according to the Prussian law.

"Such is our pleasure.

"Given at Potsdam, this twenty-fifth day of the month of August, one thousand seven hundred and seventy-three, and in the thirty-third year of our reign.

"By the King, in his Council.

---

4. Sodomites. Colonists had long complained that the British saved prison expenses by exporting their criminals to America.

5. King William III of Great Britain (r. 1689–1702); King George I (r. 1714–27); King George II (r. 1727–60).

"Rechtmaeesig, Sec."[6]

Some take this Edict to be merely one of the King's *Jeux d'Esprit:*[7] others suppose it serious, and that he means a quarrel with England; but all here think the assertion it concludes with, "that these regulations are copied from acts of the English parliament respecting their colonies," a very injurious one; it being impossible to believe, that a people distinguished for their love of liberty, a nation so wise, so liberal in its sentiments, so just and equitable towards it neighbors, should, from mean and injudicious views of petty imme-diate profit, treat its own children in a manner so arbitrary and tyrannical!

1773

Rules by Which a Great Empire May Be Reduced to a Small One

Presented to a Late Minister,
When He Entered upon His Administration.[1]

An ancient Sage boasted, that, tho' he could not fiddle, he knew how to make a *great city* of a *little one.* The science that I, a modern simpleton, am about to communicate, is the very reverse.

I address myself to all ministers who have the management of extensive dominions, which from their very greatness are become troublesome to gov-ern, because the multiplicity of their affairs leaves no time for *fiddling.*[2]

I. In the first place, gentlemen, you are to consider, that a great empire, like a great cake, is most easily diminished at the edges. Turn your attention, therefore, first to your *remotest* provinces; that, as you get rid of them, the next may follow in order.

II. That the possibility of this separation may always exist, take special care the provinces are never incorporated with the mother country; that they do not enjoy the same common rights, the same privileges in commerce; and that they are governed by *severer* laws, all of *your enacting,* without allowing them any share in the choice of the legislators. By carefully making and preserving such distinctions, you will (to keep to my simile of the cake) act like a wise gingerbread-baker, who, to facilitate a division, cuts his dough half through in those places where, when baked, he would have it *broken to pieces.*

III. Those remote provinces have perhaps been acquired, purchased, or conquered, at the *sole expence* of the settlers, or their ancestors, without the aid of the mother country. If this should happen to increase her *strength,* by their growing numbers, ready to join in her wars; her *commerce,* by their grow-ing demand for her manufactures; or her *naval power,* by greater employment for her ships and seamen, they may probably suppose some merit in this, and that it entitles them to some favor; you are therefore to *forget it all, or resent it,* as if they had done you injury. If they happen to be zealous whigs,[3] friends of liberty, nurtured in revolution principles, *remember all that* to their preju-

---

6. Legally authorized (German); secretary.
7. Witticisms (French).
1. The minister was Wills Hill, the first earl of Hills-borough and secretary of state to the colonies

(1768–72).
2. Cheating.
3. Here, American supporters of independence from Britain.

dice, and resolve to punish it; for such principles, after a revolution is thoroughly established, are of *no more use;* they are even *odious* and *abominable.*

IV. However peaceably your colonies have submitted to your government, shown their affection to your interests, and patiently borne their grievances; you are to *suppose* them always inclined to revolt, and treat them accordingly. Quarter troops among them, who by their insolence may *provoke* the rising of mobs, and by their bullets and bayonets *suppress* them. By this means, like the husband who uses his wife ill *from suspicion,* you may in time convert your *suspicions* into *realities.*

V. Remote provinces must have *Governors* and *Judges,* to represent the Royal Person, and execute everywhere the delegated parts of his office and authority. You ministers know, that much of the strength of government depends on the *opinion* of the people; and much of that opinion on the *choice of rulers* placed immediately over them. If you send them wise and good men for governors, who study the interest of the colonists, and advance their prosperity, they will think their King wise and good, and that he wishes the welfare of his subjects. If you send them learned and upright men for Judges, they will think him a lover of justice. This may attach your provinces more to his government. You are therefore to be careful whom you recommend for those offices. If you can find prodigals, who have ruined their fortunes, broken gamesters or stockjobbers,[4] these may do well as *governors;* for they will probably be rapacious, and provoke the people by their extortions. Wrangling proctors and pettifogging lawyers,[5] too, are not amiss; for they will be for ever disputing and quarrelling with their little parliaments. If withal they should be ignorant, wrong-headed, and insolent, so much the better. Attorneys' clerks and Newgate solicitors[6] will do for *Chief Justices,* especially if they hold their places *during your pleasure;*[7] and all will contribute to impress those ideas of your government, that are proper for a people *you would wish to renounce it.*

VI. To confirm these impressions, and strike them deeper, whenever the injured come to the capital with complaints of maladministration, oppression, or injustice, punish such suitors with long delay, enormous expense, and a final judgment in favor of the oppressor. This will have an admirable effect every way. The trouble of future complaints will be prevented, and Governors and Judges will be encouraged to farther acts of oppression and injustice; and thence the people may become more disaffected, and at length desperate.

VII. When such Governors have crammed their coffers, and made themselves so odious to the people that they can no longer remain among them, with safety to their persons, *recall and reward* them with pensions. You may make them *baronets*[8] too, if that respectable order should not think fit to resent it. All will contribute to encourage new governors in the same practice, and make the supreme government, *detestable.*

VIII. If, when you are engaged in war, your colonies should vie in liberal aids of men and money against the common enemy, upon your simple requisition, and give far beyond their abilities, reflect that a penny taken from them by your power is more honorable to you, than a pound presented by their benevolence; despise therefore their voluntary grants, and resolve to harass

---

4. Gamblers or speculators.
5. I.e., shysters. "Proctors": civil lawyers.
6. Solicitors are British lawyers, and Newgate was a London prison; the phrase may be akin to our "ambu-

lance chasers."
7. I.e., at your pleasure.
8. I.e., give them noble titles.

them with novel taxes. They will probably complain to your parliaments, that they are taxed by a body in which they have no representative, and that this is contrary to common right. They will petition for redress. Let the Parliaments flout their claims, reject their petitions, refuse even to suffer the reading of them, and treat the petitioners with the utmost contempt. Nothing can have a better effect in producing the alienation proposed; for though many can forgive injuries, *none ever forgave contempt*.

IX. In laying these taxes, never regard the heavy burthens those remote people already undergo, in defending their own frontiers, supporting their own provincial governments, making new roads, building bridges, churches, and other public edifices, which in old countries have been done to your hands by your ancestors, but which occasion constant calls and demands on the purses of a new people. Forget the *restraints* you lay on their trade for *your own* benefit, and the advantage a *monopoly* of this trade gives your exacting merchants. Think nothing of the wealth those merchants and your manufacturers acquire by the colony commerce; their increased ability thereby to pay taxes at home; their accumulating, in the price of their commodities, most of those taxes, and so levying them from their consuming customers; all this, and the employment and support of thousands of your poor by the colonists, you are *entirely to forget*. But remember to make your arbitrary tax more grievous to your provinces, by public declarations importing that your power of taxing them has *no limits*; so that when you take from them without their consent one shilling in the pound, you have a clear right to the other nineteen. This will probably weaken every idea of *security in their property*, and convince them, that under such a government they *have nothing they can call their own*; which can scarce fail of producing the *happiest consequences!*

X. Possibly, indeed, some of them might still comfort themselves, and say, "Though we have no property, we have yet *something* left that is valuable; we have constitutional *liberty*, both of person and of conscience. This King, these Lords, and these Commons, who it seems are too remote from us to know us, and feel for us, cannot take from us our *Habeas Corpus*[9] right, or our right of trial *by a jury of our neighbors*; they cannot deprive us of the exercise of our religion, alter our ecclesiastical constitution, and compel us to be Papists, if they please, or Mahometans." To annihilate this comfort, begin by laws to perplex their commerce with infinite regulations, impossible to be remembered and observed; ordain seizures of their property for every failure; take away the trial of such property by Jury, and give it to arbitrary Judges of your own appointing, and of the lowest characters in the country, whose salaries and emoluments[1] are to arise out of the duties or condemnations, and whose appointments are *during pleasure*. Then let there be a formal declaration of both Houses, that opposition to your edicts is *treason*, and that any person suspected of treason in the provinces may, according to some obsolete law, be seized and sent to the metropolis of the empire for trial; and pass an act, that those there charged with certain other offenses, shall be sent away in chains from their friends and country to be tried in the same manner for felony. Then erect a new Court of Inquisition among them, accompanied by an armed force, with instructions to transport[2] all such suspected persons; to be ruined

9. You shall have the body (Latin, literal trans.); the right to know with what one is charged.
1. Payments for services rendered.

2. I.e., to deport, as criminals were to the American colonies.

by the expense, if they bring over evidences to prove their innocence, or be found guilty and hanged, if they cannot afford it. And, lest the people should think you cannot possibly go any farther, pass another solemn declaratory act, "that King, Lords, Commons had, hath, and of right ought to have, full power and authority to make statutes of sufficient force and validity to bind the unrepresented provinces IN ALL CASES WHATSOEVER." This will include *spiritual* with temporal, and, taken together, must operate wonderfully to your purpose; by convincing them, that they are at present under a power something like that spoken of in the scriptures, which can not only *kill their bodies*, but *damn their souls* to all eternity, by compelling them, if it pleases, *to worship the Devil*.

XI. To make your taxes more odious, and more likely to procure resistance, send from the capital a board of officers to superintend the collection, composed of the most *indiscreet, ill-bred*, and *insolent* you can find. Let these have large salaries out of the extorted revenue, and live in open, grating luxury upon the sweat and blood of the industrious; whom they are to worry continually with groundless and expensive prosecutions before the abovementioned arbitrary revenue Judges; *all at the cost of the party prosecuted*, tho' acquitted, because *the King is to pay no costs*. Let these men, *by your order*, be exempted from all the common taxes and burthens of the province, though they and their property are protected by its laws. If any revenue offices are *suspected* of the least tenderness for the people, discard them. If others are justly complained of, protect and reward them. If any of the under officers behave so as to provoke the people to drub them, promote those to better offices: this will encourage others to procure for themselves such profitable drubbings, by multiplying and enlarging such provocations, and *all will work towards the end you aim at*.

XII. Another way to make your tax odious, is to misapply the produce of it. If it was originally appropriated for the *defense* of the provinces, the better support of government, and the administration of justice, where it may be *necessary*, then apply none of it to that *defense*, but bestow it where it is *not necessary*, in augmented salaries or pensions to every governor, who has distinguished himself by his enmity to the people, and by calumniating them to their sovereign. This will make them pay it more unwillingly, and be more apt to quarrel with those that collect it and those that imposed it, who will quarrel again with them, and all shall contribute to your *main purpose*, of making them *weary of your government*.

XIII. If the people of any province have been accustomed to support their own Governors and Judges to satisfaction, you are to apprehend that such Governors and Judges may be thereby influenced to treat the people kindly, and to do them justice. This is another reason for applying part of that revenue in larger salaries to such Governors and Judges, given, as their commissions are, *during your pleasure* only; forbidding them to take any salaries from their provinces; that thus the people may no longer hope any kindness from their Governors, or (in Crown cases)[3] any justice from their Judges. And, as the money thus misapplied in one province is extorted from all, probably *all will resent the misapplication*.

XIV. If the parliaments of your provinces should dare to claim rights, or complain of your administration, order them to be harrassed with *repeated*

---

3. Cases that were formerly appealed directly to the king.

dissolutions. If the same men are continually returned by new elections, adjourn their meetings to some country village, where they cannot be accommodated, and there keep them *during pleasure;* for this, you know, is your PREROGATIVE; and an excellent one it is, as you may manage it to promote discontents among the people, diminish their respect, and *increase their disaffection.*

XV. Convert the brave, honest officers of your *navy* into pimping tide-waiters[4] and colony officers of the *customs.* Let those, who in time of war fought gallantly in defense of the commerce of their countrymen, in peace be taught to prey upon it. Let them learn to be corrupted by great and real smugglers; but (to show their diligence) scour with armed boats every bay, harbor, river, creek, cove, or nook throughout the coast of your colonies; stop and detain every coaster, every wood-boat, every fisherman, tumble their cargoes and even their ballast inside out and upside down; and, if a penn'orth of pins is found unentered, let the whole be seized and confiscated. Thus shall the trade of your colonists suffer more from their friends in time of peace, than it did from their enemies in war. Then let these boats' crews land upon every farm in their way, rob the orchards, steal the pigs and the poultry, and insult the inhabitants. If the injured and exasperated farmers, unable to procure other justice, should attack the aggressors, drub them, and burn their boats; you are to call this *high treason and rebellion,* order fleets and armies into their country, and threaten to carry all the offenders three thousand miles to be hanged, drawn, and quartered. *O! this will work admirably!*

XVI. If you are told of discontents in your colonies, never believe that they are general, or that you have given occasion for them; therefore do not think of applying any remedy, or of changing any offensive measure. Redress no grievance, lest they should be encouraged to demand the redress of some other grievance. Grant no request that is just and reasonable, lest they should make another that is unreasonable. Take all your informations of the state of the colonies from your Governors and officers in enmity with them. Encourage and reward these *leasing-makers;*[5] secrete their lying accusations, lest they should be confuted; but act upon them as the clearest evidence; and believe nothing you hear from the friends of the people: suppose all *their* complaints to be invented and promoted by a few factious demagogues, whom if you could catch and hang, all would be quiet. Catch and hang a few of them accordingly; and the *blood of the Martyrs* shall *work miracles* in favor of your purpose.

XVII. If you see *rival nations* rejoicing at the prospect of your disunion with your provinces, and endeavoring to promote it; if they translate, publish, and applaud all the complaints of your discontented colonists, at the same time privately stimulating you to severer measures, let not that *alarm* or offend you. Why should it, since you all mean *the same thing?*

XVIII. If any colony should at their own charge erect a fortress to secure their port against the fleets of a foreign enemy, get your Governor to betray that fortress into your hands. Never think of paying what it cost the country, for that would look, at least, like some regard for justice; but turn it into a citadel to awe the inhabitants and curb their commerce. If they should have lodged in such fortress the very arms they bought and used to aid you in your

4. Customs officers who boarded a ship before it   5. I.e., liars.
docked.

conquests, seize them all; it will provoke like *ingratitude* added to *robbery*. One admirable effect of these operations will be, to discourage every other colony from erecting such defenses, and so your enemies may more easily invade them; to the great disgrace of your government, and of course *the furtherance of your project.*

XIX. Send armies into their country under pretense of protecting the inhabitants; but, instead of garrisoning the forts on their frontiers with those troops, to prevent incursions, demolish those forts, and order the troops into the heart of the country, that the savages may be encouraged to attack the frontiers, and that the troops may be protected by the inhabitants. This will seem to proceed from your ill will or your ignorance, and contribute farther to produce and strengthen an opinion among them, *that you are no longer fit to govern them.*

XX. Lastly, invest the General of your army in the provinces, with great and unconstitutional powers, and free him from the control of even your own Civil Governors. Let him have troops enow[6] under his command, with all the fortresses in his possession; and who knows but (like some provincial Generals in the Roman empire, and encouraged by the universal discontent you have produced) he may take it into his head to set up for himself? If he should, and you have carefully practiced these few *excellent rules* of mine, take my word for it, all the provinces will immediately join him; and you will that day (if you have not done it sooner) get rid of the trouble of governing them, and all the *plagues* attending their *commerce* and connection from henceforth and for ever.   Q. E. D.[7]

1773

The Sale of the Hessians[1]

From *The Count de Schaumbergh to the Baron Hohendorf, Commanding the Hessian Troops in America*

Rome, February 18, 1777.

MONSIEUR LE BARON:—On my return from Naples, I received at Rome your letter of the 27th December of last year. I have learned with unspeakable pleasure the courage our troops exhibited at Trenton, and you cannot imagine my joy on being told that of the 1,950 Hessians engaged in the fight, but 345 escaped.[2] There were just 1,605 men killed, and I cannot sufficiently commend your prudence in sending an exact list of the dead to my minister in London. This precaution was the more necessary, as the report sent to the English ministry does not give but 1,455 dead. This would make 483,450 florins instead of 643,500 which I am entitled to demand under our convention. You will comprehend the prejudice which such an error would work in my finances, and I do not doubt you will take the necessary pains to prove that Lord North's[3] list is false and yours correct.

6. Enough.
7. Abbreviation for *Quod erat demonstrandum:* Which was to be demonstrated (Latin); the usual conclusion to a geometry problem. I.e., "I have proved my point."
1. The American colonists were angry to find themselves defending their soil against German mercenaries purchased by Britain, and so Franklin's satire is based on rumors that Frederick-William II (1744–97), head of the German state of Hesse-Cassel, was paid thirty pounds each for 15,700 Hessians killed on American soil.
2. The Battle of Trenton (New Jersey) was fought on Christmas Eve 1776. In truth, Washington took 950 Hessian prisoners and between twenty and thirty Hessian soldiers were killed.
3. Frederick North, earl of Guilford and British prime minister from 1770 to 1782.

The court of London objects that there were a hundred wounded who ought not to be included in the list, nor paid for as dead; but I trust you will not overlook my instructions to you on quitting Cassel, and that you will not have tried by human succor to recall the life of the unfortunates whose days could not be lengthened but by the loss of a leg or an arm. That would be making them a pernicious present, and I am sure they would rather die than live in a condition no longer fit for my service. I do not mean by this that you should assassinate them; we should be humane, my dear Baron, but you may insinuate to the surgeons with entire propriety that a crippled man is a reproach to their profession, and that there is no wiser course than to let every one of them die when he ceases to be fit to fight.

I am about to send to you some new recruits. Don't economize them. Remember glory before all things. Glory is true wealth. There is nothing degrades the soldier like the love of money. He must care only for honor and reputation, but this reputation must be acquired in the midst of dangers. A battle gained without costing the conqueror any blood is an inglorious success, while the conquered cover themselves with glory by perishing with their arms in their hands. Do you remember that of the 300 Lacedæmonians who defended the defile[4] of Thermopylæ, not one returned? How happy should I be could I say the same of my brave Hessians?

It is true that their king, Leonidas, perished with them: but things have changed, and it is no longer the custom for princes of the empire to go and fight in America for a cause with which they have no concern. And besides, to whom should they pay the thirty guineas per man if I did not stay in Europe to receive them? Then, it is necessary also that I be ready to send recruits to replace the men you lose. For this purpose I must return to Hesse. It is true, grown men are becoming scarce there, but I will send you boys. Besides, the scarcer the commodity the higher the price. I am assured that the women and little girls have begun to till our lands, and they get on not badly. You did right to send back to Europe that Dr. Crumerus who was so successful in curing dysentery. Don't bother with a man who is subject to looseness of the bowels. That disease makes bad soldiers. One coward will do more mischief in an engagement than ten brave men will do good. Better that they burst in their barracks than fly in a battle, and tarnish the glory of our arms. Besides, you know that they pay me as killed for all who die from disease, and I don't get a farthing for runaways. My trip to Italy, which has cost me enormously, makes it desirable that there should be a great mortality among them. You will therefore promise promotion to all who expose themselves; you will exhort them to seek glory in the midst of dangers; you will say to Major Maundorff that I am not at all content with his saving the 345 men who escaped the massacre of Trenton. Through the whole campaign he has not had ten men killed in consequence of his orders. Finally, let it be your principal object to prolong the war and avoid a decisive engagement on either side, for I have made arrangements for a grand Italian opera, and I do not wish to be obliged to give it up. Meantime I pray God, my dear Baron de Hohendorf, to have you in His holy and gracious keeping.

1778

---

4. A narrow mountain gorge or pass that necessitates troops marching through only by files. The Spartans unsuccessfully defended their lands against the Persians in 480 B.C.

The Ephemera[1]

An Emblem of Human Life

You may remember, my dear friend,[2] that when we lately spent that happy day in the delightful garden and sweet society of the Moulin Joly,[3] I stopped a little in one of our walks, and stayed some time behind the company. We had been shown numberless skeletons of a kind of little fly, called an ephemera, whose successive generations, we were told, were bred and expired within the day. I happened to see a living company of them on a leaf, who appeared to be engaged in conversation. You know I understand all the inferior animal tongues: my too great application to the study of them is the best excuse I can give for the little progress I have made in your charming language. I listened through curiosity to the discourse of these little creatures; but as they, in their national vivacity, spoke three or four together, I could make but little of their conversation. I found, however, by some broken expressions that I heard now and then, they were disputing warmly on the merit of two foreign musicians, one a *cousin*, the other a *moschetto*;[4] in which dispute they spent their time, seemingly as regardless of the shortness of life as if they had been sure of living a month. Happy people! thought I, you live certainly under a wise, just, and mild government, since you have no public grievances to complain of, nor any subject of contention but the perfections and imperfections of foreign music. I turned my head from them to an old gray-headed one, who was single on another leaf, and talking to himself. Being amused with his soliloquy, I put it down in writing, in hopes it will likewise amuse her to whom I am so much indebted for the most pleasing of all amusements, her delicious company and heavenly harmony.

"It was," said he, "the opinion of learned philosophers of our race, who lived and flourished long before my time, that this vast world, the Moulin Joly, could not itself subsist more than eighteen hours; and I think there was some foundation for that opinion, since, by the apparent motion of the great luminary that gives life to all nature, and which in my time has evidently declined considerably towards the ocean at the end of our earth, it must then finish its course, be extinguished in the waters that surround us, and leave the world in cold and darkness, necessarily producing universal death and destruction. I have lived seven of those hours, a great age, being no less than four hundred and twenty minutes of time. How very few of us continue so long! I have seen generations born, flourish, and expire. My present friends are the children and grandchildren of the friends of my youth, who are now, alas, no more! And I must soon follow them; for, by the course of nature, though still in health, I cannot expect to live about seven or eight minutes longer. What now avails all my toil and labor, in amassing honey-drew on this leaf, which I cannot live to enjoy! What the political struggles I have been

---

1. Franklin printed his "Bagatelles," of which this is the first, on his own press while he was in residence in France from 1776 to 1785. This essay was printed in both English and French but the date of first publication is unknown. It was included in W. T. Franklin's edition of the *Writings* in 1818.

2. Mme. d'Hardancourt Brillon de Jouy was about thirty-five years younger than Franklin and together with the widow Catherine Helvétius was the subject of much attention on Franklin's part. Her husband seems to have shown little concern over Franklin's presence in her company every Wednesday and Saturday. She was a musician and occasionally set Franklin's verses to music.

3. An estate on an island in the river Seine.

4. Little fly (Italian, literal trans., diminutive of *mosca*). "*Cousin*": gnat (French).

engaged in, for the good of my compatriot inhabitants of this bush, or my philosophical studies for the benefit of our race in general! for, in politics, what can laws do without morals? Our present race of ephemeræ will in a course of minutes become corrupt, like those of other and older bushes, and consequently as wretched. And in philosophy how small our progress! Alas! art is long, and life is short! My friends would comfort me with the idea of a name, they say, I shall leave behind me; and they tell me I have lived long enough to nature and to glory. But what will fame be to an ephemera who no longer exists? And what will become of all history in the eighteenth hour, when the world itself, even the whole Moulin Joly, shall come to its end, and be buried in universal ruin?"

To me, after all my eager pursuits, no solid pleasures now remain, but the reflection of a long life spent in meaning well, the sensible conversation of a few good lady ephemeræ, and now and then a kind smile and a tune from the ever amiable *Brillante*.[5]

B. FRANKLIN

Information to Those Who Would Remove to America[1]

Many persons in Europe, having directly or by letters, expressed to the writer of this, who is well acquainted with North America, their desire of transporting and establishing themselves in that country; but who appear to have formed, through ignorance, mistaken ideas and expectations of what is to be obtained there; he thinks it may be useful, and prevent inconvenient, expensive, and fruitless removals and voyages of improper persons, if he gives some clearer and truer notions of that part of the world, than appear to have hitherto prevailed.

He finds it is imagined by numbers, that the inhabitants of North America are rich, capable of rewarding, and disposed to reward, all sorts of ingenuity; that they are at the same time ignorant of all the sciences, and consequently, that strangers, possessing talents in the belles-lettres, fine arts, etc., must be highly esteemed, and so well paid, as to become easily rich themselves; that there are also abundance of profitable offices to be disposed of, which the natives are not qualified to fill; and that, having few persons of family among them, strangers of birth must be greatly respected, and of course easily obtain the best of those offices, which will make all their fortunes; that the governments too, to encourage emigrations from Europe, not only pay the expense of personal transportation, but give lands gratis to strangers, with Negroes to work for them, utensils of husbandry, and stocks of cattle. These are all wild imaginations; and those who go to America with expectations founded upon them will surely find themselves disappointed.

The truth is, that though there are in that country few people so miserable as the poor of Europe, there are also very few that in Europe would be called rich; it is rather a general happy mediocrity that prevails. There are few great proprietors of the soil, and few tenants; most people cultivate their own lands,

---

5. A pun on Madame Brillon's name.
1. The title is taken from an edition of this pamphlet published in London without Franklin's permission in

1784. Franklin's title was *Advice to Such As Would Remove to America*, and he used this title when he published his own edition in France in the same year.

or follow some handicraft or merchandise; very few rich enough to live idly upon their rents or incomes, or to pay the high prices given in Europe for paintings, statues, architecture, and the other works of art, that are more curious than useful. Hence the natural geniuses, that have arisen in America with such talents, have uniformly quitted that country for Europe, where they can be more suitably rewarded. It is true, that letters and mathematical knowledge are in esteem there, but they are at the same time more common than is apprehended; there being already existing nine colleges or universities, viz., four in New England, and one in each of the provinces of New York, New Jersey, Pennsylvania, Maryland, and Virginia, all furnished with learned professors; besides a number of smaller academies; these educate many of their youth in the languages, and those sciences that qualify men for the professions of divinity, law, or physic.[2] Strangers indeed are by no means excluded from exercising those professions; and the quick increase of inhabitants everywhere gives them a chance of employ, which they have in common with the natives. Of civil offices, or employments, there are few; no superfluous ones, as in Europe; and it is a rule established in some of the states, that no office should be so profitable as to make it desirable. The 36th Article of the Constitution of Pennsylvania, runs expressly in these words: "As every freeman, to preserve his independence, (if he has not a sufficient estate) ought to have some profession, calling, trade, or farm, whereby he may honestly subsist, there can be no necessity for, nor use in, establishing offices of profit; the usual effects of which are dependence, and servility, unbecoming freemen, in the possessors and expectants; faction, contention, corruption, and disorder among the people. Wherefore, whenever an office, through increase of fees or otherwise, becomes so profitable, as to occasion many to apply for it, the profits ought to be lessened by the legislature."

These ideas prevailing more or less in all the United States, it cannot be worth any man's while, who has a means of living at home, to expatriate himself, in hopes of obtaining a profitable civil office in America; and, as to military offices, they are at an end with the war,[3] the armies being disbanded. Much less is it advisable for a person to go thither, who has no other quality to recommend him but his birth. In Europe it has indeed its value; but it is a commodity that cannot be carried to a worse market than that of America, where people do not inquire concerning a stranger, *what is he?* but, *what can he do?* If he has any useful art, he is welcome; and if he exercises it, and behaves well, he will be respected by all that know him; but a mere man of quality, who, on that account, wants to live upon the public, by some office or salary, will be despised and disregarded. The husbandman[4] is in honor there, and even the mechanic,[5] because their employments are useful. The people have a saying, that God Almighty is Himself a mechanic, the greatest in the universe; and He is respected and admired more for the variety, ingenuity, and utility of His handyworks, than for the antiquity of His family. They are pleased with the observation of a Negro, and frequently mention it, that *Boccarorra* (meaning the white men) *make de black man workee, make de horse workee, make de ox workee, make eberyting workee; only de hog. He, de hog, no workee; he eat, he drink, he walk about, he go to sleep when he please; he libb like a gentleman.* According to these opinions of the Americans, one of

2. Medicine.
3. I.e., the Revolutionary War.
4. Farmer.
5. Manual laborer.

them would think himself more obliged to a genealogist, who could prove for him that his ancestors and relations for ten generations had been plowmen, smiths, carpenters, turners, weavers, tanners,[6] or even shoemakers, and consequently that they were useful members of society; than if he could only prove that they were gentlemen, doing nothing of value, but living idly on the labor of others, mere *fruges consumere nati*,[7] and otherwise *good for nothing*, till by their death their estates, like the carcass of the Negro's gentleman hog, come to be *cut up*.

With regard to encouragements for strangers from government, they are really only what are derived from good laws and liberty. Strangers are welcome, because there is room enough for them all, and therefore the old inhabitants are not jealous of them; the laws protect them sufficiently, so that they have no need for the patronage of great men; and every one will enjoy securely the profits of his industry. But, if he does not bring a fortune with him, he must work and be industrious to live. One or two years' residence gives him all the rights of a citizen; but the government does not at present, whatever it may have done in former times, hire people to become settlers, by paying their passages, giving land, Negroes, utensils, stock, or any other kind of emolument whatsoever. In short, America is the land of labor, and by no means what the English call *Lubberland*,[8] and the French Pays de Cocagne,[9] where the streets are said to be paved with half-peck loaves, the houses tiled with pancakes, and where the fowls fly about ready roasted, crying *come eat me!*

Who then are the kind of persons to whom an emigration to America may be advantageous? And what are the advantages they may reasonably expect?

Land being cheap in that country, from the vast forests still void of inhabitants, and not likely to be occupied in an age to come, insomuch that the property of an hundred acres of fertile soil full of wood may be obtained near the frontiers, in many places, for eight or ten guineas, hearty young laboring men, who understand the husbandry of corn and cattle, which is nearly the same in that country as in Europe, may easily establish themselves there. A little money saved of the good wages they receive there, while they work for others, enables them to buy the land and begin their plantation,[1] in which they are assisted by the good will of their neighbors, and some credit. Multitudes of poor people from England, Ireland, Scotland, and Germany, have by this means in a few years become wealthy farmers, who, in their own countries, where all the lands are fully occupied, and the wages of labor low, could never have emerged from the poor condition wherein they were born.

From the salubrity of the air, the healthiness of the climate, the plenty of good provisions, and the encouragement to early marriages by the certainty of subsistence in cultivating the earth, the increase of inhabitants by natural generation is very rapid in America, and becomes still more so by the accession of strangers; hence there is a continual demand for more artisans of all the necessary and useful kinds, to supply those cultivators of the earth with houses, and with furniture and utensils of the grosser sorts, which cannot so well be brought from Europe. Tolerably good workmen in any of those mechanic arts are sure to find employ, and to be well paid for their work, there being no restraints preventing strangers from exercising any art they understand, nor any

6. Those who convert hides into leather.
7. " '. . . born / Merely to eat up the corn.'—Watts" [Franklin's note].
8. A land of laziness.
9. I.e., never-never land.
1. Farm.

permission necessary. If they are poor, they begin first as servants or jour-neymen;[2] and if they are sober, industrious, and frugal, they soon become masters, establish themselves in business, marry, raise families, and become respectable citizens.

Also, persons of moderate fortunes and capitals, who, having a number of children to provide for, as desirous of bringing them up to industry,[3] and to secure estates for their posterity, have opportunities of doing it in America, which Europe does not afford. There they may be taught and practice profit-able mechanic arts, without incurring disgrace on that account, but on the contrary acquiring respect by such abilities. There small capitals laid out in lands, which daily become more valuable by the increase of people, afford a solid prospect of ample fortunes thereafter for those children. The writer of this has known several instances of large tracts of land, bought, on what was then the frontier of Pennsylvania, for ten pounds per hundred acres, which after 20 years, when the settlements had been extended far beyond them, sold readily, without any improvement made upon them, for three pounds per acre. The acre in America is the same with the English acre, or the acre of Normandy.

Those, who desire to understand the state of government in America, would do well to read the constitutions of the several states, and the Articles of Con-federation that binds the whole together for general purposes, under the direc-tion of one assembly, called the Congress. These constitutions have been printed, by order of Congress, in America; two editions of them have also been printed in London; and a good translation of them into French has lately been published at Paris.

Several of the princes of Europe having of late years, from an opinion of advantage to arise by producing all commodities and manufactures within their own dominions, so as to diminish or render useless their importations, have endeavored to entice workmen from other countries by high salaries, privileges, etc. Many persons, pretending to be skilled in various great manu-factures, imagining that America must be in want of them, and that the Con-gress would probably be disposed to imitate the prince above mentioned, have proposed to go over, on condition of having their passages paid, lands given, salaries appointed, exclusive privileges for terms of years, etc. Such persons, on reading the Articles of Confederation, will find, that the Congress have no power committed to them, or money out into their hands, for such purposes; and that if any such encouragement is given, it must be by the government of some separate state. This, however, has rarely been done in America; and, when it has been done, it has rarely succeeded, so as to establish a manufac-ture, which the country was not yet so ripe for as to encourage private persons to set it up; labor being generally too dear there, and hands difficult to be kept together, every one desiring to be a master, and the cheapness of lands inclin-ing many to leave trades for agriculture. Some indeed have met with success, and are carried on to advantage; but they are generally such as require only a few hands, or wherein great part of the work is performed by machines. Things that are bulky, and of so small value as not well to bear the expense of freight, may often be made cheaper in the country, than they can be imported; and the manufacture of such things will be profitable wherever there is a sufficient

2. Those who have served their apprenticeship and are paid by the day.

3. To be skillful in whatever they undertake in the way of a vocation.

demand. The farmers in America produce indeed a good deal of wool and flax; and none is exported, it is all worked up; but it is in the way of domestic manufacture, for the use of the family. The buying up quantities of wool and flax, with the design to employ spinners, weavers, etc., and form great establishments, producing quantities of linen and woollen goods for sale, has been several times attempted in different provinces; but those projects have generally failed, goods of equal value being imported cheaper. And when the governments have been solicited to support such schemes by encouragements, in money, or by imposing duties on importation of such goods, it has been generally refused, on this principle, that, if the country is ripe for the manufacture, it may be carried on by private persons to advantage; and if not, it is a folly to think of forcing Nature. Great establishments of manufacture require great numbers of poor to do the work for small wages; these poor are to be found in Europe, but will not be found in America, till the lands are all taken up and cultivated, and the excess of people, who cannot get land, want employment. The manufacture of silk, they say, is natural in France, as that of cloth in England, because each country produces in plenty the first material; but if England will have a manufacture of silk as well as that of cloth, and France one of cloth as well as that of silk, these unnatural operations must be supported by mutual prohibitions, or high duties on the importation of each other's goods; by which means the workmen are enabled to tax the home consumer by greater prices, while the higher wages they receive makes them neither happier nor richer, since they only drink more and work less. Therefore the governments in America do nothing to encourage such projects. The people, by this means, are not imposed on, either by the merchant or mechanic. If the merchant demands too much profit on imported shoes, they buy of the shoemaker; and if he asks too high a price, they take them of the merchant; thus the two professions are checks on each other. The shoemaker, however, has, on the whole, considerable profit upon his labor in America, beyond what he had in Europe, as he can add to his price a sum nearly equal to all the expenses of freight and commission, risk or insurance, etc., necessarily charged by the merchant. And the case is the same with the workmen in every other mechanic art. Hence it is, that artisans generally live better and more easily in America than in Europe; and such as are good economists[4] make a comfortable provision for age, and for their children. Such may, therefore, remove with advantage to America.

In the long-settled countries of Europe, all arts, trades, professions, farms, etc., are so full, that it is difficult for a poor man, who has children, to place them where they may gain, or learn to gain, a decent livelihood. The artisans, who fear creating future rivals in business, refuse to take apprentices, but upon conditions of money, maintenance, or the like, which the parents are unable to comply with. Hence the youth are dragged up in ignorance of every gainful art, and obliged to become soldiers, or servants, or thieves, for a subsistence. In America, the rapid increase of inhabitants takes away that fear of rivalship, and artisans willingly receive apprentices from the hope of profit by their labor, during the remainder of the time stipulated, after they shall be instructed. Hence it is easy for poor families to get their children instructed; for the artisans are so desirous of apprentices, that many of them will even give money to the

4. Providers.

parents, to have boys from ten to fifteen years of age bound apprentices to them till the age of twenty-one; and many poor parents have, by that means, on their arrival in the country, raised money enough to buy land sufficient to establish themselves, and to subsist the rest of their family by agriculture. These contracts for apprentices are made before a magistrate, who regulates the agreement according to reason and justice, and, having in view the formation of a future useful citizen, obliges the master to engage by a written indenture, not only that, during the time of service stipulated, the apprentice shall be duly provided with meat, drink, apparel, washing, and lodging, and, at its expiration, with a complete new suit of clothes, but also that he shall be taught to read, write, and cast accounts;[5] and that he shall be well instructed in the art or profession of his master, or some other, by which he may afterwards gain a livelihood, and be able in his turn to raise a family. A copy of this indenture is given to the apprentice or his friends, and the magistrate keeps a record of it, to which recourse may be had, in case of failure by the master in any point of performance. This desire among the masters, to have more hands employed in working for them, induces them to pay the passages of young persons, of both sexes, who, on their arrival, agree to serve them one, two, three, or four years; those, who have already learned a trade, agreeing for a shorter term, in proportion to their skill, and the consequent immediate value of their service; and those, who have none, agreeing for a longer term, in consideration of being taught an art their poverty would not permit them to acquire in their own country.

The almost general mediocrity of fortune that prevails in America obliging its people to follow some business for subsistence, those vices, that arise usually from idleness, are in a great measure prevented. Industry and constant employment are great preservatives of the morals and virtue of a nation. Hence bad examples to youth are more rare in America, which must be a comfortable consideration to parents. To this may be truly added, that serious religion, under its various denominations, is not only tolerated, but respected and practiced. Atheism is unknown there; infidelity rare and secret; so that persons may live to a great age in that country, without having their piety shocked by meeting with either an atheist or an infidel. And the Divine Being seems to have manifested His approbation of the mutual forbearance and kindness with which the different sects treat each other, by the remarkable prosperity with which He has been pleased to favor the whole country.

1782   1784

Remarks Concerning the Savages of North America

Savages we call them, because their manners differ from ours, which we think the perfection of civility; they think the same of theirs.

Perhaps, if we could examine the manners of different nations with impartiality, we should find no people so rude, as to be without any rules of politeness; nor any so polite, as not to have some remains of rudeness.

The Indian men, when young, are hunters and warriors; when old, counsel-

5. Calculate; add up the figures in a column.

ors; for all their government is by counsel of the sages; there is no force, there are no prisons, no officers to compel obedience, or inflict punishment. Hence they generally study oratory, the best speaker having the most influence. The Indian women till the ground, dress the food, nurse and bring up the children, and preserve and hand down to posterity the memory of public transactions. These employments of men and women are accounted natural and honorable. Having few artificial wants, they have abundance of leisure for improvement by conversation. Our laborious manner of life, compared with theirs, they esteem slavish and base; and the learning, on which we value ourselves, they regard as frivolous and useless. An instance of this occurred at the Treaty of Lancaster, in Pennsylvania, *anno* 1744, between the government of Virginia and the Six Nations.[1] After the principal business was settled, the commissioners from Virginia acquainted the Indians by a speech, that there was at Williamsburg a college, with a fund for educating Indian youth; and that, if the Six Nations would send down half a dozen of their young lads to that college, the government would take care that they should be well provided for, and instructed in all the learning of the white people. It is one of the Indian rules of politeness not to answer a public proposition the same day that it is made; they think it would be treating it as a light matter, and that they show it respect by taking time to consider it, as of a matter important. They therefore deferred their answer till the day following; when their speaker began, by expressing their deep sense of the kindness of the Virginia government, in making them that offer; "for we know," says he, "that you highly esteem the kind of learning taught in those Colleges, and that the maintenance of our young men, while with you, would be very expensive to you. We are convinced, therefore, that you mean to do us good by your proposal; and we thank you heartily. But you, who are wise, must know that different nations have different conceptions of things; and you will therefore not take it amiss, if our ideas of this kind of education happen not to be the same with yours. We have had some experience of it; several of our young people were formerly brought up at the colleges of the northern provinces; they were instructed in all your sciences; but, when they came back to us, they were bad runners, ignorant of every means of living in the woods, unable to bear either cold or hunger, knew neither how to build a cabin, take a deer, or kill an enemy, spoke our language imperfectly, were therefore neither fit for hunters, warriors, nor counselors; they were totally good for nothing. We are however not the less obliged by your kind offer, though we decline accepting it; and, to show our grateful sense of it, if the gentlemen of Virginia will send us a dozen of their sons, we will take great care of their education, instruct them in all we know, and make *men* of them."

Having frequent occasions to hold public councils, they have acquired great order and decency in conducting them. The old men sit in the foremost ranks, that warriors in the next, and the women and children in the hindmost. The business of the women is to take exact notice of what passes, imprint it in their memories (for they have no writing), and communicate it to their children. They are the records of the council, and they preserve traditions of the stipulations in treaties 100 years back; which, when we compare with our writings, we always find exact. He that would speak, rises. The rest observe a profound silence. When he has finished and sits down, they leave him 5 or 6 minutes

---

1. A confederation of Iroquois tribes: Seneca, Cayuga, Oneida, Onondaga, Mohawk, and Tuscarora.

to recollect, that, if he has omitted anything he intended to say, or has anything to add, he may rise again and deliver it. To interrupt another, even in
common conversation, is reckoned highly indecent. How different this from
the conduct of a polite British House of Commons, where scarce a day passes
without some confusion, that makes the speaker hoarse in calling to *order*; and
how different from the mode of conversation in many polite companies of
Europe, where, if you do not deliver your sentence with great rapidity, you
are cut off in the middle of it by the impatient loquacity of those you converse
with, and never suffered to finish it!

The politeness of these savages in conversation is indeed carried to excess,
since it does not permit them to contradict or deny the truth of what is asserted
in their presence. By this means they indeed avoid disputes; but then it
becomes difficult to know their minds, or what impression you make upon
them. The missionaries who have attempted to convert them to Christianity,
all complain of this as one of the great difficulties of their mission. The Indians
hear with patience the truths of the Gospel explained to them, and give their
usual tokens of assent and approbation; you would think they were convinced.
No such matter. It is mere civility.

A Swedish minister, having assembled the chiefs of the Susquehanah Indians, made a sermon to them, acquainting them with the principal historical
facts on which our religion is founded; such as the fall of our first parents by
eating an apple, the coming of Christ to repair the mischief, His miracles and
suffering, etc. When he had finished, an Indian orator stood up to thank him.
"What you have told us," he says, "is all very good. It is indeed bad to eat
apples. It is better to make them all into cider. We are much obliged by your
kindness in coming so far, to tell us these things which you have heard from
your mothers. In return, I will tell you some of those we have heard from
ours. In the beginning, our fathers had only the flesh of animals to subsist on;
and if their hunting was unsuccessful, they were starving. Two of our young
hunters, having killed a deer, made a fire in the woods to broil some part of it.
When they were about to satisfy their hunger, they beheld a beautiful young
woman descend from the clouds, and seat herself on that hill, which you see
yonder among the blue mountains. They said to each other, it is a spirit that
has smelled our broiling vension, and wishes to eat of it; let us offer some to
her. They presented her with the tongue; she was pleased with the taste of it,
and said, 'Your kindness shall be rewarded; come to this place after thirteen
moons, and you shall find something that will be of great benefit in nourishing
you and your children to the latest generations.' They did so, and, to their
surprise, found plants they had never seen before; but which, from that ancient
time, have been constantly cultivated among us, to our great advantage.
Where her right hand had touched the ground, they found maize; where her
left hand had touched it, they found kidney-beans; and where her backside
had sat on it, they found tobacco." The good missionary, disgusted with this
idle tale, said, "What I delivered to you were sacred truths; but what you tell
me is mere fable, fiction, and falsehood." The Indian, offended, replied, "My
brother, it seems your friends have not done you justice in your education;
they have not well instructed you in the rules of common civility. You saw
that we, who understand and practice those rules, believed all your stories;
why do you refuse to believe ours?"

When any of them come into our towns, our people are apt to crowd round them, gaze upon them, and incommode them, where they desire to be private; this they esteem great rudeness, and the effect of the want of instruction in the rules of civility and good manners. "We have," say they, "as much curiosity as you, and when you come into our towns, we wish for opportunities of looking at you, but for this purpose we hide ourselves behind bushes, where you are to pass, and never intrude ourselves into your company."

Their manner of entering one another's village has likewise its rules. It is reckoned uncivil in traveling strangers to enter a village abruptly, without giving notice of their approach. Therefore, as soon as they arrive within hearing, they stop and hollow,[2] remaining there till invited to enter. Two old men usually come out to them, and lead them in. There is in every village a vacant dwelling, called *the stranger's house*. Here they are placed, while the old men go round from hut to hut, acquainting the inhabitants, that strangers are arrived, who are probably hungry and weary; and every one sends them what he can spare of victuals, and skins to repose on. When the strangers are refreshed, pipes and tobacco are brought; and then, but not before, conversation begins, with inquiries who they are, whither bound, what news, etc.; and it usually ends with offers of service, if the strangers have occasion of guides, or any necessaries for continuing their journey; and nothing is exacted for the entertainment.

The same hospitality, esteemed among them as a principal virtue, is practiced by private persons; of which Conrad Weiser, our interpreter, gave me the following instances. He had been naturalized among the Six Nations, and spoke well the Mohawk language. In going through the Indian country, to carry a message from our Governor to the Council at Onondaga, he called at the habitation of Canassatego, an old acquaintance, who embraced him, spread furs for him to sit on, placed before him some boiled beans and venison, and mixed some rum and water for his drink. When he was well refreshed, and had lit his pipe, Canassatego began to converse with him; asked how he had fared the many years since they had seen each other; whence he then came; what occasioned the journey, etc. Conrad answered all his questions; and when the discourse began to flag, the Indian, to continue it, said, "Conrad, you have lived long among the white people, and know something of their customs; I have been sometimes at Albany, and have observed, that once in seven days they shut up their shops, and assemble all in the great house; tell me what it is for? What do they do there?" "They meet there," says Conrad, "to hear and learn *good things*." "I do not doubt," says the Indian, "that they tell you so; they have told me the same; but I doubt the truth of what they say, and I will tell you my reasons. I went lately to Albany to sell my skins and buy blankets, knives, powder, rum, etc. You know I used generally to deal with Hans Hanson; but I was a little inclined this time to try some other merchant. However, I called first upon Hans, and asked him what he would give for beaver. He said he could not give any more than four shillings a pound; 'but,' says he, 'I cannot talk on business now; this is the day when we meet together to learn *good things*, and I am going to the meeting.' So I thought to myself, 'Since we cannot do any business today, I may as well go to the meeting too,' and I went with him. There stood up a man in black, and began to talk to the people very angrily. I did not understand what he said;

2. Cry out; announce themselves.

but, perceiving that he looked much at me and at Hanson, I imagined he was angry at seeing me there; so I went out, sat down near the house, struck fire, and lit my pipe, waiting till the meeting should break up. I thought too, that the man had mentioned something of beaver, and I suspected it might be the subject of their meeting. So, when they came out, I accosted my merchant. 'Well, Hans,' says I, 'I hope you have agreed to give more than four shillings a pound.' 'No,' says he, 'I cannot give so much; I cannot give more than three shillings and sixpence.' I then spoke to several other dealers, but they all sung the same song,—three and sixpence,—three and sixpence. This made it clear to me, that my suspicion was right; and, that whatever they pretended of meeting to learn *good things*, the real purpose was to consult how to cheat Indians in the price of beaver. Consider but a little, Conrad, and you must be of my opinion. If they met so often to learn *good things*, they would certainly have learned some before this time. But they are still ignorant. You know our practice. If a white man, in traveling through our country, enters one of our cabins, we all treat him as I treat you; we dry him if he is wet, we warm him if he is cold, we give him meat and drink, that he may allay his thirst and hunger; and we spread soft furs for him to rest and sleep on; we demand nothing in return. But, if I go into a white man's house at Albany, and ask for victuals and drink, they say, 'Where is your money?' and if I have none, they say, 'Get out, you Indian dog.' You see they have not yet learned those little *good things*, that we need no meetings to be instructed in, because our mothers taught them to us when we were children; and therefore it is impossible their meetings should be, as they say, for any such purpose, or have any such effect; they are only to contrive *the cheating of Indians in the price of beaver.*"[3]

1784

Speech in the Convention, at the Conclusion of Its Deliberations[1]

Mr. President,

I confess, that I do not entirely approve of this Constitution at present; but, Sir, I am not sure I shall never approve it; for, having lived long, I have experienced many instances of being obliged, by better information or fuller consideration, to change my opinions even on important subjects, which I once thought right, but found to be otherwise. It is therefore that, the older I grow, the more apt I am to doubt my own judgment of others. Most men, indeed, as well as most sects in religion, think themselves in possession of all truth, and that wherever others differ from them, it is so far error. Steele,[2] a Protestant, in a dedication, tells the Pope, that the only difference between our two churches in their opinions of the certainty of their doctrine, is, the

---

3. "It is remarkable that in all ages and countries hospitality has been allowed as the virtue of those whom the civilized were pleased to call barbarians. The Greeks celebrated the Scythians for it. The Saracens possessed it eminently, and it is to this day the reigning virtue of the wild Arabs. St. Paul, too, in the relation of his voyage and shipwreck on the island of Melité says the barbarous people showed us no little kindness; for they kindled a fire, and received us every one, because of the present rain, and because of the cold" [Franklin's note]. St. Paul's account of his visit to Melita may be found in Acts 28. The Scythians were nomadic tribes of southeastern Europe known for their plundering.

1. James Wilson of the Pennsylvania delegation read Franklin's speech on the final day of the Constitutional Convention, September 17, 1787.

2. Sir Richard Steele (1672–1729), English essayist.

Romish Church is *infallible*, and the Church of England is *never in the wrong*. But, though many private Persons think almost as highly of their own infallibility as of that of their Sect, few express it so naturally as a certain French Lady, who, in a little dispute with her sister, said, "But I meet with nobody but myself that is *always* in the right." *"Je ne trouve que moi qui aie toujours raison."*

In these sentiments, Sir, I agree to this Constitution, with all its faults,—if they are such; because I think a general Government necessary for us, and there is no *form* of government but what may be a blessing to the people, if well administered; and I believe, farther, that this is likely to be well administered for a course of years, and can only end in despotism, as other forms have done before it, when the people shall become so corrupted as to need despotic government, being incapable of any other. I doubt, too, whether any other Convention we can obtain, may be able to make a better constitution; for, when you assemble a number of men, to have the advantage of their joint wisdom, you inevitably assemble with those men all their prejudices, their passions, their errors of opinion, their local interests, and their selfish views. From such an assembly can a *perfect* production be expected? It therefore astonishes me, Sir, to find this system approaching so near to perfection as it does; and I think it will astonish our enemies, who are waiting with confidence to hear, that our councils are confounded like those of the builders of Babel,[3] and that our States are on the point of separation, only to meet hereafter for the purpose of cutting one another's throats. Thus I consent, Sir, to this Constitution, because I expect no better, and because I am not sure that it is not the best. The opinions I have had of its *errors* I sacrifice to the public good. I have never whispered a syllable of them abroad. Within these walls they were born, and here they shall die. If every one of us, in returning to our Constituents, were to report the objections he has had to it, and endeavor to gain Partisans in support of them, we might prevent its being generally received, and thereby lose all the salutary effects and great advantages resulting naturally in our favor among foreign nations, as well as among ourselves, from our real or apparent unanimity. Much of the strength and efficiency of any government, in procuring and securing happiness to the people, depends on *opinion*, on the general opinion of the goodness of that government, as well as of the wisdom and integrity of its governors. I hope, therefore, for our own sakes, as a part of the people, and for the sake of our posterity, that we shall act heartily and unanimously in recommending this Constitution, wherever our Influence may extend, and turn our future thoughts and endeavors to the means of having it *well administered*.

On the whole, Sir, I cannot help expressing a wish, that every member of the Convention who may still have objections to it, would with me on this occasion doubt a little of his own infallibility, and, to make *manifest* our *unanimity*, put his name to this Instrument.

1787   1837

---

3. Builders of the Tower of Babel, whose pride the Lord punished by confounding their language (Genesis 11.1–9).

Letters

To Josiah Franklin[1]

[FORMING OPINIONS]

Philadelphia, April 13, 1738.

Honored Father,

    I have your favors[2] of the 21st of March, in which you both seem concerned lest I have imbibed some erroneous opinions. Doubtless I have my share; and when the natural weakness and imperfection of human understanding is considered, the unavoidable influence of education, custom, books, and company upon our ways of thinking, I imagine a man must have a good deal of vanity who believes, and a good deal of boldness who affirms, that all the doctrines he holds are true, and all he rejects are false. And perhaps the same may be justly said of every sect, church, and society of men, when they assume to themselves that infallibility, which they deny to the Pope and councils.

    I think opinions should be judged of by their influences and effects; and, if a man holds none that tend to make him less virtuous or more vicious, it may be concluded he holds none that are dangerous; which I hope is the case with me.

    I am sorry you should have any uneasiness on my account; and if it were a thing possible for one to alter his opinions in order to please another, I know none whom I ought more willingly to oblige in that respect than yourselves. But, since it is no more in a man's power to *think* than to *look* like another, methinks all that should be expected from me is to keep my mind open to conviction, to hear patiently and examine attentively, whatever is offered me for that end; and, if after all I continue in the same errors, I believe your usual charity will induce you to rather pity and excuse, than blame me. In the mean time your care and concern for me is what I am very thankful for.

    My mother grieves, that one of her sons is an Arian, another an Arminian.[3] What an Arminian or an Arian is, I cannot say that I very well know. The truth is, I make such distinctions very little my study. I think vital religion has always suffered, when orthodoxy is more regarded than virtue; and the Scriptures assure me, that at the last day we shall not be examined what we *thought*, but what we *did*; and our recommendation will not be, that we said, *Lord! Lord!* but that we did good to our fellow creatures. See Matt. xxv.[4]

    As to the freemasons,[5] I know no way of giving my mother a better account of them than she seems to have at present, since it is not allowed that women should be admitted into that secret society. She has, I must confess, on that account some reason to be displeased with it; but for any thing else, I must entreat her to suspend her judgment till she is better informed, unless she will believe me, when I assure her that they are in general a very harmless sort of people, and have no principles or practices that are inconsistent with religion and good manners.

    We have had great rains here lately, which, with the thawing of snow on the mountains back of our country, have made vast floods in our rivers, and,

---

1. Josiah Franklin (1655–1744) came to Boston from England in 1685.
2. Letters.
3. Arians deny the divinity of Jesus; Arminians are opposed to the doctrine of predestination and argue for the freedom of the will.
4. "Then shall he answer them, saying, Verily I say unto you, Inasmuch as ye did it not to one of the least of these, ye did it not to me" (Matthew 25.45).
5. A secret fraternity.

by carrying away bridges, boats, etc., made traveling almost impracticable for a week past; so that our post has entirely missed making one trip.

I hear nothing of Dr. Crook, nor can I learn any such person has ever been here.

I hope my sister Jenny's child is by this time recovered. I am your dutiful son.

B. FRANKLIN.

1738   1834

To Peter Collinson[6]

[WHIRLWINDS]

Philadelphia, Aug. 25, 1755.

Dear Sir,—

As you have my former papers on Whirlwinds, etc., I now send you an account of one which I had lately an opportunity of seeing and examining myself.

Being in *Maryland*, riding with Colonel *Tasker*, and some other gentlemen to his country-seat, where I and my son were entertained by that amiable and worthy man with great hospitality and kindness, we saw in the vale below us, a small whirlwind beginning in the road, and showing itself by the dust it raised and contained. It appeared in the form of a sugar-loaf,[7] spinning on its point, moving up the hill towards us, and enlarging as it came forward. When it passed by us, its smaller part near the ground, appeared no bigger than a common barrel, but widening upwards, it seemed, at 40 or 50 feet high, to be 20 or 30 feet in diameter. The rest of the company stood looking after it, but my curiosity being stronger, I followed it, riding close by its side, and observed its licking up, in its progress, all the dust that was under its smaller part. As it is a common opinion that a shot, fired through a water-spout,[8] will break it, I tried to break this little whirlwind, by striking my whip frequently through it, but without any effect. Soon after, it quitted the road and took into the woods, growing every moment larger and stronger, raising, instead of dust, the old dry leaves with which the ground was thick covered, and making a great noise with them and the branches of the trees, bending some tall trees round in a circle swiftly and very surprisingly, though the progressive motion of the whirl was not so swift but that a man on foot might have kept pace with it; but the circular motion was amazingly rapid. By the leaves it was now filled with, I could plainly perceive that the current of air they were driven by, moved upwards in a spiral line; and when I saw the trunks and bodies of large trees enveloped in the passing whirl, which continued entire after it had left them I no longer wondered that my whip had no effect on it in its smaller state. I accompanied it about three quarters of a mile, till some limbs of dead trees, broken off by the whirl, flying about and falling near me, made me more apprehensive of danger; and then I stopped, looking at the top of it as it went on, which was visible, by means of the leaves contained in it, for a very great height above the trees. Many of the leaves, as they got loose from the upper

6. English scientist and friend of Franklin's (d. 1768). He had Franklin's *Experiments and Observations on Electricity* printed in 1751; it was Franklin's first pub- lished pamphlet.
7. A cone shape.
8. Geyser.

and widest part, were scattered in the wind; but so great was their height in the
air, that they appeared no bigger than flies. My son, who was by this time
come up with me, followed the whirlwind till it left the woods, and crossed an
old tobacco-field, where, finding neither dust nor leaves to take up, it gradually
became invisible below as it went away over that field. The course of the
general wind then blowing was along with us as we traveled, and the progressive motion of the whirlwind was in a direction nearly opposite, though it did
not keep a straight line, nor was its progressive motion uniform, it making
little sallies on either hand as it went, proceeding sometimes faster and sometimes slower, and seeming sometimes for a few seconds almost stationary, then
starting forward pretty fast again. When we rejoined the company, they were
admiring the vast height of the leaves now brought by the common wind, over
our heads. These leaves accompanied us as we traveled, some falling now and
then round about us, and some not reaching the ground till we had gone near
three miles from the place where we first saw the whirlwind begin. Upon
my asking Colonel *Tasker* if such whirlwinds were common in *Maryland*, he
answered pleasantly, "No, not at all common; but we got this on purpose to
treat Mr. Franklin." And a very high treat it was, to
                         Dear Sir,
             Your affectionate friend and humble servant,
                                                        B. F[RANKLIN.]

1755   1769

                         To Mrs. Jane Mecom

                    [INTERPRETING AN ACROSTIC]

                                       London, September 16, 1758.
Dear Sister,
    I received your favor of June 17. I wonder you have had no letter from me
since my being in England. I have wrote you at least two, and I think a third
before this, and what was next to waiting on you in person, sent you my
picture. In June last I sent Benny a trunk of books, and wrote to him; I hope
they are come to hand, and that he meets with encouragement in his business.
I congratulate you on the conquest of Cape Breton,[9] and hope as your people
took it by praying, the first time, you will now pray that it may never be given
up again, which you then forgot. Billy[1] is well, but in the country. I left him
at Tunbridge Wells, where we spent a fortnight, and he is now gone with some
company to see Portsmouth. We have been together over a great part of
England this summer, and among other places, visited the town our father
was born in, and found some relations in that part of the country still living.
    Our cousin Jane Franklin, daughter of our uncle John, died about a year
ago. We saw her husband, Robert Page, who gave us some old letters to his
wife, from Uncle Benjamin. In one of them, dated Boston, July 4, 1723, he
writes that your uncle Josiah has a daughter Jane, about twelve years old, a
good-humored child. So keep up to your character, and don't be angry when
you have no letters. In a little book he sent her, called "None but Christ," he

9. Fort Louisburg on Cape Breton Island, Nova Scotia, was founded by the French in 1713. It was lost to
the British in 1745 and returned to France. In 1758
the English, under Lord Jeffrey Amherst and Admiral
Boscawen, once more claimed it for the Crown.
1. Franklin's son.

wrote an acrostick[2] on her name, which for namesake's sake, as well as the good advice it contains, I transcribe and send you, viz.,

> "Illuminated from on high,
> And shining brightly in your sphere,
> Ne'er faint, but keep a steady eye,
> Expecting endless pleasures there.

> "Flee vice as you'd a serpent flee;
> Raise *faith* and *hope* three stories higher,
> And let Christ's endless love to thee
> Ne'er cease to make thy love aspire.
> Kindness of heart by words express,
> Let your obedience be sincere,
> In prayer and praise your God address,
> Nor cease, till he can cease to hear."

After professing truly that I had a great esteem and veneration for the pious author, permit me a little to play the commentator and critic on these lines. The meaning of *three stories higher* seems somewhat obscure. You are to understand, then, that *faith, hope,* and *charity* have been called the three steps of Jacob's ladder,[3] reaching from earth to heaven; our author calls them *stories,* likening religion to a building, and these are the three stories of the Christian edifice. Thus improvement in religion is called *building up* and *edification.* *Faith* is then the ground floor, *hope* is up one pair of stairs. My dear beloved Jenny, don't delight so much to dwell in those lower rooms, but get as fast as you can into the garret, for in truth the best room in the house is *charity.* For my part, I wish the house was turned upside down; 'tis so difficult (when one is fat) to go up stairs; and not only so, but I imagine *hope* and *faith* may be more firmly built upon *charity,* than *charity* upon *faith* and *hope.* However that may be, I think it the better reading to say—

> "Raise faith and hope one story higher."

Correct it boldly, and I'll support the alteration; for, when you are up two stories already, if you raise your building three stories higher you will make five in all, which is two more than there should be, you expose your upper rooms more to the winds and storms; and, besides, I am afraid the foundation will hardly bear them, unless indeed you build with such light stuff as straw and stubble, and that, you know, won't stand fire. Again, where the author says,

> "Kindness of heart by words express,"

strike out *words,* and put in *deeds.* The world is too full of compliments already. They are the rank growth of every soil, and choke the good plants of benevolence, and beneficence; nor do I pretend to be the first in this comparison of words and actions to plants; you may remember an ancient poet, whose works we have all studied and copied at school long ago.

---

2. A poem in which the first letter in each line spells out a name; in the printing of the time, *i* and *j* were often used interchangeably, as here.
3. In Genesis 28.12, the patriarch sees in his dream a ladder leading to heaven, with angels ascending and descending. Cf. also 1 Corinthians 13.13: "And now abideth faith, hope, charity, these three; but the greatest of these is charity."

> "A man of words and not of deeds
> Is like a garden full of weeds."

'Tis a pity that good works, among some sorts of people, are so little valued, and good words admired in their stead:[4] I mean seemingly pious discourses, instead of humane benevolent actions. Those they almost put out of countenance, by calling morality *rotten morality*, righteousness *ragged righteousness*, and even filthy rags—and when you mention virtue, pucker up their noses as if they smelt a stink; at the same time that they eagerly snuff up an empty canting[5] harangue, as if it was a posey of the choicest flowers: So they have inverted the good old verse, and say now

> "A man of deeds and not of words
> Is like a garden full of——"

I have forgot the rhyme, but remember 'tis something the very reverse of perfume. So much by way of commentary.

My wife will let you see my letter, containing an account of our travels, which I would have you read to Sister Dowse, and give my love to her. I have no thoughts of returning till next year, and then may possibly have the pleasure of seeing you and yours; taking Boston in my way home. My love to brother and all your children, concludes at this time from, dear Jenny, your affectionate brother,

B. FRANKLIN.

1758   1817

To Lord Kames[6]

[PARLIAMENT AND THE COLONIES]

London, April 11, 1767.

My dear Lord,—

I received your obliging favor of January the 19th. You have kindly relieved me from the pain I had long been under. You are goodness itself. I ought to have answered yours of December 25. 1765. I never received a letter that contained sentiments more suitable to my own. It found me under much agitation of mind on the very important subject it treated. It fortified me greatly in the judgment I was inclined to form (though contrary to the general vogue) on the then delicate and critical situation of affairs between Great Britain and her Colonies, and on that weighty point, their *Union*. You guessed aright in supposing that I would not be a *mute*[7] *in that play*. I was extremely busy, attending Members of both Houses, informing, explaining, consulting, disputing, in a continual hurry from morning to night, till the affair was happily ended. During the course of it, being called before the House of Commons, I spoke my mind pretty freely. Enclosed I send you the imperfect account that was taken of that examination. You will there see how entirely we agree, except in a point of fact, of which you could not but be misinformed; the papers at that time being full of mistaken assertions, that the colonies had been the cause of the war, and had ungratefully refused to bear any part of the expense of it.

4. I.e., in their place.
5. Affectedly pious or righteous.
6. Henry Home, Lord Kames (1696–1782), a Scottish

jurist and philosopher.
7. Nonspeaking actor.

I send it you now, because I apprehend some late incidents are likely to revive the contest between the two countries. I fear it will be a mischievous one. It becomes a matter of great importance that clear ideas should be formed on solid principles, both in Britain and America, of the true political relation between them, and the mutual duties belonging to that relation. Till this is done, they will be often jarring. I know none whose knowledge, sagacity and impartiality qualify him so thoroughly for such a service, as yours do you. I wish therefore you would consider it. You may thereby be the happy instrument of great good to the nation, and of preventing much mischief and bloodshed. I am fully persuaded with you, that a *Consolidating Union*, by a fair and equal representation of all the parts of this empire in Parliament, is the only firm basis on which its political grandeur and prosperity can be founded. Ireland once wished it, but now rejects it. The time has been, when the colonies might have been pleased with it: they are now *indifferent* about it; and if it is much longer delayed, they too will *refuse* it. But the pride of this people cannot bear the thought of it, and therefore it will be delayed. Every man in England seems to consider himself as a piece of a sovereign over America; seems to jostle himself into the throne with the King, and talks of *our subjects in the Colonies*. The Parliament cannot well and wisely make laws suited to the Colonies, without being properly and truly informed of their circumstances, abilities, temper, etc. This it cannot be, without representatives from thence: and yet it is fond of this power, and averse to the only means of acquiring the necessary knowledge for exercising it; which is desiring to be *omnipotent*, without being *omniscient*.

I have mentioned that the contest is likely to be revived. It is on this occasion. In the same session with the stamp act, an act was passed to regulate the quartering[8] of soldiers in America; when the bill was first brought in, it contained a clause, empowering the officers to quarter their soldiers in private houses: this we warmly opposed, and got it omitted. The bill passed, however, with a clause, that empty houses, barns, etc., should be hired for them, and that the respective provinces where they were should pay the expense and furnish firing,[9] bedding, drink, and some other articles to the soldiers *gratis*. There is no way for any province to do this, but by the Assembly's making a law to raise the money. The Pennsylvania Assembly has made such a law: the New York Assembly has refused to do it: and now all the talk here is of sending a force to compel them.

The reasons given by the Assembly to the Governor, for the refusal, are, that they understand the act to mean the furnishing such things to soldiers, only while on their march through the country, and not to great bodies of soldiers, to be fixt as at present, in the province; the burthen in the latter case being greater than the inhabitants can bear: That it would put it in the power of the Captain-General to oppress the province at pleasure, etc. But there is supposed to be another reason at bottom, which they intimate, though they do not plainly express it; to wit, that it is of the nature of an *internal tax* laid on them by Parliament, which has no right so to do. Their refusal is here called *Rebellion*, and punishment is thought of.

Now waiving that point of right, and supposing the Legislatures in America

---

8. Lodging. The Stamp Act of 1765 was the first direct tax levied on the American colonies by Parliament. It required that stamps be purchased and attached to legal documents and most printed items, like newspapers and magazines.
9. Fuel.

subordinate to the Legislature of Great Britain, one might conceive, I think, a power in the superior Legislature to forbid the inferior Legislatures making particular laws; but to enjoin it to make a particular law contrary to its own judgment, seems improper; an Assembly or Parliament not being an *executive* officer of Government, whose duty it is, in law-making, to obey orders, but a *deliberative* body, who are to consider what comes before them, its propriety, practicability, or possibility, and to determine accordingly: The very nature of a Parliament seems to be destroyed, by supposing it may be bound, and compelled by a law of a superior Parliament, to make a law contrary to its own judgment.

Indeed, the act of Parliament in question has not, as in other acts, when a duty is enjoined, directed a penalty on neglect or refusal, and a mode of recovering that penalty. It seems, therefore, to the people in America as a mere requisition, which they are at liberty to comply with or not, as it may suit or not suit the different circumstances of different provinces. Pennsylvania has therefore voluntarily complied. New York, as I said before, has refused. The Ministry that made the act, and all their adherents, call for vengeance. The present Ministry are perplext, and the measures they will finally take on the occasion, are yet unknown. But sure I am, that, if *Force* is used, great mischief will ensue; the affections of the people of America to this country will be alienated; your commerce will be diminished; and a total separation of interests be the final consequence.

It is a common, but mistaken notion here, that the Colonies were planted at the expense of Parliament, and that therefore the Parliament has a right to tax them, etc. The truth is, they were planted at the expense of private adventurers, who went over there to settle, with leave of the King, given by charter. On receiving this leave,[1] and those charters, the adventurers voluntarily engaged to remain the King's subjects, though in a foreign country; a country which had not been conquered by either King or Parliament, but was possessed by a free people.

When our planters arrived, they purchased the lands of the natives, without putting King or Parliament to any expense. Parliament had no hand in their settlement, was never so much as consulted about their constitution, and took no kind of notice of them, till many years after they were established. I except only the two modern Colonies, or rather attempts to make Colonies, (for they succeed but poorly, and as yet hardly deserve the name of Colonies), I mean Georgia and Nova Scotia, which have hitherto been little better than Parliamentary jobs.[2] Thus all the colonies acknowledge the King as their sovereign; his Governors there represent his person: Laws are made by their Assemblies or little Parliaments, with the Governor's assent, subject still to the King's pleasure to confirm or annul them: Suits arising in the Colonies, and differences between Colony and Colony, are determined by the King in Council. In this view, they seem so many separate little states, subject to the same Prince. The *sovereignty of the* King is therefore easily understood. But nothing is more common here than to talk of the *sovereignty of* PARLIAMENT, and the *sovereignty of* THIS NATION over the Colonies; a kind of sovereignty, the idea of which is not so clear, nor does it clearly appear on what foundation it is established. On the other hand, it seems necessary for the common good of the

1. Permission.
2. Colonies that have served members of Parliament for their own personal gain or party advantage.

empire, that a power be lodged somewhere, to regulate its general commerce: this can be placed nowhere so properly as in the Parliament of Great Britain; and therefore, though that power has in some instances been executed with great partiality to Britain, and prejudice to the Colonies, they have nevertheless always submitted to it. Custom-houses are established in all of them, by virtue of laws made here, and the duties constantly paid, except by a few smugglers, such as are here and in all countries; but internal taxes laid on them by Parliament, are still and ever will be objected to, for the reasons that you will see in the mentioned Examination.

Upon the whole, I have lived so great a part of my life in Britain, and have formed so many friendships in it, that I love it, and sincerely wish it prosperity; and therefore wish to see that Union, on which alone I think it can be secured and established. As to America, the advantages of such a union to her are not so apparent. She may suffer at present under the arbitrary power of this country; she may suffer for a while in a separation from it; but these are temporary evils that she will outgrow. Scotland and Ireland are differently circumstanced. Confined by the sea, they can scarcely increase in numbers, wealth and strength, so as to overbalance England. But America, an immense territory, favored by Nature with all advantages of climate, soil, great navigable rivers, and lakes, etc., must become a great country, populous and mighty; and will, in a less time than is generally conceived, be able to shake off any shackles that may be imposed on her, and perhaps place them on the imposers. In the mean time, every act of oppression will sour their tempers, lessen greatly, if not annihilate the profits of your commerce with them, and hasten their final revolt; for the seeds of liberty are universally found there, and nothing can eradicate them. And yet, there remains among that people, so much respect, veneration and affection for Britain, that, if cultivated prudently, with kind usage, and tenderness for their privileges, they might be easily governed still for ages, without force, or any considerable expense. But I do not see here a sufficient quantity of the wisdom, that is necessary to produce such a conduct, and I lament the want of it.

I borrowed at Millar's the new edition of your *Principles of Equity*, and have read with great pleasure the preliminary discourse on the Principles of Morality. I have never before met with any thing so satisfactory on the subject. While reading it, I made a few remarks as I went along. They are not of much importance, but I send you the paper.

I know the lady you mention;[3] having, when in England before, met her once or twice at Lord Bath's. I remember I then entertained the same opinion of her that you express. On the strength of your kind recommendation, I purpose soon to wait on[4] her.

This is unexpectedly grown a long letter. The visit to Scotland, and the *Art of Virtue*, we will talk of hereafter. It is now time to say, that I am, with increasing esteem and affection, my dear friend, yours ever,

B. FRANKLIN.

1767   1807

3. Lady Mary Wortley Montagu (1689–1762), well   4. Make a formal call on.
known in England as a poet and letter writer.

To Joseph Priestley[5]

[RESOLVING DIFFICULT CASES]

London, Sept. 19, 1772.

Dear Sir,

In the Affair of so much Importance to you, wherein you ask my Advice, I cannot for want of sufficient Premises, advise you *what* to determine, but if you please I will tell you *how*. When those difficult Cases occur, they are difficult, chiefly because while we have them under Consideration, all the Reasons *pro* and *con* are not present to the Mind at the same time; but sometimes one Set present themselves, and at other times another, the first being out of Sight. Hence the various Purposes or Inclinations that alternately prevail, and the Uncertainty that perplexes us.

To get over this, my Way is, to divide half a Sheet of Paper by a Line into two Columns; writing over the one *Pro*, and over the other *Con*. Then during three or four Days Consideration, I put down under the different Heads short Hints of the different Motives, that at different Times occur to me, *for* or *against* the Measure. When I have thus got them all together in one View, I endeavour to estimate their respective Weights; and where I find two, one on each side, that seem equal, I strike them both out. If I find a Reason *pro* equal to some *two* Reasons *con*, I strike out the three. If I judge some *two* Reasons *con*, equal to some three Reasons *pro*, I strike out the five; and thus proceeding I find at length where the Balance lies; and if after a Day or two of farther Consideration, nothing new that is of Importance occurs on either side, I come to a Determination accordingly. And, tho' the Weight of Reasons cannot be taken with the Precision of Algebraic Quantities, yet, when each is thus considered, separately and comparatively, and the whole lies before me, I think I can judge better, and am less liable to make a rash Step; and in fact I have found great Advantage from this kind of Equation, in what may be called *Moral* or *Prudential Algebra*.

Wishing sincerely that you may determine for the best, I am ever, my dear Friend, yours most affectionately,

B. FRANKLIN.

1772　　　　　　　　　　　　　　　　　　　　　　　　　　　　1907

To Miss Georgiana Shipley[6]

[IN MEMORY OF HER PET SQUIRREL]

London, September 26, 1772.

Dear Miss,

I lament with you most sincerely the unfortunate end of poor MUNGO. Few squirrels were better accomplished; for he had had a good education, had traveled far, and seen much of the world. As he had the honor of being, for his virtues, your favorite, he should not go, like common skuggs,[7] without an elegy or an epitaph. Let us give him one in the monumental style and mea-

---

5. English clergyman and scientist (1733–1804), author of *The History of the Present State of Electricity* (1767).

6. Daughter of the bishop of Saint Asaph.

7. Squirrels.

sure, which, being neither prose nor verse, is perhaps the properest for grief; since to use common language would look as if we were not affected, and to make rhymes would seem trifling in sorrow.

EPITAPH.

Alas! poor MUNGO!
Happy wert thou, hadst thou known
Thy own felicity.
Remote from the fierce bald eagle,
Tyrant of thy native woods,
Thou hadst nought to fear from his piercing talons,
Nor from the murdering gun
Of the thoughtless sportsman.
Safe in thy wired castle,
GRIMALKIN[8] never could annoy thee.
Daily wert thou fed with the choicest viands,
By the fair hand of an indulgent mistress;
But, discontented,
Thou wouldst have more freedom.
Too soon, alas! didst thou obtain it;
And wandering,
Thou art fallen by the fangs of wanton, cruel RANGER!

Learn hence,
Ye who blindly seek more liberty,
Whether subjects, sons, squirrels or daughters,
That apparent restraint may be real protection;
Yielding peace and plenty
With security.

You see, my dear Miss, how much more decent and proper this broken style is, than if we were to say, by way of epitaph,

Here SKUGG
Lies snug,
As a bug
In a rug.

and yet, perhaps, there are people in the world of so little feeling as to think that this would be a good-enough epitaph for poor Mungo.

If you wish it, I shall procure another to succeed him; but perhaps you will now choose some other amusement.

Remember me affectionately to all the good family, and believe me ever,
Your affectionate friend,

B. FRANKLIN.

1772   1907

---

8. A cat.

To Charles de Weissenstein[9]

[AGAINST PROPOSALS FROM A SECRET AGENT]

Passy, July 1, 1778.

Sir,

I received your letter, dated at Brussels the 16th past. My vanity might possibly be flattered by your expressions of compliment to my understanding, if your *proposals* did not more clearly manifest a mean opinion of it.

You conjure me, in the name of the omniscient and just God, before whom I must appear, and by my hopes of future fame, to consider if some expedient cannot be found to put a stop to the desolation of America, and prevent the miseries of a general war. As I am conscious of having taken every step in my power to prevent the breach, and no one to widen it, I can appear cheerfully before that God, fearing nothing from his justice in this particular, though I have much occasion for his mercy in many others. As to my future fame, I am content to rest it on my past and present conduct, without seeking an addition to it in the crooked, dark paths, you propose to me, where I should most certainly lose it. This your solemn address would therefore have been more properly made to your sovereign and his venal Parliament. He and they, who wickedly began, and madly continue, a war for the desolation of America, are alone accountable for the consequences.

You endeavor to impress me with a bad opinion of French faith; but the instances of their friendly endeavors to serve a race of weak princes, who, by their own imprudence, defeated every attempt to promote their interest, weigh but little with me, when I consider the steady friendship of France to the Thirteen United States of Switzerland,[1] which has now continued inviolate two hundred years. You tell me, that she will certainly cheat us, and that she despises us already. I do not believe that she will cheat us, and I am not certain that she despises us; but I see clearly that you are endeavoring to cheat us by your conciliatory bills;[2] that you actually despised our understandings, when you flattered yourselves those artifices would succeed; and that not only France, but all Europe, yourselves included, most certainly and for ever would despise us, if we were weak enough to accept your insidious propositions.

Our expectations of the future grandeur of America are not so magnificent, and therefore not so vain or visionary, as you represent them to be. The body of our people are not merchants, but humble husbandmen,[3] who delight in the cultivation of their lands, which, from their fertility and the variety of our climates, are capable of furnishing all the necessaries and conveniences of life without external commerce; and we have too much land to have the least temptation to extend our territory by conquest from peaceable neighbors, as well as too much justice to think of it. Our militia, you find by experience, are sufficient to defend our lands from invasion; and the commerce with us will be defended by all the nations who find an advantage in it. We, therefore, have not the occasion you imagine, of fleets or standing armies, but may leave those expensive machines to be maintained for the pomp of princes, and the wealth of ancient states. We propose, if possible, to live in peace with all

9. Pseudonym of a British secret agent, never identified, who wrote to Franklin from Brussels on June 16, 1778, urging secret correspondence to realize his plan for a new British/American government.

1. I.e., its then cantons.
2. Petitions.
3. Farmers.

mankind; and after you have been convinced, to your cost, that there is nothing to be got by attacking us, we have reason to hope, that no other power will judge it prudent to quarrel with us, lest they divert us from our own quiet industry, and turn us into corsairs[4] preying upon theirs. The weight therefore of an independent empire, which you seem certain of our inability to bear, will not be so great as you imagine. The expense of our civil government we have always borne, and can easily bear, because it is small. A virtuous and laborious people may be cheaply governed. Determining, as we do, to have no offices of profit, nor any sinecures or useless appointments, so common in ancient or corrupted states, we can govern ourselves a year, for the sum you pay in a single department, or for what one jobbing contractor, by the favor of a minister, can cheat you out of in a single article.[5]

You think we flatter ourselves, and are deceived into an opinion that England *must* acknowledge our independency. We, on the other hand, think you flatter yourselves in imagining such an acknowledgment a vast boon, which we strongly desire, and which you may gain some great advantage by granting or withholding. We have never asked it of you; we only tell you, that you can have no treaty with us but as an independent state; and you may please yourselves and your children with the rattle of your right to govern us, as long as you have done with that of your King's being King of France, without giving us the least concern, if you do not attempt to exercise it. That this pretended right is indisputable, as you say, we utterly deny. Your Parliament never had a right to govern us, and your King has forfeited it by his bloody tyranny. But I thank you for letting me know a little of your mind, that, even if the Parliament should acknowledge our independency, the act would not be binding to posterity, and that your nation would resume and prosecute the claim as soon as they found it convenient from the influence of your passions, and your present malice against us. We suspected before, that you would not be actually bound by your conciliatory acts, longer than till they had served their purpose of inducing us to disband our forces; but we were not certain, that you were knaves by principle, and that we ought not to have the least confidence in your offers, promises, or treaties, though confirmed by Parliament.

I now indeed recollect my being informed, long since, when in England, that a certain very great personage, then young, studied much a certain book, called *Arcana Imperii*.[6] I had the curiosity to procure the book and read it. There are sensible and good things in it, but some bad ones; for, if I remember rightly, a particular king is applauded for his politically exciting a rebellion among his subjects, at a time when they had not strength to support it, that he might, in subduing them, take away their privileges, which were troublesome to him; and a question is formally stated and discussed, *Whether a prince, who, to appease a revolt, makes promises of indemnity to the revolters, is obliged to fulfil those promises.* Honest and good men would say, Ay; but this politician says, as you say, No. And he gives this pretty reason, that, though it was right to make the promises, because otherwise the revolt would not be suppressed, yet it would be wrong to keep them, because revolters ought to be punished to deter from future revolts.

---

4. Pirates.
5. Clause. "Jobbing": swindling.
6. The full title was *Arcana imperii detecta* (The se-

crets of the empire revealed), a translation of Mark Zuirius Boxhorn's *Disquisitiones politicae* (Political inquiry) (1701).

If these are the principles of your nation, no confidence can be placed in you; it is in vain to treat with you; and the wars can only end in being reduced to an utter inability of continuing them.

One main drift of your letter seems to be, to impress me with an idea of your own impartiality, by just censures of your ministers and measures, and to draw from me propositions of peace, or approbations of those you have enclosed to me which you intimate may by your means be conveyed to the King directly, without the intervention of those ministers. You would have me give them to, or drop them for, a stranger, whom I may find next Monday in the church of Notre Dame, to be known by a rose in his hat. You yourself, Sir, are quite unknown to me; you have not trusted me with your true name. Our taking the least step towards a treaty with England through you, might, if you are an enemy, be made use of to ruin us with our new and good friends. I may be indiscreet enough in many things; but certainly, if I were disposed to make propositions (which I cannot do, having none committed to me to make), I should never think of delivering them to the Lord knows who, to be carried to the Lord knows where, to serve no one knows what purposes. Being at this time one of the most remarkable[7] figures in Paris, even my appearance in the church of Notre Dame, where I cannot have any conceivable business, and especially being seen to leave or drop any letter to any person there, would be a matter of some speculation, and might, from the suspicions it must naturally give, have very mischievous consequences to our credit here.

The very proposing of a correspondence so to be managed, in a manner not necessary where fair dealing is intended, gives just reason to suppose you intend the contrary. Besides, as your court has sent Commissioners to treat with the Congress, with all the powers that could be given them by the crown under the act of Parliament, what good purpose can be served by privately obtaining propositions from us? Before those Commissioners went, we might have treated in virtue of our general powers, (with the knowledge, advice, and approbation of our friends), upon any propositions made to us. But, under the present circumstances, for us to make propositions, while a treaty is supposed to be actually on foot with the Congress, would be extremely improper, highly presumptuous with regard to our constituents, and answer no good end whatever.

I write this letter to you, notwithstanding; (which I think I can convey in a less mysterious manner, and guess it may come to your hands;) I write it because I would let you know our sense of your procedure, which appears as insidious as that of your conciliatory bills. Your true way to obtain peace, if your ministers desire it, is, to propose openly to the Congress fair and equal terms, and you may possibly come sooner to such a resolution, when you find, that personal flatteries, general cajolings, and panegyrics on our *virtue* and *wisdom* are not likely to have the effect you seem to expect; the persuading us to act basely and foolishly, in betraying our country and posterity into the hands of our most bitter enemies, giving up or selling our arms and warlike stores, dismissing our ships of war and troops, and putting those enemies in possession of our forts and ports.

This proposition of delivering ourselves, bound and gagged, ready for hanging, without even a right to complain, and without a friend to be found after-

---

7. I.e., noticeable.

wards among all mankind, you would have us embrace upon the faith of an act of Parliament! Good God! an act of your Parliament! This demonstrates that you do not yet know us, and that you fancy we do not know you; but it is not merely this flimsy faith, that we are to act upon; you offer us *hope*, the hope of PLACES, PENSIONS,[8] and PEERAGES. These, judging from yourselves, you think are motives irresistible. This offer to corrupt us, Sir, is with me your credential, and convinces me that you are not a private volunteer in your application. It bears the stamp of British court character. It is even the signature of your King. But think for a moment in what light it must be viewed in America. By PLACES, you mean places among us, for you take care by a special article to secure your own to yourselves. We must then pay the salaries in order to enrich ourselves with these places. But you will give us PENSIONS, probably to be paid too out of your expected American revenue, and which none of us can accept without deserving, and perhaps obtaining, a SUS-*pension*. PEERAGES! alas! Sir, our long observation of the vast servile majority of your peers, voting constantly for every measure proposed by a minister, however weak or wicked, leaves us small respect for that title. We consider it as a sort of *tar-and-feather* honor, or a mixture of foulness and folly, which every man among us, who should accept it from your King, would be obliged to renounce, or exchange for that conferred by the mobs of their own country, or wear it with everlasting infamy. I am, Sir, your humble servant,

B. FRANKLIN.

1778   1907

To Madame Brillon[9]

[PAYING TOO MUCH FOR A WHISTLE]

Passy, November 10, 1779.

I received my dear friend's two letters, one for Wednesday and one for Saturday. This is again Wednesday. I do not deserve one for today, because I have not answered the former. But, indolent as I am, and averse to writing, the fear of having no more of your pleasing epistles, if I do not contribute to the correspondence, obliges me to take up my pen; and as Mr. B. has kindly sent me word, that he sets out tomorrow to see you, instead of spending this Wednesday evening as I have done its namesakes, in your delightful company, I sit down to spend it in thinking of you, in writing to you, and in reading over and over again your letters.

I am charmed with your description of Paradise, and with your plan of living there; and I approve much of your conclusion, that, in the mean time, we should draw all the good we can from this world. In my opinion, we might all draw more good from it than we do, and suffer less evil, if we would take care not to give too much for *whistles*. For to me it seems, that most of the unhappy people we meet with, are become so by neglect of that caution.

You ask what I mean? You love stories, and will excuse my telling one of myself.

When I was a child of seven years old, my friends, on a holiday, filled my pocket with coppers. I went directly to a shop where they sold toys for children;

---

8. I.e., government grants. "Places": i.e., at court or in the government.

9. Anne-Louise Boivin d'Hardancourt Brillon de Jouy (1744–1824), one of Franklin's favorite French friends.

and, being charmed with the sound of a *whistle,* that I met by the way in the hands of another boy, I voluntarily offered and gave all my money for one. I then came home, and went whistling all over the house, much pleased with my *whistle,* but disturbing all the family. My brothers, and sisters, and cousins, understanding the bargain I had made, told me I had given four times as much for it as it was worth; put me in mind what good things I might have bought with the rest of the money; and laughed at me so much for my folly, that I cried with vexation; and the reflection gave me more chagrin than the *whistle* gave me pleasure.

This however was afterwards of use to me, the impression continuing on my mind; so that often, when I was tempted to buy some unnecessary thing, I said to myself, *Don't give too much for the whistle;* and I saved my money.

As I grew up, came into the world, and observed the actions of men, I thought I met with many, very many, who *gave too much for the whistle.*

When I saw one too ambitious of court favor, sacrificing his time in attendance on levees,[1] his repose, his liberty, his virtue, and perhaps his friends, to attain it, I have said to myself, *This man gives too much for his whistle.*

When I saw another fond of popularity, constantly employing himself in political bustles, neglecting his own affairs, and running them by that neglect, *He pays, indeed,* said I, *too much for his whistle.*

If I knew a miser, who gave up every kind of comfortable living, all the pleasure of doing good to others, all the esteem of his fellow-citizens, and the joys of benevolent friendship, for the sake of accumulating wealth, *Poor man,* said I, *you pay too much for your whistle.*

When I met with a man of pleasure, sacrificing every laudable improvement of the mind, or of his fortune, to mere corporeal sensations, and ruining his health in their pursuit, *Mistaken man,* said I, *you are providing pain for yourself, instead of pleasure; you give too much for your whistle.*

If I see one fond of appearance, or fine clothes, fine houses, fine furniture, fine equipages,[2] all above his fortune, for which he contracts debts, and ends his career in a prison, *Alas!* say I, *he has paid dear, very dear, for his whistle.*

When I see a beautiful, sweet-tempered girl married to all ill-natured brute of a husband, *What a pity,* say I, *that she should pay so much for a whistle!*

In short, I conceive that great part of the miseries of mankind are brought upon them by the false estimates they have made of the value of things, and by their *giving too much for their whistles.*

Yet I ought to have charity for these unhappy people, when I consider, that, with all this wisdom of which I am boasting, there are certain things in the world so tempting, for example, the apples of King John,[3] which happily are not to be bought; for if they were put to sale by auction, I might very easily be led to ruin myself in the purchase, and find that I had once more given too much for the *whistle.*

Adieu, my dear friend, and believe me ever yours very sincerely and with unalterable affection,

B. FRANKLIN.

1779   1907

---

1. I.e., receptions at court.
2. Horse-drawn carriages.

3. Probably King John of England (1199–1216), but the reference to his apples is unclear.

To Samuel Mather[4]

[DOING GOOD]

Passy, May 12, 1784

Revd Sir,

I received your kind letter, with your excellent advice to the people of the United States, which I read with great pleasure, and hope it will be duly regarded. Such writings, though they may be lightly passed over by many readers, yet, if they make a deep impression on one active mind in a hundred, the effects may be considerable. Permit me to mention one little instance, which, though it relates to myself, will not be quite uninteresting to you. When I was a boy, I met with a book, entitled "*Essays to do Good,*" which I think was written by your father. It had been so little regarded by a former possessor, that several leaves of it were torn out; but the remainder gave me such a turn of thinking, as to have an influence on my conduct through life; for I have always set a greater value on the character of a *doer of good*, than on any other kind of reputation; and if I have been, as you seem to think, a useful citizen, the public owes the advantage of it to that book.

You mention your being in your 78th year; I am in my 79th; we are grown old together. It is now more than 60 years since I left Boston, but I remember well both your father and grandfather, having heard them both in the pulpit, and seen them in their houses. The last time I saw your father was in the beginning of 1724, when I visited him after my first trip to Pennsylvania. He received me in his library, and on my taking leave showed me a shorter way out of the house through a narrow passage, which was crossed by a beam over head. We were still talking as I withdrew, he accompanying me behind, and I turning partly towards him, when he said hastily, "*Stoop, stoop!*" I did not understand him, till I felt my head hit against the beam. He was a man that never missed any occasion of giving instruction, and upon this he said to me, "*You are young, and have the world before you;* STOOP *as you go through it, and you will miss many hard thumps.*" This advice, thus beat into my head, has frequently been of use to me; and I often think of it, when I see pride mortified, and misfortunes brought upon people by their carrying their heads too high.

I long much to see again my native place, and to lay my bones there. I left it in 1723; I visited it in 1733, 1743, 1753, and 1763. In 1773 I was in England; in 1775 I had a sight of it, but could not enter; it being in possession of the enemy.[5] I did hope to have been there in 1783, but could not obtain my dismission from this employment here; and now I fear I shall never have that happiness. My best wishes however attend my dear country. *Esto perpetua.*[6] It is now blest with an excellent constitution; may it last for ever!

This powerful monarchy continues its friendship for the United States. It is a friendship of the utmost importance to our security, and should be carefully cultivated. Britain has not yet well digested the loss of its dominion over us, and has still at times some flattering hopes of recovering it. Accidents may increase those hopes, and encourage dangerous attempts. A breach between us and France would infallibly bring the English again upon our backs; and

4. The Reverend Samuel Mather (1706–1785) was the son of Cotton Mather (1663–1728) and the grandson of Increase Mather (1639–1723). All were ministers at the Second Church, Boston.
5. Boston was besieged in October 1775 by the British.
6. Let her be (Latin).

yet we have some wild heads among our countrymen, who are endeavoring to weaken that connection! Let us preserve our reputation by performing our engagements; our credit by fulfilling our contracts; and friends by gratitude and kindness; for we know not how soon we may again have occasion for all of them. With great and sincere esteem, I have the honor to be, etc.

B. FRANKLIN.

1784   1907

To Ezra Stiles[7]

[MY RELIGION]

Philadelphia, March 9, 1790

Reverend and Dear Sir,

I received your kind letter of January 28, and am glad you have at length received the portrait of Governor Yale[8] from his family, and deposited it in the college library. He was a great and good man, and had the merit of doing infinite service to your country by his munificence to that institution. The honor you propose doing me by placing mine in the same room with his is much too great for my deserts; but you always had a partiality for me, and to that it must be ascribed. I am however too much obliged to Yale College, the first learned society that took notice of me[9] and adorned me with its honors, to refuse a request that comes from it through so esteemed a friend. But I do not think any one of the portraits you mention, as in my possession, worthy of the place and company you propose to place it in. You have an excellent artist lately arrived. If he will undertake to make one for you, I shall cheerfully pay the expense; but he must not delay setting about it, or I may slip through his fingers, for I am now in my eighty-fifty year, and very infirm.[1]

I send with this a very learned work, as it seems to me, on the ancient Samaritan coins, lately printed in Spain, and at least curious for the beauty of the impression. Please to accept it for your college library. I have subscribed for the Encyclopædia[2] now printing here, with the intention of presenting it to the college. I shall probably depart before the work is finished, but shall leave directions for its continuance to the end. With this you will receive some of the first numbers.

You desire to know something of my religion. It is the first time I have been questioned upon it. But I cannot take your curiosity amiss, and shall endeavor in a few words to gratify it. Here is my creed. I believe in one God, Creator of the Universe. That He governs it by His providence. That He ought to be worshiped. That the most acceptable service we render to Him is doing good to His other children. That the soul of man is immortal, and will be treated

---

7. Ezra Stiles (1727–95) was the grandson of the poet Edward Taylor and president of Yale College. He wrote to Franklin on January 28, 1780, asking Franklin to provide him with some information about his "religious sentiments" and his opinion "concerning Jesus of Nazareth." Stiles hoped Franklin would not think his inquiry an "impertinence" because he revered Franklin with an affection "bordering on adoration." The text used here is from *The Writings of Benjamin Franklin*, Vol. 10, edited by Albert Henry Smyth (1907).
8. Elihu Yale (1649–1721) was an official in the East India Company, and governor of Fort Saint George. Yale College was named for him after the receipt from London of books and goods in 1714 and 1718.
9. Franklin was awarded an honorary master's degree from Yale in 1753.
1. Franklin died on April 17, 1790.
2. The 3rd edition of the *Encyclopaedia Britannica*, printed in the United States for the first time. It was customary in undertaking expensive publishing ventures to get customers to subscribe for future volumes and ensure the success of the undertaking.

with justice in another life respecting its conduct in this. These I take to be the fundamental principles of all sound religion, and I regard them as you do in whatever sect I meet with them.

As to Jesus of Nazareth, my opinion of whom you particularly desire, I think the system of morals and his religion, as he left them to us, the best the world ever saw or is likely to see; but I apprehend it has received various corrupting changes, and I have with most of the present dissenters in England, some doubts as to his divinity; though it is question I do not dogmatize upon, having never studied it, and think it needless to busy myself with it now, when I expect soon an opportunity of knowing the truth with less trouble. I see no harm, however, in its being believed, if that belief has the good consequence, as probably it has, of making his doctrines more respected and better observed; especially as I do not perceive, that the Supreme takes it amiss, by distinguishing the unbelievers in His government of the world with any peculiar marks of His displeasure.

I shall only add, respecting myself, that, having experienced the goodness of that Being in conducting me prosperously through a long life, I have no doubt of its continuance in the next, though without the smallest conceit of meriting such goodness. My sentiments on this head you will see in the copy of an old letter enclosed, which I wrote in answer to one from a zealous religionist, whom I had relieved in a paralytic case by electricity, and who, being afraid I should grow proud upon it, sent me his serious though rather impertinent caution. I send you also the copy of another letter,[3] which will show something of my disposition relating to religion. With great and sincere esteem and affection, I am, your obliged old friend and most obedient humble servant,

B. FRANKLIN.

1790   1907

P.S. Had not your college some present of books from the King of France? Please to let me know, if you had an expectation given you of more, and the nature of that expectation? I have a reason for the inquiry.

I confide, that you will not expose me to criticism and censure by publishing any part of this communication to you. I have ever let others enjoy their religious sentiments, without reflecting on them for those that appeared to me unsupportable and even absurd. All sects here, and we have a great variety, have experienced my good will in assisting them with subscriptions for building their new places of worship; and, as I have never opposed any of their doctrines, I hope to go out of the world in peace with them all.

1790   1840

The Autobiography   Franklin turned to the manuscript of *The Autobiography* on four different occasions over a period of nineteen years. The first part, addressed to his son William Franklin (c. 1731–1813), who was governor of New Jersey when Franklin was writing this section, was composed while Franklin was visiting the country home of Bishop Jonathan Shipley at Twyford, a village about fifty miles from London. It was begun on July 30 and concluded on or about

---

3. It has been suggested that this letter was addressed to Thomas Paine.

August 13, 1771. Franklin did not work on the manuscript again until he was living in France and was minister of the newly formed United States, about thirteen years later. The last two sections were written in August 1788 and the winter of 1789–90, when Franklin stopped because of illness. Before he died he carried his life up to the year 1758. The account ends, therefore, before Franklin's great triumphs as a diplomat and public servant.

The first part of *The Autobiography* was published in 1791 by Jacques Buisson in a French translation; William Temple Franklin, Franklin's grandson, published an edition of *The Autobiography* in 1818, but he did not possess the last section that his grandfather wrote because he unwittingly exchanged it for the French translator's Part One. It was not until 1868 that John Bigelow published *The Autobiography* as we know it, with all four sections complete.

The text for *The Autobiography* here reprinted is entirely new; it is the first to have been taken directly from the manuscript itself (all other editors have merely corrected earlier printed texts). The text was established by J. A. Leo Lemay and Paul Zall for their Norton Critical Edition of *The Autobiography*, and is here reprinted with their kind permission. The text has been only slightly modernized. All manuscript abbreviations and symbols have been expanded. The editors note that they have omitted short dashes, which Franklin often wrote after sentences, and punctuation marks that "have been clearly superseded by revisions or additions." Careless slips have been corrected silently but may be found in their section on emendations in their complete text. Professors Lemay and Zall have been very generous in letting us see their footnotes and biographical sketches. Every student of Franklin's *Autobiography* must also acknowledge the extremely helpful edition of Leonard W. Labaree et al. (1964).

The Autobiography

[Part One]

Twyford, at the Bishop of St. Asaph's 1771.

Dear Son,

I have ever had a Pleasure in obtaining any little Anecdotes of my Ancestors. You may remember the Enquiries I made among the Remains[1] of my Relations when you were with me in England; and the Journey I took for that purpose. Now imagining it may be equally agreeable to you to know the Circumstances of *my* Life, many of which you are yet unacquainted with; and expecting a Week's uninterrupted Leisure in my present Country Retirement, I sit down to write them for you. To which I have besides some other Inducements. Having emerg'd from the Poverty and Obscurity in which I was born and bred, to a State of Affluence and some Degree of Reputation in the World, and having gone so far thro' Life with a considerable Share of Felicity, the conducting Means I made use of, which, with the Blessing of God, so well succeeded, my Posterity may like to know, as they may find some of them suitable to their own Situations, and therefore fit to be imitated. That Felicity, when I reflected on it, has induc'd me sometimes to say, that were it offer'd to my Choice, I should have no Objection to a Repetition of the same Life from its Beginning, only asking the Advantage Authors have in a second Edition to correct some Faults of the first. So would I if I might, besides correcting the

---

1. I.e., the remaining representatives of a family. Franklin and his son toured England in 1758 and visited ancestral homes at Ecton and Banbury, Northhamptonshire, England.

Faults, change some sinister Accidents and Events of it for others more favorable, but tho' this were denied, I should still accept the Offer. However, since such a Repetition is not to be expected, the Thing most like living one's Life over again, seems to be a *Recollection* of that Life; and to make that Recollection as durable as possible, the putting it down in Writing. Hereby, too, I shall indulge the Inclination so natural in old Men, to be talking of themselves and their own past Actions, and I shall indulge it, without being troublesome to others who thro' respect to Age might think themselves oblig'd to give me a Hearing, since this may be read or not as any one pleases. And lastly, (I may as well confess it, since my Denial of it will be believ'd by no body) perhaps I shall a good deal gratify my own V*anity*. Indeed I scarce ever heard or saw the introductory Words, *Without Vanity I may say*, etc. but some vain thing immediately follow'd. Most People dislike Vanity in others whatever Share they have of it themselves, but I give it fair Quarter wherever I meet with it, being persuaded that it is often productive of Good to the Possessor and to others that are within his Sphere of Action: And therefore in many Cases it would not be quite absurd if a Man were to thank God for his Vanity among the other Comforts of Life.

And now I speak of thanking God, I desire with all Humility to acknowledge, that I owe the mention'd Happiness of my past Life to his kind Providence, which led me to the Means I us'd and gave them Success. My Belief of This, induces me to *hope*, tho' I must not *presume*, that the same Goodness will still be exercis'd towards me in continuing that Happiness, or in enabling me to bear a fatal Reverso,[2] which I may experience as others have done, the Complexion of my future Fortune being known to him only: and in whose Power it is to bless to us even our Afflictions.

The Notes one of my Uncles (who had the same kind of Curiosity in collecting Family Anecdotes) once put into my Hands, furnish'd me with several Particulars, relating to our Ancestors. From those Notes I learned that the Family had liv'd in the same Village, Ecton in Northamptonshire, for 300 Years, and how much longer he knew not, (perhaps from the Time when the Name *Franklin* that before was the Name of an Order of People,[3] was assum'd by them for a Surname, when others took Surnames all over the Kingdom)[4] on a Freehold of about 30 Acres, aided by the Smith's Business which had continued in the Family till his Time, the eldest Son being always bred to that Business. A Custom which he and my Father both followed as to their eldest Sons. When I search'd the Register at Ecton, I found an Account of their Births, Marriages and Burials, from the Year 1555 only, there being no Register kept in that Parish at any time preceding. By that Register I perceiv'd that I was the youngest Son of the youngest Son for 5 Generations back. My Grandfather Thomas, who was born in 1598, lived at Ecton till he grew too old to follow Business longer, when he went to live with his Son John, a Dyer at Banbury in Oxfordshire, with whom my Father serv'd an Apprenticeship. There my Grandfather died and lies buried. We saw his Gravestone in 1758. His eldest Son Thomas liv'd in the House at Ecton, and left it with the Land to his only Child, a Daughter, who with her Husband, one Fisher of Wellingborough, sold it to Mr. Isted, now Lord of the Manor there.

My Grandfather had 4 Sons that grew up, viz., Thomas, John, Benjamin

---

2. I.e., a backhanded stroke, a word used in dueling with rapiers.
3. A "franklin" was a freeholder—an individual who owned land but was not of noble birth.
4. "Here a note" [Franklin intended to insert a note here, but did not].

and Josiah. I will give you what Account I can of them at this distance from my Papers, and if those are not lost in my Absence, you will among them find many more Particulars. Thomas was bred a Smith under his Father, but being ingenious, and encourag'd in Learning (as all his Brothers likewise were,) by an Esquire[5] Palmer then the principal Gentleman in that Parish, he qualified himself for the Business of Scrivener,[6] became a considerable Man in the County Affairs, was a chief Mover of all public Spirited Undertakings for the County or Town of Northampton and his own Village, of which many Instances were told us at Ecton, and he was much taken Notice of and patroniz'd by the then Lord Halifax. He died in 1702, Jan. 6, old Stile,[7] just 4 Years to a Day before I was born. The Account we receiv'd of his Life and Character from some old People at Ecton, I remember struck you as something extraordinary from its Similarity to what you knew of mine. Had he died on the same Day, you said one might have suppos'd a Transmigration.[8]

John was bred a Dyer, I believe of Woollens. Benjamin was bred a Silk Dyer, serving an Apprenticeship at London. He was an ingenious Man. I remember him well, for when I was a Boy he came over to my Father in Boston, and lived in the House with us some Years. He lived to a great Age. His Grandson Samuel Franklin now lives in Boston. He left behind him two Quarto[9] Volumes, Manuscript of his own Poetry, consisting of little occasional Pieces address'd to his Friends and Relations, of which the following sent to me, is a Specimen.[1] He had form'd a Shorthand of his own, which he taught me, but never practicing it I have now forgot it. I was nam'd after this Uncle, there being a particular Affection between him and my Father. He was very pious, a great Attender of Sermons of the best Preachers, which he took down in his Shorthand and had with him many Volumes of them. He was also much of a Politician, too much perhaps for his Station. There fell lately into my Hands in London a Collection he had made of all the principal Pamphlets relating to Public Affairs from 1641 to 1717. Many of the Volumes are wanting, as appears by the Numbering, but there still remains 8 Volumes Folio, and 24 in Quarto and Octavo. A Dealer in old Books met with them, and knowing me by my sometimes buying of him, he brought them to me. It seems my Uncle must have left them here when he went to America, which was above 50 Years since. There are many of his Notes in the Margins.

This obscure Family of ours was early in the Reformation, and continu'd Protestants thro' the Reign of Queen Mary,[2] when they were sometimes in Danger of Trouble on Account of their Zeal against Popery. They had got an English Bible,[3] and to conceal and secure it, it was fastened open with Tapes under and within the Frame of a Joint Stool.[4] When my Great Great Grandfa-

---

5. An honorific originally extended to a young man of gentle birth, but extended as a courtesy to any gentleman.

6. A professional copier of documents.

7. Until September 1752 England used the Julian calendar, in which the New Year began on March 25. Because the Julian calendar did not have leap years, the English skipped eleven days (September 3 to September 13, 1752) when adopting the Gregorian calendar. Franklin's birthday is either January 6, 1705–6 "old Stile" or January 17, 1706, New Style.

8. The passage of the soul to another's body upon death.

9. The terms *folio*, *quarto*, and *octavo* designate book

sizes from large to small. A single sheet folded once makes a folio, or four sides for printing; a quarto is obtained if the sheet is folded again; an octavo is the sheet folded once more.

1. "Here insert it" [Franklin's note, but the example was not included].

2. From 1553 to 1558, Mary, the older sister of Elizabeth I, tried to restore Roman Catholicism as the national church.

3. A Bible known as the "Geneva" version, translated by Reformed English Protestants living in Switzerland; this version, used by the Puritans, was outlawed by the Church of England.

4. A small four-legged stool.

ther read in it to his Family, he turn'd up the Joint Stool upon his Knees, turning over the Leaves then under the Tapes. One of the Children stood at the Door to give Notice if he saw the Apparitor[5] coming, who was an Officer of the Spiritual Court. In that Case the Stool was turn'd down again upon its feet, when the Bible remain'd conceal'd under it as before. This Anecdote I had from my Uncle Benjamin. The Family continu'd all of the Church of England till about the End of Charles the Second's Reign,[6] when some of the Ministers that had been outed for Nonconformity, holding Conventicles[7] in Northamptonshire, Benjamin and Josiah adher'd to them, and so continu'd all their Lives. The rest of the Family remain'd with the Episcopal Church.

Josiah, my Father, married young, and carried his Wife with three Children unto New England, about 1682.[8] The Conventicles having been forbidden by Law, and frequently disturbed, induced some considerable Men of his Acquaintance to remove to that Country, and he was prevail'd with to accompany them thither, where they expected to enjoy their Mode of Religion with Freedom. By the same Wife he had 4 Children more born there, and by a second Wife ten more, in all 17, of which I remember 13 sitting at one time at his Table, who all grew up to be Men and Women, and married. I was the youngest Son and the youngest Child but two, and was born in Boston, New England.

My Mother the second Wife was Abiah Folger, a Daughter of Peter Folger, one of the first Settlers of New England, of whom honorable mention is made by Cotton Mather, in his Church History of that Country, (entitled Magnalia Christi Americana) as a *godly learned Englishman*, if I remember the Words rightly.[9] I have heard that he wrote sundry small occasional Pieces, but only one of them was printed which I saw now many Years since. It was written in 1675, in the homespun Verse of that Time and People, and address'd to those then concern'd in the Government there. It was in favor of Liberty of Conscience, and in behalf of the Baptists, Quakers, and other Sectaries,[1] that had been under Persecution; ascribing the Indian Wars and other Distresses that had befallen the Country to that Persecution, as so many Judgments of God, to punish so heinous an Offence; and exhorting a Repeal of those uncharitable Laws. The whole appear'd to me as written with a good deal of Decent Plainness and manly Freedom. The six last concluding Lines I remember, tho' I have forgotten the two first of the Stanza, but the Purport of them was that his Censures proceeded from *Goodwill*, and therefore he would be known as the Author,

> because to be a Libeler, (says he)
> I hate it with my Heart.
> From Sherburne Town[2] where now I dwell,
> My Name I do put here,
> Without Offence, your real Friend,
> It is Peter Folgier.

5. An officer of an ecclesiastical court, in this case a court established to eliminate heresy.
6. Charles II (1630–1685) reigned from 1660 to 1685.
7. Secret and illegal meetings of Nonconformists, outlawed in 1664. Nonconformists refused to adopt the rituals and acknowledge the hierarchy of the Church of England.
8. More correctly, October 1683.

9. Cotton Mather's ecclesiastical history *The Wonderful Work of Christ in America*, which was published in London in 1702; the quotation is properly "an Able Godly Englishman."
1. Believers or followers of a particular religious teaching.
2. "In the Island of Nantucket" [Franklin's note].

My elder Brothers were all put Apprentices to different Trades. I was put to the Grammar School at Eight Years of Age, my Father intending to devote me as the Tithe[3] of his Sons to the Service of the Church. My early Readiness in learning to read (which must have been very early, as I do not remember when I could not read) and the Opinion of all his Friends that I should certainly make a good Scholar, encourag'd him in this Purpose of his. My Uncle Benjamin too approv'd of it, and propos'd to give me all his Shorthand Volumes of Sermons, I suppose as a Stock to set up with, if I would learn his Character.[4] I continu'd however at the Grammar School not quite one Year, tho' in that time I had risen gradually from the Middle of the Class of that Year to be the Head of it, and farther was remov'd into the next Class above it, in order to go with that into the third at the End of the Year. But my Father in the meantime, from a View of the Expense of a College Education which, having so large a Family, he could not well afford, and the mean Living many so educated were afterwards able to obtain, Reasons that he gave to his Friends in my Hearing, altered his first Intention, took me from the Grammar School, and sent me to a School for Writing and Arithmetic kept by a then famous Man, Mr. George Brownell, very successful in his Profession generally, and that by mild encouraging Methods. Under him I acquired fair Writing pretty soon, but I fail'd in the Arithmetic, and made no Progress in it.

At Ten Years old, I was taken home to assist my Father in his Business, which was that of a Tallow Chandler and Soap-Boiler.[5] A Business he was not bred to, but had assumed on his Arrival in New England and on finding his Dying Trade would not maintain his Family, being in little Request. Accordingly I was employed in cutting Wick for the Candles, filling the Dipping Mold, and the Molds for cast Candles, attending the Shop, going of Errands, etc. I dislik'd the Trade and had a strong Inclination for the Sea; but my Father declar'd against it; however, living near the Water, I was much in and about it, learned early to swim well, and to manage Boats, and when in a Boat or Canoe with other Boys I was commonly allow'd to govern,[6] especially in any case of Difficulty; and upon other Occasions I was generally a Leader among the Boys, and sometimes led them into Scrapes, of which I will mention one Instance, as it shows an early projecting public Spirit, tho' not then justly conducted. There was a Salt Marsh that bounded part of the Mill Pond, on the Edge of which at Highwater, we us'd to stand to fish for Minnows. By much Trampling, we had made it a mere Quagmire. My Proposal was to build a Wharf there fit for us to stand upon, and I show'd my Comrades a large Heap of Stones which were intended for a new House near the Marsh, and which would very well suit our Purpose. Accordingly in the Evening when the Workmen were gone, I assembled a Number of my Playfellows, and working with them diligently like so many Emmets,[7] sometimes two or three to a Stone, we brought them all away and built our little Wharf. The next Morning the Workmen were surpris'd at Missing the Stones; which were found in our Wharf; Enquiry was made after the Removers; we were discovered and complain'd of; several of us were corrected by our Fathers; and tho' I pleaded the Usefulness of the Work, mine convinc'd me that nothing was useful which was not honest.

3. I.e., as if he were the tenth part of his income, traditionally given to the church.
4. Here, his system of shorthand.
5. Maker of candles and soap.
6. Steer.
7. Ants.

I think you may like to know something of his Person and Character. He had an excellent Constitution of Body, was of middle Stature, but well set and very strong. He was ingenious, could draw prettily, was skill'd a little in Music and had a clear pleasing Voice, so that when he play'd Psalm Tunes on his Violin and sung withal as he some times did in an Evening after the Business of the Day was over, it was extremely agreeable to hear. He had a mechanical Genius too, and on occasion was very handy in the Use of other Tradesmen's Tools. But his great Excellence lay in a sound Understanding, and solid Judgment in prudential Matters, both in private and public Affairs. In the latter indeed he was never employed, the numerous Family he had to educate and the Straitness of his Circumstances, keeping him close to his Trade, but I remember well his being frequently visited by leading People, who consulted him for his Opinion on Affairs of the Town or of the Church he belong'd to and show'd a good deal of Respect for his Judgment and Advice. He was also much consulted by private Persons about their Affairs when any Difficulty occur'd, and frequently chosen an Arbitrator between contending Parties. At his Table he lik'd to have as often as he could, some sensible Friend or Neighbor, to converse with, and always took care to start some ingenious or useful Topic for Discourse, which might tend to improve the Minds of his Children. By this means he turn'd our Attention to what was good, just, and prudent in the Conduct of Life; and little or no Notice was ever taken of what related to the Victuals on the Table, whether it was well or ill drest, in or out of season, of good or bad flavor, preferable or inferior to this or that other thing of the kind; so that I was brought up in such a perfect Inattention to those Matters as to be quite Indifferent what kind of Food was set before me; and so unobservant of it, that to this Day, if I am ask'd I can scarce tell, a few Hours after Dinner, what I din'd upon. This has been a Convenience to me in traveling, where my Companions have been sometimes very unhappy for want of a suitable Gratification of their more delicate because better instructed Tastes and Appetites.

My Mother had likewise an excellent Constitution. She suckled all her 10 Children. I never knew either my Father or Mother to have any Sickness but that of which they died, he at 89 and she at 85 Years of age. They lie buried together at Boston, where I some Years since plac'd a Marble stone over their Grave with this Inscription:

> Josiah Franklin
> And Abiah his Wife
> Lie here interred.
> They lived lovingly together in Wedlock
> Fifty-five Years.
> Without an Estate or any gainful Employment,[8]
> By constant Labor and Industry,
> With God's Blessing,
> They maintained a large Family
> Comfortably;
> And brought up thirteen Children,
> And seven Grandchildren
> Reputably.

8. Privileged employment.

From this Instance, Reader,
Be encouraged to Diligence in thy Calling,
And distrust not Providence.
He was a pious and prudent Man,
She a discreet and virtuous Woman.
Their youngest Son,
In filial Regard to their Memory,
Places this Stone.
J.F. born 1655—Died 1744. Ætat[9] 89
A.F. born 1667—died 1752——85.

By my rambling Digressions I perceive myself to be grown old. I us'd to write more methodically. But one does not dress for private Company as for a public Ball. 'Tis perhaps only Negligence.

To return. I continu'd thus employ'd in my Father's Business for two Years, that is till I was 12 Years old; and my Brother John[1] who was bred to that Business having left my Father, married and set up for himself at Rhode Island, there was all Appearance that I was destin'd to supply his Place and be a Tallow Chandler. But my Dislike to the Trade continuing, my Father was under Apprehensions that if he did not find one for me more agreeable, I should break away and get to Sea, as his Son Josiah had done to his great Vexation. He therefore sometimes took me to walk with him, and see Joiners, Bricklayers, Turners, Braziers,[2] etc. at their Work, that he might observe my Inclination, and endeavor to fix it on some Trade or other on Land. It has ever since been a Pleasure to me to see good Workmen handle their Tools; and it has been useful to me, having learned so much by it, as to be able to do little Jobs myself in my House, when a Workman could not readily be got; and to construct little Machines for my Experiments while the Intention of making the Experiment was fresh and warm in my Mind. My Father at last fix'd upon the Cutler's Trade, and my Uncle Benjamin's Son Samuel who was bred to that Business in London being about that time establish'd in Boston, I was sent to be with him some time on liking. But his Expectations of a Fee with me displeasing my Father, I was taken home again.

From a Child I was fond of Reading, and all the little Money that came into my Hands was ever laid out in Books. Pleas'd with the Pilgrim's Progress, my first Collection was of John Bunyan's[3] Works, in separate little Voumes. I afterwards sold them to enable me to buy R. Burton's[4] Historical Collections; they were small Chapmen's Books[5] and cheap, 40 or 50 in all. My Father's little Library consisted chiefly of Books in polemic Divinity, most of which I read, and have since often regretted, that at a time when I had such a Thirst for Knowledge, more proper Books had not fallen in my Way, since it was now resolv'd I should not be a Clergyman. Plutarch's Lives[6] there was, in which I read abundantly, and I still think that time spent to great Advantage.

---

9. Aged.
1. John Franklin (1690–1756), Franklin's favorite brother; he was to become postmaster of Boston.
2. Woodworkers, bricklayers, latheworkers, brassworkers.
3. John Bunyan (1628–1688) published *Pilgrim's Progress* in 1678; his works were enormously popular and available in cheap one-shilling editions. The book is an allegory in which the hero, Christian, flees the City of Destruction and makes his way to the Celestial City with the help of Mr. Worldly-Wiseman, Faithful, Hopeful, etc.
4. "Burton" was a pseudonym for Nathaniel Crouch (1632?–1725?), a popularizer of British history.
5. Peddlers' books, hence inexpensive.
6. Plutarch (A.D. 46?–120?), Greek biographer who wrote *Parallel Lives* of noted Greek and Roman figures.

There was also a Book of Defoe's called an Essay on Projects[7] and another of Dr. Mather's call'd Essays to do Good,[8] which perhaps gave me a Turn of Thinking that had an Influence on some of the principal future Events of my Life.

This Bookish Inclination at length determin'd my Father to make me a Printer, tho' he had already one Son, (James) of that Profession. In 1717 my Brother James return'd from England with a Press and Letters[9] to set up his Business in Boston. I lik'd it much better than that of my Father, but still had a Hankering for the Sea. To prevent the apprehended Effect of such an Inclination, my Father was impatient to have me bound[1] to my Brother. I stood out some time, but at last was persuaded and signed the Indentures,[2] when I was yet but 12 Years old. I was to serve as an Apprentice till I was 21 Years of Age, only I was to be allow'd Journeyman's Wages[3] during the last Year. In a little time I made great Proficiency in the Business, and became a useful Hand to my Brother. I now had Access to better Books. An Acquaintance with the Apprentices of Booksellers enabled me sometimes to borrow a small one, which I was careful to return soon and clean. Often I sat up in my Room reading the greatest Part of the Night, when the Book was borrow'd in the Evening and to be return'd early in the Morning lest it should be miss'd or wanted. And after some time an ingenious Tradesman[4] who had a pretty[5] Collection of Books, and who frequented our Printing-House, took Notice of me, invited me to his Library, and very kindly lent me such Books as I chose to read. I now took a Fancy to Poetry, and made some little Pieces. My Brother, thinking it might turn to account encourag'd me, and put me on composing two occasional Ballads. One was called the *Light House Tragedy*, and contain'd an Account of the drowning of Capt. Worthilake with his Two Daughters; the other was a Sailor Song on the Taking of *Teach* or Blackbeard the Pirate.[6] They were wretched Stuff, in the Grubstreet Ballad Style,[7] and when they were printed he sent me about the Town to sell them. The first sold wonderfully, the Event being recent, having made a great Noise. This flatter'd my Vanity. But my Father discourag'd me, by ridiculing my Performances, and telling me Verse-makers were generally Beggars; so I escap'd being a Poet, most probably a very bad one. But as Prose Writing has been of great Use to me in the Course of my Life, and was a principal Means of my Advancement, I shall tell you how in such a Situation I acquir'd what little Ability I have in that Way.

There was another Bookish Lad in the Town, John Collins by Name, with whom I was intimately acquainted. We sometimes disputed, and very fond we were of Argument, and very desirous of confuting one another. Which disputatious Turn, by the way, is apt to become a very bad Habit, making People often extremely disagreeable in Company, by the Contradiction that is necessary to bring it into Practice, and thence, besides souring and spoiling

7. Daniel Defoe's (1659?–1731) *Essay on Projects* (1697) offered suggestions for economic improvement (see also n. 2, p. 501).
8. Cotton Mather published *Bonifacius: An Essay upon the Good* in 1710.
9. Type.
1. Apprenticed.
2. A contract binding him to work for his brother for nine years. James Franklin (1697–1735) had learned the printer's trade in England.
3. I.e., be paid for each day's work, having served his apprenticeship.
4. "Mr. Matthew Adams" [Franklin's note].
5. Exceptionally fine.
6. The full texts of these ballads cannot be found; George Worthylake, lighthouse keeper on Beacon Island, Boston Harbor, and his wife and daughter were drowned on November 3, 1718; the pirate Blackbeard, Edward Teach, was killed off the Carolina coast on November 22, 1718.
7. Grub Street in London was inhabited by poor literary hacks who capitalized on poems of topical interest.

the Conversation, is productive of Disgusts and perhaps Enmities where you may have occasion for Friendship. I had caught it by reading my Father's Books of Dispute about Religion. Persons of good Sense, I have since observ'd, seldom fall into it, except Lawyers, University Men, and Men of all Sorts that have been bred at Edinburgh.[8] A Question was once some how or other started between Collins and me, of the Propriety of educating the Female Sex in Learning, and their Abilities for Study. He was of Opinion that it was improper; and that they were naturally unequal to it. I took the contrary Side, perhaps a little for Dispute sake. He was naturally more eloquent, had a ready Plenty of Words, and sometimes as I thought bore me down more by his Fluency than by the Strength of his Reasons. As we parted without settling the Point, and were not to see one another again for some time, I sat down to put my Arguments in Writing, which I copied fair and sent to him. He answer'd and I replied. Three or four Letters of a Side had pass'd, when my Father happen'd to find my Papers, and read them. Without entering into the Discussion, he took occasion to talk to me about the Manner of my Writing, observ'd that tho' I had the Advantage of my Antagonist in correct Spelling and pointing[9] (which I ow'd to the Printing-House) I fell far short in elegance of Expression, in Method and in Perspicuity, of which he convinc'd me by several Instances. I saw the Justice of his Remarks, and thence grew more attentive to the *Manner* in Writing, and determin'd to endeavor at Improvement.

About this time I met with an odd Volume of the Spectator.[1] I had never before seen any of them. I bought it, read it over and over, and was much delighted with it. I thought the Writing excellent, and wish'd if possible to imitate it. With that View, I took some of the Papers, and making short Hints of the Sentiment in each Sentence, laid them by a few Days, and then without looking at the Book, tried to complete the Papers again, by expressing each hinted Sentiment at length and as fully as it had been express'd before, in any suitable Words that should come to hand.

Then I compar'd my Spectator with the Original, discover'd some of my Faults and corrected them. But I found I wanted a Stock of Words or a Readiness in recollecting and using them, which I thought I should have acquir'd before that time, if I had gone on making Verses, since the continual Occasion for Words of the same Import but of different Length, to suit the Measure,[2] or of different Sound for the Rhyme, would have laid me under a constant Necessity of searching for Variety, and also have tended to fix that Variety in my Mind, and make me Master of it. Therefore I took some of the Tales and turn'd them into Verse: And after a time, when I had pretty well forgotten the Prose, turn'd them back again. I also sometimes jumbled my Collections of Hints into Confusion, and after some Weeks, endeavor'd to reduce them into the best Order, before I began to form the full Sentences, and complete the Paper. This was to teach me Method in the Arrangement of Thoughts. By comparing my Work afterwards with the original, I discover'd many faults and amended them; but I sometimes had the Pleasure of Fancying that in certain Particulars of small Import, I had been lucky enough to improve the Method

8. Scottish Presbyterians were noted for their argumentative nature.
9. Punctuation. Spelling and punctuation were not standardized at this time.
1. An English periodical published daily from March 1, 1711, to December 6, 1712, and revived in 1714. It contained esays by Joseph Addison (1672–1719) and Richard Steele (1672–1729). It addressed itself primarily to matters of literature and morality. Its aim was to "enliven morality with wit" and "temper wit with morality."
2. Meter.

or the Language and this encourag'd me to think I might possibly in time come to be a tolerable English Writer, of which I was extremely ambitious.

My Time for these Exercises and for Reading, was at Night after Work, or before Work began in the Morning; or on Sundays, when I contrived to be in the Printing-House alone, evading as much as I could the common Attendance on public Worship, which my Father used to exact of me when I was under his Care: And which indeed I still thought a Duty; tho' I could not, as it seemed to me, afford the Time to practice it.

When about 16 Years of Age, I happen'd to meet with a Book written by one Tryon,[3] recommending a Vegetable Diet. I determined to go into it. My Brother being yet unmarried, did not keep House, but boarded himself and his Apprentices in another Family. My refusing to eat Flesh occasioned an Inconveniency, and I was frequently chid for my singularity. I made myself acquainted with Tryon's Manner of preparing some of his Dishes, such as Boiling Potatoes or Rice, making Hasty Pudding,[4] and a few others, and then propos'd to my Brother, that if he would give me Weekly half the Money he paid for my Board, I would board myself. He instantly agreed to it, and I presently found that I could save half what he paid me. This was an additional Fund for buying Books: But I had another Advantage in it. My Brother and the rest going from the Printing-House to their Meals, I remain'd there alone, and dispatching presently my light Repast, (which often was no more than a Biscuit or a Slice of Bread, a Handful of Raisins or a Tart from the Pastry Cook's, and a Glass of Water) had the rest of the Time till their Return, for Study, in which I made the greater Progress from that greater Clearness of Head and quicker Apprehension which usually attend Temperance in Eating and Drinking. And now it was that being on some Occasion made asham'd of my Ignorance in Figures, which I had twice fail'd in learning when at School, I took Cocker's Book of Arithmetic,[5] and went thro' the whole by myself with great Ease. I also read Seller's and Sturmy's Books of Navigation,[6] and became acquainted with the little Geometry they contain, but never proceeded far in that Science. And I read about this Time Locke on Human Understanding and the Art of Thinking by Messrs. du Port Royal.[7]

While I was intent on improving my Language, I met with an English Grammar (I think it was Greenwood's[8]) at the End of which there were two little Sketches of the Arts of Rhetoric and Logic, the latter finishing with a Specimen of a Dispute in the Socratic Method.[9] And soon after I procur'd Xenophon's Memorable Things of Socrates,[1] wherein there are many Instances of the same Method. I was charm'd with it, adopted it, dropped my abrupt Contradiction and positive Argumentation, and put on the humble Enquirer and Doubter. And being then, from reading Shaftesbury and Collins,[2] became a real Doubter in many Points of our Religious Doctrine, I

3. Thomas Tryon, whose *Way to Health, Wealth, and Happiness* appeared in 1682; a digest titled *Wisdom's Dictates* appeared in 1691.
4. I.e., cornmeal or oatmeal mush.
5. Edward Cocker's *Arithmetic*, published in 1677, was reprinted twenty times by 1700.
6. John Seller published *An Epitome of the Art of Navigation* in 1681. Samuel Sturmy published *The Mariner's Magazine: Or Sturmy's Mathematical and Practical Arts* in 1699.
7. John Locke (1632–1704) published *An Essay Concerning Human Understanding* in 1690. Antoine Ar-

nauld (1612–94) and Pierre Nicole (1625?–95), of Port Royal, published the English edition of *Logic: Or the Art of Thinking* in 1687. It was originally published in Latin in 1662.
8. James Greenwood, *An Essay towards a Practical English Grammar* (1711).
9. I.e., in the form of a debate.
1. Xenophon's (434?–355 B.C.) *The Memorable Things of Socrates* was translated by Edward Bysshe in 1712.
2. Anthony Ashley Cooper, third earl of Shaftesbury (1671–1713), was a religious skeptic. Anthony Collins (1676–1729) argued that the world could satisfactorily

found this Method safest for myself and very embarrassing to those against whom I used it, therefore I took a Delight in it, practic'd it continually and grew very artful and expert in drawing People even of superior Knowledge into Concessions the Consequences of which they did not foresee, entangling them in Difficulties out of which they could not extricate themselves, and so obtaining Victories that neither myself nor my Cause always deserved. I continu'd this Method some few Years, but gradually left it, retaining only the Habit of expressing myself in Terms of modest Diffidence, never using when I advance any thing that may possibly be disputed, the Words, *Certainly*, *undoubtedly*, or any others that give the Air of Positiveness to an Opinion; but rather say, *I conceive*, or *I apprehend* a Thing to be so or so, *It appears to me*, or *I should think it so or so for such and such Reasons*, or *I imagine* it to be so, or *it is so if I am not mistaken*. This Habit I believe has been of great Advantage to me, when I have had occasion to inculcate my Opinions and persuade Men into Measures that I have been from time to time engag'd in promoting. And as the chief Ends of Conversation are to *inform*, or to be *informed*, to *please* or to *persuade*, I wish well-meaning sensible Men would not lessen their Power of doing Good by a Positive assuming Manner that seldom fails to disgust, tends to create Opposition, and to defeat every one of those Purposes for which Speech was given us, to wit, giving or receiving Information, or Pleasure: For If you would *inform*, a positive dogmatical Manner in advancing your Sentiments, may provoke Contradiction and prevent a candid Attention. If you wish Information and Improvement from the Knowledge of others and yet at the same time express yourself as firmly fix'd in your present Opinions, modest sensible Men, who do not love Disputation, will probably leave you undisturb'd in the Possession of your Error; and by such a Manner you can seldom hope to recommend yourself in *pleasing* your Hearers, or to persuade those whose Concurrence you desire. Pope says, judiciously.

> *Men should be taught as if you taught them not,*
> *And things unknown propos'd as things forgot,*

farther recommending it to us,

> *To speak tho' sure, with seeming Diffidence.*[3]

And he might have coupled with this Line that which he has coupled with another, I think less properly,

> *For want of Modesty is want of Sense.*

If you ask why *less properly*, I must repeat the Lines;

> "Immodest Words admit of *no* Defence;
> *For* Want of Modesty is Want of Sense."[4]

Now is not *Want of Sense*, (where a Man is so unfortunate as to want it) some Apology for his *Want of Modesty*? and would not the Lines stand more justly thus?

---

be explained in terms of itself. Perhaps Franklin read Shaftesbury's *Characteristics of Men, Manners, Opinions, Times* (1711) and Collins's *A Discourse of Free Thinking* (1713).

3. From Alexander Pope's *An Essay on Criticism* (1711), lines 574–75 and 567, respectively. Franklin is quoting from memory. The first line should read, "Men must be taught as if you taught them not," and

the third, "And speak, tho' sure, with seeming diffidence."

4. Franklin is mistaken here: the lines are from Wentworth Dillon, fourth earl of Roscommon (1633?–1685), from his *Essay on Translated Verse* (1684), lines 113–14. The second line should read, "For want of decency is want of sense." "Want": lack.

Immodest Words admit *but this* Defence,
That Want of Modesty is Want of Sense.

This however I should submit to better Judgments.

My Brother had in 1720 or 21, begun to print a Newspaper. It was the second[5] that appear'd in America, and was called *The New England Courant.* The only one before it, was *The Boston News Letter.* I remember his being dissuaded by some of his Friends from the Undertaking, as not likely to succeed, one Newspaper being in their Judgment enough for America. At this time 1771 there are not less than five and twenty. He went on however with the Undertaking, and after having work'd in composing the Types and printing off the Sheets I was employ'd to carry the Papers thro' the Streets to the Customers. He had some ingenious Men among his Friends who amus'd themselves by writing little Pieces for this Paper, which gain'd it Credit, and made it more in Demand; and these Gentlemen often visited us. Hearing their Conversations, and their Accounts of the Approbation their Papers were receiv'd with, I was excited to try my Hand among them. But being still a Boy, and suspecting that my Brother would object to printing any Thing of mine in his Paper if he knew it to be mine, I contriv'd to disguise my Hand, and writing an anonymous Paper I put it in at Night under the Door of the Printing-House.

It was found in the Morning and communicated to his Writing Friends when they call'd in as Usual. They read it, commented on it in my Hearing, and I had the exquisite Pleasure, of finding it met with their Approbation, and that in their different Guesses at the Author none were named but Men of some Character among us for Learning and Ingenuity. I suppose now that I was rather lucky in my Judges: And that perhaps they were not really so very good ones as I then esteem'd them. Encourag'd however by this, I wrote and convey'd in the same Way to the Press several more Papers,[6] which were equally approv'd, and I kept my Secret till my small Fund of Sense for such Performances was pretty well exhausted, and then I discovered[7] it; when I began to be considered a little more by my Brother's Acquaintance, and in a manner that did not quite please him, as he thought, probably with reason, that it tended to make me too vain. And perhaps this might be one Occasion of the Differences that we began to have about this Time. Tho' a Brother, he considered himself as my Master, and me as his Apprentice; and accordingly expected the same Services from me as he would from another; while I thought he demean'd me too much in some he requir'd of me, who from a Brother expected more Indulgence, Our Disputes were often brought before our Father, and I fancy I was either generally in the right, or else a better Pleader, because the Judgment was generally in my favor. But my Brother was passionate and had often beaten me, which I took extremely amiss; and thinking my Apprenticeship very tedious, I was continually wishing for some Opportunity of shortening it, which at length offered in a manner unexpected.[8]

One of the Pieces in our Newspaper, on some political Point which I have now forgotten, gave Offence to the Assembly. He was taken up, censur'd and imprison'd[9] for a Month by the Speaker's Warrant, I suppose because he would not discover his Author. I too was taken up and examin'd before the

5. Actually the fifth; James Franklin's paper appeared on August 7, 1721.
6. *The Silence Dogood Letters* (April 12–October 8, 1722) were the earliest essay series in America.
7. Revealed.
8. "I fancy his harsh and tyrannical Treatment of me,

might be a means of impressing me with that Aversion to arbitrary Power that has stuck to me thro' my whole Life" [Franklin's note].
9. On June 11, 1722, the *Courant* hinted that there was collusion between local authorities and pirates raiding off Boston Harbor. James Franklin was jailed

Council; but tho' I did not give them any Satisfaction, they contented themselves with admonishing me, and dismiss'd me; considering me perhaps as an Apprentice who was bound to keep his Master's Secrets. During my Brother's Confinement, which I resented a good deal, notwithstanding our private Differences, I had the Management of the Paper, and I made bold to give our Rulers some Rubs[1] in it, which my Brother took very kindly, while others began to consider me in an unfavorable Light, as a young Genius that had a Turn for Libeling and Satire.[2] My Brother's Discharge was accompanied with an Order of the House, (a very odd one) *that James Franklin should no longer print the Paper called the New England Courant.* There was a Consultation held in our Printing-House among his Friends what he should do in this Case. Some propos'd to evade the Order by changing the Name of the Paper; but my Brother seeing Inconveniences in that, it was finally concluded on as a better Way, to let it be printed for the future under the Name of *Benjamin Franklin.* And to avoid the Censure of the Assembly that might fall on him, as still printing it by his Apprentice, the Contrivance was, that my old Indenture should be return'd to me with a full Discharge on the Back of it, to be shown on Occasion; but to secure to him the Benefit of my Service I was to sign new Indentures for the Remainder of the Term, which were to be kept private. A very flimsy Scheme it was, but however it was immediately executed, and the Paper went on accordingly under my Name for several Months.[3] At length a fresh Difference arising between my Brother and me, I took upon me to assert my Freedom, presuming that he would not venture to produce the new Indentures. It was not fair in me to take this Advantage, and this I therefore reckon one of the first Errata[4] of my Life: But the Unfairness of it weigh'd little with me, when under the Impressions of Resentment, for the Blows his Passion too often urg'd him to bestow upon me. Tho' he was otherwise not an ill-natur'd Man: Perhaps I was too saucy and provoking.

When he found I would leave him, he took care to prevent my getting Employment in any other Printing-House of the Town, by going round and speaking to every Master, who accordingly refus'd to give me Work. I then thought of going to New York as the nearest Place where there was a Printer: and I was the rather inclin'd to leave Boston, when I reflected that I had already made myself a little obnoxious to the governing Party; and from the arbitrary Proceedings of the Assembly in my Brother's Case it was likely I might if I stay'd soon bring myself into Scrapes; and farther that my indiscreet Disputations about Religion began to make me pointed at with Horror by good People, as an Infidel or Atheist; I determin'd on the Point: but my Father now siding with my Brother, I was sensible that if I attempted to go openly, Means would be used to prevent me. My Friend Collins therefore undertook to manage a little for me. He agreed with the Captain of a New York Sloop for my Passage, under the Notion of my being a young Acquaintance of his that had got a naughty Girl with Child, whose Friends would compel me to marry her, and therefore I could not appear or come away publicly. So I sold some of my Books to raise a little Money, was taken on board privately, and as we had a fair Wind, in three Days I found myself in New York near 300 Miles from

from June 12 to July 7. "Assembly": Massachusetts legislative body; the lower house, with representatives elected by towns of the Massachusetts general court.
1. Insults, annoyances.

2. Satirizing.
3. The paper continued under Franklin's name until 1726, nearly three years after he left Boston.
4. Printer's term for errors (Latin).

home, a Boy of but 17, without the least Recommendation to or Knowledge of any Person in the Place, and with very little Money in my Pocket.

My Inclinations for the Sea, were by this time worn out, or I might now have gratified them. But having a Trade, and supposing myself a pretty good Workman, I offer'd my Service to the Printer of the Place, old Mr. William Bradford.[5] He could give me no Employment, having little to do, and Help enough already: But, says he, my Son at Philadelphia has lately lost his principal Hand, Aquila Rose, by Death. If you go thither I believe he may employ you. Philadelphia was 100 Miles farther. I set out, however, in a Boat for Amboy;[6] leaving my Chest and Things to follow me round by Sea. In crossing the Bay we met with a Squall that tore our rotten Sails to pieces, prevented our getting into the Kill,[7] and drove us upon Long Island. In our Way a drunken Dutchman, who was a Passenger too, fell overboard; when he was sinking I reach'd thro' the Water to his shock Pate[8] and drew him up so that we got him in again. His Ducking sober'd him a little, and he went to sleep, taking first out of his Pocket a Book which he desir'd I would dry for him. It prov'd to be my old favorite Author Bunyan's Pilgrim's Progress[9] in Dutch, finely printed on good Paper with copper Cuts,[1] a Dress better than I had ever seen it wear in its own Language. I have since found that it has been translated into most of the Languages of Europe, and suppose it has been more generally read than any other Book except perhaps the Bible. Honest John was the first that I know of who mix'd Narration and Dialogue, a Method of Writing very engaging to the Reader, who in the most interesting Parts finds himself as it were brought into the Company, and present at the Discourse. Defoe in his Crusoe, his Moll Flanders, Religious Courtship, Family Instructor, and other Pieces, has imitated it with Success.[2] And Richardson has done the same in his Pamela,[3] etc.

When we drew near the Island we found it was at a Place where there could be no Landing, there being a great Surf on the stony Beach. So we dropped Anchor and swung round towards the Shore. Some People came down to the Water Edge and hallow'd to us, as we did to them. But the Wind was so high and the Surf so loud, that we could not hear so as to understand each other. There were Canoes on the Shore, and we made Signs and hallow'd that they should fetch us, but they either did not understand us, or thought it impracticable. So they went away, and Night coming on, we had no Remedy but to wait till the Wind should abate, and in the mean time the Boatman and I concluded to sleep if we could, and so crowded into the Scuttle[4] with the Dutchman who was still wet, and the Spray beating over the Head of our Boat, leak'd thro' to us, so that we were soon almost as wet as he. In this Manner we lay all Night with very little Rest. But the Wind abating the next Day, we made a Shift to reach Amboy before Night, having been 30 hours on the

5. William Bradford (1663–1752), one of the first American printers and father of Andrew Bradford (1686–1742), Franklin's future competitor in Philadelphia.
6. Perth Amboy, New Jersey.
7. The narrow channel with separates Staten Island, New York, from New Jersey.
8. Shaggy head of hair.
9. See n. 3, p. 494.
1. Engravings.

2. Daniel Defoe (1659?–1731) published Robinson Crusoe in 1719, Moll Flanders in 1722, Religious Courtship in 1772, and The Family Instructor in 1715–18.
3. Samuel Richardson (1689–1761) published his novel Pamela: Or Virtue Rewarded in 1740. Franklin reprinted Richardson's first novel in 1744 and in doing so published the first novel in America.
4. A hole or opening in a ship's deck provided with a movable cover or lid.

Water without Victuals, or any Drink but a Bottle of filthy Rum: The Water
we sail'd on being salt.

In the Evening I found myself very feverish, and went ill to Bed. But having
read somewhere that cold Water drank plentifully was good for a Fever, I
follow'd the Prescription, sweat plentifully most of the Night, my Fever left
me, and in the Morning crossing the Ferry, proceeded on my Journey, on
foot, having 50 Miles to Burlington,[5] where I was told I should find Boats that
would carry me the rest of the Way to Philadelphia.

It rain'd very hard all the Day, I was thoroughly soak'd, and by Noon a good
deal tir'd, so I stopped at a poor Inn, where I stayed all Night, beginning now
to wish I had never left home. I cut so miserable a Figure too, that I found by
the Questions ask'd me I was suspected to be some runaway Servant, and in
danger of being taken up on that Suspicion. However I proceeded the next
Day, and got in the Evening to an Inn within 8 or 10 Miles of Burlington,
kept by one Dr. Browne.[6]

He entered into Conversation with me while I took some Refreshment, and
finding I had read a little, became very sociable and friendly. Our Acquaintance continu'd as long as he liv'd. He had been, I imagine, an itinerant
Doctor, for there was no Town in England, or Country in Europe, of which
he could not give a very particular Account. He had some Letters,[7] and was
ingenious, but much of an Unbeliever, and wickedly undertook some Years
after to travesty the Bible in doggerel Verse as Cotton had done Virgil.[8] By this
means he set many of the Facts in a very ridiculous Light, and might have
hurt weak minds if his Work had been publish'd: but it never was. At his
House I lay that Night, and the next Morning reach'd Burlington.—But had
the Mortification to find that the regular Boats were gone a little before my
coming, and no other expected to go till Tuesday, this being Saturday. Wherefore I return'd to an old Woman in the Town of whom I had bought Ginger-
bread to eat on the Water, and ask'd her Advice; she invited me to lodge at her
House till a Passage by Water should offer; and being tired with my foot Traveling, I accepted the Invitation. She understanding I was a Printer, would have
had me stay at that Town and follow my Business, being ignorant of the Stock
necessary to begin with. She was very hospitable, gave me a Dinner of Ox
Cheek with great Goodwill, accepting only of a Pot of Ale in return. And I
thought myself fix'd till Tuesday should come. However walking in the Evening by the Side of the River a Boat came by, which I found was going towards
Philadelphia with several People in her. They took me in, and as there was no
Wind, we row'd all the Way; and about Midnight not having yet seen the
City, some of the Company were confident we must have pass'd it, and would
row no farther, the others knew not where we were, so we put towards the
Shore, got into a Creek, landed near an old Fence with the Rails of which we
made a Fire, the Night being cold, in October, and there we remain'd till
Daylight. Then one of the Company knew the Place to be Cooper's Creek a
little above Philadelphia, which we saw as soon as we got out of the Creek,

5. Then the capital of West Jersey, about eighteen
miles north of Philadelphia.
6. Dr. John Browne (c. 1667–1737), innkeeper in
Burlington, and a noted religious skeptic as well as physician.

7. I.e., education.
8. Charles Cotton (1630–87), who parodied the first
and fourth books of the *Aeneid* in his *Scarronides*
(1664). The opening lines are: "I sing the Man (read it
who list), / A Trojan true as ever pissed."

and arriv'd there about 8 or 9 aClock, on the Sunday morning, and landed at the Market Street Wharf.[9]

I have been the more particular in this Description of my Journey, and shall be so of my first Entry into that City, that you may in your Mind compare such unlikely Beginning with the Figure I have since made there. I was in my working Dress, my best Clothes being to come round by Sea. I was dirty from my Journey; my Pockets were stuff'd out with Shirts and Stockings; I knew no Soul, nor where to look for Lodging. I was fatigu'd with Traveling, Rowing and Want of Rest. I was very hungry, and my whole Stock of Cash consisted of a Dutch Dollar and about a Shilling in Copper. The latter I gave the People of the Boat for my Passage, who at first refus'd it on Account of my Rowing; but I insisted on their taking it, a Man being sometimes more generous when he has but a little Money than when he has plenty, perhaps thro' Fear of being thought to have but little. Then I walk'd up the Street, gazing about, till near the Market House I met a Boy with Bread. I had made many a Meal on Bread, and inquiring where he got it, I went immediately to the Baker's he directed me to in Second Street; and ask'd for Biscuit, intending such as we had in Boston, but they it seems were not made in Philadelphia, then I ask'd for a three-penny Loaf, and was told they had none such: so not considering or knowing the Difference of Money and the greater Cheapness nor the Names of his Bread, I bad him give me three pennyworth of any sort. He gave me accordingly three great Puffy Rolls. I was surpris'd at the Quantity, but took it, and having no Room in my Pockets, walk'd off, with a Roll under each Arm, and eating the other. Thus I went up Market Street as far as Fourth Street, passing by the Door of Mr. Read, my future Wife's Father, when she standing at the Door saw me, and thought I made as I certainly did a most awkward ridiculous Appearance. Then I turn'd and went down Chestnut Street and part of Walnut Street, eating my Roll all the Way, and coming round found myself again at Market Street Wharf, near the Boat I came in, to which I went for a Drought of the River Water, and being fill'd with one of my Rolls, gave the other two to a Woman and her Child that came down the River in the Boat with us and were waiting to go farther. Thus refresh'd I walk'd again up the Street, which by this time had many clean dress'd People in it who were all walking the same Way; I join'd them, and thereby was led into the great Meeting House of the Quakers near the Market. I sat down among them, and after looking round a while and hearing nothing said, being very drowsy thro' Labor and want of Rest the preceding Night, I fell fast asleep, and continu'd so till the Meeting broke up, when one was kind enough to rouse me. This was therefore the first House I was in or slept in, in Philadelphia.

Walking again down towards the River, and looking in the Faces of People, I met a young Quaker Man whose Countenance I lik'd, and accosting him requested he would tell me where a Stranger could get Lodging. We were then near the Sign of the Three Mariners. Here, says he, is one Place that entertains Strangers, but it is not a reputable House; if thee wilt walk with me, I'll show thee a better. He brought me to the Crooked Billet in Water Street. Here I got a Dinner. And while I was eating it, several sly Questions were ask'd me, as it seem'd to be suspected from my youth and Appearance, that I might be some Runaway. After Dinner my Sleepiness return'd: and being shown to a Bed, I

9. October 6, 1723.

lay down without undressing, and slept till Six in the Evening; was call'd to Supper; went to Bed again very early and slept soundly till the next Morning. Then I made myself as tidy as I could, and went to Andrew Bradford the Printer's. I found in the Shop the old Man his Father, whom I had seen at New York, and who traveling on horse back had got to Philadelphia before me. He introduc'd me to his Son, who receiv'd me civilly, gave me a Breakfast, but told me he did not at present want a Hand, being lately supplied with one. But there was another Printer in town lately set up, one Keimer,[1] who perhaps might employ me; if not, I should be welcome to lodge at his House, and he would give me a little Work to do now and then till fuller Business should offer.

The old Gentleman said, he would go with me to the new Printer: And when we found him, Neighbor, says Bradford, I have brought to see you a young Man of your Business, perhaps you may want such a One. He ask'd me a few Questions, put a Composing Stick[2] in my Hand to see how I work'd, and then said he would employ me soon, tho' he had just then nothing for me to do. And taking old Bradford whom he had never seen before, to be one of the Townspeople that had a Goodwill for him, enter'd into a Conversation on his present Undertaking and Prospects; while Bradford not discovering that he was the other Printer's Father; on Keimer's Saying he expected soon to get the greatest Part of the Business into his own Hands, drew him on by artful Questions and starting little Doubts, to explain all his Views, what Interest he relied on, and in what manner he intended to proceed. I who stood by and heard all, saw immediately that one of them was a crafty old Sophister,[3] and the other a mere Novice. Bradford left me with Keimer, who was greatly surpris'd when I told him who the old Man was.

Keimer's Printing-House I found, consisted of an old shatter'd Press and one small worn-out Font of English,[4] which he was then using himself, composing in it an Elegy on Aquila Rose[5] before-mentioned, an ingenious young Man of excellent Character much respected in the Town, Clerk of the Assembly,[6] and a pretty Poet. Keimer made Verses, too, but very indifferently. He could not be said to write them, for his Manner was to compose them in the Types directly out of his Head; so there being no Copy, but one Pair of Cases,[7] and the Elegy likely to require all the Letter, no one could help him. I endeavor'd to put his Press (which he had not yet us'd, and of which he understood nothing) into Order fit to be work'd with; and promising to come and print off his Elegy as soon as he should have got it ready, I return'd to Bradford's who gave me a little Job to do for the present, and there I lodged and dieted.[8] A few Days after Keimer sent for me to print off the Elegy. And now he had got another Pair of Cases, and a Pamphlet to reprint, on which he set me to work.

These two Printers I found poorly qualified for their Business. Bradford had not been bred to it, and was very illiterate; and Keimer tho' something of a Scholar, was a mere Compositor, knowing nothing of Presswork. He had been one of the French Prophets[9] and could act their enthusiastic Agitations. At

1. Samuel Keimer (c. 1688–1742) was a printer in London before coming to Philadelphia.
2. An instrument of adjustable width in which type is set before being put on a galley.
3. Trickster, rationalizer.
4. An oversized type, not practicable for books and newspapers.
5. Journeyman printer (c. 1695–1723) for Andrew Bradford; his son Joseph apprenticed with Franklin.

6. One who has charge of the records, documents, and correspondence of any organized body; here, the Pennsylvania legislative council.
7. Two shallow trays that contain uppercase and lowercase type.
8. Boarded.
9. An English sect that preached doomsday and cultivated emotional fits.

this time he did not profess any particular Religion, but something of all on occasion; was very ignorant of the World, and had, as I afterwards found, a good deal of the Knave in his Composition. He did not like my Lodging at Bradford's while I work'd with him. He had a House indeed, but without Furniture, so he could not lodge me: But he got me a Lodging at Mr. Read's before-mentioned, who was the Owner of his House. And my Chest and Clothes being come by this time, I made rather a more respectable Appearance in the Eyes of Miss Read, than I had done when she first happen'd to see me eating my Roll in the Street.

I began now to have some Acquaintance among the young People of the Town, that were Lovers of Reading with whom I spent my Evenings very pleasantly and gaining Money by my Industry and Frugality, I lived very agreeably, forgetting Boston as much as I could, and not desiring that any there should know where I resided except my Friend Collins who was in my Secret, and kept it when I wrote to him. At length an Incident happened that sent me back again much sooner than I had intended.

I had a Brother-in-law, Robert Homes,[1] Master of a Sloop that traded between Boston and Delaware. He being at New Castle 40 Miles below Philadelphia, heard there of me, and wrote me a Letter, mentioning the Concern of my Friends in Boston at my abrupt Departure, assuring me of their Goodwill to me, and that everything would be accommodated to my Mind if I would return, to which he exhorted me very earnestly. I wrote an Answer to his Letter, thank'd him for his Advice, but stated my Reasons for quitting Boston fully, and in such a Light as to convince him I was not so wrong as he had apprehended. Sir William Keith[2] Governor of the Province, was then at New Castle, and Captain Homes happening to be in Company with him when my Letter came to hand, spoke to him of me, and show'd him the Letter. The Governor read it, and seem'd surpris'd when he was told my Age. He said I appear'd a young Man of promising Parts, and therefore should be encouraged: The Printers at Philadelphia were wretched ones, and if I would set up there, he made no doubt I should succeed; for his Part, he would procure me the public Business, and do me every other Service in his Power. This my Brother-in-Law afterwards told me in Boston. But I knew as yet nothing of it; when one Day Keimer and I being at Work together near the Window, we saw the Governor and another Gentleman (which prov'd to be Colonel French, of New Castle) finely dress'd, come directly across the Street to our House, and heard them at the Door.

Keimer ran down immediately, thinking it a Visit to him. But the Governor enquir'd for me, came up, and with a Condescension and Politeness I had been quite unus'd to, made me many Compliments, desired to be acquainted with me, blam'd me kindly for not having made myself known to him when I first came to the Place, and would have me away with him to the Tavern where he was going with Colonel French to taste as he said some excellent Madeira. I was not a little surpris'd, and Keimer star'd like a Pig poison'd. I went however with the Governor and Colonel French, to a Tavern the Corner of Third Street, and over the Madeira he propos'd my Setting up my Business, laid before me the Probabilities of Success, and both he and Colonel French assur'd me I should have their Interest and Influence in procuring the Public-

1. Husband of Franklin's sister Mary, and a ship's captain (d. before 1743).
2. Keith (1680–1749) was governor of Pennsylvania from 1717 to 1726; he fled to England in 1728 to escape debtor's prison.

Business of both Governments. On my doubting whether my Father would assist me in it, Sir William said he would give me a Letter to him, in which he would state the Advantages, and he did not doubt of prevailing with him. So it was concluded I should return to Boston in the first Vessel with the Governor's Letter recommending me to my Father.

In the meantime the Intention was to be kept secret, and I went on working with Keimer as usual, the Governor sending for me now and then to dine with him, a very great Honor I thought it, and conversing with me in the most affable, familiar, and friendly manner imaginable. About the End of April 1724, a little Vessel offer'd for Boston. I took Leave of Keimer as going to see my Friends. The Governor gave me an ample Letter, saying many flattering things of me to my Father, and strongly recommending the Project of my setting up at Philadelphia, as a Thing that must make my Fortune. We struck on a Shoal in going down the Bay and sprung a Leak, we had a blustring time at Sea, and were oblig'd to pump almost continually, at which I took my Turn. We arriv'd safe however at Boston in about a Fortnight. I had been absent Seven Months and my Friends had heard nothing of me, for my Brother Homes was not yet return'd; and had not written about me. My unexpected Appearance surpris'd the Family; all were however very glad to see me and made me Welcome, except my Brother.

I went to see him at his Printing-House: I was better dress'd than ever while in his Service, having a genteel new Suit from Head to foot, a Watch, and my Pockets lin'd with near Five Pounds Sterling in Silver. He receiv'd me not very frankly, look'd me all over, and turn'd to his Work again. The Journeymen were inquisitive where I had been, what sort of a Country it was, and how I lik'd it? I prais'd it much, and the happy Life I led in it; expressing strongly my Intention of returning to it; and one of them asking what kind of Money we had there, I produc'd a handful of Silver and spread it before them, which was a kind of Raree-Show[3] they had not been us'd to, Paper being the Money of Boston. Then I took an Opportunity of letting them see my Watch: and lastly, (my Brother still grum and sullen) I gave them a Piece of Eight to drink[4] and took my Leave. This Visit of mine offended him extremely. For when my Mother some time after spoke to him of a Reconciliation, and of her Wishes to see us on good Terms together, and that we might live for the future as Brothers, he said, I had insulted him in such a Manner before his People that he could never forget or forgive it. In this however he was mistaken.

My Father receiv'd the Governor's Letter with some apparent Surprise; but said little of it to me for some Days; when Captain Homes returning, he show'd it to him, ask'd if he knew Keith, and what kind of a Man he was: Adding his Opinion that he must be of small Discretion, to think of setting a Boy up in Business who wanted yet 3 Years of being at Man's Estate. Homes said what he could in favor of the Project; but my Father was clear in the Impropriety of it; and at last gave a flat Denial to it. Then he wrote a civil Letter to Sir William thanking him for the Patronage he had so kindly offered me, but declining to assist me as yet in Setting up, I being in his Opinion too young to be trusted with the Management of a Business so important; and for which the Preparation must be so expensive.

My Friend and Companion Collins, who was a Clerk at the Post-Office,

---

3. A sidewalk peep show; silver coins were rare in the colonies.

4. A Spanish dollar with which they could buy drinks.

pleas'd with the Account I gave him of my new Country, determin'd to go thither also: And while I waited for my Father's Determination,[5] he set out before me by Land to Rhode Island, leaving his Books which were a pretty Collection of Mathematics and Natural Philosophy,[6] to come with mine and me to New York where he propos'd to wait for me. My Father, tho' he did not approve Sir William's Proposition, was yet pleas'd that I had been able to obtain so advantageous a Character from a Person of such Note where I had resided, and that I had been so industrious and careful as to equip myself so handsomely in so short a time: therefore seeing no Prospect of an Accommodation between my Brother and me, he gave his Consent to my Returning again to Philadelphia, advis'd me to behave respectfully to the People there, endeavor to obtain the general Esteem, and avoid lampooning and libeling to which he thought I had too much Inclination; telling me, that by steady Industry and a prudent Parsimony, I might save enough by the time I was One and Twenty to set me up, and that if I came near the Matter he would help me out with the Rest. This was all I could obtain, except some small Gifts as Tokens of his and my Mother's Love, when I embark'd again for New York, now with their Approbation and their Blessing.

The Sloop putting in at Newport, Rhode Island, I visited my Brother John, who had been married and settled there some Years. He received me very affectionately, for he always lov'd me. A Friend of his, one Vernon, having some Money due to him in Pennsylvania, about 35 Pounds Currency, desired I would receive it for him, and keep it till I had his Directions what to remit it in. Accordingly he gave me an Order. This afterwards occasion'd me a good deal of Uneasiness. At Newport we took in a Number of Passengers for New York: Among which were two young Women, Companions, and a grave, sensible Matron-like Quaker-Woman with her Attendants. I had shown an obliging Readiness to do her some little Services which impress'd her I suppose with a degree of Goodwill towards me. Therefore when she saw a daily growing Familiarity between me and the two Young Women, which they appear'd to encourage, she took me aside and said, Young Man, I am concern'd for thee, as thou has no Friend with thee, and seems not to know much of the World, or of the Snares Youth is expos'd to; depend upon it those are very bad Women, I can see it in all their Actions, and if thee art not upon thy Guard, they will draw thee into some Danger: they are Strangers to thee, and I advise thee in a friendly Concern for thy Welfare, to have no Acquaintance with them. As I seem'd at first not to think so ill of them as she did, she mention'd some Things she had observ'd and heard that had escap'd my Notice; but now convinc'd me she was right. I thank'd her for her kind Advice, and promis'd to follow it. When we arriv'd at New York, they told me where they liv'd, and invited me to come and see them: but I avoided it. And it was well I did: For the next Day, the Captain miss'd a Silver Spoon and some other Things that had been taken out of his Cabin, and knowing that these were a Couple of Strumpets, he got a Warrant to search their Lodgings, found the stolen Goods, and had the Thieves punish'd. So tho' we had escap'd a sunken Rock which we scrap'd upon in the Passage, I thought this Escape of rather more Importance to me.

At New York I found my Friend Collins, who had arriv'd there some Time

5. Decision.

6. I.e., natural science.

before me. We had been intimate from[7] Children, and had read the same Books together. But he had the Advantage of more time for Reading, and Studying and a wonderful Genius for Mathematical Learning in which he far outstripped me. While I liv'd in Boston most of my Hours of Leisure for Conversation were spent with him, and he continu'd a sober as well as an industrious Lad; was much respected for his Learning by several of the Clergy and other Gentlemen, and seem'd to promise making a good Figure in Life: but during my Absence he had acquir'd a Habit of Sotting[8] with Brandy; and I found by his own Account and what I heard from others, that he had been drunk every day since his Arrival at New York, and behav'd very oddly. He had gam'd too and lost his Money, so that I was oblig'd to discharge[9] his Lodgings, and defray his Expences to and at Philadelphia: Which prov'd extremely inconvenient to me. The then Governor of New York, Burnet,[1] Son of Bishop Burnet, hearing form the Captain that a young Man, one of his Passengers, had a great many Books, desired he would bring me to see him. I waited upon him accordingly, and should have taken Collins with me but that he was not sober. The Governor treated me with great Civility, show'd me his Library, which was a very large one, and we had a good deal of Conversation about Books and Authors. This was the second Governor who had done me the Honor to take Notice of me, which to a poor Boy like me was very pleasing.

We proceeded to Philadelphia. I received on the Way Vernon's Money, without which we could hardly have finish'd our Journey. Collins wish'd to be employ'd in some Counting House; but whether they discover'd his Dramming by his Breath, or by his Behavior, tho' he had some Recommendations, he met with no Success in any Application, and continu'd Lodging and Boarding at the same House with me and at my Expense. Knowing I had that Money of Vernon's he was continually borrowing of me, still promising Repayment as soon as he should be in Business. At length he had got so much of it, that I was distress'd to think what I should do, in case of being call'd on to remit it. His Drinking continu'd, about which we sometimes quarrel'd, for when a little intoxicated he was very fractious. Once in a Boat on the Delaware with some other young Men, he refused to row in his Turn: I will be row'd home, says he. We will not row you, says I. You must, says he, or stay all Night on the Water, just as you please. The others said, Let us row; What signifies it? But my Mind being soured with his other Conduct, I continu'd to refuse. So he swore he would make me row, or throw me overboard; and coming along stepping on the Thwarts[2] towards me, when he came up and struck at me, I clapped my Hand under his Crotch, and rising, pitch'd him headforemost into the River. I knew he was a good Swimmer, and so was under little Concern about him; but before he could get round to lay hold of the Boat, we had with a few Strokes pull'd her out of his Reach. And ever when he drew near the Boat, we ask'd if he would row, striking a few Strokes to slide her away from him. He was ready to die with Vexation, and obstinately would not promise to row; however seeing him at last beginning to tire, we lifted him in; and brought him home dripping wet in the Evening. We hardly exchang'd a civil Word afterwards; and a West India Captain who had a Commission to procure a Tutor for the Sons of a Gentleman at Barbados,[3] happening to meet with

7. I.e., since.
8. Getting stupefied on.
9. To release him from debt by paying his bills.
1. William Burnet (1688–1729), governor of New York and New Jersey from 1720 to 1728, and governor of Massachusetts from 1728 to 1729.
2. The seat on which an oarsman sits.
3. Island in the British West Indies.

him, agreed to carry him thither. He left me then, promising to remit me the first Money he should receive in order to discharge the Debt. But I never heard of him after.

The Breaking into this Money of Vernon's was one of the first great Errata of my Life. And this Affair show'd that my Father was not much out in his Judgment when he suppos'd me too Young to manage Business of Importance. But Sir William, on reading his Letter, said he was too prudent. There was great Difference in Persons, and Discretion did not always accompany Years, nor was Youth always without it. And since he will not set you up, says he, I will do it myself. Give me an Inventory of the Things necessary to be had from England, and I will send for them. You shall repay me when you are able; I am resolv'd to have a good Printer here, and I am sure you must succeed. This was spoken with such an Appearance of Cordiality, that I had not the least doubt of his meaning what he said. I had hitherto kept the Proposition of my Setting up a Secret in Philadelphia, and I still kept it. Had it been known that I depended on the Governor, probably some Friend that knew him better would have advis'd me not to rely on him, as I afterwards heard it as his known Character to be liberal of Promises which he never meant to keep. Yet unsolicited as he was by me, how could I think his generous Offers insincere? I believ'd him one of the best Men in the World.

I presented him an Inventory of a little Printing-House, amounting by my Computation to about 100 Pounds Sterling. He lik'd it, but ask'd me if my being on the Spot in England to choose the Types and see that everything was good of the kind, might not be of some Advantage. Then, says he, when there, you may make Acquaintances and establish Correspondences in the Bookselling, and Stationery Way. I agreed that this might be advantageous. Then says he, get yourself ready to go with Annis;[4] which was the annual Ship, and the only one at that Time usually passing between London and Philadelphia. But it would be some Months before Annis sail'd, so I continu'd working with Keimer, fretting about the Money Collins had got from me, and in daily Apprehensions of being call'd upon by Vernon, which however did not happen for some Years after.

I believe I have omitted mentioning that in my first Voyage from Boston, being becalm'd off Block Island,[5] our People set about catching Cod and haul'd up a great many. Hitherto I had stuck to my Resolution of not eating animal Food; and on this Occasion, I consider'd with my Master Tryon, the taking every Fish as a kind of unprovok'd Murder, since none of them had or ever could do us any Injury that might justify the Slaughter. All this seem'd very reasonable. But I had formerly been a great Lover of Fish, and when this came hot out of the Frying Pan, it smelt admirably well. I balanc'd some time between Principle and Inclination: till I recollected, that when the Fish were opened, I saw smaller Fish taken out of their Stomachs: Then, thought I, if you eat one another, I don't see why we mayn't eat you. So I din'd upon Cod very heartily and continu'd to eat with other People, returning only now and then occasionally to a vegetable Diet. So convenient a thing it is to be a *reasonable Creature*, since it enables one to find or make a Reason for everything one has a mind to do.

Keimer and I liv'd on a pretty good familiar Footing and agreed tolerably well: for he suspected nothing of my Setting up. He retain'd a great deal of

4. Thomas Annis, captain of the *London Hope*, the packet boat on which Franklin sailed to London in 1724.

5. Off the coast of Rhode Island.

his old Enthusiasms, and lov'd an Argumentation. We therefore had many Disputations. I us'd to work him so with my Socratic Method, and had trapann'd[6] him so often by Questions apparently so distant from any Point we had in hand, and yet by degrees led to the Point, and brought him into Difficulties and Contradictions, that at last he grew ridiculously cautious, and would hardly answer me the most common Question, without asking first, *What do you intend to infer from that?* However it gave him so high an Opinion of my Abilities in the Confuting Way, that he seriously propos'd my being his Colleague in a Project he had of setting up a new Sect. He was to preach the Doctrines, and I was to confound all Opponents. When he came to explain with me upon the Doctrines, I found several Conundrums[7] which I objected to, unless I might have my Way a little too, and introduce some of mine. Keimer wore his Beard at full Length, because somewhere in the Mosaic Law it is said, *thou shalt not mar the Corners of thy Beard.*[8] He likewise kept the seventh-day Sabbath; and these two Points were Essentials with him. I dislik'd both, but agreed to admit them upon Condition of his adopting the Doctrine of using no animal Food. I doubt, says he, my Constitution will not bear that. I assur'd him it would, and that he would be the better for it. He was usually a great Glutton, and I promis'd myself some Diversion in half-starving him. He agreed to try the Practice if I would keep him Company. I did so and we held it for three Months. We had our Victuals dress'd and brought to us regularly by a Woman in the Neighborhood, who had from me a List of 40 Dishes to be prepar'd for us at different times, in all which there was neither Fish Flesh nor Fowl, and the Whim suited me the better at this time from the Cheapness of it, not costing us about 18 Pence Sterling each, per Week. I have since kept several Lents most strictly, leaving the common Diet for that, and that for the common, abruptly, without the least Inconvenience: So that I think there is little in the Advice of making those Changes by easy Gradations. I went on pleasantly, but Poor Keimer suffer'd grievously, tir'd of the Project, long'd for the Flesh Pots of Egypt,[9] and order'd a roast Pig. He invited me and two Women Friends to dine with him, but it being brought too soon upon table, he could not resist the Temptation, and ate it all up before we came.

I had made some Courtship during this time to Miss Read. I had a great Respect and Affection for her, and had some Reason to believe she had the same for me: but as I was about to take a long Voyage, and we were both very young, only a little above 18, it was thought most prudent by her Mother to prevent our going too far at present, as a Marriage if it was to take place would be more convenient after my Return, when I should be as I expected set up in my Business. Perhaps too she thought my Expectations not so well founded as I imagined them to be.

My chief Acquaintances at this time were, Charles Osborne, Joseph Watson, and James Ralph;[1] All Lovers of Reading. The two first were Clerks to an eminent Scrivener or Conveyancer in the Town, Charles Brockden;[2] the other

---

6. Trapped.
7. Puzzles, difficult questions.
8. "Ye shall not round the corners of your heads, neither shalt thou mar the corners of thy beard" (Leviticus 19.27). Keimer probably also wore his hair long.
9. "And the whole congregation of the children of Israel murmured against Moses and Aaron in the wilderness: And the children of Israel said unto them, Would to God we had died by the hand of the Lord in the land of Egypt, when we sat by the flesh pots, and when we did eat bread to the full" (Exodus 16.2–3).

1. Charles Osborne's dates are unknown. Joseph Watson died about 1728. James Ralph (c. 1695–1762) became well known as a political journalist.
2. Brockden (1683–1769) came to Philadelphia in 1706. "Conveyancer": one who draws up leases and deeds.

was Clerk to a Merchant. Watson was a pious sensible young Man, of great integrity. The others rather more lax in their Principles of Religion, particularly Ralph, who as well as Collins had been unsettled by me, for which they both made me suffer. Osborne was sensible, candid, frank, sincere, and affectionate to his Friends; but in literary Matters too fond of Criticizing. Ralph, was ingenious, genteel in his Manners, and extremely eloquent; I think I never knew a prettier Talker. Both of them great Admirers of Poetry, and began to try their Hands in little Pieces. Many pleasant Walks we four had together, on Sundays into the Woods near Skuylkill,[3] where we read to one another and conferr'd on what we read. Ralph was inclin'd to pursue the Study of Poetry, not doubting but he might become eminent in it and make his Fortune by it, alledging that the best Poets must when they first began to write, make as many Faults as he did. Osborne dissuaded him, assur'd him he had no Genius for Poetry, and advis'd him to think of nothing beyond the Business he was bred to; that in the mercantile way tho' he had no Stock, he might by his Diligence and Punctuality recommend himself to Employment as a Factor,[4] and in time acquire wherewith to trade on his own Account. I approv'd the amusing oneself with Poetry now and then, so far as to improve one's Language, but no farther. On this it was propos'd that we should each of us at our next Meeting produce a Piece of our own Composing, in order to improve by our mutual Observations, Criticisms and Corrections. As Language and Expression was what we had in View, we excluded all Considerations of Invention,[5] by agreeing that the Task should be a Version of the 18th Psalm, which describes the Descent of a Deity.[6] When the Time of our Meeting drew nigh, Ralph call'd on me first, and let me know his Piece was ready. I told him I had been busy, and having little Inclination had done nothing. He then show'd me his Piece for my Opinion; and I much approv'd it, as it appear'd to me to have great Merit. Now, says he, Osborne never will allow the least Merit in any thing of mine, but makes 1000 Criticisms out of mere Envy. He is not so jealous of you. I wish therefore you would take this Piece, and produce it as yours. I will pretend not to have had time, and so produce nothing. We shall then see what he will say to it. It was agreed, and I immediately transcrib'd it that it might appear in my own hand. We met.

Watson's Performance was read: there were some Beauties in it: but many Defects. Osborne's was read: It was much better. Ralph did it Justice, remark'd some Faults, but applauded the Beauties. He himself had nothing to produce. I was backward, seem'd desirous of being excus'd, had not had sufficient Time to correct; etc., but no Excuse could be admitted, produce I must. It was read and repeated; Watson and Osborne gave up the Contest; and join'd in applauding it immoderately. Ralph only made some Criticisms and propos'd some Amendments, but I defended my Text. Osborne was against Ralph, and told him he was no better a Critic than Poet; so he dropped the Argument. As they two went home together, Osborne express'd himself still more strongly in favor of what he thought my Production, having restrain'd himself before as he said, lest I should think it Flattery. But who would have imagin'd, says he, that Franklin had been capable of such a Performance; such Painting, such Force! such Fire! He has even improv'd the Original! In his common Conver-

---

3. Schuylkill River, at Philadelphia.
4. Business agent.
5. I.e., originality.

6. "He bowed the heavens also, and came down: and darkness was under his feet" (Psalm 18.9).

sation, he seems to have no Choice of Words; he hesitates and blunders; and yet, good God, how he writes!

When we next met, Ralph discover'd the Trick we had played him, and Osborne was a little laughed at. This Transaction fix'd Ralph in his Resolution of becoming a Poet. I did all I could to dissuade him from it, but he continu'd scribbling Verses, till *Pope*[7] cur'd him. He became however a pretty good Prose Writer. More of him hereafter. But as I may not have occasion again to mention the other two, I shall just remark here, that Watson died in my Arms a few Years after, much lamented, being the best of our Set. Osborne went to the West Indies, where he became an eminent Lawyer and made Money, but died young. He and I had made a serious Agreement, that the one who happen'd first to die, should if possible make a friendly Visit to the other, and acquaint him how he found things in that separate State. But he never fulfill'd his Promise.

The Governor, seeming to like my Company, had me frequently to his House; and his Setting me up was always mention'd as a fix'd thing. I was to take with me Letters recommendatory to a Number of his Friends, besides the Letter of Credit to furnish me with the necessary Money for purchasing the Press and Types, Paper, etc. For these Letters I was appointed to call at different times, when they were to be ready, but a future time was still[8] named. Thus we went on till the ship whose Departure too had been several times postponed was on the Point of sailing. Then when I call'd to take my Leave and receive the Letters, his Secretary, Dr. Bard,[9] came out to me and said the Governor was extremely busy, in writing, but would be down at New Castle[1] before the Ship, and there the Letters would be delivered to me.

Ralph, tho' married and having one Child, had determined to accompany me in this Voyage. It was thought he intended to establish a Correspondence, and obtain Goods to sell on Commission. But I found afterwards, that thro' some Discontent with his Wife's Relations, he purposed to leave her on their Hands, and never return again. Having taken leave of my Friends, and interchang'd some Promises with Miss Read, I left Philadelphia in the Ship, which anchor'd at New Castle. The Governor was there. But when I went to his Lodging, the Secretary came to me from him with the civilest Message in the World, that he could not then see me being engag'd in Business of the utmost Importance, but should send the Letters to me on board, wish'd me heartily a good Voyage and a speedy Return, etc. I return'd on board, a little puzzled, but still not doubting.

Mr. Andrew Hamilton,[2] a famous Lawyer of Philadelphia, had taken Passage in the same Ship for himself and Son: and with Mr. Denham[3] a Quaker Merchant, and Messrs. Onion and Russel Masters of an Iron Work in Maryland, had engag'd the Great Cabin; so that Ralph and I were forc'd to take up

---

7. In the 2nd edition of the *Dunciad* (1728), a poem that attacks ignorance of all kinds, Alexander Pope responded to Ralph's slur against him in *Sawney:* "Silence, ye Wolves: while Ralph to Cynthia howls. / And makes Night hideous—Answer him ye Owls" (book 3, lines 159–60). In the 1742 edition Pope included another dig at Ralph: "And see: The very Gazeteers give o'er, / Ev'n Ralph repents" (book 1, lines 215–16).
8. Always.
9. Patrick Bard, or Baird, resided in Philadelphia as port physician after 1720.

1. Delaware.
2. Andrew Hamilton (c. 1678–1741), American-born lawyer; his successful defense of John Peter Zenger against a charge of libel established freedom of the press in the colonies and earned for Hamilton the sobriquet "the Philadelphia Lawyer." His son James Hamilton (c. 1710–1783) was governor of Pennsylvania four times between 1748 and 1773.
3. Thomas Denham (d. 1728), merchant and benefactor, left Bristol, England, in 1715.

with a Berth in the Steerage: And none on board knowing us, were considered as ordinary Persons. But Mr. Hamilton and his Son (it was James, since Governor) return'd from New Castle to Philadelphia the Father being recall'd by a great Fee to plead for a seized Ship. And just before we sail'd Colonel French coming on board, and showing me great Respect, I was more taken Notice of, and with my Friend Ralph invited by the other Gentlemen to come into the Cabin, there being now Room. Accordingly we remov'd thither.

Understanding that Colonel French had brought on board the Governor's Dispatches, I ask'd the Captain for those Letters that were to be under my Care. He said all were put into the Bag together; and he could not then come at them; but before we landed in England, I should have an Opportunity of picking them out. So I was satisfied for the present, and we proceeded on our Voyage. We had a sociable Company in the Cabin, and lived uncommonly well, having the Addition of all Mr. Hamilton's Stores, who had laid in plentifully. In this Passage Mr. Denham contracted a Friendship for me that continued during his Life. The Voyage was otherwise not a pleasant one, as we had a great deal of bad Weather.

When we came into the Channel, the Captain kept his Word with me, and gave me an Opportunity of examining the Bag for the Governor's Letters. I found none upon which my Name was put, as under my Care; I pick'd out 6 or 7 that by the Handwriting I thought might be the promis'd Letters, especially as one of them was directed to Basket[4] the King's Printer, and another to some Stationer. We arriv'd in London the 24th of December, 1724. I waited upon the Stationer who came first in my Way, delivering the Letter as from Governor Keith. I don't know such a Person, says he: but opening the Letter, O, this is from Riddlesden;[5] I have lately found him to be a complete Rascal, and I will have nothing to do with him, nor receive any Letters from him. So putting the Letter into my Hand, he turn'd on his Heel and left me to serve some Customer. I was surprised to find these were not the Governor's Letters. And after recollecting and comparing Circumstances, I began to doubt his Sincerity. I found my Friend Denham, and opened the whole Affair to him. He let me into Keith's Character, told me there was not the least Probability that he had written any Letters for me, that no one who knew him had the smallest Dependence on him, and he laughed at the Notion of the Governor's giving me a Letter of Credit, having as he said no Credit to give. On my expressing some Concern about what I should do: He advis'd me to endeavor getting some Employment in the Way of my Business. Among the Printers here, says he, you will improve yourself; and when you return to America, you will set up to greater Advantage.

We both of us happen'd to know, as well as the Stationer, that Riddlesden the Attorney, was a very Knave. He had half ruin'd Miss Read's Father by drawing him in to be bound[6] for him. By his Letter it appear'd, there was a secret Scheme on foot to the Prejudice of Hamilton, (Suppos'd to be then coming over with us,) and that Keith was concern'd in it with Riddlesden. Denham, who was a Friend of Hamilton's, thought he ought to be acquainted with it. So when he arriv'd in England, which was soon after, partly from Resentment and Ill-Will to Keith and Riddlesden, and partly from Goodwill

---

4. John Baskett (d. 1742).
5. William Riddlesden (d. before 1733), well known in Maryland as a man of "infamy."

6. I.e., as a cosigner of a document and legally bound to be responsible for his debts.

to him: I waited on him, and gave him the Letter. He thank'd me cordially, the Information being of Importance to him. And from that time he became my Friend, greatly to my Advantage afterwards on many Occasions.

But what shall we think of a Governor's playing such pitiful Tricks, and imposing so grossly on a poor ignorant Boy! It was a Habit he had acquired. He wish'd to please everybody; and having little to give, he gave Expectations. He was otherwise an ingenious sensible Man, a pretty good Writer, and a good Governor for the People, tho' not for his Constituents the Proprietaries,[7] whose Instructions he sometimes disregarded. Several of our best Laws were of his Planning, and pass'd during his Administration.

Ralph and I were inseparable Companions. We took Lodgings together in Little Britain[8] at 3 shillings 6 pence per Week, as much as we could then afford. He found some Relations, but they were poor and unable to assist him. He now let me know his Intentions of remaining in London, and that he never meant to return to Philadelphia. He had brought no Money with him, the whole he could muster having been expended in paying his Passage. I had 15 Pistoles.[9] So he borrowed occasionally of me, to subsist while he was looking out for Business. He first endeavor'd to get into the Playhouse, believing himself qualified for an Actor; but Wilkes,[1] to whom he applied, advis'd him candidly not to think of that Employment, as it was impossible he should succeed in it. Then he propos'd to Roberts, a Publisher in Paternoster Row,[2] to write for him a Weekly Paper like the Spectator, on certain Conditions, which Roberts did not approve. Then he endeavor'd to get Employment as a Hackney Writer[3] to copy for the Stationers and Lawyers about the Temple[4] but could find no Vacancy.

I immediately got into Work at Palmer's, then a famous Printing-House in Bartholomew Close;[5] and here I continu'd near a Year. I was pretty diligent; but spent with Ralph a good deal of my Earnings in going to Plays and other Places of Amusement. We had together consum'd all my Pistoles, and now just rubb'd[6] on from hand to mouth. He seem'd quite to forget his Wife and Child, and I by degrees my Engagements with Miss Read, to whom I never wrote more than one Letter, and that was to let her know I was not likely soon to return. This was another of the great Errata of my Life, which I should wish to correct if I were to live it over again. In fact, by our Expenses, I was constantly kept unable to pay my Passage.

At Palmer's I was employ'd in Composing for the second Edition of Wollaston's Religion of Nature.[7] Some of his Reasonings not appearing to me well-founded, I wrote a little metaphysical Piece, in which I made Remarks on them. It was entitled, A Dissertation on Liberty and Necessity, Pleasure and Pain.[8] I inscrib'd it to my Friend Ralph. I printed a small Number. I occa-

7. Members of the Penn family were the Proprietors of Pennsylvania and the legal owners of the state. "Constituents": those who appointed him their representative; in this case, the Penn family, which retained control of Pennsylvania until the Revolution.
8. A street in London near St. Paul's Cathedral.
9. A Spanish gold coin worth approximately eighteen shillings.
1. Robert Wilks (1665?–1732), an Irish actor, dominated London theater life from 1709 to 1730.
2. The center of the London printing business.
3. A copyist.
4. The Inner and Middle Temples were two of four

buildings in London that were centers for the legal profession.
5. Just off Little Britain, and a square known for its printers and typesetters.
6. Proceeded with difficulty.
7. William Wollaston's Religion of Nature was first published in 1725. Franklin set the type for the 4th edition, which appeared in April 1726.
8. Franklin's pamphlet, of which only four copies are known to survive. By denying the existence of virtue and vice Franklin laid himself open to accusations of atheism.

sion'd my being more consider'd by Mr. Palmer, as a young Man of some Ingenuity, tho' he seriously expostulated with me upon the Principles of my Pamplet which to him appear'd abominable. My printing this Pamphlet was another Erratum.

While I lodg'd in Little Britain I made an Acquaintance with one Wilcox a Bookseller, whose Shop was at the next Door. He had an immense Collection of second-hand Books. Circulating Libraries were not then in Use; but we agreed that on certain reasonable Terms which I have now forgotten, I might take, read and return any of his Books. This I esteem'd a great Advantage, and I made as much Use of it as I could.

My Pamphlet by some means falling into the Hands of one Lyons,[9] a Surgeon, Author of a Book entitled *The Infallibility of Human Judgment*, it occasioned an Acquaintance between us; he took great Notice of me, call'd on me often, to converse on these Subjects, carried me to the Horns a pale Ale-House in [blank] Lane, Cheapside, and introduc'd me to Dr. Mandeville,[1] Author of the Fable of the Bees who had a Club there, of which he was the Soul, being a most facetious entertaining Companion. Lyons too introduc'd me to Dr. Pemberton, at Batson's Coffee House,[2] who promis'd to give me an Opportunity some time or other of seeing Sir Isaac Newton,[3] of which I was extremely desirous; but this never happened.

I had brought over a few Curiosities among which the principal was a Purse made of the Asbestos, which purifies by Fire. Sir Hans Sloane[4] heard of it, came to see me, and invited me to his House in Bloomsbury Square; where he show'd me all his Curiosities, and persuaded me to let him add that to the Number, for which he paid me handsomely.

In our House there lodg'd a young Woman, a Millener, who I think had a shop in the Cloisters.[5] She had been genteelly bred, was sensible and lively, and of most pleasing Conversation. Ralph read Plays to her in the Evenings, they grew intimate, she took another Lodging, and he follow'd her. They liv'd together some time, but he being still out of Business, and her Income not sufficient to maintain them with her Child, he took a Resolution of going from London, to try for a Country School, which he thought himself well qualified to undertake, as he wrote an excellent Hand, and was a Master of Arithmetic and Accounts. This however he deem'd a Business below him, and confident of future better Fortune when he should be unwilling to have it known that he once was so meanly employ'd, he chang'd his Name, and did me the Honor to assume mine. For I soon after had a Letter from him, acquainting me, that he was settled in a small Village in Berkshire, I think it was, where he taught reading and writing to 10 or a dozen Boys at 6 pence each per Week, recommending Mrs. T. to my Care, and desiring me to write to him directing for Mr. Franklin Schoolmaster at such a Place. He continu'd to write frequently, sending me large Specimens of an Epic Poem, which he was then composing, and desiring my Remarks and Corrections. These I gave

9. William Lyons, a surgeon and author of *The Infallibility, Dignity, and Excellence of Human Judgment* (1719).
1. Bernard Mandeville (c. 1670–1733), a Dutch physician and man of letters residing in London. His *Fable of the Bees* was published in 1714.
2. Batson's in Cornhill was a favorite meeting place of physicians. Henry Pemberton (1694–1771) was a friend of Isaac Newton's and a member of the Royal

Society.
3. Isaac Newton (1642–1727), best known for explaining the theories of gravity, light, and color, president of the Royal Society 1703–27.
4. Physician and naturalist (1660–1753), was the successor to Newton as president of the Royal Society; his library and museum served as the basis for the present collection at the British Museum.
5. Probably near St. Bartholomew's Church, London.

him from time to time, but endeavor'd rather to discourage his Proceeding. One of Young's Satires was then just publish'd.[6] I copied and sent him a great Part of it, which set in a strong Light the Folly of pursuing the Muses with any Hope of Advancement by them. All was in vain. Sheets of the Poem continu'd to come by every Post. In the mean time Mrs. T. having on his Account lost her Friends and Business, was often in Distresses, and us'd to send for me, and borrow what I could spare to help her out of them. I grew fond of her Company, and being at this time under no Religious Restraints, and presuming on my Importance to her, I attempted Familiarities, (another Erratum) which she repuls'd with a proper Resentment, and acquainted him with my Behavior. This made a Breach between us, and when he return'd again to London, he let me know he thought I had cancel'd all the Obligations he had been under to me. So I found I was never to expect his Repaying me what I lent to him or advanc'd for him. This was however not then of much Consequence, as he was totally unable. And in the Loss of his Friendship I found myself reliev'd from a Burden. I now began to think of getting a little Money beforehand; and expecting better Work, I left Palmer's to work at Watts's[7] near Lincoln's Inn Fields, a still greater Printing-House. Here I continu'd all the rest of my Stay in London.

At my first Admission into this Printing-House, I took to working at Press, imagining I felt a Want of the Bodily Exercise I had been us'd to in America, where Presswork is mix'd with Composing. I drank only Water; the other Workmen, near 50 in Number, were great Guzzlers of Beer. On occasion I carried up and down Stairs a large Form of Types[8] in each hand, when others carried but one in both Hands. They wonder'd to see from this and several Instances that the Water-American as they call'd me was *stronger* than themselves who drunk *strong*[9] Beer. We had an Alehouse Boy who attended always in the House to supply the Workmen. My Companion at the Press drank every day a Pint before Breakfast, a Pint at Breakfast with his Bread and Cheese; a Pint between Breakfast and Dinner; a Pint at Dinner; a Pint in the Afternoon about Six o'clock, and another when he had done his Day's Work. I thought it a detestable Custom. But it was necessary, he suppos'd, to drink *strong* Beer that he might be *strong* to labor. I endeavor'd to convince him that the Bodily Strength afforded by Beer could only be in proportion to the Grain or Flour of the Barley dissolved in the Water of which it was made; that there was more Flour in a Penny-worth of Bread, and therefore if he would eat that with a Pint of Water, it would give him more Strength than a Quart of Beer. He drank on however, and had 4 or 5 Shillings to pay out of his Wages every Saturday Night for that muddling Liquor; an Expense I was free from. And thus these poor Devils keep themselves always under.[1]

Watts after some Weeks desiring to have me in the Composing-Room, I left the Pressmen. A new *Bienvenu*[2] or Sum for Drink, being 5 Shillings, was demanded of me by the Compositors.[3] I thought it an Imposition, as I had paid below. The Master thought so too, and forbad my Paying it. I stood out two or three Weeks, was accordingly considered as an Excommunicate, and had so many little Pieces of private Mischief done me, by mixing my Sorts,[4]

6. Edward Young (1683–1765) published the first four parts of *Love of Fame, the Universal Passion* in 1725.
7. John Watts (c. 1678–1763).
8. Type set and locked in metal frames.
9. Intoxicating.

1. I.e., in poverty.
2. Welcome (French, literal trans.).
3. Typesetters.
4. Type, letters.

transposing my Pages, breaking my Matter,[5] etc., etc. if I were ever so little out of the Room, and all ascrib'd to the Chapel[6] Ghost, which they said ever haunted those not regularly admitted, that notwithstanding the Master's Protection, I found myself oblig'd to comply and pay the Money; convinc'd of the Folly of being on ill Terms with those one is to live with continually. I was now on a fair Footing with them, and soon acquir'd considerable Influence. I propos'd some reasonable Alterations in their Chapel Laws, and carried them against all Opposition. From my Example a great Part of them, left their muddling Breakfast of Beer and Bread and Cheese, finding they could with me be supplied from a neighboring House with a large Porringer of hot Water-gruel, sprinkled with Pepper, crumb'd with Bread, and a Bit of Butter in it, for the Price of a Pint of Beer, viz., three halfpence. This was a more comfortable as well as cheaper Breakfast, and kept their Heads clearer. Those who continu'd sotting with Beer all day, were often, by not paying, out of Credit at the Alehouse, and us'd to make Interest with me to get Beer, *their Light*, as they phras'd it, *being out*. I watch'd the Pay table on Saturday Night, and collected what I stood engag'd for them, having to pay some times near Thirty Shillings a Week on their Accounts. This and my being esteem'd a pretty good Riggite,[7] that is a jocular verbal Satirist, supported my Consequence in the Society. My constant Attendance, (I never making a St. Monday),[8] recommended me to the Master; and my uncommon Quickness at Composing, occasion'd my being put upon all Work of Dispatch, which was generally better paid. So I went on now very agreeably.

My Lodging in Little Britain being too remote, I found another in Duke Street opposite to the Romish Chapel.[9] It was two pair of Stairs backwards at an Italian Warehouse. A Widow Lady kept the House; she had a Daughter and a Maid Servant, and a Journeyman who attended the Warehouse, but lodg'd abroad. After sending to enquire my Character at the House where I last lodg'd, she agreed to take me in at the same Rate, 3 Shillings 6 Pence per Week, cheaper as she said from the Protection she expected in having a Man lodge in the House. She was a Widow, an elderly Woman, had been bred a Protestant, being a Clergyman's Daughter, but was converted to the Catholic Religion by her Husband, whose Memory she much revered, had lived much among People of Distinction, and knew a 1000 Anecdotes of them as far back as the Times of Charles the second. She was lame in her Knees with the Gout, and therefore seldom stirr'd out of her Room, so sometimes wanted Company; and hers was so highly amusing to me that I was sure to spend an Evening with her whenever she desired it. Our Supper was only half an Anchovy each, on a very little Strip of Bread and Butter, and half a Pint of Ale between us. But the Entertainment was in her Conversation. My always keeping good Hours, and giving little Trouble in the Family, made her unwilling to part with me; so that when I talk'd of a Lodging I had heard of, nearer my Business, for 2 Shillings a Week, which, intent as I now was on saving Money, made some Difference; she bid me not think of it, for she would abate me two Shillings a Week for the future, so I remain'd with her at 1 Shilling 6 Pence as long as I stayed in London.

5. Type set up for printing.
6. "A Printing House is always called a Chappel by the Workmen" [Franklin's note]. The workers set their own customs, practices, and fines.

7. One who makes fun of others.
8. Taking Monday off as if it were a religious holiday.
9. The Roman Catholic Chapel of St. Anselm and St. Cecilia.

In a Garret of her House there lived a Maiden Lady of 70 in the most retired Manner, of whom my Landlady gave me this Account, that she was a Roman Catholic, had been sent abroad when young and lodg'd in a Nunnery with an Intent of becoming a Nun: but the Country not agreeing with her, she return'd to England, where there being no Nunnery, she had vow'd to lead the Life of a Nun as near as might be done in those Circumstances: Accordingly She had given all her Estate to charitable Uses, reserving only Twelve Pounds a year to live on, and out of this Sum she still gave a great deal in Charity, living herself on Watergruel only, and using no Fire but to boil it. She had lived many Years in that Garret, being permitted to remain there gratis by successive catholic Tenants of the House below, as they deem'd it a Blessing to have her there. A Priest visited her, to confess her every Day. I have ask'd her, says my Landlady, how she, as she liv'd, could possibly find so much Employment for a Confessor? O, says she, it is impossible to avoid *vain Thoughts*. I was permitted once to visit her: She was cheerful and polite, and convers'd pleasantly. The Room was clean, but had no other Furniture than a Mattress, a Table with a Crucifix and Book, a Stool, which she gave me to sit on, and a Picture over the Chimney of *St. Veronica*,[1] displaying her Handkerchief with the miraculous Figure of Christ's bleeding Face on it, which she explain'd to me with great Seriousness. She look'd pale, but was never sick, and I give it as another Instance on how small an Income Life and Health may be supported.

At Watts's Printing-House I contracted an Acquaintance with an ingenious young Man, one Wygate, who having wealthy Relations, had been better educated than most Printers, was a tolerable Latinist, spoke French, and lov'd Reading. I taught him, and a Friend of his, to swim at twice going into the River, and they soon became good Swimmers. They introduc'd me to some Gentlemen from the Country who went to Chelsea by Water to see the College and Don Saltero's Curiosities.[2] In our Return, at the Request of the Company, whose Curiosity Wygate had excited, I stripped and leaped into the River, and swam from near Chelsea to Blackfriars,[3] performing on the Way many Feats of Activity both upon and under Water, that surpris'd and pleas'd those to whom they were Novelties. I had from a Child been ever delighted with this Exercise, had studied and practic'd all Thevenot's[4] Motions and Positions, added some of my own, aiming at the graceful and easy, as well as the Useful. All these I took this Occasion of exhibiting to the Company, and was much flatter'd by their Admiration. And Wygate, who was desirous of becoming a Master, grew more and more attach'd to me on that account, as well as from the Similarity of our Studies. He at length propos'd to me traveling all over Europe together, supporting ourselves every where by working at our Business. I was once inclin'd to it. But mentioning it to my good Friend Mr. Denham, with whom I often spent an Hour when I had Leisure, he dissuaded me from it; advising me to think only of returning to Pennsylvania, which he was now about to do.

I must record one Trait of this good Man's Character. He had formerly been in Business at Bristol, but fail'd in Debt to a Number of People, compounded[5]

1. According to tradition, as Christ bore the cross, St. Veronica wiped his face with a cloth that miraculously retained the image of his face.

2. James Salter was a former barber of Sir Hans Sloane; he kept supposed curios, like Job's tears and pieces of the True Cross, on view. He was dubbed Don

Saltero by the *Tatler*. "College": i.e., Chelsea Hospital, erected on the site of the former Chelsea College.

3. I.e., more than three miles.

4. Melchisédeck de Thevenot, *The Art of Swimming* (1699).

5. Settled part payment on his debts.

and went to America. There, by a close Application to Business as a Merchant, he acquir'd a plentiful Fortune in a few Years. Returning to England in the Ship with me, He invited his old Creditors to an Entertainment, at which he thank'd them for the easy Composition[6] they had favor'd him with, and when they expected nothing but the Treat, every Man at the first Remove[7] found under his Plate an Order on a Banker for the full Amount of the unpaid Remainder with Interest.

He now told me he was about to return to Philadelphia, and should carry over a great Quantity of Goods in order to open a Store there: He propos'd to take me over as his Clerk, to keep his Books (in which he would instruct me), copy his Letters, and attend the Store. He added, that as soon as I should be acquainted with mercantile Business he would promote me by sending me with a Cargo of Flour and Bread, etc., to the West Indies, and procure me Commissions from others; which would be profitable, and if I manag'd well, would establish me handsomely. The Thing pleas'd me, for I was grown tired of London, remember'd with Pleasure the happy Months I had spent in Pennsylvania, and wish'd again to see it. Therefore I immediately agreed, on the Terms of Fifty Pounds a Year, Pennsylvania Money; less indeed than my then Gettings as a Compositor, but affording a better Prospect.

I now took Leave of Printing, as I thought for ever, and was daily employ'd in my new Business; going about with Mr. Denham among the Tradesmen, to purchase various Articles, and see them pack'd up, doing Errands, calling upon Workmen to dispatch, etc., and when all was on board, I had a few Days' Leisure. On one of these Days I was to my Surprise sent for by a great Man I knew only by Name, a Sir William Wyndham and I waited upon him. He had heard by some means or other of my Swimming from Chelsey to Blackfriars, and of my teaching Wygate and another young Man to swim in a few Hours. He had two Sons about to set out on their Travels; he wish'd to have them first taught Swimming; and propos'd to gratify me handsomely if I would teach them. They were not yet come to Town and my Stay was uncertain, so I could not undertake it. But from this Incident I thought it likely, that if I were to remain in England and open a Swimming School, I might get a good deal of Money. And it struck me so strongly, that had the Overture been sooner made me, probably I should not so soon have returned to America. After Many Years, you and I had something of more Importance to do with one of these Sons of Sir William Wyndham,[8] become Earl of Egremont, which I shall mention in its Place.[9]

Thus I spent about 18 Months in London. Most Part of the Time, I work'd hard at my Business, and spent but little upon myself except in seeing Plays, and in Books. My Friend Ralph had kept me poor. He owed me about 27 Pounds; which I was now never likely to receive; a great Sum out of my small Earnings. I lov'd him notwithstanding, for he had many amiable Qualities. Tho' I had by no means improv'd my Fortune, I had pick'd up some very ingenious Acquaintance whose Conversation was of great Advantage to me, and I had read considerably.

We sail'd from Gravesend on the 23d of July 1726. For The Incidents of

6. Conditions for accepting a declaration of bankruptcy.
7. I.e., the first time the plates were cleared.
8. Chancellor of the exchequer and Tory leader in Parliament (1687–1740).
9. Franklin does not mention Charles Wyndham (1710–1763) again.

the Voyage, I refer you to my Journal, where you will find them all minutely related. Perhaps the most important Part of that Journal is the *Plan*[1] to be found in it which I formed at Sea for regulating my future Conduct in Life. It is the more remarkable, as being form'd when I was so young, and yet being pretty faithfully adhered to quite thro' to old Age. We landed in Philadelphia the 11th of October, where I found sundry Alterations. Keith was no longer Governor, being superseded by Major Gordon:[2] I met him walking the Streets as a common Citizen. He seem'd a little asham'd at seeing me, but pass'd without saying anything. I should have been as much asham'd at seeing Miss Read, had not her Friends despairing with Reason of my Return, after the Receipt of my Letter, persuaded her to marry another, one Rogers, a Potter, which was done in my Absence. With him however she was never happy, and soon parted from him, refusing to cohabit with him, or bear his Name. It being now said that he had another Wife. He was a worthless Fellow tho' an excellent Workman which was the Temptation to her Friends. He got into Debt, and ran away in 1727 or 28, went to the West Indies, and died there. Keimer had got a better House, a Shop well supplied with Stationery, plenty of new Types, a number of Hands tho' none good, and seem'd to have a great deal of Business.

Mr. Denham took a Store in Water Street, where we open'd our Goods. I attended the Business diligently, studied Accounts, and grew in a little Time expert at selling. We lodg'd and boarded together, he counsel'd me as a Father, having a sincere Regard for me: I respected and lov'd him: and we might have gone on together very happily: But in the Beginning of February 1726/7 when I had just pass'd my 21st Year, we both were taken ill. My Distemper was a Pleurisy,[3] which very nearly carried me off: I suffered a good deal, gave up the Point[4] in my own mind, and was rather disappointed when I found myself recovering; regretting in some degree that I must now sometime or other have all that disagreeable Work to do over again. I forget what his Distemper was. It held him a long time, and at length carried him off. He left me a small Legacy in a nuncupative Will,[5] as a Token of his Kindness for me, and he left me once more to the wide World. For the Store was taken into the Care of his Executors, and my Employment under him ended: My Brother-in-law Homes, being now at Philadelphia, advis'd my Return to my Business. And Keimer tempted me with an Offer of large Wages by the Year to come and take the Management of his Printing-House that he might better attend his Stationer's Shop. I had heard a bad Character of him in London, from his Wife and her Friends, and was not fond of having any more to do with him. I tried for farther Employment as a Merchant's Clerk; but not readily meeting with any, I clos'd again with Keimer.

I found in *his* House these Hands; Hugh Meredith[6] a Welsh-Pennsylvanian, 30 Years of Age, bred to Country Work: honest, sensible, had a great deal of solid Observation, was something of a Reader, but given to drink: Stephen Potts,[7] a young Country Man of full Age, bred to the Same, of uncommon natural Parts[8] and great Wit and Humor, but a little idle. These he had agreed with at extreme low Wages, per Week, to be rais'd a Shilling every 3 Months,

1. Only the "Outline" and "Preamble" of Franklin's *Plan* survive.
2. Patrick Gordon (1644–1736), governor of Pennsylvania from 1726 to 1736.
3. A disease of the lungs.
4. End; i.e., resigned himself to death.

5. An oral will.
6. Hugh Meredith (c. 1696–1749), later a business partner of Franklin's.
7. Later a bookseller and innkeeper (d. 1758).
8. I.e., handsome.

as they would deserve by improving in their Business, and the Expectation of these high Wages to come on hereafter was what he had drawn them in with. Meredith was to work at Press, Potts at Bookbinding, which he by Agreement, was to teach them, tho' he knew neither one nor t'other. John ———— a wild Irishman brought up to no Business, whose Service for 4 Years Keimer had purchas'd[9] from the Captain of a Ship. He too was to be made a Pressman. George Webb,[1] an Oxford Scholar, whose Time for 4 Years he had likewise bought, intending him for a Compositor: of whom more presently. And David Harry,[2] a Country Boy, whom he had taken Apprentice. I soon perceiv'd that the Intention of engaging me at Wages so much higher than he had been us'd to give, was to have these raw cheap Hands form'd thro' me, and as soon as I had instructed them, then, they being all articled to him, he should be able to do without me. I went on however, very cheerfully; put his Printing-House in Order, which had been in great Confusion, and brought his Hands by degrees to mind their Business and to do it better.

It was an odd Thing to find an Oxford Scholar in the Situation of a bought Servant. He was not more than 18 Years of Age, and gave me this Account of himself; that he was born in Gloucester, educated at a Grammar School there, had been distinguish'd among the Scholars for some apparent Superiority in performing his Part when they exhibited Plays; belong'd to the Witty Club there, and had written some Pieces in Prose and Verse which were printed in the Gloucester Newspapers. Thence he was sent to Oxford; there he continu'd about a Year, but not well-satisfied, wishing of all things to see London and become a Player. At length receiving his Quarterly Allowance of 15 Guineas, instead of discharging his Debts, he walk'd out of Town, hid his Gown in a Furz Bush,[3] and footed it to London, where having no Friend to advise him, he fell into bad Company, soon spent his Guineas, found no means of being introduc'd among the Players, grew necessitous, pawn'd his Clothes and wanted Bread. Walking the Street very hungry, and not knowing what to do with himself, a Crimp's Bill[4] was put into his Hand, offering immediate Entertainment and Encouragement to such as would bind themselves to serve in America. He went directly, sign'd the Indentures, was put into the Ship and came over; never writing a Line to acquaint his Friends what was become of him. He was lively, witty, good-natur'd and a pleasant Companion, but idle, thoughtless and imprudent to the last Degree.

John the Irishman soon ran away. With the rest I began to live very agreeably; for they all respected me, the more as they found Keimer incapable of instructing them, and that from me they learned something daily. We never work'd on a Saturday, that being Keimer's Sabbath. So I had two Days for Reading. My Acquaintance with ingenious People in the Town increased. Keimer himself treated me with great Civility and apparent Regard; and nothing now made me uneasy but my Debt to Vernon, which I was yet unable to pay, being hitherto but a poor Economist. He however kindly made no Demand of it.

Our Printing-House often wanted Sorts,[5] and there was no Letter Founder in America. I had seen Types cast at James's[6] in London, but without much

---

9. I.e., Keimer had paid for his passage in exchange for his service.
1. Later a member of Franklin's Junto Club and printer (1708–1736?).
2. A Welsh Quaker (1708–1760) and later first printer in the Barbados.

3. An evergreen shrub; gorse. "Gown": academic robe worn regularly by Oxford students.
4. An advertisement for free passage to the colonies for those who would work as indentured servants.
5. Letters of type.
6. Thomas James's foundry in London.

Attention to the Manner: However I now contriv'd a Mold, made use of the Letters we had as Puncheons, struck the Matrices[7] in Lead, and thus supplied in a pretty tolerable way all Deficiencies. I also engrav'd several Things on occasion. I made the Ink, I was Warehouse-man and everything, in short quite a Factotum.[8]

But however serviceable I might be, I found that my Services became every Day of less Importance, as the other Hands improv'd in the Business. And when Keimer paid my second Quarter's Wages, he let me know that he felt them too heavy, and thought I should make an Abatement. He grew by degrees less civil, put on more of the Master, frequently found Fault, was captious and seem'd ready for an Out-breaking. I went on nevertheless with a good deal of Patience, thinking that his encumber'd Circumstances were partly the Cause. At length a Trifle snapped our Connection. For a great Noise happening near the Courthouse, I put my Head out of the Window to see what was the Matter. Keimer being in the Street look'd up and saw me, call'd out to me in a loud Voice and angry Tone to mind my Business, adding some reproachful Words, that nettled me the more for their Publicity, all the Neighbors who were looking out on the same Occasion being Witnesses how I was treated. He came up immediately into the Printing-House, continu'd the Quarrel, high Words pass'd on both Sides, he gave me the Quarter's Warning we had stipulated, expressing a Wish that he had not been oblig'd to so long a Warning: I told him his Wish was unnecessary for I would leave him that Instant; and so taking my Hat walk'd out of Doors; desiring Meredith whom I saw below to take care of some Things I left, and bring them to my Lodging.

Meredith came accordingly in the Evening, when we talk'd my Affair over. He had conceiv'd a great Regard for me, and was very unwilling that I should leave the House while he remain'd in it. He dissuaded me from returning to my native Country[9] which I began to think of. He reminded me that Keimer was in debt for all he possess'd, that his Creditors began to be uneasy, that he kept his Shop miserably, sold often without Profit for ready Money, and often trusted without keeping Account. That he must therefore fail; which would make a Vacancy I might profit of. I objected my Want of Money. He then let me know, that his Father had a high Opinion of me, and from some Discourse that had pass'd between them, he was sure would advance Money to set us up, if I would enter into Partnership with him. My Time, says he, will be out with Keimer in the Spring. By that time we may have our Press and Types in from London: I am sensible I am no Workman. If you like it, Your Skill in the Business shall be set against the Stock I furnish; and we will share the Profits equally.—The Proposal was agreeable, and I consented. His Father was in Town, and approv'd of it, the more as he saw I had great Influence with his Son, had prevail'd on him to abstain long from Dramdrinking,[1] and he hop'd might break him of that wretched Habit entirely, when we came to be so closely connected. I gave an Inventory to the Father, who carried it to a Merchant; the Things were sent for; the Secret was to be kept till they should arrive, and in the mean time I was to get Work if I could at the other Printing-House. But I found no Vacancy there, and so remain'd idle a few Days, when

---

7. Molds for casting types. "Puncheons": stamping tools.
8. Jack-of-all-trades.

9. I.e., Boston.
1. Frequently drinking small measures of alcohol.

Keimer, on a Prospect of being employ'd to print some Paper-money, in New Jersey, which would require Cuts and various Types that I only could supply, and apprehending Bradford might engage me and get the Job from him, sent me a very civil Message, that old Friends should not part for a few Words, the Effect of sudden Passion, and wishing me to return. Meredith persuaded me to comply, as it would give more Opportunity for his Improvement under my daily Instructions. So I return'd, and we went on more smoothly than for some time before. The New Jersey Job was obtain'd. I contriv'd a Copper-Plate Press for it, the first that had been seen in the Country. I cut several Ornaments and Checks for the Bills. We went together to Burlington,[2] where I executed the Whole to Satisfaction, and he received so large a Sum for the Work, as to be enabled thereby to keep his Head much longer above Water.

At Burlington I made an Acquaintance with many principal People of the Province. Several of them had been appointed by the Assembly a Committee to attend the Press, and take Care that no more Bills were printed than the Law directed. They were therefore by Turns constantly with us, and generally he who attended brought with him a Friend or two for Company. My Mind having been much more improv'd by Reading than Keimer's, I suppose it was for that Reason my Conversation seem'd to be more valu'd. They had me to their Houses, introduc'd me to their Friends and show'd me much Civility, while he, tho' the Master, was a little neglected. In truth he was an odd Fish, ignorant of common Life, fond of rudely opposing receiv'd Opinions, slovenly to extreme dirtiness, enthusiastic[3] in some Points of Religion, and a little Knavish withal. We continu'd there near 3 Months, and by that time I could reckon among my acquired Friends, Judge Allen, Samuel Bustill, the Secretary of the Province, Isaac Pearson, Joseph Cooper and several of the Smiths, Members of Assembly, and Isaac Decow the Surveyor General. The latter was a shrewd sagacious old Man, who told me that he began for himself when young by wheeling Clay for the Brickmakers, learned to write after he was of Age, carried the Chain for Surveyors, who taught him Surveying, and he had now by his Industry acquir'd a good Estate; and says he, I foresee, that you will soon work this Man out of his Business and make a Fortune in it at Philadelphia. He had not then the least Intimation of my Intention to set up there or anywhere. These Friends were afterwards of great Use to me, as I occasionally was to some of them. They all continued their Regard for me as long as they lived.

Before I enter upon my public Appearance in Business, it may be well to let you know the then State of my Mind, with regard to my Principles and Morals, that you may see how far those influenc'd the future Events of my Life. My Parents had early given me religious Impressions, and brought me through my Childhood piously in the Dissenting Way.[4] But I was scarce 15 when, after doubting by turns of several Points as I found them disputed in the different Books I read, I began to doubt of Revelation itself. Some Books against Deism fell into my Hands; they were said to be the Substance of Sermons preached at Boyle's Lectures.[5] It happened that they wrought an Effect on me quite contrary to what was intended by them: For the Arguments of the Deists which

2. New Jersey.
3. Highly emotional.
4. I.e., in the Congregational or Presbyterian way, as opposed to the Church of England.
5. Robert Boyle (1627–1691), English physicist and chemist, endowed annual lectures for preaching eight sermons a year against "infidels." Deism accepts a supreme being as the author of finite existence, but denies Christian doctrines of revelation and supernaturalism.

were quoted to be refuted, appeared to me much Stronger than the Refutations. In short I soon became a thorough Deist. My Arguments perverted some others, particularly Collins and Ralph: but each of them having afterwards wrong'd me greatly without the least Compunction, and recollecting Keith's Conduct towards me, (who was another Freethinker) and my own towards Vernon and Miss Read which at Times gave me great Trouble, I began to suspect that this Doctrine tho' it might be true, was not very useful. My London pamphlet, which had for its Motto those Lines of Dryden

> ———Whatever is, is right
> Tho' purblind Man Sees but a Part of
> The Chain, the nearest Link,
> His Eyes not carrying to the equal Beam,
> That poizes all, above.[6]

And from the Attributes of God, his infinite Wisdom, Goodness and Power concluded that nothing could possibly be wrong in the World, and that Vice and Virtue were empty Distinctions, no such Things existing: appear'd now not so clever a Performance as I once thought it; and I doubted whether some Error had not insinuated itself unperceiv'd into my Argument, so as to infect all that follow'd, as is common in metaphysical Reasonings. I grew convinc'd that *Truth*, *Sincerity* and *Integrity* in Dealings between Man and Man, were of the utmost Importance to the Felicity of Life, and I form'd written Resolutions, (which still remain in my Journal Book) to practice them ever while I lived. Revelation had indeed no weight with me as such; but I entertain'd an Opinion, that tho' certain Actions might not be bad *because* they were forbidden by it, or good *because* it commanded them; yet probably those Actions might be forbidden *because* they were bad for us, or commanded *because* they were beneficial to us, in their own Natures, all the Circumstances of things considered. And this Persuasion, with the kind hand of Providence, or some guardian Angel, or accidental favorable Circumstances and Situations, or all together, preserved me (thro' this dangerous Time of Youth and the hazardous Situations I was sometimes in among Strangers, remote from the Eye and Advice of my Father) without any *willful* gross Immorality or Injustice that might have been expected from my Want of Religion. I say *willful*, because the Instances I have mentioned, had something of *Necessity* in them, from my Youth, Inexperience, and the Knavery of others. I had therefore a tolerable Character to begin the World with, I valued it properly, and determin'd to preserve it.

We had not been long return'd to Philadelphia, before the New Types arriv'd from London. We settled with Keimer, and left him by his Consent before he heard of it. We found a House to hire near the Market, and took it. To lessen the Rent, (which was then but 24 Pounds a Year tho' I have since known it let for 70) we took in Thomas Godfrey a Glazier,[7] and his Family, who were to pay a considerable Part of it to us, and we to board with them. We had scarce opened our Letters and put our Press in Order, before George House, an Acquaintance of mine, brought a Countryman to us; whom he had met in the Street enquiring for a Printer. All our Cash was now expended in the Variety of Particulars we had been obliged to procure, and this Country-

---

6. The first line is not from John Dryden (1631–1700) but from Alexander Pope's *Essay on Man* (1733), Epistle I, line 294; however, Dryden's line is close: "Whatever is, is in its Causes just." The rest of the poem is recalled accurately from Dryden's *Oedipus* (3.1.244–48).

7. A man who sets glass for windowpanes.

man's Five Shillings, being our First Fruits and coming so seasonably, gave me more Pleasure than any Crown[8] I have since earn'd; and from the Gratitude I felt towards House, has made me often more ready than perhaps I should otherwise have been to assist young Beginners.

There are Croakers in every Country always boding its Ruin. Such a one then lived in Philadelphia, a Person of Note, an elderly Man, with a wise Look and very grave Manner of Speaking. His Name was Samuel Mickle. This Gentleman, a Stranger to me, stopped one Day at my Door, and ask'd me if I was the young Man who had lately opened a new Printing-House: Being answer'd in the Affirmative; He said he was sorry for me; because it was an expensive Undertaking, and the Expense would be lost, for Philadelphia was a sinking[9] Place, the People already half Bankrupts or near being so; all Appearances of the contrary such as new Buildings and the Rise of Rents, being to his certain Knowledge fallacious, for they were in fact among the Things that would soon ruin us. And he gave me such a Detail of Misfortunes now existing or that were soon to exist, that he left me half-melancholy. Had I known him before I engag'd in this Business, probably I never should have done it. This Man continu'd to live in this decaying Place, and to declaim in the same Strain, refusing for many Years to buy a House there, because all was going to Destruction, and at last I had the Pleasure of seeing him give five times as much for one as he might have bought it for when he first began his Croaking.

I should have mention'd before, that in the Autumn of the preceding Year, I had form'd most of my ingenious Acquaintance into a Club, for mutual Improvement, which we call'd the Junto.[1] We met on Friday Evenings. The Rules I drew up, requir'd that every Member in his Turn should produce one or more Queries on any Point of Morals, Politics or Natural Philosophy, to be discuss'd by the Company, and once in three Months produce and read an Essay of his own Writing on any Subject he pleased. Our Debates were to be under the Direction of a President, and to be conducted in the sincere Spirit of Enquiry after Truth, without fondness for Dispute, or Desire of Victory; and to prevent Warmth, all expressions of Positiveness in Opinion, or of direct Contradiction, were after some time made contraband and prohibited under small pecuniary Penalties. The first Members were, Joseph Breintnall,[2] a Copier of Deeds for the Scriveners; a good-natur'd friendly middle-ag'd Man, a great Lover of Poetry, reading all he could meet with, and writing some that was tolerable; very ingenious in many little Nicknackeries, and of sensible Conversation. Thomas Godfrey,[3] a self-taught Mathematician, great in his Way, and afterwards Inventor of what is now call'd Hadley's Quadrant.[4] But he knew little out of his way, and was not a pleasing Companion, as like most Great Mathematicians I have met with, he expected unusual Precision in everything said, or was forever denying or distinguishing upon Trifles, to the Disturbance of all Conversation. He soon left us. Nicholas Scull,[5] a Surveyor, afterwards Surveyor-General, Who lov'd Books, and sometimes made a few Verses. William Parsons,[6] bred a Shoemaker, but loving Reading, had acquir'd a considerable Share of Mathematics, which he first studied with a

---

8. A coin worth five shillings.
9. Economically declining.
1. I.e., a small, select group (the name is taken from the Spanish word *junta*, or fraternity).
2. Brientnal (d. 1746) shared Franklin's interest in science.

3. Godfrey (1704–1749).
4. An instrument for measuring altitudes in navigation and astronomy.
5. Nicholas Scull II (1687–1761).
6. Became surveyor general in 1741 and librarian of the Library Company (1701–1757).

View to Astrology that he afterwards laughed at. He also became Surveyor General. William Maugridge,[7] a Joiner, and a most exquisite Mechanic, and a solid sensible Man. Hugh Meredith, Stephen Potts, and George Webb, I have Characteris'd before. Robert Grace,[8] a young Gentleman of some Fortune, generous, lively and witty, a Lover of Punning and of his Friends. And William Coleman,[9] then a Merchant's Clerk, about my Age, who had the coolest clearest Head, the best Heart, and the exactest Morals, of almost any Man I ever met with. He became afterwards a Merchant of great Note, and one of our Provincial Judges: Our Friendship continued without Interruption to his Death, upwards of 40 Years. And the Club continu'd almost as long and was the best School of Philosophy, Morals and Politics that then existed in the Province; for our Queries which were read the Week preceding their Discussion, put us on reading with Attention upon the several Subjects, that we might speak more to the purpose: and here too we acquired better Habits of Conversation, everything being studied in our Rules which might prevent our disgusting each other. From hence the long Continuance of the Club, which I shall have frequent Occasion to speak farther of hereafter; But my giving this Account of it here, is to show something of the Interest I had, everyone of these exerting themselves in recommending Business to us.

Breintnall particularly procur'd us from the Quakers, the Printing 40 Sheets of their History, the rest being to be done by Keimer: and upon this we work'd exceeding hard, for the Price was low. It was a Folio, Pro Patria Size, in Pica with Long Primer Notes.[1] I compos'd of it a Sheet a Day, and Meredith work'd it off at Press. It was often 11 at Night and sometimes later, before I had finish'd my Distribution[2] for the next day's Work: For the little Jobs sent in by our other Friends now and then put us back. But so determin'd I was to continue doing a Sheet a Day of the Folio, that one Night when having impos'd my Forms,[3] I thought my Day's Work over, one of them by accident was broken and two Pages reduc'd to Pie,[4] I immediately distributed and compos'd it over again before I went to bed. And this Industry visible to our Neighbors began to give us Character and Credit; particularly I was told, that mention being made of the new Printing Office at the Merchants' Every-night-Club, the general Opinion was that it must fail, there being already two Printers in the Place, Keimer and Bradford; but Doctor Baird (whom you and I saw many Years after at his native Place, St. Andrews in Scotland) gave a contrary Opinion; for the Industry of that Franklin, says he, is superior to anything I ever saw of the kind: I see him still at work when I go home from Club; and he is at Work again before his Neighbors are out of bed. This struck the rest, and we soon after had Offers from one of them to supply us with Stationery. But as yet we did not choose to engage in Shop Business.

I mention this Industry the more particularly and the more freely, tho' it seems to be talking in my own Praise, that those of my Posterity who shall read it, may know the Use of that Virtue, when they see its Effects in my Favor throughout this Relation.

George Webb, who had found a Friend that lent him wherewith to purchase

7. A ship's carpenter (d. 1766).
8. Franklin's landlord for thirty-seven years (1709–1766).
9. Coleman (1704–1769).
1. A book of large size, with the main text in twelve-point type and the notes in ten-point type.

2. I.e., of type, returning letters to their cases so that they may be used again.
3. Locked the type into its form and readied it for printing.
4. A confused pile.

his Time of Keimer, now came to offer himself as a Journeyman to us. We could not then employ him, but I foolishly let him know, as a Secret, that I soon intended to begin a Newspaper, and might then have Work for him. My Hopes of Success as I told him were founded on this, that the then only Newspaper,[5] printed by Bradford was a paltry thing, wretchedly manag'd, no way entertaining; and yet was profitable to him. I therefore thought a good Paper could scarcely fail of good Encouragement. I requested Webb not to mention it, but he told it to Keimer, who immediately, to be beforehand with me, published Proposals for Printing one himself, on which Webb was to be employ'd. I resented this, and to counteract them, as I could not yet begin our Paper, I wrote several Pieces of Entertainment for Bradford's Paper, under the Title of the Busy Body which Breintnall continu'd some Months.[6] By this means the Attention of the Public was fix'd on that Paper, and Keimer's Proposals which we burlesqu'd and ridicul'd, were disregarded. He began his Paper however, and after carrying it on three Quarters of a Year, with at most only 90 Subscribers, he offer'd it to me for a Trifle, and I having been ready some time to go on with it, took it in hand directly, and it prov'd in a few Years extremely profitable to me.[7]

I perceive that I am apt to speak in the singular Number, though our Partnership still continu'd. The Reason may be, that in fact the whole Management of the Business lay upon me. Meredith was no Compositor, a poor Pressman, and seldom sober. My Friends lamented my Connection with him, but I was to make the best of it.

Our first Papers made a quite different Appearance from any before in the Province, a better Type and better printed: but some spirited Remarks of my Writing on the Dispute then going on between Governor Burnet[8] and the Massachusetts Assembly, struck the principal People, occasion'd the Paper and the Manager of it to be much talk'd of, and in a few Weeks brought them all to be our Subscribers. Their Example was follow'd by many, and our Number went on growing continually. This was one of the first good Effects of my having learned a little to scribble. Another was, that the leading Men, seeing a Newspaper now in the hands of one who could also handle a Pen, thought it convenient to oblige and encourage me. Bradford still printed the Votes and Laws and other Public Business. He had printed an Address of the House[9] to the Governor in a coarse blundering manner; We reprinted it elegantly and correctly, and sent one to every Member. They were sensible of the Difference, it strengthen'd the Hands of our Friends in the House, and they voted us their Printers for the Year ensuing.

Among my Friends in the House I must not forget Mr. Hamilton[1] beforementioned, who was then returned from England and had a Seat in it. He interested himself[2] for me strongly in that Instance, as he did in many others afterwards, continuing his Patronage till his Death. Mr. Vernon about this time put me in mind of the Debt I ow'd him: but did not press me. I wrote him an ingenuous Letter of Acknowledgments, crav'd his Forbearance a little

5. The American Weekly Mercury.
6. From February 4, 1728, to September 25, 1729.
7. Franklin took over Keimer's The Universal Instructor in All Arts and Sciences: and Pennsylvania Gazette in October 1729 and shortened the name to the Pennsylvania Gazette.
8. See n. 1, p. 508.

9. I.e., the Pennsylvania Assembly.
1. Andrew Hamilton (see n. 2, p. 512).
2. "I got his Son once £500" [Franklin's note]. Franklin was able to get the legislature to pay Governor James Hamilton his salary when they were at odds with him.

longer which he allow'd me, and as soon as I was able I paid the Principal with
Interest and many Thanks. So that Erratum was in some degree corrected.

But now another Difficulty came upon me, which I had never the least
Reason to expect. Mr. Meredith's Father, who was to have paid for our Printing-House according to the Expectations given me, was able to advance only
one Hundred Pounds, Currency, which had been paid, and a Hundred more
was due to the Merchant; who grew impatient and su'd us all. We gave Bail,
but saw that if the Money could not be rais'd in time, the Suit must come to
a Judgment and Execution, and our hopeful Prospects must with us be ruined,
as the Press and Letters must be sold for Payment, perhaps at half-Price. In
this Distress two true Friends whose Kindness I have never forgotten nor ever
shall forget while I can remember anything, came to me separately unknown
to each other, and without any Application from me, offering each of them to
advance me all the Money that should be necessary to enable me to take the
whole Business upon myself if that should be practicable, but they did not like
my continuing the Partnership with Meredith, who as they said was often seen
drunk in the Streets, and playing at low Games in Alehouses, much to our
Discredit. These two Friends were *William Coleman* and *Robert Grace*.

I told them I could not propose a Separation while any Prospect remain'd
of the Merediths fulfilling their Part of our Agreement. Because I thought
myself under great Obligations to them for what they had done and would do
if they could. But if they finally fail'd in their Performance, and our Partnership must be dissolv'd, I should then think myself at Liberty to accept the
Assistance of my Friends. Thus the matter rested for some time. When I said
to my Partner, perhaps your Father is dissatisfied at the Part you have undertaken in this Affair of ours, and is unwilling to advance for you and me what
he would for you alone: If that is the Case, tell me, and I will resign the whole
to you and go about my Business. No—says he, my Father has really been
disappointed and is really unable; and I am unwilling to distress him farther. I
see this is a Business I am not fit for. I was bred a Farmer, and it was a Folly
in me to come to Town and put myself at 30 Years of Age an Apprentice to
learn a new Trade. Many of our Welsh People are going to settle in North
Carolina where Land is cheap: I am inclin'd to go with them, and follow my
old Employment. You may find Friends to assist you. If you will take the
Debts of the Company upon you, return to my Father the hundred Pound he
has advanc'd, pay my little personal Debts, and give me Thirty Pounds and a
new Saddle, I will relinquish the Partnership and leave the whole in your
Hands. I agreed to this Proposal. It was drawn up in Writing, sign'd and seal'd
immediately. I gave him what he demanded and he went soon after to Carolina; from whence he sent me next Year two long Letters, containing the best
Account that had been given of that Country, the Climate, Soil, Husbandry,
etc., for in those Matters he was very judicious. I printed them in the Papers,[3]
and they gave great Satisfaction to the Public.

As soon as he was gone, I recurr'd to my two Friends; and because I would
not give an unkind Preference to either, I took half what each had offered and
I wanted, of one, and half of the other; paid off the Company Debts, and went
on with the Business in my own Name, advertising that the Partnership was
dissolved. I think this was in or about the Year 1729.[4]

3. In the *Pennsylvania Gazette*, May 6, and 13, 1732.   4. More accurately, July 14, 1730.

About this Time there was a Cry among the People for more Paper-Money, only 15,000 Pounds being extant in the Province and that soon to be sunk.[5] The wealthy Inhabitants oppos'd any Addition, being against all Paper Currency, from an Apprehension that it would depreciate as it had done in New England to the Prejudice of all Creditors. We had discuss'd this Point in our Junto, where I was on the Side of an Addition, being persuaded that the first small Sum struck in 1723 had done much good, by increasing the Trade, Employment, and Number of Inhabitants in the Province, since I now saw all the old Houses inhabited, and many new ones building, where as I remember'd well, that when I first walk'd about the Streets of Philadelphia, eating my Roll, I saw most of the Houses in Walnut Street between Second and Front Streets with Bills[6] on their Doors, to be let; and many likewise in Chestnut Street, and other Streets; which made me then think the Inhabitants of the City were one after another deserting it. Our Debates possess'd me so fully of the Subject, that I wrote and printed an anonymous Pamphlet on it, entitled, *The Nature and Necessity of a Paper Currency*.[7] It was well receiv'd by the common People in general; but the Rich Men dislik'd it; for it increas'd and strengthen'd the Clamor for more Money; and they happening to have no Writers among them that were able to answer it, their Opposition slacken'd, and the Point was carried by a Majority in the House. My Friends there, who conceiv'd I had been of some Service, thought fit to reward me, by employing me in printing the Money,[8] a very profitable Job, and a great Help to me. This was another Advantage gain'd by my being able to write. The Utility of this Currency became by Time and Experience so evident, as never afterwards to be much disputed, so that it grew soon to 55,000 Pounds, and in 1739 to 80,000 Pounds, since which it arose during War to upwards of 350,000 Pounds—Trade, Building and Inhabitants all the while increasing. Tho' I now think there are Limits beyond which the Quantity may be hurtful.

I soon after obtain'd, thro' my Friend Hamilton, the Printing of the New Castle[9] Paper Money, another profitable Job, as I then thought it; small Things appearing great to those in small Circumstances. And these to me were really great Advantages, as they were great Encouragements. He procured me also the Printing of the Laws and Votes of that Government which continu'd in my Hands as long as I follow'd the Business.

I now open'd a little Stationer's Shop.[1] I had in it Blanks of all Sorts the correctest that ever appear'd among us, being assisted in that by my Friend Breintnall; I had also Paper, Parchment, Chapmen's Books,[2] etc. One Whitmarsh[3] a Compositor I had known in London, an excellent Workman now came to me and work'd with me constantly and diligently, and I took an Apprentice the Son of Aquila Rose. I began now gradually to pay off the Debt I was under for the Printing-House. In order to secure my Credit and Character as a Tradesman, I took care not only to be in *Reality* Industrious and frugal, but to avoid all *Appearances* of the contrary. I dressed plainly; I was seen at no

5. Destroyed. In 1723 paper money had become so scarce that the Assembly issued new money secured by real estate mortgages; when the mortgages were paid off, the bills were "sunk." But by 1729 the value of the currency was so low that the money was recalled before the mortgages were paid.
6. Signs.
7. A *Modest Inquiry into the Nature and Necessity of a Paper Currency* (April 3, 1729).

8. Franklin received the contract to print money in 1731.
9. New Castle, Delaware. Delaware had a separate legislature but the same proprietary governor as Pennsylvania.
1. In July 1730.
2. Inexpensive paper pamphlets.
3. Thomas Whitmarsh (d. 1733); the following year Whitmarsh went to South Carolina.

Places of idle Diversion; I never went out a-fishing or shooting; a Book, indeed, sometimes debauch'd me from my Work; but that was seldom, snug, and gave no Scandal: and to show that I was not above my Business, I sometimes brought home the Paper I purchas'd at the Stores, thro' the Streets on a Wheelbarrow. Thus being esteem'd an industrious thriving young Man, and paying duly for what I bought, the Merchants who imported Stationery solicited my Custom, others propos'd supplying me with Books, and I went on swimmingly. In the mean time Keimer's Credit and Business declining daily, he was at last forc'd to sell his Printing-House to satisfy his Creditors. He went to Barbados, and there lived some Years, in very poor Circumstances.

His Apprentice David Harry, whom I had instructed while I work'd with him, set up in his Place at Philadelphia, having bought his Materials. I was at first apprehensive of a powerful Rival in Harry, as his Friends were very able, and had a good deal of Interest. I therefore propos'd a Partnership to him; which he, fortunately for me, rejected with Scorn. He was very proud, dress'd like a Gentleman, liv'd expensively, took much Diversion and Pleasure abroad, ran in debt, and neglected his Business, upon which all Business left him; and finding nothing to do, he follow'd Keimer to Barbados; taking the Printing-House with him. There this Apprentice employ'd his former Master as a Journeyman. They quarrel'd often. Harry went continually behind-hand, and at length was forc'd to sell his Types, and return to his Country Work in Pennsylvania. The Person that bought them employ'd Keimer to use them, but in a few years he died. There remain'd now no Competitor with me at Philadelphia, but the old one, Bradford, who was rich and easy, did a little Printing now and then by straggling Hands, but was not very anxious about the Business. However, as he kept the Post Office, it was imagined he had better Opportunities of obtaining News, his Paper was thought a better Distributer of Advertisements than mine, and therefore had many more, which was a profitable thing to him and a Disadvantage to me. For tho' I did indeed receive and send Papers by the Post, yet the public Opinion was otherwise; for what I did send was by Bribing the Riders[4] who took them privately: Bradford being unkind enough to forbid it: which occasion'd some Resentment on my Part; and I thought so meanly of him for it, that when I afterwards came into his Situation,[5] I took care never to imitate it.

I had hitherto continu'd to board with Godfrey who lived in Part of my House with his Wife and Children, and had one Side of the Shop for his Glazier's Business, tho' he work'd little, being always absorb'd in his Mathematics. Mrs. Godfrey projected a Match for me with a Relation's Daughter, took Opportunities of bringing us often together, till a serious Courtship on my Part ensu'd, the Girl being in herself very deserving. The old Folks encourag'd me by continual Invitations to Supper, and by leaving us together, till at length it was time to explain. Mrs. Godfrey manag'd our little Treaty. I let her know that I expected as much Money with their Daughter as would pay off my Remaining Debt for the Printing-House, which I believe was not then above a Hundred Pounds.[6] She brought me Word they had no such Sum to spare. I said they might mortgage their House in the Loan Office. The Answer

---

4. I.e., the postal riders or carriers. Franklin did this to have his papers delivered on the same day as Bradford's.
5. Franklin assumed Bradford's office as postmaster of

Philadelphia in October 1737.
6. Franklin's expectations were not unusual: marriages were often arranged on agreeable financial considerations.

to this after some Days was, that they did not approve the Match; that on Enquiry of Bradford they had been inform'd the Printing Business was not a profitable one, the Types would soon be worn out and more wanted, that S. Keimer and D. Harry had fail'd one after the other, and I should probably soon follow them; and therefore I was forbidden the House, and the Daughter shut up.

Whether this was a real Change of Sentiment, or only Artifice, on a Supposition of our being too far engag'd in Affection to retract, and therefore that we should steal a Marriage, which would leave them at Liberty to give or withhold what they pleas'd, I know not: But I suspected the latter, resented it, and went no more. Mrs. Godfrey brought me afterwards some more favorable Accounts of their Disposition, and would have drawn me on again: But I declared absolutely my Resolution to have nothing more to do with that Family. This was resented by the Godfreys, we differ'd, and they removed, leaving me the whole House, and I resolved to take no more Inmates. But this Affair having turn'd my Thoughts to Marriage, I look'd round me, and made Overtures of Acquaintance in other Places; but soon found that the Business of a Printer being generally thought a poor one, I was not to expect Money with a Wife unless with such a one, as I should not otherwise think agreeable. In the mean time, that hard-to-be-govern'd Passion of Youth, had hurried me frequently into Intrigues with low Women that fell in my Way, which were attended with some Expense and great Inconvenience, besides a continual Risk to my Health by a Distemper[7] which of all Things I dreaded, tho' by great good Luck I escaped it.

A friendly Correspondence as Neighbors and old Acquaintances, had continued between me and Mrs. Read's Family who all had a Regard for me from the time of my first Lodging in their House. I was often invited there and consulted in their Affairs, wherein I sometimes was of Service. I pitied poor Miss Read's unfortunate Situation, who was generally dejected, seldom cheerful, and avoided Company. I consider'd my Giddiness and Inconstancy when in London as in a great degree the Cause of her Unhappiness; tho' the Mother was good enough to think the Fault more her own than mine, as she had prevented our Marrying before I went thither, and persuaded the other Match in my Absence. Our mutual Affection was revived, but there were now great Objections to our Union. That Match was indeed look'd upon as invalid, a preceding Wife being said to be living in England; but this could not easily be prov'd, because of the Distance, etc. And tho' there was a Report of his Death, it was not certain. Then, tho' it should be true, he had left many Debts which his Successor might be call'd upon to pay. We ventured however, over all these Difficulties, and I took her to Wife Sept. 1, 1730.[8] None of the Inconveniencies happened that we had apprehended, she prov'd a good and faithful Helpmate, assisted me much by attending the Shop, we throve together, and have ever mutually endeavor'd to make each other happy. Thus I corrected that great Erratum as well as I could.

About this Time our Club meeting, not at a Tavern, but in a little Room of Mr. Grace's set apart for that Purpose; a Proposition was made by me, that since our Books were often referr'd to in our Disquisitions upon the Queries,

7. I.e., syphilis.
8. Because there was no proof that John Rogers, Deborah Read's first husband, was dead, she and Franklin entered into a common-law marriage without civil ceremony.

it might be convenient to us to have them all together where we met, that upon Occasion they might be consulted; and by thus clubbing our Books to a common Library, we should, while we lik'd to keep them together, have each of us the Advantage of using the Books of all the other Members, which would be nearly as beneficial as if each owned the whole. It was lik'd and agreed to, and we fill'd one End of the Room with such Books as we could best spare. The Number was not so great as we expected; and tho' they had been of great Use, yet some Inconveniencies occurring for want of due Care of them, the Collection after about a Year was separated, and each took his Books home again.

And now I set on foot my first Project of a public Nature, that for a Subscription Library. I drew up the Proposals, got them put into Form by our great Scrivener Brockden, and by the help of my Friends in the Junto, procur'd Fifty Subscribers of 40 Shillings each to begin with and 10 Shillings a Year for 50 Years, the Term our Company was to continue. We afterwards obtain'd a Charter, the Company being increas'd to 100. This was the Mother of all the North American Subscription Libraries now so numerous. It is become a great thing itself, and continually increasing. These Libraries have improv'd the general Conversation of the Americans, made the common Tradesmen and Farmers as intelligent as most Gentlemen from other Countries, and perhaps have contributed in some degree to the Stand so generally made throughout the Colonies in Defense of their Privileges.

Memo.

Thus far was written with the Intention express'd in the Beginning and therefore contains several little family Anecdotes of no Importance to others. What follows was written many Years after in compliance with the Advice contain'd in these Letters, and accordingly intended for the Public. The Affairs of the Revolution occasion'd the Interruption.

[Part Two][9]

LETTER FROM MR. ABEL JAMES,[1] WITH NOTES ON MY LIFE, (RECEIVED IN PARIS)

My dear and honored Friend.

I have often been desirous of writing to thee, but could not be reconciled to the Thought that the Letter might fall into the Hands of the British,[2] lest some Printer or busy Body should publish some Part of the Contents and give our Friends Pain and myself Censure.

Some Time since there fell into my Hands to my great Joy about 23 Sheets in thy own handwriting containing an Account of the Parentage and Life of thyself, directed to thy Son ending in the Year 1730 with which there were Notes[3] likewise in thy writing, a Copy of which I enclose in Hopes it may be a means if thou continuedst it up to a later period, that the first and latter part may be put together; and if it is not yet continued, I hope thou wilt not delay it. Life is uncertain as the

9. Franklin wrote the second part of his autobiography at the Hôtel de Valentenois in Passy, a Paris suburb. He had been sent to Paris as American representative to the peace treaty, ending the war with Britain, September 3, 1783. Franklin remained in Paris until July 1785, when Thomas Jefferson replaced him as minister.

1. A Quaker merchant in Philadelphia (c. 1726–1790).
2. James's letter was written in 1782, when Britain was still at war with the colonies.
3. Franklin's outline for his *Autobiography*, written in 1771. Reprinted in the Yale University edition, 1964.

Preacher tells us, and what will the World say if kind, humane and benevolent Ben Franklin should leave his Friends and the World deprived of so pleasing and profitable a Work, a Work which would be useful and entertaining not only to a few, but to millions.

The Influence Writings under that Class have on the Minds of Youth is very great, and has no where appeared so plain as in our public Friends' Journals. It almost insensibly leads the Youth into the Resolution of endeavoring to become as good and as eminent as the Journalist. Should thine for Instance when published, and I think it could not fail of it, lead the Youth to equal the Industry and Temperance of thy early Youth, what a Blessing with that Class would such a Work be. I know of no Character living nor many of them put together, who has so much in his Power as Thyself to promote a greater Spirit of Industry and early Attention to Business, Frugality and Temperance with the American Youth. Not that I think the Work would have no other Merit and Use in the World, far from it, but the first is of such vast Importance, that I know nothing that can equal it.

The foregoing letter and the minutes accompanying it being shown to a friend, I received from him the following:

LETTER FROM MR. BENJAMIN VAUGHAN[4]

MY DEAREST SIR, Paris, January 31, 1783.

When I had read over your sheets of minutes of the principal incidents of your life, recovered for you by your Quaker acquaintance; I told you I would send you a letter expressing my reasons why I thought it would be useful to complete and publish it as he desired. Various concerns have for some time past prevented this letter being written, and I do not know whether it was worth any expectation: happening to be at leisure however at present, I shall by writing at least interest and instruct myself; but as the terms I am inclined to use may tend to offend a person of your manners, I shall only tell you how I would address any other person, who was as good and as great as yourself, but less diffident. I would say to him, Sir, I *solicit* the history of your life from the following motives.

Your history is so remarkable, that if you do not give it, somebody else will certainly give it; and perhaps so as nearly to do as much harm, as your own management of the thing might do good.

It will moreover present a table of the internal circumstances of your country, which will very much tend to invite to it settlers of virtuous and manly minds. And considering the eagerness with which such information is sought by them, and the extent of your reputation, I do not know of a more efficacious advertisement than your Biography would give.

All that has happened to you is also connected with the detail of the manners and situation of *a rising* people; and in this respect I do not think that the writings of Caesar and Tacitus[5] can be more interesting to a true judge of human nature and society.

But these, Sir, are small reasons in my opinion, compared with the chance which your life will give for the forming of future great men; and

4. The wealthy son (1751–1835) of a Jamaican merchant and Maine mother; private secretary to Lord Shelburne, and personal emissary to Franklin during the Paris peace talks (1782–85).
5. Gaius Julius Caesar (100–44 B.C.) and Publius Cornelius Tacitus (late 1st and early 2nd centuries A.D.).

in conjunction with your *Art of Virtue*,[6] (which you design to publish) of improving the features of private character, and consequently of aiding all happiness both public and domestic.

The two works I allude to, Sir, will in particular give a noble rule and example of *self-education*. School and other education constantly proceed upon false principles, and show a clumsy apparatus pointed at a false mark; but your apparatus is simple, and the mark a true one; and while parents and young persons are left destitute of other just means of estimating and becoming prepared for a reasonable course in life, your discovery that the thing is in many a man's private power, will be invaluable!

Influence upon the private character late in life, is not only an influence late in life, but a weak influence. It is in *youth* that we plant our chief habits and prejudices; it is in youth that we take our party[7] as to profession, pursuits, and matrimony. In youth therefore the turn is given; in youth the education even of the next generation is given; in youth the private and public character is determined: and the term of life extending from youth to age, life ought to begin well from youth; and more especially *before* we take our party as to our principal objects.

But your Biography will not merely teach self-education, but the education of *a wise man*; and the wisest man will receive lights and improve his progress, by seeing detailed the conduct of another wise man. And why are weaker men to be deprived of such helps, when we see our race has been blundering on in the dark, almost without a guide in this particular, from the farthest trace of time. Show then, Sir, how much is to be done, *both to sons and fathers*; and invite all wise men to become like yourself; and other men to become wise.

When we see how cruel statesmen and warriors can be to the humble race, and how absurd distinguished men can be to their acquaintance, it will be instructive to observe the instances multiply of pacific acquiescing manners; and to find how compatible it is to be great and *domestic*; enviable and yet *good-humored*.

The little private incidents which you will also have to relate, will have considerable use, as we want above all things, *rules of prudence in ordinary affairs*; and it will be curious to see how you have acted in these. It will be so far a sort of key to life, and explain many things that all men ought to have once explained to them, to give them a chance of becoming wise by foresight.

The nearest thing to having experience of one's own, is to have other people's affairs brought before us in a shape that is interesting; this is sure to happen from your pen. Your affairs and management will have an air of simplicity or importance that will not fail to strike; and I am convinced you have conducted them with as much originality as if you had been conducting discussions in politics or philosophy; and what more worthy of experiments and system, (its importance and its errors considered) than human life!

Some men have been virtuous blindly, others have speculated fantastically, and others have been shrewd to bad purposes; but you, Sir, I am

---

6. Vaughan is referring to Franklin's intention to write "a little work for the benefit of youth" to be called *The Art of Virtue*. Part Two of the *Autobiography* is, in part, an answer to Vaughan's reminder.
7. Make our decision.

sure, will give under your hand, nothing but what is at the same moment, wise, practical, and good.

Your account of yourself (for I suppose the parallel I am drawing for Dr. Franklin, will hold not only in point of character but of private history), will show that you are ashamed of no origin; a thing the more important, as you prove how little necessary all origin is to happiness, virtue, or greatness.

As no end likewise happens without a means, so we shall find, Sir, that even you yourself framed a plan by which you became considerable; but at the same time we may see that though the event is flattering, the means are as simple as wisdom could make them; that is, depending upon nature, virtue, thought, and habit.

Another thing demonstrated will be the propriety of every man's waiting for his time for appearing upon the stage of the world. Our sensations being very much fixed to the moment, we are apt to forget that more moments are to follow the first, and consequently that man should arrange his conduct so as to suit the *whole* of a life. Your attribution appears to have been applied to your *life*, and the passing moments of it have been enlivened with content and enjoyment, instead of being tormented with foolish impatience or regrets. Such a conduct is easy for those who make virtue and themselves their standard, and who try to keep themselves in countenance by examples of other truly great men, of whom patience is so often the characteristic.

Your Quaker correspondent, Sir (for here again I will suppose the subject of my letter resembling Dr. Franklin,) praised your frugality, diligence, and temperance, which he considered as a pattern for all youth: but it is singular that he should have forgotten your modesty, and your disinterestedness, without which you never could have waited for your advancement, or found your situation in the mean time comfortable; which is a strong lesson to show the poverty of glory, and the importance of regulating our minds.

If this correspondent had known the nature of your reputation as well as I do, he would have said; your former writings and measures would secure attention to your Biography, and Art of Virtue; and your Biography and Art of Virtue, in return, would secure attention to them. This is an advantage attendant upon a various character, and which brings all that belongs to it into greater play; and it is the more useful, as perhaps more persons are at a loss for the *means* of improving their minds and characters, than they are for the time or the inclination to do it.

But there is one concluding reflection, Sir, that will show the use of your life as a mere piece of biography. This style of writing seems a little gone out of vogue, and yet it is a very useful one; and your specimen of it may be particularly serviceable, as it will make a subject of comparison with the lives of various public cut-throats and intriguers, and with absurd monastic self-tormentors, or vain literary triflers. If it encourages more writings of the same kind with your own, and induces more men to spend lives fit to be written; it will be worth all Plutarch's Lives put together.

But being tired of figuring to myself a character of which every feature suits only one man in the world, without giving him the praise of it; I shall end my letter, my dear Dr. Franklin, with a personal application to your proper self.

I am earnestly desirous then, my dear Sir, that you should let the world into the traits of your genuine character, as civil broils may otherwise tend to disguise or traduce it. Considering your great age, the caution of your character, and your peculiar style of thinking, it is not likely that any one besides yourself can be sufficiently master of the facts of your life, or the intentions of your mind.

Besides all this, the immense revolution of the present period, will necessarily turn our attention towards the author of it; and when virtuous principles have been pretended in it, it will be highly important to show that such have really influenced; and, as your own character will be the principal one to receive a scrutiny, it is proper (even for its effects upon your vast and rising country, as well as upon England and upon Europe), that it should stand respectable and eternal. For the furtherance of human happiness, I have always maintained that it is necessary to prove that man is not even at present a vicious and detestable animal; and still more to prove that good management may greatly amend him; and it is for much the same reason, that I am anxious to see the opinion established, that there are fair characters existing among the individuals of the race; for the moment that all men, without exception, shall be conceived abandoned, good people will cease efforts deemed to be hopeless, and perhaps think of taking their share in the scramble of life, or at least of making it comfortable principally for themselves.

Take then, my dear Sir, this work most speedily into hand: show yourself good as you are good, temperate as you are temperate; and above all things, prove yourself as one who from your infancy have loved justice, liberty, and concord, in a way that has made it natural and consistent for you to have acted, as we have seen you act in the last seventeen years of your life. Let Englishmen be made not only to respect, but even to love you. When they think well of individuals in your native country, they will go nearer to thinking well of your country; and when your countrymen see themselves well thought of by Englishmen, they will go nearer to thinking well of England. Extend your views even further; do not stop at those who speak the English tongue, but after having settled so many points in nature and politics, think of bettering the whole race of men.

As I have not read any part of the life in question, but know only the character that lived it, I write somewhat at hazard. I am sure however, that the life, and the treatise I allude to (on the *Art of Virtue*), will necessarily fullfil the chief of my expectations; and still more so if you take up the measure of suiting these performances to the several views above stated. Should they even prove unsuccessful in all that a sanguine admirer of yours hopes from them, you will at least have framed pieces to interest the human mind; and whoever gives a feeling of pleasure that is innocent to man, has added so much to the fair side of a life otherwise too much darkened by anxiety, and too much injured by pain.

In the hope therefore that you will listen to the prayer addressed to you in this letter, I beg to subscribe myself, my dearest Sir, etc., etc.

Signed   BENJ. VAUGHAN.

CONTINUATION OF THE ACCOUNT OF MY LIFE.
BEGUN AT PASSY, 1784.

It is some time since I receiv'd the above Letters, but I have been too busy till now to think of complying with the Request they contain. It might too be much better done if I were at home among my Papers, which would aid my Memory, and help to ascertain Dates. But my Return being uncertain, and having just now a little Leisure, I will endeavor to recollect and write what I can; if I live to get home, it may there be corrected and improv'd.

Not having any Copy here of what is already written, I know not whether an Account is given of the means I used to establish the Philadelphia public Library, which from a small Beginning is now become so considerable, though I remember to have come down to near the Time of that Transaction, 1730. I will therefore begin here, with an Account of it, which may be struck out if found to have been already given.

At the time I establish'd myself in Pennsylvania, there was not a good Bookseller's Shop in any of the Colonies to the Southward of Boston. In New York and Philadelphia the Printers were indeed Stationers, they sold only Paper, etc., Almanacs, Ballads, and a few common School Books. Those who lov'd Reading were oblig'd to send for their Books from England. The Members of the Junto had each a few. We had left the Alehouse where we first met, and hired a Room to hold our Club in. I propos'd that we should all of us bring our Books to that Room, where they would not only be ready to consult in our Conferences, but become a common Benefit, each of us being at Liberty to borrow such as he wish'd to read at home. This was accordingly done, and for some time contented us. Finding the Advantage of this little Collection, I propos'd to render the Benefit from Books more common by commencing a Public Subscription Library. I drew a Sketch of the Plan and Rules that would be necessary, and got a skillful Conveyancer Mr. Charles Brockden[8] to put the whole in Form of Articles of Agreement to be subscribed, by which each Subscriber engag'd to pay a certain Sum down for the first Purchase of Books and an annual Contribution for increasing them. So few were the Readers at that time in Philadelphia, and the Majority of us so poor, that I was not able with great Industry to find more than Fifty Persons, mostly young Tradesmen, willing to pay down for this purpose Forty shillings each, and Ten Shillings per Annum. On this little Fund we began. The Books were imported. The Library was open one Day in the Week for lending them to the Subscribers, on their Promissory Notes to pay Double the Value if not duly returned. The Institution soon manifested its Utility, was imitated by other Towns and in other Provinces, the Libraries were augmented by Donations, Reading became fashionable, and our People having no public Amusements to divert their Attention from Study became better acquainted with Books, and in a few Years were observ'd by Strangers to be better instructed and more intelligent than People of the same Rank generally are in other Countries.

When we were about to sign the above-mentioned Articles, which were to be binding on us, our Heirs, etc., for fifty Years, Mr. Brockden, the Scrivener, said to us, "You are young Men, but it is scarce probable that any of you will live to see the Expiration of the Term fix'd in this Instrument." A Number of

---

8. Philadelphia's leading drafter of legal documents (1683–1769). "Conveyancer": an attorney who specializes in the transfer of real estate and property.

us, however, are yet living: But the Instrument was after a few Years rendered null by a Charter that incorporated and gave Perpetuity to the Company.

The Objections, and Reluctances I met with in Soliciting the Subscriptions, made me soon feel the Impropriety of presenting oneself as the Proposer of any useful Project that might be suppos'd to raise one's Reputation in the smallest degree above that of one's Neighbors, when one has need of their Assistance to accomplish that Project. I therefore put myself as much as I could out of sight, and stated it as a Scheme of *a Number of Friends*, who had requested me to go about and propose it to such as they thought Lovers of Reading. In this way my Affair went on more smoothly, and I ever after prac- tic'd it on such Occasions; and from my frequent Successes, can heartily rec- ommend it. The present little Sacrifice of your Vanity will afterwards be amply repaid. If it remains a while uncertain to whom the Merit belongs, someone more vain than yourself will be encourag'd to claim it, and then even Envy will be dispos'd to do you Justice, by plucking those assum'd Feathers, and restoring them to their right Owner.

This Library afforded me the Means of Improvement by constant Study, for which I set apart an Hour or two each Day; and thus repair'd in some Degree the Loss of the Learned Education my Father once intended for me. Reading was the only Amusement I allow'd myself. I spent no time in Taverns, Games, or Frolics of any kind. And my Industry in my Business continu'd as indefati- gable as it was necessary. I was in debt for my Printing-House, I had a young Family[9] coming on to be educated, and I had to contend with for Business two Printers who were establish'd in the Place before me. My Circumstances however grew daily easier: my original Habits of Frugality continuing. And My Father having among his Instructions to me when a Boy, frequently repeated a Proverb of Solomon, "*Seest thou a Man diligent in his Calling, he shall stand before Kings, he shall not stand before mean Men.*"[1] I from thence consider'd Industry as a Means of obtaining Wealth and Distinction, which encourag'd me: tho' I did not think that I should ever literally stand before Kings, which however has since happened; for I have stood before five,[2] and even had the honor of sitting down with one, the King of Denmark, to Dinner.

We have an English Proverb that says,

> He that would thrive
> Must ask his Wife,[3]

it was lucky for me that I had one as much dispos'd to Industry and Frugality as myself. She assisted me cheerfully in my Business, folding and stitching Pamphlets, tending Shop, purchasing old Linen Rags for the Paper-makers, etc., etc. We kept no idle Servants, our Table was plain and simple, our Furniture of the cheapest. For instance my Breakfast was a long time Bread and Milk, (no Tea,) and I ate it out of a two penny earthen Porringer[4] with a Pewter Spoon. But mark how Luxury will enter Families, and make a Prog- ress, in Spite of Principle. Being Call'd one Morning to Breakfast, I found it in a China[5] Bowl with a Spoon of Silver. They had been bought for me with- out my Knowledge by my Wife, and had cost her the enormous Sum of three

9. Franklin had three children: William, born c. 1731; Francis, born in 1732; Sarah, born in 1743.
1. Proverbs 22.29.
2. Louis XV and Louis XVI of France, George II and George III of England, and Christian VI of Denmark.

3. More commonly: "He that will thrive must ask leave of his wife."
4. Bowl.
5. I.e., porcelain.

and twenty Shillings, for which she had no other Excuse or Apology to make, but that she thought *her* Husband deserv'd a Silver Spoon and China Bowl as well as any of his Neighbors. This was the first Appearance of Plate[6] and China in our House, which afterwards in a Course of Years as our Wealth increas'd, augmented gradually to several Hundred Pounds in Value.

I had been religiously educated as a Presbyterian, and tho' some of the Dogmas of that Persuasion, such as the Eternal Decrees of God, Election, Reprobation,[7] etc., appear'd to me unintelligible, others doubtful, and I early absented myself from the Public Assemblies of the Sect, Sunday being my Studying-Day, I never was without some religious Principles; I never doubted, for instance, the Existence of the Deity, that he made the World, and govern'd it by his Providence; that the most acceptable Service of God was the doing Good to Man; that our Souls are immortal; and that all Crime will be punished and Virtue rewarded either here or hereafter; these I esteem'd the Essentials of every Religion, and being to be found in all the Religions we had in our Country I respected them all, tho' with different degrees of Respect as I found them more or less mix'd with other Articles which without any Tendency to inspire, promote or confirm Morality, serv'd principally to divide us and make us unfriendly to one another. This Respect to all, with an Opinion that the worst had some good Effects, induc'd me to avoid all Discourse that might tend to lessen the good Opinion another might have of his own Religion; and as our Province increas'd in People and new Places of worship were continually wanted, and generally erected by voluntary Contribution, my Mite[8] for such purpose, whatever might be the Sect, was never refused.

Tho' I seldom attended any Public Worship, I had still an Opinion of its Propriety, and of its Utility when rightly conducted, and I regularly paid my annual Subscription for the Support of the only Presbyterian Minister or Meeting we had in Philadelphia. He us'd to visit me sometimes as a Friend, and admonish me to attend his Administrations, and I was now and then prevail'd on to do so, once for five Sundays successively. Had he been, *in my Opinion*, a good Preacher perhaps I might have continued, notwithstanding the occasion I had for the Sunday's Leisure in my Course of Study: But his Discourses were chiefly either polemic Arguments, or Explications of the peculiar Doctrines of our Sect, and were all to me very dry, uninteresting and unedifying, since not a single moral Principle was inculcated or enforc'd, their Aim seeming to be rather to make us Presbyterians than good Citizens. At length he took for his Text that Verse of the 4th Chapter of Philippians, *Finally, Brethren, Whatsoever Things are true, honest, just, pure, lovely, or of good report, if there be any virtue, or any praise, think on these Things;*[9] and I imagin'd in a Sermon on such a Text, we could not miss of having some Morality: But he confin'd himself to five Points only as meant by the Apostle, viz., 1. Keeping holy the Sabbath Day. 2. Being diligent in Reading the Holy Scriptures. 3. Attending duly the Public Worship. 4. Partaking of the Sacrament. 5. Paying a due Respect to God's Ministers.—These might be all good Things, but as they were not the kind of good Things that I expected from that Text, I despaired of ever meeting with them from any other, was disgusted, and attended his Preaching no more. I had some Years before compos'd a little

---

6. Silver.
7. Punishment. "Election": God's choosing who is to be saved and who is to be damned.

8. Small contribution.
9. A paraphrase of Philippians 4.8.

Liturgy or Form of Prayer for my own private Use, viz., in 1728, entitled, *Articles of Belief and Acts of Religion.*[1] I return'd to the Use of this, and went no more to the public Assemblies. My Conduct might be blameable, but I leave it without attempting farther to excuse it, my present purpose being to relate Facts, and not to make Apologies for them.

It was about this time that I conceiv'd the bold and arduous Project of arriving at moral Perfection. I wish'd to live without committing any Fault at anytime; I would conquer all that either Natural Inclination, Custom, or Company might lead me into. As I knew, or thought I knew, what was right and wrong, I did not see why I might not *always* do the one and avoid the other. But I soon found I had undertaken a Task of more Difficulty than I had imagined: While my Care was employ'd in guarding against one Fault, I was often surpris'd by another. Habit took the Advantage of Inattention. Inclination was sometimes too strong for Reason. I concluded at length, that the mere speculative Conviction that it was our Interest to be completely virtuous, was not sufficient to prevent our Slipping, and that the contrary Habits must be broken and good Ones acquired and established, before we can have any Dependence on a steady uniform Rectitude of Conduct. For this purpose I therefore contriv'd the following Method.

In the various Enumerations of the moral Virtues I had met with in my Reading, I found the Catalog more or less numerous, as different Writers included more or fewer Ideas under the same Name. Temperance, for Example, was by some confin'd to Eating and Drinking, while by others it was extended to mean the moderating every other Pleasure, Appetite, Inclination or Passion, bodily or mental, even to our Avarice and Ambition. I propos'd to myself, for the sake of Clearness, to use rather more Names with fewer Ideas annex'd to each, than a few Names with more Ideas; and I included after Thirteen Names of Virtues all that at that time occurr'd to me as necessary or desirable, and annex'd to each a short Precept, which fully express'd the Extent I gave to its Meaning.

These Names of Virtues with their Precepts were

1. TEMPERANCE.
Eat not to Dullness. Drink not to Elevation.

2. SILENCE.
Speak not but what may benefit others or yourself. Avoiding trifling Conversation.

3. ORDER.
Let all your Things have their Places. Let each Part of your Business have its Time.

4. RESOLUTION.
Resolve to perform what you ought. Perform without fail what you resolve.

5. FRUGALITY.
Make no Expense but to do good to others or yourself: i.e., Waste nothing.

6. INDUSTRY.
Lose no Time. Be always employ'd in something useful. Cut off all unnecessary Actions.

1. Only the first part of Franklin's *Articles of Belief and Acts of Religion* survives. It can be found in *The Papers of Benjamin Franklin*, vol. 1, edited by Leonard W. Labaree et al. (1964).

7. SINCERITY.

Use no hurtful Deceit. Think innocently and justly; and, if you speak; speak accordingly.

8. JUSTICE.

Wrong none, by doing Injuries or omitting the Benefits that are your Duty.

9. MODERATION.

Avoid Extremes. Forbear resenting Injuries so much as you think they deserve.

10. CLEANLINESS.

Tolerate no Uncleanness in Body, Clothes or Habitation.

11. TRANQUILITY.

Be not disturbed at Trifles, or Accidents common or unavoidable.

12. CHASTITY.

Rarely use Venery but for Health or Offspring; Never to Dullness, Weakness, or the Injury of your own or another's Peace or Reputation.

13. HUMILITY.

Imitate Jesus and Socrates.

My intention being to acquire the *Habitude*[2] of all these Virtues, I judg'd it would be well not to distract my Attention by attempting the whole at once, but to fix it on one of them at a time, and when I should be Master of that, then to proceed to another, and so on till I should have gone thro' the thirteen. And as the previous Acquisition of some might facilitate the Acquisition of certain others, I arrang'd them with that View as they stand above. *Temperance* first, as it tends to procure that Coolness and Clearness of Head, which is so necessary where constant Vigilance was to be kept up, and Guard maintained, against the unremitting Attraction of ancient Habits, and the Force of perpetual Temptations. This being acquir'd and establish'd, *Silence* would be more easy, and my Desire being to gain Knowledge at the same time that I improv'd in Virtue, and considering that in Conversation it was obtain'd rather by the Use of the Ears than of the Tongue, and therefore wishing to break a Habit I was getting into of Prattling, Punning and Joking, which only made me acceptable to trifling Company, I gave *Silence* the second Place. This, and the next, *Order*, I expected would allow me more Time for attending to my Project and my studies; RESOLUTION once become habitual, would keep me firm in my Endeavors to obtain all the subsequent Virtues; *Frugality* and *Industry*, by freeing me from my remaining Debt, and producing Affluence and Independence would make more easy the Practice of *Sincerity* and *Justice*, etc., etc. Conceiving then that agreeable to the Advice of Pythagoras[3] in his Golden Verses, daily Examination would be necessary, I contriv'd the following Method for conducting that Examination.

I made a little Book in which I allotted a Page for each of the Virtues. I rul'd each Page with red Ink so as to have seven Columns, one for each Day of the Week, marking each Column with a Letter for the Day. I cross'd these

2. I.e., making these virtues an integral part of his nature.
3. Pythagoras (6th century B.C.) was a Greek philosopher and mathematician. Franklin added a note here: "Insert those Lines that direct it in a Note," and wished to include verses translated: "Let sleep not close your eyes till you have thrice examined the transactions of the day: where have I strayed, what have I done, what good have I omitted?"

Form of the Pages

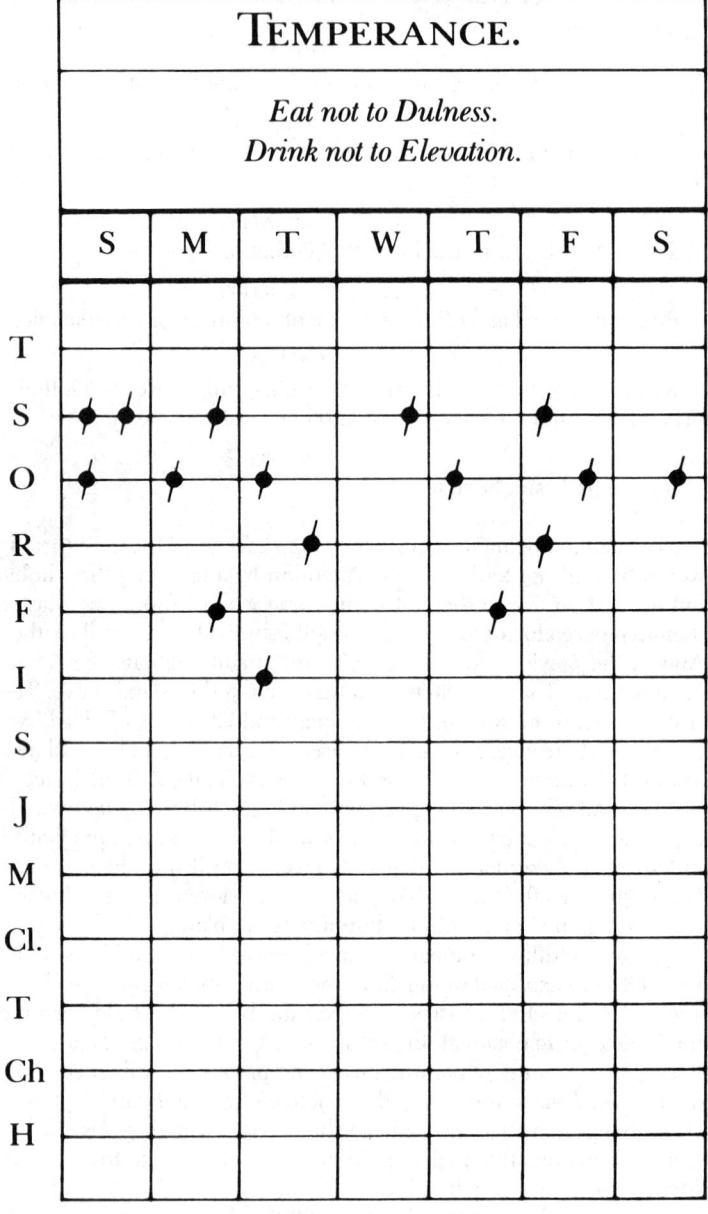

Columns with thirteen red Lines, marking the Beginning of each Line with the first Letter of one of the Virtues, on which Line and in its proper Column I might mark by a little black Spot every Fault I found upon Examination, to have been committed respecting that Virtue upon that Day.

I determined to give a Week's strict Attention to each of the Virtues successively. Thus in the first Week my great Guard was to avoid every the least Offence against Temperance, leaving the other Virtues to their ordinary Chance, only marking every Evening the Faults of the Day. Thus if in the first Week I could keep my first Line marked T clear of Spots, I suppos'd the Habit of that Virtue so much strengthen'd and its opposite weaken'd, that I might venture extending my Attention to include the next, and for the following Week keep both Lines clear of Spots. Proceeding thus to the last, I could go thro' a Course complete in Thirteen Weeks, and four Courses in a Year. And like him who having a Garden to weed, does not attempt to eradicate all the bad Herbs at once, which would exceed his Reach and his Strength, but works on one of the Beds at a time, and having accomplish'd the first proceeds to a second; so I should have, (I hoped) the encouraging Pleasure of seeing on my Pages the Progress I made in Virtue, by clearing successively my Lines of their Spots, till in the End by a Number of Courses, I should be happy in viewing a clean Book after a thirteen Weeks' daily Examination.

This my little Book had for its Motto these Lines from *Addison's Cato*,[4]

> *Here will I hold: If there is a Pow'r above us,*
> *(And that there is, all Nature cries aloud*
> *Thro' all her Works) he must delight in Virtue,*
> *And that which he delights in must be happy.*

Another from *Cicero*.[5]

> *O Vitæ Philosophia Dux! O Virtutum indagatrix, expultrixque vitiorum!*
> *Unus dies bene, et ex preceptis tuis actus, peccanti immortalitati est anteponendus.*

Another from the Proverbs of Solomon speaking of Wisdom or Virtue;

> Length of Days is in her right hand, and in her Left Hand Riches and Honors; Her Ways are Ways of Pleasantness, and all her Paths are Peace.
>
> III, 16, 17

And conceiving God to be the Fountain of Wisdom, I thought it right and necessary to solicit his Assistance for obtaining it; to this End I form'd the following little Prayer, which was prefix'd to my Tables of Examination, for daily Use.

> *O Powerful Goodness! bountiful Father! merciful Guide! Increase in me that Wisdom which discovers my truest Interests; Strengthen my Resolutions to perform what that Wisdom dictates. Accept my kind Offices to thy other Children, as the only Return in my Power for thy continual Favors to me.*

---

4. Joseph Addison, *Cato, a Tragedy* (1713; 5.1.15–18). Franklin also used these lines as an epigraph for his *Articles of Belief and Acts of Religion*.
5. Marcus Tullius Cicero (106–43 B.C.), Roman philosopher and orator. The quotation is from *Tusculan Disputations* (5.2.5), but several lines are omitted after *vitiorum:* Oh, philosophy, guide of life: Oh, searcher out of virtues and expeller of vices! . . . One day lived well and according to thy precepts is to be preferred to an eternity of sin (Latin).

The Morning Question, What Good shall I do this Day?	5 6 7	Rise, wash, and address *Powerful Goodness;* contrive Day's Business and take the Resolution of the Day; prosecute the present Study: and breakfast.—
	8 9 10 11	Work.
	12 1	Read, or overlook my Accounts, and dine.
	2 3 4 5	Work.
	6 7 8 9	Put Things in their Places, Supper, Musick, or Diversion, or Conversation, Examination of the Day.
Evening Question, What Good have I done to day?	10 11 12 1 2 3 4	Sleep.—

I us'd also sometimes a little Prayer which I took from *Thomson's*[6] Poems, viz.,

> *Father of Light and Life, thou Good supreme,*
> *O teach me what is good, teach me thy self!*
> *Save me from Folly, Vanity and Vice,*
> *From every low Pursuit, and fill my Soul*
> *With Knowledge, conscious Peace, and Virtue pure,*
> *Sacred, substantial, neverfading Bliss!*

The Precept of *Order* requiring that *every Part of my Business should have its allotted Time*, one Page in my little Book contain'd the following Scheme of Employment for the Twenty-four Hours of a natural Day.

I enter'd upon the Execution of this Plan for Self-examination, and continu'd it with occasional Intermissions for some time. I was surpris'd to find myself so much fuller of Faults than I had imagined, but I had the Satisfaction of seeing them diminish. To avoid the Trouble of renewing now and then my little Book, which by scraping out the Marks on the Paper of old Faults to make room for new Ones in a new Course, became full of Holes: I transferr'd my Tables and Precepts to the Ivory Leaves of a Memorandum Book, on which the Lines were drawn with red Ink that made a durable Stain, and on those Lines I mark'd my Faults with a black Lead Pencil, which Marks I could easily wipe out with a wet Sponge. After a while I went thro' one Course only in a Year, and afterwards only one in several Years; till at length I omitted them entirely, being employ'd in Voyages and Business abroad with a Multiplicity of Affairs, that interfered. But I always carried my little Book with me.

My Scheme of ORDER, gave me the most Trouble, and I found, that tho' it might be practicable where a Man's Business was such as to leave him the Disposition of his Time, that of a Journeyman Printer for instance, it was not possible to be exactly observ'd by a Master, who must mix with the World, and often receive People of Business at their own Hours. *Order* too, with regard to Places for Things, Papers, etc., I found extremely difficult to acquire. I had not been early accustomed to it, and having an exceeding good Memory, I was not so sensible of the Inconvenience attending Want of Method. This Article therefore cost me so much painful Attention and my Faults in it vex'd me so much, and I made so little Progress in Amendment, and had such frequent Relapses, that I was almost ready to give up the Attempt, and content myself with a faulty Character in that respect. Like the Man who in buying an Ax of a Smith my Neighbor, desired to have the whole of its Surface as bright as the Edge; the Smith consented to grind it bright for him if he would turn the Wheel. He turn'd while the Smith press'd the broad Face of the Ax hard and heavily on the Stone, which made the Turning of it very fatiguing. The Man came every now and then from the Wheel to see how the Work went on; and at length would take his Ax as it was without farther Grinding. No, says the Smith, Turn on, turn on; we shall have it bright by and by; as yet 'tis only speckled. Yes, says the Man; but—I *think I like a speckled Ax best*.—And I believe this may have been the Case with many who having for want of some such Means as I employ'd found the Difficulty of obtaining good, and breaking bad Habits, in other Points of Vice and Virtue, have given up the Struggle, and concluded that *a speckled Ax was best*. For something that pretended to

---

6. James Thomson (1700–1748), *The Seasons*, "Winter" (1726), lines 218–23.

be Reason was every now and then suggesting to me, that such extreme Nicety as I exacted of myself might be a kind of Foppery in Morals, which if it were known would make me ridiculous; that a perfect Character might be attended with the Inconvenience of being envied and hated; and that a benevolent Man should allow a few Faults in himself, to keep his Friends in Countenance.

In Truth I found myself incorrigible with respect to *Order*; and now I am grown old, and my Memory bad, I feel very sensibly the want of it. But on the whole, tho' I never arrived at the Perfection I had been so ambitious of obtaining, but fell far short of it, yet I was by the Endeavor made a better and a happier Man than I otherwise should have been, if I had not attempted it; As those who aim at perfect Writing by imitating the engraved Copies,[7] tho' they never reach the wish'd for Excellence of those Copies, their Hand is mended by the Endeavor, and is tolerable while it continues fair and legible.

And it may be well my Posterity should be informed, that to this little Artifice, with the Blessing of God, their Ancestor ow'd the constant Felicity of his Life down to his 79th Year in which this is written. What Reverses may attend the Remainder is in the Hand of Providence: But if they arrive, the Reflection on past Happiness enjoy'd ought to help his Bearing them with more Resignation. To *Temperance* he ascribes his long-continu'd Health, and what is still left to him of a good Constitution. To *Industry* and *Frugality* the early Easiness of his Circumstances, and Acquisition of his Fortune, with all that Knowledge which enabled him to be an useful Citizen, and obtain'd for him some Degree of Reputation among the Learned. To *Sincerity* and *Justice* the Confidence of his Country, and the honorable Employs it conferr'd upon him. And to the joint Influence of the whole Mass of the Virtues, even in their imperfect State he was able to acquire them, all that Evenness of Temper, and that Cheerfulness in Conversation which makes his Company still sought for, and agreeable even to his younger Acquaintance. I hope therefore that some of my Descendants may follow the Example and reap the Benefit.

It will be remark'd[8] that, tho' my Scheme was not wholly without Religion there was in it no Mark of any of the distinguishing Tenets of any particular Sect. I had purposely avoided them; for being fully persuaded of the Utility and Excellency of my Method, and that it might be serviceable to People in all Religions, and intending some time or other to publish it, I would not have anything in it that should prejudice anyone of any Sect against it. I purposed writing a little Comment on each Virtue, in which I would have shown the Advantages of possessing it, and the Mischiefs attending its opposite Vice; and I should have called my Book the ART *of Virtue*, because it would have shown the *Means and Manner* of obtaining Virtue; which would have distinguish'd it from the mere Exhortation to be good, that does not instruct and indicate the Means; but is like the Apostle's Man of verbal Charity, who only, without showing to the Naked and the Hungry *how* or where they might get Clothes or Victuals, exhorted them to be fed and clothed. *James II*, 15, 16.[9]

But it so happened that my Intention of writing and publishing this Comment was never fulfilled. I did indeed, from time to time put down short Hints of the Sentiments, Reasonings, etc., to be made use of in it; some of which I

---

7. I.e., the models in the printed book.
8. Observed.
9. "If a brother or sister be naked, and destitute of daily food, And one of you say unto them, Depart in peace, be ye warmed and filled: notwithstanding ye give them not those things which are needful to the body; what doth it profit?"

have still by me: But the necessary close Attention to private Business in the earlier part of Life, and public Business since, have occasioned my postponing it. For it being connected in my Mind with a *great and extensive Project* that required the whole Man to execute, and which an unforeseen Succession of Employs prevented my attending to, it has hitherto remain'd unfinish'd.

In this Piece it was my Design to explain and enforce this Doctrine, that vicious Actions are not hurtful because they are forbidden, but forbidden because they are hurtful, the Nature of Man alone consider'd: That it was therefore every one's Interest to be virtuous, who wish'd to be happy even in this World. And I should from this Circumstance (there being always in the World a Number of rich Merchants, Nobility, States and Princes, who have need of honest Instruments for the Management of their Affairs, and such being so rare) have endeavored to convince young Persons, that no Qualities were so likely to make a poor Man's Fortune as those of Probity and Integrity.

My List of Virtues contain'd at first but twelve: But a Quaker Friend having kindly inform'd me that I was generally thought proud; that my Pride show'd itself frequently in Conversation; that I was not content with being in the right when discussing any Point, but was overbearing and rather insolent; of which he convinc'd me by mentioning several Instances; I determined endeavoring to cure myself if I could of this Vice or Folly among the rest, and I added *Humility* to my List, giving an extensive Meaning to the Word. I cannot boast of much Success in acquiring the *Reality* of this Virtue; but I had a good deal with regard to the *Appearance* of it. I made it a Rule to forbear all direct Contradiction to the Sentiments of others, and all positive Assertion of my own. I even forbid myself, agreeable to the old Laws of our Junto, the Use of every Word or Expression in the Language that imported[1] a fix'd Opinion; such as *certainly, undoubtedly,* etc., and I adopted instead of them, I *conceive,* I *apprehend,* or I *imagine* a thing to be so or so, or it so appears to me at present. When another asserted something that I thought an Error, I denied myself the Pleasure of contradicting him abruptly, and of showing immediately some Absurdity in his Proposition; and in answering I began by observing that in certain Cases or Circumstances his Opinion would be right, but that in the present case there *appear'd* or *seem'd* to me some Difference, etc., I soon found the Advantage of this Change in my Manners. The Conversations I engag'd in went on more pleasantly. The modest way in which I propos'd my Opinions, procur'd them a readier Reception and less Contradiction; I had less Mortification when I was found to be in the wrong, and I more easily prevail'd with others to give up their Mistakes and join with me when I happen'd to be in the right. And this Mode, which I at first put on, with some violence to natural Inclination, became at length so easy and so habitual to me, that perhaps for these Fifty Years past no one has ever heard a dogmatical Expression escape me. And to this Habit (after my Character of Integrity) I think it principally owing, that I had early so much Weight with my Fellow Citizens, when I proposed new Institutions, or Alterations in the old; and so much Influence in public Councils when I became a Member. For I was but a bad Speaker, never eloquent, subject to much Hesitation in my choice of Words, hardly correct in Language, and yet I generally carried my Points.

In reality there is perhaps no one of our natural Passions so hard to subdue

---

1. Suggested.

as *Pride*. Disguise it, struggle with it, beat it down, stifle it, mortify it as much as one pleases, it is still alive, and will every now and then peep out and show itself. You will see it perhaps often in this History. For even if I could conceive that I had completely overcome it, I should probably be proud of my Humility.

Thus far written at Passy, 1784.

[*Part Three*]²

I am now about to write at home, August 1788, but cannot have the help expected from my Papers, many of them being lost in the War. I have however found the following.

Having mentioned a *great and extensive Project* which I had conceiv'd, it seems proper that some Account should be here given of that Project and its Object. Its first Rise in my Mind appears in the following little Paper, accidentally preserv'd, viz.,

OBSERVATIONS on my Reading
History in Library, May 9, 1731.
"That the great Affairs of the World, the Wars, Revolutions, etc., are carried on and effected by Parties.

"That the View of these Parties is their present general Interest, or what they take to be such.

"That the different Views of these different Parties, occasion all Confusion.

"That while a Party is carrying on a general Design, each Man has his particular private Interest in View.

"That as soon as a Party has gain'd its general Point, each Member becomes intent upon his particular Interest, which thwarting others, breaks that Party into Divisions, and occasions more Confusion.

"That few in Public Affairs act from a mere View of the Good of their Country, whatever they may pretend; and tho' their Actings bring real Good to their Country, yet Men primarily consider'd that their own and their Country's Interest was united, and did not act from a Principle of Benevolence.

"That fewer still in public Affairs act with a View to the Good of Mankind.

"There seems to me at present to be great Occasion for raising an united Party for Virtue, by forming the Virtuous and good Men of all Nations into a regular Body, to be govern'd by suitable good and wise Rules, which good and wise Men may probably be more unanimous in their Obedience to, than common People are to common Laws.

"I at present think, that whoever attempts this aright, and is well qualified, cannot fail of pleasing God, and of meeting with Success.

B.F."

Revolving this Project in my Mind, as to be undertaken hereafter when my Circumstances should afford me the necessary Leisure, I put down from time to time on Pieces of Paper such Thoughts as occur'd to me respecting it. Most of these are lost; but I find one purporting to be the Substance of an intended Creed, containing as I thought the Essentials of every known Religion, and

2. Franklin wrote the third part of his autobiography in Philadelphia, between August 1788 and the end of May 1789.

being free of everything that might shock the Professors of any Religion. It is express'd in these Words, viz.,

"That there is one God who made all things.

"That he governs the World by his Providence.

"That he ought to be worshiped by Adoration, Prayer and Thanksgiving.

"But that the most acceptable Service of God is doing Good to Man.

"That the Soul is immortal.

"And that God will certainly reward Virtue and punish Vice either here or hereafter."

My Ideas at that time were, that the Sect should be begun and spread at first among young and single Men only; that each Person to be initiated should not only declare his Assent to such Creed, but should have exercis'd himself with the Thirteen Weeks' Examination and Practice of the Virtues as in the before-mention'd Model; that the Existance of such a Society should be kept a Secret till it was become considerable, to prevent Solicitations for the Admission of improper Persons; but that the Members should each of them search among his Acquaintance for ingenuous well-disposed Youths, to whom with prudent Caution the Scheme should be gradually communicated: That the Members should engage to afford their Advice, Assistance and Support to each other in promoting one another's Interest, Business and Advancement in Life: That for Distinction we should be call'd the Society of the *Free and Easy*; Free, as being by the general Practice and Habit of the Virtues, free from the Dominion of Vice, and particularly by the Practice of Industry and Frugality, free from Debt, which exposes a Man to Confinement and a Species of Slavery to his Creditors. This is as much as I can now recollect of the Project, except that I communicated it in part to two young Men, who adopted it with some Enthusiasm. But my then narrow Circumstances, and the Necessity I was under of sticking close to my Business, occasion'd my Postponing the farther Prosecution of it at that time, and my multifarious Occupations public and private induc'd me to continue postponing, so that it has been omitted till I have no longer Strength or Activity left sufficient for such an Enterprise: Tho' I am still of Opinion that it was a practicable Scheme, and might have been very useful, by forming a great Number of good Citizens: And I was not discourag'd by the seeming Magnitude of the Undertaking, as I have always thought that one Man of tolerable Abilities may work great Changes, and accomplish great Affairs among Mankind, if he first forms a good Plan, and, cutting off all Amusements or other Employments that would divert his Attention, makes the Execution of that same Plan his sole Study and Business.

In 1732 I first published my Almanac, under the Name of *Richard Saunders*; it was continu'd by me about 25 Years, commonly call'd *Poor Richard's* Almanac. I endeavor'd to make it both entertaining and useful, and it accordingly came to be in such Demand that I reap'd considerable Profit from it, vending[3] annually near ten Thousand. And observing that it was generally read, scarce any Neighborhood in the Province being without it, I consider'd it as a proper Vehicle for conveying Instruction among the common People, who bought scarce any other Books. I therefore filled all the little Spaces that occur'd between the Remarkable Days in the Calendar, with Proverbial Sen-

---

3. Selling. *Poor Richard's Almanac* was first published on December 19, 1732. Richard Saunders was a London almanac maker of the 17th century. Franklin may also have had in mind a London almanac published from 1661 to 1776 called *Poor Robin*.

tences, chiefly such as inculcated Industry and Frugality, as the Means of procuring Wealth and thereby securing Virtue, it being more difficult for a Man in Want to act always honestly, as (to use here one of those Proverbs) *it is hard for an empty Sack to stand upright.* These Proverbs, which contained the Wisdom of many Ages and Nations, I assembled and form'd into a connected Discourse prefix'd to the Almanac of 1757, as the Harangue of a wise old Man to the People attending an Auction.[4] The bringing all these scatter'd Counsels thus into a Focus, enabled them to make greater Impression. The Piece being universally approved was copied in all the Newspapers of the Continent, reprinted in Britain on a Broadside[5] to be stuck up in Houses, two Translations were made of it in French, and great Numbers bought by the Clergy and Gentry to distribute gratis among their poor Parishioners and Tenants. In Pennsylvania, as it discouraged useless Expense in foreign Superfluities, some thought it had its share of Influence in producing that growing Plenty of Money which was observable for several Years after its Publication.

I consider'd my Newspaper also as another Means of communicating Instruction, and in that View frequently reprinted in it Extracts from the Spectator[6] and other moral Writers, and sometimes publish'd little Pieces of my own which had been first compos'd for Reading in our Junto. Of these are a Socratic Dialogue tending to prove, that, whatever might be his Parts and Abilities, a vicious Man could not properly be called a Man of Sense. And a Discourse on Self-denial, showing that Virtue was not Secure, till its Practice became a Habitude, and was free from the Opposition of contrary Inclinations. These may be found in the Papers about the beginning of 1735.[7] In the Conduct of my Newspaper I carefully excluded all Libeling and Personal Abuse, which is of late Years become so disgraceful to our Country. Whenever I was solicited to insert anything of that kind, and the Writers pleaded as they generally did, the Liberty of the Press, and that a Newspaper was like a Stage Coach in which any one who would pay had a Right to a Place, my Answer was, that I would print the Piece separately if desired, and the Author might have as many Copies as he pleased to distribute himself, but that I would not take upon me to spread his Detraction, and that having contracted with my Subscribers to furnish them with what might be either useful or entertaining, I could not fill their Papers with private Altercation in which they had no Concern without doing them manifest Injustice. Now many of our Printers make no scruple of gratifying the Malice of Individuals by false Accusations of the fairest Characters among ourselves, augmenting Animosity even to the producing of Duels, and are moreover so indiscrete as to print scurrilous Reflections on the Government of neighboring States, and even on the Conduct of our best national Allies, which may be attended with the most pernicious Consequences. These Things I mention as a Caution to young Printers, and that they may be encouraged not to pollute their Presses and disgrace their Profession by such infamous Practices, but refuse steadily; as they may see by my Example, that such a Course of Conduct will not on the whole be injurious to their Interests.

In 1733, I sent one of my Journeymen to Charleston South Carolina where

---

4. This is the famous preface to the twenty-fifth anniversary edition called *Father Abraham's Speech* or *The Way to Wealth.*

5. A sheet of paper with printing on only one side.

6. See n. 1, p. 496.

7. I.e., in the *Pennsylvania Gazette*, February 11 and 18, 1735.

a Printer was wanting. I furnish'd him with a Press and Letters, on an Agreement of Partnership, by which I was to receive One Third of the Profits of the Business, paying One Third of the Expense. He was a Man of Learning and honest, but ignorant in Matters of Account;[8] and tho' he sometimes made me Remittances, I could get no Account from him, nor any satisfactory State of our Partnership while he lived. On his Decease, the Business was continued by his Widow, who being born and bred in Holland, where as I have been inform'd the Knowledge of Accounts makes a Part of Female Education, she not only sent me as clear a State as she could find of the Transactions past, but continu'd to account with the greatest Regularity and Exactitude every Quarter afterwards; and manag'd the Business with such Success that she not only brought up reputably a Family of Children, but at the Expiration of the Term was able to purchase of me the Printing-House and establish her Son in it. I mention this affair chiefly for the Sake of recommending that Branch of Education for our young Females, as likely to be of more Use to them and their Children in Case of Widowhood than either Music or Dancing, by preserving them from Losses by Imposition of crafty Men, and enabling them to continue perhaps a profitable mercantile House with establish'd Correspondence till a Son is grown up fit to undertake and go on with it, to the lasting Advantage and enriching of the Family.

About the Year 1734, there arrived among us from Ireland, a young Presbyterian Preacher named Hemphill,[9] who delivered with a good Voice, and apparently extempore, most excellent Discourses, which drew together considerable Numbers of different Persuasions, who join'd in admiring them. Among the rest I became one of his constant Hearers, his Sermons pleasing me as they had little of the dogmatical kind, but inculcated strongly the Practice of Virtue, or what in the religious Style are called Good Works. Those however, of our Congregation, who considered themselves as orthodox Presbyterians, disapprov'd his Doctrine, and were join'd by most of the old Clergy, who arraign'd him of Heterodoxy before the Synod,[1] in order to have him silenc'd. I became his zealous Partisan, and contributed all I could to raise a Party[2] in his Favor; and we combated for him a while with some Hopes of Success. There was much Scribbling pro and con upon the Occasion; and finding that tho' an elegant Preacher he was but a poor Writer, I lent him my Pen and wrote for him two or three Pamphlets, and one Piece in the Gazette of April 1735. Those Pamphlets, as is generally the Case with controversial Writings, tho' eagerly read at the time, were soon out of Vogue, and I question whether a single Copy of them now exists.

During the Contest an unlucky Occurrence hurt his Cause exceedingly. One of our Adversaries having heard him preach a Sermon that was much admired, thought he had somewhere read that Sermon before, or at least a part of it. On Search he found that Part quoted at length in one of the British Reviews, from a Discourse of Dr. Foster's.[3] This Detection gave many of our Party Disgust, who accordingly abandoned his Cause, and occasion'd our more speedy Discomfiture in the Synod. I stuck by him, however, as I rather approv'd his giving us good Sermons compos'd by others, than bad ones of his

---

8. Bookkeeping.
9. Samuel Hemphill, Irish Presbyterian minister who preached in Philadelphia in 1734.
1. The governing body of the Presbyterian church.

2. A group of supporters.
3. James Foster (1697–1735), well-known London Baptist preacher.

own Manufacture; tho' the latter was the Practice of our common Teachers. He afterwards acknowledg'd to me that none of those he preach'd were his own; adding that his Memory was such as enabled him to retain and repeat any Sermon after one Reading only. On our Defeat he left us, in search elsewhere of better Fortune, and I quitted the Congregation, never joining it after, tho' I continu'd many Years my Subscription for the Support of its Ministers.

I had begun in 1733 to study Languages. I soon made myself so much a Master of the French as to be able to read the Books with Ease. I then undertook the Italian. An Acquaintance who was also learning it, us'd often to tempt me to play Chess with him. Finding this took up too much of the Time I had to spare for Study, I at length refus'd to play anymore, unless on this Condition, that the Victor in every Game, should have a Right to impose a Task, either in Parts of the Grammar to be got by heart, or in Translation, etc., which Tasks the Vanquish'd was to perform upon Honor before our next Meeting. As we play'd pretty equally we thus beat one another into that Language. I afterwards with a little Pains-taking acquir'd as much of the Spanish as to read their Books also.

I have already mention'd that I had only one Year's Instruction in a Latin School, and that when very young, after which I neglected that Language entirely.—But when I had attained an Acquaintance with the French, Italian and Spanish, I was surpris'd to find, on looking over a Latin Testament,[4] that I understood so much more of that Language than I had imagined; which encouraged me to apply myself again to the Study of it, and I met with the more Success, as those preceding Languages had greatly smooth'd my Way. From these Circumstances I have thought, that there is some Inconsistency in our common Mode of Teaching Languages. We are told that it is proper to begin first with the Latin, and having acquir'd that, it will be more easy to attain those modern languages which are deriv'd from it; and yet we do not begin with the Greek in order more easily to acquire the Latin. It is true, that if you can clamber[5] and get to the Top of a Staircase without using the Steps, you will more easily gain them in descending: but certainly if you begin with the lowest you will with more Ease ascend to the Top. And I would therefore offer it to the Consideration of those who superintend the Educating of our Youth, whether, since many of those who begin with the Latin, quit the same after spending some Years, without having made any great Proficiency, and what they have learned becomes almost useless, so that their time has been lost, it would not have been better to have begun them with the French, proceeding to the Italian, etc., for tho' after spending the same time they should quit the Study of Languages, and never arrive at the Latin, they would however have acquir'd another Tongue or two that being in modern Use might be serviceable to them in common Life.

After ten Years' Absence from Boston, and having become more easy in my Circumstances, I made a Journey thither to visit my Relations, which I could not sooner well afford. In returning I call'd at Newport, to see my Brother then settled there with his Printing-House. Our former Differences were forgotten, and our Meeting was very cordial and affectionate. He was fast declining in his Health, and requested of me that in case of his Death which he apprehended not far distant, I would take home his Son, then but 10 Years of Age,

---

4. I.e., a copy of the New Testament in Latin.   5. Climb with difficulty; scramble.

and bring him up to the Printing Business. This I accordingly perform'd, sending him a few Years to School before I took him into the Office. His Mother carried on the Business till he was grown up, when I assisted him with an Assortment of new Types, those of his Father being in a Manner worn out.— Thus it was that I made my Brother ample Amends for the Service I had depriv'd him of by leaving him so early.

In 1736 I lost one of my Sons,[6] a fine Boy of 4 Years old, by the Smallpox taken in the common way. I long regretted bitterly and still regret that I had not given it to him by Inoculation. This I mention for the Sake of Parents, who omit that Operation on the Supposition that they should never forgive themselves if a Child died under it; my Example showing that the Regret may be the same either way, and that therefore the safer should be chosen.

Our Club, the Junto, was found so useful, and afforded such Satisfaction to the Members, that several were desirous of introducing their Friends, which could not well be done without exceeding what we had settled as a convenient Number, viz., Twelve. We had from the Beginning made it a Rule to keep our Institution a Secret, which was pretty well observ'd. The Intention was, to avoid Applications of improper Persons for Admittance, some of whom perhaps we might find it difficult to refuse. I was one of those who were against any Addition to our Number, but instead of it made in Writing a Proposal, that every Member separately should endeavor to form a subordinate Club, with the same Rules respecting Queries,[7] etc., and without informing them of the Connection with the Junto. The Advantages propos'd were the Improvement of so many more young Citizens by the Use of our Institutions; Our better Acquaintance with the general Sentiments of the Inhabitants on any Occasion, as the Junto-Member might propose what Queries we should desire, and was to report to Junto what pass'd in his separate Club; the Promotion of our particular Interests in Business by more extensive Recommendations; and the Increase of our Influence in public Affairs and our Power of doing Good by spreading thro' the several Clubs the Sentiments of the Junto. The Project was approv'd, and every Member undertook to form his Club: but they did not all succeed. Five or six only were completed, which were call'd by different Names, as the Vine, the Union, the Band, etc. They were useful to themselves, and afforded us a good deal of Amusement, Information, and Instruction, besides answering in some considerable Degree our Views of influencing the public Opinion on particular Occasions, of which I shall give some Instances in course of time as they happened.

My first Promotion was my being chosen in 1736 Clerk of the General Assembly. The Choice was made that Year without Opposition, but the Year following when I was again propos'd (the Choice, like that of the Members being annual) a new Member made a long Speech against me in order to favor some other Candidate. I was however chosen; which was the more agreeable to me, as besides the Pay for immediate Service as Clerk, the Place gave me a better Opportunity of keeping up an Interest among the Members, which secur'd to me the Business of Printing the Votes, Laws, Paper Money, and other occasional Jobs for the Public, that on the whole were very profitable. I therefore did not like the Opposition of this new Member, who was a Gentle-

6. Francis Folger Franklin, who died from smallpox before he had been inoculated. Franklin did not have him inoculated because Francis was recovering from an intestinal disorder.

7. I.e., questions to be discussed.

man of Fortune, and Education, with Talents that were likely to give him in time great Influence in the House, which indeed afterwards happened. I did not however aim at gaining his Favor by paying any servile Respect to him, but after some time took this other Method. Having heard that he had in his Library a certain very scarce and curious Book, I wrote a Note to him expressing my Desire of perusing that Book, and requesting he would do me the Favor of lending it to me for a few Days. He sent it immediately; and I return'd it in about a Week, with another Note expressing strongly my Sense of the Favor. When we next met in the House he spoke to me, (which he had never done before) and with great Civility. And he ever afterwards manifested a Readiness to serve me on all Occasions, so that we became great Friends, and our Friendship continu'd to his Death. This is another Instance of the Truth of an old Maxim I had learned, which says, *He that has once done you a Kindness will be more ready to do you another, than he whom you yourself have obliged.* And it shows how much more profitable it is prudently to remove, than to resent, return and continue inimical Proceedings.

In 1737, Colonel Spotswood,[8] late Governor of Virginia, and then Postmaster General, being dissatisfied with the Conduct of his Deputy at Philadelphia, respecting some Negligence in rendering, and Inexactitude of his Accounts, took from him the Commission and offered it to me.[9] I accepted it readily, and found it of great Advantage; for tho' the Salary was small, it facilitated the Correspondence that improv'd my Newspaper, increas'd the Number demanded, as well as the Advertisements to be inserted, so that it came to afford me a very considerable Income. My old Competitor's Newspaper declin'd proportionably, and I was satisfied without retaliating his Refusal, while Postmaster, to permit my Papers being carried by the Riders. Thus He suffer'd greatly from his Neglect in due Accounting; and I mention it as a Lesson to those young Men who may be employ'd in managing Affairs for others that they should always render Accounts and make Remittances with great Clearness and Punctuality. The Character of observing Such a Conduct is the most powerful of all Recommendations to new Employments and Increase of Business.

I began now to turn my Thoughts a little to public Affairs, beginning however with small Matters. The City Watch[1] was one of the first Things that I conceiv'd to want Regulation. It was managed by the Constables of the respective Wards in Turn. The Constable warn'd a Number of Housekeepers to attend[2] him for the Night. Those who chose never to attend paid him Six Shillings a Year to be excus'd, which was suppos'd to be for hiring Substitutes; but was in Reality much more than was necessary for that purpose, and made the Constableship a Place of Profit. And the Constable for a little Drink often got such Ragamuffins about him as a Watch, that reputable Housekeepers did not choose to mix with. Walking the Rounds too was often neglected, and most of the Night spent in Tippling. I thereupon wrote a Paper to be read in Junto, representing these Irregularities, but insisting more particularly on the Inequality of this Six Shilling Tax of the Constables, respecting the Circumstances of those who paid it, since a poor Widow Housekeeper, all whose

8. Alexander Spotswood (1676–1740), military leader and lieutenant governor of Virginia 1710–22.
9. For the last nine years of his office, Bradford did not submit accounts; he was succeeded by Franklin in

October 1737.
1. I.e., the night watch or patrol.
2. Accompany.

Property to be guarded by the Watch did not perhaps exceed the Value of Fifty Pounds, paid as much as the wealthiest Merchant who had Thousands of Pounds worth of Goods in his Stores. On the whole I proposed as a more effectual Watch, the Hiring of proper Men to serve constantly in that Business; and as a more equitable Way of supporting the Charge, the levying a Tax that should be proportion'd to Property. This Idea being approv'd by the Junto, was communicated to the other Clubs, but as arising in each of them. And tho' the Plan was not immediately carried into Execution, yet by preparing the Minds of People for the Change, it paved the Way for the Law obtain'd a few Years after,[3] when the Members of our Clubs were grown into more Influence.

About this time I wrote a Paper, (first to be read in Junto but it was afterwards publish'd)[4] on the different Accidents and Carelessnesses by which Houses were set on fire, with Cautions against them, and Means proposed of avoiding them. This was much spoken of as a useful Piece, and gave rise to a Project, which soon followed it, of forming a Company for the more ready Extinguishing of Fires, and mutual Assistance in Removing and Securing of Goods when in Danger.[5] Associates in this Scheme were presently found amounting to Thirty. Our Articles of Agreement oblig'd every Member to keep always in good Order and fit for Use, a certain Number of Leather Buckets, with strong Bags and Baskets (for packing and transporting of Goods), which were to be brought to every Fire; and we agreed to meet once a Month and spend a social Evening together, in discoursing, and communicating such Ideas as occurr'd to us upon the Subject of Fires as might be useful in our Conduct on such Occasions. The Utility of this Institution soon appear'd, and many more desiring to be admitted than we thought convenient for one Company, they were advised to form another; which was accordingly done. And this went on, one new Company being formed after another, till they became so numerous as to include most of the Inhabitants who were Men of Property; and now at the time of my Writing this, tho' upwards of Fifty Years since its Establishment, that which I first formed, called the Union Fire Company, still subsists and flourishes, tho' the first Members are all deceas'd but myself and one who is older by a Year than I am. The small Fines that have been paid by Members for Absence at the Monthly Meetings, have been applied to the Purchase of Fire Engines, Ladders, Firehooks, and other useful Implements for each Company, so that I question whether there is a City in the World better provided with the Means of putting a Stop to beginning Conflagrations; and in fact since these Institutions, the City has never lost by Fire more than one or two Houses at a time, and the Flames have often been extinguish'd before the House in which they began has been half-consumed.

In 1739 arriv'd among us from England the Rev. Mr. Whitefield,[6] who had made himself remarkable there as an itinerant Preacher. He was at first permitted to preach in some of our Churches; but the Clergy taking a Dislike to him, soon refus'd him their Pulpits and he was oblig'd to preach in the Fields. The Multitudes of all Sects and Denominations that attended his Sermons were enormous and it was matter of Speculation to me who was one of the Number,

3. Actually, seventeen years later.
4. In the *Pennsylvania Gazette*, February 4, 1735.
5. The Union Fire Company articles of incorporation were signed in December 1736.
6. George Whitefield (1714–1770), a popular Methodist preacher whose visit to the colonies coincided with the spiritual revival known as the "Great Awakening."

to observe the extraordinary Influence of his Oratory on his Hearers, and how much they admir'd and respected him, notwithstanding his common Abuse of them, by assuring them they were naturally *half Beasts and half Devils*. It was wonderful to see the Change soon made in the Manners of our Inhabitants; from being thoughtless or indifferent about Religion, it seem'd as if all the World were growing Religious; so that one could not walk thro' the Town in an Evening without Hearing Psalms sung in different Families of every Street. And it being found inconvenient to assemble in the open Air, subject to its Inclemencies, the Building of a House to meet in was no sooner propos'd and Persons appointed to receive Contributions, but sufficient Sums were soon receiv'd to procure the Ground and erect the Building which was 100 feet long and 70 broad, about the Size of Westminster Hall;[7] and the Work was carried on with such Spirit as to be finished in a much shorter time than could have been expected. Both House and Ground were vested in Trustees, expressly for the Use of any Preacher of any religious Persuasion who might desire to say something to the People of Philadelphia, the Design in building not being to accommodate any particular Sect, but the Inhabitants in general, so that even if the Mufti of Constantinople were to send a Missionary to preach Mahometanism to us, he would find a Pulpit at his Service.[8]

Mr. Whitefield, in leaving us, went preaching all the Way thro' the Colonies to Georgia. The Settlement of that Province had lately been begun; but instead of being made with hardy industrious Husbandmen accustomed to Labor, the only People fit for such an Enterprise, it was with Families of broken[9] Shopkeepers and other insolvent Debtors, many of indolent and idle habits, taken out of the Jails, who being set down in the Woods, unqualified for clearing Land, and unable to endure the Hardships of a new Settlement, perished in Numbers, leaving many helpless Children unprovided for. The Sight of their miserable Situation inspired the benevolent Heart of Mr. Whitefield with the Idea of building an Orphan House there, in which they might be supported and educated. Returning northward he preach'd up this charity, and made large Collections;—for his Eloquence had a wonderful Power over the Hearts and Purses of his Hearers, of which I myself was an Instance. I did not disapprove of the Design, but as Georgia was then destitute of Materials and Workmen, and it was propos'd to send them from Philadelphia at a great Expense, I thought it would have been better to have built the House here and brought the Children to it. This I advis'd, but he was resolute in his first Project, and rejected my Counsel, and I thereupon refus'd to contribute.

I happened soon after to attend one of his Sermons, in the Course of which I perceived he intended to finish with a Collection, and I silently resolved he should get nothing from me. I had in my Pocket a Handful of Copper Money, three or four silver Dollars, and five Pistoles in Gold. As he proceeded I began to soften, and concluded to give the Coppers. Another Stroke of his Oratory made me asham'd of that, and determin'd me to give the Silver; and he finish'd so admirably, that I emptied my Pocket wholly into the Collector's Dish, Gold and all. At this Sermon there was also one of our Club, who being of my Sentiments respecting the Building in Georgia, and suspecting a Collection might be intended, had by Precaution emptied his Pockets before he came

---

7. In London.
8. The building was called "New Building" and was later used by the University of Pennsylvania, then called the Academy and College of Philadelphia. "Mufti": a judge who interprets Moslem religious law.
9. Bankrupt.

from home; towards the Conclusion of the Discourse however, he felt a strong Desire to give, and apply'd to a Neighbor who stood near him to borrow some Money for the Purpose. The Application was unfortunately to perhaps the only Man in the Company who had the firmness not to be affected by the Preacher. His Answer was, *At any other time, Friend Hopkinson,*[1] *I would lend to thee freely; but not now; for thee seems to be out of thy right Senses.*

Some of Mr. Whitefield's Enemies affected to suppose that he would apply these Collections to his own private Emolument; but I, who was intimately acquainted with him, (being employ'd in printing his Sermons and Journals,[2] etc.) never had the least Suspicion of his Integrity, but am to this day decidedly of Opinion that he was in all his Conduct, a perfectly *honest Man*. And methinks my Testimony in his Favor ought to have the more Weight, as we had no religious Connection. He us'd indeed sometimes to pray for my Conversion, but never had the Satisfaction of believing that his Prayers were heard. Ours was a mere civil Friendship, sincere on both Sides, and lasted to his Death.

The following Instance will show something of the Terms on which we stood. Upon one of his Arrivals from England at Boston, he wrote to me that he should come soon to Philadelphia, but knew not where he could lodge when there, as he understood his old kind Host Mr. Benezet[3] was remov'd to Germantown. My Answer was; You know my House, if you can make shift with its scanty Accommodations you will be most heartily welcome. He replied, that if I made that kind Offer for Christ's sake, I should not miss of a Reward.—And I return'd, *Don't let me be mistaken; it was not for Christ's sake, but for your sake.* One of our common Acquaintance jocosely remark'd, that knowing it to be the Custom of the Saints,[4] when they receiv'd any favor, to shift the Burthen of the Obligation from off their own Shoulders, and place it in Heaven, I had contriv'd to fix it on Earth.

The last time I saw Mr. Whitefield was in London, when he consulted me about his Orphan House Concern, and his Purpose of appropriating it to the Establishment of a College.

He had a loud and clear Voice, and articulated his Words and Sentences so perfectly that he might be heard and understood at a great Distance, especially as his Auditors, however numerous, observ'd the most exact Silence. He preach'd one Evening from the Top of the Court House Steps, which are in the Middle of Market Street, and on the West Side of Second Street which crosses it at right angles. Both Streets were fill'd with his Hearers to a considerable Distance. Being among the hindmost in Market Street, I had the Curiosity to learn how far he could be heard, by retiring backwards down the Street towards the River, and I found his Voice distinct till I came near Front Street,[5] when some Noise in that Street, obscur'd it. Imagining then a Semicircle, of which my Distance should be the Radius, and that it were fill'd with Auditors, to each of whom I allow'd two square feet, I computed that he might well be heard by more than Thirty Thousand. This reconcil'd me to the Newspaper Accounts of his having preach'd to 25,000 People in the Fields, and to the ancient Histories of Generals haranguing whole Armies, of which I had sometimes doubted.

---

1. Thomas Hopkinson (1709–1761), first president of the American Philosophical Society.
2. Franklin printed a number of Whitefield's books and journals from 1739 to 1741.
3. John Stephen Benezet (1683–1751) came to Phila-

delphia as a Quaker but became a Moravian, or a member of the Church of United Brethren, when he moved to Germantown.
4. Living church members who feel they are saved.
5. About five hundred feet from the courthouse.

By hearing him often I came to distinguish easily between Sermons newly compos'd, and those which he had often preach'd in the Course of his Travels. His Delivery of the latter was so improv'd by frequent Repetitions, that every Accent, every Emphasis, every Modulation of Voice, was so perfectly well turn'd and well plac'd, that without being interested in the Subject, one could not help being pleas'd with the Discourse, a Pleasure of much the same kind with that receiv'd from an excellent Piece of Music. This is an Advantage itinerant Preachers have over those who are stationary: as the latter cannot well improve their Delivery of a Sermon by so many Rehearsals.

His Writing and Printing from time to time gave great Advantage to his Enemies. Unguarded Expressions and even erroneous Opinions delivered in Preaching might have been afterwards explain'd, or qualified by supposing others that might have accompanied them; or they might have been denied; but *litera scripta manet*.[6] Critics attack'd his Writings violently, and with so much Appearance of Reason as to diminish the Number of his Votaries,[7] and prevent their Increase: So that I am of Opinion, if he had never written anything he would have left behind him a much more numerous and important Sect. And his Reputation might in that case have been still growing, even after his Death; as there being nothing of his Writings on which to found a Censure; and give him a lower Character, his Proselytes would be left at Liberty to feign for him as great a Variety of Excellencies, as their enthusiastic Admiration might wish him to have possessed.

My Business was now continually augmenting, and my Circumstances growing daily easier, my Newspaper having become very profitable, as being for a time almost the only one in this and the neighboring Provinces. I experienc'd too the Truth of the Observation, that *after getting the first hundred Pound, it is more easy to get the second:* Money itself being of a prolific Nature: The Partnership at Carolina having succeeded, I was encourag'd to engage in others, and to promote several of my Workmen who had behaved well, by establishing them with Printing-Houses in different Colonies, on the same Terms with that in Carolina. Most of them did well, being enabled at the End of our Term, Six Years, to purchase the Types of me; and go on working for themselves, by which means several Families were raised. Partnerships often finish in Quarrels, but I was happy in this, that mine were all carried on and ended amicably; owing I think a good deal to the Precaution of having very explicitly settled in our Articles everything to be done by or expected from each Partner, so that there was nothing to dispute, which Precaution I would therefore recommend to all who enter into Partnerships, for whatever Esteem Partners may have for and Confidence in each other at the time of the Contract, little Jealousies and Disgusts may arise, with Ideas of Inequality in the Care and Burden of the Business, etc., which are attended often with Breach of Friendship and of the Connection, perhaps with Lawsuits and other disagreeable Consequences.

I had on the whole abundant Reason to be satisfied with my being established in Pennsylvania. There were however two things that I regretted: There being no Provision for Defense, nor for a complete Education of Youth. No Militia nor any College. I therefore in 1743, drew up a Proposal[8] for establish-

6. *Vox audita perit, litera scripta manet:* The spoken word passes away, the written word remains (Latin).
7. Those devoted to him; disciples.

8. No such proposal exists, but it evidently included plans for using the "New Building" built for Whitefield.

ing an Academy; and at that time thinking the Rev. Mr. Peters,[9] who was out of Employ, a fit Person to superintend such an Institution, I communicated the Project to him. But he having more profitable Views in the Service of the Proprietor,[1] which succeeded, declin'd the Undertaking. And not knowing another at that time suitable for such a Trust, I let the Scheme lie a while dormant. I succeeded better the next Year, 1744, in proposing and establishing a Philosophical Society. The Paper I wrote for that purpose will be found among my Writings when collected.[2]

With respect to Defense, Spain having been several Years at War against Britain, and being at length join'd by France, which brought us into greater Danger,[3] and the labored and long-continued Endeavors of our Governor Thomas[4] to prevail with our Quaker Assembly to pass a Militia Law, and make other Provisions for the Security of the Province having proved abortive, I determined to try what might be done by a voluntary Association of the People. To promote this I first wrote and published a Pamphlet, entitled, PLAIN TRUTH,[5] in which I stated our defenseless Situation in strong Lights, with the Necessity of Union and Discipline for our Defense, and promis'd to propose in a few Days an Association to be generally signed for that purpose. The Pamphlet had a sudden and surprising Effect. I was call'd upon for the Instrument[6] of Association: And having settled the Draft of it with a few Friends, I appointed a Meeting of the Citizens in the large Building before-mentioned.

The House was pretty full. I had prepared a Number of printed Copies, and provided Pens and Ink dispers'd all over the Room. I harangu'd them a little on the Subject, read the Paper and explain'd it, and then distributed the Copies which were eagerly signed, not the least Objection being made. When the Company separated, and the Papers were collected we found above Twelve hundred Hands; and other Copies being dispers'd in the Country the Subscribers amounted at length to upwards of Ten Thousand. These all furnish'd themselves as soon as they could with Arms; form'd themselves into Companies, and Regiments, chose their own Officers, and met every Week to be instructed in the manual Exercise, and other Parts of military Discipline. The Women, by Subscriptions among themselves, provided Silk Colors, which they presented to the Companies, painted with different Devices and Mottos which I supplied. The Officers of the Companies composing the Philadelphia Regiment, being met, chose me for their Colonel; but conceiving myself unfit, I declin'd that Station, and recommended Mr. Lawrence,[7] a fine Person and Man of Influence, who was accordingly appointed. I then propos'd a Lottery to defray the Expense of Building a Battery[8] below the Town, and furnishing it with Cannon. It filled expeditiously and the Battery was soon erected, the

9. Richard Peters (c. 1704–1776), called "the most learned man in Pennsylvania." He was an Anglican clergyman and the provincial secretary to the Penn family.
1. Pennsylvania was granted by the Crown to William Penn as owner or Proprietor (see n. 7, p. 514).
2. A Proposal for Promoting Useful Knowledge among the British Plantations in America (May 14, 1743). The idea for the society was originally that of the naturalist John Bartram. The American Philosophical Society was the first learned society in North America.
3. War on Spain and France had been declared by Great Britain in 1739 and 1744, respectively. Colonial shipping was, therefore, subject to attack by privateers

of Spain and France. The Peace of Aix-la-Chapelle brought this fear to an end.
4. George Thomas (c. 1695–1774), governor of Pennsylvania, 1738–47.
5. Plain Truth; or, Serious Considerations on the Present State of the City of Philadelphia, and Province of Pennsylvania, by a "tradesman of Philadelphia" (November 17, 1747).
6. Charter, probably including the by-laws.
7. Thomas Lawrence (1689–1754), a native of New York, was the lieutenant colonel of the Philadelphia City Regiment.
8. Wall or platform on which guns are placed.

Merlons[9] being fram'd of Logs and fill'd with Earth. We bought some old Cannon from Boston, but these not being sufficient, we wrote to England for more, soliciting at the same Time our Proprietaries for some Assistance, tho' without much Expectation of obtaining it.

Meanwhile Colonel Lawrence, William Allen, Abraham Taylor, Esquires, and myself were sent to New York by the Associators, commission'd to borrow some Cannon of Governor Clinton. He at first refus'd us peremptorily: but at a Dinner with his Council where there was great Drinking of Madeira Wine, as the Custom at that Place then was, he soften'd by degrees, and said he would lend us Six. After a few more Bumpers[1] he advanc'd to Ten. And at length he very good-naturedly conceded Eighteen. They were fine Cannon, 18 pounders, with their Carriages, which we soon transported and mounted on our Battery, where the Associators kept a nightly Guard while the War lasted: And among the rest I regularly took my Turn of Duty there as a common Soldier.

My Activity in these Operations was agreeable to the Governor and Council; they took me into Confidence, and I was consulted by them in every Measure wherein their Concurrence was thought useful to the Association. Calling in the Aid of Religion, I propos'd to them the Proclaiming a Fast, to promote Reformation, and implore the Blessing of Heaven on our Undertaking. They embrac'd the Motion, but as it was the first Fast ever thought of in the Province, the Secretary had no Precedent from which to draw the Proclamation. My Education in New England, where a Fast is proclaim'd every Year, was here of some Advantage. I drew it in the accustomed Style, it was translated into German, printed in both Languages and divulg'd[2] thro' the Province. This gave the Clergy of the different Sects an Opportunity of Influencing their Congregations to join in the Association; and it would probably have been general among all but Quakers if the Peace had not soon interven'd.

It was thought by some of my Friends that by my Activity in these Affairs, I should offend that Sect, and thereby lose my Interest in the Assembly where they were a great Majority. A young Gentleman who had likewise some Friends in the House, and wish'd to succeed me as their Clerk, acquainted me that it was decided to displace me at the next Election, and he therefore in goodwill advis'd me to resign, as more consistent with my Honor than being turn'd out. My Answer to him was, that I had read or heard of some Public Man, who made it a Rule never to ask for an Office, and never to refuse one when offer'd to him. I approve, says I, of his Rule, and will practice it with a small Addition; I shall never *ask*, never *refuse*, nor ever *resign* an Office.[3] If they will have my Office of Clerk to dispose of to another, they shall take it from me. I will not be giving it up, lose my Right of some time or other making Reprisals on my adversaries. I heard however no more of this. I was chosen again, unanimously as usual, at the next Election. Possibly as they dislik'd my late Intimacy with the Members of Council, who had join'd the Governors in all the Disputes about military Preparations with which the House had long been harass'd, they might have been pleas'd if I would voluntarily have left them; but they did not care to displace me on Account merely of my Zeal for the Association; and they could not well give another Reason.

---

9. Battlements.
1. I.e., drinking vessels filled to the brim.
2. Made known.

3. Franklin here neglects to mention that he applied for the position of clerk of the assembly in 1736 and for the deputy postmaster generalship in 1751.

Indeed I had some Cause to believe, that the Defense of the Country was not disagreeable to any of them, provided they were not requir'd to assist in it. And I found that a much greater Number of them than I could have imagined, tho' against offensive War, were clearly for the defensive. Many Pamphlets *pro and con* were publish'd on the Subject, and some by good Quakers in favor of Defense, which I believe convinc'd most of their younger People. A Transaction in our Fire Company gave me some Insight into their prevailing Sentiments. It had been propos'd that we should encourage the Scheme for building a Battery by laying out the present Stock, then about Sixty Pounds, in Tickets of the Lottery. By our Rules no Money could be dispos'd of but at the next Meeting after the Proposal. The Company consisted of Thirty Members, of which Twenty-two were Quakers, and Eight only of other Persuasions. We eight punctually attended the Meeting; but tho' we thought that some of the Quakers would join us, we were by no means sure of a Majority. Only one Quaker, Mr. James Morris,[4] appear'd to oppose the Measure: He express'd much Sorrow that it had ever been propos'd, as he said *Friends*[5] were all against it, and it would create such Discord as might break up the Company. We told him, that we saw no Reason for that; we were the Minority, and if *Friends* were against the Measure and outvoted us, we must and should, agreeable to the Usage of all Societies, submit.

When the Hour for Business arriv'd, it was mov'd to put the Vote. He allow'd we might then do it by the Rules, but as he could assure us that a Number of Members intended to be present for the purpose of opposing it, it would be but candid to allow a little time for their appearing. While we were disputing this, a Waiter came to tell me two Gentlemen below desir'd to speak with me. I went down, and found they were two of our Quaker Members. They told me there were eight of them assembled at a Tavern just by; that they were determin'd to come and vote with us if there should be occasion, which they hop'd would not be the Case; and desir'd we would not call for their Assistance if we could do without it, as their Voting for such a Measure might embroil them with their Elders and Friends. Being thus secure of a Majority, I went up, and after a little seeming Hesitation, agreed to a Delay of another Hour. This Mr. Morris allow'd to be extremely fair. Not one of his opposing Friends appear'd, at which he express'd great Surprise; and at the Expiration of the Hour, we carried the Resolution Eight to one; And as of the 22 Quakers, Eight were ready to vote with us and, Thirteen by their Absence manifested that they were not inclin'd to oppose the Measure, I afterwards estimated the Proportion of Quakers sincerely against Defense as one to twenty-one only. For these were all regular Members of that Society, and in good Reputation among them, and had due Notice of what was propos'd at that Meeting.

The honorable and learned Mr. Logan,[6] who had always been of that Sect, was one who wrote an Address to them, declaring his Approbation of defensive War, and supporting his Opinion by many strong Arguments: He put into my Hands Sixty Pounds,[7] to be laid out in Lottery Tickets for the Battery, with Directions to apply what Prizes might be drawn wholly to that Service. He

4. James Morris (1707–1751), prominent Philadelphia Quaker, an assemblyman, and member of the Library Company, the first subscription library in North America.

5. I.e., members of the Society of Friends, or Quak-ers. Pacifism is a basic article of their faith.

6. James Logan (1674–1751) came to Philadelphia as William Penn's secretary in 1699 and oversaw Penn's business for fifty years.

7. Actually 250.

told me the following Anecdote of his old Master William Penn[8] respecting Defense. He came over from England, when a young Man, with that Proprietary, and as his Secretary. It was War Time, and their Ship was chas'd by an armed Vessel suppos'd to be an Enemy. Their Captain prepar'd for Defense, but told William Penn and his Company of Quakers, that he did not expect their Assistance, and they might retire into the Cabin; which they did, except James Logan, who chose to stay upon Deck, and was quarter'd to a Gun. The suppos'd Enemy prov'd a Friend; so there was no Fighting. But when the Secretary went down to communicate the Intelligence, William Penn rebuk'd him severely for staying upon Deck and undertaking to assist in defending the Vessel, contrary to the Principles of *Friends*, especially as it had not been required by the Captain. This Reproof being before all the Company, piqu'd the Secretary, who answer'd, *I being thy Servant, why did thee not order me to come down: but thee was willing enough that I should stay and help to fight the Ship when thee thought there was Danger.*

My being many Years in the Assembly, the Majority of which were constantly Quakers, gave me frequent Opportunities of seeing the Embarrassment given them by their Principle against War, whenever Application was made to them by Order of the Crown to grant Aids for military Purposes. They were unwilling to offend Government on the one hand, by a direct Refusal, and their Friends the Body of Quakers on the other, by a Compliance contrary to their Principles. Hence a Variety of Evasions to avoid Complying, and Modes of disguising the Compliance when it became unavoidable. The common Mode at last was to grant Money under the Phrase of its being *for the King's Use*, and never to enquire how it was applied. But if the Demand was not directly from the Crown, that Phrase was found not so proper, and some other was to be invented. As when Powder was wanting, (I think it was for the Garrison at Louisburg,)[9] and the Government of New England solicited a Grant of some from Pennsylvania, which was much urg'd on the House by Governor Thomas, they could not grant Money to buy Powder, because that was an Ingredient of War, but they voted an Aid to New England, of Three Thousand Pounds, to be put into the hands of the Governor, and appropriated it for the Purchasing of Bread, Flour, Wheat, *or other Grain*. Some of the Council desirous of giving the House still farther Embarrassment, advis'd the Governor not to accept Provision, as not being the Thing he had demanded. But he replied, "I shall take the Money, for I understand very well their Meaning; *Other Grain*, is Gunpowder"; which he accordingly bought; and they never objected to it.

It was in Allusion to this Fact, that when in our Fire Company we feared the Success of our Proposal in favor of the Lottery, and I had said to my friend Mr. Syng,[1] one of our Members, if we fail, let us move the Purchase of a Fire Engine with the Money; the Quakers can have no Objection to that: and then if you nominate me, and I you, as a Committee for that purpose, we will buy a great Gun, which is certainly a *Fire-Engine*: I see, says he, you have improv'd by being so long in the Assembly; your equivocal Project would be just a Match for their Wheat *or other grain*.

8. See n. 7, p. 514.
9. Fort Louisburg was built on Cape Breton Island to protect the St. Lawrence River approaches. It was captured in 1745 and returned to France in 1748 by the

Treaty of Aix-la-Chapelle.
1. Philip Syng (1703–1789), member of the Junto Club and a silversmith.

These Embarrassments that the Quakers suffer'd from having establish'd and publish'd it as one of their Principles, that no kind of War was lawful, and which being once published, they could not afterwards, however they might change their minds, easily get rid of, reminds me of what I think a more prudent Conduct in another Sect among us; that of the Dunkers. I was acquainted with one of its Founders, Michael Welfare,[2] soon after it appear'd. He complain'd to me that they were grievously calumniated by the Zealots of other Persuasions, and charg'd with abominable Principles and Practices to which they were utter Strangers. I told him this had always been the case with new Sects; and that to put a Stop to such Abuse, I imagin'd it might be well to publish the Articles of their Belief and the Rules of their Discipline. He said that it had been propos'd among them, but not agreed to, for this Reason; "When we were first drawn together as a Society, says he, it had pleased God to enlighten our Minds so far, as to see that some Doctrines which we once esteemed Truths were Errors, and that others which we had esteemed Errors were real Truths. From time to time he has been pleased to afford us farther Light, and our Principles have been improving, and our Errors diminishing. Now we are not sure that we are arriv'd at the End of this Progression, and at the Perfection of Spiritual or Theological Knowledge; and we fear that if we should once print our Confession of Faith, we should feel ourselves as if bound and confin'd by it, and perhaps be unwilling to receive farther Improvement; and our Successors still more so, as conceiving what we their Elders and Founders had done, to be something sacred, never to be departed from."

This Modesty in a Sect is perhaps a singular Instance in the History of Mankind, every other Sect supposing itself in Possession of all Truth, and that those who differ are so far in the Wrong: Like a Man traveling in foggy Weather: Those at some Distance before him on the Road he sees wrapped up in the Fog, as well as those behind him, and also the People in the Fields on each side; but near him all appears clear.—Tho' in truth he is as much in the Fog as any of them. To avoid this kind of Embarrassment the Quakers have of late Years been gradually declining the public Service in the Assembly and in the Magistracy.[3] Choosing rather to quit their Power than their Principle.[4]

In Order of Time I should have mentioned before, that having in 1742 invented an open Stove,[5] for the better warming of Rooms and at the same time saving Fuel, as the fresh Air admitted was warmed in Entering, I made a Present of the Model to Mr. Robert Grace, one of my early Friends, who having an Iron Furnace, found the Casting of the Plates for these Stoves a profitable Thing, as they were growing in Demand. To promote that Demand I wrote and published a Pamphlet entitled, *An Account of the New-Invented* PENNSYLVANIA FIRE PLACES: *Wherein their Construction and manner of Operation is particularly explained; their Advantages above every other Method of warming Rooms demonstrated; and all Objections that have been raised against the Use of them answered and obviated, etc.*[6] This Pamphlet had a good Effect. Governor Thomas was so pleas'd with the Construction of this Stove, as describ'd in it, that he offer'd to give me a Patent for the sole Vending

2. Michael Wolfaert or Wohlfahrt (1687–1741), leader of the Seventh Day Baptist community at Ephrata, Pennsylvania. "Dunkers": nickname for German Baptists who believed in baptism by total immersion. They came to Pennsylvania in 1719.
3. Courts.
4. In 1756 ten pacifist Quakers resigned from their assembly seats and three refused to run for reelection.
5. The stove that Franklin refers to is not the stove that we know today as the Franklin stove. None of Franklin's originals survives.
6. First advertised in 1744.

of them for a Term of Years; but I declin'd it from a Principle which has ever weigh'd with me on such Occasions, viz., *That as we enjoy great Advantages from the Inventions of Others, we should be glad of an Opportunity to serve others by any Invention of ours, and this we should do freely and generously.* An Ironmonger in London, however, after assuming[7] a good deal of my Pamphlet and working it up into his own, and making some small Changes in the Machine, which rather hurt its Operation, got a Patent for it there, and made as I was told a little Fortune by it. And this is not the only Instance of Patents taken out for my Inventions by others, tho' not always with the same success: which I never contested, as having no Desire of profiting by Patents myself, and hating Disputes. The Use of these Fireplaces in very many Houses both of this and the neighboring Colonies, has been and is a great Saving of Wood to the Inhabitants.

Peace being concluded, and the Association Business therefore at an End, I turn'd my Thoughts again to the Affair of establishing an Academy. The first Step I took was to associate in the Design a Number of active Friends, of whom the Junto furnished a good Part; the next was to write and publish a Pamphlet entitled, *Proposals relating to the Education of Youth in Pennsylvania.*[8] This I distributed among the principal Inhabitants gratis; and as soon as I could suppose their Minds a little prepared by the Perusal of it, I set on foot a Subscription for Opening and Supporting an Academy; it was to be paid in Quotas yearly for Five Years; by so dividing it I judg'd the Subscription might be larger, and I believe it was so, amounting to no less (if I remember right) than Five thousand Pounds.[9] In the Introduction to these Proposals, I stated their Publication not as an Act of mine, but of some *public-spirited Gentlemen*, avoiding as much as I could, according to my usual Rule, the presenting myself to the Public as the Author of any Scheme for their Benefit.

The Subscribers, to carry the Project into immediate Execution chose out of their Number Twenty-four Trustees, and appointed Mr. Francis, then Attorney General, and myself, to draw up Constitutions for the Government of the Academy, which being done and signed, an House was hired, Masters engag'd and the Schools opened I think in the same Year 1749.[1] The Scholars increasing fast, the House was soon found too small, and we were looking out for a Piece of Ground properly situated, with Intention to build, when Providence threw into our way a large House ready built, which with a few Alterations might well serve our purpose, this was the Building before-mentioned erected by the Hearers of Mr. Whitefield, and was obtain'd for us in the following Manner.

It is to be noted, that the Contributions to this Building being made by People of different Sects, Care was taken in the Nomination of Trustees, in whom the Building and Ground was to be vested, that a Predominancy should not be given to any Sect, lest in time that Predominancy might be a means of appropriating the whole to the Use of such Sect, contrary to the original Intention; it was therefore that one of each Sect was appointed, viz., one Church-of-England-man, one Presbyterian, one Baptist, one Moravian, etc. Those in case of Vacancy by Death were to fill it by Election from among the Contributors. The Moravian happen'd not to please his Colleagues, and on his Death,

7. Appropriating. The ironmonger, or hardware merchant, was probably one James Sharp.
8. Published in 1749.

9. Actually, two thousand pounds.
1. Actually, January 1751.

they resolved to have no other of that Sect. The Difficulty then was, how to avoid having two of some other Sect, by means of the new Choice. Several Persons were named and for that Reason not agreed to. At length one mention'd me, with the Observation that I was merely an honest Man, and of no Sect at all; which prevail'd with them to choose me.

The Enthusiasm which existed when the House was built, had long since abated, and its Trustees had not been able to procure fresh Contributions for paying the Ground Rent, and discharging some other Debts the Building had occasion'd, which embarrass'd them greatly. Being now a Member of both Sets of Trustees, that for the Building and that for the Academy, I had good Opportunity of negotiating with both, and brought them finally to an Agreement, by which the Trustees for the Building were to cede it to those of the Academy, the latter undertaking to discharge the Debt, to keep forever open in the Building a large Hall for occasional Preachers according to the original Intention, and maintain a Free School for the Instruction of poor Children. Writings were accordingly drawn, and on paying the Debts the Trustees of the Academy were put in Possession of the Premises, and by dividing the great and lofty Hall into Stories, and different Rooms above and below for the several Schools, and purchasing some additional Ground, the whole was soon made fit for our purpose, and the Scholars remov'd into the Building. The Care and Trouble of agreeing with the Workmen, purchasing Materials, and superintending the Work fell upon me, and I went thro' it the more cheerfully, as it did not then interfere with my private Business, having the Year before taken a very able, industrious and honest Partner, Mr. David Hall,[2] with whose Character I was well acquainted, as he had work'd for me four Years. He took off my Hands all Care of the Printing-Office, paying me punctually my Share of the Profits. This Partnership continued Eighteen Years, successfully for us both.

The Trustees of the Academy after a while were incorporated by a Charter from the Governor; their Funds were increas'd by Contributions in Britain, and Grants of Land from the Proprietaries, to which the Assembly has since made considerable Addition, and thus was established the present University of Philadelphia. I have been continued one of its Trustees from the Beginning, now near forty Years, and have had the very great Pleasure of seeing a Number of the Youth who have receiv'd their Education in it, distinguish'd by their improv'd Abilities, serviceable in public Stations, and Ornaments to their Country.

When I disengag'd myself as above-mentioned from private Business, I flatter'd myself that, by the sufficient tho' moderate Fortune I had acquir'd, I had secur'd Leisure during the rest of my Life, for Philosophical Studies[3] and Amusements; I purchas'd all Dr. Spencer's[4] Apparatus, who had come from England to lecture here; and I proceeded in my Electrical Experiments with great Alacrity; but the Public now considering me as a Man of Leisure, laid hold of me for their Purposes; every Part of our Civil Government, and almost at the same time, imposing some Duty upon me. The Governor put me into the Commission of the Peace; the Corporation of the City chose me of the Common Council, and soon after an Alderman; and the Citizens at large

2. David Hall (1714–1772), Franklin's partner, a Scots printer who came to Philadelphia at Franklin's invitation.

3. I.e., natural science.
4. Archibald Spencer (c. 1698–1760) was a lecturer on electricity. Franklin heard his Boston lectures in 1743.

chose me a Burgess to represent them in Assembly.[5] This latter Station was the more agreeable to me, as I was at length tired with sitting there to hear Debates in which as Clerk I could take no part, and which were often so unentertaining, that I was induc'd to amuse myself with making magic Squares, or Circles,[6] or anything to avoid Weariness. And I conceiv'd my becoming a Member would enlarge my Power of doing Good. I would not however insinuate that my Ambition was not flatter'd by all these Promotions. It certainly was. For considering my low Beginning they were great Things to me. And they were still more pleasing, as being so many spontaneous Testimonies of the public's good Opinion, and by me entirely unsolicited.

The Office of Justice of the Peace I tried a little, by attending a few Courts, and sitting on the Bench to hear Causes. But finding that more knowledge of the Common Law than I possess'd, was necessary to act in that Station with Credit, I gradually withdrew from it, excusing myself by my being oblig'd to attend the higher Duties of a Legislator in the Assembly. My Election to this Trust was repeated every Year for Ten Years, without my ever asking any Elector for his Vote, or signifying either directly or indirectly any Desire of being chosen. On taking my Seat in the House, my Son was appointed their Clerk.

The Year following, a Treaty being to be held with the Indians at Carlisle,[7] the Governor sent a Message to the House, proposing that they should nominate some of their Members to be join'd with some Members of Council as Commissioners for that purpose. The House nam'd the Speaker (Mr. Norris) and myself; and being commission'd we went to Carlisle, and met the Indians accordingly. As those People are extremely apt to get drunk, and when so are very quarrelsome and disorderly, we strictly forbad the selling any Liquor to them; and when they complain'd of this Restriction, we told them that if they would continue sober during the Treaty, we would give them Plenty of Rum when Business was over. They promis'd this; and they kept their Promise— because they could get no Liquor—and the Treaty was conducted very orderly, and concluded to mutual Satisfaction. They then claim'd and receiv'd the Rum. This was in the Afternoon. They were near 100 Men, Women and Children, and were lodg'd in temporary Cabins built in the Form of a Square just without the Town. In the Evening, hearing a great Noise among them, the Commissioners walk'd out to see what was the Matter. We found they had made a great Bonfire in the Middle of the Square. They were all drunk, Men and Women, quarreling and fighting. Their dark-color'd Bodies, half naked, seen only by the gloomy Light of the Bonfire, running after and beating one another with Firebrands, accompanied by their horrid Yellings, form'd a Scene the most resembling our Ideas of Hell that could well be imagin'd. There was no appeasing the Tumult, and we retired to our Lodging. At Midnight a Number of them came thundering at our Door, demanding more Rum; of which we took no Notice. The next Day, sensible they had misbehav'd in giving us that Disturbance, they sent three of their old Counselors to make their Apology. The Orator acknowledg'd the Fault, but laid it upon the

5. Franklin served as city councilman in 1748, justice of the peace in 1749, alderman in 1751, and assemblyman in 1751. "Burgess": representative to a legislative body sent by a town.
6. Franklin describes his magic squares and circles in letters to Peter Collinson in 1752. In a magic square numbers are arranged so that the sums of each row, whether horizontal, vertical, or diagonal, are always equal. A magic circle is a circular configuration of numbers whose additive values equal 180 or 360 when arranged in a prescribed way.
7. In Pennsylvania.

Rum; and then endeavor'd to excuse the Rum, by saying, *"The great Spirit who made all things made everything for some Use, and whatever Use he design'd anything for, that Use it should always be put to; Now, when he made Rum, he said,* LET THIS BE FOR INDIANS TO GET DRUNK WITH. *And it must be so.*—And indeed if it be the Design of Providence to extirpate these Savages in order to make room for Cultivators of the Earth, it seems not improbable that Rum may be the appointed Means. It has already annihilated all the Tribes who formerly inhabited the Seacoast.

In 1751 Dr. Thomas Bond,[8] a particular Friend of mine, conceiv'd the Idea of establishing a Hospital in Philadelphia for the Reception and Cure of poor sick Persons, whether Inhabitants of the Province or Strangers. A very beneficent Design, which has been ascrib'd to me, but was originally his. He was zealous and active in endeavoring to procure Subscriptions for it; but the Proposal being a Novelty in America, and at first not well understood, he met with small Success. At length he came to me, with the Compliment that he found there was no such thing as carrying a public-spirited Project through, without my being concern'd in it; "for, says he, I am often ask'd by those to whom I propose Subscribing, Have you consulted Franklin upon this Business? and what does he think of it? And when I tell them that I have not, (supposing it rather out of your Line,) they do not subscribe, but say they will consider of it." I enquir'd into the Nature, and probable Utility of his Scheme, and receiving from him a very satisfactory Explanation, I not only subscrib'd to it myself, but engag'd heartily in the Design of Procuring Subscriptions from others. Previous however to the Solicitation, I endeavored to prepare the Minds of the People by writing on the Subject in the Newspapers,[9] which was my usual Custom in such Cases, but which he had omitted. The Subscriptions afterwards were more free and generous, but beginning to flag, I saw they would be insufficient without some Assistance from the Assembly, and therefore propos'd to petition for it, which was done. The Country Members did not at first relish the Project. They objected that it could only be serviceable to the City, and therefore the Citizens should alone be at the Expense of it; and they doubted whether the Citizens themselves generally approv'd of it: My Allegation on the contrary, that it met with such Approbation as to leave no doubt of our being able to raise 2000 Pounds by voluntary Donations, they considered as a most extravagant Supposition, and utterly impossible. On this I form'd my Plan; and asking Leave to bring in a Bill, for incorporating the Contributors, according to the Prayers of their Petition, and granting them a blank Sum of Money, which Leave was obtain'd chiefly on the Consideration that the House could throw the Bill out if they did not like it, I drew it so as to make the important Clause a conditional One, viz., "And be it enacted by the Authority aforesaid That when the said Contributors shall have met and chosen their Managers and Treasurer, *and shall have raised by their Contributions a Capital Stock of 2000 Pounds Value,* (the yearly Interest of which is to be applied to the Accommodating of the Sick Poor in the said Hospital, free of Charge for Diet, Attendance, Advice and Medicines) and *shall make the same appear to the Satisfaction of the Speaker of the Assembly* for the time being; that *then* it shall and may be lawful for the said Speaker, and he is hereby

---

8. Thomas Bond (1712–1784) was Franklin's physician.
9. *Pennsylvania Gazette,* August 8 and 15, 1751.

Franklin also published *Some Account of the Pennsylvania Hospital* in 1754.

required to sign an Order on the Provincial Treasurer for the Payment of Two Thousand Pounds in two yearly Payments, to the Treasurer of the said Hospital, to be applied to the Founding, Building and Finishing of the same."— This Condition carried the Bill through; for the Members who had oppos'd the Grant, and now conceiv'd they might have the Credit of being charitable without the Expense, agreed to its Passage; And then in soliciting Subscriptions among the People we urg'd the conditional Promise of the Law as an additional Motive to give, since every Man's Donation would be doubled. Thus the Clause work'd both ways. The subscriptions accordingly soon exceeded the requisite Sum, and we claim'd and receiv'd the Public Gift, which enabled us to carry the Design into Execution. A convenient and handsome Building was soon erected, the Institution has by constant Experience been found useful, and flourishes to this Day. And I do not remember any of my political Maneuvers, the Success of which gave me at the time more Pleasure. Or that in after-thinking of it, I more easily excus'd myself for having made some Use of Cunning.

It was about this time that another Projector, the Revd. Gilbert Tennent,[1] came to me, with a Request that I would assist him in procuring a Subscription for erecting a new Meetinghouse. It was to be for the Use of a Congregation he had gathered among the Presbyterians who were originally Disciples of Mr. Whitefield. Unwilling to make myself disagreeable to my fellow Citizens, by too frequently soliciting their Contributions, I absolutely refus'd. He then desir'd I would furnish him with a List of the Names of Persons I knew by Experience to be generous and public-spirited. I thought it would be unbecoming in me, after their kind Compliance with my Solicitations, to mark them out to be worried by other Beggars, and therefore refus'd also to give such a List. He then desir'd I would at least give him my Advice. That I will readily do, said I; and, in the first Place, I advise you to apply to all those whom you know will give something; next to those whom you are uncertain whether they will give anything or not; and show them the List of those who have given: and lastly, do not neglect those who you are sure will give nothing; for in some of them you may be mistaken. He laugh'd, and thank'd me, and said he would take my Advice. He did so, for he ask'd of *everybody*; and he obtain'd a much larger Sum than he expected, with which he erected the capacious and very elegant Meetinghouse that stands in Arch Street.

Our City, tho' laid out with a beautiful Regularity, the Streets large, straight, and crossing each other at right Angles, had the Disgrace of suffering those Streets to remain long unpav'd, and in wet Weather the Wheels of heavy Carriages plough'd them into a Quagmire, so that it was difficult to cross them. And in dry Weather the Dust was offensive. I had liv'd near what was call'd the Jersey Market, and saw with Pain the Inhabitants wading in Mud while purchasing their Provisions. A Strip of Ground down the middle of that Market was at length pav'd with Brick, so that being once in the Market they had firm Footing, but were often over Shoes in Dirt to get there. By talking and writing on the Subject, I was at length instrumental in getting the Street pav'd with Stone between the Market and the brick'd Foot-Pavement that was on each Side next the Houses. This for some time gave an easy Access to the Market, dry-shod. But the rest of the Street not being pav'd, whenever a Car-

---

1. Presbyterian preacher (1703–1764) in New Brunswick, New Jersey, and companion of George Whitefield in the revival of 1740. "Projector": someone with a proposal in mind.

riage came out of the Mud upon this Pavement, it shook off and left its Dirt on it, and it was soon cover'd with Mire, which was not remov'd, the City as yet having no Scavengers.[2] After some Enquiry I found a poor industrious Man, who was willing to undertake keeping the Pavement clean, by sweeping it twice a week and carrying off the Dirt from before all the Neighbors' Doors, for the Sum of Sixpence per Month, to be paid by each House. I then wrote and printed a Paper, setting forth the Advantages to the Neighborhood that might be obtain'd by this small Expense; the greater Ease in keeping our Houses clean, so much Dirt not being brought in by People's Feet; the Benefit to the Shops by more Custom,[3] as Buyers could more easily get at them, and by not having in windy Weather the Dust blown in upon their Goods, etc., etc. I sent one of these Papers to each House, and in a Day or two went round to see who would subscribe an Agreement to pay these Sixpences. It was unanimously sign'd, and for a time well executed. All the Inhabitants of the City were delighted with the Cleanliness of the Pavement that surrounded the Market; it being a Convenience to all; and this rais'd a general Desire to have all the Streets paved; and made the People more willing to submit to a Tax for that purpose.

After some time I drew a Bill for Paving the City, and brought it into the Assembly. It was just before I went to England in 1757[4] and did not pass till I was gone, and then with an Alteration in the Mode of Assessment, which I thought not for the better, but with an additional Provision for lighting as well as Paving the Streets, which was a great Improvement. It was by a private Person, the late Mr. John Clifton,[5] his giving a Sample of the Utility of Lamps by placing one at his Door, that the People were first impress'd with the Idea of enlightening[6] all the City. The Honor of this public Benefit has also been ascrib'd to me, but it belongs truly to that Gentleman. I did but follow his Example; and have only some Merit to claim respecting the Form of our Lamps as differing from the Globe Lamps we at first were supplied with from London. Those we found inconvenient in these respects; they admitted no Air below, the Smoke therefore did not readily go out above, but circulated in the Globe, lodg'd on its Inside, and soon obstructed the Light they were intended to afford; giving, besides, the daily Trouble of wiping them clean: and an accidental Stroke on one of them would demolish it, and render it totally useless. I therefore suggested the composing them of four flat Panes, with a long Funnel above to draw up the Smoke,[7] and Crevices admitting Air below, to facilitate the Ascent of the Smoke. By this means they were kept clean, and did not grow dark in a few Hours as the London Lamps do, but continu'd bright till Morning; and an accidental Stroke would generally break but a single Pane, easily repair'd. I have sometimes wonder'd that the Londoners did not, from the Effect Holes in the Bottom of the Globe Lamps us'd at Vauxhall,[8] have in keeping them clean, learn to have such Holes in their Street Lamps. But those Holes being made for another purpose, viz., to communicate Flame more suddenly to the Wick, by a little Flax hanging down thro' them, the other Use of letting in Air seems not to have been thought of.—And

2. Street cleaners.
3. Business, trade.
4. Franklin went to England as an agent for the Pennsylvania Assembly to negotiate with Thomas and Richard Penn on the matter of taxing proprietary estates in common with other property.

5. Quaker apothecary (d. 1759).
6. I.e., illuminating.
7. These lamps may now be seen in Independence Square, Philadelphia.
8. A garden and amusement park near London.

therefore, after the Lamps have been lit a few Hours, the Streets of London are very poorly illuminated.

The Mention of these Improvements puts me in mind of one I propos'd when in London, to Dr. Fothergill,[9] who was among the best Men I have known, and a great Promoter of useful Projects. I had observ'd that the Streets when dry were never swept and the light Dust carried away, but it was suffer'd to accumulate till wet Weather reduc'd it to Mud, and then after lying some Days so deep on the Pavement that there was no Crossing but in Paths kept clean by poor People with Brooms, it was with great Labor rak'd together and thrown up into Carts open above, the Sides of which suffer'd some of the Slush at every jolt on the Pavement to shake out and fall, sometimes to the Annoyance of Foot-Passengers. The Reason given for not sweeping the dusty Streets was, that the Dust would fly into the Windows of Shops and Houses. An accidental Occurrence had instructed me how much Sweeping might be done in a little Time. I found at my Door in Craven Street[1] one Morning a poor Woman sweeping my Pavement with a birch Broom. She appeared very pale and feeble as just come out of a Fit of Sickness. I ask'd who employ'd her to sweep there. She said, "Nobody; but I am very poor and in Distress, and I sweeps before Gentlefolkeses Doors, and hopes they will give me something." I bid her sweep the whole Street clean and I would give her a Shilling. This was at 9 aClock. At 12 she came for the Shilling. From the Slowness I saw at first in her Working, I could scarce believe that the Work was done so soon, and sent my Servant to examine it, who reported that the whole Street was swept perfectly clean, and all the Dust plac'd in the Gutter which was in the Middle. And the next Rain wash'd it quite away, so that the Pavement and even the Kennel[2] were perfectly clean. I then judg'd that if that feeble Woman could sweep such a Street in 3 Hours, a strong active Man might have done it in half the time. And here let me remark the Convenience of having but one Gutter in such a narrow Street, running down its Middle, instead of two, one on each Side near the Footway. For Where all the Rain that falls on a Street runs from the Sides and meets in the middle, it forms there a Current strong enough to wash away all the Mud it meets with: But when divided into two Channels, it is often too weak to cleanse either, and only makes the Mud it finds more fluid, so that the Wheels of Carriages and Feet of Horses throw and dash it up on the Foot Pavement which is thereby rendered foul and slippery, and sometimes splash it upon those who are walking. My Proposal communicated to the good Doctor, was as follows.

"For the more effectual cleaning and keeping clean the Streets of London and Westminster, it is proposed,

"That the several Watchmen be contracted with to have the Dust swept up in dry Seasons, and the Mud rak'd up at other Times, each in the several Streets and Lanes of his Round.

"That they be furnish'd with Brooms and other proper Instruments for these purposes, to be kept at their respective Stands, ready to furnish the poor People they may employ in the Service.

"That in the dry Summer Months the Dust be all swept up into Heaps at

---

9. John Fothergill (1712–1780), a leader of the English Quakers and Franklin's physician when he was in London.
1. A street in London near Charing Cross where

Franklin lived from 1757 to 1762 and from 1764 to 1775.
2. Gutter.

proper Distances, before the Shops and Windows of Houses are usually opened: when the Scavengers with close-covered Carts shall also carry it all away.

"That the Mud when rak'd up be not left in Heaps to be spread abroad again by the Wheels of Carriages and Trampling of Horses; but that the Scavengers be provided with Bodies of Carts, not plac'd high upon Wheels, but low upon Sliders; with Lattice Bottoms, which being cover'd with Straw, will retain the Mud thrown into them, and permit the Water to drain from it, whereby it will become much lighter, Water making the greatest Part of its Weight. These Bodies of Carts to be plac'd at convenient Distances, and the Mud brought to them in Wheelbarrows, they remaining where plac'd till the Mud is drain'd, and then Horses brought to draw them away."

I have since had Doubts of the Practicability of the latter Part of this Proposal, on Account of the Narrowness of some Streets, and the Difficulty of placing the Draining Sleds so as not to encumber too much the Passage: But I am still of Opinion that the former, requiring the dust to be swept up and carried away before the Shops are open, is very practicable in the Summer, when the Days are long. For in walking thro' the Strand and Fleet Street one Morning at 7 aClock I observ'd there was not one shop open tho' it had been Daylight and the Sun up above three Hours. The Inhabitants of London choosing voluntarily to live much by Candle Light, and sleep by Sunshine; and yet often complain, a little absurdly, of the Duty on Candles and the high Price of Tallow.

Some may think these trifling Matters not worth minding or relating. But when they consider, that tho' Dust blown into the Eyes of a single Person or into a single Shop on a windy Day, is but of small Importance, yet the great Number of the Instances in a populous City, and its frequent Repetitions give it Weight and Consequence; perhaps they will not censure very severely those who bestow some of Attention to Affairs of this seemingly low Nature. Human Felicity is produc'd not so much by great Pieces of good Fortune that seldom happen, as by little Advantages that occur every Day. Thus if you teach a poor young Man to shave himself and keep his Razor in order, you may contribute more to the Happiness of his Life than in giving him a 1000 Guineas. The Money will be soon spent, and the Regret only remaining of having foolishly consum'd it. But in the other Case he escapes the frequent Vexation of waiting for Barbers, and of their sometimes, dirty Fingers, offensive Breaths and dull Razors. He shaves when most convenient to him, and enjoys daily the Pleasure of its being done with a good Instrument.—With these Sentiments I have hazarded the few preceding Pages, hoping they may afford Hints which some time or other may be useful to a City I love, having lived many Years in it very happily, and perhaps to some of our Towns in America.

Having been for some time employed by the Postmaster General of America, as his Comptroller, in regulating the several Offices, and bringing the Officers to account, I was upon his Death in 1753 appointed jointly with Mr. William Hunter[3] to succeed him by a Commission from the Postmaster General in England. The American Office had never hitherto paid anything to that of Britain. We were to have 600 Pounds a Year between us if we could make that Sum out of the Profits of the Office. To do this, a Variety of

---

3. Printer and publisher of the *Virginia Gazette* (d. 1761).

Improvements were necessary; some of these were inevitably at first expensive; so that in the first four Years the Office became above 900 Pounds in debt to us. But it soon after began to repay us, and before I was displac'd, by a Freak of the Minister's, of which I shall speak hereafter, we had brought it to yield *three times* as much clear Revenue to the Crown as the Post-Office of Ireland. Since that imprudent Transaction, they have receiv'd from it,—Not one Farthing.[4]

The Business of the Post-Office occasion'd my taking a Journey this Year to New England, where the College of Cambridge of their own Motion, presented me with the Degree of Master of Arts. Yale College in Connecticut, had before made me a similar Compliment.[5] Thus without studying in any College I came to partake of their Honors. They were Confer'd in Consideration of my Improvements and Discoveries in the electric Branch of Natural Philosophy.

In 1754, War with France being again apprehended,[6] a Congress of Commissioners from the different Colonies, was by an Order of the Lords of Trade, to be assembled at Albany, there to confer with the Chiefs of the Six Nations,[7] concerning the Means of defending both their Country and ours. Governor Hamilton, having receiv'd this Order, acquainted the House with it, requesting they would furnish proper Presents[8] for the Indians to be given on this Occasion; and naming the Speaker (Mr. Norris) and myself, to join Mr. Thomas Penn and Mr. Secretary Peters,[9] as Commissioners to act for Pennsylvania. The House approv'd the Nomination, and provided the Goods for the Present, tho' they did not much like treating out of the Province, and we met the other Commissioners and met at Albany about the Middle of June. In our Way thither, I projected and drew up a Plan for the Union of all the Colonies, under one Government so far as might be necessary for Defense, and other important general Purposes. As we pass'd thro' New York, I had there shown my Project to Mr. James Alexander and Mr. Kennedy,[1] two Gentlemen of great Knowledge in public Affairs, and being fortified by their Approbation I ventur'd to lay it before the Congress. It then appear'd that several of the Commissioners had form'd Plans of the same kind. A previous Question was first taken whether a Union should be established, which pass'd in the Affirmative unanimously. A Committee was then appointed, One Member from each Colony, to consider the several Plans and report. Mine happen'd to be prefer'd, and with a few Amendments was accordingly reported.

By this Plan, the general Government was to be administered by a President General appointed and supported by the Crown, and a Grand Council to be chosen by the Representatives of the People of the several Colonies met in their respective Assemblies. The Debates upon it in Congress went on daily hand in hand with the Indian Business. Many Objections and Difficulties were started, but at length they were all overcome, and the Plan was unanimously agreed to, and Copies ordered to be transmitted to the Board of Trade

4. Coin worth one-quarter of a penny.
5. Actually, Yale conferred the degree on September 12, 1753, and Harvard on July 25.
6. Because the Iroquois Indians had defected to the French.
7. The confederation of Iroquois-speaking tribes: Seneca, Cayuga, Onondaga, Oneida, Mohawk, and Tuscarora.
8. It was customary to present goods to the Indians.

9. For Peters, see n. 9, p. 439. I was actually John Penn (1729–1795), a nephew of Thomas Penn and later lieutenant governor of Pennsylvania, 1763–71, 1773–76.
1. Alexander (1691–1756), a New Yorker who held public offices in New York and, later, New Jersey. Archibald Kennedy (1685–1763) held high public office in New York and wrote *The Importance of Gaining and Preserving the Friendship of the Indians* (1751).

and to the Assemblies of the several Provinces. Its Fate was singular. The Assemblies did not adopt it, as they all thought there was too much *Prerogative* in it; and in England it was judg'd to have too much of the *Democratic*.[2] The Board of Trade therefore did not approve of it; nor recommend it for the Approbation of his Majesty; but another Scheme was form'd (suppos'd better to answer the same Purpose) whereby the Governors of the Provinces with some Members of their respective Councils were to meet and order the raising of Troops, building of Forts, etc., etc., to draw on the Treasury of Great Britain for the Expense, which was afterwards to be refunded by an Act of Parliament laying a Tax on America. My Plan, with my Reasons in support of it, is to be found among my political Papers that are printed.[3]

Being the Winter following in Boston, I had much Conversation with Governor Shirley[4] upon both the Plans. Part of what pass'd between us on the Occasion may also be seen among those Papers. The different and contrary Reasons of dislike to my Plan, makes me suspect that it was really the true Medium; and I am still of Opinion it would have been happy for both Sides the Water if it had been adopted. The Colonies so united would have been sufficiently strong to have defended themselves; there would then have been no need of Troops from England; of course the subsequent Pretense for Taxing America, and the bloody Contest it occasioned, would have been avoided. But such Mistakes are not new; History is full of the Errors of States and Princes.

> "Look round the habitable World, how few
> Know their own Good, or knowing it pursue."[5]

Those who govern, having much Business on their hands, do not generally like to take the Trouble of considering and carrying into Execution new Projects. The best public Measures are therefore seldom *adopted from previous Wisdom*, but *forc'd by the Occasion*.

The Governor of Pennsylvania in sending it down to the Assembly, express'd his Approbation of the Plan "as appearing to him to be drawn up with great Clearness and Strength of Judgment, and therefore recommended it as well worthy their closest and most serious Attention." The House however, by the Management of a certain Member, took it up when I happen'd to be absent, which I thought not very fair, and reprobated[6] it without paying any Attention to it at all, to my no small Mortification.

In my Journey to Boston this Year I met at New York with our new Governor, Mr. Morris,[7] just arriv'd there from England, with whom I had been before intimately acquainted. He brought a Commission to supersede Mr. Hamilton, who, tir'd with the Disputes his Proprietary Instructions subjected him to, had resigned. Mr. Morris ask'd me, if I thought he must expect as uncomfortable an Administration. I said, No; you may on the contrary have a very comfortable one, if you will only take care not to enter into any Dispute

2. "Too much Prerogative" means too much royal power was to be invested in the proposed governor general of all the North American colonies. "Too much Democratic" means that too much power was to be given to the proposed intercolonial legislature.
3. *Political, Miscellaneous, and Philosophical Papers* (1779). Labaree points out that Franklin has oversimplified reasons for the failure of the Albany plan. The colonies themselves feared the domination of any one colony and were wary of strong-willed colonial assemblies and reluctant to see any one strong legislature emerge.
4. William Shirley (1694–1771), governor of Massachusetts, 1741–49 and 1753–56.
5. From John Dryden's translation of Juvenal's *Tenth Satire*, lines 1–3.
6. Rejected totally.
7. Robert Hunter Morris (c. 1700–1764), governor of Pennsylvania, 1754–56.

with the Assembly; "My dear Friend, says he, pleasantly, how can you advise my avoiding Disputes. You know I love Disputing; it is one of my greatest Pleasures: However, to show the Regard I have for your Counsel, I promise you I will if possible avoid them." He had some Reason for loving to dispute, being eloquent, an acute Sophister, and therefore generally successful in argumentative Conversation. He had been brought up to it from a Boy, his Father (as I have heard) accustoming his Children to dispute with one another for his Diversion while sitting at Table after Dinner. But I think the Practice was not wise, for in the Course of my Observation, these disputing, contradicting and confuting People are generally unfortunate in their Affairs. They get Victory sometimes, but they never get Good Will, which would be of more use to them. We parted, he going to Philadelphia, and I to Boston. In returning, I met at New York with the Votes of the Assembly, by which it appear'd that notwithstanding his Promise to me, he and the House were already in high Contention, and it was a continual Battle between them, as long as he retain'd the Government.

I had my Share of it; for as soon as I got back to my Seat in the Assembly, I was put on every Committee for answering his Speeches and Messages, and by the Committees always desired to make the Drafts. Our Answers as well as his Messages were often tart, and sometimes indecently abusive. And as he knew I wrote for the Assembly, one might have imagined that when we met we could hardly avoid cutting Throats. But he was so good-natur'd a Man, that no personal Difference between him and me was occasion'd by the Contest, and we often din'd together.[8] One Afternoon in the height of this public Quarrel, we met in the Street. "Franklin, says he, you must go home with me and spend the Evening. I am to have some Company that you will like;" and taking me by the Arm he led me to his House. In gay Conversation over our Wine after Supper he told us Jokingly that he much admir'd the Idea of Sancho Panza, who when it was propos'd to give him a Government, requested it might be a Government of *Blacks*, as then, if he could not agree with his People he might sell them.[9] One of his Friends who sat next me, says, "Franklin, why do you continue to side with these damn'd Quakers? had not you better sell them? the Proprietor[1] would give you a good Price." The Governor, says I, had not yet *black'd* them enough. He had indeed labor'd hard to blacken the Assembly in all his Messages, but they wip'd off his Coloring as fast as he laid it on, and plac'd it in return thick upon his own Face; so that finding he was likely to be negrified himself, he as well as Mr. Hamilton, grew tir'd of the Contest, and quitted the Government.

These public Quarrels were all at bottom owing to the Proprietaries, our hereditary Governors; who when any Expense was to be incurr'd for the Defense of their Province, with incredible Meanness instructed their Deputies to pass no Act for levying the necessary Taxes, unless their vast Estates were in the same Act expressly excused; and they had even taken Bonds of those Deputies to observe such Instructions. The Assemblies for three Years held out against this Injustice. Tho' constrain'd to bend at last. At length Captain

8. It has often been observed that Franklin's account of Pennsylvania politics during this period is too temperate to reflect accurately some of the real bitterness.
9. A distortion of Cervantes' novel. In *Don Quixote*, part I, chap. 29, Sancho Panza grieves at the idea of governing blacks until he realizes that he could sell them.
1. Now, Thomas Penn (1702–1775), son of William Penn.

Denny,[2] who was Governor Morris's Successor, ventur'd to disobey those Instructions; how that was brought about I shall show hereafter.

But I am got forward too fast with my Story; there are still some Transactions to be mentioned that happened during the Administration of Governor Morris.

War being, in a manner, commenced with France[3] the Government of Massachusetts Bay projected an Attack upon Crown Point,[4] and sent Mr. Quincy to Pennsylvania, and Mr. Pownall,[5] afterwards Governor Pownall, to New York to solicit Assistance. As I was in the Assembly, knew its Temper, and was Mr. Quincy's Countryman, he applied to me for my Influence and Assistance. I dictated his Address to them which was well receiv'd. They voted an Aid of Ten Thousand Pounds, to be laid out in Provisions. But the Governor refusing his Assent to their Bill, (which included this with other Sums granted for the Use of the Crown) unless a Clause were inserted exempting the Proprietary Estate from bearing any Part of the Tax that would be necessary, the Assembly, tho' very desirous of making their Grant to New England effectual, were at a Loss how to accomplish it. Mr. Quincy laboured hard with the Governor to obtain his Assent, but he was obstinate. I then suggested a Method of doing the Business without the Governor, by Orders on the Trustees of the Loan-Office, which by Law the Assembly had the Right of Drawing.[6] There was indeed little or no Money at that time in the Office, and therefore I propos'd that the Orders should be payable in a Year and to bear an Interest of Five percent. With these Orders I suppos'd the Provisions might easily be purchas'd. The Assembly with very little Hesitation adopted the Proposal. The Orders were immediately printed, and I was one of the Committee directed to sign and dispose of them. The Fund for Paying them was the Interest of all the Paper Currency then extant in the Province upon Loan, together with the Revenue arising from the Excise,[7] which being known to be more than sufficient, they obtain'd instant Credit, and were not only receiv'd in Payment for the Provisions, but many money'd People who had Cash lying by them, vested it in those Orders, which they found advantageous, as they bore Interest while upon hand, and might on any Occasion be used as Money: So that they were eagerly all bought up, and in a few Weeks none of them were to be seen. Thus this important Affair was by my means completed. Mr. Quincy return'd Thanks to the Assembly in a handsome Memorial, went home highly pleas'd with the Success of his Embassy, and ever after bore for me the most cordial and affectionate Friendship.

The British Government not choosing to permit the Union of the Colonies, as propos'd at Albany, and to trust that Union with their Defense, lest they should thereby grow too military, and feel their own Strength, Suspicions and

2. William Denny (1709–1765), governor of Pennsylvania, 1756–59, a corrupt man, was pressured into signing a bill taxing proprietary estates in 1759. The assembly had failed to get the proprietors to share the expenses of government and did not attempt to tax their estates until 1775. Franklin's account remains unfinished.

3. Franklin is referring to the French and Indian War, which began in 1754 and concluded with the Treaty of Paris in 1763. The defeat of the French in these wars brought to an end the great French influence in North America.

4. Fort St. Frederick was located at Crown Point on Lake Champlain to guard the approaches to Montreal and Quebec.

5. Josiah Quincy (1710–1784), wealthy Massachusetts merchant. Thomas Pownall (1722–1805), governor of Massachusetts, 1757–60.

6. The Loan Office lent paper money authorized by legislative act and secured by mortgages on real estate. Interest was received on the loans. The assembly was empowered to direct the expenditure of these receipts.

7. A tax on articles made and used in the colonies.

Jealousies at this time being entertain'd of them, sent over General Braddock[8] with two Regiments of Regular English Troops for that purpose. He landed at Alexandria in Virginia, and thence march'd to Frederick Town[9] in Maryland, where he halted for Carriages. Our Assembly apprehending, from some Information, that he had conceived violent Prejudices against them, as averse to the Service, wish'd me to wait upon him, not as from them, but as Postmaster General, under the guise of proposing to settle with him the Mode of conducting with most Celerity and Certainty the Dispatches between him and the Governors of the several Provinces, with whom he must necessarily have continual Correspondence, and of which they propos'd to pay the Expense. My Son accompanied me on this Journey. We found the General at Frederick Town, waiting impatiently for the Return of those he had sent thro' the back Parts of Maryland and Virginia to collect Waggons. I stayed with him several Days, Din'd with him daily, and had full Opportunity of removing all his Prejudices, by the Information of what the Assembly had before his Arrival actually done and were still willing to do to facilitate his Operations.

When I was about to depart, the Returns of Waggons to be obtain'd were brought in, by which it appear'd that they amounted only to twenty-five, and not all of those were in serviceable Condition. The General and all the Officers were surpris'd, declar'd the Expedition was then at an End, being impossible, and exclaim'd against the Ministers for ignorantly landing them in a Country destitute of the Means of conveying their Stores, Baggage, etc., not less than 150 Waggons being necessary. I happen'd to say, I thought it was pity they had not been landed rather in Pennsylvania, as in that Country almost every Farmer had his Waggon. The General eagerly laid hold of my Words, and said, "Then you, Sir, who are a Man of Interest there, can probably procure them for us; and I beg you will undertake it." I ask'd what Terms were to be offer'd the Owners of the Waggons; and I was desir'd to put on Paper the Terms that appear'd to me necessary. This I did, and they were agreed to, and a Commission and Instructions accordingly prepar'd immediately. What those Terms were will appear in the Advertisement I publish'd as soon as I arriv'd at Lancaster,[1] which being, from the great and sudden Effect it produc'd, a Piece of some Curiosity, I shall insert at length, as follows.

ADVERTISEMENT

Lancaster, April 26, 1755.

WHEREAS 150 Waggons, with 4 Horses to each Waggon, and 1500 Saddle or Pack-Horses are wanted for the Service of his Majesty's Forces now about to rendezvous at *Wills's* Creek;[2] and his Excellency General *Braddock* hath been pleased to empower me to contract for the Hire of the same; I hereby give Notice, that I shall attend for that Purpose at *Lancaster* from this Time till next *Wednesday* Evening; and at *York* from next *Thursday* Morning 'till *Friday* Evening; where I shall be ready to agree for Waggons and Teams, or single Horses, on the following Terms, viz.,

1st. That there shall be paid for each Waggon with 4 good Horses and a

8. Edward Braddock (1695–1755), commander of the British forces in North America in the French and Indian War.
9. Frederick, fifty miles northwest of Annapolis, Maryland.
1. In Pennsylvania.
2. At Fort Cumberland, in the western part of Maryland.

Driver, *Fifteen Shillings* per *Diem:* And for each able Horse with a Pack-Saddle or other Saddle and Furniture,[3] *Two Shillings* per *Diem.* And for each able Horse without a Saddle, *Eighteen Pence* per *Diem.*

2dly, That the Pay commence from the Time of their joining the Forces at *Wills's* Creek (which must be on or before the twentieth of *May* ensuing) and that a reasonable Allowance be made over and above for the Time necessary for their traveling to *Wills's* Creek and home again after their Discharge.

3dly, Each Waggon and Team, and every Saddle or Pack Horse is to be valued by indifferent[4] Persons, chosen between me and the Owner, and in Case of the Loss of any Waggon, Team or other Horse in the Service, the Price according to such Valuation, is to be allowed and paid.

4thly, Seven Days' Pay is to be advanced and paid in hand by me to the Owner of each Waggon and Team, or Horse, at the Time of contracting, if required; and the Remainder to be paid by General *Braddock*, or by the Paymaster of the Army, at the Time of their Discharge, or from time to time as it shall be demanded.

5thly, No Drivers of Waggons, or Persons taking care of the hired Horses, are on any Account to be called upon to do the Duty of Soldiers, or be otherwise employ'd than in conducting or taking Care of their Carriages and Horses.

6thly, All Oats, Indian Corn or other Forage,[5] that Waggons or Horses bring to the Camp more than is necessary for the Subsistence of the Horses, is to be taken for the Use of the Army, and a reasonable Price paid for it.

Note. My Son *William Franklin*, is empowered to enter into like Contracts with any Person in *Cumberland* County.

B. FRANKLIN.

To the Inhabitants of the Counties of Lancaster,
York, *and* Cumberland.

Friends and Countrymen,
BEING occasionally at the Camp at *Frederick* a few Days since, I found the General and Officers of the Army extremely exasperated, on Account of their not being supplied with Horses and Carriages, which had been expected from this Province as most able to furnish them; but thro' the Dissensions between our Governor and Assembly, Money had not been provided nor any Steps taken for that Purpose.

It was proposed to send an armed Force immediately into these Counties, to seize as many of the best Carriages and Horses as should be wanted, and compel as many Persons into the Service as would be necessary to drive and take care of them.

I apprehended that the Progress of a Body of Soldiers thro' these Counties on such an Occasion, especially considering the Temper they are in, and their Resentment against us, would be attended with many and great Inconveniences to the Inhabitants; and therefore more willingly undertook the Trouble of trying first what might be done by fair and equitable Means.

The People of these back Counties have lately complained to the Assembly that a sufficient Currency was wanting; you have now an Opportunity of

3. Tack, harnesses.   5. Fodder.
4. Ojective.

receiving and dividing among you a very considerable Sum; for if the Service of this Expedition should continue (as it's more than probable it will) for 120 Days, the Hire of these Waggons and Horses will amount to upwards of *Thirty thousand Pounds*, which will be paid you in Silver and Gold of the King's Money.

The Service will be light and easy, for the Army will scarce march above 12 Miles per Day, and the Waggons and Baggage Horses, as they carry those Things that are absolutely necessary to the Welfare of the Army, must march with the Army and no faster, and are, for the Army's sake, always plac'd where they can be most secure, whether on a March or in Camp.

If you are really, as I believe you are, good and loyal Subjects to His Majesty, you may now do a most acceptable Service, and make it easy to yourselves; for three or four of such as cannot separately spare from the Business of their Plantations a Waggon and four Horses and a Driver, may do it together, one furnishing the Waggon, another one or two Horses, and another the Driver, and divide the Pay proportionably between you. But if you do not this Service to your King and Country voluntarily, when such good Pay and reasonable Terms are offered you, your Loyalty will be strongly suspected; the King's Business must be done; so many brave Troops, come so far for your Defense, must not stand idle, thro' your backwardness to do what may be reasonably expected from you; Waggons and Horses must be had; violent Measures will probably be used; and you will be to seek for a Recompense where you can find it, and your Case perhaps be little pitied or regarded.

I have no particular Interest in this Affair; as (except the Satisfaction of endeavouring to do Good and prevent Mischief) I shall have only my Labor for my Pains. If this Method of obtaining the Waggons and Horses is not like to succeed, I am oblig'd to send Word to the General in fourteen Days; and I suppose Sir *John St. Clair* the Hussar,[6] with a Body of Soldiers, will immediately enter the Province, for the Purpose aforesaid, of which I shall be sorry to hear, because
I am,

very sincerely and truly
your Friend and Well-wisher, B. FRANKLIN

I receiv'd of the General about 800 Pounds to be disburs'd in Advance-money to the Waggon-Owners, etc.: but that Sum being insufficient, I advanc'd upwards of 200 Pounds more, and in two Weeks, the 150 Waggons with 259 carrying Horses were on their March for the Camp. The Advertisement promised Payment according to the Valuation, in case any Waggon or Horse should be lost. The Owners however, alledging they did not know General Braddock, or what Dependance might be had on his Promise, insisted on my Bond for the Performance, which I accordingly gave them.

While I was at the Camp, supping one Evening with the Officers of Colonel Dunbar's[7] Regiment, he represented to me his Concern for the Subalterns, who he said were generally not in Affluence, and could ill afford in this dear[8] Country to lay in the Stores that might be necessary in so long a March thro'

6. Cavalryman. Sir John Sinclair (?) or St. Clair had a reputation for violence. I.e., Sinclair will requisition horses.
7. Thomas Dunbar (d. 1767), colonel who replaced

Braddock as commander of the North American forces in 1755.
8. Expensive. "Subalterns": officers below the rank of captain.

a Wilderness where nothing was to be purchas'd. I commiserated their Case, and resolved to endeavor procuring them some Relief. I said nothing however to him of my Intention, but wrote the next Morning to the Committee of Assembly, who had the Disposition of some public Money, warmly recommending the Case of these Officers to their consideration, and proposing that a Present should be sent them of Necessaries and Refreshments. My Son,[9] who had had some Experience of a Camp Life, and of its Wants, drew up a List for me, which I enclos'd in my Letter. The Committee approv'd, and used such Diligence, that conducted by my Son, the Stores arrived at the Camp as soon as the Waggons. They consisted of 20 Parcels, each containing

> 6 lb. Loaf Sugar[1]
> 6 lb. good Muscovado[2] Ditto
> 1 lb. good Green Tea
> 1 lb. good Bohea[3] Ditto
> 6 lb. good ground Coffee
> 6 lb. Chocolate
> 1/2 Hundredweight best white Biscuit
> 1/2 lb. Pepper
> 1 Quart best white Wine Vinegar
> 1 Gloucester Cheese
> 1 Keg containing 20 lb. good Butter
> 2 Doz. old Madeira Wine
> 2 Gallons Jamaica Spirits[4]
> 1 Bottle Flour of Mustard
> 2 well-cur'd Hams
> 1/2 Doz. dried Tongues
> 6 lb. Rice.
> 6 lb. Raisins.

These 20 Parcels well pack'd were plac'd on as many Horses, each Parcel with the Horse, being intended as a Present for one Officer. They were very thankfully receiv'd, and the Kindness acknowledg'd by Letters to me from the Colonels of both Regiments in the most grateful Terms. The General too was highly satisfied with my Conduct in procuring him the Waggons, etc., and readily paid my Account of Disbursements; thanking me repeatedly and requesting my farther Assistance in sending Provisions after him. I undertook this also, and was busily employ'd in it till we heard of his Defeat,[5] advancing, for the Service, of my own Money, upwards of 1000 Pounds Sterling, of which I sent him an Account. It came to his Hands luckily for me a few Days before the Battle, and he return'd me immediately an Order on the Paymaster for the round Sum of 1000 Pounds, leaving the Remainder to the next Account. I consider this Payment as good Luck; having never been able to obtain that Remainder; of which more hereafter.

This General was I think a brave Man, and might probably have made a Figure as a good Officer in some European War. But he had too much self-

9. William Franklin had been an officer in a colonial army that was brought together to resist French Canada.
1. In this period sugar was either loaf shaped or cone shaped.
2. Unrefined sugar.

3. In the 18th century, a fine black tea.
4. Rum.
5. Braddock died from wounds received in the Battle of the Wilderness, near the Monongahela River, on July 9, 1755. George Washington directed the survivors of this battle in retreat.

confidence, too high an Opinion of the Validity of Regular Troops,[6] and too mean a One of both Americans and Indians. George Croghan, our Indian Interpreter, join'd him on his March with 100 of those People, who might have been of great Use to his Army as Guides, Scouts, etc., if he had treated them kindly; but he slighted and neglected them, and they gradually left him.

In Conversation with him one day, he was giving me some Account of his intended Progress. "After taking Fort Duquesne,[7] says he, I am to proceed to Niagara; and having taken that, to Frontenac,[8] if the Season will allow time; and I suppose it will; for Duquesne can hardly detain me above three or four Days; and then I see nothing that can obstruct my March to Niagara."— Having before revolv'd in my Mind the long Line his Army must make in their March, by a very narrow Road to be cut for them thro' the Woods and Bushes; and also what I had read of a former Defeat of 1500 French who invaded the Iroquois Country,[9] I had conceiv'd some Doubts, and some Fears for the Event of the Campaign. But I ventur'd only to say, To be sure, Sir, if you arrive well before Duquesne, with these fine Troops so well provided with Artillery, that Place, not yet completely fortified, and as we hear with no very strong Garrison, can probably make but a short Resistance. The only Danger I apprehend of Obstruction to your March, is from Ambuscades of Indians, who by constant Practice are dextrous in laying and executing them. And the slender Line near four Miles long, which your Army must make, may expose it to be attack'd by Surprise in its Flanks, and to be cut like a Thread into several Pieces, which from their Distance cannot come up in time to support each other.

He smil'd at my Ignorance, and replied, "These Savages may indeed be a formidable Enemy to your raw American Militia; but, upon the King's regular and disciplin'd Troops, Sir, it is impossible they should make any Impression." I was conscious of an Impropriety in my Disputing with a military Man in Matters of his Profession, and said no more.—The Enemy however did not take the Advantage of his Army which I apprehended its long Line of March expos'd it to, but let it advance without Interruption till within 9 Miles of the Place,[1] and then when more in a Body, (for it had just pass'd a River, where the Front had halted till all were come over) and in a more open Part of the Woods than any it had pass'd, attack'd its advanc'd Guard, by a heavy Fire from behind Trees and Bushes; which was the first Intelligence the General had of an Enemy's being near him. This Guard being disordered, the General hurried the Troops up to their Assistance, which was done in great Confusion thro' Waggons, Baggage and Cattle; and presently the Fire came upon their Flank; the Officers being on Horseback were more easily distinguish'd, pick'd out as Marks, and fell very fast; and the Soldiers were crowded together in a Huddle, having or hearing no Orders, and standing to be shot at till two-thirds of them were killed, and then being seiz'd with a Panic the whole fled with Precipitation. The Waggoners took each a Horse out of his Team, and scamper'd; their Example was immediately follow'd by others, so that all the Waggons, Provisions, Artillery and Stores were left to the Enemy.

The General being wounded was brought off with Difficulty, his Secretary

6. I.e., the standing army.
7. At Pittsburgh.
8. In Quebec.
9. Franklin may have in mind the campaign of the

Marquis de Denonville against the Seneca tribe in 1687. The French were ambushed and forced to retreat.

1. I.e., Fort Duquesne.

Mr. Shirley[2] was killed by his Side, and out of 86 Officers 63 were killed or wounded, and 714 Men killed out of 1100.[3] These 1100 had been picked Men, from the whole Army, the Rest had been left behind with Colonel Dunbar, who was to follow with the heavier Part of the Stores, Provisions and Baggage. The Fliers, not being pursu'd, arriv'd at Dunbar's Camp, and the Panic they brought with them instantly seiz'd him and all his People. And tho' he had now above 1000 Men, and the Enemy who had beaten Braddock did not at most exceed 400,[4] Indians and French together; instead of Proceeding and endeavoring to recover some of the lost Honor, he order'd all the Stores, Ammunitions, etc., to be destroy'd, that he might have more Horses to assist his Flight towards the Settlements, and less Lumber[5] to remove. He was there met with Requests from the Governors of Virginia, Maryland and Pennsylvania, that he would post his Troops on the Frontiers so as to afford some Protection to the Inhabitants; but he continu'd his hasty March thro' all the Country, not thinking himself safe till he arriv'd at Philadelphia, where the Inhabitants could protect him. This whole Transaction gave us Americans the first Suspicion that our exalted Ideas of the Prowess of British Regulars had not been well founded.

In their first March too, from their Landing till they got beyond the Settlements, they had plundered and stripped the Inhabitants, totally ruining some poor Families, besides insulting, abusing and confining the People if they remonstrated. This was enough to put us out of Conceit[6] of such Defenders if we had really wanted any. How different was the Conduct of our French Friends in 1781, who during a March thro' the most inhabited Part of our Country, from Rhode Island to Virginia, near 700 Miles, occasion'd not the smallest Complaint, for the Loss of a Pig, a Chicken, or even an Apple!

Captain Orme,[7] who was one of the General's Aides Camp, and being grievously wounded was brought off with him, and continu'd with him to his Death, which happen'd in a few Days, told me, that he was totally silent, all the first Day, and at Night only said, *Who'd have thought it?* that he was silent again the following Days, only saying at last, *We shall better know how to deal with them another time*; and died a few Minutes after.

The Secretary's Papers with all the General's Orders, Instructions and Correspondence falling into the Enemy's Hands, they selected and translated into French a Number of the Articles, which they printed to prove the hostile Intentions of the British Court before the Declaration of War. Among these I saw some Letters of the General to the Ministry speaking highly of the great Service I had rendered the Army, and recommending me to their Notice. David Hume[8] too, who was some Years after Secretary to Lord Harcourt when Minister in France, and afterwards to General Conway when Secretary of State, told me he had seen among the Papers in that Office Letters from Braddock highly recommending me. But the Expedition having been unfortunate, my Service it seems was not thought of much Value, for those Recommendations were never of any Use to me.

As to Rewards from himself, I ask'd only one, which was, that he would

---

2. William Shirley, Jr. (1721–1755), son of the governor of Massachusetts.
3. More accurately, 1,469 military were engaged, 456 were killed, and 520 were wounded.
4. A more accurate estimate would be eight hundred.
5. I.e., supplies and equipment.

6. Patience.
7. Robert Orme (d. 1790).
8. Scottish philosopher and historian (1711–1776), later secretary to Francis Seymour-Conway (1719–1749), first marquis of Hertford.

give Orders to his Officers not to enlist any more of our bought servants,[9] and that he would discharge such as had been already enlisted. This he readily granted, and several were accordingly return'd to their Masters on my Application. Dunbar, when the Command devolv'd on him, was not so generous. He Being at Philadelphia on his Retreat, or rather Flight, I applied to him for the Discharge of the Servants of three poor Farmers of Lancaster County that he had enlisted, reminding him of the late General's Orders on that head. He promis'd me, that if the Masters would come to him at Trenton, where he should be in a few Days on his March to New York, he would there deliver their Men to them. They accordingly were at the Expense and Trouble of going to Trenton, and there he refus'd to perform his Promise, to their great Loss and Disappointment.

As soon as the Loss of the Waggons and Horses was generally known, all the Owners came upon me for the Valuation which I had given Bond to pay. Their Demands gave me a great deal of Trouble, my acquainting them that the Money was ready in the Paymaster's Hands, but that Orders for paying it must first be obtained from General Shirley, and my assuring them that I had applied to that General by Letter, but he being at a Distance an Answer could not soon be receiv'd, and they must have Patience; all this was not sufficient to satisfy, and some began to sue me. General Shirley at length reliev'd me from this terrible Situation, by appointing Commissioners to examine the Claims and ordering Payment. They amounted to near twenty Thousand Pound, which to pay would have ruined me.

Before we had the News of this Defeat, the two Doctors Bond came to me with a Subscription Paper,[1] for raising Money to defray the Expense of a grand Firework, which it was intended to exhibit at a Rejoicing on receipt of the News of our Taking Fort Duquesne. I looked grave and said, "it would, I thought, be time enough to prepare for the Rejoicing when we knew we should have occasion to rejoice."—They seem'd surpris'd that I did not immediately comply with their Proposal. "Why, the D—l," says one of them, "you surely don't suppose that the Fort will not be taken?" "I don't know that it will not be taken; but I know that the Events of War are subject to great Uncertainty."—I gave them the Reasons of my doubting. The Subscription was dropped, and the Projectors thereby miss'd that Mortification they would have undergone if the Firework had been prepared. Dr. Bond on some other Occasions afterwards said, that he did not like Franklin's forebodings.

Governor Morris who had continually worried the Assembly with Message after Message before the Defeat of Braddock, to beat them into the making of Acts to raise Money for the Defense of the Province without Taxing among others the Proprietary Estates, and had rejected all their Bills for not having such an exempting Clause, now redoubled his Attacks, with more hope of Success, the Danger and Necessity being greater. The Assembly however continu'd firm, believing they had Justice on their side, and that it would be giving up an essential Right, if they suffered the Governor to amend their Money-Bills. In one of the last, indeed, which was for granting 50,000 Pounds, his propos'd Amendment was only of a single Word; the Bill express'd that all Estates real and personal were to be taxed, those of the Proprietaries *not*

9. I.e., indentured servants whose masters received no compensation while they were conscripted.
1. Petition to which subscribers would agree to con-

tribute money. "Doctors Bond": Thomas Bond (1713–1784) and Phineas Bond (1717–1773), Philadelphia physicians.

excepted. His Amendment was; For *not* read *only*. A small but very material Alteration! However, when the News of this Disaster reach'd England, our Friends there whom we had taken care to furnish with all the Assembly's Answers to the Governor's Messages, rais'd a Clamor against the Proprietaries for their Meanness and Injustice in giving their Governor such Instructions, some going so far as to say that by obstructing the Defense of their Province, they forfeited their Right to it. They were intimidated by this, and sent Orders to their Receiver General to add 5000 Pounds of their Money to whatever Sum might be given by the Assembly, for such Purpose. This being notified to the House, was accepted in Lieu of their Share of a general Tax, and a new Bill was form'd with an exempting Clause which pass'd accordingly. By this Act I was appointed one of the Commissioners for disposing of the Money, 60,000 Pounds. I had been active in modelling it, and procuring its Passage: and had at the same time drawn a Bill for establishing and disciplining a voluntary Militia, which I carried thro' the House without much Difficulty, as Care was taken in it, to leave the Quakers at their Liberty.[2]

To promote the Association necessary to form the Militia, I wrote a Dialogue,[3] stating and answering all the Objections I could think of to such a Militia, which was printed and had as I thought great Effect. While the several Companies in the City and Country were forming and learning their Exercise, the Governor prevail'd with me to take Charge of our Northwestern Frontier, which was infested by the Enemy, and provide for the Defense of the Inhabitants by raising Troops, and building a Line of Forts. I undertook this military Business, tho' I did not conceive myself well-qualified for it. He gave me a Commission with full Powers and a Parcel of blank Commissions for Officers to be given to whom I thought fit. I had but little Difficulty in raising Men, having soon 560 under my Command. My Son who had in the preceding War been an Officer in the Army rais'd against Canada, was my Aide de Camp, and of great Use to me. The Indians had burned Gnadenhut,[4] a Village settled by the Moravians,[5] and massacred the Inhabitants, but the Place was thought a good Situation for one of the Forts. In order to march thither, I assembled the Companies at Bethlehem, the chief Establishment of those People. I was surprised to find it in so good a Posture of Defense. The Destruction of Gnadenhut had made them apprehend Danger. The principal Buildings were defended by a Stockade: They had purchased a Quantity of Arms and Ammunition from New York, and had even plac'd Quantities of small Paving Stones between the Windows of their high Stone Houses, for their Women to throw down upon the Heads of any Indians that should attempt to force into them. The armed Brethren too, kept Watch, and reliev'd[6] as methodically as in any Garrison Town. In Conversation with Bishop Spangenberg, I mention'd this my Surprise; for knowing they had obtain'd an Act of Parliament exempting them from military Duties in the Colonies, I had suppos'd they were conscientiously scrupulous of bearing Arms. He answer'd me, "That it

2. Franklin's bill was vetoed by the ministry on July 7, 1756. It provided exemption for conscientious objectors, made enlistment voluntary, and contained little in the way of military discipline.
3. "This Dialogue and the Militia Act are in the Gent. Magazine for February and March 1756" [Franklin's note]. *Dialogue between X, Y, and Z* first appeared in the *Pennsylvania Gazette*, December 18, 1755, and was reprinted in *Gentleman's Magazine*, March 26,

1756. The *Militia Act* appeared in *Gentleman's Magazine* in February.
4. Gnadenhutten, now Leightown, Pennsylvania, was burned on November 24, 1755; new troops stationed there were defeated on January 1, 1756.
5. Moravians were members of the Church of the United Brethren and immigrated from Saxony in 1735. Their center was at Bethlehem, Pennsylvania.
6. I.e., relieved the guard and kept careful watch.

was not one of their establish'd Principles; but that at the time of their obtaining that Act, it was thought to be a Principle with many of their People. On this Occasion, however, they to their Surprise found it adopted by but a few." It seems they were either deceiv'd in themselves, or deceiv'd the Parliament. But Common Sense aided by present Danger, will sometimes be too strong for whimsical Opinions.

It was the Beginning of January when we set out upon this Business of Building Forts. I sent one Detachment towards the Minisinks,[7] with Instructions to erect one for the Security of that upper Part of the Country; and another to the lower Part, with similar Instructions. And I concluded to go myself with the rest of my Force to Gnadenhut, where a Fort was thought more immediately necessary. The Moravians procur'd me five Waggons for our Tools, Stores, Baggage, etc. Just before we left Bethlehem, Eleven Farmers who had been driven from their Plantations by the Indians, came to me, requesting a supply of Fire Arms, that they might go back and fetch off their Cattle. I gave them each a Gun with suitable Ammunition. We had not march'd many Miles before it began to rain, and it continu'd raining all Day. There were no Habitations on the Road, to shelter us, till we arriv'd near Night, at the House of a German, where and in his Barn we were all huddled together as wet as Water could make us.[8] It was well we were not attack'd in our March, for Our Arms were of the most ordinary Sort, and our Men could not keep their Gunlocks[9] dry. The Indians are dextrous in Contrivances for that purpose, which we had not. They met that Day the eleven poor Farmers above-mentioned and kill'd Ten of them.[1] The one who escap'd inform'd that his and his Companions' Guns would not go off, the Priming being wet with the Rain.

The next Day being fair, we continu'd our March and arriv'd at the desolated Gnadenhut. There was a Saw Mill near, round which were left several Piles of Boards, with which we soon hutted ourselves; an Operation the more necessary at that inclement Season, as we had no Tents. Our first Work was to bury more effectually the Dead we found there, who had been half interr'd by the Country People. The next Morning our Fort was plann'd and mark'd out, the Circumference measuring 455 feet, which would require as many Palisades to be made of Trees one with another of a Foot Diameter each. Our Axes, of which we had 70 were immediately set to work, to cut down Trees; and our Men being dextrous in the Use of them, great Dispatch was made. Seeing the Trees fall so fast, I had the Curiosity to look at my Watch when two Men began to cut at a Pine. In 6 Minutes they had it upon the Ground; and I found it of 14 Inches Diameter. Each Pine made three Palisades of 18 Feet long, pointed at one End. While these were preparing, our other Men, dug a Trench all round of three feet deep in which the Palisades were to be planted, and our Waggons, the Body being taken off, and the fore and hind Wheels separated by taking out the Pin which united the two Parts of the Perch,[2] we had 10 Carriages with two Horses each, to bring the Palisades from the Woods to the Spot. When they were set up, our Carpenters built a Stage of Boards all round within, about 6 Feet high, for the Men to stand on when

---

7. I.e., northeastern Pennsylvania. The northern Delaware Indians were called Munsees or Minisinks.
8. The march from Bethlehem to Gnadenhutten took place from January 15 to 18, 1756.
9. The firing mechanism, which required priming powder.
1. Actually, two of the eleven escaped.
2. The wagon shaft that connects the front and rear axles.

to fire thro' the Loopholes. We had one swivel Gun which we mounted on one of the Angles; and fired it as soon as fix'd, to let the Indians know, if any were within hearing, that we had such Pieces. And thus our Fort, (if such a magnificent Name may be given to so miserable a Stockade) was finished in a Week, tho' it rain'd so hard every other Day that the Men could not work.

This gave me occasion to observe, that when Men are employ'd they are best contented. For on the Days they work'd they were good-natur'd and cheerful; and with the consciousness of having done a good Day's work they spent the Evenings jollily; but on the idle Days they were mutinous and quarrelsome, finding fault with their Pork, the Bread, etc., and in continual ill-humor: which put me in mind of a Sea-Captain, whose Rule it was to keep his Men constantly at Work; and when his Mate once told him that they had done everything, and there was nothing farther to employ them about; O, says he, *make them scour the Anchor.*

This kind of Fort, however contemptible, is a sufficient Defense against Indians who have no Cannon. Finding ourselves now posted securely, and having a Place to retreat to on Occasion, we ventur'd out in Parties to scour the adjacent Country. We met with no Indians, but we found the Places on the neighboring Hills where they had lain to watch our Proceedings. There was an Art in their Contrivance of these Places that seems worth mention. It being Winter, a Fire was necessary for them. But a common Fire on the Surface of the Ground would by its Light have discover'd their Position at a Distance. They had therefore dug Holes in the Ground about three feet Diameter, and somewhat deeper. We saw where they had with their Hatchets cut off the Charcoal from the Sides of burned Logs lying in the Woods. With these Coals they had made small Fires in the Bottom of the Holes, and we observ'd among the Weeds and Grass the Prints of their Bodies made by their laying all around with their Legs hanging down in the Holes to keep their Feet warm, which with them is an essential Point. This kind of Fire, so manag'd, could not discover them either by its Light, Flame, Sparks or even Smoke. It appear'd that their Number was not great, and it seems they saw we were too many to be attack'd by them with Prospect of Advantage.

We had for our Chaplain a zealous Presbyterian Minister, Mr. Beatty,[3] who complain'd to me that the Men did not generally attend his Prayers and Exhortations. When they enlisted, they were promis'd, besides Pay and Provisions, a Gill[4] of Rum a Day, which was punctually serv'd out to them, half in the Morning and the other half in the Evening, and I observ'd they were as punctual in attending to receive it. Upon which I said to Mr. Beatty, "It is perhaps below the Dignity of your Profession to act as Steward of the Rum. But if you were to deal it out, and only just after Prayers, you would have them all about you." He lik'd the Thought, undertook the Office, and with the help of a few hands to measure out the Liquor executed it to Satisfaction; and never were Prayers more generally and more punctually attended. So that I thought this Method preferable to the Punishments inflicted by some military Laws for Non-Attendance on Divine Service.

I had hardly finish'd this Business, and got my Fort well stor'd with Provisions, when I receiv'd a Letter from the Governor, acquainting me that he had called the Assembly, and wish'd my Attendance there, if the Posture of Affairs

3. Charles Clinton Beatty (c. 1715–1772), later pastor of the Deep Run, Pennsylvania, Presbyterian church and trustee of the College of New Jersey.
4. Quarter of a pint.

on the Frontiers was such that my remaining there was no longer necessary. My Friends too of the Assembly pressing me by their Letters to be if possible at the Meeting, and my three intended Forts being now completed,[5] and the Inhabitants contented to remain on their Farms under that Protection, I resolved to return. The more willingly as a New England Officer, Colonel Clapham,[6] experienc'd in Indian War, being on a Visit to our Establishment, consented to accept the Command. I gave him a Commission, and parading the Garrison had it read before them, and introduc'd him to them as an Officer who from his Skill in Military Affairs, was much more fit to command them than myself; and giving them a little Exhortation took my Leave. I was escorted as far as Bethlehem, where I rested a few Days, to recover from the Fatigue I had undergone. The first Night being in a good Bed, I could hardly sleep, it was so different from my hard Lodging on the Floor of our Hut at Gnaden, wrapped only in a Blanket or two.

While at Bethlehem, I enquir'd a little into the Practices of the Moravians. Some of them had accompanied me, and all were very kind to me. I found they work'd for a common Stock,[7] ate at common Tables, and slept in common Dormitories, great Numbers together. In the Dormitories I observ'd Loopholes at certain Distances all along just under the Ceiling, which I thought judiciously plac'd for Change of Air. I was at their Church, where I was entertain'd with good Music, the Organ being accompanied with Violins, Hautboys,[8] Flutes, Clarinets, etc. I understood that their Sermons were not usually preached to mix'd Congregations of Men, Women and Children, as is our common Practice; but that they assembled sometimes the married Men, at other times their Wives, then the Young Men, the young Women, and the little Children, each Division by itself. The Sermon I heard was to the latter, who came in and were plac'd in Rows on Benches, the Boys under the Conduct of a young Man their Tutor, and the Girls conducted by a young Woman. The Discourse seem'd well adapted to their Capacities, and was delivered in a pleasing familiar Manner, coaxing them as it were to be good. They behav'd very orderly, but look'd pale and unhealthy, which made me suspect they were kept too much within-doors, or not allow'd sufficient Exercise. I enquir'd concerning the Moravian Marriages, whether the Report was true that they were by Lot? I was told that Lots were us'd only in particular Cases. That generally when a young Man found himself dispos'd to marry, he inform'd the Elders of his Class, who consulted the Elder Ladies that govern'd the young Women. As these Elders of the different Sexes were well acquainted with the Tempers and Dispositions of their respective Pupils, they could best judge what Matches were suitable, and their Judgments were generally acquiesc'd in. But if for example it should happen that two or three young Women were found to be *equally* proper for the young Man, the Lot was then recurr'd to. I objected, If the Matches are not made by the mutual Choice of the Parties, some of them may chance to be very unhappy. And so they may, answer'd my Informer, if you let the Parties choose for themselves.—Which indeed I could not deny.

Being return'd to Philadelphia, I found the Association went on swim-

5. The stockade Fort Allen named by Franklin; the others were Fort Norris, about fifteen miles northeast, and Fort Franklin, about fifteen miles southwest.
6. William Clapham (d. 1763) was well known as a frontiersman; he died at Fort Pitt.
7. I.e., shared their produce communally.
8. Oboes.

mingly, the Inhabitants that were not Quakers having pretty generally come into it, form'd themselves into Companies, and chosen their Captains, Lieutenants and Ensigns[9] according to the new Law.[1] Dr. B.[2] visited me, and gave me an Account of the Pains he had taken to spread a general good Liking to the Law, and ascrib'd much to those Endeavors. I had had the Vanity to ascribe all to my Dialogue; However, not knowing but that he might be in the right, I let him enjoy his Opinion, which I take to be generally the best way in such Cases.—The Officers meeting chose me to be Colonel of the Regiment; which I this time accepted. I forget how many Companies we had, but We paraded about 1200 well-looking Men, with a Company of Artillery who had been furnish'd with 6 brass Field Pieces, which they had become so expert in the Use of as to fire twelve times in a Minute. The first Time I review'd my Regiment, they accompanied me to my House, and would salute me with some Rounds fired before my Door, which shook down and broke several Glasses of my Electrical Apparatus. And my new Honor prov'd not much less brittle; for all our Commissions were soon after broke by a Repeal of the Law in England.[3]

During the short time of my Colonelship, being about to set out on a Journey to Virginia, the Officers of my Regiment took it into their heads that it would be proper for them to escort me out of town as far as the Lower Ferry. Just as I was getting on Horseback, they came to my door, between 30 and 40, mounted, and all in their Uniforms. I had not been previously acquainted with the Project, or I should have prevented it, being naturally averse to the assuming of State on any Occasion, and I was a good deal chagrin'd at their Appearance, as I could not avoid their accompanying me. What made it worse, was, that as soon as we began to move, they drew their Swords, and rode with them naked all the way. Somebody wrote an Account of this to the Proprietor, and it gave him great Offense. No such Honor had been paid him when in the Province; nor to any of his Governors; and he said it was only proper to Princes of the Blood Royal; which may be true for aught I know, who was, and still am, ignorant of the Etiquette, in such Cases. This silly Affair, however greatly increas'd his Rancor against me, which was before not a little, on account of my Conduct in the Assembly, respecting the Exemption of his Estate from Taxation, which I had always oppos'd very warmly, and not without severe Reflections on his Meanness and Injustice in contending for it. He accus'd me to the Ministry as being the great Obstacle to the King's Service, preventing by my Influence in the House the proper Forming of the Bills for raising Money; and he instanc'd this Parade with my Officers as a Proof of my having an Intention to take the Government of the Province out of his Hands by Force. He also applied to Sir Everard Fawkener,[4] then Post Master General, to deprive me of my Office. But this had no other Effect, than to procure from Sir Everard a gentle Admonition.

Notwithstanding the continual Wrangle between the Governor and the House, in which I as a Member had so large a Share, there still subsisted a civil Intercourse between that Gentleman and myself, and we never had any

---

9. Standard-bearer; the lowest commissioned army grade.
1. The militia elections were held from December 22 to 24, and caused rioting when Governor Morris refused to accept balloting at the polls as valid.
2. Probably Thomas Bond.

3. Franklin was commissioned on February 23, 1756; Philadelphians were informed that the Militia Act had been rejected in mid-October 1756.
4. Fawkener (1684–1758) was appointed postmaster general in 1745.

personal Difference. I have sometimes since thought that his little or no Resentment against me for the Answers it was known I drew up to his Messages, might be the Effect of professional Habit, and that, being bred a Lawyer, he might consider us both as merely Advocates for contending Clients in a suit, he for the Proprietaries and I for the Assembly. He would therefore sometimes call in a friendly way to advise with me on difficult Points, and sometimes, tho' not often, take my Advice. We acted in Concert to supply Braddock's Army with Provisions, and When the shocking News arriv'd of his Defeat, the Governor sent in haste for me, to consult with him on Measures for preventing the Desertion of the back Counties. I forget now the Advice I gave, but I think it was, that Dunbar should be written to and prevail'd with if possible to post his Troops on the Frontiers for their Protection, till by Reinforcements from the Colonies, he might be able to proceed on the Expedition.—And after my Return from the Frontier, he would have had me undertake the Conduct of such an Expedition with Provincial Troops, for the Reduction of Fort Duquesne, Dunbar and his Men being otherwise employ'd; and he propos'd to commission me as General. I had not so good an Opinion of my military Abilities as he profess'd to have; and I believe his Professions must have exceeded his real Sentiments: but probably he might think that my Popularity would facilitate the Raising of the Men, and my Influence in Assembly the Grant of Money to pay them;—and that, perhaps, without taxing the Proprietary Estate. Finding me not so forward to engage as he expected, the Project was dropped: and he soon after left the Government, being superseded by Captain Denny.

Before I proceed in relating the Part I had in public Affairs under this new Governor's Administration, it may not be amiss here to give some Account of the Rise and Progress of my Philosophical[5] Reputation.

In 1746 being at Boston, I met there with a Dr. Spencer,[6] who was lately arrived from Scotland, and show'd me some electric Experiments. They were imperfectly perform'd, as he was not very expert; but being on a Subject quite new to me, they equally surpris'd and pleas'd me. Soon after my Return to Philadelphia, our Library Company receiv'd from Mr. Peter Collinson,[7] F.R.S. of London a Present of a Glass Tube,[8] with some Account of the Use of it in making such Experiments. I eagerly seiz'd the Opportunity of repeating what I had seen at Boston, and by much Practice acquir'd great Readiness in performing those also which we had an Account of from England, adding a Number of new Ones. I say much Practice, for my House was continually full for some time, with People who came to see these new Wonders. To divide a little this Incumbrance among my Friends, I caused a Number of similar Tubes to be blown at our Glass-House, with which they furnish'd themselves, so that we had at length several Performers. Among these the Principal was Mr. Kinnersley,[9] an ingenious Neighbor, who being out of Business, I encouraged to undertake showing the Experiments for Money, and drew up for him two Lectures, in which the Experiments were rang'd in such Order and accompanied with Explanations, in such Method, as that the foregoing should assist in Comprehending the following. He procur'd an elegant Apparatus for

5. Scientific.
6. Dr. Archibald Spencer, physician and natural scientist.
7. London Quaker and botanist (1694–1768), fellow of the Royal Society.

8. I.e., a solid glass rod that when rubbed with a cloth, produces electrical charges.
9. Ebenezer Kinnersley (1711–1778), Philadelphia schoolmaster who worked closely with Franklin on his experiments in electricity.

the purpose, in which all the little Machines that I had roughly made for myself, were nicely form'd by Instrument-makers. His Lectures were well attended and gave great Satisfaction; and after some time he went thro' the Colonies exhibiting them in every capital Town, and pick'd up some Money. In the West India Islands indeed it was with Difficulty the Experiments could be made, from the general Moisture of the Air.

Oblig'd as we were to Mr. Collinson for his Present of the Tube, etc., I thought it right he should be inform'd of our Success in using it, and wrote him several Letters containing Accounts of our Experiments. He got them read in the Royal Society, where they were not at first thought worth so much Notice as to be printed in their Transactions. One Paper which I wrote for Mr. Kinnersley, on the Sameness of Lightning with Electricity, I sent to Dr. Mitchel,[1] an Acquaintance of mine, and one of the Members also of that Society; who wrote me word that it had been read but was laughed at by the Connoisseurs:[2] The Papers however being shown to Dr. Fothergill,[3] he thought them of too much value to be stifled, and advis'd the Printing of them. Mr. Collinson then gave them to *Cave*[4] for publication in his Gentleman's Magazine; but he chose to print them separately in a Pamphlet, and Dr. Fothergill wrote the Preface.[5] *Cave* it seems judg'd rightly for his Profit; for by the Additions that arriv'd afterwards they swell'd to a Quarto Volume, which has had five Editions, and cost him nothing for Copy-money.[6]

It was however some time before those Papers were much taken Notice of in England. A Copy of them happening to fall into the Hands of the Count de Buffon,[7] a Philosopher deservedly of great Reputation in France, and indeed all over Europe, he prevail'd with M. Dalibard[8] to translate them into French; and they were printed at Paris. The Publication offended the Abbé Nollet, Preceptor[9] in Natural Philosophy to the Royal Family, and an able Experimenter, who had form'd and publish'd a Theory of Electricity, which then had the general Vogue. He could not at first believe that such a Work came from America, and said it must have been fabricated by his Enemies at Paris, to decry his System. Afterwards having been assur'd that there really existed such a Person as Franklin of Philadelphia, which he had doubted, he wrote and published a Volume of Letters, chiefly address'd to me, defending his Theory, and denying the Verity of my Experiments and of the Positions deduc'd from them. I once purpos'd answering the Abbé, and actually began the Answer. But on Consideration that my Writings contain'd only a Description of Experiments, which any one might repeat and verify, and if not to be verified could not be defended; or of Observations, offer'd as Conjectures, and not delivered dogmatically, therefore not laying me under any Obligation to defend them; and reflecting that a Dispute between two Persons writing in different Languages might be lengthened greatly by mistranslations, and thence misconceptions of one another's Meaning, much of one of the Abbé's

1. John Mitchell (d. 1768), English physician and mapmaker.
2. Franklin seems to have underestimated the reception of his observations by English scientists, many of whom recognized them as important.
3. Dr. John Fothergill (1712–1780).
4. Edward Cave (1691–1754), English publisher of *Gentleman's Magazine* (1731–54).
5. To Franklin's *Experiments and Observations on Electricity* (1751).
6. Copyright; money paid to authors for their manu-

script.
7. Georges Louis Leclerc, Comte de Buffon (1707–1788), French naturalist whose comments on the inferiority of North American species inspired Jefferson to write his *Notes on the State of Virginia*.
8. Thomas François Dalibard (1703–1799), well-known physician.
9. Instructor, tutor. Jean Antoine Nollet (1700–1770), French scientist whose theories of electricity were corrected by Franklin's experiments.

Letters being founded on an Error in the Translation; I concluded to let my Papers shift for themselves; believing it was better to spend what time I could spare from public Business in making new Experiments, than in Disputing about those already made. I therefore never answer'd M. Nollet; and the Event gave me no Cause to repent my Silence; for my Friend M. le Roy[1] of the Royal Academy of Sciences took up my Cause and refuted him, my Book was translated into the Italian, German and Latin Languages, and the Doctrine it contain'd was by degrees universally adopted by the Philosophers of Europe in preference to that of the Abbé, so that he liv'd to see himself the last of his Sect: except Mr. B——[2] his Elève and immediate Disciple.

What gave my Book the more sudden and general Celebrity, was the Success of one of its propos'd Experiments, made by Messrs. Dalibard and Delor, at Marly,[3] for drawing Lightning from the Clouds. This engag'd the public Attention everywhere. M. Delor, who had an Apparatus for experimental Philosophy, and lectur'd in that Branch of Science, undertook to repeat what he call'd the *Philadelphia Experiments*, and after they were performed before the King and Court, all the Curious of Paris flock'd to see them. I will not swell this Narrative with an Account of that capital Experiment, nor of the infinite Pleasure I receiv'd in the Success of a similar one I made soon after with a Kite at Philadelphia, as both are to be found in the Histories of Electricity. Dr. Wright,[4] an English Physician then at Paris, wrote to a Friend who was of the Royal Society an Account of the high Esteem my Experiments were in among the Learned abroad, and of their Wonder that my Writings had been so little noticed in England. The Society on this resum'd the Consideration of the Letters that had been read to them, and the celebrated Dr. Watson[5] drew up a summary Account of them, and of all I had afterwards sent to England on the Subject, which he accompanied with some Praise of the Writer. This Summary was then printed in their Transactions: And some Members of the Society in London, particularly the very ingenious Mr. Canton,[6] having verified the Experiment of procuring Lightning from the Clouds by a Pointed Rod, and acquainting them with the Success, they soon made me more than Amends for the Slight with which they had before treated me. Without my having made any Application for that Honor, they chose me a Member, and voted that I should be excus'd the customary Payments, which would have amounted to twenty-five Guineas, and ever since have given me their Transactions[7] gratis. They also presented me with the Gold Medal of Sir Godfrey Copley[8] for the Year 1753, the Delivery of which was accompanied by a very handsome Speech of the President Lord Macclesfield,[9] wherein I was highly honored.

1. Jean Baptiste Le Roy (1720–1800) invented the first practical generator and perfected the lightning rod.
2. Pupil (French). "Mr. B——": Mathurin Jacques Brisson (1723–1806), translator of Joseph Priestley's *History and Present State of Electricity* (1767) into French.
3. Dalibard and his associate Delor (first names unknown) performed Franklin's experiment with electricity on May 10, 1752, at Marly-la-Ville, France. Franklin began his experiments with electricity in 1746 and in 1750 suggested placing a rod on a steeple to draw "electrical fluid" from thunderclouds, thus identifying lightning and electricity.
4. Edward Wright (d. 1761), Scottish physician and

fellow of the Royal Society.
5. William Watson (1715–1787) developed a theory of electricity similar to Franklin's and nominated Franklin for membership in the Royal Society in 1756.
6. John Canton (1718–1772), schoolmaster; first person in England to try Franklin's electrical experiments.
7. Published accounts.
8. Copley (c. 1654–1709) established an annual prize to be given to one who had contributed to the advancement of knowledge.
9. George Parker, second earl of Macclesfield (c. 1697–1764), astronomer and mathematician; president of the Royal Society.

Our new Governor, Captain Denny, brought over for me the before-mentioned Medal from the Royal Society, which he presented to me at an Entertainment given him by the City. He accompanied it with very polite Expressions of his Esteem for me, having, as he said been long acquainted with my Character. After Dinner, when the Company as was customary at that time, were engag'd in Drinking, he took me aside into another Room, and acquainted me that he had been advis'd by his Friends in England to cultivate a Friendship with me, as one who was capable of giving him the best Advice, and of contributing most effectually to the making his Administration easy. That he therefore desired of all things to have a good Understanding with me; and he begg'd me to be assur'd of his Readiness on all Occasions to render me every Service that might be in his Power. He said much to me also of the Proprietor's good Dispositions toward the Province, and of the Advantage it might be to us all, and to me in particular, if the Opposition that had been so long continu'd to his Measures, were dropped, and Harmony restor'd between him and the People, in effecting which it was thought no one could be more serviceable than myself, and I might depend on adequate Acknowledgments and Recompenses, etc., etc.

The Drinkers finding we did not return immediately to the Table, sent us a Decanter of Madeira, which the Governor made liberal Use of, and in proportion became more profuse of his Solicitations and Promises. My Answers were to this purpose, that my Circumstances, Thanks to God, were such as to make Proprietary Favors unnecessary to me; and that being a Member of the Assembly I could not possibly accept of any; that however I had no personal Enmity to the Proprietary, and that whenever the public Measures he propos'd should appear to be for the Good of the People, no one should espouse and forward them more zealously than myself, my past Opposition having been founded on this, that the Measures which had been urg'd were evidently intended to serve the Proprietary Interest with great Prejudice to that of the People. That I was much obliged to him (the Governor) for his Professions of Regard to me, and that he might rely on everything in my Power to make his Administration as easy to him as possible, hoping at the same time that he had not brought with him the same unfortunate Instructions his Predecessor had been hamper'd with.[1] On this he did not then explain himself. But when he afterwards came to do Business with the Assembly they appear'd again, the Disputes were renewed, and I was as active as ever in the Opposition, being the Penman first of the Request to have a Communication of the Instructions, and then of the Remarks upon them, which may be found in the Votes of the Time, and in the Historical Review[2] I afterwards publish'd; but between us personally no Enmity arose; we were often together, he was a Man of Letters, had seen much of the World, and was very entertaining and pleasing in Conversation. He gave me the first Information that my old Friend James Ralph was still alive, that he was esteem'd one of the best political Writers in England, had been employ'd in the Dispute between Prince Frederick[3] and the King, and had

1. As proprietor, Thomas Penn gave instructions to his "governor," or deputy. The assembly distinguished between these orders and those of the British ministry, which they were willing to obey. On September 23, 1756, the assembly condemned private instructions to the "governor," and in 1757 Franklin was sent to London to "remove grievances we labor under." One particular issue involved was the appropriation of money.

2. An Historical Review of the Constitution and Government of Pennsylvania was written by Richard Jackson, but Franklin paid for its publication (1759) and supplied much of the material.

3. Frederick Louis, prince of Wales (1707–1751), led the opposition party to his father, George II (1683–1760), and was the father of George III (1738–1820).

obtain'd a Pension of Three Hundred a Year; that his Reputation was indeed small as a Poet, *Pope* having damn'd his Poetry in the Dunciad,[4] but his Prose was thought as good as any Man's.

The Assembly finally, finding the Proprietaries obstinately persisted in man-acling their Deputies with Instructions inconsistent not only with the Privileges of the People, but with the Service of the Crown, resolv'd to petition the King against them, and appointed me their Agent to go over to England to present and support the Petition. The House had sent up a Bill to the Governor grant-ing a Sum of Sixty Thousand Pounds for the King's Use, (10,000 Pounds of which was subjected to the Orders of the then General Lord Loudon,[5]) which the Governor absolutely refus'd to pass, in Compliance with his Instructions. I had agreed with Captain Morris of the Packet[6] at New York for my Passage, and my Stores were put on board, when Lord Loudon arriv'd at Philadelphia, expressly, as he told me to endeavor an Accommodation between the Gover-nor and Assembly, that his Majesty's Service might not be obstructed by their Dissensions: Accordingly he desir'd the Governor and myself to meet him, that he might hear what was to be said on both sides.

We met and discuss'd the Business. In behalf of the Assembly I urg'd all the Arguments that may be found in the public Papers of that Time, which were of my Writing, and are printed with the Minutes of the Assembly and the Governor pleaded his Instructions, the Bond he had given to observe them, and his Ruin if he disobey'd: Yet seem'd not unwilling to hazard himself if Lord Loudon would advise it. This his Lordship did not choose to do, tho' I once thought I had nearly prevail'd with him to do it; but finally he rather chose to urge the Compliance of the Assembly; and he entreated me to use my Endeavors with them for that purpose; declaring he could spare none of the King's Troops for the Defense of our Frontiers, and that if we did not continue to provide for that Defense ourselves they must remain expos'd to the Enemy. I acquainted the House with what had pass'd, and (presenting them with a Set of Resolutions I had drawn up, declaring our Rights, and that we did not relinquish our Claim to those Rights but only suspended the Exercise of them on this Occasion thro *Force*, against which we protested) they at length agreed to drop that Bill and frame another comformable to the Proprietary Instructions. This of course the Governor pass'd, and I was then at Liberty to proceed on my Voyage: but in the meantime the Packet had sail'd with my Sea-Stores, which was some Loss to me, and my only Recompense was his Lordship's Thanks for my Service, all the Credit of obtaining the Accommoda-tion falling to his Share.

He set out for New York before me; and as the Time for dispatching the Packet Boats, was in his Disposition, and there were two then remaining there, one of which he said was to sail very soon, I requested to know the precise time, that I might not miss her by any Delay of mine. His Answer was, I have given out that she is to sail on Saturday next, but I may let you know *entre nous*,[7] that if you are there by Monday morning you will be in time, but do not delay longer. By some Accidental Hindrance at a Ferry, it was Monday Noon before I arrived, and I was much afraid she might have sailed as the

4. See n. 7, p. 512.
5. John Campbell, fourth earl of Loudon (1705–1782), served as commander-in-chief of the British forces in North America after Braddock's defeat in 1755.
6. Fast ship for carrying mail. William Morris, captain of the *Halifax*.
7. Privately.

Wind was fair, but I was soon made easy by the Information that she was still in the Harbor, and would not move till the next Day.

One would imagine that I was now on the very point of Departing for Europe. I thought so; but I was not then so well acquainted with his Lordship's Character, of which *Indecision* was one of the Strongest Features. I shall give some Instances. It was about the Beginning of April that I came to New York, and I think it was near the End of June before we sail'd.[8] There were then two of the Packet Boats which had been long in Port, but were detain'd for the General's Letters, which were always to be ready tomorrow. Another Packet arriv'd, and she too was detain'd, and before we sail'd a fourth was expected. Ours was the first to be dispatch'd, as having been there longest. Passengers were engag'd in all, and some extremely impatient to be gone, and the Merchants uneasy about their Letters, and the Orders they had given for Insurance (it being War-time) and for Fall Goods. But their Anxiety avail'd nothing; his Lordship's Letters were not ready. And yet whoever waited on him found him always at his Desk, Pen in hand, and concluded he must needs write abundantly.

Going myself one Morning to pay my Respects, I found in his Antechamber one Innis,[9] a Messenger of Philadelphia, who had come from thence express, with a Packet from Governor Denny for the General. He deliver'd to me some Letters from my Friends there, which occasion'd my enquiring when he was to return and where he lodg'd, that I might send some Letters by him. He told me he was order'd to call tomorrow at nine for the General's Answer to the Governor, and should set off immediately. I put my Letters into his Hands the same Day. A Fortnight after I met him again in the same Place. So you are soon return'd, Innis! *Return'd*; No, I am not *gone* yet.—How so?—I have call'd here by Order every Morning these two Weeks past for his Lordship's Letter, and it is not yet ready.—Is it possible, when he is so great a Writer, for I see him constantly at his Scritoire.[1] Yes, says Innis, but he is like St. George on the Signs, *always on horseback, and never rides on.*[2] This Observation of the Messenger was it seems well founded; for when in England, I understood that Mr. Pitt[3] gave it as one Reason for Removing this General, and sending Amherst and Wolf,[4] *that the Ministers never heard from him, and could not know what he was doing.*

This daily Expectation of Sailing, and all the three Packets going down Sandy hook,[5] to join the Fleet there, the Passengers thought it best to be on board, lest by a sudden Order the Ships should sail, and they be left behind. There if I remember right we were about Six Weeks, consuming our Sea Stores, and oblig'd to procure more. At length the Fleet sail'd, the General and all his Army on board, bound to Louisburg[6] with Intent to besiege and take that Fortress;[7] all the Packet Boats in Company, ordered to attend the General's Ship, ready to receive his Dispatches when those should be ready. We were out 5 Days before we got a Letter with Leave to part; and then our

8. June 20, 1757.
9. James Ennis (c. 1709–1774), official courier for the government of Pennsylvania.
1. Writing desk.
2. This proverb refers to the image of St. George on horseback slaying a dragon. It was a common tavern sign.
3. William Pitt (1708–1778), prime minister of England, champion of the American cause.

4. Jeffrey Amherst (1717–1797), successor to Lord Loudon as British commander-in-chief in North America. James Wolfe (1727–1759), commander of the British campaign to seize Quebec.
5. In eastern New Jersey.
6. I.e., Fort Louisburg.
7. The earl of Loudon's attack failed because of bad weather and superior French defenses.

Ship quitted the Fleet and steered for England. The other two Packets he still detain'd, carried them with him to Halifax,[8] where he stayed some time to exercise the Men in sham Attacks upon sham Forts, then alter'd his Mind as to besieging Louisburg, and return'd to New York with all his Troops, together with the two Packets above-mentioned and all their Passengers. During his Absence the French and Savages had taken Fort George[9] on the Frontier of that Province, and the Savages had massacred many of the Garrison after Capitulation.

I saw afterwards in London, Captain Bonnell,[1] who commanded one of those Packets. He told me, that when he had been detain'd a Month, he acquainted his Lordship that his Ship was grown foul, to a degree that must necessarily hinder her fast Sailing, a Point of consequence for a Packet Boat, and requested an Allowance of Time to heave her down and clean her Bottom. He was ask'd how long time that would require. He answer'd Three Days. The General replied, If you can do it in one Day, I give leave; otherwise not; for you must certainly sail the Day after tomorrow. So he never obtain'd leave tho' detain'd afterwards from day to day during full three Months. I saw also in London one of Bonnell's Passengers, who was so enrag'd against his Lordship for deceiving and detaining him so long at New York, and then carrying him to Halifax, and back again, that he swore he would sue him for Damages. Whether he did or not I never heard; but as he represented the Injury to his Affairs it was very considerable.

On the whole I then wonder'd much, how such a Man came to be entrusted with so important a Business as the Conduct of a great Army: but having since seen more of the great World, and the means of obtaining and Motives for giving Places and Employments, my Wonder is diminished. General Shirley, on whom the Command of the Army devolved upon the Death of Braddock, would in my Opinion if continued in Place, have made a much better Campaign than that of Loudon in 1757, which was frivolous, expensive and disgraceful to our Nation beyond Conception: For tho' Shirley was not a bred Soldier, he was sensible and sagacious in himself, and attentive to good Advice from others, capable of forming judicious Plans, quick and active in carrying them into Execution. Loudon, instead of defending the Colonies with his great Army, left them totally expos'd while he paraded it idly at Halifax, by which means Fort George was lost;—besides he derang'd all our mercantile Operations, and distress'd our Trade by a long Embargo on the Exportation of Provisions, on pretense of keeping Supplies from being obtain'd by the Enemy, but in Reality for beating down their Price in Favor of the Contractors, in whose Profits it was said, perhaps from Suspicion only, he had a Share. And when at length the Embargo was taken off, by neglecting to send Notice of it to Charlestown, the Carolina Fleet was detain'd near three Months longer, whereby their Bottoms were so much damag'd by the Worm, that a great Part of them founder'd in the Passage home. Shirley was I believe sincerely glad of being reliev'd from so burdensome a Charge as the Conduct of an Army must be to a Man unacquainted with military Business. I was at the Entertainment given by the City of New York, to Lord Loudon on his taking upon him the Command. Shirley, tho' thereby superseded, was present also. There was a

8. In Nova Scotia.
9. Fort William Henry on Lake George in upper New York State.

1. John Dod Bonnell, captain of the packet *Harriott*, wounded on Loudon's Louisburg campaign.

great Company of Officers, Citizens and Strangers, and some Chairs having been borrowed in the Neighborhood, there was one among them very low which fell to the Lot of Mr. Shirley. Perceiving it as I sat by him, I said, they have given you, Sir, too low a Seat.—No Matter, says he; Mr. Franklin, I find *a low Seat* the easiest!

While I was, as afore-mention'd, detain'd at New York, I receiv'd all the Accounts of the Provisions, etc., that I had furnish'd to Braddock, some of which Accounts could not sooner be obtain'd from the different Persons I had employ'd to assist in the Business. I presented them to Lord Loudon, desiring to be paid the Balance. He caus'd them to be regularly examin'd by the proper Officer, who, after comparing every Article with its Voucher, certified them to be right, and the Balance due, for which his Lordship promis'd to give me an Order on the Paymaster. This, however, was put off from time to time, and tho' I called often for it by Appointment, I did not get it. At length, just before my Departure, he told me he had on better Consideration concluded not to mix his Accounts with those of his Predecessors. And you, says he, when in England, have only to exhibit your Accounts at the Treasury, and you will be paid immediately. I mention'd, but without Effect, the great and unexpected Expense I had been put to by being detain'd so long at New York, as a Reason for my desiring to be presently paid; and On my observing that it was not right I should be put to any farther Trouble or Delay in obtaining the Money I had advanc'd, as I charg'd no Commissions for my Service. O, Sir, says he, you must not think of persuading us that you are no Gainer. We understand better those Affairs, and know that every one concern'd in supplying the Army finds means in the doing it to fill his own Pockets. I assur'd him that was not my Case, and that I had not pocketed a Farthing: but he appear'd clearly not to believe me; and indeed I have since learned that immense Fortunes are often made in such Employments.—As to my Balance, I am not paid it to this Day, of which more hereafter.

Our Captain of the Packet had boasted much before we sail'd, of the Swiftness of his Ship. Unfortunately when we came to Sea, she proved the dullest[2] of 96 Sail, to his no small Mortification. After many Conjectures respecting the Cause, when we were near another Ship almost as dull as ours, which however gain'd upon us, the Captain order'd all hands to come aft and stand as near the Ensign Staff[3] as possible. We were, Passengers included, about forty Persons. While we stood there the Ship mended her Pace, and soon left our Neighbor far behind, which prov'd clearly what our Captain suspected, that she was loaded too much by the Head. The Casks of Water it seems had been all plac'd forward. These he therefore order'd to be remov'd farther aft; on which the Ship recover'd her Character, and prov'd the best Sailor in the Fleet.

The Captain said she had once gone at the Rate of 13 Knots, which is accounted 13 Miles per hour.[4] We had on board as a Passenger Captain Kennedy[5] of the Navy, who contended that it was impossible, that no Ship ever sailed so fast, and that there must have been some Error in the Division of the Log-Line, or some Mistake in heaving[6] the Log. A Wager ensu'd between the

---

2. Slowest.
3. The flagpole bearing the ship's flag.
4. Thirteen nautical miles, or approximately seventeen land miles per hour.

5. Archibald Kennedy, Jr. (d. 1794), son of Franklin's friend.
6. Setting up, measuring.

two Captains, to be decided when there should be sufficient Wind. Kennedy thereupon examin'd rigorously the Log-line, and being satisfied with that, he determin'd to throw the Log himself. Accordingly some Days after when the Wind blew very fair and fresh, and the Captain of the Packet (Lutwidge) said he believ'd she then went at the Rate of 13 Knots, Kennedy made the Experiment, and own'd his Wager lost.

The above Fact I give for the sake of the following Observation. It has been remark'd as an Imperfection in the Art of Shipbuilding, that it can never be known till she is tried, whether a new Ship will or will not be a good Sailor; for that the Model of a good sailing Ship has been exactly follow'd in a new One, which has prov'd on the contrary remarkably dull. I apprehend this may be partly occasion'd by the different Opinions of Seamen respecting the Modes of lading, rigging and sailing of a Ship. Each has his System. And the same Vessel laden by the Judgment and Orders of one Captain shall sail better or worse than when by the Orders of another. Besides, it scarce ever happens that a Ship is form'd, fitted for the Sea, and sail'd by the same Person. One Man builds the Hull, another rigs her, a third lades[7] and sails her. No one of these has the Advantage of knowing all the Ideas and Experience of the others, and therefore cannot draw just Conclusions from a Combination of the whole. Even in the simple Operation of Sailing when at Sea, I have often observ'd different Judgments in the Officers who commanded the successive Watches, the Wind being the same. One would have the Sails trimm'd sharper or flatter than another, so that they seem'd to have no certain Rule to govern by. Yet I think a Set of Experiments might be instituted, first to determine the most proper Form of the Hull for swift sailing; next the best Dimensions and properest Place for the Masts; then the Form and Quantity of Sail, and their Position as the Winds may be; and lastly the Disposition of her Lading. This is the Age of Experiments; and such a Set accurately made and combin'd would be of great Use. I am therefore persuaded that ere long some ingenious Philosopher will undertake it—to whom I wish Success.

We were several times chas'd on our Passage, but outsail'd everything, and in thirty Days had Soundings.[8] We had a good Observation, and the Captain judg'd himself so near our Port, (Falmouth) that if we made a good Run in the Night we might be off the Mouth of that Harbor in the Morning, and by running in the Night might escape the Notice of the Enemy's Privateers,[9] who often cruis'd near the Entrance of the Channel. Accordingly all the Sail was set that we could possibly make, and the Wind being very fresh and fair, we went right before it, and made great Way. The Captain after his Observation, shap'd his Course as he thought so as to pass wide of the Scilly Isles:[1] but it seems there is sometimes a strong Indraft setting up St. George's Channel which deceives Seamen, and caus'd the Loss of Sir Cloudsley Shovel's Squadron.[2] This Indraft was probably the Cause of what happen'd to us. We had a Watchman plac'd in the Bow to whom they often call'd, *Look well out befor'e, there*; and he as often answer'd *Aye, Aye!* But perhaps had his Eyes shut, and was half asleep at the time: they sometimes answering as is said mechanically: For he did not see a Light just before us, which had been hid by the Studding

7. Loads.
8. I.e., land on the bottom of the sea could be touched with a weighted line.
9. Armed ship in "private" hands, commissioned by a government to seize its enemies' ships.

1. Twenty-five miles southwest of England.
2. St. George's Channel is between England and Ireland. Cloudelley Shovell (1650–1707), of Queen Anne's navy, struck the rocks of the islands and went down on October 22, 1707.

Sails[3] from the Man at Helm and from the rest of the Watch; but by an accidental Yaw[4] of the Ship was discover'd, and occasion'd a great Alarm, we being very near it, the light appearing to me as big as a Cart Wheel. It was Midnight, and Our Captain fast asleep. But Captain Kennedy jumping upon Deck, and seeing the Danger, ordered the Ship to wear round, all Sails standing. An Operation dangerous to the Masts, but it carried us clear, and we escap'd Shipwreck, for we were running right upon the Rocks on which the Lighthouse was erected. This Deliverance impress'd me strongly with the Utility of Lighthouses, and made me resolve to encourage the building more of them in America, if I should live to return there.

In the Morning it was found by the Soundings, etc., that we were near our Port, but a thick Fog hid the Land from our Sight. About 9 aClock the Fog began to rise, and seem'd to be lifted up from the Water like the Curtain at a Playhouse, discovering underneath the Town of Falmouth, the Vessels in its Harbor, and the Fields that surrounded it. A most pleasing Spectacle to those who had been so long without any other Prospects, than the uniform View of a vacant Ocean! And it gave us the more Pleasure, as we were now freed from the Anxieties which the State of War occasion'd.

I set out immediately with my Son for London, and we only stopped a little by the Way to view Stonehenge[5] on Salisbury Plain, and Lord Pembroke's House and Gardens, with his very curious Antiquities at Wilton.[6]

We arriv'd in London the 27th of July 1757.[7] [Part Four] As soon as I was settled in a Lodging Mr. Charles[8] had provided for me, I went to visit Dr. Fothergill, to whom I was strongly recommended, and whose Counsel respecting my Proceedings I was advis'd to obtain. He was against an immediate Complaint to Government, and thought the Proprietaries should first be personally applied to, who might possibly be induc'd by the Interposition and Persuasion of some private Friends to accommodate Matters amicably. I then waited on my old Friend and Correspondent Mr. Peter Collinson, who told me that John Hanbury,[9] the great Virginia Merchant, had requested to be informed when I should arrive, that he might carry me to Lord Granville's,[1] who was then President of the Council, and wish'd to see me as soon as possible. I agreed to go with him the next Morning. Accordingly Mr. Hanbury called for me and took me in his Carriage to that Nobleman's, who receiv'd me with great Civility; and after some Questions respecting the present State of Affairs in America, and Discourse thereupon, he said to me, "You Americans have wrong Ideas of the Nature of your Constitution; you contend that the King's Instructions to his Governors are not Laws, and think yourselves at Liberty to regard or disregard them at your own Discretion. But those Instructions are not like the Pocket Instructions given to a Minister going abroad, for regulating his Conduct in some trifling Point of Ceremony. They are first

---

3. Small sails set at the sides of larger sails.
4. Movement.
5. The prehistoric British monument, about ten miles north of Salisbury.
6. Wilton House, home of the earls of Pembroke and one of the great manor houses of England. Sir Philip Sidney wrote his *Arcadia* there.
7. Franklin arrived at Falmouth on July 17 and reached London on the evening of July 26. This sentence concludes the third part of the *Autobiography*. It was the last sentence in the manuscript printed by Franklin's son in 1818. Part Four was written between

November 13, 1789, and Franklin's death on April 17, 1790, at age 84.
8. Robert Charles (d. 1770) returned to England in 1739 and became an agent for New York and Pennsylvania.
9. London agent for the Library Company, merchant, and correspondent to scientists (1694-1768). John Hanbury (1700-1758), London Quaker and tobacco merchant.
1. John Cartaret, first earl of Granville (1690-1763), president of the king's privy council (1751-63), which ruled on Franklin's case against the proprietors.

drawn up by Judges learned in the Laws; they are then considered, debated and perhaps amended in Council, after which they are signed by the King. They are then so far as relates to you, the *Law of the Land*: for THE KING IS THE LEGISLATOR OF THE COLONIES."

I told his Lordship this was new Doctrine to me. I had always understood from our Charters, that our Laws were to be made by our Assemblies, to be presented indeed to the King for his Royal Assent, but that being once given the King could not repeal or alter them. And as the Assemblies could not make permanent Laws without his Assent, so neither could he make a Law for them without theirs. He assur'd me I was totally mistaken. I did not think so however. And his Lordship's Conversation having a little alarm'd me as to what might be the Sentiments of the Court concerning us, I wrote it down as soon as I return'd to my Lodgings.—I recollected that about 20 Years before, a Clause in a Bill brought into Parliament by the Ministry, had propos'd to make the King's Instructions Laws in the Colonies; but the Clause was thrown out by the Commons, for which we ador'd them as our Friends and Friends of Liberty, till by their Conduct towards us in 1765, it seem'd that they had refus'd that Point of Sovereignty to the King, only that they might reserve it for themselves.[2]

After some Days, Dr. Fothergill having spoken to the Proprietaries, they agreed to a Meeting with me at Mr. J. Penn's[3] House in Spring Garden. The Conversation at first consisted of mutual Declarations of Disposition to reasonable Accommodation; but I suppose each Party had its own Ideas of what should be meant by *reasonable*. We then went into Consideration of our several Points of Complaint which I enumerated. The Proprietaries justified their Conduct as well as they could, and I the Assembly's. We now appeared very wide, and so far from each other in Our Opinions, as to discourage all Hope of Agreement. However, it was concluded that I should give them the Heads[4] of our Complaints in Writing, and they promis'd then to consider them.—I did so soon after; but they put the Paper into the Hands of their Solicitor Ferdinando John Paris,[5] who manag'd for them all their Law Business in their great Suit with the neighboring Proprietary of Maryland, Lord Baltimore,[6] who had subsisted 70 Years, and wrote for them all their Papers and Messages in their Dispute with the Assembly. He was a proud angry Man; and as I had occasionally in the Answers of the Assembly treated his Papers with some Severity, they being really weak in point of Argument, and haughty in Expression, he had conceiv'd a mortal Enmity to me, which discovering itself whenever we met, I declin'd the Proprietary's Proposal that he and I should discuss the Heads of Complaint between our two selves, and refus'd treating with anyone but them. They then by his Advice put the Paper into the Hands of the Attorney and Solicitor General for their Opinion and Counsel upon it, where it lay unanswered a Year wanting eight Days, during which time I made frequent Demands of an Answer from the Proprietaries but without obtaining any other than that they had not yet receiv'd the Opinion of the

2. After Parliament repealed the Stamp Act in 1766 it passed the Declaratory Act, which asserted the right of Parliament to legislate for the colonies without their consent.

3. Actually Thomas Penn, not John Penn, who lived in England after 1741. He remained proprietor of Pennsylvania until 1775.

4. I.e., chief points. Franklin's "Heads of Complaint"

was submitted on August 20, 1757.

5. John Ferdinand Paris (d. 1759), legal adviser to the Penns and an attorney specializing in colonial affairs.

6. Charles Calvert, the fifth Baron Baltimore (1699–1751), proprietor of Maryland. The boundary between Pennsylvania and Maryland was settled by the survey of the Mason-Dixon Line, 1763–67.

Attorney and Solicitor General: What it was when they did receive it I never learned, for they did not communicate it to me, but sent a long Message to the Assembly drawn and signed by Paris reciting my Paper, complaining of its want of Formality as a Rudeness on my part, and giving a flimsy Justification of their Conduct, adding that they should be willing to accommodate Matters, if the Assembly would send over *some Person of Candor* to treat with them for that purpose, intimating thereby that I was not such.

The want of Formality or Rudeness, was probably my not having address'd the Paper to them with their assum'd Titles of true and absolute Proprietaries of the Province of Pennsylvania, which I omitted as not thinking it necessary in a Paper the Intention of which was only to reduce to a Certainty by writing what in Conversation I had delivered *vivâ voce*.[7] But during this Delay, the Assembly having prevail'd with Governor Denny to pass an Act taxing the Proprietary Estate in common with the Estates of the People, which was the grand Point in Dispute, they omitted answering the Message.

When the Act however came over, the Proprietaries counsel'd by Paris determin'd to oppose its receiving the Royal Assent. Accordingly they petition'd the King in Council, and a Hearing was appointed, in which two Lawyers were employ'd by them against the Act, and two by me in Support of it. They alledg'd that the Act was intended to load the Proprietary Estate in order to spare those of the People, and that if it were suffer'd to continue in force, and the Proprietaries who were in Odium with the People, left to their Mercy in proportioning the Taxes, they would inevitably be ruined. We replied that the Act had no such Intention and would have no such Effect. That the Assessors were honest and discreet Men, under an Oath to assess fairly and equitably, and that any Advantage each of them might expect in lessening his own Tax by augmenting that of the Proprietaries was too trifling to induce them to perjure themselves. This is the purport of what I remember as urg'd by both Sides, except that we insisted strongly on the mischievous Consequences that must attend a Repeal; for that the Money, 100,000 Pounds, being printed and given to the King's Use, expended in his Service, and now spread among the People, the Repeal would strike it dead in their Hands to the Ruin of many, and the total Discouragement of future Grants, and the Selfishness of the Proprietors in soliciting such a general Catastrophe, merely from a groundless Fear of their Estate being taxed too highly, was insisted on in the strongest Terms.

On this Lord Mansfield,[8] one of the Council rose, and beckoning to me, took me into the Clerk's Chamber, while the Lawyers were pleading, ask'd me if I was really of Opinion that no Injury would be done the Proprietary Estate in the Execution of the Act. I said, Certainly. Then says he, you can have little Objection to enter into an Engagement to assure that Point. I answer'd None, at all. He then call'd in Paris, and after some Discourse his Lordship's Proposition was accepted on both Sides; a Paper to the purpose was drawn up by the Clerk of the Council, which I sign'd with Mr. Charles, who was also an Agent of the Province for their ordinary Affairs; when Lord Mansfield return'd to the Council Chamber where finally the Law was allowed to pass. Some Changes were however recommended and we also engag'd they should

7. Orally (Latin).
8. William Murray, first earl of Mansfield (1705–1793), chief justice of the King's Bench.

be made by a subsequent Law; but the Assembly did not think them necessary. For one Year's Tax having been levied by the Act before the Order of Council arrived, they appointed a Committee to examine the Proceedings of the Assessors, and On this Committee they put several particular Friends of the Proprietaries. After a full Enquiry they unanimously sign'd a Report that they found the Tax had been assess'd with perfect Equity.

The Assembly look'd on my entering into the first Part of the Engagement as an essential Service to the Province, since it secur'd the Credit of the Paper Money then spread over all the Country; and they gave me their Thanks in form when I return'd. But the Proprietaries were enrag'd at Governor Denny for having pass'd the Act, and turn'd him out, with Threats of suing him for Breach of Instructions which he had given Bond to observe. He however having done it at the Instance[9] of the General and for his Majesty's Service, and having some powerful Interest at Court, despis'd the Threats, and they were never put in Execution.

1771–90   1868

9. Urging.

ELIZABETH ASHBRIDGE
1713–1755

The spiritual autobiography is as old as Christianity, but in the seventeenth and eighteenth centuries Christians turned the history of their conversions into an art form of its own. In the Reverend Edward Taylor's congregation in Westfield, Massachusetts, for example, men were accustomed to describing the drama of their spiritual lives before church members to be admitted into full fellowship in the Lord's Supper. Such public accounts led to no great unveiling of the hidden private life: Taylor told the congregation that it was his sister's retelling of the story of the Creation and of Jesus's life, particularly the Christmas story, that filled him with a new devotion. Women did not customarily make public accounts of their conversions: these moments were reserved for private meetings in the minister's study.

Anyone familiar with these Congregational "relations" and their rather predictable progressions, therefore, will be struck with the decidedly more frank and novelistic account given of her life in Christ by Elizabeth Ashbridge of Mount Holly, New Jersey, who came to these shores at the age of nineteen, "a stranger in a strange land." Ashbridge found her spiritual home in America, but she soon learned that Americans were not as tolerant of religious beliefs as they sometimes claimed and were easily threatened by any religion that asserted the truth of the heart over traditional forms of masculine authority.

We know almost nothing whatsoever about Ashbridge other than what she tells us in *Some Account*. She was born in 1713 in Middlewich, Cheshire County, England, and came from a conventional home. Her father was a ship's surgeon and had little to do with her growing up. After her teenage transgression he involved himself not at all in her life, and it was her mother who cared for her. She was not an easy child to raise, for in spite of talk of her love of dancing her innocence, she clearly had a strong will and was easily pleased with herself, judgmental, and disobedient. When she was little more than fourteen she ran away with a man who died five months later. Unwanted by her father at home, she left England for Ireland, first going to Dublin, where her Quaker relatives annoyed her, and then to the west of Ireland, where country manners were more to her liking. When she met a woman going to America she joined her and indentured herself to her without knowing her at all. Kidnapped for a time, she turned around and sailed on the very ship whose captain held her prisoner. She seems to have escaped from a life of near white slavery only to find herself attached to an aggressive bully whose one redeeming grace was that he allowed her to purchase her freedom from a four-year indenture after serving three years. At twenty-two she married again, this time to a man named Sullivan (his name is not mentioned in her *Account*). He loved her for her dancing. She neither loved him nor valued him at all.

All this, of course, sounds more like the trappings of an eighteenth-century popular novel than a description of a religious conversion, but it is precisely this accumulated detail that makes Ashbridge's life so intriguing. Had she written her *Account* after becoming a successful Quaker preacher and not shortly after her third, and happy, marriage (to Aaron Ashbridge in New Jersey in 1746), we might not have been given quite so many particulars. But in concentrating on the early part of her life, Ashbridge provides us with an unfamiliar glimpse of an America, one that we are inclined to repress: its cruelty to women, its intolerance, its injustice and prejudices, its terrible city and country poverty, and its indifference to all those who lacked money and, consequently, power. Surely one reason she petitioned her community in New Jersey to permit her to return to England and Ireland in 1753 to preach was that she wanted to complete the circle of her life: to prove that the child who stood in awe of religion, who loved the poor and hated hypocrisy, and who wished that she were a boy so that she might take Holy Orders, was no longer a stranger but a saint. Ashbridge was ill almost from the moment of her arrival and died in Ireland on May 16, 1755.

Some Account of the Fore-Part of the Life of Elizabeth Ashbridge[1]

My life being attended with many uncommon occurrences, some of which I brought upon myself, which I believe were for my good, I have therefore thought proper to make some remarks on the dealings of Divine Goodness with me, having often had cause with David, to say, "It is good for me that I have been afflicted";[2] and I most earnestly desire that whosoever reads the following lines may take warning and shun the evils that through the deceitfulness of Satan I have been drawn into.

I was born in Middlewich, in Cheshire,[3] in the year 1713, of honest parents. My father's name was Thomas Sampson, he was a surgeon; my mother's name was Mary. My father was a man that bore a good character, but not so strictly religious as my mother, who was a pattern of virtue to me. I was the only child of my father, but my mother had a son and a daughter by a former husband. Soon after my birth my father took to the sea, and followed his profession on board a ship many long voyages, till I was twelve years old, about which time he settled at home; so that my education lay mostly on my mother, in which she discharged her duty by endeavoring to instill into me the princi-

---

1. The text is that of the 1st edition, published in Nantwich, England, in 1774. Some of the spelling and punctuation has been altered for easier reading.

2. Psalm 119.71.

3. A former county in the west of England.

ples of virtue during my tender age, for which I have since had cause to be thankful to the Lord, that He blessed me with such a parent, tho' her good advice and counsel have been as cast upon the water, etc.[4] In short, she was a good example to all about her, and beloved by most that knew her, tho' not of the same religious persuasion I am now of. But oh! alas, when the time came that she might reasonably have expected the benefit of her labor, and have had comfort from me, I left her, of which I shall mention in its proper place.

In my very infancy I had an awful[5] regard for religion and a great love for religious people, particularly the ministers, and sometimes grieved at my not being a boy and therefore could not be one, as I thought they were good men, and beloved of God. I also had a great love for the poor, remembering I had read they were blessed of the Lord; this I took to mean such as were poor in this world, and often went to their poor cottages to see them, and if I had any money or other things, I used to give them some, remembering that saying, that they that give to the poor lend to the Lord, and I had when very young an earnest desire to be beloved of Him. I used also to make remarks on those called gentlemen, and when I heard them swear it would grieve me much; for my mother had informed me that if I used any naughty words, God would not love me. As I grew up I took notice that there were several different religious societies, wherefore I often went alone and wept, desiring that I might be directed to the right. Thus my young years were attended with such like tender desires, tho' I was sometimes guilty of those things incident to children, but then I always found something in me that made me sorry for what I did amiss. Till I arrived at the age of fourteen years, I was as innocent as most children, about which time my sorrows began, and have continued most part of my life, through my giving way to a foolish passion, in setting my affections on a young man, who became a suitor to me, without my parent's consent, till I suffered myself (I may say with sorrow of heart) to be carried off in the night, and to be married before my parents found me; altho' as soon as they missed me all possible search was made after me, but all in vain, till too late to recover me.

This precipitate act plunged me into a vast scene of sorrow, for I was soon smote with remorse for thus leaving my parents, who had a right to have disposed of me, or at least their approbation ought to have been consulted in the affair, for I was soon chastised for my disobedience. Divine Providence let me see my error, and in five months I was stripped of the darling of my soul, and left a young and disconsolate widow.

I had then no home to fly to. My father was so displeased that he would do nothing for me, but my dear mother had some compassion towards me, and kept me amongst the neighbors for some time, till by her advice I went to Dublin,[6] to a relation of hers, in hopes that absence would help to regain my father's affection. But he continued inflexible and would not send for me, and I dared not to return without his permission.——This relation with whom I lived was one of the people called Quakers. His conduct was so different from the manner of my education, which was in the way of the Church of England, that it made my situation disagreeable; for tho', as I said, I had a religious education, yet I was allowed to sing and dance, which my cousins were against, and I having a great vivacity in my natural disposition could not bear to give way to the gloomy scene of sorrow, and conviction gave it the wrong

4. "Cast thy bread upon the waters: for thou shalt find   5. I.e., awe-inspired, reverential.
it after many days" (Ecclesiastes 11.1).   6. In Ireland.

effect, and made me more wild and airy[7] than before, for which I was often reproved. But I then thought, as a great many do now, that it was the effect of singularity[8] and therefore would not be subject to it.

I having at that time a distant relation in the west of Ireland, I left Dublin, and went there, where I was entertained, and what rendered me disagreeable in the former place was quite pleasing to the latter. Between these two relations I spent 3 years and 2 months. While I was in Ireland I contracted an intimacy with a widow and her daughter, who were Papists, with whom I used to discourse about religion, they in defense of their faith, and I of mine; and altho' I was then very wild, it made me very thoughtful. The old woman would tell me of such mighty miracles done by their priests that I began to be disturbed in my mind, and thought that if those things were so, they must be the Apostle's successors.[9] The old woman perceiving it one day, said in rapture, that if I, under God, can be instrumental to convert you to the holy Catholic faith, all the sins that ever I committed will be forgiven me. In a while it got so far that the priests came to converse with me, and I being young and my judgment weak was ready to believe what they said. And tho' wild as I was, it cost me many a tear with desires that I might be rightly directed. For some time I frequented their place of worship, but none of my relations knew I had any intention of going with them. At length I concluded never to be led darkly into their belief, and thought to myself—if their articles of faith are good, they will not be against my knowing them. Therefore the next time I had an opportunity with the priest, I told him I had some thoughts of becoming one of his flock, but I did not like to join with them till I knew all I was to agree to, and therefore desired to see their principles. He answered I must first confess my sins to him, and gave me till next day to consider of them. I was not much against that, having done nothing that any person could hurt me, and if, thought I, what the man says be true, it will be for my good. So when he came again, I told him all I could remember, which I thought bad enough; but he thought me, as he said, the most innocent creature that ever made confession to him. When he had done he took a book out of his pocket, and read all which I was to swear to, if I joined with them.

Tho' I was but young, I made my remarks as he went on, but I do not think it worth my writing, nor the reader's hearing. It was a great deal of ridiculous stuff. But what made me sick of my new intention was (I believe I should have swallowed the rest), I was to swear "I believed the Pretender to be the true heir to the crown of England, and that he was King James' son, and also, that whosoever died out of the pale[1] of the church were damned." As to the first, I did not believe it essential to salvation, whether I believed it or not, and to take an oath to any such thing would be very unsafe; and the second I saw struck directly against charity, which the Apostles preferred before all other Graces. And besides, I had a religious mother who was out of that opinion.[2] I therefore thought it would be wicked in me to believe she was damned. I therefore concluded to consider about it, but before I saw him again a sudden turn took hold of me, which put a final end to it.

7. Vivacious.

8. I.e., that the Quakers were peculiar and not to be taken seriously.

9. I.e., the true successors of Peter, who founded the (Catholic) church.

1. I.e., protection. The "Pretender" was James Fran-

cis Edward Stuart (1688–1766), son of James II and a Roman Catholic, who claimed he was the true heir to the English throne.

2. I.e., was a member of the Church of England and thus damned.

My father still keeping me at so great a distance, I thought myself quite shut out of his affections, and therefore concluded, since my absence was most agreeable he should have it, and getting acquaintance with a gentlewoman lately come from Pennsylvania, who was going back again, where I had an uncle, my mother's brother, I soon agreed with her for my passage, and being ignorant in the nature of an indenture[3] consented to be bound. As soon as this was over, she invited me to go and see the vessel we was to sail in, [to] which I readily consented, not knowing what would follow. When I came on board I found a young woman, who I afterwards understood was of a good family and had been deluded away by this creature. I was extremely glad to think I should have such an agreeable companion, but while we were in discourse, our kidnapper left us, and went ashore, and when I wanted to go was not permitted. I was kept there near three weeks, in which time the young woman's friends found her and fetched her away, by which means my friends found me, and went to the water bailiff, who brought me on shore, and our gentlewoman was obliged to conceal herself, or she would have been laid fast.[4] My friends kept me close for two weeks, but at last I found means to get away, for my thoughts being full of going to America, I was determined to proceed with my intention, and one day meeting with the captain, I inquired of him when they sailed, and entered on board the same ship that I was on board before, and I have since thought there was [a] Providential hand in it.

There was sixty Irish servants on board, and several English passengers, but none of the English, excepting myself, understood a word of the Irish language. As for me, I had been at no small pains to learn it, by which I had acquired so much as to discover anything they discoursed upon in Irish, which was of service to us all. There was on board the aforesaid gentlewoman and her husband's brother. While we were on the coast of Ireland, for the wind kept us there some time, I overheard the servants contriving how they should get their liberty when they came to America. To accomplish which they concluded to rise and kill the ship's crew, and all the English passengers on board, and the above mentioned young man was to navigate the ship. I took a private opportunity of informing the captain with their wicked intentions, and he let the English know of it. The next day they bore for the shore, and at a small distance from the Cove of Cork they lowered sail and cast anchor, under pretense of the wind not being fair to stand[5] their course, then hoisted out their boat and invited the passengers to go on shore to divert themselves. And among the rest this young man that was to be this rabble's captain went, by which our end was answered. And as soon as he was on shore the rest left him and came on board, and our captain immediately ordered to weigh anchor and hoist sail. At this there was a great outcry for the young man on shore, but the captain told them the wind was fresh up, and he would not stay, [even] if it was for his own son. So their treachery was betrayed in good time, and in a manner they did not mistrust; for it was thought most advisable to keep it private least any of them should do me a mischief. But at length they found out that I understood Irish by my smiling at a story that they were telling in that language, and from that time they devised many ways to do me hurt, for which several of them were put in irons.

---

3. A contract in which she would be bound as a servant for a specific time.
4. Arrested. "Water bailiff": officer of the court supervising matters concerning shipping.
5. Maintain.

In nine weeks from the time I left Dublin we arrived at New York, viz., on the 15 of the 7th month, 1732.[6] Now those to whom I had been instrumental to preserve life proved treacherous to me.—I was a stranger in a strange land.[7]

The captain got an indenture and demanded of me to sign it, at the same time threatening me if I refused it. I told him I could find means to satisfy him for my passage without being bound, but he told me I might take my choice: either to sign that or have the other in force which I signed in Ireland. By this time I had learned the character of the before-mentioned woman, by which she appeared to be a vile person, and I feared if ever I was in her power she would use me ill on her brother's account. I therefore in a fright signed the latter, and tho' there was no magistrate present it proved sufficient to make me a servant for four years. In two weeks time I was sold, and were it possible to convey in characters[8] a scene of the sufferings of my servitude, it would affect the most stony heart with pity for a young creature who had been so tenderly brought up. For tho' my father had no great estate yet he lived well, and I had been used to little but the school, tho' it had been better for me now if I had been brought up to greater hardships.

For a while I was pretty well used, but in a little time the scale turned, which was occasioned by a difference between my master and me, wherein I was innocent; but from that time he set himself against me, and was so inhuman that he would not suffer me to have clothes to be decent in, making me to go barefoot in the snowy weather, and to be employed in the meanest drudgery, wherein I suffered the utmost hardships that my body was able to bear, and which the rest of my troubles had like to have been my ruin to all eternity, had not Almighty God interposed. My master would seem to be a religious man, often taking the Sacrament, so called, and used to pray every night in his family, except when his prayer book was lost, for he never prayed without it as I remember, but the difference was of such a kind, that I was sick of his religion. For tho' I had but little myself, I had an idea what sort of people they should be who professed[9] much. But at length the enemy[1] by his insinuations made me believe there was no such a thing as religion, and that the convictions I had felt in my youth were nothing more than the prejudice of education, which convictions were at times so strong that I have gone and fallen on the ground, crying for mercy. But now I began to be hardened and for some months don't remember I felt any such thing, so that I was ready to conclude there was no God, and that all was priestcraft, I having a different opinion of those sort of men than what I had in my youth. And what corroborated with my atheistical opinion was this: my master's house used to be a place of great resort for the clergy, which gave me an opportunity of making my remarks on them;[2] for sometimes those that came out of the country used to lodge there, and their evening diversions often was playing at cards and singing, and in a few moments after, praying and singing psalms to Almighty God. But I thought, if there be a God, He must be a Pure Being and will not hear the prayers of polluted lips; for He hath in an abundant manner shown mercy to me as will be shown in the sequel, which did not suffer me to doubt in this

6. September was the seventh month under the old calendar. The new calendar with January as the first month began March 25, 1752. "Viz.": namely (Latin).
7. "And she bare him a son, and he called his name Gershom: for he said, I have been a stranger in a strange land" (Exodus 2.22).
8. Writing.
9. Believed.
1. Satan.
2. I.e., observing them.

manner any longer. For when my feet were near the bottomless pit, He plucked me back.

I had to one woman and no other discovered[3] the occasion of this difference, and the nature of it, which two years before had happened betwixt my master and me, and by that means he heard of it, and tho' he knew it to be true, he sent for the town whipper to correct me for it, and upon his appearing, I was called in and ordered to strip, without asking whether I deserved it or not, at which my heart was ready to burst, for I could as freely have given up my life, as suffer such ignominy. And I then said, "If there be a God, be graciously pleased to look down on one of the most unhappy creatures, and plead my cause, for Thou knowest what I have said is the truth, and had it not been from a principle more noble than he was capable of, I would have told it before his wife." Then fixing my eyes on the barbarous man, in a flood of tears, I said to him, "Sir, if you have no pity on me, yet for my father's sake spare me from this shame" (for before this he had heard of my father several ways), "and if you think I deserve such punishment do it yourself." He then took a turn about the room and bid the whipper go about his business, so I came off without a blow, which I thought something remarkable.

I now began to think my credit was gone, for they said several things of me, which (I bless God) were not true; and here I suffered so much cruelty that I knew not how to bear it, and the enemy immediately came in and put me in a way how to get rid of it all, by tempting me to end my miserable life, which I joined with, and for that purpose went into the garret in order to hang myself, at which time I was convinced there was a God, for as my feet entered the place, horror seized me to that[4] degree that I trembled much, and while I stood in amazement, it seemed as tho' I heard a voice say, "There is a hell beyond the grave," at which I was greatly astonished and convinced of an Almighty Power, to whom I prayed, saying "God be merciful and enable me to bear whatsoever Thou of Thy Providence shall bring or suffer to come upon me for my disobedience." I then went downstairs but let none know what I had been about.

Soon after this I had a dream, and tho' some may ridicule dreams, yet this seems very significant to me, therefore I shall mention it.——I thought somebody knocked at the door, which when I had opened there stood a grave[5] woman, holding in her right hand an oil lamp burning, who with a solid countenance fixed her eyes on me, and said, "I am sent to tell thee, that if thou wilt return to the Lord thy God, He will have mercy on thee, and thy lamp shall not be put out in obscure darkness"; upon which the light flamed from the lamp in a very radiant manner and the vision left me. But oh! alas, I did not give up to join with the heavenly vision, as I think I may call it; for, after all this, I was near being caught in another snare, which if I had, would probably have been my ruin, from which I was also preferred.[6]

I was accounted a fine singer and dancer, in which I took great delight, and once falling in company with some of the stage players, then at New York, they took a great fancy to me, as they said, and persuaded me to become an actress amongst them, and they would find means to get me from my servitude, and that I should live like a lady. The proposal took with me, and I used much pains to qualify myself for the stage, by reading plays, even when I

---

3. Revealed.   5. Somber.
4. I.e., such.   6. Esteemed enough to be saved.

should have slept, but after all this I found a stop in my mind, when I came to consider what my father would think when he heard of it, who had not only forgiven my disobedience in marriage, but had sent for me home, tho' my proud heart would not suffer me to return in so mean a condition I was then in, but rather chose bondage.

When I had served three years I bought the remainder of my time, and got a genteel maintenance by my needle, but alas! I was not sufficiently punished by my former servitude but got into another, and that for life; for a few months after this, I married a young man, who fell in love with me for my dancing— a poor motive for a man to choose a wife, or a woman to choose a husband.[7]

As to my part I fell in love for nothing I saw in him, and it seems unaccountable, that I, who had refused several offers, both in this country and in Ireland, should at last marry a man I had no value for.

In a week after we were married, my husband, who was a school-master, removed from New York, and took me along with him to New England, and settled at a place called Westerley, in Rhode Island government. With respect to religion, he was much like myself, without any; for when he was in drink he would use the worst of oaths. I don't mention this to expose my husband, but to show the effect it had upon me, for I now saw myself ruined, as I thought, being joined to a man I had no love for, and who was a pattern of no good to me. I therefore began to think we were like two joining hands and going to destruction, which made me conclude that if I was not forsaken of God, to alter my course of life. But to love the Divine Being, and not to love my husband, I saw was an inconfidency, and seemed impossible; therefore I requested, with tears, that my affections might increase towards my husband, and I can say in truth that my love was sincere to him. I now resolved to do my duty towards God, and expecting that I must come to the knowledge of it by reading the Scriptures, I read them with a strong resolution of following their directions, but the more I read the more uneasy I grew, especially about baptism, for altho' I had reason to believe I was sprinkled[8] in my infancy, because at the age of fourteen I passed under the bishop's hands for confirmation, as it is called, yet I could not find any precedent for that practice, and upon reading where it is said, "he that believes and is baptized, etc.,"[9] I observed that belief went before baptism, which I was not capable of when I was sprinkled, at which I grew very uneasy, and living in a neighborhood that were mostly Seventh Day Baptists, I conversed with them, and at length thinking it to be really my duty, I was baptized by one of their teachers, but did not join strictly with them, tho' I began to think the seventh-day[1] the true sabbath, and for some time kept it as such. My husband did not yet oppose me, for he saw I grew more affectionate to him, but I did not yet leave off singing and dancing so much, but I could divert him whenever he desired it.

Soon after this my husband and I concluded to go for England, and for that purpose went to Boston, where we found a ship bound for Liverpool, and agreed for our passage, expecting to sail in two weeks. But my time was not yet come, for there came one called a gentleman, who hired the ship to carry him

7. Ashbridge's second husband, like her first, is never named. She married her third husband, Aaron Ashbridge, in Burlington County, New Jersey, in 1746.
8. Baptized with holy water by the priest in infancy, as distinguished from total immersion after the age of reason.

9. "He that believeth and is baptized shall be saved; but he that believeth not shall be damned" (Mark 16.16). "Confirmation" is the ceremony admitting young adults to full church membership.
1. Saturday.

and his attendants to Philadelphia, and to take no other passengers. There being no other ship near sailing, we for that time gave it over.

We stayed several weeks at Boston, and I remained still dissatisfied as to religion, tho' I had reformed my conduct so as to be accounted by those that knew me a sober woman. But that was not sufficient; for even then I expected to find the sweets of such a change, and though several thought me religious, I dared not to think myself so, and what to do to be so, I seemed still an utter stranger to. I used to converse with people of all societies, as opportunity offered, and, like many others, had got a deal of head knowledge, and several societies thought me of their opinion, but I joined strictly with none, resolving never to leave searching till I found the TRUTH. This was in the 22d year of my age.

While we were at Boston, I went one day to the Quakers' meeting, not expecting to find what I wanted, but from a motive of curiosity. At this meeting there was a woman spoke, at which I was a little surprised, for I had never heard one before. I looked on her with pity for her ignorance, and in contempt of her practice said to myself, "I am sure you're a fool, for if ever I should turn Quaker, which will never be, I could not be a preacher." In these and such like thoughts I sat while she was speaking. After she had done, there stood up a man, which I could better bear; he spoke well, as I thought, from good Joshua's resolutions, viz., "As for me and my house we will serve the Lord."[2] After a time of silence he went to prayer, which was attended with something so awful and affecting that I was reduced to tears, yet a stranger to the cause.

Soon after this we left Boston, for my husband was given to ramble, which was very disagreeable to me, but I must submit. We went to Rhode Island, where he hired a place to keep a school. This place was mostly inhabited with Presbyterians, where I soon got acquainted with some of the most religious amongst them; for tho' I was poor, I was favored with respect amongst people of the best credit, and had frequent discourses with them, but the more I was acquainted with their principles, the worse I liked them, so that I remained dissatisfied, and the old enemy of my happiness,[3] knowing I was resolved to abandon him, assaulted me afresh, and laid a bait with which I had like to have been caught. For one day having been abroad, at my return home, I found the people, at whose house we had taken a room, had left some flax in an apartment through which I went to my own, at sight of which I was tempted to steal some to make some thread, and I went and took a small bunch in my hand, at which I was smote with remorse, and immediately laid it down, saying, "Lord help me from such a vile act as this." But the twisting serpent did not leave me yet, his assaults were so strong and prevalent that I took it into my room; when I came there horror seized me, and bursting into tears, I cried, "O God of mercy, enable me to resist this temptation," which He of His mercy did, and gave me power to say, "I will regard thy convictions." So I carried it back, and returning to my room, I was so filled with thanksgiving to God, and wrapped into such a frame as I have not words to express, neither can any guess but those who have resisted temptation, and tasted of the same sweet peace by experience.

2. "And if it seem evil unto you to serve the Lord, choose you this day whom ye will serve; whether the gods which your father served that were on the other side of the flood, or the gods of the Amorites in whose land ye dwell: but as for me and my house, we will serve the Lord" (Joshua 24.15).
3. I.e., Satan.

Soon after this my husband hired[4] a place further up the island, where we were nearer a Church of England, to which place I used to go, for tho' I disliked some of their ways, yet I approved of them the best.

At this time a new exercise fell upon me,[5] and of such a sort as I had never heard of before, and while I was under it I thought myself alone.——It was in the 2d month of the year.[6] I was sitting by a fire in company with several persons, amongst whom my husband was one; there arose a thunder gust and with the noise that struck my ear, a voice attending, even as the sound of a mighty trumpet piercing through me with these words: "Oh, eternity! eternity! the endless term of long eternity!" at which I was exceedingly surprised and sat speechless as in a trance, and in a moment saw myself in such a state as made me despair of ever being happy. I seemed to behold a roll,[7] wrote in black characters, at sight of which I heard a voice say, "These are thy sins"; and immediately followed another saying: "The Blood of Christ is not sufficient to wash them away, and this is shown thee that thou mayst confess thy damnation is just, and not in order that they should be forgiven thee."

All this while I sat speechless, but at last I got up trembling, and threw myself upon a bed. The company thought my indisposition proceeded only from the fright of the thunder, but oh! alas, it was of another kind, and from that time for several months I was in the utmost despair, for if I at any time did endeavor to hope or lay hold of a gracious promise, the old accuser[8] would come in telling me it was now too late, that I had withstood the day of mercy, and that I should add to my sins by praying for pardon and provoke the Divine Vengeance to make a monument of wrath of me.

I now was like one already in torment. My sleep departed from me, I ate little, became extremely melancholy, and took no delight in anything. Had this world been mine and the glory of it, I would gladly have given it for a glimpse of hope. My husband was shocked to see me so changed. I that once could divert him with a song, in which he took great delight, nay after I grew religious as to the outward form, and till I could do it no longer. But now my singing was turned into mourning, and my dancing into lamentations; for my nights and days were one continual scene of sorrow. I let none know my desperate condition. My husband used all means to divert my melancholy state, but all in vain; the wound was too deep to be healed with anything short of the true Balm of Gilead.[9] I durst not go much alone for fear of evil spirits, but if I would, my husband would not suffer[1] it, and if I took the Bible he would take it from me, saying, "How you are altered; you used to be agreeable company, but now I have no comfort of you." I endeavored to bear all with patience, expecting soon to bear more than man could inflict upon me.

At length I went to a priest to see if he could relieve me, but he was a stranger to my condition, and advised me to take the Sacrament, and to use some innocent diversions,[2] and sent me a book of prayers which he said was for my condition. But all was in vain. As to the Sacrament, I thought myself in a state very unfit to receive it worthily, and I then could not use my prayers, for I thought that if ever my prayers should be acceptable, I should be enabled

---

4. I.e., was hired for.
5. Absorbed my attention. "Exercise": here, spiritual struggle or trial.
6. April.
7. Scroll, document.
8. In the 1774 edition, "accuser" was misprinted as amuser.
9. "Is there no balm in Gilead; is there no physician there?" (Jeremiah 8.22).
1. Allow.
2. Amusements. "The Sacrament": Holy Communion.

to pray without a book, and diversions were burdensome, for as I said, my husband used all means tending that way to no purpose. Yet he with some others once persuaded me to the raising of a building, where much people were got, in hopes of diverting my grief. But instead of relief, it added to my sorrow; for to this place came an officer to summon a jury to inquire concerning the body of a man that had hanged himself, which as soon as I understood, it seemed to be attended with a voice, saying, "Thou shalt be the next monument of wrath, for thou art not worthy to die a natural death."

For two months after this I was daily tempted to destroy myself, and sometimes the temptation was so strong I could scarce resist, through fear of which, when I went alone I used to throw off my apron and garters, and if I had a knife, to cast it from me, crying, "Lord keep me from taking away that life Thou gave me, and which Thou wouldst have made happy, if I had joined with the offers of Thy grace, and had regarded the convictions I've had from my youth—the fault is my own, Thou, O Lord, [art] clear." And yet so great was my agony that I desired death, that I might know the worst of my torments; all this while I was so hardened that I could not shed a tear. But God in His own good time delivered my soul out of this thralldom.

For one night as I lay in my bed, my husband by me asleep, bemoaning my miserable condition, I had strength to cry, "O my God, had Thou no mercy left? Look down I beseech Thee for Christ's sake, who has promised that all manner of sin and blasphemy shall be forgiven. Therefore Lord, if Thou wilt graciously please to extend this promise to me, an unworthy creature, trembling before Thee, there is nothing Thou shalt command, but I will obey." In an instant my heart tendered and dissolved into a flood of tears, abhorring my past offenses, and admiring the mercies of God; for I was made to hope in Christ my redeemer, and enabled to look upon Him with an eye of faith, and saw fulfilled what I believed when the priest lent me his book, that if ever my prayers would be acceptable to God, I should be enabled to pray without form,[3] and so used it no more. Nevertheless I thought to join with some religious society, but met with none that I liked in everything. Yet the Church of England seemed nearest, upon which I joined with them and received the Sacrament, so called, and can say in truth that I did it with reverence and fear.

Being thus released from deep distress, I seemed like another creature, and went often alone without fear and tears flowed abundantly from my eyes; and once as I was abhorring myself, in great humility of mind, I heard a gracious voice say, "I will not forsake thee, only obey what I shall make known unto thee." I then entered into covenant,[4] saying, "My soul doth magnify Thee the God of mercy; if Thou will vouchsafe Thy Grace, the rest of my days shall be devoted to Thee, and if it be Thy will that I beg my bread, I will be content and submit to Thy Providence."

I now began to think of my relations in Pennsylvania, whom I had not yet seen, and having a great desire to see them, I got leave of my husband to go, and also a certificate from the priest, in order that if I made any stay, I might be received as a member wherever I came. Then setting out, my husband bore me company to the Blazing Star Ferry, saw me safe over, and then returned. In the way near a place called Maidenhead, I fell from my horse and was

---

3. Without reading a prayer book.   4. Formal agreement.

disabled from traveling for some time, and abode at the house of an honest Dutchman, who with his wife was very kind to me—and tho' they had much trouble in going to the doctor and waiting upon me, for I was several days unable to help myself—yet would have nothing for it, which I thought very kind, and charged me[5] if ever I came that way again to call and lodge there.— I mention this because I shall have occasion to remark this place again.

I arrived next at Trent town Ferry,[6] where I met with no small mortification upon hearing that my relations were Quakers, and what was worst of all, my aunt was a preacher. I was sorry to hear of it, for I was exceedingly prejudiced against those people, and have often wondered with what face they could call themselves Christians; and I began to repent my coming, sometimes having a mind to return back without seeing them. At last I concluded to go see them, since I was so far on my journey, tho' I expected little comfort from my visit. But see how God brings unforeseen things to pass, for by my going there I was brought to the knowledge of the TRUTH.

I went from Trent town Ferry to Philadelphia by water, and thence to my uncle's on horseback, where I met with a very kind reception; for tho' my own uncle was dead and my aunt married again, yet both she and her husband received me in a very kind manner. I had not been there 3 hours before I met with a shock, and my opinion began to alter with respect to these people; for seeing a book lie on the table, and being much given to reading, I took it up, which my aunt observing, said, "Cousin, that is a Quaker's book, Samuel Crisp's *Two Letters*,"[7] and I suppose she thought I should not like it, at perceiving that I was not one. I made her no answer, but thought to myself, "What can these people write about, for I have heard that they deny the Scripture, and have no other bible but George Foxe's *Journal*,[8] and that they deny all the holy Ordinances;" for I resolved to read a little, and had not read two pages before my very heart burned within me, and tears came into my eyes, which I was afraid would be seen. I therefore walked with the book into the garden, and the piece being small, read it through before I went in, and sometimes uttering these involuntary expressions: "My God, if ever I come to the true knowledge of the truth, must I be of this man's opinion, who has fought Thee as I have done, and join with these people that I preferred the Papists to, but a [few] hours ago. Oh! Thou the God of my salvation and of my life, who hast in an abundant manner manifested Thy long-suffering and tender mercy in redeeming me as from the lowest hell, a monument of Thy grace. Lord my soul beseeches Thee to direct me in the right way, and keep me from error; and then according to my covenant, I'll think nothing too near to part with for Thy name's sake, if these things be so. Oh! happy people thus beloved of God."

After I came a little to myself I washed my face, least any in the house should perceive I had been weeping. At night I got very little sleep, for the old enemy began to suggest that I was one of those that wavered and was not steadfast in the faith, advancing several texts of Scripture against me and them that mention in the latter days there shall be those that will deceive the very elect, and these people were them, and that I was in danger of being deluded.

5. Made me promise.
6. Trenton, New Jersey.
7. Samuel Crisp (n.d.) was an English schoolmaster and the author of *A Libeller Exposed: being a Vindication of the People Called Quaker* (1704).

8. George Fox (1624–1691), an Englishman and founder of the Society of Friends, popularly called Quakers. His *Journal* appeared in 1694, revised by a committee headed by William Penn.

Here the subtle serpent transformed himself so hiddenly that I verily thought this to be a timely caution from a good angel, so resolved to beware of these deceivers, and for some weeks did not touch any of their books.

The next day being the first of the week, I wanted to have gone to church, which was distant about four miles, but being a stranger and having nobody to go with me, was forced to give it up, and as most of the family was going to meeting, I went with them. But with this conclusion: not to like them. And so it was; for as they sat in silence, I looked over the meeting, thinking within myself, how like fools these people sit, how much better were it to stay at home and read the Bible, or some good book, than to come here and go to sleep; for I being very sleepy thought they were no better than me. Indeed, at length I fell asleep and had like to have fallen down, but this was the last time I ever fell asleep in a meeting, tho' often assaulted with it.

I now began to be lifted up with spiritual pride, and thought myself better than they, but through mercy this did not last long, for in a little time I was brought low, and saw that they were the people to whom I must join. It may seem strange that I, who had lived so long with one of this society in Dublin, should yet be so great a stranger to them. In answer, let it be considered, that during the time I was there, I never read one of their books or went to one meeting, and besides, I had heard such ridiculous stories of them as made me think they were the worst of any society of people. But God that knew the sincerity of my heart, looked with pity on my weakness, and soon let me see my error; for in a few weeks there was an afternoon's meeting held at my uncle's to which came that servant of the Lord, William Hammons,[9] who was then made instrumental in convincing me of the TRUTH more perfectly, and helping me over some great doubts, tho' I believe no one did ever sit in greater opposition than I did when he first stood up. But I was soon brought down, for he preached the Gospel with such power that I was forced to give up and confess it was the TRUTH.

As soon as meeting was ended, I endeavored to get alone, for I was not fit to be seen, being so broken; yet afterwards the restless adversary assaulted me again in the manner following. The morning before this meeting I had been disputing with my uncle about Baptism,[1] which was the subject this good man dwelt upon and which he handled so clearly as to answer all my scruples beyond objection. Yet the crooked serpent farther alleged that the sermon I had heard did not proceed from Divine Revelation, but that my uncle and aunt had acquainted the Friend[2] of me, which being strongly suggested, I fell to accusing them of it, and of which they both cleared themselves, saying they had not seen him since my coming to these parts until he came to the meeting.

I then concluded he was a messenger sent from God to me, and with fervent cries desired I might be directed right. And now I laid aside all prejudice and set my heart to receive TRUTH, and the Lord in His own good time revealed to my soul not only the beauty there is in it, and that those should shine who continued faithful to it, but also the emptiness of all shadows, which in their way were glorious, but now the Son of Glory was come to put an end to them all and establish everlasting righteousness in the room thereof, which is a work in the soul. He likewise let me see that all I had gone through was to prepare me for this day, and that the time was near that He would require me to go

9. Evidently a Quaker of some renown.   *Babylon.*
1. In the 1774 edition, "Baptism" was misprinted as   2. I.e., Hammons.

forth and declare to others what the God of mercy had done for my soul; at which I was surprised and desired I might be excused, for fear I should bring dishonor to the TRUTH, and cause His holy Name to be evil spoken of.

All this while I did not let anybody know the condition I was in, nor did appear like a Friend,[3] and feared a discovery. I now began to think of returning to my husband, but found a restraint to stay where I was. I then hired a place to keep a school, and hearing of a place for him wrote desiring him to come to me, but let him know nothing how it was with me.

I loved to go to meetings, but did not like to be seen to go on week days, and therefore to shun it used to go from my school through the woods to them. But notwithstanding all my care, the neighbors that were not Friends soon began to revile, calling me Quaker, saying they supposed I intended to be a fool and turn preacher. I then received the same censure that I, a little above a year before, had passed on[4] one of the handmaids of the Lord at Boston, and so weak was I, alas, I could not bear the reproach, and in order to change their opinions got in to greater excess in apparel than I had freedom to wear for some time before I became acquainted with Friends. In this condition I continued till my husband came, and then began the trial of my faith. Before he reached me he heard I was turned Quaker, at which he stamped, saying, I had rather have heard she had been dead, well as I love her, for if so all my comfort is gone; he then came to me, and had not seen me for four months; I got up and met him, saying, "My dear, I am glad to see thee," at which he fell in a great passion, and said, "The devil THEE thee, don't THEE me." I used all the mild means I could to pacify him, and at length got him fit to go and speak to my relations, but he was alarmed, and as soon as he got alone he said, "So I see your Quaker relations have made you one." I told him they had not, which was true, nor had I ever told them how it was with me. But he would have it that I was one, and therefore should not stay amongst them, and having found a place to his mind,[5] hired it, and came directly back to fetch me, and in one afternoon walked near thirty miles to keep me from meeting, the next day being the first-day,[6] and on the morrow took me to the aforesaid place, hired lodgings at a Church-man's house, who was one of the wardens,[7] and a bitter enemy to Friends, and would tell me a great deal of ridiculous stuff. But my judgment was too clearly convinced to believe. I still did not appear like a Friend, but they all believed I was one. When my husband and him used to be making their diversions and revilings, I used to sit in silence, but now and then an involuntary sigh would break from me, at which he would say to my husband, "There, did not I tell you your wife was a Quaker, and she will be a preacher soon," upon which my husband once in a great rage came up to me, and shaking his hand over me said, "You had better be hanged on that day." I then, Peter like,[8] in a panic denied my being a Quaker, at which great horror seized upon me, and continued for near three months, so that I again feared that by denying the Lord who bought me the heavens were shut against me; for great darkness surrounded me, and I was again plunged in despair.

I used to walk much alone in the woods, where no eye saw, or ear heard me, and there lamented my miserable condition, and have often gone from

3. I.e., did not dress in Quaker clothes.
4. I.e., the criticism that I . . . had made of.
5. Suitable to him.
6. Sunday. Quakers preferred not to use the traditional names for the days of the week because they are derived from the names of pagan gods.
7. Lay officer in the Anglican, or Episcopal, church.
8. Peter denied Christ three times in Mark 14.66–72.

morning till night without breaking my fast, with which I was brought so low that my life was a burden to me. The devil seemed to vaunt[9] [that although] the sins [of] my youth were forgiven, yet now he was sure of me, for that I had committed the unpardonable sin, and hell would inevitably be my portion, and my torments would be greater than if I had hanged myself at the first.

In this doleful condition I had now to bewail my misery, and even in the night, when I could not sleep, under the painful distress of my mind. And if my husband perceived me weeping he used to revile me for it. At last, when he and his friends thought themselves too weak to overset me, tho' I feared it was already done, he went to the priest at Chester to advise what to do with me. This man knew I was a member of the Church, for I had shown him my certificate. His advice was to take me out of Pennsylvania, and find some place where there was no Quakers, and there my opinion would wear off. To this my husband agreed, saying he did not care where he went, if he could but restore me to that liveliness of temper I was naturally of, and to that Church of which I was a member. I, on my part, had no spirit to oppose their proposals, neither much cared where I was; for I seemed to have nothing to hope for, but daily expected to be made a spectacle of Divine Wrath, and I was possessed it would be by thunder.

The time of removal came and I was not suffered[1] to bid my relations farewell. My husband was poor and kept no horse, so I must travel on foot. We came to Wilmington, 15 miles thence to Philadelphia, by water; here he took me to a tavern, where I soon became a spectacle and discourse of the company. My husband told them his wife was turned Quaker, and that he designed, if possible, to find out some place where there was none. Oh, thought I, I was once in condition of deserving that name, but now it was over with me. Oh, that I might, from a true hope, once more have an opportunity to confess to the TRUTH, tho' sure of all manner of cruelties yet I would not regard it. These were my concerns while he was entertaining the company with my story, in which he told them that I had been a good dancer, but now he could neither get me to dance nor sing; upon which one of the company starts up, saying, "I'll go fetch my fiddle and we'll have a dance," at which my husband was pleased. The fiddle came, the sight of which put me in a sad condition, for fear, if I refused, my husband would be in a great passion. However I took up this resolution not to comply whatever might be the consequence. He came to me and took me by the hand, saying, "Come my dear, shake off that gloom, let's have a civil dance, you would now and then, when you were a good Church-woman and that is better than a stiff Quaker." I, trembling, desired to be excused. But he insisted on it, and knowing his temper to be exceeding choleric, I durst not say much, but would not consent. He then pulled me round the room till tears affected my eyes, at sight of which the musician stopped, and said, "I'll play no more, let your wife alone," of which I was glad. There was also a man in [this] company who came from Freehold, in West Jersey,[2] who said, "I see your wife is a Quaker, but if you'll take my advice, you need not go so far (for my husband designed to go to Staten Island), come and live amongst us and we'll soon cure her from her Quakerism, and we want both a school-master and mistress." To which he agreed, and a happy turn it was for me as will be seen by and by, and the

9. Brag.   2. Now the western part of the state of New Jersey,
1. Allowed.   where many Quakers lived.

wonderful turn of Providence, who had not yet abandoned me, but raised a glimmering hope and afforded the answer of peace in refusing to dance, for which I was more rejoiced than if I were made a mistress of much riches, and in floods of tears, said, "Lord, I dread to ask, and yet without Thy gracious pardon I am miserable, I therefore fall down before Thy throne, imploring mercy at Thy hand. O Lord, once more I beseech Thee try my obedience, and then whatsoever Thou commands, I will obey, and not fear to confess Thee before men." Thus was my soul engaged before God in sincerity, and He of His tender mercy heard my cries, and in me has shewn that He delights not in the death of a sinner, for He again set my soul at liberty and I could praise Him.

I now again longed for an opportunity to confess to His TRUTH, which He showed me should come, tho' in what manner I did not see, but believed the words I had heard, which in a little time were fulfilled to me. My husband, as aforesaid, agreed to go to Freehold, and in our way thither came to Maidenhead, where I went to see the kind Dutchman, aforementioned, who made us welcome, and invited us to stay a few days. While we were there, there was held a great meeting of the Presbyterians, not only of worship, but business also; for one of their preachers being charged with drunkenness was this day to have his trial before a great number of priests, and we went to it, of which I was afterwards glad; for here I perceived great divisions amongst the people about who should be their shepherd, and for which I greatly pitied their condition. I now saw beyond the men-made ministers,[3] and what they preached for, and which all those at this meeting might have done, had not the prejudice of education, which is very prevalent, blinded their eyes. Some insisted to have the old offender restored; some to have a young man they had upon trial[4] some weeks; a third party was for sending for one from New England. At length one stood up, and, addressing himself to the chief speaker, said, "Sir, when we have been at the expense, which will be no small matter, of fetching this gentleman from New England, perhaps he won't stay with us." [Answered.] "Don't you know how to make him?" [Replied.] "No, Sir." "I'll tell you then," said he, to which I gave good attention: "Give him a good salary, and I'll engage he'll stay." O, thought I, these mercenary creatures, they are actuated by one and the same thing, ever the love of money, and not the regard of souls. This, [so-]called reverend gentleman, whom these poor people almost adored, to my knowledge had left his flock on Long Island and moved to Philadelphia, where he could get more money. I myself had heard some of them on the Island say that they had almost impoverished themselves to keep him, but not being able to equal Philadelphia's invitation, he left them without a shepherd. This man therefore, knowing their ministry proceeded from one cause, might be purchased with the same thing.—Surely these and such like are the shepherds that regard the fleece more than the flock, and in whose mouth are lies, saying the Lord hath sent them, and that they were Christ's ambassadors, whose command to those He sent was "Freely ye have received, freely give."[5] I durst not say anything to my husband of the remarks I had made, but laid them up in my heart, and they did help to strengthen me in my resolutions.

3. I.e., ministers without a divine calling.
4. I.e., on probation as a replacement for the accused.
5. "Heal the sick, cleanse the lepers, raise the dead, cast out devils: freely ye have received, freely give" (Matthew 10.8).

Hence we set forward for Freehold, and coming through Stony Brook, my husband turning towards me said tauntingly, "There's one of Satan's Synagogues, don't you want to be in it? I hope I shall see you carried off [by] this new religion." I made no answer but went on. In a little time we came to a large run of water, over which was no bridge, and we being strangers knew no way to get over. But through we was obliged to go. My husband carried our clothes, which we had in bundles, and I pulled off my shoes and waded through in my stockings, which served somewhat to prevent the chill of the water from [freezing] me, it being very cold and a fall of snow, in the 12th month.[6] My heart was concerned in prayer that the Lord would sanctify all my afflictions to me, and give me patience to bear whatsoever should be suffered to come upon me.

We walked most part of a mile before we came to a house, which proved to be a sort of a tavern. My husband called for some spirituous liquors, but I got some cider mulled, which when I had drank of't, the cold being struck to my heart, made me extremely sick, insomuch, that when we were a little past the house I expected I should have fainted, and not being able to stand, fell down under a fence. Which my husband observing, tauntingly said, "What's the matter now? What are you drunk? Where's your religion now?" He knew better, and at that time I believe he pitied me, yet was suffered grievously to afflict me. In a little time I grew better, and going on came to another tavern at which place we lodged. The next day I was indifferent well, and as we proceeded on our journey a young man with an empty cart overtook us, and I desired my husband to ask the young man to let us ride, which he did and it was readily granted. I now thought myself well off, and took it as a great favor, for my proud heart was humbled, and I did not regard the looks of it, tho' the time had been that I would not have been seen in a cart. This cart belonged to a man at Shrewsbury and was to go through the place that we were going to, so we rode on. We soon had the care of the team to ourselves, from a failure in the driver, to the place where I was intended to have been made a prey on. But see how unforeseen things are brought to pass by a Providential hand. It is said and answered, Shall we do evil that good may come? God forbid.[7] Yet hence good came to me. Here my husband would fain have me stay, while he went to see the team safe at home, but I told him no, since he had led me through the country like a vagabond, I would not stay behind him; so we went on, and lodged that night at the man's house who owned the cart. Next day on our return to Freehold, we met a man riding full speed, who stopped, and said to my husband, "Sir, are you a school-master?" and was answered yes. "I came to tell you," replied the stranger, "of two new school houses, and each want a master and are two miles apart." How this stranger came to hear of us, who came but the night before, I never knew, but I was glad he was not one called a Quaker, lest my husband should have thought it had been a plot. I said to my husband: "My dear, look on me with pity. If thou hast any affections left for me, which I hope thou hast, for I am not conscious of having done anything to alienate them here; here is," continued I, "an opportunity to settle us both, and I am willing to do all in my power towards an honest livelihood."

My expressions took place, and after a little pause he consented to the young

---

6. February.
7. "Shall we continue in sin, that grace may abound? God forbid" (Romans 6.1–2).

man's directions and made towards the place, and in our way we came to the house of a worthy Friend, whose wife was a preacher, tho' we did not know it. I was surprised to see the people so kind to us who were strangers. We had not been long in the house before we were invited to lodge there that night, it being the last of the week. I said nothing, but waited to hear my master speak. He soon consented, saying, "My wife has had a tedious travel, and I pity her," at which kind expressions I was greatly affected, for they were now very seldom used to me.

The Friends' kindness could not have proceeded from my appearing in the garb of a Quaker, for I had not yet altered my dress; but the woman of the house, after we had concluded to stay, fixed her eyes on me and said, I believe thou hast met with a deal of troubles, to which I made but little answer. My husband observing they were of that sort of people he had so much endeavored to shun would give us no opportunity for any discourse that night, but the next morning I let the Friend know a little how it was with me. Meeting time came, to which I longed to go, but durst not ask my husband leave, for fear of disturbing him, till we were settled, and then thought I, "If ever I am favored to be in this place, come life or death, I'll fight through, for my salvation is at stake." The Friends, getting ready for meeting, asked my husband if he would go, saying they knew who were to be his employers, and if they were at meeting, they would speak to them. He then consented to go. Then said the woman, "Friend, and wilt thou let thy wife go?" to which he denied, making several objections, all which she answered so prudently, that he could not be angry and at last he consented. With joy I went, for I had not been at one for near 4 months, and an heavenly meeting it was to me. I now renewed my covenant, and saw the word of the Lord made good, that I should have another opportunity to confess to His name, for which, "My soul did magnify the Lord, and my spirit did rejoice in the God of my salvation,"[8] who had brought strange things to pass. May I ever be preserved in humility, never forgetting His tender mercies to me.

Here according to my desire we settled, my husband got one school and I the other. We took a room at a Friend's house, a mile from each school, and 8 miles from the meeting-house. Before the next first-day we were got to our new settlement, and now I concluded to let my husband see that I was determined to join with Friends. When the first-day came I directed myself to him in this manner: "My dear, art thou willing to let me go to meeting?" at which he fell into a rage, saying, "No, you shan't." I then drew up a resolution and told him that as a dutiful wife ought, so was I ready to obey all his commands, but where they imposed on my conscience I no longer durst, for I had already done it too long, and had wronged myself by it, and tho' he was near and I loved him as a wife ought, yet God was nearer than all the world to me, and had made me sensible this was the way I ought to go, which I assured him was no small cross to my own will. Yet I had given up my heart, and hoped he that had called for it would enable me the residue of my life to keep it steadily devoted to him whatever I suffered, adding I hoped not to make him any worse a wife for it. But all I could say was in vain. I had now put my hand to the plow and resolved not to look back, so went without leave, but expected to be immediately followed and forced back. He did not follow me as I expected, so

8. "And Mary said, My soul doth magnify the Lord, and my spirit hath rejoiced in God my Savior" (Luke 1.46–47).

I went to a neighbor's and got a girl to show me the way; and then went on rejoicing and praising God in my heart who had thus far given me power, and another opportunity to confess to the TRUTH.

Thus for some time I had to go 8 miles on foot to meeting, which I never thought hard. My husband now bought a horse, but would not let me ride him, neither when my shoes were wore out would he let me have a new pair, thinking by that means to keep me from meetings. But this did not hinder me, for I have taken strings and tied round to keep them on. He now finding no hard usage could alter my resolution, neither threatening to beat me, nor denying it, for he several times struck me with sore blows, which I endeavored to bear with patience, believing the time would come when he would see I was in the right, which accordingly [he] did. He once came up to me and took out his penknife, saying, "If you offer to go to meeting to-morrow, with this knife I'll cripple you, for you shall not be a Quaker." I made him no answer but when morning came I set out as usual, and he was not suffered to hurt me.

In despair of recovering me himself, he now fled to the priest for help, and told him that I had been a very religious woman in the way of the Church of England, was a member of it, and had a good certificate from Long Island, but now was bewitched and turned Quaker, which almost broke his heart. He therefore desired, as he was one who had the care of souls, he would come and pay me a visit, and use his best endeavors to reclaim me, and he hoped by the blessing of God it would be done.

The priest consented to come, and the time was fixed, which was to be that day two weeks, for he said he could not come sooner. My husband came home extremely pleased, and told me of it, at which I smiled and said I hope to be enabled to give a reason for the hope that is in me, at the same time believing the priest would never trouble me nor he never did. Before this appointed time came it was required of me in a more public manner to confess to the world what I was, and to give up in prayer at the meeting. The fight of which and the power that attended it made me tremble, and I could not hold myself still. I now again desired death and could have freely given up my natural life as ransom. And what made it harder to me, I was not taken under the care of Friends; and what kept me from requesting it was for fear I should be overcome, and bring a scandal on the Society. I begged to be excused till I was joined, and then I would give up freely, to which I received this answer, as tho' I had heard a distinct voice, "I am a covenant-keeping God, and the words that I spoke to thee when I found thee in distress, even that I would never leave thee, nor forsake thee, if thou wouldst be obedient to what I should make known to thee, which I will assuredly make good; but if thou refuse, my Spirit shall not always strive. Fear not, I will make way for thee through all thy difficulties, which shall be many, for My name's sake, but be faithful, and I will give thee a crown of life." I then being sure it was God that spoke, said, "Thy will, O God, be done, I am in Thy hand, do with me according to Thy word." And I gave up, but after it was over the enemy came in like a flood, telling me I had done what I ought not, and should now bring dishonor to this people. But this shock did not last long.

This day, as usual, I had gone on foot. My husband, as he afterwards told me, lying on the bed, these words ran through him, "Lord where shall I fly to shun thee," at which he arose, and seeing it rain, got the horse and came to fetch me, and coming just as the meeting broke up, I got on horseback as quick as possible, least he should hear what had happened. Nevertheless he had heard, and as soon as we were got into the woods he began, saying, "What do you mean thus to make my life unhappy? could you not be a Quaker without turning fool after this manner?" I answered in tears, saying, "My dear, look on me with pity, if thou hast any; can'st thou think that I in the bloom of my days would bear all that thou knowest of, and a great deal which thou knowest not of, if I did not believe it to be my duty?" This took hold of him, and he taking my hand said, "Well, I'll even give you up, for I see it don't avail to strive. If it be of God, I cannot overthrow it, and if it be of yourself it will soon fall," and I saw the tears stand in his eyes, at which my heart was overcome with joy, and I would not have changed conditions with a queen. I already began to reap the fruit of my obedience, but my trials did not end here. The time being up that the priest was to come, but no priest appeared, my husband went to fetch him, but he would not come, saying he was busy and could not, which so displeased my husband that he'd never go near him more, and for some time went to no place of worship.

Now the Unwearied Adversary found out another scheme, and with it assaulted me so strong, that I thought all I had gone through was but little to this. It came upon me in such an unexpected manner, I hearing a woman relate a book she had read, in which it was asserted that Christ was not the Son of God. As soon as she had spoke the words, if a man had spoke I could not more distinctly have heard these words, "No more He is, it's all a fancy, and the contrivance of man," and an horror of great darkness fell upon me which continued for three weeks. The exercise[9] I was in I am not able to express, neither durst I let any one know how it was with me. I again sought desolate places, where I might make my moan, and have lain whole nights and don't know that my eyes have been shut to sleep. I again thought myself alone, but would never let go my faith in Him, after saying in my heart, I'll believe till I die, and keep a hope that He who delivered me out of the paw of the bear and from the jaws of the devouring lion would in His own good time deliver me out of this temptation also, which He of His mercy did, and let me see this was for my good in order to prepare me for further service, which He had for me to do, and that it was necessary that His ministers should be dipped into all states,[1] that thereby they might be abler to speak to all, for which my soul was thankful to Him, the God of mercies, who had at several times redeemed me out of great distress. And I found the truth of His words that all things should work for good to those that loved and feared Him, which I did with my whole heart, and I hope ever shall while I have a being.

This happened soon after my first appearance, and Friends had not been to talk with me, nor did they know what to do till I had appeared again, which was not for some time, when at the monthly meeting, four Friends came to pay me a visit, which I was glad of, and gave them such satisfaction that they left me well satisfied. I then joined with Friends, my husband went to no place of worship. One day he said, "I'd go to meeting, only I'm afraid I shall hear your clack, which I cannot bear." I used no persuasions, yet when meeting-time came he got the horse, and took me behind him and went to meeting. But for several months, if he saw me offer to rise,[2] he would go out, till one time I got up before he was aware, and then, as he afterward said, was ashamed

9. As above, spiritual struggle or trial.
1. I.e., spiritual or mental states.

2. I.e., to stand up and speak at a Quaker meeting.

to do it, and from that time never did nor hindered me from going to meeting, and tho' he, poor man, could not take up the Cross, yet his judgment was convinced, and sometimes in a flood of tears would say, "My dear, I've seen the beauty there is in the TRUTH, and that thou art in the right, and I pray God preserve thee in it, but as for me the Cross is too heavy, I cannot bear it." I told him I hoped He that had given me strength would also favor him. "Oh!" said he, "I can't bear the reproach thou dost to be called turn-coat, and become a laughing stock to the world. But I'll no longer hinder thee from it;" which I looked on as a great favor that my way was thus far made easy, and a little hope remained that my prayers would be heard on his account.

In this place he had got linked in with some that he was afraid would make game of him, which indeed they already did, asking him when he designed to commence preacher, for that they saw he intended to turn Quaker, and seemed to love his wife better since she did than before. We were now got to a little house by ourselves, which tho' mean, and little to put in it, our bed being no better than chaff,[3] yet I was truly content, and did not envy the rich their riches. The only desires I now had was my own persuasion, and to be blessed with the reformation of my husband. These men used to come to our house and there provoke my husband to sit up and drink sometimes till near day, while I have been sorrowing in a stable. As I once sat in this condition I heard my husband say to his company, "I cannot bear any longer to afflict my poor wife in this manner, for whatever you may think of her, I do believe she is a good woman," upon which he came to me, and said, "Come in, my dear, God has given thee a deal of patience, I'll put an end to this practice." And so he did, for this was the last time they sat up at nights. My husband now thought if he was in any place where it was not known that he had been so bitter against Friends he could do better than here, but I was much against his moving, fearing it would turn out to his hurt, having been for some months much altered for the better, establishing me in the TRUTH, and therefore would not have him be afflicted about that, and according to the measure of Grace received did what I could both by example and advice for his good, and my advice was for him to fight through it here, fearing he would grow weaker, and the enemy gain advantage over him, if he thus fled. But all I could say did not prevail against his moving, and hearing of a place at Burdon Town [Borden-town], [he] went there. But that did not suit. He then moved to Mount Holy [New Jersey], and there we settled. He got a good school and so did I, and here we might have done very well. We got our house pretty well furnished for poor folks. I now began to think I wanted but one thing to complete my happiness, viz., the reformation of my husband, to which also I had too much reason to doubt, for it fell out according to my fears, and he grew worse here, and took to drinking, so that it seemed as tho' my life was to be a continual scene of sorrow, and most earnestly I prayed to Almighty God, to endue me with patience to bear my afflictions, and submit to His providence, which I can say in truth I did without murmuring, or ever uttering an unsavory expression, to the best of my knowledge, except once when my husband coming home a little in drink, in which frame he was very fractious, and finding me at work by a candle, came to me, put it out, and fetching me a box on the ear said, "You don't earn your light," which unkind usage—for he had not struck me of two years before—went hard with me, and I uttered these [sic] rash

---

3. Straw. "Mean": inferior.

expressions, "Thou art a vile man," and was a little angry, but soon recovered and was sorry for it. He struck me again, which I received without so much as a word in return, and [he] went on in a distracted manner, uttering several rash expressions that bespoke despair, as that he now believed he was predestined to damnation, and he did not care how soon God would strike him dead and the like. I durst say but little, but at length I broke out in these words, "Lord look down on my afflictions, and deliver me by some means or other." I was answered I should soon be, and so I was, but in such a manner as I verily believed it would have killed me.

In a little time he went to Burlington, where he got in drink, and enlisted for a common soldier to go to Cuba, anno dom. 1740. I had drank many bitter cups, but this seemed to exceed them all; for indeed my very senses seemed shaken. I now a thousand times blamed myself for making such an undevised[4] request, fearing I had displeased God by it, and tho' He had granted it, it was in displeasure and suffered to be in this manner to punish me. But I can say I never desired his death more than my own, nay not so much. I have since had cause to believe his mind was benefited by the undertaking, which hope makes up for all I have suffered from him, being informed that he did in the army what he could not do at home, viz., suffer for the testimony of TRUTH. When they came to an engagement he refused to fight, for which he was whipped, and brought before the general, who asked him why he enlisted, if he would not fight. "I did it," said he, "in a drunken frolic, when the devil had the better of me, but my judgment is convinced, that I ought not, neither will I, whatever I suffer. I have but one life and you may take that if you please, but I'll never take up arms." They used him with much cruelty to make him yield, but could not, by means whereof he was so disabled that the general sent him to the hospital at Chelsea, near London, where in nine months he died, and I hope made a good end, for which I prayed both night and day, till I heard of his death.

Thus I thought it my duty to say what I could in his favor, as I have been obliged to say so much of his hard usage to me, all which I hope did me good, and altho' he was so bad yet had several good properties, and I never thought him the worst of men. He was one I loved, and had he let religion have its perfect work, I should have thought myself happy in the lowest state of life, and I have cause to bless God who enabled me in the station of a wife to do my duty, and now a widow, to submit to His will, always believing every thing He doth to be right. May He in all stations of life so preserve me by the arm of Divine Power, that I may never forget His tender mercies to me, the remembrance whereof doth often bow down my soul in humility before His throne, saying, "Lord, what was I, that Thou should'st have revealed to my soul the knowledge of the TRUTH, and done so much for me, who deserved Thy displeasure rather. But in me Thou hast shown Thy long-suffering and tender mercy. May Thou, O God, be glorified, and I abased, for it is Thy own works that praise Thee, and, of a truth, to the humble soul makest everything sweet."[5]

1774

4. I.e., thoughtless.
5. In an "Appendix" to the 1774 edition Aaron Ashbridge informed the reader that Elizabeth's second husband left her in debt for the sum of eighty pounds and that she repaid it with great difficulty. In 1753 she left New Jersey for Ireland, called to service abroad. She died in Ireland "the sixteenth day of the fifth month [July], 1755."

JOHN WOOLMAN

1720–1772

In a catalog of American writers John Woolman stands almost alone as a model of unqualified integrity, decency, and forthrightness. Woolman was a kind of latter-day "visible saint," a man both in the world but apart from it, who combined something of Franklin's practicality with Thoreau's passion for sincerity.

Woolman was born on his family's farm in Burlington County, New Jersey, a few miles east of Philadelphia. The nearest town was Mount Holly, New Jersey, a community settled mostly by English Quakers. It was an area close enough to Pennsylvania to benefit from William Penn's generous invitation to all persecuted believers to settle on his lands. After 1681 large numbers of Quakers, Baptists, and Mennonites settled in these regions. Although it may be argued that Quaker beliefs were a logical outgrowth of the Puritan movement for reforming the Church of England, Puritans despised Quakers because Quakers saw Christ's sacrifice as an act of redemption for all humankind. Quakers rejected Calvinist doctrines of election and predestination, and trusted in an "inner light," which Puritans saw as merely willful and antiauthoritarian. Quakers were not shy about their beliefs and, starting with George Fox (1624–1691), their founder, often found themselves in conflict with established order. This sense of alienation made Quaker communities like Mount Holly especially close knit. Woolman went to the Mount Holly village school and, until he was twenty-one, worked for his father on the family farm. He then moved to Mount Holly to tend a retail store and later set up in business for himself. Woolman's success in business was disturbing to him (mostly for what it said about human unresourcefulness), and it offended his Quaker belief in simplicity. He deliberately cut back his business and devoted himself more to tailoring. Woolman taught himself a number of other useful things: he was a surveyor, a teacher, and a farmer and he studied enough law to become adept at making wills and deeds.

It was while writing a bill of sale for a slave that Woolman first became aware of the conflict between public law and private conscience that was to absorb his life. Although he tells us that on that first occasion he remained silent, "gave way," and wrote the bill of sale, he was never to make that mistake again. The next time he informed the owner that slavery and a religious conscience were incompatible. Woolman thereafter found his true vocation in "speaking up," both to Friends in their homes and at Quaker meetings, where his gift for articulating his religious concerns qualified him to lead. Woolman was scrupulous in calling attention to all those things in daily life that are compromises with the "true ministry" of Christ. At twenty-three he set out on a number of missions to share his convictions with fellow believers. He traveled extensively from North Carolina to New Hampshire; his last call was a trip to England, where he died in York of smallpox. In all his "conversations" with Friends, Woolman warned of the dangers of a materialist society, of the exploitation of workers, of military conscription, of paying taxes to support wars, and above all, of the corruptions of slavery. He was, as the philosopher A. N. Whitehead once put it, the "first Apostle of human freedom."

Woolman's *Journal* has never been out of print since it was first published in 1774. Almost everyone who has read it has become an admirer of the man and his writing. Charles Lamb, the English essayist, once observed that it was the only American book he had ever read twice. It has been admired not only for the life and temperament it reveals but for the directness and simplicity of its style. John Greenleaf Whittier, who was himself a Quaker, tells us that Woolman "wrote as he believed, from an inward spiritual prompting; and with all his unaffected humility he evidently felt that his work was done in the clear radiance of 'the light which never was on land or sea.' "

The text used is *The Journal and Major Essays of John Woolman,* edited by Phillips P. Moulton (1971).

From The Journal of John Woolman

[Early Life and Vocation]

I have often felt a motion of love to leave some hints in writing of my experience of the goodness of God, and now, in the thirty-sixth year of my age, I begin this work. I was born in Northampton, in Burlington County in West Jersey, A.D. 1720, and before I was seven years old I began to be acquainted with the operations of divine love. Through the care of my parents, I was taught to read near as soon as I was capable of it, and as I went from school one Seventh Day,[1] I remember, while my companions went to play by the way, I went forward out of sight; and sitting down, I read the twenty-second chapter of the Revelations: "He showed me a river of water, clear as crystal, proceeding out of the throne of God and the Lamb, etc." And in reading it my mind was drawn to seek after that pure habitation which I then believed God had prepared for His servants. The place where I sat and the sweetness that attended my mind remains fresh in my memory.

This and the like gracious visitations[2] had that effect upon me, that when boys used ill language it troubled me, and through the continued mercies of God I was preserved from it. The pious instructions of my parents were often fresh in my mind when I happened amongst wicked children, and was of use to me. My parents, having a large family of children, used frequently on First Days after meeting[3] to put us to read in the Holy Scriptures or some religious books, one after another, the rest sitting by without much conversation, which I have since often thought was a good practice. From what I had read and heard, I believed there had been in past ages people who walked in uprightness before God in a degree exceeding any that I knew, or heard of, now living; and the apprehension of there being less steadiness and firmness amongst people in this age than in past ages often troubled me while I was a child.

I had a dream about the ninth year of my age as follows: I saw the moon rise near the west and run a regular course eastward, so swift that in about a quarter of an hour she reached our meridian, when there descended from her a small cloud on a direct line to the earth, which lighted on a pleasant green about twenty yards from the door of my father's house (in which I thought I stood) and was immediately turned into a beautiful green tree. The moon appeared to run on with equal swiftness and soon set in the east, at which time the sun arose at the place where it commonly does in the summer, and shining with full radiance in a serene air, it appeared as pleasant a morning as ever I saw.

All this time I stood still in the door in an awful[4] frame of mind, and I

1. I.e., Saturday. Quakers, or members of the Religious Society of Friends, substituted numbers for the days of the week both for the sake of simplicity and to discard the names of the pagan gods (e.g., Saturday was a day named in honor of Saturn).
2. I.e., similar moments when he felt God's presence

again.
3. Quakers refer to their assemblies as "meetings" and their church as a "meetinghouse." It is the custom for worshipers to remain silent until someone is moved to speak.
4. Full of awe.

observed that as heat increased by the rising sun, it wrought so powerfully on the little green tree that the leaves gradually withered; and before noon it appeared dry and dead. There then appeared a being, small of size, full of strength and resolution, moving swift from the north, southward, called a sun worm.[5]

Another thing remarkable in my childhood was that once, going to a neighbor's house, I saw on the way a robin sitting on her nest; and as I came near she went off, but having young ones, flew about and with many cries expressed her concern for them. I stood and threw stones at her, till one striking her, she fell down dead. At first I was pleased with the exploit, but after a few minutes was seized with horror, as having in a sportive way killed an innocent creature while she was careful for her young. I beheld her lying dead and thought those young ones for which she was so careful must now perish for want of their dam to nourish them; and after some painful considerations on the subject, I climbed up the tree, took all the young birds and killed them, supposing that better than to leave them to pine away and die miserably, and believed in this case that Scripture proverb was fulfilled, "The tender mercies of the wicked are cruel."[6] I then went on my errand, but for some hours could think of little else but the cruelties I had committed, and was much troubled.

Thus He whose tender mercies are over all His works hath placed a principle in the human mind which incites to exercise goodness toward every living creature; and this being singly attended to, people become tender-hearted and sympathizing, but being frequently and totally rejected, the mind shuts itself up in a contrary disposition.

About the twelfth year of my age, my father being abroad, my mother reproved me for some misconduct, to which I made an undutiful reply; and the next First Day as I was with my father returning from meeting, he told me he understood I had behaved amiss to my mother and advised me to be more careful in future. I knew myself blameable, and in shame and confusion remained silent. Being thus awakened to a sense of my wickedness, I felt remorse in my mind, and getting home I retired and prayed to the Lord to forgive me, and do not remember that I ever after that spoke unhandsomely to either of my parents, however foolish in other things.

Having attained the age of sixteen years, I began to love wanton company, and though I was preserved from profane language or scandalous conduct, still I perceived a plant in me which produced much wild grapes. Yet my merciful Father forsook me not utterly, but at times through His grace I was brought seriously to consider my ways, and the sight of my backsliding affected me with sorrow. But for want of rightly attending to the reproofs of instruction, vanity was added to vanity, and repentance to repentance; upon the whole my mind was more and more alienated from the Truth,[7] and I hastened toward destruction. While I meditate on the gulf toward which I traveled and reflect on my youthful disobedience, for these things I weep; mine eye runneth down with water.

Advancing in age the number of my acquaintance increased, and thereby my way grew more difficult. Though I had heretofore found comfort in reading the Holy Scriptures and thinking on heavenly things, I was now estranged therefrom. I knew I was going from the flock of Christ and had no resolution

5. I.e., sun snake. Woolman's creature is imaginary.   7. I.e., ultimate spiritual reality.
6. Proverbs 12.10.

to return; hence serious reflections were uneasy to me and youthful vanities and diversions my greatest pleasure. Running in this road I found many like myself, and we associated in that which is reverse to true friendship.[8]

But in this swift race it pleased God to visit me with sickness, so that I doubted of recovering. And then did darkness, horror, and amazement with full force seize me, even when my pain and distress of body was very great. I thought it would have been better for me never to have had a being than to see the day which I now saw. I was filled with confusion, and in great affliction both of mind and body I lay and bewailed myself. I had not confidence to lift up my cries to God, whom I had thus offended, but in a deep sense of my great folly I was humbled before Him, and at length that Word which is as a fire and a hammer broke and dissolved my rebellious heart. And then my cries were put up in contrition, and in the multitude of His mercies I found inward relief, and felt a close engagement that if He was pleased to restore my health, I might walk humbly before Him.

After my recovery this exercise[9] remained with me a considerable time; but by degrees giving way to youthful vanities, they gained strength, and getting with wanton[1] young people I lost ground. The Lord had been very gracious and spoke peace to me in the time of my distress, and I now most ungratefully turned again to folly, on which account at times I felt sharp reproof but did not get low enough to cry for help. I was not so hardy as to commit things scandalous, but to exceed in vanity and promote mirth was my chief study. Still I retained a love and esteem for pious people, and their company brought an awe upon me.

My dear parents several times admonished me in the fear of the Lord, and their admonition entered into my heart and had a good effect for a season, but not getting deep enough to pray rightly, the tempter when he came found entrance. I remember once, having spent a part of the day in wantonness, as I went to bed at night there lay in a window near my bed a Bible, which I opened, and first cast my eye on the text, "We lie down in our shame, and our confusion covers us."[2] This I knew to be my case, and meeting with so unexpected a reproof, I was somewhat affected with it and went to bed under remorse of conscience, which I soon cast off again.

Thus time passed on; my heart was replenished with mirth and wantonness, while pleasing scenes of vanity were presented to my imagination till I attained the age of eighteen years, near which time I felt the judgments of God in my soul like a consuming fire, and looking over my past life the prospect was moving. I was often sad and longed to be delivered from those vanities; then again my heart was strongly inclined to them, and there was in me a sore conflict. At times I turned to folly, and then again sorrow and confusion took hold of me. In a while I resolved totally to leave off some of my vanities, but there was a secret reserve in my heart of the more refined part of them, and I was not low enough to find true peace. Thus for some months I had great trouble, there remaining in me an unsubjected will which rendered my labors fruitless, till at length through the merciful continuance of heavenly visitations I was made to bow down in spirit before the Lord.

I remember one evening I had spent some time in reading a pious author,

8. I.e., those ideals basic to the Religious Society of Friends.
9. Religious experience.
1. Frivolous, unthinking.
2. Jeremiah 3.25.

and walking out alone I humbly prayed to the Lord for His help, that I might be delivered from all those vanities which so ensnared me. Thus being brought low, He helped me; and as I learned to bear the cross I felt refreshment to come from His presence; but not keeping in that strength which gave victory, I lost ground again, the sense of which greatly affected me; and I sought deserts and lonely places and there with tears did confess my sins to God and humbly craved help of Him. And I may say with reverence He was near to me in my troubles, and in those times of humiliation opened my ear to discipline.

I was now led to look seriously at the means by which I was drawn from the pure Truth, and learned this: that if I would live in the life which the faithful servants of God lived in, I must not go into company as heretofore in my own will, but all the cravings of sense must be governed by a divine principle. In times of sorrow and abasement these instructions were sealed upon me, and I felt the power of Christ prevail over selfish desires, so that I was preserved in a good degree of steadiness. And being young and believing at that time that a single life was best for me, I was strengthened to keep from such company as had often been a snare to me.

I kept steady to meetings, spent First Days after noon chiefly in reading the Scriptures and other good books, and was early convinced in my mind that true religion consisted in an inward life, wherein the heart doth love and reverence God the Creator and learn to exercise true justice and goodness, not only toward all men but also toward the brute creatures; that as the mind was moved on an inward principle to love God as an invisible, incomprehensible being, on the same principle it was moved to love Him in all His manifestations in the visible world; that as by His breath the flame of life was kindled in all animal and sensitive creatures, to say we love God as unseen and at the same time exercise cruelty toward the least creature moving by His life, or by life derived from Him, was a contradiction in itself.

I found no narrowness respecting sects and opinions, but believed that sincere, upright-hearted people in every Society who truly loved God were accepted of Him.

As I lived under the cross[3] and simply followed the openings[4] of Truth, my mind from day to day was more enlightened; my former acquaintance was left to judge of me as they would, for I found it safest for me to live in private and keep these things sealed up in my own breast.

While I silently ponder on that change wrought in me, I find no language equal to it nor any means to convey to another a clear idea of it. I looked upon the works of God in this visible creation and an awfulness covered me; my heart was tender and often contrite, and a universal love to my fellow creatures increased in me. This will be understood by such who have trodden in the same path. Some glances of real beauty may be seen in their faces who dwell in true meekness. There is a harmony in the sound of that voice to which divine love gives utterance, and some appearance of right order in their temper and conduct whose passions are fully regulated. Yet all these do not fully show forth that inward life to such who have not felt it, but this white stone and new name is known rightly to such only who have it.[5]

---

3. I.e., mindful of Christ and in humility.
4. Quakers referred to "openings" as direct messages from God; they came to those who lived in habitual expectation of them.

5. "To him that overcometh will I give to eat of the hidden manna, and will I give him a white stone, and in the stone a new name written, which no man knoweth saving he that receiveth it" (Revelation 2.17).

Now though I had been thus strengthened to bear the cross, I still found myself in great danger, having many weaknesses attending me and strong temptations to wrestle with, in the feelings whereof I frequently withdrew into private places and often with tears besought the Lord to help me, whose gracious ear was open to my cry.

All this time I lived with my parents and wrought[6] on the plantation, and having had schooling pretty well for a planter, I used to improve in winter evenings and other leisure times. And being now in the twenty-first year of my age, a man in much business shopkeeping and baking asked me if I would hire with him to tend shop and keep books. I acquainted my father with the proposal, and after some deliberation it was agreed for me to go.

At home I had lived retired, and now having a prospect of being much in the way of company, I felt frequent and fervent cries in my heart to God, the Father of Mercies, that He would preserve me from all taint and corruption, that in this more public employ I might serve Him, my gracious Redeemer, in that humility and self-denial with which I had been in a small degree exercised in a very private life.

The man who employed me furnished a shop in Mount Holly, about five miles from my father's house and six from his own, and there I lived alone and tended his shop. Shortly after my settlement here I was visited by several young people, my former acquaintance, who knew not but vanities would be as agreeable to me now as ever; and at these times I cried to the Lord in secret for wisdom and strength, for I felt myself encompassed with difficulties and had fresh occasion to bewail the follies of time past in contracting a familiarity with a libertine people. And as I had now left my father's house outwardly, I found my Heavenly Father to be merciful to me beyond what I can express.

By day I was much amongst people and had many trials to go through, but in evenings I was mostly alone and may with thankfulness acknowledge that in those times the spirit of supplication was often poured upon me, under which I was frequently exercised and felt my strength renewed.

In a few months after I came here, my master bought[7] several Scotch menservants from on board a vessel and brought them to Mount Holly to sell, one of which was taken sick and died. The latter part of his sickness he, being delirious, used to curse and swear most sorrowfully, and after he was buried I was left to sleep alone the next night in the same chamber where he died. I perceived in me a timorousness. I knew, however, I had not injured the man but assisted in taking care of him according to my capacity, and was not free to ask anyone on that occasion to sleep with me. Nature was feeble, but every trial was a fresh incitement to give myself up wholly to the service of God, for I found no helper like Him in times of trouble.

After a while my former acquaintance gave over expecting me as one of their company, and I began to be known to some whose conversation was helpful to me. And now, as I had experienced the love of God through Jesus Christ to redeem me from many pollutions and to be a succor to me through a sea of conflicts, with which no person was fully acquainted, and as my heart was often enlarged in this heavenly principle, I felt a tender compassion for the youth who remained entangled in snares like those which had entangled

6. Worked.
7. I.e., bought the indentures of menservants. It was common to pay for passage to America by contracting to work for several years as an indentured servant. These contracts were negotiable.

me. From one month to another this love and tenderness increased, and my mind was more strongly engaged for the good of my fellow creatures.

I went to meetings in an awful frame of mind and endeavored to be inwardly acquainted with the language of the True Shepherd. And one day being under a strong exercise of spirit, I stood up and said some words in a meeting, but not keeping close to the divine opening,[8] I said more than was required of me; and being soon sensible of my error, I was afflicted in mind some weeks without any light or comfort, even to that degree that I could take satisfaction in nothing. I remembered God and was troubled, and in the depth of my distress He had pity upon me and sent the Comforter. I then felt forgiveness for my offense, and my mind became calm and quiet, being truly thankful to my gracious Redeemer for His mercies. And after this, feeling the spring of divine love opened and a concern[9] to speak, I said a few words in a meeting, in which I found peace. This I believe was about six weeks from the first time, and as I was thus humbled and disciplined under the cross, my understanding became more strengthened to distinguish the language of the pure Spirit which inwardly moves upon the heart[1] and taught [me] to wait in silence sometimes many weeks together, until I felt that rise which prepares the creature to stand like a trumpet through which the Lord speaks to His flock.

From an inward purifying, and steadfast abiding under it, springs a lively operative desire for the good of others. All faithful people are not called to the public ministry, but whoever are, are called to minister of that which they have tasted and handled spiritually. The outward modes of worship are various, but wherever men are true ministers of Jesus Christ it is from the operation of His spirit upon their hearts, first purifying them and thus giving them a feeling sense of the conditions of others. This truth was early fixed in my mind, and I was taught to watch the pure opening and to take heed lest while I was standing to speak, my own will should get uppermost and cause me to utter words from worldly wisdom and depart from the channel of the true gospel ministry.

In the management of my outward affairs I may say with thankfulness I found Truth to be my support, and I was respected in my master's family, who came to live in Mount Holly within two year after my going there.

About the twenty-third year of my age, I had many fresh and heavenly openings in respect to the care and providence of the Almighty over his creatures in general, and over man as the most noble amongst those which are visible. And being clearly convinced in my judgment that to place my whole trust in God was best for me, I felt renewed engagements that in all things I might act on an inward principle of virtue and pursue worldly business no further than as Truth opened my way therein.

About the time called Christmas I observed many people from the country and dwellers in town who, resorting to the public houses, spent their time in drinking and vain sports, tending to corrupt one another, on which account I was much troubled. At one house in particular there was much disorder, and I believed it was a duty laid on me to go and speak to the master of that house. I considered I was young and that several elderly Friends in town had opportunity to see these things, and though I would gladly have been excused, yet I could not feel my mind clear.

8. I.e., he did not focus on the divine truth that inspired him to stand and speak, and spoke with "worldly wisdom."
9. For Quakers a "concern" is something that is felt so deeply that one is compelled to do something about it

almost against one's will.
1. Quakers distinguish between true inner light, which is characterized by "disciplined understanding," and mere selfish desires.

The exercise was heavy, and as I was reading what the Almighty said to Ezekiel[2] respecting his duty as a watchman, the matter was set home more clearly; and then with prayer and tears I besought the Lord for His assistance, who in loving-kindness gave me a resigned heart. Then at a suitable opportunity I went to the public house, and seeing the man amongst a company, I went to him and told him I wanted to speak with him; so we went aside, and there in the fear and dread of the Almighty I expressed to him what rested on my mind, which he took kindly, and afterward showed more regard to me than before. In a few years after, he died middle-aged, and I often thought that had I neglected my duty in that case it would have given me great trouble, and I was humbly thankful to my gracious Father, who had supported me herein.

My employer, having a Negro woman, sold her and directed me to write a bill of sale, the man being waiting who bought her. The thing was sudden, and though the thoughts of writing an instrument of slavery for one of my fellow creatures felt uneasy,[3] yet I remembered I was hired by the year, that it was my master who directed me to do it, and that it was an elderly man, a member of our Society, who bought her; so through weakness I gave way and wrote it, but at the executing it, I was so afflicted in my mind that I said before my master and the Friend that I believed slavekeeping to be a practice inconsistent with the Christian religion. This in some degree abated my uneasiness, yet as often as I reflected seriously upon it I thought I should have been clearer if I had desired to be excused from it as a thing against my conscience, for such it was. And some time after this a young man of our Society spake to me to write an instrument of slavery, he having lately taken a Negro into his house. I told him I was not easy to write it, for though many kept slaves in our Society, as in others, I still believed the practice was not right, and desired to be excused from writing [it]. I spoke to him in good will, and he told me that keeping slaves was not altogether agreeable to his mind, but that the slave being a gift made to his wife, he had accepted of her.

1774

From Some Considerations on the Keeping of Negroes

[*Part One*][1]

RECOMMENDED TO THE PROFESSORS[2] OF CHRISTIANITY OF EVERY DENOMINATION

INTRODUCTION

Customs generally approved and opinions received by youth from their superiors become like the natural produce of a soil, especially when they are suited to favorite inclinations. But as the judgments of God are without partiality, by which the state of the soul must be tried, it would be the highest wisdom to forego customs and popular opinions, and try the treasures of the soul by the infallible standard: Truth.

2. Ezekiel was a priest and prophet. "Son of man, I have made thee a watchman unto the house of Israel: therefore hear the word at my mouth, and give them warning from me" (Ezekiel 3.17).
3. I.e., he contradicted his sense of right and felt ill at ease with his conscience.
1. Woolman's essay was written after a visit to southern Maryland, Virginia, and North Carolina.
2. Believers.

Natural affection needs a careful examination. Operating upon us in a soft manner, it kindles desires of love and tenderness, and there is danger of taking it for something higher. To me it appears an instinct like that which inferior creatures have; each of them, we see, by the ties of nature love self best. That which is a part of self they love by the same tie or instinct. In them it in some measure does the offices of reason, by which, among other things, they watchfully keep and orderly feed their helpless offspring. Thus natural affection appears to be a branch of self-love, good in the animal race, in us likewise with proper limitations, but otherwise is productive of evil by exciting desires to promote some by means prejudicial to others.

Our blessed Savior seems to give a check to this irregular fondness in nature and, at the same time, a precedent for us: "Who is my mother, and who are my brethren?"—thereby intimating that the earthly ties of relationship are, comparatively, inconsiderable to such who, through a steady course of obedience, have come to the happy experience of the Spirit of God bearing witness with their spirits that they are His children: "And he stretched forth his hands toward his disciples and said, 'Behold my mother and my brethren; for whosoever shall do the will of my Father which is in heaven (arrives at the more noble part of true relationship)[3] the same is my brother, and sister, and mother.'" Matthew 12.48[–50].

This doctrine agrees well with a state truly complete, where love necessarily operates according to the agreeableness of things on principles unalterable and in themselves perfect. If endeavoring to have my children eminent amongst men after my death be that which no reasons grounded on those principles can be brought to support, then to be temperate in my pursuit after gain and to keep always within the bounds of those principles is an indispensable duty, and to depart from it a dark unfruitful toil.

In our present condition, to love our children is needful; but except this love proceeds from the true heavenly principle which sees beyond earthly treasures, it will rather be injurious than of any real advantage to them. Where the fountain is corrupt, the streams must necessarily be impure.

That important injunction of our Savior (Matthew 6.33),[4] with the promise annexed, contains a short but comprehensive view of our duty and happiness. If then the business of mankind in this life is to first seek another, if this cannot be done but by attending to the means, if a summary of the means is not to do that to another which (in like circumstances) we would not have done unto us, then these are points of moment and worthy of our most serious consideration.

What I write on this subject is with reluctance, and the hints given are in as general terms as my concern would allow. I know it is a point about which in all its branches men that appear to aim well are not generally agreed, and for that reason I chose to avoid being very particular. If I may happily have let drop anything that may excite such as are concerned in the practice to a close thinking on the subject treated of, the candid amongst them may easily do the subject such further justice as, on an impartial inquiry, it may appear to deserve; and such an inquiry I would earnestly recommend.

---

3. A phrase inserted by Woolman in the quotation from Matthew.

4. "But seek ye first the kingdom of God, and his righteousness; and all these things shall be added unto you."

SOME CONSIDERATIONS ON THE KEEPING OF NEGROES

"Forasmuch as ye did it to the least of these my brethren, ye did it unto me." Matthew 25.40.

As many times there are different motives to the same actions, and one does that from a generous heart which another does for selfish ends, the like may be said in this case.

There are various circumstances amongst them that keep Negroes, and different ways by which they fall under their care; and, I doubt not, there are many well-disposed persons amongst them who desire rather to manage wisely and justly in this difficult matter than to make gain of it. But the general disadvantage which these poor Africans lie under in an enlightened Christian country having often filled me with real sadness, and been like undigested matter on my mind, I now think it my duty, through divine aid, to offer some thoughts thereon to the consideration of others.

When we remember that all nations are of one blood (Genesis 3.20);[5] that in this world we are but sojourners; that we are subject to the like afflictions and infirmities of body, the like disorders and frailties in mind, the like temptations, the same death and the same judgment; and that the All-wise Being is judge and Lord over us all, it seems to raise an idea of a general brotherhood and a disposition easy to be touched with a feeling of each other's afflictions. But when we forget those things and look chiefly at our outward circumstances, in this and some ages past, constantly retaining on our minds the distinction betwixt us and them with respect to our knowledge and improvement in things divine, natural, and artificial, our breasts being apt to be filled with fond notions of superiority, there is danger of erring in our conduct toward them.

We allow them to be of the same species with ourselves; the odds is we are in a higher station and enjoy greater favors than they. And when it is thus that our Heavenly Father endoweth some of His children with distinguished gifts, they are intended for good ends. But if those thus gifted are thereby lifted up above their brethren, not considering themselves as debtors to the weak nor behaving themselves as faithful stewards, none who judge impartially can suppose them free from ingratitude. When a people dwell under the liberal distribution of favors from heaven, it behooves them carefully to inspect their ways and consider the purposes for which those favors were bestowed, lest through forgetfulness of God and misusing His gifts they incur His heavy displeasure, whose judgments are just and equal, who exalteth and humbleth to the dust as He seeth meet.

It appears by Holy Record that men under high favors have been apt to err in their opinions concerning others. Thus Israel, according to the description of the prophet (Isaiah 65.5), when exceedingly corrupted and degenerated, yet remembered they were the chosen people of God and could say, "Stand by thyself, come not near me, for I am holier than thou." That this was no chance language, but their common opinion of other people, more fully appears by considering the circumstances which attended when God was beginning to fulfill His precious promises concerning the gathering of the Gentiles.

---

5. "And Adam called his wife's name Eve; because she was the mother of all living."

The Most High, in a vision, undeceived Peter, first prepared his heart to believe, and at the house of Cornelius showed him of a certainty that God was no respecter of persons. The effusion of the Holy Ghost upon a people with whom they, the Jewish Christians, would not so much as eat was strange to them. All they of the circumcision were astonished to see it, and the apostles and brethren of Judea contended with Peter about it, till he having rehearsed the whole matter and fully shown that the Father's love was unlimited, they are thereat struck with admiration and cry out, "Then hath God also to the Gentiles granted repentance unto life!" [Acts 11.18]

The opinion of peculiar favors being confined to them was deeply rooted, or else the above instance had been less strange to them, for these reasons: First, they were generally acquainted with the writings of the prophets, by whom this time was repeatedly spoken of and pointed at. Secondly, our blessed Lord shortly before expressly said, "I have other sheep, not of this fold; them also must I bring," etc. [John 10.16]. Lastly, His words to them after His resurrection, at the very time of His ascension, "Ye shall be witnesses to me not only in Jerusalem, Judea, and Samaria, but to the uttermost parts of the earth" [Acts 1.8].

Those concurring circumstances, one would think, might have raised a strong expectation of seeing such a time. Yet when it came, it proved matter of offense and astonishment.

To consider mankind otherwise than brethren, to think favors are peculiar to one nation and exclude others, plainly supposes a darkness in the understanding. For as God's love is universal, so where the mind is sufficiently influenced by it, it begets a likeness of itself and the heart is enlarged towards all men. Again, to conclude a people froward,[6] perverse, and worse by nature than others (who ungratefully receive favors and apply them to bad ends), this will excite a behavior toward them unbecoming the excellence of true religion.

To prevent such error let us calmly consider their circumstance, and, the better to do it, make their case ours. Suppose, then, that our ancestors and we have been exposed to constant servitude in the most servile and inferior employments of life; that we had been destitute of the help of reading and good company; that amongst ourselves we had had few wise and pious instructors; that the religious amongst our superiors seldom took notice of us; that while others in ease have plentifully heaped up the fruit of our labor, we had received barely enough to relieve nature, and being wholly at the command of others had generally been treated as a contemptible, ignorant part of mankind. Should we, in that case, be less abject than they now are? Again, if oppression be so hard to bear that a wise man is made mad by it (Ecclesiastes 7.7), then a series of those things altering the behavior and manners of a people is what may reasonably be expected.

When our property is taken contrary to our mind by means appearing to us unjust, it is only through divine influence and the enlargement of heart from thence proceeding that we can love our reputed oppressors. If the Negroes fall short in this, an uneasy, if not a disconsolate, disposition will be awakened and remain like seeds in their minds, producing sloth and many other habits appearing odious to us, with which being free men they perhaps had not been chargeable. These and other circumstances, rightly considered, will lessen that too great disparity which some make between us and them.

6. Contrary.

Integrity of heart hath appeared in some of them, so that if we continue in the word of Christ (previous to discipleship, John 8.31)[7] and our conduct towards them be seasoned with His love, we may hope to see the good effect of it, the which, in a good degree, is the case with some into whose hands they have fallen. But that too many treat them otherwise, not seeming conscious of any neglect, is, alas! too evident.

When self-love presides in our minds our opinions are biased in our own favor. In this condition, being concerned with a people so situated that they have no voice to plead their own cause, there's danger of using ourselves to an undisturbed partiality till, by long custom, the mind becomes reconciled with it and the judgment itself infected.

To humbly apply to God for wisdom, that we may thereby be enabled to see things as they are and ought to be, is very needful; hereby the hidden things of darkness may be brought to light and the judgment made clear. We shall then consider mankind as brethren. Though different degrees and a variety of qualifications and abilities, one dependent on another, be admitted, yet high thoughts will be laid aside, and all men treated as becometh the sons of one Father, agreeable to the doctrine of Christ Jesus.

> He hath laid down the best criterion by which mankind ought to judge of their own conduct, and others judge for them of theirs, one towards another—viz., "Whatsoever ye would that men should do unto you, do ye even so to them." I take it that all men by nature are equally entitled to the equity of this rule and under the indispensable obligations of it. One man ought not to look upon another man or society of men as so far beneath him but that he should put himself in their place in all his actions towards them, and bring all to this test—viz., How should I approve of this conduct were I in their circumstance and they in mine?— Arscott's *Considerations*, Part III, Fol. 107.[8]

This doctrine, being of a moral unchangeable nature, hath been likewise inculcated in the former dispensation:[9] "If a stranger sojourn with thee in your land, ye shall not vex him; but the stranger that dwelleth with you shall be as one born amongst you, and thou shalt love him as thyself." Leviticus 19.33, 34. Had these people come voluntarily and dwelt among us, to have called them strangers would be proper. And their being brought by force, with regret and a languishing mind, may well raise compassion in a heart rightly disposed. But there is nothing in such treatment which upon a wise and judicious consideration will any ways lessen their right of being treated as strangers. If the treatment which many of them meet with be rightly examined and compared with those precepts, "Thou shalt not vex him nor oppress him; he shall be as one born amongst you, and thou shalt love him as thyself" (Leviticus 19.33; Deuteronomy 27.19), there will appear an important difference betwixt them.

It may be objected there is cost of purchase and risk of their lives to them

7. "Then said Jesus to those Jews which believed on him. If ye continue in my word, then are ye my disciples indeed."
8. "This quotation, slightly altered, is found in Alexander Arscott, *Some Considerations Relating to the Present State of the Christian Religion, wherein the Nature, End, and Design of Christianity, as well as the Principle Evidence of the Truth of it, are Explained and Recommended out of the Holy Scriptures; with a General Appeal to the Experience of all Men for Confirmation thereof*, Part III (London, 1734), 78. Arscott

(1676–1737), an Oxford graduate, was a schoolmaster. About 1700, to the great dismay of his parents, he became a Quaker. He served many years as clerk of the London Yearly Meeting. He intended this volume as an apologetic for Christianity based on both Scripture and reason, apart from the special point of view of the Friends. All three parts were reprinted in Philadelphia, the first two by Benjamin Franklin in 1732, the third by A. Bradford in 1738" [Moulton's note].
9. I.e., the Old Testament.

who possess 'em, and therefore needful that they make the best use of their time. In a practice just and reasonable such objections may have weight; but if the work be wrong from the beginning, there's little or no force in them. If I purchase a man who hath never forfeited his liberty, the natural right of freedom is in him. And shall I keep him and his posterity in servitude and ignorance? How should I approve of conduct were I in his circumstances and he in mine? It may be thought that to treat them as we would willingly be treated, our gain by them would be inconsiderable; and it were, in diverse respects, better that there were none in our country.

We may further consider that they are now amongst us, and those of our nation the cause of their being here, that whatsoever difficulty accrues thereon we are justly chargeable with, and to bear all inconveniences attending it with a serious and weighty concern of mind to do our duty by them is the best we can do. To seek a remedy by continuing the oppression because we have power to do it and see others do it, will, I apprehend, not be doing as we would be done by.

How deeply soever men are involved in the most exquisite difficulties, sincerity of heart and upright walking before God, freely submitting to His providence, is the most sure remedy. He only is able to relieve not only persons but nations in their greatest calamities. David, in a great strait when the sense of his past error and the full expectation of an impending calamity as the reward of it were united to the aggravating his distress, after some deliberation saith, "Let me fall now into the hands of the Lord, for very great are his mercies; let me not fall into the hand of man." 1 Chronicles 21.13.

To act continually with integrity of heart above all narrow or selfish motives is a sure token of our being partakers of that salvation which God hath appointed for walls and bulwarks (Isaiah 5.26; Romans 15.8), and is, beyond all contradiction, a more happy situation than can ever be promised by the utmost reach of art and power united, not proceeding from heavenly wisdom.

A supply to nature's lawful wants, joined with a peaceful, humble mind, is the truest happiness in this life. And if here we arrive to this and remain to walk in the path of the just, our case will be truly happy. And though herein we may part with or miss of some glaring shows of riches and leave our children little else but wise instructions, a good example, and the knowledge of some honest employment, these, with the blessing of providence, are sufficient for their happiness, and are more likely to prove so than laying up treasures for them which are often rather a snare than any real benefit, especially to them who, instead of being exampled to temperance, are in all things taught to prefer the getting of riches and to eye the temporal distinctions they give as the principal business of this life. These readily overlook the true happiness of man as it results from the enjoyment of all things in the fear of God, and miserably substituting an inferior good, dangerous in the acquiring and uncertain in the fruition, they are subject to many disappointments; and every sweet carries its sting.

It is the conclusion of our blessed Lord and His apostles, as appears by their lives and doctrines, that the highest delights of sense or most pleasing objects visible ought ever to be accounted infinitely inferior to that real intellectual happiness suited to man in his primitive innocence and now to be found in true renovation of mind, and that the comforts of our present life, the things most grateful to us, ought always to be received with temperance and never made the chief objects of our desire, hope, or love, but that our whole heart and affections be principally looking to that city "which hath foundations, whose maker and builder is God" [Hebrews 11.10].

Did we so improve the gifts bestowed on us that our children might have an education suited to these doctrines, and our example to confirm it, we might rejoice in hopes of their being heirs of an inheritance incorruptible. This inheritance, as Christians, we esteem the most valuable; and how then can we fail to desire it for our children? Oh, that we were consistent with ourselves in pursuing means necessary to obtain it!

It appears by experience that where children are educated in fullness,[1] ease, and idleness, evil habits are more prevalent than is common amongst such who are prudently employed in the necessary affairs of life. And if children are not only educated in the way of so great temptation, but have also the opportunity of lording it over their fellow creatures and being masters of men in their childhood, how can we hope otherwise than that their tender minds will be possessed with thoughts too high for them?—which by continuance, gaining strength, will prove like a slow current, gradually separating them from (or keeping from acquaintance with) that humility and meekness in which alone lasting happiness can be enjoyed.

Man is born to labor, and experience abundantly showeth that it is for our good. But where the powerful lay the burden on the inferior, without affording a Christian education and suitable opportunity of improving the mind, and a treatment which we in their case should approve—that themselves may live at ease and fare sumptuously and lay up riches for their posterity—this seems to contradict the design of Providence and, I doubt, is sometimes the effect of a perverted mind. For while the life of one is made grievous by the rigor of another, it entails misery on both.

Amongst the manifold works of Providence displayed in the different ages of the world, these which follow (with many others) may afford instruction:

Abraham[2] was called of God to leave his country and kindred, to sojourn amongst strangers. Through famine and danger of death he was forced to flee from one kingdom to another. He at length not only had assurance of being the father of many nations, but became a mighty prince. Genesis 23.6.

Remarkable was the dealings of God with Jacob[3] in a low estate. The just sense he retained of them after his advancement appears by his words: "I am not worthy of the least of all thy mercies." Genesis 32.10; 48.15.

The numerous afflictions of Joseph[4] are very singular, the particular providence of God therein no less manifest. He at length became governor of Egypt and famous for wisdom and virtue.

The series of troubles David[5] passed through, few amongst us are ignorant of; and yet he afterwards became as one of the great men of the earth.

Some evidences of the divine wisdom appears in those things, in that such who are intended for high stations have first been very low and dejected, that Truth might be sealed on their hearts, and that the characters there imprinted by bitterness and adversity might in after years remain, suggesting compassionate ideas and, in their prosperity, quicken their regard to those in the like

---

1. Affluence.
2. The first of the Old Testament patriarchs.
3. Old Testament patriarch and grandson of Abraham; his twelve sons became the founders of the twelve tribes of Israel.

4. One of the sons of Jacob; his brothers sold him into slavery in Egypt.
5. The second king of the Hebrews; it was he who slew the giant Goliath.

condition, which yet further appears in the case of Israel. They were well acquainted with grievous sufferings, a long and rigorous servitude, then through many notable events were made chief amongst the nations. To them we find a repetition of precepts to the purpose above-said. Though for ends agreeable to infinite wisdom they were chosen as a peculiar people for a time, yet the Most High acquaints them that his love is not confined, but extends to the stranger, and to excite their compassion, reminds them of times past: "Ye were strangers in the land of Egypt." Deuteronomy 10.19. Again, "Thou shalt not oppress a stranger, for ye know the heart of a stranger, seeing ye were strangers in the land of Egypt." Exodus 23.9.

If we call to mind our beginning, some of us may find a time wherein our fathers were under afflictions, reproaches, and manifold sufferings. Respecting our progress in this land, the time is short since our beginning was small and number few, compared with the native inhabitants. He that sleeps not by day nor night hath watched over us and kept us as the apple of His eye. His almighty arm hath been round about us and saved us from dangers.

The wilderness and solitary deserts in which our fathers passed the days of their pilgrimage are now turned into pleasant fields. The natives are gone from before us, and we establish peaceably in the possession of the land, enjoying our civil and religious liberties. And while many parts of the world have groaned under the heavy calamities of war, our habitation remains quiet and our land fruitful.

When we trace back the steps we have trodden and see how the Lord hath opened a way in the wilderness for us, to the wise it will easily appear that all this was not done to be buried in oblivion, but to prepare a people for more fruitful returns, and the remembrance thereof ought to humble us in prosperity and excite in us a Christian benevolence towards our inferiors.

If we do not consider these things aright, but through a stupid indolence conceive views of interest separate from the general good of the great brotherhood, and in pursuance thereof treat our inferiors with rigor, to increase our wealth and gain riches for our children, what then shall we do when God riseth up; and when He visiteth, what shall we answer Him? Did not He that made us make them, and "did not one fashion us in the womb?" Job 31.14[–15].

To our great Master we stand or fall; to judge or condemn is most suitable to His wisdom and authority. My inclination is to persuade and entreat, and simply give hints of my way of thinking.

If the Christian religion be considered, both respecting its doctrines and the happy influence which it hath on the minds and manners of all real Christians, it looks reasonable to think that the miraculous manifestation thereof to the world is a kindness beyond expression. Are we the people thus favored? Are we they whose minds are opened, influenced, and governed by the spirit of Christ and thereby made sons of God? Is it not a fair conclusion that we, like our Heavenly Father, ought in our degree to be active in the same great cause—of the eternal happiness of at least our whole families, and more, if thereto capacitated?

If we, by the operation of the Spirit of Christ, become heirs with Him in the kingdom of His Father, and are redeemed from the alluring counterfeit joys of this world, and the joy of Christ remain in us; to suppose that one remaining in this happy condition can, for the sake of earthly riches, not only deprive his fellow creatures of the sweetness of freedom (which, rightly used, is one of the greatest temporal blessings), but therewith neglect using proper means for their acquaintance with the Holy Scriptures and the advantage of true religion, seems, at least, a contradiction to reason.

Whoever rightly advocates the cause of some thereby promotes the good of all. The state of mankind was harmonious in the beginning; and though sin hath introduced discord, yet through the wonderful love of God in Christ Jesus our Lord, the way is open for our redemption, and means appointed to restore us to primitive harmony.

That if one suffer by the unfaithfulness of another, the mind, the most noble part of him that occasions the discord, is thereby alienated from its true and real happiness. Our duty and interest is inseparably united, and when we neglect or misuse our talents we necessarily depart from the heavenly fellowship and are in the way to the greatest of evils. Therefore, to examine and prove ourselves, to find what harmony the power presiding in us bears with the divine nature, is a duty not more incumbent and necessary than it would be beneficial.

In Holy Writ the Divine Being saith of Himself, " 'I am the Lord, which exercise loving-kindness, judgment, and righteousness in the earth; for in these things I delight,' saith the Lord." Jeremiah 9.24. Again, speaking in the way of man to show His compassion to Israel, whose wickedness had occasioned a calamity, and then being humbled under it, it is said, "His soul was grieved for their miseries." Judges 10.16.

If we consider the life of our blessed Savior when on earth, as it is recorded by His followers, we shall find that one uniform desire for the eternal and temporal good of mankind discovered itself in all His actions. If we observe men, both apostles and others in many different ages, who have really come to the unity of the spirit and the fellowship of the saints, there still appears the like disposition; and in them the desire of the real happiness of mankind has out-balanced the desire of ease, liberty, and many times life itself.

If upon a true search we find that our natures are so far renewed that to exercise righteousness and loving-kindness (according to our ability) towards all men, without respect of persons, is easy to us or is our delight; if our love be so orderly and regular that he who doth the will of our Father who is in heaven appears in our view to be our nearest relation, our brother and sister and mother; if this be our case, there is a good foundation to hope that the blessing of God will sweeten our treasures during our stay in this life, and our memory be savory when we are entered into rest.

To conclude, 'tis a truth most certain that a life guided by wisdom from above, agreeable with justice, equity, and mercy, is throughout consistent and amiable, and truly beneficial to society. The serenity and calmness of mind in it affords an unparalleled comfort in this life, and the end of it is blessed. And, no less true, that they who in the midst of high favors remain ungrateful, and under all the advantages that a Christian can desire are selfish, earthly, and sensual, do miss the true fountain of happiness and wander in a maze of dark anxiety, where all their treasures are insufficient to quiet their minds. Hence, from an insatiable craving they neglect doing good with what they have acquired, and too often add oppression to vanity, that they may compass more.

"Oh, that they were wise, that they understood this, that they would consider their latter end!" Deuteronomy 32.29.

1746

SAMSON OCCOM
1723–1792

Born in New London, Connecticut, Samson Occom was a Mohegan, a member of the northernmost branch of the Pequot Indians. Although he was certainly not the last of the Mohegans, in 1725, two years after Occom's birth, the Mohegans numbered no more than 351 people, the tribe having dwindled as a result of disease and degeneration under the stress of the colonists' encroachment. "I was born a Heathen," Occom wrote in 1768, "and brought up in Heathenism, till I was between 16 & 17 years of age." It was at that age that he first heard the sermons of Christian evangelical preachers and was moved to study the Bible. Having taught himself to read, he eventually made his way to New Lebanon, Connecticut, to study with the Reverend Eleazar Wheelock, who was committed to training young Indian men to be Christian missionaries. Occom began his schooling under Wheelock's direction in 1743.

Wheelock was following in the footsteps of other seventeenth- and early-eighteenth-century missionaries to the Indians like John Eliot of the Massachusetts Bay Colony; the Mayhews of Martha's Vineyard; James Fitch of Norwich, Connecticut; and John Sergeant (whose successor was Wheelock's contemporary Jonathan Edwards) of Stockbridge, Massachusetts. Like them, Wheelock sincerely desired to bring the Indians to Christianity, and like them as well, he was aware of the advantage to the colonists of winning Indian converts. Christian Indians served, he wrote, as "a far better defense than all our expensive Fortresses" against those native people still hostile to the settlers. With these ends in mind, Wheelock founded his Moors Indian-Charity School at New Lebanon, Connecticut, in 1754.

Occom, who came to Wheelock more than a decade before the formal establishment of the school, studied with him for four years before leaving to teach and preach among the Indians, first in New London, then Montauk, Long Island, where he remained for eleven years. It was there that he met and married Mary Fowler, a Montauk, with whom he had ten children. It was on Long Island as well that he was ordained a minister by the Presbytery of Suffolk in 1759.

Occom corresponded regularly with his mentor, Wheelock, and in 1765, Occom traveled to England along with the Reverend Nathaniel Whitaker to raise funds for Wheelock's Indian School. In England and Scotland Occom delivered some three hundred sermons and collected nearly twelve thousand pounds. Occom returned to find his family sick and in extreme poverty, although Wheelock had promised to care for them in his absence. Thus when Wheelock asked him to set out on a mission to the Iroquois, Occom refused. When he learned that Wheelock intended to use the money he had helped raise to move his school from Lebanon, Connecticut, to Hanover, New Hampshire, he angrily wrote Wheelock that the Indian school would soon "be Naturally ashamed to suckle the Tawnees [Indians] for she is already equal in Power, Honor and Authority to any College in Europe, [sic] I think your College has too much Worked by Grandeur for the Poor Indians, they'll never have much benefit of it." He was right. In very little time the school, which soon became Dartmouth College, had ceased to minister to Indian students, and Occom and Wheelock broke off their long relation.

In dire financial straits, having broken with Wheelock, and feeling vulnerable as an "Indian preacher" in the church, Occom wrote a ten-page autobiography. In it, he tells of his education and conversion and describes the many injustices he experienced himself and witnessed against other Indians. Narrating the story of a "poor Indian boy" who does his best but whose English master beats him because he is an Indian, Occom responds to his critics, saying he too has done his best and wondering whether he has been disparaged "because I am a poor Indian." Dated

September 17, 1768, the autobiography remained unpublished in the Dartmouth archives until 1982.

If the audience for Occom's autobiography was small (because it was not published in his lifetime), he soon was to have an audience as large as those his preaching had drawn in England. In December 1771, in the town of Bethany, Connecticut, Moses Paul, a Mohegan and a one-time convert to Christianity, in a drunken fury smashed the skull of a highly respected citizen of Waterbury named Moses Cook. Convicted of murder, Paul was to be hanged in September 1772, and after the custom of the times, the General Assembly of Connecticut wished to make of his execution a solemn public occasion to promote morality and condemn the ruinous effects of strong drink. Execution sermons in early New England were a familiar genre of public oratory; indeed, such eminent religious leaders as Cotton and Increase Mather had preached them. It is not known who decided Occom was the perfect man to preach at the execution of Paul—who better, after all, than an Indian preacher to condemn the sin of his drunken compatriot—but from his jail cell in New Haven, the unfortunate Paul, on July 16, 1772, signed a letter (assuredly written for him), requesting that Occom "preach a Sermon to me at my execution." It is because "we are of the same nation," Paul explained, that he had a "peculiar desire that you should preach to me upon that occasion & therefore that I may likely better receive and be more impressed with the same things said by you, than if said by any other man. . . . Have I not reason to hope & expect that you will not deny this my dying request?"

Occom did not deny it. He arrived in New Haven the night before the execution and ministered to Paul in his cell. The following morning, Wednesday, September 2, 1772, Occom preached to the crowd gathered at the First Church of New Haven. Among his audience were native people who had come from all the surrounding country.

Occom's text was from Romans 6.23 ("For the wages of sin is death; but the gift of God is eternal life through Jesus Christ our Lord"), one of the most commonly cited texts for these occasions. The sermon, which directly addresses not only the unfortunate Paul but also the Indians in the audience, was surely a memorable and powerful performance, given Occom's reputation as a preacher and the subsequent popularity of the printed version. Published that same year, in 1772, the *Sermon at the Execution of Moses Paul* ran through some nineteen editions, extending into the nineteenth century.

Occom's only further publication in his lifetime was A *Choice Collection of Hymns and Spiritual Songs, Intended for the Edification of Sincere Christians of All Denominations*, published in New London in 1774. As the colonists approached the Revolutionary War with England, it was Occom's sense that neutrality was best for the Indians, and he urged them "not to intermeddle in these Quarrils among the White People." In the years after the colonists won their independence, Occom served as a minister to the Indians at New Stockbridge; he was a teacher to the Tuscarora in New York State at the time of his death in 1792.

Sermon Preached at the Execution of Moses Paul[1]

The Preface

The world is already full of books; and the people of God are abundantly furnished with excellent books upon divine subjects; and, it seems, that every subject has been written upon over & over again: and the people in very deed have had precept upon precept, line upon line, here a little and there a little;

---

1. The text is from the 1772 edition, first published in New Haven, Connecticut.

and so in the whole, they have much, yea, very much, they have enough and more than enough. And when I come to consider these things, I am ready to say with myself, What folly and madness is it in me to suffer anything of mine to appear in print, to expose my ignorance to the world.[2]

It seems altogether unlikely that my performance will do any manner of service in the world, since the most excellent writings of worthy and learned men are disregarded. But there are two or three considerations that have induced me to be willing, to suffer my broken hints to appear in the world. One is, that the books that are in the world are written in very high and refined language; and the sermons that are delivered every sabbath in general, are in a very high and lofty stile, so that the common people understand but little of them. But I think they can't help understanding my talk; it is common, plain, every day talk; little children may understand me. And poor Negroes may plainly and fully understand my meaning; and it may be of service to them. Again, it may in a particular manner be serviceable to my poor kindred, the Indians.[3] Further, as it comes from an uncommon quarter, it may induce people to read it, because it is from an Indian. Lastly, God works where and when he pleases, and by what instruments he sees fit, and he can and has used weak and unlikely instruments to bring about his great work.

It was a stormy and very uncomfortable day,[4] when the following discourse was delivered, and about one half of it was not delivered, as it was written, and now it is a little altered and enlarged in some places.[5]

Introduction

By the melancholy providence of God, and at the earnest desire and invitation of the poor condemned criminal, I am here before this great concourse of people at this time, to give the last discourse to the poor miserable object who is to be executed this day before your eyes, for the due reward of his folly and madness, and enormous wickedness. It is an unwelcome task to me to speak upon such an occasion; but since it is the desire of the poor man himself, who is to die a shameful death—this day, in conscience I cannot deny him; I must endeavour to do the great work the dying man requests.

I conclude that this great concourse of people have come together to see the execution of justice upon this poor Indian; and I suppose the bigest part of you look upon yourselves christians, and as such I hope you will demean yourselves; and that you will have suitable commiseration towards this poor object. Tho' you can't in justice pray for his life to be continued in this world, yet you can pray earnestly for the salvation of his poor soul, consistently with the mind of God. Let this be therefore, the fervent exercise of our souls: for this is the last day we have to pray for him. As for you, that don't regard religion, it cannot be expected, that you will put up one petition for this miserable creature: yet I would intreat you seriously to consider the frailty of corrupt nature, and behave yourselves as becomes rational creatures.

---

2. Occom's opening is largely conventional, recalling Ecclesiastes 12.12: "Of making many books there is no end."

3. Occom, who is quite capable of "a very high and lofty stile" when the occasion demands it (and he uses such a style frequently, even in this sermon), here claims the particular virtue of the Indian preacher: the ability to speak in a "plain, every day" language, so that even a child can understand. The linking of "poor Negroes" and "my poor kindred, the Indians" offers an insight into the fact that both blacks and American Indians suffer the ill effects of race prejudice.

4. This is literal, not figurative: Wednesday, September 2, 1772, was in fact a very stormy day.

5. No record of the original delivery exists, so we have only Occom's word that what we are reading is an expanded revision of the sermon he actually delivered.

And in a word, let us all be suitably affected with the melancholy occasion of the day, knowing that we are all dying creatures, and accountable unto God. Tho' this poor condemned criminal will in a few minutes know more than all of us, either in unutterable joy, or in inconceivable wo, yet we shall certainly know as much as he, in a few days.

The sacred words that I have chosen to speak from upon this undesirable occasion, are found written in the epistle of St. Paul to the Romans VI.23.

> For the wages of sin is death, but the gift of God is eternal life through Jesus Christ our Lord.

Death is called the King of Terrors, and it ought to be the subject of every man and woman's thoughts daily; because it is that unto which they are liable every moment of their lives: and therefore, it cannot be unseasonable to think, speak and hear of it at any time, and especially on this mournful occasion; for we must all come to it, how soon we cannot tell; whether we are prepared or not prepared, ready or not ready, whether death is welcome or not welcome, we must feel the force of it: whether we concern ourselves with death or not, it will concern itself with us.[6] Seeing that this is the case with every one of us, what manner of persons ought we to be in all holy conversation and godliness; how ought men to exert themselves in preparation for death continually; for they know not what a day or an hour may bring forth, with respect to them. But, alas! according to the appearance of mankind in general, death is the least thought of. They go on from day to day, as if they were to live here forever, as if this was the only life. They contrive, rack their inventions, disturb their rest, and even hazard their lives in all manner of dangers, both by sea and land; yea they leave no stone unturn'd that they may live in the world, and at the same time have little or no contrivance to die well: God and their souls are neglected, and heaven and eternal happiness are disregarded; Christ and his religion are despised—yet most of these very men intend to be happy when they come to die, not considering that there must be great preparation in order to die well. Yea there is none so fit to live as those that are fit to die; those that are not fit to die are not fit to live. Life & death are nearly connected; we generally own that it is a great and solemn thing to die. If this be true, then it is a great and solemn thing to live; for as we live, so we shall die. But I say again, how little do mankind realize these things? They are busy about the things of this world as if there was no death before them. Dr. Watts[7] pictures them out to the life in his psalms:

> See the vain race of mortals move
> Like shadows o'er the plain,
> They rage and strive, desire and love,
> But all the noise is vain.

> Some walk in honor's gaudy show,
> Some dig for golden ore,
> They toil for heirs they know not who,
> And strait are seen no more.

---

6. See Jonathan Edwards's *Sinners in the Hands of an Angry God* for a particularly forceful sermon on this subject.
7. Isaac Watts (1674–1748) was an English writer and composer of hymns noted for their power and devotional force. Occom cites #613 from Watts's *The Psalms of David Imitated in the Language of the New Testament* (1719).

But on the other hand, life is the most precious thing, and ought to be the most desired by all rational creatures. It ought to be prized above all things; yet there is nothing so abused and despised as life, and nothing so neglected: I mean eternal life is shamefully disregarded by men in general, and eternal death is chosen rather than life. This is the general complaint of the bible from the beginning to the end. As long as Christ is neglected, life is refused, and as long as sin is cherished, death is chosen; and this seems to be the woful case of mankind of all nations, according to their appearance in these days; for it is too plain to be denied, that vice and immorality, and floods of iniquity are abounding every where amongst all nations, and all orders and ranks of men, and in every sect of people. Yea there is a great agreement and harmony among all nations, and from the highest to the lowest to practise sin and iniquity; and the pure religion of Jesus Christ is turned out of doors, and is dying without; or, in other words, the Lord Jesus Christ is turned out of doors by men in general, and even by his professed people. "He came to his own; and his own received him not."[8] But the devil is admitted, he has free access to the houses and hearts of the children of men: Thus life is refused and death is chosen.

But in further speaking upon our text, by divine assistence, I shall consider these two general propositions:

> I. That sin is the cause of all the miseries that befal the children of men, both as to their bodies and souls, for time and eternity.
> II. That eternal life and happiness is the free gift of God, thro' Jesus Christ our Lord.

In speaking to the first proposition I shall first consider the nature of sin; and secondly shall consider the consequences of sin, or the wages of sin, which is death.

First then, we are to describe the nature of sin.

Sin is the transgression of the law: This is the scripture definition of sin. Now the law of God being holy, just and good; sin must be altogether unholy, unjust and evil. If I was to define sin, I should call it a contrariety to God; and as such it must be the vilest thing in the world; it is full of all evil; it is the evil of evils; the only evil, in which dwells no good thing; and is most destructive to God's creation, where ever it takes effect. It was sin that transformed the very angels in heaven, into devils; and it was sin that caused hell to be made. If it had not been for sin, there never would have been such a thing as hell or devil, death or misery.

And if sin is such a thing as we have just described; it must be worse than the devils and hell itself.—Sin is full of deadly poison; it is full of malignity and hatred against God, against all his divine perfections and atributes, against his wisdom, against his power, against his holiness and goodness, against his mercy and justice, against his written law and gospel; yea, against his very being and existence. Were it in the power of sin, it would even dethrone God, and set itself on the throne.

When Christ the Son of the Most High, came down from the glorious world above, into this wretched world of sin and sorrow, to seek and to save that which was lost, sin, or sinners rose up against him, as soon as he entered our

8. John 1.11.

world and pursued him with hellish malice, night and day, for above thirty years together, till they kill'd him.

Further, sin is against the Holy Ghost; it opposes all his good and holy operations upon the children of men. When, and wherever there is the out-pouring of the Spirit of God, upon the children of men, in a way of conviction and conversion; sin will immediately prompt the devil and his children to rise up against it, and they will oppose the work with all their power, and in every shape. And if open opposition will not do, the devil will mimick the work, and thus prevent the good effect.

Thus we find by the scripture accounts, that whenever God raises up men, and uses them as instruments of conviction and conversion, the devil and his instruments will rise up to destroy both the reformers and the reformed. Thus it has been from the early days of Christianity, to this day. We have found it so in our day. In the time of the outpouring of the Spirit of God in these colonies, to the conviction and reformation of many; immediately sin and the devil influenced numbers to rise up against the good work of God, calling it delusion, and work of the devil. And thus sin also opposes every motion of the Spirit of God, in the heart of every Christian; this makes a warfare in the soul.

2. I shall endeavour to shew the sad consequences or effects of sin upon the children of men.

Sin has poison'd them, & made them distracted or fools. The Psalmist says, The fool hath said in his heart, there is no God.[9] And Solomon, thro' his Proverbs, calls ungodly sinners fools; and their sin he calls their folly, and foolishness.[1] The Apostle James says, But the tongue can no man tame, it is an unruly evil, full of deadly poison.[2] It is the heart that is in the first place full of deadly poison. The tongue is only an interpreter of the heart. Sin has viriated[3] the whole man, both soul and body; all the powers are corrupted; it has turned the minds of men against all good, towards all evil. So poisoned are they, according to the prophet Isaiah 5.20, "Wo unto them that call evil good, and good evil; that put darkness for light, and light for darkness; that put bitter for sweet, and sweet for bitter." And Christ Jesus faith in John 3.19, 20. "And this is the condemnation, that light is come into the world, and men loved darkness rather than light, because their deeds were evil. For every one that doth evil hateth the light, neither cometh to the light, lest his deeds should be reproved." Sin has stupified mankind, they are now ignorant of God their maker; neither do they enquire after him. And they are ignorant of themselves, they know not what is good for them, neither do they understand their danger; and they have no fear of God before their eyes.

Further, sin has blinded their eyes, so that they can't discern spiritual things; neither do they see the way that they should go, and they are deaf as adders, so that they cannot hear the joyful sound of the gospel that brings glad tidings of peace and pardon to sinners of mankind. Neither do they regard the Charmer charming never so wisely.—Not only so, but sin has made man proud, tho' he has nothing to be proud of; for he has lost all his excellency, his beauty and happiness; he is a bankrupt, and is excommunicated from God; he was turned out of paradise by God himself, and become a vagabond in God's world, and as such he has no right nor title to the least crumb of mercy

---

9. Psalms 14.1
1. E.g., Proverbs 12.23: "A prudent man concealeth knowledge: but the heart of fools proclaimeth fool-

ishness."
2. James 3.8.
3. Probably a misprint for *vitiated*, meaning spoiled.

in the world: yet he is proud, he is haughty, and exalts himself above God, tho' he is wretched and miserable, and poor, and blind and naked. He glories in his shame. Sin has made him beastly and devilish; yea he is sunk beneath the beasts, and is worse than the ravenous beasts of the wilderness. He is become ill-natur'd, cruel and murderous; he is contentious and quarrelsome. I said he is worse than the ravenous beasts, for wolves and bears don't devour their own kind, but man does; yea we have numberless instances of women killing their own children, such women I think are worse than she tygers.

Sin has made men dishonest and deceitful, so that he goes about cheating and defrauding and deceiving his fellow men in the world: yea, he is become a cheat himself, he goes about in a vain shew;[4] we don't know where to find man. Some times we find [him] as an angel of God; and at other times we find [him] as a devil, even one and the same man. Sin has made man a liar even from the womb; so that there is no believing nor trusting him. The royal psalmist says, "The wicked are estranged from the womb, they go astray as soon as they are born, speaking lies."[5]—His language is also corrupted. Whereas he had a pure and holy language, in his innocency, to adore and praise God his maker, he now curses, swears, and profanes the holy name of God, and curses and damns his fellow-creatures. In a word, man is a most unruly and ungovernable creature, and is become as the wild ass's colt, and is harder to tame than any of God's creatures in this world. In short, man is worse than all creatures in this lower world, his propensity is to evil and that continually; he is more like the devil than any creature we can think of: and I think it is not going beyond the word of God, to say, man is the most devilish creature in the world. Christ said to his disciples, One of you is a devil;[6] to the Jews he said, Ye are of your father the devil, and the lusts of your father ye will do.[7] Thus every unconverted soul is a child of the devil, sin has made them so.

We have given some few hints of the nature of sin, and the effects of sin on mankind.

We shall in the next place consider the wages or the reward of sin, which is death.

Sin is the cause of all the miseries that attend poor sinful man, which will finally bring him to death, death temporal and eternal. I shall first consider his temporal death.

His temporal death then begins as soon as he is born. Tho' it seems to us that he is just beginning to live, yet in fact he is just entered into a state of death; as St. Paul says, "Wherefore, as by one man sin entered into the world, and death by sin; and so death passed upon all men, for that all have sinned."[8] Man is surrounded with ten thousand instruments of death, and is liable to death every moment of his life; a thousand diseases await him on every side continually; the sentence of death is past upon them as soon as they are born: yea they are struck with death as soon as they breathe. And it seems all the enjoyments of men in this world are also poisoned with sin. For God said to Adam after he had sinned, "Cursed is the ground for thy sake, in sorrow shalt thou eat of it all the days of thy life."[9] By this we plainly see that every thing that grows out of the ground is cursed, and all creatures that God hath made

4. I.e., show.
5. Psalms 58.3.
6. John 6.70.

7. John 8.44.
8. Romans 5.12.
9. Genesis 3.17.

for man are cursed also; and whatever God curses is a cursed thing indeed. Thus death and destruction is [sic] in all the enjoyments of men in this life, every enjoyment in this world is liable to misfortune in a thousand ways, both by sea and land.

How many ships, that have been loaded with the choicest treasures of the earth, have been swallowed up in the ocean, many times just before they enter their desired haven. And vast treasures have been consumed by fire on the land, etc. And the fruits of the earth are liable to many judgments. And the dearest and nearest enjoyments of men are generally balanced with equal sorrow and grief. A man and his wife who have liv'd together in happiness for many years; that have comforted each other in various changes of life, must at last be seperated; one or the other must be taken away first by death, and then the poor survivor is drowned in tears, in sorrow, mourning and grief. And when a dear child or children are taken away by death, the bereaved parents are bowed down with sorrow and deep mourning. When Joseph[1] was sold by his brethren unto the Ishmaelites, they took his coat and rolled it in blood, and carried it to their father, and the good patriarch knew it to be Joseph's coat, and he concluded that his dear Joseph was devoured by evil beasts, and he was plunged all over in sorrow and bitter mourning, and he refused to be comforted. And so when tender parents are taken away by death, the children are left comfortless.—All this is the sad effect of sin.—These are the wages of sin.

And secondly, we are to consider man's spiritual death, while he is here in this world. We find it thus written in the word of God. "And the Lord God commanded the man, saying, of every tree of the garden thou mayest freely eat: but of the tree of the knowledge, of good and evil, thou shalt not eat of it, for in the day that thou eatest thereof thou shalt surely die."[2] And yet he did eat of it, and so he and all his posterity, are but dead men. And St. Paul to the Ephesians saith, "You hath he quickened, who were dead in trespasses and sins."[3]—The great Mr. Henry[4] says in this place, that unregenerate souls are dead in trespasses and sins. All those who are in their sins, are dead in sins; yea, in trespasses and sins; which may signify all sorts of sins, habitual and actual; sins of heart and life. Sin is the death of the soul. Wherever that prevails, there is a privation of all spiritual life. Sinners are dead in state, being destitute of the principles and powers of spiritual life; and cut off from God, the fountain of life: and they are dead in law, as a condemned malefactor is said to be a dead man. Now a dead man, in a natural sense, is unactive, and is of no service to the living; there is no correspondence between the dead and the living: there is no agreement or union between them, no fellowship at all between the dead and the living. A dead man is altogether ignorant of the intercourses amongst the living:—just so it is with men that are spiritually dead; they have no agreeable activity. Their activity in sin, is their deadness, and inactivity towards God. They are of no service to God; and they have no correspondence with heaven; and there is no agreement or fellowship between them and the living God; and they are totally ignorant of the agreable and sweet intercourse there is between God and his children here below: and they are ignorant, and know nothing of that blessed fellowship and union there is

1. The story of Joseph is told in Genesis 37–48.
2. Genesis 2.16–17.
3. Ephesians 2.1.

4. Matthew Henry (1662–1714), British theologian, whose *Exposition of the Old and New Testament* (1710) Occom had read.

among the saints here below. They are ready to say indeed, behold how they love one another! But they know nothing of that love, that the children of God enjoy. As sin is in opposition to God; so sinners are at enmity against God; there is no manner of agreement between them.

Let us consider further. God is a living God, he is all life, the fountain of life; and a sinner is a dead soul; there is nothing but death in him. And now judge ye, what agreement can there be between them? God is a holy and pure God, and a sinner is an unholy and filthy creature;—God is a righteous Being, and a sinner is an unrighteous creature; God is light, and a sinner is darkness itself, etc. Further, what agreement can there be between God and a lyar, a thief, a drunkard, a swearer, a profane creature, a whoremonger, an adulterer, and idolater, etc. No one that has any sense, dare say, that there is any agreement. Further, as sinners are dead to God, as such, they have no delight in God, and godliness; they have no taste for the religion of Jesus Christ; they have no pleasure in the holy exercises of religion. Prayer is no pleasant work with them; or if they have any pleasure in it, it is not out of love to God, but out of self-love, like the Pharisees[5] of old; they loved to pray in open view of men, that they might have praise from them. And perhaps, they were not careful to pray in secret. These were dead souls, they were unholy, rotten hypocrites, and so all their prayers and religious exercises were cold, dead, and abominable services to God. Indeed they are dead to all the duties that God requires of them; they are dead to the holy bible; to all the laws, commands, and precepts thereof; and to the ordinances of the gospel of the Lord Jesus Christ. When they read the book of God, it is like an old almanack to them, a dead book. But it is because they are dead, and as such, all their services are against God, even their best services are an abomination unto God; yea, a sinner is so dead in sin, that the threatnings of God don't move them. All the thunderings and lightnings of Mount-Sinai[6] don't stir them. And all the curses of the law are out against them; yea, every time they read those curses in the bible, they are cursing them to their faces, and to their very eyes; yet they are unconcern'd, and go on in sin without fear. And lastly here, sin has so stup-ify'd the sinner, that he will not believe his own senses; he won't believe his own eyes, nor his own ears; he reads the book of God, but he does not believe what he reads. And he hears of God and heaven, and eternal happiness, and of hell and eternal misery; but he believes none of these things; he goes on as if there were no God, nor heaven and happiness; neither has he any fear of hell and eternal torments;—and he sees his fellow men dropping away daily on every side, yet he goes on carelessly in sin, as if he never was to die. And if he at any time thinks of dying, he hardly believes his own tho'ts. Death is at great distance, so far off, that he don't concern himself about it, so as to pre-pare for it. God mournfully complains of his people, that they don't consider; O that they were wise, that they understood this, that they would consider their latter end.

The next thing I shall consider, is the actual death of the body, or seperation between soul and body. At the cessation of natural life, there is an end of all the enjoyments of this life; there is no more joy nor sorrow; no more hope nor fear, as to the body; no more contrivance and carrying on any business; no

5. A Jewish sect of Jesus' time that followed strict reli-gious laws, the members of which considered them-selves more religious and holier than other Jews.

6. Where Moses received the Ten Commandments from God (see Exodus 19).

more merchandizing and trading; no more farming; no more buying and selling; no more building of any kind, no more contrivance at all to live in the
world; no more flatteries nor frowns from the world; no more honor nor
reproach; no more praise; no more good report, nor evil report; no more learning of any trades, arts or sciences in the world; no more sinful pleasures, they
are all at an end; re-creations, visiting, tavern haunting, music and dancing,
chambering and carousing, playing at dice and cards, or any game whatsoever;
cursing and swearing, and profaning the holy name of God, drunkenness,
fighting, debauchery, lying and cheating, in this world, must cease forever.
Not only so, but they must bid an eternal farewel to all the world; bid farewel
to all their beloved sins and pleasures; and the places and possessions, that
knew them once, shall know them no more forever. And further, they must
bid adieu to all sacred and divine things. They are obliged to leave the bible,
and all the ordinances thereof; and to bid farewel to preachers, and all sermons
and all christian people, and christian conversation; they must bid a long farewel to sabbaths and seasons, and opportunities of worship; yea, an eternal
farewel to all mercy, and all hope; an eternal farewel to God the Father, Son
and Holy Ghost, and adieu to heaven and all happiness, to saints and all the
inhabitants of the upper world. At your leisure please to read the destruction
of Babylon; you will find it written in the 18th of the Revelation.

On the other hand, the poor departed soul must take up its lodging in sorrow, wo and misery, in the lake that burns with fire and brimstone, where the
worm dieth not, and the fire is not quenched; where a multitude of frightful
deformed devils dwell, and the damned ghosts of Adam's race; where darkness,
horror and despair reigns, where hope never comes, and where poor guilty
naked souls will be tormented with exquisite torments, even the wrath of the
Almighty poured out upon their damned souls; the smoke of their torments
ascending up forever and ever; their mouths and nostrils streaming forth with
living fire; and hellish groans, howlings, cries and shrieks all round them, and
merciless devils upbraiding them for their folly and madness, and tormenting
them incessantly.—And there they must endure the most unsatiable, fruitless
desire, and the most overwhelming shame and confusion, and the most horrible fear, and the most doleful sorrow, and the most racking despair. When
they cast their flaming eyes to heaven, with Dives in torments, they behold an
angry and frowning God, whose eyes are as a flaming fire, and they are struck
with ten thousand darts of pain; and the sight of the happiness of the saints
above, adds to their pains and aggravates their misery. And when they reflect
upon their past folly and madness in neglecting the great salvation in their
day, it will pierce them with ten thousand inconceivable torments; it will as it
were enkindle their hell afresh; and it will cause them to curse themselves
bitterly, and curse the day in which they were born, and curse their parents
that were the instruments of their being in the world; yea they will curse,
bitterly curse and wish that very God that gave them their being, to be in the
same condition with them in hell torments. This is what is called the second
death, and it is the last death, and an eternal death to a guilty soul.

And O eternity, eternity, eternity! Who can measure it? Who can count the
years thereof? Arithmetic must fail, the thoughts of men and angels are
drowned in it; how shall we describe eternity? To what shall we compare it?
Were it possible to employ a fly to carry off this globe by the small particles
thereof, and to carry them to such a distance that it should return once in ten

thousand years for another particle, and so continue till it has carried off all this globe, and framed them together in some unknown space, till it has made just such a world as this is: after all eternity would remain the same unexhausted duration. This must be the unavoidable portion of all impenitent sinners, let them be who they will, great or small, honorable or ignoble, rich or poor, bond or free. Negroes, Indians, English, or of what nations soever, all that die in their sins, must go to hell together, for the wages of sin is death.

The next thing that I was to consider is this:

That eternal life and happiness is the free gift of God, thro' Jesus Christ our Lord.

Under this proposition I shall endeavour to shew what this life and happiness is.

The life that is mentioned in our text is, a spiritual life: it is the life of the soul, a restoration of soul from sin, to holiness, from darkness to light, a translation from the kingdom and dominion of Satan, to the kingdom of God's grace. In other words, it is being restored to the image of God, and delivered from the image of Satan. And this life consists in union of the soul to God, and communion with God; a real participation of the divine nature, or in the apostle's words, it is Christ formed within us; I live, says he, yet not I, but Christ liveth in me.[7] And the apostle John saith, God is love,[8] and he that dwelleth in love, dwelleth in God, and God in him.[9] This is the life of the soul. It is called emphatically life, because it is a life that shall never have a period, a stable, permanent, and unchangeable life, called in the scriptures, everlasting life, or life eternal. And the happiness of this life consists in communion with God, or in the spiritual enjoyment of God. As much as a soul enjoys of God in this life, just so much of life and happiness he enjoys or possesses; yea, just so much of heaven he enjoys. A true christian, desires no other heaven, but the enjoyment of God, a full and perfect enjoyment of God, is a full and perfect heaven and happiness to a gracious soul. Further, this life is called eternal life, because God has planted a living principle in the soul; and whereas he was dead before, now he is made alive unto God; there is an active principle within him towards God, he now moves towards God in his religious devotions and exercises; is daily comfortably and sweetly walking with God, in all his ordinances and commands; his delight is in the ways of God; he breathes towards God, a living breath, in praises, prayers, adorations and thanksgivings; his prayers are now heard in the heavens, and his praises delight the ears of the Almighty, and his thanksgivings are accepted. So alive is he now to God, that it is his meat and drink, yea more than his meat and drink, to do the will of his heavenly Father. It is his delight, his happiness and pleasure to serve God. He does not drag himself to his duties now, but he does them out of choice, and with alacrity of soul. Yea, so alive is he to God, that he gives up himself and all that he has entirely to God, to be for him and none other; his whole aim is to glorify God in all things, whether by life or death, all the same to him.

We have a bright example of this in St. Paul. After he was converted, he was all alive to God; he regarded not his life, but was willing to spend, and be

---

7. Cf. Galatians 2.20: "I am crucified with Christ: nevertheless I live; yet not I, but Christ liveth in me: and the life which I now live in the flesh I live by the faith of the Son of God, who loved me, and gave him- self for me."
8. 1 John 4.8.
9. 1 John 4.16.

spent in the service of his God; he was hated, revil'd, despised, laughed at, and called by all manner of evil names; was scourged, stoned and imprisoned;—and all cou'd not stop his activity towards God. He would boldly and couragiously go on in preaching the gospel of the Lord Jesus Christ, to poor, lost, and undone sinners; he would do the work God set him about, in spite of all opposition he met with, either from men or devils, earth or hell, come death, or come life, none of these things moved him, because he was alive unto God. Tho' he suffered hunger and thirst, cold and heat, poverty & nakedness by day & by night, by sea and land, & was in danger all ways; yet he would serve God amidst all these dangers. Read his amazing account in 2 Cor. 2.23 and on.

Another instance of marvellous love towards God, we have in Daniel.[1] When there was a proclamation of prohibition, sent by the king, to all his subjects, forbidding them to call upon their gods, for thirty days; which was done by envious men, that they might find occasion against Daniel the servant of the Most High God; yet he having the life of God in his soul, regarded not the king's decree, but made his petitions to his God, as often as he used to do, tho' death was threatned to the disobedient. But he feared not the hell they had prepared; for it seems, the den resembled hell, and the lions represented the devils. And when he was actually cast into the lion's den, the ravenous beasts become meek and innocent as lambs, before the prophet, because he was alive unto God: the spirit of the Most High was in him, and the lions were afraid before him. Thus it was with Daniel and Paul: they went thro' fire and water, as the common saying is, because they had eternal life in their souls in eminent manner, and they regarded not this life, for the cause and glory of God. And thus it has been in all ages with true Christians. Many of the fore- fathers of the English, in this country, had this life, and are gone the same way, that the holy prophets and apostles went. Many of them went thro' all manner of sufferings for God; and a great number of them are gone home to heaven, in chariots of fire. I have seen the place in London, called Smith- field,[2] where numbers were burnt to death for the religion of Jesus Christ. And there is the same life in true christians now in these days; and if there should persecutions arise in our day, I verily believe, true christians would suffer with the same spirit and temper of mind, as those did, who suffered in days past.— This is the life which our text speaks of.

We proceed in the next place to shew, that this life, which we have describ'd, is the free gift of God, thro' Jesus Christ our Lord.

Sinners have forfeited all mercy into the hand of divine justice, and have merited hell and damnation to themselves; for the wages of sin is everlasting death, but heaven and happiness is a free gift; it comes by favour; and all merit is excluded: and especially if we consider that we are fallen sinful creatures, and there is nothing in us that can recommend us to the favour of God; and we can do nothing that is agreeable and acceptable to God; and the mercies we enjoy in this life are altogether from the pure mercy of God; we are unequal to them. Good old Jacob cried out, under a sense of his unworthiness, "I am less than the least of all thy mercies,"[3] and we have nothing to give unto God, if we essay to give all the service that we are capable of, we should give him

---

1. The Book of Daniel tells his story.
2. An open area of London that was the scene of burnings for heresy until 1612.

3. Cf. Genesis 32.10: "I am not worthy of the least of all the mercies, and of all the truth which thou hast shewed unto thy servant."

nothing but what was his own, and when we give up ourselves unto God, both soul and body, we give him nothing; for we were his before; he had right to do with us as he pleased, either to throw us into hell, or save us!—There is nothing that we can call our own, but our sins; and who is he that dares to say, I expect to have heaven for my sins? for our text says, that the wages of sin is death. If we are thus unequal and unworthy of the least mercy in this life, how much more are we unworthy of eternal life? yet God can find it in his heart to give it. And it is altogether unmerited; it is a free gift to undeserving and hell deserving sinners of mankind: it is altogether of God's sovereign good pleasure to give it. It is of free grace & sovereign mercy, and from the unbounded goodness of God; he was self-moved to it. And it is said that this life is given in and through the Lord Jesus Christ. It could not be given in any other way, but in and through the death and sufferings of the Lord Jesus Christ; Christ himself is the gift, and he is the christian's life. "For God so loved the world that he gave his only begotten Son, that whosoever believeth in him should not perish, but have everlasting life."[4] The word says further, "For by grace ye are saved, thro' faith, and that not of yourselves, it is the gift of God."[5] This is given thro' Jesus Christ our Lord; it is Christ that purchased it with his own blood; he prepared it with his divine and almighty power; and by the same power, and by the influence of his spirit, he prepares us for it; and by his divine grace preserves us to it. In a word, he is all in all in our eternal salvation; all this is the free gift of God.

I have now gone thro' what I proposed from my text. And I shall now make some application of the whole.

First to the criminal in particular; and then to the auditory[6] in general.

My poor unhappy brother Moses;[7]

As it was your own desire that I should preach to you this last discourse, so I shall speak plainly to you.—You are the bone of my bone, and flesh of my flesh. You are an Indian, a despised creature; but you have despised yourself; yea you have despised God more; you have trodden under foot his authority; you have despised his commands and precepts: and now, as God says, be sure your sins will find you out. And now, poor Moses, your sins have found you out, and they have overtaken you this day; the day of your death is now come, the king of terrors is at hand; you have but a very few moments to breathe in this world.—The just laws of man, and the holy law of Jehovah, call aloud for the destruction of your mortal life; God says, "Whoso sheddeth mans blood, by man shall his blood be shed."[8] This is the ancient decree of heaven, and it is to be executed by man; nor have you the least gleam of hope of escape, for the unalterable sentence is past; the terrible day of execution is come; the unwelcome guard is about you; and the fatal instruments of death are now made ready; your coffin and your grave, your last lodging, are open ready to receive you.

Alas! poor Moses, now you know, by sad, by woful experience, the living truth of our text, that the wages of sin is death. You have been already dead; yea twice dead: by nature spiritually dead. And since the awful sentence of death has been past upon you, you have been dead to all the pleasures of this life; or all the pleasures, lawful or unlawful, have been dead to you. And

4. John 3.16.   7. I.e., Moses Paul.
5. Ephesians 2.8.   8. Genesis 9.6.
6. I.e., the audience or listeners.

death, which is the wages of sin, is standing even on this side of your grave ready to put a final period to your mortal life; and just beyond the grave, eternal death awaits your poor soul, and the devils are ready to drag your miserable soul down to their bottomless den, where everlasting wo and horror reigns; the place is filled with doleful shrieks, howls and groans of the damned. Oh! to what a miserable, forlorn, and wretched condition have your extravagant folly and wickedness brought you! i.e. if you die in your sins.—And O! what manner of repentance ought you to manifest! How ought your heart to bleed for what you have done! How ought you to prostrate your soul before a bleeding God! And under self-condemnation, cry out, Ah Lord, ah Lord, what have I done!—Whatever partiality, injustice and error there may be among the judges of the earth, remember that you have deserved a thousand deaths, and a thousand hells, by reason of your sins, at the hands of a holy God. Should God come out against you in strict justice, alas! what could you say for yourself? for you have been brought up under the bright sun-shine, and plain, and loud found of the gospel; and you have had a good education; you can read and write well; and God has given you a good natural understanding: and therefore your sins are so much more aggravated. You have not sinned in such an ignorant manner as others have done; but you have sinned with both your eyes open as it were, under the light, even the glorious light of the gospel of the Lord Jesus Christ.—You have sinned against the light of your own conscience, against your knowledge and understanding; you have sinned against the pure and holy laws of God, and the just laws of men; you have sinned against heaven and earth; you have sinned against all the mercies and goodness of God; you have sinned against the whole bible, against the old and new testament; you have sinned against the blood of Christ, which is the blood of the everlasting covenant. O poor Moses, see what you have done! and now repent, repent, I say again repent; see how the blood you shed cries against you, and the Avenger of Blood is at your heels. O fly, fly to the Blood of the Lamb of God for the pardon of all your aggravated sins.[9]

But let us now turn to a more pleasant theme.—Tho' you have been a great sinner, a heaven daring sinner; yet hark and hear the joyful sound from heaven, even from the King of kings, and Lord of lords; that the gift of God is eternal life, thro' Jesus Christ our Lord. It is a free gift, and offered to the greatest sinners, and upon their true repentance towards God and faith in the Lord Jesus Christ, they shall be welcome to the life, which we have spoken of, it is offered upon free terms. He that hath no money may come; he that hath no righteousness, no goodness, may come; the call is to poor undone sinners; the call is not to the righteous, but sinners, calling them to repentance. Hear the voice of the Son of the most high God, Come unto me, all yea that labour and are heavy laden, and I will give you rest. This is a call, a gracious call to you, poor Moses, under your present burdens and distresses. And Christ alone has a right to call sinners to himself. It would be presumption for a mighty angel to call a poor sinner in this manner; and were it possible for you to apply to all God's creatures, they would with one voice tell you, that it was not in them to help you. Go to all the means of grace, they would prove miserable helps, without Christ himself. Yea, apply to all the ministers of the gospel in the world, they would all say, that it was not in them, but would only prove

9. I.e., turn to Christ and ask forgiveness.

as indexes, to point out to you, the Lord Jesus Christ, the only saviour of
sinners of mankind. Yea, go to all the angels in heaven, they would do the
same. Yea, go to God the Father himself, without Christ, he cou'd not help
you, to speak after the manner of men, he should also point to the Lord Jesus
Christ, & say this is my beloved Son, in whom I am well pleased, hear ye
him. Thus you see, poor Moses, that there is none in heaven, or on the earth,
that can help you, but Christ; he alone has power to save, and to give life.—
God the eternal Father appointed him, chose him, authorized, and fully commissioned him to save sinners. He came down from heaven, into this lower
world, and became as one of us, and stood in our room. He was the second
Adam.—And as God demanded perfect obedience of the first Adam; the second fulfil'd it; and as the first sinned, and incurred the wrath and anger of
God, the second endur'd it; he suffered in our room. As he became sin for us,
he was a man of sorrows, and acquainted with grief; all our stripes were laid
upon him; yea, he was finally condemned, because we were under condemnation; and at last was executed and put to death, for our sins; was lifted up
between the heaven and the earth, and was crucified on the accursed tree; his
blessed hands and feet were fastened there;—there he died a shameful and
ignominious death; there he finished the great work of our redemption: there
his hearts blood was shed for our cleansing: there he fully satisfied the divine
justice of God, for penitent, believing sinners, tho' they have been the chief
of sinners.—O Moses! this is good news to you, in this last day of your life;
here is a crucified Saviour at hand for your sins; his blessed hands are outstretched, all in a gore of blood for you. This is the only Saviour, an almighty
Saviour, just such as you stand in infinite and perishing need of. O, poor
Moses! hear the dying prayer of a gracious Saviour on the accursed tree,—
Father forgive them, for they know not what they do.[1] This was a prayer for
his enemies and murderers; and it is for you, if you would only repent and
believe in him. O why will you die eternally, poor Moses, since Christ has
died for sinners? Why will you go to hell from beneath the bleeding Saviour
as it were? This is the day of your execution, yet it is the accepted time, it is
the day of salvation if you will now believe in the Lord Jesus Christ. Must
Christ follow you into the prison by his servants, and there intreat you to
accept of eternal life, and will you refuse it? and must he follow you even to
the gallows, and there beseech you to accept of him, and will you refuse him?
Shall he be crucified hard by your gallows, as it were, and will you regard him
not? O, poor Moses, now believe on the Lord Jesus Christ with all your heart,
and thou shalt be saved eternally. Come just as you are, with all your sins and
abominations, with all your filthiness, with all your blood-guiltiness, with all
your condemnation, and lay hold of the hope set before you this day. This is
the last day of salvation with your soul; you will be beyond the bounds of
mercy in a few minutes more. O, what a joyful day would it be if you would
now openly believe in and receive the Lord Jesus Christ; it would be the beginning of heavenly days with your poor soul; instead of a melancholy day, it
would be a wedding day to your soul; it would cause the very angels in heaven
to rejoice, and the saints on earth to be glad; it would cause the angels to come
down from the realms above, and wait hovering about your gallows, ready to
convey your soul to the heavenly mansions, there to take the possession of

1. Luke 23.34.

eternal glory and happiness, and join the heavenly choirs in singing the songs of Moses and the Lamb: there to set down forever with Abraham, Isaac and Jacob[2] in the kingdom of God's glory; and your shame and guilt shall be forever banished from the place, and all sorrow and fear forever fly away, and tears be wip'd from your face; and there shall you forever admire the astonishing and amazing and infinite mercy of God in Christ Jesus, in pardoning such a monstrous sinner as you have been; there you will claim the highest note of praise, for the riches of free grace in Christ Jesus. But if you will not accept of a Saviour so freely offered to you in this last day of your life, you must this very day bid farewel to God the Father, Son and Holy Ghost, to heaven and all the saints and angels that are there; and you must bid all the saints in this lower world an eternal farewel, and even the whole world. And so I must leave you in the hands of God; and I must turn to the whole auditory.

Sirs, We may plainly see, from what we have heard, and from the miserable object before us, into what a doleful condition sin has brought mankind, even into a state of death and misery. We are by nature as certainly under sentence of death from God, as this miserable man is, by the just determination of man; and we are all dying creatures, and we are, or ought to be sensible[3] of it; and this is the dreadful fruit of sin. O! let us then fly from all appearance of sin; let us fight against it with all our might; let us repent and turn to our God, and believe on the Lord Jesus Christ, that we may live forever; let us all prepare for death, for we know not how soon, nor how suddenly we may be called out of the world.

Permit me in particular, reverend Gentlemen and fathers in Israel,[4] to speak a few words to you, tho' I am well sensible that I need to be taught the first principles of the oracles of God, by the least of you. But since the providence of God has so ordered it, that I must speak here on this occasion, I beg that you would not be offended nor be angry with me.

God has raised you up, from among your brethren, and has qualified, and authorized you to do his great work; and you are the servants of the Most High God, and ministers of the Lord Jesus the Son of the living God: you are Christ's ambassadors; you are called Shepherds, watchmen, overseers, or bishops, and you are rulers of the temples of God, or of the assemblies of God's people; you are God's angels, and as such you have nothing to do but to wait upon God, and to do the work the Lord Jesus Christ your blessed Lord and Master has set you about, not fearing the face of any man, nor seeking to please men, but your Master. You are to declare the whole counsel of God, and to give a portion to every soul in due season; as a physician gives a portion to his patients, according to their diseases, so you are to give a portion to every soul in due season, according to their spiritual maladies; whether it be agreeable or disagreeable to them, you must give it them; whether they will love you or hate you for it, you must do your work.—Your work is to encounter sin and Satan; this was the very end of the coming of Christ into the world, and the end of his death and sufferings; it was to make an end of sin and to destroy the works of the devil. And this is your work still, you are to fight the battles of the Lord. Therefore combine together, and be terrible as an army with banners; attack this monster sin in all its shapes and windings, and lift up your voices as trumpets and not spare, call aloud, call your people to arms

2. Biblical patriarchs. "Moses and the Lamb": i.e., the prophet Moses and Christ.

3. Aware.

4. Fathers of the church; ministers of the gospel.

against this common enemy of mankind, that sin may not be their ruin. Call upon all orders, ranks and degrees of people, to rise up against sin and Satan. Arm yourselves with fervent prayer continually, this is a terrible weapon against the kingdom of Satan. And preach the death and sufferings, and the resurrection of Jesus Christ; for nothing is so destructive to the kingdom of the devil, as this is. But what need I speak any more? Let us all attend, and hear the great Apostle of the Gentiles[5] speaking unto us in Ephesians 6 ch. from the 10th ver. and onward. Finally; my brethren, be strong in the Lord, and in the power of his might; put on the whole armour of God, that ye may be able to stand against the wiles of the devil. For we wrestle not against flesh and blood, but against principalities, against powers, against the rulers of the darkness of this world, against spiritual wickedness in high places. Wherefore take unto you the whole armour of God, that ye may be able to stand in the evil day, and having done all to stand. Stand therefore, having your loins girt about with truth, and having on the breast-plate of righteousness; and your feet shod with the preparation of the gospel of peace: above all, taking the shield of faith, wherewith ye shall be able to quench all the firy darts of the wicked; and take the helmet of salvation, and the sword of the spirit, which is the word of God: praying always with all prayer and supplication in the spirit, and watching thereunto with all perservance, and supplication for all saints.

I shall now address myself to the Indians, my brethren and kindred according to the flesh.

My poor kindred,

You see the woful consequences of sin, by seeing this our poor miserable country-man now before us, who is to die this day for his sins and great wickedness. And it was the sin of drunkenness that has brought this destruction and untimely death upon him. There is a dreadful wo denounced from the Almighty against drunkards; and it is this sin, this abominable, this beastly and accursed sin of drunkenness, that has stript us of every desirable comfort in this life; by this we are poor, miserable and wretched; by this sin we have no name nor credit in the world among polite nations; for this sin we are despised in the world, and it is all right and just, for we despise ourselves more; and if we don't regard ourselves, who will regard us? And it is for our sins, and especially for that accursed, that most develish sin of drunkenness that we suffer every day. For the love of strong drink we spend all that we have, and every thing we can get. By this sin we can't have comfortable houses, nor any thing comfortable in our houses; neither food nor raiment, nor decent utensils. We are obliged to put up any sort of shelter just to screen us from the severity of the weather; and we go about with very mean, ragged and dirty cloathes, almost naked. And we are half starved, for most of the time obliged to pick up any thing to eat.—And our poor children are suffering every day for want of the necessaries of life; they are very often crying for want of food, and we have nothing to give them; and in the cold weather they are shivering and crying, being pinched with cold.—All this is for the love of strong drink. And this is not all the misery and evil we bring on ourselves in this world; but when we are intoxicated with strong drink, we drown our rational powers, by which we are distinguished from the brutal creation; we unman ourselves, and bring ourselves not only level with the beasts of the field, but seven degrees beneath

---

5. I.e., Paul, who was an apostle *of* the Gentiles because he was not a Jewish convert to Christianity; he also was an apostle *to* the Gentiles.

them; yea we bring ourselves level with the devils; I don't know but we make ourselves worse than the devils, for I never heard of drunken devils.

My poor kindred, do consider what a dreadful abominable sin drunkenness is. God made us men, and we chuse to be beasts and devils; God made us rational creatures, and we chuse to be fools. Do consider further, and behold a drunkard, and see how he looks, when he has drowned his reason; how deformed and shameful does he appear. He dis-figures every part of him, both soul and body, which was made after the image of God. He appears with awful deformity, and his whole visage is dis-figured; if he attempts to speak he cannot bring out his words distinct, so as to be understood; if he walks he reals and staggers to and fro, and tumbles down. And see how he behaves, he is now laughing, and then he is crying; he is singing and the next minute he is mourning; and is all love to every one, and anon he is raging, & for fighting, & killing all before him, even the nearest and the dearest relations and friends: Yea nothing is too bad for a drunken man to do. He will do that, which he would not do for the world, in his right mind; he may lie with his own sister or daughter as Lot[6] did.

Further, when a person is drunk, he is just good for nothing in the world; he is of no service to himself, to his family, to his neighbours, or his country; and how much more unfit is he to serve God: yet he is just fit for the service of the devil.

Again, a man in drunkenness is in all manner of dangers, he may be kill'd by his fellow-men, by wild beasts, and tame beasts; he may fall into the fire, into the water, or into a ditch; or he may fall down as he walks along, and break his bones or his neck; he may cut himself with edge-tools.[7]—Further, if he has any money or any thing valuable, he may loose it all, or may be robb'd, or he may make a foolish bargain, and be cheated out of all he has.

I believe you know the truth of what I have just now said, many of you, by sad experience; yet you will go on still in your drunkenness. Tho' you have been cheated over and over again, and you have lost your substance by drunkenness, yet you will venture to go on in this most destructive sin. O fools when will ye be wise?—We all know the truth of what I have been saying, by what we have seen and heard of drunken deaths. How many have been drowned in our rivers, and how many frozen to death in the winter seasons! yet drunkards go on without fear and consideration: alas, alas! What will become of all such drunkards? Without doubt they must all go to hell, except they truly repent and turn to God. Drunkenness is so common amongst us, that even our young men and young women are not ashamed to get drunk. Our young men will get drunk as soon as they will eat when they are hungry.—It is generally esteemed amongst men, more abominable for a woman to be drunk, than a man; and yet there is nothing more common amongst us than female drunkards. Women ought to be more modest than men; the holy scriptures recommend modesty to women in particular:—but drunken women have no modesty at all. It is more intolerable for a woman to get drunk, if we consider further, that she is in great danger of falling into the hands of the sons of Belial, or wicked men, and being shamefully treated by them.

And here I cannot but observe, we find in scared writ, a wo denounced against men, who put their bottles to their neighbours mouth to make them

6. See Genesis 20.30–36.
7. Woodworking tools that have a cutting edge, such as chisels, gouges, and planes.

drink, that they may see their nakedness: and no doubt there are such develish men now in our day, as there were in the days of old.

And to conclude, consider my poor kindred, you that are drunkards, in to what a miserable condition you have brought yourselves. There is a dreadful wo thundering against you every day, and the Lord says, That drunkards shall not inherit the kingdom of God.

And now let me exhort you all to break off from your drunkenness, by a gospel repentance, and believe on the Lord Jesus and you shall be saved. Take warning by this doleful sight before us, and by all the dreadful judgments that have befallen poor drunkards. O let us all reform our lives, and live as becomes dying creatures, in time to come. Let us be persuaded that we are accountable creatures to God, and we must be called to an account in a few days. You that have been careless all your days now awake to righteousness, and be concerned for your poor and never dying souls. Fight against all sins, and especially the sin that easily besets you, and behave in time to come as becomes rational creatures; and above all things, receive and believe on the Lord Jesus Christ, and you shall have eternal life; and when you come to die, your souls will be received into heaven, there to be with the Lord Jesus in eternal happiness, with all the saints in glory; which, God of his infinite mercy grant, thro' Jesus Christ our Lord.

AMEN

J. HECTOR ST. JEAN DE CRÈVECOEUR
1735–1813

J. Hector St. Jean Crèvecoeur was a man with a mysterious past, and a number of details of his life have puzzled his biographers. He was born Michel-Guillaume-Jean de Crèvecoeur in Caen, Normandy, in 1735. When he was nineteen, he left home and sailed to England, where he took up residence with distant relatives. He planned to marry, but his fiancée died before the ceremony took place, and in 1755 he went to Canada; he enlisted in the Canadian militia, served the government as a surveyor and cartographer, and was wounded in the defense of Quebec. His military career came to an end in 1759, and for the next ten years Crèvecoeur traveled extensively in the colonies as a surveyor and trader with American Indians. In 1769 he bought land in Orange County, New York, and, newly married, settled into the life of an American farmer.

Given the history of Crèvecoeur's restlessness, it is hard to know whether or not he would have been happy forever at Pine Hill, but the advent of the American Revolution and his Tory sympathies were enough to determine his return to France. He claimed that he wished to reestablish ownership of family lands, and it is ironic, given his political sympathies, that he was arrested and imprisoned as a rebel spy when he tried to sail from the port of New York. Not until 1780 did Crèvecoeur succeed in reaching London. He remained in France until 1783, when he returned as French consul to New York, Connecticut, and New Jersey, only to learn that his farm had been burned in an Indian attack, his wife was dead, and his children were housed with strangers.

Crèvecoeur was a great success as a diplomat—he was made an honorary citizen of a number of American cities, and the town of St. Johnsbury, Vermont, was named in his honor—but he did not remain long in America. He returned to France in 1785 and after 1790 remained there permanently, first living in Paris and retiring, after 1793, to Normandy.

The first year that Crèvecoeur spent at Pine Hill he began to write a series of essays about America based on his travels and experience as a farmer. He brought them to London in 1780 and, suppressing those essays most unsympathetic to the American cause, sold them to the bookseller Thomas Davies. *Letters from an American Farmer* appeared in 1782 and was an immediate success. Crèvecoeur found himself a popular hero when the expanded French edition (dated 1784) appeared. Its publication followed close enough on the American Revolution to satisfy an almost insatiable demand for things American and confirmed, for most readers, a vision of a new land, rich and promising, where industry prevailed over class and fashion. George Washington said the book was "too flattering" to be true, but more careful readers of these twelve letters will take note of a more ambiguous attitude throughout: Crèvecoeur's hymn to the land does not make him blind to the ignorant frontier settlers or the calculating slaveholder. His final letter, "Distresses of a Frontiersman," affirms the possibility of a harmonious relationship with nature, but he writes from an American Indian village and with no successful historical models in mind.

From Letters from an American Farmer[1]

From *Letter III. What Is an American*

I wish I could be acquainted with the feelings and thoughts which must agitate the heart and present themselves to the mind of an enlightened Englishman, when he first lands on this continent. He must greatly rejoice that he lived at a time to see this fair country discovered and settled; he must necessarily feel a share of national pride, when he views the chain of settlements which embellishes these extended shores. When he says to himself, this is the work of my countrymen, who, when convulsed by factions,[2] afflicted by a variety of miseries and wants, restless and impatient, took refuge here. They brought along with them their national genius,[3] to which they principally owe what liberty they enjoy, and what substance they possess. Here he sees the industry of his native country displayed in a new manner, and traces in their works the embryos of all the arts, sciences, and ingenuity which flourish in Europe. Here he beholds fair cities, substantial villages, extensive fields, an immense country filled with decent houses, good roads, orchards, meadows, and bridges, where an hundred years ago all was wild, woody, and uncultivated! What a train of pleasing ideas this fair spectacle must suggest; it is a prospect which must inspire a good citizen with the most heartfelt pleasure. The difficulty consists in the manner of viewing so extensive a scene. He is arrived on a new continent; a modern society offers itself to his contemplation, different from what he had hitherto seen. It is not composed, as in Europe, of great lords who possess everything, and of a herd of people who have nothing. Here are no aristocratical families, no courts, no kings, no bishops, no ecclesiastical dominion, no invisible power giving to a few a very visible one; no great

1. From *Letters from an American Farmer*, edited by Albert Boni and Charles Boni (1925).

2. Disputes.

3. Spirit; distinctive national character.

manufacturers employing thousands, no great refinements of luxury. The rich and the poor are not so far removed from each other as they are in Europe. Some few towns excepted, we are all tillers of the earth, from Nova Scotia to West Florida. We are a people of cultivators, scattered over an immense territory, communicating with each other by means of good roads and navigable rivers, united by the silken bands of mild government, all respecting the laws, without dreading their power, because they are equitable. We are all animated with the spirit of an industry which is unfettered and unrestrained, because each person works for himself. If he travels through our rural districts he views not the hostile castle, and the haughty mansion, contrasted with the clay-built hut and miserable cabin, where cattle and men help to keep each other warm, and dwell in meanness, smoke, and indigence. A pleasing uniformity of decent competence appears throughout our habitations. The meanest of our log-houses is a dry and comfortable habitation. Lawyer or merchant are the fairest titles our towns afford; that of a farmer is the only appellation of the rural inhabitants of our country. It must take some time ere he can reconcile himself to our dictionary, which is but short in words of dignity, and names of honor. There, on a Sunday, he sees a congregation of respectable farmers and their wives, all clad in neat homespun, well mounted, or riding in their own humble wagons. There is not among them an esquire, saving the unlettered magistrate. There he sees a parson as simple as his flock, a farmer who does not riot[4] on the labor of others. We have no princes, for whom we toil, starve, and bleed; we are the most perfect society now existing in the world. Here man is free as he ought to be; nor is this pleasing equality so transitory as many others are. Many ages will not see the shores of our great lakes replenished with inland nations, nor the unknown bounds of North America entirely peopled. Who can tell how far it extends? Who can tell the millions of men whom it will feed and contain? for no European foot has as yet traveled half the extent of this mighty continent!

The next wish of this traveler will be to know whence came all these people? They are a mixture of English, Scotch, Irish, French, Dutch, Germans and Swedes. From this promiscuous breed, that race now called Americans have arisen. The eastern provinces[5] must indeed be excepted, as being the unmixed descendants of Englishmen. I have heard many wish that they had been more intermixed also: for my part, I am no wisher, and think it much better as it has happened. They exhibit a most conspicuous figure in this great and variegated picture; they too enter for a great share in the pleasing perspective displayed in these thirteen provinces. I know it is fashionable to reflect on them, but respect them for what they have done; for the accuracy and wisdom with which they have settled their territory; for the decency of their manners; for their early love of letters; their ancient college,[6] the first in this hemisphere; for their industry, which to me who am but a farmer is the criterion of everything. There never was a people, situated as they are, who with so ungrateful a soil have done more in so short a time. Do you think that the monarchical ingredients which are more prevalent in other governments have purged them from all foul stains? Their histories assert the contrary.

In this great American asylum, the poor of Europe have by some means met together, and in consequence of various causes; to what purpose should

---

4. I.e., indulge himself.   6. Harvard College was founded in 1636.
5. New England.

they ask one another what countrymen they are? Alas, two thirds of them had no country. Can a wretch who wanders about, who works and starves, whose life is a continual scene of sore affliction or pinching penury, can that man call England or any other kingdom his country? A country that had no bread for him, whose fields procured him no harvest, who met with nothing but the frowns of the rich, the severity of the laws, with jails and punishments; who owned not a single foot of the extensive surface of this planet? No! Urged by a variety of motives, here they came. Everything has tended to regenerate them; new laws, a new mode of living, a new social system; here they are become men: in Europe they were as so many useless plants, wanting vegetative mold and refreshing showers; they withered, and were mowed down by want, hunger, and war; but now by the power of transplantation, like all other plants they have taken root and flourished! Formerly they were not numbered in any civil lists[7] of their country, except in those of the poor; here they rank as citizens. By what invisible power has this surprising metamorphosis been performed? By that of the laws and that of their industry. The laws, the indulgent laws, protect them as they arrive, stamping on them the symbol of adoption; they receive ample rewards for their labors; these accumulated rewards procure them lands; those lands confer on them the title of freemen, and to that title every benefit is affixed which men can possibly require. This is the great operation daily performed by our laws. From whence proceed these laws? From our government. Whence the government? It is derived from the original genius and strong desire of the people ratified and confirmed by the crown. This is the great chain which links us all, this is the picture which every province exhibits, Nova Scotia excepted. There the crown has done all;[8] either there were no people who had genius, or it was not much attended to: the consequence is that the province is very thinly inhabited indeed; the power of the crown in conjunction with the mosquitoes has prevented men from settling there. Yet some parts of it flourished once, and it contained a mild, harmless set of people. But for the fault of a few leaders, the whole were banished. The greatest political error the crown ever committed in America was to cut off men from a country which wanted nothing but men!

What attachment can a poor European emigrant have for a country where he had nothing? The knowledge of the language, the love of a few kindred as poor as himself, were the only cords that tied him: his country is now that which gives him land, bread, protection, and consequence: *Ubi panis ibi patria*[9] is the motto of all emigrants. What then is the American, this new man? He is either a European, or the descendant of a European, hence that strange mixture of blood, which you will find in no other country. I could point out to you a family whose grandfather was an Englishman, whose wife was Dutch, whose son married a French woman, and whose present four sons have now four wives of different nations. *He* is an American, who, leaving behind him all his ancient prejudices and manners, receives new ones from the new mode of life he has embraced, the new government he obeys, and the new rank he holds. He becomes an American by being received in the broad lap of our great *Alma Mater*.[1] Here individuals of all nations are melted into

---

7. Recognized employees of the civil government: ambassadors, judges, secretaries, etc.
8. In 1755 the French Acadians were banished from Nova Scotia by the British, who took it in 1710.

9. Where there is bread, there is one's fatherland (Latin).
1. Dear mother (Latin, literal trans.).

a new race of men, whose labors and posterity will one day cause great changes in the world. Americans are the western pilgrims, who are carrying along with them that great mass of arts, sciences, vigor, and industry which began long since in the east; they will finish the great circle. The Americans were once scattered all over Europe; here they are incorporated into one of the finest systems of population which has ever appeared, and which will hereafter become distinct by the power of the different climates they inhabit. The American ought therefore to love this country much better than that wherein either he or his forefathers were born. Here the rewards of his industry follow with equal steps the progress of his labor; his labor is founded on the basis of nature, *self-interest*; can it want a stronger allurement? Wives and children, who before in vain demanded of him a morsel of bread, now, fat and frolicsome, gladly help their father to clear those fields whence exuberant crops are to arise to feed and to clothe them all; without any part being claimed, either by a despotic prince, a rich abbot, or a mighty lord. Here religion demands but little of him; a small voluntary salary to the minister, and gratitude to God; can he refuse these? The American is a new man, who acts upon new principles; he must therefore entertain new ideas, and form new opinions. From involuntary idleness, servile dependence, penury, and useless labor, he has passed to toils of a very different nature, rewarded by ample subsistence.— This is an American.

British America is divided into many provinces, forming a large association, scattered along a coast 1,500 miles extent and about 200 wide. This society I would fain examine, at least such as it appears in the middle provinces; if it does not afford that variety of tinges and gradations which may be observed in Europe, we have colors peculiar to ourselves. For instance, it is natural to conceive that those who live near the sea must be very different from those who live in the woods; the intermediate space will afford a separate and distinct class.

Men are like plants; the goodness and flavor of the fruit proceeds from the peculiar soil and exposition in which they grow. We are nothing but what we derive from the air we breathe, the climate we inhabit, the government we obey, the system of religion we profess, and the nature of our employment. Here you will find but few crimes; these have acquired as yet no root among us. I wish I was able to trace all my ideas; if my ignorance prevents me from describing them properly, I hope I shall be able to delineate a few of the outlines, which are all I propose.

Those who live near the sea feed more on fish than on flesh, and often encounter that boisterous element. This renders them more bold and enterprising; this leads them to neglect the confined occupations of the land. They see and converse with a variety of people, their intercourse with mankind becomes extensive. The sea inspires them with a love of traffic, a desire of transporting produce from one place to another; and leads them to a variety of resources which supply the place of labor. Those who inhabit the middle settlements, by far the most numerous, must be very different; the simple cultivation of the earth purifies them, but the indulgences of the government, the soft remonstrances of religion, the rank of independent freeholders, must necessarily inspire them with sentiments, very little known in Europe among people of the same class. What do I say? Europe has no such class of men; the early knowledge they acquire, the early bargains they make, give them a great degree of sagacity. As freemen they will be litigious; pride and obstinancy are often the cause of lawsuits; the nature of our laws and governments may be another. As citizens it is easy to imagine that they will carefully read the newspapers, enter into every political disquisition, freely blame or censure governors and others. As farmers they will be careful and anxious to get as much as they can, because what they get is their own. As northern men they will love the cheerful cup. As Christians, religion curbs them not in their opinions; the general indulgence leaves everyone to think for themselves in spiritual matters; the laws inspect our actions, our thoughts are left to God. Industry, good living, selfishness, litigiousness, country politics, the pride of freemen, religious indifference are their characteristics. If you recede still farther from the sea, you will come into more modern settlements; they exhibit the same strong lineaments, in a ruder appearance. Religion seems to have still less influence, and their manners are less improved.

Now we arrive near the great woods, near the last inhabited districts;[2] there men seem to be placed still farther beyond the reach of government, which in some measure leaves them to themselves. How can it pervade every corner; as they were driven there by misfortunes, necessity of beginnings, desire of acquiring large tracts of land, idleness, frequent want of economy,[3] ancient debts; the reunion of such people does not afford a very pleasing spectacle. When discord, want of unity and friendship; when either drunkenness or idleness prevail in such remote districts; contention, inactivity, and wretchedness must ensue. There are not the same remedies to these evils as in a long-established community. The few magistrates they have are in general little better than the rest; they are often in a perfect state of war; that of man against man, sometimes decided by blows, sometimes by means of the law; that of man against every wild inhabitant of these venerable woods, of which they are come to dispossess them. There men appear to be no better than carnivorous animals of a superior rank, living on the flesh of wild animals when they can catch them, and when they are not able, they subsist on grain. He who would wish to see America in its proper light, and have a true idea of its feeble beginnings and barbarous rudiments, must visit our extended line of frontiers where the last settlers dwell, and where he may see the first labors of settlement, the mode of clearing the earth, in all their different appearances; where men are wholly left dependent on their native tempers and on the spur of uncertain industry, which often fails when not sanctified by the efficacy of a few moral rules. There, remote from the power of example and check of shame, many families exhibit the most hideous parts of our society. They are a kind of forlorn hope, preceding by ten or twelve years the most respectable army of veterans which come after them. In that space, prosperity will polish some, vice and the law will drive off the rest, who uniting again with others like themselves will recede still farther; making room for more industrious people, who will finish their improvements, convert the loghouse into a convenient habitation, and rejoicing that the first heavy labors are finished, will change in a few years that hitherto barbarous country into a fine fertile, well-regulated district. Such is our progress, such is the march of the Europeans toward the interior parts of this continent. In all societies these are offcasts; this impure part serves as our precursors or pioneers; my father himself was one of

2. I.e., the frontier; the land west of the original colonies and east of the Mississippi.

3. I.e., they were improvident and spent beyond their means.

that class,[4] but he came upon honest principles, and was therefore one of the few who held fast; by good conduct and temperance, he transmitted to me his fair inheritance, when not above one in fourteen of his contemporaries had the same good fortune.

Forty years ago his smiling country was thus inhabited; it is now purged, a general decency of manners prevails throughout, and such has been the fate of our best countries.

Exclusive of those general characteristics, each province has its own, founded on the government, climate, mode of husbandry, customs, and peculiarity of circumstances. Europeans submit insensibly to these great powers, and become, in the course of a few generations, not only Americans in general, but either Pennsylvanians, Virginians, or provincials under some other name. Whoever traverses the continent must easily observe those strong differences, which will grow more evident in time. The inhabitants of Canada, Massachusetts, the middle provinces, the southern ones will be as different as their climates; their only points of unit will be those of religion and language.

As I have endeavored to show you how Europeans become Americans, it may not be disagreeable to show you likewise how the various Christian sects introduced wear out, and how religious indifference becomes prevalent. When any considerable number of a particular sect happen to dwell contiguous to each other, they immediately erect a temple, and there worship the Divinity agreeably to their own peculiar ideas. Nobody disturbs them. If any new sect springs up in Europe it may happen that many of its professors[5] will come and settle in America. As they bring their zeal with them, they are at liberty to make proselytes if they can, and to build a meeting and to follow the dictates of their consciences; for neither the government nor any other power interferes. If they are peaceable subjects, and are industrious, what is it to their neighbors how and in what manner they think fit to address their prayers to the Supreme Being? But if the sectaries are not settled close together, if they are mixed with other denominations, their zeal will cool for want of fuel, and will be extinguished in a little time. Then the Americans become as to religion what they are as to country, allied to all. In them the name of Englishman, Frenchman, and European is lost, and in like manner, the strict modes of Christianity as practiced in Europe are lost also. This effect will extend itself still farther hereafter, and though this may appear to you as a strange idea, yet it is a very true one. I shall be able perhaps hereafter to explain myself better; in the meanwhile, let the following example serve as my first justification.

Let us suppose you and I to be traveling; we observe that in this house, to the right, lives a Catholic, who prays to God as he has been taught, and believes in transubstantiation;[6] he works and raises wheat, he has a large family of children, all hale and robust; his belief, his prayers offend nobody. About one mile farther on the same road, his next neighbor may be a good honest plodding German Lutheran, who addresses himself to the same God, the God of all, agreeably to the modes he has been educated in, and believes in consubstantiation;[7] by so doing he scandalizes nobody; he also works in his fields,

4. His father never came to America.
5. Believers.
6. The doctrine followed by Roman Catholics that the substance of the bread and wine used in the sacrament of communion are changed at the consecration to the substance of the body and blood of Christ.

7. As distinguished from transubstantiation; the doctrine that affirms that Christ's body is not present in or under the elements of bread and wine, but that the bread and wine are signs of Christ's presence through faith.

embellishes the earth, clears swamps, etc. What has the world to do with his Lutheran principles? He persecutes nobody, and nobody persecutes him, he visits his neighbors, and his neighbors visit him. Next to him lives a seceder,[8] the most enthusiastic of all sectaries;[9] his zeal is hot and fiery, but separated as he is from others of the same complexion, he has no congregation of his own to resort to, where he might cabal and mingle religious pride with worldly obstinacy. He likewise raises good crops, his house is handsomely painted, his orchard is one of the fairest in the neighborhood. How does it concern the welfare of the country, or of the province at large, what this man's religious sentiments are, or really whether he has any at all? He is a good farmer, he is a sober, peaceable, good citizen: William Penn[1] himself would not wish for more. This is the visible character, the invisible one is only guessed at, and is nobody's business. Next again lives a Low Dutchman, who implicitly believes the rules laid down by the synod of Dort.[2] He conceives no other idea of a clergyman than that of a hired man; if he does his work well he will pay him the stipulated sum; if not he will dismiss him, and do without his sermons, and let his church be shut up for years. But notwithstanding this coarse idea, you will find his house and farm to be the neatest in all the country; and you will judge by his wagon and fat horses that he thinks more of the affairs of this world than of those of the next. He is sober and laborious, therefore he is all he ought to be as to the affairs of this life; as for those of the next, he must trust to the great Creator. Each of these people instruct their children as well as they can, but these instructions are feeble compared to those which are given to the youth of the poorest class in Europe. Their children will therefore grow up less zealous and more indifferent in matters of religion than their parents. The foolish vanity, or rather the fury of making proselytes, is unknown here; they have no time, the seasons call for all their attention, and thus in a few years, this mixed neighborhood will exhibit a strange religious medley, that will be neither pure Catholicism nor pure Calvinism. A very perceptible indifference, even in the first generation, will become apparent; and it may happen that the daughter of the Catholic will marry the son of the seceder, and settle by themselves at a distance from their parents. What religious education will they give their children? A very imperfect one. If there happens to be in the neighborhood any place of worship, we will suppose a Quaker's meeting; rather than not show their fine clothes, they will go to it, and some of them may perhaps attach themselves to that society. Others will remain in a perfect state of indifference; the children of these zealous parents will not be able to tell what their religious principles are, and their grandchildren still less. The neighborhood of a place of worship generally leads them to it, and the action of going thither is the strongest evidence they can give of their attachment to any sect. The Quakers are the only people who retain a fondness for their own mode of worship; for be they ever so far separated from each other, they hold a sort of communion with the society, and seldom depart from its rules, at least in this country. Thus all sects are mixed as well as all nations; thus religious indifference is imperceptibly disseminated from one end of the continent to the other; which is at present one of the strongest character-

8. A Presbyterian who has separated from the established Church of Scotland.
9. One who dissents or withdraws from an established church.
1. William Penn (1644–1718), English Quaker and founder of Pennsylvania.
2. The Synod of Dort met in Holland in 1618 and attempted to settle disputes between Protestant reformed churches. "Low Dutchman": someone from Holland, not Belgium.

istics of the Americans. Where this will reach no one can tell, perhaps it may leave a vacuum fit to receive other systems. Persecution, religious pride, the love of contradiction are the food of what the world commonly calls religion. These motives have ceased here; zeal in Europe is confined; here it evaporates in the great distance it has to travel; there it is a grain of power inclosed, here it burns away in the open air, and consumes without effect.

But to return to our back settlers. I must tell you that there is something in the proximity of the woods which is very singular. It is with men as it is with the plants and animals that grow and live in the forests; they are entirely different from those that live in the plains. I will candidly tell you all my thoughts but you are not to expect that I shall advance any reasons. By living in or near the woods, their actions are regulated by the wildness of the neighborhood. The deer often come to eat their grain, the wolves to destroy their sheep, the bears to kill their hogs, the foxes to catch their poultry. This surrounding hostility immediately puts the gun into their hands; they watch these animals, they kill some; and thus by defending their property, they soon become professed hunters; this is the progress; once hunters, farewell to the plow. The chase renders them ferocious, gloomy, and unsociable; a hunter wants no neighbor, he rather hates them, because he dreads the competition. In a little time their success in the woods makes them neglect their tillage. They trust to the natural fecundity of the earth, and therefore do little; carelessness in fencing often exposes what little they sow to destruction; they are not at home to watch; in order therefore to make up the deficiency, they go oftener to the woods. That new mode of life brings along with it a new set of manners, which I cannot easily describe. These new manners, being grafted on the old stock, produce a strange sort of lawless profligacy, the impressions of which are indelible. The manners of the Indian natives are respectable, compared with this European medley. Their wives and children live in sloth and inactivity; and having no proper pursuits, you may judge what education the latter receive. Their tender minds have nothing else to contemplate but the example of their parents; like them they grow up a mongrel breed, half civilized, half savage, except nature stamps on them some constitutional propensities. That rich, that voluptuous sentiment is gone that struck them so forcibly; the possession of their freeholds[3] no longer conveys to their minds the same pleasure and pride. To all these reasons you must add their lonely situation, and you cannot imagine what an effect on manners the great distances they live from each other has! Consider one of the last settlements in its first view: of what is it composed? Europeans who have not that sufficient share of knowledge they ought to have, in order to prosper; people who have suddenly passed from oppression, dread of government, and fear of laws into the unlimited freedom of the woods. This sudden change must have a very great effect on most men, and on that class particularly. Eating of wild meat, whatever you may think, tends to alter their temper: though all the proof I can adduce is that I have seen it: and having no place of worship to resort to, what little society this might afford is denied them. The Sunday meetings, exclusive of religious benefits, were the only social bonds that might have inspired them with some degree of emulation in neatness. Is it then surprising to see men thus situated, immersed in great and heavy labors, degenerate a little? It is rather a wonder the effect is

3. Land held outright for a specified period of time.

not more diffusive. The Moravians[4] and the Quakers are the only instances in exception to what I have advanced. The first never settle singly, it is a colony of the society which emigrates; they carry with them their forms, worship, rules, and decency: the others never begin so hard, they are always able to buy improvements, in which there is a great advantage, for by that time the country is recovered from its first barbarity. Thus our bad people are those who are half cultivators and half hunters; and the worst of them are those who have degenerated altogether into the hunting state. As old plowmen and new men of the woods, as Europeans and new-made Indians, they contract the vices of both; they adopt the moroseness and ferocity of a native, without his mildness, or even his industry at home. If manners are not refined, at least they are rendered simple and inoffensive by tilling the earth; all our wants are supplied by it, our time is divided between labor and rest, and leaves none of the commission of great misdeeds. As hunters it is divided between the toil of the chase, the idleness of repose, or the indulgence of inebriation. Hunting is but a licentious idle life, and if it does not always pervert good dispositions; yet, when it is united with bad luck, it leads to want: want stimulates that propensity to rapacity and injustice, too natural to needy men, which is the fatal gradation. After this explanation of the effects which follow by living in the woods, shall we yet vainly flatter ourselves with the hope of converting the Indians? We should rather begin with converting our back-settlers; and now if I dare mention the name of religion, its sweet accents would be lost in the immensity of these woods. Men thus placed are not fit either to receive or remember its mild instructions; they want[5] temples and ministers, but as soon as men cease to remain at home, and begin to lead an erratic life, let them be either tawny or white, they cease to be its disciples.

✻   ✻   ✻

Europe contains hardly any other distinctions but lords and tenants; this fair country alone is settled by freeholders, the possessors of the soil they cultivate, members of the government they obey, and the framers of their own laws, by means of their representatives. This is a thought which you have taught me to cherish; our difference from Europe, far from diminishing, rather adds to our usefulness and consequence as men and subjects. Had our forefathers remained there, they would only have crowded it, and perhaps prolonged those convulsions which had shook it so long. Every industrious European who transports himself here may be compared to a sprout growing at the foot of a great tree; it enjoys and draws but a little portion of sap; wrench it from the parent roots, transplant it, and it will become a tree bearing fruit also. Colonists are therefore entitled to the consideration due to the most useful subjects; a hundred families barely existing in some parts or Scotland will here in six years cause an annual exportation of 10,000 bushels of wheat; 100 bushels being but a common quantity for an industrious family to sell, if they cultivated good land. It is here then that the idle may be employed, the useless become useful, and the poor become rich; but by riches I do not mean gold and silver, we have but little of those metals; I mean a better sort of wealth,

4. The Moravians were followers of Jacob Hutter, who was executed in 1536; they were Christian family communities who gave up private property and were noted for their industry and thrift. They suffered a number of persecutions in the 17th century and emigrated to other lands.
5. Lack.

cleared lands, cattle, good houses, good clothes, and an increase of people to enjoy them.

There is no wonder that this country has so many charms, and presents to Europeans so many temptations to remain in it. A traveler in Europe becomes a stranger as soon as he quits his own kingdom; but it is otherwise here. We know, properly speaking, no strangers; this is every person's country; the variety of our soils, situations, climates, governments, and produce hath something which must please everybody. No sooner does a European arrive, no matter of what condition, than his eyes are opened upon the fair prospect; he hears his language spoken, he retraces many of his own country manners, he perpetually hears the names of families and towns with which he is acquainted; he sees happiness and prosperity in all places disseminated; he meets with hospitality, kindness, and plenty everywhere; he beholds hardly any poor; he seldom hears of punishments and executions; and he wonders at the elegance of our towns, those miracles of industry and freedom. He cannot admire enough our rural districts, our convenient roads, good taverns, and our many accommodations; he involuntarily loves a country where everything is so lovely.

*   *   *

After a foreigner from any part of Europe is arrived, and become a citizen, let him devoutly listen to the voice of our great parent, which says to him, "Welcome to my shores, distressed European; bless the hour in which thou didst see my verdant fields, my fair navigable rivers, and my green mountains!—If thou wilt work, I have bread for thee; if thou wilt be honest, sober, and industrious, I have greater rewards to confer on thee—ease and independence. I will give thee fields to feed and clothe thee; a comfortable fireside to sit by, and tell thy children by what means thou hast prospered; and a decent bed to repose on. I shall endow thee beside with the immunities of a freeman. If thou wilt carefully educate thy children, teach them gratitude to God, and reverence to that government, the philanthropic government, which has collected here so many men and made them happy. I will also provide for thy progeny; and to every good man this ought to be the most holy, the most powerful, the most earnest wish he can possibly form, as well as the most consolatory prospect when he dies. Go thou and work and till; thou shalt prosper, provided thou be just, grateful, and industrious."

From *Letter IV. Description of the Island of Nantucket, with the Manners, Customs, Policy, and Trade of the Inhabitants*

The greatest compliment that can be paid to the best of kings, to the wisest ministers, or the most patriotic rulers, is to think, that the reformation of political abuses, and the happiness of their people are the primary objects of their attention. But alas! how disagreeable must the work of reformation be; how dreaded the operation; for we hear of no amendment: on the contrary, the great number of European emigrants, yearly coming over here, informs us, that the severity of taxes, the injustice of laws, the tyranny of the rich, and the oppressive avarice of the church; are as intolerable as ever. Will these calamities have no end? Are not the great rulers of the earth afraid of losing, by degrees, their most useful subjects? This country, providentially intended for the general asylum of the world, will flourish by the oppression of their people; they will every day become better acquainted with the happiness we enjoy, and seek for the means of transporting themselves here, in spite of all obstacles and laws. To what purpose then have so many useful books and divine maxims been transmitted to us from preceding ages?—Are they all vain, all useless? Must human nature ever be the sport of the few, and its many wounds remain unhealed? How happy are we here, in having fortunately escaped the miseries which attended our fathers; how thankful ought we to be, that they reared us in a land where sobriety and industry never fail to meet with the most ample rewards! You have, no doubt, read several histories of this continent, yet there are a thousand facts, a thousand explanations overlooked. Authors will certainly convey to you a geographical knowledge of this country; they will acquaint you with the eras of the several settlements, the foundations of our towns, the spirit of our different charters, etc., yet they do not sufficiently disclose the genius of the people, their various customs, their modes of agriculture, the innumerable resources which the industrious have of raising themselves to a comfortable and easy situation. Few of these writers have resided here, and those who have, had not pervaded every part of the country, nor carefully examined the nature and principles of our association. It would be a task worthy a speculative genius, to enter intimately into the situation and characters of the people, from Nova Scotia to West Florida; and surely history cannot possibly present any subject more pleasing to behold. Sensible how unable I am to lead you through so vast a maze, let us look attentively for some small unnoticed corner; but where shall we go in quest of such an one? Numberless settlements, each distinguished by some peculiarities, present themselves on every side; all seem to realize the most sanguine wishes that a good man could form for the happiness of his race. Here they live by fishing on the most plentiful coasts in the world; there they fell trees, by the sides of large rivers, for masts and lumber; here others convert innumerable logs into the best boards; there again others cultivate the land, rear cattle, and clear large fields. Yet I have a spot in my view, where none of these occupations are performed, which will, I hope, reward us for the trouble of inspection; but though it is barren in its soil, insignificant in its extent, inconvenient in its situation, deprived of materials for building; it seems to have been inhabited merely to prove what mankind can do when happily governed! Here I can point out to you exertions of the most successful industry; instances of native sagacity unassisted by science; the happy fruits of a well directed perseverance. It is always a refreshing spectacle to me, when in my review of the various component parts of this immense *whole*, I observe the labors of its inhabitants singularly rewarded by nature; when I see them emerged out of their first difficulties, living with decency and ease, and conveying to their posterity that plentiful subsistence, which their fathers have so deservedly earned. But when their prosperity arises from the goodness of the climate, and fertility of the soil; I partake of their happiness, it is true; yet stay but a little while with them, as they exhibit nothing but what is natural and common. On the contrary, when I meet with barren spots fertilized, grass growing where none grew before; grain gathered from fields which had hitherto produced nothing better than brambles; dwellings raised where no building materials were to be found; wealth acquired by the most uncommon means: there I pause, to dwell on the favorite object of my speculative inquiries. Willingly do I leave the former to enjoy the odoriferous furrow, or their rich valleys, with anxiety repairing to the spot, where so many difficulties have been overcome; where extraordinary exertions have produced extraordinary effects, and where every natural obstacle has been removed by a vigorous industry.

I want not to record the annals of the island of Nantucket—its inhabitants have no annals, for they are not a race of warriors. My simple wish is to trace them throughout their progressive steps, from their arrival here to this present hour; to inquire by what means they have raised themselves from the most humble, the most insignificant beginnings, to the ease and the wealth they now possess; and to give you some idea of their customs, religion, manners, policy, and mode of living.

This happy settlement was not founded on intrusion, forcible entries, or blood, as so many others have been; it drew its origin from necessity on the one side, and from good will on the other; and ever since, all has been a scene of uninterrupted harmony.—Neither political, nor religious broils; neither disputes with the natives, nor any other contentions, have in the least agitated or disturbed its detached society. Yet the first founders knew nothing either of Lycurgus or Solon;[6] for this settlement has not been the work of eminent men or powerful legislators, forcing nature by the accumulated labors of art. This singular establishment has been effected by means of that native industry and perseverance common to all men, when they are protected by a government which demands but little for its protection; when they are permitted to enjoy a system of rational laws founded on perfect freedom. The mildness and humanity of such a government necessarily implies that confidence which is the source of the most arduous undertakings and permanent success. Would you believe that a sandy spot, of about twenty-three thousand acres, affording neither stones nor timber, meadows nor arable, yet can boast of an handsome town, consisting of more than 500 houses, should possess above 200 sail of vessels, constantly employ upwards of 2000 seamen, feed more than 15,000 sheep, 500 cows, 200 horses; and has several citizens worth 20,000£ sterling! Yet all these facts are uncontroverted. Who would have imagined that any people should have abandoned a fruitful and extensive continent, filled with the riches which the most ample vegetation affords; replete with good soil, enameled meadows, rich pastures, every kind of timber, and with all other materials necessary to render life happy and comfortable: to come and inhabit a little sand-bank, to which nature had refused those advantages; to dwell on a spot where there scarcely grew a shrub to announce, by the budding of its leaves, the arrival of the spring, and to warn by their fall the proximity of winter. Had this island been contiguous to the shores of some ancient monarchy, it would only have been occupied by a few wretched fishermen, who, oppressed by poverty, would hardly have been able to purchase or build little fishing barks; always dreading the weight of taxes, or the servitude of men of war. Instead of that boldness of speculation for which the inhabitants of this island are so remarkable, they would fearfully have confined themselves, within the narrow limits of the most trifling attempts; timid in their excursions, they never could have extricated themselves from their first difficulties. This island, on the contrary, contains 5000 hardy people, who boldly derive their riches from the element that surrounds them, and have been compelled by

6. Lycurgus was a 9th-century B.C. lawgiver who laid the groundwork for Sparta's military preparedness. Solon (638?–559 B.C.) was one of the seven wise men of Greece.

the sterility of the soil to seek abroad for the means of subsistence. You must not imagine, from the recital of these facts, that they enjoyed any exclusive privileges or royal charters, or that they were nursed by particular immunities in the infancy of their settlement. No, their freedom, their skill, their probity, and perseverance, have accomplished every thing, and brought them by degrees to the rank they now hold.

From this first sketch, I hope that my partiality to this island will be justified. Perhaps you hardly know that such an one exists in the neighborhood of Cape Cod. What has happened here, has and will happen everywhere else. Give mankind the full rewards of their industry, allow them to enjoy the fruit of their labor under the peaceable shade of their vines and fig trees, leave their native activity unshackled and free, like a fair stream without dams or other obstacles; the first will fertilize the very sand on which they tread, the other exhibit a navigable river, spreading plenty and cheerfulness wherever the declivity of the ground leads it. If these people are not famous for tracing the fragrant furrow on the plain, they plough the rougher ocean, they gather from its surface, at an immense distance, and with Herculean labors,[7] the riches it affords; they go to hunt and catch that huge fish which by its strength and velocity one would imagine ought to be beyond the reach of man. This island has nothing deserving of notice but its inhabitants; here you meet with neither ancient monuments, spacious halls, solemn temples, nor elegant dwellings; not a citadel, nor any kind of fortification, not even a battery[8] to rend the air with its loud peals on any solemn occasion. As for their rural improvements, they are many, but all of the most simple and useful kind.

*   *   *

Nantucket is a great nursery of seamen, pilots, coasters, and bank-fishermen; as a country belonging to the province of Massachusetts, it has yearly the benefit of a court of Common Pleas, and their appeal lies to the supreme court at Boston. I observed before, that the Friends[9] compose two thirds of the magistracy of this island; thus they are the proprietors of its territory, and the principal rulers of its inhabitants; but with all this apparatus of law, its coercive powers are seldom wanted or required. Seldom is it that any individual is amerced[1] or punished; their jail conveys no terror; no man has lost his life here judicially since the foundation of this town, which is upwards of an hundred years. Solemn tribunals, public executions, humiliating punishments, are altogether unknown. I saw neither governors, nor any pageantry of state; neither ostentatious magistrates, nor any individuals clothed with useless dignity: no artificial phantoms subsist here either civil or religious; no gibbets loaded with guilty citizens offer themselves to your view; no soldiers are appointed to bayonet their compatriots into servile compliance. But how is a society composed of 5000 individuals preserved in the bonds of peace and tranquility? How are the weak protected from the strong?—I will tell you. Idleness and poverty, the causes of so many crimes, are unknown here; each seeks in the prosecution of his lawful business that honest gain which supports them; every period of their time is full, either on shore or at sea. A probable expectation of reasonable profits, or of kindly assistance, if they fail of success,

---

7. Hercules won immortality by performing twelve labors demanded by Hera, the goddess of women and marriage and the wife of Zeus.

8. A platform on which guns are mounted.
9. Quakers.
1. Fined.

renders them strangers to licentious expedients. The simplicity of their manners shortens the catalogues of their wants; the law at a distance is ever ready to exert itself in the protection of those who stand in need of its assistance. The greatest part of them are always at sea, pursuing the whale or raising the cod from the surface of the banks: some cultivate their little farms with the utmost diligence; some are employed in exercising various trades; others again in providing every necessary resource in order to refit their vessels, or repair what misfortunes may happen, looking out for future markets, etc. Such is the rotation of those different scenes of business which fill the measure of their days; of that part of their lives at least which is enlivened by health, spirits, and vigor. It is but seldom that vice grows on a barren sand like this, which produces nothing without extreme labor. How could the common follies of society take root in so despicable a soil; they generally thrive on its exuberant juices: here there are none but those which administer to the useful, to the necessary, and to the indispensable comforts of life. This land must necessarily either produce health, temperance, and a great equality of conditions, or the most abject misery. Could the manners of luxurious countries be imported here, like an epidemical disorder they would destroy every thing; the majority of them could not exist a month, they would be obliged to emigrate. As in all societies except that of the natives, some difference must necessarily exist between individual and individual, for there must be some more exalted than the rest either by their riches or their talents; so in *this*, there are what you might call the high, the middling, and the low; and this difference will always be more remarkable among people who live by sea excursions than among those who live by the cultivation of their land. The first run greater hazard, and adventure more: the profits and the misfortunes attending this mode of life must necessarily introduce a greater disparity than among the latter, where the equal division of the land offers no short road to superior riches. The only difference that may arise among them is that of industry, and perhaps of superior goodness of soil; the gradations I observed here, are founded on nothing more than the good or ill success of their maritime enterprises, and do not proceed from education; that is the same throughout every class, simple, useful, and unadorned like their dress and their houses. This necessary difference in their fortunes does not however cause those heart burnings, which in other societies generate crimes. The sea which surrounds them is equally open to all, and presents to all an equal title to the chance of good fortune. A collector from Boston is the only king's officer who appears on these shores to receive the trifling duties which this community owes to those who protect them, and under the shadow of whose wings they navigate to all parts of the world.

From *Letter IX. Description of Charles-Town; Thoughts on Slavery; on Physical Evil; A Melancholy Scene*

Charles-Town is, in the north, what Lima is in the south; both are capitals of the richest provinces of their respective hemispheres: you may therefore conjecture, that both cities must exhibit the appearances necessarily resulting from riches. Peru abounding in gold, Lima is filled with inhabitants who enjoy all those gradations of pleasure, refinement, and luxury, which proceed from wealth. Carolina produces commodities, more valuable perhaps than gold, because they are gained by greater industry; it exhibits also on our northern stage, a display of riches and luxury, inferior indeed to the former, but far superior to what are to be seen in our northern towns. Its situation is admirable, being built at the confluence of two large rivers, which receive in their course a great number of inferior streams; all navigable in the spring, for flatboats. Here the produce of this extensive territory concenters; here therefore is the seat of the most valuable exportation; their wharfs, their docks, their magazines,[2] are extremely convenient to facilitate this great commercial business. The inhabitants are the gayest in America; it is called the center of our beau monde, and it [is] always filled with the richest planters of the province, who resort hither in a quest of health and pleasure. Here are always to be seen a great number of valetudinarians from the West Indies, seeking for the renovation of health, exhausted by the debilitating nature of their sun, air, and modes of living. Many of these West Indians have I seen, at thirty, loaded with the infirmities of old age; for nothing is more common in those countries of wealth, than for persons to lose the abilities of enjoying the comforts of life, at a time when we northern men just begin to taste the fruits of our labor and prudence. The round of pleasure, and the expenses of those citizens' tables, are much superior to what you would imagine: indeed the growth of this town and province has been astonishingly rapid. It is [a] pity that the narrowness of the neck on which it stands prevents it from increasing; and which is the reason why houses are so dear. The heat of the climate, which is sometimes very great in the interior parts of the country, is always temperate in Charles-Town; though sometimes when they have no sea breezes the sun is too powerful. The climate renders excesses of all kinds very dangerous, particularly those of the table; and yet, insensible or fearless of danger, they live on, and enjoy a short and a merry life: the rays of their sun seem to urge them irresistably to dissipation and pleasure: on the contrary, the women, from being abstemious, reach to a longer period of life, and seldom die without having had several husbands. An European at his first arrival must be greatly surprised when he sees the elegance of their houses, their sumptuous furniture, as well as the magnificence of their tables. Can he imagine himself in a country, the establishment of which is so recent?

The three principal classes of inhabitants are, lawyers, planters, and merchants; this is the province which has afforded to the first the richest spoils, for nothing can exceed their wealth, their power, and their influence. They have reached the *ne plus ultra*[3] of worldly felicity; no plantation is secured, no title is good, no will is valid, but what they dictate, regulate, and approve. The whole mass of provincial property is become tributary to this society; which, far above priests and bishops, disdain to be satisfied with the poor Mosaical portion of the tenth.[4] I appeal to the many inhabitants, who, while contending perhaps for their right to a few hundred acres, have lost by the mazes of the law their whole patrimony. These men are more properly law givers than interpreters of the law; and have united here, as well as in most other provinces, the skill and dexterity of the scribe with the power and ambition of the prince: who can tell where this may lead in a future day? The nature of our laws, and the spirit of freedom, which often tends to make us litigious, must necessarily throw the greatest part of the property of the colonies into the hands

---

2. Warehouses.
3. No more beyond (Latin, literal trans.); the point of highest achievement.

4. The law set forth in the first five books of the Old Testament that one-tenth of one's worldly goods should be offered to God.

of these gentlemen. In another century, the law will possess in the north, what now the church possesses in Peru and Mexico.

While all is joy, festivity, and happiness in Charles-Town, would you imagine that scenes of misery overspread in the country? Their ears by habit are become deaf, their hearts are hardened; they neither see, hear, nor feel for the woes of their poor slaves, from whose painful labors all their wealth proceeds. Here the horrors of slavery, the hardship of incessant toils, are unseen; and no one thinks with compassion of those showers of sweat and of tears which from the bodies of Africans, daily drop, and moisten the ground they till. The cracks of the whip urging these miserable beings to excessive labor, are far too distant from the gay capital to be heard. The chosen race eat, drink, and live happy, while the unfortunate one grubs up the ground, raises indigo, or husks the rice; exposed to a sun full as scorching as their native one; without the support of good food, without the cordials of any cheering liquor. This great contrast has often afforded me subjects of the most afflicting meditation. On the one side, behold a people enjoying all that life affords most bewitching and pleasurable, without labor, without fatigue, hardly subjected to the trouble of wishing. With gold, dug from Peruvian mountains, they order vessels to the coasts of Guinea; by virtue of that gold, wars, murders, and devastations are committed in some harmless, peaceable African neighborhood, where dwelt innocent people, who even knew not but that all men were black. The daughter torn from her weeping mother, the child from the wretched parents, the wife from the loving husband; whose families swept away and brought through storms and tempests to this rich metropolis! There, arranged like horses at a fair, they are branded like cattle, and then driven to toil, to starve, and to languish for a few years on the different plantations of these citizens. And for whom must they work? For persons they know not, and who have no other power over them than that of violence; no other right than what this accursed metal has given them! Strange order of things! Oh, Nature, where are thou?—Are not these blacks thy children as well as we? On the other side, nothing is to be seen but the most diffusive misery and wretchedness, unrelieved even in thought or wish! Day after day they drudge on without any prospect of ever reaping for themselves; they are obliged to devote their lives, their limbs, their will, and every vital exertion to swell the wealth of masters; who look not upon them with half the kindness and affection with which they consider their dogs and horses. Kindness and affection are not the portion of those who till the earth, who carry the burdens, who convert the logs into useful boards. This reward, simple and natural as one would conceive it, would border on humanity; and planters must have none of it!

*   *   *

A clergyman settled a few years ago at George-Town, and feeling as I do now, warmly recommended to the planters, from the pulpit, a relaxation of severity; he introduced the benignity of Christianity, and pathetically made use of the admirable precepts of that system to melt the hearts of his congregation into a greater degree of compassion toward their slaves than had been hitherto customary; "Sir (said one of his hearers) we pay you a genteel salary to read to us the prayers of the liturgy, and to explain to us such parts of the Gospel as the rule of the church directs; but we do not want you to teach us what we are to do with our blacks." The clergyman found it prudent to withhold any farther admonition. Whence this astonishing right, or rather this barbarous custom, for most certainly we have no kind of right beyond that of force? We are told, it is true, that slavery cannot be so repugnant to human nature as we at first imagine, because it has been practiced in all ages, and in all nations: the Lacedemonians[5] themselves, those great assertors of liberty, conquered the Helotes with the design of making them their slaves; the Romans, whom we consider as our masters in civil and military policy, lived in the exercise of the most horrid oppression; they conquered to plunder and to enslave. What a hideous aspect the face of the earth must then have exhibited! Provinces, towns, districts, often depopulated; their inhabitants driven to Rome, the greatest market in the world, and there sold by thousands! The Roman dominions were tilled by the hands of unfortunate people, who had once been, like their victors free, rich, and possessed of every benefit society can confer; until they became subject to the cruel right of war, and to lawless force. Is there then no superintending power who conducts the moral operations of the world, as well as the physical? The same sublime hand which guides the planets round the sun with so much exactness, which preserves the arrangement of the whole with such exalted wisdom and paternal care, and prevents the vast system from falling into confusion; doth it abandon mankind to all the errors, the follies, and the miseries, which their most frantic rage, and their most dangerous vices and passions can produce?

✳   ✳   ✳

Everywhere one part of the human species are taught the art of shedding the blood of the other; of setting fire to their dwellings; of leveling the works of their industry: half of the existence of nations regularly employed in destroying other nations. What little political felicity is to be met with here and there, has cost oceans of blood to purchase; as if good was never to be the portion of unhappy man. Republics, kingdoms, monarchies, founded either on fraud or successful violence, increase by pursuing the steps of the same policy, until they are destroyed in their turn, either by the influence of their own crimes, or by more successful but equally criminal enemies.

If from this general review of human nature, we descend to the examination of what is called civilized society; there the combination of every natural and artificial want, makes us pay very dear for what little share of political felicity we enjoy. It is a strange heterogeneous assemblage of vices and virtues, and of a variety of other principles, forever at war, forever jarring, forever producing some dangerous, some distressing extreme. Where do you conceive then that nature intended we should be happy? Would you prefer the state of men in the woods, to that of men in a more improved situation? Evil preponderates in both; in the first they often eat each other for want of food, and in the other they often starve each other for want of room. For my part, I think the vices and miseries to be found in the latter, exceed those of the former; in which real evil is more scarce, more supportable, and less enormous. Yet we wish to see the earth peopled; to accomplish the happiness of kingdoms, which is said to consist in numbers. Gracious God! to what end is the introduction of so many beings into a mode of existence in which they must grope amidst as many errors, commit as many crimes, and meet with as many diseases, wants, and sufferings!

The following scene will I hope account for these melancholy reflections,

---

5. Another name for Spartans, who enslaved the people of Helos, a town in Laconia.

and apologize for the gloomy thoughts with which I have filled this letter: my mind is, and always has been, oppressed since I became a witness to it. I was not long since invited to dine with a planter who lived three miles from ———, where he then resided. In order to avoid the heat of the sun, I resolved to go on foot, sheltered in a small path, leading through a pleasant wood. I was leisurely traveling along, attentively examining some peculiar plants which I had collected, when all at once I felt the air strongly agitated; though the day was perfectly calm and sultry. I immediately cast my eyes toward the cleared ground, from which I was but at a small distance, in order to see whether it was not occasioned by a sudden shower; when at that instant a sound resembling a deep rough voice, uttered, as I thought, a few inarticulate monosyllables. Alarmed and surprised, I precipitately looked all round, when I perceived at about six rods distance something resembling a cage, suspended to the limbs of a tree; all the branches of which appeared covered with large birds of prey, fluttering about, and anxiously endeavoring to perch on the cage. Actuated by an involuntary motion of my hands, more than by any design of my mind, I fired at them; they all flew to a short distance, with a most hideous noise: when, horrid to think and painful to repeat, I perceived a Negro, suspended in the cage, and left there to expire! I shudder when I recollect that the birds had already picked out his eyes, his cheek bones were bare; his arms had been attacked in several places, and his body seemed covered with a multitude of wounds. From the edges of the hollow sockets and from the lacerations with which he was disfigured, the blood slowly dropped, and tinged the ground beneath. No sooner were the birds flown, than swarms of insects covered the whole body of this unfortunate wretch, eager to feed on his mangled flesh and to drink his blood. I found myself suddenly arrested by the power of affright and terror; my nerves were convulsed; I trembled, I stood motionless, involuntarily contemplating the fate of this Negro, in all its dismal latitude. The living specter, though deprived of his eyes, could still distinctly hear, and in his uncouth dialect begged me to give him some water to allay his thirst. Humanity herself would have recoiled back with horror; she would have balanced whether to lessen such reliefless distress, or mercifully with one blow to end this dreadful scene of agonizing torture! Had I had a ball in my gun, I certainly should have dispatched him; but finding myself unable to perform so kind an office, I sought, though trembling, to relieve him as well as I could. A shell ready fixed to a pole, which had been used by some Negroes, presented itself to me; filled it with water, and with trembling hands I guided it to the quivering lips of the wretched sufferer. Urged by the irresistible power of thirst, he endeavored to meet it, as he instinctively guessed its approach by the noise it made in passing through the bars of the cage. "Tankè, you whitè man, tankè you, putè somè poison and givè me." "How long have you been hanging there?" I asked him. "Two days, and me no die; the birds, the birds; aaah me!" Oppressed with the reflections which this shocking spectacle afforded me, I mustered strength enough to walk away, and soon reached the house at which I intended to dine. There I heard that the reason for this slave being thus punished was on account of his having killed the overseer of the plantation. They told me that the laws of self-preservation rendered such executions necessary; and supported the doctrine of slavery with the arguments generally made use of to justify the practice; with the repetition of which I shall not trouble you at present.

                                                                    Adieu.

From *Letter X. On Snakes; and on the Humming Bird*

*   *   *

As I was one day sitting solitary and pensive in my primitive arbor, my attention was engaged by a strange sort of rustling noise at some paces distant. I
looked all around without distinguishing anything, until I climbed one of my
great hemp stalks; when to my astonishment, I beheld two snakes of considerable length, the one pursuing the other with great celerity through a hemp
stubble field. The aggressor was of the black kind, six feet long; the fugitive
was a water snake, nearly of equal dimensions. They soon met, and in the fury
of their first encounter, they appeared in an instant firmly twisted together;
and whilst their united tails beat the ground, they mutually tried with open
jaws to lacerate each other. What a fell[6] aspect did they present! their heads
were compressed to a very small size, their eyes flashed fire; and after this
conflict had lasted about five minutes, the second found means to disengage
itself from the first, and hurried toward the ditch. Its antagonist instantly
assumed a new posture, and half creeping and half erect, with a majestic
mein, overtook and attacked the other again, which placed itself in the same
attitude, and prepared to resist. The scene was uncommon and beautiful; for
thus opposed they fought with their jaws, biting each other with the utmost
rage; but notwithstanding this appearance of mutual courage and fury, the
water snake still seemed desirous of retreating toward the ditch, its natural
element. This was no sooner perceived by the keen-eyed black one, than twisting its tail twice round a stalk of hemp, and seizing its adversary by the throat,
not by means of its jaws, but by twisting its own neck twice round that of the
water snake, pulled it back from the ditch. To prevent a defeat the latter took
hold likewise of a stalk on the bank, and by the acquisition of that point of
resistance became a match for its fierce antagonist. Strange was this to behold;
two great snakes strongly adhering to the ground mutually fastened together by
means of the writhings which lashed them to each other, and stretched at their
full length, they pulled but pulled in vain, and in the moments of greatest
exertions that part of their bodies which was entwined, seemed extremely
small, while the rest appeared inflated, and now and then convulsed with
strong undulations, rapidly following each other. Their eyes seemed on fire,
and ready to start out of their heads; at one time the conflict seemed decided;
the water-snake bent itself into two great folds, and by that operation rendered
the other more than commonly outstretched; the next minute the new struggles of the black one gained an unexpected superiority, it acquired two great
folds likewise, which necessarily extended the body of its adversary in proportion as it had contracted its own. These efforts were alternate; victory seemed
doubtful, inclining sometimes to the one side and sometimes to the other;
until at last the stalk to which the black snake fastened, suddenly gave way,
and in consequence of this accident they both plunged into the ditch. The
water did not extinguish their vindictive rage; for by their agitations I could
trace, though not distinguish their mutual attacks. They soon reappeared on
the surface twisted together, as in their first onset; but the black snake seemed
to retain its wonted superiority, for its head was exactly fixed above that of the
other, which it incessantly pressed down under the water, until it was stifled,
and sunk. The victor no sooner perceived its enemy incapable of farther resis-

6. Evil.

tance, than abandoning it to the current, it returned on shore and disappeared.

From *Letter XII. Distresses of a Frontier Man*

I wish for a change of place; the hour is come at last, that I must fly from my house and abandon my farm! But what course shall I steer, enclosed as I am? The climate best adapted to my present situation and humor[7] would be the polar regions, where six months day and six months night divide the dull year: nay, a simple Aurora Borealis would suffice me, and greatly refresh my eyes, fatigued now by so many disagreeable objects. The severity of those climates, that great gloom, where melancholy dwells, would be perfectly analogous to the turn of my mind. Oh, could I remove my plantation to the shores of the Oby, willingly would I dwell in the hut of a Samoyede,[8] with cheerfulness would I go and bury myself in the cavern of a Laplander. Could I but carry my family along with me, I would winter at Pello, or Tobolsky,[9] in order to enjoy the peace and innocence of that country. But let me arrive under the pole, or reach the antipodes,[1] I never can leave behind me the remembrance of the dreadful scenes to which I have been a witness; therefore never can I be happy! Happy, why would I mention that sweet, that enchanting word? Once happiness was our portion; now it is gone from us, and I am afraid not to be enjoyed again by the present generation! Whichever way I look, nothing but the most frightful precipices present themselves to my view, in which hundreds of my friends and acquaintances have already perished: of all animals that live on the surface of this planet, what is man when no longer connected with society; or when he finds himself surrounded by a convulsed and a half-dissolved one? He cannot live in solitude, he must belong to some community bound by some ties, however imperfect. Men mutually support and add to the boldness and confidence of each other; the weakness of each is strengthened by the force of the whole. I had never before these calamitous times formed any such ideas; I lived on, labored and prospered, without having ever studied on what the security of my life and the foundation of my prosperity were established: I perceived them just as they left me. Never was a situation so singularly terrible as mine, in every possible respect, as a member of an extensive society, as a citizen of an inferior division of the same society, as a husband, as a father, as a man who exquisitely feels for the miseries of others as well as for his own! But alas! so much is everything now subverted among us, that the very word misery, with which we were hardly acquainted before, no longer conveys the same ideas; or rather tired with feeling for the miseries of others, everyone feels now for himself alone. When I consider myself as connected in all these characters, as bound by so many cords, all uniting in my heart, I am seized with a fever of the mind, I am transported beyond that degree of calmness which is necessary to delineate our thoughts. I feel as if my reason wanted to leave me, as if it would burst its poor weak tenement: again I try to compose myself, I grow cool, and preconceiving the dreadful loss, I endeavor to retain the useful guest.

✻   ✻   ✻

7. Temperament.
8. Siberian nomadic inhabitants of the shores of the Arctic Ocean near Tobolsk. "Oby": river in Siberia.
9. In Siberia.
1. Places opposite to each other on the globe.

Must I then bid farewell to Britain, to that renowned country? Must I renounce a name so ancient and so venerable? Alas, she herself, that once indulgent parent, forces me to take up arms against her. She herself first inspired the most unhappy citizens of our remote districts with the thoughts of shedding the blood of those whom they used to call by the name of friends and brethren. That great nation which now convulses the world; which hardly knows the extent of her Indian kingdoms; which looks toward the universal monarchy of trade, of industry, of riches, of power: why must she strew our poor frontiers with the carcasses of her friends, with the wrecks of our insignificant villages, in which there is no gold? When, oppressed by painful recollection, I revolve all these scattered ideas in my mind; when I contemplate my situation, and the thousand streams of evil with which I am surrounded; when I descend into the particular tendency even of the remedy I have proposed, I am convulsed—convulsed sometimes to that degree, as to be tempted to exclaim—Why has the master of the world permitted so much indiscriminate evil throughout every part of this poor planet, at all times, and among all kinds of people? It ought surely to be the punishment of the wicked only. I bring that cup to my lips, of which I must soon taste, and shudder at its bitterness. What then is life, I ask myself, is it a gracious gift? No, it is too bitter; a gift means something valuable conferred, but life appears to be a mere accident, and of the worst kind: we are born to be victims of diseases and passions, of mischances and death: better not to be than to be miserable.—Thus impiously I roam, I fly from one erratic thought to another, and my mind, irritated by these acrimonious reflections, is ready sometimes to lead me to dangerous extremes of violence. When I recollect that I am a father, and a husband, the return of these endearing ideas strikes deep into my heart. Alas! they once made it to glow with pleasure and with every ravishing exultation; but now they fill it with sorrow. At other times, my wife industriously rouses me out of these dreadful meditations, and soothes me by all the reasoning she is mistress of; but her endeavors only serve to make me more miserable, by reflecting that she must share with me all these calamities, the bare apprehensions of which I am afraid will subvert her reason. Nor can I with patience think that a beloved wife, my faithful helpmate, throughout all my rural schemes, the principal hand which has assisted me in rearing the prosperous fabric of ease and independence I lately possessed, as well as my children, those tenants of my heart, should daily and nightly be exposed to such a cruel fate. Self-preservation is above all political precepts and rules, and even superior to the dearest opinions of our minds; a reasonable accommodation of ourselves to the various exigencies of the times in which we live is the most irresistible precept. To this great evil I must seek some sort of remedy adapted to remove or to palliate it; situated as I am, what steps should I take that will neither injure nor insult any of the parties, and at the same time save my family from that certain destruction which awaits it if I remain here much longer. Could I insure them bread, safety, and subsistence, not the bread of idleness, but that earned by proper labor as heretofore; could this be accomplished by the sacrifice of my life, I would willingly give it up. I attest before heaven that it is only for these I would wish to live and to toil: for these whom I have brought into this miserable existence. I resemble, methinks, one of the stones of a ruined arch, still retaining that pristine form that anciently fitted the place I occupied, but the center is tumbled down; I can be nothing until I am replaced, either in the former circle or in some stronger one. I see one on a smaller scale, and at a considerable distance, but it is within my power to reach it: and since I have ceased to consider myself as a member of the ancient state now convulsed, I willingly descend into an inferior one. I will revert into a state approaching nearer to that of nature, unencumbered either with voluminous laws or contradictory codes, often galling the very necks of those whom they protect; and at the same time sufficiently remote from the brutality of unconnected savage nature. Do you, my friend, perceive the path I have found out? it is that which leads to the tenants of the great ———— village of ————, where, far removed from the accursed neighborhood of Europeans, its inhabitants live with more ease, decency, and peace than you imagine: where, though governed by no laws, yet find, in uncontaminated simple manners all that laws can afford. Their system is sufficiently complete to answer all the primary wants of man and to constitute him a social being, such as he ought to be in the great forest of nature. There it is that I have resolved at any rate to transport myself and family: an eccentric thought, you may say, thus to cut asunder all former connections, and to form new ones with a people whom nature has stamped with such different characteristics! But as the happiness of my family is the only object of my wishes, I care very little where we be, or where we go, provided that we are safe and all united together.

٭   ٭   ٭

You may therefore, by means of anticipation, behold me under the Wigwam;[2] I am so well acquainted with the principal manners of these people, that I entertain not the least apprehension from them. I rely more securely on their strong hospitality than on the witnessed compacts of many Europeans. As soon as possible after my arrival, I design to build myself a wigwam, after the same manner and size with the rest, in order to avoid being thought singular, or giving occasion for any railleries; though these people are seldom guilty of such European follies. I shall erect it hard by the lands which they propose to allot me, and will endeavor that my wife, my children, and myself may be adopted soon after our arrival. Thus becoming truly inhabitants of their village, we shall immediately occupy that rank within the pale[3] of their society which will afford us all the amends we can possibly expect for the loss we have met with by the convulsions of our own. According to their customs we shall likewise receive names from them, by which we shall always be known. My youngest children shall learn to swim and to shoot with the bow, that they may acquire such talents as will necessarily raise them into some degree of esteem among the Indian lads of their own age; the rest of us must hunt with the hunters. I have been for several years an expert marksman; but I dread lest the imperceptible charm of Indian education may seize my younger children and give them such a propensity to that mode of life as may preclude their returning to the manners and customs of their parents. I have but one remedy to prevent this great evil; and that is, to employ them in the labor of the fields as much as I can; I am even resolved to make their daily subsistence depend altogether on it. As long as we keep ourselves busy in tilling the earth, there is no fear of any of us becoming wild; it is the chase and the food it procures that have this strange effect. Excuse a simile—those hogs which range in the

2. I.e., living as an American Indian. A wigwam is a hut or lodge, usually built of poles and covered with   skins, mats, or bark.
3. Bounds.

woods, and to whom grain is given once a week, preserve their former degree of tameness; but if, on the contrary, they are reduced to live on ground nuts, and on what they can get, they soon become wild and fierce. For my part, I can plow, sow, and hunt, as occasion may require; but my wife, deprived of wool and flax, will have no room for industry,[4] what is she then to do? like the other squaws, she must cook for us the nasaump, the ninchické,[5] and such other preparations of corn as are customary among these people. She must learn to bake squashes and pumpkins under the ashes; to slice and smoke the meat of our own killing, in order to preserve it; she must cheerfully adopt the manners and customs of her neighbors, in their dress, deportment, conduct, and internal economy, in all respects. Surely if we can have fortitude enough to quit all we have, to remove so far, and to associate with people so different from us, these necessary compliances are but part of the scheme. The change of garments, when those they carry with them are worn out, will not be the least of my wife's and daughter's concerns: though I am in hopes that self-love will invent some sort of reparation. Perhaps you would not believe that there are in the woods looking-glasses, and paint of every color; and that the inhabitants take as much pains to adorn their faces and their bodies, to fix their bracelets of silver, and plait their hair, as our forefathers the Picts[6] used to do in the time of the Romans. Not that I would wish to see either my wife or daughter adopt those savage customs; we can live in great peace and harmony with them without descending to every article; the interruption of trade hath, I hope, suspended this mode of dress. My wife understands inoculation[7] perfectly well, she inoculated all our children one after another, and has successfully performed the operation on several scores of people, who, scattered here and there through our woods, were too far removed from all medical assistance. If we can persuade but one family to submit to it, and it succeeds, we shall then be as happy as our situation will admit of; it will raise her into some degree of consideration, for whoever is useful in any society will always be respected. If we are so fortunate as to carry one family through a disorder, which is the plague among these people, I trust to the force of example, we shall then become truly necessary, valued, and beloved; we indeed owe every kind office to a society of men who so readily offer to admit us into their social partnership, and to extend to my family the shelter of their village, the strength of their adoption, and even the dignity of their names. God grant us a prosperous beginning, we may then hope to be of more service to them than even missionaries who have been sent to preach to them a Gospel they cannot understand.

As to religion, our mode of worship will not suffer much by this removal from a cultivated country, into the bosom of the woods; for it cannot be much simpler than that which we have followed here these many years: and I will with as much care as I can, redouble my attention, and twice a week, retrace to them the great outlines of their duty to God and to man. I will read and expound to them some part of the decalogue,[8] which is the method I have pursued ever since I married.

*   *   *

4. Household work.
5. Varieties of cornmeal mush; "nasaump" is more commonly known as *samp*.
6. Ancient people of northern Britain.

7. I.e., vaccination; the injection of a virus or bacterium into the body to establish immunity.
8. The Ten Commandments.

Thus then in the village of ———, in the bosom of that peace it has enjoyed ever since I have known it, connected with mild hospitable people, strangers to *our* political disputes, and having none among themselves; on the shores of a fine river, surrounded with woods, abounding with game; our little society united in perfect harmony with the new adoptive one, in which we shall be incorporated, shall rest I hope from all fatigues, from all apprehensions, from our present terrors, and from our long watchings. Not a word of politics shall cloud our simple conversation; tired either with the chase or the labor of the field, we shall sleep on our mats without any distressing want, having learnt to retrench every superfluous one: we shall have but two prayers to make to the Supreme Being, that He may shed His fertilizing dew on our little crops, and that He will be pleased to restore peace to our unhappy country. These shall be the only subject of our nightly prayers, and of our daily ejaculations:[9] and if the labor, the industry, the frugality, the union of men can be an agreeable offering to Him, we shall not fail to receive His paternal blessings. There I shall contemplate Nature in her most wild and ample extent; I shall carefully study a species of society, of which I have at present but very imperfect ideas; I will endeavor to occupy with propriety that place which will enable me to enjoy the few and sufficient benefits it confers. The solitary and unconnected mode of life I have lived in my youth must fit me for this trial, I am not the first who has attempted it; Europeans did not, it is true, carry to the wilderness numerous families; they went there as merely speculators; I, as a man seeking a refuge from the desolation of war. They went there to study the manner of the aborigines; I to conform to them, whatever they are; some went as visitors, as travelers; I as a sojourner, as a fellow hunter and laborer, go determined industriously to work up among them such a system of happiness as may be adequate to my future situation, and may be a sufficient compensation for all my fatigues and for the misfortunes I have borne: I have always found it at home, I may hope likewise to find it under the humble roof of my wigwam.

O Supreme Being! if among the immense variety of planets, inhabited by Thy creative power, Thy paternal and omnipotent care deigns to extend to all the individuals they contain; if it be not beneath Thy infinite dignity to cast Thy eye on us wretched mortals; if my future felicity is not contrary to the necessary effects of those secret causes which Thou hast appointed, receive the supplications of a man, to whom in Thy kindness Thou hast given a wife and an offspring: View us all with benignity, sanctify this strong conflict of regrets, wishes, and other natural passions; guide our steps through these unknown paths, and bless our future mode of life. If it is good and well meant, it must proceed from Thee; Thou knowest, O Lord, our enterprise contains neither fraud, nor malice, nor revenge. Bestow on me that energy of conduct now become so necessary, that it may be in my power to carry the young family Thou hast given me through this great trial with safety and in Thy peace. Inspire me with such intentions and such rules of conduct as may be most acceptable to Thee. Preserve, O God, preserve the companion of my bosom, the best gift Thou hast given me: endue her with courage and strength sufficient to accomplish this perilous journey. Bless the children of our love, those portions of our hearts; I implore Thy divine assistance, speak to their tender minds, and inspire them with the love of that virtue which alone can serve as

9. Prayers.

the basis of their conduct in this world, and of their happiness with Thee. Restore peace and concord to our poor afflicted country, assuage the fierce storm which has so long ravaged it. Permit, I beseech Thee, O Father of Nature, that our ancient virtues, and our industry, may not be totally lost: and that as a reward for the great toils we have made on this new land, we may be restored to our ancient tranquillity, and enabled to fill it with successive generations, that will constantly thank Thee for the ample subsistence Thou hast given them.

The unreserved manner in which I have written must give you a convincing proof of that friendship and esteem, of which I am sure you never yet doubted. As members of the same society, as mutually bound by the ties of affection and old acquaintance, you certainly cannot avoid feeling for my distresses; you cannot avoid mourning with me over that load of physical and moral evil with which we are all oppressed. My own share of it I often overlook when I minutely contemplate all that hath befallen our native country.

c. 1769–80   1782

JOHN ADAMS   ABIGAIL ADAMS
1735–1826   1744–1818

Abigail Smith and John Adams were married on October 25, 1764, and they remained partners in marriage until Abigail's death fifty-four years later. She was the daughter of a wealthy Congregational minister from Weymouth, Massachusetts, on the South Shore, and he—a man who was to become second president of the United States—the son of a farmer from nearby Braintree (now a part of Quincy, Massachusetts). Abigail had no formal schooling of any kind because, as she often explained, she was frequently ill as a child. Although this was undoubtedly true, she observed in later years that girls and boys in her youth were not treated equally and that "daughters" were "wholly neglected in point of Literature." She grew up in her grandmother's house where "instruction and amusement" were blended together. With a remarkable native intelligence, easy access to her father's library, and a good ear for assimilating conversation heard in a parsonage, she could boast of a superior mind in spite of her remarkable spelling. She did not ever suffer fools gladly and seems early in life to have understood how politicians get ahead in the world.

John Adams graduated from Harvard College in the class of 1755. He taught school for a short time in Worcester, but the role of the teacher and the preacher were too closely joined for his taste and he was made uncomfortable by association with any "frigid" Calvinism. He took up the study of law, instead, and was admitted to the Boston bar in 1758. He met Abigail the following year. Although he preferred a country to a city law practice and treasured his Braintree farm, he found it impossible to support a growing family (the Adamses had four children) on a country clientele. In 1768 they moved to Boston. John Adams's earlier opposition to the Stamp Act of 1765 and his defense of Massachusetts radicals like John Hancock identified him as one who would support the cause of independence, and in June 1774 he was elected as a Massachusetts delegate to the first Congress of the colonies, scheduled to meet in Philadelphia, later known as the First Continental Congress. He left Braintree on August 10, and for the next twenty-six years, ten of them spent abroad, he was a famous and sometimes controversial figure in American public life. He was elected vice president for two terms (1788 and 1792) and president in 1796. After losing the election of 1800 to Thomas Jefferson, he retired to Braintree at last, anxious to lead the Arcadian life he spoke so wistfully about while holding public office. It was Abigail, as usual, who oversaw the daily life of the farm: she was always an astute manager of money, property, animals, and people.

From the time that John Adams left Massachusetts in 1774 until he returned from Paris in 1783, more than three hundred letters passed between this couple. They were lovingly saved and many of them were published by their grandson in the middle of the nineteenth century. They provide not only an extraordinary document of a long and happy marriage, but a vivid portrait of a nation seeking its identity.

From The Letters of John and Abigail Adams[1]

Abigail Adams to John Adams

[CLASSICAL PARALLELS]

Braintree August 19 1774

The great distance between us, makes the time appear very long to me. It seems already a month since you left me.[2] The great anxiety I feel for my Country, for you and for our family renders the day tedious, and the night unpleasant. The Rocks and quick Sands appear upon every Side. What course you can or will take is all wrapt in the Bosom of futurity. Uncertainty and expectation leave the mind great Scope. Did ever any Kingdom or State regain their Liberty, when once it was invaded without Blood shed? I cannot think of it without horror.

Yet we are told that all the Misfortunes of Sparta[3] were occasiond by their too great Sollicitude for present tranquility, and by an excessive love of peace they neglected the means of making it sure and lasting. They ought to have reflected says Polibius[4] that as there is nothing more desirable, or advantages than peace, when founded in justice and honour, so there is nothing more shameful and at the same time more pernicious when attained by bad measures, and purchased at the price of liberty.

I have received a most charming Letter from our Friend Mrs. W[arre]n.[5] She desires me to tell you that her best wishes attend you thro your journey both as a Friend and patriot—hopes you will have no uncommon difficulties to surmount or Hostile Movements to impeade you—but if the Locrians should interrupt you, she hop[e]s you will beware that no future Annals may say you chose an ambitious Philip for your Leader, who subverted the noble order of the American Amphyctions, and built up a Monarchy on the Ruins of the happy institution.[6]

---

1. The text used here is taken from *Adams Family Correspondence*, 2 vols., edited by L. H. Butterfield (1963). The original spelling remains unchanged. Words in angle brackets, identify the writer's earlier choice of a word.
2. In June 1774, John was chosen as one of five delegates from Massachusetts to the Continental Congress to be held in Philadelphia. He left Braintree, Massachusetts (now Quincy), on August 10. Massachusetts was in a state of near-rebellion.
3. When Philip of Macedon (see n. 6, below) invaded Greece, the Greek citizens of the city of Sparta were concerned only with protecting their own territory, and

as a consequence the country fell.
4. Polybius (205?–?125 B.C.), Greek historian and author of a history of Rome.
5. Mercy Otis Warren (1728–1814), well known as a correspondent and friend of the leading political figures of her day; wife of James Warren (1726–1808).
6. Philip II, king of Macedon (382–336 B.C.) transformed democratic Greece into a monarchy. In 338 B.C. he invaded Greece under the pretext that the Locrian town of Amphissa had resisted the authority of a neighboring council of states known as the Amphictyonic League.

I have taken a very great fondness for reading Rollin's ancient History[7] since you left me. I am determined to go thro with it if possible in these my days of solitude. I find great pleasure and entertainment from it, and I have perswaided Johnny[8] to read me a page or two every day, and hope he will from his desire to oblige me entertain a fondness for it.—We have had a charming rain which lasted 12 hours and has greatly revived the dying fruits of the earth.

I want much to hear from you. I long impatiently to have you upon the Stage of action. The first of September or the month of September, perhaps may be of as much importance to Great Britan as the Ides of March were to Ceaser.[9] I wish you every Publick as well, as private blessing, and that wisdom which is profitable both for instruction and edification to conduct you in this difficult day.—The little flock remember Pappa, and kindly wish to see him. So does your most affectionate

Abigail Adams

1774   1848

John Adams to Abigail Adams

[NEWS, LOVE, AND ADVICE FROM PRINCETON]

Prince Town New Jersey Aug. 28th. 1774

My Dr.[1]

I received your kind Letter, at New York, and it is not easy for you to imagine the Pleasure it has given me. I have not found a single Opportunity to write since I left Boston, excepting by the Post and I dont choose to write by that Conveyance, for fear of foul Play.[2] But as We are now within forty two Miles of Philadelphia, I hope there to find some private Hand by which I can convey this.

The Particulars of our Journey, I must reserve, to be communicated after my Return. It would take a Volume to describe the whole. It has been upon the whole an Agreable Jaunt, We have had Opportunities to see the World, and to form Acquaintances with the most eminent and famous Men, in the several Colonies we have passed through. We have been treated with unbounded Civility, Complaisance,[3] and Respect.

We Yesterday visited Nassau Hall Colledge,[4] and were politely treated by the Schollars, Tutors, Professors and President, whom We are, this Day to hear preach. Tomorrow We reach the Theatre of Action.[5] God Almighty grant us Wisdom and Virtue sufficient for the high Trust that is devolved upon Us. The Spirit of the People wherever we have been seems to be very favourable. They universally consider our Cause as their own, and express the firmest Resolution, to abide the Determination of the Congress.

I am anxious for our perplexed, distressed Province—hope they will be directed into the right Path. Let me intreat you, my Dear, to make yourself as easy and quiet as possible. Resignation to the Will of Heaven is our only Resource in such dangerous Times. Prudence and Caution should be our

7. Charles Rollin (1661–1741) was rector of the University of Paris. John owned the 5th edition (1768) of his *Ancient History*.
8. Their seven-year-old son.
9. Julius Caesar's (d. 44 B.C.) death fell, as predicted, on the Ides of March. In the ancient Roman calendar the Ides fell on the fifteenth of March, May, July, and October, and on the thirteenth of the remaining months.

1. Dear.
2. Letters carried by post (relays of horses and riders) were sometimes stolen and their contents published.
3. Courtesy.
4. Now Princeton University.
5. Philadelphia.

Guides. I have the strongest Hopes, that We shall yet see a clearer Sky, and better Times.

Remember my tender Love to my little Nabby.[6] Tell her she must write me a Letter and inclose it in the next you send. I am charmed with your Amusement with our little Johnny. Tell him I am glad to hear he is so good a Boy as to read to his Mamma, for her Entertainment, and to keep himself out of the Company of rude Children. Tell him I hope to hear a good Account of his Accidence and Nomenclature,[7] when I return. Kiss my little Charley and Tommy for me.[8] Tell them I shall be at Home by November, but how much sooner I know not.

Remember me to all enquiring Friends—particularly to Uncle Quincy, your Pappa and Family, and Dr. Tufts and Family. Mr. Thaxter,[9] I hope, is a good Companion, in your Solitude. Tell him, if he devotes his Soul and Body to his Books, I hope, notwithstanding the Darkness of these Days, he will not find them unprofitable Sacrifices in future.

I have received three very obliging Letters, from Tudor, Trumble, and Hill.[1] They have cheared us, in our Wanderings, and done us much Service.

My Compliments to Mr. Wibirt and Coll. Quincy,[2] when you see them.

Your Account of the Rain refreshed me. I hope our Husbandry[3] is prudently and industriously managed. Frugality must be our Support. Our Expences, in this Journey, will be very great—our only Reward will be the consolatory Reflection that We toil, spend our Time, and tempt Dangers for the public Good—happy indeed, if we do any good!

The Education of our Children is never out of my Mind. Train them to Virtue, habituate them to industry, activity, and Spirit. Make them consider every Vice, as shamefull and unmanly: fire them with Ambition to be usefull—make them disdain to be destitute of any usefull, or ornamental Knowledge or Accomplishment. Fix their Ambition upon great and solid Objects, and their Contempt upon little, frivolous, and useless ones. It is Time, my dear, for you to begin to teach them French. Every Decency, Grace, and Honesty should be inculcated upon them.

I have [kept] a few Minutes by Way of Journal, which shall be your Entertainment when I come home, but We have had so many Persons and so various Characters to converse with, and so many Objects to view, that I have not been able to be so particular as I could wish.—I am, with the tenderest Affection and Concern, your wandering

John Adams

1774   1875

6. Their nine-year-old daughter, Abigail (1765–1846).
7. (Knowledge of) inflectional endings and parts of speech.
8. Charles Adams (1770–1800) and Thomas Boylston Adams (1772–1832).
9. John Thaxter, Jr. (1755–1791), John's law clerk. Dr. Cotton Tufts (1732–1815), a cousin of Abigail's and an uncle by marriage.

1. All clerks in John's Boston law office. John Trumbull (1750–1831) went on to a distinguished career in law and letters.
2. Rev. Anthony Wibird (1729–1800) was the minister of the First Church in Braintree. Col. Josiah Quincy (1710–1784) lived in the Wollaston section of Quincy, Massachusetts.
3. Agriculture.

John Adams to Abigail Adams

[PRAYERS AT THE CONGRESS]

Phyladelphia Septr. 16. 1774

Having a Leisure Moment, while the Congress is assembling, I gladly embrace it to write you a Line.

When the Congress first met, Mr. Cushing[4] made a Motion, that it should be opened with Prayer. It was opposed by Mr. Jay of N. York and Mr. Rutledge[5] of South Carolina, because we were so divided in religious Sentiments, some Episcopalians, some Quakers, some Anabaptists, some Presbyterians, and some Congregationalists, so that We could not join in the same Act of Worship.—Mr. S. Adams[6] arose and said he was no Bigot, and could hear a Prayer from a Gentleman of Piety and Virtue, who was at the same Time a Friend to his Country. He was a Stranger in Phyladelphia, but had heard that Mr. Duchè[7] (Dushay they pronounce it) deserved that Character, and therefore he moved that Mr. Duchè, an episcopal Clergyman, might be desired, to read Prayers to the Congress, tomorrow Morning. The Motion was seconded and passed in the Affirmative. Mr. Randolph our President, waited on[8] Mr. Duchè, and received for Answer that if his Health would permit, he certainly would. Accordingly next Morning he appeared with his Clerk and in his Pontificallibus, and read several Prayers, in the established Form;[9] and then read the Collect for the seventh day of September, which was the Thirty fifth Psalm.[1]—You must remember this was the next Morning after we heard the horrible Rumour, of the Cannonade[2] of Boston.—I never saw a greater Effect upon an Audience. It seemed as if Heaven had ordained that Psalm to be read on that Morning.

After this Mr. Duchè, unexpected to every Body struck out into an extemporary Prayer, which filled the Bosom of every Man present. I must confess I never heard a better Prayer or one, so well pronounced. Episcopalian as he is, Dr. Cooper[3] himself never prayed with such fervour, such Ardor, such Earnestness and Pathos, and in Language so elegant and sublime—for America, for the Congress, for The Province of Massachusetts Bay, and especially the Town of Boston. It has had an excellent Effect upon every Body here.

I must beg you to read that Psalm. If there was any Faith in the sortes Virgilianæ, or sortes Homericæ, or especially the Sortes biblicæ, it would be thought providential.[4]

It will amuse your Friends to read this Letter and the 35th. Psalm to them. Read it to your Father and Mr. Wibirt.—I wonder what our Braintree Churchmen would think of this?—Mr. Duchè is one of the most ingenious[5]

4. Thomas Cushing (1725–1788), a Massachusetts delegate to the Continental Congress.
5. John Jay (1745–1829), jurist. John Rutledge (1739–1800), later governor of South Carolina.
6. Samuel Adams (1722–1803), a Massachusetts patriot.
7. Rev. Jacob Duché (1737–1798) assistant rector of Christ Church and St. Peter's in Philadelphia. He later supported the Crown and fled to England.
8. Made a formal call on. Peyton Randolph (1721?–1775), from Virginia, was president of the Continental Congress.
9. I.e., in the form set down by the Church of England. "Pontificallibus": priestly attire.
1. "Plead my cause, O Lord, with them that strive with me: fight against them that fight against me" (Psalm 35.1). "Collect": the prayer assigned to be read before the Epistle.
2. Bombardment.
3. Samuel Cooper (1725–1783), minister of the Brattle Street Church, Boston.
4. The Bible and the works of the Roman poet Virgil (70–19 B.C.) and of the Greek epic poet Homer were thought to have magical properties: a passage read by "sortes" (lot) had relevance to one's life and future.
5. Showing discernment.

Men, and best Characters, and greatest orators in the Episcopal order, upon this Continent—Yet a Zealous Friend of Liberty and his Country.

I long to see my dear Family. God bless, preserve and prosper it. Adieu.

John Adams

1774   1875

John Adams to Abigail Adams

[THE BUSINESS OF THE CONGRESS IS TEDIOUS]

Phyladelphia Octr. 9. 1774

My Dear

I am wearied to Death with the Life I lead. The Business of the Congress is tedious, beyond Expression. This Assembly is like no other that ever existed. Every Man in it is a great Man—an orator, a Critick, a statesman, and therefore every Man upon every Question must shew his oratory, his Criticism, and his Political Abilities.

The Consequence of this is, that Business is drawn and spun out to an immeasurable Length. I believe if it was moved and seconded that We should come to a Resolution that Three and two make five We should be entertained with Logick and Rhetorick, Law, History, Politicks and Mathematicks, concerning the Subject for two whole Days, and then We should pass the Resolution unanimously in the Affirmative.

The perpetual Round of feasting too, which we are obliged to submit to, make the Pilgrimage more tedious to me.

This Day I went to Dr. Allisons[6] Meeting in the Forenoon and heard the Dr.—a good Discourse upon the Lords Supper. This is a Presbyterian Meeting. I confess I am not fond of the Presbyterian Meetings in this Town. I had rather go to Church.[7] We have better Sermons, better Prayers, better Speakers, softer, sweeter Musick, and genteeler Company. And I must confess, that the Episcopal Church is quite as agreable to my Taste as the Presbyterian. They are both Slaves to the Domination of the Priesthood. I like the Congregational Way best—next to that the Independant.[8]

This afternoon, led by Curiosity and good Company I strolled away to Mother Church, or rather Grandmother Church, I mean the Romish Chappell.[9] Heard a good, short, moral Essay upon the Duty of Parents to their Children, founded in Justice and Charity, to take care of their Interests temporal and spiritual. This Afternoons Entertainment was to me, most awful[1] and affecting. The poor Wretches, fingering their Beads, chanting Latin, not a Word of which they understood, their Pater Nosters and Ave Maria's.[2] Their holy Water—their Crossing themselves perpetually—their Bowing to the Name of Jesus, wherever they hear it—their Bowings, and Kneelings, and Genuflections before the Altar. The Dress of the Priest was rich with Lace—his Pulpit was Velvet and Gold. The Altar Piece was very rich—little Images and Crucifixes about—Wax Candles lighted up. But how shall I describe the Picture of our Saviour in a Frame of Marble over the Altar at full Length upon the Cross, in the Agonies, and the Blood dropping and streaming from his Wounds.

6. Francis Alison (1705–1779), minister of the First Presbyterian Church in Philadelphia.
7. I.e., to a Congregational church. Adams preferred a church not too Calvinist in temper.
8. Here Baptist or "Separate."
9. St. Mary's Church, built in 1763.
1. Appalling and disturbing.
2. Our Fathers and Hail Marys.

The Musick consisting of an organ, and a Choir of singers, went all the Afternoon, excepting sermon Time, and the Assembly chanted—most sweetly and exquisitely.

Here is every Thing which can lay hold of the Eye, Ear, and Imagination. Every Thing which can charm and bewitch the simple and ignorant. I wonder how Luther[3] ever broke the spell.

Adieu.

John Adams

1774   1875

Abigail Adams to John Adams

[THE FIRST SCENE OF THE INFERNAL PLOT DISCLOSED]

Braintree october 16 1774

My Much Loved Friend

I dare not express to you at 300 hundred miles distance how ardently I long for your return. I have some very miserly Wishes; and cannot consent to your spending one hour in Town till at least I have had you 12. The Idea plays about my Heart, unnerves my hand whilst I write, awakens all the tender sentiments that years have encreased and matured, and which when with me were every day dispensing to you.[4] The whole collected stock of ⟨nine⟩ ten weeks absence knows not how to brook[5] any longer restraint, but will break forth and flow thro my pen. May the like sensations enter thy breast, and (in spite of all the weighty cares of State) Mingle themselves with those I wish to communicate, for in giving them utterance I have felt more sincere pleasure than I have known since the 10 of August.[6]—Many have been the anxious hours I have spent since that day—the threatning aspect of our publick affairs, the complicated distress of this province, the Arduous and perplexed Business in which you are engaged, have all conspired to agitate my bosom, with fears and apprehensions to which I have heretofore been [a] stranger, and far from thinking the Scene closed, it looks [as] tho the curtain was but just drawn and only the first Scene of the infernal plot disclosed and whether the end will be tragical Heaven alone knows. You cannot be, I know, nor do I wish to see you an inactive Spectator, but if the Sword be drawn I bid adieu to all domestick felicity, and look forward to that Country where there is neither wars nor rumors of War in a firm belief that thro the mercy of its Kings we shall both rejoice there together.

I greatly fear that the arm of treachery and violence is lifted over us as a Scourge and heavy punishment from heaven for our numerous offences, and for the misimprovement of our great advantages. If we expect to inherit the blessings of our Fathers, we should return a little more to their primitive Simplicity of Manners, and not sink into inglorious ease. We have too many high sounding words, and too few actions that correspond with them. I have spent one Sabbeth in Town since you left me. I saw no difference in respect to ornaments, &c. &c. but in the Country you must look for that virtue, of which you find but small Glimerings in the Metropolis. Indeed they have not the advantages, nor the resolution to encourage our own Manufactories which

---

3. Martin Luther (1483–1546), the founder of Protestantism.
4. I.e., being dispensed to you.

5. Tolerate.
6. When John left Braintree for Philadelphia.

people in the country have. To the Mercantile part, tis considerd as throwing away their own Bread; but they must retrench their expenses and be content with a small share of gain for they will find but few who will wear their Livery. As for me I will seek wool and flax and work willingly with my Hands, and indeed their is occasion for all our industry and economy.

You mention the removal of our Books &c. from Boston.[7] I believe they are safe there, and it would incommode the Gentlemen to remove them, as they would not then have a place to repair to for study. I suppose they would not chuse to be at the expence of bording out. Mr. Williams I believe keeps pretty much with his mother. Mr. Hills father had some thoughts of removing up to Braintree provided he could be accommodated with a house, which he finds very difficult.

Mr. Cranch's[8] last determination was to tarry in Town unless any thing new takes place. His Friends in Town oppose his Removal so much that he is determined to stay. The opinion you have entertaind of General Gage[9] is I believe just, indeed he professes to act only upon the Defensive. The People in the Co[untr]y begin to be very anxious for the congress to rise.[1] They have no idea of the Weighty Buisness you have to transact, and their Blood boils with indignation at the Hostile prepairations they are constant Witnesses of. Mr. Quincys so secret departure is Matter of various Specculation—some say he is deputed by the congress, others that he is gone to Holland, and the Tories says he is gone to be hanged.[2]

I rejoice at the favourable account you give me of your Health; May it be continued to you. My Health is much better than it was last fall. Some folks say I grow very fat.—I venture to write most any thing in this Letter, because I know the care of the Bearer. He will be most sadly disappointed if you should be broke up before he arrives, as he is very desirous of being introduced by you to a Number of Gentlemen of respectable characters. I almost envy him, that he should see you, before I can.

Mr. Thaxter and Rice[3] present their Regards to you. Unkle Quincy too sends his Love to you, he is very good to call and see me, and so have many other of my Friends been. Coll. Warren and Lady were here a monday, and send their Love to you. The Coll. promiss'd to write. Mrs. Warren will spend a Day or two on her return with me. I told Betsy to write to you. She says she would if you were her *Husband*.

Your Mother sends her Love to you, and all your family too numerous to name desire to be rememberd. You will receive Letters from two, who are as earnest to write to Pappa as if the welfare of a kingdom depended upon it. If you can give any guess within a month let me know when you think of returning to Your most Affectionate

Abigail Adams

1774   1848

7. The Adamses maintained a house in Boston, where John's law clerks Williams and Hills were resident.
8. Richard Cranch (1726–1811), Abigail's brother-in-law.
9. General Thomas Gage (1721–1787) was the British governor of Massachusetts in 1774. He left Boston in

1775.
1. Adjourn.
2. Josiah Quincy, Jr. (1744–1775), a lawyer, sailed secretly to England to argue the American cause to British friendly to the colonies.
3. John Thaxter, Jr. and Nathan Rice, law clerks.

Abigail Adams to John Adams

[CONTINUAL EXPECTATION OF HOSTILITIES]

June 25 1775 Braintree

Dearest Friend

My Father has been more affected with the distruction of Charlstown,[4] than with any thing which has heretofore taken place. Why should not his countanance be sad when the city, the place of his Fathers Sepulchers lieth waste, and the gates thereof are consumed with fire, scarcly one stone remaineth upon an other. But in the midst of sorrow we have abundant cause of thankfulness that so few of our Breathren are numberd with the slain, whilst our enimies were cut down like the Grass before the Sythe. But one officer of all the Welch fuzelers[5] remains to tell his story. Many poor wretches dye for want of proper assistance and care of their wounds.

Every account agrees in 14 and 15 hundred slain and wounded upon their side nor can I learn that they dissemble the number themselves. We had some Heroes that day who fought with amazing intrepidity, and courage—

> "Extremity is the trier of Spirits—
> Common chances common men will bear;
> And when the Sea is calm all boats alike
> Shew mastership in floating, but fortunes blows
> When most struck home, being bravely warded, crave
> A noble cunning."   *Shakespear.*[6]

I hear that General *How* should say the Battle upon the plains of Abram was but a Bauble[7] to this. When we consider all the circumstances attending this action we stand astonished that our people were not all cut of. They had but one hundred foot intrenched, the number who were engaged, did not exceed 800, and they [had] not half amunition enough. The reinforcements not able to get to them seasonably, the tide was up and high, so that their floating batteries[8] came upon each side of the causway and their row gallies keeping a continual fire. Added to this the fire from fort hill and from the Ship, the Town in flames all around them and the heat from the flames so intence as scarcely to be borne; the day one of the hottest we have had this season and the wind blowing the smoke in their faces—only figure to yourself all these circumstances, and then consider that we do not count 60 Men lost. My Heart overflows at the recollection.

We live in continual Expectation of Hostilities. Scarcely a day that does not produce some, but like Good Nehemiah[9] having made our prayer with God, and set the people with their Swords, their Spears and their bows we will say unto them, Be not affraid of them. Remember the Lord who is great and

---

4. Rev. William Smith (1707–1783) lived in Weymouth, Massachusetts. The Battle of Bunker Hill and the burning of Charlestown began on Saturday, June 7, 1775.
5. Soldiers armed with flintlock muskets.
6. Incorrectly quoted from William Shakespeare's (1564–1616) tragedy *Coriolanus* (4.1.3–9). The lines are

> You were us'd
> To say extremities was the trier of spirits,
> That common chances common men could bear,
> That when the sea was calm all boats alike
> Show'd mastership in floating; fortunes' blows

> When most strook home, being gentle wounded
>   craves
> A noble cunning.

7. Trifle. General Sir William Howe (1729–1814), British commander-in-chief in America. The Plains of Abraham, in Quebec, was the site of a great battle (1759) in which General Wolfe defeated the French led by General Montcalm during the French and Indian War.
8. Warships.
9. Nehemiah 4.14. During the Babylonian captivity, Nehemiah returned to Jerusalem and caused the wall to be rebuilt.

terrible, and fight for your Breathren, your sons and your daughters, your wives and your houses.

I have just received yours of the 17 of june in 7 days only. Every line from that far Country is precious. You do not tell me how you do, but I will hope better. Alass you little thought what distress we were in the day you wrote. They delight in molesting us upon the Sabbeth. Two Sabbeths we have been in such Alarms that we have had no meeting. This day we have set under our own vine in quietness, have heard Mr. Taft, from psalms. "The Lord is good to all and his tender mercies are over all his works"[1] The good man was earnest and pathetick. I could forgive his weakness for the sake of his sincerity—but I long for a *Cooper* and an *Elliot*.[2] I want a person who has feeling and sensibility who can take one up with him

"And in his Duty prompt at every call
Can watch, and weep, and pray, and feel for all."

Mr. Rice joins General Heaths regiment to morrow as adjutant.[3] Your Brother is very desirous of being in the army, but your good Mother is really voilent against it. I cannot persuaid nor reason her into a consent. Neither he nor I dare let her know that he is trying for a place. My Brother has a Captains commission, and is stationd at Cambridge.[4] I thought you had the best of inteligence[5] or I should have taken pains to have been more perticuliar. As to Boston, there are many persons yet there who would be glad to get out if they could. Mr. Boylstone and Mr. Gill the printer with his family are held upon the black list tis said. Tis certain they watch them so narrowly that they cannot escape, nor your Brother Swift and family.[6] Mr. Mather[7] got out a day or two before Charlstown was distroyed, and had lodged his papers and what else he got out at Mr. Carys, but they were all consumed. So were many other peoples, who thought they might trust their little there; till teams could be procured to remove them. The people from the Alms house and work house were sent to the lines last week, to make room for their wounded they say. Medford people are all removed. Every sea port seems in motion.—O North![8] may the Groans and cryes of the injured and oppressed Harrow up thy Soul. We have a prodigious Army, but we lack many accomadations which we need. I hope the apointment of these new Generals will give satisfaction. They must be proof against calumny. In a contest like this continual reports are circulated by our Enimies, and they catch with the unwary and the gaping croud who are ready to listen to the marvellous, without considering of consequences even tho there best Friends are injured.—I have not venturd to inquire one word of you about your return. I do not know whether I ought to wish for it— it seems as if your sitting together was absolutely necessary whilst every day is big[9] with Events.

Mr. Bowdoin called a fryday and took his leave of me desiring I would

1. Rev. Moses Taft (n.d.), a minister from Randolph, Massachusetts, took Psalm 145, verse 9, as the subject for his sermon.
2. Rev. Samuel Cooper (1725–1783), a famous Boston pulpit orator. Rev. Andrew Eliot (1718–1778), who served as pastor of the New North Church, Boston.
3. John's brother Peter Boylston Adams (1738–1823) lived with their widowed mother. Nathan Rice (n.d.), John's law clerk. Major General William Heath (1737–1814), of the Continental Army. "Adjutant": staff officer.
4. Abigail's brother was William Smith, Jr. (1746–1787).

5. News.
6. Thomas Boylston (1721–1798), first cousin of John's mother and a merchant. John Gill (n.d.) was the printer of the *Boston Gazette*. Samuel Swift was a brother lawyer and not a relative of John's. Blacklisted persons were suspected of subversion.
7. Rev. Samuel Mather (1706–1785), last of the Mather dynasty of Boston preachers, minister of the Tenth Congregational Society, Boston.
8. Lord North, prime minister of England (1770–1782), whose ruinous policies toward the colonies provoked the Revolution.
9. Pregnant.

present his affectionate regards to you. I have hopes that he will recover—he has mended a good deal. He wished he could have staid in Braintree, but his Lady was fearful.[1]

I have often heard that fear makes people loving. I never was so much noticed *by some people* as I have been since you went out of Town, or rather since the 19 of April. Mr. W[inslo]ws family are determined to be sociable. Mr. A———n are quite Friendly.—Nabby Johny Charly Tommy all send duty. Tom says I wish I could see *par*. You would laugh to see them all run upon the sight of a Letter—like chickens for a crum, when the Hen clucks. Charls says *mar* What is it any good news? and who is for us and who against us, is the continual inquiry.—Brother and Sister Cranch send their Love. He has been very well since he removed, for him, and has full employ in his Buisness. Unkel Quincy calls to hear most every day, and as for the Parson, he determines I shall not make the same complaint I did last time, for he comes every other day.

Tis exceeding dry weather. We have not had any rain for a long time. Bracket[2] has mowed the medow and over the way, but it will not be a last years crop.—Pray let me hear from you by every opportunity till I have the joy of once more meeting you. Yours ever more,

Portia[3]

P.S. Tell Bass[4] his father and family are well.

1775   1848

From *Abigail Adams to John Adams*

[OUR GENERALS. NEWS OF BOSTON AND HOME]

Braintree July 16 1775

Dearest Friend

I have this afternoon had the pleasure of receiving your Letter by your Friends Mr. Collins and Kaighn[5] and an English Gentle man his Name I do not remember. It was next to seeing my dearest Friend. Mr. Collins could tell me more perticuliarly about you and your Health than I have been able to hear since you left me. I rejoice in his account of your better Health, and of your spirits, tho he says I must not expect to see you till next spring. I hope he does not speak the truth. I know (I think I do, for am not I your Bosome Friend?) your feelings, your anxieties, your exertions, &c. more than those before whom you are obliged to wear the face of chearfulness.

I have seen your Letters to Col. Palmer and Warren.[6] I pity your Embaresments. How difficult the task to quench out the fire and the pride of private ambition, and to sacrifice ourselfs and all our hopes and expectations to the publick weal. How few have souls capable of so noble an undertaking—how often are the lawrels[7] worn by those who have had no share in earning them, but there is a future recompence of reward to which the upright man looks, and which he will most assuredly obtain provided he perseveres unto the

1. James Bowdoin (1726–1790) and his wife, Elizabeth. Bowdoin excused himself from serving in the Continental Congress.
2. The Adamses' farmhand.
3. The favorite pen name of Abigail's after her marriage to John. She took the name from the heroine-lawyer of Shakespeare's *Merchant of Venice*.
4. Joseph Bass, John's servant in Philadelphia. He was

a shoemaker from Braintree.
5. Stephen Collins (n.d.) and John Kaighn (or Cain) (n.d.) were Quakers from Philadelphia.
6. Deacon Joseph Palmer (1716–1788) was promoted to general in the Revolution. For James Warren, see n. 5, p. 684.
7. The reward for victory in classical times.

end.—The appointment of the Generals Washington and Lee,[8] gives universal satisfaction. The people have the highest opinion of Lees abilities, but you know the continuation of the popular Breath, depends much upon favorable events.

I had the pleasure of seeing both the Generals and their Aid de camps soon after their arrival and of being personally made known to them. They very politely express their regard for you. Major Miflin said he had orders from you to visit me at Braintree. I told him I should be very happy to see him there, and accordingly sent Mr. Thaxter to Cambridge with a card to him and Mr. Read[9] to dine with me. Mrs. Warren and her Son were to be with me. They very politely received the Message and lamented that they were not able to upon account of Expresses[1] which they were that day to get in readiness to send of.

I was struck with General Washington. You had prepaired me to entertain a favorable opinion of him, but I thought the one half was not told me. Dignity with ease, and complacency, the Gentleman and Soldier look agreably blended in him. Modesty marks every line and feture of his face. Those lines of Dryden[2] instantly occurd to me

> "Mark his Majestick fabrick! he's a temple
> Sacred by birth, and built by hands divine
> His Souls the Deity that lodges there.
> Nor is the pile unworthy of the God."

General Lee looks like a careless hardy Veteran and from his appearance brought to my mind his namesake Charls the 12, king of Sweeden.[3] The Elegance of his pen far exceeds that of his person. I was much pleased with your Friend Collins. I persuaded them to stay coffe with me, and he was as unreserved and social as if we had been old acquaintances, and said he was very loth to leave the house. I would have detaind them till morning, but they were very desirous of reaching Cambridge.

You have made often and frequent complaints that your Friends do not write to you. I have stired up some of them. Dr. Tufts, Col. Quincy, Mr. Tudor, Mr. Thaxter all have wrote you now, and a Lady[4] whom I am willing you should value preferable to all others save one. May not I in my turn make complaints? All the Letters I receive from you seem to be wrote in so much haste, that they scarcely leave room for a social feeling. They let me know that you exist, but some of them contain scarcely six lines. I want some sentimental Effusions of the Heart. I am sure you are not destitute of them or are they all absorbed in the great publick. Much is due to that I know, but being part of the whole I lay claim to a Larger Share than I have had. You used to be more communicative a Sundays. I always loved a Sabeth days letter, for then you had a greater command of your time—but hush to all complaints.

I am much surprized that you have not been more accurately informd of what passes in the camps. As to intelegance from Boston, tis but very seldom we are able to collect any thing that may be relied upon, and to report the

8. George Washington (1732–1799), commander-in-chief of the American forces. Major General Charles Lee (1731–1782) of the Continental Army. Lee was later severely criticized by Washington for his failure to execute his orders promptly.

9. Brigadier General Joseph Reed (1741–1785), Washington's military secretary. Major General Thomas Mifflin (1744–1800), Washington's aide-de-camp.

1. Dispatches.

2. John Dryden (1631–1700), English poet and dramatist.

3. Charles XII, king of Sweden (1682–1718), defeated in several invasions of Russia.

4. Mercy Otis Warren (see n. 5, p. 684).

vague flying rumours would be endless. I heard yesterday by one Mr. Role-stone[5] a Goldsmith who got out in a fishing Schooner, that there distress encreased upon them fast, their Beaf is all spent, their Malt and Sider all gone, all the fresh provisions they can procure they are obliged to give to the sick and wounded. 19 of our Men who were in Jail and were wounded at the Battle of Charlstown were Dead. No Man dared now to be seen talking to his Friend in the Street, they were obliged to be within every evening at ten o clock according to Martial Law, nor could any inhabitant walk any Street in Town after that time without a pass from Gage.[6] He has orderd all the melasses to be stilld up into rum for the Soldiers, taken away all Licences, and given out others obligeing to a forfeiture of ten pounds L M[7] if any rum is sold without written orders from the General. He give much the same account of the kill'd and wounded we have had from others. The Spirit he says which prevails among the Soldiers is a Spirit of Malice and revenge, there is no true courage and bravery to be observed among them, their Duty is hard allways mounting guard with their packs at their back ready for an alarm which they live in continual hazard of. Doctor Eliot[8] is not on bord a man of war, as has been reported, but perhaps was left in Town as the comfort and support of those who cannot escape, he was constantly with our prisoners. Mr. Lovel and Leach[9] with others are certainly in Jail. A poor Milch cow was last week kill'd in Town and sold for a shilling sterling per pound. The transports arrived last week from York, but every additional Man adds to their distress.—There has been a little Expidition this week to Long Island. There has been before several attempts to go on but 3 men of war lay near, and cutters all round the Island that they could not succeed. A number of whale boats lay at Germantown; 300 volenters commanded by one Capt. Tupper came on monday evening and took the boats, went on and brought of 70 odd Sheep, 15 head of cattle, and 16 prisoners 13 of whom were sent by Simple Sapling[1] to mow the Hay which they had very badly executed. They were all a sleep in the house and barn when they were taken. There were 3 women with them. Our Heroes came of in triumph not being observed by their Enimies. This spiritted up other[s]. They could not endure the thought that the House and barn should afford them any shelter. They did not distroy them the night before for fear of being discovered. Capt. Wild of this Town with about 25 of his company, Capt. Gold [Gould] of Weymouth with as many of his, and some other volent-ers to the amount of an 100, obtain leave to go on and distroy the Hay together with the House and barn and in open day in full view of the men of war they set of from the Moon so call'd coverd by a number of men who were placed there, went on, set fire to the Buildings and Hay. A number of armed cutters[2] immediately Surrounded the Island, fired upon our Men. They came of with a hot and continued fire upon them, the Bullets flying in every direc-tion and the Men of Wars boats plying them with small arms. Many in this Town who were spectators expected every moment our Men would all be sacrificed, for sometimes they were so near as to be calld to and damnd by their Enimies and orderd to surrender yet they all returnd in safty, not one Man even wounded. Upon the Moon we lost one Man from the cannon on

5. John Roulstone (n.d.), a Boston watchmaker and goldsmith.
6. See n. 9, p. 688.
7. Liquid measure.
8. Rev. Andrew Eliot.
9. James Lovell (1737–1814), a schoolmaster, and

John Leach (n.d.).
1. A character in Mercy Otis Warren's satire The Group, standing for the Loyalist Nathaniel Ray Thomas (1731–1787).
2. Small boats.

board the Man of War.[3] On the Evening of the same day a Man of War came and anchord near Great Hill, and two cutters came to Pig Rocks.[4] It occasiond an alarm in this Town and we were up all Night. They remain there yet, but have not ventured to land any men.

*   *   *

Every article here in the West india way is very scarce and dear. In six week[s] we shall not be able to purchase any article of the kind. I wish you would let Bass get me one pound of peper, and 2 yd. of black caliminco[5] for Shooes. I cannot wear leather if I go bare foot the reason I need not mention. Bass may make a fine profit if he layes in a stock for himself. You can hardly immagine how much we want many common small articles which are not manufactured amongst ourselves, but we will have them in time. Not one pin is to be purchased for love nor money. I wish you could convey me a thousand by any Friend travelling this way. Tis very provoking to have such a plenty so near us, but tantulus like[6] not able to touch. I should have been glad to have laid in a small stock of the West India articles, but I cannot get one copper. No person thinks of paying any thing, and I do not chuse to run in debt. I endeavour to live in the most frugal manner posible, but I am many times distressed.—Mr. Trot[7] I have accommodated by removeing the office into my own chamber, and after being very angry and sometimes persuaideding I obtaind the mighty concession of the Bed room, but I am now so crouded as not to have a Lodging for a Friend that calls to see me. I must beg you would give them[8] warning to seek a place before Winter. Had that house been empty I could have had an 100 a year for it. Many person[s] had applied before Mr. Trot, but I wanted some part of it my self, and the other part it seems I have no command of.—We have since I wrote you had many fine showers, and altho the crops of grass have been cut short, we have a fine prospect of Indian corn and English grain. Be not afraid, ye beasts of the field, for the pastures of the Wilderness do spring, the Tree beareth her fruit, the vine and the olive yeald their increase.

We have not yet been much distressed for grain. Every thing at present looks blooming. O that peace would once more extend her olive Branch.

> "This Day be Bread and peace my lot
> All Else beneath the Sun
> Thou knowst if best bestowed or not
> And let thy will be done."

> But is the Almighty ever bound to please
> Ruild by my wish or studious of my ease.
> Shall I determine where his frowns shall fall
> And fence my Grotto from the Lot of all?
> Prostrate his Sovereign Wisdom I adore
> Intreat his Mercy, but I dare no more.

3. These events took place July 11–12. Long Island is halfway between Quincy and Boston, and Moon Island is near Long Island.
4. Great Hill is at the extremity of Hough's Neck in present-day Quincy, Massachusetts. Pig Rock is a half mile offshore from Great Hill.
5. Or calamanco, a glossy wool fabric. For Bass, see n. 4, p. 691.

6. In Greek mythology a king condemned to Hades. He stood in water that receded when he tried to drink and beneath fruit that was always beyond his grasp.
7. George Trott, Sr. (n.d.), a jeweler and husband of John's cousin.
8. Members of the Hayden family, of which there were many in Braintree.

Our little ones send Duty to pappa. You would smile to see them all gather round mamma upon the reception of a letter to hear from pappa, and Charls with open mouth, What does par say—did not he write no more. And little Toms says I wish I could see par. Upon Mr. Rice's going into the army he asked Charls if he should get him a place, he catchd at it with great eagerness and insisted upon going. We could not put him of, he cryed and beged, no obstical we could raise was sufficent to satisfy him, till I told him he must first obtain your consent. Then he insisted that I must write about it, and has been every day these 3 weeks insisting upon my asking your consent. At last I have promised to write to you, and am obliged to be as good as my word.—I have now wrote you all I can collect from every quarter. Tis fit for no eye but yours, because you can make all necessary allowances. I cannot coppy.

There are yet in Town 4 of the Selectmen and some thousands of inhabitants tis said.—I hope to hear from you soon. Do let me know if there is any prospect of seeing you? Next Wednesday is 13 weeks since you went away.

I must bid you adieu. You have many Friends tho they have not noticed you by writing. I am sorry they have been so neglegent. I hope no share of that blame lays upon your most affectionate

                                                                            Portia
Mr. Cranch has in his possession a Barrel of Mrs. Wilkings Beer which belonged to the late Dr. Warren. He does not know what to do with it. Suppose you should take it and give credit for it, as there will be neither wine, lemmons or any thing else to be had but what we make ourselves. Write me your pleasure about it.

1775   1848

John Adams to Abigail Adams

[DR. FRANKLIN]

                                                            July 23 1775
My Dear
You have more than once in your Letters mentioned Dr. Franklin,[9] and in one intimated a Desire that I should write you something concerning him.

Dr. Franklin has been very constant in his Attendance on Congress from the Beginning. His Conduct has been composed and grave and in the Opinion of many Gentlemen very reserved. He has not assumed any Thing, nor affected to take the lead; but has seemed to choose that the Congress should pursue their own Principles and sentiments and adopt their own Plans: Yet he has not been backward: has been very usefull, on many occasions, and discovered a Disposition entirely American. He does not hesitate at our boldest Measures, but rather seems to think us, too irresolute, and backward. He thinks us at present in an odd State, neither in Peace nor War, neither dependent nor independent. But he thinks that We shall soon assume a Character more decisive.

He thinks, that We have the Power of preserving ourselves, and that even if We should be driven to the disagreable Necessity of assuming a total Independency, and set up a separate state, We could maintain it. The People of England, have thought that the Opposition in America, was wholly owing to Dr. Franklin: and I suppose their scribblers will attribute the Temper, and

9. Benjamin Franklin (1706–1790) returned to Philadelphia from England in 1775.

Proceedings of this Congress to him: but there cannot be a greater Mistake. He has had but little share farther than to co operate and assist. He is however a great and good Man. I wish his Colleagues from this City were All like him, particularly one,[1] whose Abilities and Virtues, formerly trumpeted so much in America, have been found wanting.

There is a young Gentleman from Pensylvania whose Name is Wilson, whose Fortitude, Rectitude, and Abilities too, greatly outshine his Masters. Mr. Biddle, the Speaker, has been taken off, by Sickness. Mr. Mifflin is gone to the Camp, Mr. Morton is ill too, so that this Province has suffered by the Timidity of two overgrown Fortunes.[2] The Dread of Confiscation, or Caprice, I know not what has influenced them too much: Yet they were for taking Arms and pretended to be very valiant.—This Letter must be secret my dear—at least communicated with great Discretion. Yours,

John Adams

1775   1875

John Adams to Abigail Adams

[PREJUDICE IN FAVOR OF NEW ENGLAND]

Octr. 29. 1775

There is, in the human Breast, a social Affection, which extends to our whole Species. Faintly indeed; but in some degree. The Nation, Kingdom, or Community to which We belong is embraced by it more vigorously. It is stronger still towards the Province to which we belong, and in which We had our Birth. It is stronger and stronger, as We descend to the County, Town, Parish, Neighbourhood, and Family, which We call our own.—And here We find it often so powerfull as to become partial, to blind our Eyes, to darken our Understandings and pervert our Wills.

It is to this Infirmity, in my own Heart, that I must perhaps attribute that local Attachment, that partial Fondness, that overweening Prejudice in favour of New England, which I feel very often and which I fear sometimes, leads me to expose myself to just Ridicule.

New England has in many Respects the Advantage of every other Colony in America, and indeed of every other Part of the World, that I know any Thing of.

I. The People are purer English Blood, less mixed with Scotch, Irish, Dutch, French, Danish, Swedish &c. than any other; and descended from Englishmen too who left Europe, in purer Times than the present and less tainted with Corruption than those they left behind them.

2. The Institutions in New England for the Support of Religion, Morals and Decency, exceed any other, obliging every Parish to have a Minister, and every Person to go to Meeting &c.[3]

3. The public Institutions in New England for the Education of Youth, supporting Colledges at the public Expence and obliging Towns to maintain Grammar schools, is not equalled and never was in any Part of the World.

1. John is referring to John Dickinson (1732–1808), elected to the Continental Congress by the Pennsylvania Assembly.
2. James Wilson (1742–1798), a lawyer, was elected to the Second Continental Congress by the Pennsylvania Assembly along with Thomas Willing (1732–1821), a banker, and Franklin. Edward Biddle (n.d.) and John

Morton (1724?–1777) were often ill and Thomas Mifflin (1744–1800) left for the army. The "two overgrown fortunes" referred to are those of Dickinson and Willing.
3. I.e., to attend a Congregational church unless specifically exempted.

4. The Division of our Territory, that is our Counties into Townships, empowering Towns to assemble, choose officers, make Laws, mend roads, and twenty other Things, gives every Man an opportunity of shewing and improving that Education which he received at Colledge or at school, and makes Knowledge and Dexterity at public Business common.

5. Our Laws for the Distribution of Intestate Estates[4] occasions a frequent Division of landed Property and prevents Monopolies, of Land.

But in opposition to these We have laboured under many Disadvantages. The exorbitant Prerogatives of our Governors &c. which would have overborn our Liberties, if it had not been opposed by the five preceding Particulars.

1775   1875

Abigail Adams to John Adams

[THE BUILDING UP A GREAT EMPIRE]

November 27 1775

Tis a fortnight to Night since I wrote you a line during which, I have been confined with the Jaundice, Rhumatism and a most voilent cold; I yesterday took a puke which has releived me, and I feel much better to day. Many, very many people who have had the dysentery, are now afflicted both with the Jaundice and Rhumatisim, some it has left in Hecticks, some in dropsies.[5]

The great and incessant rains we have had this fall, (the like cannot be recollected) may have occasiond some of the present disorders. The Jaundice is very prevelant in the Camp.[6] We have lately had a week of very cold weather, as cold as January, and a flight of snow, which I hope will purify the air of some of the noxious vapours. It has spoild many hundreds of Bushels of Apples, which were designd for cider, and which the great rains had prevented people from making up. Suppose we have lost 5 Barrels by it.

Col. Warren[7] returnd last week to Plymouth, so that I shall not hear any thing from you till he goes back again which will not be till the last of ⟨next⟩ this month.

He Damp'd my Spirits greatly by telling me that the Court had prolonged your Stay an other month.[8] I was pleasing myself with the thoughts that you would soon be upon your return. Tis in vain to repine. I hope the publick will reap what I sacrifice.

I wish I knew what mighty things were fabricating.[9] If a form of Goverment is to be established here what one will be assumed? Will it be left to our assemblies to chuse one? and will not many men have many minds? and shall we not run into Dissentions among ourselves?

I am more and more convinced that Man is a dangerous creature, and that power whether vested in many or a few is ever grasping, and like the grave cries give, give. The great fish swallow up the small, and he who is most strenuous for the Rights of the people, when vested with power, is as eager after the perogatives of Government. You tell me of degrees of perfection to which Humane Nature is capable of arriving, and I believe it, but at the same time lament that our admiration should arise from the scarcity of the instances.

4. The distribution of property when no will exists.
5. With fevers and an unnatural collection of water in any part of the body.
6. Army.
7. Col. James Warren.

8. On November 11, the Massachusetts House of Representatives extended the current commissions of the delegates to the Continental Congress.
9. Being made.

The Building up a Great Empire, which was only hinted at by my correspondent may now I suppose be realized even by the unbelievers. Yet will not
ten thousand Difficulties arise in the formation of it? The Reigns of Government have been so long slakned, that I fear the people will not quietly submit
to those restraints which are necessary for the peace, and security, of the community; if we seperate from Brittain, what Code of Laws will be established.
How shall we be governd so as to retain our Liberties? Can any government
be free which is not adminstred by general stated Laws? Who shall frame these
Laws? Who will give them force and energy? Tis true your Resolution[s] as a
Body have heithertoo had the force of Laws. But will they continue to have?

When I consider these things and the prejudices of people in favour of
Ancient customs and Regulations, I feel anxious for the fate of our Monarchy
or Democracy or what ever is to take place. I soon get lost in a Labyrinth of
perplexities, but whatever occurs, may justice and righteousness be the Stability of our times, and order arise out of confusion. Great difficulties may be
surmounted, by patience and perserverance.

I believe I have tired you with politicks. As to news we have not any at all.
I shudder at the approach of winter when I think I am to remain desolate.
Suppose your weather is warm yet. Mr. Mason and Thaxter[1] live with me,
and render some part of my time less disconsolate. Mr. Mason is a youth who
will please you, he has Spirit, taste and Sense. His application to his Studies
is constant and I am much mistaken if he does not make a very good figure in
his profession.

I have with me now, the only Daughter of your Brother;[2] I feel a tenderer
affection for her as she has lost a kind parent. Though too young to be sensible
of her own loss, I can pitty her. She appears to be a child of a very good
Disposition—only wants to be a little used to company.

Our Little ones send Duty to pappa and want much to see him. Tom says
he wont come home till the Battle is over—some strange notion he has got
into his head. He has got a political cread to say to him when he returns.

I must bid you good night. Tis late for one who am much of an invalid. I
was dissapointed last week in receiving a packet by the post, and upon sealing it found only four news papers. I think you are more cautious than you
need be. All Letters I believe have come safe to hand. I have Sixteen from
you, and wish I had as many more. Adieu. Yours.

1775   1848

John Adams to Abigail Adams

[THESE COLONIES ARE FREE AND INDEPENDENT STATES]

Philadelphia July 3. 1776

Your Favour of June 17. dated at Plymouth, was handed me, by Yesterdays
Post. I was much pleased to find that you had taken a Journey to Plymouth,
to see your Friends in the long Absence of one whom you may wish to see.
The Excursion will be an Amusement, and will serve your Health. How happy
would it have made me to have taken this Journey with you?

I was informed, a day or two before the Receipt of your Letter, that you was

---

1. Jonathan Mason, Jr., and John Thaxter, Jr., law   2. Susanna Adams (1766–1826), daughter of Elihu
clerks.   and Thankful Adams.

gone to Plymouth, by Mrs. Polly Palmer,[3] who was obliging enough in your Absence, to inform me, of the Particulars of the Expedition to the lower Harbour against the Men of War. Her Narration is executed, with a Precision and Perspicuity, which would have become the Pen of an accomplished Historian.

I am very glad you had so good an opportunity of seeing one of our little American Men of War. Many Ideas, new to you, must have presented themselves in such a Scene; and you will in future, better understand the Relations of Sea Engagements.

I rejoice extreamly at Dr. Bulfinches[4] Petition to open an Hospital. But I hope, the Business will be done upon a larger Scale. I hope, that one Hospital will be licensed in every County, if not in every Town. I am happy to find you resolved, to be with the Children, in the first Class. Mr. Whitney and Mrs. Katy Quincy,[5] are cleverly through Innoculation, in this City.

I have one favour to ask, and that is, that in your future Letters, you would acknowledge the Receipt of all those you may receive from me, and mention their Dates. By this Means I shall know if any of mine miscarry.

The Information you give me of our Friends refusing his Appointment, has given me much Pain, Grief and Anxiety.[6] I believe I shall be obliged to follow his Example. I have not Fortune enough to support my Family, and what is of more Importance, to support the Dignity of that exalted Station. It is too high and lifted up, for me; who delight in nothing so much as Retreat, Solitude, Silence, and Obscurity. In private Life, no one has a Right to censure me for following my own Inclinations, in Retirement, Simplicity, and Frugality: in public Life, every Man has a Right to remark as he pleases, at least he thinks so.

Yesterday the greatest Question was decided, which ever was debated in America, and a greater perhaps, never was or will be decided among Men. A Resolution was passed without one dissenting Colony "that these united Colonies, are, and of right ought to be free and independent States, and as such, they have, and of Right ought to have full Power to make War, conclude Peace, establish Commerce, and to do all the other Acts and Things, which other States may rightfully do." You will see in a few days a Declaration setting forth the Causes, which have impell'd Us to this mighty Revolution, and the Reasons which will justify it, in the Sight of God and Man.[7] A Plan of Confederation will be taken up in a few days.

When I look back to the Year 1761, and recollect the Argument concerning Writs of Assistance, in the Superiour Court, which I have hitherto considered as the Commencement of the Controversy,[8] between Great Britain and America, and run through the whole Period from that Time to this, and recollect the series of political Events, the Chain of Causes and Effects, I am surprized at the Suddenness, as well as Greatness of this Revolution. Britain has been fill'd with Folly, and America with Wisdom, at least this is my Judg-

3. Miss Mary Palmer (*Mrs.* here stands for "Mistress") (1746–1791), a niece of the Cranches'.
4. Dr. Thomas Bulfinch (n.d.) inoculated Abigail Adams against smallpox. He was the father of the architect Charles Bulfinch (1768–1844).
5. Rev. Whitney was from Massachusetts. Katherine Quincy (1733–1804) was a relative of Abigail's.
6. In an earlier letter, Abigail had informed John that James Warren had declined an appointment as associate justice of the Massachusetts Superior Court.
7. The editors of the *Adams Family Correspondence*

note that this letter "and the next one of the same date were written *between* the act of independence itself and the adoption of the statement designed to 'justify it in the sight of God and man.' "
8. Writs of assistance were general search warrants and a threat to civil liberty. When John heard James Otis (1725–1783) argue against them in Salem, Massachusetts, in 1761, he was profoundly moved and wrote in his diary that from this day forth he was ready to "take arms against writs of assistance."

ment.—Time must determine. It is the Will of Heaven, that the two Countries should be sundered forever. It may be the Will of Heaven that America shall suffer Calamities still more wasting and Distresses yet more dreadfull. If this is to be the Case, it will have this good Effect, at least: it will inspire Us with many Virtues, which We have not, and correct many Errors, Follies, and Vices, which threaten to disturb, dishonour, and destroy Us.—The Furnace of Affliction produces Refinement, in States as well as Individuals. And the new Governments we are assuming, in every Part, will require a Purification from our Vices, and an Augmentation of our Virtues or they will be no Blessings. The People will have unbounded Power. And the People are extreamly addicted to Corruption and Venality, as well as the Great.—I am not without Apprehensions from this Quarter. But I must submit all my Hopes and Fears, to an overruling Providence, in which, unfashionable as the Faith may be, I firmly believe.

1776   1792

John Adams to Abigail Adams
[REFLECTIONS ON THE DECLARATION OF INDEPENDENCE]

Philadelphia July 3d. 1776

Had a Declaration of Independency been made seven Months ago, it would have been attended with many great and glorious Effects.[9] . . . We might before this Hour, have formed Alliances with foreign States.—We should have mastered Quebec and been in Possession of Canada. . . . You will perhaps wonder, how such a Declaration would have influenced our Affairs, in Canada, but if I could write with Freedom I could easily convince you, that it would, and explain to you the manner how.—Many Gentlemen in high Stations and of great Influence have been duped, by the ministerial Bubble of Commissioners to treat. . . . And in real, sincere Expectation of this Event, which they so fondly wished, they have been slow and languid, in promoting Measures for the Reduction of that Province. Others there are in the Colonies who really wished that our Enterprise in Canada would be defeated, that the Colonies might be brought into Danger and Distress between two Fires, and be thus induced to submit. Others really wished to defeat the Expedition to Canada, lest the Conquest of it, should elevate the Minds of the People too much to hearken to those Terms of Reconciliation which they believed would be offered Us. These jarring Views, Wishes and Designs, occasioned an opposition to many salutary Measures, which were proposed for the Support of that Expedition, and caused Obstructions, Embarrassments and studied Delays, which have finally, lost Us the Province.

All these Causes however in Conjunction would not have disappointed Us, if it had not been for a Misfortune, which could not be foreseen, and perhaps could not have been prevented, I mean the Prevalence of the small Pox among our Troops. . . . This fatal Pestilence compleated our Destruction.—It is a Frown of Providence upon Us, which We ought to lay to heart.

But on the other Hand, the Delay of this Declaration to this Time, has

---

9. Here and below the ellipses are in the manuscript. On June 7, Richard Henry Lee (1732–1794), from Virginia, moved "that these United Colonies are, and of right ought to be, Free and Independent States." Lee's motion was carried on July 2 after vigorous debate. A committee was appointed to prepare a formal declaration and this document, written by Thomas Jefferson, was adopted July 4, 1776.

many great Advantages attending it.—The Hopes of Reconciliation, which were fondly entertained by Multitudes of honest and well meaning tho weak and mistaken People, have been gradually and at last totally extinguished.— Time has been given for the whole People, maturely to consider the great Question of Independence and to ripen their Judgments, dissipate their Fears, and allure their Hopes, by discussing it in News Papers and Pamphletts, by debating it, in Assemblies, Conventions, Committees of Safety and Inspection, in Town and County Meetings, as well as in private Conversations, so that the whole People in every Colony of the 13, have now adopted it, as their own Act.—This will cement the Union, and avoid those Heats and perhaps Convulsions which might have been occasioned, by such a Declaration Six Months ago.

But the Day is past. The Second Day of July 1776, will be the most memorable Epocha, in the History of America.—I am apt to believe that it will be celebrated, by succeeding Generations, as the great anniversary Festival. It ought to be commemorated, as the Day of Deliverance by solemn Acts of Devotion to God Almighty. It ought to be solemnized with Pomp and Parade, with Shews, Games, Sports, Guns, Bells, Bonfires and Illuminations from one End of this Continent to the other from this Time forward forever more.

You will think me transported with Enthusiasm but I am not.—I am well aware of the Toil and Blood and Treasure, that it will cost Us to maintain this Declaration, and support and defend these States.—Yet through all the Gloom I can see the Rays of ravishing Light and Glory. I can see that the End is more than worth all the Means. And that Posterity will tryumph in that Days Transaction, even altho We should rue it, which I trust in God We shall not.

1776   1792

Abigail Adams to John Adams

[THE DECLARATION. SMALLPOX. THE GREY HORSE]

*   *   *

Sunday july 14 [1776]

By yesterdays post I received two Letters dated 3 and 4 of July and tho your Letters never fail to give me pleasure, be the subject what it will, yet it was greatly heightned by the prospect of the future happiness and glory of our Country; nor am I a little Gratified when I reflect that a person so nearly connected with me has had the Honour of being a principal actor, in laying a foundation for its future Greatness. May the foundation of our new constitution, be justice, Truth and Righteousness. Like the wise Mans house may it be founded upon those Rocks and then neither storms or temptests will overthrow it.

I cannot but feel sorry that some of the most Manly Sentiments in the Declaration are Expunged from the printed coppy. Perhaps wise reasons induced it.

Poor Canady I lament Canady but we ought to be in some measure sufferers for the past folly of our conduct. The fatal effects of the small pox there, has led almost every person to consent to Hospitals in every Town. In many Towns, already arround Boston the Selectmen have granted Liberty for innoculation. I hope the necessity is now fully seen.

I had many dissagreable Sensations at the Thoughts of comeing myself, but to see my children thro it I thought my duty, and all those feelings vanished as soon as I was innoculated and I trust a kind providence will carry me safely thro. Our Friends from Plymouth came into Town yesterday. We have enough upon our hands in the morning. The Little folks are very sick then and puke every morning but after that they are comfortable. I shall write you now very often. Pray inform me constantly of every important transaction. Every expression of tenderness is a cordial to my Heart. Unimportant as they are to the rest of the world, to me they are *every Thing*.

We have had during all the month of June a most severe Drougth which cut of all our promising hopes of english Grain and the first crop of Grass, but since july came in we have had a plenty of rain and now every thing looks well. There is one Misfortune in our family which I have never mentioned in hopes it would have been in my power to have remedied it, but all hopes of that kind are at an end. It is the loss of your Grey Horse. About 2 months ago, I had occasion to send Jonathan[1] of an errant to my unkle Quincys (the other Horse being a plowing). Upon his return a little below the church she trod upon a rolling stone and lamed herself to that degree that it was with great difficulty that she could be got home. I immediately sent for Tirrel[2] and every thing was done for her by Baths, ointments, polticeing, Bleeding &c. that could be done. Still she continued extreem lame tho not so bad as at first. I then got her carried to Domet[3] but he pronounces her incurable, as a callous is grown upon her footlock joint. You can hardly tell, not even by your own feelings how much I lament her. She was not with foal, as you immagined, but I hope she is now as care has been taken in that Respect.

I suppose you have heard of a fleet which came up pretty near the Light and kept us all with our mouths open ready to catch them, but after staying near a week and makeing what observations they could set sail and went of to our great mortification who were [prepared?][4] for them in every respect. If our Ship of 32 Guns which [was] Built at Portsmouth and waiting only for Guns and an other of [. . .] at Plimouth in the same state, had been in readiness we should in all probability been Masters of them. Where the blame lies in that respect I know not, tis laid upon Congress, and Congress is also blamed for not appointing us a General.—But Rome was not Built in a day.

I hope the Multiplicity of cares and avocations which invellope you will not be too powerfull for you. I have many anxietyes upon that account. Nabby and Johnny send duty and desire Mamma to say that an inflamation in their Eyes which has been as much of a distemper as the small pox, has prevented their writing, but they hope soon to be able to acquaint Pappa of their happy recovery from the Distemper.—Mr. C[ranch] and wife, Sister B[etsy] and all our Friend[s] desire to be rememberd to you and foremost in that Number stands your

Portia

PS   A little India herb[5] would have been mighty agreable now.

1776   1875

---

1. Abigail's servant or farm boy.
2. A veterinarian from Braintree.
3. Another veterinarian.

4. The manuscript is torn here and below.
5. Tea, an import of the British East India company.

John Adams to Abigail Adams

[DO MY FRIENDS THINK I HAVE FORGOTTEN MY WIFE AND CHILDREN?]

Philadelphia July 20. 1776

This has been a dull day to me: I waited the Arrival of the Post with much Solicitude and Impatience, but his Arrival made me more solicitous still.— "To be left at the Post Office" in your Hand Writing, on the back of a few Lines from the Dr.[6] were all that I could learn of you, and my little Folks. If you was too busy to write, I hoped that some kind Hand would have been found to let me know something about you.

Do my Friends think that I have been a Politician so long as to have lost all feeling? Do they suppose I have forgotten my Wife and Children? Or are they so panic struck with the Loss of Canada, as to be afraid to correspond with me? Or have they forgotten that you have an Husband and your Children a Father? What have I done, or omitted to do, that I should be thus forgotten and neglected in the most tender and affecting scæne of my Life! Dont mistake me, I dont blame you. Your Time and Thoughts must have been wholly taken up, with your own and your Families situation and Necessities.—But twenty other Persons might have informed me.

I suspect, that you intended to have run slyly, through the small Pox with the family, without letting me know it, and then have sent me an Account that you were all well. This might be a kind Intention, and if the design had succeeded, would have made me very joyous. But the secret is out, and I am left to conjecture. But as the Faculty[7] have this distemper so much under Command I will flatter myself with the Hope and Expectation of soon hearing of your Recovery.

1776   1875

Abigail Adams to John Adams

[SMALLPOX. THE PROCLAMATION FOR INDEPENDENCE READ ALOUD]

July 21 1776 Boston

I have no doubt but that my dearest Friend is anxious to know how his Portia does, and his little flock of children under the opperation of a disease once so formidable.

I have the pleasure to tell him that they are all comfortable tho some of them complaining. Nabby has been very ill, but the Eruption begins to make its appearance upon her, and upon Johnny. Tommy is so well that the Dr. innoculated him again to day fearing it had not taken. Charlly has no complaints yet, tho his arm has been very soar.

I have been out to meeting this forenoon, but have so many dissagreable Sensations this afternoon that I thought it prudent to tarry at home. The Dr. says they are very good feelings. Mr. Cranch has passed thro the preparation and the Eruption is comeing out cleverly upon him without any Sickness at all. Mrs. Cranch is cleverly and so are all her children. Those who are broke out are pretty full for the new method as tis call'd, the Suttonian[8] they profess

6. Dr. Cotton Tufts (1732–1815), Abigail's uncle by marriage.
7. The medical profession.
8. Named after Daniel Sutton (1735–1819) of Essex,

Massachusetts. His method required only a small puncture instead of the customary gash to infect the subject.

to practice upon. I hope to give you a good account when I write next, but our Eyes are very weak and the Dr. is not fond of either writing or reading for his patients. But I must transgress a little.

I received a Letter from you by wedensday Post 7 of July and tho I think it a choise one in the Litterary Way, containing many usefull hints and judicious observations which will greatly assist me in the future instruction of our Little ones, yet it Lacked some essential engrediants to make it compleat. Not one word respecting yourself, your Health or your present Situation. My anxiety for your welfare will never leave me but with my parting Breath, tis of more importance to me than all this World contains besides. The cruel Seperation to which I am necessatated cuts of half the enjoyments of life, the other half are comprised in the hope I have that what I do and what I suffer may be serviceable to you, to our Little ones and our Country; I must beseach you therefore for the future never to omit what is so essential to my happiness.

Last Thursday[9] after hearing a very Good Sermon I went with the Multitude into Kings Street to hear the proclamation for independance read and proclamed. Some Field peices with the Train[1] were brought there, the troops appeard under Arms and all the inhabitants assembled there (the small pox prevented many thousand from the Country). When Col. Crafts read from the Belcona[2] of the State House the Proclamation, great attention was given to every word. As soon as he ended, the cry from the Belcona, was God Save our American States and then 3 cheers which rended the air, the Bells rang, the privateers[3] fired, the forts and Batteries, the cannon were discharged, the platoons followed and every face appeard joyfull. Mr. Bowdoin then gave a Sentiment,[4] Stability and perpetuity to American independance. After dinner the kings arms were taken down from the State House and every vestage of him from every place in which it appeard and burnt in King Street. Thus ends royall Authority in this State, and all the people shall say Amen.

I have been a little surprized that we collect no better accounts with regard to the horrid conspiricy at New York, and that so little mention has been made of it here. It made a talk for a few days but now seems all hushed in Silence. The Tories say that it was not a conspiricy but an association, and pretend that there was no plot to assasinate the General.[5] Even their hardned Hearts ⟨Blush⟩ feel————the discovery. We have in Gorge a match for a Borgia and a Catiline,[6] a Wretch Callous to every Humane feeling. Our worthy preacher told us that he believed one of our Great Sins for which a righteous God has come out in judgment against us, was our Biggoted attachment to so wicked a Man. May our repentance be sincere.

Monday morg. july 22

I omitted many things yesterday in order to be better informed. I have got Mr. Cranch to inquire and write you, concerning a French Schooner from Martineco which came in yesterday and a prize from Ireland. My own infirmities prevents my writing. A most Excruciating pain in my head and every

---

9. July 18, 1776.
1. I.e., field guns with their vehicles.
2. Balcony. Col. Thomas Crafts (n.d.).
3. Privately owned armed vessels with a government commission.
4. A personal reflection. James Bowdoin, Sr. (1726–1790), proposed by John for governor of Massa-

chusetts (1785–87).
5. George Washington.
6. King George III of England (1738–1820) is compared to the Italian statesman and cardinal Cesare Borgia (1475–1507), famous for his cruelty, and Catiline (108?–62 B.C.), Roman politician and conspirator.

Limb and joint I hope portends a speedy Eruption and prevents my saying more than that I am forever Yours.

The children are not yet broke out. Tis the Eleventh Day with us.

1776 1875

John Adams to Abigail Adams

[MY COUNTRYMEN WANT ART AND ADDRESS]

Aug. 3. 1776

The Post was later than usual to day, so that I had not yours of July 24 till this Evening. You have made me very happy, by the particular and favourable Account you give me of all the Family. But I dont understand how there are so many who have no Eruptions, and no Symptoms. The Inflammation in the Arm might do, but without that, there is no small Pox.

I will lay a Wager, that your whole Hospital have not had so much small Pox, as Mrs. Katy Quincy. Upon my Word she has had an Abundance of it, but is finely recovered, looks as fresh as a Rose, but pitted all over, as thick as ever you saw any one. I this Evening presented your Compliments and Thanks to Mr. Hancock[7] for his polite offer of his House, and likewise your Compliments to his Lady and Mrs. Katy.

Aug. 4

Went this Morning to the Baptist Meeting, in Hopes of hearing Mr. Stillman,[8] but was dissappointed. He was there, but another Gentleman preached. His Action was violent to a degree bordering on fury. His Gestures, unnatural, and distorted. Not the least Idea of Grace in his Motions, or Elegance in his Style. His Voice was vociferous and boisterous, and his Composition almost wholly destitute of Ingenuity. I wonder extreamly at the Fondness of our People for schollars educated at the Southward and for southern Preachers. There is no one Thing, in which We excell them more, than in our University, our schollars, and Preachers. Particular Gentlemen here, who have improved upon their Education by Travel, shine. But in general, old Massachusetts outshines her younger sisters, still. In several Particulars, they have more Wit, than We. They have Societies; the philosophical Society particularly, which excites a scientific Emulation, and propagates their Fame. If ever I get through this Scene of Politicks and War, I will spend the Remainder of my days, in endeavouring to instruct my Countrymen in the Art of making the most of their Abilities and Virtues, an Art, which they have hitherto, too much neglected. A philosophical society shall be established at Boston, if I have Wit and Address enough to accomplish it, sometime or other.—Pray set Brother[9] Cranch's Philosophical Head to plodding upon this Project. Many of his Lucubrations would have been published and preserved, for the Benefit of Mankind, and for his Honour, if such a Clubb had existed.

My Countrymen want Art and Address.[1] They want Knowledge of the World. They want the exteriour and superficial Accomplishments of Gentlemen, upon which the World has foolishly set so high a Value. In solid Abilities and real Virtues, they vastly excell in general, any People upon this

7. John Hancock (1737–1793), another delegate from Massachusetts.

8. Rev. Samuel Stillman (1738–1807), pastor of the First Baptist Church of Boston from 1765 to 1807.

9. I.e., brother-in-law.

1. I.e., lack skill and dexterity.

Continent. Our N. England People are Aukward and bashfull; yet they are pert, ostentatious and vain, a Mixture which excites Ridicule and gives Disgust. They have not the faculty of shewing themselves to the best Advantage, nor the Art of concealing this faculty. An Art and Faculty which some People possess in the highest degree. Our Deficiencies in these Respects, are owing wholly to the little Intercourse We have had with strangers, and to our Inexperience in the World. These Imperfections must be remedied, for New England must produce the Heroes, the statesmen, the Philosophers, or America will make no great Figure for some Time.

Our Army is rather sickly at N. York, and We live in daily Expectation of hearing of some great Event. May God almighty grant it may be prosperous for America.—Hope is an Anchor and a Cordial. Disappointment however will not disconcert me.

If you will come to Philadelphia in September, I will stay, as long as you please. I should be as proud and happy as a Bridegroom. Yours.

1776   1875

THOMAS PAINE

1737–1809

The author of two of the most popular books in eighteenth-century America, and the most persuasive rhetorician of the cause for independence that our country has ever known, Thomas Paine was born in England in 1737, the son of a Quaker father and an Anglican mother, and did not come to America until he was thirty-seven years old. Paine's early years prepared him to be a supporter of the Revolution. The discrepancy between his high intelligence and the limitations imposed on him by poverty and caste made him long for a new social order. He once said that a sermon he heard at the age of eight impressed him with the cruelty inherent in Christianity and made him a rebel forever. When he arrived in Philadelphia with letters of introduction from Benjamin Franklin, recommending him as an "ingenious, worthy young man," he had already had a remarkably full life. Until he was thirteen he went to grammar school and then was apprenticed in his father's corset shop; at nineteen he ran away from home to go to sea. From 1757 to 1774 he was a corset maker, a tobacconist and grocer, a schoolteacher, and an exciseman (a government employee who taxed goods). His efforts to organize the excisemen and make Parliament raise their salary was unprecedented. He lost his job when he admitted he had stamped as examined goods that had not been opened. His first wife died less than a year after his marriage, and he was separated from his second wife after three years. Scandals about his private life and questions about his integrity while employed as an exciseman provided his critics with ammunition for the rest of his life. Franklin was right, however, in recognizing Paine's genius; for, like Franklin himself, he was a remarkable man, self-taught and curious about everything, from the philosophy of law to natural science.

In Philadelphia he seemed to find himself as a journalist, and he made his way quickly in that city, first as a spokesman against slavery and then as the anonymous author of *Common Sense*, the first pamphlet published in this country to urge immediate independence from Britain. Paine was obviously the right man in the right place at the right time. Relations with England were at their lowest ebb: Boston was under seige, and the Second Continental Congress had convened in

Philadelphia. *Common Sense* sold almost half a million copies, and its authorship (followed by the charge of traitor) could not be kept a secret for long. Paine enlisted in the Revolutionary Army and served as an aide-de-camp in battles in New York, New Jersey, and Pennsylvania. He followed his triumph of *Common Sense* with the first of sixteen pamphlets titled *Crisis*. The first *Crisis* paper ("These are the times that try men's souls") was read to Washington's troops at Trenton and did much to shore up the spirits of the Revolutionary soldiers.

Paine received a number of political appointments as rewards for his services as a writer for the American cause, but he misused his privileges and lost the most lucrative offices. He was too indiscreet and hot tempered for public employment. In 1787 he returned to England, determined to get financial assistance to construct an iron bridge for which he had devised plans. It came to nothing. But in England he wrote his second most successful work, his *Rights of Man* (1791–92), an impassioned plea against hereditary monarchy, the traditional institution Paine never tired of arguing against. Paine was charged with treason and fled to France, where he was made a citizen and lionized as a spokesman for revolution. The horrors of the French Revolution, however, brought home to Paine the fact that the mere overthrow of monarchy did not usher in light and order. When he protested the execution of Louis XVI, he was accused of sympathy with the Crown and imprisoned. He was saved from trial by the American ambassador, James Monroe, who offered him an American citizenship and safe passage back to New York.

Paine spent the last years of his life in New York City and in New Rochelle, New York. They were unhappy, impoverished years, and his reputation suffered enormously as a result of *The Age of Reason* (1794). Paine's attempt to define his beliefs was viewed as an attack on Christianity and, by extension, on conventional society. He was ridiculed and despised. Even George Washington, who had supported Paine's early writing, thought English criticism of him was "not a bad thing." Paine had clearly outlived his time. He was buried on his farm at New Rochelle after his request for a Quaker grave site was refused. Ten years later an enthusiastic admirer exhumed his bones with the intention of having him reburied in England. The admirer's plans came to nothing, and the whereabouts of Paine's grave is, at present, unknown.

Paine's great gift as a stylist was "plainness." He said he needed no "ceremonious expressions." "It is my design," he wrote, "to make those who can scarcely read understand," to put his arguments in a language "as plain as the alphabet," and to shape everything "to fit the powers of thinking and the turn of language to the subject, so as to bring out a clear conclusion that shall hit the point in question and nothing else."

From Common Sense[1]

Introduction

Perhaps the sentiments contained in the following pages are not yet sufficiently fashionable to procure them general favor; a long habit of not thinking a thing wrong gives it a superficial appearance of being right, and raises at first a formidable outcry in defence of custom. But the tumult soon subsides. Time makes more converts than reason.

---

1. The full title is *Common Sense: Addressed to the Inhabitants of America, on the following Interesting Subjects: viz.: I. Of the Origin and Design of Government in General; with Concise Remarks on the English Constitution. II. Of Monarchy and Hereditary Succes-* sion. III. Thoughts on the Present State of American Affairs. IV. Of the Present Ability of America; with some Miscellaneous Reflections. The text used here is from *The Writings of Thomas Paine*, vol. 1, edited by M. D. Conway (1894–96).

As a long and violent abuse of power is generally the means of calling the right of it in question (and in matters too which might never have been thought of, had not the sufferers been aggravated into the inquiry), and as the King of England hath undertaken in his own right, to support the Parliament in what he calls theirs, and as the good people of this country are grievously oppressed by the combination, they have an undoubted privilege to inquire into the pretensions of both, and equally to reject the usurpation of either.

In the following sheets, the author hath studiously avoided everything which is personal among ourselves. Compliments as well as censure to individuals make no part thereof. The wise and the worthy need not the triumph of a pamphlet; and those whose sentiments are injudicious or unfriendly will cease of themselves, unless too much pains is bestowed upon their conversions.

The cause of America is in a great measure the cause of all mankind. Many circumstances have, and will, arise which are not local, but universal, and through which the principles of all lovers of mankind are affected, and in the event of which their affections are interested. The laying a country desolate with fire and sword, declaring war against the natural rights of all mankind, and extirpating the defenders thereof from the face of the earth, is the concern of every man to whom nature hath given the power of feeling; of which class, regardless of party censure, is

The Author

From III. Thoughts on the Present State of American Affairs

In the following pages I offer nothing more than simple facts, plain arguments, and common sense: and have no other preliminaries to settle with the reader, than that he will divest himself of prejudice and prepossession, and suffer his reason and his feelings to determine for themselves: that he will put on, or rather that he will not put off, the true character of a man, and generously enlarge his views beyond the present day.

Volumes have been written on the subject of the struggle between England and America. Men of all ranks have embarked in the controversy, from different motives, and with various designs; but all have been ineffectual, and the period of debate is closed. Arms as the last resource decide the contest; the appeal was the choice of the King, and the continent has accepted the challenge.

It hath been reported of the late Mr. Pelham[2] (who though an able minister was not without his faults) that on his being attacked in the House of Commons on the score that his measures were only of a temporary kind, replied, "they will last my time." Should a thought so fatal and unmanly possess the colonies in the present contest, the name of ancestors will be remembered by future generations with detestation.

The sun never shined on a cause of greater worth. 'Tis not the affair of a city, a county, a province, or a kingdom; but of a continent—of at least one eighth part of the habitable globe. 'Tis not the concern of a day, a year, or an age; posterity are virtually involved in the contest, and will be more or less affected even to the end of time, by the proceedings now. Now is the seed time of continental union, faith and honor. The least fracture now will be like a

---

2. Henry Pelham (c. 1695–1754), prime minister of Britain (1743–54).

name engraved with the point of a pin on the tender rind of a young oak; the wound would enlarge with the tree, and posterity read it in full grown characters.

By referring the matter from argument to arms, a new era for politics is struck—a new method of thinking hath arisen. All plans, proposals, etc., prior to the nineteenth of April, i.e., to the commencement of hostilities,[3] are like the almanacs of the last year; which though proper then, are superceded and useless now. Whatever was advanced by the advocates on either side of the question then, terminated in one and the same point, viz., a union with Great Britain; the only difference between the parties was the method of effecting it; the one proposing force, the other friendship; but it hath so far happened that the first hath failed, and the second hath withdrawn her influence.

As much hath been said of the advantages of reconciliation, which, like an agreeable dream, hath passed away and left us as we were, it is but right that we should examine the contrary side of the argument, and inquire into some of the many material injuries which these colonies sustain, and always will sustain, by being connected with and dependent on Great Britain. To examine that connection and dependence, on the principles of nature and common sense, to see what we have to trust to, if separated, and what we are to expect, if dependent.

I have heard it asserted by some, that as America has flourished under her former connection with Great Britain, the same connection is necessary towards her future happiness, and will always have the same effect. Nothing can be more fallacious than this kind of argument. We may as well assert that because a child has thrived upon milk, that it is never to have meat, or that the first twenty years of our lives is to become a precedent for the next twenty. But even this is admitting more than is true; for I answer roundly, that America would have flourished as much, and probably much more, had no European power taken any notice of her. The commerce by which she hath enriched herself are the necessaries of life, and will always have a market while eating is the custom of Europe.

But she has protected us, say some. That she hath engrossed[4] us is true, and defended the continent at our expense as well as her own, is admitted; and she would have defended Turkey from the same motive, viz., for the sake of trade and dominion.

Alas! we have been long led away by ancient prejudices and made large sacrifices to superstition. We have boasted the protection of Great Britain without considering that her motive was interest not attachment; and that she did not protect us from our enemies on our account; but from her enemies on her own account, from those who had no quarrel with us on any other account, and who will always be our enemies on the same account. Let Britain waive her pretensions to the continent, or the continent throw off the dependence, and we should be at peace with France and Spain, were they at war with Britain. The miseries of Hanover's last war[5] ought to warn us against connections.

3. The "Minutemen" of Lexington, Massachusetts, defended their ammunition stores against the British on April 19, 1775, and engaged in the first armed conflict of the American Revolution.
4. Dominated.
5. King George III of Great Britain was a descendant of the Prussian House of Hanover; Paine is referring to the Seven Years' War (1756–63), which originally involved Prussia and Austria and grew to involve all the major European powers. American losses in the French and Indian War were heavy, even though the war was settled in Britain's favor.

It hath lately been asserted in Parliament, that the colonies have no relation to each other but through the parent country, i.e., that Pennsylvania and the Jerseys,[6] and so on for the rest, are sister colonies by the way of England; this is certainly a very roundabout way of proving relationship, but it is the nearest and only true way of proving enmity (or enemyship, if I may so call it). France and Spain never were, nor perhaps ever will be, our enemies as Americans, but as our being the subjects of Great Britain.

But Britain is the parent country, say some. Then the more shame upon her conduct. Even brutes do not devour their young, nor savages make war upon their families; wherefore, the assertion, if true, turns to her reproach; but it happens not to be true, or only partly so, and the phrase parent or mother country hath been jesuitically[7] adopted by the King and his parasites, with a low papistical design of gaining an unfair bias on the credulous weakness of our minds. Europe, and not England, is the parent country of America. This new world hath been the asylum for the persecuted lovers of civil and religious liberty from every part of Europe. Hither have they fled, not from the tender embraces of the mother, but from the cruelty of the monster; and it is so far true of England, that the same tyranny which drove the first emigrants from home, pursues their descendants still.

In this extensive quarter of the globe, we forget the narrow limits of three hundred and sixty miles (the extent of England) and carry our friendship on a larger scale; we claim brotherhood with every European Christian, and triumph in the generosity of the sentiment.

It is pleasant to observe by what regular gradations we surmount the force of local prejudices, as we enlarge our acquaintance with the world. A man born in any town in England divided into parishes, will naturally associate most with his fellow parishioners (because their interests in many cases will be common) and distinguish him by the name of neighbor; if he meet him but a few miles from home, he drops the narrow idea of a street, and salutes him by the name of townsman; if he travel out of the county and meet him in any other, he forgets the minor divisions of street and town, and calls him countryman, i.e., countyman: but if in their foreign excursions they should associate in France, or any other part of Europe, their local remembrance would be enlarged into that of Englishmen. And by a just parity of reasoning, all Europeans meeting in America, or any other quarter of the globe, are countrymen; for England, Holland, Germany, or Sweden, when compared with the whole, stand in the same places on the larger scale, which the divisions of street, town, and county do on the smaller ones; distinctions too limited for continental minds. Not one third of the inhabitants, even of this province,[8] are of English descent. Wherefore, I reprobate the phrase of parent or mother country applied to England only, as being false, selfish, narrow and ungenerous.

But, admitting that we were all of English descent, what does it amount to? Nothing. Britain, being now an open enemy, extinguishes every other name and title: and to say that reconciliation is our duty is truly farcical. The first King of England of the present line (William the Conqueror) was a Frenchman, and half the peers of England are descendants from the same country; wherefore, by the same method of reasoning, England ought to be governed by France.

6. The colony was divided into East and West Jersey.   8. I.e., Pennsylvania.
7. I.e., cunningly.

Much hath been said of the united strength of Britain and the colonies, that in conjunction they might bid defiance to the world: but this is mere presumption; the fate of war is uncertain, neither do the expressions mean anything; for this continent would never suffer itself to be drained of inhabitants to support the British arms in either Asia, Africa, or Europe.

Besides, what have we to do with setting the world at defiance? Our plan is commerce, and that, well attended to, will secure us the peace and friendship of all Europe; because it is the interest of all Europe to have America a free port. Her trade will always be a protection, and her barrenness of gold and silver secure her from invaders.

I challenge the warmest advocate for reconciliation to show a single advantage that this continent can reap by being connected with Great Britain. I repeat the challenge; not a single advantage is derived. Our corn will fetch its price in any market in Europe, and our imported goods must be paid for buy them where we will.

But the injuries and disadvantages which we sustain by that connection, are without number; and our duty to mankind at large, as well as to ourselves, instruct us to renounce the alliance: because, any submission to, or dependence on, Great Britain tends directly to involve this continent in European wars and quarrels, and set us at variance with nations who would otherwise seek our friendship, and against whom we have neither anger nor complaint. As Europe is our market for trade, we ought to form no partial connection with any part of it. It is the true interest of America to steer clear of European contentions, which she never can do, while, by her dependence on Britain, she is made the makeweight in the scale of British politics.

Europe is too thickly planted with kingdoms to be long at peace, and whenever a war breaks out between England and any foreign power, the trade of America goes to ruin, because of her connection with Britain. The next war may not turn out like the last,[9] and should it not, the advocates for reconciliation now will be wishing for separation then, because neutrality in that case would be a safer convoy than a man of war. Everything that is right or reasonable pleads for separation. The blood of the slain, the weeping voice of nature cries, " 'Tis time to part." Even the distance at which the Almighty hath placed England and America is a strong and natural proof that the authority of the one over the other was never the design of Heaven. The time likewise at which the continent was discovered adds weight to the argument, and the manner in which it was peopled increases the force of it. The Reformation was preceded by the discovery of America: as if the Almighty graciously meant to open a sanctuary to the persecuted in future years, when home should afford neither friendship nor safety.

The authority of Great Britain over this continent is a form of government which sooner or later must have an end: and a serious mind can draw no true pleasure by looking forward, under the painful and positive conviction that what he calls "the present constitution" is merely temporary. As parents, we can have no joy, knowing that this government is not sufficiently lasting to insure anything which we may bequeath to posterity: and by a plain method of argument, as we are running the next generation into debt, we ought to do the work of it, otherwise we use them meanly and pitifully. In order to discover

9. The Seven Years' War concluded with the Treaty of Paris (1763), and Britain gained all the French territory in North America.

the line of our duty rightly, we should take our children in our hand, and fix our station a few years farther into life; that eminence will present a prospect which a few present fears and prejudices conceal from our sight.

Though I would carefully avoid giving unnecessary offense, yet I am inclined to believe that all those who espouse the doctrine of reconciliation may be included within the following descriptions.

Interested men who are not to be trusted, weak men who cannot see, prejudiced men who will not see, and a certain set of moderate men who think better of the European world than it deserves; and this last class, by an ill-judged deliberation, will be the cause of more calamities to this continent than all the other three.

It is the good fortune of many to live distant from the scene of present sorrow; the evil is not sufficiently brought to their doors to make them feel the precariousness with which all American property is possessed. But let our imaginations transport us a few moments to Boston;[1] that seat of wretchedness will teach us wisdom, and instruct us forever to renounce a power in whom we can have no trust. The inhabitants of that unfortunate city, who but a few months ago were in ease and affluence, have now no other alternative than to stay and starve, or turn out to beg. Endangered by the fire of their friends if they continue within the city, and plundered by the soldiery if they leave it, in their present situation they are prisoners without the hope of redemption, and in a general attack for their relief they would be exposed to the fury of both armies.

Men of passive tempers look somewhat lightly over the offenses of Great Britain, and, still hoping for the best, are apt to call out, "Come, come, we shall be friends again for all this." But examine the passions and feelings of mankind: bring the doctrine of reconciliation to the touchstone of nature, and then tell me whether you can hereafter love, honor, and faithfully serve the power that hath carried fire and sword into your land? If you cannot do all these, then are you only deceiving yourselves, and by your delay bringing ruin upon posterity. Your future connection with Britain, whom you can neither love nor honor, will be forced and unnatural, and, being formed only on the plan of present convenience, will in a little time fall into a relapse more wretched than the first. But if you say, you can still pass the violations over, then I ask, hath your house been burnt? Hath your property been destroyed before your face? Are your wife and children destitute of a bed to lie on, or bread to live on? Have you lost a parent or a child by their hands, and yourself the ruined and wretched survivor? If you have not, then are you not a judge of those who have. But if you have, and can still shake hands with the murderers, then are you unworthy the name of husband, father, friend, or lover, and whatever may be your rank or title in life, you have the heart of a coward, and the spirit of a sycophant.

This is not inflaming or exaggerating matters, but trying them by those feelings and affections which nature justifies, and without which we should be incapable of discharging the social duties of life, or enjoying the felicities of it. I mean not to exhibit horror for the purpose of provoking revenge, but to awaken us from fatal and unmanly slumbers, that we may pursue determinately some fixed object. 'Tis not in the power of Britain or of Europe to

---

1. Boston was under British military occupation and blockaded for six months.

conquer America, if she doth not conquer herself by delay and timidity. The present winter is worth an age if rightly employed, but if lost or neglected the whole continent will partake of the misfortune; and there is no punishment which that man doth not deserve, be he who, or what, or where he will, that may be the means of sacrificing a season so precious and useful.

'Tis repugnant to reason, to the universal order of things, to all examples from former ages, to suppose that this continent can long remain subject to any external power. The most sanguine in Britain doth not think so. The utmost stretch of human wisdom cannot, at this time, compass a plan, short of separation, which can promise the continent even a year's security. Reconciliation is now a fallacious dream. Nature hath deserted the connection, and art cannot supply her place. For, as Milton wisely expresses, "never can true reconcilement grow where wounds of deadly hate have pierced so deep."[2]

*   *   *

A government of our own is our natural right: and when a man seriously reflects on the precariousness of human affairs, he will become convinced that it is infinitely wiser and safer to form a constitution of our own in a cool deliberate manner, while we have it in our power, than to trust such an interesting event to time and chance. If we omit it now, some Massanello[3] may hereafter arise, who, laying hold of popular disquietudes, may collect together the desperate and the discontented, and by assuming to themselves the powers of government, finally sweep away the liberties of the continent like a deluge. Should the government of America return again into the hands of Britain, the tottering situation of things will be a temptation for some desperate adventurer to try his fortune; and in such a case, what relief can Britain give? Ere she could hear the news, the fatal business might be done; and ourselves suffering like the wretched Britons under the oppression of the conqueror. Ye that oppose independence now, ye know not what ye do: ye are opening a door to eternal tyranny by keeping vacant the seat of government. There are thousands and tens of thousands, who would think it glorious to expel from the continent that barbarous and hellish power, which hath stirred up the Indians and the Negroes to destroy us; the cruelty hath a double guilt: it is dealing brutally by us, and treacherously by them.

To talk of friendship with those in whom our reason forbids us to have faith, and our affections wounded through a thousand pores instruct us to detest, is madness and folly. Every day wears out the little remains of kindred between us and them; and can there be any reason to hope, that as the relationship expires, the affection will increase, or that we shall agree better when we have ten times more and greater concerns to quarrel over than ever?

Ye that tell us of harmony and reconciliation, can ye restore to us the time that is past? Can ye give to prostitution its former innocence? Neither can ye reconcile Britain and America. The last cord now is broken, the people of England are presenting addresses against us. There are injuries which nature cannot forgive; she would cease to be nature if she did. As well can the lover forgive the ravisher of his mistress, as the continent forgive the murders of

---

2. *Paradise Lost* 4.98–99.
3. "Thomas Anello, otherwise Massanello, a fisherman of Naples, who after spiriting up his countrymen in the public market place, against the oppression of the Spaniards, to whom the place was then subject, prompted them to revolt, and in the space of a day became King" [Paine's note].

Britain. The Almighty hath implanted in us these unextinguishable feelings
for good and wise purposes. They are the guardians of His image in our hearts.
They distinguish us from the herd of common animals. The social compact
would dissolve, and justice be extirpated from the earth, or have only a casual
existence were we callous to the touches of affection. The robber and the
murderer would often escape unpunished, did not the injuries which our tempers sustain provoke us into justice.

O! ye that love mankind! Ye that dare oppose not only the tyranny but the
tyrant, stand forth! Every spot of the old world is overrun with oppression.
Freedom hath been hunted round the globe. Asia and Africa have long
expelled her. Europe regards her like a stranger, and England hath given her
warning to depart. O! receive the fugitive, and prepare in time an asylum
for mankind.

1776

The Crisis,[1] No. 1

These are the times that try men's souls. The summer soldier and the sunshine patriot will, in this crisis, shrink from the service of their country; but he
that stands it now, deserves the love and thanks of man and woman. Tyranny,
like hell, is not easily conquered; yet we have this consolation with us, that
the harder the conflict, the more glorious the triumph. What we obtain too
cheap, we esteem too lightly: it is dearness only that gives everything its value.
Heaven knows how to put a proper price upon its goods; and it would be
strange indeed if so celestial an article as freedom should not be highly rated.
Britain, with an army to enforce her tyranny, has declared that she has a right
(not only to tax) but "to bind us in all cases whatsoever," and if being bound
in that manner is not slavery, then is there not such a thing as slavery upon
earth. Even the expression is impious; for so unlimited a power can belong
only to God.

Whether the independence of the continent was declared too soon, or
delayed too long, I will not now enter into as an argument; my own simple
opinion is, that had it been eight months earlier, it would have been much
better. We did not make a proper use of last winter, neither could we, while
we were in a dependent state. However, the fault, if it were one, was all our
own;[2] we have none to blame but ourselves. But no great deal is lost yet. All
that Howe[3] has been doing for this month past is rather a ravage than a conquest, which the spirit of the Jerseys,[4] a year ago, would have quickly repulsed,
and which time and a little resolution will soon recover.

I have as little superstition in me as any man living, but my secret opinion
has ever been, and still is, that God Almighty will not give up a people to

1. The first of sixteen pamphlets that appeared under
this title. Paine sometimes referred to this particular
essay as *The American Crisis*. There were three pamphlet editions in one week: one undated, one dated December 19, and the one reprinted here, dated December 23. The text used here is from *The Writings of
Thomas Paine*, vol. 1, edited by M. D. Conway
(1894–96).
2. "The present winter is worth an age, if rightly employed; but, if lost or neglected, the whole continent

will partake of the evil; and there is no punishment that
man does not deserve, be he who, or what, or where
he will, that may be the means of sacrificing a season
so precious and useful" [Paine's note, taken from *Common Sense*]. Paine wanted an immediate declaration of
independence, uniting the colonies and enlisting the
aid of France and Spain.
3. Lord William Howe (1729–1814) was commander
of the British Army in America from 1775 to 1778.
4. The colony was divided into East and West Jersey.

military destruction, or leave them unsupportedly to perish, who have so earnestly and so repeatedly sought to avoid the calamities of war, by every decent method which wisdom could invent. Neither have I so much of the infidel in me as to suppose that He has relinquished the government of the world, and given us up to the care of devils; and as I do not, I cannot see on what grounds the King of Britain can look up to heaven for help against us: a common murderer, a highwayman, or a housebreaker has as good a pretense as he.

'Tis surprising to see how rapidly a panic will sometimes run through a country. All nations and ages have been subject to them: Britain has trembled like an ague[5] at the report of a French fleet of flat-bottomed boats; and in the fourteenth[6] century the whole English army, after ravaging the kingdom of France, was driven back like men petrified with fear; and this brave exploit was performed by a few broken forces collected and headed by a woman, Joan of Arc. Would that heaven might inspire some Jersey maid to spirit up her countrymen, and save her fair fellow sufferers from ravage and ravishment! Yet panics, in some cases, have their uses; they produce as much good as hurt. Their duration is always short; the mind soon grows through them, and acquires a firmer habit than before. But their peculiar advantage is that they are the touchstones of sincerity and hypocrisy, and bring things and men to light, which might otherwise have lain forever undiscovered. In fact, they have the same effect on secret traitors, which an imaginary apparition would have upon a private murderer. They sift out the hidden thoughts of man, and hold them up in public to the world. Many a disguised tory[7] has lately shown his head, that shall penitentially solemnize with curses the day on which Howe arrived upon the Delaware.

As I was with the troops at Fort Lee, and marched with them to the edge of Pennsylvania, I am well acquainted with many circumstances, which those who live at a distance know but little or nothing of. Our situation there was exceedingly cramped, the place being a narrow neck of land between the North River[8] and the Hackensack. Our force was inconsiderable, being not one fourth so great as Howe could bring against us. We had no army at hand to have relieved the garrison, had we shut ourselves up and stood on our defense. Our ammunition, light artillery, and the best part of our stores had been removed on the apprehension that Howe would endeavor to penetrate the Jerseys, in which case Fort Lee could be of no use to us; for it must occur to every thinking man, whether in the army or not, that these kind of field forts are only for temporary purposes, and last in use no longer than the enemy directs his force against the particular object, which such forts are raised to defend. Such was our situation and condition at Fort Lee on the morning of the 20th of November, when an officer arrived with information that the enemy with 200 boats had landed about seven miles above: Major General Green,[9] who commanded the garrison, immediately ordered them under arms, and sent express to General Washington at the town of Hackensack, distant, by the way of the ferry, six miles. Our first object was to secure the bridge over the Hackensack, which laid up the river between the enemy and us, about six miles from us, and three from them. General Washington arrived

5. I.e., like one who is chilled.
6. Properly, the 15th century. Joan of Arc led the French to victory over the English in 1429.
7. I.e., supporter of the king.

8. I.e., the Hudson River.
9. Paine was aide-de-camp to Major General Nathanael Greene (1742–1786).

in about three quarters of an hour, and marched at the head of the troops towards the bridge, which place I expected we should have a brush for; however, they did not choose to dispute it with us, and the greatest part of our troops went over the bridge, the rest over the ferry, except some which passed at a mill on a small creek, between the bridge and the ferry, and made their way through some marshy grounds up to the town of Hackensack, and there passed the river. We brought off as much baggage as the wagons could contain, the rest was lost. The simple object was to bring off the garrison, and march them on till they could be strengthened by the Jersey or Pennsylvania militia, so as to be enabled to make a stand. We staid four days at Newark, collected our outposts with some of the Jersey militia, and marched out twice to meet the enemy, on being informed that they were advancing, though our numbers were greatly inferior to theirs. Howe, in my little opinion, committed a great error in generalship in not throwing a body of forces off from Staten Island through Amboy, by which means he might have seized all our stores at Brunswick, and intercepted our march into Pennsylvania; but if we believe the power of hell to be limited, we must likewise believe that their agents are under some providential control.[1]

I shall not now attempt to give all the particulars of our retreat to the Delaware; suffice it for the present to say, that both officers and men, though greatly harassed and fatigued, frequently without rest, covering, or provision, the inevitable consequences of a long retreat, bore it with a manly and martial spirit. All their wishes centered in one, which was that the country would turn out and help them to drive the enemy back. Voltaire has remarked that King William never appeared to full advantage but in difficulties and in action;[2] the same remark may be made on General Washington, for the character fits him. There is a natural firmness in some minds which cannot be unlocked by trifles, but which, when unlocked, discovers a cabinet[3] of fortitude; and I reckon it among those kind of public blessings, which we do not immediately see, that God hath blessed him with uninterrupted health, and given him a mind that can even flourish upon care.

I shall conclude this paper with some miscellaneous remarks on the state of our affairs; and shall begin with asking the following question: Why is it that the enemy have left the New England provinces, and made these middle ones the seat of war? The answer is easy: New England is not infested with tories, and we are. I have been tender in raising the cry against these men, and used numberless arguments to show them their danger, but it will not do to sacrifice a world either to their folly or their baseness. The period is now arrived, in which either they or we must change our sentiments, or one or both must fall. And what is a tory? Good God! what is he? I should not be afraid to go with a hundred whigs[4] against a thousand tories, were they to attempt to get into arms. Every tory is a coward; for servile, slavish, self-interested fear is the foundation of toryism; and a man under such influence, though he may be cruel, never can be brave.

But, before the line of irrecoverable separation be drawn between us, let us reason the matter together: Your conduct is an invitation to the enemy, yet

1. The American losses were larger than Paine implies. General Howe took three thousand prisoners and a large store of military supplies when he captured Fort Lee. Paine wrote *The Crisis, No. 1* while serving with Washington's army as it retreated through New Jersey.

2. Voltaire (1694–1778) made this remark about King William III of England (1650–1702) in his *History of Louis the Fourteenth* (1751).

3. Storehouse.

4. Supporters of the Revolution.

not one in a thousand of you has heart enough to join him. Howe is as much deceived by you as the American cause is injured by you. He expects you will all take up arms, and flock to his standard, with muskets on your shoulders. Your opinions are of no use to him, unless you support him personally, for 'tis soldiers, and not tories, that he wants.

I once felt all that kind of anger, which a man ought to feel, against the mean principles that are held by the tories: a noted one, who kept a tavern at Amboy,[5] was standing at his door, with as pretty a child in his hand, about eight or nine years old, as I ever saw, and after speaking his mind as freely as he thought was prudent, finished with this unfatherly expression, "Well! give me peace in my day." Not a man lives on the continent but fully believes that a separation must some time or other finally take place, and a generous parent should have said, "If there must be trouble, let it be in my day, that my child may have peace"; and this single reflection, well applied, is sufficient to awaken every man to duty. Not a place upon earth might be so happy as America. Her situation is remote from all the wrangling world, and she has nothing to do but to trade with them. A man can distinguish himself between temper and principle, and I am as confident, as I am that God governs the world, that America will never be happy till she gets clear of foreign dominion. Wars, without ceasing, will break out till that period arrives, and the continent must in the end be conqueror; for though the flame of liberty may sometimes cease to shine, the coal can never expire.

America did not, nor does not, want force; but she wanted a proper application of that force. Wisdom is not the purchase of a day, and it is no wonder that we should err at the first setting off. From an excess of tenderness, we were unwilling to raise an army, and trusted our cause to the temporary defense of a well-meaning militia. A summer's experience has now taught us better; yet with those troops, while they were collected, we were able to set bounds to the progress of the enemy, and thank God! they are again assembling. I always considered militia as the best troops in the world for a sudden exertion, but they will not do for a long campaign. Howe, it is probable, will make an attempt on this city;[6] should he fail on this side of the Delaware, he is ruined: if he succeeds, our cause is not ruined. He stakes all on his side against a part on ours; admitting he succeeds, the consequence will be that armies from both ends of the continent will march to assist their suffering friends in the middle states; for he cannot go everywhere, it is impossible. I consider Howe as the greatest enemy the tories have; he is bringing a war into their country, which, had it not been for him and partly for themselves, they had been clear of. Should he now be expelled, I wish with all the devotion of a Christian, that the names of whig and tory may never more be mentioned; but should the tories give him encouragement to come, or assistance if he come, I as sincerely wish that our next year's arms may expel them from the continent, and the congress appropriate their possessions to the relief of those who have suffered in well-doing. A single successful battle next year will settle the whole. America could carry on a two years' war by the confiscation of the property of disaffected persons, and be made happy by their expulsion. Say not that this is revenge; call it rather the soft resentment of a suffering people, who, having no object in view but the good of all, have staked their own all upon a seem-

5. Paine was stationed at Perth Amboy, New Jersey, while in the Continental Army.   6. I.e., Philadelphia.

ingly doubtful event. Yet it is folly to argue against determined hardness; eloquence may strike the ear, and the language of sorrow draw forth the tear of compassion, but nothing can reach the heart that is steeled with prejudice.

Quitting this class of men, I turn with the warm ardor of a friend to those who have nobly stood, and are yet determined to stand the matter out: I call not upon a few, but upon all: not on this state or that state, but on every state: up and help us; lay your shoulders to the wheel; better have too much force than too little, when so great an object is at stake. Let it be told to the future world that in the depth of winter, when nothing but hope and virtue could survive, that the city and the country, alarmed at one common danger, came forth to meet and to repulse it. Say not that thousands are gone, turn out your tens of thousands;[7] throw not the burden of the day upon Providence, but "show your faith by your works"[8] that God may bless you. It matters not where you live, or what rank of life you hold, the evil or the blessing will reach you all. The far and the near, the home counties and the back,[9] the rich and poor will suffer or rejoice alike. The heart that feels not now is dead: the blood of his children will curse his cowardice who shrinks back at a time when a little might have saved the whole, and made them happy. I love the man that can smile in trouble, that can gather strength from distress, and grow brave by reflection. 'Tis the business of little minds to shrink; but he whose heart is firm, and whose conscience approves his conduct, will pursue his principles unto death. My own line of reasoning is to myself as straight and clear as a ray of light. Not all the treasures of the world, so far as I believe, could have induced me to support an offensive war, for I think it murder; but if a thief breaks into my house, burns and destroys my property, and kills or threatens to kill me, or those that are in it, and to "bind me in all cases whatsoever"[1] to his absolute will, am I to suffer it? What signifies it to me, whether he who does it is a king or a common man; my countryman or not my countryman; whether it be done by an individual villain, or an army of them? If we reason to the root of things we shall find no difference; neither can any just cause be assigned why we should punish in the one case and pardon in the other. Let them call me rebel, and welcome, I feel no concern from it; but I should suffer the misery of devils were I to make a whore of my soul by swearing allegiance to one whose character is that of a sottish, stupid, stubborn, worthless, brutish man. I conceive likewise a horrid idea in receiving mercy from a being, who at the last day shall be shrieking to the rocks and mountains to cover him, and fleeing with terror from the orphan, the widow, and the slain of America.

There are cases which cannot be overdone by language, and this is one. There are persons, too, who see not the full extent of the evil which threatens them; they solace themselves with hopes that the enemy, if he succeed, will be merciful. It is the madness of folly to expect mercy from those who have refused to do justice; and even mercy, where conquest is the object, is only a trick of war; the cunning of the fox is as murderous as the violence of the wolf, and we ought to guard equally against both. Howe's first object is, partly by threats and partly by promises, to terrify or seduce the people to deliver up

---

7. "Saul hath slain his thousands, and David his ten thousands" (1 Samuel 18.7).
8. "Shew me thy faith without thy works, and I will shew thee my faith by my works" (James 2.18).

9. I.e., the backwoods.
1. From the Declaratory Act of Parliament, February 24, 1766, establishing British authority over the American colonies.

their arms and receive mercy. The ministry recommended the same plan to Gage,[2] and this is what the tories call making their peace, "a peace which passeth all understanding"[3] indeed! A peace which would be the immediate forerunner of a worse ruin than any we have yet thought of. Ye men of Pennsylvania, do reason upon these things! Were the back counties to give up their arms, they would fall an easy prey to the Indians, who are all armed: this perhaps is what some tories would not be sorry for. Were the home counties to deliver up their arms, they would be exposed to the resentment of the back counties, who would then have it in their power to chastise their defection at pleasure. And were any one state to give up its arms, that state must be garrisoned by all Howe's army of Britons and Hessians[4] to preserve it from the anger of the rest. Mutual fear is the principal link in the chain of mutual love, and woe be to that state that breaks the compact. Howe is mercifully inviting you to barbarous destruction, and men must be either rogues or fools that will not see it. I dwell not upon the vapors of imagination: I bring reason to your ears, and, in language as plain as A, B, C, hold up truth to your eyes.

I thank God that I fear not. I see no real cause for fear. I know our situation well, and can see the way out of it. While our army was collected, Howe dared not risk a battle; and it is no credit to him that he decamped from the White Plains,[5] and waited a mean opportunity to ravage the defenseless Jerseys; but it is great credit to us, that, with a handful of men, we sustained an orderly retreat for near an hundred miles, brought off our ammunition, all our field pieces, the greatest part of our stores, and had four rivers to pass. None can say that our retreat was precipitate, for we were near three weeks in performing it, that the country[6] might have time to come in. Twice we marched back to meet the enemy, and remained out till dark. The sign of fear was not seen in our camp, and had not some of the cowardly and disaffected inhabitants spread false alarms through the country, the Jerseys had never been ravaged. Once more we are again collected and collecting; our new army at both ends of the continent is recruiting fast, and we shall be able to open the next campaign with sixty thousand men, well armed and clothed. This is our situation, and who will may know it. By perseverance and fortitude we have the prospect of a glorious issue; by cowardice and submission, the sad choice of a variety of evils—a ravaged country—a depopulated city—habitations without safety, and slavery without hope—our homes turned into barracks and bawdyhouses for Hessians, and a future race to provide for, whose fathers we shall doubt of. Look on this picture and weep over it! and if there yet remains one thoughtless wretch who believes it not, let him suffer it unlamented.

Common Sense

1776

2. General Thomas Gage, who commanded the British armies in America from 1763 to 1775, before Howe.
3. "And the peace of God, which passeth all understanding, shall keep your hearts and minds through Christ Jesus" (Philippians 4.7).

4. German mercenaries.
5. At White Plains, New York, on October 28, 1776, General Howe successfully overcame Washington's troops, but failed to take full advantage of his victory.
6. I.e., the local volunteers.

From The Age of Reason[1]

Chapter I. The Author's Profession of Faith

It has been my intention, for several years past, to publish my thoughts upon religion; I am well aware of the difficulties that attend the subject, and from that consideration had reserved it to a more advanced period of life. I intended it to be the last offering I should make to my fellow citizens of all nations, and that at a time when the purity of the motive that induced me to it could not admit of a question, even by those who might disapprove the work.

The circumstance that has now taken place in France,[2] of the total abolition of the whole national order of priesthood, and of everything appertaining to compulsive systems of religion, and compulsive articles of faith, has not only precipitated my intention, but rendered a work of this kind exceedingly necessary lest, in the general wreck of superstition, of false systems of government, and false theology, we lose sight of morality, of humanity, and of the theology that is true.

As several of my colleagues and others of my fellow citizens of France have given me the example of making their voluntary and individual profession of faith, I also will make mine; and I do this with all that sincerity and frankness with which the mind of man communicates with itself.

I believe in one God, and no more; and I hope for happiness beyond this life.

I believe the equality of man, and I believe that religious duties consist in doing justice, loving mercy, and endeavoring to make our fellow creatures happy.

But, lest it should be supposed that I believe many other things in addition to these, I shall, in the progress of this work, declare the things I do not believe, and my reasons for not believing them.

I do not believe in the creed professed by the Jewish church, by the Roman church, by the Greek church, by the Turkish church, by the Protestant church, nor by any church that I know of. My own mind is my own church.

All national institutions of churches, whether Jewish, Christian, or Turkish, appear to me no other than human inventions set up to terrify and enslave mankind, and monopolize power and profit.

I do not mean by this declaration to condemn those who believe otherwise; they have the same right to their belief as I have to mine. But it is necessary to the happiness of man that he be mentally faithful to himself. Infidelity does not consist in believing, or in disbelieving; it consists in professing to believe what he does not believe.

It is impossible to calculate the moral mischief, if I may so express it, that mental lying has produced in society. When a man has so far corrupted and prostituted the chastity of his mind as to subscribe his professional belief to things he does not believe, he has prepared himself for the commission of every other crime. He takes up the trade of a priest for the sake of gain, and, in order to qualify himself for that trade, he begins with a perjury. Can we conceive anything more destructive to morality than this?

Soon after I had published the pamphlet *Common Sense*, in America, I saw the exceeding probability that a revolution in the system of government would

---

1. The text used here is from *The Writings of Thomas Paine*, vol. 4, edited by M. D. Conway (1894–96).
2. By 1792 leaders of the French Revolution had dis-credited the Roman Catholic Church in France and closed the churches.

be followed by a revolution in the system of religion. The adulterous connection of church and state, wherever it had taken place, whether Jewish, Christian, or Turkish, had so effectually prohibited, by pains and penalties, every discussion upon established creeds and upon first principles of religion, that until the system of government should be changed, those subjects could not be brought fairly and openly before the world; but that whenever this should be done, a revolution in the system of religion would follow. Human inventions and priestcraft would be detected; and man would return to the pure, unmixed, and unadulterated belief of one God, and no more.

Chapter II. Of Missions and Revelations

Every national church or religion has established itself by pretending some special mission from God, communicated to certain individuals. The Jews have their Moses; the Christians their Jesus Christ, their apostles and saints; and the Turks their Mahomet; as if the way to God was not open to every man alike.

Each of those churches shows certain books, which they call revelation, or the Word of God. The Jews say that their Word of God was given by God to Moses face to face; the Christians say that their Word of God came by divine inspiration; and the Turks say that their Word of God (the Koran) was brought by an angel from heaven. Each of those churches accuses the other of unbelief; and, for my own part, I disbelieve them all.

As it is necessary to affix right ideas to words, I will, before I proceed further into the subject, offer some observations on the word revelation. Revelation when applied to religion, means something communicated immediately from God to man.

No one will deny or dispute the power of the Almighty to make such a communication if He pleases. But admitting, for the sake of a case, that something has been revealed to a certain person, and not revealed to any other person, it is revelation to that person only. When he tells it to a second person, a second to a third, a third to a fourth, and so on, it ceases to be a revelation to all those persons. It is revelation to the first person only, and hearsay to every other, and, consequently, they are not obliged to believe it.

It is a contradiction in terms and ideas to call anything a revelation that comes to us at secondhand, either verbally or in writing. Revelation is necessarily limited to the first communication. After this, it is only an account of something which that person says was a revelation made to him; and though he may find himself obliged to believe it, it cannot be incumbent on me to believe it in the same manner, for it was not a revelation made to me, and I have only his word for it that it was made to him.

When Moses told the children of Israel that he received the two tables of the commandments from the hand of God, they were not obliged to believe him, because they had no other authority for it than his telling them so; and I have no other authority for it than some historian telling me so, the commandments carrying no internal evidence of divinity with them. They contain some good moral precepts such as any man qualified to be a lawgiver or a legislator could produce himself, without having recourse to supernatural intervention.[3]

When I am told that the Koran was written in Heaven, and brought to

3. "It is, however, necessary to except the declaration which says that God *visits the sins of the fathers upon the children*. This is contrary to every principle of moral justice" [Paine's note].

Mahomet by an angel, the account comes to near the same kind of hearsay evidence and secondhand authority as the former. I did not see the angel myself, and therefore I have a right not to believe it.

When also I am told that a woman, called the Virgin Mary, said, or gave out, that she was with child without any cohabitation with a man, and that her betrothed husband, Joseph, said that an angel told him so, I have a right to believe them or not: such a circumstance required a much stronger evidence than their bare word for it: but we have not even this; for neither Joseph nor Mary wrote any such matter themselves. It is only reported by others that they said so. It is hearsay upon hearsay, and I do not choose to rest my belief upon such evidence.

It is, however, not difficult to account for the credit that was given to the story of Jesus Christ being the Son of God. He was born when the heathen mythology had still some fashion and repute in the world, and that mythology had prepared the people for the belief of such a story. Almost all the extraordinary men that lived under the heathen mythology were reputed to be the sons of some of their gods. It was not a new thing at that time to believe a man to have been celestially begotten; the intercourse of gods with women was then a matter of familiar opinion. Their Jupiter,[4] according to their accounts, had cohabited with hundreds; the story therefore had nothing in it either new, wonderful, or obscene; it was conformable to the opinions that then prevailed among the people called Gentiles, or mythologists, and it was those people only that believed it. The Jews, who had kept strictly to the belief of one god, and no more, and who had always rejected the heathen mythology, never credited the story.

It is curious to observe how the theory of what is called the Christian Church, sprung out of the tail of the heathen mythology. A direct incorporation took place in the first instance, by making the reputed founder to be celestially begotten. The trinity of gods that then followed was no other than a reduction of the former plurality, which was about twenty or thirty thousand. The statue of Mary succeeded the statue of Diana of Ephesus.[5] The deification of heroes changed into the canonization of saints. The mythologists had gods for everything; the Christian mythologists had saints for everything. The church became as crowded with the one, as the Pantheon[6] had been with the other; and Rome was the place of both. The Christian theory is little else than the idolatry of the ancient mythologists, accommodated to the purposes of power and revenue; and it yet remains to reason and philosophy to abolish the amphibious fraud.

Chapter XI. Of the Theology of the Christians, and the True Theology

As to the Christian system of faith, it appears to me as a species of atheism; a sort of religious denial of God. It professes to believe in a man rather than in God. It is a compound made up chiefly of man-ism with but little deism, and is as near to atheism as twilight is to darkness. It introduces between man and his Maker an opaque body, which it calls a redeemer, as the moon introduces her opaque self between the earth and the sun, and it produces by this means a religious or an irreligious eclipse of light. It has put the whole orbit of reason into shade.

4. Roman god of the heavens.
5. There was a temple built to honor the goddess Diana at Ephesus, an Ionian city in Asia Minor, which was one of the seven wonders of the ancient world. Diana of Ephesus was worshiped as a fertility goddess.
6. A temple in Rome dedicated to all the gods.

The effect of this obscurity has been that of turning everything upside down, and representing it in reverse; and among the revolutions it has thus magically produced, it has made a revolution in theology.

That which is now called natural philosophy, embracing the whole circle of science, of which astronomy occupies the chief place, is the study of the works of God, and of the power and wisdom of God in His works, and is the true theology.

As to the theology that is now studied in its place, it is the study of human opinions and of human fancies concerning God. It is not the study of God Himself in the works that He has made, but in the works or writings that man has made; and it is not among the least of the mischiefs that the Christian system has done to the world, that it has abandoned the original and beautiful system of theology, like a beautiful innocent, to distress and reproach, to make room for the hag of superstition.

The Book of Job and the 19th Psalm, which even the church admits to be more ancient than the chronological order in which they stand in the book called the Bible,[7] are theological orations conformable to the original system of theology. The internal evidence of those orations proves to a demonstration that the study and contemplation of the works of creation, and of the power and wisdom of God revealed and manifested in those works, made a great part of the religious devotion of the times in which they were written; and it was this devotional study and contemplation that led to the discovery of the principles upon which what are now called sciences are established; and it is to the discovery of these principles that almost all the arts that contribute to the convenience of human life owe their existence. Every principal art has some science for its parent, though the person who mechanically performs the work does not always, and but very seldom, perceive the connection.

It is a fraud of the Christian system to call the sciences human inventions; it is only the application of them that is human. Every science has for its basis a system of principles as fixed and unalterable as those by which the universe is regulated and governed. Man cannot make principles; he can only discover them.

For example: every person who looks at an almanac sees an account when an eclipse will take place, and he sees also that it never fails to take place according to the account there given. This shows that man is acquainted with the laws by which the heavenly bodies move. But it would be something worse than ignorance, were any church on earth to say that those laws are an human invention.

It would also be ignorance, or something worse, to say that the scientific principles, by the aid of which man is enabled to calculate and foreknow when an eclipse will take place, are an human invention. Man cannot invent anything that is eternal and immutable; and the scientific principles he employs for this purpose must, and are, of necessity, as eternal and immutable as the laws by which the heavenly bodies move, or they could not be used as they are to ascertain the time when, and the manner how, an eclipse will take place.

The scientific principles that man employs to obtain the foreknowledge of

---

7. In the order of the Old Testament, Job comes before the Book of Psalms, but the author of Job alludes to some lines of the Psalms, which must have come earlier. Paine thinks that both Job and Psalm 19 ("The heavens declare the glory of God; and the firmament sheweth his handiwork") conform "to the original system of theology," because they are about immediate responses to the world that God made.

an eclipse, or of anything else relating to the motion of the heavenly bodies, are contained chiefly in that part of science that is called trigonometry, or the properties of a triangle, which, when applied to the study of the heavenly bodies, is called astronomy; when applied to direct the course of a ship on the ocean, it is called navigation; when applied to the construction of figures drawn by a rule and compass, it is called geometry; when applied to the construction of plans of edifices, it is called architecture; when applied to the measurement of any portion of the surface of the earth, it is called land surveying. In fine, it is the soul of science. It is an eternal truth: it contains the mathematical demonstration of which man speaks, and the extent of its uses are unknown.

It may be said, that man can make or draw a triangle, and therefore a triangle is an human invention.

But the triangle, when drawn, is no other than the image of the principle: it is a delineation to the eye, and from thence to the mind, of a principle that would otherwise be imperceptible. The triangle does not make the principle any more than a candle taken into a room that was dark makes the chairs and tables that before were invisible. All the properties of a triangle exist independently of the figure, and existed before any triangle was drawn or thought of by man. Man had no more to do in the formation of those properties or principles than he had to do in making the laws by which the heavenly bodies move; and therefore the one must have the same divine origin as the other.

In the same manner as, it may be said, that man can make a triangle, so also, may it be said, he can make the mechanical instrument called a lever. But the principle by which the lever acts is a thing distinct from the instrument, and would exist if the instrument did not; it attaches itself to the instrument after it is made; the instrument, therefore, can act no otherwise than it does act; neither can all the efforts of human invention make it act otherwise. That which, in all such cases, man calls the effect, is no other than the principle itself rendered perceptible to the senses.

Since, then, man cannot make principles, from whence did he gain a knowledge of them, so as to be able to apply them, not only to things on earth, but to ascertain the motion of bodies so immensely distant from him as all the heavenly bodies are? From whence, I ask, could he gain that knowledge, but from the study of the true theology?

It is the structure of the universe that has taught this knowledge to man. That structure is an ever-existing exhibition of every principle upon which every part of mathematical science is founded. The offspring of this science is mechanics; for mechanics is no other than the principles of science applied practically. The man who proportions the several parts of a mill uses the same scientific principles as if he had the power of constructing an universe, but as he cannot give to matter that invisible agency by which all the component parts of the immense machine of the universe have influence upon each other, and act in motional unison together, without any apparent contact, and to which man has given the name of attraction, gravitation, and repulsion, he supplies the place of that agency by the humble imitation of teeth and cogs. All the parts of man's microcosm must visibly touch. But could he gain a knowledge of that agency, so as to be able to apply it in practice, we might then say that another canonical book[8] of the word of God had been discovered.

---

8. I.e., a book that would form a part of Scripture.

If man could alter the properties of the lever, so also could he alter the properties of the triangle: for a lever (taking that sort of lever which is called a steelyard, for the sake of explanation) forms, when in motion, a triangle. The line it descends from (one point of that line being in the fulcrum), the line it descends to, and the chord of the arc, which the end of the lever describes in the air, are the three sides of a triangle. The other arm of the lever describes also a triangle; and the corresponding sides of those two triangles, calculated scientifically, or measured geometrically—and also the sines, tangents, and secants generated from the angles, and geometrically measured—have the same proportions to each other as the different weights have that will balance each other on the lever, leaving the weight of the lever out of the case.

It may also be said that man can make a wheel and axis; that he can put wheels of different magnitudes together, and produce a mill. Still the case comes back to the same point, which is, that he did not make the principle that gives the wheels those powers. This principle is as unalterable as in the former cases, or rather it is the same principle under a different appearance to the eye.

The power that two wheels of different magnitudes have upon each other is in the same proportion as if the semidiameter of the two wheels were joined together and made into that kind of lever I have described, suspended at the part where the semidiameters join; for the two wheels, scientifically considered, are no other than the two circles generated by the motion of the compound lever.

It is from the study of the true theology that all our knowledge of science is derived; and it is from that knowledge that all the arts have originated.

The Almighty lecturer, by displaying the principles of science in the structure of the universe, has invited man to study and to imitation. It is as if He had said to the inhabitants of this globe that we call ours, "I have made an earth for man to dwell upon, and I have rendered the starry heavens visible, to teach him science and the arts. He can now provide for his own comfort, and learn from my munificence to all, to be kind to each other."

Of what use is it, unless it be to teach man something, that his eye is endowed with the power of beholding, to an incomprehensible distance, an immensity of worlds revolving in the ocean of space? Or of what use is it that this immensity of worlds is visible to man? What has man to do with the Pleiades, with Orion, with Sirius, with the star he calls the North Star, with the moving orbs he has named Saturn, Jupiter, Mars, Venus, and Mercury, if no uses are to follow from their being visible? A less power of vision would have been sufficient for man, if the immensity he now possesses were given only to waste itself, as it were, on an immense desert of space glittering with shows.

It is only by contemplating what he calls the starry heavens, as the book and school of science, that he discovers any use in their being visible to him, or any advantage resulting from his immensity of vision. But when he contemplates the subject in this light, he sees an additional motive for saying, that nothing was made in vain; for in vain would be this power of vision if it taught man nothing.

1793   1794

THOMAS JEFFERSON
1743–1826

President of the United States, first secretary of state, and minister to France, governor of Virginia, and congressman, Thomas Jefferson once said that he wished to be remembered for only three things: drafting the Declaration of Independence, writing and supporting the Virginia Statute for Religious Freedom (1786), and founding the University of Virginia. Jefferson might well have included a number of other accomplishments in this list: he was a remarkable architect and designed the Virginia state capital, his residence Monticello, and the original buildings for the University of Virginia; he farmed thousands of acres and built one of the most beautiful plantations in America; he had a library of some ten thousand volumes, which served as the basis for the Library of Congress, and a collection of paintings and sculpture that made him America's greatest patron of the arts; and was known the world over for his spirit of scientific inquiry and as the creator of a number of remarkable inventions. The three acts for which he wished to be remembered, however, have this in common: they all testify to Jefferson's lifelong passion to liberate the human mind from tyranny, whether imposed by the state, the church, or our own ignorance.

Jefferson was born at Shadwell, in what is now Albermarle County, Virginia. His mother, Jane Randolph, came from one of the most distinguished families in Virginia. Peter Jefferson, his father, was a county official and surveyor. He made the first accurate map of Virginia, something of which Jefferson was always proud. When his father died Thomas was only fourteen. Peter Jefferson left his son 2,750 acres of land, and Jefferson added to this acreage until he died; at one time he owned almost ten thousand acres. Jefferson tells us in his *Autobiography* that his father's education had been "quite neglected" but that he was always "eager after information" and determined to improve himself. In 1760, when Jefferson entered William and Mary College in Williamsburg, Virginia, he had mastered Latin and Greek, played the violin respectably, and was a skilled horseman. He was tall and a bit awkward looking, but a good companion. Williamsburg was the capital of Virginia as well as a college town, and Jefferson was fortunate enough to make the acquaintance of three men who strongly influenced his life: Governor Francis Fauquier, a fellow of the Royal Society; George Wythe, one of the best teachers of law in the country; and Dr. William Small, an emigrant from Scotland who taught mathematics and philosophy and who introduced Jefferson, as Garry Wills has put it, "to the invigorating realm of the Scottish Enlightenment," especially the work of Francis Hutcheson, author of *An Inquiry into the Original of Our Ideas of Beauty and Virtue* (1725), and Lord Kames (Henry Home), author of *Essays on the Principles of Morality and Natural Religion* (1751). Jefferson flourished in Williamsburg, and it is hard to imagine a city in America where his natural interests and talents could have been more sympathetically encouraged.

Jefferson stayed on in Williamsburg to read law after graduation and was admitted to the bar. In 1769 he was elected to the Virginia House of Burgesses and began a distinguished career in the legislature. In 1774 he wrote an influential and daring pamphlet called *A Summary View of the Rights of British America*, denying all parliamentary authority over America and arguing that ties to the British monarchy were voluntary and not irrevocable. Jefferson's reputation as a writer preceded him to Philadelphia, where he was a delegate to the Second Continental Congress, and on June 11, 1776, he was elected to join Benjamin Franklin, John Adams, Roger Sherman, and Robert Livingston in drafting a declaration of independence. Although committee members made suggestions, the draft was very much Jefferson's own. As Garry Wills has recently shown, Jefferson was unhappy with the changes made by Congress to his draft, and rightly so; for congressional changes went contrary to some of his basic arguments. Jefferson wished to place the British *people* on record as the ultimate cause of the Revolution, because they tolerated a corrupt parliament and king; and he wished to include a strong statement against slavery. Congress tolerated neither passage. Jefferson was justified, however, in asking that he be remembered as the author of the Declaration. It was, as Dumas Malone, Jefferson's biographer, once put it, a "dangerous but glorious opportunity." Whether as the result of these frustrations or merely Jefferson's wish to be nearer his family, he left the Congress in September 1776, and entered the Virginia House of Delegates. In 1779 he was elected governor, and although reelected the following year, Jefferson's term of office came to an ignominious end when he resigned. After the British captured Richmond in 1781, Jefferson and the legislature moved to Charlottesville, and he and the legislators barely escaped imprisonment when the pursuing British army descended on them at Monticello. Jefferson's resignation and the lack of preparations for the defense of the city were held against him, and it was some time before he regained the confidence of Virginians.

From 1781 to 1784 Jefferson withdrew from public life and remained at Monticello, completing his only book, *Notes on the State of Virginia*. In 1784 he was appointed minister to France and served with Benjamin Franklin on the commission that signed the Treaty of Paris, ending the Revolutionary War. He returned to Monticello in 1789, and in 1790 Washington appointed him the first secretary of state under the newly adopted Constitution. After three years he announced his plans for retirement once again and withdrew to Monticello, where he rotated his crops and built a grist mill. But Jefferson's political blood was too thick for retirement, and in 1796 he ran for the office of president, losing to John Adams and taking the office of vice president instead. In 1800 he was elected president, the first to be inaugurated in Washington. He named Benjamin Latrobe surveyor of public buildings, and he worked with Latrobe in planning a great city.

When Jefferson returned to Monticello in 1809, he knew that this time his public life was over. For the final seventeen years of his life he kept a watchful eye on everything that grew in Monticello. But Jefferson was never far from the world. He rose every morning to attack his voluminous correspondence. The Library of Congress holds more than fifty-five thousand Jefferson manuscripts and letters, and the most recent edition of his writings will run to sixty volumes. Jefferson left no treatise on political philosophy and, in a sense, was no political thinker. He was always more interested in the practical consequences of ideas. He remained an agrarian aristocrat all his life, and it is to the liberty of mind and the values of the land that he always returned. As Dumas Malone puts it: he was a "homely aristocrat in manner of life and personal tastes; he distrusted all rulers and feared the rise of an industrial proletariat, but more than any of his eminent contemporaries, he trusted the common man, if measurably enlightened and kept in rural virtue." Jefferson died a few hours before John Adams on the Fourth of July, 1826.

From The Autobiography of Thomas Jefferson[1]

From *The Declaration of Independence*

* * *

It appearing in the course of these debates, that the colonies of New York, New Jersey, Pennsylvania, Delaware, Maryland, and South Carolina were not

1. On June 7, 1776, Richard Henry Lee of Virginia proposed to the Second Continental Congress, meeting in Philadelphia, that "these united Colonies are, and of a right ought to be, free and independent states." On

yet matured for falling from the parent stem, but that they were fast advancing to that state, it was thought most prudent to wait a while for them, and to postpone the final decision to July 1st; but, that this might occasion as little delay as possible, a committee was appointed to prepare a Declaration of Independence. The committee were John Adams, Dr. Franklin, Roger Sherman, Robert R. Livingston, and myself. Committees were also appointed, at the same time, to prepare a plan of confederation for the colonies, and to state the terms proper to be proposed for foreign alliance. The committee for drawing the Declaration of Independence, desired me to do it. It was accordingly done, and being approved by them, I reported it to the House on Friday, the 28th of June, when it was read, and ordered to lie on the table. On Monday, the 1st of July, the House resolved itself into a committee of the whole, and resumed the consideration of the original motion made by the delegates of Virginia, which, being again debated through the day, was carried in the affirmative by the votes of New Hampshire, Connecticut, Massachusetts, Rhode Island, New Jersey, Maryland, Virginia, North Carolina and Georgia. South Carolina and Pennsylvania voted against it. Delaware had but two members present, and they were divided. The delegates from New York declared they were for it themselves, and were assured their constituents were for it; but that their instructions having been drawn near a twelve-month before, when reconciliation was still the general object, they were enjoined by them to do nothing which should impede that object. They, therefore, thought themselves not justifiable in voting on either side, and asked leave to withdraw from the question: which was given them. The committee rose and reported their resolution to the House. Mr. Edward Rutledge, of South Carolina, then requested the determination might be put off to the next day, as he believed his colleagues, though they disapproved of the resolution, would then join in it for the sake of unanimity. The ultimate question, whether the House would agree to the resolution of the committee, was accordingly postponed to the next day, when it was again moved, and South Carolina concurred in voting for it. In the meantime, a third member had come post[2] from the Delaware counties, and turned the vote of that colony in favor of the resolution. Members of a different sentiment attending that morning from Pennsylvania also, her vote was changed, so that the whole twelve colonies who were authorized to vote at all, gave their voices for it; and, within a few days, the convention of New York approved of it, and thus supplied the void occasioned by the withdrawing of her delegates from the vote.

Congress proceeded the same day to consider the Declaration of Independence, which had been reported and lain on the table the Friday preceding, and on Monday referred to a committee of the whole. The pusillanimous idea that we had friends in England worth keeping terms with, still haunted the minds of many. For this reason, those passages which conveyed censures on the people of England were struck out, lest they should give them offense. The clause too, reprobating the enslaving the inhabitants of Africa, was struck out

June 11, a committee of five—John Adams of Massachusetts, Benjamin Franklin of Pennsylvania, Roger Sherman of Connecticut, Robert Livingston of New York, and Thomas Jefferson of Virginia—was instructed to draft a declaration of independence. The draft presented to Congress on June 28 was primarily the work of Jefferson. Lee's resolution was passed on July 2, and the Declaration was adopted on July 4 with the changes noted by Jefferson in this text, taken from his *Autobiography*. On August 2 a copy in parchment was signed by all the delegates but three, and they signed later. The text used here is from *The Writings of Thomas Jefferson*, edited by A. A. Lipscomb and A. E. Bergh (1903).

2. Speedily, posthaste.

in complaisance to South Carolina and Georgia, who had never attempted to restrain the importation of slaves, and who, on the contrary, still wished to continue it. Our northern brethren also, I believe, felt a little tender under those censures; for though their people had very few slaves themselves, yet they had been pretty considerable carriers of them to others. The debates, having taken up the greater parts of the 2d, 3d, and 4th days of July, were, on the evening of the last, closed; the Declaration was reported by the committee, agreed to by the House, and signed by every member present, except Mr. Dickinson.[3] As the sentiments of men are known not only by what they receive, but what they reject also, I will state the form of the Declaration as originally reported. The parts struck out by Congress shall be distinguished by a black line drawn under them, and those inserted by them shall be placed in the margin, or in a concurrent column.

A DECLARATION BY THE REPRESENTATIVES OF THE UNITED STATES OF AMERICA, IN GENERAL CONGRESS ASSEMBLED.

When, in the course of human events, it becomes necessary for one people to dissolve the political bands which have connected them with another, and to assume among the powers of the earth the separate and equal station to which the laws of nature and of nature's God entitle them, a decent respect to the opinions of mankind requires that they should declare the causes which impel them to the separation.

We hold these truths to be self evident: that all men are created equal;[4] that they are endowed by their Creator with <u>inherent and</u>   certain inalienable rights; that among these are life, liberty, and the pursuit of happiness;[5] that to secure these rights, governments are instituted among men, deriving their just powers from the consent of the governed; that whenever any form of government becomes destructive of these ends, it is the right of the people to alter or to abolish it, and to institute new government, laying its foundation on such principles, and organizing its powers in such form, as to them shall seem most likely to effect their safety and happiness. Prudence, indeed, will dictate that governments long established should not be changed for light and transient causes; and accordingly all experience hath shown that mankind are more disposed to suffer while evils are sufferable, than to right themselves by abolishing the forms to which they are accustomed. But when a long train of abuses and usurpations, <u>begun at a distinguished[6] period and</u> pursuing invariably the same object, evinces a design

3. John Dickinson of Pennsylvania, who opposed it.
4. Garry Wills, in his study of the Declaration (*Inventing America*, 1978), tells us that Jefferson means *equal* in possessing a moral sense: "The moral sense is not only man's *highest* faculty, but the one that is *equal* to all men."
5. In his *Second Treatise on Government* (1689) John Locke defined man's natural rights to "life, liberty, and property." Jefferson's substitution of "pursuit of happiness" has puzzled a number of critics. Wills suggests that Jefferson was less influenced by Locke than the Scottish philosophers, particularly Francis Hutcheson

and his *Inquiry into the Original of Our Ideas of Beauty and Virtue* (1725). Wills tells us that "the pursuit of happiness is a phenomenon both obvious and paradoxical. It supplies us with the ground of human right and the goal of human virtue. It is the basic drive of the self, and the only means given for transcending the self. . . . Men in the eighteenth century felt they could become conscious of their freedom only by discovering how they were bound: When they found what they *must* pursue, they knew they had a *right* to pursue it."
6. I.e., discernible.

to reduce them under absolute despotism, it is their right, it is their duty to throw off such government, and to provide new guards for their future security. Such has been the patient sufferance of these colonies; and such is now the necessity which constrains them to <u>expunge</u> their former systems of government. The history of the present king of Great Britain[7] is a history of <u>unremitting</u> injuries and usurpations, <u>among which appears no solitary fact to contradict the uniform tenor of the rest, but all have</u> in direct object the establishment of an absolute tyranny over these states. To prove this, let facts be submitted to a candid world <u>for the truth of which we pledge a faith yet unsullied by falsehood.</u>

     alter
     repeated
     all having

He has refused his assent to laws the most wholesome and necessary for the public good.

He has forbidden his governors to pass laws of immediate and pressing importance, unless suspended in their operation till his assent should be obtained; and, when so suspended, he has utterly neglected to attend to them.

He has refused to pass other laws for the accommodation of large districts of people, unless those people would relinquish the right of representation in the legislature, a right inestimable to them, and formidable to tyrants only.

He has called together legislative bodies at places unusual, uncomfortable, and distant from the depository of their public records, for the sole purpose of fatiguing them into compliance with his measures.

He has dissolved representative houses repeatedly <u>and continually</u> for opposing with manly firmness his invasions on the rights of the people.

He has refused for a long time after such dissolutions to cause others to be elected, whereby the legislative powers, incapable of annihilation, have returned to the people at large for their exercise, the state remaining, in the meantime, exposed to all the dangers of invasion from without and convulsions within.

He has endeavored to prevent the population of these states; for that purpose obstructing the laws for naturalization of foreigners, refusing to pass others to encourage their migrations hither, and raising the conditions of new appropriations of lands.

He has <u>suffered</u> the administration of justice <u>totally to cease in some of these states</u> refusing his assent to laws for establishing judiciary powers.

     obstructed
     by

He has made <u>our</u> judges dependent on his will alone for the tenure of their offices, and the amount and payment of their salaries.

He has erected a multitude of new offices, <u>by a self-assumed power</u> and sent hither swarms of new officers to harass our people and eat out their substance.

He has kept among us in times of peace standing armies <u>and ships of war</u> without the consent of our legislatures.

---

7. King George III (1738–1820).

He has affected to render the military independent of, and superior to, the civil power.

He has combined with others[8] to subject us to a jurisdiction foreign to our constitutions and unacknowledged by our laws, giving his assent to their acts of pretended legislation for quartering large bodies of armed troops among us; for protecting them by a mock trial from punishment for any murders which they should commit on the inhabitants of these states; for cutting off our trade with all parts of the world; for imposing taxes on us without our consent; for depriving us [*in many cases*] of the benefits of trial by jury; for transporting us beyond seas to be tried for pretended offenses; for abolishing the free system of English laws in a neighboring province,[9] establishing therein an arbitrary government, and enlarging its boundaries, so as to render it at once an example and fit instrument for introducing the same absolute rule into these states; for *colonies;* taking away our charters, abolishing our most valuable laws, and altering fundamentally the forms of our governments; for suspending our own legislatures, and declaring themselves invested with power to legislate for us in all cases whatsoever.

He has abdicated government here withdrawing his governors, and declaring us out of his allegiance and protection. *by declaring us out of his protection, and waging war against us.*

He has plundered our seas, ravaged our coasts, burnt our towns, and destroyed the lives of our people.

He is at this time transporting large armies of foreign mercenaries[1] to complete the works of death, desolation and tyranny already begun with circumstances of cruelty and perfidy [ ] unworthy the head of a civilized nation. *scarcely paralleled in the most barbarous ages, and totally*

He has constrained our fellow citizens taken captive on the high seas, to bear arms against their country, to become the executioners of their friends and brethren, or to fall themselves by their hands.

He has [ ] endeavored to bring on the inhabitants of our frontiers, the merciless Indian savages, whose known rule of warfare is an undistinguished destruction of all ages, sexes and conditions of existence. *excited domestic insurrection among us, and has*

He has incited treasonable insurrections of our fellow citizens, with the allurements of forfeiture and confiscation of our property.

He has waged cruel war against human nature itself, violating its most sacred rights of life and liberty in the persons of a distant people who never offended him, captivating and carrying them into slavery in another hemisphere, or to incur miserable death in their transportation thither. This piratical warfare, the opprobrium of INFIDEL powers, is the warfare of the CHRISTIAN king of Great Britain. Determined to keep open a market where MEN should be bought and sold, he has prostituted his negative for suppressing every legislative attempt to prohibit or to restrain this

---

8. I.e., the British Parliament.
9. The Quebec Act of 1774 recognized the Roman Catholic religion in Quebec and extended the borders of the province to the Ohio River; it restored French civil law and thus angered the New England colonies. It was often referred to as one of the "intolerable acts."
1. German soldiers hired by the king for colonial service.

execrable commerce. And that this assemblage of horrors might want no fact of distinguished die, he is now exciting those very people to rise in arms among us, and to purchase that liberty of which he has deprived them, by murdering the people on whom he also obtruded them: thus paying off former crimes committed against the LIBERTIES of one people, with crimes which he urges them to commit against the LIVES of another.

In every stage of these oppressions we have petitioned for redress in the most humble terms: our repeated petitions have been answered only by repeated injuries.

A prince whose character is thus marked by every act which may define a tyrant is unfit to be the ruler of a [ ] people who mean to be free. Future ages will scarcely believe that the hardiness of one man adventured, within the short compass of twelve years only, to lay a foundation ·so broad and so undisguised for tyranny over a people fostered and fixed in principles of freedom. *free*

Nor have we been wanting in attentions to our British brethren. We have warned them from time to time of attempts by their legislature to extend a jurisdiction over these our states. We have reminded them of the circumstances of our emigration and settlement here, no one of which could warrant so strange a pretension: that these were effected at the expense of our own blood and treasure, unassisted by the wealth or the strength of Great Britain: that in constituting indeed our several forms of government, we had adopted one common king, thereby laying a foundation for perpetual league and amity with them: but that submission to their parliament was no part of our constitution, nor ever in idea, if history may be credited: and, we [ ] appealed to their native justice and magnanimity as well as to the ties of our common kindred to disavow these usurpations which were likely to interrupt our connection and correspondence. They too have been deaf to the voice of justice and of consanguinity, and when occasions have been given them, by the regular course of their laws, of removing from their councils the disturbers of our harmony, they have, by their free election, reestablished them in power. At this very time too, they are permitting their chief magistrate to send over not only soldiers of our common blood, but Scotch and foreign mercenaries to invade and destroy us. These facts have given the last stab to agonizing affection, and manly spirit bids us to renounce forever these unfeeling brethren. We must endeavor to forget our former love for them, and hold them as we hold the rest of mankind, enemies in war, in peace friends. We might have been a free and a great people together; but a communication of grandeur and of freedom, it seems, is below their dignity. Be it so, since they will have it. The road to happiness and to glory is open to us, too. We will tread it apart from them, and acquiesce in the necessity which denounces[2] our eternal separation [ ]!

an unwarrantable us

have and we have conjured them by would inevitably

We must therefore

and hold them as we hold the rest of mankind, enemies in war, in peace friends.

2. Proclaims.

We therefore the representatives of the United States of America in General Congress assembled, do in the name, and by the authority of the good people of these <u>states reject and renounce all allegiance and subjection to the kings of Great Britain and all others who may hereafter claim by, through or under them; we utterly dissolve all political connection which may heretofore have subsisted between us and the people or parliament of Great Britain: and finally we do assert and declare these colonies to be free and independent states,</u> and that as free and independent states, they have full power to levy war, conclude peace, contract alliances, establish commerce, and to do all other acts and things which independent states may of right do.

And for the support of this declaration, we mutually pledge to each other our lives, our fortunes, and our sacred honor.

We, therefore, the representatives of the United States of America in

General Congress assembled, appealing to the supreme judges of the world for the rectitude of our intentions, do in the name, and by the authority of the good people of these colonies, solemnly publish and declare, that these united colonies are, and of right ought to be free and independent states; that they are absolved from all allegiance to the British crown, and that all political connection between them and the state of Great Britain is, and ought to be, totally dissolved; and that as free and independent states, they have full power to levy war, conclude peace, contract alliances, establish commerce, and to do all other acts and things which independent states may of right do.

And for the support of this declaration, with a firm reliance on the protection of divine providence, we mutually pledge to each other our lives, our fortunes, and our sacred honor.

The Declaration thus signed on the 4th, on paper, was engrossed on parchment, and signed again on the 2d of August.

1821   1829

From Notes on the State of Virginia[1]

From *Query* V. *Cascades*

* * *

NATURAL BRIDGE[2]

The *Natural bridge*, the most sublime of Nature's works, though not comprehended under the present head,[3] must not be pretermitted.[4] It is on the ascent of a hill, which seems to have been cloven through its length by some

1. In 1781, the year Jefferson retired as governor of Virginia, he received a request from the Marquis de Barbé-Marbois, secretary of the French legation at Philadelphia, to answer twenty-three questions concerning the geographical boundaries, the ecology, and the social history of Virginia. Jefferson took the occasion to make some observations on slavery, manufacturing, and government. He wanted especially to counter the notion, prevalent among European naturalists, that species in North America had degenerated and were inferior to Old World types. Jefferson's replies were published privately in 1784–85. The threat of an unauthorized French translation prompted Jefferson to publish an authorized edition in London in 1787. The text used here is from the Norton edition, edited by William Peden (1954).
2. Jefferson owned the land near Lexington, Virginia, on which the Natural Bridge stands.
3. I.e., it is not a cascade.
4. Omitted.

great convulsion. The fissure, just at the bridge, is by some admeasurements, 270 feet deep, by others only 205. It is about 45 feet wide at the bottom, and 90 feet at the top; this of course determines the length of the bridge, and its height from the water. Its breadth in the middle, is about 60 feet, but more at the ends, and the thickness of the mass at the summit of the arch, about 40 feet. A part of this thickness is constituted by a coat of earth, which gives growth to many large trees. The residue, with the hill on both sides, is one solid rock of limestone. The arch approaches the Semi-elliptical form; but the larger axis of the ellipsis, which would be the cord of the arch, is many times longer than the semi-axis which gives its height. Though the sides of this bridge are provided in some parts with a parapet of fixed rocks, yet few men have resolution to walk to them and look over into the abyss. You involuntarily fall on your hands and feet, creep to the parapet and peep over it. Looking down from this height about a minute gave me a violent headache. This painful sensation is relieved by a short, but pleasing view of the Blue ridge along the fissure downwards, and upwards by that of the Short hills, which, with the Purgatory mountain is a divergence from the North ridge; and, descending then to to the valley below, the sensation becomes delightful in the extreme. It is impossible for the emotions, arising from the sublime, to be felt beyond what they are here: so beautiful an arch, so elevated, so light, and springing, as it were, up to heaven, the rapture of the Spectator is really indescribable! The fissure continues deep and narrow and, following the margin of the stream upwards about three eighths of a mile you arrive at a limestone cavern, less remarkable, however, for height and extent than those before described. Its entrance into the hill is but a few feet above the bed of the stream. This bridge is in the county of Rockbridge, to which it has given name, and affords a public and commodious passage over a valley, which cannot be crossed elsewhere for a considerable distance. The stream passing under it is called Cedar Creek. It is a water of James River, and sufficient in the driest seasons to turn a grist-mill, though its fountain is not more than two miles above.

From *Query VI. Productions Mineral, Vegetable, and Animal*

*　　*　　*

The opinion advanced by the Count de Buffon[5] is 1. That the animals common both to the old and new world are smaller in the latter. 2. That those peculiar to the new are on a smaller scale. 3. That those which have been domesticated in both have degenerated in America. and 4. That on the whole it exhibits fewer species. And the reason he thinks is that the heats of America are less; that more waters are spread over its surface by nature, and fewer of these drained off by the hand of man. In other words, that *heat* is friendly, and *moisture* adverse to the production and development of large quadrupeds. I will not meet this hypothesis on its first doubtful ground, whether the climate of America be comparatively more humid? Because we are not furnished with observations sufficient to decide this question. And though, till it be decided, we are as free to deny, as others are to affirm, the fact, yet for a moment let it be supposed. The hypothesis, after this supposition, proceeds to another; that *moisture* is unfriendly to animal growth. The truth of this is inscrutable to us

5. Georges Louis Leclerc de Buffon (1707–1788), French naturalist and keeper of the Royal Gardens. Buffon suggested that North American species were degenerate in his *Natural History* (1749–88).

by reasonings a priori.[6] Nature has hidden from us her modus agendi.[7] Our only appeal on such questions is to experience; and I think that experience is against the supposition. It is by the assistance of *heat* and *moisture* that vegetables are elaborated from the elements of earth, air, water, and fire. We accordingly see the more humid climates produce the greater quantity of vegetables. Vegetables are mediately or immediately the food of every animal: and in proportion to the quantity of food, we see animals not only multiplied in their numbers, but improved in their bulk, as far as the laws of their nature will admit. Of this opinion is the Count de Buffon himself in another part of his work: "in general it seems that somewhat cold countries are better suited to our oxen than hot countries, and they are the heavier and bigger in proportion as the climate is damper and more abounding in pasture lands. The oxen of Denmark, of Podolie,[8] of the Ukraine, and of Tartary which is inhabited by the Calmouques,[9] are the largest of all." Here then a race of animals, and one of the largest too, has been increased in its dimensions by *cold* and *moisture*, in direct opposition to the hypothesis, which supposes that these two circumstances diminish animal bulk, and that it is their contraries *heat* and *dryness* which enlarge it. But when we appeal to experience, we are not to rest satisfied with a single fact. Let us therefore try our question on more general ground. Let us take our portions of the earth, Europe and America for instance, sufficiently extensive to give operation to general causes; let us consider the circumstances peculiar to each, and observe their effect on animal nature. America, running through the torrid as well as temperate zone, has more *heat*, collectively taken, than Europe. But Europe, according to our hypothesis, is the *dryest*. They are equally adapted then to animal productions; each being endowed with one of those causes which befriend animal growth, and with one which opposes it. If it be thought unequal to compare Europe with America, which is so much larger, I answer, not more so than to compare America with the whole world. Besides, the purpose of the comparison is to try an hypothesis, which makes the size of animals depend on the *heat* and *moisture* of climate. If therefore we take a region, so extensive as to comprehend a sensible distinction of climate, and so extensive too as that local accidents, or the intercourse of animals on its borders, may not materially affect the size of those in its interior parts, we shall comply with those conditions which the hypothesis may reasonably demand. The objection would be the weaker in the present case, because any intercourse of animals which may take place on the confines of Europe and Asia, is to the advantage of the former, Asia producing certainly larger animals than Europe. * * *

Hitherto I have considered this hypothesis as applied to brute animals only, and not in its extension to the man of America, whether aboriginal or transplanted. It is the opinion of Mons. de Buffon that the former furnishes no exception to it: "Although the savage of the new world is about the same height as man in our world, this does not suffice for him to constitute an exception to the general fact that all living nature has become smaller on that continent. The savage is feeble, and has small organs of generation; he has neither hair nor beard, and no ardor whatever for his female; although swifter than the European because he is better accustomed to running, he is, on the other

6. Assumptions; previously held ideas (Latin).
7. The mode by which a thing acts or operates (Latin).
8. A village in northeast India.

9. More commonly spelled "Kalmucks," a nomadic Mongol tribe.

hand, less strong in body; he is also less sensitive, and yet more timid and cowardly; he has no vivacity, no activity of mind; the activity of his body is less an exercise, a voluntary motion, than a necessary action caused by want; relieve him of hunger and thirst, and you deprive him of the active principle of all his movements; he will rest stupidly upon his legs or lying down entire days. There is no need for seeking further the cause of the isolated mode of life of these savages and their repugnance for society: the most precious spark of the fire of nature has been refused to them; they lack ardor for their females, and consequently have no love for their fellow men: not knowing this strongest and most tender of all affections, their other feelings are also cold and languid; they love their parents and children but little; the most intimate of all ties, the family connection, binds them therefore but loosely together; between family and family there is no tie at all; hence they have no communion, no common-wealth, no state of society. Physical love constitutes their only morality; their heart is icy, their society cold, and their rule harsh. They look upon their wives only as servants for all work, or as beasts of burden, which they load without consideration with the burden of their hunting, and which they com-pel without mercy, without gratitude, to perform tasks which are often beyond their strength. They have only few children, and they take little care of them. Everywhere the original defect appears: they are indifferent because they have little sexual capacity, and this indifference to the other sex is the fundamental defect which weakens their nature, prevents its development, and—destroying the very germs of life—uproots society at the same time. Man is here no excep-tion to the general rule. Nature, by refusing him the power of love, has treated him worse and lowered him deeper than any animal." An afflicting picture indeed, which, for the honor of human nature, I am glad to believe has no original. Of the Indian of South America I know nothing; for I would not honor with the appelation of knowledge, what I derive from the fables pub-lished of them. These I believe to be just as true as the fables of Aesop.[1] This belief is founded on what I have seen of man, white, red, and black, and what has been written of him by authors, enlightened themselves, and writing amidst an enlightened people. The Indian of North America being more within our reach, I can speak of him somewhat from my own knowledge, but more from the information of others better acquainted with him, and on whose truth and judgment I can rely. From these sources I am able to say, in contradiction to this representation, that he is neither more defective in ardor, nor more impotent with his female, than the white reduced to the same diet and exercise: that he is brave, when an enterprise depends on bravery; educa-tion with him making the point of honor consist in the destruction of an enemy by stratagem, and in the preservation of his own person free from injury; or perhaps this is nature; while it is education which teaches us to honor force more than finesse; that he will defend himself against an host of enemies, always choosing to be killed, rather than to surrender, though it be to the whites, who he knows will treat him well: that in other situations also he meets death with more deliberation, and endures tortures with a firmness unknown almost to religious enthusiasm with us: that he is affectionate to his children, careful of them, and indulgent in the extreme: that his affections comprehend his other connections, weakening, as with us, from circle to cir-

---

1. A Greek slave (c. 620–560 B.C.), reported to be the author of fables.

cle, as they recede from the center: that his friendships are strong and faithful to the uttermost extremity: that his sensibility is keen, even the warriors weeping most bitterly on the loss of their children, though in general they endeavor to appear superior to human events: that his vivacity and activity of mind is equal to ours in the same situation; hence his eagerness for hunting, and for games of chance. The women are submitted to unjust drudgery. This I believe is the case with every barbarous people. With such, force is law. The stronger sex therefore imposes on the weaker. It is civilization alone which replaces women in the enjoyment of their natural equality. That first teaches us to subdue the selfish passions, and to respect those rights in others which we value in ourselves. Were we in equal barbarism, our females would be equal drudges. The man with them is less strong than with us, but their woman stronger than ours; and both for the same obvious reason; because our man and their woman is habituated to labor, and formed by it. With both races the sex which is indulged with ease is least athletic. An Indian man is small in the hand and wrist for the same reason for which a sailor is large and strong in the arms and shoulders, and a porter in the legs and thighs.—They raise fewer children than we do. The causes of this are to be found, not in a difference of nature, but of circumstance. The women are frequently attending the men in their parties of war and of hunting, childbearing becomes extremely inconvenient to them. It is said, therefore, that they have learnt the practice of procuring abortion by the use of some vegetable; and that it even extends to prevent conception for a considerable time after. During these parties they are exposed to numerous hazards, to excessive exertions, to the greatest extremities of hunger. Even at their homes the nation depends for food, through a certain part of every year, on the gleanings of the forest: that is, they experience a famine once in every year. With all animals, if the female be badly fed, or not fed at all, her young perish: and if both male and female be reduced to like want, generation becomes less active, less productive. To the obstacles then of want and hazard, which nature has opposed to the multiplication of wild animals, for the purpose of restraining their numbers within certain bounds, those of labor and of voluntary abortion are added with the Indian. No wonder then if they multiply less than we do. Where food is regularly supplied, a single farm will show more of cattle, than a whole country of forests can of buffaloes. The same Indian women, when married to white traders, who feed them and their children plentifully and regularly, who exempt them from excessive drudgery, who keep them stationary and unexposed to accident, produce and raise as many children as the white women. Instances are known, under these circumstances, of their rearing a dozen children. An inhuman practice once prevailed in this country of making slaves of the Indians. (This practice commenced with the Spaniards with the first discovery of America). It is a fact well known with us, that the Indian women so enslaved produced and raised as numerous families as either the whites or blacks among whom they lived.—It has been said, that Indians have less hair than the whites, except on the head. But this is a fact of which fair proof can scarcely be had. With them it is disgraceful to be hairy on the body. They say it likens them to hogs. They therefore pluck the hair as fast as it appears. But the traders who marry their women, and prevail on them to discontinue this practice, say, that nature is the same with them as with the whites. Nor, if the fact be true, is the consequence necessary which has been drawn from it. Negroes have notoriously less hair than the whites; yet they are more ardent. But if cold and moisture be the agents of nature for diminishing the races of animals, how comes she all at once to suspend their operation as to the physical man of the new world, whom the Count acknowledges to be "about the same size as the man of our hemisphere," and to let loose their influence on his moral faculties? How has this "combination of the elements and other physical causes, so contrary to the enlargement of animal nature in this new world, these obstacles to the development and formation of great germs," been arrested and suspended, so as to permit the human body to acquire its just dimensions, and by what inconceivable process has their action been directed on his mind alone? To judge of the truth of this, to form a just estimate of their genius and mental powers, more facts are wanting, and great allowance to be made for those circumstances of their situation which call for a display of particular talents only. This done, we shall probably find that they are formed in mind as well as in body, on the same module with the "Homo sapiens Europæus."[2] The principles of their society forbidding all compulsion, they are to be led to duty and to enterprise by personal influence and persuasion. Hence eloquence in council, bravery and address in war, become the foundations of all consequence with them. To these acquirements all their faculties are directed. Of their bravery and address in war we have multiplied proofs, because we have been the subjects on which they were exercised. Of their eminence in oratory we have fewer examples, because it is displayed chiefly in their own councils. Some, however, we have of very superior luster. I may challenge the whole orations of Demosthenes and Cicero,[3] and of any more eminent orator, if Europe has furnished more eminent, to produce a single passage, superior to the speech of Logan, a Mingo chief, to Lord Dunmore,[4] when governor of this state. And, as a testimony of their talents in this line, I beg leave to introduce it, first stating the incidents necessary for understanding it. In the spring of the year 1774, a robbery was committed by some Indians on certain land-adventurers on the river Ohio. The whites in that quarter, according to their custom, undertook to punish this outrage in a summary way. Captain Michael Cresap,[5] and a certain Daniel Great-house, leading on these parties, surprised, at different times, traveling and hunting parties of the Indians, having their women and children with them, and murdered many. Among these were unfortunately the family of Logan, a chief celebrated in peace and war, and long distinguished as the friend of the whites. This unworthy return provoked his vengeance. He accordingly signalized himself in the war which ensued. In the autumn of the same year a decisive battle was fought at the mouth of the Great Kanhaway, between the collected forces of the Shawanese, Mingoes, and Delawares, and a detachment of the Virginia militia. The Indians were defeated, and sued for peace. Logan however disdained to be seen among the suppliants. But, lest the sincerity of a treaty should be distrusted, from which so distinguished a chief absented himself, he sent by a messenger the following speech to be delivered to Lord Dunmore.

"I appeal to any white man to say, if ever he entered Logan's cabin hungry, and he gave him not meat; if ever he came cold and naked, and he clothed

---

2. European man (Latin).
3. Demosthenes (385?–322 B.C.) was an Athenian orator. Cicero (106–43 B.C.) was a Roman orator and statesman.

4. John Murray, earl of Dunmore (1732–1809), was the colonial governor of Virginia from 1771 to 1775. "Mingo": an Iroquois tribe.
5. A Maryland soldier and frontiersman (1742–1775).

him not. During the course of the last long and bloody war, Logan remained idle in his cabin, an advocate for peace. Such was my love for the whites, that my countrymen pointed as they passed, and said, 'Logan is the friend of white men.' I had even thought to have lived with you, but for the injuries of one man. Col. Cresap, the last spring, in cold blood, and unprovoked, murdered all the relations of Logan, not sparing even my women and children. There runs not a drop of my blood in the veins of any living creature. This called on me for revenge. I have sought it: I have killed many: I have fully glutted my vengeance. For my country, I rejoice at the beams of peace. But do not harbor a thought that mine is the joy of fear. Logan never felt fear. He will not turn on his heel to save his life. Who is there to mourn for Logan?—Not one."

Before we condemn the Indians of this continent as wanting genius,[6] we must consider that letters have not yet been introduced among them. Were we to compare them in their present state with the Europeans North of the Alps, when the Roman arms and arts first crossed those mountains, the comparison would be unequal, because, at that time, those parts of Europe were swarming with numbers; because numbers produce emulation, and multiply the chances of improvement, and one improvement begets another. Yet I may safely ask, How many good poets, how many able mathematicians, how many great inventors in arts or sciences had Europe North of the Alps then produced? And it was sixteen centuries after this before a Newton[7] could be formed. I do not mean to deny, that there are varieties in the race of man, distinguished by their powers both of body and mind. I believe there are, as I see to be the case in the races of other animals. I only mean to suggest a doubt, whether the bulk and faculties of animals depend on the side of the Atlantic on which their food happens to grow, or which furnishes the elements of which they are compounded? Whether nature has enlisted herself as a Cis[8] or transatlantic partisan? I am induced to suspect, there has been more eloquence than sound reasoning displayed in support of this theory; that it is one of those cases where the judgment has been seduced by a glowing pen: and whilst I render every tribute of honor and esteem to the celebrated zoologist, who has added, and is still adding, so many precious things to the treasures of science, I must doubt whether in this instance he has not cherished error also, by lending her for a moment his vivid imagination and bewitching language. * * *

Query XVII. Religion

The first settlers in this country were emigrants from England, of the English church, just at a point of time when it was flushed with complete victory over the religious of all other persuasions. Possessed, as they became, of the powers of making, administering, and executing the laws, they showed equal intolerance in this country with their Presbyterian brethren, who had emigrated to the northern government. The poor Quakers were flying from persecution in England. They cast their eyes on these new countries as asylums of civil and religious freedom; but they found them free only for the reigning sect. Several acts of the Virginia assembly of 1659, 1662, and 1693,

6. Lacking intelligence.
7. Sir Isaac Newton (1642–1727), English philosopher and mathematician, most frequently identified with his theory of gravitation.
8. On this side.

had made it penal in parents to refuse to have their children baptized; had prohibited the unlawful assembling of Quakers; had made it penal for any master of a vessel to bring a Quaker into the state; had ordered those already here, and such as should come thereafter, to be imprisoned till they should abjure the country; provided a milder punishment for their first and second return, but death for their third; had inhibited all persons from suffering their meetings in or near their houses, entertaining them individually, or disposing of books which supported their tenets. If no capital execution took place here, as did in New England, it was not owing to the moderation of the church, or spirit of the legislature, as may be inferred from the law itself; but to historical circumstances which have not been handed down to us. The Anglicans retained full possession of the country about a century. Other opinions began then to creep in, and the great care of the government to support their own church, having begotten an equal degree of indolence in its clergy, two-thirds of the people had become dissenters at the commencement of the present revolution. The laws indeed were still oppressive on them, but the spirit of the one party had subsided into moderation, and of the other had risen to a degree of determination which commanded respect.

The present state of our laws on the subject of religion is this. The convention of May 1776, in their declaration of rights, declared it to be a truth, and a natural right, that the exercise of religion should be free; but when they proceeded to form on that declaration the ordinance of government, instead of taking up every principle declared in the bill of rights, and guarding it by legislative sanction, they passed over that which asserted our religious rights, leaving them as they found them.[9] The same convention, however, when they met as a member of the general assembly in October 1776, repealed all *acts of parliament* which had rendered criminal the maintaining any opinions in matters of religion, the forbearing to repair to church, and the exercising any mode of worship; and suspended the laws giving salaries to the clergy, which suspension was made perpetual in October 1779. Statutory oppressions in religion being thus wiped away, we remain at present under those only imposed by the common law, or by our own acts of assembly. At the common law, *heresy* was a capital offense, punishable by burning. Its definition was left to the ecclesiastical judges, before whom the conviction was, till the statute of the 1 El. c. 1.[1] circumscribed it, by declaring, that nothing should be deemed heresy, but what had been so determined by authority of the canonical scriptures, or by one of the four first general councils, or by some other council having for the grounds of their declaration the express and plain words of the scriptures. Heresy, thus circumscribed, being an offense at the common law, our act of assembly of October 1777, c. 17. gives cognizance of it to the general court, by declaring, that the jurisdiction of that court shall be general in all matters at the common law. The execution is by the writ De *hæretico comburendo*.[2] By our own act of assembly of 1705, c. 30, if a person brought up in the Christian religion denies the being of a God, or the Trinity, or asserts there are more Gods than one, or denies the Christian religion to be true, or the scriptures to be of divine authority, he is punishable on the first offense by incapacity to hold any office or employment ecclesiastical, civil, or military; on the second by disability to sue, to take any gift or legacy, to be guardian,

9. Jefferson is referring to Article XVI of Virginia's Declaration of Rights.
1. The first year in the reign of Queen Elizabeth of

England, 1558–59.
2. Of the burning of a heretic (Latin).

executor, or administrator, and by three years' imprisonment, without bail. A father's right to the custody of his own children being founded in law on his right of guardianship, this being taken away, they may of course be severed from him, and put, by the authority of a court, into more orthodox hands. This is a summary view of that religious slavery, under which a people have been willing to remain, who have lavished their lives and fortunes for the establishment of their civil freedom.

The error seems not sufficiently eradicated, that the operations of the mind, as well as the acts of the body, are subject to the coercion of the laws.[3] But our rulers can have authority over such natural rights only as we have submitted to them. The rights of conscience we never submitted, we could not submit. We are answerable for them to our God. The legitimate powers of government extend to such acts only as are injurious to others. But it does me no injury for my neighbor to say there are twenty gods, or no god. It neither picks my pocket nor breaks my leg. If it be said, his testimony in a court of justice cannot be relied on, reject it then, and be the stigma on him. Constraint may make him worse by making him a hypocrite, but it will never make him a truer man. It may fix him obstinately in his errors, but will not cure them. Reason and free enquiry are the only effectual agents against error. Give a loose to them, they will support the true religion, by bringing every false one to their tribunal, to the test of their investigation. They are the natural enemies of error, and of error only. Had not the Roman government permitted free inquiry, Christianity could never have been introduced. Had not free inquiry been indulged, at the era of the Reformation, the corruptions of Christianity could not have been purged away. If it be restrained now, the present corruptions will be protected, and new ones encouraged. Was the government to prescribe to us our medicine and diet, our bodies would be in such keeping as our souls are now. Thus in France the emetic was once forbidden as a medicine, and the potato as an article of food. Government is just as infallible too when it fixes systems in physics. Galileo[4] was sent to the Inquisition for affirming that the earth was a sphere: the government had declared it to be as flat as a trencher, and Galileo was obliged to abjure his error. This error however at length prevailed, the earth became a globe, and Descartes[5] declared it was whirled round its axis by a vortex. The government in which he lived was wise enough to see that this was no question of civil jurisdiction, or we should all have been involved by authority in vortices. In fact, the vortices have been exploded, and the Newtonian principle of gravitation is now more firmly established, on the basis of reason, than it would be were the government to step in, and to make it an article of necessary faith. Reason and experiment have been indulged, and error has fled before them. It is error alone which needs the support of government. Truth can stand by itself. Subject opinion to coercion: whom will you make your inquisitors? Fallible men; men governed by bad passions, by private as well as public reasons. And why subject it to coercion? To produce uniformity. But is uniformity of opinion desirable? No more than of face and stature. Introduce the bed of Procrustes[6] then, and as there is danger that the large men may beat the small, make us all of a size, by lopping the former and stretching the latter. Difference of opinion is

3. "Furneaux passim" [Jefferson's note]. Philip Furneaux (1726–1783), English minister and author of *Letters to the Honorable Mr. Justice Blackstone* (1770).
4. Galileo (1564–1642) taught mathematics at Padua and appeared before the Inquisition in 1632.

5. René Descartes (1596–1650), French scientist and philosopher.
6. Procrustes was a highwayman in classical mythology who either stretched or cut off the legs of his captors to fit his iron bed.

advantageous in religion. The several sects perform the office of a Censor morum[7] over each other. Is uniformity attainable? Millions of innocent men, women, and children, since the introduction of Christianity, have been burnt, tortured, fined, imprisoned; yet we have not advanced one inch towards uniformity. What has been the effect of coercion? To make one half the world fools, and the other half hypocrites. To support roguery and error all over the earth. Let us reflect that it is inhabited by a thousand millions of people. That these profess probably a thousand different systems of religion. That ours is but one of that thousand. That if there be but one right, and ours that one, we should wish to see the 999 wandering sects gathered into the fold of truth. But against such a majority we cannot effect this by force. Reason and persuasion are the only practicable instruments. To make way for these, free inquiry must be indulged; and how can we wish others to indulge it while we refuse it ourselves. But every state, says an inquisitor, has established some religion. No two, say I, have established the same. Is this a proof of the infallibility of establishments? Our sister states of Pennsylvania and New York, however, have long subsisted without any establishment at all. The experiment was new and doubtful when they made it. It has answered beyond conception. They flourish infinitely. Religion is well supported; of various kinds, indeed, but all good enough; all sufficient to preserve peace and order: or if a sect arises, whose tenets would subvert morals, good sense has fair play, and reasons and laughs it out of doors, without suffering the state to be troubled with it. They do not hang more malefactors than we do. They are not more disturbed with religious dissensions. On the contrary, their harmony is unparalleled, and can be ascribed to nothing but their unbounded tolerance, because there is no other circumstance in which they differ from every nation on earth. They have made the happy discovery, that the way to silence religious disputes, is to take no notice of them. Let us too give this experiment fair play, and get rid, while we may, of those tyrannical laws. It is true, we are as yet secured against them by the spirit of the times. I doubt whether the people of this country would suffer an execution for heresy, or a three years' imprisonment for not comprehending the mysteries of the Trinity. But is the spirit of the people an infallible, a permanent reliance? Is it government? Is this the kind of protection we receive in return for the rights we give up? Besides, the spirit of the times may alter, will alter. Our rulers will become corrupt, our people careless. A single zealot may commence persecutor, and better men be his victims. It can never be too often repeated, that the time for fixing every essential right on a legal basis is while our rulers are honest, and ourselves united. From the conclusion of this war we shall be going downhill. It will not then be necessary to resort every moment to the people for support. They will be forgotten, therefore, and their rights disregarded. They will forget themselves, but in the sole faculty of making money, and will never think of uniting to effect a due respect for their rights. The shackles, therefore, which shall not be knocked off at the conclusion of this war, will remain on us long, will be made heavier and heavier, till our rights shall revive or expire in a convulsion.

Query XIX. Manufactures

We never had an interior trade of any importance. Our exterior commerce has suffered very much from the beginning of the present contest. During this

---

7. Critic of morals or customs (Latin).

time we have manufactured within our families the most necessary articles of clothing. Those of cotton will bear some comparison with the same kinds of manufacture in Europe; but those of wool, flax and hemp are very coarse, unsightly, and unpleasant: and such is our attachment to agriculture, and such our preference for foreign manufactures, that be it wise or unwise, our people will certainly return as soon as they can, to the raising raw materials, and exchanging them for finer manufactures than they are able to execute themselves.

The political economists of Europe have established it as a principle that every state should endeavor to manufacture for itself: and this principle, like many others, we transfer to America, without calculating the difference of circumstance which should often produce a difference of result. In Europe the lands are either cultivated, or locked up against the cultivator. Manufacture must therefore be resorted to of necessity not of choice, to support the surplus of their people. But we have an immensity of land courting the industry of the husbandman.[8] Is it best then that all our citizens should be employed in its improvement, or that one half should be called off from that to exercise manufactures and handicraft arts for the other? Those who labor in the earth are the chosen people of God, if ever He had a chosen people, whose breasts He has made his peculiar deposit for substantial and genuine virtue. It is the focus in which He keeps alive that sacred fire, which otherwise might escape from the face of the earth. Corruption of morals in the mass of cultivators is a phenomenon of which no age nor nation has furnished an example. It is the mark set on those, who not looking up to heaven, to their own soil and industry, as does the husbandman, for their subsistence, depend for it on the casualties and caprice of customers. Dependence begets subservience and venality, suffocates the germ of virtue, and prepares fit tools for the designs of ambition. This, the natural progress and consequence of the arts, has sometimes perhaps been retarded by accidental circumstances: but, generally speaking, the proportion which the aggregate of the other classes of citizens bears in any state to that of its husbandmen is the proportion of its unsound to its healthy parts, and is a good enough barometer whereby to measure its degree of corruption. While we have land to labor then, let us never wish to see our citizens occupied at a workbench, or twirling a distaff.[9] Carpenters, masons, smiths are wanting in husbandry: but, for the general operations of manufacture, let our workshops remain in Europe. It is better to carry provisions and materials to workmen there, than bring them to the provisions and materials, and with them their manners and principles. The loss by the transportation of commodities across the Atlantic will be made up in happiness and permanence of government. The mobs of great cities add just so much to the support of pure government as sores do to the strength of the human body. It is the manners and spirit of a people which preserve a republic in vigor. A degeneracy in these is a canker which soon eats to the heart of its laws and constitution.

1780–81   1787

---

8. Farmer.   9. A short stick on which wool or flax is wound.

Letter to Peter Carr[1]

[A Young Man's Education]

Paris, August 10, 1787

Dear Peter,—I have received your two letters of December the 30th and April the 18th, and am very happy to find by them, as well as by letters from Mr. Wythe,[2] that you have been so fortunate as to attract his notice and good will; I am sure you will find this to have been one of the most fortunate events of your life, as I have ever been sensible it was of mine. I enclose you a sketch of the sciences to which I would wish you to apply, in such order as Mr. Wythe shall advise; I mention, also, the books in them worth your reading, which submit to his correction. Many of these are among your father's books, which you should have brought to you. As I do not recollect those of them not in his library, you must write to me for them, making out a catalog of such as you think you shall have occasion for, in eighteen months from the date of your letter, and consulting Mr. Wythe on the subject. To this sketch, I will add a few particular observations:

1. Italian. I fear the learning this language will confound your French and Spanish. Being all of them degenerated dialects of the Latin, they are apt to mix in conversation. I have never seen a person speaking the three languages, who did not mix them. It is a delightful language, but late events having rendered the Spanish more useful, lay it aside to prosecute that.

2. Spanish. Bestow great attention on this, and endeavor to acquire an accurate knowledge of it. Our future connections with Spain and Spanish America, will render that language a valuable acquisition. The ancient history of that part of America, too, is written in that language. I send you a dictionary.

3. Moral Philosophy. I think it lost time to attend lectures on this branch. He who made us would have been a pitiful bungler, if he had made the rules of our moral conduct a matter of science. For one man of science, there are thousands who are not. What would have become of them? Man was destined for society. His morality, therefore, was to be formed to this object. He was endowed with a sense of right and wrong, merely relative to this. This sense is as much a part of his nature, as the sense of hearing, seeing, feeling; it is the true foundation of morality, and not the το καλοι,[3] truth, etc., as fanciful writers have imagined. The moral sense, or conscience, is as much a part of man as his leg or arm. It is given to all human beings in a stronger or weaker degree, as force of members is given them in a greater or less degree. It may be strengthened by exercise, as may any particular limb of the body. This sense is submitted, indeed, in some degree, to the guidance of reason; but it is a small stock which is required for this: even a less one than what we call common sense. State a moral case to a plowman and a professor. The former will decide it as well, and often better than the latter, because he has not been led astray by artificial rules. In this branch, therefore, read good books, because they will encourage, as well as direct your feelings. The writings of

---

1. Peter Carr was a nephew of Thomas Jefferson, the son of his fourth sister, Martha, and Dabney Carr. The text used here is from *The Writings of Thomas Jefferson*, Vol. 6, edited by A. A. Lipscomb and A. E. Bergh (1903).

2. George Wythe (1726–1806) was a close friend of Jefferson's, a self-educated man who became a distinguished Virginia lawyer and political figure.
3. The beautiful (Greek).

Sterne,[4] particularly, form the best course of morality that ever was written. Besides these, read the books mentioned in the enclosed paper; and, above all things, lose no occasion of exercising your dispositions to be grateful, to be generous, to be charitable, to be humane, to be true, just, firm, orderly, courageous, etc. Consider every act of this kind, as an exercise which will strengthen your moral faculties and increase your worth.

4. Religion. Your reason is now mature enough to examine this object. In the first place, divest yourself of all bias in favor of novelty and singularity of opinion. Indulge them in any other subject rather than that of religion. It is too important, and the consequences of error may be too serious. On the other hand, shake off all the fears and servile prejudices, under which weak minds are servilely crouched. Fix reason firmly in her seat, and call to her tribunal every fact, every opinion. Question with boldness even the existence of a God; because, if there is one, He must more approve of the homage of reason, than that of blindfolded fear. You will naturally examine first, the religion of your own country. Read the Bible, then, as you would read Livy or Tacitus.[5] The facts which are within the ordinary course of nature, you will believe on the authority of the writer, as you do those of the same kind in Livy and Tacitus. The testimony of the writer weighs in their favor, in one scale, and their not being against the laws of nature, does not weigh against them. But those facts in the Bible which contradict the laws of nature must be examined with more care, and under a variety of faces. Here you must recur to the pretensions of the writer to inspiration from God. Examine upon what evidence his pretensions are founded, and whether that evidence is so strong, as that its falsehood would be more improbable than a change in the laws of nature, in the case he relates. For example, in the book of Joshua, we are told, the sun stood still several hours.[6] Were we to read that fact in Livy or Tacitus, we should class it with their showers of blood, speaking of statues, beasts, etc. But it is said, that the writer of that book was inspired. Examine, therefore, candidly, what evidence there is of his having been inspired. The pretension is entitled to your inquiry, because millions believe it. On the other hand, you are astronomer enough to know how contrary it is to the law of nature that a body revolving on its axis, as the earth does, should have stopped, should not, by that sudden stoppage, have prostrated animals, trees, buildings, and should after a certain time have resumed its revolution, and that without a second general prostration. Is this arrest of the earth's motion, or the evidence which affirms it, most within the law of probabilities? You will next read the New Testament. It is the history of a personage called Jesus. Keep in your eye the opposite pretensions: 1, of those who say he was begotten by God, born of a virgin, suspended and reversed the laws of nature at will, and ascended bodily into heaven; and 2, of those who say he was a man of illegitimate birth, of a benevolent heart, enthusiastic mind, who set out without pretensions to divinity, ended in believing them, and was punished capitally for sedition, by being gibbeted, according to the Roman law, which punished the first commission of that offense by whipping, and the second by exile, or death *in furca*.[7] See

4. Laurence Sterne, author of *Tristram Shandy* (1760) and *A Sentimental Journey through France and Italy* (1768).
5. Livy (59 B.C.–A.D. 17) and Tacitus (55?–118?) were Roman historians.
6. "So the sun stood still in the midst of heaven and

hasted not to go down about a whole day" (Joshua 10.13).
7. The fork (Latin, literal trans.); an instrument of punishment in which the neck is placed in the tongs and the arms tied to the ends.

this law in the *Digest* [Book 48, Chapter 19, paragraph 28, sentence 3] and [the second book of] Lipsius *de cruce* [Concerning the cross], chapter 2.[8] These questions are examined in the books I have mentioned, under the head of Religion, and several others. They will assist you in your inquiries; but keep your reason firmly on the watch in reading them all. Do not be frightened from this inquiry by any fear of its consequences. If it ends in a belief that there is no God, you will find incitements to virtue in the comfort and pleasantness you feel in its exercise, and the love of others which it will procure you. If you find reason to believe there is a God, a consciousness that you are acting under his eye, and that he approves you, will be a vast additional incitement; if that there be a future state, the hope of a happy existence in that increases the appetite to deserve it; if that Jesus was also a God, you will be comforted by a belief of his aid and love. In fine,[9] I repeat, you must lay aside all prejudice on both sides, and neither believe nor reject anything, because any other persons, or description of persons, have rejected or believed it. Your own reason is the only oracle given you by heaven, and you are answerable, not for the rightness, but uprightness of the decision. I forgot to observe, when speaking of the New Testament, that you should read all the histories of Christ, as well as those whom a council of ecclesiastics have decided for us, to be Pseudo-evangelists,[1] as those they named Evangelists. Because these Pseudo-evangelists pretended to inspiration, as much as the others, and you are to judge their pretensions by your own reason, and not by the reason of those ecclesiastics. Most of these are lost. There are some, however, still extant, collected by Fabricius,[2] which I will endeavor to get and send you.

5. Traveling. This makes men wiser, but less happy. When men of sober age travel, they gather knowledge, which they may apply usefully for their country; but they are subject ever after to recollections mixed with regret; their affections are weakened by being extended over more objects; and they learn new habits which cannot be gratified when they return home. Young men, who travel, are exposed to all these inconveniences in a higher degree, to others still more serious, and do not acquire that wisdom for which a previous foundation is requisite, by repeated and just observations at home. The glare of pomp and pleasure is analogous to the motion of the blood; it absorbs all their affection and attention, they are torn from it as from the only good in this world, and return to their home as to a place of exile and condemnation. Their eyes are forever turned back to the object they have lost, and its recollection poisons the residue of their lives. Their first and most delicate passions are hackneyed on unworthy objects here, and they carry home the dregs, insufficient to make themselves or anybody else happy. Add to this, that a habit of idleness, an inability to apply themselves to business is acquired, and renders them useless to themselves and their country. These observations are founded in experience. There is no place where your pursuit of knowledge will be so little obstructed by foreign objects, as in your own country, nor any, wherein the virtues of the heart will be less exposed to be weakened. Be good, be

---

8. *"Digest"*: the *Corpus Iuris Civillis*, collected by Tribonianus for Justinian (527–565). Justus Lipsius (1547–1606) was a Flemish scholar and author of books on political theory.
9. In conclusion.
1. The pseudoevangelists were nonapostolic writers and thus disqualified for admission to the New Testament. Some of them include Clement of Rome, the author of the Shepherd of Hermas, the author of the Apocalypse of Peter, and the author of the Acts of Paul.
2. Johann Albert Fabricius (1668–1736), biblical scholar and best known for his studies of the Apocrypha.

learned, and be industrious, and you will not want the aid of traveling, to render you precious to your country, dear to your friends, happy within yourself. I repeat my advice, to take a great deal of exercise, and on foot. Health is the first requisite after morality. Write to me often, and be assured of the interest I take in your success, as well as the warmth of those sentiments of attachment with which I am, dear Peter, your affectionate friend.

Letter to John Adams[1]

[The Natural Aristocrat]

Monticello, October 28, 1813

Dear Sir,—According to the reservation between us, of taking up one of the subjects of our correspondence at a time, I turn to your letters of August the 16th and September the 2d. * * * I agree with you that there is a natural aristocracy among men. The grounds of this are virtue and talents. Formerly, bodily powers gave place among the aristoi.[2] But since the invention of gunpowder has armed the weak as well as the strong with missile death, bodily strength, like beauty, good humor, politeness and other accomplishments, has become but an auxiliary ground of distinction. There is also an artificial aristocracy, founded on wealth and birth, without either virtue or talents; for with these it would belong to the first class. The natural aristocracy I consider as the most precious gift of nature for the instruction, the trusts, and government of society. And indeed, it would have been inconsistent in creation to have formed man for the social state, and not to have provided virtue and wisdom enough to manage the concerns of the society. May we not even say that that form of government is the best which provides the most effectually for a pure selection of these natural aristoi into the offices of government? The artificial aristocracy is a mischievous ingredient in government, and provision should be made to prevent its ascendency. On the question, what is the best provision, you and I differ; but we differ as rational friends, using the free exercise of our own reason, and mutually indulging its errors. You think it best to put the pseudo-aristoi into a separate chamber of legislation, where they may be hindered from doing mischief by their co-ordinate branches, and where, also, they may be a protection to wealth against the agrarian and plundering enterprises of the majority of the people. I think that to give them power in order to prevent them from doing mischief is arming them for it, and increasing instead of remedying the evil. For if the co-ordinate branches can arrest their action, so may they that of the co-ordinates. Mischief may be done negatively as well as positively. Of this, a cabal in the Senate of the United States has furnished many proofs. Nor do I believe them necessary to protect the wealthy; because enough of these will find their way into every branch of the legislation, to protect themselves. From fifteen to twenty legislatures of our

1. Thomas Jefferson and John Adams (1735–1826) became estranged when Adams was elected second president in 1796. Adams's Federalist positions were opposed by Jefferson, who succeeded him as president in 1801. In 1812 they began to correspond and were able to debate their differences. The text used here is from *The Writings of Thomas Jefferson*, vol. 13, edited by A. A. Lipscomb and A. E. Bergh (1903).
2. The best (Greek). On July 9, 1813, Adams wrote to Jefferson that he recalled a maxim from the work of the Greek elegiac poet Theognis (6th century B.C.) that said that " 'nobility in men is worth as much as it is in horses, asses, or rams; but the meanest [i.e., poorest] blooded puppy in the world, if he gets a little money is as good a man as the best of them.' Yet birth and wealth together have prevailed over virtue and talents in all ages. The many will acknowledge no other *aristoi*."

own, in action for thirty years past, have proved that no fears of an equalization of property are to be apprehended from them. I think the best remedy is exactly that provided by all our constitutions, to leave to the citizens the free election and separation of the aristoi from the pseudo-aristoi, of the wheat from the chaff. In general they will elect the really good and wise. In some instances, wealth may corrupt, and birth blind them; but not in sufficient degree to endanger the society.

It is probable that our difference of opinion may, in some measure, be produced by a difference of character in those among whom we live. From what I have seen of Massachusetts and Connecticut myself, and still more from what I have heard, and the character given of the former by yourself,[3] who know them so much better, there seems to be in those two states a traditionary reverence for certain families, which has rendered the offices of the government nearly hereditary in those families. I presume that from an early period of your history, members of those families happening to possess virtue and talents, have honestly exercised them for the good of the people, and by their services have endeared their names to them. In coupling Connecticut with you, I mean it politically only, not morally. For having made the Bible the common law of their land, they seem to have modeled their morality on the story of Jacob and Laban.[4] But although this hereditary succession to office with you, may, in some degree, be founded in real family merit, yet in a much higher degree, it has proceeded from your strict alliance of Church and State. These families are canonized in the eyes of the people on common principles, "you tickle me, and I will tickle you." In Virginia we have nothing of this. Our clergy, before the Revolution, having been secured against rivalship by fixed salaries, did not give themselves the trouble of acquiring influence over the people. Of wealth, there were great accumulations in particular families, handed down from generation to generation, under the English law of entails.[5] But the only object of ambition for the wealthy was a seat in the King's Council.[6] All their court then was paid to the crown and its creatures; and they philippized[7] in all collisions between the King and the people. Hence they were unpopular; and that unpopularity continues attached to their names. A Randolph, a Carter, or a Burwell[8] must have great personal superiority over a common competitor to be elected by the people even at this day. At the first session of our legislature after the Declaration of Independence, we passed a law abolishing entails. And this was followed by one abolishing the privilege of primogeniture, and dividing the lands of intestates[9] equally among all their children, or other representatives. These laws, drawn by myself, laid the axe to the foot of pseudo-aristocracy. And had another which I prepared been adopted by the legislature, our work would have been complete. It was a bill for the more general diffusion of learning. This proposed to divide every county into wards of five or six miles square, like your townships; to establish in each ward a free school for reading, writing and common arithmetic; to

---

3. "Vol, 1, page 111" [Jefferson's note]. A reference to Adams's *Defense of the Constitutions of Government of the United States of America*, 3 vols. (1797). This work was first published in 1787.
4. I.e., a dynastic family, founded on the marital relations between the daughters of Jacob and Laban (Genesis 24–31).
5. An estate that cannot be willed but must pass from a proscribed list of successors.

6. The Privy Council, a select group of advisers, appointed by the king.
7. Argued against liberty for the people; spoke corrupted by their desire to please the king.
8. John Randolph, Landon Carter, and Lewis Burwell were all Virginia aristocrats.
9. Those who died without wills. "Primogeniture": a law that gives estates to the eldest son.

provide for the annual selection of the best subjects from these schools, who might receive, at the public expense, a higher degree of education at a district school; and from these district schools to select a certain number of the most promising subjects, to be completed at an university, where all the useful sciences should be taught. Worth and genius would thus have been sought out from every condition of life, and completely prepared by education for defeating the competition of wealth and birth for public trusts. My proposition had, for a further object, to impart to these wards those portions of self-government for which they are best qualified, by confiding to them the care of their poor, their roads, police, elections, the nomination of jurors, administration of justice in small cases, elementary exercises of militia; in short, to have made them little republics, with a warden at the head of each, for all those concerns which, being under their eye, they would better manage than the larger republics of the county or state. A general call of ward meetings by their wardens on the same day through the state, would at any time produce the genuine sense of the people on any required point, and would enable the state to act in mass, as your people have so often done, and with so much effect by their town meetings. The law for religious freedom,[1] which made a part of this system, having put down the aristocracy of the clergy, and restored to the citizen the freedom of the mind, and those of entails and descents nurturing an equality of condition among them, this on education would have raised the mass of the people to the high ground of moral respectability necessary to their own safety, and to orderly government; and would have completed the great object of qualifying them to select the veritable aristoi, for the trusts of government, to the exclusion of the pseudalists; and the same Theognis who has furnished the epigraphs of your two letters, assures us that "Ονδεμιαν πω, Κυρν', αγαθοι πολιν ωλεσαν ανδρε."[2] Although this law has not yet been acted on but in a small and inefficient degree, it is still considered as before the legislature, with other bills of the revised code, not yet taken up, and I have great hope that some patriotic spirit will, at a favorable moment, call it up, and make it the keystone of the arch of our government.

With respect to aristocracy, we should further consider, that before the establishment of the American states, nothing was known to history but the man of the old world, crowded within limits either small or overcharged, and steeped in the vices which that situation generates. A government adapted to such men would be one thing; but a very different one, that for the man of these states. Here every one may have land to labor for himself, if he chooses; or, preferring the exercise of any other industry, may exact for it such compensation as not only to afford a comfortable subsistence, but wherewith to provide for a cessation from labor in old age. Every one, by his property, or by his satisfactory situation, is interested in the support of law and order. And such men may safely and advantageously reserve to themselves a wholesome control over their public affairs, and a degree of freedom, which, in the hands of the canaille[3] of the cities of Europe, would be instantly perverted to the demolition and destruction of everything public and private. The history of the last twenty-five years of France,[4] and of the last forty years in America, nay of its last two hundred years, proves the truth of both parts of this observation.

1. Passed in 1786.
2. Curnis, good men have never harmed any city (Greek).
3. Mob.
4. I.e., since the French Revolution (1789).

But even in Europe a change has sensibly taken place in the mind of man. Science had liberated the ideas of those who read and reflect, and the American example had kindled feelings of right in the people. An insurrection has consequently begun, of science, talents, and courage, against rank and birth, which have fallen into contempt. It has failed in its first effort, because the mobs of the cities, the instrument used for its accomplishment, debased by ignorance, poverty, and vice, could not be restrained to rational action. But the world will recover from the panic of this first catastrophe. Science is progressive, and talents and enterprise on the alert. Resort may be had to the people of the country, a more governable power from their principles and subordination; and rank, and birth, and tinsel-aristocracy will finally shrink into insignificance, even there. This, however, we have no right to meddle with. It suffices for us, if the moral and physical condition of our own citizens qualifies them to select the able and good for the direction of their government, with a recurrence of elections at such short periods as will enable them to displace an unfaithful servant, before the mischief he meditates may be irremediable.

I have thus stated my opinion on a point on which we differ, not with a view to controversy, for we are both too old to change opinions which are the result of a long life of inquiry and reflection; but on the suggestions of a former letter of yours, that we ought not to die before we have explained ourselves to each other. We acted in perfect harmony, through a long and perilous contest for our liberty and independence. A constitution has been acquired, which, though neither of us thinks perfect, yet both consider as competent to render our fellow citizens the happiest and the securest on whom the sun has ever shone. If we do not think exactly alike as to its imperfections, it matters little to our country, which, after devoting to it long lives of disinterested labor, we have delivered over to our successors in life, who will be able to take care of it and of themselves.

Of the pamphlet on aristocracy which has been sent to you, or who may be its author, I have heard nothing but through your letter. If the person you suspect, it may be known from the quaint, mystical, and hyperbolical ideas, involved in affected, newfangled and pedantic terms which stamp his writings. Whatever it be, I hope your quiet is not to be affected at this day by the rudeness or intemperance of scribblers; but that you may continue in tranquility to live and to rejoice in the prosperity of our country, until it shall be your own wish to take your seat among the aristoi who have gone before you. Ever and affectionately yours.

From Letter to Benjamin Austin, Esq. [1]

[*Manufactures*]

Monticello, January 9, 1816

Dear Sir,—Your favor of December 21st has been received, and I am first to thank you for the pamphlet it covered. * * *

You tell me I am quoted[2] by those who wish to continue our dependence

---

1. The text used here is from *The Writings of Thomas Jefferson*, vol. 14, edited by A. A. Lipscomb and A. E. Bergh (1903). Benjamin Austin (1752–1820) was a Bostonian who wrote for the *Independent Chronicle*.

2. In *Notes on the State of Virginia*, published privately in 1784–85.

on England for manufactures. There was a time when I might have been so quoted with more candor, but within the thirty years which have since elapsed, how are circumstances changed! We were then in peace. Our independent place among nations was acknowledged. A commerce which offered the raw material in exchange for the same material after receiving the last touch of industry was worthy of welcome to all nations. It was expected that those especially to whom manufacturing industry was important, would cherish the friendship of such customers by every favor, by every inducement, and particularly cultivate their peace by every act of justice and friendship. Under this prospect the question seemed legitimate whether, with such an immensity of unimproved land, courting the hand of husbandry, the industry of agriculture, or that of manufactures would add most to the national wealth? And the doubt was entertained on this consideration chiefly, that to the labor of the husbandman a vast addition is made by the spontaneous energies of the earth on which it is employed: for one grain of wheat committed to the earth, she renders twenty, thirty, and even fifty fold, whereas to the labor of the manufacturer nothing is added. Pounds of flax, in his hands, yield, on the contrary, but pennyweights of lace. This exchange, too, laborious as it might seem, what a field did it promise for the occupations of the ocean; what a nursery for that class of citizens who were to exercise and maintain our equal rights on that element? This was the state of things in 1785, when the "Notes on Virginia" were first printed; when, the ocean being open to all nations, and their common right in it acknowledged and exercised under regulations sanctioned by the assent and usage of all, it was thought that the doubt might claim some consideration. But who in 1785 could foresee the rapid depravity which was to render the close of that century the disgrace of the history of man?[3] Who could have imagined that the two most distinguished in the rank of nations, for science and civilization, would have suddenly descended from that honorable eminence, and setting at defiance all those moral laws established by the Author of nature between nation and nation, as between man and man, would cover earth and sea with robberies and piracies, merely because strong enough to do it with temporal impunity; and that under this disbandment of nations from social order, we should have been despoiled of a thousand ships, and have thousands of our citizens reduced to Algerine slavery. Yet all this has taken place. One of these nations interdicted to our vessels all harbors of the globe without having first proceeded to some one of hers, there paid a tribute proportioned to the cargo, and obtained her license to proceed to the port of destination. The other declared them to be lawful prize if they had touched at the port, or been visited by a ship of the enemy nation. Thus were we completely excluded from the ocean. Compare this state of things with that of '85, and say whether an opinion founded in the circumstances of that day can be fairly applied to those of the present. We have experienced what we did not then believe, that there exist both profligacy and power enough to exclude us from the field of interchange with other nations: that to be independent for the comforts of life we must fabricate them ourselves. We must now place the manufacturer by the side of the agriculturist. The former question is suppressed, or rather assumes a new form. Shall we make our own comforts, or go without them, at the will of a foreign nation? He, therefore, who is now

---

3. A reference to the Reign of Terror (1793–94) which followed the French Revolution.

against domestic manufacture, must be for reducing us either to dependence on that foreign nation, or to be clothed in skins, and to live like wild beasts in dens and caverns. I am not one of these; experience has taught me that manufactures are now as necessary to our independence as to our comfort; and if those who quote me as of a different opinion will keep pace with me in purchasing nothing foreign where an equivalent of domestic fabric can be obtained, without regard to difference of price, it will not be our fault if we do not soon have a supply at home equal to our demand, and wrest that weapon of distress from the hand which has wielded it. If it shall be proposed to go beyond our own supply, the question of '85 will then recur, will our *surplus* labor be then most beneficially employed in the culture of the earth, or in the fabrications of art? We have time yet for consideration, before that question will press upon us; and the maxim to be applied will depend on the circumstances which shall then exist; for in so complicated a science as political economy, no one axiom can be laid down as wise and expedient for all times and circumstances, and for their contraries. Inattention to this is what has called for this explanation, which reflection would have rendered unnecessary with the candid, while nothing will do it with those who use the former opinion only as a stalking horse, to cover their disloyal propensities to keep us in eternal vassalage to a foreign and unfriendly people.

I salute you with assurances of great respect and esteem.

Letter to John Adams[1]

[Living One's Life Over]

Monticello, August 1, 1816

Dear Sir,—Your two philosophical letters of May 4th and 6th have been too long in my carton of "letters to be answered." To the question, indeed, on the utility of grief, no answer remains to be given. You have exhausted the subject. I see that, with the other evils of life, it is destined to temper the cup we are to drink.

> Two urns by Jove's high throne have ever stood,
> The source of evil one, and one of good;
> From thence the cup of mortal man he fills,
> Blessings to these, to those distributes ills;
> To most he mingles both.[2]

Putting to myself your question, would I agree to live my seventy-three years over again forever? I hesitate to say. With Chew's[3] limitations from twenty-five to sixty, I would say yes; and I might go further back, but not come lower down. For, at the latter period, with most of us, the powers of life are sensibly on the wane, sight becomes dim, hearing dull, memory constantly enlarging its frightful blank and parting with all we have ever seen or known, spirits evaporate, bodily debility creeps on palsying every limb, and so faculty after

---

1. The text used here is from *The Writings of Thomas Jefferson*, vol. 15, edited by A. A. Lipscomb and A. E. Bergh (1903).
2. Alexander Pope's (1688–1744) translation of Homer's *Iliad*, book 24, lines 663–67.

3. In John Adams's letter to Jefferson, May 3, 1816, Adams refers to a remark by the Philadelphia lawyer Benjamin Chew that he would like to "go back to twenty-five, to all Eternity."

faculty quits us, and where then is life? If, in its full vigor, of good as well as evil, your friend Vassall[4] could doubt its value, it must be purely a negative quantity when its evils alone remain. Yet I do not go into his opinion entirely. I do not agree that an age of pleasure is no compensation for a moment of pain. I think, with you, that life is a fair matter of account, and the balance often, nay generally, in its favor. It is not indeed easy, by calculation of intensity and time, to apply a common measure, or to fix the par between pleasure and pain; yet it exists, and is measurable. On the question, for example, whether to be cut for the stone? The young, with a longer prospect of years, think these overbalance the pain of the operation. Dr. Franklin, at the age of eighty, thought his residuum of life not worth that price. I should have thought with him, even taking the stone out of the scale. There is a ripeness of time for death, regarding others as well as ourselves, when it is reasonable we should drop off, and make room for another growth. When we have lived our generation out, we should not wish to encroach on another. I enjoy good health; I am happy in what is around me, yet I assure you I am ripe for leaving all, this year, this day, this hour. If it could be doubted whether we would go back to twenty-five, how can it be whether we would go forward from seventy-three? Bodily decay is gloomy in prospect, but of all human contemplations the most abhorrent is body without mind. Perhaps, however, I might accept of time to read Grimm[5] before I go. Fifteen volumes of anecdotes and incidents, within the compass of my own time and cognizance, written by a man of genius, of taste, of point, an acquaintance, the measure and traverses of whose mind I know, could not fail to turn the scale in favor of life during their perusal. I must write to Ticknor[6] to add it to my catalog, and hold on till it comes. There is a Mr. Van der Kemp[7] of New York, a correspondent, I believe, of yours, with whom I have exchanged some letters without knowing who he is. Will you tell me? I know nothing of the history of the Jesuits[8] you mention in four volumes. Is it a good one? I dislike, with you, their restoration because it marks a retrograde step from light towards darkness. We shall have our follies without doubt. Some one or more of them will always be afloat. But ours will be the follies of enthusiasm, not of bigotry, not of Jesuitism. Bigotry is the disease of ignorance, of morbid minds; enthusiasm of the free and buoyant. Education and free discussion are the antidotes of both. We are destined to be a barrier against the returns of ignorance and barbarism. Old Europe will have to lean on our shoulders, and to hobble along by our side, under the monkish trammels of priests and kings, as she can. What a colossus shall we be when the southern continent comes up to our mark! What a stand will it secure as a ralliance for the reason and freedom of the globe! I like the dreams of the future better than the history of the past,—so good night! I will dream on, always fancying that Mrs. Adams and yourself are by my side marking the progress and the obliquities of ages and countries.

4. William Vassall, a Massachusetts attorney.

5. Baron Friedrich Melchior von Grimm (1723–1807), whose *Letters, Literary, Philosophical and Critical* began to appear in 1812 and ran to seventeen volumes.

6. George Ticknor (1791–1871), educator, historian, and founder of the Boston Public Library; he visited Jefferson at Monticello as a young man.

7. Rev. Francis Adrian Van der Kemp, a Dutch émigré to New York.

8. Members of the Society of Jesus, founded by St. Ignatius Loyola in 1534 as a counteraction to the Protestant Reformation. They exerted great political influence, and the word *jesuitical* was identified with casuistry and intrigue. In 1773 they were dissolved by order of the pope and not reformed until many years later.

Letter to Nathaniel Burwell, Esq.[1]

[Women's Education]

Monticello, March 14, 1818

Dear Sir,—Your letter of February 17th found me suffering under an attack of rheumatism, which has but now left me at sufficient ease to attend to the letters I have received. A plan of female education has never been a subject of systematic contemplation with me. It has occupied my attention so far only as the education of my own daughters occasionally required. Considering that they would be placed in a country situation, where little aid could be obtained from abroad, I thought it essential to give them a solid education, which might enable them, when become mothers, to educate their own daughters, and even to direct the course for sons, should their fathers be lost, or incapable, or inattentive. My surviving daughter accordingly, the mother of many daughters as well as sons, has made their education the object of her life, and being a better judge of the practical part than myself, it is with her aid and that of one of her élèves,[2] that I shall subjoin a catalog of the books for such a course of reading as we have practiced.

A great obstacle to good education is the inordinate passion prevalent for novels, and the time lost in that reading which should be instructively employed. When this poison infects the mind, it destroys its tone and revolts it against wholesome reading. Reason and fact, plain and unadorned, are rejected. Nothing can engage attention unless dressed in all the figments of fancy, and nothing so bedecked comes amiss. The result is a bloated imagination, sickly judgment, and disgust towards all the real businesses of life. This mass of trash, however, is not without some distinction; some few modeling their narratives, although fictitious, on the incidents of real life, have been able to make them interesting and useful vehicles of a sound morality. Such, I think, are Marmontel's[3] new moral tales, but not his old ones, which are really immoral. Such are the writings of Miss Edgeworth,[4] and some of those of Madame Genlis.[5] For a like reason, too, much poetry should not be indulged. Some is useful for forming style and taste. Pope, Dryden, Thompson, Shakespeare, and of the French, Molière, Racine, the Corneilles, may be read with pleasure and improvement.

The French language, become that of the general intercourse of nations, and from their extraordinary advances, now the depository of all science, is an indispensable part of education for both sexes. In the subjoined catalog, therefore, I have placed the books of both languages indifferently, according as the one or the other offers what is best.

The ornaments too, and the amusements of life, are entitled to their portion of attention. These, for a female, are dancing, drawing, and music. The first is a healthy exercise, elegant and very attractive for young people. Every affectionate parent would be pleased to see his daughter qualified to participate with her companions, and without awkwardness at least, in the circles of festivity,

1. The text used here is from *The Writings of Thomas Jefferson*, vol. 15, edited by A. A. Lipscomb and A. E. Bergh (1903). Burwell was a distinguished Virginian.
2. Pupils (French).
3. Jean François Marmontel (1723–1799), French novelist and dramatist, whose *Moral Tales* appeared

in 1781.
4. Maria Edgeworth (1767–1849), English novelist, author of *Castle Rackrent* (1800).
5. Stéphanie Félicité du Crest de Saint-Aubin, Comtesse de Genlis (1746–1830), French novelist and educator, best known for her novel *Madame de la Vallière*.

of which she occasionally becomes a part. It is a necessary accomplishment, therefore, although of short use; for the French rule is wise, that no lady dances after marriage. This is founded in solid physical reasons, gestation and nursing leaving little time to a married lady when this exercise can be either safe or innocent. Drawing is thought less of in this country than in Europe. It is an innocent and engaging amusement, often useful, and a qualification not to be neglected in one who is to become a mother and an instructor. Music is invaluable where a person has an ear. Where they have not, it should not be attempted. It furnishes a delightful recreation for the hours of respite from the cares of the day, and lasts us through life. The taste of this country, too, calls for this accomplishment more strongly than for either of the others.

I need say nothing of household economy,[6] in which the mothers of our country are generally skilled, and generally careful to instruct their daughters. We all know its value, and that diligence and dexterity in all its processes are inestimable treasures. The order and economy of a house are as honorable to the mistress as those of the farm to the master, and if either be neglected, ruin follows, and children destitute of the means of living.

This, Sir, is offered as a summary sketch on a subject on which I have not thought much. It probably contains nothing but what has already occurred to yourself, and claims your acceptance on no other ground than as a testimony of my respect for your wishes, and of my great esteem and respect.

6. Management.

THE FEDERALIST

When Richard Henry Lee, Virginia delegate to the Continental Congress, proposed on June 7, 1776, his resolution for independence from Britain, he also suggested that a "plan of confederation be prepared and transmitted to the respective colonies for their consideration and approbation." On July 12, 1776, the Articles of Confederation were presented to Congress and debated for a year; they were ratified and adopted as the bylaws of the nation on March 1, 1781. The central question before the Constitutional Convention meeting in Philadelphia six years later was whether to try to salvage these articles by a number of complicated amendments or to draw up the framework of a new national government. Delegates to the convention decided upon the latter and, in September 1787, received copies of the proposed Constitution which they, in turn, were to submit to their state legislatures for ratification. Advocates of the new Constitution, dubbed Federalists, and their Antifederalist opponents, quickly rose to the occasion, and a great debate followed. Many were fearful at what they saw as the loss of states' rights and the power of a large, impersonal government to dominate the lives of individual citizens, and they cited the absence of a bill of rights; others thought that the Constitution favored urban over rural populations; while others bemoaned the end of the slave trade.

The debate took ten months, and in the state of New York, where adoption was not going to be automatic and a number of states' rights supporters objected to strengthening the power of the federal government, serious discussion ensued. The debate produced a number of significant documents, but none more lasting than the eighty-five essays that appeared in New York newspapers from October 1787 to April 1788, signed with the pen name Publius and later collected in two volumes called *The Federalist*. These essays were written by Alexander Hamilton (1757–1804), a brilliant and quick-tempered man who was a secretary and aide to General Washington and, later, secretary of the treasury; John Jay (1745–1829), first chief justice of the United States Supreme Court and governor of the state of New York; and James Madison (1751–1836), fourth president of the United States, a Virginian, and a lawyer of distinction. The pseudonym Publius was used for the sake of anonymity, but the authorship was generally known.

As originally conceived, *The Federalist* had only one purpose: to persuade reluctant New Yorkers to adopt the proposed new Constitution. It did not set out to define the nature of government; yet it has turned out to be more lasting than most political treatises. Its essential argument is that individuals have a natural right to "liberty, dignity, and happiness" and that to ensure these rights government must "secure the public good, and private rights, against the dangers of a majority," at the same time preserving the "spirit and form of a popular government." This difficult balancing that *The Federalist* argues goes to the very heart of American democracy.

From The Federalist[1]

No. 1 [*Alexander Hamilton*]

To the People of the State of New York.   October 27, 1787

After an unequivocal experience of the inefficacy of the subsisting[2] federal government, you are called upon to deliberate on a new Constitution for the United States of America. The subject speaks its own importance; comprehending in its consequences nothing less than the existence of the Union, the safety and welfare of the parts of which it is composed, the fate of an empire, in many respects, the most interesting in the world. It has been frequently remarked that it seems to have been reserved to the people of this country, by their conduct and example, to decide the important question whether societies of men are really capable or not of establishing good government from reflection and choice, or whether they are forever destined to depend, for their political constitutions, on accident and force. If there be any truth in the remark, the crisis at which we are arrived may with propriety be regarded as the era in which that decision is to be made; and a wrong election of the part we shall act, may, in this view, deserve to be considered as the general misfortune of mankind.

This idea will add the inducements of philanthropy to those of patriotism to heighten the solicitude, which all considerate and good men must feel for the event. Happy will it be if our choice should be directed by a judicious estimate of our true interests, unperplexed and unbiased by considerations not connected with the public good. But this is a thing more ardently to be wished than seriously to be expected. The plan offered to our deliberations affects too many particular interests, innovates[3] upon too many local institutions, not to involve in its discussion a variety of objects foreign to its merits, and of views, passions and prejudices little favorable to the discovery of truth.

Among the most formidable of the obstacles which the new Constitution will have to encounter may readily be distinguished the obvious interest of a certain class of men in every state to resist all changes which may hazard a

---

1. The text used here is from *The Federalist*, edited by Jacob E. Cooke (1961).
2. Existing; present.
3. Makes changes.

diminution of the power, emolument and consequence of the offices they hold under the state establishments—and the perverted ambition of another class of men, who will either hope to aggrandize themselves by the confusions of their country, or will flatter themselves with fairer prospects of elevation from the subdivision of the empire into several partial confederacies, than from its union under one government.

It is not, however, my design to dwell upon observations of this nature. I am well aware that it would be disingenuous to resolve indiscriminately the opposition of any set of men (merely because their situations might subject them to suspicion) into interested or ambitious views: candor will oblige us to admit, that even such men may be actuated by upright intentions; and it cannot be doubted that much of the opposition which has made its appearance, or may hereafter make its appearance, will spring from sources, blameless at least, if not respectable, the honest errors of minds led astray by preconceived jealousies and fears. So numerous indeed and so powerful are the causes, which serve to give a false bias to the judgment, that we upon many occasions see wise and good men on the wrong as well as on the right side of questions of the first magnitude to society. This circumstance, if duly attended to, would furnish a lesson of moderation to those, who are ever so much persuaded of their being in the right in any controversy. And a further reason for caution, in this respect, might be drawn from the reflection that we are not always sure that those who advocate the truth are influenced by purer principles than their antagonists. Ambition, avarice, personal animosity, party opposition, and many other motives, not more laudable than these, are apt to operate as well upon those who support as upon those who oppose the right side of a question. Were there not even these inducements to moderation, nothing could be more ill judged than that intolerant spirit, which has, at all times, characterized political parties. For, in politics as in religion, it is equally absurd to aim at making proselytes by fire and sword. Heresies in either can rarely be cured by persecution.

And yet however just these sentiments will be allowed to be, we have already sufficient indications that it will happen in this as in all former cases of great national discussion. A torrent of angry and malignant passions will be let loose. To judge from the conduct of the opposite parties, we shall be led to conclude that they will mutually hope to evince the justness of their opinions, and to increase the number of their converts by the loudness of their declamations, and by the bitterness of their invectives. An enlightened zeal for the energy and efficiency of government will be stigmatized, as the offspring of a temper fond of despotic power and hostile to the principles of liberty. An overscrupulous jealousy of danger to the rights of the people, which is more commonly the fault of the head than of the heart, will be represented as mere pretense and artifice; the bait for popularity at the expense of public good. It will be forgotten, on the one hand, that jealousy is the usual concomitant of violent love, and that the noble enthusiasm of liberty is too apt to be infected with a spirit of narrow and illiberal distrust. On the other hand, it will be equally forgotten that the vigor of government is essential to the security of liberty; that in the contemplation of a sound and well-informed judgment, their interest can never be separated; and that a dangerous ambition more often lurks behind the specious mask of zeal for the rights of the people than under the forbidding appearance of zeal for the firmness and efficiency of government. History will teach us that the former has been found a much more certain road to the introduction of despotism than the latter, and that of those men who have overturned the liberties of republics the greatest number have begun their career by paying an obsequious court to the people, commencing demagogues and ending tyrants.

In the course of the preceding observations I have had an eye, my fellow citizens, to putting you upon your guard against all attempts, from whatever quarter, to influence your decision in a matter of the utmost moment to your welfare by any impressions other than those which may result from the evidence of truth. You will, no doubt, at the same time, have collected from the general scope of them that they proceed from a source not unfriendly to the new Constitution. Yes, my countrymen, I own to you, that, after having given it an attentive consideration, I am clearly of opinion it is your interest to adopt it. I am convinced that this is the safest course for your liberty, your dignity, and your happiness. I effect not reserves, which I do not feel. I will not amuse you with an appearance of deliberation, when I have decided. I frankly acknowledge to you my convictions, and I will freely lay before you the reasons on which they are founded. The consciousness of good intentions disdains ambiguity. I shall not however multiply professions on this head. My motives must remain in the depository of my own breast: my arguments will be open to all, and may be judged of by all. They shall at least be offered in a spirit which will not disgrace the cause of truth.

I propose in a series of papers to discuss the following interesting particulars—the utility of the Union to your political prosperity—the insufficiency of the present confederation to preserve that Union—the necessity of a government at least equally energetic with the one proposed to the attainment of this object—the conformity of the proposed constitution to the true principles of republican government—its analogy to your own state constitution—and lastly, the additional security which its adoption will afford to the preservation of that species of government, to liberty and to property.

In the progress of this discussion I shall endeavor to give a satisfactory answer to all the objections which shall have made their appearance that may seem to have any claim to your attention.

It may perhaps be thought superfluous to offer arguments to prove the utility of the Union, a point, no doubt, deeply engraved on the hearts of the great body of the people in every state, and one, which it may be imagined, has no adversaries. But the fact is that we already hear it whispered in the private circles of those who oppose the new constitution that the thirteen states are of too great extent for any general system, and that we must of necessity resort to separate confederacies of distinct portions of the whole.[4] This doctrine will, in all probability, be gradually propagated, till it has votaries enough to countenance an open avowal of it. For nothing can be more evident, to those who are able to take an enlarged view of the subject, than the alternative of an adoption of the new Constitution, or a dismemberment of the Union. It will therefore be of use to begin by examining the advantages of that Union, the certain evils and the probable dangers to which every state will be exposed from its dissolution. This shall accordingly constitute the subject of my next address.

Publius[5]

---

4. "The same idea, tracing the arguments to their consequences, is held out in several of the late publications against the new Constitution" [Publius's note].

5. A Latin proper name and collective pseudonym adopted by Hamilton, Madison, and Jay as the authors of *The Federalist*; its identity was well known.

No. 10 [*James Madison*]

To the People of the State of New York.　　　　　November 22, 1787

Among the numerous advantages promised by a well-constructed Union, none deserves to be more accurately developed than its tendency to break and control the violence of faction. The friend of popular governments never finds himself so much alarmed for their character and fate as when he contemplates their propensity to this dangerous vice. He will not fail therefore to set a due value on any plan which, without violating the principles to which he is attached, provides a proper cure for it. The instability, injustice and confusion introduced into the public councils have in truth been the mortal diseases under which popular governments have everywhere perished; as they continue to be the favorite and fruitful topics from which the adversaries to liberty derive their most specious declamations. The valuable improvements made by the American constitutions on the popular models, both ancient and modern, cannot certainly be too much admired; but it would be an unwarrantable partiality to contend that they have as effectually obviated the danger on this side as was wished and expected. Complaints are everywhere heard from our most considerate and virtuous citizens, equally the friends of public and private faith and of public and personal liberty; that our governments are too unstable; that the public good is disregarded in the conflicts of rival parties; and that measures are too often decided not according to the rules of justice and the rights of the minor party, but by the superior force of an interested and overbearing majority. However anxiously we may wish that these complaints had no foundation, the evidence of known facts will not permit us to deny that they are in some degree true. It will be found indeed, on a candid review of our situation, that some of the distresses under which we labor have been erroneously charged on the operation of our governments; but it will be found, at the same time, that other causes will not alone account for many of our heaviest misfortunes; and particularly, for that prevailing and increasing distrust of public engagements, and alarm for private rights, which are echoed from one end of the continent to the other. These must be chiefly, if not wholly, effects of the unsteadiness and injustice with which a factious spirit has tainted our public administrations.

By a faction I understand a number of citizens, whether amounting to a majority or minority of the whole, who are united and actuated by some common impulse of passion or of interest, adverse to the rights of other citizens, or to the permanent and aggregate interests of the community.

There are two methods of curing the mischiefs of faction: the one, by removing its causes; the other, by controlling its effects.

There are again two methods of removing the causes of faction: the one by destroying the liberty which is essential to its existence; the other, by giving to every citizen the same opinions, the same passions, and the same interests.

It could never be more truly said than of the first remedy, that it is worse than the disease. Liberty is to faction, what air is to fire, an aliment[1] without which it instantly expires. But it could not be a less folly to abolish liberty, which is essential to political life, because it nourishes faction, than it would be to wish the annihilation of air, which is essential to animal life, because it imparts to fire its destructive agency.

---

1. Nutriment; sustenance.

The second expedient is as impracticable as the first would be unwise. As long as the reason of man continues fallible, and he is at liberty to exercise it, different opinions will be formed. As long as the connection subsists between his reason and his self-love, his opinions and his passions will have a reciprocal influence on each other; and the former will be objects to which the latter will attach themselves. The diversity in the faculties of men from which the rights of property originate is not less an insuperable obstacle to a uniformity of interests. The protection of these faculties is the first object of government. From the protection of different and unequal faculties of acquiring property, the possession of different degrees and kinds of property immediately results: and from the influence of these on the sentiments and views of the respective proprietors ensues a division of the society into different interests and parties.

The latent causes of faction are thus sown in the nature of man; and we see them everywhere brought into different degrees of activity, according to the different circumstances of civil society. A zeal for different opinions concerning religion, concerning government and many other points, as well of speculation as of practice; an attachment to different leaders ambitiously contending for pre-eminence and power; or to persons of other descriptions whose fortunes have been interesting to the human passions have in turn divided mankind into parties, inflamed them with mutual animosity, and rendered them much more disposed to vex and oppress each other than to cooperate for their common good. So strong is this propensity of mankind to fall into mutual animosities that where no substantial occasion presents itself, the most frivolous and fanciful distinctions have been sufficient to kindle their unfriendly passions and excite their most violent conflicts. But the most common and durable source of factions has been the various and unequal distribution of property. Those who hold and those who are without property have ever formed distinct interests in society. Those who are creditors and those who are debtors fall under a like discrimination. A landed interest, a manufacturing interest, a mercantile interest, a monied interest, with many lesser interests, grow up of necessity in civilized nations, and divide them into different classes, actuated by different sentiments and views. The regulation of these various and interfering interests forms the principal task of modern legislation, and involves the spirit of party and faction in the necessary and ordinary operations of government.

No man is allowed to be a judge in his own cause, because his interest would certainly bias his judgment and, not improbably, corrupt his integrity. With equal, nay with greater, reason a body of men are unfit to be both judges and parties at the same time; yet what are many of the most important acts of legislation but so many judicial determinations, not indeed concerning the rights of single persons, but concerning the rights of large bodies of citizens; and what are the different classes of legislators but advocates and parties to the causes which they determine? Is a law proposed concerning private debts? It is a question to which the creditors are parties on one side and the debtors on the other. Justice ought to hold the balance between them. Yet the parties are and must be themselves the judges; and the most numerous party, or, in other words, the most powerful faction, must be expected to prevail. Shall domestic manufactures be encouraged, and in what degree, by restrictions on foreign manufactures? are questions which would be differently decided by the landed and the manufacturing classes; and probably by neither, with a sole regard to justice and the public good. The apportionment of taxes on the various descriptions of property is an act which seems to require the most exact impartiality; yet, there is perhaps no legislative act in which greater opportunity and temptation are given to a predominant party to trample on the rules of justice. Every shilling with which they overburden the inferior number is a shilling saved to their own pockets.

It is in vain to say that enlightened statesmen will be able to adjust these clashing interests and render them all subservient to the public good. Enlightened statesmen will not always be at the helm; nor, in many cases, can such an adjustment be made at all, without taking into view indirect and remote considerations, which will rarely prevail over the immediate interest which one party may find in disregarding the rights of another, or the good of the whole.

The inference to which we are brought is that the *causes* of faction cannot be removed, and that relief is only to be sought in the means of controlling its *effects*.

If a faction consists of less than a majority, relief is supplied by the republican principle, which enables the majority to defeat its sinister views by regular vote. It may clog the administration, it may convulse the society, but it will be unable to execute and mask its violence under the forms of the Constitution. When a majority is included in a faction, the form of popular government on the other hand enables it to sacrifice to its ruling passion or interest both the public good and the rights of other citizens. To secure the public good and private rights against the danger of such a faction, and at the same time to preserve the spirit and the form of popular government, is then the great object to which our inquiries are directed. Let me add that it is the great desideratum[2] by which alone this form of government can be rescued from the opprobrium under which it has so long labored and be recommended to the esteem and adoption of mankind.

By what means is this object attainable? Evidently by one of two only. Either the existence of the same passion or interest in a majority at the same time must be prevented; or the majority, having such co-existent passion or interest, must be rendered, by their number and local situation, unable to concert and carry into effect schemes of oppression. If the impulse and the opportunity be suffered to coincide, we well know that neither moral nor religious motives can be relied on as an adequate control. They are not found to be such on the injustice and violence of individuals, and lose their efficacy in proportion to the number combined together; that is, in proportion as their efficacy becomes needful.

From this view of the subject, it may be concluded, that a pure democracy, by which I mean a society consisting of a small number of citizens who assemble and administer the government in person, can admit of no cure for the mischiefs of faction. A common passion or interest will, in almost every case, be felt by a majority of the whole; a communication and concert results from the form of government itself; and there is nothing to check the inducements to sacrifice the weaker party, or an obnoxious individual. Hence it is that such democracies have ever been spectacles of turbulence and contention; have ever been found incompatible with personal security, or the rights of property; and have in general been as short in their lives, as they have been violent in their deaths. Theoretic politicians, who have patronized this species of government,

---

2. Thing which is desired; that which is felt to be missing and needed (Latin).

have erroneously supposed that by reducing mankind to a perfect equality in their political rights, they would, at the same time, be perfectly equalized and assimilated in their possessions, their opinions, and their passions.

A republic, by which I mean a government in which the scheme of representation takes place, opens a different prospect, and promises the cure for which we are seeking. Let us examine the points in which it varies from pure democracy, and we shall comprehend both the nature of the cure, and the efficacy which it must derive from the Union.

The two great points of difference between a democracy and a republic are, first, the delegation of the government, in the latter, to a small number of citizens elected by the rest: secondly, the greater number of citizens, and greater sphere of country, over which the latter may be extended.

The effect of the first difference is, on the one hand, to refine and enlarge the public views by passing them through the medium of a chosen body of citizens, whose wisdom may best discern the true interest of their country, and whose patriotism and love of justice will be least likely to sacrifice it to temporary or partial considerations. Under such a regulation, it may well happen that the public voice pronounced by the representatives of the people will be more consonant to the public good than if pronounced by the people themselves convened for the purpose. On the other hand, the effect may be inverted. Men of factious tempers, of local prejudices, or of sinister designs may, by intrigue, by corruption or by other means, first obtain the suffrages,[3] and then betray the interests of the people. The question resulting is whether small or extensive republics are most favorable to the election of proper guardians of the public weal: and it is clearly decided in favor of the latter by two obvious considerations.

In the first place it is to be remarked that however small the republic may be, the representatives must be raised to a certain number in order to guard against the cabals[4] of a few; and that however large it may be, they must be limited to a certain number in order to guard against the confusion of a multitude. Hence the number of representatives in the two cases, not being in proportion to that of the constituents, and being proportionally greatest in the small republic, it follows, that if the proportion of fit characters be not less in the large than in the small republic, the former will present a greater option, and consequently a greater probability of a fit choice.

In the next place, as each representative will be chosen by a greater number of citizens in the large than in the small republic, it will be more difficult for unworthy candidates to practice with success the vicious arts, by which elections are too often carried; and the suffrages of the people being more free will be more likely to center on men who possess the most attractive merit, and the most diffusive and established characters.

It must be confessed that in this, as in most other cases, there is a mean, on both sides of which inconveniencies will be found to lie. By enlarging too much the number of electors, you render the representative too little acquainted with all their local circumstances and lesser interests; as by reducing it too much, you render him unduly attached to these, and too little fit to comprehend and pursue great and national objects. The federal Constitution forms a happy combination in this respect; the great and aggregate interests being referred to the national, the local, and, particular, to the state legislatures.

3. Votes.   4. Plots.

The other point of difference is the greater number of citizens and extent of territory which may be brought within the compass of republican, than of democratic[5] government; and it is this circumstance principally which renders factious combinations less to be dreaded in the former than in the latter. The smaller the society, the fewer probably will be the distinct parties and interests composing it; the fewer the distinct parties and interests, the more frequently will a majority be found of the same party; and the smaller the number of individuals composing a majority, and smaller the compass within which they are placed, the more easily will they concert and execute their plans of oppression. Extend the sphere, and you take in a greater variety of parties and interests; you make it less probable that a majority of the whole will have a common motive to invade the rights of other citizens; or if such a common motive exists, it will be more difficult for all who feel it to discover their own strength, and to act in unison with each other. Besides other impediments, it may be remarked, that where there is a consciousness of unjust or dishonorable purposes, communication is always checked by distrust, in proportion to the number whose concurrence is necessary.

Hence it clearly appears that the same advantage which a republic has over a democracy, in controling the effects of faction, is enjoyed by a large over a small republic—is enjoyed by the Union over the states composing it. Does this advantage consist in the substitution of representatives, whose enlightened views and virtuous sentiments render them superior to local prejudices, and to schemes of injustice? It will not be denied, that the representation of the Union will be most likely to possess these requisite endowments. Does it consist in the greater security afforded by a greater variety of parties, against the event of any one party being able to outnumber and oppress the rest? In an equal degree does the increased variety of parties, comprised within the Union, increase this security? Does it, in fine,[6] consist in the greater obstacles opposed to the concert and accomplishment of the secret wishes of an unjust and interested majority? Here, again, the extent of the Union gives it the most palpable advantage.

The influence of factious leaders may kindle a flame within their particular states, but will be unable to spread a general conflagration through the other states: a religious sect, may degenerate into a political faction in a part of the confederacy; but the variety of sects dispersed over the entire face of it must secure the national councils against any danger from that source: a rage for paper money, for an abolition of debts, for an equal division of property, or for any other improper or wicked project, will be less apt to pervade the whole body of the Union than a particular member of it; in the same proportion as such a malady is more likely to taint a particular county or district than an entire state.

In the extent and proper structure of the Union, therefore, we behold a republican remedy for the diseases most incident to republican government. And according to the degree of pleasure and pride we feel in being republicans, ought to be our zeal in cherishing the spirit, and supporting the character of Federalists.

Publius

1787

1788

5. Republicans are Federalists and are willing to have an elected few represent the whole; Democrats are Antifederalists and are carefully guarding the individual's right to vote.
6. In conclusion.

OLAUDAH EQUIANO

c. 1745–1797

The Interesting Narrative of the Life of Olaudah Equiano, or Gustavus Vassa, the African was published in London in 1789 and found an enthusiastic American audience when it was reprinted in New York in 1791. In the next five years it went through eight more editions and it was reprinted again in the nineteenth century. No black voice before Frederick Douglass in his *Narrative* of 1845 spoke so movingly to American readers about inhumanity. In a literature replete with self-made figures who voyage from innocence to experience—some fictive, some not—Equiano's story stands, in view of the actual horrors he suffered, in a class quite by itself. He defined himself, of course, as neither African-American (his first owner in the New World was a Virginian) nor Anglo-African (with London as his adopted home). He was "the African," even at the end of his life, a man set apart from everyone else by his color and his bondage, shaped as much by what he left behind as what he saw before him.

Equiano was born about 1745 in what is now Nigeria, in an unlocated Ibo village called Essaka; he was sold to British slavers in 1756 and transported first to the Barbadoes in the West Indies and then to a plantation in Virginia. He was with his second owner, Lt. Michael Henry Pascal, all during the Seven Years' War between England and France and was present at the siege of Fort Louisburg on Cape Breton Island in Nova Scotia. Eventually, he was sold to a Quaker merchant from Philadelphia, Robert King, who carried on much of his business in the West Indies. King often traded in "live cargo," or slaves, and Equiano saw much that made him grateful for his Quaker master's treatment of him, without having, for a moment, any illusions about what the loss of freedom entailed. He saw the ugliest side of American life in both the North and the South. Even in Philadelphia, a city built on the premise of "brotherly love," Equiano observed that the freed black was treated with profound contempt, "plundered" and "universally insulted," with no possibility of redress. King, however, did make it possible for Equiano to purchase his freedom in 1766. Once having gained his freedom by saving forty pounds—earned by his own instincts for enterprise, carrying on his own business while managing King's—he never set foot on American soil again.

It was Equiano's intention to settle in London for the rest of his life. He made his living there as a free servant, a musician (he played the French horn), and a barber. But Equiano's skill as a seaman, and his always remarkable curiosity, made him restless for new adventures, and before he died he had traveled as far as Turkey; had heard opera in Rome; and had seen Jamaica, Honduras, and Nicaragua. In 1783 Equiano brought the case of the infamous ship *Zong* to the British public: the owners had thrown overboard 132 shackled slaves and later made insurance claims against their loss. He lectured widely on the abolition of slavery and approved a project to resettle poor blacks in Sierra Leone, Africa. He was, in fact, given an official post in this undertaking, but lost it after he made accusations of misdeeds against some officials. Although he always spoke about his desire to return to the place of his birth, Africa always lay beyond his reach. In a letter written to his hosts in Birmingham, England, after lecturing there, he wrote:

> These acts of kindness and hospitality have filled me with a longing desire to see these worthy friends on my own estate in Africa, where the richest produce of it should be devoted to their entertainment. There they should partake of the luxuriant pineapples, and the well-flavored virgin palm-wine, and to heighten the bliss I would burn a certain tree, that would afford us light as clear and brilliant as the virtue of my guests.

In 1792 Equiano married Susanna Cullen, and their marriage was duly noticed in the London *Gentleman's Magazine*. He died on March 31, 1797, and his only child, a daughter, died shortly after him.

From The Interesting Narrative of the Life of Olaudah Equiano, or Gustavas Vassa, the African, Written by Himself[1]

From *Chapter I*

I believe it is difficult for those who publish their own memoirs to escape the imputation of vanity; nor is this the only disadvantage under which they labor: it is also their misfortune, that what is uncommon is rarely, if ever, believed, and what is obvious we are apt to turn from with disgust, and to charge the writer with impertinence. People generally think those memoirs only worthy to be read or remembered which abound in great or striking events; those, in short, which in a high degree excite either admiration or pity: all others they consign to contempt and oblivion. It is therefore, I confess, not a little hazardous in a private and obscure individual, and a stranger too, thus to solicit the indulgent attention of the public; especially when I own[2] I offer here the history of neither a saint, a hero, nor a tyrant. I believe there are few events in my life, which have not happened to many: it is true the incidents of it are numerous; and, did I consider myself an European, I might say my sufferings were great: but when I compare my lot with that of most of my countrymen, I regard myself as a *particular favorite of Heaven*, and acknowledge the mercies of Providence in every occurrence of my life. If, then, the following narrative does not appear sufficiently interesting to engage general attention, let my motive be some excuse for its publication. I am not so foolishly vain as to expect from it either immortality or literary reputation. If it affords any satisfaction to my numerous friends, at whose request it has been written, or in the smallest degree promotes the interests of humanity, the ends for which it was undertaken will be fully attained, and every wish of my heart gratified. Let it therefore be remembered, that, in wishing to avoid censure, I do not aspire to praise.

That part of Africa, known by the name of Guinea, to which the trade for slaves is carried on, extends along the coast above 3400 miles, from Senegal to Angola, and includes a variety of kingdoms. Of these the most considerable is the kingdom of Benin, both as to extent and wealth, the richness and cultivation of the soil, the power of its king, and the number and warlike disposition of the inhabitants. It is situated nearly under the line,[3] and extends along the coast about 170 miles, but runs back into the interior part of Africa to a distance hitherto, I believe, unexplored by any traveler; and seems only terminated at length by the empire of Abyssinnia, near 1500 miles from its beginning. This kingdom is divided into many provinces or districts: in one of the most remote and fertile of which, I was born, in the year 1745, situated in a charming fruitful vale, named Essaka. The distance of this province from

1. The text used here is taken from the 1st edition, published in two volumes for the author in London in 1789. The original paragraphing has been altered to facilitate reading.
2. Acknowledge.
3. I.e., the equator.

the capital of Benin and the sea coast must be very considerable: for I had never heard of white men or Europeans, nor of the sea; and our subjection to the king of Benin was little more than nominal; for every transaction of the government, as far as my slender observation extended, was conducted by the chief or elders of the place. The manners and government of a people who have little commerce with other countries, are generally very simple; and the history of what passes in one family or village, may serve as a specimen of the whole nation. My father was one of those elders or chiefs I have spoken of, and was styled Embrenche; a term, as I remember, importing the highest distinction, and signifying in our language a *mark* of grandeur. This mark is conferred on the person entitled to it, by cutting the skin across at the top of the forehead, and drawing it down to the eyebrows: and while it is in this situation applying a warm hand, and rubbing it until it shrinks up into a thick *weal* across the lower part of the forehead. Most of the judges and senators were thus marked; my father had long borne it: I had seen it conferred on one of my brothers, and I also was *destined* to receive it by my parents. Those Embrenche or chief men, decided disputes and punished crimes; for which purpose they always assembled together. The proceedings were generally short: and in most cases the law of retaliation prevailed. * * *

We are almost a nation of dancers, musicians and poets. Thus every great event, such as a triumphant return from battle, or other cause of public rejoicing, is celebrated in public dances, which are accompanied with songs and music suited to the occasion. The assembly is separated into four divisions, which dance either apart or in succession, and each with a character peculiar to itself. The first division contains the married men, who in their dances frequently exhibit feats of arms, and the representation of a battle. To these succeed the married women, who dance in the second division. The young men occupy the third: and the maidens the fourth. Each represents some interesting scene of real life, such as a great achievement, domestic employment, a pathetic story, or some rural sport; and as the subject is generally founded on some recent event, it is therefore ever new. This gives our dances a spirit and variety which I have scarcely seen elsewhere.[4]

* * *

Chapter II

I hope the reader will not think I have trespassed on his patience in introducing myself to him, with some account of the manners and customs of my country. They had been implanted in me with great care, and made an impression on my mind, which time could not erase, and which all the adversity and variety of fortune I have since experienced, served only to rivet and record; for, whether the love of one's country be real or imaginary, or a lesson of reason, or an instinct of nature, I still look back with pleasure on the first scenes of my life, though that pleasure has been for the most part mingled with sorrow.

I have already acquainted the reader with the time and place of my birth. My father, besides many slaves, had a numerous family, of which seven lived to grow up, including myself and a sister, who was the only daughter. As I was the youngest of the sons, I became, of course, the greatest favorite with my

---

4. "When I was in Smyrna I have frequently seen the Greeks dance after this manner" [Equiano's note].

mother, and was always with her; and she used to take particular pains to form my mind. I was trained up from my earliest years in the art of war: my daily exercise was shooting and throwing javelins; and my mother adorned me with emblems, after the manner of our greatest warriors. In this way I grew up till I was turned the age of eleven, when an end was put to my happiness in the following manner:—generally when the grown people in the neighborhood were gone far in the fields to labor, the children assembled together in some of the neighboring premises to play; and commonly some of us used to get up a tree to look out for any assailant, or kidnapper, that might come upon us— for they sometimes took those opportunities of our parents' absence, to attack and carry off as many as they could seize. One day as I was watching at the top of a tree in our yard, I saw one of those people come into the yard of our next neighbor but one to kidnap, there being many stout[5] young people in it. Immediately on this I gave the alarm of the rogue, and he was surrounded by the stoutest of them, who entangled him with cords, so that he could not escape till some of the grown people came and secured him. But, alas! ere long it was my fate to be thus attacked, and to be carried off, when none of the grown people were nigh. One day, when all our people were gone out to their works as usual, and only I and my dear sister were left to mind the house, two men and a woman got over our walls, and in a moment seized us both, and, without giving us time to cry out, or make resistance, they stopped our mouths, and ran off with us into the nearest wood. Here they tied our hands, and continued to carry us as far as they could, till night came on, when we reached a small house, where the robbers halted for refreshment, and spent the night. We were then unbound, but were unable to take any food; and, being quite overpowered by fatigue and grief, our only relief was some sleep, which allayed our misfortune for a short time. The next morning we left the house, and continued traveling all the day. For a long time we had kept the woods, but at last we came into a road which I believed I knew. I had now some hopes of being delivered; for we had advanced but a little way before I discovered some people at a distance, on which I began to cry out for their assistance; but my cries had no other effect than to make them tie me faster and stop my mouth, and then they put me into a large sack. They also stopped my sister's mouth, and tied her hands; and in this manner we proceeded till we were out of sight of these people. When we went to rest the following night, they offered us some victuals, but we refused it; and the only comfort we had was in being in one another's arms all that night, and bathing each other with our tears. But alas! we were soon deprived of even the small comfort of weeping together. The next day proved a day of greater sorrow than I had yet experienced; for my sister and I were then separated, while we lay clasped in each other's arms. It was in vain that we besought them not to part us; she was torn from me, and immediately carried away, while I was left in a state of distraction not to be described. I cried and grieved continually; and for several days did not eat any thing but what they forced into my mouth. At length, after many days traveling, during which I had often changed masters, I got into the hands of a chieftain, in a very pleasant country. This man had two wives and some children, and they all used me extremely well, and did all they could to comfort me; particularly the first wife, who was something like

5. Strong.

my mother. Although I was a great many days' journey from my father's house, yet these people spoke exactly the same language with us. This first master of mine, as I may call him, was a smith,[6] and my principal employment was working his bellows, which were the same kind as I had seen in my vicinity. They were in some respects not unlike the stoves here in gentlemen's kitchens, and were covered over with leather; and in the middle of that leather a stick was fixed, and a person stood up, and worked it in the same manner as is done to pump water out of a cask with a hand pump. I believe it was gold he worked, for it was of a lovely bright yellow color, and was worn by the women on their wrists and ankles. I was there I suppose about a month, and they at last used to trust me some little distance from the house. This liberty I used in embracing every opportunity to inquire the way to my own home; and I also sometimes, for the same purpose, went with the maidens, in the cool of the evenings, to bring pitchers of water from the springs for the use of the house. I had also remarked where the sun rose in the morning, and set in the evening, as I had traveled along; and I had observed that my father's house was towards the rising of the sun. I therefore determined to seize the first opportunity of making my escape, and to shape my course for that quarter; for I was quite oppressed and weighed down by grief after my mother and friends; and my love of liberty, ever great, was strengthened by the mortifying circumstance of not daring to eat with the free-born children, although I was mostly their companion. While I was projecting my escape one day, an unlucky event happened, which quite disconcerted my plan, and put an end to my hopes. I used to be sometimes employed in assisting an elderly slave to cook and take care of the poultry; and one morning, while I was feeding some chickens, I happened to toss a small pebble at one of them, which hit it on the middle, and directly killed it. The old slave, having soon after missed the chicken, inquired after it; and on my relating the accident (for I told her the truth, for my mother would never suffer me to tell a lie), she flew into a violent passion, and threatened that I should suffer for it; and, my master being out, she immediately went and told her mistress what I had done. This alarmed me very much, and I expected an instant flogging, which to me was uncommonly dreadful, for I had seldom been beaten at home. I therefore resolved to fly; and accordingly I ran into a thicket that was hard by, and hid myself in the bushes. Soon afterwards my mistress and the slave returned, and, not seeing me, they searched all the house, but not finding me, and I not making answer when they called to me, they thought I had run away, and the whole neighborhood was raised in the pursuit of me. In that part of the country, as in ours, the houses and villages were skirted with woods, or shrubberies, and the bushes were so thick that a man could readily conceal himself in them, so as to elude the strictest search. The neighbors continued the whole day looking for me, and several times many of them came within a few yards of the place where I lay hid. I expected every moment, when I heard a rustling among the trees, to be found out, and punished by my master; but they never discovered me, though they were often so near that I even heard their conjectures as they were looking about for me; and I now learned from them that any attempts to return home would be hopeless. Most of them supposed I had fled towards home; but the distance was so great, and the way so intricate, that they thought I could

6. A metalworker; here, a goldsmith.

never reach it, and that I should be lost in the woods. When I heard this I was seized with a violent panic, and abandoned myself to despair. Night, too, began to approach, and aggravated all my fears. I had before entertained hopes of getting home, and had determined when it should be dark to make the attempt; but I was now convinced it was fruitless, and began to consider that, if possibly I could escape all other animals, I could not those of the human kind; and that, not knowing the way, I must perish in the woods. Thus was I like the hunted deer—

> —"Every leaf and every whisp'ring breath,
> Convey'd a foe, and every foe a death."

I heard frequent rustlings among the leaves, and being pretty sure they were snakes, I expected every instant to be stung by them. This increased my anguish, and the horror of my situation became now quite insupportable. I at length quitted the thicket, very faint and hungry, for I had not eaten or drank any thing all the day, and crept to my master's kitchen, from whence I set out at first, which was an open shed, and laid myself down in the ashes with an anxious wish for death, to relieve me from all my pains. I was scarcely awake in the morning, when the old woman slave, who was the first up, came to light the fire, and saw me in the fire place. She was very much surprised to see me, and could scarcely believe her own eyes. She now promised to intercede for me, and went for her master, who soon after came, and, having slightly reprimanded me, ordered me to be taken care of, and not ill treated.

Soon after this, my master's only daughter, and child by his first wife, sickened and died, which affected him so much that for some time he was almost frantic, and really would have killed himself, had he not been watched and prevented. However, in short time afterwards he recovered, and I was again sold. I was now carried to the left of the sun's rising, through many dreary wastes and dismal woods, amidst the hideous roarings of wild beasts. The people I was sold to used to carry me very often, when I was tired, either on their shoulders or on their backs. I saw many convenient well built sheds along the road, at proper distances, to accommodate the merchants and travelers, who lay in those buildings along with their wives, who often accompany them; and they always go well armed.

From the time I left my own nation, I always found somebody that understood me till I came to the sea coast. The languages of different nations did not totally differ, nor were they so copious as those of the Europeans, particularly the English. They were therefore, easily learned; and, while I was journeying thus through Africa, I acquired two or three different tongues. In this manner I had been traveling for a considerable time, when, one evening, to my great surprise, whom should I see brought to the house where I was but my dear sister! As soon as she saw me, she gave a loud shriek, and ran into my arms—I was quite overpowered: neither of us could speak; but, for a considerable time, clung to each other in mutual embraces, unable to do any thing but weep. Our meeting affected all who saw us; and, indeed, I must acknowledge, in honor of those sable destroyers of human rights, that I never met with any ill treatment, or saw any offered to their slaves, except tying them, when necessary, to keep them from running away. When these people knew we were brother and sister, they indulged us to be together; and the man, to whom I supposed we belonged, lay with us, he in the middle, while she and I held one another by the hands across his breast all night; and thus for a while we forgot our misfortunes, in the joy of being together; but even this small comfort was soon to have an end; for scarcely had the fatal morning appeared when she was again torn from me forever! I was now more miserable, if possible, than before. The small relief which her presence gave me from pain was gone, and the wretchedness of my situation was redoubled by my anxiety after her fate, and my apprehensions lest her sufferings should be greater than mine, when I could not be with her to alleviate them. Yes, thou dear partner of all my childish sports! thou sharer of my joys and sorrows! happy should I have ever esteemed myself to encounter every misery for you and to procure your freedom by the sacrifice of my own.—Though you were early forced from my arms, your image has been always riveted in my heart, from which neither time nor fortune have been able to remove it; so that, while the thoughts of your sufferings have damped my prosperity, they have mingled with adversity and increased its bitterness. To that Heaven which protects the weak from the strong, I commit the care of your innocence and virtues, if they have not already received their full reward, and if your youth and delicacy have not long since fallen victims to the violence of the African trader, the pestilential stench of a Guinea ship, the seasoning in the European colonies, or the lash and lust of a brutal and unrelenting overseer.

  I did not long remain after my sister. I was again sold, and carried through a number of places, till after traveling a considerable time, I came to a town called Tinmah, in the most beautiful country I had yet seen in Africa. It was extremely rich, and there were many rivulets which flowed through it, and supplied a large pond in the center of the town, where the people washed. Here I first saw and tasted cocoa nuts, which I thought superior to any nuts I had ever tasted before; and the trees which were loaded, were also interspersed among the houses, which had commodious shades adjoining, and were in the same manner as ours, the insides being neatly plastered and whitewashed. Here I also saw and tasted for the first time, sugar cane. Their money consisted of little white shells, the size of the finger nail. I was sold here for one hundred and seventy-two of them, by a merchant who lived and brought me there. I had been about two or three days at his house, when a wealthy widow, a neighbor of his, came there one evening, and brought with her an only son, a young gentleman about my own age and size. Here they saw me; and, having taken a fancy to me, I was bought of the merchant, and went home with them. Her house and premises were situated close to one of those rivulets I have mentioned, and were the finest I ever saw in Africa: they were very extensive, and she had a number of slaves to attend her. The next day I was washed and perfumed, and when mealtime came, I was led into the presence of my mistress, and ate and drank before her with her son. This filled me with astonishment; and I could scarce help expressing my surprise that the young gentleman should suffer[7] me, who was bound, to eat with him who was free; and not only so, but that he would not at any time either eat or drink till I had taken first, because I was the eldest, which was agreeable to our custom. Indeed, every thing here, and all their treatment of me, made me forget that I was a slave. The language of these people resembled ours so nearly, that we understood each other perfectly. They had also the very same customs as we. There were

7. Allow.

likewise slaves daily to attend us, while my young master and I, with other boys, sported with our darts and bows and arrows, as I had been used to do at home. In this resemblance to my former happy state, I passed about two months; and I now began to think I was to be adopted into the family, and was beginning to be reconciled to my situation, and to forget by degrees my misfortunes, when all at once the delusion vanished; for, without the least previous knowledge, one morning early, while my dear master and companion was still asleep, I was awakened out of my reverie to fresh sorrow, and hurried away even amongst the uncircumcised.

Thus, at the very moment I dreamed of the greatest happiness, I found myself most miserable; and it seemed as if fortune wished to give me this taste of joy only to render the reverse more poignant.—The change I now experienced, was as painful as it was sudden and unexpected. It was a change indeed, from a state of bliss to a scene which is inexpressible by me, as it discovered to me an element I had never before beheld, and till then had no idea of, and wherein such instances of hardship and cruelty continually occurred, as I can never reflect on but with horror.

All the nations and people I had hitherto passed through, resembled our own in their manners, customs, and language: but I came at length to a country, the inhabitants of which differed from us in all those particulars. I was very much struck with this difference, especially when I came among a people who did not circumcise, and ate without washing their hands. They cooked also in iron pots, and had European cutlasses and cross bows, which were unknown to us, and fought with their fists among themselves. Their women were not so modest as ours, for they ate, and drank, and slept with their men. But above all, I was amazed to see no sacrifices or offerings among them. In some of those places the people ornamented themselves with scars, and likewise filed their teeth very sharp. They wanted sometimes to ornament me in the same manner, but I would not suffer them; hoping that I might some time be among a people who did not thus disfigure themselves, as I thought they did. At last I came to the banks of a large river which was covered with canoes, in which the people appeared to live with their household utensils, and provisions of all kinds. I was beyond measure astonished at this, as I had never before seen any water larger than a pond or a rivulet: and my surprise was mingled with no small fear when I was put into one of these canoes, and we began to paddle and move along the river. We continued going on thus till night, and when we came to land, and made fires on the banks, each family by themselves; some dragged their canoes on shore, others stayed and cooked in theirs, and laid in them all night. Those on the land had mats, of which they made tents, some in the shape of little houses; in these we slept; and after the morning meal, we embarked again and proceeded as before. I was often very much astonished to see some of the women, as well as the men, jump into the water, dive to the bottom, come up again, and swim about.—Thus I continued to travel, sometimes by land, sometimes by water, through different countries and various nations, till, at the end of six or seven months after I had been kidnapped, I arrived at the sea coast. It would be tedious and uninteresting to relate all the incidents which befell me during this journey, and which I have not yet forgotten; of the various hands I passed through, and the manners and customs of all the different people among whom I lived—I shall therefore only observe, that in all the places where I was, the soil was exceedingly rich; the pumpkins, eadas,[8] plaintains, yams, etc., etc., were in great abundance, and of incredible size. There were also vast quantities of different gums, though not used for any purpose, and every where a great deal of tobacco. The cotton even grew quite wild, and there was plenty of red-wood. I saw no mechanics[9] whatever in all the way, except such as I have mentioned. The chief employment in all these countries was agriculture, and both the males and females, as with us, were brought up to it, and trained in the arts of war.

The first object which saluted my eyes when I arrived on the coast, was the sea, and a slave ship, which was then riding at anchor, and waiting for its cargo. These filled me with astonishment, which was soon converted into terror, when I was carried on board. I was immediately handled, and tossed up to see if I were sound, by some of the crew; and I was now persuaded that I had gotten into a world of bad spirits, and that they were going to kill me. Their complexions, too, differing so much from ours, their long hair, and the language they spoke (which was very different from any I had ever heard), united to confirm me in this belief. Indeed, such were the horrors of my views and fears at the moment, that, if ten thousand worlds had been my own, I would have freely parted with them all to have exchanged my condition with that of the meanest slave in my own country. When I looked round the ship too, and saw a large furnace of copper boiling, and a multitude of black people of every description chained together, every one of their countenances expressing dejection and sorrow, I no longer doubted of my fate; and, quite overpowered with horror and anguish, I fell motionless on the deck and fainted. When I recovered a little, I found some black people about me, who I believed were some of those who had brought me on board, and had been receiving their pay; they talked to me in order to cheer me, but all in vain. I asked them if we were not to be eaten by those white men with horrible looks, red faces, and long hair. They told me I was not: and one of the crew brought me a small portion of spirituous liquor in a wine glass, but, being afraid of him, I would not take it out of his hand. One of the blacks, therefore, took it from him and gave it to me, and I took a little down my palate, which, instead of reviving me, as they thought it would, threw me into the greatest consternation at the strange feeling it produced, having never tasted any such liquor before. Soon after this, the blacks who brought me on board went off, and left me abandoned to despair.

I now saw myself deprived of all chance of returning to my native country, or even the least glimpse of hope of gaining the shore, which I now considered as friendly; and I even wished for my former slavery in preference to my present situation, which was filled with horrors of every kind, still heightened by my ignorance of what I was to undergo. I was not long suffered to indulge my grief; I was soon put down under the decks, and there I received such a salutation in my nostrils as I had never experienced in my life: so that, with the loathsomeness of the stench, and crying together, I became so sick and low that I was not able to eat, nor had I the least desire to taste any thing. I now wished for the last friend, death, to relieve me; but soon, to my grief, two of the white men offered me eatables; and, on my refusing to eat, one of them held me fast by the hands, and laid me across, I think the windlass, and tied my feet, while the other flogged me severely. I had never experienced any thing of this kind

8. More commonly spelled "eddoes": edible roots   9. Artisans, manual workers.
found in the tropics.

before, and although not being used to the water, I naturally feared that element the first time I saw it, yet, nevertheless, could I have got over the nettings, I would have jumped over the side, but I could not; and besides, the crew used to watch us very closely who were not chained down to the decks, lest we should leap into the water; and I have seen some of these poor African prisoners most severely cut, for attempting to do so, and hourly whipped for not eating. This indeed was often the case with myself. In a little time after, amongst the poor chained men, I found some of my own nation, which in a small degree gave ease to my mind. I inquired of these what was to be done with us? They gave me to understand we were to be carried to these white people's country to work for them. I then was a little revived, and thought, if it were no worse than working, my situation was not so desperate; but still I feared I should be put to death, the white people looked and acted, as I thought, in so savage a manner; for I had never seen among any people such instances of brutal cruelty; and this not only shown towards us blacks, but also to some of the whites themselves. One white man in particular I saw, when we were permitted to be on deck, flogged so unmercifully with a large rope near the foremast, that he died in consequence of it; and they tossed him over the side as they would have done a brute. This made me fear these people the more; and I expected nothing less than to be treated in the same manner. I could not help expressing my fears and apprehensions to some of my countrymen; I asked them if these people had no country, but lived in this hollow place (the ship)? They told me they did not, but came from a distant one. "Then," said I, "how comes it in all our country we never heard of them?" They told me because they lived so very far off. I then asked where were their women? had they any like themselves? I was told they had. "And why," said I, "do we not see them?" They answered, because they were left behind. I asked how the vessel could go? they told me they could not tell; but that there was cloth put upon the masts by the help of the ropes I saw, and then the vessel went on; and the white men had some spell or magic they put in the water when they liked, in order to stop the vessel. I was exceedingly amazed at this account, and really thought they were spirits. I therefore wished much to be from amongst them, for I expected they would sacrifice me; but my wishes were vain—for we were so quartered that it was impossible for any of us to make our escape.

While we stayed on the coast I was mostly on deck; and one day, to my great astonishment, I saw one of these vessels coming in with the sails up. As soon as the whites saw it, they gave a great shout, at which we were amazed; and the more so, as the vessel appeared larger by approaching nearer. At last, she came to an anchor in my sight, and when the anchor was let go, I and my countrymen who saw it, were lost in astonishment to observe the vessel stop— and were now convinced it was done by magic. Soon after this the other ship got her boats out, and they came on board of us, and the people of both ships seemed very glad to see each other.—Several of the strangers also shook hands with us black people, and made motions with their hands, signifying I suppose, we were to go to their country, but we did not understand them.

At last, when the ship we were in had got in all her cargo, they made ready with many fearful noises, and we were all put under deck, so that we could not see how they managed the vessel. But this disappointment was the least of my sorrow. The stench of the hold while we were on the coast was so intolerably loathsome, that it was dangerous to remain there for any time, and some of us had been permitted to stay on the deck for the fresh air; but now that the whole ship's cargo were confined together, it became absolutely pestilential. The closeness of the place, and the heat of the climate, added to the number in the ship, which was so crowded that each had scarcely room to turn himself, almost suffocated us. This produced copious perspirations, so that the air soon became unfit for respiration, from a variety of loathsome smells, and brought on a sickness among the slaves, of which many died—thus falling victims to the improvident avarice, as I may call it, of their purchasers. This wretched situation was again aggravated by the galling of the chains, now become insupportable, and the filth of the necessary tubs, into which the children often fell, and were almost suffocated. The shrieks of the women, and the groans of the dying, rendered the whole a scene of horror almost inconceivable. Happily perhaps, for myself, I was soon reduced so low here that it was thought necessary to keep me almost always on deck; and from my extreme youth I was not put in fetters. In this situation I expected every hour to share the fate of my companions, some of whom were almost daily brought upon deck at the point of death, which I began to hope would soon put an end to my miseries. Often did I think many of the inhabitants of the deep much more happy than myself. I envied them the freedom they enjoyed, and as often wished I could change my condition for theirs. Every circumstance I met with, served only to render my state more painful, and heightened my apprehensions, and my opinion of the cruelty of the whites.

One day they had taken a number of fishes; and when they had killed and satisfied themselves with as many as they thought fit, to our astonishment who were on deck, rather than give any of them to us to eat, as we expected, they tossed the remaining fish into the sea again, although we begged and prayed for some as well as we could, but in vain; and some of my countrymen, being pressed by hunger, took an opportunity, when they thought no one saw them, of trying to get a little privately; but they were discovered, and the attempt procured them some very severe floggings. One day, when we had a smooth sea and moderate wind, two of my wearied countrymen who were chained together (I was near them at the time), preferring death to such a life of misery, somehow made through the nettings and jumped into the sea: immediately, another quite dejected fellow, who, on account of his illness, was suffered to be out of irons, also followed their example; and I believe many more would very soon have done the same, if they had not been prevented by the ship's crew, who were instantly alarmed. Those of us that were the most active, were in a moment put down under the deck, and there was such a noise and confusion amongst the people of the ship as I never heard before, to stop her, and get the boat out to go after the slaves. However, two of the wretches were drowned, but they got the other, and afterwards flogged him unmercifully, for thus attempting to prefer death to slavery. In this manner we continued to undergo more hardships than I can now relate, hardships which are inseparable from this accursed trade. Many a time we were near suffocation from the want of fresh air, which we were often without for whole days together. This, and the stench of the necessary tubs, carried off many.

During our passage, I first saw flying fishes, which surprised me very much; they used frequently to fly across the ship, and many of them fell on the deck. I also now first saw the use of the quadrant; I had often with astonishment seen the mariners make observations with it, and I could not think what it meant. They at last took notice of my surprise; and one of them, willing to increase it, as well as to gratify my curiosity, made me one day look through it. The clouds appeared to me to be land, which disappeared as they passed along. This heightened my wonder; and I was now more persuaded than ever, that I was in another world, and that every thing about me was magic. At last, we came in sight of the island of Barbadoes,[1] at which the whites on board gave a great shout, and made many signs of joy to us. We did not know what to think of this; but as the vessel drew nearer, we plainly saw the harbor, and other ships of different kinds and sizes, and we soon anchored amongst them, off Bridgetown. Many merchants and planters now came on board, though it was in the evening. They put us in separate parcels,[2] and examined us attentively. They also made us jump, and pointed to the land, signifying we were to go there. We thought by this, we should be eaten by these ugly men, as they appeared to us; and, when soon after we were all put down under the deck again, there was much dread and trembling among us, and nothing but bitter cries to be heard all the night from these apprehensions, insomuch, that at last the white people got some old slaves from the land to pacify us. They told us we were not to be eaten, but to work, and were soon to go on land, where we should see many of our country people. This report eased us much. And sure enough, soon after we were landed, there came to us Africans of all languages.

We were conducted immediately to the merchant's yard, where we were all pent up together, like so many sheep in a fold, without regard to sex or age. As every object was new to me, every thing I saw filled me with surprise. What struck me first, was, that the houses were built with bricks and stories,[3] and in every other respect different from those I had seen in Africa; but I was still more astonished on seeing people on horseback. I did not know what this could mean; and, indeed, I thought these people were full of nothing but magical arts. While I was in this astonishment, one of my fellow prisoners spoke to a countryman of his, about the horses, who said they were the same kind they had in their country. I understood them, though they were from a distant part of Africa; and I thought it odd I had not seen any horses there; but afterwards, when I came to converse with different Africans, I found they had many horses amongst them, and much larger than those I then saw.

We were not many days in the merchant's custody, before we were sold after their usual manner, which is this:—On a signal given (as the beat of a drum), the buyers rush at once into the yard where the slaves are confined, and make choice of that parcel they like best. The noise and clamor with which this is attended, and the eagerness visible in the countenances of the buyers, serve not a little to increase the apprehension of terrified Africans, who may well be supposed to consider them as the ministers of that destruction to which they think themselves devoted. In this manner, without scruple, are relations and friends separated, most of them never to see each other again. I remember, in the vessel in which I was brought over, in the men's apartment, there were several brothers, who, in the sale, were sold in different lots; and it was very moving on this occasion, to see and hear their cries at parting. O, ye nominal Christians![4] might not an African ask you—Learned you this from

---

1. In the West Indies.
2. Groups.

3. I.e., the buildings were two storied.
4. Christians in name only.

your God, who says unto you, Do unto all men as you would men should do unto you? Is it not enough that we are torn from our country and friends, to toil for your luxury and lust of gain? Must every tender feeling be likewise sacrificed to your avarice? Are the dearest friends and relations, now rendered more dear by their separation from their kindred, still to be parted from each other, and thus prevented from cheering the gloom of slavery, with the small comfort of being together, and mingling their sufferings and sorrows? Why are parents to lose their children, brothers their sisters, or husbands their wives? Surely, this is a new refinement in cruelty, which, while it has no advantage to atone for it, thus aggravates distress, and adds fresh horrors even to the wretchedness of slavery.

From *Chapter III*

I now totally lost the small remains of comfort I had enjoyed in conversing with my countrymen; the women too, who used to wash and take care of me were all gone different ways, and I never saw one of them afterwards.

I stayed in this island for a few days; I believe it could not be above a fortnight; when I, and some few more slaves, that were not salable amongst the rest, from very much fretting, were shipped off in a sloop for North America. On the passage we were better treated than when we were coming from Africa, and we had plenty of rice and fat pork. We were landed up a river a good way from the sea, about Virginia county, where we saw few or none of our native Africans, and not one soul who could talk to me. I was a few weeks weeding grass, and gathering stones in a plantation; and at last all my companions were distributed different ways, and only myself was left. I was now exceedingly miserable, and thought myself worse off than any of the rest of my companions; for they could talk to each other, but I had no person to speak to that I could understand. In this state, I was constantly grieving and pining,[5] and wishing for death rather than any thing else. While I was in this plantation, the gentleman, to whom I suppose the estate belonged, being unwell, I was one day sent for to his dwelling house to fan him; when I came into the room where he was I was very much affrighted at some things I saw, and the more so as I had seen a black woman slave as I came through the house, who was cooking the dinner, and the poor creature was cruelly loaded with various kinds of iron machines; she had one particularly on her head, which locked her mouth so fast that she could scarcely speak; and could not eat nor drink. I was much astonished and shocked at this contrivance, which I afterwards learned was called the iron muzzle. Soon after I had a fan put in my hand, to fan the gentleman while he slept; and so I did indeed with great fear. While he was fast asleep I indulged myself a great deal in looking about the room, which to me appeared very fine and curious. The first object that engaged my attention was a watch which hung on the chimney, and was going. I was quite surprised at the noise it made, and was afraid it would tell the gentleman any thing I might do amiss; and when I immediately after observed a picture hanging in the room, which appeared constantly to look at me, I was still more affrighted, having never seen such things as these before. At one time I thought it was something relative to magic; and not seeing it move, I thought it might

5. Suffering.

be some way the whites had to keep their great men when they died, and offer them libations as we used to do our friendly spirits. In this state of anxiety I remained till my master awoke, when I was dismissed out of the room, to my no small satisfaction and relief; for I thought that these people were all made up of wonders. In this place I was called Jacob; but on board the African Snow, I was called Michael. I had been some time in this miserable forlorn, and much dejected state, without having any one to talk to, which made my life a burden, when the kind and unknown hand of the Creator (who in very deed leads the blind in a way they know not) now began to appear, to my comfort; for one day the captain of a merchant ship, called the Industrious Bee, came on some business to my master's house. This gentleman, whose name was Michael Henry Pascal, was a lieutenant in the royal navy, but now commanded this trading ship, which was somewhere in the confines of the county many miles off. While he was at my master's house, it happened that he saw me, and liked me so well that he made a purchase of me. I think I have often heard him say he gave thirty or forty pounds sterling for me; but I do not remember which. However, he meant me for a present to some of his friends in England: and as I was sent accordingly from the house of my then master (one Mr. Campbell), to the place where the ship lay; I was conducted on horseback by an elderly black man (a mode of traveling which appeared very odd to me). When I arrived I was carried on board a fine large ship, loaded with tobacco, etc., and just ready to sail for England. I now thought my condition much mended; I had sails to lie on, and plenty of good victuals to eat; and everybody on board used me very kindly, quite contrary to what I had seen of any white people before; I therefore began to think that they were not all of the same disposition. A few days after I was on board we sailed for England. I was still at a loss to conjecture my destiny. By this time, however, I could smatter a little imperfect English; and I wanted to know as well as I could where we were going. Some of the people of the ship used to tell me they were going to carry me back to my own country, and this made me very happy. I was quite rejoiced at the idea of going back; and thought if I could get home what wonders I should have to tell. But I was reserved for another fate, and was soon undeceived when we came within sight of the English coast. While I was on board this ship, my captain and master named me *Gustavus Vassa*. I at that time began to understand him a little, and refused to be called so, and told him as well as I could that I would be called Jacob; but he said I should not, and still called me Gustavus: and when I refused to answer to my new name, which I at first did, it gained me many a cuff; so at length I submitted, and by which I have been known ever since. The ship had a very long passage; and on that account we had very short allowance of provisions. Towards the last, we had only one pound and a half of bread per week, and about the same quantity of meat, and one quart of water a day. We spoke with only one vessel the whole time we were at sea, and but once we caught a few fishes. In our extremities the captain and people told me in jest they would kill and eat me; but I thought them in earnest, and was depressed beyond measure, expecting every moment to be my last. While I was in this situation, one evening they caught, with a good deal of trouble, a large shark, and got it on board. This gladdened my poor heart exceedingly, as I thought it would serve the people to eat instead of their eating me; but very soon, to my astonishment, they cut off a small part of the tail, and tossed the rest over the side. This renewed my consternation; and I did not know what to think of these white people, though I very much feared they would kill and eat me. There was on board the ship a young lad who had never been at sea before, about four or five years older than myself: his name was Richard Baker. He was a native of America, had received an excellent education, and was of a most amiable temper. Soon after I went on board, he showed me a great deal of partiality and attention, and in return I grew extremely fond of him. We at length became inseparable; and, for the space of two years, he was of very great use to me, and was my constant companion and instructor. Although this dear youth had many slaves of his own, yet he and I have gone through many sufferings together on shipboard; and we have many nights lain in each other's bosoms when we were in great distress. Thus such a friendship was cemented between us as we cherished till his death, which, to my very great sorrow, happened in the year 1759, when he was up the Archipelago, and on board his Majesty's ship the Preston: an event which I have never ceased to regret, as I lost at once a kind interpreter, an agreeable companion, and a faithful friend; who, at the age of fifteen, discovered a mind superior to prejudice; and who was not ashamed to notice, to associate with, and to be the friend and instructor of one who was ignorant, a stranger, of a different complexion, and a slave!

* * *

From *Chapter IV*

It was now between two and three years since I first came to England, a great part of which I had spent at sea; so that I became inured[6] to that service, and began to consider myself as happily situated, for my master treated me always extremely well; and my attachment and gratitude to him were very great. From the various scenes I had beheld on shipboard, I soon grew a stranger to terror of every kind, and was, in that respect at least, almost an Englishman. I have often reflected with surprise that I never felt half the alarm at any of the numerous dangers I have been in, that I was filled with at the first sight of the Europeans, and at every act of theirs, even the most trifling, when I first came among them, and for some time afterwards. That fear, however, which was the effect of my ignorance, wore away as I began to know them. I could now speak English tolerably well, and I perfectly understood every thing that was said. I not only felt myself quite easy with these new countrymen, but relished their society and manners. I no longer looked upon them as spirits, but as men superior to us; and therefore I had the stronger desire to resemble them, to imbibe their spirit, and imitate their manners. I therefore embraced every occasion of improvement, and every new thing that I observed I treasured up in my memory. I had long wished to be able to read and write; and for this purpose I took every opportunity to gain instruction, but had made as yet very little progress. However, when I went to London with my master, I had soon an opportunity of improving myself, which I gladly embraced. Shortly after my arrival, he sent me to wait upon the Miss Guerins, who had treated me with much kindness when I was there before; and they sent me to school.

While I was attending these ladies, their servants told me I could not go to

6. Accustomed.

Heaven unless I was baptized. This made me very uneasy, for I had now some faint idea of a future state. Accordingly I communicated my anxiety to the eldest Miss Guerin, with whom I was become a favorite, and pressed her to have me baptized; when to my great joy, she told me I should. She had formerly asked my master to let me be baptized, but he had refused. However she now insisted on it; and he being under some obligation to her brother, complied with her request. So I was baptized in St. Margaret's church, Westminster, in February, 1759, by my present name. The clergyman at the same time, gave me a book, called a Guide to the Indians, written by the Bishop of Sodor and Man.[7] On this occasion, Miss Guerin did me the honor to stand as god-mother, and afterwards gave me a treat. I used to attend these ladies about the town, in which service I was extremely happy; as I had thus many opportunities of seeing London, which I desired of all things. I was sometimes, however, with my master at his rendezvous house,[8] which was at the foot of Westminster bridge. Here I used to enjoy myself in playing about the bridge stairs, and often in the waterman's wherries,[9] with other boys. On one of these occasions there was another boy with me in a wherry, and we went out into the current of the river; while we were there, two more stout boys came to us in another wherry, and abusing us for taking the boat, desired me to get into the other wherry boat. Accordingly, I went to get out of the wherry I was in, but just as I had got one of my feet into the other boat, the boys shoved it off, so that I fell into the Thames; and, not being able to swim, I should unavoidably have been drowned, but for the assistance of some watermen who providentially came to my relief.

The Namur being again got ready for sea, my master, with his gang,[1] was ordered on board; and, to my no small grief, I was obliged to leave my schoolmaster, whom I liked very much, and always attended while I stayed in London, to repair on board with my master. Nor did I leave my kind patronesses, the Miss Guerins, without uneasiness and regret. They often used to teach me to read, and took great pains to instruct me in the principles of religion and the knowledge of God. I therefore parted from those amiable ladies with reluctance, after receiving from them many friendly cautions how to conduct myself, and some valuable presents.

When I came to Spithead,[2] I found we were destined for the Mediterranean, with a large fleet, which was now ready to put to sea. We only waited for the arrival of the Admiral, who soon came on board. And about the beginning of the spring of 1759, having weighed anchor, and got under way, sailed for the Mediterranean; and in eleven days, from the Land's End, we got to Gibralter. While we were here I used to be often on shore, and got various fruits in great plenty, and very cheap.

I had frequently told several people, in my excursions on shore, the story of my being kidnapped with my sister, and of our being separated, as I have related before; and I had as often expressed my anxiety for her fate, and my sorrow at having never met her again. One day, when I was on shore, and mentioning these circumstances to some persons, one of them told me he knew where my sister was, and if I would accompany him, he would bring me to her. Improbable as this story was, I believed it immediately, and agreed to

7. Present-day Hebrides and the Isle of Man.
8. Private residence.
9. Small rowboats.

1. I.e., crew.
2. On the southern coast of England; a common rendezvous for the British fleet.

go with him, while my heart leaped for joy; and, indeed, he conducted me to a black young woman, who was so like my sister, that at first sight, I really thought it was her; but I was quickly undeceived. And, on talking to her, I found her to be of another nation.

While we lay here, the Preston came in from the Levant.[3] As soon as she arrived, my master told me I should now see my old companion, Dick, who was gone in her when she sailed for Turkey. I was much rejoiced at this news, and expected every minute to embrace him; and when the captain came on board of our ship, which he did immediately after, I ran to inquire after my friend; but, with inexpressible sorrow, I learned from the boat's crew that the dear youth was dead! and that they had brought his chest, and all his other things, to my master. These he afterwards gave to me, and I regarded them as a memorial of my friend, whom I loved, and grieved for, as a brother.

* * *

After our ship was fitted out again for service, in September she went to Guernsey,[4] where I was very glad to see my old hostess, who was now a widow, and my former little charming companion, her daughter. I spent some time here very happily with them, till October, when we had orders to repair to Portsmouth. We parted from each other with a great deal of affection; and I promised to return soon, and see them again, not knowing what all powerful fate had determined for me. Our ship having arrived at Portsmouth, we went into the harbor, and remained there till the latter end of November, when we heard great talk about a peace;[5] and, to our very great joy, in the beginning of December we had orders to go up to London with our ship, to be paid off. We received this news with loud huzzas, and every other demonstration of gladness; and nothing but mirth was to be seen throughout every part of the ship. I, too, was not without my share of the general joy on this occasion. I thought now of nothing but being freed, and working for myself, and thereby getting money to enable me to get a good education; for I always had a great desire to be able at least to read and write; and while I was on ship-board, I had endeavored to improve myself in both. While I was in the Etna,[6] particularly, the captain's clerk taught me to write, and gave me a smattering of arithmetic, as far as the Rule of Three.[7] There was also one Daniel Queen, about forty years of age, a man very well educated, who messed[8] with me on board this ship, and he likewise dressed and attended the captain. Fortunately this man soon became very much attached to me, and took very great pains to instruct me in many things. He taught me to shave and dress hair a little, and also to read in the Bible, explaining many passages to me, which I did not comprehend. I was wonderfully surprised to see the laws and rules of my own country written almost exactly here; a circumstance which I believe tended to impress our manners and customs more deeply on my memory. I used to tell him of this resemblance, and many a time we have sat up the whole night together at this employment. In short, he was like a father to me, and some even used to call me after his name; they also styled me the black Christian. Indeed, I almost loved him with the affection of a son. Many things I have denied myself that

3. The eastern shore of the Mediterranean.
4. One of the Channel Islands in the English Channel.
5. The Seven Years' War between England and France began in 1756.

6. The name of a ship.
7. A method of finding a fourth (unknown) number from three given numbers.
8. Took meals.

he might have them; and when I used to play at marbles, or any other game, and won a few half-pence, or got any little money, which I sometimes did, for shaving any one, I used to buy him a little sugar or tobacco, as far as my stock of money would go. He used to say, that he and I never should part; and that when our ship was paid off, as I was as free as himself, or any other man on board, he would instruct me in his business, by which I might gain a good livelihood. This gave me new life and spirits; and my heart burned within me, while I thought the time long till I obtained my freedom. For though my master had not promised it to me, yet, besides the assurances I had received, that he had no right to detain me, he always treated me with the greatest kindness, and reposed in me an unbounded confidence; he even paid attention to my morals, and would never suffer me to deceive him, or tell lies, of which he used to tell me the consequences; and that if I did so, God would not love me. So that, from all this tenderness, I had never once supposed, in all my dreams of freedom, that he would think of detaining me any longer than I wished.

In pursuance of our orders, we sailed from Portsmouth for the Thames, and arrived at Deptford the 10th of December, where we cast anchor just as it was high water. The ship was up about half an hour, when my master ordered the barge to be manned; and all in an instant, without having before given me the least reason to suspect any thing of the matter, he forced me into the barge, saying, I was going to leave him, but he would take care I should not. I was so struck with the unexpectedness of this proceeding, that for some time I did not make a reply, only I made an offer to go for my books and chest of clothes, but he swore I should not move out of his sight, and if I did, he would cut my throat, at the same time taking his hanger.[9] I began, however, to collect myself, and plucking up courage, I told him I was free, and he could not by law serve me so. But this only enraged him the more: and he continued to swear, and said he would soon let me know whether he would or not, and at that instant sprung himself into the barge from the ship, to the astonishment and sorrow of all on board. The tide, rather unluckily for me, had just turned downward, so that we quickly fell down the river along with it, till we came among some outward-bound West Indiamen; for he was resolved to put me on board the first vessel he could get to receive me. The boat's crew, who pulled against their will, became quite faint, different times, and would have gone ashore, but he would not let them. Some of them strove then to cheer me, and told me he could not sell me, and that they would stand by me, which revived me a little, and I still entertained hopes; for, as they pulled along, he asked some vessels to receive me, but they would not. But, just as we had got a little below Gravesend, we came along side of a ship which was going away the next tide for the West Indies. Her name was the Charming Sally. Captain James Doran, and my master went on board, and agreed with him for me; and in a little time I was sent for into the cabin. When I came there, Captain Doran asked me if I knew him. I answered that I did not. "Then," said he, "you are now my slave." I told him my master could not sell me to him, nor to any one else. "Why," said he, "did not your master buy you?" I confessed he did. "But I have served him," said I, "many years, and he has taken all my wages and prize money, for I had only got one sixpence

9. Small sword.

during the war; besides this I have been baptized, and by the laws of the land no man has a right to sell me." And I added that I had heard a lawyer and others at different times tell my master so. They both then said that those people who told me so were not my friends; but I replied, "It was very extraordinary that other people did not know the law as well as they." Upon this, Captain Doran said I talked too much English; and if I did not behave myself well, and be quiet, he had a method on board to make me. I was too well convinced of his power over me to doubt what he said; and my former sufferings in the slave ship presenting themselves to my mind, the recollection of them made me shudder. However, before I retired I told them that, as I could not get any right among men here, I hoped I should hereafter in Heaven; and I immediately left the cabin, filled with resentment and sorrow. The only coat I had with me my master took away him with him, and said, "If your prize money had been £10,000, I had a right to it all, and would have taken it." I had about nine guineas, which, during my long seafaring life, I had scraped together from trifling perquisites and little ventures; and I hid it at that instant, lest my master should take that from me likewise, still hoping that by some means or other I should make my escape to the shore; and indeed some of my old shipmates told me not to despair, for they would get me back again; and that, as soon as they could get their pay, they would immediately come to Portsmouth to me, where the ship was going. But, alas! all my hopes were baffled, and the hour of my deliverance as was yet far off. My master, having soon concluded his bargain with the captain, came out of the cabin, and he and his people got into the boat and put off. I followed them with aching eyes as long as I could, and when they were out of sight I threw myself on the deck, with a heart ready to burst with sorrow and anguish.

From *Chapter* V

*   *   *

About the middle of May, when the ship was got ready to sail for England, I all the time believing that fate's blackest clouds were gathering over my head, and expecting their bursting would mix me with the dead, Captain Doran sent for me ashore one morning, and I was told by the messenger that my fate was then determined. With trembling steps and fluttering heart, I came to the captain, and found with him one Mr. Robert King, a Quaker, and the first merchant in the place. The captain then told me my former master had sent me there to be sold; but that he had desired him to get me the best master he could, as he told him I was a very deserving boy, which Captain Doran said he found to be true; and if he were to stay in the West Indies, he would be glad to keep me himself; but he could not venture to take me to London, for he was very sure that when I came there I would leave him. I at that instant burst out a crying, and begged much of him to take me to England with him, but all to no purpose. He told me he had got me the very best master in the whole island, with whom I should be as happy as if I were in England, and for that reason he chose to let him have me, though he could sell me to his own brother-in-law for a great deal more money than what he got from this gentleman. Mr. King, my new master, then made a reply, and said the reason he had bought me was on account of my good character; and as he had not the least doubt of my good behavior, I should be very well off with him. He also told me he did not live in the West Indies, but at Philadelphia, where he was going soon; and, as I understood something of the rules of arithmetic, when we got there he would put me to school, and fit me for a clerk. This conversation relieved my mind a little, and I left those gentlemen considerably more at ease in myself than when I came to them; and I was very thankful to Captain Doran, and even to my old master, for the character they had given me. A character which I afterwards found of infinite service to me. I went on board again, and took leave of all my shipmates, and the next day the ship sailed. When she weighed anchor, I went to the waterside and looked at her with a very wishful and aching heart, and followed her with my eyes until she was totally out of sight. I was so bowed down with grief, that I could not hold up my head for many months; and if my new master had not been kind to me, I believe I should have died under it at last. And, indeed, I soon found that he fully deserved the good character which Captain Doran gave me of him; for he possessed a most amiable disposition and temper, and was very charitable and humane. If any of his slaves behaved amiss he did not beat or use them ill, but parted with them. This made them afraid of disobliging him; and as he treated his slaves better than any other man on the island, so he was better and more faithfully served by them in return. By this kind treatment I did at last endeavor to compose myself; and with fortitude, though moneyless, determined to face whatever fate had decreed for me. Mr. King soon asked me what I could do; and at the same time said he did not mean to treat me as a common slave. I told him I knew something of seamanship, and could shave and dress hair pretty well; and I could refine wines, which I had learned on shipboard, where I had often done it; and that I could write, and understood arithmetic tolerably well, as far as the Rule of Three. He then asked me if I knew any thing of guaging; and, on my answering that I did not, he said one of his clerks should teach me to guage.[1]

Mr. King dealt in all manner of merchandize, and kept from one to six clerks. He loaded many vessels in a year; particularly to Philadelphia, where he was born; and was connected with a great mercantile house in that city. He had, besides, many vessels and droggers,[2] of different sizes, which used to go about the island; and others, to collect rum, sugar, and other goods. I understood pulling and managing those boats very well. And this hard work, which was the first that he set me to, in the sugar seasons used to be my constant employment. I have rowed the boat, and slaved at the oars, from one hour to sixteen in the twenty-four; during which I had fifteen pence sterling per day to live on, though sometimes only ten pence. However, this was considerably more than was allowed to other slaves that used to work often with me, and belonged to other gentlemen on the island. Those poor souls had never more than nine-pence per day, and seldom more than six-pence, from their masters or owners, though they earned them three or four pistareens.[3] For it is a common practice in the West Indies for men to purchase slaves, though they have not plantations themselves, in order to let them out to planters and merchants at so much a piece by the day, and they give what allowance they choose out of this product of their daily work to their slaves, for subsistence; this allowance is often very scanty. My master often gave the owners of the slaves two and a half of these pieces per day, and found the poor fellows in victuals himself,

1. To measure the depth of a vessel when fully loaded.
2. Slow West Indian coasting vessels.
3. "These pistareens are of a value of a shilling" [Equiano's note].

because he thought their owners did not feed them well enough according to the work they did.

*   *   *

Once, for a few days, I was let out to fit a vessel, and I had no victuals allowed me by either party; at last I told my master of this treatment, and he took me away from it. In many of the estates, on the different islands where I used to be sent for rum or sugar, they would not deliver it to me, or any other negro; he was therefore obliged to send a white man along with me to those places; and then he used to pay him from six to ten pistareens a day. From being thus employed, during the time I served Mr. King, in going about the different estates on the island,[4] I had all the opportunity I could wish for, to see the dreadful usage of the poor men; usage that reconciled me to my situation, and made me bless God for the hands into which I had fallen.

I had the good fortune to please my master in every department in which he employed me; and there was scarcely any part of his business, or household affairs, in which I was not occasionally engaged. I often supplied the place of a clerk, in receiving and delivering cargoes to the ships, in tending stores, and delivering goods. And besides this, I used to shave and dress my master when convenient, and take care of his horse; and when it was necessary, which was very often, I worked likewise on board of different vessels of his. By these means I became very useful to my master, and saved him, as he used to acknowledge, above a hundred pounds a year. Nor did he scruple to say I was of more advantage to him than any of his clerks; though their usual wages in the West Indies are from sixty to a hundred pounds current a year.

I have sometimes heard it asserted that a Negro cannot earn his master the first cost; but nothing can be further from the truth. I suppose ninetenths of the mechanics throughout the West Indies are Negro slaves; and I well know the coopers[5] among them earn two dollars a day, the carpenters the same, and often times more; as also the masons, smiths, and fisherman, etc. And I have known many slaves whose masters would not take a thousand pounds current for them. But surely this assertion refutes itself; for, if it be true, why do the planters and merchants pay such a price for slaves? And, above all, why do those who make this assertion exclaim the most loudly against the abolition of the slave trade? So much are men blinded, and to such inconsistent arguments are they driven by mistaken interest! I grant, indeed, that slaves are sometimes, by half-feeding, half-clothing, over-working and stripes,[6] reduced so low, that they are turned out as unfit for service, and left to perish in the woods, or expire on the dunghill.

My master was several times offered, by different gentlemen, one hundred guineas for me, but he always told them he would not sell me, to my great joy. And I used to double my diligence and care, for fear of getting into the hands of those men who did not allow a valuable slave the common support of life. Many of them even used to find fault with my master for feeding his slaves so well as he did; although I often went hungry, and an Englishman might think my fare very indifferent;[7] but he used to tell them he always would do it, because the slaves thereby looked better and did more work.

---

4. Equiano remained in the West Indies from 1763   6. Lashes.
to 1766.   7. Poor, unsatisfactory.
5. Barrel makers.

While I was thus employed by my master, I was often a witness to cruelties of every kind, which were exercised on my unhappy fellow slaves. I used frequently to have different cargoes of new Negroes in my care for sale; and it was almost a constant practice with our clerks, and other whites, to commit violent depredations on the chastity of the female slaves; and these I was, though with reluctance, obliged to submit to at all times, being unable to help them. When we have had some of these slaves on board my master's vessels, to carry them to other islands, or to America, I have known our mates to commit these acts most shamefully, to the disgrace, not of Christians only, but of men. I have even known them to gratify their brutal passion with females not ten years old; and these abominations, some of them practiced to such scandalous excess, that one of our captains discharged the mate and others on that account. And yet in Montserrat[8] I have seen a Negro man staked to the ground, and cut most shockingly, and then his ears cut off bit by bit, because he had been connected with a white woman, who was a common prostitute. As if it were no crime in the whites to rob an innocent African girl of her virtue; but most heinous in a black man only to gratify a passion of nature, where the temptation was offered by one of a different color, though the most abandoned woman of her species.

Another Negro man was half hanged, and then burnt, for attempting to poison a cruel overseer. Thus, by repeated cruelties, are the wretched first urged to despair, and then murdered, because they still retain so much of human nature about them as to wish to put an end to their misery, and retaliate on their tyrants! These overseers are indeed for the most part persons of the worst character of any denomination of men in the West Indies. Unfortunately, many humane gentlemen, but not residing on their estates, are obliged to leave the management of them in the hands of these human butchers, who cut and mangle the slaves in a shocking manner on the most trifling occasions, and altogether treat them in every respect like brutes. They pay no regard to the situation of pregnant women, nor the least attention to the lodging of the field Negroes. Their huts, which ought to be well covered, and the place dry where they take their little repose, are often open sheds, built in damp places; so that when the poor creatures return tired from the toils of the field, they contract many disorders, from being exposed to the damp air in this uncomfortable state, while they are heated, and their pores are open. This neglect certainly conspires with many others to cause a decrease in the births as well as in the lives of the grown Negroes. I can quote many instances of gentlemen who reside on their estates in the West Indies, and then the scene is quite changed; the Negroes are treated with lenity and proper care, by which their lives are prolonged, and their masters profited. To the honor of humanity, I knew several gentlemen who managed their estates in this manner, and they found that benevolence was their true interest. And, among many I could mention in several of the islands, I knew one in Montserrat whose slaves looked remarkably well, and never needed any fresh supplies of Negroes; and there are many other estates, especially in Barbadoes, which, from such judicious treatment, need no fresh stock of Negroes at any time. I have the honor of knowing a most worthy and humane gentleman, who is a native of Barbadoes, and his estates there.[9] This gentleman has written a treatise on the

8. An island in the West Indies seven miles from Antigua.

9. Two of Equiano's notes identifying these men are omitted.

usage of his own slaves. He allows them two hours of refreshment at midday, and many other indulgencies and comforts, particularly in their lodging; and, besides this, he raises more provisions on his estate than they can destroy; so that by these attentions he saves the lives of his Negroes, and keeps them healthy, and as happy as the condition of slavery can admit. I myself, as shall appear in the sequel,[1] managed an estate, where, by those attentions, the Negroes were uncommonly cheerful and healthy, and did more work by half than by the common mode of treatment they usually do. For want,[2] therefore, of such care and attention to the poor Negroes, and otherwise oppressed as they are, it is no wonder that the decrease should require 20,000 new Negroes annually, to fill up the vacant places of the dead.

＊　＊　＊

From *Chapter VI*

In the preceding chapter I have set before the reader a few of those many instances of oppression, extortion, and cruelty, which I have been a witness to in the West Indies; but were I to enumerate them all, the catalog would be tedious and disgusting. The punishments of the slaves on every trifling occasion are so frequent, and so well known, together with the different instruments with which they are tortured, that it cannot any longer afford novelty to recite them; and they are too shocking to yield delight either to the writer or the reader. I shall therefore hereafter only mention such as incidentally befell myself in the course of my adventures.

＊　＊　＊

Some time in the year 1763, kind Providence seemed to appear rather more favorable to me. One of my master's vessels, a Bermudas sloop, about sixty tons burthen, was commanded by one captain Thomas Farmer, an Englishman, a very alert and active man, who gained my master a great deal of money by his good management in carrying passengers from one island to another; but very often his sailors used to get drunk and run away from the vessel, which hindered him in his business very much. This man had taken a liking to me, and many times begged of my master to let me go a trip with him as a sailor; but he would tell him he could not spare me, though the vessel sometimes could not go for want of hands, for sailors were generally very scarce in the island. However, at last, from necessity or force, my master was prevailed on, though very reluctantly, to let me go with this captain; but he gave him great charge to take care that I did not run away, for if I did he would make him pay for me. This being the case, the captain had for some time a sharp eye upon me whenever the vessel anchored; and as soon as she returned I was sent for on shore again. Thus was I slaving, as it were, for life, sometimes at one thing, and sometimes at another. So that the captain and I were nearly the most useful men in my master's employment. I also became so useful to the captain on ship-board, that many times, when he used to ask for me to go with him, though it should be but for twenty-four hours, to some of the islands near us, my master would answer he could not spare me, at which the captain would swear, and would not go the trip, and tell my master I was better to him on board than any three white men he had; for they used to behave ill in many

1. I.e., later.　　　　　　　　2. Lack.

respects, particularly in getting drunk; and then they frequently got the boat stove,[3] so as to hinder the vessel from coming back as soon as she might have done. This my master knew very well; and at last, by the captain's constant entreaties, after I had been several times with him, one day to my great joy, told me the captain would not let him rest, and asked whether I would go aboard as a sailor, or stay on shore and mind the stores, for he could not bear any longer to be plagued in this manner. I was very happy at this proposal, for I immediately thought I might in time stand some chance by being on board to get a little money, or possibly make my escape if I should be used ill. I also expected to get better food, and in greater abundance; for I had oftentimes felt much hunger, though my master treated his slaves, as I have observed, uncommonly well. I therefore, without hesitation, answered him, that I would go and be a sailor if he pleased. Accordingly I was ordered on board directly. Nevertheless, between the vessel and the shore, when she was in port, I had little or no rest, as my master always wished to have me along with him. Indeed he was a very pleasant gentleman, and but for my expectations on shipboard, I should not have thought of leaving him. But the captain liked me also very much, and I was entirely his right hand man. I did all I could to deserve his favor, and in return I received better treatment from him than any other, I believe, ever met with in the West Indies, in my situation.

After I had been sailing for some time with this captain, at length I endeavored to try my luck, and commence merchant. I had but a very small capital to begin with; for one single half bit,[4] which is equal to three pence in England, made up my whole stock. However, I trusted to the Lord to be with me; and at one of our trips to St. Eustatia,[5] a Dutch island, I bought a glass tumbler with my half bit, and when I came to Montserrat, I sold it for a bit, or six pence. Luckily we made several successive trips to St. Eustatia (which was a general mart for the West Indies, about twenty leagues from Montserrat), and in our next, finding my tumbler so profitable, with this one bit I bought two tumblers more; and when I came back, I sold them for two bits, equal to a shilling sterling. When we went again, I bought with these two bits four more of these glasses, which I sold for four bits on our return to Montserrat. And in our next voyage to St. Eustatia, I bought two glasses with one bit, and with the other three I bought a jug of Geneva,[6] nearly about three pints in measure. When we came to Montserrat, I sold the gin for eight bits, and the tumblers for two, so that my capital now amounted in all to a dollar, well husbanded[7] and acquired in the space of a month or six weeks, when I blessed the Lord that I was so rich. As we sailed to different islands, I laid this money out in various things occasionally, and it used to turn out to very good account, especially when we went to Guadaloupe, Grenada, and the rest of the French islands. Thus was I going all about the islands upwards of four years, and ever trading as I went, during which I experienced many instances of ill usage, and have seen many injuries done to other Negroes in our dealings with whites. And, amidst our recreations, when we have been dancing and merry-making, they, without cause, have molested and insulted us. Indeed, I was more than once obliged to look up to God on high, as I had advised the poor fisherman

---

3. Put a hole in it.
4. In the West Indies a small silver coin a fraction of the Spanish dollar.
5. St. Eustatius is one of the Leeward Islands in the West Indies.
6. A liquor distilled from grain and flavored with juniper berries.
7. Managed.

some time before. And I had not been long trading for myself in the manner I have related above, when I experienced the like trial in company with him as follows:—This man, being used to the water, was upon an emergency put on board of us by his master, to work as another hand, on a voyage to Santa Cruz; and at our sailing he had brought his little all for a venture, which consisted of six bits' worth of limes and oranges in a bag; I had also my whole stock, which was about twelve bits' worth of the same kind of goods, separate in two bags, for we had heard these fruits sold well in that island. When we came there, in some little convenient time, he and I went ashore to sell them; but we had scarcely landed, when we were met by two white men, who presently took our three bags from us. We could not at first guess what they meant to do, and for some time we thought they were jesting with us; but they too soon let us know otherwise, for they took our ventures immediately to a house hard by, and adjoining the fort, while we followed all the way begging of them to give us our fruits, but in vain. They not only refused to return them, but swore at us, and threatened if we did not immediately depart they would flog us well. We told them these three bags were all we were worth in the world, and that we brought them with us to sell when we came from Montserrat, and showed them the vessel. But this was rather against us, as they now saw we were strangers, as well as slaves. They still therefore swore, and desired us to be gone, and even took sticks to beat us; while we, seeing they meant what they said, went off in the greatest confusion and despair. Thus, in the very minute of gaining more by three times than I ever did by any venture in my life before, was I deprived of every farthing I was worth. An unsupportable misfortune! but how to help ourselves we knew not. In our consternation we went to the commanding officer of the fort, and told him how we had been served by his people, but we obtained not the least redress. He answered our complaints only by a volley of imprecations against us, and immediately took a horse-whip, in order to chastise us, so that we were obliged to turn out much faster than we came in. I now, in the agony of distress and indignation, wished that the ire of God in his forked lightning might transfix these cruel oppressors among the dead. Still, however, we persevered; went back again to the house, and begged and besought them again and again for our fruits, till at last some other people that were in the house asked if we would be contented if they kept one bag and gave us the other two. We, seeing no remedy whatever, consented to this; and they, observing one bag to have both kinds of fruit in it, which belonged to my companion, kept that; and the other two, which were mine, they gave us back. As soon as I got them, I ran as fast as I could, and got the first Negro man I could to help me off. My companion, however, stayed a little longer to plead; he told them the bag they had was his, and likewise all that he was worth in the world; but this was of no avail, and he was obliged to return without it. The poor old man wringing his hands, cried bitterly for his loss; and, indeed, he then did look up to God on high, which so moved me in pity for him, that I gave him nearly one-third of my fruits. We then proceeded to the markets to sell them; and Providence was more favorable to us than we could have expected, for we sold our fruits uncommonly well; I got for mine about thirty-seven bits. Such a surprising reverse of fortune in so short a space of time seemed like a dream, and proved no small encouragement for me to trust the Lord in any situation. My captain afterwards frequently used to take my part, and get me my right, when I have been plundered or used ill by these tender Christian depredators; among whom I have shuddered to observe the unceasing blasphemous execrations which are wantonly thrown out by persons of all ages and conditions, not only without occasion, but even as if they were indulgencies and pleasure.

＊   ＊   ＊

The reader cannot but judge of the irksomeness of this situation to a mind like mine, in being daily exposed to new hardships and impositions, after having seen many better days, and been, as it were, in a state of freedom and plenty; added to which, every part of the world I had hitherto been in, seemed to me a paradise in comparison to the West Indies. My mind was therefore hourly replete with inventions and thoughts of being freed, and, if possible, by honest and honorable means; for I always remembered the old adage, and I trust it has ever been my ruling principle, that "honesty is the best policy;" and likewise that other golden precept—"To do unto all men as I would they should do unto me." However, as I was from early years a predestinarian, I thought whatever fate had determined must ever come to pass; and, therefore, if ever it were my lot to be freed, nothing could prevent me, although I should at present see no means or hope to obtain my freedom; on the other hand, if it were my fate not to be freed, I never should be so, and all my endeavors for that purpose would be fruitless. In the midst of these thoughts, I therefore looked up with prayers anxiously to God for my liberty; and at the same time used every honest means, and did all that was possible on my part to obtain it. In process of time, I became master of a few pounds, and in a fair way of making more, which my friendly captain knew very well; this occasioned him sometimes to take liberties with me; but whenever he treated me waspishly, I used plainly to tell him my mind, and that I would die before I would be imposed upon as other Negroes were, and that to my life had lost its relish when liberty was gone. This I said, although I foresaw my then well-being or future hopes of freedom (humanly speaking) depended on this man. However, as he could not bear the thoughts of my not sailing with him, he always became mild on my threats. I therefore continued with him; and, from my great attention to his orders and his business, I gained him credit, and through his kindness to me, I at last procured my liberty. While I thus went on, filled with the thoughts of freedom, and resisting oppression as well as I was able, my life hung daily in suspense, particularly in the surfs I have formerly mentioned, as I could not swim. These are extremely violent throughout the West Indies, and I was ever exposed to their howling rage and devouring fury in all the islands. I have seen them strike and toss a boat right up on end, and maim several on board. Once in the Grenada islands, when I and about eight others were pulling a large boat with two puncheons[8] of water in it, a surf struck us, and drove the boat, and all in it, about half a stone's throw, among some trees, and above the high water mark. We were obliged to get all the assistance we could from the nearest estate to mend the boat, and launch it into the water again. At Montserrat, one night, in pressing hard to get off the shore on board, the punt[9] was overset with us four times, the first time I was very near being drowned; however, the jacket I had on kept me up above water a little space of time, when I called on a man near me, who was a good swimmer, and told

8. Large casks.   9. Narrow flat-bottomed boat.

him I could not swim; he then made haste to me, and, just as I was sinking, he caught hold of me, and brought me to sounding,[1] and then he went and brought the punt also. As soon as we had turned the water out of her, lest we should be used ill for being absent, we attempted again three times more, and as often the horrid surfs served us as at first; but at last, the fifth time we attempted, we gained our point, at the imminent hazard of our lives. One day also, at Old Road, in Montserrat, our captain, and three men besides myself, were going in a large canoe in quest of rum and sugar, when a single surf tossed the canoe an amazing distance from the water, and some of us, near a stone's throw from each other. Most of us were very much bruised; so that I and many more often said, and really thought, that there was not such another place under the heavens as this. I longed, therefore, much to leave it, and daily wished to see my master's promise performed, of going to Philadelphia.

While we lay in this place, a very cruel thing happened on board our sloop, which filled me with horror; though I found afterwards such practices were frequent. There was a very clever and decent free young mulatto man, who sailed a long time with us; he had a free woman for his wife, by whom he had a child, and she was then living on shore, and all very happy. Our captain and mate, and other people on board, and several elsewhere, even the natives of Bermudas, all knew this young man from a child that he was always free, and no one had ever claimed him as their property. However, as might too often overcomes right in these parts, it happened that a Bermudas captain, whose vessel lay there for a few days in the road, came on board of us, and seeing the mulatto man, whose name was Joseph Clipson, he told him he was not free, and that he had orders from his master to bring him to Bermudas. The poor man could not believe the captain to be in earnest, but he was very soon undeceived, his men laying violent hands on him; and although he showed a certificate of his being born free in St. Kitts, and most people on board knew that he served his time to[2] boat building, and always passed for a free man, yet he was forcibly taken out of our vessel. He then asked to be carried ashore before the Secretary or Magistrates, and these infernal invaders of human rights promised him he should; but instead of that, they carried him on board of the other vessel. And the next day, without giving the poor man any hearing on shore, or suffering him even to see his wife or child, he was carried away, and probably doomed never more in this world to see them again. Nor was this the only instance of this kind of barbarity I was a witness to. I have since often seen in Jamaica and other islands, free men, whom I have known in America, thus villainously trepanned[3] and held in bondage. I have heard of two similar practices even in Philadelphia. And were it not for the benevolence of the Quakers in that city, many of the sable[4] race, who now breathe the air of liberty, would, I believe, be groaning indeed under some planter's chains. These things opened my mind to a new scene of horror, to which I had been before a stranger. Hitherto I had thought slavery only dreadful, but the state of a free negro appeared to me now equally so at least, and in some respects even worse, for they live in constant alarm for their liberty; which is but nominal, for they are universally insulted and plundered, without the possibility of redress; for such is the equity of the West Indian laws, that no free Negro's evidence will be admitted in their courts of justice. In this situation, is it

1. I.e., to where the water's depth could be measured.   3. Beguiled.
2. Was apprenticed at.   4. Black.

surprising that slaves, when mildly treated, should prefer even the misery of slavery to such a mockery of freedom? I was now completely disgusted with the West Indies, and thought I never should be entirely free until I had left them.

* * *

About the latter end of the year 1764, my master bought a larger sloop, called the Prudence, about seventy or eighty tons, of which my captain had the command. I went with him in this vessel, and we took a load of new slaves for Georgia and Charlestown. My master now left me entirely to the captain, though he still wished me to be with him; but I, who always much wished to lose sight of the West Indies, was not a little rejoiced at the thoughts of seeing any other country. Therefore, relying on the goodness of my captain, I got ready all the little venture I could; and, when the vessel was ready, we sailed, to my great joy. When we got to our destined places, Georgia and Charlestown, I expected I should have an opportunity of selling my little property to advantage. But here, particularly in Charlestown, I met with buyers, white men, who imposed on me as in other places. Notwithstanding, I was resolved to have fortitude, thinking no lot or trial too hard when kind Heaven is the rewarder.

We soon got loaded again, and returned to Montserrat; and there, amongst the rest of the islands, I sold my goods well; and in this manner I continued trading during the year 1764—meeting with various scenes of imposition, as usual. After this, my master fitted out his vessel for Philadelphia, in the year 1765; and during the time we were loading her, and getting ready for the voyage, I worked with redoubled alacrity, from the hope of getting money enough by these voyages to buy my freedom, in time, if it should please God; and also to see the town of Philadelphia, which I had heard a great deal about for some years past. Besides which, I had always longed to prove my master's promise the first day I came to him. In the midst of these elevated ideas, and while I was about getting my little stock of merchandize in readiness, one Sunday my master sent for me to his house. When I came there, I found him and the captain together; and, on my going in, I was struck with astonishment at his telling me he heard that I meant to run away from him when I got to Philadelphia. "And therefore," said he, "I must tell you again, you cost me a great deal of money, no less than forty pounds sterling; and it will not do to lose so much. You are a valuable fellow," continued he, "and I can get any day for you one hundred guineas, from many gentlemen in this island." And then he told me of Captain Doran's brother-in-law, a severe master, who ever wanted to buy me to make me his overseer. My captain also said he could get much more than a hundred guineas for me in Carolina. This I knew to be a fact; for the gentleman that wanted to buy me came off several times on board of us, and spoke to me to live with him, and said he would use me well. When I asked him what work he would put me to, he said, as I was a sailor, he would make me a captain of one of his rice vessels. But I refused; and fearing at the same time, by a sudden turn I saw in the captain's temper, he might mean to sell me, I told the gentleman I would not live with him on any condition, and that I certainly would run away with his vessel: but he said he did not fear that, as he would catch me again, and then he told me how cruelly he would serve me if I should do so. My captain, however, gave him to understand that I knew something of navigation, so he thought better of it; and, to my great joy, he went away. I now told my master, I did not say I would run away in Philadelphia; neither did I mean it, as he did not use me ill, nor yet the captain; for if they did, I certainly would have made some attempts before now; but as I thought that if it were God's will I ever should be freed, it would be so, and, on the contrary, if it was not his will, it would not happen. So I hoped if ever I were freed, whilst I was used well, it should be by honest means; but as I could not help myself, he must do as he pleased, I could only hope and trust to the God of Heaven; and at that instant my mind was big with inventions, and full of schemes to escape. I then appealed to the captain, whether he ever saw any sign of my making the least attempt to run away, and asked him if I did not always come on board according to the time for which he gave me liberty; and, more particularly, when all our men left us at Guade-loupe, and went on board of the French fleet, and advised me to go with them, whether I might not, and that he could not have got me again. To my no small surprise, and very great joy, the captain confirmed every syllable that I had said, and even more; for he said he had tried different times to see if I would make any attempt of this kind, both at St. Eustatia and in America, and he never found that I made the smallest; but, on the contrary, I always came on board according to his orders; and he did really believe, if I ever meant to run away, that, as I could never have had a better opportunity, I would have done it the night the mate and all the people left our vessel at Guadeloupe. The captain then informed my master, who had been thus imposed on by our mate (though I did not know who was my enemy), the reason the mate had for imposing this lie upon him; which was, because I had acquainted the captain of the provisions the mate had given away or taken out of the vessel. This speech of the captain was like life to the dead to me, and instantly my soul glorified God; and still more so, on hearing my master immediately say that I was a sensible fellow, and he never did intend to use me as a common slave; and that but for the entreaties of the captain, and his character of me, he would not have let me go from the shores about as I had done. That also, in so doing, he thought by carrying one little thing or other to different places to sell, I might make money. That he also intended to encourage me in this, by crediting me with half a puncheon of rum and half a hogshead[5] of sugar at a time; so that, from being careful, I might have money enough, in some time, to purchase my freedom; and, when that was the case, I might depend upon it he would let me have it for forty pounds sterling money, which was only the same price he gave for me. This sound gladdened my poor heart beyond measure; though indeed it was no more than the very idea I had formed in my mind of my master long before, and I immediately made him this reply: "Sir, I always had that very thought of you, indeed I had, and that made me so diligent in serving you." He then gave me a large piece of silver coin, such as I never had seen or had before, and told me to get ready for the voyage, and he would credit me with a tierce[6] of sugar, and another of rum; he also said that he had two amiable sisters in Philadelphia, from whom I might get some necessary things. Upon this my noble captain desired me to go aboard; and, knowing the African metal,[7] he charged me not to say any thing of this matter to any body; and he promised that the lying mate should not go with him any more. This was a change indeed: in the same hour to feel

5. Large barrel.   7. I.e., character.
6. A third of a barrel.

the most exquisite pain, and in the turn of a moment the fullest joy. It caused in me such sensations as I was only able to express in my looks; my heart was so overpowered with gratitude, that I could have kissed both of their feet. When I left the room, I immediately went, or rather flew, to the vessel; which being loaded, my master, as good as his word, trusted me with a tierce of rum, and another of sugar, when we sailed, and arrived safe at the elegant town of Philadelphia. I sold my goods here pretty well; and in this charming place I found every thing plentiful and cheap.

While I was in this place, a very extraordinary occurrence befell me. I had been told one evening of a wise woman, a Mrs. Davis, who revealed secrets, foretold events, etc., etc. I put little faith in this story at first, as I could not conceive that any mortal could foresee the future disposals of Providence, nor did I believe in any other revelation than that of the Holy Scriptures; however, I was greatly astonished at seeing this woman in a dream that night, though a person I never before beheld in my life. This made such an impression on me, that I could not get the idea the next day out of my mind, and I then became as anxious to see her as I was before indifferent. Accordingly in the evening, after we left off working, I inquired where she lived, and being directed to her, to my inexpressible surprise, beheld the very woman in the very same dress she appeared to me to wear in the vision. She immediately told me I had dreamed of her the preceding night; related to me many things that had happened with a correctness that astonished me, and finally told me I should not be long a slave. This was the more agreeable news; as I believed it the more readily from her having so faithfully related the past incidents of my life. She said I should be twice in very great danger of my life within eighteen months, which, if I escaped, I should afterwards go on well. So, giving me her blessing, we parted. After staying here sometime till our vessel was loaded, and I had bought in my little traffic, we sailed from this agreeable spot for Montserrat, once more to encounter the raging surfs.

* * *

We soon came to Georgia, where we were to complete our landing, and here worse fate than ever attended me; for one Sunday night, as I was with some negroes in their master's yard, in the town of Savannah, it happened that their master, one Doctor Perkins, who was a very severe and cruel man, came in drunk; and not liking to see any strange negroes in his yard, he and a ruffian of a white man, he had in his service, beset me in an instant, and both of them struck me with the first weapons they could get hold of. I cried out as long as I could for help and mercy; but, though I gave a good account of myself, and he knew my captain, who lodged hard by him,[8] it was to no purpose, They beat and mangled me in a shameful manner, leaving me near dead. I lost so much blood from the wounds I received, that I lay quite motionless, and was so benumbed that I could not feel any thing for many hours. Early in the morning, they took me away to the jail. As I did not return to the ship all night, my captain, not knowing where I was, and being uneasy that I did not then make my appearance, made inquiry after me; and having found where I was, immediately came to me. As soon as the good man saw me so cut and mangled, he could not forbear weeping; he soon got me out of

8. I.e., close by him.

jail to his lodgings, and immediately sent for the best doctors in the place, who at first declared it as their opinion that I could not recover. My captain on this went to all the lawyers in the town for their advice, but they told him they could do nothing for me as I was a negro. He then went to Doctor Perkins, the hero who had vanquished me, and menaced him, swearing he would be revenged on him, and challenged him to fight.—But cowardice is ever the companion of cruelty—and the Doctor refused. However, by the skillfullness of one Dr. Brady of that place, I began at last to amend; but, although I was so sore and bad with the wounds I had all over me, that I could not rest in any posture, yet I was in more pain on account of the captain's uneasiness about me, than I otherwise should have been. The worthy man nursed and watched me all the hours of the night; and I was, through his attention and that of the doctor, able to get out of bed in about sixteen or eighteen days. All this time I was very much wanted on board, as I used frequently to go up and down the river for rafts, and other parts of our cargo, and stow them, when the mate was sick or absent. In about four weeks, I was able to go on duty, and in a fortnight after, having got in all our lading, our vessel set sail for Montserrat; and in less than three weeks we arrived there safe towards the end of the year. This ended my adventures in 1764, for I did not leave Montserrat again till the beginning of the following year.

From *Chapter VII*

Every day now brought me nearer my freedom, and I was impatient till we proceeded again to sea, that I might have an opportunity of getting a sum large enough to purchase it. I was not long ungratified; for, in the beginning of the year 1766, my master bought another sloop, named the Nancy, the largest I had ever seen. She was partly laden, and was to proceed to Philadelphia; our captain had his choice of three, and I was well pleased he chose this, which was the largest; for, from his having a large vessel, I had more room, and could carry a larger quantity of goods with me. Accordingly, when we had delivered our old vessel, the Prudence, and completed the lading of the Nancy, having made near three hundred per cent. by four barrels of pork I brought from Charlestown, I laid in as large a cargo as I could, trusting to God's providence to prosper my undertaking. With these views I sailed for Philadelphia. On our passage, when we drew near the land, I was for the first time surprised at the sight of some whales, having never seen any such large sea monsters before; and as we sailed by the land, one morning, I saw a puppy whale close by the vessel; it was about the length of a wherry boat, and it followed us all the day till we got within the Capes. We arrived safe, and in good time at Philadelphia, and I sold my goods there chiefly to the Quakers. They always appeared to be a very honest, discreet sort of people, and never attempted to impose on me; I therefore liked them, and ever after chose to deal with them in preference to any others.

One Sunday morning, while I was here, as I was going to church, I chanced to pass a meetinghouse. The doors being open, and the house full of people, it excited my curiosity to go in. When I entered the house, to my great surprise, I saw a very tall woman standing in the midst of them, speaking in an audible voice something which I could not understand. Having never seen any thing of this kind before, I stood and stared about me for some time, wondering at this odd scene. As soon as it was over, I took an opportunity to make inquiry about the place and people, when I was informed they were called Quakers. I particularly asked what that woman I saw in the midst of them had said, but none of them were pleased to satisfy me; so I quitted them, and soon after, as I was returning, I came to a church crowded with people; the churchyard was full likewise, and a number of people were even mounted on ladders looking in at the windows. I thought this a strange sight, as I had never seen churches, either in England or the West Indies, crowded in this manner before. I therefore made bold to ask some people the meaning of all this, and they told me the Rev. Mr. George Whitefield was preaching. I had often heard of this gentleman, and had wished to see and hear him; but I never before had an opportunity. I now therefore resolved to gratify myself with the sight, and pressed in amidst the multitude. When I got into the church, I saw this pious man exhorting the people with the greatest fervor and earnestness, and sweating as much as I ever did while in slavery on Montserrat beach. I was very much struck and impressed with this; I thought it strange I had never seen divines exert themselves in this manner before, and was no longer at a loss to account for the thin congregations they preached to.

When we had discharged our cargo here, and were loaded again, we left this fruitful land once more, and set sail for Montserrat. My traffic had hitherto succeeded so well with me, that I thought, by selling my goods when we arrived at Montserrat, I should have enough to purchase my freedom. But as soon as our vessel arrived there, my master came on board, and gave orders for us to go to St. Eustatia, and discharge our cargo there, and from thence proceed for Georgia. I was much disappointed at this; but thinking, as usual, it was of no use to encounter with the decrees of fate, I submitted without repining, and we went to St. Eustatia. After we had discharged our cargo there, we took in a live cargo (as we call a cargo of slaves). Here I sold my goods tolerably well; but, not being able to lay out all my money in this small island to as much advantage as in many other places, I laid out only part, and the remainder I brought away with me net. We sailed from hence for Georgia, and I was glad when we got there, though I had not much reason to like the place from my last adventure in Savannah; but I longed to get back to Montserrat and procure my freedom, which I expected to be able to purchase when I returned. As soon as we arrived here, I waited on my careful doctor, Mr. Brady, to whom I made the most grateful acknowledgments in my power, for his former kindness and attention during my illness.

*   *   *

When we had unladen the vessel, and I had sold my venture, finding myself master of about forty-seven pounds—I consulted my true friend, the captain, how I should proceed in offering my master the money for my freedom. He told me to come on a certain morning, when he and my master would be at breakfast together. Accordingly, on that morning I went, and met the captain there, as he had appointed. When I went in I made my obeisance to my master, and with my money in my hand, and many fears in my heart, I prayed him to be as good as his offer to me, when he was pleased to promise me my freedom as soon as I could purchase it. This speech seemed to confound him, he began to recoil, and my heart that instant sunk within me. "What," said he, "give you your freedom? Why, where did you get the money? Have you got forty pounds sterling?" "Yes, sir," I answered. "How did you get it?" replied he. I told him, very honestly. The captain then said he knew I got the money honestly, and with much industry, and that I was particularly careful. On which my master replied, I got money much faster than he did; and said he would not have made me the promise he did if he had thought I should have got the money so soon. "Come, come," said my worthy captain, clapping my master on the back, "Come, Robert (which was his name), I think you must let him have his freedom;—you have laid your money out very well; you have received a very good interest for it all this time, and here is now the principal at last. I know Gustavus has earned you more than a hundred a year, and he will save you money, as he will not leave you.—Come, Robert, take the money." My master then said he would not be worse than his promise; and, taking the money, told me to go to the Secretary at the Register Office, and get my manumission[9] drawn up. These words of my master were like a voice from Heaven to me. In an instant all my trepidation was turned into unutterable bliss; and I most reverently bowed myself with gratitude, unable to express my feelings, but by the overflowing of my eyes, and a heart replete with thanks to God, while my true and worthy friend, the captain, congratulated us both with a peculiar degree of heart-felt pleasure. As soon as the first transports of my joy were over, and that I had expressed my thanks to these my worthy friends, in the best manner I was able, I rose with a heart full of affection and reverence, and left the room, in order to obey my master's joyful mandate of going to the Register Office. As I was leaving the house I called to mind the words of the Psalmist, in the 126th Psalm, and like him, "I glorified God in my heart, in whom I trusted." These words had been impressed on my mind from the very day I was forced from Deptford to the present hour, and I now saw them, as I thought, fulfilled and verified. My imagination was all rapture as I flew to the Register Office; and, in this respect, like the apostle Peter[1] (whose deliverance from prison was so sudden and extraordinary, that he thought he was in a vision), I could scarcely believe I was awake. Heavens! who could do justice to my feelings at this moment! Not conquering heroes themselves, in the midst of a triumph—Not the tender mother who has just regained her long lost infant, and presses it to her heart—Not the weary hungry, mariner, at the sight of the desired friendly port—Not the lover, when he once more embraces his beloved mistress, after she has been ravished from his arms! All within my breast was tumult, wildness, and delirium! My feet scarcely touched the ground, for they were winged with joy; and, like Elijah, as he rose to Heaven,[2] they "were with lightning sped as I went on." Every one I met I told of my happiness, and blazed about the virtue of my amiable master and captain.

When I got to the office and acquainted the Register with my errand, he congratulated me on the occasion, and told me he would draw up my manumission for half price, which was a guinea. I thanked him for his kindness; and, having received it, and paid him, I hastened to my master to get him to sign it, that I might be fully released. Accordingly he signed the manumission that day; so that, before night, I, who had been a slave in the morning, trembling at the will of another, was become my own master, and completely

---

9. Document declaring his freedom.
1. "Acts xii.9" [Equiano's note]. "And he went out and followed him; and wist not that it was true which

was done by the angel; but thought he saw a vision."
2. The Lord takes Elijah into heaven in 2 Kings 2.11.

free. I thought this was the happiest day I had ever experienced; and my joy was still heightened by the blessings and prayers of many of the sable race, particularly the aged, to whom my heart had ever been attached with reverence.

* * *

As the form of my manumission has something peculiar in it, and expresses the absolute power and dominion one man claims over his fellow, I shall beg leave to present it before my readers at full length:

Montserrat.—To all men unto whom these presents shall come: I, Robert King, of the parish of St. Anthony, in the said island, merchant, send greeting. Know ye, that I, the aforesaid Robert King, for and in consideration of the sum of seventy pounds current money of the said island,[3] to me in hand paid, and to the intent that a negro man slave, named Gustavus Vassa, shall and may become free, having manumitted, emancipated, enfranchised, and set free, and by these presents do manumit, emancipate, enfranchise, and set free, the aforesaid negro man slave, named Gustavus Vassa, for ever; hereby giving, granting, and releasing unto him, the said Gustavus Vassa, all right, title, dominion, sovereignty, and property, which, as lord and master over the aforesaid Gustavus Vassa, I had, or now have, or by any means whatsoever I may or can hereafter possibly have over him, the aforesaid negro, for ever. In witness whereof, I, the above said Robert King, have unto these presents set my hand and seal, this tenth day of July, in the year of our Lord one thousand seven hundred and sixty-six.

ROBERT KING.

Signed, sealed, and delivered in the presence of Terry Legay, Montserrat.

Registered the within manumission at full length, this eleventh day of July, 1766, in liber D.[4]

TERRY LEGAY, Register.

* * *

1789

3. The exchange rate favored the West Indians in this period: forty pounds sterling equaling seventy pounds in "local" currency.
4. In book D (Latin).

PHILIP FRENEAU
1752–1832

Philip Freneau had all the advantages that wealth and social position could bestow, and the Freneau household in Manhattan was frequently visited by well-known writers and painters. Philip received a good education at the hands of tutors and at fifteen entered the sophomore class at the College of New Jersey (now Princeton University). There he became fast friends with his roommate, James Madison, a future president, and a classmate, Hugh Henry Brackenridge, who was to become a successful novelist. In their senior year Freneau and Brackenridge composed an ode on *The Rising Glory of America*, and Brackenridge read the poem at commencement. It establishes early in Freneau's career his recurrent vision of a glorious future in which America would fulfill the collective hope of humankind:

> Paradise anew
> Shall flourish, by no second Adam lost,
> No dangerous tree with deadly fruit shall grow,
> No tempting serpent to allure the soul
> From native innocence. . . . The lion and the lamb
> In mutual friendship linked, shall browse the shrub,
> And timorous deer with softened tigers stray
> O'er mead, or lofty hill, or grassy plain . . .

For a short time Freneau taught school and hoped to make a career as a writer, but it was an impractical wish. When he was offered a position as secretary on a plantation in the West Indies in 1776, he sailed to Santa Cruz and remained there almost three years. It was in that country, where "Sweet orange groves in lonely valleys rise," that Freneau wrote some of his most sensuous lyrics, but as he tells us in *To Sir Toby*, he could not talk of "blossoms" and an "endless spring" forever in a land that abounded in poverty and misery and where the owners grew wealthy on a slave economy. In 1778 he returned home and enlisted as a seaman on a blockade runner; two years later he was captured at sea and imprisoned on the British ship *Scorpion*, anchored in New York harbor. He was treated brutally, and when he was exchanged from the hospital ship *Hunter* his family feared for his life.

Freneau was to spend ten more years of his life at sea, first as a master of a merchant ship in 1784, and again in 1803, but immediately after he regained his health, he moved to Philadelphia to work in the post office, and it was in that city that he gained his reputation as a satirist, journalist, and poet. As editor of the *Freeman's Journal*, Freneau wrote impassioned verse in support of the American Revolution and turned all his rhetorical gifts against anyone who was thought to be in sympathy with the British monarchy. It was during this period in his life that he became identified as the "Poet of the American Revolution." In 1791, after he returned from duties at sea, Jefferson, as secretary of state, offered him a position as translator in his department, understanding that Freneau would have plenty of free time to devote to his newspaper, the *National Gazette*. Like Thomas Paine, Freneau was a strong supporter of the French Revolution, and he had a sharp eye for anyone not sympathetic to the democratic cause. He had a special grudge against Alexander Hamilton, secretary of the treasury, as chief spokesman for the Federalists. President Washington thought it was ironic that "that rascal Freneau" should be employed by his administration when he attacked it so outspokenly.

The *National Gazette* ceased publication in 1793, and after Jefferson resigned his office, Freneau left Philadelphia for good, alternating between ship's captain and newspaper editor in New York and New Jersey. He spent his last years on his New Jersey farm, unable to make it self-supporting and with no hope of further employment. Year after year he sold off the land he inherited from his father and was finally reduced to applying for a pension as a veteran of the American Revolution. He died impoverished and unknown, lost in a blizzard.

Freneau's biographer, Lewis Leary, subtitled his book A *Study in Literary Failure* and began that work by observing that "Philip Freneau failed in almost everything he attempted." Freneau's most sympathetic readers have always believed that he was born in a time not ripe for poetry and that his genuine lyric gifts were always in conflict with his political pamphleteering. Had he been born fifty years later, perhaps he could have joined Cooper and Irving in a life devoted exclusively to letters. There is no doubt that he did much to pave the way for these later writers.

Freneau is not "the father of American poetry" (as his readers, anxious for an advocate for a national literary consciousness, liked to call him), but his obsession with the beautiful, transient things of nature and the conflict in his art between the sensuous and the didactic are central to the concerns of American poetry.

Texts used are *The Poems of Philip Freneau*, edited by F. L. Pattee (1902); *The Poems of Freneau*, edited by H. H. Clark (1929); and *The Last Poems of Philip Freneau*, edited by Lewis Leary (1945).

From The House of Night

From A *Vision*

Advertisement——This Poem is founded upon the authority of Scripture, inasmuch as these sacred books assert, that *the last enemy that shall be conquered is Death.*[1] For the purposes of poetry he is here personified, and represented as on his dying bed. The scene is laid at a solitary palace, (the time midnight), which, though before beautiful and joyous, is now become sad and gloomy, as being the abode and receptacle of Death. Its owner, an amiable, majestic youth, who had lately lost a beloved consort,[2] nevertheless with a noble philosophical fortitude and humanity, entertains him in a friendly manner, and by employing Physicians, endeavors to restore him to health, although an enemy; convinced of the excellence and propriety of that divine precept, *If thine enemy hunger, feed him; if he thirst, give him drink.*[3] He nevertheless, as if by a spirit of prophecy, informs this (fictitiously) wicked being of the certainty of his doom, and represents to him in a pathetic manner the vanity of his expectations, either of a reception into the abodes of the just, or continuing longer to make havoc of mankind upon earth. The patient finding his end approaching, composes his epitaph, and orders it to be engraved on his tombstone, hinting to us thereby, that even Death and Distress have vanity; and would be remembered with honor after he is no more, although his whole life has been spent in deeds of devastation and murder. He dies at last in the utmost agonies of despair, after agreeing with the avaricious Undertaker to intomb his bones. This reflects upon the inhumanity of those men, who, not to mention an enemy, would scarcely cover a departed friend with a little dust, without certainty of a reward for so doing. The circumstances of his funeral are then recited, and the visionary and fabulous part of the poem disappears. It concludes with a few reflections on the impropriety of a too great attachment to the present life, and incentives to such moral virtue as may assist in conducting us to a better.

1

Trembling I write my dream, and recollect
A fearful vision at the midnight hour;
So late, Death o'er me spread his sable wings,
Painted with fancies of malignant power!

*   *   *

1. 1 Corinthians 15.26.   3. Romans 12.20.
2. Wife and companion.

3
Let others draw from smiling skies their theme,
And tell of climes that boast unfading light,   10
I draw a darker scene, replete with gloom,
I sing the horrors of the House of Night.
4
Stranger, believe the truth experience tells,
Poetic dreams are of a finer cast
Than those which o'er the sober brain diffused,   15
Are but a repetition of some action past.
5
Fancy, I own[4] thy power—when sunk in sleep
Thou play'st thy wild delusive part so well
You lift me into immortality,
Depict new heavens, or draw the scenes of hell.   20
6
By some sad means, when Reason holds no sway,
Lonely I roved at midnight o'er a plain
Where murmuring streams and mingling rivers flow,
Far to their springs, or seek the sea again.
7
Sweet vernal May! though then thy woods in bloom   25
Flourished, yet nought of this could Fancy see,
No wild pinks blessed the meads,[5] no green the fields,
And naked seemed to stand each lifeless tree:

                    *   *   *

11
At last, by chance and guardian fancy led,
I reached a noble dome, raised fair and high,
And saw the light from upper windows flame,
Presage of mirth and hospitality.
12
And by that light around the dome appeared   45
A mournful garden of autumnal hue,
Its lately pleasing flowers all drooping stood
Amidst high weeds that in rank plenty grew.
13
The primrose there, the violet darkly blue,
Daisies and fair narcissus ceased to rise,   50
Gay spotted pinks their charming bloom withdrew,
And polyanthus quenched its thousand dyes.
14
No pleasant fruit or blossom gaily smiled.
Nought but unhappy plants or trees were seen,
The yew, the myrtle, and the church-yard elm,   55
The cypress, with its melancholy green.[6]
15
There cedars dark, the osier, and the pine,
Shorn tamarisks, and weeping willows grew,

---

4. Acknowledge. "Fancy": imagination.
5. Meadows.
6. All the trees and plants mentioned here and in the

lines following are identified in mythology with sleep
and death.

The poplar tall, the lotos, and the lime,
And pyracantha did her leaves renew.   60

16

The poppy there, companion to repose,
Displayed her blossoms that began to fall,
And here the purple amaranthus rose
With mint strong-scented, for the funeral.

17

And here and there with laurel shrubs between   65
A tombstone lay, inscribed with strains of woe,
And stanzas sad, throughout the dismal green,
Lamented for the dead that slept below.

18

Peace to this awful dome!—when straight[7] I heard
The voice of men in a secluded room,   70
Much did they talk of death, and much of life,
Of coffins, shrouds, and horrors of a tomb.

19

Pathetic were their words, and well they aimed
To explain the mystic paths of providence,
Learned were they all, but there remained not I   75
To hear the upshot of their conference.

20

Meantime from an adjoining chamber came
Confuséd murmurings, half distinguished sounds,
And as I nearer drew, disputes arose
Of surgery, and remedies for wounds.   80

*   *   *

23

Then up three winding stairs my feet were brought
To a high chamber, hung with mourning sad,   90
The unsnuffed candles glared with visage dim,
'Midst grief, in ecstasy of woe run mad.

24

A wide leafed table stood on either side,
Well fraught with phials, half their liquids spent,
And from a couch, behind the curtain's veil,   95
I heard a hollow voice of loud lament.

25

Turning to view the object whence it came,
My frighted eyes a horrid form surveyed;
Fancy, I own thy power—Death on the couch,
With fleshless limbs, at rueful length, was laid.   100

*   *   *

28

Sad was his countenance, if we can call
That countenance, where only bones were seen   110
And eyes sunk in their sockets, dark and low,
And teeth, that only showed themselves to grin.

7. Immediately. "Awful": awesome.

29

Reft was his skull of hair, and no fresh bloom
Of cheerful mirth sate[8] on his visage hoar:
Sometimes he raised his head, while deep-drawn groans   115
Were mixed with words that did his fate deplore.

30

Oft did he wish to see the daylight spring,
And often toward the window leaned to hear,
Forerunner of the scarlet-mantled morn,
The early note of wakeful chanticleer.[9]   120

31

Thus he—But at my hand a portly[1] youth
Of comely countenance, began to tell,
"That this was Death upon his dying bed,
"Sullen, morose, and peevish to be well;

32

"Fixed is his doom—the miscreant reigns no more   125
"The tyrant of the dying or the dead;
"This night concludes his all-consuming reign,
"Pour out, ye heav'ns, your vengeance on his head."

*　*　*

47

But now this man of hell toward me turned,   185
And straight, in hideous tone, began to speak,
Long held he sage discourse, but I forebore
To answer him, much less his news to seek.

48

He talked of tombstones and of monuments,
Of equinoctial climes[2] and India shores,   190
He talked of stars that shed their influence,
Fevers and plagues, and all their noxious stores.

*　*　*

50

Much spoke he of the myrtle and the yew,
Of ghosts that nightly walk the church-yard o'er
Of storms that through the wint'ry ocean blow
And dash the well-manned galley on the shore,   200

51

Of broad-mouthed cannons, and the thunderbolt,
Of sieges and convulsions, dearth and fire,
Of poisonous weeds—but seemed to sneer at these
Who by the laurel o'er him did aspire.

52

Then with a hollow voice thus went he on,   205
"Get up, and search, and bring, when found, to me,
"Some cordial, potion, or some pleasant draught,
"Sweet, slumb'rous poppy, or the mild Bohea.[3]

8. Sat.
9. Rooster.
1. Dignified.

2. Places beneath the equator.
3. Tea.

53

"But hark, my pitying friend!—and, if you can,
"Deceive the grim physician at the door— 210
"Bring half the mountain springs—ah! hither bring
"The cold rock water from the shady bower.

54

"For till this night such thirst did ne'er invade,
"A thirst provoked by heav'n's avenging hand;

"Hence bear me, friends, to quaff, and quaff again 215
"The cool wave bubbling from the yellow sand.

55

"To these dark walls with stately step I came,
"Prepared your drugs and doses to defy;
"Smit with the love of never dying fame,
"I came, alas! to conquer—not to die!" 220

*   *   *

88

Up rushed a band, with compasses and scales
To measure his slim carcass, long and lean— 350
"Be sure," said he, "to frame my coffin strong,
"You, master workman, and your men, I mean:

89

"For if the Devil, so late my trusty friend,
"Should get one hint where I am laid, from you,
"Not with my soul content, he'd seek to find 355
"That moldering mass of bones, my body, too!

90

"Of hardest ebon let the plank be found,
"With clamps and ponderous bars secured around,
"That if the box by Satan should be stormed,
"It may be able for resistance found." 360

*   *   *

125

At distance far approaching to the tomb,
By lamps and lanterns guided through the shade,
A coal-black chariot hurried through the gloom,
Specters attending, in black weeds arrayed, 500

126

Whose woeful forms yet chill my soul with dread,
Each wore a vest in Stygian[4] chambers wove,
Death's kindred all—Death's horses they bestrode,
And galloped fiercely, as the chariot drove.

127

Each horrid face a grisly mask concealed, 505
Their busy eyes shot terror to my soul
As now and then, by the pale lantern's glare,
I saw them for their parted friend condole.

---

4. Hellish; from the name of the river Styx, over which, in Greek mythology, the souls of the dead must cross.

128

Before the hearse Death's chaplain seemed to go,
Who strove to comfort, what he could, the dead;   510
Talked much of Satan, and the land of woe,
And many a chapter from the scriptures read.

129

At last he raised the swelling anthem high,
In dismal numbers seemed he to complain;
The captive tribes that by Euphrates[5] wept,   515
Their song was jovial to his dreary strain.

130

That done, they placed the carcass in the tomb,
To dust and dull oblivion now resigned,
Then turned the chariot toward the House of Night,
Which soon flew off, and left no trace behind.   520

131

But as I stooped to write the appointed[6] verse,
Swifter than thought the airy scene decayed;
Blushing the morn arose, and from the east
With her gay streams of light dispelled the shade.

132

What is this Death, ye deep read sophists,[7] say?—   525
Death is no more than one unceasing change;
New forms arise, while other forms decay,
Yet all is Life throughout creation's range.

133

The towering Alps, the haughty Appenine,
The Andes, wrapt in everlasting snow,   530
The Appalachian and the Ararat[8]
Sooner or later must to ruin go.

134

Hills sink to plains, and man returns to dust,
That dust supports a reptile or a flower;
Each changeful atom by some other nursed   535
Takes some new form, to perish in an hour.

135

Too nearly joined to sickness, toils, and pains,
(Perhaps for former crimes imprisoned here)
True to itself the immortal soul remains,
And seeks new mansions in the starry sphere.   540

136

When Nature bids thee from the world retire,
With joy thy lodging leave, a fated guest;
In Paradise, the land of thy desire,
Existing always, always to be blest.

1777–78   1779, 1786

---

5. The Euphrates is one of the rivers of paradise (Genesis 2.14) and marked the northern limit of the land promised to the Israelites. Here those Israelites in bondage to the Babylonians weep for the land they have lost. Cf. Psalm 137.
6. Required.
7. Teachers of philosophy.

8. The highest mountain in Turkey. "Alps": the mountains of south central Europe. "Appenine": mountains in Italy. "Andes": mountains of South America. "Appalachian": eastern North American mountain range that runs from Newfoundland to Alabama.

On the Emigration to America and Peopling the Western Country

To western woods, and lonely plains,
Palemon[1] from the crowd departs,
Where Nature's wildest genius reigns,
To tame the soil, and plant the arts—
What wonders there shall freedom show, 5
What mighty states successive grow!

From Europe's proud, despotic shores
Hither the stranger takes his way,
And in our new found world explores
A happier soil, a milder sway, 10
Where no proud despot holds him down,
No slaves insult him with a crown.

What charming scenes attract the eye,
On wild Ohio's savage stream!
There Nature reigns, whose works outvie 15
The boldest pattern art can frame;
There ages past have rolled away,
And forests bloomed but to decay.

From these fair plains, these rural seats,
So long concealed, so lately known, 20
The unsocial Indian far retreats,
To make some other clime his own,
Where other streams, less pleasing flow,
And darker forests round him grow.

Great sire[2] of floods! whose varied wave 25
Through climes and countries takes its way,
To whom creating Nature gave
Ten thousand streams to swell thy sway!
No longer shall *they* useless prove,
Nor idly through the forests rove; 30

Nor longer shall your princely flood
From distant lakes be swelled in vain,
Nor longer through a darksome wood
Advance, unnoticed, to the main,[3]
Far other ends, the heavens decree— 35
And commerce plans new freights for thee.

While virtue warms the generous breast,
There heaven-born freedom shall reside,
Nor shall the voice of war molest,
Nor Europe's all-aspiring pride— 40

1. Conventionally, any young man setting out on a journey. Palemon appears in Chaucer's *Knight's Tale*, an adaptation of Boccaccio's *Teseide*.
2. "Mississippi" [Freneau's note].
3. Ocean.

There Reason shall new laws devise,
And order from confusion rise.

Forsaking kings and regal state,
With all their pomp and fancied bliss,
The traveler owns,[4] convinced though late,   45
No realm so free, so blessed as this—
The east is half to slaves consigned,
Where kings and priests enchain the mind.

O come the time, and haste the day,
When man shall man no longer crush,   50
When Reason shall enforce her sway,
Nor these fair regions raise our blush,
Where still the *African* complains,
And mourns his yet unbroken chains.

Far brighter scenes a future age,   55
The muse predicts, these states will hail,
Whose genius may the world engage,
Whose deeds may over death prevail,
And happier systems bring to view,
Than all the eastern sages knew.   60

1785

The Wild Honey Suckle

Fair flower, that dost so comely grow,
Hid in this silent, dull retreat,
Untouched thy honeyed blossoms blow,[1]
Unseen thy little branches greet:
   No roving foot shall crush thee here,   5
   No busy hand provoke a tear.

By Nature's self in white arrayed,
She bade thee shun the vulgar[2] eye,
And planted here the guardian shade,
And sent soft waters murmuring by;   10
   Thus quietly thy summer goes,
   Thy days declining to repose.

Smit with those charms, that must decay,
I grieve to see your future doom;
They died—nor were those flowers more gay,   15
The flowers that did in Eden bloom;
   Unpitying frosts, and Autumn's power
   Shall leave no vestige of this flower.

---

4. Admits.   2. Common; unfeeling.
1. Bloom.

From morning suns and evening dews
At first thy little being came: 20
If nothing once, you nothing lose,
For when you die you are the same;
    The space between, is but an hour,
    The frail duration of a flower.

                                           1786

The Indian Burying Ground

In spite of all the learned have said,
I still my old opinion keep;
The *posture*, that *we* give the dead,
Points out the soul's eternal sleep.

Not so the ancients of these lands—   5
The Indian, when from life released,
Again is seated[1] with his friends,
And shares again the joyous feast.

His imaged birds, and painted bowl,
And venison, for a journey dressed,   10
Bespeak the nature of the soul,
Activity, that knows no rest.

His bow, for action ready bent,
And arrows, with a head of stone,
Can only mean that life is spent,   15
And not the old ideas gone.

Thou, stranger, that shalt come this way,
No fraud upon the dead commit—
Observe the swelling turf, and say
They do not *lie*, but here they *sit*.   20

Here still a lofty rock remains,
On which the curious eye may trace
(Now wasted, half, by wearing rains)
The fancies of a ruder race.

Here still an agéd elm aspires,   25
Beneath whose far-projecting shade
(And which the shepherd still admires)
The children of the forest played!

There oft a restless Indian queen
(Pale Sheba,[2] with her braided hair)   30

1. "The North American Indians bury their dead in a
sitting posture; decorating the corpse with wampum,
the images of birds, quadrupeds, etc.: And (if that of a
warrior) with bows, arrows, tomhawks and other military weapons" [Freneau's note].
2. Sheba is the queen who visited Solomon to test his
wisdom (1 Kings 10.1–13).

And many a barbarous form is seen
To chide the man that lingers there.

By midnight moons, o'er moistening dews,
In habit for the chase arrayed,
The hunter still the deer pursues,   35
The hunter and the deer, a shade!

And long shall timorous fancy see
The painted chief, and pointed spear,
And Reason's self shall bow the knee
To shadows and delusions here.   40

1788

To Sir Toby[1]

*A Sugar Planter in the Interior Parts of Jamaica, Near the City of San
Jago de la Vega, (Spanish Town) 1784*

> *"The motions of his spirit are black as night,
> And his affections dark as Erebus."*
> —Shakespeare[2]

If there exists a hell—the case is clear—
Sir Toby's slaves enjoy that portion here:
Here are no blazing brimstone lakes—'tis true;
But kindled rum too often burns as blue;
In which some fiend, whom nature must detest,   5
Steeps Toby's brand, and marks poor Cudjoe's[3] breast.
  Here whips on whips excite perpetual fears,
And mingled howlings vibrate on my ears:
Here Nature's plagues abound, to fret and tease,
Snakes, scorpions, despots, lizards, centipedes—   10
No art, no care escapes the busy lash;
All have their dues—and all are paid in cash—
The eternal driver keeps a steady eye
On a black herd, who would his vengeance fly,
But chained, imprisoned, on a burning soil,   15
For the mean avarice of a tyrant toil![4]
The lengthy cart-whip guards this monster's reign—
And cracks, like pistols, from the fields of cane.
  Ye powers! who formed these wretched tribes, relate,
What had they done, to merit such a fate!   20
Why were they brought from Eboe's[5] sultry waste,
To see that plenty which they must not taste—
Food, which they cannot buy, and dare not steal;

---

1. First published in the *Daily Advertiser*, February 1, 1791, titled *The Island Field Negro*. The text used here is the 1809 version.
2. *The Merchant of Venice* 5.1.79. Freneau has substituted the word *black* for "dull." "Erebus": in Greek mythology the region beneath the earth through which the dead must pass before entering Hades.
3. "Cudge" or "Cudjoe" was a common name for a

slave. "This passage has a reference to the West Indian custom (sanctioned by law) of branding a newly imported slave on the breast, with a red hot iron, as evidence of the purchaser's property" [Freneau's note].
4. Lines 13–16 were added in 1809.
5. "A small Negro kingdom near the river Senegal" [Freneau's note].

Yams and potatoes—many a scanty meal!—
One, with a gibbet[6] wakes his negro's fears,   25
One to the windmill nails him by the ears;
One keeps his slave in darkened dens, unfed,
One puts the wretch in pickle ere he's dead:
This, from a tree suspends him by the thumbs,
that, from his table grudges even the crumbs!   30
  O'er yond' rough hills a tribe of females go,
Each with her gourd,[7] her infant, and her hoe;
Scorched by a sun that has no mercy here,
Driven by a devil, whom men call overseer—
In chains, twelve wretches to their labors haste;   35
Twice twelve I saw, with iron collars graced!—
  Are such the fruits that spring from vast domains?
Is wealth, thus got, Sir Toby, worth your pains!—
Who would your wealth on terms, like these, possess,
Where all we see is pregnant with distress—   40
Angola's[8] natives scourged by ruffian hands,
And toil's hard product shipped to foreign lands.
  Talk not of blossoms, and your endless spring;
What joy, what smile, can scenes of misery bring?—
Though Nature, here, has every blessing spread,   45
Poor is the laborer—and how meanly fed!—
  Here Stygian[9] paintings light and shade renew,
Pictures of hell, that Virgil's[1] pencil drew:
Here, surly Charons[2] make their annual trip,
And ghosts arrive in every Guinea ship,[3]   50
To find what beasts these western isles afford,
Plutonian[4] scourges, and despotic lords:—
  Here, they, of stuff determined to be free,
Must climb the rude cliffs of the Liguanee;[5]
Beyond the clouds, in sculking haste repair,   55
And hardly safe from brother traitors[6] there.—

1784   1791, 1809

On Mr. Paine's Rights of Man[1]

Thus briefly sketched the sacred rights of man,
How inconsistent with the royal plan!

6. Gallows.
7. Water cup.
8. West African Portuguese colony.
9. Hellish; taken from the river Styx over which, in Greek mythology, souls of the dead must cross.
1. "See *Aeneid*, Book 6th.—and Fenelon's Telemachus, Book 18" [Freneau's note]. Aeneas descends to the underworld in the sixth book of the Latin poet Virgil's (70–19 B.C.) epic. Francois de Salignac de la Mothe-Fénelon (1651–1715) was a theologian and the author of *Télémaque* (1699), a didactic romance concerning the son of Ulysses as he searches for his father.
2. In Greek mythology, Charon ferries the souls of the dead over the river Styx to Hades.
3. Slave ships from West Africa.

4. Hellish; in Greek mythology Pluto was the god of the underworld.
5. "The mountains northward of the kingdom" [Freneau's note].
6. "Alluding to the *Independent* negroes in the blue mountains, who, for a stipulated reward, deliver up every fugitive that falls into their hands, to the English Government" [Freneau's note].
1. The original title was *To a Republican with Mr. Paine's Rights of Man.* Paine read Edmund Burke's *Reflections on the French Revolution* (1790), a defense of monarchy and an attack on revolution, when he was living in England. In his *Rights of Man* (1791–92) Paine argued for the overthrow of monarchy and the right of the people to govern themselves.

Which for itself exclusive honor craves,
Where some are masters born, and millions slaves.
With what contempt must every eye look down   5
On that base, childish bauble called a *crown*,
The gilded bait, that lures the crowd, to come,
Bow down their necks, and meet a slavish doom;
The source of half the miseries men endure,
The quack[2] that kills them, while it seems to cure,   10
   Roused by the reason of his manly page,
Once more shall Paine a listening world engage:
From Reason's source, a bold reform he brings,
In raising up *mankind*, he pulls down *kings*,
Who, source of discord, patrons of all wrong,   15
On blood and murder have been fed too long:
Hid from the world, and tutored to be base,
The curse, the scourge, the ruin of our race,
Their's was the task, a dull designing few,
To shackle beings that they scarcely knew,   20
Who made this globe the residence of slaves,
And built their thrones on systems formed by knaves
—Advance, bright years, to work their final fall,
And haste the period that shall crush them all.
   Who, that has read and scanned the historic page   25
But glows, at every line, with kindling rage,
To see by them the rights of men aspersed,
Freedom restrained, and Nature's law reversed,
Men, ranked with beasts, by monarchs willed away,
And bound young fools, or madmen to obey: 30
Now driven to wars, and now oppressed at home,
Compelled in crowds o'er distant seas to roam,
From India's climes the plundered prize to bring
To glad the strumpet, or to glut the king.
   Columbia, hail! immortal be thy reign: 35
Without a king, we till the smiling plain;
Without a king, we trace the unbounded sea,
And traffic round the globe, through each degree;
Each foreign clime our honored flag reveres,
Which asks no monarch, to support the stars: 40
Without a *king*, the laws maintain their sway,
While honor bids each generous heart obey.
Be ours the task the ambitious to restrain,
And this great lesson teach—that kings are vain;
That warring realms to certain ruin haste,   45
That kings subsist by war, and wars are waste:
So shall our nation, formed on Virtue's plan,
Remain the guardian of the Rights of Man,
A vast republic, famed through every clime,
Without a king, to see the end of time.   50

                                              1795

---

2. False physician.

On the Religion of Nature

The power, that gives with liberal hand
   The blessings man enjoys, while here,
And scatters through a smiling land
   Abundant products of the year;
      That power of nature, ever blessed,   5
      Bestowed religion with the rest.

Born with ourselves, her early sway
   Inclines the tender mind to take
The path of right, fair virtue's way
   Its own felicity to make.   10
      This universally extends
      And leads to no mysterious ends.

Religion, such as nature taught,
   With all divine perfection suits;
Had all mankind this system sought   15
   Sophists[1] would cease their vain disputes,
      And from this source would nations know
      All that can make their heaven below.

This deals not curses on mankind,
   Or dooms them to perpetual grief,   20
If from its aid no joys they find,
   It damns them not for unbelief;
      Upon a more exalted plan
      Creatress nature dealt with man—

Joy to the day, when all agree   25
   On such grand systems to proceed,
From fraud, design, and error free,
   And which to truth and goodness lead:
      Then persecution will retreat
      And man's religion be complete.   30

1815

On Observing a Large Red-streak Apple

In spite of ice, in spite of snow,
In spite of all the winds that blow,
In spite of hail and biting frost,
Suspended here I see you tossed
You still retain your wonted[2] hold   5
Though days are short and nights are cold.

---

1. Teachers of philosophy.   2. Accustomed.

Amidst this system of decay
How could you have one wish to stay?
If fate or fancy kept you there
They meant you for a solitaire.[3]   10
Were it not better to descend,
Or in the cider mill to end
Than thus to shiver in the storm
And not a leaf to keep you warm—
A moment, then, had buried all,   15
Nor you have doomed so late a fall.

But should the stem to which you cling
Uphold you to another spring,
Another race would round you rise
And view the *stranger* with surprise,   20
And, peeping from the blossoms say
Away, old dotard,[4] get away!

Alas! small pleasure can there be
To dwell, a hermit, on the tree—
Your old companions, all, are gone,   25
Have dropped, and perished, every one;
You only stay to face the blast,
A sad memento of the past.

Would fate or nature hear my prayer,
I would your bloom of youth repair   30
I would the wrongs of time restrain
And bring your blossom state again:
But fate and nature both say no;
And you, though late must perish too.

What can we say, what can we hope?   35
Ere from the branch I see you drop,
All I can do, all in my power
Will be to watch your parting hour:
When from the branch I see you fall,
A grave we dig a-south the wall.   40
There you shall sleep till from your core,
Of youngsters rises three or four;
These shall salute the coming spring
And red-streaks to perfection bring
When years have brought them to their prime   45
And they shall have their summer's time:
This, this is all you can attain,
And thus, I bid you, live again!

1822, 1945

3. I.e., an isolated example.   4. Feebleminded old person.

To a New England Poet

Though skilled in Latin and in Greek,
And earning fifty cents a week,
Such knowledge, and the income, too,
Should teach you better what to do:
    The meanest drudges, kept in pay,   5
    Can pocket fifty cents a day.

Why stay in such a tasteless land,
Where all must on a level stand,
(Excepting people, at their ease,
Who choose the level where they please:)   10
    See Irving[1] gone to Britain's court
    To people of another sort,
He will return, with wealth and fame,
While Yankees hardly know your name.

Lo! he has kissed a Monarch's—hand!   15
Before a prince I see him stand,
And with the glittering nobles mix,
Forgetting times of seventy-six,[2]
While you with terror meet the frown
Of Bank Directors of the town,   20
    The home-made nobles of our times,
    Who hate the bard, and spurn his rhymes.

Why pause?—like Irving, haste away,
To England your addresses pay;
And England will reward you well,   25
When you some pompous story tell
    Of British feats, and British arms,
    The maids of honor, and their charms.

Dear bard, I pray you, take the hint,
In England what you write and print,   30
Republished here in shop, or stall,
Will perfectly enchant us all:
    It will assume a different face,
    And post your name at every place,
    From splendid domes of first degree   35
    Where ladies meet, to sip their tea;
    From marble halls, where lawyers plead,
    Or Congress-men talk loud, indeed,
    To huts, where evening clubs appear,
    And 'squires resort—to guzzle Beer.   40

1823, 1945

1. Washington Irving (1783–1859) was the first American writer to gain an international reputation; Freneau objects to his success because in works like *Bracebridge Hall* (1822) Irving idealized English country life and often wrote as an American tourist awed by England's past.
2. The American Revolution of 1776.

PHILLIS WHEATLEY
c. 1753–1784

Phillis Wheatley was either nineteen or twenty years old when her *Poems on Various Subjects, Religious and Moral* was published in London in 1773. At the time of their publication she was the object of considerable public attention because, in addition to being a child prodigy, Wheatley was a black slave, born in Africa (probably in present-day Senegal or Gambia), and brought to Boston in 1761. She had been purchased by a wealthy tailor, John Wheatley, for his wife, Susannah, probably as a companion, and named for the vessel that carried her to our shores. Wheatley was fortunate in her surroundings, for Susannah Wheatley was sympathetic toward this very frail and remarkably intelligent child. In an age in which few white women were given an education, Wheatley was taught to read and write, and in a short time began to read Latin writers. She came to know the Bible well, and three English poets—Milton, Pope, and Gray—touched her deeply and exerted a strong influence on her verse. The Wheatleys moved in a circle of enlightened Boston Christians and Phillis, as James Levernier has recently shown, was introduced early on to a community that challenged the role of slavery as incompatible with Christian life. Wheatley's poem on the death of the Reverend George Whitefield, the great egalatarian English evangelist who frequently toured New England, made her famous. In June 1773, she arrived in London with her manuscript in the company of the Wheatleys' son Nathaniel. She came to England partly for reasons of health and partly to seek support for her first book. Benjamin Franklin and the lord mayor of London were among those who paid their respects. Her literary gifts, intelligence, and piety were a striking example to her English and American admirers of the triumph of the human spirit over the circumstances of birth. Her poems appeared early in September and the governor of Massachusetts, along with John Wheatley and John Hancock, were among the eighteen prominent citizens testifying that "under the Disadvantage of serving as a Slave in a Family in this Town," Wheatley "had been examined and thought qualified to write them."

Wheatley did not remain long enough in London to witness their publication; for she was called back to Boston with the news that Susannah Wheatley was dying. Early in the fall of 1773 she was manumitted. Susannah Wheatley died in 1774 and John Wheatley, four years later. In that same year, 1778, she married John Peters, a freedman, about whom almost nothing is known other than that the Wheatleys did not like him, that he petitioned for a license to sell liquor in 1784, and that he may have been in debtor's prison when Wheatley died, having endured poverty and the loss of two children in her last years. On her deathbed her third child lay ill beside her and succumbed shortly after Wheatley herself. They were buried together in an unmarked grave. Five years earlier, and only one year after her marriage, a proposal appeared for a second volume of poetry to include thirteen letters and thirty-three poems. The volume was never published and most of the poems and letters have yet to be found.

Wheatley's poetry was rediscovered in the 1830s by the New England abolitionists, but it is no exaggeration to say that she has never been better understood than at the present. Her recent critics have not only corrected a number of biographical errors but, more important, have provided a context in which her work can be best read and her life understood. This reconsideration shows Wheatley to be a bold and canny spokesperson for her faith and her politics; she early on joined the cause of American independence and the abolition of slavery, anticipating her friend the Reverend Samuel Hopkins's complaint that when American Negroes first heard the "sons of liberty" cry for freedom they were shocked by indifference to their own "abject slavery and utter wretchedness." It doesn't take a philosopher, Wheatley told Samson Occom, a Presbyterian minister and Mohegan tribesman, to see that the exercise of slavery cannot be reconciled with a "principle" that God has implanted in every human breast, "Love of Freedom." She was mistaken in thinking that the conservative earl of Dartmouth (William Legge) might be sympathetic to the American cause but correct in reminding him that there could be no justice anywhere if people in authority were deaf to the history of human sorrow:

> Should you, my lord, while you peruse my song,
> Wonder from whence my love of *Freedom* sprung,
> Whence flow these wishes for the common good,
> By feeling hearts best understood,
> I, young in life, by seeming cruel fate
> Was snatched from *Afric's* fancied happy seat:
> What pangs excruciating must molest,
> What sorrows labor in my parent's breast?
> Steeled was that soul and by no misery moved
> That from a father seized his babe beloved:
> Such, such my case. And can I then but pray
> Others may never feel tyrannic sway?

With the publication of Wheatley's *Poems*, Henry Louis Gates, Jr., has argued, "Wheatley launched two traditions at once—the black American literary tradition *and* the black woman's literary tradition. It is extraordinary that not just one but both of these traditions were founded simultaneously by a black woman—certainly an event unique in the history of literature—it is also ironic that this important fact of common, coterminous literary origin seems to have escaped most scholars."

The text used here for both the letters and the poems is from *The Poems of Phillis Wheatley*, edited by Julian D. Mason, Jr. (1966, rev. 1989). Wheatley's letters retain her original spelling.

On Being Brought from Africa to America

> 'Twas mercy brought me from my pagan land,
> Taught my benighted soul to understand
> That there's a God, that there's a Savior too:
> Once I redemption neither sought nor knew.
> Some view our sable[1] race with scornful eye.   5
> "Their color is a diabolic dye."
> Remember, Christians, Negroes, black as Cain,[2]
> May be refined, and join the angelic train.

1773

To the University of Cambridge, in New England[1]

> While an intrinsic ardor prompts to write,
> The muses promise to assist my pen;

1. Black.
2. Cain slew his brother Abel and was "marked" by God for doing so. This mark has sometimes been taken to be the origin of dark-skinned peoples (Genesis 4.1–15).

1. Harvard.

'Twas not long since I left my native shore
The land of errors,[2] and Egyptian gloom:[3]
Father of mercy, 'twas Thy gracious hand   5
Brought me in safety from those dark abodes.

    Students, to you 'tis given to scan the heights
Above, to traverse the ethereal space,
And mark the systems of revolving worlds.
Still more, ye sons of science[4] ye receive   10
The blissful news by messengers from Heav'n,
How Jesus' blood for your redemption flows.
See Him with hands outstretched upon the cross;
Immense compassion in His bosom glows;
He hears revilers, nor resents their scorn: 15
What matchless mercy in the Son of God!
When the whole human race by sin had fall'n,
He deigned to die that they might rise again,
And share with Him in the sublimest skies,
Life without death, and glory without end.   20

    Improve your privileges while they stay,
Ye pupils, and each hour redeem, that bears
Or good or bad report of you to Heav'n.
Let sin, that baneful evil to the soul,
By you be shunned, nor once remit your guard;   25
Suppress the deadly serpent in its egg.
Ye blooming plants of human race divine,
An Ethiop[5] tells you 'tis your greatest foe;
Its transient sweetness turns to endless pain,
And in immense perdition sinks the soul.   30

1767   1773

On the Death of the
Rev. Mr. George Whitefield, 1770[1]

Hail, happy saint, on thine immortal throne,
Possessed of glory, life, and bliss unknown;
We hear no more the music of thy tongue,
Thy wonted[2] auditories cease to throng.
Thy sermons in unequaled accents flowed,   5
And every bosom with devotion glowed;
Thou didst in strains of eloquence refined
Inflame the heart, and captivate the mind.

---

2. I.e., theological errors, because Africa was unconverted.
3. "And Moses stretched forth his hand toward
heaven; and there was a thick darkness in all the land
of Egypt three days" (Exodus 10.22).
4. Knowledge.
5. Ethiopian. In Wheatley's time "Ethiopian" was a
conventional name for the black peoples of Africa.

1. George Whitefield (1714–1770), an English follower of John Wesley, was the best-known revivalist in
the 18th century. He made several visits to America
and died in Newburyport, Massachusetts. This was
Wheatley's first published poem, and it made her
famous.
2. Accustomed.

Unhappy we the setting sun deplore,
So glorious once, but ah! it shines no more.   10

Behold the prophet in his towering flight!
He leaves the earth for heav'n's unmeasured height,}
And worlds unknown receive him from our sight.
There Whitefield wings with rapid course his way,
And sails to Zion[3] through vast seas of day.   15
Thy prayers, great saint, and thine incessant cries
Have pierced the bosom of thy native skies.
Thou moon hast seen, and all the stars of light,
How he has wrestled with his God by night.
He prayed that grace in every heart might dwell,   20
He longed to see America excel;
He charged[4] its youth that every grace divine
Should with full luster in their conduct shine;
That Savior, which his soul did first receive,
The greatest gift that ev'n a God can give,   25
He freely offered to the numerous throng,
That on his lips with listening pleasure hung.

"Take Him, ye wretched, for your only good,
Take Him ye starving sinners, for your food;
Ye thirsty, come to this life-giving stream,   30
Ye preachers, take Him for your joyful theme;
Take Him my dear Americans," he said,
"Be your complaints on His kind bosom laid:
Take Him, ye Africans, He longs for you,
Impartial Savior is His title due: 35
Washed in the fountain of redeeming blood,
You shall be sons, and kings, and priests to God."

Great *Countess*,[5] we Americans revere
Thy name, and mingle in thy grief sincere;
New England deeply feels, the orphans mourn,   40
Their more than father will no more return.

But, though arrested by the hand of death,
Whitefield no more exerts his laboring breath,
Yet let us view him in the eternal skies,
Let every heart to this bright vision rise;   45
While the tomb safe retains its sacred trust,
Till life divine re-animates his dust.

1770   1770, 1773

---

3. Here, the heavenly city of God.
4. Exhorted.
5. Selina Shirley Hastings (1707–1791), countess of

Huntington, was a strong supporter of George
Whitefield and active in Methodist church affairs.
Wheatley visited her in England in 1773.

Thoughts on the Works of Providence

Arise, my soul, on wings enraptured, rise
To praise the monarch of the earth and skies,
Whose goodness and beneficence appear
As round its center moves the rolling year,
Or when the morning glows with rosy charms,   5
Or the sun slumbers in the ocean's arms:
Of light divine by a rich portion lent
To guide my soul, and favor my intent.
Celestial muse, my arduous flight sustain,
And raise my mind to a seraphic[1] strain!   10

    Adored forever be the God unseen,
Which round the sun revolves this vast machine,
Though to His eye its mass a point appears:
Adored the God that whirls surrounding spheres,
Which first ordained that mighty Sol[2] should reign   15
The peerless monarch of the ethereal train:
Of miles twice forty millions is his height,
And yet his radiance dazzles mortal sight
So far beneath—from him the extended earth
Vigor derives, and every flowery birth: 20
Vast through her orb she moves with easy grace
Around her Phœbus[3] in unbounded space;
True to her course the impetuous storm derides,
Triumphant o'er the winds, and surging tides.

    Almighty, in these wond'rous works of Thine,   25
What Power, what Wisdom, and what Goodness shine!
And are Thy wonders, Lord, by men explored,
And yet creating glory unadored!

    Creation smiles in various beauty gay,
While day to night, and night succeeds to day: 30
That wisdom, which attends Jehovah's ways,
Shines most conspicuous in the solar rays:
Without them, destitute of heat and light,
This world would be the reign of endless night:
In their excess how would our race complain,   35
Abhorring life! how hate its lengthened chain!
From air adust[4] what numerous ills would rise?
What dire contagion taint the burning skies?
What pestilential vapors, fraught with death,
Would rise, and overspread the lands beneath?   40

    Hail, smiling morn, that from the orient main[5]
Ascending dost adorn the heavenly plain!
So rich, so various are thy beauteous dyes,

---

1. Angelic.   4. Dried up.
2. The sun.   5. Ocean. "Orient": eastern.
3. Apollo, the Greek sun god.

That spread through all the circuit of the skies,
That, full of thee, my soul in rapture soars,   45
And thy great God, the cause of all adores.

O'er beings infinite His love extends,
His wisdom rules them, and His power defends.
When tasks diurnal[6] tire the human frame,
The spirits faint, and dim the vital flame,   50
Then too that ever active bounty shines,
Which not infinity of space confines.
The sable veil, that night in silence draws,
Conceals effects, but shows the almighty cause;
Night seals in sleep the wide creation fair,   55
And all is peaceful but the brow of care.
Again, gay Phœbus, as the day before,
Wakes every eye, but what shall wake no more;
Again the face of nature is renewed,
Which still appears harmonious, fair, and good.   60
May grateful strains salute the smiling morn,
Before its beams the eastern hills adorn!

Shall day to day, and night to night conspire
To show the goodness of the Almighty Sire?
This mental voice shall man regardless hear,   65
And never, never raise the filial prayer?
Today, O hearken, nor your folly mourn
For time misspent, that never will return.

But see the sons of vegetation rise,
And spread their leafy banners to the skies.   70
All-wise Almighty providence we trace
In trees, and plants, and all the flowery race;
As clear as in the nobler frame of man,
All lovely copies of the Maker's plan.
The power the same that forms a ray of light,   75
That called creation from eternal night.
"Let there be light," He said: from His profound[7]
Old Chaos heard, and trembled at the sound:
Swift as the word, inspired by power divine,
Behold the light around its maker shine,   80
The first fair product of the omnific God,
And now through all His works diffused abroad.

As reason's powers by day our God disclose,
So we may trace Him in the night's repose:
Say what is sleep? and dreams how passing strange!   85
When action ceases, and ideas range
Licentious and unbounded o'er the plains,
Where Fancy's[8] queen in giddy triumph reigns.
Hear in soft strains the dreaming lover sigh

6. Daily.
7. A place in the depths of the ocean. "And God said,   Let there be light: and there was light" (Genesis 1.3).
8. The imagination in its image-making aspect.

To a kind fair, or rave in jealousy;   90
On pleasure now, and now on vengeance bent,
The laboring passions struggle for a vent.
What power, O man! thy reason then restores,
So long suspended in nocturnal hours?
What secret hand returns the mental train,   95
And gives improved thine active powers again?
From thee, O man, what gratitude should rise!
And, when from balmy sleep thou op'st thine eyes,⎫
Let thy first thoughts be praises to the skies. ⎭
How merciful our God who thus imparts   100
O'erflowing tides of joy to human hearts,
When wants and woes might be our righteous lot,
Our God forgetting, by our God forgot!

     Among the mental powers a question rose,
"What most the image of the Eternal shows?"   105
When thus to Reason (so let Fancy rove)
Her great companion spoke, immortal Love.

     "Say, mighty power, how long shall strife prevail,
And with its murmurs load the whispering gale?
Refer the cause to Recollection's shrine,   110
Who loud proclaims my origin divine,
The cause whence heaven and earth began to be,
And is not man immortalized by me?
Reason let this most causeless strife subside."
Thus Love pronounced, and Reason thus replied.   115

     "Thy birth, celestial queen! 'tis mine to own,
In thee resplendent is the Godhead shown;
Thy words persuade, my soul enraptured feels
Resistless beauty which thy smile reveals."
Ardent she spoke, and, kindling at her charms,   120
She clasped the blooming goddess in her arms.

     Infinite Love wher'er we turn our eyes
Appears: this every creature's wants supplies;
This most is heard in Nature's constant voice,
This makes the morn, and this is the eve rejoice;   125
This bids the fostering rains and dews descend
To nourish all, to serve one general end,
The good of man: yet man ungrateful pays
But little homage, and but little praise.
To Him, whose works arrayed with mercy shine,   130
What songs should rise, how constant, how divine!

                                                        1773

To S.M.,[1] a Young African Painter, on Seeing His Works

To show the laboring bosom's deep intent,
And thought in living characters to paint,
When first thy pencil did those beauties give,
And breathing figures learnt from thee to live,
How did those prospects give my soul delight,   5
A new creation rushing on my sight?
Still, wond'rous youth! each noble path pursue,
On deathless glories fix thine ardent view:
Still may the painter's and the poet's fire
To aid thy pencil, and thy verse conspire!   10
And may the charms of each seraphic[2] theme
Conduct thy footsteps to immortal fame!
High to the blissful wonders of the skies
Elate thy soul, and raise thy wishful eyes.
Thrice happy, when exalted to survey   15
That splendid city, crowned with endless day,
Whose twice six gates[3] on radiant hinges ring:
Celestial Salem[4] blooms in endless spring.

Calm and serene thy moments glide along,
And may the muse inspire each future song!   20
Still, with the sweets of contemplation blest,
May peace with balmy wings your soul invest!
But when these shades of time are chased away,
And darkness ends in everlasting day,
On what seraphic pinions shall we move,   25
And view the landscape in the realms above?
There shall thy tongue in heavenly murmurs flow,
And there my muse with heavenly transport glow:
No more to tell of Damon's[5] tender sighs,
Or rising radiance of Aurora's[6] eyes,   30
For nobler themes demand a nobler strain,
And purer language on the ethereal plain.
Cease, gentle muse! the solemn gloom of night
Now seals the fair creation from my sight.

1773

To His Excellency General Washington[1]

Sir. I have taken the freedom to address your Excellency in the enclosed poem, and entreat your acceptance, though I am not insensible of its inaccura-

---

1. Scipio Moorhead, a servant to the Rev. John Moorhead of Boston.
2. Angelic.
3. Heaven, like the city of Jerusalem, is thought to have had twelve gates (as many gates as tribes of Israel).
4. Heavenly Jerusalem.
5. In classical mythology Damon pledged his life for his friend Pythias.
6. The Roman goddess of the dawn.
1. This poem was first published in the *Pennsylvania Magazine* when Thomas Paine was editor. Washington invited Wheatley to meet him in Cambridge, Massachusetts, in February 1776, after reading it.

cies. Your being appointed by the Grand Continental Congress to be Generalissimo of the armies of North America, together with the fame of your virtues,
excite sensations not easy to suppress. Your generosity, therefore, I presume,
will pardon the attempt. Wishing your Excellency all possible success in the
great cause you are so generously engaged in. I am,

Your Excellency's most obedient humble servant,
Phillis Wheatley

Providence, Oct. 26, 1775.
His Excellency Gen. Washington.

> Celestial choir! enthroned in realms of light,
>   Columbia's[2] scenes of glorious toils I write.
> While freedom's cause her anxious breast alarms,
> She flashes dreadful in refulgent arms.
> See mother earth her offspring's fate bemoan,   5
> And nations gaze at scenes before unknown!
> See the bright beams of heaven's revolving light
> Involved in sorrows and the veil of night!
>   The goddess comes, she moves divinely fair,
> Olive and laurel[3] binds her golden hair: 10
> Wherever shines this native of the skies,
> Unnumbered charms and recent graces rise.
>   Muse! bow propitious while my pen relates
> How pour her armies through a thousand gates,
> As when Eolus[4] heaven's fair face deforms,   15
> Enwrapped in tempest and a night of storms;
> Astonished ocean feels the wild uproar,
> The refluent surges beat the sounding shore;
> Or thick as leaves in Autumn's golden reign,
> Such, and so many, moves the warrior's train.   20
> In bright array they seek the work of war,
> Where high unfurled the ensign[5] waves in air.
> Shall I to Washington their praise recite?
> Enough thou know'st them in the fields of fight.
> Thee, first in place and honors—we demand   25
> The grace and glory of thy martial band.
> Famed for thy valor, for thy virtues more,
> Heart every tongue thy guardian aid implore!
>   One century scarce performed its destined round,
> When Gallic[6] powers Columbia's fury found;   30
> And so may you, whoever dares disgrace
> The land of freedom's heaven-defended race!
> Fixed are the eyes of nations on the scales,
> For in their hopes Columbia's arm prevails.
> Anon Britannia droops the pensive head,   35
> While round increase the rising hills of dead.

---

2. This reference to America as "the land Columbus found" is believed to be the first in print.
3. Emblems of victory.
4. Keeper of the winds.

5. Flag or banner.
6. The French and Indian War (1754–63) comprised four wars between France and England, which actually ended the French colonial empire in North America.

Ah! cruel blindness to Columbia's state!
Lament thy thirst of boundless power too late.
  Proceed, great chief, with virtue on thy side,
Thy every action let the goddess guide.   Th)T40
A crown, a mansion, and a throne that shine,
With gold unfading, WASHINGTON! be thine.

1775–76   1776, 1834

Letters

To John Thornton,[1] London

[THE BIBLE MY CHIEF STUDY]

[Boston, April 21, 1772]

Hon'd, Sir

I rec'd your instructive fav[r2] of Feb. 29, for which, return you ten thousand thanks, I did not flatter myself with the tho'ts of your honouring me with an Answer to my letter, I thank you for recommending the Bible to be my chief Study, I find and Acknowledge it the best of Books, it contains an endless treasure of wisdom, and knowledge. O that my eyes were more open'd to see the real worth, and true excellence of the word of truty, my flinty heart Soften'd with the grateful dews of divine grace and the Stubborn will, and affections, bent on God alone their proper object, and the vitiated palate may be corrected to relish heav'nly things. It has pleas'd God to lay me on a bed of Sickness, and I knew not but my deathbed, but he has been graciously pleas'd to restore me in a great measure. I beg your prayers, that I may be made thankful for his paternal corrections, and that I may make a proper use of them to the glory of his grace. I am Still very weak & the Physicians, seem to think there is danger of a consumpsion. And O that when my flesh and my heart fail me God would be my strength and portion for ever. that I might put my whole trust and Confidence in him, who has promis'd never to forsake those who Seek him with the whole heart. You could not, I am sure have express greater tenderness and affection for me, than by being a welwisher to my Soul, the friends of Souls bear Some resemblance to the father of Spirits and are made partakers of his divine Nature.

I am affraid I have entruded on your patient, but if I had not tho't it ungrateful to omit writing in answer to your favour Should not have troubl'd you, but I can't expect you to answer this,

I am Sir with greatest respect,
your very hum. sert.
Phillis Wheatley

---

1. A London merchant (1720–1790), who was a devout Anglican and lived outside London at Clapham, where a small group of Christians were committed to helping the poor and abolishing slavery. He was a friend of John and Susannah Wheatley and sent them money to be used for work among the American Indians.
2. Favor, i.e., letter.

To Arbour Tanner,[3] Newport, Rhode Island

[A SENSE OF THE BEAUTIES AND EXCELLENCE OF THE CRUCIFIED
SAVIOUR]

[Boston, May 19, 1772]

Dear Sister

I rec'd your favour of February 6th for which I give you my sincere thanks,
I greatly rejoice with you in that realizing view,[4] and I hope experience, of the
Saving change which you So emphatically describe. Happy were it for us if we
could arrive to that evangelical Repentance, and the true holiness of heart
which you mention. Inexpressibly happy Should we be could we have a due
Sense of the Beauties and excellence of the Crucified Saviour. In his Crucifixion may be seen marvellous displays of Grace and Love, Sufficient to draw
and invite us to the rich and endless treasures of his mercy, let us rejoice in
and adore the wonders of God's infinite Love in bringing us from a land Sem-
blant of darkness itself, and where the divine light of revelation (being
obscur'd) is as darkness. Here, the knowledge of the true God and eternal life
are made manifest; But there, profound ignorance overshadows the Land,
Your observation is true, namely, that there was nothing in us to recommend
us to God. Many of our fellow creatures are pass'd by, when the bowels[5] of
divine love expanded towards us. May this goodness & long Suffering of God
lead us to unfeign'd repentance

It gives me very great pleasure to hear of so many of my Nation, Seeking
with eagerness the way to true felicity, O may we all meet at length in that
happy mansion. I hope the correspondence between us will continue, (my
being much indispos'd this winter past was the reason of my not answering
yours before now) which correspondence I hope may have the happy effect of
improving our mutual friendship. Till we meet in the regions of consummate
blessedness, let us endeavor by the assistance of divine grace, to live the life,
and we Shall die the death of the Righteous. May this be our happy case and
of those who are travelling to the region of Felicity is the earnest request of
your affectionate

Friend & hum. Sert.   Phillis Wheatley

To John Thornton, London

[THE GIFT OF GOD IS ETERNAL LIFE]

[Boston, December 1, 1773]

Hon'd Sir

It is with great satisfaction, I acquaint you with my experience of the goodness of God in safely conducting my passage over the mighty waters, and
returning me in safety to my American Friends.[6] I presume you will Join with
them and m[e] in praise to God for so distinguishing a favour, it was amazing
Mercy, altogether unmerited by me: and if possible it is augmented by the
consideration of the bitter r[e]verse, which is the deserved wages of my evil

---

3. There are more extant Wheatley letters to Arbour
(sometimes spelled "Obour") Tanner, a black servant
in the family of James Tanner, than to any other
person.
4. I.e., to a new realization of Christianity.

5. The seat of compassion.
6. Wheatley accompanied John Wheatley to London
in the spring of 1773 and returned to Boston hurriedly
when they received news of Susannah Wheatley's illness. They arrived in Boston on September 13.

doings. The Apostle Paul, tells us that the wages of Sin is death.[7] I don't imagine he excepted any sin whatsoever being equally hateful in its nature in the sight of God, who is essential Purity.

Should we not sink hon'd Sir, under this Sentence of Death, pronounced on every Sin, from the comparatively least to the greatest, were not this blessed Co[n]trast annexed to it, "But the Gift of God is eternal Life,["] through Jesus Christ our Lord? It is his Gift. O let us be thankful for it! What a load is taken from the Sinner's Shoulder when he thinks that Jesus has done that work for him which he could never have done, and Suffer'd, that punishment of his imputed Rebellions, for which a long Eternity of Torments could not have made sufficient expiation. O that I could meditate continually on this work of wonde[r] in Deity itself. This, which Kings & Prophets have desir'd to see, & have not See[n]. This, which Angels are continually exploring, et are not equal to the search,—Millions of Ages shall roll away, and they may try in vain to find out to perfection, the sublime mysteries of Christ's Incarnation. Nor will this desir[e] to look into the deep things of God, cease, in the Breasts of glorified Saints & Angels. It's duration will be coeval with Eternity. This Eternity how dreadf[ul,] how delightful! Delightful to those who have an interest in the Crucifi[ed] Saviour, who has dignified our Nature, by seating it at the Right Hand of the divine Majesty.—They alone who are thus interested have Cause to rejoi[ce] even on the brink of that Bottomless Profound: and I doubt not (without the [lea]st Adulation) that you are one of that happy number. O pray that I may be one also, who Shall Join with you in Songs of praise at the Throne of him, who is no respecter of Persons: being equally the great Maker of all:—Therefor disdain not to be called the Father of Humble Africans and Indians; though despisd on earth on account of our colour, we have this Consolation, if he enables us to deserve it. "That God dwells in the humble & contrite heart." O that I were more & more possess'd of this inestimable blessing; to be directed by the immediate influence of the divine Spirit in my daily walk & Conversation.

Do you, my hon'd Sir, who have abundant Reason to be thankful for the great Share you possess of it, be always mindful in your Closet, of those who want it—of me in particular.— When I first arrivd at home my mistress was so bad as not to be expected to live above two or three days, but through the goodness of God She is still alive, but remains in a very weak & languishing Condition, She begs a continued interest in your most earnest prayers, that she may be surly prepar'd for that great Change which [She] is likely Soon to undergo; She intreats you, as her Son is Still in England, that you would take all opportun[i]ties to advise & counsel him; She says she is going to leave him & desires you'd be a Spiritual Fath[er] to hi[m]. She will take it very kind. *She thanks you heartily for the kind notice you took of me while in England.* Pleas[e] to give my best Respects to Mrs. & miss Thornton, and masters Henry and Robert who held with me a long conversation on many subjects which Mrs. Drinkwater[8] knows very well, hope she is in better Health than when I left her. Please to remember me to your whole family & I than[k] them for their kindness to me. begging Still an interest in your best hours
I am Hon'd Sir

most respectfully your Humble Servt.
Phillis Wheatley

7. "The wages of sin is death; but the gift of God is eternal life" (Romans 6.23).   8. A mutual friend.

I have written to Mrs. Wilberforce[9] Sometime since Please to give my duty to her; Since writing the above the Rev'd Mr. Moorhead[1] has made his Exit from this world, in whom we lament the loss of the Zealous Pious & true christian

To Rev. Samson Occom,[2] New London, Connecticut

[THE NATURAL RIGHTS OF NEGROES]

[February 11, 1774]

"Rev'd and honor'd Sir,

I have this Day received your obliging kind Epistle, and am greatly satisfied with your Reasons respecting the Negroes, and think highly reasonable what you offer in Vindication of their natural Rights: Those that invade them cannot be insensible that the divine Light is chasing away the thick Darkness[3] which broods over the Land of Africa; and the Chaos which has reign'd so long, is converting into beautiful Order, and [r]eveals more and more clearly, the glorious Dispensation of civil and religious Liberty, which are so inseparably united, that there is little or no Enjoyment of one without the other: Otherwise, perhaps, the Israelites had been less solicitous for their Freedom from Egyptian slavery; I do not say they would have been contented without it, by no means, for in every human Breast, God has implanted a Principle, which we call Love of Freedom; it is impatient of Oppression, and pants for Deliverance; and by the Leave of our modern Egyptians I will assert, that the same Principle lives in us. God grant Deliverance in his own Way and Time, and get him honour upon all those whose Avarice impels them to countenance and help forward the Calamities of their fellow Creatures. This I desire not for their Hurt, but to convince them of the strange Absurdity of their Conduct whose Words and Actions are so diametrically opposite. How well the Cry for Liberty, and the reverse Disposition for the exercise of oppressive Power over others agree,—I humbly think it does not require the Penetration of a philosopher to determine."—

To John Thornton, London

[THE DEATH OF MRS. WHEATLEY]

[Boston, March 29, 1774]

Much honoured Sir,

I should not so soon have troubled you with the 2d. Letter, but the mournful *Occasion* will sufficiently Apologize. It is the death of Mrs. Wheatley. She has been labouring under a languishing illness for many months past and has at length took he flight from hence to those blissful regions, which need not the light of any, but the Sun of Righteousness. O could you have been present, to See how She long'd to drop the tabernacle of Clay, and to be freed from the cumbrous Shackles of a mortal Body, which had so many Times retarded her desires when Soaring upward. She has often told me how your Letters hav[e] quicken'd her in her spiritual Course: when She has been in darkness of mind

9. Thornton's sister.
1. The Rev. John Moorhead (d. 1773) came to Boston from Scotland in 1730 and was the pastor of a Scotch Presbyterian church near the Wheatley home. Wheatley wrote an elegy on his death and dedicated it to his daughter Mary.
2. A Mohegan Indian (1723–1792) born and living in New London; he was in England from 1766 to 1767.

Mason notes that Occom, an ordained Presbyterian minister and friend of the Wheatleys, suggested to Wheatley that she go to Africa as a missionary, but she rejected the idea.
3. "And Moses stretched forth his hand toward heaven; and there was a thick darkness in all the land of Egypt three days" (Exodus 10.22).

they have rais'd and enliven'd her insomuch, that She went on, with chearful-n[ess] and alacrity in the path of her duty. She did truely, *run with patience the race that was Set before her,*[4] and hath, at length obtained the celestial Goal. She is now Sure, that the afflictions of this present time, were not wor-thy to be compared to the Glory, which is now, revealed in her, Seeing they have wrought out for her, *a far more exceeding and eternal weight of Glory:*[5] This, Sure, is Sufficient encouragement under the bitterest Sufferings, which we can endure.—About half an hour before her Death, She Spoke with a more audible voice, than She had for 3 months before. She calld. her friends & relations around her, and charg'd them not to leave their great work undone till *that* hour, but to fear God, and keep his Commandments. being ask'd if her faith faild her She answer'd, No. Then Spr[ead] out her arms crying come! come quickly! come, come! O pray for an eas[y] and quick Passage! She eagerly longed to depart to be with Christ. She retaind her Senses till the very last moment when "fare well, fare well." with a very low voice, were the last words She utter'd. I sat the whole time by her bed Side, and Saw with Grief and Wonder, the Effects of Sin on the human race. Had not Christ taken away the envenom'd Sting, where had been our hopes? what might we not have fear'd, what might we not have expectd from the dreadful King of Ter-rors? But *this* is matter of endless praise, to the King eternal immortal, invisi-ble, that, *it is finished.* I hope her Son will be interested in Your Closet duties,[6] & that the prayers which she was continually putting up, & wch. are recorded before God, in the Book of his remembrance for her Son & for me may be answer'd, I can Scarcely think that an Object of so many prayers, will fail of the Blessings implor'd for him ever Since he was born. I intreat the same Interest in your best thoughts for my Self, that her prayers, in my behalf, may be favour'd with an Answer of *Peace.* We received and forwarded your Letter to the rev'd Mr. Occom, but first, took the freedom to peruse it, and am exceeding glad, that you have order'd him to draw immediately for £25. for I really think he is in absolute necessity for that and as much more, he is so loth to run in debt for fear he Shall not be able to repay, that he has not the Least Shelter for his Creatures to defend them from the inclemencies of the weather, and he has lost some already for want of it, His hay is quite as defenceless, thus the former are in a fair way of being lost, and the latter to be wasted; It were to be wished that his *dwelling house* was like the Ark, with appartments, to contain the beasts and their provision; He said Mrs. Wheatley and the rev'd Mr. Moorhead were his best friends in Boston, But alass! they are gone. I trust gone to recieve the rewards promis'd to those, who Offer a Cup of cold water in the name & for the sake of Jesus—They have both been very instrum[ental in meetin]g the wants of that child of God, Mr. Occom— but I fear your pa[tience has been] exhausted, it remains only that we thank you for your kind Letter to my mistress it came above a fortnight after her Death.—Hoping for an interest in your prayers for these [and then] Sanctifici-ation of this bereaving Providence, I am hon'd Sir with dutiful respect ever your obliged

and devoted Humble Servant   Phillis Wheatley

---

4. "Wherefore seeing we also are compassed about with so great a cloud of witnesses, let us lay aside every weight, and the sin which doth so easily beset us, and let us run with patience the race that is set before us" (Hebrews 12.1).

5. "For our light affliction, which is but for a moment, worketh for us a far more exceeding and eternal weight of glory" (2 Corinthians 4.17).

6. I.e., his meditations and prayers.

JOEL BARLOW
1754–1812

In 1779 Joel Barlow wrote to his former Yale College roommate Noah Webster that "The American Republic is a fine theater for the display of merit of every kind. If ever virtue is to be rewarded, it is in America." Barlow spent most of his life affirming the virtues of America, and one feels something of the exuberance and confidence of the early years of the Republic in almost all his verse.

Barlow was the son of a wealthy Connecticut farmer, and he seems to have done everything he pleased. He was brought up on the family farm in Redding and attended the Morris School in Hanover, New Hampshire, enrolling at Dartmouth for a few months before entering the freshman class at Yale. In the summer of 1776 he fought on the side of the American Revolutionary Army at the battle of Long Island, returning to Yale in the fall and graduating in 1778. Shortly after graduation he moved to Hartford, Connecticut, where he helped to edit a newspaper and ran a stationery business. It was in Hartford that he joined a literary circle that became known as the "Hartford" or "Connecticut Wits," a group of nine ambitious young writers who wished to celebrate American literary independence and keep a critical eye on the follies of democracy. Next to Barlow the most famous of this group were Timothy Dwight (1752–1817), president of Yale, and John Trumbull (1750–1831), author of a satire on American education called *The Progress of Dullness*.

Barlow was always restless in his occupations, and when the *American Mercury* ceased publication he made plans to leave Hartford. In 1778 Barlow and his wife left for Europe, and they remained there seventeen years. Barlow became a wealthy man as an agent for American landholding companies, overseeing the sale of farmland to potential immigrants. It was while living abroad that Barlow changed from a political conservative to an ardent spokesman for the French Revolution. In 1791, when Thomas Paine was imprisoned in Paris, it was Barlow who saw to the publication of *The Age of Reason*. His own collection of essays in favor of the natural rights of man, *Advice to Privileged Orders* (1792), reflects the influence of Paine, and its publication in London forced Barlow to leave that city for Paris.

Barlow was a popular figure in France and was made an honorary citizen. He was serious enough about French politics to run for election as deputy to the French National Assembly. It was while in Savoy, campaigning, that he was served a bowl of hasty pudding, and he took that occasion as the subject of his most famous poem, a mock epic (that is, a poem that brings to a trivial subject all the literary conventions usually brought to bear on a poem treating a monumental event) that celebrates the glories of American simplicity over the sophisticated decadence of courtly Europe.

On Barlow's return to America in 1805, he established his family in a beautiful home in Washington, D.C., and set about completing the second revision of *The Vision of Columbus*, a poem he had first published almost twenty years before. *The Columbiad*, as the poem was now called, turned out to be a very patriotic poem (almost unreadable today), in which the glories of the American future are sharply contrasted with Europe's past. The poem had many famous admirers, including George Washington and Thomas Paine, and it made Barlow a national figure, able to travel in the most influential national political circles.

Barlow was working on a history of the United States when President James Madison appointed him minister to France. Barlow's special task was to get a commitment from Emperor Napoleon for more favorable treatment of American commerce, and Barlow set out to meet the emperor in Poland, only to learn, by the time he had caught up with him, of Napoleon's defeat and long death-march home. Barlow wrote *Advice to a Raven in Russia* just before he himself turned back toward Paris. Before he could begin his journey he caught pneumonia and died in a village near Cracow, where he is buried.

The Hasty Pudding[1]

A *Poem, in Three Cantos*

WRITTEN AT CHAMBERY, IN SAVOY,[2] JANUARY, 1793

Omne tulit punctum qui miscuit utile dulci.[3]
He makes a good breakfast who mixes pudding with molasses.

PREFACE

A simplicity in diet, whether it be considered with reference to the happiness of individuals or the prosperity of a nation, is of more consequence than we are apt to imagine. In recommending so important an object to the rational part of mankind, I wish it were in my power to do it in such a manner as would be likely to gain their attention. I am sensible that it is one of those subjects in which example has infinitely more power than the most convincing arguments or the highest charms of poetry. Goldsmith's *Deserted Village*,[4] though possessing these two advantages in a greater degree than any other work of the kind, has not prevented villages in England from being deserted. The apparent interest of the rich individuals, who form the taste as well as the laws in that country, has been against him; and with that interest it has been vain to contend.

The vicious habits which in this little piece I endeavor to combat, seem to me not so difficult to cure. No class of people has any interest in supporting them; unless it be the interest which certain families may feel in vying with each other in sumptuous entertainments. There may indeed be some instances of depraved appetites, which no arguments will conquer; but these must be rare. There are very few persons but what would always prefer a plain dish for themselves, and would prefer it likewise for their guests, if there were no risk of reputation in the case. This difficulty can only be removed by example; and the example should proceed from those whose situation enables them to take the lead in forming the manners of a nation. Persons of this description in America, I should hope, are neither above nor below the influence of truth and reason, when conveyed in language suited to the subject.

Whether the manner I have chosen to address my arguments to them be such as to promise any success is what I cannot decide. But I certainly had hopes of doing some good, or I should not have taken the pains of putting so many rhymes together. The example of domestic virtues has doubtless a great effect. I only wish to rank simplicity of diet among the virtues. In that case I should hope it will be cherished and more esteemed by others than it is at present.

The Author

1. A breakfast dish often made from flour and milk but in America made from Indian corn and water. The text used here is from that published by Fellow and Adam (1796).
2. France.
3. He who combines the useful and the pleasing wins the approval of all (Latin; Horace *Ars Poetica*, line 343).
4. *The Deserted Village*, by Oliver Goldsmith (1728–1774), is a poem that idealizes English rural life as young people leave the farms and move to industrial centers.

CANTO I

Ye Alps audacious, through the heavens that rise,
To cramp the day and hide me from the skies;
Ye Gallic flags,[5] that o'er their heights unfurled,
Bear death to kings, and freedom to the world,
I sing not you. A softer theme I choose,   5
A virgin theme, unconscious of the muse,
But fruitful, rich, well suited to inspire
The purest frenzy of poetic fire.
    Despise it not, ye bards to terror steeled,
Who hurl your thunders round the epic field;   10
Nor ye who strain your midnight throats to sing
Joys that the vineyard and the stillhouse[6] bring;
Or on some distant fair your notes employ,
And speak of raptures that you ne'er enjoy.
I sing the sweets I know, the charms I feel,   15
My morning incense, and my evening meal,
The sweets of Hasty Pudding. Come, dear bowl,
Glide o'er my palate, and inspire my soul.
The milk beside thee, smoking from the kine,[7]
Its substance mingled, married in with thine,   20
Shall cool and temper thy superior heat,
And save the pains of blowing while I eat.
    Oh! could the smooth, the emblematic song
Flow like thy genial juices o'er my tongue,
Could those mild morsels in my numbers chime,   25
And, as they roll in substance, roll in rhyme,
No more thy awkward unpoetic name
Should shun the muse, or prejudice thy fame;
But rising grateful to the accustomed ear,
All bards should catch it, and all realms revere!   30
    Assist me first with pious toil to trace
Through wrecks of time thy lineage and thy race;
Declare what lovely squaw, in days of yore,
(Ere great Columbus sought thy native shore)
First gave thee to the world; her works of fame   35
Have lived indeed, but lived without a name.
Some tawny Ceres,[8] goddess of her days,
First learned with stones to crack the well-dried maize,
Through the rough sieve to shake the golden shower,
In boiling water stir the yellow flour: 40
The yellow flour, bestrewed and stirred with yeast,
Swells in the flood and thickens to a paste,
Then puffs and wallops,[9] rises to the brim,
Drinks the dry knobs that on the surface swim;
The knobs at last the busy ladle breaks,   45
And the whole mass its true consistence takes.
    Could but her sacred name, unknown so long,
Rise, like her labors, to the son of song,

---

5. Savoy, which was once a part of the kingdom of
Sardinia, was annexed by France in 1792.
6. Distillery.

7. Cattle.
8. Roman goddess of agriculture.
9. Bubbles.

To her, to them, I'd consecrate my lays,
And blow her pudding with the breath of praise.   50
If 'twas Oella, whom I sang before,
I here ascribe her one great virtue more.
Not through the rich Peruvian realms alone
The fame of Sol's[1] sweet daughter should be known,
But o'er the world's wide climes should live secure,   55
Far as his rays extend, as long as they endure.

    Dear Hasty Pudding, what unpromised joy
Expands my heart, to meet thee in Savoy!
Doomed o'er the world through devious paths to roam,
Each clime my country, and each house my home,   60
My soul is soothed, my cares have found an end,
I greet my long-lost, unforgotten friend.

    For thee through Paris, that corrupted town,
How long in vain I wandered up and down,
Where shameless Bacchus,[2] with his drenching hoard,   65
Cold from his cave usurps the morning board.
London is lost in smoke and steeped in tea;
No Yankee there can lisp the name of thee;
The uncouth word, a libel on the town,
Would call a proclamation from the crown.[3]   70
For climes oblique, that fear the sun's full rays,
Chilled in their fogs, exclude the generous maize;
A grain whose rich luxuriant growth requires
Short gentle showers, and bright ethereal fires.

    But here, though distant from our native shore,   75
With mutual glee we meet and laugh once more.
The same! I know thee by that yellow face,
That strong complexion of true Indian race,
Which time can never change, nor soil impair,
Nor Alpine snows, nor Turkey's morbid air;   80
For endless years, through every mild domain,
Where grows the maize, there thou art sure to reign.

    But man, more fickle, the bold license claims,
In different realms to give thee different names.
Thee the soft nations round the warm Levant[4]   85
Polanta call, the French of course *Polenta;*[5]
Ev'n in thy native regions, how I blush
To hear the Pennsylvanians call thee *mush!*
On Hudson's banks, while men of Belgic spawn[6]
Insult and eat thee by the name *suppawn.*[7]   90
All spurious appellations, void of truth;
I've better known thee from my earliest youth,
Thy name is *Hasty Pudding!* thus our sires
Were wont to greet thee fuming from their fires;

1. The sun. "Oella": legendary Inca princess, daughter of Sol and the inventor of spinning; referred to by Barlow in his *Vision of Columbus* (1787).
2. Roman god of wine.
3. "A certain king, at the time when this was written, was publishing proclamations to prevent American principles from being propagated in his country" [Barlow's note]. The king referred to is England's George III.
4. The coastlands of the eastern Mediterranean.
5. Italian and French for cooked cornmeal.
6. I.e., Dutch ancestry.
7. An approximation of the eastern American Indian word for cornmeal mush.

And while they argued in thy just defense   95
With logic clear, they thus explained the sense:
"In *haste* the boiling cauldron, o'er the blaze,
Receives and cooks the ready-powdered maize;
In *haste* 'tis served, and then in equal *haste*,
With cooling milk, we make the sweet repast.   100
No carving to be done, no knife to grate
The tender ear, and wound the stony plate;
But the smooth spoon, just fitted to the lip,
And taught with art the yielding mass to dip,
By frequent journeys to the bowl well stored,   105
Performs the hasty honors of the board."
Such is thy name, significant and clear,
A name, a sound to every Yankee dear,
But most to me, whose heart and palate chaste
Preserve my pure hereditary taste.   110
          There are who strive to stamp with disrepute
The luscious food, because it feeds the brute;
In tropes[8] of high-strained wit, while gaudy prigs
Compare thy nursling man to pampered pigs;
With sovereign scorn I treat the vulgar jest,   115
Nor fear to share thy bounties with the beast.
What though the generous cow gives me to quaff
The milk nutritious; am I then a calf?
Or can the genius of the noisy swine,
Though nursed on pudding, thence lay claim to mine?   120
Sure the sweet song, I fashion to thy praise,
Runs more melodious than the notes they raise.
          My song resounding in its grateful glee,
No merit claims; I praise myself in thee.
My father loved thee through his length of days;   125
For thee his fields were shaded o'er with maize;
From thee what health, what vigor he possessed,
Ten sturdy freemen from his loins attest;
Thy constellation ruled my natal morn,
And all my bones were made of Indian corn.   130
Delicious grain! whatever form it take,
To roast or boil, to smother or to bake,
In every dish 'tis welcome still to me,
But most, my Hasty Pudding, most in thee.
          Let the green succotash with thee contend,   135
Let beans and corn their sweetest juices blend,
Let butter drench them in its yellow tide,
And a long slice of bacon grace their side;
Not all the plate, how famed soe'er it be,
Can please my palate like a bowl of thee.   140
          Some talk of hoe-cake, fair Virginia's pride,
Rich Johnny-cake this mouth has often tried;
Both please me well, their virtues much the same,
Alike their fabric, as allied their fame,
Except in dear New England, where the last   145

8. Figures of speech.

Receives a dash of pumpkin in the paste,
To give it sweetness and improve the taste.
But place them all before me, smoking hot,
The big round dumpling rolling from the pot;
The pudding of the bag, whose quivering breast,   150
With suet lined, leads on the Yankee feast;
The charlotte brown, within whose crusty sides
A belly soft the pulpy apple hides;
The yellow bread, whose face like amber glows,
And all of Indian that the bakepan knows   155
You tempt me not—my favorite greets my eyes,
To that loved bowl my spoon by instinct flies.

CANTO II

To mix the food by vicious rules of art,
To kill the stomach and to sink the heart,
To make mankind to social virtue sour,   160
Cram o'er each dish, and be what they devour;
For this the kitchen muse first framed her book,
Commanding sweat to stream from every cook;
Children no more their antic gambols tried,
And friends to physic[9] wondered why they died.   165
Not so the Yankee—his abundant feast,
With simples furnished, and with plainness dressed,
A numerous offspring gathers round the board,
And cheers alike the servant and the lord;
Whose well-bought hunger prompts the joyous taste,   170
And health attends them from the short repast.
While the full pail rewards the milkmaid's toil,
The mother sees the morning cauldron boil;
To stir the pudding next demands their care,
To spread the table and the bowls prepare;   175
To feed the children, as their portions cool,
And comb their heads, and send them off to school.
Yet may the simplest dish some rules impart,
For nature scorns not all the aids of art.
Ev'n Hasty Pudding, purest of all food,   180
May still be bad, indifferent, or good,
As sage experience the short process guides,
Or want of skill, or want of care presides,
Whoe'er would form it on the surest plan,
To rear the child and long sustain the man;   185
To shield the morals while it mends the size,
And all the powers of every food supplies,
Attend the lessons that the muse shall bring.
Suspend your spoons, and listen while I sing.
But since, O man! thy life and health demand   190
Not food alone, but labor from thy hand,
First in the field, beneath the sun's strong rays,
Ask of thy mother earth the needful maize;

9. Science.

She loves the race that courts her yielding soil,
And gives her bounties to the sons of toil.   195
When now the ox, obedient to thy call,
Repays the loan that filled the winter stall,
Pursue his traces o'er the furrowed plain,
And plant in measured hills the golden grain.
But when the tender germ begins to shoot,   200

And the green spire declares the sprouting root,
Then guard your nursling from each greedy foe,
The insidious worm, the all-devouring crow.
A little ashes, sprinkled round the spire,
Soon steeped in rain, will bid the worm retire;   205
The feathered robber with his hungry maw
Swift flies the field before your man of straw,
A frightful image, such as schoolboys bring
When met to burn the Pope or hang the King.[1]
   Thrice in the season, through each verdant row   210
Wield the strong plowshare and the faithful hoe;
The faithful hoe, a double task that takes,
To till the summer corn, and roast the winter cakes.
   Slow springs the blade, while checked by chilling rains,
Ere yet the sun the seat of Cancer[2] gains;   215
But when his fiercest fires emblaze the land,
Then start the juices, then the roots expand;
Then, like a column of Corinthian mold,[3]
The stalk struts upward, and the leaves unfold;
The bushy branches all the ridges fill,   220
Entwine their arms, and kiss from hill to hill.
Here cease to vex them, all your cares are done;
Leave the last labors to the parent sun;
Beneath his genial smiles the well-dressed field,
When autumn calls, a plenteous crop shall yield.   225
   Now the strong foliage bears the standards high,
And shoots the tall top-gallants[4] to the sky;
The suckling ears their silky fringes bend,
And pregnant grown, their swelling coats distend;
The loaded stalk, while still the burden grows,   230
O'erhangs the space that runs between the rows;
High as a hop-field waves the silent grove,
A safe retreat for little thefts of love,
When the pledged roasting ears invite the maid,
To meet her swain beneath the new-formed shade;   235
His generous hand unloads the cumbrous hill,
And the green spoils her ready basket fill;
Small compensation for the two-fold bliss,

---

1. The English celebrate Guy Fawkes Day on November 5, the anniversary of the day in 1605 when a Roman Catholic plot to blow up Parliament and assassinate the king was discovered. In New England it was called Pope Day (or Pope Night), and schoolboys burned effigies of the Pope. Gradually, anti-Catholic sentiment was transformed to antimonarchial protests.
2. The sign of the zodiac that begins on June 21, the summer solstice.
3. An ornate Greek column with leaves on the capital.
4. Upper masts and sails on a full-rigged ship.

The promised wedding and the present kiss.
  Slight depredations these; but now the moon   240
Calls from his hollow tree the sly raccoon;
And while by night he bears his prize away,
The bolder squirrel labors through the day.
Both thieves alike, but provident of time,
A virtue rare, that almost hides their crime.   245
Then let them steal the little stores they can,
And fill their granaries from the toils of man;
We've one advantage where they take no part,
With all their wiles they ne'er have found the art
To boil the Hasty Pudding; here we shine   250
Superior far to tenants of the pine;
This envied boon to man shall still belong,
Unshared by them in substance or in song.
At last the closing season browns the plain,
And ripe October gathers in the grain;   255
Deep loaded carts the spacious corn-house fill,
The sack distended marches to the mill;
The laboring mill beneath the burthen groans,
And showers the future pudding from the stones;
Till the glad housewife greets the powdered gold,   260
And the new crop exterminates the old.

CANTO III

  The days grow short; but though the falling sun
To the glad swain proclaims his day's work done,
Night's pleasant shades his various tasks prolong,
And yield new subjects to my various song.   265
For now, the corn-house filled, the harvest home,
The invited neighbors to the husking[5] come;
A frolic scene, where work, and mirth, and play,
Unite their charms, to chase the hours away.
  Where the huge heap lies centered in the hall,   270
The lamp suspended from the cheerful wall,
Brown corn-fed nymphs, and strong hard-handed beaux,
Alternate ranged, extend in circling rows,
Assume their seats, the solid mass attack;
The dry husks rustle, and the corncobs crack;   275
The song, the laugh, alternate notes resound,
And the sweet cider trips in silence round.
  The laws of husking every wight[6] can tell;
And sure no laws he ever keeps so well:
For each red ear a general kiss he gains,   280
With each smut ear he smuts the luckless swains;[7]
But when to some sweet maid a prize is cast,
Red as her lips, and taper as her waist,
She walks the round, and culls one favored beau,
Who leaps the luscious tribute to bestow.   285

5. A party for husking corn.
6. Individual.

7. Marks the young men with ears of fungus-blackened corn.

Various the sports, as are the wits and brains
Of well-pleased lasses and contending swains;
Till the vast mound of corn is swept away,
And he that gets the last ear wins the day.
    Meanwhile the housewife urges all her care,   290
The well-earned feast to hasten and prepare.
The sifted meal already waits her hand,
The milk is strained, the bowls in order stand,
The fire flames high; and, as a pool (that takes
The headlong stream that o'er the milldam breaks)   295
Foams, roars, and rages with incessant toils,
So the vexed cauldron rages, roars, and boils.
    First with clean salt she seasons well the food,
Then strews the flour, and thickens all the flood.
Long o'er the simmering fire she lets it stand;   300
To stir it well demands a stronger hand;
The husband takes his turn; and round and round
The ladle flies: at last the toil is crowned;
When to the board the thronging huskers pour,
And take their seats as at the corn before.   305
    I leave them to their feast. There still belong
More copious matters to my faithful song.
For rules there are, though ne'er unfolded yet,
Nice[8] rules and wise, how pudding should be ate.
    Some with molasses line the luscious treat,   310
And mix, like bards, the useful with the sweet.
A wholesome dish, and well deserving praise,
A great resource in those bleak wintry days,
When the chilled earth lies buried deep in snow,
And raging Boreas[9] drives the shivering cow.   315
    Blessed cow! thy praise shall still my notes employ,
Great source of health, the only source of joy;
Mother of Egypt's God[1]—but sure, for me,
Were I to leave my God, I'd worship thee.
How oft thy teats these pious hands have pressed!   320
How oft thy bounties proved my only feast!
How oft I've fed thee with my favorite grain!
And roared, like thee, to find thy children slain!
    Ye swains who know her various worth to prize,
Ah! house her well from winter's angry skies.   325
Potatoes, pumpkins, should her sadness cheer,
Corn from your crib, and mashes from your beer;
When spring returns she'll well acquaint the loan,
And nurse at once your infants and her own.
    Milk then with pudding I should always choose;   330
To this in future I confine my Muse,
Till she in haste some further hints unfold,
Well for the young, nor useless to the old.
First in your bowl the milk abundant take,
Then drop with care along the silver lake   335

8. Precise; subtle.
9. In Greek mythology the north wind.

1. The goddess Nut, mother of Osiris, was sometimes depicted as a cow.

Your flakes of pudding; these at first will hide
Their little bulk beneath the swelling tide;
But when their growing mass no more can sink,
When the soft island looms above the brink,
Then check your hand; you've got the portion's due,   340
So taught our sires, and what they taught is true.
    There is a choice in spoons. Though small appear
The nice distinction, yet to me 'tis clear.
The deep-bowled Gallic spoon, contrived to scoop
In ample draughts the thin diluted soup,   345
Performs not well in those substantial things,
Whose mass adhesive to the metal clings;
Where the strong labial muscles must embrace,
The gentle curve, and sweep the hollow space.
With ease to enter and discharge the freight,   350
A bowl less concave but still more dilate,
Becomes the pudding best. The shape, the size,
A secret rests unknown to vulgar eyes.
Experienced feeders can alone impart
A rule so much above the lore of art.   355
These tuneful lips that thousand spoons have tried,
With just precision could the point decide,
Though not in song; the Muse but poorly shines
In cones, and cubes, and geometric lines;
Yet the true form, as near as she can tell,   360
Is that small section of a goose-egg shell,
Which in two equal portions shall divide
The distance from the center to the side.
    Fear not to slaver; 'tis no deadly sin.
Like the free Frenchman, from your joyous chin   365
Suspend the ready napkin; or, like me,
Poise with one hand your bowl upon your knee;
Just in the zenith your wise head project,
Your full spoon, rising in a line direct,
Bold as a bucket, heeds no drops that fall,   370
The wide-mouthed bowl will surely catch them all.

1793   1796

Advice to a Raven in Russia[1]

December 1812

Black fool, why winter here? These frozen skies,
Worn by your wings and deafened by your cries,
Should warn you hence, where milder suns invite,
And day alternates with his mother night.

1. Barlow wrote this poem as he witnessed the retreat of Napoleon's army from Russia in 1812. Napoleon invaded Russia in June 1812, after almost all of Europe was in his power. He reached Moscow in September only to have the Russians burn the city. He saw the futility of his campaign and began his retreat in Octo- ber, leaving his troops open to guerrilla attack. Of the six hundred thousand troops involved in the retreat, only twenty-four thousand returned in formation. The text used here is from Leon Howard, "Joel Barlow and Napoleon," *Huntington Library Quarterly* 2 (1938).

You fear perhaps your food will fail you there,   5
Your human carnage, that delicious fare
That lured you hither, following still your friend
The great Napoleon to the world's bleak end.
You fear, because the southern climes poured forth
Their clustering nations to infest the north,   10
Bavarians, Austrians, those who drink the Po[2]
And those who skirt the Tuscan seas below,
With all Germania, Neustria, Belgia, Gaul,[3]
Doomed here to wade through slaughter to their fall,
You fear he left behind no wars, to feed   15
His feathered cannibals and nurse the breed.
      Fear not, my screamer, call your greedy train,
Sweep over Europe, hurry back to Spain,
You'll find his legions there; the valiant crew
Please best their master when they toil for you.   20
Abundant there they spread the country o'er.
And taint the breeze with every nation's gore,
Iberian, Lusian,[4] British widely strown,
But still more wide and copious flows their own.
      Go where you will; Calabria,[5] Malta, Greece,   25
Egypt and Syria still his fame increase,
Domingo's[6] fattened isle and India's plains
Glow deep with purple drawn from Gallic veins.
No raven's wing can stretch the flight so far
As the torn bandrols[7] of Napoleon's war.   30
Choose then your climate, fix your best abode,
He'll make you deserts and he'll bring you blood.
      How could you fear a dearth? have not mankind,
Though slain by millions, millions left behind?
Has not conscription still the power to wield   35
Her annual falchion[8] o'er the human field?
A faithful harvester! or if a man
Escape that gleaner, shall he scape the ban?[9]
The triple ban, that like the hound of hell[1]
Gripes with three joles,[2] to hold his victim well.   40
      Fear nothing then, hatch fast your ravenous brood,
Teach them to cry to Bonaparte for food;
They'll be like you, of all his suppliant train,
The only class that never cries in vain.
For see what mutual benefits you lend!   45
(The surest way to fix the mutual friend)
While on his slaughtered troops your tribes are fed,
You cleanse his camp and carry off his dead.
Imperial scavenger! but now you know
Your work is vain amid these hills of snow.   50

2. River in Italy flowing from the Alps to the Adriatic.
3. France. "Germania": Germany. "Neustria": northern France. "Belgia": the Netherlands.
4. Lusitania is almost identical with present-day Portugal. "Iberian": Spanish.
5. In southern Italy.
6. The West Indies.
7. Flags carried in war.

8. Sickle or sword.
9. Curse. In French military parlance, a list of young
people eligible for conscription to the National Guard.
The youngest possible draftees would appear on the
third ban or list (see line 39).
1. Three-headed Cerberus guards the gates of Hades.
2. Jaws.

His tentless troops are marbled through with frost
And change to crystal when the breath is lost.
Mere trunks of ice, though limbed like human frames
And lately warmed with life's endearing flames,
They cannot taint the air, the world impest,[3]   55
Nor can you tear one fiber from their breast.
No! from their visual sockets, as they lie,
With beak and claws you cannot pluck an eye.
The frozen orb, preserving still its form,
Defies your talons as it braves the storm,   60
But stands and stares to God, as if to know
In what cursed hands He leaves His world below.
    Fly then, or starve; though all the dreadful road
From Minsk[4] to Moscow with their bodies strowed
May count some myriads, yet they can't suffice   65
To feed you more beneath these dreary skies.
Go back, and winter in the wilds of Spain;
Feast there awhile, and in the next campaign
Rejoin your master; for you'll find him then,
With his new million of the race of men,   70
Clothed in his thunders, all his flags unfurled,
Raging and storming o'er the prostrate world.
    War after war his hungry soul requires,
State after state shall sink beneath his fires,
Yet other Spains in victim smoke shall rise   75
And other Moscows suffocate the skies,
Each land lie reeking with its people's slain
And not a stream run bloodless to the main.
Till men resume their souls, and dare to shed
Earth's total vengeance on the monster's head,   80
Hurl from his blood-built throne this king of woes,
Dash him to dust, and let the world repose.

1812   1938

3. Infect.   4. City four hundred miles southwest of Moscow.

ROYALL TYLER
1757–1826

The colonial period was by no means conducive to English-speaking theater—let alone drama—and it says something about the theater's strength as an institution that it was able to exist at all. For one thing, settlers were too busy wresting a life from soil to be entertained; more important, both Puritans and Quakers disapproved in principle of what Jonathan in *The Contrast* calls "the devil's drawing-room." Nevertheless, some British acting companies occasionally toured the principal cities, some amateur theatricals were staged in southern colonies, and college students performed dramatic readings. Even those activities virtually ceased during the Revolution, when Americans were too busy fighting for their new country.

After the Revolution, however, as the theater historian Walter J. Meserve has pointed out, "it became clear that the theatre was to be part of a new nation and that a playwright might even elicit some slight fame and fortune," for a national drama would be part of the search for a cultural identity. Antidrama bans were lifted, older acting companies returned, and new ones were formed to occupy the new playhouses. One of the few new playwrights to emerge was Royall Tyler, whose play *The Contrast* was performed in 1787. It was our first English-speaking comedy and an immediate hit.

Tyler was not a dramatist with a mission, but an accomplished young man with a flair for letters. He earned degrees simultaneously at both Harvard College and Yale College in 1776. He served in the Revolutionary War; he enjoyed playing man about town (in this case, Boston); he paid court to Abigail Adams, John and Abigail's daughter. At length he became a lawyer, and an intelligent and successful one; in his later years, he was both chief justice of the Supreme Court of Vermont and professor of law at the University of Vermont. He also—in the same year as *The Contrast* was produced—was a member of the militia that put down Shays's Rebellion, an incident mentioned twice in the play. And he dashed off *The Contrast* in three weeks.

Although its author was an amateur, the play, most readers agree, reads like a polished professional product of the time. It is based, to be sure, on Richard Brinsley Sheridan's famous comedy *The School for Scandal* (1777), which Tyler saw produced in New York in 1787. From Sheridan's play Tyler took the basic story line that contrasts a mean and shallow fashionable demimonde with a world of honest and wholesome sentiment: the latter, of course, triumphs. He repays his debt handsomely in the scene where the comic Jonathan thinks he has witnessed real life in a private home but has actually been watching *The School for Scandal* itself.

What was revolutionary was that Tyler totally Americanized the story. His fashionable New Yorkers ape British modes—most especially the deceitful villain, a young man who runs his life according to Lord Chesterfield's dictates. The hero, Captain Manly, is a model of thoughtful rectitude; a veteran of the Revolution, he may well embody the idea, current at the time, that these officer veterans were America's best hope. His servant Jonathan is one of the first examples of an enduring dramatic type, the comic Yankee: he is the butt of fun because of his ignorance of city ways, but he is also shrewd, honorable, and squarely on the side of homespun good. The critic William L. Hedges notes that Manly and Jonathan embody two American myths—"Publius and Yankee Doodle teamed up to save American virtue from the seductions of British luxury." "Contrasts" run throughout the play.

Tyler continued to write during the rest of his life: other plays, satirical essays, verses, and a picaresque novel, *The Algerine Captive* (1797), one of the first works by an American to be also published in England. None, however, equals *The Contrast*, with its good humor and its brash, sunny nationalism:

> Exult each patriot heart!—this night is shewn
> A piece, which we may fairly call our own.

The new country wanted a national literature, and in Tyler's play got an excellent example of it. Moreover, because social comedy is so topical, we can also read *The Contrast* for a vivid idea of what it was like to be an American when this country was still young.

The Contrast[1]

Prologue

[*Written by a* YOUNG GENTLEMAN *of New York, and Spoken by* MR. WIGNELL]

Exult each patriot heart!—this night is shewn
A piece, which we may fairly call our own;
Where the proud titles of "My Lord! Your Grace!"
To humble Mr. and plain Sir give place.
Our Author pictures not from foreign climes
The fashions, or the follies of the times;
But has confin'd the subject of his work
To the gay scenes—the circles of New York.
On native themes his Muse displays her pow'rs;
If ours the faults, the virtues too are ours.
Why should our thoughts to distant countries roam,
When each refinement may be found at home?
Who travels now to ape the rich or great,
To deck an equipage and roll in state;
To court the graces,[2] or to dance with ease,
Or by hypocrisy to strive to please?
Our free-born ancestors such arts despis'd;
Genuine sincerity alone they priz'd;
Their minds, with honest emulation fir'd.
To solid good—-not ornament—aspir'd;
Or, if ambition rous'd a bolder flame,
Stern virtue throve, where indolence was shame.

But modern youths, with imitative sense,
Deem taste in dress the proof of excellence;
And spurn the meanness of your homespun arts,
Since homespun habits would obscure their parts;
Whilst all, which aims at splendor and parade,
Must come from Europe, and be ready made.
Strange! we should thus our native worth disclaim,
And check the progress of our rising fame.
Yet one, whilst imitation bears the sway,
Aspires to nobler heights, and points the way,
Be rous'd, my friends! his bold example view;
Let your own Bards be proud to copy you!
Should rigid critics reprobate our play,
At least the patriotic heart will say,
"Glorious our fall, since in a noble cause.
"The bold attempt alone demands applause."
Still may the wisdom of the Comic Muse
Exalt your merits, or your faults accuse.
But think not, 'tis her aim to be severe;—

---

1. First performed in 1787, it was published in 1790 by Thomas Wignell, which is the source of our text. Wignell, a prominent comic actor and George Washington's favorite comedian, later ran one of the new country's most successful theaters, the Chestnut Street Theatre, in Philadelphia. He played the part of Jonathan in New York.
2. Greek goddesses, personifications of loveliness or grace. "Equipage": coach.

We all are mortals, and as mortals err.
If candor pleases, we are truly blest;
Vice trembles, when compell'd to stand confess'd.
Let not light Censure on your faults offend,
Which aims not to expose them, but amend.
Thus does our Author to your candor trust;
Conscious, the free are generous, as just.

Act First

SCENE 1. *An apartment at* CHARLOTTE's.

[CHARLOTTE *and* LETITIA *discovered.*]

LETITIA.   And so, Charlotte, you really think the pocket-hoop[1] unbecoming.

CHARLOTTE.   No, I don't say so: It may be very becoming to saunter round the house of a rainy day; to visit my grand-mamma, or go to Quakers' meeting: but to swim in a minuet, with the eyes of fifty well-dressed beaux upon me, to trip it in the Mall, or walk on the battery,[2] give me the luxurious, jaunty, flowing, bell-hoop. It would have delighted you to have seen me the last evening, my charming girl! I was dangling o'er the battery with Billy Dimple; a knot of young fellows were upon the platform; as I passed them I faultered with one of the most bewitching false steps you ever saw, and then recovered myself with such a pretty confusion, flirting my hoop to discover a jet black shoe and brilliant buckle. Gad! how my little heart thrilled to hear the confused raptures of—"Demme,[3] Jack, what a delicate foot!" "Ha! General, what a well-turn'd—"

LETITIA.   Fie! fie! Charlotte [*stopping her mouth*], I protest you are quite a libertine.

CHARLOTTE.   Why, my dear little prude, are we not all such libertines? Do you think, when I sat tortured two hours under the hands of my friseur, and an hour more at my toilet,[4] that I had any thoughts of my aunt Susan, or my cousin Betsey? though they are both allowed to be critical judges of dress.

LETITIA.   Why, who should we dress to please, but those who are judges of its merits?

CHARLOTTE.   Why a creature who does not know *Buffon* from *Souflee*[5]—Man!—my Letitia—Man! for whom we dress, walk, dance, talk, lisp, languish, and smile. Does not the grave Spectator[6] assure us, that even our much bepraised diffidence, modesty, and blushes, are all directed to make ourselves good wives and mothers as fast as we can. Why, I'll undertake with one flirt of this hoop to bring more beaux to my feet in one week, than the grave Maria, and her sentimental circle, can do, by sighing sentiment till their hairs are grey.

LETITIA.   Well, I won't argue with you; you always out talk me; let us change the subject. I hear that Mr. Dimple and Maria are soon to be married.

CHARLOTTE.   You hear true. I was consulted in the choice of the wedding

1. Hoopskirts became fashionable about 1700; the "pocket hoop," confined to the hips, was smaller than the "bell hoop," mentioned a few lines later.
2. Area at the southernmost tip of Manhattan Island (formerly a Dutch fortification, hence the name). "Beaux": i.e., dandies. "The Mall": fashionable promenade.
3. Affected version of *Damn me.*
4. Dressing table, vanity. "Friseur": hairdresser.

5. I.e., soufflé, a puffy dish made with eggs and sauce. "Buffon": a pun on Georges Buffon, 18th-century French naturalist, and "bouffant," puffed out, as in a hairdo.
6. A popular periodical written and published by Joseph Addison and Richard Steele, which provided "a wholesome and pleasant regimen" of essays on morals, manners, and literature.

clothes. She is to be married in a delicate white satin, and has a monstrous pretty brocaded lutestring[7] for the second day. It would have done you good to have seen with what an affected indifference the dear sentimentalist turned over a thousand pretty things, just as if her heart did not palpitate with her approaching happiness, and at last made her choice, and arranged her dress with such apathy, as if she did not know that plain white satin, and a simple blond lace, would shew her clear skin, and dark hair, to the greatest advantage.

LETITIA.   But they say her indifference to dress, and even to the gentleman himself, is not entirely affected.

CHARLOTTE.   How?

LETITIA.   It is whispered, that if Maria gives her hand to Mr. Dimple, it will be without her heart.

CHARLOTTE.   Though the giving the heart is one of the last of all laughable considerations in the marriage of a girl of spirit, yet I should like to hear what antiquated notions the dear little piece of old fashioned prudery has got in her head.

LETITIA.   Why you know that old Mr. John-Richard-Robert-Jacob-Isaac-Abraham-Cornelius Van Dumpling, Billy Dimple's father (for he has thought fit to soften his name, as well as manners, during his English tour) was the most intimate friend of Maria's father. The old folks, about a year before Mr. Van Dumpling's death, proposed this match: the young folks were accordingly introduced, and told they must love one another. Billy was then a good natured, decent, dressing young fellow, with a little dash of the coxcomb,[8] such as our young fellows of fortune usually have. At this time, I really believe she thought she loved him; and had they then been married, I doubt not, they might have jogged on, to the end of the chapter, a good kind of a sing-song lack-a-daysaical life, as other honest married folks do.

CHARLOTTE.   Why did they not then marry?

LETITIA.   Upon the death of his father, Billy went to England to see the world, and rub off a little of the patroon rust.[9] During his absence, Maria like a good girl, to keep herself constant to her *nown*[1] *true-love*, avoided company, and betook herself, for her amusement, to her books, and her dear Billy's letters. But, alas! how many ways has the mischievous demon of inconstancy of stealing into a woman's heart! Her love was destroyed by the very means she took to support it.

CHARLOTTE.   How?—Oh! I have it—some likely young beau found the way to her study.

LETITIA.   Be patient, Charlotte—your head so runs upon beaux.—Why she read Sir Charles Grandison, Clarissa Harlow, Shenstone, and the Sentimental Journey;[2] and between whiles, as I said, Billy's letters. But as her taste improved, her love declined. The contrast was so striking betwixt the good sense of her books, and the flimsiness of her love-letters, that she discovered she had unthinkingly engaged her hand without her heart; and then the whole transaction managed by the old folks, now appeared so unsentimental, and looked so like bargaining for a bale of goods, that she found she ought to have rejected, according to every rule of romance, even

7. A glossy silk.
8. Conceitedness.
9. I.e., old-fashioned country style or manners.
1. I.e., "own" (probably from a popular song).
2. All sentimental works of the 18th century: *Sir*

Charles Grandison and *Clarissa* (Harlowe) are novels by Samuel Richardson, and *A Sentimental Journey* is by Laurence Sterne. William Shenstone was a popular poet. Novel reading was then considered a woman's occupation.

the man of her choice, if imposed upon her in that manner—Clary Harlow would have scorned such a match.

CHARLOTTE.   Well, how was it on Mr. Dimple's return? Did he meet a more favorable reception than his letters?

LETITIA.   Much the same. She spoke of him with respect abroad, and with contempt in her closet.[3] She watched his conduct and conversation, and found that he had by traveling acquired the wickedness of Lovelace[4] without his wit, and the politeness of Sir Charles Grandison without his generosity. The ruddy youth who washed his face at the cistern every morning, and swore and looked eternal love and constancy, was now metamorphosed into a flippant, palid, polite beau, who devotes the morning to his toilet, reads a few pages of Chesterfield's letters,[5] and then minces out, to put the infamous principles in practice upon every woman he meets.

CHARLOTTE.   But, if she is so apt at conjuring up these sentimental bugbears, why does she not discard him at once?

LETITIA.   Why, she thinks her word too sacred to be trifled with. Besides, her father, who has a great respect for the memory of his deceased friend, is ever telling her how he shall renew his years in their union, and repeating the dying injunctions of old Van Dumpling.

CHARLOTTE.   A mighty pretty story! And so you would make me believe, that the sensible Maria would give up Dumpling manor, and the all-accomplished Dimple as a husband, for the absurd, ridiculous reason, forsooth, because she despises and abhors him. Just as if a lady could not be privileged to spend a man's fortune, ride in his carriage, be called after his name, and call him her *nown dear lovee* when she wants money, without loving and respecting the great he-creature. Oh! my dear girl, you are a monstrous prude.

LETITIA.   I don't say what I would do; I only intimate how I suppose she wishes to act.

CHARLOTTE.   No, no, no! A fig for sentiment. If she breaks, or wishes to break, with Mr. Dimple, depend upon it, she has some other man in her eye. A woman rarely discards one lover, until she is sure of another.— Letitia little thinks what a clue I have to Dimple's conduct. The generous man submits to render himself disgusting to Maria, in order that she may leave him at liberty to address me. I must change the subject [*Aside, and rings a bell.*]

   [*Enter* SERVANT.]

Frank, order the horses to.—Talking of marriage—did you hear that Sally Bloomsbury is going to be married next week to Mr. Indigo, the rich Carolinian?

LETITIA.   Sally Bloomsbury married!—Why, she is not yet in her teens.

CHARLOTTE.   I do not know how that is, but, you may depend upon it, 'tis a done affair. I have it from the best authority. There is my aunt Wyerley's Hannah (you know Hannah—though a black, she is a wench that was never caught in a lie in her life); now Hannah has a brother who courts Sarah, Mrs. Catgut the milliner's girl, and she told Hannah's brother, and Hannah, who, as I said before, is a girl of undoubted veracity, told it directly to me, that Mrs. Catgut was making a new cap for Miss Bloomsbury, which, as it was very dressy, it is very probable is designed for a wedding cap: now,

3. Private apartment or room.
4. The handsome dashing villain in *Clarissa*.
5. Letters written to his illegitimate son by Philip Stanhope, earl of Chesterfield, on deportment and manners in polite society; published in 1774, they were described by Samuel Johnson as teaching "the morals of a whore and the manners of a dancing master."

as she is to be married, who can it be to, but to Mr. Indigo? Why, there is
no other gentleman that visits at her papa's.

LETITIA.   Say not a word more, Charlotte. Your intelligence[6] is so direct and
well grounded, it is almost a pity that it is not a piece of scandal.

CHARLOTTE.   Oh! I am the pink of prudence. Though I cannot charge myself
with ever having discredited a tea-party by my silence, yet I take care never
to report any thing of my acquaintance, especially if it is to their credit,—
discredit, I mean—until I have searched to the bottom of it. It is true, there
is infinite pleasure in this charitable pursuit. Oh! how delicious to go and
condole with the friends of some backsliding sister, or to retire with some
old dowager or maiden aunt of the family, who love scandal so well, that
they cannot forbear gratifying their appetite at the expence of the reputation
of their nearest relations! And then to return full fraught with a rich collection of circumstances, to retail to the next circle of our acquaintance under
the strongest injunctions of secrecy,—ha, ha, ha!—interlarding the melancholy tale with so many doleful shakes of the head, and more doleful, "Ah!
who would have thought it! so amiable, so prudent a young lady, as we all
thought her, what a monstrous pity! well, I have nothing to charge myself
with; I acted the part of a friend, I warned her of the principles of that rake,[7]
I told her what would be the consequence; I told her so, I told her so."—
Ha, ha, ha!

LETITIA.   Ha, ha, ha! Well, but Charlotte, you don't tell me what you think
of Miss Bloombury's match.

CHARLOTTE.   Think! why I think it is probable she cried for a plaything, and
they have given her a husband. Well, well, well, the puling chit[8] shall not
be deprived of her plaything: 'tis only exchanging London dolls for American babies—Apropos, of babies, have you heard what Mrs. Affable's high-
flying notions of delicacy have come to?

LETITIA.   Who, she that was Miss Lovely?

CHARLOTTE.   The same; she married Bob Affable of Schenectady. Don't you
remember?

[Enter SERVANT.]

SERVANT.   Madam, the carriage is ready.

LETITIA.   Shall we go to the stores first, or visiting?

CHARLOTTE.   I should think it rather too early to visit; especially Mrs. Prim:
you know she is so particular.

LETITIA.   Well, but what of Mrs. Affable?

CHARLOTTE.   Oh, I'll tell you as we go; come, come, let us hasten. I hear
Mrs. Catgut has some of the prettiest caps arrived, you ever saw. I shall die
if I have not the first sight of them. [Exeunt.]

SCENE 2. A room in VAN ROUGH's
house.

[MARIA sitting disconsolate at a Table, with Books, etc.]

Song

I

The sun sets in night, and the stars shun the day;
But glory remains when their lights fade away!

6. I.e., news.
7. Or "rakehell," a libertine or dissolute man.
8. Whimpering child or young woman.

Begin, ye tormentors! your threats are in vain,
For the son of Alknomook[9] shall never complain.
                        II
Remember the arrows he shot from his bow;
Remember your chiefs by his hatchet laid low:
Why so slow?—do you wait till I shrink from the pain?
No—the son of Alknomook will never complain.
                       III
Remember the wood where in ambush we lay;
And the scalps which we bore from your nation away:
Now the flame rises fast, you exult in my pain;
But the son of Alknomook can never complain.
                       IV
I go to the land where my father is gone;
His ghost shall rejoice in the fame of his son:
Death comes like a friend, he relieves me from pain;
And thy son, Oh Alknomook! has scorn'd to complain.

There is something in this song which ever calls forth my affections. The manly virtue of courage, that fortitude which steels the heart against the keenest misfortunes, which interweaves the laurel of glory amidst the instruments of torture and death, displays something so noble, so exalted, that in despite of the prejudices of education, I cannot but admire it, even in a savage. The prepossession which our sex is supposed to entertain for the character of a soldier, is, I know, a standing piece of raillery among the wits. A cockade, a lapel'd coat, and a feather,[1] they will tell you, are irresistible by a female heart. Let it be so.—Who is it that considers the helpless situation of our sex, that does not see we each moment stand in need of a protector, and that a brave one too. Formed of the more delicate materials of nature, endowed only with the softer passions, incapable, from our ignorance of the world, to guard against the wiles of mankind, our security for happiness often depends upon their generosity and courage:—Alas! how little of the former do we find. How inconsistent! that man should be leagued to destroy that honor, upon which, solely rests his respect and esteem. Ten thousand temptations allure us, ten thousand passions betray us; yet the smallest deviation from the path of rectitude is followed by the contempt and insult of man, and the more remorseless pity of woman: years of penitence and tears cannot wash away the stain, nor a life of virtue obliterate its remembrance. Reputation is the life of woman; yet courage to protect it, is masculine and disgusting; and the only safe asylum a woman of delicacy can find, is in the arms of a man of honor. How naturally then, should we love the brave, and the generous; how gratefully should we bless the arm raised for our protection, when nerv'd by virtue, and directed by honor! Heaven grant that the man with whom I may be connected—may be connected!—Whither has my imagination transported me—whither does it now lead me?—Am I not indissolubly engaged by every obligation of honor, which my own consent, and my father's approbation can give, to a man who can never share my affections, and whom a few days hence, it will be criminal for me to disapprove—to disapprove! would to heaven that were all—to

9. An Indian name. The authorship of the song is unknown.

1. I.e., military dress. "Cockade": badge worn on a hat.

despise. For, can the most frivolous manners, actuated by the most depraved heart, meet, or merit, anything but contempt from every woman of delicacy and sentiment?

  [VAN ROUGH, *without.*] Mary!

MARIA. Ha, my father's voice—Sir!

  [*Enter* VAN ROUGH.]

VAN ROUGH. What, Mary, always singing doleful ditties, and moping over these plaguy[2] books.

MARIA. I hope, Sir, that it is not criminal to improve my mind with books; or to divert my melancholy with singing at my leisure hours.

VAN ROUGH. Why, I don't know that, child; I don't know that. They us'd to say when I was a young man, that if a woman knew how to make a pudding, and to keep herself out of fire and water, she knew enough for a wife. Now, what good have these books done you? have they not made you melancholy? as you call it. Pray, what right has a girl of your age to be in the dumps? haven't you every thing your heart can wish; ain't you going to be married to a young man of great fortune; ain't you going to have the quit-rent[3] of twenty miles square?

MARIA. One hundredth part of the land, and a lease for life of the heart of a man I could love, would satisfy me.

VAN ROUGH. Pho, pho, pho! child; nonsense, downright nonsense, child. This comes of your reading your story-books; your Charles Grandisons, your Sentimental Journals, and your Robinson Crusoes, and such other trumpery.[4] No, no, no! child, it is money makes the mare go; keep your eye upon the main chance,[5] Mary.

MARIA. Marriage, Sir, is, indeed, a very serious affair.

VAN ROUGH. You are right, child; you are right. I am sure I found it so to my cost.

MARIA. I mean, Sir, that as marriage is a portion for life, and so intimately involves our happiness, we cannot be too considerate in the choice of our companion.

VAN ROUGH. Right, child; very right. A young woman should be very sober when she is making her choice, but when she has once made it, as you have done, I don't see why she should not be as merry as a grig;[6] I am sure she has reason enough to be so—Solomon says, that "there is a time to laugh, and a time to weep";[7] now a time for a young woman to laugh is when she has made sure of a good rich husband. Now a time to cry, according to you, Mary, is when she is making choice of him: but, I should think, that a young woman's time to cry was, when she despaired of *getting* one.—Why, there was your mother now; to be sure when I popp'd the question to her, she did look a little silly; but when she had once looked down on her apron-strings, as all modest young women us'd to do, and drawled out ye-s, she was as brisk and as merry as a bee.

MARIA. My honored mother, Sir, had no motive to melancholy; she married the man of her choice.

VAN ROUGH. The man of her choice! And pray, Mary, ain't you going to marry the man of your choice—what trumpery notion is this?—It is these vile books [*throwing them away*]. I'd have you to know, Mary, if you won't

---

2. Annoying, irritating.
3. Small fixed rent.
4. Worthless nonsense. *Robinson Crusoe* was published by Daniel Defoe in 1719.

5. I.e., the biggest advantage.
6. Lighthearted young person.
7. "A time to weep, and a time to laugh" (Ecclesiastes 3.4); Ecclesiastes is thought to be written by Solomon.

make young Van Dumpling the man of *your* choice, you shall marry him as the man of *my* choice.

MARIA.   You terrify me, Sir. Indeed, Sir, I am all submission. My will is yours.

VAN ROUGH.   Why, that is the way your mother us'd to talk. "My will is yours, my dear Mr. Van Rough, my will is yours": but she took special care to have her own way though for all that.

MARIA.   Do not reflect upon my mother's memory, Sir—

VAN ROUGH.   Why not, Mary, why not? She kept me from speaking my mind all *her* life, and do you think she shall henpeck me now she is *dead* too? Come, come; don't go to sniveling: be a good girl, and mind the main chance. I'll see you well settled in the world.

MARIA.   I do not doubt your love, Sir; and it is my duty to obey you.—I will endeavor to make my duty and inclination go hand in hand.

VAN ROUGH.   Well, well, Mary; do you be a good girl, mind the main chance, and never mind inclination.—Why, do you know that I have been down in the cellar this very morning to examine a pipe of Madeira[8] which I purchased the week you were born, and mean to tap on your wedding day.— That pipe cost me fifty pounds sterling. It was well worth sixty pounds; but I over-reached Ben Bulkhead, the supercargo:[9] I'll tell you the whole story. You must know that—

   [*Enter* SERVANT.]

SERVANT.   Sir, Mr. Transfer, the broker, is below. [*Exit.*]

VAN ROUGH.   Well, Mary, I must go.—Remember, and be a good girl, and mind the main chance. [*Exit.*]

MARIA [*alone*].   How deplorable is my situation! How distressing for a daughter to find her heart militating with her filial duty! I know my father loves me tenderly, why then do I reluctantly obey him? Heaven knows! with what reluctance I should oppose the will of a parent, or set an example of filial disobedience; at a parent's command I could wed awkwardness and deformity. Were the heart of my husband good, I would so magnify his good qualities with the eye of conjugal affection, that the defects of his person and manners should be lost in the emanation of his virtues. At a father's command, I could embrace poverty. Were the poor man my husband, I would learn resignation to my lot; I would enliven our frugal meal with good humor, and chase away misfortune from our cottage with a smile. At a father's command, I could almost submit, to what every female heart knows to be the most mortifying, to marry a weak man, and blush at my husband's folly in every company I visited.—But to marry a depraved wretch, whose only virtue is a polished exterior; who is actuated by the unmanly ambition of conquering the defenceless; whose heart, insensible to the emotions of patriotism, dilates at the plaudits of every unthinking girl: whose laurels are the sighs and tears of the miserable victims of his specious behavior.—Can he, who has no regard for the peace and happiness of other families, ever have a due regard for the peace and happiness of his own? Would to heaven that my father were not so hasty in his temper! Surely, if I were to state my reasons for declining this match, he would not compel me to marry a man—whom, though my lips may solemnly promise to honor, I find my heart must ever despise. [*Exit.*]

8. Big cask of wine.
9. Officer or merchant ship concerned with the voyage's commercial aspects.

Act Second

SCENE 1. CHARLOTTE'*s* apartment.

[*Enter* CHARLOTTE *and* LETITIA.]

CHARLOTTE [*at entering*].   Betty, take those things out of the carriage and
carry them to my chamber; see that you don't tumble[1] them.—My dear, I
protest, I think it was the homeliest of the whole. I declare I was almost
tempted to return and change it.

LETITIA.   Why would you take it?

CHARLOTTE.   Didn't Mrs. Catgut say it was the most fashionable?

LETITIA.   But, my dear, it will never sit becomingly on you.

CHARLOTTE.   I know that; but did not you hear Mrs. Catgut say it was fashionable?

LETITIA.   Did you see that sweet airy cap with the white sprig?

CHARLOTTE.   Yes, and I longed to take it; but, my dear, what could I do?—
Did not Mrs. Catgut say it was the most fashionable; and if I had not taken
it, was not that awkward gawky, Sally Slender, ready to purchase it immediately?

LETITIA.   Did you observe how she tumbled over the things at the next shop,
and then went off without purchasing any thing, nor even thanking the poor
man for his trouble?—But of all the awkward creatures, did you see Miss
Blouze, endeavoring to thrust her unmerciful arm into those small kid
gloves?

CHARLOTTE.   Ha, ha, ha, ha!

LETITIA.   Then did you take notice, with what an affected warmth of friendship she and Miss Wasp met? when all their acquaintances know how much
pleasure they take in abusing each other in every company?

CHARLOTTE.   Lud![2] Letitia, is that so extraordinary? Why, my dear, I hope
you are not going to turn sentimentalist.—Scandal, you know, is but amusing ourselves with the faults, foibles, follies and reputations of our friends;—
indeed, I don't know why we should have friends, if we are not at liberty to
make use of them. But no person is so ignorant of the world as to suppose,
because I amuse myself with a lady's faults, that I am obliged to quarrel
with her person, every time we meet; believe me, my dear, we should have
very few acquaintances at that rate.

[SERVANT *enters and delivers a letter to* CHARLOTTE, *and exits.*]

CHARLOTTE.   You'll excuse me, my dear. [*Opens and reads to herself.*]

LETITIA.   Oh, quite excusable.

CHARLOTTE.   As I hope to be married, my brother Henry is in the city.

LETITIA.   What, your brother, Colonel Manly?

CHARLOTTE.   Yes, my dear; the only brother I have in the world.

LETITIA.   Was he never in this city?

CHARLOTTE.   Never nearer than Harlem Heights,[3] where he lay with his regiment.

LETITIA.   What sort of a being is this brother of yours? If he is as chatty, as
pretty, as sprightly as you, half the belles in the city will be pulling caps[4]
for him.

CHARLOTTE.   My brother is the very counterpart and reverse of me: I am gay,
he is grave; I am airy, he is solid; I am ever selecting the most pleasing
objects for my laughter, he has a tear for every pitiful one. And thus, whilst

1. Rumple, disorder.
2. I.e., Lord.
3. Then north of New York City and site of a Revolutionary War battle.
4. I.e., setting their caps.

he is plucking the briars and thorns from the path of the unfortunate, I am strewing on my own path with roses.

LETITIA.   My sweet friend, not quite so poetical, and little more particular.

CHARLOTTE.   Hands off, Letitia. I feel the rage of simile[5] upon me; I can't talk to you in any other way. My brother has a heart replete with the noblest sentiments, but then, it is like—it is like—Oh! you provoking girl, you have deranged all my ideas—it is like—Oh! I have it—his heart is like an old maiden lady's band-box;[6] it contains many costly things, arranged with the most scrupulous nicety, yet the misfortune is, that they are too delicate, costly, and antiquated, for common use.

LETITIA.   By what I can pick out of your flowery description, your brother is no beau.

CHARLOTTE.   No, indeed; he makes no pretension to the character. He'd ride, or rather fly, an hundred miles to relieve a distressed object, or to do a gallant act in the service of his country: but, should you drop your fan or bouquet in his presence, it is ten to one that some beau at the farther end of the room would have the honor of presenting it to you, before he had observed that it fell. I'll tell you one of his antiquated, anti-gallant notions.—He said once in my presence, in a room full of company—would you believe it—in a large circle of ladies, that the best evidence a gentleman could give a young lady of his respect and affection, was, to endeavor in a friendly manner to rectify her foibles. I protest I was crimson to the eyes, upon reflecting that I was known as his sister.

LETITIA.   Insupportable creature! tell a lady of her faults! If he is so grave, I fear I have no chance of captivating him.

CHARLOTTE.   His conversation is like a rich old fashioned brocade,[7] it will stand alone; every sentence is a sentiment. Now you may judge what a time I had with him in my twelve months' visit to my father. He read me such lectures, out of pure brotherly affection, against the extremes of fashion, dress, flirting, and coquetry, and all the other dear things which he knows I doat upon, that, I protest, his conversation made me as melancholy as if I had been at church; and heaven knows, though I never prayed to go there but on one occasion, yet I would have exchanged his conversation for a psalm and a sermon. Church is rather melancholy, to be sure; but then I can ogle the beaux, and be regaled with "here endeth the first lesson"; but his brotherly *here*, you would think had no end. You captivate him! Why, my dear, he would as soon fall in love with a box of Italian flowers. There is Maria now, if she were not engaged, she might do something.—Oh, how I should like to see that pair of pensorosos[8] together, looking as grave as two sailors' wives of a stormy night, with a flow of sentiment meandering through their conversation like purling streams in modern poetry.

LETITIA.   Oh! my dear fanciful—

CHARLOTTE.   Hush! I hear some person coming through the entry.

          [*Enter* SERVANT.]

SERVANT.   Madam, there's a gentleman below who calls himself Colonel Manly; do you chuse to be at home?

CHARLOTTE.   Shew him in. [*Exit* SERVANT.] Now for a sober face.

          [*Enter* COLONEL MANLY.]

---

5. I.e., desire to make poetic comparisons.
6. Cylindrical box for clothes: its lid was held on by a band of ribbon.
7. Rich stiff fabric.

8. Melancholy, thoughtful people (from the title of John Milton's poem about such a person, *Il Penseroso*).

MANLY.   My dear Charlotte, I am happy that I once more enfold you within the arms of fraternal affection. I know you are going to ask (amiable impatience!) how our parents do,—the venerable pair transmit you their blessing by me—they totter on the verge of a well-spent life, and wish only to see their children settled in the world, to depart in peace.

CHARLOTTE.   I am very happy to hear that they are well. [*Coolly.*] Brother, will you give me leave to introduce you to our uncle's ward, one of my most intimate friends.

MANLY [*saluting* LETITIA].   I ought to regard your friends as my own.

CHARLOTTE.   Come, Letitia, do give us a little dash of your vivacity; my brother is so sentimental, and so grave, that I protest he'll give us the vapors.[9]

MANLY.   Though sentiment and gravity, I know, are banished the polite world, yet, I hoped, they might find some countenance in the meeting of such near connections as brother and sister.

CHARLOTTE.   Positively, brother, if you go one step further in this strain, you will set me crying, and that, you know, would spoil my eyes; and then I should never get the husband which our good papa and mamma have so kindly wished me—never be established in the world.

MANLY.   Forgive me, my sister—I am no enemy to mirth; I love your sprightliness; and I hope it will one day enliven the hours of some worthy man; but when I mention the respectable authors of my existence,—the cherishers and protectors of my helpless infancy, whose hearts glow with such fondness and attachment, that they would willingly lay down their lives for my welfare, you will excuse me, if I am so unfashionable as to speak of them with some degree of respect and reverence.

CHARLOTTE.   Well, well, brother; if you won't be gay, we'll not differ; I will be as grave as you wish. [*Affects gravity.*] And so, brother, you have come to the city to exchange some of your commutation notes[1] for a little pleasure.

MANLY.   Indeed, you are mistaken; my errand is not of amusement, but business; and as I neither drink nor game, my expences will be so trivial, I shall have no occasion to sell my notes.

CHARLOTTE.   Then you won't have occasion to do a very good thing. Why, there was the Vermont General—he came down some time since, sold all his musty notes at one stroke, and then laid the cash out in trinkets for his dear Fanny. I want a dozen pretty things myself; have you got the notes with you?

MANLY.   I shall be ever willing to contribute as far as it is in my power, to adorn, or in any way to please my sister; yet, I hope, I shall never be obliged for this, to sell my notes. I may be romantic, but I preserve them as a sacred deposit. Their full amount is justly due to me, but as embarrassments, the natural consequences of a long war, disable my country from supporting its credit, I shall wait with patience until it is rich enough to discharge them. If that is not in my day, they shall be transmitted as an honorable certificate to posterity, that I have humbly imitated our illustrious WASHINGTON, in having exposed my health and life in the service of my country, without reaping any other reward than the glory of conquering in so arduous a contest.

CHARLOTTE.   Well said heroics. Why, my dear Henry, you have such a lofty

---

9. I.e., depress us.
1. Notes given to Continental Army officers after the Revolution, promising payment of a pension when the notes came due; they could be cashed in earlier, for less than the face amount.

way of saying things, that I protest I almost tremble at the thought of introducing you to the polite circles in the city. The belles would think you were
a player[2] run mad, with your head filled with old scraps of tragedy: and, as
to the beaux, they might admire, because they would not understand you.—
But, however, I must, I believe, venture to introduce you to two or three
ladies of my acquaintance.

LETITIA.   And that will make him acquainted with thirty or forty beaux.

CHARLOTTE.   Oh! brother, you don't know what a fund of happiness you have
in store.

MANLY.   I fear, sister, I have not refinement sufficient to enjoy it.

CHARLOTTE.   Oh! you cannot fail being pleased.

LETITIA.   Our ladies are so delicate and dressy.

CHARLOTTE.   And our beaux so dressy and delicate.

LETITIA.   Our ladies chat and flirt so agreeably.

CHARLOTTE.   And our beaux simper and bow so gracefully.

LETITIA.   With their hair so trim and neat.

CHARLOTTE.   And their faces so soft and sleek.

LETITIA.   Their buckles so tonish[3] and bright.

CHARLOTTE.   And their hands so slender and white.

LETITIA.   I vow, Charlotte, we are quite poetical.

CHARLOTTE.   And then, brother, the faces of the beaux are of such a lily white
hue! None of that horrid robustness of constitution, that vulgar corn-fed
glow of health, which can only serve to alarm an unmarried lady with apprehensions, and prove a melancholy memento to a married one, that she can
never hope for the happiness of being a widow. I will say this to the credit
of our city beaux, that such is the delicacy of their complexion, dress, and
address, that, even had I no reliance upon the honor of the dear Adonises,[4]
I would trust myself in any possible situation with them, without the least
apprehensions of rudeness.

MANLY.   Sister Charlotte!

CHARLOTTE.   Now, now, now brother [interrupting him], now don't go to
spoil my mirth with a dash of your gravity; I am so glad to see you, I am in
tip-top spirits. Oh! that you could be with us at a little snug party. There is
Billy Simper, Jack Chassé, and Colonel Van Titter, Miss Promonade, and
the two Miss Tambours, sometimes make a party, with some other ladies,
in a side-box[5] at the play. Everything is conducted with such decorum,—
first we bow round to the company in general, then to each one in particular, then we have so many inquiries after each other's health, and we are so
happy to meet with each other, and it is so many ages since we last had that
pleasure, and, if a married lady is in company, we have such a sweet dissertation upon her son Bobby's chin-cough, then the curtain rises, then our
sensibility[6] is all awake, and then by the mere force of apprehension, we
torture some harmless expression into a double meaning, which the poor
author never dreamt of, and then we have recourse to our fans, and then
we blush, and then the gentlemen jog one another, peep under the fan, and
make the prettiest remarks; and then we giggle and they simper, and they
giggle and we simper, and then the curtain drops, and then for nuts and
oranges, and then we bow, and it's pray Ma'am take it, and pray Sir keep it,
and oh! not for the world, Sir: and then the curtain rises again, and then we

2. Actor.
3. Smart, fashionable (from the French *ton*).
4. I.e., handsome youths, named for the beautiful
young man beloved by Venus in classical myth. "Ad-

dress": bearing.
5. Fashionable box seats, near the stage.
6. Responsiveness. "Chin-cough": whooping cough.

blush, and giggle, and simper, and bow, all over again. Oh! the sentimental charms of a side-box conversation! [*All laugh.*]

MANLY.   Well, sister, I join heartily with you in the laugh; for, in my opinion, it is as justifiable to laugh at folly, as it is reprehensible to ridicule misfortune.

CHARLOTTE.   Well, but brother, positively, I can't introduce you in these clothes: why, your coat looks as if it were calculated for the vulgar purpose of keeping yourself comfortable.

MANLY.   This coat was my regimental coat in the late war. The public tumults of our state[7] have induced me to buckle on the sword in support of that government which I once fought to establish. I can only say, sister, that there was a time when this coat was respectable, and some people even thought that those men who had endured so many winter campaigns in the service of their country, without bread, clothing, or pay, at least deserved that the poverty of their appearance should not be ridiculed.

CHARLOTTE.   We agree in opinion entirely, brother, though it would not have done for me to have said it: it is the coat makes the man respectable. In the time of the war, when we were almost frightened to death, why, your coat was respectable, that is, fashionable; now another kind of coat is fashionable, that is, respectable. And pray direct the taylor to make yours the height of the fashion.

MANLY.   Though it is of little consequence to me of what shape my coat is, yet, as to the height of the fashion, there you will please to excuse me, sister. You know my sentiments on that subject. I have often lamented the advantage which the French have over us in the particular. In Paris, the fashions have their dawnings, their routine and declensions,[8] and depend as much upon the caprice of the day as in other countries; but there every lady assumes a right to deviate from the general *ton*, as far as will be of advantage to her own appearance. In America, the cry is, what is the fashion? and we follow it, indiscriminately, because it is so.

CHARLOTTE.   Therefore it is, that when large hoops are in fashion, we often see many a plump girl lost in the immensity of a hoop petticoat, whose want of height and *em-bon-point*[9] would never have been remarked in any other dress. When the high head-dress is the mode, how then do we see a lofty cushion, with a profusion of gauze, feathers, and ribband, supported by a face no bigger than an apple; whilst a broad full-faced lady, who really would have appeared tolerably handsome in a large head-dress, looks with her smart *chapeau*[1] as masculine as a soldier.

MANLY.   But remember, my dear sister, and I wish all my fair country-women would recollect, that the only excuse a young lady can have for going extravagantly into a fashion, is, because it makes her look extravagantly handsome.—Ladies, I must wish you a good morning.

CHARLOTTE.   But, brother, you are going to make home with us.

MANLY.   Indeed, I cannot. I have seen my uncle, and explained that matter.

CHARLOTTE.   Come and dine with us, then. We have a family dinner about half past four o'clock.

MANLY.   I am engaged to dine with the Spanish ambassador. I was introduced to him by an old brother officer; and instead of freezing me with a cold card

---

7. The young nation's problems, especially the financial ones, were by no means solved by the Revolution. Manly may be referring specifically to Shays's Rebellion (1787) in Massachusetts. Daniel Shays, a war veteran, led an armed protest against high taxes and the lack of paper money; it was quickly put down by the militia, of which Tyler was at the time a member.
8. I.e., pattern and fall.
9. Stoutness. "Want": lack.
1. Hat.

of compliment[2] to dine with him ten days hence, he, with the true old Castilian frankness, in a friendly manner, asked me to dine with him to-day—an honor I could not refuse. Sister, adieu—Madam, your most obedient—[*Exit.*]

CHARLOTTE.   I will wait upon you to the door, brother; I have something particular to say to you. [*Exit.*]

LETITIA [*alone*].   What a pair!—She the pink of flirtation, he the essence of everything that is *outré*[3] and gloomy.—I think I have completely deceived Charlotte by my manner of speaking of Mr. Dimple; she's too much the friend of Maria to be confided in. He is certainly rendering himself disagreeable to Maria, in order to break with her and proffer his hand to me. This is what the delicate fellow hinted in our last conversation. [*Exit.*]

SCENE 2. The Mall.

[*Enter* JESSAMY.]

JESSAMY.   Positively this Mall is a very pretty place. I hope the city won't ruin it by repairs. To be sure, it won't do to speak of in the same day with Ranelagh or Vauxhall;[4] however, it's a fine place for a young fellow to display his person to advantage. Indeed, nothing is lost here; the girls have taste, and I am very happy to find they have adopted the elegant London fashion of looking back, after a genteel fellow like me has passed them. Ah! who comes here! This, by his awkwardness, must be the Yankee colonel's servant. I'll accost him.

[*Enter* JONATHAN.]

V*otre très*—humble *serviteur*, Monsieur.[5] I understand Colonel Manly, the Yankee officer, has the honor of your services.

JONATHAN.   Sir!—

JESSAMY.   I say, Sir, I understand that Colonel Manly has the honor of having you for a servant.

JONATHAN.   Servant! Sir, do you take me for a neger,—I am Colonel Manly's waiter.[6]

JESSAMY.   A true Yankee distinction egad, without a difference. Why, Sir, do you not perform all the offices of a servant? Do you not even blacken his boots?

JONATHAN.   Yes; I do grease them a bit sometimes; but I am a true blue son of liberty, for all that. Father said I should come as Colonel Manly's waiter to see the world, and all that; but no man shall master me: my father has as good a farm as the colonel.

JESSAMY.   Well, Sir, we will not quarrel about terms upon the eve of an acquaintance, from which I promise myself so much satisfaction,—therefore *sans ceremonie*[7]—

JONATHAN.   What?—

JESSAMY.   I say, I am extremely happy to see Colonel Manly's waiter.

JONATHAN.   Well, and I vow, too, I am pretty considerably glad to see you—but what the dogs need of all this outlandish lingo? Who may you be, Sir, if I may be so bold?

JESSAMY.   I have the honor to be Mr. Dimple's servant, or, if you please, waiter. We lodge under the same roof, and should be glad of the honor of your acquaintance.

---

2. Invitation card.
3. Bizarre (French).
4. London pleasure gardens.

5. Your very humble servant, sir (French).
6. Valet, manservant.
7. Without ceremony (French).

JONATHAN.   You a waiter! By the living jingo, you look so topping, I took you for one of the agents to Congress.[8]

JESSAMY.   The brute has discernment notwithstanding his appearance.—Give me leave to say I wonder then at your familiarity.

JONATHAN.   Why, as to the matter of that, Mr.—pray, what's your name?

JESSAMY.   Jessamy, at your service.

JONATHAN.   Why, I swear we don't make any great matter of distinction in our state, between quality and other folks.

JESSAMY.   This is, indeed, a leveling principle. I hope, Mr. Jonathan, you have not taken part with the insurgents.

JONATHAN.   Why, since General Shays has sneaked off, and given us the bag to hold, I don't care to give my opinion; but you'll promise not to tell— put your ear this way—you won't tell?—I vow, I did think the sturgeons[9] were right.

JESSAMY.   I thought, Mr. Jonathan, you Massachusetts men always argued with a gun in your hand.—Why didn't you join them?

JONATHAN.   Why, the colonel is one of those folks called the Shin—shin— dang it all, I can't speak them *lignum vitæ* words—you know who I mean— there is a company of them—they wear a China goose at their buttonhole— a kind of gilt thing.[1]—Now the colonel told father and brother,—you must know there are, let me see—there is Elnathan, Silas, and Barnabas, Tabi- tha—no, no, she's a she—tarnation, now I have it—there's Elnathan, Silas, Barnabas, Jonathan, that's I—seven of us, six went into the wars, and I staid at home to take care of mother. Colonel said that it was a burning shame for the true blue Bunker-hill sons of liberty, who had fought Governor Hutchinson, Lord North,[2] and the Devil, to have any hand in kicking up a cursed dust against a government, which we had every mother's son of us a hand in making.

JESSAMY.   Bravo!—Well, have you been abroad in the city since your arrival? What have you seen that is curious and entertaining?

JONATHAN.   Oh! I have seen a power of fine sights. I went to see two marble- stone men and a leaden horse, that stands out in doors in all weathers; and when I came where they was, one had got no head, and t'other wer'nt there. They said as how the leaden man was a damn'd tory,[3] and that he took wit in his anger and rode off in the time of the troubles.

JESSAMY.   But this was not the end of your excursion.

JONATHAN.   Oh, no; I went to a place they call Holy Ground. Now I counted this was a place where folks go to meeting;[4] so I put my hymn-book in my pocket, and walked softly and grave as a minister; and when I came there, the dogs a bit of a meeting-house could I see. At last I spied a young gentle- woman standing by one of the seats, which they have here at the doors—I took her to be the deacon's daughter, and she looked so kind, and so oblig- ing, that I thought I would go and ask her the way to lecture, and would you think it—she called me dear, and sweeting, and honey, just as if we were married; by the living jingo, I had a month's mind to buss[5] her.

8. Ambassador.
9. Jonathan's awkward mispronunciation of Jessamy's *insurgents*, above; being from Massachusetts, he is on Shays' side.
1. The badge of the Society of the Cincinnati, a Revo- lutionary officers fraternal group, was a gold eagle. "*Lignum vitae*": staff of life (Latin, literal trans.); here, the tough wood of a tropical tree recently introduced into New England.
2. Lord Frederick North was prime minister of En-

gland from 1770 to 1782. Bunker Hill, then outside of Boston, was the site of the first engagement in the Revolution. Thomas Hutchinson was British governor of Massachusetts from 1771 to 1774.
3. British Loyalist.
4. Church service. "Holy Ground": New York's whorehouse district, apparently so-called because Trinity Church owned much of the land.
5. Kiss.

JESSAMY.   Well, but how did it end?

JONATHAN.   Why, as I was standing talking with her, a parcel of sailor men and boys got round me, the snarl headed curs fell a-kicking and cursing of me at such a tarnal[6] rate, that, I vow, I was glad to take to my heels and split home, right off, tail on end like a stream of chalk.

JESSAMY.   Why, my dear friend, you are not acquainted with the city; that girl you saw was a—[*Whispers.*]

JONATHAN.   Mercy on my soul! was that young woman a harlot!—Well, if this is New York Holy Ground, what must the Holy-day Ground be!

JESSAMY.   Well, you should not judge of the city too rashly. We have a number of elegant fine girls here, that make a man's leisure hours pass very agreeably. I would esteem it an honor to announce[7] you to some of them.— Gad! that announce is a select word; I wonder where I picked it up.

JONATHAN.   I don't want to know them.

JESSAMY.   Come, come, my dear friend, I see that I must assume the honor of being the director of your amusements. Nature has given us passions, and youth and opportunity stimulate to gratify them. It is no shame, my dear Blueskin,[8] for a man to amuse himself with a little gallantry.

JONATHAN.   Girl huntry! I don't altogether understand. I never played at that game. I know how to play hunt the squirrel, but I can't play anything with the girls; I am as good as married.

JESSAMY.   Vulgar, horrid brute! Married, and above a hundred miles from his wife, and think that an objection to his making love to every woman he meets! He never can have read, no, he never can have been in a room with a volume of the divine Chesterfield.—So you are married?

JONATHAN.   No, I don't say so; I said I was as good as married, a kind of promise.

JESSAMY.   As good as married!—

JONATHAN.   Why, yes; there's Tabitha Wymen, the deacon's daughter, at home, she and I have been courting a great while, and folks say as how we are to be married; and so I broke a piece of money with her when we parted,[9] and she promised not to spark it with Solomon Dyer while I am gone. You wouldn't have me false to my true love, would you?

JESSAMY.   May be you have another reason for constancy; possibly the young lady has a fortune? Ha! Mr. Jonathan, the solid charms; the chains of love are never so binding as when the links are made of gold.

JONATHAN.   Why, as to fortune, I must needs say her father is pretty dumb rich; he went representative for our town last year. He will give her—let me see—four times seven is—seven times four—nought and carry one;—he will give her twenty acres of land—somewhat rocky though—a Bible, and a cow.

JESSAMY.   Twenty acres of rock, a Bible, and a cow! Why, my dear Mr. Jonathan, we have servant maids, or, as you would more elegantly express it, wait'resses, in this city, who collect more in one year from their mistress' cast[1] clothes.

JONATHAN.   You don't say so!—

JESSAMY.   Yes, and I'll introduce you to one of them. There is a little lump of flesh and delicacy that lives at next door, wait'ress to Miss Maria; we often see her on the stoop.

---

6. Mild oath (from *eternal*). "Parcel": pack.
7. Present.
8. I.e., Yankee (from the blue of the Revolutionary Army uniform); also, possibly, mulatto.

9. A country custom: a coin was broken by a parting couple, and each kept one of the pieces.
1. I.e., cast-off.

JONATHAN.   But are you sure she would be courted by me?

JESSAMY.   Never doubt it; remember a faint heart never[2]—blisters of my tongue—I was going to be guilty of a vile proverb; flat against the authority of Chesterfield.—I say there can be no doubt, that the brilliancy of your merit will secure you a favorable reception.

JONATHAN.   Well, but what must I say to her?

JESSAMY.   Say to her! why, my dear friend, though I admire your profound knowledge on every other subject, yet, you will pardon my saying, that your want of opportunity has made the female heart escape the poignancy of your penetration. Say to her!—Why, when a man goes a-courting, and hopes for success, he must begin with doing, and not saying.

JONATHAN.   Well, what must I do?

JESSAMY.   Why, when you are introduced you must make five or six elegant bows.

JONATHAN.   Six elegant bows! I understand that; six, you say? Well—

JESSAMY.   Then you must press and kiss her hand; then press and kiss, and so on to her lips and cheeks; then talk as much as you can about hearts, darts, flames, nectar and ambrosia—the more incoherent the better.

JONATHAN.   Well, but suppose she should be angry with I?

JESSAMY.   Why, if she should pretend—please to observe, Mr. Jonathan—if she should pretend to be offended, you must—But I'll tell you how my master acted in such a case: He was seated by a young lady of eighteen upon a sofa, plucking with a wanton hand the blooming sweets of youth and beauty. When the lady thought it necessary to check his ardor, she called up a frown upon her lovely face, so irresistably alluring, that it would have warmed the frozen bosom of age: remember, said she, putting her delicate arm upon his, remember your character and my honor. My master instantly dropped upon his knees, with eyes swimming with love, cheeks glowing with desire, and in the gentlest modulation of voice, he said—My dear Caroline, in a few months our hands will be indissolubly united at the altar; our hearts I feel are already so—the favors you now grant as evidence of your affection, are favors indeed; yet when the ceremony is once past, what will now be received with rapture, will then be attributed to duty.

JONATHAN.   Well, and what was the consequence?

JESSAMY.   The consequence!—Ah! forgive me, my dear friend, but you New England gentlemen have such a laudable curiosity of seeing the bottom of every thing;—why, to the honest, I confess I saw the blooming cherub of a consequence smiling in its angelic mother's arms, about ten months afterwards.

JONATHAN.   Well, if I follow all your plans, make them six bows, and all that; shall I have such little cherubim consequences?

JESSAMY.   Undoubtedly.—What are you musing upon?

JONATHAN.   You say you'll certainly make me acquainted?—Why, I was thinking then how I should contrive to pass this broken piece of silver—won't it buy a sugar-dram?[3]

JESSAMY.   What is that, the love-token from the deacon's daughter?—You come on bravely. But I must hasten to my master. Adieu, my dear friend.

JONATHAN.   Stay, Mr. Jessamy—must I buss her when I am introduced to her?

JESSAMY.   I told you, you must kiss her.

JONATHAN.   Well, but must I buss her?

2. I.e., faint heart never won fair lady.   3. I.e., a small amount of sugar.

JESSAMY.   Why, kiss and buss, and buss and kiss, is all one.

JONATHAN.   Oh! my dear friend, though you have a profound knowledge of all, a pugnancy[4] of tribulation, you don't know everything. [*Exit.*]

JESSAMY [*alone*].   Well, certainly I improve; my master could not have insinuated himself with more address into the heart of a man he despised.—Now will this blundering dog sicken Jenny with his nauseous pawings, until she flies into my arms for very ease. How sweet will the contrast be, between the blundering Jonathan, and the courtly and accomplished Jessamy.

Act Third

SCENE 1. DIMPLE's *room.*

[DIMPLE *discovered at a Toilet,*[5] *reading.*]

DIMPLE.   "Women have in general but one object, which is their beauty." Very true, my lord; positively very true. "Nature has hardly formed a woman ugly enough to be insensible to flattery upon her person." Extremely just, my lord; every day's delightful experience confirms this. "If her face is so shocking, that she must, in some degree, be conscious of it, her figure and air, she thinks, make ample amends for it." The sallow Miss Wan is a proof of this.—Upon my telling the distasteful wretch, the other day, that her countenance spoke the pensive language of sentiment, and that Lady Wortley Montague[6] declared, that if the ladies were arrayed in the garb of innocence, the face would be the last part which would be admired as Monsieur Milton expresses it, she grin'd horribly a ghastly smile.[7] "If her figure is deformed, she thinks her face counterbalances it."

[*Enter* JESSAMY *with letters.*]

DIMPLE.   Where got you these, Jessamy?

JESSAMY.   Sir, the English packet[8] is arrived.

[DIMPLE *opens and reads a letter enclosing notes.*]

"SIR,

"I have drawn bills on you in favor of Messrs. Van Cash and Co. as per margin. I have taken up your note to Col. Piquet, and discharged your debts to my Lord Lurcher and Sir Harry Rook. I herewith enclose you copies of the bills, which I have no doubt will be immediately honored. On failure, I shall empower some lawyer in your country to recover the amounts.

"I am, Sir,

"Your most humble servant,

"JOHN HAZARD."

Now, did not my lord expressly say, that it was unbecoming a well-bred man to be in a passion, I confess I should be ruffled. [*Reads.*] "There is no accident so unfortunate, which a wise man may not turn to his advantage; nor any accident so fortunate, which a fool will not turn to his disadvantage." True, my lord: but how advantage can be derived from this, I can't see. Chesterfield himself, who made, however, the worst practice of the most excellent precepts, was never in so embarrassing a situation. I love the person of Charlotte, and it is necessary I should command the fortune of

---

4. Another awkward mispronunciation—of Jessemy's *poignancy*, above.
5. I.e., revealed sitting at a dressing table. He is reading Chesterfield's *Letters.*

6. English poet and letter writer (1689–1762).
7. "Death / Grinned horrible a ghastly smile," *Paradise Lost* 2.845–46, by John Milton (1608–1674).
8. Passenger boat carrying mail and cargo.

Letitia. As to Maria!—I doubt not by my *sang-froid*[9] behavior I shall compel
her to decline the match; but the blame must not fall upon me. A prudent
man, as my lord says, should take all the credit of a good action to himself,
and throw the discredit of a bad one upon others. I must break with Maria,
marry Letitia, and as for Charlotte—why, Charlotte must be a companion
to my wife.—Here, Jessamy!

    [*Enter* JESSAMY.]

    [DIMPLE *folds and seals two letters.*]

DIMPLE.   Here, Jessamy, take this letter to my love. [*Gives one.*]

JESSAMY.   To which of your honor's loves?—Oh! [*reading*] to Miss Letitia,
your honor's rich love.

DIMPLE.   And this [*delivers another*] to Miss Charlotte Manly. See that you
deliver them privately.

JESSAMY.   Yes, your honor. [*Going.*]

DIMPLE.   Jessamy, who are these strange lodgers that came to the house last
night?

JESSAMY.   Why, the master is a Yankee colonel; I have not seen much of him;
but the man is the most unpolished animal your honor ever disgraced your
eyes by looking upon. I have had one of the most *outré* conversations with
him!—He really has a most prodigious effect upon my risibility.

DIMPLE.   I ought, according to every rule of Chesterfield, to wait on him[1] and
insinuate myself into his good graces.—Jessamy, wait on the colonel with
my compliments, and if he is disengaged, I will do myself the honor of
paying him my respects.—Some ignorant unpolished boor—

    [JESSAMY *goes off and returns.*]

JESSAMY.   Sir, the colonel is gone out, and Jonathan, his servant, says that he
is gone to stretch his legs upon the Mall—Stretch his legs! what an indelicacy of diction!

DIMPLE.   Very well. Reach me my hat and sword. I'll accost him there, in
my way to Letitia's, as by accident; pretend to be struck with his person and
address, and endeavor to steal into his confidence. Jessamy, I have no business for you at present. [*Exit.*]

JESSAMY [*taking up the book*].   My master and I obtain our knowledge from
the same source;—though, gad! I think myself much the prettier fellow of
the two. [*Surveying himself in the glass.*] That was a brilliant thought, to
insinuate that I folded my master's letters for him; the folding is so neat,
that it does honor to the operator. I once intended to have insinuated that I
wrote his letters too; but that was before I saw them; it won't do now! no
honor there, positively.—"Nothing looks more vulgar [*reading affectedly*],
ordinary, and illiberal, than ugly, uneven, and ragged nails; the ends of
which should be kept even and clean, not tipped with black, and cut in
small segments of circles"—Segments of circles! surely my lord did not consider that he wrote for the beaux. Segments of circles! what a crabbed term!
Now I dare answer, that my master, with all his learning, does not know
that this means, according to the present mode, to let the nails grow long,
and then cut them off even at top. [*Laughing without.*] Ha! that's Jenny's
titter. I protest I despair of ever teaching that girl to laugh; she has something
so execrably natural in her laugh, that I declare it absolutely discomposes
my nerves. How came she into our house!—[*Calls.*] Jenny!

    [*Enter* JENNY.]

JESSAMY.   Prythee, Jenny, don't spoil your fine face with laughing.

---

9. Cool, unperturbable (French).   1. Pay him a formal call.

JENNY. Why, mustn't I laugh, Mr. Jessamy?

JESSAMY. You may smile; but, as my lord says, nothing can authorize a laugh.[2]

JENNY. Well, but I can't help laughing—Have you seen him, Mr. Jessamy? Ha, ha, ha!

JESSAMY. Seen whom?—

JENNY. Why, Jonathan, the New England colonel's servant. Do you know he was at the play last night, and the stupid creature don't know where he has been. He would not go to a play for the world; he thinks it was a show, as he calls it.

JESSAMY. As ignorant and unpolished as he is, do you know, Miss Jenny, that I propose to introduce him to the honor of your acquaintance.

JENNY. Introduce him to me! for what?

JESSAMY. Why, my lovely girl, that you may take him under your protection, as Madam Ramboulliet did young Stanhope; that you may, by your plastic[3] hand, mould this uncouth cub into a gentleman. He is to make love to you.

JENNY. Make love to me!—

JESSAMY. Yes, Mistress Jenny, make love to you; and, I doubt not, when he shall become domesticated in your kitchen, that this boor, under your auspices, will soon become *un aimable petit Jonathan*.[4]

JENNY. I must say, Mr. Jessamy, if he copies after me, he will be vastly monstrously polite.

JESSAMY. Stay here one moment, and I will call him.—Jonathan!—Mr. Jonathan!—[*Calls.*]

JONATHAN [*within*]. Holla! there—[*Enters.*] You promise to stand by me— six bows you say. [*Bows.*]

JESSAMY. Mrs. Jenny, I have the honor of presenting Mr. Jonathan, Colonel Manly's waiter, to you. I am extremely happy that I have it in my power to make two worthy people acquainted with each other's merit.

JENNY. So, Mr. Jonathan, I hear you were at the play last night.

JONATHAN. At the play! why, did you think I went to the devil's drawing-room!

JENNY. The devil's drawing-room!

JONATHAN. Yes; why ain't cards and dice the devil's device; and the play-house the shop where the devil hangs out the vanities of the world, upon the tenterhooks of temptation. I believe you have not heard how they were acting the old boy one night, and the wicked one came among them sure enough; and went right off in a storm, and carried one quarter of the play-house with him. Oh! no, no, no! you won't catch me at a play-house, I warrant you.

JENNY. Well, Mr. Jonathan, though I don't scruple your veracity, I have some reasons for believing you were there; pray, where were you about six o'clock?

JONATHAN. Why, I went to see one Mr. Morrison, the *hocus pocus* man; they said as how he could eat a café knife.[5]

JENNY. Well, and how did you find the place?

JONATHAN. As I was going about here and there, to and again, to find it, I saw a great croud of folks going into a long entry, that had lantherns over

2. "To my mind, there is nothing so illiberal and so ill-bred, as audible laughter"—Chesterfield's *Letters*.
3. Creative.
4. A well-behaved little Jonathan (French).

5. I.e., a restaurant knife: Morrison was evidently not only a conjurer ("*hocus-pocus* man") but also a sword-swallower.

the door; so I asked a man, whether that was not the place where they played *hocus pocus?* He was a very civil kind man, though he did speak like the Hessians;[6] he lifted up his eyes and said—"they play *hocus pocus* tricks enough there, Got knows, mine friend."

JENNY. Well—

JONATHAN. So I went right in, and they shewed me away clean up to the garret, just like a meeting-house gallery. And so I saw a power of topping folks, all sitting round in little cabins,[7] just like father's corncribs;—and then there was such a squeaking with the fiddles, and such a tarnal blaze with the lights, my head was near turned. At last the people that sat near me set up such a hissing—hiss—like so many mad cats; and then they went thump, thump, thump, just like our Peleg threshing wheat, and stampt away, just like the nation;[8] and called out for one Mr. Langolee,—I suppose he helps act the tricks.

JENNY. Well, and what did you do all this time?

JONATHAN. Gor, I—I liked the fun, and so I thumpt away, and hiss'd as lustily as the best of 'em. One sailor-looking man that sat by me, seeing me stamp, and knowing I was a cute fellow, because I could make a roaring noise, clapt me on the shoulder and said, you are a d——d hearty cock, smite my timbers! I told him so I was, but I thought he need not swear so, and make use of such naughty words.

JESSAMY. The savage!—Well, and did you see the man with his tricks?

JONATHAN. Why, I vow, as I was looking out for him, they lifted up a great green cloth, and let us look right into the next neighbor's house. Have you a good many houses in New York made so in that 'ere way?

JENNY. Not many: but did you see the family?

JONATHAN. Yes, swamp it; I see'd the family.

JENNY. Well, and how did you like them?

JONATHAN. Why, I vow they were pretty much like other families;—there was a poor, good natured, curse of a husband, and a sad rantipole[9] of a wife.

JENNY. But did you see no other folks?

JONATHAN. Yes. There was one youngster, they called him Mr. Joseph; he talked as sober and as pious as a minister; but like some ministers that I know, he was a fly tike[1] in his heart for all that: He was going to ask a young woman to spark it with him, and—the Lord have mercy on my soul!—she was another man's wife!

JESSAMY. The Wabash![2]

JENNY. And did you see any more folks?

JONATHAN. Why they came on as thick as mustard. For my part, I thought the house was haunted. There was a soldier fellow, who talked about his row de dow dow, and courted a young woman:[3] but of all the cute folk I saw, I liked one little fellow—

JENNY. Aye! who was he?

JONATHAN. Why, he had red hair, and a little round plump face like mine,

---

6. Germans, especially from Hesse, had been hired by the British as mercenary troops for the Revolutionary War.
7. I.e., in boxes in the theater.
8. I.e., damnation.
9. Unruly, wild person.
1. I.e., artful kid. The "rantipole" wife and the "pious" Joseph had by this time clued in contemporary audiences to the fact that the play Jonathan has taken for real life is Richard Brinsley Sheridan's *The School*

for Scandal (1777), which had been performed in New York the previous month—a production that Tyler saw.
2. Perhaps "the scoundrel."
3. As there is no "soldier fellow" in *The School for Scandal*, Jonathan is probably now talking about *The Poor Soldier* (1783), a comic opera played on the same bill as Sheridan's play. "Row de dow dow": noisy disturbance.

only not altogether so handsome. His name was Darby:—that was his bap-
tizing name, his other name I forgot. Oh! it was, Wig—Wag—Wagall,
Darby Wag-all;[4]—pray, do you know him?—I should like to take a fling[5]
with him, or a drap of cyder with a pepper-pod in it, to make it warm
and comfortable.

JENNY.   I can't say I have that pleasure.

JONATHAN.   I wish you did, he is a cute fellow. But there was one thing I
didn't like in that Mr. Darby; and that was, he was afraid of some of them
'ere shooting irons, such as your troopers wear on training days. Now, I'm
a true born Yankee American son of liberty, and I never was afraid of a gun
yet in all my life.

JENNY.   Well, Mr. Jonathan, you were certainly at the play-house.

JONATHAN.   I at the play-house!—Why didn't I see the play then?

JENNY.   Why, the people you saw were players.

JONATHAN.   Mercy on my soul! did I see the wicked players?—Mayhap that
'ere Darby that I liked so, was the old serpent himself, and had his cloven
foot in his pocket. Why, I vow, now I come to think on 't, the candles
seemed to burn blue, and I am sure where I sat it smelt tarnally of brimstone.

JESSAMY.   Well, Mr. Jonathan, from your account, which I confess is very
accurate, you must have been at the play-house.

JONATHAN.   Why, I vow I began to smell a rat. When I came away, I went to
the man for my money again: you want your money, says he; yes, says I; for
what, says he; why, says I, no man shall jocky me out of my money; I paid
my money to see sights, and the dogs a bit of a sight have I seen, unless you
call listening to people's private business a sight. Why says he, it is the
School for Scandalization.—The School for Scandalization—Oh, ho! no
wonder you New York folks are so cute at it, when you go to school to learn
it: and so I jogged off.[6]

JESSAMY.   My dear Jenny, my master's business drags me from you; would to
heaven I knew no other servitude than to your charms.

JONATHAN.   Well, but don't go; you won't leave me so.—

JESSAMY.   Excuse me.—Remember the cash. [*Aside to him, and—Exit.*]

JENNY.   Mr. Jonathan, won't you please to sit down. Mr. Jessamy tells me
you wanted to have some conversation with me.

      [*Having brought forward two chairs, they sit.*]

JONATHAN.   Ma'am!—

JENNY.   Sir!—

JONATHAN.   Ma'am!—

JENNY.   Pray, how do you like the city, Sir?

JONATHAN.   Ma'am!—

JENNY.   I say, Sir, how do you like New York?

JONATHAN.   Ma'am!—

JENNY.   The stupid creature! but I must pass some little time with him, if it
is only to endeavor to learn, whether it was his master that made such an
abrupt entrance into our house, and my young mistress's heart, this morning. [*Aside.*] As you don't seem to like to talk, Mr. Jonathan—do you
sing?

JONATHAN.   Gor, I—I am glad she asked that, for I forgot what Mr. Jessamy

---

4. I.e., Thomas Wignell, one of whose famous parts   5. Other texts read "sling"—an alcoholic drink.
was Darby in *The Poor Soldier*.   6. Trotted off.

bid me say, and I dare as well be hanged as act what he bid me do, I'm so ashamed. [*Aside.*] Yes, Ma'am, I can sing—I can sing Mear, Old Hundred, and Bangor.[7]

JENNY. Oh, I don't mean psalm tunes. Have you no little song to please the ladies; such as Roslin Castle, or the Maid of the Mill?[8]

JONATHAN. Why, all my tunes go to meeting tunes, save one, and I count you won't altogether like that 'ere.

JENNY. What is it called?

JONATHAN. I am sure you have heard folks talk about it, it is called Yankee Doodle.

JENNY. Oh! it is the tune I am fond of; and, if I know anything of my mistress, she would be glad to dance to it. Pray, sing?

JONATHAN [*sings*].

Father and I went to camp,—
Along with Captain Goodwin;
And there we saw the men and boys,
As thick as hasty pudding.[9]
     Yankee Doodle do, etc.

And there we saw a swamping gun,
Big as log of maple,
On a little deuced cart,
A load for father's cattle.[1]
     Yankee Doodle do, etc.

And every time they fired it off,
It took a horn of powder,
It made a noise—like father's gun,
Only a nation louder.
     Yankee Doodle do, etc.

There was a man in our town,
His name was—

No, no, that won't do. Now, if I was with Tabitha Wymen and Jemima Cawley, down at father Chase's, I shouldn't mind singing this all out before them—you would be affronted if I was to sing that, though that's a lucky thought; if you should be affronted, I have something dang'd cute, which Jessamy told me to say to you.

JENNY. Is that all! I assure you I like it of all things.

JONATHAN. No, no; I can sing more, some other time, when you and I are better acquainted, I'll sing the whole of it—no, no—that's a fib—I can't sing but a hundred and ninety verses: our Tabitha at home can sing it all.—
                                [*Sings.*]

Marblehead's a rocky place,
And Cape-Cod is sandy;
Charleston is burnt down,

7. Popular names for hymn tunes: "Mear" is probably "Meae Animae Amator" (Jesus, lover of my soul); "Old Hundred" is "All People That on Earth Do Dwell"; "Bangor" is "Eternal God, We Look to Thee."

8. Popular songs of the time.
9. Breakfast dish made from Indian corn and water (see also *Hasty Pudding*, p. 831).
1. I.e., oxen. "Swamping": big, overwhelming.

Boston is the dandy.
    Yankee Doodle do, etc.

I vow, my own town song has put me into such topping spirits, that I believe I'll begin to do a little, as Jessamy says we must when we go a courting— [*Runs and kisses her.*] Burning rivers! cooling flames! red hot roses! pig-nuts! hasty-pudding and ambrosia!

JENNY.   What means this freedom! you insulting wretch. [*Strikes him.*]

JONATHAN.   Are you affronted?

JENNY.   Affronted! with what looks shall I express my anger?

JONATHAN.   Looks! why, as to the matter of looks, you look as cross as a witch.

JENNY.   Have you no feeling for the delicacy of my sex?

JONATHAN.   Feeling! Gor, I—I feel the delicacy of your sex pretty smartly [*rubbing his cheek*], though, I vow, I thought when you city ladies courted and married, and all that, you put feeling out of the question. But I want to know whether you are really affronted, or only pretend to be so? 'Cause, if you are certainly right down affronted, I am at the end of my tether;— Jessamy didn't tell me what to say to you.

JENNY.   Pretend to be affronted!

JONATHAN.   Aye, aye, if you only pretend, you shall hear how I'll go to work to make cherubim consequences.[2] [*Runs up to her.*]

JENNY.   Begone, you brute!

JONATHAN.   That looks like mad; but I won't lose my speech. My dearest Jenny—your name is Jenny, I think? My dearest Jenny, though I have the highest esteem for the sweet favors you have just now granted me—Gor, that's a fib though, but Jessamy says it is not wicked to tell lies to the women. [*Aside.*] I say, though I have the highest esteem for the favors you have just now granted me, yet, you will consider, that as soon as the dissolvable knot is tied, they will no longer be favors, but only matters of duty, and matters of course.

JENNY.   Marry you! you audacious monster! get out of my sight, or rather let me fly from you. [*Exit hastily.*]

JONATHAN.   Gor! she's gone off in a swinging passion, before I had time to think of consequences. If this is the way with your city ladies, give me the twenty acres of rocks, the Bible, the cow, and Tabitha, and a little peaceable bundling.[3]

SCENE 2. *The Mall.*

[*Enter* MANLY.]

MANLY.   It must be so, Montague! and it is not at all the tribe of Mandevilles[4] shall convince me, that a nation, to become great, must first become dissipated. Luxury is surely the bane of a nation: Luxury! which enervates both soul and body, by opening a thousand new sources of enjoyment, opens, also, a thousand new sources of contention and want: Luxury! which renders a people weak at home, and accessible to bribery, corruption, and force from abroad. When the Grecian states knew no other tools than the axe and the saw, the Grecians were a great, a free, and a happy people. The kings of Greece devoted their lives to the service of their country, and her senators

"Deuced": i.e., damned.
2. Cf. p. 859.
3. An old courtship custom, in which a couple occupied the same bed without undressing.

4. Edward Montague and Bernard Mandeville, 18th-century authors of books on the decline of civilizations and the folly of mankind.

knew no other superiority over their fellow-citizens than a glorious preeminence in danger and virtue. They exhibited to the world a noble spectacle,—a number of independent states united by a similarity of language, sentiment, manners, common interest, and common consent, in one grand mutual league of protection.—And, thus united, long might they have continued the cherishers of arts and sciences, the protectors of the oppressed, the scourge of tyrants, and the safe asylum of liberty: But when foreign gold, and still more pernicious, foreign luxury, had crept among them, they sapped the vitals of their virtue. The virtues of their ancestors were only found in their writings. Envy and suspicion, the vices of little minds, possessed them. The various states engendered jealousies of each other; and, more unfortunately, growing jealous of their great federal council, the Amphictyons,[5] they forgot that their common safety had existed, and would exist, in giving them an honorable extensive prerogative. The common good was lost in the pursuit of private interest; and that people, who, by uniting, might have stood against the world in arms, by dividing, crumbled into ruin;—their name is now only known in the page of the historian, and what they once were, is all we have left to admire. Oh! that America! Oh! that my country, would in this her day, learn the things which belong to her peace!

     [*Enter* DIMPLE.]

DIMPLE.   You are Colonel Manly, I presume?

MANLY.   At your service, Sir.

DIMPLE.   My name is Dimple, Sir. I have the honor to be a lodger in the same house with you, and hearing you were in the Mall, came hither to take the liberty of joining you.

MANLY.   You are very obliging, Sir.

DIMPLE.   As I understand you are a stranger here, Sir, I have taken the liberty to introduce myself to your acquaintance, as possibly I may have it in my power to point out some things in this city worthy your notice.

MANLY.   An attention to strangers is worthy a liberal mind, and must ever be gratefully received. But to a soldier, who has no fixed abode, such attentions are particularly pleasing.

DIMPLE.   Sir, there is no character so respectable as that of a soldier. And, indeed, when we reflect how much we owe to those brave men who have suffered so much in the service of their country, and secured to us those inestimable blessings that we now enjoy, our liberty and independence, they demand every attention which gratitude can pay. For my own part, I never meet an officer, but I embrace him as my friend, nor a private in distress, but I insensibly extend my charity to him.—I have hit the Bumpkin[6] off very tolerably. [*Aside.*]

MANLY.   Give me your hand, Sir! I do not proffer this hand to everybody; but you steal into my heart. I hope I am as insensible to flattery as most men; but I declare (it may be my weak side), that I never hear the name of soldier mentioned with respect, but I experience a thrill of pleasure, which I never feel on any other occasion.

DIMPLE.   Will you give me leave, my dear colonel, to confer an obligation on myself, by shewing you some civilities during your stay here, and giving a similar opportunity to some of my friends?

MANLY.   Sir, I thank you; but I believe my stay in this city will be very short.

---

5. Religious associations of Greek states.   6. Rustic.

DIMPLE.   I can introduce you to some men of excellent sense, in whose company you will esteem yourself happy; and, by way of amusement, to some
fine girls, who will listen to your soft things with pleasure.

MANLY.   Sir, I should be proud of the honor of being acquainted with those
gentlemen;—but, as for the ladies, I don't understand you.

DIMPLE.   Why, Sir, I need not tell you, that when a young gentleman is
alone with a young lady, he must say some soft things to her fair cheek—
indeed the lady will expect it. To be sure, there is not much pleasure, when
a man of the world and a finished coquette meet, who perfectly know each
other; but how delicious is it to excite the emotions of joy, hope, expectation, and delight, in the bosom of a lovely girl, who believes every tittle of
what you say to be serious.

MANLY.   Serious, Sir! In my opinion, the man, who, under pretensions of
marriage, can plant thorns in the bosom of an innocent, unsuspecting girl,
is more detestable than a common robber, in the same proportion, as private
violence is more despicable than open force, and money of less value than
happiness.

DIMPLE.   How he awes me by the superiority of his sentiments. [Aside.] As
you say, Sir, a gentleman should be cautious how he mentions marriage.

MANLY.   Cautious, Sir! No person more approves of an intercourse between
the sexes than I do. Female conversation softens our manners, whilst our
discourse, from the superiority of our literary advantages, improves their
minds. But, in our young country, where there is no such thing as gallantry,
when a gentleman speaks of love to a lady, whether he mentions marriage,
or not, she ought to conclude, either that he meant to insult her, or, that
his intentions are the most serious and honorable. How mean, how cruel,
is it, by a thousand tender assiduities, to win the affections of an amiable
girl, and though you leave her virtue unspotted, to betray her into the
appearance of so many tender partialities, that every man of delicacy would
suppress his inclination towards her, by supposing her heart engaged! Can
any man, for the trivial gratification of his leisure hours, affect the happiness
of a whole life! His not having spoken of marriage, may add to his perfidy,
but can be no excuse for his conduct.

DIMPLE.   Sir, I admire your sentiments;—they are mine. The light observations that fell from me, were only a principle of the tongue; they came not
from the heart—my practice has ever disapproved these principles.

MANLY.   I believe you, Sir. I should with reluctance suppose that those pernicious sentiments could find admittance into the heart of a gentleman.

DIMPLE.   I am now, Sir, going to visit a family, where, if you please, I will
have the honor of introducing you. Mr. Manly's ward, Miss Letitia, is a
young lady of immense fortune; and his niece, Miss Charlotte Manly is a
young lady of great sprightliness and beauty.

MANLY.   That gentleman, Sir, is my uncle, and Miss Manly my sister.

DIMPLE.   The devil she is! [Aside.] Miss Manly your sister, Sir? I rejoice to
hear it, and feel a double pleasure in being known to you.—Plague on him!
I wish he was at Boston again with all my soul. [Aside.]

MANLY.   Come, Sir, will you go?

DIMPLE.   I will follow you in a moment, Sir. [Exit MANLY.]
Plague on it! this is unlucky. A fighting brother is a cursed appendage to a
fine girl. Egad! I just stopped in time; had he not discovered himself, in two
minutes more I should have told him how well I was with his sister.—
Indeed, I cannot see the satisfaction of an intrigue, if one can't have the
pleasure of communicating it to our friends. [Exit.]

Act Fourth

SCENE 1. CHARLOTTE'S *apartment.*

[CHARLOTTE *leading in* MARIA.]

CHARLOTTE.   This is so kind, my sweet friend, to come to see me at this moment. I declare, if I were going to be married in a few days, as you are, I should scarce have found time to visit my friends.

MARIA.   Do you think then that there is an impropriety in it?—How should you dispose of your time?

CHARLOTTE.   Why, I should be shut up in my chamber; and my head would so run upon—upon—upon the solemn ceremony that I was to pass through—I declare it would take me above two hours merely to learn that little monosyllable—*Yes.* Ah! my dear, your sentimental imagination does not conceive what that little tiny word implies.

MARIA.   Spare me your raillery, my sweet friend; I should love your agreeable vivacity at any other time.

CHARLOTTE.   Why this is the very time to amuse you. You grieve me to see you look so unhappy.

MARIA.   Have I not reason to look so?

CHARLOTTE.   What new grief distresses you?

MARIA.   Oh! how sweet it is, when the heart is borne down with misfortune, to recline and repose on the bosom of friendship! Heaven knows, that, although it is improper for a young lady to praise a gentleman, yet I have ever concealed Mr. Dimple's foibles, and spoke of him as of one whose reputation I expected would be linked with mine: but his late conduct towards me, has turned my coolness into contempt. He behaves as if he meant to insult and disgust me; whilst my father, in the last conversation on the subject of our marriage, spoke of it as a matter which laid near his heart, and in which he would not bear contradiction.

CHARLOTTE.   This works well: oh! the generous Dimple. I'll endeavor to excite her to discharge him. [*Aside.*] But, my dear friend, your happiness depends on yourself:—Why don't you discard him? Though the match has been of long standing, I would not be forced to make myself miserable: no parent in the world should oblige me to marry the man I did not like.

MARIA.   Oh! my dear, you never lived with your parents, and do not know what influence a father's frowns have upon a daughter's heart. Besides, what have I to allege against Mr. Dimple, to justify myself to the world? He carries himself so smoothly, that every one would impute the blame to me, and call me capricious.

CHARLOTTE.   And call her capricious! Did ever such an objection start into the heart of woman? For my part, I wish I had fifty lovers to discard, for no other reason, than because I did not fancy them. My dear Maria, you will forgive me; I know your candor and confidence in me; but I have at times, I confess, been led to suppose, that some other gentleman was the cause of your aversion to Mr. Dimple.

MARIA.   No, my sweet friend, you may be assured, that though I have seen many gentlemen I could prefer to Mr. Dimple, yet I never saw one that I thought I could give my hand to, until this morning.

CHARLOTTE.   This morning!

MARIA.   Yes;—one of the strangest accidents in the world. The odious Dimple, after disgusting me with his conversation, had just left me, when a gentleman, who, it seems, boards in the same house with him, saw him coming out of our door, and the houses looking very much alike, he came into our house instead of his lodgings; nor did he discover his mistake until he got into the parlor, where I was: he then bowed so gracefully; made such a genteel apology, and looked so manly and noble!—

CHARLOTTE.	I see some folks, though it is so great an impropriety, can praise a gentleman, when he happens to be the man of their fancy. [*Aside.*]

MARIA.	I don't know how it was,—I hope he did not think me indelicate—but I asked him, I believe, to sit down, or pointed to a chair. He sat down and instead of having recourse to observations upon the weather, or hackneyed criticisms upon the theater, he entered readily into a conversation worthy a man of sense to speak, and a lady of delicacy and sentiment to hear. He was not strictly handsome, but he spoke the language of sentiment, and his eyes looked tenderness and honor.

CHARLOTTE.	Oh! [*eagerly*] you sentimental grave girls, when your hearts are once touched, beat us rattles a bar's length. And so, you are quite in love with this he-angel?

MARIA.	In love with him! How can you rattle so, Charlotte? am I not going to be miserable? [*Sighs.*] In love with a gentleman I never saw but one hour in my life, and don't know his name!—No: I only wished that the man I shall marry, may look, and talk, and act, just like him. Besides, my dear, he is a married man.

CHARLOTTE.	Why, that was good natured.—He told you so, I suppose, in mere charity, to prevent your falling in love with him?

MARIA.	He didn't tell me so [*peevishly*]; he looked as if he was married.

CHARLOTTE.	How, my dear, did he look sheepish?

MARIA.	I am sure he has a susceptible heart, and the ladies of his acquaintance must be very stupid not to—

TITLE & MSPP:

CHARLOTTE.	Hush! I hear some person coming.

		[*Enter* LETITIA.]

LETITIA.	My dear Maria, I am happy to see you. Lud! what a pity it is that you purchased your wedding clothes.

MARIA.	I think so. [*Sighing.*]

LETITIA.	Why, my dear, there is the sweetest parcel of silks come over you ever saw. Nancy Brilliant has a full suit come; she sent over her measure, and it fits her to a hair; it is immensely dressy, and made for a court-hoop. I thought they said the large hoops were going out of fashion.

CHARLOTTE.	Did you see the hat?—Is it a fact, that the deep laces round the border is still the fashion?

DIMPLE [*within*].	Upon my honor, Sir!

MARIA.	Ha! Dimple's voice! My dear, I must take leave of you. There are some things necessary to be done at our house.—Can't I go through the other room?

		[*Enter* DIMPLE *and* MANLY.]

DIMPLE.	Ladies, your most obedient.

CHARLOTTE.	Miss Van Rough, shall I present my brother Henry to you? Colonel Manly, Maria,—Miss Van Rough, brother.

MARIA.	Her brother! [*Turns and sees* MANLY.] Oh! my heart! The very gentleman I have been praising.

MANLY.	The same amiable girl I saw this morning!

CHARLOTTE.	Why, you look as if you were acquainted.

MANLY.	I unintentionally intruded into this lady's presence this morning, for which she was so good as to promise me her forgiveness.

CHARLOTTE.	Oh! ho! is that the case! Have these two penserosos been together? Were they Henry's eyes that looked so tenderly? [*Aside.*] And so you promised to pardon him? and could you be so good natured?—have you really forgiven him? I beg you would do it for my sake. [*Whispering loud to* MARIA.] But, my dear, as you are in such haste, it would be cruel to detain you: I can show you the way through the other room.

MARIA.   Spare me, sprightly friend.

MANLY.   The lady does not, I hope, intend to deprive us of the pleasure of her company so soon.

CHARLOTTE.   She has only a mantua-maker[7] who waits for her at home. But, as I am to give my opinion of the dress, I think she cannot go yet. We were talking of the fashions when you came in; but I suppose the subject must be changed to something of more importance now.—Mr. Dimple, will you favor us with an account of the public entertainments?

DIMPLE.   Why, really, Miss Manly, you could not have asked me a question more *mal-apropos.*[8] For my part, I must confess, that to a man who has traveled, there is nothing that is worthy the name of amusement to be found in this city.

CHARLOTTE.   Except visiting the ladies.

DIMPLE.   Pardon me, Madam; that is the avocation of a man of taste. But, for amusement, I positively know of nothing that can be called so, unless you dignify with that title the hopping once a fortnight to the sound of two or three squeaking fiddles, and the clattering of the old tavern windows, or sitting to see the miserable mummers, whom you call actors, murder comedy, and make a farce of tragedy.

MANLY.   Do you never attend the theater, Sir?

DIMPLE.   I was tortured there once.

CHARLOTTE.   Pray, Mr. Dimple, was it a tragedy or a comedy?

DIMPLE.   Faith, Madam, I cannot tell; for I sat with my back to the stage all the time, admiring a much better actress than any there;—a lady who played the fine woman to perfection;—though, by the laugh of the horrid creatures around me, I suppose it was comedy. Yet, on second thoughts, it might be some hero in a tragedy, dying so comically as to set the whole house in an uproar.—Colonel, I presume you have been in Europe?

MANLY.   Indeed, Sir, I was never ten leagues from the continent.

DIMPLE.   Believe me, Colonel, you have an immense pleasure to come; and when you shall have seen the brilliant exhibitions of Europe, you will learn to despise the amusements of this country as much as I do.

MANLY.   Therefore I do not wish to see them; for I can never esteem that knowledge valuable, which tends to give me a distaste for my native country.

DIMPLE.   Well, Colonel, though you have not traveled, you have read.

MANLY.   I have, a little: and by it have discovered that there is a laudable partiality, which ignorant, untraveled men entertain for everything that belongs to their native country. I call it laudable;—it injures no one; adds to their own happiness; and, when extended, becomes the noble principle of patriotism. Traveled gentlemen rise superior, in their own opinion, to this: but, if the contempt which they contract for their country is the most valuable acquisition of their travels, I am far from thinking that their time and money are well spent.

MARIA.   What noble sentiments!

CHARLOTTE.   Let my brother set out from where he will in the fields of conversation, he is sure to end his tour in the temple of gravity.

---

7. I.e., dressmaker.   8. Inappropriate (French).

MANLY.   Forgive me, my sister. I love my country; it has its foibles undoubtedly;—some foreigners will with pleasure remark them—but such remarks
fall very ungracefully from the lips of her citizens.

DIMPLE.   You are perfectly in the right, Colonel—America has her faults.

MANLY.   Yes, Sir; and we, her children, should blush for them in private,
and endeavor, as individuals, to reform them. But, if our country has its
errors in common with other countries, I am proud to say America, I mean
the United States, have displayed virtues and achievements which modern
nations may admire, but of which they have seldom set us the example.

CHARLOTTE.   But, brother, we must introduce you to some of our gay folks,
and let you see the city, such as it is. Mr. Dimple is known to almost every
family in town;—he will doubtless take a pleasure in introducing you.

DIMPLE.   I shall esteem every service I can render your brother an honor.

MANLY.   I fear the business I am upon will take up all my time, and my family
will be anxious to hear from me.

MARIA.   His family! But what is it to me that he is married! [Aside.]
Pray, how did you leave your lady, Sir?

CHARLOTTE.   My brother is not married [observing her anxiety]; it is only an
odd way he has of expressing himself.—Pray, brother, is this business which
you make your continual excuse, a secret?

MANLY.   No, sister, I came hither to solicit the honorable Congress that a
number of my brave old soldiers may be put upon the pension-list, who
were, at first, not judged to be so materially wounded as to need the public
assistance.—My sister says true: [To MARIA.] I call my late soldiers my family.—Those who were not in the field in the late glorious contest, and those
who were, have their respective merits; but, I confess, my old brother-
soldiers are dearer to me than the former description. Friendships made in
adversity are lasting; our countrymen may forget us; but that is no reason
why we should forget one another. But I must leave you; my time of engagement approaches.

CHARLOTTE.   Well, but brother, if you will go, will you please to conduct my
fair friend home? You live in the same street;—I was to have gone with her
myself—[Aside.] A lucky thought.

MARIA.   I am obliged to your sister, Sir, and was just intending to go. [Going.]

MANLY.   I shall attend her with pleasure.

[Exit with MARIA, followed by DIMPLE and CHARLOTTE.]

MARIA.   Now, pray don't betray me to your brother.

CHARLOTTE [just as she sees him make a motion to take his leave].   One word
with you, brother, if you please. [Follows them out.]
    [Manent DIMPLE and LETITIA.[9]

DIMPLE.   You received the billet[1] I sent you, I presume?

LETITIA.   Hush!—Yes.

DIMPLE.   When shall I pay my respects to you?

LETITIA.   At eight I shall be unengaged.
    [Reenter CHARLOTTE.]

DIMPLE.   Did my lovely angel receive my billet? [To CHARLOTTE.]

CHARLOTTE.   Yes.

DIMPLE.   What hour shall I expect with impatience?

CHARLOTTE.   At eight I shall be at home, unengaged.

DIMPLE.   Unfortunate! I have a horrid engagement of business at that hour.—
Can't you finish your visit earlier, and let six be the happy hour?

CHARLOTTE.   You know your influence over me. [Exeunt severally.]

---

9. I.e., Dimple and Letitia remain.   1. Letter, note.

SCENE 2. VAN ROUGH's *house.*

[VAN ROUGH, *alone.*]

VAN ROUGH. It cannot possibly be true! The son of my old friend can't have acted so unadvisedly. Seventeen thousand pounds! in bills!—Mr. Transfer must have been mistaken. He always appeared so prudent, and talked so well upon money-matters, and even assured me that he intended to change his dress for a suit of clothes which would not cost so much, and look more substantial, as soon as he married. No, no, no! it can't be; it cannot be.— But, however, I must look out sharp. I did not care what his principles or his actions were, so long as he minded the main chance. Seventeen thousand pounds!—If he had lost it in trade, why the best men may have ill-luck; but to game it away, as Transfer says—why, at this rate, his whole estate may go in one night, and, what is ten times worse, mine into the bargain. No, no; Mary is right. Leave women to look out in these matters; for all they look as if they didn't know a journal from a ledger, when their interest is concerned, they know what's what; they mind the main chance as well as the best of us.—I wonder Mary did not tell me she knew of his spending his money so foolishly. Seventeen thousand pounds! Why, if my daughter was standing up to be married, I would forbid the banns, if I found it was to a man who did not mind the main chance.—Hush! I hear somebody coming. 'Tis Mary's voice: a man with her too! I shouldn't be surprized if this should be the other string to her bow.—Aye, aye, let them alone; women under- stand the main chance.—Though, i' faith, I'll listen a little. [*Retires into a closet.*]

[MANLY *leading in* MARIA.]

MANLY. I hope you will excuse my speaking upon so important a subject, so abruptly; but the moment I entered your room, you struck me as the lady whom I had long loved in imagination, and never hoped to see.

MARIA. Indeed, Sir, I have been led to hear more upon this subject than I ought.

TITLE & MSPP:

MANLY. Do you then disapprove my suit, Madam, or the abruptness of my introducing it? If the latter, my peculiar situation, being obliged to leave the city in a few days, will, I hope, be my excuse; if the former, I will retire: for I am sure I would not give a moment's inquietude to her, whom I could devote my life to please. I am not so indelicate as to seek your immediate approbation; permit me only to be near you, and by a thousand tender assiduities to endeavor to excite a grateful return.

MARIA. I have a father, whom I would die to make happy—he will disap- prove—

MANLY. Do you think me so ungenerous as to seek a place in your esteem without his consent? You must—you ever ought to consider that man as unworthy of you, who seeks an interest in your heart, contrary to a father's approbation. A young lady should reflect, that the loss of a lover may be supplied, but nothing can compensate for the loss of a parent's affection. Yet, why do you suppose your father would disapprove? In our country, the affections are not sacrificed to riches, or family aggrandizement:—should you approve, my family is decent, and my rank honorable.

MARIA. You distress me, Sir.

MANLY. Then I will sincerely beg your excuse for obtruding so disagreeable a subject and retire. [*Going.*]

MARIA. Stay, Sir! Your generosity and good opinion of me deserve a return; but why must I declare what, for these few hours, I have scarce suffered myself to think?—I am—

MANLY. What?—

MARIA. Engaged, Sir;—and, in a few days, to be married to the gentleman you saw at your sister's.

MANLY. Engaged to be married! And have I been basely invading the rights of another? Why have you permitted this—Is this the return for the partiality I declared for you?

MARIA. You distress me, Sir. What would you have me say? You are too generous to wish the truth: ought I to say that I dared not suffer myself to think of my engagement, and that I am going to give my hand without my heart?—Would you have me confess a partiality for you? If so, your triumph is complete; and can be only more so, when days of misery, with the man I cannot love, will make me think of him whom I could prefer.

MANLY [after a pause]. We are both unhappy; but it is your duty to obey your parent,—mine to obey my honor. Let us, therefore, both follow the path of rectitude; and of this we may be assured, that if we are not happy, we shall, at least deserve to be so. Adieu! I dare not trust myself longer with you. [Exeunt severally.²]

Act Fifth
SCENE 1. DIMPLE's lodgings.

[JESSAMY meeting JONATHAN.]

JESSAMY. Well, Mr. Jonathan, what success with the fair?

JONATHAN. Why, such a tarnal cross tike³ you never saw!—You would have counted she had lived upon crabapples and vinegar for a fortnight. But what the rattle makes you look so tarnation glum?

JESSAMY. I was thinking, Mr. Jonathan, what could be the reason of her carrying herself so coolly to you.

JONATHAN. Coolly, do you call it? Why, I vow, she was fire-hot angry: may be it was because I buss'd her.

JESSAMY. No, no, Mr. Jonathan; there must be some other cause: I never yet knew a lady angry at being kissed.

JONATHAN. Well, if it is not the young woman's bashfulness, I vow I can't conceive why she shou'd n't like me.

JESSAMY. May be it is because you have not the Graces, Mr. Jonathan.

JONATHAN. Grace! Why, does the young woman expect I must be converted before I court her?⁴

JESSAMY. I mean graces of person; for instance, my lord tells us that we must cut off our nails even at top, in small segments of circles;—though you won't understand that—In the next place, you must regulate your laugh.

JONATHAN. Maple-log seize it! don't I laugh natural?

JESSAMY. That's the very fault, Mr. Jonathan. Besides, you absolutely misplace it. I was told by a friend of mine that you laughed outright at the play the other night, when you ought only to have tittered.

JONATHAN. Gor! I—what does one go to see fun for if they can't laugh?

JESSAMY. You may laugh;—but you must laugh by rule.

JONATHAN. Swamp it—laugh by rule! Well, I should like that tarnally.

JESSAMY. Why you know, Mr. Jonathan, that to dance, a lady to play with her fan, or a gentleman with his cane, and all other natural motions, are

2. Separately.
3. Here, churlish person. "The fair": i.e., the fair sex.
4. Jonathan takes "grace" in its religious sense.

regulated by art. My master has composed an immensely pretty gamut,[5] by which any lady, or gentleman, with a few years' close application, may learn to laugh as gracefully as if they were born and bred to it.

JONATHAN.   Mercy on my soul! A gamut for laughing—just like fa, la, sol?

JESSAMY.   Yes. It comprises every possible display of jocularity, from an *affetuoso* smile to a *piano* titter, or full chorus *fortissimo*[6] ha, ha, ha! My master employs his leisure-hours in marking out the plays, like a cathedral chanting-book,[7] that the ignorant may know where to laugh; and that pit, box, and gallery[8] may keep time together, and not have a snigger in one part of the house, a broad grin in the other, and a d——d grum[9] look in the third. How delightful to see the audience all smile together, then look on their books, then twist their mouths into an agreeable simper, then altogether shake the house with a general ha, ha, ha! loud as a full chorus of Handel's, at an Abbey-commemoration.[1]

JONATHAN.   Ha, ha, ha! that's dang'd cute, I swear.

JESSAMY.   The gentlemen, you see, will laugh the tenor; the ladies will play the counter-tenor; the beaux will squeak the treble; and our jolly friends in the gallery a thorough bass,[2] ho, ho, ho!

JONATHAN.   Well, can't you let me see that gamut?

JESSAMY.   Oh! yes, Mr. Jonathan; here it is. [*Takes out a book.*] Oh! no, this is only a titter with its variations. Ah, here it is. [*Takes out another.*] Now you must know, Mr. Jonathan, this is a piece written by Ben Jonson,[3] which I have set to my master's gamut. The places where you must smile, look grave, or laugh outright, are marked below the line. Now look over me.— "There was a certain man"—now you must smile.

JONATHAN.   Well, read it again; I warrant I'll mind my eye.

JESSAMY.   "There was a certain man, who had a sad scolding wife,"—now you must laugh.

JONATHAN.   Tarnation! That's no laughing matter, though.

JESSAMY.   "And she lay sick a-dying";—now you must titter.

JONATHAN.   What, snigger when the good woman's a-dying! Gor, I—

JESSAMY.   Yes; the notes say you must—"And she asked her husband leave to make a will,"—now you must begin to look grave;—"and her husband said"—

JONATHAN.   Ay, what did her husband say?—Something dang'd cute, I reckon.

JESSAMY.   "And her husband said, you have had your will all your life time, and would you have it after you are dead too?"

JONATHAN.   Ho, ho, ho! There the old man was even with her; he was up to the notch—ha, ha, ha!

JESSAMY.   But, Mr. Jonathan, you must not laugh so. Why, you ought to have tittered *piano*, and you have laughed *fortissimo*. Look here; you see these marks, A. B. C. and so on; these are the references to the other part of the book. Let us turn to it, and you will see the directions how to manage the muscles. This [*turns over*] was note D you blundered at.—"You must purse the mouth into a smile, then titter, discovering the lower part of the three front upper teeth."

5. Full range (of musical notes).

6. Very loud. "*Affetuoso*": passionate. "*Piano*": soft. These are all musical terms.

7. I.e., hymnal.

8. I.e., balcony. "Pit": playhouse area nearest the stage.

9. Surly, grim.

1. I.e., in an oratorio by George Frederick Handel (1685–1759), British composer, performed at Westminster Abbey in London.

2. In Baroque music, the bass part.

3. British comic dramatist (1572–1637).

JONATHAN.   How! read it again.

JESSAMY.   "There was a certain man"—very well!—"who had a sad scolding wife,"—why don't you laugh?

JONATHAN.   Now, that scolding wife sticks in my gizzard so pluckily, that I can't laugh for the blood and nowns[4] of me. Let me look grave here, and I'll laugh your belly full where the old creature's a-dying.—

JESSAMY.   "And she asked her husband"—[*Bell rings.*] My master's bell! he's returned, I fear—Here, Mr. Jonathan, take this gamut; and, I make no doubt but with a few years' close application, you may be able to smile gracefully. [*Exeunt severally.*]

SCENE 2.   CHARLOTTE'S *apartment.*

[*Enter* MANLY.]

MANLY.   What, no one at home? How unfortunate to meet the only lady my heart was ever moved by, to find her engaged to another, and confessing her partiality for me! Yet engaged to a man, who, by her intimation, and his libertine conversation with me, I fear, does not merit her. Aye! there's the sting; for, were I assured that Maria was happy, my heart is not so selfish, but that it would dilate in knowing it, even though it were with another.— But to know she is unhappy!—I must drive these thoughts from me. Charlotte has some books; and this is what I believe she calls her little library. [*Enters a closet.*]

[*Enter* DIMPLE *leading* LETITIA.]

LETITIA.   And will you pretend to say, now, Mr. Dimple, that you propose to break with Maria? Are not the banns published?[5] Are not the clothes purchased? Are not the friends invited? In short, is it not a done affair?

DIMPLE.   Believe me, my dear Letitia, I would not marry her.

LETITIA.   Why have you not broke with her before this, as you all along deluded me by saying you would?

DIMPLE.   Because I was in hopes she would ere this have broke with me.

LETITIA.   You could not expect it.

DIMPLE.   Nay, but be calm a moment; 'twas from my regard to you that I did not discard her.

LETITIA.   Regard to me!

DIMPLE.   Yes; I have done everything in my power to break with her, but the foolish girl is so fond of me, that nothing can accomplish it. Besides, how can I offer her my hand, when my heart is indissolubly engaged to you?—

LETITIA.   There may be reason in this; but why so attentive to Miss Manly?

DIMPLE.   Attentive to Miss Manly! For heaven's sake, if you have no better opinion of my constancy, pay not so ill a compliment to my taste.

LETITIA.   Did I not see you whisper her to-day?

DIMPLE.   Possibly I might—but something of so very trifling a nature, that I have already forgot what it was.

LETITIA.   I believe, she has not forgot it.

DIMPLE.   My dear creature, how can you for a moment suppose I should have any serious thoughts of that trifling, gay, flighty coquette, that disagreeable—

[*Enter* CHARLOTTE.]

---

4. From the oath, "God's blood and wounds." "Pluckily" may be a pun to go with "gizzard," for *pluck* means not only courage but also the heart, liver, and lungs of a slaughtered animal.

5. I.e., the marriage been publicly announced.

DIMPLE.   My dear Miss Manly, I rejoice to see you; there is a charm in your
conversation that always marks your entrance into company as fortunate.

LETITIA.   Where have you been, my dear?

CHARLOTTE.   Why, I have been about to twenty shops, turning over pretty
things, and so have left twenty visits unpaid. I wish you would step into the
carriage and whisk round, make my apology, and leave my cards where our
friends are not at home; that you know will serve as a visit. Come, do go.

LETITIA.   So anxious to get me out! but I'll watch you. [*Aside.*] Oh! yes, I'll
go; I want a little exercise.—Positively [DIMPLE *offering to accompany her*],
Mr. Dimple, you shall not go, why, half my visits are cake and caudle[6]
visits; it won't do, you know, for you to go.—

[*Exit, but returns to the door in the back scene and listens.*]

DIMPLE.   This attachment of your brother to Maria is fortunate.

CHARLOTTE.   How did you come to the knowledge of it?

DIMPLE.   I read it in their eyes.

CHARLOTTE.   And I had it from her mouth. It would have amused you to
have seen her! She that thought it so great an impropriety to praise a gentleman, that she could not bring out one word in your favor, found a redun-
dancy to praise him.

DIMPLE.   I have done everything in my power to assist his passion there: your
delicacy, my dearest girl, would be shocked at half the instances of neglect
and misbehavior.

CHARLOTTE.   I don't know how I should bear neglect; but Mr. Dimple must
misbehave himself indeed, to forfeit my good opinion.

DIMPLE.   Your good opinion, my angel, is the pride and pleasure of my heart;
and if the most respectful tenderness for you and an utter indifference for
all your sex besides, can make me worthy of your esteem, I shall richly
merit it.

CHARLOTTE.   All my sex besides, Mr. Dimple—you forgot your *tête-à-tête*[7]
with Letitia.

DIMPLE.   How can you, my lovely angel, cast a thought on that insipid, wry-
mouthed, ugly creature!

CHARLOTTE.   But her fortune may have charms?

DIMPLE.   Not to a heart like mine. The man who has been blessed with the
good opinion of my Charlotte, must despise the allurements of fortune.

CHARLOTTE.   I am satisfied.

DIMPLE.   Let us think no more on the odious subject, but devote the present
hour to happiness.

CHARLOTTE.   Can I be happy, when I see the man I prefer going to be married
to another?

DIMPLE.   Have I not already satisfied my charming angel that I can never
think of marrying the puling Maria. But, even if it were so, could that be
any bar to our happiness; for, as the poet sings—

> Love, free as air, at sight of human ties,
> Spreads his light wings, and in a moment flies.[8]

Come then, my charming angel! why delay our bliss! The present moment
is ours; the next is in the hand of fate. [*Kissing her.*]

6. Warm ale or wine, mixed with bread, sugar, eggs,
and spices.
7. Private conversation of two people.

8. "Eloisa to Abelard" (1717), lines 75–76, by Alexander Pope, British poet.

CHARLOTTE. Begone, Sir! By your delusions you had almost lulled my honour asleep.

DIMPLE. Let me lull the demon to sleep again with kisses. [*He struggles with her; she screams.*]

[*Enter* MANLY.]

MANLY. Turn, villain! and defend yourself.—

[*Draws.* VAN ROUGH *enters and beats down their swords.*]

VAN ROUGH. Is the devil in you? are you going to murder one another? [*Holding* DIMPLE.]

DIMPLE. Hold him, hold him,—I can command my passion.

[*Enter* JONATHAN.]

JONATHAN. What the rattle ails you? Is the old one[9] in you? Let the colonel alone, can't you? I feel chock full of fight,—do you want to kill the colonel?—

MANLY. Be still, Jonathan; the gentleman does not want to hurt me.

JONATHAN. Gor! I—I wish he did; I'd shew him Yankee boys play, pretty quick—Don't you see you have frightened the young woman into the *hystrikes*?[1]

VAN ROUGH. Pray, some of you explain this; what has been the occasion of all this racket?

MANLY. That gentleman can explain it to you; it will be a very diverting story for an intended father-in-law to hear.

VAN ROUGH. How was this matter, Mr. Van Dumpling?

DIMPLE. Sir, upon my honor—all I know is, that I was talking to this young lady, and this gentleman broke in on us, in a very extraordinary manner.

VAN ROUGH. Why, all this is nothing to the purpose: can you explain it, Miss? [*To* CHARLOTTE.]

[*Enter* LETITIA *through the back scene.*[2]]

LETITIA. I can explain it to that gentleman's confusion. Though long betrothed to your daughter [*to* VAN ROUGH], yet allured by my fortune, it seems (with shame do I speak it), he has privately paid his addresses to me. I was drawn in to listen to him by his assuring me that the match was made by his father without his consent, and that he proposed to break with Maria, whether he married me or not. But whatever were his intentions respecting your daughter, Sir, even to me he was false; for he has repeated the same story, with some cruel reflections upon my person, to Miss Manly.

JONATHAN. What a tarnal curse!

LETITIA. Nor is this all, Miss Manly. When he was with me this very morning, he made the same ungenerous reflections upon the weakness of your mind as he has so recently done upon the defects of my person.

JONATHAN. What a tarnal curse and damn too!

DIMPLE. Ha! since I have lost Letitia, I believe I had as good make it up with Maria—Mr. Van Rough, at present I cannot enter into particulars; but, I believe I can explain everything to your satisfaction in private.

VAN ROUGH. There is another matter, Mr. Van Dumpling, which I would have you explain:—pray, Sir, have Messrs. Van Cash and Co. presented you those bills for acceptance?

DIMPLE. The deuce! Has he heard of those bills! Nay, then, all's up with Maria, too; but an affair of this sort can never prejudice me among the ladies; they will rather long to know what the dear creature possesses to make him so agreeable. [*Aside.*] Sir, you'll hear from me. [*To* MANLY.]

9. I.e., the devil.   2. I.e., from the rear of the acting area.
1. Awkward pronunciation of *hysterics.*

MANLY.   And you from me, Sir.—

DIMPLE.   Sir, you wear a sword.—

MANLY.   Yes, Sir:—This sword was presented to me by that brave Gallic hero, the Marquis De La Fayette.[3] I have drawn it in the service of my country, and in private life, on the only occasion where a man is justified in drawing his sword, in defence of a lady's honor. I have fought too many battles in the service of my country to dread the imputation of cowardice.—Death from a man of honor would be a glory you do not merit; you shall live to bear the insult of man, and the contempt of that sex, whose general smiles afforded you all your happiness.

DIMPLE.   You won't meet me, Sir?— Then I'll post you[4] a coward.

MANLY.   I'll venture that, Sir.—The reputation of my life does not depend upon the breath of a Mr. Dimple. I would have you to know, however, Sir, that I have a cane to chastise the insolence of a scoundrel, and a sword and the good laws of my country, to protect me from the attempts of an assassin.—

DIMPLE.   Mighty well! Very fine, indeed!—ladies and gentlemen, I take my leave, and you will please to observe, in the case of my deportment, the contrast between a gentleman, who has read Chesterfield and received the polish of Europe, and an unpolished, untraveled American. [*Exit.*]

[*Enter* MARIA.]

MARIA.   Is he indeed gone?—

LETITIA.   I hope never to return.

VAN ROUGH.   I am glad I heard of those bills; though it's plaguy unlucky; I hoped to see Mary married before I died.

MANLY.   Will you permit a gentleman, Sir, to offer himself as a suitor to your daughter? Though a stranger to you, he is not altogether so to her, or unknown in this city. You may find a son-in-law of more fortune, but you can never meet with one who is richer in love for her, or respect for you.

VAN ROUGH.   Why, Mary, you have not let this gentleman make love to[5] you without my leave?

MANLY.   I did not say, Sir—

MARIA.   Say, Sir!—I—the gentleman, to be sure, met me accidentally.

VAN ROUGH.   Ha, ha, ha! Mark me, Mary; young folks think old folks to be fools; but old folks know young folks to be fools.—Why, I knew all about this affair:—This was only a cunning way I had to bring it about—Hark ye! I was in the closet when you and he were at our house. [*Turns to the company.*] I heard that little baggage say she loved her old father, and would die to make him happy! Oh! how I loved the little baggage!—And you talked very prudently, young man. I have inquired into your character, and find you to be a man of punctuality and mind the main chance. And so, as you love Mary, and Mary loves you, you shall have my consent immediately to be married. I'll settle my fortune on you, and go and live with you the remainder of my life.

MANLY.   Sir, I hope—

VAN ROUGH.   Come, come, no fine speeches; mind the main chance, young man, and you and I shall always agree.

LETITIA.   I sincerely wish you joy [*advancing to* MARIA]; and hope your pardon for my conduct.

MARIA.   I thank you for your congratulations, and hope we shall at once forget

---

3. French statesman and general who fought on behalf of the Continental Army in 1780 and 1781.

4. I.e., denounce you as.

5. I.e., court.

the wretch who has given us so much disquiet, and the trouble that he has occasioned.

CHARLOTTE.   And I, my dear Maria,—how shall I look up to you for forgiveness? I, who, in the practice of the meanest arts, have violated the most sacred rights of friendship? I can never forgive myself, or hope charity from the world, but I confess I have much to hope from such a brother! and I am happy that I may soon say, such a sister.—

MARIA.   My dear, you distress me; you have all my love.

MANLY.   And mine.

CHARLOTTE.   If repentance can entitle me to forgiveness, I have already much merit; for I despise the littleness of my past conduct. I now find, that the heart of any worthy man cannot be gained by invidious attacks upon the rights and characters of others;—by countenancing the addresses of a thousand;—or that the finest assemblage of features, the greatest taste in dress, the genteelest address, or the most brilliant wit, cannot eventually secure a coquette from contempt and ridicule.

MANLY.   And I have learned that probity, virtue, honor, though they should not have received the polish of Europe, will secure to an honest American the good graces of his fair countrywoman, and, I hope, the applause of THE PUBLIC.

[*curtain*]

1787, 1790

American Literature
1820-1865

In a painting popular during the late nineteenth century, Christian Schussele reverentially depicted *Washington Irving and His Literary Friends at Sunnyside.* Working in 1863, four years after Irving's death, Schussele portrayed an astonishing number of elegantly clad notables in Irving's snug study in his Gothic cottage-castle on the Hudson River, north of New York City. Among them were several writers in this anthology: Irving himself, Oliver Wendell Holmes, Nathaniel Hawthorne, Henry Wadsworth Longfellow, Ralph Waldo Emerson, William Cullen Bryant, and James Fenimore Cooper. Intermingled with these men were poets and novelists now seldom read: William Gilmore Simms, Fitz-Greene Halleck, Nathaniel Parker Willis, James Kirke Paulding, John Pendleton Kennedy, and Henry T. Tuckerman, along with the historians William H. Prescott and George Bancroft. The Schussele painting was a pious hoax, for these guests never assembled together at one time, at Sunnyside or anywhere else, and while a few of those depicted were indeed among Irving's friends, he barely knew some of them and never met others at all. But in several ways the scene is profoundly true to American literary history.

As Schussele's painting suggests, Irving, beloved by ordinary readers and by most of his fellow writers, was the central figure in the American literary world between 1809 (the year of his parody *History of New York*) and the Civil War, especially after he demonstrated in *The Sketch Book* (1819–20) that memorable fiction—*Rip Van Winkle* and *The Legend of Sleepy Hollow*—could be set in the United States; he also proved, by the book's international success, that an American writer could win a British and Continental audience. Irving's legion of imitators included several of the men in the painting, and among his fellow writers Irving's reputation was enhanced by his generosity, as in his gallantly relinquishing the subject of the conquest of Mexico to Prescott or in urging the publisher George P. Putnam to bring out an American edition of the first book by the unknown Herman Melville. Although James Fenimore Cooper's fame as a fiction writer rivaled Irving's in the 1820s and 1830s, his influence never approached the breadth of Irving's. Nor did the influence of Ralph Waldo Emerson, despite his profoundly provocative effects on such writers as Margaret Fuller, Henry David Thoreau, Walt Whitman, Herman Melville, and Emily Dickinson—effects that make modern literary historians see him as the seminal writer of the century.

Mentioning the names of Fuller, Thoreau, Melville, and Dickinson suggests still another way the Schussele painting is exemplary. Because the painter set out to depict representative literary men (not literary women) as much as to depict genuine intimates of Irving, it is striking that he omitted writers who now seem among the most important of the century: Edgar Allan Poe, Thoreau, Whitman, Melville, John Greenleaf Whittier (who was frowned on as a militant abolitionist until 1866, when *Snow-Bound* made him seem a safe poet to admire), and Dickinson (in the 1860s an all but unpublished recluse). The painter would probably have considered Augustus Baldwin Longstreet, George Washington Harris, and other southern or backwoods humorists in this volume to be subliterary, despite the fact that Irving had influenced such writing and had delighted in reading it.

THE SMALL WORLD OF AMERICAN WRITERS

Perhaps most important, paintings like the one by Schussele (and the similar wishful fad of depicting famous literary people in cozy association through the then-new technique of composite photography) capture the fact that in the nineteenth century the American literary world was very small indeed, so small that most of the writers in this period knew each other, often intimately, or else knew much about each other. They lived, if not in each other's pockets, at least in each other's houses, or boardinghouses: Lemuel Shaw, from 1830 to 1860 chief justice of the Massachusetts Supreme Court, and Herman Melville's father-in-law after 1847, for a time stayed in a Boston boardinghouse run by Ralph Waldo Emerson's widowed mother; the Longfellows summered in the 1840s at the Pittsfield boardinghouse run by Melville's cousin, a house where Melville had stayed in his early teens; in Pittsfield and Lenox, Hawthorne and Melville paid each other overnight visits, in Concord the Hawthornes rented the Old Manse, the Emerson ancestral home, and later bought a house there from the educator Bronson Alcott and made it famous as the Wayside; in Concord the Emersons welcomed many guests, including Margaret Fuller, and when the master was away Thoreau sometimes stayed in the house to help Mrs. Emerson with the children and the property. The popular Manhattan hostess Anne Lynch assigned the young travel-writer Bayard Taylor to write a valentine for a slightly older travel-writer, Herman Melville, in 1848, and three years later, apparently with matchmaking in mind, brought together Taylor's intimate friend R. H. Stoddard and Elizabeth Barstow, a distant relative of Hawthorne. In 1853 Hawthorne received at Wayside young Mr. Stoddard, by then husband of Elizabeth Barstow, and pulled wires to get him a job in the New York Custom House, Hawthorne having the year before written the campaign biography for his old friend, the candidate for president, Franklin Pierce. (When Melville finally got his own appointment to the Custom House in 1866, Stoddard was on desk duty to welcome him; Stoddard kept Melville from being fired once, but Melville outlasted him many years in that nest of corruption.) On a visit to Washington after the Civil War had broken out, the still reclusive, and ailing, Hawthorne seriously considered making the hazardous trip to Wheeling to meet the extraordinary new contributor to the *Atlantic Monthly*, Rebecca Harding; later he welcomed her at Wayside. At Litchfield, Connecticut, the young Georgian Longstreet greatly admired one of the minister Lyman Beecher's daughters (not Harriet, then a small child).

Many of the writers of this period came together casually for dining and drinking, the hospitality at the editor Evert A. Duyckinck's house in New York being famous, open to southerners like Simms as well as New Yorkers like Melville and Bostonians like the elder Richard Henry Dana. In the late 1850s a Bohemian group of newspaper and theater people and writers drank together at Pfaff's saloon on Broadway above Bleecker Street; for a time Whitman was a fixture there. Of the clubs formed by writers, artists, and other notables (usually male), the four most memorable are the Bread and Cheese Club, which Cooper organized in 1824 in the back room of his publisher's Manhattan bookstore; the Transcendental Club, started in Boston in 1836 and lasting four years; the Saturday Club, a more convivial Boston group formed in 1856; and the Authors Club, founded in New York in 1882. Members of the Bread and Cheese Club included the poet William Cullen Bryant, Samuel F. B. Morse (the painter who later invented the telegraph), the poet Fitz-Greene Halleck, and Thomas Cole (the English-born painter of the American landscape). Emerson was the leading spirit of the Transcendental Club, but other members included Bronson Alcott, later Margaret Fuller, and George

Ripley (the organizer of the Transcendental commune at Brook Farm, near Roxbury). Among the members of the Saturday Club were Emerson, James Russell
Lowell, Henry Wadsworth Longfellow, Oliver Wendell Holmes, and the historians John Lothrop Motley and William H. Prescott; Nathaniel Hawthorne attended
some meetings. Brander Matthews cofounded the Authors Club, from the first a
beloved resource for the literary establishment, which included dominant magazine editors of the time such as Richard Watson Gilder and critics and poets such
as R. H. Stoddard and Edmund Clarence Stedman (an intimate of Samuel L.
Clemens and William Dean Howells who also befriended Melville in his last years
and whose son Arthur became Melville's literary executor); Matthews recalled that
once or twice "the shy and elusive Herman Melville dropped in for an hour or
two."

THE SMALL COUNTRY

Such intimacy was inevitable in a country that had only a few literary and publishing centers, all of them along the Atlantic seaboard. Despite the acquisition of the
Louisiana Territory from France in 1803 and the vast Southwest from Mexico in
1848, most of the writers we still read lived all their lives in the original thirteen
states, except for trips abroad, and their practical experience was of a compact
country: in 1840 the "northwestern" states were those covered by the Northwest
Ordinance of 1787 (Ohio, Indiana, Illinois, and Michigan; Wisconsin was still a
territory), while the "southwestern" humor writers such as George Washington
Harris, Thomas Bangs Thorpe, and Johnson Jones Hooper wrote in the region
bounded by Georgia, Louisiana, and Tennessee.

Improvements in transportation were shrinking the country even while territorial
gains were enlarging it. When Irving went from Manhattan to Albany in 1800,
steamboats had not yet been invented, although William Longstreet, the father of
the writer, had been planning one for a decade; the Hudson voyage was slow and
dangerous, and in 1803 the wagons of Irving's Canada-bound party barely made it
through the bogs beyond Utica. The Erie Canal, completed in 1825, changed
things: in the 1830s and 1840s Hawthorne, Melville, and Fuller took the canal
boats in safety, suffering only from crowded and stuffy sleeping conditions. When
Irving went buffalo hunting in Indian territory (now Oklahoma) in 1832 he left the
steamboat at St. Louis and went on horseback, camping out at night except when
his party reached one of the line of missions built to accommodate whites who were
Christianizing the Plains Indians. By the 1840s railroads had replaced stagecoaches
between many eastern towns, although to get to New Orleans in 1848 Whitman
had to change from railroad to stagecoach to steamboat. Despite frequent train
wrecks, steamboat explosions, and Atlantic shipwrecks, by the 1850s travel had
ceased to be the hazardous adventure it had been. But the few American writers
who saw much of the country were still provincials in their practical attitude toward
their literary careers, for their publishers and purchasers were concentrated mainly
in or near New York, Philadelphia, and Boston.

And the New York, Philadelphia, and Boston of this period were themselves
tiny in comparison to their modern size. The site of Brook Farm, now long since
a victim of urban sprawl, was chosen because it was nine miles remote from Boston
and two miles away from the nearest farm. The population of New York City at
the start of the 1840s was only a third of a million and was concentrated in lower
Manhattan: Union Square was the edge of town. Horace Greeley, the editor of the
New York Tribune, escaped the bustle of the city by living on a ten-acre farm up
the East River on Turtle Bay, where the East Fifties are now; there he and his wife
provided a bucolic retreat for Margaret Fuller when she was his literary critic and
metropolitan reporter. In 1853 the Crystal Palace, an exposition of arts, crafts, and
sciences, created in imitation of the great Crystal Palace at the London World's
Fair of 1851, failed—largely because it was too far out of town, up west of the new

Croton Water Reservoir that had recently brought running water to the city. The reservoir was on the spot where the New York Public Library now stands, at Forty-second Street and Fifth Avenue, and the Crystal Palace was on the site of the modern Bryant Park, named for the nature poet.

THE ECONOMICS OF AMERICAN LETTERS

Geography and modes of transportation bore directly on publishing procedures in the United States of this period. For a long time writers who wanted to publish a book carried the manuscript to a local printer and paid job rates to have it printed and bound. Longfellow worked in this fashion with a firm in Brunswick, Maine, when he printed his translation of *Elements of French Grammar* and other text-books during his first years as a teacher. Fiction was also sometimes sent to a local printer, as when Longstreet had his own firm in Augusta print *Georgia Scenes* or when Johnson Jones Hooper paid a firm in Tuscaloosa, Alabama, to print *A Ride with Old Kit Kuncker* before having it brought out the next year by a regular Philadelphia publisher. However, the true publishing centers were major seaports that could receive the latest British books by the fastest ships and, hastily reprinting them, distribute them inland by river traffic as well as in coastal cities. After 1820 the leading publishing towns were New York and Philadelphia, with the Erie Canal soon giving New York an advantage in the Ohio trade. Boston remained only a provincial publishing center until after 1850, when publishers realized the value of the new railroad connections to the West. Despite the aggressive merchandising techniques of a few firms, the creation of a national book-buying market for literature, especially American literature, was long delayed.

The problem was that the economic interests of American publisher-booksellers were antithetical to the interests of American writers. A national copyright law became effective in the United States in 1790, but it was 1891 before American writers had international protection and foreign writers received protection in the United States. Until the end of the century, American printers routinely pirated English writers, paying nothing to Sir Walter Scott or Charles Dickens for their novels, which were rushed into print and sold very cheaply in New York, Philadelphia, and other cities. American readers benefited from the situation, for they could buy the best British—and Continental—writings cheaply, but American writers suffered, because if they were to receive royalties, their books had to be priced above the prices charged for works of the most famous British writers. American publishers were willing to carry a few native novelists and poets as prestige items for a while, but they were businesspeople, not philanthropists.

To compound the problem, Irving's apparent conquest of the British publishing system, by which he received large sums for *The Sketch Book* and succeeding volumes, proved delusory. Cooper and others followed in Irving's track and were paid by magnanimous British publishers under a system whereby works first printed in Great Britain were presumed to hold a British copyright. But this practice was ruled illegal by a British judge in 1849, and the British market dried up for American writers.

Throughout this period, making a serious American contribution to the literature of the world was no guarantee at all of monetary rewards. Except possibly for a few authors of sentimental best-sellers, including what Hawthorne jealously called "that damned mob of scribbling women," the United States was not a country in which one could make a living by writing. It was not even a place where the best authors could always publish what they wrote. The only writers who could consistently find a publisher were Irving and Cooper, who kept their appeal on the basis of early success (though more copies had to be sold to make the same profit) and the magazine or newspaper editors who could fill some of their own columns when they wanted. These editors included (for various periods of time) Poe, Longstreet, Harris, Thorpe, Hooper, Lowell, and four other notable examples: Fuller, who for several years reported for the *New York Tribune* at home and from Europe; Whitman, who for much of the 1840s and 1850s was free to editorialize in one Brooklyn or Manhattan newspaper or another; Whittier, who for more than two decades before the Civil War was corresponding editor of the *Washington National Era*; and most conspicuous, Bryant, long-time owner of the *New York Evening Post*. Whitman was his own publisher for most editions of *Leaves of Grass* and filled mail orders himself, as Thoreau also did when an occasional request came for one of the seven hundred copies of his first book, which the publisher had turned back to him. At crucial moments in his career Melville was balked from writing what he wanted to write, as when he sacrificed his literary aspirations after the failure of *Mardi* and wrote *Redburn* and *White-Jacket*, which he regarded as mere drudgery; and at other times he was "prevented from publishing" works he had written, including at least one that was subsequently destroyed. Ironically, the writer freest to pursue literary greatness in this period was probably Emily Dickinson, whose "letter to the world" remained unmailed during her lifetime.

THE QUEST FOR AN AMERICAN LITERARY DESTINY

In the first half of the nineteenth century, lobbying for the existence of an American literature in magazines seemed to take up more space than the literature itself. Especially after the War of 1812 confirmed American independence, theorists called for a great literature that would match the emerging political greatness of the nation. Huckstering critics soon developed specific notions as to the subjects that would-be writers should choose: preferably the distant colonial past (the nearest we could hope to come to the medieval settings that were serving Sir Walter Scott so well), or possibly American Indian legends, or still less desirable (because too near the mundane present), subjects from the recent Revolutionary past. Such exhortations were the stock-in-trade of commencement speakers and literary critics in the 1820s and 1830s. But in *The Poet* (1842) Emerson boldly called for a poet who would write of the United States as it was, not as it might have been:

> We have yet had no genius in America, with tyrannous eye, which knew the value of our incomparable materials, and saw, in the barbarism and materialism of the times, another carnival of the same gods whose picture he so much admires in Homer; then in the middle age; then in Calvinism. Banks and tariffs, the newspaper and caucus, methodism and unitarianism, are flat and dull to dull people, but rest on the same foundations of wonder as the town of Troy, and the temple of Delphos, and are as swiftly passing away. Our logrolling, our stumps and their politics, our fisheries, our Negroes, and Indians, our boasts, and our repudiations, the wrath of rogues, and the pusillanimity of honest men, the northern trade, the southern planting, the western clearing, Oregon, and Texas, are yet unsung. Yet America is a poem in our eyes; its ample geography dazzles the imagination, and it will not wait long for metres.

Later Whitman was to say that he had remained simmering, simmering, until Emerson brought him to a boil.

During the 1840s Evert A. Duyckinck and other New York literary men and women (primarily through the columns of the *Democratic Review* and the *Literary World*) mustered a squad of promoters of the great literature that was to come. The propagandists perfected the rhetorical strategy of linking literary destiny to geography and political destiny: the "great nation of futurity" must have a literature to match Niagara Falls and the Rocky Mountains. Herman Melville for several years was associated with Duyckinck's magazines, and he half-champions and half-spoofs the chauvinistic rhetoric in the essay on Hawthorne that he wrote for the *Literary World* in 1850. An American, he proclaimed, was "bound to carry republican progressiveness into Literature, as well as into Life," even to the point of believing that sooner or later American writers would rival Shakespeare, whom a generation of Bardolators regarded as unapproachable. This was literary manifest destiny with a vengeance, warranted only because as he wrote the essay Melville had already written his way well into what he later titled *Moby-Dick*.

None of the American writers of the period was chauvinistic enough to think that a great American literature could be written without reference to past English and European literature. As Cooper protested in *Notions of the Americans* (1828), writers in the United States possessed the same literary heritage that writers in Great Britain did. Shakespeare, Spenser, Milton, Bunyan, Addison, Pope, Fielding, Johnson, and Burns, along with many others (especially some now neglected writers of the eighteenth century) were the possession of all educated Americans born in the late eighteenth century or early in the nineteenth. Americans were not long behind the British in responding to the Romantics Wordsworth and Coleridge, then to Byron, Moore, and Scott. By the 1830s Carlyle was a force in the lives of several American writers through his translations of recent German philosophical works and his own jeremiads against contemporary British values. Americans had access to the latest British and continental discussions of art, religion, politics, and science, for British magazines, especially the quarterly reviews, were imported promptly and widely reprinted. Nineteenth-century American writing reveals its full meanings only in the light of European influences and parallel developments.

THE NEW AMERICANNESS OF AMERICAN LITERATURE

Despite the cultural cross-connections with Europe, the best literature that emerged in the United States was distinctively new, and a few perceptive critics very early began trying to define its special quality. This analysis from the review of *The Whale* (the English title of *Moby-Dick*) in the London *Leader* had currency in America as well, for the popular *Harper's New Monthly Magazine* quoted it approvingly:

> Want [lack] of originality has long been the just and standing reproach to American literature; the best of its writers were but second-hand Englishmen. Of late some have given evidence of originality, not *absolute* originality, but such genuine outcomings of the American intellect as can be safely called national. Edgar Poe, Nathaniel Hawthorne, Herman Melville are assuredly no British offshoots; nor is Emerson—the *German* American that he is! The observer of this commencement of an American literature, properly so called, will notice as significant that these writers have a wild and mystic love of the supersensual, peculiarly their own. To move a horror skilfully, with something of the earnest faith in the Unseen, and with weird imagery to shape these Phantasms so vividly that the most incredulous mind is hushed, absorbed—to do this no European pen has apparently any longer the power— to do this American literature is without a rival. What *romance* writer can be named with Hawthorne? Who knows the terrors of the seas like Herman Melville?"

Plainly, this was meant as praise, but to employ "weird imagery" to "move a horror skilfully" was hardly the ambition of any American writer of the period besides Poe; for their part Hawthorne and Melville were not concerned with the supernatural except as stage devices for heightening their psychological analyses.

But literary historians have not improved much on the reviewer in the *Leader* in deciding what was American about American literature. American writers were not achieving originality in form: Irving's sentences were accepted as models of English prose style precisely because they were themselves modeled on the sentences of Addison and Goldsmith, long the prime exemplars of decorous English prose. Melville's sentences often looked like those of whatever powerful master of the English language he had most recently been reading—Shakespeare, Milton, Burton, Taylor, Sterne, De Quincey, or Carlyle. Nor was the content of the best American writing of this period original in anything like an "absolute" sense. Modern scholars have shown that in his most "American" stories, *Rip Van Winkle* and *The Legend of Sleepy Hollow*, Irving drew on, and even closely translated, parts of German tales. In *Moby-Dick* Melville's metaphysics are recognizably of the generation of Goethe, Byron, and Carlyle. Thoreau's recurrent ideas came mainly from Emerson (at least Emerson himself insisted they did), but Emerson had picked them up from dozens of ancient and modern philosophers.

Yet, as everyone in the country sensed by the 1850s, there was some elusive quality about its new literature that was *American*. Irving's German-influenced stories were profoundly moving to Americans, who knew more than most Britons what it was to feel the trauma of rapid change, especially to experience repeated physical uprootings, and Americans found in the ne'er-do-well Rip a model for making a success of failure. In Cooper's novels was a sense of the immensity of physical nature and the power of human beings to destroy nature that most European writers could experience only vicariously. In Melville's *Moby-Dick* was a sense (long suppressed in European consciousness) of the grandeur of the physical universe and of the place of human beings in that universe. In *Leaves of Grass* Whitman undertook another elemental task—to become the national poet of a new people on a new continent. What proved most enduringly "American" about Emerson was his wide streak of Yankee individualism best displayed in *Self-Reliance*, which became an inspiration to thousands of Americans who were determined to hitch their wagons, as Emerson said, to a star. Even Thoreau's *Walden*, which many contemporaries took merely as an American counterpart of the English naturalist Gilbert White's *Natural History and Antiquities of Selbourne*, was in fact consciously an American counterscripture, a Franklinesque retort to Poor Richard, a how-to book on getting a living by working at what you love. At a time when grandiloquence in political rhetoric was often taken for eloquence, Abraham Lincoln mastered both the majestic cadences of the King James Version of the Bible and the extravagant toughness of backwoods tall talk. Dickinson's poems in their minute intensity were as ambitious as Whitman's, magnificent attempts to define her experience at whatever cost in wrenched syntax and rhyme. At best, beyond question, American writers were accomplishing things yet unattempted in the English language.

THE AESTHETICS OF A NATIONAL LITERATURE

The great writers of the period for the most part defined their aesthetic problems by themselves, though Emerson's *The Poet* aided some of the others. The primary difficulty of how to keep from being secondhand English writers had not been squarely faced by the theorists of nationality in literature, who most often seemed to think that adoption of an American setting or, more vaguely, the infusion of an American "spirit" guaranteed Americanness. Insofar as the issues had been addressed by Americans before the 1840s, it was primarily by painters and sculptors, the most prominent of whom had received their training abroad but then had found it impossible to reconcile their European notions of noble subject and style with Americanness. The Hudson River school of painters, led by Thomas Cole (one of whose notable followers was Asher B. Durand, the painter of *Kindred Spirits*, a detail of which is reproduced on the cover of this volume), found a pantheistic majesty in American landscapes not anticipated by the history-filled landscapes of European painting. Some of Cole's own work was marred by a tendency to allegorize as inveterate as Hawthorne's own, but others of the Hudson River school, including Frederic Edwin Church, faced in North—and South—America a New World, a landscape with primeval power both to awe and destroy.

Artistic tributes could be as clichéd as Whitman's catalogs (everyone from Church to T. B. Thorpe painted inevitable Niagaras), but Church's rediscovered *Icebergs* (1861) is only a decade away from *Moby-Dick*, a work by a spirit that was in truth kindred. Other Americans, notably Martin Johnson Heade, born the same year as Melville, found compelling mystery not only in the exotica of South America but also in the salt hay marshes and low coasts of New England. The genre painters who formed so conspicuous a part of the artistic establishment—Melville's and Whitman's acquaintance William Sidney Mount, for instance—were pleasantly but unchallengingly continuing the familiar Dutch tradition—familiar from paintings brought across the Atlantic by Dutch settlers as well as those more recently brought over. Of the major writers of the period Whitman, from his friendships with the members of the Brooklyn Art Union in the early 1850s, was exposed to controversies in art in time to have them affect his poetry—his own aesthetic statements reflect Horatio Greenough's championship of the nude and his disparagement of mere embellishment. Most of the writers, despite the theorizing about painting and sculpting and the actual painting and sculpting available for them to see, were pretty much on their own when they were solving their crucial aesthetic problems—such as Hawthorne's attempts to strike a balance between the allegorical and the realistic, Emerson's difficulty in achieving unity from the mutually repellent particles of his thought, Thoreau's attempts to unite the Transcendentalist and the naturalist in himself, Whitman's struggle to domesticate the epic catalog without falling into self-parody, Melville's attempt to create a tragedy in a democracy, and Dickinson's attempt to walk the hairline between mere coyness and psychological precision.

THE WRITERS AND THEIR AMERICA

When the great American writers of the mid-nineteenth century took stock of their country, they sometimes caught the contagion of an ebullient, expansionist mood that struck many observers as the dominant one of the time, and even Thoreau, the most relentless critic of the values of his society, insisted that to some extent he counted himself among "those who find their encouragement and inspiration in precisely the present condition of things, and cherish it with the fondness and enthusiasm of lovers." But often they felt a profound alienation. Emerson was a preacher who had renounced his pulpit, and the other great writers—also preachers without pulpits—devoted much of their artistic effort to analyzing conditions of life in America and to exhorting their fellow citizens to live more wisely.

CONFORMITY, MATERIALISM, AND THE ECONOMY

The eccentricity of Americans, especially in rural areas and smaller towns, was notorious among visitors from abroad and was recorded in some of its aspects by writers as diverse as Longstreet, Harris, Melville, and Stowe. In Stowe's novels of the late 1850s and early 1860s there is a gallery of portraits of such mentally angular or gnarled characters. In Amherst, Emily Dickinson out-Thoreaued Thoreau in her resolute privacy, idiosyncracies, and individuality. But she could be understood in relation to real and fictional characters. The night her correspondent Thomas Wentworth Higginson met her in 1870 he strove to convey her character in a letter to his wife without staying up too late; "if you had read Mrs. Stoddard's novels you could understand a house where each member runs his or her own selves." Despite such powerful individualists, it seemed to some of the writers that Americans, even while deluding themselves that they were the most self-reliant populace in the world, were systematically selling out their individuality. Emerson sounded the alarm: "Society everywhere is in conspiracy against the manhood of every one of its members. Society is a joint-stock company in which the members agree for the better securing of his bread to each shareholder, to surrender the liberty and culture of the eater. The virtue in most request is conformity." In *The Celestial Railroad*

Hawthorne satirically described the condition at the Vanity Fair of modern America, where there was a "species of machine for the wholesale manufacture of individual morality." He went on: "This excellent result is effected by societies for all manner of virtuous purposes; with which a man has merely to connect himself, throwing, as it were, his quota of virtue into the common stock; and the president and directors will take care that the aggregate amount be well applied." Thoreau repeatedly satirized America as a nation of joiners that tried to force every new-comer "to belong to their desperate odd-fellow society": to Thoreau, members of the Odd Fellows and other social organizations were simply not odd *enough*, not individual enough.

But none of the writers found anything comical in the wholesale loss of Yankee individualism as both men and women deserted worn-out farms for factories, where many began to feel what Emerson called "the disproportion between their faculties and the work offered them." Far too often, the search for a better life had degenerated into a desire to possess factory-made objects. "Things are in the sad-dle," Emerson said sweepingly, "and ride mankind." In elaboration of that accusa-tion, Thoreau wrote *Walden* as a treatise on expanding the spiritual life by simplifying material wants. Informing Thoreau's outrage at the materialism of his time was the bitter knowledge that even the most impoverished were being led to waste their money (and, therefore, their lives) on trumpery. In a vocabulary echo-ing Benjamin Franklin, he condemned the emerging consumer economy that was devoted, even in the infancy of advertising, to the creation of "artificial wants" for things that were unneeded or outright pernicious. And to counter the loss of an archetypal Yankee virtue, he made himself into a jack-of-all-trades and strong mas-ter of one, the art of writing. In strangely different ways the four to speak out most profoundly about the emerging American economic system were Melville, Stowe, Whitman, and Harding.

SEX AND SEXUAL ROLES

At a time when sex was banished from the magazines and from almost all books except medical treatises, Whitman alone called for a healthy sense of the relation between body and soul and created a forum for discussing sexual joy and anguish. The other male writers made no challenge to conventional sexual roles; when Emerson, for instance, said that society "is in conspiracy against the manhood of every one of its members," he meant "*man*hood," not "manhood and woman-hood." Only Whitman among the male authors regularly employed what we would call nonsexist language, and only Whitman rejected the opinion that woman's proper "sphere" was a limited, subservient, supportive one. While the attitudes of most male—and female—writers of the time reflected and embodied the prevailing sexism, Whitman rejected the "empty dish, gallantry" as a degraded attitude: "This tepid wash, this diluted deferential love, as in songs, fictions, and so forth, is enough to make a man vomit." Instead, he insisted on equality: "Women in These States approach the day of that organic equality with me, with-out which, I see, men cannot have organic equality among themselves." Of the other writers only Margaret Fuller thought so deeply about sexual roles. Ironically, as the mother of a tardily acknowledged child (and perhaps not the wife of its Italian father), Fuller was an incalculable threat to the little Boston literary society in the months before her death by shipwreck prevented her arrival home. Of the women writers of the time, Dickinson, who never married, was the most bitterly ironic observer of the sacrifices marriage often required of a woman, as in her depiction of the bride who "rose to His Requirement—dropt / The Playthings of Her Life / To take the honorable Work / Of Woman, and of Wife," and Elizabeth Stoddard, overshadowed by her husband, wrote controlled, ironic analyses of the restricted roles women were allowed to assume. But women had no monopoly on sexual anguish. Melville, who as a young man had known the pagan Eden of the

South Seas, found that the claims of his intellect and imagination, his pursuit of a literary career, could not be met while also meeting the claims of his wife and children. And Whitman, the only writer of the period to advance a "Programme" for honest depiction of sex in literature, privately recorded the torments he endured from his homoerotic longings.

NATURE

In "a new country," Thoreau said, "fuel is an encumbrance," and his generation acted as if trees existed to be burned (and mountains to be graded and wild animals to be slaughtered). But while Thoreau faced the possibility that like villains we might grub our forests all up, "poaching on our own national domains," he had no deep anxiety that primeval nature like the Maine woods would be destroyed. Melville was likewise sure that the whale would not perish: "hunted from the savannas and glades of the middle seas, the whale-bone whales can at last resort to their Polar citadels, and diving under the ultimate glassy barriers and walls there, come up among icy fields and floes; and in a charmed circle of everlasting December, bid defiance to all pursuit from man." Of the major writers of the period, Emerson, Thoreau, and Whitman felt an intensity of communion with nature that warrants their being called nature-mystics, and Dickinson, bounded by town lots and fields near her house in Amherst, found a profoundly un-Christian, "Druidic difference" that enhanced nature for her with a sense of harmony between it and human beings. The writers diverged in their wider views of the universe, Melville describing in *Moby-Dick* the maddening of a cabin boy abandoned in the immensity of ocean, and Thoreau, by contrast, insisting that he was not lonely at Walden. "Why should I feel lonely? is not our planet in the Milky Way?" But whatever their sense of the place of human beings in the cosmos, they all found nature a force in their lives in ways out of keeping with the times, when the Romantic sense of nature as restorer and healer of humankind seemed to persist, as Thoreau pointed out, in the absurd form of uneasy rest-day strollers anxious to pass their allotted time in the woods and return to town.

ORTHODOX RELIGION AND TRANSCENDENTALISM

All the major writers found themselves at odds with the dominant religion of their time, a nominal Protestant Christianity that exerted practical control over what could be printed in books and magazines. This church, Emerson said, acted "as if God were dead." Whitman was more bitter still: "The churches are one vast lie; the people do not believe them, and they do not believe themselves." The writers all came of Protestant backgrounds in which Calvinism was more or less watered down (less in the cases of Melville and Dickinson), but they tended to apply absolute standards toward what passed for Christianity. In *The Celestial Railroad* Hawthorne memorably satirized the American urge to be progressive and liberal in theology as well as in politics, and Melville extended the satire throughout an entire book, *The Confidence-Man*.

Awareness of the fact of religious ecstasy was not at issue. Emerson, for instance, showed in *The Over-Soul* a clinical sense of the varieties of religious experience, the "varying forms of that shudder of awe and delight with which the individual soul always mingles with the universal soul." Similarly, Thoreau acknowledged the validity of the "second birth and peculiar religious experience" available to the "solitary hired man on a farm in the outskirts of Concord" but felt that any religious denomination in America would pervert that mystical experience into something available only under its auspices and something to be brought into line with its particular doctrines. Like Thoreau, Whitman saw all religious ecstasy as equally valid and came forth in *Song of Myself* outbidding "the old cautious hucksters" like Jehovah, Kronos, Zeus, and Hercules, gods who held too low an estimate of the value of men and women. Among these writers Melville was alone in his anguish at the realization that Christianity was impracticable. Melville also felt the brutal power of the Calvinistic Jehovah with special keenness: human beings were "god-bullied" even as the hull of the *Pequod* was in *Moby-Dick*, and the best way people had of demonstrating their own divinity lay in defying the omnipotent tyrant. To Dickinson also God was a bully—a "Mastiff," whom subservience might, or might not, appease. In a series of novels Harriet Beecher Stowe best described the way rigid Calvinism could cripple young minds.

Transcendentalism in the late 1830s and early 1840s was treated in newspapers and magazines as something between a national laughingstock and a clear menace to organized religion. The running journalistic joke, which Hawthorne echoed in *The Celestial Railroad*, was that no one could define the term, other than that it was highfalutin, foreign, and obscurely dangerous. The conservative Christian view is well represented by a passage that appeared in Stowe's newspaper serialization of *Uncle Tom's Cabin* (1851) but was omitted from the book version, a sarcastic indictment of the reader who might find it hard to believe that Tom could be stirred by a passage in the Bible: "I mention this, of course, philosophic friend, as a psychological phenomenon. Very likely it would do no such a thing for you, because you are an enlightened man, and have out-grown the old myths of past centuries. But then you have Emerson's Essays and Carlyle's Miscellanies, and other productions of the latter day, suited to your advanced development." Such early observers understood well enough that Transcendentalism was more pantheistic than Christian. The "defiant Pantheism" infusing Thoreau's shorter pieces helped keep them out of the magazines, and James Russell Lowell for the *Atlantic Monthly* publication of a section of *The Maine Woods* censored a sentence in which Thoreau declared that a pine tree was as immortal as he was and perchance would "go to as high a heaven."

Melville also was at least once kept from publication by the religious scruples of the magazines, and often he was harshly condemned for what he had managed to publish. For years he bore the wrath of reviewers such as the one who denounced him for writing *Moby-Dick* and the Harpers for publishing it: "The Judgment day will hold him liable for not turning his talents to better account, when, too, both authors and publishers of injurious books will be cojointly answerable for the influence of those books upon the wide circle of immortal minds on which they have written their mark. The book-maker and the book-publisher had better do their work with a view to the trial it must undergo at the bar of God." The ultimate result was that Melville was silenced. This was extreme, but Emerson, Thoreau, and Whitman all suffered in comparable ways for transgressing the code of the Doctors of Divinity (Thoreau said he wished it were not the D.D.'s but the chickadee-dees who acted as censors). Lowell himself indiscriminately censored Thoreau, Whitman, and Stoddard.

IMMIGRATION AND XENOPHOBIA

However threatened conservative Protestants felt by Transcendentalism and by religious speculations like Melville's, they felt far more threatened by Catholicism when refugees from the Napoleonic Wars were followed by refugees from oppressed and famine-struck Ireland. In Boston, Lyman Beecher, father of Harriet Beecher Stowe, thundered out antipapist sermons, then professed dismay when in 1834 a mob in Charlestown, across the Charles River from Boston, burned the Ursuline Convent School where daughters of many wealthy families were educated. Through the 1830s and 1840s and long afterward, the country was saturated with lurid books and pamphlets purporting to reveal the truth about sexual practices in nunneries and monasteries (accounts of how priests and nuns disposed of their babies were specially prized) and about the pope's schemes to take over the Mississippi Valley (Samuel F. B. Morse and others warned that Jesuits were prowling the Ohio Valley, in disguise). An extreme of xenophobia was reached in the summer of 1844, when rioters in Philadelphia (the city, everyone pointed out, of brotherly love) burned Catholic churches and a seminary. Melville was replying to the current hostility when he followed a description of the pestilent conditions of steerage passengers in emigrant ships with this plea: "Let us waive that agitated national topic, as to whether such multitudes of foreign poor should be landed on our American shores; let us waive it, with the one only thought, that if they can get here, they have God's right to come; though they bring all Ireland and her miseries with them. For the whole world is the patrimony of the whole world; there is no telling who does not own a stone in the Great Wall of China."

For all his humanitarian eloquence, Melville, like the other writers, realized that the new immigrants were changing the country from the cozy, homogeneous land it had been, or had seemed to be. By the end of the Civil War many native Americans shared Stowe's profound nostalgia for the days before the railroads, before the influx of Catholics, before the even more alien influx of immigrants from Southern and Eastern Europe, few of whom spoke English and many of whom were not Christian at all. The view of many in the literary establishment was reflected by Thomas Bailey Aldrich in *The Stillwater Tragedy* (1880): what you do with the widow and children of the unionizing Italian (once he has conveniently and agonizingly died) is ship them back to Italy.

POLITICS AND WARS

The major writers of the period lived with the anguishing paradox that the most idealistic nation in the world was implicated in continuing national sins: the near-genocide of the American Indians (whole tribes in colonial times had already become, in Melville's phrase for the Massachusetts Pequods, as extinct as the ancient Medes), the enslavement of blacks, and (partly a by-product of slavery) the staged "Executive's War" against Mexico, started by President Polk before being declared by Congress. Emerson was an exception, but most writers were silent about the successive removal of eastern Indian tribes to less desirable lands west of the Mississippi River, as legislated by the Indian Removal Act of 1830. American destiny plainly required a little practical callousness, most whites felt, in a secular version of the colonial notion that God had willed the extirpation of the American Indian. The imperialistic Mexican War was so gaudily exotic—and so distant— that only a small minority of American writers voiced more than perfunctory opposition; an exception was Thoreau, who spent a night in the Concord jail in symbolic protest against being taxed to support the war.

It was black slavery, what Melville called "man's foulest crime," which most stirred the consciences of the white writers, and in describing his own enslavement, the fugitive Frederick Douglass developed a notable capacity to stir readers as well as audiences in the lecture halls. When the Fugitive Slave Law was enforced in Boston in 1851 (by Melville's father-in-law, Chief Justice Shaw), Thoreau worked his outrage into his journals; then after another famous case in 1854 he combined the experiences into his most scathing speech, *Slavery in Massachusetts*, for delivery at a Fourth of July countercelebration at which a copy of the Constitution was burned because slavery was written into it. In that speech Thoreau summed up the disillusionment that many of his generation shared. He had felt a vast but indefinite loss after the 1854 case, he said: "I did not know at first what ailed me. At last it occurred to me that what I had lost was a country." (Successive generations of American writers would experience the same trauma: Howells, Twain, and others when the United States turned from savior to conqueror in the Philippines after the Spanish-American War; Robert Lowell and many others after it became clear that the involvement of the United States in Vietnam was not purely a gesture of compassion toward a grateful, beleaguered nation.) More obliquely than Thoreau, Melville explored black slavery in *Benito Cereno* as an index to the emerging national character. At his bitterest, he felt in the mid-1850s that "free Ameriky" was "intrepid, unprincipled, reckless, predatory, with boundless ambition, civilized in externals but a savage at heart."

John Brown's raid on Harpers Ferry in 1859, immediately repudiated by the new Republican party, drew from the now tubercular Thoreau a passionate defense. During the Civil War itself, Lincoln found the genius to suit diverse occasions with right language and length of utterance, but the major writers fell silent. When the war began on April 12, 1861, with the firing of Confederate guns on Fort Sumter, in Charleston harbor, Irving, Cooper, Poe, and Fuller were dead (the younger two earlier than the older two), and before Robert E. Lee's surrender to Ulysses S. Grant at Appomattox, Virginia, on April 9, 1865, Thoreau had been dead three years and Hawthorne one. Some writers in this anthology had in their ways, directly and indirectly, helped to bring the war on: Lincoln was not wholly jesting if in fact he called Stowe "the little woman who had started the big war"; Whittier had by 1861 devoted decades of his life to the struggle against slavery, arousing furious resistance to him both in the North and in the South; and Douglass's oratory had revealed to many white Northerners a sense of the evils of slavery and the humanness of those of another race (or of mixed races). Firebrand Yankees such as Thoreau and firebrand Southerners such as G. W. Harris had roused the passions of at least some members of their own communities and regions. When the war came, most Northern writers were slow to have a sense of its reality. As Rebecca Harding saw during her visit to Concord in 1862, fresh from a portion of a slave state that had chosen to stay with the Union, Emerson had no notion what suffering was involved. Hawthorne, who received her with enthusiasm, had faced the start of the war as a Southern sympathizer in a village that had welcomed John Brown, then had seen Washington in wartime, and retained, as he always did, a practical politician's sense of things. It was for many Northerners an oddly informal war. A man did not have to go when he was drafted: Dickinson's brother Austin was drafted in 1864 but paid five hundred dollars for a substitute to be hired. Dickinson, who at first felt the war as "an oblique place," worried about the wounding of the "preceptor" she had not yet seen, Thomas Wentworth Higginson, earlier a co-conspirator with John Brown, then in 1862 the commander of the first black regiment, the First South Carolina Volunteers. When his son Charley ran away to join the Union Army, Longfellow had Senator Charles Sumner forward boxes to the boy and was baffled if they did not arrive promptly; he fussed about Charley's not having his rubber overcoat, and sent him a servant and two horses. Melville went down to camp to see a soldier cousin and, borrowing a flannel shirt, went along on a scouting party. Henry James's brother Wilkinson, injured at Charleston when Colonel Robert Gould Shaw's black regiment was half-slaughtered in July 1863, was saved by the civilian father of his closest friend, who did not find the son he was hunting for among the wounded, but found Wilky and delivered him on a stretcher to the James home in Newport. Whitman went to seek his wounded brother, passing piles of amputated limbs on his way to the field hospital, and stayed, nursing the wounded in Washington hospitals, in the single most courageous sacrifice any of these writers made to the war. All the Northern writers felt the reality before the war was over. James Russell Lowell was not a greatly exceptional case in losing three nephews.

Simply because the South was almost exclusively the battlefield, Southerners lived more immediately with the horrors of wounding and death than did most Northerners, and because the South became effectively blockaded from medical supplies and other necessities, Southern civilians suffered directly in deprivation of food, disruption of livelihoods, forced evacuations, and destroyed property as well as deaths of friends and family members. Harris and Longstreet were made refugees; Simms's magnificent library at Woodlands was burned by stragglers from Sherman's army, with the loss (among other riches) of many letters from Poe and many letters from Evert Duyckinck (which must have contained mentions of Poe,

Melville, and other writers, especially New Yorkers and Southerners).

None of the writers in this anthology fought in the war, though Thorpe held federal office in occupied New Orleans. A younger Connecticut writer, John William DeForest, recruited a company of volunteers at New Haven and served through the war as their captain. His *The First Time under Fire*, published in the September 1864 *Harper's*, deserves to be better known and may find a place in some future edition of this anthology; surely in the opening of the nineteenth-century canon his *Miss Ravenel's Conversion from Secession to Loyalty* will be taught in survey courses as a supplemental text. Samuel L. Clemens after a brief fling at patrolling in Missouri (an episode he later winsomely if speciously recorded in *The Private History of a Campaign that Failed*) saw the war out safely in the west; William Dean Howells sat it out in Venice; and Henry James, seeing both younger brothers off to the war, the opening of which coincided with his suffering what he called an "obscure" injury, spent the war years in Newport and Cambridge. No writer really escaped it, and for most of them, as for most citizens, it was a chasm in personal and national history. In *Clarel* (1876) Melville called the winter of 1860–61 a "sad arch between contrasted eras"; his modern critics have forgivably misapplied the words to the years 1861–65.

DeForest's masterpiece aside, the war did not soon evoke great fiction, but Melville's uneven *Battle-Pieces* (1866) included some remarkable meditative poems as well as the technically interesting *Donelson*, in which he conveyed vividly the anxiety of civilians awaiting news during a prolonged and dubious battle and eagerly reading aloud the latest bulletins posted outside the telegraph office. (His contemporaries such as Richard Henry Stoddard liked best the brisk derivative poems such as *Sheridan's Ride*.) Whitman's *Drum-Taps* (1865) also is uneven but contains several great poems. After a few copies had been dispersed, Whitman held back the edition for a "Sequel" mainly consisting of newly written poems on Lincoln, among them *When Lilacs Last in the Dooryard Bloom'd*, the greatest literary work to come out of the war and one of the world's great elegies. Both volumes summed up the national experience. Both writers looked ahead as well as backward, Whitman calling "reconciliation" the "word over all," and Melville urging in a prose "Supplement" that the victorious North "be Christians toward our fellow-whites, as well as philanthropists toward the blacks, our fellow-men." Later in *Specimen Days* Whitman made a memorable attempt to do the impossible—to put the real war realistically into a book.

Both Whitman and Melville, especially in their later years, saw American politics cease to be concerned with great national struggles over momentous issues; rather, politics meant corruption, on a petty or a grand scale. Melville lived out the Gilded Age as an employee at the notoriously corrupt Custom House in New York City. In *Clarel*, foreseeing a descent from the present "civic barbarism" to "the Dark Ages of Democracy," he portrayed his American pilgrims to the Holy Land as recognizing sadly that the time might come to honor the God of Limitations in what had been the Land of Opportunity, a time when Americans might cry: "To Terminus build fanes! / Columbus ended earth's romance: / No New World to mankind remains!"

THE HEROISM OF AMERICAN WRITERS

Against a society that often lost sight of principles, whether aesthetic, social, or political, Emerson offered the challenge that the other great writers took up: "Let us affront and reprimand the smooth mediocrity and squalid contentment of the times, and hurl in the face of custom, and trade, and office, the fact which is the upshot of all history, that there is a great responsible Thinker and Actor moving wherever moves a man: that a true man belongs to no other time or place, but is the centre of things." In the same spirit Melville looked bravely at the risks that lay beyond the imitation of Irving:

But the graceful writer, who perhaps of all Americans has received the most plaudits from his own country for his productions,—that very popular and amiable writer, however good, and self-reliant in many things, perhaps owes his chief reputation to the self-acknowledged imitation of a foreign model, and to the studied avoidance of all topics but smooth ones. But it is better to fail in originality, than to succeed in imitation. He who has never failed somewhere, that man can not be great. Failure is the true test of greatness.

In the same spirit Whitman commanded his readers: "Re-examine all you have been told at school or church or in any book, dismiss whatever insults your own soul, and your very flesh shall be a great poem and have the richest fluency not only in its words but in the silent lines of its lips and face and between the lashes of your eyes and in every motion and joint of your body." As Emerson had warned them they must, the great writers of this time relinquished "display and immediate fame" to wrestle, in Melville's phrase, "with the angel—Art," making their writings into classics from which later generations, and sometimes even their own, would date eras in their lives. As the selections in this volume demonstrate, all of Emerson's great fellow writers fervently shared his conviction that "nothing is of any value in books, excepting the transcendental and extraordinary."

WASHINGTON IRVING
1783–1859

Washington Irving, the first American to achieve an international literary reputation, was born in New York City on April 3, 1783, the last of eleven children of a Scottish-born father and English-born mother. Well into his thirties his brothers routinely tried to make plans for him, and his own devotion to his family was a dominant emotion throughout his life. He read widely in English literature at home, modeling his early prose on the graceful *Spectator* papers by Joseph Addison, but delighted by many other writers, including Shakespeare, Oliver Goldsmith, and Laurence Sterne. His brothers enjoyed writing poems and essays as pleasant, companionable recreation, and at nineteen Irving wrote a series of satirical essays on the theater and New York society for his brother Peter's newspaper, the *Morning Courier*.

When Irving showed signs of tuberculosis in 1804, his brothers sent him abroad for a two-year tour of Europe, where in his notebooks he steadily became an acute observer and felicitous recorder of what he witnessed. On his return, he began studying law with Judge Josiah Hoffman, but more important for his career, he and his brother William (along with William's brother-in-law, James Kirke Paulding) started an anonymous satirical magazine, *Salmagundi* (the name of a spicy hash), which ran through 1807 with sketches and poems on politics and drama as well as familiar essays on a great range of topics. Then in 1808 Irving began work on *A History of New York*, at first conceiving it as a parody of Samuel Latham Mitchell's pompously titled *The Picture of New-York; or The Traveller's Guide through the Commercial Metropolis of the United States*, then taking on a variety of satiric targets, including President Jefferson, whom he portrayed as an early Dutch governor of New Amsterdam, William the Testy. Exuberant, broadly comic, the *History* spoofed historians' pedantries but was itself the result of many months of antiquarian reading in local libraries, where his researches gave Irving refuge from grief over the sudden death of Judge Hoffman's daughter Matilda, to whom he had become engaged. Then the *History* was launched by a charming publicity campaign. First a newspaper noted the disappearance of a "small elderly gentleman, dressed in an old black coat and cocked hat, by the name of KNICK-ERBOCKER," adding that there were "some reasons for believing he is not entirely in his right mind." After further "news" items the old man's fictitious landlord announced that he had found in Knickerbocker's room a *"very curious kind of a written book"* which he intended to dispose of to pay the bill that was owed him, and the book at last appeared, ascribed to Diedrich Knickerbocker. With its publication Irving became an American celebrity. Reprinted in England, the *History* reached Sir Walter Scott, who declared that it made his sides hurt from laughter. Like all but the rarest of topical satires, however, it has become increasingly inaccessible to later generations of readers, who can hardly comprehend Irving's strategies and targets without precisely the sort of antiquarian footnotes he found delight in mocking.

During the War of 1812 Irving was editor of the *Analectic Magazine*, which he filled mainly with essays from British periodicals but where he printed his own timely series of patriotic biographical sketches of American naval heroes. Toward the end of the war he was made a colonel in the New York State Militia. Then in May 1815, a major break occurred in his life: he left for Europe and stayed away for seventeen years. At first he worked in Liverpool with his brother Peter, an importer of English hardware. In 1818 Peter went bankrupt, shortly after their mother died in New York; profoundly grieved and shamed, Irving once again took refuge in writing. During his work on *The Sketch Book* he met Scott, who buoyed him by admiration for the *History* and helpfully directed Irving's attention to the wealth of unused literary material in German folktales; there, as scholars have shown, Irving found the source for *Rip Van Winkle*, some passages of which are close paraphrases of the original. In 1819 Irving began sending *The Sketch Book* to the United States for publication in installments. When the full version was printed in England the next year, it made Irving famous and brought him the friendship of many of the leading British writers of the time. His new pseudonym, Geoffrey Crayon, became universally recognized, and over the next years selections from *The Sketch Book* entered the classroom as models of English prose just as selections from Addison had long been used. As Irving knew, part of his British success derived from general astonishment that a man born in the United States could write in such an English way about English scenes: Addison lay behind the sketches of English country life, just as Oliver Goldsmith's essays on the Boar's-head Tavern in Eastcheap and on Westminster Abbey lay behind Irving's on the same topics. But in among the graceful, tame tributes to English scenes and characters were two vigorous tales set in rural New York, *Rip Van Winkle* and *The Legend of Sleepy Hollow*. Everyone who read them knew instantly that they were among the literary treasures of the language, and it very soon became hard to remember that they had not always been among the English classics.

Irving's next book, *Bracebridge Hall* (1822), a worshipful tribute to old-fashioned English country life, was, as the author realized, a feeble follow-up, and *Tales of a Traveller* (1824) was widely taken as a sign that he had written himself out. At a loss to sustain his career, Irving gambled on accepting an invitation from an acquaintance, the American minister to Spain: he was to come to Spain as an attaché of the legation (a device for giving him entrée into manuscript collections) and translate Martín Fernández de Navarrete's new compilation of accounts of the voyages of Columbus, including Columbus's own lost journals as copied by an earlier historian. Helped by the American consul in Madrid, Obadiah Rich, who owned a magnificent collection of books and manuscripts on Spanish and Latin American history, Irving worked intensely and in 1828 published *The Life and Voyages of Christopher Columbus*, not a translation of Navarrete (though the Spaniard's volume supplied most of the facts) but a biography of Irving's own, shaped by his skill at evocative re-creation of history. Out of these Spanish years came also

The Conquest of Granada (1829), *Voyages and Discoveries of the Companions of Columbus* (1831), and *The Alhambra* (1832), which became known as "the Spanish *Sketch Book*."

In 1829 Irving was appointed secretary to the American legation in London, where he became a competent, hardworking diplomat, aided by his access to the highest levels of British society. No longer the latest rage, Irving by now was a solidly established author. On his return to the United States in 1832 his reputation was in need of redemption from a different charge—that of becoming too Europeanized. As if in an effort to make amends, Irving turned to three studies of the American West: *A Tour on the Prairies* (1835), based on his horseback journey into what is now Oklahoma; *Astoria* (1836), an account of John Jacob Astor's fur-trading colony in Oregon, written in Astor's own library and based on published accounts as well as research in Astor's archives (in which task Irving was assisted by his nephew Peter); and *The Adventures of Captain Bonneville, U.S.A.* (1837), an account of a Frenchman's explorations in the Rockies and the Far West.

In the late 1830s Irving bought and began refurbishing a house near Tarrytown, along the Hudson north of New York City, just where he had dreamed of settling down in *The Legend of Sleepy Hollow*. At Sunnyside he made a home for several members of his family, including as many as five nieces at a time, but he wrote little. From this somewhat purposeless stage of his life he was rescued by appointment as minister to Spain in 1842; he served four years in Madrid with great success. After his return he arranged with G. P. Putnam to publish a collected edition of his writings and took the occasion to revise some of them. Using essays he had written years before, he also prepared for the edition a derivative biography of Oliver Goldsmith (1849), after which critics more than ever compared him to the Irish prince of hack writers. Irving's main work after 1851 was his long-contemplated life of George Washington. He worked in libraries, read old newspapers, studied government records, and visited battlefields, but once again he drew very heavily on published biographies, especially the recent one by Jared Sparks. He forced himself, in the most heroic effort of his career, to complete the successive five volumes, the first of which was published in 1855. Just after finishing the last he collapsed, and died a few months later, on November 28, 1859.

Decades before his death, Irving had achieved the status of a classic writer; in his own country he had no rival as a stylist. As schoolboys, Hawthorne and Longfellow were inspired by the success of *The Sketch Book*, and their prose, as well as that of a horde of now-unread writers, owed much to Irving. Although Melville, in his essay on Hawthorne's *Mosses from an Old Manse*, declared his preference for creative geniuses over adept imitators like Irving, he could not escape Irving's influence, which emerges both in his short stories and in a late poem, *Rip Van Winkle's Lilacs*, which showed he saw Rip as an archetypal artist figure. (Melville's debt was even more tangible, for early in 1846 Irving had passed the word to Putnam that *Typee* was worth reprinting in New York, but then Irving had been generous to younger writers all his life, as in his supervision of the London publication of Bryant's poems in 1832.) The southwestern humorists of the 1840s, whom Irving read and enjoyed, were much more robust than Irving in his mature years, yet they learned from him that realistic details of rural life in America could be worked memorably into fiction. From the beginning, Americans identified with Rip as a counterhero, an anti-Franklinian who made a success of failure, and successive generations have responded profoundly to Irving's pervasive theme of mutability, especially as localized in his portrayal of the bewildering and destructive rapidity of change in American life.

The Author's Account of Himself[1]

"I am of this mind with Homer, that as the snaile that crept out of her shel was turned eftsoones into a toad, and thereby was forced to make a stoole to sit on; so the traveller that stragleth from his owne country is in a short time transformed into so monstrous a shape, that he is faine to alter his mansion with his manners, and to live where he can, not where he would."

—*Lyly's Euphues*[2]

I was always fond of visiting new scenes, and observing strange characters and manners. Even when a mere child I began my travels, and made many tours of discovery into foreign parts and unknown regions of my native city, to the frequent alarm of my parents, and the emolument of the town-crier.[3] As I grew into boyhood, I extended the range of my observations. My holiday afternoons were spent in rambles about the surrounding country. I made myself familiar with all its places famous in history or fable. I knew every spot where a murder or robbery had been committed, or a ghost been seen. I visited the neighbouring villages, and added greatly to my stock of knowledge, by noting their habits and customs, and conversing with their sages and great men. I even journeyed one long summer's day to the summit of the most distant hill, from whence I stretched my eye over many a mile of terra incognita,[4] and was astonished to find how vast a globe I inhabited.

This rambling propensity strengthened with my years. Books of voyages and travels became my passion, and in devouring their contents, I neglected the regular exercises of the school. How wistfully would I wander about the pier heads in fine weather, and watch the parting ships, bound to distant climes—with what longing eyes would I gaze after their lessening sails, and waft myself in imagination to the ends of the earth.

Farther reading and thinking, though they brought this vague inclination into more reasonable bounds, only served to make it more decided. I visited various parts of my own country; and had I been merely a lover of fine scenery, I should have felt little desire to seek elsewhere for its gratification: for on no country have the charms of nature been more prodigally lavished. Her mighty lakes, like oceans of liquid silver; her mountains, with their bright aerial tints; her valleys, teeming with wild fertility; her tremendous cataracts, thundering in their solitudes; her boundless plains, waving with spontaneous verdure; her broad deep rivers, rolling in solemn silence to the ocean; her trackless forests, where vegetation puts forth all its magnificence; her skies, kindling with the magic of summer clouds and glorious sunshine:—no, never need an American look beyond his own country for the sublime and beautiful of natural scenery.

But Europe held forth all the charms of storied and poetical association. There were to be seen the masterpieces of art, the refinements of highly cultivated society, the quaint peculiarities of ancient and local custom. My native country was full of youthful promise; Europe was rich in the accumulated treasures of age. Her very ruins told the history of times gone by, and every

---

1. Irving sent a tentative batch of sketches from England to his brothers in New York in March 1819. This group, which included *The Author's Account of Himself* and *Rip Van Winkle*, was published in New York (by C. S. Van Winkle) in May 1819 as *The Sketch Book of Geoffrey Crayon, Gent.*, no. 1, the source of the text printed here. In 1820, after a total of seven installments had been printed separately, the publisher bound them together.

2. In *Euphues and His England* (1580), by John Lyly

(1554?—1606), this is what Euphues reports that the hermit Caffander (once a great traveler) says to his nephew Callimachus to discourage him from traveling. A phrase is omitted: the original has "was forced to make a stoole to sit on, disdaining hir own house: so the Travailer. . . ."

3. The man hired (in this case) to spread the word that a child was lost.

4. Unknown land (Latin), as designated on early maps.

mouldering stone was a chronicle. I longed to wander over the scenes of renowned achievement—to tread, as it were, in the footsteps of antiquity—to loiter about the ruined castle—to meditate on the falling tower—to escape, in short, from the commonplace realities of the present, and lose myself among the shadowy grandeurs of the past.

I had, beside all this, an earnest desire to see the great men of the earth. We have, it is true, our great men in America: not a city but has an ample share of them. I have mingled among them in my time, and been almost withered by the shade into which they cast me; for there is nothing so baleful to a small man as the shade of a great one, particularly the great man of a city. But I was anxious to see the great men of Europe; for I had read in the works of various philosophers, that all animals degenerated in America, and man among the number.[5] A great man of Europe, therefore, thought I, must be as superior to a great man of America, as a peak of the Alps to a highland of the Hudson; and in this idea I was confirmed, by observing the comparative importance and swelling magnitude of many English travellers among us; who, I was assured, were very little people in their own country.[6] I will visit this land of wonders, therefore, thought I, and see the gigantic race from which I am degenerated.

It has been either my good or evil lot to have my roving passion gratified. I have wandered through different countries, and witnessed many of the shifting scenes of life. I cannot say that I have studied them with the eye of a philosopher, but rather with the sauntering gaze with which humble lovers of the picturesque stroll from the window of one print shop to another; caught sometimes by the delineations of beauty, sometimes by the distortions of caricature, and sometimes by the loveliness of landscape. As it is the fashion for modern tourists to travel pencil in hand, and bring home their port folios filled with sketches, I am disposed to get up a few for the entertainment of my friends. When I look over, however, the hints and memorandums I have taken down for the purpose, my heart almost fails me to find how my idle humour has led me aside from the great objects studied by every regular traveller who would make a book. I fear I shall give equal disappointment with an unlucky landscape painter, who had travelled on the continent, but following the bent of his vagrant inclination, had sketched in nooks, and corners, and by-places. His sketch book was accordingly crowded with cottages, and landscapes, and obscure ruins; but he had neglected to paint St. Peter's, or the Coliseum; the cascade of Terni,[7] or the bay of Naples; and had not a single glacier or volcano in his whole collection.

1819

Rip Van Winkle[1]

[The following Tale was found among the papers of the late Diedrich Knickerbocker, an old gentleman of New-York, who was very curious in the Dutch

5. The French scientist Georges Louis Leclerc, Count de Buffon (1707–1788) had theorized that the climate in America would cause the descendants of European emigrants to decline in physical stature and force.
6. English travelers in the United States had already begun to publish their scornful accounts of conditions in the former colonies.
7. St. Peter's, in Rome, is the world's largest church, built largely according to plans of Bramante. The Coli-

seum, in Rome, in part still standing, was built by Vespasian and Titus around A.D. 80. The cascade of Terni, famous waterfall in the Apennines, was created when a Roman consul altered the course of a river in the 3rd century B.C.
1. Rip Van Winkle was the last of the sketches printed in the May 1819 first installment of The Sketch Book, the source of the present text.

history of the province, and the manners of the descendants from its primitive
settlers. His historical researches, however, did not lay so much among books,
as among men; for the former are lamentably scanty on his favourite topics;
whereas he found the old burghers, and still more, their wives, rich in that
legendary lore, so invaluable to true history. Whenever, therefore, he happened upon a genuine Dutch family, snugly shut up in its low-roofed farm
house, under a spreading sycamore, he looked upon it as a little clasped volume of black-letter,[2] and studied it with the zeal of a bookworm.

The result of all these researches was a history of the province, during the
reign of the Dutch governors, which he published some years since. There
have been various opinions as to the literary character of his work, and, to tell
the truth, it is not a whit better than it should be. Its chief merit is its scrupulous accuracy, which, indeed, was a little questioned, on its first appearance,
but has since been completely established;[3] and it is now admitted into all
historical collections, as a book of unquestionable authority.

The old gentleman died shortly after the publication of his work, and now,
that he is dead and gone, it cannot do much harm to his memory, to say, that
his time might have been much better employed in weightier labours. He,
however, was apt to ride his hobby his own way; and though it did now and
then kick up the dust a little in the eyes of his neighbours, and grieve the spirit
of some friends, for whom he felt the truest deference and affection; yet his
errors and follies are remembered "more in sorrow than in anger,"[4] and it
begins to be suspected, that he never intended to injure or offend. But however
his memory may be appreciated by critics, it is still held dear among many
folk, whose good opinion is well worth having; particularly certain biscuit
bakers, who have gone so far as to imprint his likeness on their new year cakes,
and have thus given him a chance for immortality, almost equal to being
stamped on a Waterloo medal, or a Queen Anne's farthing.[5]]

Rip Van Winkle
A Posthumous Writing of Diedrich Knickerbocker

> By Woden, God of Saxons,
> From whence comes Wensday, that is Wodensday,
> Truth is a thing that ever I will keep
> Unto thylke day in which I creep into
> My sepulchre—
>
> —*Cartwright*[6]

Whoever has made a voyage up the Hudson, must remember the Kaatskill
mountains. They are a dismembered branch of the great Appalachian family,
and are seen away to the west of the river, swelling up to a noble height, and

2. Typeface in early printed books, resembling medieval script; such books, because of their value, were
often equipped with clasps so they could be shut tightly
and even locked.
3. Irving knew that most of his first readers would remember with delight the wildly inaccurate Knickerbocker *History*. He is also echoing Cervantes' humorous assurance of accuracy at the outset of *Don Quixote*.
4. Shakespeare's *Hamlet* 1.1.231–32. To this quotation Irving appended the following footnote: "Vide
[see] the excellent discourse of G. C. Verplanck, Esq.
before the New-York Historical Society." If Irving's

friend Gulian C. Verplanck ever made such an address, it was in fun.
5. Irving's irony cuts in different directions: Waterloo
medals were minted liberally after the defeat of Napoleon in 1815, whereas farthings (tiny coins) from the
reign of Queen Anne of England (1702–14) were commonly, though wrongly, considered rare, one story saying only three were minted.
6. In this quotation from *The Ordinary*, 3.1.1050–54,
a play by the English writer William Cartwright
(1611–1643), the speaker is a pedant named Moth.
"Woden": Norse god of war.

lording it over the surrounding country. Every change of season, every change
of weather, indeed, every hour of the day, produces some change in the magical hues and shapes of these mountains, and they are regarded by all the good
wives, far and near, as perfect barometers. When the weather is fair and settled, they are clothed in blue and purple, and print their bold outlines on the
clear evening sky; but some times, when the rest of the landscape is cloudless,
they will gather a hood of gray vapours about their summits, which, in the last
rays of the setting sun, will glow and light up like a crown of glory.

   At the foot of these fairy mountains, the voyager may have descried the light
smoke curling up from a village, whose shingle roofs gleam among the trees,
just where the blue tints of the upland melt away into the fresh green of the
nearer landscape. It is a little village of great antiquity, having been founded
by some of the Dutch colonists, in the early times of the province, just about
the beginning of the government of the good Peter Stuyvesant,[7] (may he rest
in peace!) and there were some of the houses of the original settlers standing
within a few years, with lattice windows, gable fronts surmounted with weathercocks, and built of small yellow bricks brought from Holland.

   In that same village, and in one of these very houses, (which, to tell the
precise truth, was sadly time worn and weather beaten,) there lived many years
since, while the country was yet a province of Great Britain, a simple good
natured fellow, of the name of Rip Van Winkle. He was a descendant of the
Van Winkles who figured so gallantly in the chivalrous days of Peter Stuyvesant, and accompanied him to the siege of Fort Christina. He inherited, however, but little of the martial character of his ancestors. I have observed that
he was a simple good natured man; he was moreover a kind neighbour, and
an obedient, henpecked husband. Indeed, to the latter circumstance might be
owing that meekness of spirit which gained him such universal popularity; for
those men are most apt to be obsequious and conciliating abroad, who are
under the discipline of shrews at home. Their tempers, doubtless, are rendered
pliant and malleable in the fiery furnace of domestic tribulation, and a curtain
lecture[8] is worth all the sermons in the world for teaching the virtues of
patience and long suffering. A termagant wife may, therefore, in some
respects, be considered a tolerable blessing; and if so, Rip Van Winkle was
thrice blessed.

   Certain it is, that he was a great favourite among all the good wives of the
village, who, as usual with the amiable sex, took his part in all family squab-
bles, and never failed, whenever they talked those matters over in their evening
gossippings, to lay all the blame on Dame Van Winkle. The children of the
village, too, would shout with joy whenever he approached. He assisted at
their sports, made their playthings, taught them to fly kites and shoot marbles,
and told them long stories of ghosts, witches, and Indians. Whenever he went
dodging about the village, he was surrounded by a troop of them, hanging on
his skirts, clambering on his back, and playing a thousand tricks on him with
impunity; and not a dog would bark at him throughout the neighbourhood.

   The great error in Rip's composition was an insuperable aversion to all kinds
of profitable labour. It could not be for the want of assiduity or perseverance;
for he would sit on a wet rock, with a rod as long and heavy as a Tartar's lance,

---

7. Peter Stuyvesant (1592–1672), last governor of the
Dutch province of New Netherlands, in 1655 (as mentioned below) defeated Swedish colonists at Fort Christina, near what is now Wilmington, Delaware.
8. Tirade delivered by a wife after the curtains around
the four-poster bed have been drawn for the night.

and fish all day without a murmur, even though he should not be encouraged by a single nibble. He would carry a fowling piece on his shoulder, for hours together, trudging through woods and swamps, and up hill and down dale, to shoot a few squirrels or wild pigeons. He would never even refuse to assist a neighbour in the roughest toil, and was a foremost man at all country frolics for husking Indian corn, or building stone fences; the women of the village, too, used to employ him to run their errands, and to do such little odd jobs as their less obliging husbands would not do for them;—in a word, Rip was ready to attend to any body's business but his own; but as to doing family duty, and keeping his farm in order, it was impossible.

In fact, he declared it was no use to work on his farm; it was the most pestilent little piece of ground in the whole country; every thing about it went wrong, and would go wrong, in spite of him. His fences were continually falling to pieces; his cow would either go astray, or get among the cabbages; weeds were sure to grow quicker in his fields than any where else; the rain always made a point of setting in just as he had some out-door work to do. So that though his patrimonial estate had dwindled away under his management, acre by acre, until there was little more left than a mere patch of Indian corn and potatoes, yet it was the worst conditioned farm in the neighbourhood.

His children, too, were as ragged and wild as if they belonged to nobody. His son Rip, an urchin begotten in his own likeness, promised to inherit the habits, with the old clothes of his father. He was generally seen trooping like a colt at his mother's heels, equipped in a pair of his father's cast-off galligas-kins,[9] which he had much ado to hold up with one hand, as a fine lady does her train in bad weather.

Rip Van Winkle, however, was one of those happy mortals, of foolish, well-oiled dispositions, who take the world easy, eat white bread or brown, which ever can be got with least thought or trouble, and would rather starve on a penny than work for a pound. If left to himself, he would have whistled life away, in perfect contentment; but his wife kept continually dinning in his ears about his idleness, his carelessness, and the ruin he was bringing on his family. Morning, noon, and night, her tongue was incessantly going, and every thing he said or did was sure to produce a torrent of household eloquence. Rip had but one way of replying to all lectures of the kind, and that, by frequent use, had grown into a habit. He shrugged his shoulders, shook his head, cast up his eyes, but said nothing. This, however, always provoked a fresh volley from his wife, so that he was fain to draw off his forces, and take to the outside of the house—the only side which, in truth, belongs to a henpecked husband.

Rip's sole domestic adherent was his dog Wolf, who was as much henpecked as his master; for Dame Van Winkle regarded them as companions in idleness, and even looked upon Wolf with an evil eye, as the cause of his master's so often going astray. True it is, in all points of spirit befitting an honourable dog, he was as courageous an animal as ever scoured the woods—but what courage can withstand the ever-during and all-besetting terrors of a woman's tongue? The moment Wolf entered the house, his crest fell, his tail drooped to the ground, or curled between his legs, he sneaked about with a gallows air, casting many a sidelong glance at Dame Van Winkle, and at the least flourish of a broomstick or ladle, would fly to the door with yelping precipitation.

9. Loose, wide breeches.

Times grew worse and worse with Rip Van Winkle as years of matrimony rolled on; a tart temper never mellows with age, and a sharp tongue is the only edge tool that grows keener by constant use. For a long while he used to console himself, when driven from home, by frequenting a kind of perpetual club of the sages, philosophers, and other idle personages of the village, that held its sessions on a bench before a small inn, designated by a rubicund portrait of his majesty George the Third. Here they used to sit in the shade, of a long lazy summer's day, talk listlessly over village gossip, or tell endless sleepy stories about nothing. But it would have been worth any statesman's money to have heard the profound discussions that sometimes took place, when by chance an old newspaper fell into their hands, from some passing traveller. How solemnly they would listen to the contents, as drawled out by Derrick Van Bummel, the schoolmaster, a dapper learned little man, who was not to be daunted by the most gigantic word in the dictionary; and how sagely they would deliberate upon public events some months after they had taken place.

The opinions of this junto[1] were completely controlled by Nicholas Vedder, a patriarch of the village, and landlord of the inn, at the door of which he took his seat from morning till night, just moving sufficiently to avoid the sun, and keep in the shade of a large tree; so that the neighbours could tell the hour by his movements as accurately as by a sun dial. It is true, he was rarely heard to speak, but smoked his pipe incessantly. His adherents, however, (for every great man has his adherents,) perfectly understood him, and knew how to gather his opinions. When any thing that was read or related displeased him, he was observed to smoke his pipe vehemently, and send forth short, frequent, and angry puffs; but when pleased, he would inhale the smoke slowly and tranquilly, and emit it in light and placid clouds, and sometimes taking the pipe from his mouth, and letting the fragrant vapour curl about his nose, would gravely nod his head in token of perfect approbation.

From even this strong hold the unlucky Rip was at length routed by his termagant wife, who would suddenly break in upon the tranquillity of the assemblage, call the members all to nought, nor was that august personage, Nicholas Vedder himself, sacred from the daring tongue of this terrible virago, who charged him outright with encouraging her husband in habits of idleness.

Poor Rip was at last reduced almost to despair; and his only alternative to escape from the labour of the farm and the clamour of his wife, was to take gun in hand, and stroll away into the woods. Here he would sometimes seat himself at the foot of a tree, and share the contents of his wallet[2] with Wolf, with whom he sympathised as a fellow sufferer in persecution. "Poor Wolf," he would say, "thy mistress leads thee a dogs' life of it; but never mind, my lad, while I live thou shalt never want a friend to stand by thee!" Wolf would wag his tail, look wistfully in his master's face, and if dogs can feel pity, I verily believe he reciprocated the sentiment with all his heart.

In a long ramble of the kind on a fine autumnal day, Rip had unconsciously scrambled to one of the highest parts of the Kaatskill mountains. He was after his favourite sport of squirrel shooting, and the still solitudes had echoed and re-echoed with the reports of his gun. Panting and fatigued, he threw himself, late in the afternoon, on a green knoll, covered with mountain herbage, that

1. Ruling committee (Spanish). 2. Knapsack.

crowned the brow of a precipice. From an opening between the trees, he could overlook all the lower country for many a mile of rich woodland. He saw at a distance the lordly Hudson, far, far below him, moving on its silent but majestic course, the reflection of a purple cloud, or the sail of a lagging bark, here and there sleeping on its glassy bosom, and at last losing itself in the blue highlands.

On the other side he looked down into a deep mountain glen, wild, lonely, and shagged, the bottom filled with fragments from the impending cliffs, and scarcely lighted by the reflected rays of the setting sun. For some time Rip lay musing on this scene, evening was gradually advancing, the mountains began to throw their long blue shadows over the valleys, he saw that it would be dark long before he could reach the village, and he heaved a heavy sigh when he thought of encountering the terrors of Dame Van Winkle.

As he was about to descend, he heard a voice from a distance, hallooing, "Rip Van Winkle! Rip Van Winkle!" He looked around, but could see nothing but a crow winging its solitary flight across the mountain. He thought his fancy must have deceived him, and turned again to descend, when he heard the same cry ring through the still evening air; "Rip Van Winkle! Rip Van Winkle!"—at the same time Wolf bristled up his back, and giving a low growl, skulked to his master's side, looking fearfully down into the glen. Rip now felt a vague apprehension stealing over him; he looked anxiously in the same direction, and perceived a strange figure slowly toiling up the rocks, and bending under the weight of something he carried on his back. He was surprised to see any human being in this lonely and unfrequented place, but supposing it to be some one of the neighbourhood in need of his assistance, he hastened down to yield it.

On nearer approach, he was still more surprised at the singularity of the stranger's appearance. He was a short square built old fellow, with thick bushy hair, and a grizzled beard. His dress was of the antique Dutch fashion—a cloth jerkin[3] strapped round the waist—several pair of breeches, the outer one of ample volume, decorated with rows of buttons down the sides, and bunches at the knees. He bore on his shoulder a stout keg, that seemed full of liquor, and made signs for Rip to approach and assist him with the load. Though rather shy and distrustful of this new acquaintance, Rip complied with his usual alacrity, and mutually relieving each other, they clambered up a narrow gully, apparently the dry bed of a mountain torrent. As they ascended, Rip every now and then heard long rolling peals, like distant thunder, that seemed to issue out of a deep ravine, or rather cleft between lofty rocks, toward which their rugged path conducted. He paused for an instant, but supposing it to be the muttering of one of those transient thunder showers which often take place in mountain heights, he proceeded. Passing through the ravine, they came to a hollow, like a small amphitheatre, surrounded by perpendicular precipices, over the brinks of which impending trees shot their branches, so that you only caught glimpses of the azure sky, and the bright evening cloud. During the whole time, Rip and his companion had laboured on in silence; for though the former marvelled greatly what could be the object of carrying a keg of liquor up this wild mountain, yet there was something strange and incomprehensible about the unknown, that inspired awe, and checked familiarity.

3. Jacket fitted tightly at the waist.

On entering the amphitheatre, new objects of wonder presented themselves. On a level spot in the centre was a company of odd-looking personages playing at nine-pins. They were dressed in a quaint, outlandish fashion: some wore short doublets,[4] others jerkins, with long knives in their belts, and most had enormous breeches, of similar style with that of the guide's. Their visages, too, were peculiar: one had a large head, broad face, and small piggish eyes; the face of another seemed to consist entirely of nose, and was surmounted by a white sugarloaf hat, set off with a little red cockstail. They all had beards, of various shapes and colours. There was one who seemed to be the commander. He was a stout old gentleman, with a weather-beaten countenance; he wore a laced doublet, broad belt and hanger,[5] high crowned hat and feather, red stockings, and high heeled shoes, with roses in them. The whole group reminded Rip of the figures in an old Flemish painting, in the parlour of Dominie[6] Van Schaick, the village parson, and which had been brought over from Holland at the time of the settlement.

What seemed particularly odd to Rip, was, that though these folks were evidently amusing themselves, yet they maintained the gravest faces, the most mysterious silence, and were, withal, the most melancholy party of pleasure he had ever witnessed. Nothing interrupted the stillness of the scene, but the noise of the balls, which, whenever they were rolled, echoed along the mountains like rumbling peals of thunder.

As Rip and his companion approached them, they suddenly desisted from their play, and stared at him with such fixed statue-like gaze, and such strange, uncouth, lack lustre countenances, that his heart turned within him, and his knees smote together. His companion now emptied the contents of the keg into large flagons, and made signs to him to wait upon the company. He obeyed with fear and trembling; they quaffed the liquor in profound silence, and then returned to their game.

By degrees, Rip's awe and apprehension subsided. He even ventured, when no eye was fixed upon him, to taste the beverage, which he found had much of the flavour of excellent Hollands.[7] He was naturally a thirsty soul, and was soon tempted to repeat the draught. One taste provoked another, and he re-iterated his visits to the flagon so often, that at length his senses were overpowered, his eyes swam in his head, his head gradually declined, and he fell into a deep sleep.

On awaking, he found himself on the green knoll from whence he had first seen the old man of the glen. He rubbed his eyes—it was a bright sunny morning. The birds were hopping and twittering among the bushes, and the eagle was wheeling aloft, and breasting the pure mountain breeze. "Surely," thought Rip, "I have not slept here all night." He recalled the occurrences before he fell asleep. The strange man with the keg of liquor—the mountain ravine—the wild retreat among the rocks—the wo-begone party at nine-pins—the flagon—"Oh! that flagon! that wicked flagon!" thought Rip—"what excuse shall I make to Dame Van Winkle?"

He looked round for his gun, but in place of the clean well-oiled fowling-piece, he found an old firelock lying by him, the barrel encrusted with rust, the lock falling off, and the stock worm-eaten. He now suspected that the grave

---

4. Male garment covering from neck to upper thighs, where it hooked to hose.
5. Short, curved sword.
6. Minister.
7. Kind of gin.

roysters of the mountain had put a trick upon him, and having dosed him with liquor, had robbed him of his gun. Wolf, too, had disappeared, but he might have strayed away after a squirrel or partridge. He whistled after him, shouted his name, but all in vain; the echoes repeated his whistle and shout, but no dog was to be seen.

He determined to revisit the scene of the last evening's gambol, and if he met with any of the party, to demand his dog and gun. As he arose to walk he found himself stiff in the joints, and wanting in his usual activity. "These mountain beds do not agree with me," thought Rip, "and if this frolick should lay me up with a fit of the rheumatism, I shall have a blessed time with Dame Van Winkle." With some difficulty he got down into the glen: he found the gully up which he and his companion had ascended the preceding evening, but to his astonishment a mountain stream was now foaming down it, leaping from rock to rock, and filling the glen with babbling murmurs. He, however, made shift to scramble up its sides, working his toilsome way through thickets of birch, sassafras, and witch hazle, and sometimes tripped up or entangled by the wild grape vines that twisted their coils and tendrils from tree to tree, and spread a kind of network in his path.

At length he reached to where the ravine had opened through the cliffs, to the amphitheatre; but no traces of such opening remained. The rocks presented a high impenetrable wall, over which the torrent came tumbling in a sheet of feathery foam, and fell into a broad deep basin, black from the shadows of the surrounding forest. Here, then, poor Rip was brought to a stand. He again called and whistled after his dog; he was only answered by the cawing of a flock of idle crows, sporting high in air about a dry tree that overhung a sunny precipice; and who, secure in their elevation, seemed to look down and scoff at the poor man's perplexities. What was to be done? the morning was passing away, and Rip felt famished for his breakfast. He grieved to give up his dog and gun; he dreaded to meet his wife; but it would not do to starve among the mountains. He shook his head, shouldered the rusty firelock, and, with a heart full of trouble and anxiety, turned his steps homeward.

As he approached the village, he met a number of people, but none that he knew, which somewhat surprised him, for he had thought himself acquainted with every one in the country round. Their dress, too, was of a different fashion from that to which he was accustomed. They all stared at him with equal marks of surprise, and whenever they cast eyes upon him, invariably stroked their chins. The constant recurrence of this gesture, induced Rip, involuntarily, to do the same, when, to his astonishment, he found his beard had grown a foot long!

He had now entered the skirts of the village. A troop of strange children ran at his heels, hooting after him, and pointing at his gray beard. The dogs, too, not one of which he recognized for his old acquaintances, barked at him as he passed. The very village seemed altered: it was larger and more populous. There were rows of houses which he had never seen before, and those which had been his familiar haunts had disappeared. Strange names were over the doors—strange faces at the windows—every thing was strange. His mind now began to misgive him, that both he and the world around him were bewitched. Surely this was his native village, which he had left but the day before. There stood the Kaatskill mountains—there ran the silver Hudson at a distance—there was every hill and dale precisely as it had always been—Rip was sorely perplexed—"That flagon last night," thought he, "has addled my poor head sadly!"

It was with some difficulty he found the way to his own house, which he approached with silent awe, expecting every moment to hear the shrill voice of Dame Van Winkle. He found the house gone to decay—the roof fallen in, the windows shattered, and the doors off the hinges. A half starved dog, that looked like Wolf, was skulking about it. Rip called him by name, but the cur snarled, showed his teeth, and passed on. This was an unkind cut indeed— "My very dog," sighed poor Rip, "has forgotten me!"

He entered the house, which, to tell the truth, Dame Van Winkle had always kept in neat order. It was empty, forlorn, and apparently abandoned. This desolateness overcame all his connubial fears—he called loudly for his wife and children—the lonely chambers rung for a moment with his voice, and then all again was silence.

He now hurried forth, and hastened to his old resort, the little village inn— but it too was gone. A large ricketty wooden building stood in its place, with great gaping windows, some of them broken, and mended with old hats and petticoats, and over the door was painted, "The Union Hotel, by Jonathan Doolittle." Instead of the great tree that used to shelter the quiet little Dutch inn of yore, there now was reared a tall naked pole, with something on top that looked like a red night cap,[8] and from it was fluttering a flag, on which was a singular assemblage of stars and stripes—all this was strange and incomprehensible. He recognised on the sign, however, the ruby face of King George, under which he had smoked so many a peaceful pipe, but even this was singularly metamorphosed. The red coat was changed for one of blue and buff,[9] a sword was stuck in the hand instead of a sceptre, the head was decorated with a cocked hat, and underneath was painted in large characters, GENERAL WASHINGTON.

There was, as usual, a crowd of folk about the door, but none that Rip recollected. The very character of the people seemed changed. There was a busy, bustling, disputatious tone about it, instead of the accustomed phlegm and drowsy tranquillity. He looked in vain for the sage Nicholas Vedder, with his broad face, double chin, and fair long pipe, uttering clouds of tobacco smoke instead of idle speeches; or Van Bummel, the schoolmaster, doling forth the contents of an ancient newspaper. In place of these, a lean bilious looking fellow, with his pockets full of handbills, was haranguing vehemently about rights of citizens—election—members of congress—liberty—Bunker's hill—heroes of seventy-six—and other words, that were a perfect Babylonish jargon[1] to the bewildered Van Winkle.

The appearance of Rip, with his long grizzled beard, his rusty fowling piece, his uncouth dress, and the army of women and children that had gathered at his heels, soon attracted the attention of the tavern politicians. They crowded around him, eyeing him from head to foot, with great curiosity. The orator bustled up to him, and drawing him partly aside, inquired "which side he voted?" Rip stared in vacant stupidity. Another short but busy little fellow pulled him by the arm, and raising on tiptoe, inquired in his ear, "whether he

---

8. Limp, close-fitting cap adopted during the French Revolution as a symbol of liberty; the pole is a "liberty pole"—i.e., a tall flagstaff topped by a liberty cap.
9. Colors of the Revolutionary uniform. Irving's joke is that the new proprietor, being a Yankee, is so parsi-

monious that he will only touch up the sign, not replace it with a true portrait of Washington.
1. Cf. Genesis 11.1–9, Babel being confused with Babylon.

was Federal or Democrat."[2] Rip was equally at a loss to comprehend the question; when a knowing, self-important old gentleman, in a sharp cocked hat, made his way through the crowd, putting them to the right and left with his elbows as he passed, and planting himself before Van Winkle, with one arm akimbo, the other resting on his cane, his keen eyes and sharp hat penetrating, as it were, into his very soul, demanded, in an austere tone, "what brought him to the election with a gun on his shoulder, and a mob at his heels, and whether he meant to breed a riot in the village?" "Alas! gentlemen," cried Rip, somewhat dismayed, "I am a poor quiet man, a native of the place, and a loyal subject of the King, God bless him!"

Here a general shout burst from the bystanders—"A tory! a tory! a spy! a refugee! hustle him! away with him!" It was with great difficulty that the self-important man in the cocked hat restored order; and having assumed a tenfold austerity of brow, demanded again of the unknown culprit, what he came there for, and whom he was seeking. The poor man humbly assured them that he meant no harm; but merely came there in search of some of his neighbours, who used to keep about the tavern.

"Well—who are they?—name them."

Rip bethought himself a moment, and inquired, "where's Nicholas Vedder?"

There was a silence for a little while, when an old man replied, in a thin piping voice, "Nicholas Vedder? why he is dead and gone these eighteen years! There was a wooden tombstone in the church yard that used to tell all about him, but that's rotted and gone too."

"Where's Brom Dutcher?"

"Oh he went off to the army in the beginning of the war; some say he was killed at the battle of Stoney-Point—others say he was drowned in a squall, at the foot of Antony's Nose.[3] I don't know—he never came back again."

"Where's Van Bummel, the schoolmaster?"

"He went off to the wars too, was a great militia general, and is now in Congress."

Rip's heart died away, at hearing of these sad changes in his home and friends, and finding himself thus alone in the world. Every answer puzzled him, too, by treating of such enormous lapses of time, and of matters which he could not understand: war—congress—Stoney-Point;—he had no courage to ask after any more friends, but cried out in despair, "does nobody here know Rip Van Winkle?"

"Oh, Rip Van Winkle!" exclaimed two or three, "Oh, to be sure! that's Rip Van Winkle yonder, leaning against the tree."

Rip looked, and beheld a precise counterpart of himself, as he went up the mountain: apparently as lazy, and certainly as ragged. The poor fellow was now completely confounded. He doubted his own identity, and whether he was himself or another man. In the midst of his bewilderment, the man in the cocked hat demanded who he was, and what was his name?

"God knows," exclaimed he, at his wit's end; "I'm not myself—I'm somebody else—that's me yonder—no—that's somebody else, got into my shoes—

2. Political parties that developed in the Washington administrations, Alexander Hamilton leading the Federalists and Thomas Jefferson, the Democrats.
3. A mountain near West Point. "Stoney Point": on the west bank of the Hudson south of West Point, captured by General Anthony Wayne (1745–1796) during the Revolution.

I was myself last night, but I fell asleep on the mountain, and they've changed my gun, and every thing's changed, and I'm changed, and I can't tell what's my name, or who I am!"

The bystanders began now to look at each other, nod, wink significantly, and tap their fingers against their foreheads. There was a whisper, also, about securing the gun, and keeping the old fellow from doing mischief. At the very suggestion of which, the self-important man in the cocked hat retired with some precipitation. At this critical moment a fresh likely woman pressed through the throng to get a peep at the graybearded man. She had a chubby child in her arms, which, frightened at his looks, began to cry. "Hush, Rip," cried she, "hush, you little fool, the old man wont hurt you." The name of the child, the air of the mother, the tone of her voice, all awakened a train of recollections in his mind.

"What is your name, my good woman?" asked he.

"Judith Gardenier."

"And your father's name?"

"Ah, poor man, his name was Rip Van Winkle; it's twenty years since he went away from home with his gun, and never has been heard of since—his dog came home without him; but whether he shot himself, or was carried away by the Indians, nobody can tell. I was then but a little girl."

Rip had but one question more to ask; but he put it with a faltering voice:

"Where's your mother?"

Oh, she too had died but a short time since; she broke a blood vessel in a fit of passion at a New-England pedlar.

There was a drop of comfort, at least, in this intelligence. The honest man could contain himself no longer.—He caught his daughter and her child in his arms.—"I am your father!" cried he—"Young Rip Van Winkle once—old Rip Van Winkle now!—Does nobody know poor Rip Van Winkle!"

All stood amazed, until an old woman, tottering out from among the crowd, put her hand to her brow, and peering under it in his face for a moment, exclaimed, "Sure enough! it is Rip Van Winkle—it is himself. Welcome home again, old neighbour—Why, where have you been these twenty long years?"

Rip's story was soon told, for the whole twenty years had been to him but as one night. The neighbours stared when they heard it; some were seen to wink at each other, and put their tongues in their cheeks; and the self-important man in the cocked hat, who, when the alarm was over, had returned to the field, screwed down the corners of his mouth, and shook his head—upon which there was a general shaking of the head throughout the assemblage.

It was determined, however, to take the opinion of old Peter Vanderdonk, who was seen slowly advancing up the road. He was a descendant of the historian of that name,[4] who wrote one of the earliest accounts of the province. Peter was the most ancient inhabitant of the village, and well versed in all the wonderful events and traditions of the neighbourhood. He recollected Rip at once, and corroborated his story in the most satisfactory manner. He assured the company that it was a fact, handed down from his ancestor the historian, that the Kaatskill mountains had always been haunted by strange beings. That it was affirmed that the great Hendrick Hudson, the first discoverer of the river

4. Adriaen Van der Donck (1620–1655?) wrote a history of New Netherlands (1655).

and country, kept a kind of vigil there every twenty years, with his crew of the Half-moon, being permitted in this way to revisit the scenes of his enterprize, and keep a guardian eye upon the river, and the great city[5] called by his name. That his father had once seen them in their old Dutch dresses playing at nine pins in a hollow of the mountain; and that he himself had heard, one summer afternoon, the sound of their balls, like long peals of thunder.

To make a long story short, the company broke up, and returned to the more important concerns of the election. Rip's daughter took him home to live with her; she had a snug, well-furnished house, and a stout cheery farmer for a husband, whom Rip recollected for one of the urchins that used to climb upon his back. As to Rip's son and heir, who was the ditto of himself, seen leaning against the tree, he was employed to work on the farm; but evinced an hereditary disposition to attend to any thing else but his business.

Rip now resumed his old walks and habits; he soon found many of his former cronies, though all rather the worse for the wear and tear of time; and preferred making friends among the rising generation, with whom he soon grew into great favour.

Having nothing to do at home, and being arrived at that happy age when a man can do nothing with impunity, he took his place once more on the bench, at the inn door, and was reverenced as one of the patriarchs of the village, and a chronicle of the old times "before the war." It was some time before he could get into the regular track of gossip, or could be made to comprehend the strange events that had taken place during his torpor. How that there had been a revolutionary war—that the country had thrown off the yoke of old England—and that, instead of being a subject of his Majesty George the Third, he was now a free citizen of the United States. Rip, in fact, was no politician; the changes of states and empires made but little impression on him. But there was one species of despotism under which he had long groaned, and that was—petticoat government. Happily, that was at an end; he had got his neck out of the yoke of matrimony, and could go in and out whenever he pleased, without dreading the tyranny of Dame Van Winkle. Whenever her name was mentioned, however, he shook his head, shrugged his shoulders, and cast up his eyes; which might pass either for an expression of resignation to his fate, or joy at his deliverance.

He used to tell his story to every stranger that arrived at Mr. Doolittle's hotel. He was observed, at first, to vary on some points every time he told it, which was, doubtless, owing to his having so recently awaked. It at last settled down precisely to the tale I have related, and not a man, woman, or child in the neighbourhood, but knew it by heart. Some always pretended to doubt the reality of it, and insisted that Rip had been out of his head, and that this was one point on which he always remained flighty. The old Dutch inhabitants, however, almost universally gave it full credit. Even to this day they never hear a thunder storm of a summer afternoon, about the Kaatskill, but they say Hendrick Hudson and his crew are at their game of nine pins; and it is a common wish of all henpecked husbands in the neighbourhood, when life hangs heavy on their hands, that they might have a quieting draught out of Rip Van Winkle's flagon.

---

5. Henry Hudson (d. 1611), English navigator in the service of the Dutch. "Great city" is ironic, for the town named for him on the east bank of the Hudson River was flourishing but not a metropolis.

NOTE

The foregoing tale, one would suspect, had been suggested to Mr. Knicker-bocker by a little German superstition about Charles V.[6] and the Kypphauser mountain; the subjoined note, however, which he had appended to the tale, shows that it is an absolute fact, narrated with his usual fidelity:

"The story of Rip Van Winkle may seem incredible to many, but neverthe-less I give it my full belief, for I know the vicinity of our old Dutch settlements to have been very subject to marvellous events and appearances. Indeed, I have heard many stranger stories than this, in the villages along the Hudson; all of which were too well authenticated to admit of a doubt. I have even talked with Rip Van Winkle myself, who, when last I saw him, was a very venerable old man, and so perfectly rational and consistent on every other point, that I think no conscientious person could refuse to take this into the bargain; nay, I have seen a certificate on the subject taken before a country justice, and signed with a cross, in the justice's own hand writing. The story, therefore, is beyond the possibility of doubt.   D.K."

1819

The Legend of Sleepy Hollow

(Found among the Papers of the Late Diedrich Knickerbocker)[1]

A pleasing land of drowsy head it was,
Of dreams that wave before the half-shut eye;
And of gay castles in the clouds that pass,
Forever flushing round a summer sky.
            —Castle of Indolence[2]

In the bosom of one of the spacious coves which indent the eastern shore of the Hudson, at that broad expansion of the river denominated by the ancient Dutch navigators the Tappaan Zee,[3] and where they always prudently short-ened sail, and implored the protection of St. Nicholas when they crossed, there lies a small market town or rural port, which by some is called Greensburgh, but which is more universally and properly known by the name of Tarry Town. This name was given it, we are told, in former days, by the good housewives of the adjacent country, from the inveterate propensity of their husbands to linger about the village tavern on market days. Be that as it may, I do not vouch for the fact, but merely advert to it, for the sake of being precise and authentic. Not far from this village, perhaps about three miles, there is a little valley, or rather lap of land among high hills, which is one of the quietest places in the whole world. A small brook glides through it, with just murmur enough to lull you to repose, and the occasional whistle of a

---

6. Later Irving changed "Charles V." (Holy Roman emperor 1519–1556) to "The Emperor Frederick der Rothbart" (i.e., Frederick Barbarossa; Holy Roman emperor 1152–1190). ("Rothbart" and "Barbarossa" both mean "redbeard.") In either form, the allusion is a red herring, a disarming way of suggesting indebted-ness to a German source while concealing the most specific source, the story of Peter Klaus in the folktales of J. C. C. N. Otmar.

1. The Legend of Sleepy Hollow was the last of three pieces printed in February 1820 as the sixth installment of The Sketch Book, the source of the present text.

2. By the Scottish poet James Thomson (1700–1748), 1.46–49.

3. Wide "sea" in the Hudson near Tarrytown.

quail, or tapping of a woodpecker, is almost the only sound that ever breaks in upon the uniform tranquillity.

I recollect that when a stripling, my first exploit in squirrel shooting was in a grove of tall walnut trees that shades one side of the valley. I had wandered into it at noon time, when all nature is peculiarly quiet, and was startled by the roar of my own gun, as it broke the sabbath stillness around, and was prolonged and reverberated by the angry echoes. If ever I should wish for a retreat, whither I might steal from the world and its distractions, and dream quietly away the remnant of a troubled life, I know of none more promising than this little valley.

From the listless repose of the place, and the peculiar character of its inhabitants, who are descendants from the original Dutch settlers, this sequestered glen has long been known by the name of SLEEPY HOLLOW, and its rustic lads are called the Sleepy Hollow Boys throughout all the neighbouring country. A drowsy, dreamy influence seems to hang over the land, and pervade the very atmosphere. Some say that the place was bewitched by a high German[4] doctor during the early days of the settlement; others, that an old Indian chief, the prophet or wizard of his tribe, held his powwows there before the country was discovered by Master Hendrick Hudson.[5] Certain it is, the place still continues under the sway of some witching power, that holds a spell over the minds of the good people, causing them to walk in a continual reverie. They are given to all kinds of marvellous beliefs; have trances and visions, and see strange sights, and hear music and voices in the air. The whole neighbourhood abounds with local tales, haunted spots, and twilight superstitions; stars shoot and meteors glare oftener across the valley than in any other part of the country, and the night-mare, with her whole nine fold,[6] seems to make it the favourite scene of her gambols.

The dominant spirit, however, that haunts this enchanted region, and seems to be commander of all the powers of the air, is the apparition of a figure on horseback without a head. It is said by some to be the ghost of a Hessian[7] trooper, whose head had been carried away by a cannon-ball, in some nameless battle during the revolutionary war, and who is ever and anon seen by various of the country people, hurrying along in the gloom of night, as if on the wings of the wind. His haunts are not confined to the valley, but extend at times to the adjacent roads, and especially to the vicinity of a church that is at no great distance. Indeed, certain of the most authentic historians of those parts, who have been careful in collecting and collating the floating facts concerning this spectre, allege, that the body of the trooper having been buried in the church-yard, the ghost rides forth to the scene of battle in nightly quest of his head, and the rushing speed with which he sometimes passes along the hollow, like a midnight blast, is owing to his being belated, and in a hurry to get back to the church-yard before day-break.

Such is the general purport of this legendary superstition, which has furnished materials for many a wild story in that region of shadows; and the spectre is known, at all the country firesides, by the name of The Headless Horseman of Sleepy Hollow.

4. I.e., from southern Germany.
5. Henry Hudson (d. 1611), English navigator in the service of the Dutch.
6. I.e., the nine foals of the demonic night mare who "rides" her sleeping victims. Cf. Shakespeare's *King Lear* 3.4.128.

7. German mercenaries from Hesse were hired by the British to fight against the colonists in the American Revolution.

It is remarkable, that the visionary turn I have mentioned is not confined to the native inhabitants of the valley, but is imperceptibly acquired by every one who resides there for a time. However wide awake they may have been before they entered that sleepy region, they are sure, in a little time, to imbibe the witching influence of the air, and begin to grow imaginative—to dream dreams, and see apparitions.

I mention this peaceful spot with all possible laud; for it is in such little retired Dutch valleys, found here and there embosomed in the great state of New-York, that populations, manners, and customs, remained fixed, while the great torrent of emigration and improvement, which is making such incessant changes in other parts of this restless country, sweeps by them unobserved. They are like those little nooks of still water, which border a rapid stream, where we may see the straw and bubble riding quietly at anchor, or slowly revolving in their mimic harbour, undisturbed by the rushing of the passing current. Though many years have elapsed since I trod the drowsy shades of Sleepy Hollow, yet I question whether I should not still find the same trees and the same families vegetating in its sheltered bosom.

In this by-place of nature there abode, in a remote period of American history, that is to say, some thirty years since, a worthy wight of the name of Ichabod Crane, who sojourned, or, as he expressed it, "tarried," in Sleepy Hollow, for the purpose of instructing the children of the vicinity. He was a native of Connecticut, a state which supplies the Union with pioneers for the mind as well as the forest, and sends forth yearly its legions of frontier woodmen and country schoolmasters. The cognomen of Crane was not inapplicable to his person. He was tall, but exceedingly lank, with narrow shoulders, long arms and legs, hands that dangled a mile out of his sleeves, feet that might have served for shovels, and his whole frame most loosely hung together. His head was small, and flat at top, with huge ears, large green glassy eyes, and a long snipe nose, so that it might have been mistaken for a weathercock perched upon his spindle neck, to tell which way the wind blew. To see him striding along the profile of a hill on a windy day, with his clothes bagging and fluttering about him, one might have mistaken him for the genius[8] of famine descending upon the earth, or some scarecrow eloped from a cornfield.

His school-house was a low building of one large room, rudely constructed of logs; the windows partly glazed, and partly patched with leaves of old copy books. It was most ingeniously secured at vacant hours, by a withe[9] twisted in the handle of the door, and stakes set against the window shutters; so that though a thief might get in with perfect ease, he would find some embarrassment in getting out; an idea most probably borrowed by the architect, Yost Van Houten, from the mystery of an eelpot.[1] The school-house stood in rather a lonely but a pleasant situation, just at the foot of a woody hill, with a brook running close by, and a formidable birch tree growing at one end of it. From hence the low murmur of his pupils' voices conning over their lessons, might be heard of a drowsy summer's day, like the hum of a bee-hive; interrupted now and then by the authoritative voice of the master, giving menace or command, or, peradventure, the appalling sound of the birch, as he urged some tardy loiterer along the flowery path of knowledge. Truth to say, he was a

8. I.e., image; an echo of Shakespeare's 2 *Henry IV* 3.2, Falstaff's description of the youthful Justice Shallow.

9. Slender, flexible branch (usually from a willow), used in place of rope.

1. Eel trap.

conscientious man, that ever bore in mind the golden maxim, "spare the rod and spoil the child."[2]—Ichabod Crane's scholars certainly were not spoiled.

I would not have it imagined, however, that he was one of those cruel potentates of the school, who joy in the smart[3] of their subjects; on the contrary, he administered justice with discrimination rather than severity; taking the burthen off the backs of the weak, and laying it on those of the strong. Your mere puny stripling, that winced at the least flourish of the rod, was passed by with indulgence; but the claims of justice were satisfied, by giving a double portion to some little, tough, wrong-headed, broad-skirted Dutch urchin, who sulked and swelled and grew dogged and sullen beneath the birch. All this he called "doing his duty by their parents;" and he never inflicted a chastisement without following it by the assurance, so consolatory to the smarting urchin, that he would remember it and thank him for it the longest day he had to live.

When school hours were over, he was even the companion and playmate of his larger boys; and would convoy some of the smaller ones home of a holyday, who happened to have pretty sisters, or good housewives for mothers, noted for the comforts of the cupboard. Indeed, it behooved him to keep on good terms with his pupils. The revenue arising from his school was small, and would have been scarcely sufficient to furnish him with daily bread, for he was a huge feeder,[4] and though lank, had the dilating powers of an Anaconda; but to help out his maintenance, he was, according to country custom in those parts, boarded and lodged at the houses of the farmers, whose children he instructed. With these he lived alternately a week at a time, thus going the rounds of the neighbourhood, with all his worldly effects tied up in a cotton handkerchief.

That all this might not be too onerous on the purses of his rustic patrons, who are apt to consider the costs of schooling a grievous burthen, and schoolmasters mere drones, he had various ways of rendering himself both useful and agreeable. He assisted the farmers occasionally in the light labours of their farms, helped to make hay, mended the fences, took the horses to water, drove the cows from pasture, and cut wood for the winter fire. He laid aside, too, all the dominant dignity and absolute sway, with which he lorded it in his little empire, the school, and became wonderfully gentle and ingratiating. He found favour in the eyes of the mothers, by petting the children, particularly the youngest, and like the lion bold, which whilome[5] so magnanimously the lamb did hold,[6] he would sit with a child on one knee, and rock a cradle with his foot, for whole hours together.

In addition to his other vocations, he was the singing-master of the neighbourhood, and picked up many bright shillings by instructing the young folks in psalmody.[7] It was a matter of no little vanity to him on Sundays, to take his station in front of the church gallery, with a band of chosen singers; where, in his own mind, he completely carried away the palm from the parson. Certain it is, his voice resounded far above all the rest of the congregation, and there are peculiar quavers still to be heard in that church, and which may even be

2. *Hudibras* 2.843 (1664), by the English poet Samuel Butler (1612–1680); ultimately from Proverbs 13.24.
3. Pain.
4. Cf. Shylock's description of Launcelot Gobbo in Shakespeare's *Merchant of Venice* 2.5.46.
5. Formerly.

6. In the *New England Primer*, a long-lived double-duty text that taught the Bible along with the alphabet, the letter *L* consists of an illustration depicting Isaiah 11.6–9 and the rhyme "The lion bold / The lamb doth hold."
7. Singing of rhymed versions of the Psalms.

heard half-a-mile off, quite to the opposite side of the mill-pond, of a still Sunday morning, which are said to be legitimately descended from the nose of Ichabod Crane. Thus, by diverse little make shifts, in that ingenious way which is commonly denominated "by hook and by crook,"[8] the worthy peda-gogue got on tolerably enough, and was thought, by all those who understood nothing of the labour of headwork, to have a wonderful easy life of it.

The schoolmaster is generally a man of some importance in the female circle of a rural neighbourhood, being considered a kind of idle gentleman-like personage, of vastly superior taste and accomplishments to the rough country swains, and, indeed, inferior in learning only to the parson. His appearance, therefore, is apt to occasion some little stir at the tea-table of a farm-house, and the addition of a supernumerary dish of cakes or sweetmeats, or, peradventure, the parade of a silver tea-pot. Our man of letters, therefore, was peculiarly happy in the smiles of all the country damsels. How he would figure among them in the church-yard, between services on Sundays; gather-ing grapes for them from the wild vines that overrun the surrounding trees; reciting for them all the epitaphs on the tomb-stones, or sauntering, with a whole bevy of them, along the banks of the adjacent mill-pond; while the more bashful country bumpkins hung sheepishly back, envying his superior elegance and address.

From his half itinerant life, also, he was a kind of travelling gazette, carrying the whole budget of local gossip from house to house; so that his appearance was always greeted with satisfaction. He was, moreover, esteemed by the women as a man of great erudition, for he had read several books quite through, and was a perfect master of Cotton Mather's History of New-England Witchcraft,[9] in which, by the way, he most firmly and potently believed.

He was, in fact, an odd mixture of small shrewdness and simple credulity. His appetite for the marvellous, and his powers of digesting it, were equally extraordinary; and both had been increased by his residence in this spell-bound region. No tale was too gross or monstrous for his capacious swallow. It was often his delight, after his school was dismissed of an afternoon, to stretch himself on the rich bed of clover, bordering the little brook that whimpered past his school-house, and there con over old Mather's direful tales, until the gathering dusk of evening made the printed page a mere mist before his eyes. Then, as he wended his way, by swamp and stream and awful[1] woodland, to the farm-house where he happened to be quartered, every sound of nature, at that witching hour, fluttered his excited imagination: the moan of the whip-poor-will from the hill side; the boding cry of the tree-toad, that harbinger of storm; the dreary hooting of the screech-owl; or the sudden rustling in the thicket, of birds frightened from their roost. The fire-flies, too, which sparkled most vividly in the darkest places, now and then startled him, as one of uncommon brightness would stream across his path; and if, by chance, a huge blockhead of a beetle came winging his blundering flight against him, the poor varlet was ready to give up the ghost, with the idea that he was struck with a witch's token. His only resource on such occasions, either to drown thought, or drive away evil spirits, was to sing psalm tunes;—and the good people of Sleepy Hollow, as they sat by their doors of an evening, were often filled with

8. From *Colin Clout* (1523) by the English poet John Skelton (1460?–1529).
9. Cotton Mather (1663–1728) wrote *Memorable* *Providences, Relating to Witchcrafts and Possessions* (1689) and *The Wonders of the Invisible World* (1693).
1. Terrifying.

awe, at hearing his nasal melody, "in linked sweetness long drawn out,"[2] floating from the distant hill, or along the dusky road.

Another of his sources of fearful pleasure was, to pass long winter evenings with the old Dutch wives, as they sat spinning by the fire, with a row of apples roasting and sputtering along the hearth, and listen to their marvellous tales of ghosts and goblins, and haunted fields and haunted brooks, and haunted bridges and haunted houses, and particularly of the headless horseman, or galloping Hessian of the Hollow, as they sometimes called him. He would delight them equally by his anecdotes of witchcraft, and of the direful omens and portentous sights and sounds in the air, which prevailed in the earlier times of Connecticut; and would frighten them wofully with speculations upon comets and shooting stars, and with the alarming fact that the world did absolutely turn round, and that they were half the time topsy-turvy!

But if there was a pleasure in all this, while snugly cuddling in the chimney corner of a chamber that was all of a ruddy glow from the crackling wood fire, and where, of course, no spectre dare to show its face, it was dearly purchased by the terrors of his subsequent walk homewards. What fearful shapes and shadows beset his path, amidst the dim and ghostly glare of a snowy night!— With what wistful look did he eye every trembling ray of light streaming across the waste fields from some distant window!—How often was he appalled by some shrub covered with snow, which like sheeted spectre beset his very path!—How often did he shrink with curdling awe at the sound of his own steps on the frosty crust beneath his feet; and dread to look over his shoulder, lest he should behold some uncouth being tramping close behind him!—and how often was he thrown into complete dismay by some rushing blast, howling among the trees, in the idea that it was the gallopping Hessian on one of his nightly scourings.

All these, however, were mere terrors of the night, phantoms of the mind, that walk in darkness; and though he had seen many spectres in his time, and been more than once beset by Satan in diverse shapes, in his lonely perambulations, yet day-light put an end to all these evils; and he would have passed a pleasant life of it, in despite of the Devil and all his works, if his path had not been crossed by a being that causes more perplexity to mortal man, than ghosts, goblins, and the whole race of witches put together, and that was— a woman.

Among the musical disciples who assembled, one evening in each week, to receive his instructions in psalmody, was Katrina Van Tassel, the daughter and only child of a substantial Dutch farmer. She was a blooming lass of fresh eighteen; plump as a partridge; ripe and melting and rosy-cheeked as one of her father's peaches, and universally famed, not merely for her beauty, but her vast expectations. She was withal a little of a coquette, as might be perceived even in her dress, which was a mixture of ancient and modern fashions, as most suited to set off her charms. She wore the ornaments of pure yellow gold, which her great-great-grandmother had brought over from Saardam; the tempting stomacher[3] of the olden time, and withal a provokingly short petticoat, to display the prettiest foot and ankle in the country round.

Ichabod Crane had a soft and foolish heart toward the sex; and it is not to be wondered at, that so tempting a morsel soon found favour in his eyes, more

2. *L'Allegro*, line 140, by the English poet John Milton (1608–1674).

3. Wide, ornamental waistband worn over a dress. "Saardam": now Zaandam, near Amsterdam

especially after he had visited her in her paternal mansion. Old Baltus Van Tassel was a perfect picture of a thriving, contented, liberal-hearted farmer. He seldom, it is true, sent either his eyes or his thoughts beyond the boundaries of his own farm; but within those every thing was snug, happy, and well-conditioned. He was satisfied with his wealth, but not proud of it, and piqued himself upon the hearty abundance, rather than the style in which he lived. His strong hold was situated on the banks of the Hudson, in one of those green, sheltered, fertile nooks, into which the Dutch farmers are so fond of nestling. A great elm tree spread its broad branches over it, at the foot of which bubbled up a spring of the softest and sweetest water, in a little kind of well, formed of a barrel, and then stole sparkling away through the grass, to a neighbouring brook, that babbled along among elders and dwarf willows. Hard by the farmhouse was a vast barn, that might have served for a church; every window and crevice of which seemed bursting forth with the treasures of the farm; the flail was busily resounding within it; swallows and martins skimmed twittering about the eaves, and rows of pigeons, some with one eye turned up, as if watching the weather, some with their heads under their wings, or buried in their bosoms, and others, swelling, and cooing, and bowing about their dames, were enjoying the sunshine on the roof. Sleek unwieldy porkers were grunting in the repose and abundance of their pens, from whence sallied forth, now and then, troops of sucking pigs, as if to snuff the air. A stately squadron of snowy geese were riding in an adjoining pond, convoying whole fleets of ducks; regiments of turkeys were gobbling about the farm yard, and guinea fowls fretting like ill-tempered housewives, with their peevish discontented cry. Before the barn door strutted the gallant cock, that pattern of a husband, a warrior, and a fine gentleman, clapping his burnished wings, and crowing in the pride and gladness of his heart—sometimes tearing up the earth with his feet, and then generously calling his ever-hungry family of wives and children to enjoy the rich morsel he had discovered.

The pedagogue's mouth watered, as he looked upon this sumptuous promise of luxurious winter fare. In his devouring mind's eye, he pictured to himself every roasting pig running about with a pudding in its belly,[4] and an apple in its mouth; the pigeons were snugly put to bed in a comfortable pie, and tucked in with a coverlet of crust; the geese were swimming in their own gravy; and the ducks pairing cosily in dishes, like snug married couples, with a decent competency of onion sauce; in the porkers he saw carved out the future sleek side of bacon, and juicy relishing ham; not a turkey, but he beheld daintily trussed up, with its gizzard under its wing, and, peradventure, a necklace of savoury sausages; and even bright chanticleer[5] himself lay sprawling on his back, in a side dish, with uplifted claws, as if craving that quarter,[6] which his chivalrous spirit disdained to ask while living.

As the enraptured Ichabod fancied all this, and as he rolled his great green eyes over the fat meadow lands, the rich fields of wheat, of rye, of buckwheat, and Indian corn, and the orchards burthened with ruddy fruit, which surrounded the warm tenement[7] of Van Tassel, his heart yearned after the damsel who was to inherit these domains, and his imagination expanded with the idea, how they might be readily turned into cash, and the money invested in

4. Cf. "that roasted Manningtree ox with the pudding in his belly" (Shakespeare's *1 Henry IV* 2.4).
5. Rooster.
6. I.e., clemency.
7. I.e., residence.

immense tracts of wild land, and shingle palaces in the wilderness. Nay, his busy fancy already put him in possession of his hopes, and presented to him the blooming Katrina, with a whole family of children, mounted on the top of a waggon loaded with household trumpery, with pots and kettles dangling beneath; and he beheld himself bestriding a pacing mare, with a colt at her heels, setting out for Kentucky, Tennessee, or the Lord knows where!

When he entered the house, the conquest of his heart was complete. It was one of those spacious farm-houses, with high-ridged, but lowly-sloping roofs, built in the style handed down from the first Dutch settlers. The low, projecting eaves formed a piazza along the front, capable of being closed up in bad weather. Under this were hung flails, harness, various utensils of husbandry, and nets for fishing in the neighbouring river. Benches were built along the sides for summer use; and a great spinning wheel at one end, and a churn at the other, showed the various uses to which this important porch might be devoted. From this piazza the wondering Ichabod entered the hall, which formed the centre of the mansion, and the place of usual residence. Here, rows of resplendent pewter, ranged on a long dresser, dazzled his eyes. In one corner stood a huge bag of wool ready to be spun; in another a quantity of linsey-woolsey just from the loom; ears of Indian corn, and strings of dried apples and peaches, hung in gay festoons along the walls, mingled with the gaud of red peppers; and a door left ajar, gave him a peep into the best parlour, where the claw-footed chairs, and dark mahogany tables, shone like mirrors; andirons, with their accompanying shovel and tongs, glistened from their covert of asparagus tops; mock oranges[8] and conch shells decorated the mantlepiece; strings of various coloured birds' eggs were suspended above it; a great ostrich egg was hung from the centre of the room, and a corner cupboard, knowingly left open, displayed immense treasures of old silver and well-mended china.

From the moment Ichabod laid his eyes upon these regions of delight, the peace of his mind was at an end, and his only study was how to gain the affections of the peerless daughter of Van Tassel. In this enterprize, however, he had more real difficulties than generally fell to the lot of a knight-errant of yore, who seldom had any thing but giants, enchanters, fiery dragons, and such like easily conquered adversaries, to contend with; and had to make his way merely through gates of iron and brass, and walls of adamant,[9] to the castle keep, where the lady of his heart was confined; all which he achieved as easily as a man would carve his way to the centre of a Christmas pie, and then the lady gave him her hand as a matter of course. Ichabod, on the contrary, had to win his way to the heart of a country coquette, beset with a labyrinth of whims and caprices, which were for ever presenting new difficulties and impediments, and he had to encounter a host of fearful adversaries of real flesh and blood, the numerous rustic admirers, who beset every portal to her heart, keeping a watchful and angry eye upon each other, but ready to fly out in the common cause against any new competitor.

Among these, the most formidable, was a burly, roaring, roystering blade, of the name of Abraham, or, according to the Dutch abbreviation, Brom Van Brunt, the hero of the country round, which rung with his feats of strength and hardihood. He was broad shouldered and double jointed, with short curly

---

8. Probably, gourds in the size and shape of oranges.   9. Fabled stone of impenetrable hardness.

black hair, and a bluff, but not unpleasant countenance, having a mingled air of fun and arrogance. From his Herculean frame and great powers of limb, he had received the nick-name of BROM BONES, by which he was universally known. He was famed for great knowledge and skill in horsemanship, being as dexterous on horseback as a Tartar. He was foremost at all races and cock-fights, and with the ascendancy which bodily strength always acquires in rustic life, was the umpire in all disputes, setting his hat on one side, and giving his decisions with an air and tone that admitted of no gainsay or appeal. He was always ready for either a fight or a frolick; had more mischief than ill-will in his composition; and with all his overbearing roughness, there was a strong dash of waggish good humour at bottom. He had three or four boon companions of his own stamp, who regarded him as their model, and at the head of whom he scoured the country, attending every scene of feud or merriment for miles round. In cold weather he was distinguished by a fur cap, surmounted with a flaunting fox's tail, and when the folks at a country gathering descried this well-known crest at a distance, whisking about among a squad of hard riders, they always stood by for a squall. Sometimes his crew would be heard dashing along past the farm-houses at midnight, with whoop and halloo, like a troop of Don Cossacks,[1] and the old dames, startled out of their sleep, would listen for a moment till the hurry scurry had clattered by, and then exclaim, "aye, there goes Brom Bones and his gang!" The neighbours looked upon him with a mixture of awe, admiration, and good-will; and when any mad-cap prank, or rustic brawl, occurred in the vicinity, always shook their heads, and warranted Brom Bones was at the bottom of it.

This rantipole[2] hero had for some time singled out the blooming Katrina for the object of his uncouth gallantries, and though his amorous toyings were something like the gentle caresses and endearments of a bear, yet it was whispered that she did not altogether discourage his hopes. Certain it is, his advances were signals for rival candidates to retire, who felt no inclination to cross a lion in his amours; insomuch, that when his horse was seen tied to Van Tassel's paling,[3] of a Sunday night, (a sure sign that his master was courting, or, as it is termed, "sparking," within,) all other suitors passed by in despair, and carried the war into other quarters.

Such was the formidable rival with whom Ichabod Crane had to contend, and, considering all things, a stouter man than he would have shrunk from the competition, and a wiser man would have despaired. He had, however, a happy mixture of pliability and perseverance in his nature; he was in form and spirit like a supple jack[4]—yielding, but tough; though he bent, he never broke; and though he bowed beneath the slightest pressure, yet, the moment it was away—jerk!—he was as erect, and carried his head as high as ever.

To have taken the field openly against his rival, would have been madness; for he was not a man to be thwarted in his amours, any more than that stormy lover, Achilles.[5] Ichabod, therefore, made his advances in a quiet and gently-insinuating manner. Under cover of his character of singing master, he made frequent visits at the farm-house; not that he had any thing to apprehend from the meddlesome interference of parents, which is so often a stumbling block

1. Russian cavalry ranging the area around the Don River.
2. Wild, unruly.
3. Fence.
4. Cane made from a climbing plant with tough, pli-

ant stems.
5. In book 1 of Homer's *Iliad* King Agamemnon takes the captive maiden Briseis from the warrior Achilles, who thereupon sulks in his tent during the Trojan War until he is roused to avenge his favorite, Patroclus.

in the path of lovers. Balt Van Tassel was an easy indulgent soul; he loved his daughter better even than his pipe, and like a reasonable man, and an excellent father, let her have her way in every thing. His notable little wife too, had enough to do to attend to her housekeeping and manage the poultry, for, as she sagely observed, ducks and geese are foolish things, and must be looked after, but girls can take care of themselves. Thus while the busy dame bustled about the house, or plied her spinning wheel at one end of the piazza, honest Balt would sit smoking his evening pipe at the other, watching the achievements of a little wooden warrior, who, armed with a sword in each hand, was most valiantly fighting the wind on the pinnacle of the barn. In the mean time, Ichabod would carry on his suit with the daughter by the side of the spring under the great elm, or sauntering along in the twilight, that hour so favourable to the lover's eloquence.

I profess not to know how women's hearts are wooed and won. To me they have always been matters of riddle and admiration. Some seem to have but one vulnerable point, or door of access; while others have a thousand avenues, and may be captured a thousand different ways. It is a great triumph of skill to gain the former, but a still greater proof of generalship to maintain possession of the latter, for a man must battle for his fortress at every door and window. He that wins a thousand common hearts, is therefore entitled to some renown; but he who keeps undisputed sway over the heart of a coquette, is indeed a hero. Certain it is, this was not the case with the redoubtable Brom Bones; and from the moment Ichabod Crane made his advances, the interests of the former evidently declined; his horse was no longer seen tied at the palings on Sunday nights, and a deadly feud gradually arose between him and the preceptor of Sleepy Hollow.

Brom, who had a degree of rough chivalry in his nature, would fain have carried matters to open warfare, and settled their pretensions to the lady, according to the mode of those most concise and simple reasoners, the knights-errant of yore—by single combat: but Ichabod was too conscious of the superior might of his adversary to enter the lists against him; he had overheard the boast of Bones, that he would "double the schoolmaster up, and put him on a shelf;" and he was too wary to give him an opportunity. There was something extremely provoking in this obstinately pacific system; it left Brom no alternative but to draw upon the funds of rustic waggery in his disposition, and play off boorish practical jokes upon his rival. Ichabod became the object of whimsical persecution to Bones, and his gang of rough riders. They harried his hitherto peaceful domains; smoked out his singing school, by stopping up the chimney; broke into the school-house at night, in spite of its formidable fastenings of withe and window stakes, and turned every thing topsy-turvy, so that the poor schoolmaster began to think all the witches in the country held their meetings there. But what was still more annoying, Brom took all opportunities of turning him into ridicule in presence of his mistress, and had a scoundrel dog, whom he taught to whine in the most ludicrous manner, and introduced as a rival of Ichabod's, to instruct her in psalmody.

In this way, matters went on for some time, without producing any material effect on the relative situations of the contending powers. On a fine autumnal afternoon, Ichabod, in pensive mood, sat enthroned on the lofty stool from whence he usually watched all the concerns of his little literary realm. In his hand he swayed a ferule, that sceptre of despotic power; the birch of justice reposed on three nails, behind the throne, a constant terror to evil doers; while on the desk before him might be seen sundry contraband articles and prohibited weapons, detected upon the persons of idle urchins, such as half-munched apples, popguns, whirligigs,[6] fly-cages, and whole legions of rampant little paper game cocks. Apparently there had been some appalling act of justice recently inflicted, for his scholars were all busily intent upon their books, or slyly whispering behind them with one eye kept upon the master; and a kind of buzzing stillness reigned throughout the school-room. It was suddenly interrupted by the appearance of a negro in tow-cloth jacket and trowsers, a round crowned fragment of a hat, like the cap of Mercury,[7] and mounted on the back of a ragged, wild, half-broken colt, which he managed with a rope by way of halter. He came clattering up to the school door with an invitation to Ichabod to attend a merry-making, or "quilting frolick," to be held that evening at Mynheer Van Tassel's, and having delivered his message with that air of importance, and effort at fine language, which a negro is apt to display on petty embassies of the kind, he dashed over the brook, and was seen scampering away up the hollow, full of the importance and hurry of his mission.

All was now bustle and hubbub in the late quiet school room. The scholars were hurried through their lessons, without stopping at trifles; those who were nimble, skipped over half with impunity, and those who were tardy, had a smart application now and then in the rear, to quicken their speed, or help them over a tall word. Books were flung aside, without being put away on the shelves; inkstands were overturned, benches thrown down, and the whole school turned loose an hour before the usual time; bursting forth like a legion of young imps, yelping and racketing about the green, in joy at their early emancipation.

The gallant Ichabod now spent at least an extra half hour at his toilet, brushing and furbishing up his best, and indeed only suit of rusty black, and arranging his looks by a bit of broken looking glass, that hung up in the school house. That he might make his appearance before his mistress in the true style of a cavalier, he borrowed a horse from the farmer with whom he was domiciliated, a choleric old Dutchman, of the name of Hans Van Ripper, and thus gallantly mounted, issued forth like a knight-errant in quest of adventures. But it is meet[8] I should, in the true spirit of romantic story, give some account of the looks and equipments of my hero and his steed.[9] The animal he bestrode was a broken-down plough horse, that had outlived almost every thing but his viciousness. He was gaunt and shagged, with a ewe neck and hammer head; his rusty mane and tail were tangled and knotted with burrs; one eye had lost its pupil, and was glaring and spectral, but the other had the gleam of a genuine devil in it. Still he must have had fire and mettle in his day, if we may judge from his name, which was Gunpowder. He had, in fact, been a favourite steed of his master's, the cholerick Van Ripper, who was a furious rider, and had infused, very probably, some of his own spirit into the animal, for, old and broken-down as he looked, there was more lurking deviltry in him than in any young filly in the country.

6. Child's toy, spun like a top.
7. A winged cap symbolized the speed of Mercury, messenger of the gods. Slavery was legal in New York into the first years of the 19th century.
8. Fitting.
9. The description recalls Cervantes's portrayal of Don Quixote and his horse Rosinante. Part of Irving's anti-Yankee fun comes from his playing off Cotton Mather's solemn books, which confuse the schoolmaster's brains, against the romances of chivalry, which are the source of Don Quixote's delusions.

Ichabod was a suitable figure for such a steed. He rode with short stirrups, which brought his knees nearly up to the pommel of the saddle; his sharp elbows stuck out like grasshoppers'; he carried his whip perpendicularly in his hand, like a sceptre, and as the horse jogged on, the motion of his arms was not unlike the flapping of a pair of wings. A small wool hat rested on the top of his nose, for so his scanty strip of forehead might be called, and the skirts of his black coat fluttered out almost to the horse's tail. Such was the appearance of Ichabod and his steed, as they shambled out of the gate of Hans Van Ripper, and it was altogether such an apparition as is seldom to be met with in broad day light.

It was, as I have said, a fine autumnal day, the sky was clear and serene, and nature wore that rich and golden livery which we always associate with the idea of abundance. The forests had put on their sober brown and yellow, while some trees of the tenderer kind had been nipped by the frosts into brilliant dyes of orange, purple, and scarlet. Streaming files of wild ducks began to make their appearance high in the air; the bark of the squirrel might be heard from the groves of beech and hickory nuts, and the pensive whistle of the quail at intervals from the neighbouring stubble field.

The small birds were taking their farewell banquets. In the fullness of their revelry, they fluttered, chirping and frolicking, from bush to bush, and tree to tree, capricious from the very profusion and variety around them. There was the honest cock-robin, the favourite game of stripling sportsmen, with its loud querulous note; and the twittering blackbirds flying in sable clouds; and the golden winged woodpecker, with his crimson crest, his broad black gorget,[1] and splendid plumage; and the cedar bird, with its red tipt wings and yellow tipt tail, and its little monteiro cap[2] of feathers; and the blue jay, that noisy coxcomb, in his gay light blue coat and white under clothes, screaming and chattering, nodding, and bobbing, and bowing, and pretending to be on good terms with every songster of the grove.

As Ichabod jogged slowly on his way, his eye, ever open to every symptom of culinary abundance, ranged with delight over the treasures of jolly autumn. On all sides he beheld vast store of apples, some hanging in oppressive opulence on the trees, some gathered into baskets and barrels for the market, others heaped up in rich piles for the cider-press. Further on he beheld great fields of Indian corn, with its golden ears peeping from their leafy coverts, and holding out the promise of cakes and hasty pudding; and the yellow pumpkins lying beneath them, turning up their fair round bellies[3] to the sun, and giving ample prospects of the most luxurious of pies; and anon he passed the fragrant buckwheat fields, breathing the odour of the bee-hive, and as he beheld them, soft anticipations stole over his mind of dainty slap-jacks, well buttered, and garnished with honey or treacle,[4] by the delicate little dimpled hand of Katrina Van Tassel.

Thus feeding his mind with many sweet thoughts and "sugared suppositions," he journeyed along the sides of a range of hills which look out upon some of the goodliest scenes of the mighty Hudson. The sun gradually wheeled his broad disk down into the west. The wide bosom of the Tappaan Zee lay motionless and glassy, excepting that here and there a gentle undulation waved and prolonged the blue shadow of the distant mountain: a few amber clouds

1. Throat.   3. Cf. Shakespeare's *As You Like It* 2.7.154.
2. Hunting cap with a flap at the front.   4. Molasses.

floated in the sky, without a breath of air to move them. The horizon was of a fine golden tint, changing gradually into a pure apple green, and from that into a deep blue of the mid-heaven. A slanting ray lingered on the woody crests of the precipices that overhung some parts of the river, giving greater depth to the dark grey and purple of their rocky sides. A sloop was loitering in the distance, dropping slowly down with the tide, her sail hanging uselessly against the mast, and as the reflection of the sky gleamed along the still water, it seemed as if the vessel was suspended in the air.

It was toward evening that Ichabod arrived at the castle of the Heer Van Tassel, which he found thronged with the pride and flower of the adjacent country. Old farmers, a spare, leathern-faced race, in homespun coats and small clothes, blue stockings, huge shoes and magnificent pewter buckles. Their brisk withered little dames in close crimped caps, long waisted short gowns, homespun petticoats, with scissors and pincushions, and gay calico pockets, hanging on the outside. Buxom lasses, almost as antiquated as their mothers, excepting where a straw hat, a fine ribband, or perhaps a white frock, gave symptoms of city innovations. The sons, in short square-skirted coats with rows of stupendous brass buttons, and their hair generally queued in the fashion of the times, especially if they could procure an eel-skin for the purpose, it being esteemed throughout the country as a potent nourisher and strengthener of the hair.

Brom Bones, however, was the hero of the scene, having come to the gathering on his favourite steed Daredevil, a creature, like himself, full of mettle and mischief, and which no one but himself could manage. He was in fact noted for preferring vicious animals, given to all kinds of tricks, which kept the rider in constant risk of his neck, and held a tractable well-broken horse as unworthy a lad of spirit.

Fain would I pause to dwell upon the world of charms that burst upon the enraptured gaze of my hero, as he entered the state parlour of Van Tassel's mansion. Not those of the bevy of buxom lasses, with their luxurious display of red and white: but the ample charms of a genuine Dutch country tea-table, in the sumptuous time of autumn. Such heaped up platters of cakes of various and almost indescribable kinds, known only to experienced Dutch housewives. There was the doughty dough-nut, the tenderer oly koek,[5] and the crisp and crumbling cruller; sweet cakes and short cakes, ginger cakes and honey cakes, and the whole family of cakes. And then there were apple pies and peach pies and pumpkin pies; not to mention slices of ham and smoked beef, together with broiled shad and roasted chickens; besides delectable dishes of preserved plums, and peaches, and pears, and quinces; with bowls of milk and cream, all mingled higgledy-piggledy, pretty much as I have enumerated them, with the motherly tea-pot sending up its clouds of vapour from the midst—Heaven bless the mark! I want[6] breath and time to discuss this banquet as it deserves, and am too eager to get on with my story. Happily, Ichabod Crane was not in so great a hurry as his historian, but did ample justice to every dainty.

He was a kind and thankful toad, whose heart dilated in proportion as his skin was filled with good cheer, and whose spirits rose with eating, as some men's do with drink. He could not help, too, rolling his large eyes round him as he eat, and chuckling with the possibility that he might one day be lord of

5. Kind of cruller or doughnut.   6. Lack.

all this scene of almost unimaginable luxury and splendour. Then, he thought, how soon he'd turn his back upon the old school house; snap his fingers in the face of Hans Van Ripper, and every other niggardly patron, and kick any itinerant pedagogue out of doors that dared to call him comrade!

Old Baltus Van Tassel moved about among his guests with a face dilated with content and good humour, round and jolly as the harvest moon. His hospitable attentions were brief, but expressive, being confined to a shake of the hand, a slap on the shoulder, a loud laugh, and a pressing invitation to "reach to, and help themselves."

And now the sound of the music from the common room or hall, summoned to the dance. The musician was an old grey-headed negro, who had been the itinerant orchestra of the neighbourhood for more than half a century. His instrument was as old and battered as himself. The greater part of the time he scraped away on two or three strings, accompanying every movement of the bow with a motion of the head; bowing almost to the ground, and stamping with his foot whenever a fresh couple were to start.

Ichabod prided himself upon his dancing as much as upon his vocal powers. Not a limb, not a fibre about him was idle, and to have seen his loosely hung frame in full motion, and clattering about the room, you would have thought Saint Vitus[7] himself, that blessed patron of the dance, was figuring before you in person. He was the admiration of all the negroes, who, having gathered, of all ages and sizes, from the farm and the neighbourhood, stood forming a pyramid of shining black faces at every door and window, gazing with delight at the scene, rolling their white eye-balls, and showing grinning rows of ivory from ear to ear. How could the flogger of urchins be otherwise than animated and joyous; the lady of his heart was his partner in the dance; she smiled graciously in reply to all his amorous oglings, while Brom Bones, sorely smitten with love and jealousy, sat brooding by himself in one corner.

When the dance was at an end, Ichabod was attracted to a knot of the sager folks, who, with old Van Tassel, sat smoking at one end of the piazza, gossiping over former times, and drawling out long stories about the war.

This neighbourhood, at the time of which I am speaking, was one of those highly favoured places which abound with chronicle and great men. The British and American line had run near it during the war; it had, therefore, been the scene of marauding, and been infested with refugees, cow boys,[8] and all kind of border chivalry. Just sufficient time had elapsed to enable each story teller to dress up his tale with a little becoming fiction, and in the indistinctness of his recollection, to make himself the hero of every exploit.

There was the story of Doffue Martling, a large, blue-bearded Dutchman, who had nearly taken a British frigate with an old iron nine-pounder from a mud breastwork,[9] only that his gun burst at the sixth discharge. And there was an old gentleman who shall be nameless, being too rich a mynheer to be lightly mentioned, who in the battle of Whiteplains,[1] being an excellent master of defence, parried a musket ball with a small sword, insomuch that he absolutely felt it whiz round the blade, and glance off at the hilt: in proof of which, he was ready at any time to show the sword, with the hilt a little bent.

7. Early Christian martyr prayed to by Catholics suffering from chorea, epilepsy, or other nervous disorders.
8. Tory guerrillas (i.e., British partisans) who raided the Tarrytown area during the Revolution.

9. Hastily erected fortification. "Nine-pounder": small cannon firing nine-pound weights.
1. The British general William Howe defeated George Washington at the battle of White Plains, near New York City, in 1776.

There were several more who had been equally great in the field, not one of whom but was persuaded that he had a considerable hand in bringing the war to a happy termination.

But all these were nothing to the tales of ghosts and apparitions that succeeded. The neighbourhood is rich in legendary treasures of the kind. Local tales and superstitions thrive best in these sheltered, long settled retreats; but they are trampled under foot, by the shifting throng that forms the population of most of our country places. Besides, there is no encouragement for ghosts in the generality of our villages, for they have scarce had time to take their first nap, and turn themselves in their graves, before their surviving friends have travelled away from the neighbourhood, so that when they turn out of a night to walk the rounds, they have no acquaintance left to call upon. This is perhaps the reason why we so seldom hear of ghosts excepting in our long-established Dutch communities.

The immediate cause, however, of the prevalence of supernatural stories in these parts, was doubtless owing to the vicinity of Sleepy Hollow. There was a contagion in the very air that blew from that haunted region; it breathed forth an atmosphere of dreams and fancies infecting all the land. Several of the Sleepy Hollow people were present at Van Tassel's, and, as usual, were doling out their wild and wonderful legends. Many dismal tales were told about funeral trains, and mournful cries and wailings heard and seen about the great tree where the unfortunate Major André[2] was taken, and which stood in the neighbourhood. Some mention was made also of the woman in white, that haunted the dark glen at Raven Rock, and was often heard to shriek on winter nights before a storm, having perished there in the snow. The chief part of the stories, however, turned upon the favourite spectre of Sleepy Hollow, the headless horseman, who had been heard several times of late, patroling the country; and it was said, tethered his horse nightly among the graves in the church-yard.

The sequestered situation of this church seems always to have made it a favourite haunt of troubled spirits. It stands on a knoll, surrounded by locust trees and lofty elms, from among which its decent, whitewashed walls shine modestly forth, like Christian purity, beaming through the shades of retirement. A gentle slope descends from it to a silver sheet of water, bordered by high trees, between which, peeps may be caught at the blue hills of the Hudson. To look upon its grass-grown yard, where the sunbeams seem to sleep so quietly, one would think that here at least the dead might rest in peace. On one side of the church extends a wide woody dell, along which raves a large brook among broken rocks and trunks of fallen trees. Over a deep black part of the stream, not far from the church, was formerly thrown a wooden bridge; the road that led to it, and the bridge itself, were thickly shaded by overhanging trees, which cast a gloom about it, even in the day time; but occasioned a fearful darkness at night. Such was one of the favourite haunts of the headless horseman, and the place where he was most frequently encountered. The tale was told of old Brouwer, a most heretical disbeliever in ghosts, that he met the horseman returning from his foray into Sleepy Hollow, and was obliged to get up behind him; that they gallopped over bush and brake, over hill and swamp, until they reached the bridge, when the horseman suddenly turned into a

2. John André (1751–1780), brave British spy arrested at Tarrytown and executed at Tappan, across the Hudson; he carried documents proving that Benedict Arnold had betrayed the colonial army.

skeleton, threw old Brouwer into the brook, and sprang away over the tree-tops with a clap of thunder.

This story was immediately matched by a thrice marvellous adventure of Brom Bones, who made light of the gallopping Hessian as an errant jockey.[3] He affirmed, that on returning one night from the neighbouring village of Sing-Sing,[4] he had been overtaken by this midnight trooper; that he had offered to race with him for a bowl of punch, and would have won it too, for Daredevil beat the goblin horse all hollow, but just as they came to the church bridge, the Hessian bolted, and vanished in a flash of fire.

All these tales, told in that drowsy under tone with which men talk in the dark, the countenances of the listeners only now and then receiving a casual gleam from the glare of a pipe, sunk deep in the mind of Ichabod. He repaid them in kind with large extracts from his invaluable author, Cotton Mather, and added many very marvellous events that had taken place in his native state of Connecticut, and fearful sights which he had seen in his nightly walks about Sleepy Hollow.

The revel now gradually broke up. The old farmers gathered together their families in their wagons, and were heard for some time rattling along the hollow roads, and over the distant hills. Some of the damsels, mounted on pillions[5] behind their favourite swains, and their light-hearted laughter min-gling with the clatter of hoofs, echoed along the silent woodlands, sounding fainter and fainter until they gradually died away—and the late scene of noise and frolick was all silent and deserted. Ichabod only lingered behind, according to the custom of country lovers, to have a tête-a-tête[6] with the heir-ess; fully convinced that he was now on the high road to success. What passed at this interview I will not pretend to say, for in fact I do not know. Something, however, I fear me, must have gone wrong, for he certainly sallied forth, after no very great interval, with an air quite desolate and chopfallen—Oh these women! these women! Could that girl have been playing off any of her coquettish tricks?—Was her encouragement of the poor pedagogue all a mere sham to secure her conquest of his rival?—Heaven only knows, not I!—Let it suffice to say, Ichabod stole forth with the air of one who had been sacking a hen roost, rather than a fair lady's heart. Without looking to the right or left to notice the scene of rural wealth, on which he had so often gloated, he went straight to the stable, and with several hearty cuffs and kicks, roused his steed most uncourteously from the comfortable quarters in which he was soundly sleeping, dreaming of mountains of corn and oats, and whole valleys of timo-thy and clover.

It was the very witching time of night[7] that Ichabod, heavyhearted and bedrooped, pursued his travel homewards, along the sides of the lofty hills which rise above Tarry Town, and which he had traversed so cheerily in the afternoon. The hour was as dismal as himself. Far below him the Tappaan Zee spread its dusky and indistinct waste of waters, with here and there the tall mast of a sloop, riding quietly at anchor under the land. In the dead hush of midnight, he could even hear the barking of the watch-dog from the opposite shore of the Hudson; but it was so vague and faint as only to give an idea of his distance from this faithful companion of man. Now and then, too, the

3. Fraud.
4. Ossining.
5. Pad behind a saddle for a second rider.

6. Head to head (French, literal trans.); i.e., a confidential conversation.
7. Cf. Shakespeare's *Hamlet* 3.2.406.

long-drawn crowing of a cock, accidentally awakened, would sound far, far off, from some farm house away among the hills—but it was like a dreaming sound in his ear. No signs of life occurred near him, but occasionally the melancholy chirp of a cricket, or perhaps the guttural twang of a bull frog, from a neighbouring marsh, as if sleeping uncomfortably, and turning suddenly in his bed.

All the stories of ghosts and goblins that Ichabod had heard in the afternoon, now came crowding upon his recollection. The night grew darker and darker; the stars seemed to sink deeper in the sky, and driving clouds occasionally hid them from his sight. He had never felt so lonely and dismal. He was, moreover, approaching the very place where many of the scenes of the ghost stories had been laid. In the centre of the road stood an enormous tulip tree, which towered like a giant above all the other trees of the neighbourhood, and formed a kind of land-mark. Its limbs were vast, gnarled, and fantastic, twisting down almost to the earth, and rising again into the air, and they would have formed trunks for ordinary trees. It was connected with the tragical story of the unfortunate André, who had been taken prisoner hard by it, and it was universally known by the name of Major André's tree. The common people regarded it with a mixture of respect and superstition, partly out of sympathy for the memory of its ill-starred namesake, and partly from the tales, strange sights, and doleful lamentations, told concerning it.

As Ichabod approached this fearful tree, he began to whistle; he thought his whistle was answered: it was but a blast sweeping sharply through the dry branches. As he approached a little nearer, he thought he saw something white, hanging in the midst of the tree: he paused and ceased whistling; but on looking more narrowly, perceived that it was a place where the tree had been scathed by lightning, and the white wood laid bare. Suddenly he heard a groan—his teeth chattered, and his knees smote against the saddle: it was but the rubbing of one huge bough upon another, as they were swayed about by the breeze. He passed the tree in safety, but new perils lay still before him.

About two hundred yards from the tree, a small brook crossed the road, and ran into a marshy and thickly wooded glen, known by the name of Wiley's Swamp. A few rough logs, laid side by side, served for a bridge over this stream. On that side of the road where the brook entered the wood, a group of oaks and chestnuts, matted thick with wild grape vines, threw a cavernous gloom over it. To pass this bridge, was the severest trial. It was at this identical spot that the unfortunate André was captured, and under the covert of those chestnuts and vines were the sturdy yeomen concealed who surprised him. This has ever since been considered a haunted stream, and fearful are the feelings of the schoolboy who has to pass it alone after dark.

As he approached the stream, his heart began to thump; he, however, summoned up all his resolution, gave his horse half a score of kicks in the ribs, and attempted to dash briskly across the bridge; but instead of starting forward, the perverse old animal made a lateral movement, and ran broadside against the fence. Ichabod, whose fears increased with the delay, jerked the reins on the other side, and kicked lustily with the contrary foot: it was all in vain; his steed started, it is true, but it was only to plunge to the opposite side of the road into a thicket of brambles and alder bushes. The schoolmaster now bestowed both whip and heel upon the starvelling ribs of old Gunpowder, who dashed forward, snuffling and snorting, but came to a stand just by the bridge with a suddenness that had nearly sent his rider sprawling over his head. Just at this moment a plashy tramp by the side of the bridge caught the sensitive ear of Ichabod. In the dark shadow of the grove, on the margin of the brook, he beheld something huge, misshapen, black and towering. It stirred not, but seemed gathered up in the gloom, like some gigantic monster ready to spring upon the traveller.

The hair of the affrighted pedagogue rose upon his head with terror. What was to be done? To turn and fly was now too late; and besides, what chance was there of escaping ghost or goblin, if such it was, which can ride upon the wings of the wind? Summoning up, therefore, a show of courage, he demanded in stammering accents—"who are you?" He received no reply. He repeated his demand in a still more agitated voice.—Still there was no answer. Once more he cudgelled the sides of the inflexible Gunpowder, and shutting his eyes, broke forth with involuntary fervour into a psalm tune. Just then the shadowy object of alarm put itself in motion, and with a scramble and a bound, stood at once in the middle of the road. Though the night was dark and dismal, yet the form of the unknown might now in some degree be ascertained. He appeared to be a horseman of large dimensions, and mounted on a black horse of powerful frame. He made no offer of molestation or sociability, but kept aloof on one side of the road, jogging along on the blind side of old Gunpowder, who had now got over his fright and waywardness.

Ichabod, who had no relish for this strange midnight companion, and bethought himself of the adventure of Brom Bones with the galloping Hessian, now quickened his steed, in hopes of leaving him behind. The stranger, however, quickened his horse to an equal pace; Ichabod pulled up, and fell into a walk, thinking to lag behind—the other did the same. His heart began to sink within him; he endeavoured to resume his psalm tune, but his parched tongue clove to the roof of his mouth, and he could not utter a stave.[8] There was something in the moody and dogged silence of this pertinacious companion, that was mysterious and appalling. It was soon fearfully accounted for. On mounting a rising ground, which brought the figure of his fellow traveller in relief against the sky, gigantic in height, and muffled in a cloak, Ichabod was horror-struck, on perceiving that he was headless! but his horror was still more increased, on observing, that the head, which should have rested on his shoulders, was carried before him on the pommel of the saddle! His terror rose to desperation; he rained a shower of kicks and blows upon Gunpowder, hoping, by a sudden movement, to give his companion the slip—but the spectre started full jump with him. Away, then, they dashed, through thick and thin; stones flying, and sparks flashing, at every bound. Ichabod's flimsy garments fluttered in the air, as he stretched his long lank body away over his horse's head, in the eagerness of his flight.

They had now reached the road which turns off to Sleepy Hollow; but Gunpowder, who seemed possessed with a demon, instead of keeping up it, made an opposite turn, and plunged headlong down hill to the left. This road leads through a sandy hollow shaded by trees for about a quarter of a mile, where it crosses the bridge famous in goblin story, and just beyond swells the green knoll on which stands the whitewashed church.

As yet the panic of the steed had given his unskilful rider an apparent advan-

8. Verse.

tage in the chace, but just as he had got half way through the hollow, the girths of the saddle gave way, and he felt it slipping from under him; he seized it by the pommel, and endeavoured to hold it firm, but in vain; and had just time to save himself by clasping old Gunpowder round the neck, when the saddle fell to the earth, and he heard it trampled under foot by his pursuer. For a moment of terror of Hans Van Ripper's wrath passed across his mind— for it was his Sunday saddle; but this was no time for petty fears: the goblin was hard on his haunches; and, unskilful rider that he was! he had much-ado to maintain his seat; sometimes slipping on one side, sometimes on another, and sometimes jolted on the high ridge of his horse's back bone, with a violence that he verily feared would cleave him asunder.

An opening in the trees now cheered him with the hopes that the Church Bridge was at hand. The wavering reflection of a silver star in the bosom of the brook told him that he was not mistaken. He saw the walls of the church dimly glaring under the trees beyond. He recollected the place where Brom Bones' ghostly competitor had disappeared. "If I can but reach that bridge," thought Ichabod, "I am safe."[9] Just then he heard the black steed panting and blowing close behind him; he fancied he felt his hot breath. Another convulsive kick in the ribs, and old Gunpowder sprung upon the bridge; he thundered over the resounding planks; he gained the opposite side, and now Ichabod cast a look behind to see if his pursuer should vanish, according to rule, in a flash of fire and brimstone. Just then he saw the goblin rising in his stirrups, and in the very act of hurling his head at him. Ichabod endeavoured to dodge the horrible missile, but too late. It encountered his cranium with a tremendous crash—he was tumbled headlong into the dust, and Gunpowder, the black steed, and the goblin rider, passed by like a whirlwind.——

The next morning the old horse was found without his saddle, and the bridle under his feet, soberly cropping the grass at his master's gate. Ichabod did not make his appearance at breakfast—dinner-hour came, but no Ichabod. The boys assembled at the schoolhouse, and strolled idly about the banks of the brook; but no schoolmaster. Hans Van Ripper now began to feel some uneasiness about the fate of poor Ichabod, and his saddle. An inquiry was set on foot, and after diligent investigation they came upon his traces. In one part of the road leading to the church, was found the saddle trampled in the dirt; the tracks of horses' hoofs deeply dented in the road, and evidently at furious speed, were traced to the bridge, beyond which, on the bank of a broad part of the brook, where the water ran deep and black, was found the hat of the unfortunate Ichabod, and close beside it a shattered pumpkin.

The brook was searched, but the body of the schoolmaster was not to be discovered. Hans Van Ripper, as executor of his estate, examined the bundle which contained all his worldly effects. They consisted of two old shirts and a half; two stocks[1] for the neck; a pair of worsted stockings with holes in them; an old pair of corduroy small-clothes; a book of psalm tunes full of dog's ears; a pitch pipe out of order; a rusty razor; a small pot of bear's grease for the hair, and a cast-iron comb. As to the books and furniture of the schoolhouse, they belonged to the community, excepting Cotton Mather's History of Witchcraft, a New-England Almanack, and a book of dreams and fortune telling, in which last was a sheet of foolscap much scribbled and blotted, by several fruitless

9. Superstition held that spirits could not cross water.   1. Wide bands or cravats.

attempts to make a copy of verses in honour of the heiress of Van Tassel. These magic books and the poetic scrawl were forthwith consigned to the flames by Hans Van Ripper, who from that time forward determined to send his children no more to school, observing, that he never knew any good come of this same reading and writing. Whatever money the schoolmaster possessed, and he had received his quarter's pay but a day or two before, he must have had about his person at the time of his disappearance.

The mysterious event caused much speculation at the Church on the following Sunday. Knots of gazers and gossips were collected in the church-yard, at the bridge, and at the spot where the hat and pumpkin had been found. The stories of Brouwer, of Bones, and a whole budget of others, were called to mind; and when they had diligently considered them all, and compared them with the symptoms of the present case, they shook their heads, and came to the conclusion, that Ichabod had been carried off by the gallopping Hessian. As he was a bachelor, and in nobody's debt, nobody troubled his head any more about him, the school was removed to a different quarter of the hollow, and another pedagogue reigned in his stead.

It is true, an old farmer, who had been down to New-York on a visit several years after, and from whom this account of the ghostly adventure was received, brought home the intelligence that Ichabod Crane was still alive; that he had left the neighbourhood partly through fear of the goblin and Hans Van Ripper, and partly in mortification at having been suddenly dismissed by the heiress; that he had changed his quarters to a distant part of the country; had kept school and studied law at the same time; had been admitted to the bar, turned politician, electioneered, written for the newspapers, and finally had been made a Justice of the Ten Pound Court.[2] Brom Bones too, who, shortly after his rival's disappearance, conducted the blooming Katrina in triumph to the altar, was observed to look exceedingly knowing whenever the story of Ichabod was related, and always burst into a hearty laugh at the mention of the pumpkin; which led some to suspect that he knew more about the matter than he chose to tell.

The old country wives, however, who are the best judges of these matters, maintain to this day, that Ichabod was spirited away by supernatural means; and it is a favourite story often told about the neighbourhood round the winter evening fire. The bridge became more than ever an object of superstitious awe, and that may be the reason why the road has been altered of late years, so as to approach the church by the border of the millpond. The schoolhouse being deserted, soon fell to decay, and was reported to be haunted by the ghost of the unfortunate pedagogue; and the plough boy, loitering homeward of a still summer evening, has often fancied his voice at a distance, chanting a melancholy psalm tune among the tranquil solitudes of Sleepy Hollow.

POSTSCRIPT, FOUND IN THE HANDWRITING OF MR. KNICKERBOCKER

The preceding Tale is given, almost in the precise words in which I heard it related at the corporation meeting of the ancient city of the Manhattoes, at which were present many of its sagest and most illustrious burghers. The narrator was a pleasant, shabby, gentlemanly old fellow, in pepper and salt

2. Small claims court.

clothes, with a sadly humourous face, and one whom I strongly suspected of being poor, he made such efforts to be entertaining. When his story was concluded, there was much laughter and approbation, particularly from two or three deputy aldermen, who had been asleep the greater part of the time. There was, however, one tall, dry-looking old gentleman, with beetling eyebrows, who maintained a grave and rather severe face throughout; now and then folding his arms, inclining his head, and looking down upon the floor, as if turning a doubt over in his mind. He was one of your wary men, who never laugh but upon good grounds—when they have reason and the law on their side. When the mirth of the rest of the company had subsided, and silence was restored, he leaned one arm on the elbow of his chair, and sticking the other a-kimbo, demanded, with a slight, but exceedingly sage motion of the head, and contraction of the brow, what was the moral of the story, and what it went to prove.

The story-teller, who was just putting a glass of wine to his lips, as a refreshment after his toils, paused for a moment, looked at his inquirer with an air of infinite deference, and lowering the glass slowly to the table, observed, that the story was intended most logically to prove,

"That there is no situation in life but has its advantages and pleasures, provided we will but take a joke as we find it:

"That, therefore, he that runs races with goblin troopers, is likely to have rough riding of it:

"Ergo, for a country schoolmaster to be refused the hand of a Dutch heiress, is a certain step to high preferment in the state."

The cautious old gentleman knit his brows tenfold closer after this explanation, being sorely puzzled by the ratiocination of the syllogism; while methought the one in pepper and salt eyed him with something of a triumphant leer. At length he observed, that all this was very well, but still he thought the story a little on the extravagant—there were one or two points on which he had his doubts.

"Faith, sir," replied the story-teller, "as to that matter, I don't believe one half of it myself."   D.K.

1820

JAMES FENIMORE COOPER
1789–1851

James Fenimore Cooper, the first successful American novelist, was born on September 15, 1789, in Burlington, New Jersey, but taken in infancy to Cooperstown, on Otsego Lake in central New York, where his wealthy father owned great tracts of land. A few years before, the region had been wilderness, but during Cooper's boyhood there were few of the early backwoods settlers left, and fewer American Indians; in his novels the information about Indian tribes came from older people and from books. In 1801 his father sent him to study in Albany in preparation for Yale, where he spent two years in his midteens before being expelled for pranks, thereby acquiring a lifelong distaste for New Englanders. He became a sailor in 1806, then two years later a midshipman in the navy. At twenty he inherited a fortune from his father and married Susan De Lancey, whose family had lost possessions by siding with the British in the Revolution but still owned lands in West-chester County. For several years Cooper and his wife wavered between Scarsdale and Otsego as a permanent home. Wherever they settled, Cooper seemed certain to live as a landed gentleman. His first book, *Precaution* (1820), a novel dealing with English high society, was the result of his casual bet with his wife that he could write a better book than the one he had been reading to her. Following that insignificant start, he wrote *The Spy* (1821), the first important historical romance of the Revolution, and on its success he moved to New York City to take up his new career. From the first his faults (such as syntactical awkwardness, arbitrary plotting, and heavy-handed attempts at humor) were obvious enough, but so were his genuine achievements in opening up new American scenes and themes for fiction. Founding the Bread and Cheese Club, he became the center of a circle that included notable painters of the Hudson River school as well as writers (William Cullen Bryant among them) and professionals. In 1823 he published *The Pioneers*, the first of what eventually consisted of five books about Natty Bumppo, known collectively as the *Leather-Stocking Tales*; the second, *The Last of the Mohicans*, followed in 1826. Cooper has other claims to fame—the virtual creation of the sea novel (starting with *The Pilot*, 1824), authorship of the first serious American novels of manners and the first American sociopolitical novels—but with Natty Bumppo, the aged hunter, he had created one of the most popular characters in world literature.

In 1826, at the height of his fame, Cooper sailed for Europe. In Paris, where he became intimate with the aged Lafayette, he wrote *The Prairie* (1827) and *Notions of the Americans* (1828), a defense of the United States against the attacks of European travelers. Smarting under the half-complimentary, half-patronizing epithet of "The American Scott," he wrote three historical novels set in medieval Europe as a realistic corrective to Sir Walter Scott's glorifications of the past. On his return to the United States in 1833 Cooper was so stung by a review of one of these novels that he renounced novel writing in the angry *Letter to His Countrymen* (1834). Then at Cooperstown he gave notice that a point of land on Otsego Lake where the townspeople had been picnicking was private property and not to be used without permission. Newspapers began attacking him as a would-be aristocrat poisoned by his residence abroad, and for years Cooper embroiled himself in lawsuits designed not to gain damages for the journalistic libels but to tame the irresponsible press. Legally in the right, Cooper sacrificed his peace of mind to establish the principle that reviewers must work within the bounds of truth when they deal with the author rather than the book. Even as he was becoming the great national scold of his time, Cooper managed to write book after book—social and political satires growing out of his experiences with the press, a reactionary primer, *The American Democrat* (1838), and despite his avowal in 1834, a series of sociopolitical novels and two more *Leather-Stocking Tales: The Pathfinder* (1840), and *The Deerslayer* (1841). His monumental *History of the Navy of the United States of America* (1839) became the focus of new quarrels and a new lawsuit.

When Cooper died on September 14, 1851, a day before his sixty-second birth-day, he was a byword for litigiousness and social pretentiousness. A lifelong defender of American democracy as he knew it in his youth against European aristocracy and then against what American democracy had become, he was out of step with his countrypeople. Yet throughout the century and into the next his *Leather-Stocking Tales* had an incalculable vogue in the United States and abroad. In his own time and shortly afterward major European writers as diverse as Honoré de Balzac and Leo Tolstoy were profoundly moved by *The Pioneers* and the subsequent Natty Bumppo novels, but gradually the *Leather-Stocking Tales* became something only schoolchildren read. Not until the 1920s did scholars begin to see Cooper's value as the country's first great social critic. It now seems clear that no revolution in taste will lead to widespread admiration of Cooper as a literary artist, but he will always be a major source for the student of ideas in America. Some of his opinions now seem hopelessly reactionary, as when he defends American slavery as legal and, after all, mild ("physical suffering cannot properly be enumerated among its evils") or when he deplores the dangers of universal manhood suffrage and argues for restricting voting on certain issues to property owners, who have the greater stake in society. What most appeals to modern readers are his profoundly ambivalent dramatizations of such enduring American conflicts as natural right versus legal right, order versus change, primeval wilderness versus civilization. And new readers will always encounter the *Leather-Stocking Tales* with a sense of something long known and loved, for if Cooper is no longer read even by children, everyone has read books—and seen films—that are directly and indirectly influenced by his grand conception of Natty Bumppo.

From The Pioneers

[*The Slaughter of the Pigeons*][1]

"Men, boys, and girls.
Desert th' unpeopled village; and wild crowds
Spread o'er the plain, by the sweet frenzy driven."[2]
—Somerville

From this time to the close of April, the weather continued to be a succession of great and rapid changes. One day, the soft airs of spring would seem to be stealing along the valley, and, in unison with an invigorating sun, attempting, covertly, to rouse the dormant powers of the vegetable world; while on the next, the surly blasts from the north would sweep across the lake, and erase every impression left by their gentle adversaries. The snow, however, finally disappeared, and the green wheat fields were seen in every direction, spotted with the dark and charred stumps that had, the preceding season, supported some of the proudest trees of the forest.[3] Ploughs were in motion, wherever those useful implements could be used, and the smokes of the sugar-camps[4] were no longer seen issuing from the summits of the woods of maple. The lake had lost all the characteristic beauty of a field of ice, but still a dark and gloomy covering concealed its waters, for the absence of currents left them yet hid under a porous crust, which, saturated with the fluid, barely retained enough of its strength to preserve the contiguity of its parts. Large flocks of wild geese were seen passing over the country, which would hover, for a time, around the hidden sheet of water, apparently searching for an opening, where they might obtain a resting-place; and then, on finding themselves excluded by the chill covering, would soar away to the north, filling the air with their

1. *The Pioneers, or The Sources of the Susquehanna; A Descriptive Tale* (1823) is the first of five Cooper novels in which Natty Bumppo is the major character. The text is that of the 1st edition, chap. 3 (chap. 22 in later one-volume editions). *The Pioneers* begins in December 1793 at the settlement of Templeton (modeled on Cooperstown) at Otsego Lake in central New York, some fifty miles west of Albany. The episode reprinted here occurs in the spring of 1794. Natty Bumppo is in his early seventies, six feet tall (then a great height), gray-eyed, with lank, sandy hair, sunburned, robust, but thin almost to emaciation. One yellow tooth survives in his enormous mouth, and he gives forth a remarkable kind of inward laugh. He wears a foxskin hat and is clad in deerskin—coat, moccasins, and even the leggings, which fasten over the knees of his buckskin breeches and give him the nickname of Leather-stocking. For his old and unusually long rifle he carries gunpowder in an enormous ox horn slung over his shoulder by a strap of deerskin. This was the unprepossessing figure who captured the imagination of the United States and Europe.
2. From *The Chace*, 2.197–99, by the English poet William Somerville (1675–1742). The last word should be *seized*, not "driven."
3. The practice was to chop timber down in the spring, let it dry through the summer, then burn the cleared area so that only blackened logs and stumps remained. Nothing was salvaged except some ashes used as the basis for potash.
4. Where sugar was made from maple sap.

discordant screams, as if venting their complaints at the tardy operations of nature.

For a week, the dark covering of the Otsego was left to the undisturbed possession of two eagles, who alighted on the centre of its field, and sat proudly eyeing the extent of their undisputed territory. During the presence of these monarchs of the air, the flocks of migrating birds avoided crossing the plain of ice, by turning into the hills, and apparently seeking the protection of the forests, while the white and bald heads of the tenants of the lake were turned upward, with a look of majestic contempt, as if penetrating to the very heavens, with the acuteness of their vision. But the time had come, when even these kings of birds were to be dispossessed. An opening had been gradually increasing, at the lower extremity of the lake, and around the dark spot where the current of the river had prevented the formation of ice, during even the coldest weather; and the fresh southerly winds, that now breathed freely up the valley, obtained an impression on the waters. Mimic waves begun to curl over the margin of the frozen field, which exhibited an outline of crystallizations, that slowly receded towards the north. At each step the power of the winds and the waves increased, until, after a struggle of a few hours, the turbulent little billows succeeded in setting the whole field in an undulating motion, when it was driven beyond the reach of the eye, with a rapidity, that was as magical as the change produced in the scene by this expulsion of the lingering remnant of winter. Just as the last sheet of agitated ice was disappearing in the distance, the eagles rose over the border of crystals, and soared with a wide sweep far above the clouds, while the waves tossed their little caps of snow into the air, as if rioting in their release from a thraldom of five months duration.

The following morning Elizabeth[5] was awakened by the exhilarating sounds of the martins, who were quarrelling and chattering around the little boxes which were suspended above her windows, and the cries of Richard,[6] who was calling, in tones as animating as the signs of the season itself—

"Awake! awake! my lady fair! the gulls are hovering over the lake already, and the heavens are alive with the pigeons. You may look an hour before you can find a hole, through which, to get a peep at the sun. Awake! awake! lazy ones! Benjamin[7] is overhauling the ammunition, and we only wait for our breakfasts, and away for the mountains and pigeon-shooting."

There was no resisting this animated appeal, and in a few minutes Miss Temple and her friend[8] descended to the parlour. The doors of the hall were thrown open, and the mild, balmy air of a clear spring morning was ventilating the apartment, where the vigilance of the ex-steward had been so long maintaining an artificial heat, with such unremitted diligence. All of the gentlemen, we do not include Monsieur Le Quoi,[9] were impatiently waiting their morning's repast, each being equipt in the garb of a sportsman. Mr. Jones made many visits to the southern door, and would cry—

"See, cousin Bess! see, 'duke![1] the pigeon-roosts of the south have broken up! They are growing more thick every instant. Here is a flock that the eye

---

5. Elizabeth Temple, daughter of Judge Marmaduke Temple, the founder of Templeton and its chief landowner; at the outset of the story she returns from four years at school.

6. Richard (Dickon) Jones, the sheriff, a cousin of Judge Temple; he superintends "all the minor concerns of Temple's business."

7. Benjamin Penguillan (called Ben Pump), a Cornishman and former sailor, majordomo, or steward

under Jones. In the next paragraph Pump is called "the ex-steward" because he had been the steward to the captain in his seagoing years. One of his charges at the Templeton house is to keep the stove in the parlor hot in winter.

8. Louisa Grant, daughter of the Episcopal minister.

9. Once a West Indian planter, now a refugee because of the French Revolution.

1. Short for "Marmaduke," the judge.

cannot see the end of. There is food enough in it to keep the army of Xerxes[2] for a month, and feathers enough to make beds for the whole county. Xerxes, Mr. Edwards,[3] was a Grecian king, who—no, he was a Turk, or a Persian, who wanted to conquer Greece, just the same as these rascals will overrun our wheat-fields, when they come back in the fall.—Away! away! Bess; I long to pepper them from the mountain."

In this wish both Marmaduke and young Edwards seemed equally to participate, for really the sight was most exhilarating to a sportsman; and the ladies soon dismissed the party, after a hasty breakfast.

If the heavens were alive with pigeons, the whole village seemed equally in motion, with men, women, and children. Every species of fire-arms, from the French ducking-gun, with its barrel of near six feet in length, to the common horseman's pistol, was to be seen in the hands of the men and boys; while bows and arrows, some made of the simple stick of a walnut sapling, and others in a rude imitation of the ancient cross-bows, were carried by many of the latter.

The houses, and the signs of life apparent in the village, drove the alarmed birds from the direct line of their flight, towards the mountains, along the sides and near the bases of which they were glancing in dense masses, that were equally wonderful by the rapidity of their motion, as by their incredible numbers.

We have already said, that across the inclined plane which fell from the steep ascent of the mountain to the banks of the Susquehanna, ran the highway, on either side of which a clearing of many acres had been made, at a very early day. Over those clearings, and up the eastern mountain, and along the dangerous path that was cut into its side, the different individuals posted themselves, as suited their inclinations; and in a few moments the attack commenced.

Amongst the sportsmen was to be seen the tall, gaunt form of Leather-stocking,[4] who was walking over the field, with his rifle hanging on his arm, his dogs following close at his heels, now scenting the dead or wounded birds, that were beginning to tumble from the flocks, and then crouching under the legs of their master, as if they participated in his feelings, at this wasteful and unsportsmanlike execution.

The reports of the fire-arms became rapid, whole volleys rising from the plain, as flocks of more than ordinary numbers darted over the opening, covering the field with darkness, like an interposing cloud; and then the light smoke of a single piece would issue from among the leafless bushes on the mountain, as death was hurled on the retreat of the affrighted birds, who would rise from a volley, for many feet into the air, in a vain effort to escape the attacks of man. Arrows, and missiles of every kind, were seen in the midst of the flocks; and so numerous were the birds, and so low did they take their flight, that even long poles, in the hands of those on the sides of the mountain, were used to strike them to the earth.

During all this time, Mr. Jones, who disdained the humble and ordinary means of destruction used by his companions, was busily occupied, aided by Benjamin, in making arrangements for an assault of a more than ordinarily fatal character. Among the relics of the old military excursions, that occasionally are discovered throughout the different districts of the western part of New-

2. Xerxes the Great (519?–465 B.C.) was king of Persia (486–65 B.C.).   3. Oliver Edwards, a mysterious young stranger.   4. I.e., Natty Bumppo.

York, there had been found in Templeton, at its settlement, a small swivel,[5] which would carry a ball of a pound weight. It was thought to have been deserted by a war-party of the whites, in one of their inroads into the Indian settlements, when, perhaps, their convenience or their necessities induced them to leave such an encumbrance to the rapidity of their march, behind them in the woods. This miniature cannon had been released from the rust, and mounted on little wheels, in a state for actual service. For several years, it was the sole organ for extraordinary rejoicings that was used in those mountains. On the mornings of the Fourth of July, it would be heard, with its echoes ringing among the hills, and telling forth its sounds, for thirteen times, with all the dignity of a two-and-thirty pounder; and even Captain Hollister,[6] who was the highest authority in that part of the country on all such occasions, affirmed that, considering its dimensions, it was no despicable gun for a salute. It was somewhat the worse for the service it had performed, it is true, there being but a trifling difference in size between the touch-hole and the muzzle.[7] Still, the grand conceptions of Richard had suggested the importance of such an instrument, in hurling death at his nimble enemies. The swivel was dragged by a horse into a part of the open space, that the sheriff thought most eligible for planting a battery of the kind, and Mr. Pump proceeded to load it. Several handfuls of duck-shot were placed on top of the powder, and the Major-domo soon announced that his piece was ready for service.

The sight of such an implement collected all the idle spectators to the spot, who, being mostly boys, filled the air with their cries of exultation and delight. The gun was pointed on high, and Richard, holding a coal of fire in a pair of tongs, patiently took his seat on a stump, awaiting the appearance of a flock that was worthy of his notice.

So prodigious was the number of the birds, that the scattering fire of the guns, with the hurling of missiles, and the cries of the boys, had no other effect than to break off small flocks from the immense masses that continued to dart along the valley, as if the whole creation of the feathered tribe were pouring through that one pass. None pretended to collect the game, which lay scattered over the fields in such profusion, as to cover the very ground with the fluttering victims.

Leather-stocking was a silent, but uneasy spectator of all these proceedings, but was able to keep his sentiments to himself until he saw the introduction of the swivel into the sports.

"This comes of settling a country" he said—"here have I known the pigeons to fly for forty long years, and, till you made your clearings, there was nobody to scare or to hurt them. I loved to see them come into the woods, for they were company to a body; hurting nothing; being, as it was, as harmless as a garter-snake. But now it gives me sore thoughts when I hear the frighty things whizzing through the air, for I know it's only a motion to bring out all the brats in the village at them. Well! the Lord won't see the waste of his creaters for nothing, and right will be done to the pigeons, as well as others, by-and-by.—There's Mr. Oliver, as bad as the rest of them, firing into the flocks as if he was shooting down nothing but the Mingo[8] warriors."

5. Small cannon capable of being swung higher or lower.
6. The landlord of the major village inn, The Bold Dragoon; his rank comes from his having been an early commander of local militia.
7. Ordinarily the muzzle (or mouth) would be consid-
erably larger than the touchhole, the vent by which fire is communicated to the powder.
8. In the *Leather-Stocking* novels set in New York, the Mingos (Iroquois) are made out to be the "bad Indians," whereas the Delawares are the "good Indians."

Among the sportsmen was Billy Kirby,[9] who, armed with an old musket, was loading, and, without even looking into the air, was firing, and shouting as his victims fell even on his own person. He heard the speech of Natty, and took upon himself to reply—

"What's that, old Leather-stocking!" he cried; "grumbling at the loss of a few pigeons! If you had to sow your wheat twice, and three times, as I have done, you wouldn't be so massyfully[1] feeling'd to'ards the divils.—Hurrah, boys! scatter the feathers. This is better than shooting at a turkey's head[2] and neck, old fellow."

"It's better for you, maybe, Billy Kirby," returned the indignant old hunter, "and all them as don't know how to put a ball down a rifle-barrel, or how to bring it up ag'in with a true aim; but it's wicked to be shooting into flocks in this wastey manner; and none do it, who know how to knock over a single bird. If a body has a craving for pigeon's flesh, why! it's made the same as all other creaters, for man's eating, but not to kill twenty and eat one. When I want such a thing, I go into the woods till I find one to my liking, and then I shoot him off the branches without touching a feather of another, though there might be a hundred on the same tree. But you couldn't do such a thing, Billy Kirby—you couldn't do it if you tried."

"What's that you say, you old, dried cornstalk! you sapless stub!" cried the wood-chopper. "You've grown mighty boasting, sin[3] you killed the turkey; but if you're for a single shot, here goes at that bird which comes on by himself."

The fire from the distant part of the field had driven a single pigeon below the flock to which it had belonged, and, frightened with the constant reports of the muskets, it was approaching the spot where the disputants stood, darting first from one side, and then to the other, cutting the air with the swiftness of lightning, and making a noise with its wings, not unlike the rushing of a bullet. Unfortunately for the wood-chopper, notwithstanding his vaunt, he did not see his bird until it was too late for him to fire as it approached, and he pulled his trigger at the unlucky moment when it was darting immediately over his head. The bird continued its course with incredible velocity.

Natty had dropped his piece from his arm, when the challenge was made, and, waiting a moment, until the terrified victim had got in a line with his eyes, and had dropped near the bank of the lake, he raised his rifle with uncommon rapidity, and fired. It might have been chance, or it might have been skill, that produced the result; it was probably a union of both; but the pigeon whirled over in the air, and fell into the lake, with a broken wing. At the sound of his rifle, both his dogs started from his feet, and in a few minutes the "slut"[4] brought out the bird, still alive.

The wonderful exploit of Leather-stocking was noised through the field with great rapidity, and the sportsmen gathered in to learn the truth of the report.

"What," said young Edwards, "have you really killed a pigeon on the wing, Natty, with a single ball?"

"Haven't I killed loons before now, lad, that dive at the flash?" returned the hunter. "It's much better to kill only such as you want, without wasting your powder and lead, than to be firing into God's creaters in such a wicked manner. But I come out for a bird, and you know the reason why I like small game, Mr. Oliver, and now I have got one I will go home, for I don't like to

9. A woodchopper.
1. Mercifully.
2. In an earlier chapter Natty Bumppo had beaten

Kirby in a turkey-shooting contest.
3. Since.
4. Bitch, female dog.

see these wasty ways that you are all practysing, as if the least thing was not made for use, and not to destroy."

"Thou sayest well, Leather-stocking," cried Marmaduke, "and I begin to think it time to put an end to this work of destruction."

"Put an ind, Judge, to your clearings. An't the woods his work as well as the pigeons? Use, but don't waste. Wasn't the woods made for the beasts and birds to harbour in? and when man wanted their flesh, their skins, or their feathers, there's the place to seek them. But I'll go to the hut with my own game, for I wouldn't touch one of the harmless things that kiver the ground here, looking up with their eyes at me, as if they only wanted tongues to say their thoughts."

With this sentiment in his mouth, Leather-stocking threw his rifle over his arm, and, followed by his dogs, stepped across the clearing with great caution, taking care not to tread on one, of the hundreds of the wounded birds that lay in his path. He soon entered the bushes on the margin of the lake, and was hid from view.

Whatever might be the impression the morality of Natty made on the Judge, it was utterly lost on Richard. He availed himself of the gathering of the sportsmen, to lay a plan for one "fell swoop"[5] of destruction. The musket-men were drawn up in battle array, in a line extending on each side of his artillery, with orders to await the signal of firing from himself.

"Stand by, my lads," said Benjamin, who acted as an aid-de-camp on this momentous occasion, "stand by, my hearties, and when Squire Dickens heaves out the signal for to begin the firing, d'ye see, you may open upon them in a broadside. Take care and fire low, boys, and you'll be sure to hull the flock."

"Fire low!" shouted Kirby—"hear the old fool! If we fire low, we may hit the stumps, but not ruffle a pigeon."

"How should you know, you lubber?"[6] cried Benjamin, with a very unbecoming heat, for an officer on the eve of battle—"how should you know, you grampus? Havn't I sailed aboard of the Boadishy[7] for five years? and wasn't it a standing order to fire low, and to hull your enemy? Keep silence at your guns, boys, and mind the order that is passed."

The loud laughs of the musketmen were silenced by the authoritative voice of Richard, who called to them for attention and obedience to his signals.

Some millions of pigeons were supposed to have already passed, that morning, over the valley of Templeton; but nothing like the flock that was now approaching had been seen before. It extended from mountain to mountain in one solid blue mass, and the eye looked in vain over the southern hills to find its termination. The front of this living column was distinctly marked by a line, but very slightly indented, so regular and even was the flight. Even Marmaduke forgot the morality of Leather-stocking as it approached, and, in common with the rest, brought his musket to his shoulder.

"Fire!" cried the Sheriff, clapping his coal to the priming of the cannon. As half of Benjamin's charge escaped through the touch-hole, the whole volley of the musketry preceded the report of the swivel. On receiving this united discharge of small-arms, the front of the flock darted upward, while, at the same instant, myriads of those in their rear rushed with amazing rapidity into their places, so that when the column of white smoke gushed from the mouth of the little cannon, an accumulated mass of objects was gliding over its point

5. Shakespeare's *Macbeth* 4.3.219, in Macduff's lament for his dead wife and children.

6. Landlubber, clumsy fellow.

7. The *Boadicea*, a ship named for the British queen

of direction. The roar of the gun echoed along the mountains, and died away to the north, like distant thunder, while the whole flock of alarmed birds seemed, for a moment, thrown into one disorderly and agitated mass. The air was filled with their irregular flights, layer rising over layer, far above the tops of the highest pines, none daring to advance beyond the dangerous pass; when, suddenly, some of the leaders of the feathered tribe shot across the valley, taking their flight directly over the village, and the hundreds of thousands in their rear followed their example, deserting the eastern side of the plain to their persecutors and the fallen.

"Victory!" shouted Richard, "victory! we have driven the enemy from the field."

"Not so, Dickon," said Marmaduke; "the field is covered with them; and, like the Leather-stocking, I see nothing but eyes, in every direction, as the innocent sufferers turn their heads in terror, to examine my movements. Full one half of those that have fallen are yet alive: and I think it is time to end the sport; if sport it be."

"Sport!" cried the Sheriff; "it is princely sport. There are some thousands of the blue-coated boys on the ground, so that every old woman in the village may have a pot-pie for the asking."

"Well, we have happily frightened the birds from this pass," said Marmaduke, "and our carnage must of necessity end, for the present.—Boys, I will give thee sixpence a hundred for the pigeons' heads only; so go to work, and bring them into the village, when I will pay thee."

This expedient produced the desired effect, for every urchin on the ground went industriously to work to wring the necks of the wounded birds. Judge Temple retired towards his dwelling with that kind of feeling, that many a man has experienced before him, who discovers, after the excitement of the moment has passed, that he has purchased pleasure at the price of misery to others. Horses were loaded with the dead; and, after this first burst of sporting, the shooting of pigeons became a business, for the remainder of the season, more in proportion to the wants of the people.[8] Richard, however, boasted for many a year, of his shot with the "cricket;"[9] and Benjamin gravely asserted, that he thought that they killed nearly as many pigeons on that day, as there were Frenchmen destroyed on the memorable occasion of Rodney's victory.[1]

1823

From Notions of the Americans[1]

[*The Literature and the Arts of the United States*]

TO THE ABBATE GIROMACHI, &C. &C., FLORENCE

Washington,———

You ask me to write freely on the subject of the literature and the arts of the United States. The subjects are so meagre as to render it a task that would

who led a rebellion against the Roman rulers in A.D. 62. "Grampus": variety of small whale, used here as a term of contempt.
8. The pigeons described in this chapter—the passenger pigeons—are extinct, the last known specimen dying in 1914 at the Cincinnati Zoological Garden.
9. I.e., the little cannon.
1. The British admiral George Brydges, Baron Rodney

(1719–1792), defeated the French off Dominica, in the West Indies, in April 1782. Penguillan's nickname comes from his tall tale about manning the pumps to keep the ship from sinking after Rodney's victory.
1. *Notions of the Americans: Picked Up by a Travelling Bachelor* is Cooper's model for a travel book—the sort of book British tourists in America should have been writing instead of the hasty, opinionated, erroneous ac-

require no small portion of the talents necessary to figure in either, in order to render them of interest. Still, as the request has come in so urgent a form, I shall endeavour to oblige you.

The Americans have been placed, as respects moral and intellectual advancement, different from all other infant nations. They have never been without the wants of civilization, nor have they ever been entirely without the means of a supply. Thus pictures, and books, and statuary, and every thing else which appertains to elegant life, have always been known to them in an abundance, and of a quality exactly proportioned to their cost. Books, being the cheapest, and the nation having great leisure and prodigious zest for information, are not only the most common, as you will readily suppose, but they are probably more common than among any other people. I scarcely remember ever to have entered an American dwelling, however humble, without finding fewer or more books. As they form the most essential division of the subject, not only on account of their greater frequency, but on account of their far greater importance, I shall give them the first notice in this letter.

Unlike the progress of the two professions in the countries of our hemisphere, in America the printer came into existence before the author. Reprints of English works gave the first employment to the press. Then came almanacks, psalm-books, religious tracts, sermons, journals, political essays, and even rude attempts at poetry. All these preceded the revolution. The first journal was established in Boston at the commencement of the last century.[2] There are several original polemical works of great originality and power that belong to the same period. I do not know that more learning and talents existed at that early day in the states of New England than in Virginia, Maryland and the Carolinas, but there was certainly a stronger desire to exhibit them.

The colleges or universities, as they were somewhat prematurely called, date very far back in the brief history of the country. There is no stronger evidence of the intellectual character, or of the judicious ambition of these people, than what this simple fact furnishes. Harvard College, now the university of Cambridge—(it better deserves the title at this day)—was founded in 1638; within less than *twenty years* after the landing of the first settlers in New England! Yale (in Connecticut) was founded in 1701. Columbia (in the city of New York) was founded in 1754. Nassau Hall (in New Jersey) in 1738; and William and Mary (in Virginia) as far back as 1691.[3] These are the oldest literary institutions in the United States, and all but the last are in flourishing conditions to the present hour. The first has given degrees to about five thousand graduates, and rarely has less than three hundred and fifty or four hundred students. Yale is about as well attended. The others contain from a hundred and fifty to two hundred under-graduates. But these are not a moiety[4] of the present colleges, or universities, (as they all aspire to be called,) existing in the country. There is no state, except a few of the newest, without at least one, and several have two or three.

counts that were being printed every year. *Notions* is in the form of letters written by a young Englishman from the United States to several English and continental members of a club of learned bachelors; it is loosely structured around General Lafayette's triumphal tour of the United States in 1824–25. The book is dedicated to a fictional "John Cadwallader, of Cadwallader, in the State of New York, United States of America," who is at last judged worthy of joining the club as replacement for a member who has succumbed to matrimony. Written in Paris partly at the urging of Lafayette himself, *Notions* was first published in London (1828), the source of the present selections, the sixth and seventh "letters" in the second volume (or chap. 23 and 24 in one-volume editions), both addressed to Giromachi, an Italian "abbate," or priest.

2. The first American newspaper, the Boston *Publick Occurrences*, lasted four days in September 1690.

3. Harvard was actually founded in 1636; Nassau Hall (Princeton), in 1746; and William and Mary, in 1693.

4. Half.

Less attention is paid to classical learning here than in Europe; and, as the term of residence rarely exceeds four years, profound scholars are by no means common. This country possesses neither the population nor the endowments to maintain a large class of learned idlers, in order that one man in a hundred may contribute a mite to the growing stock of general knowledge. There is a luxury in this expenditure of animal force, to which the Americans have not yet attained. The good is far too problematical and remote, and the expense of man too certain, to be prematurely sought. I have heard, I will confess, an American legislator quote Horace and Cicero;[5] but it is far from being the humour of the country. I thought the taste of the orator questionable. A learned quotation is rarely of any use in an argument, since few men are fools enough not to see that the application of any maxim to politics is liable to a thousand practical objections, and, nine times in ten, they are evidences of the want[6] of a direct, natural, and vigorous train of thought. They are the affectations, but rarely the ebullitions of true talent. When a man feels strongly, or thinks strongly, or speaks strongly, he is just as apt to do it in his native tongue as he is to laugh when he is tickled, or to weep when in sorrow. The Americans are strong speakers and acute thinkers, but no great quoters of the morals and axioms of a heathen age, because they happen to be recorded in Latin.

The higher branches of learning are certainly on the advance in this country. The gentlemen of the middle[7] and southern states, before the revolution, were very generally educated in Europe, and they were consequently, in this particular, like our own people. Those who came into life during the struggle, and shortly after, fared worse. Even the next generation had little to boast of in the way of instruction. I find that boys entered the colleges so late as the commencement of the present century, who had read a part of the Greek Testament, and a few books of Cicero and Virgil,[8] with perhaps a little of Horace. But great changes have been made, and are still making, in the degree of previous qualification.

Still, it would be premature to say that there is any one of the American universities where classical knowledge, or even science is profoundly attained, even at the present day. Some of the professors push their studies, for a life, certainly; and you well know, after all, that little short of a life, and a long one too, will make any man a good general scholar. In 1820, near eight thousand graduates of the twelve oldest colleges of this country (according to their catalogues) were then living. Of this number, 1,406 were clergymen. As some of the catalogues consulted were several years old, this number was, of necessity, greatly within the truth. Between the years 1800 and 1810, it is found that of 2,792 graduates, four hundred and fifty-three became clergymen. Here is pretty good evidence that religion is not neglected in America, and that its ministers are not, as a matter of course, absolutely ignorant.

But the effects of the literary institutions of the United States are somewhat peculiar. Few men devote their lives to scholarship. The knowledge that is actually acquired, is perhaps quite sufficient for the more practical and useful pursuits. Thousands of young men, who have read the more familiar classics, who have gone through enough of mathematics to obtain a sense of their own tastes, and of the value of precision, who have cultivated *belles lettres* to a

5. Roman orator and statesman (106–43 B.C.). Horace was a Roman poet and satirist (65–8 B.C.).
6. Lack.
7. I.e., the Middle Atlantic states: Pennsylvania, New Jersey, Delaware, and Maryland.
8. Roman poet (70–19 B.C.).

reasonable extent, and who have been moderately instructed in the arts of composition, and in the rules of taste, are given forth to the country to mingle in its active employments. I am inclined to believe that a class of American graduates carries away with it quite as much general and diversified knowledge, as a class from one of our own universities. The excellence in particular branches is commonly wanting; but the deficiency is more than supplied by variety of information. The youth who has passed four years within the walls of a college, goes into the office of a lawyer for a few more. The profession of the law is not subdivided in America. The same man is counsellor, attorney, and conveyancer.[9] Here the student gets a general insight into the principles, and a familiarity with the practice of the law, rather than an acquaintance with the study as a science. With this instruction he enters the world as a practitioner. Instead of existing in a state of dreaming retrospection, lost in a maze of theories, he is at once turned loose into the jostlings of the world. If perchance he encounters an antagonist a little more erudite than himself, he seizes the natural truth for his sheet anchor, and leaves precedent and quaint follies to him who has made them his study and delight. No doubt he often blunders, and is frequently, of necessity, defeated. But in the course of this irreverent treatment, usages and opinions, which are bottomed in no better foundation than antiquity, and which are as inapplicable to the present state of the world, as the present state of the world is, or ought to be, unfavourable to all feudal absurdities, come to receive their death warrants. In the mean time, by dint of sheer experience, and by the collision of intellects, the practitioner gets a stock of learning, that is acquired in the best possible school; and, what is of far more importance, the laws themselves get a dress which brings them within the fashions of the day. This same man becomes a legislator perhaps, and, if particularly clever, he is made to take an active part in the framing of laws that are not to harmonize with the other parts of an elaborate theory, but which are intended to make men comfortable and happy. Now, taken with more or less qualification, this is the history of thousands in this country, and it is also an important part of the history of the country itself.

In considering the course of instruction in the United States, you are always to commence at the foundation. The common schools, which so generally exist, have certainly elevated the population above that of any other country, and are still elevating it higher, as they improve and increase in numbers. Law is getting every day to be more of a science, but it is a science that is forming rules better adapted to the spirit of the age. Medicine is improving, and in the cities it is perhaps now, in point of practice, quite on a level with that of Europe. Indeed, the well-educated American physician very commonly enjoys an advantage that is little known in Europe. After obtaining a degree in his own country, he passes a few years in London, Edinburgh, Paris, and frequently in Germany, and returns with his gleanings from their several schools. This is not the case with one individual, but with many, annually. Indeed, there is so much of a fashion in it, and the custom is attended by so many positive advantages, that its neglect would be a serious obstacle to any very eminent success. Good operators[1] are by no means scarce, and as surgery and medicine are united in the same person, there is great judgment in their prac-

---

9. A lawyer who draws up deeds to "convey" or transfer property. In England the profession is divided into barristers, who plead cases in the courtroom, and solic-itors, who advise clients outside the courtroom.
1. I.e., surgeons.

tice. Human life is something more valuable in America than in Europe, and I think a critical attention to patients more common here than with us, especially when the sufferer belongs to an inferior condition in life. The profession is highly respectable; and in all parts of the country the better sort of its practitioners mingle, on terms of perfect equality, with the highest classes of society. There are several physicians in congress, and a great many in the different state legislatures.

Of the ministry it is unnecessary to speak. The clergy are of all denominations, and they are educated, or not, precisely as they belong to sects which consider the gift of human knowledge of any importance. You have already seen how large a proportion of the graduates of some of the colleges enter the desk.[2]

As respects authorship, there is not much to be said. Compared to the books that are printed and read, those of native origin are few indeed. The principal reason of this poverty of original writers, is owing to the circumstance that men are not yet driven to their wits for bread. The United States are the first nation that possessed institutions, and, of course, distinctive opinions of its own, that was ever dependant on a foreign people for its literature. Speaking the same language as the English, and long in the habit of importing their books from the mother country, the revolution effected no immediate change in the nature of their studies, or mental amusements. The works were reprinted, it is true, for the purposes of economy, but they still continued English. Had the latter nation used this powerful engine with tolerable address, I think they would have secured such an ally in this country as would have rendered their own decline not only more secure, but as illustrious as had been their rise. There are many theories entertained as to the effect produced in this country by the falsehoods and jealous calumnies which have been undeniably uttered in the mother country, by means of the press, concerning her republican descendant. It is my own opinion that, like all other ridiculous absurdities, they have defeated themselves, and that they are now more laughed at and derided, even here, than resented. By all that I can learn, twenty years ago, the Americans were, perhaps, far too much disposed to receive the opinions and to adopt the prejudices of their relatives; whereas, I think it is very apparent that they are now beginning to receive them with singular distrust. It is not worth our while to enter further into this subject, except as it has had, or is likely to have, an influence on the national literature.[3]

It is quite obvious, that, so far as taste and forms alone are concerned, the literature of England and that of America must be fashioned after the same models. The authors, previously to the revolution, are common property, and it is quite idle to say that the American has not just as good a right to claim Milton, and Shakspeare, and all the old masters of the language, for his countrymen, as an Englishman. The Americans having continued to cultivate, and to cultivate extensively, an acquaintance with the writers of the mother country, since the separation, it is evident they must have kept pace with the trifling changes of the day. The only peculiarity that can, or ought to be expected in

2. I.e., pulpit.

3. "The writer might give, in proof of this opinion, one fact. He is led to believe that, so lately as within ten years, several English periodical works were reprinted, and much read in the United States, and that now they patronize their own, while the former are far less sought, though the demand, by means of the increased population, should have been nearly doubled. Some of the works are no longer even re-printed" [Cooper's note].

their literature, is that which is connected with the promulgation of their distinctive political opinions. They have not been remiss in this duty, as any one may see, who chooses to examine their books. But we will devote a few minutes to a more minute account of the actual condition of American literature.

The first, and the most important, though certainly the most familiar branch of this subject, is connected with the public journals. It is not easy to say how many newspapers are printed in the United States. The estimated number varies from six hundred to a thousand. In the State of New York there are more than fifty counties. Now, it is rare that a county, in a state as old as that of New York (especially in the more northern parts of the country), does not possess one paper at least. The cities have many. The smaller towns sometimes have three or four, and very many of the counties four or five. There cannot be many less than one hundred and fifty journals in the state of New York alone. Pennsylvania is said to possess eighty. But we will suppose that these two states publish two hundred journals. They contain about 3,000,000 of inhabitants. As the former is an enlightened state, and the latter rather below the scale of the general intelligence of the nation, it may not be a very bad average of the whole population. This rate would give eight hundred journals for the United States, which is probably something within the truth. I confess, however, this manner of equalizing estimates in America, is very uncertain in general, since a great deal, in such a question, must depend on the progress of society in each particular section of the country.

As might be expected, there is nearly every degree of merit to be found in these journals. No one of them has the benefit of that collected talent which is so often enlisted in the support of the more important journals of Europe. There is not often more than one editor to the best; but he is usually some man who has seen, in his own person, enough of men and things to enable him to speak with tolerable discretion on passing events. The usefulness of the American journals, however, does not consist in their giving the tone to the public mind, in politics and morals, but in imparting facts. It is certain that, could the journals agree, they might, by their united efforts, give a powerful inclination to the common will. But, in point of fact, they do not agree on any one subject or set of subjects, except, perhaps, on those which directly affect their own interests. They, consequently, counteract, instead of aiding each other, on all points of disputed policy; and it is in the bold and sturdy discussions that follow, that men arrive at the truth. The occasional union in their own favour, is a thing too easily seen through to do either good or harm. So far, then, from the journals succeeding in leading the public opinion astray, they are invariably obliged to submit to it. They serve to keep it alive, by furnishing the means for its expression, but they rarely do more. Of course, the influence of each particular press is in proportion to the constancy and the ability with which is found to support what is thought to be sound principles; but those principles must be in accordance with the private opinions of men, or most of their labour is lost.

The public press in America is rather more decent than that of England, and less decorous than that of France. The tone of the nation, and the respect for private feelings, which are, perhaps, in some measure, the consequence of a less artificial state of society, produce the former; and the liberty, which is a necessary attendant of fearless discussion, is, I think, the cause of the latter. The affairs of an individual are rarely touched upon in the journals of this country; never, unless it is thought they have a direct connection with the public interests, or from a wish to do him good. Still there is a habit, getting into use in America, no less than in France, that is borrowed from the English, which proves that the more unworthy feelings of our nature are common to men under all systems, and only need opportunity to find encouragement. I allude to the practice of repeating the proceedings of the courts of justice, in order to cater to a vicious appetite for amusement in the public.

It is pretended that, as a court of justice is open to the world, there can be no harm in giving the utmost publicity to its proceedings. It is strange the courts should act so rigidly on the principle, that it is better a dozen guilty men should go free, than that one innocent man should suffer, and yet permit the gross injustice that is daily done by means of this practice. One would think, that if a court of justice is so open to the world, that it should be the business of the people of the world to enter it, in order that they might be certain that the information they crave should be without colouring or exaggeration. It is idle to say that the reports are accurate, and that he who reads is enabled to do justice to the accused, by comparing the facts that are laid before him. A reporter may give the expression of the tongue; but can he convey that of the eye, of the countenance, or of the form?—without regarding all of which no man is perfectly master of the degree of credibility that is due to any witness of whose character he is necessarily ignorant. But every man has an infallible means of assuring himself of the value of these reports. Who has ever read a dozen of them without meeting with one (or perhaps more), in which the decision of the court and jury is to him a matter of surprise? It is true he assumes, that those who were present knew best, and as he has no great interest in the matter, he is commonly satisfied. But how is it with the unfortunate man who is wrongfully brought out of his retirement to repel an unjust attack against his person, his property, or his character? If he be a man of virtue, he is a man of sensibility; and not only he, but, what is far worse, those tender beings, whose existence is wrapped up in his own, are to be wounded daily and hourly, for weeks at a time, in order that a depraved appetite should be glutted. It is enough for justice that her proceedings should be so public as to prevent the danger of corruption; but we pervert a blessing to a curse, in making that which was intended for our protection, the means of so much individual misery. It is an unavoidable evil of the law that it necessarily works some wrong, in order to do much good; but it is cruel that even the acquittal of a man should be unnecessarily circulated, in a manner to make all men remember that he had been accused. We have proof of the consequences of this practice in England. Men daily shrink from resistance to base frauds, rather than expose themselves to the observations and comments of those who enliven their breakfasts by sporting with these exhibitions of their fellow creatures. There are, undoubtedly, cases of that magnitude which require some sacrifice of private feelings, in order that the community should reap the advantage; but the regular books are sufficient for authorities—the decisions of the courts are sufficient for justice—and the utmost possible oblivion should prove as nearly sufficient as may be to serve the ends of a prudent and a righteous humanity.

Nothing can be more free than the press of this country, on all subjects connected with politics. Treason cannot be written, unless by communicating with an open enemy. There is no other protection to a public man than that which is given by an independent jury, which punishes, of course, in proportion to the dignity and importance of the injured party. But the utmost lenity is always used in construing the right of the press to canvass the public acts of public men. Mere common place charges defeat themselves, and get into discredit so soon as to be lost, while graver accusations are met by grave replies. There is no doubt that the complacency of individuals is sometimes disturbed by these liberties; but they serve to keep the officers of the government to their work, while they rarely do any lasting, or even temporary injury. Serious and criminal accusations against a public man, if groundless, are, by the law of reason, a crime against the community, and, as such, they are punished. The general principle observed in these matters is very simple. If A. accuse B. of an act that is an offence against law, he may be called on for his proof, and if he fail he must take the consequences. But an editor of a paper, or any one else, who should bring a criminal charge, no matter how grave, against the president, and who could prove it, is just as certain of doing it with impunity, as if he held the whole power in his own hands. He would be protected by the invincible shield of public opinion, which is not only in consonance with the law, but which, in this country, makes law.

Actions for injuries done by the press, considering the number of journals, are astonishingly rare in America.[4] When one remembers the usual difficulty of obtaining legal proof, which is a constant temptation, even to the guilty, to appeal to the courts; and, on the other hand, the great freedom of the press, which is a constant temptation to abuse the trust, this fact, in itself, furnishes irresistible evidence of the general tone of decency which predominates in this nation. The truth is, that public opinion, among its other laws, has imperiously prescribed that, amidst the utmost latitude of discussion, certain limits shall not be passed; and public opinion, which is so completely the offspring of a free press, must be obeyed in this, as well as in other matters.

Leaving the journals, we come to those publications which make their appearance periodically. Of these there are a good many, some few of which are well supported. There are several scientific works, that are printed monthly, or quarterly, of respectable merit, and four or five reviews. Magazines of a more general character are not much encouraged. England, which is teeming with educated men, who are glad to make their bread by writing for these works, still affords too strong a competition for the success of any American attempts, in this species of literature. Though few, perhaps no English magazine is actually republished in America, a vast number are imported and read in the towns, where the support for any similar original production must first be found.

The literature of the United States has, indeed, two powerful obstacles to conquer before (to use a mercantile expression) it can ever enter the markets of its own country on terms of perfect equality with that of England. Solitary and individual works of genius may, indeed, be occasionally brought to light, under the impulses of the high feeling which has conceived them; but, I fear, a good, wholesome, profitable, and continued pecuniary support is the applause that talent most craves. The fact, that an American publisher can get an English work without money, must, for a few years longer (unless legislative protection shall be extended to their own authors), have a tendency to repress a national literature.[5] No man will pay a writer for an epic, a tragedy, a sonnet, a history, or a romance, when he can get a work of equal merit for nothing. I

---

4. A decade later Cooper took to the courts in a personal crusade against scurrilous newspaper editors.

5. The lack of an international copyright law handicapped American writers until 1891.

have conversed with those who are conversant on the subject, and, I confess, I have been astonished at the information they imparted.

A capital American publisher has assured me that there are not a dozen writers in this country, whose works he should feel confidence in publishing at all, while he reprints hundreds of English books without the least hesitation. This preference is by no means so much owing to any difference in merit, as to the fact that, when the price of the original author is to be added to the uniform hazard which accompanies all literary speculations, the risk becomes too great. The general taste of the reading world in this country is better than that of England.[6] The fact is both proved and explained by the circumstance that thousands of works that are printed and read in the mother country, are not printed and read here. The publisher on this side of the Atlantic has the advantage of seeing the reviews of every book he wishes to print, and, what is of far more importance, he knows, with the exception of books that he is sure of selling, by means of a name, the decision of the English critics before he makes his choice. Nine times in ten, popularity, which is all he looks for, is a sufficient test of general merit. Thus, while you find every English work of character, or notoriety, on the shelves of an American book-store, you may ask in vain for most of the trash that is so greedily devoured in the circulating libraries of the mother country, and which would be just as eagerly devoured here, had not a better taste been created by a compelled abstinence. That taste must now be overcome before such works could be sold at all.

When I say that books are not rejected here, from any want of talent in the writers, perhaps I ought to explain. I wish to express something a little different. Talent is sure of too many avenues to wealth and honours, in America, to seek, unnecessarily, an unknown and hazardous path. It is better paid in the ordinary pursuits of life, than it would be likely to be paid by an adventure in which an extraordinary and skilful, because practised, foreign competition is certain. Perhaps high talent does not often make the trial with the American bookseller; but it is precisely for the reason I have named.

The second obstacle against which American literature has to contend is in the poverty of materials. There is scarcely an ore which contributes to the wealth of the author, that is found, here, in veins as rich as in Europe. There are no annals for the historian; no follies (beyond the most vulgar and common place) for the satirist; no manners for the dramatist; no obscure fictions for the writer of romance; no gross and hardy offences against decorum for the moralist; nor any of the rich artificial auxiliaries of poetry. The weakest hand can extract a spark from the flint, but it would baffle the strength of a giant to attempt kindling a flame with a pudding stone.[7] I very well know there are theorists who assume that the society and institutions of this country are, or ought to be, particularly favourable to novelties and variety. But the experience of one month, in these states, is sufficient to show any observant man the falsity of their position. The effect of a promiscuous assemblage any where, is to create a standard of deportment; and great liberty permits every one to aim at its attainment. I have never seen a nation so much alike in my life, as the people of the United States, and what is more, they are not only like each other, but they are remarkably like that which common sense tells them they ought to resemble. No doubt, traits of character that are a little peculiar, with-

6. "The writer does not mean that the best taste of America is better than that of England; perhaps it is not quite so good; but, as a whole, the American reading world requires better books than the whole of the English reading world" [Cooper's note].
7. Soft, sandy rock unfit to serve as a flintstone.

out, however, being either very poetical, or very rich, are to be found in remote districts; but they are rare, and not always happy exceptions. In short, it is not possible to conceive a state of society in which more of the attributes of plain good sense, or fewer of the artificial absurdities of life, are to be found, than here. There is no costume for the peasant, (there is scarcely a peasant at all,) no wig for the judge, no baton for the general, no diadem for the chief magistrate. The darkest ages of their history are illuminated by the light of truth; the utmost efforts of their chivalry are limited by the laws of God; and even the deeds of their sages and heroes are to be sung in a language that would differ but little from a version of the ten commandments. However useful and respectable all this may be in actual life, it indicates but one direction to the man of genius.

It is very true there are a few young poets now living in this country, who have known how to extract sweets from even these wholesome, but scentless native plants. They have, however, been compelled to seek their inspiration in the universal laws of nature, and they have succeeded, precisely in proportion as they have been most general in their application. Among these gifted young men, there is one (Halleck)[8] who is remarkable for an exquisite vein of ironical wit, mingled with a fine, poetical, and, frequently, a lofty expression. This gentleman commenced his career as a satirist in one of the journals of New York. Heaven knows, his materials were none of the richest; and yet the melody of his verse, the quaintness and force of his comparisons, and the exceeding humour of his strong points, brought him instantly into notice. He then attempted a general satire, by giving the history of the early days of a *belle*.[9] He was again successful, though every body, at least every body of any talent, felt that he wrote in leading-strings.[1] But he happened, shortly after the appearance of the little volume just named (Fanny), to visit England. Here his spirit was properly excited, and, probably on a rainy day, he was induced to try his hand at a *jeu d'esprit*,[2] in the mother country. The result was one of the finest semi-heroic ironical descriptions to be found in the English language.[3] This simple fact, in itself, proves the truth of a great deal of what I have just been writing, since it shews the effect a superiority of material can produce on the efforts of a man of true genius.

Notwithstanding the difficulties of the subject, talent has even done more than in the instance of Mr. Halleck. I could mention several other young poets of this country of rare merit. By mentioning Bryant, Percival, and Sprague,[4] I shall direct your attention to the names of those whose works would be most likely to give you pleasure. Unfortunately they are not yet known in Italian, but I think even you would not turn in distaste from the task of translation which the best of their effusions will invite.

The next, though certainly an inferior branch of imaginative writing, is fictitious composition. From the facts just named, you cannot expect that the novelists, or romance writers of the United States, should be very successful. The same reason will be likely, for a long time to come, to repress the ardour of dramatic genius. Still, tales and plays are no novelties in the literature of this country. Of the former, there are many as old as soon after the revolution;

---

8. Fitz-Greene Halleck (1790–1867), New York writer.
9. This book is *Fanny* (1819), a satire of society in New York City.
1. I.e., in a state of dependence or subservient imitation; from "leading-strings" used to support and guide children learning to walk.

2. A clever, playful little work (French).
3. "This little *morceau* of pleasant irony is called Alnwick Castle" [Cooper's note]. *Morceau* is French for morsel, or bit. *Alnwick Castle* was published in 1827.
4. William Cullen Bryant (1794–1878). James Gates Percival (1795–1856). Charles Sprague (1791–1875).

and a vast number have been published within the last five years. One of their authors of romance, who curbed his talents by as few allusions as possible to actual society, is distinguished for power and comprehensiveness of thought. I remember to have read one of his books (Wieland)[5] when a boy, and I take it to be a never-failing evidence of genius, that, amid a thousand similar pictures which have succeeded, the images it has left still stand distinct and prominent in my recollection. This author (Mr. Brockden Brown) enjoys a high reputation among his countrymen, whose opinions are sufficiently impartial, since he flattered no particular prejudice of the nation in any of his works.

The reputation of Irving[6] is well known to you. He is an author distinguished for a quality (humour) that has been denied his countrymen; and his merit is the more rare, that it has been shewn in a state of society so cold and so restrained. Besides these writers, there are many others of a similar character, who enjoy a greater or less degree of favour in their own country. The works of two or three have even been translated (into French) in Europe, and a great many are reprinted in England. Though every writer of fiction in America has to contend against the difficulties I have named, there is a certain interest in the novelty of the subject, which is not without its charm. I think, however, it will be found that they have all been successful, or the reverse, just as they have drawn warily, or freely, on the distinctive habits of their own country. I now speak of their success purely as writers of romance. It certainly would be possible for an American to give a description of the manners of his own country, in a book that he might choose to call a romance, which should be read, because the world is curious on the subject, but which would certainly never be read for that nearly indefinable poetical interest which attaches itself to a description of manners less bald and uniform. All the attempts to blend history with romance in America, have been comparative failures, (and perhaps fortunately,) since the subjects are too familiar to be treated with the freedom that the imagination absolutely requires. Some of the descriptions of the progress of society on the borders,[7] have had a rather better success, since there is a positive, though no very poetical, novelty in the subject; but, on the whole, the books which have been best received, are those in which the authors have trusted most to their own conceptions of character, and to qualities that are common to the rest of the world and to human nature. This fact, if its truth be admitted, will serve to prove that the American writer must seek his renown in the exhibition of qualities that are general, while he is confessedly compelled to limit his observations to a state of society that has a wonderful tendency not only to repress passion, but to equalize humours.

The Americans have always been prolific writers on polemics and politics. Their sermons and fourth of July orations are numberless. Their historians, without being very classical or very profound, are remarkable for truth and good sense. There is not, perhaps, in the language a closer reasoner in metaphysics than Edwards;[8] and their theological writers find great favour among the sectarians of their respective schools.

The stage of the United States is decidedly English. Both plays and players, with few exceptions, are imported. Theatres are numerous, and they are to be found in places where a traveller would little expect to meet them. Of course

5. *Wieland, or The Transformation* (1798), by Charles Brockden Brown (1771–1810).
6. Washington Irving (1783–1859). In private Cooper had only contemptuous remarks to make of Irving, whom he regarded as overpaid for his writings and alto- gether too flexible in his political allegiances.
7. The most famous such work was Cooper's own *The Pioneers* (1823).
8. Jonathan Edwards (1703–1758), American theologian.

they are of all sizes and of every degree of decoration and architectural beauty known in Europe, below the very highest. The façade of the principal theatre in Philadelphia is a chaste specimen in marble, of the Ionic, if my memory is correct. In New York, there are two theatres about as large as the Théâtre Français[9] (in the interior), and not much inferior in embellishments. Besides these, there is a very pretty little theatre, where lighter pieces are performed, and another with a vast stage for melo-dramas. There are also one or two other places of dramatic representation in this city, in which horses and men contend for the bays.

The Americans pay well for dramatic talent. Cooke,[1] the greatest English tragedian of our age, died on this side of the Atlantic; and there are few players of eminence in the mother country who are not tempted, at some time or other, to cross the ocean. Shakspeare, is of course, the great author of America, as he is of England, and I think he is quite as well relished here as there. In point of taste, if all the rest of the world be any thing against England, that of America is the best, since it unquestionably approaches nearest to that of the continent of Europe. Nearly one half of the theatrical taste of the English is condemned by their own judgments, since the stage is not much supported by those who have had an opportunity of seeing any other. You will be apt to ask me how it happens, then, that the American taste is better? Because the people, being less exaggerated in their habits, are less disposed to tolerate caricatures, and because the theatres are not yet sufficiently numerous (though that hour is near) to admit of a representation that shall not be subject to the control of a certain degree of intelligence. I have heard an English player complain that he never saw such a dull audience as the one before which he had just been exhibiting; and I heard the same audience complain that they never listened to such dull jokes. Now, there was talent enough in both parties; but the one had formed his taste in a coarse school, and the others had formed theirs under the dominion of common sense. Independently of this peculiarity, there is a vast deal of acquired, travelled taste in this country. English tragedy, and high English comedy, both of which, you know, are excellent, never fail here, if well played; that is, they never fail under the usual limits of all amusement. One will cloy of sweets. But the fact of the taste and judgment of these people, in theatrical exhibitions, is proved by the number of their good theatres, compared to their population.

Of dramatic writers there are none, or next to none. The remarks I have made in respect to novels apply with double force to this species of composition. A witty and successful American comedy could only proceed from extraordinary talent. There would be less difficulty, certainly, with a tragedy; but still, there is rather too much foreign competition, and too much domestic employment in other pursuits, to invite genius to so doubtful an enterprise. The very baldness of ordinary American life is in deadly hostility to scenic representation. The character must be supported solely by its intrinsic power. The judge, the footman, the clown, the lawyer, the belle, or the beau, can receive no great assistance from dress. Melo-dramas, except the scene should be laid in the woods, are out of the question. It would be necessary to seek the great clock, which is to strike the portentous twelve blows, in the nearest church; a vaulted passage would degenerate into a cellar; and, as for ghosts,

9. Great national theater in Paris.
1. George Frederick Cooke (1756–1811), English Shakespearean actor.

the country was discovered, since their visitations have ceased.[2] The smallest departure from the incidents of ordinary life would do violence to every man's experience; and, as already mentioned, the passions which belong to human nature must be delineated, in America, subject to the influence of that despot—common sense.

Notwithstanding the overwhelming influence of British publications, and all the difficulties I have named, original books are getting to be numerous in the United States. The impulses of talent and intelligence are bearing down a thousand obstacles. I think the new works will increase rapidly, and that they are destined to produce a powerful influence on the world. We will pursue this subject another time.—Adieu.

2. The too-sweeping assertion is a little obscured by the syntax: i.e., Europeans had ceased to believe in ghosts by the time they landed in America.

THE CHEROKEE MEMORIALS

In 1829, gold was discovered at Dahlonega, on the western boundary of the Cherokee Nation, in the state of Georgia. Georgia had for some time wished to rid itself of its Indian population; now, the desire to mine Cherokee gold, and the fact that Andrew Jackson had been elected president the previous year, spurred Georgians to press for Indian removal. Jackson, having made his national reputation as an Indian fighter, had made it clear that he favored removing the American Indians from the eastern states to lands west of the Mississippi River. It was also his position, consistent with that of Georgia, that independent governments (like that of the Cherokee Nation) should not exist within the borders of any of the states.

In 1830, the Indian Removal Act, authorizing the president to relocate eastern Indians to lands west of the Mississippi, was passed in the Senate by a vote of 28 to 20, and then in the House, by a vote of 103 to 97. As Representative Henry Storrs of New York noted, we might now "break up [the Indians'] society, dissolve their institutions, and drive them into the wilderness." Jackson signed the bill into law on May 28, 1830. According to Alexis de Tocqueville, the French social observer, who visited the United States in 1831,

> The Spaniards by unparalleled atrocities which brand them with indelible shame, did not succeed in exterminating the Indian race and could not even prevent them from sharing their rights; the United States Americans have attained both these results without spilling blood and without violating a single one of the great principles of morality in the eyes of the world. It is impossible to destroy men with more respect to the laws of humanity.

The Cherokee were well aware of the intentions of Georgia and of President Jackson. Able to write their own language in the syllabary devised by the mixed-blood Sequoyah (George Guess) in 1821, and with substantial numbers of the population literate in English, the Cherokee took up the pen to fight for their traditional homelands. In 1828, the Cherokee Buck Watie, who had taken the name of Elias Boudinot, founded and edited *The Cherokee Phoenix*, which, according to the Cherokee scholar Rennard Strickland, "contain[ed] the most articulate presentation of the Cherokee position" against removal. Editorials in the *Phoenix* were reprinted in newspapers in New Orleans, New York, Philadelphia, and Baltimore in the fight against passage of the Removal Act.

The Cherokee also engaged directly with the courts, the Congress, and the various officers of the federal government, sending letters, briefs, and petitions. In addition, they presented to Congress "memorials," documents that, in the nineteenth century, had approximately the status of a petition. Bills for the removal of the Cherokee had been introduced into both houses of Congress early in 1830, and debate on the Removal Bill had begun in the House on February 24. On March 15, the Cherokee Council, led by Principal Chief John Ross, aided by Clerk of Council John Ridge and Delegate Lewis Ross, offered an official document, along with twelve other memorials from "the native citizens of the nation themselves."

The official document of the council, probably authored mainly by Ridge, opens with what must be an intentional, although unstated, reference to the Declaration of Independence. Where the Declaration made known the "long train of abuses and usurpations" for which the British king George III was responsible, the Cherokee memorial establishes the wrongs done by his namesake state, Georgia, petitioning the Congress of the United States, the same body that had adopted the Declaration, for redress of grievances. But where the colonists had found it necessary to *declare* their independence, the Cherokee find themselves compelled, instead, to *affirm* their independence. The writers of the memorial exploit the irony that the Declaration of Independence, the document that had proclaimed the sovereignty of the United States of America, should now be used (as President Jackson and members of his cabinet had done) to undermine the sovereignty of an indigenous nation. Acknowledging that Georgia and the president have the power to force them to unfamiliar lands west of the Mississippi, the Cherokee Council insists that the use of such power would lead to a sorry end. The memorial of the council imagines for the Cherokee a happier fate than forced removal. In the florid language of the period, the Cherokee Council offers a vision of the further advancement of the Cherokee people "in civilized life . . . science and Christian knowledge," on the lands which they have for long occupied.

The memorial of the Cherokee citizens is less formal that that of the Cherokee Council. Its rhetorical strategies invoke, in some degree, traditional Cherokee oratorical practices. For example, in the third paragraph, the Cherokee citizens employ a language of kinship: "Brothers—we address you according to usage adopted by our forefathers." This form of familial address, "brother to brother" rather than child to father, returns to the habits of *eighteenth*-century Indian oratory, when indigenous people and settlers treated one another more nearly as equals ("brother to brother") rather than as inferior to superior ("red *children* to their white *fathers*"). Neither the rhetorical sophistication of the official memorial's textual references nor the more oral mode of the citizens's memorial kept the Cherokee from being driven from their homelands.

After passage of the Removal Act, the government continued to exert pressure on the Cherokee *voluntarily* to remove. In 1835, Elias Boudinot, his uncle Major Ridge, and cousin John Ridge, along with other Cherokee who had reluctantly concluded that further resistance was futile, signed the Treaty of New Echota, agreeing to the cession of Cherokee lands in the east in exchange for lands west of the Mississippi. But a majority of the Cherokee nation still did not wish to go. Finally, in the winter of 1838–9, federal troops under the command of General Winfield Scott were sent to enforce the treaty. Some twelve thousand Cherokee people were driven westward on the infamous Trail of Tears. One-third, fully four thousand people, died en route before the survivors reached Indian Country in what would eventually become Oklahoma.

All the selections printed here are from the 21st Congress, 1st session, report 311.

[Note on the Accompanying Memorials, February 15, 1830][1]

Brown's Hotel, Washington City

Hon. Speaker of the House of Representatives:

Sir: The accompanying memorials you will please lay before the House over which you preside; the one from the late General Council of our nation, and signed by all the members of that body, and principal chief, in behalf of the Cherokee nation, relative to the present unpleasant state of affairs[1] in consequence of certain causes therein stated; the others, twelve in number, are from the native citizens of the nation themselves, and adopted throughout the country, and to which are appended upwards of three thousand names. They have been forwarded to us by mail, to be laid before Congress. Their object, as will appear, is to prove to that honorable body, that the many reports of late circulated by officers of the Government, that a greater portion of the Cherokees are favorably disposed to a removal Westward, and are only restrained by the threats and tyranny of their chiefs, are erroneous, and entirely unfounded. They wish to speak of their wishes and determination in that respect themselves, and to be heard by the representatives of the United States; they wish them to be convinced, that, to know their feelings and interests, is to know that they ardently desire to remain in peace and quietude upon their ancient territory, and to enjoy the comforts and advantages of civilization; that the great mass of our citizens are opposed to removal, (as has been plainly demonstrated by the offers and inducements lately held out to them) and that it is not the fear of chiefs that has forced upon them their determination to remain; but that it has been produced by causes no less than convincing evidence, that their only and best hopes of preservation and advancement in moral and civil improvement is to remain where their Great Father alone placed them. There they wish to pursue agriculture, and to educate their sons and daughters in the sciences and knowledge of things which pertain to their future happiness. With these remarks, we submit the memorials for the consideration of Congress, humbly hoping that the grievances of our nation will be heard, and duly considered.

[Memorial of the Cherokee Council, November 5, 1829]

To the Honorable Senate and House of Representatives of the United States of America in Congress assembled.

We, the representatives of the people of the Cherokee nation, in general council convened, compelled by a sense of duty we owe to ourselves and nation, and confiding in the justice of your honorable bodies, address and make known to you the grievances which disturb the quiet repose and harmony of our citizens, and the dangers by which we are surrounded. Extraordinary as this course may appear to you, the circumstances that have imposed

1. Refers to the introduction of the Removal Bill into the House and Senate and to Georgia's passage of legislation that would bring any Cherokee who remained in Georgia under Georgia's laws, a situation that would effectively destroy Cherokee sovereignty as a nation.

upon us this duty we deem sufficient to justify the measure; and our safety as individuals, and as a nation, require that we should be heard by the immediate representatives of the people of the United States, whose humanity and magnanimity, by permission and will of Heaven, may yet preserve us from ruin and extinction.

The authorities of Georgia have recently and unexpectedly assumed a doctrine, horrid in its aspect, and fatal in its consequences to us, and utterly at variance with the laws of nations, of the United States, and the subsisting treaties between us, and the known history of said State, of this nation, and of the United States. She claims the exercise of sovereignty over this nation; and has threatened and decreed the extension of her jurisdictional limits over our people. The Executive of the United States, through the Secretary of War,[1] in a letter to our delegation of the 18th April last, has recognised this right to be abiding in, and possessed by, the State of Georgia; by the Declaration of Independence, and the treaty of peace concluded between the United States and Great Britain in 1783; and which it is urged vested in her all the rights of sovereignty pertaining to Great Britain, and which, in time previously, she claimed and exercised, within the limits of what constituted the "thirteen United States." It is a subject of vast importance to know whether the power of self-government abided in the Cherokee nation at the discovery of America, three hundred and thirty-seven years ago; and whether it was in any manner affected or destroyed by the charters of European potentates. It is evident from facts deducible from known history, that the Indians were found here by the white man, in the enjoyment of plenty and peace, and all the rights of soil and domain, inherited from their ancestors from time immemorial, well furnished with kings, chiefs, and warriors, the bulwarks of liberty, and the pride of their race. Great Britain established with them relationships of friendship and alliance, and at no time did she treat them as subjects, and as tenants at will, to her power. In war she fought them as a separate people, and they resisted her as a nation. In peace, she spoke the language of friendship, and they replied in the voice of independence, and frequently assisted her as allies, at their choice to fight her enemies in their own way and discipline, subject to the control of their own chiefs, and unaccountable to European officers and military law. Such was the connexion of this nation to Great Britain, to wit, that of friendship, and not allegiance, to the period of the declaration of Independence by the United States, and during the Revolutionary contest, down to the treaty of peace between the United States and Great Britain, forty-six years ago, when she abandoned all hopes of conquest, and at the same time abandoned her Cherokee allies to the difficulties in which they had been involved, either to continue the war, or procure peace on the best terms they could, and close the scenes of carnage and blood, that had so long been witnessed and experienced by both parties. Peace was at last concluded at Hopewell, in '85, under the administration of Washington, by "the Commissioners, Plenipotentiaries of the United States in Congress assembled:" and the Cherokees were received "into the favor and protection of the United States of America." It remains to be proved, under a view of all these circumstances, and the knowledge we have of history, how our right to self-government was affected and destroyed by the Declaration of Independence, which never

1. I.e., John Eaton. President Andrew Jackson (the "Executive of the United States") believed that treating the Indians as sovereign nations was a mistake and that Indian occupancy of lands within the United States was simply owing to the generosity and goodwill of the federal government and the states in question.

noticed the subject of Cherokee sovereignty; and the treaty of peace, in '83, between Great Britain and the United States, to which the Cherokees were not a party; but maintained hostilities on their part to the treaty of Hopewell, afterwards concluded. If, as it is stated by the Hon. Secretary of War, that the Cherokees were mere tenants at will,[2] and only permitted to enjoy possession of the soil to pursue game; and if the States of North Carolina and Georgia were sovereigns in truth and in right over us; why did President Washington send "Commissioners Plenipotentiaries" to treat with the subjects of those States? Why did they permit the chiefs and warriors to enter into treaty, when, if they were subjects, they had grossly rebelled and revolted from their allegiance? And why did not those sovereigns make their lives pay the forfeit of their guilt, agreeably to the laws of said States? The answer must be plain— they were not subjects, but a distinct nation, and in that light viewed by Washington, and by all the people of the Union, at that period. In the first and second articles of the Hopewell treaty, and the third article of the Holston treaty,[3] the United States and the Cherokee nation were bound to a mutual exchange of prisoners taken during the war; which incontrovertibly proves the possession of sovereignty by *both* contracting parties. It ought to be remembered too, in the conclusions of the treaties to which we have referred, and most of the treaties subsisting between the United States and this nation, that the phraseology, composition, etc. was always written by the Commissioners, on the part of the United States, for obvious reasons: as the Cherokees were unacquainted with letters. Again, in the Holston treaty, eleventh article, the following remarkable evidence is contained that our nation is not under the jurisdiction of any State: "If any citizen or inhabitant of the Untied States, or of either of the territorial districts of the United States, shall go into any town, settlement, or territory, belonging to the Cherokees, and shall there commit any crime upon, or trespass against, the person or property of any peaceable and friendly Indian or Indians, which, *if committed within the jurisdiction of any State, or within the jurisdiction of either of the said districts*, against a citizen or any white inhabitant thereof, would be punishable by the laws of such State or district, such offender or offenders shall be proceeded against in the same manner as if the offence had been committed *within the jurisdiction of the State or district* to which he or they may belong, against a citizen or white inhabitant thereof." The power of a State may put our national existence under its feet, and coerce us into her jurisdiction; but it would be contrary to legal right, and the plighted faith of the United States' Government. It is said by Georgia and the Honorable Secretary of War, that one sovereignty cannot exist within another, and, therefore, we must yield to the stronger power; but is not this doctrine favorable to our Government, which does not interfere with that of any other? Our sovereignty and right of enforcing legal enactments, extend no further than our territorial limits, and that of Georgia is, and

2. I.e., the will of the states and the federal government "to allow" the Cherokee to live on their own ancestral lands. These lands came into the possession of the United States as a result of the Declaration of Independence and victory in the Revolutionary War. The Treaty of Hopewell, signed November 28, 1785, was the first treaty between the Cherokee and the United States enacted after the Revolutionary War. It established the boundaries of Cherokee lands and was negotiated as an agreement between two sovereign nations. The Cherokee refer to the treaty to show that they were once recognized as an independent nation

and should still be treated as such.
3. Signed July 2, 1791, this treaty gave the federal government (not the states) exclusive right to regulate all citizens' trade with the Cherokee and redrew the boundaries, much encroached on by the settlers, of Cherokee lands. It also affirmed "Perpetual peace between the United States and the Cherokee Nation," and forbade non-Cherokee persons from hunting on or traversing Cherokee lands without a passport issued by the federal government. The Cherokee cite this as further evidence of their having been treated as a sovereign nation in the past.

has always terminated at, her limits. The constitution of the United States (article 6) contains these words: "All treaties made under the authority of the United States shall be the supreme law of the land, and the judges in every State shall be bound thereby, any thing in the laws or constitution of any State to the contrary notwithstanding." The sacredness of treaties, made under the authority of the United States, is paramount and supreme, stronger than the laws and constitution of any State. The jurisdiction, then, of our nation over its soil is settled by the laws, treaties, and constitution of the United States, and has been exercised from time out of memory.

Georgia has objected to the adoption, on our part, of a constitutional form of government, and which has in no wise violated the intercourse and connexion which bind us to the United States, its constitution, and the treaties thereupon founded, and in existence between us. As a distinct nation, notwithstanding any unpleasant feelings it might have created to a neighboring State, we had a right to improve our Government, suitable to the moral, civil, and intellectual advancement of our people; and had we anticipated any notice of it, it was the voice of encouragement by an approving world. We would, also, while on this subject, refer your attention to the memorial and protest submitted before your honorable bodies, during the last session of Congress, by our delegation then at Washington.

Permit us, also, to make known to you the aggrieved and unpleasant situation under which we are placed by the claim which Georgia has set up to a large portion of our territory, under the treaty of the Indian Springs concluded with the late General M'Intosh[4] and his party; and which was declared void, and of no effect, by a subsequent treaty between the Creek Nation and the United States, at Washington City. The President of the United States, through the Secretary of War, assured our delegation, that, so far as he understood the Cherokees had rights, protection should be afforded; and, respecting the intrusions on our lands, he had been advised, "and instructions had been forwarded to the agent of the Cherokees, directing him to cause their removal; and earnestly hoped, that, on this matter, all cause for future complaint would cease, and the order prove effectual." In consequence of the agent's neglecting to comply with the instructions, and a suspension of the order made by the Secretary afterwards, our border citizens are at this time placed under the most unfortunate circumstances, by the intrusions of citizens of the United States, and which are almost daily increasing, in consequence of the suspension of the once contemplated "effectual order." Many of our people are experiencing all the evils of personal insult, and, in some instances, expulsion from their homes, and loss of property, from the unrestrained intruders let loose upon us, and the encouragement they are allowed to enjoy, under the last order to the agent for this nation, which amounts to a suspension of the force of treaties, and the wholesome operation of the intercourse laws[5] of the United States. The reason alleged by the War Department for this suspension is, that it had been requested so to do, until the claim the State of Georgia has made to a portion of the Cherokee country be determined; and the intruders are to remain unmolested within the border limits of this nation. We beg leave to protest against this unprecedented procedure. If the State of Georgia has a

4. General William McIntosh was a Creek Indian leader who signed the Treaty of Indian Springs on February 12, 1785, The treaty ceded Creek lands to the state of Georgia and agreed to the removal of the Creek to west of the Mississippi. But the Creek had earlier denied McIntosh's right to act on their behalf and did not honor the treaty. McIntosh was assassinated, and John Ridge and David Vann were engaged to negotiate a new treaty, the "subsequent treaty" referred to below.
5. Laws regulating trade.

claim to any portion of our lands, and is entitled by law and justice to them, let her seek through a legal channel to establish it; and we do hope that the United States will not suffer her to take possession of them forcibly, and investigate her claim afterwards.

Arguments to effect the emigration of our people, and to escape the troubles and disquietudes incident to a residence contiguous to the whites, have been urged upon us, and the arm of protection has been withheld, that we may experience still deeper and ampler proofs of the correctness of the doctrine; but we still adhere to what is right and agreeable to ourselves; and our attachment to the soil of our ancestors is too strong to be shaken. We have been invited to a retrospective view of the past history of Indians, who have melted away before the light of civilization, and the mountains of difficulties that have opposed our race in their advancement in civilized life. We have done so; and, while we deplore the fate of thousands of our complexion and kind, we rejoice that our nation stands and grows a lasting monument of God's mercy, and a durable contradiction to the misconceived opinion that the aborigines are incapable of civilization. The opposing mountains, that cast fearful shadows in the road of Cherokee improvement, have dispersed into vernal clouds; and our people stand adorned with the flowers of achievement flourishing around them, and are encouraged to secure the attainment of all that is useful in science and Christian knowledge.

Under the fostering care of the United States we have thus prospered; and shall we expect approbation, or shall we sink under the displeasure and rebukes of our enemies?

We now look with earnest expectation to your honorable bodies for redress, and that our national existence may not be extinguished before a prompt and effectual interposition is afforded in our behalf. The faith of your Government is solemnly pledged for our protection against all illegal oppressions, so long as we remain firm to our treaties; and that we have, for a long series of years, proved to be true and loyal friends, the known history of past events abundantly proves. Your Chief Magistrate himself has borne testimony of our devotedness in supporting the cause of the United States, during their late conflict with a foreign foe. It is with reluctant and painful feelings that circumstances have at length compelled us to seek from you the promised protection, for the preservation of our rights and privileges. This resort to us is a last one, and nothing short of the threatening evils and dangers that beset us could have forced it upon the nation but it is a right we surely have, and in which we cannot be mistaken—that of appealing for justice and humanity to the United States, under whose kind and fostering care we have been led to the present degree of civilization, and the enjoyment of its consequent blessings. Having said thus much, with patience we shall await the final issue of your wise deliberations.

[Memorial of the Cherokee Citizens, December 18, 1829]

To the Honorable Senate and House of Representatives of the United States of America in Congress assembled:

The undersigned memorialists humbly make known to your honorable bodies, that they are free citizens of the Cherokee nation. Circumstances of late occurrence have troubled our hearts, and induced us at this time to appeal to you, knowing that you are generous and just. As weak and poor children are accustomed to look to their guardians and patrons for protection, so we would come and make our grievances known. Will you listen to us? Will you have pity upon us? You are great and renowned—the nation which you represent is like a mighty man who stands in his strength. But we are small—our name is not renowned. You are wealthy, and have need of nothing; but we are poor in life, and have not the arm and power of the rich.

By the will of our Father in Heaven, the Governor of the whole world, the red man of America has become small, and the white man great and renowned. When the ancestors of the people of these United States first came to the shores of America, they found the red man strong—though he was ignorant and savage, yet he received them kindly, and gave them dry land to rest their weary feet. They met in peace, and shook hands in token of friendship. Whatever the white man wanted and asked of the Indian, the latter willingly gave. At that time the Indian was the lord, and the white man the suppliant. But now the scene has changed. The strength of the red man has become weakness. As his neighbors increased in numbers, his power became less and less, and now, of the many and powerful tribes who once covered these United States, only a few are to be seen—a few whom a sweeping pestilence[1] has left. The Northern tribes, who were once so numerous and powerful, are now nearly extinct. Thus it has happened to the red man of America. Shall we, who are remnants, share the same fate?

Brothers—we address you according to usage adopted by our forefathers, and the great and good men who have successfully directed the Councils of the nation you represent. We now make known to you our grievances. We are troubled by some of your own people. Our neighbor, the State of Georgia, is pressing hard upon us, and urging us to relinquish our possessions for her benefit. We are told, if we do not leave the country which we dearly love, and betake ourselves to the Western wilds, the laws of the State will be extended over us, and the time, 1st of June, 1830, is appointed for the execution of the edict. When we first heard of this, we were grieved, and appealed to our father the President, and begged that protection might be extended over us. But we were doubly grieved when we understood from a letter of the Secretary of War to our Delegation, dated March of the present year, that our father the President had refused us protection, and that he had decided in favor of the extension of the laws of the State over us. This decision induces us to appeal to the immediate Representatives of the American people. We love, we dearly love our country, and it is due to your honorable bodies, as well as to us, to make known why we think the country is ours, and why we wish to remain in peace where we are.

The land on which we stand we have received as an inheritance from our fathers, who possessed it from time immemorial, as a gift from our common Father in Heaven. We have already said, that, when the white man came to the shores of America, our ancestors were found in peaceable possession of this very land. They bequeathed it to us as their children, and we have sacredly kept it, as containing the remains of our beloved men. This right of inheritance we have *never ceded*, nor ever *forfeited*. Permit us to ask, what better

---

1. This pestilence is both literal and figurative. Native populations were severely diminished by exposure to diseases to which the Europeans had developed immunities. The figurative reference is to the equally devastating effects of conflict with settlers who persistently ventured onto Indian lands, taking the law into their own hands, and rarely answering to any governmental authority.

right can the people have to a country, than the right of *inheritance* and *immemorial peaceable possession?* We know it is said of late by the State of Georgia, and by the Executive of the United States, that we have forfeited this right—but we think this is said gratuitously. At what time have we made the forfeit? What great crime have we committed, whereby we must forever be divested of our country and rights? Was it when we were hostile to the United States, and took part with the King of Great Britain, during the struggle for Independence? If so, why was not this forfeiture declared in the first treaty of peace between the United States and our beloved men? Why was not such an article as the following inserted in the treaty: "The United States give peace to the Cherokees, but, for the part they took in the late war, declare them to be but tenants at will, to be removed, when the convenience of the States within whose chartered limits they live, shall require it." That was the proper time to assume such a possession. But it was not thought of, nor would our forefathers have agreed to any treaty, whose tendency was to deprive them of their rights and their country. All that they have conceded and relinquished are inserted in the treaties, open to the investigation of all people. We would repeat, then, the right of inheritance and peaceable possession which we claim, we have never ceded nor forfeited.

In addition to that first of all first, the right of inheritance and peaceable possession, we have the faith and pledge of the United States, repeated over and over again, in treaties made at various times. By these treaties, our rights as a separate people are distinctly acknowledged, and guaranties given that they shall be secured and protected. So we have always understood the treaties. The conduct of the Government towards us from its organization until very lately, the talks given to our beloved men by the Presidents of the United States, and the speeches of the Agents and Commissioners, all concur to show that we are not mistaken in our interpretation. Some of our beloved men who signed the treaties are still living, and their testimony tends to the same conclusion. We have always supposed that this understanding of the treaties was in concordance with the views of the Government, nor have we ever imagined that any body would interpret them otherwise. In what light shall we view the conduct of the United States and Georgia, in their intercourse with us, in urging us to enter into treaties, and cede lands? If we were but tenants at will, why was it necessary that our consent must first be obtained, before these Governments could take lawful possession of our lands? The answer is obvious. These Governments perfectly understood our rights—our right to the country, and our right to self Government. Our understanding of the treaties is further supported by the intercourse law of the United States, which prohibits all encroachments upon our territory. The undersigned memorialists humbly represent, that if their interpretation of the treaties has been different from that of the Government, then they have ever been deceived as to how the Government regarded them, and what she has asked and promised. Moreover, they have uniformly misunderstood their own acts.

In view of the strong ground upon which their rights are founded, your memorialists solemnly protest against being considered as tenants at will, or as mere occupants of the soil, without possessing the sovereignty. We have already stated to your honorable bodies, that our forefathers were found in possession of this soil in full sovereignty, by the first European settlers; and as we have never ceded nor forfeited the occupancy of the soil, and the sovereignty over it, we do solemnly protest against being forced to leave it, either by direct or indirect measures. To the land, of which we are now in possession, we are attached. It is our fathers' gift; it contains their ashes; it is the land of our nativity, and the land of our intellectual birth. We cannot consent to abandon it for another *far inferior*, and which holds out to us no inducements. We do moreover protest against the arbitrary measures of our neighbor, the State of Georgia, in her attempt to extend her laws over us, in surveying our lands without our consent, and in direct opposition to the treaties and the intercourse law of the United States, and interfering with our municipal regulations in such a manner as to derange the regular operation of our own laws. To deliver and protect them from all these and every encroachment upon their rights, the undersigned memorialists do most earnestly pray your honorable bodies. Their existence and future happiness are at stake. Divest them of their liberty and country, and you sink them in degradation, and put a check, if not a final stop, to their present progress in the arts of civilized life, and in the knowledge of the Christian religion. Your memorialists humbly conceive, that such an act would be in the highest degree oppressive. From the people of these United States, who, perhaps, of all men under heaven, are the most religious and free, it cannot be expected. Your memorialists, therefore, cannot anticipate such a result. You represent a virtuous, intelligent, and Christian nation. To you they willingly submit their cause for your righteous decision.

AUGUSTUS BALDWIN LONGSTREET

1790–1870

Augustus Baldwin Longstreet was born on September 22, 1790, in Augusta, Georgia, of parents from New Jersey; his ancestry was primarily English, French, and Dutch ("Langstraet"); in his time, as later, Georgia had a high percentage of emigrants from Northern states. After attending a notable school in Willington, South Carolina, he consciously followed John C. Calhoun's path, graduating from Yale in 1813 (his teachers included some of the "Connecticut Wits"), then studying law in Litchfield, Connecticut, and passing the Georgia bar examination in 1815. Two years later he married and shared an exceptionally happy family life despite suffering the loss of young children and much later the trauma of the Civil War, until his wife's death in 1868. Longstreet was elected to the state's General Assembly in 1821 and was elected judge of the superior court in 1822; in 1824 he abandoned the race for Congress when his first son died. He became a Methodist minister (licensed to preach in 1829); owned and edited the Augusta *State Rights' Sentinel* from 1834 to 1836; and then in 1839 became president of Emory College, still in Oxford, Georgia, and only two years old. In 1849 he became president of Centenary College in Jackson, Louisiana, then of the University of Mississippi (his second time at a town named Oxford), and in 1858 president of South Carolina College in Columbia (now the University of South Carolina). In the war he was a refugee, never without funds but piteous because of his age; during the occupation of Oxford, Mississippi, Grant's soldiers burned his house down, destroying his library and private papers.

In the early 1830s, recalling his experiences in traveling through the seven counties of his judicial district (and still other counties, when filling in for a fellow judge) and drawing on his already well-known skill at tale telling, Longstreet began writing realistic, occasionally humorous, sketches for newspaper publication under two pseudonyms: Hall, the name put to stories mainly about men, was taken from a Georgian who signed the Declaration of Independence, and Baldwin, the name put to stories about women, was his own middle name and the name of a Georgian who signed the Constitution. When Longstreet bought his own newspaper he republished some earlier stories as well as new ones, and in 1835, at his own newspaper press but without sufficient supervision, he printed, anonymously, *Georgia Scenes, Characters, Incidents, &c., in the First Half Century of the Republic. By a Native Georgian.* It had, throughout the country, remarkable success; Poe praised it in a long review in the *Southern Literary Messenger.* In the late 1830s and early 1840s Longstreet wrote more stories, some of which he published in his friend William Tappan Thompson's *Augusta Mirror* and *Southern Miscellany,* others in Simms's *The Magnolia,* always keeping in mind an enlarged edition he never found time to complete. By 1840, when his authorship was an open secret, the popular demand for the book in the North led the Harpers to reprint it prefaced by a rueful complaint that they had not been able to prevail on the author to revise the work.

Neglected but never forgotten, Longstreet has been, as James B. Meriwether explains, mislabeled as "a Southwestern humorist," when he was not a Southwesterner and not primarily a humorist but rather a social historian, an early literary realist as keenly aware as Irving of the mutability of American lives and American landscapes. Longstreet had insisted in his preface: "The following sketches were written rather in the hope that chance would bring them to light when time would give them an interest, than in the belief that they would afford any interest to the readers of the present day." A letter he wrote to T. W. White, the publisher of the *Southern Literary Messenger* (whom Longstreet assumed had written the review in that magazine), makes clear that that original purpose also applies to the augmented volume he hoped to publish: "The leading object of the Georgia Scenes, is to enable those who came after us, to see us *precisely as we are.* If my life be spared; they will [be] carried through all ranks of society. I have often desired to see the Greeks and Romans, as they saw each other. . . . The time will come perhaps, when the same desire will be felt to know all about us; and to gratify that desire, I am now writing."

Among those who knew Georgia, the authenticity of the sketches was never doubted, but Longstreet remained, as Meriwether says, "a rather lonely pioneer of literary realism." Yet his influence was enormous. In his own time, he made possible, as much as Irving, the writing of George Washington Harris, and his influence on the young Samuel L. Clemens was strong, as, much later, was his influence on William Faulkner. (The young Faulkner read his way around the library in the home of his friend Phil Stone, the house where Longstreet's son-in-law L. C. Q. Lamar had lived; some of Longstreet's books were still in the house, and Phil Stone had as a boy outraged General James Longstreet, the nephew of the writer, by asking about the general's much disputed delay in obeying Lee's orders at Gettysburg—graphic evidence of how the Civil War impinged on Southern lives into the middle of this century. A. B. Longstreet and William Faulkner are buried not far from each other in St. Peter's Cemetery, in Oxford, Mississippi, fitting proximity for two men who wrote the best horse-swapping stories in our literature.)

Literary scholars are at last giving Longstreet the attention he deserves. Meriwether and Leo Lemay have refined the author's own distinctions between the two personas used in the sketches, and James M. Cox has called *Georgia Scenes* "as 'good' a book as Hawthorne's *Twice-Told Tales,* published two years later. It has as much art, imagination, perception, and insight as Hawthorne's early work possesses." In our search for an aesthetically, historically, and socially honest canon of American literature (especially for the nineteenth century) we are only beginning to challenge the hegemony of the Bearded Poets and New England prose masters; regional prejudice is as real as sexual and racial prejudice, and sometimes as subtle.

The Horse-Swap[1]

During the session of the Supreme Court, in the village of——, about three weeks ago, when a number of people were collected in the principal street of the village, I observed a young man riding up and down the street, as I supposed, in a violent passion. He galloped this way, then that, and then the other; spurred his horse to one group of citizens, then to another; then dashed off at half speed, as if fleeing from danger; and, suddenly checking his horse, returned—first in a pace, then in a trot, and then in a canter.[2] While he was performing these various evolutions, he cursed, swore, whooped, screamed, and tossed himself in every attitude which man could assume on horse back. In short, he *cavorted* most magnanimously, (a term which, in our tongue, expresses all that I have described, and a little more), and seemed to be setting all creation at defiance. As I like to see all that is passing, I determined to take a position a little nearer to him, and to ascertain if possible, what it was that affected him so sensibly.[3] Accordingly I approached a crowd before which he had stopt for a moment, and examined it with the strictest scrutiny.—But I could see nothing in it that seemed to have any thing to do with the cavorter. Every man appeared to be in good humor, and all minding their own business. Not one so much as noticed the principal figure. Still he went on. After a semicolon pause, which my appearance seemed to produce (for he eyed me closely as I approached) he fetched a whoop, and swore that "he could out-swap any live man, woman, or child that ever walked these hills, or that ever straddled horse flesh since the days of old daddy Adam. "Stranger," said he to me, "did you ever see the *Yallow* Blossom from Jasper?"

"No," said I, "but I have often heard of him."

"I'm the boy," continued he; "perhaps a *leetle*, jist a *leetle* of the best man at a horse swap, that ever trod shoe-leather."

I began to feel my situation a little awkward, when I was relieved by a man somewhat advanced in years, who stept up and began to survey the "*Yallow Blossom's*" horse with much apparent interest. This drew the rider's attention, and he turned the conversation from me to the stranger.

"Well, my old coon," said he, "do you want to swap *hosses?*"

"Why, I don't know," replied the stranger; "I believe I've got a beast I'd trade with you for that one, if you like him."

"Well, fetch up your nag, my old cock; you're jist the lark[4] I wanted to get hold of. I am perhaps a *leetle*, jist a *leetle*, of the best man at a horse swap that ever stole *cracklins* out of his mammy's fat gourd.[5] Where's your *hoss?*"

"I'll bring him presently; but I want to examine your horse a little."

---

1. The sketch was first printed in the Milledgeville, Georgia, *Southern Recorder* of November 13, 1833, and collected in *Georgia Scenes* (1835), the source of the present text, which has been silently emended to correct the sort of "typographical errors" Longstreet deplored in his preface. In reprinting the book in 1840 the Harpers regretted that they had been unable "to prevail upon the author to revise the work," and took it on themselves to correct the text at many points.
2. A three-beat gait in which the horse's feet touch in this order beginning with the right hind leg—right hind, left hind and right fore (almost at once), then for a moment all four feet are off the ground before the left foreleg touches. "Pace": gait in which the legs move in

lateral pairs, the horse being supported alternately on the right and the left side. "Trot": a pace of two-time in which the legs move in diagonal pairs (near fore and off hind, off fore and near hind), but not quite simultaneously.
3. Obviously, keenly.
4. A wild fellow, a "rattlepate."
5. "Cracklins": the crisp residue after a hog's skin, fatty pieces, and well-washed intestines have been rendered down to make lard, comparable in snack function to our packaged potato chips and flavored corn chips but more chewy, greasy, and strong. The dried shell of the gourd holds lard (and some cracklings) ready for use, while greater quantities are stored in a crock.

"Oh! look at him," said the Blossom, alighting and hitting him a cut; "look at him. He's the best piece of *hoss* flesh in the thirteen united univarsal worlds.[6] There's no sort o' mistake in little Bullet. He can pick up miles on his feet, and fling 'em behind him as fast as the next man's *hoss,* I don't care where he comes from.—And he can keep at it as long as the sun can shine without resting."

During this harangue, little Bullet looked as if he understood it all, believed it, and was ready at any moment to verify it. He was a horse of goodly countenance, rather expressive of vigilance than fire; though an unnatural appearance of fierceness was thrown into it, by the loss of his ears, which had been cropt pretty close to his head. Nature had done but little for Bullet's head and neck; but he managed, in a great measure, to hide their defects, by bowing perpetually. He had obviously suffered severely for corn; but if his ribs and hip bones had not disclosed the fact, *he* never would have done it; for he was in all respects, as cheerful and happy, as if he commanded all the corn-cribs and fodder stacks in Georgia. His height was about twelve hands;[7] but as his shape partook somewhat of that of the giraffe, his haunches stood much lower. They were short, strait,[8] peaked, and concave. Bullet's tail, however, made amends for all his defects. All that the artist could do to beautify it, had been done; and all that horse could do to compliment the artist, Bullet did. His tail was nicked in superior style, and exhibited the line of beauty in so many directions, that it could not fail to hit the most fastidious taste in some of them. From the root it dropt into a graceful festoon; then rose in a handsome curve; then resumed its first direction; and then mounted suddenly upwards like a cypress knee[9] to a perpendicular of about two and a half inches. The whole had a careless and bewitching inclination to the right. Bullet obviously knew where his beauty lay, and took all occasions to display it to the best advantage. If a stick cracked, or if any one moved suddenly about him, or coughed, or hawked,[1] or spoke a little louder than common, up went Bullet's tail like lightning; and if the *going up* did not please, the *coming down* must of necessity, for it was as different from the other movement, as was its direction. The first, was a bold and rapid flight upward; usually to an angle of forty-five degrees. In this position he kept his interesting appendage, until he satisfied himself that nothing in particular was to be done; when he commenced dropping it by half inches, in second beats—then in triple time[2]—then faster and shorter, and faster and shorter still; until it finally died away imperceptibly into its natural position. If I might compare sights to sounds, I should say, its *settling,* was more like the note of a locust[3] than any thing else in nature.

Either from native sprightliness of disposition, from uncontrolable activity, or from an unconquerable habit of removing flies by the stamping of the feet,

---

6. The original states.
7. Forty-eight inches high, counting a handbreadth as four inches.
8. Narrow.
9. The knobbed slanting formation found at the base of cypress trees.
1. Cleared throat (noisily) before spitting. Mark Twain marked through "or hawked" as he prepared to anthologize this story, violating the spirit of Longstreet's last paragraph in the preface to *Georgia Scenes:* "I cannot conclude these introductory remarks, without reminding those who have taken exceptions to the

coarse, inelegant, and sometimes ungrammatical language, which the writer represents himself as occasionally using; *that it is language accommodated to the capacity of the person to whom he represents himself as speaking.*"
2. The horse's tail is compared to a conductor's baton, first waving up and down in double time, then waving faster, back and forth, in triple time.
3. Cicada or seventeen-year locust, large flying insect; the males have vibrating membranes on the underside of the abdomen that produce long, shrill noises.

Bullet never stood still; but always kept up a gentle fly-scaring movement of his limbs, which was peculiarly interesting.

"I tell you, man," proceeded the Yellow Blossom, "he's the best live hoss that ever trod the grit of Georgia. Bob Smart knows the hoss. Come here, Bob, and mount this hoss, and show Bullet's motions." Here Bullet bristled up, and looked as if he had been hunting for Bob all day long, and had just found him. Bob sprang on his back. "Boo-oo-oo!" said Bob, with a fluttering noise of the lips; and away went Bullet, as if in a quarter race,[4] with all his beauties spread in handsome style.

"Now fetch him back," said Blossom. Bullet turned and came in pretty much as he went out.

"Now trot him by." Bullet reduced his tail to "*customary*"—sidled to the right and left airily, and exhibited at least three varieties of trot, in the short space of fifty yards.

"Make him pace!" Bob commenced twitching the bridle and kicking at the same time. These inconsistent movements obviously (and most naturally) disconcerted Bullet; for it was impossible for him to learn, from them, whether he was to proceed or stand still. He started to trot—and was told that wouldn't do. He attempted a canter—and was checked again. He stopt and was urged to go on. Bullet now rushed into the wide field of experiment, and struck out a gait of his own, that completely turned the tables upon his rider, and certainly deserved a patent. It seemed to have derived its elements from the jig, the minuet, and the cotillon.[5] If it was not a pace, it certainly had *pace* in it; and no man would venture to call it any thing else; so it passed off to the satisfaction of the owner.

"Walk him!" Bullet was now at home again; and he walked as if money was staked on him.

The stranger, whose name I afterward learned was Peter Ketch, having examined Bullet to his heart's content, ordered his son Neddy to go and bring up Kit. Neddy soon appeared upon Kit; a well formed sorrel[6] of the middle size, and in good order. His *tout ensemble*[7] threw Bullet entirely in the shade, though a glance was sufficient to satisfy any one that Bullet had the decided advantage of him in point of intellect.

"Why man," said Blossom, "do you bring such a hoss as that to trade for Bullet? Oh, I see you're no notion of trading."

"Ride him off, Neddy!" said Peter. Kit put off at a handsome lope.[8]

"Trot him back!" Kit came in at a long, sweeping trot, and stopt suddenly at the crowd.

"Well," said Blossom, "let me look at him; may be he'll do to plough."

"Examine him!" said Peter, taking hold of the bridle close to the mouth; "he's nothing but a tacky.[9] He an't as *pretty* a horse as Bullet, I know; but he'll do. Start 'em together for a hundred and fifty *mile*; and if Kit an't twenty mile ahead of him at the coming out, any man may take Kit for nothing. But he's a monstrous mean horse, gentlemen; any man may see that. He's the scariest horse, too, you ever saw. He won't do to hunt on, no how. Stranger, will you

---

4. A race a quarter of a mile long.
5. A ballroom dance for couples, resembling the quadrille. "Jig": a lively dance in triple rhythm. "Minuet": a slow, graceful dance, consisting of a coupé (a quick changing of one foot for the other), a high step, and a balance (the reciprocal movement of dancers toward and back from each other).
6. A horse of a light chestnut color.
7. Entire aspect (French).
8. A smooth gait in which the horse canters in front and trots behind.
9. A "weedy" horse, a sorry-looking beast.

let Neddy have your rifle to shoot off him? Lay the rifle between his ears, Neddy, and shoot at the blaze[1] in that stump. Tell me when his head is high enough."

Ned fired, and hit the blaze; and Kit did not move a hair's breadth.

"Neddy, take a couple of sticks, and beat on that hogshead[2] at Kit's tail."

Ned made a tremendous rattling, at which Bullet took fright, broke his bridle, and dashed off in grand style; and would have stopt all farther negotiations, by going home in disgust, had not a traveller arrested him and brought him back; but Kit did not move.

"I tell you, gentlemen," continued Peter, "he's the scariest horse you ever saw. He an't as gentle as Bullet, but he won't do any harm if you watch him. Shall I put him in a cart, gig,[3] or wagon for you, stranger? He'll cut the same capers there he does here. He's a monstrous mean horse."

During all this time Blossom was examining him with the nicest scrutiny. Having examined his frame and limbs, he now looked at his eyes.

"He's got a curious look out of his eyes," said Blossom.

"Oh yes, sir," said Peter, "just as blind as a bat. Blind horses always have clear eyes. Make a motion at his eyes, if you please, sir."

Blossom did so, and Kit threw up his head rather as if something pricked him under the chin, than as if fearing a blow. Blossom repeated the experiment, and Kit jerked back in considerable astonishment.

"Stone blind, you see, gentlemen," proceeded Peter; "but he's just as good to travel of a dark night as if he had eyes."

"Blame my buttons," said Blossom, "if I like them eyes."

"No," said Peter, "nor I neither. I'd rather have 'em made of diamonds; but they'll do, if they don't show as much white as Bullet's."

"Well," said Blossom, "make a pass[4] at me."

"No," said Peter; "you made the banter, now make your pass."

"Well, I'm never afraid to price my hosses. You must give me twenty-five dollars boot."[5]

"Oh, certainly; say fifty, and my saddle and bridle in. Here, Neddy, my son, take away daddy's horse."

"Well," said Blossom, "I've made my pass, now you make yours."

"I'm for short talk in a horse swap, and therefore always tell a gentleman, at once, what I mean to do. You must give me ten dollars."

Blossom swore absolutely, roundly, and profanely, that he never would give boot.

"Well," said Peter, "I didn't care about trading; but you cut such high shines, that I thought I'd like to back you out, and I've done it. Gentlemen, you see I've brought him to a hack."[6]

"Come, old man," said Blossom, "I've been joking with you. I begin to think you do want to trade; therefore, give me five dollars and take Bullet. I'd rather lose ten dollars any time, than not make a trade; though I hate to fling away a good hoss."

"Well," said Peter, "I'll be as clever[7] as you are. Just put the five dollars on Bullet's back and hand him over, it's a trade."

1. Mark made by chipping off a section with an ax, originally to mark a trail.
2. Barrel, containing 100 to 140 gallons.
3. A light one-horse carriage.
4. Sally, offer.
5. Bonus, above the exchange of horses.
6. Halt.
7. Good-natured, agreeable.

Blossom swore again, so roundly as before, that he would not give boot; and, said he, "Bullet wouldn't hold five dollars on his back, no how. But, as I bantered you, if you say an even swap, here's at you."

"I told you," said Peter, "I'd be as clever as you; therefore, here goes two dollars more, just for trade[8] sake. Give me three dollars, and it's a bargain."

Blossom repeated his former assertion; and here the parties stood for a long time, and the by-standers (for many were now collected,) began to taunt both parties. After some time, however, it was pretty unanimously decided that the old man had backed Blossom out.

At length Blossom swore he "never would be backed out, for three dollars, after bantering a man;" and accordingly they closed the trade.

"Now," said Blossom, as he handed Peter the three dollars, "I'm a man, that when he makes a bad trade, makes the most of it until he can make a better. I'm for no rues and after-claps."[9]

"That's just my way," said Peter; "I never goes to law to mend my bargains."

"Ah, you're the kind of boy I love to trade with. Here's your hoss, old man. Take the saddle and bridle off him, and I'll strip yours; but lift up the blanket easy from Bullet's back, for he's a mighty tenderbacked hoss."

The old man removed the saddle, but the blanket stuck fast. He attempted to raise it, and Bullet bowed himself, switched his tail, danced a little, and gave signs of biting.

"Don't hurt him, old man," said Blossom, archly; "take it off easy. I am, perhaps, a leetle of the best man at a horse-swap that ever catched a coon."

Peter continued to pull at the blanket more and more roughly; and Bullet became more and more *cavortish*: in so much that when the blanket came off, he had reached the *kicking* point in good earnest.

The removal of the blanket, disclosed a sore on Bullet's backbone that seemed to have defied all medical skill. It measured six full inches in length, and four in breadth; and had as many features as Bullet had motions. My heart sickened at the sight; and I felt that the brute who had been riding him in that situation deserved the halter.[1]

The prevailing feeling, however, was that of mirth. The laugh became loud and general, at the old man's expense, and rustic witticisms were liberally bestowed upon him and his late purchase. These, Blossom continued to provoke by various remarks. He asked the old man "if he thought Bullet would let five dollars lie on his back." He declared most seriously, that he had owned that horse three months, and had never discovered before, that he had a sore back, "or he never should have thought of trading him," &c., &c.

The old man bore it all with the most philosophic composure. He evinced no astonishment at his late discovery, and made no replies. But his son, Neddy, had not disciplined his feelings quite so well. His eyes opened, wider and wider, from the first to the last pull of the blanket; and when the whole sore burst upon his view, astonishment and fright seemed to contend for the mastery of his countenance. As the blanket disappeared, he stuck his hands in his breeches pockets, heaved a deep sigh, and lapsed into a profound revery, from which he was only roused by the cuts at his father. He bore them as long as he could; and, when he could contain himself no longer, he began, with a certain wildness of expression, which gave a peculiar interest to what he

---

8. I.e., trade's.
9. Regrets or belated complaints following a suppos-

edly closed or settled deal.
1. Hangman's noose.

uttered: "His back's mighty bad off; but dod drot my soul, if he's put it to daddy as bad as he thinks he has, for old Kit's both blind and *deef*, I'll be dod drot if he eint."

"The devil he is," said Blossom.

"Yes, dod drot my soul if he *eint*. You walk him and see if he *eint*. His eyes don't look like it; but he'd *jist as leve*[2] go *agin* the house with you, or in a ditch, as any how. Now you go try him." The laugh was now turned on Blossom; and many rushed to test the fidelity of the little boy's report. A few experiments established its truth beyond controversy.

"Neddy" said the old man, "you oughtn't to try and make people discontented with their things." "Stranger, don't mind what the little boy says. If you can only get Kit rid of them little failings, you'll find him all sorts of a horse. You are a *leetle* the best man at a horse swap, that ever I got hold of; but don't fool away Kit. Come, Neddy, my son, let's be moving; the stranger seems to be getting snappish."

HALL

1833, 1835

A Sage Conversation[1]

I love the aged matrons of our land. As a class, they are the most pious, the most benevolent, the most useful, and the most harmless of the human family. Their life, is a life of good offices. At home, they are patterns of industry, care, economy, and hospitality; abroad, they are ministers of comfort, peace, and consolation. Where affliction is, there are they, to mitigate its pangs; where sorrow is, there are they to assuage its pains. Nor night, nor day, nor summer's heat, nor winter's cold, nor angry elements, can deter them from scenes of suffering and distress. They are the first at the fevered couch, and the last to leave it. They hold the first and last cup to the parched lip. They bind the aching head, close the dying eye, and linger in the death-stricken habitation, to pour the last drop of consolation into the afflicted bosoms of the bereaved. I cannot, therefore, ridicule them myself, nor bear to hear them ridiculed in my presence. And yet, I am often amused at their conversations; and have amused *them* with a rehearsal[2] of their own conversations, taken down by me when they little dreamed that I was listening to them. Perhaps my reverence for their character, conspiring with a native propensity to extract amusement

---

2. Soon.

1. A *Sage Conversation* was first printed in the Augusta *State Rights Sentinel* of March 17, 1835, and was included in *Georgia Scenes* (1835), the source of the present text; some small changes have been adopted from the Harper text (1840) or made independently. The short sketch belongs in the tradition of humorous accounts of the accommodations travelers had to content themselves with (contemporaries would have known that the Spouter Inn section of *Moby-Dick* was in the same genre). It also belongs to, and to some extent sets, the tradition of recording the conversation of women—a tradition to which Eudora Welty and Flannery O'Connor have made triumphant contributions. Julia Penelope Stanley and Susan J. Wolfe in "Toward

a Feminist Aesthetic," *Chrysalis* 6 (1978), have tried to define a connection between women's conversation and women's writing styles, women being more "expressive" than men, using "run-on, infinite syntax" and a "discursive, conjunctive style." Such theory risks treating women reductively. Longstreet does not patronize women, and his follower Samuel L. Clemens delighted in recording male command of such talk as occurs in this story. James B. Meriwether has done his best to gain the story new readers: "Homosexuality, transvestitism, seduction and betrayal are the dark underlying themes of this sketch, skillfully and delicately handled."

2. Repetition.

from all that passes under my observation, has accustomed me to pay a uniformly strict attention to all they say in my presence.

This much in extraordinary courtesy to those who cannot distinguish between a simple narrative of an amusing interview, and ridicule of the parties to it. Indeed I do not know that the conversation which I am about to record, will be considered amusing by any of my readers. Certainly the amusement of the readers of my own times, is not the leading object of it, or of any of the "Georgia Scenes;" forlorn as may be the hope that their main object will ever be answered.

When I seated myself to the sheet now before me, my intention was merely to detail a conversation between three ladies, which I heard many years since; confining myself to only so much of it as sprung from the ladies' own thoughts, unawakened by the suggestions of others; but, as the manner of its introduction will perhaps interest some of my readers, I will give it.

I was travelling with my old friend, Ned Brace,[3] when we stopped at the dusk of the evening at a house on the road side, for the night. Here we found three nice, tidy, aged matrons, the youngest of whom could not have been under sixty; one of them of course was the lady of the house, whose husband, old as he was, had gone from home upon a land exploring expedition. She received us hospitably, had our horses well attended to, and soon prepared for us a comfortable supper. While these things were doing, Ned and I engaged the other two in conversation; in the course of which, Ned deported himself with becoming seriousness. The kind lady of the house occasionally joined us, and became permanently one of the party, from the time the first dish was placed on the table. At the usual hour, we were summoned to supper; and as soon as we were seated, Ned, unsolicited, and most unexpectedly to me, said grace.—I knew full well that this was a prelude to some trick, I could not conjecture what. His explanation (except so much as I discovered myself) was, that he knew that one of us would be asked to say grace, and he thought he might as well save the good ladies the trouble of asking. The matter was, however, more fully explained just before the moment of our retiring to bed arrived. To this moment the conversation went round between the good ladies and ourselves, with mutual interest to all.—It was much enlivened by Ned, who was capable, as the reader has been heretofore informed, of making himself extremely agreeable in all company; and who, upon this occasion, was upon his very best behaviour. It was immediately after I had looked at my watch in token of my disposition to retire for the night, that the conversation turned upon marriages, happy and unhappy, strange, unequal, runaways, &c. Ned rose in the midst of it, and asked the landlady where we should sleep. She pointed to an open shed-room adjoining the room in which we were sitting, and separated from it by a log partition, between the spaces of which might be seen all that passed in the dining room; and so close to the fireplace of this apartment, that a loud whisper might be easily heard from one to the other.

"The strangest match," said Ned, resuming the conversation with a parson's gravity, "that ever I heard of, was that of George Scott and David Snow: two

3. Brace is first introduced in *The Character of a Native Georgian* as a satirist of the "beau in the presence of his mistress, the fop, the pedant, the purse-proud, the over-fastidious and sensitive" but also as what we would identify as a consummate put-on artist who plays his roles for the pleasure of his own performance and the observation of his audiences.

most excellent men, who became so much attached to each other that they actually got married—"

"The lackaday!" exclaimed one of the ladies.

"And was it really a fact?" enquired another.

"Oh, yes, ma'am," continued Ned; "I knew them very well, and often went to their house; and no people could have lived happier or managed better than they did. And they raised a lovely parcel of children—as fine a set as I ever saw, except their youngest son, Billy: he was a little wild, but, upon the whole, a right clever boy himself.—Come, friend Baldwin, we're setting up too late for travellers." So saying, Ned moved to the shed-room, and I followed him.

The ladies were left in silent amazement; and Ned, suspecting, doubtless, that they were listening for a laugh from our chamber as we entered it, continued the subject with unabated gravity, thus: "You knew those two men, didn't you?"

"Where did they live!" enquired I, not a little disposed to humor him.

"Why, they lived down there, on Cedar Creek, close by Jacob Denman's— Oh, I'll tell you who their daughter Nancy married—she married John Clarke—you knew *him* very well."

"Oh, yes," said I, "I knew John Clarke very well.—*His* wife *was* a most excellent woman."

"Well, the boys were just as clever, for boys, as she was for a girl, except Bill; and I never heard any thing *very* bad of him, unless it was his laughing in church; that put me more out of conceit of him than any thing I ever knew of him.———Now, Baldwin, when I go to bed, I go to bed to *sleep*, and not to talk; and, therefore, from the time my head touches the pillow, there must be no more talking. Besides, we must take an early start to-morrow, and I'm tired." So saying, he hopped into his bed, and I obeyed his injunctions.

Before I followed his example, I could not resist the temptation of casting an eye through the cracks of the partition, to see the effect of Ned's wonderful story upon the kind ladies. Mrs. Barney (it is time to give their names) was setting in a thoughtful posture; her left hand supporting her chin, and her knee supporting her left elbow. Her countenance was that of one who suffers from a slight tooth-ache. Mrs. Shad leaned forward, resting her fore-arm on her knees, and looking into the fire as if she saw *groups of children* playing in it. Mrs. Reed, the landlady, who was the fattest of the three, was thinking and laughing alternately at short intervals. From my bed, it required but a slight change of position to see any one of the group at pleasure.

I was no sooner composed on my pillow, than the old ladies drew their chairs close together, and began the following colloquy in a low undertone, which rose as it progressed:

Mrs. Barney. Didn't that man say them was two *men* that got married to one another?

Mrs. Shad. It seemed to me so.

Mrs. Reed. Why to be sure he did.—I know he said so; for he said what their names was.

Mrs. B. Well, in the name o' sense, what did the man mean by saying they raised a fine pa'cel of children?

Mrs. R. Why, bless your heart and soul, honey! that's what I've been thinkin' about. It seems mighty curious to me some how or other. I can't study it out, no how.

Mrs. S. The man must be jokin', certainly.

Mrs. R. No, he wasn't jokin'; for I looked at him, and he was just as much in yearnest as any body I ever *seed:* and besides, no *Christian* man would tell such a story in that solemn way. And didn't you hear that other man say he knew their da'ter Nancy?

Mrs. S. But, la messy! Mis' Reed, it can't be so. It doesn't stand to reason; don't you know it don't?

Mrs. R. Well; I wouldn't think so; but it's hard for me some how to dispute a *Christian* man's word.

Mrs. B. I've been thinking the thing all over in my mind, and I reckon— now I don't say it is so, for I don't know nothing at all about it—but I reckon that one o'them men was a woman dress'd in men's clothes; for I've often hearn o' women doin' them things, and following their true-love to the wars, and bein' a waitin'-boy to 'em, and all sich.

Mrs. S. Well, may be it's some how in that way—but, la' me! 'twould o' been obliged to been found out; don't you know it would? Only think how many children she had. Now it stands to reason, that at some time or other it must have been found out.

Mrs. R. Well, I'm an old woman any how, and I reckon the good man won't mind what an old woman says to him; so bless the Lord, if I live to see the morning, I'll ask him about it.

I knew that Ned was surpassed by no man living in extricating himself from difficulties; but how he was to escape from this, with even tolerable credit to himself, I could not devise.

The ladies here took leave of Ned's marvellous story, drew themselves closely round the fire, lighted their pipes, and proceeded as follows:

Mrs. B. Jist before me and my old man was married, there was a gal name Nancy Mountcastle (puff——puff,) and she was a mighty likely gal——(puff) I know'd her mighty well—she dressed herself up in men's clothes—(puff, puff,) and followed Jemmy Darden from P'ankatank, in KING AND QUEEN— (puff) clean up to LOUDON.[4]

Mrs. S. (puff, puff, puff, puff, puff.) And did he marry her?

Mrs. B. (sighing deeply). No: Jemmy didn't marry her—pity he hadn't, poor thing.

Mrs. R. Well, I know'd a gal on Tar river,[5] done the same thing—(puff, puff, puff.) She followed Moses Rusher 'way down somewhere in the South State—(puff, puff.)

Mrs. S. (puff, puff, puff, puff.) And what did he do?

Mrs. R. Ah—(puff, puff,) Lord bless your soul, honey, I can't tell you what he did. Bad enough.

Mrs. B. Well, now it seems to me—I don't know much about it—but it seems to me men don't like to marry gals that take on that way. It looks like it puts 'em out o'concait[6] of 'em.

Mrs. S. I know'd one man that married a woman that followed him from Car'lina to this State; but she didn't dress herself in men's clothes. You both know 'em.—You know Simpson Trotty's sister and Rachæl's son Reuben. 'Twas him and his wife.

---

4. Village on the Piankatank River, in King and Queen County, eastern Virginia; Loudon County is in northern Virginia. (The emphasis on county as a his-torical-geographical unit persists from English termi-nology.)
5. In northeast North Carolina; it flows southeast into the Pemlico.
6. Conceit, favorable opinion.

Mrs. R. and Mrs. B. Oh yes, I know 'em mighty well.

Mrs. S. Well, it was his wife—she followed him out to this State.

Mrs. B. I know'd 'em all mighty well. Her da'ter Lucy was the littlest teeny bit of a thing when it was born I ever did see. But they tell me that when I was born—now I don't know any thing about it myself—but the old folks used to tell me, that when I was born, they put me in a quart-mug, and mought o' covered me up in it.

Mrs. S. The lackaday!

Mrs. R. What ailment did Lucy die of, Mis Barney?

Mrs. B. Why, first she took the ager[7] and fever, and took a 'bundance o' doctor's means for that. And then she got a powerful bad cough, and it kept gittin' worse and worse, till at last it turned into a consumption, and she jist nat'ly wasted away, till she was nothing but skin and bone, and she died; but, poor creater, she died mighty happy, and I think in my heart, she made the prettiest corpse, considerin', of anybody I most ever seed.

Mrs. R. and Mrs. S. Emph! (solemnly.)

Mrs. R. What did the doctors give her for the fever and ager?

Mrs. B. Oh, they gin' her a 'bundance o' truck[8]—I don't know what all; and none of 'em holp her at all. But at last she got over it, some how or other. If they'd have just gin' her a sweat o' bitter yerbs,[9] jist as the spell was comin' on, it would have cured her right away.

Mrs. R. Well, I reckon sheep-saffron[1] the onliest thing in nater for the ager.

Mrs. B. I've always hearn it was wonderful in hives, and measly ailments.

Mrs. R. Well, it's jist as good for an ager—it's a powerful sweat. Mrs. Clarkson told me, that her cousin Betsey's aunt Sally's Nancy was cured sound and well by it, of a hard shakin' ager.

Mrs. S. Why, you don't tell me so!

Mrs. R. Oh bless your heart, honey, it's every word true; for she told me so with her own mouth.

Mrs. S. "A hard, hard shakin' ager!!"

Mrs. R. Oh yes, honey, it's the truth.

Mrs. S. Well, I'm told that if you'll wrap the inside skin of an egg round your little finger, and go three days reg'lar to a young persimmon,[2] and tie a string round it, and every day tie three knots in it, and then not go agin for three days, that the ager will leave you.

Mrs. B. I've often hearn o' that, but I don't know about it. Some people don't believe in it.

Mrs. S. Well, Davy Cooper's wife told me, she didn't believe in it; but she tried it, and it cured her sound and well.

Mrs. R. I've hearn of many folks bein' cured in that way. And what did they do for Lucy's cough, Mis' Barney.

Mrs. B. Oh, dear me, they gin' her a powerful chance o' truck. I reckon, first and last, she took at least a pint o'lodimy.[3]

Mrs. S. and Mrs. R. The law!

Mrs. S. Why that ought to have killed her, if nothing else. If they'd jist gin' her a little cumfry and alecampane,[4] stewed in honey, or sugar, or molasses,

---

7. Ague.
8. Stuff.
9. Herbs.
1. Probably bastard saffron or safflower, used in medicine as a substitute for saffron.
2. I.e., a persimmon tree.

3. Laudanum, a tincture of opium.
4. I.e., elecampane; the root of this herb was once used as a remedy for pulmonary diseases. "Cumfry": i.e., comfrey; this herb was once used to stem internal bleeding, heal bones, and curb coughing.

with a little lump o' mutton suet or butter in it: it would have cured her in two days sound and well.

Mrs. B. I've always counted cumfry and alecampane the lead of all yerbs for colds.

Mrs. S. Horehound and sugar's mazin good.

Mrs. B. Mighty good—mighty good.

Mrs. R. Powerful good. I take mightily to a sweat of sage-tea, in desperate bad colds.

Mrs. S. And so do I, Mis' Reed. Indeed I have a great leanin' to sweats of yerbs, in all ailments sich as colds, and rheumaty pains, and pleurisies, and sich—they're wonderful good. Old brother Smith came to my house from Bethany meeting, in a mighty bad way, with a cold, and cough, and his throat and nose all stopt up; seemed like it would 'most take his breath away, and it was dead o' winter, and I had nothin' but dried yerbs, sich as camomile, sage, pennyryal, catmint, horehound,[5] and sich; so I put a hot rock to his feet, and made him a large bowl o' catmint tea, and I reckon he drank most two quarts of it through the night, and it put him in a mighty fine sweat, and loosened all the *phleem*, and opened all his head; and the next morning, says he to me, says he, sister Shad—you know he's a mighty kind spoken man, and always was so 'fore he joined society;[6] and the old man likes a joke yet right well, the old man does; but he's a mighty good man, and I think he prays with greater libity,[7] than most any one of his age I most ever seed—don't you think he does, Mis' Reed?

Mrs. R. Powerful.

Mrs. B. Who did he marry?

Mrs. S. Why, he married—stop, I'll tell you directly————Why, what does make my old head forget so?

Mrs. B. Well, it seems to me I don't remember like I used to. Didn't he marry a Ramsbottom?

Mrs. R. No. Stay, I'll tell you who he married presently—Oh, stay! why I'll tell you who he married!—He married old daddy Johnny Hooer's da'ter, Mournin'.

Mrs. S. Why, la! messy on me, so he did!

Mrs. B. Why, did he marry a Hooer?

Mrs. S. Why, to be sure he did.—You knew Mournin'.

Mrs. B. Oh, mighty well; but I'd forgot that brother Smith married her: I really thought he married a Ramsbottom.

Mrs. R. Oh no, bless your soul, honey, he married Mournin'.

Mrs. B. Well, the law me, I'm clear beat!

Mrs. S. Oh, it's so, you may be sure it is.

Mrs. B. Emp, emph, emph, emph! And brother Smith married Mournin' Hooer! Well, I'm clear put out! Seems to me I'm gittin' mighty forgetful, some how.

5. A European mint whose hoary (whitish) leaves are used to make cough remedies and stomach tonics and also used as an anthelmintic (a drug used to kill or expel intestinal worms). "Camomile": the foliage and flower heads of this herb are strongly scented and are used as antispasmodics and diaphoretics (drugs that increase perspiration). "Sage": this common kitchen herb is an antiseptic that has been used as a general tonic.

"Pennyryal": i.e., pennyroyal; this mint was used as a culicifuge, or mosquito killer. "Catmint": i.e., catnip; this herb was used as a cough remedy and a diaphoretic.
6. Technical term from Congregationalism; here, the communicants enrolled in a particular church.
7. Liberty, facility.

Mrs. S. Oh yes, he married Mournin', and I saw her when she joined society.

Mrs. B. Why, you don't tell me so!

Mrs. S. Oh, it's the truth. She didn't join till after she was married, and the church took on mightily about his marrying one out of society. But after she joined they all got satisfied.

Mrs. R. Why, la! me, the seven stars[8] is 'way over here!

Mrs. B. Well, let's light our pipes, and take a short smoke, and go to bed. How did you come on raisin' chickens, this year, Mis' Shad?

Mrs. S. La messy, honey! I have had mighty bad luck. I had the prettiest pa'sel you most ever seed till the varment took to killin' 'em.

Mrs. R. and Mrs. B. The varment!!

Mrs. S. Oh dear, yes. The hawk catched a powerful sight of them; and then the varment took to 'em and nat'ly took 'em fore and aft, bodily, till they left most none at all hardly. Sucky counted 'em up t'other day, and there warn't but thirty-nine, she said, countin' in the old speckle hen's chickens that jist come off of her nest.

Mrs. R. and Mrs. B. Humph-h-h-h!

Mrs. R. Well, I've had bad luck too. Billy's hound-dogs broke up most all my nests.

Mrs. B. Well, so they did me, Mis' Reed. I always did despise a hound-dog upon the face of yea'th.[9]

Mrs. R. Oh, they're the bawllinest, squallinest, thievishest things ever was about one; but Billy will have 'em, and I think in my soul his old Troup's the beat of all creaters I ever seed in all my born days a suckin' o' hen's eggs—He's clean most broke me up entirely.

Mrs. S. The lackaday!

Mrs. R. And them that was hatched out, some took to takin' the gaps, and some the pip,[1] and one ailment or other, till they most all died.

Mrs. S. Well I reckon there must be somethin' in the season this year that an't good for fowls: for Larkin Goodman's brother Jimmie's wife aunt Penny, told me, she lost most all her fowls with different sorts of ailments, the like of which she never seed before—They'd jist go 'long lookin' right well, and tilt right over backwards, (*Mrs. B.* The law!) and die right away, (*Mrs. R.* Did you ever!) with a sort o' somethin' like the blind staggers.

Mrs. B. and Mrs. R. Messy on me!

Mrs. B. I reckon they must have eat[2] somethin' didn't agree with them.

Mrs. S. No, they didn't, for she fed 'em every mornin' with her own hand.

Mrs. B. Well, it's mighty curious!

A short pause ensued, which was broken by Mrs. Barney, with—"And brother Smith married Mournin' Hooer!" It came like an opiate upon my senses, and I dropt asleep.

The next morning, when we rose from our beds, we found the good ladies sitting round the fire just as I left them, for they rose long before us.

Mrs. Barney was just in the act of ejaculating, "And brother Smith married Mournin' "—when she was interrupted by our entry into the dining room. We

---

8. The Big Dipper.
9. Earth.
1. I.e., roup, disease of fowls in which scales form on the dry tip of the tongue. "Gaps": disease of fowls char-

acterized by gaping (yawning), caused by the gape-worm, a parasitic nematode infesting the trachea and bronchi.
2. Past tense, pronounced to rhyme with *yet*.

were hardly seated, before Mrs. Reed began to verify her promise. "Mr. ———,"
said she to Ned, "didn't you say last night, that them was two *men* that got
married to one another?"

"Yes, madam," said Ned.

"And didn't you say they raised a fine pa'cel of children?"

"Yes, madam, except Billy.—I said, you know, that he was a little wild."

"Well, yes; I know you said Billy wasn't as clever as the rest of them. But
we old women were talking about it last night after you went out, and none of
us could make it out, how they could have children; and I said, I reckoned
you wouldn't mind an old woman's chat; and, therefore, that I would ask you
how it could be? I suppose you won't mind telling an old woman how it was."

"Certainly not, madam. They were both widowers before they fell in love
with each other and got married."

"The lack-a-day! I wonder none of us thought o' that. And they had children
before they got married?"

"Yes, madam; they had none afterwards that I heard of."

We were here informed that our horses were in waiting, and we bade the
good ladies farewell.

BALDWIN.

1835

WILLIAM CULLEN BRYANT
1794–1878

William Cullen Bryant was born in the backwoods of Massachusetts, at Cumming-
ton, but his father was a physician who loved the classics, and Cullen, as the boy
was called, was trained early in Greek and Latin. For religion he was taught a
harsh Calvinism that held that the Fall of Adam and Eve had brought about the
Fall of Nature as well. But Bryant's first published poem was political, not about
nature and religion: when he wrote an anti-Jefferson lampoon, *The Embargo*, his
Federalist father printed it as a pamphlet (1808). Bryant entered Williams College
in 1810 but dropped out after a few months with the expectation of entering Yale.
His father could not afford that expense, and instead Bryant read for the law, being
admitted to practice in 1815. Meanwhile, in 1813 or 1814, Bryant wrote the first,
shorter version of *Thanatopsis*, the poem by which he is best remembered. Since
his early teens Bryant had been reading the melancholy and sometimes scarifying
meditations of the British "graveyard poets" of the previous decades, especially
Robert Blair (*The Grave*), Thomas Gray (*Elegy Written in a Country Churchyard*),
Bishop Beilby Porteus (*Death*), and various poems by Henry Kirke White. Such
poems by their luxurious sonorousness tempered the Calvinism instilled in the
boy, but they often poeticized religious doctrine, as in Blair's account of the resurrection at the Judgment Day: "The time draws on / When not a single spot of
burial-earth, / Whether on land, or on the spacious sea, / But must give back its
long-committed dust / Inviolate" (*The Grave*). In 1810 or soon afterward Bryant
read *Lyrical Ballads* and responded strongly to Wordsworth's near-pantheistic view
of nature. *Thanatopsis* as published in the *North American Review* in 1817 is
nondoctrinally meditative. The fuller version of 1821 concludes with a fervent
injunction to trust in something or someone who remains unspecified: Bryant's

Calvinistic earnestness was outliving his commitment to particular doctrines. (Symptomatically, a reference to the Fall of Nature in the first version of *The Prairies*, 1834, was later removed.) *Thanatopsis* won Bryant immediate acknowledgment in 1817, but a full-time career as a poet was economically impossible. In 1820, the year his father died, Bryant was appointed as justice of the peace in Berkshire County. Early in 1821 he married Frances Fairchild in Great Barrington, Massachusetts, and later that year published the very slim volume *Poems*.

Stirred by the conflict between his literary ambition and his need to support his family, Bryant in 1825 chanced a move to New York City as an editor of the *New-York Review and Atheneum Magazine*. He was welcomed as a literary celebrity and quickly fitted into metropolitan life, becoming an early member of James Fenimore Cooper's Bread and Cheese Club. His magazine failed, as almost all periodicals did at that time, but Bryant stayed on in New York as editorial assistant on the *Evening Post* (1826), then soon became part owner and editor-in-chief. Bryant was not immune to the pettier temptations of the then-brawling occupation of journalism, but over the decades he made the *Evening Post* one of the most respected newspapers in the country, mainly through editorials in which he argued out his position on many momentous issues. A deeply committed Jacksonian Democrat, despite his youthful Federalism, Bryant rarely let party loyalty interfere with principle. He led the antislavery Free-Soil movement within the Democratic party as long as this seemed a feasible way of achieving his ends, then helped to form the Republican party. In 1860 he was an influential advocate of Abraham Lincoln.

As he prospered with his newspaper, Bryant became a great traveler, at home and abroad, and through his letters to the *Evening Post* he helped to shape a sense of the world for his countrypeople. *Letters of a Traveller* appeared in 1850; *Letters of a Traveller, Second Series*, in 1859; and *Letters from the East* (that is, the Mideast) in 1869. His community service took many forms, most tangibly in his campaign for the creation of Central Park. His private life was happy. In 1844 he moved his family to a fine old farmhouse on the Sound in then-rural Long Island, and for many years he relieved his strenuous urban activity with peaceful respites at his estate, Cedarmere. Left a widower in 1866, Bryant continued to work at the *Evening Post*. Blessed with patriarchal fame and great wealth as well as astonishing health, which owed much to a daily set of vigorous exercises, Bryant in his seventies undertook the remarkably ambitious task of translating Homer. His version of the *Iliad* was published in 1870, and that of the *Odyssey* two years later. Together with the 1876 printing of his *Poems* (a new accumulation of many old and a few new verses), these translations crowned his career.

Bryant died of the consequences of a fall suffered after he gave a speech at the unveiling of a statue of the Italian patriot Joseph Mazzini in Central Park. In New York City flags were lowered to half mast, and he was mourned throughout the country as a great poet and editor.

Bryant had, in fact, written very little poetry; his translations from Homer are many times as long as his own verses. And his poems, early and late, are for the most part limited to a few subjects treated in ways that soon become predictable. His collected poetry consists of accurately rhymed or sonorously unrhymed blank verse on landscapes, flora, meteorological phenomena, historical personages and events, friends, Indian legends, and a few other topics. Yet the country's response showed plainly that he was providing what it needed at a time of national self-consciousness about the scarcity of talented poets—a loftiness of diction that at best seemed securely Miltonic, a way of making American landscapes and subjects as worthy of celebration as Old World scenes and topics, and a moral stance that blended ecumenical vagueness with didactic earnestness. Bryant's fame as a poet was accurately analyzed by his early biographer, W. A. Bradley: "He appeared much more remarkable to his early contemporaries than he ever can to us, because of the contrast which he presented with what had gone before. And later, after a period in which he suffered somewhat of an eclipse through the rise of new schools and new poets to contest with him the palm of supremacy, his great age, the traditions of an earlier day which he represented, his personality which so perfectly embodied the prophetic and seer-like aspect of the poetic ideal, and finally local pride in the possession of a poet whom New York could produce to oppose the claims of its rival, Boston, to literary supremacy,—all these tended to create a regard for Bryant that was rather personal than literary." On the strength of a few— mainly very early—poems and a notable public life, Bryant passed into what seemed, to his own time, literary immortality. Only as historians describe his part in the great political issues of his time is he passing into a perhaps truer immortality as a man who may not have been a great American poet but who led a great American life.

Thanatopsis[1]

To him who in the love of Nature holds
Communion with her visible forms, she speaks
A various language; for his gayer hours
She has a voice of gladness, and a smile
And eloquence of beauty, and she glides   5
Into his darker musings, with a mild
And gentle sympathy, that steals away
Their sharpness, ere he is aware. When thoughts
Of the last bitter hour come like a blight
Over thy spirit, and sad images   10
Of the stern agony, and shroud, and pall,
And breathless darkness, and the narrow house,
Make thee to shudder, and grow sick at heart;—
Go forth under the open sky, and list
To Nature's teachings, while from all around—   15
Earth and her waters, and the depths of air,—
Comes a still voice—Yet a few days, and thee
The all-beholding sun shall see no more
In all his course; nor yet in the cold ground,
Where thy pale form was laid, with many tears,   20
Nor in the embrace of ocean shall exist
Thy image. Earth, that nourished thee, shall claim
Thy growth, to be resolv'd to earth again;
And, lost each human trace, surrend'ring up
Thine individual being, shalt thou go   25
To mix forever with the elements,
To be a brother to th' insensible rock
And to the sluggish clod, which the rude swain
Turns with his share,[2] and treads upon. The oak
Shall send his roots abroad, and pierce thy mould.   30
Yet not to thy eternal resting place
Shalt thou retire alone—nor couldst thou wish
Couch more magnificent. Thou shalt lie down
With patriarchs of the infant world—with kings

---

1. The text is that of the first full printing, in Bryant's *Poems* (1821). The title ("Meditation on death") was supplied by an editor for the central section of the poem (lines 17–73) when that section was printed in the *North American Review* (September 1817).
2. Plowshare. "Swain": farmer.

The powerful of the earth—the wise, the good,   35
Fair forms, and hoary seers of ages past,
All in one mighty sepulchre.—The hills
Rock-ribb'd and ancient as the sun,—the vales
Stretching in pensive quietness between;
The venerable woods—rivers that move   40
In majesty, and the complaining brooks
That make the meadows green; and pour'd round all,
Old ocean's grey and melancholy waste,—
Are but the solemn decorations all
Of the great tomb of man. The golden sun,   45
The planets, all the infinite host of heaven,
Are shining on the sad abodes of death,
Through the still lapse of ages. All that tread
The globe are but a handful to the tribes
That slumber in its bosom.—Take the wings   50
Of morning—and the Barcan desert[3] pierce,
Or lose thyself in the continuous woods
Where rolls the Oregan,[4] and hears no sound,
Save his own dashings—yet—the dead are there,
And millions in those solitudes, since first   55
The flight of years began, have laid them down
In their last sleep—the dead reign there alone.—
So shalt thou rest—and what if thou shalt fall
Unnoticed by the living—and no friend
Take note of thy departure? All that breathe   60
Will share thy destiny. The gay will laugh
When thou art gone, the solemn brood of care
Plod on, and each one as before will chase
His favourite phantom; yet all these shall leave
Their mirth and their employments, and shall come,   65
And make their bed with thee. As the long train
Of ages glide away, the sons of men,
The youth in life's green spring, and he who goes
In the full strength of years, matron, and maid,
The bow'd with age, the infant in the smiles   70
And beauty of its innocent age cut off,—
Shall one by one be gathered to thy side,
By those, who in their turn shall follow them.
So live, that when thy summons comes to join
The innumerable caravan, that moves   75
To the pale realms of shade, where each shall take
His chamber in the silent halls of death,
Thou go not, like the quarry-slave at night,
Scourged to his dungeon, but sustain'd and sooth'd
By an unfaltering trust, approach thy grave,   80
Like one who wraps the drapery of his couch
About him, and lies down to pleasant dreams.

c. 1814   1821

3. In Barca (northeast Libya).
4. An early variant spelling of Oregon; now the Columbia River. (For his distant examples Bryant ranges
across the Atlantic and then westward across the North
American continent.)

The Yellow Violet[1]

When beechen buds begin to swell,
        And woods the blue-bird's warble know,
The yellow violet's modest bell
        Peeps from the last year's leaves below.

Ere russet fields their green resume,   5
        Sweet flower! I love in forest bare,
To meet thee, when thy faint perfume
        Alone is in the virgin air.

Of all her train, the hands of Spring
        First plant thee in the watery mould;   10
And I have seen thee blossoming
        Beside the snow-bank's edges cold.

Thy Parent Sun, who bade thee view
        Pale skies, and chilling moisture sip,
Has bathed thee in his own bright hue,   15
        And streak'd with jet thy glowing lip.

Yet slight thy form, and low thy seat,
        And earthward bent thy gentle eye,
Unapt the passing view to meet,
        When loftier flowers are flaunting nigh.   20

Oft, in the sunless April day,
        Thy early smile has staid my walk;
But midst the gorgeous blooms of May
        I pass'd thee on thy humble stalk.

So they, who climb to wealth, forget   25
        The friends in darker fortunes tried;
I copied them—but I regret
        That I should ape the ways of pride.

And when again the genial hour
        Awakes the painted tribes of light,   30
I'll not o'erlook the modest flower
        That made the woods of April bright.

1815   1821

To a Waterfowl[2]

Whither, 'midst falling dew,
While glow the heavens with the last steps of day,

---

1. The text is that of the first printing, in *Poems* (1821);
it was written around 1815.
2. The text is that of the printing in *Poems* (1821); the

poem was drafted in Bridgewater, Massachusetts, during July 1815.

Far, through their rosy depths, dost thou pursue
            Thy solitary way?

        Vainly the fowler's eye   5
Might mark thy distant flight to do thee wrong,
As, darkly painted on the crimson sky,
            Thy figure floats along.

        Seek'st thou the plashy[3] brink
Of weedy lake, or marge of river wide,   10
Or where the rocking billows rise and sink
            On the chafed ocean side?

        There is a Power whose care
Teaches thy way along that pathless coast,—
The desert and illimitable air,—   15
            Lone wandering, but not lost.

        All day thy wings have fann'd
At that far height, the cold thin atmosphere:

Yet stoop not, weary, to the welcome land,
            Though the dark night is near.   20

        And soon that toil shall end,
Soon shalt thou find a summer home, and rest,
And scream among thy fellows; reeds shall bend
            Soon o'er thy sheltered nest.

        Thou'rt gone, the abyss of heaven   25
Hath swallowed up thy form; yet, on my heart
Deeply hath sunk the lesson thou hast given,
            And shall not soon depart.

        He, who, from zone to zone,
Guides through the boundless sky thy certain
flight,   30
In the long way that I must tread alone,
            Will lead my steps aright.

1815   1821

Sonnet—To an American Painter
Departing for Europe[1]

Thine eyes shall see the light of distant skies:
    Yet, Cole! thy heart shall bear to Europe's strand

---

3. Marshy; a plash is a pool.
1. From *Poems* (1832). Thomas Cole (1801–1848), English-born painter of the American landscape, was a companion of Bryant's in walking expeditions into the Catskills. Cole was a leader of the Hudson River school of painters whose celebrations of the romantic beauty of American scenery complemented Bryant's similar attempts in poetry.

A living image of thy native land,[2]
Such as on thy own glorious canvass lies.
Lone lakes—savannahs where the bison roves—   5
     Rocks rich with summer garlands—solemn streams—
     Skies, where the desert eagle wheels and screams—
Spring bloom and autumn blaze of boundless groves.
Fair scenes shall greet thee where thou goest—fair,
     But different—every where the trace of men,   10
     Paths, homes, graves, ruins, from the lowest glen
To where life shrinks from the fierce Alpine air.
     Gaze on them, till the tears shall dim thy sight,
     But keep that earlier, wilder image bright.

1829   1832

The Prairies[1]

These are the Gardens of the Desert, these
The unshorn fields, boundless and beautiful,
And fresh as the young earth, ere man had sinned—
The Prairies. I behold them for the first,
And my heart swells, while the dilated sight   5
Takes in the encircling vastness. Lo! they stretch
In airy undulations, far away,
As if the ocean, in his gentlest swell,
Stood still, with all his rounded billows fixed,
And motionless for ever.—Motionless?—   10
No—they are all unchained again. The clouds
Sweep over with their shadows, and beneath
The surface rolls and fluctuates to the eye;
Dark hollows seem to glide along and chase
The sunny ridges. Breezes of the South!   15
Who toss the golden and the flame-like flowers,
And pass the prairie-hawk that, poised on high,
Flaps his broad wings, yet moves not—ye have played
Among the palms of Mexico and vines
Of Texas, and have crisped the limpid brooks   20
That from the fountains of Sonora[2] glide
Into the calm Pacific—have ye fanned
A nobler or a lovelier scene than this?
Man hath no part in all this glorious work:
The hand that built the firmament hath heaved   25
And smoothed these verdant swells, and sown their slopes
With herbage, planted them with island groves,
And hedged them round with forests. Fitting floor
For this magnificent temple of the sky—

2. Bryant seems to have thought Cole was a native-born American. He later learned better and altered this line to "A living image of our own bright land."
1. From the first printing in *Poems* (1834). Bryant wrote the poem over a year after visiting his brothers in Illinois during 1832. Later he removed the reference to the Fall of Adam and Eve by substituting this as the third line: "For which the speech of England has no name—" (alluding to the fact that the word *prairies* was adopted from French explorers and trappers).
2. River in northwest Mexico.

With flowers whose glory and whose multitude   30
Rival the constellations! The great heavens
Seem to stoop down upon the scene in love,—
A nearer vault, and of a tenderer blue,
Than that which bends above the eastern hills.
    As o'er the verdant waste I guide my steed,   35
Among the high rank grass that sweeps his sides,
The hollow beating of his footstep seems
A sacrilegious sound. I think of those
Upon whose rest he tramples. Are they here—
The dead of other days!—and did the dust   40
Of these fair solitudes once stir with life
And burn with passion? Let the mighty mounds[3]
That overlook the rivers, or that rise
In the dim forest crowded with old oaks,
Answer. A race, that long has passed away,   45
Built them;—a disciplined and populous race
Heaped, with long toil, the earth, while yet the Greek
Was hewing the Pentelicus[4] to forms
Of symmetry, and rearing on its rock
The glittering Parthenon. These ample fields   50
Nourished their harvests, here their herds were fed,
When haply by their stalls the bison lowed,
And bowed his maned shoulder to the yoke.
All day this desert murmured with their toils,
Till twilight blushed and lovers walked, and wooed   55
In a forgotten language, and old tunes,
From instruments of unremembered form,
Gave the soft winds a voice. The red man came—
The roaming hunter tribes, warlike and fierce,
And the mound-builders vanished from the earth.   60
The solitude of centuries untold
Has settled where they dwelt. The prairie wolf
Hunts in their meadows, and his fresh dug den
Yawns by my path. The gopher mines the ground
Where stood their swarming cities. All is gone—   65
All—save the piles of earth that hold their bones—
The platforms where they worshipped unknown gods—
The barriers which they builded from the soil
To keep the foe at bay—till o'er the walls
The wild beleaguerers broke, and, one by one,   70
The strong holds of the plain were forced, and heaped
With corpses. The brown vultures of the wood
Flocked to those vast uncovered sepulchres,
And sat, unscared and silent, at their feast.
Haply some solitary fugitive,   75
Lurking in marsh and forest, till the sense
Of desolation and of fear became

3. The burial mounds common in Illinois; Bryant follows a contemporary theory that they were built by a
culture older than the American Indians.
4. Greek mountain from which a fine white marble

was quarried, including that used in building the Parthenon, the temple of Athena on the Acropolis in
Athens.

Bitterer than death, yielded himself to die.
Man's better nature triumphed. Kindly words
Welcomed and soothed him; the rude conquerors   80
Seated the captive with their chiefs. He chose
A bride among their maidens. And at length
Seemed to forget,—yet ne'er forgot,—the wife
Of his first love, and her sweet little ones
Butchered, amid their shrieks, with all his race.   85
    Thus change the forms of being. Thus arise
Races of living things, glorious in strength,
And perish, as the quickening breath of God
Fills them, or is withdrawn. The red man too—
Has left the blooming wilds he ranged so long,   90
And, nearer to the Rocky Mountains, sought
A wider hunting ground. The beaver builds
No longer by these streams, but far away,
On waters whose blue surface ne'er gave back
The white man's face—among Missouri's springs,   95
And pools whose issues swell the Oregan,[5]
He rears his little Venice.[6] In these plains
The bison feeds no more. Twice twenty leagues
Beyond remotest smoke of hunter's camp,
Roams the majestic brute, in herds that shake   100
The earth with thundering steps—yet here I meet
His ancient footprints stamped beside the pool.
    Still this great solitude is quick with life.
Myriads of insects, gaudy as the flowers
They flutter over, gentle quadrupeds,   105
And birds, that scarce have learned the fear of man
Are here, and sliding reptiles of the ground,
Startlingly beautiful. The graceful deer
Bounds to the wood at my approach. The bee,
A more adventurous colonist than man,   110
With whom he came across the eastern deep,
Fills the savannas with his murmurings,
And hides his sweets, as in the golden age,
Within the hollow oak. I listen long
To his domestic hum, and think I hear   115
The sound of that advancing multitude
Which soon shall fill these deserts. From the ground
Comes up the laugh of children, the soft voice
Of maidens, and the sweet and solemn hymn
Of Sabbath worshippers. The low of herds   120
Blends with the rustling of the heavy grain
Over the dark-brown furrows. All at once
A fresher wind sweeps by, and breaks my dream,
And I am in the wilderness alone.

1833   1834

---

5. The Columbia River.   6. I.e., builds a city in the water.

The Poet[1]

Thou, who wouldst wear the name
   Of poet mid thy brethren of mankind,
And clothe in words of flame
   Thoughts that shall live within the general mind!
Deem not the framing of a deathless lay   5
The pastime of a drowsy summer day.

But gather all thy powers,
   And wreak them on the verse that thou dost weave,
And in thy lonely hours,   10
   At silent morning or at wakeful eve,
While the warm current tingles through thy veins,
Set forth the burning words in fluent strains.

No smooth array of phrase,
   Artfully sought and ordered though it be,
Which the cold rhymer lays   15
   Upon his page with languid industry,
Can wake the listless pulse to livelier speed,
Or fill with sudden tears the eyes that read.

The secret wouldst thou know
   To touch the heart or fire the blood at will?
Let thine own eyes o'erflow;   20
   Let thy lips quiver with the passionate thrill;
Seize the great thought, ere yet its power be past,
And bind, in words, the fleet emotion fast.

Then, should thy verse appear   25
   Halting and harsh, and all unaptly wrought,
Touch the crude line with fear,
   Save in the moment of impassioned thought;
Then summon back the original glow and mend
The strain with rapture that with fire was penned.   30

Yet let no empty gust
   Of passion find an utterance in thy lay,
A blast that whirls the dust
   Along the howling street and dies away;
But feelings of calm power and mighty sweep,   35
Like currents journeying through the windless deep.

Seek'st thou, in living lays,
   To limn[2] the beauty of the earth and sky?
Before thine inner gaze
   Let all that beauty in clear vision lie;   40
Look on it with exceeding love, and write
The words inspired by wonder and delight.

1. The text is that of the first printing in *Thirty Poems*   2. Paint.
(1863).

Of tempests wouldst thou sing,
   Or tell of battles—make thyself a part
Of the great tumult; cling   45
   To the tossed wreck with terror in thy heart;
Scale, with the assaulting host, the rampart's height,
And strike and struggle in the thickest fight.

So shalt thou frame a lay
   That haply may endure from age to age,   50
And they who read shall say:
   What witchery hangs upon this poet's page!
What art is his the written spells to find
That sway from mood to mood the willing mind!

1863

Abraham Lincoln[1]

Oh, slow to smite and swift to spare,
   Gentle and merciful and just!
Who, in the fear of God, didst bear
   The sword of power, a nation's trust!

In sorrow by thy bier we stand,   5
   Amid the awe that hushes all,
And speak the anguish of a land
   That shook with horror at thy fall.

Thy task is done; the bond are free;
   We bear thee to an honored grave,   10
Whose proudest monument shall be
   The broken fetters of the slave.

Pure was thy life; its bloody close
   Hath placed thee with the sons of light,
Among the noble host of those   15
   Who perished in the cause of Right.

1865

1. Lincoln was assassinated on April 14, 1865; this poem was read to a great crowd of mourners at Union Square in New York City on April 24, 1865. The text is that of the first printing, in the New York *Evening Post*, April 26, 1865.

WILLIAM APESS
1798–1839

Little is known of William Apess's life other than what he tells us in A *Son of the Forest* (1829), the first extensive autobiography published by a Native American.

His grandfather, says Apess, was a white man who married the granddaughter of the Wampanoag leader King Philip, or Metacom, the loser, in 1678, of "King Philip's War." Philip increasingly occupied Apess's thoughts during his lifetime, serving as the subject of his last published work. Apess's father was of mixed blood, but he joined the Pequot tribe and married a full-blood Indian woman. Born in Colrain, Massachusetts, Apess drops from public record after 1838. Only recently have obituaries in the New York *Sun* and the New York *Observer* been found recording his death, from alcoholism, in New York, in the spring of 1839.

In *A Son of the Forest*, Apess details the pains of his early life: at three he was taken into the home of his poor, alcoholic maternal grandparents; he was severely beaten and, at four or five, sold as an indentured laborer. His first master allowed him to attend school for six years, which constituted his entire formal education; he also introduced Apess to Christianity. Apess served as a soldier in the abortive American attack on Montreal in the War of 1812 and converted to evangelical Methodism after leaving the army. At the conclusion of *A Son of the Forest*, Apess writes that he achieved an "exhorter's" license from his church, enabling him to earn a living as an itinerant preacher; only later would he realize his goal of ordination as a Methodist minister.

A fervent Christian, Apess early understood Christianity as incompatible with any form of race prejudice, sounding a note that presages Christian abolitionists later in the nineteenth century. In 1833, Apess went to preach at Mashpee, the only remaining Indian town in Massachusetts. There he became involved in the Mashpees' struggle to preserve their resources and rights, which were threatened by the overseers imposed on them by the Commonwealth of Massachusetts. The Mashpee eventually drew up petitions, probably composed by Apess, requiring that no whites cut wood or hay on Mashpee lands without the Indians' consent for "we, as a tribe, will rule ourselves, and have the right to do so; for all men are born free and equal, says the Constitution of the Country." Such unprecedented assertiveness on the part of the Indians alarmed the governor of Massachusetts, who announced his readiness to put down the unrest with troops. Apess's version of the controversy appears in his *Indian Nullification of the Unconstitutional Laws of Massachusetts Relative to the Marshpee* [sic] *Tribe; or, The Pretended Riot Explained* (1835). A year before the book appeared, its case was won when the state legislature granted the Mashpee the same rights of self-governance that other Massachusetts townships possessed.

Apess's career as a preacher and an author comes to a close with his *Eulogy on King Philip*, delivered in 1836 at the Odeon in Boston, one of the city's largest public lecture halls, and published that same year. In the *Eulogy* Apess meditated on his distant relation, naming Philip the foremost man that America had thus far produced. He reminds his audience, descendants of the Pilgrims, of the crimes of their ancestors, although "you and I have to rejoice that we have not to answer for our fathers' crimes; neither shall we do right to charge them one to another." Nonetheless, he notes, "in vain have I looked for the Christian to take me by the hand and bid me welcome to his cabin, as my fathers did them [the Christians], before we were born." Apess concludes that a "different course must be pursued. . . . And while you ask yourselves, 'What do they, the Indians, want?' you have only to look at the unjust laws made for them and say, 'They want what I want' ": justice and Christian fellowship.

Our selection comes from *The Experiences of Five Christian Indians of the Pequot Tribe*, published in 1833, the year Apess came to Mashpee. The first of these "experiences" is Apess's own, an account of his life and conversion that repeats some of the material in *A Son of the Forest* but intensifies considerably the condemnation of Euro-American treatment of native peoples. Apess concludes this book with the text anthologized here, *An Indian's Looking Glass for the White Man*, a searing indictment of race prejudice against people of color generally and

Native Americans particularly. The forceful beginning of *Indian's Looking Glass* is marked by the hortatory style of the practiced preacher as well as by a remembered sense of the power of the spoken word in native cultures. Although his punctuation and syntax do not conform to the conventions of standard written English, Apess writes in a style that powerfully imitates oral performance. His provocative, ironic voice calls to mind that of the later moralist and orator for justice, Henry David Thoreau.

An Indian's Looking-Glass for the White Man[1]

Having a desire to place a few things before my fellow creatures who are traveling with me to the grave, and to that God who is the maker and preserver both of the white man and the Indian, whose abilities are the same and who are to be judged by one God, who will show no favor to outward appearances but will judge righteousness. Now I ask if degradation has not been heaped long enough upon the Indians? And if so, can there not be a compromise? Is it right to hold and promote prejudices? If not, why not put them all away? I mean here, among those who are civilized. It may be that many are ignorant of the situation of many of my brethren within the limits of New England. Let me for a few moments turn your attention to the reservations in the different states of New England, and, with but few exceptions, we shall find them as follows: the most mean, abject, miserable race of beings in the world—a complete place of prodigality and prostitution.

Let a gentleman and lady of integrity and respectability visit these places, and they would be surprised; as they wandered from one hut to the other they would view, with the females who are left alone, children half-starved and some almost as naked as they came into the world. And it is a fact that I have seen them as much so—while the females are left without protection, and are seduced by white men, and are finally left to be common prostitutes for them and to be destroyed by that burning, fiery curse, that has swept millions, both of red and white men, into the grave with sorrow and disgrace—rum. One reason why they are left so is because their most sensible and active men are absent at sea. Another reason is because they are made to believe they are minors and have not the abilities given them from God to take care of themselves, without it is to see to a few little articles, such as baskets and brooms. Their land is in common stock, and they have nothing to make them enterprising.

Another reason is because those men who are Agents,[2] many of them are unfaithful and care not whether the Indians live or die; they are much imposed upon by their neighbors, who have no principle. They would think it no crime to go upon Indian lands and cut and carry off their most valuable timber, or anything else they chose; and I doubt not but they think it clear gain. Another reason is because they have no education to take care of themselves; if they had, I would risk them to take care of their own property.

Now I will ask if the Indians are not called the most ingenious people among us. And are they not said to be men of talents? And I would ask: Could there

---

1. The text is from *The Experiences of Five Christian Indians of the Pequot Tribe* (1833) reprinted in *On Our Own Ground: The Complete Writings of William Apess, a Pequot*, edited by Barry O'Connell (1992).

2. Those appointed by the Commonwealth of Massachusetts to oversee Indian affairs in such towns as Mashpee.

be a more efficient way to distress and murder them by inches than the way they have taken? And there is no people in the world but who may be destroyed in the same way. Now, if these people are what they are held up in our view to be, I would take the liberty to ask why they are not brought forward and pains taken to educate them, to give them all a common education, and those of the brightest and first-rate talents put forward and held up to office. Perhaps some unholy, unprincipled men would cry out, "The skin was not good enough"; but stop, friends—I am not talking about the skin but about principles. I would ask if there cannot be as good feelings and principles under a red skin as there can be under a white. And let me ask: Is it not on the account of a bad principle that we who are red children have had to suffer so much as we have? And let me ask: Did not this bad principle proceed from the whites or their forefathers? And I would ask: Is it worthwhile to nourish it any longer? If not, then let us have a change, although some men no doubt will spout their corrupt principles against it, that are in the halls of legislation and elsewhere. But I presume this kind of talk will seem surprising and horrible. I do not see why it should so long as they (the whites) say that they think as much of us as they do of themselves.

This I have heard repeatedly, from the most respectable gentlemen and ladies—and having heard so much precept, I should now wish to see the example. And I would ask who has a better right to look for these things than the naturalist[3] himself—the candid man would say none.

I know that many say that they are willing, perhaps the majority of the people, that we should enjoy our rights and privileges as they do. If so, I would ask, Why are not we protected in our persons and property throughout the Union? Is it not because there reigns in the breast of many who are leaders a most unrighteous, unbecoming, and impure black principle, and as corrupt and unholy as it can be—while these very same unfeeling, self-esteemed characters pretend to take the skin as a pretext to keep us from our unalienable and lawful rights? I would ask you if you would like to be disfranchised from all your rights, merely because your skin is white, and for no other crime. I'll venture to say, these very characters who hold the skin to be such a barrier in the way would be the first to cry out, "Injustice! awful injustice!"

But, reader, I acknowledge that this is a confused world, and I am not seeking for office, but merely placing before you the black inconsistency that you place before me—which is ten times blacker than any skin that you will find in the universe. And now let me exhort you to do away that principle, as it appears ten times worse in the sight of God and candid men than skins of color—more disgraceful than all the skins that Jehovah ever made. If black or red skins or any other skin of color is disgraceful to God, it appears that he has disgraced himself a great deal—for he has made fifteen colored people to one white and placed them here upon this earth.

Now let me ask you, white man, if it is a disgrace for to eat, drink, and sleep with the image of God, or sit, or walk and talk with them. Or have you the folly to think that the white man, being one in fifteen or sixteen, are the only beloved images of God? Assemble all nations together in your imagination, and then let the whites be seated among them, and then let us look for the whites, and I doubt not it would be hard finding them; for to the rest of the

---

3. I.e., the American Indian; a play on the view of Indians as children of nature (or "sons of the forest").

nations, they are still but a handful. Now suppose these skins were put together, and each skin had its national crimes written upon it—which skin do you think would have the greatest? I will ask one question more. Can you charge the Indians with robbing a nation almost of their whole continent, and murdering their women and children, and then depriving the remainder of their lawful rights, that nature and God require them to have? And to cap the climax, rob another nation to till their grounds and welter out their days under the lash with hunger and fatigue under the scorching rays of a burning sun?[4] I should look at all the skins, and I know that when I cast my eye upon that white skin, and if I saw those crimes written upon it, I should enter my protest against it immediately and cleave to that which is more honorable. And I can tell you that I am satisfied with the manner of my creation, fully—whether others are or not.

But we will strive to penetrate more fully into the conduct of those who profess to have pure principles and who tell us to follow Jesus Christ and imitate him and have his Spirit. Let us see if they come anywhere near him and his ancient disciples. The first thing we are to look at are his precepts, of which we will mention a few. "Thou shalt love the Lord thy God with all thy heart, with all thy soul, with all thy mind, and with all thy strength. The second is like unto it. Thou shalt love thy neighbor as thyself. On these two precepts hang all the law and the prophets" (Matthew 22.37, 38, 39, 40). "By this shall all men know that they are my disciples, if ye have love one to another" (John 13.35). Our Lord left this special command with his followers, that they should love one another.

Again, John in his Epistles says, "He who loveth God loveth his brother also" (1 John 4.21). "Let us not love in word but in deed" (1 John 3.18). "Let your love be without dissimulation. See that ye love one another with a pure heart fervently" (1 Peter 1.22). "If any man say, I love God, and hateth his brother, he is a liar" (1 John 4.20). "Whosoever hateth his brother is a murderer, and no murderer hath eternal life abiding in him" (1 John 3.15). The first thing that takes our attention is the saying of Jesus, "Thou shalt love," etc. The first question I would ask my brethren in the ministry, as well as that of the membership: What is love, or its effects? Now, if they who teach are not essentially affected with pure love, the love of God, how can they teach as they ought? Again, the holy teachers of old said, "Now if any man have not the spirit of Christ, he is none of his" (Romans 8.9). Now, my brethren in the ministry, let me ask you a few sincere questions. Did you ever hear or read of Christ teaching his disciples that they ought to despise one because his skin was different from theirs? Jesus Christ being a Jew, and those of his Apostles certainly were not whites—and did not he who completed the plan of salvation complete it for the whites as well as for the Jews, and others? And were not the whites the most degraded people on the earth at that time? And none were more so, for they sacrificed their children to dumb idols![5] And did not St. Paul labor more abundantly for building up a Christian nation among you than any of the Apostles? And you know as well as I that you are not indebted to a principle beneath a white skin for your religious services but to a colored one.

What then is the matter now? Is not religion the same now under a colored

---

4. The reference is to the "nation" of Africa, many of whose people were brought to the United States as slaves.

5. The ancient Hebrews considered various Mideastern peoples idolators whose practices presumably included child sacrifice.

skin as it ever was? If so, I would ask, why is not a man of color respected? You may say, as many say, we have white men enough. But was this the spirit of Christ and his Apostles? If it had been, there would not have been one white preacher in the world—for Jesus Christ never would have imparted his grace or word to them, for he could forever have withheld it from them. But we find that Jesus Christ and his Apostles never looked at the outward appearances. Jesus in particular looked at the hearts, and his Apostles through him, being discerners of the spirit, looked at their fruit without any regard to the skin, color, or nation; as St. Paul himself speaks, "Where there is neither Greek nor Jew, circumcision nor uncircumcision, Barbarian nor Scythian, bond nor free—but Christ is all, and in all" (Colossians 3.11). If you can find a spirit like Jesus Christ and his Apostles prevailing now in any of the white congregations, I should like to know it. I ask: Is it not the case that everybody that is not white is treated with contempt and counted as barbarians? And I ask if the word of God justifies the white man in so doing. When the prophets prophesied, of whom did they speak? When they spoke of heathens, was it not the whites and others who were counted Gentiles? And I ask if all nations with the exception of the Jews were not counted heathens. And according to the writings of some, it could not mean the Indians, for they are counted Jews. And now I would ask: Why is all this distinction made among these Christian societies? I would ask: What is all this ado about missionary societies, if it be not to Christianize those who are not Christians? And what is it for? To degrade them worse, to bring them into society where they must welter out their days in disgrace merely because their skin is of a different complexion. What folly it is to try to make the state of human society worse than it is. How astonished some may be at this—but let me ask: Is it not so? Let me refer you to the churches only. And, my brethren, is there any agreement? Do brethren and sisters love one another? Do they not rather hate one another? Outward forms and ceremonies, the lusts of the flesh, the lusts of the eye, and pride of life is of more value to many professors[6] than the love of God shed abroad in their hearts, or an attachment to his altar, to his ordinances, or to his children. But you may ask: Who are the children of God? Perhaps you may say, none but white. If so, the word of the Lord is not true.

I will refer you to St. Peter's precepts (Acts 10): "God is no respecter of persons," etc. Now if this is the case, my white brother, what better are you than God? And if no better, why do you, who profess his Gospel and to have his spirit, act so contrary to it? Let me ask why the men of a different skin are so despised. Why are not they educated and placed in your pulpits? I ask if his services well performed are not as good as if a white man performed them. I ask if a marriage or a funeral ceremony or the ordinance of the Lord's house would not be as acceptable in the sight of God as though he was white. And if so, why is it not to you? I ask again: Why is it not as acceptable to have men to exercise their office in one place as well as in another? Perhaps you will say that if we admit you to all of these privileges you will want more. I expect that I can guess what that is—Why, say you, there would be intermarriages. How that would be I am not able to say—and if it should be, it would be nothing strange or new to me; for I can assure you that I know a great many that have intermarried, both of the whites and the Indians—and many are their sons

---

6. I.e., those who profess the Christian faith.

and daughters and people, too, of the first respectability. And I could point to some in the famous city of Boston and elsewhere. You may look now at the disgraceful act in the statute law passed by the legislature of Massachusetts, and behold the fifty-pound fine levied upon any clergyman or justice of the peace that dare to encourage the laws of God and nature by a legitimate union in holy wedlock between the Indians and whites. I would ask how this looks to your lawmakers. I would ask if this corresponds with your sayings—that you think as much of the Indians as you do of the whites. I do not wonder that you blush, many of you, while you read; for many have broken the ill-fated laws made by man to hedge up the laws of God and nature. I would ask if they who have made the law have not broken it—but there is no other state in New England that has this law but Massachusetts; and I think, as many of you do not, that you have done yourselves no credit.

But as I am not looking for a wife, having one of the finest cast, as you no doubt would understand while you read her experience and travail of soul in the way to heaven, you will see that it is not my object. And if I had none, I should not want anyone to take my right from me and choose a wife for me; for I think that I or any of my brethren have a right to choose a wife for themselves as well as the whites—and as the whites have taken the liberty to choose my brethren, the Indians, hundreds and thousands of them, as partners in life, I believe the Indians have a much right to choose their partners among the whites if they wish. I would ask you if you can see anything inconsistent in your conduct and talk about the Indians. And if you do, I hope you will try to become more consistent. Now, if the Lord Jesus Christ, who is counted by all to be a Jew—and it is well known that the Jews are a colored people,[7] especially those living in the East, where Christ was born—and if he should appear among us, would he not be shut out of doors by many, very quickly? And by those too who profess religion?

By what you read, you may learn how deep your principles are. I should say they were skin-deep. I should not wonder if some of the most selfish and ignorant would spout a charge of their principles now and then at me. But I would ask: How are you to love your neighbors as yourself? Is it to cheat them? Is it to wrong them in anything? Now, to cheat them out of any of their rights is robbery. And I ask: Can you deny that you are not robbing the Indians daily, and many others? But at last you may think I am what is called a hard and uncharitable man. But not so. I believe there are many who would not hesitate to advocate our cause; and those too who are men of fame and respectability— as well as ladies of honor and virtue. There is a Webster, an Everett, and a Wirt,[8] and many others who are distinguished characters—besides a host of my fellow citizens, who advocate our cause daily. And how I congratulate such noble spirits—how they are to be prized and valued; for they are well calculated to promote the happiness of mankind. They well know that man was made for society, and not for hissing-stocks[9] and outcasts. And when such a principle as this lies within the hearts of men, how much it is like its God—

7. Referring to the belief that Moses and the biblical Hebrews, including Jesus, were people of color.
8. William Wirt (1772–1834), lawyer, politician, orator, and writer; he served as attorney general under President James Monroe and was nominated by the Whig party for president. Daniel Webster (1782–1852), orator, legislator, statesman, and interpreter of the Constitution; he served as congressman from New Hampshire, senator from Massachusetts, and secretary of state under President William Henry Harrison. Edward Everett (1794–1865), the first Eliot Professor of Greek at Harvard and the editor of the prestigious *North American Review*; he served in Congress and as governor of Massachusetts.
9. Those who are laughed at or hissed at (cf. laughing-stocks).

and how it honors its Maker—and how it imitates the feelings of the Good Samaritan, that had his wounds bound up, who had been among thieves and robbers.

Do not get tired, ye noble-hearted—only think how many poor Indians want their wounds done up daily; the Lord will reward you, and pray you stop not till this tree of distinction shall be leveled to the earth, and the mantle of prejudice torn from every American heart—then shall peace pervade the Union.[1]

1. "In the 1837 edition, *Experience of Five Christian Indians*, Apess removed this entire essay and substituted the following (entitled 'An Indian's Thought') in its place and thus ended the book: 'He would ask the white Christian thus: How can you let your light shine among Indians unless you do it by example? Proof of the Savior's light. Not by precept only, that he loved the world, but by example. Such as doing all manner of cures, by working miracles, to the astonishment of all the world; and to test his love for them, he laid down his life for them, even while they were enemies. Now, if we have his spirit, as we profess to have, we shall most certainly want the indigent of all classes made confortable. And who that understands the history of the world, does not know that ignorance is the cause of the major part of the vices that exist in the world. Now, does not the white man know that it is his duty to educate the Indians, to help them build houses of worship, and such like, in order to raise them up and make them comfortable as yourselves? And do you not know it was the intent of Christ's dying to make you and them equal with himself in holiness and peace? Now, this is just the way you ought to feel toward all the race of mankind. And you can never make ignorant people know that you love them, unless you do something for them. And be it known to all men, that your light can never shine unless you do it by works of righteousness. Judge ye, what that is.—William Apess' " [O'Connell's note]

RALPH WALDO EMERSON
1803–1882

Ralph Waldo Emerson was a man who had no personal excesses such as doomed Poe, no mysterious decade such as lent glamor to Hawthorne, no exotic adventures such as Melville founded his career on, no dramatic struggles for artistic recognition such as Whitman waged, no local notoriety as a crank and extremist such as Thoreau acquired. He led a respectable, conventional life as a family man and decent, solid citizen. Yet in both literature and philosophy this man of conventional life became the American writer with whom every other significant writer of his time had to come to terms. At one extreme, Melville reacted so hostilely to the optimistic side of Emerson's thought that he satirized him in *The Confidence-Man* as a great American philosophical con man. At the other extreme, without Emerson's inspiration the writings of Thoreau are all but unthinkable and Whitman's great poetry might never have been written. Emerson's persisting influence on twentieth-century American writers is evident in astonishing permutations, on writers as diverse as Theodore Dreiser, Robert Frost, Wallace Stevens, his namesake Ralph Waldo Ellison, and A. R. Ammons.

Emerson was born in Boston on May 25, 1803, son of a Unitarian minister and the second of five surviving boys. He was eight years old when the death of his father left the family to the meager charity of the church. Determined to send four sons to Harvard (another son, mentally retarded, was cared for by rural relatives), Emerson's mother kept a succession of boardinghouses. Emerson grew up in the city, protected from the lower-class "rough boys" in his early years and sent at nine to the Boston Public Latin School. So poorly clothed that two brothers had to make do at times with one coat, the boys were encouraged by a brilliant eccentric aunt, Mary Moody Emerson, to regard deprivation as ecstatic self-denial. Emerson showed no remarkable literary promise either in his early prose exercises or in his adolescent satires in imitation of Alexander Pope. His Harvard years, 1817–21, were frugal, industrious, and undistinguished. After graduation he served, he said, as "a hopeless Schoolmaster," unable to impose his authority on his pupils. Escaping into the study of theology in 1825, he began preaching in October 1826, and early in 1829 was ordained as junior pastor of Boston's Second Church, where Increase Mather and Cotton Mather had preached a century and more before.

Biographers have pointed out that Emerson's dedication to the ministry at the age of twenty-one was to a life of public service through eloquence, not to a life of preserving and disseminating religious dogma. In any case, Boston was no longer a Puritan stronghold. Boston Unitarianism, led in the 1820s by William Ellery Channing, still accepted the Bible as the revelation of God's intentions for humankind, but no longer held that human beings were innately depraved or that Jesus was more than the highest type of mortal individual. Emerson's skepticism toward Christianity was strengthened by his exposure to the German "higher criticism," which heretically interpreted biblical miracles in the light of comparable stories in other cultures. Emerson was gradually developing a faith greater in individual moral sentiment than in revealed religion. Around 1830–31 his reading of Samuel Taylor Coleridge's *Aids to Reflection* provided him with a basic terminology in his postulation of an intuitive "Reason," which is superior to the mere "Understanding," or ordinary rationality operating on the materials of sense experience. Undogmatic about Christianity as he became, Emerson nevertheless seems to have undergone an intense religious experience around these same years, 1830 or 1831, something comparable with the sweet inward burning that the Calvinist Jonathan Edwards had delighted in describing. Emerson's knowledge of this emotion is clear from his later essay *The Over-Soul*, but he felt no impulse to account for it according to the tenets of a particular church.

In the year of his ordination, Emerson married a young woman from New Hampshire, Ellen Tucker. She died sixteen months later of tuberculosis, the disease that had already infected Emerson and others in his family. Early in 1832 Emerson notified his church that he had become so skeptical of the validity of the Lord's Supper that he could no longer administer it. A few months later he resigned, keeping the sober goodwill of many in his flock, and embarked on a leisurely European tour, which constituted a postgraduate education in art and natural science. In the custom of that time, he called on well-known writers, meeting Walter Savage Landor in Italy, listening to Coleridge converse with such cogent volubility that he seemed to be reading aloud, and hearing William Wordsworth recite his poetry. Most important for his intellectual growth and for his reputation was his visit to Thomas Carlyle at Craigenputtock in Scotland, beginning a lifelong alliance in which each helped to publish and create an audience for the other.

In 1834 Emerson drifted into a quiet retreat at Concord, Massachusetts, where generations of his ancestors had been ministers. That year he received the first installment of his wife's legacy. Soon he was assured of more than a thousand dollars annually, enough so that he did not need to hold a steady job again. He continued to preach occasionally and began lecturing at New England lyceums, the public halls that brought a variety of speakers and performers both to the cities and to smaller towns. In 1835, after a prudent courtship, he married Lydia Jackson of Plymouth, having explained to her his work and the conditions under which he must pursue it. One condition was that he must live in rural Concord rather than move into the bustle of Plymouth. His assessment of his accomplishments was focused on his being a "poet," even when writing prose: "I am a poet, of a low class without doubt yet a poet. That is my nature & vocation. My singing be sure is very 'husky,' & is for the most part in prose. Still am I a poet in the sense of a perceiver & dear lover of the harmonies that are in the soul & in matter, & specially of the correspondences between these & those. A sunset, a forest, a snow storm, a certain river-view, are more to me than many friends & do ordinarily divide my day with books. Wherever I go therefore I guard & study my rambling propensities with a care that is ridiculous to people, but to me is the care of my high calling."

At this time, before *Nature* was published and before his essays were written, Emerson may well have hoped to gain his literary fame by his verse, and in fact the poems he had written thus far were not so husky or unmelodious as he implied. His main problem as a poet was not the huskiness he complained of but the more serious failure first to arrive at, then to apply, his great insight: that in true poetry the thought creates its own meter, the content creates its own form. Emerson's first little book, *Nature* (1836), did not establish him as an important American writer (for one thing, it was anonymous, and not every reviewer was in on what became an open secret around Boston), but it did confirm his future as a prose writer, however poetic that prose might be. One reviewer noticed the influence of Wordsworth and Coleridge in the tendency to "look on Nature with the spiritual eye," so that one creates Nature in perceiving it. Another found that the author had adopted "the Berkeleyan system" of philosophy, which denies "the outward and real existence" of Nature, and noticed also that the new school of philosophy called Transcendentalism was "a revival of the Old Platonic school" in rejecting a scientific attitude toward Nature. Yet another reviewer stressed the influence of Wordsworth's *Immortality* ode and of Coleridge's *Dejection: An Ode* in the author's concept of Nature. Another hailed the book as revealing a mind cognate with Thomas Carlyle's, "however inferior in energies and influences," and defined the philosophy of the book as "an Idealistic Pantheism" like that of Carlyle's *Sartor Resartus* (1834). A Swedenborgian writer in London took *Nature* as self-evidently the work of an American Swedenborgian, especially in "the beautiful and heart-cheering doctrine of correspondences" between moods of Nature and moods of human beings. As all these reviewers understood, *Nature* was not a Christian book but one influenced by a range of idealistic philosophies, ancient and very modern, Transcendentalism being merely the latest name for an old way of thinking. Although the favorable reception of the book in England encouraged some American journalists, hitherto skeptical, to take Emerson more seriously as a force in modern thought, Emerson's immediate reward was having the book become the unofficial manifesto for "the Symposium" or the Transcendental Club, which held its first meeting only a few days after *Nature* was published.

The Transcendental Club had influences, on Emerson and on the intellectual life of the country, out of proportion to its small membership and its short life of four years. It was composed mainly of ministers who were repelled by John Locke's views that the mind is a passive receiver of sense impressions and enthusiastic about Coleridge's alternative view of the mind as creative in perception. Among the members were the educator Bronson Alcott, the abolitionist and Unitarian minister Theodore Parker, and the Unitarian minister Orestes A. Brownson (later a major force in American Catholicism). Such friends were welcome, for during the early 1830s deaths broke up the close-knit band of Emerson brothers. Emerson himself had gone south to recover from tuberculosis in 1826–27; weakened by the same disease, Edward Emerson became mentally deranged in 1827 and died in 1834; and the youngest brother, Charles, died in 1836. There was compensation for Emerson in the circle of admirers who began forming about him at the time of his second marriage and the publication of *Nature*. Alcott, Margaret Fuller, and others sought him out, some paying him frequent and prolonged visits or even settling in Concord to be near him.

Nature reached a smaller audience than did many of his lectures, which were often reported by newspapers in substantial part; his formal Harvard addresses to the Phi Beta Kappa Society in 1837 on the American scholar and to the Divinity School graduates in 1838 on the state of Christianity were both printed as pamphlets, according to the custom of the time. The second of these speeches occasioned a brief, virulent series of attacks in the press for its heresies, giving Emerson a notoriety that barred him from speaking at Harvard for three decades. His unsigned contributions to the Transcendentalists' magazine *The Dial* did not enhance his reputation; indeed, he sometimes was attacked in newspapers as the author of Alcott's *Orphic Sayings*, which jocular contemporaries took as the ultimate of transcendental gibberish. Only with the publication of *Essays* (1841) did Emerson's lasting reputation begin. Far more than *Nature*, this book was directed to a popular audience. The essays had been tried out, in whole or large part, in his lectures, so that their final form was shaped by the responses of many audiences.

By the early 1840s, Emerson's life had settled into its enduring routine. He gave intermittent lectures in Boston and made lecture tours in the Northeast and, later, in the Middle Atlantic states to supplement the income from his legacy. Early in 1842 his first son, Waldo, died at the age of five, the last of the untimely deaths in Emerson's immediate family; after that Emerson devoted himself more and more to the personal problems of his circle of family and friends. His editing of *The Dial* from 1842 till 1844, for instance, was undertaken mainly to support his friends, especially Margaret Fuller. He worked steadily at a succession of essays, usually derived from his extensive journals by way of one or more intervening lectures. *Essays* (1841) was followed by *Essays: Second Series* (1844). The second collection demonstrated even more thoroughly than the first that Emerson's intellect had sharpened in the years since *Nature*. In *The Poet* especially his grappling with aesthetic problems was more incisive; he spoke from practical experience as well as theoretical speculation in defining the present state of literature in America, and he brilliantly foretold the nature of the great national poets to come. In *Experience* and other essays he resolutely and realistically faced the conflict between idealism and ordinary life. The deferential minister and the once-tentative lecturer had become a confident American prophet. Emerson slowly gained recognition for his poems, which he collected at the end of 1846. A second trip to Europe (1847–48) capped his secure middle age. He became something of a country squire, buying up many pieces of property in and around Concord. Always aware that there was a certain coldness in his disposition, he deliberately set out to make himself into a more sociable man, taking part in Boston club life (and smoking cigars to mask his diffidence). As his reputation expanded, he widened his lecture tours into the Midwest. His newer books, among them *Representative Men* (1849) and *Conduct of Life* (1860), were less forceful than his earlier ones, though they sold better because of the enlarged market and his established fame. After long resisting attempts by reformers to gain his support for various social issues, Emerson became a fervent advocate in the 1850s for abolitionism, though his efforts were too late and too local to make him a national leader. The rest of Emerson's writing, like the rest of his life, was a slow anticlimax to the intellectual ferment of the years between the mid-1830s and the mid-1840s, though it was only during these later decades that his earlier work first won general recognition. Emerson's memory began to fail more than ten years before his death, and he declined into a benign senility during which the English-speaking world, and even many who read him in translation, continued to honor the intellectual liberator that he had been in his middle life.

Although Emerson's contemporary reputation rested on his essays, he had all along been writing another masterpiece, his journals, which were not published in full until the 1960s and 1970s under the title *Journals and Miscellaneous Notebooks*. It will take time before readers fully grasp the importance of these writings as the historical record of a response to people and events, the most thorough documentation we possess of the growth of a nineteenth-century American writer, and the remarkable account of a spiritual life. A large number of important journal entries is reprinted here, interspersed with some of Emerson's more memorable letters so as to present a picture of his day-to-day life.

A critic said that Emerson wanted to get his whole philosophy into each essay; more than that, he got as much of it as he could into everything he wrote. Emerson's point of view may shift from one pole of a subject to the other even within a single work, for his mind moved like that of a dramatist who embodies felt or imagined moods in various characters, but the subject remains Emersonian. In this there is challenge for the new reader to find pattern in diversity. And for those who have already cherished Emerson through the various stages of life there is the warmth of familiarity, however unsettling this mild-mannered man always remains to any receptive reader.

Nature   Since its anonymous publication (1836), a little book paid for by the author himself, *Nature* has been recognized as a major document in American Romanticism and Transcendentalism. Merton M. Sealts, Jr., and Alfred R. Ferguson in their *Emerson's "Nature"—Origin, Growth, Meaning* point out "how wide the divergence has been over how to read such a work—whether as doctrine or mysticism, philosophy or poetry." In an earlier Norton anthology, *Eight American Writers* (1963), one of the most conscientious Emersonians, the late Stephen E. Whicher, took the book as "an audacious attempt to rescue nature from the natural scientists and to sketch instead a human or poetical science"; he took Emerson's question "To what end is nature?" as asking how nature can help "to restore our confidence and release our powers, as the fact of historical religion once did." Underlying many passages in *Nature* is the defensiveness of a man who has chosen to be a thinker rather than taking what his contemporaries would have seen as an active role in affairs, a defensiveness, in the sexist terminology which he regularly employed, against the charge of "effeminancy." For modern readers there is inescapable pain at Emerson's confidence that wild nature is inexhaustible and invulnerable and at the undreamed-of consequences of the belief that nature is created for human benefit.

We have drawn on the Sealts-Ferguson list of emendations for the corrections of a few obvious typographical errors and have followed Sealts and Ferguson in two corrections Emerson made in presentation copies at the beginning of Chapter 4, but we have left several oddities of punctuation, spelling, and rough-and-ready subject-verb agreements. The text is thus the one Emerson offered to his circle of American and British friends in the fall of 1836 as his first bid for a national and international reputation.

The Sealts-Ferguson volume is indispensable to serious study of *Nature* for, among other virtues, its printing of source passages in the Harvard University Press edition of *The Journals and Miscellaneous Notebooks of Ralph Waldo Emerson* (abbreviated here *JMN*). We have given the journal and lecture citations only when they reveal Emerson's literary borrowings (which are as often as not second-hand—a quotation from a Greek philosopher in a work by Samuel Taylor Coleridge, for example).

Nature

> "Nature is but an image or imitation of wisdom, the last thing of the soul; nature being a thing which doth only do, but not know."
>
> —Plotinus[1]

Introduction

Our age is retrospective. It builds the sepulchres of the fathers. It writes biographies, histories, and criticism. The foregoing generations beheld God

---

1. Emerson found the motto from the Roman philosopher Plotinus (205?–270?) in his copy of Ralph Cudworth's *The True Intellectual System of the Universe* (1820).

and nature face to face; we, through their eyes. Why should not we also enjoy an original relation to the universe? Why should not we have a poetry and philosophy of insight and not of tradition, and a religion by revelation to us, and not the history of theirs? Embosomed for a season in nature, whose floods of life stream around and through us, and invite us by the powers they supply, to action proportioned to nature, why should we grope among the dry bones of the past,[2] or put the living generation into masquerade out of its faded wardrobe? The sun shines to-day also. There is more wool and flax in the fields. There are new lands, new men, new thoughts. Let us demand our own works and laws and worship.

Undoubtedly we have no questions to ask which are unanswerable. We must trust the perfection of the creation so far, as to believe that whatever curiosity the order of things has awakened in our minds, the order of things can satisfy. Every man's condition is a solution in hieroglyphic to those inquiries he would put. He acts it as life, before he apprehends it as truth. In like manner, nature is already, in its forms and tendencies, describing its own design. Let us interrogate the great apparition, that shines so peacefully around us. Let us inquire, to what end is nature?

All science has one aim, namely, to find a theory of nature. We have theories of races and of functions, but scarcely yet a remote approximation to an idea of creation. We are now so far from the road to truth, that religious teachers dispute and hate each other, and speculative men are esteemed unsound and frivolous. But to a sound judgment, the most abstract truth is the most practical. Whenever a true theory appears, it will be its own evidence. Its test is, that it will explain all phenomena. Now many are thought not only unexplained but inexplicable; as language, sleep, dreams, beasts, sex.

Philosophically considered, the universe is composed of Nature and the Soul. Strictly speaking, therefore, all that is separate from us, all which Philosophy distinguishes as the NOT ME,[3] that is, both nature and art, all other men and my own body, must be ranked under this name, NATURE. In enumerating the values of nature and casting up their sum, I shall use the word in both senses;—in its common and in its philosophical import. In inquiries so general as our present one, the inaccuracy is not material; no confusion of thought will occur. *Nature*, in the common sense, refers to essences unchanged by man; space, the air, the river, the leaf. *Art* is applied to the mixture of his will with the same things, as in a house, a canal, a statue, a picture. But his operations taken together are so insignificant, a little chipping, baking, patching, and washing, that in an impression so grand as that of the world on the human mind, they do not vary the result.

Chapter I. Nature

To go into solitude, a man needs to retire as much from his chamber as from society. I am not solitary whilst I read and write, though nobody is with me. But if a man would be alone, let him look at the stars. The rays that come

---

2. An echo of Ezekiel 37.1–14, esp. 37.4, where God tells Ezekiel to "Prophesy upon these bones, and say unto them, O ye dry bones, hear the word of the Lord." Emerson had left the ministry but was still writing as a prophet.

3. Emerson takes "not me" from Thomas Carlyle's *Sartor Resartus* (1833–34), where it appears as a translation of the recent German philosophical term for everything but the self.

from those heavenly worlds, will separate between him and vulgar things. One might think the atmosphere was made transparent with this design, to give man, in the heavenly bodies, the perpetual presence of the sublime. Seen in the streets of cities, how great they are! If the stars should appear one night in a thousand years, how would men believe and adore; and preserve for many generations the remembrance of the city of God which had been shown! But every night come out these preachers of beauty, and light the universe with their admonishing smile.

The stars awaken a certain reverence, because though always present, they are always inaccessible; but all natural objects make a kindred impression, when the mind is open to their influence. Nature never wears a mean appearance. Neither does the wisest man extort all her secret, and lose his curiosity by finding out all her perfection. Nature never became a toy to a wise spirit. The flowers, the animals, the mountains, reflected all the wisdom of his best hour, as much as they had delighted the simplicity of his childhood.

When we speak of nature in this manner, we have a distinct but most poetical sense in the mind. We mean the integrity of impression made by manifold natural objects. It is this which distinguishes the stick of timber of the wood-cutter, from the tree of the poet. The charming landscape which I saw this morning, is indubitably made up of some twenty or thirty farms. Miller owns this field, Locke that, and Manning the woodland beyond. But none of them owns the landscape. There is a property in the horizon which no man has but he whose eye can integrate all the parts, that is, the poet. This is the best part of these men's farms, yet to this their land-deeds give them no title.[4]

To speak truly, few adult persons can see nature. Most persons do not see the sun. At least they have a very superficial seeing. The sun illuminates only the eye of the man, but shines into the eye and the heart of the child. The lover of nature is he whose inward and outward senses are still truly adjusted to each other; who has retained the spirit of infancy even into the era of manhood.[5] His intercourse with heaven and earth, becomes part of his daily food. In the presence of nature, a wild delight runs through the man, in spite of real sorrows. Nature says,—he is my creature, and maugre[6] all his impertinent griefs, he shall be glad with me. Not the sun or the summer alone, but every hour and season yields its tribute of delight; for every hour and change corresponds to and authorizes a different state of the mind, from breathless noon to grimmest midnight. Nature is a setting that fits equally well a comic or a mourning piece. In good health, the air is a cordial of incredible virtue. Crossing a bare common, in snow puddles, at twilight, under a clouded sky, without having in my thoughts any occurrence of special good fortune, I have enjoyed a perfect exhilaration. Almost I fear to think how glad I am. In the woods too, a man casts off his years, as the snake his slough, and at what period soever of life, is always a child. In the woods, is perpetual youth. Within these plantations of God, a decorum and sanctity reign, a perennial festival is dressed, and the guest sees not how he should tire of them in a thousand years. In the woods, we return to reason and faith. There I feel that nothing can befal me in life,—no disgrace, no calamity, (leaving me my eyes,) which nature cannot

4. Cf., *Where I Lived, and What I Lived For* (p. 1791) in the opening paragraphs of Thoreau's *Walden*.
5. An echo of Samuel Taylor Coleridge's *Biographia Literaria*, chap. 4, in which Coleridge defines the character and privilege of genius as the ability to carry the feelings of childhood into the powers of adulthood.
6. Despite.

repair. Standing on the bare ground,—my head bathed by the blithe air, and uplifted into infinite space,—all mean egotism vanishes. I become a transparent eye-ball.[7] I am nothing. I see all. The currents of the Universal Being circulate through me; I am part or particle of God. The name of the nearest friend sounds then foreign and accidental. To be brothers, to be acquaintances,—master or servant, is then a trifle and a disturbance. I am the lover of uncontained and immortal beauty. In the wilderness, I find something more dear and connate[8] than in streets or villages. In the tranquil landscape, and especially in the distant line of the horizon, man beholds somewhat as beautiful as his own nature.

The greatest delight which the fields and woods minister, is the suggestion of an occult relation between man and the vegetable. I am not alone and unacknowledged. They nod to me and I to them. The waving of the boughs in the storm, is new to me and old. It takes me by surprise, and yet is not unknown. Its effect is like that of a higher thought or a better emotion coming over me, when I deemed I was thinking justly or doing right.

Yet it is certain that the power to produce this delight, does not reside in nature, but in man, or in a harmony of both. It is necessary to use these pleasures with great temperance. For, nature is not always tricked in holiday attire, but the same scene which yesterday breathed perfume and glittered as for the frolic of the nymphs, is overspread with melancholy today. Nature always wears the colors of the spirit.[9] To a man laboring under calamity, the heat of his own fire hath sadness in it. Then, there is a kind of contempt of the landscape felt by him who has just lost by death a dear friend. The sky is less grand as it shuts down over less worth in the population.

Chapter II. Commodity[1]

Whoever considers the final cause[2] of the world, will discern a multitude of uses that enter as parts into that result. They all admit of being thrown into one of the following classes; Commodity; Beauty; Language; and Discipline.

Under the general name of Commodity, I rank all those advantages which our senses owe to nature. This, of course, is a benefit which is temporary and mediate, not ultimate, like its service to the soul. Yet although low, it is perfect in its kind, and is the only use of nature which all men apprehend. The misery of man appears like childish petulance, when we explore the steady and prodigal provision that has been made for his support and delight on this green ball which floats him through the heavens. What angels invented these splendid ornaments, these rich conveniences, this ocean of air above, this ocean of water beneath, this firmament of earth between? this zodiac of lights, this tent of dropping clouds, this striped coat of climates, this fourfold year? Beasts, fire, water, stones, and corn serve him. The field is at once his floor, his work-yard, his play-ground, his garden, and his bed.

---

7. The most famous phrase in the essay, endlessly ridiculed and explicated. As Sealts says in *The Composition of Nature*, Emerson is not "merely repeating what he had already said about the implications of the preceding sentence on the bare common." When the speaker leaves the village for the woods, "the level of discourse is significantly shifted along with the setting, and the ensuing episode takes place on what Emerson would later call another 'platform' of experience."
8. Related.
9. See Emerson's maturer broodings on subjectivity in *Experience* (p. 1088).
1. Usefulness.
2. In the sense of "purpose."

"More servants wait on man
Than he'll take notice of."[3]——

Nature, in its ministry to man, is not only the material, but is also the process and the result. All the parts incessantly work into each other's hands for the profit of man. The wind sows the seed; the sun evaporates the sea; the wind blows the vapor to the field; the ice, on the other side of the planet, condenses rain on this; the rain feeds the plant; the plant feeds the animal; and thus the endless circulations of the divine charity nourish man.

The useful arts are but reproductions or new combinations by the wit of man, of the same natural benefactors. He no longer waits for favoring gales, but by means of steam, he realizes the fable of Æolus's bag,[4] and carries the two and thirty winds in the boiler of his boat. To diminish friction, he paves the road with iron bars, and, mounting a coach with a ship-load of men, animals, and merchandise behind him, he darts through the country, from town to town, like an eagle or a swallow through the air. By the aggregate of these aids, how is the face of the world changed, from the era of Noah to that of Napoleon! The private poor man hath cities, ships, canals, bridges, built for him. He goes to the post-office, and the human race run on his errands; to the book-shop, and the human race read and write of all that happens, for him; to the court-house, and nations repair his wrongs. He sets his house upon the road, and the human race go forth every morning, and shovel out the snow, and cut a path for him.

But there is no need of specifying particulars in this class of uses. The catalogue is endless, and the examples so obvious, that I shall leave them to the reader's reflection, with the general remark, that this mercenary benefit is one which has respect to a farther good. A man is fed, not that he may be fed, but that he may work.

Chapter III. Beauty

A nobler want of man is served by nature, namely, the love of Beauty.

The ancient Greeks called the world κοσμο,[5] beauty. Such is the constitution of all things, or such the plastic[6] power of the human eye, that the primary forms, as the sky, the mountain, the tree, the animal, give us a delight *in and for themselves*; a pleasure arising from outline, color, motion, and grouping. This seems partly owing to the eye itself. The eye is the best of artists. By the mutual action of its structure and of the laws of light, perspective is produced, which integrates every mass of objects, of what character soever, into a well colored and shaded globe, so that where the particular objects are mean and unaffecting, the landscape which they compose, is round and symmetrical. And as the eye is the best composer, so light is the first of painters. There is no object so foul that intense light will not make beautiful. And the stimulus it affords to the sense, and a sort of infinitude which it hath, like space and time, make all matter gay. Even the corpse hath its own beauty. But beside this general grace diffused over nature, almost all the individual forms are

---

3. From *Man*, by the English poet George Herbert (1593–1633), quoted at length in chap. 8, "Prospects."
4. In the *Odyssey* 10, Aeolus, the god of winds, gives Odysseus a bag containing favorable winds, but they create a storm when his unwary sailors let them all out

at once; here, Emerson refers only to the harnessing of the powers of nature by human beings. "Realizes": brings into real existence.
5. Cosmos, or order.
6. Creative.

agreeable to the eye, as is proved by our endless imitations[7] of some of them, as the acorn, the grape, the pine-cone, the wheat-ear, the egg, the wings and forms of most birds, the lion's claw, the serpent, the butterfly, sea-shells, flames, clouds, buds, leaves, and the forms of many trees, as the palm.

For better consideration, we may distribute the aspects of Beauty in a three-fold manner.

1. First, the simple perception of natural forms is a delight. The influence of the forms and actions in nature, is so needful to man, that, in its lowest functions, it seems to lie on the confines of commodity and beauty. To the body and mind which have been cramped by noxious work or company, nature is medicinal and restores their tone. The tradesman, the attorney comes out of the din and craft[8] of the street, and sees the sky and the woods, and is a man again. In their eternal calm, he finds himself. The health of the eye seems to demand a horizon. We are never tired, so long as we can see far enough.

But in other hours, Nature satisfies the soul purely by its loveliness, and without any mixture of corporeal benefit. I have seen the spectacle of morning from the hill-top over against my house, from day-break to sun-rise, with emotions which an angel might share. The long slender bars of cloud float like fishes in the sea of crimson light. From the earth, as a shore, I look out into that silent sea. I seem to partake its rapid transformations: the active enchantment reaches my dust, and I dilate and conspire with[9] the morning wind. How does Nature deify us with a few and cheap elements! Give me health and a day, and I will make the pomp of emperors ridiculous. The dawn is my Assyria; the sun-set and moon-rise my Paphos, and unimaginable realms of faerie, broad noon shall be my England of the senses and the understanding; the night shall be my Germany of mystic philosophy and dreams.[1]

Not less excellent, except for our less susceptibility in the afternoon, was the charm, last evening, of a January sunset. The western clouds divided and subdivided themselves into pink flakes modulated with tints of unspeakable softness; and the air had so much life and sweetness, that it was a pain to come within doors. What was it that nature would say? Was there no meaning in the live repose of the valley behind the mill, and which Homer or Shakspeare could not re-form for me in words? The leafless trees become spires of flame in the sunset, with the blue east for their background, and the stars of the dead calices of flowers, and every withered stem and stubble rimed[2] with frost, contribute something to the mute music.

The inhabitants of cities suppose that the country landscape is pleasant only half the year. I please myself with observing the graces of the winter scenery, and believe that we are as much touched by it as by the genial[3] influences of summer. To the attentive eye, each moment of the year has its own beauty, and in the same field, it beholds, every hour, a picture which was never seen before, and which shall never be seen again. The heavens change every moment, and reflect their glory or gloom on the plains beneath. The state of the crop in the surrounding farms alters the expression of the earth from week

---

7. As in architectural and furniture design and decoration.

8. Craftiness, materialism.

9. Breathe with.

1. "Assyria": the ancient Near Eastern empire. "Paphos": the ancient city in Cyprus (site of worship of Aphrodite). In the next part of the passage Emerson is contrasting the Scottish Common Sense philosophy with German post-Kantian idealism.

2. Coated. "Calices": i.e., calyxes; the outer whorls of leaves or sepals at the bases of flowers.

3. Generative, creative.

to week. The succession of native plants in the pastures and roadsides, which make the silent clock by which time tells the summer hours, will make even the divisions of the day sensible to a keen observer. The tribes of birds and insects, like the plants punctual to their time, follow each other, and the year has room for all. By water-courses, the variety is greater. In July, the blue pontederia or pickerel-weed blooms in large beds in the shallow parts of our pleasant river,[4] and swarms with yellow butterflies in continual motion. Art cannot rival this pomp of purple and gold. Indeed the river is a perpetual gala, and boasts each month a new ornament.

But this beauty of Nature which is seen and felt as beauty, is the least part. The shows of day, the dewy morning, the rainbow, mountains, orchards in blossom, stars, moonlight, shadows in still water, and the like, if too eagerly hunted, become shows merely, and mock us with their unreality. Go out of the house to see the moon, and 't is mere tinsel; it will not please as when its light shines upon your necessary journey. The beauty that shimmers in the yellow afternoons of October, who ever could clutch it? Go forth to find it, and it is gone: 't is only a mirage as you look from the windows of the diligence.

2. The presence of a higher, namely, of the spiritual element is essential to its perfection. The high and divine beauty which can be loved without effeminacy, is that which is found in combination with the human will, and never separate. Beauty is the mark God sets upon virtue. Every natural action is graceful. Every heroic act is also decent,[5] and causes the place and the bystanders to shine. We are taught by great actions that the universe is the property of every individual in it. Every rational creature has all nature for his dowry and estate. It is his, if he will. He may divest himself of it; he may creep into a corner, and abdicate his kingdom, as most men do, but he is entitled to the world by his constitution. In proportion to the energy of his thought and will, he takes up the world into himself. "All those things for which men plough, build, or sail, obey virtue;" said an ancient historian.[6] "The winds and waves," said Gibbon,[7] "are always on the side of the ablest navigators." So are the sun and moon and all the stars of heaven. When a noble act is done,—perchance in a scene of great natural beauty; when Leonidas and his three hundred martyrs consume one day in dying, and the sun and moon come each and look at them once in the steep defile of Thermopylæ; when Arnold Winkelried,[8] in the high Alps, under the shadow of the avalanche, gathers in his side a sheaf of Austrian spears to break the line for his comrades; are not these heroes entitled to add the beauty of the scene to the beauty of the deed? When the bark of Columbus nears the shore of America;—before it, the beach lined with savages, fleeing out of all their huts of cane; the sea behind; and the purple mountains of the Indian Archipelago around, can we separate the man from the living picture? Does not the New World clothe his form with her palm-groves and savannahs as fit drapery? Ever does natural beauty steal in like air, and envelope great actions. When Sir Harry Vane[9] was dragged up the Tower-hill, sitting on a sled, to suffer death, as the champion

4. The Concord River.
5. Beautiful.
6. Sallust (1st century B.C.), Roman historian, in *The Conspiracy of Cataline*, chap. 2.
7. Edward Gibbon (1737–1794), English historian, from *The Decline and Fall of the Roman Empire*, chap. 68 (*JMN* 5.108).

8. Arnold von Winkelried, a Swiss hero, was killed (1386) in a battle against the Austrians at Sempach. Leonidas, king of Sparta, was killed (c. 480 B.C.) defending the pass at Thermopylae against the Persian army led by Xerxes.
9. A Puritan, once colonial governor of Massachusetts; he was executed for treason in 1662.

of the English laws, one of the multitude cried out to him, "You never sate on so glorious a seat." Charles II., to intimidate the citizens of London, caused the patriot Lord Russel[1] to be drawn in an open coach, through the principal streets of the city, on his way to the scaffold. "But," to use the simple narrative of his biographer, "the multitude imagined they saw liberty and virtue sitting by his side." In private places, among sordid objects, an act of truth or heroism seems at once to draw to itself the sky as its temple, the sun as its candle. Nature stretcheth out her arms to embrace man, only let his thoughts be of equal greatness. Willingly does she follow his steps with the rose and the violet, and bend her lines of grandeur and grace to the decoration of her darling child. Only let his thoughts be of equal scope, and the frame will suit the picture. A virtuous man, is in unison with her works, and makes the central figure of the visible sphere. Homer, Pindar, Socrates, Phocion,[2] associate themselves fitly in our memory with the whole geography and climate of Greece. The visible heavens and earth sympathize with Jesus. And in common life, whosoever has seen a person of powerful character and happy genius, will have remarked how easily he took all things along with him,—the persons, the opinions, and the day, and nature became ancillary to a man.

3. There is still another aspect under which the beauty of the world may be viewed, namely, as it becomes an object of the intellect. Beside the relation of things to virtue, they have a relation to thought. The intellect searches out the absolute order of things as they stand in the mind of God, and without the colors of affection.[3] The intellectual and the active powers seem to succeed each other in man, and the exclusive activity of the one, generates the exclusive activity of the other. There is something unfriendly in each to the other, but they are like the alternate periods of feeding and working in animals; each prepares and certainly will be followed by the other. Therefore does beauty, which, in relation to actions, as we have seen comes unsought, and comes because it is unsought, remain for the apprehension and pursuit of the intellect; and then again, in its turn, of the active power. Nothing divine dies. All good is eternally reproductive. The beauty of nature reforms itself in the mind, and not for barren contemplation, but for new creation.

All men are in some degree impressed by the face of the world. Some men even to delight. This love of beauty is Taste. Others have the same love in such excess, that, not content with admiring, they seek to embody it in new forms. The creation of beauty is Art.

The production of a work of art throws a light upon the mystery of humanity. A work of art is an abstract or epitome of the world. It is the result or expression of nature, in miniature. For although the works of nature are innumerable and all different, the result or the expression of them all is similar and single. Nature is a sea of forms radically alike and even unique.[4] A leaf, a sunbeam, a landscape, the ocean, make an analogous impression on the mind. What is common to them all,—that perfectness and harmony, is beauty. Therefore the standard of beauty, is the entire circuit of natural forms,—the totality of nature; which the Italians expressed by defining beauty "il piu nell'

1. William, Lord Russel (b. 1639) was executed for treason in 1683 after perjurous testimony. *JMN* (5.76) cites Emerson's source as Alexander Chalmer's *General Biographical Dictionary*.
2. Athenian statesman and general of the 4th century B.C., of whom Emerson knew from Plutarch's *Lives*.

Homer was the legendary Greek author of *The Iliad* and *The Odyssey*. Pindar was a Greek lyric poet of the 5th and 6th centuries B.C. Socrates was a Greek philosopher of the 5th century B.C.
3. Modifying emotions.
4. Similar to the point of being identical.

uno."[5] Nothing is quite beautiful alone: nothing but is beautiful in the whole. A single object is only so far beautiful as it suggests this universal grace. The poet, the painter, the sculptor, the musician, the architect seek each to concentrate this radiance of the world on one point, and each in his several work to satisfy the love of beauty which stimulates him to produce. Thus is Art, a nature passed through the alembic[6] of man. Thus in art, does nature work through the will of a man filled with the beauty of her first works.

The world thus exists to the soul to satisfy the desire of beauty. Extend this element to the uttermost, and I call it an ultimate end. No reason can be asked or given why the soul seeks beauty. Beauty, in its largest and profoundest sense, is one expression for the universe. God is the all-fair. Truth, and goodness, and beauty, are but different faces of the same All. But beauty in nature is not ultimate. It is the herald of inward and eternal beauty, and is not alone a solid and satisfactory good. It must therefore stand as a part and not as yet the last or highest expression of the final cause of Nature.

Chapter IV. Language

A third use which Nature subserves to man is that of Language. Nature is the vehicle of thought, and in a simple, double, and threefold degree.

1. Words are signs of natural facts.
2. Particular natural facts are symbols of particular spiritual facts.
3. Nature is the symbol of spirit.

1. Words are signs of natural facts. The use of natural history is to give us aid in supernatural history. The use of the outer creation is to give us language for the beings and changes of the inward creation. Every word which is used to express a moral or intellectual fact, if traced to its root, is found to be borrowed from some material appearance. *Right* originally means *straight*; *wrong* means *twisted*. *Spirit* primarily means *wind*; *transgression*, the crossing of a *line*; *supercilious*, the *raising of the eye-brow*. We say the *heart* to express emotion, the *head* to denote thought; and *thought* and *emotion* are, in their turn, words borrowed from sensible things, and now appropriated to spiritual nature. Most of the process by which this transformation is made, is hidden from us in the remote time when language was framed; but the same tendency may be daily observed in children. Children and savages use only nouns or names of things, which they continually convert into verbs, and apply to analogous mental acts.

2. But this origin of all words that convey a spiritual import,—so conspicuous a fact in the history of language,—is our least debt to nature. It is not words only that are emblematic; it is things which are emblematic. Every natural fact is a symbol of some spiritual fact.[7] Every appearance in nature corresponds to some state of the mind, and that state of the mind can only be described by presenting that natural appearance as its picture. An enraged man is a lion, a cunning man is a fox, a firm man is a rock, a learned man is a torch. A lamb is innocence; a snake is subtle spite; flowers express to us the delicate affections. Light and darkness are our familiar expression for knowl-

---

5. The many in one (a borrowing from Coleridge).
6. A distilling apparatus.
7. This passage owes much to the Swedish theologian and mystic Emanuel Swedenborg (1688–1772), whose doctrine of correspondence between the inner and outer worlds underlies much of Emerson's thought.

edge and ignorance; and heat for love. Visible distance behind and before us, is respectively our image of memory and hope.

Who looks upon a river in a meditative hour, and is not reminded of the flux of all things? Throw a stone into the stream, and the circles that propagate themselves are the beautiful type of all influence. Man is conscious of a universal soul within or behind his individual life, wherein, as in a firmament, the natures of Justice, Truth, Love, Freedom, arise and shine. This universal soul, he calls Reason: it is not mine or thine or his, but we are its; we are its property and men.[8] And the blue sky in which the private earth is buried, the sky with its eternal calm, and full of everlasting orbs, is the type of Reason. That which, intellectually considered, we call Reason, considered in relation to nature, we call Spirit. Spirit is the Creator. Spirit hath life in itself. And man in all ages and countries, embodies it in his language, as the FATHER.

It is easily seen that there is nothing lucky or capricious in these analogies, but that they are constant, and pervade nature. These are not the dreams of a few poets, here and there, but man is an analogist, and studies relations in all objects. He is placed in the centre of beings, and a ray of relation passes from every other being to him. And neither can man be understood without these objects, nor these objects without man. All the facts in natural history taken by themselves, have no value, but are barren like a single sex. But marry it to human history, and it is full of life. Whole Floras, all Linnæus' and Buffon's[9] volume, are but dry catalogues of facts; but the most trivial of these facts, the habit of a plant, the organs, or work, or noise of an insect, applied to the illustration of a fact in intellectual philosophy, or, in any way associated to human nature, affects us in the most lively and agreeable manner. The seed of a plant,—to what affecting analogies in the nature of man, is that little fruit made use of, in all discourse, up to the voice of Paul, who calls the human corpse a seed,—"It is sown a natural body; it is raised a spiritual body."[1] The motion of the earth round its axis, and round the sun, makes the day, and the year. These are certain amounts of brute light and heat. But is there no intent of an analogy between man's life and the seasons? And do the seasons gain no grandeur or pathos from that analogy? The instincts of the ant are very unimportant considered as the ant's; but the moment a ray of relation is seen to extend from it to man, and the little drudge is seen to be a monitor, a little body with a mighty heart, then all its habits, even that said to be recently observed, that it never sleeps, become sublime.

Because of this radical[2] correspondence between visible things and human thoughts, savages, who have only what is necessary, converse in figures. As we go back in history, language becomes more picturesque, until its infancy, when it is all poetry; or, all spiritual facts are represented by natural symbols.[3] The same symbols are found to make the original elements of all languages. It has moreover been observed, that the idioms of all languages approach each other in passages of the greatest eloquence and power. And as this is the first language, so is it the last. This immediate dependence of language upon nature, this conversion of an outward phenomenon into a type of somewhat

8. As he regularly does, Emerson uses *reason* to mean something like what we think of as the intuitive powers of the mind and *understanding* to mean the rational powers.

9. French naturalist (1707–1788). "Linnaeus": Carl von Linné (1707–1778), Swedish botanist.

1. 1 Corinthians 15.44.

2. Fundamental (literally "from the root").

3. The superseded theory of language was a Romantic commonplace, familiar to Emerson from Percy Bysshe Shelley's A *Defense of Poetry* (1821): "In the infancy of society every author is necessarily a poet."

in human life, never loses its power to affect us. It is this which gives that piquancy to the conversation of a strong-natured farmer or back-woodsman, which all men relish.

Thus is nature an interpreter, by whose means man converses with his fellow men. A man's power to connect his thought with its proper symbol, and so utter it, depends on the simplicity of his character, that is, upon his love of truth and his desire to communicate it without loss. The corruption of man is followed by the corruption of language. When simplicity of character and the sovereignty of ideas is broken up by the prevalence of secondary desires, the desire of riches, the desire of pleasure, the desire of power, the desire of praise,—and duplicity and falsehood take place of simplicity and truth, the power over nature as an interpreter of the will, is in a degree lost; new imagery ceases to be created, and old words are perverted to stand for things which are not; a paper currency is employed when there is no bullion in the vaults. In due time, the fraud is manifest, and words lose all power to stimulate the understanding or the affections. Hundreds of writers may be found in every long-civilized nation, who for a short time believe, and make others believe, that they see and utter truths, who do not of themselves clothe one thought in its natural garment, but who feed unconsciously upon the language created by the primary writers of the country, those, namely, who hold primarily on nature.

But wise men pierce this rotten diction and fasten words again to visible things; so that picturesque language is at once a commanding certificate that he who employs it, is a man in alliance with truth and God. The moment our discourse rises above the ground line of familiar facts, and is inflamed with passion or exalted by thought, it clothes itself in images. A man conversing in earnest, if he watch his intellectual processes, will find that always a material image, more or less luminous, arises in his mind, contemporaneous with every thought, which furnishes the vestment of the thought. Hence, good writing and brilliant discourse are perpetual allegories. This imagery is spontaneous. It is the blending of experience with the present action of the mind. It is proper creation. It is the working of the Original Cause through the instruments he has already made.

These facts may suggest the advantage which the country-life possesses for a powerful mind, over the artificial and curtailed life of cities. We know more from nature than we can at will communicate. Its light flows into the mind evermore, and we forget its presence. The poet, the orator, bred in the woods, whose scenes have been nourished by their fair and appeasing changes, year after year, without design and without heed,—shall not lose their lesson altogether, in the roar of cities or the broil of politics. Long hereafter, amidst agitation and terror in national councils,—in the hour of revolution,—these solemn images shall reappear in their morning lustre, as fit symbols and words of the thoughts which the passing events shall awaken. At the call of a noble sentiment, again the woods wave, the pines murmur, the river rolls and shines, and the cattle low upon the mountains, as he saw and heard them in his infancy. And with these forms, the spells of persuasion, the keys of power are put into his hands.

3. We are thus assisted by natural objects in the expression of particular meanings. But how great a language to convey such pepper-corn informations! Did it need such noble races of creatures, this profusion of forms, this host of

orbs in heaven, to furnish man with the dictionary and grammar of his municipal speech? Whilst we use this grand cipher to expedite the affairs of our pot
and kettle, we feel that we have not yet put it to its use, neither are able. We
are like travellers using the cinders of a volcano to roast their eggs. Whilst we
see that it always stands ready to clothe what we would say, we cannot avoid
the question, whether the characters are not significant of themselves. Have
mountains, and waves, and skies, no significance but what we consciously
give them, when we employ them as emblems of our thoughts? The world is
emblematic. Parts of speech are metaphors because the whole of nature is a
metaphor of the human mind. The laws of moral nature answer to those of
matter as face to face in a glass. "The visible world and the relation of its parts,
is the dial plate of the invisible."[4] The axioms of physics translate the laws of
ethics.[5] Thus, "the whole is greater than its part;" "reaction is equal to action;"
"the smallest weight may be made to lift the greatest, the difference of weight
being compensated by time;" and many the like propositions, which have an
ethical as well as physical sense. These propositions have a much more extensive and universal sense when applied to human life, than when confined to
technical use.

In like manner, the memorable words of history, and the proverbs of
nations, consist usually of a natural fact, selected as a picture or parable of a
moral truth. Thus; A rolling stone gathers no moss; A bird in the hand is worth
two in the bush; A cripple in the right way, will beat a racer in the wrong;
Make hay whilst the sun shines; 'T is hard to carry a full cup even; Vinegar is
the son of wine; The last ounce broke the camel's back; Long-lived trees make
roots first;—and the like.[6] In their primary sense these are trivial facts, but we
repeat them for the value of their analogical import. What is true of proverbs,
is true of all fables, parables, and allegories.

This relation between the mind and matter is not fancied by some poet, but
stands in the will of God, and so is free to be known by all men. It appears to
men, or it does not appear. When in fortunate hours we ponder this miracle,
the wise man doubts, if, at all other times, he is not blind and deaf;

> ——"Can these things be,
> And overcome us like a summer's cloud,
> Without our special wonder?"[7]

for the universe becomes transparent, and the light of higher laws than its
own, shines through it. It is the standing problem which has exercised the
wonder and the study of every fine genius since the world began; from the era
of the Egyptians and the Brahmins, to that of Pythagoras, of Plato, of Bacon,
of Leibnitz, of Swedenborg.[8] There sits the Sphinx at the road-side, and from
age to age, as each prophet comes by, he tries his fortune at reading her riddle.[9] There seems to be a necessity in spirit to manifest itself in material forms;

4. Emerson copied the Swedenborg quotation from
the *New Jerusalem Magazine* (July 1832), 437 (*JMN*
4.33).
5. Adapted from Mme. De Stael's *Germany* (1813):
"Not a mathematical axiom but is a moral rule"
(*JMN* 3.255).
6. A list of proverbs in *JMN* (6.138–41) includes several of these, the one about the cripple in the race being attributed to Francis Bacon's *The Advancement of
Learning*, II, and the one about the full cup being attributed to Robert Leighton's *Select Works*.

7. *Macbeth*, 3.4.110–12 (Emerson misquotes "these"
for "such").
8. For Emerson, representatives of "every fine genius
since the world began" (*Early Lectures*, 1.224).
9. In Greek mythology, the winged monster with a
lion's body and the head and breasts of a woman
perched on a rock near Thebes and challenged every
passerby with a riddle; if they answered incorrectly, she
killed them. When Oedipus answered it correctly, she
killed herself.

and day and night, river and storm, beast and bird, acid and alkali, preëxist in necessary Ideas in the mind of God, and are what they are by virtue of preceding affections,[1] in the world of spirit. A Fact is the end or last issue of spirit. The visible creation is the terminus or the circumference of the invisible world. "Material objects," said a French philosopher, "are necessarily kinds of *scoriæ* of the substantial thoughts of the Creator, which must always preserve an exact relation to their first origin; in other words, visible nature must have a spiritual and moral side."[2]

This doctrine is abstruse, and though the images of "garment," "scoriæ," "mirror," &c., may stimulate the fancy, we must summon the aid of subtler and more vital expositors to make it plain. "Every scripture is to be interpreted by the same spirit which gave it forth,"—is the fundamental law of criticism.[3] A life in harmony with nature, the love of truth and of virtue, will purge the eyes to understand her text. By degrees we may come to know the primitive sense of the permanent objects of nature, so that the world shall be to us an open book, and every form significant of its hidden life and final cause.

A new interest surprises us, whilst, under the view now suggested, we contemplate the fearful extent and multitude of objects; since "every object rightly seen, unlocks a new faculty of the soul."[4] That which was unconscious truth, becomes, when interpreted and defined in an object, a part of the domain of knowledge,—a new amount to the magazine[5] of power.

Chapter V. Discipline[6]

In view of this significance of nature, we arrive at once at a new fact, that nature is a discipline. This use of the world includes the preceding uses, as parts of itself.

Space, time, society, labor, climate, food, locomotion, the animals, the mechanical forces, give us sincerest lessons, day by day, whose meaning is unlimited. They educate both the Understanding and the Reason. Every property of matter is a school for the understanding,—its solidity or resistance, its inertia, its extension, its figure, its divisibility. The understanding adds, divides, combines, measures, and finds everlasting nutriment and room for its activity in this worthy scene. Meantime, Reason transfers all these lessons into its own world of thought, by perceiving the analogy that marries Matter and Mind.

1. Nature is a discipline of the understanding in intellectual truths. Our dealing with sensible objects is a constant exercise in the necessary lessons of difference, of likeness, of order, of being and seeming, of progressive arrangement;[7] of ascent from particular to general; of combination to one end of manifold forces. Proportioned to the importance of the organ to be formed, is

---

1. Modifying emotions.
2. Guillaume Oegger, *The True Messiah* (1829), which Emerson had seen in a manuscript translation, perhaps by Elizabeth Peabody. "Scoriæ": i.e., scoria; slag or refuse left after metal has been smelted from ore.
3. From the English Quaker, George Fox (1624–91) (*JMN* 4.31).
4. From Coleridge's *Aids to Reflection* (1829), 150–51 (*JMN* 5.189).
5. Storehouse.

6. Whicher quotes the American literature anthologists Bradley, Beatty, and Long for their caution about the term *discipline*: "A trained ecclesiastic, Emerson utilizes the dualism of this word, signifying at once a controlled obedience to the absolute, and, secondly, the ecclesiastical discipline of practical rules affecting conduct."
7. A borrowing from Coleridge's *The Friend* (1818). Emerson made a note on "what Coleridge defines Method, viz. progressive arrangement" (*JMN* 3.299).

the extreme care with which its tuition is provided,—a care pretermitted[8] in no single case. What tedious training, day after day, year after year, never ending, to form the common sense; what continual reproduction of annoyances, inconveniences, dilemmas; what rejoicing over us of little men; what disputing of prices, what reckonings of interest,—and all to form the Hand of the mind;—to instruct us that "good thoughts are no better than good dreams, unless they be executed!"[9]

The same good office is performed by Property and its filial systems of debt and credit. Debt, grinding debt, whose iron face the widow, the orphan, and the sons of genius fear and hate;—debt, which consumes so much time, which so cripples and disheartens a great spirit with cares that seem so base, is a preceptor whose lessons cannot be foregone, and is needed most by those who suffer from it most. Moreover, property, which has been well compared to snow,—"if it fall level to-day, it will be blown into drifts tomorrow,"—is merely the surface action of internal machinery, like the index on the face of a clock. Whilst now it is the gymnastics of the understanding, it is hiving in the foresight of the spirit, experience in profounder laws.

The whole character and fortune of the individual is affected by the least inequalities in the culture of the understanding; for example, in the perception of differences. Therefore is Space, and therefore Time, that man may know that things are not huddled and lumped, but sundered and individual. A bell and a plough have each their use, and neither can do the office of the other. Water is good to drink, coal to burn, wool to wear; but wool cannot be drunk, nor water spun, nor coal eaten. The wise man shows his wisdom in separation, in gradation, and his scale of creatures and of merits, is as wide as nature. The foolish have no range in their scale, but suppose every man is as every other man. What is not good they call the worst, and what is not hateful, they call the best.

In like manner, what good heed, nature forms in us! She pardons no mistakes. Her yea is yea, and her nay, nay.

The first steps in Agriculture, Astronomy, Zoölogy, (those first steps which the farmer, the hunter, and the sailor take,) teach that nature's dice are always loaded; that in her heaps and rubbish are concealed sure and useful results.

How calmly and genially the mind apprehends one after another the laws of physics! What noble emotions dilate the mortal as he enters into the counsels of the creation, and feels by knowledge the privilege to BE His insight refines him. The beauty of nature shines in his own breast. Man is greater that he can see this, and the universe less, because Time and Space relations vanish as laws are known.

Here again we are impressed and even daunted by the immense Universe to be explored. 'What we know, is a point to what we do not know.'[1] Open any recent journal of science, and weigh the problems suggested concerning Light, Heat, Electricity, Magnetism, Physiology, Geology, and judge whether the interest of natural science is likely to be soon exhausted.

Passing by many particulars of the discipline of nature we must not omit to specify two.

8. Neglected. "Tuition": guardianship.
9. Adapted from Francis Bacon's essay *Of Great Place* (*JMN* 5.136).
1. A saying ascribed both to Sir Isaac Newton

(1642–1727), English mathematician and philosopher, and to Bishop Joseph Butler (1692– 1752), the moralist.

The exercise of the Will or the lesson of power is taught in every event. From the child's successive possession of his several senses up to the hour when he saith, "thy will be done!"[2] he is learning the secret, that he can reduce under his will, not only particular events, but great classes, nay the whole series of events, and so conform all facts to his character. Nature is thoroughly mediate. It is made to serve. It receives the dominion of man as meekly as the ass on which the Saviour rode.[3] It offers all its kingdoms to man as the raw material which he may mould into what is useful. Man is never weary of working it up. He forges the subtile and delicate air into wise and melodious words, and gives them wing as angels of persuasion and command. More and more, with every thought, does his kingdom stretch over things, until the world becomes, at last, only a realized will,—the double of the man.

2. Sensible objects conform to the premonitions of Reason and reflect the conscience. All things are moral; and in their boundless changes have an unceasing reference to spiritual nature. Therefore is nature glorious with form, color, and motion, that every globe in the remotest heaven; every chemical change from the rudest crystal up to the laws of life; every change of vegetation from the first principle of growth in the eye of a leaf, to the tropical forest and antediluvian[4] coal-mine; every animal function from the sponge up to Hercules,[5] shall hint or thunder to man the laws of right and wrong, and echo the Ten Commandments. Therefore is nature always the ally of Religion: lends all her pomp and riches to the religious sentiment. Prophet and priest, David, Isaiah, Jesus, have drawn deeply from this source.

This ethical character so penetrates the bone and marrow of nature, as to seem the end for which it was made. Whatever private purpose is answered by any member or part, this is its public and universal function, and is never omitted. Nothing in nature is exhausted in its first use. When a thing has served an end to the uttermost, it is wholly new for an ulterior service. In God, every end is converted into a new means. Thus the use of Commodity, regarded by itself, is mean and squalid. But it is to the mind an education in the great doctrine of Use, namely, that a thing is good only so far as it serves; that a conspiring of parts and efforts to the production of an end, is essential to any being. The first and gross manifestation of this truth, is our inevitable and hated training in values and wants, in corn and meat.

It has already been illustrated, in treating of the significance of material things, that every natural process is but a version of a moral sentence. The moral law lies at the centre of nature and radiates to the circumference. It is the pith and marrow of every substance, every relation, and every process. All things with which we deal, preach to us. What is a farm but a mute gospel? The chaff and the wheat, weeds and plants, blight, rain, insects, sun,—it is a sacred emblem from the first furrow of spring to the last stack which the snow of winter overtakes in the fields. But the sailor, the shepherd, the miner, the merchant, in their several resorts, have each an experience precisely parallel and leading to the same conclusions. Because all organizations are radically alike. Nor can it be doubted that this moral sentiment which thus scents the air, and grows in the grain, and impregnates the waters of the world, is caught by man and sinks into his soul. The moral influence of nature upon every

---

2. Matthew 6.10 and 26.42.
3. Matthew 21.5.
4. Before the Flood, which destroyed all living crea-

tures not in Noah's ark (Genesis 6–9).
5. In Greek mythology the hero renowned for feats of strength.

individual is that amount of truth which it illustrates to him. Who can estimate this? Who can guess how much firmness the sea-beaten rock has taught the fisherman? how much tranquillity has been reflected to man from the azure sky, over whose unspotted deeps the winds forevermore drive flocks of stormy clouds, and leave no wrinkle or stain? how much industry and providence and affection we have caught from the pantomime of brutes? What a searching preacher of self-command is the varying phenomenon of Health!

Herein is especially apprehended the Unity of Nature,—the Unity in Variety,—which meets us everywhere. All the endless variety of things make a unique, an identical impression. Xenophanes[6] complained in his old age, that, look where he would, all things hastened back to Unity. He was weary of seeing the same entity in the tedious variety of forms. The fable of Proteus has a cordial[7] truth. Every particular in nature, a leaf, a drop, a crystal, a moment of time is related to the whole, and partakes of the perfection of the whole. Each particle is a microcosm, and faithfully renders the likeness of the world.

Not only resemblances exist in things whose analogy is obvious, as when we detect the type of the human hand in the flipper of the fossil saurus, but also in objects wherein there is great superficial unlikeness. Thus architecture is called 'frozen music,' by De Stael and Goethe.[8] 'A Gothic church,' said Coleridge,[9] 'is a petrified religion.' Michael Angelo maintained, that, to an architect, a knowledge of anatomy is essential.[1] In Haydn's[2] oratorios, the notes present to the imagination not only motions, as, of the snake, the stag, and the elephant, but colors also; as the green grass. The granite is differenced in its laws only by the more or less of heat, from the river that wears it away. The river, as it flows, resembles the air that flows over it; the air resembles the light which traverses it with more subtile currents; the light resembles the heat which rides with it through Space. Each creature is only a modification of the other; the likeness in them is more than the difference, and their radical law is one and the same. Hence it is, that a rule of one art, or a law of one organization, holds true throughout nature. So intimate is this Unity, that, it is easily seen, it lies under the undermost garment of nature, and betrays its source in universal Spirit. For, it pervades Thought also. Every universal truth which we express in words, implies or supposes every other truth. *Omne verum vero consonat.*[3] It is like a great circle on a sphere, comprising all possible circles; which, however, may be drawn, and comprise it, in like manner. Every such truth is the absolute Ens[4] seen from one side. But it has innumerable sides.

The same central Unity is still more conspicuous in actions. Words are finite organs of the infinite mind. They cannot cover the dimensions of what is in truth. They break, chop, and impoverish it. An action is the perfection and publication of thought. A right action seems to fill the eye, and to be

---

6. Greek philosopher of 5th and 6th centuries B.C. who taught the unity of all existence (*JMN* 3.369 and 5.136).
7. Vital, heartwarming. "Proteus": sea god who could change his shape so as to evade any captor.
8. Johann Wolfgang von Goethe (1749–1832), in his *Conversations with Eckermann* (*JMN* 4.337). Mme. de Stael (1766–1817), in *Corinne*, book 4, chap. 3 (*JMN* 4.40).
9. In his *Lecture on the General Character of the*

Gothic Mind in the Middle Ages (1836) (*JMN* 5.36).
1. From the sketch of Michelangelo in *Lives of Eminent Persons* (1833), p. 57 (*JMN* 5.367–68).
2. Franz Joseph Haydn (1732–1809), Austrian composer (*JMN* 5.137).
3. Every truth agrees with every other truth (Latin). "We say every truth supposes or implies every other truth" (*JMN* 4.376).
4. Abstract being.

related to all nature. "The wise man, in doing one thing, does all; or, in the one thing he does rightly, he sees the likeness of all which is done rightly."[5]

Words and actions are not the attributes of mute and brute nature. They introduce us to that singular form which predominates over all other forms. This is the human. All other organizations appear to be degradations of the human form. When this organization appears among so many that surround it, the spirit prefers it to all others. It says, 'From such as this, have I drawn joy and knowledge. In such as this, have I found and beheld myself. I will speak to it. It can speak again. It can yield me thought already formed and alive.' In fact, the eye,—the mind,—is always accompanied by these forms, male and female; and these are incomparably the richest informations[6] of the power and order that lie at the heart of things. Unfortunately, every one of them bears the marks as of some injury; is marred and superficially defective. Nevertheless, far different from the deaf and dumb nature around them, these all rest like fountain-pipes on the unfathomed sea of thought and virtue whereto they alone, of all organizations, are the entrances.

It were a pleasant inquiry to follow into detail their ministry to our education, but where would it stop? We are associated in adolescent and adult life with some friends, who, like skies and waters, are coextensive with our idea; who, answering each to a certain affection of the soul, satisfy our desire on that side; whom we lack power to put at such focal distance from us, that we can mend or even analyze them. We cannot chuse but love them. When much intercourse with a friend has supplied us with a standard of excellence, and has increased our respect for the resources of God who thus sends a real person to outgo our ideal; when he has, moreover, become an object of thought, and, whilst his character retains all its unconscious effect, is converted in the mind into solid and sweet wisdom,—it is a sign to us that his office is closing, and he is commonly withdrawn from our sight in a short time.

Chapter VI. Idealism

Thus is the unspeakable but intelligible and practicable meaning of the world conveyed to man, the immortal pupil, in every object of sense. To this one end of Discipline, all parts of nature conspire.

A noble doubt perpetually suggests itself, whether this end be not the Final Cause of the Universe; and whether nature outwardly exists. It is a sufficient account of that Appearance we call the World, that God will teach a human mind, and so makes it the receiver of a certain number of congruent sensations, which we call sun and moon, man and woman, house and trade. In my utter impotence to test the authenticity of the report of my senses, to know whether the impressions they make on me correspond with outlying objects, what difference does it make, whether Orion is up there in heaven, or some god paints the image in the firmament of the soul? The relations of parts and the end of the whole remaining the same, what is the difference, whether land and sea interact, and worlds revolve and intermingle without number or end,—deep yawning under deep,[7] and galaxy balancing galaxy, throughout absolute space, or, whether, without relations of time and space, the same

---

5. Paraphrase of Goethe's *Wilhelm Meister* from Carlyle's translation (*JMN* 4.75).
6. Products of the inward, form-giving capacity.

7. From Psalm 42.7: "Deep calleth unto deep at the noise of thy waterspouts: all thy waves and thy billows are gone over me."

appearances are inscribed in the constant faith of man. Whether nature enjoy a substantial existence without, or is only in the apocalypse[8] of the mind, it is alike useful and alike venerable to me. Be it what it may, it is ideal to me, so long as I cannot try the accuracy of my senses.

The frivolous make themselves merry with the Ideal theory,[9] as if its consequences were burlesque; as if it affected the stability of nature. It surely does not. God never jests with us, and will not compromise the end of nature, by permitting any inconsequence in its procession. Any distrust of the permanence of laws, would paralyze the faculties of man. Their permanence is sacredly respected, and his faith therein is perfect. The wheels and springs of man are all set to the hypothesis of the permanence of nature. We are not built like a ship to be tossed, but like a house to stand. It is a natural consequence of this structure, that, so long as the active powers predominate over the reflective, we resist with indignation any hint that nature is more short-lived or mutable than spirit. The broker, the wheelwright, the carpenter, the tollman, are much displeased at the intimation.

But whilst we acquiesce entirely in the permanence of natural laws, the question of the absolute existence of nature, still remains open. It is the uniform effect of culture on the human mind, not to shake our faith in the stability of particular phenomena, as of heat, water, azote;[1] but to lead us to regard nature as a phenomenon, not a substance; to attribute necessary existence to spirit; to esteem nature as an accident and an effect.

To the senses and the unrenewed understanding, belongs a sort of instinctive belief in the absolute existence of nature. In their view, man and nature are indissolubly joined. Things are ultimates, and they never look beyond their sphere. The presence of Reason mars this faith. The first effort of thought tends to relax this despotism of the senses, which binds us to nature as if we were a part of it, and shows us nature aloof, and, as it were, afloat. Until this higher agency intervened, the animal eye sees, with wonderful accuracy, sharp outlines and colored surfaces. When the eye of Reason opens, to outline and surface are at once added, grace and expression. These proceed from imagination and affection, and abate somewhat of the angular distinctness of objects. If the Reason be stimulated to more earnest vision, outlines and surfaces become transparent, and are no longer seen; causes and spirits are seen through them. The best, the happiest moments of life, are these delicious awakenings of the higher powers, and the reverential withdrawing of nature before its God.

Let us proceed to indicate the effects of culture. 1. Our first institution[2] in the Ideal philosophy is a hint from nature herself.

Nature is made to conspire with spirit to emancipate us. Certain mechanical changes, a small alteration in our local position apprizes us of a dualism. We are strangely affected by seeing the shore from a moving ship, from a balloon, or through the tints of an unusual sky. The least change in our point of view, gives the whole world a pictorial air. A man who seldom rides, needs only to get into a coach and traverse his own town, to turn the street into a puppet-show. The men, the women,—talking, running, bartering, fighting,—the earnest mechanic, the lounger, the beggar, the boys, the dogs, are unrealized[3] at

---

8. Revelation.
9. Emerson uses Bishop George Berkeley (1685–1753) as representative of the notion that we can only know ideas in the mind and cannot know material things in themselves.

1. Nitrogen.
2. Instruction. "Effects of culture": in the sense of the effects of awakening thought.
3. Made unsubstantial. "Mechanic": manual laborer.

once, or, at least, wholly detached from all relation to the observer, and seen as apparent, not substantial beings. What new thoughts are suggested by seeing a face of country quite familiar, in the rapid movement of the rail-road car! Nay, the most wonted objects, (make a very slight change in the point of vision,) please us most. In a camera obscura,[4] the butcher's cart, and the figure of one of our own family amuse us. So a portrait of a well-known face gratifies us. Turn the eyes upside down, by looking at the landscape through your legs, and how agreeable is the picture, though you have seen it any time these twenty years!

In these cases, by mechanical means, is suggested the difference between the observer and the spectacle,—between man and nature. Hence arises a pleasure mixed with awe; I may say, a low degree of the sublime is felt from the fact, probably, that man is hereby apprized, that, whilst the world is a spectacle, something in himself is stable.

2. In a higher manner, the poet communicates the same pleasure. By a few strokes he delineates, as on air, the sun, the mountain, the camp, the city, the hero, the maiden, not different from what we know them, but only lifted from the ground and float before the eye. He unfixes the land and the sea, makes them revolve around the axis of his primary thought, and disposes them anew. Possessed himself by a heroic passion, he uses matter as symbols of it. The sensual man conforms thoughts to things; the poet conforms things to his thoughts.[5] The one esteems nature as rooted and fast; the other, as fluid, and impresses his being thereon. To him, the refractory world is ductile and flexible; he invests dusts and stones with humanity and makes them the words of the Reason. The imagination may be defined to be, the use which the Reason makes of the material world. Shakspeare possesses the power of subordinating nature for the purposes of expression, beyond all poets. His imperial muse tosses the creation like a bauble from hand to hand, to embody any capricious shade of thought that is uppermost in his mind. The remotest spaces of nature are visited, and the farthest sundered things are brought together, by a subtle spiritual connexion. We are made aware that magnitude of material things is merely relative, and all objects shrink and expand to serve the passion of the poet. Thus, in his sonnets, the lays of birds, the scents and dyes of flowers, he finds to be the *shadow* of his beloved; time, which keeps her from him, is his *chest*; the suspicion she has awakened, is her *ornament*;[6]

> The ornament of beauty is Suspect,
> A crow which flies in heaven's sweetest air.[7]

His passion is not the fruit of chance; it swells, as he speaks, to a city, or a state.

---

4. Dark chamber or box with a lens or opening through which an image is projected in natural colors onto an opposite surface.

5. From Bacon's *The Advancement of Learning* (2.4.2), but more directly from William Hazlitt's adaptation (*JMN* 6.227).

6. Emerson summarizes Shakespeare's *Sonnet 98*:

From you have I been absent in the spring,
When proud-pied April, dress'd in all his trim,
Hath put a spirit of youth in every thing,
That heavy Saturn laugh'd and leap'd with him.
Yet nor the lays of birds, nor the sweet smell
Of different flowers in odour and in hue,

Could make me any summer's story tell,
Or from their proud lap pluck them where they grew;
Nor did I wonder at the lily's white,
Nor praise the deep vermilion in the rose:
They were but sweet, but figures of delight.
Drawn after you, you pattern of all
    those.
Yet seemed it winter still, and you away,
As with your shadow I with these did play.

Then Emerson refers to *Sonnet 65* ("Shall Time's best jewel from Time's chest lie hid?")

7. Shakespeare's *Sonnet 70*.

No, it was builded far from accident;
It suffers not in smiling pomp, nor falls
Under the brow of thralling discontent;
It fears not policy, that heretic,
That works on leases of short numbered hours,
But all alone stands hugely politic.[8]

In the strength of his constancy, the Pyramids[9] seem to him recent and transitory. And the freshness of youth and love dazzles him with its resemblance to morning.

Take those lips away
Which so sweetly were forsworn;
And those eyes,—the break of day,
Lights that do mislead the morn.[1]

The wild beauty of this hyperbole, I may say, in passing, it would not be easy to match in literature.

This transfiguration which all material objects undergo through the passion of the poet,—this power which he exerts, at any moment, to magnify the small, to micrify the great,—might be illustrated by a thousand examples from his Plays. I have before me the Tempest, and will cite only these few lines.

PROSPERO.   The strong based promontory
Have I made shake, and by the spurs plucked up
The pine and cedar.[2]

Prospero calls for music to sooth the frantic Alonzo, and his companions;

A solemn air, and the best comforter
To an unsettled fancy, cure thy brains
Now useless, boiled within thy skull.

Again;

The charm dissolves space
And, as the morning steals upon the night,
Melting the darkness, so their rising senses
Begin to chase the ignorant fumes that mantle
Their clearer reason.

Their understanding
Begins to swell: and the approaching tide
Will shortly fill the reasonable shores
That now lie foul and muddy.

The perception of real affinities between events, (that is to say, of *ideal* affinities, for those only are real,) enables the poet thus to make free with the most imposing forms and phenomena of the world, and to assert the predominance of the soul.

3. Whilst thus the poet delights us by animating[3] nature like a creator, with

---

8. Shakespeare's *Sonnet 124.*
9. Shakespeare's *Sonnet 123:* "No, Time, thou shalt not boast that I do change: / Thy pyramids built up with newer might / To me are nothing novel, nothing strange: / They are but dressings of a former sight."
1. From Shakespeare's *Measure for Measure* (5.1.1–4).

2. *The Tempest* 5.1.46–48 (the 1836 text says "Ariel" instead of Prospero, a careless slip not preserved here): later quotations are from 5.1.58–60, 64–68, and 79–82.
3. Giving life to.

his own thoughts, he differs from the philosopher only herein, that the one proposes Beauty as his main end; the other Truth. But, the philosopher, not less than the poet, postpones the apparent order and relations of things to the empire of thought. "The problem of philosophy," according to Plato, "is, for all that exists conditionally, to find a ground unconditioned and absolute."[4] It proceeds on the faith that a law determines all phenomena, which being known, the phenomena can be predicted. That law, when in the mind, is an idea. Its beauty is infinite. The true philosopher and the true poet are one, and a beauty, which is truth, and a truth, which is beauty, is the aim of both. Is not the charm of one of Plato's or Aristotle's definitions, strictly like that of the Antigone of Sophocles?[5] It is, in both cases, that a spiritual life has been imparted to nature; that the solid seeming block of matter has been pervaded and dissolved by a thought; that this feeble human being has penetrated the vast masses of nature with an informing soul, and recognised itself in their harmony, that is, seized their law. In physics, when this is attained, the memory disburthens itself of its cumbrous catalogues of particulars, and carries centuries of observation in a single formula.

Thus even in physics, the material is ever degraded before the spiritual. The astronomer, the geometer, rely on their irrefragable analysis, and disdain the results of observation. The sublime remark of Euler[6] on his law of arches, "This will be found contrary to all experience, yet it is true;" had already transferred nature into the mind, and left matter like an outcast corpse.

4. Intellectual science has been observed to beget invariably a doubt of the existence of matter. Turgot[7] said, "He that has never doubted the existence of matter, may be assured he has no aptitude for metaphysical inquiries." It fastens the attention upon immortal necessary uncreated natures, that is, upon Ideas; and in their beautiful and majestic presence, we feel that our outward being is a dream and a shade. Whilst we wait in this Olympus of gods, we think of nature as an appendix to the soul. We ascend into their region, and know that these are the thoughts of the Supreme Being. "These are they who were set up from everlasting, from the beginning, or ever the earth was. When he prepared the heavens, they were there; when he established the clouds above, when he strengthened the fountains of the deep. Then they were by him, as one brought up with him. Of them took he counsel."[8]

Their influence is proportionate. As objects of science, they are accessible to few men. Yet all men are capable of being raised by piety or by passion, into their region. And no man touches these divine natures, without becoming, in some degree, himself divine. Like a new soul, they renew the body. We become physically nimble and lightsome; we tread on air; life is no longer irksome, and we think it will never be so. No man fears age or misfortune or death, in their serene company, for he is transported out of the district of change. Whilst we behold unveiled the nature of Justice and Truth, we learn the difference between the absolute and the conditional or relative. We apprehend the absolute. As it were, for the first time, *we exist*. We become immor-

---

4. Emerson draws this quotation from Coleridge's *The Friend* (1818) (*JMN* 6.202).
5. Greek dramatist of the 5th century B.C., wrote the tragedy *Antigone* in which the title character chooses death rather than violate her sacred duty to perform funeral rites for her slain brother.
6. Leonhard Euler (1707–1783), Swiss mathematician

and physicist; Emerson took the quotation from Coleridge's *Aids to Reflection* (1829) (*JMN* 4.327, 332).
7. Anne Robert Jacques Turgot (1727–1781), French economist and author of a book on proofs of the existence of God (*JMN* 2.212–13).
8. Cf. Proverbs 8.23–30.

tal, for we learn that time and space are relations of matter; that, with a perception of truth, or a virtuous will, they have no affinity.[9]

5. Finally, religion and ethics, which may be fitly called,—the practice of ideas, or the introduction of ideas into life,—have an analogous effect with all lower culture, in degrading nature and suggesting its dependence on spirit. Ethics and religion differ herein; that the one is the system of human duties commencing from man; the other, from God. Religion includes the personality of God; Ethics does not. They are one to our present design. They both put nature under foot. The first and last lesson of religion is, "The things that are seen, are temporal; the things that are unseen are eternal."[1] It puts an affront upon nature. It does that for the unschooled, which philosophy does for Berkeley and Viasa.[2] The uniform language that may be heard in the churches of the most ignorant sects, is,—'Contemn the unsubstantial shows of the world; they are vanities, dreams, shadows, unrealities; seek the realities of religion.' The devotee flouts nature. Some theosophists[3] have arrived at a certain hostility and indignation towards matter, as the Manichean and Plotinus. They distrusted in themselves any looking back to these flesh-pots of Egypt. Plotinus was ashamed of his body.[4] In short, they might all better say of matter, what Michael Angelo said of external beauty, "it is the frail and weary weed, in which God dresses the soul, which he has called into time."[5]

It appears that motion, poetry, physical and intellectual science, and religion, all tend to affect our convictions of the reality of the external world. But I own there is something ungrateful in expanding too curiously the particulars of the general proposition, that all culture tends to imbue us with idealism. I have no hostility to nature, but a child's love to it. I expand and live in the warm day like corn and melons. Let us speak her fair. I do not wish to fling stones at my beautiful mother, nor soil my gentle nest. I only wish to indicate the true position of nature in regard to man, wherein to establish man, all right education tends; as the ground which to attain is the object of human life, that is, of man's connexion with nature. Culture inverts the vulgar views of nature, and brings the mind to call that apparent, which it uses to call real, and that real, which it uses to call visionary. Children, it is true, believe in the external world. The belief that it appears only, is an afterthought, but with culture, this faith will as surely arise on the mind as did the first.

The advantage of the ideal theory over the popular faith, is this, that it presents the world in precisely that view which is most desirable to the mind. It is, in fact, the view which Reason, both speculative and practical, that is, philosophy and virtue, take. For, seen in the light of thought, the world always is phenomenal;[6] and virtue subordinates it to the mind. Idealism sees the world in God. It beholds the whole circle of persons and things, of actions and events, of country and religion, not as painfully accumulated, atom after atom, act after act, in an aged creeping Past, but as one vast picture, which

9. An echo of Socrates' speech in the *Symposium*.
1. 2 Corinthians 4.18.
2. Reputed author of the Vedas, the ancient sacred literature of Hinduism (*JMN* 5.123). George Berkeley (1685–1753), Irish idealist philosopher.
3. In the broad sense of those who attempt to establish direct contact with divine principle through contemplation and revelation.
4. Plotinus, Greek neoplatonical philosopher of the 3rd century, was not so much "ashamed of his body" as of the fact that his soul had to be contained in a body

(*JMN* 3.251). (Neoplatonism is a mystical religious system, combining features of Platonic and other Greek philosophies with features of Judaism and Christianity.) The Israelites yearned for the fleshpots of Egypt while in the wilderness (Exodus 16.3). "Manichean": from Mani or Manes, 3rd-century Persian, who founded a religion based on the dualism of good and evil.
5. Michelangelo's *Sonnet 51* (Emerson's *Early Lectures*, 1.229).
6. Only an appearance.

God paints on the instant eternity, for the contemplation of the soul. Therefore the soul holds itself off from a too trivial and microscopic study of the universal tablet. It respects the end too much, to immerse itself in the means. It sees something more important in Christianity, than the scandals of ecclesiastical history or the niceties of criticism; and, very incurious concerning persons or miracles, and not at all disturbed by chasms of historical evidence, it accepts from God the phenomenon, as it finds it, as the pure and awful form of religion in the world. It is not hot and passionate at the appearance of what it calls its own good or bad fortune, at the union or opposition of other persons. No man is its enemy. It accepts whatsoever befalls, as part of its lesson. It is a watcher more than a doer, and it is a doer, only that it may the better watch.

Chapter VII. Spirit

It is essential to a true theory of nature and of man, that it should contain somewhat progressive. Uses that are exhausted or that may be, and facts that end in the statement, cannot be all that is true of this brave lodging wherein man is harbored, and wherein all his faculties find appropriate and endless exercise. And all the uses of nature admit of being summed in one, which yields the activity of man an infinite scope. Through all its kingdoms, to the suburbs and outskirts of things, it is faithful to the cause whence it had its origin. It always speaks of Spirit. It suggests the absolute. It is a perpetual effect. It is a great shadow pointing always to the sun behind us.

The aspect of nature is devout. Like the figure of Jesus, she stands with bended head, and hands folded upon the breast. The happiest man is he who learns from nature the lesson of worship.

Of that ineffable essence which we call Spirit, he that thinks most, will say least. We can foresee God in the coarse and, as it were, distant phenomena of matter; but when we try to define and describe himself, both language and thought desert us, and we are as helpless as fools and savages. That essence refuses to be recorded in propositions, but when man has worshipped him intellectually, the noblest ministry of nature is to stand as the apparition[7] of God. It is the great organ through which the universal spirit speaks to the individual, and strives to lead back the individual to it.

When we consider Spirit, we see that the views already presented do not include the whole circumference of man. We must add some related thoughts.

Three problems are put by nature to the mind; What is matter? Whence is it? and Whereto? The first of these questions only, the ideal theory answers. Idealism saith: matter is a phenomenon, not a substance. Idealism acquaints us with the total disparity between the evidence of our own being, and the evidence of the world's being. The one is perfect, the other, incapable of any assurance; the mind is a part of the nature of things; the world is a divine dream, from which we may presently awake to the glories and certainties of day. Idealism is a hypothesis to account for nature by other principles than those of carpentry and chemistry. Yet, if it only deny the existence of matter, it does not satisfy the demands of the spirit. It leaves God out of me. It leaves me in the splendid labyrinth of my perceptions, to wander without end. Then the heart resists it, because it baulks the affections in denying substantive being

7. Visible state.

to men and women. Nature is so pervaded with human life, that there is something of humanity in all, and in every particular. But this theory makes nature foreign to me, and does not account for that consanguinity which we acknowledge to it.

Let it stand then, in the present state of our knowledge, merely as a useful introductory hypothesis, serving to apprize us of the eternal distinction between the soul and the world.

But when, following the invisible steps of thought, we come to inquire, Whence is matter? and Whereto? many truths arise to us out of the recesses of consciousness. We learn that the highest is present to the soul of man, that the dread universal essence, which is not wisdom, or love, or beauty, or power, but all in one, and each entirely, is that for which all things exist, and that by which they are; that spirit creates; that behind nature, throughout nature, spirit is present; that spirit is one and not compound; that spirit does not act upon us from without, that is, in space and time, but spiritually, or through ourselves. Therefore, that spirit, that is, the Supreme Being, does not build up nature around us, but puts it forth through us, as the life of the tree puts forth new branches and leaves through the pores of the old. As a plant upon the earth, so a man rests upon the bosom of God: he is nourished by unfailing fountains, and draws, at his need, inexhaustible power. Who can set bounds to the possibilities of man? Once inspire the infinite, by being admitted to behold the absolute natures of justice and truth, and we learn that man has access to the entire mind of the Creator, is himself the creator in the finite. This view, which admonishes me where the sources of wisdom and power lie, and points to virtue as to

> "The golden key
> When opes the palace of eternity,"[8]

carries upon its face the highest certificate of truth, because it animates me to create my own world through the purification of my soul.

The world proceeds from the same spirit as the body of man. It is a remoter and inferior incarnation of God, a projection of God in the unconscious. But it differs from the body in one important respect. It is not, like that, now subjected to the human will. Its serene order is inviolable by us. It is therefore, to us, the present expositor of the divine mind. It is a fixed point whereby we may measure our departure. As we degenerate, the contrast between us and our house is more evident. We are as much strangers in nature, as we are aliens from God. We do not understand the notes of the birds. The fox and the deer run away from us; the bear and tiger rend us. We do not know the uses of more than a few plants, as corn and the apple, the potato and the vine. Is not the landscape, every glimpse of which hath a grandeur, a face of him? Yet this may show us what discord is between man and nature, for you cannot freely admire a noble landscape, if laborers are digging in the field hard by. The poet finds something ridiculous in his delight, until he is out of the sight of men.

Chapter VIII. Prospects

In inquiries respecting the laws of the world and the frame of things, the highest reason is always the truest. That which seems faintly possible—it is so

8. John Milton's *Comus*, 13–14.

refined, is often faint and dim because it is deepest seated in the mind among the eternal verities. Empirical science is apt to cloud the sight, and, by the very knowledge of functions and processes, to bereave the student of the manly contemplation of the whole. The savant[9] becomes unpoetic. But the best read naturalist who lends an entire and devout attention to truth, will see that there remains much to learn of his relation to the world, and that it is not to be learned by any addition or subtraction or other comparison of known quantities, but is arrived at by untaught sallies of the spirit, by a continual self-recovery, and by entire humility. He will perceive that there are far more excellent qualities in the student than preciseness and infallibility; that a guess is often more fruitful than an indisputable affirmation, and that a dream may let us deeper into the secret of nature than a hundred concerted experiments.

For, the problems to be solved are precisely those which the physiologist and the naturalist omit to state. It is not so pertinent to man to know all the individuals of the animal kingdom, as it is to know whence and whereto is this tyrannizing unity in his constitution, which evermore separates and classifies things, endeavouring to reduce the most diverse to one form. When I behold a rich landscape, it is less to my purpose to recite correctly the order and superposition of the strata, than to know why all thought of multitude is lost in a tranquil sense of unity. I cannot greatly honor minuteness in details, so long as there is no hint to explain the relation between things and thoughts; no ray upon the *metaphysics* of conchology, of botany, of the arts, to show the relation of the forms of flowers, shells, animals, architecture, to the mind, and build science upon ideas. In a cabinet[1] of natural history, we become sensible of a certain occult recognition and sympathy in regard to the most bizarre forms of beast, fish, and insect. The American who has been confined, in his own country, to the sight of buildings designed after foreign models, is surprised on entering York Minister or St. Peter's at Rome, by the feeling that these structures are imitations also,—faint copies of an invisible archetype. Nor has science sufficient humanity, so long as the naturalist overlooks that wonderful congruity which subsists between man and the world; of which he is lord, not because he is the most subtile inhabitant, but because he is its head and heart, and finds something of himself in every great and small thing, in every mountain stratum, in every new law of color, fact of astronomy, or atmospheric influence which observation or analysis lay open. A perception of this mystery inspires the muse of George Herbert, the beautiful psalmist of the seventeenth century. The following lines are part of his little poem on Man[2]

> "Man is all symmetry,
> Full of proportions, one limb to another,
> And to all the world besides.
> Each part may call the farthest, brother;
> For head with foot hath private amity,
> And both with moons and tides.
>
> "Nothing hath got so far
> But man hath caught and kept it as his prey;
> His eyes dismount the highest star;
> He is in little all the sphere.

9. Learned person.
1. Display case, or room containing many display cases.
2. Herbert's *Man* (stanzas 1–4 and 6).

Herbs gladly cure our flesh, because that they
    Find their acquaintance there.

"For us, the winds do blow.
The earth doth rest, heaven move, and fountains flow;
    Nothing we see, but means our good,
        As our delight, or as our treasure;
    The whole is either our cupboard of food,
        Or cabinet of pleasure.

"The stars have us to bed;
Night draws the curtain; which the sun withdraws.
    Music and light attend our head.
    All things unto our flesh are kind,
In their descent and being; to our mind,
    In their ascent and cause.

"More servants wait on man
Than he'll take notice of. In every path,
    He treads down that which doth befriend him
    When sickness makes him pale and wan.
Oh mighty love! Man is one world, and hath
    Another to attend him."

The perception of this class of truths makes the eternal attraction which draws men to science, but the end is lost sight of in attention to the means. In view of this half-sight of science, we accept the sentence of Plato, that, "poetry comes nearer to vital truth than history."[3] Every surmise and vaticination[4] of the mind is entitled to a certain respect, and we learn to prefer imperfect theories, and sentences, which contain glimpses of truth, to digested systems which have no one valuable suggestion. A wise writer will feel that the ends of study and composition are best answered by announcing undiscovered regions of thought, and so communicating, through hope, new activity to the torpid spirit.

I shall therefore conclude this essay with some traditions of man and nature, which a certain poet[5] sang to me; and which, as they have always been in the world, and perhaps reappear to every bard, may be both history and prophecy.

The foundations of man are not in matter, but in spirit. But the element of spirit is eternity. To it, therefore, the longest series of events, the oldest chronologies are young and recent. In the cycle of the universal man, from whom the known individuals proceed, centuries are points, and all history is but the epoch of one degradation.

'We distrust and deny inwardly our sympathy with nature. We own and disown our relation to it, by turns. We are, like Nebuchadnezzar, dethroned, bereft of reason, and eating grass like an ox.[6] But who can set limits to the remedial force of spirit?

---

3. In copying two quotations from the *Edinburgh Review* Emerson blurred the attributions; here he quotes not from Plato but from section 9 of Aristotle's *Poetics* (*JMN* 4.261 and 173).
4. Foretelling, prophesying.
5. The poet is Emerson himself, in the same sort of private joke that he later uses in *The Poet*, but before writing this passage he had been seeing his neighbor, the arch-Transcendentalist and idealist Bronson Alcott, who was full of his own "Orphic Sayings," so the device is a little joke with Alcott, one of the first readers and admirers of *Nature*.
6. See Daniel 4.31–33.

'A man is a god in ruins. When men are innocent, life shall be longer, and shall pass into the immortal, as gently as we awake from dreams. Now, the world would be insane and rabid, if these disorganizations should last for hundreds of years. It is kept in check by death and infancy. Infancy is the perpetual Messiah, which comes into the arms of fallen men, and pleads with them to return to paradise.

'Man is the dwarf of himself. Once he was permeated and dissolved by spirit. He filled nature with his overflowing currents. Out from him sprang the sun and moon; from man, the sun; from woman, the moon. The laws of his mind, the periods of his actions externized themselves into day and night, into the year and the seasons. But, having made for himself this huge shell, his waters retired; he no longer fills the veins and veinlets; he is shrunk to a drop. He sees, that the structure still fits him, but fits him colossally. Say, rather, once it fitted him, now it corresponds to him from far and on high. He adores timidly his own work. Now is man the follower of the sun, and woman the follower of the moon. Yet sometimes he starts in his slumber, and wonders at himself and his house, and muses strangely at the resemblance betwixt him and it. He perceives that if his law is still paramount, if still he have elemental power, "if his word is sterling yet in nature," it is not conscious power, it is not inferior but superior to his will. It is Instinct.' Thus my Orphic poet sang.

At present, man applies to nature but half his force. He works on the world with his understanding alone. He lives in it, and masters it by a penny-wisdom; and he that works most in it, is but a half-man and whilst his arms are strong and his digestion good, his mind is imbruted and he is a selfish savage. His relation to nature, his power over it, is through the understanding; as by manure; the economic use of fire, wind, water, and the mariner's needle; steam, coal, chemical agriculture; the repairs of the human body by the dentist and the surgeon. This is such a resumption of power, as if a banished king should buy his territories inch by inch, instead of vaulting at once into his throne. Meantime, in the thick darkness, there are not wanting gleams of a better light,—occasional examples of the action of man upon nature with his entire force,—with reason as well as understanding. Such examples are; the traditions of miracles in the earliest antiquity of all nations; the history of Jesus Christ; the achievements of a principle, as in religious and political revolutions, and in the abolition of the Slave-trade; the miracles of enthusiasm,[7] as those reported of Swedenborg, Hohenlohe, and the Shakers;[8] many obscure and yet contested facts, now arranged under the name of Animal Magnetism;[9] prayer; eloquence, self-healing; and the wisdom of children. These are examples of Reason's momentary grasp of the sceptre, the exertions of a power which exists not in time or space, but an instantaneous in-streaming causing power. The difference between the actual and the ideal force of man is happily figured by the schoolmen,[1] in saying, that the knowledge of man is an evening knowledge, *vespertina cognitio*, but that of God is a morning knowledge, *matutina cognitio*.

The problem of restoring to the world original and eternal beauty, is solved by the redemption of the soul. The ruin or the blank, that we see when we look at nature, is in our own eye. The axis of vision is not coincident with the

7. Those in a supernatural ecstasy or possession.
8. An offshoot of the Quakers; the group believed in miraculous cures. Leopold Franz Emmerich, prince of

Hohnlohe (1794–1849), reputed miracle healer.
9. Hypnotism.
1. Medieval scholastic philosophers (see *JMN* 6.179).

axis of things, and so they appear not transparent but opake. The reason why the world lacks unity, and lies broken and in heaps, is, because man is disunited with himself. He cannot be a naturalist, until he satisfies all the demands of the spirit. Love is as much its demand, as perception. Indeed, neither can be perfect without the other. In the uttermost meaning of the words, thought is devout, and devotion is thought. Deep calls unto deep.[2] But in actual life, the marriage is not celebrated. There are innocent men who worship God after the tradition of their fathers, but their sense of duty has not yet extended to the use of all their faculties. And there are patient naturalists, but they freeze their subject under the wintry light of the understanding. Is not prayer also a study of truth,—a sally of the soul into the unfound infinite? No man ever prayed heartily, without learning something. But when a faithful thinker, resolute to detach every object from personal relations, and see it in the light of thought, shall, at the same time, kindle science with the fire of the holiest affections, then will God go forth anew into the creation.

It will not need, when the mind is prepared for study, to search for objects. The invariable mark of wisdom is to see the miraculous in the common. What is a day? What is a year? What is summer? What is woman? What is a child? What is sleep? To our blindness, these things seem unaffecting. We make fables to hide the baldness of the fact and conform it, as we say, to the higher law of the mind. But when the fact is seen under the light of an idea, the gaudy fable fades and shrivels. We behold the real higher law. To the wise, therefore, a fact is true poetry, and the most beautiful of fables. These wonders are brought to our own door. You also are a man. Man and woman, and their social life, poverty, labor, sleep, fear, fortune, are known to you. Learn that none of these things is superficial, but that each phenomenon hath its roots in the faculties and affections of the mind. Whilst the abstract question occupies your intellect, nature brings it in the concrete to be solved by your hands. It were a wise inquiry for the closet,[3] to compare, point by point, especially at remarkable crises in life, our daily history, with the rise and progress of ideas in the mind.

So shall we come to look at the world with new eyes. It shall answer the endless inquiry of the intellect,—What is truth? and of the affections,—What is good? by yielding itself passive to the educated Will. Then shall come to pass what my poet said; 'Nature is not fixed but fluid. Spirit alters, moulds, makes it. The immobility or bruteness of nature, is the absence of spirit; to pure spirit, it is fluid, it is volatile, it is obedient. Every spirit builds itself a house; and beyond its house, a world; and beyond its world, a heaven. Know then, that the world exists for you. For you is the phenomenon perfect. What we are, that only can we see. All that Adam had, all that Cæsar could, you have and can do. Adam called his house, heaven and earth; Cæsar called his house, Rome; you perhaps call yours, a cobler's trade; a hundred acres of ploughed land; or a scholar's garret. Yet line for line and point for point, your dominion is as great as theirs, though without fine names. Build, therefore your own world. As fast as you can conform your life to the pure idea in your mind, that will unfold its great proportions. A correspondent revolution in things will attend the influx of the spirit. So fast will disagreeable appearances, swine, spiders, snakes, pests, mad-houses, prisons, enemies, vanish; they are

2. Psalm 42.7.   3. The scholar's private workroom.

temporary and shall be no more seen. The sordor and filths of nature, the sun shall dry up, and the wind exhale. As when the summer comes from the south, the snow-banks melt, and the face of the earth becomes green before it, so shall the advancing spirit create its ornaments along its path, and carry with it the beauty it visits, and the song which enchants it; it shall draw beautiful faces, and warm hearts, and wise discourse, and heroic acts, around its way, until evil is no more seen. The kingdom of man over nature, which cometh not with observation,[4]—a dominion such as now is beyond his dream of God,—he shall enter without more wonder than the blind man feels who is gradually restored to perfect sight.'

1836

The American Scholar[1]

Mr. President, and Gentlemen,

I greet you on the re-commencement of our literary year. Our anniversary is one of hope, and, perhaps, not enough of labor. We do not meet for games of strength or skill, for the recitation of histories, tragedies and odes, like the ancient Greeks; for parliaments of love and poesy, like the Troubadours;[2] nor for the advancement of science, like our cotemporaries in the British and European capitals. Thus far, our holiday has been simply a friendly sign of the survival of the love of letters amongst a people too busy to give to letters any more. As such, it is precious as the sign of an indestructible instinct. Perhaps the time is already come, when it ought to be, and will be something else; when the sluggard intellect of this continent will look from under its iron lids and fill the postponed expectation of the world with something better than the exertions of mechanical skill. Our day of dependence, our long apprentice-ship to the learning of other lands, draws to a close. The millions that around us are rushing into life, cannot always be fed on the sere remains of foreign harvests. Events, actions arise, that must be sung, that will sing themselves. Who can doubt that poetry will revive and lead in a new age, as the star in the constellation Harp which now flames in our zenith, astronomers announce, shall one day be the pole-star for a thousand years.

In the light of this hope, I accept the topic which not only usage, but the nature of our association, seem to prescribe to this day,—the AMERICAN SCHOLAR. Year by year, we come up hither to read one more chapter of his biography. Let us inquire what new lights, new events and more days have thrown on his character, his duties and his hopes.

It is one of those fables, which out of an unknown antiquity, convey an unlooked for wisdom, that the gods, in the beginning, divided Man into men, that he might be more helpful to himself;[3] just as the hand was divided into fingers, the better to answer its end.

The old fable covers a doctrine ever new and sublime; that there is One

4. Luke 17.20

1. The text printed here is that of the first publication (1837) as a pamphlet titled An Oration, Delivered before the Phi Beta Kappa Society at Cambridge, August 31, 1837. By altering the title to The American Scholar when he republished it in Essays (1841), Emerson expanded the application to all American college students and all others who dedicate themselves to thought.

2. Courtly poets of southern France, especially Provence, in the 12th and 13th centuries.

3. One such fable Emerson knew from Plato's Symposium.

Man,—present to all particular men only partially, or through one faculty; and that you must take the whole society to find the whole man. Man is not a farmer, or a professor, or an engineer, but he is all. Man is priest, and scholar, and statesman, and producer, and soldier. In the *divided* or social state, these functions are parcelled out to individuals, each of whom aims to do his stint of the joint work, whilst each other performs his. The fable implies that the individual to possess himself, must sometimes return from his own labor to embrace all the other laborers. But unfortunately, this original unit, this fountain of power, has been so distributed to multitudes, has been so minutely subdivided and peddled out, that it is spilled into drops, and cannot be gathered. The state of society is one in which the members have suffered amputation from the trunk, and strut about so many walking monsters,—a good finger, a neck, a stomach, an elbow, but never a man.

Man is thus metamorphosed into a thing, into many things. The planter, who is Man sent out into the field to gather food, is seldom cheered by any idea of the true dignity of his ministry. He sees his bushel and his cart, and nothing beyond, and sinks into the farmer, instead of Man on the farm. The tradesman scarcely ever gives an ideal worth to his work, but is ridden by the routine of his craft, and the soul is subject to dollars. The priest becomes a form; the attorney, a statute-book; the mechanic, a machine; the sailor, a rope of a ship.

In this distribution of functions, the scholar is the delegated intellect. In the right state, he is, *Man Thinking*. In the degenerate state, when the victim of society, he tends to become a mere thinker, or, still worse, the parrot of other men's thinking.

In this view of him, as Man Thinking, the whole theory of his office[4] is contained. Him nature solicits, with all her placid, all her monitory pictures. Him the past instructs. Him the future invites. Is not, indeed, every man a student, and do not all things exist for the student's behoof? And, finally, is not the true scholar the only true master? But, as the old oracle said, "All things have two handles. Beware of the wrong one." In life, too often, the scholar errs with mankind and forfeits his privilege. Let us see him in his school, and consider him in reference to the main influences he receives.

I. The first in time and the first in importance of the influences upon the mind is that of nature. Every day, the sun; and, after sunset, night and her stars. Ever the winds blow; ever the grass grows. Every day, men and women, conversing, beholding and beholden. The scholar must needs stand wistful and admiring before this great spectacle. He must settle its value in his mind. What is nature to him? There is never a beginning, there is never an end to the inexplicable continuity of this web of God, but always circular power returning into itself. Therein it resembles his own spirit, whose beginning, whose ending he never can find—so entire, so boundless. Far, too, as her splendors shine, system on system shooting like rays, upward, downward, without centre, without circumference,—in the mass and in the particle nature hastens to render account of herself to the mind. Classification begins. To the young mind, every thing is individual, stands by itself. By and by, it finds how to join two things, and see in them one nature; then three, then three thousand; and so, tyrannized over by its own unifying instinct, it goes on

4. Function.

tying things together, diminishing anomalies, discovering roots running under ground, whereby contrary and remote things cohere, and flower out from one stem. It presently learns, that, since the dawn of history, there has been a constant accumulation and classifying of facts. But what is classification but the perceiving that these objects are not chaotic, and are not foreign, but have a law which is also a law of the human mind? The astronomer discovers that geometry, a pure abstraction of the human mind, is the measure of planetary motion. The chemist finds proportions and intelligible method throughout matter: and science is nothing but the finding of analogy, identity in the most remote parts. The ambitious soul sits down before each refractory fact; one after another, reduces all strange constitutions, all new powers, to their class and their law, and goes on forever to animate the last fibre of organization, the outskirts of nature, by insight.

Thus to him, to this school-boy under the bending dome of day, is suggested, that he and it proceed from one root; one is leaf and one is flower; relation, sympathy, stirring in every vein. And what is that Root? Is not that the soul of his soul?—A thought too bold—a dream too wild. Yet when this spiritual light shall have revealed the law of more earthly natures,—when he has learned to worship the soul, and to see that the natural philosophy that now is, is only the first gropings of its gigantic hand, he shall look forward to an ever expanding knowledge as to a becoming creator. He shall see that nature is the opposite of the soul, answering to it part for part. One is seal, and one is print. Its beauty is the beauty of his own mind. Its laws are the laws of his own mind. Nature then becomes to him the measure of his attainments. So much of nature as he is ignorant of, so much of his own mind does he not yet possess. And, in fine, the ancient precept, "Know thyself," and the modern precept, "Study nature," become at last one maxim.

II. The next great influence[5] into the spirit of the scholar, is, the mind of the Past,—in whatever form, whether of literature, of art, of institutions, that mind is inscribed. Books are the best type of the influence of the past, and perhaps we shall get at the truth—learn the amount of this influence more conveniently—by considering their value alone.

The theory of books is noble. The scholar of the first age received into him the world around; brooded thereon; gave it the new arrangement of his own mind, and uttered it again. It came into him—life; it went out from him— truth. It came to him—short-lived actions; it went out from him—immortal thoughts. It came to him—business; it went from him—poetry. It was—dead fact; now, it is quick[6] thought. It can stand, and it can go. It now endures, it now flies, it now inspires.[7] Precisely in proportion to the depth of mind from which it issued, so high does it soar, so long does it sing.

Or, I might say, it depends on how far the process had gone, of transmuting life into truth. In proportion to the completeness of the distillation, so will the purity and imperishableness of the product be. But none is quite perfect. As no air-pump can by any means make a perfect vacuum, so neither can any artist entirely exclude the conventional, the local, the perishable from his book, or write a book of pure thought that shall be as efficient, in all respects, to a remote posterity, as to cotemporaries, or rather to the second age. Each

5. Inflowing.
6. Living. "Business": busyness, activity.

7. Breathes in. "Go": walk.

age, it is found, must write its own books; or rather, each generation for the next succeeding. The books of an older period will not fit this.

Yet hence arises a grave mischief. The sacredness which attaches to the act of creation,—the act of thought,—is instantly transferred to the record. The poet chanting, was felt to be a divine man. Henceforth the chant is divine also. The writer was a just and wise spirit. Henceforward it is settled, the book is perfect; as love of the hero corrupts into worship of his statue. Instantly, the book becomes noxious. The guide is a tyrant. We sought a brother, and lo, a governor. The sluggish and perverted mind of the multitude, always slow to open to the incursions of Reason, having once so opened, having once received this book, stands upon it, and makes an outcry, if it is disparaged. Colleges are built on it. Books are written on it by thinkers, not by Man Thinking; by men of talent, that is, who start wrong, who set out from accepted dogmas, not from their own sight of principles. Meek young men grow up in libraries, believing it their duty to accept the views which Cicero, which Locke, which Bacon have given, forgetful that Cicero, Locke and Bacon were only young men in libraries when they wrote these books.[8]

Hence, instead of Man Thinking, we have the bookworm. Hence, the book-learned class, who value books, as such; not as related to nature and the human constitution, but as making a sort of Third Estate[9] with the world and the soul. Hence, the restorers of readings, the emendators, the bibliomaniacs of all degrees.

This is bad; this is worse than it seems. Books are the best of things, well used; abused, among the worst. What is the right use? What is the one end which all means go to effect? They are for nothing but to inspire. I had better never see a book than to be warped by its attraction clean out of my own orbit, and made a satellite instead of a system. The one thing in the world of value, is, the active soul,—the soul, free, sovereign, active. This every man is entitled to; this every man contains within him, although in almost all men, obstructed, and as yet unborn. The soul active sees absolute truth; and utters truth, or creates. In this action, it is genius; not the privilege of here and there a favorite, but the sound estate of every man. In its essence, it is progressive. The book, the college, the school of art, the institution of any kind, stop with some past utterance of genius. This is good, say they,—let us hold by this. They pin me down. They look backward and not forward. But genius always looks forward. The eyes of man are set in his forehead, not in his hindhead. Man hopes. Genius creates. To create,—to create,—is the proof of a divine presence. Whatever talents may be, if the man create not, the pure efflux[1] of the Deity is not his:—cinders and smoke, there may be, but not yet flame. There are creative manners, there are creative actions, and creative words; manners, actions, words, that is, indicative of no custom or authority, but springing spontaneous from the mind's own sense of good and fair.

On the other part, instead of being its own seer, let it receive always from another mind its truth, though it were in torrents of light, without periods of

---

8. These examples are not especially apt, since none of the three wrote books at an unusually precocious age. As a young man Marcus Tullius Cicero (106–143 B.C., Roman statesman, was best known for his oratory. John Locke (1632–1704), English philosopher and political thinker, wrote *Essay Concerning Human Understanding* (1690) before he was forty. Sir Francis Bacon (1561–1626), English statesman and philosopher, wrote his *Essays*.

9. On the analogy of the three-part division of estates of the realm, in which the third estate is the common people; the first estate is the nobility and the second, the clergy.

1. Flowing forth.

solitude, inquest and self-recovery, and a fatal disservice is done. Genius is always sufficiently the enemy of genius by over-influence. The literature of every nation bear me witness. The English dramatic poets have Shakspearized now for two hundred years.

Undoubtedly, there is a right way of reading,—so it be sternly subordinated. Man Thinking must not be subdued by his instruments. Books are for the scholar's idle times. When he can read God directly, the hour is too precious to be wasted in other mens' transcripts of their readings. But when the intervals of darkness come, as come they must,—when the soul seeth not, when the sun is hid, and the stars withdraw their shining,—we repair to the lamps which were kindled by their ray to guide our steps to the East again, where the dawn is. We hear that we may speak. The Arabian proverb says, "A fig tree looking on a fig tree, becometh fruitful."

It is remarkable, the character of the pleasure we derive from the best books. They impress us ever with the conviction that one nature wrote and the same reads. We read the verses of one of the great English poets, of Chaucer, of Marvell, of Dryden, with the most modern joy,—with a pleasure, I mean, which is in great part caused by the abstraction of all *time* from their verses. There is some awe mixed with the joy of our surprise, when this poet, who lived in some past world, two or three hundred years ago, says that which lies close to my own soul, that which I also had well nigh thought and said. But for the evidence thence afforded to the philosophical doctrine of the identity of all minds, we should suppose some pre-established harmony, some foresight of souls that were to be, and some preparation of stores for their future wants, like the fact observed in insects, who lay up food before death for the young grub they shall never see.

I would not be hurried by any love of system, by any exaggeration of instincts, to underrate the Book. We all know, that as the human body can be nourished on any food, though it were boiled grass and the broth of shoes, so the human mind can be fed by any knowledge. And great and heroic men have existed, who had almost no other information than by the printed page. I only would say, that it needs a strong head to bear that diet. One must be an inventor to read well. As the proverb says, "He that would bring home the wealth of the Indies, must carry out the wealth of the Indies." There is then creative reading, as well as creative writing. When the mind is braced by labor and invention, the page of whatever book we read becomes luminous with manifold allusion. Every sentence is doubly significant, and the sense of our author is as broad as the world. We then see, what is always true, that as the seer's hour of vision is short and rare among heavy days and months, so is its record, perchance, the least part of his volume. The discerning will read in his Plato or Shakspeare, only that least part,—only the authentic utterances of the oracle,—and all the rest he rejects, were it never so many times Plato's and Shakspeare's.

Of course, there is a portion of reading quite indispensable to a wise man. History and exact science he must learn by laborious reading. Colleges, in like manner, have their indispensable office,—to teach elements. But they can only highly serve us, when they aim not to drill, but to create; when they gather from far every ray of various genius to their hospitable halls, and, by the concentrated fires, set the hearts of their youth on flame. Thought and knowledge are natures in which apparatus and pretension avail nothing.

Gowns, and pecuniary foundations, though of towns of gold, can never countervail the least sentence or syllable of wit. Forget this, and our American colleges will recede in their public importance whilst they grow richer every year.

III. There goes in the world a notion that the scholar should be a recluse, a valetudinarian,—as unfit for any handiwork or public labor, as a penknife for an axe. The so called "practical men" sneer at speculative men, as if, because they speculate or *see*, they could do nothing. I have heard it said that the clergy,—who are always more universally than any other class, the scholars of their day,—are addressed as women: that the rough, spontaneous conversation of men they do not hear, but only a mincing and diluted speech. They are often virtually disfranchised; and, indeed, there are advocates for their celibacy. As far as this is true of the studious classes, it is not just and wise. Action is with the scholar subordinate, but it is essential. Without it, he is not yet man. Without it, thought can never ripen into truth. Whilst the world hangs before the eye as a cloud of beauty, we can not even see its beauty. Inaction is cowardice, but there can be no scholar without the heroic mind. The preamble of thought, the transition through which it passes from the unconscious to the conscious, is action. Only so much do I know, as I have lived. Instantly, we know whose words are loaded with life, and whose not.

The world,—this shadow of the soul, or *other me*, lies wide around. Its attractions are the keys which unlock my thoughts and make me acquainted with myself. I launch eagerly into this resounding tumult. I grasp the hands of those next me, and take my place in the ring to suffer and to work, taught by an instinct that so shall the dumb abyss be vocal with speech. I pierce its order; I dissipate its fear; I dispose of it within the circuit of my expanding life. So much only of life as I know by experience, so much of the wilderness have I vanquished and planted, or so far have I extended my being, my dominion. I do not see how any man can afford, for the sake of his nerves and his nap, to spare any action in which he can partake. It is pearls and rubies to his discourse. Drudgery, calamity, exasperation, want, are instructers in eloquence and wisdom. The true scholar grudges every opportunity of action past by, as a loss of power.

It is the raw material out of which the intellect moulds her splendid products. A strange process too, this, by which experience is converted into thought, as a mulberry leaf is converted into satin. The manufacture goes forward at all hours.

The actions and events of our childhood and youth are now matters of calmest observation. They lie like fair pictures in the air. Not so with our recent actions,—with the business which we now have in hand. On this we are quite unable to speculate. Our affections as yet circulate through it. We no more feel or know it, than we feel the feet, or the hand, or the brain of our body. The new deed is yet a part of life,—remains for a time immersed in our unconscious life. In some contemplative hour, it detaches itself from the life like a ripe fruit, to become a thought of the mind. Instantly, it is raised, transfigured; the corruptible has put on incorruption.[2] Always now it is an object of beauty, however base its origin and neighborhood. Observe, too, the impossibility of antedating this act. In its grub state, it cannot fly, it cannot shine,—

2. "For this corruptible must put on incorruption, and this mortal must put on immortality" (I Corinthians 15.53).

it is a dull grub. But suddenly, without observation, the selfsame thing unfurls beautiful wings, and is an angel of wisdom. So is there no fact, no event, in our private history, which shall not, sooner or later, lose its adhesive inert form, and astonish us by soaring from our body into the empyrean.[3] Cradle and infancy, school and playground, the fear of boys, and dogs, and ferules,[4] the love of little maids and berries, and many another fact that once filled the whole sky, are gone already; friend and relative, profession and party, town and country, nation and world, must also soar and sing.

Of course, he who has put forth his total strength in fit actions, has the richest return of wisdom. I will not shut myself out of this globe of action and transplant an oak into a flower pot, there to hunger and pine; nor trust the revenue of some single faculty, and exhaust one vein of thought, much like those Savoyards,[5] who, getting their livelihood by carving shepherds, shepherdesses, and smoking Dutchmen, for all Europe, went out one day to the mountain to find stock, and discovered that they had whittled up the last of their pine trees. Authors we have in numbers, who have written out their vein, and who, moved by a commendable prudence, sail for Greece or Palestine, follow the trapper into the prairie, or ramble round Algiers to replenish their merchantable stock.[6]

If it were only for a vocabulary the scholar would be covetous of action. Life is our dictionary. Years are well spent in country labors; in town—in the insight into trades and manufactures; in frank intercourse with many men and women; in science; in art; to the one end of mastering in all their facts a language, by which to illustrate and embody our perceptions. I learn immediately from any speaker how much he has already lived, through the poverty or the splendor of his speech. Life lies behind us as the quarry from whence we get tiles and copestones for the masonry of to-day. This is the way to learn grammar. Colleges and books only copy the language which the field and the workyard made.

But the final value of action, like that of books, and better than books, is, that it is a resource. That great principle of Undulation in nature, that shows itself in the inspiring and expiring of the breath; in desire and satiety; in the ebb and flow of the sea, in day and night, in heat and cold, and as yet more deeply ingrained in every atom and every fluid, is known to us under the name of Polarity,—these "fits of easy transmission and reflection," as Newton[7] called them, are the law of nature because they are the law of spirit.

The mind now thinks; now acts; and each fit reproduces the other. When the artist has exhausted his materials, when the fancy no longer paints, when thoughts are no longer apprehended, and books are a weariness,—he has always the resource to *live*. Character is higher than intellect. Thinking is the function. Living is the functionary. The stream retreats to its source. A great soul will be strong to live, a well as strong to think. Does he lack organ or medium to impart his truths? He can still fall back on this elemental force of living them. This is a total act. Thinking is a partial act. Let the grandeur of justice shine in his affairs. Let the beauty of affection cheer his lowly roof.

3. The highest reaches of heaven.
4. Rods used for punishing children.
5. Savoy is in the western Alps, where France, Italy, and Switzerland converge.
6. Emerson's contemporaries would have understood a reference to writers now unread, such as Nathaniel Parker Willis, as well as to two still-famous writers, James Fenimore Cooper, author of *The Prairie* (1827), and Washington Irving, author of *A Tour on the Prairies* (1835).
7. From the *Optics* (1704) of Sir Isaac Newton (1642–1727), English scientist and mathematician.

Those "far from fame" who dwell and act with him, will feel the force of his constitution in the doings and passages of the day better than it can be measured by any public and designed display. Time shall teach him that the scholar loses no hour which the man lives. Herein he unfolds the sacred germ of his instinct screened from influence. What is lost in seemliness is gained in strength. Not out of those on whom systems of education have exhausted their culture, comes the helpful giant to destroy the old or to build the new, but out of unhandselled[8] savage nature, out of terrible Druids and Berserkirs, come at last Alfred[9] and Shakspear.

I hear therefore with joy whatever is beginning to be said of the dignity and necessity of labor to every citizen. There is virtue yet in the hoe and the spade, for learned as well as for unlearned hands. And labor is every where welcome; always we are invited to work; only be this limitation observed, that a man shall not for the sake of wider activity sacrifice any opinion to the popular judgments and modes of action.

I have now spoken of the education of the scholar by nature, by books, and by action. It remains to say somewhat of his duties.

They are such as become Man Thinking. They may all be comprised in self-trust. The office of the scholar is to cheer, to raise, and to guide men by showing them facts amidst appearances. He plies the slow, unhonored, and unpaid task of observation. Flamsteed and Herschel, in their glazed[1] observatory, may catalogue the stars with the praise of all men, and the results being splendid and useful, honor is sure. But he, in his private observatory, cataloguing obscure and nebulous stars of the human mind, which as yet no man has thought of as such,—watching days and months, sometimes, for a few facts; correcting still his old records;—must relinquish display and immediate fame. In the long period of his preparation, he must betray often an ignorance and shiftlessness in popular arts, incurring the disdain of the able who shoulder him aside. Long he must stammer in his speech; often forego the living for the dead. Worse yet, he must accept—how often! poverty and solitude. For the ease and pleasure of treading the old road, accepting the fashions, the education, the religion of society, he takes the cross of making his own, and, of course, the self accusation, the faint heart, the frequent uncertainty and loss of time which are the nettles and tangling vines in the way of the self-relying and self-directed; and the state of virtual hostility in which he seems to stand to society, and especially to educated society. For all this loss and scorn, what offset? He is to find consolation in exercising the highest functions of human nature. He is one who raises himself from private considerations, and breathes and lives on public and illustrious thoughts. He is the world's eye. He is the world's heart. He is to resist the vulgar prosperity that retrogrades ever to barbarism, by preserving and communicating heroic sentiments, noble biographies, melodious verse, and the conclusions of history. Whatsoever oracles the human heart in all emergencies, in all solemn hours has uttered as its commentary on the world of actions,—these he shall receive and impart. And whatsoever new verdict Reason from her inviolable seat pronounces on the passing men and events of to-day,—this he shall hear and promulgate.

8. A handsel is a gift to express good wishes at the outset of some enterprise; apparently Emerson uses the word to mean something like unauspicious.
9. The enlightened 9th-century king of the West Saxons. "Terrible Druids and Berserkirs": uncivilized Celts and Anglo-Saxons.

1. Glass-roofed. John Flamsteed (1646–1719), English astronomer, first royal astronomer at Greenwich Observatory. Sir William Herschel (1738–1822), German-born English astronomer, founder of sideral astronomy.

These being his functions, it becomes him to feel all confidence in himself, and to defer never to the popular cry. He and he only knows the world. The world of any moment is the merest appearance. Some great decorum, some fetish of a government, some ephemeral trade, or war, or man, is cried up by half mankind and cried down by the other half, as if all depended on this particular up or down. The odds are that the whole question is not worth the poorest thought which the scholar has lost in listening to the controversy. Let him not quit his belief that a popgun is a popgun, though the ancient and honorable of the earth affirm it to be the crack of doom. In silence, in steadiness, in severe abstraction, let him hold by himself; add observation to observation; patient of neglect, patient of reproach, and bide his own time,—happy enough if he can satisfy himself alone that this day he has seen something truly. Success treads on every right step. For the instinct is sure that prompts him to tell his brother what he thinks. He then learns that in going down into the secrets of his own mind, he has descended into the secrets of all minds. He learns that he who has mastered any law in his private thoughts, is master to that extent of all men whose language he speaks, and of all into whose language his own can be translated. The poet in utter solitude remembering his spontaneous thoughts and recording them, is found to have recorded that which men in "cities vast" find true for them also. The orator distrusts at first the fitness of his frank confessions,—his want of knowledge of the persons he addresses,—until he finds that he is the complement of his hearers;—that they drink his words because he fulfils for them their own nature; the deeper he dives into his privatest secretest presentiment,—to his wonder he finds, this is the most acceptable, most public, and universally true. The people delight in it; the better part of every man feels, This is my music: this is myself.

In self-trust, all the virtues are comprehended. Free should the scholar be,—free and brave. Free even to the definition of freedom, "without any hindrance that does not arise out of his own constitution." Brave; for fear is a thing which a scholar by his very function puts behind him. Fear always springs from ignorance. It is a shame to him if his tranquillity, amid dangerous times, arise from the presumption that like children and women, his is a protected class; or if he seek a temporary peace by the diversion of his thoughts from politics or vexed questions, hiding his head like an ostrich in the flowering bushes, peeping into microscopes, and turning rhymes, as a boy whistles to keep his courage up. So is the danger a danger still: so is the fear worse. Manlike let him turn and face it. Let him look into its eye and search its nature, inspect its origin—see the whelping of this lion,—which lies no great way back; he will then find in himself a perfect comprehension of its nature and extent; he will have made his hands meet on the other side, and can henceforth defy it, and pass on superior. The world is his who can see through its pretension. What deafness, what stone-blind custom, what overgrown error you behold, is there only by sufferance,—by your sufferance. See it to be a lie, and you have already dealt it its mortal blow.

Yes, we are the cowed,—we the trustless. It is a mischievous notion that we are come late into nature; that the world was finished a long time ago. As the world was plastic and fluid in the hands of God, so it is ever to so much of his attributes as we bring to it. To ignorance and sin, it is flint. They adapt themselves to it as they may; but in proportion as a man has anything in him divine, the firmament flows before him, and takes his signet[2] and form. Not he is

2. Seal.

great who can alter matter, but he who can alter my state of mind. They are the kings of the world who give the color of their present thought to all nature and all art, and persuade men by the cheerful serenity of their carrying the matter, that this thing which they do, is the apple which the ages have desired to pluck, now at last ripe, and inviting nations to the harvest. The great man makes the great thing. Wherever Macdonald sits, there is the head of the table.[3] Linnæus makes botany the most alluring of studies and wins it from the farmer and the herb-woman. Davy, chemistry: and Cuvier,[4] fossils. The day is always his, who works in it with serenity and great aims. The unstable estimates of men crowd to him whose mind is filled with a truth, as the heaped waves of the Atlantic follow the moon.

For this self-trust, the reason is deeper than can be fathomed,—darker than can be enlightened. I might not carry with me the feeling of my audience in stating my own belief. But I have already shown the ground of my hope, in adverting to the doctrine that man is one. I believe man has been wronged: he has wronged himself. He has almost lost the light that can lead him back to his prerogatives. Men are become of no account. Men in history, men in the world of to-day are bugs, are spawn, and are called "the mass" and "the herd." In a century, in a millenium, one or two men; that is to say—one or two approximations to the right state of every man. All the rest behold in the hero or the poet their own green and crude being—ripened; yes, and are content to be less, so *that* may attain to its full stature. What a testimony—full of grandeur, full of pity, is borne to the demands of his own nature, by the poor clansman, the poor partisan, who rejoices in the glory of his chief. The poor and the low find some amends to their immense moral capacity, for their acquiescence in a political and social inferiority. They are content to be brushed like flies from the path of a great person, so that justice shall be done by him to that common nature which it is the dearest desire of all to see enlarged and glorified. They sun themselves in the great man's light, and feel it to be their own element. They cast the dignity of man from their downtrod selves upon the shoulders of a hero, and will perish to add one drop of blood to make that great heart beat, those giant sinews combat and conquer. He lives for us, and we live in him.

Men such as they are, very naturally seek money or power; and power because it is as good as money,—the "spoils," so called, "of office." And why not? for they aspire to the highest, and this, in their sleep-walking, they dream is highest. Wake them, and they shall quit the false good and leap to the true, and leave government to clerks and desks. This revolution is to be wrought by the gradual domestication of the idea of Culture. The main enterprise of the world for splendor, for extent, is the upbuilding of a man. Here are the materials strown along the ground. The private life of one man shall be a more illustrious monarchy,—more formidable to its enemy, more sweet and serene in its influence to its friend, than any kingdom in history. For a man, rightly viewed, comprehendeth the particular natures of all men. Each philosopher, each bard, each actor, has only done for me, as by a delegate, what one day I can do for myself. The books which once we valued more than the apple of

3. An old proverb says, "Where Macgregor sits, there is the head of the table"; Emerson substitutes another typical name for a Scottish chief.
4. Georges Cuvier (1769–1832), French pioneer in comparative anatomy and paleontology. Carl von Linné ("Linnaeus") (1707–1778), Swedish botanist. Sir Humphry Davy (1778–1829), English chemist.

the eye, we have quite exhausted. What is that but saying that we have come up with the point of view which the universal mind took through the eyes of that one scribe; we have been that man, and have passed on. First, one; then another; we drain all cisterns, and waxing greater by all these supplies, we crave a better and more abundant food. The man has never lived that can feed us ever. The human mind cannot be enshrined in a person who shall set a barrier on any one side to this unbounded, unboundable empire. It is one central fire which flaming now out of the lips of Etna, lightens the capes of Sicily; and now out of the throat of Vesuvius, illuminates the towers and vineyards of Naples.[5] It is one light which beams out of a thousand stars. It is one soul which animates all men.

But I have dwelt perhaps tediously upon this abstraction of the Scholar. I ought not to delay longer to add what I have to say, of nearer reference to the time and to this country.

Historically, there is thought to be a difference in the ideas which predominate over successive epochs, and there are data for marking the genius of the Classic, of the Romantic, and now of the Reflective or Philosophical age.[6] With the views I have intimated of the oneness or the identity of the mind through all individuals, I do not much dwell on these differences. In fact, I believe each individual passes through all three. The boy is a Greek; the youth, romantic; the adult, reflective. I deny not, however, that a revolution in the leading idea may be distinctly enough traced.

Our age is bewailed as the age of Introversion. Must that needs be evil? We, it seems, are critical. We are embarrassed with second thoughts. We cannot enjoy any thing for hankering to know whereof the pleasure consists. We are lined with eyes. We see with our feet. The time is infected with Hamlet's unhappiness,—

"Sicklied o'er with the pale cast of thought."[7]

Is it so bad then? Sight is the last thing to be pitied. Would we be blind? Do we fear lest we should outsee nature and God, and drink truth dry? I look upon the discontent of the literary class as a mere announcement of the fact that they find themselves not in the state of mind of their fathers, and regret the coming state as untried; as a boy dreads the water before he has learned that he can swim. If there is any period one would desire to be born in,—is it not the age of Revolution; when the old and the new stand side by side, and admit of being compared; when the energies of all men are searched by fear and by hope; when the historic glories of the old, can be compensated by the rich possibilities of the new era? This time, like all times, is a very good one, if we but know what to do with it.

I read with joy some of the auspicious signs of the coming days as they glimmer already through poetry and art, through philosophy and science, through church and state.

One of these signs is the fact that the same movement which effected the elevation of what was called the lowest class in the state, assumed in literature a very marked and as benign an aspect. Instead of the sublime and beautiful, the near, the low, the common, was explored and poetised. That which had

5. Active volcanoes in eastern Sicily and western Italy.
6. Emerson proceeds to refute the self-excusing notion that his age was merely a time for criticism, not for genuinely creative achievements.
7. Shakespeare's *Hamlet* (3.1.85–87).

been negligently trodden under foot by those who were harnessing and provisioning themselves for long journies into far countries, is suddenly found to be richer than all foreign parts. The literature of the poor, the feelings of the child, the philosophy of the street, the meaning of household life, are the topics of the time. It is a great stride. It is a sign—is it not? of new vigor, when the extremities are made active, when currents of warm life run into the hands and the feet. I ask not for the great, the remote, the romantic; what is doing in Italy or Arabia; what is Greek art, or Provencal Minstrelsy; I embrace the common, I explore and sit at the feet of the familiar, the low. Give me insight into to-day, and you may have the antique and future worlds. What would we really know the meaning of? The meal in the firkin; the milk in the pan; the ballad in the street; the news of the boat; the glance of the eye; the form and the gait of the body;—show me the ultimate reason of these matters;—show me the sublime presence of the highest spiritual cause lurking, as always it does lurk, in these suburbs and extremities of nature; let me see every trifle bristling with the polarity that ranges it instantly on an eternal law; and the shop, the plough, and the ledger, referred to the like cause by which light undulates and poets sing;—and the world lies no longer a dull miscellany and lumber room,[8] but has form and order; there is no trifle; there is no puzzle; but one design unites and animates the farthest pinnacle and the lowest trench.

This idea has inspired the genius of Goldsmith, Burns, Cowper, and in a newer time, of Goethe, Wordsworth, and Carlyle. This idea they have differently followed and with various success. In contrast with their writing, the style of Pope, of Johnson, of Gibbon, looks cold and pedantic.[9] This writing is blood-warm. Man is surprised to find that things near are not less beautiful and wondrous than things remote. The near explains the far. The drop is a small ocean. A man is related to all nature. This perception of the worth of the vulgar, is fruitful in discoveries. Goethe, in this very thing the most modern of the moderns, has shown us, as none ever did, the genius of the ancients.

There is one man of genius who has done much for this philosophy of life, whose literary value has never yet been rightly estimated;—I mean Emanuel Swedenborg.[1] The most imaginative of men, yet writing with the precision of a mathematician, he endeavored to engraft a purely philosophical Ethics on the popular Christianity of his time. Such an attempt, of course, must have difficulty which no genius could surmount. But he saw and showed the connexion between nature and the affections of the soul. He pierced the emblematic or spiritual character of the visible, audible, tangible world. Especially did his shade-loving muse hover over and interpret the lower parts of nature; he showed the mysterious bond that allies moral evil to the foul material forms, and has given in epical parables a theory of insanity, of beasts, of unclean and fearful things.

Another sign of our times, also marked by an analogous political movement is, the new importance given to the single person. Every thing that tends to insulate the individual,—to surround him with barriers of natural respect, so that each man shall feel the world is his, and man shall treat with man as a

---

8. Junk room.

9. Himself nurtured on such "cold and pedantic" writers as Alexander Pope, Samuel Johnson, and Edward Gibbon, in this passage Emerson conventionally contrasts them with the so-called pre-Romantics like Oliver Goldsmith, Robert Burns, and William Cowper and Romantics like Goethe, Wordsworth, and Carlyle,

supposedly marked by greater attention to aspects of ordinary life.

1. No important critic after Emerson has taken up this advocacy of literary greatness in Swedenborg (1688–1772), Swedish scientist and theologian. He was a passion of Emerson's because of his intellectual and spiritual affinities not his intrinsic literary merit.

sovereign state with a sovereign state;—tends to true union as well as greatness. "I learned," said the melancholy Pestalozzi,[2] "that no man in God's wide earth is either willing or able to help any other man." Help must come from the bosom alone. The scholar is that man who must take up into himself all the ability of the time, all the contributions of the past, all the hopes of the future. He must be an university of knowledges. If there be one lesson more than another which should pierce his ear, it is, The world is nothing, the man is all; in yourself is the law of all nature, and you know not yet how a globule of sap ascends; in yourself slumbers the whole of Reason; it is for you to know all, it is for you to dare all. Mr. President and Gentlemen, this confidence in the unsearched might of man, belongs by all motives, by all prophecy, by all preparation, to the American Scholar. We have listened too long to the courtly muses of Europe. The spirit of the American freeman is already suspected to be timid, imitative, tame. Public and private avarice make the air we breathe thick and fat. The scholar is decent, indolent, complaisant.[3] See already the tragic consequence. The mind of this country taught to aim at low objects, eats upon itself. There is no work for any but the decorous and the complaisant. Young men of the fairest promise, who begin life upon our shores, inflated by the mountain winds, shined upon by all the stars of God, find the earth below not in unison with these,—but are hindered from action by the disgust which the principles on which business is managed inspire, and turn drudges, or die of disgust,—some of them suicides. What is the remedy? They did not yet see, and thousands of young men as hopeful now crowding to the barriers for the career, do not yet see, that if the single man plant himself indomitably on his instincts, and there abide, the huge world will come round to him. Patience—patience;—with the shades of all the good and great for company; and for solace, the perspective of your own infinite life; and for work, the study and the communication of principles, the making those instincts prevalent, the conversion of the world. Is it not the chief disgrace in the world, not to be an unit;—not to be reckoned one character;—not to yield that peculiar fruit which each man was created to bear, but to be reckoned in the gross, in the hundred, or the thousand, of the party, the section, to which we belong; and our opinion predicted geographically, as the north, or the south. Not so, brothers and friends,—please God, ours shall not be so. We will walk on our own feet; we will work with our own hands; we will speak our own minds. Then shall man be no longer a name for pity, for doubt, and for sensual indulgence. The dread of man and the love of man shall be a wall of defence and a wreath of love around all. A nation of men will for the first time exist, because each believes himself inspired by the Divine Soul which also inspires all men.

1837

The Divinity School Address[1]

In this refulgent summer it has been a luxury to draw the breath of life. The grass grows, the buds burst, the meadow is spotted with fire and gold in the

---

2. Johann Heinrich Pestalozzi (1746–1827), Swiss educator and benefactor of poor children, whose ideas on education influenced Emerson's friends Bronson Alcott and Elizabeth Peabody.

3. Too ready to please others.

1. *An Address Delivered before the Senior Class in Divinity College, Cambridge, Sunday Evening 15 July, 1838* was published as a pamphlet in Boston soon after

tint of flowers. The air is full of birds, and sweet with the breath of the pine, the balm-of-Gilead,[2] and the new hay. Night brings no gloom to the heart with its welcome shade. Through the transparent darkness pour the stars their almost spiritual rays. Man under them seems a young child, and his huge globe a toy. The cool night bathes the world as with a river, and prepares his eyes again for the crimson dawn. The mystery of nature was never displayed more happily. The corn and the wine have been freely dealt to all creatures, and the never-broken silence with which the old bounty goes forward, has not yielded yet one word of explanation. One is constrained to respect the perfection of this world, in which our senses converse. How wide; how rich; what invitation from every property it gives to every faculty of man! In its fruitful soils; in its navigable sea; in its mountains of metal and stone; in its forests of all woods; in its animals; in its chemical ingredients; in the powers and path of light, heat, attraction, and life, is it well worth the pith and heart of great men to subdue and enjoy it. The planters, the mechanics, the inventors, the astronomers, the builders of cities, and the captains, history delights to honor.

But the moment the mind opens, and reveals the laws which traverse the universe, and make things what they are, then shrinks the great world at once into a mere illustration and fable of this mind. What am I? and What is? asks the human spirit with a curiosity new-kindled, but never to be quenched. Behold these outrunning laws, which our imperfect apprehension can see tend this way and that, but not come full circle. Behold these infinite relations, so like, so unlike; many, yet one. I would study, I would know, I would admire forever. These works of thought have been the entertainments of the human spirit in all ages.

A more secret, sweet, and overpowering beauty appears to man when his heart and mind open to the sentiment of virtue. Then instantly he is instructed in what is above him. He learns that his being is without bound; that, to the good, to the perfect, he is born, low as he now lies in evil and weakness. That which he venerates is still his own, though he has not realized it yet. *He ought.* He knows the sense of that grand word, though his analysis fails entirely to render account of it. When in innocency, or when by intellectual perception, he attains to say,—'I love the Right; Truth is beautiful within and without, forevermore. Virtue, I am thine: save me: use me: thee will I serve, day and night, in great, in small, that I may be not virtuous, but virtue;'—then is the end of the creation answered, and God is well pleased.

The sentiment of virtue is a reverence and delight in the presence of certain divine laws. It perceives that this homely game of life we play, covers, under what seem foolish details, principles that astonish. The child amidst his baubles, is learning the action of light, motion, gravity, muscular force; and in the game of human life, love, fear, justice, appetite, man, and God, interact. These laws refuse to be adequately stated. They will not by us or for us be written out on paper, or spoken by the tongue. They elude, evade our perse-

it was given. That original text is followed here, though with the title used in *Essays* (1841). Outraged attacks appeared in newspapers and pamphlets, and Emerson cautioned himself in his journal to remain "steady." (Perry Miller, in *The Transcendentalists* [1950], reprints some of the documents in this brief furor, including the most notorious attack on Emerson, Andrews Norton's *The Latest Form of Infidelity*.)

Emerson retracted nothing privately or publicly and was not invited back to Harvard for three decades, after the university had become more secular and Emerson's own international reputation had muted the charges against him.

2. An aromatic evergreen tree, named for the curative resin associated with Gilead in Jeremiah 8.22: "Is there no balm in Gilead; is there no physician there?"

vering thought, and yet we read them hourly in each other's faces, in each other's actions, in our own remorse. The moral traits which are all globed into every virtuous act and thought,—in speech, we must sever, and describe or suggest by painful enumeration of many particulars. Yet, as this sentiment is the essence of all religion, let me guide your eyes to the precise objects of the sentiment, by an enumeration of some of those classes of facts in which this element is conspicuous.

The intuition of the moral sentiment is an insight of the perfection of the laws of the soul. These laws execute themselves. They are out of time, out of space, and not subject to circumstance. Thus; in the soul of man there is a justice whose retributions are instant and entire. He who does a good deed, is instantly ennobled himself. He who does a mean deed, is by the action itself contracted. He who puts off impurity, thereby puts on purity. If a man is at heart just, then in so far is he God; the safety of God, the immortality of God, the majesty of God do enter into that man with justice. If a man dissemble, deceive, he deceives himself, and goes out of acquaintance with his own being. A man in the view of absolute goodness, adores, with total humility. Every step so downward, is a step upward. The man who renounces himself, comes to himself by so doing.

See how this rapid intrinsic energy worketh everywhere, righting wrongs, correcting appearances, and bringing up facts to a harmony with thoughts. Its operation in life, though slow to the senses, is, at last, as sure as in the soul. By it, a man is made the Providence to himself, dispensing good to his goodness, and evil to his sin. Character is always known. Thefts never enrich; alms never impoverish; murder will speak out of stone walls. The least admixture of a lie,—for example, the smallest mixture of vanity, the least attempt to make a good impression, a favorable appearance,—will instantly vitiate the effect. But speak the truth, and all nature and all spirits help you with unexpected furtherance. Speak the truth, and all things alive or brute are vouchers, and the very roots of the grass underground there, do seem to stir and move to bear you witness. See again the perfection of the Law as it applies itself to the affections, and becomes the law of society. As we are, so we associate. The good, by affinity, seek the good; the vile, by affinity, the vile. Thus of their own volition, souls proceed into heaven, into hell.

These facts have always suggested to man the sublime creed, that the world is not the product of manifold power, but of one will, of one mind; and that one mind is everywhere, in each ray of the star, in each wavelet of the pool, active; and whatever opposes that will, is everywhere baulked and baffled, because things are made so, and not otherwise. Good is positive. Evil is merely privative,[3] not absolute. It is like cold, which is the privation of heat. All evil is so much death or nonentity. Benevolence is absolute and real. So much benevolence as a man hath, so much life hath he. For all things proceed out of this same spirit, which is differently named love, justice, temperance, in its different applications, just as the ocean receives different names on the several shores which it washes. All things proceed out of the same spirit, and all things conspire with it. Whilst a man seeks good ends, he is strong by the whole strength of nature. In so far as he roves from these ends, he bereaves himself of power, of auxiliaries; his being shrinks out of all remote channels, he

---

3. I.e., not an active power, but the absence of a power.

becomes less and less, a mote, a point, until absolute badness is absolute death.

The perception of this law of laws always awakens in the mind a sentiment which we call the religious sentiment, and which makes our highest happiness. Wonderful is its power to charm and to command. It is a mountain air. It is the embalmer of the world. It is myrrh and storax, and chlorine and rosemary.[4] It makes the sky and the hills sublime, and the silent song of the stars is it. By it, is the universe made safe and habitable, not by science or power. Thought may work cold and intransitive in things, and find no end or unity. But the dawn of the sentiment of virtue on the heart, gives and is the assurance that Law is sovereign over all natures; and the worlds, time, space, eternity, do seem to break out into joy.

This sentiment is divine and deifying. It is the beatitude of man. It makes him illimitable. Through it, the soul first knows itself. It corrects the capital mistake of the infant man, who seeks to be great by following the great, and hopes to derive advantages *from another*,—by showing the fountain of all good to be in himself, and that he, equally with every man, is a door into the deeps of Reason. When he says, "I ought;" when love warms him; when he chooses, warned from on high, the good and great deed; then, deep melodies wander through his soul from Supreme Wisdom. Then he can worship, and be enlarged by his worship; for he can never go behind this sentiment. In the sublimest flights of the soul, rectitude is never surmounted, love is never outgrown.

This sentiment lies at the foundation of society, and successively creates all forms of worship. The principle of veneration never dies out. Man fallen into superstition, into sensuality, is never wholly without the visions of the moral sentiment. In like manner, all the expressions of this sentiment are sacred and permanent in proportion to their purity. The expressions of this sentiment affect us deeper, greatlier, than all other compositions. The sentences of the oldest time, which ejaculate this piety, are still fresh and fragrant. This thought dwelled always deepest in the minds of men in the devout and contemplative East; not alone in Palestine, where it reached its purest expression, but in Egypt, in Persia, in India, in China. Europe has always owed to oriental genius, its divine impulses. What these holy bards said, all sane men found agreeable and true. And the unique impression of Jesus upon mankind, whose name is not so much written as ploughed into the history of this world, is proof of the subtle virtue of this infusion.

Meantime, whilst the doors of the temple stand open, night and day, before every man, and the oracles of this truth cease never, it is guarded by one stern condition; this, namely; It is an intuition. It cannot be received at second hand. Truly speaking, it is not instruction, but provocation, that I can receive from another soul. What he announces, I must find true in me, or wholly reject; and on his word, or as his second, be he who he may, I can accept nothing. On the contrary, the absence of this primary faith is the presence of degradation. As is the flood so is the ebb. Let this faith depart, and the very words it spake, and the things it made, become false and hurtful. Then falls the church, the state, art, letters, life. The doctrine of the divine nature being

---

4. An aromatic evergeen shrub of Southern Europe and Asia Minor, used in cookery and perfumery. "Myrrh": one of the gifts the wise men brought to Je- sus, a perfume made from aromatic resins. "Storax": an aromatic resin. "Chlorine": in this sense, a greenish yellow gas used for purification.

forgotten, a sickness infects and dwarfs the constitution. Once man was all; now he is an appendage, a nuisance. And because the indwelling Supreme Spirit cannot wholly be got rid of, the doctrine of it suffers this perversion, that the divine nature is attributed to one or two persons, and denied to all the rest, and denied with fury. The doctrine of inspiration is lost; the base doctrine of the majority of voices, usurps the place of the doctrine of the soul. Miracles, prophecy, poetry, the ideal life, the holy life, exist as ancient history merely; they are not in the belief, nor in the aspiration of society; but, when suggested, seem ridiculous. Life is comic or pitiful, as soon as the high ends of being fade out of sight, and man becomes near-sighted, and can only attend to what addresses the senses.

These general views, which, whilst they are general, none will contest, find abundant illustration in the history of religion, and especially in the history of the Christian church. In that, all of us have had our birth and nurture. The truth contained in that, you, my young friends, are now setting forth to teach. As the Cultus, or established worship of the civilized world, it has great historical interest for us. Of its blessed words, which have been the consolation of humanity, you need not that I should speak. I shall endeavor to discharge my duty to you, on this occasion, by pointing out two errors in its administration, which daily appear more gross from the point of view we have just now taken.

Jesus Christ belonged to the true race of prophets. He saw with open eye the mystery of the soul. Drawn by its severe harmony, ravished with its beauty, he lived in it, and had his being there. Alone in all history, he estimated the greatness of man. One man was true to what is in you and me. He saw that God incarnates himself in man, and evermore goes forth anew to take possession of his world. He said, in this jubilee of sublime emotion, 'I am divine. Through me, God acts; through me, speaks. Would you see God, see me; or, see thee, when thou also thinkest as I now think.' But what a distortion did his doctrine and memory suffer in the same, in the next, and the following ages! There is no doctrine of the Reason which will bear to be taught by the Understanding.[5] The understanding caught this high chant from the poet's lips, and said, in the next age, 'This was Jehovah come down out of heaven. I will kill you, if you say he was a man.' The idioms of his language, and the figures of his rhetoric, have usurped the place of his truth; and churches are not built on his principles, but on his tropes. Christianity became a Mythus,[6] as the poetic teaching of Greece and of Egypt, before. He spoke of miracles; for he felt that man's life was a miracle, and all that man doth, and he knew that this daily miracle shines, as the man is diviner. But the very word Miracle, as pronounced by Christian churches, gives a false impression; it is Monster. It is not one with the blowing clover and the falling rain.

He felt respect for Moses and the prophets; but no unfit tenderness at postponing their initial revelations, to the hour and the man that now is; to the eternal revelation in the heart. Thus was he a true man. Having seen that the law in us is commanding, he would not suffer it to be commanded. Boldly, with hand, and heart, and life, he declared it was God. Thus was he a true man. Thus is he, as I think, the only soul in history who has appreciated the worth of a man.

---

5. Emerson reverses the common meaning of *reason*, using it in the sense of intuitive, suprarational knowledge, while by *understanding* he means knowledge ar- rived at through a logical reasoning process.
6. A cult deliberately fostered.

1. In thus contemplating Jesus, we become very sensible of the first defect of historical Christianity. Historical Christianity has fallen into the error that corrupts all attempts to communicate religion. As it appears to us, and as it has appeared for ages, it is not the doctrine of the soul, but an exaggeration of the personal, the positive, the ritual. It has dwelt, it dwells, with noxious exaggeration about the *person* of Jesus. The soul knows no persons. It invites every man to expand to the full circle of the universe, and will have no preferences but those of spontaneous love. But by this eastern monarchy of a Christianity, which indolence and fear have built, the friend of man is made the injurer of man. The manner in which his name is surrounded with expressions, which were once sallies of admiration and love, but are now petrified into official titles, kills all generous sympathy and liking. All who hear me, feel, that the language that describes Christ to Europe and America, is not the style of friendship and enthusiasm to a good and noble heart, but is appropriated and formal,—paints a demigod, as the Orientals or the Greeks would describe Osiris or Apollo.[7] Accept the injurious impositions of our early catachetical instruction, and even honesty and self-denial were but splendid sins, if they did not wear the Christian name. One would rather be

'A pagan suckled in a creed outworn,'[8]

than to be defrauded of his manly right in coming into nature, and finding not names and places, not land and professions, but even virtue and truth foreclosed and monopolized. You shall not be a man even. You shall not own the world; you shall not dare, and live after the infinite Law that is in you, and in company with the infinite Beauty which heaven and earth reflect to you in all lovely forms; but you must subordinate your nature to Christ's nature; you must accept our interpretations; and take his portrait as the vulgar draw it.

That is always best which gives me to myself. The sublime is excited in me by the great stoical doctrine, Obey thyself. That which shows God in me, fortifies me. That which shows God out of me, makes me a wart and a wen. There is no longer a necessary reason for my being. Already the long shadows of untimely oblivion creep over me, and I shall decease forever.

The divine bards are the friends of my virtue, of my intellect, of my strength. They admonish me, that the gleams which flash across my mind, are not mine, but God's; that they had the like, and were not disobedient to the heavenly vision.[9] So I love them. Noble provocations go out from them, inviting me also to emancipate myself; to resist evil; to subdue the world; and to Be. And thus by his holy thoughts, Jesus serves us, and thus only. To aim to convert a man by miracles, is a profanation of the soul. A true conversion, a true Christ, is now, as always, to be made, by the reception of beautiful sentiments. It is true that a great and rich soul, like his, falling among the simple, does so preponderate, that, as his did, it names the world. The world seems to them to exist for him, and they have not yet drunk so deeply of his sense, as to see that only by coming again to themselves, or to God in themselves, can they grow forevermore. It is a low benefit to give me something; it is a high benefit to enable me to do somewhat of myself. The time is coming when all men will see, that the gift of God to the soul is not a vaunting,

7. Emerson associates Egypt (where Osiris was a fertility god) with the Orient and associates Greece (where Apollo was the god of the sun) with European culture.
8. From Wordsworth's sonnet *The World Is Too Much with Us.*
9. "I was not disobedient unto the heavenly vision" (Acts 26.19).

overpowering, excluding sanctity, but a sweet, natural goodness, a goodness like thine and mine, and that so invites thine and mine to be and to grow.

The injustice of the vulgar tone of preaching is not less flagrant to Jesus, than it is to the souls which it profanes. The preachers do not see that they make his gospel not glad, and shear him of the locks of beauty and the attributes of heaven. When I see a majestic Epaminondas,[1] or Washington; when I see among my contemporaries, a true orator, an upright judge, a dear friend; when I vibrate to the melody and fancy of a poem; I see beauty that is to be desired. And so lovely, and with yet more entire consent of my human being, sounds in my ear the severe music of the bards that have sung of the true God in all ages. Now do not degrade the life and dialogues of Christ out of the circle of this charm, by insulation and peculiarity. Let them lie as they befel, alive and warm, part of human life, and of the landscape, and of the cheerful day.

2. The second defect of the traditionary and limited way of using the mind of Christ is a consequence of the first; this, namely; that the Moral Nature, that Law of laws, whose revelations introduce greatness,—yea, God himself, into the open soul, is not explored as the fountain of the established teaching in society. Men have come to speak of the revelation as somewhat long ago given and done, as if God were dead. The injury to faith throttles the preacher; and the goodliest of institutions becomes an uncertain and inarticulate voice.

It is very certain that it is the effect of conversation with the beauty of the soul, to beget a desire and need to impart to others the same knowledge and love. If utterance is denied, the thought lies like a burden on the man. Always the seer is a sayer. Somehow his dream is told. Somehow he publishes it with solemn joy. Sometimes with pencil on canvas; sometimes with chisel on stone; sometimes in towers and aisles of granite, his soul's worship is builded; sometimes in anthems of indefinite music; but clearest and most permanent, in words.

The man enamored of this excellency, becomes its priest or poet. The office is coeval with the world. But observe the condition, the spiritual limitation of the office. The spirit only can teach. Not any profane man, not any sensual, not any liar, not any slave can teach, but only he can give, who has; he only can create, who is. The man on whom the soul descends, through whom the soul speaks, alone can teach. Courage, piety, love, wisdom, can teach; and every man can open his door to these angels, and they shall bring him the gift of tongues. But the man who aims to speak as books enable, as synods use, as the fashion guides, and as interest commands, babbles. Let him hush.

To this holy office, you propose to devote yourselves. I wish you may feel your call in throbs of desire and hope. The office is the first in the world. It is of that reality, that it cannot suffer the deduction of any falsehood. And it is my duty to say to you, that the need was never greater of new revelation than now. From the views I have already expressed, you will infer the sad conviction, which I share, I believe, with numbers, of the universal decay and now almost death of faith in society. The soul is not preached. The Church seems to totter to its fall, almost all life extinct. On this occasion, any complaisance, would be criminal, which told you, whose hope and commission it is to preach the faith of Christ, that the faith of Christ is preached.

It is time that this ill-suppressed murmur of all thoughtful men against the

---

1. Theban general (418?–362 B.C) whose military innovations helped end Sparta's dominance in Greece.

famine of our churches; this moaning of the heart because it is bereaved of the consolation, the hope, the grandeur, that come alone out of the culture of the moral nature; should be heard through the sleep of indolence, and over the din of routine. This great and perpetual office of the preacher is not discharged. Preaching is the expression of the moral sentiment in application to the duties of life. In how many churches, by how many prophets, tell me, is man made sensible that he is an infinite Soul; that the earth and heavens are passing into his mind; that he is drinking forever the soul of God? Where now sounds the persuasion, that by its very melody imparadises my heart, and so affirms its own origin in heaven? Where shall I hear words such as in elder ages drew men to leave all and follow,—father and mother, house and land, wife and child?[2] Where shall I hear these august laws of moral being so pronounced, as to fill my ear, and I feel ennobled by the offer of my uttermost action and passion? The test of the true faith, certainly, should be its power to charm and command the soul, as the laws of nature control the activity of the hands,—so commanding that we find pleasure and honor in obeying. The faith should blend with the light of rising and of setting suns, with the flying cloud, the singing bird, and the breath of flowers. But now the priest's Sabbath has lost the splendor of nature; it is unlovely; we are glad when it is done; we can make, we do make, even sitting in our pews, a far better, holier, sweeter, for ourselves.

Whenever the pulpit is usurped by a formalist, then is the worshipper defrauded and disconsolate. We shrink as soon as the prayers begin, which do not uplift, but smite and offend us. We are fain to wrap our cloaks about us, and secure, as best we can, a solitude that hears not. I once heard a preacher who sorely tempted me to say, I would go to church no more. Men go, thought I, where they are wont to go, else had no soul entered the temple in the afternoon. A snowstorm was falling around us. The snowstorm was real; the preacher merely spectral; and the eye felt the sad contrast in looking at him, and then out of the window behind him, into the beautiful meteor of the snow. He had lived in vain. He had no one word intimating that he had laughed or wept, was married or in love, had been commended, or cheated, or chagrined. If he had ever lived and acted, we were none the wiser for it. The capital secret of his profession, namely, to convert life into truth, he had not learned. Not one fact in all his experience, had he yet imported into his doctrine. This man had ploughed, and planted, and talked, and bought, and sold; he had read books; he had eaten and drunken; his head aches; his heart throbs; he smiles and suffers; yet was there not a surmise, a hint, in all the discourse, that he had ever lived at all. Not a line did he draw out of real history. The true preacher can always be known by this, that he deals out to the people his life,—life passed through the fire of thought. But of the bad preacher, it could not be told from his sermon, what age of the world he fell in; whether he had a father or a child; whether he was a freeholder or a pauper; whether he was a citizen or a countryman; or any other fact of his biography.

It seemed strange that the people should come to church. It seemed as if their houses were very unentertaining, that they should prefer this thoughtless

2. See Matthew 19.28–29: "And Jesus said unto them, Verily I say unto you, That ye which have followed me, in the regeneration when the Son of man shall sit in the throne of his glory, ye also shall sit upon twelve thrones, judging the twelve tribes of Israel. And every one that hath forsaken houses, or brethren, or sisters, or father, or mother, or wife, or children, or lands, for my name's sake, shall receive an hundredfold, and shall inherit everlasting life."

clamor. It shows that there is a commanding attraction in the moral sentiment, that can lend a faint tint of light to dulness and ignorance, coming in its name and place. The good hearer is sure he has been touched sometimes; is sure there is somewhat to be reached, and some word that can reach it. When he listens to these vain words, he comforts himself by their relation to his remembrance of better hours, and so they clatter and echo unchallenged.

I am not ignorant that when we preach unworthily, it is not always quite in vain. There is a good ear, in some men, that draws supplies to virtue out of very indifferent nutriment. There is poetic truth concealed in all the common-places of prayer and of sermons, and though foolishly spoken, they may be wisely heard; for, each is some select expression that broke out in a moment of piety from some stricken or jubilant soul, and its excellency made it remembered. The prayers and even the dogmas of our church, are like the zodiac of Denderah,[3] and the astronomical monuments of the Hindoos, wholly insulated from anything now extant in the life and business of the people. They mark the height to which the waters once rose. But this docility is a check upon the mischief from the good and devout. In a large portion of the community, the religious service gives rise to quite other thoughts and emotions. We need not chide the negligent servant. We are struck with pity, rather, at the swift retribution of his sloth. Alas for the unhappy man that is called to stand in the pulpit, and *not* give bread of life. Everything that befals, accuses him. Would he ask contributions for the missions, foreign or domestic? Instantly his face is suffused with shame, to propose to his parish, that they should send money a hundred or a thousand miles, to furnish such poor fare as they have at home, and would do well to go the hundred or the thousand miles, to escape. Would he urge people to a godly way of living;—and can he ask a fellow creature to come to Sabbath meetings, when he and they all know what is the poor uttermost they can hope for therein? Will he invite them privately to the Lord's Supper? He dares not. If no heart warm this rite, the hollow, dry, creaking formality is too plain, than that he can face a man of wit and energy, and put the invitation without terror. In the street, what has he to say to the bold village blasphemer? The village blasphemer sees fear in the face, form, and gait of the minister.

Let me not taint the sincerity of this plea by any oversight of the claims of good men. I know and honor the purity and strict conscience of numbers of the clergy. What life the public worship retains, it owes to the scattered company of pious men, who minister here and there in the churches, and who, sometimes accepting with too great tenderness the tenet of the elders, have not accepted from others, but from their own heart, the genuine impulses of virtue, and so still command our love and awe, to the sanctity of character. Moreover, the exceptions are not so much to be found in a few eminent preachers, as in the better hours, the truer inspirations of all,—nay, in the sincere moments of every man. But with whatever exception, it is still true, that tradition characterizes the preaching of this country; that it comes out of the memory, and not out of the soul; that it aims at what is usual, and not at what is necessary and eternal; that thus, historical Christianity destroys the power of preaching, by withdrawing it from the exploration of the moral nature of man, where the sublime is, where are the resources of astonishment and

3. At Dandarah, a village in Upper Egypt, the ceiling of a ruined ancient temple is sculpted with astronomical scenes.

power. What a cruel injustice it is to that Law, the joy of the whole earth, which alone can make thought dear and rich; that Law whose fatal sureness the astronomical orbits poorly emulate, that it is travestied and depreciated, that it is behooted and behowled, and not a trait, not a word of it articulated. The pulpit in losing sight of this Law, loses all its inspiration, and gropes after it knows not what. And for want of this culture, the soul of the community is sick and faithless. It wants nothing so much as a stern, high, stoical, Christian discipline, to make it know itself and the divinity that speaks through it. Now man is ashamed of himself; he skulks and sneaks through the world, to be tolerated, to be pitied, and scarcely in a thousand years does any man dare to be wise and good, and so draw after him the tears and blessings of his kind.

Certainly there have been periods when, from the inactivity of the intellect on certain truths, a greater faith was possible in names and persons. The Puritans in England and America, found in the Christ of the Catholic Church, and in the dogmas inherited from Rome, scope for their austere piety, and their longings for civil freedom. But their creed is passing away, and none arises in its room. I think no man can go with his thoughts about him, into one of our churches, without feeling that what hold the public worship had on men, is gone or going. It has lost its grasp on the affection of the good, and the fear of the bad. In the country,—neighborhoods, half parishes are *signing off*,—to use the local term. It is already beginning to indicate character and religion to withdraw from the religious meetings. I have heard a devout person, who prized the Sabbath, say in bitterness of heart, "On Sundays, it seems wicked to go to church." And the motive, that holds the best there, is now only a hope and a waiting. What was once a mere circumstance, that the best and the worst men in the parish, the poor and the rich, the learned and the ignorant, young and old, should meet one day as fellows in one house, in sign of an equal right in the soul,—has come to be a paramount motive for going thither.

My friends, in these two errors, I think, I find the causes of that calamity of a decaying church and a wasting unbelief, which are casting malignant influences around us, and making the hearts of good men sad. And what greater calamity can fall upon a nation, than the loss of worship? Then all things go to decay. Genius leaves the temple, to haunt the senate, or the market. Literature becomes frivolous. Science is cold. The eye of youth is not lighted by the hope of other worlds, and age is without honor. Society lives to trifles, and when men die, we do not mention them.

And now, my brothers, you will ask, What in these desponding days can be done by us? The remedy is already declared in the ground of our complaint of the Church. We have contrasted the Church with the Soul. In the soul, then, let the redemption be sought. In one soul, in your soul, there are resources for the world. Wherever a man comes, there comes revolution. The old is for slaves. When a man comes, all books are legible, all things transparent, all religions are forms. He is religious. Man is the wonderworker. He is seen amid miracles. All men bless and curse. He saith yea and nay, only. The stationariness of religion; the assumption that the age of inspiration is past, that the Bible is closed; the fear of degrading the character of Jesus by representing him as a man; indicate with sufficient clearness the falsehood of our theology. It is the office of a true teacher to show us that God is, not was; that He speaketh, not spake. The true Christianity,—a faith like Christ's in the infinitude of man,—is lost. None believeth in the soul of man, but only in some man or person old and departed. Ah me! no man goeth alone. All men go in flocks to this saint or that poet, avoiding the God who seeth in secret. They cannot see in secret; they love to be blind in public. They think society wiser than their soul, and know not that one soul, and their soul, is wiser than the whole world. See how nations and races flit by on the sea of time, and leave no ripple to tell where they floated or sunk, and one good soul shall make the name of Moses, or of Zeno, or of Zoroaster,[4] reverend forever. None assayeth the stern ambition to be the Self of the nation, and of nature, but each would be an easy secondary to some Christian scheme, or sectarian connexion, or some eminent man. Once leave your own knowledge of God, your own sentiment, and take secondary knowledge, as St. Paul's, or George Fox's, or Swedenborg's,[5] and you get wide from God with every year this secondary form lasts, and if, as now, for centuries,—the chasm yawns to that breadth, that men can scarcely be convinced there is in them anything divine.

Let me admonish you, first of all, to go alone; to refuse the good models, even those most sacred in the imagination of men, and dare to love God without mediator or veil. Friends enough you shall find who will hold up to your emulation Wesleys and Oberlins,[6] Saints and Prophets. Thank God for these good men, but say, 'I also am a man.' Imitation cannot go above its model. The imitator dooms himself to hopeless mediocrity. The inventor did it, because it was natural to him, and so in him it has a charm. In the imitator, something else is natural, and he bereaves himself of his own beauty, to come short of another man's.

Yourself a newborn bard of the Holy Ghost,—cast behind you all conformity, and acquaint men at first hand with Deity. Be to them a man. Look to it first and only, that you are such; that fashion, custom, authority, pleasure, and money are nothing to you,—are not bandages over your eyes, that you cannot see,—but live with the privilege of the immeasurable mind. Not too anxious to visit periodically all families and each family in your parish connexion,—when you meet one of these men or women, be to them a divine man; be to them thought and virtue; let their timid aspirations find in you a friend; let their trampled instincts be genially tempted out in your atmosphere; let their doubts know that you have doubted, and their wonder feel that you have wondered. By trusting your own soul, you shall gain a greater confidence in other men. For all our penny-wisdom, for all our soul-destroying slavery to habit, it is not to be doubted, that all men have sublime thoughts; that all men do value the few real hours of life; they love to be heard; they love to be caught up into the vision of principles. We mark with light in the memory the few interviews, we have had in the dreary years of routine and of sin, with souls that made our souls wiser; that spoke what we thought; that told us what we knew; that gave us leave to be what we inly were. Discharge to men the priestly office, and, present or absent, you shall be followed with their love as by an angel.

And, to this end, let us not aim at common degrees of merit. Can we not

---

4. Iranian religious reformer (6 century B.C.), founder of religion still practiced by the Parsees. Moses, Hebrew lawgiver who led the exodus from Egypt. Zeno (342?–270? B.C.), Greek philosopher and founder of Stoicism.
5. Emanuel Swedenborg (1688–1772), Swedish scientist and theologian. St. Paul, the apostle to the Gentiles, hero of the Book of Acts, and author of other books of the New Testament. George Fox

(1624–1691), English founder of the Society of Friends (Quakers).
6. Jean Frédéric Oberlin (1740–1826), Alsatian Lutheran clergyman and philanthropist, innovator in children's education; the town and college in Ohio are named in his honor. John Wesley (1703–1791) and his brother Charles (1707–1788) founded the Methodist movement in the Church of England.

leave, to such as love it, the virtue that glitters for the commendation of society, and ourselves pierce the deep solitudes of absolute ability and worth? We easily come up to the standard of goodness in society. Society's praise can be cheaply secured, and almost all men are content with those easy merits; but the instant effect of conversing with God, will be, to put them away. There are sublime merits; persons who are not actors, not speakers, but influences; persons too great for fame, for display; who disdain eloquence; to whom all we call art and artist, seems too nearly allied to show and by-ends, to the exaggeration of the finite and selfish, and loss of the universal. The orators, the poets, the commanders encroach on us only as fair women do, by our allowance and homage. Slight them by preoccupation of mind, slight them, as you can well afford to do, by high and universal aims, and they instantly feel that you have right, and that it is in lower places that they must shine. They also feel your right; for they with you are open to the influx of the all-knowing Spirit, which annihilates before its broad noon the little shades and gradations of intelligence in the compositions we call wiser and wisest.

In such high communion, let us study the grand strokes of rectitude: a bold benevolence, an independence of friends, so that not the unjust wishes of those who love us, shall impair our freedom, but we shall resist for truth's sake the freest flow of kindness, and appeal to sympathies far in advance; and,— what is the highest form in which we know this beautiful element,—a certain solidity of merit, that has nothing to do with opinion, and which is so essentially and manifestly virtue, that it is taken for granted, that the right, the brave, the generous step will be taken by it, and nobody thinks of commending it. You would compliment a coxcomb doing a good act, but you would not praise an angel. The silence that accepts merit as the most natural thing in the world, is the highest applause. Such souls, when they appear, are the Imperial Guard of Virtue, the perpetual reserve, the dictators of fortune. One needs not praise their courage,—they are the heart and soul of nature. O my friends, there are resources in us on which we have not drawn. There are men who rise refreshed on hearing a threat; men to whom a crisis which intimidates and paralyzes the majority—demanding not the faculties of prudence and thrift, but comprehension, immovableness, the readiness of sacrifice,—comes graceful and beloved as a bride. Napoleon said of Massena,[7] that he was not himself until the battle began to go against him; then, when the dead began to fall in ranks around him, awoke his powers of combination, and he put on terror and victory as a robe. So it is in rugged crises, in unwearied endurance, and in aims which put sympathy out of question, that the angel is shown. But these are heights that we can scarce remember and look up to, without contrition and shame. Let us thank God that such things exist.

And now let us do what we can to rekindle the smouldering, nigh quenched fire on the altar. The evils of that church that now is, are manifest. The question returns. What shall we do? I confess, all attempts to project and establish a Cultus with new rites and forms, seem to me vain. Faith makes us, and not we it, and faith makes its own forms. All attempts to contrive a system, are as cold as the new worship introduced by the French to the goddess of Reason,[8]—today, pasteboard and fillagree, and ending to-morrow in madness and murder. Rather let the breath of new life be breathed by you through the

---

7. André Masséna (1758–1817), marshal of the empire under Napoleon; the anecdote is taken from Barry Edward O'Meara's *Napoleon in Exile* (1823).

8. A reference to the French "worship of Reason" promulgated in 1793 during the Reign of Terror.

forms already existing. For, if once you are alive, you shall find they shall become plastic[9] and new. The remedy to their deformity is, first, soul, and second, soul, and evermore, soul. A whole popedom[1] of forms, one pulsation of virtue can uplift and vivify. Two inestimable advantages Christianity has given us; first; the Sabbath, the jubilee of the whole world; whose light dawns welcome alike into the closet of the philosopher, into the garret of toil, and into prison cells, and everywhere suggests, even to the vile, a thought of the dignity of spiritual being. Let is stand forevermore, a temple, which new love, new faith, new sight shall restore to more than its first splendor to mankind. And secondly, the institution of preaching;—the speech of man to men,— essentially the most flexible of all organs, of all forms. What hinders that now, everywhere, in pulpits, in lecture-rooms, in houses, in fields, wherever the invitation of men or your own occasions lead you, you speak the very truth, as your life and conscience teach it, and cheer the waiting, fainting hearts of men with new hope and new revelation.

I look for the hour when that supreme Beauty, which ravished the souls of those Eastern men, and chiefly of those Hebrews, and through their lips spoke oracles to all time, shall speak in the West also. The Hebrew and Greek Scriptures contain immortal sentences, that have been bread of life to millions. But they have no epical integrity; are fragmentary; are not shown in their order to the intellect. I look for the new Teacher, that shall follow so far those shining laws, that he shall see them come full circle; shall see their rounding complete grace; shall see the world to be the mirror of the soul; shall see the identity of the law of gravitation with purity of heart; and shall show that the Ought, that Duty, is one thing with Science, with Beauty, and with Joy.

1838, 1841

Self-Reliance[1]

Ne te quæsiveris extra.[2]

*"Man is his own star, and the soul that can
Render an honest and a perfect man,
Command all light, all influence, all fate,
Nothing to him falls early or too late.
Our acts our angels are, or good or ill,
Our fatal shadows that walk by us still."*
    —Epilogue to Beaumont and Fletcher's *Honest Man's Fortune*[3]

*Cast the bantling[4] on the rocks,
Suckle him with the she-wolf's teat:
Wintered with the hawk and fox,
Power and speed be hands and feet.*

I read the other day some verses written by an eminent painter which were original and not conventional. Always the soul hears an admonition in such

---

9. Receptive to influences, capable of receiving new shapes.
1. I.e., rigid hierarchy.
1. *Self-Reliance*, first published in *Essays* (1841), the source of the present text, is even more than most of Emerson's essays a collection of thoughts from his journals, often by way of various lectures over a period of years. The earliest of the journal entries reused in this essay is from 1832, the year Emerson renounced

his pulpit, and numerous other reused journal entries and lecture reworkings are from the years 1838–40, when *The Divinity School Address* provided a major test of his own self-trust.
2. Persius, *Satire* 1.7: "Do not search outside yourself" (Latin), i.e., meaning do not imitate.
3. 1613.
4. Baby. The stanza is Emerson's.

lines, let the subject be what it may. The sentiment they instil is of more value than any thought they may contain. To believe your own thought, to believe that what is true for you in your private heart, is true for all men,—that is genius. Speak your latent conviction and it shall be the universal sense; for always the inmost becomes the outmost,—and our first thought is rendered back to us by the trumpets of the Last Judgment. Familiar as the voice of the mind is to each, the highest merit we ascribe to Moses, Plato, and Milton, is that they set at naught books and traditions, and spoke not what men but what they thought. A man should learn to detect and watch that gleam of light which flashes across his mind from within, more than the lustre of the firmament of bards and sages. Yet he dismisses without notice his thought, because it is his. In every work of genius we recognize our own rejected thoughts: they come back to us with a certain alienated majesty. Great works of art have no more affecting lesson for us than this. They teach us to abide by our spontaneous impression with good humored inflexibility then most when the whole cry of voices is on the other side. Else, to-morrow a stranger will say with masterly good sense precisely what we have thought and felt all the time, and we shall be forced to take with shame our own opinion from another.

There is a time in every man's education when he arrives at the conviction that envy is ignorance; that imitation is suicide; that he must take himself for better, for worse, as his portion; that though the wide universe is full of good, no kernel of nourishing corn can come to him but through his toil bestowed on that plot of ground which is given to him to till. The power which resides in him is new in nature, and none but he knows what that is which he can do, nor does he know until he has tried. Not for nothing one face, one character, one fact makes much impression on him, and another none. It is not without preëstablished harmony, this sculpture in the memory. The eye was placed where one ray should fall, that it might testify of that particular ray. Bravely let him speak the utmost syllable of his confession. We but half express ourselves, and are ashamed of that divine idea which each of us represents. It may be safely trusted as proportionate and of good issues, so it be faithfully imparted, but God will not have his work made manifest by cowards. It needs a divine man to exhibit any thing divine. A man is relieved and gay when he has put his heart into his work and done his best; but what he has said or done otherwise, shall give him no peace. It is a deliverance which does not deliver. In the attempt his genius deserts him; no muse befriends; no invention, no hope.

Trust thyself: every heart vibrates to that iron string. Accept the place the divine Providence has found for you; the society of your contemporaries, the connexion of events. Great men have always done so and confided themselves childlike to the genius of their age, betraying their perception that the Eternal was stirring at their heart, working through their hands, predominating in all their being. And we are now men, and must accept in the highest mind the same transcendent destiny; and not pinched in a corner, not cowards fleeing before a revolution, but redeemers and benefactors, pious aspirants to be noble clay plastic under the Almighty effort, let us advance and advance on Chaos and the Dark.

What pretty oracles nature yields us on this text in the face and behavior of children, babes and even brutes. That divided and rebel mind, that distrust of a sentiment because our arithmetic has computed the strength and means opposed to our purpose, these have not. Their mind being whole, their eye is as yet unconquered, and when we look in their faces, we are disconcerted. Infancy conforms to nobody: all conform to it, so that one babe commonly makes four or five out of the adults who prattle and play to it. So God has armed youth and puberty and manhood no less with its own piquancy and charm, and made it enviable and gracious and its claims not to be put by, if it will stand by itself. Do not think the youth has no force because he cannot speak to you and me. Hark! in the next room, who spoke so clear and emphatic? Good Heaven! it is he! it is that very lump of bashfulness and phlegm which for weeks has done nothing but eat when you were by, that now rolls out these words like bell-strokes. It seems he knows how to speak to his contemporaries. Bashful or bold, then, he will know how to make us seniors very unnecessary.

The nonchalance of boys who are sure of a dinner, and would disdain as much as a lord to do or say aught to conciliate one, is the healthy attitude of human nature. How is a boy the master of society; independent, irresponsible, looking out from his corner on such people and facts as pass by, he tries and sentences them on their merits, in the swift summary way of boys, as good, bad, interesting, silly, eloquent, troublesome. He cumbers himself never about consequences, about interests: he gives an independent, genuine verdict. You must court him: he does not court you. But the man is, as it were, clapped into jail by his consciousness. As soon as he has once acted or spoken with eclat, he is a committed person, watched by the sympathy or the hatred of hundreds whose affections must now enter into his account. There is no Lethe[5] for this. Ah, that he could pass again into his neutral, godlike independence! Who can thus lose all pledge, and having observed, observe again from the same unaffected, unbiased, unbribable, unaffrighted innocence, must always be formidable, must always engage the poet's and the man's regards. Of such an immortal youth the force would be felt. He would utter opinions on all passing affairs, which being seen to be not private but necessary, would sink like darts into the ear of men, and put them in fear.

These are the voices which we hear in solitude, but they grow faint and inaudible as we enter into the world. Society everywhere is in conspiracy against the manhood of every one of its members. Society is a joint-stock company[6] in which the members agree for the better securing of his bread to each shareholder, to surrender the liberty and culture of the eater. The virtue in most request is conformity. Self-reliance is its aversion. It loves not realities and creators, but names and customs.

Whoso would be a man must be a nonconformist. He who would gather immortal palms must not be hindered by the name of goodness, but must explore if it be goodness. Nothing is at last sacred but the integrity of our own mind. Absolve you to yourself, and you shall have the suffrage of the world. I remember an answer which when quite young I was prompted to make to a valued adviser who was wont to importune me with the dear old doctrines of the church. On my saying, What have I to do with the sacredness of traditions, if I live wholly from within? my friend suggested—"But these impulses may be from below, not from above." I replied, 'They do not seem to me to be

---

5. Oblivion-producing water from the river of the underworld in Greek mythology.

6. Business for which the capital is held by its joint owners in transferable shares.

such; but if I am the devil's child, I will live then from the devil.' No law can be sacred to me but that of my nature. Good and bad are but names very readily transferable to that or this; the only right is what is after my constitution, the only wrong what is against it. A man is to carry himself in the presence of all opposition as if every thing were titular and ephemeral but he. I am ashamed to think how easily we capitulate to badges and names, to large societies and dead institutions. Every decent and well-spoken individual affects and sways me more than is right. I ought to go upright and vital, and speak the rude truth in all ways. If malice and vanity wear the coat of philanthropy, shall that pass? If an angry bigot assumes this bountiful cause of Abolition, and comes to me with his last news from Barbadoes,[7] why should I not say to him, 'Go love thy infant; love thy wood-chopper: be good-natured and modest: have that grace; and never varnish your hard, uncharitable ambition with this incredible tenderness for black folk a thousand miles off. Thy love afar is spite at home.' Rough and graceless would be such greeting, but truth is handsomer than the affectation of love. Your goodness must have some edge to it—else it is none. The doctrine of hatred must be preached as the counteraction of the doctrine of love when that pules and whines. I shun father and mother and wife and brother, when my genius calls me.[8] I would write on the lintels of the door-post, Whim.[9] I hope it is somewhat better than whim at last, but we cannot spend the day in explanation. Expect me not to show cause why I seek or why I exclude company. Then, again, do not tell me, as a good man did to-day, of my obligation to put all poor men in good situations. Are they *my* poor? I tell thee, thou foolish philanthropist, that I grudge the dollar, the dime, the cent I give to such men as do not belong to me and to whom I do not belong. There is a class of persons to whom by all spiritual affinity I am bought and sold; for them I will go to prison, if need be; but your miscellaneous popular charities; the education at college of fools; the building of meeting-houses to the vain end to which many now stand; alms to sots; and the thousandfold Relief Societies;—though I confess with shame I sometimes succumb and give the dollar, it is a wicked dollar which by-and-by I shall have the manhood to withhold.

Virtues are in the popular estimate rather the exception than the rule. There is the man *and* his virtues. Men do what is called a good action, as some piece of courage or charity, much as they would pay a fine in expiation of daily non-appearance on parade. Their works are done as an apology or extenuation of their living in the world,—as invalids and the insane pay a high board. Their virtues are penances. I do not wish to expiate, but to live. My life is not an apology, but a life. It is for itself and not for a spectacle. I much prefer that it should be of a lower strain, so it be genuine and equal, than that it should be glittering and unsteady. I wish it to be sound and sweet, and not to need diet and bleeding.[1] My life should be unique; it should be an alms, a battle, a conquest, a medicine. I ask primary evidence that you are a man, and refuse this appeal from the man to his actions. I know that for myself it makes no

---

7. Island in the eastern Caribbean where slavery was officially abolished in 1834 and all slaves freed by 1838.
8. For shunning family to obey a divine command see Matthew 10.34–37.
9. See Exodus 12 for God's instructions to Moses on marking with blood the "two side posts" and the "upper door post" (or lintel) of houses so that God would spare those within when he passed through to "smite all the firstborn in the land of Egypt, both man and beast." Emerson equates importunate distractions from other people with a death threat to his intellectual and spiritual life.
1. The old medical treatment of bloodletting.

difference whether I do or forbear those actions which are reckoned excellent. I cannot consent to pay for a privilege where I have intrinsic right. Few and mean as my gifts may be, I actually am, and do not need for my own assurance or the assurance of my fellows any secondary testimony.

What I must do, is all that concerns me, not what the people think. This rule, equally arduous in actual and in intellectual life, may serve for the whole distinction between greatness and meanness. It is the harder, because you will always find those who think they know what is your duty better than you know it. It is easy in the world to live after the world's opinion; it is easy in solitude to live after our own; but the great man is he who in the midst of the crowd keeps with perfect sweetness the independence of solitude.

The objection to conforming to usages that have become dead to you, is, that it scatters your force. It loses your time and blurs the impression of your character. If you maintain a dead church, contribute to a dead Bible-Society, vote with a great party either for the Government or against it, spread your table like base housekeepers,—under all these screens, I have difficulty to detect the precise man you are. And, of course, so much force is withdrawn from your proper life. But do your thing, and I shall know you. Do your work, and you shall reinforce yourself. A man must consider what a blindman's-buff is this game of conformity. If I know your sect, I anticipate your argument. I hear a preacher announce for his text and topic the expediency of one of the institutions of his church. Do I not know beforehand that not possibly can he say a new and spontaneous word? Do I not know that with all this ostentation of examining the grounds of the institution, he will do no such thing? Do I not know that he is pledged to himself not to look but at one side; the permitted side, not as a man, but as a parish minister? He is a retained attorney, and these airs of the bench are the emptiest affectation. Well, most men have bound their eyes with one or another handkerchief, and attached themselves to some one of these communities of opinion. This conformity makes them not false in a few particulars, authors of a few lies, but false in all particulars. Their every truth is not quite true. Their two is not the real two, their four not the real four: so that every word they say chagrins us, and we know not where to begin to set them right. Meantime nature is not slow to equip us in the prison-uniform of the party to which we adhere. We come to wear one cut of face and figure, and acquire by degrees the gentlest asinine expression. There is a mortifying experience in particular which does not fail to wreak itself also in the general history; I mean, "the foolish face of praise,"[2] the forced smile which we put on in company where we do not feel at ease in answer to conversation which does not interest us. The muscles, not spontaneously moved, but moved by a low usurping wilfulness, grow tight about the outline of the face and make the most disagreeable sensation, a sensation of rebuke and warning which no brave young man will suffer twice.

For non-conformity the world whips you with its displeasure. And therefore a man must know how to estimate a sour face. The bystanders look askance on him in the public street or in the friend's parlor. If this aversation had its origin in contempt and resistance like his own, he might well go home with a sad countenance; but the sour faces of the multitude, like their sweet faces, have no deep cause,—disguise no god, but are put on and off as the wind

2. Alexander Pope, *Epistle to Dr. Arbuthnot*, line 212.

blows, and a newspaper directs. Yet is the discontent of the multitude more formidable than that of the senate and the college. It is easy enough for a firm man who knows the world to brook the rage of the cultivated classes. Their rage is decorous and prudent, for they are timid as being very vulnerable themselves. But when to their feminine rage the indignation of the people is added, when the ignorant and the poor are aroused, when the unintelligent brute force that lies at the bottom of society is made to growl and mow, it needs the habit of magnanimity and religion to treat it godlike as a trifle of no concernment.

The other terror that scares us from self-trust is our consistency; a reverence for our past act or word, because the eyes of others have no other data for computing our orbit than our past acts, and we are loath to disappoint them.

But why should you keep your head over your shoulder? Why drag about this monstrous corpse of your memory, lest you contradict somewhat you have stated in this or that public place? Suppose you should contradict yourself; what then? It seems to be a rule of wisdom never to rely on your memory alone, scarcely even in acts of pure memory, but bring the past for judgment into the thousand-eyed present, and live ever in a new day. Trust your emotion. In your metaphysics you have denied personality to the Deity: yet when the devout motions of the soul come, yield to them heart and life, though they should clothe God with shape and color. Leave your theory as Joseph his coat in the hand of the harlot, and flee.[3]

A foolish consistency is the hobgoblin of little minds, adored by little statesmen and philosophers and divines. With consistency a great soul has simply nothing to do. He may as well concern himself with his shadow on the wall. Out upon your guarded lips! Sew them up with packthread, do. Else, if you would be a man, speak what you think to-day in words as hard as cannon balls, and to-morrow speak what to-morrow thinks in hard words again, though it contradict every thing you said to-day. Ah, then, exclaim the aged ladies, you shall be sure to be misunderstood. Misunderstood! It is a right fool's word. Is it so bad then to be misunderstood? Pythagoras was misunderstood, and Socrates, and Jesus, and Luther, and Copernicus, and Galileo, and Newton, and every pure and wise spirit that ever took flesh. To be great is to be misunderstood.

I suppose no man can violate his nature. All the sallies of his will are rounded in by the law of his being as the inequalities of Andes and Himmaleh[4] are insignificant in the curve of the sphere. Nor does it matter how you guage and try him. A character is like an acrostic or Alexandrian stanza;[5]—read it forward, backward, or across, it still spells the same thing. In this pleasing contrite wood-life which God allows me, let me record day by day my honest thought without prospect or retrospect, and, I cannot doubt, it will be found symmetrical, though I mean it not, and see it not. My book should smell of pines and resound with the hum of insects. The swallow over my window should interweave that thread or straw he carries in his bill into my web also. We pass for what we are. Character teaches above our wills. Men imagine that they communicate their virtue or vice only by overt actions and do not see that virtue or vice emit a breath every moment.

---

3. The story of Joseph and Potiphar's wife is in Genesis 39.
4. Mountain ranges in South America and Asia, the latter (now spelled Himalayas) separates India from China.
5. A palindrome, reading the same backward as forward.

Fear never but you shall be consistent in whatever variety of actions, so they be each honest and natural in their hour. For of one will, the actions will be harmonious, however unlike they seem. These varieties are lost sight of when seen at a little distance, at a little height of thought. One tendency unites them all. The voyage of the best ship is a zigzag line of a hundred tacks. This is only microscopic criticism. See the line from a sufficient distance, and it straightens itself to the average tendency. Your genuine action will explain itself and will explain your other genuine actions. Your conformity explains nothing. Act singly, and what you have already done singly, will justify you now. Greatness always appeals to the future. If I can be great enough now to do right and scorn eyes, I must have done so much right before, as to defend me now. Be it how it will, do right now. Always scorn appearances, and you always may. The force of character is cumulative. All the foregone days of virtue work their health into this. What makes the majesty of the heroes of the senate and the field, which so fills the imagination? The consciousness of a train of great days and victories behind. There they all stand and shed an united light on the advancing actor. He is attended as by a visible escort of angels to every man's eye. That is it which throws thunder into Chatham's voice, and dignity into Washington's port, and America into Adams's[6] eye. Honor is venerable to us because it is no ephemeris. It is always ancient virtue. We worship it to-day, because it is not of to-day. We love it and pay it homage, because it is not a trap for our love and homage, but is self-dependent, self-derived, and therefore of an old immaculate pedigree, even if shown in a young person.

I hope in these days we have heard the last of conformity and consistency. Let the words be gazetted and ridiculous henceforward.[7] Instead of the gong for dinner, let us hear a whistle from the Spartan fife.[8] Let us bow and apologize never more. A great man is coming to eat at my house. I do not wish to please him: I wish that he should wish to please me. I will stand here for humanity, and though I would make it kind, I would made it true. Let us affront and reprimand the smooth mediocrity and squalid contentment of the times, and hurl in the face of custom, and trade, and office, the fact which is the upshot of all history, that there is a great responsible Thinker and Actor moving wherever moves a man; that a true man belongs to no other time or place, but is the centre of things. Where he is, there is nature. He measures you, and all men, and all events. You are constrained to accept his standard. Ordinarily every body in society reminds us of somewhat else or of some other person. Character, reality, reminds you of nothing else. It takes place of the whole creation. The man must be so much that he must make all circumstances indifferent,—put all means into the shade. This all great men are and do. Every true man is a cause, a country, and an age; requires infinite spaces and numbers and time fully to accomplish his thought;—and posterity seem to follow his steps as a procession. A man Cæsar is born, and for ages after, we have a Roman Empire. Christ is born, and millions of minds so grow and cleave to his genius, that he is confounded with virtue and the possible of man.

---

6. Adams may be Samuel Adams (1722–1803), leader of Revolutionary movement in Massachusetts or, more likely, his younger relative John Quincy Adams (1767–1848), sixth president of the United States and, afterward, long-time member of the House of Representatives, known as "Old Man Eloquence." William Pitt, first earl of Chatham (1708–1778), English states-man and great orator. George Washington (1732–1799), first president of the United States. "Port": carriage or physical bearing.

7. Labeled in public as not to be used henceforth.

8. Emerson is associating the gong with lax ease and the Spartan fife with disciplined alertness.

An institution is the lengthened shadow of one man; as, the Reformation, of Luther; Quakerism, of Fox; Methodism, of Wesley; Abolition, of Clarkson.[9] Scipio,[1] Milton called "the height of Rome;" and all history resolves itself very easily into the biography of a few stout and earnest persons.

Let a man then know his worth, and keep things under his feet. Let him not peep or steal, or skulk up and down with the air of a charity-boy, a bastard, or an interloper, in the world which exists for him. But the man in the street finding no worth in himself which corresponds to the force which built a tower or sculptured a marble god, feels poor when he looks on these. To him a palace, a statue, or a costly book have an alien and forbidding air, much like a gay equipage, and seem to say like that, 'Who are you, sir?' Yet they all are his, suitors for his notice, petitioners to his faculties that they will come out and take possession. The picture waits for my verdict: it is not to command me, but I am to settle its claims to praise. That popular fable of the sot who was picked up dead drunk in the street, carried to the duke's house, washed and dressed and laid in the duke's bed, and, on his waking, treated with all obsequious ceremony like the duke, and assured that he had been insane,[2]— owes its popularity to the fact, that it symbolizes so well the state of man, who is in the world a sort of sot, but now and then wakes up, exercises his reason, and finds himself a true prince.

Our reading is mendicant and sycophantic. In history, our imagination makes fools of us, plays us false. Kingdom and lordship, power and estate are a gaudier vocabulary than private John and Edward in a small house and common day's work: but the things of life are the same to both: the sum total of both is the same. Why all this deference to Alfred, and Scanderbeg, and Gustavus?[3] Suppose they were virtuous: did they wear out virtue? As great a stake depends on your private act to-day, as followed their public and renowned steps. When private men shall act with vast views, the lustre will be transferred from the actions of kings to those of gentlemen.

The world has indeed been instructed by its kings, who have so magnetized the eyes of nations. It has been taught by this colossal symbol the mutual reverence that is due from man to man. The joyful loyalty with which men have every where suffered the king, the noble, or the great proprietor to walk among them by a law of his own, make his own scale of men and things, and reverse theirs, pay for benefits not with money but with honor, and represent the Law in his person, was the hieroglyphic by which they obscurely signified their consciousness of their own right and comeliness, the right of every man.

The magnetism which all original action exerts is explained when we inquire the reason of self-trust. Who is the Trustee? What is the aboriginal Self on which a universal reliance may be grounded? What is the nature and power of that science-baffling star, without parallax,[4] without calculable elements, which shoots a ray of beauty even into trivial and impure actions, if the least mark of independence appear? The inquiry leads us to that source, at once the essence of genius, the essence of virtue, and the essence of life, which

---

9. These founders are Martin Luther (1483–1546), George Fox (1624–1691), John Wesley (1703–1791), and Thomas Clarkeson (1760–1846).
1. Scipio Africanus (237–183 B.C.), the conqueror of Carthage.
2. The best-known version of the fable is in the "Induction" to Shakespeare's *The Taming of the Shrew*.

3. National heroes: Alfred (849–899), of England; Scanderbeg (1404?–1468), of Albania; and Gustavis (1594–1632), of Sweden.
4. An apparent change in the direction of an object caused by a change in the position from which it is observed. Apparently Emerson means without an observational position.

we call Spontaneity or Instinct. We denote this primary wisdom as Intuition, whilst all later teachings are tuitions. In that deep force, the last fact behind which analysis cannot go, all things find their common origin. For the sense of being which in calm hours rises, we know not how, in the soul, is not diverse from things, from space, from light, from time, from man, but one with them, and proceedeth obviously from the same source whence their life and being also proceedeth. We first share the life by which things exist, and afterwards see them as appearances in nature, and forget that we have shared their cause. Here is the fountain of action and the fountain of thought. Here are the lungs of that inspiration which giveth man wisdom, of that inspiration of man which cannot be denied without impiety and atheism. We lie in the lap of immense intelligence, which makes us organs of its activity and receivers of its truth. When we discern justice, when we discern truth, we do nothing of ourselves, but allow a passage to its beams. If we ask whence this comes, if we seek to pry into the soul that causes,—all metaphysics, all philosophy is at fault. Its presence or its absence is all we can affirm. Every man discerns between the voluntary acts of his mind, and his involuntary perceptions. And to his involuntary perceptions, he knows a perfect respect is due. He may err in the expression of them, but he knows that these things are so, like day and night, not to be disputed. All my wilful actions and acquisitions are but roving;—the most trivial reverie, the faintest native emotion are domestic and divine. Thoughtless people contradict as readily the statement of perceptions as of opinions, or rather much more readily; for, they do not distinguish between perception and notion. They fancy that I choose to see this or that thing. But perception is not whimsical, but fatal. If I see a trait, my children will see it after me, and in course of time, all mankind,—although it may chance that no one has seen it before me. For my perception of it is as much a fact as the sun.

The relations of the soul to the divine spirit are so pure that it is profane to seek to interpose helps. It must be that when God speaketh, he should communicate not one thing, but all things; should fill the world with his voice; should scatter forth light, nature, time, souls from the centre of the present thought; and new date and new create the whole. Whenever a mind is simple, and receives a divine wisdom, then old things pass away,—means, teachers, texts, temples fall; it lives now and absorbs past and future into the present hour. All things are made sacred by relation to it,—one thing as much as another. All things are dissolved to their centre by their cause, and in the universal miracle petty and particular miracles disappear. This is and must be. If, therefore, a man claims to know and speak of God, and carries you backward to the phraseology of some old mouldered nation in another country, in another world, believe him not. Is the acorn better than the oak which is its fulness and completion? Is the parent better than the child into whom he has cast his ripened being? Whence then this worship of the past? The centuries are conspirators against the sanity and majesty of the soul. Time and space are but physiological colors which the eye maketh, but the soul is light; where it is, is day; where it was, is night; and history is an impertinence and an injury, if it be anything more than a cheerful apologue or parable of my being and becoming.

Man is timid and apologetic. He is not longer upright. He dares not say 'I think,' 'I am,' but quotes some saint or sage. He is ashamed before the blade of grass or the blowing rose. These roses under my window make no reference to former roses or to better ones; they are for what they are; they exist with God to-day. There is no time to them. There is simply the rose; it is perfect in every moment of its existence. Before a leaf-bud has burst, its whole life acts; in the full-blown flower, there is no more; in the leafless root, there is no less. Its nature is satisfied, and it satisfies nature, in all moments alike. There is no time to it. But man postpones or remembers; he does not live in the present, but with reverted eye laments the past, or, heedless of the riches that surround him, stands on tiptoe to foresee the future. He cannot be happy and strong until he too lives with nature in the present, above time.

This should be plain enough. Yet see what strong intellects dare not yet hear God himself, unless he speak the phraseology of I know not what David, or Jeremiah, or Paul.[5] We shall not always set so great a price on a few texts, on a few lines. We are like children who repeat by rote the sentences of grandames and tutors, and, as they grow older, of the men of talents and character they chance to see,—painfully recollecting the exact words they spoke; afterwards, when they come into the point of view which those had who uttered these sayings, they understand them, and are willing to let the words go; for, at any time, they can use words as good, when occasion comes. So was it with us, so will it be, if we proceed. If we live truly, we shall see truly. It is as easy for the strong man to be strong, as it is for the weak to be weak. When we have new perception, we shall gladly disburthen the memory of its hoarded treasures as old rubbish. When a man lives with God, his voice shall be as sweet as the murmur of the brook and the rustle of the corn.

And now at last the highest truth on this subject remains unsaid; probably, cannot be said; for all that we say is the far off remembering of the intuition. That thought, by what I can now nearest approach to say it, is this. When good is near you, when you have life in yourself,—it is not by any known or appointed way; you shall not discern the foot-prints of any other; you shall not see the face of man; you shall not hear any name;—the way, the thought, the good shall be wholly strange and new. It shall exclude all other being. You take the way from man not to man. All persons that ever existed are its fugitive ministers. There shall be no fear in it. Fear and hope are alike beneath it. It asks nothing. There is somewhat low even in hope. We are then in vision. There is nothing that can be called gratitude nor properly joy. The soul is raised over passion. It seeth identity and eternal causation. It is a perceiving that Truth and Right are. Hence it becomes a Tranquillity out of the knowing that all things go well. Vast spaces of nature; the Atlantic Ocean, the South Sea; vast intervals of time, years, centuries, are of no account. This which I think and feel, underlay that former state of life and circumstances, as it does underlie my present, and will always all circumstance, and what is called life, and what is called death.

Life only avails, not the having lived. Power ceases in the instant of repose; it resides in the moment of transition from a past to a new state; in the shooting of the gulf; in the darting to an aim. This one fact the world hates, that the soul *becomes*; for, that forever degrades the past; turns all riches to poverty; all reputation to a shame; confounds the saint with the rogue; shoves Jesus and Judas equally aside. Why then do we prate of self-reliance? Inasmuch as the soul is present, there will be power not confident but agent. To talk of reliance,

---

5. Biblical authors of the Book of Psalms, the Book of Jeremiah, and various New Testament Epistles, respectively.

is a poor external way of speaking. Speak rather of that which relies, because it works and is. Who has more soul than I, masters me, though he should not raise his finger. Round him I must revolve by the gravitation of spirits; who has less, I rule with like facility. We fancy it rhetoric when we speak of eminent virtue. We do not yet see that virtue is Height, and that a man or a company of men plastic and permeable to principles, by the law of nature must overpower and ride all cities, nations, kings, rich men, poets, who are not.

This is the ultimate fact which we so quickly reach on this as on every topic, the resolution of all into the ever blessed ONE. Virtue is the governor, the creator, the reality. All things real are so by so much of virtue as they contain. Hardship, husbandry, hunting, whaling, war, eloquence, personal weight, are somewhat, and engage my respect as examples of the soul's presence and impure action. I see the same law working in the nature for conservation and growth. The poise of a planet, the bended tree recovering itself from the strong wind, the vital resources of every vegetable and animal, are also demonstrations of the self-sufficing, and therefore self-relying soul. All history from its highest to its trivial passages is the various record of this power.

Thus all concentrates; let us not rove; let us sit at home with the cause. Let us stun and astonish the intruding rabble of men and books and institutions by a simple declaration of the divine fact. Bid them take the shoes from off their feet,[6] for God is here within. Let our simplicity judge them, and our docility to our own law demonstrate the poverty of nature and fortune beside our native riches.

But now we are a mob. Man does not stand in awe of man, nor is the soul admonished to stay at home, to put itself in communication with the internal ocean, but it goes abroad to beg a cup of water of the urns of men. We must go alone. Isolation must precede true society. I like the silent church before the service begins, better than any preaching. How far off, how cool, how chaste the persons look, begirt each one with a precinct or sanctuary. So let us always sit. Why should we assume the faults of our friend, or wife, or father, or child, because they sit around our hearth, or are said to have the same blood? All men have my blood, and I have all men's. Not for that will I adopt their petulance or folly, even to the extent of being ashamed of it. But your isolation must not be mechanical, but spiritual, that is, must be elevation. At times the whole world seems to be in conspiracy to importune you with emphatic trifles. Friend, client, child, sickness, fear, want, charity, all knock at once at thy closet door and say, 'Come out unto us.'—Do not spill thy soul; do not all descend; keep thy state; stay at home in thine own heaven; come not for a moment into their facts, into their hubbub of conflicting appearances, but let in the light of thy law on their confusion. The power men possess to annoy me, I give them by a weak curiosity. No man can come near me but through my act. "What we love that we have, but by desire we bereave ourselves of the love."

If we cannot at once rise to the sanctities of obedience and faith, let us at least resist our temptations, let us enter into the state of war, and wake Thor and Woden,[7] courage and constancy in our Saxon breasts. This is to be done in our smooth times by speaking the truth. Check this lying hospitality and

6. Exodus 3.5.
7. Norse gods, here taken as ancestral gods of the Anglo-Saxon as well, associated respectively with courage and endurance. Emerson took seriously the idea of racial traits.

lying affection. Live no longer to the expectation of these deceived and deceiving people with whom we converse. Say to them, O father, O mother, O wife, O brother, O friend, I have lived with you after appearances hitherto. Henceforward I am the truth's. Be it known unto you that henceforward I obey no law less than the external law. I will have no covenants but proximities. I shall endeavor to nourish my parents, to support my family, to be the chaste husband of one wife,—but these relations I must fill after a new and unprecedented way. I appeal from your customs. I must be myself. I cannot break myself any longer for you, or you. If you can love me for what I am, we shall be the happier. If you cannot, I will still seek to deserve that you should. I must be myself. I will not hide my tastes or aversions. I will so trust that what is deep is holy, that I will do strongly before the sun and moon whatever inly rejoices me, and the heart appoints. If you are noble, I will love you; if you are not, I will not hurt you and myself by hypocritical attentions. If you are true, but not in the same truth with me, cleave to your companions; I will seek my own. I do this not selfishly, but humbly and truly. It is alike your interest and mine and all men's, however long we have dwelt in lies, to live in truth. Does this sound harsh to-day? You will soon love what is dictated by your nature as well as mine, and if we follow the truth, it will bring us out safe at last.—But so you may give these friends pain. Yes, but I cannot sell my liberty and my power, to save their sensibility. Besides, all persons have their moments of reason when they look out into the region of absolute truth; then will they justify me and do the same thing.

The populace think that your rejection of popular standards is a rejection of all standard, and mere antinomianism;[8] and the bold sensualist will use the name of philosophy to gild his crimes. But the law of consciousness abides. There are two confessionals, in one or the other of which we must be shriven. You may fulfil your round of duties by clearing yourself in the *direct*, or, in the *reflex* way. Consider whether you have satisfied your relations to father, mother, cousin, neighbor, town, cat, and dog; whether any of these can upbraid you. But I may also neglect this reflex standard, and absolve me to myself. I have my own stern claims and perfect circle. It denies the name of duty to many offices that are called duties. But if I can discharge its debts, it enables me to dispense with the popular code. If any one imagines that this law is lax, let him keep its commandment one day.

And truly it demands something godlike in him who has cast off the common motives of humanity, and has ventured to trust himself for a task-master. High be his heart, faithful his will, clear his sight, that he may in good earnest be doctrine, society, law to himself, that a simple purpose may be to him as strong as iron necessity is to others.

If any man consider the present aspects of what is called by distinction *society*, he will see the need of these ethics. The sinew and heart of man seem to be drawn out, and we are become timorous desponding whimperers. We are afraid of truth, afraid of fortune, afraid of death, and afraid of each other. Our age yields no great and perfect persons. We want men and women who shall renovate life and our social state, but we see that most natures are insolvent; cannot satisfy their own wants, have an ambition out of all proportion to their practical force, and so do lean and beg day and night continually. Our

---

8. Rejection of moral and religious laws.

housekeeping is mendicant, our arts, our occupations, our marriages, our religion we have not chosen, but society has chosen for us. We are parlor soldiers. The rugged battle of fate, where strength is born, we shun.

If our young men miscarry in their first enterprizes, they lose all heart. If the young merchant fails, men say he is *ruined.* If the finest genius studies at one of our colleges, and is not installed in an office within one year afterwards in the cities or suburbs of Boston or New York, it seems to his friends and to himself that he is right in being disheartened and in complaining the rest of his life. A sturdy lad from New Hampshire or Vermont, who in turn tries all the professions, who *teams it, farms it, peddles,* keeps a school, preaches, edits a newspaper, goes to Congress, buys a township, and so forth, in successive years, and always, like a cat, falls on his feet, is worth a hundred of these city dolls.[9] He walks abreast with his days, and feels no shame in not 'studying a profession,' for he does not postpone his life, but lives already. He has not one chance, but a hundred chances. Let a stoic arise who shall reveal the resources of man, and tell men they are not leaning willows, but can and must detach themselves; that with the exercise of self-trust, new powers shall appear; that a man is the word made flesh, born to shed healing to the nations, that he should be ashamed of our compassion, and that the moment he acts from himself, tossing the laws, the books, idolatries, and customs out of the window,—we pity him no more but thank and revere him,—and that teacher shall restore the life of man to splendor, and make his name dear to all History.

It is easy to see that a greater self-reliance,—a new respect for the divinity in man,—must work a revolution in all the offices and relations of men; in their religion; in their education; in their pursuits; their modes of living; their association; in their property; in their speculative views.

1. In what prayers do men allow themselves! That which they call a holy office, is not so much as brave and manly. Prayer looks abroad and asks for some foreign addition to come through some foreign virtue, and loses itself in endless mazes of natural and supernatural, and mediatorial and miraculous. Prayer that craves a particular commodity—any thing less than all good, is vicious. Prayer is the contemplation of the facts of life from the highest point of view. It is the soliloquy of a beholding and jubilant soul. It is the spirit of God pronouncing his works good. But prayer as a means to effect a private end, is theft and meanness. It supposes dualism and not unity in nature and consciousness. As soon as the man is at one with God, he will not beg. He will then see prayer in all action. The prayer of the farmer kneeling in his field to weed it, the prayer of the rower kneeling with the stroke of his oar, are true prayers heard throughout nature, though for cheap ends. Caratach, in Fletcher's *Bonduca,* when admonished to inquire the mind of the god Audate, replies,

> "His hidden meaning lies in our endeavors,
> Our valors are our best gods."[1]

Another sort of false prayers are our regrets. Discontent is the want of self-reliance; it is infirmity of will. Regret calamities, if you can thereby help the sufferer; if not, attend your own work, and already the evil begins to be repaired. Our sympathy is just as base. We come to them who weep foolishly,

---

9. Emerson's journal entry for May 27, 1839, shows that this passage was originally modeled on the young

Thoreau.
1. Lines 1294–95, slightly misquoted.

and sit down and cry for company, instead of imparting to them truth and
health in rough electric shocks, putting them once more in communication
with the soul. The secret of fortune is joy in our hands. Welcome evermore
to gods and men is the self-helping man. For him all doors are flung wide.
Him all tongues greet, all honors crown, all eyes follow with desire. Our love
goes out to him and embraces him, because he did not need it. We solicitously
and apologetically caress and celebrate him, because he held on his way and
scorned our disapprobation. The gods love him because men hated him. "To
the persevering mortal," said Zoroaster,[2] "the blessed Immortals are swift."

    As men's prayers are a disease of the will, so are their creeds a disease of the
intellect. They say with those foolish Israelites, 'Let not God speak to us, lest
we die. Speak thou, speak any man with us, and we will obey.'[3] Everywhere I
am bereaved of meeting God in my brother, because he has shut his own
temple doors, and recites fables merely of his brother's, or his brother's
brother's God. Every new mind is a new classification. If it prove a mind of
uncommon activity and power, a Locke, a Lavoisier, a Hutton, a Bentham, a
Spurzheim,[4] it imposes its classification on other men, and lo! a new system.
In proportion always to the depth of the thought, and so to the number of the
objects it touches and brings within reach of the pupil, is his complacency. But
chiefly is this apparent in creeds and churches, which are also classifications of
some powerful mind acting on the great elemental thought of Duty, and man's
relation to the Highest. Such is Calvinism, Quakerism, Swedenborgianism.[5]
The pupil takes the same delight in subordinating every thing to the new terminology that a girl does who has just learned botany, in seeing a new earth and
new seasons thereby. It will happen for a time, that the pupil will feel a real
debt to the teacher,—will find his intellectual power has grown by the study
of his writings. This will continue until he has exhausted his master's mind.
But in all unbalanced minds, the classification is idolized, passes for the end,
and not for a speedily exhaustible means, so that the walls of the system blend
to their eye in the remote horizon with the walls of the universe; the luminaries
of heaven seem to them hung on the arch their master built. They cannot
imagine how you aliens have any right to see,—how you can see; 'It must be
somehow that you stole the light from us.' They do not yet perceive, that, light
unsystematic, indomitable, will break into any cabin, even into theirs. Let
them chirp awhile and call it their own. If they are honest and do well, presently their neat new pinfold will be too strait and low, will crack, will lean,
will rot and vanish, and the immortal light, all young and joyful, million-
orbed, million-colored, will beam over the universe as on the first morning.

    2. It is for want of self-culture that the idol of Travelling, the idol of Italy,
of England, of Egypt, remains for all educated Americans. They who made
England, Italy, or Greece venerable in the imagination, did so not by rambling
round creation as a moth round a lamp, but by sticking fast where they were,

2. Religious prophet of ancient Persia.
3. See the fearful words of the Hebrews after God has
given Moses the Ten Commandments, Exodus 20.19:
"And they said unto Moses, Speak thou with us, and
we will hear: but let not God speak with us, lest we
die."
4. These innovators are John Locke (1632–1704), English philosopher; Antoine Lavoisier (1726–1797),
French chemist; James Hutton (1726–1797), Scottish
geologist; Jeremy Bentham (1748–1832), English phi-

losopher; and Johann Kaspar Spurzheim (1776–1832),
German physician whose work led to the pseudoscience of phrenology, reading character by the bumps on
the skull.
5. Three widely varying religious movements founded
by or based on the teachings of, respectively, John Calvin (1509–1564), French theologian; George Fox
(1624–1691), English clergyman; and Emanuel Swedenborg (1688–1772), Swedish scientist and theologian.

like an axis of the earth. In manly hours, we feel that duty is our place, and that the merrymen of circumstance should follow as they may. The soul is no traveller: the wise man stays at home with the soul, and when his necessities, his duties, on any occasion call him from his house, or into foreign lands, he is at home still, and is not gadding abroad from himself, and shall make men sensible by the expression of his countenance, that he goes the missionary of wisdom and virtue, and visits cities and men like a sovereign, and not like an interloper or a valet.

I have no churlish objection to the circumnavigation of the globe, for the purposes of art, of study, and benevolence, so that the man is first domesticated, or does not go abroad with the hope of finding somewhat greater than he knows. He who travels to be amused, or to get somewhat which he does not carry, travels away from himself, and grows old even in youth among old things. In Thebes, in Palmyra, his will and mind have become old and dilapidated as they. He carries ruins to ruins.

Travelling is a fool's paradise. We owe to our first journeys the discovery that place is nothing. At home I dream that at Naples, at Rome, I can be intoxicated with beauty, and lose my sadness. I pack my trunk, embrace my friends, embark on the sea, and at last wake up in Naples, and there beside me is the stern Fact, the sad self, unrelenting, identical, that I fled from. I seek the Vatican, and the palaces. I affect to be intoxicated with sights and suggestions, but I am not intoxicated. My giant goes with me wherever I go.

3. But the rage of travelling is itself only a symptom of a deeper unsoundness affecting the whole intellectual action. The intellect is vagabond, and the universal system of education fosters restlessness. Our minds travel when our bodies are forced to stay at home. We imitate; and what is imitation but the travelling of the mind? Our houses are built with foreign taste; our shelves are garnished with foreign ornaments; our opinions, our tastes, our whole minds lean, and follow the Past and the Distant, as the eyes of a maid follow her mistress. The soul created the arts wherever they have flourished. It was in his own mind that the artist sought his model. It was an application of his own thought to the thing to be done and the conditions to be observed. And why need we copy the Doric or the Gothic model?[6] Beauty, convenience, grandeur of thought, and quaint expression are as near to us as to any, and if the American artist will study with hope and love the precise thing to be done by him, considering the climate, the soil, the length of the day, the wants of the people, the habit and form of the government, he will create a house in which all these will find themselves fitted, and taste and sentiment will be satisfied also.

Insist on yourself; never imitate. Your own gift you can present every moment with the cumulative force of a whole life's cultivation; but of the adopted talent of another, you have only an extemporaneous, half possession. That which each can do best, none but his Maker can teach him. No man yet knows what it is, nor can, till that person has exhibited it. Where is the master who could have taught Shakspeare? Where is the master who could have instructed Franklin, or Washington, or Bacon, or Newton. Every great man is an unique. The Scipionism[7] of Scipio is precisely that part he could not borrow. If any body will tell me whom the great man imitates in the original crisis when he performs a great act, I will tell him who else than himself can

6. I.e., Greek or medieval architecture.   7. I.e., the essence of the man.

teach him. Shakspeare will never be made by the study of Shakspeare. Do that which is assigned thee, and thou canst not hope too much or dare too much. There is at this moment, there is for me an utterance bare and grand as that of the colossal chisel of Phidias,[8] or trowel of the Egyptians, or the pen of Moses, or Dante, but different from all these. Now possibly will the soul all rich, all eloquent, with thousand-cloven tongue, deign to repeat itself; but if I can hear what these patriarchs say, surely I can reply to them in the same pitch of voice: for the ear and the tongue are two organs of one nature. Dwell up there in the simple and noble regions of thy life, obey thy heart, and thou shalt reproduce the Foreworld again.

4. As our Religion, our Education, our Art look abroad, so does our spirit of society. All men plume themselves on the improvement of society, and no man improves.

Society never advances. It recedes as fast on one side as it gains on the other. Its progress is only apparent, like the workers of a treadmill. It undergoes continual changes: it is barbarous, it is civilized, it is christianized, it is rich, it is scientific; but this change is not amelioration. For every thing that is given, something is taken. Society acquires new arts and loses old instincts. What a contrast between the well-clad, reading, writing, thinking American, with a watch, a pencil, and a bill of exchange in his pocket, and the naked New Zealander, whose property is a club, a spear, a mat, and an undivided twentieth of a shed to sleep under. But compare the health of the two men, and you shall see that his aboriginal strength the white man has lost. If the traveller tell us truly, strike the savage with a broad axe, and in a day or two the flesh shall unite and heal as if you struck the blow into soft pitch, and the same blow shall send the white to his grave.

The civilized man has built a coach, but has lost the use of his feet. He is supported on crutches, but loses so much support of muscle. He has got a fine Geneva watch, but he has lost the skill to tell the hour by the sun. A Greenwich nautical almanac he has, and so being sure of the information when he wants it, the man in the street does not know a star in the sky. The solstice he does not observe; the equinox he knows as little; and the whole bright calendar of the year is without a dial in his mind. His notebooks impair his memory; his libraries overload his wit; the insurance office increases the number of accidents; and it may be a question whether machinery does not encumber; whether we have not lost by refinement some energy, by a christianity entrenched in establishments and forms, some vigor of wild virtue. For every stoic was a stoic;[9] but in Christendom where is the Christian?

There is no more deviation in the moral standard than in the standard of height or bulk. No greater men are now than ever were. A singular equality may be observed between the great men of the first and of the last ages; nor can all the science, art, religion and philosophy of the nineteenth century avail to educate greater men than Plutarch's heroes,[1] three or four and twenty centuries ago. Not in time is the race progressive. Phocion, Socrates, Anaxagoras, Diogenes,[2] are great men, but they leave no class. He who is really of

---

8. Greek sculptor of 5th century B.C.
9. Emerson refers particularly to the Stoics, members of the Greek school of philosophy founded by Zeno about 308 B.C. It taught the ideal of a calm, passionless existence in which any occurrence is accepted as inevitable.

1. The lives of famous Greeks and Romans written by Plutarch (46?–120?), Greek biographer.
2. Four Greek philosophers: Phocion (402?–317 B.C.), Socrates (470?–399 B.C.), Anaxagoras (500?–428 B.C.), and Diogenes (412?–323 B.C.).

their class will not be called by their name, but be wholly his own man, and, in his turn the founder of a sect. The arts and inventions of each period are only its costume, and do not invigorate men. The harm of the improved machinery may compensate its good. Hudson and Behring[3] accomplished so much in their fishing-boats, as to astonish Parry and Franklin,[4] whose equipment exhausted the resources of science and art. Galileo, with an opera-glass, discovered a more splendid series of facts than any one since. Columbus found the New world in an undecked boat. It is curious to see the periodical disuse and perishing of means and machinery which were introduced with loud laudation, a few years or centuries before. The great genius returns to essential man. We reckoned the improvements of the art of war among the triumphs of science, and yet Napoleon conquered Europe by the Bivouac, which consisted of falling back on naked valor, and disencumbering it of all aids. The Emperor held it impossible to make a perfect army, says Las Cases,[5] "without abolishing our arms, magazines, commissaries, and carriages, until in imitation of the Roman custom, the soldier should receive his supply of corn, grind it in his hand-mill, and bake his bread himself."

Society is a wave. The wave moves onward, but the water of which it is composed, does not. The same particle does not rise from the valley to the ridge. Its unity is only phenomenal. The persons who make up a nation today, next year die, and their experience with them.

And so the reliance on Property, including the reliance on governments which protect it, is the want of self-reliance. Men have looked away from themselves and at things so long, that they have come to esteem what they call the soul's progress, namely, the religious, learned, and civil institutions, as guards of property, and they deprecate assaults on these, because they feel them to be assaults on property. They measure their esteem of each other, by what each has, and not by what each is. But a cultivated man becomes ashamed of his property, ashamed of what he has, out of new respect for his being. Especially, he hates what he has, if he see that it is accidental,—came to him by inheritance, or gift, or crime; then he feels that it is not having; it does not belong to him, has no root in him, and merely lies there, because no revolution or no robber takes it away. But that which a man is, does always by necessity acquire, and what the man acquires is permanent and living property, which does not wait the beck of rulers, or mobs, or revolutions, or fire, or storm, or bankruptcies, but perpetually renews itself wherever the man is put. "Thy lot or portion of life," said the Caliph Ali,[6] "is seeking after thee; therefore be at rest from seeking after it." Our dependence on these foreign goods leads us to our slavish respect for numbers. The political parties meet in numerous conventions; the greater the concourse, and with each new uproar of announcement, The delegation from Essex![7] The Democrats from New Hampshire! The Whigs of Maine! the young patriot feels himself stronger than before by a new thousand of eyes and arms. In like manner the reformers summon conventions, and vote and resolve in multitude. But not so, O friends! will the God deign to enter and inhabit you, but by a method precisely

---

3. Vitus Jonassen Bering (1680–1741), Danish navigator who explored the northern Pacific Ocean. Henry Hudson (d. 1611) English navigator (sometimes in service of the Dutch).
4. Sir William Edward Perry (1790–1855) and Sir John Franklin (1786–1847), English explorers of the

Arctic.
5. Comte Emmanuel de Las Cases (1766–1842), author of a book recording his conversations with the exiled Napoleon at St. Helena.
6. Fourth Moslem caliph of Mecca (602?–661).
7. County in Massachusetts.

the reverse. It is only as a man puts off from himself all external support, and stands alone, that I see him to be strong and to prevail. He is weaker by every recruit to his banner. Is not a man better than a town? Ask nothing of men, and in the endless mutation, thou only firm column must presently appear the upholder of all that surrounds thee. He who knows that power is in the soul, that he is weak only because he has looked for good out of him and elsewhere, and so perceiving, throws himself unhesitatingly on his thought, instantly rights himself, stands in the erect position, commands his limbs, works miracles; just as a man who stands on his feet is stronger than a man who stands on his head.

So use all that is called Fortune. Most men gamble with her, and gain all, and lose all, as her wheel rolls. But do thou leave as unlawful these winnings, and deal with Cause and Effect, the chancellors of God. In the Will work and acquire, and thou hast chained the wheel of Chance, and shalt always drag her after thee. A political victory, a rise of rents, the recovery of your sick, or the return of your absent friend, or some other quite external event, raises your spirits, and you think good days are preparing for you. Do not believe it. It can never be so. Nothing can bring you peace but yourself. Nothing can bring you peace but the triumph of principles.

1841

The Over-Soul[1]

There is a difference between one and another hour of life, in their authority and subsequent effect. Our faith comes in moments; our vice is habitual. Yet is there a depth in those brief moments, which constrains us to ascribe more reality to them than to all other experiences. For this reason, the argument, which is always forthcoming to silence those who conceive extraordinary hopes of man, namely, the appeal to experience, is forever invalid and vain. A mightier hope abolishes despair. We give up the past to the objector, and yet we hope. He must explain this hope. We grant that human life is mean; but how did we find out that it was mean? What is the ground of this uneasiness of ours; of this old discontent? What is the universal sense of want and ignorance, but the fine inuendo[2] by which the great soul makes its enormous claim? Why do men feel that the natural history of man has never been written, but always he is leaving behind what you have said of him, and it becomes old, and books of metaphysics worthless? The philosophy of six thousand years has not searched the chambers and magazines of the soul. In its experiments there has always remained, in the last analysis, a residuum it could not resolve. Man is a stream whose source is hidden. Always our being is descending into us from we know not whence. The most exact calculator has no prescience that somewhat incalculable may not baulk the very next moment. I am constrained every moment to acknowledge a higher origin for events than the will I call mine.

1. *The Over-Soul*, reprinted here from its first appearance in *Essays* (1841), is Emerson's most comprehensive and sensitive analysis of the varieties of religious experience. In his *Journals* (7.412) Emerson gives a partial definition of the term that serves as title of the essay: *Oversoul or The Highest Thou Always Unknown.*

Another definition is in the third paragraph of the essay. Had Emerson used the word *God*, his readers would have interpreted him as meaning merely the Jehovah of Judaism and Christianity, not the power that lies behind all religions.

2. An acceptable spelling in Emerson's day.

As with events, so is it with thoughts. When I watch that flowing river, which, out of regions I see not, pours for a season its streams into me,—I see that I am a pensioner,—not a cause, but a surprised spectator of this ethereal water; that I desire and look up, and put myself in the attitude of reception, but from some alien energy the visions come.

The Supreme Critic on all the errors of the past and the present, and the only prophet of that which must be, is that great nature in which we rest, as the earth lies in the soft arms of the atmosphere; that Unity, that Over-Soul, within which every man's particular being is contained and made one with all other; that common heart, of which all sincere conversation is the worship, to which all right action is submission; that overpowering reality which confutes our tricks and talents, and constrains every one to pass for what he is, and to speak from his character and not from his tongue; and which evermore tends and aims to pass into our thought and hand, and become wisdom, and virtue, and power, and beauty. We live in succession, in division, in parts, in particles. Meantime within man is the soul of the whole; the wise silence; the universal beauty, to which every part and particle is equally related; the eternal ONE. And this deep power in which we exist, and whose beatitude is all accessible to us, is not only self-sufficing and perfect in every hour, but the act of seeing, and the thing seen, the seer and the spectacle, the subject and the object, are one. We see the world piece by piece, as the sun, the moon, the animal, the tree; but the whole, of which these are the shining parts, is the soul. It is only by the vision of that Wisdom, that the horoscope of the ages can be read, and it is only by falling back on our better thoughts, by yielding to the spirit of prophecy which is innate in every man, that we can know what it saith. Every man's words, who speaks from that life, must sound vain to those who do not dwell in the same thought on their own part. I dare not speak for it. My words do not carry its august sense; they fall short and cold. Only itself can inspire whom it will, and behold! their speech shall be lyrical, and sweet, and universal as the rising of the wind. Yet I desire, even by profane words, if sacred I may not use, to indicate the heaven of this deity, and to report what hints I have collected of the transcendent simplicity and energy of the Highest Law.

If we consider what happens in conversation, in reveries, in remorse, in times of passion, in surprises, in the instructions of dreams wherein often we see ourselves in masquerade,—the droll disguises only magnifying and enhancing a real element, and forcing it on our distinct notice,—we shall catch many hints that will broaden and lighten into knowledge of the secret of nature. All goes to show that the soul in man is not an organ, but animates and exercises all the organs; is not a function, like the power of memory, of calculation, of comparison,—but uses these as hands and feet; is not a faculty, but a light; is not the intellect or the will, but the master of the intellect and the will;—is the vast back-ground of our being, in which they lie,—an immensity not possessed and that cannot be possessed. From within or from behind, a light shines through us upon things, and makes us aware that we are nothing, but the light is all. A man is the façade of a temple wherein all wisdom and all good abide. What we commonly call man, the eating, drinking, planting, counting man, does not, as we know him, represent himself, but misrepresents himself. Him we do not respect, but the soul, whose organ he is, would he let it appear through his action, would make our knees bend. When it breathes through his intellect, it is genius; when it breathes through his will, it is virtue; when it flows through his affection, it is love. And the blindness of the intellect begins, when it would be something of itself. The weakness of the will begins when the individual would be something of himself. All reform aims, in some one particular, to let the great soul have its way through us; in other words, to engage us to obey.

Of this pure nature every man is at some time sensible. Language cannot paint it with his colors. It is too subtle. It is undefinable, unmeasureable, but we know that it pervades and contains us. We know that all spiritual being is in man. A wise old proverb says, "God comes to see us without bell:" that is, as there is no screen or ceiling between our heads and the infinite heavens, so is there no bar or wall in the soul where man, the effect, ceases, and God, the cause, begins. The walls are taken away. We lie open on one side to the deeps of spiritual nature, to all the attributes of God. Justice we see and know, Love, Freedom, Power. These natures no man ever got above, but always they tower over us, and most in the moment when our interests tempt us to wound them.

The sovereignty of this nature whereof we speak, is made known by its independency of those limitations which circumscribe us on every hand. The soul circumscribeth all things. As I have said, it contradicts all experience. In like manner it abolishes time and space. The influence of the senses has, in most men, overpowered the mind to that degree, that the walls of time and space have come to look solid, real and insurmountable; and to speak with levity of these limits, is, in the world, the sign of insanity. Yet time and space are but inverse measures of the force of the soul. A man is capable of abolishing them both. The spirit sports with time—

> "Can crowd eternity into an hour,
> Or stretch an hour to eternity."[3]

We are often made to feel that there is another youth and age than that which is measured from the year of our natural birth. Some thoughts always find us young and keep us so. Such a thought is the love of the universal and eternal beauty. Every man parts from that contemplation with the feeling that it rather belongs to ages than to mortal life. The least activity of the intellectual powers redeems us in a degree from the influences of time. In sickness, in languor, give us a strain of poetry or a profound sentence, and we are refreshed; or produce a volume of Plato, or Shakspeare, or remind us of their names, and instantly we come into a feeling of longevity. See how the deep, divine thought demolishes centuries, and millenniums, and makes itself present through all ages. Is the teaching of Christ less effective now than it was when first his mouth was opened? The emphasis of facts and persons to my soul has nothing to do with time. And so, always, the soul's scale is one; the scale of the senses and the understanding is another. Before the great revelations of the soul, Time, Space and Nature shrink away. In common speech, we refer all things to time, as we habitually refer the immensely sundered stars to one concave sphere. And so we say that the Judgment is distant or near, that the Millennium[4] approaches, that a day of certain political, moral, social reforms

---

3. Adapted from William Blake's *Auguries of Innocence:* "To see a World in a Grain of Sand / And a Heaven in a Wild Flower, / Hold Infinity in the palm of your hand / And Eternity in an hour."
4. From the reference in Revelation 20.2 to the "thousand years" during which Satan will be bound and Je-

sus will reign on earth; Emerson has in mind the extraordinary publicity—and hysteria—created by the prediction of the American preacher William Miller (1782–1849) that the Second Coming of Jesus would occur in 1843.

is at hand, and the like, when we mean, that in the nature of things, one of the facts we contemplate is external and fugitive, and the other is permanent and connate with the soul. The things we now esteem fixed, shall, one by one, detach themselves, like ripe fruit, from our experience, and fall. The wind shall blow them none knows whither.[5] The landscape, the figures, Boston, London, are facts as fugitive as any institution past, or any whiff of mist or smoke, and so is society, and so is the world. The soul looketh steadily forwards, creating a world alway before her, and leaving worlds alway behind her. She has no dates, nor rites, nor persons, nor specialties, nor men. The soul knows only the soul. All else is idle weeds[6] for her wearing.

After its own law and not by arithmetic is the rate of its progress to be computed. The soul's advances are not made by gradation, such as can be represented by motion in a straight line; but rather by ascension of state, such as can be represented by metamorphosis,—from the egg to the worm, from the worm to the fly. The growths of genius are of a certain *total* character, that does not advance the elect individual first over John, then Adam, then Richard, and give to each the pain of discovered inferiority, but by every throe of growth, the man expands there where he works, passing, at each pulsation, classes, populations of men. With each divine impulse the mind rends the thin rinds of the visible and finite, and comes out into eternity, and inspires and expires its air. It converses with truths that have always been spoken in the world, and becomes conscious of a closer sympathy with Zeno and Arrian,[7] than with persons in the house.

This is the law of moral and of mental gain. The simple rise as by specific levity, not into a particular virtue, but into the region of all the virtues. They are in the spirit which contains them all. The soul is superior to all the particulars of merit. The soul requires purity, but purity is not it; requires justice, but justice is not that; requires beneficence, but is somewhat better: so that there is a kind of descent and accommodation felt when we leave speaking of moral nature, to urge a virtue which it enjoins. For, to the soul in her pure action, all the virtues are natural, and not painfully acquired. Speak to his heart, and the man becomes suddenly virtuous.

Within the same sentiment is the germ of intellectual growth, which obeys the same law. Those who are capable of humility, of justice, of love, of aspiration, are already on a platform that commands the sciences and arts, speech and poetry, action and grace. For whoso dwells in this moral beatitude, does already anticipate those special powers which men prize so highly; just as love does justice to all the gifts of the object beloved. The lover has no talent, no skill, which passes for quite nothing with his enamored maiden, however little she may possess of related faculty. And the heart, which abandons itself to the Supreme Mind, finds itself related to all its works and will travel a royal road to particular knowledges and powers. For, in ascending to this primary and aboriginal sentiment, we have come from our remote station on the circumference instantaneously to the centre of the world, where, as in the closet of God, we see causes, and anticipate the universe, which is but a slow effect.

One mode of the divine teaching is the incarnation of the spirit in a form,—

---

5. "The wind bloweth where it listeth, and thou hearest the sound thereof, but canst not tell whence it cometh, and whither it goeth: so is every one that is born of the Spirit" (John 3.8).
6. Black mourning garments.
7. Emerson's point is not only that these are men of

the distant past and, therefore, difficult to feel affinity with but also that as the founder of Stoicism and the biographer of another Stoic, Epictetus, these two men would take a philosophical stand against the cultivation of a close, sympathetic relationship.

in forms, like my own. I live in society; with persons who answer to thoughts in my own mind, or outwardly express to me a certain obedience to the great instincts to which I live. I see its presence to them. I am certified of a common nature; and so these other souls, these separated selves, draw me as nothing else can. They stir in me the new emotions we call passion; of love, hatred, fear, admiration, pity; thence comes conversation, competition, persuasion, cities, and war. Persons are supplementary to the primary teaching of the soul. In youth we are mad for persons. Childhood and youth see all the world in them. But the larger experience of man discovers the identical nature appearing through them all. Persons themselves acquaint us with the impersonal. In all conversation between two persons, tacit reference is made as to a third party, to a common nature. That third party or common nature is not social; it is impersonal; is God. And so in groups where debate is earnest, and especially on great questions of thought, the company become aware of their unity; aware that the thought rises to an equal height in all bosoms, that all have a spiritual property in what was said, as well as the sayer. They all wax wiser than they were. It arches over them like a temple, this unity of thought, in which every heart beats with nobler sense of power and duty, and thinks and acts with unusual solemnity. All are conscious of attaining to a higher self-possession. It shines for all. There is a certain wisdom of humanity which is common to the greatest men with the lowest, and which our ordinary education often labors to silence and obstruct. The mind is one, and the best minds who love truth for its own sake, think much less of property in truth. Thankfully they accept it everywhere, and do not label or stamp it with any man's name, for it is theirs long beforehand. It is theirs from eternity. The learned and the studious of thought have no monopoly on wisdom. Their violence of direction in some degree disqualifies them to think truly. We owe many valuable observations to people who are not very acute or profound, and who say the thing without effort, which we want and have long been hunting in vain. The action of the soul is oftener in that which is felt and left unsaid, than in that which is said in any conversation. It broods over every society, and they unconsciously seek for it in each other. We know better than we do. We do not yet possess ourselves, and we know at the same time that we are much more. I feel the same truth how often in my trivial conversation with my neighbors, that somewhat higher in each of us overlooks this by-play, and Jove nods to Jove from behind each of us.

Men descend to meet. In their habitual and mean service to the world, for which they forsake their native nobleness, they resemble those Arabian Sheikhs, who dwell in mean houses and affect an external poverty, to escape the rapacity of the Pacha, and reserve all their display of wealth for their interior and guarded retirements.

As it is present in all persons, so it is in every period of life. It is adult already in the infant man. In my dealing with my child, my Latin and Greek, my accomplishments and my money, stead me nothing. They are all lost on him: but as much soul as I have, avails. If I am merely wilful, he gives me a Rowland for an Oliver,[8] sets his will against mine, one for one, and leaves me, if I please, the degradation of beating him by my superiority of strength. But if I

---

8. Emerson is playing on the proverbial expression to give "a Rowland for an Oliver," or to match one incredible lie with another. (Roland and Oliver were among Charlemagne's Twelve Peers and became heroes of medieval romances.)

renounce my will, and act for the soul, setting that up as umpire between us two, out of his young eyes looks the same soul; he reveres and loves with me.

The soul is the perceiver and revealer of truth. We know truth when we see it, let skeptic and scoffer say what they choose. Foolish people ask you, when you have spoken what they do not wish to hear, 'How do you know it is truth, and not an error of your own?' We know truth when we see it, from opinion, as we know when we are awake that we are awake. It was a grand sentence of Emanuel Swedenborg,[9] which would alone indicate the greatness of that man's perception,—"It is no proof of a man's understanding to be able to affirm whatever he pleases, but to be able to discern that what is true is true, and that what is false is false, this is the mark and character of intelligence." In the book I read, the good thought returns to me, as every truth will, the image of the whole soul. To the bad thought which I find in it, the same soul becomes a discerning, separating sword and lops it away. We are wiser than we know. If we will not interfere with our thought, but will act entirely, or see how the thing stands in God, we know the particular thing, and every thing, and every man. For, the Maker of all things and all persons, stands behind us, and casts his dread omniscience through us over things.

But beyond this recognition of its own in particular passages of the individual's experience, it also reveals truth. And here we should seek to reinforce ourselves by its very presence, and to speak with a worthier, loftier strain of that advent. For the soul's communication of truth is the highest event in nature, for it then does not give somewhat from itself, but it gives itself, or passes into and becomes that man whom it enlightens; or in proportion to that truth he receives, it takes him to itself.

We distinguish the announcements of the soul, its manifestations of its own nature, by the term *Revelation*. These are always attended by the emotion of the sublime. For this communication is an influx of the Divine mind into our mind. It is an ebb of the individual rivulet before the flowing surges of the sea of life. Every distinct apprehension of this central commandment agitates men with awe and delight. A thrill passes through all men at the reception of new truth, or at the performance of a great action, which comes out of the heart of nature. In these communications, the power to see, is not separated from the will to do, but the insight proceeds from obedience, and the obedience proceeds from a joyful perception. Every moment when the individual feels himself invaded by it, is memorable. Always, I believe, by the necessity of our constitution, a certain enthusiasm attends the individual's consciousness of that divine presence. The character and duration of this enthusiasm varies with the state of the individual, from an extasy and trance and prophetic inspiration,—which is its rarer appearance, to the faintest glow of virtuous emotion, in which form it warms, like our household fires, all the families and associations of men, and makes society possible. A certain tendency to insanity has always attended the opening of the religious sense in men, as if "blasted with excess of light."[1] The trances of Socrates; the "union" of Plotinus; the vision of Porphyry; the conversion of Paul; the aurora of Behmen; the convulsions of George Fox and his Quakers; the illumination of Swedenborg; are of this kind.[2] What was in the case of these remarkable persons a ravishment, has, in

---

9. Swedish theologian and statesman (1688–1772), Emerson's favorite example of a mystic.
1. From *The Progress of Poesy* (3.2.7), by Thomas

Gray (1716–1771), English poet.
2. I.e., whatever the particular vocabulary, the same psychological phenomenon unites the experiences of

innumerable instances in common life, been exhibited in less striking manner. Everywhere the history of religion betrays a tendency to enthusiasm. The rapture of the Moravian and Quietist; the opening of the internal sense of the Word, in the language of the New Jerusalem Church; the revival of the Calvinistic Churches; the experiences of the Methodists,[3] are varying forms of that shudder of awe and delight with which the individual soul always mingles with the universal soul.

The nature of these revelations is always the same: they are perceptions of the absolute law. They are solutions of the soul's own questions. They do not answer the questions which the understanding asks. The soul answers never by words, but by the thing itself that is inquired after.

Revelation is the disclosure of the soul. The popular notion of a revelation, is, that it is a telling of fortunes. In past oracles of the soul, the understanding seeks to find answers to sensual questions, and undertakes to tell from God how long men shall exist, what their hands shall do, and who shall be their company, adding even names, and dates and places. But we must pick no locks. We must check this low curiosity. An answer in words is delusive; it is really no answer to the questions you ask. Do not ask a description of the countries towards which you sail. The description does not describe them to you, and to-morrow you arrive there, and know them by inhabiting them. Men ask of the immortality of the soul, and the employments of heaven, and the state of the sinner, and so forth. They even dream that Jesus has left replies to precisely these interrogatories. Never a moment did that sublime spirit speak in their *patois*.[4] To truth, justice, love, the attributes of the soul, the idea of immutableness is essentially associated. Jesus, living in these moral sentiments, heedless of sensual fortunes, heeding only the manifestations of these, never made the separation of the idea of duration from the essence of these attributes; never uttered a syllable concerning the duration of the soul. It was left to his disciples to sever duration from the moral elements and to teach the immortality of the soul as a doctrine, and maintain it by evidences. The moment the doctrine of the immortality is separately taught, man is already fallen. In the flowing of love, in the adoration of humility, there is no question of continuance. No inspired man ever asks this question, or condescends to these evidences. For the soul is true to itself, and the man in whom it is shed abroad, cannot wander from the present, which is infinite, to a future, which would be finite.

These questions which we lust to ask about the future, are a confession of sin. God has no answer for them. No answer in words can reply to a question of things. It is not in an arbitrary "decree of God," but in the nature of man that a veil shuts down on the facts of to-morrow: for the soul will not have us read any other cipher but that of cause and effect. By this veil, which curtains events, it instructs the children of men to live in to-day. The only mode of obtaining an answer to these questions of the senses, is, to forego all low curi-

---

the pagan Greek philosopher (Socrates), two neoplatonic Greek philosophers of the early Christian era (Plotinus and Porphyry), the apostle Paul, the German theosophist Behmen or Böhme (1575–1624), the English 17th-century founder of Quakerism (Fox), and an 18th-century Swedish mystic (Swedenborg). (Neoplatonism is a mystical religious system, combining features of Platonic and other Greek philosophies with features of Judaism and Christianity.)
3. Methodists began as an 18th-century offshoot of the Church of England. The Moravians were exiles from

Czechoslovakia, members of a Protestant sect in Saxony in the 18th-century. Quietists were 17th-century believers in perfection through passivity of the soul, condemned as heretics by the Roman Catholic church. Members of the New Jerusalem Church in Emerson's time were followers of Swedenborg. Calvinist churches, including the Presbyterian and Congregational, would emphasize innate depravity. Once again Emerson's point is that whatever the terminology, the experience is the same.
4. Dialect; here, within their circumscribed limits.

osity, and, accepting the tide of being which floats us into the secret of nature, work and live, work and live, and all unawares, the advancing soul has built and forged for itself a new condition, and the question and the answer are one.

Thus is the soul the perceiver and revealer of truth. By the same fire, serene, impersonal, perfect, which burns until it shall dissolve all things into the waves and surges of an ocean of light,—we see and know each other, and what spirit each is of. Who can tell the grounds of his knowledge of the character of the several individuals in his circle of friends? No man. Yet their acts and words do not disappoint him. In that man, though he knew no ill of him, he put no trust. In that other, though they had seldom met, authentic signs had yet passed, to signify that he might be trusted as one who had an interest in his own character. We know each other very well,—which of us has been just to himself, and whether that which we teach or behold, is only an aspiration, or is our honest effort also.

We are all discerners of spirits. That diagnosis lies aloft in our life or unconscious power, not in the understanding. The whole intercourse of society, its trade, its religion, its friendships, its quarrels,—is one wide, judicial investigation of character. In full court, or in small committee, or confronted face to face, accuser and accused, men offer themselves to be judged. Against their will they exhibit those decisive trifles by which character is read. But who judges? and what? Not our understanding. We do not read them by learning or craft. No; the wisdom of the wise man consists herein, that he does not judge them; he lets them judge themselves, and merely reads and records their own verdict.

By virtue of this inevitable nature, private will is overpowered, and, maugre[5] our efforts, or our imperfections, your genius will speak from you, and mine from me. That which we are, we shall teach, not voluntarily, but involuntarily. Thoughts come into our minds by avenues which we never left open, and thoughts go out of our minds through avenues which we never voluntarily opened. Character teaches over our head. The infallible index of true progress is found in the tone the man takes. Neither his age, nor his breeding, nor company, nor books, nor actions, nor talents, nor all together, can hinder him from being deferential to a higher spirit than his own. If he have not found his home in God, his manners, his forms of speech, the turn of his sentences, the build, shall I say, of all his opinions will involuntarily confess it, let him brave it out how he will. If he have found his centre, the Deity will shine through him, through all the disguises of ignorance, of ungenial temperament, of unfavorable circumstance. The tone of seeking, is one, and the tone of having is another.

The great distinction between teachers sacred or literary; between poets like Herbert, and poets like Pope; between philosophers like Spinoza, Kant, and Coleridge,—and philosophers like Locke, Paley, Mackintosh, and Stewart;[6] between men of the world who are reckoned accomplished talkers, and here

---

5. Malgré, despite.

6. Emerson's oppositions pit the religious poet George Herbert (1593–1633) against the more worldly Alexander Pope (1688–1744). The metaphysically minded Dutch philosopher Baruch Spinoza (1632–1677), the German philosopher Immanuel Kant (1724–1804), and the English poet-philosopher S. T. Coleridge (1772–1834) are pitted against the rational, pragmatic English writers John Locke (1632–1704), author of *Essay Concerning Human Understanding* (1690), which argued that knowledge comes only from sense experience and subsequent reflection on such experience, and William Paley (1743–1805), who in *Principles of Moral and Political Philosophy* (1785) took a utilitarian view of Christianity, as well as two Scottish philosophers, Sir James Mackintosh (1765–1832), advocate of a version of utilitarianism, and Dugald Stewart (1753–1828), a member of the Scottish Common Sense school of philosophy.

and there a fervent mystic, prophesying half-insane under the infinitude of his thought, is, that one class speak *from within,* or from experience, as parties and possessors of the fact; and the other class, *from without,* as spectators merely, or perhaps as acquainted with the fact, on the evidence of third persons. It is of no use to preach to me from without. I can do that too easily myself. Jesus speaks always from within, and in a degree that transcends all others. In that, is the miracle. That includes the miracle. My soul believes beforehand that it ought so to be. All men stand continually in the expectation of the appearance of such a teacher. But if a man do not speak from within the veil, where the word is one with that it tells of, let him lowly confess it.

The same Omniscience flows into the intellect, and makes what we call genius. Much of the wisdom of the world is not wisdom, and the most illuminated class of men are no doubt superior to literary fame, and are not writers. Among the multitude of scholars and authors, we feel no harrowing presence; we are sensible of a knack and skill rather than of inspiration; they have a light, and know not whence it comes, and call it their own: their talent is some exaggerated faculty, some overgrown member, so that their strength is a disease. In these instances, the intellectual gifts do not make the impression of virtue, but almost of vice; and we feel that a man's talents stand in the way of his advancement in truth. But genius is religious. It is a larger imbibing of the common heart. It is not anomalous, but more like, and not less like other men. There is in all great poets, a wisdom of humanity, which is superior to any talents they exercise. The author, the wit, the partisan, the fine gentleman, does not take place of the man. Humanity shines in Homer, in Chaucer, in Spenser, in Shakspeare, in Milton. They are content with truth. They use the positive degree. They seem frigid and phlegmatic to those who have been spiced with the frantic passion and violent coloring of inferior, but popular writers. For, they are poets by the free course which they allow to the informing soul, which, though their eyes beholdeth again, and blesseth the things which it hath made. The soul is superior to its knowledge; wiser than any of its works. The great poet makes us feel our own wealth, and then we think less of his compositions. His greatest communication to our mind, is, to teach us to despise all he has done. Shakspeare carries us to such a lofty strain of intelligent activity, as to suggest a wealth which beggars his own; and we then feel that the splendid works which he has created, and which in other hours, we extol as a sort of self-existent poetry, take no stronger hold of real nature than the shadow of a passing traveller on the rock. The inspiration which uttered itself in Hamlet and Lear, could utter things as good from day to day, forever. Why then should I make account of Hamlet and Lear, as if we had not the soul from which they fell as syllables from the tongue?

This energy does not descend into individual life, on any other condition than entire possession. It comes to the lowly and simple; it comes to whomsoever will put off what is foreign and proud; it comes as insight; it comes as serenity and grandeur. When we see those whom it inhabits, we are apprised of new degrees of greatness. From that inspiration the man comes back with a changed tone. He does not talk with men, with an eye to their opinion. He tries them. It requires of us to be plain and true. The vain traveller attempts to embellish his life by quoting my Lord, and the Prince, and the Countess, who thus said or did to *him.* The ambitious vulgar,[7] show you their spoons, and

---

7. Common people.

brooches, and rings, and preserve their cards and compliments. The more cultivated, in their account of their own experience, cull out the pleasing poetic circumstance; the visit to Rome; the man of genius they saw; the brilliant friend they know; still further on, perhaps, the gorgeous landscape, the mountain lights, the mountain thoughts, they enjoyed yesterday,—and so seek to throw a romantic color over their life. But the soul that ascendeth to worship the great God, is plain and true; has no rose color; no fine friends; no chivalry; no adventures; does not want admiration; dwells in the hour that now is, in the earnest experience of the common day,—by reason of the present moment, and the mere trifle having become porous to thought, and bibulous of the sea of light.

Converse with a mind that is grandly simple, and literature looks like word-catching. The simplest utterances are worthiest to be written, yet are they so cheap, and so things of course, that in the infinite riches of the soul, it is like gathering a few pebbles off the ground, or bottling a little air in a phial, when the whole earth, and the whole atmosphere are ours. The mere author, in such society, is like a pickpocket among gentlemen, who has come in to steal a gold button or a pin. Nothing can pass there, or make you one of the circle, but the casting aside your trappings, and dealing man to man in naked truth, plain confession and omniscient affirmation.

Souls, such as these, treat you as gods would; walk as gods in the earth, accepting without any admiration, your wit, your bounty, your virtue, even, say rather your act of duty, for your virtue they own as their proper blood, royal as themselves, and over-royal, and the father of the gods. But what rebuke their plain fraternal bearing casts on the mutual flattery with which authors solace each other, and wound themselves! These flatter not. I do not wonder that these men go to see Cromwell, and Christina, and Charles II., and James I., and the Grand Turk.[8] For they are in their own elevation, the fellows of kings, and must feel the servile tone of conversation in the world. They must always be a godsend to princes, for they confront them, a king to a king, without ducking or concession, and give a high nature the refreshment and satisfaction of resistance, of plain humanity, of even companionship, and of new ideas. They leave them wiser and superior men. Souls like these make us feel that sincerity is more excellent than flattery. Deal so plainly with man and woman, as to constrain the utmost sincerity, and destroy all hope of trifling with you. It is the highest compliment you can pay. Their "highest praising," said Milton, "is not flattery, and their plainest advice is a kind of praising."[9]

Ineffable is the union of man and God in every act of the soul. The simplest person, who in his integrity worships God, becomes God; yet forever and ever the influx of this better and universal self is new and unsearchable. Ever it inspires awe and astonishment. How dear, how soothing to man, arises the idea of God, peopling the lonely place, effacing the scars of our mistakes and disappointments! When we have broken our god of tradition, and ceased from our god of rhetoric, then may God fire the heart with his presence. It is the doubling of the heart itself, nay, the infinite enlargement of the heart with a power of growth to a new infinity on every side. It inspires in man an infallible

---

8. As the peculiar unchronological order shows, Emerson primarily means any rulers, not only rulers especially receptive to unusual common people, although he may have been thinking of Descartes's welcome at the court of Queen Christina of Sweden or Milton's services to Cromwell.
9. The *Areopagitica* (1644), third paragraph, slightly adapted.

trust. He has not the conviction, but the sight that the best is the true, and may in the thought easily dismiss all particular uncertainties and fears, and adjourn to the sure revelation of time, the solution of his private riddles. He is sure that his welfare is dear to the heart of being. In the presence of law to his mind, he is overflowed with a reliance so universal, that it sweeps away all cherished hopes and the most stable projects of mortal condition in its flood. He believes that he cannot escape from his good. The things that are really for thee, gravitate to thee. You are running to seek your friend. Let your feet run, but your mind need not. If you do not find him, will you not acquiesce that it is best you should not find him? for there is a power, which, as it is in you, is in him also, and could therefore very well bring you together, if it were for the best. You are preparing with eagerness to go and render a service to which your talent and your taste invite you, the love of men, and the hope of fame. Has it not occurred to you, that you have no right to go, unless you are equally willing to be prevented from going? O believe, as thou livest, that every sound that is spoken over the round world, which thou oughtest to hear, will vibrate on thine ear. Every proverb, every book, every by-word that belongs to thee for aid or comfort, shall surely come home through open or winding passages. Every friend whom not thy fantastic will, but the great and tender heart in thee craveth, shall lock thee in his embrace. And this, because the heart in thee is the heart of all; not a valve, not a wall, not an intersection is there any where in nature, but one blood rolls uninterruptedly, an endless circulation through all men, as the water of the globe is all one sea, and, truly seen, its tide is one.

Let man then learn the revelation of all nature, and all thought to his heart; this, namely; that the Highest dwells with him; that the sources of nature are in his own mind, if the sentiment of duty is there. But if he would know what the great God speaketh, he must 'go into his closet and shut the door,' as Jesus said.[1] God will not make himself manifest to cowards. He must greatly listen to himself, withdrawing himself from all the accents of other men's devotion. Their prayers even are hurtful to him, until he have made his own. The soul makes no appeal from itself. Our religion vulgarly stands on numbers of believers. Whenever the appeal is made,—no matter how indirectly,—to numbers, proclamation is then and there made, that religion is not. He that finds God a sweet, enveloping thought to him, never counts his company. When I sit in that presence, who shall dare to come in? When I rest in perfect humility, when I burn with pure love,—what can Calvin or Swedenborg say?

It makes no difference whether the appeal is to numbers or to one. The faith that stands on authority is not faith. The reliance on authority, measures the decline of religion, the withdrawal of the soul. The position men have given to Jesus, now for many centuries of history, is a position of authority. It characterizes themselves. It cannot alter the eternal facts. Great is the soul, and plain. It is no flatterer, it is no follower; it never appeals from itself. It always believes in itself. Before the immense possibilities of man, all mere experience, all past biography, however spotless and sainted, shrinks away. Before that holy heaven which our presentiments foreshow us, we cannot easily praise any form of life we have seen or read of. We not only affirm that we have few great men, but absolutely speaking, that we have none; that we have no history, no

1. Matthew 6.6.

record of any character or mode of living, that entirely contents us. The saints and demigods whom history worships, we are constrained to accept with a grain of allowance. Though in our lonely hours, we draw a new strength out of their memory, yet pressed on our attention, as they are by the thoughtless and customary, they fatigue and invade. The soul gives itself alone, original, and pure, to the Lonely, Original and Pure, who, on that condition, gladly inhabits, leads, and speaks through it. Then it is glad, young, and nimble. It is not wise, but it sees through all things. It is not called religious, but it is innocent. It calls the light its own, and feels that the grass grows, and the stone falls by a law inferior to, and dependent on its nature. Behold, it saith, I am born into the great, the universal mind. I the imperfect, adore my own Perfect. I am somehow receptive of the great soul, and thereby I do overlook the sun and the stars, and feel them to be but the fair accidents and effects which change and pass. More and more the surges of everlasting nature enter into me, and I become public and human in my regards and actions. So come I to live in thoughts, and act with energies which are immortal. Thus revering the soul, and learning, as the ancient said, that "its beauty is immense," man will come to see that the world is the perennial miracle which the soul worketh, and be less astonished at particular wonders; he will learn that there is no profane history; that all history is sacred; that the universe is represented in an atom, in a moment of time. He will weave no longer a spotted life of shreds and patches, but he will live with a divine unity. He will cease from what is base and frivolous in his own life, and be content with all places and any service he can render. He will calmly front the morrow in the negligency of that trust which carries God with it, and so hath already the whole future in the bottom of the heart.

1841

The Poet[1]

A moody child and wildly wise
Pursued the game with joyful eyes,
Which chose, like meteors, their way,
And rived the dark with private ray:
They overleapt the horizon's edge,
Searched with Apollo's privilege;
Through man, and woman, and sea, and star,
Saw the dance of nature forward far;
Through worlds, and races, and terms, and times,
Saw musical order, and pairing rhymes.

Olympian bards who sung
Divine ideas below,
Which always find us young,
And always keep us so.

Those who are esteemed umpires of taste, are often persons who have acquired some knowledge of admired pictures or sculptures, and have an incli-

1. First published in *Essays, Second Series* (1844), the source of the present text, *The Poet* contains the fullest elaboration of Emerson's aesthetic ideas and his most incisive comments on contemporary poetry and criticism. The first prefatory poem is from one of Emerson's own uncompleted poems, and the second is from his *Ode to Beauty*.

nation for whatever is elegant; but if you inquire whether they are beautiful souls, and whether their own acts are like fair pictures, you learn that they are selfish and sensual. Their cultivation is local, as if you should rub a log of dry wood in one spot to produce fire, all the rest remaining cold. Their knowledge of the fine arts is some study of rules and particulars, or some limited judgment of color or form, which is exercised for amusement or for show. It is a proof of the shallowness of the doctrine of beauty, as it lies in the minds of our amateurs, that men seem to have lost the perception of the instant dependence of form upon soul. There is no doctrine of forms in our philosophy. We were put into our bodies, as fire is put into a pan, to be carried about; but there is no accurate adjustment between the spirit and the organ, much less is the latter the germination of the former. So in regard to other forms, the intellectual men do not believe in any essential dependence of the material world on thought and volition. Theologians think it a pretty air-castle to talk of the spiritual meaning of a ship or a cloud, of a city or a contract, but they prefer to come again to the solid ground of historical evidence; and even the poets are contented with a civil and conformed manner of living, and to write poems from the fancy, at a safe distance from their own experience. But the highest minds of the world have never ceased to explore the double meaning, or, shall I say, the quadruple, or the centuple, or much more manifold meaning, of every sensuous fact: Orpheus, Empedocles, Heraclitus, Plato, Plutarch, Dante, Swedenborg,[2] and the masters of sculpture, picture, and poetry. For we are not pans and barrows, nor even porters of the fire and torchbearers, but children of the fire, made of it, and only the same divinity transmuted, and at two or three removes, when we know least about it. And this hidden truth, that the foundations whence all this river of Time, and its creatures, floweth, are intrinsically ideal and beautiful, draws us to the consideration of the nature and functions of the Poet, or the man of Beauty, to the means and materials he uses, and to the general aspect of the art in the present time.

The breadth of the problem is great, for the poet is representative. He stands among partial men for the complete man, and apprises us not of his wealth, but of the commonwealth. The young man reveres men of genius, because, to speak truly, they are more himself than he is. They receive of the soul as he also receives, but they more. Nature enhances her beauty, to the eye of loving men, from their belief that the poet is beholding her shows at the same time. He is isolated among his contemporaries, by truth and by his art, but with this consolation in his pursuits, that they will draw all men sooner or later. For all men live by truth, and stand in need of expression. In love, in art, in avarice, in politics, in labor, in games, we study to utter our painful secret. The man is only half himself, the other half is his expression.

Notwithstanding this necessity to be published, adequate expression is rare. I know not how it is that we need an interpreter; but the great majority of men seem to be minors, who have not yet come into possession of their own, or mutes, who cannot report the conversation they have had with nature. There is no man who does not anticipate a supersensual utility in the sun, and stars, earth, and water. These stand and wait to render him a peculiar service. But there is some obstruction, or some excess of phlegm in our constitution, which

2. Emanuel Swedenborg (1688–1772), Swedish scientist and mystic. Orpheus, a legendary Greek poet. Empedocles (5th century B.C.), Heraclitus (6th century B.C.), and Plato (4th century B.C.) were Greek philosophers. Plutarch (1st century), Greek biographer. Dante (1265–1321), Italian poet.

does not suffer them to yield the due effect. Too feeble fall the impressions of nature on us to make us artists. Every touch should thrill. Every man should be so much an artist, that he could report in conversation what had befallen him. Yet, in our experience, the rays or appulses have sufficient force to arrive at the senses, but not enough to reach the quick, and compel the reproduction of themselves in speech. The poet is the person in whom these powers are in balance, the man without impediment, who sees and handles that which others dream of, traverses the whole scale of experience, and is its representative of man, in virtue of being the largest power to receive and to impart.

For the Universe has three children, born at one time, which reappear, under different names, in every system of thought, whether they be called cause, operation, and effect; or, more poetically, Jove, Pluto, Neptune; or, theologically, the Father, the Spirit, and the Son; but which we will call here, the Knower, the Doer, and the Sayer. These stand respectively for the love of truth, for the love of good, and for the love of beauty. These three are equal. Each is that which he is essentially, so that he cannot be surmounted or analyzed, and each of these three has the power of the others latent in him, and his own patent.

The poet is the sayer, the namer, and represents beauty. He is a sovereign, and stands on the centre. For the world is not painted or adorned, but is from the beginning beautiful; and God has not made some beautiful things, but Beauty is the creator of the universe. Therefore the poet is not any permissive potentate, but is emperor in his own right. Criticism is infested with a cant of materialism, which assumes that manual skill and activity is the first merit of all men, and disparages such as say and do not, overlooking the fact that some men, namely, poets, are natural sayers, sent into the world to the end of expression, and confounds them with those whose province is action, but who quit it to imitate the sayers. But Homer's words are as costly and admirable to Homer, as Agamemnon's victories are to Agamemnon.[3] The poet does not wait for the hero or the sage, but, as they act and think primarily, so he writes primarily what will and must be spoken, reckoning the others, though primaries also, yet, in respect to him, secondaries and servants; as sitters or models in the studio of a painter, or as assistants who bring building materials to an architect.

For poetry was all written before time was, and whenever we are so finely organized that we can penetrate into that region where the air is music, we hear those primal warblings, and attempt to write them down, but we lose ever and anon a word, or a verse, and substitute something of our own, and thus miswrite the poem. The men of more delicate ear write down these cadences more faithfully, and these transcripts, though imperfect, become the songs of the nations. For nature is as truly beautiful as it is good, or as it is reasonable, and must as much appear, as it must be done, or be known. Words and deeds are quite indifferent modes of the divine energy. Words are also actions, and actions are a kind of words.

The sign and credentials of the poet are, that he announces that which no man foretold. He is the true and only doctor;[4] he knows and tells; he is the only teller of news, for he was present and privy to the appearance which he describes. He is a beholder of ideas, and an utterer of the necessary and causal.

3. Emerson is comparing the author (Homer) with his character (Agamemnon, in *The Iliad*).   4. Teacher.

For we do not speak now of men of poetical talents, or of industry and skill in metre, but of the true poet. I took part in a conversation the other day, concerning a recent writer of lyrics, a man of subtle mind, whose head appeared to be a music-box of delicate tunes and rhythms, and whose skill, and command of language, we could not sufficiently praise. But when the question arose, whether he was not only a lyrist, but a poet, we were obliged to confess that he is plainly a contemporary, not an eternal man. He does not stand out of our low limitations, like a Chimborazo under the line,[5] running up from the torrid base through all the climates of the globe, with belts of the herbage of every latitude on its high and mottled sides; but this genius is the landscape-garden of a modern house, adorned with fountains and statues, with well-bred men and women standing and sitting in the walks and terraces. We hear, through all the varied music, the ground-tone of conventional life. Our poets are men of talents who sing, and not the children of music. The argument is secondary, the finish of the versus is primary.

For it is not metres, but a metre-making argument, that makes a poem,—a thought so passionate and alive, that, like the spirit of a plant or an animal, it has an architecture of its own, and adorns nature with a new thing. The thought and the form are equal in the order of time, but in the order of genesis the thought is prior to the form. The poet has a new thought: he has a whole new experience to unfold; he will tell us how it was with him, and all men will be the richer in his fortune. For, the experience of each new age requires a new confession, and the world seems always waiting for its poet. I remember, when I was young, how much I was moved one morning by tidings that genius had appeared in a youth who sat near me at table. He had left his work, and gone rambling none knew whither, and had written hundreds of lines, but could not tell whether that which was in him was therein told: he could tell nothing but that all was changed,—man, beast, heaven, earth, and sea. How gladly we listened! how credulous! Society seemed to be compromised. We sat in the aurora of a sunrise which was to put out all the stars. Boston seemed to be at twice the distance it had the night before, or was much farther than that. Rome,—what was Rome! Plutarch and Shakspeare were in the yellow leaf, and Homer no more should be heard of. It is much to know that poetry has been written this very day, under this very roof, by your side. What! that wonderful spirit has not expired! these stony moments are still sparkling and animated! I had fancied that the oracles were all silent, and nature had spent her fires, and behold! all night, from every pore, these fine auroras have been streaming. Every one has some interest in the advent of the poet, and no one knows how much it may concern him. We know that the secret of the world is profound, but who or what shall be our interpreter, we know not. A mountain ramble, a new style of face, a new person, may put the key into our hands. Of course, the value of genius to us is in the veracity of its report. Talent may frolic and juggle; genius realizes and adds. Mankind, in good earnest, have availed so far in understanding themselves and their work, that the foremost watchman on the peak announces his news. It is the truest word ever spoken, and the phrase will be the fittest, most musical, and the unerring voice of the world for that time.

All that we call sacred history attests that the birth of a poet is the principal

---

5. Equator. "Chimborazo": a mountain in Ecuador.

event in chronology. Man, never so often deceived, still watches for the arrival of a brother who can hold him steady to a truth, until he has made it his own. With what joy I begin to read a poem, which I confide in as an inspiration! And now my chains are to be broken; I shall mount above these clouds and opaque airs in which I live,—opaque, though they seem transparent,—and from the heaven of truth I shall see and comprehend my relations. That will reconcile me to life, and renovate nature, to see trifles animated by a tendency, and to know what I am doing. Life will no more be a noise; now I shall see men and women, and know the signs by which they may be discerned from fools and satans. This day shall be better than my birth-day: then I became an animal: now I am invited into the science of the real. Such is the hope, but the fruition is postponed. Oftener it falls, that this winged man, who will carry me into the heaven, whirls me into the clouds, then leaps and frisks about with me from cloud to cloud, still affirming that he is bound heavenward; and I, being myself a novice, am slow in perceiving that he does not know the way into the heavens, and is merely bent that I should admire his skill to rise, like a fowl or a flying fish, a little way from the ground or the water; but the all-piercing, all-feeding, and ocular[6] air of heaven, that man shall never inhabit. I tumble down again soon into my old nooks, and lead the life of exaggerations as before, and have lost my faith in the possibility of any guide who can lead me thither where I would be.

But leaving these victims of vanity, let us, with new hope, observe how nature, by worthier impulses, has ensured the poet's fidelity to his office of announcement and affirming, namely, by the beauty of things, which becomes a new, and higher beauty, when expressed. Nature offers all her creatures to him as a picture-language. Being used as a type, a second wonderful value appears in the object, far better than its old value, as the carpenter's stretched cord, if you hold your ear close enough, is musical in the breeze. "Things more excellent than every image," says Jamblichus,[7] "are expressed through images." Things admit of being used as symbols, because nature is a symbol, in the whole, and in every part. Every line we can draw in the sand, has expression; and there is no body without its spirit or genius. All form is an effect of character; all condition, of the quality of the life; all harmony, of health; (and, for this reason, a perception of beauty should be sympathetic, or proper only to the good.) The beautiful rests on the foundations of the necessary. The soul makes the body, as the wise Spenser teaches:—

> "So every spirit, as it is most pure,
> And hath in it the more of heavenly light,
> So it the fairer body doth procure
> To habit in, and it more fairly dight,
> With cheerful grace and amiable sight.
> For, of the soul, the body form doth take,
> For soul is form, and doth the body make."[8]

Here we find ourselves, suddenly, not in a critical speculation, but in a holy place, and should go very warily and reverently. We stand before the secret of

---

6. Visible.
7. Neoplatonic philosopher of the 4th century A.D. (Neoplatonism is a mystical religious system, combining features of Platonic and other Greek philosophies

with features of Judaism and Christianity.)
8. *An Hymn in Honour of Beauty* (1596), by the English poet Edmund Spenser (1552–1599).

the world, there where Being passes into Appearance, and Unity into Variety.

The Universe is the externisation of the soul. Wherever the life is, that bursts into appearance around it. Our science is sensual, and therefore superficial. The earth, and the heavenly bodies, physics, and chemistry, we sensually treat, as if they were self-existent; but these are the retinue of that Being we have. "The mighty heaven," said Proclus,[9] "exhibits, in its transfigurations, clear images of the splendor of intellectual perceptions; being moved in conjunction with the unapparent periods of intellectual natures." Therefore, science always goes abreast with the just elevation of the man, keeping step with religion and metaphysics; or, the state of science is an index of our self-knowledge. Since everything in nature answers to a moral power, if any phenomenon remains brute and dark, it is that the corresponding faculty in the observer is not yet active.

No wonder, then, if these waters be so deep, that we hover over them with a religious regard. The beauty of the fable proves the importance of the sense; to the poet, and to all others; or, if you please, every man is so far a poet as to be susceptible of these enchantments of nature: for all men have the thoughts whereof the universe is the celebration. I find that the fascination resides in the symbol. Who loves nature? Who does not? Is it only poets, and men of leisure and cultivation, who live with her? No; but also hunters, farmers, grooms, and butchers, though they express their affection in their choice of life, and not in their choice of words. The writer wonders what the coachman or the hunter values in riding, in horses, and dogs. It is not superficial qualities. When you talk with him, he holds these at as slight a rate as you. His worship is sympathetic; he has no definitions, but he is commanded in nature, by the living power which he feels to be there present. No imitation, or playing of these things, would content him; he loves the earnest of the northwind, of rain, of stone, and wood, and iron. A beauty not explicable, is dearer than a beauty which we can see to the end of. It is nature the symbol, nature certifying the supernatural, body overflowed by life, which he worships, with coarse, but sincere rites.

The inwardness, and mystery, of this attachment, drives men of every class to the use of emblems. The schools of poets, and philosophers, are not more intoxicated with their symbols, than the populace with theirs. In our political parties, compute the power of badges and emblems. See the great ball which they roll from Baltimore to Bunker hill! In the political processions, Lowell goes in a loom, and Lynn in a shoe, and Salem in a ship.[1] Witness the ciderbarrel, the log-cabin, the hickory-stick, the palmetto, and all the cognizances of party. See the power of national emblems. Some stars, lilies, leopards, a crescent, a lion, an eagle, or other figure, which came into credit God knows how, on an old rag of bunting, blowing in the wind, on a fort, at the ends of the earth, shall make the blood tingle under the rudest, or the most conventional exterior. The people fancy they hate poetry, and they are all poets and mystics!

Beyond this universality of the symbolic language, we are apprised of the divineness of this superior use of things, whereby the world is a temple, whose walls are covered with emblems, pictures, and commandments of the Deity, in this, that there is no fact in nature which does not carry the whole sense of

9. Greek neoplatonic philosopher (411–485).
1. Towns are symbolized by major products. "The great ball": a recent political stunt.

nature; and the distinctions which we make in events, and in affairs, of low and high, honest and base, disappear when nature is used as a symbol. Thought makes every thing fit for use. The vocabulary of an omniscient man would embrace words and images excluded from polite conversation. What would be base, or even obscene, to the obscene, becomes illustrious, spoken in a new connexion of thought. The piety of the Hebrew prophets purges their grossness. The circumcision is an example of the power of poetry to raise the low and offensive. Small and mean things serve as well as great symbols. The meaner the type by which a law is expressed, the more pungent it is, and the more lasting in the memories of men: just as we choose the smallest box, or case, in which any needful utensil can be carried. Bare lists of words are found suggestive, to an imaginative and excited mind; as it is related of Lord Chatham,[2] that he was accustomed to read in Bailey's Dictionary,[2] when he was preparing to speak in Parliament. The poorest experience is rich enough for all the purposes of expressing thought. Why covet a knowledge of new facts? Day and night, house and garden, a few books, a few actions, serve us as well as would all trades and all spectacles. We are far from having exhausted the significance of the few symbols we use. We can come to use them yet with a terrible simplicity. It does not need that a poem should be long. Every word was once a poem. Every new relation is a new word. Also, we use defects and deformaties to a sacred purpose, so expressing our sense that the evils of the world are such only to the evil eye. In the old mythology, mythologists observe, defects are ascribed to divine natures, as lameness to Vulcan, blindness to Cupid, and the like, to signify exuberances.

For, as it is dislocation and detachment from the life of God, that makes things ugly, the poet, who re-attaches things to nature and the Whole,—re-attaching even artificial things, and violations of nature, to nature, by a deeper insight,—disposes very easily of the most disagreeable facts. Readers of poetry see the factory-village, and the railway, and fancy that the poetry of the landscape is broken up by these; for these works of art are not yet consecrated in their reading; but the poet sees them fall within the great Order not less than the bee-hive, or the spider's geometrical web. Nature adopts them very fast into her vital circles, and the gliding train of cars she loves like her own. Besides, in a centred mind, it signifies nothing how many mechanical inventions you exhibit. Though you add millions, and never so surprising, the fact of mechanics has not gained a grain's weight. The spiritual fact remains unalterable, by many or by few particulars; as no mountain is of any appreciable height to break the curve of the sphere. A shrewd country-boy goes to the city for the first time, and the complacent citizen is not satisfied with his little wonder. It is not that he does not see all the fine houses, and know that he never saw such before, but he disposes of them as easily as the poet finds place for the railway. The chief value of the new fact, is to enhance the great and constant fact of Life, which can dwarf any and every circumstance, and to which the belt of wampum, and the commerce of America, are alike.

The world being thus put under the mind for verb and noun, the poet is he who can articulate it. For, though life is great, and fascinates, and absorbs,— and though all men are intelligent of the symbols through which it is

2. Nathan (or Nathaniel) Bailey (d. 1742) published *An Universal Etymological English Dictionary* (1721), which ran through many editions. "Lord Chatham": William Pitt (1708–1778), English statesman, famous for his oratory.

named,—yet they cannot originally use them. We are symbols, and inhabit symbols; workmen, work, and tools, words and things, birth and death, all are emblems; but we sympathize with the symbols, and, being infatuated with the economical uses of things, we do not know that they are thoughts. The poet, by an ulterior intellectual perception, gives them a power which makes their old use forgotten, and puts eyes, and a tongue, into every dumb and inanimate object. He perceives the independence of the thought on the symbol, the stability of the thought, the accidency and fugacity of the symbol. As the eyes of Lyncæus[3] were said to see through the earth, so the poet turns the world to glass, and shows us all things in their right series and procession. For, through that better perception, he stands one step nearer to things, and sees the flowing or metamorphosis; perceives that thought is multiform; that within the form of every creature is a force impelling it to ascend into a higher form; and, following with his eyes the life, uses the forms which express that life, and so his speech flows with the flowing of nature. All the facts of the animal economy, sex, nutriment, gestation, birth, growth, are symbols of the passage of the world into the soul of man, to suffer there a change, and reappear a new and higher fact. He uses forms according to the life, and not according to the form. This is true science. The poet alone knows astronomy, chemistry, vegetation, and animation, for he does not stop at these facts, but employs them as signs. He knows why the plain, or meadow of space, was strown with these flowers we call suns, and moons, and stars; why the great deep is adorned with animals, with men, and gods; for, in every word he speaks he rides on them as the horses of thought.

By virtue of this science the poet is the Namer, or Language-maker, naming things sometimes after their appearance, sometimes after their essence, and giving to every one its own name and not another's, thereby rejoicing the intellect, which delights in detachment or boundary. The poets made all the words, and therefore language is the archives of history, and, if we must say it, a sort of tomb of the muses. For, though the origin of most of our words is forgotten, each word was at first a stroke of genius, and obtained currency, because for the moment it symbolized the world to the first speaker and to the hearer. The etymologist finds the deadest word to have been once a brilliant picture. Language is fossil poetry. As the limestone of the continent consists of infinite masses of the shells of animalcules, so language is made up of images, or tropes, which now, in their secondary use, have long ceased to remind us of their poetic origin. But the poet names the thing because he sees it, or comes one step nearer to it than any other. This expression, or naming, is not art, but a second nature, grown out of the first, as a leaf out of a tree. What we call nature, is a certain self-regulated motion, or change; and nature does all things by her own hands, and does not leave another to baptise her, but baptises herself; and this through the metamorphosis again. I remember that a certain poet[4] described it to me thus:

> Genius is the activity which repairs the decays of things, whether wholly or partly of a material and finite kind. Nature, through all her kingdoms, insures herself. Nobody cares for planting the poor fungus: so she shakes down from the gills of one agaric countless spores, any one of

3. In Greek mythology, the keenest-sighted crewman on the *Argo*, in which Jason sailed in search of the

Golden Fleece.
4. A private joke: the poet is Emerson himself.

which, being preserved, transmits new billions of spores to-morrow or next day. The new agaric of this hour has a chance which the old one had not. This atom of seed is thrown into a new place, not subject to the accidents which destroyed its parent two rods off. She makes a man; and having brought him to ripe age, she will no longer run the risk of losing this wonder at a blow, but she detaches from him a new self, that the kind may be safe from accidents to which the individual is exposed. So when the soul of the poet has come to ripeness of thought, she detaches and sends away from it its poems or songs,—a fearless, sleepless, deathless progeny, which is not exposed to the accidents of the weary kingdom of time: a fearless, vivacious offspring, clad with wings (such was the virtue of the soul out of which they came), which carry them fast and far, and infix them irrecoverably into the hearts of men. These wings are the beauty of the poet's soul. The songs, thus flying immortal from their mortal parent, are pursued by clamorous flights of censures, which swarm in far greater numbers, and threaten to devour them; but these last are not winged. At the end of a very short leap they fall plump down, and rot, having received from the souls out of which they came no beautiful wings. But the melodies of the poet ascend, and leap, and pierce into the deeps of infinite time.

So far the bard taught me, using his freer speech. But nature has a higher end, in the production of new individuals, than security, namely, *ascension,* or, the passage of the soul into higher forms. I knew, in my younger days, the sculptor who made the statue of the youth which stands in the public garden. He was, as I remember, unable to tell directly, what made him happy, or unhappy, but by wonderful indirections he could tell. He rose one day, according to his habit, before the dawn, and saw the morning break, grand as the eternity out of which it came, and, for many days after, he strove to express this tranquillity, and, lo! his chisel had fashioned out of marble the form of a beautiful youth, Phosphorus,[5] whose aspect is such, that, it is said, all persons who look on it become silent. The poet also resigns himself to his mood, and that thought which agitated him is expressed, but *alter idem,*[6] in a manner totally new. The expression is organic, or, the new type which things themselves take when liberated. As, in the sun, objects paint their images on the retina of the eye, so they, sharing the aspiration of the whole universe, tend to paint a far more delicate copy of their essence in his mind. Like the metamorphosis of things into higher organic forms, is their change into melodies. Over everything stands its dæmon, or soul, and, as the form of the thing is reflected by the eye, so the soul of the thing is reflected by a melody. The sea, the mountain-ridge, Niagara, and every flower-bed, pre-exist, or super-exist, in pre-cantations, which sail like odors in the air, and when any man goes by with an ear sufficiently fine, he overhears them, and endeavors to write down the notes, without diluting or depraving them. And herein is the legitimation of criticism, in the mind's faith, that the poems are a corrupt version of some text in nature, with which they ought to be made to tally. A rhyme in one of our sonnets should not be less pleasing than the iterated nodes of a seashell, or the resembling difference of a group of flowers. The pairing of the birds is an idyl, not tedious as our idyls are; a tempest is a rough ode, without falsehood

5. The Greek god associated with the morning star.   6. The same, yet different (Latin).

or rant: a summer, with its harvest sown, reaped, and stored, is an epic song, subordinating how many admirably executed parts. Why should not the symmetry and truth that modulate these, glide into our spirits, and we participate the invention of nature?

This insight, which expresses itself by what is called Imagination, is a very high sort of seeing, which does not come by study, but by the intellect being where and what it sees, by sharing the path, or circuit of things through forms, and so making them translucid to others. The path of things is silent. Will they suffer a speaker to go with them? A spy they will not suffer; a lover, a poet, is the transcendency of their own nature,—him they will suffer. The condition of true naming, on the poet's part, is his resigning himself to the divine aura[7] which breathes through forms, and accompanying that.

It is a secret which every intellectual man quickly learns, that, beyond the energy of his possessed and conscious intellect, he is capable of a new energy (as of an intellect doubled on itself), by abandonment to the nature of things; that, beside his privacy of power as an individual man, there is a great public power, on which he can draw, by unlocking, at all risks, his human doors, and suffering the ethereal tides to roll and circulate through him: then he is caught up into the life of the Universe, his speech is thunder, his thought is law, and his words are universally intelligible as the plants and animals. The poet knows that he speaks adequately, then, only when he speaks somewhat wildly, or, "with the flower of the mind;" not with the intellect, used as an organ, but with the intellect released from all service, and suffered to take its direction from its celestial life; or, as the ancients were wont to express themselves, not with intellect alone, but with the intellect inebriated by nectar. As the traveller who has lost his way, throws his reins on his horse's neck, and trusts to the instinct of the animal to find his road, so must we do with the divine animal who carries us through this world. For if in any manner we can stimulate this instinct, new passages are opened for us into nature, the mind flows into and through things hardest and highest, and the metamorphosis is possible.

This is the reason why bards love wine, mead, narcotics, coffee, tea, opium, the fumes of sandal-wood and tobacco, or whatever other species of animal exhilaration. All men avail themselves of such means as they can, to add this extraordinary power to their normal powers; and to this end they prize conversation, music, pictures, sculpture, dancing, theatres, travelling, war, mobs, fires, gaming, politics, or love, or science, or animal intoxication, which are several coarser or finer quasi-mechanical substitutes for the true nectar, which is the ravishment of the intellect by coming nearer to the fact. These are auxiliaries to the centrifugal tendency of a man, to his passage out into free space, and they help him to escape the custody of that body in which he is pent up, and of that jail-yard of individual relations in which he is enclosed. Hence a great number of such as were professionally expressors of Beauty, as painters, poets, musicians, and actors, have been more than others wont to lead a life of pleasure and indulgence; all but the few who received the true nectar; and, as it was a spurious mode of attaining freedom, as it was an emancipation not into the heavens, but into the freedom of baser places, they were punished for that advantage they won, by a dissipation and deteriora-

7. Distinctive quality.

tion. But never can any advantage be taken of nature by a trick. The spirit of the world, the great calm presence of the creator, comes not forth to the sorceries of opium or of wine. The sublime vision comes to the pure and simple soul in a clean and chaste body. That is not an inspiration which we owe to narcotics, but some counterfeit excitement and fury. Milton says, that the lyric poet may drink wine and live generously, but the epic poet, he who shall sing of the gods, and their descent unto men, must drink water out of a wooden bowl.[8] For poetry is not 'Devil's wine,' but God's wine. It is with this as it is with toys. We fill the hands and nurseries of our children with all manner of dolls, drums, and horses, withdrawing their eyes from the plain face and sufficing objects of nature, the sun, and moon, the animals, the water, and stones, which should be their toys. So the poet's habit of living should be set on a key so low and plain, that the common influences should delight him. His cheerfulness should be the gift of the sunlight; the air should suffice for his inspiration, and he should be tipsy with water. That spirit which suffices quiet hearts, which seems to come forth to such from every dry knoll of sere grass, from every pine-stump, and half-imbedded stone, on which the dull March sun shines, comes forth to the poor and hungry, and such as are of simple taste. If thou fill thy brain with Boston and New York, with fashion and covetousness, and wilt stimulate thy jaded senses with wine and French coffee, thou shalt find no radiance of wisdom in the lonely waste of the pine-woods.

If the imagination intoxicates the poet, it is not inactive in other men. The metamorphosis excites in the beholder an emotion of joy. The use of symbols has a certain power of emancipation and exhilaration for all men. We seem to be touched by a wand, which makes us dance and run about happily, like children. We are like persons who come out of a cave or cellar into the open air. This is the effect on us of tropes,[9] fables, oracles, and all poetic forms. Poets are thus liberating gods. Men have really got a new sense, and found within their world, another world, or nest of worlds; for, the metamorphosis once seen, we divine that it does not stop. I will not now consider how much this makes the charm of algebra and the mathematics, which also have their tropes, but it is felt in every definition; as, when Aristotle defines *space* to be an immovable vessel, in which things are contained;—or, when Plato defines a *line* to be a flowing point; or, *figure* to be a bound of solid; and many the like. What a joyful sense of freedom we have, when Vitruvius announces the old opinion of artists, that no architect can build any house well, who does not know something of anatomy. When Socrates, in Charmides, tells us that the soul is cured of its maladies by certain incantations, and that these incantations are beautiful reasons, from which temperance is generated in souls; when Plato calls the world an animal; and Timæus affirms that the plants also are animals; or affirms a man to be a heavenly tree, growing with his root, which is his head, upward; and, as George Chapman, following him, writes,—

> "So in our tree of man, whose nervie root
> Springs in his top;"

when Orpheus speaks of hoariness as "that white flower which marks extreme old age;" when Proclus calls the universe the statue of the intellect; when

8. In Milton's *Sixth Latin Elegy*.   9. Figures of speech.

Chaucer, in his praise of 'Gentilesse,' compares good blood in mean condition to fire, which, though carried to the darkest house betwixt this and the mount of Caucasus, will yet hold its natural office, and burn as bright as if twenty thousand men did it behold; when John saw, in the apocalypse, the ruin of the world through evil, and the stars fall from heaven, as the figtree casteth her untimely fruit; when Æsop reports the whole catalogue of common daily relations through the masquerade of birds and beasts;—we take the cheerful hint of the immortality of our essence, and its versatile habit and escapes, as when the gypsies say, "it is in vain to hang them, they cannot die."[1]

The poets are thus liberating gods. The ancient British bards had for the title of their order, "Those who are free throughout the world." They are free, and they make free. An imaginative book renders us much more service at first, by stimulating us through its tropes, than afterward, when we arrive at the precise sense of the author. I think nothing is of any value in books, excepting the transcendental and extraordinary. If a man is inflamed and carried away by his thought, to that degree that he forgets the authors and the public, and heeds only this one dream, which holds him like an insanity, let me read his paper, and you may have all the arguments and histories and criticism. All the value which attaches to Pythagoras, Paracelsus, Cornelius Agrippa, Cardan, Kepler, Swedenborg, Schelling, Oken,[2] or any other who introduces questionable facts into his cosmogony, as angels, devils, magic, astrology, palmistry, mesmerism,[3] and so on, is the certificate we have of departure from routine, and that here is a new witness. That also is the best success in conversation, the magic of liberty, which puts the world, like a ball, in our hands. How cheap even the liberty then seems; how mean to study, when an emotion communicates to the intellect the power to sap and upheave nature; how great the perspective! nations, times, systems, enter and disappear, like threads in tapestry of large figure and many colors; dream delivers us to dream, and, while the drunkenness lasts, we will sell our bed, our philosophy, our religion, in our opulence.

There is good reason why we should prize this liberation. The fate of the poor shepherd, who, blinded and lost in the snowstorm, perishes in a drift within a few feet of his cottage door, is an emblem of the state of man. On the brink of the waters of life and truth, we are miserably dying. The inaccessibleness of every thought but that we are in, is wonderful. What if you come near to it,—you are as remote, when you are nearest, as when you are farthest. Every thought is also a prison; every heaven is also a prison. Therefore we love the poet, the inventor, who in any form, whether in an ode, or in an action, or in looks and behavior, has yielded us a new thought. He unlocks our chains, and admits us to a new scene.

This emancipation is dear to all men, and the power to impart it, as it must come from greater depth and scope of thought, is a measure of intellect.

---

1. Emerson's freewheeling allusiveness embodies the liberation he is celebrating: *Charmides* and *Timaeus* are two of Plato's Dialogues. The Chapman quotation is from his dedication to his translation of Homer. Chaucer's praise of "gentilesse" is in *The Wife of Bath's Tale*. John's vision is in Revelation 6.13. The Greek Aesop in the 6th century B.C. wrote beast fables, which commented on human foibles. The saying attributed to gypsies is unlocated.
2. Lorenz Oken (1779–1851), German naturalist. Py-

thagoras (6th century B.C.), Greek mathematician and mystic philosopher. Paracelsus (1493–1541), German alchemist. Agrippa (1486–1535), German physician. Girolamo Cardano (1501–1576), Italian mathematician. Johann Kepler (1571–1630), German astronomer. Swedenborg, see n. 2, p. 1074. Friedrich Wilhelm Joseph von Schelling (1775–1854), German philosopher.
3. Hypnotism.

Therefore all books of the imagination endure, all which ascend to that truth, that the writer sees nature beneath him, and uses it as his exponent.[4] Every verse or sentence, possessing this virtue, will take care of its own immortality. The religions of the world are the ejaculations[5] of a few imaginative men.

But the quality of the imagination is to flow, and not to freeze. The poet did not stop at the color, or the form, but read their meaning; neither may he rest in this meaning, but he makes the same objects exponents of his new thought. Here is the difference betwixt the poet and the mystic, that the last nails a symbol to one sense, which was a true sense for a moment, but soon becomes old and false. For all symbols are fluxional; all language is vehicular and transitive, and is good, as ferries and horses are, for conveyance, not as farms and houses are, for homestead. Mysticism consists in the mistake of an accidental and individual symbol for an universal one. The morning-redness happens to be the favorite meteor to the eyes of Jacob Behmen,[6] and comes to stand to him for truth and faith; and he believes should stand for the same realities to every reader. But the first reader prefers as naturally the symbol of a mother and child, or a gardener and his bulb, or a jeweller polishing a gem. Either of these, or of a myriad more, are equally good to the person to whom they are significant. Only they must be held lightly, and be very willingly translated into the equivalent terms which others use. And the mystic must be steadily told,—All that you say is just as true without the tedious use of that symbol as with it. Let us have a little algebra, instead of this trite rhetoric,— universal signs, instead of these village symbols,—and we shall both be gain- ers. The history of hierarchies seems to show, that all religious error consisted in making the symbol too stark and solid, and, at last, nothing but an excess of the organ of language.

Swedenborg, of all men in the recent ages, stands eminently for the transla- tor of nature into thought. I do not know the man in history to whom things stood so uniformly for words. Before him the metamorphosis continually plays. Everything on which his eye rests, obeys the impulses of moral nature. The figs become grapes whilst he eats them. When some of his angels affirmed a truth, the laurel twig which they held blossomed in their hands. The noise which, at a distance, appeared like gnashing and thumping, on coming nearer was found to be the voice of disputants. The men, in one of his visions, seen in heavenly light, appeared like dragons, and seemed in darkness: but, to each other, they appeared as men, and, when the light from heaven shone into their cabin, they complained of the darkness, and were compelled to shut the window that they might see.

There was this perception in him, which makes the poet or seer, an object of awe and terror, namely, that the same man, or society of men, may wear one aspect to themselves and their companions, and a different aspect to higher intelligences. Certain priests, whom he describes as conversing very learnedly together, appeared to the children, who were at some distance, like dead horses: and many the like misappearances. And instantly the mind inquires, whether these fishes under the bridge, yonder oxen in the pasture, those dogs in the yard, are immutably fishes, oxen, and dogs, or only so appear to me, and perchance to themselves appear upright men; and whether I appear as a man to all eyes. The Bramins and Pythagoras propounded the same ques-

4. Means of expounding his beliefs.   6. German mystic (1575–1624).
5. Throwings forth.

tion, and if any poet has witnessed the transformation, he doubtless found it in harmony with various experiences. We have all seen changes as considerable in wheat and caterpillars. He is the poet, and shall draw us with love and terror, who sees, through the flowing vest, the firm nature, and can declare it.

I look in vain for the poet whom I describe. We do not, with sufficient plainness, or sufficient profoundness, address ourselves to life, nor dare we chaunt our own times and social circumstance. If we filled the day with bravery, we should not shrink from celebrating it. Time and nature yield us many gifts, but not yet the timely man, the new religion, the reconciler, whom all things await. Dante's praise is, that he dared to write his autobiography in colossal cipher, or into universality. We have yet had no genius in America, with tyrannous eye, which knew the value of our incomparable materials, and saw, in the barbarism and materialism of the times, another carnival of the same gods whose picture he so much admires in Homer; then in the middle age; then in Calvinism. Banks and tariffs, the newspaper and caucus, methodism and unitarianism, are flat and dull to dull people, but rest on the same foundations of wonder as the town of Troy, and the temple of Delphos,[7] and are as swiftly passing away. Our logrolling, our stumps and their politics,[8] our fisheries, our Negroes, and Indians, our boasts, and our repudiations, the wrath of rogues, and the pusillanimity of honest men, the northern trade, the southern planting, the western clearing, Oregon, and Texas, are yet unsung. Yet America is a poem in our eyes; its ample geography dazzles the imagination, and it will not wait long for metres. If I have not found that excellent combination of gifts in my countrymen which I seek, neither could I aid myself to fix the idea of the poet by reading now and then in Chalmers's collection of five centuries of English poets.[9] These are wits, more than poets, though there have been poets among them. But when we adhere to the ideal of the poet, we have our difficulties even with Milton and Homer. Milton is too literary, and Homer too literal and historical.

But I am not wise enough for a national criticism, and must use the old largeness a little longer, to discharge my errand from the muse to the poet concerning his art.

Art is the path of the creator to his work. The paths, or methods, are ideal and eternal, though few men ever see them, not the artist himself for years, or for a lifetime, unless he comes into the conditions. The painter, the sculptor, the composer, the epic rhapsodist, the orator, all partake one desire, namely, to express themselves symmetrically and abundantly, not dwarfishly and fragmentarily. They found or put themselves in certain conditions, as, the painter and sculptor before some impressive human figures; the orator, into the assembly of the people; and the others, in such scenes as each has found exciting to his intellect; and each presently feels the new desire. He hears a voice, he sees a beckoning. Then he is apprised, with wonder, what herds of dæmons hem him in. He can no more rest; he says, with the old painter, "By God, it is in me, and must go forth of me." He pursues a beauty, half seen, which flies

7. The home of the Delphic oracle, or prophetess, in Greece. Troy is the site of the Trojan War in Asia Minor.
8. "Boasts" is the common correction for the 1st edition's "boats." "Logrolling" seems to be used in the metaphorical sense of exchanging political favors. "Stumps" refers to the practice political orators had of addressing audiences from any makeshift platform, even a tree stump. Emerson is contrasting the optimism of the states as they sold bonds here and abroad with their seemingly blithe repudiation of states' debts when grandiose projects fell through.
9. A commonly used set compiled by Alexander Chalmers (1759–1834), Scottish journalist and biographer.

before him. The poet pours out verses in every solitude. Most of the things he says are conventional, no doubt; but by and by he says something which is original and beautiful. That charms him. He would say nothing else but such things. In our way of talking, we say, "That is yours, this is mine;' but the poet knows well that it is not his; that it is as strange and beautiful to him as to you; he would fain hear the like eloquence at length. Once having tasted this immortal ichor,[1] he cannot have enough of it, and, as an admirable creative power exists in these intellections, it is of the last importance that these things get spoken. What a little of all we know is said! What drops of all the sea of our science are bailed up! and by what accident it is that these are exposed, when so many secrets sleep in nature! Hence the necessity of speech and song; hence these throbs and heart-beatings in the orator, at the door of the assembly, to the end, namely, that thought may be ejaculated as Logos, or Word.

Doubt not, O Poet, but persist. Say, 'It is in me, and shall out.' Stand there, baulked and dumb, stuttering and stammering, hissed and hooted, stand and strive, until, at last, rage draw out of thee that *dream*-power which every night shows thee is thine own; a power transcending all limit and privacy, and by virtue of which a man is the conductor of the whole river of electricity. Nothing walks, or creeps, or grows, or exists, which must not in turn arise and walk before him as exponent of his meaning. Comes he to that power, his genius is no longer exhaustible. All the creatures, by pairs and by tribes, pour into his mind as into a Noah's ark, to come forth again to people a new world. This is like the stock of air for our respiration, or for the combustion of our fireplace, not a measure of gallons, but the entire atmosphere if wanted. And therefore the rich poets, as Homer, Chaucer, Shakspeare, and Raphael, have obviously no limits to their works, except the limits of their lifetime, and resemble a mirror carried through the street, ready to render an image of every created thing.

O poet! a new nobility is conferred in groves and pastures, and not in castles, or by the sword-blade, any longer. The conditions are hard, but equal. Thou shalt leave the world, and know the muse only. Thou shalt not know any longer the times, customs, graces, politics, or opinions of men, but shalt take all from the muse. For the time of towns is tolled from the world by funereal chimes, but in nature the universal hours are counted by succeeding tribes of animals and plants, and by growth of joy on joy. God wills also that thou abdicate a manifold and duplex life, and that thou be content that others speak for thee. Others shall be thy gentlemen, and shall represent all courtesy and worldly life for thee; others shall do the great and resounding actions also. Thou shalt lie close hid with nature, and canst not be afforded to the Capitol or the Exchange.[2] The world is full of renunciations and apprenticeships, and this is thine: thou must pass for a fool and a churl for a long season. This is the screen and sheath in which Pan[3] has protected his well-beloved flower, and thou shalt be known only to thine own, and they shall console thee with tenderest love. And thou shalt not be able to rehearse the names of thy friends in thy verse, for an old shame before the holy ideal. And this is the reward: that the ideal shall be real to thee; and the impressions of the actual world shall fall like summer rain, copious, but not troublesome, to thy invulnerable

1. In Greek myth, blood of the gods, but Emerson may mean nectar, the drink of the gods.
2. Stock exchange.

3. In Greek myth, the god of woods and fields, represented with goat's legs, horns, and ears.

essence. Thou shalt have the whole land for thy park and manor, the sea for thy bath and navigation, without tax and without envy; the woods and the rivers thou shalt own; and thou shalt possess that wherein others are only tenants and boarders. Thou true land-lord! sea-lord! air-lord! Wherever snow falls, or water flows, or birds fly, wherever day and night meet in twilight, wherever the blue heaven is hung by clouds, or sown with stars, wherever are forms with transparent boundaries, wherever are outlets into celestial space, wherever is danger, and awe, and love, there is Beauty, plenteous as rain, shed for thee, and though thou shouldest walk the world over, thou shalt not be able to find a condition inopportune or ignoble.

1844

Experience[1]

> The lords of life, the lords of life,—
> I saw them pass,
> In their own guise,
> Like and unlike,
> Portly and grim,
> Use and Surprise,
> Surface and Dream,
> Succession swift, and spectral Wrong,
> Temperament without a tongue,
> And the inventor of the game
> Omnipresent without name;—
> Some to see, some to be guessed,
> They marched from east to west:
> Little man, least of all,
> Among the legs of his guardians tall,
> Walked about with puzzled look:—
> Him by the hand dear nature took;
> Dearest nature, strong and kind,
> Whispered, 'Darling, never mind!
> Tomorrow they will wear another face,
> The founder thou! these are thy race!"

Where do we find ourselves? In a series of which we do not know the extremes, and believe that it has none. We wake and find ourselves on a stair; there are stairs below us, which we seem to have ascended; there are stairs above us, many a one, which go upward and out of sight. But the Genius[2] which, according to the old belief, stands at the door by which we enter, and gives us the lethe[3] to drink, that we may tell no tales, mixed the cup too strongly, and we cannot shake off the lethargy now at noonday. Sleep lingers all our lifetime about our eyes; as night hovers all day in the boughs of the fir-tree. All things swim and glitter. Our life is not so much threatened as our perception. Ghostlike we glide through nature, and should not know our place

1. First published in *Essays, Second Series* (1844), *Experience* emerged in 1843 and 1844 during Emerson's broodings following the death of his young son Waldo in January 1842, rather than being derived from a lecture, as most of his essays were. David W. Hill has shown that some of the more optimistic passages derive from journal entries made after Waldo's death, while some of the darker passages were first drafted before 1842, so no simple autobiographical reading is tenable.

Still, it is the intensity of concentration following Waldo's death and the new and ruthless determination to tell the truth as he saw it that give the essay a strong claim to being Emerson's masterpiece. The epigraph is by Emerson.
2. Governing or guardian spirit.
3. Water from the river of forgetfulness in the underworld of Greek myth.

again. Did our birth fall in some fit of indigence and frugality in nature, that she was so sparing of her fire and so liberal of her earth, that it appears to us that we lack the affirmative principle, and though we have health and reason, yet we have no superfluity of spirit for new creation? We have enough to live and bring the year about, but not an ounce to impart or to invest. Ah that our Genius were a little more of a genius! We are like millers on the lower levels of a stream, when the factories above them have exhausted the water. We too fancy that the upper people must have raised their dams.

If any of us knew what we were doing, or where we are going, then when we think we best know! We do not know today whether we are busy or idle. In times when we thought ourselves indolent, we have afterwards discovered, that much was accomplished, and much was begun in us. All our days are so unprofitable while they pass, that 'tis wonderful where or when we ever got anything of this which we call wisdom, poetry, virtue. We never got it on any dated calendar day. Some heavenly days must have been intercalated some-where, like those that Hermes won with dice of the Moon, that Osiris[4] might be born. It is said, all martyrdoms looked mean when they were suffered. Every ship is a romantic object, except that we sail in. Embark, and the romance quits our vessel, and hangs on every other sail in the horizon. Our life looks trivial, and we shun to record it. Men seem to have learned of the horizon the art of perpetual retreating and reference. 'Yonder uplands are rich pasturage, and my neighbor has fertile meadow, but my field,' says the queru-lous farmer, 'only holds the world together.' I quote another man's saying; unluckily, that other withdraws himself in the same way, and quotes me. 'Tis the trick of nature thus to degrade today; a good deal of buzz, and somewhere a result slipped magically in. Every roof is agreeable to the eye, until it is lifted; then we find tragedy and moaning women, and hard-eyed husbands, and del-uges of lethe, and the men ask, 'What's the news?' as if the old were so bad. How many individuals can we count in society? how many actions? how many opinions? So much of our time is preparation, so much is routine, and so much retrospect, that the pith of each man's genius contracts itself to a very few hours. The history of literature—take the net result of Tiraboschi, Warton, or Schlegel,[5]—is a sum of very few ideas, and of very few original tales,—all the rest being variation of these. So in this great society wide lying around us, a critical analysis would find very few spontaneous actions. It is almost all custom and gross sense. There are even few opinions, and these seem organic in the speakers, and do not disturb the universal necessity.

What opium is instilled into all disaster! It shows formidable as we approach it, but there is at last no rough rasping friction, but the most slippery sliding surfaces. We fall soft on a thought. *Ate Dea*[6] is gentle,

> "Over men's heads walking aloft,
> With tender feet treading so soft."[7]

People grieve and bemoan themselves, but it is not half so bad with them as they say. There are moods in which we court suffering, in the hope that here,

---

4. Chief Egyptian god. The following story is told in Plutarch's *Morals*: the sun god forbade his wife, Rhea, to give birth on any day of the year, but Hermes won five new days from the moon, during which Osiris could be born.
5. Either Friedrich von Schlegel (1772–1829) or his brother August Wilhelm von Schlegel (1767–1845), historians of European literature. Girolamo Tiraboschi (1731–1794), historian of Italian literature. Thomas Warton (1728–1790), historian of British literature.
6. The goddess of mischief or fatal recklessness.
7. *The Iliad*, book 19.

at least, we shall find reality, sharp peaks and edges of truth. But it turns out to be scene-painting and counterfeit. The only thing grief has taught me, is to know how shallow it is. That, like all the rest, plays about the surface, and never introduces me into the reality, for contact with which, we would even pay the costly price of sons and lovers. Was it Boscovich[8] who found out that bodies never come in contact? Well, souls never touch their objects. An innavigable sea washes with silent waves between us and the things we aim at and converse with. Grief too will make us idealists. In the death of my son, now more than two years ago, I seem to have lost a beautiful estate,—no more. I cannot get it nearer to me. If tomorrow I should be informed of the bankruptcy of my principal debtors, the loss of my property would be a great inconvenience to me, perhaps, for many years; but it would leave me as it found me,—neither better nor worse. So is it with this calamity: it does not touch me: some thing which I fancied was a part of me, which could not be torn away without tearing me, nor enlarged without enriching me, falls off from me, and leaves no scar. It was caducous.[9] I grieve that grief can teach me nothing, nor carry me one step into real nature. The Indian who was laid under a curse, that the wind should not blow on him, nor water flow to him, nor fire burn him, is a type of us all. The dearest events are summer-rain, and we the Para coats[1] that shed every drop. Nothing is left us now but death. We look to that with a grim satisfaction, saying, there at least is reality that will not dodge us.

I take this evanescence and lubricity of all objects, which lets them slip through our fingers then when we clutch hardest, to be the most unhandsome part of our condition. Nature does not like to be observed, and likes that we should be her fools and playmates. We may have the sphere for our cricket-ball, but not a berry for our philosophy. Direct strokes she never gave us power to make; all our blows glance, all our hits are accidents. Our relations to each other are oblique and casual.

Dream delivers us to dream, and there is no end to illusion. Life is a train of moods like a string of beads, and, as we pass through them, they prove to be many-colored lenses which paint the world their own hue, and each shows only what lies in its focus. From the mountain you see the mountain. We animate what we can, and we see only what we animate. Nature and books belong to the eyes that see them. It depends on the mood of the man, whether he shall see the sunset or the fine poem. There are always sunsets, and there is always genius; but only a few hours so serene that we can relish nature or criticism. The more or less depends on structure or temperament. Temperament is the iron wire on which the beads are strung. Of what use is fortune or talent to a cold and defective nature? Who cares what sensibility or discrimination a man has at some time shown, if he falls asleep in his chair? or if he laugh and giggle? or if he apologize? or is affected with egotism? or thinks of his dollar? or cannot go by food? or has gotten a child in his boyhood? Of what use is genius, if the organ is too convex or too concave, and cannot find a focal distance within the actual horizon of human life? Of what use, if the brain is too cold or too hot, and the man does not care enough for results, to

8. Ruggiero Giuseppe Boscovich (1711–1787), Italian physicist who advanced a molecular theory of matter.

9. Not long lasting.
1. Rubber overcoats.

stimulate him to experiment, and hold him up in it? or if the web is too finely woven, too irritable by pleasure and pain, so that life stagnates from too much reception, without due outlet? Of what use to make heroic vows of amendment, if the same old law-breaker is to keep them? What cheer can the religious sentiment yield, when that is suspected to be secretly dependent on the seasons of the year, and the state of the blood? I knew a witty physician who found theology in the biliary duct, and used to affirm that if there was disease in the liver, the man became a Calvinist, and if that organ was sound, he became a Unitarian. [2] Very mortifying is the reluctant experience that some unfriendly excess or imbecility neutralizes the promise of genius. We see young men who owe us a new world, so readily and lavishly they promise, but they never acquit the debt; they die young and dodge the account: or if they live, they lose themselves in the crowd.

Temperament also enters fully into the system of illusions, and shuts us in a prison of glass which we cannot see. There is an optical illusion about every person we meet. In truth, they are all creatures of given temperament, which will appear in a given character, whose boundaries they will never pass: but we look at them, they seem alive, and we presume there is impulse in them. In the moment it seems impulse; in the year, in the lifetime, it turns out to be a certain uniform tune which the revolving barrel of the music-box must play. Men resist the conclusion in the morning, but adopt it as the evening wears on, that temper prevails over everything of time, place, and condition, and is inconsumable in the flames of religion. Some modifications the moral sentiment avails to impose, but the individual texture holds its dominion, if not to bias the moral judgments, yet to fix the measure of activity and of enjoyment.

I thus express the law as it is read from the platform of ordinary life, but must not leave it without noticing the capital exception. For temperament is a power which no man willingly hears any one praise but himself. On the platform of physics, we cannot resist the contracting influences of so-called science. Temperament puts all divinity to rout. I know the mental proclivity of physicians. I hear the chuckle of the phrenologists. [3] Theoretic kidnappers and slave-drivers, they esteem each man the victim of another, who winds him round his finger by knowing the law of his being, and by such cheap signboards as the color of his beard, or the slope of his occiput, reads the inventory of his fortunes and character. The grossest ignorance does not disgust like this impudent knowingness. The physicians say, they are not materialists; but they are:—Spirit is matter reduced to an extreme thinness: O so thin!— But the definition of *spiritual* should be, *that which is its own evidence.* What notions do they attach to love! what to religion! One would not willingly pronounce these words in their hearing, and give them the occasion to profane them. I saw a gracious gentleman who adapts his conversation to the form of the head of the man he talks with! I had fancied that the value of life lay in its inscrutable possibilities; in the fact that I never know, in addressing myself to a new individual, what may befall me. I carry the keys of my castle in my hand, ready to throw them at the feet of my lord, whenever and in what disguise soever he shall appear. I know he is in the neighborhood hidden

---

2. I.e., the Calvinistic sense of Original Sin is seen as an intellectual manifestation of a bodily disease; the Unitarian view of humanity has none of the Calvinistic preoccupation with eternal damnation for all but the select few, the elect.

3. Pseudoscientists who claimed to read character by bumps on the skull.

among vagabonds. Shall I preclude my future, by taking a high seat, and kindly adapting my conversation to the shape of heads? When I come to that, the doctors shall buy me for a cent.——'But, sir, medical history; the report to the Institute; the proven facts!'—I distrust the facts and the inferences. Temperament is the veto or limitation-power in the constitution, very justly applied to restrain an opposite excess in the constitution, but absurdly offered as a bar to original equity. When virtue is in presence, all subordinate powers sleep. On its own level, or in view of nature, temperament is final. I see not, if one be once caught in this trap of so-called sciences, any escape for the man from the links of the chain of physical necessity. Given such an embryo, such a history must follow. On this platform, one lives in a sty of sensualism, and would soon come to suicide. But it is impossible that the creative power should exclude itself. Into every intelligence there is a door which is never closed, through which the creator passes. The intellect, seeker of absolute truth, or the heart, lover of absolute good, intervenes for our succor, and at one whisper of these high powers, we awake from ineffectual struggles with this nightmare. We hurl it into its own hell, and cannot again contract ourselves to so base a state.

The secret of the illusoriness is in the necessity of a succession of moods or objects. Gladly we would anchor, but the anchorage is quicksand. This onward trick of nature is too strong for us: *Pero si muove.*[4] When, at night, I look at the moon and stars, I seem stationary, and they to hurry. Our love of the real draws us to permanence, but health of body consists in circulation, and sanity of mind in variety or facility of association. We need change of objects. Dedication to one thought is quickly odious. We house with the insane, and must humor them; then conversation dies out. Once I took such delight in Montaigne, that I thought I should not need any other book; before that, in Shakspeare; then in Plutarch; then in Plotinus; at one time in Bacon; afterwards in Goethe; even in Bettine;[5] but now I turn the pages of either of them languidly, whilst I still cherish their genius. So with pictures; each will bear an emphasis of attention once, which it cannot retain, though we fain would continue to be pleased in that manner. How strongly I have felt of pictures, that when you have seen one well, you must take your leave of it; you shall never see it again. I have had good lessons from pictures, which I have since seen without emotion or remark. A deduction must be made from the opinion, which even the wise express of a new book or occurrence. Their opinion gives me tidings of their mood, and some vague guess at the new fact, but is nowise to be trusted as the lasting relation between that intellect and that thing. The child asks, 'Mamma, why don't I like the story as well as when you told it me yesterday?' Alas, child, it is even so with the oldest cherubim of knowledge. But will it answer thy question to say, Because thou wert born to a whole, and this story is a particular? The reason of the pain this discovery

---

4. It moves, all the same (Italian); Galileo's muttered protest after the Inquisition (tribunal of the Roman Catholic church charged with suppressing heresy) had forced him to retract the idea that the earth revolves around the sun.

5. Elizabeth ("Bettine") von Arnim (1785–1859), whose purported correspondence with Goethe was published in 1835. Michel de Montaigne (1533–1592), French essayist. Plutarch (46?–120?),

Greek biographer of famous Greeks and Romans. Plotinus (205?–270?), Egyptian-born Roman neoplatonist philosopher. (Neoplatonism is a mystic religious system, combining features of Platonic and other Greek philosophies with features of Judaism and Christianity.) Sir Francis Bacon (1561–1626), English essayist, philosopher, and statesman. Johann Wolfgang von Goethe (1749–1832), German poet and dramatist.

causes us (and we make it late in respect to works of art and intellect), is the plaint of tragedy which murmurs from it in regard to persons, to friendship and love.

That immobility and absence of elasticity which we find in the arts, we find with more pain in the artist. There is no power of expansion in men. Our friends early appear to us as representatives of certain ideas, which they never pass or exceed. They stand on the brink of the ocean of thought and power, but they never take the single step that would bring them there. A man is like a bit of Labrador spar,[6] which has no lustre as you turn it in your hand, until you come to a particular angle; then it shows deep and beautiful colors. There is no adaptation or universal applicability in men, but each has his special talent, and the mastery of successful men consists in adroitly keeping themselves where and when that turn shall be oftenest to be practised. We do what we must, and call it by the best names we can, and would fain have the praise of having intended the result which ensues. I cannot recall any form of man who is not superfluous sometimes. But is not this pitiful? Life is not worth the taking, to do tricks in.

Of course, it needs the whole society, to give the symmetry we seek. The parti-colored wheel must revolve very fast to appear white. Something is learned too by conversing with so much folly and defect. In fine, whoever loses, we are always of the gaining party. Divinity is behind our failures and follies also. The plays of children are nonsense, but very educative nonsense. So it is with the largest and solemnest things, with commerce, government, church, marriage, and so with the history of every man's bread, and the ways by which he is to come by it. Like a bird which alights nowhere, but hops perpetually from bough to bough, is the Power which abides in no man and in no woman, but for a moment speaks from this one, and for another moment from that one.

But what help from these fineries or pedantries? What help from thought? Life is not dialectics. We, I think, in these times, have had lessons enough of the futility of criticism. Our young people have thought and written much on labor and reform, and for all that they have written, neither the world nor themselves have got on a step. Intellectual tasting of life will not supersede muscular activity. If a man should consider the nicety of the passage of a piece of bread down his throat, he would starve. At Education-Farm,[7] the noblest theory of life sat on the noblest figures of young men and maidens, quite powerless and melancholy. It would not rake or pitch a ton of hay; it would not rub down a horse; and the men and maidens it left pale and hungry. A political orator wittily compared our party promises to western roads, which opened stately enough, with planted trees on either side, to tempt the traveller, but soon became narrow and narrower, and ended in a squirrel-track, and ran up a tree. So does culture with us; it ends in head-ache. Unspeakably sad and barren does life look to those, who a few months ago were dazzled with the splendor of the promise of the times. "There is now no longer any right course of action, nor any self-devotion left among the Iranis."[8] Objections and criticism we have had our fill of. There are objections to every course of life and

6. Labradorite, crystalline rock.
7. Brook Farm, the Transcendentalist commune at West Roxbury, Massachusetts.

8. From the Persian *Desatir*, ancient scriptures credited to Zoroaster (6th century B.C.), founder of the Parsee religion.

action, and the practical wisdom infers an indifferency, from the omnipresence of objection. The whole frame of things preaches indifferency. Do not
craze yourself with thinking, but go about your business anywhere. Life is not
intellectual or critical, but sturdy. Its chief good is for well-mixed people who
can enjoy what they find, without question. Nature hates peeping and our
mothers speak her very sense when they say, "Children, eat your victuals, and
say no more of it." To fill the hour,—that is happiness; to fill the hour, and
leave no crevice for a repentance or an approval. We live amid surfaces, and
the true art of life is to skate well on them. Under the oldest mouldiest conventions, a man of native force prospers just as well as in the newest world, and
that by skill of handling and treatment. He can take hold anywhere. Life itself
is a mixture of power and form, and will not bear the least excess of either. To
finish the moment, to find the journey's end in every step of the road, to live
the greatest number of good hours, is wisdom. It is not the part of men, but of
fanatics, or of mathematicians, if you will, to say, that, the shortness of life
considered, it is not worth caring whether for so short a duration we were
sprawling in want, or sitting high. Since our office is with moments, let us
husband them. Five minutes of today are worth as much to me, as five
minutes in the next millennium. Let us be poised, and wise, and our own,
today. Let us treat the men and women well: treat them as if they were real:
perhaps they are. Men live in their fancy, like drunkards whose hands are too
soft and tremulous for successful labor. It is a tempest of fancies, and the only
ballast I know, is a respect to the present hour. Without any shadow of doubt
amidst this vertigo of shows and politics, I settle myself ever the firmer in the
creed, that we should not postpone and refer and wish, but do broad justice
where we are, by whomsoever we deal with, accepting our actual companions
and circumstances, however humble or odious, as the mystic officials to whom
the universe has delegated its whole pleasure for us. If these are mean and
malignant, their contentment, which is the last victory of justice, is a more
satisfying echo to the heart, than the voice of poets and the casual sympathy
of admirable persons. I think that however a thoughtful man may suffer from
the defects and absurdities of his company, he cannot without affectation deny
to any set of men and women, a sensibility to extraordinary merit. The coarse
and frivolous have an instinct of superiority, if they have not a sympathy, and
honor it in their blind capricious way with sincere homage.

The fine young people despise life, but in me, and in such as with me are
free from dyspepsia, and to whom a day is a sound and solid good, it is a great
excess of politeness to look scornful and to cry for company. I am grown by
sympathy a little eager and sentimental, but leave me alone, and I should
relish every hour and what it brought me, the potluck of the day, as heartily
as the oldest gossip in the bar-room. I am thankful for small mercies. I compared notes with one of my friends who expects everything of the universe,
and is disappointed when anything is less than the best, and I found that I
begin at the other extreme, expecting nothing, and am always full of thanks
for moderate goods. I accept the clangor and jangle of contrary tendencies. I
find my account in sots and bores also. They give a reality to the circumjacent
picture, which such a vanishing meteorous appearance can ill spare. In the
morning I awake, and find the old world, wife, babes, and mother, Concord
and Boston, the dear old spiritual world, and even the dear old devil not far
off. If we will take the good we find, asking no questions, we shall have heap-

ing measures. The great gifts are not got by analysis. Everything good is on the highway. The middle region of our being is the temperate zone. We may climb into the thin and cold realm of pure geometry and lifeless science, or sink into that of sensation. Between these extremes is the equator of life, of thought, of spirit, of poetry,—a narrow belt. Moreover, in popular experience, everything good is on the highway. A collector peeps into all the picture-shops of Europe, for a landscape of Poussin, a crayon-sketch of Salvator; but the Transfiguration, the Last Judgment, the Communion of St. Jerome, and what are as transcendent as these, are on the walls of the Vatican, the Uffizii, or the Louvre, where every footman may see them;[9] to say nothing of nature's pictures in every street, of sunsets and sunrises every day, and the sculpture of the human body never absent. A collector recently bought at public auction, in London, for one hundred and fifty-seven guineas,[1] an autograph of Shakspeare: but for nothing a school-boy can read Hamlet, and can detect secrets of highest concernment yet unpublished therein. I think I will never read any but the commonest books,—the Bible, Homer, Dante, Shakspeare, and Milton. Then we are impatient of so public a life and planet, and run hither and thither for nooks and secrets. The imagination delights in the woodcraft of Indians, trappers, and bee-hunters. We fancy that we are strangers, and not so intimately domesticated in the planet as the wild man, and the wild beast and bird. But the exclusion reaches them also; reaches the climbing, flying, gliding, feathered and four-footed man. Fox and woodchuck, hawk and snipe, and bittern, when nearly seen, have no more root in the deep world than man, and are just such superficial tenants of the globe. Then the new molecular philosophy shows astronomical interspaces betwixt atom and atom, shows that the world is all outside: it has no inside.

The mid-world is best. Nature, as we know her, is no saint. The lights of the church, the ascetics, Gentoos and Grahamites,[2] she does not distinguish by any favor. She comes eating and drinking and sinning. Her darlings, the great, the strong, the beautiful, are not children of our law, do not come out of the Sunday School, nor weigh their food, nor punctually keep the commandments. If we will be strong with her strength, we must not harbor such disconsolate consciences, borrowed too from the consciences of other nations. We must set up the strong present tense against all the rumors of wrath, past or to come. So many things are unsettled which it is of the first importance to settle,—and, pending their settlement, we will do as we do. Whilst the debate goes forward on the equity of commerce, and will not be closed for a century or two, New and Old England may keep shop. Law of copyright and international copyright[3] is to be discussed, and, in the interim, we will sell our books for the most we can. Expediency of literature, reason of literature, lawfulness of writing down a thought, is questioned; much is to say on both sides, and, while the fight waxes hot, thou, dearest scholar, stick to thy foolish task, add a line every hour, and between whiles add a line. Right

---

9. I.e., the collector hunts for minor paintings in out-of-the-way shops while the great paintings are in museums where anyone may see them. Nicolas Poussin (1594–1665), French painter. Salvator Rosa (1615–1673), Italian painter of wild landscapes. The *Transfiguration* is that by Raphael, in Rome. The *Last Judgment* is Michelangelo's, in Florence. The *Communion of St. Jerome* is that by Il Domenichino in Paris.

1. British gold coin worth one shilling more than a pound.
2. Contemporary food-faddists; from Sylvester Graham (1794–1851), vegetarian whose efforts at food reform are memorialized in the graham cracker. "Gentoos": Hindu sectarians.
3. Not passed by the American Congress until 1891.

to hold land, right of property, is disputed, and the conventions convene, and before the vote is taken, dig away in your garden, and spend your earnings as a waif or godsend to all serene and beautiful purposes. Life itself is a bubble and a skepticism, and a sleep within a sleep. Grant it, and as much more as they will—but thou, God's darling! heed thy private dream: thou wilt not be missed in the scorning and skepticism: there are enough of them: stay there in thy closet, and toil, until the rest are agreed what to do about it. Thy sickness, they say, and thy puny habit, require that thou do this or avoid that, but know that thy life is a flitting state, a tent for a night, and do thou, sick or well, finish that stint. Thou art sick, but shalt not be worse, and the universe, which holds thee dear, shall be the better.

Human life is made up of the two elements, power and form, and the proportion must be invariably kept, if we would have it sweet and sound. Each of these elements in excess makes a mischief as hurtful as its defect. Everything runs to excess: every good quality is noxious, if unmixed, and, to carry the danger to the edge of ruin, nature causes each man's peculiarity to super-abound. Here, among the farms, we adduce the scholars as examples of this treachery. They are nature's victims of expression. You who see the artist, the orator, the poet, too near, and find their life no more excellent than that of mechanics or farmers, and themselves victims of partiality, very hollow and haggard, and pronounce them failures,—not heroes, but quacks,—conclude very reasonably, that these arts are not for man, but are disease. Yet nature will not bear you out. Irresistible nature made men such, and makes legions more of such, every day. You love the boy reading in a book, gazing at a drawing, or a cast: yet what are these millions who read and behold, but incipient writers and sculptors? Add a little more of that quality which now reads and sees, and they will seize the pen and chisel. And if one remembers how innocently he began to be an artist, he perceives that nature joined with his enemy. A man is a golden impossibility. The line he must walk is a hair's breadth. The wise through excess of wisdom is made a fool.

How easily, if fate would suffer it, we might keep forever these beautiful limits, and adjust ourselves, once for all, to the perfect calculation of the kingdom of known cause and effect. In the street and in the newspapers, life appears so plain a business, that manly resolution and adherence to the multiplication-table through all weathers, will insure success. But ah! presently comes a day, or is it only a half-hour, with its angel-whispering,—which discomfits the conclusions of nations and of years! Tomorrow again, everything looks real and angular, the habitual standards are reinstated, common sense is as rare as genius,—is the basis of genius, and experience is hands and feet to every enterprise;—and yet, he who should do his business on this understanding, would be quickly bankrupt. Power keeps quite another road than the turnpikes of choice and will, namely, the subterranean and invisible tunnels and channels of life. It is ridiculous that we are diplomatists, and doctors, and considerate people: there are no dupes like these. Life is a series of surprises, and would not be worth taking or keeping, if it were not. God delights to isolate us every day, and hide from us the past and the future. We would look about us, but with grand politeness he draws down before us an impenetrable screen of purest sky, and another behind us of purest sky. 'You will not remember,' he seems to say, 'and you will not expect.' All good conversation, manners, and action, come from a spontaneity which forgets usages, and makes the moment great. Nature hates calculators; her methods are saltatory and impulsive. Man lives by pulses; our organic movements are such; and the chemical and ethereal agents are undulatory and alternate; and the mind goes antagonizing on, and never prospers but by fits. We thrive by casualties. Our chief experiences have been casual. The most attractive class of people are those who are powerful obliquely, and not by the direct stroke: men of genius, but not yet accredited: one gets the cheer of their light, without paying too great a tax. Theirs is the beauty of the bird, or the morning light, and not of art. In the thought of genius there is always a surprise; and the moral sentiment is well called "the newness," for it is never other; as new to the oldest intelligence as to the young child.—"the kingdom that cometh without observation."[4] In like manner, for practical success, there must not be too much design. A man will not be observed in doing that which he can do best. There is a certain magic about his properest action, which stupefies your powers of observation, so that though it is done before you, you wist not of it. The art of life has a pudency, and will not be exposed. Every man is an impossibility, until he is born; every thing impossible, until we see a success. The ardors of piety agree at last with the coldest skepticism,—that nothing is of us or our works,—that all is of God. Nature will not spare us the smallest leaf of laurel. All writing comes by the grace of God, and all doing and having. I would gladly be moral, and keep due metes and bounds, which I dearly love, and allow the most to the will of man, but I have set my heart on honesty in this chapter, and I can see nothing at last, in success or failure, than more or less of vital force supplied from the Eternal. The results of life are uncalculated and uncalculable. The years teach much which the days never know. The persons who compose our company, converse, and come and go, and design and execute many things, and somewhat comes of it all, but an unlooked for result. The individual is always mistaken. He designed many things, and drew in other persons as coadjutors, quarrelled with some or all, blundered much, and something is done; all are a little advanced, but the individual is always mistaken. It turns out somewhat new, and very unlike what he promised himself.

The ancients, stuck with this irreducibleness of the elements of human life to calculation, exalted Chance into a divinity, but that is to stay too long at the spark,—which glitters truly at one point,—but the universe is warm with the latency of the same fire. The miracle of life which will not be expounded, but will remain a miracle, introduces a new element. In the growth of the embryo, Sir Everard Home,[5] I think, noticed that the evolution was not from one central point, but co-active from three or more points. Life has no memory. That which proceeds in succession might be remembered, but that which is co-existent, or ejaculated from a deeper cause, as yet far from being conscious, knows not its own tendency. So it is with us, now skeptical, or without unity, because immersed in forms and effects all seeming to be of equal yet hostile value, and now religious, whilst in the reception of spiritual law. Bear with these distractions, with this coetaneous growth of the parts: they will one day be *members*, and obey one will. On that one will, on that secret cause,

4. Luke 17.20.   5. Scottish surgeon (1756–1832).

they nail our attention and hope. Life is hereby melted into an expectation or a religion. Underneath the inharmonious and trivial particulars, is a musical perfection, the Ideal journeying always with us, the heaven without rent or seam. Do but observe the mode of our illumination. When I converse with a profound mind, or if at any time being alone I have good thoughts, I do not at once arrive at satisfactions, as when, being thirsty, I drink water, or go to the fire, being cold: no! but I am at first apprised of my vicinity to a new and excellent region of life. By persisting to read or to think, this region gives further sign of itself, as it were in flashes of light, in sudden discoveries of its profound beauty and repose, as if the clouds that covered it parted at intervals, and showed the approaching traveller the inland mountains, with the tranquil eternal meadows spread at their base, whereon flocks graze, and shepherds pipe and dance. But every insight from this realm of thought is felt as initial, and promises a sequel. I do not make it; I arrive there, and behold what was there already. I make! O no! I clap my hands in infantine joy and amazement, before the first opening to me of this august magnificence, old with the love and homage of innumerable ages, young with the life of life, the sunbright Mecca of the desert. And what a future it opens! I feel a new heart beating with the love of the new beauty. I am ready to die out of nature, and be born again into this new yet unapproachable America I have found in the West.

> "Since neither now nor yesterday began
> These thoughts, which have been ever, nor yet can
> A man be found who their first entrance knew."[6]

If I have described life as a flux of moods, I must now add, that there is that in us which changes not, and which ranks all sensations and states of mind. The consciousness in each man is a sliding scale, which identifies him now with the First Cause, and now with the flesh of his body; life above life, in infinite degrees. The sentiment from which it sprung determines the dignity of any deed, and the question ever is, not, what you have done or forborne, but, at whose command you have done or forborne it.

Fortune, Minerva,[7] Muse, Holy Ghost,—these are quaint names, too narrow to cover this unbounded substance. The baffled intellect must still kneel before this cause, which refuses to be named—ineffable cause, which every fine genius has essayed to represent by some emphatic symbol, as, Thales by water, Anaximenes by air, Anaxagoras by (Noῦς) thought, Zoroaster[8] by fire, Jesus and the moderns by love: and the metaphor of each has become a national religion. The Chinese Mencius[9] has not been the least successful in his generalization. "I fully understand language," he said, "and nourish well my vast-flowing vigor."—"I beg to ask what you call vast-flowing vigor?"—said his companion. "The explanation," replied Mencius, "is difficult. This vigor is supremely great, and in the highest degree unbending. Nourish it correctly, and do it no injury, and it will fill up the vacancy between heaven and earth. This vigor accords with and assists justice and reason, and leaves no hunger."—In our more correct writing, we give to this generalization the name of Being, and thereby confess that we have arrived as far as we can go. Suffice it

---

6. A free translation of the conclusion of one of the heroine's speeches in Sophocles' *Antigone* (lines 456–57).
7. Roman goddess of wisdom.
8. The 6th-century Persian founder of the fire worship of the Parsees. Thales (7th century B.C.), Anaximenes (6th century B.C.), and Anaxagoras (5th century B.C.), Greek philosophers.
9. Meng-tsu (3rd century B.C.), compiler of doctrines of Confucianism.

for the joy of the universe, that we have not arrived at a wall, but at interminable oceans. Our life seems not present, so much as prospective; not for the affairs on which it is wasted, but as a hint of this vast-flowing vigor. Most of life seems to be mere advertisement of faculty: information is given us not to sell ourselves cheap; that we are very great. So, in particulars, our greatness is always in a tendency or direction, not in an action. It is for us to believe in the rule, not in the exception. The noble are thus known from the ignoble. So in accepting the leading of the sentiments, it is not what we believe concerning the immortality of the soul, or the like, but *the universal impulse to believe*, that is the material circumstance, and is the principal fact in the history of the globe. Shall we describe this cause as that which works directly? The spirit is not helpless or needful of mediate organs. It has plentiful powers and direct effects. I am explained without explaining, I am felt without acting, and where I am not. Therefore all just persons are satisfied with their own praise. They refuse to explain themselves, and are content that new actions should do them that office. They believe that we communicate without speech, and above speech, and that no right action of ours is quite unaffecting to our friends, at whatever distance; for the influence of action is not to be measured by miles. Why should I fret myself, because a circumstance has occurred, which hinders my presence where I was expected? If I am not at the meeting, my presence where I am, should be as useful to the commonwealth of friendship and wisdom, as would be my presence in that place. I exert the same quality of power in all places. Thus journeys the mighty Ideal before us; it never was known to fall into the rear. No man ever came to an experience which was satiating, but his good is tidings of a better. Onward and onward! In liberated moments, we know that a new picture of life and duty is already possible; the elements already exist in many minds around you, of a doctrine of life which shall transcend any written record we have. The new statement will comprise the skepticisms, as well as the faiths of society, and out of unbeliefs a creed shall be formed. For, skepticisms are not gratuitous or lawless, but are limitations of the affirmative statement, and the new philosophy must take them in, and make affirmations outside of them, just as much as it must include the oldest beliefs.

It is very unhappy, but too late to be helped, the discovery we have made, that we exist. That discovery is called the Fall of Man. Ever afterwards, we suspect our instruments. We have learned that we do not see directly, but mediately, and that we have no means of correcting these colored and distorting lenses which we are, or of computing the amount of their errors. Perhaps these subject-lenses have a creative power; perhaps there are no objects. Once we lived in what we saw; now, the rapaciousness of this new power, which threatens to absorb all things, engages us. Nature, art, persons, letters, religions,—objects, successively tumble in, and God is but one of its ideas. Nature and literature are subjective phenomena; every evil and every good thing is a shadow which we cast. The street is full of humiliations to the proud. As the fop contrived to dress his bailiffs in his livery, and make them wait on his guests at table, so the chagrins[1] which the bad heart gives off as bubbles, at once take form as ladies and gentlemen in the street, shopmen or barkeepers in hotels, and threaten or insult whatever is threatenable and insultable in us.

1. Ill-humored feelings.

'Tis the same with our idolatries. People forget that it is the eye which makes the horizon, and the rounding mind's eye which makes this or that man a type or representative of humanity with the name of hero or saint. Jesus the "providential man," is a good man on whom many people are agreed that these optical laws shall take effect. By love on one part, and by forbearance to press objection on the other part, it is for a time settled, that we will look at him in the centre of the horizon, and ascribe to him the properties that will attach to any man so seen. But the longest love or aversion has a speedy term. The great and crescive[2] self, rooted in absolute nature, supplants all relative existence, and ruins the kingdom of mortal friendship and love. Marriage (in what is called the spiritual world) is impossible, because of the inequality between every subject and every object. The subject is the receiver of God-head, and at every comparison must feel his being enhanced by that cryptic might. Though not in energy, yet by presence, this magazine[3] of substance cannot be otherwise than felt: nor can any force of intellect attribute to the object the proper deity which sleeps or wakes forever in every subject. Never can love make consciousness and ascription equal in force. There will be the same gulf between every me and thee, as between the original and the picture. The universe is the bride of the soul. All private sympathy is partial. Two human beings are like globes, which can touch only in a point, and, whilst they remain in contact, all other points of each of the spheres are inert; their turn must also come, and the longer a particular union lasts, the more energy of appetency[4] the parts not in union acquire.

Life will be imaged, but cannot be divided nor doubled. Any invasion of its unity would be chaos. The soul is not twin-born, but the only begotten, and though revealing itself as child in time, child in appearance, is of a fatal and universal power, admitting no co-life. Every day, every act betrays the ill-concealed deity. We believe in ourselves, as we do not believe in others. We permit all things to ourselves, and that which we call sin in others, is experiment for us. It is an instance of our faith in ourselves, that men never speak of crime as lightly as they think: or, every man thinks a latitude safe for himself, which is nowise to be indulged to another. The act looks very differently on the inside, and on the outside; in its quality, and in its consequences. Murder in the murderer is no such ruinous thought as poets and romancers will have it; it does not unsettle him, or fright him from his ordinary notice of trifles: it is an act quite easy to be contemplated, but in its sequel, it turns out to be a horrible jangle and confounding of all relations. Especially the crimes that spring from love, seem right and fair from the actor's point of view, but, when acted, are found destructive of society. No man at last believes that he can be lost, nor that the crime in him is as black as in the felon. Because the intellect qualifies in our own case the moral judgments. For there is no crime to the intellect. That is antinomian or hypernomian,[5] and judges law as well as fact. "It is worse than a crime, it is a blunder," said Napoleon, speaking the language of the intellect. To it, the world is a problem in mathematics or the science of quantity, and it leaves out praise and blame, and all weak emotions. All stealing is comparative. If you come to absolutes, pray who does not steal? Saints are sad, because they behold sin, (even when they speculate,) from the point of view of the conscience, and not of the intellect; a confusion of

2. Increasing.
3. Stored supply.
4. Strong impulse toward union.
5. Against or beyond the control of law.

thought. Sin seen from the thought, is a diminution or *less:* seen from the conscience or will, it is pravity or *bad*. The intellect names it shade, absence of light, and no essence. The conscience must feel it as essence, essential evil. This it is not: it has an objective existence, but no subjective.

Thus inevitably does the universe wear our color, and every object fall successively into the subject itself. The subject exists, the subject enlarges; all things sooner or later fall into place. As I am, so I see; use what language we will, we can never say anything but what we are; Hermes, Cadmus, Columbus, Newton, Buonaparte, are the mind's ministers.[6] Instead of feeling a poverty when we encounter a great man, let us treat the new comer like a travelling geologist, who passes through our estate, and shows us good slate, or limestone, or anthracite, in our brush pasture. The partial action of each strong mind in one direction, is a telescope for the objects on which it is pointed. But every other part of knowledge is to be pushed to the same extravagance, ere the soul attains her due sphericity. Do you see that kitten chasing so prettily her own tail? If you could look with her eyes, you might see her surrounded with hundreds of figures performing complex dramas, with tragic and comic issues, long conversations, many characters, many ups and downs of fate,—and meantime it is only puss and her tail. How long before our masquerade will end its noise of tamborines, laughter, and shouting, and we shall find it was a solitary performance?—A subject and an object,—it takes so much to make the galvanic circuit complete, but magnitude adds nothing. What imports it whether it is Kepler and the sphere; Columbus and America; a reader and his book; or puss with her tail?

It is true that all the muses and love and religion hate these developments, and will find a way to punish the chemist, who publishes in the parlor the secrets of the laboratory. And we cannot say too little of our constitutional necessity of seeing things under private aspects, or saturated with our humors. And yet is the God the native of these bleak rocks. That need makes in morals the capital virtue of self-trust. We must hold hard to this poverty, however scandalous, and by more vigorous self-recoveries, after the sallies of action, possess our axis more firmly. The life of truth is cold, and so far mournful; but it is not the slave of tears, contritions, and perturbations. It does not attempt another's work, nor adopt another's facts. It is a main lesson of wisdom to know your own from another's. I have learned that I cannot dispose of other people's facts; but I possess such a key to my own, as persuades me against all their denials, that they also have a key to theirs. A sympathetic person is placed in the dilemma of a swimmer among drowning men, who all catch at him, and if he give so much as a leg or a finger, they will drown him. They wish to be saved from the mischiefs of their vices, but not from their vices. Charity would be wasted on this poor waiting on the symptoms. A wise and hardy physician will say, *Come out of that*, as the first condition of advice.

In this our talking America, we are ruined by our good nature and listening on all sides. This compliance takes away the power of being greatly useful. A man should not be able to look other than directly and forthright. A preoccupied attention is the only answer to the importunate frivolity of other people:

6. I.e., great gods or men of legend and history are servants of the human mind because our subjectivity uses them to light up areas of our own being. Hermes is the Greek god of invention. Cadmus is the mythical inventor of the alphabet and creator of the Thebans by sowing dragon's teeth. Columbus sailed to America. Newton discovered the law of gravity. Napoleon Bonaparte in Emerson's childhood was the conquerer of much of Europe.

an attention, and to an aim which makes their wants frivolous. This is a divine answer, and leaves no appeal, and no hard thoughts. In Flaxman's drawing of the Eumenides of Æschylus, Orestes supplicates Apollo, whilst the Furies sleep on the threshold.[7] The face of the god expresses a shade of regret and compassion, but calm with the conviction of the irreconcilableness of the two spheres. He is born into other politics, into the eternal and beautiful. The man at his feet asks for his interest in turmoils of the earth, into which his nature cannot enter. And the Eumenides there lying express pictorially this disparity. The god is surcharged with his divine destiny.

Illusion, Temperament, Succession, Surface, Surprise, Reality, Subjectiveness,—these are threads on the loom of time, these are the lords of life. I dare not assume to give their order, but I name them as I find them in my way. I know better than to claim any completeness for my picture. I am a fragment, and this is a fragment of me. I can very confidently announce one or another law, which throws itself into relief and form, but I am too young yet by some ages to compile a code. I gossip for my hour concerning the eternal politics. I have seen many fair pictures not in vain. A wonderful time I have lived in. I am not the novice I was fourteen, nor yet seven years ago. Let who will ask, where is the fruit? I find a private fruit sufficient. This is a fruit,—that I should not ask for a rash effect from meditations, counsels, and the hiving of truths. I should feel it pitiful to demand a result on this town and county, an overt effect on the instant month and year. The effect is deep and secular[8] as the cause. It works on periods in which mortal lifetime is lost. All I know is reception; I am and I have: but I do not get, and when I have fancied I had gotten anything, I found I did not. I worship with wonder the great Fortune. My reception has been so large, that I am not annoyed by receiving this or that superabundantly. I say to the Genius, if he will pardon the proverb, *In for a mill, in for a million.* When I receive a new gift, I do not macerate my body to make the account square, for, if I should die, I could not make the account square. The benefit overran the merit the first day, and has overran the merit ever since. The merit itself, so-called, I reckon part of the receiving.

Also, that hankering after an overt or practical effect seems to me an apostasy. In good earnest, I am willing to spare this most unnecessary deal of doing. Life wears to me a visionary face. Hardest, roughest action is visionary also. It is but a choice between soft and turbulent dreams. People disparage knowing and the intellectual life, and urge doing. I am very content with knowing, if only I could know. That is an august entertainment, and would suffice me a great while. To know a little, would be worth the expense of this world. I hear always the law of Adrastia,[9] "that every soul which had acquired any truth, should be safe from harm until another period."

I know that the world I converse with in the city and in the farms, is not the world I *think.* I observe that difference, and shall observe it. One day, I shall know the value and law of this discrepance. But I have not found that much was gained by manipular attempts to realize the world of thought. Many eager

---

7. John Flaxman (1755–1826), English illustrator. In the clearer modern usage, the title of Aeschylus's play *The Eumenides* would be italicized; in the scene depicted by Flaxman, the Furies, or Eumenides, who have pursued Orestes since his murder of his adulterous mother, are temporarily lulled by the power of Apollo, who sanctioned the murder.
8. Lasting from century to century.
9. Another name for Nemesis or Destiny. The quotation is from the *Phaedrus* by Plato.

persons successively make an experiment in this way, and make themselves ridiculous. They acquire democratic manners, they foam at the mouth, they hate and deny. Worse, I observe, that, in the history of mankind, there is never a solitary example of success,—taking their own tests of success. I say this polemically, or in reply to the inquiry, why not realize your world? But far be from me the despair which prejudges the law by a paltry empiricism,— since there never was a right endeavor, but it succeeded. Patience and patience, we shall win at the last. We must be very suspicious of the deceptions of the element of time. It takes a good deal of time to eat or to sleep, or to earn a hundred dollars, and a very little time to entertain a hope and an insight which becomes the light of our life. We dress our garden, eat our dinners, discuss the household with our wives, and these things make no impression, are forgotten next week; but in the solitude to which every man is always returning, he has a sanity and revelations, which in his passage into new worlds he will carry with him. Never mind the ridicule, never mind the defeat: up again, old heart!—it seems to say,—there is victory yet for all justice; and the true romance which the world exists to realize, will be the transformation of genius into practical power.

1844

Fate[1]

Delicate omens traced in air
To the lone bard true witness bare;
Birds with auguries on their wings
Chanted undeceiving things
Him to beckon, him to warn;
Well might then the poet scorn
To learn of scribe or courier
Hints writ in vaster character;
And on his mind, at dawn of day,
Soft shadows of the evening lay.
For the prevision is allied
Unto the thing so signified;
Or say, the foresight that awaits
Is the same Genius that creates.[2]

It chanced during one winter, a few years ago, that our cities were bent on discussing the theory of the Age. By an odd coincidence, four or five noted men were each reading a discourse to the citizens of Boston or New York, on the Spirit of the Times.[3] It so happened that the subject had the same prominence in some remarkable pamphlets and journals issued in London in the same season.[4] To me, however, the question of the times resolved itself into a practical question of the conduct of life. How shall I live? We are incompetent to solve the times. Our geometry cannot span the huge orbits of the prevailing

1. The text is from *The Conduct of Life*, first printing (1860), 1–42. At some stage the work existed in 1851, when Emerson delivered a lecture on fate. He worked intermittently on it over the next decade, making some alterations just before publication.
2. The opening poem is Emerson's.
3. Emerson himself lectured on that theme in New York City on January 29, 1851.

4. Several well-known English writers had published works with this title or a close variation of it over the last three decades; among them were William Hazlitt, John Stuart Mill, Chandos Leigh, and R. H. Horne. In the United States both a Democratic newspaper in Philadelphia and the great New York City sporting magazine were called *The Spirit of the Times*.

ideas, behold their return, and reconcile their opposition. We can only obey our own polarity. 'Tis fine for us to speculate and elect our course, if we must accept an irresistible dictation.

In our first steps to gain our wishes, we come upon immovable limitations. We are fired with the hope to reform men. After many experiments, we find that we must begin earlier,—at school. But the boys and girls are not docile; we can make nothing of them. We decide that they are not of good stock. We must begin our reform earlier still,—at generation: that is to say, there is Fate, or laws of the world.

But if there be irresistible dictation, this dictation understands itself. If we must accept Fate, we are not less compelled to affirm liberty, the significance of the individual, the grandeur of duty, the power of character. This is true, and that other is true. But our geometry cannot span these extreme points, and reconcile them. What to do? By obeying each thought frankly, by harping, or, if you will, pounding on each string, we learn at last its power. By the same obedience to other thoughts, we learn theirs, and then comes some reasonable hope of harmonizing them. We are sure, that, though we know not how, necessity does comport with liberty, the individual with the world, my polarity with the spirit of the times. The riddle of the age has for each a private solution. If one would study his own time, it must be by this method of taking up in turn each of the leading topics which belong to our scheme of human life, and, by firmly stating all that is agreeable to experience on one, and doing the same justice to the opposing facts in the others, the true limitations will appear. Any excess of emphasis, on one part, would be corrected, and a just balance would be made.

But let us honestly state the facts. Our America has a bad name for superficialness. Great man, great nations, have not been boasters and buffoons, but perceivers of the terror of life, and have manned themselves to face it. The Spartan, embodying his religion in his country, dies before its majesty without a question. The Turk, who believes his doom is written on the iron leaf in the moment when he entered the world, rushes on the enemy's sabre with undivided will. The Turk, the Arab, the Persian, accepts the foreordained fate.

> "On two days, it steads not to run from thy grave,
> The appointed, and the unappointed day;
> On the first, neither balm nor physician can save,
> Nor thee, on the second, the Universe slay."[5]

The Hindoo, under the wheel, is as firm. Our Calvinists, in the last generation, had something of the same dignity.[6] They felt that the weight of the Universe held them down to their place. What could *they* do? Wise men feel that there is something which cannot be talked or voted away,—a strap or belt which girds the world.

> "The Destiny, minister general,
> That executeth in the world o'er all,
> The purveyance which God hath seen beforne,
> So strong it is, that tho' the world had sworn

---

5. Emerson's translation of a German translation of a Persian poet, which he found in *Geschichte der schönen Redekunste Persiens*. In his *Journals* (11.103) he ascribes the poem to "Pindar of Rei in Cuhistan."

6. That is, 18th-century New England Calvinists who still believed in the doctrine of election, God's arbitrary choice of who was to be saved or damned.

The contrary of a thing by yea or nay,
Yet sometime it shall fallen on a day
That falleth not oft in a thousand year;
For, certainly, our appetités here,
Be it of war, or peace, or hate, or love,
All this is ruled by the sight above."
    —CHAUCER: *The Knighte's Tale*.[7]

The Greek Tragedy expressed the same sense: "Whatever is fated, that will take place. The great immense mind of Jove is not to be transgressed."[8]

Savages cling to a local god of one tribe or town. The broad ethics of Jesus were quickly narrowed to village theologies, which preach an election or favoritism. And, now and then, an amiable parson, like Jung Stilling, or William Huntington, believes in a pistareen-Providence,[9] which, whenever the good man wants a dinner, makes that somebody shall knock at his door, and leave a half-dollar. But Nature is no sentimentalist,—does not cosset or pamper us. We must see that the world is rough and surly, and will not mind drowning a man or a woman; but swallows your ship like a grain of dust. The cold, inconsiderate of persons, tingles your blood, benumbs your feet, freezes a man like an apple. The diseases, the elements, fortune, gravity, lightning, respect no persons. The way of Providence is a little rude. The habit of snake and spider, the snap of the tiger and other leapers and bloody jumpers, the crackle of the bones of his prey in the coil of the anaconda,—these are in the system, and our habits are like theirs. You have just dined, and, however scrupulously the slaughter-house is concealed in the graceful distance of miles, there is complicity,—expensive races,—race living at the expense of race. The planet is liable to shocks from comets, perturbations from planets, rendings from earthquake and volcano, alterations of climate, precessions of equinoxes. Rivers dry up by opening of the forest. The sea changes its bed. Towns and counties fall into it. At Lisbon, an earthquake[1] killed men like flies. At Naples, three years ago, ten thousand persons were crushed in a few minutes.[2] The scurvy at sea; the sword of the climate in the west of Africa, at Cayenne, at Panama, at New Orleans, cut off men like a massacre. Our western prairie shakes with fever and ague. The cholera, the small-pox, have proved as mortal to some tribes, as a frost to the crickets, which, having filled the summer with noise, are silenced by a fall of the temperature of one night. Without uncovering what does not concern us, or counting how many species of parasites hang on a bombyx; or groping after intestinal parasites, or infusory biters, or the obscurities of alternate generation;—the forms of the shark, the *labrus*, the jaw of the sea-wolf paved with crushing teeth, the weapons of the grampus,[3] and other warriors hidden in the sea,—are hints of ferocity in the interiors of nature. Let us not deny it up and down. Providence has a wild, rough, incalculable road to its end, and it is of no use to try to whitewash its huge, mixed instrumentalities, or to dress up that terrific benefactor in a clean shirt and white neckcloth of a student in divinity.

---

7. Lines 805–14, somewhat altered.
8. Aeschylus, *The Suppliants*, lines 1047–49.
9. A God who troubles himself with trivial handouts to the needy. Johann Heinrich Jung (1740–1817), who used the name Heinrich Stilling, was a German physician, mystic, and friend of Goethe, in whose autobiography, *Poetry and Truth*, Emerson read of him. The 1st edition has "Robert Huntington," a slip for William

Huntington (1745–1813), English coal heaver turned eccentric minister; he signed himself "William Huntington, S. S.," meaning "Sinner Saved."
1. The terrible earthquake of 1755.
2. On December 17, 1857.
3. The killer whale. "Bombyx": silkworm moth. "Biters": microscopic marine animals. "Labrus": thick-lipped predatory fish.

Will you say, the disasters which threaten mankind are exceptional, and one need not lay his account for cataclysms every day? Aye, but what happens once, may happen again, and so long as these strokes are not to be parried by us, they must be feared.

But these shocks and ruins are less destructive to us, than the stealthy power of other laws which act on us daily. An expense of ends to means is fate;—organization tyrannizing over character. The menagerie, or forms and powers of the spine, is a book of fate:[4] the bill of the bird, the skull of the snake, determines tyrannically its limits. So is the scale of races, of temperaments;[5] so is sex; so is climate; so is the reaction of talents imprisoning the vital power in certain directions. Every spirit makes its house; but afterwards the house confines the spirit.

The gross lines are legible to the dull: the cabman is phrenologist so far: he looks in your face to see if his shilling is sure. A dome of brow denotes one thing; a pot-belly another; a squint, a pugnose, mats of hair, the pigment of the epidermis, betray character. People seem sheathed in their tough organization. Ask Spurzheim, ask the doctors, ask Quetelet,[6] if temperaments decide nothing? or if there be anything they do not decide? Read the description in medical books of the four temperaments, and you will think you are reading your own thoughts which you had not yet told. Find the part which black eyes, and which blue eyes, play severally in the company. How shall a man escape from his ancestors, or draw off from his veins the black drop which he drew from his father's or his mother's life? It often appears in a family, as if all the qualities of the progenitors were potted in several jars,—some ruling quality in each son or daughter of the house,—and sometimes the unmixed temperament, the rank unmitigated elixir, the family vice, is drawn off in a separate individual, and the others are proportionally relieved. We sometimes see a change of expression in our companion, and say, his father, or his mother, comes to the windows of his eyes, and sometimes a remote relative. In different hours, a man represents each of several of his ancestors, as if there were seven or eight of us rolled up in each man's skin,—seven or eight ancestors at least,—and they constitute the variety of notes for that new piece of music which his life is. At the corner of the street, you read the possibility of each passenger, in the facial angle, in the complexion, in the depth of his eye. His parentage determines it. Men are what their mothers made them. You may as well ask a loom which weaves huckaback,[7] why it does not make cashmere, as expect poetry from this engineer, or a chemical discovery from that jobber. Ask the digger in the ditch to explain Newton's laws: the fine organs of his brain have been pinched by overwork and squalid poverty from father to son, for a hundred years. When each comes forth from his mother's womb, the gate of gifts closes behind him. Let him value his hands and feet, he has but one pair. So he has but one future, and that is already predetermined in his lobes, and described in that little fatty face, pig-eye, and squat form. All the privilege and all the legislation of the world cannot meddle or help to make a poet or a prince of him.

---

4. That is, one can read in varying physical construction of animals an index to their behavior.
5. The four different humors in ancient and medieval physiology were blood, phlegm, choler, and melancholy; the varying mixtures in different people determined their temperaments.
6. Lambert Quételet (1796–1874), Belgian mathema-

tician, creator of the science of statistics. Johann Kaspar Spurzheim (1776–1832), popularizer of the pseudoscience of phrenology, which claimed to judge character by the bumps on the skull. He died in Boston, where he had lectured in his last year of life.
7. Rough linen used for toweling.

Jesus said, "When he looketh on her, he hath committed adultery."[8] But he is an adulterer before he has yet looked on the woman, by the superfluity of animal, and the defect of thought, in his constitution. Who meets him, or who meets her, in the street, sees that they are ripe to be each other's victim.

In certain men, digestion and sex absorb the vital force, and the stronger these are, the individual is so much weaker. The more of these drones perish, the better for the hive. If, later, they give birth to some superior individual, with force enough to add to this animal a new aim, and a complete apparatus to work it out, all the ancestors are gladly forgotten. Most men and most women are merely one couple more. Now and then, one has a new cell or camarilla[9] opened in his brain,—an architectural, a musical, or a philological knack, some stray taste or talent for flowers, or chemistry, or pigments, or story-telling, a good hand for drawing, a good foot for dancing, an athletic frame for wide journeying, &c.—which skill nowise alters rank in the scale of nature, but serves to pass the time, the life of sensation going on as before. At last, these hints and tendencies are fixed in one, or in a succession. Each absorbs so much food and force, as to become itself a new centre. The new talent draws off so rapidly the vital force, that not enough remains for the animal functions, hardly enough for health; so that, in the second generation, if the like genius appear, the health is visibly deteriorated, and the generative force impaired.

People are born with the moral or with the material bias;—uterine brothers with this diverging destination: and I suppose, with high magnifiers, Mr. Frauenhofer or Dr. Carpenter[1] might come to distinguish in the embryo at the fourth day, this is a Whig, and that a Free-soiler.[2]

It was a poetic attempt to lift this mountain of Fate, to reconcile this despotism of race with liberty, which led the Hindoos to say, "Fate is nothing but the deeds committed in a prior state of existence."[3] I find the coincidence of the extremes of eastern and western speculation in the daring statement of Schelling,[4] "there is in every man a certain feeling, that he has been what he is from all eternity, and by no means became such in time." To say it less sublimely,—in the history of the individual is always an account of his condition, and he knows himself to be a party to his present estate.

A good deal of our politics is physiological. Now and then, a man of wealth in the heyday of youth adopts the tenet of broadest freedom. In England, there is always some man of wealth and large connection planting himself, during all his years of health, on the side of progress, who, as soon as he begins to die, checks his forward play, calls in his troops, and becomes conservative. All conservatives are such from personal defects. They have been effeminated by position or nature, born halt and blind, through luxury of their parents, and can only, like invalids, act on the defensive. But strong natures, backwoodsmen, New Hampshire giants, Napoleons, Burkes, Broughams, Web-

<hr>

8. "But I say unto you, That whosoever looketh on a woman to lust after her hath committed adultery with her already in his heart" (Matthew 5.28).
9. Small chamber.
1. William B. Carpenter (1813–1885), English biologist and writer on the uses of the microscope. Joseph von Frauenhofer (1787–1826), German optician, improver of the telescope.
2. The anti-Democratic party and the antislavery faction of the Democratic party at the time Emerson be-

gan lecturing on fate; both terms were superseded by the time the essay was published.
3. Apparently not a direct quotation but a distillation of the idea of karma.
4. Friedrich Wilhelm Joseph von Schelling (1775–1854), German philosopher. The quotation is probably from James Elliot Cabot's translation of *Philosophical Search for the Ways of Human Happiness*, which Emerson read in manuscript.

sters, Kossuths,[5] are inevitable patriots, until their life ebbs, and their defects and gout, palsy and money, warp them.

The strongest idea incarnates itself in majorities and nations, in the healthiest and strongest. Probably, the election goes by avoirdupois weight, and, if you could weigh bodily the tonnage of any hundred of the Whig and the Democratic party in a town, on the Dearborn balance,[6] as they passed the hayscales, you could predict with certainty which party would carry it. On the whole, it would be rather the speediest way of deciding the vote, to put the selectmen or the mayor and aldermen at the hayscales.

In science, we have to consider two things: power and circumstance. All we know of the egg, from each successive discovery, is, *another vesicle*,[7] and if, after five hundred years, you get a better observer, or a better glass, he finds within the last observed another. In vegetable and animal tissue, it is just alike, and all that the primary power or spasm operates, is, still, vesicles, vesicles. Yes,—but the tyrannical Circumstance! A vesicle in new circumstances, a vesicle lodged in darkness, Oken[8] thought, became animal; in light, a plant. Lodged in the parent animal, it suffers changes, which end in unsheathing miraculous capability in the unaltered vesicle, and it unlocks itself to fish, bird, or quadruped, head and foot, eye and claw. The Circumstance is Nature. Nature is, what you may do. There is much you may not. We have two things,—the circumstance, and the life. Once we thought, positive power was all. Now we learn, that negative power, or circumstance, is half. Nature is the tyrannous circumstance, the thick skull, the sheathed snake, the ponderous, rock-like jaw; necessitated activity; violent direction; the conditions of a tool, like the locomotive, strong enough on its track, but which can do nothing but mischief off of it; or skates, which are wings on the ice, but fetters on the ground.

The book of Nature is the book of Fate. She turns the gigantic pages,—leaf after leaf,—never re-turning one. One leaf she lays down, a floor of granite; then a thousand ages, and a bed of slate; a thousand ages, and a measure of coal; a thousand ages, and a layer of marl and mud: vegetable forms appear; her first misshapen animals, zoophyte, trilobium, fish; then, saurians,—rude forms, in which she has only blocked her future statue, concealing under these unwieldy monsters the fine type of her coming king. The face of the planet cools and dries, the races meliorate, and man is born. But when a race has lived its term, it comes no more again.

The population of the world is a conditional population; not the best, but the best that could live now; and the scale of tribes, and the steadiness with which victory adheres to one tribe, and defeat to another, is as uniform as the superposition of strata. We know in history what weight belongs to race. We see the English, French, and Germans planting themselves on every shore and market of America and Australia, and monopolizing the commerce of these countries. We like the nervous and victorious habit of our own branch

5. Lajos Kossuth (1802–1894), Hungarian patriot who led a fight for freedom in 1848 and made a triumphal tour of the United States in 1851 and 1852; Emerson officially welcomed him to Concord in May 1852. Napoleon Bonaparte (1769–1821), French emperor 1804–15. Edmund Burke (1729–1797), British statesman and philosopher. Henry Peter Brougham (1778–1868), English statesman, supporter of the Re-

form Act of 1832. Daniel Webster (1782–1852), Massachusetts politician, leader of the Whig party.
6. Spring balance invented by Henry Dearborn.
7. Small fluid-filled bladder or sac.
8. Lorenz Oken (1779–1851), German naturalist who argued in *Procreation* that all organisms derive from cells or vesicles.

of the family. We follow the step of the Jew, of the Indian, of the Negro. We see how much will has been expended to extinguish the Jew, in vain. Look at the unpalatable conclusions of Knox,[9] in his "Fragment of Races,"—a rash and unsatisfactory writer, but charged with pungent and unforgetable truths. "Nature respects race, and not hybrids." "Every race has its own *habitat*." "Detach a colony from the race, and it deteriorates to the crab."[1] See the shades of the picture. The German and Irish millions, like the Negro, have a great deal of guano[2] in their destiny. They are ferried over the Atlantic, and carted over America, to ditch and to drudge, to make corn cheap, and then to lie down prematurely to make a spot of green grass on the prairie.

One more fagot of these adamantine bandages is, the new science of Statistics. It is a rule, that the most casual and extraordinary events—if the basis of population is broad enough—become matter of fixed calculation. It would not be safe to say when a captain like Bonaparte, a singer like Jenny Lind, or a navigator like Bowditch,[3] would be born in Boston: but, on a population of twenty or two hundred millions, something like accuracy may be had.[4]

'Tis frivolous to fix pedantically the date of particular inventions. They have all been invented over and over fifty times. Man is the arch machine, of which all these shifts drawn from himself are toy models. He helps himself on each emergency by copying or duplicating his own structure, just so far as the need is. 'Tis hard to find the right Homer, Zoroaster, or Manu,[5] harder still to find the Tubal Cain, or Vulcan, or Cadmus, or Copernicus, or Fust, or Fulton,[6] the indisputable inventor. There are scores and centuries of them. "The air is full of men." This kind of talent so abounds, this constructive tool-making efficiency, as if it adhered to the chemic atoms, as if the air he breathes were made of Vaucansons, Franklins, and Watts.[7]

Doubtless, in every million there will be an astronomer, a mathematician, a comic poet, a mystic. No one can read the history of astronomy, without perceiving that Copernicus, Newton, Laplace,[8] are not new men, or a new kind of men, but that Thales, Anaximenes, Hipparchus, Empedocles, Aris-

9. Robert Knox (1791–1862), Scottish anatomist and ethnologist, in *The Races of Men, a Fragment* (1850). His "ethnology" was a way of justifying racial prejudice scientifically. He thought, for example, that colonies die away unless kept strong by continual immigration from the mother country: "Already the United States man differs in appearance from the European: the ladies early lose their teeth; * * * the muscles become stringy, and show themselves; the tendons appear on the surface; symptoms of premature decay manifest themselves."

1. I.e., degenerates the way apple trees degenerate to crabapples when abandoned to nature.

2. Dung of sea birds and bats, used as fertilizer.

3. Nathaniel Bowditch (1773–1838), American mathematician and astronomer, author of *The New American Practical Navigator* (1802). Jenny Lind (1820–1887), popular Swedish-born British coloratura soprano.

4. " 'Everything which pertains to the human species, considered as a whole, belongs to the order of physical facts. The greater the number of individuals, the more does the influence of the individual will disappear, leaving predominance to a series of general facts dependent on causes by which society exists, and is pre-

served.'—QUETELET" [Emerson's note].

5. Reputed author of the Hindu *Laws of Manu*. Homer, legendary Greek epic poet, credited with the authorship of *The Iliad* and *The Odyssey*. Zoroaster (6th century B.C.), Persian prophet.

6. Robert Fulton (1765–1815), American inventor, designed early steamboats. In Genesis 4.22 Tubal-cain is "an instructer of every artificer in brass and iron," an obvious parallel to Vulcan, the Roman god of metalworking. Cadmus was a Phoenician prince who strewed the ground with the teeth of a dragon he had slain, from the teeth sprang up an army. Nicolaus Copernicus (1473–1543), Polish astronomer, realized that the earth revolves around the sun. Johann Fust (1400?–1466?), German printer associated with Johann Gutenberg, inventor of movable type.

7. James Watt (1736–1819), Scottish engineer, inventor of modern steam engine. Jacques de Vaucanson (1709–1782), French mathematician and inventor of automata. Benjamin Franklin (1706–1790), American writer, scientist, and statesman.

8. Pierre Simon, Marquis de Laplace (1749–1827), French mathematician and astronomer. Sir Isaac Newton (1642–1727), English mathematician, originator of the theory of universal gravitation.

tarchus, Pythagoras, Œnopides,[9] had anticipated them; each had the same tense geometrical brain, apt for the same vigorous computation and logic, a mind parallel to the movement of the world. The Roman mile probably rested on a measure of a degree of the meridian. Mahometan and Chinese know what we know of leap-year, of the Gregorian calendar,[1] and of the precession of the equinoxes. As, in every barrel of cowries, brought to New Bedford, there shall be one *orangia*,[2] so there will, in a dozen millions of Malays and Mahometans, be one or two astronomical skulls.[3] In a large city, the most casual things, and things whose beauty lies in their casuality, are produced as punctually and to order as the baker's muffin for breakfast. Punch[4] makes exactly one capital joke a week; and the journals[5] contrive to furnish one good piece of news every day.

And not less work the laws of repression, the penalties of violated functions. Famine, typhus, frost, war, suicide, and effete races, must be reckoned calculable parts of the system of the world.

These are pebbles from the mountain, hints of the terms by which our life is walled up, and which show a kind of mechanical exactness, as of a loom or mill, in what we call casual or fortuitous events.

The force with which we resist these torrents of tendency looks so ridiculously inadequate, that it amounts to little more than a criticism or a protest made by a minority of one, under compulsion of millions. I seemed, in the height of a tempest, to see men overboard struggling in the waves, and driven about here and there. They glanced intelligently at each other, but 'twas little they could do for one another; 'twas much if each could keep afloat alone. Well, they had a right to their eyebeams, and all the rest was Fate.

We cannot trifle with this reality, this cropping-out in our planted gardens of the core of the world. No picture of life can have any veracity that does not admit the odious facts. A man's power is hooped in by a necessity, which, by many experiments, he touches on every side, until he learns its arc.

The element running through entire nature, which we popularly call Fate, is known to us as limitation. Whatever limits us, we call Fate. If we are brute and barbarous, the fate takes a brute and dreadful shape. As we refine, our checks become finer. If we rise to spiritual culture, the antagonism takes a spiritual form. In the Hindoo fables, Vishnu follows Maya[6] through all her ascending changes, from insect and crawfish up to elephant; whatever form she took, he took the male form of that kind, until she became at last woman and goddess, and he a man and a god. The limitations refine as the soul purifies, but the ring of necessity is always perched at the top.

When the gods in the Norse heaven were unable to bind the Fenris Wolf[7] with steel or with weight of mountains,—the one he snapped and the other he

---

9. Thales (640?–546 B.C.), Greek philosopher and geometrician who held that the earth is globular and that the moon borrows its light from the sun. Anaximenes (6th century B.C.), Greek philosopher who argued that air is the soul. Hipparchus (2nd century B.C.), Greek astronomer. Empedocles (5th century B.C.), Greek philosopher and medical theorist. Aristarchus of Samos (3rd century B.C.), Greek astronomer who anticipated Copernicus in arguing that the earth moves around the sun. Pythagoras (6th century B.C.), Greek philosopher who vied with Oenopides of Chios for claim to have discovered the obliquity of the ecliptic.

1. The modern calendar, in use since 1582, adopted by England and its American colonies in 1752.
2. A spectacular tropical seashell. "Cowries": tropical marine mollusks having brightly marked shells.
3. I.e., brains fitted for astronomical speculation.
4. British satirical weekly.
5. Daily newspapers.
6. The Hindu goddess of illusion. Vishnu is one of the three gods of the Hindu trinity, savior of humankind.
7. Monster in Norse mythology, finally enchained by the frailest-looking of bonds, but he might at any moment be loosed upon the world.

spurned with his heel,—they put round his foot a limp band softer than silk or cobweb, and this held him: the more he spurned it, the stiffer it drew. So soft and so stanch is the ring of Fate. Neither brandy, nor nectar, nor sulphuric ether, nor hell-fire, no ichor,[8] nor poetry, nor genius, can get rid of this limp band. For if we give it the high sense in which the poets use it, even thought itself is not above Fate: that too must act according to eternal laws, and all that is wilful and fantastic in it is in opposition to its fundamental essence.

And, last of all, high over thought, in the world of morals, Fate appears as vindicator, levelling the high, lifting the low, requiring justice in man, and always striking soon or late, when justice is not done. What is useful will last; what is hurtful will sink. "The doer must suffer," said the Greeks: "you would soothe a Deity not to be soothed." "God himself cannot procure good for the wicked," said the Welsh triad.[9] "God may consent, but only for a time," said the bard of Spain. The limitation is impassable by any insight of man. In its last and loftiest ascensions, insight itself, and the freedom of the will, is one of its obedient members. But we must not run into generalizations too large, but show the natural bounds or essential distinctions, and seek to do justice to the other elements as well.

Thus we trace Fate, in matter, mind, and morals,—in race, in retardations of strata, and in thought and character as well. It is everywhere bound or limitation. But Fate has its lord; limitation its limits; is different seen from above and from below; from within and from without. For, though Fate is immense, so is power, which is the other fact in the dual world, immense. If Fate follows and limits power, power attends and antagonizes Fate. We must respect Fate as natural history, but there is more than natural history. For who and what is this criticism that pries into the matter? Man is not order of nature, sack and sack, belly and members,[1] link in a chain, nor any ignominious baggage, but a stupendous antagonism, a dragging together of the poles of the Universe. He betrays his relation to what is below him,—thick-skulled, small-brained, fishy, quadrumanous,[2]—quadruped ill-disguised, hardly escaped into biped, and has paid for the new powers by loss of some of the old ones. But the lightning which explodes and fashions planets, maker of planets and suns, is in him. On one side, elemental order, sandstone and granite, rock-ledges, peat-bog, forest, sea and shore; and, on the other part, thought, the spirit which composes and decomposes nature,—here they are, side by side, god and devil, mind and matter, king and conspirator, belt and spasm, riding peacefully together in the eye and brain of every man.

Nor can he blink the freewill. To hazard the contradiction,—freedom is necessary. If you please to plant yourself on the side of Fate, and say, Fate is all; then we say, a part of Fate is the freedom of man. Forever wells up the impulse of choosing and acting in the soul. Intellect annuls Fate. So far as a man thinks, he is free. And though nothing is more disgusting than the crowing about liberty by slaves, as most men are, and the flippant mistaking for freedom of some paper preamble like a "Declaration of Independence," or the statute right to vote, by those who have never dared to think or to act, yet it is

8. The rarefied fluid that runs in the veins of the gods.
9. This would be part of a triad, not the whole (in Welsh poetics the triad consisted of an arrangement of subjects or statements in groups of three). The particular triad, like the sources of the Greek and Spanish say-

ings that follow, is unidentified.
1. The fable of the belly and other parts of the body is in Shakespeare's *Coriolanus* 1.1.99ff.
2. Having four feet with opposable first digits, as in nonhuman primates.

wholesome to man to look not at Fate, but the other way: the practical view is the other. His sound relation to these facts is to use and command, not to cringe to them. "Look not on nature, for her name is fatal," said the oracle. The too much contemplation of these limits induces meanness. They who talk much of destiny, their birth-star, &c., are in a lower dangerous plane, and invite the evils they fear.

I cited the instinctive and heroic races as proud believers in Destiny. They conspire with it; a loving resignation is with the event. But the dogma makes a different impression, when it is held by the weak and lazy. 'Tis weak and vicious people who cast the blame on Fate. The right use of Fate is to bring up our conduct to the loftiness of nature. Rude and invincible except by themselves are the elements. So let man be. Let him empty his breast of his windy conceits, and show his lordship by manners and deeds on the scale of nature. Let him hold his purpose as with the tug of gravitation. No power, no persuasion, no bribe shall make him give up his point. A man ought to compare advantageously with a river, an oak, or a mountain. He shall have not less the flow, the expansion, and the resistance of these.

'Tis the best use of Fate to teach a fatal courage. Go face the fire at sea, or the cholera in your friend's house, or the burglar in your own, or what danger lies in the way of duty, knowing you are guarded by the cheribum of Destiny. If you believe in Fate to your harm, believe it, at least, for your good.

For, if Fate is so prevailing, man also is part of it, and can confront fate with fate. If the Universe have these savage accidents, our atoms are as savage in resistance. We should be crushed by the atmosphere, but for the reaction of the air within the body. A tube made of a film of glass can resist the shock of the ocean, if filled with the same water. If there be omnipotence in the stroke, there is omnipotence of recoil.

1. But Fate against Fate is only parrying and defence: there are, also, the noble creative forces. The revelation of Thought takes man out of servitude into freedom. We rightly say of ourselves, we were born, and afterward we were born again, and many times. We have successive experiences so important, that the new forgets the old, and hence the mythology of the seven or the nine heavens. The day of days, the great day of the feast of life, is that in which the inward eye opens to the Unity in things, to the omnipresence of law;—sees that what is must be, and ought to be, or is the best. This beatitude dips from on high down on us, and we see. It is not in us so much as we are in it. If the air come to our lungs, we breathe and live; if not, we die. If the light come to our eyes, we see; else not. And if truth come to our mind, we suddenly expand to its dimensions, as if we grew to worlds. We are as lawgivers; we speak for Nature; we prophesy and divine.

This insight throws us on the party and interest of the Universe, against all and sundry; against ourselves, as much as others. A man speaking from insight affirms of himself what is true of the mind: seeing its immortality, he says, I am immortal; seeing its invincibility, he says, I am strong. It is not in us, but we are in it. It is of the maker, not of what is made. All things are touched and changed by it. This uses, and is not used. It distances those who share it, from those who share it not. Those who share it not are flocks and herds. It dates from itself;—not from former men or better men,—gospel, or constitution, or college, or custom. Where it shines, Nature is no longer intrusive, but all things make a musical or pictorial impression. The world of men show like a comedy without laughter:—populations, interests, government, history;—'tis all toy figures in a toy house. It does not overvalue particular truths. We hear eagerly every thought and word quoted from an intellectual man. But, in his presence, our own mind is roused to activity, and we forget very fast what he says, much more interested in the new play of our own thought, than in any thought of his. 'Tis the majesty into which we have suddenly mounted, the impersonality, the scorn of egotisms, the sphere of laws, that engage us. Once we were stepping a little this way, and a little that way; now, we are as men in a balloon, and do not think so much of the point we have left, or the point we would make, as of the liberty and glory of the way.

Just as much intellect as you add, so much organic power. He who sees through the design, presides over it, and must will that which must be. We sit and rule, and, though we sleep, our dream will come to pass. Our thought, though it were only an hour old, affirms an oldest necessity, not to be separated from thought, and not to be separated from will. They must always have coëxisted. It apprises us of its sovereignty and godhead, which refuse to be severed from it. It is not mine or thine, but the will of all mind. It is poured into the souls of all men, as the soul itself which constitutes them men. I know not whether there be, as is alleged, in the upper region of our atmosphere, a permanent westerly current, which carries with it all atoms which rise to that height, but I see, that when souls reach a certain clearness of perception, they accept a knowledge and motive above selfishness. A breath of will blows eternally through the universe of souls in the direction of the Right and Necessary. It is the air which all intellects inhale and exhale, and it is the wind which blows the worlds into order and orbit.

Thought dissolves the material universe, by carrying the mind up into a sphere where all is plastic. Of two men, each obeying his own thought, he whose thought is deepest will be the strongest character. Always one man more than another represents the will of Divine Providence to the period.

2. If thought makes free, so does the moral sentiment. The mixtures of spiritual chemistry refuse to be analyzed. Yet we can see that with the perception of truth is joined the desire that it shall prevail. That affection is essential to will. Moreover, when a strong will appears, it usually results from a certain unity of organization, as if the whole energy of body and mind flowed in one direction. All great force is real and elemental. There is no manufacturing a strong will. There must be a pound to balance a pound. Where power is shown in will, it must rest on the universal force. Alaric[3] and Bonaparte must believe they rest on a truth, or their will can be bought or bent. There is a bribe possible for any finite will. But the pure sympathy with universal ends is an infinite force, and cannot be bribed or bent. Whoever has had experience of the moral sentiment cannot choose but believe in unlimited power. Each pulse from that heat is an oath from the Most High. I know not what the word *sublime* means, if it be not the intimations in this infant of a terrific force. A text of heroism, a name and anecdote of courage, are not arguments, but sallies of freedom. One of these is the verse of the Persian Hafiz,[4] " 'Tis written on the gate of Heaven, 'Wo unto him who suffers himself to be betrayed by Fate!' " Does the reading of history make us fatalists? What courage does not

3. Alaric (370?–410), king of the Visigoths and conqueror of Rome in 410.

4. Persian poet of the 14th century.

the opposite opinion show! A little whim of will to be free gallantly contending against the universe of chemistry.

But insight is not will, nor is affection will. Perception is cold, and goodness dies in wishes; as Voltaire[5] said, 'tis the misfortune of worthy people that they are cowards; "*un des plus grands malheurs des honnêtes gens c'est qu'ils sont des lâches.*" There must be a fusion of these two to generate the energy of will. There can be no driving force, except through the conversion of the man into his will, making him the will, and the will him. And one may say boldly, that no man has a right perception of any truth, who has not been reacted on by it, so as to be ready to be its martyr.

The one serious and formidable thing in nature is a will. Society is servile from want of will, and therefore the world wants saviours and religions. One way is right to go: the hero sees it, and moves on that aim, and has the world under him for root and support. He is to others as the world. His approbation is honor; his dissent, infamy. The glance of his eye has the force of sunbeams. A personal influence towers up in memory only worthy, and we gladly forget numbers, money, climate, gravitation, and the rest of Fate.

We can afford to allow the limitation, if we know it is the meter of the growing man. We stand against Fate, as children stand up against the wall in their father's house, and notch their height from year to year. But when the boy grows to man, and is master of the house, he pulls down that wall, and builds a new and bigger. 'Tis only a question of time. Every brave youth is in training to ride and rule this dragon. His science is to make weapons and wings of these passions and retarding forces. Now whether, seeing these two things, fate and power, we are permitted to believe in unity? The bulk of mankind believe in two gods. They are under one dominion here in the house, as friend and parent, in social circles, in letters, in art, in love, in religion: but in mechanics, in dealing with steam and climate, in trade, in politics, they think they come under another; and that it would be a practical blunder to transfer the method and way of working of one sphere, into the other. What good, honest, generous men at home, will be wolves and foxes on change![6] What pious men in the parlor will vote for what reprobates at the polls! To a certain point, they believe themselves the care of a Providence. But, in a steamboat, in an epidemic, in war, they believe a malignant energy rules.

But relation and connection are not somewhere and sometimes, but everywhere and always. The divine order does not stop where their sight stops. The friendly power works on the same rules, in the next farm, and the next planet. But, where they have not experience, they run against it, and hurt themselves. Fate, then, is a name for facts not yet passed under the fire of thought;—for causes which are unpenetrated.

But every jet of chaos which threatens to exterminate us, is convertible by intellect into wholesome force. Fate is unpenetrated causes. The water drowns ship and sailor, like a grain of dust. But learn to swim, trim your bark,[7] and the wave which drowned it, will be cloven by it, and carry it, like its own foam, a plume and a power. The cold is inconsiderate of persons, tingles your blood, freezes a man like a dew-drop. But learn to skate, and the ice will give

5. Pen name of François Marie Arouet (1694–1778), French writer. Emerson gives the English translation before he quotes the French.

6. Stock exchange.
7. Boat.

you a graceful, sweet, and poetic motion. The cold will brace your limbs and brain to genius, and make you foremost men of time. Cold and sea will train an imperial Saxon race, which nature cannot bear to lose, and, after cooping it up for a thousand years in yonder England, gives a hundred Englands, a hundred Mexicos. All the bloods it shall absorb and domineer: and more than Mexicos,—the secrets of water and steam, the spasms of electricity, the ductility of metals, the chariot of the air, the ruddered balloon are awaiting you.

The annual slaughter from typhus far exceeds that of war; but right drainage destroys typhus. The plague in the sea-service from scurvy is healed by lemon juice and other diets portable or procurable: the depopulation by cholera and small-pox is ended by drainage and vaccination; and every other pest is not less in the chain of cause and effect, and may be fought off. And, whilst art draws out the venom, it commonly extorts some benefit from the vanquished enemy. The mischievous torrent is taught to drudge for man: the wild beasts he makes useful for food, or dress, or labor; the chemic explosions are controlled like his watch. These are now the steeds on which he rides. Man moves in all modes, by legs of horses, by wings of wind, by steam, by gas of balloon, by electricity, and stands on tiptoe threatening to hunt the eagle in his own element. There's nothing he will not make his carrier.

Steam was, till the other day, the devil which we dreaded. Every pot made by any human potter or brazier had a hole in its cover, to let off the enemy, lest he should lift pot and roof, and carry the house away. But the Marquis of Worcester,[8] Watt, and Fulton bethought themselves, that, where was power, was not devil, but was God; that it must be availed of, and not by any means let off and wasted. Could he lift pots and roofs and houses so handily? he was the workman they were in search of. He could be used to lift away, chain, and compel other devils, far more reluctant and dangerous, namely, cubic miles of earth, mountains, weight or resistance of water, machinery, and the labors of all men in the world; and time he shall lengthen, and shorten space.

It has not fared much otherwise with higher kinds of steam. The opinion of the million was the terror of the world, and it was attempted, either to dissipate it, by amusing nations, or to pile it over with strata of society,—a layer of soldiers; over that, a layer of lords; and a king on the top; with clamps and hoops of castles, garrisons, and police. But, sometimes, the religious principle would get in, and burst the hoops, and rive every mountain laid on top of it. The Fultons and Watts of politics, believing in unity, saw that it was a power, and, by satisfying it, (as justice satisfies everybody,) through a different disposition of society,—grouping it on a level, instead of piling it into a mountain,— they have contrived to make of this terror the most harmless and energetic form of a State.

Very odious, I confess, are the lessons of Fate. Who likes to have a dapper phrenologist pronouncing on his fortunes? Who likes to believe that he has hidden in his skull, spine, and pelvis, all the vices of a Saxon or Celtic race, which will be sure to pull him down,—with what grandeur of hope and resolve he is fired,—into a selfish, huckstering, servile, dodging animal? A learned physician tells us, the fact is invariable with the Neapolitan, that, when mature, he assumes the forms of the unmistakable scoundrel. That is a little overstated,—but may pass.

8. Edward Somerset, marquis of Worcester (1601–1667), avid student of mechanics who wrote a book in which he describes something like a basic steam engine.

But these are magazines[9] and arsenals. A man must thank his defects, and stand in some terror of his talents. A transcendent talent draws so largely on his forces, as to lame him; a defect pays him revenues on the other side. The sufferance, which is the badge of the Jew, has made him, in these days, the ruler of the rulers of the earth.[1] If Fate is ore and quarry, if evil is good in the making, if limitation is power that shall be, if calamities, oppositions, and weights are wings and means,—we are reconciled.

Fate involves the melioration. No statement of the Universe can have any soundness, which does not admit its ascending effort. The direction of the whole, and of the parts, is toward benefit, and in proportion to the health. Behind every individual, closes organization: before him, opens liberty,—the Better, the Best. The first and worst races are dead. The second and imperfect races are dying out, or remain for the maturing of higher. In the latest race, in man, every generosity, every new perception, the love and praise he extorts from his fellows, are certificates of advance out of fate into freedom. Liberation of the will from the sheaths and clogs of organization which he has outgrown, is the end and aim of this world. Every calamity is a spur and valuable hint; and where his endeavors do not yet fully avail, they tell as tendency. The whole circle of animal life,—tooth against tooth,—devouring war, war for food, a yelp of pain and a grunt of triumph, until, at last, the whole menagerie, the whole chemical mass is mellowed and refined for higher use,— pleases at a sufficient perspective.

But to see how fate slides into freedom, and freedom into fate, observe how far the roots of every creature run, or find, if you can, a point where there is no thread of connection. Our life is consentaneous[2] and far-related. This knot of nature is so well tied, that nobody was ever cunning enough to find the two ends. Nature is intricate, overlapped, interweaved, and endless. Christopher Wren said of the beautiful King's College chapel,[3] "that, if anybody would tell him where to lay the first stone, he would build such another." But where shall we find the first atom in this house of man, which is all consent, inosculation,[4] and balance of parts?

The web of relation is shown in *habitat*, shown in hybernation. When hybernation was observed, it was found, that, whilst some animals became torpid in winter, others were torpid in summer: hybernation then was a false name. The *long sleep* is not an effect of cold, but is regulated by the supply of food proper to the animal. It becomes torpid when the fruit or prey it lives on is not in season, and regains its activity when its food is ready.

Eyes are found in light; ears in auricular[5] air; feet on land; fins in water; wings in air; and, each creature where it was meant to be, with a mutual fitness. Every zone has its own *Fauna*. There is adjustment between the animal and its food, its parasite, its enemy. Balances are kept. It is not allowed to diminish in numbers, nor to exceed. The like adjustments exist for man. His food is cooked, when he arrives; his coal in the pit; the house ventilated; the mud of the deluge dried; his companions arrived at the same hour, and awaiting him with love, concert, laughter, and tears. These are coarse adjustments, but the invisible are not less. There are more belongings to every creature than his air and his food. His instincts must be met, and he has

---

9. Storehouses.
1. By control of certain banks.
2. Consistent.
3. At Cambridge University. Christopher Wren

(1632–1732), English architect.
4. The uniting of blood vessels, nerve fibers, or the like by small openings.
5. Having to do with hearing.

predisposing power that bends and fits what is near him to his use. He is not possible until the invisible things are right for him, as well as the visible. Of what changes, then, in sky and earth, and in finer skies and earths, does the appearance of some Dante or Columbus[6] apprise us!

How is this effected? Nature is no spendthrift, but takes the shortest way to her ends. As the general says to his soldiers, "if you want a fort, build a fort," so nature makes every creature do its own work and get its living,—is it planet, animal, or tree. The planet makes itself. The animal cell makes itself;—then, what it wants. Every creature,—wren or dragon,—shall make its own lair. As soon as there is life, there is self-direction, and absorbing and using of material. Life is freedom,—life in the direct ratio of its amount. You may be sure, the new-born man is not inert. Life works both voluntarily and supernaturally in its neighborhood. Do you suppose, he can be estimated by his weight in pounds, or, that he is contained in his skin,—this reaching, radiating, jaculating[7] fellow? The smallest candle fills a mile with its rays, and the papillæ[8] of a man run out to every star.

When there is something to be done, the world knows how to get it done. The vegetable eye makes leaf, pericarp,[9] root, bark, or thorn, as the need is; the first cell converts itself into stomach, mouth, nose, or nail, according to the want: the world throws its life into a hero or a shepherd; and puts him where he is wanted. Dante and Columbus were Italians, in their time: they would be Russians or Americans to-day. Things ripen, new men come. The adaptation is not capricious. The ulterior aim, the purpose beyond itself, the correlation by which planets subside and crystallize, then animate beasts and men, will not stop, but will work into finer particulars, and from finer to finest.

The secret of the world is, the tie between person and event. Person makes event, and event person. The "times," "the age," what is that, but a few profound persons and a few active persons who epitomize the times?—Goethe, Hegel, Metternich, Adams, Calhoun, Guizot, Peel, Cobden, Kossuth, Rothschild, Astor, Brunel,[1] and the rest. The same fitness must be presumed between a man and the time and event, as between the sexes, or between a race of animals and the food it eats, or the inferior races it uses. He thinks his fate alien, because the copula is hidden. But the soul contains the event that shall befall it, for the event is only the actualization of its thoughts; and what we pray to ourselves for is always granted. The event is the print of your form. It fits you like your skin. What each does is proper to him. Events are the children of his body and mind. We learn that the soul of Fate is the soul of us, as Hafiz sings,

> Alas! till now I had not known.
> My guide and fortune's guide are one.

---

6. Italian navigator (1451–1506) who opened the New World to exploration. Dante (1265–1321), Italian poet and author of *The Divine Comedy*.
7. Hurling.
8. Nipplelike protuberances.
9. Seed vessel of a fruit.
1. Isambard Brunel (1806–1859), designer of the first Atlantic steamer, the *Great Western*. Johann Wolfgang von Goethe (1749–1832), German poet and dramatist. Georg Wilhelm Friedrich Hegel (1770–1831), German philosopher. Prince Klemens von Metternich (1773–1859), Austrian statesman. John Adams (1735–1826), second president of the United States. John C. Calhoun (1782–1850), vice president of the United States 1825–32 and long-time politician. François Guizot (1787–1874), French historian and statesman. Robert Peel (1788–1850), prime minister of Great Britain 1834–35 and 1841–46. Richard Cobden (1804–1865), British economist and politician. Lajos Kossuth (1802–1894), Hungarian patriot and statesman. Meyer Rothschild (1743–1812), German-Jewish banker (or his sons). John Jacob Astor (1763–1848), German-born American fur trader, major capitalist of his time.

All the toys that infatuate men, and which they play for,—houses, land, money, luxury, power, fame, are the selfsame thing, with a new gauze or two of illusion overlaid. And of all the drums and rattles by which men are made willing to have their heads broke, and are led out solemnly every morning to parade,—the most admirable is this by which we are brought to believe that events are arbitrary, and independent of actions. At the conjuror's, we detect the hair by which he moves his puppet, but we have not eyes sharp enough to descry the thread that ties cause and effect.

Nature magically suits the man to his fortunes, by making these the fruit of his character. Ducks take to the water, eagles to the sky, waders to the sea margin, hunters to the forest, clerks to counting-rooms, soldiers to the frontier. Thus events grow on the same stem with persons; are sub-persons. The pleasure of life is according to the man that lives it, and not according to the work or the place. Life is an ecstasy. We know what madness belongs to love,— what power to paint a vile object in hues of heaven. As insane persons are indifferent to their dress, diet, and, other accommodations, and, as we do in dreams, with equanimity, the most absurd acts, so, a drop more of wine in our cup of life will reconcile us to strange company and work. Each creature puts forth from itself its own condition and sphere, as the slug sweats out its slimy house on the pear-leaf, and the woolly aphides on the apple perspire their own bed, and the fish its shell. In youth, we clothe ourselves with rainbows, and go as brave as the zodiac. In age, we put out another sort of perspiration,—gout, fever, rheumatism, caprice, doubt, fretting, and avarice.

A man's fortunes are the fruit of his character. A man's friends are his magnetisms. We go to Herodotus and Plutarch[2] for examples of Fate; but we are examples. "*Quisque suos patimur manes.*"[3] The tendency of every man to enact all that is in his constitution is expressed in the old belief, that the efforts which we make to escape from our destiny only serve to lead us into it: and I have noticed, a man likes better to be complimented on his position, as the proof of the last or total excellence, than on his merits.

A man will see his character emitted in the events that seem to meet, but which exude from and accompany him. Events expand with the character. As once he found himself among toys, so now he plays a part in colossal systems, and his growth is declared in his ambition, his companions, and his performance. He looks like a piece of luck, but is a piece of causation;—the mosaic, angulated[4] and ground to fit into the gap he fills. Hence in each town there is some man who is, in his brain and performance, an explanation of the tillage, production, factories, banks, churches, ways of living, and society, of that town. If you do not chance to meet him, all that you see will leave you a little puzzled: if you see him, it will become plain. We know in Massachusetts who built New Bedford, who built Lynn, Lowell, Lawrence, Clinton, Fitchburg, Holyoke, Portland, and many another noisy mart. Each of these men, if they were transparent, would seem to you not so much men, as walking cities, and, wherever you put them, they would build one.

History is the action and reaction of these two,—Nature and Thought;— two boys pushing each other on the curb-stone of the pavement. Everything is

2. Greek biographer and philosopher (46?–120?). Herodotus (5th century B.C.), Greek historian.
3. Each person undergoes his special penalty (Latin). From Anchises' speech to his son Aeneas in the Under-world, whither Aeneas has gone to learn from his father what destiny awaits him and sees the pageant of Roman heroes to come in the future (*Aeneid* 6.743).
4. Built with corners.

pusher or pushed: and matter and mind are in perpetual tilt and balance, so. Whilst the man is weak, the earth takes up him. He plants his brain and affections. By and by he will take up the earth, and have his gardens and vineyards in the beautiful order and productiveness of his thought. Every solid in the universe is ready to become fluid on the approach of the mind, and the power to flux it is the measure of the mind. If the wall remain adamant, it accuses the want of thought. To a subtler force, it will stream into new forms, expressive of the character of the mind. What is the city in which we sit here, but an aggregate of incongruous materials, which have obeyed the will of some man? The granite was reluctant, but his hands were stronger, and it came. Iron was deep in the ground, and well combined with stone; but could not hide from his fires. Wood, lime, stuffs, fruits, gums,[5] were dispersed over the earth and sea, in vain. Here they are, within reach of every man's day-labor,— what he wants of them. The whole world is the flux of matter over the wires of thought to the poles or points where it would build. The races of men rise out of the ground preoccupied with a thought which rules them, and divided into parties ready armed and angry to fight for this metaphysical abstraction. The quality of the thought differences the Egyptian and the Roman, the Austrian and the American. The men who come on the stage at one period are all found to be related to each other. Certain ideas are in the air. We are all impressionable, for we are made of them; all impressionable, but some more than others, and these first express them. This explains the curious contemporaneousness of inventions and discoveries. The truth is in the air, and the most impressionable brain will announce it first, but all will announce it a few minutes later. So women, as most susceptible, are the best index of the coming hour. So the great man, that is, the man most imbued with the spirit of the time, is the impressionable man,—of a fibre irritable and delicate, like iodine to light. He feels the infinitesimal attractions. His mind is righter than others, because he yields to a current so feeble as can be felt only by a needle delicately poised.

The correlation is shown in defects. Möller,[6] in his Essay on Architecture, taught that the building which was fitted accurately to answer its end, would turn out to be beautiful, though beauty had not been intended. I find the like unity in human structures rather virulent and pervasive; that a crudity in the blood will appear in the argument; a hump in the shoulder will appear in the speech and handiwork. If his mind could be seen, the hump would be seen. If a man has a seesaw in his voice, it will run into his sentences, into his poem, into the structure of his fable, into his speculation, into his charity. And, as every man is hunted by his own dæmon,[7] vexed by his own disease, this checks all his activity.

So each man, like each plant, has his parasites. A strong, astringent, bilious nature has more truculent enemies than the slugs and moths that fret my leaves. Such an one has curculios, borers, knifeworms: a swindler ate him first, then a client, then a quack, then smooth, plausible gentlemen, bitter and selfish as Moloch.[8]

5. Various viscous substances exuded by certain trees or plants.
6. Georg Moller (1784–1852), German architect and author of Essay on the Origin and Progress of Gothic Architecture (1825).
7. His own spirit.

8. Phoenician god to whom children were burned in sacrifice. In Paradise Lost, 2.44–45, he is described as "the strongest and fiercest Spirit / That fought in Heav'n." This passage originated in Emerson's journals as a meditation on how a "strong, astringent, bilious nature"—that of his brother-in-law Dr. Charles T.

This correlation really existing can be divined. If the threads are there, thought can follow and show them. Especially when a soul is quick and docile; as Chaucer sings,

"Or if the soul of proper kind
Be so perfect as men find,
That it wot what is to come,
And that he warneth all and some
Of every of their aventures,
By previsions or figures;
But that our flesh hath not might
It to understand aright
For it is warned too darkly."[9]—

Some people are made up of rhyme, coincidence, omen, periodicity, and presage: they meet the person they seek; what their companion prepares to say to them, they first say to him; and a hundred signs apprise them of what is about to befall.

Wonderful intricacy in the web, wonderful constancy in the design this vagabond life admits. We wonder how the fly finds its mate, and yet year after year we find two men, two women, without legal or carnal tie, spend a great part of their best time within a few feet of each other. And the moral is, that what we seek we shall find;[1] what we flee from flees from us; as Goethe said, "what we wish for in youth, comes in heaps on us in old age,"[2] too often cursed with the granting of our prayer: and hence the high caution, that, since we are sure of having what we wish, we beware to ask only for high things.

One key, one solution to the mysteries of human condition, one solution to the old knots of fate, freedom, and foreknowledge, exists, the propounding, namely, of the double consciousness. A man must ride alternately on the horses of his private and his public nature, as the equestrians in the circus throw themselves nimbly from horse to horse, or plant one foot on the back of one, and the other foot on the back of the other. So when a man is the victim of his fate, has sciatica in his loins, and cramp in his mind; a club-foot and a club in his wit; a sour face, and a selfish temper; a strut in his gait, and a conceit in his affection; or is ground to powder by the vice of his race; he is to rally on his relation to the Universe, which his ruin benefits. Leaving the dæmon who suffers, he is to take sides with the Deity who secures universal benefit by his pain.

To offset the drag of temperament and race, which pulls down, learn this lesson, namely, that by the cunning co-presence of two elements, which is throughout nature, whatever lames or paralyzes you, draws in with it the divinity, in some form, to repay. A good intention clothes itself with sudden power. When a god wishes to ride, any chip or pebble will bud and shoot out winged feet, and serve him for a horse.

Let us build altars to the Blessed Unity which holds nature and souls in

Jackson—had become surrounded by enemies. The "curculio" or weevil was Dr. Henry J. Bigelow of Massachusetts General Hospital, who attacked Jackson's claims to have invented the use of ether as an anesthetic. Two borers were John W. Foster and Josiah D. Whitney, associates of Jackson's on a geological survey who became highly critical of him. The swindler was Charles Brown, a brother-in-law of Jackson's. The cli-ent was Samuel F. B. Morse, whom Jackson charged with stealing from him the principles of telegraphy. The quack was Dr. William T. G. Morton, who took credit for discovering the use of ether as an anesthetic.

9. *The House of Fame*, Poem, lines 43–51.
1. Matthew 7.7.
2. The epigraph of the second part of Goethe's *Poetry and Truth*.

perfect solution, and compels every atom to serve an universal end. I do not wonder at a snow-flake, a shell, a summer landscape, or the glory of the stars; but at the necessity of beauty under which the universe lies; that all is and must be pictorial; that the rainbow, and the curve of the horizon, and the arch of the blue vault are only results from the organism of the eye. There is no need for foolish amateurs to fetch me to admire a garden of flowers, or a sun-gilt cloud, or a waterfall, when I cannot look without seeing splendor and grace. How idle to choose a random sparkle here or there, when the indwelling necessity plants the rose of beauty on the brow of chaos, and discloses the central intention of Nature to be harmony and joy.

Let us build altars to the Beautiful Necessity. If we thought men were free in the sense, that, in a single exception one fantastical will could prevail over the law of things, it were all one as if a child's hand could pull down the sun. If, in the least particular, one could derange the order of nature,—who would accept the gift of life?

Let us build altars to the Beautiful Necessity, which secures that all is made of one piece; that plaintiff and defendant, friend and enemy, animal and planet, food and eater, are of one kind. In astronomy, is vast space, but no foreign system; in geology, vast time, but the same laws as to-day. Why should we be afraid of Nature, which is no other than "philosophy and theology, embodied"? Why should we fear to be crushed by savage elements, we who are made up of the same elements? Let us build to the Beautiful Necessity, which makes man brave in believing that he cannot shun a danger that is appointed, nor incur one that is not; to the Necessity which rudely or softly educates him to the perception that there are no contingencies; that Law rules throughout existence, a Law which is not intelligent but intelligence,—not personal nor impersonal,—it disdains words and passes understanding; it dissolves persons; it vivifies nature; yet solicits the pure in heart to draw on all its omnipotence.

1860

Thoreau[1]

Henry David Thoreau was the last male descendant of a French ancestor who came to this country from the Isle of Guernsey.[2] His character exhibited occasional traits drawn from this blood in singular combination with a very strong Saxon genius.

He was born in Concord, Massachusetts, on the 12th of July, 1817. He was graduated at Harvard College in 1837, but without any literary distinction. An iconoclast in literature, he seldom thanked colleges for their service to him, holding them in small esteem, whilst yet his debt to them was important. After

1. On May 9, 1862, Emerson read an address at Thoreau's funeral; in a longer form (but still retaining the stance of one eulogizing a neighbor) it was published in the August 1862 *Atlantic Monthly*, the text reprinted here. The essay is permeated with Emerson's conviction that Thoreau, lacking ambition, had drifted into an unsatisfactory course of life as one of the most valuable but most exasperating citizens of Concord. Emerson reveals little sense that his crotchety but no-ble-minded disciple had set himself the high ambition of becoming a great writer and had bravely devoted his life to achieving that aim. Partial portrait that it is, the essay is indispensable, the fruit of Emerson's quarter century of intimate knowledge and the source for many of Thoreau's sayings, which otherwise would have been lost.
2. Island in the English Channel. Emerson's racial assumptions are typical of the period.

leaving the University, he joined his brother in teaching a private school, which he soon renounced. His father was a manufacturer of lead-pencils, and Henry applied himself for a time to this craft, believing he could make a better pencil than was then in use. After completing his experiments, he exhibited his work to chemists and artists in Boston, and having obtained their certificates to its excellence and to its equality with the best London manufacture, he returned home contented. His friends congratulated him that he had now opened his way to fortune. But he replied, that he should never make another pencil. "Why should I? I would not do again what I have done once." He resumed his endless walks and miscellaneous studies, making every day some new acquaintance with Nature, though as yet never speaking of zoölogy or botany, since, though very studious of natural facts, he was incurious of technical and textual science.

At this time, a strong, healthy youth, fresh from college, whilst all his companions were choosing their profession, or eager to begin some lucrative employment, it was inevitable that his thoughts should be exercised on the same question, and it required rare decision to refuse all the accustomed paths, and keep his solitary freedom at the cost of disappointing the natural expectations of his family and friends: all the more difficult that he had a perfect probity, was exact in securing his own independence, and in holding every man to the like duty. But Thoreau never faltered. He was a born protestant. He declined to give up his large ambition of knowledge and action for any narrow craft or profession, aiming at a much more comprehensive calling, the art of living well. If he slighted and defied the opinions of others, it was only that he was more intent to reconcile his practice with his own belief. Never idle or self-indulgent, he preferred, when he wanted money, earning it by some piece of manual labor agreeable to him, as building a boat or a fence, planting, grafting, surveying, or other short work, to any long engagements. With his hardy habits and few wants, his skill in wood-craft, and his powerful arithmetic, he was very competent to live in any part of the world. It would cost him less time to supply his wants than another. He was therefore secure of his leisure.

A natural skill for mensuration,[3] growing out of his mathematical knowledge, and his habit of ascertaining the measures and distance of objects which interested him, the size of trees, the depth and extent of ponds and rivers, the height of mountains, and the air-line distance of his favorite summits,—this, and his intimate knowledge of the territory about Concord, made him drift into the profession of land-surveyor. It had the advantage for him that it led him continually into new and secluded grounds, and helped his studies of Nature. His accuracy and skill in this work were readily appreciated, and he found all the employment he wanted.

He could easily solve the problems of the surveyor, but he was daily beset with graver questions, which he manfully confronted. He interrogated every custom, and wished to settle all his practice on an ideal foundation. He was a protestant à l'outrance,[4] and few lives contain so many renunciations. He was bred to no profession; he never married; he lived alone; he never went to church; he never voted; he refused to pay a tax to the State; he ate no flesh, he drank no wine, he never knew the use of tobacco; and, though a naturalist,

---

3. Measuring.   4. I.e., the extremest sort of protestor (French).

he used neither trap nor gun. He chose, wisely, no doubt, for himself, to be the bachelor of thought and Nature. He had no talent for wealth, and knew how to be poor without the least hint of squalor or inelegance. Perhaps he fell into his way of living without forecasting it much, but approved it with later wisdom. "I am often reminded," he wrote in his journal, "that, if I had bestowed on me the wealth of Crœsus,[5] my aims must be still the same, and my means essentially the same." He had no temptations to fight against,—no appetites, no passions, no taste for elegant trifles. A fine house, dress, the manners and talk of highly cultivated people were all thrown away on him. He much preferred a good Indian, and considered these refinements as impediments to conversation, wishing to meet his companion on the simplest terms. He declined invitations to dinner-parties, because there each was in every one's way, and he could not meet the individuals to any purpose. "They make their pride," he said, "in making their dinner cost much; I make my pride in making my dinner cost little." When asked at table what dish he preferred, he answered, "The nearest." He did not like the taste of wine, and never had a vice in his life. He said,—"I have a faint recollection of pleasure derived from smoking dried lily-stems, before I was a man. I had commonly a supply of these. I have never smoked anything more noxious."

He chose to be rich by making his wants few, and supplying them himself. In his travels, he used the railroad only to get over so much country as was unimportant to the present purpose, walking hundreds of miles, avoiding taverns, buying a lodging in farmers' and fishermen's houses, as cheaper, and more agreeable to him, and because there he could better find the men and the information he wanted.

There was somewhat military in his nature not to be subdued, always manly and able, but rarely tender, as if he did not feel himself except in opposition. He wanted a fallacy to expose, a blunder to pillory, I may say required a little sense of victory, a roll of the drum, to call his powers into full exercise. It cost him nothing to say No; indeed, he found it much easier than to say Yes. It seemed as if his first instinct on hearing a proposition was to controvert it, so impatient was he of the limitations of our daily thought. This habit, of course, is a little chilling to the social affections; and though the companion would in the end acquit him of any malice or untruth, yet it mars conversation. Hence, no equal companion stood in affectionate relations with one so pure and guileless. "I love Henry," said one of his friends, "but I cannot like him; and as for taking his arm, I should as soon think of taking the arm of an elm-tree."

Yet, hermit and stoic as he was, he was really fond of sympathy, and threw himself heartily and childlike into the company of young people whom he loved, and whom he delighted to entertain, as he only could, with the varied and endless anecdotes of his experiences by field and river. And he was always ready to lead a huckleberry-party or a search for chestnuts or grapes. Talking, one day, of a public discourse, Henry remarked, that whatever succeeded with the audience was bad. I said, "Who would not like to write something which all can read, like 'Robinson Crusoe'? and who does not see with regret that his page is not solid with a right materialistic treatment, which delights everybody?" Henry objected, of course, and vaunted the better lectures which reached only a few persons. But, at supper, a young girl, understanding that

5. King of Lydia (6th century B.C.), in Asia Minor, fabled to have been the richest man in the world.

he was to lecture at the Lyceum,[6] sharply asked him, "whether his lecture would be a nice, interesting story, such as she wished to hear, or whether it was one of those old philosophical things that she did not care about." Henry turned to her, and bethought himself, and, I saw, was trying to believe that he had matter that might fit her and her brother, who were to sit up and go to the lecture, if it was a good one for them.

He was a speaker and actor of the truth,—born such,—and was ever running into dramatic situations from this cause. In any circumstance, it interested all bystanders to know what part Henry would take, and what he would say; and he did not disappoint expectation, but used an original judgment on each emergency. In 1845 he built himself a small framed house on the shores of Walden Pond, and lived there two years alone, a life of labor and study. This action was quite native and fit for him. No one who knew him would tax him with affectation. He was more unlike his neighbors in his thought than in his action. As soon as he had exhausted the advantages of that solitude, he abandoned it. In 1847, not approving some uses to which the public expenditure was applied, he refused to pay his town tax, and was put in jail. A friend[7] paid the tax for him, and he was released. The like annoyance was threatened the next year. But, as his friends paid the tax, notwithstanding his protest, I believe he ceased to resist. No opposition or ridicule had any weight with him. He coldly and fully stated his opinion without affecting to believe that it was the opinion of the company. It was of no consequence, if every one present held the opposite opinion. On one occasion he went to the University Library to procure some books. The librarian refused to lend them. Mr. Thoreau repaired to the President, who stated to him the rules and usages, which permitted the loan of books to resident graduates, to clergymen who were alumni, and to some others resident within a circle of ten miles' radius from the College. Mr. Thoreau explained to the President that the railroad had destroyed the old scale of distances,—that the library was useless, yes, and President and College useless, on the terms of his rules,—that the one benefit he owed to the College was its library,—that, at this moment, not only his want of books was imperative, but he wanted a large number of books, and assured him that he, Thoreau, and not the librarian, was the proper custodian of these. In short, the President found the petitioner so formidable, and the rules getting to look so ridiculous, that he ended by giving him a privilege which in his hands proved unlimited thereafter.

No truer American existed than Thoreau. His preference of his country and condition was genuine, and his aversation from English and European manners and tastes almost reached contempt. He listened impatiently to news or *bon mots* gleaned from London circles; and though he tried to be civil, these anecdotes fatigued him. The men were all imitating each other, and on a small mould. Why can they not live as far apart as possible, and each be a man by himself? What he sought was the most energetic nature; and he wished to go to Oregon, not to London. "In every part of Great Britain," he wrote in his diary, "are discovered traces of the Romans, their funereal urns, their camps, their roads, their dwellings. But New England, at least, is not based on any Roman ruins. We have not to lay the foundations of our houses on the ashes of a former civilization."

6. Public hall where lectures were given.
7. The friend is variously identified. The year was actually 1846.

But, idealist as he was, standing for abolition of slavery, abolition of tariffs, almost for abolition of government, it is needless to say he found himself not only unrepresented in actual politics, but almost equally opposed to every class of reformers. Yet he paid the tribute of his uniform respect to the Anti-Slavery party. One man, whose personal acquaintance he had formed, he honored with exceptional regard. Before the first friendly word had been spoken for Captain John Brown,[8] he sent notices to most houses in Concord, that he would speak in a public hall on the condition and charter of John Brown, on Sunday evening, and invited all people to come. The Republican Committee, the Abolitionist Committee, sent him word that it was premature and not advisable. He replied,—"I did not send to you for advice, but to announce that I am to speak." The hall was filled at an early hour by people of all parties, and his earnest eulogy of the hero was heard by all respectfully, by many with a sympathy that surprised themselves.

It was said of Plotinus[9] that he was ashamed of his body, and 't is very likely he had good reason for it,—that his body was a bad servant, and he had not skill in dealing with the material world, as happens often to men of abstract intellect. But Mr. Thoreau was equipped with a most adapted and serviceable body. He was of short stature, firmly built, of light complexion, with strong, serious blue eyes, and a grave aspect,—his face covered in the late years with a becoming beard. His senses were acute, his frame well-knit and hardy, his hands strong and skilful in the use of tools. And there was a wonderful fitness of body and mind. He could pace sixteen rods more accurately than another man could measure them with rod and chain. He could find his path in the woods at night, he said, better by his feet than his eyes. He could estimate the measure of a tree very well by his eye; he could estimate the weight of a calf or a pig, like a dealer. From a box containing a bushel or more of loose pencils, he could take up with his hands fast enough just a dozen pencils at every grasp. He was a good swimmer, runner, skater, boatman, and would probably outwalk most countrymen in a day's journey. And the relation of body to mind was still finer than we have indicated. He said he wanted every stride his legs made. The length of his walk uniformly made the length of his writing. If shut up in the house, he did not write at all.

He had a strong common sense, like that which Rose Flammock,[1] the weaver's daughter, in Scott's romance, commends in her father, as resembling a yardstick, which, whilst it measures dowlas and diaper, can equally well measure tapestry and cloth of gold. He had always a new resource. When I was planting forest-trees, and had procured half a peck of acorns, he said that only a small portion of them would be sound, and proceeded to examine them, and select the sound ones. But finding this took time, he said, "I think, if you put them all into water, the good ones will sink"; which experiment we tried with success. He could plan a garden, or a house, or a barn; would have been competent to lead a "Pacific Exploring Expedition"; could give judicious counsel in the gravest private or public affairs.

He lived for the day, not cumbered and mortified by his memory. If he brought you yesterday a new proposition, he would bring you to-day another

---

8. The American abolitionist (1800–1859), executed after seizing Harpers Ferry late in 1859.
9. Roman philosopher (205?–270), exemplar of neoplatonism, the religious system made up from teach-ings of Plato and other Greeks mixed with Judeo-Christian and other doctrines.
1. Character in Sir Walter Scott's *The Betrothed* (1825).

not less revolutionary. A very industrious man, and setting, like all highly organized men, a high value on his time, he seemed the only man of leisure in town, always ready for any excursion that promised well, or for conversation prolonged into late hours. His trenchant sense was never stopped by his rules of daily prudence, but was always up to the new occasion. He liked and used the simplest food, yet, when someone urged a vegetable diet, Thoreau thought all diets a very small matter, saying that "the man who shoots the buffalo lives better than the man who boards at the Graham House."[2] He said,—"You can sleep near the railroad, and never be disturbed: Nature knows very well what sounds are worth attending to, and has made up her mind not to hear the railroad-whistle. But things respect the devout mind, and a mental ecstasy was never interrupted." He noted, what repeatedly befell him, that, after receiving from a distance a rare plant, he would presently find the same in his own haunts. And those pieces of luck which happen only to good players happened to him. One day, walking with a stranger, who inquired where Indian arrow-heads could be found, he replied, "Everywhere," and, stooping forward, picked one on the instant from the ground. At Mount Washington, in Tuckerman's Ravine, Thoreau had a bad fall, and sprained his foot. As he was in the act of getting up from his fall, he saw for the first time the leaves of the *Arnica mollis*.[3]

His robust common sense, armed with stout hands, keen perceptions, and strong will, cannot yet account for the superiority which shone in his simple and hidden life. I must add the cardinal fact, that there was an excellent wisdom in him, proper to a rare class of men, which showed him the material world as a means and symbol. This discovery, which sometimes yields to poets a certain casual and interrupted light, serving for the ornament of their writing, was in him an unsleeping insight; and whatever faults or obstructions of temperament might cloud it, he was not disobedient to the heavenly vision. In his youth, he said, one day, "The other world is all my art: my pencils will draw no other; my jack-knife will cut nothing else; I do not use it as a means." This was the muse and genius that ruled his opinions, conversation, studies, work, and course of life. This made him a searching judge of men. At first glance he measured his companion, and, though insensible to some fine traits of culture, could very well report his weight and calibre. And this made the impression of genius which his conversation sometimes gave.

He understood the matter in hand at a glance, and saw the limitations and poverty of those he talked with, so that nothing seemed concealed from such terrible eyes. I have repeatedly known young men of sensibility converted in a moment to the belief that this was the man they were in search of, the man of men, who could tell them all they should do. His own dealing with them was never affectionate, but superior, didactic,—scorning their petty ways,—very slowly conceding, or not conceding at all, the promise of his society at their houses, or even at his own. "Would he not walk with them?" "He did not know. There was nothing so important to him as his walk; he had no walks to throw away on company." Visits were offered him from respectful parties, but he declined them. Admiring friends offered to carry him at their own cost to the Yellow-Stone River,—to the West Indies,—to South America. But though

2. Boston boardinghouse run on Sylvester Graham's dietary system (one part of which remains in the na- tional diet as the graham cracker).
3. Thistle used medicinally.

nothing could be more grave or considered than his refusals, they remind one in quite new relations of that fop Brummel's[4] reply to the gentleman who offered him his carriage in a shower, "But where will *you* ride, then?"—and what accusing silences, and what searching and irresistible speeches, battering down all defences, his companions can remember!

Mr. Thoreau dedicated his genius with such entire love to the fields, hills, and waters of his native town, that he made them known and interesting to all reading Americans, and to people over the sea. The river on whose banks he was born and died he knew from its springs to its confluence with the Merrimack. He had made summer and winter observations on it for many years, and at every hour of the day and the night. The result of the recent survey of the Water Commissioners appointed by the State of Massachusetts he had reached by his private experiments, several years earlier. Every fact which occurs in the bed, on the banks, or in the air over it; the fishes, and their spawning and nests, their manners, their food; the shad-flies which fill the air on a certain evening once a year, and which are snapped at by the fishes so ravenously that many of these die of repletion; the conical heaps of small stones on the river-shallows, one of which heaps will sometimes overfill a cart,—these heaps the huge nests of small fishes; the birds which frequent the stream, heron, duck, sheldrake, loon, osprey; the snake, muskrat, otter, woodchuck, and fox, on the banks; the turtle, frog, hyla, and cricket, which make the banks vocal,—were all known to him, and, as it were, townsmen and fellow-creatures; so that he felt an absurdity or violence in any narrative of one of these by itself apart, and still more of its dimensions on an inch-rule, or in the exhibition of its skeleton, or the specimen of a squirrel or a bird in brandy. He liked to speak of the manners of the river, as itself a lawful creature, yet with exactness, and always to an observed fact. As he knew the river, so the ponds in this region.

One of the weapons he used, more important than microscope or alcohol-receiver to other investigators, was a whim which grew on him by indulgence, yet appeared in gravest statement, namely, of extolling his own town and neighborhood as the most favored centre for natural observation. He remarked that the Flora of Massachusetts embraced almost all the important plants of America,—most of the oaks, most of the willows, the best pines, the ash, the maple, the beech, the nuts. He returned Kane's[5] "Arctic Voyage" to a friend of whom he had borrowed it, with the remark, that "most of the phenomena noted might be observed in Concord." He seemed a little envious of the Pole, for the coincident sunrise and sunset, or five minutes' day after six months: a splendid fact, which Annursnuc[6] had never afforded him. He found red snow in one of his walks, and told me that he expected to find yet the *Victoria regia*[7] in Concord. He was the attorney of the indigenous plants, and owned to a preference of the weeds to the imported plants, as of the Indian to the civilized man,—and noticed, with pleasure, that the willow bean-poles of his neighbor had grown more than his beans. "See these weeds," he said, "which have been hoed at by a million farmers all spring and summer, and yet have prevailed, and just now come out triumphant over all lanes, pastures, fields, and gardens, such is their vigor. We have insulted them with low names, too,—as Pigweed,

---

4. George ("Beau") Brummell (1778–1840), British dandy.
5. Elisha Kent Kane (1820–1857), American naval of-

ficer and explorer of a route to the North Pole.
6. A Concord hill.
7. South American water lily.

Wormwood, Chickweed, Shad-Blossom." He says, "They have brave names, too,—Ambrosia, Stellaria, Amelanchia, Amaranth, etc."

I think his fancy for referring everything to the meridian of Concord did not grow out of any ignorance or depreciation of other longitudes or latitudes, but was rather a playful expression of his conviction of the indifferency of all places, and that the best place for each is where he stands. He expressed it once in this wise:—"I think nothing is to be hoped from you, if this bit of mould under your feet is not sweeter to you to eat than any other in this world, or in any world."

The other weapon with which he conquered all obstacles in science was patience. He knew how to sit immovable, a part of the rock he rested on, until the bird, the reptile, the fish, which had retired from him, should come back, and resume its habits, nay, moved by curiosity, should come to him and watch him.

It was a pleasure and a privilege to walk with him. He knew the country like a fox or a bird, and passed through it as freely by paths of his own. He knew every track in the snow or on the ground, and what creature had taken this path before him. One must submit abjectly to such a guide, and the reward was great. Under his arm he carried an old music-book to press plants; in his pocket, his diary and pencil, a spy-glass for birds, microscope, jack-knife, and twine. He wore straw hat, stout shoes, strong gray trousers, to brave shrub-oaks and smilax, and to climb a tree for a hawk's or a squirrel's nest. He waded into the pool for the water-plants, and his strong legs were no insignificant part of his armor. On the day I speak of he looked for the Menyanthes,[8] detected it across the wide pool, and, on examination of the florets, decided that it had been in flower five days. He drew out of his breast-pocket his diary, and read the names of all the plants that should bloom on this day, whereof he kept account as a banker when his notes fall due. The Cypripedium[9] not due till to-morrow. He thought, that, if waked up from a trance, in this swamp, he could tell by the plants what time of the year it was within two days. The redstart was flying about, and presently the fine grosbeaks, whose brilliant scarlet makes the rash gazer wipe his eye,[1] and whose fine clear note Thoreau compared to that of a tanager which has got rid of its hoarseness. Presently he heard a note which he called that of the night-warbler, a bird he had never identified, had been in search of twelve years, which always, when he saw it, was in the act of diving down into a tree or bush, and which it was vain to seek; the only bird that sings indifferently by night and by day. I told him he must beware of finding and booking it, lest life should have nothing more to show him. He said, "What you seek in vain for, half your life, one day you come full upon all the family at dinner. You seek it like a dream, and as soon as you find it you become its prey."

His interest in the flower or the bird lay very deep in his mind, was connected with Nature,—and the meaning of Nature was never attempted to be defined by him. He would not offer a memoir of his observations to the Natural History Society. "Why should I? To detach the description from its connections in my mind would make it no longer true or valuable to me: and they do not wish what belongs to it." His power of observation seemed to indicate

---

8. Bogbean (so-called from its growing in boglike areas) or buckbean.

9. Lady's slipper.

1. An allusion to George Herbert's *Virtue* (1633).

additional senses. He saw as with microscope, heard as with ear-trumpet, and his memory was a photographic register of all he saw and heard. And yet none knew better than he that it is not the fact that imports, but the impression or effect of the fact on your mind. Every fact lay in glory in his mind, a type of the order and beauty of the whole.

His determination on Natural History was organic. He confessed that he sometimes felt like a hound or a panther, and, if born among Indians, would have been a fell hunter. But, restrained by his Massachusetts culture, he played out the game in this mild form of botany and ichthyology. His intimacy with animals suggested what Thomas Fuller records of Butler the apiologist, that "either he had told the bees things or the bees had told him." Snakes coiled round his leg; the fishes swam into his hand, and he took them out of the water; he pulled the woodchuck out of its hole by the tail, and took the foxes under his protection from the hunters. Our naturalist had perfect magnanimity; he had no secrets: he would carry you to the heron's haunt, or even to his most prized botanical swamp,—possibly knowing that you could never find it again, yet willing to take his risks.

No college ever offered him a diploma, or a professor's chair; no academy made him its corresponding secretary, its discoverer, or even its member. Perhaps these learned bodies feared the satire of his presence. Yet so much knowledge of Nature's secret and genius few others possessed, none in a more large and religious synthesis. For not a particle of respect had he to the opinions of any man or body of men, but homage solely to the truth itself; and as he discovered everywhere among doctors some leaning of courtesy, it discredited them. He grew to be revered and admired by his townsmen, who had at first known him only as an oddity. The farmers who employed him as a surveyor soon discovered his rare accuracy and skill, his knowledge of their lands, of trees, of birds, of Indian remains, and the like, which enabled him to tell every farmer more than he knew before of his own farm; so that he began to feel a little as if Mr. Thoreau had better rights in his land than he. They felt, too, the superiority of character which addressed all men with a native authority.

Indian relics abound in Concord,—arrow-heads, stone chisels, pestles, and fragments of pottery; and on the river-bank, large heaps of clam-shells and ashes mark spots which the savages frequented. These, and every circumstance touching the Indian, were important in his eyes. His visits to Maine were chiefly for love of the Indian. He had the satisfaction of seeing the manufacture of the bark-canoe, as well as of trying his hand in its management on the rapids. He was inquisitive about the making of the stone arrow-head, and in his last days charged a youth setting out for the Rocky Mountains to find an Indian who could tell him that: "It was well worth a visit to California to learn it." Occasionally, a small party of Penobscot Indians would visit Concord, and pitch their tents for a few weeks in summer on the river-bank. He failed not to make acquaintance with the best of them; though he well knew that asking questions of Indians is like catechizing beavers and rabbits. In his last visit to Maine he had great satisfaction from Joseph Polis, an intelligent Indian of Oldtown, who was his guide for some weeks.

He was equally interested in every natural fact. The depth of his perception found likeness of law throughout Nature, and I know not any genius who so swiftly inferred universal law from the single fact. He was no pedant of a department. His eye was open to beauty, and his ear to music. He found these, not in rare conditions, but wheresoever he went. He thought the best of music was in single strains; and he found poetic suggestion in the humming of the telegraph-wire.

His poetry might be bad or good; he no doubt wanted a lyric facility and technical skill; but he had the source of poetry in his spiritual perception. He was a good reader and critic, and his judgment on poetry was to the ground of it. He could not be deceived as to the presence or absence of the poetic element in any composition, and his thirst for this made him negligent and perhaps scornful of superficial graces. He would pass by many delicate rhythms, but he would have detected every live stanza or line in a volume, and knew very well where to find an equal poetic charm in prose. He was so enamored of the spiritual beauty that he held all actual written poems in very light esteem in the comparison. He admired Æschylus and Pindar; but, when some one was commending them, he said that "Æschylus and the Greeks, in describing Apollo and Orpheus, had given no song, or no good one. They ought not to have moved trees, but to have chanted to the gods such a hymn as would have sung all their old ideas out of their heads, and new ones in." His own verses are often rude and defective. The gold does not yet run pure, is drossy and crude. The thyme and marjoram are not yet honey. But if he want lyric fineness and technical merits, if he have not the poetic temperament, he never lacks the causal thought, showing that his genius was better than his talent. He knew the worth of the Imagination for the uplifting and consolation of human life, and liked to throw every thought into a symbol. The fact you tell is of no value, but only the impression. For this reason his presence was poetic, always piqued the curiosity to know more deeply the secrets of his mind. He had many reserves, an unwillingness to exhibit to profane eyes what was still sacred in his own, and knew well how to throw a poetic veil over his experience. All readers of "Walden" will remember his mythical record of his disappointments:—

"I long ago lost a hound, a bay horse, and a turtle-dove, and am still on their trail. Many are the travellers I have spoken concerning them, describing their tracks, and what calls they answered to. I have met one or two who had heard the hound, and the tramp of the horse, and even seen the dove disappear behind a cloud; and they seemed as anxious to recover them as if they had lost them themselves."[2]

His riddles were worth the reading, and I confide, that, if at any time I do not understand the expression, it is yet just. Such was the wealth of his truth that it was not worth his while to use words in vain. His poem entitled "Sympathy" reveals the tenderness under that triple steel of stoicism, and the intellectual subtilty it could animate. His classic poem on "Smoke" suggests Simonides,[3] but is better than any poem of Simonides. His biography is in his verses. His habitual thought makes all his poetry a hymn to the Cause of causes, the Spirit which vivifies and controls his own.

> "I hearing get, who had but ears,
> And sight, who had but eyes before;
> I moments live, who lived but years;
> And truth discern, who knew but learning's lore."

---

2. See *Walden*, p. 1727.   3. Greek lyric poet of the 6th century B.C.

And still more in these religious lines:—

> "Now chiefly is my natal hour,
> And only now my prime of life;
> I will not doubt the love untold,
> Which not my worth or want hath bought,
> Which wooed me young, and wooes me old,
> And to this evening hath me brought."[4]

Whilst he used in his writings a certain petulance of remark in reference to churches or churchmen, he was a person of a rare, tender, and absolute religion, a person incapable of any profanation, by act or by thought. Of course, the same isolation which belonged to his original thinking and living detached him from the social religious forms. This is neither to be censured nor regretted. Aristotle long ago explained it, when he said, "One who surpasses his fellow-citizens in virtue is no longer a part of the city. Their law is not for him, since he is a law to himself."[5]

Thoreau was sincerity itself, and might fortify the convictions of prophets in the ethical laws by his holy living. It was an affirmative experience which refused to be set aside. A truth-speaker he, capable of the most deep and strict conversation; a physician to the wounds of any soul; a friend, knowing not only the secret of friendship, but almost worshipped by those few persons who resorted to him as their confessor and prophet, and knew the deep value of his mind and great heart. He thought that without religion or devotion of some kind nothing great was ever accomplished: and he thought that the bigoted sectarian had better bear this in mind.

His virtues, of course, sometimes ran into extremes. It was easy to trace to the inexorable demand on all for exact truth that austerity which made this willing hermit more solitary even than he wished. Himself of a perfect probity, he required not less of others. He had a disgust at crime, and no worldly success would cover it. He detected paltering as readily in dignified and prosperous persons as in beggars, and with equal scorn. Such dangerous frankness was in his dealing that his admirers called him "that terrible Thoreau," as if he spoke when silent, and was still present when he had departed. I think the severity of his ideal interfered to deprive him of a healthy sufficiency of human society.

The habit of a realist to find things the reverse of their appearance inclined him to put every statement in a paradox. A certain habit of antagonism defaced his earlier writings,—a trick of rhetoric not quite outgrown in his later, of substituting for the obvious word and thought its diametrical opposite. He praised wild mountains and winter forests for their domestic air, in snow and ice he would find sultriness, and commended the wilderness for resembling Rome and Paris. "It was so dry, that you might call it wet."

The tendency to magnify the moment, to read all the laws of Nature in the one object or one combination under your eye, is of course comic to those who do not share the philosopher's perception of identity. To him there was no such thing as size. The pond was a small ocean; the Atlantic, a large Walden Pond. He referred every minute fact to cosmical laws. Though he meant

---

4. Both quotations are from Thoreau's "Inspiration"   5. The source of this quotation remains unlocated.
in A Week on the Concord and Merrimack Rivers.

to be just, he seemed haunted by a certain chronic assumption that the science of the day pretended completeness, and he had just found out that the *savans*[6] had neglected to discriminate a particular botanical variety, had failed to describe the seeds or count the sepals. "That is to say," we replied, "the blockheads were not born in Concord; but who said they were? It was their unspeakable misfortune to be born in London, or Paris, or Rome; but, poor fellows, they did what they could, considering that they never saw Bateman's Pond, or Nine-Acre Corner, or Becky-Stow's Swamp. Besides, what were you sent into the world for, but to add this observation?"

Had his genius been only contemplative, he had been fitted to his life, but with his energy and practical ability he seemed born for great enterprise and for command; and I so much regret the loss of his rare powers of action, that I cannot help counting it a fault in him that he had no ambition. Wanting this, instead of engineering for all America, he was the captain of a huckleberry-party. Pounding beans is good to the end of pounding empires one of these days; but if, at the end of years, it is still only beans!

But these foibles, real or apparent, were fast vanishing in the incessant growth of a spirit so robust and wise, and which effaced its defeats with new triumphs. His study of Nature was a perpetual ornament to him, and inspired his friends with curiosity to see the world through his eyes, and to hear his adventures. They possessed every kind of interest.

He had many elegances of his own, whilst he scoffed at conventional elegance. Thus, he could not bear to hear the sound of his own steps, the grit of gravel; and therefore never willingly walked in the road, but in the grass, on mountains and in woods. His senses were acute, and he remarked that by night every dwelling-house gives out bad air, like a slaughterhouse. He liked the pure fragrance of melilot.[7] He honored certain plants with special regard, and, over all, the pond-lily,—then, the gentian, and the *Mikania scandens*,[8] and "life-everlasting," and a bass-tree which he visited every year when it bloomed, in the middle of July. He thought the scent a more oracular inquisition than the sight,—more oracular and trustworthy. The scent, of course, reveals what is concealed from the other senses. By it he detected earthiness. He delighted in echoes, and said they were almost the only kind of kindred voices that he heard. He loved Nature so well, was so happy in her solitude, that he became very jealous of cities, and the sad work which their refinements and artifices made with man and his dwelling. The axe was always destroying his forest. "Thank God," he said, "they cannot cut down the clouds!" "All kinds of figures are drawn on the blue ground with this fibrous white paint."

I subjoin a few sentences taken from his unpublished manuscripts, not only as records of his thought and feeling, but for their power of description and literary excellence.

"Some circumstantial evidence is very strong, as when you find a trout in the milk."

"The chub is a soft fish, and tastes like boiled brown paper salted."

"The youth gets together his materials to build a bridge to the moon, or, perchance, a palace or temple on the earth, and at length the middle-aged man concludes to build a wood-shed with them."

---

6. Learned ones (French).   8. Climbing hempweed.
7. Sweet clover.

"The locust z-ing."

"Devil's-needles zigzagging along the Nut-Meadow brook."

"Sugar is not so sweet to the palate as sound to the healthy ear."

"I put on some hemlock-boughs, and the rich salt crackling of their leaves was like mustard to the ear, the crackling of uncountable regiments. Dead trees love the fire."

"The bluebird carries the sky on his back."

"The tanager flies through the green foliage as if it would ignite the leaves."

"If I wish for a horse-hair for my compass-sight, I must go to the stable; but the hair-bird, with her sharp eyes, goes to the road."

"Immortal water, alive even to the superficies."

"Fire is the most tolerable third party."

"Nature made ferns for pure leaves, to show what she could do in that line."

"No tree has so fair a bole and so handsome an instep as the beech."

"How did these beautiful rainbow-tints get into the shell of the fresh-water clam, buried in the mud at the bottom of our dark river?"

"Hard are the times when the infant's shoes are second-foot."

"We are strictly confined to our men to whom we give liberty."

"Nothing is so much to be feared as fear. Atheism may comparatively be popular with God himself."

"Of what significance the things you can forget? A little thought is sexton[9] to all the world."

"How can we expect a harvest of thought who have not had a seed-time of character?"

"Only he can be trusted with gifts who can present a face of bronze to expectations."

"I ask to be melted. You can only ask of the metals that they be tender to the fire that melts them. To nought else can they be tender."

There is a flower known to botanists, one of the same genus with our summer plant called "Life-Everlasting," a *Gnaphalium* like that, which grows on the most inaccessible cliffs of the Tyrolese mountains, where the chamois dare hardly venture, and which the hunter, tempted by its beauty, and by his love, (for it is immensely valued by the Swiss maidens), climbs the cliffs to gather, and is sometimes found dead at the foot, with the flower in his hand. It is called by botanists the *Gnaphalium leontopodium*, but by the Swiss *Edelweisse*, which signifies *Noble Purity*. Thoreau seemed to me living in the hope to gather this plant, which belonged to him of right. The scale on which his studies proceeded was so large as to require longevity, and we were the less prepared for his sudden disappearance. The country knows not yet, or in the least part, how great a son it has lost. It seems an injury that he should leave in the midst his broken task, which none else can finish,—a kind of indignity to so noble a soul, that it should depart out of Nature before yet he has been really shown to his peers for what he is. But he, at least, is content. His soul was made for the noblest society; he had in a short life exhausted the capabilities of this world; wherever there is knowledge, wherever there is virtue, wherever there is beauty, he will find a home.

1862

9. Gravedigger.

Hymn Sung at the Completion of the Concord Monument, April 19, 1836[1]

By the rude bridge that arched the flood,
   Their flag to April's breeze unfurled,
Here once the embattled farmers stood,
   And fired the shot heard round the world.

The foe long since in silence slept;   5
   Alike the conqueror silent sleeps;
And Time the ruined bridge has swept
   Down the dark stream which seaward creeps.

On this green bank, by this soft stream,
   We set to-day a votive stone;   10
That memory may their deed redeem,
   When, like our sires, our sons are gone.

Spirit, that made those heroes dare
   To die, or leave their children free,
Bid Time and Nature gently spare   15
   The shaft we raise to them and thee.

1837   1847

Each and All

Little thinks, in the field, yon red-cloaked clown,[2]
Of thee from the hill-top looking down;
The heifer that lows in the upland farm,
Far-heard, lows not thine ear to charm;
The sexton, tolling his bell at noon,   5
Deems not that great Napoleon
Stops his horse, and lists with delight,
Whilst his files sweep round yon Alpine height;
Nor knowest thou what argument
Thy life to thy neighbor's creed has lent.   10
All are needed by each one;
Nothing is fair or good alone.
I thought the sparrow's note from heaven,
Singing at dawn on the alder bough;
I brought him home, in his nest, at even;   15
He sings the song, but it cheers not now,
For I did not bring home the river and sky;—
He sang to my ear,—they sang to my eye.
The delicate shells lay on the shore;
The bubbles of the latest wave   20

---

1. This poem was read aloud and then sung to the tune of the familiar hymn "Old Hundred" on July 4, 1837, at the dedication of the monument to the heroes of the battle against the British soldiers on April 19, 1775. Despite the title, the ceremony was on July 4, 1837. The texts of this and the following poems (except *Days*) are from Emerson's *Poems* (1847), copies of which were available in December 1846.
2. Peasant.

Fresh pearls to their enamel gave;
And the bellowing of the savage sea
Greeted their safe escape to me.
I wiped away the weeds and foam,
I fetched my sea-born treasures home;   25
But the poor, unsightly, noisome things
Had left their beauty on the shore,
With the sun, and the sand, and the wild uproar.
The lover watched his graceful maid,
As 'mid the virgin train she strayed,   30
Nor knew her beauty's best attire
Was woven still by the snow-white choir.
At last she came to his hermitage,
Like the bird from the woodlands to the cage;—
The gay enchantment was undone,   35
A gentle wife, but fairy none.
Then I said, 'I covet truth;
Beauty is unripe childhood's cheat;
I leave it behind with the games of youth.'—
As I spoke, beneath my feet   40
The ground-pine curled its pretty wreath,
Running over the club-moss burrs;
I inhaled the violet's breath;
Around me stood the oaks and firs;
Pine-cones and acorns lay on the ground,   45
Over me soared the eternal sky,
Full of light and of deity;
Again I saw, again I heard,
The rolling river, the morning bird;—
Beauty through my senses stole;   50
I yielded myself to the perfect whole.

1847

The Problem

I like a church; I like a cowl;
I love a prophet of the soul;
And on my heart monastic aisles
Fall like sweet strains, or pensive smiles;
Yet not for all his faith can see   5
Would I that cowled churchman be.

Why should the vest[1] on him allure,
Which I could not on me endure?

Not from a vain or shallow thought
His awful Jove young Phidias[2] brought;   10

---

1. Vestment.   2. Greek sculptor of the 5th century B.C.

Never from lips of cunning fell
The thrilling Delphic oracle;[3]
Out from the heart of nature rolled
The burdens of the Bible old;
The litanies of nations came,   15
Like the volcano's tongue of flame,
Up from the burning core below,—
The canticles of love and woe;
The hand that rounded Peter's dome,
And groined the aisles of Christian Rome,[4]   20
Wrought in a sad sincerity;
Himself from God he could not free;
He builded better than he knew;—
The conscious stone to beauty grew.

Know'st thou what wove yon woodbird's nest   25
Of leaves, and feathers from her breast?
Or how the fish outbuilt her shell,
Painting with morn each annual cell?
Or how the sacred pine-tree adds
To her old leaves new myriads?   30
Such and so grew these holy piles,
Whilst love and terror laid the tiles.
Earth proudly wears the Parthenon,
As the best gem upon her zone;
And Morning opes with haste her lids,   35
To gaze upon the Pyramids;
O'er England's abbeys bends the sky,
As on its friends, with kindred eye;
For, out of Thought's interior sphere,
These wonders rose to upper air;   40
And Nature gladly gave them place,
Adopted them into her race,
And granted them an equal date
With Andes and with Ararat.[5]

These temples grew as grows the grass;   45
Art might obey, but not surpass.
The passive Master lent his hand
To the vast soul that o'er him planned;
And the same power that reared the shrine,
Bestrode the tribes that knelt within.   50
Ever the fiery Pentecost[6]
Girds with one flame the countless host,
Trances the heart through chanting choirs,
And through the priest the mind inspires.
The word unto the prophet spoken   55
Was writ on tables yet unbroken;

3. The prophetess at the temple of Apollo at Delphos, in Greece.
4. Late in life the great Renaissance artist Michelangelo (1475–1564) became the chief architect of St. Peter's Cathedral in Rome.
5. Mountain in Asia Minor where Noah's ark landed after the Flood. The Andes are a mountain range in South America.
6. The Holy Spirit, whose descent is described in Acts 2.

The word by seers or sibyls told,
In groves of oak, or fanes[7] of gold,
Still floats upon the morning wind,
Still whispers to the willing mind.   60
One accent of the Holy Ghost
The heedless world hath never lost.
I know what say the fathers wise,—
The Book itself before me lies,
Old *Chrysostom*, best Augustine,[8]   65
And he who blent both in his line,
The younger *Golden Lips* or mines,
Taylor, the Shakspeare of divines.[9]
His words are music in my ear,
I see his cowled portrait dear;   70
And yet, for all his faith could see,
I would not the good bishop be.

1847

Uriel[1]

It fell in the ancient periods,
    Which the brooding soul surveys,
Or ever the wild Time coined itself
    Into calendar months and days.

This was the lapse of Uriel,   5
Which in Paradise befell.
Once, among the Pleiads walking,
SAID[2] overheard the young gods talking;
And the treason, too long pent,
To his ears was evident.   10
The young deities discussed
Laws of form, and metre just,
Orb, quintessence, and sunbeams,
What subsisteth, and what seems.
One, with low tones that decide,   15
And doubt and reverend use defied,
With a look that solved the sphere,
And stirred the devils everywhere,
Gave his sentiment divine
Against the being of a line.   20
'Line in nature is not found;
Unit and universe are round;
In vain produced, all rays return;

7. Temples.
8. St. Augustine (354–430), bishop of Hippo in Roman Africa, greatest religious thinker of early Christianity, and in early life a teacher of rhetoric. St. John Chrysostom (345?–407), patriarch of Constantinople, renowned for eloquence (his surname means "golden-mouthed"), a major force in early Christianity.
9. Preachers. Jeremy Taylor (1613–1667), Anglican clergyman and author, famous from early manhood for his eloquence.
1. Borrowed from the name of Milton's angel of the sun (*Paradise Lost* 3.648–54).
2. In later editions changed to "Seyd," adapted from the Persian poet Saadi, whom Emerson had read. Pleiades is a cluster of seven stars named in Greek mythology for the daughters of Atlas and Pleione.

Evil will bless, and ice will burn.
As Uriel spoke with piercing eye,   25
A shudder ran around the sky;
The stern old war-gods shook their heads;
The seraphs frowned from myrtle-beds;
Seemed to the holy festival
The rash word boded ill at all;   30
The balance-beam of Fate was bent;
The bounds of good and ill were rent;
Strong Hades could not keep his own,
But all slid to confusion.
A sad self-knowledge, withering, fell   35
On the beauty of Uriel;
In heaven once eminent, the god
Withdrew, that hour, into his cloud;
Whether doomed to long gyration
In the sea of generation,   40
Or by knowledge grown too bright
To hit the nerve of feebler sight.
Straightway, a forgetting wind
Stole over the celestial kind,
And their lips the secret kept,   45
If in ashes the fire-seed slept.
But now and then, truth-speaking things
Shamed the angels' veiling wings;
And, shrilling from the solar course,
Or from fruit of chemic force,   50
Procession of a soul in matter,
Or the speeding change of water,
Or out of the good of evil born,
Came Uriel's voice of cherub scorn,
And a blush tinged the upper sky,   55
And the gods shook, they knew not why.

                                                      1847

Hamatreya[1]

Minott, Lee, Willard, Hosmer, Meriam, Flint[2]
Possessed the land which rendered to their toil
Hay, corn, roots, hemp, flax, apples, wool, and wood.
Each of these landlords walked amidst his farm,
Saying, "'Tis mine, my children's, and my name's: 5
How sweet the west wind sounds in my own trees!
How graceful climb those shadows on my hill!
I fancy these pure waters and the flags[3]
Know me, as does my dog: we sympathize;

---

1. Variant of Maitreya, a character Emerson encountered in the Hindu *Vishnu Purana*, one of the late
Hindu scriptures.
2. All real local Concord names; later Emerson revised the line to "Bulkeley, Hunt, Willard, Hosmer,
Meriam, Flint."
3. Irises or similar plants.

And, I affirm, my actions smack of the soil.' 10
Where are these men? Asleep beneath their grounds;
And strangers, fond as they, their furrows plough.
Earth laughs in flowers, to see her boastful boys
Earth-proud, proud of the earth which is not theirs;
Who steer the plough, but cannot steer their feet 15
Clear of the grave.
They added ridge to valley, brook to pond,
And sighed for all that bounded their domain.
'This suits me for a pasture; that's my park;
We must have clay, lime, gravel, granite-ledge, 20
And misty lowland, where to go for peat.
The land is well,—lies fairly to the south.
'T is good, when you have crossed the sea and back,
To find the sitfast acres where you left them.'
Ah! the hot owner sees not Death, who adds 25
Him to his land, a lump of mould the more.
Hear what the Earth says:—

Earth-Song

'Mine and yours;
Mine, not yours.
Earth endures; 30
Stars abide—
Shine down in the old sea;
Old are the shores;
But where are old men?
I who have seen much, 35
Such have I never seen.

'The lawyer's deed
Ran sure,
In tail,[4]
To them, and to their heirs 40
Who shall succeed,
Without fail,
Forevermore.

'Here is the land,
Shaggy with wood, 45
With its old valley,
Mound and flood.
But the heritors?
Fled like the flood's foam,—
The lawyer, and the laws, 50
And the kingdom,
Clean swept herefrom.

'They called me theirs,
Who so controlled me;

4. Entailed: in a specific, unalterable succession.

Yet every one   55
Wished to stay, and is gone.
How am I theirs,
If they cannot hold me,
But I hold them?'

When I heard the Earth-song,   60
I was no longer brave;
My avarice cooled
Like lust in the chill of the grave.

1847

The Rhodora

On Being Asked, Whence Is the Flower?

In May, when sea-winds pierced our solitudes,
I found the fresh Rhodora in the woods,
Spreading its leafless blooms in a damp nook,
To please the desert and the sluggish brook.
The purple petals, fallen in the pool,   5
Made the black water with their beauty gay;
Here might the red-bird come his plumes to cool,
And court the flower that cheapens his array.
Rhodora! if the sages ask thee why
This charm is wasted on the earth and sky,   10
Tell them, dear, that if eyes were made for seeing,
Then Beauty is its own excuse for being:
Why thou wert there, O rival of the rose!
I never thought to ask, I never knew;
But, in my simple ignorance, suppose   15
The self-same Power that brought me there brought you.

1847

The Snow-Storm

Announced by all the trumpets of the sky,
Arrives the snow, and, driving o'er the fields,
Seems nowhere to alight: the whited air
Hides hills and woods, the river, and the heaven,
And veils the farm-house at the garden's end.   5
The sled and traveller stopped, the courier's feet
Delayed, all friends shut out, the housemates sit
Around the radiant fireplace, enclosed
In a tumultuous privacy of storm.

Come see the north wind's masonry.   10
Out of an unseen quarry evermore

Furnished with tile, the fierce artificer
Curves his white bastions with projected roof
Round every windward stake, or tree, or door.
Speeding, the myriad-handed, his wild work   15
So fanciful, so savage, nought cares he
For number or proportion. Mockingly,
On coop or kennel he hangs Parian wreaths;[1]
A swan-like form invests the hidden thorn;
Fills up the farmer's lane from wall to wall,   20
Maugre[2] the farmer's sighs; and, at the gate,
A tapering turret overtops the work.
And when his hours are numbered, and the world
Is all his own, retiring, as he were not,
Leaves, when the sun appears, astonished Art   25
To mimic in slow structures, stone by stone,
Built in an age, the mad wind's night-work,
The frolic architecture of the snow.

                                                            1847

Ode, Inscribed to W. H. Channing[1]

Though loath to grieve
The evil time's sole patriot,
I cannot leave
My honied thought
For the priest's cant,   5
Or statesman's rant.

If I refuse
My study for their politique,
Which at the best is trick,
The angry Muse   10
Puts confusion in my brain.

But who is he that prates
Of the culture of mankind,
Of better arts and life?
Go, blindworm, go,   15
Behold the famous States
Harrying Mexico
With rifle and with knife!

Or who, with accent bolder,
Dare praise the freedom-loving mountaineer?   20
I found by thee, O rushing Contoocook!

---

1. I.e., sculpted in white, from the marble quarried in the island of Paros, in the Aegean sea, for sculptors of classical Greece.
2. Despite.
1. A young clergyman, nephew of the famous Unitarian minister William Ellery Channing; as the poem makes clear, he had urged Emerson to take an overt political role in resisting the war waged by the United States against Mexico.

And in thy valleys, Agiochook![2]
The jackals of the negro-holder.

The God who made New Hampshire
Taunted the lofty land   25
With little men;—
Small bat and wren
House in the oak:—
If earth-fire cleave
The upheaved land, and bury the folk,   30
The southern crocodile would grieve.

Virtue palters; Right is hence;
Freedom praised, but hid;
Funeral eloquence
Rattles the coffin-lid.   35

What boots thy zeal,
O glowing friend,
That would indignant rend
The northland from the south?
Wherefore? to what good end?   40
Boston Bay and Bunker Hill[3]
Would serve things still;—
Things are of the snake.

The horseman serves the horse,
The neatherd serves the neat,[4]   45
The merchant serves the purse,
The eater serves his meat;
'Tis the day of the chattel,
Web to weave, and corn to grind;
Things are in the saddle,   50
And ride mankind.

There are two laws discrete,
Not reconciled,—
Law for man, and law for thing;
The last builds town and fleet,   55
But it runs wild,
And doth the man unking.

'Tis fit the forest fall,
The steep be graded,
The mountain tunnelled,   60
The sand shaded,
The orchard planted,

2. New Hampshire had gone Democratic, which
meant in effect proslavery, reason enough for Emerson
to taunt the debased inhabitants of that state with the
majesty of their rivers like Contoocook and mountains
like Agiochook.
3. Emerson does not spare his own state from accusa-

tion of materialism, whatever its heroic past memorialized in the Bunker Hill Monument. One manifestation
of that materialism was a commercial alliance between
the South, which grew cotton, and the North, which
shipped and manufactured it.
4. The cowherd serves the cow.

The glebe[5] tilled,
The prairie granted,
The steamer built.   65

Let man serve law for man;
Live for friendship, live for love,
For truth's and harmony's behoof;
The state may follow how it can,
As Olympus follows Jove.[6]   70

    Yet do not I invite[7]
The wrinkled shopman to my sounding woods,
Nor bid the unwilling senator
Ask votes of thrushes in the solitudes.
Every one to his chosen work;—   75
Foolish hands may mix and mar;
Wise and sure the issues are.
Round they roll till dark is light,
Sex to sex, and even to odd;—
The over-god   80
Who marries Right to Might,
Who peoples, unpeoples,—
He who exterminates
Races by stronger races,
Black by white faces,—   85
Knows to bring honey
Out of the lion;[8]
Grafts gentlest scion
On pirate and Turk.

The Cossack eats Poland,[9]   90
Like stolen fruit,
Her last noble is ruined,
Her last poet mute:
Straight, into double band
The victors divide;   95
Half for freedom strike and stand;—
The astonished Muse finds thousands at her side.

                                                              1847

Merlin[1]

I

    Thy trivial harp will never please
    Or fill my craving ear;

---

5. Soil.
6. As minor gods follow the supreme god.
7. Later texts read "implore."
8. A reference to the riddle (Judges 14) that Samson propounded after finding the carcass of a lion in which bees had made honey: "Out of the eater came forth

meat, and out of the strong came forth sweetness."
9. Poland had been partitioned three times in the late 18th century, with Russia (the Cossack) getting the lion's share.
1. Here, the type of a great poet (not the magician-prophet of Arthurian legend).

Its chords should ring as blows the breeze,
Free, peremptory, clear.
No jingling serenader's art,   5
Nor tinkle of piano strings,
Can make the wild blood start
In its mystic springs.
The kingly bard
Must smit the chords rudely and hard,   10
As with hammer or with mace;
That they may render back
Artful thunder, which conveys
Secrets of the solar track,
Sparks of the supersolar blaze.   15
Merlin's blows are strokes of fate,
Chiming with the forest tone,
When boughs buffet boughs in the wood;
Chiming with the gasp and moan
Of the ice-imprisoned flood;   20
With the pulse of manly hearts;
With the voice of orators;
With the din of city arts;
With the cannonade of wars;
With the marches of the brave;   25
And prayers of might from martyrs' cave.

Great is the art,
Great be the manners, of the bard.
He shall not his brain encumber
With the coil of rhythm and number;   30
But, leaving rule and pale forethought,
He shall aye[2] climb
For his rhyme.
'Pass in, pass in,' the angels say,
'In to the upper doors,   35
Nor count compartments of the floors,
But mount to paradise
By the stairway of surprise.'

Blameless master of the games,
King of sport that never shames,   40
He shall daily joy dispense
Hid in song's sweet influence.
Things[3] more cheerly live and go,
What time the subtle mind
Sings aloud the tune whereto   45
Their pulses beat,
And march their feet,
And their members are combined.

By Sybarites[4] beguiled,
He shall no task decline;   50

---

2. Always.
3. Later texts read "Forms."

4. Like people from Sybaris, the Greek city in Italy notorious for wealth and hedonistic indulgence.

Merlin's mighty line
Extremes of nature reconciled,—
Bereaved a tyrant of his will,
And made the lion mild.
Songs can the tempest still,   55
Scattered on the stormy air,
Mould the year to fair increase,
And bring in poetic peace.

He shall not seek to weave,
In weak, unhappy times,   60
Efficacious rhymes;
Wait his returning strength.
Bird, that from the nadir's floor
To the zenith's top can soar,
The soaring orbit of the muse exceeds that
       journey's length.   65
Nor profane affect to hit
Or compass that, by meddling wit,
Which only the propitious mind
Publishes when 'tis inclined.
There are open hours   70
When the God's will sallies free,
And the dull idiot might see
The flowing fortunes of a thousand years;—
Sudden, at unawares,
Self-moved, fly-to the doors   75
Nor sword of angels could reveal
What they conceal.

II

The rhyme of the poet
Modulates the king's affairs;
Balance-loving Nature   80
Made all things in pairs.
To every foot its antipode;
Each color with its counter glowed;
To every tone beat answering tones,
Higher or graver;   85
Flavor gladly blends with flavor;
Leaf answers leaf upon the bough;
And match the paired cotyledons.
Hands to hands, and feet to feet,
Coeval grooms and brides;[5]   90
Eldest rite, two married sides
In every mortal meet.
Light's far furnace shines,
Smelting balls and bars,
Forging double stars,   95

5. Later texts read "In one body grooms and brides."

Glittering twins and trines.
The animals are sick with love,
Lovesick with rhyme;
Each with all propitious time
Into chorus wove.   100

Like the dancers' ordered band,
Thoughts come also hand in hand;
In equal couples mated,
Or else alternated;
Adding by their mutual gage,   105
One to other, health and age.
Solitary fancies go
Short-lived wandering to and fro,
Most like to bachelors,
Or an ungiven maid,   110
Not ancestors,
With no posterity to make the lie afraid,
Or keep truth undecayed.
Perfect-paired as eagle's wings,
Justice is the rhyme of things;   115
Trade and counting use
The self-same tuneful muse;
And Nemesis,[6]
Who with even matches odd,
Who athwart space redresses   120
The partial wrong,
Fills the just period,
And finishes the song.

Subtle rhymes, with ruin rife,
Murmur in the house of life,   125
Sung by the Sisters[7] as they spin;
In perfect time and measure they
Build and unbuild our echoing clay,
As the two twilights of the day
Fold us music-drunken in.   130

1847

Days[1]

Daughters of Time, the hypocritic Days,
Muffled and dumb, like barefoot dervishes,[2]
And marching single in an endless file,
Bring diadems and fagots[3] in their hands.
To each they offer gifts, after his will,—   5
Bread, kingdoms, stars, or sky that holds them all.

6. Here, the imposer of order, not the personification
of divine disapproval and punishment.
7. The Fates, in Greek mythology.
1. The text is from the first printing, in the *Atlantic*

Monthly (November 1857), the inaugural issue of the
magazine.
2. Moslem ascetics.
3. Crowns and sticks: unequal portions.

I, in my pleached[4] garden, watched the pomp,
Forgot my morning wishes, hastily
Took a few herbs and apples, and the Day
Turned and departed silent. I, too late,   10
Under her solemn fillet[5] saw the scorn

1857

FROM JOURNALS AND LETTERS[1]

From Journals

Myself

"Nil fuit unquam sic dispar sibi." Hor[2]

April 18, 1824 [Canterbury (Roxbury), Massachusetts]

Sunday. I am beginning my professional studies. In a month I shall be *legally* a man. And I deliberately dedicate my time, my talents, & my hopes to the Church. Man is an animal that looks before & after; and I should be loth to reflect at a remote period that I took so solemn a step in my existence without some careful examination of my past & present life. Since I cannot alter I would not repent the resolution I have made & this page must be witness to the latest year of my life whether I have good grounds to warrant my determination.

I cannot dissemble that my abilities are below my ambition. And I find that I judged by a false criterion when I measured my powers by my ability to understand & to criticise the intellectual character of another. For men graduate their respect not by the secret wealth but by the outward use; not by the power to understand, but by the power to act. I have or had a strong imagination & consequently a keen relish for the beauties of poetry. The exercise which the practice of composition gives to this faculty is the cause of my immoderate fondness for writing, which has swelled these pages to a voluminous extent. My reasoning faculty is proportionately weak, nor can I ever hope to write a Butler's Analogy or an Essay of Hume.[3] Nor is it strange that with this confession I should choose theology, which is from everlasting to everlast-

---

4. Shaded with interlaced branches or vines.
5. Headband.
1. Emerson's journals and notebooks have been newly edited by several scholars, led by the late William H. Gilman and published meticulously by Harvard University Press as *The Journals and Miscellaneous Notebooks of Ralph Waldo Emerson.* Because the Harvard edition does not print "clear text" but shows Emerson's revisions, some of the quotations here have been simplified to show only the final readings. The six-volume edition of *The Letters of Ralph Waldo Emerson* excludes most letters previously published in one collection or another, so the letters printed here are drawn from various sources indicated in the footnotes. Passages from the journals and letters are printed chronologically, but because Emerson sometimes failed to date journal entries the date given may be merely the

first one that occurs before the entry. Annotations are light, because the selections are meant to be suggestive of the diverse contents of the journals and letters, not comprehensive, even on a topic of such enduring interest as Emerson's ambivalence toward Thoreau. Together the journal entries and the letters afford the best view of Emerson the man, in both his private and public aspects.
2. Never was a creature so inconsistent (Latin), from Horace, *Satires* 1.3.18.
3. David Hume (1711–1766), Scottish philosopher, author of *Philosophical Essays* (1748). Joseph Butler (1692–1752), English bishop and philosopher, wrote *Analogy of Religion* (1736), a defense of Christianity against deism in which an attempt is made to reconcile reason and revelation.

ing 'debateable Ground.' For, the highest species of reasoning upon divine subjects is rather the fruit of a sort of moral imagination, than of the 'Reasoning Machines' such as Locke & Clarke[4] & David Hume. Dr Channing's Dudleian Lecture[5] is the model of what I mean, and the faculty which produced this is akin to the higher flights of the fancy. I may add that the preaching most in vogue at the present day depends chiefly on imagination for its success, and asks those accomplishments which I believe are most within my grasp. I have set down little which can gratify my vanity, and I must further say that every comparison of myself with my mates that six or seven, perhaps sixteen or seventeen, years have made has convinced me that there exists a signal defect of character which neutralizes in great part the just influence my talents ought to have. Whether that defect by in the *address*, in the fault of good forms, which Queen Isabella[6] said, were like perpetual letters commendatory, or deeper seated in an absence of common *sympathies*, or even in a levity of the understanding, I cannot tell. But its bitter fruits are a sore uneasiness in the company of most men & women, a frigid fear of offending & jealousy of disrespect, an inability to lead & an unwillingness to follow the current conversation, which contrive to make me second with all those among whom chiefly I wish to be first.

Hence my bearing in the world is the direct opposite of that good humoured independence & self esteem which should mark the gentleman. Be it here remembered that there is a decent pride which is conspicuous in the perfect model of a Christian man. I am unfortunate also, as was Rienzi,[7] in a propensity to laugh or rather snicker. I am ill at ease therefore among men. I criticize with hardness; I lavishly applaud; I weakly argue; and I wonder with a foolish face of praise.

Now the profession of Law demands a good deal of personal address, an impregnable confidence in one's own powers, upon all occasions expected & unexpected, & a logical mode of thinking & speaking—which I do not possess, & may not reasonably hope to obtain. Medicine also makes large demands on the practitioner for a seducing Mannerism. And I have no taste for the pestle & mortar, for Bell on the bones or Hunter or Celsus.[8]

But in Divinity I hope to thrive. I inherit from my sire a formality of manner & speech, but I derive from him or his patriotic parent a passionate love for the strains of eloquence. I burn after the 'aliquid immensum infinitumque' which Cicero[9] desired. What we ardently love we learn to imitate. My understanding venerates & my heart loves that Cause which is dear to God & man— the laws of Morals, the Revelations which sanction, & the blood of martyrs & triumphant suffering of the saints which seal them. In my better hours, I am the believer (if not the dupe) of brilliant promises, and can respect myself as the possessor of those powers which command the reason & passions of the

---

4. Samuel Clarke (1675–1729), English theologian and philosopher who, in A *Demonstration of the Being and Attributes of God* (1705), attempted to prove the existence of God with near-mathematical certainty. John Locke (1632–1704), English philosopher, author of *An Essay Concerning Human Understanding* (1690). Emerson regarded Locke, Clarke, and Hume as rationalists.
5. William Ellery Channing preached at Harvard on the evidence of revealed religion, March 14, 1821.
6. This allusion to Queen Isabella is unlocated.
7. Cola di Rienzi (1313–1354), Italian patriot whose

plans for the restoration of Roman power ran into conflict with the pope.
8. Aulus Cornelius Celsus (1st century B.C.) wrote medical treatises. The Scottish surgeons Charles Bell (1774–1842) and John Bell (1763–1820) wrote several textbooks on anatomy, as did John Hunter (1728–1793), another Scottish physician and medical writer.
9. Roman philosopher and statesman (1st century B.C.), author of books on oratory. The Latin quotation translates as: Something great and immeasurable.

multitude. The office of a clergyman is twofold; public preaching & private influence. Entire success in the first is the lot of few, but this I am encouraged to expect. If however the individual himself lack that moral worth which is to secure the last, his studies upon the first are idly spent. The most prodigious genius, a seraph's eloquence will shamefully defeat its own end, if it has not first won the heart of the defender to the cause he defends, but the coolest reason cannot censure my choice when I oblige myself *professionally* to a life which all wise men freely & advisedly adopt. I put no great restraint on myself & can therefore claim little merit in a manner of life which chimes with inclination & habit. But I would learn to love Virtue for her own sake, I would have my pen so guided as was Milton's when a deep & enthusiastic love of goodness & of God dictated the Comus to the bard, or that prose rhapsody in the 3rd Book of Prelaty.[1] I would sacrifice inclination to the interest of mind & soul. I would remember that "Spare Fast oft with Gods doth diet," that Justinian devoted but one out of twenty four hours to sleep & this week (for instance) I will remember to curtail my dinner & supper sensibly & rise from table each day with an appetite; & so see if it be fact that I can understand more clearly.[2]

I have mentioned a defect of character; perhaps it is not one, but many. Every wise man aims at an entire conquest of himself. We applaud as possessed of extraordinary good sense, one who never makes the slightest mistake in speech or action; one in whom not only every important step of life, but every passage of conversation, every duty of the day, even every movement of every muscle—hands, feet, & tongue, are measured & dictated by deliberate reason. I am not assuredly that excellent creature. A score of words & deeds issue from me daily, of which I am not the master. They are begotten of weakness & born of shame. I cannot assume the elevation I ought,—but lose the influence I should exert among those of meaner or younger understanding, for want of sufficient *bottom* in my nature, for want of that confidence of manner which springs from an erect mind which is without fear & without reproach. In my frequent humiliation, even before women & children I am compelled to remember the poor boy who cried, "I told you, Father, they would find me out." Even those feelings which are counted noble & generous, take in me the taint of frailty. For my strong propensity to friendship, instead of working out its manly ends, degenerates to a fondness for particular casts of feature perchance not unlike the doting of old King James.[3] Stateliness & silence hang very like Mokannah's suspicious silver veil, only concealing what is best not shewn.[4] What is called a warm heart, I have not.

The stern accuser Conscience cries that the Catalogue of Confessions is not yet full. I am a lover of indolence, & of the belly. And the good have a right to ask the Neophyte who wears this garment of scarlet sin, why he comes where all are apparelled in white? Dares he hope that some patches of pure & generous feeling, some bright fragments of lofty thought, it may be of divine poesy shall charm the eye away from all the particoloured shades of his Char-

---

1. Emerson the young idealist is ignoring the Shakespearean beauties of John Milton's *Comus* (1634) in favor of its high moral preachments; Milton's third tract advocating abolition of prelates (archbishops and bishops) is *Animadversions* (1641).
2. Emerson clarified his ascetic resolution with this notation: "N.B. Till Tuesday Evg next." "Spare Fast": from Milton's *Il Penseroso*, line 46. Justinian

(483–565), Roman emperor (527–65).
3. King James I (1566–1625) of England, author of books on demonology.
4. In Thomas Moore's *Lalla Rookh*, an immensely popular narrative poem in the Romantic Oriental vogue of the early 19th century, Hashim ibn-Hakim al-Mokanna pretends that he wears a veil to conceal the divine light in his countenance.

acter? And when he is clothed in the vestments of the priest, & has inscribed on his forehead 'Holiness to the Lord', & wears on his breast the breastplate of the tribes, then can the Ethiopian change his skin & the unclean be pure? Or how shall I strenuously enforce on men the duties & habits to which I am a stranger? Physician, heal thyself.[5] I need not go far for an answer to so natural a question. I am young in my everlasting existence. I already discern the deep dye of elementary errors, which threaten to colour its infinity of duration. And I judge that if I devote my nights & days *in form*, to the service of God & the War against Sin,—I shall soon be prepared to do the same *in substance*.

I cannot accurately estimate my chances of success, in my profession, & in life. Were it just to judge the future from the past, they would be very low. In my case I think it is not. I have never expected success in my present employment.[6] My scholars are carefully instructed, my money is faithfully earned, but the instructor is little wiser. & the duties were never congenial with my disposition. Thus far the dupe of hope I have trudged on with my bundle at my back, and my eye fixed on the distant hill where my burden would fall. It may be I shall write *dupe* a long time to come & the end of life shall intervene betwixt me & the release. My trust is that my profession shall be my regeneration of mind, manners, inward & outward estate; or rather my starting point, for I have hoped to put on eloquence as a robe, and by goodness and zeal and the awfulness of virtue to press & prevail over the false judgments, the rebel passions & corrupt habits of men. We blame the past we magnify & gild the future and are not wiser for the multitude of days. Spin on, Ye of the adamantine spindle,[7] spin on, my fragile thread.

[*Always a Right Word*]

July 8, 1831 [Boston]

No man can write well who thinks there is any choice of words for him. The laws of composition are as strict as those of sculpture & architecture. There is always one line that ought to be drawn or one proportion that should be kept & every other line or proportion is wrong, & so far wrong as it deviates from this. So in writing, there is always a right word, & every other than that is wrong. There is no beauty in words except in their collocation. The effect of a fanciful word misplaced, is like that of a horn of exquisite polish growing on a human head.

[*In the Garden of Plants*]

July 13, 1833, [Paris]

I carried my ticket from Mr Warden[8] to the Cabinet of Natural History in the Garden of Plants. How much finer things are in composition than alone. 'Tis wise in man to make Cabinets.[9] When I was come into the Ornithological Chambers, I wished I had come only there. The fancy-coloured vests of these

---

5. A proverb that Jesus quotes to the skeptical towns-people of Nazareth: "Ye will surely say unto me this proverb, Physician, heal thyself: whatsoever we have heard done in Capernaum, do also here in thy country" (Luke 4.23).

6. Schoolteacher.
7. In Greek mythology, Clotho, the one of the three Fates who spins the thread of destiny.
8. David Bailie Warden, American consul in Paris.
9. A "cabinet" is a scientific collection.

elegant beings make me as pensive as the hues & forms of a cabinet of shells, formerly. It is a beautiful collection & makes the visiter as calm & genial as a bridegroom. The limits of the possible are enlarged, & the real is stranger than the imaginary. Some of the birds have a fabulous beauty. One parrot of a fellow, called *Psittacus erythropterus* from New Holland, deserves as special mention as a picture of Raphael[1] in a Gallery. He is the beau of all birds. Then the hummingbirds little & gay. Least of all is the Trochilus Niger. I have seen beetles larger. The *Trochilus pella* hath such a neck of gold & silver & fire! Trochilus Delalandi from Brazil is a glorious little tot—la mouche magnifique.

Among the birds of Paradise I remarked the Manucode or P. regia from New Guinea, the Paradisaea Apoda, & P. rubra. Forget not the Veuve à epaulettes or Emberiza longicauda, black with fine shoulder knots; nor the Ampelis cotinga nor the Phasianus Argus a peacock looking pheasant; nor the Trogon pavoninus called also Couroncou pavonin.

I saw black swans & white peacocks, the ibis the sacred & the rosy; the flamingo, with a neck like a snake, the Toucan rightly called *rhinoceros*; & a vulture whom to meet in the wilderness would make your flesh quiver[,] so like an executioner he looked.

In the other rooms I saw amber containing perfect musquitoes, grand blocks of quartz, native gold in all its forms of crystallization, threads, plates, crystals, dust; & silver black as from fire. Ah said I this is philanthropy, wisdom, taste— to form a Cabinet of natural history. Many students were there with grammar & note book & a class of boys with their tutor from some school. Here we are impressed with the inexhaustible riches of nature. The Universe is a more amazing puzzle than ever as you glance along this bewildering series of animated forms,—the hazy butterflies, the carved shells, the birds, beasts, fishes, insects, snakes,—& the upheaving principle of life everywhere incipient in the very rock aping organized forms. Not a form so grotesque, so savage, nor so beautiful but is an expression of some property inherent in man the observer,—an occult relation between the very scorpions and man. I feel the centipede in me—cayman,[2] carp, eagle, & fox. I am moved by strange sympathies, I say continually "I will be a naturalist."

There's a good collection of skulls in the Comparative anatomy chambers. The best skull seemed to be English. The skeleton of the Balena[3] looks like the frame of a schooner turned upside down.

The Garden itself is admirably arranged. They have attempted to classify all the plants *in the ground,* to put together, that is, as nearly as may be the conspicuous plants of each class on Jussieu's[4] system.

Walk down the alleys of this flower garden & you come to the enclosures of the animals where almost all that Adam named or Noah preserved are represented. Here are several lions, two great elephants walking out in open day, a camelopard[5] 17 feet high, the bison, the rhinoceros, & so forth [—] all manner of four footed things in air & sunshine, in the shades of a pleasant garden, where all people French & English may come & see without money. By the way, there is a caricature in the printshops representing the arrival of the giraffe

1. Painter of the Italian Renaissance (1483–1520).
2. Or "caiman" is the American crocodile.
3. The whale.
4. Adrien de Jussieu (1797–1853), son of Antoine

Laurent de Jussieu (1748–1836), who developed the classification system at the Garden of Plants.
5. The giraffe, from its camellike head and leopardlike spots.

in Paris, exclaiming to the mob "Messieurs, il n'y a qu'un bete de plus."[6] It is very pleasant to walk in this garden.

As I went out, I noticed a placard posted on the gates giving notice that M. Jussieu would next Sunday give a public herborisation, that is, make a botanical excursion into the country & inviting all & sundry to accompany him.

[My Savings Bank]

January 1, 1834 [Boston]

This Book is my Savings Bank. I grow richer because I have somewhere to deposit my earnings; and fractions are worth more to me because corresponding fractions are waiting here that shall be made integers by their addition.

[A White Whale]

February 19, 1834 [Boston]

A seaman in the coach told the story of an old sperm whale which he called a white whale which was known for many years by the whaleman as Old Tom & who rushed upon the boats which attacked him & crushed the boats to small chips in his jaws, the men generally escaping by jumping overboard & being picked up. A vessel was fitted out at New Bedford, he said, to take him. And he was finally taken somewhere off Payta head[7] by the Winslow or the Essex. He gave a fine account of a storm which I heard imperfectly. Only 'the whole ocean was all feather white.' A whale sometimes runs off three rolls of cord, three hundred fathom in length each one.

To Lydia Jackson[8]

[A Modulated New Love; I Am Born a Poet]

Concord, 1 February [1835]—

One of my wise masters, Edmund Burke,[9] said, 'A wise man will speak the truth with temperance that he may speak it the longer.' In this new sentiment that you awaken in me, my Lydian Queen, what might scare others pleases me, its quietness, which I accept as a pledge of permanence. I delighted myself on Friday with my quite domesticated position & the good understanding that grew all the time, yet I went & came without one vehement word—or one passionate sign. In this was nothing of design, I merely surrendered myself to the hour & to the facts. I find a sort of grandeur in the modulated expressions of a love in which the individuals, & what might seem even reasonable personal expectations, are steadily postponed to a regard for truth & the universal love. Do not think me a metaphysical lover. I am a man & hate & suspect the over refiners, & do sympathize with the homeliest pleasures & attractions by which our good foster mother Nature draws her children together. Yet am I well pleased that between us the most permanent ties should be the first formed & thereon should grow whatever others human nature will.

6. It's just another animal, gentleman (French).
7. Point on the coast of Peru.
8. Emerson's fiancée.
9. British statesman and philosopher (1729–1797).

My Mother rejoices very much & asks me all manner of questions about you, many of which I cannot answer. I dont know whether you sing, or read French, or Latin, or where you have lived, & much more. So you see there is nothing for it but that you should come here & on the Battle-Ground stand the fire of her catechism.

Under this morning's severe but beautiful light I thought dear friend that hardly should I get away from Concord. I must win you to love it. I am born a poet, of a low class without doubt yet a poet. That is my nature & vocation. My singing be sure is very 'husky,' & is for the most part in prose. Still am I a poet in the sense of a perceiver & dear lover of the harmonies that are in the soul & in matter, & specially of the correspondences between these & those. A sunset, a forest, a snow storm, a certain river-view, are more to me than many friends & do ordinarily divide my day with my books. Wherever I go therefore I guard & study my rambling propensities with a care that is ridiculous to people, but to me is the care of my high calling. Now Concord is only one of a hundred towns in which I could find these necessary objects but Plymouth I fear is not one. Plymouth is streets; I live in the wide champaign.[1]

Time enough for this however. If I succeed in preparing my lecture on Michel Angelo Buonaroti this week for Thursday, I will come to Plymouth on Friday. If I do not succeed—do not attain unto the Idea of that man—I shall read of Luther, Thursday & then I know not when I shall steal a visit.[2]—

Dearest forgive the egotism of all this letter Say they not 'The more love the more egotism.' Repay it by as much & more. Write, write to me. And please dear Lidian take that same low counsel & leave thinking for the present & let the winds of heaven blow away your dyspepsia.

Waldo E.

From Journals

[Sadness after Thirty]

August 1, 1835 [Concord]

After thirty a man wakes up sad every morning excepting perhaps five or six until the day of his death.

[Philanthropic Meetings and Holy Hurrahs]

April 26, 1838 [Concord]

As far as I notice what passes in philanthropic meetings & holy hurrahs, there is very little depth of interest. The speakers warm each other's skin & lubricate each other's tongue & the words flow, & the superlatives thicken, & the lips quiver, & the eyes moisten, & an observer new to such scenes would say, here was true fire; the assembly were all ready to be martyred, & the effect of such a spirit on the community would be irresistible. But they separate & go to the shop, to a dance, to bed, & an hour afterwards they care so little for

---

1. Plain.
2. I.e., if he finishes his new lecture on Michelangelo, he will feel justified in taking a holiday to Plymouth; if he merely repeats an old one on Luther, he will not.

the matter that on slightest temptation each one would disclaim the meeting. "Yes, he went, but they were for carrying it too far, &c. &c."

The lesson is to know that men are superficially very inflammable but that these fervors do not strike down & reach the action & habit of the man[.]

To Thomas Carlyle[3]

[I Am a Rich Man]

Concord, May 10, 1838

* * * When you publish your next book I think you must send it out to me in sheets, & let us print it here contemporaneously with the English Edition. The eclat of so new a book would help the sale very much. But a better device would be, that you should embark in the Victoria steamer, & come in a fortnight to New York, & in 24 hours more, to Concord. Your study armchair, fireplace & bed long vacant auguring expect you. Then you shall revise your proofs & dictate wit & learning to the New World. Think of it in good earnest. In aid of your friendliest purpose, I will set down some of the facts. I occupy or *improve*, as we Yankees say, two acres only of God's earth, on which is my house, my kitchen-garden, my orchard of thirty young trees, my empty barn. My house is now a very good one for comfort, & abounding in room. Besides my house, I have, I believe, $22,000, whose income in ordinary years is 6 per cent. I have no other tithe or glebe[4] except the income of my winter lectures which was last winter 800 dollars. Well, with this income, here at home, I am a rich man. I stay at home and go abroad at my own instance. I have food, warmth, leisure, books, friends. Go away from home,—I am rich no longer. I never have a dollar to spend on a fancy. As no wise man, I suppose ever was rich in the sense of *freedom to spend*, because of the inundation of claims, so neither am I, who am not wise. But at home I am rich,—rich enough for ten brothers. My wife Lidian is an incarnation of Christianity,—I call her Asia— & keeps my philosophy from Antinomianism.[5] My mother—whitest, mildest, most conservative of ladies, whose only exception to her universal preference of old things is her son; my boy, a piece of love & sunshine, well worth my watching from morning to night; these & three domestic women who cook & sew & run for us, make all my household. Here I sit & read & write with very little system & as far as regards composition with the most fragmentary result: paragraphs incompressible each sentence an infinitely repellent particle. In summer with the aid of a neighbor, I manage my garden; & a week ago I set out on the west side of my house forty young pine trees to protect me or my son from the wind of January. The ornament of the place is the occasional presence of some ten or twelve persons good & wise who visit us in the course of the year.—But my story is too long already. God grant that you will come

---

3. Thomas Carlyle (1795–1881), Scottish-born English essayist and historian; Emerson acted as agent in arranging the American publication of *The French Revolution* in 1859.
4. Sometimes merely "earth," but here in the British sense of plot of land granted a minister as part of his benefice.
5. The belief that salvation can be attained by faith without the mediation of any formal church. Lydia was

Emerson's second wife. In his biography of Emerson, Ralph L. Rusk says the nickname "Asia" "seemed suitable not only because no other New Englander he knew possessed such a depth of feeling continually called out on trival occasions but also because it symbolized Christianity and even religious conservatism. 'Palestine,' another of his names for her, expressed the latter meaning even more emphatically."

& bring that blessed wife, whose protracted illness we heartily grieve to learn, & whom a voyage & my wifes & my mothers nursing would in less than a twelvemonth restore to blooming health. My wife sends to her this mesage; "Come & I will be to you a sister." What have you to do with Italy? Your genius tendeth to the New, to the West. Come & live with me a year, & if you do not like New England well enough to stay, one of these years (when the History[6] has passed its ten editions & been translated into as many languages) I will come & dwell with you. * * *

From Journals

[*Protest; Writing; America*]

June 18, 1838 [Concord]

C[aroline]. S[turgis].[7] protests. That is a good deal. In these times you shall find a small number of persons of whom only that can be affirmed that they protest. Yet is it as divine to say no, as to say yes. You say they go too much alone. Yea, but they shun society to the end of finding society. They repudiate the false out of love of the true. Extravagance is a good token. In an Extravagance, there is hope; in Routine, none.

* * *

The art of writing consists in putting two things together that are unlike and that belong together like a horse & cart. Then have we somewhat far more goodly & efficient than either.

* * *

Ah my country! In thee is the reasonable hope of mankind not fulfilled. It should be that when all feudal straps & bandages were taken off an unfolding of the Titans[8] had followed & they had laughed & leaped young giants along the continent & ran up the mountains of the West with the errand of Genius & of love. But the utmost thou hast yet produced, is a puny love of beauty in Allston, in Greenough; in Bryant; in Everett; in Channing; in Irving; an imitative love of grace.[9] A vase of fair outline but empty, which whoso seeth may fill with what wit & character is in him but which does not like the charged cloud overflow with terrible beauty & emit lightnings on all beholders. Ah me! the cause is one; the diffidence of Ages in the Soul has crept over thee too, America. No man here believeth in the soul of man but only in some name or person old & departed. Ah me! No man goeth alone[,] all men go in flocks to this saint or that poet avoiding the God who seeth in secret. They

6. *The French Revolution.*
7. From Boston, who had been visiting the Emersons; later she was a contributor to the *Dial* under Emerson's editorship.
8. The gigantic pre-Olympian gods of Greek mythology; in revolt against their father, Uranus, they stormed heaven.
9. I.e., instead of an American artistic flourishing comparable to the revolt of the Titans there occurred only a puny stirring. Here Emerson catalogs the best the country had yet produced in the arts. The South Carolina painter Washington Allston (1779–1843) had

an enormously inflated reputation in his adopted Boston. Horatio Greenough (1805–1852) was both a sculptor and an aesthetician who made important comments on architecture. William Cullen Bryant (1794–1878) was revered as our best serious poet. Edward Everett (1794–1865) was a clergyman famous for his oratory. William Ellery Channing (1780–1842) was the leading Unitarian clergyman of Boston and a major influence on Emerson during Emerson's young manhood. Washington Irving (1783–1859) had no rival as the best-loved American fiction writer, despite the popularity of James Fenimore Cooper.

cannot see in secret. They love to be blind in public. They think society wiser than their soul, & know not that one soul, & their soul is wiser than the whole world. See how nations & races flit by on the sea of time & leave no ripple to tell where they floated or sunk, & one good soul shall make the name of Moses or of Zeno or Zoroaster[1] reverend forever. None assayeth the austere ambition to be the Man, the Self of the nation & of nature, but each would be an easy Secondary to some English Literature or Christian Scheme or American government.

[Goodies]

June 23, 1838 [Concord]

I hate goodies. I hate goodness that preaches. Goodness that preaches undoes itself. A little electricity of virtue lurks here & there in kitchens & among the obscure—chiefly women, that flashes out occasional light & makes the existence of the thing still credible. But one had as lief curse & swear as be guilty of this odious religion that watches the beef & watches the cider in the pitcher at table, that shuts the mouth hard at any remark it cannot twist nor wrench into a sermon, & preaches as long as itself & its hearer is awake. Goodies make us very bad. We should, if the race should increase, be scarce restrained from calling for bowl & dagger.[2] We will almost sin to spite them. Better indulge yourself, feed fat, drink liquors, than go strait laced for such cattle as these.

[I Decline Invitations]

August 22, 1838 [Concord]

I decline invitations to evening parties chiefly because beside the time spent, commonly ill, in the party, the hours preceding & succeeding the visit, are lost for any solid use, as I am put out of tune for writing or reading. That makes my objection to many employments that seem trifles to a bystander as packing a trunk, or any small handiwork, or correcting proof sheets, that they put me out of tune.

[Aftermath of the Divinity School Address]

August 31, 1838 [Concord]

Yesterday at φ B.K.[3] anniversary. Steady, steady. I am convinced that if a man will be a true scholar, he shall have perfect freedom. The young people & the mature hint at odium, & aversion of faces to be presently encountered in society. I say no: I fear it not. No scholar need fear it. For if it be true that

---

1. Zoroaster (6th century B.C.), a Persian prophet, founded Zoroastrianism, a major tenet of which is that forces of light and darkness are engaged in a universal struggle. Moses was the lawgiver who led the Israelites out of Egypt toward Israel, as described in Exodus. Zeno (342?–270? B.C.), a Greek philosopher, was the founder of Stoicism.
2. I.e., the prissiness of the Goodies (self-righteously moral people) tempts us to drink and brawl as a way of expressing our contempt for them.
3. Phi Beta Kappa. Emerson had delivered his oration The American Scholar at the previous celebration, but on the 1838 anniversary he was merely in the audience. The warnings of ostracism that he heard on August 30, 1838, had to do with the growing hostility toward the address he had made on July 15, 1838, to the senior class of the Divinity School.

he is merely an observer, a dispassionate reporter, no partisan, a singer merely for the love of music, his is a position of perfect immunity: to him no disgusts can attach; he is invulnerable. The vulgar[4] think he would found a sect & would be installed & made much of. He knows better & much prefers his melons & his woods. Society has no bribe for me, neither in politics, nor church, nor college, nor city. My resources are far from exhausted. If they will not hear me lecture, I shall have leisure for my book which wants me. Beside[,] it is an universal maxim worthy of all acceptation that a man may have that allowance which he takes. Take the place & attitude to which you see your unquestionable right, & all men acquiesce. Who are these murmurers, these haters, these revilers? Men of no knowledge, & therefore no stability. The scholar on the contrary is sure of his point, is fast-rooted, & can securely predict the hour when all this roaring multitude shall roar *for* him.

Analyze the chiding opposition & it is made up of such timidities, uncertainties, & no opinions, that it is not worth dispersing.

To Thomas Carlyle

[*Delayed Reactions to the Divinity School Address*]

[Concord, October 17, 1838]

* * * In a letter within a twelvemonth I have urged you to pay us a visit in America, & in Concord. I have believed that you would come, one day, & do believe it. But if, on your part, you have been generous & affectionate enough to your friends here—or curious enough concerning our society to wish to come, I think you must postpone, for the present, the satisfaction of your friendship & your curiosity. At this moment, I would not have you here, on any account. The publication of my "Address to the Divinity College," (copies of which I sent you) has been the occasion of an outcry in all our leading local newspapers against my "infidelity," "pantheism," & "atheism." The writers warn all & sundry against me, & against whatever is supposed to be related to my connexion of opinion, &c; against Transcendentalism, Goethe & *Carlyle*. I am heartily sorry to see this last aspect of the storm in our washbowl.[5] For, as Carlyle is nowise guilty, & has unpopularities of his own, I do not wish to embroil him in my parish-differences. You were getting to be a great favorite with us all here, and are daily a greater, with the American public, but just now, *in Boston*, where I am known as your editor, I fear you lose by the association. Now it is indispensable to your right influence here, that you should never come before our people as one of a clique, but as a detached, that is, universally associated man; so I am happy, as I could not have thought, that you have not yet yielded yourself to my entreaties. Let us wait a little until this foolish clam[or] be overblown. My position is fortunately such as to put me quite out of the reach of any real inconvenience from the panic strikers or the panic struck; &, indeed, so far as this uneasiness is a necessary result of mere inaction of mind, it seems very clear to me that, if I live, my neighbors must look for a great many more shocks, & perhaps harder to bear. * * *

4. The masses; ordinary, insensitive people.
5. The intense, though sporadic and local, hostility resulting from his address to the Harvard Divinity School (see n. 3, p. 1156).

From Journals

[Challenging Thoreau to Write His Opinions into Good Poetry]

November 10, 1838 [Concord]

My brave Henry Thoreau walked with me to Walden this P.M. and complained of the proprietors who compelled him to whom as much as to any the whole world belonged, to walk in a strip of road & crowded him out of all the rest of God's earth. He must not get over the fence: but to the building of that fence he was no party. Suppose, he said, some great proprietor, before he was born, had bought up the whole globe. So had he been hustled out of nature. Not having been privy to any of these arrangements he does not feel called on to consent to them & so cuts fishpoles in the woods without asking who has a better title to the wood than he. I defended of course the good Institution as a scheme not good but the best that could be hit on for making the woods & waters & fields available to Wit & Worth, & for restraining the bold bad man. At all events, I begged him, having this maggot of Freedom & Humanity in his brain, to write it out into good poetry & so clear himself of it. He replied, that he feared that that was not the best way; that in doing justice to the thought, the man did not always do justice to himself: the poem ought to sing itself: if the man took too much pains with the expression he was not any longer the Idea himself. I acceded & confessed that this was the tragedy of Art that the Artist was at the expense of the Man; & hence, in the first age, as they tell, the Sons of God printed no epics, carved no stone, painted no picture, built no railroad; for the sculpture, the poetry, the music, & architecture, were in the Man. And truly Bolts & Bars do not seem to me the most exalted or exalting of our institutions. And what other spirit reigns in our intellectual works? We have literary property. The very recording of a thought betrays a distrust that there is any more or much more as good for us. If we felt that the Universe was ours[,] that we dwelled in eternity & advance into all wisdom we should be less covetous of these sparks & cinders. Why should we covetously build a St Peter's, if we had the seeing Eye which beheld all the radiance of beauty & majesty in the matted grass & the overarching boughs? Why should a man spend years upon the carving an Apollo who looked Apollos into the landscape with every glance he threw?

[The Business of Education]

September 14, 1839 [Concord]

Yesterday Mr Mann's Address on Education.[6] It was full of the modern gloomy view of our democratical institutions, and hence the inference to the importance of Schools. But as far as it betrayed distrust, it seemed to pray, as do all our pulpits, for the consolation of Stoicism. A Life in Plutarch would be a perfect rebuke to such a sad discourse. If Christianity is effete let us try the doctrine of power to endure.

Education. Sad it was to see the death-cold convention yesterday morning

---

6. According to the *Journal* editors, the educator Horace Mann (brother-in-law of Hawthorne) "came to Concord from Lexington on Friday, September 13, to speak to the annual convention of the Middlesex County Education Association"; in his diary Mann counted "not more than thirty or forty" assembled in the morning, and "very meagre" attendance in the afternoon.

as they sat shivering, a handful of pale men & women in a large church, for it seems the Law has touched the business of Education with the point of its pen & instantly it has frozen stiff in the universal congelation of society. An education in things is not: we all are involved in the condemnation of words, an Age of words. We are shut up in schools & college recitation rooms for ten or fifteen years & come out at last with a bellyfull of words & do not know a thing. We cannot use our hands or our legs or our eyes or our arms. We do not know an edible root in the woods. We cannot tell our course by the stars nor the hour of the day by the sun. It is well if we can swim & skate. We are afraid of a horse, of a cow, of a dog, of a cat, of a spider. Far better was the Roman rule to teach a boy nothing that he could not learn standing. Now here are my wise young neighbors who instead of getting like the wordmen into a railroad-car where they have not even the activity of holding the reins, have got into a boat which they have built with their own hands, with sails which they have contrived to serve as a tent by night, & gone up the river Merrimack to live by their wits on the fish of the stream & the berries of the wood. My worthy neighbor Dr B[artlett]. expressed a true parental instinct when he desired to send his boy with them to learn something. The farm, the farm is the right school. The reason of my deep respect for the farmer is that he is a realist & not a dictionary. The farm is a piece of the world, the School house is not. The farm by training the physical rectifies & invigorates the metaphysical & moral nature.

Now so bad we are that the world is stripped of love & of terror. Here came the other night an Aurora so wonderful a curtain of red & blue & silver glory that in any other age or nation it would have moved the awe & wonder of men & mingled with the profoundest sentiments of religion & love, & we all saw it with cold arithmetical eyes, we knew how many colours shone, how many degrees it extended, how many hours it lasted, & of this heavenly flower we beheld nothing more: a primrose by the brim of the river of time. Shall we not wish back again the Seven Whistlers, the Flying Dutchman, the lucky & unlucky days, & the terrors of the Day of Doom?[7]

I lament that I find in me no enthusiasm, no resources for the instruction & guidance of the people when they shall discover that their present guides are blind. This convention of Education is cold, but I should perhaps affect a hope I do not feel if I were bidden to counsel it. I hate preaching whether in pulpits or Teachers' meetings. Preaching is a pledge & I wish to say what I think & feel today with the proviso that tomorrow perhaps I shall contradict it all. Freedom boundless I wish. I will not pledge myself not to drink wine, not to drink ink, not to lie, & not to commit adultery lest I hanker tomorrow to do these very things by reason of my having tied my hands. Besides Man is so poor he cannot afford to part with any advantages or bereave himself of the functions even of one hair. I do not like to speak to the Peace Society if so I am to restrain me in so extreme a privilege as the use of the sword & bullet. For the peace of the man who has forsworn the use of the bullet seems to me not quite peace, but a canting impotence: but with knife & pistol in my hands,

---

7. Emerson is longing for the credulous days when one could believe in stories such as the one about the spectral ship (*The Flying Dutchman*) said to cruise in storms off the Cape of Good Hope or that bulwark of Christianity, the threat of destruction detailed in Revelation 16. Emerson's irony cuts several ways, one stroke going toward his own Romantic opposition of science and beauty.

if I, from greater bravery & honor, cast them aside, then I know the glory of peace.

[The Screaming of the Mad Neighborwoman]

June 24, 1840 [Concord]

Now for near five years I have been indulged by the gracious Heaven in my long holiday in this goodly house of mine entertaining & entertained by so many worthy & gifted friends and all this time poor Nancy Barron the madwoman has been screaming herself hoarse at the poorhouse across the brook & I still hear her whenever I open my window.

[Skepticism about the Brook Farm Utopia]

October 17, 1840 [Concord]

Yesterday George & Sophia Ripley, <&> Margaret Fuller & Alcott discussed here the new social plans.[8] I wished to be convinced, to be thawed, to be made nobly mad by the kindlings before my eye of a new dawn of human piety. But this scheme was arithmetic & comfort; this was a hint borrowed from the Tremont House & U.S. Hotel;[9] a rage in our poverty & politics to live rich & gentlemanlike, an anchor to leeward against a change of weather; a prudent forecast on the probable issue of the great questions of pauperism & property. And not once could I be inflamed,—but sat aloof & thoughtless, my voice faltered & fell. It was not the cave of persecution which is the palace of spiritual power, but only a room in the Astor House hired for the Transcendentalists. I do not wish to remove from my present prison to a prison a little larger. I wish to break all prisons. I have not yet conquered my own house. It irks & repents me. Shall I raise the siege of this hencoop & march baffled away to a pretended siege of Babylon? It seems to me that so to do were to dodge the problem I am set to solve, & to hide my impotency in the thick of a crowd. I can see too afar that I should not find myself more than now,—no, not so much, in that select, but not by me selected, fraternity. Moreover, to join this body would be to traverse all my long trumpeted theory, and the instinct which spoke from it, that one man is a counterpoise to a city,—that a man is stronger than a city, that his solitude is more prevalent & beneficent than the concert of crowds.

[Swearing as the Best Rhetoric]

October 25, 1840 [Concord]

What a pity that we cannot curse & swear in good society. Cannot the stinging dialect of the sailors be domesticated? It is the best rhetoric and for a

8. Plans for the utopian community Brook Farm near West Roxbury, Massachusetts. George Ripley (1802–1880), Unitarian minister, editor, and literary critic, with his wife, Sarah Dana Ripley, was the major organizer of the community and was its president. Margaret Fuller (1810–1850), leading Transcendentalist and feminist. Bronson Alcott (1799–1888), Tran-

scendentalist and educator. Text in angle brackets was added by the *Journal* editors.
9. Celebrated hotels in Boston (the Tremont House, opened 1829, and the U.S. Hotel opened 1840) and in New York (the Astor House opened 1836), all early examples of the modern luxurious hotel.

hundred occasions those forbidden words are the only good ones. My page about "Consistency" would be better written thus; Damn Consistency. And to how many foolish canting remarks would a sophomore's ejaculation be the only suitable reply, "The devil you do;" or, "You be damned."

[Dead Sentences versus Man-Making Words]

November–December, 1841 [Concord]

All writing is by the grace of God. People do not deserve to have good writing, they are so pleased with bad. In these sentences that you show me I can find no beauty, for I see death in every clause & every word. There is a fossil or a mummy character which pervades this book. The best sepulchres, the vastest catacombs, Thebes & Cairo pyramids are sepulchres to me. I like gardens and nurseries. Give me initiative, spermatic, prophesying, man-making words.

[Young Waldo's Physical World]

January 30, 1842 [Concord]

What he[1] looked upon is better, what he looked not upon is insignificant. The morning of Friday I woke at 3 oclock, & every cock in every barnyard was shrilling with the most unnecessary noise. The sun went up the morning sky with all his light, but the landscape was dishonored by this loss. For this boy in whose remembrance I have both slept & awaked so oft, decorated for me the morning star, & the evening cloud, how much more all the particulars of daily economy; for he had touched with his lively curiosity every trivial fact & circumstance in the household the hard coal & the soft coal which I put into my stove; the wood of which he brought his little quota for grandmothers fire, the hammer, the pincers, & file, he was so eager to use; the microscope, the magnet, the little gobe, & every trinket & instrument in the study; the loads of gravel on the meadow the nests in the henhouse and many & many a little visit to the doghouse and to the barn,— For every thing he had his own name & way of thinking his own pronunciation & manner. And every word came mended from that tongue. A boy of early wisdom, of a grave & even majestic deportment, of a perfect gentleness

[Young Waldo's Human World]

January 30(?), 1842 [Concord]

The boy had his full swing in this world Never I think did a child enjoy more he had been thoroughly respected by his parents & those around him & not interfered with; and he had been the most fortunate in respect to the influences near him for his Aunt Elizabeth[2] had adopted him from his infancy & treated him ever with that plain & wise love which belongs to her and, as she boasted, had never given him sugar plums. So he was won to her & always signalized her arrival as a visit to him & left playmates playthings & all to go

1. Waldo Emerson (1836–1842), Emerson's son.
2. Elizabeth Hoar, who had been engaged to Emerson's dead brother Charles.

to her. Then Mary Russell[3] had been his friend & teacher for two summers with true love & wisdom. Then Henry Thoreau had been one of the family for the last year, & charmed Waldo by the variety of toys whistles boats popguns & all kinds of instruments which he could make & mend; & possessed his love & respect by the gentle firmness with which he always treated him. Margaret Fuller & Caroline Sturgis[4] had also marked the boy & caressed & conversed with him whenever they were here. Meantime every day his Grandmother gave him his reading lesson & had by patience taught him to read & spell; by patience & by love for she loved him dearly.

To William Emerson[5]

[What to Expect from Thoreau]

Concord, 6 May, 1843

Dear William,

I received yesterday your letter with its enclosure $47.06 which comes in good time. Yet our Concord rapacity is greater than one would look for in a quiet town, & we spend faster than the utmost generosity of cities can keep up with. I have advanced Henry Thoreau $10.00 more, since I wrote before, & this sum having been expanded in outfit, I paid him last night $7.00 for travelling expenses, so that I charge you with 17.—And now goes our brave youth into the new house, the new connexion, the new City. I am sure no truer & no purer person lives in wide New York; and he is a bold & a profound thinker though he may easily chance to pester you with some accidental crotchets and perhaps a village exaggeration of the value of facts. Yet I confide, if you should content each other, in Willie's soon coming to value him for his real power to serve & instruct him. I shall eagerly look, though not yet for some time, for tidings how you speed in this new relation. * * *

Affectionately your brother
Waldo

From Journals

[Thoreau's Fault of Unlimited Contradiction]

August 25, 1843 [Concord]

H. D. T. sends me a paper[6] with the old fault of unlimited contradiction. The trick of his rhetoric is soon learned. It consists in substituting for the obvious word & thought its diametrical antagonist. He praises wild mountains & winter forests for their domestic air; snow & ice for their warmth; villagers & wood choppers for their urbanity[;] and the wilderness for resembling Rome & Paris. With the constant inclination to dispraise cities & civilization, he yet can find no way to honour woods & woodmen except by paralleling them with towns & townsmen. W[illiam] E[llery] C[hanning]

---

3. The private teacher of Emerson's children.
4. A young Bostonian Transcendentalist, frequent guest of the Emersons.
5. Emerson's brother, the father of the "Willie" men-

tioned in the letter whom Thoreau was to tutor.
6. A *Winter Walk*, published in the *Dial*, October 1843.

declares the piece is excellent: but it makes me nervous & wretched to read it, with all its merits.

To William Emerson

[A Craze for Acquiring Property]

Concord, October 4, 1844

* * * I have lately added an absurdity or two to my usual ones, which I am impatient to tell you of. In one of my solitary wood-walks by Walden Pond, I met two or three men who told me they had come thither to sell & to buy a field, on which they wished me to bid as purchaser. As it was on the shore of the pond, & now for years I had a sort of daily occupancy in it, I bid on it, & bought it, eleven acres for $8.10 per acre. The next day I carried some of my well beloved gossips to the same place & they deciding that the field was not good for anything, if Heartwell Bigelow[7] should cut down his pine-grove, I bought, for 125 dollars more, his pretty wood lot of 3 or 4 acres, and so am landlord & waterlord of 14 acres, more or less, on the shore of Walden, & can raise my own blackberries. I am now, like other men who have hazarded a small stake, mad for more. Since Mrs Brown wishes me to build her a cottage on some land near my house; & the dreaming Alcott is here with Indian dreams that I helped him to some house & farm in the Spirit Land! These are the light headed frolics of a hack of a scribe, when released at last from months of weary tending on the printers devil! I expect to grow fat & plump now for weeks to come. My book,[8] I prayed the publisher to secure me some copies of in time to send you tomorrow but he did not seem willing to promise any before Monday or Tuesday.

Yours with love to Susan & boys!

Waldo

From Journals

[The London Literati on Male Chastity]

April 25, 1848 [London]

Dined with John Forster, Esq. Lincoln's Inn Fields, & found Carlyle, & Dickens, & young Pringle.[9] Forster, who has an obstreperous cordiality, received Carlyle with loud salutation, "My Prophet!" Forster called Carlyle's passion, Musket-worship. There were only gentlemen present, & the conversation turned on the shameful lewdness of the London streets at night. (Carlyle said, & the others agreed, that chastity for men was as good as given up in Europe.) "I hear it," he said, "I hear whoredom in the House of Commons. Disraeli betrays whoredom, & the whole H. of Commons universal incontinence, in every word they say." I said, that, when I came to Liverpool, I

---

7. The people referred to are Concord neighbors.
8. I.e., *Essays, Second Series*.
9. Aside from Emerson's old friend Carlyle, the party consisted of John Forster (1812–1876), English critic and biographer. Charles Dickens (1812–1870), already the most popular novelist of his time. "Young Pringle"

was apparently a son of the Scottish poet Thomas Pringle (1789–1834). References later in this entry are to Benjamin Disraeli (1804–1881), novelist and statesman, later the first earl of Beaconsfield, and to the poet and critic Leigh Hunt (1784–1859).

inquired whether the prostitution was always as gross in that city, as it then appeared? for, to me, it seemed to betoken a fatal rottenness in the state, & I saw not how any boy could grow up safe. But I had been told, it was not worse nor better, for years. C & D. replied, that chastity in the male sex was as good as gone in our times; &, in England, was so rare, that they could name all the exceptions. Carlyle evidently believed that the same things were true in America.—He had heard this & that, of New York, &c. I assured them that it was not so with us; that, for the most part, young men of good standing & good education with us, go virgins to their nuptial bed, as truly as their brides. Dickens replied, "that incontinence is so much the rule in England, that if his own son were particularly chaste, he should be alarmed on his account, as if he could not be in good health. Leigh Hunt," he said, "thought it indifferent."

[Tennyson as a Talkative Hawthorne]

May 6(?), 1848 [London]

I saw Tennyson, first, at the house of Coventry Patmore, where we dined together.[1] His friend Brookfield was also of the party. I was contented with him, at once. He is tall, scholastic-looking, no dandy,—but a great deal of plain strength about him, & though cultivated, quite unaffected.—Quiet sluggish sense & strength, refined, as all English are,—and good humoured. The print of his head in Horne's book is too rounded & handsome. There is in him an air of general superiority, that is very satisfactory. He lives very much with his college set * * * and has the air of one who is accustomed to be petted and indulged by those he lives with * * * Take away Hawthorne's bashfulness, & let him talk easily & fast, & you would have a pretty good Tennyson.

[Thoreau the Woodgod]

August 1848 [Concord]

Henry Thoreau is like the woodgod who solicits the wandering poet & draws him into antres vast & desarts idle,[2] & bereaves him of his memory, & leaves him naked, plaiting vines & with twigs in his hand. Very seductive are the first steps from the town to the woods, but the End is want & madness.—

* * *

I spoke of friendship, but my friends & I are fishes in their habit. As for taking T.'s arm, I should as soon take the arm of an elm tree.

[The Hypocrisy of Daniel Webster]

April 1851 [Concord]

I opened a paper today in which he [Daniel Webster] pounds on the old strings in a letter to the Washington Birth Day feasters at N. Y. "Liberty!

---

1. The dinner was on May 5, 1848. In 1850 Alfred Tennyson (1809–1892) became poet laureate of England. Other people mentioned in this entry are Coventry Patmore (1823–1896), English poet, and William Henry Brookfield (1809–1874), minister, college friend of Tennyson. Richard Henry Horne

(1803–1884) had included the "too rounded & handsome" portrait of Tennyson in A New Spirit of the Age (1844).
2. Empty wastelands. "Antres": caves. This is an echo of Othello 1.3.140, the Moor's account of how he wooed Desdemona.

liberty!" Pho! Let Mr Webster for decency's sake shut his lips once & forever on this word. The word *liberty* in the mouth of Mr Webster sounds like the word *love* in the mouth of a courtezan.[3]

[The Purist Who Refuses to Vote]

April 13, 1852 [Concord]

The Purist who refuses to vote, because the gov[ernmen]t does not content him in all points, should refuse to feed a starving beggar, lest he should feed his vices.

[Black Slavery versus Quite Other Slaves to Free]

August 1, 1852 [Concord]

I waked at night, & bemoaned myself, because I had not thrown myself into this deplorable question of Slavery, which seems to want nothing so much as a few assured voices. But then, in hours of sanity, I recover myself, & say, God must govern his own world, & knows his way out of this pit, without my desertion of my post which has none to guard it but me. I have quite other slaves to free than those negroes, to wit, imprisoned spirits, imprisoned thoughts, far back in the brain of man,—far retired in the heaven of invention, &, which, important to the republic of Man, have no watchman, or lover, or defender, but I.—

To Walter Whitman

[The Wonderful Gift of Leaves of Grass]

July 21, 1855, Concord

* * * I am not blind to the worth of the wonderful gift of "Leaves of Grass." I find it the most extraordinary piece of wit and wisdom that America has yet contributed. I am very happy in reading it, as great power makes us happy. It meets the demand I am always making of what seemed the sterile & stingy nature, as if too much handiwork or too much lymph[4] in the temperament, were making our western wits fat & mean. I give you joy of your free & brave thought. I have great joy in it. I find incomparable things said incomparably well, as they must be. I find the courage of treatment, which so delights me, and which large perception only can inspire. I greet you at the beginning of a great career, which yet must have had a long foreground somewhere, for such a start. I rubbed my eyes a little to see if this sunbeam were no illusion; but the solid sense of the book is a sober certainty. It has the best of merits, namely, of fortifying & encouraging.

I did not know until I, last night, saw the book advertised in a newspaper, that I could trust the name as real & available for a post-office. I wish to see my benefactor, & have felt much like striking my tasks, & visiting New York to pay you my respects. * * *

---

3. Antislavery New Englanders felt betrayed by Senator Daniel Webster (1782–1852) after he supported the Compromise of 1850 and particularly after one of its parts, the Fugitive Slave Law, was enforced in Boston in April 1851.

4. Here, a sluggish or phlegmatic substance.

From Journals

[*The Frustration of Trying to Talk to Thoreau*]

February 29, 1856 [Concord]

If I knew only Thoreau, I should think cooperation of good men impossible. Must we always talk for victory, & never once for truth, for comfort, & joy? Centrality he has, & penetration, strong understanding, & the higher gifts,— the insight of the real or from the real, & the moral rectitude that belongs to it; but all this & all his resources of wit & invention are lost to me in every experiment, year after year, that I make, to hold intercourse with his mind. Always some weary captious paradox to fight you with, & the time & temper wasted.

To Thomas Carlyle

[*Second Thoughts on the Nondescript Monster,* Leaves of Grass]

May 6, 1856, Concord

* * * One book, last summer, came out in New York, a nondescript monster which yet has terrible eyes & buffalo strength, & was indisputably American,—which I thought to send you; but the book throve so badly with the few to whom I showed it, & wanted good morals so much, that I never did. Yet I believe now again, I shall. It is called "Leaves of Grass,"—was written & printed by a journeyman printer in Brooklyn, N. Y. named Walter Whitman; and after you have looked into it, if you think, as you may, that it is only an auctioneer's inventory of a warehouse, you can light your pipe with it. * * *

From Journals

[*Thoreau: Why He Fancied Whitman*]

February 1862 [Concord]

Thoreau. Perhaps his fancy for Walt Whitman grew out of his taste for wild nature, for an otter, a woodchuck, or a loon. He loved sufficiency, hated a sum that would not prove; loved Walt and hated Alcott.[5]

"It were well if the false preacher of Christianity were always met and balked by a superior, more living, and elastic faith in his audience, just as some missionaries in India are balked by the easiness with which the Hindoos believe every word of miracle and prophecy, only surprised that they are much less wonderful than those of their own scriptures, which also they implicitly believe."

—H. D. T.

T——[6] came to see Thoreau on business, but Thoreau at once perceived that he had been drinking, and advised him to go home and cut his throat,

---

5. As the editors of this passage said in 1913, Emerson lets his rhetorical neatness distort the truth: Thoreau became impatient with Alcott, as did everyone who knew him, but did not hate him.

6. Alex Therien, the French-Canadian woodchopper introduced in *Walden,* "Visitors."

and that speedily. T—— did not well know what to make of it, but went away, and Thoreau said he learned that he had been repeating it about town, which he was glad to hear, and hoped that by this time he had begun to understand what it meant.

[Seeing Himself Furthered in Thoreau's Journals]

June 1863 [Concord]

In reading Henry Thoreau's journal, I am very sensible of the vigour of his constitution. That oaken strength which I noted whenever he walked, or worked, or surveyed wood-lots, the same unhesitating hand with which a field-labourer accosts a piece of work, which I should shun as a waste of strength, Henry shows in his literary task. He has muscle, and ventures on and performs feats which I am forced to decline. In reading him, I find the same thought, the same spirit that is in me, but he takes a step beyond, and illustrates by excellent images that which I should have conveyed in a sleepy generality. 'T is as if I went into a gymnasium, and saw youths leap, climb, and swing with a force unapproachable,—though their feats are only continuations of my initial grapplings and jumps.

[Taking Lincoln with His Faults]

1863 [Concord]

Lincoln. We must accept the results of universal suffrage, and not try to make it appear that we can elect fine gentlemen. We shall have coarse men, with a fair chance of worth and manly ability, but not polite men, not men to please the English or French.

You cannot refine Mr. Lincoln's taste, extend his horizon, or clear his judgment; he will not walk dignifiedly through the traditional part of the President of America, but will pop out his head at each railroad station and make a little speech, and get into an argument with Squire A. and Judge B. He will write letters to Horace Greeley,[7] and any editor or reporter or saucy party committee that writes to him, and cheapen himself.

But this we must be ready for, and let the clown appear, and hug ourselves that we are well off, if we have got good nature, honest meaning, and fidelity to public interest, with bad manners,—instead of an elegant *roué* and malignant self-seeker.

[The Burial of Hawthorne—After Waiting Too Long to Get to Know Him]

May 24, 1864 [Concord]

Yesterday, May 23, we buried Hawthorne in Sleepy Hollow, in a pomp of sunshine and verdure, and gentle winds. James Freeman Clarke read the ser-

---

7. Horace Greeley (1881–1872), long-time editor of the *New York Tribune*, recipient of the famous letter of August 22, 1862, in which Lincoln wrote: "If I could save the Union without freeing any slaves, I would do it; and if I could save it by freeing all the slaves, I would do it; and if I could save it by freeing some and leaving others alone, I would also do that."

vice in the church and at the grave. Longfellow, Lowell, Holmes, Agassiz, Hoar, Dwight, Whipple, Norton, Alcott, Hillard, Fields, Judge Thomas, and I attended the hearse as pallbearers. Franklin Pierce[8] was with the family. The church was copiously decorated with white flowers delicately arranged. The corpse was unwillingly shown,—only a few moments to this company of his friends. But it was noble and serene in its aspect,—nothing amiss,—a calm and powerful head. A large company filled the church and the grounds of the cemetery. All was so bright and quiet that pain or mourning was hardly suggested, and Holmes said to me that it looked like a happy meeting.

Clarke in the church said that Hawthorne had done more justice than any other to the shades of life, shown a sympathy with the crime in our nature, and, like Jesus, was the friend of sinners.

I thought there was a tragic element in the event, that might be more fully rendered,—in the painful solitude of the man, which, I suppose, could not longer be endured, and he died of it.

I have found in his death a surprise and disappointment. I thought him a greater man than any of his works betray, that there was still a great deal of work in him, and that he might one day show a purer power. Moreover, I have felt sure of him in his neighbourhood, and in his necessities of sympathy and intelligence,—that I could well wait his time,—his unwillingness and caprice,—and might one day conquer a friendship. It would have been a happiness, doubtless to both of us, to have come into habits of unreserved intercourse. It was easy to talk with him,—there were no barriers,—only, he said so little, that I talked too much, and stopped only because, as he gave no indications, I feared to exceed. He showed no egotism or self-assertion, rather a humility, and, at one time, a fear that he had written himself out. One day, when I found him on the top of his hill, in the woods, he paced back the path to his house, and said, "This path is the only rememberance of me that will remain." Now it appears that I waited too long.

Lately he had removed himself the more by the indignation his perverse politics and unfortunate friendship for that paltry Franklin Pierce awakened, though it rather moved pity for Hawthorne, and the assured belief that he would outlive it, and come right at last.

[A Mystery about Reading]

July 2, 1867 [Concord]

Reading. I suppose every old scholar has had the experience of reading something in a book which was significant to him, but which he could never

---

8. Most of the pallbearers were, like Emerson, members of the Saturday Club, which met at the Parker House in Boston the last Saturday of every month. Clubmen were the poets Longfellow, Lowell, and Holmes; the Harvard scientist Louis Agassiz (1807–1873), an immigrant from Switzerland; Judge Ebenezer Rockwood Hoar (1816–1895), brother of Charles Emerson's fiancée Elizabeth Hoar; John S. Dwight (1813–1893), Transcendentalist and music critic; Edwin Percy Whipple (1819–1886), literary critic; Charles Eliot Norton (1827–1908), then a contributor to the *Atlantic Monthly*, later Lowell's successor at Harvard; and James T. Fields (1817–1881), Haw-

thorne's publisher. A subsequent member of the Saturday Club was James Freeman Clarke (1810–88), Unitarian minister and theological writer who had officiated at the marriage of Sophia Peabody and Nathaniel Hawthorne (the Boston world was small: he also gave communion to Elizabeth Shaw the day she married Herman Melville). Other pallbearers were Bronson Alcott (1799–1888), educator and Transcendentalist philosopher; George Hillard (1808–1879), lawyer and writer; and B. F. Thomas (1813–1878), Boston jurist and antiquarian. Franklin Pierce (1804–1869), Hawthorne's college friend, was president of the United States 1853–57.

find again. Sure he is that he read it there; but no one else ever read it, nor can he find it again, though he buy the book, and ransack every page.

[The Scientific Splendors of This Age]

June 1871 [Concord]

The splendors of this age outshine all other recorded ages. In my lifetime have been wrought five miracles,—namely, 1, the Steamboat; 2, the Railroad; 3, the Electric Telegraph; 4, the application of the Spectroscope to astronomy; 5, the Photograph;—five miracles which have altered the relations of nations to each other. Add cheap postage; and the mowing-machine and the horse-rake. A corresponding power has been given to manufactures by the machine for pegging shoes, and the power-loom, and the power-press of the printers. And in dentistry and in surgery, Dr. Jackson's discovery of Anæsthesia. It only needs to add the power which, up to this hour, eludes all human ingenuity, namely, a rudder to the balloon, to give us the dominion of the air, as well as of the sea and the land. But the account is not complete until we add the discovery of Oersted, of the identity of Electricity and Magnetism, and the generalization of that conversion by its application to light, heat, and gravitation. The geologist has found the correspondence of the age of stratified remains to the ascending scale of structure in animal life. Add now, the daily predictions of the weather for the next twenty-four hours for North America, by the Observatory at Washington.[9]

9. After four decades of active experimentation, regular Atlantic steam crossings between England and the United States began in 1838. From the 1820s, railroads had been used as public transportation. The electric telegraph became available for public use in the 1840s. Astronomical spectroscopy, the science of using prisms to gain information about the chemical elements of the sun and other stars, began with Isaac Newton in 1666, but modern spectroscopy dates from 1814, when Joseph von Fraunhofer combined the use of telescope and prism. Modern photography began with the work of the Frenchman Joseph Niepce in 1822; by the 1830s and 1840s daguerreotyping was common. Emerson's brother-in-law Charles Thomas Jackson (1805–1880) was a pioneer in the use of ether in anesthesia, although William Morton received most of the public credit. The Danish chemist Hans Christian Oersted (1777–1851) discovered the identity of electricity and magnetism in 1820.

NATHANIEL HAWTHORNE
1804–1864

Nathaniel Hawthorne was born on Independence Day, 1804, in Salem, Massachusetts, a descendant of Puritan immigrants; one ancestor had been a judge in the Salem witchcraft trials. The family, like the seaport town, was on the decline. When his sea-captain father died in Dutch Guiana in 1808, his mother's brothers took responsibility for his education. In his early teens he lived three years as free as "a bird of the air" at Sebago Lake, in Maine (then still a part of Massachusetts), acquiring a love of tramping, which he always kept. By his mid-teens he was reading eighteenth-century novelists like Henry Fielding, Tobias Smollett, and Horace Walpole as well as contemporary writers like William Godwin and Sir Walter Scott and forming an ambition to be a writer himself. At Bowdoin College shyness caused him to try to evade the obligatory public declamations, but in social clubs he formed smoking, card-playing, and drinking friendships; two fellow members of the Democratic literary society, Horatio Bridge and Franklin Pierce, later president, became lifelong friends; Longfellow, another classmate, belonged to the rival Federalist society. Hawthorne kept outdoors a good deal at the bucolic college but managed, as he later said, to read "desultorily right and left." At the graduation ceremonies in 1825, Longfellow spoke optimistically on the possibility that "Our Native Writers" could achieve lasting fame. Hawthorne went home to Salem and became a writer, but he was agonizingly slow in winning acclaim.

Hawthorne's years between 1825 and 1837 have fascinated his biographers and critics. Hawthorne himself took pains to propagate the notion that he had lived as a hermit who left his upstairs room only for nighttime walks and hardly communicated even with his mother and sisters. Twentieth-century scholars have shown that although in fact Hawthorne was intensely committed to his writing and was steeping himself in colonial history more than the political issues of his time, he socialized in Salem, had several more or less serious flirtations, kept in touch with Pierce and Bridge, among others, and spent most of the summers knocking about all over New England (an uncle owned stage lines). He even got as far as Detroit one year. Often called his apprenticeship, these dozen years in fact encompassed as well his period of finest creativity. The first surviving piece of his true apprenticework is the historical novel *Fanshawe*, which Hawthorne paid to have published in 1828 and then quickly suppressed.

Over the next several years Hawthorne tried unsuccessfully to find a publisher for collections of the tales he was writing. In chagrin he burned *Seven Tales of My Native Land* (including one or two stories of witchcraft) although at least one of the seven, *Alice Doane's Appeal*, survives in an altered form. By 1829 he was negotiating—again fruitlessly—for the publication of a volume called *Provincial Tales*, which included *The Gentle Boy* as well, apparently, as *Roger Malvin's Burial* and *My Kinsman, Major Molineux*. In tales like these he had found his special—though highly unsatisfactory—outlets for publication: magazines and the literary annuals that were issued each fall as genteel Christmas gifts. For his tales Hawthorne got a few dollars each and no fame at all, since publication in the annuals was anonymous. He continued to strive to interest a bookseller in his tales, offering what could have been a remarkable volume called *The Story Teller*, in which the title character wandered about New England telling his stories in dramatic settings and circumstances. One story, *Mr. Higginbotham's Catastrophe*, reached print in its narrative frame, but the editor of the *New-England Magazine* scrapped the frame for *Young Goodman Brown* and others that are now known as isolated items instead of interrelated elements in a larger whole. The biographer Randall Stewart plausibly suggests that "*The Story Teller* would have united in one work Hawthorne's imaginative and reportorial faculties as none of his published writings quite do." In 1836 Hawthorne turned to literary hackwork, making an encyclopedia for the Boston publisher Samuel G. Goodrich, whose annual, *The Token*, had become the regular market for his tales. In the same year Bridge secretly persuaded Goodrich to publish a collection of Hawthorne's tales by promising to repay any losses. *Twice-Told Tales* appeared in March 1837, with Hawthorne's name on the title page; the title was a self-deprecating allusion to Shakespeare's *King John* 3.4: "Life is as tedious as a twice-told tale / Vexing the dull eare of a drowsie man." The book was reviewed in England as well as the United States, and opened up what Hawthorne called "an intercourse with the world." A notebook entry written sometime in 1836 was only a little premature: "In this dismal and sordid chamber FAME was won."

Throughout the early stories, both those collected in *Twice-Told Tales* and those he left for later gleaning, Hawthorne mused obsessively over a small range of psychological themes: the consequences of pride, selfishness, and secret guilt; the conflict between lighthearted and somber attitudes toward life; the difficulty of preventing isolation from leading to coldness of heart; the impingement of the past (especially the Puritan past) on the present; the futility of comprehensive social reforms; and the impossibility of eradicating sin from the human heart. Above all, his theme was curiosity about the recesses of other men's and women's beings. About this theme he was always ambivalent, for he knew that his success as a writer depended on his keen psychological analysis of people he met, while he could never forget that invasion of the sanctity of another's personality may harden the heart even as it enriches the mind. He knew that there was "something of the hawk-eye" about him and that the line was vague between prurient curiosity and legitimate artistic study of character. At his best, he was a master of psychological insight, and some of his power of psychological burrowing remained with him throughout his career, even in the romances that were left unfinished at his death.

The year 1837 was the start of Hawthorne's public literary career; it also marked the end of his single-minded dedication to his work. In the fall of 1838 Elizabeth Peabody, a Salemite who was to become a major force in American educational reform, sought out the new local celebrity. When Hawthorne met her sister Sophia, twenty-nine and an invalid, his life abruptly changed course. Within a few months he and Sophia were engaged. To save money for marriage, Hawthorne worked as salt and coal measurer in the Boston Custom House during 1839 and 1840, then the next year invested in the utopian community Brook Farm, more as a business venture than as a philosophical gesture; the only return, however, was the locale he later used for *The Blithedale Romance* (1852). During his engagement, Hawthorne's main literary productions were letters to Sophia—full of ironical self-deprecation, satirical reportage, and romantic effusions. In December 1841, he wrote Evert A. Duyckinck and Cornelius Mathews, New York magazine editors, that his early stories had grown out of quietude and seclusion, the lack of which would probably prevent him from writing any more. Marriage, not literature, became Hawthorne's new career long before the actual ceremony in July 1842. As he rather severely put it, "when a man has taken upon himself to beget children, he has no longer any right to a life of his own."

The first three years of marriage, spent at the Old Manse in Concord, the home of Emerson's ancestors, seemed idyllic to the Hawthornes, but a hoped-for novel never materialized. By now comfortably familiar with accounts of the Puritan and Revolutionary past, he wrote a child's history of colonial and revolutionary New England, *Grandfather's Chair* (1841), and four years later produced a rewriting of Bridge's *Journal of an African Cruiser. Mosses from an Old Manse* (1846) consisted mainly of new tales, but among the early ones first collected in it were *Roger Malvin's Burial* and *Young Goodman Brown*. His literary earnings were not rising, but his reputation was, partly through his own shrewd creation of a public persona. Knowing that certain readers who delight in realism would be disturbed by the shadowiness of some of his stories, he anticipated the worst that could be said, declaring in the whimsical survey of his career in the headnote to *Rappaccini's Daughter* that "M. de l'Aubépine" (French for "Hawthorne") had "an inveterate love of allegory, which is apt to invest his plots and characters with the aspect of scenery and people in the clouds, and to steal away the human warmth out of his conceptions." Any hostility, of course, was disarmed by such self-criticism, and in the introductory essay for *Mosses from an Old Manse* Hawthorne pursued his strategy of evoking for himself an equivalent of the Miltonic fit audience though few, yet enlarging that audience without letting his readers feel they were part of a mob. Hawthorne insisted winningly both on his ultimate reserve—his refusal to "serve up" his own heart delicately fried—and on his eagerness to communicate with his chosen audience. Even after he attained a large readership, he knew the value of trading on his own early obscurity so as to make a reader feel like a special discoverer of a rarity yet unshared by the many. In the 1851 edition of *Twice-Told Tales*, Hawthorne observed that the author, "on the internal evidence of his sketches, came to be regarded as a mild, shy, gentle, melancholic, exceedingly sensitive, and not very forcible man, hiding his blushes under an assumed name, the quaintness of which was supposed, somehow or other, to symbolize his personal and literary traits." While summarizing the image critics had conceived of him, he helped fix that image for a century and more as *the* Hawthorne.

Through long service to the local Democrats, Hawthorne was named Surveyor of the Port of Salem in 1846. The office was something of a sinecure, but his forenoons—always his most productive hours—had to be spent at the Custom House, and he wrote little. Hawthorne was thrown out of office by the new Whig administration in June 1849, amid a furious controversy in the newspapers. He then spent a summer of "great diversity and severity" of emotion climaxed by his mother's death. In September he was at work on *The Scarlet Letter*, which he planned as a long tale to make up half a volume called *Old Time Legends; together with Sketches, Experimental and Ideal*. Besides the long introduction, *The Custom House*, which was Hawthorne's means of revenging himself on the Salem Whigs who had ousted him, he planned to include some still-uncollected tales. James Fields, the young associate of the publisher William D. Ticknor, persuaded him that a long piece of fiction would sell better than another collection of stories, and Hawthorne obligingly omitted the stories. (Fields was the source of a false story that he also persuaded Hawthorne to expand *The Scarlet Letter* from a story to a novel.) Although it was frequently denounced as licentious or morbid, *The Scarlet Letter* (1850) was nevertheless a literary sensation in the United States and Great Britain, and Hawthorne was proclaimed as the finest American romancer. There had already been many novels set in Puritan New England, and many more followed, but *The Scarlet Letter* remains the single classic of the group, appealing to tastes of changing generations in different ways; perhaps the most powerful appeal has not changed at all: the remarkable way Hawthorne manages to evoke emotional sympathy for the heroine even when he is condemning her actions.

During a year and a half in the Berkshires of western Massachusetts, where Melville became his "not-too-distant neighbor," Hawthorne wrote *The House of the Seven Gables* (1851), assembled *The Snow Image*, mainly from very early pieces, and wrote for children A *Wonder-Book* (1852). Escaping from the rigors of the Berkshire winters, he wrote *The Blithedale Romance* (1852) in West Newton; then in the first home he had owned, the Wayside at Concord, he put together a political biography of his friend Franklin Pierce for the campaign of 1852 and worked up *The Tanglewood Tales* (1853), prettified stories from mythology. This productivity was broken when President Pierce appointed him American consul at Liverpool. The consulship came as a blessing despite the disruption of his new life at Concord, for his literary income was not enough to support his family, which now included a son and two daughters.

At Liverpool (1853–57) Hawthorne was an uncommonly industrious consul; he had always been more comfortable among businesspeople and politicians than among literary people. Tireless in sightseeing among ancient inns, castles, and other public buildings, he also set himself a rigorous course of gallery going and elaborately recorded his observations in his notebooks. Exposed to great museums for the first time, Hawthorne surprised himself with his affinity for the seventeenth-century Dutch masters of genre painting, deciding that those painters "accomplish all they aim at,—a praise, methinks, which can be given to no other men since the world began." He forced himself—fortified with liquor—to make the required public speeches, and late in his consulship let himself be lionized during an extended trip to London. A stay in Italy—starting in the miserably cold first months of 1858—ate deeply into the more than $30,000 he had earned at Liverpool, and malaria nearly killed his daughter Una. Except during her illness, he kept up his minutely detailed tourist's account as well as a record of the family's contacts with the English and American colony of painters, sculptors, and writers. Many pages of the notebooks went nearly verbatim into a book that he began in Florence in

1858 and finished late in 1859, after his return to England. This romance, suggested by the statue of a faun attributed to the classical Greek sculptor Praxiteles, was published in London (1860) as *Transformation* and in the United States under Hawthorne's preferred title, *The Marble Faun*.

The Hawthornes came home in June 1860, during the general acclaim of the new romance, and set about fitting up the Wayside; this project was a considerable drain on Hawthorne's savings, which were already depleted by prolonged residence abroad after resigning his consulship and by generous, though unwise, loans to friends. His literary stature made even his abolitionist neighbors respectful toward him, but Hawthorne was keenly aware that his sympathy for the South ran counter to the mood of neighbors such as Emerson and Thoreau. For the *Atlantic Monthly* Fields solicited a series of sketches that Hawthorne adapted from his English notebooks. Fields paid well, but he was pressing Hawthorne into overwork. Despite short excursions designed to restore his vigor, Hawthorne's physical and psychic energies waned steadily. Humiliated by his weakness, he intermittently forced himself to work on his literary projects, especially the English sketches, which he published as *Our Old Home* (1863), loyally dedicating it to Pierce, who because of his Southern sympathies was now anathema to many Northerners. Hawthorne began four romances, overlapping attempts to grapple with two major themes: an American claimant to an ancestral English estate and the search for an elixir of life. He finished none of them before his death in May 1864, while traveling in New Hampshire with Pierce. He was buried in the Sleepy Hollow Cemetery at Concord. Alcott, Emerson, Fields, Holmes, Longfellow, and Lowell were among his pallbearers.

My Kinsman, Major Molineux[1]

After the kings of Great Britain had assumed the right of appointing the colonial governors,[2] the measures of the latter seldom met with the ready and general approbation, which had been paid to those of their predecessors, under the original charters. The people looked with most jealous scrutiny to the exercise of power, which did not emanate from themselves, and they usually rewarded the rulers with slender gratitude, for the compliances, by which, in softening their instructions from beyond the sea, they had incurred the reprehension of those who gave them. The annals of Massachusetts Bay will inform us, that of six governors, in the space of about forty years from the surrender of the old charter, under James II., two were imprisoned by a popular insurrection; a third, as Hutchinson[3] inclines to believe, was driven from the province by the whizzing of a musket ball; a fourth, in the opinion of the same historian, was hastened to his grave by continual bickerings with the house of representatives; and the remaining two, as well as their successors, till the Revolution, were favored with few and brief intervals of peaceful sway. The inferior members of the court party,[4] in times of high political excitement, led scarcely a more desirable life. These remarks may serve as preface to the following adventures, which chanced upon a summer night, not far from a hundred years ago. The reader, in order to avoid a long and dry detail

---

1. The text here is that of the first printing in *The Token* for 1832, where the story is identified as being "By the Author of 'Sights from a Steeple.'"
2. I.e., after 1684, when the British government annulled the Massachusetts charter.
3. Thomas Hutchinson (1711–1780), the last royal governor. The particular annals, or year-by-year histories, that Hawthorne has in mind are *The History of the Colony and Province of Massachusetts-Bay* (1764, 1767) by Hutchinson. James II (1633–1701) reigned briefly (1685–88) before being exiled to France in the Glorious Revolution.
4. The pro-Crown party.

of colonial affairs, is requested to dispense with an account of the train of circumstances, that had caused much temporary inflammation of the popular mind.

It was near nine o'clock of a moonlight evening, when a boat crossed the ferry with a single passenger, who had obtained his conveyance, at that unusual hour, by the promise of an extra fare. While he stood on the landing-place, searching in either pocket for the means of fulfilling his agreement, the ferryman lifted a lantern, by the aid of which, and the newly risen moon, he took a very accurate survey of the stranger's figure. He was a youth of barely eighteen years, evidently country-bred, and now, as it should seem, upon his first visit to town. He was clad in a coarse grey coat, well worn, but in excellent repair; his under garments were durably constructed of leather, and sat tight to a pair of serviceable and well-shaped limbs; his stockings of blue yarn, were the incontrovertible handiwork of a mother or a sister; and on his head was a three-cornered hat, which in its better days had perhaps sheltered the graver brow of the lad's father. Under his left arm was a heavy cudgel, formed of an oak sapling, and retaining a part of the hardened root; and his equipment was completed by a wallet,[5] not so abundantly stocked as to incommode the vigorous shoulders on which it hung. Brown, curly hair, well-shaped features, and bright, cheerful eyes, were nature's gifts, and worth all that art could have done for his adornment.

The youth, one of whose names was Robin, finally drew from his pocket the half of a little province-bill[6] of five shillings, which, in the depreciation of that sort of currency, did but satisfy the ferryman's demand, with the surplus of a sexangular piece of parchment valued at three pence. He then walked forward into the town, with as light a step, as if his day's journey had not already exceeded thirty miles, and with as eager an eye, as if he were entering London city, instead of the little metropolis of a New England colony. Before Robin had proceeded far, however, it occurred to him, that he knew not whither to direct his steps; so he paused, and looked up and down the narrow street, scrutinizing the small and mean wooden buildings, that were scattered on either side.

'This low hovel cannot be my kinsman's dwelling,' thought he, 'nor yonder old house, where the moonlight enters at the broken casement; and truly I see none hereabouts that might be worthy of him. It would have been wise to inquire my way of the ferryman, and doubtless he would have gone with me, and earned a shilling from the Major for his pains. But the next man I meet will do as well.'

He resumed his walk, and was glad to perceive that the street now became wider, and the houses more respectable in their appearance. He soon discerned a figure moving on moderately in advance, and hastened his steps to overtake it. As Robin drew nigh, he saw that the passenger was a man in years, with a full periwig of grey hair, a wide-skirted coat of dark cloth, and silk stockings rolled about his knees. He carried a long and polished cane, which he struck down perpendicularly before him, at every step; and at regular intervals he uttered two successive hems, of a peculiarly solemn and sepulchral intonation. Having made these observations, Robin laid hold of the skirt of the old man's coat, just when the light from the open door and windows of a barber's shop, fell upon both their figures.

---

5. Knapsack.   6. Local paper money.

'Good evening to you, honored Sir,' said he, making a low bow, and still retaining his hold of the skirt. 'I pray you to tell me whereabouts is the dwelling of my kinsman, Major Molineux?'

The youth's question was uttered very loudly; and one of the barbers, whose razor was descending on a well-soaped chin, and another who was dressing a Ramillies wig,[7] left their occupations, and came to the door. The citizen, in the meantime, turned a long favored countenance upon Robin, and answered him in a tone of excessive anger and annoyance. His two sepulchral hems, however, broke into the very centre of his rebuke, with most singular effect, like a thought of the cold grave obtruding among wrathful passions.

'Let go my garment, fellow! I tell you. I know not the man you speak of. What! I have authority, I have—hem, hem—authority; and if this be the respect you show your betters, your feet shall be brought acquainted with the stocks,[8] by daylight, tomorrow morning!'

Robin released the old man's skirt, and hastened away, pursued by an ill-mannered roar of laughter from the barber's shop. He was at first considerably surprised by the result of his question, but, being a shrewd youth, soon thought himself able to account for the mystery.

'This is some country representative,' was his conclusion, 'who has never seen the inside of my kinsman's door, and lacks the breeding to answer a stranger civilly. The man is old, or verily—I might be tempted to turn back and smite him on the nose. Ah, Robin, Robin! even the barber's boys laugh at you, for choosing such a guide! You will be wiser in time, friend Robin.'

He now became entangled in a succession of crooked and narrow streets, which crossed each other, and meandered at no great distance from the waterside. The smell of tar was obvious to his nostrils, the masts of vessels pierced the moonlight above the tops of the buildings, and the numerous signs, which Robin paused to read, informed him that he was near the centre of business. But the streets were empty, the shops were closed, and lights were visible only in the second stories of a few dwelling-houses. At length, on the corner of a narrow lane, through which he was passing, he beheld the broad countenance of a British hero swinging before the door of an inn, whence proceeded the voices of many guests. The casement of one of the lower windows was thrown back, and a very thin curtain permitted Robin to distinguish a party at supper, round a well-furnished table. The fragrance of good cheer steamed forth into the outer air, and the youth could not fail to recollect, that the last remnant of his travelling stock of provision had yielded to his morning appetite, and that noon had found, and left him, dinnerless.

'Oh, that a parchment three-penny might give me a right to sit down at yonder table,' said Robin, with a sigh. 'But the Major will make me welcome to the best of his victuals; so I will even step boldly in, and inquire my way to his dwelling.'

He entered the tavern, and was guided by the murmur of voices, and fumes of tobacco, to the public room. It was a long and low apartment, with oaken walls, grown dark in the continual smoke, and a floor, which was thickly sanded, but of no immaculate purity. A number of persons, the larger part of whom appeared to be mariners, or in some way connected with the sea, occupied the wooden benches, or leather-bottomed chairs, conversing on various

---

7. Elaborately plaited wig named for Ramillies, Belgium.
8. Instrument of punishment having a heavy wooden frame with holes for confining the ankles and sometimes the wrists as well.

matters, and occasionally lending their attention to some topic of general interest. Three or four little groups were draining as many bowls of punch, which the great West India trade had long since made a familiar drink in the colony. Others, who had the aspect of men who lived by regular and laborious handicraft, preferred the insulated bliss of an unshared potation, and became more taciturn under its influence. Nearly all, in short, evinced a predilection for the Good Creature in some of its various shapes, for this is a vice, to which, as the Fast-day[9] sermons of a hundred years ago will testify, we have a long hereditary claim. The only guests to whom Robin's sympathies inclined him, were two or three sheepish countrymen, who were using the inn somewhat after the fashion of a Turkish Caravansary;[1] they had gotten themselves into the darkest corner of the room, and, heedless of the Nicotian[2] atmosphere, were supping on the bread of their own ovens, and the bacon cured in their own chimney-smoke. But though Robin felt a sort of brotherhood with these strangers, his eyes were attracted from them, to a person who stood near the door, holding whispered conversation with a group of ill-dressed associates. His features were separately striking almost to grotesqueness, and the whole face left a deep impression in the memory. The forehead bulged out into a double prominence, with a vale between; the nose came boldly forth in an irregular curve, and its bridge was of more than a finger's breadth; the eyebrows were deep and shaggy, and the eyes glowed beneath them like fire in a cave.

While Robin deliberated of whom to inquire respecting his kinsman's dwelling, he was accosted by the innkeeper, a little man in a stained white apron, who had come to pay his professional welcome to the stranger. Being in the second generation from a French protestant, he seemed to have inherited the courtesy of his parent nation; but no variety of circumstance was ever known to change his voice from the one shrill note in which he now addressed Robin.

'From the country, I presume, Sir?' said he, with a profound bow. 'Beg to congratulate you on your arrival, and trust you intend a long stay with us. Fine town here, Sir, beautiful buildings, and much that may interest a stranger. May I hope for the honor of your commands in respect to supper?'

'The man sees a family likeness! the rogue has guessed that I am related to the Major!' thought Robin, who had hitherto experienced little superfluous civility.

All eyes were now turned on the country lad, standing at the door, in his worn three-cornered hat, grey coat, leather breeches, and blue yarn stockings, leaning on an oaken cudgel, and bearing a wallet on his back. Robin replied to the courteous innkeeper, with such an assumption of consequence, as befitted the Major's relative.

'My honest friend,' he said, 'I shall make it a point to patronise your house on some occasion, when—' here he could not help lowering his voice—'I may have more than a parchment three-pence in my pocket. My present business,' continued he, speaking with lofty confidence, 'is merely to inquire the way to the dwelling of my kinsman, Major Molineux.'

There was a sudden and general movement in the room, which Robin inter-

---

9. Days set apart for public penitence. "Good Creature": rum; Hawthorne is playing on the warning against food fanatics in 1 Timothy 4.4: "For every creature of God is good, and nothing to be refused, if it be received with thanksgiving."

1 An inn built around a court for accommodating caravans.
2. Heavy with tobacco fumes (from Jean Nicot, who introduced tobacco into France when he was French ambassador at Lisbon).

preted as expressing the eagerness of each individual to become his guide. But the innkeeper turned his eyes to a written paper on the wall, which he read, or seemed to read, with occasional recurrences to the young man's figure.

'What have we here?' said he, breaking his speech into little dry fragments, "Left the house of the subscriber, bounden servant,[3] Hezekiah Mudge—had on when he went away, grey coat, leather breeches, master's third best hat. One pound currency reward to whoever shall lodge him in any jail in the province." 'Better trudge, boy, better trudge.'

Robin had begun to draw his hand towards the lighter end of the oak cudgel, but a strange hostility in every countenance, induced him to relinquish his purpose of breaking the courteous innkeeper's head. As he turned to leave the room, he encountered a sneering glance from the bold-featured personage whom he had before noticed; and no sooner was he beyond the door, than he heard a general laugh, in which the innkeeper's voice might be distinguished, like the dropping of small stones in a kettle.

'Now is it not strange,' thought Robin, with his usual shrewdness, 'is it not strange, that the confession of an empty pocket, should outweigh the name of my kinsman, Major Molineux? Oh, if I had one of these grinning rascals in the woods, where I and my oak sapling grew up together, I would teach him that my arm is heavy, though my purse be light!'

On turning the corner of the narrow lane, Robin found himself in a spacious street, with an unbroken line of lofty houses on each side, and a steepled building at the upper end, whence the ringing of a bell announced the hour of nine. The light of the moon, and the lamps from numerous shop windows, discovered people promenading on the pavement, and amongst them, Robin hoped to recognise his hitherto inscrutable relative. The result of his former inquiries made him unwilling to hazard another, in a scene of such publicity, and he determined to walk slowly and silently up the street, thrusting his face close to that of every elderly gentleman, in search of the Major's lineaments. In his progress, Robin encountered many gay and gallant figures. Embroidered garments, of showy colors, enormous periwigs, gold-laced hats, and silver hilted swords, glided past him and dazzled his optics. Travelled youths, imitators of the European fine gentlemen of the period, trod jauntily along, half-dancing to the fashionable tunes which they hummed, and making poor Robin ashamed of his quiet and natural gait. At length, after many pauses to examine the gorgeous display of goods in the shop windows, and after suffering some rebukes for the impertinence of his scrutiny into people's faces, the Major's kinsman found himself near the steepled building, still unsuccessful in his search. As yet, however, he had seen only one side of the thronged street; so Robin crossed, and continued the same sort of inquisition down the opposite pavement, with stronger hopes than the philosopher seeking an honest man,[4] but with no better fortune. He had arrived about midway towards the lower end, from which his course began, when he overheard the approach of some one, who struck down a cane on the flag-stones at every step, uttering, at regular intervals, two sepulchral hems.

'Mercy on us!' quoth Robin, recognising the sound.

---

3. A person bound by contract to servitude for seven years (or another set period), usually in repayment for transportation to the colonies.

4. Diogenes, the Greek philosopher (412?–323 B.C.), carried a lantern about in daytime in his search for an honest man.

Turning a corner, which chanced to be close at his right hand, he hastened to pursue his researches, in some other part of the town. His patience was now wearing low, and he seemed to feel more fatigue from his rambles since he crossed the ferry, than from his journey of several days on the other side. Hunger also pleaded loudly within him, and Robin began to balance the propriety of demanding, violently and with lifted cudgel, the necessary guidance from the first solitary passenger, whom he should meet. While a resolution to this effect was gaining strength, he entered a street of mean appearance, on either side of which, a row of ill-built houses was straggling towards the harbor. The moonlight fell upon no passenger along the whole extent, but in the third domicile which Robin passed, there was a half-opened door, and his keen glance detected a woman's garment within.

'My luck may be better here,' said he to himself.

Accordingly, he approached the door, and beheld it shut closer as he did so; yet an open space remained, sufficing for the fair occupant to observe the stranger, without a corresponding display on her part. All that Robin could discern was a strip of scarlet petticoat, and the occasional sparkle of an eye, as if the moonbeams were trembling on some bright thing.

'Pretty mistress,'—for I may call her so with a good conscience, thought the shrewd youth, since I know nothing to the contrary—'my sweet pretty mistress, will you be kind enough to tell me whereabouts I must seek the dwelling of my kinsman, Major Molineux?'

Robin's voice was plaintive and winning, and the female, seeing nothing to be shunned in the handsome country youth, thrust open the door, and came forth into the moonlight. She was a dainty little figure, with a white neck, round arms, and a slender waist, at the extremity of which her scarlet petticoat jutted out over a hoop, as if she were standing in a balloon. Moreover, her face was oval and pretty, her hair dark beneath the little cap, and her bright eyes possessed a sly freedom, which triumphed over those of Robin.

'Major Molineux dwells here,' said this fair woman.

Now her voice was the sweetest Robin had heard that night, the airy counterpart of a stream of melted silver; yet he could not help doubting whether that sweet voice spoke gospel truth. He looked up and down the mean street, and then surveyed the house before which they stood. It was a small, dark edifice of two stories, the second of which projected over the lower floor; and the front apartment had the aspect of a shop for petty commodities.

'Now truly I am in luck,' replied Robin, cunningly, 'and so indeed is my kinsman, the Major, in having so pretty a housekeeper. But I prithee trouble him to step to the door; I will deliver him a message from his friends in the country, and then go back to my lodgings at the inn.'

'Nay, the Major has been a-bed this hour or more, said the lady of the scarlet petticoat; 'and it would be to little purpose to disturb him to night, seeing his evening draught was of the strongest. But he is a kind-hearted man, and it would be as much as my life's worth, to let a kinsman of his turn away from the door. You are the good old gentleman's very picture, and I could swear that was his rainy-weather hat. Also, he has garments very much resembling those leather—But come in, I pray, for I bid you hearty welcome in his name.'

So saying, the fair and hospitable dame took our hero by the hand; and though the touch was light, and the force was gentleness, and though Robin read in her eyes what he did not hear in her words, yet the slender waisted woman, in the scarlet petticoat, proved stronger than the athletic country youth. She had drawn his half-willing footsteps nearly to the threshold, when the opening of a door in the neighborhood, startled the Major's housekeeper, and, leaving the Major's kinsman, she vanished speedily into her own domicile. A heavy yawn preceded the appearance of a man, who, like the Moonshine of Pyramus and Thisbe, carried a lantern,[5] needlessly aiding his sister luminary in the heavens. As he walked sleepily up the street, he turned his broad, dull face on Robin, and displayed a long staff, spiked at the end.

'Home, vagabond, home!' said the watchman, in accents that seemed to fall asleep as soon as they were uttered. 'Home, or we'll set you in the stocks by peep of day!'

'This is the second hint of the kind,' thought Robin. 'I wish they would end my difficulties, by setting me there to-night.'

Nevertheless, the youth felt an instinctive antipathy towards the guardian of midnight order, which at first prevented him from asking his usual question. But just when the man was about to vanish behind the corner, Robin resolved not to lose the opportunity, and shouted lustily after him—

'I say, friend! will you guide me to the house of my kinsman, Major Molineux?'

The watchman made no reply, but turned the corner and was gone; yet Robin seemed to hear the sound of drowsy laughter stealing along the solitary street. At that moment, also, a pleasant titter saluted him from the open window above his head; he looked up, and caught the sparkle of a saucy eye; a round arm beckoned to him, and next he heard light footsteps descending the staircase within. But Robin, being of the household of a New England clergyman, was a good youth, as well as a shrewd one; so he resisted temptation, and fled away.

He now roamed desperately, and at random, through the town, almost ready to believe that a spell was on him, like that, by which a wizard of his country, had once kept three pursuers wandering, a whole winter night, within twenty paces of the cottage which they sought. The streets lay before him, strange and desolate, and the lights were extinguished in almost every house. Twice, however, little parties of men, among whom Robin distinguished individuals in outlandish attire, came hurrying along, but though on both occasions they paused to address him, such intercourse did not at all enlighten his perplexity. They did but utter a few words in some language of which Robin knew nothing, and perceiving his inability to answer, bestowed a curse upon him in plain English, and hastened away. Finally, the lad determined to knock at the door of every mansion that might appear worthy to be occupied by his kinsman, trusting that perseverance would overcome the fatality which had hitherto thwarted him. Firm in this resolve, he was passing beneath the walls of a church, which formed the corner of two streets, when, as he turned into the shade of its steeple, he encountered a bulky stranger, muffled in a cloak. The man was proceeding with the speed of earnest business, but Robin planted himself full before him, holding the oak cudgel with both hands across his body, as a bar to further passage.

'Halt, honest man, and answer me a question,' said he, very resolutely,

---

5. In Shakespeare's *Midsummer Night's Dream* 5.1, the craftsmen's play within a play.

'Tell me, this instant, whereabouts is the dwelling of my kinsman, Major Molineux?'

'Keep your tongue between your teeth, fool, and let me pass,' said a deep, gruff voice, which Robin partly remembered. 'Let me pass, I say, or I'll strike you to the earth!'

'No, no, neighbor!' cried Robin, flourishing his cudgel, and then thrusting its larger end close to the man's muffled face. 'No, no, I'm not the fool you take me for, nor do you pass, till I have an answer to my question. Whereabouts is the dwelling of my kinsman, Major Molineux?'

The stranger, instead of attempting to force his passage, stept back into the moonlight, unmuffled his own face and stared full into that of Robin.

'Watch here an hour, and Major Molineux will pass by,' said he.

Robin gazed with dismay and astonishment, on the unprecedented physiognomy of the speaker. The forehead with its double prominence, the broad-hooked nose, the shaggy eyebrows, and fiery eyes, were those which he had noticed at the inn, but the man's complexion had undergone a singular, or more properly, a two-fold change. One side of the face blazed of an intense red, while the other was black as midnight, the division line being in the broad bridge of the nose; and a mouth, which seemed to extend from ear to ear, was black or red, in contrast to the color of the cheek. The effect was as if two individual devils, a fiend of fire and a fiend of darkness, had united themselves to form this infernal visage. The stranger grinned in Robin's face, muffled his party-colored features, and was out of sight in a moment.

'Strange things we travellers see!' ejaculated Robin.

He seated himself, however, upon the steps of the church-door, resolving to wait the appointed time for his kinsman's appearance. A few moments were consumed in philosophical speculations, upon the species of the *genus homo*, who had just left him, but having settled this point shrewdly, rationally, and satisfactorily, he was compelled to look elsewhere for amusement. And first he threw his eyes along the street; it was of more respectable appearance than most of those into which he had wandered, and the moon, 'creating, like the imaginative power, a beautiful strangeness in familiar objects,' gave something of romance to a scene, that might not have possessed it in the light of day. The irregular, and often quaint architecture of the houses, some of whose roofs were broken into numerous little peaks; while others ascended, steep and narrow, into a single point; and others again were square; the pure milk-white of some of their complexions, the aged darkness of others, and the thousand sparklings, reflected from bright substances in the plastered walls of many; these matters engaged Robin's attention for awhile, and then began to grow wearisome. Next he endeavored to define the forms of distant objects, starting away with almost ghostly indistinctness, just as his eye appeared to grasp them; and finally he took a minute survey of an edifice, which stood on the opposite side of the street, directly in front of the church-door, where he was stationed. It was a large square mansion, distinguished from its neighbors by a balcony, which rested on tall pillars, and by an elaborate gothic window, communicating therewith.

'Perhaps this is the very house I have been seeking,' thought Robin.

Then he strove to speed away the time, by listening to a murmur, which swept continually along the street, yet was scarcely audible, except to an unaccustomed ear like his; it was a low, dull, dreamy sound, compounded of many noises, each of which was at too great a distance to be separately heard. Robin marvelled at this snore of a sleeping town, and marvelled more, whenever its continuity was broken, by now and then a distant shout, apparently loud where it originated. But altogether it was a sleep-inspiring sound, and to shake off its drowsy influence, Robin arose, and climbed a window-frame, that he might view the interior of the church. There the moonbeams came trembling in, and fell down upon the deserted pews, and extended along the quiet aisles. A fainter, yet more awful radiance, was hovering round the pulpit, and one solitary ray had dared to rest upon the opened page of the great bible. Had Nature, in that deep hour, become a worshipper in the house, which man had builded? Or was that heavenly light the visible sanctity of this place, visible because no earthly and impure feet were within the walls? The scene made Robin's heart shiver with a sensation of loneliness, stronger than he had ever felt in the remotest depths of his native woods; so he turned away, and sat down again before the door. There were graves around the church, and now an uneasy thought obtruded into Robin's breast. What if the object of his search, which had been so often and so strangely thwarted, were all the time mouldering in his shroud? What if his kinsman should glide through yonder gate, and nod and smile to him in passing dimly by?

'Oh, that any breathing thing were here with me!' said Robin.

Recalling his thoughts from this uncomfortable track, he sent them over forest, hill, and stream, and attempted to imagine how that evening of ambiguity and weariness, had been spent by his father's household. He pictured them assembled at the door, beneath the tree, the great old tree, which had been spared for its huge twisted trunk, and venerable shade, when a thousand leafy brethren fell. There, at the going down of the summer sun, it was his father's custom to perform domestic worship, that the neighbors might come and join with him like brothers of the family, and that the wayfaring man might pause to drink at that fountain, and keep his heart pure by freshening the memory of home. Robin distinguished the seat of every individual of the little audience; he saw the good man in the midst, holding the scriptures in the golden light that shone from the western clouds; he beheld him close the book, and all rise up to pray. He heard the old thanksgivings for daily mercies, the old supplications for their continuance, to which he had so often listened in weariness, but which were now among his dear remembrances. He perceived the slight inequality of his father's voice when he came to speak of the Absent One; he noted how his mother turned her face to the broad and knotted trunk, how his elder brother scorned, because the beard was rough upon his upper lip, to permit his features to be moved; how his younger sister drew down a low hanging branch before her eyes; and how the little one of all, whose sports had hitherto broken the decorum of the scene, understood the prayer for her playmate, and burst into clamorous grief. Then he saw them go in at the door; and when Robin would have entered also, the latch tinkled into its place, and he was excluded from his home.

'Am I here, or there?' cried Robin, starting; for all at once, when his thoughts had become visible and audible in a dream, the long, wide, solitary street shone out before him.

He aroused himself, and endeavored to fix his attention steadily upon the large edifice which he had surveyed before. But still his mind kept vibrating between fancy and reality; by turns, the pillars of the balcony lengthened into the tall, bare stems of pines, dwindled down to human figures, settled again in their true shape and size, and then commenced a new succession of changes. For a single moment, when he deemed himself awake, he could have sworn that a visage, one which he seemed to remember, yet could not absolutely name as his kinsman's, was looking towards him from the Gothic window. A deeper sleep wrestled with, and nearly overcame him, but fled at the sound of footsteps along the opposite pavement. Robin rubbed his eyes, discerned a man passing at the foot of the balcony, and addressed him in a loud, peevish, and lamentable cry.

'Halloo, friend! must I wait here all night for my kinsman, Major Molineux?'

The sleeping echoes awoke, and answered the voice; and the passenger, barely able to discern a figure sitting in the oblique shade of the steeple, traversed the street to obtain a nearer view. He was himself a gentleman in his prime, of open, intelligent, cheerful and altogether prepossessing countenance. Perceiving a country youth, apparently homeless and without friends, he accosted him in a tone of real kindness, which had become strange to Robin's ears.

'Well, my good lad, why are you sitting here?' inquired he. 'Can I be of service to you in any way?'

'I am afraid not, Sir,' replied Robin, despondingly; 'yet I shall take it kindly, if you'll answer me a single question. I've been searching half the night for one Major Molineux; now, Sir, is there really such a person in these parts, or am I dreaming?'

'Major Molineux! The name is not altogether strange to me,' said the gentleman smiling. 'Have you any objection to telling me the nature of your business with him?'

Then Robin briefly related that his father was a clergyman, settled on a small salary, at a long distance back in the country, and that he and Major Molineux were brothers' children. The Major, having inherited riches, and acquired civil and military rank, had visited his cousin in great pomp a year or two before; had manifested much interest in Robin and an elder brother, and, being childless himself, had thrown out hints respecting the future establishment of one of them in life. The elder brother was destined to succeed to the farm, which his father cultivated, in the interval of sacred duties; it was therefore determined that Robin should profit by his kinsman's generous intentions, especially as he had seemed to be rather the favorite, and was thought to possess other necessary endowments.

'For I have the name of being a shrewd youth,' observed Robin, in this part of his story.

'I doubt not you deserve it,' replied his new friend, good naturedly; 'but pray proceed.'

'Well, Sir, being nearly eighteen years old, and well grown, as you see,' continued Robin, raising himself to his full height, 'I thought it high time to begin the world. So my mother and sister put me in handsome trim, and my father gave me half the remnant of his last year's salary, and five days ago I started for this place, to pay the Major a visit. But would you believe it, Sir? I crossed the ferry a little after dusk, and have yet found nobody that would show me the way to his dwelling; only an hour or two since, I was told to wait here, and Major Molineux would pass by.'

'Can you describe the man who told you this?' inquired the gentleman.

'Oh, he was a very ill-favored fellow, Sir,' replied Robin, 'with two great bumps on his forehead, a hook nose, fiery eyes, and, what struck me as the strangest, his face was of two different colors. Do you happen to know such a man, Sir?'

'Not intimately,' answered the stranger, 'but I chanced to meet him a little time previous to your stopping me. I believe you may trust his word, and that the Major will very shortly pass through this street. In the mean time, as I have a singular curiosity to witness your meeting, I will sit down here upon the steps, and bear you company.'

He seated himself accordingly, and soon engaged his companion in animated discourse. It was but of brief continuance, however, for a noise of shouting, which had long been remotely audible, drew so much nearer, that Robin inquired its cause.

'What may be the meaning of this uproar?' asked he. 'Truly, if your town be always as noisy, I shall find little sleep, while I am an inhabitant.'

'Why, indeed, friend Robin, there do appear to be three or four riotous fellows abroad to-night,' replied the gentleman. 'You must not expect all the stillness of your native woods, here in our streets. But the watch will shortly be at the heels of these lads, and—'

'Aye, and set them in the stocks by peep of day,' interrupted Robin, recollecting his own encounter with the drowsy lantern-bearer. 'But, dear Sir, if I may trust my ears, an army of watchmen would never make head against such a multitude of rioters. There were at least a thousand voices went to make up that one shout.'

'May not one man have several voices, Robin, as well as two complexions?' said his friend.

'Perhaps a man may; but heaven forbid that a woman should!' responded the shrewd youth, thinking of the seductive tones of the Major's housekeeper.

The sounds of a trumpet in some neighboring street, now became so evident and continual, that Robin's curiosity was strongly excited. In addition to the shouts, he heard frequent bursts from many instruments of discord, and a wild and confused laughter filled up the intervals. Robin rose from the steps, and looked wistfully towards a point, whither several people seemed to be hastening.

'Surely some prodigious merrymaking is going on,' exclaimed he. 'I have laughed very little since I left home, Sir, and should be sorry to lose an opportunity. Shall we just step round the corner by that darkish house, and take our share of the fun?'

'Sit down again, sit down, good Robin,' replied the gentleman, laying his hand on the skirt of the grey coat. 'You forget that we must wait here for your kinsman; and there is reason to believe that he will pass by, in the course of a very few moments.'

The near approach of the uproar had now disturbed the neighborhood; windows flew open on all sides; and many heads, in the attire of the pillow, and confused by sleep suddenly broken, were protruded to the gaze of whoever had leisure to observe them. Eager voices hailed each other from house to house, all demanding the explanation, which not a soul could give. Half-dressed men hurried towards the unknown commotion, stumbling as they went over the stone steps, that thrust themselves into the narrow foot-walk. The shouts, the laughter, and the tuneless bray, the antipodes of music, came onward with increasing din, till scattered individuals, and then denser bodies, began to appear round a corner, at a distance of a hundred yards.

'Will you recognise your kinsman, Robin, if he passes in this crowd?' inquired the gentleman.

'Indeed, I can't warrant it, Sir; but I'll take my stand here, and keep a bright look out,' answered Robin, descending to the outer edge of the pavement.

A mighty stream of people now emptied into the street, and came rolling slowly towards the church. A single horseman wheeled the corner in the midst of them, and close behind him came a band of fearful wind-instruments, sending forth a fresher discord, now that no intervening buildings kept it from the ear. Then a redder light disturbed the moonbeams, and a dense multitude of torches shone along the street, concealing by their glare whatever object they illuminated. The single horseman, clad in a military dress, and bearing a drawn sword, rode onward as the leader, and, by his fierce and variegated countenance, appeared like war personified; the red of one cheek was an emblem of fire and sword; the blackness of the other betokened the mourning which attends them. In his train, were wild figures in the Indian dress, and many fantastic shapes without a model, giving the whole march a visionary air, as if a dream had broken forth from some feverish brain, and were sweeping visibly through the midnight streets. A mass of people, inactive, except as applauding spectators, hemmed the procession in, and several women ran along the sidewalks, piercing the confusion of heavier sounds, with their shrill voices of mirth or terror.

'The double-faced fellow has his eye upon me,' muttered Robin, with an indefinite but uncomfortable idea, that he was himself to bear a part in the pageantry.

The leader turned himself in the saddle, and fixed his glance full upon the country youth, as the steed went slowly by. When Robin had freed his eyes from those fiery ones, the musicians were passing before him, and the torches were close at hand; but the unsteady brightness of the latter formed a veil which he could not penetrate. The rattling of wheels over the stones sometimes found its way to his ear, and confused traces of a human form appeared at intervals, and then melted into the vivid light. A moment more, and the leader thundered a command to halt; the trumpets vomited a horrid breath, and held their peace; the shouts and laughter of the people died away, and there remained only an universal hum, nearly allied to silence. Right before Robin's eyes was an uncovered cart. There the torches blazed the brightest, there the moon shone out like day, and there, in tar-and-feathery dignity, sate his kinsman, Major Molineux!

He was an elderly man, of large and majestic person, and strong, square features, betokening a steady soul; but steady as it was, his enemies had found the means to shake it. His face was pale as death, and far more ghastly; the broad forehead was contracted in his agony, so that the eyebrows formed one dark grey line; his eyes were red and wild, and the foam hung white upon his quivering lip. His whole frame was agitated by a quick, and continual tremor, which his pride strove to quell, even in those circumstances of overwhelming humiliation. But perhaps the bitterest pang of all was when his eyes met those of Robin; for he evidently knew him on the instant, as the youth stood witnessing the foul disgrace of a head that had grown grey in honor. They stared at each other in silence, and Robin's knees shook, and his hair bristled, with a mixture of pity and terror. Soon, however, a bewildering excitement began to seize upon his mind; the preceding adventures of the night, the unexpected appearance of the crowd, the torches, the confused din, and the hush that followed, the spectre of his kinsman reviled by that great multitude, all this, and more than all, a perception of tremendous ridicule in the whole scene, affected him with a sort of mental inebriety. At that moment a voice of sluggish merriment saluted Robin's ears; he turned instinctively, and just behind the corner of the church stood the lantern-bearer, rubbing his eyes, and drowsily enjoying the lad's amazement. Then he heard a peal of laughter like the ringing of silvery bells; a woman twitched his arm, a saucy eye met his, and he saw the lady of the scarlet petticoat. A sharp, dry cachinnation appealed to his memory, and, standing on tiptoe in the crowd, with his white apron over his head, he beheld the courteous little innkeeper. And lastly, there sailed over the heads of the multitude a great, broad laugh, broken in the midst by two deep sepulchral hems; thus—

'Haw, haw, haw—hem, hem—haw, haw, haw, haw!'

The sound proceeded from the balcony of the opposite edifice, and thither Robin turned his eyes. In front of the Gothic window stood the old citizen, wrapped in a wide gown, his grey periwig exchanged for a nightcap, which was thrust back from his forehead, and his silk stockings hanging down about his legs. He supported himself on his polished cane in a fit of convulsive merriment, which manifested itself on his solemn old features, like a funny inscription on a tomb-stone. Then Robin seemed to hear the voices of the barbers; of the guests of the inn; and of all who had made sport of him that night. The contagion was spreading among the multitude, when, all at once, it seized upon Robin, and he sent forth a shout of laughter that echoed through the street; every man shook his sides, every man emptied his lungs, but Robin's shout was the loudest there. The cloud-spirits peeped from their silvery islands, as the congregated mirth went roaring up the sky! The Man in the Moon heard the far bellow; 'Oho,' quoth he, 'the old Earth is frolicsome to-night!'

When there was a momentary calm in that tempestuous sea of sound, the leader gave the sign, and the procession resumed its march. On they went, like fiends that throng in mockery round some dead potentate, mighty no more, but majestic still in his agony. On they went, in counterfeited pomp, in senseless uproar, in frenzied merriment, trampling all on an old man's heart. On swept the tumult, and left a silent street behind.

. . . . .

'Well, Robin, are you dreaming?' inquired the gentleman, laying his hand on the youth's shoulder.

Robin started, and withdrew his arm from the stone post, to which he had instinctively clung, while the living stream rolled by him. His cheek was somewhat pale, and his eye not quite so lively as in the earlier part of the evening.

'Will you be kind enough to show me the way to the Ferry?' said he, after a moment's pause.

'You have then adopted a new subject of inquiry?' observed his companion, with a smile.

'Why, yes, Sir,' replied Robin, rather dryly. 'Thanks to you, and to my other friends, I have at last met my kinsman, and he will scarce desire to see my face again. I begin to grow weary of a town life, Sir. Will you show me the way to the Ferry?'

'No, my good friend Robin, not to-night, at least,' said the gentleman. 'Some few days hence, if you continue to wish it, I will speed you on your journey. Or, if you prefer to remain with us, perhaps, as you are a shrewd youth, you may rise in the world, without the help of your kinsman, Major Molineux.'

1832, 1837

Roger Malvin's Burial[1]

One of the few incidents of Indian warfare, naturally susceptible of the moonlight of romance, was that expedition, undertaken, for the defence of the frontiers, in the year 1725, which resulted in the well-remembered 'Lovell's Fight.'[2] Imagination, by casting certain circumstances judiciously into the shade, may see much to admire in the heroism of a little band, who gave battle to twice their number in the heart of the enemy's country. The open bravery displayed by both parties was in accordance with civilized ideas of valor, and chivalry itself might not blush to record the deeds of one or two individuals. The battle, though so fatal to those who fought, was not unfortunate in its consequences to the country; for it broke the strength of a tribe, and conduced to the peace which subsisted during several ensuing years. History and tradition are unusually minute in their memorials of this affair; and the captain of a scouting party of frontier-men has acquired as actual a military renown, as many a victorious leader of thousands. Some of the incidents contained in the following pages will be recognised, notwithstanding the substitution of fictitious names, by such as have heard, from old men's lips, the fate of the few combatants who were in a condition to retreat, after 'Lovell's Fight.'

· · · · · ·

The early sunbeams hovered cheerfully upon the tree-tops, beneath which two weary and wounded men had stretched their limbs the night before. Their bed of withered oak leaves was strewn upon the small level space, at the foot of a rock, situated near the summit of one of the gentle swells, by which the face of the country is there diversified. The mass of granite, rearing its smooth, flat surface, fifteen or twenty feet above their heads, was not unlike a gigantic grave-stone, upon which the veins seemed to form an inscription in forgotten characters. On a tract of several acres around this rock, oaks and other hardwood trees had supplied the place of the pines, which were the usual growth of the land; and a young and vigorous sapling stood close beside the travellers.

The severe wound of the elder man had probably deprived him of sleep; for, so soon as the first ray of sunshine rested on the top of the highest tree, he reared himself painfully from his recumbent posture, and sat erect. The deep lines of his countenance, and the scattered grey of his hair, marked him as past the middle age; but his muscular frame would, but for the effects of his

1. The text is that of the first printing, in *The Token* for 1832.　　2. An incident in the Penobscot War in Maine (then part of Massachusetts) during 1725.

wound, have been as capable of sustaining fatigue, as in the early vigor of life. Languor and exhaustion now sat upon his haggard features, and the despairing glance which he sent forward through the depths of the forest, proved his own conviction that his pilgrimage was at an end. He next turned his eyes to the companion, who reclined by his side. The youth, for he had scarcely attained the years of manhood, lay, with his head upon his arm, in the embrace of an unquiet sleep, which a thrill of pain from his wounds seemed each moment on the point of breaking. His right hand grasped a musket, and, to judge from the violent action of his features, his slumbers were bringing back a vision of the conflict, of which he was one of the few survivors. A shout,—deep and loud to his dreaming fancy,—found its way in an imperfect murmur to his lips, and, starting even at the slight sound of his own voice, he suddenly awoke. The first act of reviving recollection, was to make anxious inquiries respecting the condition of his wounded fellow traveller. The latter shook his head.

'Reuben, my boy,' said he, 'this rock, beneath which we sit, will serve for an old hunter's grave-stone. There is many and many a long mile of howling wilderness before us yet; nor would it avail me anything, if the smoke of my own chimney were but on the other side of that swell of land. The Indian bullet was deadlier than I thought.'

'You are weary with our three days' travel,' replied the youth, 'and a little longer rest will recruit you. Sit you here, while I search the woods for the herbs and roots, that must be our sustenance; and having eaten, you shall lean on me, and we will turn our faces homeward. I doubt not, that, with my help, you can attain to some one of the frontier garrisons.'

'There is not two days' life in me, Reuben,' said the other, calmly, 'and I will no longer burthen you with my useless body, when you can scarcely support your own. Your wounds are deep, and your strength is failing fast; yet, if you hasten onward alone, you may be preserved. For me there is no hope; and I will await death here.'

'If it must be so, I will remain and watch by you,' said Reuben, resolutely.

'No, my son, no,' rejoined his companion. 'Let the wish of a dying man have weight with you; give me one grasp of your hand, and get you hence. Think you that my last moments will be eased by the thought, that I leave you to die a more lingering death? I have loved you like a father, Reuben, and, at a time like this, I should have something of a father's authority. I charge you to be gone, that I may die in peace.'

'And because you have been a father to me, should I therefore leave you to perish, and to lie unburied in the wilderness?' exclaimed the youth. 'No; if your end be in truth approaching, I will watch by you, and receive your parting words. I will dig a grave here by the rock, in which, if my weakness overcome me, we will rest together; or, if Heaven gives me strength, I will seek my way home.'

'In the cities, and wherever men dwell,' replied the other, 'they bury their dead in the earth; they hide them from the sight of the living; but here, where no step may pass, perhaps for a hundred years, wherefore should I not rest beneath the open sky, covered only by the oak-leaves, when the autumn winds shall strew them? And for a monument, here is this grey rock, on which my dying hand shall carve the name of Roger Malvin: and the traveller in days to come will know, that here sleeps a hunter and a warrior. Tarry not, then, for a folly like this, but hasten away, if not for your own sake, for hers who will else be desolate.'

Malvin spoke the last few words in a faultering voice, and their effect upon his companion was strongly visible. They reminded him that there were other, and less questionable duties, than that of sharing the fate of a man whom his death could not benefit. Nor can it be affirmed that no selfish feeling strove to enter Reuben's heart, though the consciousness made him more earnestly resist his companion's entreaties.

'How terrible, to wait the slow approach of death, in this solitude!' exclaimed he. 'A brave man does not shrink in the battle, and, when friends stand round the bed, even women may die composedly; but here'—

'I shall not shrink, even here, Reuben Bourne;' interrupted Malvin, 'I am a man of no weak heart; and, if I were, there is a surer support than that of earthly friends. You are young, and life is dear to you. Your last moments will need comfort far more than mine; and when you have laid me in the earth, and are alone, and night is settling on the forest, you will feel all the bitterness of the death that may now be escaped. But I will urge no selfish motive to your generous nature. Leave me for my sake; that, having said a prayer for your safety, I may have space to settle my account, undisturbed by worldly sorrows.'

'And your daughter! How shall I dare to meet her eye?' exclaimed Reuben. 'She will ask the fate of her father, whose life I vowed to defend with my own. Must I tell her, that he travelled three days' march with me from the field of battle, and that then I left him to perish in the wilderness? Were it not better to lie down and die by your side, than to return safe, and say this to Dorcas?'

'Tell my daughter,' said Roger Malvin, 'that, though yourself sore wounded, and weak, and weary, you led my tottering footsteps many a mile, and left me only at my earnest entreaty, because I would not have your blood upon my soul. Tell her, that through pain and danger you were faithful, and that, if your life-blood could have saved me, it would have flowed to its last drop. And tell her, that you will be something dearer than a father, and that my blessing is with you both, and that my dying eyes can see a long and pleasant path, in which you will journey together.'

As Malvin spoke, he almost raised himself from the ground, and the energy of his concluding words seemed to fill the wild and lonely forest with a vision of happiness. But when he sank exhausted upon his bed of oak-leaves, the light, which had kindled in Reuben's eye, was quenched. He felt as if it were both sin and folly to think of happiness at such a moment. His companion watched his changing countenance, and sought, with generous art, to wile him to his own good.

'Perhaps I deceive myself in regard to the time I have to live,' he resumed. 'It may be, that, with speedy assistance, I might recover my wound. The foremost fugitives must, ere this, have carried tidings of our fatal battle to the frontiers, and parties will be out to succour those in like condition with ourselves. Should you meet one of these, and guide them hither, who can tell but that I may sit by my own fireside again?'

A mournful smile strayed across the features of the dying man, as he insinuated that unfounded hope; which, however, was not without its effect on Reuben. No merely selfish motive, nor even the desolate condition of Dorcas, could have induced him to desert his companion, at such a moment. But his wishes seized upon the thought, that Malvin's life might be preserved, and his sanguine nature heightened, almost to certainty, the remote possibility of procuring human aid.

'Surely there is reason, weighty reason, to hope that friends are not far distant,' he said, half aloud. 'There fled one coward, unwounded, in the beginning of the fight, and most probably he made good speed. Every true man on the frontier would shoulder his musket, at the news; and though no party may range so far into the woods as this, I shall perhaps encounter them in one day's march. Counsel me faithfully,' he added, turning to Malvin, in distrust of his own motives. 'Were your situation mine, would you desert me while life remained?'

'It is now twenty years,' replied Roger Malvin, sighing, however, as he secretly acknowledged the wide dissimilarity between the two cases,—'it is now twenty years, since I escaped, with one dear friend, from Indian captivity, near Montreal. We journeyed many days through the woods, till at length, overcome with hunger and weariness, my friend lay down, and besought me to leave him; for he knew, that, if I remained, we both must perish. And, with but little hope of obtaining succour, I heaped a pillow of dry leaves beneath his head, and hastened on.'

'And did you return in time to save him?' asked Reuben, hanging on Malvin's words, as if they were to be prophetic of his own success.

'I did,' answered the other, 'I came upon the camp of a hunting party, before sunset of the same day. I guided them to the spot where my comrade was expecting death; and he is now a hale and hearty man, upon his own farm, far within the frontiers, while I lie wounded here, in the depths of the wilderness.'

This example, powerful in effecting Reuben's decision, was aided, unconsciously to himself, by the hidden strength of many another motive. Roger Malvin perceived that the victory was nearly won.

'Now go, my son, and Heaven prosper you!' he said. 'Turn not back with our friends, when you meet them, lest your wounds and weariness overcome you; but send hitherward two or three, that may be spared, to search for me. And believe me, Reuben, my heart will be lighter with every step you take towards home.' Yet there was perhaps a change, both in his countenance and voice, as he spoke thus; for, after all, it was a ghastly fate, to be left expiring in the wilderness.

Reuben Bourne, but half convinced that he was acting rightly, at length raised himself from the ground, and prepared for his departure. And first, though contrary to Malvin's wishes, he collected a stock of roots and herbs, which had been their only food during the last two days. This useless supply he placed within reach of the dying man, for whom, also, he swept together a fresh bed of dry oak-leaves. Then, climbing to the summit of the rock, which on one side was rough and broken, he bent the oak-sapling downwards, and bound his handkerchief to the topmost branch. This precaution was not unnecessary, to direct any who might come in search of Malvin; for every part of the rock, except its broad, smooth front, was concealed, at a little distance, by the dense undergrowth of the forest. The handkerchief had been the bandage of a wound upon Reuben's arm; and, as he bound it to the tree, he vowed, by the blood that stained it, that he would return, either to save his companion's life, or to lay his body in the grave. He then descended, and stood, with downcast eyes, to receive Roger Malvin's parting words.

The experience of the latter suggested much and minute advice, respecting the youth's journey through the trackless forest. Upon this subject he spoke with calm earnestness, as if he were sending Reuben to the battle or the chase, while he himself remained secure at home; and not as if the human countenance, that was about to leave him, were the last he would ever behold. But his firmness was shaken, before he concluded.

'Carry my blessing to Dorcas, and say that my last prayer shall be for her and you. Bid her have no hard thoughts because you left me here'—Reuben's heart smote him—'for that your life would not have weighed with you, if its sacrifice could have done me good. She will marry you, after she has mourned a little while for her father; and Heaven grant you long and happy days! and may your children's children stand round your death-bed! And, Reuben,' added he, as the weakness of mortality made its way at last, 'return, when your wounds are healed and your weariness refreshed, return to this wild rock, and lay my bones in the grave, and say a prayer over them.'

An almost superstitious regard, arising perhaps from the customs of the Indians, whose war was with the dead, as well as the living, was paid by the frontier inhabitants to the rites of sepulture; and there are many instances of the sacrifice of life, in the attempt to bury those who had fallen by the 'sword of the wilderness.' Reuben, therefore, felt the full importance of the promise, which he most solemnly made, to return, and perform Roger Malvin's obsequies. It was remarkable, that the latter, speaking his whole heart in his parting words, no longer endeavored to persuade the youth, that even the speediest succour might avail to the preservation of his life. Reuben was internally convinced, that he should see Malvin's living face no more. His generous nature would fain have delayed him, at whatever risk, till the dying scene were past; but the desire of existence, and the hope of happiness had strengthened in his heart, and he was unable to resist them.

'It is enough,' said Roger Malvin, having listened to Reuben's promise. 'Go, and God speed you!'

The youth pressed his hand in silence, turned, and was departing. His slow and faultering steps, however, had borne him but a little way, before Malvin's voice recalled him.

'Reuben, Reuben,' said he, faintly; and Reuben turned and knelt down by the dying man.

'Raise me and let me lean against the rock,' was his last request. 'My face will be turned towards home, and I shall see you a moment longer, as you pass among the trees.'

Reuben, having made the desired alteration in his companion's posture, again began his solitary pilgrimage. He walked more hastily at first, than was consistent with his strength; for a sort of guilty feeling, which sometimes torments men in their most justifiable acts, caused him to seek concealment from Malvin's eyes. But, after he had trodden far upon the rustling forest-leaves, he crept back, impelled by a wild and painful curiosity, and, sheltered by the earthy roots of an uptorn tree, gazed earnestly at the desolate man. The morning sun was unclouded, and the trees and shrubs imbibed the sweet air of the month of May; yet there seemed a gloom on Nature's face, as if she sympathized with mortal pain and sorrow. Roger Malvin's hands were uplifted in a fervent prayer, some of the words which stole through the stillness of the woods, and entered Reuben's heart, torturing it with an unutterable pang.

They were the broken accents of a petition for his own happiness and that of Dorcas; and, as the youth listened, conscience, or something in its similitude, pleaded strongly with him to return, and lie down again by the rock. He felt how hard was the doom of the kind and generous being whom he had deserted in his extremity. Death would come, like the slow approach of a corpse, stealing gradually towards him through the forest, and showing its ghastly and motionless features from behind a nearer, and yet a nearer tree. But such must have been Reuben's own fate, had he tarried another sunset; and who shall impute blame to him, if he shrank from so useless a sacrifice? As he gave a parting look, a breeze waved the little banner upon the sapling-oak, and reminded Reuben of his vow.

· · · · ·

Many circumstances contributed to retard the wounded traveller, in his way to the frontiers. On the second day, the clouds, gathering densely over the sky, precluded the possibility of regulating his course by the position of the sun; and he knew not but that every effort of his almost exhausted strength, was removing him farther from the home he sought. His scanty sustenance was supplied by the berries, and other spontaneous products of the forest. Herds of deer, it is true, sometimes bounded past him, and partridges frequently whirred up before his footsteps; but his ammunition had been expended in the fight, and he had no means of slaying them. His wounds, irritated by the constant exertion in which lay the only hope of life; wore away his strength, and at intervals confused his reason. But, even in the wanderings of intellect, Reuben's young heart clung strongly to existence, and it was only through absolute incapacity of motion, that he at last sank down beneath a tree, compelled there to await death. In this situation he was discovered by a party, who, upon the first intelligence of the fight, had been despatched to the relief of the survivors. They conveyed him to the nearest settlement, which chanced to be that of his own residence.

Dorcas, in the simplicity of the olden time, watched by the bed-side of her wounded lover, and administered all those comforts, that are in the sole gift of woman's heart and hand. During several days, Reuben's recollection strayed drowsily among the perils and hardships through which he had passed, and he was incapable of returning definite answers to the inquiries, with which many were eager to harass him. No authentic particulars of the battle had yet been circulated; nor could mothers, wives, and children tell, whether their loved ones were detained by captivity, or by the stronger chain of death. Dorcas nourished her apprehensions in silence, till one afternoon, when Reuben awoke from an unquiet sleep, and seemed to recognise her, more perfectly than at any previous time. She saw that his intellect had become composed, and she could no longer restrain her filial anxiety.

'My father, Reuben?' she began; but the change in her lover's countenance made her pause.

The youth shrank, as if with a bitter pain, and the blood gushed vividly into his wan and hollow cheeks. His first impulse was to cover his face; but, apparently with a desperate effort, he half raised himself, and spoke vehemently, defending himself against an imaginary accusation.

'Your father was sore wounded in the battle, Dorcas, and he bade me not burthen myself with him, but only to lead him to the lakeside, that he might quench his thirst and die. But I would not desert the old man in his extremity, and, though bleeding myself, I supported him; I gave him half my strength, and led him away with me. For three days we journeyed on together, and your father was sustained beyond my hopes; but, awaking at sunrise on the fourth day, I found him faint and exhausted,—he was unable to proceed,—his life had ebbed away fast,—and'—

'He died!' exclaimed Dorcas, faintly.

Reuben felt it impossible to acknowledge, that his selfish love of life had hurried him away, before her father's fate was decided. He spoke not; he only bowed his head; and, between shame and exhaustion, sank back and hid his face in the pillow. Dorcas wept, when her fears were thus confirmed; but the shock, as it had been long anticipated, was on that account the less violent.

'You dug a grave for my poor father, in the wilderness, Reuben?' was the question by which her filial piety manifested itself.

'My hands were weak, but I did what I could,' replied the youth in a smothered tone. 'There stands a noble tomb-stone above his head, and I would to Heaven I slept as soundly as he!'

Dorcas, perceiving the wildness of his latter words, inquired no farther at that time; but her heart found ease in the thought, that Roger Malvin had not lacked such funeral rites as it was possible to bestow. The tale of Reuben's courage and fidelity lost nothing, when she communicated it to her friends; and the poor youth, tottering from his sick chamber to breathe the sunny air, experienced from every tongue the miserable and humiliating torture of unmerited praise. All acknowledged that he might worthily demand the hand of the fair maiden, to whose father he had been 'faithful unto death;' and, as my tale is not of love, it shall suffice to say, that, in the space of two years, Reuben became the husband of Dorcas Malvin. During the marriage ceremony, the bride was covered with blushes, but the bridegroom's face was pale.

There was now in the breast of Reuben Bourne an incommunicable thought; something which he was to conceal most heedfully from her whom he most loved and trusted. He regretted, deeply and bitterly, the moral cowardice that had restrained his words, when he was about to disclose the truth to Dorcas; but pride, the fear of losing her affection, the dread of universal scorn, forbade him to rectify this falsehood. He felt, that, for leaving Roger Malvin, he deserved no censure. His presence, the gratuitous sacrifice of his own life, would have added only another, and a needless agony to the last moments of the dying man. But concealment had imparted to a justifiable act, much of the secret effect of guilt; and Reuben, while reason told him that he had done right, experienced in no small degree, the mental horrors, which punish the perpetrator of undiscovered crime. By a certain association of ideas, he at times almost imagined himself a murderer. For years, also, a thought would occasionally recur, which, though he perceived all its folly and extravagance, he had not power to banish from his mind; it was a haunting and torturing fancy, that his father-in-law was yet sitting at the foot of the rock, on the withered forest-leaves, alive, and awaiting his pledged assistance. These mental deceptions, however, came and went, nor did he ever mistake them for realities; but in the calmest and clearest moods of his mind, he was conscious that he had a deep vow unredeemed, and that an unburied corpse was calling to him, out of the wilderness. Yet, such was the consequence of his prevarication, that he could not obey the call. It was now too late to require the assistance of Roger Malvin's friends, in performing his long-deferred sepulture; and superstitious fears, of which none were more susceptible than the people of the outward settlements, forbade Reuben to go alone. Neither did he know where, in the pathless and illimitable forest, to seek that smooth and lettered rock, at the base of which the body lay; his remembrance of every portion of his travel thence was indistinct, and the latter part had left no impression upon his mind. There was, however, a continual impulse, a voice audible only to himself, commanding him to go forth and redeem his vow; and he had a strange impression, that, were he to make the trial, he would be led straight to Malvin's bones. But, year after year, that summons, unheard but felt, was disobeyed. His one secret thought, became like a chain, binding down his spirit, and, like a serpent, gnawing into his heart; and he was transformed into a sad and downcast, yet irritable man.

In the course of a few years after their marriage, changes began to be visible in the external prosperity of Reuben and Dorcas. The only riches of the former had been his stout heart and strong arm; but the latter, her father's sole heiress, had made her husband master of a farm, under older cultivation, larger, and better stocked than most of the frontier establishments. Reuben Bourne, however, was a neglectful husbandman; and while the lands of the other settlers became annually more fruitful, his deteriorated in the same proportion. The discouragements to agriculture were greatly lessened by the cessation of Indian war, during which men held the plough in one hand, and the musket in the other; and were fortunate if the products of their dangerous labor were not destroyed, either in the field or in the barn, by the savage enemy. But Reuben did not profit by the altered condition of the country; nor can it be denied, that his intervals of industrious attention to his affairs were but scantily rewarded with success. The irritability, by which he had recently become distinguished, was another cause of his declining prosperity, as it occasioned frequent quarrels, in his unavoidable intercourse with the neighboring settlers. The results of these were innumerable law-suits; for the people of New England, in the earliest stages and wildest circumstances of the country, adopted, whenever attainable, the legal mode of deciding their differences. To be brief, the world did not go well with Reuben Bourne, and, though not till many years after his marriage, he was finally a ruined man, with but one remaining expedient against the evil fate that had pursued him. He was to throw sunlight into some deep recess of the forest, and seek subsistence from the virgin bosom of the wilderness.

The only child of Reuben and Dorcas was a son, now arrived at the age of fifteen years, beautiful in youth, and giving promise of a glorious manhood. He was peculiarly qualified for, and already began to excel in, the wild accomplishments of frontier life. His foot was fleet, his aim true, his apprehension quick, his heart glad and high; and all, who anticipated the return of Indian war, spoke of Cyrus Bourne as a future leader in the land. The boy was loved by his father, with a deep and silent strength, as if whatever was good and happy in his own nature had been transferred to his child, carrying his affections with it. Even Dorcas, though loving and beloved, was far less dear to him; for Reuben's secret thoughts and insulated emotions had gradually made him a selfish man; and he could no longer love deeply, except where he saw, or imagined, some reflection or likeness of his own mind. In Cyrus he recognised what he had himself been in other days; and at intervals he seemed to partake of the boy's spirit, and to be revived with a fresh and happy life. Reuben was accompanied by his son in the expedition, for the purpose of selecting a tract of land, and felling and burning the timber, which necessarily preceded the removal of the household gods.[3] Two months of autumn were thus occupied; after which Reuben Bourne and his young hunter returned, to spend their last winter in the settlements.

. . . . .

It was early in the month of May, that the little family snapped asunder whatever tendrils of affection had clung to inanimate objects, and bade farewell to the few, who, in the blight of fortune, called themselves their friends. The sadness of the parting moment had, to each of the pilgrims, its peculiar alleviations. Reuben, a moody man, and misanthropic because unhappy, strode onward, with his usual stern brow and downcast eye, feeling few regrets, and disdaining to acknowledge any. Dorcas, while she wept abundantly over the broken ties by which her simple and affectionate nature had bound itself to everything, felt that the inhabitants of her inmost heart moved on with her, and that all else would be supplied wherever she might go. And the boy dashed one tear-drop from his eye, and thought of the adventurous pleasures of the untrodden forest. Oh! who, in the enthusiasm of a day-dream, has not wished that he were a wanderer in a world of summer wilderness, with one fair and gentle being hanging lightly on his arm? In youth, his free and exulting step would know no barrier but the rolling ocean or the snow-topt mountains; calmer manhood would choose a home, where Nature had strewn a double wealth, in the vale of some transparent stream; and when hoary age, after long, long years of that pure life, stole on and found him there, it would find him the father of a race, the patriarch of a people, the founder of a mighty nation yet to be. When death, like the sweet sleep which we welcome after a day of happiness, came over him, his far descendants would mourn over the venerated dust. Enveloped by tradition in mysterious attributes, the men of future generations would call him godlike; and remote posterity would see him standing, dimly glorious, far up the valley of a hundred centuries!

The tangled and gloomy forest, through which the personages of my tale were wandering, differed widely from the dreamer's Land of Fantasië; yet there was something in their way of life that Nature asserted as her own; and the gnawing cares, which went with them from the world, were all that now obstructed their happiness. One stout and shaggy steed, the bearer of all their wealth, did not shrink from the added weight of Dorcas; although her hardy breeding sustained her, during the larger part of each day's journey, by her husband's side. Reuben and his son, their muskets on their shoulders, and their axes slung behind them, kept an unwearied pace, each watching with a hunter's eye for the game that supplied their food. When hunger bade, they halted and prepared their meal on the bank of some unpolluted forest-brook, which, as they knelt down with thirsty lips to drink, murmured a sweet unwillingness, like a maiden, at love's first kiss. They slept beneath a hut of branches, and awoke at peep of light, refreshed for the toils of another day. Dorcas and the boy went on joyously, and even Reuben's spirit shone at intervals with an outward gladness; but inwardly there was a cold, cold sorrow, which he com-

---

3. I.e., prized possessions, because of the value placed on personal idols in many cultures. In Genesis 31.19 Rachel, without telling her husband, Jacob, steals her father's household gods.

pared to the snow-drifts, lying deep in the glens and hollows of the rivulets, while the leaves were brightly green above.

Cyrus Bourne was sufficiently skilled in the travel of the woods, to observe, that his father did not adhere to the course they had pursued, in their expedition of the preceding autumn. They were now keeping farther to the north, striking out more directly from the settlements, and into a region, of which savage beasts and savage men were as yet the sole possessors. They boy sometimes hinted his opinions upon the subject, and Reuben listened attentively, and once or twice altered the direction of their march in accordance with his son's counsel. But having so done, he seemed ill at ease. His quick and wandering glances were sent forward, apparently in search of enemies lurking behind the tree-trunks; and seeing nothing there, he would cast his eyes backward, as if in fear of some pursuer. Cyrus, perceiving that his father gradually resumed the old direction, forbore to interfere; nor, though something began to weigh upon his heart, did his adventurous nature permit him to regret the increased length and the mystery of their way.

On the afternoon of the fifth day, they halted and made their simple encampment, nearly an hour before sunset. The face of the country, for the last few miles, had been diversified by swells of land, resembling huge waves of a petrified sea; and in one of the corresponding hollows, a wild and romantic spot, had the family reared their hut, and kindled their fire. There is something chilling, and yet heart-warming, in the thought of three, united by strong bands of love, and insulated from all that breathe beside. The dark and gloomy pines looked down upon them, and, as the wind swept through their tops, a pitying sound was heard in the forest; or did those old trees groan, in fear that men were come to lay the axe to their roots at last? Reuben and his son, while Dorcas made ready their meal, proposed to wander out in search of game, of which that day's march had afforded no supply. The boy, promising not to quit the vicinity of the encampment, bounded off with a step as light and elastic as that of the deer he hoped to slay; while his father, feeling a transient happiness as he gazed after him, was about to pursue an opposite direction. Dorcas, in the meanwhile, had seated herself near their fire of fallen branches, upon the moss-grown and mouldering trunk of a tree, uprooted years before. Her employment, diversified by an occasional glance at the pot, now beginning to simmer over the blaze, was the perusal of the current year's Massachusetts Almanac, which, with the exception of an old black-letter[4] Bible, comprised all the literary wealth of the family. None pay a greater regard to arbitrary divisions of time, than those who are excluded from society; and Dorcas mentioned, as if the information were of importance, that it was now the twelfth of May. Her husband started.

'The twelfth of May! I should remember it well,' muttered he, while many thoughts occasioned a momentary confusion in his mind. 'Where am I? Whither am I wandering? Where did I leave him?'

Dorcas, too well accustomed to her husband's wayward moods to note any peculiarity of demeanor, now laid aside the Almanac, and addressed him in that mournful tone, which the tender-hearted appropriate to griefs long cold and dead.

'It was near this time of the month, eighteen years ago, that my poor father

---

4. Printed in early type resembling the shapes of letters used by medieval and early Renaissance scribes.

left this world for a better. He had a kind arm to hold his head, and a kind
voice to cheer him, Reuben, in his last moments; and the thought of the
faithful care you took of him, has comforted me, many a time since. Oh!
death would have been awful to a solitary man, in a wild place like this!'

'Pray Heaven, Dorcas,' said Reuben, in a broken voice, 'pray Heaven, that
neither of us three die solitary, and lie unburied, in this howling wilderness!'
And he hastened away, leaving her to watch the fire, beneath the gloomy
pines.

Reuben Bourne's rapid pace gradually slackened, as the pang, unintentionally inflicted by the words of Dorcas, became less acute. Many strange reflections, however, thronged upon him; and, straying onward, rather like a sleep-
walker than a hunter, it was attributable to no care of his own, that his devious
course kept him in the vicinity of the encampment. His steps were imperceptibly led almost in a circle, nor did he observe that he was on the verge of a tract
of land heavily timbered, but not with pine-trees. The place of the latter was
here supplied by oaks, and other of the harder woods; and around their roots
clustered a dense and bushy undergrowth, leaving, however, barren spaces
between the trees, thick-strewn with withered leaves. Whenever the rustling of
the branches, or the creaking of the trunks made a sound, as if the forest were
waking from slumber, Reuben instinctively raised the musket that rested on
his arm, and cast a quick, sharp glance on every side; but, convinced by a
partial observation that no animal was near, he would again give himself up
to his thoughts. He was musing on the strange influence, that had led him
away from his premeditated course, and so far into the depths of the wilderness. Unable to penetrate to the secret place of his soul, where his motives lay
hidden, he believed that a supernatural voice had called him onward, and that
a supernatural power had obstructed his retreat. He trusted that it was Heaven's
intent to afford him an opportunity of expiating his sin; he hoped that he might
find the bones, so long unburied; and that, having laid the earth over them,
peace would throw its sunlight into the sepulchre of his heart. From these
thoughts he was aroused by a rustling in the forest, at some distance from the
spot to which he had wandered. Perceiving the motion of some object behind
a thick veil of undergrowth, he fired, with the instinct of a hunter, and the
aim of a practised marksman. A low moan, which told his success, and by
which even animals can express their dying agony, was unheeded by Reuben
Bourne. What were the recollections now breaking upon him?

The thicket, into which Reuben had fired, was near the summit of a swell
of land, and was clustered around the base of a rock, which, in the shape and
smoothness of one of its surfaces, was not unlike a gigantic gravestone. As if
reflected in a mirror, its likeness was in Reuben's memory. He even recognised
the veins which seemed to form an inscription in forgotten characters; everything remained the same, except that a thick covert of bushes shrouded the
lower part of the rock, and would have hidden Roger Malvin, had he still been
sitting there. Yet, in the next moment, Reuben's eye was caught by another
change, that time had effected, since he last stood, where he was now standing
again, behind the earthy roots of the uptorn tree. The sapling, to which he
had bound the blood-stained symbol of his vow, had increased and strengthened into an oak, far indeed from its maturity, but with no mean spread of
shadowy branches. There was one singularity, observable in this tree, which
made Reuben tremble. The middle and lower branches were in luxuriant life,
and an excess of vegetation had fringed the trunk, almost to the ground; but a

blight had apparently stricken the upper part of the oak, and the very topmost bough was withered, sapless, and utterly dead. Reuben remembered how the little banner had fluttered on that topmost bough, when it was green and lovely, eighteen years before. Whose guilt had blasted it?

. . . . .

Dorcas, after the departure of the two hunters, continued her preparations for their evening repast. Her sylvan table was the moss-covered trunk of a large fallen tree, on the broadest part of which she had spread a snow-white cloth, and arranged what were left of the bright pewter vessels, that had been her pride in the settlements. It had a strange aspect—that one little spot of homely comfort, in the desolate heart of Nature. The sunshine yet lingered upon the higher branches of the trees that grew on rising ground; but the shades of evening had deepened into the hollow, where the encampment was made; and the fire-light began to redden as it gleamed up the tall trunks of the pines, or hovered on the dense and obscure mass of foliage, that circled round the spot. The heart of Dorcas was not sad; for she felt that it was better to journey in the wilderness, with two whom she loved, than to be a lonely woman in a crowd that cared not for her. As she busied herself in arranging seats of mouldering wood, covered with leaves, for Reuben and her son, her voice danced through the gloomy forest, in the measure of a song that she had learned in youth. The rude melody, the production of a bard who won no name, was descriptive of a winter evening in a frontier-cottage, when, secured from savage inroad by the high-piled snow-drifts, the family rejoiced by their own fire-side. The whole song possessed that nameless charm, peculiar to unborrowed thought; but four continually-recurring lines shone out from the rest, like the blaze of the hearth whose joys they celebrated. Into them, working magic with a few simple words, the poet had instilled the very essence of domestic love and household happiness, and they were poetry and picture joined in one. As Dorcas sang, the walls of her forsaken home seemed to encircle her; she no longer saw the gloomy pines, nor heard the wind, which still, as she began each verse, sent a heavy breath through the branches, and died away in a hollow moan, from the burthen of the song. She was aroused by the report of a gun, in the vicinity of the encampment; and either the sudden sound, or her loneliness by the glowing fire, caused her to tremble violently. The next moment, she laughed in the pride of a mother's heart.

'My beautiful young hunter! my boy has slain a deer!' she exclaimed, recol- lecting that, in the direction whence the shot proceeded, Cyrus had gone to the chase.

She waited a reasonable time, to hear her son's light step bounding over the rustling leaves, to tell of his success. But he did not immediately appear, and she sent her cheerful voice among the trees, in search of him.

'Cyrus! Cyrus!'

His coming was still delayed, and she determined, as the report of the gun had apparently been very near, to seek for him in person. Her assistance, also, might be necessary in bringing home the venison, which she flattered herself he had obtained. She therefore set forward, directing her steps by the long-past sound, and singing as she went, in order that the boy might be aware of her approach, and run to meet her. From behind the trunk of every tree, and from every hiding place in the thick foliage of the undergrowth, she hoped to dis- cover the countenance of her son, laughing with the sportive mischief that is born of affection. The sun was now beneath the horizon, and the light that came down among the trees was sufficiently dim to create many illusions in her expecting fancy. Several times she seemed indistinctly to see his face gazing out from among the leaves; and once she imagined that he stood beckoning to her, at the base of a craggy rock. Keeping her eyes on this object, however, it proved to be no more than the trunk of an oak, fringed to the very ground with little branches, one of which, thrust out farther than the rest, was shaken by the breeze. Making her way round the foot of the rock, she suddenly found herself close to her husband, who had approached in another direction. Leaning upon the butt of his gun, the muzzle of which rested upon the withered leaves, he was apparently absorbed in the contemplation of some object at his feet.

'How is this, Reuben? Have you slain the deer, and fallen asleep over him?' exclaimed Dorcas, laughing cheerfully, on her first slight observation of his posture and appearance.

He stirred not, neither did he turn his eyes towards her; and a cold, shuddering fear, indefinite in its source and object, began to creep into her blood. She now perceived that her husband's face was ghastly pale, and his features were rigid, as if incapable of assuming any other expression than the strong despair which had hardened upon them. He gave not the slightest evidence that he was aware of her approach.

'For the love of Heaven, Reuben, speak to me!' cried Dorcas, and the strange sound of her own voice affrighted her even more than the dead silence.

Her husband started, stared into her face; drew her to the front of the rock, and pointed with his finger.

Oh! there lay the boy, asleep, but dreamless, upon the fallen forest-leaves! His cheek rested upon his arm, his curled locks were thrown back from his brow, his limbs were slightly relaxed. Had a sudden weariness overcome the youthful hunter? Would his mother's voice arouse him? She knew that it was death.

'This broad rock is the grave-stone of your near kindred, Dorcas,' said her husband. 'Your tears will fall at once over your father and your son.'

She heard him not. With one wild shriek, that seemed to force its way from the suffer's inmost soul, she sank insensible by the side of her dead boy. At that moment, the withered topmost bough of the oak loosened itself, in the stilly air, and fell in soft, light fragments upon the rock, upon the leaves, upon Reuben, upon his wife and child, and upon Roger Malvin's bones. Then Reuben's heart was stricken, and the tears gushed out like water from a rock. The vow that the wounded youth had made, the blighted man had come to redeem. His sin was expiated, the curse was gone from him; and, in the hour, when he had shed blood dearer to him than his own, a prayer, the first for years, went up to Heaven from the lips of Reuben Bourne.

1832   1846

Young Goodman Brown[1]

Young goodman Brown came forth, at sunset, into the street of Salem village, but put his head back, after crossing the threshold, to exchange a parting

---

1. The text followed here is that of the first publication, in the *New-England Magazine* (April 1835); the story was ascribed to "the author of 'The Gray Champion,'" which had appeared in the same magazine

kiss with his young wife. And Faith, as the wife was aptly named, thrust her own pretty head into the street, letting the wind play with the pink ribbons of her cap, while she called to goodman Brown.

'Dearest heart,' whispered she, softly and rather sadly, when her lips were close to his ear, 'pr'y thee, put off your journey until sunrise, and sleep in your own bed to-night. A lone woman is troubled with such dreams and such thoughts, that she's afeard of herself, sometimes. Pray, tarry with me this night, dear husband, of all nights in the year!'

'My love and my Faith,' replied young goodman Brown, 'of all nights in the year, this one night must I tarry away from thee. My journey, as thou callest it, forth and back again, must needs be done 'twixt now and sunrise. What, my sweet, pretty wife, dost thou doubt me already, and we but three months married!'

'Then, God bless you!' and Faith, with the pink ribbons, 'and may you find all well, when you come back.'

'Amen!' cried goodman Brown. 'Say thy prayers, dear Faith, and go to bed at dusk, and no harm will come to thee.'

So they parted; and the young man pursued his way, until, being about to turn the corner by the meeting-house, he looked back, and saw the head of Faith still peeping after him, with a melancholy air, in spite of her pink ribbons.

'Poor little Faith!' thought he, for his heart smote him. 'What a wretch am I, to leave her on such an errand! She talks of dreams, too. Methought, as she spoke, there was trouble in her face, as if a dream had warned her what work is to be done to-night. But, no, no! 't would kill her to think it. Well; she's a blessed angel on earth; and after this one night, I'll cling to her skirts and follow her to Heaven.'

With this excellent resolve for the future, goodman Brown felt himself justified in making more haste on his present evil purpose. He had taken a dreary road, darkened by all the gloomiest trees of the forest, which barely stood aside to let the narrow path creep through, and closed immediately behind. It was all as lonely as could be; and there is this peculiarity in such a solitude, that the traveler knows not who may be concealed by the innumerable trunks and the thick boughs overhead; so that, with lonely footsteps, he may yet be passing through an unseen multitude.

'There may be a devilish Indian behind every tree,' said goodman Brown, to himself; and he glanced fearfully behind him, as he added, 'What if the devil himself should be at my very elbow!'

His head being turned back, he passed a crook of the road, and looking forward again, beheld the figure of a man, in grave and decent attire, seated at the foot of an old tree. He arose, at goodman Brown's approach, and walked onward, side by side with him.

'You are late, goodman Brown,' said he. 'The clock of the Old South was striking as I came through Boston; and that is full fifteen minutes agone.'[2]

'Faith kept me back awhile,' replied the young man, with a tremor in his voice, caused by the sudden appearance of his companion, though not wholly unexpected.

---

three months earlier. "Goodman": Hawthorne puns on the title used to address a man of humble birth and the moral implications of "good man"; what with "Brown"

as a surname, the hero is equivalent to Young Mister Anybody.
2. This speed could only be supernatural.

It was now deep dusk in the forest, and deepest in that part of it where these two were journeying. As nearly as could be discerned, the second traveler was about fifty years old, apparently in the same rank of life as goodman Brown, and bearing a considerable resemblance to him, though perhaps more in expression than features. Still, they might have been taken for father and son. And yet, though the elder person was as simply clad as the younger, and as simple in manner too, he had an indescribable air of one who knew the world, and would not have felt abashed at the governor's dinner-table, or in king William's[3] court, were it possible that his affairs should call him thither. But the only thing about him, that could be fixed upon as remarkable, was his staff, which bore the likeness of a great black snake, so curiously wrought, that it might almost be seen to twist and wriggle itself, like a living serpent. This, of course, must have been an ocular deception, assisted by the uncertain light.

'Come, goodman Brown!' cried his fellow-traveler, 'this is a dull pace for the beginning of a journey. Take my staff, if you are so soon weary.'

'Friend,' said the other, exchanging his slow pace for a full stop, 'having kept covenant by meeting thee here, it is my purpose now to return whence I came. I have scruples, touching the matter thou wot'st of.'

'Sayest thou so?' replied he of the serpent, smiling apart. 'Let us walk on, nevertheless, reasoning as we go, and if I convince thee not, thou shalt turn back. We are but a little way in the forest, yet.'

'Too far, too far!' exclaimed the goodman, unconsciously resuming his walk. 'My father never went into the woods on such an errand, nor his father before him. We have been a race of honest men and good Christians, since the days of the martyrs.[4] And shall I be the first of the name of Brown, that ever took this path, and kept'—

'Such company, thou wouldst say,' observed the elder person, interpreting his pause. 'Good, goodman Brown! I have been as well acquainted with your family as with ever a one among the Puritans; and that's no trifle to say. I helped your grandfather, the constable, when he lashed the Quaker woman so smartly through the streets of Salem. And it was I that brought your father a pitch-pine knot, kindled at my own hearth, to set fire to an Indian village, in king Philip's[5] war. They were my good friends, both; and many a pleasant walk have we had along this path, and returned merrily after midnight. I would fain be friends with you, for their sake.'

'If it be as thou sayest,' replied goodman Brown, 'I marvel they never spoke of these matters. Or, verily, I marvel not, seeing that the least rumor of the sort would have driven them from New-England. We are a people of prayer, and good works, to boot, and abide no such wickedness.'

'Wickedness or not,' said the traveler with the twisted staff, 'I have a very general acquaintance here in New-England. The deacons of many a church have drunk the communion wine with me; the selectmen, of divers towns, make me their chairman; and a majority of the Great and General Court[6]

3. William of Orange, first cousin and husband of Queen Mary II, with whom he jointly ruled England, 1689–1702.
4. I.e., during the reign of the Catholic Mary Tudor of England (1553–58), called "Bloody Mary" for her persecution of Protestants. Common reading in New England was John Foxe's *Acts and Monuments* (1563),

soon known as the *Book of Martyrs*; it concluded with horrifically detailed accounts of martyrdoms under Mary.
5. Leader of the Wampanoag Indians who waged war (1675–76) against the New England colonists.
6. The legislature.

are firm supporters of my interest. The governor and I, too—but these are state-secrets.'

'Can this be so!' cried goodman Brown, with a stare of amazement at his undisturbed companion. 'Howbeit, I have nothing to do with the governor and council; they have their own ways, and are no rule for a simple husband-man,[7] like me. But, were I to go on with thee, how should I meet the eye of that good old man, our minister, at Salem village? Oh, his voice would make me tremble, both Sabbath-day and lecture-day!'[8]

Thus far, the elder traveler had listened with due gravity, but now burst into a fit of irrepressible mirth, shaking himself so violently, that his snake-like staff actually seemed to wriggle in sympathy.

'Ha! ha! ha!' shouted he, again and again; then composing himself, 'Well, go on, goodman Brown, go on; but, pr'y thee, don't kill me with laughing!'

'Well, then, to end the matter at once,' said goodman Brown, considerably nettled, 'there is my wife, Faith. It would break her dear little heart; and I'd rather break my own!'

'Nay, if that be the case,' answered the other, 'e'en go thy ways, goodman Brown. I would not, for twenty old women like the one hobbling before us, that Faith should come to any harm.'

As he spoke, he pointed his staff at a female figure on the path, in whom goodman Brown recognized a very pious and exemplary dame, who had taught him his catechism, in youth, and was still his moral and spiritual adviser, jointly with the minister and deacon Gookin.

'A marvel, truly, that goody Cloyse[9] should be so far in the wilderness, at night-fall!' said he. 'But, with your leave, friend, I shall take a cut through the woods, until we have left this Christian woman behind. Being a stranger to you, she might ask whom I was consorting with, and whither I was going.'

'Be it so,' said his fellow-traveler. 'Betake you to the woods, and let me keep the path.'

Accordingly, the young man turned aside, but took care to watch his com-panion, who advanced softly along the road, until he had come within a staff's length of the old dame. She, meanwhile, was making the best of her way, with singular speed for so aged a woman, and mumbling some indistinct words, a prayer, doubtless, as she went. The traveler put forth his staff, and touched her withered neck with what seemed the serpent's tail.

'The devil!' screamed the pious old lady.

'Then goody Cloyse knows her old friend?' observed the traveler, confront-ing her, and leaning on his writhing stick.

'Ah, forsooth, and is it your worship, indeed?' cried the good dame. 'Yea, truly is it, and in the very image of my old gossip, goodman Brown, the grand-father of the silly fellow that now is. But, would your worship believe it? my broomstick hath strangely disappeared, stolen, as I suspect, by that unhanged witch, goody Cory, and that, too, when I was all anointed with the juice of smallage and cinque-foil and wolf's-bane'[1]—

---

7. Usually, farmer; here, man of ordinary status.
8. Midweek sermon day, Wednesday or Thursday.
9. Hawthorne uses historical names of people involved in the Salem witchcraft trials. "Goody": i.e., "good-wife"; the polite title for a married woman of humble rank.

1. Plants associated with witchcraft. "Smallage": wild celery or parsley. "Cinque-foil": a five-lobed plant of the rose family (from the Latin for "five fingers"). "Wolf's-bane": hooded, poisonous plant known as monkshood (*bane* means "poison").

'Mingled with fine wheat and the fat of a new-born babe,' said the shape of old goodman Brown.

'Ah, your worship knows the receipt,' cried the old lady, cackling aloud. 'So, as I was saying, being all ready for the meeting, and no horse to ride on, I made up my mind to foot it; for they tell me, there is a nice young man to be taken into communion to-night. But now your good worship will lend me your arm, and we shall be there in a twinkling.'

'That can hardly be,' answered her friend. 'I may not spare you my arm, goody Cloyse, but here is my staff, if you will.'

So saying, he threw it down at her feet, where, perhaps, it assumed life, being one of the rods which its owner had formerly lent to the Egyptian Magi.[2] Of this fact, however, goodman Brown could not take cognizance. He had cast up his eyes in astonishment, and looking down again, beheld neither goody Cloyse nor the serpentine staff, but his fellow-traveler alone, who waited for him as calmly as if nothing had happened.

'That old woman taught me my catechism!' said the young man; and there was a world of meaning in this simple comment.

They continued to walk onward, while the elder traveler exhorted his companion to make good speed and persevere in the path, discoursing so aptly, that his arguments seemed rather to spring up in the bosom of his auditor, than to be suggested by himself. As they went, he plucked a branch of maple, to serve for a walking-stick, and began to strip it of the twigs and little boughs, which were wet with evening dew. The moment his fingers touched them, they became strangely withered and dried up, as with a week's sunshine. Thus the pair proceeded, at a good free pace, until suddenly, in a gloomy hollow of the road, goodman Brown sat himself down on the stump of a tree, and refused to go any farther.

'Friend,' said he, stubbornly, 'my mind is made up. Not another step will I budge on this errand. What if a wretched old woman do choose to go to the devil, when I thought she was going to Heaven! Is that any reason why I should quit my dear Faith, and go after her?'

'You will think better of this, by-and-by,' said his acquaintance, composedly. 'Sit here and rest yourself awhile; and when you feel like moving again, there is my staff to help you along.'

Without more words, he threw his companion the maple stick, and was as speedily out of sight, as if he had vanished into the deepening gloom. The young man sat a few moments, by the roadside, applauding himself greatly, and thinking with how clear a conscience he should meet the minister, in his morning-walk, nor shrink from the eye of good old deacon Gookin. And what calm sleep would be his, that very night, which was to have been spent so wickedly, but purely and sweetly now, in the arms of Faith! Amidst these pleasant and praiseworthy meditations, goodman Brown heard the tramp of horses along the road, and deemed it advisable to conceal himself within the verge of the forest, conscious of the guilty purpose that had brought him thither, though now so happily turned from it.

On came the hoof-tramps and the voices of the riders, two grave old voices, conversing soberly as they drew near. These mingled sounds appeared to pass along the road, within a few yards of the young man's hiding-place; but owing,

2. See Exodus 7.11 for the magicians of Egypt who duplicated Aaron's feat of casting down his rod before Pharaoh and making it turn into a serpent.

doubtless, to the depth of the gloom, at that particular spot, neither the travelers nor their steeds were visible. Though their figures brushed the small boughs by the way-side, it could not be seen that they intercepted, even for a moment, the faint gleam from the strip of bright sky, athwart which they must have passed. Goodman Brown alternately crouched and stood on tip-toe, pulling aside the branches, and thrusting forth his head as far as he durst, without discerning so much as a shadow. It vexed him the more, because he could have sworn, were such a thing possible, that he recognized the voices of the minister and deacon Gookin, jogging along quietly, as they were wont to do, when bound to some ordination or ecclesiastical council. While yet within hearing, one of the riders stopped to pluck a switch.

'Of the two, reverend Sir,' said the voice like the deacon's, 'I had rather miss an ordination-dinner than to-night's meeting. They tell me that some of our community are to be here from Falmouth and beyond, and others from Connecticut and Rhode-Island; besides several of the Indian powows,[3] who, after their fashion, know almost as much deviltry as the best of us. Moreover, there is a goodly young woman to be taken into communion.'

'Mighty well, deacon Gookin!' replied the solemn old tones of the minister. 'Spur up, or we shall be late. Nothing can be done, you know, until I get on the ground.'

The hoofs clattered again, and the voices, talking so strangely in the empty air, passed on through the forest, where no church had ever been gathered, nor solitary Christian prayed. Whither, then, could these holy men be journeying, so deep into the heathen wilderness? Young goodman Brown caught hold of a tree, for support, being ready to sink down on the ground, faint and overburthened with the heavy sickness of his heart. He looked up to the sky, doubting whether there really was a Heaven above him. Yet, there was the blue arch, and the stars brightening in it.

'With Heaven above, and Faith below, I will yet stand firm against the devil!' cried goodman Brown.

While he still gazed upward, into the deep arch of the firmament, and had lifted his hands to pray, a cloud, though no wind was stirring, hurried across the zenith, and hid the brightening stars. The blue sky was still visible, except directly overhead, where this black mass of cloud was sweeping swiftly northward. Aloft in the air, as if from the depths of the cloud, came a confused and doubtful sound of voices. Once, the listener fancied that he could distinguish the accents of town's-people of his own, men and women, both pious and ungodly, many of whom he had met at the communion-table, and had seen others rioting at the tavern. The next moment, so indistinct were the sounds, he doubted whether he had heard aught but the murmur of the old forest, whispering without a wind. Then came a stronger swell of those familiar tones, heard daily in the sunshine, at Salem village, but never, until now, from a cloud of night. There was one voice, of a young woman, uttering lamentations, yet with an uncertain sorrow, and entreating for some favor, which, perhaps, it would grieve her to obtain. And all the unseen multitude, both saints and sinners, seemed to encourage her onward.

'Faith!' shouted goodman Brown, in a voice of agony and desperation; and

3. Medicine men. Usually spelled "pow-wow" and later used to refer to any conference or gathering. Falmouth is a town on Cape Cod, about seventy miles from Salem.

the echoes of the forest mocked him, crying—'Faith! Faith!' as if bewildered wretches were seeking her, all through the wilderness.

The cry of grief, rage, and terror, was yet piercing the night, when the unhappy husband held his breath for a response. There was a scream, drowned immediately in a louder murmur of voices, fading into far-off laughter, as the dark cloud swept away, leaving the clear and silent sky above goodman Brown. But something fluttered lightly down through the air, and caught on the branch of a tree. The young man seized it, and beheld a pink ribbon.

'My Faith is gone!' cried he, after one stupefied moment. 'There is no good on earth; and sin is but a name. Come, devil! for to thee is this world given.'

And maddened with despair, so that he laughed loud and long, did goodman Brown grasp his staff and set forth again, at such a rate, that he seemed to fly along the forest-path, rather than to walk or run. The road grew wilder and drearier, and more faintly traced, and vanished at length, leaving him in the heart of the dark wilderness, still rushing onward, with the instinct that guides mortal man to evil. The whole forest was peopled with frightful sounds; the creaking of the trees, the howling of wild beasts, and the yell of Indians; while, sometimes, the wind tolled like a distant church-bell, and sometimes gave a broad roar around the traveler, as if all Nature were laughing him to scorn. But he was himself the chief horror of the scene, and shrank not from its other horrors.

'Ha! ha! ha!' roared goodman Brown, when the wind laughed at him. 'Let us hear which will laugh loudest! Think not to frighten me with your deviltry! Come witch, come wizard, come Indian powow, come devil himself! and here comes goodman Brown. You may as well fear him as he fear you!'

In truth, all through the haunted forest, there could be nothing more frightful than the figure of goodman Brown. On he flew, among the black pines, brandishing his staff with frenzied gestures, now giving vent to an inspiration of horrid blasphemy, and now shouting forth such laughter, as set all the echoes of the forest laughing like demons around him. The fiend in his own shape is less hideous, than when he rages in the breast of man. Thus sped the demoniac on his course, until, quivering among the trees, he saw a red light before him, as when the felled trunks and branches of a clearing have been set on fire, and throw up their lurid blaze against the sky, at the hour of midnight. He paused, in a lull of the tempest that had driven him onward, and heard the swell of what seemed a hymn, rolling solemnly from a distance, with the weight of many voices. He knew the tune; it was a familiar one in the choir of the village meeting-house. The verse died heavily away, and was lengthened by a chorus, not of human voices, but of all the sounds of the benighted wilderness, pealing in awful harmony together. Goodman Brown cried out; and his cry was lost to his own ear, by its unison with the cry of the desert.

In the interval of silence, he stole forward, until the light glared full upon his eyes. At one extremity of an open space, hemmed in by the dark wall of the forest, arose a rock, bearing some rude, natural resemblance either to an altar or a pulpit, and surrounded by four blazing pines, their tops a flame, their stems untouched, like candles at an evening meeting. The mass of foliage, that had overgrown the summit of the rock, was all on fire, blazing high into the night, and fitfully illuminating the whole field. Each pendent twig and leafy festoon was in a blaze. As the red light arose and fell, a numerous congregation alternately shone forth, then disappeared in shadow, and again grew, as it were, out of the darkness, peopling the heart of the solitary woods at once.

'A grave and dark-clad company!' quoth goodman Brown.

In truth, they were such. Among them, quivering to-and-fro, between gloom and splendor, appeared faces that would be seen, next day, at the council-board of the province, and others which, Sabbath after Sabbath, looked devoutly heavenward, and benignantly over the crowded pews, from the holiest pulpits in the land. Some affirm, that the lady of the governor was there. At least, there were high dames well known to her, and wives of honored husbands, and widows, a great multitude, and ancient maidens, all of excellent repute, and fair young girls, who trembled, lest their mothers should espy them. Either the sudden gleams of light, flashing over the obscure field, bedazzled goodman Brown, or he recognized a score of the church-members of Salem village, famous for their especial sanctity. Good old deacon Gookin had arrived, and waited at the skirts of that venerable saint, his revered pastor. But, irreverently consorting with these grave, reputable, and pious people, these elders of the church, these chaste dames and dewy virgins, there were men of dissolute lives and women of spotted fame, wretches given over to all mean and filthy vice, and suspected even of horrid crimes. It was strange to see, that the good shrank not from the wicked, nor were the sinners abashed by the saints. Scattered, also, among their pale-faced enemies, were the Indian priests, or powows, who had often scared their native forest with more hideous incantations than any known to English witchcraft.

'But, where is Faith?' thought goodman Brown; and, as hope came into his heart, he trembled.

Another verse of the hymn arose, a slow and solemn strain, such as the pious love, but joined to words which expressed all that our nature can conceive of sin, and darkly hinted at far more. Unfathomable to mere mortals is the lore of fiends. Verse after verse was sung, and still the chorus of the desert swelled between, like the deepest tone of a mighty organ. And, with the final peal of that dreadful anthem, there came a sound, as if the roaring wind, the rushing streams, the howling beasts, and every other voice of the unconverted wilderness, were mingling and according with the voice of guilty man, in homage to the prince of all. The four blazing pines threw up a loftier flame, and obscurely discovered shapes and visages of horror on the smoke-wreaths, above the impious assembly. At the same moment, the fire on the rock shot redly forth, and formed a glowing arch above its base, where now appeared a figure. With reverence be it spoken, the apparition bore no slight similitude, both in garb and manner, to some grave divine of the New-England churches.

'Bring forth the converts!' cried a voice, that echoed through the field and rolled into the forest.

At the word, goodman Brown stept forth from the shadow of the trees, and approached the congregation, with whom he felt a loathful brotherhood, by the sympathy of all that was wicked in his heart. He could have well nigh sworn, that the shape of his own dead father beckoned him to advance, looking downward from a smoke-wreath, while a woman, with dim features of despair, threw out her hand to warn him back. Was it his mother? But he had no power to retreat one step, nor to resist, even in thought, when the minister and good old deacon Gookin, seized his arms, and led him to the blazing rock. Thither came also the slender form of a veiled female, led between Goody Cloyse, that pious teacher of the catechism, and Martha Carrier, who had received the devil's promise to be queen of hell. A rampant hag was she! And there stood the proselytes, beneath the canopy of fire.

'Welcome, my children,' said the dark figure, 'to the communion of your race![4] Ye have found, thus young, your nature and your destiny. My children, look behind you!"

They turned; and flashing forth, as it were, in a sheet of flame, the fiend-worshippers were seen; the smile of welcome gleamed darkly on every visage.

'There,' resumed the sable form, 'are all whom ye have reverenced from youth. Ye deemed them holier than yourselves, and shrank from your own sin, contrasting it with their lives of righteousness, and prayerful aspirations heavenward. Yet, here are they all, in my worshipping assembly! This night it shall be granted you to know their secret deeds; how hoary-bearded elders of the church have whispered wanton words to the young maids of their households; how many a woman, eager for widow's weeds, has given her husband a drink at bed-time, and let him sleep his last sleep in her bosom; how beardless youths have made haste to inherit their fathers' wealth; and how fair damsels—blush not, sweet ones!—have dug little graves in the garden, and bidden me, the sole guest, to an infant's funeral. By the sympathy of your human hearts for sin, ye shall scent out all the places—whether in church, bed-chamber, street, field, or forest—where crime has been committed, and shall exult to behold the whole earth one stain of guilt, one mighty blood-spot. Far more than this! It shall be your's to penetrate, in every bosom, the deep mystery of sin, the fountain of all wicked arts, and which, inexhaustibly supplies more evil impulses than human power—than my power, at its utmost!—can make manifest in deeds. And now, my children, look upon each other.'

They did so; and, by the blaze of the hell-kindled torches, the wretched man beheld his Faith, and the wife her husband, trembling before that unhallowed altar.

'Lo! there ye stand, my children,' said the figure, in a deep and solemn tone, almost sad, with its despairing awfulness, as if his once angelic nature could yet mourn for our miserable race. 'Depending upon one another's hearts, ye had still hoped, that virtue were not all a dream. Now are ye undeceived! Evil is the nature of mankind. Evil must be your only happiness. Welcome, again, my children, to the communion of your race!'

'Welcome!' repeated the fiend-worshippers, in one cry of despair and triumph.

And there they stood, the only pair, as it seemed, who were yet hesitating on the verge of wickedness, in this dark world. A basin was hollowed, naturally, in the rock. Did it contain water, reddened by the lurid light? or was it blood? or, perchance, a liquid flame? Herein did the Shape of Evil dip his hand, and prepare to lay the mark of baptism upon their foreheads, that they might be partakers of the mystery of sin, more conscious of the secret guilt of others, both in deed and thought, than they could now be of their own. The husband cast one look at his pale wife, and Faith at him. What polluted wretches would the next glance shew them to each other, shuddering alike at what they disclosed and what they saw!

'Faith! Faith!' cried the husband. 'Look up to Heaven, and resist the Wicked One!'

Whether Faith obeyed, he knew not. Hardly had he spoken, when he found himself amid calm night and solitude, listening to a roar of the wind, which died heavily away through the forest. He staggered against the rock and felt it

---

4. The *New-England Magazine* erroneously printed "grave," corrected to "race" in *Mosses from an Old Manse* (1846).

chill and damp, while a hanging twig, that had been all on fire, besprinkled his cheek with the coldest dew.

The next morning, young goodman Brown came slowly into the street of Salem village, staring around him like a bewildered man. The good old minister was taking a walk along the graveyard, to get an appetite for breakfast and meditate his sermon, and bestowed a blessing, as he passed, on goodman Brown. He shrank from the venerable saint, as if to avoid an anathema. Old deacon Gookin was at domestic worship, and the holy words of his prayer were heard through the open window. 'What God doth the wizard pray to?' quoth goodman Brown. Goody Cloyse, that excellent old Christian, stood in the early sunshine, at her own lattice, catechising a little girl, who had brought her a pint of morning's milk. Goodman Brown snatched away the child, as from the grasp of the fiend himself. Turning the corner by the meeting-house, he spied the head of Faith, with the pink ribbons, gazing anxiously forth, and bursting into such joy at sight of him, that she skipt along the street, and almost kissed her husband before the whole village. But, goodman Brown looked sternly and sadly into her face, and passed on without a greeting.

Had goodman Brown fallen asleep in the forest, and only dreamed a wild dream of a witch-meeting?

Be it so, if you will. But, alas! it was a dream of evil omen for young goodman Brown. A stern, a sad, a darkly meditative, a distrustful, if not a desperate man, did he become, from the night of that fearful dream. On the Sabbath-day, when the congregation were singing a holy psalm, he could not listen, because an anthem of sin rushed loudly upon his ear, and drowned all the blessed strain. When the minister spoke from the pulpit, with power and fervid eloquence, and, with his hand on the open bible, of the sacred truths of our religion, and of saint-like lives and triumphant deaths, and of future bliss or misery unutterable, then did goodman Brown turn pale, dreading, lest the roof should thunder down upon the gray blasphemer and his hearers. Often, awakening suddenly at midnight, he shrank from the bosom of Faith, and at morning or eventide, when the family knelt down at prayer, he scowled, and muttered to himself, and gazed sternly at his wife, and turned away. And when he had lived long, and was borne to his grave, a hoary corpse, followed by Faith, an aged woman, and children and grand-children, a goodly procession, besides neighbors, not a few, they carved no hopeful verse upon his tombstone; for his dying hour was gloom.

1835

The May-Pole of Merry Mount[1]

There is an admirable foundation for a philosophic romance, in the curious history of the early settlement of Mount Wallaston, or Merry Mount. In the slight sketch here attempted, the facts, recorded on the grave pages of our New England annalists, have wrought themselves, almost spontaneously, into a sort of allegory. The masques, mummeries, and festive customs, described in the text, are in accordance with the manners of the age. Authority, on these points may be found in Strutt's Book of English Sports and Pastimes.[2]

1. The text is that of the first printing in *The Token* (1836), where the story is ascribed to "the Author of 'The Gentle Boy.'" "May-pole": in English tradition the tall pole placed in a prominent site in a village where on May 1 flower-bedecked young people could dance around it after a night of gathering new vegetation and blossoms in the woods. Puritans condemned the custom as a sexual orgy.
2. Joseph Strutt, *The Sports and Pastimes of the People of England* (1801). Hawthorne also knew Nathaniel

Bright were the days at Merry Mount, when the May-Pole was the banner-staff of that gay colony! They who reared it, should their banner be triumphant, were to pour sun-shine over New England's rugged hills, and scatter flower-seeds throughout the soil. Jollity and gloom were contending for an empire. Midsummer eve[3] had come, bringing deep verdure to the forest, and roses in her lap, of a more vivid hue than the tender buds of Spring. But May, or her mirthful spirit, dwelt all the year round at Merry Mount, sporting with the Summer months, and revelling with Autumn, and basking in the glow of Winter's fireside. Through a world of toil and care, she flitted with a dreamlike smile, and came hither to find a home among the lightsome hearts of Merry Mount.

Never had the May-Pole been so gaily decked as at sunset on mid-summer eve. This venerated emblem was a pine tree, which had preserved the slender grace of youth, while it equalled the loftiest height of the old wood monarchs. From its top streamed a silken banner, colored like the rainbow. Down nearly to the ground, the pole was dressed with birchen boughs, and others of the liveliest green, and some with silvery leaves, fastened by ribbons that fluttered in fantastic knots of twenty different colors, but no sad ones. Garden flowers, and blossoms of the wilderness, laughed gladly forth amid the verdure, so fresh and dewy, that they must have grown by magic on that happy pine tree. Where this green and flowery splendor terminated, the shaft of the May-Pole was stained with the seven brilliant hues of the banner at its top. On the lowest green bough hung an abundant wreath of roses, some that had been gathered in the sunniest spots of the forest, and others, of still richer blush, which the colonists had reared from English seed. Oh, people of the Golden Age, the chief of your husbandry, was to raise flowers!

But what was the wild throng that stood hand in hand about the May-Pole? It could not be, that the Fauns and Nymphs, when driven from their classic groves and homes of ancient fable, had sought refuge, as all the persecuted did, in the fresh woods of the West. These were Gothic monsters, though perhaps of Grecian ancestry. On the shoulders of a comely youth, uprose the head and branching antlers of a stag; a second, human in all other points, had the grim visage of a wolf; a third, still with the trunk and limbs of a mortal man, showed the beard and horns of a venerable he-goat. There was the likeness of a bear erect, brute in all but his hind legs, which were adorned with pink silk stockings. And here again, almost as wondrous, stood a real bear of the dark forest, lending each of his fore paws to the grasp of a human hand, and as ready for the dance as any in that circle. This inferior nature rose half-way, to meet his companions as they stooped. Other faces wore the similitude of man or woman, but distorted or extravagant, with red noses pendulous before their mouths, which seemed of awful depth, and stretched from ear to ear in an eternal fit of laughter. Here might be seen the Salvage Man,[4] well known in heraldry, hairy as a baboon, and girdled with green leaves. By his side, a nobler figure, but still a counterfeit, appeared an Indian hunter, with feathery crest and wampum belt. Many of this strange company wore fools-caps, and had little bells appended to their garments, tinkling with a silvery sound, responsive to the inaudible music of their gleesome spirits. Some

---

Morton's *New England Memorial* (1669), which drew on William Bradford's manuscript history *Of Plymouth Plantation.*

3. June 20, the day before the longest day of the year.
4. Person clad in foliage to represent a savage, as in medieval and Renaissance pageantry.

youths and maidens were of soberer garb, yet well maintained their places in
the irregular throng, by the expression of wild revelry upon their features.
Such were the colonists of Merry Mount, as they stood in the broad smile of
sunset, round their venerated May-Pole.

Had a wanderer, bewildered in the melancholy forest, heard their mirth,
and stolen a half-affrighted glance, he might have fancied them the crew of
Comus,[5] some already transformed to brutes, some midway between man and
beast, and the others rioting in the flow of tipsey jollity that foreran the change.
But a band of Puritans, who watched the scene, invisible themselves, compared the masques to those devils and ruined souls, with whom their superstition peopled the black wilderness.

Within the ring of monsters, appeared the two airiest forms, that had ever
trodden on any more solid footing than a purple and golden cloud. One was a
youth, in glistening apparel, with a scarf of the rainbow pattern crosswise on
his breast. His right hand held a gilded staff, the ensign[6] of high dignity among
the revellous, and his left grasped the slender fingers of a fair maiden, not less
gaily decorated than himself. Bright roses glowed in contrast with the dark and
glossy curls of each, and were scattered round their feet, or had sprung up
spontaneously there. Behind this lightsome couple, so close to the May-Pole
that its boughs shaded his jovial face, stood the figure of an English priest,
canonically dressed, yet decked with flowers, in Heathen fashion, and wearing
a chaplet of the native vine leaves. By the riot of his rolling eye, and the pagan
decorations of his holy garb, he seemed the wildest monster there, and the
very Comus of the crew.

'Votaries of the May-Pole,' cried the flower-decked priest, 'merrily, all day
long, have the woods echoed to your mirth. But be this your merriest hour,
my hearts! Lo, here stand the Lord and Lady of the May, whom I, a clerk[7] of
Oxford, and high priest of Merry Mount, am presently to join in holy matrimony. Up with your nimble spirits, ye morrice-dancers, green-men, and glee-
maidens,[8] bears and wolves, and horned gentlemen! Come; a chorus now,
rich with the old mirth of Merry England, and the wilder glee of this fresh
forest; and then a dance, to show the youthful pair what life is made of, and
how airily they should go through it! All ye that love the May-Pole, lend your
voices to the nuptial song of the Lord and Lady of the May!'

This wedlock was more serious than most affairs of Merry Mount, where
jest and delusion, trick and fantasy, kept up a continual carnival. The Lord
and Lady of the May, though their titles must be laid down at sunset, were
really and truly to be partners for the dance of life, beginning the measure that
same bright eve. The wreath of roses, that hung from the lowest green bough
of the May-Pole, had been twined for them, and would be thrown over both
their heads, in symbol of their flowery union. When the priest had spoken,
therefore, a riotous uproar burst from the rout of monstrous figures.

'Begin you the stave,[9] reverend Sir,' cried they all; 'and never did the woods
ring to such a merry peal, as we of the May-Pole shall send up!'

Immediately a prelude of pipe, cittern,[1] and viol, touched with practised
minstrelsy, began to play from a neighboring thicket, in such a mirthful

5. The god of revelry, here associated with Milton's
Comus (1634).
6. Sign, token.
7. In Anglican usage, lay minister who assists the parish clergyman.

8. Participants in an English folk dance, which was
originally "Moorish dance." "Green-men": men bedecked in greenery. "Glee-maidens": girl singers.
9. Stanza.
1. Guitar with pear-shaped body.

cadence, that the boughs of the May-Pole quivered to the sound. But the May Lord, he of the gilded staff, chancing to look into his Lady's eyes, was wonderstruck at the almost pensive glance that met his own.

'Edith, sweet Lady of the May,' whispered he, reproachfully, 'is your wreath of roses a garland to hang above our graves, that you look so sad? Oh, Edith, this is our golden time! Tarnish it not by any pensive shadow of the mind; for it may be, that nothing of futurity will be brighter than the mere remembrance of what is now passing.'

'That was the very thought that saddened me! How came it in your mind too?' said Edith, in a still lower tone than he; for it was high treason to be sad at Merry Mount. 'Therefore do I sigh amid this festive music. And besides, dear Edgar, I struggle as with a dream, and fancy that these shapes of our jovial friends are visionary, and their mirth unreal, and that we are no true Lord and Lady of the May. What is the mystery in my heart?'

Just then, as if a spell had loosened them, down came a little shower of withering rose leaves from the May-Pole. Alas, for the young lovers! No sooner had their hearts glowed with real passion, than they were sensible of something vague and unsubstantial in their former pleasures, and felt a dreary presentiment of inevitable change. From the moment that they truly loved, they had subjected themselves to earth's doom of care, and sorrow, and troubled joy, and had no more a home at Merry Mount. That was Edith's mystery. Now leave we the priest to marry them, and the masquers to sport round the May-Pole, till the last sunbeam be withdrawn from its summit, and the shadows of the forest mingle gloomily in the dance. Meanwhile, we may discover who these gay people were.

Two hundred years ago, and more, the old world and its inhabitants became mutually weary of each other. Men voyaged by thousands to the West; some to barter glass beads, and such like jewels, for the furs of the Indian hunter; some to conquer virgin empires; and one stern band to pray. But none of these motives had much weight with the colonists of Merry Mount. Their leaders were men who had sported so long with life, that when Thought and Wisdom came, even these unwelcome guests were led astray, by the crowd of vanities which they should have put to flight. Erring Thought and perverted Wisdom were made to put on masques, and play the fool. The men of whom we speak, after losing the heart's fresh gaiety, imagined a wild philosophy of pleasure, and came hither to act out their latest day-dream. They gathered followers from all that giddy tribe, whose whole life is like the festal days of soberer men. In their train were minstrels, not unknown in London streets; wandering players, whose theatres had been the halls of noblemen; mummeries, rope-dancers, and mountebanks,[2] who would long be missed at wakes, church-ales, and fairs; in a word, mirth-makers of every sort, such as abounded in that age, but now began to be discountenanced by the rapid growth of Puritanism. Light had their footsteps been on land, and as lightly they came across the sea. Many had been maddened by their previous troubles into a gay despair; others were as madly gay in the flush of youth, like the May Lord and his Lady; but whatever might be the quality of their mirth, old and young were gay at Merry Mount. The young deemed themselves happy. The elder spirits, if they knew that mirth was but the counterfeit of happiness, yet followed the false shadow

---

2. Showmen who "climb on a bench" to hawk medicines or (as here) to tell stories or do tricks. "Mummeries": masked actors. "Rope-dancers": tightrope walkers.

wilfully, because at least her garments glittered brightest. Sworn triflers of a life-time, they would not venture among the sober truths of life, not even to be truly blest.

All the hereditary pastimes of Old England were transplanted hither. The King of Christmas was duly crowned, and the Lord of Misrule[3] bore potent sway. On the eve of Saint John,[4] they felled whole acres of the forest to make bonfires, and danced by the blaze all night, crowned with garlands, and throwing flowers into the flame. At harvest time, though their crop was of the smallest, they made an image with the sheaves of Indian corn, and wreathed it with autumnal garlands, and bore it home triumphantly. But what chiefly characterized the colonists of Merry Mount, was their veneration for the May-Pole. It has made their true history a poet's tale. Spring decked the hallowed emblem with young blossoms and fresh green boughs; Summer brought roses of the deepest blush, and the perfected foliage of the forest; Autumn enriched it with that red and yellow gorgeousness, which converts each wildwood leaf into a painted flower; and Winter silvered it with sleet, and hung it round with icicles, till it flashed in the cold sunshine, itself a frozen sunbeam. Thus each alternate season did homage to the May-Pole, and paid it a tribute of its own richest splendor. Its votaries danced round it, once, at least, in every month; sometimes they called it their religion, or their altar; but always, it was the banner-staff of Merry Mount.

Unfortunately, there were men in the new world, of a sterner faith than these May-Pole worshippers. Not far from Merry Mount was a settlement of Puritans, most dismal wretches, who said their prayers before daylight, and then wrought in the forest or the cornfield, till evening made it prayer time again. Their weapons were always at hand, to shoot down the straggling savage. When they met in conclave, it was never to keep up the old English mirth, but to hear sermons three hours long, or to proclaim bounties on the heads of wolves and the scalps of Indians. Their festivals were fast-days, and their chief pastime the singing of psalms. Woe to the youth or maiden, who did but dream of a dance! The selectman nodded to the constable; and there sat the light-heeled reprobate in the stocks; or if he danced, it was round the whipping-post, which might be termed the Puritan May-Pole.

A party of these grim Puritans, toiling through the difficult woods, each with a horse-load of iron armor to burthen his footsteps, would sometimes draw near the sunny precincts of Merry Mount. There were the silken colonists, sporting round their May-Pole; perhaps teaching a bear to dance, or striving to communicate their mirth to the grave Indian; or masquerading in the skins of deer and wolves, which they had hunted for that especial purpose. Often, the whole colony were playing at blindman's bluff, magistrates and all with their eyes bandaged, except a single scape-goat, whom the blinded sinners pursued by the tinkling of the bells at his garments. Once, it is said, they were seen following a flower-decked corpse, with merriment and festive music, to his grave. But did the dead man laugh? In their quietest times, they sang ballads and told tales, for the edification of their pious visiters; or perplexed them with juggling tricks; or grinned at them through horse-collars; and when sport itself grew wearisome, they made game of their own stupidity, and began a yawning match. At the very least of these enormities, the men of iron shook

---

3. Master of the traditional Christmas revelry.   4. Midsummer eve.

their heads and frowned so darkly, that the revellers looked up, imagining that a momentary cloud had overcast the sunshine, which was to be perpetual there. On the other hand, the Puritans affirmed, that, when a psalm was pealing from their place of worship, the echo, which the forest sent them back, seemed often like the chorus of a jolly catch, closing with a roar of laughter. Who but the fiend, and his fond slaves, the crew of Merry Mount, had thus disturbed them! In due time, a feud arose, stern and bitter on one side, and as serious on the other as any thing could be, among such light spirits as had sworn allegiance to the May-Pole. The future complexion of New England was involved in this important quarrel. Should the grisly saints establish their jurisdiction over the gay sinners, then would their spirits darken all the clime, and make it a land of clouded visages, of hard toil, of sermon and psalm, forever. But should the banner-staff of Merry Mount be fortunate, sunshine would break upon the hills, and flowers would beautify the forest, and late posterity do homage to the May-Pole!

After these authentic passages from history, we return to the nuptials of the Lord and Lady of the May. Alas! we have delayed too long, and must darken our tale too suddenly. As we glanced again at the May-Pole, a solitary sunbeam is fading from the summit, and leaves only a faint golden tinge, blended with the hues of the rain bow banner. Even that dim light is now withdrawn, relinquishing the whole domain of Merry Mount to the evening gloom, which has rushed so instantaneously from the black surrounding woods. But some of these black shadows have rushed forth in human shape.

Yes: with the setting sun, the last day of mirth had passed from Merry Mount. The ring of gay masquers was disordered and broken; the stag lowered his antlers in dismay; the wolf grew weaker than a lamb; the bells of the morrice dancers tinkled with tremulous affright. The Puritans had played a characteristic part in the May-Pole mummeries. Their darksome figures were intermixed with the wild shapes of their foes, and made the scene a picture of the moment, when waking thoughts start up amid the scattered fantasies of a dream. The leader of the hostile party stood in the centre of the circle, while the rout of monsters cowered around him, like evil spirits in the presence of a dread magician. No fantastic foolery could look him in the face. So stern was the energy of his aspect, that the whole man, visage, frame, and soul, seemed wrought of iron, gifted with life and thought, yet all of one substance with his head-piece and breast-plate. It was the Puritan of Puritans; it was Endicott[5] himself!

'Stand off, priest of Baal!' said he, with a grim frown, and laying no reverent hand upon the surplice. 'I know thee, Claxton![6] Thou art the man, who couldst not abide the rule even of thine own corrupted church,[7] and hast come hither to preach iniquity, and to give example of it in thy life. But now shall it be seen that the Lord hath sanctified this wilderness for his peculiar people. Woe unto them that would defile it! And first for this flower-decked abomination, the altar of thy worship!'

And with his keen sword, Endicott assaulted the hallowed May-Pole. Nor long did it resist his arm. It groaned with a dismal sound; it showered leaves

5. John Endicott (1589?–1665), several times governor of the Massachusetts colony.
6. "Did Governor Endicott speak less positively, we should suspect a mistake here. The Reverend Mr. Claxton, though an eccentric, is not known to have been an immoral man. We rather doubt his identity with the priest of Merry Mount" [Hawthorne's note].
For the slaying of the prophets of the fertility god Baal, see 1 Kings 18.
7. I.e., the Anglican church.

and rose-buds upon the remorseless enthusiast; and finally, with all its green boughs, and ribbons, and flowers, symbolic of departed pleasures, down fell the banner-staff of Merry Mount. As it sank, tradition says, the evening sky grew darker, and the woods threw forth a more sombre shadow.

'There,' cried Endicott, looking triumphantly on his work, 'there lies the only May-Pole in New-England! The thought is strong within me, that, by its fall, is shadowed forth the fate of light and idle mirth-makers, amongst us and our posterity. Amen, saith John Endicott!'

'Amen!' echoed his followers.

But the votaries of the May-Pole gave one groan for their idol. At the sound, the Puritan leader glanced at the crew of Comus, each a figure of broad mirth, yet, at this moment, strangely expressive of sorrow and dismay.

'Valiant captain,' quoth Peter Palfrey, the Ancient[8] of the band, 'what order shall be taken with the prisoners?'

'I thought not to repent me of cutting down a May-Pole,' replied Endicott, 'yet now I could find in my heart to plant it again, and give each of these bestial pagans one other dance round their idol. It would have served rarely for a whipping-post!'

'But there are pine trees enow,' suggested the lieutenant.

'True, good Ancient,' said the leader. 'Wherefore, bind the heathen crew, and bestow on them a small matter of stripes apiece, as earnest of our future justice. Set some of the rogues in the stocks to rest themselves, so soon as Providence shall bring us to one of our own well-ordered settlements, where such accommodations may be found. Further penalties, such as branding and cropping of ears, shall be thought of hereafter.'

'How many stripes for the priest?' inquired Ancient Palfrey.

'None as yet,' answered Endicott, bending his iron frown upon the culprit. 'It must be for the Great and General Court[9] to determine, whether stripes and long imprisonment, and other grievous penalty, may atone for his transgressions. Let him look to himself! For such as violate our civil order, it may be permitted us to show mercy. But woe to the wretch that troubleth our religion!'

'And this dancing bear,' resumed the officer. 'Must he share the stripes of his fellows?'

'Shoot him through the head!' said the energetic Puritan. 'I suspect witchcraft in the beast.'

'Here be a couple of shining ones,' continued Peter Palfrey, pointing his weapon at the Lord and Lady of the May. 'They seem to be of high station among these mis-doers. Methinks their dignity will not be fitted with less than a double share of stripes.'

Endicott rested on his sword, and closely surveyed the dress and aspect of the hapless pair. There they stood, pale, downcast, and apprehensive. Yet there was an air of mutual support, and of pure affection, seeking aid and giving it, that showed them to be man and wife, with the sanction of a priest upon their love. The youth, in the peril of the moment, had dropped his gilded staff, and thrown his arm about the Lady of the May, who leaned against his breast, too lightly to burthen him, but with weight enough to express that their destinies were linked together, for good or evil. They looked

8. Lieutenant.   9. Massachusetts legislature.

first at each other, and then into the grim captain's face. There they stood, in the first hour of wedlock, while the idle pleasures, of which their companions were the emblems, had given place to the sternest cares of life, personified by the dark Puritans. But never had their youthful beauty seemed so pure and high, as when its glow was chastened by adversity.

'Youth,' said Endicott, 'ye stand in an evil case, thou and thy maiden wife. Make ready presently; for I am minded that ye shall both have a token to remember your wedding-day!'

'Stern man,' exclaimed the May Lord, 'How can I move thee? Were the means at hand, I would resist to the death. Being powerless, I entreat! Do with me as thou wilt; but let Edith go untouched!'

'Not so,' replied the immitigable zealot. 'We are not wont to show an idle courtesy to that sex, which requireth the stricter discipline. What sayest thou, maid? Shall thy silken bridegroom suffer thy share of the penalty, besides his own?'

'Be it death,' said Edith, 'and lay it all on me!'

Truly, as Endicott had said, the poor lovers stood in a woeful case. Their foes were triumphant, their friends captive and abased, their home desolate, the benighted wilderness around them, and a rigorous destiny, in the shape of the Puritan leader, their only guide. Yet the deepening twilight could not altogether conceal, that the iron man was softened; he smiled, at the fair spectacle of early love; he almost sighed, for the inevitable blight of early hopes.

'The troubles of life have come hastily on this young couple,' observed Endicott. 'We will see how they comport themselves under their present trials, ere we burthen them with greater. If, among the spoil, there be any garments of a more decent fashion, let them be put upon this May Lord and his Lady, instead of their glistening vanities. Look to it, some of you.'

'And shall not the youth's hair be cut?' asked Peter Palfrey, looking with abhorrence at the love-lock and long glossy curls of the young man.

'Crop it forthwith, and that in the true pumpkin shell fashion,'[1] answered the captain. 'Then bring them along with us, but more gently than their fellows. There be qualities in the youth, which may make him valiant to fight, and sober to toil, and pious to pray; and in the maiden, that may fit her to become a mother in our Israel,[2] bringing up babes in better nurture than her own hath been. Nor think ye, young ones, that they are the happiest, even in our lifetime of a moment, who misspend it in dancing round a May-Pole!'

And Endicott, the severest Puritan of all who laid the rock-foundation of New England, lifted the wreath of roses from the ruin of the May-Pole, and threw it, with his own gauntleted hand, over the heads of the Lord and Lady of the May. It was a deed of prophecy. As the moral gloom of the world overpowers all systematic gaiety, even so was their home of wild mirth made desolate amid the sad forest. They returned to it no more. But, as their flowery garland was wreathed of the brightest roses that had grown there, so, in the tie that united them, were intertwined all the purest and best of their early joys. They went heavenward, supporting each other along the difficult path which it was their lot to tread, and never wasted one regretful thought on the vanities of Merry Mount.

1835

---

1. Roundhead style, close-cropped in Puritan fashion.
2. Endicott makes the standard 17th-century Puritan

identification of the New England settlers with the Jews, another persecuted, God-chosen minority.

Wakefield[1]

In some old magazine or newspaper, I recollect a story, told as truth, of a man—let us call him Wakefield—who absented himself for a long time, from his wife. The fact, thus abstractedly stated, is not very uncommon, nor—without a proper distinction of circumstances—to be condemned either as naughty or nonsensical. Howbeit, this, though far from the most aggravated, is perhaps the strangest instance, on record, of marital delinquency; and, moreover, as remarkable a freak as may be found in the whole list of human oddities. The wedded couple lived in London. The man, under pretence of going a journey, took lodgings in the next street to his own house, and there, unheard of by his wife or friends, and without the shadow of a reason for such self-banishment, dwelt upwards of twenty years. During that period, he beheld his home every day, and frequently the forlorn Mrs. Wakefield. And after so great a gap in his matrimonial felicity—when his death was reckoned certain, his estate settled, his name dismissed from memory, and his wife, long, long ago, resigned to her autumnal widowhood—he entered the door one evening, quietly, as from a day's absence, and became a loving spouse until death.

This outline is all that I remember. But the incident, though of the purest originality, unexampled, and probably never to be repeated, is one, I think, which appeals to the general sympathies of mankind. We know, each for himself, that none of us would perpetrate such a folly, yet feel as if some other might. To my own contemplations, at least, it has often recurred, always exciting wonder, but with a sense that the story must be true, and a conception of its hero's character. Whenever any subject so forcibly affects the mind, time is well spent in thinking of it. If the reader choose, let him do his own meditation; or if he prefer to ramble with me through the twenty years of Wakefield's vagary, I bid him welcome; trusting that there will be a pervading spirit and a moral, even should we fail to find them, done up neatly, and condensed into the final sentence. Thought has always its efficacy, and every striking incident its moral.

What sort of a man was Wakefield? We are free to shape out our own idea, and call it by his name. He was now in the meridian of life; his matrimonial affections, never violent, were sobered into a calm, habitual sentiment; of all husbands, he was likely to be the most constant, because a certain sluggishness would keep his heart at rest, wherever it might be placed. He was intellectual, but not actively so; his mind occupied itself in long and lazy musings, that tended to no purpose, or had not vigor to attain it; his thoughts were seldom so energetic as to seize hold of words. Imagination, in the proper meaning of the term, made no part of Wakefield's gifts. With a cold, but not depraved nor wandering heart, and a mind never feverish with riotous thoughts, nor perplexed with originality, who could have anticipated, that our friend would entitle himself to a foremost place among the doers of eccentric deeds? Had his acquaintances been asked, who was the man in London, the surest to perform nothing to-day which should be remembered on the morrow, they would have thought of Wakefield. Only the wife of his bosom might have hesitated. She, without having analyzed his character, was partly aware of a quiet selfishness, that had rusted into his inactive mind—of a peculiar sort of vanity, the most uneasy attribute about him—of a disposition to craft, which

1. The text is from the first publication, in the *New-England Magazine* (May 1835).

had seldom produced more positive effects than the keeping of petty secrets, hardly worth revealing—and, lastly, of what she called a little strangeness, sometimes, in the good man. This latter quality is indefinable, and perhaps non-existent.

Let us now imagine Wakefield bidding adieu to his wife. It is the dusk of an October evening. His equipment is a drab great-coat, a hat covered with an oil-cloth, top-boots, an umbrella in one hand and a small portmanteau in the other. He has informed Mrs. Wakefield that he is to take the night-coach into the country. She would fain inquire the length of his journey, its object, and the probable time of his return; but, indulgent to his harmless love of mystery, interrogates him only by a look. He tells her not to expect him positively by the return coach, nor to look alarmed should he tarry three or four days; but, at all events, to look for him at supper on Friday evening. Wakefield himself, be it considered, has no suspicion of what is before him. He holds out his hand; she gives her own, and meets his parting kiss, in the matter-of-course way of a ten years' matrimony; and forth goes the middle-aged Mr. Wakefield, almost resolved to perplex his good lady by a whole week's absence. After the door has closed behind him, she perceives it thrust partly open, and a vision of her husband's face, through the aperture, smiling on her, and gone in a moment. For the time, this little incident is dismissed without a thought. But, long afterwards, when she has been more years a widow than a wife, that smile recurs, and flickers across all her reminiscences of Wakefield's visage. In her many musings, she surrounds the original smile with a multitude of fantasies, which make it strange and awful; as, for instance, if she imagines him in a coffin, that parting look is frozen on his pale features; or, if she dreams of him in Heaven, still his blessed spirit wears a quiet and crafty smile. Yet, for its sake, when all others have given him up for dead, she sometimes doubts whether she is a widow.

But, our business is with the husband. We must hurry after him, along the street, ere he lose his individuality, and melt into the great mass of London life. It would be vain searching for him there. Let us follow close at his heels, therefore, until, after several superfluous turns and doublings, we find him comfortably established by the fireside of a small apartment, previously be-spoken. He is in the next street to his own, and at his journey's end. He can scarcely trust his good fortune, in having got thither unperceived—recollecting that, at one time, he was delayed by the throng, in the very focus of a lighted lantern; and, again, there were foot-steps, that seemed to tread behind his own, distinct from the multitudinous tramp around him; and, anon, he heard a voice shouting afar, and fancied that it called his name. Doubtless, a dozen busy-bodies had been watching him, and told his wife the whole affair. Poor Wakefield! Little knowest thou thine own insignificance in this great world! No mortal eye but mine has traced thee. Go quietly to thy bed, foolish man; and, on the morrow, if thou wilt be wise, get thee home to good Mrs. Wake-field, and tell her the truth. Remove not thyself, even for a little week, from thy place in her chaste bosom. Were she, for a single moment, to deem thee dead, or lost, or lastingly divided from her, thou wouldst be woefully conscious of a change in thy true wife, forever after. It is perilous to make a chasm in human affections; not that they gape so long and wide—but so quickly close again!

Almost repenting of his frolic, or whatever it may be termed, Wakefield lies down betimes, and starting from his first nap, spreads forth his arms into the wide and solitary waste of the unaccustomed bed. 'No'—thinks he, gathering the bed-clothes about him—'I will not sleep alone another night.'

In the morning, he rises earlier than usual, and sets himself to consider what he really means to do. Such are his loose and rambling modes of thought, that he has taken this very singular step, with the consciousness of a purpose, indeed, but without being able to define it sufficiently for his own contemplation. The vagueness of the project, and the convulsive effort with which he plunges into the execution of it, are equally characteristic of a feeble-minded man. Wakefield sifts his ideas, however, as minutely as he may, and finds himself curious to know the progress of matters at home—how his exemplary wife will endure her widowhood, of a week; and, briefly, how the little sphere of creatures and circumstances, in which he was a central object, will be affected by his removal. A morbid vanity, therefore, lies nearest the bottom of the affair. But, how is he to attain his ends? Not, certainly, by keeping close in this comfortable lodging, where, though he slept and awoke in the next street to his home, he is as effectually abroad, as if the stage-coach had been whirling him away all night. Yet, should he reappear, the whole project is knocked in the head. His poor brains being hopelessly puzzled with this dilemma, he at length ventures out, partly resolving to cross the head of the street, and send one hasty glance towards his forsaken domicile. Habit—for he is a man of habits—takes him by the hand, and guides him, wholly unaware, to his own door, where, just at the critical moment, he is aroused by the scraping of his foot upon the step. Wakefield! whither are you going?

At that instant, his fate was turning on the pivot. Little dreaming of the doom to which his first backward step devotes him, he hurries away, breathless with agitation hitherto unfelt, and hardly dares turn his head, at the distant corner. Can it be, that nobody caught sight of him? Will not the whole household—the decent Mrs. Wakefield, the smart maid-servant, and the dirty little foot-boy—raise a hue-and-cry, through London streets, in pursuit of their fugitive lord and master? Wonderful escape! He gathers courage to pause and look homeward, but is perplexed with a sense of change about the familiar edifice, such as affects us all, when, after a separation of months or years, we again see some hill or lake, or work of art, with which we were friends, of old. In ordinary cases, this indescribable impression is caused by the comparison and contrast between our imperfect reminiscences and the reality. In Wakefield, the magic of a single night has wrought a similar transformation, because, in that brief period, a great moral change has been effected. But this is a secret from himself. Before leaving the spot, he catches a far and momentary glimpse of his wife, passing athwart the front window, with her face turned towards the head of the street. The crafty nincompoop takes to his heels, scared with the idea, that, among a thousand such atoms of mortality, her eye must have detected him. Right glad is his heart, though his brain be somewhat dizzy, when he finds himself by the coal-fire of his lodgings.

So much for the commencement of this long whim-wham. After the critical conception, and the stirring up of the man's sluggish temperament to put it in practice, the whole matter evolves itself in a natural train. We may suppose him, as the result of deep deliberation, buying a new wig, of reddish hair, and selecting sundry garments, in a fashion unlike his customary suit of brown, from a Jew's old-clothes bag. It is accomplished. Wakefield is another man.

The new system being now established, a retrograde movement to the old would be almost as difficult as the step that placed him in his unparalleled position. Furthermore, he is rendered obstinate by a sulkiness, occasionally incident to his temper, and brought on, at present, by the inadequate sensation which he conceived to have been produced in the bosom of Mrs. Wakefield. He will not go back until she be frightened half to death. Well; twice or thrice has she passed before his sight, each time with a heavier step, a paler cheek, and more anxious brow; and, in the third week of his non-appearance, he detects a portent of evil entering the house, in the guise of an apothecary. Next day, the knocker is muffled. Towards night-fall, comes the chariot of a physician, and deposits its big-wigged and solemn burthen at Wakefield's door, whence, after a quarter of an hour's visit, he emerges, perchance the herald of a funeral. Dear woman! Will she die? By this time, Wakefield is excited to something like energy of feeling, but still lingers away from his wife's bedside, pleading with his conscience, that she must not be disturbed at such a juncture. If aught else restrains him, he does not know it. In the course of a few weeks, she gradually recovers; the crisis is over; her heart is sad, perhaps, but quiet; and, let him return soon or late, it will never be feverish for him again. Such ideas glimmer through the mist of Wakefield's mind, and render him indistinctly conscious that an almost impassible gulf divides his hired apartment from his former home. 'It is but in the next street!' he sometimes says. Fool! it is in another world. Hitherto, he has put off his return from one particular day to another; henceforward, he leaves the precise time undetermined. Not to-morrow—probably next week—pretty soon. Poor man! The dead have nearly as much chance of re-visiting their earthly homes, as the self-banished Wakefield.

Would that I had a folio to write, instead of a brief article in the New-England! Then might I exemplify how an influence, beyond our control, lays its strong hand on every deed which we do, and weaves its consequences into an iron tissue of necessity. Wakefield is spell-bound. We must leave him, for ten years or so, to haunt around his house, without once crossing the threshold, and to be faithful to his wife, with all the affection of which his heart is capable, while he is slowly fading out of hers. Long since, it must be remarked, he has lost the perception of singularity in his conduct.

Now for a scene! Amid the throng of a London street, we distinguish a man, now waxing elderly, with few characteristics to attract careless observers, yet bearing, in his whole aspect, the hand-writing of no common fate, for such as have the skill to read it. He is meagre; his low and narrow forehead is deeply wrinkled; his eyes, small and lustreless, sometimes wander apprehensively about him, but oftener seem to look inward. He bends his head, and moves with an indescribable obliquity of gait, as if unwilling to display his full front to the world. Watch him, long enough to see what we have described, and you will allow, that circumstances—which often produce remarkable men from nature's ordinary handiwork—have produced one such here. Next, leaving him to sidle along the foot-walk, cast your eyes in the opposite direction, where a portly female, considerably in the wane of life, with a prayer-book in her hand, is proceeding to yonder church. She has the placid mien of settled widowhood. Her regrets have either died away, or have become so essential to her heart, that they would be poorly exchanged for joy. Just as the lean man and well conditioned woman are passing, a slight obstruction occurs, and brings these two figures directly in contact. Their hands touch; the pressure of the crowd forces her bosom against his shoulder; they stand, face to face, staring into each other's eyes. After a ten years' separation, thus Wakefield meets his wife!

The throng eddies away, and carries them asunder. The sober widow, resuming her former pace, proceeds to church, but pauses in the portal, and throws a perplexed glance along the street. She passes in, however, opening her prayer-book as she goes. And the man? With so wild a face, that busy and selfish London stands to gaze after him, he hurries to his lodgings, bolts the door, and throws himself upon the bed. The latent feelings of years break out; his feeble mind acquires a brief energy from their strength; all the miserable strangeness of his life is revealed to him at a glance; and he cries out, passionately—'Wakefield! Wakefield! You are mad!'

Perhaps he was so. The singularity of his situation must have so moulded him to itself, that, considered in regard to his fellow-creatures and the business of life, he could not be said to possess his right mind. He had contrived, or rather he had happened, to dissever himself from the world—to vanish—to give up his place and privileges with living men, without being admitted among the dead. The life of a hermit is nowise parallel to his. He was in the bustle of the city, as of old; but the crowd swept by, and saw him not; he was, we may figuratively say, always beside his wife, and at his hearth, yet must never feel the warmth of the one, nor the affection of the other. It was Wakefield's unprecedented fate, to retain his original share of human sympathies, and to be still involved in human interests, while he had lost his reciprocal influence on them. It would be a most curious speculation, to trace out the effect of such circumstances on his heart and intellect, separately, and in unison. Yet, changed as he was, he would seldom be conscious of it, but deem himself the same man as ever; glimpses of the truth, indeed, would come, but only for the moment; and still he would keep saying—'I shall soon go back!'— nor reflect, that he had been saying so for twenty years.

I conceive, also, that these twenty years would appear, in the retrospect, scarcely longer than the week to which Wakefield had at first limited his absence. He would look on the affair as no more than an interlude in the main business of his life. When, after a little while more, he should deem it time to re-enter his parlor, his wife would clap her hands for joy, on beholding the middle-aged Mr. Wakefield. Alas, what a mistake! Would Time but await the close of our favorite follies, we should be young men, all of us, and till Doom's Day.

One evening, in the twentieth year since he vanished, Wakefield is taking his customary walk towards the dwelling which he still calls his own. It is a gusty night of autumn, with frequent showers, that patter down upon the pavement, and are gone, before a man can put up his umbrella. Pausing near the house, Wakefield discerns, through the parlor-windows of the second floor, the red glow, and the glimmer and fitful flash, of a comfortable fire. On the ceiling, appears a grotesque shadow of good Mrs. Wakefield. The cap, the nose and chin, and the broad waist, form an admirable caricature, which dances, moreover, with the up-flickering and down-sinking blaze, almost too merrily for the shade of an elderly widow. At this instant, a shower chances to fall, and is driven, by the unmannerly gust, full into Wakefield's face and bosom. He is quite penetrated with its autumnal chill. Shall he stand, wet and shivering here, when his own hearth has a good fire to warm him, and his own wife will run to fetch the gray coat and small-clothes, which, doubtless, she has kept carefully in the closet of their bed-chamber? No! Wakefield is no such fool. He ascends the steps—heavily!—for twenty years have stiffened his legs, since he came down—but he knows it not. Stay, Wakefield! Would you go to the sole home that is left you? Then step into your grave! The door opens. As he passes in, we have a parting glimpse of his visage, and recognize the crafty smile, which was the precursor of the little joke, that he has ever since been playing off at his wife's expense. How unmercifully has he quizzed the poor woman! Well; a good night's rest to Wakefield!

This happy event—supposing it to be such—could only have occurred at an unpremeditated moment. We will not follow our friend across the threshold. He has left us much food for thought, a portion of which shall lend its wisdom to a moral, and be shaped into a figure. Amid the seeming confusion of our mysterious world, individuals are so nicely adjusted to a system, and systems to one another, and to a whole, that, by stepping aside for a moment, a man exposes himself to a fearful risk of losing his place forever. Like Wakefield, he may become, as it were, the Outcast of the Universe.

1835

The Minister's Black Veil

A Parable[1]

BY THE AUTHOR OF 'SIGHTS FROM A STEEPLE'

The sexton stood in the porch of Milford meeting-house, pulling lustily at the bell-rope. The old people of the village came stooping along the street. Children, with bright faces, tript merrily beside their parents, or mimicked a graver gait, in the conscious dignity of their sunday clothes. Spruce bachelors looked sidelong at the pretty maidens, and fancied that the sabbath sunshine made them prettier than on week-days. When the throng had mostly streamed into the porch, the sexton began to toll the bell, keeping his eye on the Reverend Mr. Hooper's door. The first glimpse of the clergyman's figure was the signal for the bell to cease its summons.

'But what has good Parson Hooper got upon his face?' cried the sexton in astonishment.

All within hearing immediately turned about, and beheld the semblance of Mr. Hooper, pacing slowly his meditative way towards the meeting-house. With one accord they started, expressing more wonder than if some strange minister were coming to dust the cushions of Mr. Hooper's pulpit.

'Are you sure it is our parson?' inquired Goodman Gray of the sexton.

'Of a certainty it is good Mr. Hooper,' replied the sexton. 'He was to have exchanged pulpits with Parson Shute of Westbury; but Parson Shute sent to excuse himself yesterday, being to preach a funeral sermon.'

---

1. The text is that of the first printing in *The Token* (1836). "Another clergyman in New-England, Mr. Joseph Moody, of York, Maine, who died about eighty years since, made himself remarkable by the same eccentricity that is here related of the Reverend Mr. Hooper. In his case, however, the symbol had a different import. In early life he had accidentally killed a beloved friend; and from that day till the hour of his own death, he hid his face from men" [Hawthorne's note].

The cause of so much amazement may appear sufficiently slight. Mr. Hooper, a gentlemanly person of about thirty, though still a bachelor, was dressed with due clerical neatness, as if a careful wife had starched his band, and brushed the weekly dust from his Sunday's garb. There was but one thing remarkable in his appearance. Swathed about his forehead, and hanging down over his face, so low as to be shaken by his breath, Mr. Hooper had on a black veil. On a nearer view, it seemed to consist of two folds of crape, which entirely concealed his features, except the mouth and chin, but probably did not intercept his sight, farther than to give a darkened aspect to all living and inanimate things. With this gloomy shade before him, good Mr. Hooper walked onward, at a slow and quiet pace, stooping somewhat and looking on the ground, as is customary with abstracted men, yet nodding kindly to those of his parishioners who still waited on the meeting-house steps. But so wonder-struck were they, that his greeting hardly met with a return.

'I can't really feel as if good Mr. Hooper's face was behind that piece of crape,' said the sexton.

'I don't like it,' muttered an old woman, as she hobbled into the meeting-house. 'He has changed himself into something awful, only by hiding his face.'

'Our parson has gone mad!' cried Goodman Gray, following him across the threshhold.

A rumor of some unaccountable phenomenon had preceded Mr. Hooper into the meeting-house, and set all the congregation astir. Few could refrain from twisting their heads towards the door; many stood upright, and turned directly about; while several little boys clambered upon the seats, and came down again with a terrible racket. There was a general bustle, a rustling of the women's gowns and shuffling of the men's feet, greatly at variance with that hushed repose which should attend the entrance of the minister. But Mr. Hooper appeared not to notice the perturbation of his people. He entered with an almost noiseless step, bent his head mildly to the pews on each side, and bowed as he passed his oldest parishioner, a white-haired great-grandsire, who occupied an arm-chair in the centre of the aisle. It was strange to observe, how slowly this venerable man became conscious of something singular in the appearance of his pastor. He seemed not fully to partake of the prevailing wonder, till Mr. Hooper had ascended the stairs, and showed himself in the pulpit, face to face with his congregation, except for the black veil. That mysterious emblem was never once withdrawn. It shook with his measured breath as he gave out the psalm; it threw its obscurity between him and the holy page, as he read the Scriptures; and while he prayed, the veil lay heavily on his uplifted countenance. Did he seek to hide it from the dread Being whom he was addressing?

Such was the effect of this simple piece of crape, that more than one woman of delicate nerves was forced to leave the meeting-house. Yet perhaps the pale-faced congregation was almost as fearful a sight to the minister, as his black veil to them.

Mr. Hooper had the reputation of a good preacher, but not an energetic one: he strove to win his people heavenward, by mild persuasive influences, rather than to drive them thither, by the thunders of the Word. The sermon which he now delivered, was marked by the same characteristics of style and manner, as the general series of his pulpit oratory. But there was something, either in the sentiment of the discourse itself, or in the imagination of the auditors, which made it greatly the most powerful effort that they had ever heard from their pastor's lips. It was tinged, rather more darkly than usual, with the gentle gloom of Mr. Hooper's temperament. The subject had reference to secret sin, and those sad mysteries which we hide from our nearest and dearest, and would fain conceal from our own consciousness, even forgetting that the Omniscient can detect them. A subtle power was breathed into his words. Each member of the congregation, the most innocent girl, and the man of hardened breast, felt as if the preacher had crept upon them, behind his awful veil, and discovered their hoarded iniquity of deed or thought. Many spread their clasped hands on their bosoms. There was nothing terrible in what Mr. Hooper said; at least, no violence; and yet, with every tremor of his melancholy voice, the hearers quaked. An unsought pathos came hand in hand with awe. So sensible were the audience of some unwonted attribute in their minister, that they longed for a breath of wind to blow aside the veil, almost believing that a stranger's visage would be discovered, though the form, gesture, and voice were those of Mr. Hooper.

At the close of the services, the people hurried out with indecorous confusion, eager to communicate their pent-up amazement, and conscious of lighter spirits, the moment they lost sight of the black veil. Some gathered in little circles, huddled closely together, with their mouths all whispering in the centre; some went homeward alone, wrapt in silent meditation; some talked loudly, and profaned the Sabbath-day with ostentatious laughter. A few shook their sagacious heads, intimating that they could penetrate the mystery; while one or two affirmed that there was no mystery at all, but only that Mr. Hooper's eyes were so weakened by the midnight lamp, as to require a shade. After a brief interval, forth came good Mr. Hooper also, in the rear of his flock. Turning his veiled face from one group to another, he paid due reverence to the hoary heads, saluted the middle-aged with kind dignity, as their friend and spiritual guide, greeted the young with mingled authority and love, and laid his hands on the little children's heads to bless them. Such was always his custom on the Sabbath-day. Strange and bewildered looks repaid him for his courtesy. None, as on former occasions, aspired to the honor of walking by their pastor's side. Old Squire Saunders, doubtless by an accidental lapse of memory, neglected to invite Mr. Hooper to his table, where the good clergyman had been wont to bless the food, almost every Sunday since his settlement. He returned, therefore, to the parsonage, and, at the moment of closing the door, was observed to look back upon the people, all of whom had their eyes fixed upon the minister. A sad smile gleamed faintly from beneath the black veil, and flickered about his mouth, glimmering as he disappeared.

'How strange,' said a lady, 'that a simple black veil, such as any woman might wear on her bonnet, should become such a terrible thing on Mr. Hooper's face!'

'Something must surely be amiss with Mr. Hooper's intellects,' observed her husband, the physician of the village. 'But the strangest part of the affair is the effect of this vagary, even on a sober-minded man like myself. The black veil, though it covers only our pastor's face, throws its influence over his whole person, and makes him ghost-like from head to foot. Do you not feel it so?'

'Truly do I,' replied the lady; 'and I would not be alone with him for the world. I wonder he is not afraid to be alone with himself!'

'Men sometimes are so,' said her husband.

The afternoon service was attended with similar circumstances. At its conclusion, the bell tolled for the funeral of a young lady. The relatives and friends were assembled in the house, and the more distant acquaintances stood about the door, speaking of the good qualities of the deceased, when their talk was interrupted by the appearance of Mr. Hooper, still covered with his black veil. It was now an appropriate emblem. The clergyman stepped into the room where the corpse was laid, and bent over the coffin, to take a last farewell of his deceased parishioner. As he stooped, the veil hung straight down from his forehead, so that, if her eye-lids had not been closed for ever, the dead maiden might have seen his face. Could Mr. Hooper be fearful of her glance, that he so hastily caught back the black veil? A person, who watched the interview between the dead and living, scrupled not to affirm, that, at the instant when the clergyman's features were disclosed, the corpse had slightly shuddered, rustling the shroud and muslin cap, though the countenance retained the composure of death. A superstitious old woman was the only witness of this prodigy. From the coffin, Mr. Hooper passed into the chambers of the mourners, and thence to the head of the staircase, to make the funeral prayer. It was a tender and heart-dissolving prayer, full of sorrow, yet so imbued with celestial hopes, that the music of a heavenly harp, swept by the fingers of the dead, seemed faintly to be heard among the saddest accents of the minister. The people trembled, though they but darkly understood him, when he prayed that they, and himself, and all of mortal race, might be ready, as he trusted this young maiden had been, for the dreadful hour that should snatch the veil from their faces. The bearers went heavily forth, and the mourners followed, saddening all the street, with the dead before them, and Mr. Hooper in his black veil behind.

'Why do you look back?' said one in the procession to his partner.

'I had a fancy,' replied she, 'that the minister and the maiden's spirit were walking hand in hand.'

'And so had I, at the same moment,' said the other.

That night, the handsomest couple in Milford village were to be joined in wedlock. Though reckoned a melancholy man, Mr. Hooper had a placid cheerfulness for such occasions, which often excited a sympathetic smile, where livelier merriment would have been thrown away. There was no quality of his disposition which made him more beloved than this. The company at the wedding awaited his arrival with impatience, trusting that the strange awe, which had gathered over him throughout the day, would now be dispelled. But such was not the result. When Mr. Hooper came, the first thing that their eyes rested on was the same horrible black veil, which had added deeper gloom to the funeral, and could portend nothing but evil to the wedding. Such was its immediate effect on the guests, that a cloud seemed to have rolled duskily from beneath the black crape, and dimmed the light of the candles. The bridal pair stood up before the minister. But the bride's cold fingers quivered in the tremulous hand of the bridegroom, and her death-like paleness caused a whisper, that the maiden who had been buried a few hours before, was come from her grave to be married. If ever another wedding were so dismal, it was that famous one, where they tolled the wedding-knell.[2] After performing the cere-

2. A reference to Hawthorne's own *The Wedding Knell*, which appeared in *The Token* for 1836 along with this story.

mony, Mr. Hooper raised a glass of wine to his lips, wishing happiness to the new-married couple, in a strain of mild pleasantry that ought to have brightened the features of the guests, like a cheerful gleam from the hearth. At that instant, catching a glimpse of his figure in the looking-glass, the black veil involved his own spirit in the horror with which it overwhelmed all others. His frame shuddered—his lips grew white—he spilt the untasted wine upon the carpet—and rushed forth into the darkness. For the Earth, too, had on her Black Veil.

The next day, the whole village of Milford talked of little else than Parson Hooper's black veil. That, and the mystery concealed behind it, supplied a topic for discussion between acquaintances meeting in the street, and good women gossiping at their open windows. It was the first item of news that the tavern-keeper told to his guests. The children babbled of it on their way to school. One imitative little imp covered his face with an old black handkerchief, thereby so affrighting his playmates, that the panic seized himself, and he well nigh lost his wits by his own waggery.

It was remarkable, that, of all the busy-bodies and impertinent people in the parish, not one ventured to put the plain question to Mr. Hooper, wherefore he did this thing. Hitherto, whenever there appeared the slightest call for such interference, he had never lacked advisers, nor shown himself averse to be guided by their judgment. If he erred at all, it was by so painful a degree of self-distrust, that even the mildest censure would lead him to consider an indifferent action as a crime. Yet, though so well acquainted with this amiable weakness, no individual among his parishioners chose to make the black veil a subject of friendly remonstrance. There was a feeling of dread, neither plainly confessed nor carefully concealed, which caused each to shift the responsibility upon another, till at length it was found expedient to send a deputation of the church, in order to deal with Mr. Hooper about the mystery, before it should grow into a scandal. Never did an embassy so ill discharge its duties. The minister received them with friendly courtesy, but became silent, after they were seated, leaving to his visitors the whole burthen[3] of introducing their important business. The topic, it might be supposed, was obvious enough. There was the black veil, swathed round Mr. Hooper's forehead, and concealing every feature above his placid mouth, on which, at times, they could perceive the glimmering of a melancholy smile. But that piece of crape, to their imagination, seemed to hang down before his heart, the symbol of a fearful secret between him and them. Were the veil but cast aside, they might speak freely of it, but not till then. Thus they sat a considerable time, speechless, confused, and shrinking uneasily from Mr. Hooper's eye, which they felt to be fixed upon them with an invisible glance. Finally, the deputies returned abashed to their constituents, pronouncing the matter too weighty to be handled, except by a council of the churches, if, indeed, it might not require a general synod.

But there was one person in the village, unappalled by the awe with which the black veil had impressed all beside herself. When the deputies returned without an explanation, or even venturing to demand one, she, with the calm energy of her character, determined to chase away the strange cloud that appeared to be settling round Mr. Hooper, every moment more darkly than before. As his plighted wife, it should be her privilege to know what the black

---

3. Burden.

veil concealed. At the minister's first visit, therefore, she entered upon the subject, with a direct simplicity, which made the task easier both for him and her. After he had seated himself, she fixed her eyes steadfastly upon the veil, but could discern nothing of the dreadful gloom that had so overawed the multitude: it was but a double fold of crape, hanging down from his forehead to his mouth, and slightly stirring with his breath.

'No,' said she aloud, and smiling, 'there is nothing terrible in this piece of crape, except that it hides a face which I am always glad to look upon. Come, good sir, let the sun shine from behind the cloud. First lay aside your black veil: then tell me why you put it on.'

Mr. Hooper's smile glimmered faintly.

'There is an hour to come,' said he, 'when all of us shall cast aside our veils. Take it not amiss, beloved friend, if I wear this piece of crape till then.'

'Your words are a mystery too,' returned the young lady. 'Take away the veil from them, at least.'

'Elizabeth, I will,' said he, 'so far as my vow may suffer me. Know, then, this veil is a type[4] and a symbol, and I am bound to wear it ever, both in light and darkness, in solitude and before the gaze of multitudes, and as with strangers, so with my familiar friends. No mortal eye will see it withdrawn. This dismal shade must separate me from the world: even you, Elizabeth, can never come behind it!'

'What grievous affliction hath befallen you,' she earnestly inquired, 'that you should thus darken your eyes for ever?'

'If it be a sign of mourning,' replied Mr. Hooper, 'I, perhaps, like most other mortals, have sorrows dark enough to be typified by a black veil.'

'But what if the world will not believe that it is the type of an innocent sorrow?' urged Elizabeth. 'Beloved and respected as you are, there may be whispers, that you hide your face under the consciousness of secret sin. For the sake of your holy office, do away this scandal!'

The color rose into her cheeks, as she intimated the nature of the rumors that were already abroad in the village. But Mr. Hooper's mildness did not forsake him. He even smiled again—that same sad smile, which always appeared like a faint glimmering of light, proceeding from the obscurity beneath the veil.

'If I hide my face for sorrow, there is cause enough,' he merely replied; 'and if I cover it for secret sin, what mortal might not do the same?'

And with this gentle, but unconquerable obstinacy, did he resist all her entreaties. At length Elizabeth sat silent. For a few moments she appeared lost in thought, considering, probably, what new methods might be tried, to withdraw her lover from so dark a fantasy, which, if it had no other meaning, was perhaps a symptom of mental disease. Though of a firmer character than his own, the tears rolled down her cheeks. But, in an instant, as it were, a new feeling took the place of sorrow: her eyes were fixed insensibly on the black veil, when, like a sudden twilight in the air, its terrors fell around her. She arose, and stood trembling before him.

'And do you feel it then at last?' said he mournfully.

She made no reply, but covered her eyes with her hand, and turned to leave the room. He rushed forward and caught her arm.

'Have patience with me, Elizabeth!' cried he passionately. 'Do not desert

4. Symbol (the phrase "a type and a symbol" is redundant).

me, though this veil must be between us here on earth. Be mine, and hereafter there shall be no veil over my face, no darkness between our souls! It is but a mortal veil—it is not for eternity! Oh, you know not how lonely I am and how frightened to be alone behind my black veil. Do not leave me in this miserable obscurity for ever!'

'Lift the veil but once, and look me in the face,' said she.

'Never! It cannot be!' replied Mr. Hooper.

'Then, farewell!' said Elizabeth.

She withrew her arm from his grasp, and slowly departed, pausing at the door, to give one long, shuddering gaze, that seemed almost to penetrate the mystery of the black veil. But, even amid his grief, Mr. Hooper smiled to think that only a material emblem had separated him from happiness, though the horrors which it shadowed forth, must be drawn darkly between the fondest of lovers.

From that time no attempts were made to remove Mr. Hooper's black veil, or, by a direct appeal, to discover the secret which it was supposed to hide. By persons who claimed a superiority to popular prejudice, it was reckoned merely an eccentric whim, such as often mingles with the sober actions of men otherwise rational, and tinges them all with its own semblance of insanity. But with the multitude, good Mr. Hooper was irreparably a bugbear.[5] He could not walk the street with any peace of mind, so conscious was he that the gentle and timid would turn aside to avoid him, and that others would make it a point of hardihood to throw themselves in his way. The impertinence of the latter class compelled him to give up his customary walk, at sunset, to the burial ground; for when he leaned pensively over the gate, there would always be faces behind the grave-stones, peeping at his black veil. A fable went the rounds, that the stare of the dead people drove him thence. It grieved him, to the very depth of his kind heart, to observe how the children fled from his approach, breaking up their merriest sports, while his melancholy figure was yet afar off. Their instinctive dread caused him to feel, more strongly than aught else, that a preternatural horror was interwoven with the threads of the black crape. In truth, his own antipathy to the veil was known to be so great, that he never willingly passed before a mirror, nor stooped to drink at a still fountain, lest, in its peaceful bosom, he should be affrighted by himself. This was what gave plausibility to the whispers, that Mr. Hooper's conscience tortured him for some great crime, too horrible to be entirely concealed, or otherwise than so obscurely intimated. Thus, from beneath the black veil, there rolled a cloud into the sunshine, an ambiguity of sin or sorrow, which enveloped the poor minister, so that love or sympathy could never reach him. It was said, that ghost and fiend consorted with him there. With self-shudderings and outward terrors, he walked continually in its shadow, groping darkly within his own soul, or gazing through a medium that saddened the whole world. Even the lawless wind, it was believed, respected his dreadful secret, and never blew aside the veil. But still good Mr. Hooper sadly smiled, at the pale visages of the worldly throng as he passed by.

Among all its bad influences, the black veil had the one desirable effect, of making its wearer a very efficient clergyman. By the aid of his mysterious emblem—for there was no other apparent cause—he became a man of awful

5. Object of dread.

power, over souls that were in agony for sin. His converts always regarded him with a dread peculiar to themselves, affirming, though but figuratively, that, before he brought them to celestial light, they had been with him behind the black veil. Its gloom, indeed, enabled him to sympathize with all dark affections. Dying sinners cried aloud for Mr. Hooper, and would not yield their breath till he appeared; though ever, as he stooped to whisper consolation, they shuddered at the veiled face so near their own. Such were the terrors of the black veil, even when death had bared his visage! Strangers came long distances to attend service at his church, with the mere idle purpose of gazing at his figure, because it was forbidden them to behold his face. But many were made to quake ere they departed! Once, during Governor Belcher's administration, Mr. Hooper was appointed to preach the election sermon.[6] Covered with his black veil, he stood before the chief magistrate, the council, and the representatives, and wrought so deep an impression, that the legislative measures of that year, were characterized by all the gloom and piety of our earliest ancestral sway.

In this manner Mr. Hooper spent a long life, irreproachable in outward act, yet shrouded in dismal suspicions; kind and loving, though unloved, and dimly feared; a man apart from men, shunned in their health and joy, but ever summoned to their aid in mortal anguish. As years wore on, shedding their snows above his sable veil, he acquired a name throughout the New-England churches, and they called him Father Hooper. Nearly all his parishioners, who were of mature age when he was settled, had been borne away by many a funeral: he had one congregation in the church, and a more crowded one in the church-yard; and having wrought so late into the evening, and done his work so well, it was now good Father Hooper's turn to rest.

Several persons were visible by the shaded candlelight, in the death-chamber of the old clergyman. Natural connections he had none. But there was the decorously grave, though unmoved physician, seeking only to mitigate the last pangs of the patient whom he could not save. There were the deacons, and other eminently pious members of his church. There, also, was the Reverend Mr. Clark, of Westbury, a young and zealous divine, who had ridden in haste to pray by the bed-side of the expiring minister. There was the nurse, no hired handmaiden of death, but one whose calm affection had endured thus long, in secrecy, in solitude, amid the chill of age, and would not perish, even at the dying hour. Who, but Elizabeth! And there lay the hoary head of good Father Hooper upon the death-pillow, with the black veil still swathed about his brow and reaching down over his face, so that each more difficult gasp of his faint breath caused it to stir. All through life that piece of crape had hung between him and the world: it had separated him from cheerful brotherhood and woman's love, and kept him in that saddest of all prisons, his own heart; and still it lay upon his face, as if to deepen the gloom of his darksome chamber, and shade him from the sunshine of eternity.

For some time previous, his mind had been confused, wavering doubtfully between the past and the present, and hovering forward, as it were, at intervals, into the indistinctness of the world to come. There had been feverish turns, which tossed him from side to side, and wore away what little strength he had.

6. A sermon was preached at the installing of each new governor (in this case, at one of Belcher's installations for a new term). Jonathan Belcher (1682–1757) was governor of Massachusetts and New Hampshire (1730–41).

But in his most convulsive struggles, and in the wildest vagaries of his intellect, when no other thought retained its sober influence, he still showed an awful solicitude lest the black veil should slip aside. Even if his bewildered soul could have forgotten, there was a faithful woman at his pillow, who, with averted eyes, would have covered that aged face, which she had last beheld in the comeliness of manhood. At length the death-stricken old man lay quietly in the torpor of mental and bodily exhaustion, with an imperceptible pulse, and breath that grew fainter and fainter, except when a long, deep, and irregular inspiration seemed to prelude the flight of his spirit.

The minister of Westbury approached the bedside.

'Venerable Father Hooper,' said he, 'the moment of your release is at hand. Are you ready for the lifting of the veil, that shuts in time from eternity?'

Father Hooper at first replied merely by a feeble motion of his head; then, apprehensive, perhaps, that his meaning might be doubtful, he exerted himself to speak.

'Yea,' said he, in faint accents, 'my soul hath a patient weariness until that veil be lifted.'

'And is it fitting,' resumed the Reverend Mr. Clark, 'that a man so given to prayer, of such a blameless example, holy in deed and thought, so far as mortal judgment may pronounce; is it fitting that a father in the church should leave a shadow on his memory, that may seem to blacken a life so pure? I pray you, my venerable brother, let not this thing be! Suffer us to be gladdened by your triumphant aspect, as you go to your reward. Before the veil of eternity be lifted, let me cast aside this black veil from your face!'

And thus speaking, the reverend Mr. Clark bent forward to reveal the mystery of so many years. But, exerting a sudden energy, that made all the beholders stand aghast, Father Hooper snatched both his hands from beneath the bed-clothes, and pressed them strongly on the black veil, resolute to struggle, if the minister of Westbury would contend with a dying man.

'Never!' cried the veiled clergyman. 'On earth, never!'

'Dark old man!' exclaimed the affrighted minister, 'with what horrible crime upon your soul are you now passing to the judgment?'

Father Hooper's breath heaved; it rattled in his throat; but, with a mighty effort, grasping forward with his hands, he caught hold of life, and held it back till he should speak. He even raised himself in bed; and there he sat, shivering with the arms of death around him, while the black veil hung down, awful, at that last moment, in the gathered terrors of a life-time. And yet the faint, sad smile, so often there, now seemed to glimmer from its obscurity, and linger on Father Hooper's lips.

'Why do you tremble at me alone?' cried he, turning his veiled face round the circle of pale spectators. 'Tremble also at each other! Have men avoided me, and women shown no pity, and children screamed and fled, only for my black veil? What, but the mystery which it obscurely typifies, has made this piece of crape so awful? When the friend shows his inmost heart to his friend; the lover to his best-beloved; when man does not vainly shrink from the eye of his Creator, loathsomely treasuring up the secret of his sin; then deem me a monster, for the symbol beneath which I have lived, and die! I look around me, and lo! on every visage a black veil!'

While his auditors shrank from one another, in mutual affright, Father Hooper fell back upon his pillow, a veiled corpse, with a faint smile lingering on the lips. Still veiled, they laid him in his coffin, and a veiled corpse they bore him to the grave. The grass of many years has sprung up and withered on that grave, the burial-stone is moss-grown, and good Mr. Hooper's face is dust; but awful is still the thought, that it mouldered beneath the black veil!

1836

Rappaccini's Daughter[1]

Writings of Aubépine

We do not remember to have seen any translated specimens of the productions of M. de l'Aubépine;[2] a fact the less to be wondered at, as his very name is unknown to many of his own countrymen, as well as to the student of foreign literature. As a writer, he seems to occupy an unfortunate position between the Transcendentalists (who, under one name or another, have their share in all the current literature of the world), and the great body of pen-and-ink men who address the intellect and sympathies of the multitude. If not too refined, at all events too remote, too shadowy and unsubstantial in his modes of development, to suit the taste of the latter class, and yet too popular to satisfy the spiritual or metaphysical requisitions of the former, he must necessarily find himself without an audience; except here and there an individual, or possibly an isolated clique. His writings, to do them justice, are not altogether destitute of fancy and originality; they might have won him greater reputation but for an inveterate love of allegory, which is apt to invest his plots and characters with the aspect of scenery and people in the clouds, and to steal away the human warmth out of his conceptions. His fictions are sometimes historical, sometimes of the present day, and sometimes, so far as can be discovered, have little or no reference either to time or space. In any case, he generally contents himself with a very slight embroidery of outward manners,—the faintest possible counterfeit of real life,—and endeavors to create an interest by some less obvious peculiarity of the subject. Occasionally, a breath of nature, a rain-drop of pathos and tenderness, or a gleam of humor, will find its way into the midst of his fantastic imagery, and make us feel as if, after all, we were yet within the limits of our native earth. We will only add to this very cursory notice, that M. de l'Aubépine's productions, if the reader chance to take them in precisely the proper point of view, may amuse a leisure hour as well as those of a brighter man; if otherwise, they can hardly fail to look excessively like nonsense.

Our author is voluminous; he continues to write and publish with as much praiseworthy and indefatigable prolixity, as if his efforts were crowned with the brilliant success that so justly attends those of Eugene Sue.[3] His first appearance was by a collection of stories, in a long series of volumes, entitled "Contes deux fois racontées."[4] The titles of some of his more recent works (we quote from memory) are as follows:—"Le Voyage Céleste à Chemin de Fer," 3 tom.

1. The text is from the first publication in *The Democratic Review* (December 1844).
2. French for "Hawthorne." What follows is a facetious account of Hawthorne's own career.
3. French novelist (1804–1857), author of *The Wan-*
dering Jew and other popular works.
4. *Twice-Told Tales* (French), Hawthorne's first volume (1837), except for the anonymous and suppressed *Fanshawe*.

1838. *"Le nouveau père Adam et la nouvelle mère Eve,"* 2 tom. 1839. *"Roderic; ou le Serpent à l'estomac,"* 2 tom. 1840. *"Le Culte du Feu,"* a folio volume of ponderous research into the religion and ritual of the old Persian Ghebers, published in 1841. *"La Soirée du Château en Espagne,"* 1 tom. 8vo. 1842; and *"L'Artiste du Beau; ou le Papillon Mécanique,"* 5 tom. 4to. 1843.[5] Our somewhat wearisome persual of this startling catalogue of volumes has left behind it a certain personal affection and sympathy, though by no means admiration, for M. de l'Aubépine; and we would fain do the little in our power towards introducing him favorably to the American public. The ensuing tale is a translation of his *"Béatrice; ou La Belle Empoisonneuse,"* recently published in *"La Revue Anti-Aristocratique."* This journal, edited by the Comte de Bearhaven,[6] has, for some years past, led the defence of liberal principles and popular rights, with a faithfulness and ability worthy of all praise.

Rappaccini's Daughter

A young man, named Giovanni Guasconti, came, very long ago, from the more southern region of Italy, to pursue his studies at the University of Padua. Giovanni, who had but a scanty supply of gold ducats in his pocket, took lodgings in a high and gloomy chamber of an old edifice, which looked not unworthy to have been the palace of a Paduan noble, and which, in fact, exhibited over its entrance the armorial bearings of a family long since extinct. The young stranger, who was not unstudied in the great poem of his country, recollected that one of the ancestors of this family, and perhaps an occupant of this very mansion, had been pictured by Dante as a partaker of the immortal agonies of his Inferno. These reminiscences and associations, together with the tendency to heart-break natural to a young man for the first time out of his native sphere, caused Giovanni to sigh heavily, as he looked around the desolate and ill-furnished apartment.

"Holy Virgin, signor," cried old dame Lisabetta, who, won by the youth's remarkable beauty of person, was kindly endeavoring to give the chamber a habitable air, "what a sigh was that to come out of a young man's heart! Do you find this old mansion gloomy? For the love of heaven, then, put your head out of the window, and you will see as bright sunshine as you have left in Naples."

Guasconti mechanically did as the old woman advised, but could not quite agree with her that the Lombard sunshine was as cheerful as that of southern Italy. Such as it was, however, it fell upon a garden beneath the window, and expended its fostering influences on a variety of plants, which seemed to have been cultivated with exceeding care.

"Does this garden belong to the house?" asked Giovanni.

"Heaven forbid, signor!—unless it were fruitful of better pot-herbs than any that grow there now," answered old Lisabetta. "No: that garden is cultivated by the own hands of Signor Giacomo Rappaccini, the famous Doctor, who, I warrant him, has been heard of as far as Naples. It is said he distils these plants

---

5. In these mock bibliographical citations "tom." (French abbreviation for *tome,* "volume") and "8vo" (octavo) and "4vo" (quarto) are jokes: Hawthorne's tales took up only a few magazine pages each. All but one of these French titles refer to stories by Hawthorne. In order, the titles are *The Celestial Railroad, The New*

Adam and Eve, Egotism: or, the Boston-Serpent, Fire-Worship, Evening in a Castle in Spain (imaginary), and *The Artist of the Beautiful.*
6. Hawthorne's friend, John O'Sullivan, editor of *The Democratic Review* (here, *"La Revue Anti-Aristocratique"*).

into medicines that are as potent as a charm. Oftentimes you may see the
signor Doctor at work, and perchance the signora his daughter, too, gathering
the strange flowers that grow in the garden."

The old woman had now done what she could for the aspect of the chamber, and, commending the young man to the protection of the saints, took
her departure.

Giovanni still found no better occupation than to look down into the garden
beneath his window. From its appearance, he judged it to be one of those
botanic gardens, which were of earlier date in Padua than elsewhere in Italy,
or in the world. Or, not improbably, it might once have been the pleasure-
place of an opulent family; for there was the ruin of a marble fountain in the
centre, sculptured with rare art, but so wofully shattered that it was impossible
to trace the original design from the chaos of remaining fragments. The water,
however, continued to gush and sparkle into the sunbeams as cheerfully as
ever. A little gurgling sound ascended to the young man's window, and made
him feel as if the fountain were an immortal spirit, that sung its song unceasingly, and without heeding the vicissitudes around it; while one century
embodied it in marble, and another scattered the garniture on the soil. All
about the pool into which the water subsided, grew various plants, that seemed
to require a plentiful supply of moisture for the nourishment of gigantic leaves,
and, in some instances, flowers gorgeously magnificent. There was one shrub
in particular, set in a marble vase in the midst of the pool, that bore a profusion of purple blossoms, each of which had the lustre and richness of a gem;
and the whole together made a show so resplendent that it seemed enough to
illuminate the garden, even had there been no sunshine. Every portion of the
soil was peopled with plants and herbs, which, if less beautiful, still bore tokens
of assiduous care; as if all had their individual virtues, known to the scientific
mind that fostered them. Some were placed in urns, rich with old carving,
and others in common garden-pots; some crept serpent-like along the ground,
or climbed on high, using whatever means of ascent was offered them. One
plant had wreathed itself round a statue of Vertumnus,[7] which was thus quite
veiled and shrouded in a drapery of hanging foliage, so happily arranged that
it might have served a sculptor for a study.

While Giovanni stood at the window, he heard a rustling behind a screen
of leaves, and became aware that a person was at work in the garden. His
figure soon emerged into view, and showed itself to be that of no common
laborer, but a tall, emaciated, sallow, and sickly-looking man, dressed in a
scholar's garb of black. He was beyond the middle term of life, with grey hair,
a thin grey beard, and a face singularly marked with intellect and cultivation,
but which could never, even in his more youthful days, have expressed much
warmth of heart.

Nothing could exceed the intentness with which this scientific gardener
examined every shrub which grew in his path; it seemed as if he was looking
into their inmost nature, making observations in regard to their creative
essence, and discovering why one leaf grew in this shape, and another in that,
and wherefore such and such flowers differed among themselves in hue and
perfume. Nevertheless, in spite of the deep intelligence on his part, there was
no approach to intimacy between himself and these vegetable existences. On

---

7. The god of the seasons (and vegetation produced by the changing seasons).

the contrary, he avoided their actual touch, or the direct inhaling of their odors, with a caution that impressed Giovanni most disagreeably; for the man's demeanor was that of one walking among malignant influences, such as savage beasts, or deadly snakes, or evil spirits, which, should he allow them one moment of license, would wreak upon him some terrible fatality. It was strangely frightful to the young man's imagination, to see this air of insecurity in a person cultivating a garden, that most simple and innocent of human toils, and which had been alike the joy and labor of the unfallen parents of the race. Was this garden, then, the Eden of the present world?—and this man, with such a perception of harm in what his own hands caused to grow, was he the Adam?

The distrustful gardener, while plucking away the dead leaves or pruning the too luxuriant growth of the shrubs, defended his hands with a pair of thick gloves. Nor were these his only armor. When, in his walk through the garden, he came to the magnificent plant that hung its purple gems beside the marble fountain, he placed a kind of mask over his mouth and nostrils, as if all this beauty did but conceal a deadlier malice. But finding his task still too danger-ous, he drew back, removed the mask, and called loudly, but in the infirm voice of a person affected with inward disease:

"Beatrice!—Beatrice!"

"Here am I, my father! What would you?" cried a rich and youthful voice from the window of the opposite house; a voice as rich as a tropical sunset, and which made Giovanni, though he knew not why, think of deep hues of purple or crimson, and of perfumes heavily delectable.—"Are you in the garden?"

"Yes, Beatrice," answered the gardener, "and I need your help."

Soon there emerged from under a sculptured portal the figure of a young girl, arrayed with as much richness of taste as the most splendid of the flowers, beautiful as the day, and with a bloom so deep and vivid that one shade more would have been too much. She looked redundant with life, health, and energy; all of which attributes were bound down and compressed, as it were, and girdled tensely, in their luxuriance, by her virgin zone.[8] Yet Giovanni's fancy must have grown morbid, while he looked down into the garden; for the impression which the fair stranger made upon him was as if here were another flower, the human sister of those vegetable ones, as beautiful as they—more beautiful than the richest of them—but still to be touched only with a glove, nor to be approached without a mask. As Beatrice came down the garden-path, it was observable that she handled and inhaled the odor of several of the plants, which her father had most sedulously avoided.

"Here, Beatrice," said the latter,—"see how many needful offices require to be done to our chief treasure. Yet, shattered as I am, my life might pay the penalty of approaching it so closely as circumstances demand. Henceforth, I fear, this plant must be consigned to your sole charge."

"And gladly will I undertake it," cried again the rich tones of the young lady, as she bent towards the magnificent plant, and opened her arms as if to embrace it. "Yes, my sister, my splendor, it shall be Beatrice's task to nurse and serve thee; and thou shalt reward her with thy kisses and perfumed breath, which to her is as the breath of life!"

8. Wide girdlelike belt customarily worn by unmarried girls.

Then, with all the tenderness in her manner that was so strikingly expressed in her words, she busied herself with such attentions as the plant seemed to require; and Giovanni, at his lofty window, rubbed his eyes, and almost doubted whether it were a girl tending her favorite flower, or one sister performing the duties of affection to another. The scene soon terminated. Whether Doctor Rappaccini had finished his labors in the garden, or that his watchful eye had caught the stranger's face, he now took his daughter's arm and retired. Night was already closing in; oppressive exhalations seemed to proceed from the plants, and steal upward past the open window; and Giovanni, closing the lattice, went to his couch, and dreamed of a rich flower and beautiful girl. Flower and maiden were different and yet the same, and fraught with some strange peril in either shape.

But there is an influence in the light of morning that tends to rectify whatever errors of fancy, or even of judgment, we may have incurred during the sun's decline, or among the shadows of the night, or in the less wholesome glow of moonshine. Giovanni's first movement on starting from sleep, was to throw open the window, and gaze down into the garden which his dreams had made so fertile of mysteries. He was surprised, and a little ashamed, to find how real and matter-of-fact an affair it proved to be, in the first rays of the sun, which gilded the dew-drops that hung upon leaf and blossom, and, while giving a brighter beauty to each rare flower, brought everything within the limits of ordinary experience. The young man rejoiced, that, in the heart of the barren city, he had the privilege of overlooking this spot of lovely and luxuriant vegetation. It would serve, he said to himself, as a symbolic language, to keep him in communion with nature. Neither the sickly and thought-worn Doctor Giacomo Rappaccini, it is true, nor his brilliant daughter were now visible; so that Giovanni could not determine how much of the singularity which he attributed to both, was due to their own qualities, and how much to his wonder-working fancy. But he was inclined to take a most rational view of the whole matter.

In the course of the day, he paid his respects to Signor Pietro Baglioni, professor of medicine in the University, a physician of eminent repute, to whom Giovanni had brought a letter of introduction. The professor was an elderly personage, apparently of genial nature, and habits that might almost be called jovial; he kept the young man to dinner, and made himself very agreeable by the freedom and liveliness of his conversation, especially when warmed by a flask or two of Tuscan wine. Giovanni, conceiving that men of science, inhabitants of the same city, must needs be on familiar terms with one another, took an opportunity to mention the name of Dr. Rappaccini. But the professor did not respond with so much cordiality as he had anticipated.

"Ill would it become a teacher of the divine art of medicine," said Professor Pietro Baglioni, in answer to a question of Giovanni, "to withhold due and well-considered praise of a physician so eminently skilled as Rappaccini. But, on the other hand, I should answer it but scantily to my conscience, were I to permit a worthy youth like yourself, Signor Giovanni, the son of an ancient friend, to imbibe erroneous ideas respecting a man who might hereafter chance to hold your life and death in his hands. The truth is, our worshipful Doctor Rappaccini has as much science as any member of the faculty—with perhaps one single exception—in Padua, or all Italy. But there are certain grave objections to his professional character."

"And what are they?" asked the young man.

"Has my friend Giovanni any disease of body or heart, that he is so inquisitive about physicians?" said the Professor, with a smile. "But as for Rappaccini, it is said of him—and I, who know the man well, can answer for its truth—that he cares infinitely more for science than for mankind. His patients are interesting to him only as subjects for some new experiment. He would sacrifice human life, his own among the rest, or whatever else was dearest to him, for the sake of adding so much as a grain of mustard-seed to the great heap of his accumulated knowledge."

"Methinks he is an awful[9] man, indeed," remarked Guasconti, mentally recalling the cold and purely intellectual aspect of Rappaccini. "And yet, worshipful Professor, is it not a noble spirit? Are there many men capable of so spiritual a love of science?"

"God forbid," answered the Professor, somewhat testily—"at least, unless they take sounder views of the healing art than those adopted by Rappaccini. It is his theory, that all medicinal virtues are comprised within those substances which we term vegetable poisons. These he cultivates with his own hands, and is said even to have produced new varieties of poison, more horribly deleterious than Nature, without the assistance of this learned person, would ever have plagued the world with. That the signor Doctor does less mischief than might be expected, with such dangerous substances, is undeniable. Now and then, it must be owned, he has effected—or seemed to effect—a marvellous cure. But, to tell you my private mind, Signor Giovanni, he should receive little credit for such instances of success—they being probably the work of chance—but should be held strictly accountable for his failures, which may justly be considered his own work."

The youth might have taken Baglioni's opinions with many grains of allowance, had he known that there was a professional warfare of long continuance between him and Doctor Rappaccini, in which the latter was generally thought to have gained the advantage. If the reader be inclined to judge for himself, we refer him to certain black-letter tracts on both sides, preserved in the medical department of the University of Padua.

"I know not, most learned Professor," returned Giovanni, after musing on what had been said of Rappaccini's exclusive zeal for science—"I know not how dearly this physician may love his art; but surely there is one object more dear to him. He has a daughter."

"Aha!" cries the Professor with a laugh. "So now our friend Giovanni's secret is out. You have heard of this daughter, whom all the young men in Padua are wild about, though not half a dozen have ever had the good hap to see her face. I know little of the Signora Beatrice, save that Rappaccini is said to have instructed her deeply in his science, and that, young and beautiful as fame reports her, she is already qualified to fill a professor's chair. Perchance her father destines her for mine! Other absurd rumors there be, not worth talking about, or listening to. So now, Signor Giovanni, drink off your glass of Lacryma."[1]

Guasconti returned to his lodgings somewhat heated with the wine he had quaffed, and which caused his brain to swim with strange fantasies in reference to Doctor Rappaccini and the beautiful Beatrice. On his way, happening to pass by a florist's, he bought a fresh bouquet of flowers.

9. The word carries some of the sense of "awe-striking."   1. A still Italian wine grown near Vesuvius.

Ascending to his chamber, he seated himself near the window, but within the shadow thrown by the depth of the wall, so that he could look down into the garden with little risk of being discovered. All beneath his eye was a solitude. The strange plants were basking in the sunshine, and now and then nodding gently to one another, as if in acknowledgment of sympathy and kindred. In the midst, by the shattered fountain, grew the magnificent shrub, with its purple gems clustering all over it; they glowed in the air, and gleamed back again out of the depths of the pool, which thus seemed to overflow with colored radiance from the rich reflection that was steeped in it. At first, as we have said, the garden was a solitude. Soon, however,—as Giovanni had half-hoped, half-feared, would be the case,—a figure appeared beneath the antique sculptured portal, and came down between the rows of plants, inhaling their various perfumes, as if she were one of those beings of old classic fable, that lived upon sweet odors. On again beholding Beatrice, the young man was even startled to perceive how much her beauty exceeded his recollection of it; so brilliant, so vivid in its character, that she glowed amid the sunlight, and, as Giovanni whispered to himself, positively illuminated the more shadowy intervals of the garden path. Her face being now more revealed than on the former occasion, he was struck by its expression of simplicity and sweetness; qualities that had not entered into his idea of her character, and which made him ask anew, what manner of mortal she might be. Nor did he fail again to observe, or imagine, an analogy between the beautiful girl and the gorgeous shrub that hung its gem-like flowers over the fountain; a resemblance which Beatrice seemed to have indulged a fantastic humor in heightening, both by the arrangement of her dress and the selection of its hues.

Approaching the shrub, she threw open her arms, as with a passionate ardor, and drew its branches into an intimate embrace; so intimate, that her features were hidden in its leafy bosom, and her glistening ringlets all intermingled with the flowers.

"Give me thy breath, my sister," exclaimed Beatrice; "for I am faint with common air! And give me this flower of thine, which I separate with gentlest fingers from the stem, and place it close beside my heart."

With these words, the beautiful daughter of Rappaccini plucked one of the richest blossoms of the shrub, and was about to fasten it in her bosom. But now, unless Giovanni's draughts of wine had bewildered his senses, a singular incident occurred. A small orange-colored reptile of the lizard or chameleon species, chanced to be creeping along the path, just at the feet of Beatrice. It appeared to Giovanni—but, at the distance from which he gazed, he could scarcely have seen anything so minute—it appeared to him, however, that a drop or two of moisture from the broken stem of the flower descended upon the lizard's head. For an instant, the reptile contorted itself violently, and then lay motionless in the sunshine. Beatrice observed this remarkable phenomenon, and crossed herself, sadly, but without surprise; nor did she therefore hesitate to arrange the fatal flower in her bosom. There it blushed, and almost glimmered with the dazzling effect of a precious stone, adding to her dress and aspect the one appropriate charm, which nothing else in the world could have supplied. But Giovanni, out of the shadow of his window bent forward and shrank back, and murmured and trembled.

"Am I awake? Have I my senses?" said he to himself. "What is this being?—beautiful, shall I call her?—or inexpressibly terrible?"

Beatrice now strayed carelessly through the garden, approaching closer beneath Giovanni's window, so that he was compelled to thrust his head quite out of its concealment in order to gratify the intense and painful curiosity which she excited. At this moment, there came a beautiful insect over the garden wall; it had perhaps wandered through the city and found no flowers nor verdure among those antique haunts of men, until the heavy perfumes of Doctor Rappaccini's shrubs had lured it from afar. Without alighting on the flowers, this winged brightness seemed to be attracted by Beatrice, and lingered in the air and fluttered about her head. Now here it could not be but that Giovanni Guasconti's eyes deceived him. Be that as it might, he fancied that while Beatrice was gazing at the insect with childish delight, it grew faint and fell at her feet!—its bright wings shivered! it was dead!—from no cause that he could discern, unless it were the atmosphere of her breath. Again Beatrice crossed herself and sighed heavily, as she bent over the dead insect.

An impulsive movement of Giovanni drew her eyes to the window. There she beheld the beautiful head of the young man—rather a Grecian than an Italian head, with fair, regular features, and a glistening of gold among his ringlets—gazing down upon her like a being that hovered in mid-air. Scarcely knowing what he did, Giovanni threw down the bouquet which he had hitherto held in his hand.

"Signora," said he, "there are pure and healthful flowers. Wear them for the sake of Giovanni Guasconti!"

"Thanks, Signor," replied Beatrice, with her rich voice, that came forth as it were like a gush of music; and with a mirthful expression half childish and half woman-like. "I accept your gift, and would fain recompense it with this precious purple flower; but if I toss it into the air, it will not reach you. So Signor Guasconti must even content himself with my thanks."

She lifted the bouquet from the ground, and then as if inwardly ashamed at having stepped aside from her maidenly reserve to respond to a stranger's greeting, passed swiftly homeward through the garden. But, few as the moments were, it seemed to Giovanni when she was on the point of vanishing beneath the sculptured portal, that his beautiful bouquet was already beginning to wither in her grasp. It was an idle thought; there could be no possibility of distinguishing a faded flower from a fresh one at so great a distance.

For many days after the incident, the young man avoided the window that looked into Doctor Rappaccini's garden, as if something ugly and monstrous would have blasted his eye-sight, had he been betrayed into a glance. He felt conscious of having put himself, to a certain extent, within the influence of an unintelligible power, by the communication which he had opened with Beatrice. The wisest course would have been, if his heart were in any real danger, to quit his lodgings and Padua itself, at once; the next wiser, to have accustomed himself, as far as possible, to the familiar and day-light view of Beatrice; thus bringing her rigidly and systematically within the limits of ordinary experience. Least of all, while avoiding her sight, should Giovanni have remained so near this extraordinary being, that the proximity and possibility even of intercourse, should give a kind of substance and reality to the wild vagaries which his imagination ran riot continually in producing. Guasconti had not a deep heart—or at all events, its depths were not sounded now—but he had a quick fancy, and an ardent southern temperament, which rose every instant to a higher fever-pitch. Whether or no Beatrice possessed those terrible attributes—that fatal breath—the affinity with those so beautiful and deadly flowers—which were indicated by what Giovanni had witnessed, she had at least instilled a fierce and subtle poison into his sytem. It was not love, although her rich beauty was a madness to him; nor horror, even while he fancied her spirit to be imbued with the same baneful essence that seemed to pervade her physical frame; but a wild offspring of both love and horror that had each parent in it, and burned like one and shivered like the other. Giovanni knew not what to dread; still less did he know what to hope; *hope* and *dread* kept a continual warfare in his breast, alternately vanquishing one another and starting up afresh to renew the contest. Blessed are all simple emotions, be they dark or bright! It is the lurid intermixture of the two that produces the illuminating blaze of the infernal regions.

Sometimes he endeavored to assuage the fever of his spirit by a rapid walk through the streets of Padua, or beyond its gates; his footsteps kept time with the throbbings of his brain, so that the walk was apt to accelerate itself to a race. One day, he found himself arrested; his arm was seized by a portly personage who had turned back on recognizing the young man, and expended much breath in overtaking him.

"Signor Giovanni!—stay, my young friend!" cried he. "Have you forgotten me? That might well be the case, if I were as much altered as yourself."

It was Baglioni, whom Giovanni had avoided, ever since their first meeting, from a doubt that the professor's sagacity would look too deeply into his secrets. Endeavoring to recover himself, he stared forth wildly from his inner world into the outer one, and spoke like a man in a dream:

"Yes; I am Giovanni Guasconti. You are Professor Pietro Baglioni. Now let me pass!"

"Not yet—not yet, Signor Giovanni Guasconti," said the Professor, smiling, but at the same time scrutinizing the youth with an earnest glance.—"What; did I grow up side by side with your father, and shall his son pass me like a stranger, in these old streets of Padua? Stand still, Signor Giovanni; for we must have a word or two, before we part."

"Speedily, then, most worshipful Professor, speedily!" said Giovanni, with feverish impatience. "Does not your worship see that I am in haste?"

Now, while he was speaking, there came a man in black along the street, stooping and moving feebly, like a person in inferior health. His face was all overspread with a most sickly and sallow hue, but yet so pervaded with an expression of piercing and active intellect, that an observer might easily have overlooked the merely physical attributes, and have seen only this wonderful energy. As he passed, this person exchanged a cold and distant salutation with Baglioni, but fixed his eyes upon Giovanni with an intentness that seemed to bring out whatever was within him worthy of notice. Nevertheless, there was a peculiar quietness in the look, as if taking merely a speculative, not a human interest, in the young man.

"It is Doctor Rappaccini!" whispered the Professor, when the stranger had passed.—"Has he ever seen your face before?"

"Not that I know," answered Giovanni, starting at the name.

"He *has* seen you!—he must have seen you!" said Baglioni, hastily. "For some purpose or other, this man of science is making a study of you. I know that look of his! It is the same that coldly illuminates his face, as he bends over a bird, a mouse, or a butterfly, which, in pursuance of some experiment, he has killed by the perfume of a flower;—a look as deep as nature itself, but without nature's warmth of love. Signor Giovanni, I will stake my life upon it, you are the subject of one of Rappaccini's experiments!"

"Will you make a fool of me?" cried Giovanni, passionately. "*That*, Signor Professor, were an untoward experiment."

"Patience, patience!" replied the imperturbable Professor.—"I tell thee, my poor Giovanni, that Rappaccini has a scientific interest in thee. Thou hast fallen into fearful hands! And the Signora Beatrice? What part does she act in this mystery?"

But Guasconti, finding Baglioni's pertinacity intolerable, here broke away, and was gone before the Professor could again seize his arm. He looked after the young man intently, and shook his head.

"This must not be," said Baglioni to himself. "The youth is the son of my old friend, and should not come to any harm from which the arcana of medical science can preserve him. Besides, it is too insufferable an impertinence in Rappaccini, thus to snatch the bud out of my own hands, as I may say, and make use of him for his infernal experiments. This daughter of his! It shall be looked to. Perchance, most learned Rappaccini, I may foil you where you little dream of it!"

Meanwhile, Giovanni had pursued a circuitous route, and at length found himself at the door of his lodgings. As he crossed the threshold, he was met by old Lisabetta, who smirked and smiled, and was evidently desirous to attract his attention; vainly, however, as the ebullition of his feelings had momentarily subsided into a cold and dull vacuity. He turned his eyes full upon the withered face that was puckering itself into a smile, but seemed to behold it not. The old dame, therefore, laid her grasp upon his cloak.

"Signor!—Signor!" whispered she, still with a smile over the whole breadth of her visage, so that it looked not unlike a grotesque carving in wood, darkened by centuries—"Listen, Signor! There is a private entrance into the garden!"

"What do you say?" exclaimed Giovanni, turning quickly about, as if an inanimate thing should start into feverish life.—"A private entrance into Doctor Rappaccini's garden!"

"Hush! hush!—not so loud!" whispered Lisabetta, putting her hand over his mouth. "Yes; into the worshipful Doctor's garden, where you may see all his fine shrubbery. Many a young man in Padua would give gold to be admitted among those flowers."

Giovanni put a piece of gold into her hand.

"Show me the way," said he.

A surmise, probably excited by his conversation with Baglioni, crossed his mind, that this interposition of old Lisabetta might perchance be connected with the intrigue, whatever were its nature, in which the Professor seemed to suppose that Doctor Rappaccini was involving him. But such a suspicion, though it disturbed Giovanni, was inadequate to restrain him. The instant he was aware of the possibility of approaching Beatrice, it seemed an absolute necessity of his existence to do so. It mattered not whether she were angel or demon; he was irrevocably within her sphere, and must obey the law that whirled him onward, in ever lessening circles, towards a result which he did not attempt to foreshadow. And yet, strange to say, there came across him a sudden doubt, whether this intense interest on his part were not delusory—whether it were really of so deep and positive a nature as to justify him in now

thrusting himself into an incalculable position—whether it were not merely
the fantasy of a young man's brain, only slightly, or not at all, connected with
his heart!

He paused—hesitated—turned half about—but again went on. His withered
guide led him along several obscure passages, and finally undid a door,
through which, as it was opened, there came the sight and sound of rustling
leaves, with the broken sunshine glimmering among them. Giovanni stepped
forth, and forcing himself through the entanglement of a shrub that wreathed
its tendrils over the hidden entrance, he stood beneath his own window, in
the open area of Doctor Rappaccini's garden.

How often is it the case, that, when impossibilities have come to pass, and
dreams have condensed their misty substance into tangible realities, we find
ourselves calm, and even coldly self-possessed, amid circumstances which it
would have been a delirium of joy or agony to anticipate! Fate delights to
thwart us thus. Passion will choose his own time to rush upon the scene, and
lingers sluggishly behind, when an appropriate adjustment of events would
seem to summon his appearance. So was it now with Giovanni. Day after day,
his pulses had throbbed with feverish blood, at the improbable idea of an
interview with Beatrice, and of standing with her, face to face, in this very
garden, basking in the oriental sunshine of her beauty, and snatching from her
full gaze the mystery which he deemed the riddle of his own existence. But
now there was a singular and untimely equanimity within his breast. He threw
a glance around the garden to discover if Beatrice or her father were present,
and perceiving that he was alone, began a critical observation of the plants.

The aspect of one and all of them dissatisfied him; their gorgeousness
seemed fierce, passionate, and even unnatural. There was hardly an individual
shrub which a wanderer, straying by himself through a forest, would not have
been startled to find growing wild, as if an unearthly face had glared at him
out of the thicket. Several, also, would have shocked a delicate instinct by an
appearance of artificialness, indicating that there had been such commixture,
and, as it were, adultery of various vegetable species, that the production was
no longer of God's making, but the monstrous offspring of man's depraved
fancy, glowing with only an evil mockery of beauty. They were probably the
result of experiment, which, in one or two cases, had succeeded in mingling
plants individually lovely into a compound possessing the questionable and
ominous character that distinguished the whole growth of the garden. In fine,
Giovanni recognized but two or three plants in the collection, and those of a
kind that he well knew to be poisonous. While busy with these contemplations, he heard the rustling of a silken garment, and turning, beheld Beatrice
emerging from beneath the sculptured portal.

Giovanni had not considered with himself what should be his deportment;
whether he should apologize for his intrusion into the garden, or assume that
he was there with the privity, at least, if not the desire of Doctor Rappaccini
or his daughter. But Beatrice's manner placed him at his ease, though leaving
him still in doubt by what agency he had gained admittance. She came lightly
along the path, and met him near the broken fountain. There was surprise in
her face, but brightened by a simple and kind expression of pleasure.

"You are a connoisseur in flowers, Signor," said Beatrice with a smile,
alluding to the bouquet which he had flung her from the window. "It is no
marvel, therefore, if the sight of my father's rare collection has tempted you to

take a nearer view. If he were here, he could tell you many strange and interesting facts as to the nature and habits of these shrubs, for he has spent a lifetime in such studies, and this garden is his world."

"And yourself, lady"—observed Giovanni—"if fame says true—you, likewise, are deeply skilled in the virtues indicated by these rich blossoms, and these spicy perfumes. Would you deign to be my instructress, I should prove an apter scholar than under Signor Rappaccini himself."

"Are there such idle rumors?" asked Beatrice, with the music of a pleasant laugh. "Do people say that I am skilled in my father's science of plants? What a jest is there! No; though I have grown up among these flowers, I know no more of them than their hues and perfume; and sometimes, methinks I would fain rid myself of even that small knowledge. There are many flowers here, and those not the least brilliant, that shock and offend me, when they meet my eye. But, pray, Signor, do not believe these stories about my science. Believe nothing of me save what you see with your own eyes."

"And must I believe all that I have seen with my own eyes?" asked Giovanni pointedly, while the recollection of former scenes made him shrink. "No, Signora, you demand too little of me. Bid me believe nothing, save what comes from your own lips."

It would appear that Beatrice understood him. There came a deep flush to her cheek; but she looked full into Giovanni's eyes, and responded to his gaze of uneasy suspicion with a queen-like haughtiness.

"I do so bid you, Signor!" she replied. "Forget whatever you may have fancied in regard to me. If true to the outward senses, still it may be false in its essence. But the words of Beatrice Rappaccini's lips are true from the heart outward. Those you may believe!"

A fervor glowed in her whole aspect, and beamed upon Giovanni's consciousness like the light of truth itself. But while she spoke, there was a fragrance in the atmosphere around her, rich and delightful, though evanescent, yet which the young man, from an indefinable reluctance, scarcely dared to draw into his lungs. It might be the odor of the flowers. Could it be Beatrice's breath, which thus embalmed her words with a strange richness, as if by steeping them in her heart? A faintness passed like a shadow over Giovanni, and flitted away; he seemed to gaze through the beautiful girl's eyes into her transparent soul, and felt no more doubt or fear.

The tinge of passion that had colored Beatrice's manner vanished; she became gay, and appeared to derive a pure delight from her communion with the youth, not unlike what the maiden of a lonely island might have felt, conversing with a voyager from the civilized world. Evidently her experience of life had been confined within the limits of that garden. She talked now about matters as simple as the day-light or summer-clouds, and now asked questions in reference to the city, or Giovanni's distant home, his friends, his mother, and his sisters; questions indicating such seclusion, and such lack of familiarity with modes and forms, that Giovanni responded as if to an infant. Her spirit gushed out before him like a fresh rill, that was just catching its first glimpse of the sunlight, and wondering at the reflections of earth and sky which were flung into its bosom. There came thoughts, too, from a deep source, and fantasies of a gem-like brilliancy, as if diamonds and rubies sparkled upward among the bubbles of the fountain. Ever and anon, there gleamed across the young man's mind a sense of wonder, that he should be walking side by side with the being who had so wrought upon his imagination—whom he had idealized in such hues of terror—in whom he had positively witnessed such manifestations of dreadful attributes—that he should be conversing with Beatrice like a brother, and should find her so human and so maiden-like. But such reflections were only momentary; the effect of her character was too real, not to make itself familiar at once.

In this free intercourse, they had strayed through the garden, and now, after many turns among its avenues, were come to the shattered fountain, beside which grew the magnificent shrub with its treasury of glowing blossoms. A fragrance was diffused from it, which Giovanni recognized as identical with that which he had attributed to Beatrice's breath, but incomparably more powerful. As her eyes fell upon it, Giovanni beheld her press her hand to her bosom, as if her heart were throbbing suddenly and painfully.

"For the first time in my life," murmured she, addressing the shrub, "I had forgotten thee!"

"I remember, Signora," said Giovanni, "that you once promised to reward me with one of these living gems for the bouquet, which I had the happy boldness to fling to your feet. Permit me now to pluck it as a memorial of this interview."

He made a step towards the shrub, with extended hand. But Beatrice darted forward, uttering a shriek that went through his heart like a dagger. She caught his hand, and drew it back with the whole force of her slender figure. Giovanni felt her touch thrilling through his fibres.

"Touch it not!" exclaimed she, in a voice of agony. "Not for thy life! It is fatal!"

Then, hiding her face, she fled from him, and vanished beneath the sculptured portal. As Giovanni followed her with his eyes, he beheld the emaciated figure and pale intelligence of Doctor Rappaccini, who had been watching the scene, he knew not how long, within the shadow of the entrance.

No sooner was Guasconti alone in his chamber, than the image of Beatrice came back to his passionate musings, invested with all the witchery that had been gathering around it ever since his first glimpse of her, and now likewise imbued with a tender warmth of girlish womanhood. She was human: her nature was endowed with all gentle and feminine qualities; she was worthiest to be worshipped; she was capable, surely, on her part, of the height and heroism of love. Those tokens, which he had hitherto considered as proofs of a frightful peculiarity in her physical and moral system, were now either forgotten, or, by the subtle sophistry of passion, transmuted into a golden crown of enchantment, rendering Beatrice the more admirable, by so much as she was the more unique. Whatever had looked ugly, was now beautiful; or, if incapable of such a change, it stole away and hid itself among those shapeless half-ideas, which throng the dim region beyond the day-light of our perfect consciousness. Thus did Giovanni spend the night, nor fell asleep, until the dawn had begun to awake the slumbering flowers in Doctor Rappaccini's garden, whither his dreams doubtless led him. Up rose the sun in his due season, and flinging his beams upon the young man's eyelids, awoke him to a sense of pain. When thoroughly aroused, he became sensible of a burning and tingling agony in his hand—in his right hand—the very hand which Beatrice had grasped in her own, when he was on the point of plucking one of the gem-like flowers. On the back of that hand there was now a purple print, like that of four small fingers, and the likeness of a slender thumb upon his wrist.

Oh, how stubbornly does love—or even that cunning semblance of love which flourishes in the imagination, but strikes no depth of root into the heart—how stubbornly does it hold its faith, until the moment come, when it is doomed to vanish into thin mist! Giovanni wrapt a handkerchief about his hand, and wondered what evil thing had stung him, and soon forgot his pain in a reverie of Beatrice.

After the first interview, a second was in the inevitable course of what we call fate. A third; a fourth; and a meeting with Beatrice in the garden was no longer an incident in Giovanni's daily life, but the whole space in which he might be said to live; for the anticipation and memory of that ecstatic hour made up the remainder. Nor was it otherwise with the daughter of Rappaccini. She watched for the youth's appearance, and flew to his side with confidence as unreserved as if they had been playmates from early infancy—as if they were such playmates still. If, by any unwonted chance, he failed to come at the appointed moment, she stood beneath the window, and sent up the rich sweetness of her tones to float around him in his chamber, and echo and reverberate throughout his heart—"Giovanni! Giovanni! Why tarriest thou? Come down!"—And down he hastened into that Eden of poisonous flowers.

But, with all this intimate familiarity, there was still a reserve in Beatrice's demeanor, so rigidly and invariably sustained, that the idea of infringing it scarcely occurred to his imagination. By all appreciable signs, they loved; they had looked love, with eyes that conveyed the holy secret from the depths of one soul into the depths of the other, as if it were too sacred to be whispered by the way; they had even spoken love, in those gushes of passion when their spirits darted forth in articulated breath, like tongues of long-hidden flame; and yet there had been no seal of lips, no clasp of hands, nor any slightest caress, such as love claims and hallows. He had never touched one of the gleaming ringlets of her hair; her garment—so marked was the physical barrier between them—had never been waved against him by a breeze. On the few occasions when Giovanni had seemed tempted to overstep the limit, Beatrice grew so sad, so stern, and withal wore such a look of desolate separation, shuddering at itself, that not a spoken word was requisite to repel him. At such times, he was startled at the horrible suspicions that rose, monster-like, out of the caverns of his heart, and stared him in the face; his love grew thin and faint as the morning-mist; his doubts alone had substance. But when Beatrice's face brightened again, after the momentary shadow, she was transformed at once from the mysterious, questionable being, whom he had watched with so much awe and horror; she was now the beautiful and unsophisticated girl, whom he felt that his spirit knew with a certainty beyond all other knowledge.

A considerable time had now passed since Giovanni's last meeting with Baglioni. One morning, however, he was disagreeably surprised by a visit from the Professor, whom he had scarcely thought of for whole weeks, and would willingly have forgotten still longer. Given up, as he had long been, to a pervading excitement, he could tolerate no companions, except upon condition of their perfect sympathy with his present state of feeling. Such sympathy was not to be expected from Professor Baglioni.

The visitor chatted carelessly, for a few moments, about the gossip of the city and the University, and then took up another topic.

"I have been reading an old classic author lately," said he, "and met with a story[2] that strangely interested me. Possibly you may remember it. It is of an

---

2. In Sir Thomas Browne's *Vulgar Errors* (1646) or elsewhere.

Indian prince, who sent a beautiful woman as a present to Alexander the
Great. She was as lovely as the dawn, and gorgeous as the sunset; but what
especially distinguished her was a certain rich perfume in her breath—richer
than a garden of Persian roses. Alexander, as was natural to a youthful conqueror, fell in love at first sight with this magnificent stranger. But a certain
sage physician, happening to be present, discovered a terrible secret in regard
to her."

"And what was that?" asked Giovanni, turning his eyes downward to avoid
those of the Professor.

"That this lovely woman," continued Baglioni, with emphasis, "had been
nourished with poisons from her birth upward, until her whole nature was so
imbued with them, that she herself had become the deadliest poison in existence. Poison was her element of life. With that rich perfume of her breath,
she blasted the very air. Her love would have been poison!—her embrace
death! Is not this a marvellous tale?"

"A childish fable," answered Giovanni, nervously starting from his chair.
"I marvel how your worship finds time to read such nonsense, among your
graver studies."

"By the by," said the Professor, looking uneasily about him, "what singular
fragrance is this in your apartment? Is it the perfume of your gloves? It is faint,
but delicious, and yet, after all, by no means agreeable. Were I to breathe it
long, methinks it would make me ill. It is like the breath of a flower—but I
see no flowers in the chamber."

"Nor are there any," replied Giovanni, who had turned pale as the Professor
spoke; "nor, I think, is there any fragrance, except in your worship's imagination. Odors, being a sort of element combined of the sensual and the spiritual,
are apt to deceive us in this manner. The recollection of a perfume—the bare
idea of it—may easily be mistaken for a present reality."

"Aye; but my sober imagination does not often play such tricks," said Baglioni; "and were I to fancy any kind of odor, it would be that of some vile
apothecary drug, wherewith my fingers are likely enough to be imbued. Our
worshipful friend Rappaccini, as I have heard, tinctures his medicaments with
odors richer than those of Araby. Doubtless, likewise, the fair and learned
Signora Beatrice would minister to her patients with draughts as sweet as a
maiden's breath. But wo to him that sips them!"

Giovanni's face evinced many contending emotions. The tone in which the
Professor alluded to the pure and lovely daughter of Rappaccini was a torture
to his soul; and yet, the intimation of a view of her character, opposite to his
own, gave instantaneous distinctness to a thousand dim suspicions, which now
grinned at him like so many demons. But he strove hard to quell them, and
to respond to Baglioni with a true lover's perfect faith.

"Signor Professor," said he, "you were my father's friend—perchance, too,
it is your purpose to act a friendly part towards his son. I would fain feel
nothing towards you, save respect and deference. But I pray you to observe,
Signor, that there is one subject on which we must not speak. You know not
the Signora Beatrice. You cannot, therefore, estimate the wrong—the blasphemy, I may even say—that is offered to her character by a light or injurious word."

"Giovanni!—my poor Giovanni!" answered the Professor, with a calm
expression of pity, "I know this wretched girl far better than yourself. You shall
hear the truth in respect to the poisoner Rappaccini, and his poisonous daugh-

ter. Yes; poisonous as she is beautiful! Listen; for even should you do violence to my grey hairs, it shall not silence me. That old fable of the Indian woman has become a truth, by the deep and deadly science of Rappaccini, and in the person of the lovely Beatrice!"

Giovanni groaned and hid his face.

"Her father," continued Baglioni, "was not restrained by natural affection from offering up his child, in this horrible manner, as the victim of his insane zeal for science. For—let us do him justice—he is as true a man of science as ever distilled his own heart in an alembic. What, then, will be your fate? Beyond a doubt, you are selected as the material of some new experiment. Perhaps the result is to be death—perhaps a fate more awful still! Rappaccini, with what he calls the interest of science before his eyes, will hesitate at nothing."

"It is a dream!" muttered Giovanni to himself, "surely it is a dream!"

"But," resumed the professor, "be of good cheer, son of my friend! It is not yet too late for the rescue. Possibly, we may even succeed in bringing back this miserable child within the limits of ordinary nature, from which her father's madness has estranged her. Behold this little silver vase! It was wrought by the hands of the renowned Benvenuto Cellini,[3] and is well worthy to be a love-gift to the fairest dame in Italy. But its contents are invaluable. One little sip of this antidote would have rendered the most virulent poisons of the Borgias[4] innocuous. Doubt not that it will be as efficacious against those of Rappaccini. Bestow the vase, and the precious liquid within it, on your Beatrice, and hopefully await the result."

Baglioni laid a small, exquisitely wrought silver phial on the table, and withdrew, leaving what he had said to produce its effect upon the young man's mind.

"We will thwart Rappaccini yet!" thought he, chuckling to himself, as he descended the stairs. "But, let us confess the truth of him, he is a wonderful man!—a wonderful man indeed! A vile empiric, however, in his practice, and therefore not to be tolerated by those who respect the good old rules of the medical profession!"

Throughout Giovanni's whole acquaintance with Beatrice, he had occasionally, as we have said, been haunted by dark surmises as to her character. Yet, so thoroughly had she made herself felt by him as a simple, natural, most affectionate and guileless creature, that the image now held up by Professor Baglioni, looked as strange and incredible, as if it were not in accordance with his own original conception. True, there were ugly recollections connected with his first glimpses of the beautiful girl; he could not quite forget the bouquet that withered in her grasp, and the insect that perished amid the sunny air, by no ostensible agency, save the fragrance of her breath. These incidents, however, dissolving in the pure light of her character, had no longer the efficacy of facts, but were acknowledged as mistaken fantasies, by whatever testimony of the senses they might appear to be substantiated. There is something truer and more real, than what we can see with the eyes, and touch with the finger. On such better evidence, had Giovanni founded his confidence in Beatrice, though rather by the necessary force of her high attributes, than by any deep and generous faith, on his part. But, now, his spirit was incapable of

3. Italian goldsmith and sculptor (1500–1571).
4. Renaissance Italian family influential in church and government and notorious for cruelty and licentiousness.

sustaining itself at the height to which the early enthusiasm of passion had exalted it; he fell down, grovelling among earthly doubts, and defiled therewith the pure whiteness of Beatrice's image. Not that he gave her up; he did but distrust. He resolved to institute some decisive test that should satisfy him, once for all, whether there were those dreadful peculiarities in her physical nature, which could not be supposed to exist without some corresponding monstrosity of soul. His eyes, gazing down afar, might have deceived him as to the lizard, the insect, and the flowers. But if he could witness, at the distance of a few paces, the sudden blight of one fresh and healthful flower in Beatrice's hand, there would be room for no further question. With this idea, he hastened to the florist's, and purchased a bouquet that was still gemmed with the morning dew-drops.

It was now the customary hour of his daily interview with Beatrice. Before descending into the garden, Giovanni failed not to look at his figure in the mirror; a vanity to be expected in a beautiful young man, yet, as displaying itself at that troubled and feverish moment, the token of a certain shallowness of feeling and insincerity of character. He did gaze, however, and said to himself, that his features had never before possessed so rich a grace, nor his eyes such vivacity, nor his cheeks so warm a hue of superabundant life.

"At least," thought he, "her poison has not yet insinuated itself into my system. I am no flower to perish in her grasp!"

With that thought, he turned his eyes on the bouquet, which he had never once laid aside from his hand. A thrill of indefinable horror shot through his frame, on perceiving that those dewy flowers were already beginning to droop; they wore the aspect of things that had been fresh and lovely, yesterday. Giovanni grew white as marble, and stood motionless before the mirror, staring at his own reflection there, as at the likeness of something frightful. He remembered Baglioni's remark about the fragrance that seemed to pervade the chamber. It must have been the poison in his breath! Then he shuddered— shuddered at himself! Recovering from his stupor, he began to watch, with curious eye, a spider that was busily at work, hanging its web from the antique cornice of the apartment, crossing and re-crossing the artful system of interwoven lines, as vigorous and active a spider as ever dangled from an old ceiling. Giovanni bent towards the insect, and emitted a deep, long breath. The spider suddenly ceased its toil; the web vibrated with a tremor originating in the body of the small artizan. Again Giovanni sent forth a breath, deeper, longer, and imbued with a venomous feeling out of his heart; he knew not whether he were wicked or only desperate. The spider made a convulsive gripe with his limbs, and hung dead across the window.

"Accursed! Accursed!" muttered Giovanni, addressing himself. "Hast thou grown so poisonous, that this deadly insect perishes by the breath?"

At that moment, a rich, sweet voice came floating up from the garden:—

"Giovanni! Giovanni! It is past the hour! Why tarriest thou! Come down!"

"Yes," muttered Giovanni again. "She is the only being whom my breath may not slay! Would that it might!"

He rushed down, and in an instant, was standing before the bright and loving eyes of Beatrice. A moment ago, his wrath and despair had been so fierce that he could have desired nothing so much as to wither her by a glance. But, with her actual presence, there came influences which had too real an existence to be at once shaken off; recollections of the delicate and benign power of her feminine nature, which had so often enveloped him in a religious calm; recollections of many a holy and passionate outgush of her heart, when the pure fountain had been unsealed from its depths, and made visible in its transparency to his mental eye; recollections which, had Giovanni known how to estimate them, would have assured him that all this ugly mystery was but an earthly illusion, and that, whatever mist of evil might seem to have gathered over her, the real Beatrice was a heavenly angel. Incapable as he was of such high faith, still her presence had not utterly lost its magic. Giovanni's rage was quelled into an aspect of sullen insensibility. Beatrice, with a quick spiritual sense, immediately felt that there was a gulf of blackness between them, which neither he nor she could pass. They walked on together, sad and silent, and came thus to the marble fountain, and to its pool of water on the ground, in the midst of which grew the shrub that bore gem-like blossoms. Giovanni was affrighted at the eager enjoyment—the appetite, as it were—with which he found himself inhaling the fragrance of the flowers.

"Beatrice," asked he abruptly, "whence came this shrub?"

"My father created it," answered she, with simplicity.

"Created it! created it!" repeated Giovanni. "What mean you, Beatrice?"

"He is a man fearfully acquainted with the secrets of nature," replied Beatrice; "and, at the hour when I first drew breath, this plant sprang from the soil, the offspring of his science, of his intellect, while I was but his earthly child. "Approach it not!" continued she, observing with terror that Giovanni was drawing nearer to the shrub. "It has qualities that you little dream of. But I, dearest Giovanni,—I grew up and blossomed with the plant, and was nourished with its breath. It was my sister, and I loved it with a human affection: for—alas! hast thou not suspected it? there was an awful doom."

Here Giovanni frowned so darkly upon her that Beatrice paused and trembled. But her faith in his tenderness re-assured her, and made her blush that she had doubted for an instant.

"There was an awful doom," she continued,—"the effect of my father's fatal love of science—which estranged me from all society of any kind. Until Heaven sent thee, dearest Giovanni, Oh! how lonely was thy poor Beatrice!"

"Was it a hard doom?" asked Giovanni, fixing his eyes upon her.

"Only of late have I known how hard it was," answered she tenderly. "Oh, yes; but my heart was torpid, and therefore quiet."

Giovanni's rage broke forth from his sullen gloom like a lightning-flash out of a dark cloud.

"Accursed one!" cried he, with venomous scorn and anger. "And finding thy solitude wearisome, thou hast severed me, likewise, from all the warmth of life, and enticed me into thy region of unspeakable horror!"

"Giovanni!" exclaimed Beatrice, turning her large bright eyes upon his face. The force of his words had not found its way into her mind; she was merely wonder-struck.

"Yes, poisonous thing!" repeated Giovanni, beside himself with passion. "Thou has done it! Thou has blasted me! Thou hast filled my veins with poison! Thou hast made me as hateful, as ugly, as loathsome and deadly a creature as thyself,—a world's wonder of hideous monstrosity! Now—if our breath be happily as fatal to ourselves as to all others—let us join our lips in one kiss of unutterable hatred, and so die!"

"What has befallen me?" murmured Beatrice, with a low moan out of her heart. "Holy Virgin pity me, a poor heart-broken child!"

"Thou! Dost thou pray?" cried Giovanni, still with the same fiendish scorn. "Thy very prayers, as they come from thy lips, taint the atmosphere with death. Yes, yes; let us pray! Let us to church, and dip our fingers in the holy water at the portal! They that come after us will perish as by a pestilence. Let us sign crosses in the air! It will be scattering curses abroad in the likeness of holy symbols!"

"Giovanni," said Beatrice calmly, for her grief was beyond passion, "why dost thou join thyself with me thus in those terrible words? I, it is true, am the horrible thing thou namest me. But thou!—what hast thou to do, save with one other shudder at my hideous misery, to go forth out of the garden and mingle with thy race, and forget that there ever crawled on earth such a monster as poor Beatrice?"

"Dost thou pretend ignorance?" asked Giovanni, scowling upon her. "Behold! This power have I gained from the pure daughter of Rappaccini!"

There was a swarm of summer-insects flitting through the air, in search of the food promised by the flower-odors of the fatal garden. They circled round Giovanni's head, and were evidently attracted towards him by the same influence which had drawn them, for an instant, within the sphere of several of the shrubs. He sent forth a breath among them, and smiled bitterly at Beatrice, as at least a score of the insects fell dead upon the ground.

"I see it! I see it!" shrieked Beatrice. "It is my father's fatal science! No, no, Giovanni; it was not I! Never, never! I dreamed only to love thee, and be with thee a little time, and so to let thee pass away, leaving but thine image in mine heart. For, Giovanni—believe it—though my body be nourished with poison, my spirit is God's creature, and craves love as its daily food. But my father!—he has united us in this fearful sympathy. Yes; spurn me!—tread upon me!—kill me! Oh, what is death, after such words as thine? But it was not I! Not for a world of bliss would I have done it!"

Giovanni's passion had exhausted itself in its outburst from his lips. There now came across a sense, mournful, and not without tenderness, of the intimate and peculiar relationship between Beatrice and himself. They stood, as it were, in an utter solitude, which would be made none the less solitary by the densest throng of human life. Ought not, then, the desert of humanity around them to press this insulated pair close together? If they should be cruel to one another, who was there to be kind to them? Besides, thought Giovanni, might there not still be a hope of his returning within the limits of ordinary nature, and leading Beatrice—the redeemed Beatrice—by the hand? Oh, weak, and selfish, and unworthy spirit, that could dream of an earthly union and earthly happiness as possible, after such deep love had been so bitterly wronged as was Beatrice's love by Giovanni's blighting words! No, no; there could be no such hope. She must pass heavily, with that broken heart, across the borders—she must bathe her hurts in some fount of Paradise, and forget her grief in the light of immortality—and *there* be well!

But Giovanni did not know it.

"Dear Beatrice," said he, approaching her, while she shrank away, as always at his approach, but now with a different impulse—"dearest Beatrice, our fate is not yet so desperate. Behold! There is a medicine, potent, as a wise physician has assured me, and almost divine in its efficacy. It is composed of ingredients the most opposite to those by which thy awful father has brought this calamity upon thee and me. It is distilled of blessed herbs. Shall we not quaff it together, and thus be purified from evil?"

"Give it me!" said Beatrice, extending her hand to receive the little silver phial which Giovanni took from his bosom. She added, with a peculiar emphasis; "I will drink—but do thou await the result."

She put Baglioni's antidote to her lips; and, at the same moment, the figure of Rappaccini emerged from the portal, and came slowly towards the marble fountain. As he drew near, the pale man of science seemed to gaze with a triumphant expression at the beautiful youth and maiden, as might an artist who should spend his life in achieving a picture or a group of statuary, and finally be satisfied with his success. He paused—his bent form grew erect with conscious power, he spread out his hand over them, in the attitude of a father imploring a blessing upon his children. But those were the same hands that had thrown poison into the stream of their lives! Giovanni trembled. Beatrice shuddered nervously, and pressed her hand upon her heart.

"My daughter," said Rappaccini, "thou art no longer lonely in the world! Pluck one of those precious gems from thy sister shrub, and bid thy bridegroom wear it in his bosom. It will not harm him now! My science, and the sympathy between thee and him, have so wrought within his system, that he now stands apart from common men, as thou dost, daughter of my pride and triumph, from ordinary women. Pass on, then, through the world, most dear to one another, and dreadful to all besides!"

"My father," said Beatrice, feebly—and still, as she spoke, she kept her hand upon her heart—"wherefore didst thou inflict this miserable doom upon thy child?"

"Miserable!" exclaimed Rappaccini. "What mean you, foolish girl? Dost thou deem it misery to be endowed with marvellous gifts, against which no power nor strength could avail an enemy? Misery, to be able to quell the mightiest with a breath? Misery, to be as terrible as thou art beautiful? Wouldst thou, then, have preferred the condition of a weak woman, exposed to all evil, and capable of none?"

"I would fain have been loved, not feared," murmured Beatrice, sinking down upon the ground.—"But now it matters not; I am going, father, where the evil, which thou hast striven to mingle with my being, will pass away like a dream—like the fragrance of these poisonous flowers, which will no longer taint my breath among the flowers of Eden. Farewell, Giovanni! Thy words of hatred are like lead within my heart—but they, too, will fall away as I ascend. Oh, was there not, from the first, more poison in thy nature than in mine?"

To Beatrice—so radically had her earthly part been wrought upon by Rappaccini's skill—as poison had been life, so the powerful antidote was death. And thus the poor victim of man's ingenuity and of thwarted nature, and of the fatality that attends all such efforts of perverted wisdom, perished there, at the feet of her father and Giovanni. Just at that moment, Professor Pietro Baglioni looked forth from the window, and called loudly, in a tone of triumph mixed with horror, to the thunder-stricken man of science:

"Rappaccini! Rappaccini! And is *this* the upshot of your experiment?"

1844

The Scarlet Letter[1]

The Custom-House

INTRODUCTORY TO "THE SCARLET LETTER"

It is a little remarkable, that—though disinclined to talk overmuch of myself and my affairs at the fireside, and to my personal friends—an autobiographical impulse should twice in my life[2] have taken possession of me, in addressing the public. The first time was three or four years since, when I favored the reader—inexcusably, and for no earthly reason, that either the indulgent reader or the intrusive author could imagine—with a description of my way of life in the deep quietude of an Old Manse. And now—because, beyond my deserts, I was happy enough to find a listener or two on the former occasion—I again seize the public by the button, and talk of my three years' experience in a Custom-House. The example of the famous "P. P., Clerk of this Parish,"[3] was never more faithfully followed. The truth seems to be, however, that, when he casts his leaves forth upon the wind, the author addresses, not the many who will fling aside his volume, or never take it up, but the few who will understand him, better than most of his schoolmates and lifemates. Some authors, indeed, do far more than this, and indulge themselves in such confidential depths of revelation as could fittingly be addressed, only and exclusively, to the one heart and mind of perfect sympathy; as if the printed book, thrown at large on the wide world, were certain to find out the divided segment of the writer's own nature, and complete his circle of existence by bringing him into communion with it. It is scarcely decorous, however, to speak all, even where we speak impersonally. But—as thoughts are frozen and utterance benumbed, unless the speaker stand in some true relation with his audience— it may be pardonable to imagine that a friend, a kind and apprehensive, though not the closest friend, is listening to our talk; and then, a native reserve being thawed by this genial consciousness, we may prate of the circumstances that lie around us, and even of ourself, but still keep the inmost Me behind its veil. To this extent and within these limits, an author, methinks, may be autobiographical, without violating either the reader's rights or his own.

It will be seen, likewise, that this Custom-House sketch has a certain propriety, of a kind always recognized in literature, as explaining how a large portion of the following pages came into my possession, and as offering proofs of the authenticity of a narrative therein contained. This, in fact,—a desire to put myself in my true position as editor, or very little more, of the most prolix among the tales that make up my volume,[4]—this, and no other, is my true reason for assuming a personal relation with the public. In accomplishing the main purpose, it has appeared allowable, by a few extra touches, to give a faint representation of a mode of life not heretofore described, together with some of the characters that move in it, among whom the author happened to make one.

---

1. The source of this text is the 1st edition (1850).
2. The "first time" was in "The Author Makes the Reader Acquainted with his Abode," the introduction to *Mosses from an Old Manse* (1846).
3. An anonymous early-18th-century mock autobiog-
raphy spoofing Bishop Gilbert Burnet's egocentric view in his *History of My Own Time* (1724).
4. A vestige of an earlier plan to print several shorter tales in the same volume with *The Scarlet Letter*.

In my native town of Salem, at the head of what, half a century ago, in the days of old King Derby,[5] was a bustling wharf,—but which is now burdened with decayed wooden warehouses, and exhibits few or no symptoms of commercial life; except, perhaps, a bark or brig, half-way down its melancholy length, discharging hides; or, nearer at hand, a Nova Scotia schooner, pitching out her cargo of firewood,—at the head, I say, of this dilapidated wharf, which the tide often overflows, and along which, at the base and in the rear of the row of buildings, the track of many languid years is seen in a border of unthrifty grass,—here, with a view from its front windows adown this not very enlivening prospect, and thence across the harbour, stands a spacious edifice of brick. From the loftiest point of its roof, during precisely three and a half hours of each forenoon, floats or droops, in breeze or calm, the banner of the republic; but with the thirteen stripes turned vertically, instead of horizontally, and thus indicating that a civil, and not a military post of Uncle Sam's government, is here established. Its front is ornamented with a portico of half a dozen wooden pillars, supporting a balcony, beneath which a flight of wide granite steps descends towards the street. Over the entrance hovers an enormous specimen of the American eagle, with outspread wings, a shield before her breast, and, if I recollect aright, a bunch of intermingled thunderbolts and barbed arrows in each claw. With the customary infirmity of temper that characterizes this unhappy fowl, she appears, by the fierceness of her beak and eye and the general truculency of her attitude, to threaten mischief to the inoffensive community; and especially to warn all citizens, careful of their safety, against intruding on the premises which she overshadows with her wings. Nevertheless, vixenly as she looks, many people are seeking, at this very moment, to shelter themselves under the wing of the federal eagle; imagining, I presume, that her bosom has all the softness and snugness of an eider-down pillow. But she has no great tenderness, even in her best of moods, and, sooner or later,— oftener soon than late,—is apt to fling off her nestlings with a scratch of her claw, a dab of her beak, or a rankling wound from her barbed arrows.

The pavement round about the above-described edifice—which we may as well name at once as the Custom-House of the port—has grass enough growing in its chinks to show that it has not, of late days, been worn by any multitudinous resort of business. In some months of the year, however, there often chances a forenoon when affairs move onward with a livelier tread. Such occasions might remind the elderly citizen of that period, before the last war with England,[6] when Salem was a port by itself; not scorned, as she is now, by her own merchants and ship-owners, who permit her wharves to crumble to ruin, while their ventures go to swell, needlessly and imperceptibly, the mighty flood of commerce at New York or Boston. On some such morning, when three or four vessels happen to have arrived at once,—usually from Africa or South America,—or to be on the verge of their departure thitherward, there is a sound of frequent feet, passing briskly up and down the granite steps. Here, before his own wife has greeted him, you may greet the sea-flushed shipmaster, just in port, with his vessel's papers under his arm in a tarnished tin box. Here, too, comes his owner, cheerful or sombre, gracious or in the sulks, accordingly as his scheme of the now accomplished voyage has been realized in merchandise that will readily be turned to gold, or has buried him under a

5. Elias Hasket Derby (1739–99), rich Salem ship-   6. The War of 1812.
owner.

bulk of incommodities, such as nobody will care to rid him of. Here, like-wise,—the germ of the wrinkle-browed, grizzly-bearded, careworn mer-chant,—we have the smart young clerk, who gets the taste of traffic as a wolf-cub does of blood, and already sends adventures in his master's ships, when he had better be sailing mimic boats upon a mill-pond. Another figure in the scene is the outward-bound sailor, in quest of a protection;[7] or the recently arrived one, pale and feeble, seeking a passport to the hospital. Nor must we forget the captains of the rusty little schooners that bring firewood from the British provinces; a rough-looking set of tarpaulins, without the alertness of the Yankee aspect, but contributing an item of no slight importance to our decaying trade.

Cluster all these individuals together, as they sometimes were, with other miscellaneous ones to diversify the group, and, for the time being, it made the Custom-House a stirring scene. More frequently, however, on ascending the steps, you would discern—in the entry, if it were summer time, or in their appropriate rooms, if wintry or inclement weather—a row of venerable figures, sitting in old-fashioned chairs, which were tipped on their hind legs back against the wall. Oftentimes they were asleep, but occasionally might be heard talking together, in voices between speech and a snore, and with that lack of energy that distinguishes the occupants of alms-houses, and all other human beings who depend for subsistence on charity, on monopolized labor, or any thing else but their own independent exertions. These old gentlemen—seated, like Matthew, at the receipt of custom, but not very liable to be summoned thence, like him, for apostolic errands—were Custom-House officers.[8]

Furthermore, on the left hand as you enter the front door, is a certain room or office, about fifteen feet square, and of a lofty height; with two of its arched windows commanding a view of the aforesaid dilapidated wharf, and the third looking across a narrow lane, and along a portion of Derby Street. All three give glimpses of the shops of grocers, block-makers, slop-sellers, and ship-chandlers; around the doors of which are generally to be seen, laughing and gossiping, clusters of old salts, and such other wharf-rats as haunt the Wap-ping[9] of a seaport. The room itself is cobwebbed, and dingy with old paint; its floor is strewn with gray sand, in a fashion that has elsewhere fallen into long disuse; and it is easy to conclude, from the general slovenliness of the place, that this is a sanctuary into which womankind, with her tools of magic, the broom and mop, has very infrequent access. In the way of furniture, there is a stove with a voluminous funnel; an old pine desk, with a three-legged stool beside it; two or three wooden-bottom chairs, exceedingly decrepit and infirm; and,—not to forget the library,—on some shelves, a score or two of volumes of the Acts of Congress, and a bulky Digest of the Revenue Laws. A tin pipe ascends through the ceiling, and forms a medium of vocal communication with other parts of the edifice. And here, some six months ago,—pacing from corner to corner, or lounging on the long-legged stool, with his elbow on the desk, and his eyes wandering up and down the columns of the morning newspaper,—you might have recognized, honored reader, the same individual who welcomed you into his cheery little study, where the sunshine glimmered

---

7. A passport.
8. "And as Jesus passed forth from thence, he saw a man, named Matthew, sitting at the receipt of custom: and he saith unto him, Follow me. And he arose, and followed him" (Matthew 9.9). The joke involves the perennial suspicion that customs officers are corrupt.
9. Rundown area of any seaport, from an area of the London wharves. "Block-makers": pulley makers. "Slop-sellers": clothiers. "Ship-chandlers": general outfitters for ship supplies.

so pleasantly through the willow branches, on the western side of the Old Manse. But now, should you go thither to seek him, you would inquire in vain for the Loco-foco Surveyor. The besom[1] of reform has swept him out of office; and a worthier successor wears his dignity and pockets his emoluments.

This old town of Salem—my native place, though I have dwelt much away from it, both in boyhood and maturer years—possesses, or did possess, a hold on my affections, the force of which I have never realized during my seasons of actual residence here. Indeed, so far as its physical aspect is concerned, with its flat, unvaried surface, covered chiefly with wooden houses, few or none of which pretend to architectural beauty,—its irregularity, which is neither picturesque nor quaint, but only tame,—its long and lazy street, lounging wearisomely through the whole extent of the peninsula, with Gallows Hill and New Guinea at one end, and a view of the alms-house at the other,—such being the features of my native town, it would be quite as reasonable to form a sentimental attachment to a disarranged checkerboard. And yet, though invariably happiest elsewhere, there is within me a feeling for old Salem, which, in lack of a better phrase, I must be content to call affection. The sentiment is probably assignable to the deep and aged roots which my family has struck into the soil. It is now nearly two centuries and a quarter since the original Briton, the earliest emigrant of my name,[2] made his appearance in the wild and forest-bordered settlement, which has since become a city. And here his descendants have been born and died, and have mingled their earthy substance with the soil; until no small portion of it must necessarily be akin to the mortal frame wherewith, for a little while, I walk the streets. In part, therefore, the attachment which I speak of is the mere sensuous sympathy of dust for dust. Few of my countrymen can know what it is; nor, as frequent transplantation is perhaps better for the stock, need they consider it desirable to know.

But the sentiment has likewise its moral quality. The figure of that first ancestor, invested by family tradition with a dim and dusky grandeur, was present to my boyish imagination, as far back as I can remember. It still haunts me, and induces a sort of home-feeling with the past, which I scarcely claim in reference to the present phase of the town. I seem to have a stronger claim to a residence here on account of this grave, bearded, sable-cloaked, and steeple-crowned progenitor,—who came so early, with his Bible and his sword, and trode the unworn street with such a stately port, and made so large a figure, as a man of war and peace,—a stronger claim than for myself, whose name is seldom heard and my face hardly known. He was a soldier, legislator, judge; he was a ruler in the Church; he had all the Puritanic traits, both good and evil. He was likewise a bitter persecutor; as witness the Quakers, who have remembered him in their histories, and relate an incident of his hard severity towards a woman of their sect, which will last longer, it is to be feared, than any record of his better deeds, although these were many. His son, too, inherited the persecuting spirit, and made himself so conspicuous in the martyrdom of the witches, that their blood may fairly be said to have left a stain upon

---

1. Bundle of twigs bound to a handle and used as a broom. "Loco-foco": the Whig term of ridicule for any Democrat, although properly it applies to a liberal faction of the New York Democrats who in 1835 carried on a meeting after lights were doused by producing the then-new lucifer matches ("locofocos") and burning them during the rest of the meeting. "Surveyor": supervisor.

2. William Hathorne (Nathaniel Hawthorne added the w), who emigrated from England in 1630. He figures as a villain in William Sewel's *History of the Christian People Called Quakers* (1722).

him.[3] So deep a stain, indeed, that his old dry bones, in the Charter Street burial-ground, must still retain it, if they have not crumbled utterly to dust! I know not whether these ancestors of mine bethought themselves to repent, and ask pardon of Heaven for their cruelties; or whether they are now groaning under the heavy consequences of them, in another state of being. At all events, I, the present writer, as their representative, hereby take shame upon myself for their sakes, and pray that any curse incurred by them—as I have heard, and as the dreary and unprosperous condition of the race, for many a long year back, would argue to exist—may be now and henceforth removed.

Doubtless, however, either of these stern and black-browed Puritans would have thought it quite a sufficient retribution for his sins, that, after so long a lapse of years, the old trunk of the family tree, with so much venerable moss upon it, should have borne, as its topmost bough, an idler like myself. No aim, that I have ever cherished, would they recognize as laudable; no success of mine—if my life, beyond its domestic scope, had ever been brightened by success—would they deem otherwise than worthless, if not positively disgraceful. "What is he?" murmurs one gray shadow of my forefathers to the other. "A writer of story-books! What kind of a business in life,—what mode of glorifying God, or being serviceable to mankind in his day and generation,—may that be? Why, the degenerate fellow might as well have been a fiddler!" Such are the compliments bandied between my great-grandsires and myself, across the gulf of time! And yet, let them scorn me as they will, strong traits of their nature have intertwined themselves with mine.

Planted deep, in the town's earliest infancy and childhood, by these two earnest and energetic men, the race has ever since subsisted here; always, too, in respectability; never, so far as I have known, disgraced by a single unworthy member; but seldom or never, on the other hand, after the first two generations, performing any memorable deed, or so much as putting forward a claim to public notice. Gradually, they have sunk almost out of sight; as old houses, here and there about the streets, get covered half-way to the eaves by the accumulation of new soil. From father to son, for above a hundred years, they followed the sea; a gray-headed shipmaster, in each generation, retiring from the quarter-deck to the homestead, while a boy of fourteen took the hereditary place before the mast, confronting the salt spray and the gale, which had blustered against his sire and grandsire. The boy, also, in due time, passed from the forecastle to the cabin,[4] spent a tempestuous manhood, and returned from his world-wanderings, to grow old, and die, and mingle his dust with the natal earth. This long connection of a family with one spot, as its place of birth and burial, creates a kindred between the human being and the locality, quite independent of any charm in the scenery or moral circumstances that surround him. It is not love, but instinct. The new inhabitant—who came himself from a foreign land, or whose father or grandfather came—has little claim to be called a Salemite; he has no conception of the oyster-like tenacity with which an old settler, over whom his third century is creeping, clings to the spot where his successive generations have been imbedded. It is no matter that the place is joyless for him; that he is weary of the old wooden houses, the mud and dust, the dead level of site and sentiment, the chill east wind, and the chillest of social atmospheres;—all these, and whatever faults besides he

3. John Hathorne, judge during the Salem witchcraft trials in 1692.   4. I.e., from ordinary seaman to captain.

may see or imagine, are nothing to the purpose. The spell survives, and just as powerfully as if the natal spot were an earthly paradise. So has it been in my case. I felt it almost as a destiny to make Salem my home; so that the mould of features and cast of character which had all along been familiar here—ever, as one representative of the race lay down in his grave, another assuming, as it were, his sentry-march along the Main Street—might still in my little day be seen and recognized in the old town. Nevertheless, this very sentiment is an evidence that the connection, which has become an unhealthy one, should at last be severed. Human nature will not flourish, any more than a potato, if it be planted and replanted, for too long a series of generations, in the same worn-out soil. My children have had other birthplaces, and, so far as their fortunes may be within my control, shall strike their roots into unaccustomed earth.

On emerging from the Old Manse, it was chiefly this strange, indolent, unjoyous attachment for my native town, that brought me to fill a place in Uncle Sam's brick edifice,[5] when I might as well, or better, have gone somewhere else. My doom was on me. It was not the first time, nor the second, that I had gone away,—as it seemed, permanently,—but yet returned, like the bad half-penny; or as if Salem were for me the inevitable centre of the universe. So, one fine morning, I ascended the flight of granite steps, with the President's commission in my pocket, and was introduced to the corps of gentlemen who were to aid me in my weighty responsibility, as chief executive officer of the Custom-House.

I doubt greatly—or rather, I do not doubt at all—whether any public functionary of the United States, either in the civil or military line, has ever had such a patriarchal body of veterans under his orders as myself. The whereabouts of the Oldest Inhabitant was at once settled, when I looked at them. For upwards of twenty years before this epoch, the independent position of the Collector had kept the Salem Custom-House out of the whirlpool of political vicissitude, which makes the tenure of office generally so fragile. A soldier,— New England's most distinguished soldier,[6]—he stood firmly on the pedestal of his gallant services; and, himself secure in the wise liberality of the successive administrations through which he had held office, he had been the safety of his subordinates in many an hour of danger and heart-quake. General Miller was radically conservative; a man over whose kindly nature habit had no slight influence; attaching himself strongly to familiar faces, and with difficulty moved to change, even when change might have brought unquestionable improvement. Thus, on taking charge of my department, I found few but aged men. They were ancient sea-captains, for the most part, who, after being tost on every sea, and standing up sturdily against life's tempestuous blast, had finally drifted into this quiet nook; where, with little to disturb them, except the periodical terrors of a Presidential election, they one and all acquired a new lease of existence. Though by no means less liable than their fellow-men to age and infirmity, they had evidently some talisman or other that kept death at bay. Two or three of their number, as I was assured, being gouty and rheumatic, or perhaps bed-ridden, never dreamed of making their appearance at the Custom-House, during a large part of the year; but, after a torpid winter, would creep out into the warm sunshine of May or June, go lazily about what

---

5. The custom house.   6. General James F. Miller, hero of the War of 1812.

they termed duty, and, at their own leisure and convenience, betake themselves to bed again. I must plead guilty to the charge of abbreviating the official
breath of more than one of these venerable servants of the republic. They were
allowed, on my representation, to rest from their arduous labors, and soon
afterwards—as if their sole principle of life had been zeal for their country's
service; as I verily believe it was—withdrew to a better world. It is a pious
consolation to me, that, through my interference, a sufficient space was
allowed them for repentance of the evil and corrupt practices, into which, as
a matter of course, every Custom-House officer must be supposed to fall. Neither the front nor the back entrance of the Custom-House opens on the road
to Paradise.

The greater part of my officers were Whigs.[7] It was well for their venerable
brotherhood, that the new Surveyor was not a politician, and, though a faithful Democrat in principle, neither received nor held his office with any reference to political services. Had it been otherwise,—had an active politician
been put into this influential post, to assume the easy task of making head
against a Whig Collector, whose infirmities withheld him from the personal
administration of his office,—hardly a man of the old corps would have drawn
the breath of official life, within a month after the exterminating angel had
come up the Custom-House steps. According to the received code in such
matters, it would have been nothing short of duty, in a politician, to bring
every one of those white heads under the axe of the guillotine. It was plain
enough to discern, that the old fellows dreaded some such discourtesy at my
hands. It pained, and at the same time amused me, to behold the terrors that
attended my advent; to see a furrowed cheek, weather-beaten by half a century
of storm, turn ashy pale at the glance of so harmless an individual as myself;
to detect, as one or another addressed me, the tremor of a voice, which, in
long-past days, had been wont to bellow through a speaking-trumpet, hoarsely
enough to frighten Boreas[8] himself to silence. They knew, these excellent old
persons, that, by all established rule,—and, as regarded some of them,
weighed by their own lack of efficiency for business,—they ought to have given
place to younger men, more orthodox in politics, and altogether fitter than
themselves to serve our common Uncle. I knew it too, but could never quite
find in my heart to act upon the knowledge. Much and deservedly to my own
discredit, therefore, and considerably to the detriment of my official conscience, they continued, during my incumbency, to creep about the wharves,
and loiter up and down the Custom-House steps. They spent a good deal of
time, also, asleep in their accustomed corners, with their chairs tilted back
against the wall; awaking, however, once or twice in a forenoon, to bore one
another with the several thousandth repetition of old sea-stories, and mouldy
jokes, that had grown to be pass-words and countersigns among them.

The discovery was soon made, I imagine, that the new Surveyor had no
great harm in him. So, with lightsome hearts, and the happy consciousness of
being usefully employed,—in their own behalf, at least, if not for our beloved
country,—these good old gentlemen went through the various formalities of
office. Sagaciously, under their spectacles, did they peep into the holds of
vessels! Mighty was their fuss about little matters, and marvellous, sometimes,
the obtuseness that allowed greater ones to slip between their fingers! When-

7. The party that opposed the Democrats between the   and the rise of the Republican party in the 1850s.
demise of the National Republicans in the early 1830s   8. God of the north wind.

ever such a mischance occurred,—when a wagon-load of valuable merchandise had been smuggled ashore, at noonday, perhaps, and directly beneath their unsuspicious noses,—nothing could exceed the vigilance and alacrity with which they proceeded to lock, and double-lock, and secure with tape and sealing-wax, all the avenues of the delinquent vessel. Instead of a reprimand for their previous negligence, the case seemed rather to require an eulogium on their praiseworthy caution, after the mischief had happened; a grateful recognition of the promptitude of their zeal, the moment that there was no longer any remedy!

Unless people are more than commonly disagreeable, it is my foolish habit to contract a kindness for them. The better part of my companion's character, if it have a better part, is that which usually comes uppermost in my regard, and forms the type whereby I recognize the man. As most of these old Custom-House officers had good traits, and as my position in reference to them, being paternal and protective, was favorable to the growth of friendly sentiments, I soon grew to like them all. It was pleasant, in the summer forenoons,—when the fervent heat, that almost liquefied the rest of the human family, merely communicated a genial warmth to their half-torpid systems,—it was pleasant to hear them chatting in the back entry, a row of them all tipped against the wall, as usual; while the frozen witticisms of past generations were thawed out, and came bubbling with laughter from their lips. Externally, the jollity of aged men has much in common with the mirth of children; the intellect, any more than a deep sense of humor, has little to do with the matter; it is, with both, a gleam that plays upon the surface, and imparts a sunny and cheery aspect alike to the green branch, and gray, mouldering trunk. In one case, however, it is real sunshine; in the other, it more resembles the phosphorescent glow of decaying wood.

It would be sad injustice, the reader must understand, to represent all my excellent old friends as in their dotage. In the first place, my coadjutors were not invariably old; there were men among them in their strength and prime, of marked ability and energy, and altogether superior to the sluggish and dependent mode of life on which their evil stars had cast them. Then, moreover, the white locks of age were sometimes found to be the thatch of an intellectual tenement in good repair. But, as respects the majority of my corps of veterans, there will be no wrong done, if I characterize them generally as a set of wearisome old souls, who had gathered nothing worth preservation from their varied experience of life. They seemed to have flung away all the golden grain of practical wisdom, which they had enjoyed so many opportunities of harvesting, and most carefully to have stored their memories with the husks. They spoke with far more interest and unction of their morning's breakfast, or yesterday's, to-day's, or to-morrow's dinner, than of the shipwreck of forty or fifty years ago, and all the world's wonders which they had witnessed with their youthful eyes.

The father of the Custom-House—the patriarch, not only of this little squad of officials, but, I am bold to say, of the respectable body of tide-waiters[9] all over the United States—was a certain permanent Inspector. He might truly be termed a legitimate son of the revenue system, dyed in the wool, or rather, born in the purple; since his sire, a Revolutionary colonel, and formerly col-

---

9. Custom officers who board incoming ships at harbor.

lector of the port, had created an office for him, and appointed him to fill it, at a period of the early ages which few living men can now remember. This Inspector, when I first knew him, was a man of fourscore years, or thereabouts, and certainly one of the most wonderful specimens of winter-green that you would be likely to discover in a lifetime's search. With his florid cheek, his compact figure, smartly arrayed in a bright-buttoned blue coat, his brisk and vigorous step, and his hale and hearty aspect, altogether, he seemed—not young, indeed—but a kind of new contrivance of Mother Nature in the shape of man, whom age and infirmity had no business to touch. His voice and laugh, which perpetually reëchoed through the Custom-House, had nothing of the tremulous quaver and cackle of an old man's utterance; they came strutting out of his lungs, like the crow of a cock, or the blast of a clarion. Looking at him merely as an animal,—and there was very little else to look at,—he was a most satisfactory object, from the thorough healthfulness and wholesomeness of his system, and his capacity, at that extreme age, to enjoy all, or nearly all, the delights which he had ever aimed at, or conceived of. The careless security of his life in the Custom-House, on a regular income, and with but slight and infrequent apprehensions of removal, had no doubt contributed to make time pass lightly over him. The original and more potent causes, however, lay in the rare perfection of his animal nature, the moderate proportion of intellect, and the very trifling admixture of moral and spiritual ingredients; these latter qualities, indeed, being in barely enough measure to keep the old gentleman from walking on all-fours. He possessed no power of thought, no depth of feeling, no troublesome sensibilities; nothing, in short, but a few commonplace instincts, which, aided by the cheerful temper that grew inevitably out of his physical well-being, did duty very respectably, and to general acceptance, in lieu of a heart. He had been the husband of three wives, all long since dead; the father of twenty children, most of whom, at every age of childhood or maturity, had likewise returned to dust. Here, one would suppose, might have been sorrow enough to imbue the sunniest disposition, through and through, with a sable tinge. Not so with our old Inspector! One brief sigh sufficed to carry off the entire burden of these dismal reminiscences. The next moment, he was as ready for sport as any unbreeched infant; far readier than the Collector's junior clerk, who, at nineteen years, was much the elder and graver man of the two.

I used to watch and study this patriarchal personage with, I think, livelier curiosity than any other form of humanity there presented to my notice. He was, in truth, a rare phenomenon; so perfect in one point of view; so shallow, so delusive, so impalpable, such an absolute nonentity, in every other. My conclusion was that he had no soul, no heart, no mind; nothing, as I have already said, but instincts; and yet, withal, so cunningly had the few materials of his character been put together, that there was no painful perception of deficiency, but, on my part, an entire contentment with what I found in him. It might be difficult—and it was so—to conceive how he should exist hereafter, so earthy and sensuous did he seem; but surely his existence here, admitting that it was to terminate with his last breath, had been not unkindly given; with no higher moral responsibilities than the beasts of the field, but with a larger scope of enjoyment than theirs, and with all their blessed immunity from the dreariness and duskiness of age.

One point, in which he had vastly the advantage over his four-footed brethren, was his ability to recollect the good dinners which it had made no small portion of the happiness of his life to eat. His gourmandism was a highly agreeable trait; and to hear him talk of roast-meat was as appetizing as a pickle or an oyster. As he possessed no higher attribute, and neither sacrificed nor vitiated any spiritual endowment by devoting all his energies and ingenuities to subserve the delight and profit of his maw, it always pleased and satisfied me to hear him expatiate on fish, poultry, and butcher's meat, and the most eligible methods of preparing them for the table. His reminiscences of good cheer, however ancient the date of the actual banquet, seemed to bring the savor of pig or turkey under one's very nostrils. There were flavors on his palate, that had lingered there not less than sixty or seventy years, and were still apparently as fresh as that of the mutton-chop which he had just devoured for his breakfast. I have heard him smack his lips over dinners, every guest at which, except himself, had long been food for worms. It was marvellous to observe how the ghosts of bygone meals were continually rising up before him; not in anger or retribution, but as if grateful for his former appreciation, and seeking to reduplicate an endless series of enjoyment, at once shadowy and sensual. A tenderloin of beef, a hind-quarter of veal, a spare-rib of pork, a particular chicken, or a remarkably praiseworthy turkey, which had perhaps adorned his board in the days of the elder Adams,[1] would be remembered; while all the subsequent experience of our race, and all the events that brightened or darkened his individual career, had gone over him with as little permanent effect as the passing breeze. The chief tragic event of the old man's life, so far as I could judge, was his mishap with a certain goose, which lived and died some twenty or forty years ago; a goose of most promising figure, but which, at table, proved so inveterately tough that the carving-knife would make no impression on its carcass; and it could only be divided with an axe and handsaw.

But it is time to quit this sketch; on which, however, I should be glad to dwell at considerably more length, because, of all men whom I have ever known, this individual was fittest to be a Custom-House officer. Most persons, owing to causes which I may not have space to hint at, suffer moral detriment from this peculiar mode of life. The old Inspector was incapable of it, and, were he to continue in office to the end of time, would be just as good as he was then, and sit down to dinner with just as good an appetite.

There is one likeness, without which my gallery of Custom-House portraits would be strangely incomplete; but which my comparatively few opportunities for observation enable me to sketch only in the merest outline. It is that of the Collector, our gallant old General, who, after his brilliant military service, subsequently to which he had ruled over a wild Western territory,[2] had come hither, twenty years before, to spend the decline of his varied and honorable life. The brave soldier had already numbered, nearly or quite, his threescore years and ten, and was pursuing the remainder of his earthly march, burdened with infirmities which even the martial music of his own spirit-stirring recollections could do little towards lightening. The step was palsied now, that had been foremost in the charge. It was only with the assistance of a servant, and by leaning his hand heavily on the iron balustrade, that he could slowly and painfully ascend the Custom-House steps, and, with a toilsome progress across

1. I.e., from 1797 to 1801, the term of John Adams, the second president, father of John Quincy Adams, the sixth president.
2. Miller was governor of Arkansas Territory 1819–25.

the floor, attain his customary chair beside the fireplace. There he used to sit, gazing with a somewhat dim serenity of aspect at the figures that came and went; amid the rustle of papers, the administering of oaths, the discussion of business, and the casual talk of the office; all which sounds and circumstances seemed but indistinctly to impress his senses, and hardly to make their way into his inner sphere of contemplation. His countenance, in this repose, was mild and kindly. If his notice was sought, an expression of courtesy and interest gleamed out upon his features; proving that there was light within him, and that it was only the outward medium of the intellectual lamp that obstructed the rays in their passage. The closer you penetrated to the substance of his mind, the sounder it appeared. When no longer called upon to speak, or listen, either of which operations cost him an evident effort, his face would briefly subside into its former not uncheerful quietude. It was not painful to behold this look; for, though dim, it had not the imbecility of decaying age. The framework of his nature, originally strong and massive, was not yet crumbled into ruin.

To observe and define his character, however, under such disadvantages, was as difficult a task as to trace out and build up anew, in imagination, an old fortress, like Ticonderoga,[3] from a view of its gray and broken ruins. Here and there, perchance, the walls may remain almost complete; but elsewhere may be only a shapeless mound, cumbrous with its very strength, and overgrown, through long years of peace and neglect, with grass and alien weeds.

Nevertheless, looking at the old warrior with affection,—for, slight as was the communication between us, my feeling towards him, like that of all bipeds and quadrupeds who knew him, might not improperly be termed so,—I could discern the main points of his portrait. It was marked with the noble and heroic qualities which showed it to be not by a mere accident, but of good right, that he had won a distinguished name. His spirit could never, I conceive, have been characterized by an uneasy activity; it must, at any period of his life, have required an impulse to set him in motion; but, once stirred up, with obstacles to overcome, and an adequate object to be attained, it was not in the man to give out or fail. The heat that had formerly pervaded his nature, and which was not yet extinct, was never of the kind that flashes and flickers in a blaze, but, rather, a deep, red glow, as of iron in a furnace. Weight, solidity, firmness; this was the expression of his repose, even in such decay as had crept untimely over him, at the period of which I speak. But I could imagine, even then, that, under some excitement which should go deeply into his consciousness,—roused by a trumpet-peal, loud enough to awaken all of his energies that were not dead, but only slumbering,—he was yet capable of flinging off his infirmities like a sick man's gown, dropping the staff of age to seize a battlesword, and starting up once more a warrior. And, in so intense a moment, his demeanour would have still been calm. Such an exhibition, however, was but to be pictured in fancy; not to be anticipated, nor desired. What I saw in him—as evidently as the indestructible ramparts of Old Ticonderoga, already cited as the most appropriate simile—were the features of stubborn and ponderous endurance, which might well have amounted to obstinacy in his earlier days; of integrity, that, like most of his other endowments, lay in a somewhat heavy mass, and was just as unmalleable and unmanageable as a ton of iron

---

3. Ethan Allen and Benedict Arnold (not yet a traitor) captured Ticonderoga from the British in 1775.

ore; and of benevolence, which, fiercely as he led the bayonets on at Chippewa or Fort Erie,[4] I take to be of quite as genuine a stamp as what actuates any or all the polemical philanthropists of the age. He had slain men with his own hand, for aught I know;—certainly, they had fallen, like blades of grass at the sweep of the scythe, before the charge to which his spirit imparted its triumphant energy;—but, be that as it might, there was never in his heart so much cruelty as would have brushed the down off a butterfly's wing. I have not known the man, to whose innate kindliness I would more confidently make an appeal.

Many characteristics—and those, too, which contribute not the least forcibly to impart resemblance in a sketch—must have vanished, or been obscured, before I met the General. All merely graceful attributes are usually the most evanescent; nor does Nature adorn the human ruin with blossoms of new beauty, that have their roots and proper nutriment only in the chinks and crevices of decay, as she sows wall-flowers over the ruined fortress of Ticonderoga. Still, even in respect of grace and beauty, there were points well worth noting. A ray of humor, now and then, would make its way through the veil of dim obstruction, and glimmer pleasantly upon our faces. A trait of native elegance, seldom seen in the masculine character after childhood or early youth, was shown in the General's fondness for the sight and fragrance of flowers. An old soldier might be supposed to prize only the bloody laurel on his brow; but here was one, who seemed to have a young girl's appreciation of the floral tribe.

There, beside the fireplace, the brave old General used to sit; while the Surveyor—though seldom, when it could be avoided, taking upon himself the difficult task of engaging him in conversation—was fond of standing at a distance, and watching his quiet and almost slumberous countenance. He seemed away from us, although we saw him but a few yards off; remote, though we passed close beside his chair; unattainable, though we might have stretched forth our hands and touched his own. It might be, that he lived a more real life within his thoughts, than amid the unappropriate environment of the Collector's office. The evolutions of the parade; the turmoil of the battle; the flourish of old, heroic music, heard thirty years before;—such scenes and sounds, perhaps, were all alive before his intellectual sense. Meanwhile, the merchants and ship-masters, the spruce clerks, and uncouth sailors, entered and departed; the bustle of this commercial and Custom-House life kept up its little murmur round about him; and neither with the men nor their affairs did the General appear to sustain the most distant relation. He was as much out of place as an old sword—now rusty, but which had flashed once in the battle's front, and showed still a bright gleam along its blade—would have been, among the inkstands, paper-folders, and mahogany rulers, on the Deputy Collector's desk.

There was one thing that much aided me in renewing and re-creating the stalwart soldier of the Niagara frontier,—the man of true and simple energy. It was the recollection of those memorable words of his,—"I'll try, Sir!"[5]— spoken on the very verge of a desperate and heroic enterprise, and breathing the soul and spirit of New England hardihood, comprehending all perils, and encountering all. If, in our country, valor were rewarded by heraldic honor,

4. Decisive battles on the Niagara front in 1814.
5. Miller's words in response to General Winfield
Scott's order to take a British battery at Lundy's Lane in Ontario, near Niagara Falls.

this phrase—which it seems so easy to speak, but which only he, with such a task of danger and glory before him, has ever spoken— would be the best and fittest of all mottoes for the General's shield of arms.

It contributes greatly towards a man's moral and intellectual health, to be brought into habits of companionship with individuals unlike himself, who care little for his pursuits, and whose sphere and abilities he must go out of himself to appreciate. The accidents of my life have often afforded me this advantage, but never with more fulness and variety than during my continuance in office. There was one man, especially, the observation of whose character gave me a new idea of talent. His gifts were emphatically those of a man of business; prompt, acute, clear-minded; with an eye that saw through all perplexities, and a faculty of arrangement that made them vanish, as by the waving of an enchanter's wand. Bred up from boyhood in the Custom-House, it was his proper field of activity; and the many intricacies of business, so harassing to the interloper, presented themselves before him with the regularity of a perfectly comprehended system. In my contemplation, he stood as the ideal of his class. He was, indeed, the Custom-House in himself; or, at all events, the main-spring that kept its variously revolving wheels in motion; for, in an institution like this, where its officers are appointed to subserve their own profit and convenience, and seldom with a leading reference to their fitness for the duty to be performed, they must perforce seek elsewhere the dexterity which is not in them. Thus, by an inevitable necessity, as a magnet attracts steel-filings, so did our man of business draw to himself the difficulties which everybody met with. With an easy condescension, and kind forbearance towards our stupidity,—which, to his order of mind, must have seemed little short of crime,—would he forthwith, by the merest touch of his finger, make the incomprehensible as clear as daylight. The merchants valued him not less than we, his esoteric friends. His integrity was perfect; it was a law of nature with him, rather than a choice or a principle; nor can it be otherwise than the main condition of an intellect so remarkably clear and accurate as his, to be honest and regular in the administration of affairs. A stain on his conscience, as to any thing that came within the range of his vocation, would trouble such a man very much in the same way, though to a far greater degree, than an error in the balance of an account, or an ink-blot on the fair page of a book of record. Here, in a word,—and it is a rare instance in my life,—I had met with a person thoroughly adapted to the situation which he held.

Such were some of the people with whom I now found myself connected. I took it in good part at the hands of Providence, that I was thrown into a position so little akin to my past habits; and set myself seriously to gather from it whatever profit was to be had. After my fellowship of toil and impracticable schemes, with the dreamy brethren of Brook Farm; after living for three years within the subtile influence of an intellect like Emerson's; after those wild, free days on the Assabeth,[6] indulging fantastic speculations beside our fire of fallen boughs, with Ellery Channing; after talking with Thoreau about pine-trees and Indian relics, in his hermitage at Walden; after growing fastidious by sympathy with the classic refinement of Hillard's culture; after becoming imbued with poetic sentiment at Longfellow's hearth-stone;—it was time, at

6. A tributary that joins the Concord River near Concord. "Brook Farm": the Transcendental agricultural commune near Boston that Hawthorne participated in during 1841 and that provided some of the setting for *The Blithedale Romance* (1852).

length, that I should exercise other faculties of my nature, and nourish myself with food for which I had hitherto had little appetite. Even the old Inspector was desirable, as a change of diet, to a man who had known Alcott.[7] I looked upon it as an evidence, in some measure, of a system naturally well balanced, and lacking no essential part of a thorough organization, that, with such associates to remember, I could mingle at once with men of altogether different qualities, and never murmur at the change.

Literature, its exertions and objects, were now of little moment in my regard. I cared not, at this period, for books; they were apart from me. Nature,—except it were human nature,—the nature that is developed in earth and sky, was, in one sense, hidden from me; and all the imaginative delight, wherewith it had been spiritualized, passed away out of my mind. A gift, a faculty, if it had not departed, was suspended and inanimate within me. There would have been something sad, unutterably dreary, in all this, had I not been conscious that it lay at my own option to recall whatever was valuable in the past. It might be true, indeed, that this was a life which could not, with impunity, be lived too long; else, it might make me permanently other than I had been, without transforming me into any shape which it would be worth my while to take. But I never considered it as other than a transitory life. There was always a prophetic instinct, a low whisper in my ear, that, within no long period, and whenever a new change of custom should be essential to my good, a change would come.

Meanwhile, there I was, a Surveyor of the Revenue, and, so far as I have been able to understand, as good a Surveyor as need be. A man of thought, fancy, and sensibility, (had he ten times the Surveyor's proportion of those qualities,) may, at any time, be a man of affairs, if he will only choose to give himself the trouble. My fellow-officers, and the merchants and sea-captains with whom my official duties brought me into any manner of connection, viewed me in no other light, and probably knew me in no other character. None of them, I presume, had ever read a page of my inditing, or would have cared a fig the more for me, if they had read them all; nor would it have mended the matter, in the least, had those same unprofitable pages been written with a pen like that of Burns or of Chaucer,[8] each of whom was a Custom-House officer in his day, as well as I. It is a good lesson—though it may often be a hard one—for a man who has dreamed of literary fame, and of making for himself a rank among the world's dignitaries by such means, to step aside out of the narrow circle in which his claims are recognized, and to find how utterly devoid of significance, beyond that circle, is all that he achieves, and all he aims at. I know not that I especially needed the lesson, either in the way of warning or rebuke; but, at any rate, I learned it thoroughly; nor, it gives me pleasure to reflect, did the truth, as it came home to my perception, ever cost me a pang, or require to be thrown off in a sigh. In the way of literary talk, it is true, the Naval Officer—an excellent fellow, who came into office with me, and went out only a little later—would often engage me in a discussion about

7. Bronson Alcott (1799–1888), innovative educator and (the point of Hawthorne's double-edge joke) abstruse and much-ridiculed idealist, whom Hawthorne knew in Concord. Emerson, Thoreau, and the irresponsible writer Channing (1818–1901) also lived in Concord. In Boston Hawthorne could visit his friend and lawyer the philanthropist George Stillman Hillard

(1808–1879), and at Cambridge he could visit his old acquaintance and newer friend Henry Wadsworth Longfellow, who lived in opulent fashion.
8. Geoffrey Chaucer (1340?–1400) was controller of customs in London 1374–86. Robert Burns was collector of excise taxes (1789–91) in Dumfries, Scotland.

one or the other of his favorite topics, Napoleon or Shakspeare. The Collector's junior clerk, too,—a young gentleman who, it was whispered, occasionally covered a sheet of Uncle Sam's letter-paper with what, (at the distance of a few yards,) looked very much like poetry,—used now and then to speak to me of books, as matters with which I might possibly be conversant. This was my all of lettered intercourse; and it was quite sufficient for my necessities.

No longer seeking nor caring that my name should be blazoned abroad on title-pages, I smiled to think that it had now another kind of vogue. The Custom-House marker imprinted it, with a stencil and black paint, on pepper-bags, and baskets of anatto,[9] and cigar-boxes, and bales of all kinds of dutiable merchandise, in testimony that these commodities had paid the impost, and gone regularly through the office. Borne on such queer vehicle of fame, a knowledge of my existence, so far as a name conveys it, was carried where it had never been before, and, I hope, will never go again.

But the past was not dead. Once in a great while, the thoughts, that had seemed so vital and so active, yet had been put to rest so quietly, revived again. One of the most remarkable occasions, when the habit of bygone days awoke in me, was that which brings it within the law of literary propriety to offer the public the sketch which I am now writing.

In the second story of the Custom-House, there is a large room, in which the brick-work and naked rafters have never been covered with panelling and plaster. The edifice—originally projected on a scale adapted to the old commercial enterprise of the port, and with an idea of subsequent prosperity destined never to be realized—contains far more space than its occupants know what to do with. This airy hall, therefore, over the Collector's apartments, remains unfinished to this day, and, in spite of the aged cobwebs that festoon its dusky beams, appears still to await the labor of the carpenter and mason. At one end of the room, in a recess, were a number of barrels, piled one upon another, containing bundles of official documents. Large quantities of similar rubbish lay lumbering[1] the floor. It was sorrowful to think how many days, and weeks, and months, and years of toil, had been wasted on these musty papers, which were now only an encumbrance of earth, and were hidden away in this forgotten corner, never more to be glanced at by human eyes. But, then, what reams of other manuscripts—filled, not with the dulness of official formalities, but with the thought of inventive brains and the rich effusion of deep hearts—had gone equally to oblivion; and that, moreover, without serving a purpose in their day, as these heaped up papers had, and—saddest of all—without purchasing for their writers the comfortable livelihood which the clerks of the Custom-House had gained by these worthless scratchings of the pen! Yet not altogether worthless, perhaps, as materials of local history. Here, no doubt, statistics of the former commerce of Salem might be discovered, and memorials of her princely merchants,—old King Derby,—old Billy Gray,—old Simon Forrester,[2]—and many another magnate in his day; whose powdered head, however, was scarcely in the tomb, before his mountain-pile of wealth began to dwindle. The founders of the greater part of the families which now compose the aristocracy of Salem might here be traced, from the

9. Yellowish red dyestuff from the pulp of seeds of a tropical American tree (usually spelled "annatto"). The trowel-shaped stencil was daubed with paint to imprint Hawthorne's name on goods passing through the port.

1. Cluttering.
2. Captain Simon Forrester (1776–1851), rich relative of the Hawthornes. William Gray (1750–1825) had become lieutenant governor of Massachusetts.

petty and obscure beginnings of their traffic, at periods generally much poste-
rior to the Revolution, upward to what their children look upon as long-established rank.

Prior to the Revolution, there is a dearth of records; the earlier documents
and archives of the Custom-House having, probably, been carried off to Halifax, when all the King's officials accompanied the British army in its flight
from Boston.[3] It has often been a matter of regret with me; for, going back,
perhaps, to the days of the Protectorate,[4] those papers must have contained
many references to forgotten or remembered men, and to antique customs,
which would have affected me with the same pleasure as when I used to pick
up Indian arrow-heads in the field near the Old Manse.

But, one idle and rainy day, it was my fortune to make a discovery of some
little interest. Poking and burrowing into the heaped-up rubbish in the corner;
unfolding one and another document, and reading the names of vessels that
had long ago foundered at sea or rotted at the wharves, and those of merchants,
never heard of now on 'Change,[5] nor very readily decipherable on their mossy
tombstones; glancing at such matters with the saddened, weary, half-reluctant
interest which we bestow on the corpse of dead activity,—and exerting my
fancy, sluggish with little use, to raise up from these dry bones an image of the
old town's brighter aspect, when India was a new region, and only Salem knew
the way thither,—I chanced to lay my hand on a small package, carefully
done up in a piece of ancient yellow parchment. This envelope had the air of
an official record of some period long past, when clerks engrossed their stiff
and formal chirography on more substantial materials than at present. There
was something about it that quickened an instinctive curiosity, and made me
undo the faded red tape, that tied up the package, with the sense that a treasure
would here be brought to light. Unbending the rigid folds of the parchment
cover, I found it to be a commission, under the hand and seal of Governor
Shirley, in favor of one Jonathan Pue,[6] as Surveyor of his Majesty's Customs
for the port of Salem, in the Province of Massachusetts Bay. I remembered to
have read (probably in Felt's Annals) a notice of the decease of Mr. Surveyor
Pue, about fourscore years ago; and likewise, in a newspaper of recent times,
an account of the digging up of his remains in the little grave-yard of St. Peter's
Church,[7] during the renewal of that edifice. Nothing, if I rightly call to mind,
was left of my respected predecessor, save an imperfect skeleton, and some
fragments of apparel, and a wig of majestic frizzle; which, unlike the head that
it once adorned, was in very satisfactory preservation. But, on examining the
papers which the parchment commission served to envelop, I found more
traces of Mr. Pue's mental part, and the internal operations of his head, than
the frizzled wig had contained of the venerable skull itself.

They were documents, in short, not official, but of a private nature, or, at
least, written in his private capacity, and apparently with his own hand. I
could account for their being included in the heap of Custom-House lumber
only by the fact, that Mr. Pue's death had happened suddenly; and that these

3. General Howe had evacuated the British troops to
Halifax, Nova Scotia, when Washington besieged Boston in 1776, but his transfer of the Salem records is un-
documented.
4. The years 1653–60, when Oliver Cromwell and
then his son Richard ruled as Lord Protector of England.

5. Exchange, equivalent of the modern stock exchange.
6. A real name that Hawthorne found in Joseph B.
Felt's Annals of Salem (1827). William Shirley, royal
governor of Massachusetts 1741–49 and 1753–56.
7. The first Anglican church in Salem, begun 1633.

papers, which he probably kept in his official desk, had never come to the knowledge of his heirs, or were supposed to relate to the business of the revenue. On the transfer of the archives to Halifax, this package, proving to be of no public concern, was left behind, and had remained ever since unopened.

The ancient Surveyor—being little molested, I suppose, at that early day, with business pertaining to his office—seems to have devoted some of his many leisure hours to researches as a local antiquarian, and other inquisitions of a similar nature. These supplied material for petty activity to a mind that would otherwise have been eaten up with rust. A portion of his facts, by the by, did me good service in the preparation of the article entitled "MAIN STREET," included in the present volume.[8] The remainder may perhaps be applied to purposes equally valuable, hereafter; or not impossibly may be worked up, so far as they go, into a regular history of Salem, should my veneration for the natal soil ever impel me to so pious a task. Meanwhile, they shall be at the command of any gentleman, inclined, and competent, to take the unprofitable labor off my hands. As a final disposition, I contemplate depositing them with the Essex Historical Society.[9]

But the object that most drew my attention, in the mysterious package, was a certain affair of fine red cloth, much worn and faded. There were traces about it of gold embroidery, which, however, was greatly frayed and defaced; so that none, or very little, of the glitter was left. It had been wrought, as was easy to perceive, with wonderful skill of needlework; and the stitch (as I am assured by ladies conversant with such mysteries) gives evidence of a now forgotten art, not to be recovered even by the process of picking out the threads. This rag of scarlet cloth,—for time, and wear, and a sacrilegious moth, had reduced it to little other than a rag,—on careful examination, assumed the shape of a letter. It was the capital letter A. By an accurate measurement, each limb proved to be precisely three inches and a quarter in length. It had been intended, there could be no doubt, as an ornamental article of dress; but how it was to be worn, or what rank, honor, and dignity, in by-past times, were signified by it, was a riddle which (so evanescent are the fashions of the world in these particulars) I saw little hope of solving. And yet it strangely interested me. My eyes fastened themselves upon the old scarlet letter, and would not be turned aside. Certainly, there was some deep meaning in it, most worthy of interpretation, and which, as it were, streamed forth from the mystic symbol, subtly communicating itself to my sensibilities, but evading the analysis of my mind.

While thus perplexed,—and cogitating, among other hypotheses, whether the letter might not have been one of those decorations which the white men used to contrive, in order to take the eyes of Indians,—I happened to place it on my breast. It seemed to me,—the reader may smile, but must not doubt my word,—it seemed to me, then, that I experienced a sensation not altogether physical, yet almost so, as of burning heat; and as if the letter were not of red cloth, but red-hot iron. I shuddered, and involuntarily let it fall upon the floor.

In the absorbing contemplation of the scarlet letter, I had hitherto neglected to examine a small roll of dingy paper, around which it had been twisted. This

8. Another vestige of the earlier intention to publish several stories and sketches along with *The Scarlet Letter*, which had been conceived as a shorter work.

9. A real institution, which does not contain Hawthorne's imaginary documents.

I now opened, and had the satisfaction to find, recorded by the old Surveyor's pen, a reasonably complete explanation of the whole affair. There were several foolscap sheets,[1] containing many particulars respecting the life and conversation of one Hester Prynne, who appeared to have been rather a noteworthy personage in the view of our ancestors. She had flourished during a period between the early days of Massachusetts and the close of the seventeenth century. Aged persons, alive in the time of Mr. Surveyor Pue, and from whose oral testimony he had made up his narrative, remembered her, in their youth, as a very old, but not decrepit woman, of a stately and solemn aspect. It had been her habit, from an almost immemorial date, to go about the country as a kind of voluntary nurse, and doing whatever miscellaneous good she might; taking upon herself, likewise, to give advice in all matters, especially those of the heart; by which means, as a person of such propensities inevitably must, she gained from many people the reverence due to an angel, but, I should imagine, was looked upon by others as an intruder and a nuisance. Prying farther into the manuscript, I found the record of other doings and sufferings of this singular woman, for most of which the reader is referred to the story[2] entitled THE SCARLET LETTER"; and it should be borne carefully in mind, that the main facts of that story are authorized and authenticated by the document of Mr. Surveyor Pue. The original papers, together with the scarlet letter itself,—a most curious relic,—are still in my possession, and shall be freely exhibited to whomsoever, induced by the great interest of the narrative, may desire a sight of them. I must not be understood as affirming, that, in the dressing up of the tale, and imagining the motives and modes of passion that influenced the characters who figure in it, I have invariably confined myself within the limits of the old Surveyor's half a dozen sheets of foolscap. On the contrary, I have allowed myself, as to such points, nearly or altogether as much license as if the facts had been entirely of my own invention. What I contend for is the authenticity of the outline.

This incident recalled my mind, in some degree, to its old track. There seemed to be here the groundwork of a tale. It impressed me as if the ancient Surveyor, in his garb of a hundred years gone by, and wearing his immortal wig,—which was buried with him, but did not perish in the grave,—had met me in the deserted chamber of the Custom-House. In his port was the dignity of one who had borne his Majesty's commission, and who was therefore illuminated by a ray of the splendor that shone so dazzlingly about the throne. How unlike, alas! the hang-dog look of a republican official, who, as the servant of the people, feels himself less than the least, and below the lowest, of his masters. With his own ghostly hand, the obscurely seen, but majestic, figure had imparted to me the scarlet symbol, and the little roll of explanatory manuscript. With his own ghostly voice, he had exhorted me, on the sacred consideration of my filial duty and reverence towards him,—who might reasonably regard himself as my official ancestor,—to bring his mouldy and moth-eaten lucubrations[3] before the public. "Do this," said the ghost of Mr. Surveyor Pue, emphatically nodding the head that looked so imposing within its memorable wig, "do this, and the profit shall be all your own! You will

---

1. Sheets of paper 13 x 16 inches, unfolded; often folded to make four 13 x 8 pages.
2. Not "romance" or "novel"; this essay may have been written before *The Scarlet Letter* reached its full

length.
3. Laborious or pedantic writing (from the Latin for working by candlelight, at night).

shortly need it; for it is not in your days as it was in mine, when a man's office was a life-lease, and oftentimes an heirloom. But, I charge you, in this matter of old Mistress Pyrnne, give to your predecessor's memory the credit which will be rightfully its due!" And I said to the ghost of Mr. Surveyor Pue,— "I will!"

On Hester Prynne's story, therefore, I bestowed much thought. It was the subject of my meditations for many an hour, while pacing to and fro across my room, or traversing, with a hundredfold repetition, the long extent from the front-door of the Custom-House to the side-entrance, and back again. Great were the weariness and annoyance of the old Inspector and the Weighers and Gaugers, whose slumbers were disturbed by the unmercifully lengthened tramp of my passing and returning footsteps. Remembering their own former habits, they used to say that the Surveyor was walking the quarter-deck. They probably fancied that my sole object—and, indeed, the sole object for which a sane man could ever put himself into voluntary motion—was, to get an appetite for dinner. And to say the truth, an appetite, sharpened by the east-wind that generally blew along the passage, was the only valuable result of so much indefatigable exercise. So little adapted is the atmosphere of a Custom-House to the delicate harvest of fancy and sensibility, that, had I remained there through ten Presidencies yet to come, I doubt whether the tale of "The Scarlet Letter" would ever have been brought before the public eye. My imagination was a tarnished mirror. It would not reflect, or only with miserable dimness, the figures with which I did my best to people it. The characters of the narrative would not be warmed and rendered malleable, by any heat that I could kindle at my intellectual forge. They would take neither the glow of passion nor the tenderness of sentiment, but retained all the rigidity of dead corpses, and stared me in the face with a fixed and ghastly grin of contemptuous defiance. "What have you to do with us?" that expression seemed to say. "The little power you might once have possessed over the tribe of unrealities is gone! You have bartered it for a pittance of the public gold. Go, then, and earn your wages!" In short, the almost torpid creatures of my own fancy twitted me with imbecility, and not without fair occasion.

It was not merely during the three hours and a half which Uncle Sam claimed as his share of my daily life, that this wretched numbness held possession of me. It went with me on my sea-shore walks and rambles into the country, whenever—which was seldom and reluctantly—I bestirred myself to seek that invigorating charm of Nature, which used to give me such freshness and activity of thought, the moment that I stepped across the threshold of the Old Manse. The same torpor, as regarded the capacity for intellectual effort, accompanied me home, and weighed upon me in the chamber which I most absurdly termed my study. Nor did it quit me, when, late at night, I sat in the deserted parlour, lighted only by the glimmering coal-fire and the moon, striving to picture forth imaginary scenes, which, the next day, might flow out on the brightening page in many-hued description.

If the imaginative faculty refused to act at such an hour, it might well be deemed a hopeless case. Moonlight, in a familiar room, falling so white upon the carpet, and showing all its figures so distinctly,—making every object so minutely visible, yet so unlike a morning or noontide visibility,—is a medium the most suitable for a romance-writer to get acquainted with his illusive guests. There is the little domestic scenery of the well-known apartment; the chairs, with each its separate individuality; the centre-table, sustaining a work-basket, a volume or two, and an extinguished lamp; the sofa; the book-case; the picture on the wall;—all these details, so completely seen, are so spiritual-ized by the unusual light, that they seem to lose their actual substance, and become things of intellect. Nothing is too small or too trifling to undergo this change, and acquire dignity thereby. A child's shoe; the doll, seated in her little wicker carriage; the hobby-horse;—whatever, in a word, has been used or played with, during the day, is now invested with a quality of strangeness and remoteness, though still almost as vividly present as by daylight. Thus, therefore, the floor of our familiar room has become a neutral territory, some-where between the real world and fairy-land, where the Actual and the Imagi-nary may meet, and each imbue itself with the nature of the other. Ghosts might enter here, without affrighting us. It would be too much in keeping with the scene to excite surprise, were we to look about us and discover a form, beloved, but gone hence, now sitting quietly in a streak of this magic moon-shine, with an aspect that would make us doubt whether it had returned from afar, or had never once stirred from our fireside.

The somewhat dim coal-fire has an essential influence in producing the effect which I would describe. It throws its unobtrusive tinge throughout the room, with a faint ruddiness upon the walls and ceiling, and a reflected gleam from the polish of the furniture. This warmer light mingles itself with the cold spirituality of the moonbeams, and communicates, as it were, a heart and sensibilities of human tenderness to the forms which fancy summons up. It converts them from snow-images into men and women. Glancing at the look-ing-glass, we behold—deep within its haunted verge—the smouldering glow of the half-extinguished anthracite, the white moonbeams on the floor, and a repetition of all the gleam and shadow of the picture, with one remove farther from the actual, and nearer to the imaginative. Then, at such an hour, and with this scene before him, if a man, sitting all alone, cannot dream strange things, and make them look like truth, he need never try to write romances.

But, for myself, during the whole of my Custom-House experience, moon-light and sunshine, and the glow of fire-light, were just alike in my regard; and neither of them was of one whit more avail than the twinkle of a tallow-candle. An entire class of susceptibilities, and a gift connected with them,—of no great richness or value, but the best I had,—was gone from me.

It is my belief, however, that, had I attempted a different order of composi-tion, my faculties would not have been found so pointless and inefficacious. I might, for instance, have contented myself with writing out the narratives of a veteran shipmaster, one of the Inspectors, whom I should be most ungrateful not to mention; since scarcely a day passed that he did not stir me to laughter and admiration by his marvellous gifts as a story-teller. Could I have preserved the picturesque force of his style, and the humorous coloring which nature taught him how to throw over his descriptions, the result, I honestly believe, would have been something new in literature. Or I might readily have found a more serious task. It was a folly, with the materiality of this daily life pressing so intrusively upon me, to attempt to fling myself back into another age; or to insist on creating the semblance of a world out of airy matter, when, at every moment, the impalpable beauty of my soap-bubble was broken by the rude contact of some actual circumstance. The wiser effort would have been, to diffuse thought and imagination through the opaque substance of to-day, and thus to make it a bright transparency; to spiritualize the burden that began to weigh so heavily; to seek, resolutely, the true and indestructible value that lay hidden in the petty and wearisome incidents, and ordinary characters, with which I was now conversant. The fault was mine. The page of life that was spread out before me seemed dull and commonplace, only because I had not fathomed its deeper import. A better book than I shall ever write was there; leaf after leaf presenting itself to me, just as it was written out by the reality of the flitting hour, and vanishing as fast as written, only because my brain wanted the insight and my hand the cunning to transcribe it. At some future day, it may be, I shall remember a few scattered fragments and broken paragraphs, and write them down, and find the letters turn to gold upon the page.

These perceptions have come too late. At the instant, I was only conscious that what would have been a pleasure once was now a hopeless toil. There was no occasion to make much moan about this state of affairs. I had ceased to be a writer of tolerably poor tales and essays, and had become a tolerably good Surveyor of the Customs. That was all. But, nevertheless, it is any thing but agreeable to be haunted by a suspicion that one's intellect is dwindling away; or exhaling, without your consciousness, like ether out of a phial; so that, at every glance, you find a smaller and less volatile residuum. Of the fact, there could be no doubt; and, examining myself and others, I was led to conclusions in reference to the effect of public office on the character, not very favorable to the mode of life in question. In some other form, perhaps, I may hereafter develop these effects. Suffice it here to say, that a Custom-House officer, of long continuance, can hardly be a very praiseworthy or respectable personage, for many reasons; one of them, the tenure by which he holds his situation, and another, the very nature of his business, which—though, I trust, an honest one—is of such a sort that he does not share in the united effort of mankind.

An effect—which I believe to be observable, more or less, in every individual who has occupied the position—is, that, while he leans on the mighty arm of the Republic, his own proper strength departs from him. He loses, in an extent proportioned to the weakness or force of his original nature, the capability of self-support. If he possess an unusual share of native energy, or the enervating magic of place do not operate too long upon him, his forfeited powers may be redeemable. The ejected officer—fortunate in the unkindly shove that sends him forth betimes, to struggle amid a struggling world—may return to himself, and become all that he has ever been. But this seldom happens. He usually keeps his ground just long enough for his own ruin, and is then thrust out, with sinews all unstrung, to totter along the difficult footpath of life as he best may. Conscious of his own infirmity,—that his tempered steel and elasticity are lost,—he for ever afterwards looks wistfully about him in quest of support external to himself. His pervading and continual hope—a hallucination, which, in the face of all discouragement, and making light of impossibilities, haunts him while he lives, and, I fancy, like the convulsive throes of the cholera, torments him for a brief space after death—is, that, finally, and in no long time, by some happy coincidence of circumstances, he shall be restored to office. This faith, more than any thing else, steals the pith and availability out of whatever enterprise he may dream of undertaking. Why should he toil and moil, and be at so much trouble to pick himself up out of the mud, when, in a little while hence, the strong arm of his Uncle will raise and support him? Why should he work for his living here, or go to dig gold in California,[4] when he is so soon to be made happy, at monthly intervals, with a little pile of glittering coin out of his Uncle's pocket? It is sadly curious to observe how slight a taste of office suffices to infect a poor fellow with this singular disease. Uncle Sam's gold—meaning no disrespect to the worthy old gentleman—has, in this respect, a quality of enchantment like that of the Devil's wages. Whoever touches it should look well to himself, or he may find the bargain to go hard against him, involving, if not his soul, yet many of its better attributes; its sturdy force, its courage and constancy, its truth, its self-reliance, and all that gives the emphasis to manly character.

Here was a fine prospect in the distance! Not that the Surveyor brought the lesson home to himself, or admitted that he could be so utterly undone, either by continuance in office, or ejectment. Yet my reflections were not the most comfortable. I began to grow melancholy and restless; continually prying into my mind, to discover which of its poor properties were gone, and what degree of detriment had already accrued to the remainder. I endeavoured to calculate how much longer I could stay in the Custom-House, and yet go forth a man. To confess the truth, it was my greatest apprehension,—as it would never be a measure of policy to turn out so quiet an individual as myself, and it being hardly in the nature of a public officer to resign,—it was my chief trouble, therefore, that I was likely to grow gray and decrepit in the Surveyorship, and become much such another animal as the old Inspector. Might it not, in the tedious lapse of official life that lay before me, finally be with me as it was with this venerable friend,—to make the dinner-hour the nucleus of the day, and to spend the rest of it, as an old dog spends it, asleep in the sunshine or the shade? A dreary look-forward this, for a man who felt it to be the best definition of happiness to live throughout the whole range of his faculties and sensibilities! But, all this while, I was giving myself very unnecessary alarm. Providence had meditated better things for me than I could possibly imagine for myself.

A remarkable event of the third year of my Surveyorship—to adopt the tone of "P.P."—was the election of General Taylor to the Presidency.[5] It is essential, in order to a complete estimate of the advantages of official life, to view the incumbent at the in-coming of a hostile administration. His position is then one of the most singularly irksome, and, in every contingency, disagreeable, that a wretched mortal can possibly occupy; with seldom an alternative of good, on either hand, although what presents itself to him as the worst event may very probably be the best. But it is a strange experience, to a man of pride and sensibility, to know that his interests are within the control of individuals who neither love nor understand him, and by whom, since one or the other must needs happen, he would rather be injured than obliged. Strange, too, for one who has kept his calmness throughout the contest, to observe the bloodthirstiness that is developed in the hour of triumph, and to be conscious that he is himself among its objects! There are few uglier traits of human nature than this tendency—which I now witnessed in men no worse than their neighbours—to grow cruel, merely because they possessed the power of

---

4. This essay was written in 1849, the year of the Gold Rush.
5. Zachary Taylor (1784–1850), Whig president whose election brought about Hawthorne's dismissal,

was still alive when this was written; he died July 9, 1850, a few months after *The Scarlet Letter* was published.

inflicting harm. If the guillotine, as applied to office-holders, were a literal fact, instead of one of the most apt of metaphors, it is my sincere belief, that the active members of the victorious party were sufficiently excited to have chopped off all our heads, and have thanked Heaven for the opportunity! It appears to me—who have been a calm and curious observer, as well in victory as defeat—that this fierce and bitter spirit of malice and revenge has never distinguished the many triumphs of my own party as it now did that of the Whigs. The Democrats take the offices, as a general rule, because they need them, and because the practice of many years has made it the law of political warfare, which, unless a different system be proclaimed, it were weakness and cowardice to murmur at. But the long habit of victory has made them gener-ous. They know how to spare, when they see occasion; and when they strike, the axe may be sharp, indeed, but its edge is seldom poisoned with ill-will; nor is it their custom ignominiously to kick the head which they have just struck off.

In short, unpleasant as was my predicament, at best, I saw much reason to congratulate myself that I was on the losing side, rather than the triumphant one. If, heretofore, I had been none of the warmest of partisans, I began now, at this season of peril and adversity, to be pretty acutely sensible with which party my predilections lay; nor was it without something like regret and shame, that, according to a reasonable calculation of chances, I saw my own prospect of retaining office to be better than those of my Democratic brethren.[6] But who can see an inch into futurity, beyond his nose? My own head was the first that fell!

The moment when a man's head drops off is seldom or never, I am inclined to think, precisely the most agreeable of his life. Nevertheless, like the greater part of our misfortunes, even so serious a contingency brings its remedy and consolation with it, if the sufferer will but make the best, rather than the worst, of the accident which has befallen him. In my particular case, the consolatory topics were close at hand, and, indeed, had suggested themselves to my medi-tations a considerable time before it was requisite to use them. In view of my previous weariness of office, and vague thoughts of resignation, my fortune somewhat resembled that of a person who should entertain an idea of commit-ting suicide, and, altogether beyond his hopes, meet with the good hap to be murdered. In the Custom-House, as before in the Old Manse, I had spent three years; a term long enough to rest a weary brain; long enough to break off old intellectual habits, and make room for new ones; long enough, and too long, to have lived in an unnatural state, doing what was really of no advantage nor delight to any human being, and withholding myself from toil that would, at least, have stilled an unquiet impulse in me. Then, moreover, as regarded his unceremonious ejectment, the late Surveyor was not altogether ill-pleased to be recognized by the Whigs as an enemy; since his inactivity in political affairs,—his tendency to roam, at will, in that broad and quiet field where all mankind may meet, rather than confine himself to those narrow paths where brethren of the same household must diverge from one another,—had some-times made it questionable with his brother Democrats whether he was a friend. Now, after he had won the crown of martyrdom, (though with no longer a head to wear it on,) the point might be looked upon as settled. Finally,

6. Perhaps literally true, but the comedy of Hawthorne's highly partisan satire against the Whigs turns on his self-portrayal as a political naif, a portrayal not justified by the facts.

little heroic as he was, it seemed more decorous to be overthrown in the down-fall of the party with which he had been content to stand, than to remain a forlorn survivor, when so many worthier men were falling; and, at last, after subsisting for four years on the mercy of a hostile administration, to be com-pelled then to define his position anew, and claim the yet more humiliating mercy of a friendly one.

Meanwhile, the press had taken up my affair, and kept me, for a week or two, careering through the public prints, in my decapitated state, like Irving's Headless Horseman;[7] ghastly and grim, and longing to be buried, as a politi-cally dead man ought. So much for my figurative self. The real human being, all this time, with his head safely on his shoulders, had brought himself to the comfortable conclusion, that every thing was for the best; and, making an investment in ink, paper, and steel-pens, had opened his long-disused writing-desk, and was again a literary man.

Now it was, that the lucubrations of my ancient predecessor, Mr. Surveyor Pue, came into play. Rusty through long idleness, some little space was requi-site before my intellectual machinery could be brought to work upon the tale, with an effect in any degree satisfactory. Even yet, though my thoughts were ultimately much absorbed in the task, it wears, to my eye, a stern and sombre aspect; too much ungladdened by genial sunshine; too little relieved by the tender and familiar influences which soften almost every scene of nature and real life, and, undoubtedly, should soften every picture of them. This uncapti-vating effect is perhaps due to the period of hardly accomplished revolution, and still seething turmoil, in which the story shaped itself. It is no indication, however, of a lack of cheerfulness in the writer's mind; for he was happier, while straying through the gloom of these sunless fantasies, than at any time since he had quitted the Old Manse. Some of the briefer articles, which con-tribute to make up the volume, have likewise been written since my involun-tary withdrawal from the toils and honors of public life, and the remainder are gleaned from annuals and magazines, of such antique date that they have gone round the circle, and come back to novelty again.[8] Keeping up the metaphor of the political guillotine, the whole may be considered as the POSTHUMOUS PAPERS OF A DECAPITATED SURVEYOR; and the sketch which I am now bringing to a close, if too autobiographical for a modest person to publish in his life-time, will readily be excused in a gentleman who writes from beyond the grave. Peace be with all the world! My blessing on my friends! My forgiveness to my enemies! For I am in the realm of quiet!

The life of the Custom-House lies like a dream behind me. The old Inspec-tor,—who, by the by, I regret to say, was overthrown and killed by a horse, some time ago; else he would certainly have lived for ever,—he, and all those other venerable personages who sat with him at the receipt of custom, are but shadows in my view; white-headed and wrinkled images, which my fancy used to sport with, and has now flung aside for ever. The merchants,—Pingree, Phillips, Shepard, Upton, Kimball, Bertram, Hunt,—these, and many other names, which had such a classic familiarity for my ear six months ago,—these men of traffic, who seemed to occupy so important a position in the world,— how little time has it required to disconnect me from them all, not merely in

---

7. In *The Legend of Sleepy Hollow.* "Careering": run-ning headlong.
8. "At the time of writing this article, the author in-tended to publish, along with 'The Scarlet Letter,' sev-eral shorter tales and sketches. These it has been thought advisable to defer" [Hawthorne's note].

act, but recollection! It is with an effort that I recall the figures and appellations of these few. Soon, likewise, my old native town will loom upon me through the haze of memory, a mist brooding over and around it; as if it were no portion of the real earth, but an overgrown village in cloud-land, with only imaginary inhabitants to people its wooden houses, and walk its homely lanes, and the unpicturesque prolixity of its main street. Henceforth, it ceases to be a reality of my life. I am a citizen of somewhere else. My good townspeople will not much regret me; for—though it has been as dear an object as any, in my literary efforts, to be of some importance in their eyes, and to win myself a pleasant memory in this abode and burial-place of so many of my fore-fathers—there has never been, for me, the genial atmosphere which a literary man requires, in order to ripen the best harvest of his mind. I shall do better amongst other faces; and these familiar ones, it need hardly be said, will do just as well without me.

It may be, however,—O, transporting and triumphant thought!—that the great-grandchildren of the present race may sometimes think kindly of the scribbler of bygone days, when the antiquary of days to come, among the sites memorable in the town's history, shall point out the locality of THE TOWN-PUMP![9]

The Scarlet Letter

I. THE PRISON-DOOR

A throng of bearded men, in sad-colored garments and gray, steeple-crowned hats, intermixed with women, some wearing hoods, and others bare-headed, was assembled in front of a wooden edifice, the door of which was heavily timbered with oak, and studded with iron spikes.

The founders of a new colony, whatever Utopia of human virtue and happi-ness they might originally project, have invariably recognized it among their earliest practical necessities to allot a portion of the virgin soil as a cemetery, and another portion as the site of a prison. In accordance with this rule, it may safely be assumed that the forefathers of Boston had built the first prison-house, somewhere in the vicinity of Cornhill, almost as seasonably as they marked out the first burial-ground, on Isaac Johnson's lot and round about his grave, which subsequently became the nucleus of all the congregated sepul-chres in the old church-yard of King's Chapel. Certain it is, that, some fifteen or twenty years[1] after the settlement of the town, the wooden jail was already marked with weather-stains and other indications of age, which gave a yet darker aspect to its beetle-browed and gloomy front. The rust on the ponderous iron-work of its oaken door looked more antique than any thing else in the new world. Like all that pertains to crime, it seemed never to have known a youthful era. Before this ugly edifice, and between it and the wheel-track of the street, was a grass-plot, much overgrown with burdock, pig-weed, apple-peru, and such unsightly vegetation, which evidently found something conge-nial in the soil that had so early borne the black flower of civilized society, a

9. A *Rill from the Town-Pump* (1835), one of Haw-thorne's best-known sketches.
1. "Some fifteen or twenty years" would mean roughly 1645–50, but Hawthorne's use of Governor Win-throp's death in chap. 12 suggests that the action of the novel (except the "Conclusion") covers 1642 to 1649; excessive precision of this sort goes counter to Haw-thorne's suggestive rather than historically exact use of actual names and events. Isaac Johnson (1601–1630) died in the first year of the settlement of Boston; his land went to public uses. Kings Chapel was the first Anglican church in Boston, built in 1688.

prison. But, on one side of the portal, and rooted almost at the threshold, was a wild rose-bush, covered, in this month of June, with its delicate gems, which might be imagined to offer their fragrance and fragile beauty to the prisoner as he went in, and to the condemned criminal as he came forth to his doom, in token that the deep heart of Nature could pity and be kind to him.

This rose-bush, by a strange chance, has been kept alive in history; but whether it had merely survived out of the stern old wilderness, so long after the fall of the gigantic pines and oaks that originally overshadowed it,—or whether, as there is fair authority for believing, it had sprung up under the footsteps of the sainted Ann Hutchinson,[2] as she entered the prison-door,—we shall not take upon us to determine. Finding it so directly on the threshold of our narrative, which is now about to issue from that inauspicious portal, we could hardly do otherwise than pluck one of its flowers and present it to the reader. It may serve, let us hope, to symbolize some sweet moral blossom, that may be found along the track, or relieve the darkening close of a tale of human frailty and sorrow.

II. THE MARKET-PLACE

The grass-plot before the jail, in Prison Lane, on a certain summer morning, not less than two centuries ago, was occupied by a pretty large number of the inhabitants of Boston; all with their eyes intently fastened on the iron-clamped oaken door. Amongst any other population, or at a later period in the history of New England, the grim rigidity that petrified the bearded physiognomies of these good people would have augured some awful business in hand. It could have betokened nothing short of the anticipated execution of some noted culprit, on whom the sentence of a legal tribunal had but confirmed the verdict of public sentiment. But, in that early severity of the Puritan character, an inference of this kind could not so indubitably be drawn. It might be that a sluggish bond-servant, or an undutiful child, whom his parents had given over to the civil authority, was to be corrected at the whipping-post. It might be, that an Antinomian, a Quaker, or other heterodox religionist, was to be scourged out of the town, or an idle and vagrant Indian, whom the white man's fire-water had made riotous about the streets, was to be driven with stripes into the shadow of the forest. It might be, too, that a witch, like old Mistress Hibbins,[3] the bitter-tempered widow of the magistrate, was to die upon the gallows. In either case, there was very much the same solemnity of demeanour on the part of the spectators; as befitted a people amongst whom religion and law were almost identical, and in whose character both were so thoroughly interfused, that the mildest and the severest acts of public discipline were alike made venerable and awful. Meagre, indeed, and cold, was the sympathy that a transgressor might look for, from such bystanders at the scaffold. On the other hand, a penalty which, in our days, would infer a degree of mocking infamy and ridicule, might then be invested with almost as stern a dignity as the punishment of death itself.

It was a circumstance to be noted, on the summer morning when our story

2. Hutchinson (1591–1643) was exiled from Massachusetts for teaching antinomianism (that is, holding that salvation came through grace rather than good works); she founded Portsmouth, Rhode Island, and was later killed by American Indians.
3. A real Ann Hibbins was tried for witchcraft in 1655 and executed in 1656.

begins its course, that the women, of whom there were several in the crowd, appeared to take a peculiar interest in whatever penal infliction might be expected to ensue. The age had not so much refinement, that any sense of impropriety restrained the wearers of petticoat and farthingale[4] from stepping forth into the public ways, and wedging their not unsubstantial persons, if occasion were, into the throng nearest to the scaffold at an execution. Morally, as well as materially, there was a coarser fibre in those wives and maidens of old English birth and breeding, than in their fair descendants, separated from them by a series of six or seven generations; for, throughout that chain of ancestry, every successive mother has transmitted to her child a fainter bloom, a more delicate and briefer beauty, and a slighter physical frame, if not a character of less force and solidity, than her own. The women, who were now standing about the prison-door, stood within less than half a century of the period when the man-like Elizabeth[5] had been the not altogether unsuitable representative of the sex. They were her countrywomen; and the beef and ale of their native land, with a moral diet not a whit more refined, entered largely into their composition. The bright morning sun, therefore, shone on broad shoulders and well-developed busts, and on round and ruddy cheeks, that had ripened in the far-off island, and had hardly yet grown paler or thinner in the atmosphere of New England. There was, moreover, a boldness and rotundity of speech among these matrons, as most of them seemed to be, that would startle us at the present day, whether in respect to its purport or its volume of tone.

"Goodwives," said a hard-featured dame of fifty, "I'll tell ye a piece of my mind. It would be greatly for the public behoof,[6] if we women, being of mature age and church-members in good repute, should have the handling of such malefactresses as this Hester Prynne. What think ye, gossips?[7] If the hussy stood up for judgment before us five, that are now here in a knot together, would she come off with such a sentence as the worshipful magistrates have awarded? Marry, I trow[8] not!"

"People say," said another, "that the Reverend Master Dimmesdale, her godly pastor, takes it very grievously to heart that such a scandal should have come upon his congregation."

"The magistrates are God-fearing gentlemen, but merciful overmuch,— that is a truth," added a third autumnal matron. "At the very least, they should have put the brand of a hot iron on Hester Prynne's forehead. Madam Hester would have winced at that, I warrant me. But she,—the naughty baggage,— little will she care what they put upon the bodice of her gown! Why, look you, she may cover it with a brooch, or such like heathenish adornment, and so walk the streets as brave as ever!"

"Ah, but," interposed, more softly, a young wife, holding a child by the hand, "let her cover the mark as she will, the pang of it will be always in her heart."

"What do we talk of marks and brands, whether on the bodice of her gown, or the flesh of her forehead?" cried another female, the ugliest as well as the most pitiless of these self-constituted judges. "This woman has brought shame upon us all, and ought to die. Is there not law for it? Truly there is, both in

4. Hoop skirt.
5. Queen Elizabeth I reigned 1558–1603.
6. Benefit.
7. Friends or companions (female); originally, kins-people.
8. Think, suppose.

the Scripture[9] and the statute-book. Then let the magistrates, who have made it of no effect, thank themselves if their own wives and daughters go astray!"

"Mercy on us, goodwife," exclaimed a man in the crowd, "is there no virtue in woman, save what springs from a wholesome fear of the gallows? That is the hardest word yet! Hush, now, gossips; for the lock is turning in the prison-door, and here comes Mistress Prynne herself."

The door of the jail being flung open from within, there appeared, in the first place, like a black shadow emerging into the sunshine, the grim and grisly presence of the town-beadle, with a sword by his side and his staff of office in his hand. The personage prefigured and represented in his aspect the whole dismal severity of the Puritanic code of law, which it was his business to administer in its final and closest application to the offender. Stretching forth the official staff in his left hand, he laid his right upon the shoulder of a young woman, whom he thus drew forward; until, on the threshold of the prison-door, she repelled him, by an action marked with natural dignity and force of character, and stepped into the open air, as if by her own free-will. She bore in her arms a child, a baby of some three months old, who winked and turned aside its little face from the too vivid light of day; because its existence, hereto-fore, had brought it acquainted only with the gray twilight of a dungeon, or other darksome apartment of the prison.

When the young woman—the mother of this child—stood fully revealed before the crowd, it seemed to be her first impulse to clasp the infant closely to her bosom; not so much by an impulse of motherly affection, as that she might thereby conceal a certain token, which was wrought or fastened into her dress. In a moment, however, wisely judging that one token of her shame would but poorly serve to hide another, she took the baby on her arm, and, with a burning blush, and yet a haughty smile, and a glance that would not be abashed, looked around at her townspeople and neighbours. On the breast of her gown, in fine red cloth, surrounded with an elaborate embroidery and fantastic flourishes of gold thread, appeared the letter A. It was so artistically done, and with so much fertility and gorgeous luxuriance of fancy, that it had all the effect of a last and fitting decoration to the apparel which she wore; and which was of a splendor in accordance with the taste of the age, but greatly beyond what was allowed by the sumptuary regulations of the colony.

The young woman was tall, with a figure of perfect elegance, on a large scale. She had dark and abundant hair, so glossy that it threw off the sunshine with a gleam, and a face which, besides being beautiful from regularity of feature and richness of complexion, had the impressiveness belonging to a marked brow and deep black eyes. She was lady-like, too, after the manner of the feminine gentility of those days; characterized by a certain state and dig-nity, rather than by the delicate, evanescent, and indescribable grace, which is now recognized as its indication. And never had Hester Prynne appeared more lady-like, in the antique interpretation of the term, than as she issued from the prison. Those who had before known her, and had expected to behold her dimmed and obscured by a disastrous cloud, were astonished, and even startled, to perceive how her beauty shone out, and made a halo of the misfortune and ignominy in which she was enveloped. It may be true, that, to a sensitive observer, there was something exquisitely painful in it. Her attire,

9. "And the man that committeth adultery with another man's wife, even he that committeth adultery with his neighbor's wife, the adulterer and the adulteress shall surely be put to death" (Leviticus 20.10).

which, indeed, she had wrought for the occasion, in prison, and had modelled much after her own fancy, seemed to express the attitude of her spirit, the desperate recklessness of her mood, by its wild and picturesque peculiarity. But the point which drew all eyes, and, as it were, transfigured the wearer,— so that both men and women, who had been familiarly acquainted with Hester Prynne, were now impressed as if they beheld her for the first time,—was that SCARLET LETTER, so fantastically embroidered and illuminated upon her bosom. It had the effect of a spell, taking her out of the ordinary relations with humanity, and inclosing her in a sphere by herself.

"She hath good skill at her needle, that's certain," remarked one of the female spectators; "but did ever a woman, before this brazen hussy, contrive such a way of showing it! Why, gossips, what is it but to laugh in the faces of our godly magistrates, and make a pride out of what they, worthy gentlemen, meant for a punishment?"

"It were well," muttered the most iron-visaged of the old dames, "if we stripped Madam Hester's rich gown off her dainty shoulders; and as for the red letter, which she hath stitched so curiously, I'll bestow a rag of mine own rheumatic flannel, to make a fitter one!"

"O, peace, neighbours, peace!" whispered their youngest companion. "Do not let her hear you! Not a stitch in that embroidered letter, but she has felt it in her heart."

The grim beadle now made a gesture with his staff.

"Make way, good people, make way, in the King's name," cried he. "Open a passage; and, I promise ye, Mistress Prynne shall be set where man, woman, and child may have a fair sight of her brave apparel, from this time till an hour past meridian. A blessing on the righteous Colony of the Massachusetts, where iniquity is dragged out into the sunshine! Come along, Madam Hester, and show your scarlet letter in the market-place!"

A lane was forthwith opened through the crowd of spectators. Preceded by the beadle, and attended by an irregular procession of stern-browed men and unkindly-visaged women, Hester Prynne set forth towards the place appointed for her punishment. A crowd of eager and curious schoolboys, understanding little of the matter in hand, except that it gave them a half-holiday, ran before her progress, turning their heads continually to stare into her face, and at the winking baby in her arms, and at the ignominious letter on her breast. It was no great distance, in those days, from the prison-door to the market-place. Measured by the prisoner's experience, however, it might be reckoned a journey of some length; for, haughty as her deameanour was, she perchance underwent an agony from every footstep of those that thronged to see her, as if her heart had been flung into the street for them all to spurn and trample upon. In our nature, however, there is a provision, alike marvellous and merciful, that the sufferer should never know the intensity of what he endures by its present torture, but chiefly by the pang that rankles after it. With almost a serene deportment, therefore, Hester Prynne passed through this portion of her ordeal, and came to a sort of scaffold, at the western extremity of the market-place. It stood nearly beneath the eaves of Boston's earliest church, and appeared to be a fixture there.

In fact, this scaffold constituted a portion of a penal machine, which now, for two or three generations past, has been merely historical and traditionary among us, but was held, in the old time, to be as effectual an agent in the promotion of good citizenship, as ever was the guillotine among the terrorists of France.[1] It was, in short, the platform of the pillory; and above it rose the framework of that instrument of discipline, so fashioned as to confine the human head in its tight grasp, and thus hold it up to the public gaze. The very ideal of ignominy was embodied and made manifest in this contrivance of wood and iron. There can be no outrage, methinks, against our common nature,—whatever be the delinquencies of the individual,—no outrage more flagrant than to forbid the culprit to hide his face for shame; as it was the essence of this punishment to do. In Hester Prynne's instance, however, as not unfrequently in other cases, her sentence bore, that she should stand a certain time upon the platform, but without undergoing that gripe about the neck and confinement of the head, the proneness to which was the most devilish characteristic of this ugly engine. Knowing well her part, she ascended a flight of wooden steps, and was thus displayed to the surrounding multitude, at about the height of a man's shoulders above the street.

Had there been a Papist among the crowd of Puritans, he might have seen in this beautiful woman, so picturesque in her attire and mien, and with the infant at her bosom, an object to remind him of the image of Divine Maternity, which so many illustrious painters have vied with one another to represent; something which should remind him, indeed, but only by contrast, of that sacred image of sinless motherhood, whose infant was to redeem the world. Here, there was the taint of deepest sin in the most sacred quality of human life, working such effect, that the world was only the darker for this woman's beauty, and the more lost for the infant that she had borne.

The scene was not without a mixture of awe, such as must always invest the spectacle of guilt and shame in a fellow-creature, before society shall have grown corrupt enough to smile, instead of shuddering, at it. The witnesses of Hester Prynne's disgrace had not yet passed beyond their simplicity. They were stern enough to look upon her death, had that been the sentence, without a murmur at its severity, but had none of the heartlessness of another social state, which would find only a theme for jest in an exhibition like the present. Even had there been a disposition to turn the matter into ridicule, it must have been repressed and overpowered by the solemn presence of men no less dignified than the Governor, and several of his counsellors, a judge, a general, and the ministers of the town; all of whom sat or stood in a balcony of the meeting-house, looking down upon the platform. When such personages could constitute a part of the spectacle, without risking the majesty or reverence of rank and office, it was safely to be inferred that the infliction of a legal sentence would have an earnest and effectual meaning. Accordingly, the crowd was sombre and grave. The unhappy culprit sustained herself as best a woman might, under the heavy weight of a thousand unrelenting eyes, all fastened upon her, and concentred at her bosom. It was almost intolerable to be borne. Of an impulsive and passionate nature, she had fortified herself to encounter the stings and venomous stabs of public contumely, wreaking itself in every variety of insult; but there was a quality so much more terrible in the solemn mood of the popular mind, that she longed rather to behold all those rigid countenances contorted with scornful merriment, and herself the object. Had a roar of laughter burst from the multitude,—each man, each woman,

---

1. During the Reign of Terror (1793–94).

each little shrill-voiced child, contributing their individual parts,—Hester Prynne might have repaid them all with a bitter and disdainful smile. But, under the leaden infliction which it was her doom to endure, she felt, at moments, as if she must needs shriek out with the full power of her lungs, and cast herself from the scaffold down upon the ground, or else go mad at once.

Yet there were intervals when the whole scene, in which she was the most conspicuous object, seemed to vanish from her eyes, or, at least, glimmered indistinctly before them, like a mass of imperfectly shaped and spectral images. Her mind, and especially her memory, was preternaturally active, and kept bringing up other scenes than this roughly hewn street of a little town, on the edge of the Western wilderness; other faces than were lowering upon her from beneath the brims of those steeple-crowned hats. Reminiscences, the most trifling and immaterial, passages of infancy and school-days, sports, childish quarrels, and the little domestic traits of her maiden years, came swarming back upon her, intermingled with recollections of whatever was gravest in her subsequent life; one picture precisely as vivid as another; as if all were of similar importance, or all alike a play. Possibly, it was an instinctive device of her spirit, to relieve itself, by the exhibition of these phantasmagoric forms, from the cruel weight and hardness of the reality.

Be that as it might, the scaffold of the pillory was a point of view that revealed to Hester Prynne the entire track along which she had been treading, since her happy infancy. Standing on that miserable eminence, she saw again her native village, in Old England, and her paternal home; a decayed house of gray stone, with a poverty-stricken aspect, but retaining a half-obliterated shield of arms over the portal, in token of antique gentility. She saw her father's face, with its bald brow, and reverend white beard, that flowed over the old-fashioned Elizabethan ruff;[2] her mother's, too, with the look of heedful and anxious love which it always wore in her remembrance, and which, even since her death, had so often laid the impediment of a gentle remonstrance in her daughter's pathway. She saw her own face, glowing with girlish beauty, and illuminating all the interior of the dusky mirror in which she had been wont to gaze at it. There she beheld another countenance, of a man well stricken in years, a pale, thin, scholar-like visage, with eyes dim and bleared by the lamp-light that had served them to pore over many ponderous books. Yet those same bleared optics had a strange, penetrating power, when it was their owner's purpose to read the human soul. This figure of the study and the cloister, as Hester Prynne's womanly fancy failed not to recall, was slightly deformed, with the left shoulder a trifle higher than the right. Next rose before her, in memory's picture-gallery, the intricate and narrow thoroughfares, the tall, gray houses, the huge cathedrals, and the public edifices, ancient in date and quaint in architecture, of a Continental city,[3] where a new life had awaited her, still in connection with the misshapen scholar; a new life, but feeding itself on time-worn materials, like a tuft of green moss on a crumbling wall. Lastly, in lieu of these shifting scenes, came back the rude market-place of the Puritan settlement, with all the townspeople assembled and levelling their stern regards at Hester Prynne,—yes, at herself,—who stood on the scaffold of the pillory, an infant on her arm, and the letter A, in scarlet, fantasti-

2. Elaborate, stiffly starched collar worn by the wealthier classes (men and women) in the 16th and 17th centuries.

3. I.e., as the next chapter shows, Amsterdam, where many English Separatists and Puritans gathered before gaining permission to settle in the colonies.

cally embroidered with gold thread, upon her bosom!

Could it be true? She clutched the child so fiercely to her breast, that it sent forth a cry; she turned her eyes downward at the scarlet letter, and even touched it with her finger, to assure herself that the infant and the shame were real. Yes!—these were her realities,—all else had vanished!

III. THE RECOGNITION

From this intense consciousness of being the object of severe and universal observation, the wearer of the scarlet letter was at length relieved by discerning, on the outskirts of the crowd, a figure which irresistibly took possession of her thoughts. An Indian, in his native garb, was standing there; but the red men were not so infrequent visitors of the English settlements, that one of them would have attracted any notice from Hester Prynne, at such a time; much less would he have excluded all other objects and ideas from her mind. By the Indian's side, and evidently sustaining a companionship with him, stood a white man, clad in a strange disarray of civilized and savage costume.

He was small in stature, with a furrowed visage, which, as yet, could hardly be termed aged. There was a remarkable intelligence in his features, as of a person who had so cultivated his mental part that it could not fail to mould the physical to itself, and become manifest by unmistakable tokens. Although, by a seemingly careless arrangement of his heterogeneous garb, he had endeavoured to conceal or abate the peculiarity, it was sufficiently evident to Hester Prynne, that one of this man's shoulders rose higher than the other. Again, at the first instant of perceiving that thin visage, and the slight deformity of the figure, she pressed her infant to her bosom, with so convulsive a force that the poor babe uttered another cry of pain. But the mother did not seem to hear it.

At his arrival in the market-place, and some time before she saw him, the stranger had bent his eyes on Hester Prynne. It was carelessly, at first, like a man chiefly accustomed to look inward, and to whom external matters are of little value and import, unless they bear relation to something within his mind. Very soon, however, his look became keen and penetrative. A writhing horror twisted itself across his features, like a snake gliding swiftly over them, and making one little pause, with all its wreathed intervolutions in open sight. His face darkened with some powerful emotion, which, nevertheless, he so instantaneously controlled by an effort of his will, that, save at a single moment, its expression might have passed for calmness. After a brief space, the convulsion grew almost imperceptible, and finally subsided into the depths of his nature. When he found the eyes of Hester Prynne fastened on his own, and saw that she appeared to recognize him, he slowly and calmly raised his finger, made a gesture with it in the air, and laid it on his lips.

Then, touching the shoulder of a townsman who stood next to him, he addressed him in a formal and courteous manner.

"I pray you, good Sir," said he, "who is this woman?—and wherefore is she here set up to public shame?"

"You must needs be a stranger in this region, friend," answered the townsman, looking curiously at the questioner and his savage companion; "else you would surely have heard of Mistress Hester Prynne, and her evil doings. She hath raised a great scandal, I promise you, in godly Master Dimmesdale's church."

"You say truly," replied the other. "I am a stranger, and have been a wanderer, sorely against my will. I have met with grievous mishaps by sea and land, and have been long held in bonds among the heathen-folk, to the southward; and am now brought hither by this Indian, to be redeemed out of my captivity. Will it please you, therefore, to tell me of Hester Prynne's,—have I her name rightly?—of this woman's offences, and what has brought her to yonder scaffold?"

"Truly, friend, and methinks it must gladden your heart, after your troubles and sojourn in the wilderness," said the townsman, "to find yourself, at length, in a land where iniquity is searched out, and punished in the sight of rulers and people; as here in our godly New England. Yonder woman, Sir, you must know, was the wife of a certain learned man, English by birth, but who had long dwelt in Amsterdam, whence, some good time agone, he was minded to cross over and cast in his lot with us of the Massachusetts. To this purpose, he sent his wife before him, remaining himself to look after some necessary affairs. Marry, good Sir, in some two years, or less, that the woman has been a dweller here in Boston, no tidings have come of this learned gentleman, Master Prynne; and his young wife, look you, being left to her own misguidance——"

"Ah!—aha!—I conceive you," said the stranger, with a bitter smile. "So learned a man as you speak of should have learned this too in his books. And who, by your favor, Sir, may be the father of yonder babe—it is some three or four months old, I should judge—which Mistress Prynne is holding in her arms?"

"Of a truth, friend, that matter remaineth a riddle; and the Daniel who shall expound it is yet a-wanting,"[4] answered the townsman. "Madam Hester absolutely refuseth to speak, and the magistrates have laid their heads together in vain. Peradventure the guilty one stands looking on at this sad spectacle, unknown of man, and forgetting that God sees him."

"The learned man," observed the stranger, with another smile, "should come himself to look into the mystery."

"It behooves him well, if he be still in life," responded the townsman. "Now, good Sir, our Massachusetts magistracy, bethinking themselves that this woman is youthful and fair, and doubtless was strongly tempted to her fall;—and that, moreover, as is most likely, her husband may be at the bottom of the sea;—they have not been bold to put in force the extremity of our righteous law against her. The penalty thereof is death. But, in their great mercy and tenderness of heart, they have doomed Mistress Prynne to stand only a space of three hours on the platform of the pillory, and then and thereafter, for the remainder of her natural life, to wear a mark of shame upon her bosom."

"A wise sentence!" remarked the stranger, gravely bowing his head. "Thus she will be a living sermon against sin, until the ignominious letter be engraved upon her tombstone. It irks me, nevertheless, that the partner of her iniquity should not, at least, stand on the scaffold by her side. But he will be known!—he will be known!—he will be known!"

He bowed courteously to the communicative townsman, and, whispering a few words to his Indian attendant, they both made their way through the crowd.

---

4. See Daniel 5 for the prophet's interpretation of the handwriting on the wall during Belshazzar's great feast.

While this passed, Hester Prynne had been standing on her pedestal, still with a fixed gaze towards the stranger; so fixed a gaze, that, at moments of intense absorption, all other objects in the visible world seemed to vanish, leaving only him and her. Such an interview, perhaps, would have been more terrible than even to meet him as she now did, with the hot, midday sun burning down upon her face, and lighting up its shame; with the scarlet token of infamy on her breast; with the sin-born infant in her arms; with a whole people, drawn forth as to a festival, staring at the features that should have been seen only in the quiet gleam of the fireside, in the happy shadow of a home, or beneath a matronly veil, at church. Dreadful as it was, she was conscious of a shelter in the presence of these thousand witnesses. It was better to stand thus, with so many betwixt him and her, than to greet him, face to face, they two alone. She fled for refuge, as it were, to the public exposure, and dreaded the moment when its protection should be withdrawn from her. Involved in these thoughts, she scarcely heard a voice behind her, until it had repeated her name more than once, in a loud and solemn tone, audible to the whole multitude.

"Hearken unto me, Hester Prynne!" said the voice.

It has already been noticed, that directly over the platform on which Hester Prynne stood was a kind of balcony, or open gallery, appended to the meeting-house. It was the place whence proclamations were wont to be made, amidst an assemblage of the magistracy, with all the ceremonial that attended such public observances in those days. Here, to witness the scene which we are describing, sat Governor Bellingham himself with four sergeants about his chair, bearing halberds,[5] as a guard of honor. He wore a dark feather in his hat, a border of embroidery on his cloak, and a black velvet tunic beneath; a gentleman advanced in years, and with a hard experience written in his wrinkles. He was not ill fitted to be the head and representative of a community, which owed its origin and progress, and its present state of development, not to the impulses of youth, but to the stern and tempered energies of manhood, and the sombre sagacity of age; accomplishing so much, precisely because it imagined and hoped so little. The other eminent characters, by whom the chief ruler was surrounded, were distinguished by a dignity of mien, belonging to a period when the forms of authority were felt to possess the sacredness of divine institutions. They were, doubtless, good men, just, and sage. But, out of the whole human family, it would not have been easy to select the same number of wise and virtuous persons, who should be less capable of sitting in judgment on an erring woman's heart, and disentangling its mesh of good and evil, than the sages of rigid aspect towards whom Hester Prynne now turned her face. She seemed conscious, indeed, that whatever sympathy she might expect lay in the larger and warmer heart of the multitude; for, as she lifted her eyes towards the balcony, the unhappy woman grew pale and trembled.

The voice which had called her attention was that of the reverend and famous John Wilson,[6] the eldest clergyman of Boston, a great scholar, like most of his contemporaries in the profession, and withal a man of kind and genial spirit. This last attribute, however, had been less carefully developed

---

5. Long-handled weapons with an ax on one side and a steel spike on the other. The historical Richard Bellingham (c. 1592–1672) came to Boston in 1634 and was governor in 1641, 1654, and 1665–72.

6. The historical John Wilson (c. 1591–1667) was a Congregational minister who came to Boston with the first settlers, in 1630.

than his intellectual gifts, and was, in truth, rather a matter of shame than self-congratulation with him. There he stood, with a border of grizzled locks beneath his skull-cap; while his gray eyes, accustomed to the shaded light of his study, were winking, like those of Hester's infant, in the unadulterated sunshine. He looked like the darkly engraved portraits which we see prefixed to old volumes of sermons; and had no more right than one of those portraits would have, to step forth, as he now did, and meddle with a question of human guilt, passion, and anguish.

"Hester Prynne," said the clergyman, "I have striven with my young brother here, under whose preaching of the word you have been privileged to sit,"— here Mr. Wilson laid his hand on the shoulder of a pale young man beside him,—"I have sought, I say, to persuade this godly youth, that he should deal with you, here in the face of Heaven, and before these wise and upright rulers, and in hearing of all the people, as touching the vileness and blackness of your sin. Knowing your natural temper better than I, he could the better judge what arguments to use, whether of tenderness or terror, such as might prevail over your hardness and obstinacy; insomuch that you should no longer hide the name of him who tempted you to this grievous fall. But he opposes to me, (with a young man's oversoftness, albeit wise beyond his years,) that it were wronging the very nature of woman to force her to lay open her heart's secrets in such broad daylight, and in presence of so great a multitude. Truly, as I sought to convince him, the shame lay in the commission of the sin, and not in the showing of it forth. What say you to it, once again, brother Dimmesdale? Must it be thou or I that shall deal with this poor sinner's soul?"

There was a murmur among the dignified and reverend occupants of the balcony; and Governor Bellingham gave expression to its purport, speaking in an authoritative voice, although tempered with respect towards the youthful clergyman whom he addressed.

"Good Master Dimmesdale," said he, "the responsibility of this woman's soul lies greatly with you. It behooves you, therefore, to exhort her to repentance, and to confession, as a proof and consequence thereof."

The directness of this appeal drew the eyes of the whole crowd upon the Reverend Mr. Dimmesdale; a young clergyman, who had come from one of the great English universities, bringing all the learning of the age into our wild forest-land. His eloquence and religious fervor had already given the earnest of high eminence in his profession. He was a person of very striking aspect, with a white, lofty, and impending brow, large, brown, melancholy eyes, and a mouth which, unless when he forcibly compressed it, was apt to be tremulous, expressing both nervous sensibility and a vast power of self-restraint. Notwithstanding his high native gifts and scholar-like attainments, there was an air about this young minister,—an apprehensive, a startled, a half-frightened look,—as of a being who felt himself quite astray and at a loss in the pathway of human existence, and could only be at ease in some seclusion of his own. Therefore, so far as his duties would permit, he trode in the shadowy by-paths, and thus kept himself simple and childlike; coming forth, when occasion was, with a freshness, and fragrance, and dewy purity of thought, which, as many people said, affected them like the speech of an angel.

Such was the young man whom the Reverend Mr. Wilson and the Governor had introduced so openly to the public notice, bidding him speak, in the hearing of all men, to that mystery of a woman's soul, so sacred even in its pollution. The trying nature of his position drove the blood from his cheek, and made his lips tremulous.

"Speak to the woman, my brother," said Mr. Wilson. "It is of moment to her soul, and therefore, as the worshipful Governor says, momentous to thine own, in whose charge hers is. Exhort her to confess the truth!"

The Reverend Mr. Dimmesdale bent his head, in silent prayer, as it seemed, and then came forward.

"Hester Prynne," said he, leaning over the balcony, and looking down steadfastly into her eyes, "thou hearest what this good man says, and seest the accountability under which I labor. If thou feelest it to be for thy soul's peace, and that thy earthly punishment will thereby be made more effectual to salvation, I charge thee to speak out the name of thy fellow-sinner and fellow sufferer! Be not silent from any mistaken pity and tenderness for him; for, believe me, Hester, though he were to step down from a high place, and stand there beside thee, on thy pedestal of shame, yet better were it so, than to hide a guilty heart through life. What can thy silence do for him, except it tempt him—yea, compel him, as it were—to add hypocrisy to sin? Heaven hath granted thee an open ignominy, that thereby thou mayest work out an open triumph over the evil within thee, and the sorrow without. Take heed how thou deniest to him—who, perchance, hath not the courage to grasp it for himself—the bitter, but wholesome, cup that is now presented to thy lips!"

The young pastor's voice was tremulously sweet, rich, deep, and broken. The feeling that it so evidently manifested, rather than the direct purport of the words, caused it to vibrate within all hearts, and brought the listeners into one accord of sympathy. Even the poor baby, at Hester's bosom, was affected by the same influence; for it directed its hitherto vacant gaze towards Mr. Dimmesdale, and held up its little arms, with half pleased, half plaintive murmur. So powerful seemed the minister's appeal, that the people could not believe but that Hester Prynne would speak out the guilty name; or else that the guilty one himself, in whatever high or lowly place he stood, would be drawn forth by an inward and inevitable necessity, and compelled to ascend the scaffold.

Hester shook her head.

"Woman, transgress not beyond the limits of Heaven's mercy!" cried the Reverend Mr. Wilson, more harshly than before. "That little babe hath been gifted with a voice, to second and confirm the counsel which thou hast heard. Speak out the name! That, and thy repentance, may avail to take the scarlet letter off thy breast."

"Never!" replied Hester Prynne, looking, not at Mr. Wilson, but into the deep and troubled eyes of the younger clergyman. "It is too deeply branded. Ye cannot take it off. And would that I might endure his agony, as well as mine!"

"Speak, woman!" said another voice, coldly and sternly, proceeding from the crowd about the scaffold. "Speak; and give your child a father!"

"I will not speak!" answered Hester, turning pale as death, but responding to this voice, which she too surely recognized. "And my child must seek a heavenly Father; she shall never know an earthly one!"

"She will not speak!" murmured Mr. Dimmesdale, who, leaning over the balcony, with his hand upon his heart, had awaited the result of his appeal. He now drew back, with a long respiration. "Wondrous strength and generosity of a woman's heart! She will not speak!"

Discerning the impracticable state of the poor culprit's mind, the elder clergyman, who had carefully prepared himself for the occasion, addressed to the multitude a discourse on sin, in all its branches, but with continual reference to the ignominious letter. So forcibly did he dwell upon this symbol, for the hour or more during which his periods were rolling over the people's heads, that it assumed new terrors in their imagination, and seemed to derive its scarlet hue from the flames of the infernal pit. Hester Prynne, meanwhile, kept her place upon the pedestal of shame, with glazed eyes, and an air of weary indifference. She had borne, that morning, all that nature could endure; and as her temperament was not of the order that escapes from too intense suffering by a swoon, her spirit could only shelter itself beneath a stony crust of insensibility, while the faculties of animal life remained entire. In this state, the voice of the preacher thundered remorselessly, but unavailingly, upon her ears. The infant, during the latter portion of her ordeal, pierced the air with its wailings and screams; she strove to hush it, mechanically, but seemed scarcely to sympathize with its trouble. With the same hard demeanour, she was led back to prison, and vanished from the public gaze within its iron-clamped portal. It was whispered, by those who peered after her, that the scarlet letter threw a lurid gleam along the dark passage-way of the interior.

IV. THE INTERVIEW

After her return to the prison, Hester Prynne was found to be in a state of nervous excitement that demanded constant watchfulness, lest she should perpetrate violence on herself, or do some half-frenzied mischief to the poor babe. As night approached, it proving impossible to quell her insubordination by rebuke or threats of punishment, Master Brackett, the jailer, thought fit to introduce a physician. He described him as a man of skill in all Christian modes of physical science, and likewise familiar with whatever the savage people could teach, in respect to medicinal herbs and roots that grew in the forest. To say the truth, there was much need of professional assistance, not merely for Hester herself, but still more urgently for the child; who, drawing its sustenance from the maternal bosom, seemed to have drank in with it all the turmoil, the anguish, and despair, which pervaded the mother's system. It now writhed in convulsions of pain, and was a forcible type,[7] in its little frame, of the moral agony which Hester Prynne had borne throughout the day.

Closely following the jailer into the dismal apartment, appeared that individual, of singular aspect, whose presence in the crowd had been of such deep interest to the wearer of the scarlet letter. He was lodged in the prison, not as suspected of any offence, but as the most convenient and suitable mode of disposing of him, until the magistrates should have conferred with the Indian sagamores[8] respecting his ransom. His name was announced as Roger Chillingworth. The jailer, after ushering him into the room, remained a moment, marvelling at the comparative quiet that followed his entrance; for Hester Prynne had immediately become as still as death, although the child continued to moan.

"Prithee, friend, leave me alone with my patient," said the practitioner. "Trust me, good jailer, you shall briefly have peace in your house; and, I

7. Symbol.   8. Subordinate chiefs.

promise you, Mistress Prynne shall hereafter be more amenable to just authority than you may have found her heretofore."

"Nay, if your worship can accomplish that," answered Master Brackett, "I shall own you for a man of skill indeed! Verily, the woman hath been like a possessed one; and there lacks little, that I should take in hand to drive Satan out of her with stripes."

The stranger had entered the room with the characteristic quietude of the profession to which he announced himself as belonging. Nor did his demeanour change, when the withdrawal of the prison-keeper left him face to face with the woman, whose absorbed notice of him, in the crowd, had intimated so close a relation between himself and her. His first care was given to the child; whose cries, indeed, as she lay writhing on the trundle-bed, made it of peremptory necessity to postpone all other business to the task of soothing her. He examined the infant carefully, and then proceeded to unclasp a leathern case, which he took from beneath his dress. It appeared to contain certain medical preparations, one of which he mingled with a cup of water.

"My old studies in alchemy," observed he, "and my sojourn, for above a year past, among a people well versed in the kindly properties of simples,[9] have made a better physician of me than many that claim the medical degree. Here, woman! The child is yours,—she is none of mine,—neither will she recognize my voice or aspect as a father's. Administer this draught, therefore, with thine own hand."

Hester repelled the offered medicine, at the same time gazing with strongly marked apprehension into his face.

"Wouldst thou avenge thyself on the innocent babe?" whispered she.

"Foolish woman!" responded the physician, half coldly, half soothingly. "What should ail me to harm this misbegotten and miserable babe? The medicine is potent for good; and were it my child,—yea, mine own, as well as thine!—I could do no better for it."

As she still hesitated, being, in fact, in no reasonable state of mind, he took the infant in his arms, and himself administered the draught. It soon proved its efficacy, and redeemed the leech's[1] pledge. The moans of the little patient subsided; its convulsive tossings gradually ceased; and in a few moments, as is the custom of young children after relief from pain, it sank into a profound and dewy slumber. The physician, as he had a fair right to be termed, next bestowed his attention on the mother. With calm and intent scrutiny, he felt her pulse, looked into her eyes,—a gaze that made her heart shrink and shudder, because so familiar, and yet so strange and cold,—and, finally, satisfied with his investigation, proceeded to mingle another draught.

"I know not Lethe nor Nepenthe," remarked he; "but I have learned many new secrets in the wilderness, and here is one of them,—a recipe that an Indian taught me, in requital of some lessons of my own, that were as old as Paracelsus.[2] Drink it! It may be less soothing than a sinless conscience. That I cannot give thee. But it will calm the swell and heaving of thy passion, like oil thrown on the waves of a tempestuous sea."

He presented the cup to Hester, who received it with a slow, earnest look

9. Drugs consisting of elementary ingredients obtained from medicinal plants.
1. Doctor; from the use of leeches, aquatic worms, in drawing blood from patients at a time when bloodletting was commonly prescribed for many illnesses.

2. Swiss alchemist (1493–1541). In Greek mythology the water of Lethe, river in the Underworld, induced oblivion. "Nepenthe": an ancient drug (perhaps opium) that induced forgetfulness of pain.

into his face; not precisely a look of fear, yet full of doubt and questioning, as to what his purposes might be. She looked also at her slumbering child.

"I have thought of death," said she,—"have wished for it,—would even have prayed for it, were it fit that such as I should pray for any thing. Yet, if death be in this cup, I bid thee think again, ere thou beholdest me quaff it. See! It is even now at my lips."

"Drink, then," replied he, still with the same cold composure. "Dost thou know me so little, Hester Prynne? Are my purposes wont to be so shallow? Even if I imagine a scheme of vengeance, what could I do better for my object than to let thee live,—than to give thee medicines against all harm and peril of life,—so that this burning shame may still blaze upon thy bosom?"—As he spoke, he laid his long forefinger on the scarlet letter, which forthwith seemed to scorch into Hester's breast, as if it had been red-hot. He noticed her involuntary gesture, and smiled.—"Live, therefore, and bear about thy doom with thee, in the eyes of men and women,—in the eyes of him whom thou didst call thy husband,—in the eyes of yonder child! And, that thou mayest live, take off this draught."

Without further expostulation or delay, Hester Prynne drained the cup, and, at the motion of the man of skill, seated herself on the bed where the child was sleeping; while he drew the only chair which the room afforded, and took his own seat beside her. She could not but tremble at these preparations; for she felt that—having now done all that humanity, or principle, or, if so it were, a refined cruelty, impelled him to do, for the relief of physical suffering—he was next to treat with her as the man whom she had most deeply and irreparably injured.

"Hester," said he, "I ask not wherefore, nor how, thou hast fallen into the pit, or say rather, thou hast ascended to the pedestal of infamy, on which I found thee. The reason is not far to seek. It was my folly, and thy weakness. I,—a man of thought,—the bookworm of great libraries,—a man already in decay, having given my best years to feed the hungry dream of knowledge,—what had I to do with youth and beauty like thine own! Misshapen from my birth-hour, how could I delude myself with the idea that intellectual gifts might veil physical deformity in a young girl's fantasy! Men call me wise. If sages were ever wise in their own behoof, I might have foreseen all this. I might have known that, as I came out of the vast and dismal forest, and entered this settlement of Christian men, the very first object to meet my eyes would be thyself, Hester Prynne, standing up, a statue of ignominy, before the people. Nay, from the moment when we came down the old church-steps together, a married pair, I might have beheld the bale-fire[3] of that scarlet letter blazing at the end of our path!"

"Thou knowest," said Hester,—for, depressed as she was, she could not endure this last quiet stab at the token of her shame,—"thou knowest that I was frank with thee. I felt no love, nor feigned any."

"True!" replied he. "It was my folly! I have said it. But, up to that epoch of my life, I had lived in vain. The world had been so cheerless! My heart was a habitation large enough for many guests, but lonely and chill, and without a household fire. I longed to kindle one! It seemed not so wild a dream,—old as I was, and sombre as I was, and misshapen as I was,—that the simple bliss,

3. Originally, funeral pyre; here, something like "hellish fire."

which is scattered far and wide, for all mankind to gather up, might yet be mine. And so, Hester, I drew thee into my heart, into its innermost chamber, and sought to warm thee by the warmth which thy presence made there!"

"I have greatly wronged thee," murmured Hester.

"We have wronged each other," answered he. "Mine was the first wrong, when I betrayed thy budding youth into a false and unnatural relation with my decay. Therefore, as a man who has not thought and philosophized in vain, I seek no vengeance, plot no evil against thee. Between thee and me, the scale hangs fairly balanced. But, Hester, the man lives who has wronged us both! Who is he?"

"Ask me not!" replied Hester Prynne, looking firmly into his face. "That thou shalt never know!"

"Never, sayest thou?" rejoined he, with a smile of dark and self-relying intelligence. "Never know him! Believe me, Hester, there are few things,— whether in the outward world, or, to a certain depth, in the invisible sphere of thought,—few things hidden from the man, who devotes himself earnestly and unreservedly to the solution of a mystery. Thou mayest cover up thy secret from the prying multitude. Thou mayest conceal it, too, from the ministers and magistrates, even as thou didst this day, when they sought to wrench the name out of thy heart, and give thee a partner on thy pedestal. But, as for me, I come to the inquest with other senses than they possess. I shall seek this man, as I have sought truth in books; as I have sought gold in alchemy. There is a sympathy that will make me conscious of him. I shall see him tremble. I shall feel myself shudder, suddenly and unawares. Sooner or later, he must needs be mine!"

The eyes of the wrinkled scholar glowed so intensely upon her, that Hester Prynne clasped her hands over her heart, dreading lest he should read the secret there at once.

"Thou wilt not reveal his name? Not the less he is mine," resumed he, with a look of confidence, as if destiny were at one with him. "He bears no letter of infamy wrought into his garment, as thou dost; but I shall read it on his heart. Yet fear not for him! Think not that I shall interfere with Heaven's own method of retribution, or, to my own loss, betray him to the gripe[4] of human law. Neither do thou imagine that I shall contrive aught against his life, no, nor against his fame; if, as I judge, he be a man of fair repute. Let him live! Let him hide himself in outward honor, if he may! Not the less he shall be mine!"

"Thy acts are like mercy," said Hester, bewildered and appalled. "But thy words interpret thee as a terror!"

"One thing, thou that wast my wife, I would enjoin upon thee," continued the scholar. "Thou hast kept the secret of thy paramour. Keep, likewise, mine! There are none in this land that know me. Breathe not, to any human soul, that thou didst ever call me husband! Here, on this wild outskirt of the earth, I shall pitch my tent; for, elsewhere a wanderer, and isolated from human interests, I find here a woman, a man, a child, amongst whom and myself there exist the closest ligaments. No matter whether of love or hate; no matter whether of right or wrong! Thou and thine, Hester Prynne, belong to me. My home is where thou art, and where he is. But betray me not!"

4. Variant spelling of "grip."

"Wherefore dost thou desire it?" inquired Hester, shrinking, she hardly knew why, from this secret bond. "Why not announce thyself openly, and cast me off at once?"

"It may be," he replied, "because I will not encounter the dishonor that besmirches the husband of a faithless woman. It may be for other reasons. Enough, it is my purpose to live and die unknown. Let, therefore, thy husband be to the world as one already dead, and of whom no tidings shall ever come. Recognize me not, by word, by sign, by look! Breathe not the secret, above all, to the man thou wottest[5] of. Shouldst thou fail me in this, beware! His fame, his position, his life, will be in my hands. Beware!"

"I will keep thy secret, as I have his," said Hester.

"Swear it!" rejoined he.

And she took the oath.

"And now, Mistress Prynne," said old Roger Chillingworth, as he was hereafter to be named, "I leave thee alone; alone with thy infant, and the scarlet letter! How is it, Hester? Doth thy sentence bind thee to wear the token in thy sleep? Art thou not afraid of nightmares and hideous dreams?"

"Why dost thou smile so at me?" inquired Hester, troubled at the expression of his eyes. "Art thou like the Black Man[6] that haunts the forest round about us? Hast thou enticed me into a bond that will prove the ruin of my soul?"

"Not thy soul," he answered, with another smile. "No, not thine!"

V. HESTER AT HER NEEDLE

Hester Prynne's term of confinement was now at an end. Her prison-door was thrown open, and she came forth into the sunshine, which, falling on all alike, seemed, to her sick and morbid heart, as if meant for no other purpose than to reveal the scarlet letter on her breast. Perhaps there was a more real torture in her first unattended footsteps from the threshold of the prison, than even in the procession and spectacle that have been described, where she was made the common infamy, at which all mankind was summoned to point its finger. Then, she was supported by an unnatural tension of the nerves, and by all the combative energy of her character, which enabled her to convert the scene into a kind of lurid triumph. It was, moreover, a separate and insulated event, to occur but once in her lifetime, and to meet which, therefore, reckless of economy, she might call up the vital strength that would have sufficed for many quiet years. The very law that condemned her—a giant of stern features, but with vigor to support, as well as to annihilate, in his iron arm—had held her up, through the terrible ordeal of her ignominy. But now, with this unattended walk from her prison-door, began the daily custom, and she must either sustain and carry it forward by the ordinary resources of her nature, or sink beneath it. She could no longer borrow from the future, to help her through the present grief. To-morrow would bring its own trial with it; so would the next day, and so would the next; each its own trial, and yet the very same that was now so unutterably grievous to be borne. The days of the far-off future would toil onward, still with the same burden for her to take up, and bear along with her, but never to fling down; for the accumulating days, and added years, would pile up their misery upon the heap of shame. Throughout them

5. Knowest.   6. Devil.

all, giving up her individuality, she would become the general symbol at which the preacher and moralist might point, and in which they might vivify and embody their images of woman's frailty and sinful passion. Thus the young and pure would be taught to look at her, with the scarlet letter flaming on her breast,—at her, the child of honorable parents,—at her, the mother of a babe, that would hereafter be a woman,—at her, who had once been innocent,—as the figure, the body, the reality of sin. And over her grave, the infamy that she must carry thither would be her only monument.

It may seem marvellous, that, with the world before her,—kept by no restrictive clause of her condemnation within the limits of the Puritan settlement, so remote and so obscure,—free to return to her birthplace, or to any other European land, and there hide her character and identity under a new exterior, as completely as if emerging into another state of being,—and having also the passes of the dark, inscrutable forest open to her, where the wildness of her nature might assimilate itself with a people whose customs and life were alien from the law that had condemned her,—it may seem marvellous, that this woman should still call that place her home, where, and where only, she must needs be the type of shame. But there is a fatality, a feeling so irresistible and inevitable that it has the force of doom, which almost invariably compels human beings to linger around and haunt, ghost-like, the spot where some great and marked event has given the color to their lifetime; and still the more irresistibly, the darker the tinge that saddens it. Her sin, her ignominy, were the roots which she had struck into the soil. It was as if a new birth, with stronger assimilations than the first, had converted the forest-land, still so uncongenial to every other pilgrim and wanderer, into Hester Prynne's wild and dreary, but life-long home. All other scenes of earth—even that village of rural England, where happy infancy and stainless maidenhood seemed yet to be in her mother's keeping, like garments put off long ago—were foreign to her, in comparison. The chain that bound her here was of iron links, and galling to her inmost soul, but never could be broken.

It might be, too,—doubtless it was so, although she hid the secret from herself, and grew pale whenever it struggled out of her heart, like a serpent from its hole,—it might be that another feeling kept her within the scene and pathway that had been so fatal. There dwelt, there trode the feet of one with whom she deemed herself connected in a union, that, unrecognized on earth, would bring them together before the bar of final judgment, and make that their marriage-altar, for a joint futurity of endless retribution. Over and over again, the tempter of souls had thrust this idea upon Hester's contemplation, and laughed at the passionate and desperate joy with which she seized, and then strove to cast it from her. She barely looked the idea in the face, and hastened to bar it in its dungeon. What she compelled herself to believe,— what, finally, she reasoned upon, as her motive for continuing a resident of New England,—was half a truth, and half a self-delusion. Here, she said to herself, had been the scene of her guilt, and here should be the scene of her earthly punishment; and so, perchance, the torture of her daily shame would at length purge her soul, and work out another purity than that which she had lost; more saint-like, because the result of martyrdom.

Hester Prynne, therefore, did not flee. On the outskirts of the town, within the verge of the peninsula, but not in close vicinity to any other habitation, there was a small thatched cottage. It had been built by an earlier settler, and abandoned, because the soil about it was too sterile for cultivation, while its comparative remoteness put it out of the sphere of that social activity which already marked the habits of the emigrants. It stood on the shore, looking across a basin of the sea at the forest-covered hills, towards the west. A clump of scrubby trees, such as alone grew on the peninsula, did not so much conceal the cottage from view, as seem to denote that here was some object which would fain have been, or at least ought to be, concealed. In this little, lonesome dwelling, with some slender means that she possessed, and by the license of the magistrates, who still kept an inquisitorial watch over her, Hester established herself, with her infant child. A mystic shadow of suspicion immediately attached itself to the spot. Children, too young to comprehend wherefore this woman should be shut out from the sphere of human charities, would creep nigh enough to behold her plying her needle at the cottage-window, or standing in the door-way, or laboring in her little garden, or coming forth along the pathway that led townward; and, discerning the scarlet letter on her breast, would scamper off, with a strange, contagious fear.

Lonely as was Hester's situation, and without a friend on earth who dared to show himself, she, however, incurred no risk of want. She possessed an art that sufficed, even in a land that afforded comparatively little scope for its exercise, to supply food for her thriving infant and herself. It was the art—then, as now, almost the only one within a woman's grasp—of needle-work. She bore on her breast, in the curiously embroidered letter, a specimen of her delicate and imaginative skill, of which the dames of a court might gladly have availed themselves, to add the richer and more spiritual adornment of human ingenuity to their fabrics of silk and gold. Here, indeed, in the sable simplicity that generally characterized the Puritanic modes of dress, there might be an infrequent call for the finer productions of her handiwork. Yet the taste of the age, demanding whatever was elaborate in compositions of this kind, did not fail to extend its influence over our stern progenitors, who had cast behind them so many fashions which it might seem harder to dispense with. Public ceremonies, such as ordinations, the installation of magistrates, and all that could give majesty to the forms in which a new government manifested itself to the people, were, as a matter of policy, marked by a stately and well-conducted ceremonial, and a sombre, but yet a studied magnificence. Deep ruffs, painfully wrought bands, and gorgeously embroidered gloves, were all deemed necessary to the official state of men assuming the reins of power; and were readily allowed to individuals dignified by rank or wealth, even while sumptuary laws[7] forbade these and similar extravagances to the plebeian order. In the array of funerals, too,—whether for the apparel of the dead body, or to typify, by manifold emblematic devices of sable cloth and snowy lawn,[8] the sorrow of the survivors,—there was a frequent and characteristic demand for such labor as Hester Prynne could supply. Baby-linen—for babies then wore robes of state—afforded still another possibility of toil and emolument.

By degrees, nor very slowly, her handiwork became what would now be termed the fashion. Whether from commiseration for a woman of so miserable a destiny; or from the morbid curiosity that gives a fictitious value even to common or worthless things; or by whatever other intangible circumstance was then, as now, sufficient to bestow, on some persons, what others might

---

7. Laws governing elaborateness of apparel allowed to various social ranks.

8. I.e., white lawn; fine, light cotton or linen fabric. "Sable cloth": black cloth, of any kind.

seek in vain; or because Hester really filled a gap which must otherwise have remained vacant; it is certain that she had ready and fairly requited employment for as many hours as she saw fit to occupy with her needle. Vanity, it may be, chose to mortify itself, by putting on, for ceremonials of pomp and state, the garments that had been wrought by her sinful hands. Her needlework was seen on the ruff of the Governor; military men wore it on their scarfs, and the minister on his band; it decked the baby's little cap; it was shut up, to be mildewed and moulder away, in the coffins of the dead. But it is not recorded that, in a single instance, her skill was called in aid to embroider the white veil which was to cover the pure blushes of a bride. The exception indicated the ever relentless vigor with which society frowned upon her sin.

Hester sought not to acquire any thing beyond a subsistence, of the plainest and most ascetic description, for herself, and a simple abundance for her child. Her own dress was of the coarsest materials and the most sombre hue; with only that one ornament,—the scarlet letter,—which it was her doom to wear. The child's attire, on the other hand, was distinguished by a fanciful, or, we might rather say, a fantastic ingenuity, which served, indeed, to heighten the airy charm that early began to develop itself in the little girl, but which appeared to have also a deeper meaning. We may speak further of it hereafter. Except for that small expenditure in the decoration of her infant, Hester bestowed all her superfluous means in charity, on wretches less miserable than herself, and who not unfrequently insulted the hand that fed them. Much of the time, which she might readily have applied to the better efforts of her art, she employed in making coarse garments for the poor. It is probable that there was an idea of penance in this mode of occupation, and that she offered up a real sacrifice of enjoyment, in devoting so many hours to such rude handiwork. She had in her nature a rich, voluptuous, Oriental characteristic,—a taste for the gorgeously beautiful, which, save in the exquisite productions of her needle, found nothing else, in all the possibilities of her life, to exercise itself upon. Women derive a pleasure, incomprehensible to the other sex, from the delicate toil of the needle. To Hester Prynne it might have been a mode of expressing, and therefore soothing, the passion of her life. Like all other joys, she rejected it as sin. This morbid meddling of conscience with an immaterial matter betokened, it is to be feared, no genuine and stedfast penitence, but something doubtful, something that might be deeply wrong, beneath.

In this manner, Hester Prynne came to have a part to perform in the world. With her native energy of character, and rare capacity, it could not entirely cast her off, although it had set a mark upon her, more intolerable to a woman's heart than that which branded the brow of Cain.[9] In all her intercourse with society, however, there was nothing that made her feel as if she belonged to it. Every gesture, every word, and even the silence of those with whom she came in contact, implied, and often expressed, that she was banished, and as much alone as if she inhabited another sphere, or communicated with the common nature by other organs and senses than the rest of human kind. She stood apart from mortal interests, yet close beside them, like a ghost that revisits the familiar fireside, and can no longer make itself seen or felt; no more smile with the household joy, nor mourn with the kindred sorrow; or,

9. "And the Lord set a mark upon Cain, lest any finding him should kill him" (Genesis 4.15).

should it succeed in manifesting its forbidden sympathy, awakening only terror and horrible repugnance. These emotions, in fact, and its bitterest scorn besides, seemed to be the sole portion that she retained in the universal heart. It was not an age of delicacy; and her position, although she understood it well, and was in little danger of forgetting it, was often brought before her vivid self-perception, like a new anguish, by the rudest touch upon the tenderest spot. The poor, as we have already said, whom she sought out to be the objects of her bounty, often reviled the hand that was stretched forth to succor them. Dames of elevated rank, likewise, whose doors she entered in the way of her occupation, were accustomed to distil drops of bitterness into her heart; sometimes through that alchemy of quiet malice, by which women can concoct a subtile poison from ordinary trifles; and sometimes, also, by a coarser expression, that fell upon the sufferer's defenceless breast like a rough blow upon an ulcerated wound. Hester had schooled herself long and well; she never responded to these attacks, save by a flush of crimson that rose irrepressibly over her pale cheek, and again subsided into the depths of her bosom. She was patient,—a martyr, indeed,—but she forbore to pray for her enemies; lest, in spite of her forgiving aspirations, the words of the blessing should stubbornly twist themselves into a curse.

Continually, and in a thousand other ways, did she feel the innumerable throbs of anguish that had been so cunningly contrived for her by the undying, the ever-active sentence of the Puritan tribunal. Clergymen paused in the street to address words of exhortation, that brought a crowd, with its mingled grin and frown, around the poor, sinful woman. If she entered a church, trusting to share the Sabbath smile of the Universal Father, it was often her mishap to find herself the text of the discourse. She grew to have a dread of children; for they had imbibed from their parents a vague idea of something horrible in this dreary woman, gliding silently through the town, with never any companion but one only child. Therefore, first allowing her to pass, they pursued her at a distance with shrill cries, and the utterance of a word that had no distinct purport to their own minds, but was none the less terrible to her, as proceeding from lips that babbled it unconsciously. It seemed to argue so wide a diffusion of her shame, that all nature knew of it; it could have caused her no deeper pang, had the leaves of the trees whispered the dark story among themselves,—had the summer breeze murmured about it,—had the wintry blast shrieked it aloud! Another peculiar torture was felt in the gaze of a new eye. When strangers looked curiously at the scarlet letter,—and none ever failed to do so,—they branded it afresh into Hester's soul; so that, oftentimes, she could scarcely refrain, yet always did refrain, from covering the symbol with her hand. But then, again, an accustomed eye had likewise its own anguish to inflict. Its cool stare of familiarity was intolerable. From first to last, in short, Hester Prynne had always this dreadful agony in feeling a human eye upon the token; the spot never grew callous; it seemed, on the contrary, to grow more sensitive with daily torture.

But sometimes, once in many days, or perchance in many months, she felt an eye—a human eye—upon the ignominious brand, that seemed to give a momentary relief, as if half of her agony were shared. The next instant, back it all rushed again, with still a deeper throb of pain; for, in that brief interval, she had sinned anew. Had Hester sinned alone?

Her imagination was somewhat affected, and, had she been of a softer moral

and intellectual fibre, would have been still more so, by the strange and solitary anguish of her life. Walking to and fro, with those lonely footsteps, in the
little world with which she was outwardly connected, it now and then appeared
to Hester,—if altogether fancy, it was nevertheless too potent to be resisted,—
she felt or fancied, then, that the scarlet letter had endowed her with a new
sense. She shuddered to believe, yet could not help believing, that it gave her
a sympathetic knowledge of the hidden sin in other hearts. She was terror-
stricken by the revelations that were thus made. What were they? Could they
be other than the insidious whispers of the bad angel,[1] who would fain have
persuaded the struggling woman, as yet only half his victim, that the outward
guise of purity was but a lie, and that, if truth were everywhere to be shown, a
scarlet letter would blaze forth on many a bosom besides Hester Prynne's? Or,
must she receive those intimations—so obscure, yet so distinct—as truth? In
all her miserable experience, there was nothing else so awful and so loathsome
as this sense. It perplexed, as well as shocked her, by the irreverent inoppor-
tuneness of the occasions that brought it into vivid action. Sometimes, the red
infamy upon her breast would give a sympathetic throb, as she passed near a
venerable minister or magistrate, the model of piety and justice, to whom that
age of antique reverence looked up, as to a mortal man in fellowship with
angels. "What evil thing is at hand?" would Hester say to herself. Lifting her
reluctant eyes, there would be nothing human within the scope of view, save
the form of this earthly saint! Again, a mystic sisterhood would contuma-
ciously assert itself, as she met the sanctified frown of some matron, who,
according to the rumor of all tongues, had kept cold snow within her bosom
throughout life. That unsunned snow in the matron's bosom, and the burning
shame on Hester Prynne's,—what had the two in common? Or, once more,
the electric thrill would give her warning,—"Behold, Hester, here is a companion!"—and, looking up, she would detect the eyes of a young maiden
glancing at the scarlet letter, shyly and aside, and quickly averted, with a faint,
chill crimson in her cheeks; as if her purity were somewhat sullied by that
momentary glance. O Fiend, whose talisman was that fatal symbol, wouldst
thou leave nothing, whether in youth or age, for this poor sinner to revere?—
Such loss of faith is ever one of the saddest results of sin. Be it accepted as a
proof that all was not corrupt in this poor victim of her own frailty, and man's
hard law, that Hester Prynne yet struggled to believe that no fellow-mortal was
guilty like herself.[2]

The vulgar, who, in those dreary old times, were always contributing a
grotesque horror to what interested their imaginations, had a story about the
scarlet letter which we might readily work up into a terrific legend. They
averred, that the symbol was not mere scarlet cloth, tinged in an earthly dye-
pot, but was red-hot with infernal fire, and could be seen glowing all alight,
whenever Hester Prynne walked abroad in the night-time. And we must needs
say, it seared Hester's bosom so deeply, that perhaps there was more truth in
the rumor than our modern incredulity may be inclined to admit.

VI. PEARL

We have as yet hardly spoken of the infant; that little creature, whose innocent life had sprung, by the inscrutable decree of Providence, a lovely and

---

1. Satan.
2. In *Young Goodman Brown* Hawthorne is less ex-   plicit in indicating that loss of faith in others is a result
of one's own sins.

immortal flower, out of the rank luxuriance of a guilty passion. How strange it seemed to the sad woman, as she watched the growth, and the beauty that became every day more brilliant, and the intelligence that threw its quivering sunshine over the tiny features of this child! Her Pearl!—For so had Hester called her; not as a name expressive of her aspect, which had nothing of the calm, white, unimpassioned lustre that would be indicated by the comparison. But she named the infant "Pearl," as being of great price,[3] purchased with all she had,—her mother's only treasure! How strange, indeed! Man had marked this woman's sin by a scarlet letter, which had such potent and disastrous efficacy that no human sympathy could reach her, save it were sinful like herself. God, as a direct consequence of the sin which man thus punished, had given her a lovely child, whose place was on that same dishonored bosom, to connect her parent for ever with the race and descent of mortals, and to be finally a blessed soul in heaven! Yet these thoughts affected Hester Prynne less with hope than apprehension. She knew that her deed had been evil; she could have no faith, therefore, that its result would be for good. Day after day, she looked fearfully into the child's expanding nature; ever dreading to detect some dark and wild peculiarity, that should correspond with the guiltiness to which she owed her being.

Certainly, there was no physical defect. By its perfect shape, its vigor, and its natural dexterity in the use of all its untried limbs, the infant was worthy to have been brought forth in Eden; worthy to have been left there, to be the plaything of the angels, after the world's first parents were driven out. The child had a native grace which does not invariably coexist with faultless beauty; its attire, however simple, always impressed the beholder as if it were the very garb that precisely became it best. But little Pearl was not clad in rustic weeds. Her mother, with a morbid purpose that may be better understood hereafter, had bought the richest tissues that could be procured, and allowed her imaginative faculty its full play in the arrangement and decoration of the dresses which the child wore, before the public eye. So magnificent was the small figure, when thus arrayed, and such was the splendor of Pearl's own proper beauty, shining through the gorgeous robes which might have extinguished a paler loveliness, that there was an absolute circle of radiance around her, on the darksome cottage-floor. And yet a russet gown, torn and soiled with the child's rude play, made a picture of her just as perfect. Pearl's aspect was imbued with a spell of infinite variety; in this one child there were many children, comprehending the full scope between the wild-flower prettiness of a peasant-baby, and the pomp, in little, of an infant princess. Throughout all, however, there was a trait of passion, a certain depth of hue, which she never lost; and if, in any of her changes, she had grown fainter or paler, she would have ceased to be herself;—it would have been no longer Pearl!

This outward mutability indicated, and did not more than fairly express, the various properties of her inner life. Her nature appeared to possess depth, too, as well as variety; but—or else Hester's fears deceived her—it lacked reference and adaptation to the world into which she was born. The child could not be made amenable to rules. In giving her existence, a great law had been broken; and the result was a being, whose elements were perhaps beautiful and brilliant, but all in disorder; or with an order peculiar to themselves, amidst which the point of variety and arrangement was difficult or impossible to be discov-

---

3. "Again, the kingdom of heaven is like unto a merchant man, seeking goodly pearls: Who, when he had found one pearl of great price, went and sold all that he had, and bought it" (Matthew 13.45–46).

ered. Hester could only account for the child's character—and even then, most vaguely and imperfectly—by recalling what she herself had been, during that momentous period while Pearl was imbibing her soul from the spiritual world, and her bodily frame from its material of earth. The mother's impassioned state had been the medium through which were transmitted to the unborn infant the rays of its moral life; and, however white and clear originally, they had taken the deep stains of crimson and gold, the fiery lustre, the black shadow, and the untempered light, of the intervening substance. Above all, the warfare of Hester's spirit, at that epoch, was perpetuated in Pearl. She could recognize her wild, desperate, defiant mood, the flightiness of her temper, and even some of the very cloud-shapes of gloom and despondency that had brooded in her heart. They were now illuminated by the morning radiance of a young child's disposition, but, later in the day of earthly existence, might be prolific of the storm and whirlwind.

The discipline of the family, in those days, was of a far more rigid kind than now. The frown, the harsh rebuke, the frequent application of the rod, enjoined by Scriptural authority,[4] were used, not merely in the way of punishment for actual offences, but as a wholesome regimen for the growth and promotion of all childish virtues. Hester Prynne, nevertheless, the lonely mother of this one child, ran little risk of erring on the side of undue severity. Mindful, however, of her own errors and misfortunes, she early sought to impose a tender, but strict, control over the infant immortality that was committed to her charge. But the task was beyond her skill. After testing both smiles and frowns, and proving that neither mode of treatment possessed any calculable influence, Hester was ultimately compelled to stand aside, and permit the child to be swayed by her own impulses. Physical compulsion or restraint was effectual, of course, while it lasted. As to any other kind of discipline, whether addressed to her mind or heart, little Pearl might or might not be within its reach, in accordance with the caprice that ruled the moment. Her mother, while Pearl was yet an infant, grew acquainted with a certain peculiar look, that warned her when it would be labor thrown away to insist, persuade, or plead. It was a look so intelligent, yet inexplicable, so perverse, sometimes so malicious, but generally accompanied by a wild flow of spirits, that Hester could not help questioning, at such moments, whether Pearl was a human child. She seemed rather an airy sprite, which, after playing its fantastic sports for a little while upon the cottage-floor, would flit away with a mocking smile. Whenever that look appeared in her wild, bright, deeply black eyes, it invested her with a strange remoteness and intangibility; it was as if she were hovering in the air and might vanish, like a glimmering light that comes we know not whence, and goes we know not whither. Beholding it, Hester was constrained to rush towards the child,—to pursue the little elf in the flight which she invariably began,—to snatch her to her bosom, with a close pressure and earnest kisses,—not so much from overflowing love, as to assure herself that Pearl was flesh and blood, and not utterly delusive. But Pearl's laugh, when she was caught, though full of merriment and music, made her mother more doubtful than before.

Heart-smitten at this bewildering and baffling spell, that so often came between herself and her sole treasure, whom she had bought so dear, and

4. "He that spareth his rod hateth his son: but he that loveth him chasteneth him betimes" (Proverbs 13:24).

who was all her world, Hester sometimes burst into passionate tears. Then, perhaps,—for there was no foreseeing how it might affect her,—Pearl would frown, and clench her little fist, and harden her small features into a stern, unsympathizing look of discontent. Not seldom, she would laugh anew, and louder than before, like a thing incapable and unintelligent of human sorrow. Or—but this more rarely happened—she would be convulsed with a rage of grief, and sob out her love for her mother, in broken words, and seem intent on proving that she had a heart, by breaking it. Yet Hester was hardly safe in confiding herself to that gusty tenderness; it passed, as suddenly as it came. Brooding over all these matters, the mother felt like one who has evoked a spirit, but, by some irregularity in the process of conjuration, has failed to win the master-word that should control this new and incomprehensible intelligence. Her only real comfort was when the child lay in the placidity of sleep. Then she was sure of her, and tasted hours of quiet, sad, delicious happiness; until—perhaps with that perverse expression glimmering from beneath her opening lids—little Pearl awoke!

How soon—with what strange rapidity, indeed!—did Pearl arrive at an age that was capable of social intercourse, beyond the mother's ever-ready smile and nonsense-words! And then what a happiness would it have been, could Hester Prynne have heard her clear, bird-like voice mingling with the uproar of other childish voices, and have distinguished and unravelled her own darling's tones, amid all the entangled outcry of a group of sportive children! But this could never be. Pearl was a born outcast of the infantile world. An imp of evil, emblem and product of sin, she had no right among christened infants. Nothing was more remarkable than the instinct, as it seemed, with which the child comprehended her loneliness; the destiny that had drawn an inviolable circle round about her; the whole peculiarity, in short, of her position in respect to other children. Never, since her release from prison, had Hester met the public gaze without her. In all her walks about the town, Pearl, too, was there; first as the babe in arms, and afterwards as the little girl, small companion of her mother, holding a forefinger with her whole grasp, and tripping along at the rate of three or four footsteps to one of Hester's. She saw the children of the settlement, on the grassy margin of the street, or at the domestic thresholds, disporting themselves in such grim fashion as the Puritanic nurture would permit; playing at going to church, perchance; or at scourging Quakers; or taking scalps in a sham-fight with the Indians; or scaring one another with freaks of imitative witchcraft. Pearl saw, and gazed intently, but never sought to make acquaintance. If spoken to, she would not speak again. If the children gathered about her, as they sometimes did, Pearl would grow positively terrible in her puny wrath, snatching up stones to fling at them, with shrill, incoherent exclamations that made her mother tremble, because they had so much the sound of a witch's anathemas in some unknown tongue.

The truth was, that the little Puritans, being of the most intolerant brood that ever lived, had got a vague idea of something outlandish, unearthly, or at variance with ordinary fashions, in the mother and child; and therefore scorned them in their hearts, and not unfrequently reviled them with their tongues. Pearl felt the sentiment, and requited it with the bitterest hatred that can be supposed to rankle in a childish bosom. These outbreaks of a fierce temper had a kind of value, and even comfort, for her mother; because there was at least an intelligible earnestness in the mood, instead of the fitful caprice that so often thwarted her in the child's manifestations. It appalled her, nevertheless, to discern here, again, a shadowy reflection of the evil that had existed in herself. All this enmity and passion had Pearl inherited, by inalienable right, out of Hester's heart. Mother and daughter stood together in the same circle of seclusion from human society; and in the nature of the child seemed to be perpetuated those unquiet elements that had distracted Hester Prynne before Pearl's birth, but had since begun to be soothed away by the softening influences of maternity.

At home, within and around her mother's cottage, Pearl wanted not a wide and various circle of acquaintance. The spell of life went forth from her ever creative spirit, and communicated itself to a thousand objects, as a torch kindles a flame wherever it may be applied. The unlikeliest materials, a stick, a bunch of rags, a flower, were the puppets of Pearl's witchcraft, and, without undergoing any outward change, became spiritually adapted to whatever drama occupied the stage of her inner world. Her one baby-voice served a multitude of imaginary personages, old and young, to talk withal. The pine-trees, aged, black, and solemn, and flinging groans and other melancholy utterances on the breeze, needed little transformation to figure as Puritan elders; the ugliest weeds of the garden were their children, whom Pearl smote down and uprooted, most unmercifully. It was wonderful, the vast variety of forms into which she threw her intellect, with no continuity, indeed, but darting up and dancing, always in a state of preternatural activity,—soon sinking down, as if exhausted by so rapid and feverish a tide of life,—and succeeded by other shapes of a similar wild energy. It was like nothing so much as the phantasmagoric play of the northern lights. In the mere exercise of the fancy, however, and the sportiveness of a growing mind, there might be little more than was observable in other children of bright faculties; except as Pearl, in the dearth of human playmates, was thrown more upon the visionary throng which she created. The singularity lay in the hostile feelings with which the child regarded all these offspring of her own heart and mind. She never created a friend, but seemed always to be sowing broadcast the dragon's teeth, whence sprung a harvest of armed enemies, against whom she rushed to battle.[5] It was inexpressibly sad—then what depth of sorrow to a mother, who felt in her own heart the cause!—to observe, in one so young, this constant recognition of an adverse world, and so fierce a training of the energies that were to make good her cause, in the contest that must ensue.

Gazing at Pearl, Hester Prynne often dropped her work upon her knees, and cried out, with an agony which she would fain have hidden, but which made utterance for itself, betwixt speech and a groan,—"O Father in Heaven,—if Thou art still my Father,—what is this being which I have brought into the world!" And Pearl, overhearing the ejaculation, or aware, through some more subtle channel, of those throbs of anguish, would turn her vivid and beautiful little face upon her mother, smile with sprite-like intelligence, and resume her play.

One peculiarity of the child's deportment remains yet to be told. The very first thing which she had noticed, in her life, was—what?—not the mother's smile, responding to it, as other babies do, by that faint, embryo smile of the little mouth, remembered so doubtfully afterwards, and with such fond

5. In Greek mythology, Jason underwent a test of courage in which he cut down armed men who attacked him after springing up from dragon teeth he had cast into furrows like seed corn.

discussion whether it were indeed a smile. By no means! But that first object of which Pearl seemed to become aware was—shall we say it?—the scarlet letter on Hester's bosom! One day, as her mother stooped over the cradle, the infant's eyes had been caught by the glimmering of the gold embroidery about the letter; and, putting up her little hand, she grasped at it, smiling, not doubtfully, but with a decided gleam that gave her face the look of a much older child. Then, gasping for breath, did Hester Prynne clutch the fatal token, instinctively endeavouring to tear it away; so infinite was the torture inflicted by the intelligent touch of Pearl's baby-hand. Again, as if her mother's agonized gesture were meant only to make sport for her, did little Pearl look into her eyes, and smile! From that epoch, except when the child was asleep, Hester had never felt a moment's safety; not a moment's calm enjoyment of her. Weeks, it is true, would sometimes elapse, during which Pearl's gaze might never once be fixed upon the scarlet letter; but then, again, it would come at unawares, like the stroke of sudden death, and always with that peculiar smile, and odd expression of the eyes.

Once, this freakish, elvish cast came into the child's eyes, while Hester was looking at her own image in them, as mothers are fond of doing; and, suddenly,—for women in solitude, and with troubled hearts, are pestered with unaccountable delusions,—she fancied that she beheld, not her own miniature portrait, but another face in the small black mirror of Pearl's eye. It was a face, fiend-like, full of smiling malice, yet bearing the semblance of features that she had known full well, though seldom with a smile, and never with malice, in them. It was as if an evil spirit possessed the child, and had just then peeped forth in mockery. Many a time afterwards had Hester been tortured, though less vividly, by the same illusion.

In the afternoon of a certain summer's day, after Pearl grew big enough to run about, she amused herself with gathering handfuls of wild-flowers, and flinging them, one by one, at her mother's bosom; dancing up and down, like a little elf, whenever she hit the scarlet letter. Hester's first motion had been to cover her bosom with her clasped hands. But, whether from pride or resignation, or a feeling that her penance might best be wrought out by this unutterable pain, she resisted the impulse, and sat erect, pale as death, looking sadly into little Pearl's wild eyes. Still came the battery of flowers, almost invariably hitting the mark, and covering the mother's breast with hurts for which she could find no balm in this world, nor knew how to seek it in another. At last, her shot being all expended, the child stood still and gazed at Hester, with that little, laughing image of a fiend peeping out—or, whether it peeped or no, her mother so imagined it—from the unsearchable abyss of her black eyes.

"Child, what art thou?" cried the mother.

"O, I am your little Pearl!" answered the child.

But, while she said it, Pearl laughed and began to dance up and down with the humorsome gesticulation of a little imp, whose next freak[6] might be to fly up the chimney.

"Art thou my child, in very truth?" asked Hester.

Nor did she put the question altogether idly, but, for the moment, with a portion of genuine earnestness; for, such was Pearl's wonderful intelligence,

6. Sudden, impulsive act or gesture.

that her mother half doubted whether she were not acquainted with the secret spell of her existence, and might not now reveal herself.

"Yes; I am little Pearl!" repeated the child, continuing her antics.

"Thou art not my child! Thou art no Pearl of mine!" said the mother, half playfully; for it was often the case that a sportive impulse came over her, in the midst of her deepest suffering. "Tell me, then, what thou art, and who sent thee hither?"

"Tell me, mother!" said the child, seriously, coming up to Hester, and pressing herself close to her knees. "Do thou tell me!"

"Thy Heavenly Father sent thee!" answered Hester Prynne.

But she said it with a hesitation that did not escape the acuteness of the child. Whether moved only by her ordinary freakishness, or because an evil spirit prompted her, she put up her small forefinger, and touched the scarlet letter.

"He did not send me!" cried she, positively. "I have no Heavenly Father!"

"Hush, Pearl, hush! Thou must not talk so!" answered the mother, suppressing a groan. "He sent us all into this world. He sent even me, thy mother. Then, much more, thee! Or, if not, thou strange and elfish child, whence didst thou come?"

"Tell me! Tell me!" repeated Pearl, no longer seriously, but laughing, and capering about the floor. "It is thou that must tell me!"

But Hester could not resolve the query, being herself in a dismal labyrinth of doubt. She remembered—betwixt a smile and a shudder—the talk of the neighbouring townspeople; who, seeking vainly elsewhere for the child's paternity, and observing some of her odd attributes, had given out that poor little Pearl was a demon offspring; such as, ever since old Catholic times[7] had occasionally been seen on earth, through the agency of their mothers' sin, and to promote some foul and wicked purpose. Luther,[8] according to the scandal of his monkish enemies, was a brat of that hellish breed; nor was Pearl the only child to whom this inauspicious origin was assigned, among the New England Puritans.

VII. THE GOVERNOR'S HALL

Hester Prynne went, one day, to the mansion of Governor Bellingham, with a pair of gloves, which she had fringed and embroidered to his order, and which were to be worn on some great occasion of state; for, though the chances of a popular election had caused this former ruler to descend a step or two from the highest rank, he still held an honorable and influential place among the colonial magistracy.

Another and far more important reason than the delivery of a pair of embroidered gloves impelled Hester, at this time, to seek an interview with a personage of so much power and activity in the affairs of the settlement. It had reached her ears, that there was a design on the part of some of the leading inhabitants, cherishing the more rigid order of principles in religion and government, to deprive her of her child. On the supposition that Pearl, as already hinted, was of demon origin, these good people not unreasonably argued that a Christian interest in the mother's soul required them to remove such a stum-

---

7. Before the 16th century when Protestant churches broke away from the Roman Catholic Church.

8. Martin Luther (1483–1546), leader of the Reformation in Germany.

bling-block from her path. If the child, on the other hand, were really capable of moral and religious growth, and possessed the elements of ultimate salvation, then, surely, it would enjoy all the fairer prospect of these advantages by being transferred to wiser and better guardianship than Hester Prynne's. Among those who promoted the design, Governor Bellingham was said to be one of the most busy. It may appear singular, and, indeed, not a little ludicrous, that an affair of this kind, which, in later days, would have been referred to no higher jurisdiction than that of the selectmen of the town, should then have been a question publicly discussed, and on which statesmen of eminence took sides. At that epoch of pristine simplicity, however, matters of even slighter public interest, and of far less intrinsic weight than the welfare of Hester and her child, were strangely mixed up with the deliberations of legislators and acts of state. The period was hardly, if at all, earlier than that of our story, when a dispute concerning the right of property in a pig, not only caused a fierce and bitter contest in the legislative body of the colony, but resulted in an important modification of the framework itself of the legislature.[9]

Full of concern, therefore,—but so conscious of her own right, that it seemed scarcely an unequal match between the public, on the one side, and a lonely woman, backed by the sympathies of nature, on the other,—Hester Prynne set forth from her solitary cottage. Little Pearl, of course, was her companion. She was now of an age to run lightly along by her mother's side, and, constantly in motion from morn till sunset, could have accomplished a much longer journey than that before her. Often, nevertheless, more from caprice than necessity, she demanded to be taken up in arms, but was soon as imperious to be set down again, and frisked onward before Hester on the grassy pathway, with many a harmless trip and tumble. We have spoken of Pearl's rich and luxuriant beauty; a beauty that shone with deep and vivid tints; a bright complexion, eyes possessing intensity both of depth and glow, and hair already of a deep, glossy brown, and which, in after years, would be nearly akin to black. There was fire in her and throughout her; she seemed the unpremeditated offshoot of a passionate moment. Her mother, in contriving the child's garb, had allowed the gorgeous tendencies of her imagination their full play; arraying her in a crimson velvet tunic, of a peculiar cut, abundantly embroidered with fantasies and flourishes of gold thread. So much strength of coloring, which must have given a wan and pallid aspect to cheeks of a fainter bloom, was admirably adapted to Pearl's beauty, and made her the very brightest little jet of flame that ever danced upon the earth.

But it was a remarkable attribute of this guard, and, indeed, of the child's whole appearance, that it irresistably and inevitably reminded the beholder of the token which Hester Prynne was doomed to wear upon her bosom. It was the scarlet letter in another form; the scarlet letter endowed with life! The mother herself—as if the red ignominy were so deeply scorched into her brain, that all her conceptions assumed its form—had carefully wrought out the similitude; lavishing many hours of morbid ingenuity, to create an analogy between the object of her affection, and the emblem of her guilt and torture. But, in truth, Pearl was the one, as well as the other; and only in consequence of that identity had Hester contrived so perfectly to represent the scarlet letter in her appearance.

9. The "Sow Case" (*Shearman v. Keayne*, 1642–43) led to the unicameral legislature's dividing into two houses in 1644.

As the two wayfarers came within the precincts of the town, the children of the Puritans looked up from their play,—or what passed for play with those sombre little urchins,—and spake gravely one to another:—

"Behold, verily, there is the woman of the scarlet letter; and, of a truth, moreover, there is the likeness of the scarlet letter running along by her side! Come, therefore, and let us fling mud at them!"

But Pearl, who was a dauntless child, after frowning, stamping her foot, and shaking her little hand with a variety of threatening gestures, suddenly made a rush at the knot of her enemies, and put them all to flight. She resembled, in her fierce pursuit of them, an infant pestilence,—the scarlet fever, or some such half-fledged angel of judgment,—whose mission was to punish the sins of the rising generation. She screamed and shouted, too, with a terrific volume of sound, which doubtless caused the hearts of the fugitives to quake within them. The victory accomplished, Pearl returned quietly to her mother, and looked up smiling into her face.

Without further adventure, they reached the dwelling of Governor Bellingham. This was a large wooden house, built in a fashion of which there are specimens still extant in the streets of our elder towns; now moss-grown, crumbling to decay, and melancholy at heart with the many sorrowful or joyful occurrences remembered or forgotten, that have happened, and passed away, within their dusky chambers. Then, however, there was the freshness of the passing year on its exterior, and the cheerfulness, gleaming forth from the sunny windows, of a human habitation into which death had never entered. It had indeed a very cheery aspect; the walls being overspread with a kind of stucco, in which fragments of broken glass were plentifully intermixed; so that, when the sunshine fell aslant-wise over the front of the edifice, it glittered and sparkled as if diamonds had been flung against it by the double handful. The brilliancy might have befitted Aladdin's palace, rather than the mansion of a grave old Puritan ruler. It was further decorated with strange and seemingly cabalistic[1] figures and diagrams, suitable to the quaint taste of the age, which had been drawn in the stucco when newly laid on, and had now grown hard and durable, for the admiration of after times.

Pearl, looking at this bright wonder of a house, began to caper and dance, and imperatively required that the whole breadth of sunshine should be stripped off its front, and given her to play with.

"No, my little Pearl!" said her mother. "Thou must gather thine own sunshine. I have none to give thee!"

They approached the door; which was of an arched form, and flanked on each side by a narrow tower or projection of the edifice, in both of which were lattice-windows, with wooden shutters to close over them at need. Lifting the iron hammer that hung at the portal, Hester Prynne gave a summons, which was answered by one of the Governor's bond-servants; a free-born Englishman, but now a seven years' slave. During that term he was to be the property of his master, and as much a commodity of bargain and sale as an ox, or a joint-stool. The serf wore the blue coat, which was the customary garb of serving-men at that period, and long before, in the old hereditary halls of England.

"Is the worshipful Governor Bellingham within?" inquired Hester.

"Yea, forsooth," replied the bond-servant, staring with wide-open eyes at the scarlet letter, which, being a new-comer in the country, he had never

1.Occult. "Aladdin's palace": in *Arabian Nights,* the palace of the boy who acquires a magic lamp and ring with which he can summon a genie to do whatever he wishes.

before seen. "Yea, his honorable worship is within. But he hath a godly minister or two with him, and likewise a leech. Ye may not see his worship now."

"Nevertheless, I will enter," answered Hester Prynne; and the bond-servant, perhaps judging from the decision of her air and the glittering symbol in her bosom, that she was a great lady in the land, offered no opposition.

So the mother and little Pearl were admitted into the hall of entrance. With many variations, suggested by the nature of his building-materials, diversity of climate, and a different mode of social life, Governor Bellingham had planned his new habitation after the residences of gentlemen of fair estate in his native land. Here, then, was a wide and reasonably lofty hall, extending through the whole depth of the house, and forming a medium of general communication, more or less directly, with all the other apartments. At one extremity, this spacious room was lighted by the windows of the two towers, which formed a small recess on either side of the portal. At the other end, though partly muffled by a curtain, it was more powerfully illuminated by one of those embowed hall-windows which we read of in old books, and which was provided with a deep and cushioned seat. Here, on the cushion, lay a folio tome, probably of the Chronicles of England,[2] or other such substantial literature; even as, in our own days, we scatter gilded volumes on the centre-table, to be turned over by the casual guest. The furniture of the hall consisted of some ponderous chairs, the backs of which were elaborately carved with wreaths of oaken flowers; and likewise a table in the same taste; the whole being of the Elizabethan age, or perhaps earlier, and heirlooms, transferred hither from the Governor's paternal home. On the table—in token that the sentiment of old English hospitality had not been left behind—stood a large pewter tankard, at the bottom of which, had Hester or Pearl peeped into it, they might have seen the frothy remnant of a recent draught of ale.

On the wall hung a row of portraits, representing the forefathers of the Bellingham lineage, some with armour on their breasts, and others with stately ruffs and robes of peace. All were characterized by the sternness and severity which old portraits so invariably put on; as if they were the ghosts, rather than the pictures, of departed worthies, and were gazing with harsh and intolerant criticism at the pursuits and enjoyments of living men.

At about the centre of the oaken panels, that lined the hall, was suspended a suit of mail, not, like the pictures, an ancestral relic, but of the most modern date; for it had been manufactured by a skilful armorer in London, the same year in which Governor Bellingham came over to New England. There was a steel head-piece, a cuirass, a gorget, and greaves,[3] with a pair of gauntlets and a sword hanging beneath; all, and especially the helmet and breastplate, so highly burnished as to glow with white radiance, and scatter an illumination everywhere about upon the floor. This bright panoply was not meant for mere idle show, but had been worn by the Governor on many a solemn muster and training field, and had glittered, moreover, at the head of a regiment in the Pequod[4] war. For, though bred a lawyer, and accustomed to speak of Bacon, Coke, Noye, and Finch,[5] as his professional associates, the exigencies of this

2. Raphael Holinshed's *Chronicles of England, Scotland, and Ireland* (1577).
3. Parts of armor. "Cuirass": breastplate. "Gorget": collar. "Greaves": shin protector.
4. Indian tribe in eastern Connecticut nearly annihilated by the British in 1637; the survivors were enslaved or otherwise scattered.
5. Sir John Finch (1584–1660), speaker of the House of Commons and chief justice. Francis Bacon (1561–1626), lord chancellor of England. Sir Edward Coke (1552–1634), lord chief justice. William Noye (1577–1634), attorney general.

new country had transformed Governor Bellingham into a soldier, as well as a statesman and ruler.

Little Pearl—who was as greatly pleased with the gleaming armour as she had been with the glittering frontispiece of the house—spent some time looking into the polished mirror of the breastplate.

"Mother," cried she, "I see you here. Look! Look!"

Hester looked, by way of humoring the child; and she saw that, owing to the peculiar effect of this convex mirror, the scarlet letter was represented in exaggerated and gigantic proportions, so as to be greatly the most prominent feature of her appearance. In truth, she seemed absolutely hidden behind it. Pearl pointed upward, also, at a similar picture in the head-piece; smiling at her mother, with the elfish intelligence that was so familiar an expression on her small physiognomy. That look of naughty merriment was likewise reflected in the mirror, with so much breadth and intensity of effect, that it made Hester Prynne feel as if it could not be the image of her own child, but of an imp who was seeking to mould itself into Pearl's shape.

"Come along, Pearl!" said she, drawing her away. "Come and look into this fair garden. It may be, we shall see flowers there; more beautiful ones than we find in the woods."

Pearl, accordingly, ran to the bow-window, at the farther end of the hall, and looked along the vista of a garden-walk, carpeted with closely shaven grass, and bordered with some rude and immature attempt at shrubbery. But the proprietor appeared already to have relinquished, as hopeless, the effort to perpetuate on this side of the Atlantic, in a hard soil and amid the close struggle for subsistence, the native English taste for ornamental gardening. Cabbages grew in plain sight; and a pumpkin vine, rooted at some distance, had run across the intervening space, and deposited one of its gigantic products directly beneath the hall-window; as if to warn the Governor that this great lump of vegetable gold was as rich an ornament as New England earth would offer him. There were a few rose-bushes, however, and a number of apple-trees, probably the descendants of those planted by the Reverend Mr. Blackstone,[6] the first settler of the peninsula; that half mythological personage who rides through our early annals, seated on the back of a bull.

Pearl, seeing the rose-bushes, began to cry for a red rose, and would not be pacified.

"Hush, child, hush!" said her mother earnestly. "Do not cry, dear little Pearl! I hear voices in the garden. The Governor is coming, and gentlemen along with him!"

In fact, adown the vista of the garden-avenue, a number of persons were seen approaching towards the house. Pearl, in utter scorn of her mother's attempt to quiet her, gave an eldritch[7] scream, and then became silent; not from any notion of obedience, but because the quick and mobile curiosity of her disposition was excited by the appearance of these new personages.

VIII. THE ELF-CHILD AND THE MINISTER

Governor Bellingham, in a loose gown and easy cap,—such as elderly gentlemen loved to indue themselves with, in their domestic privacy,—walked foremost, and appeared to be showing off his estate, and expatiating on his

6. Anglican minister who settled at Boston before the arrival of the Puritans, then moved on into American Indian lands.
7. Weird, unearthly.

projected improvements. The wide circumference of an elaborate ruff, beneath his gray beard, in the antiquated fashion of King James's reign, caused his head to look not a little like that of John the Baptist in a charger.[8] The impression made by his aspect, so rigid and severe, and frost-bitten with more than autumnal age, was hardly in keeping with the appliances of worldly enjoyment wherewith he had evidently done his utmost to surround himself. But it is an error to suppose that our grave forefathers—though accustomed to speak and think of human existence as a state merely of trial and warfare, and though unfeignedly prepared to sacrifice goods and life at the behest of duty— made it a matter of conscience to reject such means of comfort, or even luxury, as lay fairly within their grasp. This creed was never taught, for instance, by the venerable pastor, John Wilson, whose beard, white as a snow-drift, was seen over Governor Bellingham's shoulder; while its wearer suggested that pears and peaches might yet be naturalized in the New England climate, and that purple grapes might possibly be compelled to flourish, against the sunny garden-wall. The old clergyman, nurtured at the rich bosom of the English Church, had a long established and legitimate taste for all good and comfortable things; and however stern he might show himself in the pulpit, or in his public reproof of such transgressions as that of Hester Prynne, still, the genial benevolence of his private life had won him warmer affection than was accorded to any of his professional contemporaries.

Behind the Governor and Mr. Wilson came two other guests; one, the Reverend Arthur Dimmesdale, whom the reader may remember, as having taken a brief and reluctant part in the scene of Hester Prynne's disgrace; and, in close companionship with him, old Roger Chillingworth, a person of great skill in physic, who, for two or three years past, had been settled in the town. It was understood that this learned man was the physician as well as friend of the young minister, whose health had severely suffered, of late, by his too unreserved self-sacrifice to the labors and duties of the pastoral relation.

The Governor, in advance of his visitors, ascended one or two steps, and, throwing open the leaves of the great hall window, found himself close to little Pearl. The shadow of the curtain fell on Hester Prynne, and partially concealed her.

"What have we here?" said Governor Bellingham, looking with surprise at the scarlet little figure before him. "I profess, I have never seen the like, since my days of vanity, in old King James's time, when I was wont to esteem it a high favor to be admitted to a court mask! There used to be a swarm of these small apparitions, in holiday-time; and we called them children of the Lord of Misrule.[9] But how gat such a guest into my hall?"

"Ay, indeed!" cried good old Mr. Wilson. "What little bird of scarlet plumage may this be? Methinks I have seen just such figures, when the sun has been shining through a richly painted window, and tracing out the golden and crimson images across the floor. But that was in the old land. Prithee, young one, who art thou, and what has ailed thy mother to bedizen thee in this strange fashion? Art thou a Christian child,—ha? Dost know thy catechism? Or art thou one of those naughty elfs or fairies, whom we thought to have left behind us, with other relics of Papistry, in merry old England?"

"I am mother's child," answered the scarlet vision, "and my name is Pearl!"

8. Platter. James I reigned in England 1603–25. For the decapitation of John the Baptist, see Matthew 14.1–12.

9. Master of the Christmas revels in England before the dominance of the Puritans.

"Pearl?—Ruby, rather!—or Coral!—or Red Rose, at the very least, judging from thy hue!" responded the old minister, putting forth his hand in a vain attempt to pat little Pearl on the cheek. "But where is this mother of thine? Ah! I see," he added; and, turning to Governor Bellingham, whispered,— "This is the selfsame child of whom we have held speech together; and behold here the unhappy woman, Hester Prynne, her mother!"

"Sayest thou so?" cried the Governor. "Nay, we might have judged that such a child's mother must needs be a scarlet woman, and a worthy type of her of Babylon![1] But she comes at a good time; and we will look into this matter forthwith."

Governor Bellingham stepped through the window into the hall, followed by his three guests.

"Hester Prynne," said he, fixing his naturally stern regard on the wearer of the scarlet letter, "there hath been much question concerning thee, of late. The point hath been weightily discussed, whether we, that are of authority and influence, do well discharge our consciences by trusting an immortal soul, such as there is in yonder child, to the guidance of one who hath stumbled and fallen, amid the pitfalls of this world. Speak thou, the child's own mother! Were it not, thinkest thou, for thy little one's temporal and eternal welfare, that she be taken out of thy charge, and clad soberly, and disciplined strictly, and instructed in the truths of heaven and earth? What canst thou do for the child, in this kind?"

"I can teach my little Pearl what I have learned from this!" answered Hester Prynne, laying her finger on the red token.

"Woman, it is thy badge of shame!" replied the stern magistrate. "It is because of the stain which that letter indicates, what we would transfer thy child to other hands."

"Nevertheless," said the mother calmly, though growing more pale, "this badge hath taught me,—it daily teaches me,—it is teaching me at this moment,—lessons whereof my child may be the wiser and better, albeit they can profit nothing to myself."

"We will judge warily," said Bellingham, "and look well what we are about to do. Good Master Wilson, I pray you, examine this Pearl,—since that is her name,—and see whether she hath had such Christian nurture as befits a child of her age."

The old minister seated himself in an arm-chair, and made an effort to draw Pearl betwixt his knees. But the child, unaccustomed to the touch or familiarity of any but her mother, escaped through the open window and stood on the upper step, looking like a wild, tropical bird, of rich plumage, ready to take flight into the upper air. Mr. Wilson, not a little astonished at this outbreak,— for he was a grandfatherly sort of personage, and usually a vast favorite with children,—essayed, however, to proceed with the examination.

"Pearl," said he, with great solemnity, "thou must take heed to instruction, that so, in due season, thou mayest wear in thy bosom the pearl of great price.[2] Canst thou tell me, my child, who made thee?"

---

1. "So he carried me away in the spirit into the wilderness: and I saw a woman sit upon a scarlet colored beast, full of names of blasphemy, having seven heads and ten horns. And the woman was arrayed in purple and scarlet color, and decked with gold and precious stones and pearls, having a golden cup in her hand full of abominations and filthiness of her fornications: And upon her forehead, was a name written, MYSTERY, BABYLON THE GREAT, "THE MOTHER OF HARLOTS AND ABOMINATIONS OF THE EARTH" (Revelation 17.3–5).
2. See n. 3, p. 1295.

Now Pearl knew well enough who made her; for Hester Prynne, the daughter of a pious home, very soon after her talk with the child about her Heavenly Father, had begun to inform her of those truths which the human spirit, at whatever stage of immaturity, imbibes with such eager interest. Pearl, therefore, so large were the attainments of her three years' lifetime, could have borne a fair examination in the New England Primer, or the first column of the Westminster Catechism,[3] although unacquainted with the outward form of either of those celebrated works. But that perversity, which all children have more or less of, and of which little Pearl had a tenfold portion, now, at the most inopportune moment, took thorough possession of her, and closed her lips, or impelled her to speak words amiss. After putting her finger in her mouth, with many ungracious refusals to answer good Mr. Wilson's question, the child finally announced that she had not been made at all, but had been plucked by her mother off the bush of wild roses, that grew by the prison-door.

This fantasy was probably suggested by the near proximity of the Governor's red roses, as Pearl stood outside of the window; together with her recollection of the prison rose-bush, which she had passed in coming hither.

Old Roger Chillingworth, with a smile on his face, whispered something in the young clergyman's ear. Hester Prynne looked at the man of skill, and even then, with her fate hanging in the balance, was startled to perceive what a change had come over his features,—how much uglier they were,—how his dark complexion seemed to have grown duskier, and his figure more misshapen,—since the days when she had familiarly known him. She met his eyes for an instant, but was immediately constrained to give all her attention to the scene now going forward.

"This is awful!" cried the Governor, slowly recovering from the astonishment into which Pearl's response had thrown him. "Here is a child of three years old, and she cannot tell who made her! Without question, she is equally in the dark as to her soul, its present depravity, and future destiny! Methinks, gentlemen, we need inquire no further."

Hester caught hold of Pearl, and drew her forcibly into her arms, confronting the old Puritan magistrate with almost a fierce expression. Alone in the world, cast off by it, and with this sole treasure to keep her heart alive, she felt that she possessed indefeasible rights against the world, and was ready to defend them to the death.

"God gave me the child!" cried she. "He gave her, in requital of all things else, which ye had taken from me. She is my happiness!—she is my torture, none the less! Pearl keeps me here in life! Pearl punishes me too! See ye not, she is the scarlet letter, only capable of being loved, and so endowed with a million-fold the power of retribution for my sin! Ye shall not take her! I will die first!"

"My poor woman," said the not unkind old minister, "the child shall be well cared for!—far better than thou canst do it."

"God gave her into my keeping," repeated Hester Prynne, raising her voice almost to a shriek. "I will not give her up!"—And here, by a sudden impulse, she turned to the young clergyman, Mr. Dimmesdale, at whom, up to this

---

3. Question-and-answer compendium of Calvinistic doctrine adopted in 1648 by Presbyterians and Congregationalists, as well as other sects, based on principles adopted at Westminster, England, 1645–47. "New England Primer": booklet for teaching alphabet through moralizing woodcuts and pious verses such as (for the letter A) "In Adam's fall we sinnéd all."

moment, she had seemed hardly so much as once to direct her eyes.—"Speak thou for me!" cried she. "Thou wast my pastor, and hadst charge of my soul, and knowest me better than these men can. I will not lose the child! Speak for me! Thou knowest,—for thou hast sympathies which these men lack!—thou knowest what is in my heart, and what are a mother's rights, and how much the stronger they are, when that mother has but her child and the scarlet letter! Look thou to it! I will not lose the child! Look to it!"

At this wild and singular appeal, which indicated that Hester Prynne's situation had provoked her to little less than madness, the young minister at once came forward, pale, and holding his hand over his heart, as was his custom whenever his peculiarly nervous temperament was thrown into agitation. He looked now more careworn and emaciated than as we described him at the scene of Hester's public ignominy; and whether it were his failing health, or whatever the cause might be, his large dark eyes had a world of pain in their troubled and melancholy depth.

"There is truth in what she says," began the minister, with a voice sweet, tremulous, but powerful, insomuch that the hall reëchoed, and the hollow armour rang with it,—"truth in what Hester says, and in the feeling which inspires her! God gave her the child, and gave her, too, an instinctive knowledge of its nature and requirements,—both seemingly so peculiar,—which no other mortal being can possess. And, moreover, is there not a quality of awful sacredness in the relation between this mother and this child?"

"Ay!—how is that, good Master Dimmesdale?" interrupted the Governor. "Make that plain, I pray you!"

"It must be even so," resumed the minister. "For, if we deem it otherwise, do we not thereby say that the Heavenly Father, the Creator of all flesh, hath lightly recognized a deed of sin, and made of no account the distinction between unhallowed lust and holy love? This child of its father's guilt and its mother's shame hath come from the hand of God, to work in many ways upon her heart, who pleads so earnestly, and with such bitterness of spirit, the right to keep her. It was meant for a blessing; for the one blessing of her life! It was meant, doubtless, as the mother herself hath told us, for a retribution too; a torture, to be felt at many an unthought of moment; a pang, a sting, an ever-recurring agony, in the midst of a troubled joy! Hath she not expressed this thought in the garb of the poor child, so forcibly reminding us of that red symbol which sears her bosom?"

"Well said, again!" cried good Mr. Wilson. "I feared the woman had no better thought than to make a mountebank of her child!"

"O, not so!—not so!" continued Mr. Dimmesdale. "She recognizes, believe me, the solemn miracle which God hath wrought, in the existence of that child. And may she feel, too,—what, methinks, is the very truth,—that this boon was meant, above all things else, to keep the mother's soul alive, and to preserve her from blacker depths of sin into which Satan might else have sought to plunge her! Therefore it is good for this poor, sinful woman that she hath an infant immortality, a being capable of eternal joy or sorrow, confided to her care,—to be trained up by her to righteousness,—to remind her, at every moment, of her fall,—but yet to teach her, as it were by the Creator's sacred pledge, that, if she bring the child to heaven, the child also will bring its parent thither! Herein is the sinful mother happier than the sinful father. For Hester Prynne's sake, then, and no less for the poor child's sake, let us leave them as Providence hath seen fit to place them!"

"You speak, my friend, with a strange earnestness," said old Roger Chillingworth, smiling at him.

"And there is weighty import in what my young brother hath spoken,"
added the Reverend Mr. Wilson. "What say you, worshipful Master Bellingham? Hath he not pleaded well for the poor woman?"

"Indeed hath he," answered the magistrate, "and hath adduced such arguments, that we will even leave the matter as it now stands; so long, at least, as
there shall be no further scandal in the woman. Care must be had, nevertheless, to put the child to due and stated examination in the catechism at thy
hands or Master Dimmesdale's. Moreover, at a proper season, the tithing-
men[4] must take heed that she go both to school and to meeting."

The young minister, on ceasing to speak, had withdrawn a few steps from
the group, and stood with his face partially concealed in the heavy folds of the
window-curtain; while the shadow of his figure, which the sunlight cast upon
the floor, was tremulous with the vehemence of his appeal. Pearl, that wild
and flighty little elf, stole softly towards him, and taking his hand in the grasp
of both her own, laid her cheek against it; a caress so tender, and withal so
unobtrusive, that her mother, who was looking on, asked herself,—"Is that
my Pearl?" Yet she knew that there was love in the child's heart, although it
mostly revealed itself in passion, and hardly twice in her lifetime had been
softened by such gentleness as now. The minister,—for, save the long-sought
regards of woman, nothing is sweeter than these marks of childish preference,
accorded spontaneously by a spiritual instinct, and therefore seeming to imply
in us something truly worthy to be loved,—the minister looked round, laid his
hand on the child's head, hesitated an instant, and then kissed her brow. Little
Pearl's unwonted mood of sentiment lasted no longer; she laughed, and went
capering down the hall, so airily, that old Mr. Wilson raised a question
whether even her tiptoes touched the floor.

"The little baggage hath witchcraft in her, I profess," said he to Mr. Dimmesdale. "She needs no old woman's broomstick to fly withal!"

"A strange child!" remarked old Roger Chillingworth. "It is easy to see the
mother's part in her. Would it be beyond a philosopher's research, think ye,
gentlemen, to analyze the child's nature, and, from its make and mould, to
give a shrewd guess at the father?"

"Nay; it would be sinful, in such a question, to follow the clew of profane
philosophy," said Mr. Wilson. "Better to fast and pray upon it; and still better,
it may be, to leave the mystery as we find it, unless Providence reveal it of its
own accord. Thereby, every good Christian man hath a title to show a father's
kindness towards the poor, deserted babe."

The affair being so satisfactorily concluded, Hester Prynne, with Pearl,
departed from the house. As they descended the steps, it is averred that the
lattice of a chamber-window was thrown open, and forth into the sunny day
was thrust the face of Mistress Hibbins, Governor Bellingham's bitter-tempered sister, and the same who, a few years later, was executed as a witch.

"Hist, hist!" said she, while her ill-omened physiognomy seemed to cast a
shadow over the cheerful newness of the house. "Wilt thou go with us to-
night? There will be a merry company in the forest; and I wellnigh promised
the Black Man that comely Hester Prynne should make one."

"Make my excuse to him, so please you!" answered Hester, with a trium-

---

4. Parish officers.

phant smile. "I must tarry at home, and keep watch over my little Pearl. Had they taken her from me, I would willingly have gone with thee into the forest, and signed my name in the Black Man's book too, and that with mine own blood!"

"We shall have thee there anon!" said the witch-lady, frowning, as she drew back her head.

But here—if we suppose this interview betwixt Mistress Hibbins and Hester Prynne to be authentic, and not a parable—was already an illustration of the young minister's argument against sundering the relation of a fallen mother to the offspring of her frailty. Even thus early had the child saved her from Satan's snare.

IX. THE LEECH

Under the appellation of Roger Chillingworth, the reader will remember, was hidden another name, which its former wearer had resolved should never more be spoken. It has been related, how, in the crowd that witnessed Hester Prynne's ignominious exposure, stood a man, elderly, travel-worn, who, just emerging from the perilous wilderness, beheld the woman, in whom he hoped to find embodied the warmth and cheerfulness of home, set up as a type of sin before the people. Her matronly fame was trodden under all men's feet. Infamy was babbling around her in the public marketplace. For her kindred, should the tidings ever reach them, and for the companions of her unspotted life, there remained nothing but the contagion of her dishonor; which would not fail to be distributed in strict accordance and proportion with the intimacy and sacredness of their previous relationship. Then why—since the choice was with himself—should the individual, whose connection with the fallen woman had been the most intimate and sacred of them all, come forward to vindicate his claim to an inheritance so little desirable? He resolved not to be pilloried beside her on her pedestal of shame. Unknown to all but Hester Prynne, and possessing the lock and key of her silence, he chose to withdraw his name from the roll of mankind, and, as regarded his former ties and interests, to vanish out of life as completely as if he indeed lay at the bottom of the ocean, whither rumor had long ago consigned him. This purpose once effected, new interests would immediately spring up, and likewise a new purpose; dark, it is true, if not guilty, but of force enough to engage the full strength of his faculties.

In pursuance of this resolve, he took up his residence in the Puritan town, as Roger Chillingworth, without other introduction than the learning and intelligence of which he possessed more than a common measure. As his studies, at a previous period of his life, had made him extensively acquainted with the medical science of the day, it was as a physician that he presented himself, and as such was cordially received. Skilful men, of the medical and chirurgical[5] profession, were of rare occurrence in the colony. They seldom, it would appear, partook of the religious zeal that brought other emigrants across the Atlantic. In their researches into the human frame, it may be that the higher and more subtile faculties of such men were materialized, and that they lost the spiritual view of existence amid the intricacies of that wondrous

5. I.e., surgical.

mechanism, which seemed to involve art enough to comprise all of life within itself. At all events, the health of the good town of Boston, so far as medicine had aught to do with it, had hitherto lain in the guardianship of an aged deacon and apothecary, whose piety and godly deportment were stronger testimonials in his favor, than any that he could have produced in the shape of a diploma. The only surgeon was one who combined the occasional exercise of that noble art with the daily and habitual flourish of a razor. To such a professional body Roger Chillingworth was a brilliant acquisition. He soon manifested his familiarity with the ponderous and imposing machinery of antique physic; in which every remedy contained a multitude of far-fetched and heterogeneous ingredients, as elaborately compounded as if the proposed result had been the Elixir of Life.[6] In his Indian captivity, moreover, he had gained much knowledge of the properties of native herbs and roots; nor did he conceal from his patients, that these simple medicines, Nature's boon to the untutored savage, had quite as large a share of his own confidence as the European pharmacopœia,[7] which so many learned doctors had spent centuries in elaborating.

This learned stranger was exemplary, as regarded at least the outward forms of a religious life, and, early after his arrival, had chosen for his spiritual guide the Reverend Mr. Dimmesdale. The young divine, whose scholar-like renown still lived in Oxford, was considered by his more fervent admirers as little less than a heaven-ordained apostle, destined, should he live and labor for the ordinary term of life, to do as great deeds for the now feeble New England Church, as the early Fathers had achieved for the infancy of the Christian faith. About this period, however, the health of Mr. Dimmesdale had evidently begun to fail. By those best acquainted with his habits, the paleness of the young minister's cheek was accounted for by his too earnest devotion to study, his scrupulous fulfilment of parochial duty, and, more than all, by the fasts and vigils of which he made a frequent practice, in order to keep the grossness of this earthly state from clogging and obscuring his spiritual lamp. Some declared, that, if Mr. Dimmesdale were really going to die, it was cause enough, that the world was not worthy to be any longer trodden by his feet. He himself, on the other hand, with characteristic humility, avowed his belief, that, if Providence should see fit to remove him, it would be because of his own unworthiness to perform its humblest mission here on earth. With all this difference of opinion as to the cause of his decline, there could be no question of the fact. His form grew emaciated; his voice, though still rich and sweet, had a certain melancholy prophecy of decay in it; he was often observed, on any slight alarm or other sudden accident, to put his hand over his heart, with first a flush and then a paleness, indicative of pain.

Such was the young clergyman's condition, and so imminent the prospect that his dawning light would be extinguished, all untimely, when Roger Chillingworth made his advent to the town. His first entry on the scene, few people could tell whence, dropping down, as it were, out of the sky, or starting from the nether earth, had an aspect of mystery, which was easily heightened to the miraculous. He was now known to be a man of skill; it was observed that he gathered herbs, and the blossoms of wild-flowers, and dug up roots and plucked off twigs from the forest-trees, like one acquainted with hidden virtues

6. Here, substance thought capable of prolonging life indefinitely.   7. Collection of approved drugs.

in what was valueless to common eyes. He was heard to speak of Sir Kenelm Digby,[8] and other famous men,—whose scientific attainments were esteemed hardly less than supernatural,—as having been his correspondents or associates. Why, with such rank in the learned world, had he come hither? What could he, whose sphere was in great cities, be seeking in the wilderness? In answer to this query, a rumor gained ground,—and, however absurd, was entertained by some very sensible people,—that Heaven had wrought an absolute miracle, by transporting an eminent Doctor of Physic, from a German university, bodily through the air, and setting him down at the door of Mr. Dimmesdale's study! Individuals of wiser faith, indeed, who knew that Heaven promotes its purposes without aiming at the stage-effect of what is called miraculous interposition, were inclined to see a providential hand in Roger Chillingworth's so opportune arrival.

This idea was countenanced by the strong interest which the physician ever manifested in the young clergyman; he attached himself to him as a parishioner, and sought to win a friendly regard and confidence from his naturally reserved sensibility. He expressed great alarm at his pastor's state of health, but was anxious to attempt the cure, and, if early undertaken, seemed not despondent of a favorable result. The elders, the deacons, the motherly dames, and the young and fair maidens, of Mr. Dimmesdale's flock, were alike importunate that he should make trial of the physician's frankly offered skill. Mr. Dimmesdale gently repelled their entreaties.

"I need no medicine," said he.

But how could the young minister say so, when, with every successive Sabbath, his cheek was paler and thinner, and his voice more tremulous than before,—when it had now become a constant habit, rather than a casual gesture, to press his hand over his heart? Was he weary of his labors? Did he wish to die? These questions were solemnly propounded to Mr. Dimmesdale by the elder ministers of Boston and the deacons of his church, who, to use their own phrase, "dealt with him" on the sin of rejecting the aid which Providence so manifestly held out. He listened in silence, and finally promised to confer with the physician.

"Were it God's will," said the Reverend Mr. Dimmesdale, when, in fulfilment of this pledge, he requested old Roger Chillingworth's professional advice, "I could be well content, that my labors, and my sorrows, and my sins, and my pains, should shortly end with me, and what is earthly of them be buried in my grave, and the spiritual go with me to my eternal state, rather than that you should put your skill to the proof in my behalf."

"Ah," replied Roger Chillingworth, with that quietness which, whether imposed or natural, marked all his deportment, "it is thus that a young clergyman is apt to speak. Youthful men, not having taken a deep root, give up their hold of life so easily! And saintly men, who walk with God on earth, would fain be away, to walk with him on the golden pavements of the New Jerusalem."[9]

"Nay, rejoined the young minister, putting his hand to his heart, with a flush of pain flitting over his brow, "were I worthier to walk there, I could be better content to toil here."

8. English naval officer, diplomat, and scientist (1603–1665).
9. The city John saw "coming down from God out of

heaven, prepared as a bride adorned for her husband" (Revelation 21.2).

"Good men ever interpret themselves too meanly," said the physician.

In this manner, the mysterious old Roger Chillingworth became the medical adviser of the Reverend Mr. Dimmesdale. As not only the disease interested the physician, but he was strongly moved to look into the character and qualities of the patient, these two men, so different in age, came gradually to spend much time together. For the sake of the minister's health, and to enable the leech to gather plants with healing balm in them, they took long walks on the seashore, or in the forest; mingling various talk with the plash and murmur of the waves, and the solemn wind-anthem among the tree-tops. Often, likewise, one was the guest of the other, in his place of study and retirement. There was a fascination for the minister in the company of the man of science, in whom he recognized an intellectual cultivation of no moderate depth or scope; together with a range and freedom of ideas, that he would have vainly looked for among the members of his own profession. In truth, he was startled, if not shocked, to find this attribute in the physician. Mr. Dimmesdale was a true priest, a true religionist, with the reverential sentiment largely developed, and an order of mind that impelled itself powerfully along the track of a creed, and wore its passage continually deeper with the lapse of time. In no state of society would he have been what is called a man of liberal views; it would always be essential to his peace to feel the pressure of a faith about him, supporting, while it confined him within its iron framework. Not the less, however, though with a tremulous enjoyment, did he feel the occasional relief of looking at the universe through the medium of another kind of intellect than those with which he habitually held converse. It was as if a window were thrown open, admitting a freer atmosphere into the close and stifled study, where his life was wasting itself away, amid lamp-light, or obstructed daybeams, and the musty fragrance, be it sensual or moral, that exhales from books. But the air was too fresh and chill to be long breathed, with comfort. So the minister, and the physician with him, withdrew again within the limits of what their church defined as orthodox.

Thus Roger Chillingworth scrutinized his patient carefully, both as he saw him in his ordinary life, keeping an accustomed pathway in the range of thoughts familiar to him, and as he appeared when thrown amidst other moral scenery, the novelty of which might call out something new to the surface of his character. He deemed it essential, it would seem, to know the man, before attempting to do him good. Wherever there is a heart and an intellect, the diseases of the physical frame are tinged with the peculiarities of these. In Arthur Dimmesdale, thought and imagination were so active, and sensibility so intense, that the bodily infirmity would be likely to have its ground-work there. So Roger Chillingworth—the man of skill, the kind and friendly physician—strove to go deep into his patient's bosom, delving among his principles, prying into his recollections, and probing every thing with a cautious touch, like a treasure-seeker in a dark cavern. Few secrets can escape an investigator, who has opportunity and license to undertake such a quest, and skill to follow it up. A man burdened with a secret should especially avoid the intimacy of his physician. If the latter possess native sagacity, and a nameless something more,—let us call it intuition; if he show no intrusive egotism, nor disagreeably prominent characteristics of his own; if he have the power, which must be born with him, to bring his mind into such affinity with his patient's, that this last shall unawares have spoken what he imagines himself only to have thought; if such revelations be received without tumult, and acknowledged not so often by an uttered sympathy, as by silence, an inarticulate breath, and here and there a word, to indicate that all is understood; if, to these qualifications of a confidant be joined the advantages afforded by his recognized character as a physician;—then, at some inevitable moment, will the soul of the sufferer be dissolved, and flow forth in a dark, but transparent stream, bringing all its mysteries into the daylight.

Roger Chillingworth possessed all, or most, of the attributes above enumerated. Nevertheless, time went on; a kind of intimacy, as we have said, grew up between these two cultivated minds, which had as wide a field as the whole sphere of human thought and study, to meet upon; they discussed every topic of ethics and religion, of public affairs, and private character; they talked much, on both sides, of matters that seemed personal to themselves; and yet no secret, such as the physician fancied must exist there, ever stole out of the minister's consciousness into his companion's ear. The latter had his suspicions, indeed, that even the nature of Mr. Dimmesdale's bodily disease had never fairly been revealed to him. It was a strange reserve!

After a time, at a hint from Roger Chillingworth, the friends of Mr. Dimmesdale effected an arrangement by which the two were lodged in the same house; so that every ebb and flow of the minister's life-tide might pass under the eye of his anxious and attached physician. There was much joy throughout the town, when this greatly desirable object was attained. It was held to be the best possible measure for the young clergyman's welfare; unless, indeed, as often urged by such as felt authorized to do so, he had selected some one of the many blooming damsels, spiritually devoted to him, to become his devoted wife. This latter step, however, there was no present prospect that Arthur Dimmesdale would be prevailed upon to take; he rejected all suggestions of the kind, as if priestly celibacy were one of his articles of church-discipline. Doomed by his own choice, therefore, as Mr. Dimmesdale so evidently was, to eat his unsavory morsel always at another's board, and endure the life-long chill which must be his lot who seeks to warm himself only at another's fireside, it truly seemed that this sagacious, experienced, benevolent, old physician, with his concord of paternal and reverential love for the young pastor, was the very man, of all mankind, to be constantly within reach of his voice.

The new abode of the two friends was with a pious widow, of good social rank, who dwelt in a house covering pretty nearly the site on which the venerable structure of King's Chapel has since been built. It had the grave-yard, originally Isaac Johnson's home-field, on one side, and so was well adapted to call up serious reflections, suited to their respective employments, in both minister and man of physic. The motherly care of the good widow assigned to Mr. Dimmesdale a front apartment, with a sunny exposure, and heavy window-curtains to create a noontide shadow, when desirable. The walls were hung round with tapestry, said to be from the Gobelin looms,[1] and, at all events, representing the Scriptural story of David and Bathsheba, and Nathan the Prophet, in colors still unfaded, but which made the fair woman of the scene almost as grimly picturesque as the woe-denouncing seer. Here, the pale clergyman piled up his library, rich with parchment-bound folios of the

---

1. I.e., looms of the great Parisian tapestry-making family.

Fathers,[2] and the lore of Rabbis, and monkish erudition, of which the Protestant divines, even while they vilified and decried that class of writers, were yet constrained often to avail themselves. On the other side of the house, old Roger Chillingworth arranged his study and laboratory; not such as a modern man of science would reckon even tolerably complete, but provided with a distilling apparatus, and the means of compounding drugs and chemicals, which the practised alchemist knew well how to turn to purpose. With such commodiousness of situation, these two learned persons sat themselves down, each in his own domain, yet familiarly passing from one apartment to the other, and bestowing a mutual and not incurious inspection into one another's business.

And the Reverend Arthur Dimmesdale's best discerning friends, as we have intimated, very reasonably imagined that the hand of Providence had done all this, for the purpose—besought in so many public, and domestic, and secret prayers—of restoring the young minister to health. But—it must now be said—another portion of the community had latterly begun to take its own view of the relation betwixt Mr. Dimmesdale and the mysterious old physician. When an uninstructed multitude attempts to see with its eyes, it is exceedingly apt to be deceived. When, however, it forms its judgment, as it usually does, on the intuitions of its great and warm heart, the conclusions thus attained are often so profound and so unerring, as to possess the character of truths supernaturally revealed. The people, in the case of which we speak, could justify its prejudice against Roger Chillingworth by no fact or argument worthy of serious refutation. There was an aged handicraftsman, it is true, who had been a citizen of London at the period of Sir Thomas Overbury's murder, now some thirty years agone; he testified to having seen the physician, under some other name, which the narrator of the story had now forgotten, in company with Doctor Forman, the famous old conjurer, who was implicated in the affair of Overbury.[3] Two or three individuals hinted, that the man of skill, during his Indian captivity, had enlarged his medical attainments by joining in the incantations of the savage priests; who were universally acknowledged to be powerful enchanters, often performing seemingly miraculous cures by their skill in the black art. A large number—and many of these were persons of such sober sense and practical observation, that their opinions would have been valuable, in other matters—affirmed that Roger Chillingworth's aspect had undergone a remarkable change while he had dwelt in town, and especially since his abode with Mr. Dimmesdale. At first, his expression had been calm, meditative, scholar-like. Now, there was something ugly and evil in his face, which they had not previously noticed, and which grew still the more obvious to sight, the oftener they looked upon him. According to the vulgar idea, the fire in his laboratory had been brought from the lower regions, and was fed with infernal fuel; and so, as might be expected, his visage was getting sooty with the smoke.

To sum up the matter, it grew to be a widely diffused opinion, that the Reverend Arthur Dimmesdale, like many other personages of especial sanctity,

2. Christians in early centuries after Jesus' death who formulated Christian doctrines and observances. For the biblical story of adultery and punishment, see 2 Samuel 11 and 12.
3. Sir Thomas Overbury (1581–1613), author of *Characters* (1614), poisoned in the Tower of London by Ann Turner (mentioned later), at the instigation of the licentious countess of Essex; earlier Dr. Simon Forman (1552–1611), keeper of a historically valuable diary, had connived with the countess in seeking Overbury's death by witchcraft.

in all ages of the Christian world, was haunted either by Satan himself, or Satan's emissary, in the guise of old Roger Chillingworth. This diabolical agent had the Divine permission, for a season, to burrow into the clergyman's intimacy, and plot against his soul. No sensible man, it was confessed, could doubt on which side the victory would turn. The people looked, with an unshaken hope, to see the minister come forth out of the conflict, transfigured with the glory which he would unquestionably win. Meanwhile, nevertheless, it was sad to think of the perchance mortal agony through which he must struggle towards his triumph.

Alas, to judge from the gloom and terror in the depths of the poor minister's eyes, the battle was a sore one, and the victory any thing but secure!

X. THE LEECH AND HIS PATIENT

Old Roger Chillingworth, throughout life, had been calm in temperament, kindly, though not of warm affections, but ever, and in all his relations with the world, a pure and upright man. He had begun an investigation, as he imagined, with the severe and equal integrity of a judge, desirous only of truth, even as if the question involved no more than the air-drawn lines and figures of a geometrical problem, instead of human passions, and wrongs inflicted on himself. But, as he proceeded, a terrible fascination, a kind of fierce, though still calm, necessity seized the old man within its gripe, and never set him free again, until he had done all its bidding. He now dug into the poor clergyman's heart, like a miner searching for gold; or, rather, like a sexton[4] delving into a grave, possibly in quest of a jewel that had been buried on the dead man's bosom, but likely to find nothing save mortality and corruption. Alas for his own soul, if these were what he sought!

Sometimes, a light glimmered out of the physician's eyes, burning blue and ominous, like the reflection of a furnace, or, let us say, like one of those gleams of ghastly fire that darted from Bunyan's awful doorway in the hill-side,[5] and quivered on the pilgrim's face. The soil where this dark miner was working had perchance shown indications that encouraged him.

"This man," said he, at one such moment, to himself, "pure as they deem him,—all spiritual as he seems,—hath inherited a strong animal nature from his father or his mother. Let us dig a little farther in the direction of this vein!"

Then, after long search into the minister's dim interior, and turning over many precious materials, in the shape of high aspirations for the welfare of his race, warm love of souls, pure sentiments, natural piety, strengthened by thought and study, and illuminated by revelation,—all of which invaluable gold was perhaps no better than rubbish to the seeker,—he would turn back, discouraged, and begin his quest towards another point. He groped along as stealthily, with as cautious a tread, and as wary an outlook, as a thief entering a chamber where a man lies only half asleep,—or, it may be, broad awake,— with purpose to steal the very treasure which this man guards as the apple of his eye. In spite of his premeditated carefulness, the floor would now and then creak; his garments would rustle; the shadow of his presence, in a forbidden

---

4. Man in charge of maintaining a church, especially responsible for digging graves in the churchyard and supervising burials there.

5. In John Bunyan's *Pilgrim's Progress* (1678), the eighth stage of Christian's pilgrimage, the "by-way to hell" through which hypocrites enter.

proximity, would be thrown across his victim. In other words, Mr. Dimmesdale, whose sensibility of nerve often produced the effect of spiritual intuition, would become vaguely aware that something inimical to his peace had thrust itself into relation with him. But old Roger Chillingworth, too, had perceptions that were almost intuitive; and when the minister threw his startled eyes towards him, there the physician sat; his kind, watchful, sympathizing, but never intrusive friend.

Yet Mr. Dimmesdale would perhaps have seen this individual's character more perfectly, if a certain morbidness, to which sick hearts are liable, had not rendered him suspicious of all mankind. Trusting no man as his friend, he could not recognize his enemy when the latter actually appeared. He therefore still kept up a familiar intercourse with him, daily receiving the old physician in his study; or visiting the laboratory, and, for recreation's sake, watching the processes by which weeds were converted into drugs of potency.

One day, leaning his forehead on his hand, and his elbow on the sill of the open window, that looked towards the grave-yard, he talked with Roger Chillingworth, while the old man was examining a bundle of unsightly plants.

"Where," asked he, with a look askance at them,—for it was the clergyman's peculiarity that he seldom, now-a-days, looked straightforth at any object, whether human or inanimate,—"Where, my kind doctor, did you gather those herbs, with such a dark, flabby leaf?"

"Even in the grave-yard, here at hand" answered the physician, continuing his employment. "They are new to me. I found them growing on a grave, which bore no tombstone, nor other memorial of the dead man, save these ugly weeds that have taken upon themselves to keep him in remembrance. They grew out of his heart, and typify, it may be, some hideous secret that was buried with him, and which he had done better to confess during his lifetime."

"Perchance," said Mr. Dimmesdale, "he earnestly desired it, but could not."

"And wherefore?" rejoined the physician. "Wherefore not; since all the powers of nature call so earnestly for the confession of sin, that these black weeds have sprung up out of a buried heart, to make manifest an unspoken crime?"

"That, good Sir, is but a fantasy of yours," replied the minister. "There can be, if I forebode aright, no power, short of the Divine mercy, to disclose, whether by uttered words, or by type or emblem, the secrets that may be buried with a human heart. The heart, making itself guilty of such secrets, must perforce hold them, until the day when all hidden things shall be revealed. Nor have I so read or interpreted Holy Writ, as to understand that the disclosure of human thoughts and deeds, then to be made, is intended as a part of the retribution. That, surely, were a shallow view of it. No; these revelations, unless I greatly err, are meant merely to promote the intellectual satisfaction of all intelligent beings, who will stand waiting, on that day, to see the dark problem of this life made plain. A knowledge of men's hearts will be needful to the completest solution of that problem. And I conceive, moreover, that the hearts holding such miserable secrets as you speak of will yield them up, at that last day,[6] not with reluctance, but with a joy unutterable."

"Then why not reveal them here?" asked Roger Chillingworth, glancing

6. Judgment day.

quietly aside at the minister. "Why should not the guilty ones sooner avail themselves of this unutterable solace?"

"They mostly do," said the clergyman, griping hard at his breast, as if afflicted with an importunate throb of pain. "Many, many a poor soul hath given its confidence to me, not only on the deathbed, but while strong in life, and fair in reputation. And ever, after such an outpouring, O, what a relief have I witnessed in those sinful brethren! even as in one who at last draws free air, after long stifling with his own polluted breath. How can it be otherwise? Why should a wretched man, guilty, we will say, of murder, prefer to keep the dead corpse buried in his own heart, rather than fling it forth at once, and let the universe take care of it!"

"Yet some men bury their secrets thus," observed the calm physician.

"True; there are such men," answered Mr. Dimmesdale. "But, not to suggest more obvious reasons, it may be that they are kept silent by the very constitution of their nature. Or,—can we not suppose it?—guilty as they may be, retaining, nevertheless, a zeal for God's glory and man's welfare, they shrink from displaying themselves black and filthy in the view of men; because, thenceforward, no good can be achieved by them; no evil of the past be redeemed by better service. So, to their own unutterable torment, they go about among their fellow-creatures, looking pure as new-fallen snow; while their hearts are all speckled and spotted with iniquity of which they cannot rid themselves."

"These men deceive themselves," said Roger Chillingworth, with somewhat more emphasis than usual, and making a slight gesture with his forefinger. "They fear to take up the shame that rightfully belongs to them. Their love for man, their zeal for God's service,—these holy impulses may or may not coexist in their hearts with the evil inmates to which their guilt has unbarred the door, and which must needs propagate a hellish breed within them. But, if they seek to glorify God, let them not lift heavenward their unclean hands! If they would serve their fellow-men, let them do it by making manifest the power and reality of conscience, in constraining them to penitential self-abasement! Wouldst thou have me to believe, O wise and pious friend, that a false show can be better—can be more for God's glory, or man's welfare—than God's own truth? Trust me, such men deceive themselves!"

"It may be so," said the young clergyman indifferently, as waiving a discussion that he considered irrelevant or unseasonable. He had a ready faculty, indeed, of escaping from any topic that agitated his too sensitive and nervous temperament.—"But, now, I would ask of my well-skilled physician, whether, in good sooth, he deems me to have profited by his kindly care of this weak frame of mine?"

Before Roger Chillingworth could answer, they heard the clear, wild laughter of a young child's voice, proceeding from the adjacent burial-ground. Looking instinctively from the open window,—for it was summer-time,—the minister beheld Hester Prynne and little Pearl passing along the footpath that traversed the inclosure. Pearl looked as beautiful as the day, but was in one of those moods of perverse merriment which, whenever they occurred, seemed to remove her entirely out of the sphere of sympathy or human contact. She now skipped irreverently from one grave to another; until, coming to the broad flat, armorial tombstone of a departed worthy,—perhaps of Isaac Johnson himself,—she began to dance upon it. In reply to her mother's command and entreaty that she would behave more decorously, little Pearl paused to gather the prickly burrs from a tall burdock, which grew beside the tomb. Taking a handful of these, she arranged them along the lines of the scarlet letter that decorated the maternal bosom, to which the burrs, as their nature was, tenaciously adhered. Hester did not pluck them off.

Roger Chillingworth had by this time approached the window, and smiled grimly down.

"There is no law, nor reverence for authority, no regard for human ordinances or opinions, right or wrong, mixed up with that child's composition," remarked he, as much to himself as to his companion. "I saw her, the other day, bespatter the Governor himself with water, at the cattle-trough in Spring Lane. What, in Heaven's name, is she? Is the imp altogether evil? Hath she affections? Hath she any discoverable principle of being?"

"None,—save the freedom of a broken law," answered Mr. Dimmesdale, in a quiet way, as if he had been discussing the point within himself. "Whether capable of good, I know not."

The child probably overheard their voices; for, looking up to the window, with a bright, but naughty smile of mirth and intelligence, she threw one of the prickly burrs at the Reverend Mr. Dimmesdale. The sensitive clergyman shrunk, with nervous dread, from the light missile. Detecting his emotion, Pearl clapped her little hands in the most extravagant ecstasy. Hester Prynne, likewise, had involuntarily looked up; and all these four persons, old and young, regarded one another in silence, till the child laughed aloud, and shouted,—"Come away, mother! Come away, or yonder old Black Man will catch you! He hath got hold of the minister already. Come away, mother, or he will catch you! But he cannot catch little Pearl!"

So she drew her mother away, skipping, dancing, and frisking fantastically among the hillocks of the dead people, like a creature that had nothing in common with a bygone and buried generation, nor owned herself akin to it. It was as if she had been made afresh, out of new elements, and must perforce be permitted to live her own life, and be a law unto herself, without her eccentricities being reckoned to her for a crime.

"There goes a woman," resumed Roger Chillingworth, after a pause, "who, be her demerits what they may, hath none of that mystery of hidden sinfulness which you deem so grievous to be borne. Is Hester Prynne the less miserable, think you, for that scarlet letter on her breast?"

"I do verily believe it," answered the clergyman. "Nevertheless, I cannot answer for her. There was a look of pain in her face, which I would gladly have been spared the sight of. But still, methinks, it must needs be better for the sufferer to be free to show his pain, as this poor woman Hester is, than to cover it all up in his heart."

There was another pause; and the physician began anew to examine and arrange the plants which he had gathered.

"You inquired of me, a little time agone," said he, at length, "my judgment as touching your health."

"I did," answered the clergyman, "and would gladly learn it. Speak frankly, I pray you, be it for life or death."

"Freely, then, and plainly," said the physician, still busy with his plants, but keeping a wary eye on Mr. Dimmesdale, "the disorder is a strange one; not so much in itself, nor as outwardly manifested,—in so far, at least, as the symptoms have been laid open to my observation. Looking daily at you, my good Sir, and watching the tokens of your aspect, now for months gone by, I should deem you a man sore sick, it may be, yet not so sick but that an instructed and watchful physician might well hope to cure you. But—I know not what to say—the disease is what I seem to know, yet know it not."

"You speak in riddles, learned Sir," said the pale minister, glancing aside out of the window.

"Then, to speak more plainly," continued the physician, "and I crave pardon, Sir,—should it seem to require pardon,—for this needful plainness of my speech. Let me ask,—as your friend,—as one having charge, under Providence, of your life and physical well-being,—hath all the operation of this disorder been fairly laid open and recounted to me?"

"How can you question it?" asked the minister. "Surely, it were child's play to call in a physician, and then hide the sore!"

"You would tell me, then, that I know all?" said Roger Chillingworth, deliberately, and fixing an eye, bright with intense and concentrated intelligence, on the minister's face. "Be it so! But, again! He to whom only the outward and physical evil is laid open knoweth, oftentimes, but half the evil which he is called upon to cure. A bodily disease, which we look upon as whole and entire within itself, may, after all, be but a symptom of some ailment in the spiritual part. Your pardon, once again, good Sir, if my speech give the shadow of offence. You, Sir, of all men whom I have known, are he whose body is the closest conjoined, and imbued, and identified, so to speak, with the spirit whereof it is the instrument."

"Then I need ask no further," said the clergyman, somewhat hastily rising from his chair. "You deal not, I take it, in medicine for the soul!"

"Thus, a sickness," continued Roger Chillingworth, going on, in an unaltered tone, without heeding the interruption,—but standing up, and confronting the emaciated and white-cheeked minister with his low, dark, and misshapen figure,—"a sickness, a sore place, if we may so call it, in your spirit, hath immediately its appropriate manifestation in your bodily frame. Would you, therefore, that your physician heal the bodily evil? How may this be, unless you first lay open to him the wound or trouble in your soul?"

"No!—not to thee!—not to an earthly physician!" cried Mr. Dimmesdale, passionately, and turning his eyes, full and bright, and with a kind of fierceness, on old Roger Chillingworth. "Not to thee! But, if it be the soul's disease, then do I commit myself to the one Physician of the soul! He, if it stand with his good pleasure, can cure; or he can kill! Let him do with me as, in his justice and wisdom, he shall see good. But who art thou, that meddlest in this matter?—that dares thrust himself between the sufferer and his God?"

With a frantic gesture, he rushed out of the room.

"It is as well to have made this step," said Roger Chillingworth to himself, looking after the minister with a grave smile. "There is nothing lost. We shall be friends again anon. But see, now, how passion takes hold upon this man, and hurrieth him out of himself! As with one passion, so with another! He hath done a wild thing ere now, this pious Master Dimmesdale, in the hot passion of his heart!"

It proved not difficult to reëstablish the intimacy of the two companions, on the same footing and in the same degree as heretofore. The young clergyman, after a few hours of privacy, was sensible that the disorder of his nerves had hurried him into an unseemly outbreak of temper, which there had been nothing in the physician's words to excuse or palliate. He marvelled, indeed, at the violence with which he had thrust back the kind old man, when merely proffering the advice which it was his duty to bestow, and which the minister himself had expressly sought. With these remorseful feelings, he lost no time in making the amplest apologies, and besought his friend still to continue the care, which, if not successful in restoring him to health, had, in all probability, been the means of prolonging his feeble existence to that hour. Roger Chillingworth readily assented, and went on with his medical supervision of the minister; doing his best for him, in all good faith, but always quitting the patient's apartment, at the close of a professional interview, with a mysterious and puzzled smile upon his lips. This expression was invisible in Mr. Dimmesdale's presence, but grew strongly evident as the physician crossed the threshold.

"A rare case!" he muttered. "I must needs look deeper into it. A strange sympathy betwixt soul and body! Were it only for the art's sake, I must search this matter to the bottom!"

It came to pass, not long after the scene above recorded, that the Reverend Mr. Dimmesdale, at noon-day, and entirely unawares, fell into a deep, deep slumber, sitting in his chair, with a large black-letter[7] volume open before him on the table. It must have been a work of vast ability in the somniferous school of literature. The profound depth of the minister's repose was the more remarkable; inasmuch as he was one of those persons whose sleep, ordinarily, is as light, as fitful, and as easily scared away, as a small bird hopping on a twig. To such an unwonted remoteness, however, had his spirit now withdrawn into itself, that he stirred not in his chair, when old Roger Chillingworth, without any extraordinary precaution, came into the room. The physician advanced directly in front of his patient, laid his hand upon his bosom, and thrust aside the vestment, that, hitherto, had always covered it even from the professional eye.

Then, indeed, Mr. Dimmesdale shuddered, and slightly stirred.

After a brief pause, the physician turned away.

But with what a wild look of wonder, joy, and horror! With what a ghastly rapture, as it were, too mighty to be expressed only by the eye and features, and therefore bursting forth through the whole ugliness of his figure, and making itself even riotously manifest by the extravagant gestures with which he threw up his arms towards the ceiling, and stamped his foot upon the floor! Had a man seen old Roger Chillingworth, at that moment of his ecstacy, he would have had no need to ask how Satan comports himself, when a precious human soul is lost to heaven, and won into his kingdom.

But what distinguished the physician's ecstasy from Satan's was the trait of wonder in it!

XI. THE INTERIOR OF A HEART

After the incident last described, the intercourse between the clergyman and the physician, though externally the same, was really of another character than it had previously been. The intellect of Roger Chillingworth had now a

---

7. An early typeface modeled on medieval script.

sufficiently plain path before it. It was not, indeed, precisely that which he had laid out for himself to tread. Calm, gentle, passionless, as he appeared, there was yet, we fear, a quiet depth of malice, hitherto latent, but active now, in this unfortunate old man, which led him to imagine a more intimate revenge than any mortal had ever wreaked upon an enemy. To make himself the one trusted friend, to whom should be confided all the fear, the remorse, the agony, the ineffectual repentance, the backward rush of sinful thoughts, expelled in vain! All that guilty sorrow, hidden from the world, whose great heart would have pitied and forgiven, to be revealed to him, the Pitiless, to him, the Unforgiving! All that dark treasure to be lavished on the very man, to whom nothing else could so adequately pay the debt of vengeance!

The clergyman's shy and sensitive reserve had balked this scheme. Roger Chillingworth, however, was inclined to be hardly, if at all, less satisfied with the aspect of affairs, which Providence—using the avenger and his victim for its own purposes, and, perchance, pardoning, where it seemed most to punish—had substituted for his black devices. A revelation, he could almost say, had been granted to him. It mattered little, for his object, whether celestial, or from what other region. By its aid, in all the subsequent relations betwixt him and Mr. Dimmesdale, not merely the external presence, but the very inmost soul of the latter seemed to be brought out before his eyes, so that he could see and comprehend its every movement. He became, thenceforth, not a spectator only, but a chief actor, in the poor minister's interior world. He could play upon him as he chose. Would he arouse him with a throb of agony? The victim was for ever on the rack; it needed only to know the spring that controlled the engine;—and the physician knew it well! Would he startle him with sudden fear? As at the waving of a magician's wand, uprose a grisly phantom,—uprose a thousand phantoms,—in many shapes, of death, or more awful shame, all flocking round about the clergyman, and pointing with their fingers at his breast!

All this was accomplished with a subtlety so perfect, that the minister, though he had constantly a dim perception of some evil influence watching over him, could never gain a knowledge of its actual nature. True, he looked doubtfully, fearfully,—even, at times, with horror and the bitterness of hatred,—at the deformed figure of the old physician. His gestures, his gait, his grizzled beard, his slightest and most indifferent acts, the very fashion of his garments, were odious in the clergyman's sight; a token, implicitly to be relied on, of a deeper antipathy in the breast of the latter than he was willing to acknowledge to himself. For, as it was impossible to assign a reason for such distrust and abhorrence, so Mr. Dimmesdale, conscious that the poison of one morbid spot was infecting his heart's entire substance, attributed all his presentiments to no other cause. He took himself to task for his bad sympathies in reference to Roger Chillingworth, disregarded the lesson that he should have drawn from them, and did his best to root them out. Unable to accomplish this, he nevertheless, as a matter of principle, continued his habits of social familiarity with the old man, and thus gave him constant opportunities for perfecting the purpose to which—poor, forlorn creature that he was, and more wretched than his victim—the avenger had devoted himself.

While thus suffering under bodily disease, and gnawed and tortured by some black trouble of the soul, and given over to the machinations of his deadliest enemy, the Reverend Mr. Dimmesdale had achieved a brilliant popularity in his sacred office. He won it, indeed, in great part, by his sorrows. His intellectual gifts, his moral perceptions, his power of experiencing and communicating emotion, were kept in a state of preternatural activity by the prick and anguish of his daily life. His fame, though still on its upward slope, already overshadowed the soberer reputations of his fellow-clergymen, eminent as several of them were. There were scholars among them, who had spent more years in acquiring abstruse lore, connected with the divine profession, than Mr. Dimmesdale had lived; and who might well, therefore, be more profoundly versed in such solid and valuable attainments than their youthful brother. There were men, too, of a sturdier texture of mind than his, and endowed with a far greater share of shrewd, hard, iron or granite understanding; which, duly mingled with a fair proportion of doctrinal ingredient, constitutes a highly respectable, efficacious, and unamiable variety of the clerical species. There were others, again, true saintly fathers, whose faculties had been elaborated by weary toil among their books, and by patient thought, and etherealized, moreover, by spiritual communications with the better world, into which their purity of life had almost introduced these holy personages, with their garments of mortality still clinging to them. All that they lacked was the gift that descended upon the chosen disciples, at Pentecost, in tongues of flame;[8] symbolizing, it would seem, not the power of speech in foreign and unknown languages, but that of addressing the whole human brotherhood in the heart's native language. These fathers, otherwise so apostolic, lacked Heaven's last and rarest attestation of their office, the Tongue of Flame. They would have vainly sought—had they ever dreamed of seeking—to express the highest truths through the humblest medium of familiar words and images. Their voices came down, afar and indistinctly, from the upper heights where they habitually dwelt.

Not improbably, it was to this latter class of men that Mr. Dimmesdale, by many of his traits of character, naturally belonged. To their high mountain-peaks of faith and sanctity he would have climbed, had not the tendency been thwarted by the burden, whatever it might be, of crime or anguish, beneath which it was his doom to totter. It kept him down, on a level with the lowest; him, the man of ethereal attributes, whose voice the angels might else have listened to and answered! But this very burden it was, that gave him sympathies so intimate with the sinful brotherhood of mankind; so that his heart vibrated in unison with theirs, and received their pain into itself, and sent its own throb of pain through a thousand other hearts, in gushes of sad, persuasive eloquence. Oftenest persuasive, but sometimes terrible! The people knew not the power that moved them thus. They deemed the young clergyman a miracle of holiness. They fancied him the mouth-piece of Heaven's messages of wisdom, and rebuke, and love. In their eyes, the very ground on which he trod was sanctified. The virgins of his church grew pale around him, victims of a passion so imbued with religious sentiment that they imagined it to be all religion, and brought it openly, in their white bosoms, as their most acceptable sacrifice before the altar. The aged members of his flock, beholding Mr. Dimmesdale's frame so feeble, while they were themselves so rugged in their infirmity, believed that he would go heavenward before them, and enjoined it upon their children, that their old bones should be buried close to their young pastor's

---

8. See Acts 2.3 for the descent of the Holy Spirit to the disciples in the form of "cloven tongues like as of fire."

holy grave. And, all this time, perchance, when poor Mr. Dimmesdale was thinking of his grave, he questioned with himself whether the grass would ever grow on it, because an accursed thing must there be buried!

It is inconceivable, the agony with which this public veneration tortured him! It was his genuine impulse to adore the truth, and to reckon all things shadow-like, and utterly devoid of weight or value, that had not its divine essence as the life within their life. Then, what was he?—a substance?—or the dimmest of all shadows? He longed to speak out, from his own pulpit, at the full height of his voice, and tell the people what he was. "I, whom you behold in these black garments of the priesthood,—I, who ascend the sacred desk, and turn my pale face heavenward, taking upon myself to hold communion, in your behalf, with the Most High Omniscience,—I, in whose daily life you discern the sanctity of Enoch,[9]—I, whose footsteps, as you suppose, leave a gleam along my earthly track, whereby the pilgrims that shall come after me may be guided to the regions of the blest,—I, who have laid the hand of baptism upon your children,—I, who have breathed the parting prayer over your dying friends, to whom the Amen sounded faintly from a world which they had quitted,—I, your pastor, whom you so reverence and trust, am utterly a pollution and a lie!"

More than once, Mr. Dimmesdale had gone into the pulpit, with a purpose never to come down its steps, until he should have spoken words like the above. More than once, he had cleared his throat, and drawn in the long, deep, and tremulous breath, which, when sent forth again, would come burdened with the black secret of his soul. More than once—nay, more than a hundred times—he had actually spoken! Spoken! But how? He had told his hearers that he was altogether vile, a viler companion of the vilest, the worst of sinners, an abomination, a thing of unimaginable iniquity; and that the only wonder was, that they did not see his wretched body shrivelled up before their eyes, by the burning wrath of the Almighty! Could there be plainer speech than this? Would not the people start up in their seats, by a simultaneous impulse, and tear him down out of the pulpit which he defiled? Not so, indeed! They heard it all, and did but reverence him the more. They little guessed what deadly purport lurked in those self-condemning words. "The godly youth!" said they among themselves. "The saint on earth! Alas, if he discern such sinfulness in his own white soul, what horrid spectacle would he behold in thine or mine!" The minister well knew—subtle, but remorseful hypocrite that he was!—the light in which his vague confession would be viewed. He had striven to put a cheat upon himself[1] by making the avowal of a guilty conscience, but had gained only one other sin, and a self-acknowledged shame, without the momentary relief of being self-deceived. He had spoken the very truth, and transformed it into the veriest falsehood. And yet, by the constitution of his nature, he loved the truth, and loathed the lie, as few men ever did. Therefore, above all things else, he loathed his miserable self!

His inward trouble drove him to practices, more in accordance with the old, corrupted faith of Rome, than with the better light of the church in which he had been born and bred. In Mr. Dimmesdale's secret closet, under lock and key, there was a bloody scourge.[2] Oftentimes, this Protestant and Puritan

---

9. In Genesis 5.21–24 Enoch is said to have "walked with God," a passage interpreted by the Apostle Paul in Hebrews 11.5 as meaning that God "translated" En-

och to heaven without his having died.
1. Label himself as a cheat.
2. Whip.

divine had plied it on his own shoulders; laughing bitterly at himself the while, and smiting so much the more pitilessly, because of that bitter laugh. It was his custom, too, as it has been that of many other pious Puritans, to fast,—not, however, like them, in order to purify the body and render it the fitter medium of celestial illumination,—but rigorously, and until his knees trembled beneath him, as an act of penance. He kept vigils, likewise, night after night, sometimes in utter darkness; sometimes with a glimmering lamp; and sometimes, viewing his own face in a looking-glass, by the most powerful light which he could throw upon it. He thus typified the constant introspection wherewith he tortured, but could not purify, himself. In these lengthened vigils, his brain often reeled, and visions seemed to flit before him; perhaps seen doubtfully, and by a faint light of their own, in the remote dimness of the chamber, or more vividly, and close beside him, within the looking-glass. Now it was a herd of diabolic shapes, that grinned and mocked at the pale minister, and beckoned him away with them; now a group of shining angels, who flew upward heavily, as sorrow-laden, but grew more ethereal as they rose. Now came the dead friends of his youth, and his white-bearded father, with a saint-like frown, and his mother, turning her face away as she passed by. Ghost of a mother, thinnest fantasy of a mother,—methinks she might yet have thrown a pitying glance towards her son! And now, through the chamber which these spectral thoughts had made so ghastly, glided Hester Prynne, leading along little Pearl, in her scarlet garb, and pointing her forefinger, first, at the scarlet letter on her bosom, and then at the clergyman's own breast.

None of these visions ever quite deluded him. At any moment, by an effort of his will, he could discern substances through their misty lack of substance, and convince himself that they were not solid in their nature, like yonder table of carved oak, or that big, square leathern-bound and brazen-clasped volume of divinity. But, for all that, they were, in one sense, the truest and most substantial things which the poor minister now dealt with. It is the unspeakable misery of a life so false as his, that it steals the pith and substance out of whatever realities there are around us, and which were meant by Heaven to be the spirit's joy and nutriment. To the untrue man, the whole universe is false,—it is impalpable,—it shrinks to nothing within his grasp. And he himself, in so far as he shows himself in a false light, becomes a shadow, or, indeed, ceases to exist. The only truth, that continued to give Mr. Dimmesdale a real existence on this earth, was the anguish in his inmost soul, and the undissembled expression of it in his aspect. Had he once found power to smile, and wear a face of gayety, there would have been no such man!

On one of those ugly nights, which we have faintly hinted at, but forborne to picture forth, the minister started from his chair. A new thought had struck him. There might be a moment's peace in it. Attiring himself with as much care as if it had been for public worship, and precisely in the same manner, he stole softly down the staircase, undid the door, and issued forth.

XII. THE MINISTER'S VIGIL

Walking in the shadow of a dream, as it were, and perhaps actually under the influence of a species of somnambulism, Mr. Dimmesdale reached the spot, where, now so long since, Hester Prynne had lived through her first hour of public ignominy. The same platform or scaffold, black and weather-stained with the storm or sunshine of seven long years, and footworn, too, with the tread of many culprits who had since ascended it, remained standing beneath the balcony of the meeting-house. The minister went up the steps.

It was an obscure night of early May. An unvaried pall of cloud muffled the whole expanse of sky from zenith to horizon. If the same multitude which had stood as eyewitnesses while Hester Prynne sustained her punishment could now have been summoned forth, they would have discerned no face above the platform, nor hardly the outline of a human shape, in the dark gray of the midnight. But the town was all asleep. There was no peril of discovery. The minister might stand there, if it so pleased him, until morning should redden in the east, without other risk than that the dank and chill night-air would creep into his frame, and stiffen his joints with rheumatism, and clog his throat with catarrh and cough; thereby defrauding the expectant audience of to-morrow's prayer and sermon. No eye could see him, save that ever-wakeful one which had seen him in his closet, wielding the bloody scourge. Why, then, had he come hither? Was it but the mockery of penitence? A mockery, indeed, but in which his soul trifled with itself! A mockery at which angels blushed and wept, while fiends rejoiced, with jeering laughter! He had been driven hither by the impulse of that Remorse which dogged him everywhere, and whose own sister and closely linked companion was that Cowardice which invariably drew him back, with her tremulous gripe, just when the other impulse had hurried him to the verge of a disclosure. Poor, miserable man! what right had infirmity like his to burden itself with crime? Crime is for the iron-nerved, who have their choice either to endure it, or, if it press too hard, to exert their fierce and savage strength for a good purpose, and fling it off at once! This feeble and most sensitive of spirits could do neither, yet continually did one thing or another, which intertwined, in the same inextricable knot, the agony of heaven-defying guilt and vain repentance.

And thus, while standing on the scaffold, in this vain show of expiation, Mr. Dimmesdale was overcome with a great horror of mind, as if the universe were gazing at a scarlet token on his naked breast, right over his heart. On that spot, in very truth, there was, and there had long been, the gnawing and poisonous tooth of bodily pain. Without any effort of his will, or power to restrain himself, he shrieked aloud; an outcry that went pealing through the night, and was beaten back from one house to another, and reverberated from the hills in the background; as if a company of devils, detecting so much misery and terror in it, had made a plaything of the sound, and were bandying it to and fro.

"It is done!" muttered the minister, covering his face with his hands. "The whole town will awake, and hurry forth, and find me here!"

But it was not so. The shriek had perhaps sounded with a far greater power, to his own startled ears, than it actually possessed. The town did not awake; or, if it did, the drowsy slumberers mistook the cry either for something frightful in a dream, or for the noise of witches; whose voices, at that period, were often heard to pass over the settlements or lonely cottages, as they rode with Satan through the air. The clergyman, therefore, hearing no symptoms of disturbance, uncovered his eyes and looked about him. At one of the chamber-windows of Governor Bellingham's mansion, which stood at some distance, on the line of another street, he beheld the appearance of the old magistrate himself, with a lamp in his hand, a white night-cap on his head, and a long white gown enveloping his figure. He looked like a ghost, evoked unseasonably from the grave. The cry had evidently startled him. At another window of the same house, moreover, appeared old Mistress Hibbins, the Governor's sister, also with a lamp, which, even thus far off, revealed the expression of her sour and discontented face. She thrust forth her head from the lattice, and looked anxiously upward. Beyond the shadow of a doubt, this venerable witch-lady had heard Mr. Dimmesdale's outcry, and interpreted it, with its multitudinous echoes and reverberations, as the clamor of the fiends and night-hags, with whom she was well known to make excursions into the forest.

Detecting the gleam of Governor Bellingham's lamp, the old lady quickly extinguished her own, and vanished. Possibly, she went up among the clouds. The minister saw nothing further of her motions. The magistrate, after a wary observation of the darkness—into which, nevertheless, he could see but little farther than he might into a mill-stone—retired from the window.

The minister grew comparatively calm. His eyes, however, were soon greeted by a little, glimmering light, which, at first a long way off, was approaching up the street. It threw a gleam of recognition on here a post, and there a garden-fence, and here a latticed windowpane, and there a pump, with its full trough of water, and here, again, an arched door of oak, with an iron knocker, and a rough log for the door-step. The Reverend Mr. Dimmesdale noted all these minute particulars, even while firmly convinced that the doom of his existence was stealing onward, in the footsteps which he now heard; and that the gleam of the lantern would fall upon him, in a few moments more, and reveal his long-hidden secret. As the light drew nearer, he beheld, within its illuminated circle, his brother clergyman,—or, to speak more accurately, his professional father, as well as highly valued friend,—the Reverend Mr. Wilson; who, as Mr. Dimmesdale now conjectured, had been praying at the bedside of some dying man. And so he had. The good old minister came freshly from the death-chamber of Governor Winthrop, who had passed from earth to heaven within that very hour.[3] And now, surrounded, like the saint-like personages of olden times, with a radiant halo, that glorified him amid this gloomy night of sin,—as if the departed Governor had left him an inheritance of his glory, or as if he had caught upon himself the distant shine of the celestial city, while looking thitherward to see the triumphant pilgram pass within its gates,—now, in short, good Father Wilson was moving homeward, aiding his footsteps with a lighted lantern! The glimmer of this luminary suggested the above conceits to Mr. Dimmesdale, who smiled,—nay, almost laughed at them,—and then wondered if he were going mad.

As the Reverend Mr. Wilson passed beside the scaffold, closely muffling his Geneva cloak[4] about him with one arm, and holding the lantern before his breast with the other, the minister could hardly restrain himself from speaking.

"A good evening to you, venerable Father Wilson! Come up hither, I pray you, and pass a pleasant hour with me!"

Good heavens! Had Mr. Dimmesdale actually spoken? For one instant, he believed that these words had passed his lips. But they were uttered only within his imagination. The venerable Father Wilson continued to step slowly onward, looking carefully at the muddy pathway before his feet, and never once turning his head towards the guilty platform. When the light of the glim-

---

3. The historical John Winthrop died in March (not May) 1649 (see also n. 1, p. 1273).

4. Black ministerial cloak named for Geneva, Switzerland, where John Calvin spent his last years.

mering lantern had faded quite away, the minister discovered, by the faintness which came over him, that the last few moments had been a crisis of terrible anxiety; although his mind had made an involuntary effort to relieve itself by a kind of lurid playfulness.

Shortly afterwards, the like grisly sense of the humorous again stole in among the solemn phantoms of his thought. He felt his limbs growing stiff with the unaccustomed chilliness of the night, and doubted whether he should be able to descend the steps of the scaffold. Morning would break, and find him there. The neighbourhood would begin to rouse itself. The earliest riser, coming forth in the dim twilight, would perceive a vaguely defined figure aloft on the place of shame; and, half crazed betwixt alarm and curiosity, would go, knocking from door to door, summoning all the people to behold the ghost— as he needs must think it—of some defunct transgressor. A dusky tumult would flap its wings from one house to another. Then—the morning light still waxing stronger—old patriarchs would rise up in great haste, each in his flannel gown, and matronly dames, without pausing to put off their night-gear. The whole tribe of decorous personages, who had never heretofore been seen with a single hair of their heads awry, would start into public view, with the disorder of a nightmare in their aspects. Old Governor Bellingham would come grimly forth, with his King James's ruff fastened askew; and Mistress Hibbins, with some twigs of the forest clinging to her skirts, and looking sourer than ever, as having hardly got a wink of sleep after her night ride; and good Father Wilson, too, after spending half the night at a death-bed, and liking ill to be disturbed, thus early, out of his dreams about the glorified saints. Hither, likewise, would come the elders and deacons of Mr. Dimmesdale's church, and the young virgins who so idolized their minister, and had made a shrine for him in their white bosoms; which, now, by the by, in their hurry and confusion, they would scantly have given themselves time to cover with their kerchiefs. All people, in a word, would come stumbling over their thresholds, and turning up their amazed and horror-stricken visages around the scaffold. Whom would they discern there, with the red eastern light upon his brow? Whom, but the Reverend Arthur Dimmesdale, half frozen to death, overwhelmed with shame, and standing where Hester Prynne had stood!

Carried away by the grotesque horror of this picture, the minister, unawares, and to his own infinite alarm, burst into a great peal of laughter. It was immediately responded to by a light, airy, childish laugh, in which, with a thrill of the heart,—but he knew not whether of exquisite pain, or pleasure as acute,— he recognized the tones of little Pearl.

"Pearl! Little Pearl!" cried he, after a moment's pause; then, suppressing his voice,—"Hester! Hester Prynne! Are you there?"

"Yes; it is Hester Prynne!" she replied, in a tone of surprise; and the minister heard her footsteps approaching from the sidewalk, along which she had been passing.—"It is I, and my little Pearl."

"Whence come you, Hester?" asked the minister. "What sent you hither?"

"I have been watching at a death-bed," answered Hester Prynne;—"at Governor Winthrop's death-bed, and have taken his measure for a robe, and am now going homeward to my dwelling."

"Come up hither, Hester, thou and little Pearl," said the Reverend Mr. Dimmesdale. "Ye have both been here before, but I was not with you. Come up hither once again, and we will stand all three together!"

She silently ascended the steps, and stood on the platform, holding little Pearl by the hand. The minister felt for the child's other hand, and took it. The moment that he did so, there came what seemed a tumultuous rush of new life, other life than his own, pouring like a torrent into his heart, and hurrying through all his veins, as if the mother and the child were communicating their vital warmth to his half-torpid system. The three formed an electric chain.

"Minister!" whispered little Pearl.

"What wouldst thou say, child?" asked Mr. Dimmesdale.

"Wilt thou stand here with mother and me, to-morrow noontide?" inquired Pearl.

"Nay; not so, my little Pearl!" answered the minister; for, with the new energy of the moment, all the dread of public exposure, that had so long been the anguish of his life, had returned upon him; and he was already trembling at the conjunction in which—with a strange joy, nevertheless—he now found himself. "Not so, my child. I shall, indeed, stand with thy mother and thee one other day, but not to-morrow!"

Pearl laughed, and attempted to pull away her hand. But the minister held it fast.

"A moment longer, my child!" said he.

"But wilt thou promise," asked Pearl, "to take my hand, and mother's hand, to-morrow noontide?"

"Not then, Pearl," said the minister, "but another time!"

"And what other time?" persisted the child.

"At the great judgment day!" whispered the minister,—and, strangely enough, the sense that he was a professional teacher of the truth impelled him to answer the child so. "Then, and there, before the judgment-seat, thy mother, and thou, and I, must stand together! But the daylight of this world shall not see our meeting!"

Pearl laughed again.

But, before Mr. Dimmesdale had done speaking, a light gleamed far and wide over all the muffled sky. It was doubtless caused by one of those meteors, which the night-watcher may so often observe burning out to waste, in the vacant regions of the atmosphere. So powerful was its radiance, that it thoroughly illuminated the dense medium of cloud betwixt the sky and earth. The great vault brightened, like the dome of an immense lamp. It showed the familiar scene of the street, with the distinctness of mid-day, but also with the awfulness that is always imparted to familiar objects by an unaccustomed light. The wooden houses, with their jutting stories and quaint gable-peaks; the door-steps and thresholds, with the early grass springing up about them; the garden-plots, black with freshly turned earth; the wheel-track, little worn, and, even in the market-place, margined with green on either side;—all were visible, but with a singularity of aspect that seemed to give another moral interpretation to the things of this world than they had ever borne before. And there stood the minister, with his hand over his heart; and Hester Prynne, with the embroidered letter glimmering on her bosom; and little Pearl, herself a symbol, and the connecting link between these two. They stood in the noon of that strange and solemn splendor, as if it were the light that is to reveal all secrets, and the daybreak that shall unite all who belong to one another.

There was witchcraft in little Pearl's eyes; and her face, as she glanced upward at the minister, wore that naughty smile which made its expression frequently so elvish. She withdrew her hand from Mr. Dimmesdale's, and pointed across the street. But he clasped both his hands over his breast, and cast his eyes towards the zenith.

Nothing was more common, in those days, than to interpret all meteoric appearances, and other natural phenomena, that occurred with less regularity than the rise and set of sun and moon, as so many revelations from a supernatural source. Thus, a blazing spear, a sword of flame, a bow, or a sheaf of arrows, seen in the midnight sky, prefigured Indian warfare. Pestilence was known to have been foreboded by a shower of crimson light. We doubt whether any marked event, for good or evil, ever befell New England, from its settlement down to Revolutionary times, of which the inhabitants had not been previously warned by some spectacle of this nature. Not seldom, it had been seen by multitudes. Oftener, however, its credibility rested on the faith of some lonely eyewitness, who beheld the wonder through the colored, magnifying, and distorting medium of his imagination, and shaped it more distinctly in his after-thought. It was, indeed, a majestic idea, that the destiny of nations should be revealed, in these awful hieroglyphics, on the cope[5] of heaven. A scroll so wide might not be deemed too expensive for Providence to write a people's doom upon. The belief was a favorite one with our forefathers, as betokening that their infant commonwealth was under a celestial guardianship of peculiar intimacy and strictness. But what shall we say, when an individual discovers a revelation, addressed to himself alone, on the same vast sheet of record! In such a case, it could only be the symptom of a highly disordered mental state, when a man, rendered morbidly self-contemplative by long, intense, and secret pain, had extended his egotism over the whole expanse of nature, until the firmament itself should appear no more than a fitting page for his soul's history and fate.

We impute it, therefore, solely to the disease in his own eye and heart, that the minister, looking upward to the zenith, beheld there the appearance of an immense letter,—the letter A,—marked out in lines of dull red light. Not but the meteor may have shown itself at that point, burning duskily through a veil of cloud; but with no such shape as his guilty imagination gave it; or, at least, with so little definiteness, that another's guilt might have seen another symbol in it.

There was a singular circumstance that characterized Mr. Dimmesdale's psychological state, at this moment. All the time that he gazed upward to the zenith, he was, nevertheless, perfectly aware that little Pearl was pointing her finger towards old Roger Chillingworth, who stood at no great distance from the scaffold. The minister appeared to see him, with the same glance that discerned the miraculous letter. To his features, as to all other objects, the meteoric light imparted a new expression; or it might well be that the physician was not careful then, as at all other times, to hide the malevolence with which he looked upon his victim. Certainly, if the meteor kindled up the sky, and disclosed the earth, with an awfulness that admonished Hester Prynne and the clergyman of the day of judgment, then might Roger Chillingworth have passed with them for the arch-fiend, standing there, with a smile and scowl, to claim his own. So vivid was the expression, or so intense the minister's

5. Canopy.

perception of it, that it seemed still to remain painted on the darkness, after the meteor had vanished, with an effect as if the street and all things else were at once annihilated.

"Who is that man, Hester?" gasped Mr. Dimmesdale, overcome with terror. "I shiver at him! Dost thou know the man? I hate him, Hester!"

She remembered her oath, and was silent.

"I tell thee, my soul shivers at him," muttered the minister again, "Who is he? Who is he? Canst thou do nothing for me? I have a nameless horror of the man."

"Minister," said little Pearl, "I can tell thee who he is!"

"Quickly, then, child!" said the minister, bending his ear close to her lips. "Quickly!—and as low as thou canst whisper."

Pearl mumbled something into his ear, that sounded, indeed, like human language, but was only such gibberish as children may be heard amusing themselves with, by the hour together. At all events, if it involved any secret information in regard to old Roger Chillingworth, it was in a tongue unknown to the erudite clergyman, and did but increase the bewilderment of his mind. The elvish child then laughed aloud.

"Dost thou mock me now?" said the minister.

"Thou wast not bold!—thou wast not true!" answered the child. "Thou wouldst not promise to take my hand, and mother's hand, tomorrow noontide!"

"Worthy Sir," said the physician, who had now advanced to the foot of the platform. "Pious Master Dimmesdale! can this be you? Well, well, indeed! We men of study, whose heads are in our books, have need to be straitly looked after! We dream in our waking moments, and walk in our sleep. Come, good Sir, and my dear friend, I pray you, let me lead you home!"

"How knewest thou that I was here?" asked the minister, fearfully.

"Verily, and in good faith," answered Roger Chillingworth, "I knew nothing of the matter. I had spent the better part of the night at the bedside of the worshipful Governor Winthrop, doing what my poor skill might to give him ease. He going home to a better world, I, likewise, was on my way homeward, when this strange light shone out. Come with me, I beseech you, Reverend Sir; else you will be poorly able to do Sabbath duty to-morrow. Aha! see now, how they trouble the brain,—these books!—these books! You should study less, good Sir, and take a little pastime; or these night-whimseys will grow upon you!"

"I will go home with you," said Mr. Dimmesdale.

With a chill despondency, like one awaking, all nerveless, from an ugly dream, he yielded himself to the physician, and was led away.

The next day, however, being the Sabbath, he preached a discourse which was held to be the richest and most powerful, and the most replete with heavenly influences, that had ever proceeded from his lips. Souls, it is said, more souls than one, were brought to the truth by the efficacy of that sermon, and vowed within themselves to cherish a holy gratitude towards Mr. Dimmesdale throughout the long hereafter. But, as he came down the pulpit-steps, the gray-bearded sexton met him, holding up a black glove, which the minister recognized as his own.

"It was found," said the sexton, "this morning, on the scaffold, where evildoers are set up to public shame. Satan dropped it there, I take it, intending a scurrilous jest against your reverence. But, indeed, he was blind and foolish, as he ever and always is. A pure hand needs no glove to cover it!"

"Thank you, my good friend," said the minister gravely, but startled at heart; for, so confused was his remembrance, that he had almost brought himself to look at the events of the past night as visionary. "Yes, it seems to be my glove indeed!"

"And, since Satan saw fit to steal it, your reverence must needs handle him without gloves, henceforward," remarked the old sexton, grimly smiling, "But did your reverence hear of the portent that was seen last night? A great red letter in the sky,—the letter A,—which we interpret to stand for Angel. For, as our good Governor Winthrop was made an angel this past night, it was doubtless held fit that there should be some notice thereof!"

"No," answered the minister, "I had not heard of it."

XIII. ANOTHER VIEW OF HESTER

In her late singular interview with Mr. Dimmesdale, Hester Prynne was shocked at the condition to which she found the clergyman reduced. His nerve seemed absolutely destroyed. His moral force was abased into more than childish weakness. It grovelled helpless on the ground, even while his intellectual faculties retained their pristine strength, or had perhaps acquired a morbid energy, which disease only could have given them. With her knowledge of a train of circumstances hidden from all others, she could readily infer, that, besides the legitimate action of his own conscience, a terrible machinery had been brought to bear, and was still operating, on Mr. Dimmesdale's well-being and repose. Knowing what this poor, fallen man had once been, her whole soul was moved by the shuddering terror with which he had appealed to her,— the outcast woman,—for support against his instinctively discovered enemy. She decided, moreover, that he had a right to her utmost aid. Little accustomed, in her long seclusion from society, to measure her ideas of right and wrong by any standard external to herself, Hester saw—or seemed to see—that there lay a responsibility upon her, in reference to the clergyman, which she owed to no other, nor to the whole world besides. The links that united her to the rest of human kind—links of flowers, or silk, or gold, or whatever the material—had all been broken. Here was the iron link of mutual crime, which neither he nor she could break. Like all other ties, it brought along with it its obligations.

Hester Prynne did not now occupy precisely the same position in which we beheld her during the earlier periods of her ignominy. Years had come, and gone. Pearl was now seven years old. Her mother, with the scarlet letter on her breast, glittering in its fantastic embroidery, had long been a familiar object to the townspeople. As is apt to be the case when a person stands out in any prominence before the community, and, at the same time, interferes neither with public nor individual interests and convenience, a species of general regard had ultimately grown up in reference to Hester Prynne. It is to the credit of human nature, that, except where its selfishness is brought into play, it loves more readily than it hates. Hatred, by a gradual and quiet process, will even be transformed to love, unless the change be impeded by a continually new irritation of the original feeling of hostility. In this matter of Hester Prynne, there was neither irritation nor irksomeness. She never battled with the public, but submitted uncomplainingly to its worst usage; she made no claim upon it, in requital for what she suffered; she did not weigh upon its sympathies. Then, also, the blameless purity of her life, during all these years in which she had been set apart to infamy, was reckoned largely in her favor. With nothing now to lose, in the sight of mankind, and with no hope, and seemingly no wish, of gaining any thing, it could only be a genuine regard for virtue that had brought back the poor wanderer to its paths.

It was perceived, too, that, while Hester never put forward even the humblest title to share in the world's privileges,—farther than to breathe the common air, and earn daily bread for little Pearl and herself by the faithful labor of her hands,—she was quick to acknowledge her sisterhood with the race of man, whenever benefits were to be conferred. None so ready as she to give of her little substance to every demand of poverty; even though the bitter-hearted pauper threw back a gibe in requital of the food brought regularly to his door, or the garments wrought for him by the fingers that could have embroidered a monarch's robe. None so self-devoted as Hester, when pestilence stalked through the town. In all seasons of calamity, indeed, whether general or of individuals, the outcast of society at once found her place. She came, not as a guest, but as a rightful inmate, into the household that was darkened by trouble; as if its gloomy twilight were a medium in which she was entitled to hold intercourse with her fellow-creatures. There glimmered the embroidered letter, with comfort in its unearthly ray. Elsewhere the token of sin, it was the taper of the sick-chamber. It had even thrown its gleam, in the sufferer's hard extremity, across the verge of time. It had shown him where to set his foot, while the light of earth was fast becoming dim, and ere the light of futurity could reach him. In such emergencies, Hester's nature showed itself warm and rich; a well-spring of human tenderness, unfailing to every real demand, and inexhaustible by the largest. Her breast, with its badge of shame, was but the softer pillow for the head that needed one. She was self-ordained a Sister of Mercy; or, we may rather say, the world's heavy hand had so ordained her, when neither the world nor she looked forward to this result. The letter was the symbol of her calling. Such helpfulness was found in her,—so much power to do, and power to sympathize,—that many people refused to interpret the scarlet A by its original signification. They said that it meant Able; so strong was Hester Prynne, with a woman's strength.

It was only the darkened house that could contain her. When sunshine came again, she was not there. Her shadow had faded across the threshold. The helpful inmate had departed, without one backward glance to gather up the meed[6] of gratitude, if any were in the hearts of those whom she had served so zealously. Meeting them in the street, she never raised her head to receive their greeting. If they were resolute to accost her, she laid her finger on the scarlet letter, and passed on. This might be pride, but was so like humility, that it produced all the softening influence of the latter quality on the public mind. The public is despotic in its temper; it is capable of denying common justice, when too strenuously demanded as a right; but quite as frequently it awards more than justice, when the appeal is made, as despots love to have it made, entirely to its generosity. Interpreting Hester Prynne's deportment as an appeal of this nature, society was inclined to show its former victim a more

6. Merited gift or reward.

benign countenance than she cared to be favored with, or, perchance, than she deserved.

The rulers, and the wise and learned men of the community, were longer in acknowledging the influence of Hester's good qualities than the people. The prejudices which they shared in common with the latter were fortified in themselves by an iron framework of reasoning, that made it a far tougher labor to expel them. Day by day, nevertheless, their sour and rigid wrinkles were relaxing into something which, in the due course of years, might grow to be an expression of almost benevolence. Thus it was with the men of rank, on whom their eminent position imposed the guardianship of the public morals. Individuals in private life, meanwhile, had quite forgiven Hester Prynne for her frailty; nay, more, they had begun to look upon the scarlet letter as the token, not of that one sin, for which she had borne so long and dreary a penance, but of her many good deeds since. "Do you see that woman with the embroidered badge?" they would say to strangers. "It is our Hester,—the town's own Hester,—who is so kind to the poor, so helpful to the sick, so comfortable to the afflicted!" Then, it is true, the propensity of human nature to tell the very worst of itself, when embodied in the person of another, would constrain them to whisper the black scandal of bygone years. It was none the less a fact, however, that, in the eyes of the very men who spoke thus, the scarlet letter had the effect of the cross on a nun's bosom. It imparted to the wearer a kind of sacredness, which enabled her to walk securely amid all peril. Had she fallen among thieves, it would have kept her safe. It was reported, and believed by many, that an Indian had drawn his arrow against the badge, and that the missile struck it, but fell harmless to the ground.

The effect of the symbol—or rather, of the position in respect to society that was indicated by it—on the mind of Hester Prynne herself, was powerful and peculiar. All the light and graceful foliage of her character had been withered up by this red-hot brand, and had long ago fallen away, leaving a bare and harsh outline, which might have been repulsive, had she possessed friends or companions to be repelled by it. Even the attractiveness of her person had undergone a similar change. It might be partly owing to the studied austerity of her dress, and partly to the lack of demonstration in her manners. It was a sad transformation, too, that her rich and luxuriant hair had either been cut off, or was so completely hidden by a cap, that not a shining lock of it ever once gushed into the sunshine. It was due in part to all these causes, but still more to something else, that there seemed to be no longer any thing in Hester's face for Love to dwell upon; nothing in Hester's form, though majestic and statue-like, that Passion would ever dream of clasping in its embrace; nothing in Hester's bosom, to make it ever again the pillow of Affection. Some attribute had departed from her, the permanence of which had been essential to keep her a woman. Such is frequently the fate, and such the stern development, of the feminine character and person, when the woman has encountered, and lived through, an experience of peculiar severity. If she be all tenderness, she will die. If she survive, the tenderness will either be crushed out of her, or— and the outward semblance is the same—crushed so deeply into her heart that it can never show itself more. The latter is perhaps the truest theory. She who has once been woman, and ceased to be so, might at any moment become a woman again, if there were only the magic touch to effect the transfiguration. We shall see whether Hester Prynne were ever afterwards so touched, and so transfigured.

Much of the marble coldness of Hester's impression was to be attributed to the circumstance that her life had turned, in a great measure, from passion and feeling, to thought. Standing alone in the world,—alone, as to any dependence on society, and with little Pearl to be guided and protected,—alone, and hopeless of retrieving her position, even had she not scorned to consider it desirable,—she cast away the fragments of a broken chain. The world's law was no law for her mind. It was an age in which the human intellect, newly emancipated, had taken a more active and a wider range than for many centuries before. Men of the sword had overthrown nobles and kings. Men bolder than these had overthrown and rearranged—not actually, but within the sphere of theory, which was their most real abode—the whole system of ancient prejudice, wherewith was linked much of ancient principle. Hester Prynne imbibed this spirit. She assumed a freedom of speculation, then common enough on the other side of the Atlantic, but which our forefathers, had they known of it, would have held to be a deadlier crime than that stigmatized by the scarlet letter. In her lonesome cottage, by the seashore, thoughts visited her, such as dared to enter no other dwelling in New England; shadowy guests, that would have been as perilous as demons to their entertainer, could they have been seen so much as knocking at her door.

It is remarkable, that persons who speculate the most boldly often conform with the most perfect quietude to the external regulations of society. The thought suffices them, without investing itself in the flesh and blood of action. So it seemed to be with Hester. Yet, had little Pearl never come to her from the spiritual world, it might have been far otherwise. Then, she might have come down to us in history, hand in hand with Ann Hutchinson, as the foundress of a religious sect. She might, in one of her phases, have been a prophetess. She might, and not improbably would, have suffered death from the stern tribunals of the period, for attempting to undermine the foundations of the Puritan establishment. But, in the education of her child, the mother's enthusiasm of thought had something to wreak itself upon. Providence, in the person of this little girl, had assigned to Hester's charge the germ and blossom of womanhood, to be cherished and developed amid a host of difficulties. Every thing was against her. The world was hostile. The child's own nature had something wrong in it, which continually betokened that she had been born amiss,—the effluence of her mother's lawless passion,—and often impelled Hester to ask, in bitterness of heart, whether it were for ill or good that the poor little creature had been born at all.

Indeed, the same dark question often rose into her mind, with reference to the whole race of womanhood. Was existence worth accepting, even to the happiest among them? As concerned her own individual existence, she had long ago decided in the negative, and dismissed the point as settled. A tendency to speculation, though it may keep woman quiet, as it does man, yet makes her sad. She discerns, it may be, such a hopeless task before her. As a first step, the whole system of society is to be torn down, and built up anew. Then, the very nature of the opposite sex, or its long hereditary habit, which has become like nature, is to be essentially modified, before woman can be allowed to assume what seems a fair and suitable position. Finally, all other difficulties being obviated, woman cannot take advantage of these preliminary reforms, until she herself shall have undergone a still mightier change; in which, perhaps, the ethereal essence, wherein she has her truest life, will be found to have evaporated. A woman never overcomes these problems by any exercise of thought. They are not to be solved, or only in one way. If her heart chance to come uppermost, they vanish. Thus, Hester Prynne, whose heart had lost its regular and healthy throb, wandered without a clew in the dark labyrinth of mind; now turned aside by an insurmountable precipice; now starting back from a deep chasm. There was wild and ghastly scenery all around her, and a home and comfort nowhere. At times, a fearful doubt strove to possess her soul, whether it were not better to send Pearl at once to heaven, and go herself to such futurity as Eternal Justice should provide.

The scarlet letter had not done its office.

Now, however, her interview with the Reverend Mr. Dimmesdale, on the night of his vigil, had given her a new theme of reflection, and held up to her an object that appeared worthy of any exertion and sacrifice for its attainment. She had witnessed the intense misery beneath which the minister struggled, or, to speak more accurately, had ceased to struggle. She saw that he stood on the verge of lunacy, if he had not already stepped across it. It was impossible to doubt, that, whatever painful efficacy there might be in the secret sting of remorse, a deadlier venom had been infused into it by the hand that proffered relief. A secret enemy had been continually by his side, under the semblance of a friend and helper, and had availed himself of the opportunities thus afforded for tampering with the delicate springs of Mr. Dimmesdale's nature. Hester could not but ask herself, whether there had not originally been a defect of truth, courage, and loyalty, on her own part, in allowing the minister to be thrown into a position where so much evil was to be foreboded, and nothing auspicious to be hoped. Her only justification lay in the fact, that she had been able to discern no method of rescuing him from a blacker ruin than had overwhelmed herself, except by acquiescing in Roger Chillingworth's scheme of disguise. Under that impulse, she had made her choice, and had chosen, as it now appeared, the more wretched alternative of the two. She determined to redeem her error, so far as it might yet be possible. Strengthened by years of hard and solemn trial, she felt herself no longer so inadequate to cope with Roger Chillingworth as on that night, abased by sin, and half maddened by the ignominy that was still new, when they had talked together in the prison-chamber. She had climbed her way, since then, to a higher point. The old man, on the other hand, had brought himself nearer to her level, or perhaps below it, by the revenge which he had stooped for.

In fine, Hester Prynne resolved to meet her former husband, and do what might be in her power for the rescue of the victim on whom he had so evidently set his gripe. The occasion was not long to seek. One afternoon, walking with Pearl in a retired part of the peninsula, she beheld the old physician, with a basket on one arm, and a staff in the other hand, stooping along the ground, in quest of roots and herbs to concoct his medicines withal.

XIV. HESTER AND THE PHYSICIAN

Hester bade little Pearl run down to the margin of the water, and play with the shells and tangled seaweed, until she should have talked awhile with yonder gatherer of herbs. So the child flew away like a bird, and, making bare her small white feet, went pattering along the moist margin of the sea. Here and there, she came to a full stop, and peeped curiously into a pool, left by the retiring tide as a mirror for Pearl to see her face in. Forth peeped at her, out of the pool, with dark, glistening curls around her head, and an elf-smile in her eyes, the image of a little maid, whom Pearl, having no other playmate, invited to take her hand and run a race with her. But the visionary little maid, on her part, beckoned likewise, as if to say,—"This is a better place! Come thou into the pool!" And Pearl, stepping in, mid-leg deep, beheld her own white feet at the bottom; while, out of a still lower depth, came the gleam of a kind of fragmentary smile, floating to and fro in the agitated water.

Meanwhile, her mother had accosted the physician.

"I would speak a word with you," said she,—"a word that concerns us much."

"Aha! And is it Mistress Hester that has a word for old Roger Chillingworth?" answered he, raising himself from his stooping posture. "With all my heart! Why, Mistress, I hear good tidings of you on all hands! No longer ago than yester-eve, a magistrate, a wise and godly man, was discoursing of your affairs, Mistress Hester, and whispered me that there had been question concerning you in the council. It was debated whether or no, with safety to the common weal, yonder scarlet letter might be taken off your bosom. On my life, Hester, I made my entreaty to the worshipful magistrate that it might be done forthwith!"

"It lies not in the pleasure of the magistrates to take off this badge," calmly replied Hester. "Were I worthy to be quit of it, it would fall away of its own nature, or be transformed into something that should speak a different purport."

"Nay, then, wear it, if it suit you better," rejoined he. "A woman must needs follow her own fancy, touching the adornment of her person. The letter is gayly embroidered, and shows right bravely on your bosom!"

All this while, Hester had been looking steadily at the old man, and was shocked, as well as wonder-smitten, to discern what a change had been wrought upon him within the past seven years. It was not so much that he had grown older; for though the traces of advancing life were visible, he bore his age well, and seemed to retain a wiry vigor and alertness. But the former aspect of an intellectual and studious man, calm and quiet, which was what she best remembered in him, had altogether vanished, and been succeeded by an eager, searching, almost fierce, yet carefully guarded look. It seemed to be his wish and purpose to mask this expression with a smile; but the latter played him false, and flickered over his visage so derisively, that the spectator could see his blackness all the better for it. Ever and anon, too, there came a glare of red light out of his eyes; as if the old man's soul were on fire, and kept on smouldering duskily within his breast, until, by some casual puff of passion, it was blown into a momentary flame. This he repressed as speedily as possible, and strove to look as if nothing of the kind had happened.

In a word, old Roger Chillingworth was a striking evidence of man's faculty of transforming himself into a devil, if he will only, for a reasonable space of time, undertake a devil's office. This unhappy person had effected such a transformation by devoting himself, for seven years, to the constant analysis of a heart full of torture, and deriving his enjoyment thence, and adding fuel to those fiery tortures which he analyzed and gloated over.

The scarlet letter burned on Hester Prynne's bosom. Here was another ruin, the responsibility of which came partly home to her.

"What see you in my face," asked the physician, "that you look at it so earnestly?"

"Something that would make me weep, if there were any tears bitter enough for it," answered she. "But let it pass! It is of yonder miserable man that I would speak."

"And what of him?" cried Roger Chillingworth eagerly, as if he loved the topic, and were glad of an opportunity to discuss it with the only person of whom he could make a confidant. "Not to hide the truth, Mistress Hester, my thoughts happen just now to be busy with the gentleman. So speak freely; and I will make answer."

"When we last spake together," said Hester, "now seven years ago, it was your pleasure to extort a promise of secrecy, as touching the former relation betwixt yourself and me. As the life and good fame of yonder man were in your hands, there seemed no choice to me, save to be silent, in accordance with your behest. Yet it was not without heavy misgivings that I thus bound myself; for, having cast off all duty towards other human beings, there remained a duty towards him; and something whispered me that I was betraying it, in pledging myself to keep your counsel. Since that day, no man is so near to him as you. You tread behind his every footstep. You are beside him, sleeping and waking. You search his thoughts. You burrow and rankle in his heart! Your clutch is on his life, and you cause him to die daily a living death; and still he knows you not. In permitting this, I have surely acted a false part by the only man to whom the power was left me to be true!"

"What choice had you?" asked Roger Chillingworth. "My finger, pointed at this man, would have hurled him from his pulpit into a dungeon,—thence, peradventure, to the gallows!"

"It had been better so!" said Hester Prynne.

"What evil have I done the man?" asked Roger Chillingworth again. "I tell thee, Hester Prynne, the richest fee that ever physician earned from monarch could not have brought such care as I have wasted on this miserable priest! But for my aid, his life would have burned away in torments, within the first two years after the perpetration of his crime and thine. For, Hester, his spirit lacked the strength that could have borne up, as thine has, beneath a burden like thy scarlet letter. O, I could reveal a goodly secret! But enough! What art can do, I have exhausted on him. That he now breathes, and creeps about on earth, is owing all to me!"

"Better he had died at once!" said Hester Prynne.

"Yea, woman, thou sayest truly!" cried old Roger Chillingworth, letting the lurid fire of his heart blaze out before her eyes. "Better had he died at once! Never did mortal suffer what this man has suffered. And all, all, in the sight of his worst enemy! He has been conscious of me. He has felt an influence dwelling always upon him like a curse. He knew, by some spiritual sense,—for the Creator never made another being so sensitive as this,—he knew that no friendly hand was pulling at his heart-strings, and that an eye was looking curiously into him, which sought only evil, and found it. But he knew not that the eye and hand were mine! With the superstition common to his brotherhood, he fancied himself given over to a fiend, to be tortured with frightful dreams, and desperate thoughts, the sting of remorse, and despair of pardon; as a foretaste of what awaits him beyond the grave. But it was the constant shadow of my presence!—the closest propinquity of the man whom he had most vilely wronged!—and who had grown to exist only by this perpetual poison of the direst revenge! Yea, indeed!—he did not err!—there was a fiend at his elbow! A mortal man, with once a human heart, has become a fiend for his especial torment!"

The unfortunate physician, while uttering these words, lifted his hands with a look of horror, as if he had beheld some frightful shape, which he could not recognize, usurping the place of his own image in a glass. It was one of those moments—which sometimes occur only at the interval of years—when a man's moral aspect is faithfully revealed to his mind's eye. Not improbably, he had never before viewed himself as he did now.

"Hast thou not tortured him enough?" said Hester, noticing the old man's look. "Has he not paid thee all?"

"No!—no!—He has but increased the debt!" answered the physician; and, as he proceeded, his manner lost its fiercer characteristics, and subsided into gloom. "Dost thou remember me, Hester, as I was nine years agone? Even then, I was in the autumn of my days, nor was it the early autumn. But all my life had been made up of earnest, studious, thoughtful, quiet years, bestowed faithfully for the increase of mine own knowledge, and faithfully, too, though this latter object was but casual to the other,—faithfully, for the advancement of human welfare. No life had been more peaceful and innocent than mine; few lives so rich with benefits conferred. Dost thou remember me? Was I not, though you might deem me cold, nevertheless a man thoughtful for others, craving little for himself,—kind, true, just, and of constant, if not warm affections? Was I not all this?"

"All this, and more," said Hester.

"And what am I now?" demanded he, looking into her face, and permitting the whole evil within him to be written on his features. "I have already told thee what I am! A fiend! Who made me so?"

"It was myself!" cried Hester, shuddering. "It was I, not less than he. Why hast thou not avenged thyself on me?"

"I have left thee to the scarlet letter," replied Roger Chillingworth. "If that have not avenged me, I can do no more!"

He laid his finger on it, with a smile.

"It has avenged thee!" answered Hester Prynne.

"I judged no less," said the physician. "And now, what wouldst thou with me touching this man?"

"I must reveal the secret," answered Hester, firmly. "He must discern thee in thy true character. What may be the result, I know not. But this long debt of confidence, due from me to him, whose bane and ruin I have been, shall at length be paid. So far as concerns the overthrow or preservation of his fair fame and his earthly state, and perchance his life, he is in thy hands. Nor do I,—whom the scarlet letter has disciplined to truth, though it be the truth of red-hot iron, entering into the soul,—nor do I perceive such advantage in his living any longer a life of ghastly emptiness, that I shall stoop to implore thy mercy. Do with him as thou wilt! There is no good for him,—no good for me,—no good for thee! There is no good for little Pearl! There is no path to guide us out of this dismal maze!"

"Woman, I could wellnigh pity thee!" said Roger Chillingworth, unable to restrain a thrill of admiration too; for there was a quality almost majestic in the despair which she expressed. "Thou hadst great elements. Peradventure, hadst thou met earlier with a better love than mine, this evil had not been. I pity thee, for the good that has been wasted in thy nature!"

"And I thee," answered Hester Prynne, "for the hatred that has transformed a wise and just man to a fiend! Wilt thou yet purge it out of thee, and be once more human? If not for his sake, then doubly for thine own! Forgive, and leave his further retribution to the Power that claims it! I said, but now, that there could be no good event for him, or thee, or me, who are here wandering together in this gloomy maze of evil, and stumbling, at every step, over the guilt wherewith we have strewn our path. It is not so! There might be good for thee, and thee alone, since thou hast been deeply wronged, and hast it at thy will to pardon. Wilt thou give up that only privilege? Wilt thou reject that priceless benefit?"

"Peace, Hester, peace!" replied the old man, with gloomy sternness. "It is not granted me to pardon. I have no such power as thou tellest me of. My old faith, long forgotten, comes back to me, and explains all that we do, and all we suffer. By thy first step awry, thou didst plant the germ of evil; but, since that moment, it has all been a dark necessity. Ye that have wronged me are not sinful, save in a kind of typical illusion; neither am I fiend-like, who have snatched a fiend's office from his hands. It is our fate. Let the black flower blossom as it may! Now go thy ways, and deal as thou wilt with yonder man."

He waved his hand, and betook himself again to his employment of gathering herbs.

XV. HESTER AND PEARL

So Roger Chillingworth—a deformed old figure, with a face that haunted men's memories longer than they liked—took leave of Hester Prynne, and went stooping away along the earth. He gathered here and there an herb, or grubbed up a root, and put it into the basket on his arm. His gray beard almost touched the ground, as he crept onward. Hester gazed after him a little while, looking with a half-fantastic curiosity to see whether the tender grass of early spring would not be blighted beneath him, and show the wavering track of his footsteps, sere and brown, across its cheerful verdure. She wondered what sort of herbs they were, which the old man was so sedulous to gather. Would not the earth, quickened to an evil purpose by the sympathy of his eye, greet him with poisonous shrubs, of species hitherto unknown, that would start up under his fingers? Or might it suffice him, that every wholesome growth should be converted into something deleterious and malignant at his touch? Did the sun, which shone so brightly everywhere else, really fall upon him? Or was there, as it rather seemed, a circle of ominous shadow moving along with his deformity, whichever way he turned himself? And whither was he now going? Would he not suddenly sink into the earth, leaving a barren and blasted spot, where in due course of time, would be seen deadly nightshade, dogwood, henbane,[7] and whatever else of vegetable wickedness the climate could produce, all flourishing with hideous luxuriance? Or would he spread bat's wings and flee away, looking so much the uglier, the higher he rose towards heaven?

"Be it sin or no," said Hester Prynne bitterly, as she still gazed after him, "I hate the man!"

She upbraided herself for the sentiment, but could not overcome or lessen it. Attempting to do so, she thought of those long-past days, in a distant land, when he used to emerge at eventide from the seclusion of his study, and sit down in the fire-light of their home, and in the light of her nuptial smile. He needed to bask himself in that smile, he said, in order that the chill of so many

7. Plants that are poisonous, produce poison, or are otherwise associated with witchcraft.

lonely hours among his books might be taken off the scholar's heart. Such scenes had once appeared not otherwise than happy, but now, as viewed through the dismal medium of her subsequent life, they classed themselves among her ugliest remembrances. She marvelled how such scenes could have been! She marvelled how she could ever have been wrought upon to marry him! She deemed it her crime most to be repented of, that she had ever endured, and reciprocated, the lukewarm grasp of his hand, and had suffered the smile of her lips and eyes to mingle and melt into his own. And it seemed a fouler offence committed by Roger Chillingworth, than any which had since been done him, that, in the time when her heart knew no better, he had persuaded her to fancy herself happy by his side.

"Yes, I hate him!" repeated Hester, more bitterly than before. "He betrayed me! He has done me worse wrong than I did him!"

Let men tremble to win the hand of woman, unless they win along with it the utmost passion of her heart! Else it may be their miserable fortune, as it was Roger Chillingworth's, when some mightier touch than their own may have awakened all her sensibilities, to be reproached even for the calm content, the marble image of happiness, which they will have imposed upon her as the warm reality. But Hester ought long ago to have done with this injustice. What did it betoken? Had seven long years, under the torture of the scarlet letter, inflicted so much of misery, and wrought out no repentance?

The emotions of that brief space, while she stood gazing after the crooked figure of old Roger Chillingworth, threw a dark light on Hester's state of mind, revealing much that she might not otherwise have acknowledged to herself.

He being gone, she summoned back her child.

"Pearl! Little Pearl! Where are you?"

Pearl, whose activity of spirit never flagged, had been at no loss for amusement while her mother talked with the old gatherer of herbs. At first, as already told, she had flirted fancifully with her own image in a pool of water, beckoning the phantom forth, and—as it declined to venture—seeking a passage for herself into its sphere of impalpable earth and unattainable sky. Soon finding, however, that either she or the image was unreal, she turned elsewhere for better pastime. She made little boats out of birch-bark, and freighted them with snail-shells, and sent out more ventures on the mighty deep than any merchant in New England; but the larger part of them foundered near the shore. She seized a live horseshoe by the tail, and made prize of several five-fingers,[8] and laid out a jelly-fish to melt in the warm sun. Then she took up the white foam, that streaked the line of the advancing tide, and threw it upon the breeze, scampering after it with winged footsteps, to catch the great snow-flakes ere they fell. Perceiving a flock of beach-birds, that fed and fluttered along the shore, the naughty child picked up her apron full of pebbles, and, creeping from rock to rock after these small sea-fowl, displayed remarkable dexterity in pelting them. One little gray bird, with a white breast, Pearl was almost sure, had been hit by a pebble, and fluttered away with a broken wing. But then the elf-child sighed, and gave up her sport; because it grieved her to have done harm to a little being that was as wild as the sea-breeze, or as wild as Pearl herself.

Her final employment was to gather sea-weed, of various kinds, and make

8. Five-rayed starfish. "Horseshoe": horseshoe crab.

herself a scarf, or mantle, and a head-dress, and thus assume the aspect of a little mermaid. She inherited her mother's gift for devising drapery and costume. As the last touch to her mermaid's garb, Pearl took some eel-grass, and imitated, as best she could, on her own bosom, the decoration with which she was so familiar on her mother's. A letter,—the letter A,—but freshly green, instead of scarlet! The child bent her chin upon her breast, and contemplated this device with strange interest; even as if the one only thing for which she had been sent into the world was to make out its hidden import.

"I wonder if mother will ask me what it means!" thought Pearl.

Just then, she heard her mother's voice, and, flitting along as lightly as one of the little sea-birds, appeared before Hester Prynne, dancing, laughing, and pointing her finger to the ornament upon her bosom.

"My little Pearl," said Hester, after a moment's silence, "the green letter, and on thy childish bosom, has no purport. But dost thou know, my child, what this letter means which thy mother is doomed to wear?"

"Yes, mother," said the child. "It is the great letter A. Thou hast taught it me in the horn-book."[9]

Hester looked steadily into her little face; but, though there was that singular expression which she had so often remarked in her black eyes, she could not satisfy herself whether Pearl really attached any meaning to the symbol. She felt a morbid desire to ascertain the point.

"Dost thou know, child, wherefore thy mother wears this letter?"

"Truly do I!" answered Pearl, looking brightly into her mother's face. "It is for the same reason that the minister keeps his hand over his heart!"

"And what reason is that?" asked Hester, half smiling at the absurd incongruity of the child's observation; but, on second thoughts, turning pale. "What has the letter to do with any heart, save mine?"

"Nay, mother, I have told all I know," said Pearl, more seriously than she was wont to speak. "Ask yonder old man whom thou hast been talking with! It may be he can tell. But in good earnest now, mother dear, what does this scarlet letter mean?—and why dost thou wear it on they bosom?—and why does the minister keep his hand over his heart?"

She took her mother's hand in both her own, and gazed into her eyes with an earnestness that was seldom seen in her wild and capricious character. The thought occurred to Hester, that the child might really be seeking to approach her with childlike confidence, and doing what she could, and as intelligently as she knew how, to establish a meeting-point of sympathy. It showed Pearl in an unwonted aspect. Heretofore, the mother, while loving her child with the intensity of a sole affection, had schooled herself to hope for little other return than the waywardness of an April breeze; which spends its time in airy sport, and has its gusts of inexplicable passion, and is petulant in its best of moods, and chills oftener than caresses you, when you take it to your bosom; in requital of which misdemeanours, it will sometimes, of its own vague purpose, kiss your cheek with a kind of doubtful tenderness, and play gently with your hair, and then begone about its other idle business, leaving a dreamy pleasure at your heart. And this, moreover, was a mother's estimate of the child's disposition. Any other observer might have seen few but unamiable traits, and have given them a far darker coloring. But now the idea came strongly into Hester's

---

9. A child's "first reader" consisting of a single page protected by a transparent sheet of horn.

mind, that Pearl, with her remarkable precocity and acuteness, might already have approached the age when she could be made a friend, and intrusted with as much of her mother's sorrows as could be imparted, without irreverence either to the parent or the child. In the little chaos of Pearl's character, there might be seen emerging—and could have been, from the very first—the steadfast principles of an unflinching courage,—an uncontrollable will,—a sturdy pride, which might be disciplined into self-respect,—and a bitter scorn of many things, which, when examined, might be found to have the taint of falsehood in them. She possessed affections, too, though hitherto acrid and disagreeable, as are the richest flavors of unripe fruit. With all these sterling attributes, thought Hester, the evil which she inherited from her mother must be great indeed, if a noble woman do not grow out of this elfish child.

Pearl's inevitable tendency to hover about the enigma of the scarlet letter seemed an innate quality of her being. From the earliest epoch of her conscious life, she had entered upon this as her appointed mission. Hester had often fancied that Providence had a design of justice and retribution, in endowing the child with this marked propensity; but never, until now, had she bethought herself to ask, whether, linked with that design, there might not likewise be a purpose of mercy and beneficence. If little Pearl were entertained with faith and trust, as a spirit-messenger no less than an earthly child, might it not be her errand to soothe away the sorrow that lay cold in her mother's heart, and converted it into a tomb?—and to help her to overcome the passion, once so wild, and even yet neither dead nor asleep, but only imprisoned within the same tomb-like heart?

Such were some of the thoughts that now stirred in Hester's mind, with as much vivacity of impression as if they had actually been whispered into her ear. And there was little Pearl, all this while, holding her mother's hand in both her own, and turning her face upward, while she put these searching questions, once, and again, and still a third time.

"What does the letter mean, mother?—and why dost thou wear it?—and why does the minister keep his hand over his heart?"

"What shall I say?" thought Hester to herself.—"No! If this be the price of the child's sympathy, I cannot pay it!"

Then she spoke aloud.

"Silly Pearl," said she, "what questions are these? There are many things in this world that a child must not ask about. What know I of the minister's heart? And as for the scarlet letter, I wear it for the sake of its gold thread!"

In all the seven bygone years, Hester Prynne had never before been false to the symbol on her bosom. It may be that it was the talisman of a stern and severe, but yet a guardian spirit, who now forsook her; as recognizing that, in spite of his strict watch over her heart, some new evil had crept into it, or some old one had never been expelled. As for little Pearl, the earnestness soon passed out of her face.

But the child did not see fit to let the matter drop. Two or three times, as her mother and she went homeward, and as often at supper-time, and while Hester was putting her to bed, and once after she seemed to be fairly asleep, Pearl looked up, with mischief gleaming in her black eyes.

"Mother," said she, "what does the scarlet letter mean?"

And the next morning, the first indication the child gave of being awake was by popping up her head from the pillow, and making that other inquiry, which she had so unaccountably connected with her investigations about the scarlet letter:—

"Mother!—Mother!—Why does the minister keep his hand over his heart?"

"Hold thy tongue, naughty child!" answered her mother, with an asperity that she had never permitted to herself before. "Do not tease me; else I shall shut thee into the dark closet!"

XVI. A FOREST WALK

Hester Prynne remained constant in her resolve to make known to Mr. Dimmesdale, at whatever risk of present pain or ulterior consequences, the true character of the man who had crept into his intimacy. For several days, however, she vainly sought an opportunity of addressing him in some of the meditative walks which she knew him to be in the habit of taking, along the shores of the peninsula, or on the wooded hills of the neighbouring country. There would have been no scandal, indeed, nor peril to the holy whiteness of the clergyman's good fame, had she visited him in his own study; where many a penitent, ere now, had confessed sins of perhaps as deep a die as the one betokened by the scarlet letter. But, partly that she dreaded the secret or undisguised interference of old Roger Chillingworth, and partly that her conscious heart imputed suspicion where none could have been felt, and partly that both the minister and she would need the whole wide world to breathe in, while they talked together,—for all these reasons, Hester never thought of meeting him in any narrower privacy than beneath the open sky.

At last, while attending in a sick-chamber, whither the Reverend Mr. Dimmesdale had been summoned to make a prayer, she learnt that he had gone, the day before, to visit the Apostle Eliot,[1] among his Indian converts. He would probably return, by a certain hour, in the afternoon of the morrow. Betimes, therefore, the next day, Hester took little Pearl,—who was necessarily the companion of all her mother's expeditions, however inconvenient her presence,—and set forth.

The road, after the two wayfarers had crossed from the peninsula to the mainland, was no other than a footpath. It straggled onward into the mystery of the primeval forest. This hemmed it in so narrowly, and stood so black and dense on either side, and disclosed such imperfect glimpses of the sky above, that, to Hester's mind, it imaged not amiss the moral wilderness in which she had so long been wandering. The day was chill and sombre. Overhead was a gray expanse of cloud, slightly stirred, however, by a breeze; so that a gleam of flickering sunshine might now and then be seen at its solitary play along the path. This flitting cheerfulness was always at the farther extremity of some long vista through the forest. The sportive sunlight—feebly sportive, at best, in the predominant pensiveness of the day and scene—withdrew itself as they came nigh, and left the spots where it had danced the drearier, because they had hoped to find them bright.

"Mother," said little Pearl, "the sunshine does not love you. It runs away and hides itself, because it is afraid of something on your bosom. Now, see! There it is, playing, a good way off. Stand you here, and let me run and catch it. I am but a child. It will not flee from me; for I wear nothing on my bosom yet!"

1. The historical John Eliot (1604–1690), missionary to American Indian tribes.

"Nor ever will, my child, I hope," said Hester.

"And why not, mother?" asked Pearl, stopping short, just at the beginning of her race. "Will not it come of its own accord, when I am a woman grown?"

"Run away, child," answered her mother, "and catch the sunshine! It will soon be gone."

Pearl set forth, at a great pace, and, as Hester smiled to perceive, did actually catch the sunshine, and stood laughing in the midst of it, all brightened by its splendor, and scintillating with the vivacity excited by rapid motion. The light lingered about the lonely child, as if glad of such a playmate, until her mother had drawn almost nigh enough to step into the magic circle too.

"It will go now!" said Pearl, shaking her head.

"See!" answered Hester, smiling. "Now I can stretch out my hand, and grasp some of it."

As she attempted to do so, the sunshine vanished; or, to judge from the bright expression that was dancing on Pearl's features, her mother could have fancied that the child had absorbed it into herself, and would give it forth again, with a gleam about her path, as they should plunge into some gloomier shade. There was no other attribute that so much impressed her with a sense of new and untransmitted vigor in Pearl's nature, as this never-failing vivacity of spirits; she had not the disease of sadness, which almost all children, in these latter days, inherit, with the scrofula,[2] from the troubles of their ancestors. Perhaps this too was a disease, and but the reflex of the wild energy with which Hester had fought against her sorrows, before Pearl's birth. It was certainly a doubtful charm, imparting a hard, metallic lustre to the child's character. She wanted—what some people want throughout life—a grief that should deeply touch her, and thus humanize and make her capable of sympathy. But there was time enough yet for little Pearl!

"Come, my child!" said Hester, looking about her, from the spot where Pearl had stood still in the sunshine. "We will sit down a little way within the wood, and rest ourselves."

"I am not aweary, mother," replied the little girl. "But you may sit down, if you will tell me a story meanwhile."

"A story, child!" said Hester. "And about what?"

"O, a story about the Black Man!" answered Pearl, taking hold of her mother's gown, and looking up, half earnestly, half mischievously, into her face. "How he haunts this forest, and carries a book with him,—a big, heavy book, with iron clasps; and how this ugly Black Man offers his book and an iron pen to every body that meets him here among the trees; and they are to write their names with their own blood. And then he sets his mark on their bosoms! Didst thou ever meet the Black Man, mother?"

"And who told you this story, Pearl?" asked her mother, recognizing a common superstition of the period.

"It was the old dame in the chimney-corner, at the house where you watched last night," said the child. "But she fancied me asleep while she was talking of it. She said that a thousand and a thousand people had met him here, and had written in his book, and have his mark on them. And that ugly-tempered lady, old Mistress Hibbins, was one. And, mother, the old dame said that this scarlet letter was the Black Man's mark on thee, and that it glows

2. Pretubercular condition affecting tissues in the young.

like a red flame when thou meetest him at midnight, here in the dark wood. Is it true, mother? And dost thou go to meet him in the night-time?"

"Didst thou ever awake, and find thy mother gone?" asked Hester.

"Not that I remember," said the child. "If thou fearest to leave me in our cottage, thou mightest take me along with thee. I would very gladly go! But, mother, tell me now! Is there such a Black Man? And didst thou ever meet him? And is this his mark?"

"Wilt thou let me be at peace, if I once tell thee?" asked her mother.

"Yes, if thou tellest me all," answered Pearl.

"Once in my life I met the Black Man!" said her mother. "This scarlet letter is his mark!"

Thus conversing, they entered sufficiently deep into the wood to secure themselves from the observation of any casual passenger along the forest-track. Here they sat down on a luxuriant heap of moss; which, at some epoch of the preceding century, had been a gigantic pine, with its roots and trunk in the darksome shade, and its head aloft in the upper atmosphere. It was a little dell where they had seated themselves, with a leaf-strewn bank rising gently on either side, and a brook flowing through the midst, over a bed of fallen and drowned leaves. The trees impending over it had flung down great branches, from time to time, which choked up the current, and compelled it to form eddies and black depths at some points; while, in its swifter and livelier passages, there appeared a channel-way of pebbles, and brown, sparkling sand. Letting the eyes follow along the course of the stream, they could catch the reflected light from its water, at some short distance within the forest, but soon lost all traces of it amid the bewilderment of tree-trunks and underbrush, and here and there a huge rock, covered over with gray lichens. All these giant trees and boulders of granite seemed intent on making a mystery of the course of this small brook; fearing, perhaps, that, with its never-ceasing loquacity, it should whisper tales out of the heart of the old forest whence it flowed, or mirror its revelations on the smooth surface of a pool. Continually, indeed, as it stole onward, the streamlet kept up a babble, kind, quiet, soothing, but melancholy, like the voice of a young child that was spending its infancy without playfulness, and knew not how to be merry among sad acquaintance and events of sombre hue.

"O brook! O foolish and tiresome little brook!" cried Pearl, after listening awhile to its talk. "Why art thou so sad? Pluck up a spirit, and do not be all the time sighing and murmuring!"

But the brook, in the course of its little lifetime among the forest-trees, had gone through so solemn an experience that it could not help talking about it, and seemed to have nothing else to say. Pearl resembled the brook, inasmuch as the current of her life gushed from a well-spring as mysterious, and had flowed through scenes shadowed as heavily with gloom. But, unlike the little stream, she danced and sparkled, and prattled airily along her course.

"What does this sad little brook say, mother?" inquired she.

"If thou hadst a sorrow of thine own, the brook might tell thee of it," answered her mother, "even as it is telling me of mine! But now, Pearl, I hear a footstep along the path, and the noise of one putting aside the branches. I would have thee betake thyself to play, and leave me to speak with him that comes yonder."

"Is it the Black Man?" asked Pearl.

"Wilt thou go and play, child?" repeated her mother. "But do not stray far into the wood. And take heed that thou come at my first call."

"Yes, mother," answered Pearl. "But, if it be the Black Man, wilt thou not let me stay a moment, and look at him, with his big book under his arm?"

"Go, silly child!" said her mother, impatiently. "It is no Black Man! Thou canst see him now through the trees. It is the minister!"

"And so it is!" said the child. "And, mother, he has his hand over his heart! Is it because, when the minister wrote his name in the book, the Black Man set his mark in that place? But why does he not wear it outside his bosom, as thou dost, mother?"

"Go now, child, and thou shalt tease me as thou wilt another time," cried Hester Prynne. "But do not stray far. Keep where thou canst hear the babble of the brook."

The child went singing away, following up the current of the brook, and striving to mingle a more lightsome cadence with its melancholy voice. But the little stream would not be comforted, and still kept telling its unintelligible secret of some very mournful mystery that had happened—or making a prophetic lamentation about something that was yet to happen—within the verge of the dismal forest. So Pearl, who had enough of shadow in her own little life, chose to break off all acquaintance with this repining brook. She set herself, therefore, to gathering violets and wood-anemones, and some scarlet columbines that she found growing in the crevices of a high rock.

When her elf-child had departed, Hester Prynne made a step or two towards the track that led through the forest, but still remained under the deep shadow of the trees. She beheld the minister advancing along the path, entirely alone, and leaning on a staff which he had cut by the way-side. He looked haggard and feeble, and betrayed a nerveless despondency in his air, which had never so remarkably characterized him in his walks about the settlement, nor in any other situation where he deemed himself liable to notice. Here it was wofully visible, in this intense seclusion of the forest, which of itself would have been a heavy trial to the spirits. There was a listlessness in his gait; as if he saw no reason for taking one step farther, nor felt any desire to do so, but would have been glad, could he be glad of any thing, to fling himself down at the root of the nearest tree, and lie there passive for evermore. The leaves might bestrew him, and the soil gradually accumulate and form a little hillock over his frame, no matter whether there were life in it or no. Death was too definite an object to be wished for, or avoided.

To Hester's eye, the Reverend Mr. Dimmesdale exhibited no symptom of positive and vivacious suffering, except that, as little Pearl had remarked, he kept his hand over his heart.

XVII. THE PASTOR AND HIS PARISHIONER

Slowly as the minister walked, he had almost gone by, before Hester Prynne could gather voice enough to attract his observation. At length, she succeeded.

"Arthur Dimmesdale!" she said, faintly at first; then louder, but hoarsely. "Arthur Dimmesdale!"

"Who speaks?" answered the minister.

Gathering himself quickly up, he stood more erect, like a man taken by surprise in a mood to which he was reluctant to have witnesses. Throwing his eyes anxiously in the direction of the voice, he indistinctly beheld a form under the trees, clad in garments so sombre, and so little relieved from the gray twilight into which the clouded sky and the heavy foliage had darkened the noontide, that he knew not whether it were a woman or a shadow. It may be, that his pathway through life was haunted thus, by a spectre that had stolen out from among his thoughts.

He made a step nigher, and discovered the scarlet letter.

"Hester! Hester Prynne!" said he. "Is it thou? Art thou in life?"

"Even so!" she answered. "In such life as has been mine these seven years past! And thou, Arthur Dimmesdale, dost thou yet live?"

It was no wonder that they thus questioned one another's actual and bodily existence, and even doubted of their own. So strangely did they meet, in the dim wood, that it was like the first encounter, in the world beyond the grave, of two spirits who had been intimately connected in their former life, but now stood coldly shuddering, in mutual dread; as not yet familiar with their state, nor wonted to the companionship of disembodied beings. Each a ghost, and awe-stricken at the other ghost! They were awe-stricken likewise at themselves; because the crisis flung back to them their consciousness, and revealed to each heart its history and experience, as life never does, except at such breathless epochs. The soul beheld its features in the mirror of the passing moment. It was with fear, and tremulously, and, as it were, by a slow, reluctant necessity, that Arthur Dimmesdale put forth his hand, chill as death, and touched the chill hand of Hester Prynne. The grasp, cold as it was, took away what was dreariest in the interview. They now felt themselves, at least, inhabitants of the same sphere.

Without a word more spoken,—neither he nor she assuming the guidance, but with an unexpressed consent,—they glided back into the shadow of the woods, whence Hester had emerged, and sat down on the heap of moss where she and Pearl had before been sitting. When they found voice to speak, it was, at first, only to utter remarks and inquiries such as any two acquaintance might have made, about the gloomy sky, the threatening storm, and, next, the health of each. Thus they went onward, not boldly, but step by step, into the themes that were brooding deepest in their hearts. So long estranged by fate and cir-cumstances, they needed something slight and casual to run before, and throw open the doors of intercourse, so that their real thoughts might be led across the threshold.

After a while, the minister fixed his eyes on Hester Prynne's.

"Hester," said he, "hast thou found peace?"

She smiled drearily, looking down upon her bosom.

"Hast thou?" she asked.

"None!—nothing but despair!" he answered. "What else could I look for, being what I am, and leading such a life as mine? Were I an atheist,—a man devoid of conscience,—a wretch with coarse and brutal instincts,—I might have found peace, long ere now. Nay, I never should have lost it! But, as matters stand with my soul, whatever of good capacity there originally was in me, all of God's gifts that were the choicest have become the ministers of spiritual torment. Hester, I am most miserable!"

"The people reverence thee," said Hester. "And surely thou workest good among them! Doth this bring thee no comfort?"

"More misery, Hester!—only the more misery!" answered the clergyman, with a bitter smile. "As concerns the good which I may appear to do, I have no faith in it. It must needs be a delusion. What can a ruined soul, like mine, effect towards the redemption of other souls!—or a polluted soul, towards their purification? And as for the people's reverence, would that it were turned to scorn and hatred! Canst thou deem it, Hester, a consolation, that I must stand up in my pulpit, and meet so many eyes turned upward to my face, as if the light of heaven were beaming from it!—must see my flock hungry for the truth, and listening to my words as if a tongue of Pentecost were speaking!— and then look inward, and discern the black reality of what they idolize? I have laughed, in bitterness and agony of heart, at the contrast between what I seem and what I am! And Satan laughs at it!"

"You wrong yourself in this," said Hester, gently. "You have deeply and sorely repented. Your sin is left behind you, in the days long past. Your present life is not less holy, in very truth, than it seems in people's eyes. Is there no reality in the penitence thus sealed and witnessed by good works? And wherefore should it not bring you peace?"

"No, Hester, no!" replied the clergyman. "There is no substance in it! It is cold and dead, and can do nothing for me! Of penance I have had enough! Of penitence there has been none! Else, I should long ago have thrown off these garments of mock holiness, and have shown myself to mankind as they will see me at the judgment-seat. Happy are you, Hester, that wear the scarlet letter openly upon your bosom! Mine burns in secret! Thou little knowest what a relief it is, after the torment of a seven years' cheat, to look into an eye that recognizes me for what I am! Had I one friend,—or were it my worst enemy!—to whom, when sickened with the praises of all other men, I could daily betake myself, and be known as the vilest of all sinners, methinks my soul might keep itself alive thereby. Even thus much of truth would save me! But, now, it is all falsehood!—all emptiness!—all death!"

Hester Prynne looked into his face, but hesitated to speak. Yet, uttering his long-restrained emotions so vehemently as he did, his words here offered her the very point of circumstances in which to interpose what she came to say. She conquered her fears, and spoke.

"Such a friend as thou hast even now wished for," said she, "with whom to weep over thy sin, thou hast in me, the partner of it!"—Again she hesitated, but brought out the words with an effort.—"Thou hast long had such an enemy, and dwellest with him under the same roof!"

The minister started to his feet, gasping for breath, and clutching at his heart as if he would have torn it out of his bosom.

"Ha! What sayest thou?" cried he. "An enemy! And under mine own roof! What mean you?"

Hester Prynne was now fully sensible of the deep injury for which she was responsible to this unhappy man, in permitting him to lie for so many years, or, indeed, for a single moment, at the mercy of one, whose purposes could not be other than malevolent. The very contiguity of his enemy, beneath whatever mask the latter might conceal himself, was enough to disturb the magnetic sphere of a being so sensitive as Arthur Dimmesdale. There had been a period when Hester was less alive to this consideration; or, perhaps, in the misanthropy of her own trouble, she left the minister to bear what she might picture to herself as a more tolerable doom. But of late, since the night of his vigil, all her sympathies towards him had been both softened and invigorated. She now read his heart more accurately. She doubted not, that the continual presence of Roger Chillingworth,—the secret poison of his malignity, infecting all the air about him,—and his authorized interference, as a physician, with the minister's physical and spiritual infirmities,—that these bad opportunities had been turned to a cruel purpose. By means of them, the sufferer's conscience had been kept in an irritated state, the tendency of which was, not to cure by wholesome pain, but to disorganize and corrupt his spiritual being. Its result, on earth, could hardly fail to be insanity, and hereafter, that eternal alienation from the Good and True, of which madness is perhaps the earthly type.

Such was the ruin to which she had brought the man, once,—nay, why should we not speak it?—still so passionately loved! Hester felt that the sacrifice of the clergyman's good name, and death itself, as she had already told Roger Chillingworth, would have been infinitely preferable to the alternative which she had taken upon herself to choose. And now, rather than have had this grievous wrong to confess, she would gladly have lain down on the forest-leaves, and died there, at Arthur Dimmesdale's feet.

"O Arthur," cried she, "forgive me! In all things else, I have striven to be true! Truth was the one virtue which I might have held fast, and did hold fast through all extremity; save when thy good,—thy life,—thy fame,—were put in question! Then I consented to a deception. But a lie is never good, even though death threaten on the other side! Dost thou not see what I would say? That old man!—the physician!—he whom they call Roger Chillingworth!— he was my husband!"

The minister looked at her, for an instant, with all that violence of passion, which—intermixed, in more shapes than one, with his higher, purer, softer qualities—was, in fact, the portion of him which the Devil claimed, and through which he sought to win the rest. Never was there a blacker or a fiercer frown, than Hester now encountered. For the brief space that it lasted, it was a dark transfiguration. But his character had been so much enfeebled by suffering, that even its lower energies were incapable of more than a temporary struggle. He sank down on the ground, and buried his face in his hands.

"I might have known it!" murmured he. "I did know it! Was not the secret told me in the natural recoil of my heart, at the first sight of him, and as often as I have seen him since? Why did I not understand? O Hester Prynne, thou little, little knowest all the horror of this thing! And the shame!—the indelicacy!—the horrible ugliness of this exposure of a sick and guilty heart to the very eye that would gloat over it! Woman, woman, thou art accountable for this! I cannot forgive thee!"

"Thou shalt forgive me!" cried Hester, flinging herself on the fallen leaves beside him. "Let God punish! Thou shalt forgive!"

With sudden and desperate tenderness, she threw her arms around him, and pressed his head against her bosom; little caring though his cheek rested on the scarlet letter. He would have released himself, but strove in vain to do so. Hester would not set him free, lest he should look her sternly in the face. All the world had frowned on her,—for seven long years had it frowned upon this lonely woman,—and still she bore it all, nor ever once turned away her firm, sad eyes. Heaven, likewise, had frowned upon her, and she had not died. But the frown of this pale, weak, sinful, and sorrow-stricken man was what Hester could not bear, and live!

"Wilt thou yet forgive me?" she repeated, over and over again. "Wilt thou not frown? Wilt thou forgive?"

"I do forgive you, Hester," replied the minister, at length, with a deep utterance out of an abyss of sadness, but no anger. "I freely forgive you now. May God forgive us both! We are not, Hester, the worst sinners in the world. There is one worse than even the polluted priest! That old man's revenge has been blacker than my sin. He has violated, in cold blood, the sanctity of a human heart. Thou and I, Hester, never did so!"

"Never, never!" whispered she. "What we did had a consecration of its own. We felt it so! We said so to each other! Hast thou forgotten it!"

"Hush, Hester!" said Arthur Dimmesdale, rising from the ground. "No; I have not forgotten!"

They sat down again, side by side, and hand clasped in hand, on the mossy trunk of the fallen tree. Life had never brought them a gloomier hour; it was the point whither their pathway had so long been tending, and darkening ever, as it stole along;—and yet it inclosed a charm that made them linger upon it, and claim another, and another, and, after all, another moment. The forest was obscure around them, and creaked with a blast that was passing through it. The boughs were tossing heavily above their heads; while one solemn old tree groaned dolefully to another, as if telling the sad story of the pair that sat beneath, or constrained to forebode evil to come.

And yet they lingered. How dreary looked the forest-track that led backward to the settlement, where Hester Prynne must take up again the burden of her ignominy, and the minister the hollow mockery of his good name! So they lingered an instant longer. No golden light had ever been so precious as the gloom of this dark forest. Here, seen only by his eyes, the scarlet letter need not burn into the bosom of the fallen woman! Here, seen only by her eyes, Arthur Dimmesdale, false to God and man, might be, for one moment, true!

He started at a thought that suddenly occurred to him.

"Hester," cried he, "here is a new horror! Roger Chillingworth knows your purpose to reveal his true character. Will he continue, then, to keep our secret? What will now be the course of his revenge?"

"There is a strange secrecy in his nature," replied Hester, thoughtfully; "and it has grown upon him by the hidden practices of his revenge. I deem it not likely that he will betray the secret. He will doubtless seek other means of satiating his dark passion."

"And I!—how am I to live longer, breathing the same air with this deadly enemy?" exclaimed Arthur Dimmesdale, shrinking within himself, and pressing his hand nervously against his heart,—a gesture that had grown involuntary with him. "Think for me, Hester! Thou art strong. Resolve for me!"

"Thou must dwell no longer with this man," said Hester, slowly and firmly. "Thy heart must be no longer under his evil eye!"

"It were far worse than death!" replied the minister. "But how to avoid it? What choice remains to me? Shall I lie down again on these withered leaves, where I cast myself when thou didst tell me what he was? Must I sink down there, and die at once?"

"Alas, what a ruin has befallen thee!" said Hester, with the tears gushing into her eyes. "Wilt thou die for very weakness? There is no other cause!"

"The judgment of God is on me," answered the conscience-stricken priest. "It is too mighty for me to struggle with!"

"Heaven would show mercy," rejoined Hester, "hadst thou but the strength to take advantage of it."

"Be thou strong for me!" answered he. "Advise me what to do."

"Is the world then so narrow?" exclaimed Hester Prynne, fixing her deep eyes on the minister's, and instinctively exercising a magnetic power over a spirit so shattered and subdued, that it could hardly hold itself erect. "Doth the universe lie within the compass of yonder town, which only a little time ago was but a leaf-strewn desert, as lonely as this around us? Whither leads yonder forest-track? Backward to the settlement, thou sayest! Yes; but onward, too! Deeper it goes, and deeper, into the wilderness, less plainly to be seen at every step; until, some few miles hence, the yellow leaves will show no vestige of the white man's tread. There thou art free! So brief a journey would bring thee from a world where thou hast been most wretched, to one where thou mayest still be happy! Is there not shade enough in all this boundless forest to hide thy heart from the gaze of Roger Chillingworth?"

"Yes, Hester; but only under the fallen leaves!" replied the minister, with a sad smile.

"Then there is the broad pathway of the sea!" continued Hester. "It brought thee hither. If thou so choose, it will bear thee back again. In our native land, whether in some remote rural village or in vast London,—or, surely, in Germany, in France, in pleasant Italy,—thou wouldst be beyond his power and knowledge! And what hast thou to do with all these iron men, and their opinions? They have kept thy better part in bondage too long already!"

"It cannot be!" answered the minister, listening as if he were called upon to realize a dream. "I am powerless to go. Wretched and sinful as I am, I have had no other thought than to drag on my earthly existence in the sphere where Providence hath placed me. Lost as my own soul is, I would still do what I may for other human souls! I dare not quit my post, though an unfaithful sentinel, whose sure reward is death and dishonor, when his dreary watch shall come to an end!"

"Thou art crushed under this seven years' weight of misery," replied Hester, fervently resolved to buoy him up with her own energy. "But thou shalt leave it all behind thee! It shall not cumber thy steps, as thou treadest along the forest-path; neither shalt thou freight the ship with it, if thou prefer to cross the sea. Leave this wreck and ruin here where it hath happened! Meddle no more with it! Begin all anew! Hast thou exhausted possibility in the failure of this one trial? Not so! The future is yet full of trial and success. There is happiness to be enjoyed! There is good to be done! Exchange this false life of thine for a true one. Be, if thy spirit summon thee to such a mission, the teacher and apostle of the red men. Or,—as is more thy nature,—be a scholar and a sage among the wisest and the most renowned of the cultivated world. Preach! Write! Act! Do any thing, save to lie down and die! Give up this name of Arthur Dimmesdale, and make thyself another, and a high one, such as thou canst wear without fear or shame. Why shouldst thou tarry so much as one other day in the torments that have so gnawed into thy life!—that have made thee feeble to will and to do!—that will leave thee powerless even to repent! Up, and away!"

"O Hester!" cried Arthur Dimmesdale, in whose eyes a fitful light, kindled by her enthusiasm, flashed up and died away, "thou tellest of running a race to a man whose knees are tottering beneath him! I must die here. There is not the strength or courage left me to venture into the wide, strange, difficult world, alone!"

It was the last expression of the despondency of a broken spirit. He lacked energy to grasp the better fortune that seemed within his reach.

He repeated the word.

"Alone, Hester!"

"Thou shalt not go alone!" answered she, in a deep whisper.

Then, all was spoken!

XVIII. A FLOOD OF SUNSHINE

Arthur Dimmesdale gazed into Hester's face with a look in which hope and joy shone out, indeed, but with fear betwixt them, and a kind of horror at her boldness, who had spoken what he vaguely hinted at, but dared not speak.

But Hester Prynne, with a mind of native courage and activity, and for so long a period not merely estranged, but outlawed, from society, had habituated herself to such latitude of speculation as was altogether foreign to the clergyman. She had wandered, without rule or guidance, in a moral wilderness; as vast, as intricate and shadowy, as the untamed forest, amid the gloom of which they were now holding a colloquy that was to decide their fate. Her intellect and heart had their home, as it were, in desert places, where she roamed as freely as the wild Indian in his woods. For years past she had looked from this estranged point of view at human institutions, and whatever priests or legislators had established; criticizing all with hardly more reverence than the Indian would feel for the clerical band, the judicial robe, the pillory, the gallows, the fireside, or the church. The tendency of her fate and fortunes had been to set her free. The scarlet letter was her passport into regions where other women dared not tread. Shame, Despair, Solitude! These had been her teachers,— stern and wild ones,—and they had made her strong, but taught her much amiss.

The minister, on the other hand, had never gone through an experience calculated to lead him beyond the scope of generally received laws; although, in a single instance, he had so fearfully transgressed one of the most sacred of them. But this had been a sin of passion, not of principle, nor even purpose. Since that wretched epoch, he had watched, with morbid zeal and minuteness, not his acts,—for those it was easy to arrange,—but each breath of emotion, and his every thought. At the head of the social system, as the clergymen of that day stood, he was only the more trammelled by its regulations, its principles, and even its prejudices. As a priest, the framework of his order inevitably hemmed him in. As a man who had once sinned, but who kept his conscience all alive and painfully sensitive by the fretting of an unhealed wound, he might have been supposed safer within the line of virtue, than if he had never sinned at all.

Thus, we seem to see that, as regarded Hester Prynne, the whole seven years of outlaw and ignominy had been little other than a preparation for this very hour. But Arthur Dimmesdale! Were such a man once more to fall, what plea could be urged in extenuation of his crime? None; unless it avail him some- what, that he was broken down by long and exquisite suffering; that his mind was darkened and confused by the very remorse which harrowed it; that, between fleeing as an avowed criminal, and remaining as a hypocrite, conscience might find it hard to strike the balance; that it was human to avoid the peril of death and infamy, and the inscrutable machinations of an enemy; that, finally, to this poor pilgrim, on his dreary and desert path, faint, sick, miserable, there appeared a glimpse of human affection and sympathy, a new life, and a true one, in exchange for the heavy doom which he was now expiating. And be the stern and sad truth spoken, that the breach which guilt has once made into the human soul is never, in this mortal state, repaired. It may be watched and guarded; so that the enemy shall not force his way again into the citadel, and might even, in his subsequent assaults, select some other avenue, in preference to that where he had formerly succeeded. But there is still the ruined wall, and, near it, the stealthy tread of the foe that would win over again his unforgotten triumph.

The struggle, if there were one, need not be described. Let it suffice, that the clergyman resolved to flee, and not alone.

"If, in all these past seven years," thought he, "I could recall one instant of peace or hope, I would yet endure, for the sake of that earnest of Heaven's mercy. But now,—since I am irrevocably doomed,—wherefore should I not snatch the solace allowed to the condemned culprit before his execution? Or, if this be the path to a better life, as Hester would persuade me, I surely give up no fairer prospect by pursuing it! Neither can I any longer live without her companionship; so powerful is she to sustain,—so tender to soothe! O Thou to whom I dare not lift mine eyes, wilt Thou yet pardon me!"

"Thou wilt go!" said Hester calmly, as he met her glance.

The decision once made, a glow of strange enjoyment threw its flickering brightness over the trouble of his breast. It was the exhilarating effect—upon a prisoner just escaped from the dungeon of his own heart—of breathing the wild, free atmosphere of an unredeemed, unchristianized, lawless region. His spirit rose, as it were, with a bound, and attained a nearer prospect of the sky, than throughout all the misery which had kept him grovelling on the earth. Of a deeply religious temperament, there was inevitably a tinge of the devotional in his mood.

"Do I feel joy again?" cried he, wondering at himself. "Methought the germ of it was dead in me! O Hester, thou art my better angel! I seem to have flung myself—sick, sin-stained, and sorrow-blackened—down upon these forest-leaves, and to have risen up all made anew, and with new powers to glorify Him that hath been merciful! This is already the better life! Why did we not find it sooner?"

"Let us not look back," answered Hester Prynne. "The past is gone! Wherefore should we linger upon it now? See! With this symbol, I undo it all, and make it as it had never been!"

So speaking, she undid the clasp that fastened the scarlet letter, and, taking it from her bosom, threw it to a distance among the withered leaves. The mystic token alighted on the hither verge of the stream. With a hand's breadth farther flight it would have fallen into the water, and have given the little brook another woe to carry onward, besides the unintelligible tale which it still kept murmuring about. But there lay the embroidered letter, glittering like a lost jewel, which some ill-fated wanderer might pick up, and thenceforth be haunted by strange phantoms of guilt, sinkings of the heart, and unaccountable misfortune.

The stigma gone, Hester heaved a long, deep sigh, in which the burden of shame and anguish departed from her spirit. O exquisite relief! She had not known the weight, until she felt the freedom! By another impulse, she took off the formal cap that confined her hair; and down it fell upon her shoulders, dark and rich, with at once a shadow and a light in its abundance, and imparting the charm of softness to her features. There played around her mouth, and beamed out of her eyes, a radiant and tender smile, that seemed gushing from the very heart of womanhood. A crimson flush was glowing on her cheek, that had been long so pale. Her sex, her youth, and the whole richness of her beauty, came back from what men call the irrevocable past, and clustered themselves, with her maiden hope, and a happiness before unknown, within the magic circle of this hour. And, as if the gloom of the earth and sky had been but the effluence of these two mortal hearts, it vanished with their sorrow. All at once, as with a sudden smile of heaven, forth burst the sunshine, pouring a very flood into the obscure forest, gladdening each green leaf, transmuting the yellow fallen ones to gold, and gleaming adown the gray trunks of the solemn trees. The objects that had made a shadow hitherto, embodied the brightness now. The course of the little brook might be traced by its merry gleam afar into the wood's heart of mystery, which had become a mystery of joy.

Such was the sympathy of Nature—that wild, heathen Nature of the forest, never subjugated by human law, nor illumined by higher truth—with the bliss of these two spirits! Love, whether newly born, or aroused from a deathlike slumber, must always create a sunshine, filling the heart so full of radiance, that it overflows upon the outward world. Had the forest still kept its gloom, it would have been bright in Hester's eyes, and bright in Arthur Dimmesdale's!

Hester looked at him with the thrill of another joy.

"Thou must know Pearl!" said she. "Our little Pearl! Thou hast seen her,— yes, I know it!—but thou wilt see her now with other eyes. She is a strange child! I hardly comprehend her! But thou wilt love her dearly, as I do, and wilt advise me how to deal with her."

"Dost thou think the child will be glad to know me?" asked the minister, somewhat uneasily. "I have long shrunk from children, because they often show a distrust,—a backwardness to be familiar with me. I have even been afraid of little Pearl!"

"Ah, that was sad!" answered the mother. "But she will love thee dearly, and thou her. She is not far off. I will call her! Pearl! Pearl!"

"I see the child," observed the minister. "Yonder she is, standing in a streak of sunshine, a good way off, on the other side of the brook. So thou thinkest the child will love me?"

Hester smiled, and again called to Pearl, who was visible, at some distance, as the minister had described her, like a bright-apparelled vision, in a sunbeam, which fell down upon her through an arch of boughs. The ray quivered to and fro, making her figure dim or distinct,—now like a real child, now like a child's spirit,—as the splendor went and came again. She heard her mother's voice, and approached slowly through the forest.

Pearl had not found the hour pass wearisomely, while her mother sat talking with the clergyman. The great black forest—stern as it showed itself to those who brought the guilt and troubles of the world into its bosom—became the playmate of the lonely infant, as well as it knew how. Sombre as it was, it put on the kindest of its moods to welcome her. It offered her the partridge-berries, the growth of the preceding autumn, but ripening only in the spring, and now red as drops of blood upon the withered leaves. These Pearl gathered, and was pleased with their wild flavor. The small denizens of the wilderness hardly took pains to move out of her path. A partridge, indeed, with a brood of ten behind her, ran forward threateningly, but soon repented of her fierceness, and clucked to her young ones not to be afraid. A pigeon, alone on a low branch, allowed Pearl to come beneath, and uttered a sound as much of greeting as alarm. A squirrel, from the lofty depths of his domestic tree, chattered either in anger or merriment,—for a squirrel is such a choleric and humorous little personage that it is hard to distinguish between his moods,—so he chattered at the child, and flung down a nut upon her head. It was a last year's nut, and already gnawed by his sharp tooth. A fox, startled from his sleep by her light foot-step on the leaves, looked inquisitively at Pearl, as doubting whether it were better to steal off, or renew his nap on the same spot. A wolf, it is said,—but here the tale has surely lapsed into the improbable,—came up, and smelt of Pearl's robe, and offered his savage head to be patted by her hand. The truth seems to be, however, that the mother-forest, and these wild things which it nourished, all recognized a kindred wildness in the human child.

And she was gentler here than in the grassy-margined streets of the settlement, or in her mother's cottage. The flowers appeared to know it; and one and another whispered, as she passed, "Adorn thyself with me, thou beautiful child, adorn thyself with me!"—and, to please them, Pearl gathered the violets, and anemones, and columbines, and some twigs of the freshest green, which the old trees held down before her eyes. With these she decorated her hair, and her young waist, and became a nymph-child, or an infant dryad,[3] or whatever else was in closest sympathy with the antique wood. In such guise had Pearl adorned herself, when she heard her mother's voice, and came slowly back.

Slowly; for she saw the clergyman!

XIX. THE CHILD AT THE BROOK-SIDE

"Thou wilt love her dearly," repeated Hester Prynne, as she and the minister sat watching little Pearl. "Dost thou not think her beautiful? And see with what natural skill she has made those simple flowers adorn her! Had she gathered pearls, and diamonds, and rubies, in the wood, they could not have become her better. She is a splendid child! But I know whose brow she has!"

"Dost thou know, Hester," said Arthur Dimmesdale, with an unquiet smile, "that this dear child, tripping about always at thy side, hath caused me many an alarm? Methought—O Hester, what a thought is that, and how terrible to dread it!—that my own features were partly repeated in her face, and so strikingly that the world might see them! But she is mostly thine!"

"No, no! Not mostly!" answered the mother with a tender smile. "A little longer, and thou needest not to be afraid to trace whose child she is. But how strangely beautiful she looks, with those wild flowers in her hair! It is as if one of the fairies, whom we left in our dear old England, had decked her out to meet us."

It was with a feeling which neither of them had ever before experienced,

3. Wood nymph.

that they sat and watched Pearl's slow advance. In her was visible the tie that united them. She had been offered to the world, these seven years past, as the living hieroglyphic, in which was revealed the secret they so darkly sought to hide,—all written in this symbol,—all plainly manifest,—had there been a prophet or magician skilled to read the character of flame! And Pearl was the oneness of their being. Be the foregone evil what it might, how could they doubt that their earthly lives and future destinies were conjoined, when they beheld at once the material union, and the spiritual idea, in whom they met, and were to dwell immortally together? Thoughts like these—and perhaps other thoughts, which they did not acknowledge or define—threw an awe about the child, as she came onward.

"Let her see nothing strange—no passion nor eagerness—in thy way of accosting her," whispered Hester. "Our Pearl is a fitful and fantastic little elf, sometimes. Especially, she is seldom tolerant of emotion, when she does not fully comprehend the why and wherefore. But the child hath strong affections! She loves me, and will love thee!"

"Thou canst not think," said the minister, glancing aside at Hester Prynne, "how my heart dreads this interview, and yearns for it! But, in truth, as I already told thee, children are not readily won to be familiar with me. They will not climb my knee, nor prattle in my ear, nor answer to my smile; but stand apart, and eye me strangely. Even little babes, when I take them in my arms, weep bitterly. Yet Pearl, twice in her little lifetime, hath been kind to me! The first time,—thou knowest it well! The last was when thou ledst her with thee to the house of yonder stern old Governor."

"And thou didst plead so bravely in her behalf and mine!" answered the mother. "I remember it; and so shall little Pearl. Fear nothing! She may be strange and shy at first, but will soon learn to love thee!"

By this time Pearl had reached the margin of the brook, and stood on the farther side, gazing silently at Hester and the clergyman, who still sat together on the mossy tree-trunk, waiting to receive her. Just where she had paused the brook chanced to form a pool, so smooth and quiet that it reflected a perfect image of her little figure, with all the brilliant picturesqueness of her beauty, in its adornment of flowers and wreathed foliage, but more refined and spiritualized than the reality. This image, so nearly identical with the living Pearl, seemed to communicate somewhat of its own shadowy and intangible quality to the child herself. It was strange, the way in which Pearl stood, looking so stedfastly at them through the dim medium of the forest-gloom; herself, meanwhile, all glorified with a ray of sunshine, that was attracted thitherward as by a certain sympathy. In the brook beneath stood another child,—another and the same,—with likewise its ray of golden light. Hester felt herself, in some indistinct and tantalizing manner, estranged from Pearl; as if the child, in her lonely ramble through the forest, had strayed out of the sphere in which she and her mother dwelt together, and was now vainly seeking to return to it.

There was both truth and error in the impression; the child and mother were estranged, but through Hester's fault, not Pearl's. Since the latter rambled from her side, another inmate had been admitted within the circle of the mother's feelings, and so modified the aspect of them all, that Pearl, the returning wanderer, could not find her wonted place, and hardly knew where she was.

"I have a strange fancy," observed the sensitive minister, "that this brook is the boundary between two worlds, and that thou canst never meet thy Pearl again. Or is she an elfish spirit, who, as the legends of our childhood taught us, is forbidden to cross a running stream? Pray hasten her; for this delay has already imparted a tremor to my nerves."

"Come, dearest child!" said Hester encouragingly, and stretching out both her arms. "How slow thou art! When hast thou been so sluggish before now? Here is a friend of mine, who must be thy friend also. Thou wilt have twice as much love, henceforward, as thy mother alone could give thee! Leap across the brook and come to us. Thou canst leap like a young deer!"

Pearl, without responding in any manner to these honey-sweet expressions, remained on the other side of the brook. Now she fixed her bright, wild eyes on her mother, now on the minister, and now included them both in the same glance; as if to detect and explain to herself the relation which they bore to one another. For some unaccountable reason, as Arthur Dimmesdale felt the child's eyes upon himself, his hand—with that gesture so habitual as to have become involuntary—stole over his heart. At length, assuming a singular air of authority, Pearl stretched out her hand, with the small forefinger extended, and pointing evidently towards her mother's breast. And beneath, in the mirror of the brook, there was the flower-girdled and sunny image of little Pearl, pointing her small forefinger too.

"Thou strange child, why dost thou not come to me?" exclaimed Hester.

Pearl still pointed with her forefinger; and a frown gathered on her brow; the more impressive from the childish, the almost baby-like aspect of the features that conveyed it. As her mother still kept beckoning to her, and arraying her face in a holiday suit of unaccustomed smiles, the child stamped her foot with a yet more imperious look and gesture. In the brook, again, was the fantastic beauty of the image, with its reflected frown, its pointed finger, and imperious gesture, giving emphasis to the aspect of little Pearl.

"Hasten, Pearl; or I shall be angry with thee!" cried Hester Prynne, who, however inured to such behaviour on the elf-child's part at other seasons, was naturally anxious for a more seemly deportment now. "Leap across the brook, naughty child, and run hither! Else I must come to thee!"

But Pearl, not a whit startled at her mother's threats, any more than mollified by her entreaties, now suddenly burst into a fit of passion, gesticulating violently, and throwing her small figure into the most extravagant contortions. She accompanied this wild outbreak with piercing shrieks, which the woods reverberated on all sides; so that, alone as she was in her childish and unreasonable wrath, it seemed as if a hidden multitude were lending her their sympathy and encouragement. Seen in the brook, once more, was the shadowy wrath of Pearl's image, crowned and girdled with flowers, but stamping its foot, wildly gesticulating, and, in the midst of all, still pointing its small forefinger at Hester's bosom!

"I see what ails the child," whispered Hester to the clergyman, and turning pale in spite of a strong effort to conceal her trouble and annoyance. "Children will not abide any, the slightest, change in the accustomed aspect of things that are daily before their eyes. Pearl misses something which she has always seen me wear!"

"I pray you," answered the minister, "if thou hast any means of pacifying the child, do it forthwith! Save it were the cankered wrath of an old witch, like Mistress Hibbins," added he, attempting to smile. "I know nothing that I would not sooner encounter than this passion in a child. In Pearl's young beauty, as in the wrinkled witch, it has a preternatural effect. Pacify her, if thou lovest me!"

Hester turned again towards Pearl, with a crimson blush upon her cheek, a conscious glance aside at the clergyman, and then a heavy sigh; while, even before she had time to speak, the blush yielded to a deadly pallor.

"Pearl," said she, sadly, "look down at thy feet! There!—before thee!—on the hither side of the brook!"

The child turned her eyes to the point indicated; and there lay the scarlet letter, so close upon the margin of the stream, that the gold embroidery was reflected in it.

"Bring it hither!" said Hester.

"Come thou and take it up!" answered Pearl.

"Was ever such a child!" observed Hester aside to the minister. "O, I have much to tell thee about her. But, in very truth, she is right as regards this hateful token. I must bear its torture yet a little longer,—only a few days longer,—until we shall have left this region, and look back hither as to a land which we have dreamed of. The forest cannot hide it! The mid-ocean shall take it from my hand, and swallow it up for ever!"

With these words, she advanced to the margin of the brook, took up the scarlet letter, and fastened it again into her bosom. Hopefully, but a moment ago, as Hester had spoken of drowning it in the deep sea, there was a sense of inevitable doom upon her, as she thus received back this deadly symbol from the hand of fate. She had flung it into infinite space!—she had drawn an hour's free breath!—and here again was the scarlet misery, glittering on the old spot! So it ever is, whether thus typified or no, that an evil deed invests itself with the character of doom. Hester next gathered up the heavy tresses of her hair, and confined them beneath her cap. As if there were a withering spell in the sad letter, her beauty, the warmth and richness of her womanhood, departed, like fading sunshine; and a gray shadow seemed to fall across her.

When the dreary change was wrought, she extended her hand to Pearl.

"Dost thou know thy mother now, child!" asked she, reproachfully, but with a subdued tone. "Wilt thou come across the brook, and own thy mother, now that she has her shame upon her,—now that she is sad?"

"Yes; now I will!" answered the child, bounding across the brook, and clasping Hester in her arms. "Now thou art my mother indeed! And I am thy little Pearl!"

In a mood of tenderness that was not usual with her, she drew down her mother's head, and kissed her brow and both her cheeks. But then—by a kind of necessity that always impelled this child to alloy whatever comfort she might chance to give with a throb of anguish—Pearl put up her mouth, and kissed the scarlet letter too!

"That was not kind!" said Hester. "When thou hast shown me a little love, thou mockest me!"

"Why doth the minister sit yonder?" asked Pearl.

"He waits to welcome thee," replied her mother. "Come thou, and entreat his blessing! He loves thee, my little Pearl, and loves thy mother too. Wilt thou not love him? Come! he longs to greet thee!"

"Doth he love us?" said Pearl, looking up with acute intelligence into her mother's face. "Will he go back with us, hand in hand, we three together, into the town?"

"Not now, dear child," answered Hester. "But in days to come he will walk hand in hand with us. We will have a home and fireside of our own; and thou shalt sit upon his knee; and he will teach thee many things, and love thee dearly. Thou wilt love him; wilt thou not?"

"And will he always keep his hand over his heart?" inquired Pearl.

"Foolish child, what a question is that!" exclaimed her mother. "Come and ask his blessing!"

But, whether influenced by the jealousy that seems instinctive with every petted child towards a dangerous rival, or from whatever caprice of her freakish nature, Pearl would show no favor to the clergyman. It was only by an exertion of force that her mother brought her up to him, hanging back, and manifesting her reluctance by odd grimaces; of which, ever since her babyhood, she had possessed a singular variety, and could transform her mobile physiognomy into a series of different aspects, with a new mischief in them, each and all. The minister—painfully embarrassed, but hoping that a kiss might prove a talisman to admit him into the child's kindlier regards—bent forward, and impressed one on her brow. Hereupon, Pearl broke away from her mother, and running to the brook, stooped over it, and bathed her forehead, until the unwelcome kiss was quite washed off, and diffused through a long lapse of the gliding water. She then remained apart, silently watching Hester and the clergyman; while they talked together, and made such arrangements as were suggested by their new position, and the purposes soon to be fulfilled.

And now this fateful interview had come to a close. The dell was to be left a solitude among its dark, old trees, which, with their multitudinous tongues, would whisper long of what had passed there, and no mortal be the wiser. And the melancholy brook would add this other tale to the mystery with which its little heart was already overburdened, and whereof it still kept up a murmuring babble, with not a whit more cheerfulness of tone than for ages heretofore.

XX. THE MINISTER IN A MAZE

As the minister departed, in advance of Hester Prynne and little Pearl, he threw a backward glance; half expecting that he should discover only some faintly traced features or outline of the mother and the child, slowly fading into the twilight of the woods. So great a vicissitude in his life could not at once be received as real. But there was Hester, clad in her gray robe, still standing beside the tree-trunk, which some blast had overthrown a long antiquity ago, and which time had ever since been covering with moss, so that these two fated ones, with earth's heaviest burden on them, might there sit down together, and find a single hour's rest and solace. And there was Pearl, too, lightly dancing from the margin of the brook,—now that the intrusive third person was gone,—and taking her old place by her mother's side. So the minister had not fallen asleep, and dreamed!

In order to free his mind from this indistinctness and duplicity of impression, which vexed it with a strange disquietude, he recalled and more thoroughly defined the plans which Hester and himself had sketched for their departure. It had been determined between them, that the Old World, with its crowds and cities, offered them a more eligible shelter and concealment than the wilds of New England, or all America, with its alternatives of an Indian wigwam, or the few settlements of Europeans, scattered thinly along the seaboard. Not to speak of the clergyman's health, so inadequate to sustain the hardships of a forest life, his native gifts, his culture, and his entire development would secure him a home only in the midst of civilization and refinement; the higher the state, the more delicately adapted to it the man. In furtherance of this choice, it so happened that a ship lay in the harbour; one of those questionable cruisers, frequent at that day, which, without being absolutely outlaws of the deep, yet roamed over its surface with a remarkable irresponsibility of character. This vessel had recently arrived from the Spanish Main, and, within three days' time, would sail for Bristol.[4] Hester Prynne—whose vocation, as a self-enlisted Sister of Charity, had brought her acquainted with the captain and crew—could take upon herself to secure the passage of two individuals and a child, with all the secrecy which circumstances rendered more than desirable.

The minister had inquired of Hester, with no little interest, the precise time at which the vessel might be expected to depart. It would probably be on the fourth day from the present. "That is most fortunate!" he had then said to himself. Now, why the Reverend Mr. Dimmesdale considered it so very fortunate, we hesitate to reveal. Nevertheless,—to hold nothing back from the reader,—it was because, on the third day from the present, he was to preach the Election Sermon;[5] and, as such an occasion formed an honorable epoch in the life of a New England clergyman, he could not have chanced upon a more suitable mode and time of terminating his professional career. "At least, they shall say of me," thought this exemplary man, "that I leave no public duty unperformed, nor ill performed!" Sad, indeed, that an introspection so profound and acute as this poor minister's should be so miserably deceived! We have had, and may still have, worse things to tell of him; but none, we apprehend, so pitiably weak; no evidence, at once so slight and irrefragable,[6] of a subtle disease, that had long since begun to eat into the real substance of his character. No man, for any considerable period, can wear one face to himself, and another to the multitude, without finally getting bewildered as to which may be the true.

The excitement of Mr. Dimmesdale's feelings, as he returned from his interview with Hester, lent him unaccustomed physical energy, and hurried him townward at a rapid pace. The pathway among the woods seemed wilder, more uncouth with its rude natural obstacles, and less trodden by the foot of man, than he remembered it on his outward journey. But he leaped across the plashy places, thrust himself through the clinging underbrush, climbed the ascent, plunged into the hollow, and overcame, in short, all the difficulties of the track, with an unweariable activity that astonished him. He could not but recall how feebly, and with what frequent pauses for breath, he had toiled over the same ground only two days before. As he drew near the town, he took an impression of change from the series of familiar objects that presented themselves. It seemed not yesterday, not one, nor two, but many days, or even years ago, since he had quitted them. There, indeed, was each former trace of the street, as he remembered it, and all the peculiarities of the houses, with the due multitude of gable-peaks, and a weathercock at every point where his memory suggested one. Not the less, however, came this importunately obtrusive sense of change. The same was true as regarded the acquaintances whom he met, and all the well-known shapes of human life, about the little town.

4. In western England.
5. Sermon preached at the installation of each new

governor.
6. Stiff, rigid.

They looked neither older nor younger, now; the beards of the aged were no whiter, nor could the creeping babe of yesterday walk on his feet today; it was impossible to describe in what respect they differed from the individuals on whom he had so recently bestowed a parting glance; and yet the minister's deepest sense seemed to inform him of their mutability. A similar impression struck him most remarkably, as he passed under the walls of his own church. The edifice had so very strange, and yet so familiar, an aspect, that Mr. Dimmesdale's mind vibrated between two ideas; either that he had seen it only in a dream hitherto, or that he was merely dreaming about it now.

This phenomenon, in the various shapes which it assumed, indicated no external change, but so sudden and important a change in the spectator of the familiar scene, that the intervening space of a single day had operated on his consciousness like the lapse of years. The minister's own will, and Hester's will, and the fate that grew between them, had wrought this transformation. It was the same town as heretofore; but the same minister returned not from the forest. He might have said to the friends who greeted him,—"I am not the man for whom you take me! I left him yonder in the forest, withdrawn into a secret dell, by a mossy tree-trunk, and near a melancholy brook! Go, seek your minister, and see if his emaciated figure, his thin cheek, his white, heavy, pain-wrinkled brow, be not flung down there like a cast-off garment!" His friends, no doubt, would still have insisted with him,—"Thou art thyself the man!"—but the error would have been their own, not his.

Before Mr. Dimmesdale reached home, his inner man gave him other evidences of a revolution in the sphere of thought and feeling. In truth, nothing short of a total change of dynasty and moral code, in that interior kingdom, was adequate to account for the impulses now communicated to the unfortunate and startled minister. At every step he was incited to do some strange, wild, wicked thing or other, with a sense that it would be at once involuntary and intentional; in spite of himself, yet growing out of a profounder self than that which opposed the impulse. For instance, he met one of his own deacons. The good old man addressed him with the paternal affection and patriarchal privilege, which his venerable age, his upright and holy character, and his station in the Church, entitled him to use; and, conjoined with this, the deep, almost worshipping respect, which the minister's professional and private claims alike demanded. Never was there a more beautiful example of how the majesty of age and wisdom may comport with the obeisance and respect enjoined upon it, as from a lower social rank and inferior order of endowment, towards a higher. Now, during a conversation of some two or three moments between the Reverend Mr. Dimmesdale and this excellent and hoary-bearded deacon, it was only by the most careful self-control that the former could refrain from uttering certain blasphemous suggestions that rose into his mind, respecting the communion-supper. He absolutely trembled and turned pale as ashes, lest his tongue should wag itself, in utterance of these horrible matters, and plead his own consent for so doing, without his having fairly given it. And, even with this terror in his heart, he could hardly avoid laughing to imagine how the sanctified old patriarchal deacon would have been petrified by his minister's impiety!

Again, another incident of the same nature. Hurrying along the street, the Reverend Mr. Dimmesdale encountered the eldest female member of his church; a most pious and exemplary old dame; poor, widowed, lonely, and with a heart as full of reminiscences about her dead husband and children, and her dead friends of long ago, as a burial-ground is full of storied grave-stones. Yet all this, which would else have been such heavy sorrow, was made almost a solemn joy to her devout old soul by religious consolations and the truths of Scripture, wherewith she had fed herself continually for more than thirty years. And, since Mr. Dimmesdale had taken her in charge, the good grandam's chief earthly comfort—which, unless it had been likewise a heav-enly comfort, could have been none at all—was to meet her pastor, whether casually, or of set purpose, and be refreshed with a word of warm, fragrant, heaven-breathing Gospel truth from his beloved lips into her dulled, but rap-turously attentive ear. But, on this occasion, up to the moment of putting his lips to the old woman's ear, Mr. Dimmesdale, as the great enemy of souls would have it, could recall no text of Scripture, nor aught else, except a brief, pithy, and, as it then appeared to him, unanswerable argument against the immortality of the human soul. The instilment thereof into her mind would probably have caused this aged sister to drop down dead, at once, as by the effect of an intensely poisonous infusion. What he really did whisper, the minister could never afterwards recollect. There was, perhaps, a fortunate dis-order in his utterance, which failed to impart any distinct idea to the good widow's comprehension, or which Providence interpreted after a method of its own. Assuredly, as the minister looked back, he beheld an expression of divine gratitude and ecstasy that seemed like the shine of the celestial city on her face, so wrinkled and ashy pale.

Again, a third instance. After parting from the old church-member, he met the youngest sister of them all. It was a maiden newly won—and won by the Reverend Mr. Dimmesdale's own sermon, on the Sabbath after his vigil—to barter the transitory pleasures of the world for the heavenly hope, that was to assume brighter substance as life grew dark around her, and which would gild the utter gloom with final glory. She was fair and pure as a lily that had bloomed in Paradise. The minister knew well that he was himself enshrined within the stainless sanctity of her heart, which hung its snowy curtains about his image, imparting to religion the warmth of love, and to love a religious purity. Satan, that afternoon, had surely led the poor young girl away from her mother's side, and thrown her into the pathway of this sorely tempted, or—shall we not rather say?—this lost and desperate man. As she drew nigh, the arch-fiend whispered him to condense into small compass and drop into her tender bosom a germ of evil that would be sure to blossom darkly soon, and bear black fruit betimes. Such was his sense of power over this virgin soul, trusting him as she did, that the minister felt potent to blight all the field of innocence with but one wicked look, and develop all its opposite with but a word. So—with a mightier struggle than he had yet sustained—he held his Geneva cloak before his face, and hurried onward, making no sign of recogni-tion, and leaving the young sister to digest his rudeness as she might. She ransacked her conscience,—which was full of harmless little matters, like her pocket or her work-bag,—and took herself to task, poor thing, for a thousand imaginary faults; and went about her household duties with swollen eyelids the next morning.

Before the minister had time to celebrate his victory over this last tempta-tion, he was conscious of another impulse, more ludicrous, and almost as horrible. It was,—we blush to tell it,—it was to stop short in the road, and teach some very wicked words to a knot of little Puritan children who were playing there, and had but just begun to talk. Denying himself this freak, as unworthy of his cloth, he met a drunken seaman, one of the ship's crew from the Spanish Main. And, here, since he had so valiantly forborne all other wickedness, poor Mr. Dimmesdale longed, at least, to shake hands with the tarry blackguard, and recreate himself with a few improper jests, such as dissolute sailors so abound with, and a volley of good, round, solid, satisfactory, and heaven-defying oaths! It was not so much a better principle, as partly his natural good taste, and still more his buckramed[5] habit of clerical decorum, that carried him safely through the latter crisis.

"What is it that haunts and tempts me thus?" cried the minister to himself, at length, pausing in the street, and striking his hand against his forehead. "Am I mad? or am I given over utterly to the fiend? Did I make a contract with him in the forest, and sign it with my blood? And does he now summon me to its fulfilment, by suggesting the performance of every wickedness which his most foul imagination can conceive?"

At the moment when the Reverend Mr. Dimmesdale thus communed with himself, and struck his forehead with his hand, old Mistress Hibbins, the reputed witch-lady, is said to have been passing by. She made a very grand appearance; having on a high head-dress, a rich gown of velvet, and a ruff done up with the famous yellow starch, of which Ann Turner, her especial friend, had taught her the secret, before this last good lady had been hanged for Sir Thomas Overbury's murder. Whether the witch had read the minister's thoughts, or no, she came to a full stop, looked shrewdly into his face, smiled craftily, and—though little given to converse with clergymen—began a conversation.

"So, reverend Sir, you have made a visit into the forest," observed the witch-lady, nodding her high head-dress at him. "The next time, I pray you to allow me only a fair warning, and I shall be proud to bear you company. Without taking overmuch upon myself, my good word will go far towards gaining any strange gentleman a fair reception from yonder potentate you wot of!"

"I profess, madam," answered the clergyman, with a grave obeisance, such as the lady's rank demanded, and his own good-breeding made imperative,— "I profess, on my conscience and character, that I am utterly bewildered as touching the purport of your words! I went not into the forest to seek a potentate; neither do I, at any future time, design a visit thither, with a view to gaining the favor of such personage. My one sufficient object was to greet that pious friend of mine, the Apostle Eliot, and rejoice with him over the many precious souls he hath won from heathendom!"

"Ha, ha, ha!" cackled the old witch-lady, still nodding her high head-dress at the minister. "Well, well, we must needs talk thus in the daytime! You carry it off like an old hand! But at midnight, and in the forest, we shall have other talk together!"

She passed on with her aged stateliness, but often turning back her head and smiling at him, like one willing to recognize a secret intimacy of connection.

"Have I then sold myself," thought the minister, "to the fiend whom, if men say true, this yellow-starched and velveted old hag has chosen for her prince and master!"

The wretched minister! He had made a bargain very like it! Tempted by a dream of happiness, he had yielded himself with deliberate choice, as he had never done before, to what he knew was deadly sin. And the infectious poison of that sin had been thus rapidly diffused throughout his moral system. It had stupefied all blessed impulses, and awakened into vivid life the whole brotherhood of bad ones. Scorn, bitterness, unprovoked malignity, gratuitous desire of ill, ridicule of whatever was good and holy, all awoke, to tempt, even while they frightened him. And his encounter with old Mistress Hibbins, if it were a real incident, did but show his sympathy and fellowship with wicked mortals and the world of perverted spirits.

He had by this time reached his dwelling, on the edge of the burial-ground, and, hastening up the stairs, took refuge in his study. The minister was glad to have reached this shelter, without first betraying himself to the world by any of those strange and wicked eccentricities to which he had been continually impelled while passing through the streets. He entered the accustomed room, and looked around him on its books, its windows, its fireplace, and the tapestried comfort of the walls, with the same perception of strangeness that had haunted him throughout his walk from the forest-dell into the town, and thitherward. Here he had studied and written; here, gone through fast and vigil, and come forth half alive; here, striven to pray; here, borne a hundred thousand agonies! There was the Bible, in its rich old Hebrew, with Moses and the Prophets speaking to him, and God's voice through all! There, on the table, with the inky pen beside it, was an unfinished sermon, with a sentence broken in the midst, where his thoughts had ceased to gush out upon the page two days before. He knew that it was himself, the thin and white-cheeked minister, who had done and suffered these things, and written thus far into the Election Sermon! But he seemed to stand apart, and eye this former self with scornful, pitying, but half-envious curiosity. That self was gone! Another man had returned out of the forest; a wiser one; with a knowledge of hidden mysteries which the simplicity of the former never could have reached. A bitter kind of knowledge that!

While occupied with these reflections, a knock came at the door of the study, and the minister said, "Come in!"—not wholly devoid of an idea that he might behold an evil spirit. And so he did! It was old Roger Chillingworth that entered. The minister stood, white and speechless, with one hand on the Hebrew Scriptures, and the other spread upon his breast.

"Welcome home, reverend Sir!" said the physician. "And how found you that godly man, the Apostle Eliot? But methinks, dear Sir, you look pale; as if the travel through the wilderness had been too sore for you. Will not my aid be requisite to put you in heart and strength to preach your Election Sermon?"

"Nay, I think not so," rejoined the Reverend Mr. Dimmesdale. "My journey, and the sight of the holy Apostle yonder, and the free air which I have breathed, have done me good, after so long confinement in my study. I think to need no more of your drugs, my kind physician, good though they be, and administered by a friendly hand."

All this time, Roger Chillingworth was looking at the minister with the grave and intent regard of a physician towards his patient. But, in spite of this outward show, the latter was almost convinced of the old man's knowledge, or, at least, his confident suspicion, with respect to his own interview with Hester Prynne. The physician knew, then, that, in the minister's regard, he was no longer a trusted friend, but his bitterest enemy. So much being known, it would appear natural that a part of it should be expressed. It is singular, however, how long a time often passes before words embody things; and with what security two persons, who choose to avoid a certain subject, may approach its very verge, and retire without disturbing it. Thus, the minister felt no apprehension that Roger Chillingworth would touch, in express words, upon the real position which they sustained towards one another. Yet did the physician, in his dark way, creep frightfully near the secret.

"Were it not better," said he, "that you use my poor skill to-night? Verily, dear Sir, we must take pains to make you strong and vigorous for this occasion of the Election discourse. The people look for great things from you; apprehending that another year may come about, and find their pastor gone."

"Yea, to another world," replied the minister, with pious resignation. "Heaven grant it be a better one; for, in good sooth, I hardly think to tarry with my flock through the flitting seasons of another year! But, touching your medicine, kind Sir, in my present frame of body I need it not."

"I joy to hear it," answered the physician. "It may be that my remedies, so long administered in vain, begin now to take due effect. Happy man were I, and well deserving of New England's gratitude, could I achieve this cure!"

"I thank you from my heart, most watchful friend," said the Reverend Mr. Dimmesdale, with a solemn smile. "I thank you, and can but requite your good deeds with my prayers."

"A good man's prayers are golden recompense!" rejoined old Roger Chillingworth, as he took his leave. "Yea, they are the current gold coin of the New Jerusalem, with the King's own mint-mark on them!"

Left alone, the minister summoned a servant of the house, and requested food, which, being set before him, he ate with ravenous appetite. Then, flinging the already written pages of the Election Sermon into the fire, he forthwith began another, which he wrote with such an impulsive flow of thought and emotion, that he fancied himself inspired; and only wondered that Heaven should see fit to transmit the grand and solemn music of its oracles through so foul an organ-pipe as he. However, leaving that mystery to solve itself, or go unsolved for ever, he drove his task onward, with earnest haste and ecstasy. Thus the night fled away, as if it were a winged steed, and he careering on it; morning came, and peeped blushing through the curtains; and at last sunrise threw a golden beam into the study, and laid it right across the minister's bedazzled eyes. There he was, with the pen still between his fingers, and a vast, immeasurable tract of written space behind him!

XXI. THE NEW ENGLAND HOLIDAY

Betimes[7] in the morning of the day on which the new Governor was to receive his office at the hands of the people, Hester Prynne and little Pearl came into the market-place. It was already thronged with the craftsmen and other plebeian inhabitants of the town, in considerable numbers; among whom, likewise, were many rough figures, whose attire of deer-skins marked them as belonging to some of the forest settlements, which surrounded the little metropolis of the colony.

On this public holiday, as on all other occasions, for seven years past, Hester was clad in a garment of coarse gray cloth. Not more by its hue than by some indescribable peculiarity in its fashion, it had the effect of making her fade

7. Early.

personally out of sight and outline; while, again, the scarlet letter brought her back from this twilight indistinctness, and revealed her under the moral aspect of its own illumination. Her face, so long familiar to the townspeople, showed the marble quietude which they were accustomed to behold there. It was like a mask; or rather, like the frozen calmness of a dead woman's features; owing this dreary resemblance to the fact that Hester was actually dead, in respect to any claim of sympathy, and had departed out of the world with which she still seemed to mingle.

It might be, on this one day, that there was an expression unseen before, nor, indeed, vivid enough to be detected now; unless some preternaturally gifted observer should have first read the heart, and have afterwards sought a corresponding development in the countenance and mien. Such a spiritual seer might have conceived, that, after sustaining the gaze of the multitude through seven miserable years as a necessity, a penance, and something which it was a stern religion to endure, she now, for one last time more, encountered it freely and voluntarily, in order to convert what had so long been agony into a kind of triumph. "Look your last on the scarlet letter and its wearer!"—the people's victim and life-long bond-slave, as they fancied her, might say to them. "Yet a little while, and she will be beyond your reach! A few hours longer, and the deep, mysterious ocean will quench and hide for ever the symbol which ye have caused to burn upon her bosom!" Nor were it an inconsistency too improbable to be assigned to human nature, should we suppose a feeling of regret in Hester's mind, at the moment when she was about to win her freedom from the pain which had been thus deeply incorporated with her being. Might there not be an irresistible desire to quaff a last, long, breathless draught of the cup of wormwood and aloes, with which nearly all her years of womanhood had been perpetually flavored? The wine of life, henceforth to be presented to her lips, must be indeed rich, delicious, and exhilarating, in its chased and golden beaker; or else leave an inevitable and weary languor, after the lees of bitterness wherewith she had been drugged, as with a cordial of intensest potency.

Pearl was decked out with airy gayety. It would have been impossible to guess that this bright and sunny apparition owed its existence to the shape of gloomy gray; or that a fancy, at once so gorgeous and so delicate as must have been requisite to contrive the child's apparel, with the same that had achieved a task perhaps more difficult, in imparting so distinct a peculiarity to Hester's simple robe. The dress, so proper was it to little Pearl, seemed an effluence, or inevitable development and outward manifestation of her character, no more to be separated from her than the many-hued brilliancy from a butterfly's wing, or the painted glory from the leaf of a bright flower. As with these, so with the child; her garb was all of one idea with her nature. On this eventful day, moreover, there was a certain singular inquietude and excitement in her mood, resembling nothing so much as the shimmer of a diamond, that sparkles and flashes with the varied throbbings of the breast on which it is displayed. Children have always a sympathy in the agitations of those connected with them; always, especially, a sense of any trouble or impending revolution, of whatever kind, in domestic circumstances; and therefore Pearl, who was the gem on her mother's unquiet bosom, betrayed, by the very dance of her spirits, the emotions which none could detect in the marble passiveness of Hester's brow.

This effervescence made her flit with a bird-like movement, rather than

walk by her mother's side. She broke continually into shouts of a wild, inarticulate, and sometimes piercing music. When they reached the market-place,
she became still more restless, on perceiving the stir and bustle that enlivened
the spot; for it was usually more like the broad and lonesome green before a
village meeting-house, than the centre of a town's business.

"Why, what is this, mother?" cried she. "Wherefore have all the people left
their work to-day? Is it a play-day for the whole world. See, there is the blacksmith! He has washed his sooty face, and put on his Sabbath-day clothes, and
looks, as if he would gladly be merry, if any kind body would only teach him
how! And there is Master Brackett, the old jailer, nodding and smiling at me.
Why does he do so, mother?"

"He remembers thee a little babe, my child," answered Hester.

"He should not nod and smile at me, for all that,—the black, grim, ugly-
eyed old man!" said Pearl. "He may nod at thee if he will; for thou are clad in
gray, and wearest the scarlet letter. But, see, mother, how many faces of
strange people, and Indians among them, and sailors! What have they all
come to do here in the market-place?"

"They wait to see the procession pass," said Hester. "For the Governor and
the magistrates are to go by, and the ministers, and all the great people and
good people, with the music, and the soldiers marching before them."

"And will the minister be there?" asked Pearl. "And will he hold out both
his hands to me, as when thou ledst me to him from the brook-side?"

"He will be there, child," answered her mother. "But he will not greet thee
to-day; nor must thou greet him."

"What a strange, sad man is he!" said the child, as if speaking partly to
herself. "In the dark night-time, he calls us to him, and holds thy hand and
mine, as when we stood with him on the scaffold yonder! And in the deep
forest, where only the old trees can hear, and the strip of sky see it, he talks
with thee, sitting on a heap of moss! And he kisses my forehead, too, so that
the little brook would hardly wash it off! But here in the sunny day, and among
all the people, he knows us not; nor must we know him! A strange, sad man
is he, with his hand always over his heart!"

"Be quiet, Pearl! Thou understandest not these things," said her mother.
"Think not now of the minister, but look about thee, and see how cheery is
every body's face to-day. The children have come from their schools, and the
grown people from their workshops and their fields, on purpose to be happy.
For, to-day, a new man is beginning to rule over them; and so—as has been
the custom of mankind ever since a nation was first gathered—they make
merry and rejoice; as if a good and golden year were at length to pass over the
poor old world!"

It was as Hester said, in regard to the unwonted jollity that brightened the
faces of the people. Into this festal season of the year—as it already was, and
continued to be during the greater part of two centuries—the Puritans compressed whatever mirth and public joy they deemed allowable to human
infirmity; thereby so far dispelling the customary cloud, that, for the space of
a single holiday, they appeared scarcely more grave than most other communities at a period of general affliction.

But we perhaps exaggerate the gray or sable tinge, which undoubtedly characterized the mood and manners of the age. The persons now in the market-
place of Boston had not been born to an inheritance of Puritanic gloom. They
were native Englishmen, whose fathers had lived in the sunny richness of the

Elizabethan epoch; a time when the life of England, viewed as one great mass, would appear to have been as stately, magnificent, and joyous, as the world has ever witnessed. Had they followed their hereditary taste, the New England settlers would have illustrated all events of public importance by bonfires, banquets, pageantries, and processions. Nor would it have been impracticable, in the observance of majestic ceremonies, to combine mirthful recreation with solemnity, and give, as it were, a grotesque and brilliant embroidery to the great robe of state, which a nation, at such festivals, puts on. There was some shadow of an attempt of this kind in the mode of celebrating the day on which the political year of the colony commenced. The dim reflection of a remembered splendor, a colorless and manifold diluted repetition of what they had beheld in proud old London,—we will not say at a royal coronation, but at a Lord Mayor's show,[8]—might be traced in the customs which our forefathers instituted, with reference to the annual installation of magistrates. The fathers and founders of the commonwealth—the statesman, the priest, and the soldier—deemed it a duty then to assume the outward state and majesty, which, in accordance with antique style, was looked upon as the proper garb of public or social eminence. All came forth, to move in procession before the people's eye, and thus impart a needed dignity to the simple framework of a government so newly constructed.

Then, too the people were countenanced, if not encouraged, in relaxing the severe and close application to their various modes of rugged industry, which, at all other times, seemed of the same piece and material with their religion. Here, it is true, were none of the appliances which popular merriment would so readily have found in the England of Elizabeth's time, or that of James,[9]—no rude shows of a theatrical kind; no minstrel with his harp and legendary ballad, nor gleeman, with an ape dancing to his music; no juggler, with his tricks of mimic witchcraft; no Merry Andrew,[1] to stir up the multitude with jests, perhaps hundreds of years old, but still effective, by their appeals to the very broadest sources of mirthful sympathy. All such professors of the several branches of jocularity would have been sternly repressed, not only by the rigid discipline of law, but by the general sentiment which gives law its vitality. Not the less, however, the great, honest face of the people smiled, grimly, perhaps, but widely too. Nor were sports wanting, such as the colonists had witnessed, and shared in, long ago, at the country fairs and on the village-greens of England; and which it was thought well to keep alive on this new soil, for the sake of the courage and manliness that were essential in them. Wrestling-matches, in the differing fashions of Cornwall and Devonshire, were seen here and there about the market-place; in one corner, there was a friendly bout at quarterstaff; and—what attracted most interest of all—on the platform of the pillory, already so noted on our pages, two masters of defence were commencing an exhibition with the buckler[2] and broadsword. But, much to the disappointment of the crowd, this latter business was broken off by the interposition of the town beadle, who had no idea of permitting the majesty of the law to be violated by such an abuse of one of its consecrated places.

It may not be too much to affirm, on the whole, (the people being then in

8. Procession and other ceremonies in honor of the inauguration of the lord mayor of London.
9. Elizabeth reigned 1558–1603; James I, 1603–25.
1. Jester or clown.

2. Small round shield, either carried or worn on the arm. "Quartershaft": long wooden staff, used as a weapon.

the first stages of joyless deportment, and the offspring of sires who had known how to be merry, in their day,) that they would compare favorably, in point of holiday keeping, with their descendants, even at so long an interval as ourselves. Their immediate posterity, the generation next to the early emigrants, wore the blackest shade of Puritanism, and so darkened the national visage with it, that all the subsequent years have not sufficed to clear it up. We have yet to learn again the forgotten art of gayety.

The picture of human life in the market-place, though its general tint was the sad gray, brown, or black of the English emigrants, was yet enlivened by some diversity of hue. A party of Indians—in their savage finery of curiously embroidered deer-skin robes, wampum-belts, red and yellow ochre, and feathers, and armed with the bow and arrow and stone-headed spear—stood apart, with countenances of inflexible gravity, beyond what even the Puritan aspect could attain. Nor, wild as were these painted barbarians, were they the wildest feature of the scene. This distinction could more justly be claimed by some mariners,—a part of the crew of the vessel from the Spanish Main,—who had come ashore to see the humors of Election Day. They were rough-looking desperadoes, with sun-blackened faces, and an immensity of beard; their wide, short trousers were confined about the waist by belts, often clasped with a rough plate of gold, and sustaining always a long knife, and, in some instances, a sword. From beneath their broad-brimmed hats of palm-leaf, gleamed eyes which, even in good nature and merriment, had a kind of animal ferocity. They transgressed, without fear or scruple, the rules of behaviour that were binding on all others; smoking tobacco under the beadle's very nose, although each whiff would have cost a townsman a shilling; and quaffing, at their pleasure, draughts of wine or aqua-vitæ[3] from pocket-flasks, which they freely tendered to the gaping crowd around them. It remarkably characterized the incomplete morality of the age, rigid as we call it, that a license was allowed the seafaring class, not merely for their freaks on shore, but for far more desperate deeds on their proper element. The sailor of that day would go near to be arraigned as a pirate in our own. There could be little doubt, for instance, that this very ship's crew, though no unfavorable specimens of the nautical brotherhood, had been guilty, as we should phrase it, of depredations on the Spanish commerce, such as would have perilled all their necks in a modern court of justice.

But the sea, in those old times, heaved, swelled, and foamed very much at its own will, or subject only to the tempestuous wind, with hardly any attempts at regulation by human law. The buccaneer on the wave might relinquish his calling, and become at once, if he chose, a man of probity and piety on land; nor, even in the full career of his reckless life, was he regarded as a personage with whom it was disreputable to traffic, or casually associate. Thus, the Puritan elders, in their black cloaks, starched bands, and steeple-crowned hats, smiled not unbenignantly at the clamor and rude deportment of these jolly seafaring men; and it excited neither surprise nor animadversion when so reputable a citizen as old Roger Chillingworth, the physician, was seen to enter the market-place, in close and familiar talk with the commander of the questionable vessel.

The latter was by far the most showy and gallant figure, so far as apparel

3. Brandy.

went, anywhere to be seen among the multitude. He wore a profusion of ribbons on his garment, and gold lace on his hat, which was also encircled by a gold chain, and surmounted with a feather. There was a sword at his side, and a sword-cut on his forehead, which, by the arrangement of his hair, he seemed anxious rather to display than hide. A landsman could hardly have worn this garb and shown this face, and worn and shown them both with such a galliard[4] air, without undergoing stern question before a magistrate, and probably incurring fine or imprisonment, or perhaps an exhibition in the stocks. As regarded the shipmaster, however, all was looked upon as pertaining to the character, as to a fish his glistening scales.

After parting from the physician, the commander of the Bristol ship strolled idly through the market-place; until, happening to approach the spot where Hester Prynne was standing, he appeared to recognize, and did not hesitate to address her. As was usually the case wherever Hester stood, a small, vacant area—a sort of magic circle—had formed itself about her, into which, though the people were elbowing one another at a little distance, none ventured, or felt disposed to intrude. It was a forcible type of the moral solitude in which the scarlet letter enveloped its fated wearer; partly by her own reserve, and partly by the instinctive, though no longer so unkindly, withdrawal of her fellow-creatures. Now, if never before, it answered a good purpose, by enabling Hester and the seaman to speak together without risk of being overheard; and so changed was Hester Prynne's repute before the public, that the matron in town most eminent for rigid morality could not have held such intercourse with less result of scandal than herself.

"So, mistress," said the mariner, "I must bid the steward make ready one more berth than you bargained for! No fear of scurvy or ship-fever, this voyage! What with the ship's surgeon and this other doctor, our only danger will be from drug or pill; more by token, as there is a lot of apothecary's stuff aboard, which I traded for with a Spanish vessel."

"What mean you?" inquired Hester, startled more than she permitted to appear. "Have you another passenger?"

"Why, know you not," cried the shipmaster, "that this physician here—Chillingworth, he calls himself—is minded to try my cabin-fare with you? Ay, ay, you must have known it; for he tells me he is of your party, and a close friend to the gentleman you spoke of,—he that is in peril from these sour old Puritan rulers!"

"They know each other well, indeed," replied Hester, with a mien of calmness, though in the utmost consternation. "They have long dwelt together."

Nothing further passed between the mariner and Hester Prynne. But, at that instant, she beheld old Roger Chillingworth himself, standing in the remotest corner of the market-place, and smiling on her; a smile which—across the wide and bustling square, and through all the talk and laughter, and various thoughts, moods, and interests of the crowd—conveyed secret and fearful meaning.

XXII. THE PROCESSION

Before Hester Prynne could call together her thoughts, and consider what was practicable to be done in this new and startling aspect of affairs, the sound

4. Lively.

of military music was heard approaching along a contiguous street. It denoted the advance of the procession of magistrates and citizens, on its way towards the meeting-house; where, in compliance with a custom thus early established, and ever since observed, the Reverend Mr. Dimmesdale was to deliver an Election Sermon.

Soon the head of the procession showed itself, with a slow and stately march, turning a corner, and making its way across the market-place. First came the music. It comprised a variety of instruments, perhaps imperfectly adapted to one another, and played with no great skill, but yet attaining the great object for which the harmony of drum and clarion addresses itself to the multitude,—that of imparting a higher and more heroic air to the scene of life that passes before the eye. Little Pearl at first clapped her hands, but then lost, for an instant, the restless agitation that had kept her in a continual effervescence throughout the morning; she gazed silently, and seemed to be borne upward, like a floating sea-bird, on the long heaves and swells of sound. But she was brought back to her former mood by the shimmer of the sunshine on the weapons and bright armour of the military company, which followed after the music, and formed the honorary escort of the procession. This body of soldiery[5]—which still sustains a corporate existence, and marches down from past ages with an ancient and honorable fame—was composed of no mercenary materials. Its ranks were filled with gentlemen, who felt the stirrings of martial impulse, and sought to establish a kind of College of Arms,[6] where, as in an association of Knights Templars,[7] they might learn the science, and, so far as peaceful exercise would teach them, the practices of war. The high estimation then placed upon the military character might be seen in the lofty port of each individual member of the company. Some of them, indeed, by their services in the Low Countries[8] and on other fields of European warfare, had fairly won their title to assume the name and pomp of soldiership. The entire array, moreover, clad in burnished steel, and with plumage nodding over their bright morions,[9] had a brilliancy of effect which no modern display can aspire to equal.

And yet the men of civil eminence, who came immediately behind the military escort, were better worth a thoughtful observer's eye. Even in outward demeanour they showed a stamp of majesty that made the warrior's haughty stride look vulgar, if not absurd. It was an age when what we call talent had far less consideration than now, but the massive materials which produce stability and dignity of character a great deal more. The people possessed, by hereditary right, the quality of reverence; which, in their descendants, if it survive at all, exists in smaller proportion, and with a vastly diminished force in the selection and estimate of public men. The change may be for good or ill, and is partly, perhaps, for both. In that old day, the English settler on these rude shores,—having left king, nobles, and all degrees of awful rank behind, while still the faculty and necessity of reverence were strong in him,—bestowed it on the white hair and venerable brow of age; on long-tried integrity; on solid wisdom and sad-colored experience; on endowments of that grave and weighty order, which gives the idea of permanence, and comes under the

5. The Ancient and Honorable Artillery Company of Massachusetts.
6. "College of Arms": i.e., like the Herald's College, the royal corporation instituted in 15th-century England to keep record of genealogies and coats of arms.
7. A 12th-century order of crusaders.
8. I.e., Belgium, the Netherlands, and Luxembourg.
9. Crested metal helmets with curved beaks at front and back.

general definition of respectability. These primitive statesmen, therefore,—Bradstreet, Endicott, Dudley,[1] Bellingham, and their compeers,—who were elevated to power by the early choice of the people, seem to have been not often brilliant, but distinguished by a ponderous sobriety, rather than activity of intellect. They had fortitude and self-reliance, and, in time of difficulty or peril, stood up for the welfare of the state like a line of cliffs against a tempestuous tide. The traits of character here indicated were well represented in the square cast of countenance and large physical development of the new colonial magistrates. So far as a demeanour of natural authority was concerned, the mother country need not have been ashamed to see these foremost men of an actual democracy adopted into the House of Peers,[2] or made the Privy Council of the sovereign.

Next in order to the magistrates came the young and eminently distinguished divine, from whose lips the religious discourse of the anniversary was expected. His was the profession, at that era, in which intellectual ability displayed itself far more than in political life; for—leaving a higher motive out of the question—it offered inducements powerful enough, in the almost worshipping respect of the community, to win the most aspiring ambition into its service. Even political power—as in the case of Increase Mather[3]—was within the grasp of a successful priest.

It was the observation of those who beheld him now, that never, since Mr. Dimmesdale first set his foot on the New England shore, had he exhibited such energy as was seen in the gait and air with which he kept his pace in the procession. There was no feebleness of step, as at other times; his frame was not bent; nor did his hand rest ominously upon his heart. Yet, if the clergyman were rightly viewed, his strength seemed not of the body. It might be spiritual, and imparted to him by angelic ministrations. It might be the exhilaration of that potent cordial, which is distilled only in the furnace-glow of earnest and long-continued thought. Or, perchance, his sensitive temperament was invigorated by the loud and piercing music, that swelled heavenward, and uplifted him on its ascending wave. Nevertheless, so abstracted was his look, it might be questioned whether Mr. Dimmesdale even heard the music. There was his body, moving onward, and with an unaccustomed force. But where was his mind? Far and deep in its own region, busying itself, with preternatural activity, to marshal a procession of stately thoughts that were soon to issue thence; and so he saw nothing, heard nothing, knew nothing, of what was around him; but the spiritual element took up the feeble frame, and carried it along, unconscious of the burden, and converting it to spirit like itself. Men of uncommon intellect, who have grown morbid, possess this occasional power of mighty effort, into which they throw the life of many days, and then are lifeless for as many more.

Hester Prynne, gazing steadfastly at the clergyman, felt a dreary influence come over her, but wherefore or whence she knew not; unless that he seemed so remote from her own sphere, and utterly beyond her reach. One glance of recognition, she had imagined, must needs pass between them. She thought of the dim forest, with its little dell of solitude, and love, and anguish, and the

1. Early governors of New England colonies: Simon Bradstreet (1603–1697), John Endicott (1588–1665), Thomas Dudley (1576–1653).
2. House of Lords, the upper house in the British parliament.
3. One of the persecutors of witches at Salem (1639–1723).

mossy tree-trunk, where, sitting hand in hand, they had mingled their sad and passionate talk with the melancholy murmur of the brook. How deeply had they known each other then! And was this the man? She hardly knew him now! He, moving proudly past, enveloped, as it were, in the rich music, with the procession of majestic and venerable fathers; he, so unattainable in his worldly position, and still more so in that far vista of his unsympathizing thoughts, through which she now beheld him! Her spirit sank with the idea that all must have been a delusion, and that, vividly as she had dreamed it, there could be no real bond betwixt the clergyman and herself. And thus much of woman was there in Hester, that she could scarcely forgive him,—least of all now, when the heavy footstep of their approaching Fate might be heard, nearer, nearer, nearer!—for being able so completely to withdraw himself from their mutual world; while she groped darkly, and stretched forth her cold hands, and found him not.

Pearl either saw and responded to her mother's feelings, or herself felt the remoteness and intangibility that had fallen around the minister. While the procession passed, the child was uneasy, fluttering up and down, like a bird on the point of taking flight. When the whole had gone by, she looked up into Hester's face.

"Mother," said she, "was that the same minister that kissed me by the brook?"

"Hold thy peace, dear little Pearl!" whispered her mother. "We must not always talk in the market-place of what happens to us in the forest."

"I could not be sure that it was he; so strange he looked," continued the child. "Else I would have run to him, and bid him kiss me now, before all the people; even as he did yonder among the dark old trees. What would the minister have said, mother? Would he have clapped his hand over his heart, and scowled on me, and bid me begone?"

"What should he say, Pearl," answered Hester, "save that it was no time to kiss, and that kisses are not to be given in the marketplace? Well for thee, foolish child, that thou didst not speak to him!"

Another shade of the same sentiment, in reference to Mr. Dimmesdale, was expressed by a person whose eccentricities—or insanity, as we should term it—led her to do what few of the townspeople would have ventured on; to begin a conversation with the wearer of the scarlet letter, in public. It was Mistress Hibbins, who, arrayed in great magnificence, with a triple ruff, a broidered stomacher, a gown of rich velvet, and a gold-headed cane, had come forth to see the procession. As this ancient lady had the renown (which subsequently cost her no less a price than her life) of being a principal actor in all the works of necromancy that were continually going forward, the crowd gave way before her, and seemed to fear the touch of her garment, as if it carried the plague among its gorgeous folds. Seen in conjunction with Hester Prynne,—kindly as so many now felt towards the latter,—the dread inspired by Mistress Hibbins was doubled, and caused a general movement from that part of the market-place in which the two women stood.

"Now, what mortal imagination could conceive it!" whispered the old lady confidentially to Hester. "Yonder divine man! That saint on earth, as the people uphold him to be, and as—I must needs say—he really looks! Who, now, that saw him pass in the procession, would think how little while it is since he went forth out of his study,—chewing a Hebrew text of Scripture in his mouth, I warrant,—to take an airing in the forest! Aha! we know what that means, Hester Prynne! But, truly, forsooth, I find it hard to believe him the same man. Many a church-member saw I, walking behind the music, that has danced in the same measure with me, when Somebody was fiddler, and, it might be, an Indian powwow[4] or a Lapland wizard changing hands with us! That is but a trifle, when a woman knows the world. But this minister! Couldst thou surely tell, Hester, whether he was the same man that encountered thee on the forest-path!"

"Madam, I know not of what you speak," answered Hester Prynne, feeling Mistress Hibbins to be of infirm mind; yet strangely startled and awe-stricken by the confidence with which she affirmed a personal connection between so many persons (herself among them) and the Evil One. "It is not for me to talk lightly of a learned and pious minister of the Word, like the Reverend Mr. Dimmesdale!"

"Fie, woman, fie!" cried the old lady, shaking her finger at Hester. "Dost thou think I have been to the forest so many times, and have yet no skill to judge who else has been there? Yea; though no leaf of the wild garlands, which they wore while they danced, be left in their hair! I know thee, Hester; for I behold the token. We may all see it in the sunshine; and it glows like a red flame in the dark. Thou wearest it openly; so there need be no question about that. But this minister! Let me tell thee, in thine ear! When the Black Man sees one of his own servants, signed and sealed, so shy of owning to the bond as is the Reverend Mr. Dimmesdale, he hath a way of ordering matters so that the mark shall be disclosed in open daylight to the eyes of the world! What is it that the minister seeks to hide, with his hand always over his heart? Ha, Hester Prynne!"

"What is it, good Mistress Hibbins?" eagerly asked little Pearl. "Hast thou seen it?"

"No matter, darling!" responded Mistress Hibbins, making Pearl a profound reverence. "Thou thyself wilt see it, one time or another. They say, child, thou art of the lineage of the Prince of the Air![5] Wilt thou ride with me, some fine night, to see thy father? Then thou shalt know wherefore the minister keeps his hand over his heart!"

Laughing so shrilly that all the market-place could hear her, the weird old gentlewoman took her departure.

By this time the preliminary prayer had been offered in the meeting-house, and the accents of the Reverend Mr. Dimmesdale were heard commencing his discourse. An irresistible feeling kept Hester near the spot. As the sacred edifice was too much thronged to admit another auditor, she took up her position close beside the scaffold of the pillory. It was in sufficient proximity to bring the whole sermon to her ears, in the shape of an indistinct, but varied, murmur and flow of the minister's very peculiar voice.

This vocal organ was in itself a rich endowment; insomuch that a listener, comprehending nothing of the language in which the preacher spoke, might still have been swayed to and fro by the mere tone and cadence. Like all other music, it breathed passion and pathos, and emotions high or tender, in a tongue native to the human heart, wherever educated. Muffled as the sound was by its passage through the church-walls, Hester Prynne listened with such

---

4. Here, medicine man.
5. Satan, described in Ephesians 2.2 as "the prince of

the power of the air, the spirit that now worketh in the children of disobedience."

intentness, and sympathized so intimately, that the sermon had throughout a meaning for her, entirely apart from its indistinguishable words. These, perhaps, if more distinctly heard, might have been only a grosser medium, and have clogged the spiritual sense. Now she caught the low undertone, as of the wind sinking down to repose itself; then ascended with it, as it rose through progressive gradations of sweetness and power, until its volume seemed to envelop her with an atmosphere of awe and solemn grandeur. And yet, majestic as the voice sometimes became, there was for ever in it an essential character of plaintiveness. A loud or low expression of anguish,—the whisper, or the shriek, as it might be conceived, of suffering humanity, that touched a sensibility in every bosom! At times this deep strain of pathos was all that could be heard, and scarcely heard, sighing amid a desolate silence. But even when the minister's voice grew high and commanding,—when it gushed irrepressibly upward,—when it assumed its utmost breadth and power, so overfilling the church as to burst its way through the solid walls, and diffuse itself in the open air,—still, if the auditor listened intently, and for the purpose, he could detect the same cry of pain. What was it? The complaint of a human heart, sorrow-laden, perchance guilty, telling its secret, whether of guilt or sorrow, to the great heart of mankind; beseeching its sympathy or forgiveness,—at every moment,—in each accent,—and never in vain! It was this profound and continual undertone that gave the clergyman his most appropriate power.

During all this time Hester stood, statue-like, at the foot of the scaffold. If the minister's voice had not kept her there, there would nevertheless have been an inevitable magnetism in that spot, whence she dated the first hour of her life of ignominy. There was a sense within her,—too ill-defined to be made a thought, but weighing heavily on her mind,—that her whole orb of life, both before and after, was connected with this spot, as with the one point that gave it unity.

Little Pearl, meanwhile, had quitted her mother's side, and was playing at her own will about the market-place. She made the sombre crowd cheerful by her erratic and glistening ray; even as a bird of bright plumage illuminates a whole tree of dusky foliage by darting to and fro, half seen and half concealed, amid the twilight of the clustering leaves. She had an undulating, but, oftentimes, a sharp and irregular movement. It indicated the restless vivacity of her spirit, which to-day was doubly indefatigable in its tiptoe dance, because it was played upon and vibrated with her mother's disquietude. Whenever Pearl saw any thing to excite her ever active and wandering curiosity, she flew thitherward, and, as we might say, seized upon that man or thing as her own property, so far as she desired it; but without yielding the minutest degree of control over her motions in requital. The Puritans looked on, and, if they smiled, were none the less inclined to pronounce the child a demon offspring, from the indescribable charm of beauty and eccentricity that shone through her little figure, and sparkled with its activity. She ran and looked the wild Indian in the face; and he grew conscious of a nature wilder than his own. Thence, with native audacity, but still with a reserve as characteristic, she flew into the midst of a group of mariners, the swarthy-cheeked wild men of the ocean, as the Indians were of the land; and they gazed wonderingly and admiringly at Pearl, as if a flake of the sea-foam had taken the shape of a little maid, and were gifted with a soul of the sea-fire, that flashes beneath the prow in the night-time.

One of these seafaring men—the shipmaster, indeed, who had spoken to Hester Prynne—was so smitten with Pearl's aspect, that he attempted to lay hands upon her, with purpose to snatch a kiss. Finding it as impossible to touch her as to catch a humming-bird in the air, he took from his hat the gold chain that was twisted about it, and threw it to the child. Pearl immediately twined it around her neck and waist, with such happy skill, that, once seen there, it became a part of her, and it was difficult to imagine her without it.

"Thy mother is yonder woman with the scarlet letter," said the seaman. "Wilt thou carry her a message from me?"

"If the message pleases me I will," answered Pearl.

"Then tell her," rejoined he, "that I spake again with the black-a-visaged, hump-shouldered old doctor, and he engages to bring his friend, the gentleman she wots of, aboard with him. So let thy mother take no thought, save for herself and thee. Wilt thou tell her this, thou witch-baby?"

"Mistress Hibbins says my father is the Prince of the Air!" cried Pearl, with her naughty smile. "If thou callest me that ill name, I shall tell him of thee; and he will chase thy ship with a tempest!"

Pursuing a zigzag course across the market-place, the child returned to her mother, and communicated what the mariner had said. Hester's strong, calm, steadfastly enduring spirit almost sank, at last, on beholding this dark and grim countenance of an inevitable doom, which—at the moment when a passage seemed to open for the minister and herself out of their labyrinth of misery—showed itself, with an unrelenting smile, right in the midst of their path.

With her mind harrassed by the terrible perplexity in which the shipmaster's intelligence involved her, she was also subjected to another trial. There were many people present, from the country roundabout, who had often heard of the scarlet letter, and to whom it had been made terrific by a hundred false or exaggerated rumors, but who had never beheld it with their own bodily eyes. These, after exhausting other modes of amusement, now thronged about Hester Prynne with rude and boorish intrusiveness. Unscrupulous as it was, however, it could not bring them nearer than a circuit of several yards. At that distance they accordingly stood, fixed there by the centrifugal force of the repugnance which the mystic symbol inspired. The whole gang of sailors, likewise, observing the press of spectators, and learning the purport of the scarlet letter, came and thrust their sunburnt and desperado-looking faces into the ring. Even the Indians were affected by a sort of cold shadow of the white man's curiosity, and, gliding through the crowd, fastened their snake-like black eyes on Hester's bosom; conceiving, perhaps, that the wearer of this brilliantly embroidered badge must needs be a personage of high dignity among her people. Lastly, the inhabitants of the town (their own interest in this worn-out subject languidly reviving itself, by sympathy with what they saw others feel) lounged idly to the same quarter, and tormented Hester Prynne, perhaps more than all the rest, with their cool, well-acquainted gaze at her familiar shame. Hester saw and recognized the self-same faces of that group of matrons, who had awaited her forthcoming from the prison-door, seven years ago; all save one, the youngest and only compassionate among them, whose burial-robe she had since made. At the final hour, when she was so soon to fling aside the burning letter, it had strangely become the centre of more remark and excitement, and was thus made to sear her breast more painfully than at any time since the first day she put it on.

While Hester stood in that magic circle of ignominy, where the cunning cruelty of her sentence seemed to have fixed her for ever, the admirable preacher was looking down from the sacred pulpit upon an audience, whose very inmost spirits had yielded to his control. The sainted minister in the church! The woman of the scarlet letter in the market-place! What imagination would have been irreverent enough to surmise that the same scorching stigma was on them both?

XXIII. THE REVELATION OF THE SCARLET LETTER

The eloquent voice, on which the souls of the listening audience had been borne aloft, as on the swelling waves of the sea, at length came to a pause. There was a momentary silence, profound as what should follow the utterance of oracles. Then ensued a murmur and half-hushed tumult; as if the auditors, released from the high spell that had transported them into the region of another's mind, were returning into themselves, with all their awe and wonder still heavy on them. In a moment more, the crowd began to gush forth from the doors of the church. Now that there was an end, they needed other breath, more fit to support the gross and earthly life into which they relapsed, than that atmosphere which the preacher had converted into words of flame, and had burdened with the rich fragrance of his thought.

In the open air their rapture broke into speech. The street and the market-place absolutely babbled, from side to side, with applauses of the minister. His hearers could not rest until they had told one another of what each knew better than he could tell or hear. According to their united testimony, never had man spoken in so wise, so high, and so holy a spirit, as he that spake this day; nor had inspiration ever breathed through mortal lips more evidently than it did through his. Its influence could be seen, as it were, descending upon him, and possessing him, and continually lifting him out of the written discourse that lay before him, and filling him with ideas that must have been as marvellous to himself as to his audience. His subject, it appeared, had been the relation between the Deity and the communities of mankind, with a special reference to the New England which they were here planting in the wilderness. And, as he drew towards the close, a spirit as of prophecy had come upon him, constraining him to its purpose as mightily as the old prophets of Israel were constrained; only with this difference, that, whereas the Jewish seers had denounced judgments and ruin on their country, it was his mission to foretell a high and glorious destiny for the newly gathered people of the Lord. But, throughout it all, and through the whole discourse, there had been a certain deep, sad undertone of pathos, which could not be interpreted otherwise than as the natural regret of one soon to pass away. Yes; their minister whom they so loved—and who so loved them all, that he could not depart heavenward without a sigh—had the foreboding of untimely death upon him, and would soon leave them in their tears! This idea of his transitory stay on earth gave the last emphasis to the effect which the preacher had produced; it was as if an angel, in his passage to the skies, had shaken his bright wings over the people for an instant,—at once a shadow and a splendor,—and had shed down a shower of golden truths upon them.

Thus, there had come to the Reverend Mr. Dimmesdale—as to most men, in their various spheres, though seldom recognized until they see it far behind them—an epoch of life more brilliant and full of triumph than any previous one, or than any which could hereafter be. He stood, at this moment, on the very proudest eminence of superiority, to which the gifts of intellect, rich lore, prevailing eloquence, and a reputation of whitest sanctity, could exalt a clergyman in New England's earliest days, when the professional character was of itself a lofty pedestal. Such was the position which the minister occupied, as he bowed his head forward on the cushions of the pulpit, at the close of his Election Sermon. Meanwhile, Hester Prynne was standing beside the scaffold of the pillory, with the scarlet letter still burning on her breast!

Now was heard again the clangor of the music, and the measured tramp of the military escort, issuing from the church-door. The procession was to be marshalled thence to the town-hall, where a solemn banquet would complete the ceremonies of the day.

Once more, therefore, the train of venerable and majestic fathers was seen moving through a broad pathway of the people, who drew back reverently, on either side, as the Governor and magistrates, the old and wise men, the holy ministers, and all that were eminent and renowned, advanced into the midst of them. When they were fairly in the market-place, their presence was greeted by a shout. This—though doubtless it might acquire additional force and volume from the childlike loyalty which the age awarded to its rulers—was felt to be an irrepressible outburst of the enthusiasm kindled in the auditors by that high strain of eloquence which was yet reverberating in their ears. Each felt the impulse in himself, and, in the same breath, caught it from his neighbour. Within the church, it had hardly been kept down; beneath the sky, it pealed upward to the zenith. There were human beings enough, and enough of highly wrought and symphonious feeling, to produce that more impressive sound than the organ-tones of the blast, or the thunder, or the roar of the sea; even that mighty swell of many voices, blended into one great voice by the universal impulse which makes likewise one vast heart out of the many. Never, from the soil of New England, had gone up such a shout! Never, on New England soil, had stood the man so honored by his mortal brethren as the preacher.

How fared it with him then? Were there not the brilliant particles of a halo in the air about his head? So etherealized by spirit as he was, and so apotheosized by worshipping admirers, did his footsteps in the procession really tread upon the dust of earth?

As the ranks of military men and civil fathers moved onward, all eyes were turned towards the point where the minister was seen to approach among them. The shout died into a murmur, as one portion of the crowd after another obtained a glimpse of him. How feeble and pale he looked amid all his triumph! The energy—or say, rather, the inspiration which had held him up, until he should have delivered the sacred message that brought its own strength along with it from heaven—was withdrawn, now that it had so faithfully performed its office. The glow, which they had just before beheld burning on his cheek, was extinguished, like a flame that sinks down hopelessly among the late-decaying embers. It seemed hardly the face of a man alive, with such a deathlike hue; it was hardly a man with life in him, that tottered on his path so nervelessly, yet tottered, and did not fall!

One of his clerical brethren,—it was the venerable John Wilson,—observing the state in which Mr. Dimmesdale was left by the retiring wave of intellect and sensibility, stepped forward hastily to offer his support. The minister tremulously, but decidedly, repelled the old man's arm. He still walked onward, if that movement could be so described, which rather resembled the wavering effort of an infant, with its mother's arms in view, outstretched to tempt him forward. And now, almost imperceptible as were the latter steps of his progress, he had come opposite the well-remembered and weather-darkened scaffold, where, long since, with all that dreary lapse of time between, Hester Prynne had encountered the world's ignominious stare. There stood Hester, holding little Pearl by the hand! And there was the scarlet letter on her breast! The minister here made a pause; although the music still played the stately and rejoicing march to which the procession moved. It summoned him onward,—onward to the festival!—but here he made a pause.

Bellingham, for the last few moments, had kept an anxious eye upon him. He now left his own place in the procession, and advanced to give assistance; judging from Mr. Dimmesdale's aspect that he must otherwise inevitably fall. But there was something in the latter's expression that warned back the magistrate, although a man not readily obeying the vague intimations that pass from one spirit to another. The crowd, meanwhile, looked on with awe and wonder. This earthly faintness was, in their view, only another phase of the minister's celestial strength; nor would it have seemed a miracle too high to be wrought for one so holy, had he ascended before their eyes, waxing dimmer and brighter, and fading at last into the light of heaven!

He turned towards the scaffold, and stretched forth his arms.

"Hester," said he, "come hither! Come, my little Pearl!"

It was a ghastly look with which he regarded them; but there was something at once tender and strangely triumphant in it. The child, with the bird-like motion which was one of her characteristics, flew to him, and clasped her arms about his knees. Hester Prynne—slowly, as if impelled by inevitable fate, and against her strongest will—likewise drew near, but paused before she reached him. At this instant old Roger Chillingworth thrust himself through the crowd,—or, perhaps, so dark, disturbed, and evil was his look, he rose up out of some nether region,—to snatch back his victim from what he sought to do! Be that as it might, the old man rushed forward and caught the minister by the arm.

"Madman, hold! What is your purpose?" whispered he. "Wave back that woman! Cast off this child! All shall be well! Do not blacken your fame, and perish in dishonor! I can yet save you! Would you bring infamy on your sacred profession?"

"Ha, tempter! Methinks thou art too late!" answered the minister, encountering his eye, fearfully, but firmly. "Thy power is not what it was! With God's help, I shall escape thee now!"

He again extended his hand to the woman of the scarlet letter.

"Hester Prynne," cried he, with a piercing earnestness, "in the name of Him, so terrible and so merciful, who gives me grace, at this last moment, to do what—for my own heavy sin and miserable agony—I withheld myself from doing seven years ago, come hither now, and twine thy strength about me! Thy strength, Hester; but let it be guided by the will which God hath granted me! This wretched and wronged old man is opposing it with all his might!—with all his own might and the fiend's! Come, Hester, come! Support me up yonder scaffold!"

The crowd was in a tumult. The men of rank and dignity, who stood more immediately around the clergyman, were so taken by surprise, and so perplexed as to the purport of what they saw,—unable to receive the explanation which most readily presented itself, or to imagine any other,—that they remained silent and inactive spectators of the judgment which Providence seemed about to work. They beheld the minister, leaning on Hester's shoulder and supported by her arm around him, approach the scaffold, and ascend its steps; while still the little hand of the sin-born child was clasped in his. Old Roger Chillingworth followed, as one intimately connected with the drama of guilt and sorrow in which they had all been actors, and well entitled, therefore, to be present at its closing scene.

"Hadst thou sought the whole earth over," said he, looking darkly at the clergyman, "there was no one place so secret,—no high place nor lowly place, where thou couldst have escaped me,—save on this very scaffold!"

"Thanks be to Him who hath led me hither!" answered the minister.

Yet he trembled, and turned to Hester with an expression of doubt and anxiety in his eyes, not the less evidently betrayed, that there was a feeble smile upon his lips.

"Is not this better," murmured he, "than what we dreamed of in the forest?"

"I know not! I know not!" she hurriedly replied. "Better? Yea; so we may both die, and little Pearl die with us!"

"For thee and Pearl, be it as God shall order," said the minister; "and God is merciful! Let me now do the will which he hath made plain before my sight. For, Hester, I am a dying man. So let me make haste to take my shame upon me."

Partly supported by Hester Prynne, and holding one hand of little Pearl's, the Reverend Mr. Dimmesdale turned to the dignified and venerable rulers; to the holy ministers, who were his brethren; to the people, whose great heart was thoroughly appalled, yet overflowing with tearful sympathy, as knowing that some deep life-matter—which, if full of sin, was full of anguish and repentance likewise—was now to be laid open to them. The sun, but little past its meridian, shone down upon the clergyman, and gave a distinctness to his figure, as he stood out from all the earth to put in his plea of guilty at the bar of Eternal Justice.

"People of New England!" cried he, with a voice that rose over them, high, solemn, and majestic,—yet had always a tremor through it, and sometimes a shriek, struggling up out of a fathomless depth of remorse and woe,—"ye, that have loved me!—ye, that have deemed me holy!—behold me here, the one sinner of the world! At last!—at last!—I stand upon the spot where, seven years since, I should have stood; here, with this woman, whose arm, more than the little strength wherewith I have crept hitherward, sustains me, at this dreadful moment, from grovelling down upon my face! Lo, the scarlet letter which Hester wears! Ye have all shuddered at it! Wherever her walk hath been,—wherever, so miserably burdened, she may have hoped to find repose,—it hath cast a lurid gleam of awe and horrible repugnance round about her. But there stood one in the midst of you, at whose brand of sin and infamy ye have not shuddered!"

It seemed, at this point, as if the minister must leave the remainder of his secret undisclosed. But he fought back the bodily weakness,—and, still more, the faintness of heart,—that was striving for the mastery with him. He threw off all assistance, and stepped passionately forward a pace before the woman and the child.

"It was on him!" he continued, with a kind of fierceness; so determined was he to speak out the whole. "God's eye beheld it! The angels were for ever pointing at it! The Devil knew it well, and fretted it continually with the touch of his burning finger! But he hid it cunningly from men, and walked among you with the mien of a spirit, mournful, because so pure in a sinful world!— and sad, because he missed his heavenly kindred! Now, at the death-hour, he stands up before you! He bids you look again at Hester's scarlet letter! He tells you, that, with all its mysterious horror, it is but the shadow of what he bears on his own breast, and that even this, his own red stigma, is no more than the type of what has seared his inmost heart! Stand any here that question God's judgment on a sinner? Behold! Behold a dreadful witness of it!"

With a convulsive motion he tore away the ministerial band from before his breast. It was revealed! But it were irreverent to describe that revelation. For an instant the gaze of the horror-stricken multitude was concentrated on the ghastly miracle; while the minister stood with a flush of triumph in his face, as one who, in the crisis of acutest pain, had won a victory. Then, down he sank upon the scaffold! Hester partly raised him, and supported his head against her bosom. Old Roger Chillingworth knelt down beside him, with a blank, dull countenance, out of which the life seemed to have departed.

"Thou hast escaped me!" he repeated more than once. "Thou hast escaped me!"

"May God forgive thee!" said the minister. "Thou, too, hast deeply sinned!"

He withdrew his dying eyes from the old man, and fixed them on the woman and the child.

"My little Pearl," said he feebly,—and there was a sweet and gentle smile over his face, as of a spirit sinking into deep repose; nay, now that the burden was removed, it seemed almost as if he would be sportive with the child,— "dear little Pearl, wilt thou kiss me now? Thou wouldst not yonder, in the forest! But now thou wilt?"

Pearl kissed his lips. A spell was broken. The great scene of grief, in which the wild infant bore a part, had developed all her sympathies; and as her tears fell upon her father's cheek, they were the pledge that she would grow up amid human joy and sorrow, nor for ever do battle with the world, but be a woman in it. Towards her mother, too, Pearl's errand as a messenger of anguish was all fulfilled.

"Hester," said the clergyman, "farewell!"

"Shall we not meet again?" whispered she, bending her face down close to his. "Shall we not spend our immortal life together? Surely, surely, we have ransomed one another, with all this woe! Thou lookest far into eternity, with those bright dying eyes! Then tell me what thou seest?"

"Hush, Hester, hush!" said he, with tremulous solemnity. "The law we broke!—the sin here so awfully revealed!—let these alone be in thy thoughts! I fear! I fear! It may be, that, when we forgot our God,—when we violated our reverence each for the other's soul,—it was thenceforth vain to hope that we could meet hereafter, in an everlasting and pure reunion. God knows; and He is merciful! He hath proved his mercy, most of all, in my afflictions. By giving me this burning torture to bear upon my breast! By sending yonder dark and terrible old man, to keep the torture always at red-heat! By bringing me hither, to die this death of triumphant ignominy before the people! Had either of these agonies been wanting, I had been lost for ever! Praised be his name! His will be done! Farewell!"

That final word came forth with the minister's expiring breath. The multitude, silent till then, broke out in a strange, deep voice of awe and wonder, which could not as yet find utterance, save in this murmur that rolled so heavily after the departed spirit.

XXIV. CONCLUSION

After many days, when time sufficed for the people to arrange their thoughts in reference to the foregoing scene, there was more than one account of what had been witnessed on the scaffold.

Most of the spectators testified to having seen, on the breast of the unhappy minister, a SCARLET LETTER—the very semblance of that worn by Hester Prynne—imprinted in the flesh. As regarded its origin, there were various explanations, all of which must necessarily have been conjectural. Some affirmed that the Reverend Mr. Dimmesdale, on the very day when Hester Prynne first wore her ignominious badge, had begun a course of penance,—which he afterwards, in so many futile methods, followed out,—by inflicting a hideous torture on himself. Others contended that the stigma had not been produced until a long time subsequent, when old Roger Chillingworth, being a potent necromancer, had caused it to appear, through the agency of magic and poisonous drugs. Others, again,—and those best able to appreciate the minister's peculiar sensibility, and the wonderful operation of his spirit upon the body,—whispered their belief, that the awful symbol was the effect of the ever active tooth of remorse, gnawing from the inmost heart outwardly, and at last manifesting Heaven's dreadful judgment by the visible presence of the letter. The reader may choose among these theories. We have thrown all the light we could acquire upon the portent, and would gladly, now that it has done its office, erase its deep print out of our own brain; where long meditation has fixed it in very undesirable distinctness.

It is singular, nevertheless, that certain persons, who were spectators of the whole scene, and professed never once to have removed their eyes from the Reverend Mr. Dimmesdale, denied that there was any mark whatever on his breast, more than on a new-born infant's. Neither, by their report, had his dying words acknowledged, nor even remotely implied, any, the slightest connection, on his part, with the guilt for which Hester Prynne had so long worn the scarlet letter. According to these highly respectable witnesses, the minister, conscious that he was dying,—conscious, also, that the reverence of the multitude placed him already among saints and angels,—had desired, by yielding up his breath in the arms of that fallen woman, to express to the world how utterly nugatory is the choicest of man's own righteousness. After exhausting life in his efforts for mankind's spiritual good, he had made the manner of his death a parable, in order to impress on his admirers the mighty and mournful lesson, that, in the view of Infinite Purity, we are sinners all alike. It was to teach them, that the holiest among us has but attained so far above his fellows as to discern more clearly the Mercy which looks down, and repudiate more utterly the phantom of human merit, which would look aspiringly upward. Without disputing a truth so momentous, we must be allowed to consider this version of Mr. Dimmesdale's story as only an instance of that stubborn fidelity with which a man's friends—and especially a clergyman's—will sometimes uphold his character; when proofs, clear as the mid-day sunshine on the scarlet letter, establish him a false and sin-stained creature of the dust.

The authority which we have chiefly followed—a manuscript of old date, drawn up from the verbal testimony of individuals, some of whom had known Hester Prynne, while others had heard the tale from contemporary witnesses— fully confirms the view taken in the foregoing pages. Among many morals which press upon us from the poor minister's miserable experience, we put only this into a sentence:—"Be true! Be true! Be true! Show freely to the world, if not your worst, yet some trait whereby the worst may be inferred!"

Nothing was more remarkable than the change which took place, almost immediately after Mr. Dimmesdale's death, in the appearance and demeanour of the old man known as Roger Chillingworth. All his strength and energy— all his vital and intellectual force—seemed at once to desert him; insomuch that he positively withered up, shrivelled away, and almost vanished from mortal sight, like an uprooted weed that lies wilting in the sun. This unhappy man had made the very principle of his life to consist in the pursuit and systematic exercise of revenge; and when, by its completest triumph and consummation, that evil principle was left with no further material to support it,— when, in short, there was no more devil's work on earth for him to do, it only remained for the unhumanized mortal to betake himself whither his Master would find him tasks enough, and pay him his wages duly. But, to all these shadowy beings, so long our near acquaintances,—as well Roger Chillingworth as his companions,—we would fain be merciful. It is a curious subject of observation and inquiry, whether hatred and love be not the same thing at bottom. Each, in its utmost development, supposes a high degree of intimacy and heart-knowledge; each renders one individual dependent for the food of his affections and spiritual life upon another; each leaves the passionate lover, or the no less passionate hater, forlorn and desolate by the withdrawal of his object. Philosophically considered, therefore, the two passions seem essentially the same, except that one happens to be seen in a celestial radiance, and the other in a dusky and lurid glow. In the spiritual world, the old physician and the minister—mutual victims as they have been—may, unawares, have found their earthly stock of hatred and antipathy transmuted into golden love.

Leaving this discussion apart, we have a matter of business to communicate to the reader. At old Roger Chillingworth's decease (which took place within the year), and by his last will and testament, of which Governor Bellingham and the Reverend Mr. Wilson were executors, he bequeathed a very considerable amount of property, both here and in England, to little Pearl, the daughter of Hester Prynne.

So Pearl—the elf-child,—the demon offspring, as some people, up to that epoch, persisted in considering her—became the richest heiress of her day, in the New World. Not improbably, this circumstance wrought a very material change in the public estimation; and, had the mother and child remained here, little Pearl, at a marriageable period of life, might have mingled her wild blood with the lineage of the devoutest Puritan among them all. But, in no long time after the physician's death, the wearer of the scarlet letter disappeared, and Pearl along with her. For many years, though a vague report would now and then find its way across the sea,—like a shapeless piece of driftwood tost ashore, with the initials of a name upon it,—yet no tidings of them unquestionably authentic were received. The story of the scarlet letter grew into a legend. Its spell, however, was still potent, and kept the scaffold awful where the poor minister had died, and likewise the cottage by the sea-shore, where Hester Prynne had dwelt. Near this latter spot, one afternoon, some children were at play, when they beheld a tall woman, in a gray robe, approach the cottage-door. In all those years it had never once been opened; but either she unlocked it, or the decaying wood and iron yielded to her hand, or she glided shadow-like through these impediments,—and, at all events, went in.

On the threshold she paused,—turned partly round,—for, perchance, the idea of entering, all alone, and all so changed, the home of so intense a former life, was more dreary and desolate than even she could bear. But her hesitation was only for an instant, though long enough to display a scarlet letter on her breast.

And Hester Prynne had returned, and taken up her long-forsaken shame. But where was little Pearl? If still alive, she must now have been in the flush and bloom of early womanhood. None knew—nor ever learned, with the ful-ness of perfect certainty—whether the elf-child had gone thus untimely to a maiden grave; or whether her wild, rich nature had been softened and sub-dued, and made capable of a woman's gentle happiness. But, through the remainder of Hester's life, there were indications that the recluse of the scarlet letter was the object of love and interest with some inhabitant of another land. Letters came, with armorial seals upon them, though of bearings unknown to English heraldry. In the cottage there were articles of comfort and luxury, such as Hester never cared to use, but which only wealth could have purchased, and affection have imagined for her. There were trifles, too, little ornaments, beautiful tokens of a continual remembrance, that must have been wrought by delicate fingers, at the impulse of a fond heart. And, once, Hester was seen embroidering a baby-garment, with such a lavish richness of golden fancy as would have raised a public tumult, had any infant, thus apparelled, been shown to our sobre-hued community.

In fine, the gossips of that day believed,—and Mr. Surveyor Pue, who made investigations a century later, believed,—and one of his recent successors in office, moreover, faithfully believes,—that Pearl was not only alive, but mar-ried, and happy, and mindful of her mother; and that she would most joyfully have entertained that sad and lonely mother at her fireside.

But there was a more real life for Hester Prynne, here, in New England, than in that unknown region where Pearl had found a home. Here had been her sin; here, her sorrow; and here was yet to be her penitence. She had returned, therefore, and resumed,—of her own free will, for not the sternest magistrate of that iron period would have imposed it,—resumed the symbol of which we have related so dark a tale. Never afterwards did it quit her bosom. But, in the lapse of the toilsome, thoughtful, and self-devoted years that made up Hester's life, the scarlet letter ceased to be a stigma which attracted the world's scorn and bitterness, and became a type of something to be sorrowed over, and looked upon with awe, yet with reverence too. And, as Hester Prynne had no selfish ends, nor lived in any measure for her own profit and enjoyment, people brought all their sorrows and perplexities, and besought her counsel, as one who had herself gone through a mighty trouble. Women, more especially,—in the continually recurring trials of wounded, wasted, wronged, misplaced, or erring and sinful passion,—or with the dreary burden of a heart unyielded, because unvalued and unsought,—came to Hester's cottage, demanding why they were so wretched, and what the remedy! Hester comforted and counselled them, as best she might. She assured them, too, of her firm belief, that, at some brighter period, when the world should have grown ripe for it, in Heaven's own time, a new truth would be revealed, in order to establish the whole relation between man and woman on a surer ground of mutual happiness. Earlier in life, Hester had vainly imagined that she herself might be the destined prophetess, but had long since recognized the impossibility that any mission of divine and mysterious truth should be confided to a woman stained with sin, bowed down with shame, or even burdened with a life-long sorrow. The angel and apostle of the coming revelation must be a woman, indeed, but lofty, pure, and beautiful; and wise, moreover, not through dusky grief, but the ethereal medium of joy; and showing how sacred love should make us happy, by the truest test of a life successful to such an end!

So said Hester Prynne, and glanced her sad eyes downward at the scarlet letter. And, after many, many years, a new grave was delved, near an old and sunken one, in that burial-ground beside which King's Chapel has since been built. It was near that old and sunken grave, yet with a space between, as if the dust of the two sleepers had no right to mingle. Yet one tombstone served for both. All around, there were monuments carved with armorial bearings; and on this simple slab of slate—as the curious investigator may still discern, and perplex himself with the purport—there appeared the semblance of an engraved escutcheon.[6] It bore a device, a herald's wording of which might serve for a motto and brief description of our now concluded legend; so sombre is it, and relieved only by one ever-glowing point of light gloomier than the shadow:—

"ON A FIELD, SABLE, THE LETTER A, GULES."[7]

The End

1850

Preface to *The House of the Seven Gables*[1]

When a writer calls his work a Romance, it need hardly be observed that he wishes to claim a certain latitude, both as to its fashion and material, which he would not have felt himself entitled to assume, had he professed to be writing a Novel. The latter form of composition is presumed to aim at a very minute fidelity, not merely to the possible, but to the probable and ordinary course of man's experience. The former—while, as a work of art, it must rigidly subject itself to laws, and while it sins unpardonably so far as it may swerve aside from the truth of the human heart—has fairly a right to present that truth under circumstances, to a great extent, of the writer's own choosing

---

6. A shield-shaped emblem.
7. I.e., on a black background, the letter A, in red.

1. The text is from *The House of the Seven Gables: A Romance* (1851).

or creation. If he think fit, also, he may so manage his atmospherical medium as to bring out or mellow the lights, and deepen and enrich the shadows, of the picture. He will be wise, no doubt, to make a very moderate use of the privileges here stated, and, especially, to mingle the Marvellous rather as a slight, delicate, and evanescent flavor, than as any portion of the actual substance of the dish offered to the public. He can hardly be said, however, to commit a literary crime, even if he disregard this caution.

In the present work, the author has proposed to himself—but with what success, fortunately, it is not for him to judge—to keep undeviatingly within his immunities. The point of view in which this tale comes under the Romantic definition lies in the attempt to connect a by-gone time with the very present that is flitting away from us. It is a legend, prolonging itself, from an epoch now gray in the distance, down into our own broad daylight, and bringing along with it some of its legendary mist, which the reader, according to his pleasure, may either disregard, or allow it to float almost imperceptibly about the characters and events, for the sake of a picturesque effect. The narrative, it may be, is woven of so humble a texture as to require this advantage, and, at the same time, to render it the more difficult of attainment.

Many writers lay very great stress upon some definite moral purpose, at which they profess to aim their works. Not to be deficient in this particular, the author has provided himself with a moral;—the truth, namely, that the wrong-doing of one generation lives into the successive ones, and, divesting itself of every temporary advantage, becomes a pure and uncontrollable mischief;—and he would feel it a singular gratification, if this romance might effectually convince mankind—or, indeed, any one man—of the folly of tumbling down an avalanche of ill-gotten gold, or real estate, on the heads of an unfortunate posterity, thereby to maim and crush them, until the accumulated mass shall be scattered abroad in its original atoms. In good faith, however, he is not sufficiently imaginative to flatter himself with the slightest hope of this kind. When romances do really teach anything, or produce any effective operation, it is usually through a far more subtle process than the ostensible one. The author has considered it hardly worth his while, therefore, relentlessly to impale the story with its moral, as with an iron rod,—or, rather as by sticking a pin through a butterfly,—thus at once depriving it of life, and causing it to stiffen in an ungainly and unnatural attitude. A high truth, indeed, fairly, finely, and skilfully wrought out, brightening at every step, and crowning the final development of a work of fiction, may add an artistic glory, but is never any truer, and seldom any more evident, at the last page than at the first.

The reader may perhaps choose to assign an actual locality to the imaginary events of this narrative. If permitted by the historical connection,—which, though slight, was essential to his plan,—the author would very willingly have avoided anything of this nature. Not to speak of other objections, it exposes the romance to an inflexible and exceedingly dangerous species of criticism, by bringing his fancy-pictures almost into positive contact with the realities of the moment. It has been no part of his object, however, to describe local manners, nor in any way to meddle with the characteristics of a community for whom he cherishes a proper respect and a natural regard. He trusts not to be considered as unpardonably offending, by laying out a street that infringes upon nobody's private rights, and appropriating a lot of land which had no visible owner, and building a house, of materials long in use for constructing

castles in the air. The personages of the tale—though they give themselves out
to be of ancient stability and considerable prominence—are really of the
author's own making, or, at all events, of his own mixing; their virtues can
shed no lustre, nor their defects redound, in the remotest degree, to the discredit of the venerable town[2] of which they profess to be inhabitants. He would
be glad, therefore, if—especially in the quarter to which he alludes—the book
may be read strictly as a Romance, having a great deal more to do with the
clouds overhead than with any portion of the actual soil of the County of
Essex.

LENOX, *January 27, 1851.*

[A Gallery of Hawthorne's Word-Portraits][1]

[Henry D. Thoreau][2]

Thursday, September 1st, [1842]

Mr. Thorow dined with us yesterday. He is a singular character—a young
man with much of wild original nature still remaining in him; and so far as he
is sophisticated, it is in a way and method of his own. He is as ugly as sin,
long-nosed, queer-mouthed, and with uncouth and somewhat rustic,
although courteous manners, corresponding very well with such an exterior.
But his ugliness is of an honest and agreeable fashion, and becomes him much
better than beauty. He was educated, I believe, at Cambridge, and formerly
kept school in this town; but for two or three years back, he has repudiated all
regular modes of getting a living, and seems inclined to lead a sort of Indian
life among civilized men—an Indian life, I mean, as respects the absence of
any systematic effort for a livelihood. He has been for sometime an inmate of
Mr. Emerson's family; and, in requital, he labors in the garden, and performs
such other offices as may suit him—being entertained by Mr. Emerson for the
sake of what true manhood there is in him. Mr. Thorow is a keen and delicate
observer of nature—a genuine observer, which, I suspect, is almost as rare a
character as even an original poet; and Nature, in return for his love, seems to
adopt him as her especial child, and shows him secrets which few others are
allowed to witness. He is familiar with beast, fish, fowl, and reptile, and has
strange stories to tell of adventures, and friendly passages with these lower
brethren of mortality. Herb and flower, likewise, wherever they grow, whether
in garden or wild wood, are his familiar friends. He is also on intimate terms
with the clouds, and can tell the portents of storms. It is a characteristic trait,
that he has a great regard for the memory of the Indian tribes, whose wild life
would have suited him so well; and strange to say, he seldom walks over a
ploughed field without picking up an arrow-point, a spear-head, or other relic
of the red men—as if their spirits willed him to be the inheritor of their simple wealth.

2. Salem, Massachusetts.
1. The gallery of characters shows Hawthorne as acute
observer of actions and speculator about motives and
puts his much-emphasized relationship with Melville
in perspective.
2. From Nathaniel Hawthorne, *The American Note-*

books, edited by Claude M. Simpson (1972). Hawthorne's spelling is one of the indications that Thoreau's name was accented on the first syllable, not the
second, and was probably pronounced about like
thorough.

With all this he has more than a tincture of literature—a deep and true taste for poetry, especially the elder poets, although more exclusive than is desirable, like all other Transcendentalists, so far as I am acquainted with them. He is a good writer—at least, he has written one good article, a rambling disquisition on Natural History in the last Dial,[3]—which, he ways, was chiefly made up from journals of his own observations. Methinks this article gives a very fair image of his mind and character—so true, minute, and literal in observation, yet giving the spirit as well as letter of what he sees, even as a lake reflects its wooded banks, showing every leaf, yet giving the wild beauty of the whole scene;—then there are passages in the article of cloudy and dreamy metaphysics, partly affected, and partly the natural exhalations of his intellect;—and also passages where his thoughts seem to measure and attune themselves into spontaneous verse, as they rightfully may, since there is real poetry in him. There is a basis of good sense and moral truth, too, throughout the article, which also is a reflection of his character; for he is not unwise to think and feel, however imperfect in his own mode of action. On the whole, I find him a healthy and wholesome man to know.

After dinner (at which we cut the first water-melon and musk melon that our garden has ripened) Mr. Thorow and I walked up the bank of the river; and, at a certain point, he shouted for his boat. Forthwith, a young man paddled it across the river, and Mr. Thorow and I voyaged further up the stream, which soon became more beautiful than any picture, with its dark and quiet sheet of water, half shaded, half sunny, between high and wooded banks. The late rains have swollen the stream so much, that many trees are standing up to their knees, as it were, in the water; and boughs, which lately swung high in air, now dip and drink deep of the passing wave. As to the poor cardinals, which glowed upon the bank, a few days since, I could see only a few of their scarlet caps, peeping above the water. Mr. Thorow managed the boat so perfectly, either with two paddles or with one, that it seemed instinct with his own will, and to require no physical effort to guide it. He said that, when some Indians visited Concord a few years since, he found that he had acquired, without a teacher, their precise method of propelling the steering a canoe. Nevertheless, being in want of money, the poor fellow was desirous of selling the boat, of which he is so fit a pilot, and which was built by his own hands; so I agreed to give him his price (only seven dollars) and accordingly became possessor of the Musketaquid. I wish I could acquire the aquatic skill of its original owner at as reasonable a rate.

* * * I was interrupted by a visit from Mr. Thoreau, who came to return a book, and to announce his purpose of going to reside at Staten Island, as private tutor in the family of Mr. Emerson's brother. We had some conversation upon this subject, and upon the spiritual advantages of change of place, and upon the Dial, and upon Mr. Alcott,[4] and other kindred or concatenated subjects. I am glad, on Mr. Thoreau's own account, that he is going away; as he is physically out of health, and, morally and intellectually, seems not to have found exactly the guiding clue; and in all these respects, he may be benefitted by his removal;—also, it is one step towards a circumstantial posi-

---

3. The Transcendentalists' magazine, edited by Margaret Fuller at this time, but soon taken over by Emerson.

4. Bronson Alcott (1799–1888), philosopher and edu-cator. This paragraph is from *The American Notebooks*, the entry for April 7, 1843. William Emerson was a lawyer.

tion in the world. On my account, I should like to have him remain here; he being one of the few persons, I think, with whom to hold intercourse is like hearing the wind among the boughs of a forest-tree; and with all this wild freedom, there is high and classic cultivation in him too. He says that Ellery Channing[5] is coming back to Concord, and that he (Mr. Thoreau) has concluded a bargain, in his behalf, for the hire of a small house, with land attached, at $55 per year. I am rather glad than otherwise; but Ellery, so far as he has been developed to my observation, is but a poor substitute for Mr. Thoreau.

[Edmund Hosmer—Emerson's Ideal Farmer][6]

Monday, August 15, [1842]

* * * About nine o'clock, Hillard[7] and I set out for a walk to Walden Pond, calling by the way at Mr. Emerson's, to obtain his guidance or directions. He, from the scruple of his external conscience, detained us till after the people had got into church, and then accompanied us in his own illustrious person. We turned aside a little from our way to visit a Mr. Edmund Hosmer, a yeoman of whose homely and self-acquired wisdom Mr. Emerson has a very high opinion. We found him walking in his fields—a short, but stalwart and sturdy personage of middle age,[8] somewhat uncouth and ugly to look at, but with a face of shrewd and kind expression, and manners of natural courtesy. He seemed to have a very free flow of talk, and not much diffidence about his own opinions; for, with a little induction from Mr. Emerson, he began to discourse about the state of the nation, agriculture, and business in general— uttering thoughts that had come to him at the plough, and which had a sort of flavor and smell of the fresh earth about them. I was not impressed with any remarkable originality in his views; but they were sensible and characteristic, and had grown in the soil where we found them. Methought, however, the good yeoman was not quite so natural as he may have been at a former period; the simplicity of his character has probably suffered, in some degree, by his detecting the impression which he makes on those around him. There is a circle, I suppose, who look up to him as an oracle; and so he inevitably assumes the oracular manner, and speaks as if truth and wisdom were uttering themselves by his voice. Mr. Emerson has risked the doing him much mischief, by putting him in print—a trial which few persons can sustain, without losing their unconsciousness. But, after all, a man gifted with thought and expression, whatever his rank in life, and his mode of uttering himself, whether by pen or tongue, cannot be expected to go through the world, without finding himself out—and as all such self-discoveries are partial and imperfect, they do more harm than good to the character. Mr. Hosmer is more natural than ninety-nine men out of a hundred; and he is certainly a man of intellectual and moral substance, a sturdy fact, a reality, something to be felt and touched. It would be amusing to draw a parallel between him and his admirer, Mr. Emerson—the mystic, stretching his hand out of cloud-land, in

---

5. William Ellery Channing (1818–1901), engaging but unreliable nephew of the Unitarian leader William Ellery Channing (1780–1842).
6. From *The American Notebooks.*

7. George Hillard (1808–1879), Boston friend of Hawthorne's, and his lawyer.
8. Hosmer was born in 1798.

vain search for something real; and the man of sturdy sense, all whose ideas seem to be dug out of his mind, hard and substantial, as he digs potatoes, beets, carrots, and turnips, out of the earth. Mr. Emerson is a great searcher for facts; but they seem to melt away and become unsubstantial in his grasp.

After leaving Mr. Hosmer, we proceeded through wood-paths to Walden Pond, picking blackberries of enormous size along the way. The pond itself was beautiful and refreshing to my soul, after such long and exclusive familiarity with our tawny and sluggish river. It lies embosomed among wooded hills, not very extensive, but large enough for waves to dance upon its surface, and to look like a piece of blue firmament, earth-encircled. The shore has a narrow, pebbly strand, which it was worth a day's journey to look at, for the sake of the contrast between it and the weedy, slimy, oozy margin of the river. Farther within its depths, you perceive a bottom of pure white sand, sparkling through the transparent water, which, methought, was the very purest liquid in the world. After Mr. Emerson left us, Hillard and I bathed in the pond; and it does really seem as if not only my corporeal person, but my moral self, had received a cleansing from that bath. A good deal of mud and river-slime had accumulated on my soul; but those bright waters washed it all away.

[Walden Pond][9]

Friday, October 6th, [1843]

Yesterday afternoon (leaving wifie with my sister Louisa, who has been with us two or three days) I took a solitary walk to Walden Pond. It was a cool, north-west windy day, with heavy clouds rolling and tumbling about the sky, but still a prevalence of genial autumn sunshine. The fields are still green, and the great masses of the woods have not yet assumed their many-colored garments; but here and there, are solitary oaks of a deep, substantial red, or maples of a more brilliant hue, or chestnuts, either yellow or of a tenderer green than in summer. Some trees seem to return to their hue of May or early June, before they put on the brighter autumnal tints. In some places, along the borders of low and moist land, a whole range of trees were clothed in the perfect gorgeousness of autumn, of all shades of brilliant color, looking like the palette on which Nature was arranging the tints wherewith to paint a picture. These hues appeared to be thrown together without design; and yet there was perfect harmony among them, and a softness and delicacy made up of a thousand different brightnesses. There is not, I think, so much contrast among these colors as might at first appear; the more you consider them, the more they seem to have one element among them all—which is the reason that the most brilliant display of them soothes the observer, instead of exciting him. And I know not whether it be more a moral effect, or a physical one operating merely on the eye, but it is a pensive gaiety, which causes a sigh often, but never a smile. We never fancy, for instance, that these gaily-clad trees should be changed into young damsels in holiday attire, and betake themselves to dancing on the plain. If they were to undergo such a transformation, they would surely arrange themselves in a funeral procession, and go sadly along with their purple, and scarlet, and golden garments trailing over the withering

9. From *The American Notebooks.*

grass. When the sunshine falls upon them, they seem to smile; but it is as if they were heartbroken. But it is in vain for me to attempt to describe these autumnal brilliancies, or to convey the impression which they make on me. I have tried a thousand times, and always without the slightest self-satisfaction. Luckily, there is no need of such a record; for Nature renews the scene, year after year; and even when we shall have passed away from the world, we can spiritually create these scenes; so that we may dispense now and hereafter with all further efforts to put them into words.

Walden Pond was clear and beautiful, as usual. It tempted me to bathe; and though the water was thrillingly cold, it was like the thrill of a happy death. Never was there such transparent water as this. I threw sticks into it, and saw them float suspended on an almost invisible medium; it seemed as if the pure air was beneath them, as well as above. If I were to be baptized, it should be in this pond; but then one would not wish to pollute it by washing off his sins into it. None but angels should bathe there. It would be a fit bathing-place for my little wife; and sometime or other, I hope, our blessed baby shall be dipt into its bosom.

In a small and secluded dell, that opens upon the most beautiful cove of the whole lake, there is a little hamlet of huts or shanties, inhabited by the Irish people who are at work upon the rail-road. There are three or four of these habitations, the very rudest, I should imagine, that civilized men ever made for themselves, constructed of rough boards, with protruding ends. Against some of them the earth is heaped up to the roof, or nearly so; and when the grass has had time to sprout upon them, they will look like small natural hillocks, or a species of ant-hill, or something in which Nature has a larger share than man. These huts are placed beneath the trees, (oaks, walnuts, and white pines) wherever the trunks give them space to stand; and by thus adapting themselves to natural interstices instead of making new ones, they do not break or disturb the solitude and seclusion of the place. Voices are heard, and the shouts and laughter of children, who play about like the sunbeams that come down through the branches. Women are washing beneath the trees, and long lines of whitened clothes are extended from tree to tree, fluttering and gambol-ling in the breeze. A pig, in a stye even more extemporary than the shanties, is grunting, and poking his snout through the clefts of his habitation. The household pots and kettles are seen at the doors, and a glance within shows the rough benches that serve for chairs, and the bed upon the floor. The visiter's nose takes note of the fragrance of a pipe. And yet, with all these homely items, the repose and sanctity of the old wood do not seem to be destroyed or prophaned; she overshadows these poor people, and assimilates them, somehow or other, to the character of her natural inhabitants. Their presence did not shock me, any more than if I had merely discovered a squir-rel's nest in a tree. To be sure, it is a torment to see the great, high, ugly embankment of the rail-road, which is here protruding itself into the lake, or along its margin, in close vicinity to this picturesque little hamlet. I have seldom seen anything more beautiful than the cove, on the border of which the huts are situated; and the more I looked, the lovelier it grew. The trees overshadowed it deeply; but on one side there was some brilliant shrubbery which seemed to light up the whole picture with the effect of a sweet and melancholy smile. I felt as if spirits were there—or as if these shrubs had a spiritual life—in short, the impression was undefinable; and after gazing and musing a good while, I retraced my steps through the Irish hamlet, and plodded on along a wood-path.

According to my invariable custom, I mistook my way, and emerging upon a road, I turned my back, instead of my face, towards Concord, and walked on very diligently, till a guideboard informed me of my mistake. I then turned about, and was shortly overtaken by an old yeoman in a chaise, who kindly offered me a ride, and shortly set me down in the village.

[*Herman Melville*][1]

[Lenox, Massachusetts, August 1, 1851]

* * * Returning to the Post office, I got Mr. Tappan's[2] mail and my own, and proceeded homeward, but clambered over the fence and sat down in Love Grove, to read the papers. While thus engaged, a cavalier on horseback came along the road, and saluted me in Spanish; to which I replied by touching my hat; and went on with the newspaper. But the cavalier renewing his salutation, I regarded him more attentively, and saw that it was Herman Melville! So, hereupon, Julian[3] and I hastened to the road, where ensued a greeting, and we all went homeward together, talking as we went. Soon, Mr. Melville alighted, and put Julian into the saddle; and the little man was highly pleased, and sat on the horse with the freedom and fearlessness of an old equestrian, and had a ride of at least a mile homeward.

I asked Mrs. Peters[4] to make some tea for Herman Melville; and so she did, and he drank a cup, but was afraid to drink much, because it would keep him awake. After supper, I put Julian to bed; and Melville and I had a talk about time and eternity, things of this world and of the next, and books, and publishers, and all possible and impossible matters, that lasted pretty deep into the night; and if truth must be told, we smoked cigars even within the sacred precincts of the sitting-room. At last, he arose, and saddled his horse (whom we had put into the barn) and rode off for his own domicile; and I hastened to make the most of what little sleeping-time remained for me. * * *

[Southport, England] November 20th, [1856], Thursday[5]

A week ago last Monday, Herman Melville came to see me at the Consulate, looking much as he used to do (a little paler, and perhaps a little sadder), in a rough outside coat, and with his characteristic gravity and reserve of manner. He had crossed from New York to Glasgow in a screw steamer, about a fortnight before, and had since been seeing Edinburgh and other interesting places. I felt rather awkward at first; because this is the first time I have met him since my ineffectual attempt to get him a consular appointment from General Pierce. However, I failed only from real lack of power to serve him; so there was no reason to be ashamed, and we soon found ourselves on pretty much our former terms of sociability and confidence. Melville has not been well, of late; he has been affected with neuralgic complaints in his head and

1. From *The American Notebooks.*
2. W. A. Tappan, Hawthorne's neighbor and landlord. A minor confrontation with Tappan over rights to fruit on the rented property led to Hawthorne's moving to West Newton, Massachusetts, in November 1851.
3. The Hawthornes' young son, born in June 1846.
4. The Hawthornes' housekeeper.
5. From Nathaniel Hawthorne, *The English Notebooks,* edited by Randall Stewart (1941).

limbs, and no doubt has suffered from too constant literary occupation, pursued without much success, latterly; and his writings, for a long while past, have indicated a morbid state of mind. So he left his place at Pittsfield, and has established his wife and family, I believe, with his father-in-law in Boston, and is thus far on his way to Constantinople. I do not wonder that he found it necessary to take an airing through the world, after so many years of toilsome pen-labor and domestic life, following upon so wild and adventurous a youth as he was. I invited him to come and stay with us at Southport, as long as he might remain in this vicinity; and, accordingly, he did come, the next day, taking with him, by way of baggage, the least little bit of a bundle, which, he told me, contained a night-shirt and a tooth-brush. He is a person of very gentlemanly instincts in every respect, save that he is a little heterodox in the matter of clean linen.

He stayed with us from Tuesday till Thursday; and, on the intervening day, we took a pretty long walk together, and sat down in a hollow among the sand hills (sheltering ourselves from the high, cool wind) and smoked a cigar. Melville, as he always does, began to reason of Providence and futurity, and of everything that lies beyond human ken, and informed me that he had "pretty much made up his mind to be annihilated"; but still he does not seem to rest in that anticipation; and, I think, will never rest until he gets hold of a definite belief. It is strange how he persists—and has persisted ever since I knew him, and probably long before—in wandering to-and-fro over these deserts, as dismal and monotonous as the sand hills amid which we were sitting. He can neither believe, nor be comfortable in his unbelief; and he is too honest and courageous not to try to do one or the other. If he were a religious man, he would be one of the most truly religious and reverential; he has a very high and noble nature, and better worth immortality than most of us.

[Abraham Lincoln][6]

[March–April, 1862]

By and by there was a little stir on the staircase and in the passage-way, and in lounged a tall, loose-jointed figure, of an exaggerated Yankee port and demeanor, whom (as being about the homeliest man I ever saw, yet by no means repulsive or disagreeable) it was impossible not to recognize as Uncle Abe.

Unquestionably, Western man though he be, and Kentuckian by birth, President Lincoln is the essential representative of all Yankees, and the veritable specimen, physically, of what the world seems determined to regard as our characteristic qualities. It is the strangest and yet the fittest thing in the jumble of human vicissitudes, that he, out of so many millions, unlooked for, unse-

---

6. From James T. Fields, *Yesterdays with Authors* (1871). Before publishing Hawthorne's *Chiefly about War-Matters* in the *Atlantic Monthly* for July 1862, Fields had insisted that this "portrait of a living man" was not "wise or tasteful to print." Hawthorne, sure of the "historical value" of his portrait, complained to Fields, "What a terrible thing it is to try to let off a little bit of truth into this miserable humbug of a world!"

With Hawthorne and Lincoln both dead, Fields felt free to enhance his own recollections with the portrait.

Here is Fields's account of the occasion of Hawthorne's meeting Lincoln: "Hawthorne and his party had gone into the President's room, annexed, as he says, as supernumeraries to a deputation from a Massachusetts whip-factory, with a present of a splendid whip to the Chief Magistrate."

lected by any intelligible process that could be based upon his genuine qualities, unknown to those who chose him, and unsuspected of what endowments
may adapt him for his tremendous responsibility, should have found the way
open for him to fling his lank personality into the chair of state,—where, I
presume, it was his first impulse to throw his legs on the council-table, and
tell the Cabinet Ministers a story. There is no describing his lengthy awkwardness, nor the uncouthness of his movement; and yet it seemed as if I had been
in the habit of seeing him daily, and had shaken hands with him a thousand
times in some village street; so true was he to the aspect of the pattern American, though with a certain extravagance which, possibly, I exaggerated still
further by the delighted eagerness with which I took it in. If put to guess his
calling and livelihood, I should have taken him for a country schoolmaster as
soon as anything else. He was dressed in a rusty black frock-coat and pantaloons, unbrushed, and worn so faithfully that the suit had adapted itself to the
curves and angularities of his figure, and had grown to be an outer skin of the
man. He had shabby slippers on his feet. His hair was black, still unmixed
with gray, stiff, somewhat bushy, and had apparently been acquainted with
neither brush nor comb that morning, after the disarrangement of the pillow;
and as to a nightcap, Uncle Abe probably knows nothing of such effeminacies.
His complexion is dark and sallow, betokening, I fear, an insalubrious atmosphere around the White House; he has thick black eyebrows and an
impending brow; his nose is large, and the lines about his mouth are very
strongly defined.

The whole physiognomy is as coarse a one as you would meet anywhere in
the length and breadth of the States; but, withal, it is redeemed, illuminated,
softened, and brightened by a kindly though serious look out of his eyes, and
an expression of homely sagacity, that seems weighted with rich results of
village experience. A great deal of native sense; no bookish cultivation, no
refinement; honest at heart, and thoroughly so, and yet, in some sort, sly—at
least, endowed with a sort of tact and wisdom that are akin to craft, and would
impel him, I think, to take an antagonist in flank, rather than to make a bull-
run at him right in front. But, on the whole, I liked this sallow, queer, sagacious visage, with the homely human sympathies that warmed it; and, for my
small share in the matter, would as lief have Uncle Abe for a ruler as any man
whom it would have been practicable to put in his place.

Immediately on his entrance the President accosted our member of Congress, who had us in charge, and, with a comical twist of his face, made some
jocular remark about the length of his breakfast. He then greeted us all round,
not waiting for an introduction, but shaking and squeezing everybody's hand
with the utmost cordiality, whether the individual's name was announced to
him or not. His manner towards us was wholly without pretence, but yet had
a kind of natural dignity, quite sufficient to keep the forwardest of us from
clapping him on the shoulder and asking for a story. A mutual acquaintance
being established, our leader took the whip out of its case, and began to read
the address of presentation. The whip was an exceedingly long one, its handle
wrought in ivory (by some artist in the Massachusetts State Prison, I believe),
and ornamented with a medallion of the President, and other equally beautiful
devices; and along its whole length there was a succession of golden bands and
ferrules. The address was shorter than the whip, but equally well made, consisting chiefly of an explanatory description of these artistic designs, and clos-

ing with a hint that the gift was a suggestive and emblematic one, and that the President would recognize the use to which such an instrument should be put.

This suggestion gave Uncle Abe rather a delicate task in his reply, because, slight as the matter seemed, it apparently called for some declaration, or intimation, or faint foreshadowing of policy in reference to the conduct of the war, and the final treatment of the Rebels. But the President's Yankee aptness and not-to-be-caughtness stood him in good stead, and he jerked or wiggled himself out of the dilemma with an uncouth dexterity that was entirely in character; although, without his gesticulation of eye and mouth,—and especially the flourish of the whip, with which he imagined himself touching up a pair of fat horses,—I doubt whether his words would be worth recording, even if I could remember them. The gist of the reply was, that he accepted the whip as an emblem of peace, not punishment; and, this great affair over, we retired out of the presence in high good-humor, only regretting that we could not have seen the President sit down and fold up his legs (which is said to be a most extraordinary spectacle), or have heard him tell one of those delectable stories for which he is so celebrated. A good many of them are afloat upon the common talk of Washington, and are certainly the aptest, pithiest, and funniest little things imaginable; though, to be sure, they smack of the frontier freedom, and would not always bear repetition in a drawing-room, or on the immaculate page of the Atlantic.

HENRY WADSWORTH LONGFELLOW
1807–1882

Henry Wadsworth Longfellow was born in Portland, Maine (then still a part of Massachusetts), on February 27, 1807, and died on March 24, 1882, in Cambridge, Massachusetts, the most beloved American poet of his time. His father sent him to Bowdoin, thinking that he would become a lawyer. Instead, Longfellow became so proficient a student of languages that Bowdoin created for him a professorship of modern languages, then one of only a handful in the country. With support from his father, Longfellow studied languages in Europe for three years before taking up his work at Bowdoin in 1829. In Spain, Washington Irving was hospitable, and Longfellow's prose romance *Outre-Mer* (1833–35) was in loving imitation of *The Sketch-Book*. Having concentrated on the Romance languages during his first European stay, Longfellow returned to perfect himself in Germanic languages, a condition for his becoming a professor at Harvard late in 1836. He took teaching seriously, although in the early years he spent most of his time instilling the rudiments of foreign languages (for which he wrote and published his own textbooks) without being able to teach the literatures. Later, at Harvard, he taught an extraordinary range of European literatures of many periods and thereby became an incalculable force in American cultural life. It would be hard, also, to overestimate the importance of his anthology *The Poets and Poetry of Europe* (1845) in bringing home to the ordinary reader the rich variety of European literatures. His own poetry became a means of teaching readers of his day something of the possible range of poetic subject matter and techniques, ancient, medieval, and modern. Irving had been notably successful in domesticating European subject matter while employing a British prose style; now Longfellow domesticated European meters, as in his adaptation of classical Greek meters to tell the story of Evangeline Bellefontaine, set in the recent North American past or in using Finnish folk meter in his celebration of American Indian legends in *Hiawatha*. Longfellow became a great teacher of the masses. If his worst fault is that he made poetry seem so easy to write that anyone could do it, his greatest virtue is that he made poetry seem worth reading and worth writing.

Longfellow married in 1831, during his professorship at Bowdoin, but in 1835, during his second European trip, his wife died after miscarrying. Longfellow stayed on, fulfilling his commitment to Harvard, and before he returned home he had met Fanny Appleton, the Boston heiress who was to become his second wife. She was slow to return his affection, and he embarrassed her by the transparent account of their meeting in the prose romance *Hyperion* (1839), but after their marriage in 1843 their life was idyllic. Longfellow's father-in-law bought the couple, as a wedding gift, Craigie House in Cambridge, a mansion George Washington had used as headquarters and where Longfellow himself had been renting rooms. Their life was elegant. Emerson, who lived amply enough in Concord, was intimidated: "If Socrates were here, we could go and talk with him; but Longfellow we cannot go and talk with; there is a palace, and servants, and a row of bottles of different colored wines, and wine glasses, and fine coats." But the sumptuousness proved supportive and encouraging to Longfellow's poetry and to his work at Harvard until he resigned in 1854. Popular as he was, Longfellow could not make a living from his poetry. In 1855 and 1856, for instance, the phenomenal sales of *Hiawatha* brought his total earnings from poetry to around $3,700 and $7,400, but in the 1840s and 1850s his average annual income from poetry hardly exceeded his Harvard salary of $1,500 ($1,800 after 1845). In 1861 Fanny Longfellow was fatally burned as she was sealing up locks of her daughters' hair. In his grief Longfellow turned to translating the entire *Divine Comedy* of Dante, making the labor the occasion for regular meetings with friends such as James Russell Lowell and the young William Dean Howells, who had lived in Venice. Longfellow's last decades were uneventful, except for one final visit to Europe in 1868–69, during which Queen Victoria gave him a private audience. His seventy-fifth birthday was celebrated nationally. Of his death his brother and official biographer wrote: "The long, busy, blameless life was ended. The loneliness of separation was over. He was dead. But the world was better and happier for his having lived."

A Psalm of Life[1]

> 'Life that shall send
> A challenge to its end,
> And when it comes, say, 'Welcome, friend.'[2]

What the Heart of the Young Man Said to the Psalmist

I

Tell me not, in mournful numbers,[3]
Life is but an empty dream!
For the soul is dead that slumbers,
And things are not what they seem.

---

1. The text is that of the first publication, in the *Knickerbocker or New-York Monthly Magazine* (September 1838). The poem was collected in *Voices of the Night* (1839).
2. Slightly misquoted from *Wishes to His Supposed Mistress* by the English poet Richard Crashaw (c. 1613–1649). Longfellow included the Crashaw poem in a volume he edited, *The Waif: A Collection of Poems* (1845).
3. Meters, rhythms.

II

Life is real—life is earnest—   5
    And the grave is not its goal:
Dust thou art, to dust returnest,
    Was not spoken of the soul.

III

Not enjoyment, and not sorrow,
    Is our destin'd end or way;   10
But to *act*, that each to-morrow
    Find us farther than to-day.

IV

Art is long, and time is fleeting,[4]
    And our hearts, though stout and brave,
Still, like muffled drums, are beating   15
    Funeral marches to the grave.

V

In the world's broad field of battle,
    In the bivouac of Life,
Be not like dumb, driven cattle!
    Be a hero in the strife!   20

VI

Trust no Future, howe'er pleasant!
    Let the dead Past bury its dead!
Act—act in the glorious Present!
    Heart within, and God o'er head!

VII

Lives of great men all remind us   25
    We can make *our* lives sublime,
And, departing, leave behind us
    Footsteps on the sands of time.

VIII

Footsteps, that, perhaps another,
    Sailing o'er life's solemn main,   30
A forlorn and shipwreck'd brother,
    Seeing, shall take heart again.

IX

Let us then be up and doing,
    With a heart for any fate;
Still achieving, still pursuing,   35
    Learn to labor and to wait.

                                                            1838, 1839

Excelsior[1]

The shades of night were falling fast,
As through an Alpine village passed
A youth, who bore, 'mid snow and ice.

---

4. A paraphrase of Seneca's complaint, "*Vita brevis est, ars longa*" (*De Brevitate vitae* 1.1). The meaning of *ars* or *art* is clearer in Chaucer's *The Parliament of Fowls*, line 1: "The lyf so short, the craft so long to lerne."

1. The text is that of the first printing in *Ballads and Other Poems* (1842), actually published late in 1841. The title means "Higher!" or "Upward!" and came from the motto on the shield of the state of New York.

A banner with the strange device[2]
   Excelsior!   5

His brow was sad; his eye beneath,
Flashed like a faulchion[3] from its sheath,
And like a silver clarion rung
The accents of that unknown tongue,
   Excelsior!   10

In happy homes he saw the light
Of household fires gleam warm and bright;
Above, the spectral glaciers shone,
And from his lips escaped a groan,
   Excelsior!   15

"Try not the Pass!" the old man said;
"Dark lowers the tempest overhead,
The roaring torrent is deep and wide!"
And loud that clarion voice replied
   Excelsior!   20

"O stay," the maiden said, "and rest
Thy weary head upon this breast!"
A tear stood in his bright blue eye,
But still he answered, with a sigh,
   Excelsior!   25

"Beware the pine-tree's withered branch!
Beware the awful avalanche!"
This was the peasant's last Good-night,
A voice replied, far up the height,
   Excelsior!   30

At break of day, as heavenward
The pious monks of Saint Bernard
Uttered the oft-repeated prayer,
A voice cried through the startled air
   Excelsior!   35

A traveller, by the faithful hound,[4]
Half-buried in the snow was found,
Still grasping in his hand of ice
That banner with the strange device
   Excelsior!   40

There in the twilight cold and gray,
Lifeless, but beautiful, he lay,
And from the sky, serene and far,
A voice fell, like a falling star,
   Excelsior!   45

1842

---

2. Emblematic design.
3. A broad-bladed, slightly curved sword.
4. I.e., rescue dog (St. Bernard), from the monastery.

Mezzo Cammin[1]

Boppard on the Rhine. August 25, 1842

Half of my life is gone, and I have let
   The years slip from me and have not fulfilled
   The aspiration of my youth, to build
   Some tower of song with lofty parapet.
Not indolence, nor pleasure, nor the fret   5
   Of restless passions that would not be stilled,
   But sorrow, and a care that almost killed,
   Kept me from what I may accomplish yet;
Though, half-way up the hill, I see the Past
   Lying beneath me with its sounds and sights,—   10
   A city in the twilight dim and vast,
With smoking roofs, soft bells, and gleaming lights,—
   And hear above me on the autumnal blast
   The cataract of Death far thundering from the heights.

1842   1886

The Slave's Dream[2]

Beside the ungathered rice he lay,
   His sickle in his hand;
His breast was bare, his matted hair
   Was buried in the sand.
Again, in the mist and shadow of sleep,   5
   He saw his Native Land.

Wide through the landscape of his dreams
   The lordly Niger[3] flowed;
Beneath the palm-trees on the plain
   Once more a king he strode;   10
And heard the tinkling caravans
   Descend the mountain-road.

He saw once more his dark-eyed queen
   Among her children stand;
They clasped his neck, they kissed his cheeks,   15
   They held him by the hand!—
A tear burst from the sleeper's lids
   And fell into the sand.

1. The text is that of the first printing in *Life of Henry Wadsworth Longfellow*, edited by Samuel Longfellow (1886). The sonnet was evidently too personal an assessment for Longfellow to publish it in his lifetime. The title comes from the opening line of Dante's *Inferno: Nel mezzo del cammin di nostra vita*" (Midway in the journey of our life), i.e., thirty-five years old, half the biblical ideal of threescore years and ten, according to Psalm 90.10.
2. From the first printing, in *Poems on Slavery* (1842),

a little volume that marked the high point of Longfellow's public concern over slavery in the United States. Longfellow's contemporaries reacted variously. Whittier thought the poems had been "of important service" to the cause of abolitionism, while a more objective observer found them "perfect dish water" compared with Whittier's own poems against slavery. The majority, North and South, deplored the publication of the poems.
3. Great African river.

And then at furious speed he rode
    Along the Niger's bank;   20
His bridle-reins were golden chains,
    And, with a martial clank,
At each leap he could feel his scabbard of steel
    Smiting his stallion's flank.

Before him, like a blood-red flag,   25
    The bright flamingoes flew;
From morn till night he followed their flight,
    O'er plains where the tamarind grew,
Till he saw the roofs of Caffre[4] huts,
    And the ocean rose to view.   30

At night he heard the lion roar,
    And the hyena scream,
And the river-horse,[5] as he crushed the reeds
    Beside some hidden stream;
And it passed, like a glorious roll of drums,   35
    Through the triumph of his dream.

The forests, with their myriad tongues,
    Shouted of liberty;
And the Blast of the Desert cried aloud,
    With a voice so wild and free,   40
That he started in his sleep and smiled
    At their tempestuous glee.

He did not feel the driver's whip,
    Nor the burning heat of day;
For Death had illumined the Land of Sleep,   45
    And his lifeless body lay
A worn-out fetter, that the soul
    Had broken and thrown away!

                                        1842

The Fire of Drift-wood[1]

We sat within the farm-house old,
    Whose windows, looking o'er the bay,
Gave to the sea-breeze, damp and cold,
    An easy entrance, night and day.

Not far away we saw the port,—   5
    The strange, old-fashioned, silent town,—

---

4. Kaffir, used here to mean non-Mohammedan Africans.
5. Hippopotamus.
1. The text is that of the first printing, in *The Seaside* and the Fireside (1849). The poem was inspired by a day the Longfellows spent in September 1846 at Devereaux Farm, near Marblehead, a town on the Atlantic near Salem, Massachusetts.

The light-house,—the dismantled fort,—
  The wooden houses, quaint and brown.

We sat and talked until the night,
  Descending, filled the little room;   10
Our faces faded from the sight,
  Our voices only broke the gloom.

We spake of many a vanished scene,
  Of what we once had thought and said,
Of what had been, and might have been,   15
  And who was changed, and who was dead;

And all that fills the hearts of friends,
  When first they feel, with secret pain,
Their lives thenceforth have separate ends,
  And never can be one again;   20

The first slight swerving of the heart,
  That words are powerless to express,
And leave it still unsaid in part,
  Or say it in too great excess.

The very tones in which we spake   25
  Had something strange, I could but mark;
The leaves of memory seemed to make
  A mournful rustling in the dark.

Oft died the words upon our lips,
  As suddenly, from out the fire   30
Built of the wreck of stranded ships,
  The flames would leap and then expire.

And, as their splendor flashed and failed,
  We thought of wrecks upon the main,—
Of ships dismasted, that were hailed   35
  And sent no answer back again.

The windows, rattling in their frames,—
  The ocean, roaring up the beach,—
The gusty blast,—the bickering flames,—
  All mingled vaguely in our speech;   40

Until they made themselves a part
  Of fancies floating through the brain,—
The long-lost ventures of the heart,
  That send no answers back again.

O flames that glowed! O hearts that yearned!   45
  They were indeed too much akin,
The drift-wood fire without that burned,
  The thoughts that burned and glowed within.

                                                         1849

From The Building of the Ship[1]

[*Conclusion*]

Then the master,   340
With a gesture of command,
Waved his hand;
And at the word,
Loud and sudden there was heard,
All around them and below,   345
The sound of hammers, blow on blow,
Knocking away the shores and spurs.
And see! she stirs!
She starts,—she moves,—she seems to feel
The thrill of life along her keel,   350
And, spurning with her foot the ground,
With one exulting, joyous bound,
She leaps into the ocean's arms!

And lo! from the assembled crowd
There rose a shout, prolonged and loud,   355
That to the ocean seemed to say,—
"Take her, O bridegroom, old and gray,
Take her to thy protecting arms,
With all her youth and all her charms!"

How beautiful she is! How fair   360
She lies within those arms, that press
Her form with many a soft caress
Of tenderness and watchful care!
Sail forth into the sea, O ship!
Through wind and wave, right onward steer!   365
The moistened eye, the trembling lip,
Are not the signs of doubt or fear.

Sail forth into the sea of life,
O gentle, loving, trusting wife,
And safe from all adversity   370
Upon the bosom of that sea
Thy comings and thy goings be!
For gentleness and love and trust
Prevail o'er angry wave and gust;
And in the wreck of noble lives   375
Something immortal still survives!

Thou, too, sail on, O Ship of State!
Sail on O UNION, strong and great!
Humanity with all its fears,
With all the hopes of future years,   380

1. From the first printing in *The Seaside and the Fire-side* (1850), which appeared late in 1849. The part of the poem reprinted here had especially great patriotic significance for most of the early readers, because the majority of Americans hoped that the measures then being debated (and adopted as the Compromise of 1850) would reduce the fierce sectional antagonisms threatening to destroy the country. The poem outraged some abolitionists, including William Lloyd Garrison, who denounced it in his *Liberator* as a sellout.

Is hanging breathless on thy fate!
We know what Master laid thy keel,
What Workmen wrought thy ribs of steel,
Who made each mast, and sail, and rope,
What anvils rang, what hammers beat,   385
In what a forge and what a heat
Were shaped the anchors of thy hope!
Fear not each sudden sound and shock,
'T is of the wave and not the rock;
'T is but the flapping of the sail,   390
And not a rent made by the gale!
In spite of rock and tempest roar,
In spite of false lights on the shore,
Sail on, nor fear to breast the sea!
Our hearts, our hopes, are all with thee,   395
Our hearts, our hopes, our prayers, our
tears,
Our faith triumphant o'er our fears,
Are all with thee,—are all with thee!

                                                               1850

My Lost Youth[1]

Often I think of the beautiful town
    That is seated by the sea;
Often in thought go up and down
The pleasant streets of that dear old town,
    And my youth comes back to me.   5
        And a verse of a Lapland song
        Is haunting my memory still:
    "A boy's will is the wind's will,
And the thoughts of youth are long, long thoughts."

I can see the shadowy lines of its trees,   10
    And catch, in sudden gleams,
The sheen of the far-surrounding seas,
And islands that were the Hesperides[2]
    Of all my boyish dreams.
        And the burden of that old song,   15
        It murmurs and whispers still:
    "A boy's will is the wind's will,
And the thoughts of youth are long, long thoughts."

I remember the black wharves and the slips,
    And the sea-tides tossing free;   20

---

1. Longfellow wrote this poem about his hometown of
Portland, Maine, in March 1855, at Cambridge, deriving the refrain from lines in John Scheffer's *The History
of Lapland* (1674): "A Youth's desire is the desire of the
wind, / All his essaies / Are long delaies, / No issue can
they find." ("Essaies," or essays, means attempts and
"issue" means outlet.) The text is that of the first printing in *Putnam's Monthly Magazine,* vol. 6 (August
1855). It was reprinted in *The Courtship of Miles
Standish and Other Poems* (1858).
2. In Greek mythology, fabled islands where the
golden apples grew.

And Spanish sailors with bearded lips,
And the beauty and mystery of the ships,
   And the magic of the sea.
     And the voice of that wayward song
     Is singing and saying still: 25
"A boy's will is the wind's will,
And the thoughts of youth are long, long thoughts."

I remember the bulwarks by the shore,
   And the fort upon the hill;
The sun-rise gun, with its hollow roar,   30
The drum-beat repeated o'er and o'er,
   And the bugle wild and shrill.
     And the music of that old song
     Throbs in my memory still:
"A boy's will is the wind's will,   35
And the thoughts of youth are long, long thoughts."

I remember the sea-fight far away,
   How it thundered o'er the tide![3]
And the dead captains, as they lay
In their graves, o'erlooking the tranquil bay,   40
   Where they in battle died.
     And the sound of that mournful song
     Goes through me with a thrill:
"A boy's will is the wind's will,
And the thoughts of youth are long, long thoughts."   45

I can see the breezy dome of groves,
   The shadows of Deering's Woods;
And the friendships old and the early loves
Come back with a Sabbath sound, as of doves
   In quiet neighborhoods.   50
     And the verse of that sweet old song,
     It flutters and murmurs still:
"A boy's will is the wind's will,
And the thoughts of youth are long, long thoughts."

I remember the gleams and glooms that dart   55
   Across the schoolboy's brain;
The song and the silence in the heart,
That in part are prophecies, and in part
   Are longings wild and vain.
     And the voice of that fitful song   60
     Sings on, and is never still:
"A boy's will is the wind's will,
And the thoughts of youth are long, long thoughts."

There are things of which I may not speak;
   There are dreams that cannot die;   65

---

3. The American *Enterprise* and the British *Boxer* fought near Portland in 1813. Both captains were killed and carried ashore for burial.

There are thoughts that make the strong heart weak,
And bring a pallor into the cheek,
   And a mist before the eye.
     And the words of that fatal song
     Come over me like a chill: 70
"A boy's will is the wind's will,
And the thoughts of youth are long, long thoughts."

Strange to me now are the forms I meet
   When I visit the dear old town;
But the native air is pure and sweet,   75
And the trees that o'ershadow each well-known street,
   As they balance up and down,
     Are singing the beautiful song,
     Are sighing and whispering still:
"A boy's will is the wind's will,   80
And the thoughts of youth are long, long thoughts."

And Deering's Woods are fresh and fair,
   And with joy that is almost pain
My heart goes back to wander there,
And among the dreams of the days that were,   85
   I find my lost youth again.
     And the strange and beautiful song,
     The groves are repeating it still:
"A boy's will is the wind's will,
And the thoughts of youth are long, long thoughts."   90

1855   1855

Aftermath[1]

When the Summer fields are mown,
When the birds are fledged and flown,
   And the dry leaves strew the path;
With the falling of the snow,
With the cawing of the crow,   5
Once again the fields we mow
   And gather in the aftermath.

Not the sweet, new grass with flowers
Is this harvesting of ours;
   Not the upland clover bloom;   10
But the rowen[2] mixed with weeds,
Tangled tufts from marsh and meads,
Where the poppy drops its seeds
   In the silence and the gloom.

1873

---

1. The text is that of the first printing in *Aftermath* (1873). Longfellow is playing on the different meanings of *aftermath*, the common figurative meaning of "consequences" and the literal meaning of "second mowing," a late cutting of hay from grasses that have grown back after the main harvesting.
2. A synonym of *aftermath*, meaning grasses in the second mowing.

JOHN GREENLEAF WHITTIER
1807–1892

John Greenleaf Whittier was born on December 17, 1807, on a farm near Haverhill, Massachusetts, of a Quaker family. No longer persecuted in New England, Quakers were still a people apart, and Whittier grew up with a sense of being different from most of his neighbors. Labor on the debt-ridden farm overstrained his health in adolescence, and thereafter throughout his long life he suffered from intermittent physical collapses. At fourteen, having had only meager education in a household suspicious of non-Quaker literature, he found in the Scottish poet Robert Burns a model for imitation, one using a regional dialect, dealing with homely subjects, and displaying a strong social conscience. His first poem was published in 1826 in a local newspaper run by another young man, William Lloyd Garrison, whose dedication to the antislavery movement was to affect Whittier's life profoundly. In 1827 Garrison helped persuade Whittier's father that the young poet deserved more education, and Whittier supported himself through two terms at Haverhill Academy. During this time and later Whittier was near serious courtships, but like many of his relatives, he never married; among the obstacles were his Quakerism, his poverty, and his commitment to abolitionism. In 1836, six years after his father's death, Whittier and his mother and sisters moved from the farm to the house in nearby Amesbury, Massachusetts, which he owned until his death.

In his twenties Whittier became editor of various newspapers, some of regional importance. He was elected for a term to the Massachusetts legislature (1835) and became a behind-the-scenes force in the Whig party and, later, in the antislavery Liberty party, which he helped to found in 1839. The turning point in his career came in 1833 with the publication of his abolitionist manifesto *Justice and Expediency*, in which Whittier concluded that there was only one practicable and just scheme of emancipation: "Immediate abolition of slavery; an immediate acknowledgment of the great truth, that man cannot hold property in man; an immediate surrender of baneful prejudice to Christian love; an immediate practical obedience to the command of Jesus Christ: 'Whatsoever ye would that men should do unto you, do ye even so to them.' " Over the next three decades Whittier paid for his principles in many ways, some subtle, some as overt as being mobbed and stoned in 1835. The climactic danger came in 1838 when Whittier, in disguise, joined a mob to save some of his papers as his office was ransacked and burned.

From the 1830s through the 1850s Whittier was a working editor associated with abolitionist papers, becoming the sort of man he was to describe in *The Tent on the Beach* (1867): A "dreamer born, / Who, with a mission to fulfil, / Had left the Muses' haunts to turn / The crank of an opinion-mill, / Making his rustic reed of song / A weapon in the war with wrong." Yet he continued to write about his own region, one legacy from his family being a rich oral history. His first book, *Legends of New England* (1831), had included stories in both prose and poetry. His first book of poetry was *Lays of My Home* (1843), and the prose *Supernaturalism of New England* followed in 1847. *Leaves from Margaret Smith's Journal* (1849) is a fictional re-creation of colonial life in the form of the diary of a young woman. Through his fictional and historical prose and through his poetry Whittier was setting a very early example of faithful treatment of American village and rural life that later local colorists and regionalists were to follow: the elderly Whittier's paternal interest in the career of Sarah Orne Jewett epitomizes this influence. But from the beginning a crucial problem for Whittier had been how to be true to the occasional beauty of rural life without portraying it in the sentimental manner that prevailed at the time. Whittier succeeded best in some late poems, especially *Snow-Bound* (1866) and the Prelude to *Among the Hills* (1868). Whittier's reputation began undergoing a change in the late 1850s, when abolitionism had ceased to be almost as much abhorred in the North as in the South; partly the new favor he received was a result of the founding in 1857 of the *Atlantic Monthly*, which was always hospitable to his poems, humorous folk legends as well as militant odes. *Snow-Bound* brought Whittier extraordinary acclaim and immediate financial security; although one of the themes of the poem was his sense of his own approaching death, Whittier ironically lived another quarter century, during which he was revered as a great American poet. He died on September 7, 1892.

Ichabod![1]

So fallen! so lost! the light withdrawn
    Which once he wore!
The glory from his gray hairs gone
    Forevermore!

Revile him not—the Tempter hath   5
    A snare for all;
And pitying tears, not scorn and wrath,
    Befit his fall!

Oh! dumb be passion's stormy rage,
    When he who might   10
Have lighted up and led his age,
    Falls back in night.

Scorn! would the angels laugh, to mark
    A bright soul driven,
Fiend-goaded, down the endless dark,   15
    From hope and heaven!

Let not the land, once proud of him,
    Insult him now,
Nor brand with deeper shame his dim,
    Dishonored brow.   20

But let its humbled sons, instead,
    From sea to lake,
A long lament, as for the dead,
    In sadness make.

Of all we loved and honored, nought   25
    Save power remains—
A fallen angel's pride of thought,
    Still strong in chains.

1. *Ichabod!* is an attack on the statesman Daniel Webster, whose championing of the Fugitive Slave Bill (the part of the Compromise of 1850 which provided that Northern states must return runaway slaves caught within their borders) made him anathema to the abolitionists. The title is from 1 Samuel 4.21: "And she named the child Ichabod, saying, The glory is departed from Israel." The text is that of the first printing in *Songs of Labor, and Other Poems* (1850).

All else is gone; from those great eyes
    The soul has fled:
When faith is lost, when honor dies,   30
    The man is dead!

Then, pay the reverence of old days
    To his dead fame;
Walk backward, with averted gaze,   35
    And hide the shame![2]

                                    1850

Snow-Bound: A Winter Idyl[1]

To the memory of the household it describes, this poem is dedicated by the author

The inmates of the family at the Whittier homestead who are referred to in the poem were my father, mother, my brother and two sisters, and my uncle and aunt both unmarried. In addition, there was the district school-master who boarded with us. The "not unfeared, half-welcome guest" was Harriet Livermore, daughter of Judge Livermore, of New Hampshire, a young woman of fine natural ability, enthusiastic, eccentric, with slight control over her violent temper, which sometimes made her religious profession doubtful. She was equally ready to exhort in school-house prayer-meetings and dance in a Washington ball-room, while her father was a member of Congress. She early embraced the doctrine of the Second Advent,[2] and felt it her duty to proclaim the Lord's speedy coming. With this message she crossed the Atlantic and spent the greater part of a long life in travelling over Europe and Asia. She lived some time with Lady Hester Stanhope,[3] a woman as fantastic and mentally strained as herself, on the slope of Mt. Lebanon, but finally quarrelled with her in regard to two white horses with red marks on their backs which suggested the idea of saddles, on which her titled hostess expected to ride into Jerusalem with the Lord. A friend of mine found her, when quite an old woman, wandering in Syria with a tribe of Arabs, who with the Oriental notion that madness is inspiration, accepted her as their prophetess and leader. At the time referred to in *Snow-Bound* she was boarding at the Rocks Village about two miles from us.

In my boyhood, in our lonely farm-house, we had scanty sources of information; few books and only a small weekly newspaper. Our only annual was the Almanac. Under such circumstances story-telling was a necessary resource in the long winter evenings. My father when a young man had traversed the wilderness to Canada, and could tell us of his adventures with Indians and

---

2. By this allusion to Genesis 9.20–25 Whittier equates Webster's shame to that of Noah after the Flood, who in drunkenness sprawled naked in his cave.
1. This poem was begun in 1864 and completed in October 1865. The text followed here is that of the 1st edition (1866), although the prefatory note on the "'inmates of the family" is taken from its first printing in the 1892 (published 1891) edition of *Snow-Bound*.
2. Second Coming. During the early 19th century many individual Christians as well as certain Christian

sects believed that Jesus would return to earth in their lifetimes.
3. Notable English eccentric (1776–1839), led a brilliant life in London as companion of her uncle William Pitt the Younger before his death in 1806. In 1810 she settled in Lebanon, where she became despot over a small area (using a mace to punish her many local retainers). She held court to famous travelers who sought her out and indulged her beliefs in transmigration of the soul and astrology.

wild beasts, and of his sojourn in the French villages. My uncle was ready with his record of hunting and fishing and, it must be confessed, with stories which he at least half believed, of witchcraft and apparitions. My mother, who was born in the Indian-haunted region of Somersworth, New Hampshire, between Dover and Portsmouth, told us of the inroads of the savages, and the narrow escape of her ancestors. She described strange people who lived on the Piscataqua and Cocheco,[4] among whom was Bantam the sorcerer. I have in my possession the wizard's "conjuring book," which he solemnly opened when consulted. It is a copy of Cornelius Agrippa's *Magic* printed in 1651, dedicated to Dr. Robert Child, who, like Michael Scott,[5] had learned

"the art of glammorie
In Padua beyond the sea,"[6]

and who is famous in the annals of Massachusetts, where he was at one time a resident, as the first man who dared petition the General Court for liberty of conscience. The full title of the book is *Three Books of Occult Philosophy, by Henry Cornelius Agrippa, Knight, Doctor of both Laws, Counsellor to Cæsar's Sacred Majesty and Judge of the Prerogative Court.*

> "As the Spirits of Darkness be stronger in the dark, so Good Spirits which be Angels of Light are augmented not only by the Divine light of the Sun, but also by our common Wood Fire: and as the celestial Fire drives away dark spirits, so also this our Fire of Wood doth the same."
> —Cor. Agrippa, *Occult Philosophy*, Book I. chap. v.

> "Announced by all the trumpets of the sky,
> Arrives the snow; and, driving o'er the fields,
> Seems nowhere to alight; the whited air
> Hides hills and woods, the river and the heaven,
> And veils the farm-house at the garden's end.
> The sled and traveller stopped, the courier's feet
> Delayed, all friends shut out, the housemates sit
> Around the radiant fireplace, enclosed
> In a tumultuous privacy of storm."
> —Emerson[7]

The sun that brief December day
Rose cheerless over hills of gray,
And, darkly circled, gave at noon
A sadder light than waning moon.
Slow tracing down the thickening sky   5
Its mute and ominous prophecy,
A portent seeming less than threat,
It sank from sight before it set.

---

4. The Cocheco River flows through Dover, New Hampshire, then joins the Piscataqua and flows by Portsmouth, New Hampshire, into the Atlantic.
5. A Scottish scholar and linguist (1175–1234), court astrologer to Frederick II of Germany. Legend transformed him into a magician as well as an astrologer. Agrippa (1486–1535) was a German physician and student of the occult. Child was an Englishman (called "doctor" because he had studied physic in Padua). He moved to Massachusetts and in 1646 petitioned the general court that the colony was failing to acknowledge the supremacy of the laws of England when it denied civil and religious rights to members of

churches not recognized as orthodox. He and a few allies signed a petition to the commissioners of plantations in London, but the Massachusetts authorities searched Child's baggage, seized the petition, and fined him and his friends severely. Child tried to get redress in England, but the dictator, Oliver Cromwell, was staunchly in favor of the Puritans.
6. Whittier is adapting Sir Walter Scott's *The Lay of the Last Minstrel*, I.11: "He learned the art, that none may name, / In Padua, far beyond the sea." (The lines are not about Michael Scott.) "Glammorie": magic. Padua was thought of as a seat of necromancy.
7. The opening of Emerson's *The Snow-Storm*.

A chill no coat, however stout,
Of homespun stuff could quite shut out,   10
A hard, dull bitterness of cold,
 That checked, mid-vein, the circling race
 Of life-blood in the sharpened face,
The coming of the snow-storm told.

The wind blew east:[8] we heard the roar   15
Of Ocean on his wintry shore,
And felt the strong pulse throbbing there
Beat with low rhythm our inland air.

Meanwhile we did our nightly chores,—
Brought in the wood from out of doors,   20
Littered the stalls, and from the mows
Raked down the herd's-grass for the cows;
Heard the horse whinnying for his corn;
And, sharply clashing horn on horn,
Impatient down the stanchion rows   25
The cattle shake their walnut bows;[9]
While, peering from his early perch
Upon the scaffold's pole of birch,
The cock his crested helmet bent
And down his querulous challenge sent.   30

Unwarmed by any sunset light
The gray day darkened into night,
A night made hoary with the swarm
And whirl-dance of the blinding storm,
As zigzag wavering to and fro   35
Crossed and recrossed the wingéd snow:
And ere the early bed-time came
The white drift piled the window-frame,
And through the glass the clothes-line posts
Looked in like tall and sheeted ghosts.   40

So all night long the storm roared on:
The morning broke without a sun;
In tiny spherule traced with lines
Of Nature's geometric signs,
In starry flake, and pellicle,[1]   45
All day the hoary meteor fell;
And, when the second morning shone,
We looked upon a world unknown,
On nothing we could call our own.
Around the glistening wonder bent   50
The blue walls of the firmament,

---

8. From the east, bringing the sound of the Atlantic.
9. Stanchions (here made of walnut and shaped like a bow) are adjustable braces set a few inches from stationary posts; they are pulled aside at the top to let a cow's head pass, then fixed against the neck so the cow cannot back out while being milked or fed.

1. In a letter to his publisher, James T. Fields, during the preparation of the poem, Whittier revised this passage slightly and explained one revision: "The word 'pellicle'—a thin film or crust or crystallization—exactly expresses the thing."

No cloud above, no earth below,—
A universe of sky and snow!
The old familiar sights of ours
Took marvellous shapes; strange domes and towers   55
Rose up where sty or corn-crib stood,
Or garden wall, or belt of wood;
A smooth white mound the brush-pile showed,
A fenceless drift what once was road;
The bridle-post an old man sat   60
With loose-flung coat and high cocked hat;
The well-curb had a Chinese roof;
And even the long sweep,[2] high aloof,
In its slant splendor, seemed to tell
Of Pisa's leaning miracle.   65

A prompt, decisive man, no breath
Our father wasted: "Boys, a path!"
Well pleased, (for when did farmer boy
Count such a summons less than joy?)
Our buskins[3] on our feet we drew;   70
    With mittened hands, and caps drawn low,
    To guard our necks and ears from snow,
We cut the solid whiteness through.
And, where the drift was deepest, made
A tunnel walled and overlaid   75
With dazzling crystal: we had read
Of rare Aladdin's wondrous cave,
And to our own his name we gave,
With many a wish the luck were ours
To test his lamp's supernal powers.   80
We reached the barn with merry din,
And roused the prisoned brutes within.
The old horse thrust his long head out,
And grave with wonder gazed about;
The cock his lusty greeting said,   85
And forth his speckled harem led;
The oxen lashed their tails, and hooked,
And mild reproach of hunger looked;
The hornéd patriarch of the sheep,
Like Egypt's Amun[4] roused from sleep,   90
Shook his sage head with gesture mute,
And emphasized with stamp of foot.

All day the gusty north-wind bore
The loosening drift its breath before;
Low circling round its southern zone,   95
The sun through dazzling snow-mist shone.
No bell the hush of silence broke,
No neighboring chimney's social smoke
Curled over woods of snow-hung oak.

2. I.e., a well sweep; a pole attached to a pivot, with a   3. Here, high-cut shoes, like a half boot.
bucket at one end for raising water.   4. Egyptian god with a ram's head.

A solitude made more intense   100
By dreary voicéd elements,
The shrieking of the mindless wind,
The moaning tree-boughs swaying blind,
And on the glass the unmeaning beat
Of ghostly finger-tips of sleet.   105
Beyond the circle of our hearth
No welcome sound of toil or mirth
Unbound the spell, and testified
Of human life and thought outside.
We minded that the sharpest ear   110
The buried brooklet could not hear,
The music of whose liquid lip
Had been to us companionship,
And, in our lonely life, had grown
To have an almost human tone.   115

As night drew on, and, from the crest
Of wooded knolls that ridged the west,
The sun, a snow-blown traveller, sank
From sight beneath the smothering bank,
We piled, with care, our nightly stack   120
Of wood against the chimney-back,—
The oaken log, green, huge, and thick,
And on its top the stout back-stick;
The knotty forestick laid apart,
And filled between with curious art   125
The ragged brush; then, hovering near,
We watched the first red blaze appear,
Heard the sharp crackle, caught the gleam
On whitewashed wall and sagging beam,
Until the old, rude-furnished room   130
Burst, flower-like, into rosy bloom;
While radiant with a mimic flame
Outside the sparkling drift became,
And through the bare-boughed lilac-tree
Our own warm hearth seemed blazing free.   135
The crane and pendent trammels showed,
The Turks' heads[5] on the andirons glowed;
While childish fancy, prompt to tell
The meaning of the miracle,
Whispered the old rhyme: "*Under the tree,*   140
When fire outdoors burns merrily,
There the witches are making tea."

The moon above the eastern wood
Shone at its full; the hill-range stood
Transfigured in the silver flood,   145
Its blown snows flashing cold and keen,
Dead white, save where some sharp ravine

---

5. A favorite ornamentation, turbanlike knots in wrought iron. "Trammels": pot hooks hanging from the crane, or movable arm.

Took shadow, or the sombre green
Of hemlocks turned to pitchy black
Against the whiteness at their back.   150
For such a world and such a night
Most fitting that unwarming light,
Which only seemed where'er it fell
To make the coldness visible.

Shut in from all the world without,   155
We sat the clean-winged hearth about.
Content to let the north-wind roar
In baffled rage at pane and door,
While the red logs before us beat
The frost-line back with tropic heat;   160
And ever, when a louder blast
Shook beam and rafter as it passed,
The merrier up its roaring draught
The great throat of the chimney laughed.
The house-dog on his paws outspread   165
Laid to the fire his drowsy head,
The cat's dark silhouette on the wall
A couchant[6] tiger's seemed to fall;
And, for the winter fireside meet,
Between the andirons' straddling feet,   170
The mug of cider simmered slow,
The apples sputtered in a row,
And, close at hand, the basket stood
With nuts from brown October's wood.

What matter how the night behaved?   175
What matter how the north-wind raved?
Blow high, blow low, not all its snow
Could quench our hearth-fire's ruddy glow.
O Time and Change!—with hair as gray
As was my sire's that winter day,   180
How strange it seems, with so much gone
Of life and love, to still live on!
Ah, brother! only I and thou
Are left of all that circle now,—
The dear home faces whereupon   185
That fitful firelight paled and shone.
Henceforward, listen as we will,
The voices of that hearth are still;
Look where we may, the wide earth o'er,
Those lighted faces smile no more.   190
We tread the paths their feet have worn,
    We sit beneath their orchard-trees,
    We hear, like them, the hum of bees
And rustle of the bladed corn;
We turn the pages that they read,   195
    Their written words we linger o'er,

6. Term from heraldry: lying down with the head raised.

But in the sun they cast no shade,
No voice is heard, no sign is made,
  No step is on the conscious floor!
Yet Love will dream, and Faith will trust,   200
(Since He who knows our need is just,)
That somehow, somewhere, meet we must.
Alas for him who never sees
The stars shine through his cypress-trees!
Who, hopeless, lays his dead away,   205
Nor looks to see the breaking day
Across the mournful marbles[7] play!
Who hath not learned, in hours of faith,
  The truth to flesh and sense unknown,
That Life is ever lord of Death,   210
  And Love can never lose its own!

We sped the time with stories old,
Wrought puzzles out, and riddles told,
Or stammered from our school-book lore
"The Chief of Gambia's golden shore."[8]   215
How often since, when all the land
Was clay in Slavery's shaping hand,
As if a trumpet called, I've heard
Dame Mercy Warren's rousing word:
"Does not the voice of reason cry,   220
  Claim the first right which Nature gave,
From the red scourge of bondage fly,
  Nor deign to live a burdened slave!"
Our father rode again his ride
On Memphremagog's wooded side;   225
Sat down again to moose and samp[9]
In trapper's hut and Indian camp;
Lived o'er the old idyllic ease
Beneath St. François'[1] hemlock-trees;
Again for him the moonlight shone   230
On Norman cap and bodiced zone;[2]
Again he heard the violin play
Which led the village dance away,
And mingled in its merry whirl
The grandam and the laughing girl.   235
Or, nearer home, our steps he led
Where Salisbury's[3] level marshes spread
  Mile-wide as flies the laden bee;
Where merry mowers, hale and strong,

---

7. I.e., the gravestones.
8. From *The African Chief*, a widely reprinted early antislavery poem by the Bostonian Sarah Wentworth Morton (1759–1846). In lines 220–3 Whittier quotes the poem but misremembers the author as Mercy Otis Warren (1728–1814), Massachusetts historian, author of a three-volume *History of * * * the American Revolution* (1805).

9. Cornmeal mush. Memphremagog is a lake between Vermont and Quebec.
1. North of Lake Memphremagog.
2. Whittier's father is recalling the dress of women in French-Canadian settlements, the cap like those worn by women in Normandy and bodices that emphasized the waist.
3. Nearby town in northeastern Massachusetts.

Swept, scythe on scythe, their swaths along 240
    The low green prairies of the sea.
We shared the fishing off Boar's Head,
    And round the rocky Isles of Shoals[4]
    The hake-broil on the drift-wood coals;
The chowder on the sand-beach made, 245
Dipped by the hungry, steaming hot,
With spoons of clam-shell from the pot.
We heard the tales of witchcraft old,
And dream and sign and marvel told
To sleepy listeners as they lay 250
Stretched idly on the salted hay,
Adrift along the winding shores,
When favoring breezes deigned to blow
The square sail of the gundalow[5]
And idle lay the useless oars. 255

Our mother, while she turned her wheel
Or run the new-knit stocking-heel,
Told how the Indian hordes came down
At midnight on Cochecho[6] town,
And how her own great-uncle bore 260
His cruel scalp-mark to fourscore.
Recalling, in her fitting phrase,
    So rich and picturesque and free,
    (The common unrhymed poetry
Of simple life and country ways,) 265
The story of her early days,—
She made for us the sunset shine
Aslant the tall columnar pine;
The river at her father's door
Its rippled moanings whispered o'er; 270
We heard the hawks at twilight play,
The boat-horn on Piscataqua,[7]
The loon's weird laughter far away.
So well she gleaned from earth and sky
That harvest of the ear and eye, 275
We almost felt the gusty air
That swept her native wood-paths bare,
Heard the far thresher's rhythmic flail,
The flapping of the fisher's sail,
Or saw, in sheltered cove and bay, 280
The ducks' black squadron anchored lay,
Or heard the wild geese calling loud
Beneath the gray November cloud.

Then, haply, with a look more grave,
And soberer tone, some tale she gave 285

---

4. Off the New Hampshire coast.
5. Flat-bottomed boat.
6. Settlement near Dover, New Hampshire, on the

Cocheco River.
7. I.e., foghorn on the Piscataqua River.

From painful Sewell's[8] ancient tome,
Beloved in every Quaker home,
Of faith fire-winged by martyrdom,
Or Chalkley's Journal, old and quaint,—
Gentlest of skippers, rare sea-saint!—   290
Who, when the dreary calms prevailed,
And water-butt and bread-cask failed,
And cruel, hungry eyes pursued
His portly presence mad for food,
With dark hints muttered under breath   295
Of casting lots for life or death,
Offered, if Heaven withheld supplies,
To be himself the sacrifice.
Then, suddenly, as if to save
The good man from his living grave,   300
A ripple on the water grew,
A school of porpoise flashed in view.[9]
"Take, eat," he said, "and be content;[1]
These fishes in my stead are sent
By Him who gave the tangled ram   305
To spare the child of Abraham."[2]
Our uncle, innocent of books,
But rich in lore of fields and brooks,
The ancient teachers never dumb
Of Nature's unhoused lyceum,[3]   310
In moons and tides and weather wise,
He read the clouds as prophecies,
And foul or fair could well divine,
By many an occult hint and sign,
Holding the cunning-warded keys[4]   315
To all the woodcraft mysteries;
Himself to Nature's heart so near
That all her voices in his ear
Of beast or bird had meanings clear,
Like Apollonius of old,   320
Who knew the tales the sparrows told,

8. William Sewell or Sewel (1650–1725), author of a history of the Quakers published in the year of his death; Whittier had an American edition of 1823. The history made painful reading because of the severe persecution and outright martyrdoms many Quakers had suffered; see Hawthorne's *The Gentle Boy*.
9. The *Journal* of Thomas Chalkley (1675–1741) was published in 1747. The passage referred to runs: "To stop their murmuring, I told them they should not need to cast lots, which was usual in such cases, which of us should die first, for I would freely offer up my life to do them good. One said, 'God bless you! I will not eat any of you.' Another said, 'He would die before he would eat any of me;' and so said several. I can truly say, on that occasion, at that time, my life was not dear to me, and that I was serious and ingenuous in my proposition: and as I was leaning over the side of the vessel, thoughtfully considering my proposal to the company, and looking in my mind to Him that made me, a very large dolphin came up towards the top or surface of the water, and looked me in the face; and I called the people to put a hook into the sea, and take him, for here is one come to redeem me (I said to them). And they put a hook into the sea, and the fish readily took it, and they caught him. He was longer than myself. I think he was about six feet long, and the largest that ever I saw. This plainly showed us that we ought not to distrust the providence of the Almighty. The people were quieted by this act of Providence, and murmured no more. We caught enough to eat plentifully of, till we got into the capes of Delaware."
1. Matthew 26.26: "Take, eat: this is my body" (Jesus' words at Passover).
2. The story of Abraham's willingness to obey God even if it meant sacrificing his son Isaac is in Genesis 22.13.
3. Lecture hall.
4. Carefully guarded (i.e., guarded by Nature from superficial observers).

Or Hermes,[5] who interpreted
What the sage cranes of Nilus[6] said;
A simple, guileless, childlike man,
Content to live where life began;   325
Strong only on his native grounds,
The little world of sights and sounds
Whose girdle was the parish bounds,
Whereof his fondly partial pride
The common features magnified,   330
As Surrey hills to mountains grew
In White of Selborne's[7] loving view,—
He told how teal and loon he shot,
And how the eagle's eggs he got,
The feats on pond and river done,   335
The prodigies of rod and gun;
Till, warming with the tales he told,
Forgotten was the outside cold,
The bitter wind unheeded blew,
From ripening corn the pigeons flew,   340
The partridge drummed i' the wood, the mink
Went fishing down the river-brink.
In fields with bean or clover gay,
The woodchuck, like a hermit gray,
Peered from the doorway of his cell;   345
The muskrat plied the mason's trade,
And tier by tier his mud-walls laid;
And from the shagbark overhead
The grizzled squirrel dropped his shell.

Next, the dear aunt, whose smile of cheer   350
And voice in dreams I see and hear,—
The sweetest woman ever Fate
Perverse denied a household mate,
Who, lonely, homeless, not the less
Found peace in love's unselfishness,   355
And welcome wheresoe'er she went,
A calm and gracious element,
Whose presence seemed the sweet income
And womanly atmosphere of home,—
Called up her girlhood memories,   360
The huskings and the apple-bees,
The sleigh-rides and the summer sails,
Weaving through all the poor details
And homespun warp of circumstance
A golden woof-thread of romance.   365
For well she kept her genial mood
And simple faith of maidenhood;
Before her still a cloud-land lay,

5. Hermes Trismegistus (3rd century A.D.), legendary author of Egyptian books of magic. Apollonius (1st century A.D.), Greek mytstic.
6. Nile River.
7. Gilbert White (1720–1793), English naturalist who lived in the county of Surrey, in southern England, and wrote *The Natural History and Antiquities of Selborne* (1789), a book to which Thoreau's reviewers often compared *Walden*.

The mirage loomed across her way;
The morning dew, that dries so soon   370
With others, glistened at her noon;
Through years of toil and soil and care
From glossy tress to thin gray hair,
All unprofaned she held apart
The virgin fancies of the heart.   375
Be shame to him of woman born
Who hath for such but thought of scorn.
There, too, our elder sister plied
Her evening task the stand beside;
A full, rich nature, free to trust,   380
Truthful and almost sternly just,
Impulsive, earnest, prompt to act,
And make her generous thought a fact,
Keeping with many a light disguise
The secret of self-sacrifice.   385
O heart sore-tried! thou hast the best
That Heaven itself could give thee,—rest,—
Rest from all bitter thoughts and things!
    How many a poor one's blessing went
    With thee beneath the low green tent   390
Whose curtain never outward swings!

As one who held herself a part
Of all she saw, and let her heart
    Against the household bosom lean,
Upon the motley-braided mat   395
Our youngest and our dearest sat,
Lifting her large, sweet, asking eyes,
    Now bathed within the fadeless green
And holy peace of Paradise.
O, looking from some heavenly hill,   400
    Or from the shade of saintly palms,
    Or silver reach of river calms,
Do those large eyes behold me still?
With me one little year ago:—
The chill weight of the winter snow   405
    For months upon her grave has lain;
And now, when summer south-winds blow
    And brier and harebell bloom again,
I tread the pleasant paths we trod,
I see the violet-sprinkled sod   410
Whereon she leaned, too frail and weak
The hillside flowers she loved to seek,
Yet following me where'er I went
With dark eyes full of love's content.
The birds are glad; the brier-rose fills   415
The air with sweetness; all the hills
Stretch green to June's unclouded sky;
But still I wait with ear and eye
For something gone which should be nigh,

A loss in all familiar things,   420
In flower that blooms, and bird that sings.
And yet, dear heart! remembering thee,
    Am I not richer than of old?
Safe in thy immortality,
    What change can reach the wealth I hold?   425
    What chance can mar the pearl and gold
Thy love hath left in trust with me?
And while in life's late afternoon,
    Where cool and long the shadows grow,
I walk to meet the night that soon   430
    Shall shape and shadow overflow,
I cannot feel that thou art far,
Since near at need the angels are;
And when the sunset gates unbar,
    Shall I not see thee waiting stand,   435
And, white against the evening star,
    The welcome of thy beckoning hand?

Brisk wielder of the birch and rule,
The master of the district school
Held at the fire his favored place,   440
Its warm glow lit a laughing face
Fresh-hued and fair, where scarce appeared
The uncertain prophecy of beard.
He played the old and simple games
Our modern boyhood scarcely names,   445
Sang songs, and told us what befalls
In classic Dartmouth's college halls.
Born the wild Northern hills among,
From whence his yeoman father wrung
By patient toil subsistence scant,   450
Not competence and yet not want,
He early gained the power to pay

His cheerful, self-reliant way;
Could doff at ease his scholar's gown
To peddle wares from town to town;   455
Or through the long vacation's reach
In lonely lowland districts teach,
Where all the droll experience found
At stranger hearths in boarding round,
The moonlit skater's keen delight,   460
The sleigh-drive through the frosty night,
The rustic party, with its rough
Accompaniment of blind-man's-buff,
And whirling plate,[8] and forfeits paid,
His winter task a pastime made.   465
Happy the snow-locked homes wherein
He tuned his merry violin,
Or played the athlete in the barn,

---

8. Simple game the object of which is to keep a pewter plate spinning on edge longer than others can do.

Or held the good dame's winding yarn,
Or mirth-provoking versions told   470
Of classic legends rare and old,
Wherein the scenes of Greece and Rome
Had all the commonplace of home,
And little seemed at best the odds
'Twixt Yankee pedlers and old gods;   475
Where Pindus-born Araxes took
The guise of any grist-mill brook,
And dread Olympus[9] at his will
Became a huckleberry hill.

A careless boy that night he seemed;   480
    But at his desk he had the look
And air of one who wisely schemed,
    And hostage from the future took
    In trainéd thought and lore of book.
Large-brained, clear-eyed,—of such as he   485
Shall Freedom's young apostles be,
Who, following in War's bloody trail,
Shall every lingering wrong assail;
All chains from limb and spirit strike,
Uplift the black and white alike;   490
Scatter before their swift advance
The darkness and the ignorance,
The pride, the lust, the squalid sloth,
Which nurtured Treason's monstrous growth,
Made murder pastime, and the hell   495
Of prison-torture possible;
The cruel lie of caste refute,
Old forms recast, and substitute
For Slavery's lash the freeman's will,
For blind routine, wise-handed skill;   500
A school-house plant on every hill,
Stretching in radiate nerve-lines thence
The quick wires of intelligence;[1]
Till North and South together brought
Shall own the same electric thought,   505
In peace a common flag salute,
And, side by side in labor's free
And unresentful rivalry,
Harvest the fields wherein they fought.

Another guest[2] that winter night   510
Flashed back from lustrous eyes the light.
Unmarked by time, and yet not young,
The honeyed music of her tongue
And words of meekness scarcely told

9. Mount Olympus: home of the gods in Greek mythology. "Araxes": Greek river, "born" in the Pindus
Mountains.
1. Information, communication (the imagery is from
the telegraph, then still a recent development).
2. As Whittier's prefatory note says, Harriet Livermore.

A nature passionate and bold,   515
Strong, self-concentred, spurning guide,
Its milder features dwarfed beside
Her unbent will's majestic pride.
She sat among us, at the best,
A not unfeared, half-welcome guest,   520
Rebuking with her cultured phrase
Our homeliness of words and ways.
A certain pard-like,[3] treacherous grace
    Swayed the lithe limbs and drooped the lash,
    Lent the white teeth their dazzling flash;   525
    And under low brows, black with night,
    Rayed out at times a dangerous light;
The sharp heat-lightnings of her face
Presaging ill to him whom Fate
Condemned to share her love or hate.   530
A woman tropical, intense
In thought and act, in soul and sense,
She blended in a like degree
The vixen and the devotee,
Revealing with each freak or feint   535
    The temper of Petruchio's Kate,
The raptures of Siena's saint.[4]
Her tapering hand and rounded wrist
Had facile power to form a fist;
The warm, dark languish of her eyes   540
Was never safe from wrath's surprise.
Brows saintly calm and lips devout
Knew every change of scowl and pout;
And the sweet voice had notes more high
And shrill for social battle-cry.   545

Since then what old cathedral town
Has missed her pilgrim staff and gown,
What convent-gate has held its lock
Against the challenge of her knock!
Through Smyrna's plague-husked thoroughfares,   550
Up sea-set Malta's rocky stairs,
Gray olive slopes of hills that hem
Thy tombs and shrines, Jerusalem,
Or startling on her desert throne
The crazy Queen of Lebanon[5]   555
With claims fantastic as her own,
Her tireless feet have held their way;
And still, unrestful, bowed, and gray,
She watches under Eastern skies,
    With hope each day renewed and fresh,   560
    The Lord's quick coming in the flesh,
Whereof she dreams and prophesies!

---

3. Leopard-like.
4. St. Catharine (1347–1380), of Siena, in Tuscany,
Italy. "Petruchio's Kate" is the heroine of Shake-

speare's *Taming of the Shrew*.
5. Lady Hester Stanhope (see n. 3, p. 1409).

Where'er her troubled path may be,
  The Lord's sweet pity with her go!
The outward wayward life we see,   565
  The hidden springs we may not know.
Nor is it given us to discern
    What threads the fatal sisters[6] spun,
    Through what ancestral years has run
The sorrow with the woman born,   570
What forged her cruel chain of moods,
What set her feet in solitudes,
  And held the love within her mute,
What mingled madness in the blood,
    A life-long discord and annoy,   575
    Water of tears with oil of joy,
And hid within the folded bud
    Perversities of flower and fruit.
It is not ours to separate
The tangled skein of will and fate,   580
To show what metes and bounds should stand
Upon the soul's debatable land,
And between choice and Providence
Divide the circle of events;
But He who knows our frame is just,[7]   585
  Merciful, and compassionate,
And full of sweet assurances
And hope for all the language is,
That He remembereth we are dust!

At last the great logs, crumbling low,   590
Sent out a dull and duller glow,
The bull's-eye watch[8] that hung in view,
Ticking its weary circuit through,
Pointed with mutely-warning sign
Its black hand to the hour of nine.   595
That sign the pleasant circle broke:
My uncle ceased his pipe to smoke,
Knocked from its bowl the refuse gray
And laid it tenderly away,
Then roused himself to safely cover   600
The dull red brands with ashes over.
And while, with care, our mother laid
The work aside, her steps she stayed
One moment, seeking to express
Her grateful sense of happiness   605
For food and shelter, warmth and health,
And love's contentment more than wealth,
With simple wishes (not the weak,
Vain prayers which no fulfilment seek,
But such as warm the generous heart,

---

6. In Greek mythology the goddesses of destiny, the Fates.
7. Psalm 103.14: "For he knoweth our frame; he re-membereth that we are dust."
8. Nearly globular watch with a thick glass face.

O'er-prompt to do with Heaven its part)
That none might lack, that bitter night,
For bread and clothing, warmth and light.

Within our beds awhile we heard
The wind that round the gables roared,
With now and then a ruder shock,
Which made our very bedsteads rock.
We heard the loosened clapboards tost,
The board-nails snapping in the frost;
And on us, through the unplastered wall,
Felt the light sifted snow-flakes fall.
But sleep stole on, as sleep will do
When hearts are light and life is new;
Faint and more faint the murmurs grew,
Till in the summer-land of dreams
They softened to the sound of streams,
Low stir of leaves, and dip of oars,
And lapsing waves on quiet shores.

Next morn we wakened with the shout
Of merry voices high and clear;
And saw the teamsters drawing near
To break the drifted highways out.
Down the long hillside treading slow
We saw the half-buried oxen go,
Shaking the snow from heads uptost,
Their straining nostrils white with frost.
Before our door the straggling train
Drew up, an added team to gain.
The elders threshed their hands a-cold,
　　Passed, with the cider-mug, their jokes
　　From lip to lip; the younger folks
Down the loose snow-banks, wrestling, rolled,
Then toiled again the cavalcade
　　O'er windy hill, through clogged ravine,
　　And woodland paths that wound between
Low drooping pine-boughs winter-weighed.
From every barn a team afoot,
At every house a new recruit,
Where, drawn by Nature's subtlest law,
Haply the watchful young men saw
Sweet doorway pictures of the curls
And curious eyes of merry girls,
Lifting their hands in mock defence
Against the snow-ball's compliments,
And reading in each missive tost
The charm with Eden never lost.
We heard once more the sleigh-bells' sound;
　　And, following where the teamsters led,
The wise old Doctor went his round,
Just pausing at our door to say,

In the brief autocratic way
Of one who, prompt at Duty's call,
Was free to urge her claim on all,
   That some poor neighbor sick abed
At night our mother's aid would need.   665
For, one in generous thought and deed,
   What mattered in the sufferer's sight
   The Quaker matron's inward light,
The Doctor's mail[9] of Calvin's creed?
All hearts confess the saints elect   670
   Who, twain in faith, in love agree,
And melt not in an acid sect
   The Christian pearl of charity!

So days went on: a week had passed
Since the great world was heard from last.   675
The Almanac we studied o'er,
Read and reread our little store,
Of books and pamphlets, scarce a score;
One harmless novel, mostly hid
From younger eyes, a book forbid,   680
And poetry, (or good or bad,
A single book was all we had,)
Where Ellwood's meek, drab-skirted Muse,
   A stranger to the heathen Nine,[1]
   Sang, with a somewhat nasal whine,   685
The wars of David and the Jews.
At last the floundering carrier bore
The village paper to our door.
Lo! broadening outward as we read,
To warmer zones the horizon spread;   690
In panoramic length unrolled
We saw the marvels that it told.
Before us passed the painted Creeks,[2]
   And daft McGregor on his raids
   In dim Floridian everglades.[3]   695
And up Taygetos winding slow
Rode Ypsilanti's Mainote Greeks,
A Turk's head at each saddle-bow![4]
Welcome to us its week-old news,
Its corner for the rustic Muse,   700
   Its monthly gauge of snow and rain,
   Its record, mingling in a breath

9. Armor. John Calvin's doctrines of predestination, Original Sin, and so on being impenetrable and less humane than the "whole armor of God" which Paul enjoins Christians to put on in Ephesians 6.11–17.
1. Thomas Ellwood (1639–1714), English Quaker, wrote the *Davideis* (1712). Whittier has an essay on him in *Old Portraits and Modern Sketches* (1850). Here, Ellwood's source of inspiration wears Quaker drab, brownish yellow homespun, and knows nothing of the nine Greek goddesses who traditionally inspire artists and scientists.

2. Alabama tribe of American Indians subdued by Andrew Jackson and driven onto a reservation.
3. The Scottish adventurer Gregor McGregor fought with Simón Bolívar for the liberation of Venezuela from Spain, then in 1817 took possession of the Spanish-owned Amelia Island, off the Florida coast.
4. The Greek Revolutionary patriot Alexander Ypsilanti (1792–1828) defeated the Turks at Mount Taygetos in 1820; his saddle ornaments are heads of Turkish soldiers, not the fanciful knots imitated in the andirons referred to earlier.

The wedding knell and dirge of death;
Jest, anecdote, and love-lorn tale,
The latest culprit sent to jail;   705
Its hue and cry of stolen and lost,
Its vendue[5] sales and goods at cost,
    And traffic calling loud for gain.
We felt the stir of hall and street,
The pulse of life that round us beat;   710
The chill embargo of the snow
Was melted in the genial glow;
Wide swung again our ice-locked door,
And all the world was ours once more!

Clasp, Angel of the backward look   715
    And folded wings of ashen gray
    And voice of echoes far away,
The brazen covers of thy book;
The weird palimpsest[6] old and vast,
Wherein thou hid'st the spectral past;   720
Where, closely mingling, pale and glow
The characters of joy and woe;
The monographs of outlived years,
Or smile-illumed or dim with tears,
    Green hills of life that slope to death,   725
And haunts of home, whose vistaed trees
Shade off to mournful cypresses
    With the white amaranths[7] underneath.
Even while I look, I can but heed
    The restless sands' incessant fall,   730
Importunate hours that hours succeed,
Each clamorous with its own sharp need,
    And duty keeping pace with all.
Shut down and clasp the heavy lids;
I hear again the voice that bids   735
The dreamer leave his dream midway
For larger hopes and graver fears:
Life greatens in these later years,
The century's aloe[8] flowers to-day!

Yet, haply, in some lull of life,   740
Some Truce of God which breaks its strife,
The worldling's eyes shall gather dew,
    Dreaming in throngful city ways
Of winter joys his boyhood knew;
And dear and early friends—the few   745
Who yet remain—shall pause to view
    These Flemish pictures[9] of old days;

---

5. Auction.
6. Parchment with earlier writing visible beneath later writing.
7. Associated with immortality in flower symbolism.
8. The century plant, fabled to bloom only once every hundred years.

9. Realistic homely scenes. As a commonplace 19th-century term of literary criticism, "Dutch fidelity" or "Dutch realism" meant the minute photographic realism of many 17th-century painters such as David Teniers (both the Elder and the Younger of that name).

Sit with me by the homestead hearth,
And stretch the hands of memory forth
    To warm them at the wood-fire's blaze!   750
And thanks untraced to lips unknown
Shall greet me like the odors blown
From unseen meadows newly mown,
Or lilies floating in some pond,
Wood-fringed, the wayside gaze beyond;   755
The traveller owns the grateful sense
Of sweetness near, he knows not whence,
And, pausing, takes with forehead bare
The benediction of the air.

1866

Prelude to *Among the Hills*[1]

Along the roadside, like the flowers of gold
That tawny Incas[2] for their gardens wrought,
Heavy with sunshine droops the golden-rod,
And the red pennons of the cardinal-flowers
Hang motionless upon their upright staves.   5
The sky is hot and hazy, and the wind,
Wing-weary with its long flight from the south,
Unfelt; yet, closely scanned, yon maple leaf
With faintest motion, as one stirs in dreams,
Confesses it. The locust by the wall   10
Stabs the noon-silence with his sharp alarm.
A single hay-cart down the dusty road
Creaks slowly, with its driver fast asleep
On the load's top. Against the neighboring hill,
Huddled along the stone wall's shady side,   15
The sheep show white, as if a snow-drift still
Defied the dog-star.[3] Through the open door
A drowsy smell of flowers—gay heliotrope,
And white sweet-clover, and shy mignonette—
Comes faintly in, and silent chorus lends   20
To the pervading symphony of peace.

No time is this for hands long overworn
To task their strength; and (unto Him be praise
Who giveth quietness!) the stress and strain
Of years that did the work of centuries   25
Have ceased, and we can draw our breath once more
Freely and full. So, as yon harvesters
Make glad their nooning underneath the elms
With tale and riddle and old snatch of song,
I lay aside grave themes, and idly turn   30

1. From the first printing, in *Among the Hills, and Other Poems* (1869).
2. An allusion to the belief that gold was so plentiful among the Inca Indians of Peru that they fashioned golden ornamental flowers for their gardens.
3. Sirius, star visible near the sun at dawn during the torrid "dog days" of August.

The leaves of Memory's sketch-book, dreaming o'er
Old summer pictures of the quiet hills,
And human life, as quiet, at their feet.

And yet not idly all. A farmer's son,
Proud of field-lore and harvest craft, and feeling   35
All their fine possibilities, how rich
And restful even poverty and toil
Become when beauty, harmony, and love
Sit at their humble hearth as angels sat
At evening in the patriarch's tent, when man   40
Makes labor noble, and his farmer's frock
The symbol of a Christian chivalry
Tender and just and generous to her
Who clothes with grace all duty; still, I know
Too well the picture has another side,—   45
How wearily the grind of toil goes on
Where love is wanting, how the eye and ear
And heart are starved amidst the plenitude
Of nature, and how hard and colorless
Is life without an atmosphere. I look   50
Across the lapse of half a century,
And call to mind old homesteads, where no flower
Told that the spring had come, but evil weeds,
Nightshade and rough-leaved burdock in the place
Of the sweet doorway greeting of the rose   55
And honeysuckle, where the house walls seemed
Blistering in sun, without a tree or vine
To cast the tremulous shadow of its leaves
Across the curtainless windows from whose panes
Fluttered the signal rags of shiftlessness;   60
Within, the cluttered kitchen-floor, unwashed
(Broom-clean I think they called it); the best room
Stifling with cellar damp, shut from the air
In hot midsummer, bookless, pictureless
Save the inevitable sampler hung   65
Over the fireplace, or a mourning-piece,[4]
A green-haired woman, peony-cheeked, beneath
Impossible willows; the wide-throated hearth
Bristling with faded pine-boughs half concealing
The piled-up rubbish at the chimney's back;   70
And, in sad keeping with all things about them,
Shrill, querulous women, sour and sullen men,
Untidy, loveless, old before their time,
With scarce a human interest save their own
Monotonous round of small economies,[5]   75
Or the poor scandal of the neighborhood;
Blind to the beauty everywhere revealed,
Treading the May-flowers with regardless feet;
For them the song-sparrow and the bobolink

4. A piece of art in memory of a departed relative.   involving the budget.
5. Management of domestic affairs, particularly those

Sang not, nor winds made music in the leaves; 80
For them in vain October's holocaust
Burned, gold and crimson, over all the hills,
The sacramental mystery of the woods.
Church-goers, fearful of the unseen Powers,
But grumbling over pulpit-tax and pew-rent,[6] 85
Saving, as shrewd economists, their souls
And winter pork with the least possible outlay
Of salt and sanctity; in daily life
Showing as little actual comprehension
Of Christian charity and love and duty, 90
As if the Sermon on the Mount[7] had been
Outdated like a last year's almanac:
Rich in broad woodlands and in half-tilled fields,
And yet so pinched and bare and comfortless,
The veriest straggler limping on his rounds, 95
The sun and air his sole inheritance,
Laughed at a poverty that paid its taxes,
And hugged his rags in self-complacency!

Not such should be the homesteads of a land
Where whoso wisely wills and acts may dwell 100
As king and lawgiver, in broad-acred state,
With beauty, art, taste, culture, books, to make
His hour of leisure richer than a life
Of fourscore to the barons of old time,
Our yeoman[8] should be equal to his home 105
Set in the fair, green valleys, purple walled,
A man to match his mountains, not to creep
Dwarfed and abased below them. I would fain
In this light way (of which I needs must own
With the knife-grinder of whom Canning sings, 110
"Story, God bless you! I have none to tell you!")[9]
Invite the eye to see and heart to feel
The beauty and the joy within their reach,—
Home, and home loves, and the beatitudes
Of nature free to all. Haply in years 115
That wait to take the places of our own,
Heard where some breezy balcony looks down
On happy homes, or where the lake in the moon
Sleeps dreaming of the mountains, fair as Ruth,
In the old Hebrew pastoral, at the feet 120
Of Boaz,[1] even this simple lay of mine
May seem the burden of a prophecy,

6. Fees to support the minister and pay for the use of a pew.
7. Matthew 5–7, Jesus' fullest statement of the absolute behavior he expects of his followers in contrast to the conventional ways of this world.
8. Farmer.
9. During the 1790s, as a way of turning English public opinion against the French Revolution, the statesman George Canning (1770–1827) wrote for *The Anti-Jacobin*, a paper, as its title says, opposed to the most radical French faction. Canning's *The Friend of Humanity and the Knife-Grinder*, extremely popular in Whittier's time, is a satire of misplaced humanitarianism and bleeding-heart liberalism. The line Whittier quotes is the drink-loving knife-grinder's brusque retort to the torrential address of the would-be philanthropist.
1. See Ruth 3 for the story of how the young widow, an ancestor of David, reminded Boaz of his family obligation to marry her.

Finding its late fulfilment in a change
Slow as the oak's growth, lifting manhood up
Through broader culture, finer manners, love,   125
And reverence, to the level of the hills.

O Golden Age, whose light is of the dawn,
And not of sunset, forward, not behind,
Flood the new heavens and earth, and with thee bring
All the old virtues, whatsoever things   130
Are pure and honest and of good repute,
But add thereto whatever bard has sung
Or seer has told of when in trance and dream
They saw the Happy Isles of prophecy!
Let Justice hold her scale, and Truth divide   135
Between the right and wrong; but give the heart
The freedom of its fair inheritance;
Let the poor prisoner, cramped and starved so long,
At Nature's table feast his ear and eye
With joy and wonder; let all harmonies   140
Of sound, form, color, motion, wait upon
The princely guest, whether in soft attire
Of leisure clad, or the coarse frock of toil.
And, lending life to the dead form of faith,
Give human nature reverence for the sake   145
Of One who bore it, making it divine
With the ineffable tenderness of God;
Let common need, the brotherhood of prayer,
The heirship of an unknown destiny,
The unsolved mystery round about us, make   150
A man more precious than the gold of Ophir.[2]
Sacred, inviolate, unto whom all things
Should minister, as outward types and signs
Of the eternal beauty which fulfils
The one great purpose of creation, Love,   155
The sole necessity of Earth and Heaven!

                                                                  1869

2. Source of treasures of gold brought to King Solomon (1 Kings 10.1).

EDGAR ALLAN POE
1809–1849

The life of Edgar Allan Poe is the most melodramatic of any of the major American writers of his generation. Determining the facts has proved difficult, as lurid legend became entwined with fact even before he died. Some legends were spread by Poe himself. Given to claiming that he was born in 1811 or 1813 and had written

certain poems far earlier than he had, Poe also exaggerated the length of his attendance at the University of Virginia and, in imitation of Lord Byron, fabricated a
"quixotic expedition to join the Greeks, then struggling for liberty." Two days
after Poe's death his supposed friend Rufus Griswold, a prominent anthologizer
of American literature, began a campaign of character assassination in which he
ultimately rewrote Poe's correspondence so as to alienate many of his friends who
could only assume that Poe had treacherously maligned them behind their backs.
Griswold's forgeries went unexposed for many years, poisoning every biographer's
image of Poe, and legend still feeds on half-truth in much writing on him.

Yet biographers now possess a great deal of factual evidence about most periods
of Poe's life. His mother, Elizabeth Arnold, had been an actress, prominent among
the wandering seaport players in a profession that was then considered disreputable.
She was a teenage widow when she married David Poe, Jr., in 1806. Poe, also an
actor, worked up to choice supporting roles before liquor destroyed his career.
Edgar, the Poes' second child, was born in Boston on January 19, 1809; a year
later David Poe deserted the family. In December 1811, Elizabeth Poe died at
twenty-four while acting in Richmond, Virginia, and her husband disappeared
completely, probably dying soon afterward at the age of twenty-seven.

The disruptions of Poe's first two years were followed by apparent security, for
John Allan, a young Richmond merchant, took him in as the children were par-
celed out. As "Master Allan," Poe accompanied the family to England in 1815,
where he attended good schools. On their return in 1820 the boy continued in
school, but under his own last name. During Poe's adolescence, uncertainty about
his future and shameful certainty about his past affected his feelings—and those of
his prosperous playmates. Around 1824, Allan's attitude toward the boy changed;
one rumor suggests that Edgar took the side of his foster mother in a quarrel. Poe
spent most of 1826 at the new University of Virginia, doing well in his studies,
although he was already drinking. Under the pretext that Allan had not provided
him an adequate allowance, he gambled, and lost some two thousand dollars—
"debts of honor," which a gentleman must repay. Allan had just inherited a fortune
of several hundred thousand dollars (with purchasing power of several million
today), but he refused to pay Poe's debts. After a quarrel with Allan in March 1827,
Poe looked up his father's relatives in Baltimore and then went on to his birthplace,
where he paid for the printing of *Tamerlane and Other Poems*, "By a Bostonian."
Before its publication, "Edgar A. Perry" had joined the army. Poe was partially
reconciled with Allan in March 1829, just after Mrs. Allan died. Released from
the army with the rank of sergeant major, Poe sought Allan's influence to gain him
an appointment to West Point, although he was past the age limit for admission.

While he was waiting for the appointment, Poe shortened *Tamerlane*, revised
other poems, and added new ones to make up a second volume, *Al Aaraaf, Tamerlane, and Minor Poems*, published at Baltimore in December 1829. He entered
West Point in June 1830, but felt he could not fit into life at the academy without
supplemental income, and Allan was interested in his own life, not Poe's. Just after
Poe went to West Point a woman in Richmond bore Allan twin sons. In October
1830 Allan married again and within a month his new wife was pregnant. Losing
any remaining hope that if he dutifully pursued a military career he might become
Allan's heir, Poe got himself expelled by missing classes and roll calls. Supportive
friends among the cadets made up a subscription for his *Poems*, published in May
1831. In this third volume Poe revised some earlier poems and for the first time
included versions of both *To Helen* (the famous "Helen, thy beauty is to me," not
a later, inferior poem of the same title) and *Israfel*.

Poe's mature career—from his twenty-first year to his death in his fortieth year—
was spent in four literary centers: Baltimore, Richmond, Philadelphia, and New
York. The Baltimore years—mid-1831 to late 1835—were marked by great industry and comparative sobriety. Poe lived in sordid poverty among his once-prosper-

ous relatives, including his poetaster brother who died in 1831; his grandmother Poe, whose death in 1835 cut off a Revolutionary widow's pension of $240 per annum on which the household relied; his aunt Maria Poe Clemm; and her daughter Virginia, whom Poe secretly married in 1835, when she was thirteen. Poe's first story, *Metzengerstein* (later subtitled *In Imitation of the German*), was published in the Philadelphia *Saturday Courier*, anonymously, in January 1832, and other stories appeared in the same paper through the year. By early 1833 Poe was projecting a volume of eleven stories, *Tales of the Folio Club*, never published under that title. In May 1833 he sent the *New-England Magazine* one of a set of *Eleven Tales of the Arabesque*—apparently the same eleven; a postscript added to the manuscript said simply, "I am poor." With his *Tales of the Folio Club*, Poe impressed all three judges of a contest in the Baltimore *Saturday Visiter*. One judge, the novelist John P. Kennedy, became a loyal mentor, offering timely money and advice.

Poe returned to Richmond in 1835, twenty-six years old, as assistant editor of T. L. White's new *Southern Literary Messenger*, at a salary of $540 a year, subsistence wages even in the 1830s. Allan was dead, survived by three small legitimate sons, and Poe had no contact with the widow. From the start, White deplored what he called Poe's tendency to "sip the juice" and gave him editorial duties without commensurate recognition or authority, even though the circulation of the magazine rose swiftly under Poe's guidance. The *Messenger* published stories by Poe, but it was through his critical pieces that he gained a national reputation as a reviewer in the virulently sarcastic British manner—a literary hatchetman.

Fired from the *Messenger* early in 1837, Poe took his aunt and his wife (whom he had publicly remarried in May 1836) to New York City, where for two years he lived hand to mouth on the fringes of the publishing world, selling a few stories and reviews. He had written a short novel, *The Narrative of Arthur Gordon Pym*, in Richmond, where White ran two installments in the *Messenger* early in 1837. *Harper's* finally brought it out in July 1838, but it earned him no money, because it purported only to be edited by Poe, and not much reputation either. In 1838 Poe moved to Philadelphia, where for weeks the family survived on bread and molasses. But he continued writing, and *Ligeia* appeared in the Baltimore *American Museum* in September 1838, where other stories and poems followed. Resorting to literary hackwork just as Hawthorne was doing, Poe put his name on *The Conchologist's First Book* (1839). In May 1839 he got his first steady job in over two years, as coeditor of *Burton's Gentleman's Magazine*. There he published book reviews and stories, among them *The Fall of the House of Usher* and *William Wilson*. Late in 1839, a Philadelphia firm published *Tales of the Grotesque and Arabesque*, but it sold badly. Poe was now at the height of his powers as a writer of tales, though his personal life continued unstable, as did his career as an editor. William Burton fired him for drinking in May 1840 but recommended him to George Graham, who carried on Burton's magazine as *Graham's*. Throughout 1841, Poe was with *Graham's* as coeditor, courting subscribers by articles on cryptography and on character as revealed in handwriting. In January 1842, Virginia Poe, not yet twenty, burst a blood vessel in her throat (she lived only five more years). Leaving *Graham's* in some unhappiness, Poe revived a project for his own magazine, now to be called *The Stylus*. In 1843 he worked at times for the Philadelphia weekly *Saturday Museum*. On a trip to Washington seeking a patronage job (and subscriptions to *The Stylus*) he reportedly was so drunk when he called on President Tyler that he wore his cloak inside out.

In April 1844 Poe moved his family to New York City, where he wrote for newspapers and worked as subeditor on the *Sunday Times*. Poe's most successful year was 1845. The February issue of *Graham's* contained James Russell Lowell's complimentary article on Poe, and *The Raven* appeared in the February *American Review* after advance publication in the New York *Evening Mirror*. Capitalizing on the sensation the poem created, Poe lectured on "Poets of America" and became a principal reviewer for the new weekly, the *Broadway Journal*. *The Raven* won him entrée into the literary life of New York. One new literary acquaintance, Evert A. Duyckinck, soon to be Melville's friend also, selected a dozen of Poe's stories for a collection brought out by Wiley & Putnam in June and arranged for the same firm to publish *The Raven and Other Poems* in November. Having acquired critical clout despite a growing number of enemies, Poe had great hopes for the *Broadway Journal*, of which he became sole owner; but it failed early in 1846. Meanwhile Poe was marring his new opportunities by drinking.

With fame the tempo of Poe's life spun into a blur of literary feuds, flirtations with literary ladies, and drinking bouts that ended in quarrels. Virginia's death in January 1847 slowed the tempo: during much of that year Poe was seriously ill himself—perhaps with a brain lesion—and drinking steadily. He worked away at *Eureka*, a prose statement of a theory of the universe, and soon after Virginia's death he wrote *Ulalume*. The year 1848 was frenetic, culminating in a brief engagement to Helen Power Whitman of Providence; his letters to her are effusively hysterical. He flirted with Mrs. Nancy Richmond of Lowell, Massachusetts, in equally desperate letters, and may—as he wrote her—have tried to commit suicide by taking laudanum. He managed to write a little still, the story *Hop-Frog* and the poem *Annabel Lee*. While headed south in June 1849, he drank on the train and got off in Philadelphia to seek asylum, he said, from two men who were trying to kill him. In Richmond he spent two improbably happy months, being received into society by his childhood friends and becoming engaged to the sweetheart of his teens, the now-widowed Elmira Royster Shelton. He gave lectures and readings, and joined the Sons of Temperance. On the way to accept a hundred dollars for editing the poems of a Philadelphia woman, he stopped off in Baltimore, broke his temperance pledge, and was found senseless near a polling place on an Election Day (October 3). Taken to a hospital, he died on October 7, 1849, "of congestion of the brain."

If Poe had disappeared from the American literary scene after publishing his third volume of poems in 1831, a literary historian grubbing among privately printed nineteenth-century collections of poetry would have classified him (once his authorship of the anonymous *Tamerlane* had been established) as an odd American imitator of major British Romantics like Lord Byron and Percy Bysshe Shelley as well as then-popular ones like Thomas Moore. In both form and content Poe's early poetry is typically Romantic, although of an unusually limited range. Well before his twenty-first birthday he had earned the right to call himself a poet, but by British standards he was not an important one.

It was the handful of poems that Poe wrote a decade and a half later that made him famous as a poet. *The Raven* brought him international celebrity, and poems like *Ulalume* and *The Bells* soon enhanced that fame among Poe's constantly enlarging posthumous audience. These poems became standard declamation pieces in schools and remained so well into the present century. In subject matter they progress little beyond the Romantic gothicism of Poe's early years, but in technique they are remarkable. Innumerable young people have learned to love poetry from them and have continued to love poetry even after they stopped loving only Poe. There could be worse fates for a man who started out as a belated, second-rate imitator of first- and second-rate British Romantics.

But the bulk of Poe's collected writings consists of his criticism, and his most abiding ambition was to become a powerful critic. Just as he had modeled his poems and first tales on British examples (or British imitations of the German), he took his critical concepts from treatises on aesthetics by late-eighteenth-century Scottish Common Sense philosophers (later modified by his borrowings from A. W. Schlegel and Coleridge) and took his stance as a reviewer from the slashing critics of the British quarterlies. Poe's employers were often uneasy about their reviewer, both because his virulence brought reproaches (though it was good for business) and because they suspected that for all his stress on aesthetic principles, Poe's reviews were apt to be unjust to writers he was jealous of and laudatory toward others he wished to curry favor with. But Poe's basic critical principles were consistent enough, however he deviated from them in his reviewing. He thought poetry should appeal only to the sense of beauty, not truth; informational poetry, poetry of ideas, or any sort of didactic poetry was illegitimate. Holding that the true poetic emotion was a vague sensory state, he set himself against realistic details in poetry, although the prose tale, with truth as one object, could profit from the discreet use of specifics. Both poems and tales should be short enough to be read in one sitting; otherwise the unity of effect would be dissipated. In Poe's view, good writers calculate their effects precisely. At a time when even famous poets such as Longfellow rarely wrote a poem of sustained coherence, Poe's reaction, with the stress on forethought, seems understandable. But his criticism is often dogmatic and self-serving, weakened partly because it was applied to some of the most wretched writing a reviewer ever had to discuss, for Poe never had the luxury of reviewing only worthwhile volumes.

Poe's first tales have proved hard to classify—are they burlesques of popular kinds of fiction or serious attempts at contributing to or somehow altering those genres? Poe's own comments tend to becloud his intentions rather than to clarify them. In 1836 his benefactor John P. Kennedy wrote him: "Some of your *bizarreries* have been mistaken for satire—and admired too in that character. *They* deserved it, but *you* did not, for you did not intend them so. I like your grotesque—it is of the very best stamp; and I am sure you will do wonders for yourself in the comic—I mean the seriotragicomic." Poe's reply is tantalizing: "You are nearly, but not altogether right in relation to the satire of some of my Tales. Most of them were *intended* for half banter, half satire—although I might not have fully acknowledged this to be their aim even to myself." The problem of determining the nature of a given work—imitation? satire? spoof? hoax?—is crucial in Poe criticism.

At the core of Poe's defenses of his stories is the hardheadedness of a professional writer who wanted to crack the popular market. Such stories, he claimed, were the products of superior minds disciplining themselves to the task at hand, not the indulgences of Romantic genius. Poe worked hard at structuring his tales of aristocratic madmen, self-tormented murderers, neurasthenic necrophiliacs, and other deviant types so as to produce the greatest possible horrific effects on the reader. In the detective story, which Poe created when he was thirty-two, with all its major conventions complete, the structuring was equally contrived, although the effect desired was one of awe at the brilliance of his preternatural logician-hero. Seriously as he took the writing of his tales, Poe never claimed that prose writing was for him, as he said poetry was, a "passion," not merely a "purpose."

Other American writers, from Poe's time to ours, have often been uneasy about him. The "jingle man," Ralph Waldo Emerson is supposed to have called him, and Henry James thought that enthusiasm for Poe was "the mark of a decidedly primitive stage of reflection," while T. S. Eliot said Poe's intellect was that of "a highly gifted young person before puberty." Yet no other American writer, except possibly Mark Twain, has been so thoroughly absorbed by later writers—writers as diverse as E. A. Robinson, Frank Norris, Theodore Dreiser, and William Faulkner, as well as the great Russian-American player of complex Poesque games, Vladimir Nabokov. Some American literary critics and historians have always been hard pressed to understand why foreign writers like Charles Baudelaire and Stéphane Mallarmé could idolize Poe and translate his works lovingly, why the French Symbolist poets could draw on him for their aesthetic ideas, how August Strindberg could fantasize that because he was born in 1849 Poe's spirit had passed to him, how the influence of someone so childish could seem profound when it came back to English indirectly, through foreigners Poe had influenced. Some American critics have often felt reproached when British writers such as Dante Gabriel Rosetti, Algernon Swinburne, Robert Louis Stevenson, Arthur Conan Doyle, and George Bernard Shaw expressed delight in Poe or indebtedness to him. More than a century and a quarter after his death, American critics are still taking sides about Poe, hailing him as a pioneering aesthetician, psychological investigator, and literary technician, or else reviling him as an absurd fraud, a subliterary vulgarian. But whatever his influence on artists of the past and present, and whatever his status with literary critics and historians, Poe's reputation with the reading public—through the whole range of literacy—is more assured than that of any other major American writer of his century, again with the possible exception of Mark Twain. For the professional writer that Poe struggled to be, that is probably a fate even better than being precisely understood and logically classified.

The Lake[1]

In youth's spring, it was my lot
To haunt of the wide earth a spot
The which I could not love the less;
So lovely was the loneliness
Of a wild lake, with black rock bound,   5
And the tall pines that tower'd around.
But when the night had thrown her pall
Upon that spot—as upon all,
And the wind would pass me by
In its still melody,   10
My infant spirit would awake
To the terror of that lone lake.
Yet that terror was not fright—
But a tremulous delight,
And a feeling undefin'd,   15
Springing from a darken'd mind.
Death was in that poison'd wave
And in its gulf a fitting grave
For him who thence could solace bring
To his dark imagining;   20
Whose wild'ring thought could even make
An Eden of that dim lake.

1827, 1845

Preface[2]

1

Romance who loves to nod and sing
With drowsy head and folded wing
Among the green leaves as they shake

---

1. The text is that of *Tamerlane and Other Poems* (1827), the first printing.
2. *Preface* is the title of this poem as published in 1829, where it preceded a section of "Miscellaneous Poems"; the text is also that of 1829. The now-familiar title *To Romance* was first used in an 1845 *Broadway Journal* reprinting.

Far down within some shadowy lake
To me a painted paroquet   5
Hath been—a most familiar bird—
Taught me my alphabet to say—
To lisp my very earliest word
While in the wild wood I did lie
A child—with a most knowing eye.   10

2

Of late, eternal Condor years
So shake the very air on high
With tumult, as they thunder by,
I hardly have had time for cares
Thro' gazing on th' unquiet sky!   15
And, when an hour with calmer wings
Its down upon my spirit flings—
That little time with lyre and rhyme
To while away—forbidden things!
My heart would feel to be a crime   20
Did it not tremble with the strings!

1829, 1845

Introduction[1]

Romance, who loves to nod and sing,
With drowsy head and folded wing,
Among the green leaves as they shake
Far down within some shadowy lake,
To me a painted paroquet   5
Hath been—a most familiar bird—
Taught me my alphabet to say—
To lisp my very earliest word
While in the wild-wood I did lie
A child—with a most knowing eye.   10

Succeeding years, too wild for song,
Then roll'd like tropic storms along,
Where, tho' the garish lights that fly
Dying along the troubled sky.
Lay bare, thro' vistas thunder-riven,   15
The blackness of the general Heaven,
That very blackness yet doth fling
Light on the lightning's silver wing.

1. This expanded version of the previous poem introduced the entire 1831 *Poems*. It is a charmingly self-
mocking portrait of the young poet as an imitator of
Thomas Moore (1779–1852), the vastly popular author
of *Irish Melodies* and the most notable contemporary
writer of Anacreontic verse (light, graceful poems in
celebration of wine and love, in imitation of those by
Anacreon, Greek poet of the 6th and 5th centuries
B.C.). The Romantic theme of the loss of creative
power (found in such poems as Coleridge's *Dejection:
An Ode* and Wordsworth's *Elegiac Stanzas* and *Composed upon an Evening of Extraordinary Splendor and
Beauty*) is fused at the end of the poem with a theatrical
defiance that owes much to the poetic posturings of
some heroes in poems by the English Romantic
George Gordon, Lord Byron (1788–1824).

For, being an idle boy lang syne,[2]
Who read Anacreon, and drank wine,   20
I early found Anacreon rhymes
Were almost passionate sometimes—
And by strange alchemy of brain
His pleasures always turn'd to pain—
His naivete to wild desire—   25
His wit to love—his wine to fire—
And so, being young and dipt in folly
I fell in love with melancholy,
And used to throw my earthly rest
And quiet all away in jest—   30
I could not love except where Death
Was mingling his with Beauty's breath—
Or Hymen,[3] Time, and Destiny
Were stalking between her and me.

O, then the eternal Condor years   35
So shook the very Heavens on high,
With tumult as they thunder'd by;
I had no time for idle cares,
Thro' gazing on the unquiet sky!
Or if an hour with calmer wing   40
Its down did on my spirit fling,
That little hour with lyre and rhyme
To while away—forbidden thing!
My heart half fear'd to be a crime
Unless it trembled with the string.   45

But *now* my soul hath too much room—
Gone are the glory and the gloom—
The black hath mellow'd into grey,
And all the fires are fading away.

My draught of passion hath been deep—   50
I revell'd, and I now would sleep—
And after-drunkenness of soul
Succeeds the glories of the bowl—
An idle longing night and day
To dream my very life away.   55

But dreams—of those who dream as I,
Aspiringly, are damned, and die:
Yet should I swear I mean alone,
By notes so very shrilly blown,
To break upon Time's monotone,   60
While yet my vapid joy and grief
Are tintless of the yellow leaf—
Why not an imp the greybeard hath,
Will shake his shadow in my path—

2. Long since, the days long ago.   3. Greek god of marriage.

And even the greybeard will o'erlook   65
Connivingly my dreaming-book.

1831, 1845

Sonnet—To Science[1]

SCIENCE! meet daughter of old Time thou art
   Who alterest all things with thy peering eyes!
Why prey'st thou thus upon the poet's heart,
   Vulture! whose wings are dull realities!
How should he love thee—or how deem thee wise   5
   Who woulds't not leave him, in his wandering,
To seek for treasure in the jewell'd skies
   Albeit, he soar with an undaunted wing?
Hast thou not dragg'd Diana from her car,
   And driv'n the Hamadryad from the wood   10
To seek a shelter in some happier star?
   The gentle Naiad[2] from her fountain-flood?
The elfin from the green grass? and from me
   The summer dream beneath the shrubbery?

1829, 1845

Fairyland[1]

Dim vales—and shadowy floods—
And cloudy-looking woods,
Whose forms we can't discover
For the tears that drip all over.
Huge moons there wax and wane—   5
Again—again—again—
Ev'ry moment of the night—
For ever changing places—
And they put out the star-light
With the breath from their pale faces;   10
About twelve by the moon-dial
One, more *filmy* than the rest
[A sort which, upon trial,
They have found to be the best][2]
Comes down—still down—and down   15
With its centre on the crown

1. The text is from *The Raven and Other Poems* (1845). Both in 1829 and 1831 the sonnet, untitled, was printed as a proem to *Al Aaraaf*; in 1845 the poem retained its place but carried the title first used in an 1843 reprinting. *Sonnet—To Science* is built on the Romantic commonplace that the scientific spirit destroys beauty, a notion well exemplified by Wordsworth's *The Tables Turned* ("Sweet is the lore which Nature brings; / Our medling intellect / Misshapes the beauteous forms of things:— / We murder to dissect") and by Keats's *Lamia* ("Philosophy will clip an angel's wings").
2. Nymph living in brooks or fountains. "Diana": Roman goddess of the moon (imaged as a chariot or car that she drives through the sky). "Hamadryad": wood nymph in Greek and Roman mythology, often thought of as living within a tree and perishing with it.
1. Poe is assessing his debts to Thomas Moore. An expanded version in the 1831 volume lacks the humor.
2. These square brackets may be part of the whimsical eccentricity of the poem.

Of a mountain's eminence,
While its wide circumference
In easy drapery falls
Over hamlets, and rich halls,   20
Wherever they may be—
O'er the strange woods—o'er the sea—
Over spirits on the wing
Over every drowsy thing—
And buries them up quite   25
In a labyrinth of light—
And then, how deep! O! deep!
Is the passion of their sleep!
In the morning they arise,
And their moony covering   30
Is soaring in the skies,
With the tempests as they toss,
Like——almost any thing—[3]
Or a yellow Albatross.
They use that moon no more   35
For the same end as before—
Videlicet[4] a tent—
Which I think extravagant:
It atomies, however,
Into a shower dissever,   40
Of which those butterflies,
Of Earth, who seek the skies,
And so come down again,
[The unbelieving things!]
Have brought a specimen   45
Upon their quivering wings.

                                    1829, 1845

To Helen[1]

Helen, thy beauty is to me
    Like those Nicéan barks[2] of yore,
That gently, o'er a perfumed sea,
    The weary, way-worn wanderer bore
    To his own native shore.   5

On desperate seas long wont to roam,
    Thy hyacinth hair, thy classic face,
Thy Naiad[3] airs have brought me home

---

3. In the original this line begins with an asterisk, signaling the following footnote: "Plagiarism—see the works of Thomas Moore—passim—*Edr.*" The "editor" is presumably Poe himself.
4. That is, namely.
1. The text is that of 1845, with two errors of indentation corrected. The poem was first published in 1831 where, among other differences, lines 9 and 10 read:

"To the beauty of fair Greece, / And the grandeur of old Rome."
2. Variously annotated by Poe scholars, the Nicéan boats are more important for their musicality and vaguely classical suggestiveness than for their vaguely Mediterranean reference.
3. Nymphlike, fairylike.

To the glory that was Greece,
And the grandeur that was Rome.   10

Lo! in yon brilliant window-niche
How statue-like I see thee stand,
The agate lamp within thy hand!
Ah, Psyche,[4] from the regions which
Are Holy-Land!   15

1831, 1845

Israfel[1]

In Heaven a spirit doth dwell
  "Whose heart-strings are a lute;"
None sing so wildly well
As the angel Israfel,
And the giddy stars (so legends tell)   5
Ceasing their hymns, attend the spell
  Of his voice, all mute.

Tottering above
  In her highest noon,
  The enamoured moon   10
Blushes with love,
  While, to listen, the red levin
  (With the rapid Pleiads,[2] even,
  Which were seven,)
Pauses in Heaven.   15

And they say (the starry choir
  And the other listening things)
That Israfeli's fire
Is owing to that lyre
  By which he sits and sings—   20
The trembling living wire
  Of those unusual strings.

But the skies that angel trod,
  Where deep thoughts are a duty—
Where Love's a grown-up God—   25
  Where the Houri[3] glances are
Imbued with all the beauty
  Which we worship in a star.

Therefore, thou art not wrong,
  Israfeli, who despisest   30

4. Goddess of the soul.
1. "And the angel Israfel, whose heartstrings are a lute, and who has the sweetest voice of all God's creatures.—KORAN" [Poe's note]. A version of this poem appeared in the 1831 volume; the present text is from 1845. In 1831 the footnote to the title read (correctly): "And the angel Israfel, who has the sweetest voice of all God's creatures.—KORAN." Poe later expanded the quotation. Parallels among English Romantic poems include Coleridge's *Kubla Khan*, where glimpses of heavenly song also inspire but ultimately frustrate the speaker.
2. In Greek mythology the seven daughters of Atlas became stars, making up a constellation.
3. Beautiful virgin waiting in paradise for the devout Mohammedan.

An unimpassioned song;
To thee the laurels belong,
    Best bard, because the wisest!
Merrily live, and long!

The ecstasies above   35
    With thy burning measures suit—
Thy grief, thy joy, thy hate, thy love,
    With the fervour of thy lute—
    Well may the stars be mute!

Yes, Heaven is thine; but this   40
    Is a world of sweets and sours;
    Our flowers are merely—flowers,
And the shadow of thy perfect bliss
    Is the sunshine of ours.

If I could dwell   45
Where Israfel
    Hath dwelt, and he where I,
He might not sing so wildly well
    A mortal melody,
While a bolder note than this might swell   50
    From my lyre within the sky.

                                    1831, 1845

The City in the Sea[1]

Lo! Death has reared himself a throne
In a strange city lying alone
Far down within the dim West,
Where the good and the bad and the worst
        and the best
Have gone to their eternal rest.   5
There shrines and palaces and towers
(Time-eaten towers that tremble not!)
Resemble nothing that is ours.
Around, by lifting winds forgot,
Resignedly beneath the sky   10
The melancholy waters lie.

No rays from the holy heaven come down
On the long night-time of that town;
But light from out the lurid sea
Streams up the turrets silently—   15
Gleams up the pinnacles far and free—
Up domes—up spires—up kingly halls—
Up fanes[2]—up Babylon-like walls—
Up shadowy long-forgotten bowers

---

1. The text is that of 1845; it was first published in   2. Temples.
1831 as *The Doomed City*.

Of sculptured ivy and stone flowers—   20
Up many and many a marvellous shrine
Whose wreathéd friezes intertwine
The viol, the violet, and the vine.
Resignedly beneath the sky
The melancholy waters lie.   25
So blend the turrets and shadows there
That all seem pendulous in air,
While from a proud tower in the town
Death looks gigantically down.

There open fanes and gaping graves   30
Yawn level with the luminous waves;
But not the riches there that lie
In each idol's diamond eye—
Not the gaily-jewelled dead
Tempt the waters from their bed;   35
For no ripples curl, alas!
Along that wilderness of glass—
No swellings tell that winds may be
Upon some far-off happier sea—
No heavings hint that winds have been   40
On seas less hideously serene.

But lo, a stir is in the air!
The wave—there is a movement there!
As if the towers had thrust aside,
In slightly sinking, the dull tide—   45
As if their tops had feebly given
A void within the filmy Heaven.
The waves have now a redder glow—
The hours are breathing faint and low—
And when, amid no earthly moans,   50
Down, down that town shall settle hence,
Hell, rising from a thousand thrones,
Shall do it reverence.

                                                    1831, 1845

The Sleeper[1]

At midnight, in the month of June,
I stand beneath the mystic moon.
An opiate vapour, dewy, dim,
Exhales from out her golden rim,
And, softly dripping, drop by drop,   5
Upon the quiet mountain top,
Steals drowsily and musically
Into the universal valley.
The rosemary nods upon the grave;

---

1. The text is that of 1845; an earlier version titled *Irene* appeared in 1831.

The lily lolls upon the wave;   10
Wrapping the fog about its breast,
The ruin moulders into rest;
Looking like Lethe,[2] see! the lake
A conscious slumber seems to take,
And would not, for the world, awake.   15
All Beauty sleeps!—and lo! where lies
(Her casement open to the skies)
Irene, with her Destinies!

Oh, lady bright! can it be right—
This window open to the night?   20
The wanton airs, from the tree-top,
Laughingly through the lattice drop—
The bodiless airs, a wizard rout,
Flit through thy chamber in and out,
And wave the curtain canopy   25
So fitfully—so fearfully—
Above the closed and fringed lid
'Neath which thy slumb'ring soul lies hid,
That, o'er the floor and down the wall,
Like ghosts the shadows rise and fall!   30
Oh, lady dear, hast thou no fear?
Why and what art thou dreaming here?
Sure thou art come o'er far-off seas,
A wonder to these garden trees!
Strange is thy pallor! strange thy dress!   35
Strange, above all, thy length of tress,
And this all solemn silentness!

The lady sleeps! Oh, may her sleep,
Which is enduring, so be deep!
Heaven have her in its sacred keep!   40
This chamber changed for one more holy,
This bed for one more melancholy,
I pray to God that she may lie
Forever with unopened eye,
While the pale sheeted ghosts go by!   45

My love, she sleeps! Oh, may her sleep,
As it is lasting, so be deep!
Soft may the worms about her creep!
Far in the forest, dim and old,
For her may some tall vault unfold—   50
Some vault that oft hath flung its black
And winged pannels fluttering back,
Triumphant, o'er the crested palls,
Of her grand family funerals—
Some sepulchre, remote, alone,   55
Against whose portal she hath thrown,
In childhood, many an idle stone—

2. The river of forgetfulness in Hades, the Greek underworld.

Some tomb from out whose sounding door
She ne'er shall force an echo more,
Thrilling to think, poor child of sin!   60
It was the dead who groaned within.

1831, 1845

The Valley of Unrest[1]

Once it smiled a silent dell
Where the people did not dwell;
They had gone unto the wars,
Trusting to the mild-eyed stars,
Nightly, from their azure towers,   5
To keep watch above the flowers,
In the midst of which all day
The red sun-light lazily lay.
Now each visiter shall confess
The sad valley's restlessness.   10
Nothing there is motionless—
Nothing save the airs that brood
Over the magic solitude.
Ah, by no wind are stirred those trees
That palpitate like the chill seas   15
Around the misty Hebrides![2]
Ah, by no wind those clouds are driven
That rustle through the unquiet Heaven
Uneasily, from morn till even,
Over the violets there that lie   20
In myriad types of the human eye—
Over the lilies there that wave
And weep above a nameless grave!
They wave:—from out their fragrant tops
Eternal dews come down in drops.   25
They weep:—from off their delicate stems
Perennial tears descend in gems.

1831, 1845

Alone[1]

From childhood's hour I have not been
As others were—I have not seen
As others saw—I could not bring
My passions from a common spring—
From the same source I have not taken   5
My sorrow—I could not awaken

---

1. The text is that of 1845; the poem was first published as *The Valley Nis* in the 1831 volume.
2. Islands off the west coast of Scotland.

1. Presumably written in the early 1830s, *Alone* was
first printed in *Scribner's Monthly Magazine* 12 (September 1875).

My heart to joy at the same tone—
And all I lov'd—*I* lov'd alone—
Then—in my childhood—in the dawn
Of a most stormy life—was drawn   10
From ev'ry depth of good and ill
The mystery which binds me still—
From the torrent, or the fountain—
From the red cliff of the mountain—
From the sun that round me roll'd   15
In its autumn tint of gold—
From the lightning in the sky
As it pass'd me flying by—
From the thunder, and the storm—
And the cloud that took the form   20
(When the rest of Heaven was blue)
Of a demon in my view—

                                        1875

Dream-land[1]

By a route obscure and lonely,
Haunted by ill angels only,
Where an Eidolon,[2] named NIGHT,
On a black throne reigns upright,
I have reached these lands but newly   5
From an ultimate dim Thule[3]—
From a wild weird clime, that lieth, sublime,
        Out of SPACE—out of TIME.

Bottomless vales and boundless floods,
And chasms, and caves, and Titan[4] woods,   10
With forms that no man can discover
For the dews that drip all over;
Mountains toppling evermore
Into seas without a shore;
Seas that restlessly aspire,   15
Surging, unto skies of fire;
Lakes that endlessly outspread
Their lone waters, lone and dead,—
Their still waters, still and chilly
With the snows of the lolling lily.   20

By a route obscure and lonely,
Haunted by ill angels only,
Where an Eidolon, named NIGHT,
On a black throne reigns upright,

1. This version, from *Graham's Magazine* 25 (June 1844), 256, contains three repetitions of the refrain; the 1845 volume text prints those lines only once, as the last stanza.
2. Phantom.

3. A fabled island located north of Britain by ancient geographers and thought of as the northernmost habitable region.
4. I.e., enormous, as were the Titans, the children of Heaven and Earth, deposed by the gods of Olympus.

I have reached my home but newly   25
From this ultimate dim Thule.

By the lakes that thus outspread
Their lone waters, lone and dead,—
Their sad waters, sad and chilly
With the snows of the lolling lily,—   30
By the mountain—near the river
Murmuring lowly, murmuring ever,—
By the gray woods,—by the swamp
Where the toad and the newt encamp,—
By the dismal tarns and pools   35
        Where dwell the Ghouls,—
By each spot the most unholy—
In each nook most melancholy,—
There the traveler meets aghast
Sheeted Memories of the Past—   40
Shrouded forms that start and sigh
As they pass the wanderer by—
White-robed forms of friends long given,
In agony, to the worms, and Heaven.

By a route obscure and lonely,   45
Haunted by ill angels only,
Where an Eidolon, named NIGHT,
On a black throne reigns upright,
I have journeyed home but newly
From this ultimate dim Thule.   50

For the heart whose woes are legion
'T is a peaceful, soothing region—
For the spirit that walks in shadow
'T is—oh 't is an Eldorado!⁵
But the traveler, traveling through it,   55
May not—dare not openly view it;
Never its mysteries are exposed
To the weak human eye unclosed;
So wills the King, who hath forbid
The uplifting of the fringéd lid;   60
And thus the sad Soul that here passes
Beholds it but through darkened glasses.

By a route obscure and lonely,
Haunted by ill angels only,
Where an Eidolon, named NIGHT,   65
On a black throne reigns upright,
I have wandered home but newly
From this ultimate dim Thule.

                                    1844, 1845

---

5. Legendary golden country sought by Spanish conquerors of South America.

The Raven[1]

By——Quarles

[*The following lines from a correspondent—besides the deep quaint strain of the sentiment, and the curious introduction of some ludicrous touches amidst the serious and impressive, as was doubtless intended by the author—appear to us one of the most felicitous specimens of unique rhyming which has for some time met our eye. The resources of English rhythm for varieties of melody, measure, and sound, producing corresponding diversities of effect, have been thoroughly studied, much more perceived, by very few poets in the language. While the classic tongues, especially the Greek, possess, by power of accent, several advantages for versification over our own, chiefly through greater abundance of spondaic feet,[2] we have other and very great advantages of sound by the modern usage of rhyme. Alliteration is nearly the only effect of that kind which the ancients had in common with us. It will be seen that much of the melody of "The Raven" arises from alliteration, and the studious use of similar sounds in unusual places. In regard to its measure, it may be noted that if all the verses were like the second, they might properly be placed merely in short lines, producing a not uncommon form; but the presence in all the others of one line—mostly the second in the verse—which flows continuously, with only an aspirate pause in the middle, like that before the short line in the Sapphic Adonic,[3] while the fifth has at the middle pause no similarity of sound with any part besides, gives the versification an entirely different effect. We could wish the capacities of our noble language, in prosody, were better understood.—ED. AM. REV.*]

Once upon a midnight dreary, while I pondered, weak and weary,
Over many a quaint and curious volume of forgotten lore,
While I nodded, nearly napping, suddenly there came a tapping,
As of some one gently rapping, rapping at my chamber door.
" 'Tis some visiter," I muttered, "tapping at my chamber door—   5
                                    Only this, and nothing more."

Ah, distinctly I remember it was in the bleak December,
And each separate dying ember wrought its ghost upon the floor.
Eagerly I wished the morrow;—vainly I had tried to borrow
From my books surcease of sorrow—sorrow for the lost Lenore—   10
For the rare and radiant maiden whom the angels name Lenore—
                                  Nameless here for evermore.

And the silken sad uncertain rustling of each purple curtain
Thrilled me—filled me with fantastic terrors never felt before;
So that now, to still the beating of my heart, I stood repeating   15
" 'Tis some visiter entreating entrance at my chamber door—
Some late visiter entreating entrance at my chamber door;—
                                  This it is, and nothing more."

Presently my soul grew stronger; hesitating then no longer,
"Sir," said I, "or Madam, truly your forgiveness I implore;

1. This printing of Poe's most famous poem is taken from the *American Review: A Whig Journal of Politics, Literature, Art and Science* 1 (February 1845), where it was first set in type; the New York *Evening Mirror* printed the poem, on January 29, 1845, from the pages of the *American Review*. The prefatory paragraph, signed as if it were by the editor of the *American Review*, is retained here because Poe most likely had a hand in it, if he did not write it all. Many minor variations appear in later texts.
2. A spondee is a metrical foot consisting of two stressed syllables.
3. A Greek lyric form. In prosody an adonic is a dactyl (a foot with one long syllable and two short ones) followed by a spondee.

20

But the fact is I was napping, and so gently you came rapping,
And so faintly you came tapping, tapping at my chamber door,
That I scarce was sure I heard you"—here I opened wide the door;—
                                    Darkness there, and nothing more.

Deep into that darkness peering, long I stood there wondering, fearing,   25
Doubting, dreaming dreams no mortal ever dared to dream before;
But the silence was unbroken, and the darkness gave no token,
And the only word there spoken was the whispered word, "Lenore!"
This *I* whispered, and an echo murmured back the word, "Lenore!"
                                    Merely this, and nothing more. 30

Then into the chamber turning, all my soul within me burning,
Soon I heard again a tapping somewhat louder than before.
"Surely," said I, "surely that is something at my window lattice;
Let me see, then, what thereat is, and this mystery explore—
Let my heart be still a moment and this mystery explore;—   35
                                    'Tis the wind, and nothing more!"

Open here I flung the shutter, when, with many a flirt and flutter,
In there stepped a stately raven of the saintly days of yore;
Not the least obeisance made he; not an instant stopped or stayed he;
But, with mien of lord or lady, perched above my chamber door—   40
Perched upon a bust of Pallas[4] just above my chamber door—
                                    Perched, and sat, and nothing more.

Then this ebony bird beguiling my sad fancy into smiling,
By the grave and stern decorum of the countenance it wore,
"Though thy crest be shorn and shaven, thou," I said, "art sure no craven,   45
Ghastly grim and ancient raven wandering from the Nightly shore—
Tell me what thy lordly name is on the Night's Plutonian[5] shore!"
                                    Quoth the raven, "Nevermore."

Much I marvelled this ungainly fowl to hear discourse so plainly,
Though its answer little meaning—little relevancy bore;   50
For we cannot help agreeing that no sublunary[6] being
Ever yet was blessed with seeing bird above his chamber door—
Bird or beast upon the sculptured bust above his chamber door,
                                    With such name as "Nevermore."

But the raven, sitting lonely on the placid bust, spoke only   55
That one word, as if his soul in that one word he did outpour.
Nothing farther then he uttered—not a feather then he fluttered—
Till I scarcely more than muttered, "Other friends have flown before—
On the morrow *he* will leave me, as my hopes have flown before."
                                    Quoth the raven, "Nevermore." 60

Wondering at the stillness broken by reply so aptly spoken,
"Doubtless," said I, "what it utters is its only stock and store,
Caught from some unhappy master whom unmerciful Disaster

4. Athena, the Greek goddess of wisdom and the arts.   6. Earthly, beneath the moon.
5. Black, as in the underworld of Greek mythology.

Followed fast and followed faster—so, when Hope he would adjure,
Stern Despair returned, instead of the sweet Hope he dared adjure—   65
                    That sad answer, "Nevermore!"[7]

But the raven still beguiling all my sad soul into smiling,
Straight I wheeled a cushioned seat in front of bird, and bust, and door;
Then upon the velvet sinking, I betook myself to linking
Fancy unto fancy, thinking what this ominous bird of yore—
                                                 70
What this grim, ungainly, ghastly, gaunt, and ominous bird of yore
                    Meant in croaking "Nevermore."

This I sat engaged in guessing, but no syllable expressing
To the fowl whose fiery eyes now burned into my bosom's core;
This and more I sat divining, with my head at ease reclining   75
On the cushion's velvet lining that the lamplight gloated o'er,
But whose velvet violet lining with the lamplight gloating o'er,
                    She shall press, ah, nevermore!

Then, methought, the air grew denser, perfumed from an unseen censer
Swung by angels whose faint foot-falls tinkled on the tufted floor.   80
"Wretch," I cried, "thy God hath lent thee—by these angels he hath sent thee
Respite—respite and Nepenthe[8] from thy memories of Lenore!
Let me quaff this kind Nepenthe and forget this lost Lenore!"
                    Quoth the raven, "Nevermore."

"Prophet!" said I, "thing of evil!—prophet still, if bird or devil!—   85
Whether Tempter sent, or whether tempest tossed thee here ashore,
Desolate, yet all undaunted, on this desert land enchanted—
On this home by Horror haunted—tell me truly, I implore—
Is there—*is* there balm in Gilead?[9]—tell me—tell me, I implore!"
                    Quoth the raven, "Nevermore."   90

"Prophet!" said I, "thing of evil!—prophet still, if bird or devil!
By that Heaven that bends above us—by that God we both adore—
Tell this soul with sorrow laden if, within the distant Aidenn,[1]
It shall clasp a sainted maiden whom the angels name Lenore—
Clasp a rare and radiant maiden whom the angels name Lenore."   95
                    Quoth the raven, "Nevermore."

"Be that word our sign of parting, bird or fiend!" I shrieked, upstarting—
"Get thee back into the tempest and the Night's Plutonian shore!
Leave no black plume as a token of that lie thy soul hath spoken!
Leave my loneliness unbroken—quit the bust above my door!   100
Take thy beak from out my heart, and take thy form from off my door!"
                    Quoth the raven, "Nevermore."

7. This stanza concluded in the 1845 volume with these lines: "Followed fast and followed faster till his songs one burden bore— / Till the dirges of his Hope that melancholy burden bore of 'Never—nevermore.' "
8. Drug that induces oblivion.
9. An echo of the ironic words in Jeremiah 8.22: "Is there no balm in Gilead; is there no physician there?" Gilead is a mountainous area east of the Jordan River between the Sea of Galilee and the Dead Sea; evergreens growing there were an ample source of medicinal resins.
1. One of Poe's vaguely evocative place names, designed to suggest Eden.

And the raven, never flitting, still is sitting, still is sitting
On the pallid bust of Pallas just above my chamber door;
And his eyes have all the seeming of a demon that is dreaming,   105
And the lamp-light o'er him streaming throws his shadow on the floor;
And my soul from out that shadow that lies floating on the floor
                                            Shall be lifted—nevermore!

                                                                        1845

To ―― ―― ――.[1] Ulalume: A Ballad

        The skies they were ashen and sober;
                The leaves they were crispéd and sere—
                The leaves they were withering and sere;
        It was night in the lonesome October
                Of my most immemorial year;   5
        It was hard by the dim lake of Auber,
                In the misty mid region of Weir[2]—
        It was down by the dank tarn[3] of Auber.
                In the ghoul-haunted woodland of Weir.

        Here once, through an alley Titanic,[4]   10
                Of cypress, I roamed with my Soul—
                Of cypress, with Psyche, my Soul.
        These were days when my heart was volcanic

                As the scoriac rivers[5] that roll—
                As the lavas that restlessly roll   15
        Their sulphurous currents down Yaanek
                In the ultimate climes of the pole—
        That groan as they roll down Mount Yaanek
                In the realms of the boreal pole.[6]

        Our talk had been serious and sober,   20
                But our thoughts they were palsied and sere—
                Our memories were treacherous and sere—
        For we knew not the month was October,
                And we marked not the night of the year—
                (Ah, night of all nights in the year!)   25
        We noted not the dim lake of Auber—
                (Though once we had journeyed down here)—
        We remembered not the dank tarn of Auber,
                Nor the ghoul-haunted woodland of Weir.

        And now, as the night was senescent   30
                And star-dials pointed to morn—

---

1. This is the longer version of the poem; Poe some-times dropped the tenth stanza. The source is the *American Review* 6 (December 1847), 599–600, the first printing.
2. "Auber" and "Weir" are surnames Poe probably knew; as place names they are chosen for their rhyme value and connotative suggestions ("Weir," for in-stance, suggesting "weird").
3. A small mountain lake.
4. The alley—the pathway—is titanic because the cypress trees on either side are enormous, on a scale to match that of the pre-Olympian Greek gods.
5. Rivers of lava.
6. North pole.

As the star-dials hinted of morn—
At the end of our path a liquescent
    And nebulous lustre was born,
Out of which a miraculous crescent   35
    Arose with a duplicate horn—
Astarte's[7] bediamonded crescent
    Distinct with its duplicate horn.

And I said—"She is warmer than Dian:[8]
    She rolls through an ether of sighs—   40
    She revels in a region of sighs:
She has seen that the tears are not dry on
    These cheeks, where the worm never dies,
And has come past the stars of the Lion[9]
    To point us the path to the skies—   45
    To the Lethean[1] peace of the skies—
Come up, in despite of the Lion,
    To shine on us with her bright eyes—
Come up through the lair of the Lion
    With Love in her luminous eyes."   50

But Psyche,[2] uplifting her finger,
    Said—"Sadly this star I mistrust—
    Her pallor I strangely mistrust:—
Oh, hasten!—oh, let us not linger!
    Oh, fly!—let us fly!—for we must."   55
In terror she spoke, letting sink her
    Wings till they trailed in the dust—
In agony sobbed, letting sink her
    Plumes till they trailed in the dust—
    Till they sorrowfully trailed in the dust.   60

I replied—"This is nothing but dreaming:
    Let us on by this tremulous light!
    Let us bathe in this crystalline light!
Its Sybillic[3] splendor is beaming
    With Hope and in Beauty to-night:—   65
    See!—it flickers up the sky through the night!
Ah, we safely may trust to its gleaming,
    And be sure it will lead us aright—
We safely may trust to a gleaming
    That cannot but guide us aright,   70
    Since it flickers up to Heaven through the night."

Thus I pacified Psyche and kissed her,
    And tempted her out of her gloom—
    And conquered her scruples and gloom:
And we passed to the end of the vista,   75
    And were stopped by the door of a tomb—

---

7. Phoenician fertility goddess, here described as a moon goddess; the horns are the ends of a new moon.
8. The chaste Roman goddess of the moon.
9. The constellation Leo.

1. Absolute peace, as if bathed in the oblivion-giving waters of Lethe.
2. The soul, imaged as a butterfly.
3. Mysterious prophetic—now spelled "sibyllic."

By the door of a legended tomb;
And I said—"What is written, sweet sister,
   On the door of this legended tomb?"
She replied—"Ulalume—Ulalume—   80
'Tis the vault of thy lost Ulalume!"

Then my heart it grew ashen and sober
   As the leaves that were crispéd and sere—
   As the leaves that were withering and sere,
And I cried—"It was surely October   85
   On *this* very night of last year
   That I journeyed—I journeyed down here—
   That I brought a dread burden down here—
   On this night of all nights in the year,
   Oh, what demon has tempted me here?   90
Well I know, now, this dim lake of Auber—
   This misty mid region of Weir—
Well I know, now, this dank tarn of Auber,
   In the ghoul-haunted woodland of Weir."

Said *we*, then—the two, then—"Ah, can it   95
   Have been that the woodlandish ghouls—
   The pitiful, the merciful ghouls—
To bar up our way and to ban it
   From the secret that lies in these wolds—
   From the thing that lies hidden in these wolds—   100
Had drawn up the spectre of a planet
   From the limbo of lunary souls—
This sinfully scintillant[4] planet
   From the Hell of the planetary souls?"

                                     1847

Annabel Lee[1]

It was many and many a year ago,
   In a kingdom by the sea
That a maiden there lived whom you may know.
   By the name of ANNABEL LEE;
And this maiden she lived with no other thought   5
   Than to love and be loved by me.

I was a child and *she* was a child,
   In this kingdom by the sea;
But we loved with a love that was more than love—
   I and my ANNABEL LEE—   10
With a love that the wingèd seraphs of heaven
   Coveted her and me.

---

4. Sparkling, shining.
1. The text is that of the first printing, in Rufus Griswold's article in the New York *Tribune* (October 9,
   1849), signed "Ludwig."

And this was the reason that, long ago,
    In this kingdom by the sea,
A wind blew out of a cloud, chilling
    My beautiful ANNABEL LEE;   15
So that her highborn kinsmen came
    And bore her away from me,
To shut her up in a sepulchre
    In this kingdom by the sea.   20

The angels, not half so happy in heaven,
    Went envying her and me—
Yes!—that was the reason (as all men know,
    In this kingdom by the sea)
That the wind came out of the cloud by night,   25
    Chilling and killing my ANNABEL LEE.

But our love it was stronger by far than the love
    Of those who were older than we—
    Of many far wiser than we—
And neither the angels in heaven above,   30
    Nor the demons down under the sea,
Can ever dissever my soul from the soul
    Of the beautiful ANNABEL LEE:

For the moon never beams, without bringing me dreams
    Of the beautiful ANNABEL LEE;   35
And the stars never rise, but I feel the bright eyes
    Of the beautiful ANNABEL LEE:
And so, all the night tide, I lie down by the side
Of my darling—my darling—my life and my bride,
    In her sepulchre there by the sea—   40
    In her tomb by the sounding sea.

1849

Ligeia[1]

And the will therein lieth, which dieth not. Who knoweth the mysteries of the will, with its vigour? For God is but a great will pervading all things by nature of its intentness. Man doth not yield himself to the angels, nor unto death utterly, save only through the weakness of his feeble will.

        —Joseph Glanvill[2]

I cannot, for my soul, remember how, when, or even precisely where I first became acquainted with the lady Ligeia. Long years have since elapsed, and my memory is feeble through much suffering: or, perhaps, I cannot *now* bring these points to mind, because, in truth, the character of my beloved, her rare

---

1. *Ligeia* was first published in the *American Museum* 1 (September 1838), the source of the present text. Poe later revised the tale slightly and added to it the poem *The Conqueror Worm*.
2. Like others of Poe's epigraphs (often added after first publication), this one is fabricated to fit the desired effect. Joseph Glanvill (1636–1680) was one of the Cambridge Platonists, 17th-century English religious philosophers who tried to reconcile Christianity and Renaissance science.

learning, her singular yet placid cast of beauty, and the thrilling and enthralling eloquence of her low, musical language, made their way into my heart by
paces, so steadily and stealthily progressive, that they have been unnoticed and
unknown. Yet I know that I met her most frequently in some large, old,
decaying city near the Rhine. Of her family—I have surely heard her speak—
that they are of a remotely ancient date cannot be doubted. Ligeia! Buried in
studies of a nature, more than all else, adapted to deaden impressions of the
outward world, it is by that sweet word alone—by Ligeia, that I bring before
mine eyes in fancy the image of her who is no more. And now, while I write,
a recollection flashes upon me that I have *never known* the paternal name of
her who was my friend and my betrothed, and who became the partner of my
studies, and eventually the wife of my bosom. Was it a playful charge on the
part of my Ligeia? or was it a test of my strength of affection that I should
institute no inquiries upon this point? or was it rather a caprice of my own—a
wildly romantic offering on the shrine of the most passionate devotion? I but
indistinctly recall the fact itself—what wonder that I have utterly forgotten the
circumstances which originated or attended it? And indeed, if ever that spirit
which is entitled *Romance*—if ever she, the wan, and the misty-winged *Ashto-
phet*[3] of idolatrous Egypt, presided, as they tell, over marriages illomened,
then most surely she presided over mine.

　　There is one dear topic, however, on which my memory faileth me not. It
is the person of Ligeia. In stature she was tall, somewhat slender, and in her
latter days even emaciated. I would in vain attempt to pourtray the majesty,
the quiet ease of her demeanour, or the incomprehensible lightness and elasticity of her footfall. She came and departed like a shadow. I was never made
aware of her entrance into my closed study save by the dear music of her low
sweet voice, as she placed her delicate hand upon my shoulder. In beauty of
face no maiden ever equalled her. It was the radiance of an opium dream—
an airy and spirit-lifting vision more wildly divine than the phantasies which
hovered about the slumbering souls of the daughters of Delos.[4] Yet her features were not of that regular mould which we have been falsely taught to
worship in the classical labors of the Heathen. "There is no exquisite[5] beauty,"
saith Verülam, Lord Bacon, speaking truly of all the forms and *genera* of
beauty, "without some *strangeness* in the proportions." Yet, although I saw
that the features of Ligeia were not of classic regularity, although I perceived
that her loveliness was indeed "exquisite," and felt that there was much of
"strangeness" pervading it, yet I have tried in vain to detect the irregularity,
and to trace home my own perception of "the strange." I examined the contour
of the lofty and pale forehead—it was faultless—how cold indeed that word
when applied to a majesty so divine! The skin rivaling the purest ivory, the
commanding breadth and repose, the gentle prominence of the regions above
the temples, and then the raven-black, the glossy, the luxuriant and naturally-
curling tresses, setting forth the full force of the Homeric epithet, "hyacin-
thine;" I looked at the delicate outlines of the nose—and nowhere but in the
graceful medallions of the Hebrews had I beheld a similar perfection. There
was the same luxurious smoothness of surface, the same scarcely perceptible

3. Variant of Ashtoreth, Phoenician goddess of fertility.
4. Probably the maidens attending Artemis, goddess of
wild nature and the hunt; she was born on Delos,
among the Cyclades in the Aegean Sea.
5. In his essay *Of Beauty* Francis Bacon, Baron Verulam (1561–1626), wrote "excellent," not "exquisite."

tendency to the aquiline, the same harmoniously curved nostril speaking the free spirit. I regarded the sweet mouth. Here was indeed the triumph of all things heavenly—the magnificent turn of the short upper lip—the soft, volup-tuous repose of the under—the dimples which sported, and the colour which spoke—the teeth glancing back, with a brilliancy almost startling, every ray of the holy light which fell upon them in her serene, and placid, yet most exultingly radiant of all smiles. I scrutinized the formation of the chin—and here, too, I found the gentleness of breadth, the softness and the majesty, the fulness and the spirituality, of the Greek, the contour which the God Apollo revealed but in a dream to Cleomenes, the son of the Athenian.[6] And then I peered into the large eyes of Ligeia.

For eyes we have no models in the remotely antique. It might have been, too, that in these eyes of my beloved lay the secret to which Lord Verülam alludes. They were, I must believe, far larger than the ordinary eyes of our race. They were even far fuller than the fullest of the Gazelle eyes of the tribe of the valley of Nourjahad.[7] Yet it was only at intervals—in moments of intense excitement—that this peculiarity became more than slightly noticeable in Ligeia. And at such moments was her beauty—in my heated fancy thus it appeared perhaps—the beauty of beings either above or apart from the earth—the beauty of the fabulous Houri[8] of the Turk. The colour of the orbs was the most brilliant of black, and far over them hung jetty lashes of great length. The brows, slightly irregular in outline, had the same hue. The "strangeness," however, which I have found in the eyes of my Ligeia was of a nature distinct from the formation, or the colour, or the brilliancy of the feature, and must, after all, be referred to the *expression*. Ah, word of no meaning! behind whose vast latitude of mere sound we intrench our ignorance of so much of the spiritual. The expression of the eyes of Ligeia! How, for long hours have I pondered upon it! How have I, through the whole of a mid-summer night, struggled to fathom it! What was it—that something more profound than the well of Democritus[9]—which lay far within the pupils of my beloved? What *was* it? I was possessed with a passion to discover. Those eyes! those large, those shining, those divine orbs! they became to me twin stars of Leda,[1] and I to them devoutest of astrologers. Not for a moment was the unfathomable meaning of their glance, by day or by night, absent from my soul.

There is no point, among the many incomprehensible anomalies of the science of mind, more thrillingly exciting than the fact—never, I believe noticed in the schools—that in our endeavours to recall to memory something long forgotten we often find ourselves *upon the very verge* of remembrance without being able, in the end, to remember. And thus, how frequently, in my intense scrutiny of Ligeia's eyes, have I felt approaching the full knowledge of the secret of their expression—felt it approaching—yet not quite be mine—and so at length utterly depart. And (strange, oh strangest mystery of all!) I found, in the commonest objects of the universe, a circle of analogies to that

6. Classical Greek sculptor whose name (possibly forged) is signed to the Venus de' Medici. The god Apollo was the patron of artists.
7. Frances Sheridan (1724–1766) wrote *The History of Nourjahad*, an Oriental romance.
8. Beautiful virgin waiting in paradise for the devout Mohammedan.
9. The Greek "laughing philosopher" (5th century

B.C.); Greece; one of his proverbs is "Truth lies at the bottom of a well."
1. Queen of Sparta whom Zeus, in the form of a swan, raped, thereby begetting Helen of Troy and (according to some versions) the twin sons Castor and Pollux, whom their father transformed into the constellation Gemini.

expression. I mean to say that, subsequently to the period when Ligeia's beauty passed into my spirit, there dwelling as in a shrine, I derived from many existences in the material world, a sentiment, such as I felt always aroused within me by her large and luminous orbs. Yet not the more could I define that sentiment, or analyze, or even steadily view it. I recognized it, let me repeat, sometimes in the commonest objects of the universe. It has flashed upon me in the survey of a rapidly-growing vine—in the contemplation of a moth, a butterfly, a chrysalis, a stream of running water. I have felt it in the ocean, in the falling of a meteor. I have felt it in the glances of unusually aged people. And there are one or two stars in heaven—(one especially, a star of the sixth magnitude, double and changeable, to be found near the large star in Lyra)[2] in a telescopic scrutiny of which I have been made aware of the feeling. I have been filled with it by certain sounds from stringed instruments, and not unfrequently by passages from books. Among innumerable other instances, I well remember something in a volume of Joseph Glanvill, which, perhaps merely from its quaintness—who shall say? never failed to inspire me with the sentiment.—"And the will therein lieth, which dieth not. Who knoweth the mysteries of the will, with its vigor? For God is but a great will pervading all things by nature of its intentness. Man doth not yield him to the angels, nor unto death utterly, but only through the weakness of his feeble will."

Length of years, and subsequent reflection, have enabled me to trace, indeed, some remote connexion between this passage in the old English moralist and a portion of the character of Ligeia. An *intensity* in thought, action, or speech was possibly, in her, a result, or at least an index, of that gigantic volition which, during our long intercourse, failed to give other and more immediate evidence of its existence. Of all women whom I have ever known, she, the outwardly calm, the ever placid Ligeia, was the most violently a prey to the tumultuous vultures of stern passion. And of such passion I could form no estimate, save by the miraculous expansion of those eyes which at once so delighted and appalled me, by the almost magical melody, modulation, distinctness and placidity of her very low voice, and by the fierce energy, (rendered doubly effective by contrast with her manner of utterance) of the words which she uttered.

I have spoken of the learning of Ligeia: it was immense—such as I have never known in woman. In all the classical tongues was she deeply proficient, and as far as my own acquaintance extended in regard to the modern dialects of Europe, I have never known her at fault. Indeed upon any theme of the most admired, because simply the most abstruse, of the boasted erudition of the academy, have I *ever* found Ligeia at fault? How singularly, how thrillingly, this one point in the nature of my wife has forced itself, at this late period, only, upon my attention! I said her knowledge was such as I had never known in woman. Where breathes the man who, like her, has traversed, and successfully, *all* the wide areas of moral, natural, and mathematical science? I saw not then what I now clearly perceive, that the acquisitions of Ligeia were gigantic, were astounding—yet I was sufficiently aware of her infinite supremacy to resign myself, with a childlike confidence, to her guidance through the chaotic world of metaphysical investigation at which I was most busily occupied during the earlier years of our marriage. With how vast a

2. The lesser star is Epsilon Lyrae, the large one Vega or Alpha Lyrae.

triumph—with how vivid a delight—with how much of all that is ethereal in hope—did I *feel*, as she bent over me, in studies but little sought for—but less known that delicious vista by slow but very perceptible degrees expanding before me, down whose long, gorgeous, and all untrodden path I might at length pass onward to the goal of a wisdom too divinely precious not to be forbidden!

How poignant, then, must have been the grief with which, after some years, I beheld my well-grounded expectations take wings to themselves and flee away! Without Ligeia I was but as a child groping benighted. Her presence, her readings alone, rendered vividly luminous the many mysteries of the transcendentalism in which we were immersed. Letters, lambent and golden, grew duller than Saturnian[3] lead wanting the radiant lustre of her eyes. And now those eyes shone less and less frequently upon the pages over which I poured. Ligeia grew ill. The wild eye blazed with a too—too glorious effulgence; the pale fingers became of the transparent waxen hue of the grave—and the blue veins upon the lofty forehead swelled and sunk impetuously with the tides of the most gentle emotion. I saw that she must die—and I struggled desperately in spirit with the grim Azrael.[4] And the struggles of the passionate Ligeia were, to my astonishment, even more energetic than my own. There had been much in her stern nature to impress me with the belief that, to her, death would have come without its terrors—but not so. Words are impotent to convey any just idea of the fierceness of resistance with which Ligeia wrestled with the dark shadow. I groaned in anguish at the pitiable spectacle. I would have soothed—I would have reasoned; but in the intensity of her wild desire for life—for life—*but* for life, solace and reason were alike the uttermost of folly. Yet not for an instant, amid the most convulsive writhings of her fierce spirit, was shaken the external placidity of her demeanor. Her voice grew more gentle—grew more low—yet I would not wish to dwell upon the wild meaning of the quietly-uttered words. My brain reeled as I hearkened, entranced, to a melody more than mortal—to assumptions and aspirations which mortality had never before known.

That Ligeia loved me, I should not have doubted; and I might have been easily aware that, in a bosom such as hers, love would have reigned no ordinary passion. But in death only, was I fully impressed with the intensity of her affection. For long hours, detaining my hand, would she pour out before me the overflowings of a heart whose more than passionate devotion amounted to idolatry. How had I deserved to be so blessed by such confessions.—How had I deserved to be so cursed with the removal of my beloved in the hour of her making them? But upon this subject I cannot bear to dilate. Let me say only, that in Ligeia's more than womanly abandonment to a love, alas, all unmerited, all unworthily bestowed; I at length recognised the principle of her longing, with so wildly earnest a desire for the life which was now fleeing so rapidly away. It is this wild longing—it is this eager intensity of desire for life—*but* for life—that I have no power to pourtray—no utterance capable to express. Methinks I again behold the terrific struggles of her lofty, her nearly idealized nature, with the might and the terror, and the majesty of the great Shadow. But she perished. The giant *will* succumbed to a power more stern. And I thought, as I gazed upon the corpse, of the wild passage in Joseph Glanvill.

3. Sluggish; in alchemy *saturnus* is the name for lead.
4. The Angel of Death (in Judaism and Mohammedanism).

"The will therein lieth, which dieth not. Who knoweth the mysteries of the will, with its vigor? For God is but a great will pervading all things by nature of its intentness. Man doth not yield him to the angels, *nor unto death utterly*, save only through the weakness of his feeble will."

She died—and I, crushed into the very dust with sorrow, could no longer endure the lonely desolation of my dwelling in the dim and decaying city by the Rhine. I had no lack of what the world terms wealth—Ligeia had brought me far more, very far more, than falls ordinarily to the lot of mortals. After a few months, therefore, of weary and aimless wandering, I purchased, and put in some repair, an abbey, which I shall not name, in one of the wildest and least frequented portions of fair England. The gloomy and dreary grandeur of the building, the almost savage aspect of the domain, the many melancholy and time-honored memories connected with both, had much in unison with the feelings of utter abandonment which had driven me into that remote and musical region of the country. Yet, although the external abbey, with its verdant decay hanging about it suffered but little alteration, I gave way with a child-like perversity, and perchance with a faint hope of alleviating my sorrows, to a display of more than regal magnificence within. For such follies even in childhood I had imbibed a taste, and now they came back to me as if in the dotage of grief. Alas, I now feel how much even of incipient madness might have been discovered in the gorgeous and fantastic draperies, in the solemn carvings of Egypt, in the wild cornices and furniture of Arabesque, in the bedlam patterns of the carpets of tufted gold! I had become a bounden slave in the trammels of opium, and my labors and my orders had taken a colouring from my dreams. But these absurdities I must not pause to detail. Let me speak only of that one chamber, ever accursed, whither, in a moment of mental alienation, I led from the altar as my bride—as the successor of the unforgotten Ligeia—the fair-haired and blue-eyed lady Rowena Trevanion, of Tremaine.

There is not any individual portion of the architecture and decoration of that bridal chamber which is not now visibly before me. Where were the souls of the haughty family of the bride, when, through thirst of gold, they permitted to pass the threshold of an apartment so bedecked, a maiden and a daughter so beloved? I have said that I minutely remember the details of the chamber—yet I am sadly forgetful on topics of deep moment—and here there was no system, no keeping, in the fantastic display, to take hold upon the memory. The room lay in a high turret of the castellated abbey, was pentagonal in shape, and of capacious size. Occupying the whole southern face of the pentagon was the sole window—an immense sheet of unbroken glass from Venice—a single pane, and tinted of a leaden hue, so that the rays of either the sun or moon, passing through it, fell with a ghastly lustre upon the objects within. Over the upper portion of this huge window extended the open trellice-work of an aged vine which clambered up the massy walls of the turret. The ceiling, of gloomy-looking oak, was excessively lofty, vaulted, and elaborately fretted with the wildest and most grotesque specimens of a semi-Gothic, semi-druidical device. From out the most central recess of this melancholy vaulting, depended, by a single chain of gold, with long links, a huge censer of the same metal, Arabesque in pattern, and with many perforations so contrived that there writhed in and out of them, as if endued with a serpent vitality, a continual succession of parti-coloured fires. Some few ottomans and golden candelabras of Eastern figure were in various stations about—and there was the couch, too, the bridal couch, of an Indian model, and low, and sculptured of solid ebony, with a canopy above. In each of the angles of the chamber, stood on end a gigantic sarcophagus of black granite, from the tombs of the kings over against Luxor,[5] with their aged lids full of immemorial sculpture. But in the draping of the apartment lay, alas! the chief phantasy of all. The lofty walls— gigantic in height—even unproportionally so, were hung from summit to foot, in vast folds with a heavy and massy looking tapestry—tapestry of a material which was found alike as a carpet on the floor, as a covering for the ottomans, and the ebony bed, as a canopy for the bed, and as the gorgeous volutes[6] of the curtains which partially shaded the window. This material was the richest cloth of gold. It was spotted all over, at irregular intervals, with Arabesque figures, of about a foot in diameter, and wrought upon the cloth in patterns of the most jetty black. But these figures partook of the true character of the Arabesque only when regarded from a single point of view. By a contrivance now common, and indeed traceable to a very remote period of antiquity, they were made changeable in aspect. To one entering the room they bore the appearance of ideal monstrosities; but, upon a farther advance, this appearance suddenly departed; and, step by step, as the visitor moved his station in the chamber, he saw himself surrounded by an endless succession of the ghastly forms which belong to the superstition of the Northman, or arise in the guilty slumbers of the monk. The phantasmagoric effect was vastly heightened by the artificial introduction of a strong continual current of wind behind the draperies—giving a hidious and uneasy vitality to the whole.

In halls such as these—in a bridal chamber such as this, I passed, with the lady of Tremaine, the unhallowed hours of the first month of our marriage— passed them with but little disquietude. That my wife dreaded the fierce mood-iness of my temper—that she shunned me, and loved me but little, I could not help perceiving—but it gave me rather pleasure than otherwise. I loathed her with a hatred belonging more to demon than to man. My memory flew back, (oh, with what intensity of regret!) to Ligeia, the beloved, the beautiful, the entombed. I revelled in recollections of her purity, of her wisdom, of her lofty, her ethereal nature, of her passionate, her idolatrous love. Now, then, did my spirit fully and freely burn with more than all the fires of her own. In the excitement of my opium dreams (for I was habitually fettered in the iron shackles of the drug)[7] I would call aloud upon her name, during the silence of the night, or among the sheltered recesses of the glens by day, as if, by the wild eagerness, the solemn passion, the consuming intensity of my longing for the departed Ligeia, I could restore the departed Ligeia to the pathways she had abandoned upon earth.

About the commencement of the second month of the marriage, the lady Rowena was attacked with sudden illness from which her recovery was slow. The fever which consumed her, rendered her nights uneasy, and, in her per-turbed state of half-slumber, she spoke of sounds, and of motions, in and about the chamber of the turret which had no origin save in the distemper of her fancy, or, perhaps, in the phantasmagoric influences of the chamber itself. She became at length convalescent—finally well. Yet but a brief period

5. In middle Egypt, near Thebes; site of famous ruins, including the temple of Amun.
6. Scroll-like ornaments.

7. The *American Museum* has no punctuation after "dreams" or "drug" in this sentence; parentheses are added to the present text.

elapsed, ere a second more violent disorder again threw her upon a bed of suffering—and from this attack her frame, at all times feeble, never altogether recovered. Her illnesses were, after this period, of alarming character, and of more alarming recurrence, defying alike the knowledge and the great exertions of her medical men. With the increase of the chronic disease which had thus, apparently, taken too sure hold upon her constitution to be eradicated by human means, I could not fail to observe a similar increase in the nervous irritability of her temperament, and in her excitability by trivial causes of fear. Indeed reason seemed fast tottering from her throne. She spoke again, and now more frequently and pertinaciously, of the sounds, of the slight sounds, and of the unusual motions among the tapestries, to which she had formerly alluded. It was one night near the closing in of September, when she pressed this distressing subject with more than usual emphasis upon my attention. She had just awakened from a perturbed slumber, and I had been watching, with feelings half of anxiety, half of a vague terror, the workings of her emaciated countenance. I sat by the side of her ebony bed, upon one of the ottomans of India. She partly arose, and spoke, in an earnest low whisper, of sounds which she *then* heard, but which I could not hear, of motions which she *then* saw, but which I could not perceive. The wind was rushing hurriedly behind the tapestries, and I wished to show her (what, let me confess it, I could not *all* believe) that those faint, almost articulate, breathings, and the very gentle variations of the figures upon the wall, were but the natural effects of that customary rushing of the wind. But a deadly pallor overspreading her face, had proved to me that my exertions to re-assure her would be fruitless. She appeared to be fainting, and no attendants were within call. I remembered where was deposited a decanter of some light wine which had been ordered by her physicians, and hastened across the chamber to procure it. But, as I stepped beneath the light of the censer, two circumstances of a startling nature attracted my attention. I had felt that some palpable object had passed lightly by my person; and I saw that there lay a faint, indefinite shadow upon the golden carpet in the very middle of the rich lustre, thrown from the censer. But I was wild with the excitement of an immoderate dose of opium, and heeded these things but little, nor spoke of them to Rowena. Finding the wine, I re-crossed the chamber, and poured out a goblet-ful, which I held to the lips of the fainting lady. But she had now partially recovered, and took, herself, the vessel, while I sank upon the ottoman near me, with my eyes rivetted upon her person. It was then that I became distinctly aware of a gentle foot-fall upon the carpet, and near the couch; and, in a second thereafter, as Rowena was in the act of raising the wine to her lips, I saw, or may have dreamed that I saw, fall within the goblet, as if from some invisible spring in the atmosphere of the room, three or four large drops of a brilliant and ruby colored fluid. If this I saw—not so Rowena. She swallowed the wine unhesitatingly, and I forbore to speak to her of a circumstance which must, after all, I considered, have been but the suggestion of a vivid imagination, rendered morbidly active by the terror of the lady, by the opium, and by the hour.

Yet I cannot conceal it from myself, after this period, a rapid change for the worse took place in the disorder of my wife, so that, on the third subsequent night, the hands of her menials prepared her for the tomb, and on the fourth, I sat alone, with her shrouded body, in that fantastical chamber which had received her as my bride. Wild visions, opium engendered, flitted, shadow-like, before me. I gazed with unquiet eye upon the sarcophagi in the angles of the room, upon the varying figures of the drapery, and upon the writhing of the parti-colored fires in the censer overhead. My eyes then fell, as I called to mind the circumstances of a former night, to the spot beneath the glare of the censer where I had beheld the faint traces of the shadow. It was there, however, no longer, and, breathing with greater freedom, I turned my glances to the pallid and rigid figure upon the bed. Then rushed upon me a thousand memories of Ligeia—and then came back upon my heart, with the turbulent violence of a flood, the whole of that unutterable woe with which I had regarded *her* thus enshrouded. The night waned; and still, with a bosom full of bitter thoughts of the one only and supremely beloved, I remained with mine eyes rivetted upon the body of Rowena.

It might have been midnight, or perhaps earlier, or later, for I had taken no note of time, when a sob, low, gentle, but very distinct, startled me from my revery. I *felt* that it came from the bed of ebony—the bed of death. I listened in an agony of superstitious terror—but there was no repetition of the sound; I strained my vision to detect any motion in the corpse, but there was not the slightest perceptible. Yet I could not have been deceived. I had heard the noise, however faint, and my whole soul was awakened within me, as I resolutely and perseveringly kept my attention rivetted upon the body. Many minutes elapsed before any circumstance occurred tending to throw light upon the mystery. At length it became evident that a slight, a very faint, and barely noticeable tinge of colour had flushed up within the cheeks, and along the sunken small veins of the eyelids. Through a species of unutterable horror and awe, for which the language of mortality has no sufficiently energetic expression, I felt my brain reel, my heart cease to beat, my limbs grow rigid where I sat. Yet a sense of duty finally operated to restore my self-possession. I could no longer doubt that we had been precipitate in our preparations for interment—that Rowena still lived. It was necessary that some immediate exertion be made; yet the turret was altogether apart from the portion of the Abbey tenanted by the servants—there were none within call, and I had no means of summoning them to my aid without leaving the room for many minutes— and this I could not venture to do. I therefore struggled alone in my endeavors to call back the spirit still hovering. In a short period it became evident however, that a relapse had taken place; the color utterly disappeared from both eyelid and cheek, leaving a wanness even more than that of marble; the lips became doubly shrivelled and pinched up in the ghastly expression of death; a coldness surpassing that of ice, overspread rapidly the surface of the body, and all the usual rigorous stiffness immediately supervened. I fell back with a shudder upon the ottoman from which I had been so startlingly aroused, and again gave myself up to passionate waking visions of Ligeia.

An hour thus elapsed when, (could it be possible?) I was a second time aware of some vague sound issuing from the region of the bed. I listened—in extremity of horror. The sound came again—it was a sigh. Rushing to the corpse, I saw—distinctly saw—a tremor upon the lips. In a minute after they slightly relaxed, disclosing a bright line of the pearly teeth. Amazement now struggled in my bosom with the profound awe which had hitherto reigned therein alone. I felt that my vision grew dim, that my brain wandered, and it was only by a convulsive effort that I at length succeeded in nerving myself to the task which duty thus, once more, had pointed out. There was now a partial glow upon the forehead, upon the cheek and throat—a perceptible warmth pervaded the whole frame—there was even a slight pulsation at the heart. The lady lived; and with redoubled ardour I betook myself to the task of restoration. I chafed, and bathed the temples, and the hands, and used every exertion which experience, and no little medical reading, could suggest. But in vain. Suddenly, the colour fled, the pulsation ceased, the lips resumed the expression of the dead, and, in an instant afterwards, the whole body took upon itself the icy chillness, the livid hue, the intense rigidity, the sunken outline, and each and all of the loathsome peculiarities of that which has been, for many days, a tenant of the tomb.

And again I sunk into visions of Ligeia—and again (what marvel that I shudder while I write?) *again* there reached my ears a low sob from the region of the ebony bed. But why shall I minutely detail the unspeakable horrors of that night? Why shall I pause to relate how, time after time, until near the period of the grey dawn, this hideous drama of revivification was repeated, and how each terrific relapse was only into a sterner and apparently more irredeemable death? Let me hurry to a conclusion.

The greater part of the fearful night had worn away, and the corpse of Rowena once again stirred—and now more vigorously than hitherto, although arousing from a dissolution more appalling in its utter hopelessness than any. I had long ceased to struggle or to move, and remained sitting rigidly upon the ottoman, a helpless prey to a whirl of violent emotions, of which extreme awe was perhaps the least terrible, the least consuming. The corpse, I repeat, stirred, and now more vigorously than before. The hues of life flushed up with unwonted energy into the countenance—the limbs relaxed—and, save that the eyelids were yet pressed heavily together, and that the bandages and draperies of the grave still imparted their charnel character to the figure, I might have dreamed that Rowena had indeed shaken off, utterly, the fetters of Death. But if this idea was not, even then, altogether adopted, I could, at least, doubt no longer, when, arising from the bed, tottering, with feeble steps, with closed eyes, and with the air of one bewildered in a dream, the lady of Tremaine stood bodily and palpably before me.

I trembled not—I stirred not—for a crowd of unutterable fancies connected with the air, the demeanour of the figure, rushing hurriedly through my brain, sent the purple blood ebbing in torrents from the temples to the heart. I stirred not—but gazed upon her who was before me. There was a mad disorder in my thoughts—a tumult unappeasable. Could it, indeed, be the *living* Rowena who confronted me? Why, *why* should I doubt it? The bandage lay heavily about the mouth—but then it was the mouth of the breathing lady of Tremaine. And the cheeks—there were the roses as in her noon of health—yes, these were indeed the fair cheeks of the living lady of Tremaine. And the chin, with its dimples, as in health, was it not hers?—but—but *had she then grown taller since her malady?* What inexpressible madness seized me with that thought? One bound, and I had reached her feet! Shrinking from my touch, she let fall from her head, unloosened, the ghastly cerements which had confined it, and there streamed forth, into the rushing atmosphere of the chamber, huge masses of long and dishevelled hair. *It was blacker than the raven wings of the midnight!* And now the eyes opened of the figure which stood before me. "Here then at least," I shrieked aloud, "can I never—can I never be mistaken—these are the full, and the black, and the wild eyes of the lady—of the lady Ligeia!"

1838

The Fall of the House of Usher[1]

During the whole of a dull, dark, and soundless day in the autumn of the year, when the clouds hung oppressively low in the heavens, I had been passing alone, on horseback, through a singularly dreary tract of country; and at length found myself, as the shades of the evening drew on, within view of the melancholy House of Usher. I know not how it was—but, with the first glimpse of the building, a sense of insufferable gloom pervaded my spirit. I say insufferable; for the feeling was unrelieved by any of that half-pleasurable, because poetic, sentiment, with which the mind usually receives even the sternest natural images of the desolate or terrible. I looked upon the scene before me—upon the mere house, and the simple landscape features of the domain—upon the bleak walls—upon the vacant eye-like windows—upon a few rank sedges—and upon a few white trunks of decayed trees—with an utter depression of soul which I can compare to no earthly sensation more properly than to the after-dream of the reveller upon opium—the bitter lapse into common life—the hideous dropping off of the veil. There was an iciness, a sinking, a sickening of the heart—an unredeemed dreariness of thought which no goading of the imagination could torture into aught of the sublime. What was it— I paused to think—what was it that so unnerved me in the contemplation of the House of Usher? It was a mystery all insoluble; nor could I grapple with the shadowy fancies that crowded upon me as I pondered. I was forced to fall back upon the unsatisfactory conclusion, that while, beyond doubt, there *are* combinations of very simple natural objects which have the power of thus affecting us, still the reason, and the analysis, of this power, lie among considerations beyond our depth. It was possible, I reflected, that a mere different arrangement of the particulars of the scene, of the details of this picture, would be sufficient to modify, or perhaps to annihilate its capacity for sorrowful impression; and, acting upon this idea, I reined my horse to the precipitous brink of a black and lurid tarn[2] that lay in unruffled lustre by the dwelling, and gazed down—but with a shudder even more thrilling than before—upon the re-modelled and inverted images of the gray sedge, and the ghastly tree-stems, and the vacant and eye-like windows.

Nevertheless, in this mansion of gloom I now proposed to myself a sojourn of some weeks. Its proprietor, Roderick Usher, had been one of my boon companions in boyhood; but many years had elapsed since our last meeting. A letter, however, had lately reached me in a distant part of the country—a letter from him—which, in its wildly importunate nature, had admitted of no other than a personal reply. The MS. gave evidence of nervous agitation. The writer spoke of acute bodily illness—of a pitiable mental idiosyncrasy which oppressed him—and of an earnest desire to see me, as his best, and indeed, his only personal friend, with a view of attempting, by the cheerfulness of my society, some alleviation of his malady. It was the manner in which all this, and much more, was said—it was the apparent *heart* that went with his request—which allowed me no room for hesitation—and I accordingly obeyed, what I still considered a very singular summons, forthwith.

Although, as boys, we had been even intimate associates, yet I really knew little of my friend. His reserve had been always excessive and habitual. I was aware, however, that his very ancient family had been noted, time out of

1. The text is that of the first publication in *Burton's Gentleman's Magazine, and American Monthly Re-* view 5 (September 1839).
2. A small lake, normally in the mountains.

mind, for a peculiar sensibility of temperament, displaying itself, through long ages, in many works of exalted art, and manifested, of late, in repeated deeds of munificent yet unobtrusive charity, as well as in a passionate devotion to the intricacies, perhaps even more than to the orthodox and easily recognizable beauties, of musical science. I had learned, too, the very remarkable fact, that the stem of the Usher race, all time-honored as it was, had put forth, at no period, any enduring branch; in other words, that the entire family lay in the direct line of descent, and had always, with very trifling and very temporary variation, so lain. It was this deficiency, I considered, while running over in thought the perfect keeping of the character of the premises with the accredited character of the people, and while speculating upon the possible influence which the one, in the long lapse of centuries, might have exercised upon the other—it was this deficiency, perhaps, of collateral issue, and the consequent undeviating transmission, from sire to son, of the patrimony with the name, which had, at length, so identified the two as to merge the original title of the estate in the quaint and equivocal appellation of the "House of Usher"—an appellation which seemed to include, in the minds of the peasantry who used it, both the family and the family mansion.

I have said that the sole effect of my somewhat childish experiment, of looking down within the tarn, had been to deepen the first singular impression. There can be no doubt that the consciousness of the rapid increase of my superstition—for why should I not so term it?—served mainly to accelerate the increase itself. Such, I have long known, is the paradoxical law of all sentiments having terror as a basis. And it might have been for this reason only, that, when I again uplifted my eyes to the house itself, from its image in the pool, there grew in my mind a strange fancy—a fancy so ridiculous, indeed, that I but mention it to show the vivid force of the sensations which oppressed me. I had so worked upon my imagination as really to believe that around about the whole mansion and domain there hung an atmosphere peculiar to themselves and their immediate vicinity—an atmosphere which had no affinity with the air of heaven, but which had reeked up from the decayed trees, and the gray walls, and the silent tarn, in the form of an inelastic vapor or gas—dull, sluggish, faintly discernible, and leaden-hued. Shaking off from my spirit what *must* have been a dream, I scanned more narrowly the real aspect of the building. Its principal feature seemed to be that of an excessive antiquity. The discoloration of ages had been great. Minute fungi overspread the whole exterior, hanging in a fine tangled web-work from the eaves. Yet all this was apart from any extraordinary dilapidation. No portion of the masonry had fallen; and there appeared to be a wild inconsistency between its still perfect adaptation of parts, and the utterly porous, and evidently decayed condition of the individual stones. In this there was much that reminded me of the specious totality of old wood-work which has rotted for long years in some neglected vault, with no disturbance from the breath of the external air. Beyond this indication of extensive decay, however, the fabric gave little token of instability. Perhaps the eye of a scrutinizing observer might have discovered a barely perceptible fissure, which, extending from the roof of the building in front, made its way down the wall in a zigzag direction, until it became lost in the sullen waters of the tarn.

Noticing these things, I rode over a short causeway to the house. A servant in waiting took my horse, and I entered the Gothic archway of the hall. A valet, of stealthy step, thence conducted me, in silence, through many dark and intricate passages in my progress to the studio of his master. Much that I encountered on the way contributed, I know not how, to heighten the vague sentiments of which I have already spoken. While the objects around me— while the carvings of the ceilings, the sombre tapestries of the walls, the ebon blackness of the floors, and the phantasmagoric armorial trophies which rattled as I strode, were but matters to which, or to such as which, I had been accustomed from my infancy—while I hesitated not to acknowledge how familiar was all this—I still wondered to find how unfamiliar were the fancies which ordinary images were stirring up. On one of the staircases, I met the physician of the family. His countenance, I thought, wore a mingled expression of low cunning and perplexity. He accosted me with trepidation and passed on. The valet now threw open a door and ushered me into the presence of his master.

The room in which I found myself was very large and excessively lofty. The windows were long, narrow, and pointed, and at so vast a distance from the black oaken floor as to be altogether inaccessible from within. Feeble gleams of encrimsoned light made their way through the trelliced panes, and served to render sufficiently distinct the more prominent objects around; the eye, however, struggled in vain to reach the remoter angles of the chamber, or the recesses of the vaulted and fretted ceiling. Dark draperies hung upon the walls. The general furniture was profuse, comfortless, antique, and tattered. Many books and musical instruments lay scattered about, but failed to give any vitality to the scene. I felt that I breathed an atmosphere of sorrow. An air of stern, deep, and irredeemable gloom hung over and pervaded all.

Upon my entrance, Usher arose from a sofa upon which he had been lying at full length, and greeted me with a vivacious warmth which had much in it, I at first thought of an overdone cordiality—of the constrained effort of the ennuyé[3] man of the world. A glance, however, at his countenance convinced me of his perfect sincerity. We sat down; and for some moments, while he spoke not, I gazed upon him with a feeling half of pity, half of awe. Surely, man had never before so terribly altered, in so brief a period, as had Roderick Usher! It was with difficulty that I could bring myself to admit the identity of the wan being before me with the companion of my early boyhood. Yet the character of his face had been at all times remarkable. A cadaverousness of complexion; an eye large, liquid, and luminous beyond comparison; lips somewhat thin and very pallid, but of a surpassingly beautiful curve; a nose of a delicate Hebrew model, but with a breadth of nostril unusual in similar formations; a finely moulded chin, speaking, in its want of prominence, of a want of moral energy; hair of a more than web-like softness and tenuity; these features, with an inordinate expansion above the regions of the temple, made up altogether a countenance not easily to be forgotten. And now in the mere exaggeration of the prevailing character of these features, and of the expression they were wont to convey, lay so much of change that I doubted to whom I spoke. The now ghastly pallor of the skin, and the now miraculous lustre of the eye, above all things startled and even awed me. The silken hair, too, had been suffered to grow all unheeded, and as, in its wild gossamer texture, it floated rather than fell about the face, I could not, even with effort, connect its arabesque expression with any idea of simple humanity.

3. Bored (from French).

In the manner of my friend I was at once struck with an incoherence—an inconsistency; and I soon found this to arise from a series of feeble and futile struggles to overcome an habitual trepidancy, an excessive nervous agitation. For something of this nature I had indeed been prepared, no less by his letter, than by reminiscences of certain boyish traits, and by conclusions deduced from his peculiar physical conformation and temperament. His action was alternately vivacious and sullen. His voice varied rapidly from a tremulous indecision (when the animal spirits seemed utterly in abeyance) to that species of energetic concision—that abrupt, weighty, unhurried, and hollow-sounding enunciation—that leaden, self-balanced and perfectly modulated guttural utterance, which may be observed in the moments of the intensest excitement of the lost drunkard, or the irreclaimable eater of opium.

It was thus that he spoke of the object of my visit, of his earnest desire to see me, and of the solace he expected me to afford him. He entered, at some length, into what he conceived to be the nature of his malady. It was, he said, a constitutional and a family evil, and one for which he despaired to find a remedy—a mere nervous affection, he immediately added, which would undoubtedly soon pass off. It displayed itself in a host of unnatural sensations. Some of these, as he detailed them, interested and bewildered me—although, perhaps, the terms, and the general manner of the narration had their weight. He suffered much from a morbid acuteness of the senses; the most insipid food was alone endurable; he could wear only garments of certain texture; the odors of all flowers were oppressive; his eyes were tortured by even a faint light; and there were but peculiar sounds, and these from stringed instruments, which did not inspire him with horror.

To an anomalous species of terror I found him a bounden slave. "I shall perish," said he, "I *must* perish in this deplorable folly. Thus, thus, and not otherwise, shall I be lost. I dread the events of the future, not in themselves, but in their results. I shudder at the thought of any, even the most trivial, incident, which may operate upon this intolerable agitation of soul. I have, indeed, no abhorrence of danger, except in its absolute effect—in terror. In this unnerved—in this pitiable condition—I feel that I must inevitably abandon life and reason together in my struggles with some fatal demon of fear."

I learned, moreover, at intervals, and through broken and equivocal hints, another singular feature of his mental condition. He was enchained by certain superstitious impressions in regard to the dwelling which he tenanted, and from which, for many years, he had never ventured forth—in regard to an influence whose supposititious force was conveyed in terms too shadowy here to be restated—an influence which some peculiarities in the mere form and substance of his family mansion, had, by dint of long sufferance, he said, obtained over his spirit—an effect which the *physique* of the gray walls and turrets, and of the dim tarn into which they all looked down, had, at length, brought about upon the *morale* of his existence.

He admitted, however, although with hesitation, that much of the peculiar gloom which thus afflicted him could be traced to a more natural and far more palpable origin—to the severe and long-continued illness—indeed to the evidently approaching dissolution—of a tenderly beloved sister; his sole companion for long years—his last and only relative on earth. "Her decease," he said, with a bitterness which I can never forget, "would leave him (him the hopeless and the frail) the last of the ancient race of the Ushers." As he spoke, the lady Madeline (for so was she called) passed slowly through a remote portion of the apartment, and, without having noticed my presence, disappeared. I regarded her with an utter astonishment not unmingled with dread. Her figure, her air, her features—all, in their very minutest development were those—were identically (I can use no other sufficient term) were identically those of the Roderick Usher who sat beside me. A feeling of stupor oppressed me, as my eyes followed her retreating steps. As a door, at length, closed upon her exit, my glance sought instinctively and eagerly the countenance of the brother—but he had buried his face in his hands, and I could only perceive that a far more than ordinary wanness had overspread the emaciated fingers through which trickled many passionate tears.

The disease of the lady Madeline had long baffled the skill of her physicians. A settled apathy, a gradual wasting away of the person, and frequent although transient affections of a partially cataleptical character, were the unusual diagnosis. Hitherto she had steadily borne up against the pressure of her malady, and had not betaken herself finally to bed; but, on the closing in of the evening of my arrival at the house, she succumbed, as her brother told me at night with inexpressible agitation, to the prostrating power of the destroyer—and I learned that the glimpse I had obtained of her person would thus probably be the last I should obtain—that the lady, at least while living, would be seen by me no more.

For several days ensuing, her name was unmentioned by either Usher or myself; and, during this period, I was busied in earnest endeavors to alleviate the melancholy of my friend. We painted and read together—or I listened, as if in a dream, to the wild improvisations of his speaking guitar. And thus, as a closer and still closer intimacy admitted me more unreservedly into the recesses of his spirit, the more bitterly did I perceive the futility of all attempt at cheering a mind from which darkness, as if an inherent positive quality, poured forth upon all objects of the moral and physical universe, in one unceasing radiation of gloom.

I shall ever bear about me, as Moslemin their shrouds at Mecca; a memory of the many solemn hours I thus spent alone with the master of the House of Usher. Yet I should fail in any attempt to convey an idea of the exact character of the studies, or of the occupations, in which he involved me, or led me the way. An excited and highly distempered ideality threw a sulphurous lustre over all. His long improvised dirges will ring for ever in my ears. Among other things, I bear painfully in mind a certain singular perversion and amplification of the wild air of the last waltz of Von Weber.[4] From the paintings over which his elaborate fancy brooded, and which grew, touch by touch, into vaguenesses at which I shuddered the more thrillingly, because I shuddered knowing not why, from these paintings (vivid as their images now are before me) I would in vain endeavor to educe more than a small portion which should lie within the compass of merely written words. By the utter simplicity, by the nakedness, of his designs, he arrested and over-awed attention. If ever mortal painted an idea, that mortal was Roderick Usher. For me at least—in the circumstances then surrounding me—there arose out of the pure abstractions which the hypochondriac contrived to throw upon his canvas, an inten-

---

4. Karl Maria von Weber (1786–1826) established Romanticism in German opera; *The Last Waltz of Von Weber* was composed by Karl Gottlieb Reissiger (1798–1859).

sity of intolerable awe, no shadow of which felt I ever yet in the contemplation of the certainly glowing yet too concrete reveries of Fuseli.[5]

One of the phantasmagoric conceptions of my friend, partaking not so rigidly of the spirit of abstraction, may be shadowed forth, although feebly, in words. A small picture presented the interior of an immensely long and rectangular vault or tunnel, with low walls, smooth, white, and without interruption or device. Certain accessory points of the design served well to convey the idea that this excavation lay at an exceeding depth below the surface of the earth. No outlet was observed in any portion of its vast extent, and no torch, or other artificial source of light was discernible—yet a flood of intense rays rolled throughout, and bathed the whole in a ghastly and inappropriate splendor.

I have just spoken of that morbid condition of the auditory nerve which rendered all music intolerable to the sufferer, with the exception of certain effects of stringed instruments. It was, perhaps, the narrow limits to which he thus confined himself upon the guitar, which gave birth, in great measure, to the fantastic character of his performances. But the fervid *facility* of his impromptus could not be so accounted for. They must have been, and were, in the notes, as well as in the words of his wild fantasias, (for he not unfrequently accompanied himself with rhymed verbal improvisations,) the result of that intense mental collectedness and concentration to which I have previously alluded as observable only in particular moments of the highest artificial excitement. The words of one of these rhapsodies I have easily borne away in memory. I was, perhaps, the more forcibly impressed with it, as he gave it, because, in the under or mystic current of its meaning, I fancied that I perceived, and for the first time, a full consciousness on the part of Usher, of the tottering of his lofty reason upon her throne. The verses, which were entitled "The Haunted Palace," ran very nearly, if not accurately, thus:[6]

I

In the greenest of our valleys,
 By good angels tenanted,
Once a fair and stately palace—
 Snow-white palace—reared its head.
In the monarch Thought's dominion—
 It stood there!
Never seraph spread a pinion
 Over fabric half so fair.

II

Banners yellow, glorious, golden,
 On its roof did float and flow;
(This—all this—was in the olden
 Time long ago)
And every gentle air that dallied,
 In that sweet day,
Along the ramparts plumed and pallid,
 A winged odor went away.

5. Henry Fuseli (1741–1825), Swiss painter who made his reputation in London; noted for his interest in the supernatural.
6. In the original printing this note appeared at the end of the story: "The ballad of 'The Haunted Palace,' introduced in this tale, was published separately, some months ago, in the Baltimore 'Museum.' "

III

Wanderers in that happy valley
　Through two luminous windows saw
Spirits moving musically
　To a lute's well-tunéd law,
Round about a throne, where sitting
　(Porphyrogene!)[7]
In state his glory well befitting,
　The sovereign of the realm was seen.

IV

And all with pearl and ruby glowing
　Was the fair palace door,
Through which came flowing, flowing, flowing,
　And sparkling evermore,
A troop of Echoes whose sole duty
　Was but to sing,
In voices of surpassing beauty,
　The wit and wisdom of their king.

V

But evil things, in robes of sorrow,
　Assailed the monarch's high estate;
(Ah, let us mourn, for never morrow
　Shall dawn upon him, desolate!)
And, round about his home, the glory
　That blushed and bloomed
Is but a dim-remembered story
　Of the old time entombed.

VI

And travellers now within that valley,
　Through the red-litten windows, see
Vast forms that move fantastically
　To a discordant melody;
While, like a rapid ghastly river,
　Through the pale door,
A hideous throng rush out forever,
　And laugh—but smile no more.

I well remember that suggestions arising from this ballad led us into a train of thought wherein there became manifest an opinion of Usher's which I mention not so much on account of its novelty, (for other men have thought thus,) as on account of the pertinacity with which he maintained it. This opinion, in its general form, was that of the sentience of all vegetable things. But, in his disordered fancy, the idea had assumed a more daring character, and trespassed, under certain conditions, upon the kingdom of inorganization. I lack words to express the full extent, or the earnest *abandon* of his persuasion. The belief, however, was connected (as I have previously hinted) with the gray stones of the home of his forefathers. The condition of the sentience had been here, he imagined, fulfilled in the method of collocation of these stones—in the order of their arrangement, as well as in that of the many fungi which overspread them, and of the decayed trees which stood around—above all, in

7. Born to the purple, of royal birth.

the long undisturbed endurance of this arrangement, and in its reduplication in the still waters of the tarn. Its evidence—the evidence of the sentience—was to be seen, he said, (and I here started as he spoke,) in *the gradual yet certain condensation of an atmosphere of their own about the waters and the walls.* The result was discoverable, he added, in that silent, yet importunate and terrible influence which for centuries had moulded the destinies of his family, and which made *him* what I now saw him—what he was. Such opinions need no comment, and I will make none.

Our books—the books which, for years, had formed no small portion of the mental existence of the invalid—were, as might be supposed, in strict keeping with this character of phantasm. We pored together over such works as the Ververt et Chartreuse of Gresset; the Belphegor of Machiavelli; the Selenography of Brewster; the Heaven and Hell of Swedenborg; the Subterranean Voyage of Nicholas Klimm de Holberg; the Chiromancy of Robert Flud, of Jean d'Indaginé, and of De la Chambre; the Journey into the Blue Distance of Tieck; and the City of the Sun of Campanella. One favorite volume was a small octavo edition of the Directorium Inquisitorium, by the Dominican Eymeric de Gironne; and there were passages in Pomponius Mela, about the old African Satyrs and Œgipans, over which Usher would sit dreaming for hours. His chief delight, however, was found in the earnest and repeated perusal of an exceedingly rare and curious book in quarto Gothic—the manual of a forgotten church—the *Vigilae Mortuorum secundum Chorum Ecclesiae Maguntinae.*[8]

I could not help thinking of the wild ritual of this work, and of its probable influence upon the hypochondriac, when, one evening, having informed me abruptly that the lady Madeline was no more, he stated his intention of preserving her corpse for a fortnight, previously to its final interment, in one of the numerous vaults within the main walls of the building. The worldly reason, however, assigned for this singular proceeding, was one which I did not feel at liberty to dispute. The brother had been led to his resolution (so he told me) by considerations of the unusual character of the malady of the deceased, of certain obtrusive and eager inquiries on the part of her medical men, and of the remote and exposed situation of the burial ground of the family. I will not deny that when I called to mind the sinister countenance of the person whom I met upon the staircase, on the day of my arrival at the house, I had no desire to oppose what I regarded as at best but a harmless, and not by any means an unnatural precaution.[9]

8. The titles are real, although the way they sound in the narrator's inventory is at least as important as their precise contents. Jean Baptiste Gresset (1709–1777) wrote the anticlerical Vairvert and Ma Chartreuse. In Belphegor, by Niccolò Machiavelli (1469–1527), a demon comes to earth to prove that women damn men to hell. Sir David Brewster (1781–1868), Scotish physicist who studied optics and polarized light. Emanuel Swedenborg (1688–1772), Swedish scientist and mystic, presents a fantastically precise anatomy of living conditions in heaven and hell, seeing the two places as mutually attractive opposites. Ludwig Holberg (1684–1754), Danish dramatist and historian, deals with a voyage to the land of death and back. Robert Flud (1574–1637), English physician and noted Rosicrucian (the Rosicrucians then being a new organization of esoteric philosophy and theology that purported to be based on ancient lore from the Middle East), and two Frenchmen, Jean D'Indaginé (fl. early 16th cen-

tury) and Maria Cireau de la Chambre (1594–1669), all wrote on chiromancy (palm reading). The German Ludwig Tieck (1773–1853) wrote Das Alte Buch; oder Reise ins Blaue hinein, which deals with a journey to another world. The City of the Sun by the Italian Tommaso Campanella (1568–1639) is a famous utopian work. Nicholas Eymeric de Gerone, who was inquisitor-general for Castile in 1356, recorded procedures for torturing heretics. Pomponius Mela (1st century) was a Roman whose widely used book on geography (printed in Italy in 1471) described strange beasts ("oegipans" are African goat-men). A book called The Vigils of the Dead, According to the Church-Choir of Mayence was printed in Basel around 1500.

9. The shortage of corpses for dissection had led to the new profession of "resurrection men," who dug up fresh corpses and sold them to medical students and surgeons.

At the request of Usher, I personally aided him in the arrangements for the temporary entombment. The body having been encoffined, we two alone bore it to its rest. The vault in which we placed it (and which had been so long unopened that our torches, half smothered in its oppressive atmosphere, gave us little opportunity for investigation) was small, damp, and utterly without means of admission for light; lying, at great depth, immediately beneath that portion of the building in which was my own sleeping apartment. It had been used, apparently, in remote feudal times, for the worst purposes of a donjon-keep, and, in later days, as a place of deposit for powder, or other highly combustible substance, as a portion of its floor, and the whole interior of a long archway through which we reached it, were carefully sheathed with copper. The door, of massive iron, had been, also, similarly protected. Its immense weight caused an unusually sharp grating sound, as it moved upon its hinges.

Having deposited our mournful burden upon tressels within this region of horror, we partially turned aside the yet unscrewed lid of the coffin, and looked upon the face of the tenant. The exact similitude between the brother and sister even here again startled and confounded me. Usher, divining, perhaps, my thoughts, murmured out some few words from which I learned that the deceased and himself had been twins, and that sympathies of a scarcely intelligible nature had always existed between them. Our glances, however, rested not long upon the dead—for we could not regard her unawed. The disease which had thus entombed the lady in the maturity of youth, had left, as usual in all maladies of a strictly cataleptical character, the mockery of a faint blush upon the bosom and the face, and that suspiciously lingering smile upon the lip which is so terrible in death. We replaced and screwed down the lid, and, having secured the door of iron, made our way, with toil, into the scarcely less gloomy apartments of the upper portion of the house.

And now, some days of bitter grief having elapsed, an observable change came over the features of the mental disorder of my friend. His ordinary manner had vanished. His ordinary occupations were neglected or forgotten. He roamed from chamber to chamber with hurried, unequal, and objectless step. The pallor of his countenance had assumed, if possible, a more ghastly hue—but the luminousness of his eye had utterly gone out. The once occasional huskiness of his tone was heard no more; and a tremulous quaver, as if of extreme terror, habitually characterized his utterance.—There were times, indeed, when I thought his unceasingly agitated mind was laboring with an oppressive secret, to divulge which he struggled for the necessary courage. At times, again, I was obliged to resolve all into the mere inexplicable vagaries of madness, as I beheld him gazing upon vacancy for long hours, in an attitude of the profoundest attention, as if listening to some imaginary sound. It was no wonder that his condition terrified—that it infected me. I felt creeping upon me, by slow yet certain degrees, the wild influences of his own fantastic yet impressive superstitions.

It was, most especially, upon retiring to bed late in the night of the seventh or eighth day after the entombment of the lady Madeline, that I experienced the full power of such feelings. Sleep came not near my couch—while the hours waned and waned away. I struggled to reason off the nervousness which had dominion over me. I endeavored to believe that much, if not all of what I felt, was due to the phantasmagoric influence of the gloomy furniture of the room—of the dark and tattered draperies, which, tortured into motion by the breath of a rising tempest, swayed fitfully to and fro upon the walls, and rustled uneasily about the decorations of the bed. But my efforts were fruitless. An irrepressible tremor gradually pervaded my frame; and, at length, there sat upon my very heart an incubus[1] of utterly causeless alarm. Shaking this off with a gasp and a struggle, I uplifted myself upon the pillows, and, peering earnestly within the intense darkness of the chamber, harkened—I know not why, except that an instinctive spirit prompted me—to certain low and indefinite sounds which came, through the pauses of the storm, at long intervals, I knew not whence. Overpowered by an intense sentiment of horror, unaccountable yet unendurable, I threw on my clothes with haste, for I felt that I should sleep no more during the night, and endeavored to arouse myself from the pitiable condition into which I had fallen, by pacing rapidly to and fro through the apartment.

I had taken but few turns in this manner, when a light step on an adjoining staircase arrested my attention. I presently recognized it as that of Usher. In an instant afterwards he rapped, with a gentle touch, at my door, and entered, bearing a lamp. His countenance was, as usual, cadaverously wan—but there was a species of mad hilarity in his eyes—an evidently restrained hysteria in his whole demeanor. His air appalled me—but any thing was preferable to the solitude which I had so long endured, and I even welcomed his presence as a relief.

"And you have not seen it?" he said abruptly, after having stared about him for some moments in silence—"you have not then seen it?—but, stay! you shall." Thus speaking, and having carefully shaded his lamp, he hurried to one of the gigantic casements, and threw it freely open to the storm.

The impetuous fury of the entering gust nearly lifted us from our feet. It was, indeed, a tempestuous yet sternly beautiful night, and one wildly singular in its terror and its beauty. A whirlwind had apparently collected its force in our vicinity; for there were frequent and violent alterations in the direction of the wind; and the exceeding density of the clouds (which hung so low as to press upon the turrets of the house) did not prevent our perceiving the life-like velocity with which they flew careering from all points against each other, without passing away into the distance. I say that even their exceeding density did not prevent our perceiving this—yet we had no glimpse of the moon or stars—nor was there any flashing forth of the lightning. But the under surfaces of the huge masses of agitated vapor, as well as all terrestrial objects immediately around us, were glowing in the unnatural light of a faintly luminous and distinctly visible gaseous exhalation which hung about and enshrouded the mansion.

"You must not—you shall not behold this!" said I, shudderingly, to Usher, as I led him, with a gentle violence, from the window to a seat. "These appearances, which bewilder you, are merely electrical phenomena not uncommon—or it may be that they have their ghastly origin in the rank miasma of the tarn. Let us close this casement—the air is chilling and dangerous to your frame. Here is one of your favorite romances. I will read, and you shall listen—and so we will pass away this terrible night together."

The antique volume which I had taken up was the "Mad Trist" of Sir Launcelot Canning[2]—but I had called it a favorite of Usher's more in sad jest

1. An evil spirit supposed to lie upon people in their sleep.
2. Not a real book. "Trist" here means simply meet-

ing, or prearranged or fated encounter, not the lovers' meeting implied in the modern use of "tryst."

than in earnest; for, in truth, there is little in its uncouth and unimaginative prolixity which could have had interest for the lofty and spiritual ideality of my friend. It was, however, the only book immediately at hand; and I indulged a vague hope that the excitement which now agitated the hypochondriac might find relief (for the history of mental disorder is full of similar anomalies) even in the extremeness of the folly which I should read. Could I have judged, indeed, by the wild, overstrained air of vivacity with which he harkened, or apparently harkened, to the words of the tale, I might have well congratulated myself upon the success of my design.

I had arrived at that well-known portion of the story where Ethelred, the hero of the Trist, having sought in vain for peaceable admission into the dwelling of the hermit, proceeds to make good an entrance by force. Here, it will be remembered, the words of the narrative run thus—

"And Ethelred, who was by nature of a doughty heart, and who was now mighty withal, on account of the powerfulness of the wine which he had drunken, waited no longer to hold parley with the hermit, who, in sooth, was of an obstinate and maliceful turn, but, feeling the rain upon his shoulders, and fearing the rising of the tempest, uplifted his mace outright, and, with blows, made quickly room in the plankings of the door for his gauntleted hand, and now pulling therewith sturdily, he so cracked, and ripped, and tore all asunder, that the noise of the dry and hollow-sounding wood alarummed and reverberated throughout the forest."

At the termination of this sentence I started, and, for a moment, paused; for it appeared to me (although I at once concluded that my excited fancy had deceived me)—it appeared to me that, from some very remote portion of the mansion or of its vicinity, there came, indistinctly, to my ears, what might have been, in its exact similarity of character, the echo (but a stifled and dull one certainly) of the very cracking and ripping sound which Sir Launcelot had so particularly described. It was, beyond doubt, the coincidence alone which had arrested my attention; for, amid the rattling of the sashes of the casements, and the ordinary commingled noises of the still increasing storm, the sound, in itself, had nothing, surely, which should have interested or disturbed me. I continued the story.

"But the good champion Ethelred, now entering within the door, was sore enraged and amazed to perceive no signal of the maliceful hermit; but, in the stead thereof, a dragon of scaly and prodigious demeanor, and of a fiery tongue, which sate in guard before a palace of gold, with a floor of silver; and upon the wall there hung a shield of shining brass with this legend enwritten—

Who entereth herein, a conqueror hath bin,
Who slayeth the dragon, the shield he shall win.

And Ethelred uplifted his mace, and struck upon the head of the dragon, which fell before him, and gave up his pesty breath, with a shriek so horrid and harsh, and withal so piercing, that Ethelred had fain to close his ears with his hands against the dreadful noise of it, the like whereof was never before heard."

Here again I paused abruptly, and now with a feeling of wild amazement— for there could be no doubt whatever that, in this instance, I did actually hear (although from what direction it proceeded I found it impossible to say) a low and apparently distant, but harsh, protracted, and most unusual screaming or grating sound—the exact counterpart of what my fancy had already conjured up as the sound of the dragon's unnatural shriek as described by the romancer.

Oppressed, as I certainly was, upon the occurrence of this second and most extraordinary coincidence, by a thousand conflicting sensations, in which wonder and extreme terror were predominant, I still retained sufficient presence of mind to avoid exciting, by any observation, the sensitive nervousness of my companion. I was by no means certain that he had noticed the sounds in question; although, assuredly, a strange alteraton had, during the last few minutes, taken place in his demeanor. From a position fronting my own, he had gradually brought round his chair, so as to sit with his face to the door of the chamber, and thus I could but partially perceive his features, although I saw that his lips trembled as if he were murmuring inaudibly. His head had dropped upon his breast—yet I knew that he was not asleep, from the wide and rigid opening of the eye, as I caught a glance of it in profile. The motion of his body, too, was at variance with his idea—for he rocked from side to side with a gentle yet constant and uniform sway. Having rapidly taken notice of all this, I resumed the narrative of Sir Launcelot, which thus proceeded:—

"And now, the champion, having escaped from the terrible fury of the dragon, bethinking himself of the brazen shield, and of the breaking up of the enchantment which was upon it, removed the carcass from out of the way before him, and approached valorously over the silver pavement of the castle to where the shield was upon the wall; which in sooth tarried not for his full coming, but fell down at his feet upon the silver floor, with a mighty great and terrible ringing sound."

No sooner had these syllables passed my lips, than—as if a shield of brass had indeed, at the moment, fallen heavily upon a floor of silver—I became aware of a distinct, hollow, metallic, and clangorous, yet apparently muffled reverberation. Completely unnerved, I started convulsively to my feet, but the measured rocking movement of Usher was undisturbed. I rushed to the chair in which he sat. His eyes were bent fixedly before him, and throughout his whole countenance there reigned a more than stony rigidity. But, as I laid my hand upon his shoulder, there came a strong shudder over his frame; a sickly smile quivered about his lips; and I saw that he spoke in a low, hurried, and gibbering murmur, as if unconscious of my presence. Bending closely over his person, I at length drank in the hideous import of his words.

"Not hear it?—yes, I hear it, and *have* heard it. Long—long—long—many minutes, many hours, many days, have I heard it—yet I dared not—oh, pity me, miserable wretch that I am!—I dared not—I *dared* not speak! *We have put her living in the tomb!* Said I not that my senses were acute?—I *now* tell you that I heard her first feeble movements in the hollow coffin. I heard them—many, many days ago—yet I dared not—*I dared not speak!* And now—to-night—Ethelred—ha! ha!—the breaking of the hermit's door, and the death-cry of the dragon, and the clangor of the shield—say, rather, the rending of the coffin, and the grating of the iron hinges, and her struggles within the coppered archway of the vault! Oh wither shall I fly? Will she not be here anon? Is she not hurrying to upbraid me for my haste? Have I not heard her footsteps on the stair? Do I not distinguish that heavy and horrible beating of her heart? Madman!"—here he sprung violently to his feet, and shrieked out his syllables, as if in the effort he were giving up his soul—"Madman! *I tell you that she now stands without the door!*"

As if in the superhuman energy of his utterance there had been found the potency of a spell—the huge antique pannels to which the speaker pointed, threw slowly back, upon the instant, their ponderous and ebony jaws. It was the work of the rushing gust—but then without those doors there *did* stand the lofty and enshrouded figure of the lady Madeline of Usher. There was blood upon her white robes, and the evidence of some bitter struggle upon every portion of her emaciated frame. For a moment she remained trembling and reeling to and fro upon the threshold—then, with a low moaning cry, fell heavily inward upon the person of her brother, and in her horrible and now final death-agonies, bore him to the floor a corpse, and a victim to the terrors he had dreaded.

From that chamber, and from that mansion, I fled aghast. The storm was still abroad in all its wrath as I found myself crossing the old causeway. Suddenly there shot along the path a wild light, and I turned to see whence a gleam so unusual could have issued—for the vast house and its shadows were alone behind me. The radiance was that of the full, setting, and blood-red moon, which now shone vividly through that once barely-discernible fissure, of which I have before spoken, as extending from the roof of the building, in a zig-zag direction, to the base. While I gazed, this fissure rapidly widened—there came a fierce breath of the whirlwind—the entire orb of the satellite burst at once upon my sight—my brain reeled as I saw the mighty walls rushing asunder—there was a long tumultuous shouting sound like the voice of a thousand waters—and the deep and dank tarn at my feet closed sullenly and silently over the fragments of the *"House of Usher."*

1839

William Wilson. A Tale[1]

> *What say of it? what say of* conscience *grim,*
> *That spectre in my path?*
> —*Chamberlaine's Pharronida*[2]

Let me call myself, for the present, William Wilson. The fair page now lying before me need not be sullied with my real appellation. This has been already too much an object for the scorn, for the horror, for the detestation of my race. To the uttermost regions of the globe have not the indignant winds bruited its unparalleled infamy? oh, outcast of all outcasts most abandoned! To the earth art thou not for ever dead? to its honours, to its flowers, to its golden aspirations? and a cloud, dense, dismal, and limitless, does it not hang eternally between thy hopes and heaven?

I would not, if I could, here or to-day, embody a record of my later years of unspeakable misery, and unpardonable crime. This epoch—these later years—took unto themselves a sudden elevation in turpitude, whose origin

---

1. This tale is reprinted from its first appearance in the Philadelphia annual *The Gift*, dated 1840 but published in September 1839. Into it Poe worked some memories of the school he attended at Stoke-Newington (Bransby was the name of his own principal there). January 19 is Poe's own birthday as well as William Wilson's, and in different printings of the story Wil-

son's birth year appears as 1809, 1811, and 1813, the latter two dates being those Poe also used in autobiographical accounts to make him even more precocious than he was.
2. The epigraph is not in this 1659 poem by William Chamberlayne.

alone it is my present purpose to assign. Men usually grow base by degrees. From me, in an instant, all virtue dropped bodily as a mantle. I shrouded my nakedness in triple guilt. From comparatively trivial wickedness I passed, with the stride of a giant, into more than the enormities of an Elah-Gabalus.[3] What chance, what one event brought this evil thing to pass, bear with me while I relate. Death approaches; and the shadow which foreruns him has thrown a softening influence over my spirit. I long, in passing through the dim valley, for the sympathy—I had nearly said for the pity— of my fellow-men. I would fain have them believe that I have been, in some measure, the slave of circumstances beyond human control. I would wish them to seek out for me, in the details I am about to give, some little oasis of *fatality* amid a wilderness of error. I would have them allow—what they cannot refrain from allowing— that, although temptation may have erewhile existed as great, man was never *thus*, at least, tempted before—certainly, never *thus* fell. And therefore has he never thus suffered. Have I not indeed been living in a dream? And am I not now dying a victim to the horror and the mystery of the wildest of all sublunary visions?

I am come of a race whose imaginative and easily excitable temperament has at all times rendered them remarkable; and, in my earliest infancy, I gave evidence of having fully inherited the family character. As I advanced in years it was more strongly developed; becoming, for many reasons, a cause of serious disquietude to my friends, and of positive injury to myself. I grew self-willed, addicted to the wildest caprices, and a prey to the most ungovernable passions. Weak-minded, and beset with constitutional infirmities akin to my own, my parents could do but little to check the evil propensities which distinguished me. Some feeble and ill-directed efforts resulted in complete failure on their part, and of course, in total triumph on mine. Thenceforward my voice was a household law; and at an age when few children have abandoned their leading-strings, I was left to the guidance of my own will, and became, in all but name, the master of my own actions.

My earliest recollections of a school-life are connected with a large, rambling, cottage-built, and somewhat decayed building in a misty-looking village of England, where were a vast number of gigantic and gnarled trees, and where all the houses were excessively ancient and inordinately tall. In truth, it was a dream-like and spirit-soothing place, that venerable old town. At this moment, in fancy, I feel the refreshing chilliness of its deeply-shadowed avenues, inhale the fragrance of its thousand shrubberies, and thrill anew with undefinable delight, at the deep, hollow note of the church-bell, breaking each hour, with sullen and sudden roar, upon the stillness of the dusky atmosphere in which the old, fretted, Gothic steeple lay imbedded and asleep.

It gives me, perhaps, as much of pleasure as I can now in any manner experience, to dwell upon minute recollections of the school and its concerns. Steeped in misery as I am—misery, alas! only too real—I shall be pardoned for seeking relief, however slight and temporary, in the weakness of a few rambling details. These, moreover, utterly trivial, and even ridiculous in themselves, assume, to my fancy, adventitious importance as connected with a period and a locality, when and where I recognise the first ambiguous moni-

3. Elagabalus (b. 204), boy emperor of Rome (218–222), murdered by his imperial guards. Among the "enormities" were the imposition of the worship of Baal, the Semitic fertility god, and the favor displayed toward handsome homosexual boys.

tions of the destiny which afterwards so fully overshadowed me. Let me then remember.

The house, I have said, was old, irregular, and cottage-built. The grounds were extensive, and an enormously high and solid brick wall, topped with a bed of mortar and broken glass, encompassed the whole. This prison-like rampart formed the limit of our domain; beyond it we saw but thrice a week— once every Saturday afternoon, when, attended by two ushers,[4] we were permitted to take brief walks in a body through some of the neighbouring fields— and twice during Sunday, when we were paraded in the same formal manner to the morning and evening service in the one church of the village. Of this church the principal of our school was pastor. With how deep a spirit of wonder and perplexity was I wont to regard him from our remote pew in the gallery, as, with step solemn and slow he ascended the pulpit! This reverend man, with countenance so demurely benign, with robes so glossy and so clerically flowing, with wig so minutely powdered, so rigid and so vast—could this be he who of late, with sour visage, and in snuffy habiliments, administered, ferule in hand, the Draconian[5] laws of the academy? Oh, gigantic paradox too utterly monstrous for solution!

At an angle of the ponderous wall frowned a more ponderous gate. It was riveted and studded with iron bolts, and surmounted with jagged iron spikes. What impressions of deep awe it inspired! It was never opened save for the three periodical egressions and ingressions already mentioned; then, in every creak of its mighty hinges we found a plenitude of mystery, a world of matter for solemn remark, or for far more solemn meditation.

The extensive enclosure was irregular in form, having many capacious recesses. Of these, three or four of the largest constituted the play-ground. It was level, and covered with fine hard gravel. I well remember it had no trees, nor benches, nor any thing similar within it. Of course it was in the rear of the house. In front lay a small parterre, planted with box and other shrubs; but through this sacred division we passed only upon rare occasions indeed, such as a first advent or final departure from school, or perhaps, when a parent or friend having called for us, we joyfully took our way home for the Christmas or Mid-summer holydays.

But the house—how quaint an old building was this!—to me how veritably a palace of enchantment! There was really no end to its windings, to its incomprehensible sub-divisions. It was impossible, at any given time, to say with certainty upon which of its two stories one happened to be. From each room to every other there were sure to be found three or four steps either in ascent or descent. Then the lateral branches were innumerable—inconceivable, and so returning in upon themselves, that our most exact ideas in regard to the whole mansion were not very far different from those with which we pondered upon infinity. During the five years of my residence here I was never able to ascertain with precision, in what remote locality lay the little sleeping apartment assigned to myself and some eighteen or twenty other scholars.

The school-room was the largest in the house—I could not help thinking, in the world. It was very long, narrow, and dismally low, with pointed Gothic windows and a ceiling of oak. In a remote and terror-inspiring angle was a square enclosure of eight or ten feet, comprising the sanctum, "during hours,"

---

4. Assistant schoolmasters.
5. Merciless, from Draco, Athenian lawgiver, whose code (621? B.C.) set death as the penalty for numerous crimes.

of our principal, the Reverend Dr. Bransby. It was a solid structure, with massy door, sooner than open which in the absence of "the Dominie,"[6] we would all have willingly perished by the *peine forte et dure*.[7] In other angles were two other similar boxes, far less reverenced, indeed, but still greatly matters of awe. One of these was the pulpit of "the classical" usher, one of the "English and mathematical." Interspersed about the room, crossing and recrossing in endless irregularity, were innumerable benches and desks, black, ancient, and time-worn, piled desperately with much-bethumbed books, and so beseamed with initial letters, names at full length, meaningless gashes, grotesque figures, and other multiplied efforts of the knife, as to have utterly lost what little of original form might have been their portion in days long departed. A huge bucket with water stood at one extremity of the room, and a clock of stupendous dimensions at the other.

Encompassed by the massy walls of this venerable academy I passed, yet not in tedium or disgust, the years of the third lustrum[8] of my life. The teeming brain of childhood requires no external world of incident to occupy or amuse it, and the apparently dismal monotony of a school, was replete with more intense excitement than my riper youth has derived from luxury, or my full manhood from crime. Yet I must believe that my first mental developement had in it much of the uncommon, even much of the *outré*.[9] Upon mankind at large the events of very early existence rarely leave in mature age any definite impression. All is gray shadow—a weak and irregular remembrance—an indistinct regathering of feeble pleasures and phantasmagoric pains. With me this is not so. In childhood I must have felt with the energy of a man what I now find stamped upon memory in lines as vivid, as deep, and as durable as the exergues of the Carthaginian medals.[1]

Yet in fact—in the fact of the world's view—how little was there to remember! The morning's awakening, the nightly summons to bed; the connings,[2] the recitations; the periodical half-holidays and perambulations; the playground, with its broils, its pastimes, its intrigues—these, by a mental sorcery long forgotten, were made to involve a wilderness of sensation, a world of rich incident, an universe of varied emotion, of excitement the most passionate and spirit-stirring. *"Oh, le bon temps, que ce siecle de fer!"*[3]

In truth, the ardency, the enthusiasm, and the imperiousness of my disposition soon rendered me a marked character among my schoolmates, and by slow but natural gradations, gave me an ascendency over all not greatly older than myself—over all with one single exception. This exception was found in the person of a scholar, who although no relation, bore the same Christian and surname as myself—a circumstance, in truth, little remarkable, for, notwithstanding a noble descent, mine was one of those every-day appellations which seem, by prescriptive right, to have been, time out of mind, the common property of the mob. In this narrative I have therefore designated myself as William Wilson—a fictitious title not very dissimilar to the real. My namesake alone, of those who in school phraseology constituted "our set," presumed

6. Minister or schoolteacher (Bransby was both).
7. Pressing to death, as with large flat rocks (French).
8. Five-year period.
9. Extreme, exaggerated (French).
1. Perhaps Poe has in mind no particular medal of Carthage (the ancient sea power on the Mediterranean near modern Tunis, defeated by Rome in the 2nd cen-

tury B.C.). "Exergues": the spaces beneath the central design on the reverse of coins.
2. Memorizings.
3. From Voltaire's *Le Mondain* (1736): "Oh, this age of iron is a good time" (French). Iron implies dull utilitarianism in contrast to the fabled heroic age of gold.

to compete with me in the studies of the class, in the sports and broils of the play-ground—to refuse implicit belief in my assertions, and submission to my will—indeed to interfere with my arbitrary dictation in any respect whatsoever. If there be on earth a supreme and unqualified despotism, it is the despotism of a master mind in boyhood over the less energetic spirits of his companions.

Wilson's rebellion was to me a source of the greatest embarrassment—the more so as, in spite of the bravado with which in public I made a point of treating him and his pretensions, I secretly felt that I feared him, and could not help thinking the equality which he maintained so easily with myself a proof of his true superiority, since not to be overcome cost me a perpetual struggle. Yet this superiority—even this equality—was in truth acknowledged by no one but myself; our companions, by some unaccountable blindness, seemed not even to suspect it. Indeed, his competition, his resistance, and especially his impertinent and dogged interference with my purposes, were not more pointed than private. He appeared to be utterly destitute alike of the ambition which urged, and of the passionate energy of mind which enabled me to excel. In his rivalry he might have been supposed actuated solely by a whimsical desire to thwart, astonish, or mortify myself; although there were times when I could not help observing, with a feeling made up of wonder, abasement, and pique, that he mingled with his injuries, his insults, or his contradictions, a certain most inappropriate, and assuredly most unwelcome *affectionateness* of manner. I could only conceive this singular behaviour to arise from a consummate self-conceit assuming the vulgar airs of patronage and protection.

Perhaps it was this latter trait in Wilson's conduct, conjoined with our identity of name, and the mere accident of our having entered the school upon the same day, which set afloat the notion that we were brothers, among the senior classes in the academy. These do not usually inquire with much strictness into the affairs of their juniors. I have before said, or should have said, that Wilson was not, in the most remote degree, connected with my family. But assuredly if we *had* been brothers we must have been twins, for, since leaving Dr. Bransby's, I casually learned that my namesake—a somewhat remarkable coincidence—was born on the nineteenth of January, 1811—and this is precisely the day of my own nativity.

It may seem strange that in spite of the continual anxiety occasioned me by the rivalry of Wilson, and his intolerable spirit of contradiction, I could not bring myself to hate him altogether. We had, to be sure, nearly every day a quarrel, in which, yielding me publicly the palm of victory, he, in some manner, contrived to make me feel that it was he who had deserved it; yet a sense of pride upon my part, and a veritable dignity upon his own, kept us always upon what are called "speaking terms," while there were many points of strong congeniality in our tempers, operating to awake in me a sentiment which our position alone, perhaps, prevented from ripening into friendship. It is difficult, indeed, to define, or even to describe, my real feelings towards him. They were formed of a heterogeneous mixture—some petulant animosity, which was not yet hatred, some esteem, more respect, much fear, with a world of uneasy curiosity. To the moralist fully acquainted with the minute springs of human action, it will be unnecessary to say, in addition, that Wilson and myself were the most inseparable of companions.

It was no doubt the anomalous state of affairs existing between us which turned all my attacks upon him, and they were many, either open or covert, into the channel of banter or practical joke (giving pain while assuming the aspect of mere fun) rather than into that of a more serious and determined hostility. But my endeavours on this head were by no means uniformly successful, even when my plans were the most wittily concocted; for my namesake had much about him, in character, of that unassuming and quiet austerity which, while enjoying the poignancy of its own jokes, has no heel of Achilles[4] in itself, and absolutely refuses to be laughed at. I could find, indeed, but one vulnerable point, and that, lying in a personal peculiarity arising, perhaps, from constitutional disease, would have been spared by any antagonist less at his wit's end than myself—my rival had a weakness in the faucial or guttural organs which precluded him from raising his voice at any time *above a very low whisper*. Of this defect I did not fail to take what poor advantage lay in my power.

Wilson's retaliations in kind were many, and there was one form of his practical wit that disturbed me beyond measure. How his sagacity first discovered at all that so petty a thing would vex me is a question I never could solve—but, having discovered, he habitually practised the annoyance. I had always felt aversion to my uncourtly patronymic, and its very common, if not plebeian, praenomen. The words were venom in my ears; and when, upon the day of my arrival, a second William Wilson came also to the academy, I felt angry with him for bearing the name, and doubly disgusted with the name because a stranger bore it who would be the cause of its twofold repetition, who would be constantly in my presence, and whose concerns, in the ordinary routine of the school business, must, inevitably, on account of the detestable coincidence, be often confounded with my own.

The feeling of vexation thus engendered, grew stronger with every circumstance tending to show resemblance, moral or physical, between my rival and myself. I had not then discovered the remarkable fact that we were of the same age; but I saw that we were of the same height, and I perceived that we were not altogether unlike in general contour of person and outline of feature. I was galled, too, by the rumour touching a relationship which had grown current in the upper forms. In a word, nothing could more seriously disturb me, (although I scrupulously concealed such disturbance,) than any allusion to a similarity of mind, person, or condition existing between us. But, in truth, I had no reason to believe that (with the exception of the matter of relationship, and in the case of Wilson himself,) this similarity had ever been made a subject of comment, or even observed at all by our schoolfellows. That *he* observed it in all its bearings, and as fixedly as I, was apparent, but that he could discover in such circumstances so fruitful a field of annoyance for myself can only be attributed, as I said before, to his more than ordinary penetration.

His cue, which was to perfect an imitation of myself, lay both in words and in actions; and most admirably did he play his part. My dress it was an easy matter to copy; my gait and general manner were, without difficulty, appropriated; in spite of his constitutional defect, even my voice did not escape him. My louder tones were, of course, unattempted, but then the key, it was identical; *and his singular whisper, it grew the very echo of my own.*

---

4. I.e., no vulnerable spot. The mother of Achilles, the hero of Homer's *Iliad*, tried to make her son immortal by dipping him into the river Styx. But no water touched the heel she held him by, and in that heel he received his death wound.

How greatly this most exquisite portraiture harassed me, (for it could not justly be termed a caricature,) I will not now venture to describe. I had but one consolation—in the fact that the imitation, apparently, was noticed by myself alone, and that I had to endure only the knowing and strangely sarcastic smiles of my namesake himself. Satisfied with having produced in my bosom the intended effect, he seemed to chuckle in secret over the sting he had inflicted, and was characteristically disregardful of the public applause which the success of his witty endeavours might have so easily elicited. That the school, indeed, did not feel his design, perceive its accomplishment, and participate in his sneer, was, for many anxious months, a riddle I could not resolve. Perhaps the *gradation* of his copy rendered it not so readily perceptible, or, more possibly, I owed my security to the masterly air of the copyist, who, disdaining the letter, which in a painting is all the obtuse can see, gave but the full spirit of his original for my individual contemplation and chagrin.

I have already more than once spoken of the disgusting air of patronage which he assumed towards me, and of his frequent officious interference with my will. This interference often took the ungracious character of advice; advice not openly given, but hinted or insinuated. I received it with a repugnance which gained strength as I grew in years. Yet, at this distant day, let me do him the simple justice to acknowledge that I can recall no occasion when the suggestions of my rival were on the side of those errors or follies so usual to his immature age, and seeming inexperience; that his moral sense, at least, if not his general talents and worldly wisdom, was far keener than my own; and that I might, to-day, have been a better, and thus a happier man, had I more seldom rejected the counsels embodied in those meaning whispers which I then but too cordially hated, and too bitterly derided.

As it was, I at length grew restive in the extreme, under his distasteful supervision, and daily resented more and more openly what I considered his intolerable arrogance. I have said that, in the first years of our connexion as schoolmates, my feelings in regard to him might have been easily ripened into friendship; but, in the latter months of my residence at the academy, although the intrusion of his ordinary manner had, beyond doubt, in some measure, abated, my sentiments, in nearly similar proportion, partook very much of positive hatred. Upon one occasion he saw this, I think, and afterwards avoided, or made a show of avoiding me.

It was about the same period, if I remember aright, that, in an altercation of violence with him, in which he was more than usually thrown off his guard, and spoke and acted with an openness of demeanour rather foreign to his nature, I discovered, or fancied I discovered, in his accent, his air, and general appearance, a something which first startled, and then deeply interested me, by bringing to mind dim visions of my earliest infancy; wild, confused, and thronging memories of a time when memory herself was yet unborn. I cannot better describe the sensation which oppressed me than by saying that I could with difficulty shake off the belief that myself and the being who stood before me had been acquainted at some epoch very long ago; some point of the past even infinitely remote. The delusion, however, faded rapidly as it came; and I mention it at all but to define the day of the last conversation I there held with my singular namesake.

The huge old house, with its countless subdivisions, had several enormously large chambers communicating with each other, where slept the greater number of the students. There were, however, as must necessarily happen in a building so awkwardly planned, many little nooks or recesses, the odds and ends of the structure; and these the economic ingenuity of Dr. Bransby had also fitted up as dormitories—although, being the merest closets, they were capable of accommodating only a single individual. One of these small apartments was occupied by Wilson.

It was upon a gloomy and tempestuous night of an early autumn, about the close of my fifth year at the school, and immediately after the altercation just mentioned, that, finding every one wrapped in sleep, I arose from bed, and, lamp in hand, stole through a wilderness of narrow passages from my own bed-room to that of my rival. I had been long plotting one of those ill-natured pieces of practical wit at his expense in which I had hitherto been so uniformly unsuccessful. It was my intention, now, to put my scheme in operation, and I resolved to make him feel the whole extent of the malice with which I was imbued. Having reached his closet, I noiselessly entered, leaving the lamp with a shade over it, on the outside. I advanced a step, and listened to the sound of his tranquil breathing. Assured of his being asleep, I returned, took the light, and with it again approached the bed. Close curtains were around it, which, in the prosecution of my plan, I slowly and quietly withdrew, when the bright rays fell vividly upon the sleeper, and my eyes, at the same moment upon his countenance. I looked, and a numbness, an iciness of feeling instantly pervaded my frame. My breast heaved, my knees tottered, my whole spirit became possessed with an objectless yet intolerable horror. Gasping for breath, I lowered the lamp in still nearer proximity to the face. Were these—*these* the lineaments of William Wilson? I saw, indeed, that they were his, but I shook as with a fit of the ague in fancying they were not. What *was* there about them to confound me in this manner? I gazed—while my brain reeled with a multitude of incoherent thoughts. Not thus he appeared—assuredly not *thus*—in the vivacity of his waking hours. The same name; the same contour of person; the same day of arrival at the academy! And then his dogged and meaningless imitation of my gait, my voice, my habits, and my manner! Was it, in truth, within the bounds of human possibility that *what I now witnessed* was the result of the habitual practice of this sarcastic imitation? Awe-stricken, and with a creeping shudder, I extinguished the lamp, passed silently from the chamber, and left, at once, the halls of that old academy, never to enter them again.

After a lapse of some months, spent at home in mere idleness, I found myself a student at Eton. The brief interval had been sufficient to enfeeble my remembrance of the events at Dr. Bransby's, or at least, to effect a material change in the nature of the feelings with which I remembered them. The truth—the tragedy—of the drama was no more. I could now find room to doubt the evidence of my senses; and seldom called up the subject at all but with wonder at the extent of human credulity, and a smile at the vivid force of the imagination which I hereditarily possessed. Neither was this species of scepticism likely to be diminished by the character of the life I led at Eton. The vortex of thoughtless folly into which I there so immediately and so recklessly plunged, washed away all but the froth of my past hours—engulfed, at once, every solid or serious impression, and left to memory only the veriest levities of a former existence.

I do not wish, however, to trace the course of my miserable profligacy here—a profligacy which set at defiance the laws, while it eluded the vigilance of the institution. Three years of folly, passed without profit, had but given me rooted habits of vice, and added, in a somewhat unusual degree, to my bodily stature, when, after a week of soulless dissipation, I invited a small party of the most dissolute students to a secret carousal in my chamber. We met at a late hour of the night, for our debaucheries were to be faithfully protracted until morning. The wine flowed freely, and there were not wanting other, perhaps more dangerous, seductions; so that the gray dawn had already faintly appeared in the east, while our delirious extravagance was at its height. Madly flushed with cards and intoxication, I was in the act of insisting upon a toast of more than intolerable profanity, when my attention was suddenly diverted by the violent, although partial unclosing of the door of the apartment, and by the eager voice from without of a servant. He said that some person, apparently in great haste, demanded to speak with me in the hall.

Wildly excited with the potent *Vin de Barac*, the unexpected interruption rather delighted than surprised me. I staggered forward at once, and a few steps brought me to the vestibule of the building. In this low and small room there hung no lamp; and now no light at all was admitted, save that of the exceedingly feeble dawn which made its way through a semicircular window. As I put my foot over the threshold I became aware of the figure of a youth about my own height, and (what then peculiarly struck my mad fancy) habited in a white cassimere morning frock, cut in the novel fashion of the one I myself wore at the moment. This the faint light enabled me to perceive—but the features of his face I could not distinguish. Immediately upon my entering he strode hurriedly up to me, and, seizing me by the arm with a gesture of petulant impatience, whispered the words "William Wilson!" in my ear. I grew perfectly sober in an instant.

There was that in the manner of the stranger, and in the tremulous shake of his uplifted finger, as he held it between my eyes and the light, which filled me with unqualified amazement—but it was not this which had so violently moved me. It was the pregnancy of solemn admonition in the singular, low, hissing utterance; and, above all, it was the character, the tone, *the key*, of those few, simple, and familiar, yet whispered, syllables, which came with a thousand thronging memories of by-gone days, and struck upon my soul with the shock of a galvanic battery. Ere I could recover the use of my senses he was gone.

Although this event failed not of a vivid effect upon my disordered imagination, yet was it evanescent as vivid. For some weeks, indeed, I busied myself in earnest inquiry, or was wrapped in a cloud of morbid speculation. I did not pretend to disguise from my perception the identity of the singular individual who thus perseveringly interfered with my affairs, and harassed me with his insinuated counsel. But who and what was this Wilson?—and whence came he?—and what were his purposes? Upon neither of these points could I be satisfied—merely ascertaining, in regard to him, that a sudden accident in his family had caused his removal from Dr. Bransby's Academy on the afternoon of the day in which I myself had eloped. But in a brief period I ceased to think upon the subject; my attention being all absorbed in a contemplated departure for Oxford. Thither I soon went; the uncalculating vanity of my parents furnished me with an outfit, and annual establishment, which would enable me to indulge at will in the luxury already so dear to my heart—to vie in profuseness of expenditure with the haughtiest heirs of the wealthiest earldoms in Great Britain.

Excited by such appliances to vice, my constitutional temperament broke forth with redoubled ardour, and I spurned even the common restraints of decency in the mad infatuation of my revels. But it were absurd to pause in the detail of my extravagance. Let it suffice, that among spendthrifts I out-heroded Herod,[5] and that, giving name to a multitude of novel follies, I added no brief appendix to the long catalogue of vices then usual in the most disso-lute university of Europe.

It could hardly be credited, however, that I had, even here, so utterly fallen from the gentlemanly estate as to seek acquaintance with the vilest arts of the gambler by profession, and, having become an adept in his despicable science, to practise it habitually as a means of increasing my already enormous income at the expense of the weak-minded among my fellow-collegians. Such, never-theless, was the fact. And the very enormity of this offence against all manly and honourable sentiment proved, beyond doubt, the main, if not the sole reason of the impunity with which it was committed. Who, indeed, among my most abandoned associates, would not rather have disputed the clearest evidence of his senses, than have suspected of such courses the gay, the frank, the generous William Wilson—the noblest and most liberal commoner at Oxford—him whose follies (said his parasites) were but the follies of youth and unbridled fancy—whose errors but inimitable whim—whose darkest vice but a careless and dashing extravagance.

I had been now two years successfully busied in this way, when there came to the university a young *parvenu* nobleman, Glendinning—rich, said report, as Herodes Atticus[6]—his riches, too, as easily acquired. I soon found him of weak intellect, and, of course, marked him as a fitting subject for my skill. I frequently engaged him in play, and contrived, with a gambler's usual art, to let him win considerable sums, the more effectually to entangle him in my snares. At length, my schemes being ripe, I met him (with the full intention that this meeting should be final and decisive) at the chambers of a fellow-commoner, (Mr. Preston,) equally intimate with both, but who, to do him justice, entertained not even a remote suspicion of my design. To give to this a better colouring, I had contrived to have assembled a party of some eight or ten, and was solicitously careful that the introduction of cards should appear accidental, and originate in the proposal of my contemplated dupe himself. To be brief upon a vile topic, none of the low finesse was omitted, so custom-ary upon similar occasions that it is a just matter for wonder how any are still found so besotted as to fall its victim.

We had protracted our sitting far into the night, and I had at length effected the manœuvre of getting Glendinning as my sole antagonist. The game, too, was my favourite écarté. The rest of the company, interested in the extent of our play, had abandoned their own cards, and were standing around us as spectators. The *parvenu*, who had been induced by my artifices in the early part of the evening to drink deeply, now shuffled, dealt, or played with a wild nervousness of manner for which his intoxication, I thought, might partially,

5. I.e., exceeded excesses, from Hamlet's advice to the players in Shakespeare's *Hamlet* 3.2. In medieval mys-tery plays a favorite luridly acted villain was Herod (73–4 B.C.), the cruel king of Judea (see Matthew 2).

6. Athenian rhetorician (2nd century), proverbial for his extreme wealth. "*Parvenu*": upstart, newly rich (French).

but could not altogether, account. In a very short period he had become my debtor to a large amount of money, when, having taken a long draught of port, he did precisely what I had been cooly anticipating, proposed to double our already extravagant stakes. With a well feigned show of reluctance, and not until after my repeated refusal had seduced him into some angry words which gave a colour of *pique* to my compliance, did I finally comply. The result, of course, did but prove how entirely the prey was in my toils—in less than a single hour he had quadrupled his debt. For some time his countenance had been losing the florid tinge lent it by the wine—but now, to my astonishment, I perceived that it had grown to a pallor truly fearful. I say to my astonishment. Glendinning had been represented to my eager inquiries as immeasurably wealthy; and the sums which he had as yet lost, although in themselves vast, could not, I supposed, very seriously annoy, much less so violently affect him. That he was overcome by the wine just swallowed, was the idea which most readily presented itself; and, rather with a view to the preservation of my own character in the eyes of my associates, than from any less interested motive, I was about to insist, peremptorily, upon a discontinuance of the play, when some expressions at my elbow from among the company, and an ejaculation evincing utter despair on the part of Glendinning, gave me to understand that I had effected his total ruin under circumstances which, rendering him an object for the pity of all, should have protected him from the ill offices of a fiend.

What now might have been my conduct it is difficult to say. The pitiable condition of my dupe had thrown an air of embarrassed gloom over all, and, for some moments, a profound and unbroken silence was maintained, during which I could not help feeling my cheeks tingle with the many burning glances of scorn or reproach cast upon me by the less abandoned of the party. I will even own that an intolerable weight of anxiety was for a brief instant lifted from my bosom by the sudden and extraordinary interruption which ensued. The wide, heavy folding doors of the apartment were all at once thrown open, to their full extent, with a vigorous and rushing impetuosity that extinguished, as if by magic, every candle in the room. Their light, in dying, enabled us just to perceive that a stranger had entered of about my own height, and closely muffled in a cloak. The darkness, however, was now total; and we could only feel that he was standing in our midst. Before any one of us could recover from the extreme astonishment into which this rudeness had thrown all, we heard the voice of the intruder.

"Gentlemen"—he said, in a low, distinct, and never-to-be-forgotten *whisper* which thrilled to the very marrow of my bones—"Gentlemen, I make no apology for this behaviour, because in thus behaving I am but fulfilling a duty. You are, beyond doubt, uninformed of the true character of the person who has to-night won at écarté a large sum of money from Lord Glendinning. I will therefore put you upon an expeditious and decisive plan of obtaining this very necessary information. Please to examine, at your leisure, the inner linings of the cuff of his left sleeve, and the several little packages which may be found in the somewhat capacious pockets of his embroidered morning wrapper."

While he spoke, so profound was the stillness that one might have heard a pin dropping upon the floor. In ceasing, he at once departed, and as abruptly as he had entered. Can I—shall I describe my sensations?—must I say that I

felt all the horrors of the damned? Most assuredly I had but little time given
for reflection. Many hands roughly seized me upon the spot, and lights were
immediately reprocured. A search ensued. In the lining of my sleeve were
found all of the court-cards essential in écarté, and, in the pockets of my
wrapper, a number of packs, fac-similes of those used at our sittings, with the
single exception that mine were of the species called, technically, *arrondé*; the
honours[7] being slightly convex at the ends, the lower cards slightly convex at
the sides. In this disposition, the dupe who cuts, as customary, at the breadth
of the pack, will invariably find that he cuts his antagonist an honour; while
the gambler, cutting at the length, will, as certainly, cut nothing for his victim
which may count in the records of the game.

Any outrageous burst of indignation upon this shameful discovery would
have affected me less than the silent contempt, or the sarcastic composure
with which it was received.

"Mr. Wilson," said our host, stooping to remove from beneath his feet an
exceedingly luxurious cloak of rare furs, "Mr. Wilson, this is your property."
(The weather was cold; and, upon quitting my own room, I had thrown a
cloak over my dressing wrapper, putting it off upon reaching the scene of play.)
"I presume it is supererogatory to seek here (eyeing the folds of the garment
with a bitter smile,) for any farther evidence of your skill. Indeed we have had
enough. You will see the necessity, I hope, of quitting Oxford—at all events,
of quitting, instantly, my chambers."

Abased, humbled to the dust as I then was, it is probable that I should have
resented this galling language by immediate personal violence, had not my
whole attention been immediately arrested, by a fact of the most startling character. The cloak which I had worn was of a rare description of fur; how rare,
how extravagantly costly, I shall not venture to say. Its fashion, too, was of my
own fantastic invention; for I was fastidious, to a degree of absurd coxcombry,
in matters of this frivolous nature. When, therefore, Mr. Preston reached me
that which he had picked up upon the floor, and near the folding doors of the
apartment, it was with an astonishment nearly bordering upon terror, that I
perceived my own already hanging on my arm, (where I had no doubt unwittingly placed it,) and that the one presented me was but its exact counterpart
in every, in even the minutest possible particular. The singular being who had
so disastrously exposed me, had been muffled, I remembered, in a cloak; and
none had been worn at all by any of the members of our party with the exception of myself. Retaining some presence of mind, I took the one offered me by
Preston, placed it, unnoticed, over my own, left the apartment with a resolute
scowl of defiance, and, next morning ere dawn of day, commenced a hurried
journey from Oxford to the continent, in a perfect agony of horror and of
shame.

I fled in vain. My evil destiny pursued me as if in exultation, and proved,
indeed, that the exercise of its mysterious dominion had as yet only begun.
Scarcely had I set foot in Paris ere I had fresh evidence of the detestable interest
taken by this Wilson in my concerns. Years flew, while I experienced no relief.
Villain!—at Rome, with how untimely, yet with how spectral an officiousness,
stepped he in between me and my ambition! At Vienna, too, at Berlin, and at
Moscow! Where, in truth, had I *not* bitter cause to curse him within my heart?

---

7. Face cards.

From his inscrutable tyranny did I at length flee, panic-stricken, as from a pestilence; and to the very ends of the earth I *fled in vain.*

And again, and again, in secret communion with my own spirit, would I demand the questions "Who is he?—whence came he?—and what are his objects?" But no answer was there found. And now I scrutinized, with a minute scrutiny, the forms, and the methods, and the leading traits of his impertinent supervision. But even here there was very little upon which to base a conjecture. It was noticeable, indeed, that, in no one of the multiplied instances in which he had of late crossed my path, had he so crossed it except to frustrate those schemes, or to disturb those actions, which, fully carried out, might have resulted in bitter mischief. Poor justification this, in truth, for an authority so imperiously assumed! Poor indemnity for natural rights of self-agency so pertinaciously, so insultingly denied!

I had also been forced to notice that my tormentor, for a very long period of time, (while scrupulously and with miraculous dexterity maintaining his whim of an identity of apparel with myself,) had so contrived it, in the execution of his varied interference with my will, that I saw not, at any moment, the features of his face. Be Wilson what he might, *this*, at least, was but the veriest of affection, or of folly. Could he, for an instant, have supposed that, in my admonisher at Eton, in the destroyer of my honour at Oxford, in him who thwarted my ambition at Rome, my revenge in Paris, my passionate love at Naples, or what he falsely termed my avarice in Egypt, that in this, my arch-enemy and evil genius, I could fail to recognize the William Wilson of my schoolboy days, the namesake, the companion, the rival, the hated and dreaded rival at Dr. Bransby's? Impossible!—But let me hasten to the last eventful scene of the drama.

Thus far I had succumbed supinely to this imperious domination. The sentiments of deep awe with which I habitually regarded the elevated character, the majestic wisdom, the apparent omnipresence and omnipotence of Wilson, added to a feeling of even terror, with which certain other traits in his nature and assumptions inspired me, had operated, hitherto, to impress me with an idea of my own utter weakness and helplessness, and to suggest an implicit, although bitterly reluctant submission to his arbitrary will. But, of late days, I had given myself up entirely to wine; and its maddening influency upon my hereditary temper rendered me more and more impatient of control. I began to murmur, to hesitate, to resist. And was it only fancy which induced me to believe that, with the increase of my own firmness, that of my tormentor underwent a proportional diminution? Be this as it may, I now began to feel the inspirations of a burning hope, and at length nurtured in my secret thoughts a stern and desperate resolution that I would submit no longer to be enslaved.

It was at Rome, during the carnival of 18—, that I attended a masquerade in the palazzo of the Neapolitan Duke Di Broglio. I had indulged more freely than usual in the excesses of the wine-table; and now the suffocating atmosphere of the crowded rooms irritated me beyond endurance. The difficulty, too, of forcing my way through the mazes of the company contributed not a little to the ruffling of my temper; for I was anxiously seeking, let me not say with what unworthy motive, the young, the gay, the beautiful wife of the aged and doting Di Broglio. With a too unscrupulous confidence she had previously communicated to me the secret of the costume in which she would be habited, and now, having caught a glimpse of her person, I was hurrying to make my way into her presence. At this moment I felt a light hand laid upon my shoulder, and that ever-remembered, low, damnable whisper within my ear.

In a perfect whirlwind of wrath, I turned at once upon him who had thus interrupted me, and seized him violently by the collar. He was attired, as I expected, like myself; wearing a large Spanish cloak, and a mask of black silk which entirely covered his features.

"Scoundrel!" I said, in a voice husky with rage, while every syllable I uttered seemed as new fuel to my fury, "scoundrel! impostor! accursed villain! you shall not—you *shall not* dog me unto death! Follow me, or I stab you where I stand," and I broke my way from the room into a small antechamber adjoining, dragging him unresistingly with me as I went.

Upon entering, I thrust him furiously from me. He staggered against the wall, while I closed the door with an oath, and commanded him to draw. He hesitated but for an instant, then, with a slight sigh, drew in silence, and put himself upon his defence.

The contest was brief indeed. I was frantic with every species of wild excitement, and felt within my single arm the energy and the power of a multitude. In a few seconds I forced him by sheer strength against the wainscoting, and thus, getting him at mercy, plunged my sword, with brute ferocity, repeatedly through and through his bosom.

At this instant some person tried the latch of the door. I hastened to prevent an intrusion, and then immediately returned to my dying antagonist. But what human language can adequately portray *that* astonishment, *that* horror which possessed me at the spectacle then presented to view. The brief moment in which I averted my eyes had been sufficient to produce, apparently, a material change in the arrangements at the upper or farther end of the room. A large mirror, it appeared to me, now stood where none had been perceptible before; and, as I stepped up to it in extremity of terror, mine own image, but with features all pale and dabbled in blood, advanced, with a feeble and tottering gait, to meet me.

Thus it appeared, I say, but was not. It was my antagonist—it was Wilson, who then stood before me in the agonies of his dissolution. Not a line in all the marked and singular lineaments of that face which was not, even identically, mine own! His mask and cloak lay, where he had thrown them, upon the floor.

It was Wilson, but he spoke no longer in a whisper, and I could have fancied that I myself was speaking while he said—

"You have conquered, and I yield. Yet, henceforward art thou also dead—dead to the world and its hopes. In me didst thou exist—and, in my death, see by this image, which is thine, how utterly thou hast murdered thyself."

1839

The Man of the Crowd[1]

Ce grand malheur, de ne pouvoir etre seul.
—La Bruyere[2]

It was well said of a certain German book that *"er lasst sich nicht lesen"*—it does not permit itself to be read. There are some secrets which do not permit themselves to be told. Men die nightly in their beds, wringing the hands of ghostly confessors, and looking them piteously in the eyes—die with despair of heart and convulsion of throat, on account of the hideousness of mysteries which will not *suffer themselves* to be revealed. Now and then, alas, the conscience of man takes up a burthen so heavy in horror that it can be thrown down only into the grave. And thus the essence of all crime is undivulged.

Not long ago, about the closing in of an evening in autumn, I sat at the large bow window of the D——Coffee-House in London. For some months I had been ill in health, but was now convalescent, and, with returning strength, found myself in one of those happy moods which are so precisely the converse of *ennui*[3]—moods of the keenest appetency, when the film from the mental vision departs—the αχλμ. ο. πζιυ εππευ[4]—and the intellect, electrified, surpasses as greatly its every-day condition, as does the vivid, yet candid reason of Combe, the mad and flimsy rhetoric of Gorgias.[5] Merely to breathe was enjoyment; and I derived positive pleasure even from many of the legitimate sources of pain. I felt a calm but inquisitive interest in every thing. With a cigar in my mouth and a newspaper in my lap, I had been amusing myself for the greater part of the afternoon, now in poring over advertisements, now in observing the promiscuous company in the room, and now in peering through the smoky panes into the street.

This latter is one of the principal thoroughfares of the city, and had been very much crowded during the whole day. But, as the darkness came on, the throng momently increased; and by the time the lamps were well litten two dense and continuous tides of population were rushing past the door. At this particular period of the evening I had never before been in a similar situation, and the tumultuous sea of human heads filled me, therefore, with a delicious novelty of emotion. I gave up at length all care of things within the hotel, and became absorbed in contemplation of the scene without. At first my observations took an abstract and generalizing turn. I looked at the passengers in masses, and thought of them in their aggregate relations. Soon, however, I descended to details, and regarded with minute interest the innumerable varieties of figure, dress, air, gait, visage, and expression of countenance.

By far the greater number of those who went by had a satisfied business-like

1. *The Man of the Crowd*, reprinted here from its first appearance in *Graham's Magazine* 7 (December 1840), 267–70, is in a tradition of stories about mysterious strangers. A well-known comic precedent is Irving's *The Stout Gentleman*, where, as in this story, an arresting figure is singled out by the observer in a mundane setting. But behind Poe's conception also lies the legend of the Wandering Jew, who refused to let Jesus (then carrying his cross to Calvary) rest outside his house, and whom Jesus punished by dooming him to wander the earth until the Second Coming; and in the repeated references to the stranger's going "to and fro" Poe may intend an allusion to Satan, the archtypal criminal who according to Job 1.7 has a way of "going to and fro in the earth," and "walking up and down in it."

2. The misery of being unable to be alone (French). Adapted from *Characters*, by Jean de La Bruyère (1645–1696).

3. Boredom (French).

4. The mist that was upon it before (Greek), from Homer's *Iliad* book 5.

5. Greek skeptic (4th century B.C.), known for a kind of rhetoric that preened itself at the expense of reason. William Combe (1741–1823), English writer of a series of books about the adventures of a clergyman-teacher, "Dr. Syntax."

demeanor, and seemed to be thinking only of making their way through the press. Their brows were knit, and their eyes rolled quickly, when pushed against by fellow-wayfarers they evinced no symptom of impatience, but adjusted their clothes and hurried on. Others, still a numerous class, were restless in their movements, had flushed faces, and talked and gesticulated to themselves, as if feeling in solitude on account of the very denseness of the company around. When impeded in their progress these people suddenly ceased muttering, but redoubled their gesticulations, and awaited, with an absent and overdone smile upon the lips, the course of the persons impeding them. If jostled, they bowed profusely to the jostlers, and appeared over-whelmed with confusion.—There was nothing very distinctive about these two large classes beyond what I have noted. Their habiliments belonged to that order which is pointedly termed the decent. They were undoubtedly noblemen, merchants, attorneys, tradesmen, stockjobbers—the Eupatrids[6] and the common-places of society—men of leisure and men actively engaged in affairs of their own—conducting business upon their own responsibility. They did not greatly excite my attention.

The tribe of clerks was an obvious one, and here I discerned two remarkable divisions. There were the junior clerks of flash houses—young gentlemen with tight coats, bright boots, well-oiled hair, and supercilious lips. Setting aside a certain dapperness of carriage which may be termed deskism for want of a better word, the manner of these persons seemed to me an exact fac-simile of what had been the perfection of *bon ton*[7] about twelve or eighteen months before. They wore the cast-off graces of the gentry—and this, I believe, involves the best definition of the class.

The division of the upper clerks of staunch firms, or of the "steady old fellows," it was not possible to mistake. These were known by their coats and pantaloons of black or brown, made to sit comfortably, with white cravats and waistcoats, broad solid-looking shoes, and thick hose, or gaiters.—They had all slightly bald heads, from which the right ears, long used to pen-holding, had an odd habit of standing off on end. I observed that they always removed or settled their hats with both hands, and wore watches, with short, gold chains of a substantial and ancient pattern. Theirs was the affectation of respectabil-ity—if indeed there be an affectation so honorable.

There were many individuals of dashing appearance, whom I easily set down as belonging to the race of swell pick-pockets, with which all great cities are infested. I watched these gentry with much inquisitiveness, and found it difficult to imagine how they should ever be mistaken for gentlemen by gentle-men themselves. Their voluminousness of wristband, with an air of excessive frankness, should betray them at once.

The gamblers, of whom I described not a few, were still more easily recogni-sable. They wore every variety of dress, from that of the desperate thimble-rig[8] bully, with velvet waistcoat, fancy neckerchief, gilt chains, and fillagreed buttons, to that of the scrupulously inornate clergyman, than which nothing could be less liable to suspicion. Still all were distinguished by a certain sodden swarthiness of complexion, a filmy dimness of eye, and pallor and compression of lip. There were two other traits, moreover, by which I could always detect them—a guarded lowness of tone in conversation, and a more than ordinary

6. Aristocrats.   8. Shell game, a favorite trick of con artists.
7. Fashion (French).

extension of the thumb in a direction at right angles with the fingers.—Very often in company with these sharpers I observed an order of men somewhat different in habits, but still birds of kindred feather. They may be defined as the gentlemen who live by their wits. They seem to prey upon the public in two battalions—that of the dandies and that of the military men. Of the first grade the leading features are long locks and smiles; of the second frogged coats and frowns.

Descending in the scale of what is termed gentility, I found darker and deeper themes for speculation. I saw Jew pedlars, with hawk eyes flashing from countenances whose every other feature wore only an expression of abject humility; sturdy professional street beggars scowling upon mendicants of a better stamp, whom despair alone had driven forth into the night for charity; feeble and ghastly invalids, upon whom death had placed a sure hand, and who sidled and tottered through the mob looking every one beseechingly in the face, as if in search of some chance consolation, some lost hope; modest young girls returning from long and late labor to a cheerless home, and shrinking more tearfully than indignantly from the glances of ruffians, whose direct contact even could not be avoided; women of the town of all kinds and of all ages—the unequivocal beauty in the prime of her womanhood, putting one in mind of the statue of Lucian, with the surface of Parian marble, and the interior filled with filth[9]—the loathsome and utterly lost leper in rags—the wrinkled, bejewelled and paint-begrimed beldame, making a last effort at youth—the mere child of immature form, yet, from long association, an adept in the dreadful coquetries of her trade, and burning with a rabid ambition to be ranked the equal of her elders in vice; drunkards innumerable and indescribable—some in shreds and patches, reeling, inarticulate, with bruised visage and lack-lustre eyes—some in whole although filthy garments, with a slightly unsteady swagger, thick sensual lips, and hearty-looking rubicund faces—others clothed in materials which had once been good, and which even now were scrupulously well-brushed—men who walked with a more than naturally firm and springy step, but whose countenances were fearfully pale, whose eyes hideously wild and red, and who clutched with quivering fingers, as they strode through the crowd, at every object which came within their reach; beside these, pie-men, porters, coal-heavers, sweeps; organ-grinders, monkey-exhibiters and ballad mongers, those who vended with those who sang; ragged artizans and exhausted laborers of every description, and still all full of a noisy and inordinate vivacity which jarred discordantly upon the ear, and gave an aching sensation to the eye.

As the night deepened, so deepened to me the interest of the scene; for not only did the general character of the crowd materially alter (its gentler features retiring in the gradual withdrawal of the more orderly portion of the people, and its harsher ones coming out into bolder relief as the late hour brought forth every species of infamy from its den,) but the rays of the gas-lamps, feeble at first in their struggle with the dying day, had now at length gained ascendency, and threw over every thing a fitful and garish lustre. All was dark yet splendid—as that ebony to which has been likened the style of Tertullian.[1] The wild effects of the light enchained me to an examination of individual

9. Paraphrased from *The Cock*, by the Greek satirist Lucian (125?–200?). Parian marble (from the island of Paros, in the Cyclades) was used in the best classical statuary.

1. Quintus Septimius Florens Tertullianus (160?–230?), Carthaginian church writer.

faces; and although the rapidity with which the world of life flitted before the window prevented me from casting more than a glance upon each visage, still it seemed that, in my then peculiar mental state, I could frequently read, even in that brief interval of a glance, the history of long years. With my brow to the glass, I was thus occupied in scrutinising the mob, when suddenly there came into view a countenance (that of a decrepid old man, some sixty-five or seventy years of age,) a countenance which at once arrested and absorbed my whole attention, on account of the absolute idiosyncrasy of its expression. Any thing even remotely resembling that expression I had never seen before. I well remember that my first thought, upon beholding it, was that Retzch,[2] had he viewed it, would have greatly preferred it to his own pictural incarnations of the fiend. As I endeavored, during the brief minute of my original survey, to form some analysis of the meaning conveyed, there arose confusedly and paradoxically within my mind the ideas of vast mental power, of caution, of penuriousness, of avarice, of coolness, of malice, of blood-thirstiness, of tri-umph, of merriment, of excessive terror, of intense, of supreme despair. I felt singularly aroused, startled, fascinated. "How wild a history," I said to myself, "is written within that bosom!" Then came a craving desire to keep the man in view—to know more of him. Hurriedly putting on an overcoat, and seizing my hat and cane, I made my way into the street, and pushed through the crowd in the direction which I had seen him take; for he had already disap-peared. With some little difficulty I at length came within sight of him, approached, and followed him closely, yet cautiously, so as not to attract his attention.

I had now a good opportunity of examining his person. He was short in stature, very thin, and apparently very feeble. His clothes, generally, were filthy and ragged; but as he came, now and then, within the strong glare of a lamp, I perceived that his linen, although dirty, was of beautiful texture; and my vision deceived me, or, through a rent in a closely-buttoned, and evidently second-handed roquelaire[3] which enveloped him, I caught a glimpse either of a diamond, or of a dagger. These observations heightened my curiosity, and I resolved to follow the stranger whithersoever he should go.

It was now fully night-fall, and a thick humid fog hung over the city, threat-ening to end in a settled and heavy rain. This change of weather had an odd effect upon the crowd, the whole of which was at once put into new commo-tion, and overshadowed by a world of umbrellas. The waver, the jostle, and the hum increased in a tenfold degree. For my own part I did not much regard the rain—the lurking of an old fever in my system rending the moisture somewhat too dangerously pleasant. Tying a handkerchief about my mouth I kept on. For half an hour the old man held his way with difficulty along the great thoroughfare; and I here walked close at his elbow through fear of losing sight of him. Never once turning his head to look back, he did not observe me. By and bye he passed into a cross street, which, although densely filled with people, was not quite so much thronged as the main one he had quitted. Here a change in his demeanor became evident. He walked more slowly and with less object than before—more hesitatingly. He crossed and re-crossed the street way repeatedly without apparent aim; and the press was still so thick that at every such movement I was obliged to follow him closely. The street was a narrow and long one, and his course lay within it for nearly an hour, during

---

2. Moritz Retzsch (1779–1857), German etcher.   3. Cloak.

which the passengers had gradually diminished to about that number which is ordinarily seen at noon in Broadway near the Park—so vast a difference is there between a London populace and that of the most frequented American city. A second turn brought us into a square, brilliantly litten, and overflowing with life. The old manner of the stranger re-appeared. His chin fell upon his breast, while his eyes rolled wildly from under his knit brows in every direction upon those who hemmed him in. He urged his way steadily and perseveringly. I was surprised, however, to find, upon his having made the circuit of the square, that he turned and retraced his steps.—Still more was I astonished to see him repeat the same walk several times—once nearly detecting me as he came round with a sudden movement.

In this exercise he spent about an hour, at the end of which we met with far less interruption from passengers than at first. The rain fell fast; the air grew cool; and the people were retiring to their homes. With a gesture of what seemed to be petulant impatience, the wanderer passed into a bye-street comparatively deserted. Down this, some quarter of a mile long, he rushed with an activity I could not have dreamed of seeing in one so aged, and which put me to much trouble in pursuit. A few minutes brought us to a large and busy bazaar, with the localities of which the stranger appeared well acquainted, and where his original demeanor again became apparent, as he forced his way to and fro, without aim, among the host of buyers and sellers.

During the hour and a half, or thereabouts, which we passed in this place, it required much caution on my part to keep him within reach without attracting his observation. Luckily I wore a pair of gum[4] over-shoes and could move about in perfect silence. At no moment did he see that I watched him. He entered shop after shop, priced nothing, spoke no word, and looked at all objects with a wild and vacant stare. I was now utterly amazed at his behavior, and firmly resolved that we should not part until I had satisfied myself in some measure respecting him.

A loud-toned clock struck eleven, and the company were fast deserting the bazaar. A shopkeeper, in putting up a shutter, jostled the old man, and at the instant I saw a strong shudder come over his frame. He hurried into the street, looked anxiously around him for an instant, and then ran with incredible swiftness through many crooked and people-less lanes, until we emerged once more upon the great thoroughfare whence we had started—the street of the D—— Hotel. It no longer wore, however, the same aspect. It was still brilliant with gas; but the rain fell fiercely, and there were few persons to be seen. The stranger grew deadly pale. He walked moodily some paces up the once populous avenue, then, with a heavy sigh, turned in the direction of the river, and, plunging through a great variety of devious ways, came out at length in view of one of the principal theatres. It was about being closed, and the audience were thronging from the doors. I saw the old man gasp as if for breath while he threw himself amid the crowd; but I thought that the intense agony of his countenance had, in some measure, abated. His head again fell upon his breast; he appeared as I had seen him at first. I observed that he now took the course in which had gone the greater number of the audience—but, upon the whole, I was at a loss to comprehend the waywardness of his actions.

As he proceeded, the company grew more scattered, and his old uneasiness and vacillation were resumed. For some time he followed closely a party of

4. Rubber.

some ten or twelve roisterers; but from this number one by one dropped off, until three only remained together in a narrow and gloomy lane little frequented. The stranger paused, and, for a moment, seemed lost in thought; then, with every mark of agitation, pursued rapidly a route which brought us to the verge of the city, amid regions very different from those we had hitherto traversed. It was the most noisome[5] quarter of London, where every thing wore the worst impress of the most deplorable poverty, and of the most desperate crime. By the dim light of an accidental lamp, tall, antique, worm-eaten, wooden tenements were seen tottering to their fall in directions so many and capricious that scarce the semblance of a passage was discernible between them. The paving-stones lay at random, displaced from their beds by the rankly-growing grass. Horrible filth festered in the dammed-up gutters. The whole atmosphere teemed with desolation. Yet, as we proceeded, the sounds of human life revived by sure degrees, and at length large bands of the most abandoned of a London populace were seen reeling to and fro. The spirits of the old man again flickered up, as a lamp which is near its death-hour.—Once more he strode onward with elastic tread. Suddenly a corner was turned, a blaze of light burst upon our sight, and we stood before one of the huge suburban temples of Intemperance—one of the palaces of the fiend, Gin.

It was now nearly day-break; but a number of wretched inebriates still pressed in and out of the flaunting entrance. With a half shriek of joy the old man forced a passage within, resumed at once his original bearing, and stalked backward and forward, without apparent object, among the throng. He had not been thus long occupied, however, before a rush to the doors gave token that the host was closing them for the night. It was something even more intense than despair that I then observed upon the countenance of the singular being whom I had watched so pertinaciously. Yet he did not hesitate in his career, but with a mad energy retraced his steps at once, to the heart of the mighty London. Long and swiftly he fled, while I followed him in the wildest amazement, resolute not to abandon a scrutiny in which I now felt an interest all-absorbing. The sun arose while we proceeded, and, when we had once again reached that most thronged mart of the populous town, the street of the D—— Hotel, it presented an appearance of human bustle and activity scarcely inferior to what I had seen on the evening before. And here, long, amid the momently increasing confusion, did I persist in my pursuit of the stranger. But, as usual, he walked to and fro, and during the day did not pass from out the turmoil of that street. And, as the shades of the second evening come on, I grew wearied unto death, and, stopping fully in front of the wanderer, gazed at him steadfastly in the face. He noticed me not, but resumed his solemn walk, while I, ceasing to follow, remained absorbed in contemplation. "This old man," I said at length, "is the type and the genius of deep crime. He refuses to be alone. *He is the man of the crowd.* It will be in vain to follow; for I shall learn no more of him, nor of his deeds. The worst heart of the world is a grosser book than the 'Hortulus Animæ,' and perhaps it is but one of the great mercies of God that *'er lasst sich nicht lesen.'* "[6]

1840

5. Stinking.
6. See the opening lines of the story. "Hortulus Animæ": a book by John Grunninger printed in Ger-

many around 1500; Poe's idea of it comes from Isaac Disraeli's *Curiosities of Literature*, where it is instanced as containing offensive religious illustrations.

The Black Cat[1]

For the most wild, yet most homely narrative which I am about to pen, I neither expect nor solicit belief. Mad indeed would I be to expect it, in a case where my very senses reject their own evidence. Yet, mad am I not—and very surely do I not dream. But to-morrow I die, and to-day I would unburthen my soul. My immediate purpose is to place before the world, plainly, succinctly, and without comment, a series of mere household events. In their consequences, these events have terrified—have tortured—have destroyed me. Yet I will not attempt to expound them. To me, they have presented little but Horror—to many they will seem less terrible than *baroques*.[2] Hereafter, perhaps, some intellect may be found which will reduce my phantasm to the common-place—some intellect more calm, more logical, and far less excitable than my own, which will perceive, in the circumstances I detail with awe, nothing more than an ordinary succession of very natural causes and effects.

From my infancy I was noted for the docility and humanity of my disposition. My tenderness of heart was even so conspicuous as to make me the jest of my companions. I was especially fond of animals, and was indulged by my parents with a great variety of pets. With these I spent most of my time, and never was so happy as when feeding and caressing them. This peculiarity of character grew with my growth, and, in my manhood, I derived from it one of my principal sources of pleasure. To those who have cherished an affection for a faithful and sagacious dog, I need hardly be at the trouble of explaining the nature or the intensity of the gratification thus derivable. There is something in the unselfish and self-sacrificing love of a brute, which goes directly to the heart of him who has had frequent occasion to test the paltry friendship and gossamer fidelity of mere *Man*.

I married early, and was happy to find in my wife a disposition not uncongenial with my own. Observing my partiality for domestic pets, she lost no opportunity of procuring those of the most agreeable kind. We had birds, gold-fish, a fine dog, rabbits, a small monkey, and *a cat*.

This latter was a remarkably large and beautiful animal, entirely black, and sagacious to an astonishing degree. In speaking of his intelligence, my wife, who at heart was not a little tinctured with superstition, made frequent allusion to the ancient popular notion, which regarded all black cats as witches in disguise. Not that she was ever *serious* upon this point—and I mention the matter at all for no better reason than that it happens, just now, to be remembered.

Pluto[3]—this was the cat's name—was my favorite pet and playmate. I alone fed him, and he attended me wherever I went about the house. It was even with difficulty that I could prevent him from following me through the streets.

Our friendship lasted, in this manner, for several years, during which my general temperament and character—through the instrumentality of the Fiend Intemperance—had (I blush to confess it) experienced a radical alteration for the worse. I grew, day by day, more moody, more irritable, more regardless of the feelings of others. I suffered myself to use intemperate language to my

---

1. *The Black Cat* was first published August 19, 1843, in the *United States Saturday Post*, a Philadelphia paper. In a letter to James Russell Lowell (July 2, 1844) Poe listed it as one of his eight best tales. The present text is that of the *Tales* (1845).
2. Baroque, bizarre.
3. Appropriate because in Roman mythology Pluto is the god of the dead and the ruler of the underworld.

wife. At length, I even offered her personal violence. My pets, of course, were made to feel the change in my disposition. I not only neglected, but ill-used them. For Pluto, however, I still retained sufficient regard to restrain me from maltreating him, as I made no scruple of maltreating the rabbits, the monkey, or even the dog, when by accident, or through affection, they came in my way. But my disease grew upon me—for what disease is like Alcohol!—and at length even Pluto, who was now becoming old, and consequently somewhat peevish—even Pluto began to experience the effects of my ill temper.

One night, returning home, much intoxicated, from one of my haunts about town, I fancied that the cat avoided my presence. I seized him; when, in his fright at my violence, he inflicted a slight wound upon my hand with his teeth. The fury of a demon instantly possessed me. I knew myself no longer. My original soul seemed, at once, to take its flight from my body; and a more than fiendish malevolence, gin-nurtured, thrilled every fibre of my frame. I took from my waistcoat-pocket a pen-knife, opened it, grasped the poor beast by the throat, and deliberately cut one of its eyes from the socket! I blush, I burn, I shudder, while I pen the damnable atrocity.

When reason returned with the morning—when I had slept off the fumes of the night's debauch—I experienced a sentiment half of horror, half of remorse, for the crime of which I had been guilty; but it was, at best, a feeble and equivocal feeling, and the soul remained untouched. I again plunged into excess, and soon drowned in wine all memory of the deed.

In the meantime the cat slowly recovered. The socket of the lost eye presented, it is true, a frightful appearance, but he no longer appeared to suffer any pain. He went about the house as usual, but, as might be expected, fled in extreme terror at my approach. I had so much of my old heart left, as to be at first grieved by this evident dislike on the part of a creature which had once so loved me. But this feeling soon gave place to irritation. And then came, as if to my final and irrevocable overthrow, the spirit of PERVERSENESS.[4] Of this spirit philosophy takes no account. Yet I am not more sure that my soul lives, than I am that perverseness is one of the primitive impulses of the human heart—one of the indivisible primary faculties, or sentiments, which give direction to the character of Man. Who has not, a hundred times, found himself committing a vile or a silly action, for no other reason than because he knows he should *not*? Have we not a perpetual inclination, in the teeth of our best judgment, to violate that which is *Law*, merely because we understand it to be such? This spirit of perverseness, I say, came to my final overthrow. It was this unfathomable longing of the soul *to vex itself*—to offer violence to its own nature—to do wrong for the wrong's sake only—that urged me to continue and finally to consummate the injury I had inflicted upon the unoffending brute. One morning, in cool blood, I slipped a noose about its neck and hung it to the limb of a tree;—hung it with the tears streaming from my eyes, and with the bitterest remorse at my heart;—hung it *because* I knew that it had loved me, and *because* I felt it had given me no reason of offence;— hung it *because* I knew that in so doing I was committing a sin—a deadly sin that would so jeopardize my immortal soul as to place it—if such a thing were

---

4. Poe's story *The Imp of the Perverse* is built around the notion that there is "an innate and primitive principle of human action, a paradoxical something, which we may call *perverseness*, for want of a more characteristic term."

possible—even beyond the reach of the infinite mercy of the Most Merciful and Most Terrible God.

On the night of the day on which this cruel deed was done, I was aroused from sleep by the cry of fire. The curtains of my bed were in flames. The whole house was blazing. It was with great difficulty that my wife, a servant, and myself, made our escape from the conflagration. The destruction was complete. My entirely worldly wealth was swallowed up, and I resigned myself thenceforward to despair.

I am above the weakness of seeking to establish a sequence of cause and effect, between the disaster and the atrocity. But I am detailing a chain of facts—and wish not to leave even a possible link imperfect. On the day succeeding the fire, I visited the ruins. The walls, with one exception, had fallen in. This exception was found in a compartment wall, not very thick, which stood about the middle of the house, and against which had rested the head of my bed. The plastering had here, in great measure, resisted the action of the fire—a fact which I attributed to its having been recently spread. About this wall a dense crowd were collected, and many persons seemed to be examining a particular portion of it with very minute and eager attention. The words "strange!" "singular!" and other similar expression, excited my curiosity. I approached and saw, as if graven in *bas relief* upon the white surface, the figure of a gigantic *cat*. The impression was given with an accuracy truly marvellous. There was a rope about the animal's neck.

When I first beheld this apparition—for I could scarcely regard it as less—my wonder and my terror were extreme. But at length reflection came to my aid. The cat, I remembered, had been hung in a garden adjacent to the house. Upon the alarm of the fire, this garden had been immediately filled by the crowd—by some one of whom the animal must have been cut from the tree and thrown, through an open window, into my chamber. This had probably been done with the view of arousing me from sleep. The falling of other walls had compressed the victim of my cruelty into the substance of the freshly-spread plaster; the lime of which, with the flames and the *ammonia* from the carcass, had then accomplished the portraiture as I saw it.

Although I thus readily accounted to my reason, if not altogether to my conscience, for the startling fact just detailed, it did not the less fail to make a deep impression upon my fancy. For months I could not rid myself of the phantasm of the cat; and, during this period, there came back into my spirit a half-sentiment that seemed, but was not, remorse. I went so far as to regret the loss of the animal, and to look about me, among the vile haunts which I now habitually frequented, for another pet of the same species, and of somewhat similar appearance, with which to supply its place.

One night as I sat, half stupified, in a den of more than infamy, my attention was suddenly drawn to some black object, reposing upon the head of one of the immense hogsheads[5] of Gin, or of Rum, which constituted the chief furniture of the apartment. I had been looking steadily at the top of this hogshead for some minutes, and what now caused me surprise was the fact that I had not sooner perceived the object thereupon. I approached it, and touched it with my hand. It was a black cat—a very large one—fully as large as Pluto, and closely resembling him in every respect but one. Pluto had not a white

---

5. Large barrels or casks, usually holding sixty-three gallons.

hair upon any portion of his body; but this cat had a large, although indefinite splotch of white, covering nearly the whole region of the breast.

Upon my touching him, he immediately arose, purred loudly, rubbed against my hand, and appeared delighted with my notice. This, then, was the very creature of which I was in search. I at once offered to purchase it of the landlord; but this person made no claim to it—knew nothing of it—had never seen it before.

I continued my caresses, and, when I prepared to go home, the animal evinced a disposition to accompany me. I permitted it to do so; occasionally stooping and patting it as I proceeded. When it reached the house it domesticated itself at once, and became immediately a great favorite with my wife.

For my own part, I soon found a dislike to it arising within me. This was just the reverse of what I had anticipated; but—I know not how or why it was—its evident fondness for myself rather disgusted and annoyed. By slow degrees, these feelings of disgust and annoyance rose into the bitterness of hatred. I avoided the creature; a certain sense of shame, and the remembrance of my former deed of cruelty, preventing me from physically abusing it. I did not, for some weeks, strike, or otherwise violently ill use it; but gradually—very gradually—I came to look upon it with unutterable loathing, and to flee silently from its odious presence, as from the breath of a pestilence.

What added, no doubt, to my hatred of the beast, was the discovery, on the morning after I brought it home, that, like Pluto, it also had been deprived of one of its eyes. This circumstance, however, only endeared it to my wife, who, as I have already said, possessed, in a high degree, that humanity of feeling which had once been my distinguishing trait, the source of many of my simplest and purest pleasures.

With my aversion to this cat, however, its partiality for myself seemed to increase. It followed my footsteps with a pertinacity which it would be difficult to make the reader comprehend. Whenever I sat, it would crouch beneath my chair, or spring upon my knees, covering me with its loathsome caresses. If I arose to walk it would get between my feet and thus nearly throw me down, or, fastening its long and sharp claws in my dress, clamber, in this manner, to my breast. At such times, although I longed to destroy it with a blow, I was yet withheld from so doing, partly by a memory of my former crime, but chiefly—let me confess it at once—by absolute *dread* of the beast.

This dread was not exactly a dread of physical evil—and yet I should be at a loss how otherwise to define it. I am almost ashamed to own—yes, even in this felon's cell, I am almost ashamed to own—that the terror and horror with which the animal inspired me, had been heightened by one of the merest chimæras[6] it would be possible to conceive. My wife had called my attention, more than once, to the character of the mark of white hair, of which I have spoken, and which constituted the sole visible difference between the strange beast and the one I had destroyed. The reader will remember that this mark, although large, had been originally very indefinite; but, by slow degrees—degrees nearly imperceptible, and which for a long time my Reason struggled to reject as fanciful—it had, at length, assumed a rigorous distinctness of outline. It was now the representation of an object that I shudder to name—and for this, above all, I loathed, and dreaded, and would have rid myself of the

6, Foolish, impossible fancyings.

monster *had I dared*—it was now, I say, the image of a hideous—of a ghastly thing—of the GALLOWS—oh, mournful and terrible engine of Horror and of Crime—of Agony and of Death!

And now was I indeed wretched beyond the wretchedness of mere Humanity. And *a brute beast*—whose fellow I had contemptuously destroyed—*a brute beast* to work out for *me*—for me a man, fashioned in the image of the High God—so much of insufferable wo! Alas! neither by day nor by night knew I the blessing of Rest any more! During the former the creature left me no moment alone; and, in the latter, I started, hourly, from dreams of unutterable fear, to find the hot breath of *the thing* upon my face, and its vast weight—an incarnate Night-Mare that I had no power to shake off—incumbent eternally upon my *heart!*

Beneath the pressure of torments such as these, the feeble remnant of the good within me succumbed. Evil thoughts became my sole intimates—the darkest and most evil of thoughts. The moodiness of my usual temper increased to hatred of all things and of all mankind; while, from the sudden, frequent, and ungovernable outbursts of a fury to which I now blindly abandoned myself, my uncomplaining wife, alas! was the most usual and the most patient of sufferers.

One day she accompanied me, upon some household errand, into the cellar of the old building which our poverty compelled us to inhabit. The cat followed me down the steep stairs, and, nearly throwing me headlong, exasperated me to madness. Uplifting an axe, and forgetting, in my wrath, the childish dread which had hitherto stayed my hand, I aimed a blow at the animal which, of course, would have proved instantly fatal had it descended as I wished. But this blow was arrested by the hand of my wife. Goaded, by the interference, into a rage more than demoniacal, I withdrew my arm from her grasp and buried the axe in her brain. She fell dead upon the spot, without a groan.

This hideous murder accomplished, I set myself forthwith, and with entire deliberation, to the task of concealing the body. I knew that I could not remove it from the house, either by day or by night, without the risk of being observed by the neighbors. Many projects entered my mind. At one period I thought of cutting the corpse into minute fragments, and destroying them by fire. At another, I resolved to dig a grave for it in the floor of the cellar. Again, I deliberated about casting it in the well in the yard—about packing it in a box, as if merchandize, with the usual arrangements, and so getting a porter to take it from the house. Finally I hit upon what I considered a far better expedient than either of these. I determined to wall it up in the cellar—as the monks of the middle ages are recorded to have walled up their victims.

For a purpose such as this the cellar was well adapted. Its walls were loosely constructed, and had lately been plastered throughout with a rough plaster, which the dampness of the atmosphere had prevented from hardening. Moreover, in one of the walls was a projection, caused by a false chimney, or fireplace, that had been filled up, and made to resemble the rest of the cellar. I made no doubt that I could readily displace the bricks at this point, insert the corpse, and wall the whole up as before, so that no eye could detect any thing suspicious.

And in this calculation I was not deceived. By means of a crow-bar I easily dislodged the bricks, and, having carefully deposited the body against the inner wall, I propped it in that position, while, with little trouble, I re-laid the whole structure as it originally stood. Having procured mortar, sand, and hair, with every possible precaution, I prepared a plaster which could not be distinguished from the old, and with this I very carefully went over the new brickwork. When I had finished, I felt satisfied that all was right. The wall did not present the slightest appearance of having been disturbed. The rubbish on the floor was picked up with the minutest care. I looked around triumphantly, and said to myself—"Here at least, then, my labor has not been in vain."

My next step was to look for the beast which had been the cause of so much wretchedness; for I had, at length, firmly resolved to put it to death. Had I been able to meet with it, at the moment, there could have been no doubt of its fate; but it appeared that the crafty animal had been alarmed at the violence of my previous anger, and forebore to present itself in my present mood. It is impossible to describe, or to imagine, the deep, the blissful sense of relief which the absence of the detested creature occasioned in my bosom. It did not make its appearance during the night—and thus for one night at least, since its introduction into the house, I soundly and tranquilly slept; aye, *slept* even with the burden of murder upon my soul!

The second and the third day passed, and still my tormentor came not. Once again I breathed as a freeman. The monster, in terror, had fled the premises forever! I should behold it no more! My happiness was supreme! The guilt of my dark deed disturbed me but little. Some few inquiries had been made, but these had been readily answered. Even a search had been instituted—but of course nothing was to be discovered. I looked upon my future felicity as secured.

Upon the fourth day of the assassination, a party of the police came, very unexpectedly, into the house, and proceeded again to make rigorous investigation of the premises. Secure, however, in the inscrutability of my place of concealment, I felt no embarrassment whatever. The officers bade me accompany them in their search. They left no nook or corner unexplored. At length, for the third or fourth time, they descended into the cellar. I quivered not in a muscle. My heart beat calmly as that of one who slumbers in innocence. I walked the cellar from end to end. I folded my arms upon my bosom, and roamed easily to and fro. The police were thoroughly satisfied and prepared to depart. The glee at my heart was too strong to be restrained. I burned to say if but one word, by way of triumph, and to render doubly sure their assurance of my guiltlessness.

"Gentlemen," I said at last, as the party ascended the steps, "I delight to have allayed your suspicions. I wish you all health, and a little more courtesy. By the bye, gentlemen, this—this is a very well constructed house." [In the rabid desire to say something easily, I scarcely knew what I uttered at all.]—"I may say an *excellently* well constructed house. These walls—are you going, gentlemen?—these walls are solidly put together;" and here, through the mere phrenzy of bravado, I rapped heavily, with a cane which I held in my hand, upon that very portion of the brick-work behind which stood the corpse of the wife of my bosom.

But may God shield and deliver me from the fangs of the Arch-Fiend! No sooner had the reverberation of my blows sunk into silence, than I was answered by a voice from within the tomb!—by a cry, at first muffled and broken, like the sobbing of a child, and then quickly swelling into one long, loud, and continuous scream, utterly anomalous and inhuman—a howl—a wailing shriek, half of horror and half of triumph, such as might have arisen only out of hell, conjointly from the throats of the damned in their agony and of the demons that exult in the damnation.

Of my own thoughts it is folly to speak. Swooning, I staggered to the opposite wall. For one instant the party upon the stairs remained motionless, through extremity of terror and of awe. In the next, a dozen stout arms were toiling at the wall. It fell bodily. The corpse, already greatly decayed and clotted with gore, stood erect before the eyes of the spectators. Upon its head, with red extended mouth and solitary eye of fire, sat the hideous beast whose craft had seduced me into murder, and whose informing voice had consigned me to the hangman. I had walled the monster up within the tomb!

1843

The Purloined Letter[1]

At Paris, just after dark one gusty evening in the autumn of 18—, I was enjoying the twofold luxury of meditation and a meerschaum, in company with my friend C. Auguste Dupin, in his little back library, or book-closet, *au troisiême*,[2] No. 33, *Rue Dunôt, Faubourg St. Germain*. For one hour at least we had maintained a profound silence; while each, to any casual observer, might have seemed intently and exclusively occupied with the curling eddies of smoke that oppressed the atmosphere of the chamber. For myself, however, I was mentally discussing certain topics which had formed matter for conversation between us at an earlier period of the evening; I mean the affair of the Rue Morgue, and the mystery attending the murder of Marie Roget. I looked upon it, therefore, as something of coincidence, when the door of our apartment was thrown open and admitted our old acquaintance, Monsieur G——, the Prefect of the Parisian police.

We gave him a hearty welcome; for there was nearly half as much of the entertaining as of the contemptible about the man, and we had not seen him for several years. We had been sitting in the dark, and Dupin now arose for the purpose of lighting a lamp, but sat down again, without doing so, upon G.'s saying that he had called to consult us, or rather to ask the opinion of my friend, about some official business which had occasioned a great deal of trouble.

"If it is any point requiring reflection," observed Dupin, as he forebore to enkindle the wick, "we shall examine it to better purpose in the dark."

"That is another of your odd notions," said the Prefect, who had a fashion

1. The text is that of the first publication in *The Gift*, a Philadelphia annual dated 1845 but for sale late in 1844. Historians of detective fiction usually cite Poe's three stories about C. Auguste Dupin as the first of the genre. This is the third Dupin story, the others being *The Murders in the Rue Morgue* (1841) and *The Mystery of Marie Rôget* (1842). Here the criminal is known from the beginning and the solution comes from Dupin's analytical powers. In *The Murders in the Rue Morgue*, however, Poe is at some pains to stress that Dupin's powers are not of mere "calculation," rather "the analyst throws himself into the spirit of his opponent, identifies himself therewith, and not unfre-

quently sees thus, at a glance, the sole methods (sometimes indeed absurdly simple ones) by which he may seduce into error or hurry into miscalculation."

2. Actually the fourth floor (because the French do not count the first, the *rez-de-chaussée*). In *The Murders in the Rue Morgue* the narrator describes his and Dupin's quarters, "a time-eaten and grotesque mansion, long deserted through superstitions," "tottering to its fall in a retired and desolate portion of the Faubourg St. Germain," but meanwhile furnished "in a style which suited the rather fantastic gloom" of their common temperament.

of calling every thing "odd" that was beyond his comprehension, and thus lived amid an absolute legion of "oddities."

"Very true," said Dupin, as he supplied his visiter with a pipe, and rolled towards him a very comfortable chair.

"And what is the difficulty now?" I asked. "Nothing more in the assassination way, I hope?"

"Oh no; nothing of that nature. The fact is, the business is *very* simple indeed, and I make no doubt that we can manage it sufficiently well ourselves; but then I thought Dupin would like to hear the details of it, because it is so excessively *odd*."

"Simple and odd," said Dupin.

"Why, yes; and not exactly that, either. The fact is, we have all been a good deal puzzled because the affair *is* so simple, and yet baffles us altogether."

"Perhaps it is the very simplicity of the thing which puts you at fault," said my friend.

"What nonsense you *do* talk!" replied the Prefect, laughing heartily.

"Perhaps the mystery is a little *too* plain," said Dupin.

"Oh, good heavens! who ever heard of such an idea?"

"A little *too* self-evident."

"Ha! ha! ha!—ha! ha! ha!—ho! ho! ho!" roared out our visiter, profoundly amused, "oh, Dupin, you will be the death of me yet!"

"And what, after all, *is* the matter on hand?" I asked.

"Why, I will tell you," replied the Prefect, as he gave a long, steady, and contemplative puff, and settled himself in his chair. "I will tell you in a few words; but, before I begin, let me caution you that this is an affair demanding the greatest secrecy, and that I should most probably lose the position I now hold, were it known that I confided it to any one."

"Proceed," said I.

"Or not," said Dupin.

"Well, then; I have received personal information, from a very high quarter, that a certain document of the last importance, has been purloined from the royal apartments. The individual who purloined it is known; this beyond a doubt; he was seen to take it. It is known, also, that it still remains in his possession."

"How is this known?" asked Dupin.

"It is clearly inferred," replied the Prefect, "from the nature of the document, and from the non-appearance of certain results which would at once arise from its passing *out* of the robber's possession;—that is to say, from his employing it as he must design in the end to employ it."

"Be a little more explicit," I said.

"Well, I may venture so far as to say that the paper gives its holder a certain power in a certain quarter where such power is immensely valuable." The Prefect was fond of the cant of diplomacy.

"Still I do not quite understand," said Dupin.

"No? Well; the disclosure of the document to a third person, who shall be nameless, would bring in question the honour of a personage of most exalted station; and this fact gives the holder of the document an ascendancy over the illustrious personage whose honour and peace are so jeopardized."

"But this ascendancy," I interposed, "would depend upon the robber's knowledge of the loser's knowledge of the robber. Who would dare—"

"The thief," said G, "is the—Minister D——, who dares all things, those unbecoming as well as those becoming a man. The method of the theft was not less ingenious than bold. The document in question—a letter, to be frank—had been received by the personage robbed while alone in the royal *boudoir*. During its perusal she was suddenly interrupted by the entrance of the other exalted personage from whom especially it was her wish to conceal it. After a hurried and vain endeavour to thrust it in a drawer, she was forced to place it, open as it was, upon a table. The address, however, was uppermost, and the contents thus unexposed, the letter escaped notice. At this juncture enters the Minister D——. His lynx eye immediately perceives the paper, recognises the handwriting of the address, observes the confusion of the personage addressed, and fathoms her secret. After some business transactions, hurried through in his ordinary manner, he produces a letter somewhat similar to the one in question, opens it, pretends to read it, and then places it in close juxtaposition to the other. Again he converses, for some fifteen minutes, upon the public affairs. At length, in taking leave, he takes also from the table the letter to which he had no claim. Its rightful owner saw, but, of course, dared not call attention to the act, in the presence of the third personage who stood at her elbow. The minister decamped; leaving his own letter—one of no importance—upon the table."

"Here, then," said Dupin to me, "you have precisely what you demand to make the ascendancy complete—the robber's knowledge of the loser's knowledge of the robber."

"Yes," replied the Prefect; "and the power thus attained has, for some months past, been wielded, for political purposes, to a very dangerous extent. The personage robbed is more thoroughly convinced, every day, of the necessity of reclaiming her letter. But this, of course, cannot be done openly. In fine, driven to despair, she has committed the matter to me."

"Than whom," said Dupin, amid a perfect whirlwind of smoke, "no more sagacious agent could, I suppose, be desired, or even imagined."

"You flatter me," replied the Prefect; "but it is possible that some such opinion may have been entertained."

"It is clear," said I, "as you observe, that the letter is still in possession of the minister; since it is this possession, and not any employment, of the letter, which bestows the power. With the employment the power departs."

"True," said G——; "and upon this conviction I proceeded. My first care was to make thorough search of the minister's hotel; and here my chief embarrassment lay in the necessity of searching without his knowledge. Beyond all things, I have been warned of the danger which would result from giving him reason to suspect our design."

"But," said I, "you are quite *au fait*[3] in these investigations. The Parisian police have done this thing often before."

"O yes; and for this reason I did not despair. The habits of the minister gave me, too, a great advantage. He is frequently absent from home all night. His servants are by no means numerous. They sleep at a distance from their master's apartments, and, being chiefly Neapolitans, are readily made drunk. I have keys, as you know, with which I can open any chamber or cabinet in Paris. For three months a night has not passed, during the greater part of

3. At home, expert (French).

which I have not been engaged, personally, in ransacking the D—— Hotel. My honour is interested, and, to mention a great secret, the reward is enormous. So I did not abandon the search until I had become fully satisfied that the thief is a more astute man than myself. I fancy that I have investigated every nook and corner of the premises in which it is possible that the paper can be concealed."

"But is it not possible," I suggested, "that although the letter may be in possession of the minister, as it unquestionably is, he may have concealed it elsewhere than upon his own premises?"

"This is barely possible," said Dupin. "The present peculiar condition of affairs at court, and especially of those intrigues in which D—— is known to be involved, would render the instant availability of the document—its susceptibility of being produced at a moment's notice—a point of nearly equal importance with its possession."

"Its susceptibility of being produced?" said I.

"That is to say, of being *destroyed*," said Dupin.

"True," I observed; "the paper is clearly then upon the premises. As for its being upon the person of the minister, we may consider that as out of the question."

"Entirely," said the Prefect. "He has been twice waylaid, as if by footpads, and his person rigorously searched under my own inspection."

"You might have spared yourself this trouble," said Dupin. "D——, I presume, is not altogether a fool, and, if not, must have anticipated these waylayings, as a matter of course."

"Not *altogether* a fool," said G——, "but then he's a poet, which I take to be only one remove from a fool."

"True;" said Dupin, after a long and thoughtful whiff from his meerschaum, "although I have been guilty of certain doggerel myself."

"Suppose you detail," said I, "the particulars of your search."

"Why the fact is, we took our time, and we searched *every where*. I have had long experience in these affairs. I took the entire building, room by room; devoting the nights of a whole week to each. We examined, first, the furniture of each apartment. We opened every possible drawer; and I presume you know that, to a properly trained police agent, such a thing as a *secret* drawer is impossible. Any man is a dolt who permits a 'secret' drawer to escape him in a search of this kind. The thing is *so* plain. There is a certain amount of bulk—of space—to be accounted for in every cabinet. Then we have accurate rules. The fiftieth part of a line could not escape us. After the cabinets we took the chairs. The cushions we probed with the fine long needles you have seen me employ. From the tables we removed the tops."

"Why so?"

"Sometimes the top of a table, or other similarly arranged piece of furniture, is removed by the person wishing to conceal an article; then the leg is excavated, the article deposited within the cavity, and the top replaced. The bottoms and tops of bed-posts are employed in the same way."

"But could not the cavity be detected by sounding?" I asked.

"By no means, if, when the article is deposited, a sufficient wadding of cotton be placed around it. Besides, in our case, we were obliged to proceed without noise."

"But you could not have removed—you could not have taken to pieces *all* articles of furniture in which it would have been possible to make a deposit in the manner you mention. A letter may be compressed into a thin spiral roll, not differing much in shape or bulk from a large knitting-needle, and in this form it might be inserted into the rung of a chair, for example. You did not take to pieces all the chairs?"

"Certainly not; but we did better—we examined the rungs of every chair in the hotel, and, indeed, the jointings of every description of furniture, by the aid of a most powerful microscope.[4] Had there been any traces of recent disturbance we should not have failed to detect it *instanter*.[5] A single grain of gimlet-dust, or sawdust, for example, would have been as obvious as an apple. Any disorder in the glueing—any unusual gaping in the joints—would have sufficed to insure detection."

"Of course you looked to the mirrors, between the boards and the plates, and you probed the beds and the bed-clothes, as well as the curtains and carpets."

"That of course; and when we had absolutely completed every particle of the furniture in this way, then we examined the house itself. We divided its entire surface into compartments, which we numbered, so that none might be missed; then we scrutinized each individual square inch throughout the premises, including the two houses immediately adjoining, with the microscope, as before."

"The two houses adjoining!" I exclaimed; "you must have had a great deal of trouble."

"We had; but the reward offered is prodigious."

"You include the *grounds* about the houses?"

"All the grounds are paved with brick. They gave us comparatively little trouble. We examined the moss between the bricks, and found it undisturbed."

"And the roofs?"

"We surveyed every inch of the external surface, and probed carefully beneath every tile."

"You looked among D——'s papers, of course, and into the books of the library?"

"Certainly; we opened every package and parcel; we not only opened every book, but we turned over every leaf in each volume, not contenting ourselves with a mere shake, according to the fashion of some of our police officers. We also measured the thickness of every book-*cover*, with the most accurate admeasurement, and applied to them the most jealous scrutiny of the microscope. Had any of the bindings been recently meddled with, it would have been utterly impossible that the fact should have escaped observation. Some five or six volumes, just from the hands of the binder, we carefully probed, longitudinally, with the needles."

"You explored the floors beneath the carpets?"

"Beyond doubt. We removed every carpet, and examined the boards with the microscope."

"And the paper on the walls?"

"Yes."

"You looked into the cellars?"

---

4. I.e., a powerful magnifying glass.   5. Instantly.

"We did; and, as time and labour were no objects, we dug up every one of them to the depth of four feet."

"Then," I said, "you have been making a miscalculation, and the letter is *not* upon the premises, as you suppose."

"I fear you are right there," said the Prefect. "And now, Dupin, what would you advise me to do?"

"To make a thorough re-search of the premises."

"That is absolutely needless," replied G——. "I am not more sure that I breathe than I am that the letter is not at the Hotel."

"I have no better advice to give you," said Dupin. "You have, of course, an accurate description of the letter?"

"Oh yes!"—And here the Prefect, producing a memorandum-book, proceeded to read aloud a minute account of the internal, and especially of the external, appearance of the missing document. Soon after finishing the perusal of this description, he took his departure, more entirely depressed in spirits than I had ever known the good gentleman before.

In about a month afterwards he paid us another visit, and found us occupied very nearly as before. He took a pipe and a chair, and entered into some ordinary conversation. At length I said,—

"Well, but G——, what of the purloined letter? I presume you have at last made up your mind that there is no such thing as overreaching the Minister?"

"Confound him, say I—yes; I made the re-examination, however, as Dupin suggested—but it was all labour lost, as I knew it would be."

"How much was the reward offered, did you say?" asked Dupin.

"Why, a very great deal—a *very* liberal reward—I don't like to say how much, precisely; but one thing I *will* say, that I wouldn't mind giving my individual check for fifty thousand francs to any one who could obtain me that letter. The fact is, it is becoming of more and more importance every day; and the reward has been lately doubled. If it were trebled, however, I could do no more than I have done."

"Why, yes," said Dupin, drawlingly, between the whiffs of his meerschaum, "I really—think, G——, you have not exerted yourself—to the utmost in this matter. You might—do a little more, I think, eh?"

"How?—in what way?"

"Why—puff, puff—you might—puff, puff—employ counsel in the matter, eh?—puff, puff, puff. Do you remember the story they tell of Abernethy?"

"No; hang Abernethy!"

"To be sure! hang him and welcome. But, once upon a time, a certain rich miser conceived the design of spunging upon this Abernethy for a medical opinion. Getting up, for this purpose, an ordinary conversation in a private company, he insinuated his case to the physician, as that of an imaginary individual.

" 'We will suppose,' said the miser, 'that his symptoms are such and such; now, doctor, what would *you* have directed him to take?'

" 'Take!' said Abernethy, 'why, take *advice*, to be sure.' "

"But," said the Prefect, a little discomposed, "I am *perfectly* willing to take advice, and to pay for it. I would *really* give fifty thousand francs, every *centime* of it, to any one who would aid me in the matter!"

"In that case," replied Dupin, opening a drawer, and producing a checkbook, "you may as well fill me up a check for the amount mentioned. When you have signed it, I will hand you the letter."

I was astounded. The Prefect appeared absolutely thunder-stricken. For some minutes he remained speechless and motionless, looking incredulously at my friend with open mouth, and eyes that seemed starting from their sockets; then, apparently recovering himself in some measure, he seized a pen, and after several pauses and vacant stares, finally filled up and signed a check for fifty thousand francs, and handed it across the table to Dupin. The latter examined it carefully and deposited it in his pocket-book; then, unlocking an *escritoire*,[6] took thence a letter and gave it to the Prefect. This functionary grasped it in a perfect agony of joy; opened it with a trembling hand, cast a rapid glance at its contents, and then, scrambling and struggling to the door, rushed at length unceremoniously from the room and from the house, without having uttered a solitary syllable since Dupin had requested him to fill up the check.

When he had gone, my friend entered into some explanations.

"The Parisian police," he said, "are exceedingly able in their way. They are persevering, ingenious, cunning, and thoroughly versed in the knowledge which their duties seem chiefly to demand. Thus when G—— detailed to us his mode of searching the premises at the Hotel D——, I felt the entire confidence in his having made a satisfactory investigation—so far as his labours extended."

"So far as his labours extended?" said I.

"Yes," said Dupin. "The measures adopted were not only the best of their kind, but carried out to absolute perfection. Had the letter been deposited within the range of their search, these fellows would, beyond a question, have found it."

I merely laughed—but he seemed quite serious in all that he said.

"The measures, then," he continued, "were good in their kind, and well executed; their defect lay in their being inapplicable to the case, and to the man. A certain set of highly ingenious resources are, with the Prefect, a sort of Procrustean bed,[7] to which he forcibly adapts his designs. But he perpetually errs by being too deep or too shallow, for the matter in hand; and many a schoolboy is a better reasoner than he. I knew one about eight years of age, whose success at guessing in the game of 'even and odd' attracted universal admiration. This game is simple, and is played with marbles. One player holds in his hand a number of these toys; and demands of another whether that number is even or odd. If the guess is right, the guesser wins one; if wrong, he loses one. The boy to whom I allude won all the marbles of the school. Of course he had some principle of guessing; and this lay in mere observation and admeasurement of the astuteness of his opponents. For example, an arrant simpleton is his opponent, and, holding up his closed hand, asks, 'are they even or odd?' Our schoolboy replies 'odd,' and loses; but upon the second trial he wins, for he then says to himself, 'the simpleton had them even upon the first trial, and his amount of cunning is just sufficient to make him have them odd upon the second; I will therefore guess odd;'—he guesses odd, and wins. Now, with a simpleton a degree above the first, he would have reasoned thus: 'this fellow finds that in the first instance I guessed odd, and, in the second, he will propose to himself, upon the first impulse, a simple variation from even to odd, as did the first simpleton; but then a second thought will suggest

6. Writing desk (French) now spelled *écritoire*.
7. Procrustes, legendary Greek bandit, made his victims fit the bed he bound them to, either by stretching them to the required length or by hacking off any surplus length in the feet and legs.

that this is too simple a variation, and finally he will decide upon putting it even as before. I will therefore guess even;'—he guesses even, and wins. Now this mode of reasoning in the schoolboy, whom his fellows termed 'lucky,'—what, in its last analysis, is it?"

"It is merely," I said, "an identification of the reasoner's intellect with that of his opponent."

"It is," said Dupin; "and, upon inquiring of the boy by what means he effected the *thorough* identification in which his success consisted, I received answer as follows: 'When I wish to find out how wise, or how stupid, or how good, or how wicked is any one, or what are his thoughts at the moment, I fashion the expression of my face, as accurately as possible, in accordance with the expression of his, and then wait to see what thoughts or sentiments arise in my mind or heart, as if to match or correspond with the expression.' This response of the schoolboy lies at the bottom of all the spurious profundity which has been attributed to Rochefoucault, to La Bruyère, to Machiavelli, and to Campanella."[8]

"And the identification," I said, "of the reasoner's intellect with that of his opponent, depends, if I understand you aright, upon the accuracy with which the opponent's intellect is admeasured."

"For its practical value it depends upon this," replied Dupin; "and the Prefect and his cohort fail so frequently, first, by default of this identification, and, secondly, by ill-admeasurement, or rather through non-admeasurement, of the intellect with which they are engaged. They consider only their *own* ideas of ingenuity; and, in searching for any thing hidden, advert only to the modes in which *they* would have hidden it. They are right in this much—that their own ingenuity is a faithful representative of that of *the mass*; but when the cunning of the individual felon is diverse in character from their own, the felon foils them, of course. This always happens when it is above their own, and very usually when it is below. They have no variation of principle in their investigations; at best, when urged by some unusual emergency—by some extraordinary reward—they extend or exaggerate their old modes of *practice*, without touching their principles. What, for example, in this case of D——, has been done to vary the principle of action? What is all this boring, and probing, and sounding, and scrutinizing with the microscope, and dividing the surface of the building into registered square inches—what is it all but an exaggeration *of the application* of the one principle or set of principles of search, which are based upon the one set of notions regarding human ingenuity, to which the Prefect, in the long routine of his duty, has been accustomed? Do you not see he has taken it for granted that *all* men proceed to conceal a letter,—not exactly in a gimlet-hole bored in a chair-leg—but, at least, in *some* out-of-the-way hole or corner suggested by the same tenor of thought which would urge a man to secrete a letter in a gimlet-hole bored in a chair-leg? And do you not see also, that such *recherches*[9] nooks for concealment are adapted only for ordinary occasions, and would be adopted only by ordinary intellects; for, in all cases of concealment, a disposal of the article concealed—a disposal of it in this *recherché* manner,—is, in the very first instance, presumed and presumable; and thus its discovery depends, not at all upon the

---

8. An oddly assorted group of moralists and political and religious philosophers, all denigrated by Dupin. The original reads "La Bougive," probably a printer's

error.

9. Out of the ordinary, esoteric (French) then permissible without the acute accent or with it, as just below.

acumen, but altogether upon the mere care, patience, and determination of the seekers; and where the case is of importance—or, what amounts to the same thing in the policial eyes, when the reward is of magnitude, the qualities in question have *never* been known to fail. You will now understand what I meant in suggesting that, had the purloined letter been hidden any where within the limits of the Prefect's examination—in other words, had the principle of its concealment been comprehended within the principles of the Prefect—its discovery would have been a matter altogether beyond question. This functionary, however, has been thoroughly mystified; and the remote source of his defeat lies in the supposition that the Minister is a fool, because he has acquired renown as a poet. All fools are poets; this the Prefect *feels*; and he is merely guilty of a *non distributio medii*[1] in thence inferring that all poets are fools."

"But is this really the poet?" I asked. "There are two brothers, I know; and both have attained reputation in letters. The Minister I believe has written learnedly on the Differential Calculus. He is a mathematician, and no poet."

"You are mistaken; I know him well; he is both. As poet *and* mathematician, he would reason well; as poet, profoundly; as mere mathematician, he could not have reasoned at all, and thus would have been at the mercy of the Prefect."

"You surprise me," I said, "by these opinions, which have been contradicted by the voice of the world. You do not mean to set at naught the well-digested idea of centuries. The mathematical reason has been long regarded as *the* reason *par excellence*."

" 'Il y a à parièr,' replied Dupin, quoting from Chamfort, 'que toute idée publique, toute convention reçue, est une sottise, car elle a convenue au plus grand nombre.'[2] The mathematicians, I grant you, have done their best to promulgate the popular error to which you allude, and which is none the less an error for its promulgation as truth. With an art worthy a better cause, for example, they have insinuated the term 'analyis' into application to algebra. The French are the originators of this particular deception; but if a term is of any importance—if words derive any value from applicability—then 'analysis' conveys 'algebra' about as much as, in Latin, *'ambitus'* implies 'ambition,' *'religio'* 'religion,' or *'homines honesti,'* a set of *honourable* men."

"You have a quarrel on hand, I see," said I, "with some of the algebraists of Paris; but proceed."

"I dispute the availability, and thus the value, of that reason which is cultivated in any especial form other than the abstractly logical. I dispute, in particular, the reason educed by mathematical study. The mathematics are the science of form and quantity; mathematical reasoning is merely logic applied to observation upon form and quantity. The great error lies in supposing that even the truths of what is called *pure* algebra, are abstract or general truths. And this error is so egregious that I am confounded at the universality with which it has been received. Mathematical axioms are *not* axioms of general truth. What is true of *relation*—of form and quantity—is often grossly false in

---

1. A fallacy in logic in which neither premise of a syllogism "distributes" (i.e., conveys information about every member of the class) the middle term. According to Dupin, the Prefect does not allow for the possibility that some poets are not fools.

2. The odds are that every common notion, every accepted convention, is nonsense, precisely because it has suited itself to the majority (French). Sébastian Roch Nicolas Chamfort (1741–1794), author of *Maximes et Pensées.*

regard to morals, for example. In this latter science it is very usually *un*true that the aggregated parts are equal to the whole. In chemistry also the axiom fails. In the consideration of motive it fails; for two motives, each of a given value, have not, necessarily, a value when united, equal to the sum of their values apart. There are numerous other mathematical truths which are only truths within the limits of *relation*. But the mathematician argues, from his *finite truths*, through habit, as if they were of absolutely general applicability— as the world indeed imagines them to be. Bryant,[3] in his very learned 'Mythology,' mentions an analogous source of error, when he says that 'although the Pagan fables are not believed, yet we forget ourselves continually, and make inferences from them as existing realities.' With the algebraist, however, who are Pagans themselves, the 'Pagan fables' *are* believed, and the inferences are made, not so much through lapse of memory, as through an unaccountable addling of the brains. In short, I never yet encountered the mere mathematician who could be trusted out of equal roots, or one who did not clandestinely hold it as a point of his faith $x^2 + px$ was absolutely and unconditionally equal to q. Say to one of these gentlemen, by way of experiment, if you please, that you believe occasions may occur where $x^2 + px$ is *not* altogether equal to q, and, having made him understand what you mean, get out of his reach as speedily as convenient, for, beyond doubt, he will endeavour to knock you down.

"I mean to say," continued Dupin, while I merely laughed at his last observations, "that if the Minister had been no more than a mathematician, the Prefect would have been under no necessity of giving me this check. Had he been no more than a poet, I think it probable that he would have foiled us all. I knew him, however, as both mathematician and poet, and my measures were adapted to his capacity, with reference to the circumstances by which he was surrounded. I knew him as a courtier, too, and as a bold *intriguant*. Such a man, I considered, could not fail to be aware of the ordinary policial modes of action. He could not have failed to anticipate—and events have proved that he did not fail to anticipate—the waylayings to which he was subjected. He must have foreseen, I reflected, the secret investigations of his premises. His frequent absences from home at night, which were hailed by the Prefect as certain aids to his success, I regarded only as *ruses*, to afford opportunity for thorough search to the police, and thus the sooner to impress them with the conviction to which G——, in fact, did finally arrive—the conviction that the letter was not upon the premises. I felt, also, that the whole train of thought, which I was at some pains in detailing to you just now, concerning the invariable principle of policial action in searches for articles concealed—I felt that this whole train of thought would necessarily pass through the mind of the Minister. It would imperatively lead him to despise all the ordinary *nooks* of concealment. *He* could not, I reflected, be so weak as not to see that the most intricate and remote recess of his hotel would be as open as his commonest closets to the eyes, to the probes, to the gimlets, and to the microscopes of the Prefect. I saw, in fine, that he would be driven, as a matter of course, to *simplicity*, if not deliberately induced to it as a matter of choice. You will remember, perhaps how desperately the Prefect laughed when I suggested,

3. Jacob Bryant (1715–1804), English scholar who wrote *A New System, or an Analysis of Antient Mythology* (1774–76).

upon our first interview, that it was just possible this mystery troubled him so much on account of its being so *very* self-evident."

"Yes," said I, "I remember his merriment well. I really thought he would have fallen into convulsions."

"The material world," continued Dupin, "abounds with very strict analogies to the immaterial; and thus some colour of truth has been given to the rhetorical dogma, that metaphor, or simile, may be made to strengthen an argument, as well as to embellish a description. The principle of the *vis inertiæ*,[4] for example, with the amount of *momentum* proportionate with it and consequent upon it, seems to be identical in physics and metaphysics. It is not more true in the former, that a large body is with more difficulty set in motion than a smaller one, and that its subsequent *impetus* is commensurate with this difficulty, than it is, in the latter, that intellects of the vaster capacity, while more forcible, more constant, and more eventful in their movements than those of inferior grade, are yet the less readily moved, and more embarrassed and full of hesitation in the first few steps of their progress. Again: have you ever noticed which of the street signs, over the shop-doors, are the most attractive of attention?"

"I have never given the matter a thought," I said.

"There is a game of puzzles," he resumed, "which is played upon a map. One party playing requires another to find a given word—the name of town, river, state, or empire—any word, in short, upon the motley and perplexed surface of the chart. A novice in the game generally seeks to embarrass his opponents by giving them the most minutely lettered names; but the adept selects such words as stretch, in large characters, from one end of the chart to the other. These, like the over-largely lettered signs and placards of the street, escape observation by dint of being excessively obvious; and here the physical oversight is precisely analogous with the moral inapprehension by which the intellect suffers to pass unnoticed those considerations which are too obtrusively and too palpably self-evident. But this is a point, it appears, somewhat above or beneath the understanding of the Prefect. He never once thought it probable, or possible, that the Minister had deposited the letter immediately beneath the nose of the whole world, by way of best preventing any portion of that world from perceiving it.

"But the more I reflected upon the daring, dashing, and discriminating ingenuity of D——; upon the fact that the document must always have been *at hand*, if he intended to use it to good purpose; and upon the decisive evidence, obtained by the Prefect, that it was not hidden within the limits of that dignitary's ordinary search—the more satisfied I became that, to conceal this letter, the Minister had resorted to the comprehensive and sagacious expedient of not attempting to conceal it at all.

"Full of these ideas, I prepared myself with a pair of green spectacles, and called one fine morning, quite by accident, at the ministerial hotel. I found D—— at home, yawning, lounging, and dawdling as usual, and pretending to be in the last extremity of *ennui*.[5] He is, perhaps, the most really energetic human being now alive—but that is only when nobody sees him.

"To be even with him, I complained of my weak eyes, and lamented the necessity of the spectacles, under cover of which I cautiously and thoroughly

---

4. The power of inertia (Latin).   5. Boredom (French).

surveyed the whole apartment, while seemingly intent only upon the conversation of my host.

"I paid especial attention to a large writing-table near which he sat, and upon which lay confusedly, some miscellanous letters and other papers, with one or two musical instruments and a few books. Here, however, after a long and very deliberate scrutiny, I saw nothing to excite particular suspicion.

"At length my eyes, in going the circuit of the room, fell upon a trumpery fillagree card-rack of pasteboard, that hung dangling by a dirty blue riband, from a little brass knob just beneath the middle of the mantel-piece. In this rack, which had three or four compartments, were five or six visiting-cards, and a solitary letter. This last was much soiled and crumpled. It was torn nearly in two, across the middle—as if a design, in the first instance, to tear it entirely up as worthless, had been altered, or stayed, in the second. It had a large black seal, bearing the D—— cipher *very* conspicuously, and was addressed, in a diminutive female hand, to D——, the minister himself. It was thrust carelessly, and even, as it seemed, contemptuously, into one of the uppermost divisions of the rack.

"No sooner had I glanced at this letter, than I concluded it to be that of which I was in search. To be sure, it was, to all appearance, radically different from the one of which the Prefect had read us so minute a description. Here the seal was large and black, with the D—— cipher; there, it was small and red, with the ducal arms of the S—— family. Here, the address, to the minister, was diminutive and feminine; there, the superscription, to a certain royal personage, was markedly bold and decided; the size alone formed a point of correspondence. But, then, the *radicalness* of these differences, which was excessive; the dirt, the soiled and torn condition of the paper, so inconsistent with the *true* methodical habits of D——, and so suggestive of a design to delude the beholder into an idea of the worthlessness of the document; these things, together with the hyper-obtrusive situation of this document, full in the view of every visiter, and thus exactly in accordance with the conclusions to which I had previously arrived; these things, I say, were strongly corroborative of suspicion, in one who came with the intention to suspect.

"I protracted my visit as long as possible, and, while I maintained a most animated discussion with the minister, upon a topic which I knew well had never failed to interest and excite him, I kept my attention really riveted upon the letter. In this examination, I committed to memory its external appearance and arrangement in the rack; and also fell, at length, upon a discovery which set at rest whatever trivial doubt I might have entertained. In scrutinizing the edges of the paper, I observed them to be more *chafed* than seemed necessary. They presented the *broken* appearance which is manifested when a stiff paper, having been once folded and pressed with a folder, is refolded in a reversed direction, in the same creases or edges which had formed the original fold. This discovery was sufficient. It was clear to me that the letter had been turned, as a glove, inside out, re-directed, and re-sealed. I bade the minister good morning and took my departure at once, leaving a gold snuff-box upon the table.

"The next morning I called for the snuff-box, when we resumed, quite eagerly, the conversation of the preceding day. While thus engaged, however, a loud report, as if of a pistol, was heard immediately beneath the windows of the hotel, and was succeeded by a series of fearful screams, and the shoutings of a terrified mob. D—— rushed to a casement, threw it open, and looked out. In the meantime, I stepped to the card-rack, took the letter, put it in my pocket, and replaced it by a *fac-simile*, which I had carefully prepared at my lodgings—imitating the D—— cipher, very readily, by means of a seal formed of bread.

"The disturbance in the street had been occasioned by the frantic behaviour of a man with a musket. He had fired it among a crowd of women and children. It proved, however, to have been without ball, and the fellow was suffered to go his way as a lunatic or a drunkard. When he had gone, D—— came from the window, whither I had followed him immediately upon securing the object in view. Soon afterwards I bade him farewell. The pretended lunatic was a man in my own pay."

"But what purpose had you," I asked, "in replacing the letter by a *fac-simile*? Would it not have been better, at the first visit, to have seized it openly, and departed?"

"D——," replied Dupin, "is a desperate man, and a man of nerve. His hotel, too, is not without attendants devoted to his interests. Had I made the wild attempt you suggest, I should never have left the ministerial presence alive. The good people of Paris would have heard of me no more. But I had an object apart from these considerations. You know my political prepossessions. In this matter, I act as a partisan of the lady concerned. For eighteen months the minister has had her in his power. She has now him in hers—since, being unaware that the letter is not in his possession, he will proceed with his exactions as if it was. Thus will he inevitably commit himself, at once, to his political destruction. His downfall, too, will not be more precipitate than awkward. It is all very well to talk about the *facilis descensus Averni;*[6] but in all kinds of climbing, as Catalini[7] said of singing, it is far more easy to get up than to come down. In the present instance I have no sympathy—at least no pity for him who descends. He is that *monstrum horrendum,*[8] an unprincipled man of genius. I confess, however, that I should like very well to know the precise character of his thoughts, when, being defied by her whom the Prefect terms 'a certain personage,' he is reduced to opening the letter which I left for him in the card-rack."

"How? did you put any thing particular in it?"

"Why—it did not seem altogether right to leave the interior blank—that would have been insulting. To be sure, D——, at Vienna once, did me an evil turn, which I told him, quite good-humouredly, that I should remember. So, as I knew he would feel some curiosity in regard to the identity of the person who had outwitted him, I thought it a pity not to give him a clue. He is well acquainted with my MS., and I just copied into the middle of the blank sheet the words—

> " '—Un dessein si funeste,
> S'il n'est digne d'Atrée, est digne de Thyeste.'

They are to be found in Crébillon's 'Atrée.' "[9]

1844

---

6. Slightly misquoted from Virgil's *Aeneid* book 6: "The descent to Avernus [Hell] is easy."
7. Angelica Catalani (1780-1849), Italian singer.
8. "Dreadful monstrosity" (Virgil's epithet for Polyphemus, the one-eyed man-eating giant).
9. Prosper Jolyot de Crébillon wrote *Atrée et Thyeste*

(1707), in which Thyestes seduces the wife of his brother Atreus, the king of Mycenae; in revenge Atreus murders the sons of Thyestes and serves them to their father at a feast. The quotation reads: So baneful a scheme, if not worthy of Atreus, is worthy of Thyestes (French).

The Imp of the Perverse[1]

In the consideration of the faculties and impulses—of the *prima mobilia* of the human soul, the phrenologists[2] have failed to make room for a propensity which, although obviously existing as a radical, primitive, irreducible sentiment, has been equally overlooked by the moralists who have preceded them. In the pure arrogance of the reason we have all overlooked it. We have suffered its existence to escape our senses solely through want of belief—of faith— whether it be faith in Revelation[3] or faith in the inner teachings of the spirit. Its idea has not occurred to us, simply because of its seeming supererogation. We saw no *need* for the propensity in question. We could not perceive its necessity. We could not understand—that is to say, we could not have understood, had the notion of the *primum mobile* ever obtruded itself—in what manner it might be made to further the objects of humanity, either temporal or eternal. It cannot be denied that all metaphysicianism has been concocted *à priori*.[4] The intellectual or logical man, rather than the understanding or observant man, set himself to imagine designs—to dictate purposes to God. Having thus fathomed to his satisfaction the intentions of Jehovah, out of these intentions he reared his innumerable systems of Mind. In the matter of Phrenology, for example, we first determined, naturally enough, that it was the design of Deity that man should eat. We then assigned to man an organ of Alimentiveness, and this organ is the scourge by which Deity compels man to his food. Again, having settled it to be God's will that man should continue his species, we discovered an organ of Amativeness forthwith. And so with Combativeness, with Ideality, with Causality, with Constructiveness; so, in short, with every organ, whether representing a propensity, a moral sentiment, or a faculty of the pure intellect. And in these arrangements of the *principia* of human action, the Spurzheimites,[5] whether right or wrong, in part, or upon the whole, have but followed, in principle, the footsteps of their predecessors; deducing and establishing every thing from the preconceived destiny of man, and upon the ground of the *objects* of his Creator.

It would have been safer—if classify we must—to classify upon the basis of what man usually or occasionally did, and was always occasionally doing, rather than upon the basis of what we took it for granted the Deity intended him to do. If we cannot comprehend God in his visible works, how then in his inconceivable thoughts that call the works into being? If we cannot understand him in his objective creatures, how then in his substantive moods and phases of creation?

Induction *à posteriori*[6] would have brought Phrenology to admit, as an innate and primitive principle of human action, a paradoxical something which, for want of a better term, we may call *Perverseness*. In the sense I intend, it is, in fact, a *mobile* without motive—a motive not *motivirt*.[7]

1. The text is that of the first publication in *Graham's Magazine* (July 1845). Through most of the piece— part disquisition, part story—Poe treats perversity as a psychological trait without associating it with a theological condition such as Original Sin.
2. Phrenology was a popular pseudoscience in which character and intelligence were diagnosed from the shapes of different parts of the skull. "*Prima mobilia*": initial compelling force or source of energy (Latin).
3. Here, not the biblical Book of Revelation but ancient scripture (as opposed to impulses from within an individual).
4. Arrived at deductively, not through experience (Latin).
5. Johann Kaspar Spurzheim (1776–1832), Austrian physician and co-founder of phrenology. "*Principia*": principles (Latin).
6. Reasoning from the particular to the general (Latin).
7. Motivated.

Through its promptings we act without comprehensible object. Or if this shall be understood as a contradiction in terms, we may so far modify the proposition as to say that through its promptings we act for the reason that we should *not*. In theory, no reason can be more unreasonable, but in reality there is none so strong. With certain minds, under certain circumstances, it becomes absolutely irresistible. I am not more sure that I breathe, than that the conviction of the wrong or impolicy of an action is often the one unconquerable *force* which impels us, and alone impels us, to its prosecution. Nor will this overwhelming tendency to do wrong for the wrong's sake, admit of analysis, or resolution into ulterior elements. It is a radical, a primitive impulse—elementary. It will be said, I am aware, that when we persist in acts because we feel that we should *not* persist in them, our conduct is but a modification of that which ordinarily springs from the Combativeness of Phrenology. But a glance will show the fallacy of this idea. The phrenological Combativeness has for its essence the necessity of self-defence. It is our safeguard against injury. Its principle regards our well-being; and thus the desire to be well must be excited simultaneously with any principle which shall be merely a modification of Combativeness. But in the case of that something which I term Perverseness, the desire to be well is not only *not* aroused, but a strongly antagonistical sentiment prevails.

An appeal to one's own heart is, after all, the best reply to the sophistry just noticed. No one who trustingly consults his own soul will be disposed to deny the entire radicalness of the propensity in question. It is not more incomprehensible than distinct. There lives no man who, at some period, has not been tormented, for example, by an earnest desire to tantalize a listener by circumlocution. The speaker, in such case, is aware that he displeases; he has every intention to please; he is usually curt, precise, and clear; the most laconic and luminous language is struggling for utterance upon his tongue; it is only with difficulty that he restrains himself from giving it flow; he dreads and deprecates the anger of him whom he addresses; yet a shadow seems to flit across the brain, and suddenly the thought strikes that, by certain involutions and parentheses, anger may be engendered. That single thought is enough. The impulse increases to a wish—the wish to a desire—the desire to an uncontrollable longing—and the longing, in defiance of all consequences, is indulged.

Again:—We have a task before us which must be speedily performed. We know that it will be ruinous to make delay. The most important crisis of our life calls, trumpet-tongued, for immediate energy and action. We glow—we are consumed with eagerness to commence the work, and our whole souls are on fire with anticipation of the glorious result. It must—it shall be undertaken to-day—and yet we put it off until to-morrow. And why? There is no answer except that we feel *perverse*—employing the word with no comprehension of the principle. To-morrow arrives, and with it a more impatient anxiety to do our duty; but with this very increase of anxiety arrives, also, a nameless—a positively fearful, because unfathomable, craving for delay. This craving gathers strength as the moments fly. The last hour for action is at hand. We tremble with the violence of the conflict within us—of the definite with the indefinite—of the Substance with the Shadow; but, if the contest have proceeded thus far, it is the Shadow which prevails. We struggle in vain. The clock strikes and is the knell of our welfare, but at the same time is the chanticleer-note to the Thing that has so long overawed us. It flies. It disappears.

We are free. The old energy returns. We will labor *now*—alas, it is *too late!*

And yet again:—We stand upon the brink of a precipice. We peer into the abyss. We grow sick and dizzy. Our first impulse is to shrink from the danger, and yet, unaccountably, we remain. By slow degrees our sickness, and dizziness, and horror, become merged in a cloud of unnameable feeling. By gradations still more imperceptible this cloud assumes shape, as did the vapor from the bottle out of which arose the Genius[8] in the Arabian Nights. But out of this *our* cloud on the precipice's edge, there grows into palpability a shape far more terrible than any Genius or any Demon of a tale. And yet it is but a *Thought*, although one which chills the very marrow of our bones with the fierceness of the delight of its horror. It is merely the idea of what would be our sensations during the sweeping precipitancy of a fall from such a height. And this fall—this rushing annihilation—for the very reason that it involves that one most ghastly and loathsome to all the most ghastly and loathsome images of death and suffering which have ever presented themselves to our imagination—*for this very cause* do we now the most impetuously desire it. And because our reason most strenuously deters us from the brink, *therefore* do we the more unhesitatingly approach it. There is no passion in Nature of so demoniac an impatience as the passion of him who, shuddering upon the edge of a precipice, thus meditates a plunge. To indulge, even for a moment, in any attempt at *thought*, is to be inevitably lost; for reflection but urges us to forbear, and *therefore* it is, I say, that we *cannot*. If there be no friendly arm to check us, or if we fail in a sudden effort to throw ourselves backward from the danger, and so out of its sight, we plunge and are destroyed.

Examine these and similar actions as we will, we shall find them resulting solely from the spirit of the *Perverse*. We perpetrate them merely because we feel that we should *not*. Beyond or behind this there is no principle that men, in their fleshly nature, can understand; and were it not occasionally known to operate in furtherance of good, we might deem the anomalous feeling a direct instigation of the Arch-fiend.

I have premised thus much that I may be able, in some degree, to give an intelligible answer to your queries—that I may explain to you why I am here— that I may assign something like a reason for my wearing these fetters and tenanting the cell of the condemned. Had I not been thus prolix, you might either have misunderstood me altogether, or, with the rabble, you might have fancied me mad.

It is impossible that any deed could have been wrought with more thorough deliberation. For weeks—for months—I pondered upon the means of the murder. I rejected a thousand schemes because their accomplishment involved a *chance* of detection. At length, in reading some French memoirs, I found an account of a nearly fatal illness that occurred to Madame Pilau, through the agency of a candle accidentally poisoned. The idea struck my fancy at once. I knew my victim's habit of reading in bed. I knew, too, that his apartment was narrow and ill-ventilated. But I need not vex you with impertinent details. I need not describe the easy artifices by which I substituted, in his candle-stand, a wax-light of my own making for the one which I there found. The next morning he was dead in his bed, and the verdict was "Death by the visitation of God."

8. Genie.

Having inherited his estate, all went merrily with me for years. The idea of detection never obtruded itself. Of the remains of the fatal taper I had myself carefully disposed, nor had I left the shadow of a clue by which it would be possible to convict or even to suspect me of the crime.

It is inconceivable how rich a sentiment of satisfaction arose in my bosom as I reflected upon my *absolute* security. For a very long period of time I reveled in this sentiment. It afforded me, I believe, more real delight than all the mere worldly advantages accruing from my sin.

There arrived at length an epoch, after which this pleasurable feeling took to itself a new tone, and grew, by scarcely perceptible gradations, into a haunting and harassing thought—a thought that harassed because it haunted.

I could scarcely get rid of it for an instant. It is quite a common thing to be thus annoyed by the ringing in our ears, or memories, of the burden of an ordinary song, or some unimpressive snatches from an opera. Nor will we be the less tormented though the song in itself be good, or the opera-air meritorious. In this manner, at last, I would perpetually find myself pondering upon my impunity and security, and very frequently would catch myself repeating, in a low, under-tone, the phrases "I am safe—I am safe."

One day, while sauntering listlessly about the streets, I arrested myself in the act of murmuring, half aloud, these customary syllables. In a fit of petulance at my indiscretion I remodeled them thus:—"I am safe—I am safe—yes, *if I do not prove fool enough to make open confession.*"

No sooner had I uttered these words, than I felt an icy chill creep to my heart. I had had (long ago, during childhood) some experience in those fits of Perversity whose nature I have been at so much trouble in explaining, and I remembered that in no instance had I successfully resisted their attacks. And now my own casual self-suggestion—that I might possibly prove fool enough to make open confession—confronted me, as if the very ghost of him I had murdered, and beckoned me on to death.

At first I made strong effort to shake off this nightmare of the soul. I whistled—I laughed aloud—I walked vigorously—faster and still faster. At length I saw—or fancied that I saw—a vast and formless shadow that seemed to dog my footsteps, approaching me from behind, with a cat-like and stealthy pace. It was then that I *ran*. I felt a wild desire to shriek aloud. Every succeeding wave of thought overwhelmed me with new terror—for alas! I understood too well that *to think*, in my condition, was to be undone. I still quickened my steps. I bounded like a madman through the crowded thoroughfares. But now the populace took alarm and pursued. Then—then I felt the consummation of my Fate. Could I have torn out my tongue I would have done it. But a rough voice from some member of the crowd now resounded in my ears, and a rougher grasp seized me by the arm. I turned—I gasped for breath. For a moment I experienced all the pangs of suffocation—I became blind, and deaf, and giddy—and at this instant it was no mortal hand, I knew, that struck me violently with a broad and massive palm upon the back. At that blow the long imprisoned secret burst forth from my soul.

They say that I spoke with distinct enunciation, but with emphasis and passionate hurry, as if in dread of interruption before concluding the brief but pregnant sentences that consigned me to the hangman and to Hell.

1842

The Cask of Amontillado[1]

The thousand injuries of Fortunato I had borne as I best could, but when he ventured upon insult I vowed revenge. You, who so well know the nature of my soul, will not suppose, however, that I gave utterance to a threat. At *length* I would be avenged; this was a point definitively settled—but the very definitiveness with which it was resolved precluded the idea of risk. I must not only punish but punish with impunity. A wrong is unredressed when retribution overtakes its redresser. It is equally unredressed when the avenger fails to make himself felt as such to him who has done the wrong.

It must be understood that neither by word nor deed had I given Fortunato cause to doubt my good will. I continued, as was my wont, to smile in his face, and he did not perceive that my smile *now* was at the thought of his immolation.

He had a weak point—this Fortunato—although in other regards he was a man to be respected and even feared. He prided himself upon his connoisseurship in wine. Few Italians have the true virtuoso spirit. For the most part their enthusiasm is adopted to suit the time and opportunity, to practice imposture upon the British and Austrian *millionaires*. In painting and gemmary, Fortunato, like his countrymen, was a quack, but in the matter of old wines he was sincere. In this respect I did not differ from him materially;—I was skilful in the Italian vintages myself, and bought largely whenever I could.

It was about dusk, one evening during the supreme madness of the carnival season, that I encountered my friend. He accosted me with excessive warmth, for he had been drinking much. The man wore motley.[2] He had on a tight-fitting parti-striped dress, and his head was surmounted by the conical cap and bells. I was so pleased to see him that I thought I should never have done wringing his hand.

I said to him—"My dear Fortunato, you are luckily met. How remarkably well you are looking to-day. But I have received a pipe of what passes for Amontillado,[3] and I have my doubts."

"How?" said he. "Amontillado? A pipe? Impossible! And in the middle of the carnival!"

"I have my doubts," I replied; "and I was silly enough to pay the full Amontillado price without consulting you in the matter. You were not to be found, and I was fearful of losing a bargain."

"Amontillado!"

"I have my doubts."

"Amontillado!"

"And I must satisfy them."

"Amontillado!"

"As you are engaged, I am on my way to Luchresi. If any one has a critical turn it is he. He will tell me——"

"Luchresi cannot tell Amontillado from Sherry."

"And yet some fools will have it that his taste is a match for your own."

"Come, let us go."

"Whither?"

"To your vaults."

---

1. The text is that of the first publication, in *Godey's Magazine and Lady's Book* 33 (November 1846).

2. Fool's varicolored costume.

3. A light Spanish sherry. "Pipe": a large barrel.

"My friend, no; I will not impose upon your good nature. I perceive you have an engagement. Luchresi——"

"I have no engagement;—come."

"My friend, no. It is not the engagement, but the severe cold with which I perceive you are afflicted. The vaults are insufferably damp. They are encrusted with nitre."[4]

"Let us go, nevertheless. The cold is merely nothing. Amontillado! You have been imposed upon. And as for Luchresi, he cannot distinguish Sherry from Amontillado."

Thus speaking, Fortunato possessed himself of my arm; and putting on a mask of black silk and drawing a *roquelaire*[5] closely about my person, I suffered him to hurry me to my palazzo.

There were no attendants at home; they had absconded to make merry in honour of the time. I had told them that I should not return until the morning, and had given them explicit orders not to stir from the house. These orders were sufficient, I well knew, to insure their immediate disappearance, one and all, as soon as my back was turned.

I took from their sconces two flambeaux, and giving one to Fortunato, bowed him through several suites of rooms to the archway that led into the vaults. I passed down a long and winding staircase, requesting him to be cautious as he followed. We came at length to the foot of the descent, and stood together upon the damp ground of the catacombs of the Montresors.

The gait of my friend was unsteady, and the bells upon his cap jingled as he strode.

"The pipe," said he.

"It is farther on," said I; "but observe the white web-work which gleams from these cavern walls."

He turned towards me, and looked into my eyes with two filmy orbs that distilled the rheum of intoxication.

"Nitre?" he asked, at length.

"Nitre," I replied. "How long have you had that cough?"

"Ugh! ugh! ugh!—ugh! ugh! ugh!—ugh! ugh !ugh!—ugh! ugh! ugh!—ugh! ugh! ugh!"

My poor friend found it impossible to reply for many minutes.

"It is nothing," he said, at last.

"Come," I said, with decision, "we will go back; your health is precious. You are rich, respected, admired, beloved; you are happy, as once I was. You are a man to be missed. For me it is no matter. We will go back; you will be ill, and I cannot be responsible. Besides, there is Luchresi——"

"Enough," he said; "the cough is a mere nothing; it will not kill me. I shall not die of a cough."

"True—true," I replied; "and, indeed, I had no intention of alarming you unneccessarily—but you should use all proper caution. A draught of this Medoc[6] will defend us from the damps."

Here I knocked off the neck of a bottle which I drew from a long row of its fellows that lay upon the mould.

"Drink," I said, presenting him the wine.

---

4. Saltpeter, the whitish mineral potassium nitrate.   6. A claret from near Bordeaux.
5. A knee-length cloak.

He raised it to his lips with a leer. He paused and nodded to me familiarly, while his bells jingled.

"I drink," he said, "to the buried that repose around us."

"And I to your long life."

He again took my arm, and we proceeded.

"These vaults," he said, "are extensive."

"The Montresors," I replied, "were a great and numerous family."

"I forget your arms."

"A huge human foot d'or, in a field azure; the foot crushes a serpent rampant whose fangs are imbedded in the heel."[7]

"And the motto?"

"*Nemo me impune lacessit.*"[8]

"Good!" he said.

The wine sparkled in his eyes and the bells jingled. My own fancy grew warm with the Medoc. We had passed through long walls of piled skeletons, with casks and puncheons intermingling, into the inmost recesses of the catacombs. I paused again, and this time I made bold to seize Fortunato by an arm above the elbow.

"The nitre!" I said; "see, it increases. It hangs like moss upon the vaults. We are below the river's bed. The drops of moisture trickle among the bones. Come, we will go back ere it is too late. Your cough——"

"It is nothing," he said; "let us go on. But first, another draught of the Medoc."

I broke and reached him a flaçon of De Grâve.[9] He emptied it at a breath. His eyes flashed with a fierce light. He laughed and threw the bottle upwards with a gesticulation I did not understand.

I looked at him in surprise. He repeated the movement—a grotesque one.

"You do not comprehend?" he said.

"Not I," I replied.

"Then you are not of the brotherhood."

"How?"

"You are not of the masons."

"Yes, yes," I said; "yes, yes."

"You? Impossible! A mason?"

"A mason," I replied.

"A sign," he said, "a sign."

"It is this," I answered, producing from beneath the folds of my *roquelaire* a trowel.

"You jest," he exclaimed, recoiling a few paces. "But let us proceed to the Amontillado."

"Be it so," I said, replacing the tool beneath the cloak and again offering him my arm. He leaned upon it heavily. We continued our rout in search of the Amontillado. We passed through a range of low arches, descended, passed on, and descending again, arrived at a deep crypt, in which the foulness of the air caused our flambeaux rather to glow than flame.

At the most remote end of the crypt there appeared another less spacious. Its walls had been lined with human remains, piled to the vault overhead, in

---

7. On the coat of arms the golden foot is in a blue background; the foot crushes a serpent whose head is reared up.

8. No one insults me with impunity (Latin).

9. A white Bordeaux wine.

the fashion of the great catacombs of Paris. Three sides of this interior crypt were still ornamented in this manner. From the fourth side the bones had been thrown down, and lay promiscuously upon the earth, forming at one point a mound of some size. Within the wall thus exposed by the displacing of the bones, we perceived a still interior crypt or recess, in depth about four feet, in width three, in height six or seven. It seemed to have been constructed for no especial use within itself, but formed merely the interval between two of the colossal supports of the roof of the catacombs, and was backed by one of their circumscribing walls of solid granite.

It was in vain that Fortunato, uplifting his dull torch, endeavoured to pry into the depth of the recess. Its termination the feeble light did not enable us to see.

"Proceed," I said; "herein is the Amontillado. As for Luchresi——"

"He is an ignoramus," interrupted my friend, as he stepped unsteadily forward, while I followed immediately at his heels. In an instant he had reached the extremity of the niche, and finding his progress arrested by the rock, stood stupidly bewildered. A moment more and I had fettered him to the granite. In its surface were two iron staples, distant from each other about two feet, horizontally. From one of these depended a short chain, from the other a padlock. Throwing the links about his waist, it was but the work of a few seconds to secure it. He was too much astounded to resist. Withdrawing the key I stepped back from the recess.

"Pass your hand," I said, "over the wall; you cannot help feeling the nitre. Indeed, it is *very* damp. Once more let me *implore* you to return. No? Then I must positively leave you. But I will first render you all the little attentions in my power."

"The Amontillado!" ejaculated my friend, not yet recovered from his astonishment.

"True," I replied; "the Amontillado."

As I said these words I busied myself among the pile of bones of which I have before spoken. Throwing them aside, I soon uncovered a quantity of building stone and mortar. With these materials and with the aid of my trowel, I began vigorously to wall up the entrance of the niche.

I had scarcely laid the first tier of the masonry when I discovered that the intoxication of Fortunato had in great measure worn off. The earliest indication I had of this was a low moaning cry from the depth of the recess. It was *not* the cry of a drunken man. There was then a long and obstinate silence. I laid the second tier, and the third, and the fourth; and then I heard the furious vibration of the chain. The noise lasted for several minutes, during which, that I might hearken to it with the more satisfaction, I ceased my labours and sat down upon the bones. When at last the clanking subsided, I resumed the trowel, and finished without interruption the fifth, the sixth, and the seventh tier. The wall was now nearly upon a level with my breast. I again paused, and holding the flambeaux over the mason-work, threw a few feeble rays upon the figure within.

A succession of loud and shrill screams, bursting suddenly from the throat of the chained form, seemed to thrust me violently back. For a brief moment I hesitated, I trembled. Unsheathing my rapier, I began to grope with it about the recess; but the thought of an instant reassured me. I placed my hand upon the solid fabric of the catacombs and felt satisfied. I reapproached the wall. I replied to the yells of him who clamoured. I re-echoed, I aided, I surpassed them in volume and in strength. I did this, and the clamourer grew still.

It was now midnight, and my task was drawing to a close. I had completed the eighth, the ninth and the tenth tier. I had finished a portion of the last and the eleventh; there remained but a single stone to be fitted and plastered in. I struggled with its weight; I placed it partially in its destined position. But now there came from out the niche a low laugh that erected the hairs upon my head. It was succeeded by a sad voice, which I had difficulty in recognizing as that of the noble Fortunato. The voice said—

"Ha! ha! ha!—he! he! he!—a very good joke, indeed—an excellent jest. We will have many a rich laugh about it at the palazzo—he! he! he!—over our wine—he! he! he!"

"The Amontillado!" I said.

"He! he! he!—he! he! he!—yes, the Amontillado. But is it not getting late? Will not they be awaiting us at the palazzo—the Lady Fortunato and the rest? Let us be gone."

"Yes," I said, "let us be gone."

"*For the love of God, Montresor!*"

"Yes," I said, "for the love of God!"

But to these words I hearkened in vain for a reply. I grew impatient. I called aloud—

"Fortunato!"

No answer. I called again—

"Fortunato!"

No answer still. I thrust a torch through the remaining aperture and let it fall within. There came forth in return only a jingling of the bells. My heart grew sick; it was the dampness of the catacombs that made it so. I hastened to make an end of my labour. I forced the last stone into its position; I plastered it up. Against the new masonry I re-erected the old rampart of bones. For the half of a century no mortal has disturbed them. *In pace requiescat!*[1]

1846

Letter to Mr. ———— ————[1]

West Point,——1831

Dear B————.

• • • • • •

Believing only a portion of my former volume to be worthy a second edition—that small portion I thought it as well to include in the present book as to republish by itself. I have, therefore, herein combined Al Aaraaf and Tamerlane with other Poems hitherto unprinted. Nor have I hesitated to insert from the "Minor Poems," now omitted, whole lines, and even passages, to the end that being placed in a fairer light, and the trash shaken from them in which they were imbedded, they may have some chance of being seen by posterity.

---

1. May he rest in peace! (Latin).

1. This letter introduced the 2nd edition of Poe's poems (1831), the source of the present text. The essay is better known under its later title, *Letter to B——*, the *B* possibly standing for the publisher, Bliss. The essay is unreliable in comparing the relation of the 2nd edition to the 1st, but it is of great interest for what it shows of Poe's very early attempts to establish his independence of two great English poets of his time, Coleridge and, especially, Wordsworth. The ellipses are probably Poe's stratagem for creating the illusion that portions of his treatise had been omitted.

⋅ ⋅ ⋅ ⋅ ⋅ ⋅

It has been said, that a good critique on a poem may be written by one who is no poet himself. This, according to *your* idea and *mine* of poetry, I feel to be false—the less poetical the critic, the less just the critique, and the converse. On this account, and because there are but few B——s in the world, I would be as much ashamed of the world's good opinion as proud of your own. Another than yourself might here observe "Shakspeare is in possession of the world's good opinion, and yet Shakspeare is the greatest of poets. It appears then that the world judge correctly, why should you be ashamed of their favorable judgment?" The difficulty lies in the interpretation of the word "judgment" or "opinion." The opinion is the world's, truly, but it may be called theirs as a man would call a book his, having bought it; he did not write the book, but it is his; they did not originate the opinion, but it is theirs. A fool, for example, thinks Shakspeare a great poet—yet the fool has never read Shakspeare. But the fool's neighbor, who is a step higher on the Andes of the mind, whose head (that is to say his more exalted thought) is too far above the fool to be seen or understood, but whose feet (by which I mean his every day actions) are sufficiently near to be discerned, and by means of which that superiority is ascertained, which *but* for them would never have been discovered—this neighbor asserts that Shakspeare is a great poet—the fool believes him, and it is henceforward his *opinion*. This neighbor's own opinion has, in like manner, been adopted from one above *him*, and so, ascendingly, to a few gifted individuals, who kneel around the summit, beholding, face to face, the master spirit who stands upon the pinnacle.

⋅ ⋅ ⋅ ⋅ ⋅ ⋅

You are aware of the great barrier in the path of an American writer. He is read, if at all, in preference to the combined and established wit of the world. I say established; for it is with literature as with law or empire—an established name is an estate in tenure, or a throne in possession. Besides, one might suppose that books, like their authors, improve by travel—their having crossed the sea is, with us, so great a distinction. Our antiquaries abandon time for distance; our very fops glance from the binding to the bottom of the title-page, where the mystic characters which spell London, Paris, or Genoa, are precisely so many letters of recommendation.

⋅ ⋅ ⋅ ⋅ ⋅

I mentioned just now a vulgar error as regards criticism. I think the notion that no poet can form a correct estimate of his own writings is another. I remarked before, that in proportion to the poetical talent, would be the justice of a critique upon poetry. Therefore, a bad poet would, I grant, make a false critique, and his self-love would infallibly bias his little judgment in his favor; but a poet, who is indeed a poet, could not, I think, fail of making a just critique. Whatever should be deducted on the score of self-love, might be replaced on account of his intimate acquaintance with the subject; in short, we have more instances of false criticism than of just, where one's own writings are the test, simply because we have more bad poets than good. There are of course many objections to what I say: Milton is a great example of the contrary; but his opinion with respect to the Paradise Regained,[2] is by no means fairly

---

2. Milton's "brief epic" (1671) on Jesus' temptation by Satan, as described in Luke 4; having written *Paradise* *Lost* four years before, Milton now elaborated on how Paradise was to be refound.

ascertained. By what trivial circumstances men are often led to assert what they do not really believe! Perhaps an inadvertent word has descended to posterity. But, in fact, the Paradise Regained is little, if at all, inferior to the Paradise Lost, and is only supposed so to be because men do not like epics, whatever they may say to the contrary, and reading those of Milton in their natural order, are too much wearied with the first to derive any pleasure from the second.

I dare say Milton preferred Comus[3] to either—if so—justly. · · · · ·

As I am speaking of poetry, it will not be amiss to touch slightly upon the most singular heresy in its modern history—the heresy of what is called very foolishly, the Lake School.[4] Some years ago I might have been induced, by an occasion like the present, to attempt a formal refutation of their doctrine; at present it would be a work of supererogation. The wise must bow to the wisdom of such men as Coleridge and Southey, but being wise, have laughed at poetical theories so prosaically exemplified.

Aristotle, with singular assurance, has declared poetry the most philosophical of all writing[5]—but it required a Wordsworth to pronounce it the most metaphysical. He seems to think that the end of poetry is, or should be, instruction—yet it is a truism that the end of our existence is happiness; if so, the end of every separate part of our existence—every thing connected with our existence should be still happiness. Therefore the end of instruction should be happiness; and happiness is another name for pleasure;—therefore the end of instruction should be pleasure; yet we see the above mentioned opinion implies precisely the reverse.

To proceed: ceteris paribus,[6] he who pleases, is of more importance to his fellow men than he who instructs, since utility is happiness, and pleasure is the end already obtained which instruction is merely the means of obtaining.

I see no reason, then, why our metaphysical[7] poets should plume themselves so much on the utility of their works, unless indeed they refer to instruction with eternity in view; in which case, sincere respect for their piety would not allow me to express my contempt for their judgment; contempt which it would be difficult to conceal, since their writings are professedly to be understood by the few, and it is the many who stand in need of salvation. In such case I should no doubt be tempted to think of the devil in Melmoth,[8] who labors indefatigably through three octavo volumes, to accomplish the destruction of one or two souls, while any common devil would have demolished one or two thousand.

· · · · ·

Against the subtleties which would make poetry a study—not a passion—it becomes the metaphysician to reason—but the poet to protest. Yet Wordsworth and Coleridge are men in years; the one imbued in contemplation from

3. The common title of A Mask Presented at Ludlow-Castle, 1634, &c. Poe's judgment of the relative merits of Milton's poems is his, not Milton's. Poe's main point is the brevity of Comus compared to that of even the "brief epic."

4. Poets of the Lake District, in three English counties: Cumberland, Lancashire, and Westmorland. Wordsworth drew Coleridge there, who in turn drew Robert Southey (1774-1843), his brother-in-law and poet laureate 1813-43. Thomas De Quincey also became associated with the Lake School.

5. "Spoudaiotaton kai philosophikotaton genos" [Poe's note]. The passage in Aristotle's Poetics 9.3 says that poetry is more philosophical than history because poetry expresses the universal, history the particular. Poe is echoing Wordsworth's allusion to Aristotle in the Preface to the 2nd edition of the Lyrical Ballads (1800).

6. Other things being equal (Latin).

7. Here, moralistic, educational.

8. Melmoth the Wanderer (1820), gothic novel by Charles Robert Maturin, an Irish clergyman.

his childhood, the other a giant in intellect and learning. The diffidence, then, with which I venture to dispute their authority would be overwhelming, did I not feel, from the bottom of my heart, that learning has little to do with the imagination—intellect with the passions—or age with poetry.

> "Trifles, like straws, upon the surface flow,
> He who would search for pearls must dive below,"[9]

are lines which have done much mischief. As regards the greater truths, men oftener err by seeking them at the bottom than at the top; the depth lies in the huge abysses where wisdom is sought—not in the palpable palaces where she is found. The ancients were not always right in hiding the goddess in a well: witness the light which Bacon[1] has thrown upon philosophy; witness the principles of our divine faith—that moral mechanism by which the simplicity of a child may overbalance the wisdom of a man.

Poetry, above all things, is a beautiful painting whose tints, to minute inspection, are confusion worse confounded, but start boldly out to the cursory glance of the connoisseur.

We see an instance of Coleridge's liability to err in his Biographia Litteraria—professedly his literary life and opinions, but, in fact, a treatise *de omni scibili et quibusdam aliis*.[2] He goes wrong by reason of his very profundity, and of his error we have a natural type in the contemplation of a star. He who regards it directly and intensely sees, it is true, the star, but it is the star without a ray—while he who surveys it less inquisitively is conscious of all for which the star is useful to us below—its brilliancy and its beauty.

. . . . . .

As to Wordsworth, I have no faith in him: That he had, in youth, the feelings of a poet, I believe—for there are glimpses of extreme delicacy in his writings—(and delicacy is the poet's own kingdom—his *El Dorado*[3])—but they have the appearance of a better day recollected; and glimpses, at best, are little evidence of present poetic fire—we know that a few straggling flowers spring up daily in the crevices of the Avalanche.

He was to blame in wearing away his youth in contemplation with the end of poetizing in his manhood. With the increase of his judgment the light which should make it apparent has faded away. His judgment consequently is too correct. This may not be understood, but the old Goths of Germany would have understood it, who used to debate matters of importance to their State twice, once when drunk, and once when sober—sober that they might not be deficient in formality—drunk lest they should be destitute of vigor.

The long wordy discussions by which he tries to reason us into admiration of his poetry, speak very little in his favor: they are full of such assertions as this—(I have opened one of his volumes at random) "Of genius the only proof is the act of doing well what is worthy to be done, and what was never done before"[4]—indeed! then it follows that in doing what is *unworthy* to be done, or what *has* been done before, no genius can be evinced: yet the picking of

---

9. Adapted from the prologue to John Dryden's *All for Love* (1677); Dryden wrote "Errors," not "Trifles."
1. Francis Bacon (1561-1626), English essayist, philosopher, and statesman.
2. On everything that can be written about, and cer-

tain other things besides (Latin).
3. City of gold, paradise.
4. From Wordsworth's *Essay, Supplementary to the Preface* (1815).

pockets is an unworthy act, pockets have been picked time immemorial, and Barrington,[5] the pick-pocket, in point of genius, would have thought hard of a comparison with William Wordsworth, the poet.

Again—in estimating the merit of certain poems, whether they be Ossian's or M'Pherson's,[6] can surely be of little consequence, yet, in order to prove their worthlessness, Mr. W. has expended many pages in the controversy. *Tantæne animis?*[7] Can great minds descend to such absurdity? But worse still: that he may bear down every argument in favor of these poems, he triumphantly drags forward a passage in his abomination of which he expects the reader to sympathize. It is the beginning of the epic poem *"Temora."* "The blue waves of Ullin roll in light; the green hills are covered with day; trees shake their dusky heads in the breeze." And this—this gorgeous, yet simple imagery—where all is alive and panting with immortality—than which earth has nothing more grand, nor paradise more beautiful—this—William Wordsworth, the author of Peter Bell, has *selected* to dignify with his imperial contempt. We shall see what better he, in his own person, has to offer. Imprimis:[8]

> "And now she's at the poney's head,
> And now she's at the poney's tail,
> On that side now, and now on this,
> And almost stifled with her bliss—
> A few sad tears does Betty shed,
> She pats the poney where or when
> She knows not: happy Betty Foy!
> O Johnny! never mind the Doctor!"

Secondly:

> "The dew was falling fast, the—stars began to blink,
> I heard a voice, it said—drink, pretty creature, drink;
> And looking o'er the hedge, be—fore me I espied
> A snow-white mountain lamb with a—maiden at its side.
> No other sheep were near, the lamb was all alone.
> And by a slender cord was—tether'd to a stone."

Now we have no doubt this is all true; we *will* believe it, indeed we will, Mr. W. Is it sympathy for the sheep you wish to excite? I love a sheep from the bottom of my heart.

· · · · ·

But there *are* occasions, dear B——, there are occasions when even Wordsworth is reasonable. Even Stamboul,[9] it is said, shall have an end, and the most unlucky blunders must come to a conclusion. Here is an extract from his preface.

"Those who have been accustomed to the phraseology of modern writers, if

---

5. Otherwise known as George Waldron (1775–1840), Irish writer and pickpocket.

6. I.e., whether they be wonderful bits of ancient poetry or a forgery. In Poe's youth the controversy was still raging over whether James Macpherson (1736–1796) had accomplished the feat of forging *Fingal, an Ancient Epic Poem* and *Temora, an Epic Poem* (collected in *The Poems of Ossian*) or had faithfully translated surviving fragments of Gaelic epic poetry. Poe echoes a frequently expressed view that the poems

are great, whoever wrote them.

7. Why all the fuss? (Latin).

8. Poe first scorns *Peter Bell*, one of Wordsworth's much-ridiculed, humorous verse narratives about rustics, then savages an early version of *The Idiot Boy* and sabotages a third early poem, *The Pet Lamb*, by inserting a succession of dashes.

9. The ancient city of Constantinople or Istanbul, founded in the 7th century B.C. as Byzantium.

they persist in reading this book to a conclusion (*impossible!*) will, no doubt, have to struggle with feelings of awkwardness; (ha! ha! ha!) they will look round for poetry (ha! ha! ha! ha!) and will be induced to inquire by what species of courtesy these attempts have been permitted to assume that title." Ha! ha! ha! ha! ha!

Yet let not Mr. W. despair; he has given immortality to a wagon, and the bee Sophocles has eternalized a sore toe, and dignified a tragedy with a chorus of turkeys.[1]

* * * * *

Of Coleridge I cannot speak but with reverence. His towering intellect! his gigantic power! To use an author quoted by himself, "Jai trouve souvent que la plupart des sectes ont raison dans une bonne partie de ce quelles avancent, mais non pas en ce quelles nient,"[2] and, to employ his own language, he has imprisoned his own conceptions by the barrier he has erected against those of others. It is lamentable to think that such a mind should be buried in metaphysics, and, like the Nyctanthes,[3] waste its perfume upon the night alone. In reading that man's poetry I tremble, like one who stands upon a volcano, conscious, from the very darkness bursting from the crater, of the fire and the light that are weltering below.

* * * * *

What is Poetry? Poetry! that Proteus-like idea, with as many appellations as the nine-titled Corcyra![4] Give me, I demanded of a scholar some time ago, give me a definition of poetry? "Tres volontiers,"[5]—and he proceeded to his library, brought me a Dr. Johnson, and overwhelmed me with a definition. Shade of the immortal Shakspeare! I imagined to myself the scowl of your spiritual eye upon the profanity of that scurrilous Ursa Major. Think of poetry, dear B——, think of poetry, and then think of—Dr. Samuel Johnson![6] Think of all that is airy and fairy-like, and then of all that is hideous and unwieldy; think of his huge bulk, the Elephant! and then—and then think of the Tempest—the Midsummer Night's Dream—Prospero—Oberon—and Titania![7]

* * * * *

A poem, in my opinion,[8] is opposed to a work of science by having, for its *immediate* object, pleasure, not truth; to romance, by having for its object an *indefinite* instead of a *definite* pleasure, being a poem only so far as this object is attained: romance presenting perceptible images with definite, poetry with *indefinite* sensations, to which end music is an *essential*, since the compre-

---

1. Wordsworth wrote *The Waggoner*. Plato, not Sophocles, was known as the "Attic Bee" (from the purity and sweetness of his style), but Poe is apparently thinking either of Sophocles' *Oedipus Rex* (*Oedipus* means "swollen foot") or *Philoctetes* (in which the hero has an agonizingly injured foot). The turkeys have not been explained.
2. I have often found that most sects are right in a large part of what they affirm, but not in what they deny (French); slightly misquoted form Coleridge's *Biographia Literaria*, chap. 12, where it is quoted from Leibniz's *Trois Lettres à M. Remond de Mont-mort* (1741).
3. Night-blooming flowers.
4. One of the many (nine, says Poe) names for the

modern Corfu, a Greek island. Proteus is the Greek sea god who could change his shape at will.
5. Gladly (French).
6. English lexicographer, biographer, critic, and editor (1709–1784). "A Dr. Johnson": i.e., a dictionary by Johnson. The Ursa Major or Big Bear of Poe's little diatribe is Johnson, not the constellation. Although excessively phrased, Poe's repudiation of what he sees as Johnson's values is typically Romantic.
7. Oberon and Titania are the king and queen of the fairies in Shakespeare's *Midsummer Night's Dream*. Prospero is the benign master of spirits in *The Tempest*.
8. Poe's youthful "opinion" is deeply indebted to Coleridge's definition of poetry in the *Biographia Literaria*, chap. 14.

hension of sweet sound is our most indefinite conception. Music, when combined without a pleasurable idea, is poetry; music without the idea is simply music; the idea without the music is prose from its very definitiveness.

What was meant by the invective against him who had no music in his soul?

. . . . .

To sum up this long rigmarole, I have, dear B——, what you no doubt perceive, for the metaphysical poets, *as* poets, the most sovereign contempt. That they have followers proves nothing—

> No Indian prince has to his palace
> More followers than a thief to the gallows.[9]

1831

[Reviews of Hawthorne's *Twice-Told Tales*][1]

[*April*]

TWICE-TOLD TALES BY NATHANIEL HAWTHORNE.
JAMES MUNROE & CO.: BOSTON

We have always regarded the *Tale* (using this word in its popular acceptation) as affording the best prose opportunity for display of the highest talent. It has peculiar advantages which the novel does not admit. It is, of course, a far finer field than the essay. It has even points of superiority over the poem. An accident has deprived us, this month, of our customary space for review; and thus nipped in the bud a design long cherished of treating this subject in detail; taking Mr. Hawthorne's volumes as a text. In May we shall endeavor to carry out our intention. At present we are forced to be brief.

With rare exception—in the case of Mr. Irving's "Tales of a Traveller"[2] and a few other works of a like cast—we have had no American tales of high merit. We have had no skilful compositions—nothing which could bear examination as works of art. Of twattle called tale-making we have had, perhaps, more than enough. We have had a superabundance of the Rosa-Matilda effusions—gilt-edged papers all *couleur de rose:*[3] a full allowance of cut-and-thrust blue-blazing melodramaticisms; a nauseating surfeit of low miniature copying of low life, much in the manner, and with about half the merit, of the Dutch herrings and decayed cheeses of Van Tuyssel[4]—of all this, *eheu jam satis!*[5]

Mr. Hawthorne's volumes appear to us misnamed in two respects. In the first place they should not have been called "Twice-Told Tales"—for this is a title which will not bear *repetition*. If in the first collected edition they were

---

9. From *Hudibras* 2.1.272–73, by Samuel Butler (1613–1680).
1. Reprinted here are Poe's six-paragraph notice of *Twice-Told Tales* in *Graham's Magazine* 20 (April 1842), 254, and his longer essay in the same magazine the next month, 298–300. The second installment contains Poe's now-famous discussion of the way tales are or should be composed, with the desired effect chosen before incidents are invented. The theory as applied to poetry is exemplified in *The Philosophy of Composition*. A reworking of the *Graham's* material was published in *Godey's Lady's Book* for November 1847.
2. This 1824 collection is normally thought inferior to Irving's earlier *Sketch Book* (1819–20) and *Bracebridge Hall* (1822), but its gothic stories such as *Adventure of the German Student* may have especially appealed to Poe.
3. Rose-colored (Latin).
4. A minor Dutch painter.
5. Ugh, enough of this!

twice-told, of course now they are thrice told.—May we live to hear them told a hundred times! In the second place, these compositions are by no means *all* "Tales." The most of them are essays properly so called. It would have been wise in their author to have modified his title, so as to have had reference to all included. This point could have been easily arranged.

But under whatever titular blunders we receive this book, it is most cordially welcome. We have seen no prose composition by any American which can compare with *some* of these articles in the higher merits, or indeed in the lower; while there is not a single piece which would do dishonor to the best of the British essayists.

"The Rill from the Town Pump" which, through the *ad captandum*⁶ nature of its title, has attracted more of public notice than any one other of Mr. Hawthorne's compositions, is perhaps the *least* meritorious. Among his best, we may briefly mention "The Hollow of the Three Hills;" "The Minister's Black Veil;" "Wakefield;" "Mr. Higginbotham's Catastrophe;" "Fancy's Show-Box;" "Dr. Heidegger's Experiment;" "David Swan;" "The Wedding Knell;" and "The White Old Maid." It is remarkable that all these, with one exception, are from the first volume.

The style of Mr. Hawthorne is purity itself. His *tone* is singularly effective— wild, plaintive, thoughtful, and in full accordance with his themes. We have only to object that there is insufficient diversity in these themes themselves, or rather in their character. His *originality* both of incident and of reflection is very remarkable; and this trait alone would ensure him at least *our* warmest regard and commendation. We speak here chiefly of the tales; the essays are not so markedly novel. Upon the whole we look upon him as one of the few men of indisputable genius to whom our country has as yet given birth. As such, it will be our delight to do him honor; and lest, in these undigested and cursory remarks, without proof and without explanation, we should appear to do him *more* honor than is his due, we postpone all farther comment until a more favorable opportunity.

1842

[May]

TWICE-TOLD TALES NATHANIEL HAWTHORNE. TWO VOLUMES.
BOSTON: JAMES MUNROE AND CO.

We said a few hurried words about Mr. Hawthorne in our last number, with the design of speaking more fully in the present. We are still, however, pressed for room, and must necessarily discuss his volumes more briefly and more at random than their high merits deserve.

The book professes to be a collection of *tales*, yet is, in two respects, misnamed. These pieces are now in their third republication, and, of course, are thrice-told. Moreover, they are by no means *all* tales, either in the ordinary or in the legitimate understanding of the term. Many of them are pure essays, for example, "Sights from a Steeple," "Sunday at Home," "Little Annie's Ramble," "A Rill from the Town-Pump," "The Toll-Gatherer's Day," "The Haunted Mind," "The Sister Years," "Snow-Flakes," "Night Sketches," and "Foot-Prints on the Sea-Shore." We mention these matters chiefly on account

6. Deliberately pleasing (Latin).

of their discrepancy with that marked precision and finish by which the body of the work is distinguished.

Of the Essays just named, we must be content to speak in brief. They are each and all beautiful, without being characterised by the polish and adaptation so visible in the tales proper. A painter would at once note their leading or predominant feature, and style it *repose*. There is no attempt at effect. All is quiet, thoughtful, subdued. Yet this repose may exist simultaneously with high originality of thought; and Mr. Hawthorne has demonstrated the fact. At every turn we meet with novel combinations; yet these combinations never surpass the limits of the quiet. We are soothed as we read; and withal is a calm astonishment that ideas so apparently obvious have never occurred or been presented to us before. Herein our author differs materially from Lamb or Hunt or Hazlitt—who, with vivid originality of manner and expression, have less of the true novelty of thought than is generally supposed, and whose originality, at best, has an uneasy and meretricious quaintness, replete with startling effects unfounded in nature, and inducing trains of reflection which lead to no satisfactory result. The Essays of Hawthorne have much of the character of Irving,[7] with more of originality, and less of finish; while, compared with the Spectator, they have a vast superiority at all points.[8] The Spectator, Mr. Irving, and Mr. Hawthorne have in common that tranquil and subdued manner which we have chosen to denominate *repose*; but, in the case of the two former, this repose is attained rather by the absence of novel combination, or of originality, than otherwise, and consists chiefly in the calm, quiet, unostentatious expression of commonplace thoughts, in an unambitious unadulterated Saxon. In them, by strong effort, we are made to conceive the absence of all. In the essays before us the absence of effort is too obvious to be mistaken, and a strong under-current of *suggestion* runs continuously beneath the upper stream of the tranquil thesis. In short, these effusions of Mr. Hawthorne are the product of a truly imaginative intellect, restrained, and in some measure repressed, by fastidiousness of taste, by constitutional melancholy and by indolence.

But it is of his tales that we desire principally to speak. The tale proper, in our opinion, affords unquestionably the fairest field for the exercise of the loftiest talent, which can be afforded by the wide domains of mere prose. Were we bidden to say how the highest genius could be most advantageously employed for the best display of its own powers, we should answer, without hesitation—in the composition of a rhymed poem, not to exceed in length what might be perused in an hour. Within this limit alone can the highest order of true poetry exist. We need only here say, upon this topic, that, in almost all classes of composition, the unity of effect or impression is a point of the greatest importance. It is clear, moreover, that this unity cannot be thoroughly preserved in productions whose perusal cannot be completed at one sitting. We may continue the reading of a prose composition, from the very nature of prose itself, much longer than we can persevere, to any good purpose, in the perusal of a poem. This latter, if truly fulfilling the demands of the poetic sentiment, induces an exaltation of the soul which cannot be long

7. A good comparison is Irving's "Author's Account of Himself," prefatory to the *Sketch Book*.
8. Poe probably is thinking primarily of the essays of Joseph Addison (1672–1719) in the most admired of the 18th-century English periodicals, the *Spectator* (1711–14), although he may also mean to include Richard Steele (1672–1729), author of many of the *Spectator* essays either independently or in collaboration with Addison.

sustained. All high excitements are necessarily transient. Thus a long poem is a paradox. And, without unity of impression, the deepest effects cannot be brought about. Epics were the offspring of an imperfect sense of Art, and their reign is no more. A poem *too* brief may produce a vivid, but never an intense or enduring impression. Without a certain continuity of effort—without a certain duration or repetition of purpose—the soul is never deeply moved. There must be the dropping of the water upon the rock. De Béranger[9] has wrought brilliant things—pungent and spirit-stirring—but, like all immassive bodies, they lack *momentum*, and thus fail to satisfy the Poetic Sentiment. They sparkle and excite, but, from want of continuity, fail deeply to impress. Extreme brevity will degenerate into epigrammatism; but the sin of extreme length is even more unpardonable. *In medio tutissimus ibis.*[1]

Were we called upon however to designate that class of composition which, next to such a poem as we have suggested, should best fulfil the demands of high genius—should offer it the most advantageous field of exertion—we should unhesitatingly speak of the prose tale, as Mr. Hawthorne has here exemplified it. We allude to the short prose narrative, requiring from a half-hour to one or two hours in its perusal. The ordinary novel is objectionable, from its length, for reasons already stated in substance. As it cannot be read at one sitting, it deprives itself, of course, of the immense force derivable from *totality*. Worldly interests intervening during the pauses of perusal, modify, annul, or counteract, in a greater or less degree, the impressions of the book. But simple cessation in reading would, of itself, be sufficient to destroy the true unity. In the brief tale, however, the author is enabled to carry out the fulness of his intention, be it what it may. During the hour of perusal the soul of the reader is at the writer's control. There are no external or extrinsic influences—resulting from weariness or interruption.

A skilful literary artist has constructed a tale. If wise, he has not fashioned his thoughts to accommodate his incidents; but having conceived, with deliberate care, a certain unique or single *effect* to be wrought out, he then invents such incidents—he then combines such events as may best aid him in establishing this preconceived effect. If his very initial sentence tend not to the outbringing of this effect, then he has failed in his first step. In the whole composition there should be no word written, of which the tendency, direct or indirect, is not to the one pre-established design. And by such means, with such care and skill, a picture is at length painted which leaves in the mind of him who contemplates it with a kindred art, a sense of the fullest satisfaction. The idea of the tale has been presented unblemished, because undisturbed; and this is an end unattainable by the novel. Undue brevity is just as exceptionable here as in the poem; but undue length is yet more to be avoided.

We have said that the tale has a point of superiority even over the poem. In fact, while the *rhythm* of this latter is an essential aid in the development of the poem's highest idea—the idea of the Beautiful—the artificialities of this rhythm are an inseparable bar to the development of all points of thought or expression which have their basis in *Truth*. But Truth is often, and in very great degree, the aim of the tale. Some of the finest tales are tales of ratiocination. Thus the field of this species of composition, if not in so elevated a region on the mountain of Mind, is a table-land of far vaster extent than the domain

9. Pierre Jean de Béranger (1780–1857), popular French poet and song writer.   1. You're safer in the middle (moderate) course (Latin).

of the mere poem. Its products are never so rich, but infinitely more numerous, and more appreciable by the mass of mankind. The writer of the prose tale, in short, may bring to his theme a vast variety of modes or inflections of thought and expression—(the ratiocinative, for example, the sarcastic or the humorous) which are not only antagonistical to the nature of the poem, but absolutely forbidden by one of its most peculiar and indispensable adjuncts; we allude of course, to rhythm. It may be added, here, *par parenthèse*, that the author who aims at the purely beautiful in a prose tale is laboring at great disadvantage. For Beauty can be better treated in the poem. Not so with terror, or passion, or horror, or a multitude of such other points. And here it will be seen how full of prejudice are the usual animadversions against those *tales of effect* many fine examples of which were found in the earlier numbers of Blackwood.[2] The impressions produced were wrought in a legitimate sphere of action, and constituted a legitimate although sometimes an exaggerated interest. They were relished by every man of genius: although there were found many men of genius who condemned them without just ground. The true critic will but demand that the design intended be accomplished, to the fullest extent, by the means most advantageously applicable.

We have very few American tales of real merit—we may say, indeed, none, with the exception of "The Tales of a Traveller" of Washington Irving, and these "Twice-Told Tales" of Mr. Hawthorne. Some of the pieces of Mr. John Neal[3] abound in vigor and originality; but in general, his compositions of this class are excessively diffuse, extravagant, and indicative of an imperfect sentiment of Art. Articles at random are, now and then, met with in our periodicals which might be advantageously compared with the best effusions of the British Magazines; but, upon the whole, we are far behind our progenitors in this department of literature.

Of Mr. Hawthorne's Tales we would say, emphatically, that they belong to the highest region of Art—an Art subservient to genius of a very lofty order. We had supposed, with good reason for so supposing, that he had been thrust into his present position by one of the impudent *cliques* which beset our literature, and whose pretensions it is our full purpose to expose at the earliest opportunity; but we have been most agreeably mistaken. We know of few compositions which the critic can more honestly commend than these "Twice-Told Tales." As Americans, we feel proud of the book.

Mr. Hawthorne's distinctive trait is invention, creation, imagination, originality—a trait which, in the literature of fiction, is positively worth all the rest. But the nature of originality, so far as regards its manifestation in letters, is but imperfectly understood. The inventive or original mind as frequently displays itself in novelty of *tone* as in novelty of matter. Mr. Hawthorne is original at *all* points.

It would be a matter of some difficulty to designate the best of these tales; we repeat that, without exception, they are beautiful. "Wakefield" is remarkable for the skill with which an old idea—a well-known incident—is worked up or discussed. A man of whims conceives the purpose of quitting his wife and residing *incognito*, for twenty years, in her immediate neighborhood. Something of this kind actually happened in London. The force of Mr. Haw-

---

2. The long-lived *Blackwood's Edinburgh Magazine*, founded in 1817. One of Poe's best satiric pieces is his loving tribute to the gothic excesses of this journal, *How to Write a Blackwood Article*.

3. John Neal (1793–1876), American literary man, more important as an editor.

thorne's tale lies in the analysis of the motives which must or might have impelled the husband to such folly, in the first instance, with the possible causes of his perseverance. Upon this thesis a sketch of singular power has been constructed.

"The Wedding Knell" is full of the boldest imagination—an imagination fully controlled by taste. The most captious critic could find no flaw in this production.

"The Minister's Black Veil" is a masterly composition of which the sole defect is that to the rabble its exquisite skill will be *caviare*. The *obvious* meaning of this article will be found to smother its insinuated one. The *moral* put into the mouth of the dying minister will be supposed to convey the *true* import of the narrative; and that a crime of dark dye, (having reference to the "young lady") has been committed, is a point which only minds congenial with that of the author will perceive.

"Mr. Higginbotham's Catastrophe" is vividly original and managed most dexterously.

"Dr. Heidegger's Experiment" is exceedingly well imagined, and executed with surpassing ability. The artist breathes in every line of it.

"The White Old Maid" is objectionable, even more than the "Minister's Black Veil," on the score of its mysticism. Even with the thoughtful and analytic, there will be much trouble in penetrating its entire import.

"The Hollow of the Three Hills" we would quote in full, had we space;—not as evincing higher talent than any of the other pieces, but as affording an excellent example of the author's peculiar ability. The subject is commonplace. A witch subjects the Distant and the Past to the view of a mourner. It has been the fashion to describe, in such cases, a mirror in which the images of the absent appear; or a cloud of smoke is made to arise, and thence the figures are gradually unfolded. Mr. Hawthorne has wonderfully heightened his effect by making the ear, in place of the eye, the medium by which the fantasy is conveyed. The head of the mourner is enveloped in the cloak of the witch, and within its magic folds there arise sounds which have an all-sufficient intelligence. Throughout this article also, the artist is conspicuous—not more in positive than in negative merits. Not only is all done that should be done, but (what perhaps is an end with more difficulty attained) there is nothing done which should not be. Every word *tells*, and there is not a word which does *not* tell.

In "Howe's Masquerade" we observe something which resembles a plagiarism—but which *may be* a very flattering coincidence of thought. We quote the passage in question.

> "*With a dark flush of wrath* upon his brow they saw the general *draw his sword* and *advance to meet* the figure *in the cloak* before the latter had stepped one pace upon the floor.
> '*Villain, unmuffle yourself,*' cried he, 'you pass no farther!'"
> "The figure, without blenching a hair's breadth from the sword which was pointed at his breast, made a solemn pause, and *lowered the cape of the cloak* from his face, yet not sufficiently for the spectators to catch a glimpse of it. But Sir William Howe had evidently seen enough. The sternness of his countenance gave place to a look of wild amazement, if not horror, while he recoiled several steps from the figure, *and let fall his sword* upon the floor."—See vol. 2, page 20.

The idea here is, that the figure in the cloak is the phantom or reduplication of Sir William Howe; but in an article called "William Wilson," one of the "Tales of the Grotesque and Arabesque," we have not only the same idea, but the same idea similarly presented in several respects. We quote two paragraphs, which our readers may compare with what has been already given. We have italicized, above, the immediate particulars of resemblance.

> "The brief moment in which I averted my eyes had been sufficient to produce, apparently, a material change in the arrangement at the upper or farther end of the room. A large mirror, it appeared to me, now stood where none had been perceptible before: and as I stepped up to it in extremity of terror, mine own image, but with features all pale and dabbled in blood, *advanced* with a feeble and tottering gait to meet me.
>
> "Thus it appeared I say, but was not. It was Wilson, who then stood before me in the agonies of dissolution. Not a line in all the marked and singular lineaments of that face which was not even identically mine own. *His mask and cloak lay where he had thrown them, upon the floor.*"—Vol. 2, p. 57.

Here it will be observed that, not only are the two general conceptions identical, but there are various *points* of similarity. In each case the figure seen is the wraith or duplication of the beholder. In each case the scene is a masquerade. In each case the figure is cloaked. In each, there is a quarrel— that is to say, angry words pass between the parties. In each the beholder is enraged. In each the cloak and sword fall upon the floor. The "villain, unmuffle yourself," of Mr. H. is precisely paralleled by a passage at page 56 of "William Wilson."

In the way of objection we have scarcely a word to say of these tales. There is, perhaps, a somewhat too general or prevalent *tone*—a tone of melancholy and mysticism. The subjects are insufficiently varied. There is not so much *versatility* evinced as we might well be warranted in expecting from the high powers of Mr. Hawthorne. But beyond these trivial exceptions we have really none to make. The style is purity itself. Force abounds. High imagination gleams from every page. Mr. Hawthorne is a man of the truest genius. We only regret that the limits of our Magazine will not permit us to pay him that full tribute of commendation, which, under other circumstances, we should be so eager to pay.

1842

The Philosophy of Composition[1]

Charles Dickens, in a note now lying before me, alluding to an examination I once made of the mechanism of "Barnaby Rudge," says—"By the way, are you aware that Godwin wrote his 'Caleb Williams' backwards? He first

1. The title means something like "The Theory of Writing." Poe wrote the work as a lecture in hopes of capitalizing on the success of *The Raven*. For years in his reviews Poe had campaigned for deliberate artistry rather than uncontrolled effusions, and *The Philosophy of Composition* must be regarded as part of that campaign rather than a factual account of how Poe actually wrote *The Raven*. In a letter of August 9, 1846, Poe called the essay his "best specimen of analysis." The text here is that of the first printing, in *Graham's Magazine* 28 (April 1846), 163–67.

involved his hero in a web of difficulties, forming the second volume, and then, for the first, cast about him for some mode of accounting for what had been done."[2]

I cannot think this the *precise* mode of procedure on the part of Godwin— and indeed what he himself acknowledges, is not altogether in accordance with Mr. Dickens' idea—but the author of "Caleb Williams" was too good an artist not to perceive the advantage derivable from at least a somewhat similar process. Nothing is more clear than that every plot, worth the name, must be elaborated to its *dénouement* before any thing be attempted with the pen. It is only with the *dénouement* constantly in view that we can give a plot its indispensable air of consequence, or causation, by making the incidents, and especially the tone at all points, tend to the development of the intention.

There is a radical error, I think, in the usual mode of constructing a story. Either history affords a thesis—or one is suggested by an incident of the day— or, at best, the author sets himself to work in the combination of striking events to form merely the basis of his narrative—designing, generally, to fill in with description, dialogue, or autorial comment, whatever crevices of fact, or action, may, from page to page, render themselves apparent.

I prefer commencing with the consideration of an *effect*. Keeping originality *always* in view—for he is false to himself who ventures to dispense with so obvious and so easily attainable a source of interest—I say to myself, in the first place, "Of the innumerable effects, or impressions, of which the heart, the intellect, or (more generally) the soul is susceptible, what one shall I, on the present occasion, select?" Having chosen a novel, first, and secondly a vivid effect, I consider whether it can best be wrought by incident or tone— whether by ordinary incidents and peculiar tone, or the converse, or by peculiarity both of incident and tone—afterward looking about me (or rather within) for such combinations of event, or tone, as shall best aid me in the construction of the effect.

I have often thought how interesting a magazine paper might be written by any author who would—that is to say, who could—detail, step by step, the processes by which any one of his compositions attained its ultimate point of completion. Why such a paper has never been given to the world, I am much at a loss to say—but, perhaps, the autorial vanity has had more to do with the omission than any one other cause. Most writers—poets in especial—prefer having it understood that they compose by a species of fine frenzy[3]—an ecstatic intuition—and would positively shudder at letting the public take a peep behind the scenes, at the elaborate and vacillating crudities of thought— at the true purposes seized only at the last moment—at the innumerable glimpses of idea that arrived not at the maturity of full view—at the fully matured fancies discarded in despair as unmanageable—at the cautious selections and rejections—at the painful erasures and interpolations—in a word, at the wheels and pinions—the tackle for scene-shifting—the step-ladders and demon-traps—the cock's feathers, the red paint and the black patches, which, in ninety-nine cases out of the hundred, constitute the properties of the literary *histrio*.[4]

2. William Godwin makes this claim in his 1832 preface to *Caleb Williams* (first published in 1794).
3. Shakespeare's *Midsummer Night's Dream* 5.1.12, in Theseus's description of the poet: "The poet's eye, in a fine frenzy rolling, / Doth glance from heaven to earth, from earth to heaven / And as imagination bodies forth / The forms of things unknown, the poet's pen / Turns them to shapes, and gives to airy nothing / A local habitation and a name."
4. Artist (Latin).

I am aware, on the other hand, that the case is by no means common, in which an author is at all in condition to retrace the steps by which his conclusions have been attained. In general, suggestions, having arisen pell-mell, are pursued and forgotten in a similar manner.

For my own part, I have neither sympathy with the repugnance alluded to, nor, at any time, the least difficulty in recalling to mind the progressive steps of any of my compositions; and, since the interest of an analysis, or reconstruction, such as I have considered a *desideratum*,[5] is quite independent of any real or fancied interest in the thing analyzed, it will not be regarded as a breach of decorum on my part to show the *modus operandi*[6] by which some one of my own works was put together. I select "The Raven," as the most generally known. It is my design to render it manifest that no one point in its composition is referrible either to accident or intuition—that the work proceeded, step by step, to its completion with the precision and rigid consequence of a mathematical problem.

Let us dismiss, as irrelevant to the poem *per se*, the circumstance—or say the necessity—which, in the first place, gave rise to the intention of composing *a* poem that should suit at once the popular and the critical taste.

We commence, then, with this intention.

The initial consideration was that of extent. If any literary work is too long to be read at one sitting, we must be content to dispense with the immensely important effect derivable from unity of impression—for, if two sittings be required, the affairs of the world interfere, and every thing like totality is at once destroyed. But since, *ceteris paribus*,[7] no poet can afford to dispense with *any thing* that may advance his design, it but remains to be seen whether there is, in extent, any advantage to counterbalance the loss of unity which attends it. Here I say no, at once. What we term a long poem is, in fact, merely a succession of brief ones—that is to say, of brief poetical effects. It is needless to demonstrate that a poem is such, only inasmuch as it intensely excites, by elevating, the soul; and all intense excitements are, through a psychal necessity, brief. For this reason, at least one half of the "Paradise Lost"[8] is essentially prose—a succession of poetical excitements interspersed, *inevitably*, with corresponding depressions—the whole being deprived, through the extremeness of its length, of the vastly important artistic element, totality, or unity, of effect.

It appears evident, then, that there is a distinct limit, as regards length, to all works of literary art—the limit of a single sitting—and that, although in certain classes of prose composition, such as "Robinson Crusoe,"[9] (demanding no unity,) this limit may be advantageously overpassed, it can never properly be overpassed in a poem. Within this limit, the extent of a poem may be made to bear mathematical relation to its merit—in other words, to the excitement or elevation—again in other words, to the degree of the true poetical effect which it is capable of inducing; for it is clear that the brevity must be in direct ratio of the intensity of the intended effect:—this, with one proviso—that a certain degree of duration is absolutely requisite for the production of any effect at all.

5. Something to be desired (Latin).
6. Method of procedure (Latin).
7. Other things being equal (Latin).
8. The twelve-book blank-verse epic by John Milton, which contains some 10,500 lines, more than a hun-

dred times as many lines as Poe considered desirable in a poem.
9. Daniel Defoe's novel of shipwreck in the Caribbean (1719), based on the experiences of Alexander Selkirk.

Holding in view these considerations, as well as that degree of excitement which I deemed not above the popular, while not below the critical, taste, I reached at once what I conceived the proper *length* for my intended poem—a length of about one hundred lines. It is, in fact, a hundred and eight.

My next thought concerned the choice of an impression, or effect, to be conveyed: and here I may as well observe that, throughout the construction, I kept steadily in view the design of rendering the work *universally* appreciable. I should be carried too far out of my immediate topic were I to demonstrate a point upon which I have repeatedly insisted, and which, with the poetical, stands not in the slightest need of demonstration—the point, I mean, that Beauty is the sole legitimate province of the poem. A few words, however, in elucidation of my real meaning, which some of my friends have evinced a disposition to misrepresent. That pleasure which is at once the most intense, the most elevating, and the most pure, is, I believe, found in the contemplation of the beautiful. When, indeed, men speak of Beauty, they mean, precisely, not a quality, as is supposed, but an effect—they refer, in short, just to that intense and pure elevation of *soul*—*not* of intellect, or of heart—upon which I have commented, and which is experienced in consequence of contemplating "the beautiful." Now I designate Beauty as the province of the poem, merely because it is an obvious rule of Art that effects should be made to spring from direct causes—that objects should be attained through means best adapted for their attainment—no one as yet having been weak enough to deny that the peculiar elevation alluded to, is *most readily* attained in the poem. Now the object, Truth, or the satisfaction of the intellect, and the object, Passion, or the excitement of the heart, are, although attainable, to a certain extent, in poetry, far more readily attainable in prose. Truth, in fact, demands a precision, and Passion, a *homeliness* (the truly passionate will comprehend me) which are absolutely antagonistic to that Beauty which, I maintain, is the excitement, or pleasurable elevation, of the soul. It by no means follows from any thing here said, that passion, or even truth, may not be introduced, and even profitably introduced, into a poem—for they may serve in elucidation, or aid the general effect, as do discords in music, by contrast—but the true artist will always contrive, first, to tone them into proper subservience to the predominant aim, and, secondly, to enveil them, as far as possible, in that Beauty which is the atmosphere and the essence of the poem.

Regarding, then, Beauty as my province, my next question referred to the *tone* of its highest manifestation—and all experience has shown that this tone is one of *sadness*. Beauty of whatever kind, in its supreme development, invariably excites the sensitive soul to tears. Melancholy is thus the most legitimate of all the poetical tones.

The length, the province, and the tone, being thus determined, I betook myself to ordinary induction, with the view of obtaining some artistic piquancy which might serve me as a key-note in the construction of the poem—some pivot upon which the whole structure might turn. In carefully thinking over all the usual artistic effects—or more properly *points*, in the theatrical sense— I did not fail to perceive immediately that no one had been so universally employed as that of the *refrain*. The universality of its employment sufficed to assure me of its intrinsic value, and spared me the necessity of submitting it to analysis. I considered it, however, with regard to its susceptibility of improvement, and soon saw it to be in a primitive condition. As commonly used, the *refrain,* or burden, not only is limited to lyric verse, but depends for its impression upon the force of monotone—both in sound and thought. The pleasure is deduced solely from the sense of identity—of repetition. I resolved to diversify, and so vastly heighten, the effect, by adhering, in general, to the monotone of sound, while I continually varied that of thought: that is to say, I determined to produce continuously novel effects, by the variation *of the application* of the *refrain*—the *refrain* itself remaining, for the most part, unvaried.

These points being settled, I next bethought me of the *nature* of my *refrain.* Since its application was to be repeatedly varied, it was clear that the *refrain* itself must be brief, for there would have been an insurmountable difficulty in frequent variations of application in any sentence of length. In proportion to the brevity of the sentence, would, of course, be the facility of the variation. This led me at once to a single word as the best *refrain.*

The question now arose as to the *character* of the word. Having made up my mind to a *refrain,* the division of the poem into stanzas was, of course, a corollary: the *refrain* forming the close to each stanza. That such a close, to have force, must be sonorous and susceptible of protracted emphasis, admitted no doubt: and these considerations inevitably led me to the long *o* as the most sonorous vowel, in connection with *r* as the most producible consonant.

The sound of the *refrain* being thus determined, it became necessary to select a word embodying this sound, and at the same time in the fullest possible keeping with that melancholy which I had predetermined as the tone of the poem. In such a search it would have been absolutely impossible to overlook the word "Nevermore." In fact, it was the very first which presented itself.

The next *desideratum* was a pretext for the continuous use of the one word "nevermore." In observing the difficulty which I at once found in inventing a sufficiently plausible reason for its continuous repetition, I did not fail to perceive that this difficulty arose solely from the pre-assumption that the word was to be so continuously or monotonously spoken by *a human* being—I did not fail to perceive, in short, that the difficulty lay in the reconciliation of this monotony with the exercise of reason on the part of the creature repeating the word. Here, then, immediately arose the idea of a *non*-reasoning creature capable of speech; and, very naturally, a parrot, in the first instance, suggested itself, but was superseded forthwith by a Raven, as equally capable of speech, and infinitely more in keeping with the intended *tone.*

I had now gone so far as the conception of a Raven—the bird of ill omen—monotonously repeating the one word, "Nevermore," at the conclusion of each stanza, in a poem of melancholy tone, and in length about one hundred lines. Now, never losing sight of the object *supremeness,* or perfection, at all points, I asked myself—"Of all melancholy topics, what, according to the *universal* understanding of mankind, is the *most* melancholy?" Death—was the obvious reply. "And when," I said, "is this most melancholy of topics most poetical?" From what I have already explained at some length, the answer, here also, is obvious—"When it most closely allies itself to *Beauty*: the death, then, of a beautiful woman is, unquestionably, the most poetical topic in the world—and equally is it beyond doubt that the lips best suited for such topic are those of a bereaved lover."

I had now to combine the two ideas, of a lover lamenting his deceased mistress and a Raven continuously repeating the word "Nevermore"—I had to combine these, bearing in mind my design of varying, at every turn, the *appli-*

cation of the word repeated; but the only intelligible model of such combination is that of imagining the Raven employing the word in answer to the queries of the lover. And here it was that I saw at once the opportunity afforded for the effect on which I had been depending—that is to say, the effect of the *variation of application.* I saw that I could make the first query propounded by the lover—the first query to which the Raven should reply "Nevermore"—that I could make this first query a commonplace one—the second less so—the third still less, and so on—until at length the lover, startled from his original *nonchalance* by the melancholy character of the word itself—by its frequent repetition—and by a consideration of the ominous reputation of the fowl that uttered it—is at length excited to superstition, and wildly propounds queries of a far different character—queries whose solution he has passionately at heart—propounds them half in superstition and half in that species of despair which delights in self-torture—propounds them not altogether because he believes in the prophetic or demoniac character of the bird (which, reason assures him, is merely repeating a lesson learned by rote) but because he experiences a phrenzied pleasure in so modeling his questions as to receive from the *expected* "Nevermore" the most delicious because the most intolerable of sorrow. Perceiving the opportunity thus afforded me—or, more strictly, thus forced upon me in the progress of the construction—I first established in mind the climax, or concluding query—that to which "Nevermore" should be in the last place an answer—that in reply to which this word "Nevermore" should involve the utmost conceivable amount of sorrow and despair.

Here then the poem may be said to have its beginning—at the end, where all works of art should begin—for it was here, at this point of my preconsiderations, that I first put pen to paper in the composition of the stanza:

> "Prophet," said I, "thing of evil! prophet still if bird or devil!
> By that heaven that bends above us—by that God we both adore,
> Tell this soul with sorrow laden, if within the distant Aidenn,
> It shall clasp a sainted maiden whom the angels name Lenore—
> Clasp a rare and radiant maiden whom the angels name Lenore."
>   Quoth the raven "Nevermore."

I composed this stanza, at this point, first that, by establishing the climax, I might the better vary and graduate, as regards seriousness and importance, the preceding queries of the lover—and, secondly, that I might definitely settle the rhythm, the metre, and the length and general arrangement of the stanza—as well as graduate the stanzas which were to precede, so that none of them might surpass this in rhythmical effect. Had I been able, in the subsequent composition, to construct more vigorous stanzas, I should, without scruple, have purposely enfeebled them, so as not to interfere with the climacteric effect.

And here I may as well say a few words of the versification. My first object (as usual) was originality. The extent to which this has been neglected, in versification, is one of the most unaccountable things in the world. Admitting that there is little possibility of variety in mere *rhythm,* it is still clear that the possible varieties of metre and stanza are absolutely infinite—and yet, *for centuries, no man, in verse, has ever done, or ever seemed to think of doing, an original thing.* The fact is, originality (unless in minds of very unusual force) is by no means a matter, as some suppose, of impulse or intuition. In general, to be found, it must be elaborately sought, and although a positive merit of the highest class, demands in its attainment less of invention than negation.

Of course, I pretend to no originality in either the rhythm or metre of the "Raven." The former is trochaic—the latter is octameter acatalectic, alternating with heptameter catalectic repeated in the *refrain* of the fifth verse, and terminating with tetrameter catalectic. Less pedantically—the feet employed throughout (trochees) consist of a long syllable followed by a short: the first line of the stanza consists of eight of these feet—the second of seven and a half (in effect two-thirds)—the third of eight—the fourth of seven and a half—the fifth the same—the sixth three and a half. Now, each of these lines, taken individually, has been employed before, and what originality the "Raven" has, is in their *combination into stanza*; nothing even remotely approaching this combination has ever been attempted. The effect of this originality of combination is aided by other unusual, and some altogether novel effects, arising from an extension of the application of the principles of rhyme and alliteration.

The next point to be considered was the mode of bringing together the lover and the Raven—and the first branch of this consideration was the *locale*. For this the most natural suggestion might seem to be a forest, or the fields—but it has always appeared to me that a close *circumscription of space* is absolutely necessary to the effect of insulated incident:—it has the force of a frame to a picture. It has an indisputable moral power in keeping concentrated the attention, and, of course, must not be confounded with mere unity of place.

I determined, then, to place the lover in his chamber—in a chamber rendered sacred to him by memories of her who had frequented it. The room is represented as richly furnished—this in mere pursuance of the ideas I have already explained on the subject of Beauty, as the sole true poetical thesis.

The *locale* being thus determined, I had now to introduce the bird—and the thought of introducing him through the window, was inevitable. The idea of making the lover suppose, in the first instance, that the flapping of the wings of the bird against the shutter, is a "tapping" at the door, originated in a wish to increase, by prolonging, the reader's curiosity, and in a desire to admit the incidental effect arising from the lover's throwing open the door, finding all dark, and thence adopting the half-fancy that it was the spirit of his mistress that knocked.

I made the night tempestuous, first, to account for the Raven's seeking admission, and secondly, for the effect of contrast with the (physical) serenity within the chamber.

I made the bird alight on the bust of Pallas,[1] also for the effect of contrast between the marble and the plumage—it being understood that the bust was absolutely *suggested* by the bird—the bust of *Pallas* being chosen, first, as most in keeping with the scholarship of the lover, and, secondly, for the sonorousness of the word, Pallas, itself.

About the middle of the poem, also, I have availed myself of the force of contrast, with a view of deepening the ultimate impression. For example, an air of the fantastic—approaching as nearly to the ludicrous as was admissible—is given to the Raven's entrance. He comes in "with many a flirt and flutter."

---

1. Pallas Athena, the Greek goddess of wisdom and the arts.

Not the *least obeisance made he*—not a moment stopped or stayed he,
But with mien of lord or lady, perched above my chamber door.

In the two stanzas which follow, the design is more obviously carried out:—

Then this ebony bird beguiling my sad fancy into smiling
By the *grave and stern decorum of the countenance it wore*,
"Though thy *crest be shorn and shaven* thou," I said, "art sure no craven,
Ghastly grim and ancient Raven wandering from the nightly shore—
Tell me what thy lordly name is on the Night's Plutonian shore!"
          Quoth the Raven "Nevermore."

          —

Much I marvelled *this ungainly fowl* to hear discourse so plainly,
Though its answer little meaning—little relevancy bore;
For we cannot help agreeing that no living human being
Ever yet was blessed with seeing bird above his chamber door—
Bird or beast upon the sculptured bust above his chamber door,
          With such name as "Nevermore."

The effect of the *dénouement* being thus provided for, I immediately drop
the fantastic for a tone of the most profound seriousness:—this tone commencing in the stanza directly following the one last quoted, with the line,

     But the Raven, sitting lonely on that placid bust, spoke only, etc.

From this epoch the lover no longer jests—no longer sees any thing even of
the fantastic in the Raven's demeanor. He speaks of him as a "grim, ungainly,
ghastly, gaunt, and ominous bird of yore," and feels the "fiery eyes" burning
into his "bosom's core." This revolution of thought, or fancy, on the lover's
part, is intended to induce a similar one on the part of the reader—to bring
the mind into a proper frame for the *dénouement*—which is now brought
about as rapidly and as *directly* as possible.

With the *dénouement* proper—with the Raven's reply, "Nevermore," to the
lover's final demand if he shall meet his mistress in another world—the poem,
in its obvious phase, that of a simple narrative, may be said to have its completion. So far, every thing is within the limits of the accountable—of the real. A
raven, having learned by rote the single word "Nevermore," and having
escaped from the custody of its owner, is driven, at midnight, through the
violence of a storm, to seek admission at a window from which a light still
gleams—the chamber-window of a student, occupied half in poring over a
volume, half in dreaming of a beloved mistress deceased. The casement being
thrown open at the fluttering of the bird's wings, the bird itself perches on the
most convenient seat out of the immediate reach of the student, who, amused
by the incident and the oddity of the visiter's demeanor, demands of it, in jest
and without looking for a reply, its name. The raven addressed, answers with
its customary word, "Nevermore"—a word which finds immediate echo in the
melancholy heart of the student, who, giving utterance aloud to certain
thoughts suggested by the occasion, is again startled by the fowl's repetition of
"Nevermore." The student now guesses the state of the case, but is impelled,
as I have before explained, by the human thirst for self-torture, and in part by
superstition, to propound such queries to the bird as will bring him, the lover,
the most of the luxury of sorrow, through the anticipated answer "Nevermore." With the indulgence, to the utmost extreme, of this self-torture, the

narration, in what I have termed its first or obvious phase, has a natural termination, and so far there has been no overstepping of the limits of the real.

But in subjects so handled, however skilfully, or with however vivid an array of incident, there is always a certain hardness or nakedness, which repels the artistical eye. Two things are invariably required—first, some amount of complexity, or more properly, adaptation; and, secondly, some amount of suggestiveness—some under current, however indefinite of meaning. It is this latter, in especial, which imparts to a work of art so much of that *richness* (to borrow from colloquy a forcible term) which we are too fond of confounding with *the ideal*. It is the *excess* of the suggested meaning—it is the rendering this the upper instead of the under current of the theme—which turns into prose (and that of the very flattest kind) the so called poetry of the so called transcendentalists.

Holding these opinions, I added the two concluding stanzas of the poem—their suggestiveness being thus made to pervade all the narrative which has preceded them. The under-current of meaning is rendered first apparent in the lines—

> "Take thy beak from out *my heart,* and take thy form from off my door!"
> Quoth the Raven "Nevermore!"

It will be observed that the words, "from out my heart," involve the first metaphorical expression in the poem. They, with the answer, "Nevermore," dispose the mind to seek a moral in all that has been previously narrated. The reader begins now to regard the Raven as emblematical—but it is not until the very last line of the very last stanza, that the intention of making him emblematical of *Mournful and Never-ending Remembrance* is permitted distinctly to be seen:

> And the Raven, never flitting, still is sitting, still is sitting,
> On the pallid bust of Pallas just above my chamber door;
> And his eyes have all the seeming of a demon's that is dreaming,
> And the lamplight o'er him streaming throws his shadow on the floor;
> And my soul *from out that shadow* that lies floating on the floor
>   Shall be lifted—nevermore.

1846

The Poetic Principle[1]

In speaking of the Poetic Principle, I have no design to be either thorough or profound. While discussing, very much at random, the essentiality of what we call Poetry, my principal purpose will be to cite for consideration, some few of those minor English or American poems which best suit my own taste, or which, upon my own fancy, have left the most definite impression. By "minor poems" I mean, of course, poems of little length. And here, in the beginning, permit to say a few words in regard to a somewhat peculiar principle, which, whether rightfully or wrongfully, has always had its influence in

1. In his last two years Poe earned a few dollars now and then by delivering this lecture. It was printed in 1850 in Griswold's edition (and printed in a newspaper from advance sheets of that edition), but there is no reason to doubt that the printing in the Philadelphia *Sartain's Magazine* 7 (October 1850), 231–39, was, as the heading said, "from the unpublished manuscript." The *Sartain's* printing is followed here.

my own critical estimate of the poem. I hold that a long poem does not exist. I maintain that the phrase, "a long poem," is simply a flat contradiction in terms.

I need scarcely observe that a poem deserves its title only inasmuch as it excites, by elevating the soul. The value of the poem is in the ratio of this elevating excitement. But all excitements are, through a psychal necessity, transient. That degree of excitement which would entitle a poem to be so called at all, cannot be sustained throughout a composition of any great length. After the lapse of half an hour, at the very utmost, it flags—fails—a revulsion ensues—and then the poem is, in effect, and in fact, no longer such.

There are, no doubt, many who have found difficulty in reconciling the critical dictum that the "Paradise Lost" is to be devoutly admired throughout, with the absolute impossibility of maintaining for it, during perusal, the amount of enthusiasm which that critical dictum would demand. This great work, in fact, is to be regarded as poetical, only when, losing sight of that vital requisite in all works of Art, Unity, we view it merely as a series of minor poems. If, to preserve its Unity—its totality of effect or impression—we read it (as would be necessary) at a single sitting, the result is but a constant alternation of excitement and depression. After a passage of what we feel to be true poetry, there follows, inevitably, a passage of platitude which no critical prejudgment can force us to admire; but if, upon completing the work, we read it again, omitting the first book—that is to say, commencing with the second—we shall be surprised at now finding that admirable which we before condemned—that damnable which we had previously so much admired. It follows from all this that the ultimate, aggregate, or absolute effect of even the best epic under the sun, is a nullity:—and this is precisely the fact.

In regard to the Iliad, we have, if not positive proof, at least very good reason for believing it intended as a series of lyrics; but, granting the epic intention, I can say only that the work is based in an imperfect sense of art. The modern epic is, of the supposititious ancient model, but an inconsiderate and blindfold imitation. But the day of these artistic anomalies is over. If, at any time, any very long poem *were* popular in reality, which I doubt, it is at least clear that no very long poem will ever be popular again.

That the extent of a poetical work is, *cœteris paribus,*[2] the measure of its merit, seems undoubtedly, when we thus state it, a proposition sufficiently absurd—yet we are indebted for it to the Quarterly Reviews.[3] Surely there can be nothing in mere *size*, abstractly considered—there can be nothing in mere *bulk*, so far as a volume is concerned, which has so continuously elicited admiration from these saturnine pamphlets! A mountain, to be sure, by the mere sentiment of physical magnitude which it conveys, *does* impress us with a sense of the sublime—but no man is impressed after *this* fashion by the material grandeur of even "The Columbiad."[4] Even the Quarterlies have not instructed us to be so impressed by it. As *yet*, they have not *insisted* on our estimating Lamartine by the cubic foot, or Pollock by the pound[5]—but what

2. Other things being equal (Latin).
3. The English and Scottish quarterlies, led by the *Edinburgh Review* (founded 1802) and the *Quarterly Review* (founded in 1809, also in Edinburgh). Their literary and political postures ranged from conservative to reactionary.
4. One of the "Connecticut Wits," Joel Barlow

(1754–1812), American diplomat and writer, was widely ridiculed for his patriotic epic *The Columbiad* (1807).
5. Robert Pollok (1798–1827), Scottish Poet, author of the long *The Course of Time* (1827). Alphonse de Lamartine (1790–1869), French poet.

else are we to *infer* from their continual prating about "sustained effort?" If, by "sustained effort," any little gentleman has accomplished an epic, let us frankly commend him for the effort—if this indeed be a thing commendable— but let us forbear praising the epic on the effort's account. It is to be hoped that common sense, in the time to come, will prefer deciding upon a work of art, rather by the impression it makes, by the effect it produces, than by the time it took to impress the effect, or by the amount of "sustained effort" which had been found necessary in effecting the impression. The fact is, that perse- verance is one thing, and genius quite another; nor can all the Quarterlies in Christendom confound them. By and by, this proposition, with many which I have been just urging, will be received as self-evident. In the mean time, by being generally condemned as falsities, they will not be essentially damaged as truths.

On the other hand, it is clear that a poem may be improperly brief. Undue brevity degenerates into mere epigrammatism. A *very* short poem, while now and then producing a brilliant or vivid, never produces a profound or enduring effect. There must be the steady pressing down of the stamp upon the wax. De Béranger[6] has wrought innumerable things, pungent and spirit-stirring; but, in general, they have been too imponderous to stamp themselves deeply into the public attention; and thus, as so many feathers of fancy, have been blown aloft only to be whistled down the wind.

A remarkable instance of the effect of undue brevity in depressing a poem— in keeping it out of the popular view—is afforded by the following exquisite little Serenade.[7]

I arise from dreams of thee,
    In the first sweet sleep of night,
When the winds are breathing low,
    And the stars are shining bright.
I arise from dreams of thee,
    And a spirit in my feet
Has led me—who knows how?—
    To thy chamber-window, sweet!

The wandering airs they faint
    On the dark, the silent stream—
The champak odours fail
    Like sweet thoughts in a dream;
The nightingale's complaint,
    It dies upon her heart,
As I must die on thine,
    O, beloved as thou art!

O, lift me from the grass!
    I die, I faint, I fail!
Let thy love in kisses rain
    On my lips and eyelids pale.
My cheek is cold and white, alas!
    My heart beats loud and fast:

6. Pierre Jean de Béranger (1780–1857), French poet.
7. *The Indian Serenade* (1819) by Percy Bysshe Shelley (1792–1822).

> Oh! press it close to thine again,
> Where it will break at last!

Very few, perhaps, are familiar with these lines—yet no less a poet than Shelley is their author. Their warm, yet delicate and ethereal imagination will be appreciated by all—but by none so thoroughly as by him who has himself arisen from sweet dreams of one beloved, to bathe in the aromatic air of a southern midsummer night.

One of the finest poems by Willis[8]—the very best, in my opinion, which he has ever written—has, no doubt, through this same defect of undue brevity, been kept back from its proper position, not less in the critical than in the popular view.

> The shadows lay along Broadway,
>   'Twas near the twilight-tide—
> And slowly there a lady fair
>   Was walking in her pride.
> Alone walked she; but, viewlessly,
>   Walked spirits at her side.
>
> Peace charmed the street beneath her feet,
>   And Honour charmed the air;
> And all astir looked kind on her,
>   And called her good as fair—
> For all God ever gave to her
>   She kept with chary care.
>
> She kept with care her beauties rare
>   From lovers warm and true—
> For her heart was cold to all but gold,
>   And the rich came not to woo—
> But honoured well are charms to sell
>   If priests the selling do.
>
> Now walking there was one more fair—
>   A slight girl, lily-pale;
> And she had unseen company
>   To make the spirit quail—
> 'Twixt Want and Scorn she walked forlorn,
>   And nothing could avail.
>
> No mercy now can clear her brow
>   For this world's peace to pray;
> For, as love's wild prayer dissolved in air,
>   Her woman's heart gave way!—
> But the sin forgiven by Christ in Heaven
>   By man is cursed alway!

In this composition we find it difficult to recognize the Willis who has written so many mere "verses of society." The lines are not only richly ideal, but full of energy; while they breathe an earnestness—an evident sincerity

---

8. Nathaniel Parker Willis (1806–1867), American poet and newspaper editor (he was coeditor of the New York *Home Journal*, where this lecture was first published).

of sentiment—for which we look in vain throughout all the other works of this author.

While the epic mania—while the idea that, to merit in poetry, prolixity is indispensable—has, for some years past, been gradually dying out of the public mind, by mere dint of its own absurdity—we find it succeeded by a heresy too palpably false to be long tolerated, but one which, in the brief period it has already endured, may be said to have accomplished more in the corruption of our Poetical Literature than all its other enemies combined. I allude to the heresy of *The Didactic*. It has been assumed, tacitly and avowedly, directly and indirectly, that the ultimate object of all Poetry is Truth. Every poem, it is said, should inculcate a moral; and by this moral is the poetical merit of the work to be adjudged. We Americans, especially, have patronised this happy idea; and we Bostonians,[9] very especially, have developed it in full. We have taken it into our heads that to write a poem simply for the poem's sake, and to acknowledge such to have been our design, would be to confess ourselves radically wanting in the true Poetic dignity and force:—but the simple fact is, that, would we but permit ourselves to look into our own souls, we should immediately there discover that under the sun there neither exists nor *can* exist any work more thoroughly dignified—more supremely noble than this very poem—this poem *per se*—this poem which is a poem and nothing more—this poem written solely for the poem's sake.

With as deep a reverence for the True as ever inspired the bosom of man, I would, nevertheless, limit, in some measure, its modes of inculcation. I would limit to enforce them. I would not enfeeble them by dissipation. The demands of Truth are severe. She has no sympathy with the myrtles.[1] All *that* which is so indispensable in Song, is precisely all *that* with which *she* has nothing whatever to do. It is but making her a flaunting paradox, to wreathe her in gems and flowers. In enforcing a truth, we need severity rather than efflorescence of language. We must be simple, precise, terse. We must be cool, calm, unimpassioned. In a word, we must be in that mood which, as nearly as possible, is the exact converse of the poetical. *He* must be blind, indeed, who does not perceive the radical and chasmal differences between the truthful and the poetical modes of inculcation. He must be theory-mad beyond redemption who, in spite of these differences, shall still persist in attempting to reconcile the obstinate oils and waters of Poetry and Truth.

Dividing the world of mind into its three most immediately obvious distinctions, we have the Pure Intellect, Taste, and the Moral Sense. I place Taste in the middle, because it is just this position, which, in the mind, it occupies. It holds intimate relations with either extreme; but from the Moral Sense is separated by so faint a difference that Aristotle has not hesitated to place some of its operations among the virtues themselves. Nevertheless, we find the *offices* of the trio marked with a sufficient distinction. Just as the Intellect concerns itself with Truth, so Taste informs us of the Beautiful while the Moral Sense is regardful of Duty. Of this latter, while Conscience teaches the obligation, and Reason the expediency, Taste contents herself with displaying the charms:—waging war upon Vice solely on the ground of her deformity—her

---

9. Poe's audiences may not have known he was born in Boston, but they could hardly have avoided knowing of his contempt for Frogpondia, his name for the Boston-Cambridge axis.

1. Sensuality or beauty, myrtle being sacred to Venus, the goddess of love.

disproportion—her animosity to the fitting, to the appropriate, to the harmonious—in a word, to Beauty.

An immortal instinct, deep within the spirit of man, is thus, plainly, a sense of the Beautiful. This it is which administers to his delight in the manifold forms, and sounds, and odours, and sentiments amid which he exists. And just as the lily is repeated in the lake, or the eyes of Amaryllis[2] in the mirror, so is the mere oral or written repetition of these forms, and sounds, and colours, and odours, and sentiments, a duplicate source of delight. But this mere repetition is not poetry. He who shall simply sing, with however glowing enthusiasm, or with however vivid a truth of description, of the sights, and sounds, and odours, and colours, and sentiments, which greet *him* in common with all mankind—he, I say, has yet failed to prove his divine title. There is still a something in the distance which he has been unable to attain. We have still a thirst unquenchable, to allay which he has not shown us the crystal springs. This thirst belongs to the immortality of Man. It is at once a consequence and an indication of his perennial existence. It is the desire of the moth for the star.[3] It is no mere appreciation of the Beauty before us—but a wild effort to reach the Beauty above. Inspired by an ecstatic prescience of the glories beyond the grave, we struggle, by multiform combinations among the things and thoughts of Time, to attain a portion of that Loveliness whose very elements, perhaps, appertain to eternity alone. And thus when by Poetry—or when by Music, the most entrancing of the Poetic moods—we find ourselves melted into tears—we weep then—not as the Abbaté Gravina[4] supposes—through excess of pleasure, but through a certain, petulant, impatient sorrow at our inability to grasp *now*, wholly, here on earth, at once and for ever, those divine and rapturous joys, of which *through* the poem, or *through* the music, we attain to but brief and indeterminate glimpses.

The struggle to apprehend the supernal Loveliness—this struggle, on the part of souls fittingly constituted—has given to the world all *that* which it (the world) has ever been enabled at once to understand and to *feel* as poetic.

The Poetic Sentiment, of course, may develope itself in various modes—in Painting, in Sculpture, in Architecture, in the Dance—very especially in Music—and very peculiarly, and with a wide field, in the composition of the Landscape Garden.[5] Our present theme, however, has regard only to its manifestation in words. And here let me speak briefly on the topic of rhythm. Contenting myself with the certainty that Music, in its various modes of metre, rhythm, and rhyme, is of so vast a moment in Poetry as never to be wisely rejected—is so vitally important an adjunct, that he is simply silly who declines its assistance, I will not now pause to maintain its absolute essentiality. It is in Music, perhaps, that the soul most nearly attains the great end for which, when inspired with the Poetic Sentiment, it struggles—the creation of supernal Beauty. It *may* be, indeed, that here this sublime end is, now and then, attained *in fact*. We are often made to feel, with a shivering delight, that from an earthly harp are stricken notes which *cannot* have been unfamiliar to the angels. And thus there can be little doubt that in the Union of Poetry with

2. Common name for a beauty or sweetheart, from its use for shepherdesses in Roman pastoral poetry.
3. From Shelley's *To ———: One Word Is Too Often Profaned*.
4. Giovanni Vincenzo Gravina (1664–1718), author of a book on poetry (1718).

5. A startling inclusion even in Poe's time, despite the vogue of landscape gardening in the 18th and early 19th centuries. Poe's *The Landscape Garden* (1842) and its revision as *The Domain of Arnheim* (1847) show his fascination with the imposition of an artist's conceptions on nature.

Music in its popular sense, we shall find the widest field for the Poetic development. The old Bards and Minnesingers had advantages which we do not possess—and Thomas Moore,[6] singing his own songs, was, in the most legitimate manner, perfecting them as poems.

To recapitulate, then:—I would define, in brief, the Poetry of words as *The Rhythmical Creation of Beauty*. Its sole arbiter is Taste. With the Intellect or with the Conscience, it has only collateral relations. Unless incidentally, it has no concern whatever either with Duty or with Truth.

A few words, however, in explanation. *That* pleasure which is at once the most pure, the most elevating, and the most intense, is derived, I maintain from the contemplation of the Beautiful. In the contemplation of Beauty we alone find it possible to attain that pleasurable elevation, or excitement, *of the soul*, which we recognise as the Poetic Sentiment, and which is so easily distinguished from Truth, which is the satisfaction of the Reason, or from Passion, which is the excitement of the heart. I make Beauty, therefore—using the word as inclusive of the sublime—I make Beauty the province of the poem, simply because it is an obvious rule of Art that effects should be made to spring as directly as possible from their causes:—no one as yet having been weak enough to deny that the peculiar elevation in question is at least *most readily* attainable in the poem. It by no means follows, however, that the incitements of Passion, or the precepts of Duty, or even the lessons of Truth, may not be introduced into a poem, and with advantage; for they may subserve, incidentally, in various ways, the general purposes of the work:—but the true artist will always contrive to tone them down in proper subjection to that *Beauty* which is the atmosphere and the real essence of the poem.

I cannot better introduce the few poems which I shall present for your consideration, than by the citation of the Pröem to Mr. Longfellow's "Waif:"[7]

> The day is done, and the darkness
>   Falls from the wings of Night,
> As a feather is wafted downward
>   From an Eagle in his flight.
>
> I see the lights of the village
>   Gleam through the rain and the mist,
> And a feeling of sadness comes o'er me,
>   That my soul cannot resist;
>
> A feeling of sadness and longing,
>   That is not akin to pain,
> And resembles sorrow only
>   As the mist resembles the rain.
>
> Come, read to me some poem,
>   Some simple and heartfelt lay,
> That shall soothe this restless feeling,
>   And banish the thoughts of day.

6. Irish poet (1779–1852), major influence on Poe's early poetry. "Old Bards and Minnesingers": i.e., old English or Celtic singing poets, responsible for the preservation of the histories of their peoples, and medieval German troubadours, who also sang their poems.
7. An 1844 collection.

Not from the grand old masters,
    Not from the bards sublime,
Whose distant footsteps echo
    Through the corridors of time.

For, like strains of martial music,
    Their mighty thoughts suggest
Life's endless toil and endeavour;
    And to-night I long for rest.

Read from some humbler poet,
    Whose songs gushed from his heart,
As showers from the clouds of summer,
    Or tears from the eyelids start;

Who through long days of labour,
    And nights devoid of ease,
Still heard in his soul the music
    Of wonderful melodies.

Such songs have power to quiet
    The restless pulse of care,
And come like the benediction
    That follows after prayer.

Then read from the treasured volume
    The poem of thy choice,
And lend to the rhyme of the poet
    The beauty of thy voice.

And the night shall be filled with music,
    And the cares that infest the day,
Shall fold their tents, like the Arabs,
    As they silently steal away.

With no great range of imagination, these lines have been justly admired for their delicacy of expression. Some of the images are very effective. Nothing can be better than—

        ————The bards sublime,
    Whose distant footsteps echo
Down the corridors of Time.

The idea of the last quatrain is also very effective. The poem, on the whole, however, is chiefly to be admired for the graceful *insouciance* of its metre, so well in accordance with the character of the sentiments, and especially for the *ease* of the general manner. This "ease," or naturalness, in a literary style, it has long been the fashion to regard as ease in appearance alone—as a point of really difficult attainment. But not so:—a natural manner is difficult only to him who should never meddle with it—to the unnatural. It is but the result of writing with the understanding, or with the instinct, that *the tone*, in composition, should always be that which the mass of mankind would adopt—and must perpetually vary, of course, with the occasion. The author who, after the fashion of "The North American Review,"[8] should be, upon *all* occasions, merely "quiet," must necessarily upon *many* occasions, be simply silly, or stupid; and has no more right to be considered "easy," or "natural," than the Cockney exquisite, or than the sleeping Beauty in the wax-works.

Among the minor poems of Bryant, none has so much impressed me as the one which he entitles "June."[9] I quote only a portion of it:

> There through the long, long summer hours,
>   The golden light should lie,
> And thick young herbs and groups of flowers
>   Stand in their beauty by.
> The oriole should build and tell
> His love-tale, close beside my cell;
>   The idle butterfly
> Should rest him there, and there be heard
> The housewife-bee and humming bird.
>
> And what, if cheerful shouts at noon,
>   Come, from the village sent,
> Or songs of maids, beneath the moon,
>   With fairy laughter blent?
> And what, if in the evening light,
> Betrothed lovers walk in sight
>   Of my low monument?
> I would the lovely scene around
> Might know no sadder sight nor sound.
>
> I know, I know I should not see
>   The season's glorious show,
> Nor would its brightness shine for me,
>   Nor its wild music flow;
> But if, around my place of sleep,
> The friends I love should come to weep,
>   They might not haste to go.
> Soft airs, and song, and light, and bloom
> Should keep them lingering by my tomb.
>
> These to their softened hearts should bear
>   The thought of what has been,
> And speak of one who cannot share
>   The gladness of the scene;
> Whose part in all the pomp that fills
> The circuit of the summer hills,
>   Is—that his grave is green;
> And deeply would their hearts rejoice
> To hear again his living voice.

The rhythmical flow, here, is even voluptuous—nothing could be more melodious. The poem has always affected me in a remarkable manner. The intense melancholy which seems to well up, perforce, to the surface of all the

---

8. The most important conservative American magazine of the century.

9. William Cullen Bryant (1794–1878); *June* was first published in 1826, in the *Atlantic Souvenir*.

poet's cheerful sayings about his grave, we find thrilling us to the soul—while there is the truest poetic elevation in the thrill. The impression left is one of a pleasurable sadness.

And if, in the remaining compositions which I shall introduce to you, there be more or less of a similar tone always apparent, let me remind you that (how or why we know not) this certain tint of sadness is inseparably connected with all the higher manifestations of true Beauty. It is, nevertheless,

> A feeling of sadness and longing
> That is not akin to pain,
> And resembles sorrow only
> As the mist resembles the rain.[1]

The taint of which I speak is clearly perceptible even in a poem so full of brilliancy and spirit as the "Health" of Edward Coote Pinkney:[2]

> I fill this cup to one made up
> Of loveliness alone,
> A woman, of her gentle sex
> The seeming paragon;
> To whom the better elements
> And kindly stars have given
> A form so fair, that, like the air,
> 'Tis less of earth than heaven.
>
> Her every tone is music's own,
> Like those of morning birds,
> And something more than melody
> Dwells ever in her words;
> The coinage of her heart are they,
> And from her lips each flows
> As one may see the burdened bee
> Forth issue from the rose.
>
> Affections are as thoughts to her,
> The measures of her hours;
> Her feelings have the fragrancy,
> The freshness of young flowers;
> And lovely passions, changing oft,
> So fill her, she appears
> The image of themselves by turns,—
> The idol of past years!
>
> Of her bright face one glance will trace
> A picture on the brain,
> And of her voice in echoing hearts
> A sound must long remain;
> But memory, such as mine of her,
> So very much endears,

---

1. From Longfellow's *The Day Is Done*, already quoted at length.
2. A young southerner (1802–1828) whose poems de-

rived from the same English Romantic tradition as Poe's own.

> When death is nigh, my latest sigh
>   Will not be life's but hers.
>
> I filled this cup to one made up
>   Of loveliness alone,
> A woman, of her gentle sex
>   The seeming paragon—
> Her health! and would on earth they stood
>   Some more of such a frame,
> That life might be all poetry,
>   And weariness a name.

It was the misfortune of Mr. Pinkney to have been born too far south. Had he been a New Englander, it is probable that he would have been ranked as the first of American lyrists, by that magnanimous cabal which has so long controlled the destinies of American Letters, in conducting the thing called "The North American Review." The poem just cited is especially beautiful; but the poetic elevation which it induces, we must refer chiefly to our sympathy in the poet's enthusiasm. We pardon his hyperboles for the evident earnestness with which they are uttered.

It was by no means my design, however, to expatiate upon the *merits* of what I should read you. These will necessarily speak for themselves. Boccalini, in his "Advertisements from Parnassus," tells us that Zoilus[3] once presented Apollo a very caustic criticism upon a very admirable book:—whereupon the god asked him for the beauties of the work. He replied that he only busied himself about the errors. On hearing this, Apollo, handing him a sack of unwinnowed wheat, bade him pick out *all the chaff* for his reward.

Now this fable answers very well as a hit at the critics—but I am by no means sure that the god was in the right. I am by no means certain that the true limits of the critical duty are not grossly misunderstood. Excellence, in a poem especially, may be considered in the light of an axiom, which need only be properly *put*, to become self-evident. It is *not* excellence if it require to be demonstrated as such;—and thus, to point out too particularly the merits of a work of Art, is to admit that they are *not* merits altogether.

Among the "Melodies" of Thomas Moore, is one whose distinguished character as a poem proper, seems to have been singularly left out of view. I allude to his lines beginning—"Come, rest in this bosom."[4] The intense energy of their expression is not surpassed by anything in Byron. There are two of the lines in which a sentiment is conveyed that embodies the *all in all* of the divine passion of love—a sentiment which, perhaps, has found its echo in more, and in more passionate, human hearts than any other single sentiment ever embodied in words:

> Come, rest in this bosom, my own stricken deer,
> Though the herd have fled from thee, thy home is still here;
> Here still is the smile that no cloud can o'ercast,
> And a heart and a hand all thy own to the last.

---

3. Legendary Greek grammarian whose name is proverbial for captious and malignant criticism. Traiano Boccalini (1556–1613); the title is normally translated as *Advices from Parnassus*.
4. Thomas Moore (1779–1852); *Come, Rest in This Bosom* is in *Irish Melodies* (1834).

Oh! what was love made for, if 'tis not the same
Through joy and through torment, through glory and shame?
I know not, I ask not, if guilt's in that heart,
I but know that I love thee, whatever thou art.

Thou hast called me thy angel in moments of bliss,
And thy angel I'll be, 'mid the horrors of this,—
Through the furnace, unshrinking, thy steps to pursue,
And shield thee, and save thee,—or perish there too!

It has been the fashion, of late days, to deny Moore imagination, while granting him fancy—a distinction originating with Coleridge, than whom no man
more fully comprehended the great powers of Moore.[5] The fact is, that the
fancy of this poet so far predominates over all his other faculties, and over the
fancy of all other men, as to have induced, very naturally, the idea that he is
fanciful *only*. But never was there a greater mistake. Never was a grosser wrong
done the fame of a true poet. In the compass of the English language I can
call to mind no poem more profoundly—more weirdly *imaginative*, in the
best sense, than the lines commencing—"I would I were by that dim lake,"—
which are the composition of Thomas Moore. I regret that I am unable to
remember them.

One of the noblest—and, speaking of fancy, one of the most singularly
fanciful of modern poets, was Thomas Hood. His "Fair Ines"[6] had always, for
me, an inexpressible charm.

> O saw ye not fair Ines?
>   She's gone into the West,
> To dazzle when the sun is down,
>   And rob the world of rest;
> She took our daylight with her,
>   The smiles that we love best,
> With morning blushes on her cheek,
>   And pearls upon her breast.
>
> O turn again, fair Ines,
>   Before the fall of night,
> For fear the moon should shine alone,
>   And stars unrivalled bright;
> And blessed will the lover be
>   That walks beneath their light,
> And breathes the love against thy cheek
>   I dare not even write!
>
> Would I had been, fair Ines,
>   That gallant cavalier,
> Who rode so gaily by thy side,
>   And whispered thee so near!
> Were there no bonny dames at home,
>   Or no true lovers here,

---

5. In chap. 13 of Coleridge's *Biographia Literaria*; the distinction being that fancy is a lower mental process capable of manipulating remembered sensations but not of organic, dissolving, fusing, and genuinely creative powers restricted to the imagination.

6. *Fair Ines* (1827), by Thomas Hood (1799–1845).

That he should cross the seas to win
    The dearest of the dear?

I saw thee, lovely Ines,
    Descend along the shore,
With bands of noble gentlemen,
    And banners waved before;
And gentle youth and maidens gay,
    And snowy plumes they wore;
It would have been a beauteous dream,
    —If it had been no more!

Alas, alas, fair Ines,
    She went away with song,
With music waiting on her steps,
    And shoutings of the throng;
But some were sad and felt no mirth,
    But only Music's wrong,
In sounds that sang farewell, farewell,
    To her you've loved so long.

Farewell, farewell, fair Ines;
    That vessel never bore
So fair a lady on its deck,
    Nor danced so light before,—
Alas, for pleasure on the sea,
    And sorrow on the shore!
The smile that blest one lover's heart
    Has broken many more?

"The Haunted House," by the same author, is one of the truest poems ever written—one of the *truest*—one of the most unexceptionable—one of the most thoroughly artistic, both in its theme and in its execution. It is, moreover, powerfully ideal—imaginative. I regret that its length renders it unsuitable for the purposes of this Lecture. In place of it, permit me to offer the universally appreciated "Bridge of Sighs."

One more Unfortunate,
    Weary of breath,
Rashly Importunate,
    Gone to her death!

Take her up tenderly,
    Lift her with care:—
Fashioned so slenderly,
    Young, and so fair!

Look at her garments
Clinging like cerements
Whilst the wave constantly
Drips from her clothing;
Take her up instantly,
Loving, not loathing.—

Touch her not scornfully;
Think of her mournfully,
Gently and humanly;
Not of the stains of her,
All that remains of her
Now, is pure womanly.

Make no deep scrutiny
Into her mutiny
Rash and undutiful;
Past all dishonour,
Death has left on her
Only the beautiful.

Still, for all slips of hers,
One of Eve's family—
Wipe those poor lips of hers
Oozing so clammily.

Loop up her tresses
Escaped from the comb,
Her fair auburn tresses;
Whilst wonderment guesses
Where was her home?

Who was her father?
Who was her mother?
Had she a sister?
Had she a brother?
Or was there a dearer one
Still, and a nearer one
Yet, than all other?

Alas! for the rarity
Of Christian charity
Under the sun!
Oh! it was pitiful!
Near a whole city full,
Home she had none.

Sisterly, brotherly,
Fatherly, motherly,
Feelings had changed:
Love, by harsh evidence,
Thrown from its eminence;
Even God's providence
Seeming estranged.

Where the lamps quiver
So far in the river,
With many a light
From window and casement,

From garret to basement,
She stood, with amazement,
Houseless by night.

The bleak wind of March
Made her tremble and shiver;
But not the dark arch,
Or the black flowing river:
Mad from life's history,
Glad to death's mystery,
Swift to be hurled—
Anywhere, anywhere
Out of the world!

In she plunged boldly,
No matter how coldly
The rough river ran,—
Over the brink of it,
Picture it,—think of it,
Dissolute Man!
Lave in it, drink of it
Then, if you can!

Take her up tenderly,
Lift her with care;
Fashioned so slenderly,
Young, and so fair!
Ere her limbs frigidly
Stiffen too rigidly,
Decently,—kindly,—
Smooth, and compose them;
And her eyes, close them,
Staring so blindly!

Dreadfully staring
Through muddy impurity,
As when with the daring
Last look of despairing
Fixed on futurity.

Perishing gloomily,
Spurred by contumely,
Cold inhumanity,
Burning insanity,
Into her rest,—
Cross her hands humbly,
As if praying dumbly,
Over her breast!
Owning her weakness,
Her evil behaviour,
And leaving, with meekness,
Her sins to her Saviour!

The vigour of this poem is no less remarkable than its pathos. The versification, although carrying the fanciful to the very verge of the fantastic, is nevertheless admirably adapted to the wild insanity which is the thesis of the poem.

Among the minor poems of Lord Byron, is one[7] which has never received from the critics the praise which it undoubtedly deserves:

> Though the day of my destiny's over,
>   And the star of my fate hath declined,
> Thy soft heart refused to discover
>   The faults which so many could find;
> Though thy soul with my grief was acquainted,
>   It shrunk not to share it with me,
> And the love which my spirit hath painted
>   It never hath found but in *thee*.
>
> Then when nature around me is smiling,
>   The last smile which answers to mine,
> I do not believe it beguiling,
>   Because it reminds me of thine;
> And when winds are at war with the ocean,
>   As the breasts I believed in with me,
> If their billows excite an emotion,
>   It is that they bear me from *thee*.
>
> Though the rock of my last hope is shivered,
>   And its fragments are sunk in the wave,
> Though I feel that my soul is delivered
>   To pain—it shall not be its slave.
> There is many a pang to pursue me:
>   They may crush, but they shall not contemn—
> They may torture, but shall not subdue me—
>   'Tis of *thee* that I think—not of them.
>
> Though human, thou didst not deceive me,
>   Though woman, thou didst not forsake,
> Though loved, thou forborest to grieve me,
>   Though slandered, thou never couldst shake,—
> Though trusted, thou didst not disclaim me,
>   Though parted, it was not to fly,
> Though watchful, 'twas not to defame me,
>   Nor mute, that the world might belie.
>
> Yet I blame not the world, nor despise it,
>   Nor the war of the many with one—
> If my soul was not fitted to prize it,
>   'Twas folly not sooner to shun:
> And if dearly that error hath cost me,
>   And more than I once could foresee,
> I have found that whatever it lost me,
>   It could not deprive me of *thee*.

---

7. *Stanzas to Augusta* (1816), addressed to Augusta Leigh, Byron's half-sister.

> From the wreck of the past, which hath perished,
> Thus much I at least may recall,
> It hath taught me that which I most cherished
> Deserved to be dearest of all:
> In the desert a fountain is springing,
> In the wide waste there still is a tree,
> And a bird in the solitude singing,
> Which speaks to my spirit of *thee*.

Although the rhythm, here, is one of the most difficult, the versification could scarcely be improved. No nobler *theme* ever engaged the pen of poet. It is the soul-elevating idea, that no man can consider himself entitled to complain of Fate while, in his adversity, he still retains the unwavering love of woman.

From Alfred Tennyson—although in perfect sincerity I regard him as the noblest poet that ever lived—I have left myself time to cite only a very brief specimen. I call him, and *think* him the noblest of poets—*not* because the impressions he produces are, at *all* times, the most profound—*not* because the poetical excitement which he induces is, at *all* times, the most intense—but because it *is*, at all times, the most ethereal—in other words, the most elevating and the most pure. No poet is so little of the earth, earthy. What I am about to read is from his last long poem, "The Princess:"[8]

> Tears, idle tears, I know not what they mean,
> Tears from the depth of some divine despair
> Rise in the heart, and gather to the eyes,
> In looking on the happy Autumn-fields,
> And thinking of the days that are no more.
>
> Fresh as the first beam glittering on a sail,
> That brings our friends up from the underworld,
> Sad as the last which reddens over one
> That sinks with all we love below the verge;
> So sad, so fresh, the days that are no more.
>
> Ah, sad and strange as in dark summer dawns
> The earliest pipe of half-awakened birds
> To dying ears, when unto dying eyes
> The casement slowly grows a glimmering square;
> So sad, so strange, the days that are no more.
>
> Dear as remembered kisses after death,
> And sweet as those by hopeless fancy feigned
> On lips that are for others; deep as love,
> Deep as first love, and wild with all regret;
> O Death in Life, the days that are no more.

Thus, although in a very cursory and imperfect manner, I have endeavoured to convey to you my conception of the Poetic Principle. It has been my purpose to suggest that, while this Principle itself is, strictly and simply, the Human Aspiration for Supernal Beauty, the manifestation of the Principle is always found in *an elevating excitement of the Soul*—quite independent of

---

8. *Tears, Idle Tears*, from *The Princess* (1847) by Alfred, Lord Tennyson (1809–1892).

that passion which is the intoxication of the Heart—or of that Truth which is the satisfaction of the Reason. For, in regard to Passion, alas! its tendency is to degrade, rather than to elevate the Soul. Love, on the contrary—Love—the true, the divine Eros—the Uranian, as distinguished from the Dionæan Venus—is unquestionably the purest and truest of all poetical themes.[9] And in regard to Truth—if, to be sure, through the attainment of a truth, we are led to perceive a harmony where none was apparent before, we experience, at once, the true poetical effect—but this effect is referable to the harmony alone, and not in the least degree to the truth which merely served to render the harmony manifest.

We shall reach, however, more immediately a distinct conception of what the true Poetry is, by mere reference to a few of the simple elements which induce in the Poet himself the true poetical effect. He recognises the ambrosia which nourishes his soul, in the bright orbs that shine in Heaven—in the volutes[1] of the flower—in the clustering of low shrubberies—in the waving of the grain-fields—in the slanting of tall, Eastern trees—in the blue distance of mountains—in the grouping of clouds—in the twinkling of half-hidden brooks—in the gleaming of silver rivers—in the repose of sequestered lakes—in the star-mirroring depths of lonely wells. He perceives it in the songs of birds—in the harp of Æolus[2]—in the sighing of the night-wind—in the repining voice of the forest—in the surf that complains to the shore—in the fresh breath of the woods—in the scent of the violet—in the voluptuous perfume of the hyacinth—in the suggestive odour that comes to him, at eventide, from far-distant, undiscovered islands, over dim oceans, illimitable and unexplored. He owns it in all noble thoughts—in all unworldly motives—in all holy impulses—in all chivalrous, generous, and self-sacrificing deeds. He feels it in the beauty of woman—in the grace of her step—in the lustre of her eye—in the melody of her voice—in her soft laughter—in her sigh—in the harmony of the rustling of her robes. He deeply feels it in her winning endearments—in her burning enthusiasms—in her gentle charities—in her meek and devotional endurances—but above all—ah, far above all—he kneels to it—he worships it in the faith, in the purity, in the strength, in the altogether divine majesty—of her *love*.

Let me conclude—by the recitation of yet another brief poem—one very different in character from any that I have before quoted. It is by Motherwell, and is called "The Song of the Cavalier."[3] With our modern and altogether rational ideas of the absurdity and impiety of warfare, we are not precisely in that frame of mind best adapted to sympathize with the sentiments, and thus to appreciate the real excellence of the poem. To do this fully, we must identify ourselves, in fancy, with the soul of the old cavalier.

> Then mounte! then mounte, brave gallants, all,
>   And don your helmes amaine:
> Deathe's couriers, Fame and Honour, call
>   Us to the field againe.

---

9. Heavenly love as opposed to earthly, Dionaea being an earth goddess, mother of Venus, the goddess of sexual love, and Urania being the Greek muse of astronomy, and therefore "heavenly."
1. Spiral-shaped blossoms.

2. Keeper of the winds; the then-popular Aeolian harp responded to wind blowing across its strings.
3. William Motherwell (1797–1835), Scottish poet; the poem was collected in 1832.

No shrewish teares shall fill our eye
    When the sword-hilt is in our hand,—
Heart-whole we'll part, and no whit sighe
    For the fayrest of the land:
Let piping swaine, and craven wight,
    Thus weepe and puling crye,
Our business is like men to fight,
    And hero-like to die!

1850

LETTERS[1]

To John Allan[2]

[My Determination Is at Length Taken]

Richmond   Monday [March 19, 1827]

Sir,
    After my treatment on yesterday and what passed between us this morning,
I can hardly think you will be surprised at the contents of this letter. My
determination is at length taken—to leave your house and indeavor to find
some place in this wide world, where I will be treated—not as *you* have treated
me—This is not a hurried determination, but one on which I have long considered—and having so considered my resolution is unalterable—You may
perhaps think that I have flown off in a passion, & that I am already wishing
to return; But not so—I will give you the reason[s] which have actuated me,
and then judge—
    Since I have been able to think on any subject, my thoughts have aspired,
and they have been taught by *you* to aspire, to eminence in public life—this
cannot be attained without a good Education, such a one I cannot obtain at a
Primary school—A collegiate Education therefore was what I most ardently
desired, and I had been led to expect that it would at some future time be
granted—but in a moment of caprice—you have blasted my hope because
forsooth I disagreed with you in an opinion, which opinion I was forced to
express—Again, I have heard you say (when you little thought I was listening
and therefore must have said it in earnest) that you had no affection for me—
    You have moreover ordered me to quit your house, and are continually
upbraiding me with eating the bread of Idleness, when you yourself were the
only person to remedy the evil by placing me to some business—You take
delight in exposing me before those whom you think likely to advance my
interest in this world—
    You suffer me to be subjected to the whims & caprice, not only of your

---

1. The texts printed here are from *The Letters of Edgar
Allan Poe*, edited by J. W. Ostrom (1948; reprinted
with supplement, 1966). In the introduction to Ostrom's edition, James Southall Wilson says Poe's "letters, like his personal life, are subject to the vicissitudes
of his fortunes. They give no impression of the continuity of a peaceful and secure personal living, rather
they suggest spasmodic unrest. Many of them are the
necessary drudge-work of a hired pen, and others are
written under circumstances painful or humiliating. * * * We see more poignantly than in any story
of his life yet written the petty traffic of the literary market, the uncertainties and disappointments of his struggle, and the combination of instability and perseverance within his own personality."
2. Poe's stepfather.

white family, but the complete authority of the blacks—these grievances I could not submit to; and I am gone[.] I request that you will send me my trunk containing my clothes & books—and if you still have the least affection for me, As the last cal[l] I shall make on your bou[nty], To prevent the fulfillment of the Prediction you this morning expressed, send me as much money as will defray the expences of my passage to some of the Northern cit[i]es & then support me for one month, by whic[h] time I [sh]all be enabled to place myself [in] some situation where I may not only o[bt]ain a livelihood, but lay by a sum which one day or another will support me at the University—Send my trunk &c to the Court-house Tavern, send me I entreat you some money immediately—as I am in the greatest necessity—If you fail to comply with my request—I tremble for the consequence

Yours &c
Edgar A Poe

It depends upon yourself if hereafter you see or hear from m[e.]

To John Allan

[In the Greatest Necessity]

Richmond   Tuesday [March 20, 1827]

Dear Sir,

Be so good as to send me my trunk with my clothes—I wrote to you on yesterday explaining my reasons for leaving—I suppose by my not receiving either my trunk, or an answer to my letter, that you did not receive it—I am in the greatest necessity, not having tasted food since Yesterday morning. I have no where to sleep at night, but roam about the Streets—I am nearly exhausted—I beseech you as you wish not your prediction concerning me to be fulfilled—to send me without delay my trunk containing my clothes, and to lend if you will not give me as much money as will defray the expence of my passage to Boston (.$12,) and a little to support me there until I shall be enabled to engage in some business—I sail on Saturday—A letter will be received by me at the Court House Tavern, where be so good as to send my trunk—

Give my love to all at home
I am Your's &c.
Edgar A Poe

I have not one cent in the world to provide any food

To John P. Kennedy[3]

[I Cannot Come]

[Baltimore] Sunday, 15th [March]

Dr Sir,

Your kind invitation to dinner to day has wounded me to the quick. I cannot come—and for reasons of the most humiliating nature my personal appear-

---

3. In 1833 Kennedy, well known as the author of the novel *Swallow Barn* (1832), had been one of the three judges who awarded Poe first prize in the fiction contest held by the Baltimore *Saturday Visiter*. Earlier on the day of this letter, Poe had sent Kennedy a note asking his help in gaining an appointment as "a teacher in a Public School"—a post Poe never held at any time.

ance. You may conceive my deep mortification in making this disclosure to you—but it was necessary. If you will be my friend so far as to loan me $20 I will call on you tomorrow—otherwise it will be impossible, and I must submit to my fate.

Sincerely, Yours

E A Poe

To Thomas W. White[4]

[Berenice *Justified*]

[Baltimore, April 30, 1835]

*   *   *

A word or two in relation to Berenice. Your opinion of it is very just. The subject is by far too horrible, and I confess that I hesitated in sending it you especially as a specimen of my capabilities. The Tale originated in a bet that I could produce nothing effective on a subject so singular, provided I treated it seriously. But what I wish to say relates to the character of your Magazine more than to any articles I may offer, and I beg you to believe that I have no intention of giving you *advice*, being fully confident that, upon consideration, you will agree with me. The history of all Magazines shows plainly that those which have attained celebrity were indebted for it to articles *similar in nature—to Berenice*—although, I grant you, far superior in style and execution. I say similar in *nature*. You ask me in what does this nature consist? In the ludicrous heightened into the grotesque: the fearful coloured into the horrible: the witty exaggerated into the burlesque: the singular wrought out into the strange and mystical. You may say all this is bad taste. I have my doubts about it. Nobody is more aware than I am that simplicity is the cant of the day—but take my word for it no one cares any thing about simplicity in their hearts. Believe me also, in spite of what people say to the contrary, that there is nothing easier in the world than to be extremely simple. But whether the articles of which I speak are, or are not in bad taste is little to the purpose. To be appreciated you must be *read*, and these things are invariably sought after with avidity. They are, if you will take notice, the articles which find their way into other periodicals, and into the papers, and in this manner, taking hold upon the public mind they augment the reputation of the source where they originated. Such articles are the "M.S. found in a Madhouse" and the "Monos and Daimonos" of the London New Monthly—the "Confessions of an Opium-Eater" and the "Man in the Bell" of Blackwood. The two first were written by no less a man than Bulwer—the *Confessions* [*illegible*] universally attributed to Coleridge—although unjustly.[5] Thus the first men in [England] have not thought writings of this nature unworthy of their talents, and I have go[od]

---

4. The owner of the Richmond *Southern Literary Messenger*, who had recently published Poe's *Berenice*; Poe had not yet gone to work for White when he wrote this justification of that story, in which the hero extracts the thirty-two teeth of his cousin while she is in a catatonic sleep, presumed dead.

5. Poe is conveying an impression, not striving for perfect accuracy. Edward Bulwer-Lytton's *Monos and Daimonos* appeared in the *New Monthly*, but *M.S. Found in a Madhouse* did not. Thomas De Quincey's *Confessions* appeared in the *London Magazine*, not *Blackwood's*, which did publish *The Man in the Bell*.

reason to believe that some very high names valued themselves *principally* upon this species of literature. To be sure originality is an essential in these things—great attention must be paid to style, and much labour spent in their composition, or they will degenerate into the tugid or the absurd. If I am not mistaken you will find Mr Kennedy, whose writings you admire, and whose Swallow-Barn is unrivalled for purity of style and thought of my opinion in this matter. It is unnecessary for you to pay much attention to the many who will no doubt favour you with their critiques. In respect to Berenice individually I allow that it approaches the very verge of bad taste—but I will not sin quite so egregiously again. I propose to furnish you every month with a Tale of the nature which I have alluded to. The effect—if any—will be estimated better by the circulation of the Magazine than by any comments upon its contents. This much, however, it is necessary to premise, that no two of these Tales will have the slightest resemblance one to the other either in matter or manner—still however preserving the character which I speak of.

✻   ✻   ✻

Yours sincerely
Edgar A Poe

To Maria Clemm[6]

["*My Own Sweetest Sissy*"]

[Richmond] Aug: 29th [1835]

My dearest Aunty,

I am blinded with tears while writing thi[s] letter—I have no wish to live another hour. Amid sorrow, [MS. *torn*] and the deepest anxiety your letter reached—and you well know how little I am able to bear up under the pressure of grief. My bitterest enemy would pity me could he now read my heart—My last my last my only hold on life is cruelly torn away—I have no desire to live and *will not*. But let my duty be done. I love, *you know* I love Virginia passionately devotedly. I cannot express in words the fervent devotion I feel towards my dear little cousin—my own darling. But what can [I] say; Oh think for me for I am incapable of thinking. Al[l my] thoughts are occupied with the supposition that both you & she will prefer to go with N. Poe;[7] I do sincerely believe that your *comforts* will for the present be secured—I cannot speak as regards your peace—your happiness. You have both tender hearts—and you will always have the reflection that my agony is more than I can bear—that you have driven me to the grave—for love like mine can never be gotten over. It is useless to disguise the truth that when Virginia goes with N. P. that I shall never behold her again—that is absolutely sure. Pity me, my dear Aunty, pity me. I have no one now to fly to—I am among strangers, and my wretchedness is more than I can bear. It is useless to expect advice from me—what can I say?—Can I, in honour & in truth say—Virginia! do not go!—do not go where

<hr>

6. At the time of this letter Virginia Clemm, Maria Clemm's daughter and Poe's first cousin, was thirteen.
7. Neilson Poe, a cousin of both Virginia Clemm and Edgar Allan Poe, was the new bridegroom of Virginia's half sister. Neilson Poe had offered to have Virginia continue her education in his household. A month later the clan's interrelationships were compounded by Edgar Allan Poe's first, secret, marriage to Virginia.

you can be comfortable & perhaps happy—and on the other hand can I calmly resign my—life itself. If she had truly loved me would she not have rejected the offer with scorn? Oh God have mercy on me! If she goes with N. P. what are you to do, my own Aunty,?

I had procured a sweet little house in a retired situation on [ch]urch hill—newly done up and with a large garden and [eve]ry convenience—at only $5 per month. I have been dreaming [*MS. torn*] every day & night since of the rapture I should feel in [havi]ng my only friends—all I love on Earth with me there, [and] the pride I would take in making you both comfor[table] & in calling her my wife—But the dream is over[.] [Oh G]od have mercy on me. What have I *to live for?* Among strangers with *not one soul to love me.* * * *

The tone of your letter wounds me to the soul—Oh Aunty, Aunty you loved me once—how can you be so cruel now? You speak of Virginia acquiring accomplishments, and entering into society—you speak in so *worldly* a tone. Are you sure she would be more happy. Do you think any one could love her more dearly than I? She will have far—very far better opportunities of entering into society here than with N. P. Every one here receives me with open arms.

Adieu my dear Aunty. I *cannot advise you.* Ask Virginia. Leave it to her. Let me have, under her own hand, a letter, bidding me *good bye*—forever—and I [m]ay die—my heart will break—but I will say no more.

E A P.

Kiss her for me—a million times[.]

For Virginia,
My love, my own sweetest Sissy, my darling little wifey, thi[nk w]ell before you break the heart of your cousin. Eddy. * * *

To Philip P. Cooke[8]

[*Such Wild Matters as* Ligeia]

Philadelphia, September 21, 1839

My Dear Sir:
I received your letter this morning—and read it with more pleasure than I can well express. You wrong me, indeed, in supposing that I meant one word of mere flattery in what I said. I have an inveterate habit of speaking the truth—and had I not valued your opinion more highly than that of any man in America I should not have written you as I did.

I say that I read your letter with delight. In fact I am aware of no delight greater than that of feeling one's self appreciated (in such wild matters as "Ligeia") by those in whose judgment one has faith. You read my inmost spirit "like a book," and with the single exception of D'Israeli, I have had communication with no other person who does. Willis had a glimpse of it—Judge Tucker[9] saw about one half way through—but your ideas are the very

8. Cooke was a young Virginian poet.
9. Poe may or may not have invented complimentary letters from Benjamin Disraeli, the English novelist and politician, and Nathaniel Parker Willis, the American poet, essayist, and newspaper editor; certainly he

exaggerated the extent of Irving's praise. Nathaniel Beverley Tucker, professor of law at William and Mary, was the pseudonymous author of the political novel *The Partisan Leader* (1836); in 1835 he had flatteringly initiated a correspondence with Poe.

echo of my own. I am very far from meaning to flatter—I am flattered and honored. Beside me is now lying a letter from Washington Irving in which he speaks with enthusiasm of a late tale of mine, "The Fall of the House of Usher,"—and in which he promises to make his opinion public, upon the first opportunity,—but from the bottom of my heart I assure you, I regard his best word as but dust in the balance when weighed with those discriminating opinions of your own, which teach me that you feel and perceive.

Touching "Ligeia" you are right—all right—throughout. The *gradual* perception of the fact that Ligeia lives again in the person of Rowena is a far loftier and more thrilling idea than the one I have embodied. It offers in my opinion, the widest possible scope to the imagination—it might be rendered even sublime. And this idea was mine—had I never written before I should have adopted it—but then there is "Morella." Do you remember there the *gradual* conviction on the part of the parent that the spirit of the first Morella tenants the person of the second? It was necessary, since "Morella" was written, to modify "Ligeia." I was forced to be content with a sudden half-consciousness, on the part of the narrator, that Ligeia stood before him. One point I have not fully carried out—I should have intimated that the *will* did not perfect its intention—there should have been a relapse—a final one—and Ligeia (who had only succeeded in so much as to convey an idea of the truth to the narrator) should be at length entombed as Rowena—the bodily alterations having gradually faded away.

But since "Morella" is upon record I will suffer "Ligeia" to remain as it is. Your word that it is "intelligible" suffices—and your commentary sustains your word. As for the mob—let them talk on. I should be grieved if I thought they comprehended me here. * * *

Sincerely yours,
Edgar A. Poe

To Joseph Evans Snodgrass[1]

[My Sole Drink Is Water]

Philadelphia, April 1, 1841

* * *

So far for the matter inasmuch as it concerns Burton. I have now to thank you for your defence of myself, as stated. You are a physician, and I presume no physician can have difficulty in detecting the *drunkard* at a glance. You are, moreover, a literary man, well read in morals. You will never be brought to believe that I could write what I daily write, *as* I write it, were I as this villain would induce those who know me not, to believe. In fine, I pledge you, before God, the solemn word of a gentleman, that I am temperate even to rigor. From the hour in which I first saw this basest of calumniators to the hour in which I retired from his office in uncontrollable disgust at his chica-

---

1. Snodgrass was an editor of the Baltimore magazine *American Museum*. William E. Burton had employed Poe on his *Burton's Gentleman's Magazine* (later *Gra-* *ham's Magazine*) and after their quarrel in 1840 had apparently told various people that Poe's drunkenness had caused the break.

nery, arrogance, ignorance and brutality, *nothing stronger than water ever passed my lips.*

It is, however, due to candor that I inform you upon what foundation he has erected his slanders. At no period of my life was I ever what men call intemperate. I never was in the *habit* of intoxication. I never drunk drams, &c. But, for a brief period, while I resided in Richmond, and edited the *Messenger*, I certainly did give way, at long intervals, to the temptation held out on all sides by the spirit of Southern conviviality. My sensitive temperament could not stand an excitement which was an everyday matter to my companions. In short, it sometimes happened that I was completely intoxicated. For some days after each excess I was invariably confined to bed. But it is now quite four years since I have abandoned every kind of alcoholic drink—four years, with the exception of a single deviation, which occurred shortly *after* my leaving Burton, and when I was induced to resort to the occasional use of *cider*, with the hope of relieving a nervous attack.

You will thus see, frankly stated, the whole amount of my sin. You will also see the blackness of that heart which could *revive* a slander of this nature. Neither can you fail to perceive how desperate the malignity of the slanderer must be—how resolute he must be to slander, and how slight the grounds upon which he would build up a defamation—since he can find nothing better with which to charge me than an accusation which can be disproved by each and every man with whom I am in the habit of daily intercourse.

I have now only to repeat to you, in general, my solemn assurance that my habits are as far removed from intemperance as the day from the night. My sole drink is water. * * *

Yours most cordially,
Edgar A. Poe

To Maria Clemm[2]

[No Fear of Starving Here]

New-York, Sunday Morning
April 7. [1844] just after breakfast.

My dear Muddy,

We have just this minute done breakfast, and I now sit down to write you about everything. I can't pay for the letter, because the P.O. won't be open to-day.—In the first place, we arrived safe at Walnut S^t wharf. The driver wanted to make me pay a dollar, but I wouldn't. Then I had to pay a boy a levy to put the trunks in the baggage car. In the meantime I took Sis in the Depôt Hotel. It was only a quarter past 6, and we had to wait till 7. We saw the Ledger & Times—nothing in either—a few words of no account in the Chronicle.—We started in good spirits, but did not get here until nearly 3 o'clock. We went in the cars to Amboy about 40 miles from N. York, and then took the steamboat the rest of the way.—Sissy coughed none at all. When we got to the wharf it was raining hard. I left her on board the boat, after putting the trunks in the

<hr>

2. This letter records a sudden move from Philadelphia to New York. Sis is Poe's wife, Virginia; Kate or Catterina is the family cat. More clearly than Poe's many desperate missives, this cheerful letter illuminates his chronic state of malnutrition during much of his adult life: "No fear of starving here."

Ladies' Cabin, and set off to buy an umbrella and look for a boarding-house. I met a man selling umbrellas and bought [o]ne for 62 cents. Then I went up Greenwich S^t and soon found a boarding-house. It is just before you get to Cedar S^t on the west side going up—the left hand side. It has brown stone steps, with a porch with brown pillars. "Morrison" is the name on the door. I made a bargain in a few minutes and then got a hack and went for Sis. I was not gone more than ½ an hour, and she was quite astonished to see me back so soon. She didn't expect me for an hour. There were 2 other ladies waiting on board—so she was'nt very lonely.—When we got to the house we had to wait about ½ an hour before the room [was ready]. The house is old & looks buggy, b[*excision* t]he landlady is a nice chatty ol[*excision* g]ave us the back room on th[*excision* e]night & day & attendance, f[or 7 $—the cheapest board I] ever knew, taking into consideration the central situation and the *living*. I wish Kate could see it—she would faint. Last night, for supper, we had the nicest tea you ever drank, strong & hot—wheat bread & rye bread—cheese—tea-cakes (elegant) a great dish (2 dishes) of elegant ham, and 2 of cold veal, piled up like a mountain and large slices—3 dishes of the cakes, and every thing in the greatest profusion. No fear of starving here. The landlady seemed as if she could'nt press us enough, and we were at home directly. Her husband is living with her—a fat good-natured old soul. There are 8 or 10 boarders—2 or 3 of them ladies—2 servants.—For breakfast we had excellent-flavored cof-fee, hot & strong—not very clear & no great deal of cream—veal cutlets, elegant ham & eggs & nice bread and butter. I never sat down to a more plentiful or a nicer breakfast. I wish you could have seen the eggs—and the great dishes of meat. I ate the first hearty breakfast I have eaten since I left our little home. Sis is delighted, and we are both in excellent spirits. She has coughed hardly any and had no night sweat. She is now busy mending my pants which I tore against a nail. I went out last night and bought a skein of silk, a skein of thread, & 2 buttons a pair of slippers & a tin pan for the stove. The fire kept in all night.—We have now got 4 $ and a half left. Tomorrow I am going to try & borrow 3 $—so that I may have a fortnight to go upon. I feel in excellent spirits & have'nt drank a drop—so that I hope so[on] to get out of trouble. The very instant I scrape together enough money I will send it on. You ca'nt imagine how much we both do miss you. Sissy had a hearty cry last night, because you and Catterina weren't here. We are resolved to get 2 rooms the first moment we can. In the meantime it is impossible we could be more comfortable or more at home than we are.—It looks as if it was going to clear up now.—Be sure and go to the P.O. & have my letters forwarded. As soon as I write Lowell's article,[3] I will send it to you, & get you to get the money from Graham. Give our best loves to Catter[ina.]

[*three line excision for autograph*]

Be sure & take home the Messenger, [to Hirst].[4] We hope to send for you *very* soon.

---

3. An article on James Russell Lowell's poems, printed in *Graham's* for March 1844 (although as Poe's letter shows, the issue came out late).

4. Henry B. Hirst, a Philadelphia poet and friend of Poe's.

ABRAHAM LINCOLN
1809–1865

Abraham Lincoln's life and presidency can be seen as affirmative answers to the central question raised by the intellectual and political ferment of the late eighteenth century: Can individuals and nations rule themselves? Lincoln's career as self-made man is a paradigm of the possibilities of individual self-regulation and development within a context of freedom; his unshakable commitment to the preservation of the Union made possible the survival of a self-governing nation devoted to the principles of equality. Only by making himself independent and responsible could Lincoln be the Great Emancipator of others; only by surviving the test of civil war could the United States be the model and hope for democratic nations.

Lincoln was born on February 12, 1809, in a backwoods cabin in Hardin County, Kentucky, to nearly illiterate parents. He attended school only sporadically—probably for no more than a year all told—and was essentially self-taught. Although his access to books was limited, he absorbed and retained what he read of the King James Bible, *Aesop's Fables*, John Bunyan's *Pilgrim's Progress*, Daniel Defoe's *Robinson Crusoe*, and Mason Locke Weem's *A History of the Life and Death, Virtues, and Exploits of General George Washington*. Lincoln never lost his love of reading—adding Shakespeare, John Stuart Mill, Lord Byron, and Robert Burns to his list of favorite authors—and was always, in sensibility and by achievement, a great master of words.

Lincoln spent his impoverished youth in Kentucky and southern Indiana, where his father farmed for a living. His mother died when he was nine, but his stepmother, who soon joined the family with children of her own, seems to have singled out Abraham for special affection; he later spoke of her as his "angel mother." In 1830 the family moved to Illinois; after helping the family settle by splitting rails to fence in a new farm, young Lincoln set out on his own, making a trip to New Orleans as a flatboatman. He soon returned to settle in the tiny village of New Salem, Illinois, where he worked as storekeeper, postmaster, and surveyor. In 1832 he volunteered for service in the Black Hawk War; he was elected captain of his company but, as he later observed, saw more action against mosquitoes than he did against the Sac and Fox Indians.

Lincoln had considered blacksmithing as a trade, but decided instead in the early 1830s to prepare himself for a career in law. This he did by studying independently the basic law books of the time: Blackstone's *Commentaries*, Chitty's *Pleadings*, Greenleaf's *Evidence*, and Story's *Equity* and *Equity Pleadings*. In 1834 he was elected to the first of four terms in the state legislature, at that time a position of small influence and smaller salary. He passed the state bar examination in 1836 and moved the next year to the new state capital in Springfield. Here he entered a succession of law partnerships, the most enduring with William H. Herndon, later his biographer. By dint of hard work—which included twice-yearly sessions following the court on horseback or buggy as it moved from town to town to reach the people across the Illinois countryside—Lincoln prospered as a lawyer and earned a reputation as a shrewd, sensible, fair, and honest practitioner.

Much has been made of Lincoln's romance with Ann Rutledge, whom he had known in New Salem, but she died at nineteen years of age; so far as the records show, Lincoln's only love was Mary Todd. She came from a well-to-do Kentucky family, and the social aristocracy of Springfield to which she belonged advised her against marrying Lincoln despite his success as a lawyer and his obvious good qualities. He, too, apparently had misgivings about the prospects for the marriage, but they were married in the fall of 1842. The relationship between Mary Todd and Abraham Lincoln has been subject to endless speculation. She was witty and intense, and no doubt her temper and extravagance were often a trial to her husband, especially later in their marriage; but he was often absent from home, absorbed in his flourishing law practice, and was himself moody and sharp-tongued. On balance, the Lincolns seemed to have shared as much affection and pleasure in their union as one might reasonably expect. They certainly seem to have joined in affectionate concern for their four boys, only one of whom survived to adulthood.

The network of political and other historical events of the 1840s and 1850s that would result in Lincoln's election to the presidency in 1860 is complicated, but the central issue involved in these events is not. Very simply, the question was whether or not slavery would be permitted in the new territories, which eventually would become states. When he was elected to Congress in 1846, Lincoln voted against abolitionist measures but he insisted that the new territories must be kept free as "places for poor people to go and better their condition." He also joined in a vote of censure against President Polk for engaging in the war against Mexico (1848), a war he believed to be both unnecessary and unconstitutional. He did not run for reelection and it seemed that his political career had come to an end.

By 1854 the two major political parties of the time—the Whigs (to which Lincoln belonged) and the Democrats—had reached compromise on the extension of slavery into new territories and states. Strong antislavery elements in both parties established independent organizations, and when, in 1854, the Republican party was organized, Lincoln soon joined it. His new party lost the presidential election of 1856 to the Democrats, but in 1858 Lincoln reentered political life as the Republican candidate in the senatorial election. He opposed the Democrat Stephen A. Douglas, who had earlier sponsored the Kansas-Nebraska Bill, a bill that would have left it to new territories to establish their status as slave or free when they achieved statehood. Lincoln may have won the famous series of debates with Douglas, but he lost the election. More important for the future, though, he had gained national recognition and he found a theme commensurate with his rapidly intensifying powers of thought and expression. As the "House Divided" speech suggests, Lincoln now added to the often biting satirical humor, and to the logic and natural grace of his earlier utterances, a resonance and wisdom that mark his emergence as a national political leader and as a master of language.

This reputation was enhanced by the "Cooper Union Address" in 1860, and at the Republican convention he won nomination on the third ballot. Lincoln was elected sixteenth president of the United States in November 1860, but before he took office on March 4, 1861, seven states had seceded from the Union to form the Confederacy. Little more than a month after his inauguration, the Civil War had begun. He devoted himself to the ; eservation of the Union, without which, he believed, neither individuals nor the nation could live freely and decently. To preserve the Union he had to develop an overall war strategy, devise a workable command system, and find the right personnel to execute his plans. All of this he was to accomplish by trial and error in the early years of the war. At the same time he had to develop popular support for his purposes by using his extraordinary political skills in times of high passion and internal division. And when the war ended, leaving him and the country exhausted, he had immediately to face the monumental problems of healing a traumatized nation.

Only by degrees had Lincoln come to commit himself to the elimination of slavery throughout the country. Initially he wished only to stop the spread of slavery; then he saw that "a house divided against itself cannot stand," and finally, he took the leading role in the passage of the Thirteenth Amendment, which outlawed slavery everywhere and forever in the United States. Elected to a second term in 1864, he had served scarcely a month of his new term when he was assassinated, while attending a play, by the demented Shakespearean actor John Wilkes Booth. He died on April 15, 1865.

The texts of Lincoln's addresses are taken from Roy P. Basler's *Abraham Lincoln: His Speeches and Writings*, pp. 372–80, 734, and 792–93. Lincoln's spellings have been retained throughout. "A House Divided," delivered on June 16, 1858, was first printed in the *Illinois Journal* for June 18, 1858; the "Gettysburg Address" of November 19, 1863, is taken from the facsimiles reproduced in W. F. Barton's *Lincoln at Gettysburg* (1930); the "Second Inaugural" was delivered on March 4, 1865, and is based on photostats of the original manuscript owned by the Abraham Lincoln Association.

[The Presidential Question:]
Speech in the United States House of Representatives
July 27, 1848[1]

*   *   *

The other day, one of the gentlemen from Georgia, an eloquent man, and a man of learning, so far as I can judge, not being learned myself, came down upon us astonishingly. He spoke in what the Baltimore American calls the "scathing and withering style." At the end of his second severe flash I was struck blind, and found myself feeling with my fingers for an assurance of my continued physical existence. A little of the bone was left, and I gradually revived. He eulogized Mr. Clay[2] in high and beautiful terms, and then declared that we had deserted all our principles, and had turned Henry Clay out, like an old horse, to root. This is terribly severe. It cannot be answered by argument; at least, I cannot so answer it. I merely wish to ask the gentleman if the Whigs are the only party he can think of, who sometimes turn old horses out to root. Is not a certain Martin Van Buren[3] an old horse, which your own party have turned out to root? and is he not rooting a little to your discomfort about now? But in not nominating Mr. Clay, we deserted our principles, you say. Ah! in what? Tell us, ye men of principles, what principle we violated? We say you did violate principle in discarding Van Buren, and we can tell you how. You violated the primary, the cardinal, the one great living principle of all Democratic representative government—the principle that the representative is bound to carry out the known will of his constituents. A large majority of the Baltimore Convention of 1844 were, by their constituents, instructed to procure Van Buren's nomination if they could. In violation, in utter, glaring contempt of this, you rejected him—rejected him, as the gentleman from New York, the other day expressly admitted, for *availability*—that same "general availability" which you charge upon us, and daily chew over here, as something exceedingly odious and unprincipled. But the gentleman from Georgia gave us a second speech yesterday, all well considered and put down in writing, in which Van Buren was scathed and withered a "few" for his present position and movements. I cannot remember the gentleman's precise language, but I do remember he put Van Buren down, down, till he got him where he was finally to "stink" and "rot."

1. The speech from which this excerpt comes argues that General Zachary Taylor, the Whig candidate, is more suitable than the Democrats' candidate, General Lewis Cass, to the majority of Whigs and Democrats alike.
2. American congressman, senator, secretary of state (1777–1852).
3. Eighth president of the United States (1782–1862).

Mr. Speaker, it is no business or inclination of mine to defend Martin Van Buren. In the war of extermination now waging between him and his old admirers, I say, devil take the hindmost—and the foremost. But there is no mistaking the origin of the breach; and if the curse of "stinking" and "rotting" is to fall on the first and greatest violators of principle in the matter, I disinterestedly suggest, that the gentleman from Georgia and his present co-workers are bound to take it upon themselves.

But the gentleman from Georgia further says, we have deserted all our principles, and taken shelter under General Taylor's military coat tail; and he seems to think this is exceedingly degrading. Well, as his faith is, so be it unto him. But can he remember no other military coat tail under which a certain other party have been sheltering for near a quarter of a century? Has he no acquaintance with the ample military coat tail of General Jackson?[4] Does he not know that his own party have run the last five Presidential races under that coat tail, and that they are now running the sixth under that same cover? Yes, sir, that coat tail was used, not only for General Jackson himself, but has been clung to with the grip of death by every Democratic candidate since. You have never ventured, and dare not now venture, from under it. Your campaign papers have constantly been "Old Hickories," with rude likenesses of the old General upon them; hickory poles and hickory brooms your never-ending emblems; Mr. Polk,[5] himself, was "Young Hickory," "Little Hickory," or something so; and even now your campaign paper here is proclaiming that Cass and Butler[6] are of the true "Hickory stripe." No, sir; you dare not give it up. Like a horde of hungry ticks, you have stuck to the tail of the Hermitage lion[7] to the end of his life, and you are still sticking to it, and drawing a loathsome sustenance from it after he is dead. A fellow once advertised that he had made a discovery, by which he could make a new man out of an old one, and have enough of the stuff left to make a little yellow dog. Just such a discovery has General Jackson's popularity been to you. You not only twice made President of him out of it, but you have had enough of the stuff left to make Presidents of several comparatively small men since; and it is your chief reliance now to make still another.

Mr. Speaker, old horses and military coat tails, or tails of any sort, are not figures of speech such as I would be the first to introduce into discussions here; but as the gentleman from Georgia has thought fit to introduce them, he and you are welcome to all you have made, or can make, by them. If you have any more old horses, trot them out; any more tails, just cock them, and come at us.

I repeat, I would not introduce this mode of discussion here; but I wish gentlemen on the other side to understand, that the use of degrading figures is a game at which they may not find themselves able to take all the winnings. [We give it up.] Aye, you give it up, and well you may, but from a very different reason from that which you would have us understand. The point— the power to hurt—of all figures, consists in the *truthfulness* of their application; and understanding this, you may well give it up. They are weapons which hit you, but miss us.

---

4. Andrew Jackson (1767–1845), seventh president of the United States.
5. James K. Polk (1795–1849), eleventh president of the United States.

6. Benjamin Franklin Butler (1795–1858), American lawyer and politician.
7. Andrew Jackson's home, near Nashville, Tennessee, was known as "the Hermitage."

But, in my hurry, I was very near closing on the subject of military tails, before I was done with it. There is one entire article of the sort I have not discussed yet; I mean the military tail you Democrats are now engaged in dovetailing on to the great Michigander. Yes, sir, all his biographers (and they are legion) have him in hand, tying him to a military tail, like so many mischievous boys tying a dog to a bladder of beans. True, the material they have is very limited; but they drive at it, might and main. He *in*vaded Canada without resistance, and he *out*vaded it without pursuit. As he did both under orders, I suppose there was, to him, neither credit nor discredit in them; but they are made to constitute a large part of the tail. He was not at Hull's surrender, but he was close by. He was volunteer aid to General Harrison on the day of the battle of the Thames; and, as you said in 1840, Harrison was picking whortleberries two miles off, while the battle was fought, I suppose it is a just conclusion, with you, to say Cass was aiding Harrison to pick whortleberries. This is about all, except the mooted question of the broken sword.[8] Some authors say he broke it; some say he threw it away; and some others, who ought to know, say nothing about it. Perhaps it would be a fair historical compromise to say, if he did not break it, he did not do anything else with it.

By the way, Mr. Speaker, did you know I am a military hero? Yes, sir, in the days of the Black Hawk war, I fought, bled, and came away. Speaking of General Cass's career, reminds me of my own. I was not at Stillman's defeat, but I was about as near it as Cass was to Hull's surrender; and, like him, I saw the place very soon afterwards. It is quite certain I did not break my sword, for I had none to break; but I bent a musket pretty badly on one occasion. If Cass broke his sword, the idea is, he broke it in desperation; I bent the musket by accident. If General Cass went in advance of me in picking whortleberries, I guess I surpassed him in charges upon the wild onions. If he saw any live fighting Indians, it was more than I did, but I had a good many bloody struggles with the mosquitoes; and although I never fainted from loss of blood, I can truly say I was often very hungry.

Mr. Speaker, if I should ever conclude to doff whatever our Democratic friends may suppose there is of black-cockade Federalism about me, and, thereupon, they shall take me up as their candidate for the Presidency, I protest they shall not make fun of me, as they have of General Cass, by attempting to write me into a military hero.

*　*　*

1848

A House Divided: Speech Delivered at Springfield, Illinois, at the Close of the Republican State Convention.
June 16, 1858

If we could first know *where* we are, and *whither* we are tending, we could better judge *what* to do, and *how* to do it.

We are now far into the *fifth* year, since a policy was initiated, with the *avowed* object, and *confident* promise, of putting an end to slavery agitation.

---

8. Cass is said to have angrily broken his sword when he learned of the surrender of Detroit in the War of 1812.

Under the operation of that policy, that agitation has not only, *not ceased*, but has *constantly augmented*.

In my opinion, it *will* not cease, until a *crisis* shall have been reached, and passed—

"A house divided against itself cannot stand."[1]

I believe this government cannot endure, permanently half *slave* and half *free*.

I do not expect the Union to be *dissolved*—I do not expect the house to *fall*—but I *do* expect it will cease to be divided.

It will become *all* one thing, or *all* the other.

Either the *opponents* of slavery, will arrest the further spread of it, and place it where the public mind shall rest in the belief that it is in course of ultimate extinction; or its *advocates* will push it forward, till it shall become alike lawful in *all* the States, *old* as well as *new*—North as well as *South*.

Have we no *tendency* to the latter condition?

Let any one who doubts, carefully contemplate that now almost complete legal combination—piece of *machinery* so to speak—compounded of the Nebraska doctrine, and the Dred Scott decision.[2] Let him consider not only *what work* the machinery is adapted to do, and *how well* adapted; but also, let him study the history of its construction, and trace, if he can, or rather *fail*, if he can, to trace the evidences of design, and concert of action, among its chief bosses, from the beginning.

The new year of 1854 found slavery excluded from more than half the States by State Constitutions, and from most of the national territory by congressional prohibition.

Four days later, commenced the struggle, which ended in repealing that congressional prohibition.

This opened all the national territory to slavery; and was the first point gained.

But, so far, *Congress* only, had acted; and an *indorsement* by the people, *real* or *apparent*, was indispensible, to *save* the point already gained, and give chance for more.

This necessity had not been overlooked; but had been provided for, as well as might be, in the notable argument of "squatter sovereignty," otherwise called "*sacred right of self government*," which latter phrase, though expressive of the only rightful basis of any government, was so perverted in this attempted use of it as to amount to just this: That if any *one* man, choose to enslave *another*, no *third* man shall be allowed to object.

That argument was incorporated into the Nebraska bill itself, in the language which follows: "*It being the true intent and meaning of this act not to legislate slavery into any Territory or State, nor to exclude it therefrom; but to leave the people thereof perfectly free to form and regulate their domestic institutions in their own way, subject only to the Constitution of the United States.*"

Then opened the roar of loose declamation in favor of "Squatter Sovereignty," and "Sacred right of self government."

"But," said opposition members, "let us be more *specific*—let us *amend* the

1. Mark 3.25: "If a house be divided against itself, that house cannot stand."
2. The Kansas-Nebraska Bill of 1854 gave newly established territories autonomy in deciding whether or not to permit slavery therein; the *Dred Scott* case established the right of slaveowners to transport their slaves to the territories and to free status under the due process clause of the Fifth Amendment.

bill so as to expressly declare that the people of the Territory *may* exclude slavery." "Not we," said the friends of the measure; and down they voted the amendment.

While the Nebraska bill was passing through congress, a *law case,* involving the question of a negro's freedom, by reason of his owner having voluntarily taken him first into a free State and then a territory covered by the congressional prohibition, and held him as a slave for a long time in each, was passing through the U. S. Circuit Court for the District of Missouri; and both Nebraska bill and law suit were brought to a decision in the same month of May, 1854. The negro's name was "Dred Scott," which name now designates the decision finally made in the case.

Before the *then* next Presidential election, the law case came *to,* and was argued *in* the Supreme Court of the United States; but the *decision* of it was deferred until *after* the election. Still, *before* the election, Senator Trumbull, on the floor of the Senate, requests the leading advocate[3] of the Nebraska bill to state *his opinion* whether the people of a territory can constitutionally exclude slavery from their limits; and the latter answers, "That is a question for the Supreme Court."

The election came. Mr. Buchanan[4] was elected, and the *indorsement,* such as it was, secured. That was the *second* point gained. This indorsement, however, fell short of a clear popular majority by nearly four hundred thousand votes, and so, perhaps, was not over-whelmingly reliable and satisfactory.

The *outgoing* President, in his last annual message, as impressively as possible *echoed back* upon the people the *weight* and *authority* of the indorsement.

The Supreme Court met again; *did not* announce their decision, but ordered a re-argument.

The Presidential inauguration came, and still no decision of the court; but the *incoming* President, in his inaugural address, fervently exhorted the people to abide by the forthcoming decision, *whatever it might be.*

Then, in a few days, came the decision.

The reputed author of the Nebraska bill finds an early occasion to make a speech at this capitol indorsing the Dred Scott Decision, and vehemently denouncing all opposition to it.

The new President, too, seizes the early occasion of the Silliman letter[5] to indorse and strongly *construe* that decision, and to express his *astonishment* that any different view had ever been entertained.

At length a squabble springs up between the President and the author of the Nebraska bill, on the *mere* question of *fact,* whether the Lecompton constitution[6] was or was not, in any just sense, made by the people of Kansas; and in that quarrel the latter declares that all he wants is a fair vote for the people, and that he *cares* not whether slavery be voted *down* or voted *up.* I do not understand his declaration that he cares not whether slavery be voted down or

---

3. Stephen A. Douglas (1813–1861), Lincoln's Democratic party opponent for the Senate. Lyman Trumbull (1813–1896), Illinois senator 1855–73.
4. James Buchanan (1791–1868), fifteenth president of the United States.
5. Written by Buchanan to Benjamin Silliman (1816–1885), the representative of forty prominent Connecticut educators and preachers who had protested Buchanan's policy of support for the newly elected, largely proslavery delegates to the Kansas State constitutional convention and the laws they passed. In essence, Buchanan vowed to support the new, proslavery government of Kansas against the competing group of antislavery settlers.
6. A proposed constitution for Kansas that would have admitted it to the Union as a slave state. It was rejected by both the House of Representatives and the voters of Kansas. Lecompton was the head of the members of the slavery faction.

voted up, to be intended by him other than as an *apt definition* of the *policy* he would impress upon the public mind—the *principle* for which he declares he has suffered much, and is ready to suffer to the end.

And well may he cling to that principle. If he has any parental feeling, well may he cling to it. That principle, is the only shred left of his original Nebraska doctrine. Under the Dred Scott decision, "squatter sovereignty" squatted out of existence, tumbled down like temporary scaffolding—like the mold at the foundry served through one blast and fell back into loose sand—helped to carry an election, and then was kicked to the winds. His late *joint* struggle with the Republicans, against the Lecompton Constitution, involves nothing of the original Nebraska doctrine. That struggle was made on a point, the right of a people to make their own constitution, upon which he and the Republicans have never differed.

The several points of the Dred Scott decision, in connection with Senator Douglas' "care not" policy, constitute the piece of machinery, in its *present* state of advancement.

The *working* points of that machinery are:

First, that no negro slave, imported as such from Africa, and no descendant of such slave can ever be a *citizen* of any State, in the sense of that term as used in the Constitution of the United States.

This point is made in order to deprive the negro, in every possible event, of the benefit of that provision of the United States Constitution, which declares that—

"the citizens of each State shall be entitled to all privileges and immunities of citizens in the several States."

Secondly, that "subject to the Constitution of the United States," neither *Congress* nor a *Territorial Legislature* can exclude slavery from any United States Territory.

The point is made in order that individual men may *fill up* the territories with slaves, without danger of losing them as property, and thus enhance the chances of *permanency* to the institution through all the future.

Thirdly, that whether the holding a negro in actual slavery in a free State, makes him free, as against the holder, the United States courts will not decide, but will leave to be decided by the courts of any slave State the negro may be forced into by the master.

This point is made, not to be pressed *immediately*; but, if acquiesced in for a while, and apparently *indorsed* by the people at an election, *then* to sustain the logical conclusion that what Dred Scott's master might lawfully do with Dred Scott, in the free State of Illinois, every other master may lawfully do with any other *one* or one *thousand* slaves, in Illinois, or in any other free State.

Auxiliary to all this, and working hand in hand with it, the Nebraska doctrine, or what is left of it, is to *educate* and *mould* public opinion, at least *Northern* public opinion, to not *care* whether slavery is voted *down* or voted *up.*

This shows exactly where we now *are*; and *partially* also, whither we are tending.

It will throw additional light on the latter, to go back, and run the mind over the string of historical facts already stated. Several things will *now* appear less *dark* and *mysterious* than they did *when* they were transpiring. The people

were to be left "perfectly free" "subject only to the Constitution." What the
Constitution had to do with it, outsiders could not *then* see. Plainly enough
now, it was an exactly fitted *nitch* for the Dred Scott decision to afterward
come in, and declare that *perfect freedom* of the people, to be just no freedom
at all.

Why was the amendment, expressly declaring the right of the people to
exclude slavery, voted down? Plainly enough *now*, the adoption of it, would
have spoiled the nitch for the Dred Scott decision.

Why was the court decision held up? Why, even a Senator's individual
opinion withheld, till *after* the Presidential election? Plainly enough *now*, the
speaking out *then* would have damaged the *"perfectly free"* argument upon
which the election was to be carried.

Why the *outgoing* President's felicitation on the indorsement? Why the
delay of a reargument? Why the incoming President's *advance* exhortation in
favor of the decision?

These things *look* like the cautious *patting* and *petting* of a spirited horse,
preparatory to mounting him, when it is dreaded that he may give the rider
a fall.

And why the hasty after indorsements of the decision by the President and
others?

We cannot absolutely *know* that all these exact adaptations are the result of
preconcert. But when we see a lot of framed timbers, different portions of
which we know have been gotten out at different times and places and by
different workmen—Stephen, Franklin, Roger, and James, for instance—and
we see these timbers joined together, and see they exactly make the frame of a
house or a mill, all the tenons and mortises exactly fitting, and all the lengths
and proportions of the different pieces exactly adapted to their respective
places, and not a piece too many or too few—not omitting even scaffolding—
or, if a single piece be lacking, we see the place in the frame exactly fitted and
prepared to yet bring such piece in—in *such* a case, we find it impossible not
to *believe* that Stephen and Franklin and Roger and James all understood one
another from the beginning, and all worked upon a common *plan* or *draft*
drawn up before the first lick was struck.

It should not be overlooked that, by the Nebraska bill, the people of a *State*
as well as *Territory*, were to be left *"perfectly free"* *"subject only to the Constitution."*

Why mention a *State*? They were legislating for *territories*, and not *for* or
about States. Certainly the people of a *State are* and *ought to be* subject to the
Constitution of the United States; but why is mention of this *lugged* into this
merely *territorial* law? Why are the people of a *territory* and the people of a
state therein *lumped* together, and their relation to the Constitution therein
treated as being *precisely* the same?

While the opinion of the Court, by Chief Justice Taney, in the Dred Scott
case, and the separate opinions of all the concurring Judges, expressly declare
that the Constitution of the United States neither permits Congress nor a territorial legislature to exclude slavery from any United States territory, they all
omit to declare whether or not the same Constitution permits a state, or the
people of a State, to exclude it.

Possibly, this is a mere *omission*; but who can be *quite* sure, if McLean or
Curtis had sought to get into the opinion a declaration of unlimited power in

the people of a state to exclude slavery from their limits, just as Chase and Mace[7] sought to get such declaration, in behalf of the people of a territory, into the Nebraska bill—I ask, who can be quite *sure* that it would not have been voted down, in the one case, as it had been in the other?

The nearest approach to the point of declaring the power of a State over slavery, is made by Judge Nelson.[8] He approaches it more than once, using the precise idea, and *almost* the language too, of the Nebraska act. On one occasion his exact language is, "except in cases where the power is restrained by the Constitution of the United States, the law of the State is supreme over the subject of slavery within its jurisdiction."

In what *cases* the power of the *states* is so restrained by the U. S. Constitution is left an *open* question, precisely as the same question, as to the restraint on the power of the *territories* was left open in the Nebraska act. Put *that* and *that* together, and we have another nice little nitch, which we may, ere long, see filled with another Supreme Court decision, declaring that the Constitution of the United States does not permit a state to exclude slavery from its limits.

And this may especially be expected if the doctrine of "care not whether slavery be voted *down* or voted *up*," shall gain upon the public mind sufficiently to give promise that such a decision can be maintained when made.

Such a decision is all that slavery now lacks of being alike lawful in all the States.

Welcome or unwelcome, such decision *is* probably coming, and will soon be upon us, unless the power of the present political dynasty shall be met and overthrown. We shall *lie down* pleasantly dreaming that the people of *Missouri* are on the verge of making their State *free;* and we shall *awake to the reality,* instead, that the *Supreme* Court has made *Illinois* a *slave* State.

To meet and overthrow the power of that dynasty, is the work now before all those who would prevent that consummation.

That is *what* we have to do.

But *how* can we best do it?

There are those who denounce us *openly* to their *own* friends, and yet whisper *us softly,* that *Senator Douglas* is the *aptest* instrument there is, with which to effect that object. *They* do *not* tell us, nor has *he* told us, that he *wishes* any such object to be effected. They wish us to *infer* all, from the facts, that he now has a little quarrel with the present head of the dynasty; and that he has regularly voted with us, on a single point, upon which, he and we, have never differed.

They remind us that *he* is a *great* man, and that the largest of *us* are very small ones. Let this be granted. But "a *living dog* is better than a *dead lion.*"[9] Judge Douglas, if not a *dead* lion *for this work.* is at least a *caged* and *toothless* one. How can he oppose the advances of slavery? He don't *care* anything about it. His avowed *mission is impressing* the "public heart" to *care* nothing about it.

A leading Douglas Democratic newspaper thinks Douglas' superior talent will be needed to resist the revival of the African slave trade.

7. Daniel Mace (1811–1867), representative from Indiana 1851–57. John McLean (1785–1861), American congressman, postmaster, and jurist. Benjamin Robbins Curtis (1809–1874), American jurist. Salmon Portland Chase (1808–1873), governor of Ohio, senator, secretary of the treasury, and chief justice of the Supreme Court.

8. Rensselaer Russell Nelson (1826–1904) was appointed an associate of the territorial supreme court of Minnesota in 1857 by Buchanan.

9. Ecclesiastes 9.4.

Does Douglas believe an effort to revive that trade is approaching? He has not said so. Does he *really* think so? But if it is, how can he resist it? For years he has labored to prove it a *sacred right* of white men to take negro slaves into the new territories. Can he possibly show that it is *less* a sacred right to *buy* them where they can be bought cheapest? And, unquestionably they can be bought *cheaper* in *Africa* than in *Virginia*.

He has done all in his power to reduce the whole question of slavery to one of a mere *right of property*; and as such, how can *he* oppose the foreign slave trade—how can he refuse that trade in that "property" shall be "perfectly free"—unless he does it as a *protection* to the home production? And as the home *producers* will probably not *ask* the protection, he will be wholly without a ground of opposition.

Senator Douglas holds, we know, that a man may rightfully be *wiser to-day* than he was *yesterday*—that he may rightfully *change* when he finds himself wrong.

But, can we for that reason, run ahead, and *infer* that he *will* make any particular change, of which he, himself, has given no intimation? Can we *safely* base *our* action upon any such *vague* inference?

Now, as ever, I wish to not misrepresent Judge Douglas' *position*, question his *motives*, or do aught that can be personally offensive to him.

Whenever, *if ever*, he and we can come together on *principle* so that *our great cause* may have assistance from *his great ability*, I hope to have interposed no adventitious obstacle.

But clearly, he is not *now* with us—he does not *pretend* to be—he does not *promise* to *ever* be.

Our cause, then, must be intrusted to, and conducted by its own undoubted friends—those whose hands are free, whose hearts are in the work—who *do care* for the result.

Two years ago the Republicans of the nation mustered over thirteen hundred thousand strong.

We did this under the single impulse of resistance to a common danger, with every external circumstance against us.

Of *strange*, *discordant*, and even, *hostile* elements, we gathered from the four winds, and *formed* and fought the battle through, under the constant hot fire of a disciplined, proud, and pampered enemy.

Did we brave all *then* to *falter* now?—now—when that same enemy is *wavering*, dissevered, and belligerent?

1858

Address Delivered at the Dedication
of the Cemetery at Gettysburg
November 19, 1863

Four score and seven years ago our fathers brought forth on this continent, a new nation, conceived in Liberty, and dedicated to the proposition that all men are created equal.

Now we are engaged in a great civil war, testing whether that nation, or any nation so conceived and so dedicated, can long endure. We are met on a great battle-field of that war. We have come to dedicate a portion of that field, as a final resting place for those who here gave their lives that that nation might live. It is altogether fitting and proper that we should do this.

But, in a larger sense, we can not dedicate—we can not consecrate—we can not hallow—this ground. The brave men, living and dead, who struggled here, have consecrated it, far above our poor power to add or detract. The world will little note, nor long remember what we say here, but it can never forget what they did here. It is for us the living, rather, to be dedicated here to the unfinished work which they who fought here have thus far so nobly advanced. It is rather for us to be here dedicated to the great task remaining before us—that from these honored dead we take increased devotion to that cause for which they gave the last full measure of devotion—that we here highly resolve that these dead shall not have died in vain—that this nation, under God, shall have a new birth of freedom—and that government of the people, by the people, for the people, shall not perish from the earth.

Abraham Lincoln

1863

Second Inaugural Address
March 4, 1865

At this second appearing to take the oath of the presidential office, there is less occasion for an extended address than there was at the first. Then a statement, somewhat in detail, of a course to be pursued, seemed fitting and proper. Now, at the expiration of four years, during which public declarations have been constantly called forth on every point and phase of the great contest which still absorbs the attention, and engrosses the energies of the nation, little that is new could be presented. The progress of our arms, upon which all else chiefly depends, is as well known to the public as to myself; and it is, I trust, reasonably satisfactory and encouraging to all. With high hope for the future, no prediction in regard to it is ventured.

On the occasion corresponding to this four years ago, all thoughts were anxiously directed to an impending civil war. All dreaded it—all sought to avert it. While the inaugural address was being delivered from this place, devoted altogether to *saving* the Union without war, insurgent agents were in the city seeking to *destroy* it without war—seeking to dissol[v]e the Union, and divide effects, by negotiation. Both parties deprecated war; but one of them would *make* war rather than let the nation survive; and the other would *accept* war rather than let it perish. And the war came.

One eighth of the whole population were colored slaves, not distributed generally over the Union, but localized in the Southern part of it. These slaves constituted a peculiar and powerful interest. All knew that this interest was, somehow, the cause of the war. To strengthen, perpetuate, and extend this interest was the object for which the insurgents would rend the Union, even by war; while the government claimed no right to do more than to restrict the territorial enlargement of it. Neither party expected for the war, the magnitude, or the duration, which it has already attained. Neither anticipated that the *cause* of the conflict might cease with, or even before, the conflict itself should cease. Each looked for an easier triumph, and a result less fundamental and astounding. Both read the same Bible, and pray to the same God; and each invokes His aid against the other. It may seem strange that any men should dare to ask a just God's assistance in wringing their bread from the sweat of other men's faces; but let us judge not that we be not judged. The prayers of both could not be answered; that of neither has been answered fully. The Almighty has his own purposes. "Woe unto the world because of offences! for it must needs be that offences come; but woe to that man by whom the offence cometh!" If we shall suppose that American Slavery is one of those offences which, in the providence of God, must needs come, but which, having continued through His appointed time, He now wills to remove, and that He gives to both North and South, this terrible war, as the woe due to those by whom the offence came, shall we discern therein any departure from those divine attributes which the believers in a Living God always ascribe to Him? Fondly do we hope—fervently do we pray—that this mighty scourge of war may speedily pass away. Yet, if God wills that it continue, until all the wealth piled by the bond-man's two hundred and fifty years of unrequited toil shall be sunk, and until every drop of blood drawn with the lash, shall be paid by another drawn with the sword, as was said three thousand years ago, so still it must be said "the judgments of the Lord, are true and righteous altogether."

With malice toward none; with charity for all; with firmness in the right, as God gives us to see the right, let us strive on to finish the work we are in; to bind up the nation's wounds; to care for him who shall have borne the battle, and for his widow, and his orphan—to do all which may achieve and cherish a just and lasting peace, among ourselves, and with all nations.

1865

OLIVER WENDELL HOLMES
1809–1894

Oliver Wendell Holmes was born on August 29, 1809, in Cambridge, Massachusetts, of old, honorable stock—what Holmes himself called the Brahmin caste. At Harvard he was class poet in 1829. He studied law at Harvard, then went to Paris to study medicine (1833–35). Harvard awarded him an M.D. in 1836, the year his *Poems* was published. Holmes was professor of anatomy at Dartmouth from 1839 to 1840, then moved to Boston. A medical treatise, *Homœopathy and Its Kindred Delusions*, was published in 1843, and the next year the controversial *Contagiousness of Puerperal Fever*, which tellingly surveyed the evidence that childbed fever, then a great danger to new mothers, might be contagious (as in fact it was, being spread by unsanitary doctors and midwives). Holmes's own three children were born in the early 1840s; the first, his namesake, became the distinguished jurist. From 1847 until 1882 Holmes was professor of anatomy at Harvard, phenomenally popular with students. Until well after his retirement, literature was only a secondary interest. Aggressive in arguing his positions in medical journals, Holmes studiously avoided involvement in the social causes that agitated so many of his contemporaries, remaining always a respectable, conservative, law-abiding citizen.

Holmes became nationally famous as an essayist and a poet in the late 1850s, when the *Atlantic Monthly* serialized his humorous essays, collected in *The Autocrat of the Breakfast Table* (1858), and printed poems that at once became classroom favorites, especially *The Chambered Nautilus* and *The Deacon's Masterpiece*. In three "medicated novels," as he called them, *Elsie Venner* (1861), *The Guardian Angel* (1867), and *A Mortal Antipathy* (1885), Holmes explored genetic and psychological determinism in a series of disturbed characters and took an analytic attitude toward theological convictions; cautious reviewers warned that the fiction was not entirely safe for the impressionable to read. Modern readers are attracted by Holmes's clinical portrayals, and all three of the novels are valuable for their local color and witty discursive passages. From the 1860s through the 1880s Holmes published several volumes of poems and essays and an unsatisfying biography of Emerson (1885) which ignored his friend's radicalism; his professional writing for medical journals continued to win respect. In his last decades Holmes was an American institution, the most famous after-dinner speaker of his time and the most reliably witty writer of poems for special occasions. He died on October 7, 1894, the last of his literary generation.

Old Ironsides[1]

Ay, tear her tattered ensign down!
  Long has it waved on high,
And many an eye has danced to see
  That banner in the sky;
Beneath it rung the battle shout,   5
  And burst the cannon's roar;—
The meteor of the ocean air
  Shall sweep the clouds no more!

Her deck, once red with heroes' blood
  Where knelt the vanquished foe,   10
When winds were hurrying o'er the flood
  And waves were white below,
No more shall feel the victor's tread,
  Or know the conquered knee;—
The harpies[2] of the shore shall pluck   15
  The eagle of the sea!

O better that her shattered hulk
  Should sink beneath the wave;
Her thunders shook the mighty deep
  And there should be her grave;   20
Nail to the mast her holy flag,
  Set every thread-bare sail,
And give her to the god of storms,—
  The lightning and the gale!

1830   1836

1. Written in 1830 in response to a newspaper account of the proposed dismantling of the frigate *Constitution*, victor against the British *Guerrière* in the War of 1812. Widely reprinted, the poem was credited with saving the ship (which is still preserved in Charlestown, Massachusetts). The nickname *Ironsides* was metaphorical, ironclad ships not being used until the Civil War. The text is that of *Poems* (1836).
2. Voracious monsters, from the ravenous creatures in Greek mythology.

The Last Leaf[1]

I saw him once before
As he passed by the door,
 And again,
The pavement stones resound
As he totters o'er the ground   5
 With his cane.

They say that in his prime,
Ere the pruning knife of Time
 Cut him down,
Not a better man was found   10
By the Crier[2] on his round
 Through the town.

But now he walks the streets,
And he looks at all he meets
 So forlorn   15
As he shakes his feeble head
That it seems as if he said,
 "They are gone."

The mossy marbles rest
On the lips that he has pressed   20
 In their bloom,
And the names he loved to hear
Have been carved for many a year
 On the tomb.

My grandmamma has said—   25
Poor old lady—she is dead
 Long ago;
That he had a Roman nose,
And his cheek was like a rose
 In the snow.   30

But now his nose is thin,
And it rests upon his chin
 Like a staff,
And a crook in his back,
And a melancholy crack   35
 In his laugh.

I know it is a sin
For me to sit and grin
 At him here,
But the old three cornered hat,   40

---

1. From *The Harbinger* (1833); first printed in the *Amateur* (March 26, 1831). The subject of the poem is the Revolutionary hero Thomas Melvill (1751–1832), famous as the last man in Boston to wear a cocked hat. He was a grandfather of Herman Melville, who in the 1850s was a friend and patient of Holmes's at Pittsfield, Massachusetts, where Melville lived and where Holmes had a summer home.
2. Official charged with making public announcements around a town.

And the breeches[3]—and all that
    Are so queer!

And if I should live to be
The last leaf upon the tree
    In the spring   45
Let them smile as I do now
At the old forsaken bough
    Where I cling.

1831, 1833

The Chambered Nautilus[1]

This is the ship of pearl, which, poets feign,
    Sails the unshadowed main,—
    The venturous bark that flings
On the sweet summer wind its purpled wings
In gulfs enchanted, where the siren sings,   5
    And coral reefs lie bare,
Where the cold sea-maids rise to sun their streaming hair.

Its webs of living gauze no more unfurl;
    Wrecked is the ship of pearl!
    And every chambered cell,   10
Where its dim dreaming life was wont to dwell,
As the frail tenant shaped his growing shell,
    Before thee lies revealed,—
Its irised ceiling rent, its sunless crypt unsealed!

Year after year beheld the silent toil   15
    That spread his lustrous coil;
    Still, as the spiral grew,
He left the past year's dwelling for the new,
Stole with soft step its shining archway through,
    Built up its idle door,   20
Stretched in his last-found home, and knew the old no more.

Thanks for the heavenly message brought by thee,
    Child of the wandering sea,
    Cast from her lap, forlorn!
From thy dead lips a clearer note is born   25
Than ever Triton[2] blew from wreathéd horn!
    While on mine ear it rings,
Through the deep caves of thought I hear a voice that sings:—

3. Small clothes—breeches that came to the knee, where they fastened to hose.
1. From the first printing in the *Atlantic Monthly* (February 1858). The "nautilus" (from the Greek, "sailor") mollusk is so named because it was thought to have a membrane that served as a sail. The pearly nautilus of this poem is found in the Indian Ocean and the South Pacific Ocean.
2. In Greek mythology, a sea god who controlled the waves with a trumpet made of a conch shell. The line echoes the sonnet *The World Is Too Much with Us* by the English poet William Wordsworth (1770–1850): "Or hear old Triton blow his wreathéd horn."

Build thee more stately mansions, O my soul,
    As the swift seasons roll!   30
    Leave thy low-vaulted past!
Let each new temple, nobler than the last,
Shut thee from heaven with a dome more vast,
    Till thou at length art free,
Leaving thine outgrown shell by life's unresting sea!   35

1858

The Deacon's Masterpiece:
or The Wonderful "One-Hoss-Shay"[1]

A *Logical Story*

Have you heard of the wonderful one-hoss-shay,
That was built in such a logical way
It ran a hundred years to a day,
And then, of a sudden, it——ah, but stay,
I'll tell you what happened without delay,   5
Scaring the parson into fits,
Frightening people out of their wits,—
Have you ever heard of that, I say?

Seventeen hundred and fifty-five.
Georgius Secundus[2] was then alive,—   10
Snuffy old drone from the German hive!
That was the year when Lisbon-town
Saw the earth open and gulp her down,[3]
And Braddock's army was done so brown,
Left without a scalp to its crown.[4]   15
It was on the terrible Earthquake-day
That the Deacon finished the one-hoss-shay.

Now in building of chaises, I tell you what,
There is always *somewhere* a weakest spot,—
In hub, tire, felloe, in spring or thill,   20
In panel, or crossbar, or floor, or sill,
In screw, bolt, thoroughbrace,—lurking still
Find it somewhere you must and will,—
Above or below, or within or without,—
And that's the reason, beyond a doubt,   25
A chaise *breaks down*, but doesn't *wear out*.

But the Deacon swore (as Deacons do,
With an "I dew vum," or an "I tell *yeou*,")

---

1. The text is that of the first printing, in the *Atlantic Monthly* (September 1858). "Shay": chaise; light, open two-wheeled carriage drawn by one horse.
2. The German-born king of Great Britain and the American colonies, George II (1683–1760).
3. Lisbon, Portugal, was devastated by an earthquake on November 1, 1755.
4. Edward Braddock (1695–1755), British general, was killed with many of his men near Fort Duquesne (now Pittsburgh) when the French and Indians ambushed his army in July 1755.

He would build one shay to beat the taown
'n' the keounty 'n' all the kentry raoun';
It should be so built that it *couldn't* break daown: 30
—"Fur," said the Deacon, " 't's mighty plain
Thut the weakes' place mus' stan' the strain;
'n' the way t' fix it, uz I maintain,
          Is only jest   35
To make that place uz strong uz the rest."

So the Deacon inquired of the village folk
Where he could find the strongest oak,
That couldn't be split nor bent nor broke,—
That was for spokes and floor and sills;   40
He sent for lancewood to make the thills;
The crossbars were ash, from the straightest trees;
The panels of white-wood, that cuts like cheese,
But lasts like iron for things like these;
The hubs of logs from the "Settler's ellum,"[5]—   45
Last of its timber,—they couldn't sell 'em,—
Never an axe had seen their chips,
And the wedges flew from between their lips,
Their blunt ends frizzled like celery-tips;
Step and prop-iron, bolt and screw,   50
Spring, tire, axle, and linchpin too,
Steel of the finest, bright and blue;
Thoroughbrace bison-skin, thick and wide;
Boot, top, dasher, from tough old hide
Found in the pit when the tanner died.   55
That was the way he "put her through."—
"There!" said the Deacon, "naow she'll dew!"

Do! I tell you, I rather guess
She was a wonder, and nothing less!
Colts grew horses, beards turned gray,   60
Deacon and deaconess dropped away,
Children and grand-children—where were they?
But there stood the stout old one-hoss-shay
As fresh as on Lisbon-earthquake-day!

EIGHTEEN HUNDRED;—it came and found   65
The Deacon's Masterpiece strong and sound.
Eighteen hundred increased by ten;—
"Hahnsum kerridge" they called it then.
Eighteen hundred and twenty came;—
Running as usual; much the same.   70
Thirty and forty at last arrive,
And then come fifty, and FIFTY-FIVE.

Little of all we value here
Wakes on the morn of its hundredth year

5. Probably, elm standing when the first settlers came to New England.

Without both feeling and looking queer.   75
In fact, there's nothing that keeps its youth
So far as I know, but a tree and truth.
(This is a moral that runs at large;
Take it.—You're welcome.—No extra charge.)

FIRST OF NOVEMBER,—the Earthquake-day.—   80
There are traces of age in the one-hoss-shay,
A general flavor of mild decay,
But nothing local, as one may say.
There couldn't be,—for the Deacon's art
Had made it so like in every part   85
That there wasn't a chance for one to start.
For the wheels were just as strong as the thills,
And the floor was just as strong as the sills,
And the panels just as strong as the floor,
And the whippletree neither less nor more,   90
And the back-crossbar as strong as the fore,
And spring and axle and hub *encore*.
And yet, *as a whole*, it is past a doubt
In another hour it will be *worn out!*

First of November, 'Fifty-five!   95
This morning the parson takes a drive.
Now, small boys, get out of the way!
Here comes the wonderful one-hoss-shay,
Drawn by a rat-tailed, ewe-necked bay.[6]
"Huddup!" said the parson.—Off went they.   100

The parson was working his Sunday's text,—
Had got to *fifthly*,[7] and stopped perplexed
At what the—Moses—was coming next.
All at once the horse stood still,
Close by the meet'n'-house on the hill.   105
—First a shiver, and then a thrill,
Then something decidedly like a spill,—
And the parson was sitting upon a rock,
At half-past nine by the meet'n'-house-clock,—
Just the hour of the Earthquake-shock!   110
—What do you think the parson found,
When he got up and stared around?
The poor old chaise in a heap or mound,
As if it had been to the mill and ground!
You see, of course, if you're not a dunce,   115
How it went to pieces all at once,—
All at once, and nothing first,—
Just as bubbles do when they burst.

End of the wonderful one-hoss-shay.
Logic is logic. That's all I say.   120

1858

---

6. Long, thin-necked reddish brown horse.
7. I.e., the fifth application of the day's biblical text, the pattern being to announce the text and then item-ize ways the text applied to the lives of the congregation.

MARGARET FULLER
1810–1850

Sarah Margaret Fuller was born at Cambridgeport (now part of Cambridge), Massachusetts, on May 23, 1810. Her father supervised her education, making her a prodigy but depriving her of a childhood. After a brief, traumatic stay at a girls' school in her early teens, she returned to pursue her rigorous education at home, steeping herself in the classics and in modern languages and literatures, especially German. Accustomed to intense, lonely study, Fuller nevertheless formed lasting intellectual and emotional friendships with a few young Harvard scholars, among them her co-biographers James Freeman Clarke and W. H. Channing. A Cambridge lady, Eliza Farrar, undertook to instill some of the social graces into the father-taught Margaret. The death of her father in 1835 burdened Fuller with the education of younger brothers and sisters. Setting aside her own ambitions (including a planned trip to Europe), she taught for several years, in Boston and Providence. During this time the German novelist and dramatist Goethe became the chief influence on her religion and philosophy, and she tormented herself with the hope that she might have money, time, and ability to write his biography. In 1839 she began leading "Conversation" classes among an elite group of Boston women. Later, men participated also, and during the next years her topics included Greek mythology, the fine arts, ethics, education, demonology, creeds, and the ideal.

A close friend of Emerson's since she first sought him out in 1836, Fuller edited the Transcendentalists' magazine *The Dial* from 1840 to 1842, meanwhile continuing to translate works by and about Goethe. In 1844 *Summer on the Lakes*, an account of a trip to the Midwest, led Horace Greeley to hire her as literary critic for his New York *Tribune*, making her probably the first self-supporting American woman journalist. More than a literary reviewer, Fuller wrote a series of reports on public questions, among them the conditions of the blind, of the insane, and of female prisoners. In 1845 Greeley published her *Woman in the Nineteenth Century*, the title article of which was an expansion of a controversial *Dial* essay, *The Great Lawsuit*. This is one of the great neglected documents of American sexual liberation—not merely of feminism, for Fuller recognized that both men and women were imprisoned by social roles, although men at least had the power to make and enforce the definitions of those roles. In 1846 some of her *Tribune* pieces were collected in *Papers on Literature and Art*. In New York she fell in love with James Nathan, a German Jew who, a cosmopolite baffled by her mixture of sexual honesty and prudery, fled home in June 1845, letting the growing spaces between his letters persuade her gradually that he had rejected her.

Fuller sailed for Europe in August 1846, intending to support herself as foreign correspondent for the *Tribune*. In England one of her idols, Thomas Carlyle (then in his fifties), disappointed her by his reactionary political views and his insensitivity to the worth of others, especially the Italian revolutionary Joseph Mazzini, who had sought refuge in England. In Paris she met another idol, George Sand, who proved more satisfactory than Carlyle, and another political revolutionary, the exiled Polish poet Adam Mickiewicz. Sand's example of sexually liberated womanhood stirred Fuller profoundly, as did Mickiewicz's blunt speculation that she could not deeply respond to Europe while remaining a virgin—not the sort of comment men like Emerson and Greeley had accustomed her to. Fuller went on to Italy, then not a unified country but a collection of states—some controlled by the pope, others independent, and to the north, a third group controlled by Austria. Soon after her arrival in Rome she became the object of courtship by a Roman of the nobility, Giovanni Angelo Ossoli, almost eleven years younger than she. When she returned from summering in northern Italy, Rome was undergoing antipapal ferment, and her dispatches to the *Tribune* became more and more political. Making use of her connections with varying factions, she began an earnest accumulation of documents concerning the forthcoming revolution—newspapers, pamphlets, leaflets.

And she began a love affair with Ossoli. In December she was pregnant, with no man or woman she could confide in, either in the United States or Europe. At the start of 1848 she wrote guardedly to a friend at home: "With this year I enter upon a sphere of my destiny so difficult that at present I see no way out except through the gate of death." Marriage seemed out of the question because of the certain opposition of Ossoli's family. Through a dismal rainy season, in which she lived on pennies a day, Fuller covered for the *Tribune* such events as the popular agitation against the Jesuits. She became intimate with the Princess Belgioioso, a leader of the anti-Austrian faction who drew her still more deeply into Italian politics. When cities of northern Italy revolted against the Austrians in March, Fuller described to her New York readers the joyous response of the Roman citizens. The revolutionaries Mickiewicz and Mazzini entered Italy; both kept in touch with Fuller out of their respect for her personal commitment to their goals and their sense of her value in shaping American opinion.

That spring, 1848, Emerson wrote from England urging her to return home with him before war broke out. Still keeping her secret, she withdrew instead to the Abruzzi region to wait out her pregnancy. Ossoli had become a member of the civic guard, but he managed to be with her for the birth of Angelo on September 5. Leaving the baby in Rieti with a wet nurse, Fuller returned to Rome late in November, in time to report the flight of the pope and, early in 1849, the arrival of the Italian nationalist Giuseppe Garibaldi and the proclamation of the Roman Republic. She shared the triumph of Mazzini's arrival in Rome, but the Republic was short-lived. Anticipating the intervention of the French on behalf of the pope, Princess Belgioioso urgently wrote Fuller on April 30, 1849: "You are named Regolatrice of the Hospital of the Fate Bene Fratelli"—on an island in the Tiber. Fuller ran the hospital heroically when the French laid siege, despite her concern for Ossoli, who was fighting with the Republican forces, and her uncertainty about the baby, whom she had hardly seen since he was two months old. After Rome fell to the French on the fourth of July she made her way to Rieti, only to find that the nurse, assuming the baby had been abandoned, was allowing him to starve. Retreating to Florence with Ossoli and the baby, Fuller faced down her shocked acquaintances, including Robert and Elizabeth Barrett Browning, and began work on her history of the Roman Republic. While at Florence she may have married Ossoli, as his sister later claimed. In May 1850, she sailed for the United States with Ossoli and the baby, full of forebodings about the ship and the way they would be received at home. All three died in a shipwreck off Fire Island, New York, on July 19. The body of the baby was washed ashore as well as a trunk that contained some of Fuller's papers but not the history. Thoreau sought in vain for her body.

Emerson, Clarke, and Channing edited Fuller's *Memoirs* (1852) in a way that sanitized her personal life, denigrated her accomplishments as a writer, and slighted her lifelong activism. In 1903 her friend Julia Ward Howe published her love letters to James Nathan, thereby sealing the image of Fuller as a would-be intellectual, willful and foolish in her personal entanglements. Hawthorne's old verdict seemed confirmed: "There never was such a tragedy as her whole story; the sadder and sterner, because so much of the ridiculous was mixed up with it, and because she could bear anything better than to be ridiculous."

Sexist ridicule dies hard, and in Fuller's case its death was retarded by the long inaccessibility of most of her writings. The Fuller bibliography included in this volume shows that her writings now, in the 1980s and the 1990s, are fast coming back into print—an excellent edition of her letters, a collection of her dispatches to the *Tribune* from Europe, an annotated edition of her *Woman in the Nineteenth Century*, and a generous anthology of her writings. The substantial "popular" biography of 1990 was followed in 1992 by the meticulously researched first volume of a projected two-volume scholarly biography. The evidence is at hand that may at last establish Fuller's candidacy for serious consideration as what Hawthorne said mockingly, "the greatest, wisest, best woman of the age."

From The Great Lawsuit
MAN versus MEN. WOMAN versus WOMEN[1]

[*Two Kinds of Slavery; Miranda; No Man Is Willingly Ungenerous*]

It is worthy of remark that, as the principle of liberty is better understood and more nobly interpreted, a broader protest is made in behalf of woman. As men become aware that all men have not had their fair chance, they are inclined to say that no women have had a fair chance. The French revolution, that strangely disguised angel, bore witness in favor of woman, but interpreted her claims no less ignorantly than those of man. Its idea of happiness did not rise beyond outward enjoyment, unobstructed by the tyranny of others. The title it gave was Citoyen, Citoyenne,[2] and it is not unimportant to woman that even this species of equality was awarded her. Before, she could be condemned to perish on the scaffold for treason, but not as a citizen, but a subject. The right, with which this title then invested a human being, was that of bloodshed and license. The Goddess of Liberty was impure. Yet truth was prophesied in the ravings of that hideous fever induced by long ignorance and abuse. Europe is conning a valued lesson from the blood-stained page. The same tendencies, farther unfolded, will bear good fruit in this country.

Yet, in this country, as by the Jews, when Moses was leading them to the promised land,[3] everything has been done that inherited depravity could, to hinder the promise of heaven from its fulfilment. The cross, here as elsewhere, has been planted only to be blasphemed by cruelty and fraud. The name of the Prince of Peace has been profaned by all kinds of injustice towards the Gentile whom he said he came to save. But I need not speak of what has been done towards the red man, the black man. These deeds are the scoff of the world; and they have been accompanied by such pious words, that the gentlest would not dare to intercede with, "Father forgive them, for they know not what they do."[4]

---

1. Reprinted here from the Boston *Dial*, vol. 4 (July 1843). In 1844 Fuller published the revised, expanded version of this work under the title *Woman in the Nineteenth Century*, but the additions were hardly more than padding. This passage of her preliminary 1844 footnote makes clear her intentions for the original title of the essay: "Objections having been made to the former title, as not sufficiently easy to be understood, the present has been substituted as expressive of the main purpose of the essay; though, by myself, the other is preferred, partly for the reason others do not like it,— that is, that it requires some thought to see what it means, and might thus prepare the reader to meet me on my own ground. Besides, it offers a larger scope, and is, in that way, more just to my desire. I meant by that title to intimate the fact that, while it is the destiny of Man, in the course of the ages, to ascertain and fulfil the law of his being, so that his life shall be seen, as a whole, to be that of an angel or messenger, the action of prejudices and passions which attend, in the day, the growth of the individual, is continually obstructing the holy work that is to make earth a part of heaven.

By Men I mean both man and woman; these are the two halves of one thought. I lay no especial stress on the welfare of either. I believe that the development of the one cannot be effected without that of the other. My highest wish is that this truth should be distinctly and rationally apprehended, and the conditions of life and freedom recognized as the same for the daughters and the sons of time; twin exponents of a divine thought." Fuller's relentlessly allusive style was typical of her time. A few of her more elusive references have had to remain unglossed in this anthology.

2. Male citizen, female citizen, equal under the law— one of the most promising early achievements of the French Revolution.

3. Fuller emphasizes the irony of Moses' promulgation of a degraded role for women under Mosaic law even while leading the Israelites, male and female, out of Egypt toward their promised homeland (see Leviticus 12 and Numbers 30).

4. Jesus' words in Luke 23.34, in reference to the Roman soldiers who had just nailed him to the cross.

Here, as elsewhere, the gain of creation consists always in the growth of individual minds, which live and aspire, as flowers bloom and birds sing, in the midst of morasses; and in the continual development of that thought, the thought of human destiny, which is given to eternity to fulfil, and which ages of failure only seemingly impede. Only seemingly, and whatever seems to the contrary, this country is as surely destined to elucidate a great moral law, as Europe was to promote the mental culture of man.

Though the national independence be blurred by the servility of individuals; though freedom and equality have been proclaimed only to leave room for a monstrous display of slave dealing and slave keeping; though the free American so often feels himself free, like the Roman, only to pamper his appetites and his indolence through the misery of his fellow beings, still it is not in vain, that the verbal statement has been made, "All men are born free and equal."[5] There it stands, a golden certainty, wherewith to encourage the good, to shame the bad. The new world may be called clearly to perceive that it incurs the utmost penalty, if it rejects the sorrowful brother. And if men are deaf, the angels hear. But men cannot be deaf. It is inevitable that an external freedom, such as has been achieved for the nation, should be so also for every member of it. That, which has once been clearly conceived in the intelligence, must be acted out. It has become a law, irrevocable as that of the Medes in their ancient dominion.[6] Men will privately sin against it, but the law so clearly expressed by a leading mind of the age,

> "Tutti fatti a sembianza d' un Solo;
> Figli tutti d' un solo riscatto,
> In qual ora, in qual parte del suolo
> Trascorriamo quest' aura vital,
> Siam fratelli, siam stretti ad un patto:
> Maladetto colui che lo infrange,
> Che s' innalza sul fiacco che piange,
> Che contrista uno spirto immortal."[7]

> "All made in the likeness of the One,
> All children of one ransom,
> In whatever hour, in whatever part of the soil
> We draw this vital air,
> We are brothers, we must be bound by one compact,
> Accursed he who infringes it,
> Who raises himself upon the weak who weep,
> Who saddens an immortal spirit."

cannot fail of universal recognition.

We sicken no less at the pomp than at the strife of words. We feel that never were lungs so puffed with the wind of declamation, on moral and religious subjects, as now. We are tempted to implore these "word-heroes," these word-Catos, word-Christs,[8] to beware of cant above all things; to remember that hypocrisy is the most hopeless as well as the meanest of crimes, and that those

---

5. As in the Declaration of Independence, second paragraph, "all men are created equal."
6. Media is now part of Iran. In Fuller's notion, as in Thoreau's, real insight always leads to action.
7. "Manzoni" [Fuller's note]. Alessandro Manzoni (1785–1873), Italian poet.
8. Windy would-be reformers, whether of political and social morality like Marcus Porcius Cato (234–149 B.C.), Roman statesman, or of religion, in fancied imitation of Jesus.

must surely be polluted by it, who do not keep a little of all this morality and religion for private use.[9] We feel that the mind may "grow black and rancid in the smoke" even of altars. We start up from the harangue to go into our closet and shut the door. But, when it has been shut long enough, we remember that where there is so much smoke, there must be some fire; with so much talk about virtue and freedom must be mingled some desire for them; that it cannot be in vain that such have become the common topics of conversation among men; that the very newspapers should proclaim themselves Pilgrims, Puritans, Heralds of Holiness.[1] The king that maintains so costly a retinue cannot be a mere Count of Carabbas[2] fiction. We have waited here long in the dust; we are tired and hungry, but the triumphal procession must appear at last.

Of all its banners, none has been more steadily upheld, and under none has more valor and willingness for real sacrifices been shown, than that of the champions of the enslaved African. And this band it is, which, partly in consequence of a natural following out of principles, partly because many women have been prominent in that cause, makes, just now, the warmest appeal in behalf of woman.

Though there has been a growing liberality on this point, yet society at large is not so prepared for the demands of this party, but that they are, and will be for some time, coldly regarded as the Jacobins[3] of their day.

"It is not enough," cries the sorrowful trader, "that you have done all you could to break up the national Union, and thus destroy the prosperity of our country, but now you must be trying to break up family union, to take my wife away from the cradle, and the kitchen hearth, to vote at polls, and preach from a pulpit? Of course, if she does such things, she cannot attend to those of her own sphere. She is happy enough as she is. She has more leisure than I have, every means of improvement, every indulgence."

"Have you asked her whether she was satisfied with these indulgences?"

"No, but I know she is. She is too amiable to wish what would make me unhappy, and too judicious to wish to step beyond the sphere of her sex. I will never consent to have our peace disturbed by any such discussions."

" 'Consent'—you? it is not consent from you that is in question, it is assent from your wife."

"Am I not the head of my house?"

"You are not the head of your wife. God has given her a mind of her own."

"I am the head and she the heart."

"God grant you play true to one another then. If the head represses no natural pulse of the heart, there can be no question as to your giving your consent. Both will be of one accord, and there needs but to present any question to get a full and true answer. There is no need of precaution, of indulgence, or consent. But our doubt is whether the heart consents with the head, or only acquiesces in its decree; and it is to ascertain the truth on this point, that we propose some liberating measures."

9. "Dr. Johnson's one piece of advice should be written on every door: 'Clear your mind of cant.' But Byron, to whom it was so acceptable, in clearing away the noxious vine, shook down the building too. Stirling's emendation is noteworthy. 'Realize your cant, not cast it off' " [Fuller's note].

1. Then-common names for newspapers in Massachusetts and elsewhere.

2. Type name for a purse-proud nobleman (or fake nobleman, as in the nursery tale *Puss in Boots*).

3. Political radicals of the extreme left, from the political group founded in Paris in 1789 near the church of Saint-Jacques.

Thus vaguely are these questions proposed and discussed at present. But their being proposed at all implies much thought, and suggests more. Many women are considering within themselves what they need that they have not, and what they can have, if they find they need it. Many men are considering whether women are capable of being and having more than they are and have, and whether, if they are, it will be best to consent to improvement in their condition.

The numerous party, whose opinions are already labelled and adjusted too much to their mind to admit of any new light, strive, by lectures on some model-women of bridal-like beauty and gentleness, by writing or lending little treatises, to mark out with due precision the limits of woman's sphere, and woman's mission, and to prevent other than the rightful shepherd from climbing the wall, or the flock from using any chance gap to run astray.

Without enrolling ourselves at once on either side, let us look upon the subject from that point of view which to-day offers. No better, it is to be feared, than a high house-top. A high hill-top, or at least a cathedral spire, would be desirable.

It is not surprising that it should be the Anti-Slavery party that pleads for woman, when we consider merely that she does not hold property on equal terms with men; so that, if a husband dies without a will, the wife, instead of stepping at once into his place as head of the family, inherits only a part of his fortune, as if she were a child, or ward only, not an equal partner.

We will not speak of the innumerable instances, in which profligate or idle men live upon the earnings of industrious wives; or if the wives leave them and take with them the children, to perform the double duty of mother and father, follow from place to place, and threaten to rob them of the children, if deprived of the rights of a husband, as they call them, planting themselves in their poor lodgings, frightening them into paying tribute by taking from them the children, running into debt at the expense of these otherwise so overtasked helots.[4] Though such instances abound, the public opinion of his own sex is against the man, and when cases of extreme tyranny are made known, there is private action in the wife's favor. But if woman be, indeed, the weaker party, she ought to have legal protection, which would make such oppression impossible.

And knowing that there exists, in the world of men, a tone of feeling towards women as towards slaves, such as is expressed in the common phrase, "Tell that to women and children;" that the infinite soul can only work through them in already ascertained limits; that the prerogative of reason, man's highest portion, is allotted to them in a much lower degree; that it is better for them to be engaged in active labor, which is to be furnished and directed by those better able to think, &c. &c.; we need not go further, for who can review the experience of last week, without recalling words which imply, whether in jest or earnest, these views, and views like these? Knowing this, can we wonder that many reformers think that measures are not likely to be taken in behalf of women, unless their wishes could be publicly represented by women?

That can never be necessary, cry the other side. All men are privately influenced by women; each has his wife, sister, or female friends, and is too much biassed by these relations to fail of representing their interests. And if this is

---

4. Slaves. Fuller fairly describes the legal situation in her time.

not enough, let them propose and enforce their wishes with the pen. The beauty of home would be destroyed, the delicacy of the sex be violated, the dignity of halls of legislation destroyed, by an attempt to introduce them there. Such duties are inconsistent with those of a mother; and then we have ludicrous pictures of ladies in hysterics at the polls, and senate chambers filled with cradles.

But if, in reply, we admit as truth that woman seems destined by nature rather to the inner circle, we must add that the arrangements of civilized life have not been as yet such as to secure it to her. Her circle, if the duller, is not the quieter. If kept from excitement, she is not from drudgery. Not only the Indian carries the burdens of the camp, but the favorites of Louis the Fourteenth accompany him in his journeys, and the washerwoman stands at her tub and carries home her work at all seasons, and in all states of health.[5]

As to the use of the pen, there was quite as much opposition to woman's possessing herself of that help to free-agency as there is now to her seizing on the rostrum or the desk; and she is likely to draw, from a permission to plead her cause that way, opposite inferences to what might be wished by those who now grant it.

As to the possibility of her filling, with grace and dignity, any such position, we should think those who had seen the great actresses, and heard the Quaker preachers of modern times, would not doubt, that woman can express publicly the fulness of thought and emotion, without losing any of the peculiar beauty of her sex.

As to her home, she is not likely to leave it more than she now does for balls, theatres, meetings for promoting missions, revival meetings, and others to which she flies, in hope of an animation for her existence, commensurate with what she sees enjoyed by men. Governors of Ladies' Fairs are no less engrossed by such a charge, than the Governor of the State by his; presidents of Washingtonian societies,[6] no less away from home than presidents of conventions. If men look straitly to it, they will find that, unless their own lives are domestic, those of the women will not be. The female Greek, of our day, is as much in the street as the male, to cry, What news?[7] We doubt not it was the same in Athens of old. The women, shut out from the market-place, made up for it at the religious festivals. For human beings are not so constituted, that they can live without expansion; and if they do not get it one way, must another, or perish.

And, as to men's representing women fairly, at present, while we hear from men who owe to their wives not only all that is comfortable and graceful, but all that is wise in the arrangement of their lives, the frequent remark, "You cannot reason with a woman," when from those of delicacy, nobleness, and poetic culture, the contemptuous phrase, "Women and children," and that in no light sally of the hour, but in works intended to give a permanent statement of the best experiences, when not one man in the million, shall I say, no, not in the hundred million, can rise above the view that woman was made *for man*, when such traits as these are daily forced upon the attention, can we feel that man will always do justice to the interests of woman? Can we think that

5. In Fuller's view courtesans and washerwomen are equally enslaved, however disparate their conditions are.
6. Roughly equivalent in purpose and reputation to the modern Daughters of the American Revolution.

7. Fuller mentions only the ancient Greek males as targets of satire for their newsmongering, but it was the Latin *quid nunc?* ("What now?") that entered English as a label for male busybodies: "quidnuncs."

he takes a sufficiently discerning and religious view of her office and destiny, ever to do her justice, except when prompted by sentiment; accidentally or transiently, that is, for his sentiment will vary according to the relations in which he is placed. The lover, the poet, the artist, are likely to view her nobly. The father and the philosopher have some chance of liberality; the man of the world, the legislator for expediency, none.

Under these circumstances, without attaching importance in themselves to the changes demanded by the champions of woman, we hail them as signs of the times. We would have every arbitrary barrier thrown down. We would have every path laid open to woman as freely as to man. Were this done, and a slight temporary fermentation allowed to subside, we believe that the Divine would ascend into nature to a height unknown in the history of past ages, and nature, thus instructed, would regulate the spheres not only so as to avoid collision, but to bring forth ravishing harmony.

Yet then, and only then, will human beings be ripe for this, when inward and outward freedom for woman, as much as for man, shall be acknowledged as a right, not yielded as a concession. As the friend of the negro assumes that one man cannot, by right, hold another in bondage, should the friend of woman assume that man cannot, by right, lay even well-meant restrictions on woman. If the negro be a soul, if the woman be a soul, apparelled in flesh, to one master only are they accountable. There is but one law for all souls, and, if there is to be an interpreter of it, he comes not as man, or son of man, but as Son of God.

Were thought and feeling once so far elevated that man should esteem himself the brother and friend, but nowise the lord and tutor of woman, were he really bound with her in equal worship, arrangements as to function and employment would be of no consequence. What woman needs is not as a woman to act or rule, but as a nature to grow, as an intellect to discern, as a soul to live freely, and unimpeded to unfold such powers as were given her when we left our common home. If fewer talents were given her, yet, if allowed the free and full employment of these, so that she may render back to the giver his own with usury, she will not complain, nay, I dare to say she will bless and rejoice in her earthly birth-place, her earthly lot.

Let us consider what obstructions impede this good era, and what signs give reason to hope that it draws near.

I was talking on this subject with Miranda,[8] a woman, who, if any in the world, might speak without heat or bitterness of the position of her sex. Her father was a man who cherished no sentimental reverence for woman, but a firm belief in the equality of the sexes. She was his eldest child, and came to him at an age when he needed a companion. From the time she could speak and go[9] alone, he addressed her not as a plaything, but as a living mind. Among the few verses he ever wrote were a copy addressed to this child, when the first locks were cut from her head, and the reverence expressed on this occasion for that cherished head he never belied. It was to him the temple of immortal intellect. He respected his child, however, too much to be an indulgent parent. He called on her for clear judgment, for courage, for honor and fidelity, in short for such virtues as he knew. In so far as he possessed the keys to the wonders of this universe, he allowed free use of them to her, and by the

---

8. Fuller's own experiences are reflected in those of "Miranda."

9. Walk.

incentive of a high expectation he forbade, as far as possible, that she should let the privilege lie idle.

Thus this child was eagerly led to feel herself a child of the spirit. She took her place easily, not only in the world of organized being, but in the world of mind. A dignified sense of self-dependence was given as all her portion, and she found it a sure anchor. Herself securely anchored, her relations with others were established with equal security. She was fortunate, in a total absence of those charms which might have drawn to her bewildering flatteries, and of a strong electric nature, which repelled those who did not belong to her, and attracted those who did. With men and women her relations were noble; affectionate without passion, intellectual without coldness. The world was free to her, and she lived freely in it. Outward adversity came, and inward conflict, but that faith and self-respect had early been awakened, which must always lead at last to an outward serenity, and an inward peace.

Of Miranda I had always thought as an example, that the restraints upon the sex were insuperable only to those who think them so, or who noisily strive to break them. She had taken a course of her own, and no man stood in her way. Many of her acts had been unusual, but excited no uproar. Few helped, but none checked her; and the many men, who knew her mind and her life, showed to her confidence as to a brother, gentleness as to a sister. And not only refined, but very coarse men approved one in whom they saw resolution and clearness of design. Her mind was often the leading one, always effective.

When I talked with her upon these matters, and had said very much what I have written, she smilingly replied, And yet we must admit that I have been fortunate, and this should not be. My good father's early trust gave the first bias, and the rest followed of course. It is true that I have had less outward aid, in after years, than most women, but that is of little consequence. Religion was early awakened in my soul, a sense that what the soul is capable to ask it must attain, and that, though I might be aided by others, I must depend on myself as the only constant friend. This self-dependence, which was honored in me, is deprecated as a fault in most women. They are taught to learn their rule from without, not to unfold it from within.

This is the fault of man, who is still vain, and wishes to be more important to woman than by right he should be.

Men have not shown this disposition towards you, I said.

No, because the position I early was enabled to take, was one of self-reliance. And were all women as sure of their wants as I was, the result would be the same. The difficulty is to get them to the point where they shall naturally develop self-respect, the question how it is to be done.

Once I thought that men would help on this state of things more than I do now. I saw so many of them wretched in the connections they had formed in weakness and vanity. They seemed so glad to esteem women whenever they could!

But early I perceived that men never, in any extreme of despair, wished to be women. Where they admired any woman they were inclined to speak of her as above her sex. Silently I observed this, and feared it argued a rooted skepticism, which for ages had been fastening on the heart, and which only an age of miracles could eradicate.

Ever I have been treated with great sincerity; and I look upon it as a most signal instance of this, that an intimate friend of the other sex said in a fervent moment, that I deserved in some star to be a man. Another used as highest praise, in speaking of a character in literature, the words "a manly woman."

It is well known that of every strong woman they say she has a masculine mind.[1]

This by no means argues a willing want of generosity towards woman. Man is as generous towards her, as he knows how to be.

Wherever she has herself arisen in national or private history, and nobly shone forth in any ideal of excellence, men have received her, not only willingly, but with triumph. Their encomiums indeed are always in some sense mortifying, they show too much surprise.

In every-day life the feelings of the many are stained with vanity. Each wishes to be lord in a little world, to be superior at least over one; and he does not feel strong enough to retain a life-long ascendant over a strong nature. Only a Brutus would rejoice in a Portia. Only Theseus could conquer before he wed the Amazonian Queen. Hercules wished rather to rest from his labors with Dejanira, and received the poisoned robe, as a fit guerdon.[2] The tale should be interpreted to all those who seek repose with the weak.

But not only is man vain and fond of power, but the same want[3] of development, which thus affects him morally in the intellect, prevents his discerning the destiny of woman. The boy wants no woman, but only a girl to play ball with him, and mark his pocket handkerchief.

Thus in Schiller's Dignity of Woman,[4] beautiful as the poem is, there is no "grave and perfect man," but only a great boy to be softened and restrained by the influence of girls. Poets, the elder brothers of their race, have usually seen further; but what can you expect of every-day men, if Schiller was not more prophetic as to what women must be? Even with Richter one foremost thought about a wife was that she would "cook him something good."[5]

The sexes should not only correspond to and appreciate one another, but prophesy to one another. In individual instances this happens. Two persons love in one another the future good which they aid one another to unfold. This is very imperfectly done as yet in the general life. Man has gone but little way, now he is waiting to see whether woman can keep step with him, but instead of calling out like a good brother; You can do it if you only think so, or impersonally; Any one can do what he tries to do, he often discourages with school-boy brag; Girls cant do that, girls cant play ball. But let any one defy their taunts, break through, and be brave and secure, they rend the air with shouts.

No! man is not willingly ungenerous. He wants[6] faith and love, because he is not yet himself an elevated being. He cries with sneering skepticism; Give

---

1. The *Dial* text gives no indication where Fuller means Miranda's voice to stop, but the 1844 edition makes this sentence Miranda's last.
2. Reward. The mutual love of Brutus and Portia is now best known from Shakespeare's *Julius Caesar*, but Fuller knew the *Lives* of Greek and Roman statesmen written by the Greek biographer and philosopher Plutarch (46?–120?). The syntax does not make it entirely clear whether Fuller sees the wedding of the Greek hero Theseus and the Amazonian queen (variously identified as Hippolyte or Oreithyia) as a fit match of warlike equals or as an instance of male domination of the female. The justly jealous Dejanira innocently tried to win back Hercules' love by sending him a shirt imbued with an ointment given her by Nessus; proffered as a love potion, it was in fact a virulent poison that consumed Hercules' flesh. Fuller interprets the story as a warning against choosing a wife for docility.
3. Lack.
4. This poem by Friedrich von Schiller (1759–1805) is a tribute to the docility of women in contrast to the strong, passionate striving of men.
5. Jean Paul Richter (1763–1825), German novelist and tale writer, often portrayed women sympathetically, but his *Levana; or The Doctrine of Education* (1807) is in part a compendium of sexist notions.
6. Lacks.

us a sign. But if the sign appears, his eyes glisten, and he offers not merely approval, but homage.

＊   ＊   ＊

[Four Kinds of Equality]

Where the thought of equality has become pervasive, it shows itself in four kinds.

The household partnership. In our country the woman looks for a "smart but kind" husband, the man for a "capable, sweet-tempered" wife.

The man furnishes the house, the woman regulates it. Their relation is one of mutual esteem, mutual dependence. Their talk is of business, their affection shows itself by practical kindness. They know that life goes more smoothly and cheerfully to each for the other's aid; they are grateful and content. The wife praises her husband as a "good provider," the husband in return compliments her as a "capital housekeeper." This relation is good as far as it goes.

Next comes a closer tie which takes the two forms, either of intellectual companionship, or mutual idolatry. The last, we suppose, is to no one a pleasing subject of contemplation. The parties weaken and narrow one another; they lock the gate against all the glories of the universe that they may live in a cell together. To themselves they seem the only wise, to all others steeped in infatuation, the gods smile as they look forward to the crisis of cure, to men the woman seems an unlovely syren, to women the man an effeminate boy.

The other form, of intellectual companionship, has become more and more frequent. Men engaged in public life, literary men, and artists have often found in their wives companions and confidants in thought no less than in feeling. And, as in the course of things the intellectual development of woman has spread wider and risen higher, they have, not unfrequently, shared the same employment. As in the case of Roland and his wife, who were friends in the household and the nation's councils, read together, regulated home affairs, or prepared public documents together indifferently.

It is very pleasant, in letters begun by Roland and finished by his wife, to see the harmony of mind and the difference of nature, one thought, but various ways of treating it.

This is one of the best instances of a marriage of friendship. It was only friendship, whose basis was esteem; probably neither party knew love, except by name.

Roland was a good man, worthy to esteem and be esteemed, his wife as deserving of admiration as able to do without it. Madame Roland is the fairest specimen we have yet of her class, as clear to discern her aim, as valiant to pursue it, as Spenser's Britomart, austerely set apart from all that did not belong to her, whether as woman or as mind. She is an antetype of a class to which the coming time will afford a field, the Spartan matron, brought by the culture of a book-furnishing age to intellectual consciousness and expansion.

Self-sufficing strength and clear-sightedness were in her combined with a power of deep and calm affection. The page of her life is one of unsullied dignity.

Her appeal to posterity is one against the injustice of those who committed such crimes in the name of liberty. She makes it in behalf of herself and her husband. I would put beside it on the shelf a little volume, containing a similar appeal from the verdict of contemporaries to that of mankind, that of Godwin in behalf of his wife, the celebrated, the by most men detested Mary Wolstone-craft.[7] In his view it was an appeal from the injustice of those who did such wrong in the name of virtue.

Were this little book interesting for no other cause, it would be so for the generous affection evinced under the peculiar circumstances. This man had courage to love and honor this woman in the face of the world's verdict, and of all that was repulsive in her own past history. He believed he saw of what soul she was, and that the thoughts she had struggled to act out were noble. He loved her and he defended her for the meaning and intensity of her inner life. It was a good fact.

Mary Wolstonecraft, like Madame Dudevant[8] (commonly known as George Sand) in our day, was a woman whose existence better proved the need of some new interpretation of woman's rights, than anything she wrote. Such women as these, rich in genius, of most tender sympathies, and capable of high virtue and a chastened harmony, ought not to find themselves by birth in a place so narrow, that in breaking bonds they become outlaws. Were there as much room in the world for such, as in Spenser's poem for Britomart, they would not run their heads so wildly against its laws. They find their way at last to purer air, but the world will not take off the brand it has set upon them. The champion of the rights of woman found in Godwin one who would plead her own cause like a brother. George Sand smokes, wears male attire, wishes to be addressed as Mon frère;[9] perhaps, if she found those who were as brothers indeed, she would not care whether she were brother or sister.

We rejoice to see that she, who expresses such a painful contempt for men in most of her works, as shows she must have known great wrong from them, in La Roche Mauprat[1] depicting one raised, by the workings of love, from the depths of savage sensualism to a moral and intellectual life. It was love for a pure object, for a steadfast woman, one of those who, the Italian said, could make the stair to heaven.

Women like Sand will speak now, and cannot be silenced; their characters and their eloquence alike foretell an era when such as they shall easier learn to lead true lives. But though such forebode, not such shall be the parents of it. Those who would reform the world must show that they do not speak in the heat of wild impulse; their lives must be unstained by passionate error; they must be severe lawgivers to themselves. As to their transgressions and opinions, it may be observed, that the resolve of Eloisa to be only the mistress of Abelard, was that of one who saw the contract of marriage a seal of degradation.[2] Wher-ever abuses of this sort are seen, the timid will suffer, the bold protest. But society is in the right to outlaw them till she has revised her law, and she must be taught to do so, by one who speaks with authority, not in anger and haste.

If Godwin's choice of the calumniated authoress of the "Rights of Woman," for his honored wife, be a sign of a new era, no less so is an article of great

---

7. *Memoirs of the Author of "A Vindication of the Rights of Woman"* (1798) by William Godwin (1756–1836); Mary Wollstonecraft (1759–1797) married Godwin shortly before her death in childbirth.
8. Amandine Aurore Lucile Dudevant (1804–1876), French Romantic novelist, scandalous for her succes-sion of lovers and mannish attire but admired by those like Fuller who saw her as crusader for the liberation of women.
9. Old friend and colleague (French); my brother (lit-eral trans.).
1. Drama by George Sand.
2. In her famous letters Eloisa steadfastly refused to marry Abelard, because marriage would force him to give up his teaching of theology within the church.

learning and eloquence, published several years since in an English review, where the writer, in doing full justice to Eloisa, shows his bitter regret that she lives not now to love him, who might have known better how to prize her love than did the egotistical Abelard.

These marriages, these characters, with all their imperfections, express an onward tendency. They speak of aspiration of soul, of energy of mind, seeking clearness and freedom. Of a like promise are the tracts now publishing by Goodwyn Barmby[3] (the European Pariah as he calls himself) and his wife Catherine. Whatever we may think of their measures, we see them in wedlock, the two minds are wed by the only contract that can permanently avail, of a common faith, and a common purpose.

We might mention instances, nearer home, of minds, partners in work and in life, sharing together, on equal terms, public and private interests, and which have not on any side that aspect of offence which characterizes the attitude of the last named; persons who steer straight onward, and in our freer life have not been obliged to run their heads against any wall. But the principles which guide them might, under petrified or oppressive institutions, have made them warlike, paradoxical, or, in some sense, Pariahs. The phenomenon is different, the last the same, in all these cases. Men and women have been obliged to build their house from the very foundation. If they found stone ready in the quarry, they took it peaceably, otherwise they alarmed the country by pulling down old towers to get materials.

These are all instances of marriage as intellectual companionship. The parties meet mind to mind, and a mutual trust is excited which can buckler them against a million. They work together for a common purpose, and, in all these instances, with the same implement, the pen.

A pleasing expression in this kind is afforded by the union in the names of the Howitts.[4] William and Mary Howitt we heard named together for years, supposing them to be brother and sister; the equality of labors and reputation, even so, was auspicious, more so, now we find them man and wife. In his late work on Germany, Howitt mentions his wife with pride, as one among the constellation of distinguished English women, and in a graceful, simple manner.

In naming these instances we do not mean to imply that community of employment is an essential to union of this sort, more than to the union of friendship. Harmony exists no less in difference than in likeness, if only the same key-note govern both parts. Woman the poem, man the poet; woman the heart, man the head; such divisions are only important when they are never to be transcended. If nature is never bound down, nor the voice of inspiration stifled, that is enough. We are pleased that women should write and speak, if they feel the need of it, from having something to tell; but silence for a hundred years would be as well, if that silence be from divine command, and not from man's tradition.

While Goetz von Berlichingen[5] rides to battle, his wife is busy in the kitchen; but difference of occupation does not prevent that community of life, that perfect esteem, with which he says,

"Whom God loves, to him gives he such a wife!"

3. Minor British publisher.
4. William Howitt (1792–1879) and Mary Howitt (1799–1888), prolific British authors and translators.
5. German knight (1481–1562), a sort of Robin Hood, familiar to Fuller from Goethe's play *Göetz von Berlichingen*.

Manzoni thus dedicates his Adelchi.[6]

"To his beloved and venerated wife, Enrichetta Luigia Blondel, who, with conjugal affections and maternal wisdom, has preserved a virgin mind, the author dedicates this Adelchi, grieving that he could not, by a more splendid and more durable monument, honor the dear name and the memory of so many virtues."

The relation could not be fairer, nor more equal, if she too had written poems. Yet the position of the parties might have been the reverse as well; the woman might have sung the deeds, given voice to the life of the man, and beauty would have been the result, as we see in pictures of Arcadia[7] the nymph singing to the shepherds, or the shepherd with his pipe allures the nymphs, either makes a good picture. The sounding lyre requires not muscular strength, but energy of soul to animate the hand which can control it. Nature seems to delight in varying her arrangements, as if to show that she will be fettered by no rule, and we must admit the same varieties that she admits.

I have not spoken of the higher grade of marriage union, the religious, which may be expressed as pilgrimage towards a common shrine. This includes the others; home sympathies, and household wisdom, for these pilgrims must know how to assist one another to carry their burdens along the dusty way; intellectual communion, for how sad it would be on such a journey to have a companion to whom you could not communicate thoughts and aspirations, as they sprang to life, who would have no feeling for the more and more glorious prospects that open as we advance, who would never see the flowers that may be gathered by the most industrious traveler. It must include all these. Such a fellow pilgrim Count Zinzendorf[8] seems to have found in his countess of whom he thus writes:

"Twenty-five years' experience has shown me that just the help-mate whom I have is the only one that could suit my vocation, Who else could have so carried through my family affairs? Who lived so spotlessly before the world? Who so wisely aided me in my rejection of a dry morality? Who so clearly set aside the Pharisaism[9] which, as years passed, threatened to creep in among us? Who so deeply discerned as to the spirits of delusion which sought to bewilder us? Who would have governed my whole economy so wisely, richly, and hospitably when circumstances commanded? Who have taken indifferently the part of servant or mistress, without on the one side affecting an especial spirituality, on the other being sullied by any worldly pride? Who, in a community where all ranks are eager to be on a level, would, from wise and real causes, have known how to maintain inward and outward distinctions? Who, without a murmur, have seen her husband encounter such dangers by land and sea? Who undertaken with him and sustained such astonishing pilgrimages? Who amid such difficulties always held up her head, and supported me?

6. A tragedy (1822) by Alessandro Manzoni (1735–1873), Italian writer.
7. Pastoral district of the Peloponnesus in Greece, symbolic of rustic simplicity and contentment.
8. Nikolas Ludwig, Count von Zinzendorf (1700–1760) German leader of the Moravian church, or the Bohemian Brethren, a Protestant sect founded in Bohemia in 1457, influential both in Europe and in the Moravian settlements in the American colonies, which he visited.
9. Self-righteous hypocrites, from the Jewish sect whom Jesus condemned as whitened sepulchres (Matthew 23.27), "which indeed appear beautiful outward, but are within full of dead men's bones, and of all uncleanness."

Who found so many hundred thousands and acquitted them on her own credit? And, finally, who, of all human beings, would so well understand and interpret to others my inner and outer being as this one, of such nobleness in her way of thinking, such great intellectual capacity, and free from the theological perplexities that enveloped me?"

An observer[1] adds this testimony.

"We may in many marriages regard it as the best arrangement, if the man has so much advantage over his wife that she can, without much thought of her own, be, by him, led and directed, as by a father. But it was not so with the Count and his consort. She was not made to be a copy; she was an original; and, while she loved and honored him, she thought for herself on all subjects with so much intelligence, that he could and did look on her as a sister and friend also."

Such a woman is the sister and friend of all beings, as the worthy man is their brother and helper.

* * *

[The Great Radical Dualism]

For woman, if by a sympathy as to outward condition, she is led to aid the enfranchisement of the slave, must no less so, by inward tendency, to favor measures which promise to bring the world more thoroughly and deeply into harmony with her nature. When the lamb takes place of the lion as the emblem of nations, both women and men will be as children of one spirit, perpetual learners of the word and doers thereof, not hearers only.

A writer in a late number of the New York Pathfinder, in two articles headed "Femality," has uttered a still more pregnant word than any we have named. He views woman truly from the soul, and not from society, and the depth and leading of his thoughts is proportionably remarkable. He views the feminine nature as a harmonizer of the vehement elements, and this has often been hinted elsewhere; but what he expresses more forcibly is the lyrical, the inspiring and inspired apprehensiveness of her being.

Had I room to dwell upon this topic, I could not say anything so precise, so near the heart of the matter, as may be found in that article; but, as it is, I can only indicate, not declare, my view.

There are two aspects of woman's nature, expressed by the ancients as Muse and Minerva.[2] It is the former to which the writer in the Pathfinder looks. It is the latter which Wordsworth has in mind, when he says,

> "With a placid brow,
> Which woman ne'er should forfeit, keep thy vow."[3]

The especial genius of woman I believe to be electrical[4] in movement, intuitive in function, spiritual in tendency. She is great not so easily in classifica-

---

1. "Spangenberg" [Fuller's note]. August Gotlieb Spengenberg (1704–1792), successor to Count von Zinzendorf, bishop of the Moravian Brethren.
2. The poetical or artistic aspect, embodied in the Muses, goddesses of song and poetry and the arts and sciences, and the intellectually serene aspect, embod-

ied in Minerva, goddess of wisdom.
3. Slightly misquoted from Liberty: Sequel to the Preceding, published 1835.
4. Darting in sparklike fashion; the root in New Latin, electricus, means "like amber," from the fact that amber gives off sparks when rubbed.

tion, or re-creation, as in an instinctive seizure of causes, and a simple breathing out of what she receives that has the singleness of life, rather than the selecting or energizing of art.

More native to her is it to be the living model of the artist, than to set apart from herself any one form in objective reality; more native to inspire and receive the poem than to create it. In so far as soul is in her completely developed, all soul is the same; but as far as it is modified in her as woman, it flows, it breathes, it sings, rather than deposits soil, or finishes work, and that which is especially feminine flushes in blossom the face of earth, and pervades like air and water all this seeming solid globe, daily renewing and purifying its life. Such may be the especially feminine element, spoken of as Femality. But it is no more the order of nature that it should be incarnated pure in any form, than that the masculine energy should exist unmingled with it in any form.

Male and female represent the two sides of the great radical dualism. But, in fact, they are perpetually passing into one another. Fluid hardens to solid, solid rushes to fluid. There is no wholly masculine man, no purely feminine woman.

History jeers at the attempts of physiologists to bind great original laws by the forms which flow from them. They make a rule; they say from observation what can and cannot be. In vain! Nature provides exceptions to every rule. She sends women to battle, and sets Hercules spinning;[5] she enables women to bear immense burdens, cold, and frost; she enables the man, who feels maternal love, to nourish his infant like a mother. Of late she plays still gayer pranks. Not only she deprives organizations, but organs, of a necessary end. She enables people to read with the top of the head, and see with the pit of the stomach. Presently she will make a female Newton, and a male Syren.[6]

Man partakes of the feminine in the Apollo, woman of the masculine as Minerva.

Let us be wise and not impede the soul. Let her work as she will. Let us have one creative energy, one incessant revelation. Let it take what form it will, and let us not bind it by the past to man or woman, black or white. Jove sprang from Rhea, Pallas from Jove.[7] So let it be.

If it has been the tendency of the past remarks to call woman rather to the Minerva side,—if I, unlike the more generous writer, have spoken from society no less than the soul,—let it be pardoned. It is love that has caused this, love for many incarcerated souls, that might be freed could the idea of religious self-dependence be established in them, could the weakening habit of dependence on others be broken up.

Every relation, every gradation of nature, is incalculably precious, but only to the soul which is poised upon itself, and to whom no loss, no change, can bring dull discord, for it is in harmony with the central soul.

If any individual live too much in relations, so that he becomes a stranger to the resources of his own nature, he falls after a while into a distraction, or imbecility, from which he can only be cured by a time of isolation, which gives the renovating fountains time to rise up. With a society it is the same. Many minds, deprived of the traditionary or instinctive means of passing a

5. I.e., sets the strongest men to domestic tasks.
6. In the inversion of sexual stereotypes, a male would be as alluring as the Syrens (or Sirens), Greek sea nymphs who lured mariners into shipwreck on the rocks surrounding their island. Isaac Newton

(1642–1727), English mathematician.
7. In Greek mythology, Rhea, the sister and wife of Cronus, bore Jove. Pallas Athena sprang from Jove's skull, fully grown and fully armed.

cheerful existence, must find help in self-impulse or perish. It is therefore that while any elevation, in the view of union, is to be hailed with joy, we shall not decline celibacy as the great fact of the time. It is one from which no vow, no arrangement, can at present save a thinking mind. For now the rowers are pausing on their oars, they wait a change before they can pull together. All tends to illustrate the thought of a wise contemporary. Union is only possible to those who are units. To be fit for relations in time, souls, whether of man or woman, must be able to do without them in the spirit.

It is therefore that I would have woman lay aside all thought, such as she habitually cherishes, of being taught and led by men. I would have her, like the Indian girl, dedicate herself to the Sun, the Sun of Truth, and go no where if his beams did not make clear the path. I would have her free from compromise, from complaisance, from helplessness, because I would have her good enough and strong enough to love one and all beings, from the fulness, not the poverty of being.

Men, as at present instructed, will not help this work, because they also are under the slavery of habit. I have seen with delight their poetic impulses. A sister is the fairest ideal and how nobly Wordsworth, and even Byron, have written of a sister.[8]

There is no sweeter sight than to see a father with his little daughter. Very vulgar men become refined to the eye when leading a little girl by the hand. At that moment the right relation between the sexes seems established, and you feel as if the man would aid in the noblest purpose, if you ask him in behalf of his little daughter. Once two fine figures stood before me, thus. The father of very intellectual aspect, his falcon eye softened by affection as he looked down on his fair child, she the image of himself, only more graceful and brilliant in expression. I was reminded of Southey's Kehama,[9] when lo, the dream was rudely broken. They were talking of education, and he said.

"I shall not have Maria brought too forward. If she knows too much, she will never find a husband; superior women hardly ever can."

"Surely," said his wife, with a blush, "you wish Maria to be as good and wise as she can, whether it will help her to marriage or not."

"No," he persisted, "I want her to have a sphere and a home, and some one to protect her when I am gone."

It was a trifling incident, but made a deep impression. I felt that the holiest relations fail to instruct the unprepared and perverted mind. If this man, indeed, would have looked at it on the other side, he was the last that would have been willing to have been taken himself for the home and protection he could give, but would have been much more likely to repeat the tale of Alcibiades with his phials.

But men do *not* look at both sides, and women must leave off asking them and being influenced by them, but retire within themselves, and explore the groundwork of being till they find their peculiar secret. Then when they come forth again, renovated and baptized, they will know how to turn all dross to gold, and will be rich and free though they live in a hut, tranquil, if in a crowd. Then their sweet singing shall not be from passionate impulse, but the

8. Fuller is thinking of the various tributes by William Wordsworth to his sister Dorothy and Lord Byron to his half-sister Augusta Leigh. Only later in the century was evidence presented of Byron's incest with Augusta, and not until the late 20th century did scholars begin to debate the possibility that William and Dorothy Wordsworth might have committed incest. Fuller's examples are unfortunate, not deliberately ironic.
9. Robert Southey's *The Curse of Kehama* (1810), a rhymed Oriental tale.

lyrical overflow of a divine rapture, and a new music shall be elucidated from this many-chorded world.

Grant her then for a while the armor and the javelin.[1] Let her put from her the press of other minds and meditate in virgin loneliness. The same idea shall reappear in due time as Muse, or Ceres,[2] the all-kindly, patient Earth-Spirit.

I tire every one with my Goethean illustrations. But it cannot be helped.

Goethe, the great mind which gave itself absolutely to the leadings of truth, and let rise through him the waves which are still advancing through the century, was its intellectual prophet. Those who know him, see, daily, his thought fulfilled more and more, and they must speak of it, till his name weary and even nauseate, as all great names have in their time. And I cannot spare the reader, if such there be, his wonderful sight as to the prospects and wants of women.

As his Wilhelm grows in life and advances in wisdom, he becomes acquainted with women of more and more character, rising from Mariana to Macaria.[3]

Macaria, bound with the heavenly bodies in fixed revolutions, the centre of all relations, herself unrelated, expresses the Minerva side.

Mignon, the electrical, inspired lyrical nature.

All these women, though we see them in relations, we can think of as unrelated. They all are very individual, yet seem nowhere restrained. They satisfy for the present, yet arouse an infinite expectation.

The economist Theresa, the benevolent Natalia, the fair Saint, have chosen a path, but their thoughts are not narrowed to it. The functions of life to them are not ends, but suggestions.

Thus to them all things are important, because none is necessary. Their different characters have fair play, and each is beautiful in its minute indications, for nothing is enforced or conventional, but everything, however slight, grows from the essential life of the being.

Mignon and Theresa wear male attire when they like, and it is graceful for them to do so, while Macaria is confined to her arm chair behind the green curtain, and the Fair Saint could not bear a speck of dust on her robe.

All things are in their places in this little world because all is natural and free, just as "there is room for everything out of doors." Yet all is rounded in by natural harmony which will always arise where Truth and Love are sought in the light of freedom.

Goethe's book bodes an era of freedom like its own, of "extraordinary generous seeking," and new revelations. New individualities shall be developed in the actual world, which shall advance upon it as gently as the figures come out upon his canvass.

A profound thinker has said "no married woman can represent the female world, for she belongs to her husband. The idea of woman must be represented by a virgin."

But that is the very fault of marriage, and of the present relation between the sexes, that the woman does belong to the man, instead of forming a whole with him. Were it otherwise there would be no such limitation to the thought.

Woman, self-centred, would never be absorbed by any relation; it would be

---

1. The weapons of Athena, Greek goddess of wisdom.
2. The Roman goddess of agriculture.
3. Feminine characters in Johann Wolfgang von

Goethe's *Wilhelm Meister's Apprenticeship*; other female characters from the same book are named just below.

only an experience to her as to man. It is a vulgar error that love, *a* love to woman is her whole existence; she also is born for Truth and Love in their universal energy. Would she but assume her inheritance, Mary would not be the only Virgin Mother. Not Manzoni[4] alone would celebrate in his wife the virgin mind with the maternal wisdom and conjugal affections. The soul is ever young, ever virgin.

And will not she soon appear? The woman who shall vindicate their birthright for all women; who shall teach them what to claim, and how to use what they obtain? Shall not her name be for her era Victoria, for her country and her life Virginia?[5] Yet predictions are rash; she herself must teach us to give her the fitting name.

1843

4. Another allusion to the preface to Manzoni's *Adelchi.*
5. I.e., shall not her character include both triumphant power (such as made Victoria so fit a name for a queen) and immaculateness (whether literally virginal or not)?

HARRIET BEECHER STOWE
1811–1896

Harriet Beecher was born into a respectable family that was to become famous: her father, Lyman, was a renowned clergyman; two of her brothers, Henry Ward and Edward, were celebrated preachers; and her older sister, Catharine, pioneered in women's education. The family was dominated by the father, who ruled with the kind of wrathful severity that he imagined was the chief characteristic of the God he worshiped and feared. The boys were expected to become preachers, the girls to marry preachers.

Stowe began school in 1816 in Litchfield, Connecticut, and when Catharine established the Hartford Female Seminary in 1824, she joined her sister there. Their father became president of the recently founded Lane Theological Seminary in Cincinnati in 1832, and the sisters reluctantly rejoined the family in this "London of the West," as he described what was still a small, raw frontier town. Harriet Stowe continued to work for her domineering older sister at the Western Female Institute she initiated, and seemed headed for a lifetime as an unknown, housebound spinster. She escaped this fate in part by converting, at great personal cost given her heavy domestic duties, her lifelong interest in writing into magazine stories that in the 1830s and 1840s earned her a few welcomed dollars. In 1836 she married Calvin Ellis Stowe, one of the leading professors at Lane, and bore the first four of their seven children within four years. The fees from her writing were useful in keeping the family on the respectable side of genteel poverty.

After eighteen years living across the Ohio River from slaveholding communities—and absorbing from fugitive slaves and visits to the South a personal knowledge of the institution of slavery—Stowe returned to New England in 1850 when her husband took a professorship at Bowdoin College in Brunswick, Maine. Partly inspired by the moral outrage that greeted the Fugitive Slave Act of 1850 (that allowed owners to pursue and recover their "property" in free states), partly liberated by her return to her New England roots, perhaps—as she claimed late in life—inspired by a God-sent image of a slave suffering, being beaten, yet forgiving his tormentors, *Uncle Tom's Cabin, or The Man That Was a Thing* (as it was originally titled) was conceived early in February 1851.

The novel began serially in the *National Era* on June 5, 1851, and the last installment appeared on April 1, 1852. The *National Era* was essentially, but not exclusively, devoted to promoting abolitionist principles, but it did so with less evangelical indignation than William Lloyd Garrison's *Liberator*. Even so, Stowe did not find a book publisher easily. When the novel did appear, however, it was an overnight success. It sold 350,000 copies during the first year, and since then has been published in some forty languages and has been read by millions of people around the world. The power of the novel unquestionably comes from the investment of the author's sense of her own suffering and oppression (as well as her determination to be free) in the characters of Tom and his fellow slave Eliza, the protagonists of the book's two main plots.

Stowe did not anticipate the sensation the novel created. To cope with Southern opposition and challenges to its accuracy, she wrote the nonfiction *A Key to Uncle Tom's Cabin*, with documented case histories to support what she had portrayed fictionally. *Dred: A Tale of the Great Dismal Swamp* (1856) was another antislavery novel, which may best be understood as an unsuccessful attempt to repeat the theme and extend the argument of her masterpiece: that a society resting on slavery could not long survive.

Because *Uncle Tom's Cabin* was such a phenomenal success, it is easy to forget that Stowe was a prolific writer for another thirty-five years, publishing regularly in *Atlantic Monthly* from the time of its founding in 1857 and in other leading periodicals on a wide variety of subjects and in a great many literary forms. Indeed, many critics feel that novels such as *The Pearl of Orr's Island* (1862), in which she depicts realistically rural life in Maine, and *Oldtown Folks* (1869), which details domestic life on the north shore of Massachusetts, constitute the true basis of her claim to our attention. There can be no question that her attention to local legends and dialects, her gift for creating humorous characters, and her capacity for compelling storytelling influenced many later regional writers, including Sarah Orne Jewett and Mary Wilkins Freeman.

Stowe's life was a sharply alternating mixture of success and notoriety and personal tragedy and pain. After *Uncle Tom's Cabin* broke upon the world, she traveled widely, met heads of state such as Abraham Lincoln and Queen Victoria, and lived among the rich and famous. At the same time, two sons died very young, another was an alcoholic, and she was deeply distressed by the scandal that touched her famous brother Henry Ward (who was tried for adultery). Her seventieth birthday was something of a national event, but her husband died a few years later and she ended her life an infirm recluse.

From Uncle Tom's Cabin; or Life among the Lowly[1]

Chapter VII. *The Mother's Struggle*

It is impossible to conceive of a human creature more wholly desolate and forlorn than Eliza, when she turned her footsteps from Uncle Tom's cabin.

Her husband's sufferings and dangers, the danger of her child, all blended in her mind with a confused and stunning sense of the risk she was running in leaving the only home she had ever known, and cutting loose from the protec-

---

1. *Uncle Tom's Cabin* was first published serially; the present chapter appeared in the *National Era* (July 19, 1851), the source of the present text. Before this selection opens, Mr. Shelby has sold his slaves Uncle Tom and Harry, young son of Eliza, to Dan Haley, a slave trader. A devout Christian, Tom accepts his fate as best he can, always hoping to return to his home in Kentucky. Eliza, however, flees across the Ohio River with her son.

tion of a friend whom she loved and revered. Then there was the parting from every familiar object—the place where she had grown up, the trees under which she had played, the groves where she had walked many an evening in happier days, by the side of her young husband—everything, as it lay in the clear frosty moonlight, seemed to speak reproachfully to her, and ask her whither could she go from a home like that?

But stronger than all was maternal love, wrought into a paroxysm of frenzy by the near approach of a fearful danger. Her boy was old enough to have walked by her side, and in an indifferent case she would only have led him by the hand; but now the bare thought of putting him out of her arms made her shudder, and she strained him to her bosom with a convulsive grasp as she went rapidly forward. The frosty ground creaked beneath her feet, and she trembled at the sound; every quaking leaf and fluttering shadow sent the blood backward to her heart, and quickened her footsteps. She wondered within herself at the strength that seemed to be come upon her, for she felt the weight of her boy as if it had been a feather, and every flutter of fear seemed to increase the supernatural strength that bore her on, while from her pale lips burst forth, in frequent ejaculations, the prayer to a Friend above—"Lord, help! Lord, save me!"

If it were *your* Harry, mother, or your Willie, that were going to be torn from you by a brutal trader, to-morrow morning—if you had seen the man, and heard that the papers were signed and delivered, and you had only from twelve o'clock till morning to make good your escape, how fast could *you* walk? How many miles could you make in those few brief hours, with the darling at your bosom—the little sleepy head on your shoulder—the small, soft arms trustingly holding on to your neck?

For the child slept; at first the novelty and alarm kept him waking; but his mother so hurriedly repressed every breath or sound, and so assured him that if he were only still, she would certainly save him, that he clung quietly round her neck, only asking, as he found himself sinking to sleep—

"Mother, I don't need to keep awake, do I?"

"No, my darling; sleep if you want to."

"But mother, if I do get asleep, you won't let him get me."

"No! so may God help me!" said his mother, with a paler cheek and a brighter light in her large dark eyes.

"You're sure, ain't you, mother?"

"Yes, *sure!*" said the mother, in a voice that startled herself, for it seemed to her to come from a spirit within, that was no part of her; and the boy dropped his little weary head on her shoulder, and was soon asleep. How the touch of those warm arms, the gentle breathings that came in her neck, seemed to add fire and spirit to her movements. It seemed to her as if strength poured into her in electric streams, from every gentle touch and movement of her sleeping, confiding child. Sublime is the dominion of the mind over the body, that for a time can make flesh and nerve impregnable, and string the sinews, like steel, so that the weak become so mighty!

The boundaries of the farm, the grove, the wood-lot, passed by her dizzily as she passed on, and still she walked, leaving one familiar object after another, slacking not, pausing not, till reddening daylight found her many a long mile from all traces of any familiar objects upon the open highway.

She had often been with her mistress, to visit some connections in the little village of T———, not far from the Ohio river, and knew the road well. To go thither, to escape across the Ohio river, were the first hurried outlines of her plan of escape—beyond which she could only hope in God.

When horses and vehicles began to move along the highway, with that keen and alert perception peculiar to a state of excitement, and which seems to be a sort of inspiration, she became aware that her headlong pace and distracted air might bring on her remark and suspicion. She therefore put the boy on the ground, and, adjusting her dress and bonnet, she walked on at as rapid a pace as she thought consistent with the preservation of appearances. In her little bundle she had provided a store of cakes and apples, which she used as expedients for quickening the speed of the child—rolling the apple some yards before them, when the boy would run with all his might after it; and this ruse, often repeated, carried them over many a half mile.

After a while they came to a thick patch of woodland, through which murmured a clear brook. As the child complained of hunger and thirst, she climbed over the fence with him; and sitting down behind a large rock which concealed them from the road, she gave him a breakfast out of her little package. The boy wondered and grieved that she could not eat, and when, putting his arms around her neck, he tried to wedge some of his cake into her mouth, it seemed to her that the rising in her throat would choke her.

"No, no, Harry, darling, mother can't eat till you are safe. We must go on—on—till we come to the river." And she hurried again into the road, and again constrained herself to walk regularly and composedly forward.

She was many miles past any neighborhood where she was personally known. If she should chance to meet any who knew her, she reflected that the well-known kindness of the family would be of itself a blind to suspicion, as making it an unlikely supposition that she could be a fugitive. As she was also so white as not to be known as of colored lineage, without a critical survey, and her child was white also, it was much easier for her to pass on unsuspected.

On this presumption, she stopped at noon at a neat farm-house, to rest herself, and buy some dinner for her child and self—for as the danger decreased with the distance, the supernatural tension of the nervous system lessened, and she found herself both weary and hungry.

The good woman, kindly and gossiping, seemed rather pleased than otherwise, with having somebody come in to talk with, and accepted without examination Eliza's statement that she "was going on a little piece to spend a week with her friends"—all which she hoped in her heart might prove strictly true.

An hour before sunset she entered the village of T———, by the Ohio river, weary and footsore, but still strong in heart. Her first glance was at the river, which lay, like Jordan,[2] between her and the Canaan of liberty on the other side.

It was now early spring, and the river was swollen and turbulent; great cakes of floating ice were swinging heavily to and fro in the turbid waters. Owing to the peculiar form of the shore on the Kentucky side, the land bending far out into the water, the ice had been lodged and detained in great quantities, and the narrow channel which swept round the bend was full of ice, piled one cake over another—thus forming a temporary barrier to the descending ice,

---

2. The river in Palestine over which the Israelites crossed into Canaan, the land of milk and honey, after their forty-year exodus in the desert (Exodus 3.17).

which lodged and formed a great undulating raft, filling up the whole river, and extending almost to the Kentucky shore.

Eliza stood for a moment contemplating this unfavorable aspect of things, which she saw at once must prevent the usual ferry-boat from running, and then turned into a small public house on the bank, to make a few inquiries.

The hostess, who was busy in various fizzing and stewing operations over the fire, preparatory to the evening meal, stopped, with a fork in her hand, as Eliza's sweet and plaintive voice arrested her.

"What is it?" she said.

"Isn't there any ferry or boat that takes people over to B—— now?" she said.

"No, indeed," said the woman, "the boats has stopped running."

Eliza's look of dismay and disappointment struck the woman, and she said, inquiringly—

"May be your wanting to get over?—anybody sick? ye seem mighty anxious."

"I've got a child that's very dangerous," said Eliza. "I never heard of it till last night, and I've walked quite a piece to-day, in hopes to get to the ferry."

"Well, now, that's onlucky," said the woman, whose motherly sympathies were much aroused; "I'm re'ely consarned for ye. Solomon!" she called, from the window, towards a small back building. A man in leather apron and very dirty hands appeared at the door.

"I say, Sol," said the woman, "is that ar man going to tote them bar'ls over to-night?"

"He said he should try, if twas any way prudent," said the man.

"There's a man a piece down here, that's going over with some truck this evening, if he durs'to; he'll be in here to supper to-night, so you'd better set down and wait. That's a sweet little fellow," added the woman, offering him a cake.

But the child, wholly exhausted, cried with weariness.

"Poor fellow! he isn't used to walking, and I've hurried him on so," said Eliza.

"Well, take him into this room," said the woman, opening into a small bed-room, where stood a comfortable bed. Eliza laid the weary boy upon it, and held his hands in hers till he was fast asleep. For her there was no rest. As a fire in her bones, the thought of the pursuer urged her on, and she gazed with longing eyes on the sullen, surging waters that lay between her and liberty.

Here we must take our leave of her for the present, to follow the course of her pursuers.

Though Mrs. Shelby had promised that the dinner should be hurried on table, yet it was soon seen, as the thing has often been seen before, that it required more than one to make a bargain. So, although the order was fairly given out in Haley's hearing, and carried to Aunt Chloe[3] by at least half a dozen juvenile messengers, that dignitary only gave certain very gruff snorts, and tosses of her head, and went on with every operation in an unusually leisurely and circumstantial manner. For some singular reason, an impression seemed to reign among the servants generally, that missis would not be partic-

---

3. Uncle Tom's wife and Shelby's cook.

ularly disobliged by delay, and it was wonderful what a number of counter accidents occurred constantly, to retard the course of things. One luckless wight contrived to upset the gravy, and then gravy had to be got up *de novo*,[4] with due care and formality, Aunt Chloe watching and stirring with dogged precision, answering shortly to all suggestions of haste, that she "warnt a going to have raw gravy on the table, to help nobody's catchings."[5] One tumbled down with the water, and had to go to the spring for more; and another precipitated the butter into the path of events, and there was from time to time giggling news brought into the kitchen that mass'r Haley was mighty oneasy, and that he couldn't sit in his cheer no ways, but was a walkin and stalkin to the winders and through the porch.

"Sarves him right!" said Aunt Chloe, indignantly. "He'll get wus nor oneasy one of these days, if he don't mend his ways. *His* master'll be sending for him, and then see how he'll look."

"He'll go to torment, and no mistake," said little Jake.

"He desarves it!" said Aunt Chloe, grimly, "he's broke a many many many hearts, I tell ye all!" she said, stopping, with a fork uplifted in her hands; "it's like what mass'r George reads in Ravelations—souls a callin under the altar! and a callin on the Lord for vengeance on sich! and by and by, the Lord he'll hear em—so he will!"[6]

Aunt Chloe, who was much revered in the kitchen, was listened to with open mouth; and the dinner being now fairly sent in, the whole kitchen was at leisure to gossip with her, and to listen to her remarks.

"Sich'll be burnt up forever, and no mistake! wont ther," said Andy.

"I'd be glad to see it, I'll be boun," said little Jake.

"Chil'en!" said a voice, that made them all start. It was Uncle Tom, who had come in, and stood listening to the conversation at the door.

"Chil'en!" he said, "I'm afeard you don't know what ye're sayin. Forever is a *dre'ful* word, chil'en; its awful to think on't. You oughtenter wish that ar to any human crittur!"

"We wouldn't to anybody but the soul-drivers,"[7] said Andy; "nobody can help wishing it to them, they's so awful wicked."

"Dont natur herself kinder cry out on em?" said Aunt Chloe. "Dont dey tear der suckin baby right off his mother's breast, and sell him, and der little children as is crying and holding on by her clothes; dont dey pull em off and sells em? Dont dey tear wife and husband apart?" said Aunt Chloe, beginning to cry—"when it's jest takin the very life on em—and all the while does they feel one bit—dont dey drink and smoke, and take it oncommon easy? Lor, if the devil don't get them, what's he good for?" And Aunt Chloe covered her face with her checked apron, and began to sob in good earnest.

"Pray for them that 'spitefully use you, the good book says," says Tom.[8]

"Pray for 'em!" said Aunt Chloe; "Lor, it's too tough! I can't pray for 'em."

"It's natur, Chloe, and natur's strong," said Tom, "but the Lord's grace is stronger; besides, you oughter think what an awful state a poor crittur's soul's

---

4. Anew (Latin).
5. Referring to Dan Haley's pursuit of Eliza and Harry.
6. "And when he had opened the fifth seal, I saw under the altar the souls of them that were slain for the word of God, and for the testimony which they held" (Revelation 6.9).

7. A common term for clergymen, but here it apparently refers to the slave traders.
8. "Love your enemies, bless them that curse you, do good to them that hate you, and pray for them which despitefully use you, and persecute you" (Matthew 5.44).

in that'll do them ar things—you oughter thank God that you aint *like* him, Chloe, I'm sure I'd rather be sold ten thousand times over than to have all that ar poor crittur's got to answer for."

"So'd I, a heap," said Jake. "Lor! *shouldn't* we cotch it, Andy?"

Andy shrugged his shoulders, and gave an acquiescent whistle.

"I'm glad mass'r didn't go off this morning as he looked to," said Tom; "that ar hurt me more than the sellin—it did," said Tom. "Mebbe it might have been natural for him, but 'twould have come desp't hard on me, as has known him from a baby; but I've seen mass'r, and I begin ter feel sort o' reconciled to the Lord's will now. Mass'r couldn't help hisself; he did right, but I'm feared things will be kinder goin to rack when I'm gone. Mass'r can't be spected to be a pryin round everywhar, as Joe done, a keepin up all the ends. The boys all means well, but they's powerful careless! That ar troubles me."

The bell here rang, and Tom was summoned to the parlor.

"Tom," said his master, kindly, "I want you to notice that I give this gentleman bonds to forfeit a thousand dollars if you are not on the spot when he wants you; he's going to-day to look after his other business, and you can have the day to yourself. Go anywhere you like, boy."

"Thank you, mass'r," said Tom.

"And mind yerself," said the trader, "and don't come it over your master with any o' yer nigger tricks, for I'll take every cent out of him if you aint thar. If he'd hear to me, he wouldn't trust any on ye—slippery as eels!"

"Mass'r," said Tom—and he stood very straight—"I was just eight years old when ole missis put you into my arms, and you wasn't a year old. 'Thar,' says she, 'Tom, that's to be *your* young mass'r; take good care on him,' says she. And now I jist ask you, mass'r, have I ever broke word to you, or gone contrary to you, specially since I was a Christian?"

Mr. Shelby was fairly overcome, and the tears rose to his eyes.

"My good boy," said he, "the Lord knows you say but the truth! and if I was able to help it, all the world shouldn't buy you."

"And sure as I am a Christian woman," said Mrs. Shelby, "you shall be redeemed as soon as I can any way bring together means. Sir," she said to Haley, "take good account of who you sell him to, and let me know."

"Lor, yes, for that matter," said the trader, "I may bring him up in a year, not much the woss for wear, and trade him back."

"I'll trade with you then, and make it for your advantage," said Mrs. Shelby.

"Of course," said the trader, "all's equal with me; lives trade 'em up as down! so I does a good business. All I want is a livin, you know, ma'am—that's all any on us wants, I spose."

Mr. and Mrs. Shelby both felt annoyed and degraded by the familiar impudence of the trader, and yet both saw the absolute necessity of putting a constraint on their feelings. The more hopelessly sordid and insensible he appeared, the greater became Mrs. Shelby's dread his succeeding in recapturing Eliza and her child, and of course the greater her motive for detaining him by every female artifice. She therefore graciously smiled, assented, chatted familiarly, and did all she could to make time pass imperceptibly.

At two o'clock Sam and Andy brought the horses up to the posts, apparently greatly refreshed and invigorated by the scamper of the morning.

Sam was then new oiled from dinner, with an abundance of zealous and ready officiousness. As Haley approached, he was boasting in flourishing style to Andy of the evident and imminent success of the operation, now that he had "farly come to it."

"Your master, I spose, don't keep no dogs," said Haley, thoughtfully, as he prepared to mount.

"Heaps on 'em," said Sam, triumphantly; "thar's Bruno—he's a roarer! and besides that, bout every nigger on us keeps a pup o some natur ur uther."

"Poh!" said Haley—and he said something else, too, with regard to the said dogs, at which Sam muttered—

"I don't see no use cussin on 'em! no way."

"But your master don't keep no dogs (I pretty much know he don't) for trackin out niggers."

Sam knew exactly what he meant but he kept on a look of earnest and desperate simplicity.

"Our dogs all smells round considable sharp. I spect they's the kind, though they han't never had no practice. They's *far* dogs, though, at most anything, if you'd get 'em started. Here, Bruno," he called, whistling to the lumbering Newfoundland, who came pitching tumultuously toward them.

"You go hang!" said Haley, getting up. "Come, tumble up now."

Sam tumbled up accordingly, dexterously contriving to tickle Andy as he did so, which occasioned Andy to split out into a laugh, greatly to Haley's indignation, who made a cut at him with his riding whip.

"I's astonished at yer, Andy," said Sam, with awful gravity. "This yer's a seris bisness, Andy. Yer musn't be a makin game. Thus yer aint no way to help mass'r."

"I shall take the straight road to the river," said Haley, decidedly, after they had come to the boundaries of the estate. "I know the way of all of 'em—they makes tracks for the underground."[9]

"Sartin," said Sam, "dat's de idee. Mass'r Haley hits de thing right in de middle. Now, der's two roads to de river—de dirt road and der pike—which mass'r mean to take?"

Andy looked up innocently at Sam, surprised at hearing this new geographical fact, but instantly confirmed what he said by a vehement reiteration.

"Cause," said Sam, "I'd ruther be clined to magine that Lizy'd take de dirt road, bein it's the least travelled."

Haley, notwithstanding that he was a very old bird, and naturally inclined to be suspicious of chaff, was rather brought up by this view of the case.

"If yer warn't both on yer such cussed liars now!" he said, contemplatively, as he pondered a moment——

The pensive, reflecting tone in which this was spoken appeared to amuse Andy prodigiously, and he drew a little behind, and shook so as apparently to run a great risk of falling off his horse, while Sam's face was immovably composed into the most doleful gravity.

"Course," said Sam, "mass'r can do as he'd ruther; go the straight road, if mass'r thinks best—it's all one to us. Now, when I study pon it, I think de straight road de best, *decidedly.*"

"She would naturally go a lonesome way," said Haley, thinking aloud, and not minding Sam's remark.

9. Although many Northern sympathizers harbored runaway slaves from the South, the law strictly prohibited this practice. Therefore, the slaves fled to neutral Canada, by means of the "Underground Railroad," the clandestine organization of individuals whose homes were used as "stations" on the escape route.

"Dar aint no sayin!" said Sam; "gals is pecular; they never does nothin yer thinks they will; mose gen'lly the contrar. Gals is nat'lly made contrary; and so if you thinks they've gone one road, it is sartin you'd better go tother, and then you'll be sure to find 'em. Now, my private 'pinion is, Lizy took der dirt road, so I think we'd better take der straight one."

This profound generic view of the female sex did not seem to dispose Haley particularly to the straight road, and he announced decidedly that he should go the other, and asked Sam when they should come to it.

"A little piece ahead," said Sam, giving a wink to Andy with the eye which was on Andy's side of the head; and he added, gravely, "but I've studded on der matter, and I'm quite clar we ought not to go dat ar way. I nebber been over it no way. It's despit lonesome, and we might lose our way—whar we'd come to, de Lord only knows."

"Nevertheless," said Haley, "I shall go that way."

"Now I think on't, I think I hearn 'em tell that dat ar road was all fenced up down by der creek, and thar, an't it, Andy?"

Andy wasn't certain; he'd only "hearn tell" about that road, but never been over it. In short, he was strictly non-committal.

Haley, accustomed to strike the balance of probabilities between lies of greater or lesser magnitude, thought that it lay in favor of the dirt road afore-said. The mention of the thing, he thought he perceived was involuntary on Sam's part at first, and his confused attempts to dissuade him he sat down to a desperate lying on second thoughts, as being unwilling to implicate Eliza.

When, therefore, Sam indicated the road, Haley plunged briskly into it, followed by Sam and Andy.

Now, the road in fact was an old one that had formerly been a thoroughfare to the river, but abandoned for many years after the laying of the new pike. It was open for about an hour's ride, and after that it was cut across by various farms and fences. Sam knew this fact perfectly well—indeed, the road had been so long closed up that Andy had never heard of it. He therefore rode along with an air of dutiful submission, only groaning and vociferating occa-sionally that 'twas "desp't rough, and bad for Jerry's foot."

"Now, I jest give yer warning," said Haley, "I know yer; yer won't get me to turn off this yer road with all yer fussin—so you shet up."

"Mass'r will go his own way," said Sam, with rueful submission, at the same time winking most portentously to Andy, whose delight was now very near the explosive point.

Sam was in wonderful spirits—professed to keep a very brisk lookout—at one time exclaiming that he saw "a gal's bonnet" on the top of some distant eminence, or calling to Andy "if that thar wasn't 'Lizy' down in the hollow," always making these exclamations in some rough or craggy part of the road, where the sudden quickening of speed was a special inconvenience to all par-ties concerned, and thus keeping Haley in a state of constant commotion.

After riding about an hour in this way, the whole party made a precipi-tate and tumultuous descent into a barn-yard belonging to a large farming establishment. Not a soul was in sight, all the hands being employed in the fields; but as the barn stood conspicuously and plainly square across the road, it was evident that their journey in that direction had reached a decided finale.

"Want dat ar what I told mass'r," said Sam, with an air of injured inno-

cence. "How does strange gentlemen spect to know more about a country dan
der natives born and raised!"

"You rascal," said Haley, "you knew all about this."

"Didn't I tell yer I *knowd*, and yer wouldn't believe me. I telled mass'r
'twas all shet up, and fenced up, and I didn't spec we could get thro—Andy
heard me."

It was all too true to be disputed, and the unlucky man had to pocket his
wrath—with the best grace he was able, and all three faced to the right about,
and took up their line of march for the highway.

In consequence of all the various delays, it was only about three-quarters of
an hour after Eliza had laid her child to sleep in the village tavern, that the
party came riding into the same place. Eliza was standing by the window,
looking out in another direction, when Sam's quick eye caught a glimpse of
her. Haley and Andy were two yards behind. At this crisis, Sam contrived to
have his hat blown off, and uttered a loud and characteristic ejaculation,
which startled her at once; she drew suddenly back; the whole train swept by
the window, round to the front door.

A thousand lives seemed to be concentrated in that one moment to Eliza.
Her room opened by a side door to the river. She caught her child, and sprang
down the steps towards it. The trader caught a full glimpse of her just as she
was disappearing down the bank, and, throwing himself from his horse, calling
loudly to Sam and Andy, he was after her like a hound after a deer. In that
dizzy moment her feet to her scarce seemed to touch the ground, and a
moment brought her to the water's edge. Right on behind they came, and,
nerved with strength such as God gives only to the desperate, with one wild
cry, and flying leap, she vaulted sheer over the turbid current by the shore, on
to the raft of ice beyond. It was a desperate leap, impossible to anything but
madness and despair; and Haley, Sam, and Andy, instinctively cried out, and
lifted up their hands as she did it.

The huge green fragment of ice on which she alighted pitched and creaked
as her weight came on it, but she staid there not a moment—with wild cries
and desperate energy she leaped to another and still another cake, stumbling,
leaping, slipping, springing upwards again! Her shoes are gone, her stockings
cut from her feet, while blood marked every step—but she saw nothing, felt
nothing, till dimly as in a dream she saw the Ohio side, and a man helping
her up the bank.

"Yer a brave gal, now, whoever ye ar," said the man, with an oath.

Eliza recognised the voice and face of a man who owned a farm not far
from her old home.

"Oh, Mr. Symmes—save me—do save me—do hide me," said Eliza.

"Why, what's this?" said the man. "Why, if taint Shelby's gal."

"My child! this boy—he'd sold him! There is his mass'r," said she, pointing
to the Kentucky shore. "Oh, Mr. Symmes, you've got a little boy."

"So I have," said the man, as he roughly, but kindly, drew her up the steep
bank. "Besides, you'r a right brave gal. I like grit, wherever I see it."

When they had gained the top of the bank, the man paused.

"I'd be glad to do something for ye," said he, "but then there's nowhar I
could take ye. The best I can do is to tell you to go *thar*," said he, pointing to
a large white house which stood by itself, off the main street of the village.
"Go thar; they'r kind folks. Thar's no kind'r danger but they'll help you—
they'r up to all that sort o' thing."

"The Lord bless you," said Eliza earnestly.

"No casion, no casion in the world," said the man. "What I've done 's of no 'count."

"And, oh, surely, sir, you won't tell any one."

"Go to thunder, gal. What do you take a feller for? In course not," said the man. "Come, now, go along like a likely sensible gal, as you are. You've arnt your liberty, and you shall have it for all me."

The woman folded her child to her bosom, and walked firmly and swiftly away. The man stood and looked after her.

"Shelby, now, mebbe won't think this yer the most neighborly thing in the world, but what's a feller to do? If he catches one of my gals in the same fix, he's welcome to pay back. Somehow I never could see no kind of crittur a strivin' and pantin', and trying to clar theirselves with the dogs artur 'em, and go agin 'em. Besides, I don't see no kind of casion for me to be hunter and catcher for other folks, neither."

So spoke this poor, heathenish Kentuckian, who had not been enlightened on his constitutional relations, and consequently was betrayed into acting in a sort of Christianized manner, which, if he had been better situated and more enlightened, he would not have been left to do.

Haley had stood a perfectly amazed spectator of the scene, till Eliza had disappeared up the bank, when he turned a blank, inquiring look on Sam and Andy.

"That ar was a tolable fair stroke of business!" said Sam.

"The gal's got seven devils in her, I believe!" said Haley. "How like a wildcat she jumped!"

"Wal, now," said Sam, scratching his head, "I hope mass'r'll 'scuse us tryin dat ar road. Don't think I feels spry enough for dat ar, no way!" and Sam gave a hoarse chuckle.

"*You* laugh!" said the trader, with a growl.

"Lord bless ye, mass'r, I couldn't help it, now," said Sam, giving way to the long pent-up delight of his soul. She looked so curis—a leapin and springin, ice a crackin, and only to hear her, plump! ker chunk! kersplash! spring. Lord, how she goes it!" and Sam and Andy laughed till the tears rolled down their cheeks.

"I'll make ye laugh t'other side yer mouths," said the trader, laying about their heads with his riding whip.

Both ducked, and ran shouting up the bank, and were on their horses before he was up.

"Good evening, mass'r," said Sam, with much gravity. "I berry much spect missis be anxious bout Jerry. Mass'r Haley won't want us no longer. Missis wouldn't hear of our ridin the critturs over Lizy's bridge to-night," and, with a facetious poke into Andy's ribs, he started off, followed by the latter, at full speed—their shouts of laughter coming dimly on the wind.

1851, 1852

The Minister's Housekeeper[1]

SCENE.—The shady side of a blueberry-pasture.—Sam Lawson with the boys,
picking blueberries.—Sam, *loq.*[2]

"Wal, you see, boys, 'twas just here,—Parson Carryl's wife, she died along
in the forepart o' March: my cousin Huldy, she undertook to keep house for
him. The way on't was, that Huldy, she went to take care o' Mis' Carryl in the
fust on't, when she fust took sick. Huldy was a tailoress by trade; but then she
was one o' these 'ere facultised[3] persons that has a gift for most any thing, and
that was how Mis' Carryl come to set sech store by her, that, when she was
sick, nothin' would do for her but she must have Huldy round all the time:
and the minister, he said he'd make it good to her all the same, and she
shouldn't lose nothin' by it. And so Huldy, she staid with Mis' Carryl full three
months afore she died, and got to seein' to every thing pretty much round
the place.

"Wal, arter Mis' Carryl died, Parson Carryl, he'd got so kind o' used to
hevin' on her 'round, takin' care o' things, that he wanted her to stay along a
spell; and so Huldy, she staid along a spell, and poured out his tea, and
mended his close, and made pies and cakes, and cooked and washed and
ironed, and kep' every thing as neat as a pin. Huldy was a drefful chipper sort
o' gal; and work sort o' rolled off from her like water off a duck's back. There
war'n't no gal in Sherburne that could put sich a sight o' work through as
Huldy; and yet, Sunday mornin', she always come out in the singers' seat like
one o' these 'ere June roses, lookin' so fresh and smilin', and her voice was jest
as clear and sweet as a meadow lark's—Lordy massy! I 'member how she used
to sing some o' them 'are places where the treble and counter used to go
together: her voice kind o' trembled a little, and it sort o' went thro' and thro'
a feller! tuck him right where he lived!"

Here Sam leaned contemplatively back with his head in a clump of
sweetfern, and refreshed himself with a chew of young wintergreen. "This 'ere
young wintergreen, boys, is jest like a feller's thoughts o' things that happened
when he was young: it comes up jest so fresh and tender every year, the longest
time you hev to live; and you can't help chawin' on't thou' 'tis sort o' stingin'.
I don't never get over likin' young wintergreen."

"But about Huldah, Sam?"

"Oh yes! about Huldy. Lord massy! when a feller is Indianin'[4] round, these
'ere pleasant summer days, a feller's thoughts gits like a flock o' young partridges: they's up and down and everywhere; 'cause one place is jest about as
good as another, when they's all so kind o' comfortable and nice. Wal, about
Huldy,—as I was a-sayin'. She was jest as handsome a gal to look at as a feller
could have; and I think a nice, well-behaved young gal in the singers' seat of a
Sunday is a means o' grace: it's sort o' drawin' to the unregenerate, you know.
Why, boys, in them days, I've walked ten miles over to Sherburne of a Sunday
mornin', jest to play the bass-viol in the same singers' seat with Huldy. She
was very much respected, Huldy was; and, when she went out to tailorin', she

---

1. *The Minister's Housekeeper* was first published in
1872 in *Sam Lawson's Oldtown Fireside Stories,* the
source of the present text.
2. Sam Lawson, the garrulous narrator, is speaking

(the Latin word *loquitur* means "he speaks").
3. I.e., facultative, able to live or thrive under more
than one set of conditions.
4. Playing the Indian, being out in the woods.

was allers bespoke[5] six months ahead, and sent for in waggins up and down for ten miles round; for the young fellers was allers 'mazin' anxious to be sent after Huldy, and was quite free to offer to go for her. Wal, after Mis' Carryl died, Huldy got to be sort o' housekeeper at the minister's, and saw to every thing, and did every thing: so that there warn't a pin out o' the way.

"But you know how 'tis in parishes: there allers is women that thinks the minister's affairs belongs to them, and they ought to have the rulin' and guidin' of 'em; and, if a minister's wife dies, there's folks that allers has their eyes open on providences,—lookin' out who's to be the next one.

"Now, there was Mis' Amaziah Pipperidge, a widder with snappin' black eyes, and a hook nose,—kind o' like a hawk; and she was one o' them up-and-down commandin' sort o' women, that feel that they have a call to be seein' to every thing that goes on in the parish, and 'specially to the minister.

"Folks did say that Mis' Pipperidge sort o' sot her eye on the Parson for herself: wal, now that 'ere might a been, or it might not. Some folks thought it was a very suitable connection. You see she hed a good property of her own, right nigh to the minister's lot, and was allers kind o' active and busy; so, takin' one thing with another, I shouldn't wonder if Mis' Pipperidge should a thought that Providence p'inted that way. At any rate, she went up to Deakin[6] Blodgett's wife, and they two sort o' put their heads together a mournin' and condolin' about the way things was likely to go on at the minister's now Mis' Carryl was dead. Ye see, the parson's wife, she was one of them women who hed their eyes everywhere and on every thing. She was a little thin woman, but tough as Inger[7] rubber, and smart as a steel trap; and there warn't a hen laid an egg, or cackled, but Mis' Carryl was right there to see about it; and she hed the garden made in the spring, and the medders mowed in summer, and the cider made, and the corn husked, and the apples got in the fall; and the doctor, he hed n't nothin' to do but jest sit stock still a meditatin' on Jerusalem and Jericho and them things that ministers think about. But Lordy massy! he didn't know nothin' about where any thing he eat or drunk or wore come from or went to: his wife jest led him 'round in temporal things and took care on him like a baby.

"Wal, to be sure, Mis' Carryl looked up to him in spirituals, and thought all the world on him; for there warn't a smarter minister no where 'round. Why, when he preached on decrees and election,[8] they used to come clear over from South Parish, and West Sherburne, and Old Town to hear him; and there was sich a row o' waggins tied along by the meetin'-house that the stables was all full, and all the hitchin'-posts was full clean up to the tavern, so that folks said the doctor made the town look like a gineral trainin'-day[9] a Sunday.

"He was gret on texts, the doctor was. When he hed a p'int to prove, he'd jest go thro' the Bible, and drive all the texts ahead o' him like a flock o' sheep; and then, if there was a text that seemed agin him, why, he'd come out with his Greek and Hebrew, and kind o' chase it 'round a spell, jest as ye see a feller chase a contrary bell-wether,[1] and make him jump the fence arter the rest. I

---

5. Hired or engaged beforehand.
6. Deacon.
7. I.e., India rubber made from the India rubber tree, known for its toughness.
8. Divine choice in theology, the belief in the predestination of individuals as objects of divine mercy and

salvation.
9. A day on which a volunteer military company is called out for drill or parade according to law.
1. A belled wether (a ram, castrated sheep, or sheep) used to keep track of the flock.

tell you, there wa'n't no text in the Bible that could stand agin the doctor when his blood was up. The year arter the doctor was app'inted to preach the 'lection[2] sermon in Boston, he made such a figger that the Brattle-street Church sent a committee right down to see if they couldn't get him to Boston; and then the Sherburne folks, they up and raised his salary; ye see, there ain't nothin' wakes folks up like somebody else's wantin' what you've got. Wal, that fall they made him a Doctor o' Divinity at Cambridge College,[3] and so they sot more by him than ever. Wal, you see, the doctor, of course he felt kind o' lonesome and afflicted when Mis' Carryl was gone; but railly and truly, Huldy was so up to every thing about house, that the doctor didn't miss nothin' in a temporal way. His shirt-bosoms was pleated finer than they ever was, and them ruffles 'round his wrists was kep' like the driven snow; and there warn't a brack[4] in his silk stockin's, and his shoe buckles was kep' polished up, and his coats brushed and then there warn't no bread and biscuit like Huldy's; and her butter was like solid lumps o'gold; and there wern't no pies to equal hers; and so the doctor never felt the loss o' Mis' Carryl at table. Then there was Huldy allers oppisite to him, with her blue eyes and her cheeks like two fresh peaches. She was kind o' pleasant to look at; and the more the doctor looked at her the better he liked her; and so things seemed to be goin' on quite quiet and comfortable ef it hadn't been that Mis' Pipperidge and Mis' Deakin Blodgett and Mis' Sawin got their heads together a talkin' about things.

" 'Poor man,' says Mis' Pipperidge, 'what can that child that he's got there do towards takin' the care of all that place? It takes a mature woman,' she says, 'to tread in Mis' Carryl's shoes.'

" 'That it does,' said Mis' Blodgett; 'and, when things once get to runnin' down hill, there ain't no stoppin' on 'em,' says she.

"Then Mis' Sawin she took it up. (Ye see, Mis' Sawin used to go out to dress-makin', and was sort o' jealous, 'cause folks sot more by Huldy than they did by her). 'Well,' says she, 'Huldy Peters is well enough at her trade. I never denied that, though I do say I never did believe in her way o' makin' button-holes; and I must say, if 'twas the dearest friend I hed, that I thought Huldy tryin' to fit Mis' Kittridge's plum-colored silk was a clear piece o' presumption; the silk was jist spiled, so 'twarn't fit to come into the meetin'-house. I must say, Huldy's a gal that's always too ventersome about takin' 'sponsibilities she don't know nothin' about.'

" 'Of course she don't,' said Mis' Deakin Blodgett. 'What does she know about all the lookin' and seein' to that there ought to be in guidin' the minister's house. Huldy's well meanin', and she's good at her work, and good in the singers' seat; but Lordy massy! she hain't got no experience. Parson Carryl ought to have an experienced woman to keep house for him. There's the spring house-cleanin' and the fall house-cleanin' to be seen to, and the things to be put away from the moths; and then the gettin' ready for the association[5] and all the ministers' meetin's; and the makin' the soap and the candles, and settin' the hens and turkeys, watchin' the calves, and seein' after the hired men and the garden; and there that 'are blessed man jist sets there at home as serene, and has nobody 'round but that 'are gal, and don't even know how things must be a runnin' to waste!'

"Wal, the upshot on't was, they fussed and fuzzled and wuzzled[6] till they'd

---

2. I.e., election (see n. 8, p. 1617).
3. Harvard University in Cambridge, Massachusetts.
4. Flaw.

5. Association of the churches in the region.
6. I.e., gossiped chaotically.

drinked up all the tea in the teapot; and then they went down and called on the parson, and wuzzled him all up talkin' about this, that, and t'other that wanted lookin' to, and that it was no way to leave every thing to a young chit[7] like Huldy, and that he ought to be lookin' about for an experienced woman. The parson he thanked 'em kindly, and said he believed their motives was good, but he didn't go no further. He didn't ask Mis' Pipperidge to come and stay there and help him, nor nothin' o' that kind; but he said he'd attend to matters himself. The fact was, the parson had got such a likin' for havin' Huldy 'round, that he couldn't think o' such a thing as swappin' her off for the Widder Pipperidge.

"But he thought to himself, 'Huldy is a good girl; but I oughtn't to be a leavin' every thing to her,—it's too hard on her. I ought to be instructin' and guidin' and helpin' of her; 'cause't 'tain't everybody could be expected to know and do what Mis' Carryl did;' and so at it he went; and Lordy massy! didn't Huldy hev a time on't when the minister began to come out of his study, and want to tew[8] 'round and see to things? Huldy, you see, thought all the world of the minister, and she was 'most afraid to laugh; but she told me she couldn't, for the life of her, help it when his back was turned, for he wuzzled things up in the most singular way. But Huldy she'd jest say, 'Yes, sir,' and get him off into his study, and go on her own way.

" 'Huldy,' says the minister one day, 'you ain't experienced outdoors; and, when you want to know any thing, you must come to me.'

" 'Yes, sir,' says Huldy.

" 'Now, Huldy,' says the parson, 'you must be sure to save the turkey-eggs, so that we can have a lot of turkeys for Thanksgiving.'

" 'Yes, sir,' says Huldy; and she opened the pantry-door, and showed him a nice dishful she'd been a savin' up. Wal, the very next day the parson's hen-turkey was found killed up to old Jim Scrogg's barn. Folks said Scroggs killed it; though Scroggs, he stood to it he didn't: at any rate, the Scroggses, they made a meal on't; and Huldy she felt bad about it 'cause she'd set her heart on raisin' the turkeys; and says she, 'Oh, dear! I don't know what I shall do. I was just ready to set her.'

" 'Do, Huldy?' says the parson: 'why, there's the other turkey, out there by the door; and a fine bird, too, he is.'

Sure enough, there was the old tom-turkey a struttin' and a sidlin' and a quitterin', and a floutin' his tail-feathers in the sun, like a lively young widower, all ready to begin life over agin.

" 'But,' says Huldy, 'you know *he* can't set on eggs.'

" 'He can't? I'd like to know why,' says the parson. 'He *shall* set on eggs, and hatch 'em too.'

" 'O doctor!' says Huldy, all in a tremble; 'cause, you know, she didn't want to contradict the minister, and she was afraid she should laugh,—'I never heard that a tom-turkey would set on eggs.'

" 'Why, they ought to,' said the parson, getting quite 'arnest; 'what else be they good for? you just bring out the eggs, now, and put 'em in the nest, and I'll make him set on 'em.'

"So Huldy she thought there wern't no way to convince him but to let him try: so she took the eggs out, and fixed 'em all nice in the nest; and then she

---

7. Child or a person likened to a child, especially a pert or forward young woman.   8. To fuss or worry.

come back and found old Tom a skirmishin' with the parson pretty lively, I tell ye. Ye see, old Tom he didn't take the idee at all; and he flopped and gobbled, and fit the parson; and the parson's wig got 'round so that his cue[9] stuck straight out over his ear, but he'd got his blood up. Ye see, the old doctor was used to carryin' his p'ints o' doctrine; and he hadn't fit the Arminians and Socinians[1] to be beat by a tom-turkey; so finally he made a dive, and ketched him by the neck in spite o' his floppin', and stroked him down, and put Huldy's apron 'round him.

" 'There, Huldy,' he says, quite red in the face, 'we've got him now;' and he travelled off to the barn with him as lively as a cricket.

"Huldy came behind jist chokin' with laugh, and afraid the minister would look 'round and see her.

" 'Now, Huldy, we'll crook his legs, and set him down,' says the parson, when they got him to the nest; 'you see he is getting quiet, and he'll set there all right.'

"And the parson, he sot him down; and old Tom he sot there solemn enough, and held his head down all droopin', lookin' like a rail pious old cock, as long as the parson sot by him.

" 'There: you see how still he sets,' says the parson to Huldy.

"Huldy was 'most dyin' for fear she should laugh. 'I'm afraid he'll get up,' says she, 'when you do.'

" 'Oh, no, he won't!' says the parson, quite confident. 'There, there,' says he, layin' his hands on him, as if pronouncin' a blessin'. But when the parson riz up, old Tom he riz up too, and began to march over the eggs.

" 'Stop, now!' says the parson. 'I'll make him get down agin: hand me that corn-basket; we'll put that over him.'

"So he crooked old Tom's legs, and got him down agin; and they put the corn-basket over him, and then they both stood and waited.

" 'That'll do the thing, Huldy,' said the parson.

" 'I don't know about it,' says Huldy.

" 'Oh yes, it will, child! I understand,' says he.

"Just as he spoke, the basket riz right up and stood, and they could see old Tom's long legs.

" 'I'll make him stay down, confound him,' says the parson; for, ye see, parsons is men, like the rest on us, and the doctor had got his spunk up.

" 'You jist hold him a minute, and I'll get something that'll make him stay, I guess;' and out he went to the fence, and brought in a long, thin, flat stone, and laid it on old Tom's back.

"Old Tom he wilted down considerable under this, and looked railly as if he was goin' to give in. He stayed still there a good long spell, and the minister and Huldy left him there and come up to the house; but they hadn't more than got in the door before they see old Tom a hippin' along, as high-steppin' as ever, sayin', "Talk! talk! and quitter! quitter!' and struttin' and gobblin' as if he'd come through the Red Sea,[2] and got the victory.

---

9. I.e., queue, the braid of his wig.
1. The Socinians were members of the anti-Trinitarian theological movement of the 16th century who believed that salvation could be achieved by the imitation of Christ's virtue. The Arminians, a 17th-century sect, opposed the absolute predestination taught by Calvin and maintained the real possibility of salvation through good works.

2. In Exodus 14.19–31, Moses, guided by God, led the Israelites out of Egypt on their journey to the Promised Land. Moses stretched out his hand, causing a wind to blow so that the waters of the Red Sea were divided, and he and his people were able to cross the Red Sea. Pharoah and his Egyptians followed and were drowned when the waters came back together.

" 'Oh, my eggs!' says Huldy. 'I'm afraid he's smashed 'em!'

"And sure enough, there they was, smashed flat enough under the stone.

" 'I'll have him killed,' said the parson: 'we won't have such a critter 'round.'

"But the parson he slep' on't, and then didn't do it; he only come out next Sunday with a tip top sermon on the ' 'Riginal Cuss'[3] that was pronounced on things in gineral, when Adam fell, and showed how every thing was allowed to go contrary ever since. There was pig-weed, and pusley, and Canady this-tles, cut-worms, and bag-worms, and canker-worms,[4] to say nothin' of rattle-snakes. The doctor made it very impressive and sort o' improvin'; but Huldy, she told me, goin' home, that she hardly could keep from laughin' two or three times in the sermon when she thought of Old Tom a standin' up with the corn-basket on his back.

"Wal, next week Huldy she jist borrowed the minister's horse and side-saddle, and rode over to South Parish to her Aunt Bascome's,—Widder Bas-come's, you know, that lives there by the trout-brook,—and got a lot o' turkey-eggs o' her, and come back and set a hen on 'em, and said nothin'; and in good time there was as nice a lot o' turkey-chicks as ever ye see.

"Huldy never said a word to the minister about his experiment, and he never said a word to her; but he sort o' kep' more to his books, and didn't take it on him to advise so much.

"But not long arter he took it into his head that Huldy ought to have a pig to be a fattin' with the buttermilk. Mis' Pipperidge set him up to it; and jist then old Tim Bigelow, out to Juniper Hill, told him if he'd call over he'd give him a little pig.

"So he sent for a man, and told him to build a pig-pen right out by the well, and have it all ready when he came home with his pig.

"Huldy she said she wished he might put a curb round the well out there, because in the dark, sometimes, a body might stumble into it; and the parson, he told him he might do that.

"Wal, old Aikin, the carpenter, he didn't come till most the middle of the arternoon; and then he sort o' idled, so that he didn't get up the well-curb till sundown; and then he went off and said he'd come and do the pig-pen next day.

"Wal, arter dark, Parson Carryl he driv into the yard, full chizel,[5] with his pig. He'd tied up his mouth to keep him from squealin'; and he see what he thought was the pig-pen,—he was rather near-sighted,—and so he ran and threw piggy over; and down he dropped into the water, and the minister put out his horse and pranced off into the house quite delighted.

" 'There, Huldy, I've got you a nice little pig.'

" 'Dear me!' says Huldy: 'where have you put him?'

" 'Why, out there in the pig-pen, to be sure.'

" 'Oh dear me!' says Huldy: 'that's the well-curb. There ain't no pig-pen built,' says she.

" 'Lordy massy!' says the parson: 'then I've thrown the pig in the well!'

"Wal, Huldy she worked and worked, and finally she fished piggy out in the bucket, but he was dead as a door-nail; and she got him out o' the way quietly, and didn't say much; and the parson, he took to a great Hebrew book in his study; and says he, 'Huldy, ain't much in temporals,' says he. Huldy says she

---

3. I.e., Original Curse or Sin.
4. Various weeds and destructive insects. "Pusley":

purslane. "Canady thistles": Canadian thistles.
5. Full speed.

kind o' felt her heart go out to him, he was so sort o' meek and helpless and larned; and says she, 'Wal, Parson Carryl, don't trouble your head no more about it; I'll see to things;' and sure enough, a week arter there was a nice pen, all ship-shape, and two little white pigs that Huldy bought with the money for the butter she sold at the store.

" 'Wal, Huldy,' said the parson, 'you are a most amazin' child: you don't say nothin',' but you do more than most folks.'

"Arter that the Parson set sich store by Huldy that he come to her and asked her about every thing, and it was amazin' how everything she put her hand to prospered. Huldy planted marigolds and larkspurs, pinks and carnations, all up and down the path to the front door, and trained up mornin' glories and scarlet-runners round the windows. And she was always a gettin' a root here, and a sprig there, and a seed from somebody else,—for Huldy was one o' them that has the gift, so that ef you jist give 'em the leastest sprig of any thing they make a great bush out of it right away; so that in six months Huldy had roses and geraniums and lilies, sich as it would a took a gardener to raise. The parson, he took no notice at fust; but when the yard was all ablaze with flowers he used to come and stand in a kind o' maze[6] at the front door, and say, 'Beautiful, beautiful! Why, Huldy, I never see anything like it.' And then when her work was done arternoons, Huldy would sit with her sewin' in the porch, and sing and trill away till she'd draw the meadow-larks and the bobo-links and the orioles to answer her, and the great big elm-tree overhead would get perfectly rackety with the birds; and the parson, settin' there in his study, would git to kind o' dreamin' about the angels, and golden harps, and the New Jerusalem; but he wouldn't speak a word, 'cause Huldy she was jist like them wood-thrushes, she never could sing so well when she thought folks was hearin'. Folks noticed, about this time, that the parson's sermons got to be like Aaron's rod,[7] that budded and blossomed; there was things in 'em about flow-ers and birds, and more 'special about the music o' heaven. And Huldy she noticed, that ef there was a hymn run in her head while she was 'round a-workin' the minister was sure to give it out next Sunday. You see, Huldy was jist like a bee: she always sung when she was workin', and you could hear her trillin', now down in the corn-patch, while she was pickin' the corn; and now in the buttery, while she was workin' the butter; and now she'd go singin' down cellar, and then she'd be singin' up over head, so that she seemed to fill a house chock full o' music.

"Huldy was so sort o' chipper and fair spoken, that she got the hired men all under her thumb: they come to her and took her orders jist as meek as so many calves; and she traded at the store, and kep' the accounts, and she hed her eyes everywhere, and tied up all the ends so tight that there want no gettin' 'round her. She wouldn't let nobody put nothin' off[8] on Parson Carryl, 'cause he was a minister. Huldy was allers up to anybody that wanted to make a hard bargain; and, afore he knew jist what he was about, she'd got the best end of it, and everybody said that Huldy was the most capable gal that they'd ever traded with.

"Wal, come to the meetin' of the association, Mis' Deakin Blodgett and Mis' Pipperidge come callin' up to the parson's, all in a stew, and offerin' their services to get the house ready; but the doctor, he jist thanked 'em quite quiet,

6. In a state of bewilderment or amazement.
7. Reference to Numbers 17.8, in which the rod (staff)   of the patriarch Aaron blossomed and yielded almonds.
     8. I.e., she wouldn't let anyone cheat.

and turned 'em over to Huldy; and Huldy she told 'em that she'd got every thing ready, and showed 'em her pantries,[9] and her cakes and her pies and her puddin's, and took 'em all over the house; and they went peekin' and pokin', openin' cupboard-doors, and lookin' into drawers; and they couldn't find so much as a thread out o' the way, from garret to cellar, and so they went off quite discontented. Arter that the women set a new trouble a brewin'. Then they begun to talk that it was a year now since Mis' Carryl died; and it r'ally wasn't proper such a young gal to be stayin' there, who everybody could see was a settin' her cap for the minister.

"Mis' Pipperidge said that, so long as she looked on Huldy as the hired gal, she hadn't thought much about it; but Huldy was r'ally takin' on airs as an equal, and appearin' as mistress o' the house in a way that would make talk if it went on. And Mis' Pipperidge she driv 'round up to Deakin Abner Snow's, and down to Mis' 'Lijah Perry's, and asked them if they wasn't afraid that the way the parson and Huldy was a goin' on might make talk. And they said they hadn't thought on't before, but now, come to think on't, they was sure it would; and they all went and talked with somebody else, and asked them if they didn't think it would make talk. So come Sunday, between meetin's there warn't nothin' else talked about; and Huldy saw folks a noddin' and a winkin', and a lookin' arter her, and she begun to feel drefful sort o' disagreeable. Finally Mis' Sawin she says to her, 'My dear, didn't you never think folk would talk about you and the minister?'

" 'No: why should they?' says Huldy, quite innocent.

" 'Wal, dear,' says she, 'I think it's a shame; but they say you're tryin' to catch him, and that it's so bold and improper for you to be courtin' of him right in his own house,—you know folks will talk,—I thought I'd tell you 'cause I think so much of you,' says she.

"Huldy was a gal of spirit, and she despised the talk, but it made her drefful uncomfortable; and when she got home at night she sat down in the mornin'-glory porch, quite quiet, and didn't sing a word.

"The minister he had heard the same thing from one of his deakins that day; and, when he saw Huldy so kind o' silent, he says to her, 'Why don't you sing, my child?'

"He hed a pleasant sort o' way with him, the minister had, and Huldy had got to likin' to be with him, and it all come over her that perhaps she ought to go away; and her throat kind o' filled up so she couldn't hardly speak; and, says she, 'I can't sing to-night.'

"Says he, 'You don't know how much good you're singin' has done me, nor how much good *you* have done me in all ways, Huldy. I wish I knew how to show my gratitude.'

" 'O sir!' says Huldy, '*is* it improper for me to be here?'

" 'No dear,' says the minister, 'but ill-natured folks will talk; but there is one way we can stop it, Huldy—if you will marry me. You'll make me very happy, and I'll do all I can to make you happy. Will you?'

"Wal, Huldy never told me jist what she said to the minister,—gals never does give you the particulars of them 'are things jist as you'd like 'em,—only I know the upshot and the hull on't was, that Huldy she did a consid'able lot o' clear starchin' and ironin' the next two days; and the Friday o' next week the

9. A pantry is a room or closet adjacent to a kitchen or dining room used for storing provisions or glassware and china for serving.

minister and she rode over together to Dr. Lothrop's in Old Town; and the doctor, he jist made 'em man and wife, 'spite of envy of the Jews,' as the hymn says. Wal, you'd better believe there was a starin' and a wonderin' next Sunday mornin' when the second bell was a tollin', and the minister walked up the broad aisle with Huldy, all in white, arm in arm with him, and he opened the minister's pew, and handed her in as if she was a princess; for, you see, Parson Carryl come of a good family, and was a born gentleman, and had a sort o' grand way o' bein' polite to women-folks. Wal, I guess there was a rus'lin' among the bunnets. Mis' Pipperidge gin a great bounce, like corn poppin' on a shovel, and her eyes glared through her glasses at Huldy as if they'd 'a sot her afire; and everybody in the meetin' house was a starin', I tell yew. But they couldn't none of 'em say nothin' agin Huldy's looks; for there warn't a crimp nor a frill about her that warn't jis' so; and her frock was white as the driven snow, and she had her bunnet all trimmed up with white ribbins; and all the fellows said the old doctor had stole a march, and got the handsomest gal in the parish.

"Wal, arter meetin' they all come 'round the parson and Huldy at the door, shakin' hands and laughin'; for by that time they was about agreed that they'd got to let putty well alone.

" 'Why, Parson Carryl,' says Mis' Deakin Blodgett, 'how you've come it over us.'[1]

" 'Yes,' says the parson, with a kind o' twinkle in his eye. 'I thought,' says he, 'as folks wanted to talk about Huldy and me, I'd give 'em somethin' wuth talkin' about.' "

1871

1. I.e., "How you've gotten the better of us!"

HARRIET JACOBS
c. 1813–1897

Harriet Jacobs was born in Edenton, North Carolina, the daughter of slaves and a slave herself. Her father was a skilled carpenter who was permitted to hire himself out, and her parents were permitted to live together even though they were "owned" by different masters; therefore, as a child Jacobs was unaware that she was a slave. Her mother's death and a change of owners for both Jacobs and her father brought her into the family of Dr. and Mrs. James Norcom in 1825. There, as she grew to adulthood, she was sexually harassed by the doctor and abused by his jealous wife. As a defense against this treatment, Jacobs involved herself with an unmarried white attorney, Samuel Tredwell Sawyer, by whom she had two children: Joseph, born in 1829, and Louisa Matilda, born in 1833. When Norcom sent her to a country plantation in 1835, she escaped back to Edenton, hiding for perhaps seven years in the home of her maternal grandmother, who had been emancipated some years earlier. While Jacobs was in hiding, Sawyer purchased, but did not emancipate, their two children. Jacobs finally escaped to the North in 1842, and later both her children came North also. Life in the North was insecure and perilous, however, because slave catchers were constantly hunting down escaped slaves to return them South, which they could do more aggressively after 1850 with the Fugitive Slave Law on their side.

For much of the next two decades Jacobs worked in the family of Nathaniel Parker Willis, one of the era's most popular writers and editors. She took care of his children and became particularly close to his second wife, Cornelia Grinnell Willis, a staunch abolitionist. In 1853 Cornelia Willis arranged to purchase Jacobs from Norcom's daughter, her legal owner; then she emancipated Jacobs.

Jacobs spent much of 1849 in Rochester, New York, working for the Anti-Slavery Office run by her younger brother, who had also escaped slavery. She read through a large body of antislavery writings and also came to know a number of abolitionists, including many white women, among them Emily Post, who became a mentor to her. Jacobs wanted to contribute her life story to the abolitionist cause in a way that would capture the attention of Northern white women in particular, to show them how slavery debased and demoralized women, at once subjecting them to white male lust and depriving them of the right to make homes for and with their children. Yet this topic was difficult to discuss in an era when extreme sexual prudery was the norm, when standards of female sexual "purity" could result in blaming the unmarried slave mother rather than sympathizing with her. In *Incidents in the Life of a Slave Girl* Jacobs tried to do more than create sympathy for her plight; she also sought to win the respect and admiration of her readers for the courage with which she forestalled abuse and for the independence with which she chose a lover rather than having one forced on her. Her description of hiding in the attic, her emphasis on family life and maternal values, and her account of the difficulties of fugitive slaves in the North also differentiate the book from the numerous slave narratives produced in the twenty years before the Civil War. *Incidents* is also distinguished by its awareness of the kinds of stories written by and about white women in the same era, for it self-consciously addresses women readers and carefully distinguishes the slave woman's experiences from theirs.

Free at last, and encouraged by the success of Harriet Beecher Stowe's *Uncle Tom's Cabin* (1852)—one of whose heroines is the slave concubine Cassy—Jacobs began work on her narrative around 1853 and finished it by 1858. She was not successful in finding a publisher for it, however, until Lydia Maria Child (1802–1880), a well-known woman of letters and abolitionist, agreed to write a preface for it. Child became very interested in the project, and when the contracted publishers went bankrupt, she arranged for its publication. The book came out under the pseudonym Linda Brent in 1861; it was sold at Anti-Slavery Offices around the country, published in England in 1862, and received several favorable reviews. The outbreak of the Civil War made its message less pressing, however, and it sank from notice until the 1980s, when interest in early writings by African-American women, and superb biographical scholarship by Jean Fagin Yellin, restored the book and its author to view.

During the war and its immediate aftermath Jacobs worked in the relief effort funded by Quaker organizations. Afterward she ran a boardinghouse in Cambridge, Massachusetts, and later moved to Washington, D.C., with her daughter. She is buried in Mount Auburn Cemetery in Cambridge.

Critics and students of *Incidents* agree that the book is a unique literary document but have wondered whether to regard it as truth or fiction and whether it is primarily Jacobs's work or Child's. Yellin has shown that all the characters and events in *Incidents* are based in reality, and Child's correspondence claims that as editor she added nothing and altered fewer than fifty words in the manuscript. But Child did take what she described as "much pains" with it, "transposing sentences and pages, so as to bring the story into continuous *order*, and the remarks into *appropriate* places," thereby making the story "much more clear and entertaining." She also asked Jacobs for instances of slave abuse apart from the author's own experiences, which Jacobs supplied. Lacking the manuscript of *Incidents*, one cannot speculate on Child's specific changes, but her work on the narrative involved precisely what editors in publishing houses do today as a matter of course. To the extent that Child's reorganization gave the book a more literary shape, *Incidents* is indeed a collaborative production. So, however, are T. S. Eliot's *The Waste Land*, Theodore Dreiser's *Sister Carrie*, and Thomas Wolfe's *Look Homeward, Angel*, to name only a few well-known examples. Jacobs expressed no dissatisfaction with Child's work and clearly regarded it as her own book, taking an active role in promoting and selling it. Not for another thirty years after *Incidents* would African-American women's writing emerge as a significant strand in American literature; when it did, many of the themes that Jacobs introduced would become central to such writing.

From Incidents in the Life of a Slave Girl

I. Childhood

I was born a slave; but I never knew it till six yeas of happy childhood had passed away. My father was a carpenter, and considered so intelligent and skilful in his trade, that, when buildings out of the common line were to be erected, he was sent for from long distances, to be head workman. On condition of paying his mistress two hundred dollars a year, and supporting himself, he was allowed to work at his trade, and manage his own affairs. His strongest wish was to purchase his children; but, though he several times offered his hard earnings for that purpose, he never succeeded. In complexion my parents were a light shade of brownish yellow, and were termed mulattoes. They lived together in a comfortable home; and, though we were all slaves, I was so fondly shielded that I never dreamed I was a piece of merchandise, trusted to them for safe keeping, and liable to be demanded of them at any moment. I had one brother, William, who was two years younger than myself—a bright, affectionate child. I had also a great treasure in my maternal grandmother, who was a remarkable woman in many respects. She was the daughter of a planter in South Carolina, who, at his death, left her mother and his three children free, with money to go to St. Augustine, where they had relatives. It was during the Revolutionary War; and they were captured on their passage, carried back, and sold to different purchasers. Such was the story my grandmother used to tell me; but I do not remember all the particulars. She was a little girl when she was captured and sold to the keeper of a large hotel. I have often heard her tell how hard she fared during childhood. But as she grew older she evinced so much intelligence, and was so faithful, that her master and mistress could not help seeing it was for their interest to take care of such a valuable piece of property. She became an indispensable personage in the household, officiating in all capacities, from cook and wet nurse to seamstress. She was much praised for her cooking; and her nice crackers became so famous in the neighborhood that many people were desirous of obtaining them. In consequence of numerous requests of this kind, she asked permission of her mistress to bake crackers at night, after all the household work was done; and she obtained leave to do it, provided she would clothe herself and her children from the profits. Upon these terms, after working hard all day for her mistress, she began her midnight bakings, assisted by her two oldest children. The business proved profitable; and each year she laid by a little, which was saved for a fund to purchase her children. Her master died, and the property was divided among his heirs. The widow had her dower in the hotel, which she continued to keep open. My grandmother remained in her service as a slave; but her children were divided among her master's children. As she had five, Benjamin, the youngest one, was sold, in order that each heir might have an equal portion of dollars and cents. There was so little difference in our ages that he seemed more like my brother than my uncle. He was a bright, handsome lad, nearly white; for he inherited the complexion my grandmother had derived from Anglo-Saxon ancestors. Though only ten years old, seven hundred and twenty dollars were paid for him. His sales was a terrible blow to my grandmother; but she was naturally hopeful, and she went to work with renewed energy, trusting in time to be able to purchase some of her children. She had laid up three hundred dollars, which her mistress one day begged as a loan, promising to pay her soon. The reader probably knows that no promise or writing given to a slave is legally binding; for, according to Southern laws, a slave, *being* property, can *hold* no property. When my grandmother lent her hard earnings to her mistress, she trusted solely to her honor. The honor of a slaveholder to a slave!

To this good grandmother I was indebted for many comforts. My brother Willie and I often received portions of the crackers, cakes, and preserves, she made to sell; and after we ceased to be children we were indebted to her for many more important services.

Such were the unusually fortunate circumstances of my early childhood. When I was six years old, my mother died, and then, for the first time, I learned, by the talk around me, that I was a slave. My mother's mistress was the daughter of my grandmother's mistress. She was the foster sister of my mother; they were both nourished at my grandmother's breast. In fact, my mother had been weaned at three months old, that the babe of the mistress might obtain sufficient food. They played together as children; and, when they became women, my mother was a most faithful servant to her whiter foster sister. On her death-bed her mistress promised that her children should never suffer for any thing; and during her lifetime she kept her word. They all spoke kindly of my dead mother, who had been a slave merely in name, but in nature was noble and womanly. I grieved for her, and my young mind was troubled with the thought who would now take care of me and my little brother. I was told that my home was now to be with her mistress; and I found it a happy one. No toilsome or disagreeable duties were imposed upon me. My mistress was so kind to me that I was always glad to do her bidding, and proud to labor for her as much as my young years would permit. I would sit by her side for hours, sewing diligently, with a heart as free from care as that of any free-born white child. When she thought I was tired, she would send me out to run and jump; and away I bounded, to gather berries or flowers to decorate her room. Those were happy days—too happy to last. The slave child had no thought for the morrow; but there came that blight, which too surely waits on every human being born to be a chattel.

When I was nearly twelve years old, my kind mistress sickened and died. As I saw the cheek grow paler, and the eye more glassy, how earnestly I prayed in my heart that she might live! I loved her; for she had been almost like a mother to me. My prayers were not answered. She died, and they buried her in the little churchyard, where, day after day, my tears fell upon her grave.

I was sent to spend a week with my grandmother. I was now old enough to begin to think of the future; and again and again I asked myself what they would do with me. I felt sure I should never find another mistress so kind as the one who was gone. She had promised my dying mother that her children should never suffer for any thing; and when I remembered that, and recalled her many proofs of attachment to me, I could not help having some hopes that she had left me free. My friends were almost certain it would be so. They thought she would be sure to do it, on account of my mother's love and faithful service. But, alas! we all know that the memory of a faithful slave does not avail much to save her children from the auction block.

After a brief period of suspense, the will of my mistress was read, and we learned that she had bequeathed me to her sister's daughter, a child of five years old. So vanished our hopes. My mistress had taught me the precepts of God's Word: "Thou shalt love thy neighbor as thyself."[1] Whatsoever ye would that men should do unto you, do ye even so unto them."[2] But I was her slave, and I suppose she did not recognize me as her neighbor. I would give much to blot out from my memory that one great wrong. As a child, I loved my mistress; and, looking back on the happy days I spent with her, I try to think with less bitterness of this act of injustice. While I was with her, she taught me to read and spell; and for this privilege, which so rarely falls to the lot of a slave, I bless her memory.

She possessed but few slaves; and at her death those were all distributed among her relatives. Five of them were my grandmother's children, and had shared the same milk that nourished her mother's children. Notwithstanding my grandmother's long and faithful service to her owners, not one of her children escaped the auction block. These God-breathing machines are no more, in the sight of their masters, than the cotton they plant, or the horses they tend.

VII. The Lover

Why does the slave ever love? Why allow the tendrils of the heart to twine around objects which may at any moment be wrenched away by the hand of violence? When separations come by the hand of death, the pious soul can bow in resignation, and say, "Not my will, but thine be done, O Lord!"[3] But when the ruthless hand of man strikes the blow, regardless of the misery he causes, it is hard to be submissive. I did not reason thus when I was a young girl. Youth will be youth. I loved, and I indulged the hope that the dark clouds around me would turn out a bright lining. I forgot that in the land of my birth the shadows are too dense for light to penetrate. A land

> "Where laughter is not mirth; nor thought the mind;
> Nor words a language; no e'en men mankind.
> Where cries reply to curses, shrieks to blows,
> And each is tortured in his separate hell."[4]

There was in the neighborhood a young colored carpenter; a free born man. We had been well acquainted in childhood, and frequently met together afterwards. We became mutually attached, and he proposed to marry me. I loved him with all the ardor of a young girl's first love. But when I reflected that I

---

1. Mark 12.31.
2. Matthew 7.12.
3. Cf. Matthew 26.39: "Nevertheless not as I will, but as thou wilt."

4. From *The Lament of Tasso* 4.7–10 (1817), by the English poet George Gordon, Lord Byron (1788–1824).

was a slave, and that the laws gave no sanction to the marriage of such, my heart sank within me. My lover wanted to buy me; but I knew that Dr. Flint was too wilful and arbitrary a man to consent to that arrangement. From him, I was sure of experiencing all sorts of opposition, and I had nothing to hope from my mistress.[5] She would have been delighted to have got rid of me, but not in that way. It would have relieved her mind of a burden if she could have seen me sold to some distant state, but if I was married near home I should be just as much in her husband's power as I had previously been,—for the husband of a slave has no power to protect her.[6] Moreover, my mistress, like many others, seemed to think that slaves had no right to any family ties of their own; that they were created merely to wait upon the family of the mistress. I once heard her abuse a young slave girl, who told her that a colored man wanted to make her his wife. "I will have you peeled and pickled, my lady," said she, "if I ever hear you mention that subject again. Do you suppose that I will have you tending *my* children with the children of that nigger?" The girl to whom she said this had a mulatto child, of course not acknowledged by its father. The poor black man who loved her would have been proud to acknowledge his helpless offspring.

Many and anxious were the thoughts I revolved in my mind. I was at a loss what to do. Above all things, I was desirous to spare my lover the insults that had cut so deeply into my own soul. I talked with my grandmother about it, and partly told her my fears. I did not dare to tell her the worst. She had long suspected all was not right, and if I confirmed her suspicions I knew a storm would rise that would prove the overthrow of all my hopes.

This love-dream had been my support through many trials; and I could not bear to run the risk of having it suddenly dissipated. There was a lady in the neighborhood, a particular friend of Dr. Flint's, who often visited the house. I had a great respect for her, and she had always manifested a friendly interest in me. Grandmother thought she would have great influence with the doctor. I went to this lady, and told her my story. I told her I was aware that my lover's being a free-born man would prove a great objection; but he wanted to buy me; and if Dr. Flint would consent to that arrangement, I felt sure he would be willing to pay any reasonable price. She knew that Mrs. Flint disliked me; therefore, I ventured to suggest that perhaps my mistress would approve of my being sold, as that would rid her of me. The lady listened with kindly sympathy, and promised to do her utmost to promote my wishes. She had an interview with the doctor, and I believe she pleaded my cause earnestly; but it was all to no purpose.

How I dreaded my master now! Every minute I expected to be summoned to his presence; but the day passed, and I heard nothing from him. The next morning, a message was brought to me: "Master wants you in his study." I found the door ajar, and I stood a moment gazing at the hateful man who claimed a right to rule me, body and soul. I entered, and tried to appear calm. I did not want him to know how my heart was bleeding. He looked fixedly at me, with an expression which seemed to say, "I have half a mind to kill you on the spot." At last he broke the silence, and that was a relief to both of us.

5. Dr. Flint was the father of Emily Flint, Linda Brent's (i.e., Harriet Jacobs's) legal owner. Because Emily is a child at this time, her father and mother, whom Brent refers to as her mistress, have legal power over her slaves.
6. Dr. Flint has been harassing Brent for some time, apparently to coerce her into a sexual relationship.

"So you want to be married, do you?" said he, "and to a free nigger."

"Yes, sir."

"Well, I'll soon convince you whether I am your master, or the nigger fellow you honor so highly. If you *must* have a husband, you may take up with one of my slaves."

What a situation I should be in, as the wife of one of *his* slaves, even if my heart had been interested!

I replied, "Don't you suppose, sir, that a slave can have some preference about marrying? Do you suppose that all men are alike to her?"

"Do you love this nigger?" said he, abruptly.

"Yes, sir."

"How dare you tell me so!" he exclaimed, in great wrath. After a slight pause, he added, "I supposed you thought more of yourself; that you felt above the insults of such puppies."

I replied, "If he is a puppy I am a puppy, for we are both of the negro race. It is right and honorable for us to love each other. The man you call a puppy never insulted me, sir; and he would not love me if he did not believe me to be a virtuous woman."

He sprang upon me like a tiger, and gave me a stunning blow. It was the first time he had ever struck me; and fear did not enable me to control my anger. When I had recovered a little from the effects, I exclaimed, "You have struck me for answering you honestly. How I despise you!"

There was silence for some minutes. Perhaps he was deciding what should be my punishment; or, perhaps, he wanted to give me time to reflect on what I had said, and to whom I had said it. Finally, he asked, "Do you know what you have said?"

"Yes, sir; but your treatment drove me to it."

"Do you know that I have a right to do as I like with you,—that I can kill you, if I please?"

"You have tried to kill me, and I wish you had; but you have no right to do as you like with me."

"Silence!" he exclaimed, in a thundering voice. "By heavens, girl, you forget yourself too far! Are you mad? If you are, I will soon bring you to your senses. Do you think any other master would bear what I have borne from you this morning? Many masters would have killed you on the spot. How would you like to be sent to jail for your insolence?"

"I know I have been disrespectful, sir," I replied; "but you drove me to it; I couldn't help it. As for the jail, there would be more peace for me there than there is here."

"You deserve to go there," he said, "and to be under such treatment, that you would forget the meaning of the word *peace*. It would do you good. It would take some of your high notions out of you. But I am not ready to send you there yet, notwithstanding your ingratitude for all my kindness and forbearance. You have been the plague of my life. I have wanted to make you happy, and I have been repaid with the basest ingratitude; but though you have proved yourself incapable of appreciating my kindness, I will be lenient towards you, Linda.[7] I will give you one more chance to redeem your character. If you behave yourself and do as I require, I will forgive you and treat you

---

7. Linda Brent is the name Jacobs wrote under.

as I always have done; but if you disobey me, I will punish you as I would the meanest slave on my plantation. Never let me hear that fellow's name mentioned again. If I ever know of your speaking to him, I will cowhide you both; and if I catch him lurking about my premises, I will shoot him as soon as I would a dog. Do you hear what I say? I'll teach you a lesson about marriage and free niggers! Now go, and let this be the last time I have occasion to speak to you on this subject."

Reader, did you ever hate? I hope not. I never did but once; and I trust I never shall again. Somebody has called it "the atmosphere of hell;" and I believe it is so.

For a fortnight the doctor did not speak to me. He thought to mortify me; to make me feel that I had disgraced myself by receiving the honorable addresses of a respectable colored man, in preference to the base proposals of a white man. But though his lips disdained to address me, his eyes were very loquacious. No animal ever watched its prey more narrowly than he watched me. He knew that I could write, though he had failed to make me read his letters; and he was now troubled lest I should exchange letters with another man. After a while he became weary of silence; and I was sorry for it. One morning, as he passed through the hall, to leave the house, he contrived to thrust a note into my hand. I thought I had better read it, and spare myself the vexation of having him read it to me. It expressed regret for the blow he had given me, and reminded me that I myself was wholly to blame for it. He hoped I had become convinced of the injury I was doing myself by incurring his displeasure. He wrote that he had made up his mind to go to Louisiana; that he should take several slaves with him, and intended I should be one of the number. My mistress would remain where she was; therefore I should have nothing to fear from that quarter. If I merited kindness from him, he assured me that it would be lavishly bestowed. He begged me to think over the matter, and answer the following day.

The next morning I was called to carry a pair of scissors to his room. I laid them on the table, with the letter beside them. He thought it was my answer, and did not call me back. I went as usual to attend my young mistress to and from school. He met me in the street, and ordered me to stop at his office on my way back. When I entered, he showed me his letter, and asked me why I had not answered it. I replied, "I am your daughter's property, and it is in your power to send me, or take me, wherever you please." He said he was very glad to find me so willing to go, and that we should start early in the autumn. He had a large practice in the town, and I rather thought he had made up the story merely to frighten me. However that might be, I was determined that I would never go to Louisiana with him.

Summer passed away, and early in the autumn, Dr. Flint's eldest son was sent to Louisiana to examine the country, with a view to emigrating. That news did not disturb me. I knew very well that I should not be sent with *him*. That I had not been taken to the plantation before this time, was owing to the fact that his son was there. He was jealous of his son; and jealousy of the overseer had kept him from punishing me by sending me into the fields to work. Is it strange that I was not proud of these protectors? As for the overseer, he was a man for whom I had less respect than I had for a bloodhound.

Young Mr. Flint did not bring back a favorable report of Louisiana, and I heard no more of that scheme. Soon after this, my lover met me at the corner of the street, and I stopped to speak to him. Looking up, I saw my master watching us from his window. I hurried home, trembling with fear. I was sent for, immediately, to go to his room. He met me with a blow. "When is mistress to be married?" said he, in a sneering tone. A shower o oaths and imprecations followed. How thankful I was that my lover was a free man! that my tyrant had no power to flog him for speaking to me in the street!

Again and again I revolved in my mind how all this would end. There was no hope that the doctor would consent to sell me on any terms. He had an iron will, and was determined to keep me, and to conquer me. My lover was an intelligent and religious man. Even if he could have obtained permission to marry me while I was a slave, the marriage would give him no power to protect me from my master. It would have made him miserable to witness the insults I should have been subjected to. And then, if we had children, I knew they must "follow the condition of the mother." What a terrible blight that would be on the heart of a free, intelligent father! For *his* sake, I felt that I ought not to link his fate with my own unhappy destiny. He was going to Savannah to see about a little property left him by an uncle; and had as it was to bring my feelings to it, I earnestly entreated him not to come back. I advised him to go to the Free States, where his tongue would not be tied, and where his intelligence would be of more avail to him. He left me, still hoping the day would come when I could be bought. With me the lamp of hope had gone out. The dream of my girlhood was over. I felt lonely and desolate.

Still I was not stripped of all. I still had my good grandmother, and my affectionate brother. When he put his arms round my neck, and looked into my eyes, as if to read there the troubles I dared not tell, I felt that I still had something to love. But even that pleasant emotion was chilled by the reflection that he might be torn from me at any moment, by some sudden freak of my master. If I had known how we love each other, I think he would have exulted in separating us. We often planned together how we could get to the north. But, as William remarked, such things are easier said than done. My movements were very closely watched, and we had no means of getting any money to defray our expenses. As for grandmother, she was strongly opposed to her children's undertaking any such project. She had not forgotten poor Benjamin's sufferings[8] and she was afraid that if another child tried to escape, he would have a similar or a worse fate. To me, nothing seemed more dreadful than my present life. I said to myself, "William *must* be free. He shall go to the north, and I will follow him." Many a slave sister has formed the same plans.

X. *A Perilous Passage in the Slave Girl's Life*

After my lover went away, Dr. Flint contrived a new plan. He seemed to have an idea that my fear of my mistress was his greatest obstacle. In the blandest tones, he told me that he was going to build a small house for me, in a secluded place, four miles away from the town. I shuddered; but I was constrained to listen, while he talked of his intention to give me a home of my own, and to make a lady of me. Hitherto, I had escaped my dreaded fate, by being in the midst of people. My grandmother had already had high words

8. One of Brent's uncles, who was caught in an escape attempt, jailed and mistreated for six months, and sold away to a trader. He eventually got to New York but never saw his mother again.

with my master about me. She had told him pretty plainly what she thought of his character, and there was considerable gossip in the neighborhood about our affairs, to which the open-mouthed jealousy of Mrs. Flint contributed not a little. When my master said he was going to build a house for me, and that he could do it with little trouble and expense, I was in hopes something would happen to frustrate his scheme; but I soon heard that the house was actually begun. I vowed before my Maker that I would never enter it. I had rather toil on the plantation from dawn till dark; I had rather live and die in jail, than drag on, from day to day, though such a living death. I was determined that the master, whom I so hated and loathed, who had blighted the prospects of my youth, and made my life a desert, should not, after my long struggle with him, succeed at last in trampling his victim under his feet. I would do any thing, every thing, or the sake of defeating him. What *could* I do? I thought and thought, till I became desperate, and made a plunge into the abyss.

And now, reader, I come to a period in my unhappy life, which I would gladly forget if I could. The remembrance fills me with sorrow and shame. It pains me to tell you of it; but I have promised to tell you the truth, and I will do it honestly, let it cost me what it may. I will not try to screen myself behind the plea of compulsion from a master; for it was not so. Neither can I plead ignorance or thoughtlessness. For years, my master had done his utmost to pollute my mind with foul images, and to destroy the pure principles inculcated by my grandmother, and the good mistress of my childhood. The influences of slavery had had the same effect on me that they had on other young girls; they had made me prematurely knowing, concerning the evil ways of the world. I knew what I did, and I did it with deliberate calculation.

But, O, ye happy women, whose purity has been sheltered from childhood, who have been free to choose the objects of your affection, whose homes are protected by law, do not judge the poor desolate slave girl too severely! If slavery had been abolished, I, also, could have married the man of my choice; I could have had a home shielded by the laws; and I should have been spared the painful task of confessing what I am now about to relate; but all my prospects had been blighted by slavery. I wanted to keep myself pure; and, under the most adverse circumstances, I tried hard to preserve my self-respect; but I was struggling alone in the powerful grasp of the demon Slavery; and the monster proved too strong for me. I felt as if I was forsaken by God and man; as if all my efforts must be frustrated; and I became reckless in my despair.

I have told you that Dr. Flint's persecutions and his wife's jealousy had given rise to some gossip in the neighborhood. Among others, it chanced that a white unmarried gentleman had obtained some knowledge of the circumstances in which I was placed. He knew my grandmother, and often spoke to me in the street. He became interested for me, and asked questions about my master, which I answered in part. He expressed a great deal of sympathy, and a wish to aid me. He constantly sought opportunities to see me, and wrote to me frequently. I was a poor slave girl, only fifteen years old.

So much attention from a superior person was, of course, flattering; for human nature is the same in all. I also felt grateful for his sympathy, and encouraged by his kind words. It seemed to me a great thing to have such a friend. By degrees, a more tender feeling crept into my heart. He was an educated and eloquent gentleman; too eloquent, alas, for the poor slave girl who trusted in him. Of course I saw whither all this was tending. I knew the impassable gulf between us; but to be an object of interest to a man who is not married, and who is not her master, is agreeable to the pride and feelings of a slave, if her miserable situation has left her any pride or sentiment. It seems less degrading to give one's self, than to submit to compulsion. There is something akin to freedom in having a lover who has no control over you, except that which he gains by kindness and attachment. A master may treat you as rudely as he pleases, and you dare not speak; moreover, the wrong does not seem so great with an unmarried man, as with one who has a wife to be made unhappy. There may be sophistry in all this; but the condition of a slave confuses all principles of morality, and, in fact, renders the practice of them impossible.

When I found that my master had actually begun to build the lonely cottage, other feelings mixed with those I have described. Revenge, and calculations of interest, were added to flattered vanity and sincere gratitude for kindness. I knew nothing would enrage Dr. Flint so much as to know that I favored another; and it was something to triumph over my tyrant even in that small way. I thought he would revenge himself by selling me, and I was sure my friend, Mr. Sands, would buy me. He was a man of more generosity and feeling than my master, and I thought my freedom could be easily obtained from him. The crisis of my fate now came so near that I was desperate. I shuddered to think of being the mother of children that should be owned by my old tyrant. I knew that as soon as a new fancy took him, his victims were sold far off to get rid of them; especially if they had children. I had seen several women sold, with his babies at the breast. He never allowed his offspring by slaves to remain long in sight of himself and his wife. Of a man who was not my master I could ask to have my children well supported; and in this case, I felt confident I should obtain the boon. I also felt quite sure that they would be made free. With all these thoughts revolving in my mind, and seeing no other way of escaping the doom I so much dreaded, I made a headlong plunge. Pity me, and pardon me, O virtuous reader! You never knew what it is to be a slave; to be entirely unprotected by law or custom; to have the laws reduce you to the condition of a chattel, entirely subject to the will of another. You never exhausted your ingenuity in avoiding the snares, and eluding the power of a hated tyrant; you never shuddered at the sound of his footsteps, and trembled within hearing of his voice. I know I did wrong. No one can feel it more sensibly than I do. The painful and humiliating memory will haunt me to my dying day. Still, in looking back, calmly, on the events of my life, I feel that the slave woman ought not to be judged by the same standard as others.

The months passed on. I had many unhappy hours. I secretly mourned over the sorrow I was bringing on my grandmother, who had so tried to shield me from harm. I knew that I was the greatest comfort of her old age, and that it was a source of pride to her that I had not degraded myself, like most of the slaves. I wanted to confess to her that I was no longer worthy of her love; but I could not utter the dreaded words.

As for Dr. Flint, I had a feeling of satisfaction and triumph in the thought of telling *him*. From time to time he told me of his intended arrangements, and I was silent. At last, he came and told me the cottage was completed, and ordered me to go to it. I told him I would never enter it. He said, "I have heard enough of such talk as that. You shall go, if you are carried by force; and you shall remain there."

I replied, "I will never go there. In a few months I shall be a mother."

He stood and looked at me in dumb amazement, and left the house without a word. I thought I should be happy in my triumph over him. But now that the truth was out, and my relatives would hear of it, I felt wretched. Humble as were their circumstances, they had pride in my good character. Now, how could I look them in the face? My self-respect was gone! I had resolved that I would be virtuous, though I was a slave. I had said, "Let the storm beat! I will brave it till I die." And now, how humiliated I felt!

I went to my grandmother. My lips moved to make confession, but the words stuck in my throat. I sat down in the shade of a tree at her door and began to sew. I think she saw something unusual was the matter with me. The mother of slaves is very watchful. She knows there is no security for her children. After they have entered their teens she lives in daily expectation of trouble. This leads to many questions. If the girl is of a sensitive nature, timidity keeps her from answering truthfully, and this well-meant course has a tendency to drive her from maternal counsels. Presently, in came my mistress, like a mad woman, and accused me concerning her husband. My grandmother, whose suspicions had been previously awakened, believed what she said. She exclaimed, "O Linda! has it come to this? I had rather see you dead than to see you as you now are. You are a disgrace to your dead mother." She tore from my fingers my mother's wedding ring and her silver thimble. "Go away!" she exclaimed, "and never come to my house, again." Her reproaches fell so hot and heavy, that they left me no chance to answer. Bitter tears, such as the eyes never shed but once, were my only answer. I rose from my seat, but fell back again, sobbing. She did not speak to me; but the tears were running down her furrowed cheeks, and they scorched me like fire. She had always been so kind to me! So kind! How I longed to throw myself at her feet, and tell her all the truth! But she had ordered me to go, and never to come there again. After a few minutes, I mustered strength, and started to obey her. With what feelings did I now close that little gate, which I used to open with such an eager hand in my childhood! It closed upon me with a sound I never heard before.

Where could I go? I was afraid to return to my master's. I walked on recklessly, not caring where I went, or what would become of me. When I had gone four or five miles, fatigue compelled me to stop. I sat down on the stump of an old tree. The stars were shining through the boughs above me. How they mocked me, with their bright, calm light! The hours passed by, and as I sat there alone a chilliness and deadly sickness came over me. I sank on the ground. My mind was full of horrid thoughts. I prayed to die; but the prayer was not answered. At last, with great effort I roused myself, and walked some distance further, to the house of a woman who had been a friend of my mother. When I told her why I was there, she spoke soothingly to me; but I could not be comforted. I thought I could bear my shame if I could only be reconciled to my grandmother. I longed to open my heart to her. I thought if she could know the real state of the case, and all I had been bearing for years, she would perhaps judge me less harshly. My friend advised me to send for her. I did so; but days of agonizing suspense passed before she came. Had she utterly forsaken me? No. She came at last. I knelt before her, and told her the things that had poisoned my life; how long I had been persecuted; that I saw no way of escape; and in an hour of extremity I had become desperate. She listened in silence. I told her I would bear any thing and do any thing, if in time I had hopes of obtaining her forgiveness. I begged of her to pity me, for my dead mother's sake. And she did pity me. She did not say, "I forgive you;" but she looked at me lovingly, with her eyes full of tears. She laid her old hand gently on my head, and murmured, "Poor child! Poor child!"

XIV. *Another Link to Life*

I had not returned to my master's house since the birth of my child. The old man raved to have me thus removed from his immediate power; but his wife vowed, by all that was good and great, she would kill me if I came back; and he did not doubt her word. Sometimes he would stay away for a season. Then he would come and renew the old threadbare discourse about his forbearance and my ingratitude. He labored, most unnecessarily, to convince me that I had lowered myself. The venomous old reprobate had no need of descanting on that theme. I felt humiliated enough. My unconscious babe was the ever-present witness of my shame. I listened with silent contempt when he talked about my having forfeited *his* good opinion; but I shed bitter tears that I was no longer worthy of being respected by the good and pure. Alas! slavery still held me in its poisonous grasp. There was no chance for me to be respectable. There was no prospect of being able to lead a better life.

Sometimes, when my master found that I still refused to accept what he called his kind offers, he would threaten to sell my child. "Perhaps that will humble you," said he.

Humble *me*! Was I not already in the dust?[9] But his threat lacerated my heart. I knew the law gave him power to fulfill it; for slaveholders have been cunning enough to enact that "the child shall follow the condition of the *mother*," not of the *father*; thus taking care that licentiousness shall not interfere with avarice. This reflection made me clasp my innocent babe all the more firmly to my heart. Horrid visions passed through my mind when I thought of his liability to fall into the slave trader's hands. I wept over him, and said, "O my child! perhaps they will leave you in some cold cabin to die, and then throw you into a hole, as if you were a dog."

When Dr. Flint learned that I was again to be a mother, he was exasperated beyond measure. He rushed from the house, and returned with a pair of shears. I had a fine head of hair; and he often railed about my pride of arranging it nicely. He cut every hair close to my head, storming and swearing all the time. I replied to some of his abuse, and he struck me. Some months before, he had pitched me down stairs in a fit of passion; and the injury I received was so serious that I was unable to turn myself in bed for many days. He then said, "Linda, I swear by God I will never raise my hand against you again;" but I knew that he would forget his promise.

After he discovered my situation, he was like a restless spirit from the pit. He came every day; and I was subjected to such insults as no pen can describe. I would not describe them if I could; they were too low, too revolting. I tried to keep them from my grandmother's knowledge as much as I could. I knew she had enough to sadden her life, without having my troubles to bear. When

---

9. Cf. Job 42.6: "Wherefore I abhor myself, and repent in dust and ashes."

she saw the doctor treat me with violence, and heard him utter oaths terrible enough to palsy a man's tongue, she could not always hold her peace. It was natural and motherlike that she should try to defend me; but it only made matters worse.

When they told me my new-born babe was a girl, my heart was heavier than it had ever been before. Slavery is terrible for men; but it is far more terrible for women. Superadded to the burden common to all, *they* have wrongs, and sufferings, and mortifications peculiarly their own.

Dr. Flint had sworn that he would make me suffer, to my last day, for this new crime against *him*, as he called it; and as long as he had me in his power he kept his word. On the fourth day after the birth of my babe, he entered my room suddenly, and commanded me to rise and bring my baby to him. The nurse who took care of me had gone out of the room to prepare some nourishment, and I was alone. There was no alternative. I rose, took up my babe, and crossed the room to where he sat. "Now stand there," said he, "till I tell you to go back!" My child bore a strong resemblance to her father, and to the deceased Mrs. Sands, her grandmother. He noticed this; and while I stood before him, trembling with weakness, he heaped upon me and my little one every vile epithet he could think of. Even the grandmother in her grave did not escape his curses. In the midst of his vituperations I fainted at his feet. This recalled him to his senses. He took the baby from my arms, laid it on the bed, dashed cold water in my face, took me up, and shook me violently, to restore my consciousness before any one entered the room. Just then my grandmother came in, and he hurried out of the house. I suffered in consequence of this treatment; but I begged my friends to let me die, rather than send for the doctor. There was nothing I dreaded so much as his presence. My life was spared; and I was glad for the sake of my little ones. Had it not been for these ties to life, I should have been glad to be released by death, though I had lived only nineteen years.

Always it gave me a pang that my children had no lawful claim to a name. Their father offered his; but, if I had wished to accept the offer, I dared not while my master lived. Moreover, I knew it would not be accepted at their baptism. A Christian name they were at least entitled to; and we resolved to call my boy for our dear good Benjamin, who had gone far away from us.

My grandmother belonged to the church, and she was very desirous of having the children christened. I knew Dr. Flint would forbid it, and I did not venture to attempt it. But chance favored me. He was called to visit a patient out of town, and was obliged to be absent during Sunday. "Now is the time," said my grandmother; "we will take the children to church, and have them christened."

When I entered the church, recollections of my mother came over me, and I felt subdued in spirit. There she had presented me for baptism, without any reason to feel ashamed. She had been married, and had such legal rights as slavery allows a slave. The vows had at least been sacred to *her*, and she had never violated them. I was glad she was not alive, to know under what different circumstances her grandchildren were presented for baptism. Why had my lot been so different from my mother's? *Her* master had died when she was a child; and she remained with her mistress till she married. She was never in the power of any master; and thus she escaped one class of the evils that generally fall upon slaves.

When my baby was about to be christened, the former mistress of my father stepped up to me, and proposed to give it her Christian name. To this I added the surname of my father, who had himself no legal right to it; for my grandfather on the paternal side was a white gentleman. What tangled skeins are the genealogies of slavery! I loved my father; but it mortified me to be obliged to bestow his name on my children.

When we left the church, my father's old mistress invited me to go home with her. She clasped a gold chain around my baby's neck. I thanked her for this kindness; but I did not like the emblem. I wanted no chain to be fastened on my daughter, not even if its links were of gold. How earnestly I prayed that she might never feel the weight of slavery's chain, whose iron entereth into the soul.[1]

XXI. The Loophole of Retreat[2]

A small shed had been added to my grandmother's house years ago. Some boards were laid across the joists at the top, and between these boards and the roof was a very small garret, never occupied by any thing but rats and mice. It was a pent roof, covered with nothing but shingles, according to the southern custom for such buildings. The garret was only nine feet long and seven wide. The highest part was three feet high, and sloped down abruptly to the loose board floor. There was no admission for either light or air. My uncle Phillip, who was a carpenter, had very skilfully made a concealed trap-door, which communicated with the storeroom. He had been doing this while I was waiting in the swamp. The storeroom opened upon a piazza. To this hole I was conveyed as soon as I entered the house. The air was stifling; the darkness total. A bed had been spread on the floor. I could sleep quite comfortably on one side; but the slope was so sudden that I could not turn on the other without hitting the roof. The rats and mice ran over my bed; but I was weary, and I slept such sleep as the wretched may, when a tempest has passed over them. Morning came. I knew it only by the noises I heard; for in my small den day and night were all the same. I suffered for air even more than for light. But I was not comfortless. I heard the voices of my children. There was joy and there was sadness in the sound. It made my tears flow. How I longed to speak to them! I was eager to look on their faces; but there was no hole, no crack, through which I could peep. This continued darkness was oppressive. It seemed horrible to sit or lie in a cramped position day after day, without one gleam of light. Yet I would have chosen this, rather than my lot as a slave, though white people considered it an easy one; and it was so compared with the fate of others. I was never cruelly over-worked; I was never lacerated with the whip from head to foot; I was never so beaten and bruised that I could not turn from one side to the other; I never had my heel-strings cut to prevent my running away; I was never chained to a log and forced to drag it about, while I toiled in the fields from morning till night; I was never branded with hot iron, or torn by bloodhounds. On the contrary, I had always been kindly treated, and

1. Cf. Psalm 105.17–18: "He sent a man before them, even Joseph, who was sold for a servant: Whose feet they hurt with fetters: he was laid in iron." This and other allusions identify Jacobs's family as Episcopalians.
2. Cf. *The Task* 4.88–90, a popular long poem (1785) by the English poet William Cowper (1731–1800). At this point in the narrative Brent has escaped from the Flint household and is hiding in her grandmother's attic. The account states that she remains there for seven years.

tenderly cared for, until I came into the hands of Dr. Flint. I had never wished for freedom till then. But though my life in slavery was comparatively devoid of hardships, God pity the woman who is compelled to lead such a life!

My food was passed up to me through the trap-door my uncle had contrived; and my grandmother, my uncle Phillip, and aunt Nancy would seize such opportunities as they could, to mount up there and chat with me at the opening. But of course this was not safe in the daytime. It must all be done in darkness. It was impossible or me to move in an erect position, but I crawled about my den for exercise. One day I hit my head against something, and found it was a gimlet. My uncle had left it sticking there when he made the trap-door. I was as rejoiced as Robinson Crusoe[3] could have been at finding such a treasure. It put a lucky thought into my head. I said to myself, "Now I will have some light. Now I will see my children." I did not dare to begin my work during the daytime, for fear of attracting attention. But I groped round; and having found the side next the street, where I could frequently see my children, I struck the gimlet in and waited for evening. I bored three rows of holes, one above another; then I bored out the interstices between. I thus succeeded in making one hole about an inch long and an inch broad. I sat by it till late into the night, to enjoy the little whiff of air that floated in. In the morning I watched for my children. The first person I saw in the street was Dr. Flint. I had a shuddering, superstitious feeling that it was a bad omen. Several familiar faces passed by. At last I heard the merry laugh of children, and presently two sweet little faces were looking up at me, as though they knew I was there, and were conscious of the joy they imparted. How I longed to *tell* them I was there!

My condition was now a little improved. But for weeks I was tormented by hundreds of little red insects, fine as a needle's point, that pierced through my skin, and produced an intolerable burning. The good grandmother gave me herb teas and cooling medicines, and finally I got rid of them. The heat of my den was intense, for nothing but thin shingles protected me from the scorching summer's sun. But I had my consolations. Through my peeping-hole I could watch the children, and when they were near enough, I could hear their talk. Aunt Nancy brought me all the news she could hear at Dr. Flint's. From her I learned that the doctor had written to New York to a colored woman, who had been born and raised in our neighborhood, and had breathed his contaminating atmosphere. He offered her a reward if she could find out any thing about me. I know not what was the nature of her reply; but he soon after started for New York in haste, saying to his family that he had business of importance to transact. I peeped at him as he passed on his way to the steamboat. It was a satisfaction to have miles of land and water between us, even for a little while; and it was a still greater satisfaction to know that he believed me to be in the Free States. My little den seemed less dreary than it had done. He returned, as he did from his former journey to New York, without obtaining any satisfactory information. When he passed our house next morning, Benny was standing at the gate. He had heard them say that he had gone to find me, and he called out, "Dr. Flint, did you bring my mother home? I want to see her." The doctor stamped his foot at him in a rage, and exclaimed, "Get out of the way, you little damned rascal! If you don't, I'll cut off your head."

3. Allusion to a popular novel (1719) by the English writer Daniel Defoe (1660–1731) about a man shipwrecked on a desert island.

Benny ran terrified into the house, saying, "You can't put me in jail again. I don't belong to you now." It was well that the wind carried the words away from the doctor's ear. I told my grandmother of it, when we had our next conference at the trap-door; and begged of her not to allow the children to be impertinent to the irascible old man.

Autumn came, with a pleasant abatement of heat. My eyes had become accustomed to the dim light, and by holding my book or work in a certain position near the aperture I contrived to read and sew. That was a great relief to the tedious monotony of my life. But when winter came, the cold penetrated through the thin shingle roof, and I was dreadfully chilled. The winters there are not so long, or so severe, as in northern latitudes; but the houses are not built to shelter from cold, and my little den was peculiarly comfortless. The kind grandmother brought me bed-clothes and warm drinks. Often I was obliged to lie in bed all day to keep comfortable; but with all my precautions, my shoulders and feet were frostbitten. O, those long, gloomy days, with no object for my eye to rest upon, and no thoughts to occupy my mind, except the dreary past and the uncertain future! I was thankful when there came a day sufficiently mild for me to wrap myself up and sit at the loophole to watch the passers by. Southerners have the habit of stopping and talking in the streets, and I heard many conversations not intended to meet my ears. I heard slave-hunters planning how to catch some poor fugitive. Several times I heard allusions to Dr. Flint, myself, and the history of my children, who, perhaps, were playing near the gate. One would say, "I wouldn't move my little finger to catch her, as old Flint's property." Another would say, "I'll catch *any* nigger for the reward. A man ought to have what belongs to him, if he *is* a damned brute." The opinion was often expressed that I was in the Free States. Very rarely did any one suggest that I might be in the vicinity. Had the least suspicion rested on my grandmother's house, it would have been burned to the ground. But it was the last place they thought of. Yet there was no place, where slavery existed, that could have afforded me so good a place of concealment.

Dr. Flint and his family repeatedly tried to coax and bribe my children to tell something they had heard said about me. One day the doctor took them into a shop, and offered them some bright little silver pieces and gay handkerchiefs if they would tell where their mother was. Ellen shrank away from him, and would not speak; but Benny spoke up, and said, "Dr. Flint, I don't know where my mother is. I guess she's in New York; and when you go there again, I wish you'd ask her to come home, for I want to see her; but if you put her in jail, or tell her you'll cut her head off, I'll tell her to go right back."

XLI. Free at Last[4]

Mrs. Bruce, and every member of her family, were exceedingly kind to me. I was thankful for the blessings of my lot, yet I could not always wear a cheerful countenance. I was doing harm to no one; on the contrary, I was doing all the good I could in my small way; yet I could never go out to breathe God's free

4. This is the final chapter of *Incidents*. Brent has escaped to New York and found employment in the Bruce family, but the passage of the Fugitive Slave Law in 1850 means that she is not really free. The title alludes to a familiar spiritual.

air without trepidation at my heart. This seemed hard; and I could not think it was a right state of things in any civilized country.

From time to time I received news from my good old grandmother. She could not write; but she employed others to write for her. The following is an extract from one of her last letters:—

> "Dear Daughter: I cannot hope to see you again on earth; but I pray to God to unite us above, where pain will no more rack this feeble body of mine; where sorrow and parting from my children will be no more.[5] God has promised these things if we are faithful unto the end. My age and feeble health deprive me of going to church now; but God is with me here at home. Thank your brother for his kindness. Give much love to him, and tell him to remember the Creator in the days of his youth,[6] and strive to meet me in the Father's kingdom. Love to Ellen and Benjamin. Don't neglect him. Tell him for me, to be a good boy. Strive, my child, to train them for God's children. May he protect and provide for you, is the prayer of your loving old mother."

These letters both cheered and saddened me. I was always glad to have tidings from the kind, faithful old friend of my unhappy youth; but her messages of love made my heart yearn to see her before she died, and I mourned over the fact that it was impossible. Some months after I returned from my flight to New England, I received a letter from her, in which she wrote, "Dr. Flint is dead. He has left a distressed family. Poor old man! I hope he made his peace with God."

I remembered how he had defrauded my grandmother of the hard earnings she had loaned; how he had tried to cheat her out of the freedom her mistress had promised her, and how he had persecuted her children; and I thought to myself that she was a better Christian than I was, if she could entirely forgive him. I cannot say, with truth, that the news of my old master's death softened my feelings towards him. There are wrongs which even the grave does not bury. The man was odious to me while he lived, and his memory is odious now.

His departure from this world did not diminish my danger. He had threatened my grandmother that his heirs should hold me in slavery after he was gone; that I never should be free so long as a child of his survived. As for Mrs. Flint, I had seen her in deeper afflictions than I supposed the loss of her husband would be, for she had buried several children; yet I never saw any signs of softening in her heart. The doctor had died in embarrassed circumstances, and had little to will to his heirs, except such property as he was unable to grasp. I was well aware what I had to expect from the family of Flints; and my fears were confirmed by a letter from the south, warning me to be on my guard, because Mrs. Flint openly declared that her daughter could not afford to lose so valuable a slave as I was.

I kept close watch of the newspapers for arrivals; but one Saturday night, being much occupied, I forgot to examine the Evening Express as usual. I went down into the parlor for it, early in the morning, and found the boy

---

5. Cf. Revelation 21.4: "And God shall wipe away all tears from their eyes; and there shall be no more death, neither sorrow, nor crying, neither shall there be any more pain: for the former things are passed away."

6. Ecclesiastes 12.1. Throughout the narrative the grandmother is portrayed as a deeply pious woman with great knowledge of the Bible.

about to kindle a fire with it. I took it from him and examined the list of arrivals. Reader, if you have never been a slave, you cannot imagine the acute sensation of suffering at my heart, when I read the names of Mr. and Mrs. Dodge,[7] at a hotel in Courtland Street. It was a third-rate hotel, and that circumstance convinced me of the truth of what I had heard, that they were short of funds and had need of my value, as *they* valued me; and that was by dollars and cents. I hastened with the paper to Mrs. Bruce. Her heart and hand were always open to every one in distress, and she always warmly sympathized with mine. It was impossible to tell how near the enemy was. He might have passed and repassed the house while we were sleeping. He might at that moment be waiting to pounce upon me if I ventured out of doors. I had never seen the husband of my young mistress, and therefore I could not distinguish him from any other stranger. A carriage was hastily ordered; and, closely veiled, I followed Mrs. Bruce, taking the baby again with me into exile. After various turnings and crossings, and returnings, the carriage stopped at the house of one of Mrs. Bruce's friends, where I was kindly received. Mrs. Bruce returned immediately, to instruct the domestics what to say if any one came to inquire for me.

It was lucky for me that the evening paper was not burned up before I had a chance to examine the list of arrivals. It was not long after Mrs. Bruce's return to her house, before several people came to inquire for me. One inquired for me, another asked for my daughter Ellen, and another said he had a letter from my grandmother, which he was requested to deliver in person.

They were told, "She *has* lived here, but she has left."

"How long ago?"

"I don't know, sir."

"Do you know where she went?"

"I do not, sir." And the door was closed.

This Mr. Dodge, who claimed me as his property, was originally a Yankee pedler in the south; then he became a merchant, and finally a slaveholder. He managed to get introduced into what was called the first society, and married Miss Emily Flint. A quarrel arose between him and her brother, and the brother cowhided him. This led to a family feud, and he proposed to remove to Virginia. Dr. Flint left him no property, and his own means had become circumscribed, while a wife and children depended upon him for support. Under these circumstances, it was very natural that he should make an effort to put me into his pocket.

I had a colored friend, a man from my native place, in whom I had the most implicit confidence. I sent for him, and told him that Mr. and Mrs. Dodge had arrived in New York. I proposed that he should call upon them to make inquiries about his friends at the south, with whom Dr. Flint's family were well acquainted. He thought there was no impropriety in his doing so, and he consented. He went to the hotel, and knocked at the door of Mr. Dodge's room, which was opened by the gentleman himself, who gruffly inquired, "What brought you here? How came you to know I was in the city?"

"Your arrival was published in the evening papers, sir; and I called to ask Mrs. Dodge about my friends at home. I didn't suppose it would give any offence."

---

7. Dodge is the married name of Emily Flint, Brent's legal owner.

"Where's that negro girl, that belongs to my wife?"

"What girl, sir?"

"You know well enough. I mean Linda, that ran away from Dr. Flint's plantation, some years ago. I dare say you've seen her, and know where she is."

"Yes, sir, I've seen her, and know where she is. She is out of your reach, sir."

"Tell me where she is, or bring her to me, and I will give her a chance to buy her freedom."

"I don't think it would be of any use, sir. I have heard her say she would go to the ends of the earth, rather than pay any man or woman for her freedom, because she thinks she has a right to it. Besides, she couldn't do it, if she would, for she has spent her earnings to educate her children."

This made Mr. Dodge very angry, and some high words passed between them. My friend was afraid to come where I was; but in the course of the day I received a note from him. I supposed they had not come from the south, in the winter, for a pleasure excursion; and now the nature of their business was very plain.

Mrs. Bruce came to me and entreated me to leave the city the next morning. She said her house was watched, and it was possible that some clew to me might be obtained. I refused to take her advice. She pleaded with an earnest tenderness, that ought to have moved me; but I was in a bitter, disheartened mood. I was weary of flying from pillar to post. I had been chased during half my life, and it seemed as if the chase was never to end. There I sat, in that great city, guiltless of crime, yet not daring to worship God in any of the churches. I heard the bells ringing for afternoon service, and, with contemptuous sarcasm, I said, "Will the preachers take for their text, 'Proclaim liberty to the captive, and the opening of prison doors to them that are bound'?[8] or will they preach from the text, 'Do unto others as ye would they should do unto you'?"[9] Oppressed Poles and Hungarians could find a safe refuge in that city; John Mitchell[1] was free to proclaim in the City Hall his desire for "a plantation well stocked with slaves;" but there I sat, an oppressed American, not daring to show my face. "God forgive the black and bitter thoughts I indulged on that Sabbath day! The Scripture says, "Oppression makes even a wise man mad;"[2] and I was not wise.

I had been told that Mr. Dodge said his wife had never signed away her right to my children, and if he could not get me, he would take them. This it was, more than any thing else, that roused such a tempest in my soul. Benjamin was with his uncle William in California, but my innocent young daughter had come to spend a vacation with me. I thought of what I had suffered in slavery at her age, and my heart was like a tiger's when a hunter tries to seize her young.

Dear Mrs. Bruce! I seem to see the expression of her face, as she turned away discouraged by my obstinate mood. Finding her expostulations unavailing, she sent Ellen to entreat me. When ten o'clock in the evening arrived

---

8. Isaiah 61.1.
9. Matthew 7.12.
1. Following the unsuccessful European revolutions of 1848, many Polish and Hungarian political refugees found homes in New York City and New England. John Mitchell (1815–1875), Irish-American founder of the New York City proslavery newspaper *The Citizen*.

Throughout the pre–Civil War era, Irish-American politicians tended to portray free blacks as competing for jobs that would otherwise go to the Irish; Mitchell indeed wrote what Jacobs attributes to him here.
2. Ecclesiastes 7.7: "Surely oppression maketh a wise man mad; and a gift destroyeth the heart."

and Ellen had not returned, this watchful and unwearied friend became anxious. She came to us in a carriage, bringing a well-filled trunk for my journey—trusting that by this time I would listen to reason. I yielded to her, as I ought to have done before.

The next day, baby and I set out in a heavy snow storm, bound for New England again. I received letters from the City of Iniquity,[3] addressed to me under an assumed name. In a few days one came from Mrs. Bruce, informing me that my new master was still searching for me, and that she intended to put an end to this persecution by buying my freedom. I felt grateful for the kindness that prompted this offer, but the idea was not so pleasant to me as might have been expected. The more my mind had become enlightened, the more difficult it was for me to consider myself an article of property; and to pay money to those who had so grievously oppressed me seemed like taking from my sufferings the glory of triumph. I wrote to Mrs. Bruce, thanking her, but saying that being sold from one owner to another seemed too much like slavery; that such a great obligation could not be easily cancelled; and that I preferred to go to my brother in California.

Without my knowledge, Mrs. Bruce employed a gentleman in New York to enter into negotiations with Mr. Dodge. He proposed to pay three hundred dollars down, if Mr. Dodge would sell me, and enter into obligations to relinquish all claim to me or my children forever after. He who called himself my master said he scorned so small an offer for such a valuable servant. The gentleman replied, "You can do as you choose, sir. If you reject this offer you will never get any thing; for the woman has friends who will convey her and her children out of the country."

Mr. Dodge concluded that "half a loaf was better than no bread," and he agreed to the proffered terms. By the next mail I received this brief letter from Mrs. Bruce: "I am rejoiced to tell you that the money for your freedom has been paid to Mr. Dodge. Come home to-morrow. I long to see you and my sweet babe."

My brain reeled as I read these lines. A gentleman near me said, "It's true; I have seen the bill of sale." "The bill of sale!" Those words struck me like a blow. So I was *sold* at last! A human being *sold* in the free city of New York! The bill of sale is on record, and future generations will learn from it that women were articles of traffic in New York, late in the nineteenth century of the Christian religion. It may hereafter prove a useful document to antiquaries, who are seeking to measure the progress of civilization in the United States. I well know the value of that bit of paper; but much as I love freedom, I do not like to look upon it. I am deeply grateful to the generous friend who procured it, but I despise the miscreant who demanded payment for what never rightfully belonged to him or his.

I had objected to having my freedom bought, yet I must confess that when it was done I felt as if a heavy load had been lifted from my weary shoulders. When I rode home in the cars I was no longer afraid to unveil my face and look at people as they passed. I should have been glad to have met Daniel Dodge himself; to have had him seen me and known me, that he might have mourned over the untoward circumstances which compelled him to sell me for three hundred dollars.

---

3. Jacobs's term for New York City as the center of the business of returning fugitive slaves into bondage.

When I reached home, the arms of my benefactress were thrown round me, and our tears mingled. As soon as she could speak, she said, "O Linda, I'm so glad it's all over! You wrote to me as if you thought you were going to be transferred from one owner to another. But I did not buy you for your services. I should have done just the same, if you had been going to sail for California tomorrow. I should, at least, have the satisfaction of knowing that you left me a free woman."

My heart was exceedingly full. I remembered how my poor father had tried to buy me, when I was a small child, and how he had been disappointed. I hoped his spirit was rejoicing over me now. I remembered how my good old grandmother had laid up her earnings to purchase me in later years, and how often her plans had been frustrated. How that faithful, loving old heart would leap for joy, if she could look on me and my children now that we were free! My relatives had been foiled in all their efforts, but God had raised me up a friend among strangers, who had bestowed on me the precious, long-desired boon. Friend! It is a common word, often lightly used. Like other good and beautiful things, it may be tarnished by careless handling; but when I speak of Mrs. Bruce as my friend, the word is sacred.

My grandmother lived to rejoice in my freedom; but not long after, a letter came with a black seal. She had gone "where the wicked cease from troubling, and the weary are at rest."[4]

Time passed on, and a paper came to me from the south, containing an obituary notice of my uncle Phillip. It was the only case I ever knew of such an honor conferred upon a colored person. It was written by one of his friends, and contained these words: "Now that death has laid him low, they call him a good man and a useful citizen; but what are eulogies to the black man, when the world has faded from his vision? It does not require man's praise to obtain rest in God's kingdom." So they called a colored man a *citizen!* Strange words to be uttered in that region![5]

Reader, my story ends with freedom; not in the usual way, with marriage.[6] I and my children are now free! We are as free from the power of slaveholders as are the white people of the north; and though that, according to my ideas, is not saying a great deal, it is a vast improvement in *my* condition. The dream of my life is not yet realized. I do not sit with my children in a home of my own. I still long for a hearthstone of my own, however humble. I wish it for my children's sake far more than for my own. But God so orders circumstances as to keep me with my friend Mrs. Bruce. Love, duty, gratitude, also bind me to her side. It is a privilege to serve her who pities my oppressed people, and who has bestowed the inestimable boon of freedom on me and my children.

It has been painful to me, in many ways, to recall the dreary years I passed in bondage. I would gladly forget them if I could. Yet the retrospection is not altogether without solace; for with those gloomy recollections come tender memories of my good old grandmother, like light, fleecy clouds floating over a dark and troubled sea.

---

4. Cf. Job 3.17: "There the wicked cease from troubling; and there the weary be at rest."
5. The laws of North Carolina at this time denied the status of citizen to free blacks as well as to slaves.

6. Allusion to the fictional formula of women's novels, reminding readers that such novels are really about white women, because black women cannot share the same story while slavery threatens them.

GEORGE WASHINGTON HARRIS
1814–1869

George Washington Harris was born on March 20, 1814, in western Pennsylvania, and as a boy was apprenticed as a metalworker in his half-brother's shop in Knoxville, Tennessee. In manhood he was the complete craftsman who could make almost anything from machines to silverware and jewelry; he was an engraver; and he repaired guns, clocks, and watches. At nineteen he became captain of a steamboat, the *Knoxville*, and he married at twenty-one.

Having left steamboating for newspaper editing and metalworking in Knoxville, Harris in the early 1840s began contributing sketches to the New York *Spirit of the Times*, the great sporting journal edited by William T. Porter. A business trip to southeast Tennessee in 1854 led to tales in the *Spirit* about Sut Lovengood (a spelling later changed to Lovingood). In 1857 Harris briefly became postmaster of Knoxville; the next year he wrote more Sut stories for the Nashville *Union and American* and began planning to collect them. Instead, he was drawn into secessionist politics, and soon the Civil War disrupted his life. During the war he lived in Chattanooga, Tennessee; Decatur, Alabama; and Trenton, Georgia.

Harris's wife died in 1867, and in October 1869 he remarried. He went to Lynchburg, Virginia, two months later on business for a railroad. On the return trip he fell ill and was taken from the train at Knoxville, where he died suddenly and mysteriously: once he said, "Poisoned." At Lynchburg he had shown a printer the manuscript of a second book, to be called *High Times and Hard Times*, but the manuscript disappeared at the time of his death or later. (A modern editor has assembled some Harris pieces under that title, but the contents of the manuscript are unknown and most pieces in it are probably lost forever, although scholars continue to find more tales in newspapers.)

From Harris's time to the present some readers have been shocked by the Lovingood stories. In *Patriotic Gore* Edmund Wilson called *Sut Lovingood* "by far the most repellent book of any real literary merit in American literature." Beyond question, Sut is the archetypal male chauvinist in his unmitigated delight in irresponsible sex—as well as in talking about sex and related crudenesses. Harris's humor can be Swiftian in its bleak, bestial foulness. But his reputation has begun to burgeon among readers who feel that his triumphant creative energy puts him now and then into the company of such writers as Mark Twain and William Faulkner, both of whom delighted in Sut Lovingood.

Parson John Bullen's Lizards[1]

AIT ($8) DULLARS REW-ARD.

'TENSHUN BELEVERS AND KONSTABLES KETCH 'IM KETCH 'IM

This kash wil be pade in korn,[2] ur uther projuce, tu be kolected at ur about nex camp-meetin, *ur thararter*, by eny wun what ketches him, fur the karkus ove a sartin wun SUT LOVINGOOD, dead ur alive, ur ailin, an' safely giv over tu the purtectin care ove Parson John Bullin, ur lef' well tied, at Squire Mackjun-

---

1. The text is that of *Sut Lovingood. Yarns Spun by a "Natural Born Durn'd Fool." Warped and Wove for Public Wear* (1867).
2. I.e., corn whiskey, or other produce. The dialect spellings ordinarily come clear readily enough; when

readers bog down, the best thing to do is back up a paragraph and start reading aloud from there. A few typographical errors have been corrected, but inconsistencies (and probably some errors) remain.

kins fur the raisin ove the devil pussonely, an' permiskusly[3] discumfurtin the wimen very powerful, an' skeerin ove folks generly a heap, an' bustin up a promisin, big warm meetin, an' a makin the wickid larf, an' wus, an' wus, insultin ove the passun orful.

Test, JEHU WETHERO.

Sined by me,
JOHN BULLEN, the passun

I found written copies of the above highly intelligible and vindictive proclamation, stuck up on every blacksmith shop, doggery,[4] and store door, in the Frog Mountain Range. Its blood-thirsty spirit, its style, and above all, its chirography,[5] interested me to the extent of taking one down from a tree for preservation.

In a few days I found Sut in a good crowd in front of Capehart's Doggery, and as he seemed to be about in good tune, I read it to him.

"Yas, George, that ar dockymint am in dead yearnist sartin. Them hard shells[6] over thar dus want me the wus kine, powerful bad. *But*, I spect ait dullers won't fetch me, nither wud ait hundred, bekase thar's nun ove 'em fas' enuf tu ketch me, nither is thar hosses by the livin jingo! Say, George, much talk 'bout this fuss up whar yu're been?" For the sake of a joke I said yes, a great deal.

"Jis' es I 'spected, durn 'em, all git drunk, an' skeer thar fool sefs ni ontu deth, an' then lay hit ontu me, a poor innersent youf, an' es soun' a belever es they is. Lite, lite, ole feller an' let that roan ove yourn blow[7] a litil, an' I'll 'splain this cussed misfortnit affar: hit hes ruinated my karacter es a pius pusson in the s'ciety roun' yere, an' is a spreadin faster nur meazils. When ever yu hear eny on 'em a spreadin hit, gin hit the dam lie squar, will yu? I haint dun nuffin tu one ove 'em. Hits true, I did sorter frustrate a few lizzards a littil, but they haint members, es I knows on.

"You, see, las' year I went tu the big meetin at Rattlesnake Springs, an' wer a sittin in a nice shady place convarsin wif a frien' ove mine, intu the huckil berry thickit, jis' duin nuffin tu nobody an' makin no fuss, when, the fust thing I remembers, I woke up frum a trance what I hed been knocked inter by a four-year old hickory-stick, hilt in the paw ove old Passun Bullin, durn his alligater hide; an' he wer standin a striddil ove me, a foamin at the mouf, a-chompin his teeth—gesterin wif the hickory club—an' a-preachin tu me so you cud a-hearn him a mile, about a sartin sins gineraly, an' my wickedness pussonely; an' mensunin the name ove my frien' loud enuf tu be hearn tu the meetin 'ous. My poor innersent frien' wer dun gone an' I wer glad ove hit, fur I tho't he ment tu kill me rite whar I lay, an' I didn't want her tu see me die."

"Who was she, the friend you speak of Sut?" Sut opened his eyes wide.

"Hu the devil, an' durnashun tole *yu* that hit wer a she?"

"Why, you did, Sut"———

"I *didn't*, durn ef I did. Ole Bullin dun hit, an' I'll hev tu kill him yet, the cussed, infernel ole tale-barer!"———

"Well, well, Sut, who was she?"

3. I.e., promiscuously (which then meant generally, variously).
4. Groggery, low-class saloon.
5. Handwriting (and spelling).
6. Hard-shell Baptists, conservative fundamentalist sect.
7. Pant, cool off. "Roan": Horse of a solid color (such as black or red) with a mixture of white hairs throughout.

"Nun ove y-u-r-e b-i-s-n-i-s-s, durn yure littil ankshus picter![8] I *sees yu* a lickin ove yure lips. I *will* tell you one thing, George; that night, a neighbor gal got a all-fired, overhandid stroppin frum her mam, wif a stirrup leather, an' old Passun Bullin, hed et supper thar, an what's wus nur all, that poor innersent, skeer'd gal hed dun her levil bes' a cookin hit fur 'im. She begged him, a trimblin, an' a-cryin not tu tell on her. He et her cookin, he promised her he'd keep dark—an' then went strait an' tole her mam. Warnt that rale low down, wolf mean? The durnd infunel, hiperkritikal, pot-bellied, scaley-hided, whisky-wastin, stinkin ole groun'-hog. He'd a heap better a stole sum *man's* hoss; I'd a tho't more ove 'im. But I paid him plum up fur hit, an' I means tu keep a payin him, ontil one ur tuther, ove our toes pints up tu the roots ove the grass.

"Well, yere's the way I lifted that note ove han'.[9] At the nex big meetin at Rattilsnaik—las' week hit wer—I wer on han' es solemn es a ole hat kivver on collection day. I hed my face draw'd out intu the shape an' perporshun ove a taylwer's sleeve-board,[1] pint down. I hed put on the convicted sinner so pufeckly that an' ole obsarvin she pillar ove the church sed tu a ole he pillar, es I walked up tu my bainch:

" 'Law sakes alive, ef thar ain't that *orful* sinner, Sut Lovingood, pearced plum thru; hu's nex?'

"Yu see, by golly, George, I *hed* tu promis the ole tub ove soap-greas tu cum an' hev myself converted, jis' tu keep him frum killin me. An' es I know'd hit wudn't interfare wif the relashun I bore tu the still housis[2] roun' thar, I didn't keer a durn. I jis' wanted tu git *ni* old Bullin, onst onsuspected, an' this wer the bes' way tu du hit. I tuk a seat on the side steps ove the pulpit, an' kivvered es much ove my straitch'd face es I could wif my han's, tu prove I wer in yearnis. Hit tuck powerful—fur I hearn a sorter thankful kine ove buzzin all over the congregashun. Ole Bullin hissef looked down at me, over his old copper specks,[3] an' hit sed jis' es plain es a look cud say hit: 'Yu am thar, ar you—durn yu, hits well fur yu that yu cum.' I tho't sorter diffrent frum that. I tho't hit wud a been well fur *yu*, ef I hadent a-cum, but I didn't say hit jis' then. Thar wer a monstrus crowd in that grove, fur the weather wer fine, an' b'levers wer plenty roun' about Rattilsnaik Springs. Ole Bullin gin out, an' they sung that hyme, yu know:

> "Thar will be mournin, mournin yere, an' mournin thar,
> On that dredful day tu cum."[4]

"Thinks I, ole hoss, kin hit be possibil enybody hes tole yu what's a gwine tu happin; an' then I tho't that nobody know'd hit but me, and I wer cumf-orted. He nex tuck hisself a tex[5] pow'fly mixed wif brimstone, an' trim'd wif blue flames, an' then he open'd. He cummenced ontu the sinners; he threaten'd 'em orful, tried tu skeer 'em wif all the wust varmints he cud think ove, an' arter a while he got ontu the idear ove Hell-sarpints, and he dwelt on it sum. He tole 'em how the old Hell-sarpints wud sarve em if they didn't repent; how cold they'd crawl over thar nakid bodys, an' how like ontu pitch they'd stick tu 'em es they crawled; how they'd rap thar tails roun' thar naiks

---

8. Picture, face.
9. Promissory note.
1. Narrow ironing board designed for shaping or press-ing sleeves.

2. Sheds enclosing stills for making whiskey.
3. Copper-rimmed spectacles.
4. Southern hymn dating from the Wesleyan revival.
5. Text.

chokin clost, poke thar tungs up thar noses, an' hiss intu thar years. This wer the way they wer tu sarve men folks. Then he turned ontu the wimmen: tole 'em how they'd quile[6] intu thar buzzims, an' how they *wud* crawl down onder thar frock-strings, no odds how tite they tied 'em, an' how sum ove the oldes' an' wus ones wud crawl up thar laigs, an' travil *onder* thar garters, no odds how tight they tied *them*, an' when the two armys ove Hell-sarpents met, then——That las' remark *fotch* 'em. Ove all the screamin, an' hollerin, an' loud cryin, I ever hearn, begun all at onst, all over the hole groun' jis' es he hollered out that word 'then.' He kep on a bellerin, but I got so buisy jis' then, that I didn't listen tu him much, fur I saw that my time fur ackshun hed cum. Now yu see, George, I'd cotch seven ur eight big pot-bellied lizzards, an' hed 'em in a littil narrer bag, what I had made a-purpus. Thar tails all at the bottim, an' so crowdid fur room that they cudent turn roun'. So when he wer a-ravin ontu his tip-toes, an' a-poundin the pulpit wif his fis'—onbenowenst tu eny-body, I ontied my bag ove reptiles, put the mouf ove hit onder the bottim ove his britches-laig, an' sot intu pinchin thar tails. Quick es gunpow-der they all tuck up his bar laig, makin a nise like squirrils a-climbin a shell-bark hickory. He stop't preachin rite in the middil ove the word 'damnation,' an' looked fur a moment like he wer a listenin fur sumthin—sorter like a ole sow dus, when she hears yu a-whistlin fur the dorgs. The tarifick shape ove his feeters[7] stopp't the shoutin an' screamin; instuntly yu cud hearn a cricket chirp. I gin a long groan, an' hilt my head a-twixt my knees. He gin hisself sum orful open-handed slaps wif fust one han' an' then tuther, about the place whar yu cut the bes' steak outen a beef. Then he'd fetch a vigrus ruff rub whar a hosses tail sprouts; then he'd stomp one foot, then tuther, then bof at onst. Then he run his han' atween his waisbun an' his shut[8] an' reach'd way down, an' roun' wif hit; then he spread his big laigs, an' gin his back a good rattlin rub agin the pulpit, like a hog scratches hisself agin a stump, leanin tu hit pow'ful, an' twitchin, an' squirmin all over, es ef he'd slept in a dorg bed, ur ontu a pisant[9] hill. About this time, one ove my lizzards scared an' hurt by all this poundin' an' feelin, an' scratchin, popp'd out his head frum the passun's shut collar, an' his ole brown naik, an' wer a-surveyin the crowd, when ole Bullin struck at 'im, jis' too late, fur he'd dodged back agin. The hell desarvin old raskil's speech now cum tu 'im, an' sez he, 'Pray fur me brethren an' sistern, fur I is a-rastilin wif the great inimy rite now!' an' his voice wer the mos' pitiful, trimblin thing I ever hearn. Sum ove the wimmen fotch a painter[1] yell, an' a young docter, wif ramrod laigs, lean'd toward me monstrus knowin like, an' sez he, 'Clar case ove Delishus Tremenjus.'[2] I nodded my head an' sez I, 'Yas, spechuly the tremenjus part, an' Ise feard hit haint at hits worst.' Ole Bullin's eyes wer a-stickin out like ontu two buckeyes[3] flung agin a mud wall, an' he wer a-cuttin up more shines nor a cockroach in a hot skillet. Off went the clawhammer coat,[4] an' he flung hit ahine 'im like he wer a-gwine intu a fight; he hed no jackid tu take off, so he unbuttond his galluses, an' vigrusly flung the ainds back over his head. He fotch his shut over-handed a durnd site faster nor I got outen my pasted[5] one, an' then flung hit strait up

6. Coil.
7. Features.
8. Shirt. "Waisbun": waistband.
9. Ant; from *pismire*, but popularly associated with *piss* in southwestern humor.
1. Panther.

2. Delirium tremens.
3. Horse chestnuts.
4. Prince Albert coat, with long tails like those on a claw hammer.
5. Starched, an allusion to *Sut's New-Fangled Shirt*, an earlier story in the 1867 collection.

in the air, like he jis' wanted hit tu keep on up furever; but hit lodged ontu a black-jack,[6] an' I seed one ove my lizzards wif his tail up, a-racin about all over the ole dirty shut, skared too bad tu jump. Then he gin a sorter shake, an' a stompin kine ove twis', an' he cum outer his britches. He tuck 'em by the bottim ove the laigs, an' swung 'em roun' his head a time ur two, an' then fotch 'em down cherall-up[7] over the frunt ove the pulpit. You cud a hearn the smash a quarter ove a mile! Ni ontu fifteen shorten'd biskits, a boiled chicken, wif hits laigs crossed, a big dubbil-bladed knife, a hunk ove terbacker, a cob-pipe, sum copper ore, lots ove broken glass, a cork, a sprinkil ove whisky, a squirt,[8] an' three lizzards flew permiskusly all over that meetin-groun', outen the upper aind ove them big flax britches. One ove the smartes' ove my lizzards lit headfust intu the buzzim ove a fat 'oman, es big es a skin'd hoss, an' ni ontu es ugly, who sot thuty yards off, a fannin hersef wif a tucky-tail.[9] Smart tu the las', by golly, he imejuntly commenced runnin down the centre ove her breas'-bone, an' kep on, I speck. She wer jis' boun' tu faint; an' she did hit fust rate—flung the tucky-tail up in the air, grabbed the lap ove her gown, gin hit a big histin[1] an' fallin shake, rolled down the hill, tangled her laigs an' garters in the top ove a huckilberry bush, wif her head in the branch an' jis' lay still. She wer interestin, she wer, ontil a serious-lookin, pale-faced 'oman hung a nankeen[2] ridin skirt over the huckilberry bush. That wer all that wer dun to'ards bringin her too, that I seed. Now ole Bullin hed nuffin left ontu 'im but a par ove heavy, low quarter'd shoes, short woolen socks, an' eel-skin garters tu keep off the cramp. His skeer hed druv him plum crazy, fur he felt roun' in the air, abuv his head, like he wer huntin sumthin in the dark, an' he beller'd out, 'Brethren, brethren, take keer ove yerselves, the Hell-sarpints *hes got me!*' When this cum out, yu cud a-hearn the screams tu Halifax. He jis' spit in his han's, an' loped over the frunt ove the pulpid *kerdiff!* He lit on top ove, an' rite amung the mos' pius part ove the congregashun. Ole Misses Chaneyberry sot wif her back tu the pulpit, sorter stoopin forrid. He lit a-stradil ove her long naik, a shuttin her up wif a snap, her head atwix her knees, like shuttin up a jack-knife, an' he sot intu gittin away his levil durndest; he went in a heavy lumberin gallop, like a ole fat waggon hoss, skared at a locomotive. When he jumpt a bainch he shook the yeath. The bonnets, an' fans clar'd the way an' jerked most ove the children wif em, an' the rest he scrunched. He open'd a purfeckly clar track tu the woods, ove every livin thing. He weighed ni ontu three hundred, hed a black stripe down his back, like ontu a ole bridil rein, an' his belly wer 'bout the size, an' color ove a beef paunch, an' hit a-swingin out frum side tu side; he leand back frum hit, like a littil feller a-totin a big drum, at a muster,[3] an' I hearn hit plum tu whar I wer. Thar wer cramp-knots on his laigs es big es walnuts, an' mottled splotches on his shins; an' takin him all over, he minded ove a durnd crazy ole elephant, pussessed ove the devil, rared up on hits hind aind, an' jis' *gittin* frum sum imijut danger ur tribulashun. He did the loudest, an' skariest, an' fussiest runnin I ever seed, tu be no faster nur hit wer, since dad tried tu outrun the ho'nets.[4]

6. Common species of shortish oak tree.
7. Chest-flap first.
8. This may be an oil can or it may have some primitive medical function, such as injecting fluid into the ear. "Shorten'd biskits": biscuits made with lard, which "shortens" the dough, making the biscuits flakey. "Dubbil-bladed": double-bladed.

9. Turkey-tail fan.
1. Hoisting.
2. Firm, durable brownish yellow cloth (originally from Nanking, China).
3. Parade of a military company.
4. In the first story in the volume, *Sut Lovingood's Daddy, Acting Horse.*

"Well, he disapear'd in the thicket jis' bustin—an' ove all the noises yu ever hearn, wer made thar on that camp groun': sum wimen screamin—they wer the skeery ones; sum larfin—they wer the wicked ones; sum cryin—they wer the fool ones, (sorter my stripe yu know;) sum tryin tu git away wif thar faces red—they wer the modest ones; sum lookin arter ole Bullin—they wer the curious ones; sum hanging clost tu thar sweethearts—they wer the sweet ones; sum on thar knees wif thar eyes shot,[5] but facin the way the old mud turtil wer a-runnin—they wer the 'saitful ones; sum duin nuthin—they wer the waitin ones; an' the mos' dangerus ove all ove em by a durnd long site.

'I tuck a big skeer mysef arter a few rocks, an' sich like fruit, spattered ontu the pulpit ni ontu my head; an' es the Lovingoods, durn em! knows nuffin but tu run, when they gits skeerd, I jis' put out fur the swamp on the krick. As I started, a black bottil ove bald-face smashed agin a tree furninst[6] me, arter missin the top ove my head 'bout a inch. Sum durn'd fool professor dun this, who hed more zeal nor sence; fur I say that eny man who wud waste a quart ove even mean sperrits, fur the chance ove knockin a poor ornary devil like me down wif the bottil, is a bigger fool nor old Squire Mackmullen, an' he tried tu shoot hissef wif a onloaded hoe-handle."[7]

"Did they catch you Sut?"

"Ketch thunder! *No sir!* jis' look at these yere laigs! Skeer me, hoss, jis' skeer me, an' then watch me while I stay in site, an' yu'll never ax that fool question agin. Why, durn it, man, that's what the ait dullers am fur.

"Ole Barbelly[8] Bullin, es they calls 'im now, never preached ontil yesterday, an' he hadn't the fust durn'd 'oman tu hear 'im, *they hev seed too much ove 'im.* Passuns ginerly hev a pow'ful strong holt on wimen; but, hoss, I tell yu thar ain't meny ove em kin run start nakid over an' thru a crowd ove three hundred wimen an' not injure thar karacters *sum.* Enyhow, hits a kind ove show they'd ruther see one at a time, an' pick the passun at that. His tex' wer, 'Nakid I cum intu the world, an' nakid I'm a gwine outen hit,[9] ef I'm spard ontil then.' He sed nakidness warnt much ove a sin, purtickerly ove dark nights. That he wer a weak, frail wum ove the dus',[1] an' a heap more sich truck. Then he totch ontu me; sed I wer a livin proof ove the hell-desarvin nater ove man, an' that thar warnt grace enuf in the whole 'sociation tu saften my outside rind; that I wer 'a lost ball'[2] forty years afore I wer born'd, an' the bes' thing they cud du fur the church, wer tu turn out, an' still hunt fur me ontil I wer shot. An' he never said Hell-sarpints onst in the hole preach. I b'leve, George, the durnd fools am at hit.

"Now, I wants yu tu tell ole Barbelly this fur me, ef he'll let me an' Sall[3] alone, I'll let him alone—a-while; an' ef he don't, ef I don't lizzard him agin, I jis' wish I may be dod durnd! *Skeer him if yu ken.*

"Let's go tu the spring an' take a ho'n.[4]

---

5. Shut.
6. In front of; from *fornent,* "opposite, facing." "Bald-face": unaged homemade whiskey.
7. Perhaps a reference to a Sut story that has not survived or has not yet been located.
8. Barebelly.
9. Cf. Job 1.21: "Naked came I out of mother's womb, and naked shall I return thither"; the joke being that Parson Bullen sees himself as suffering Job-like tribulations.
1. An echo of many biblical passages. Micah 7.17 may be closest: "They shall lick the dust like a serpent, they shall move out of their holes like worms of the earth: they shall be afraid of the Lord our God, and shall fear because of thee."
2. See Isaiah 22.18: "He will surely violently turn and toss thee like a ball into a large country: there shalt thou die, and there the chariots of thy glory shall be the shame of thy lord's house."
3. Sally Yardley, who appears in *Mrs. Yardley's Quilting* (p. 1652).
4. Cow's-horn drinking cup, i.e., a drink.

"Say George, didn't that ar Hell-sarpint sermon ove his'n, hev sumthin like a Hell-sarpint aplicashun?[5] Hit looks sorter so tu me."

1867

Mrs. Yardley's Quilting[1]

"Thar's one durn'd nasty muddy job, an' I is jis' glad enuf tu take a ho'n[2] ur two, on the straingth ove hit."

"What have you been doing, Sut?"

"Helpin tu salt ole Missis Yardley down."

"What do you mean by that?"

"Fixin her fur rotten cumfurtably, kiverin her up wif sile, tu keep the buzzards frum cheatin the wurms."

"Oh, you have been helping to bury a woman."

"That's hit, by golly! Now why the devil can't I 'splain myself like yu? I ladles out my words at random, like a calf kickin at yaller-jackids[3] yu jis' rolls em out tu the pint, like a feller a-layin bricks—every one fits. How is it that bricks fits so clost enyhow? Rocks won't ni du hit."

"Becaze they'se all ove a size," ventured a man with a wen over his eye.

"The devil yu say, ho'ney-head![4] haint reapin-mersheens ove a size? I'd like tu see two ove em fit clost. Yu wait ontil yu sprouts tuther ho'n, afore yu venters tu 'splain mix'd questions.[5] George, did yu know ole Missis Yardley?"

"No."

"Well, she wer a curious 'oman in her way, an' she wore shiney specks. Now jis' listen: Whenever yu see a ole 'oman ahine a par ove *shiney* specks, yu keep yer eye skinn'd; they am dang'rus in the extreme. Thar is jis' no knowin what they ken du. I hed one a-stradil ove me onst, fur kissin her gal. She went fur my har, an' she went fur my skin, ontil I tho't she ment tu kill me, an' wud a-dun hit, ef my hollerin hadent fotch ole Dave Jordan, a *bacheler*, tu my aid. He, like a durn'd fool, cotch her by the laig, an' drug her back'ards ofen me. She jis' kivered him, an' I run, by golly! The nex time I seed him he wer bald headed, an' his face looked like he'd been a-fitin wildcats.

"Ole Missis Yardley wer a great noticer ove littil things, that nobody else ever seed. She'd say right in the middil ove sumbody's serious talk: 'Law sakes! thar goes that yaller slut ove a hen, a-flingin straws over her shoulder; she's arter settin now, an' haint laid but seven aigs. I'll disapint *her*, see ef I don't; I'll put a punkin in her nes', an' a feather in her nose. An' bless my soul! jis' look at that cow wif the wilted ho'n, a-flinging up dirt an' a-smellin the place whar hit cum frum, wif the rale ginuine still-wurim twis'[6] in her tail, too; what upon the face ove the yeath kin she be arter now, the ole fool? watch her, Sally. An' sakes alive, jis' look at that ole sow; she's a-gwine in a fas' trot, wif her empty bag a-floppin agin her sides. Thar, she hes stop't, an's a-listenin!

---

5. Application (from the text-and-applications structure of sermons).

1. The text is that of *Sut Lovingood. Yarns Spun by a "Natural Born Durn'd Fool." Warped and Wove for Public Wear* (1867).

2. Cow's-horn drinking cup, i.e., a drink.

3. Yellow jackets, small mean-tempered wasps.

4. An insult based on "wen," an encysted skin tumor.

5. Trick questions, loaded questions.

6. Twist like the coils of a still-worm, the spiral condensing tube in an apparatus for distilling whiskey.

massy on us! what a long yearnis grunt she gin; hit cum frum way back ove her kidneys. Thar she goes agin; she's arter no good, sich kerryin on means no good.'

"An' so she wud gabble, no odds who wer a-listenin. She looked like she mout been made at fust 'bout four foot long, an' the common thickness ove wimen when they's at tharsefs,[7] an' then had her har tied tu a stump, a par ove steers hitched to her heels, an' then straiched out a-mos' two foot more—mos' ove the straichin cumin outen her laigs an' naik. Her stockins, a-hangin on the clothes-line tu dry, looked like a par ove sabre scabbards, an' her naik looked like a dry beef shank smoked, an' mout been ni ontu es tough. I never felt hit myself, I didn't, I jis' jedges by looks. Her darter Sal wer bilt at fust 'bout the laingth ove her mam, but wer never straiched eny by a par ove steers an' she wer fat enuf tu kill; she wer taller lyin down than she wer a-standin up. Hit wer her who gin me the 'hump shoulder.' Jis' look at me; haint I'se got a tech[8] ove the dromedary back thar bad? haint I humpy? Well, a-stoopin tu kiss that squatty lard-stan[9] ove a gal is what dun hit tu me. She wer the fairest-lookin gal I ever seed. She allers wore thick woolin stockins 'bout six inches too long fur her laig; they rolled down over her garters, lookin like a par ove life-presarvers up thar. I tell yu she wer a tarin gal enyhow. Luved kissin, wrastlin, an' biled cabbige, an' hated tite clothes, hot weather, an' suckit-riders.[1] B'leved strong in married folk's ways, cradles, an' the remishun ove sins, an' didn't b'leve in corsets, fleas, peaners,[2] nur the fashun plates."

"What caused the death of Mrs. Yardley, Sut?"

"Nuffin, only her heart stop't beatin 'bout losin a nine dimunt[3] quilt. True, she got a skeer'd hoss tu run over her, but she'd a-got over that ef a quilt hadn't been mix'd up in the catastrophy. Yu see quilts wer wun ove her speshul gifts; she run strong on the bed-kiver question. Irish chain, star ove Texas, sun-flower, nine dimunt, saw teeth, checker board, an' shell quilts; blue, an' white, an' yaller an' black coverlids, an' callickercumfurts reigned triumphan' 'bout her hous'. They wer packed in drawers, layin in shelfs full, wer hung four dubbil on lines in the lof, packed in chists, piled on cheers, an' wer everywhar, even ontu the beds, an' wer changed every bed-makin. She told everybody she cud git tu listen tu hit that she ment tu give every durn'd one ove them tu Sal when she got married. Oh, lordy! what es fat a gal es Sal Yardley cud ever du wif half ove em, an' sleepin wif a husbun at that, is more nor I ever cud see through. Jis' think ove her onder twenty layer ove quilts in July, an' yu in thar too. Gewhillikins! George, look how I is sweatin' now, an' this is December. I'd 'bout es lief be shet up in a steam biler wif a three hundred pound bag ove lard, es tu make a bisiness ove sleepin wif that gal—'twould kill a glass-blower.[4]

"Well, tu cum tu the serious part ove this conversashun, that is how the old quilt-mersheen an' coverlid-loom cum tu stop operashuns on this yeath. She hed narrated hit thru the neighborhood that nex Saterday she'd gin a quiltin—three quilts an' one cumfurt tu tie. 'Goblers,[5] fiddils, gals, an' whisky,' wer the

7. At themselves, at their normal adult (unpregnant) girth.
8. Touch, little.
9. Big squat crock of hog fat.
1. Circuit riders, preachers who made the round (or circuit) of several settlements in turn, none being able to support a full-time minister of its own.

2. Pianos.
3. Diamond; nine diamonds is a traditional quilt pattern (other patterns are named below).
4. I.e., someone who regularly works with flame.
5. Turkeys. "Cumfurt tu tie": comforters were often finished by tying the layers of fabric together with, e.g, yarn rather than by quilting.

words she sent tu the men-folk, an' more tetchin ur wakenin words never drap't ofen an 'oman's tongue. She sed tu the gals, 'Sweet toddy, huggin, dancin, an' huggers in 'bundunce.' Them words struck the gals rite in the pit ove the stumick, an' spread a ticklin sensashun bof ways, ontil they scratched thar heads wif one han, an' thar heels wif tuther.

"Everybody, he an' she, what wer baptized b'levers in the righteousnes ove quiltins wer thar, an' hit jis' so happen'd that everybody in them parts, frum fifteen summers tu fifty winters, wer unannamus b'levers. Strange, warn't hit? Hit wer the bigges' quiltin ever Missis Yardley hilt, an' she hed hilt hundreds; everybody wer thar, 'scept the constibil an' suckit-rider, two dam easily-spared pussons; the numbers ni ontu even too; jis' a few more boys nur gals; that made hit more exhitin, fur hit gin the gals a chance tu kick an' squeal a littil, wifout runnin eny risk ove not gittin kissed at all, an' hit gin reasonabil grouns fur a few scrimmages amung the he's. Now es kissin an' fitin am the pepper an' salt ove all soshul getherins, so hit wer more espishully wif this ove ours. Es I swung my eyes over the crowd, George, I thought quiltins, managed in a morril an' sensibil way, truly am good things—good fur free drinkin, good fur free eatin, good fur free huggin, good fur free dancin, good fur free fitin, an' goodest ove all fur poperlatin a country fas'.

"Thar am a fur-seein wisdum in quiltins, ef they hes proper trimmins: 'vittils, fiddils, an' sperrits in 'bundunce.' One holesum quiltin am wuf three old pray'r-meetins on the poperlashun pint, purtickerly ef hits hilt in the dark ove the moon, an' runs intu the night a few hours, an' April ur May am the time chosen. The moon don't suit quiltins whar everybody is well acquainted an' already fur along in courtin. She dus help pow'ful tu begin a courtin match onder, but when hit draws ni ontu a head, nobody wants a moon but the ole mammys.

"The mornin cum, still, saft, sunshiney; cocks crowin, hens singin, birds chirpin, tuckeys gobblin—jis' the day tu sun quilts, kick, kiss, squeal, an' make love.

"All the plow-lines an' clothes-lines wer straiched tu every post an' tree. Quilts purvailed. Durn my gizzard ef two acres roun that ar house warn't jis' one solid quilt, all out a-sunnin, an' tu be seed. They dazzled the eyes, skeered the hosses, gin wimen the heart-burn, an' perdominated.

"To'ards sundown the he's begun tu drap in. Yearnis' needil-drivin cummenced tu lose groun; threads broke ofen, thimbils got los', an' quilts needed anuther roll. Gigglin, winkin, whisperin, smoofin ove har, an' gals a-ticklin one anuther, wer a-gainin every inch ove groun what the needils los'. Did yu ever notis, George, at all soshul getherins, when the he's begin tu gather, that the young she's begin tu tickil one anuther an' the ole maids swell thar tails, roach[6] up thar backs, an' sharpen thar nails ontu the bed-posts an' door jams, an' spit an' groan sorter like cats a-courtin? Dus hit mean *rale* rath, ur is hit a dare tu the he's, sorter kivered up wif the outside signs ove danger? I honestly b'leve that the young shes' ticklin means, 'Cum an' take this job ofen our hans.' But that swellin I jis' don't onderstan; dus yu? Hit looks skeery, an' I never tetch one ove em when they am in the swellin way. I may be mistaken'd 'bout the ticklin bisiness too; hit may be dun like a feller chaws poplar bark when he haint got eny terbacker, a-sorter better nur nun make-shif. I dus know

6. Arch.

one thing tu a certainty: that is, when the he's take hold the ticklin quits, an' ef yu gits one ove the ole maids out tu hersef, then she subsides an' is the smoofes, sleekes, saft thing yu ever seed, an' dam ef yu can't hear her purr, jis' es plain!

"But then, George, gals an' ole maids haint the things tu fool time away on. Hits widders, by golly, what am the rale sensibil, steady-goin, never-skeerin, never-kickin, willin, sperrited, smoof pacers. They cum clost up tu the hoss-block,[7] standin still wif thar purty silky years playin, an' the naik-veins a-throbbin, an' waits fur the word, which ove course yu gives, arter yu finds yer feet well in the stirrup, an' away they moves like a cradil on cushioned rockers, ur a spring buggy runnin in damp san'. A tetch ove the bridil, an' they knows yu wants em tu turn, an' they dus hit es willin es ef the idear wer thar own. I be dod rabbited ef a man can't 'propriate happiness by the skinful ef he is in contack wif sumbody's widder, an' is smart. Gin me a willin widder, the yeath over: what they dont know, haint worth larnin. They hes all been tu Jamakey an' larnt how sugar's made, an' knows how tu sweeten wif hit; an' by golly, they is always ready tu use hit. All yu hes tu du is tu find the spoon, an' then drink cumfort till yer blind. Nex tu good sperrits an' my laigs, I like a twenty-five year ole widder, wif roun ankils, an' bright eyes, honestly an' squarly lookin intu yurn, an' sayin es plainly es a partrige sez 'Bob White,'[8] 'Don't be afraid ove me; I hes been thar; yu know hit ef yu hes eny sense, an' thar's no use in eny humbug, ole feller—cum ahead!'

"Ef yu onderstans widder nater, they ken save yu a power ove troubil, onsar-tinty, an' time, an' ef yu is interprisin yu gits mons'rous well paid for hit. The very soun ove thar littil shoe-heels speak full trainin, an' hes a knowin click as they tap the floor; an' the rustil ove thar dress sez, 'I dar yu tu ax me.'

"When yu hes made up yer mind tu court one, jis' go at hit like hit wer a job ove rail-maulin.[9] Ware yer workin close, use yer common, every-day mos-huns an' words, an' abuv all, fling away yer cinamint ile vial[1] an' burn all yer love songs. No use in tryin tu fool em, fur they sees plum thru yu, a durn'd sight plainer than they dus thru thar veils. No use in a pasted[2] shut; she's been thar. No use in borrowin a cavortin fat hoss; she's been thar. No use in har-dye; she's been thar. No use in cloves, tu kill whisky breff; she's been thar. No use in buyin clost curtains fur yer bed, fur she has been thar. Widders am a speshul means, George, fur ripenin green men, killin off weak ones, an makin 'ternally happy the soun ones.

"Well, es I sed, afore I flew the track an' got ontu the widders. The fellers begun tu ride up an' walk up, sorter slow, like they warn't in a hurry, the durn'd 'saitful raskils, hitchin thar critters tu enything they cud find. One red-comb'd, long-spurr'd, dominecker feller, frum town, in a red an' white grid-iron jackid an' patent leather gaiters,[3] hitched his hoss, a wild, skeery, wall-eyed[4] devil, inside the yard palins, tu a cherry tree lim'. Thinks I, that hoss hes a skeer intu him big enuf tu run intu town, an' perhaps beyant hit, ef I kin only tetch hit off; so I sot intu thinkin.

7. Hitching post; here used with phallic connotations.
8. The partridge or quail now commonly called "bob-white" from this note, accented on the second syllable.
9. Splitting rails (for fencing) with mauls, heavy ham-mers to drive in wedges.
1. Phial of cinnamon oil (used for perfume).
2. Starched.
3. A high shoe covering the ankle and instep. Domi-

nickers, or Dominiques (from the island in the West Indies), are red-and-white barred chickens; Sut's rival wears a jacket of a similar gridiron pattern.
4. A "wall-eyed" horse has one normal eye and the other enlarged or nearsighted; such a horse is "skeery" because he is frightened by objects that appear bigger to one eye than the other. (From The Horseman's En-cyclopedia, 1963 edition.)

"One aind ove a long clothes-line, wif nine dimunt quilts ontu hit, wer tied tu the same cherry tree that the hoss wer. I tuck my knife and socked hit thru every quilt, 'bout the middil, an' jis' below the rope, an' tied them thar wif bark, so they cudent slip. Then I went tu the back aind, an' ontied hit frum the pos', knottin in a hoe-handil, by the middil, tu keep the quilts frum slippin off ef my bark strings failed, an' laid hit on the groun. Then I went tu the tuther aind: thar wer 'bout ten foot tu spar, a-lyin on the groun arter tyin tu the tree. I tuck hit atwix Wall-eye's hine laigs, an' tied hit fas' tu bof stirrups, an' then cut the cherry tree lim' betwix his bridil an' the tree, almos' off. Now, mine yu thar wer two ur three uther ropes full ove quilts atween me an' the hous', so I wer purty well hid frum thar. I jis' tore off a palin frum the fence, an' tuck hit in bof hans, an' arter raisin hit 'way up yander, I fotch hit down, es hard es I cud, flatsided to'ards the groun, an' hit acksidentally happen'd tu hit Wall-eye, 'bout nine inches ahead ove the root ove his tail. Hit landed so hard that hit made my hans tingle, an' then busted intu splinters. The first thing I did, wer tu feel ove myself, on the same spot whar hit hed hit the hoss. I cudent help duin hit tu save my life, an' I swar I felt sum ove Wall-eye's sensashun, jis' es plain. The fust thing he did, wer tu tare down the lim' wif a twenty foot jump, his head to'ards the hous'. Thinks I, now yu hev dun hit, yu durn'd wall-eyed fool! tarin down that lim' wer the beginin ove all the troubil, an' the hoss did hit hissef; my conshuns felt clar es a mountin spring, an' I wer in a frame ove mine tu observe things es they happen'd, an' they soon begun tu happen purty clost arter one anuther rite then, an' thar, an' tharabouts, clean ontu town, thru hit, an' still wer a-happenin, in the woods beyant thar ni ontu eleven mile frum ole man Yardley's gate, an' four beyant town.

"The fust line ove quilts he tried tu jump, but broke hit down; the nex one he ran onder; the rope cotch ontu the ho'n ove the saddil, broke at bof ainds, an' went along wif the hoss, the cherry tree lim' an' the fust line ove quilts, what I hed proverdensally tied fas' tu the rope. That's what I calls foresight, George. Right furnint[5] the frunt door he cum in contack wif ole Missis Yardley hersef, an' anuther ole 'oman; they wer a-holdin a nine dimunt quilt spread out, a-'zaminin hit, an' a-praisin hits purfeckshuns. The durn'd onmanerly, wall-eyed fool run plum over Missis Yardley frum ahine, stompt one hine foot through the quilt, takin hit along, a-kickin ontil he made hits corners snap like a whip. The gals screamed, the men hollered wo! an' the ole 'oman wer toted intu the hous' limber es a wet string, an' every word she sed wer, 'Oh, my preshus nine dimunt quilt!'

"Wall-eye busted thru the palins, an' Dominicker seed 'im, made a mortal rush fur his bitts, wer too late fur them, but in good time fur the strings ove flyin quilts, got tangled amung em, an' the gridiron jackid patren wer los' tu my sight amung star an' Irish chain quilts; he went frum that quiltin at the rate ove thuty miles tu the hour. Nuffin lef on the lot ove the hole consarn, but a nine biler[6] hat, a par ove gloves, an' the jack ove hearts.

"What a onmanerly, suddin way ove leavin places sum folks hev got, enyhow.

"Thinks I, well, that fool hoss, tarin down that cherry tree lim', hes dun sum good, enyhow; hit hes put the ole 'oman outen the way fur the balance

5. In front of.
6. Unidentified; perhaps a stovepipe hat or a large bowler.

ove the quiltin, an' tuck Dominicker outen the way an' outen danger, fur that gridiron jackid wud a-bred a scab on his nose[7] afore midnite; hit wer morrily boun tu du hit.

"Two months arterwards, I tracked the route that hoss tuck in his kalamatus skeer, by quilt rags, tufts ove cotton, bunches ove har, (human an' hoss,) an' scraps ove a gridiron jackid stickin ontu the bushes, an' plum at the aind ove hit, whar all signs gin out, I foun a piece ove watch chain an' a hosses head. The places what know'd Dominicker, know'd 'im no more.[8]

"Well, arter they'd tuck the ole 'oman up stairs an' camfired her tu sleep, things begun tu work agin. The widders broke the ice, an' arter a littil gigilin, goblin, an' gabblin, the kissin begun. *Smack!*—'Thar, now,' a widder sed that. *Pop!*—'Oh, don't!' *Pfip!*—'Oh, yu quit!' *Plosh!*—'Go *way* yu awkerd critter, yu kissed me in the eye!' anuther widder sed that. *Bop!* 'Now yu ar satisfied, I recon, big mouf!' *Vip!*—'That haint fair!' *Spat!*—'Oh, lordy! May, cum pull Bill away; he's a-tanglin my hair.' *Thut!*—'I jis' d-a-r-e yu tu du that agin!' a widder sed that, too. Hit sounded all 'roun that room like poppin co'n in a hot skillet, an' wer pow'ful sujestif.

"Hit kep on ontil I be durn'd ef *my* bristils didn't begin tu rise, an' sumthin like a cold buckshot wud run down the marrow in my back-bone 'bout every ten secons, an' then run up agin, tolerabil hot. I kep a swallerin wif nuthin tu swaller, an' my face felt swell'd; an' yet I wer fear'd tu make a bulge. Thinks I, I'll ketch one out tu hersef torreckly, an' then I guess we'll rastil.[9] Purty soon Sal Yardley started fur the smoke-'ous, so I jis' gin my head a few short shakes, let down one ove my wings a-trailin, an' sirkiled roun her wif a side twis' in my naik, steppin sidewise, an' a-fetchin up my hinmos' foot wif a sorter jerkin slide at every step. Sez I, 'Too coo-took a-too.' She onderstood hit, an stopt, sorter spreadin her shoulders. An' jis' es I hed pouch'd out my mouf, an' wer a-reachin forrid wif hit, fur the article hitsef, sunthin interfared wif me, hit did. George, wer yu ever ontu yer hans an' knees, an' let a hell-tarin big, mad ram, wif a ten-yard run, but[1] yu yearnis'ly, jis' onst, right squar ontu the pint ove yer back-bone?"

"No, you fool; why do you ask?"

"Kaze I wanted tu know ef yu cud hev a realizin' noshun ove my shock. Hits scarcely worth while tu try tu make yu onderstan the case by words only, onless yu hev been tetched in that way. Gr-eat golly! the fust thing I felt, I tuck hit tu be a back-ackshun[2] yeathquake; an' the fust thing I seed wer my chaw'r terbacker a-flyin' over Sal's head like a skeer'd bat. My mouf wer pouch'd out, ready fur the article hitsef, yu know, an' hit went outen the roun hole like the wad outen a pop-gun—thug! an' the fust thing I know'd, I wer a flyin over Sal's head too, an' a-gainin on the chaw'r terbacker fast. I wer straitened out strait, toes hinemos', middil finger-nails foremos', an' the fust thing I hearn wer, 'Yu dam Shanghi!'[3] Great Jerus-a-lam! I lit ontu my all fours jis' in time tu but the yard gate ofen hits hinges, an' skeer loose sum more hosses— kep on in a four-footed gallop, clean acrost the lane afore I cud straiten up, an' yere I cotch up wif my chaw'r terbacker, stickin flat agin a fence-rail. I hed

7. I.e., from a fight with Sut.
8. Job 7.9–10: "As the cloud is consumed and vanisheth away; so he that goeth down to the grave shall come up no more. He shall return no more to his house, neither shall his place know him any more."
9. Wrestle.

1. Butt (a verb).
2. Action reversing the usual direction or motion, a term from the steam engine, familiar to Harris from his steamboating years.
3. Shanghai, Asiatic domestic fowl popular in the United States for its sturdiness.

got so good a start that I thot hit a pity tu spile hit, so I jis' jump'd the fence an' tuck thru the orchurd. I tell yu I dusted these yere close, fur I tho't hit wer arter me.

"Arter runnin a spell, I ventered tu feel roun back thar, fur sum signs ove what hed happened tu me. George, arter two pow'ful hardtugs, I pull'd out the vamp an' sole ove one ove ole man Yardley's big brogans,[4] what he hed los' amung my coat-tails. Dre'ful! dre'ful! Arter I got hit away frum thar, my flesh went fas' asleep, frum abuv my kidneys tu my knees; about now, fur the fust time, the idear struck me, what hit wer that hed interfar'd wif me, an' los' me the kiss. Hit wer ole Yardley hed kicked me. I walked fur a month like I wer straddlin a thorn hedge. Sich a shock, at sich a time, an' on sich a place— jis' think ove hit! hit am tremenjus, haint hit? The place feels num, right now."

"Well, Sut, how did the quilting come out?"

"How the hell du yu 'speck me tu know? I warn't thar eny more."

1867

Hen Baily's Reformation[1]

[This truthful narrative is particularly recommended to the careful consideration of the Rev. Mr. Stiggins, and his disciples, of the Brick Lane Branch of the Grand Junction Ebenezer Temperance Association. This mode of treatment can be fully relied upon.]

We were resting by a fine cool spring, at noon, with an invitingly clean gourd hanging on a bush over the water. Sut, as usual, was at full length on the grass, intently looking at the gourd.

"Say fellers, that ar long-handil'd gourd thar, mout cum the temprince dodge[2] over sum ove yu fellers afore yu wer quite ready fur the oaf. I looks on em all es dangrus, an' that's a mons'us 'spishus lookin wun, hit hes sich a durn'd long handil. Allers 'zamin the inside ove a gourd-handil wif a sharp pinted[3] swich, afore yu drinks; hits a holesum foresight. Hen Baily—did eny ove yu know Hen?—he wer a peach wif a wurm intu hit, enyhow—a durn'd no-count, good, easy, good-fur-nuthin vagerbone,[4] big es a hoss, an' lazy es a shingle-maker, but a pow'ful b'lever, not a sarcumsised b'lever, but a lie b'lever ove the straites seck,[5] swallered everything he hearn, an' mos' everything he seed. That ar swallerin gif[6] ove his'n cum wifin a eighth ove a inch, onst, ove sendin him tu kingdum cum, an' did send him head fust intu a life-everlastin temprince s'ciety. I'd a-liked pow'ful well fur tu hearn him gin in his 'sperince, even ef he tole one half. He lov'd biled drinks orful, never wer a hour's walk frum a still-hous' ur a doggery[7] since he tuck tu warin breeches.

---

4. Coarse, heavy, high shoe. "Vamp": part of a shoe above the sole and welt.
1. The text is from *Sut Lovingood. Yarns Spun by a "Natural Born Darn'd Fool."* *Warped and Wove for Public Wear* (1867). A few obvious corrections of missing single quotation marks and the like have been made. The story of how Henry Baily went from active alcoholic to teetotaler is not for the squeamish, but lovers of Sut are hardput to find adequate praise for the delicacy with which the final stage of Hen's sufferings is described. Readers are requested not to ruin the story for anyone else by revealing the plot.
2. Temperance trick—a strategy for making the "fell-

ers" swear off the abuse of alcohol before they were ready to take the oath ("oaf").
3. Pointed; the advice is to run a twig or switch of a tree down the open handle of the gourd before drinking from it, so as to avoid ingesting an insect or other undesired trash in the handle.
4. Vagabond.
5. Sect.
6. Gift, talent.
7. Little low-class place to buy and drink bad whiskey (with none of the amenities of a "saloon"). "Still-house": building where liquor is made.

"Well, yu see the ole man Rogers up on Los' Creek wer a-paintin his hous' a-new, an' Hen wer suckilatin roun thar, jis' prospectin fur sperits, an' seed a bottil wif clar truck[8] in hit what he tuck tu be new sperrits, so when the painter's back wer turned, he jis' run hits naik down his froat. He fotch hit out wif a onder-handid jerk, flung hit ahine him an' put, sputterin an' yerkin, fur the spring, a-swabbin out his mouf wif his ole wool hat rolled up. Now, boys, hit *wer* sperrits, but orful tu think ove, hit wer sperrits ove tupentine, fresh frum the rosinny part[9] ove Noth Caliney.

"Me an' a few uther durn'd fools wer at the spring, sorter es we is now, a-mixin a few draps ove hit wif sum limber laig-whisky,[1] an' gabblin, when we seed him a-cumin jis' a-flutterin. Es he run a-pas' the wash place, he flung the hat swab away, an' snatched the wash gourd, so es tu save time. The durn'd lazy cuss wer in a rale tarin hurry; fust time I ever seed him run ur cum ni runnin in all my born'd days. His mouf wer es red es a split beef, an' the light big bubbil kine ove slobber wer a-flyin like snow frum a-runnin hosses heels. Thinks I, *sody*,[2] by the great golly! oh, yu dam fool, sum gal's cum the luv-powder game over yu purfeckly. He *wer* trubbil'd in mine, fur at the landin part ove every jump, he'd say, in souns like he hed a gob ove scaldin mush stuck tu the ruff ove his mouf, the words 'Hell-fire,' nuffin else; them wer pow'ful suitabil words tu his case. I didn't think he wer so good at pickin out talk; they 'splained his ailmint better nur a doctor cud. He soused the ole soap subs gourd intu the spring, an' then filled his mouf over mos' half ove the aidge, quicker nor flea ketchin. Es he turn'd hit up, I seed a stripid eight inch lizard cum tarin outen the handil, whar he'd been hid es *he* thought. He sot his fore paws ontu the aidge ove the gourd an' peeped over. Seein us, gin him a turnin skeer, an' he jis' darted down Hen's froat. I seed his tail fly up agin Hen's snout, es he started down hill. The rep-tile tuck his mouf tu be a prover-denshul hole in the groun, an' I dusn't wunder, fur hit wud a-fool'd a king-fisher[3] eny-time. He drap't the empty gourd, an' holdin his belly in his lock't hans, sed—

" 'Warter makes hit wus, boys.'

"Sez I, 'Hen, hits the lizard.'

"He wall'd roun his sweaty stuck out eyes at me, an' sez he—

" 'What lizard?'

" 'Why that big striped he lizard what yu let rum down yer froat jis' now, outen the gourd-handil. I speck I wer the las' pusson what seed him outside ove yu,[4] fur I seed the pint ove his tail arter hit passed the gap whar that ar frunt tooth cum out.'

"He look't a-sorter listenin look, down at the groun, fur a second, an' sot intu hoppin up an' down ontu wun laig, an' then ontu tuther, a-shakin in the air the laig what warn't imejuntly engaged in hoppin, an' mentionin 'Hell-fire,' every time he changed laigs, an' that wer every two hops. Then he fell down an' sot intu rollin, wus nur a yung dorg what hes ignurently yamped[5] a pole-cat. He kep a-tuckin his head sorter onder, like he wer tryin tu make hit roll faster nor his body. Sez he—

---

8. Clear stuff, junk.

9. Turpentine oil is made from rosin.

1. *Yarns* has "limber-laig whisky" ("laig": leg).

2. A reference to the widely reprinted story *Blown Up with Soda*, in which the treacherous Sicily Burns doses Sut with soda.

3. Handsome-crested bird (which like the lizard would have mistaken Hen's mouth for a hole in the ground).

4. Sut is punning on two meanings of *outside*: "exterior to" and "besides" or "except."

5. Clamped his teeth onto.

" 'Great fathers, boys, he's a-gallopin roun, he is by grashus!'

"Sez I, 'Hen, he's a-'zaminin yer whisky bag fur a good spot tu bild his nestes in, he means tu stay.'

" 'Oh, lordy!' yell'd Hen, 'he's dun foun hit, an's a-tarin up the linin ove my paunch tu bild hit wif,' an' he roll'd on faster nur ever. 'Sut, ef yu please, run fur a doctor; yu hes the laigs.'

" 'Yas,' sez I: 'but hits dun gone fur apas' common doctorin.'

"When he hearn that vardic, he flounced tu his feet, fotch a yell what ef et hed went thru a three-foot tin ho'n wud a-busted hit plum open frum aind tu aind, an' sot intu flingin the bes' kine ove show actor summersets[6] amung the roun rocks in the spring branch back'ards twice, forids onst, then sidewise, now a full turn an' a 'alf that wud fetch him ontu his head, now a 'alf turn, an' that wud lan' him ontu his sturn. Durnation, how he'd spatter warter when he made the three quarter turns, then clean over ontu his feet he'd cum, jis' tu yell an' fling sum more. I counted till hit got tu thuty-one, an' got outen heart, an' quit: a suckis agent[7] wud a-gin him big wages jis' then, but hed been the wust fool'd man ever born'd, onless he ment tu dose Hen wif tupentine an' lizards, an' I doubts hits movin him a secon time. Durn'd ef his kerryins on didn't mine me ove my sody misery in a minnit; hit struck me so pow'ful that I hed a vilent sarchin blow ove belly-ache rite thar. Sez I—

" 'That's hit Hen, jis' yu keep on, an' yu'll soon make that ar lizard b'leve he's tuck up lodgins in the cylinder ove a four hoss thrashin-mersheen, an' that harves time am cum. He's boun tu vacate yu; jis' rastil on, hoss; that's hit; no mortal lizard kin stan that sort ove churnin amung sich a mixin es yu ginerly totes intu yer paunch.'

" 'Oh, lordy, Sut, yu'se right, fur I raley du b'leve he's cuttin his way out now. Can't yu, (an' over he'd go agin) *du* sumthin?' (over onst more.)

" 'Yu dam fool,' sez I, 'I don't know; but ef yu means tu keep on at that rate, I wud surjis' that yu swaller a few ove these yere roun rocks, 'bout es big es goose aigs, an' dam ef he ain't a groun up rep-tile sooner nor ef he wer in a hungry goose's gizzard. He made a moshun ur two like he wer grabbin fur rocks es he lit, but jis' then he changed his mine, an' sot intu runnin roun the spring-hous', a-leanin to'ards hit an' jis' a-missin the corners. He went so fas' he looked like three ur four fellers arter each uther, groanin, hollerin, an' remarkin 'Hell-fire,' all roun thar. He's a pow'ful activ injurin man, when onder stimuluses, that's a fac'. I tuck a stan ni ontu wun corner, an' es he cum roun, I cummenced in time, an' sed—

" 'Hen, did yer take yer sody seperit?'

"Next time he cum, sez he, 'Sody seperit—h—l!' an' nex roun sez he, 'Aka-fortis,' an' the nex arter that he addid the words 'Fourth-proof[8] at that.' He wer gwine so fas' that his talkin seemed oninterrupted. The las' time he cum roun, he hollered in dispar, 'I haint a-gainin on hit a dam bit,' an' tuck hissef up a red elm. He went up by fas' jerks, jis' adzackly like a cat climbs a appil tree frum a clost cumin dorg. He locked his footsis roun the lowis lim's, an' hung hed down, swingin about, an' smackin his hans like he wer ni the shou-tin pint ove happiness at a ravin camp meetin.[9] Sez I—

---

6. Older pronunciation of *somersaults*. "Ho'n": horn for blowing to attract attention of someone out of shouting range.

7. Circus agent. The importance of traveling circuses in the South continued through Mark Twain's and William Faulkner's time.

8. Unpleasantly strong brandy. "Aka-fortis": aqua-for-tis; brandy.

9. Outdoor evangelical religious gathering, usually held in a tent.

" '*That* won't du; that's a wus idear nur sircklin the spring-hous' wer, an' don't cumpar wif yer suckis sperimint, fur the lizard went pow'fully *down hill* a-gwine intu that sloppy hole he's intu now, an' he's too smart tu start *down hill* eny more fur fear hit'll git wus; he won't cum, Hen.'

"He answered me mons'ous cross an' spiteful—

" 'Let him go up hill then, dam 'im; so he keeps gwine's all I ax.'

"The lizard wer a-tarin roun right peart, I speck, wadin an' swimin as he wer in a dark pon' ove whisky, an' tupentine, thickened wif a breakfus' ove blackberries an' mush, stirred intu a purfeck hurrycane by Hen's kerryins on. Hit warn't jis' adzackly the right place fur even a varmint tu go tu sleep in, enyhow.

"Hen soon foun that hit wud nither go up hill nur down hill, but kep a-tarin roun et[1] randum wif hits long toe-nails, so he los' all hope, let foot holts loose, an' sunk his nose up tu his years in the branch bank mud, an' by golly, lay still. I begun tu think the show wer about tu close, an I hed rights tu think so; thuty-one counted summersets, an' lots ove oncounted ones, averidgin a full turn each, a mile an' a quarter roun a spring-hous', an' nine hundred yards in rollin, not countin the small moshuns, in 'bout five minutes wer ni ontu enuf tu fetch eny man body tu lie still—an' then the lizard an' turpentine—hit wer a job ove no common kine, an' speshully fur Hen hit wer mos' wunderful. Thinks I, ole feller, yu're gwine tu make a die ove hit, an' sez I—

" 'Hen, ole feller, while yu'se a-restin thar, jis' feel ni yer trousis an' git me that half duller yu borrowed frum me las' Chrismus; feel easy fur hit an' don' skeer yer lizard.'

"He never let on like he hearn me. Sez I, 'Yere, Hen, try a littil ove this yere *whisky*.' I menshun whisky loud; dam ef even that moved the *pints* ove his fingers. Sez I, 'Boys, he's 'bout dun wif yeathly matters, he won't notis whisky, an' his herearter's wifin ten steps ove him rite now.'

"Ole Missis Rogers hearn the fuss, an' seed the crowd roun her spring-hous', an' the safety ove her milk an' butter struck her pow'ful. So yere she cum, wif her ole brass specks ridin a-straddil ove the highes pint ove her calliker cap crown; thar laigs wer a-usin two locks ove her red roan[2] har fur stirrups, away below her years. She hed a biled roasin ear mos' ove the time acrost her mouf, wif silks an' smashed grains plenty, stickin tu her ole moley chin,[3] an' her nose. Sez she—

" 'What upon yeath yu all duin yere—not holdin meetin, sure? Ah! yu am thar, am yu, laigs, yu dad-dratted draggild san-hill crane? Sum devilment on han, rite now. Clar yersefs, yu nasty, stinkin, low-lived, sheep-killin dorgs. S-n-e-a-k off, afore yu steals sum thin. Yere Rove, yere Rove, yere, yere!'

" 'Sez I, mouns'us solimn, straitenin mysef up wif foldid arms, 'Missis Rogers, afore yer dorg Rove cums, take a look at sum ove yu're work. That ar a-dyin feller bein; let jis' a few ove yer bowils[4] melt, an' pour out rite yere in pity an' rey-morse.'

"She tuck a short look at Hen. 'What ails *him?*'

1. At.
2. Mrs. Rogers's hair had been red, but now is thickly streaked with gray, like the color of a roan horse. "Laigs": legs ("temples" of the glasses).
3. Mashed kernels from the roasting ear of corn have stuck to Mrs. Rogers's chin in among the darkish growths on her skin; kernels and moles are presumably of about the same size but of contrasting colors. (Sut delicately mentions the cornsilks sticking to her chin but does not draw any parallel with facial moles, which are often hairy.) (The mole introduced later in the story is the furry burrowing mammal.)
4. In the older sense: seat of pity or tenderness.

"Sez I, wif my arms straiched strait out, 'Cholick,[5] vilent cork-screw cho-lick, one ove the cholery perswashun; he jis' tast'd yer buttermilk in thar, an' by granny, hits dun kill'd 'im, that's all, Missis Rogers.' Yu see she wer noted fur feedin the work-hans on buttermilk so sour that hit wud eat hits way outen a yeathen crock in wun nite. Sez she, wif her hans ontu her hips, an' standin wide an' strait up, 'Yu're a liar, Mister Lovingood!' I hes allers notis'd nobody ever calls me Mister Lovingood, (ef they knows me,) onless they's mad at me. 'Very well,' sez I, 'we am gwine tu strip him now, an' yu kin see fur yerself; hits et[6] hits way outen him by this time; jis' stay an' 'zamin his belly. I'll bet yu my shut agin that ar momoxed up roas'in har, that hits chawed intu dish rags, frum his waisbun[7] clean down tu——' She flung down the roas'in ear, an' put fur the hous', a-totin her frock-tail high hilt up wif bof her hans, wifout waitin fur me tu add 'his fork.' I wer gittin sorter skeer'd, an' sorry bof, fur Hen, the ornary devil, an' wer a-lookin at the groun studyin et hit warn't bes' tu knock him on the head wif a rock, an' put him outen his misery, when I seed the break an' bulge ove a mole a-plowin. A idear, the bes' idear I ever own'd, struck plum thru my head, an' I dug out the mole. Sez I—

" 'Boys, listen tu me: that ar feller's feller's mons'us ni ded; desprit cases wants desprit docterin; let's tie his galluses roun his waisbun tight, an' start this yere bline,[8] fury scramblin littil cuss up his breeches laig. When he feels the scramblin sensashun on the outside, he'll think the lizard hes got out sum-whar, an' the idear will make him feel good, enyhow, live ur ded; thar's no harm in a mole, nohow; les' try hit.'

"We turned Hen ontu his stomick, an' made the top ove his britches mole tight, an' I set the mole a-straddil ove his heel-string, an' sunk my thumb-nail intu hits tail. Away hit went up his bar laig pow'ful fas', rootin like a hog; he wanted tu go tu his trade ove diggin agin, yu know, an' wer sarchin fur a saft place. He warn't outen site very long, when Hen sorter started forrid on his stomick; that wer the fust sign ove life he'd show'd since he buried his nose in the blue mud. Sez I, wif a heap ove hope, 'Boys, things am workin; ef he wudn't notis speerits, he'a a-notisin that ar mole.' He hed a par ove foot-holts agin a root, an' he shot hissef forrid ten foot intu the branch at one lunge wifout risin four inches frum the groun. I tho't I hearn 'Hell-fire,' agin in a sorter sick whisper. He ris tu his all fours, an' shook the warter outen his years pearingly es strong es ever, an' tuck down the branch in a rale fas' cavalry lope. He made the mud an' warter fly, 'speshully when he'd kick, an' that wer every two ur three jumps. He used his hine legs jis' like a hoss a-fightin, an' as he'd fling up his shoes he'd menshun the kine ove fire I'se been tellin yu about, an' he'd wall a mons'us sarchin oneasy eye over his shoulder every time he'd kick. Sez I, 'Boys, the show ain't over yet; les' see the aind, an' git the wuf ove our munny.[9] One ur two ove the crowd dodged intu the bushes sorter des'arted; they wer fear'd tu see eny more. The res' ove us foller'd Hen. When he'd cum tu a deep hole, he'd squat intu hit up tu his years, a-sorter workin hissef roun like a hen a-fixin her nestes, gruntin orful, an' a-cussin everybody, an' every-thing in a lump; then he'd rar forrid ontu his all fours again, an' jis' travil.[1] I can't fur the life ove me think what kep him down tu his all fours. Ef hit hed

---

5. Or colic; abdominal pain.
6. Eaten.
7. Waistband. "Shut": shirt. The thought of what might be exposed drives off Mrs. Rogers, but Sut speci-fies that (whatever he might do) the grossest word he

was about to speak was "fork" (crotch).
8. Blind.
9. Let's see the end, and get our money's worth ("wuf").
1. Travel, move fast.

been my case, yu'd a seed sum ove the durn'des straites up an' down runnin ever did by eny livin mortal. P'raps the kerryins on in his in'ards warn't es sarchin in that position. At las' he gallop'd out ontu a san bank, an' sunk spread out, wif his head in a short twis', ni clean gone.

"Sez I, 'Boys, the durn'd fool hes drowndid my mole atwixt his breeches an' his hide, a-squattin in them holes, an' I hes no hopes ove him now; les' kill 'im.' Jis' then I seed him yerk, sorter vomitin way, so I straddiled him, an cotch him by the har, an' pull'd up his head tu straiten his swaller, when imejuntly yere[2] cum the lizard tarin outen his mouf, the wust skeer'd varmint I ever seed in all my born'd days. His eyes wer es big es fox grapes,[3] an' mos' all ove em outside ove his head, an' dam ef he didn't hev enuf tu skeer a lion, fur the mole hed 'im fas' by the tail, an' wer mendin his holt, an' that ar interprisin littil yeath-borer hadn't a durn'd mossel[4] ove fur left ontu his hide; hit wer all *lime'd* off; he looked rite down slick an' funny, wif a lizard a-haulin 'im fru the san, I swar he did. Wunder what *they* thought hed been happenin.

"Well, we toted Hen home, an' when he got sorter well, he jined a ole well-sot temprince s'ciety, an puts hit up that the hole thing, tupentine, lizards an' mole, wer interpersishun[5] tu save him frum turnin intu a drunkard. The cussed hippercrit! he warn't never enything else. I oughtent tu speak hard ove the misfortnit critter tho', fur he hes got the dispepsy,[6] the wust kine."

1867

2. Here.
3. Wild, edible purplish black grapes.
4. Morsel. "Yearth-borer": earth-borer.
5. Interposition: divine intervention.
6. Chronic gas, flatulence.

T. B. THORPE
1815–1878

Thomas Bangs Thorpe was born on March 1, 1815, at Westfield, Massachusetts, son of a Methodist minister who died when the boy was four. Thorpe spent his childhood in Dutch Albany, with his mother's family, and summers with his paternal grandparents in Connecticut. In 1827 he went with the family to New York City, where in 1830 he began studying with the eccentric painter John Quidor, an early illustrator of Irving. (When Thorpe first exhibited at the American Academy of Fine Arts in 1833, the subject of his painting was Ichabod Crane.) From 1834 to 1936 Thorpe attended Wesleyan University in Middletown, Connecticut, then withdrew in ill health. He went South early in 1837 and recovered his health while painting plantation families in Louisiana and Mississippi. He married in 1838, and the next year became a minor celebrity with a casual sketch of a Louisiana bee hunter published in William T. Porter's *Spirit of the Times* and widely reprinted in the United States and abroad.

During a trip to New York in 1840 Thorpe solidified his friendship with Porter and arranged to write for the *Knickerbocker Magazine*. The next year the *Spirit* published *The Big Bear of Arkansas*, and in the aftermath of this second triumph Thorpe wrote many sketches, mainly about hunting. He continued to paint, frontier scenes and animal paintings as well as portraits, while editing newspapers in Louisiana. In 1845 Porter used Thorpe's most famous story as the title of his anthology of the best southwestern humor writing he had published *(The Big Bear of Arkansas, and Other Sketches)*, and later that year Thorpe published a book of his own, *Mysteries of the Backwoods; or, Sketches of the Southwest: Including Character, Scenery, and Rural Sports.* At the outbreak of the Mexican War, Thorpe wrote and illustrated *Our Army on the Rio Grande.* Much involved with Whig politics, he failed to establish any long or profitable journalistic connection, and in 1854 returned to New York, where he wrote for *Harper's.* In 1854 he published an enlargement of his *Mysteries* volume as *The Hive of "The Bee-Hunter": A Repository of Sketches, Including Peculiar American Character, Scenery, and Rural Sports.* His wife died in 1855 and he remarried two years later, about the time he went on the staff of *Frank Leslie's Illustrated Newspaper.* From 1859 to 1861, after Porter's death, Thorpe was part owner of the *Spirit,* but he was still painting, notably a mammoth view of Niagara Falls (1860) and a view of Irving's grave (1862). In 1862 he went to occupied New Orleans, where he was put in charge of distributing food to the poor on a massive scale as well as enforcing sanitation. He served as a member of the Union-backed Louisiana constitutional convention in 1864 before returning North, where from 1869 on he worked at the New York City Custom House; in his last years he also wrote for a new magazine, *Appleton's.* Thorpe died of Bright's disease on September 20, 1878.

Restless, nervous (as Porter described him), self-effacing, Thorpe never quite brought his varied powers to fruition. Yet he has a permanent niche in American literary history for a story that gave its name to "the Big Bear School of literature."

The Big Bear of Arkansas[1]

A steamboat on the Mississippi frequently, in making her regular trips, carries between places varying from one to two thousand miles apart; and as these boats advertise to land passengers and freight at "all intermediate landings," the heterogeneous character of the passengers of one of these up-country boats can scarcely be imagined by one who has never seen it with his own eyes. Starting from New Orleans in one of these boats, you will find yourself associated with men from every State in the Union, and from every portion of the globe; and a man of observation need not lack for amusement or instruction in such a crowd, if he will take the trouble to read the great book of character so favorably opened before him. Here may be seen jostling together the wealthy Southern planter, and the pedlar of tin-ware from New England— the Northern merchant, and the Southern jockey—a venerable bishop, and a desperate gambler—the land speculator, and the honest farmer—professional men of all creeds and characters—Wolvereens, Suckers, Hoosiers, Buckeyes, and Corncrackers,[2] beside a "plentiful sprinkling" of the half-horse and half-alligator species of men,[3] who are peculiar to "old Mississippi," and who appear to gain a livelihood simply by going up and down the river. In the pursuit of pleasure or business, I have frequently found myself in such a crowd.

On one occasion, when in New Orleans, I had occasion to take a trip of a few miles up the Mississippi, and I hurried on board the well-known, "high-

1. The text is that of the first printing, in *The Spirit of the Times: A Chronicle of the Turf, Agriculture, Field Sports, Literature and the Stage* (March 27, 1841). The story was reprinted in *The Big Bear of Arkansas, and Other Sketches,* edited by William T. Porter, 1845), and in Thorpe's *The Hive of "The Bee-Hunter"* (1854).

2. I.e., people from Michigan, Illinois, Indiana, Ohio, and Kentucky, respectively.
3. The heroic, tall-talking raftsmen, the most celebrated of whom was Mike Fink (1770?–1823), known as "the last of the boatmen." See Chapter 16 of *Huckleberry Finn* (vol. 2, p. 81).

pressure-and-beat-every-thing" steamboat "Invincible," just as the last note of
the last bell was sounding, and when the confusion and bustle that is natural
to a boat's getting under way had subsided, I discovered that I was associated
in as heterogeneous a crowd as was ever got together. As my trip was to be of
a few hours duration only, I made no endeavors to become acquainted with
my fellow passengers, most of whom would be together many days. Instead of
this, I took out of my pocket the "latest paper," and more critically than usual
examined its contents; my fellow passengers at the same time disposed of themselves in little groups. While I was thus busily employed in reading, and my
companions were more busily still employed in discussing such subjects as
suited their humors best, we were startled most unexpectedly by a loud Indian
whoop, uttered in the "social hall," that part of the cabin fitted off for a bar;
then was to be heard a loud crowing, which would not have continued to have
interested us—such sounds being quite common in that *place of spirits*—had
not the hero of these windy accomplishments stuck his head into the cabin
and hallooed out, "Hurra for the Big Bar of Arkansaw!" and then might be
heard a confused hum of voices, unintelligible, save in such broken sentences
as "horse," "screamer,"[4] "lightning is slow," &c. As might have been
expected, this continued interruption attracted the attention of every one in
the cabin; all conversation dropped, and in the midst of this surprise the "Big
Bar" walked into the cabin, took a chair, put his feet on the stove, and looking
back over his shoulder, passed the general and familiar salute of "Strangers,
how are you?" He then expressed himself as much at home as if he had been
at "the Forks of Cypress," and "prehaps a little more so." Some of the company at this familiarity looked a little angry, and some astonished, but in a
moment every face was wreathed in a smile. There was something about the
intruder that won the heart on sight. He appeared to be a man enjoying perfect
health and contentment—his eyes were as sparkling as diamonds, and good
natured to simplicity. Then his perfect confidence in himself was irresistibly
droll. "Prehaps," said he, "gentlemen," running on without a person speaking,
"prehaps you have been to New Orleans often; I never made *the first visit
before*, and I don't intend to make another in a crow's life. I am thrown away
in that ar place, and useless, that ar a fact. Some of the gentlemen thar called
me *green*—well, prehaps I am, said I, *but I arn't so at home*; and if I aint off
my trail much, the heads of them perlite chaps themselves wern't much the
hardest, for according to my notion, they were *real know-nothings*, green as a
pumpkin-vine—couldn't, in farming, I'll bet, raise a crop of turnips—and as
for shooting, they'd miss a barn if the door was swinging, and that, too, with
the best rifle in the country. And then they talked to me 'bout hunting, and
laughed at my calling the principal game in Arkansaw poker, and high-low-
jack. 'Prehaps,' said I, 'you prefer checkers and rolette;'[5] at this they laughed
harder than ever, and asked me if I lived in the woods, and didn't know what
game was? At this I rather think I laughed. 'Yes,' I roared, and says, 'Strangers,
if you'd asked me *how we got our meat* in Arkansaw, I'd a told you at once,
and given you a list of varmints that would make a caravan, beginning with
the bar, and ending off with the cat; that's *meat* though, not game.' Game,
indeed, that's what city folks call it, and with them it means chippen-birds and

---

4. Something of unusual size, strength, or speed.
5. Roulette. The reading "checkers" is from the 1845 edition; the *Spirit* has "chickens," probably a misreading of the manuscript.

shite-pokes;[6] maybe such trash live in my diggings, but I arn't noticed them yet—a bird any way is too trifling. I never did shoot at but one, and I'd never forgiven myself for that had it weighed less than forty pounds; I wouldn't draw a rifle on anything less than that; and when I meet with another wild turkey of the same weight I will drap him."

"A wild turkey weighing forty pounds?" exclaimed twenty voices in the cabin at once.

"Yes, strangers, and wasn't it a whopper? You see, the thing was so fat that he couldn't fly far, and when he fell out of the tree, after I shot him, on striking the ground he bust open behind, and the way the pound gobs of tallow rolled out of the opening was perfectly beautiful."

"Where did all that happen?" asked a cynical looking hoosier.

"Happen! happened in Arkansaw; where else could it have happened, but in the creation State, the finishing-up country; a State where the *sile* runs down to the centre of the 'arth, and government gives you a title to every inch of it. Then its airs, just breath them, and they will make you snort like a horse. It's a State without a fault, it is."

"Excepting mosquitoes," cried the hoosier.

"Well, stranger, except them; for it ar a fact that they are rather *enormous*, and do push themselves in somewhat troublesome. But, stranger, they never stick twice in the same place, and give them a fair chance for a few months, and you will get as much above noticing them as an alligator. They can't hurt my feelings, for they lay under the skin; and I never knew but one case of injury resulting from them, and that was to a Yankee: and they take worse to foreigners, anyhow, than they do to natives. But the way they used that fellow up! first they punched him until he swelled up and busted, then he sup-per-a-ted, as the doctor called it, until he was raw as beef; then he took the ager,[7] owing to the warm weather, and finally he took a steamboat and left the country. He was the only man that ever took mosquitoes at heart that I know of. But mosquitoes is natur, and I never find fault with her; if they ar large, Arkansaw is large, her varmints ar large, her trees ar large, her rivers ar large, and a small mosquitoe would be of no more use in Arkansaw than preaching in a cane-brake."

This knock-down argument in favor of big mosquitoes used the hoosier up, and the logician started on a new track, to explain how numerous bear were in his "diggings," where he represented them to be "about as plenty as black-berries, and a little plentifuler."

Upon the utterance of this assertion, a timid little man near me enquired if the bear in Arkansaw ever attacked the settlers in numbers.

"No," said our hero, warming with the subject, "no, stranger, for you see it ain't the natur of bar to go in droves, but the way they squander about in pairs and single ones is edifying. And then the way I hunt them—the old black rascals know the crack of my gun as well as they know a pig's squealing. They grow thin in our parts, it frightens them so, and they do take the noise dread-fully, poor things. That gun of mine is perfect *epidemic among bar*—if not watched closely, it will go off as quick on a warm scent as my dog Bowie-knife[8] will; and then that dog, whew! why the fellow thinks that the world is full of bar, he finds them so easy. It's lucky he don't talk as well as think, for with his

6. Chipping sparrows and herons.
7. Ague.

8. Named for James Bowie (b. 1796), who was killed in the Alamo in 1836. *Bowie* rhymes with *who he*.

natural modesty, if he should suddenly learn how much he is acknowledged to be ahead of all other dogs in the universe, he would be astonished to death in two minutes. Strangers, that dog knows a bar's way as well as a horse-jockey knows a woman's; he always barks at the right time—bites at the exact place—and whips without getting a scratch. I never could tell whether he was made expressly to hunt bar, or whether bar was made expressly for him to hunt; any way, I believe they were ordained to go together as naturally as Squire Jones says a man and woman is, when he moralizes in marrying a couple. In fact, Jones once said, said he, 'Marriage according to law is a civil contract of divine origin, it's common to all countries as well as Arkansaw, and people take to it as naturally as Jim Doggett's Bowie-knife takes to bar.' "

"What season of the year do your hunts take place?" enquired a gentlemanly foreigner, who, from some peculiarities of his baggage, I suspected to be an Englishman, on some hunting expedition, probably, at the foot of the Rocky Mountains.

"The season for bar hunting, stranger," said the man of Arkansaw, "is generally all the year round, and the hunts take place about as regular. I read in history that varmints have their fat season, and their lean season. That is not the case in Arkansaw, feeding as they do upon the *spontenacious* productions of the sile, they have one continued fat season the year round—though in winter things in this way is rather more greasy than in summer, I must admit. For that reason bar with us run in warm weather, but in winter they only waddle. Fat, fat! it's an enemy to speed—it tames everything that has plenty of it. I have seen wild turkies, from its influence, as gentle as chickens. Run a bar in this fat condition, and the way it improves the critter for eating is amazing; it sort of mixes the ile up with the meat until you can't tell t'other from which. I've done this often. I recollect one perty morning in particular, of putting an old he fellow on the stretch, and considering the weight he carried, he run well. But the dogs soon tired him down, and when I came up with him wasn't he in a beautiful sweat—I might say fever; and then to see his tongue sticking out of his mouth a feet,[9] and his sides sinking and opening like a bellows, and his cheeks so fat he couldn't look cross. In this fix I blazed at him, and pitch me naked into a briar patch if the steam didn't come out of the bullet hole ten foot in a straight line. The fellow, I reckon, was made on the high-pressure system, and the lead sort of bust his biler."

"That column of steam was rather curious, or else the bear must have been *warm*,"[1] observed the foreigner, with a laugh.

"Stranger, as you observe, that bar was WARM, and the blowing off of the steam show'd it, and also how hard the varmint had been run. I have no doubt if he had kept on two miles farther his insides would have been stewed; and I expect to meet with a varmint yet of extra bottom, who will run himself into a skin full of bar's-grease: it is possible, much onlikelier things have happened."

"Where abouts are these bear so abundant?" enquired the foreigner, with increasing interest.

"Why, stranger, they inhabit the neighborhood of my settlement, one of the prettiest places on Old Mississippi—a perfect location, and no mistake; a place that had some defects until the river made the 'cut-off at 'Shirt-tail bend,' and that remedied the evil, as it brought my cabin on the edge of the

9. Perhaps a misprint for "foot."
1. Some slang usage may be involved, although the foreigner is probably employing humorous understatement.

river—a great advantage in wet weather, I assure you, as you can now roll a barrel of whiskey into my yard in high water, from a boat, as easy as falling off a log; it's a great improvement, as toting it by land in a jug, as I used to do, *evaporated* it too fast, and it became expensive. Just stop with me, stranger, a month or two, or a year if you like, and you will appreciate my place. I can give you plenty to eat, for beside hog and hominy, you can have bar ham, and bar sausages, and a mattrass of bar-skins to sleep on, and a wildcat-skin, pulled off hull, stuffed with corn-shucks, for a pillow. That bed would put you to sleep if you had the rheumatics in every joint in your body. I call that ar bed a *quietus*.[2] Then look at my land, the government ain't got another such a piece to dispose of. Such timber, and such bottom land, why you can't preserve anything natural you plant in it, unless you pick it young, things thar will grow out of shape so quick. I once planted in those diggings a few potatoes and beets, they took a fine start, and after that an ox team couldn't have kept them from growing. About that time I went off to old Kentuck on bisiness, and did not hear from them things in three months, when I accidentally stumbled on a fellow who had stopped at my place, with an idea of buying me out. 'How did you like things?' said I. 'Pretty well,' said he; 'the cabin is convenient, and the timber land is good; but that bottom land ain't worth the first red cent.' 'Why?' said I. ' 'Cause,' said he. ' 'Cause what?' said I. ' 'Cause it's full of cedar stumps and Indian mounds,' said he, 'and *it can't be cleared.*' 'Lord,' said I, 'them ar "cedar stumps" is beets, and them ar "Indian mounds" ar tater hills,'—as I expected the crop was overgrown and useless; the sile is too rich, *and planting in Arkansaw is dangerous.* I had a good sized sow killed in that same bottom land; the old thief stole an ear of corn, and took it down where she slept at night to eat; well, she left a grain or two on the ground, and lay down on them; before morning the corn shot up, and the percussion killed her dead. I don't plant any more; natur intended Arkansaw for a hunting ground, and I go according to natur."

The questioner, who thus elicited the description of our hero's settlement, seemed to be perfectly satisfied, and said no more; but the "Big Bar of Arkansaw" rambled on from one thing to another with a volubility perfectly astonishing, occasionally disputing with those around him, particularly with a "live sucker" from Illinois, who had the daring to say that our Arkansaw friend's stories "smelt rather tall."

In this manner the evening was spent, but conscious that my own association with so singular a personage would probably end before morning, I asked him if he would not give me a description of some particular bear hunt— adding that I took great interest in such things, though I was no sportsman. The desire seemed to please him, and he squared himself round towards me, saying, that he could give me an idea of a bar hunt that was never beat in this world, or in any other. His manner was so singular, that half of his story consisted in his excellent way of telling it, the great peculiarity of which was, the happy manner he had of emphasizing the prominent parts of his conversation. As near as I can recollect, I have italicized them, and given the story in his own words.

"Stranger," said he, "in bar hunts *I am numerous,* and which particular one as you say I shall tell puzzles me. There was the old she devil I shot at the

2. Final discharge from all care.

hurricane last fall—then there was the old hog thief I popped over at the Bloody Crossing, and then——Yes, I have it, I will give you an idea of a hunt, in which the greatest bar was killed that ever lived, *none excepted;* about an old fellow that I hunted, more or less, for two or three years, and if that ain't a *particular bar hunt,* I ain't got one to tell. But in the first place, stranger, let me say, I am pleased with you, because you ain't ashamed to gain information by asking, and listening, and that's what I say to Countess's pups every day when I'm home—and I have got great hopes of them ar pups, because they are continually *nosing* about, and though they stick it sometimes in the wrong place, they gain experience anyhow, and may learn something useful to boot. Well, as I was saying about this big bar, you see when I and some more first settled in our region, we were drivin to hunting naturally; we soon liked it, and after that we found it an easy matter to make the thing our business. One old chap who had pioneered 'afore us, gave us to understand that we had settled in the right place. He dwelt upon its merits until it was affecting, and showed us, to prove his assertions, more marks on the sassafras trees than I ever saw on a tavern door 'lection time.[3] 'Who keeps that ar reckoning?' said I. 'The bar,' said he. 'What for?' said I. 'Can't tell,' said he, 'but so it is, the bar bite the bark and wood too, at the highest point from the ground they can reach, and you can tell, by the marks,' said he, 'the length of the bar to an inch.' 'Enough,' said I, 'I've learned something here a'ready, and I'll put it in practice.' Well, stranger, just one month from that time I killed a bar, and told its exact length before I measured it by those very marks—and when I did that I swelled up considerable—I've been a prouder man ever since. So I went on, larning something every day, until I was reckoned a buster,[4] and allowed to be decidedly the best bar hunter in my district; and that is a reputation as much harder to earn than to be reckoned first man in Congress, as an iron ram-rod is harder than a toad-stool. Did the varmints grow over cunning by being fooled with by green-horn hunters, and by this means get troublesome, they send for me as a matter of course, and thus I do my own hunting, and most of my neighbors'. I walk into the varmints though, and it has become about as much the same to me as drinking. It is told in two sentences—a bar is started, and he is killed. The thing is somewhat monotonous now—I know just how much they will run, where they will tire, how much they will growl, and what a thundering time I will have in getting them home. I could give you this history of the chase with all particulars at the commencement, I know the signs so well. *Stranger, I'm certain.* Once I met with a match, though, and I will tell you about it, for a common hunt would not be worth relating.

"On a fine fall day, long time ago, I was trailing about for bar, and what should I see but fresh marks on the sassafras trees, about eight inches above any in the forests that I knew of. Says I, them marks is a hoax, or it indicates the d——t bar that was ever grown. In fact, stranger, I couldn't believe it was real, and I went on. Again I saw the same marks, at the same height, and *I knew the thing lived.* That conviction came home to my soul like an earthquake. Says I, here is something a-purpose for me—that bar is mine, or I give up the hunting business. The very next morning what should I see but a number of buzzards hovering over my cornfield. The rascal has been there, said I, for that sign is certain; and, sure enough, on examining, I found the

3. I.e., reckonings, drinking bills, posted on the doors of inns or taverns; drinking would be extremely heavy during an election.
4. Something stupendous, "busting" all records.

bones of what had been as beautiful a hog the day before, as was ever raised by a Buck-eye. Then I tracked the critter out of the field to the woods, and all the marks he left behind, showed me that he was *the Bar.*

"Well, stranger, the first fair chase I ever had with that big critter, I saw him no less than three distinct times at a distance, the dogs run him over eighteen miles, and broke down, my horse gave out, and I was as nearly used up as a man can be, made on *my* principle, *which is patent.* Before this adventure, such things were unknown to me as possible; but, strange as it was, that bar got me used to it, before I was done with him,—for he got so at last, that he would leave me on a long chase *quite easy.* How he did it, I never could understand. That a bar runs at all, is puzzling; but how this one could tire down, and bust up a pack of hounds and a horse, that were used to overhauling every thing they started after in no time, was past my understanding. Well, stranger, that bar finally got so sassy, that he used to help himself to a hog off my premises whenever he wanted one;—the buzzards followed after what he left, and so between *bar and buzzard,* I rather think I was *out of pork.* Well, missing that bar so often, took hold of my vitals, and I wasted away. The thing had been carried too far, and it reduced me in flesh faster than an ager. I would see that bar in every thing I did,—*he hunted me,* and that, too, like a devil, which I began to think he was. While in this fix, I made preparations to give him a last brush, and be done with it. Having completed every thing to my satisfaction, I started at sun-rise, and to my great joy, I discovered from the way the dogs run, that they were near him—finding his trail was nothing, for that had become as plain to the pack as a turnpike-road.[5] On we went, and coming to an open country, what should I see but the bar very leisurely ascending a hill, and the dogs close at his heels, either a match for him this time in speed, or else he did not care to get out of their way—I don't know which. But, wasn't he a beauty though? I loved him like a brother. On he went, until coming to a tree, the limbs of which formed a crotch about six feet from the ground,—into this crotch he got and seated himself,—the dogs yelling all around it—and there he sat eyeing them, as quiet as a pond in low water. A green-horn friend of mine, in company, reached shooting distance before me, and blazed away, hitting the critter in the centre of his forehead. The bar shook his head as the ball struck it, and then he walked down from that tree as gently as a lady would from a carriage. 'Twas a beautiful sight to see him do that,—he was in such a rage, that he seemed to be as little afraid of the dogs, as if they had been sucking pigs; and the dogs warn't slow in making a ring around him at a respectful distance, I tell you; even Bowie-knife himself stood off. Then the way his eyes flashed—why the fire of them would have singed a cat's hair; in fact, that bar was in a *wrath all over.* Only one pup came near him, and he was brushed out so totally with the bar's left paw, that he entirely disappeared; and that made the old dogs more cautious still. In the mean time, I came up, and taking deliberate aim as a man should do, at his side, just back of his foreleg, *if my gun did not snap,*[6] call me a coward, and I won't take it personal. Yes, stranger, *it snapped,* and I could not find a cap[7] about my person. While in this predicament, I turned round to my fool friend—says I, 'Bill,' says I, 'you're an ass—you're a fool—you might as well

---

5. A toll road (from the pike or spear-shaped implement that turns to permit entrance after payment).
6. I.e., the hammer fell but the gun misfired.

7. Metallic percussion cap filled with fulminating (explosive) powder.

have tried to kill that bar by barking the tree under his belly, as to have done it by hitting him in the head. Your shot has made a tiger of him, and blast me, if a dog gets killed or wounded when they come to blows, I will stick my knife into your liver, I will——' my wrath was up. I had lost my caps, my gun had snapped, the fellow with me had fired at the bar's head, and I expected every moment to see him close in with the dogs, and kill a dozen of them at least. In this thing I was mistaken, for the bar leaped over the ring formed by the dogs, and giving a fierce growl, was off—the pack of course in full cry after him. The run this time was short, for coming to the edge of a lake the varmint jumped in, and swam to a little island in the lake, which it reached just a moment before the dogs. I'll have him now, said I, for I had found my caps in the *lining of my coat*—so, rolling a log into the lake, I paddled myself across to the island, just as the dogs had cornered the bar in a thicket. I rushed up and fired—at the same time the critter leaped over the dogs and came within three feet of me, running like mad; he jumped into the lake, and tried to mount the log I had just deserted, but every time he got half his body on it, it would roll over and send him under; the dogs, too, got around him, and pulled him about, and finally Bowie-knife clenched with him, and they sunk into the lake together. Stranger, about this time I was excited, and I stripped off my coat, drew my knife, and intended to have taken a part with Bowie-knife myself when the bar rose to the surface. But the varmint staid under—Bowie-knife came up alone, more dead than alive, and with the pack came ashore. Thank God, said I, the old villain has got his deserts at last. Determined to have the body, I cut a grape-vine for a rope, and dove down where I could see the bar in the water, fastened my queer rope to his leg, and fished him, with great difficulty, ashore. Stranger, may I be chawed to death by young alligators, if the thing I looked at wasn't a *she bar, and not the old critter after all*. The way matters got mixed on that island was onaccountably curious, and thinking of it made me more than ever convinced that I was hunting the devil himself. I went home that night and took to my bed—the thing was killing me. The entire team of Arkansaw in bar-hunting, acknowledged himself used up, and the fact sunk into my feelings like a snagged boat will in the Mississippi. I grew as cross as a bar with two cubs and a sore tail. The thing got out 'mong my neighbors, and I was asked how come on that individ-u-al that never lost a bar when once started? and if that same individ-u-al didn't wear telescopes when he turned a she bar, of ordinary size, into an old he one, a little larger than a horse? Prehaps, said I, friends—getting wrathy—prehaps you want to call somebody a liar. Oh, no, said they, we only heard such things as being *rather common* of late, but we don't believe one word of it; oh, no,—and then they would ride off and laugh like so many hyenas over a dead nigger. It was too much, and I determined to catch that bar, go to Texas, or die,—and I made my preparations accordin'. I had the pack shut up and rested. I took my rifle to pieces, and iled it. I put caps in every pocket about my person, *for fear of the lining*. I then told my neighbors, that on Monday morning—naming the day—I would start THAT BAR, and bring him home with me, or they might divide my settlement among them, the owner having disappeared. Well, stranger, on the morning previous to the great day of my hunting expedition, I went into the woods near my house, taking my gun and Bowie-knife along, just *from habit*, and there sitting down also from habit, what should I see, getting over my fence, but *the bar*! Yes, the old varmint was within a hundred yards of me, and the way he walked *over that fence,*—stranger, he loomed up like a *black mist,* he seemed so large, and he walked right towards me. I raised myself, took deliberate aim, and fired. Instantly the varmint wheeled, gave a yell, and *walked through the fence* like a falling tree would through a cobweb. I started after, but was tripped up by my inexpressibles, which either from habit, or the excitement of the moment, were about my heels, and before I had really gathered myself up, I heard the old varmint groaning in a thicket near by, like a thousand sinners, and by the time I reached him he was a corpse. Stranger, it took five niggers and myself to put that carcase on a mule's back, and old long ears waddled under his load, as if he was foundered in every leg of his body, and with a common whopper of a bar, he would have trotted off, and enjoyed himself. 'Twould astonish you to know how big he was,—I made a *bed spread of his skin,* and the way it used to cover my bar mattrass, and leave several feet on each side to tuck up, would have delighted you. It was in fact a creation bar, and if it had lived in Sampson's[8] time, and had met him, in a fair fight, it would have licked him in the twinkling of a dice-box. But, stranger, I never liked the way I hunted, *and missed him.* There was something curious about it, I could never understand,—and I never was satisfied at his giving in so *easy at last.* Prehaps, he had heard of my prepara- tions to hunt him the next day, so he jist come in, like Capt. Scott's coon,[9] to save his wind to grunt with in dying; but that ain't likely. My private opinion is, that that bar was an *unhuntable bar, and died when his time come.*"

When the story was ended, our hero sat some minutes with his auditors in a grave silence; I saw there was a mystery to him connected with the bear whose death he had just related, that had evidently made a strong impression on his mind. It was also evident that there was some superstitious awe con- nected with the affair,—a feeling common with all "children of the wood," when they meet with any thing out of their every day experience. He was the first one, however, to break the silence, and jumping up he asked all present to "liquor" before going to bed,—a thing which he did, with a number of companions, evidently to his heart's content.

Long before day, I was put ashore at my place of destination, and I can only follow with the reader, in imagination, our Arkansas friend, in his adventures at the "Forks of Cypress" on the Mississippi.

1841

8. Variant spelling of "Samson," strongman and judge of Israel (Judges 13–16).
9. In a favorite anecdote of the time the fine marks- man Captain Martin Scott is taking aim at a coon when the animal recognizes that his situation is hopeless and cries out "I'm a gone coon!" or "Don't shoot, captain, I'm coming down!"

HENRY DAVID THOREAU
1817–1862

Henry David Thoreau Thoreau won his place in American literature by adventur- ing at home—traveling, as he put it, a good deal in Concord. With that kind of paradox he infuriated and inspired his Massachusetts neighbors and audiences while he lived; his writings have infuriated and inspired successive generations of readers since his death.

Of the men and women who made Concord the center of Transcendentalism, only Thoreau was born there. He lived in Concord all his life, except for a few years in early childhood, his college years at nearby Cambridge, and several months on Staten Island in 1843. He made numerous short excursions, including three to northern Maine, four to Cape Cod, others to New Hampshire, one to Quebec, and a last trip to Minnesota (1861) in a futile attempt to strengthen his tubercular lungs. Never marrying, and horrified by the one proposal that he received, his most complex personal relationship outside his family was with his older neighbor, Ralph Waldo Emerson, though the discrepancies between their rarefied ideals of friendship and the realities of social commerce finally left them frustrated with each other. Aside from Emerson, contemporary writers meant little to him except for Thomas Carlyle, whom he regarded as one of the great exhorting prophets of the generation, and Walt Whitman, although he was always a reader of any history of travel and exploration that could suggest possible ways of experimenting with life. He steeped himself in the classics—Greek, Roman, and English—and he knew in translation the sacred writings of the Hindus. He wrote constantly in his journals, which he began at Emerson's suggestion. Ultimately he made them a finished literary form, but in his early career he used them primarily as sources for his lectures, for his essays, and for both of the books that he published, *A Week on the Concord and Merrimack Rivers* (1849) and *Walden* (1854). Through his writings and lectures he attracted admirers, a few of whom must be called disciples. Much effort—and much unwonted tact—went into satisfying their demands on him while keeping them at an appropriate distance. In the 1850s, as his journals became more and more the record of his observations of nature, his scientific discoveries made him well known to important naturalists such as Louis Agassiz. During the same years, he became one of the most outspoken abolitionists. Although he was never one to affiliate himself with groups, he became known as a reliable abolitionist speaker—not as important as Wendell Phillips, William Lloyd Garrison, or Theodore Parker, but effective enough to be summoned to fill in for Frederick Douglass at a convention in Boston. Thoreau moved into the political forefront only with his defense of John Brown, immediately after the arrests at Harpers Ferry. He was forty-four when he died at Concord on May 6, 1862, in his mother's house. The little national fame he had achieved was as an eccentric Emersonian social experimenter and a firebrand champion of Brown. Emerson, himself famous as the sage of Concord, called Thoreau preeminently "*the* man of Concord," a sincere compliment that precisely delimited his sense of his younger friend as ultimately far more provincial than himself.

Thoreau's nonliterary neighbors, whom he taunted in *Walden* to compel their attention, knew him as an educated man without an occupation—an affront to a society in which few sons (and no daughters) had the privilege of going to Harvard College. Even Emerson thought that he had drifted into his odd way of life rather than choosing it deliberately. Thoreau might in fact have made a career of his first job as a Concord schoolteacher had he not quickly resigned rather than inflict corporal punishment on his students. He would have taken another teaching job, but in that depression year of 1837 could find none. He and his older brother John started their own progressive school in Concord, but it disbanded when John became ill. John died early in 1842, and Thoreau never went back to teaching. That year he became a handyman at Emerson's house in exchange for room and board, and stayed there intermittently during the 1840s, especially when Emerson was away on long trips. He tried tutoring at the Staten Island home of Emerson's brother William in 1843, but he grew miserably homesick. One long-term advantage was that the job had permitted him some contact with the New York publishing circle. He spent two years on Emerson's property at Walden Pond (1845–47) in a cabin he built himself. He first lectured at the Concord Lyceum in 1838; from the late 1840s onward he occasionally earned twenty-five dollars or so for lecturing in small towns such as New Bedford and Worcester and, less often, in Boston. Sometimes he charmed his audiences with woodlore and what reviewers called his "comical" and "highfalutin" variety of laconic Yankee wit; sometimes he infuriated them with righteous challenges to the way they lived. No critic, however friendly, claimed that Thoreau had much presence as a public speaker, except during the fury of some of his abolitionist addresses. After 1848 he earned some money now and then by surveying property. He sold a few magazine articles, but earned nothing from his two books. He worked at times in his father's pencil factory, and carried on the business when his father died in 1859, thereby aggravating his tuberculosis with the dust from graphite. His whole life, after the period of uncertainty about an occupation in his early manhood, became a calculated refusal to live by the materialistic values of the neighbors who provided him with a microcosm of the world. By simplifying his needs—an affront to what was already a consumer society devoted to arousing "artificial wants"—he succeeded, with minimal compromises, in living his life rather than wasting it, as he saw it, in earning a living.

Among Thoreau's literary acquaintances such as Bronson Alcott, Ellery Channing, and Margaret Fuller, Emerson was his first and most powerful champion. Emerson published many of Thoreau's early poems and essays in the *Dial* between 1842 and 1844, and tried to persuade publishers in Boston and New York to print Thoreau's first book. Emerson saw to it that *Week* and, later, *Walden* were known to his British friends, including Thomas Carlyle. Hawthorne, a sometime Concord resident, liked Thoreau although he thought him "the most unmalleable fellow alive." In 1845 Hawthorne discouraged Evert A. Duyckinck from looking for any popular book from Thoreau except perhaps "a book of simple observation of nature." Later, Hawthorne mentioned Thoreau in the prefaces to *Mosses from an Old Manse* (1846) and *The Scarlet Letter* (1850), and Elizabeth Peabody, Hawthorne's sister-in-law, printed *Resistance to Civil Government* in her *Aesthetic Papers* (1849). Horace Greeley, the vigorous editor of the New York *Tribune*, did more than anyone besides Emerson to make Thoreau a national figure, from 1843 onward mentioning his contributions to the *Dial*, reviewing his books, advertising his lectures, reprinting some of his writings, and aggressively forcing some of Thoreau's essays on magazine editors in New York and Philadelphia, then dunning them for payment. George William Curtis, who was one of the "raisers" of the Walden cabin, printed three parts of *A Yankee in Canada* (1866) in *Putnam's Monthly* (1853), but Thoreau withdrew the rest when Curtis wanted to modify what Greeley guessed were "very flagrant heresies (like your defiant Pantheism)." Curtis also accepted *Cape Cod* for *Putnam's Monthly*, but held it for three years before starting to print it in 1855, and even then Thoreau had to contend with Curtis's religious scruples. The *Atlantic Monthly*, founded in 1857 by men of abolitionist sympathies, ought to have become a regular outlet, but the editor, James Russell Lowell, had acquired a dislike for Thoreau, either at Harvard or during Lowell's enforced rustication at Concord. Lowell accepted part of what became *The Maine Woods* but deleted a climactic sentence about a pine tree: "It is as immortal as I am, and perchance will go to as high a heaven, there to tower above me still." Thoreau scathingly declared that the expurgation had been made in "a very mean and cowardly manner," and the *Atlantic Monthly* was closed to him until just before his death, when the new editors solicited manuscripts.

When he died, Thoreau was putting many of his works in shape for publication. His last audible words had to do with *The Maine Woods*: "moose" and "Indian." Although Thoreau had published only *Week* and *Walden* in book form, substantial sections of two posthumous books, *The Maine Woods* and *Cape Cod*, had appeared in magazines. Had they appeared as books, these two might have won Thoreau a wider reputation as a conservationist and an acute observer of people and places, but they would hardly have won him a loftier literary fame.

A Week on the Concord and Merrimack Rivers (1849) purports to be the record of a canoe excursion Thoreau and his brother took upriver. They leave Concord on a Saturday; by Thursday they are as far into New Hampshire as their canoe will go; and then they go back downstream to Concord on a Thursday and Friday (really of the next week). The book consists partly of descriptions of the fauna and flora that the brothers see, along with brief mention of people they encounter. Many pages are devoted to local history, plundered from gazetteers; Thoreau even includes a narrative of Indian captivity, which he ends with some Hawthornesque sensationalism. Poems by Thoreau and others and fragments of his translations from Greek epics and drama also take up space. The bulk of the small book, however, consists of numerous essays, spliced in hit or miss, on a variety of topics such as rivers, fish and fishing, fables, Christianity, poetry, reading, writing, reformers, Oriental scriptures, canal boats, Anacreon, quackery, pedestrian travel, Persius, the distinction between art and nature, the Concord Cattle Show, Ossian, and Chaucer. The longest essay is on friendship. Much of this, verse as well as prose, was fugitive material salvaged from issues of the *Dial*. First completed in the spring of 1846, *Week* was revised and expanded over the next years (the essay on friendship being added in 1848) before Thoreau published an edition of one thousand copies at his own expense in 1849; the true story of his having to accommodate some seven hundred unsold copies in his attic is one of the more grimly ironic episodes in the history of earning a living in America by writing. Emerson had generously assured one editor in 1846 that *Week* contained the results of years of study. That is even truer of the book in its final form, but it was never worked into a unified whole. Its great merit is that by its disastrous reception Thoreau was forced not to publish *Walden* right away (there were ads for it in *Week*). Instead, he kept the manuscript of *Walden* for several more years, reworking it many times. If *Week* had been even a modest success, *Walden* probably would not have been a literary classic.

As early as 1857, Thoreau made clear his intention to publish *The Maine Woods* as a book, though in his lifetime only the first two parts appeared. In this book there is very little satire and very little of the reflective writing shunned by magazines of the time. The most heightened passages of "Ktaadn" deal with Thoreau's realization that the Maine woods were "primeval, untamed, and forever untameable *Nature*," and his peroration would not have offended even the spoilers of nature, citing as it did the inviolable areas in America still left for exploration. Even passages on conservation are not in the voice of a nature-loving Jeremiah, though "Chesuncook" ends with the hope that we shall not, like villains, grub the forests all up, "poaching on our own national domains." These two sections, like almost all of the third, are largely straightforward descriptions of people, places, plants, and animals, with special attention paid to what woodlore could be picked up from lumbermen and American Indian guides. The book's modern editor aptly says that as Maine became a favorite hunting and resort area in the 1870s and 1880s *The Maine Woods* served as a backwoods Baedeker. The backwoods have retreated, but the book is a durable record of what a trained and resourceful observer could discover of primeval nature only a short way from Concord, a reminder that Thoreau was a frontiersman, an explorer of the primeval wilderness as well as of the higher latitudes to be found within oneself.

Thoreau also wrote *Cape Cod* as a book, but during his lifetime he was able to publish only the first four chapters. If he had managed to publish it in the early 1850s it might have gone some way toward making him a popular author. At this time Cape Cod was not fashionable, so Thoreau had a subject almost as exotic as Melville's "Encantadas" (which appeared in *Putnam's Monthly* a little earlier than the chapters from *Cape Cod*) with the added piquancy that Thoreau's unknown land was in the backyards of New York and Boston. Much of the book is vivid eyewitness reportage in the punning style of Thoreau's maturity and with a cheeriness none of his other works sustains. Many pages are openly cribbed from local histories; at best, such information is supplemented by fresh stories from the local inhabitants (who, to Thoreau's delight, often turned out to be even more cantankerous than himself) and by Thoreau's own observations. There is no rage in the book, even in the satire; much of the book is joyous tall talk. In the late twentieth century there is poignancy in reading Thoreau's concluding glance at the future of Cape Cod. The last sentence is a powerful image of Thoreau's repudiation of the worst aspects of his time: "A man may stand there [at Cape Cod] and put all America behind him."

None of the other books that Thoreau published or projected conveys anything like the image of the whole Thoreau that *Walden* does, and even his most representative short work, *Life without Principle*, contains little to suggest his cheerier humor or his love of nature. *Walden* has the meditativeness of *Week* without its diffuseness, the natural observation of *The Maine Woods* without its constriction to particular excursions, the attention to quaintnesses of person and place of *Cape Cod* without its sometimes smothering admixture of borrowed facts. The meandering of *Week* and the travelogue quality of both *The Maine Woods* and *Cape Cod* are replaced in *Walden* by an account that is both a factual record of a particular experience and a parable of all experience. The parables of *Week* are elaborated more richly and focused more memorably in *Walden*; in it the satiric verve of *Cape Cod* is focused on issues far more momentous; in it the nature study of *The Maine Woods* is infused with Thoreau's Transcendentalism. *Week* was the product of diverse impulses; *Cape Cod* and *The Maine Woods* were products of single but limited impulses—perfect of their kind but not belonging to the first order of aspiration or achievement. *Walden* was the product of a single impulse, but one of the strongest literary impulses ever felt: the determination to write a basic book on how to live wisely, a book so profoundly liberating that from the reading of it men and women would date new eras in their lives. In *Walden* Thoreau's whole character emerges. In it he becomes, in the highest sense, a public servant, offering the English-speaking public the fruits of his experience, thought, and artistic dedication.

Thoreau's early writing, even well after his college days, was undistinguished— mere educated prose, less individual, for the most part, than the thirdhand prose that Melville uneasily employed in *Typee*. Thoreau's prose ran to clichés even when the topics, such as love and friendship, were those that were to recur in memorable forms in his later writings. As late as *Week*, the writing was often pedestrianly learned, not up to the alertness of a profoundly educated walker like Thoreau. In *Walden* and a few other works of his mature years, however, Thoreau's style totally subserves his main purpose. Throughout *Walden* that purpose is to force his readers to evaluate the way they have been living and thinking. Whether with his famous aphoristic sentences, his brief fables or allegories, his thick-strewn puns, or many other rhetorical devices, Thoreau's intention always is to make the reader look beyond the obvious, routine sense of an expression to see what idea once vitalized it. He ultimately wants his readers to reevaluate any institution, from the Christian religion to the Constitution of the United States, but first he makes his readers work up their courage by reevaluating on a smaller scale. Thoreau's rhetorical devices afford the hard exercise by which a reader may learn to think freshly. The prose of *Walden*, in short, is designed as a practical course in the liberation of the reader.

Recognition of Thoreau as an important writer was slow in coming. Literary people of his own time knew well enough who he was, but the reading public did not until the publication of *Walden* occasioned comment in some widely read newspapers and magazines. What became Thoreau's most famous essay, *Resistance to Civil Government* (the posthumous title *On the Duty of Civil Disobedience*, now usually cut to the last two words, is apparently not authorial), was published anonymously and never attached to his name in print during his life, though such people as Emerson and Hawthorne knew Thoreau was the author; many decades passed before anyone explicitly acted on the essay's radical advice.

Thoreau's early essays in magazines like the *Democratic Review* and *Graham's* were anonymous, and Greeley did not mention him by name when he printed in the *Tribune* for May 25, 1848, a remarkable quotation from a Thoreau letter that was to become part of the first chapter of *Walden*. Thoreau's *Putnam's Monthly* and *Atlantic Monthly* pieces were also anonymous, according to the custom, so that most of his readers probably never knew they were reading Thoreau. Ironically, his widest-read works published under his name during his lifetime were not *Week* or even *Walden*, but *Slavery in Massachusetts* (printed in William Lloyd Garrison's *Liberator* and copied in the *Tribune*) and A *Plea for Captain John Brown* (printed in the fast-selling *Echoes of Harper's Ferry*, 1860).

Between June 1862 (the month after Thoreau's death) and November 1863, the *Atlantic Monthly* published *Walking, Autumn Tints, Wild Apples, Life without Principle*, and *Night and Moonlight* anonymously, but publicized them as Thoreau's. Ticknor and Fields reissued *Week* and *Walden* and quickly got out five new books: *Excursions* (1863), *The Maine Woods* (1864), *Cape Cod* (1864), *Letters to Various Persons* (1865), and A *Yankee in Canada, with Anti-Slavery and Reform Papers* (1866). The expanded form of Emerson's funeral speech, published in the *Atlantic Monthly* for August 1863, confirmed Thoreau's growing reputation even while unnecessarily stressing some of his less attractive traits, especially his "habit of antagonism." In the *North American Review* for October 1865, James Russell Lowell—by then the foremost American critic—had his revenge for Thoreau's scorn for his censorship. Reviewing *Letters to Various Persons*, Lowell depicted Thoreau as a mere echoer of Emerson, "surly and stoic," with "a morbid self-consciousness that pronounces the world of men empty and worthless before trying it." Perhaps most damning, Thoreau was a man who "had no humor." Even Robert Louis Stevenson's description (1880) of Thoreau as a "skulker" had a less baneful effect. In American literary histories and classroom anthologies of the next sixty years, Lowell's words were endlessly quoted or paraphrased.

With Thoreau's credit as social philosopher so thoroughly squelched, his friends began emphasizing his role as a student of nature. Channing published *Thoreau: The Poet-Naturalist* (1873), and John Burroughs's essays followed in the 1880s. Capitalizing on this new attention, Thoreau's disciple H. G. O. Blake, who had inherited the journals from Thoreau's sister Sophia, published *Early Spring in Massachusetts* (1881), *Summer* (1884), *Winter* (1887), and *Autumn* (1892). British critics became interested in Thoreau, and in 1890 an important biography was published by the socialist H. S. Salt—just in time to introduce Thoreau to many Fabians and Labour party members. Thoreau was at last becoming widely recognized as a social philosopher as well as a naturalist. In 1906 Mahatma Gandhi, in his African exile, read *Civil Disobedience* and made it—and later *Life without Principle*—major documents in his struggle for Indian independence. The publication of the journals in 1906 in chronological order (Blake had plundered the journals for seasonal passages regardless of the years in which they occurred) gave readers for the first time a nearly full body of evidence for understanding and judging Thoreau. By the 1930s, when for many "Simplify!" had become not a whim but a necessity, Thoreau had attained the status of a major American voice. Scholarly attention in the next decades began to exalt him to a literary rank higher than Emerson's, even while civil-rights leaders such as Martin Luther King, Jr., tested his tactics of civil disobedience throughout the South and sometimes into the North. In the 1960s and 1970s the counterculture's concern with experiments in living and the general American concern for ecological sanity helped establish Thoreau more firmly than ever as a great American prophet, while his potential value to the radical left remains largely untested. Oddly enough, editors and publishers have kept much of his best work from being known by frequently reprinting *Walden* and *Civil Disobedience* together while ignoring his other works. Thoreau has yet to achieve his full recognition as a great prose stylist as well as a lover of nature, a New England mystic, and a powerful social philosopher. He remains the most challenging major writer America has produced. No good reader will ever be entirely pleased with himself or herself or with the current state of culture and civilization while reading any of Thoreau's best works.

Thomas Carlyle and His Works[1]

Thomas Carlyle is a Scotchman, born about fifty years ago, "at Ecclefechan, Annandale," according to one authority.[2] "His parents 'good farmer people,' his father an elder in the Secession church[3] there, and a man of strong native sense, whose words were said to 'nail a subject to the wall.' " We also hear of his "excellent mother," still alive, and of "her fine old convenanting[4] accents, concerting with his transcendental tones." He seems to have gone to school at Annan, on the shore of the Solway Frith,[5] and there, as he himself writes, "heard of famed professors, of high matters classical, mathematical, a whole Wonderland of Knowledge," from Edward Irving,[6] then a young man "fresh from Edinburgh, with college prizes, &c."—"come to see our schoolmaster, who had also been his." From this place, they say, you can look over into Wordsworth's country.[7] Here first he may have become acquainted with Nature, with woods, such as are there, and rivers and brooks, some of whose names we have heard, and the last lapses of Atlantic billows. He got some of his education, too, more or less liberal, out of the University of Edinburgh, where, according to the same authority, he had to "support himself," partly by "private tuition, translations for the booksellers, &c.," and afterward, as we are glad to hear, "taught an academy in Dysart, at the same time that Irving was teaching in Kirkaldy," the usual middle passage of a literary life. He was destined for the church, but not by the powers that rule man's life; made his

1. Thomas Carlyle (1795–1881) was for Emerson and Thoreau (as well as Melville and Whitman) the single most influential contemporary British writer. Thoreau wrote this essay at Walden and read a version of it at the Concord Lyceum on February 4, 1846. It is included here for two reasons. First, it is the most economical way of suggesting the immense debt Thoreau owed to Carlyle (as well as to other British writers, including Burns, on whom Carlyle had written and who was one of Thoreau's own favorites). (We tend to forget that until the latter part of the century every important American writer, including Whitman, was steeped in Burns.) Second, this may be the best single text for watching the process by which Thoreau began to acquire his own literary voice, for the stylistic exuberance of Carlyle freed him to attempt the complex interplay of sentence lengths and of levels of diction that was to distinguish *Walden*. There are moments in this essay on Carlyle when Thoreau for the first time speaks in his own voice.

Aggressively serving as Thoreau's agent, Horace Greeley placed the piece with *Graham's Magazine* of Philadelphia, where, after delays that pained Thoreau, it was published in two parts, March–April 1847, the source of the present text and fuller than the text that Thoreau's editors printed in the posthumous *A Yankee in Canada* (1866). In May 1848 Greeley finally muscled $50 for Thoreau out of the recalcitrant owner of *Graham's*.

Besides being well acquainted with Carlyle's books and many of his magazine writings, Thoreau knew much about Carlyle directly from Emerson and from what Emerson had written, e.g., the prefaces to the Boston editions of *Sartor Resartus* (1836) and *Past and Present* (1843). He also had read some of the controversial essays that had appeared in British magazines during the previous decade (Emerson subscribed to some of them, and others were available in the Boston–Concord circle), for he cast his piece as a rebuttal to earlier assessments that he thought had overemphasized the Germanic influences on Carlyle's style and had underestimated Carlyle's humor. Thoreau sent the essay to Carlyle, who replied through Emerson that the "lecture" had been "carefully read, as beseemed, with due entertainment and recognition."

2. Robert Sattelmeyer has identified Thoreau's source as George Gilfillan's *Sketches of Modern Literature, and Eminent Literary Men* (1846).

3. A dissenting branch of the Presbyterian church.

4. The term *covenanter* was applied to various groups of Scottish Presbyterians who opposed English oppression.

5. Or Firth; an inlet on the border between England and Scotland.

6. Scottish minister (1792–1834) whose emphasis on the need to reestablish the primitive functions of the church may have influenced Carlyle's adoption of the role of cultural prophet. Carlyle's tribute, "Death of Edward Irving, " is in his *Critical and Miscellaneous Essays*.

7. I.e., the Lake District in the north of England.

literary début in Fraser's Magazine, long ago; read here and there in English and French, with more or less profit, we may suppose, such of us at least as are not particularly informed, and at length found some words which spoke to his condition in the German language, and set himself earnestly to unravel that mystery—with what success many readers know.

After his marriage he "resided partly at Comely Bank, Edinburgh; and for a year or two at Craigenputtock, a wild and solitary farm-house in the upper part of Dumfriesshire," at which last place, amid barren heather hills, he was visited by our countryman Emerson.[8] With Emerson he still corresponds. He was early intimate with Edward Irving, and continued to be his friend until the latter's death. Concerning this "freest, brotherliest, bravest human soul," and Carlyle's relation to him, those whom it concerns will do well to consult a notice of his death in Fraser's Magazine for 1835, reprinted in the Miscellanies. He also corresponded with Goethe. Latterly, we hear, the poet, Stirling[9] was his only intimate acquaintance in England.

He has spent the last quarter of his life in London, writing books; has the fame, as all readers know, of having made England acquainted with Germany, in late years, and done much else that is novel and remarkable in literature. He especially is the literary man of those parts. You may imagine him living in altogether a retired and simple way, with small family, in a quiet part of London, called Chelsea, a little out of the din of commerce, in "Cheyne Row,"[1] there, not far from the "Chelsea Hospital." "A little past this, and an old ivy-clad church, with its buried generations lying around it," writes one traveler, "you come to an antique street running at right angles with the Thames, and, a few steps from the river, you find Carlyle's name on the door."

"A Scotch lass ushers you into the second story front chamber, which is the spacious workship of the world maker." Here he sits a long time together, with many books and papers about him; many new books, we have been told, on the upper shelves, uncut, with the "author's respects" in them; in late months, with many manuscripts in an old English hand, and innumerable pamphlets, from the public libraries, relating to the Cromwellian period; now, perhaps, looking out into the street on brick and pavement, for a change, and now upon some rod of grass ground in the rear; or, perchance, he steps over to the British Museum,[2] and makes that his studio for the time. This is the fore part of the day; that is the way with literary men commonly; and then in the afternoon, we presume, he takes a short run[3] of a mile or so through the suburbs out into the country; we think he would run that way, though so short a trip might not take him to very sylvan or rustic places. In the meanwhile, people are calling to see him, from various quarters, very few worthy of being seen by him, "distinguished travelers from America," not a few, to all and sundry of whom he gives freely of his yet unwritten rich and flashing soliloquy, in exchange for

---

8. Emerson went to Scottland to visit Carlyle in 1833.

9. John Sterling (1806–1844), minister, follower of Coleridge; an early admirer then friend of Carlyle, who wrote a Life of him (1851). Johann Wolfgang von Goethe (1749–1832), great German Romantic poet and dramatist. Carlyle's translations of Goethe and other German writers and his polemic magazine articles on them had opened recent German literature to British and American readers. Many Americans, including Emerson, learned to recognize and cherish Carlyle by his subject matter and his style before they knew who was writing the anonymous essays on Ger-

man writers.

1. Chelsea was then a semirural part of western London, which became a fashionable literary address after D. G. Rossetti and others followed Carlyle to Cheyne Walk or neighboring streets.

2. Then as now in Bloomsbury (not by modern standards an easy stroll from Chelsea, although the reading room (which Carlyle complained about) has been replaced.

3. Thoreau means walk: many Victorians like their American counterparts were great walkers.

whatever they may have to offer; speaking his English, as they say, with a "broad Scotch accent," talking, to their astonishment and to ours, very much as he writes, a sort of Carlylese, his discourse "coming to its climaxes, ever and anon, in long, deep, chestshaking bursts of laughter."

He goes to Scotland sometimes to visit his native heath-clad hills, having some interest still in the earth there; such names as Craigenputtock and Ecclefechan, which we have already quoted, stand for habitable places there to him; or he rides to the seacoast of England in his vacations, upon his horse Yankee, bought by the sale of his books here, as we have been told.[4]

How, after all, he gets his living; what proportion of his daily bread he earns by day-labor or job-work with his pen, what he inherits, what steals—questions whose answers are so significant, and not to be omitted in his biography—we, alas! are unable to answer here. It may be worth the while to state that he is not a Reformer, in our sense of the term, eats, drinks, and sleeps, thinks and believes, professes and practices, not according to the New England standard, nor to the Old English wholly. Nevertheless, we are told that he is a sort of lion in certain quarters there, "an amicable centre for men of the most opposite opinions," and "listened to as an oracle," "smoking his perpetual pipe."

A rather tall, gaunt figure, with intent face, dark hair and complexion, and the air of a student; not altogether well in body, from sitting too long in his workhouse, he, born in the border country and descended from moss-troopers,[5] it may be. We have seen several pictures of him here; one, a full length portrait, with hat and overall, if it did not tell us much, told the fewest lies; another, we remember, was well said to have "too combed[6] a look;" one other also we have seen in which we discern some features of the man we are thinking of; but the only ones worth remembering, after all, are those which he has unconsciously drawn of himself.

When we remember how these volumes came over to us, with their encouragement and provocation from month to month, and what commotion they created in many private breasts, we wonder that the country did not ring, from shore to shore, from the Atlantic to the Pacific, with its greeting; and the Boons and Crockets[7] of the West make haste to hail him, whose wide humanity embraces them too. Of all that the packets[8] have brought over to us, has there been any richer cargo than this? What else has been English news for so long a season? What else, of late years, has been England to us—to us who read books, we mean? Unless we remembered it as the scene where the age of Wordsworth was spending itself, and a few younger muses were trying their wings, and from time to time, as the residence of Landor; Carlyle alone, since the death of Coleridge,[9] has kept the promise of England. It is the best apology for all the bustle and the sin of commerce, that it has made us acquainted with the thoughts of this man. Commerce would not concern us much if it were

---

4. Thoreau's knowledge was imperfect. When Emerson sent Carlyle money earned by sales of his books in the United States, Carlyle wrote him of plans to spend the funds on a horse fittingly to be called "Yankee," but instead a wealthy admirer from Leeds gave him a horse, which he called "Citoyenne" (i.e., female citizen in France during the revolution).

5. Marauders or raiders in the bogs at the border between England and Scotland in the 17th century. Thoreau's point is that by ancestry Carlyle should have been an outdoorsman, not a city dweller.

6. Well-groomed. "Overall": cloak.

7. I.e., the American frontier heroes Daniel Boone (1734–1820) and Davy Crockett (1786–1836).

8. Mail and passenger boats.

9. The English poet Walter Savage Landor (1775–1864) lived abroad during the whole of Thoreau's youth (Emerson visited him in Florence in 1833); later in 1833 Emerson also visited the Romantic poet and aesthetician Samuel Taylor Coleridge (1772–1834) in London.

not for such results as this. New England owes him a debt which she will be slow to recognize. His earlier essays reached us at a time when Coleridge's were the only recent words which had made any notable impression so far, and they found a field unoccupied by him, before yet any words of moment had been uttered in our midst. He had this advantage, too, in a teacher, that he stood near to his pupils; and he has no doubt afforded reasonable encouragement and sympathy to many an independent but solitary thinker. Through him, as usher, we have been latterly, in a great measure, made acquainted with what philosophy and criticism the nineteenth century had to offer— admitted, so to speak, to the privileges of the century; and what he may yet have to say, is still expected here with more interest than any thing else from that quarter.

It is remarkable, but on the whole, perhaps, not to be lamented, that the world is so unkind to a new book. Any distinguished traveler who comes to our shores, is likely to get more dinners and speeches of welcome than he can well dispose of, but the best books, if noticed at all, meet with coldness and suspicion, or, what is worse, gratuitous, off-hand criticism. It is plain that the reviewers, both here and abroad, do not know how to dispose of this man. They approach him too easily, as if he were one of the men of letters about town, who grace Mr. Somebody's administration, merely; but he already belongs to literature, and depends neither on the favor of reviewers, nor the honesty of booksellers, nor the pleasure of readers for his success. He has more to impart than to receive from his generation. He is another such a strong and finished workman in his craft as Samuel Johnson[1] was, and like him, makes the literary class respectable. As few are yet out of their apprenticeship, or even if they learn to be able writers, are at the same time able and valuable thinkers. The aged and critical eye, especially, is incapacitated to appreciate the works of this author. To such their meaning is impalpable and evanescent, and they seem to abound only in obstinate mannerisms, Germanisms, and whimsical ravings of all kinds, with now and then an unaccountably true and sensible remark. On the strength of this last, Carlyle is admitted to have what is called genius. We hardly know an old man whom these volumes are not hopelessly sealed. The language, they say, is foolishness and a stumbling-block to them; but to many a clear-headed boy, they are plainest English, and despatched with such hasty relish as his bread and milk. The fathers wonder how it is that the children take to this diet so readily, and digest it with so little difficulty. They shake their heads with mistrust at their free and easy delight, and remark that "Mr. Carlyle is a very learned man;" for they, too, not to be out of fashion, have got grammar and dictionary, if the truth were known, and with the best faith cudgelled their brains to get a little way into the jungle, and they could not but confess, as often as they found the clue, that it was as intricate as Blackstone[2] to follow, if you read it honestly. But merely reading, even with the best intentions, is not enough, you must almost have written these books yourself. Only he who has had the good fortune to read them in the nick of time, in the most perceptive and recipient season of life, can give any adequate account of them.

1. In an essay on Carlyle in the October 1839 *London and Westminster Review* (which Emerson called a "noble critique"), John Sterling singled out Carlyle's essay on Dr. Johnson (1709–1784) as reversing the recent tendency to minimize the stature of this famous lexicographer and critic.

2. Sir William Blackstone (1723–1780), British jurist, author of *Commentaries*, which generations of law students studied.

Many have tasted of this well with an odd suspicion, as if it were some fountain Arethuse[3] which had flowed under the sea from Germany, as if the materials of his books had lain in some garret there, in danger of being appropriated for waste paper. Over what German ocean, from what Hercynian[4] forest, he has been imported, piece-meal, into England, or whether he has now all arrived, we are not informed. This article is not invoiced in Hamburg, nor in London. Perhaps it was contraband. However, we suspect that this sort of goods cannot be imported in this way. No matter how skillful the stevedore, all things being got into sailing trim, wait for a Sunday, and aft wind, and then weigh anchor, and run up the main-sheet—straightway what of transcendant and permanent value is there resists the aft wind, and will doggedly stay behind that Sunday—it does not travel Sundays; while biscuit and pork make headway, and sailors cry heave-yo! it must part company, if it open a seam.[5] It is not quite safe to send out a venture in this kind, unless yourself go supercargo. Where a man goes, there he is; but the slightest virtue is immovable—it is real estate, not personal; who would keep it, must consent to be bought and sold with it.

However, we need not dwell on this charge of a German extraction, it being generally admitted, by this time, that Carlyle is English, and an inhabitant of London. He has the English for his mother tongue, though with a Scotch accent, or never so many accents, and thoughts also, which are the legitimate growth of native soil, to utter therewith. His style is eminently colloquial—and no wonder it is strange to meet with in a book. It is not literary or classical; it has not the music of poetry, nor the pomp of philosophy, but the rhythms and cadences of conversation endlessly repeated. It resounds with emphatic, natural, lively, stirring tones, muttering, rattling, exploding, like shells and shot, and with like execution. So far as it is a merit in composition, that the written answer to the spoken word, and the spoken word to a fresh and pertinent thought in the mind, as well as to the half thoughts, the tumultuary misgivings and expectancies, this author is, perhaps, not to be matched in literature. In the streets men laugh and cry, but in books, never; they "whine, put finger i' the eye, and sob" only. One would think that all books of late, had adopted the falling inflexion. "A mother, if she wishes to sing her child to sleep," say the musical men, "will always adopt the falling inflexion." Would they but choose the rising inflexion, and wake the child up for once.

He is no mystic either, more than Newton or Arkwright, or Davy[6]—and tolerates none. Not one obscure line, or half line, did he ever write. His meaning lies plain as the daylight, and he who runs may read;[7] indeed, only he who runs *can* read, and keep up with the meaning. It has the distinctness of picture to his mind, and he tells us only what he sees printed in largest English type upon the face of things. He utters substantial English thoughts in plainest

---

3. Spring in Syracuse, Sicily, associated in Milton's *Lycidas* with Roman pastoral poetry.
4. Of a mountain range in ancient Germany.
5. I.e., if it cracks a joint.
6. Britons notable for nonmystic thought: Sir Isaac Newton (1642–1727), mathematician, philosopher, and scientist who developed the theory of gravitation (later Thoreau refers to the popular account of his being stimulated to construct his theory by the falling of an apple). Sir Richard Arkwright (1732–1792), inventor of machines for spinning thread (and, therefore, in-

veighed against by Carlyle in *Past and Present* as contributing to the growth of workhouses). Sir Humphrey Davy (1778–1829), chemist, discoverer of twelve chemical elements.
7. In Habbakuk 2:2 God tells the prophet: "Write the vision, and make it plain upon tables, that he may run that readeth it," i.e., write the prophecy on the clay tablet in letters so large as to be read by one who is running past, not sitting down to read. The modern equivalent would be writing the message on billboards.

English dialects; for it must be confessed, he speaks more than one of these. All the shires of England, and all the shires of Europe, are laid under contribution to his genius; for to be English does not mean to be exclusive and narrow, and adapt one's self to the apprehension of his nearest neighbor only. And yet no writer is more thoroughly Saxon. In the translation of those fragments of Saxon poetry, we have met with the same rhythm that occurs so often in his poem on the French Revolution. And if you would know where many of those obnoxious Carlyleisms and Germanisms came from, read the best of Milton's prose, read those speeches of Cromwell which he has brought to light,[8] or go and listen once more to your mother's tongue. So much for his German extraction.

Indeed, for fluency and skill in the use of the English tongue, he is a master unrivaled. His felicity and power of expression surpass even any of his special merits as a historian and critic. Therein his experience has not failed him, but furnished him with such a store of winged, aye, and legged words, as only a London life, perchance, could give account of; we had not understood the wealth of the language before. Nature is ransacked, and all the resorts and purlieus of humanity are taxed, to furnish the fittest symbol for his thought. He does not go to the dictionary, the word-book, but to the word-manufactory itself, and has made endless work for the lexicographers—yes, he has that same English for his mother-tongue, that you have, but with him it is no dumb, muttering, mumbling faculty, concealing the thoughts, but a keen, unwearied, resistless weapon. He has such command of it as neither you nor I have; and it would be well for any who have a lost horse to advertise, or a town-meeting warrant, or a sermon, or a letter to write, to study this universal letter-writer, for he knows more than the grammar or the dictionary.

The style is worth attending to, as one of the most important features of the man which we at this distance can discern. It is for once quite equal to the matter. It can carry all its load, and never breaks down nor staggers. His books are solid and workmanlike, as all that England does; and they are graceful and readable also. They tell of huge labor done, well done, and all the rubbish swept away, like the bright cutlery which glitters in shopwindows, while the coke and ashes, the turnings, filings, dust, and borings, lie far away at Birmingham,[9] unheard of. He is a masterly clerk, scribe, reporter, and writer. He can reduce to writing most things—gestures, winks, nods, significant looks, patois, brogue, accent, pantomime, and how much that had passed for silence before, does he represent by written words. The countryman who puzzled the city lawyer, requiring him to write, among other things, his call to his horses, would hardly have puzzled him; he would have found a word for it, all right and classical, that would have started his team for him. Consider the ceaseless tide of speech forever flowing in countless cellars, garrets, *parlors:* that of the French, says Carlyle, "only ebbs toward the short hours of night," and what a drop in the bucket is the printed word. Feeling, thought, speech, writing, and we might add, poetry, inspiration—for so the circle is completed; how they gradually dwindle at length, passing through successive colanders, into your history and classics, from the roar of the ocean, the murmur of the forest, to the squeak of a mouse; so much only parsed and spelt out, and punctuated, at

8. Carlyle edited *Cromwell's Letters and Speeches* (1845). Oliver Cromwell (1599–1658) was the Puritan leader in the English Civil War.

9. English city famous for its cutlery manufacture. "Coke": fuel waste. "Turnings" and "borings": metal waste.

last. The few who can talk like a book, they only get reported commonly. But this writer reports a new "Lieferung."[1]

One wonders how so much, after all, was expressed in the old way, so much here depends upon the emphasis, tone, pronunciation, style, and spirit of the reading. No writer uses so profusely all the aids to intelligibility which the printer's art affords. You wonder how others had contrived to write so many pages without emphatic or italicised words, they are so expressive, so natural, so indispensable here, as if none had ever used the demonstrative pronouns demonstratively before. In another's sentences the thought, though it may be immortal, is, as it were, embalmed, and does not *strike* you, but here it is so freshly living, even the body of it, not having passed through the ordeal of death, that it stirs in the very extremities, and the smallest particles and pronouns are all alive with it. It is not simple dictionary *it*, yours or mine, but IT. The words did not come at the command of grammar, but of a tyrannous, inexorable meaning; not like standing soldiers,[2] by vote of parliament, but any able-bodied countryman pressed into the service, for "sire, it is not a revolt, it is a revolution."

We have never heard him speak, but we should say that Carlyle was a rare talker. He has broken the ice, and streams freely forth like a spring torrent. He does not trace back the stream of his thought, silently adventurous, up to its fountain-head, but is borne away with it, as it rushes through his brain like a torrent to overwhelm and fertilize. He holds a talk with you. His audience is such a tumultuous mob of thirty thousand, as assembled at the University of Paris,[3] before printing was invented. Philosophy, on the other hand, does not talk, but write, or, when it comes personally before an audience, lecture or read; and therefore it must be read to-morrow, or a thousand years hence. But the talker must naturally be attended to at once; he does not talk on without an audience; the winds do not long bear the sound of his voice. Think of Carlyle reading his French Revolution[4] to any audience. One might say it was never written, but spoken; and thereafter reported and printed, that those not within sound of his voice might know something about it. Some men read to you something which they have written, in a dead *language*, of course, but it may be in a living *letter*, in a Syriac, or Roman, or Runic character. Men must *speak* English who can *write* Sanscrit; and they must speak a modern language who write, perchance, an ancient and universal one. We do not live in those days when the learned used a learned language. There is no writing of Latin with Carlyle, but as Chaucer, with all reverence to Homer, and Virgil, and Messieurs the Normans, sung his poetry in the homely Saxon tongue; and Locke[5] has at least the merit of having done philosophy into English—so Carlyle has done a different philosophy still further into English, and thrown open the doors of literature and criticism to the populace.

Such a style—so diversified and variegated! It is like the face of a country; it is like a New England landscape, with farm-houses and villages, and cultivated spots, and belts of forests and blueberry-swamps round about it, with the fragrance of shad-blossoms and violets on certain winds. And as for the reading of it, it is novel enough to the reader who has used only the diligence, and old-line mailcoach. It is like traveling, sometimes on foot, sometimes in a gig

1. Supply (German).
2. I.e., conscripts awaiting orders.
3. I.e., to hear a religious debate.

4. Carlyle published his *French Revolution* in 1837.
5. John Locke (1632–1704), English empirical philosopher.

tandem;[6] sometimes in a full coach, over highways, mended and unmended, for which you will prosecute the town; on level roads, through French departments, by Simplon roads over the Alps, and now and then he hauls up for a relay, and yokes in an unbroken colt of a Pegasus for a leader, driving off by cart-paths, and across lots, by corduroy roads[7] and gridiron bridges; and where the bridges are gone, not even a string-piece left, and the reader has to set his breast and swim. You have got an expert driver this time, who has driven ten thousand miles, and was never known to upset; can drive six in hand on the edge of a precipice, and touch the leaders anywhere with his snapper.[8]

With wonderful art he grinds into paint for his picture all his moods and experiences, so that all his forces may be brought to the encounter. Apparently writing without a particular design or responsibility, setting down his soliloquies from time to time, taking advantage of all his humors,[9] when at length the hour comes to declare himself, he puts down in plain English, without quotation marks, what he, Thomas Carlyle, is ready to defend in the face of the world, and fathers the rest, often quite as defensible, only more modest, or plain spoken, or insinuating, upon "Sauerteig,"[1] or some other gentleman long employed on the subject. Rolling his subject how many ways in his mind, he meets it now face to face, wrestling with it at arm's length, and striving to get it down, or throws it over his head; and if that will not do, or whether it will do or not, tries the back-stitch and side-hug with it, and downs it again—scalps it, draws and quarters it,[2] hangs it in chains, and leaves it to the winds and dogs. With his brows knit, his mind made up, his will resolved and resistless, he advances, crashing his way through the host of weak, half-formed, *dilettante* opinions, honest and dishonest ways of thinking, with their standards raised, sentimentalities and conjectures, and tramples them all into dust. See how he prevails; you don't even hear the groans of the wounded and dying. Certainly it is not so well worth the while to look through any man's eyes at history, for the time, as through his; and his way of looking at things is fastest getting adopted by his generation.

It is not in man to determine what his style shall be. He might as well determine what his thoughts shall be. We would not have had him write always as in the chapter on Burns, and the Life of Schiller,[3] and elsewhere. No; his thoughts were ever irregular and impetuous. Perhaps as he grows older and writes more he acquires a truer expression; it is in some respects manlier, freer, struggling up to a level with its fountain-head. We think it is the richest prose style we know of.

---

6. Two-wheeled carriage drawn by horses harnessed one before the other. "Diligence": stagecoach. "Gig": light two-wheeled, one-horse carriage. Emerson had hired a gig for the trip from Glasgow to Craigenputtock.
7. Roads built of logs side by side transversely. "Simplon roads": hazardous roads like those near the Simplon Pass in the Alps between Switzerland and Italy. "Pegasus": the winged horse of Greek mythology, associated with the poetic power.
8. Whip.
9. I.e., moods.
1. One of Carlyle's favorite invented characters, Doctor Gottfried Sauerteig, author of *Aesthetische Springwurzeln*, used (like Professor Teufelsdröckh in *Sartor Resartus*) to promulgate highly debatable opinions more or less close to Carlyle's own. In the *Dial*

(July 1843) Emerson described Carlyle's "expedient for expressing those unproven opinions which he entertains but will not endorse, by summoning one of his straw men from the cell,—and the respectable Sauerteig, or Teufelsdröckh, or Dryasdust, or Picturesque Traveller, says what is put into his mouth, and disappears."
2. A reference to the punishment wherein a victim's body is drawn in four different directions by horses, thereby "quartering" the person.
3. The Scottish poet Robert Burns (1759–1796) and the German poet and dramatist Johann Christoph Friedrich von Schiller (1759–1805) are mentioned as favorites of Carlyle, who wrote a *Life of Schiller* (1825) and who ranked Burns with Johnson and Rousseau as "The Hero as Man of Letters" in *On Heroes, Hero-Worship, & the Heroic in History* (1841).

Who cares what a man's style is, so it is intelligible—as intelligible as his thought. Literally and really, the style is no more than the *stylus*, the pen he writes with—and it is not worth scraping and polishing, and gilding, unless it will write his thoughts the better for it. It is something for use, and not to look at. The question for us is not whether Pope[4] had a fine style, wrote with a peacock's feather, but whether he uttered useful thoughts. Translate a book a dozen times from one language to another, and what becomes of its style? Most books would be worn out and disappear in this ordeal. The pen which wrote it is soon destroyed, but the poem survives. We believe that Carlyle has, after all, more readers, and is better known to-day for this very originality of style, and that posterity will have reason to thank him for emancipating the language, in some measure, from the fetters which a merely conservative, aimless, and pedantic literary class had imposed upon it, and setting an example of greater freedom and naturalness. No man's thoughts are new, but the style of their expression is the never failing novelty which cheers and refreshes men. If we were to answer the question, whether the mass of men, as we know them, talk as the standard authors and reviewers write, or rather as this man writes, we should say that he alone begins to write their language at all, and that the former is, for the most part, the mere effigies of a language, not the best method of concealing one's thoughts even, but frequently a method of doing without thoughts at all.

In his graphic description of Richter's[5] style, Carlyle describes his own pretty nearly; and no doubt he first got his own tongue loosened at that fountain, and was inspired by it to equal freedom and originality. "The language," as he says of Richter, "groans with indescribable metaphors and allusions to all things, human and divine, flowing onward, not like a river, but like an inundation; circling in complex eddies, chafing and gurgling, now this way, now that;" but in Carlyle, "the proper current" never "sinks out of sight amid the boundless uproar." Again: "His very language is Titanian[6]—deep, strong, tumultuous, shining with a thousand hues, fused from a thousand elements, and winding in labyrinthic mazes."

In short, if it is desirable that a man be eloquent, that he talk much, and address himself to his own age mainly, then this is not a bad style of doing it. But if it is desired rather that he pioneer into unexplored regions of thought, and speaks to silent centuries to come, then, indeed, we could wish that he had cultivated the style of Goethe more, that of Richter less; not that Goethe's is the kind of utterance most to be prized by mankind, but it will serve for a model of the best that can be successfully cultivated.

But for style, and fine writing, and Augustan[7] ages—that is but a poor style, and vulgar writing, and a degenerate age, which allows us to remember these things. This man has something to communicate. Carlyle's are not, in the common sense, works of art in their origin and aim; and yet, perhaps, no living English writer evinces an equal literary talent. They are such works of art only as the plough, and corn-mill, and steam-engine—not as pictures and statues. Others speak with greater emphasis to scholars, as such, but none so

---

4. Alexander Pope (1688–1744), English poet.
5. Jean Paul Richter (1763–1825), German Romantic novelist, author of *The Titan*. Carlyle's defense of Richter's style in a review essay (1827) is akin to the attempts of Thoreau and others to defend his own style.

6. I.e., that of a giant (from the Titans of Greek mythology).
7. Applied to English literature from around 1700 to 1750, after Oliver Goldsmith's use of the term (1759) for the writings of the reign of Queen Anne.

earnestly and effectually to all who can read. Others give their advice, he gives his sympathy also. It is no small praise that he does not take upon himself the airs, has none of the whims, none of the pride, the nice vulgarities, the starched, impoverished isolation, and cold glitter of the spoiled children of genius. He does not need to husband[8] his pearl, but excels by a greater humanity and sincerity.

He is singularly serious and untrivial. We are every where impressed by the rugged, unwearied, and rich sincerity of the man. We are sure that he never sacrificed one jot of his honest thought to art or whim, but to utter himself in the most direct and effectual way, that is the endeavor. These are merits which will wear well. When time has worn deeper into the substance of these books, this grain will appear. No such sermons have come to us here out of England, in late years, as those of this preacher; sermons to kings, and sermons to peasants, and sermons to all intermediate classes. It is in vain that John Bull,[9] or any of his cousins, turns a deaf ear, and pretends not to hear them, nature will not soon be weary of repeating them. There are words less obviously true, more for the ages to hear, perhaps, but none so impossible for this age not to hear. What a cutting cimiter was that "past and present,"[1] going through heaps of silken stuffs, and glibly through the necks of men, too, without their knowing it, leaving no trace. He has the earnestness of a prophet. In an age of pedantry and dilettantism, he has no grain of these in his composition. There is no where else, surely, in recent readable English, or other books, such direct and effectual teaching, reproving, encouraging, stimulating, earnestly, vehemently, almost like Mahomet, like Luther; not looking behind him to see how his *Opera Omnia*[2] will look, but forward to other work to be done. His writings are a gospel to the young of this generation, they will hear his manly, brotherly speech with responsive joy, and press forward to older or newer gospels.

We should omit a main attraction in these books, if we said nothing of their humor. Of this indispensable pledge of sanity, without some leaven, of which the abstruse thinker may justly be suspected of mysticism, fanaticism, or insanity, there is a superabundance in Carlyle. Especially the transcendental philosophy needs the leaven of humor to render it light and digestible. In his later and longer works it is an unfailing accompaniment, reverberating through pages and chapters, long sustained without effort. The very punctuation, the italics, the quotation marks, the blank spaces and dashes, and the capitals, each and all are pressed into its service.

Every man, of course, has his fane, from which even the most innocent conscious humor is excluded; but in proportion as the writer's position is high above his fellows, the range of his humor is extended. To the thinker, all the institutions of men, as all imperfection, viewed from the point of equanimity, are legitimate subjects of humor. Whatever is not necessary, no matter how sad or personal, or universal a grievance, is, indeed, a jest more or less sublime.

Carlyle's humor is vigorous and Titanic, and has more sense in it than the

---

8. I.e., use sparingly.
9. Personification of England.
1. Carlyle's *Past and Present* was then new (1843). "Cimiter": i.e., scimitar, a curved Oriental sword.
2. Complete works (Latin). Mahomet (or Moham-

med) was the subject of a lecture by Carlyle on "The Hero as Prophet." Luther was one of Carlyle's examples in the lecture on "The Hero as Priest" (two of the six lectures in *Heroes and Hero-Worship*, 1841).

sober philosophy of many another. It is not to be disposed of by laughter and smiles merely; it gets to be too serious for that—only they may laugh who are not hit by it. For those who love a merry jest, this is a strange kind of fun— rather too practical joking, if they understand it. The pleasant humor which the public loves, is but the innocent pranks of the ballroom, harmless flow of animal spirits, the light plushy pressure of dandy pumps,[3] in comparison. But when an elephant takes to treading on your corns, why then you are lucky if you sit high, or wear cowhide. His humor is always subordinate to a serious purpose, though often the real charm for the reader, is not so much in the essential progress and final upshot of the chapter, as in this indirect sidelight illustration of every hue. He sketches first with strong, practical English pencil, the essential features in outline, black on white, more faithfully than Dryas- dust would have done, telling us wisely whom and what to mark, to save time, and then with brush of camel's hair, or sometimes with more expeditious swab, he lays on the bright and fast colors of his humor everywhere. One piece of solid work, be it known, we have determined to do, about which let there be no jesting, but all things else under the heavens, to the right and left of that, are for the time fair game. To us this humor is not wearisome, as almost every other is. Rabelais,[4] for instance, is intolerable; one chapter is better than a volume it may be sport to him, but it is death to us. A mere humorist, indeed, is a most unhappy man; and his readers are most unhappy also.

Humor is not so distinct a quality as for the purposes of criticism, it is commonly regarded, but allied to every, even the divinest faculty. The familiar and cheerful conversation about every hearth-side, if it be analyzed, will be found to be sweetened by this principle. There is not only a never-failing, pleasant, and earnest humor kept up there, embracing the domestic affairs, the dinner, and the scolding, but there is also a constant run upon the neigh- bors, and upon church and state, and to cherish and maintain this, in a great measure, the fire is kept burning, and the dinner provided. There will be neighbors, parties to a very genuine, even romantic friendship, whose whole audible salutation and intercourse, abstaining from the usual cordial expres- sions, grasping of hands, or affectionate farewells, consists in the mutual play and interchange of a genial and healthy humor, which excepts nothing, not even themselves, in its lawless range. The child plays continually, if you will let it, and all its life is a sort of practical humor of a very pure kind, often of so fine and ethereal a nature, that its parents, its uncles and cousins, can in no wise participate in it, but must stand aloof in silent admiration, and reverence even. The more quiet the more profound it is. Even nature is observed to have her playful moods or aspects, of which man seems sometimes to be the sport.

But, after all, we could sometimes dispense with the humor, though unquestionably incorporated in the blood, if it were replaced by this author's gravity. We should not apply to himself, without qualification, his remarks on the humor of Richter. With more repose in his inmost being, his humor would become more thoroughly genial and placid. Humor is apt to imply but a half satisfaction at best. In his pleasantest and most genial hour, man smiles but as the globe smiles, and the works of nature. The fruits *dry* ripe, and much as we relish some of them, in their green and pulpy state, we lay up for our

3. Foppish dancing slippers.
4. François Rabelais (1494?–1553), French physician and humanist, author of the great ribald works *Gar-* *gantua* and *Pantagruel*. Thoreau's prudery surfaces here; it was enough for him to deal with Carlyle's Teu- felsdröckh (politely translated as "Devil's-dung").

winter store, not out of these, but the rustling autumnal harvests. Though we never weary of this vivacious wit, while we are perusing its work, yet when we remember it from afar, we sometimes feel balked and disappointed, missing the security, the simplicity, and frankness, even the occasional magnanimity of acknowledged dullness and bungling. This never-failing success and brilliant talent become a reproach. To the most practical reader the humor is certainly too obvious and constant a quality. When we are to have dealings with a man, we prize the good faith and valor of soberness and gravity. There is always a more impressive statement than consists with those victorious comparisons. Besides, humor does not wear well. It is commonly enough said, that a joke will not bear repeating. The deepest humor will not keep. Humors do not circulate but stagnate, or circulate partially. In the oldest literature, in the Hebrew, the Hindoo, the Persian, the Chinese, it is rarely humor, even the most divine, which still survives, but the most sober and private, painful or joyous thoughts, maxims of duty, to which the life of all men may be referred. After time has sifted the literature of a people, there is left only their SCRIPTURE, for that is WRITING,[5] *par excellence*. This is as true of the poets, as of the philosophers and moralists by profession; for what subsides in any of these is the moral only, to re-appear as dry land at some remote epoch.

We confess that Carlyle's humor is rich, deep, and variegated, in direct communication with the back bone and risible muscles of the globe—and there is nothing like it; but much as we relish this jovial, this rapid and deluegeous[6] way of conveying one's views and impressions, when we would not converse but meditate, we pray for a man's diamond edition of his thought, without the colored illuminations in the margin—the fishes and dragons, and unicorns, the red or the blue ink, but its initial letter in distinct skeleton type, and the whole so clipped and condensed down to the very essence of it, that time will have little to do. We know not but we shall immigrate soon, and would fain take with us all the treasures of the east, and all kinds of *dry*, portable soups, in small tin canisters, which contain whole herds of English beeves, boiled down, will be acceptable.

The difference between this flashing, fitful writing and pure philosophy, is the difference between flame and light. The flame, indeed, yields light, but when we are so near as to observe the flame, we are apt to be incommoded by the heat and smoke. But the sun, that old Platonist,[7] is set so far off in the heavens, that only a genial summer-heat and ineffable day-light can reach us. But many a time, we confess, in wintery weather, we have been glad to forsake the sun-light, and warm us by these Promethean flames.[8]

Carlyle must undoubtedly plead guilty to the charge of mannerism. He not only has his vein, but his peculiar manner of working it. He has a style which can be imitated, and sometimes is an imitator of himself. Every man, though born and bred in the metropolis of the world, will still have some provincialism adhering to him; but in proportion as his aim is simple and earnest, he approaches at once the most ancient and the most modern men. There is no mannerism in the Scriptures. The style of proverbs, and indeed of all *maxims*, whether measured by sentences or by chapters, if they may be said to have any

---

5. "Scripture" in two senses: (1) sacred or authoritative writings; (2) writing in general.
6. Floodlike (Graham's contained the misreading "detergeous").

7. I.e., realist.
8. The Titan Prometheus stole fire from the gods and gave it to humankind.

style, is one, and as the expression of one voice, merely an account of the matter by the latest witness. It is one advantage enjoyed by men of science, that they use only formulas which are universal. The common language and the common sense of mankind, it is most uncommon to meet with in the individual. Yet liberty of thought and speech is only liberty to think the universal thought, and speak the universal language of men, instead of being enslaved to a particular mode. Of this universal speech there is very little. It is equable and sure; from a depth within man which is beyond education and prejudice.

Certainly, no critic has anywhere said what is more to the purpose, than this which Carlyle's own writings furnish, which we quote, as well for its intrinsic merit as for its pertinence here. "It is true," says he, thinking of Richter, "the beaten paths of literature lead the safeliest to the goal; and the talent pleases us most, which submits to shine with new gracefulness through old forms. Nor is the noblest and most peculiar mind too noble or peculiar for working by prescribed laws; Sophocles, Shakspeare, Cervantes, and in Richter's own age, Goethe, how little did they innovate on the given forms of composition, how much in the spirit they breathed into them! All this is true; and Richter must lose of our esteem in proportion." And again, in the chapter on Goethe, "We read Goethe for years before we come to see wherein the distinguishing peculiarity of his understanding, of his disposition, even of his way of writing, consists! It seems quite a simple style, [that of his?] remarkable chiefly for its calmness, its perspicuity, in short, its commonness; and yet it is the most uncommon of all styles." And this, too, translated for us by the same pen from Schiller, which we will apply not merely to the outward form of his works, but to their inner form and substance. He is speaking of the artist. "Let some beneficent divinity snatch him, when a suckling, from the breast of his mother, and nurse him with the milk of a better time, that he may ripen to his full stature beneath a distant Grecian sky. And having grown to manhood, let him return, a foreign shape, into his century; not, however, to delight it by his presence, but, dreadful, like the son of Agamemnon, to purify it. The matter of his works he will take from the present, but their form he will derive from a nobler time; nay, from beyond all time, from the absolute unchanging unity of his own nature."

But enough of this. Our complaint is already out of all proportion to our discontent.

Carlyle's works, it is true, have not the stereotyped success which we call classic. They are a rich but inexpensive entertainment, at which we are not concerned lest the host has strained or impoverished himself to feed his guests. It is not the most lasting word, nor the loftiest wisdom, but rather the word which comes last. For his genius it was reserved to give expression to the thoughts which were throbbing in a million breasts. He has plucked the ripest fruit in the public garden; but this fruit already least concerned the tree that bore it, which was rather perfecting the bud at the foot of the leaf stalk. His works are not to be studied, but read with a swift satisfaction. Their flavor and gust[9] is like what poets tell of the froth of wine, which can only be tasted once and hastily. On a review we can never find the pages we had read. The first impression is the truest and the deepest, and there is no reprint, no *double*

9. I.e., taste.

entendre, so to speak, for the alert reader. Yet they are in some degree true natural products in this respect. All things are but once, and never repeated. The first faint blushes of the morning, gilding the mountain tops, the pale phosphor and saffron-colored clouds do verily transport us to the morning of creation; but what avails it to travel eastward, or look again there an hour hence? We should be as far in the day ourselves, mounting toward our meridian.[1] These works were designed for such complete success that they serve but for a single occasion. It is the luxury of art, when its own instrument is manufactured for each particular and present use. The knife which slices the bread of Jove ceases to be a knife when this service is rendered.

But he is wilfully and pertinaciously unjust, even scurrilous, impolite, ungentlemanly; calls us "Imbeciles," "Dilettants," "Philistines," implying sometimes what would not sound well expressed. If he would adopt the newspaper style, and take back these hard names—but where is the reader who does not derive some benefit from these epithets, applying them to himself? Think not that with each repetition of them there is a fresh overflowing of bile; oh no! Perhaps none at all after the first time, only a faithfulness, the right name being found, to apply it—"They are the same ones we meant before"—and ofttimes with a genuine sympathy and encouragement expressed. Indeed, there appears in all his writings a hearty and manly sympathy with all misfortune and wretchedness, and not a weak and sniveling one. They who suspect a Mephistophiles,[2] or sneering, satirical devil, under all, have not learned the secret of true humor, which sympathizes with the gods themselves, in view of their grotesque, half-finished creatures.

He is, in fact, the best tempered, and not the least impartial of reviewers. He goes out of his way to do justice to profligates and quacks. There is somewhat even Christian, in the rarest and most peculiar sense, in his universal brotherliness, his simple, child-like endurance, and earnest, honest endeavor, with sympathy for the like. And this fact is not insignificant, that he is almost the only writer of biography, of the lives of men, in modern times. So kind and generous a tribute to the genius of Burns cannot be expected again, and is not needed. We honor him for his noble reverence for Luther, and his patient, almost reverent study of Goethe's genius, anxious that no shadow of his author's meaning escape him for want of trustful attention. There is nowhere else, surely, such determined and generous love of whatever is manly in history. His just appreciation of any, even inferior talent, especially of all sincerity, under whatever guise, and all true men of endeavor, must have impressed every reader. Witness the chapters on Werner, Heyne, even Cagliostro, and others.[3] He is not likely to underrate his man. We are surprised to meet with such a discriminator of kingly qualities in these republican and democratic days, such genuine loyalty all thrown away upon the world.

Carlyle, to adopt his own classification, is himself the hero, as literary man. There is no more notable working-man in England, in Manchester or Birmingham, or the mines round about. We know not how many hours a-day he toils, nor for what wages, exactly, we only know the results for us. We hear through the London fog and smoke the steady systole, diastole, and vibratory

1. I.e., noon.
2. Diabolic figure from Goethe's *Faust*.
3. The German writers Werner and Heyne were subjects of essays by Carlyle in the *Foreign Review* (1828);

he wrote on the Italian Count Cagliostro in *Fraser's* (1833). The three essays are in his *Critical and Miscellaneous Essays*.

hum, from "Somebody's Works"[4] there; the "Print Works," say some; the
"Chemicals," say others; where something, at any rate, is manufactured which
we remember to have seen in the market. This is the place, then. Literature
has come to mean, to the ears of laboring men, something idle, something
cunning and pretty merely, because the nine hundred and ninety-nine really
write for fame or for amusement. But as the laborer works, and soberly by the
sweat of his brow earns bread for his body, so this man *works* anxiously and
sadly, to get bread of life, and dispense it. We cannot do better than quote his
own estimate of labor from Sartor Resartus.

"Two men I honor, and no third. First; the toil-worn craftsman that with
earth-made implement laboriously conquers the earth, and makes her man's.
Venerable to me is the hard hand; crooked, coarse, wherein, notwithstanding,
lies a cunning virtue, indefeasibly royal, as of the sceptre of this planet. Venerable, too, is the rugged face, all weather-tanned, besoiled, with its rude intelligence; for it is the face of a man living manlike. Oh, but the more venerable
for thy rudeness, and even because we must pity as well as love thee. Hardly-
entreated brother! For us was thy back so bent, for us were thy straight limbs
and fingers so deformed; thou wert our conscript, on whom the lot fell, and
fighting our battles wert so marred. For in thee, too, lay a god-created form,
but it was not to be unfolded; encrusted must it stand with the thick adhesions
and defacements of labor; and thy body, like thy soul, was not to know freedom. Yet toil on, toil on; *thou* art in thy duty, be out of it who may; thou
toilest for the altogether indispensable, for daily bread."

"A second man I honor, and still more highly; him who is seen toiling for
the spiritually indispensable; not daily bread, but the bread of life. Is not he,
too, in his duty, endeavoring toward inward harmony, revealing this, by act
or by word, through all his outward endeavors, be they high or low? Highest
of all, when his outward and his inward endeavor are one; when we can name
him Artist; not earthly craftsman only, but inspired thinker, that with heaven-
made implement conquers heaven for us. If the poor and humble toil that we
have food, must not the high and glorious toil for him in return, that he have
light, have guidance, freedom, immortality? These two in all their degrees, I
honor; all else is chaff and dust, which let the wind blow whither it listeth."

"Unspeakably touching is it, however, when I find both dignities united;
and he that must toil outwardly for the lowest of man's wants, is also toiling
inwardly for the highest. Sublimer in this world know I nothing than a peasant
saint, could such now anywhere be met with. Such a one will take thee back
to Nazareth[5] itself; thou wilt see the splendor of heaven spring forth from the
humblest depths of earth, like a light shining in great darkness."

Notwithstanding the very genuine, admirable, and loyal tributes to Burns,
Schiller, Goethe, and others, Carlyle is not a critic of poetry. In the book of
heroes, Shakspeare, the hero, as poet, comes off rather slimly. His sympathy,
as we said, is with the men of endeavor; not using the life got, but still bravely
getting their life. "In fact," as he says of Cromwell, "every where we have to
notice the decisive, practical *eye* of this man; how he drives toward the practical and practicable; has a genuine insight into what *is* fact." You must have
very stout legs to get noticed at all by him. He is thoroughly English in his

---

4. Briticism for *factory*. "Systole, diastole": Contraction and dialation, respectively, of the heart muscle.
5. Village in Galilee where Jesus passed his child-

hood. The passage depends on knowledge of the scornful inquiry, "Can there any good thing come out of
Nazareth?" (John 1:46).

love of practical men, and dislike for cant, and ardent enthusiastic heads that are not supported by any legs. He would kindly knock them down that they may regain some vigor by touching their mother earth. We have often wondered how he ever found out Burns, and must still refer a good share of his delight in him to neighborhood and early association. The Lycidas and Comus appearing in Blackwood's Magazine, would probably go unread by him, nor lead him to expect a Paradise Lost. The condition of England question[6] is a practical one. The condition of England demands a hero, not a poet. Other things demand a poet; the poet answers other demands. Carlyle in London, with this question pressing on him so urgently, sees no occasion for minstrels and rhapsodists there. Kings may have their bards when there are any kings. Homer would *certainly* go a begging there. He lives in Chelsea, not on the plains of Hindostan, nor on the prairies of the West, where settlers are scarce, and a man must at least go *whistling* to himself.

What he says of poetry is rapidly uttered, and suggestive of a thought, rather than the deliberate development of any. He answers your question, What is poetry? by writing a special poem, as that Norse one, for instance, in the Book of Heroes, altogether wild and original;—answers your question, What is light? by kindling a blaze which dazzles you, and pales sun and moon, and not as a peasant might, by opening a shutter. And, certainly, you would say that this question never could be answered but by the grandest of poems; yet he has not dull breath and stupidity enough, perhaps, to give the most deliberate and universal answer, such as the fates wring from illiterate and unthinking men. He answers like Thor,[7] with a stroke of his hammer, whose dint makes a valley in the earth's surface.

Carlyle is not a *seer*, but a brave looker-on and *reviewer*; not the most free and catholic observer of men and events, for they are likely to find him preoccupied, but unexpectedly free and catholic when they fall within the focus of his lens. He does not live in the present hour, and read men and books as they occur for his theme, but having chosen this, he directs his studies to this end.

But if he supplies us with arguments and illustrations against himself, we will remember that we may perhaps be convicted of error from the same source—stalking on these lofty reviewer's stilts so far from the green pasturage around. If we look again at his page, we are apt to retract somewhat that we have said. Often a genuine poetic feeling dawns through it, like the texture of the earth seen through the dead grass and leaves in the spring. There is indeed more poetry in this author than criticism on poetry. He often reminds us of the ancient Scald,[8] inspired by the grimmer features of life, dwelling longer on Dante than on Shakspeare. We have not recently met with a more solid and unquestionable piece of poetic work than that episode of "The Ancient Monk," in Past and Present,[9] at once idyllic, narrative, heroic; a beautiful restoration of a past age. There is nothing like it elsewhere that we know of. The History of the French Revolution is a poem, at length got translated into prose; an Iliad, indeed, as he himself has it—"The destructive wrath of Sansculotism:[1] this is what we speak, having unhappily no voice for singing."

---

6. Carlyle's phrase for the laissez-faire economics of England, which he attacked. John Milton (1608–1674), English poet, wrote *Lycidas* (an elegiac poem), *Comus* (a dramatic poem), and *Paradise Lose* (an epic poem).
7. Norse god of thunder.
8. Or *skald*, an ancient Scandinavian or German bard or poet.

9. Jocelin of Brakelond, monk of St. Edmundsbury in Suffolk, memorialized in *Past and Present*.
1. In the French Revolution, extreme antiroyalists, because of the style of wearing pantaloons instead of the knee-breeches worn by men of the upper classes: from the French *sans*, "without," and *culotte*, "breeches."

One improvement we could suggest in this last, as indeed in most epics, that he should let in the sun oftener upon his picture. It does not often enough appear, but it is all revolution, the old way of human life turned simply bottom upward, so that when at length we are inadvertently reminded of the "Brest Shipping,"[2] a St. Domingo colony, and that anybody thinks of owning plantations, and simply turning up the soil there, and that now at length, after some years of this revolution, there is a falling off in the importation of sugar, we feel a queer surprise. Had they not sweetened their water with Revolution then? It would be well if there were several chapters headed "Work for the Month"—Revolution-work inclusive, of course—"Altitude of the Sun," "State of the Crops and Markets," "Meteorological Observations," "Attractive Industry," "Day Labor," &c., just to remind the reader that the French peasantry did something beside go without breeches, burn châteaus, get ready knotted cords, and embrace and throttle one another by turns. These things are sometimes hinted at, but they deserve a notice more in proportion to their importance. We want not only a background to the picture, but a ground under the feet also. We remark, too, occasionally, an unphilosophical habit, common enough elsewhere, in Alison's[3] History of Modern Europe, for instance, of saying, undoubtedly with effect, that if a straw had not fallen this way or that, why then—but, of course, it is as easy in philosophy to make kingdoms rise and fall as straws. The old adage is as true for our purpose, which says that a miss is as good as a mile. Who shall say how near the man came to being killed who was not killed? If an apple had not fallen then we had never heard of Newton and the law of gravitation; as if they could not have contrived to let fall a pear as well.

The poet is blithe and cheery ever, and as well as nature. Carlyle has not the simple Homeric health of Wordsworth, nor the deliberate philosophic turn of Coleridge, nor the scholastic taste of Landor, but, though sick and under restraint, the constitutional vigor of one of his old Norse heroes, struggling in a lurid light, with Jötuns[4] still, striving to throw the old woman, and "she was Time"—striving to lift the big cat—and that was "The Great World-Serpent, which, tail in mouth, girds and keeps up the whole created world." The smith, though so brawny and tough, I should not call the healthiest man. There is too much shopwork, too great extremes of heat and cold, and incessant ten-pound-ten and thrashing of the anvil, in his life. But the haymaker's is a true sunny perspiration, produced by the extreme of summer heat only, and conversant with the blast of the zephyr, not of the forge-bellows. We know very well the nature of this man's sadness, but we do not know the nature of his gladness. There sits Bull in the court all the year round, with his hoarse bark and discontented growl—not a cross dog, only a canine habit, verging to madness some think—now separated from the shuddering travelers only by the paling, now heard afar in the horizon, even melodious there; baying the moon o'nights, *baying the sun by day*, with his mastiff mouth. He never goes after the cows, nor stretches in the sun, nor plays with the children. Pray give him a longer rope, ye gods, or let him go at large, and never taste raw meat more.

The poet will maintain serenity in spite of all disappointments. He is

---

2. Thoreau refers to the mention of the defeat of the harbor Brest in book 5, chap. 4 of Carlyle's *French Revolution.*

3. Archibald Alison, *History of Europe from the Commencement of the French Revolution in 1789, to the Restoration of the Bourbons in 1815* (1842–43).

4. Giants of old Norse myth. Emerson said in the preface to *Past and Present*: "In this work, as in his former labors, Mr. Carlyle reminds us of a sick giant."

expected to preserve an unconcerned and healthy outlook over the world while he lives. *Philosophia practica est eruditionis meta*, philosophy practiced is the goal of learning; and for that other, *Oratoris est celare artem*, we might read, *Herois est celare pugnam*, the hero will conceal his struggles. Poetry is the only life got, the only work done, the only pure product and free labor of man, performed only when he has put all the world under his feet, and conquered the last of his foes.

Carlyle speaks of Nature with a certain unconscious pathos for the most part. She is to him a receded but ever memorable splendor, casting still a reflected light over all his scenery. As we read his books here in New England, where there are potatoes enough, and every man can get his living peacefully and sportively as the birds and bees, and need think no more of that, it seems to us as if by the world he often meant London, at the head of the tide upon the Thames, the sorest place on the face of the earth, the very citadel of conservatism. Possibly a South African village might have furnished a more hopeful, and more exacting audience, or in the silence of the wilderness and the desert, he might have addressed himself more entirely to his true audience posterity.

In his writings, we should say that he, as conspicuously as any, though with little enough expressed or even conscious sympathy, represents the Reformer class, and all the better for not being the acknowledged leader of any. In him the universal plaint is most settled, unappeasable and serious. Until a thousand named and nameless grievances are righted, there will be no repose for him in the lap of nature, or the seclusion of science and literature. By foreseeing it he hastens the crisis in the affairs of England, and is as good as many years added to her history.

As we said, we have no adequate word from him concerning poets—Homer, Shakspeare; nor more, we might add, of Saints—Jesus; nor philosophers— Socrates, Plato; nor mystics—Swedenborg.[5] He has no articulate sympathy at least with such as these as yet. Odin, Mahomet, Cromwell, will have justice at his hands, and we would leave him to write the eulogies of all the giants of the will, but the kings of men, whose kingdoms are wholly in the hearts of their subjects, strictly transcendent and moral greatness, what is highest and worthiest in character, he is not inclined to dwell upon or point to. To do himself justice, and set some of his readers right, he should give us some transcendent hero at length, to rule his demigods and Titans; develop, perhaps, his reserved and dumb reverence for Christ, not speaking to a London or Church of England audience merely. Let *not* "sacred silence meditate that sacred matter" forever, but let us have sacred speech and sacred scripture thereon. True reverence is not necessarily dumb, but ofttimes prattling and hilarious as children in the spring.

Every man will include in his list of worthies those whom he himself best represents. Carlyle, and our countryman Emerson, whose place and influence must ere long obtain a more distinct recognition, are, to a certain extent, the complement of each other. The age could not do with one of them, it cannot do without[6] both. To make a broad and rude distinction, to suit our present purpose, the former, as critic, deals with the men of action—Mahomet,

---

5. Emanuel Swedenborg (1688–1722), visionary Swedish philosopher and religious writer.
6. The reading in 1847 and 1866 is "with," but Tho- reau cannot be saying that the age cannot bear having both Carlyle and Emerson alive.

Luther, Cromwell; the latter with the thinkers—Plato, Shakspeare, Goethe,[7] for though both have written upon Goethe, they do not meet in him. The one has more sympathy with the heroes, or practical reformers, the other with the observers, or philosophers. Put these worthies together, and you will have a pretty fair representation of mankind; yet with one or more memorable exceptions. To say nothing of Christ, who yet awaits a just appreciation from literature, the peacefully practical hero, whom Columbus may represent, is obviously slighted; but above and after all, the Man of the Age, come to be called working-man, it is obvious that none yet speaks to his condition, for the speaker is not yet in his condition. There is poetry and prophecy to cheer him, and advice of the head and heart to the hands; but no very memorable coöperation, it must be confessed, since the Christian era, or rather since Prometheus tried it. It is even a note-worthy fact, that a man addresses effectually in another only himself still, and what he himself does and is, alone can he prompt the other to do and to become. Like speaks to like only; labor to labor, philosophy to philosophy, criticism to criticism, poetry to poetry, &c. Literature speaks how much still to the past, how little to the future, how much to the east, how little to the west—

> In the East fames are won,
> In the West deeds are done.

One more merit in Carlyle, let the subject be what it may, is the freedom of prospect he allows, the entire absence of cant and dogma. He removes many cart-loads of rubbish, and leaves open a broad highway. His writings are all enfenced on the side of the future and the possible. He does not place himself across the passage out of his books, so that none may go freely out, but rather by the entrance, inviting all to come in and go through. No gins, no net-work, no pickets[8] here, to restrain the free thinking reader. In many books called philosophical, we find ourselves running hither and thither, under and through, and sometimes quite unconsciously straddling some imaginary fence-work, which in our clairvoyance we had not noticed, but fortunately, not with such fatal consequences as happen to those birds which fly against a white-washed wall, mistaking it for fluid air. As we proceed the wreck of this dogmatic tissue collects about the organs of our perception, like cobwebs about the muzzles of hunting dogs in dewy mornings. If we look up with such eyes as these authors furnish, we see no heavens, but a low pent-roof of straw or tiles, as if we stood under a shed, with no sky-light through which to glimpse the blue.

Carlyle, though he does but inadvertently direct our eyes to the open heavens, nevertheless, lets us wander broadly underneath, and shows them to us reflected in innumerable pools and lakes. We have from him, occasionally, some hints of a possible science of astronomy even, and revelation of heavenly arcana, but nothing definite hitherto.

These volumes contain not the highest, but a very practicable wisdom, which startles and provokes, rather than informs us. Carlyle does not oblige us to think; we have thought enough for him already, but he compels us to act. We accompany him rapidly through an endless gallery of pictures, and glori-

---

7. Subjects of essays in Emerson's *Representative Men* (not published until 1850).

8. Sharp pointed stakes. "Gins": traps snares to catch small animals.

ous reminiscences of experiences unimproved. "Have you not had Moses and the prophets? Neither will ye be persuaded if one should rise from the dead."[9] There is no calm philosophy of life here, such as you might put at the end of the Almanac, to hang over the farmer's hearth, how men shall live in these winter, in these summer days. No philosophy, properly speaking, of love, or friendship, or religion, or politics, or education, or nature, or spirit; perhaps a nearer approach to a philosophy of kingship, and of the place of the literary man, than of any thing else. A rare preacher, with prayer, and psalm, and sermon, and benediction, but no contemplation of man's life from serene oriental ground, nor yet from the stirring occidental. No thanksgiving sermon for the holydays, or the Easter vacations, when all men submit to float on the full currents of life. When we see with what spirits, though with little heroism enough, wood-choppers, drovers, and apprentices, take and spend life, playing all day long, sunning themselves, shading themselves, eating, drinking, sleeping, we think that the philosophy of their life written would be such a level natural history as the Gardener's Calendar, and the works of the early botanists, inconceivably slow to come to practical conclusions; its premises away off before the first morning light, ere the heather was introduced into the British isles, and no inferences to be drawn during this noon of the day, not till after the remote evening shadows have begun to fall around.

There is no philosophy here for philosophers, only as every man is said to have his philosophy. No system but such as is the man himself; and, indeed, he stands compactly enough. No progress beyond the first assertion and challenge, as it were, with trumpet blast. One thing is certain, that we had best be doing something in good earnest, henceforth forever; that's an indispensable philosophy. The before impossible precept, *"know thyself,"* he translates into the partially possible one, *"know what thou canst work at."* Sartor Resartus is, perhaps, the sunniest and most philosophical, as it is the most autobiographical of his works, in which he drew most largely on the experience of his youth. But we miss everywhere a calm depth, like a lake, even stagnant, and must submit to rapidity and whirl, as on skates, with all kinds of skillful and antic motions, sculling, sliding, cutting punch-bowls and rings, forward and backward. The talent is very nearly equal to the genius. Sometimes it would be preferable to wade slowly through a Serbonian bog, and feel the juices of the meadow. We should say that he had not speculated far, but faithfully, living up to it. He lays all the stress still on the most elementary and initiatory maxims, introductory to philosophy. It is the experience of the religionist. He pauses at such a quotation as, "It is only with renunciation that life, properly speaking, can be said to begin;" or, "Doubt of any sort cannot be removed except by action;" or, "Do the duty which lies nearest thee." The chapters entitled, "The Everlasting No," and "The Everlasting Yea," contain what you might call the religious experience of his hero. In the latter, he assigns to him these words, brief, but as significant as any we remember in this author:—"One BIBLE, I know, of whose plenary inspiration doubt is not so much as possible; nay, with my own eyes I saw the God's-hand writing it: thereof all other Bibles are but leaves." This belongs to "The Everlasting Yea;" yet he lingers unaccountably in "The Everlasting No," under the negative pole. "Truth!" he still cries with Teufelsdröckh, "though the heavens crush me for

9. Luke 16.31: "If they hear not Moses and the prophets, neither will they be persuaded, though one rose from the dead."

following her: no falsehood! though a whole celestial Lubberland were the price of apostacy." Again, "Living without God in the world, of God's light I was not utterly bereft; if my as yet sealed eyes, with their unspeakable longing, could nowhere see Him, nevertheless, in my heart He was present, and His heaven-written law still stood legible and sacred there." Again, "Ever from that time, [*the era of his Protest*,] the temper of my misery was changed: not fear or whining sorrow was it, but indignation and grim, fire-eyed defiance." And in the "Centre of Indifference," as editor,[1] he observes, that "it was no longer a quite hopeless unrest," and then proceeds, not in his best style, "For the fire-baptized soul, long so scathed and thunder-riven, here feels its own freedom, which feeling is its Baphometic Baptism: the citadel of its whole kingdom it has thus gained by assault, and will keep inexpungable; outward from which the remaining dominions, not, indeed, without hard battling, will doubtless by degrees be conquered and pacificated."

Beside some philosophers of larger vision, Carlyle stands like an honest, half-despairing boy, grasping at some details only of their world systems. Philosophy, certainly, is some account of truths, the fragments and very insignificant parts of which man will practice in this work-shop; truths infinite and in harmony with infinity; in respect to which the very objects and ends of the so-called practical philosopher, will be mere propositions, like the rest. It would be no reproach to a philosopher, that he knew the future better than the past, or even than the present. It is better worth knowing. He will prophecy, tell what is to be, or in other words, what alone is, under appearances, laying little stress on the boiling of the pot, or the Condition of England question. He has no more to do with the condition of England than with her national debt, which a vigorous generation would not inherit. The philosopher's conception of things will, above all, be truer than other men's, and his philosophy will subordinate all the circumstances of life. To live like a philosopher, is to live, not foolishly, like other men, but wisely, and according to universal laws. In this, which was the ancient sense, we think there has been no philosopher in modern times. The wisest and most practical men of recent history, to whom this epithet has been hastily applied, have lived comparatively meagre lives, of conformity and tradition, such as their fathers transmitted to them. But a man may live in what style he can. Between earth and heaven, there is room for all kinds. If he take counsel of fear and prudence, he has already failed. One who believed, by his very constitution, some truth which a few words express, would make a revolution never to be forgotten in this world; for it needs but a fraction of truth to found houses and empires on.

However, such distinctions as poet and philosopher, do not much assist our final estimate of a man; we do not lay much stress on them. "A man's a man for a that."[2] If Carlyle does not take two steps in philosophy, are there any who take three? Philosophy having crept clinging to the rocks, so far, puts out its feelers many ways in vain. It would be hard to surprise him by the relation of any important human experience, but in some nook or corner of his works, you will find that this, too, was sometimes dreamed of in his philosophy.

To sum up our most serious objections, in a few words, we should say that Carlyle indicates a depth,—and we mean not impliedly, but distinctly,— which he neglects to fathom. We want to know more about that which he

---

1. In *Sartor Resartus*, Teufelsdröckh's remarks are supposed to have been put together by an imaginary editor.

2. Robert Burns, *For a' That and a' That*, line 12.

wants to know as well. If any luminous star, or undissolvable nebula, is visible from his station, which is not visible from ours, the interests of science require that the fact be communicated to us. The universe expects every man to do his duty in his parallel of latitude. We want to hear more of his inmost life; his hymn and prayer, more; his elegy and eulogy, less; that he should speak more from his character, and less from his talent; communicate centrally with his readers, and not by a side; that he should say what he believes, without suspecting that men disbelieve it, out of his never-misunderstood nature. Homer and Shakspeare speak directly and confidently to us. The confidence implied in the unsuspicious tone of the world's worthies, is a great and encouraging fact. Dig up some of the earth you stand on, and show that. If he gave us religiously the meagre results of his experience, his style would be less picturesque and diversified, but more attractive and impressive. His genius can cover all the land with gorgeous palaces, but the reader does not abide in them, but pitches his tent rather in the desert and on the mountain peak.

When we look about for something to quote, as the fairest specimen of the man, we confess that we labor under an unusual difficulty; for his philosophy is so little of the proverbial or sentential kind, and opens so gradually, rising insensibly from the reviewer's level, and developing its thought completely and in detail, that we look in vain for the brilliant passages, for point and antithesis, and must end by quoting his works entire. What in a writer of less breadth would have been the proposition which would have bounded his discourse, his column of victory, his Pillar of Hercules, and *ne plus ultra*,[3] is in Carlyle frequently the same thought unfolded; no Pillar of Hercules, but a considerable prospect, north and south, along the Atlantic coast. There are other pillars of Hercules, like beacons and light-houses, still further in the horizon, toward Atlantis, set up by a few ancient and modern travelers; but, so far as this traveler goes, he clears and colonizes, and all the surplus population of London is bound thither at once. What we would quote is, in fact, his vivacity, and not any particular wisdom or sense, which last is ever synonymous with sentence,[4] [*sententia*,] as in his contemporaries, Coleridge, Landor and Wordsworth.

We have not attempted to discriminate between his works, but have rather regarded them all as one work, as is the man himself. We have not examined so much as remembered them. To do otherwise, would have required a more indifferent, and perhaps even less just review, than the present. The several chapters were thankfully received, as they came out, and now we find it impossible to say which was best; perhaps each was best in its turn. They do not require to be remembered by chapters—that is a merit—but are rather remembered as a well-known strain, reviving from time to time, when it had nearly died away, and always inspiring us to worthier and more persistent endeavors.

In his last work, "The Letters and Speeches of Oliver Cromwell," Carlyle has added a chapter to the history of England; has actually written a chapter of her history, and, in comparison with this, there seems to be no other,—this, and the thirty thousand or three hundred thousand pamphlets in the British Museum, and that is all. This book is a practical comment on Universal History. What if there were a British Museum in Athens and Babylon, and nameless cities! It throws light on the history of the Iliad and the labors of

3. Not more beyond (Latin); i.e., the utmost point. The Pillars of Hercules (plural) are the headlands at the eastern end of the Strait of Gibraltar.
4. Considered opinion.

Pisistratus.[5] History is, then, an account of memorable events that have some-time transpired, and not an incredible and confused fable, quarters for scholars merely, or a gymnasium for poets and orators. We may say that he has dug up a hero, who was buried alive in his battle-field, hauled him out of his cairn,[6] on which every passer had cast a pamphlet. We had heard of their digging up Arthurs before to be sure they were there; and, to be sure they were there, their bones, seven feet of them; but they had to bury them again. Others have helped to make known Shakspeare, Milton, Herbert,[7] to give a name to such treasures as we all possessed; but, in this instance, not only a lost character has been restored to our imaginations, but palpably a living body, as it were, to our senses, to wear and sustain the former. His Cromwell's restoration, if England will read it faithfully, and addressed to New England too. Every reader will make his own application.

To speak deliberately, we think that in this instance, vague rumor and a vague history have for the first time been subjected to a rigid scrutiny, and the wheat, with at least novel fidelity, sifted from the chaff; so that there remain for result,—First, Letters and Speeches of Oliver Cromwell, now for the first time read or readable, and well nigh as complete as the fates will permit; secondly, Deeds, making an imperfect and fragmentary life, which may, with probability, be fathered upon him; thirdly, this wreck of an ancient picture, the present editor has, to the best of his ability, restored, sedulously scraping away the daubings of successive bunglers, and endeavoring to catch the spirit of the artist himself. Not the worst, nor a barely possible, but for once the most favorable construction has been put upon this evidence of the life of a man, and the result is a picture of the ideal Cromwell, the perfection of the painter's art. Possibly this was the actual man. At any rate, this only can contain the actual hero. We confess that when we read these Letters and Speeches, unquestionably Cromwell's, with open and confident mind, we get glimpses occasionally of a grandeur and heroism, which even this editor has not proclaimed. His "Speeches" make us forget modern orators, and might go right into the next edition of the Old Testament, without alteration. Cromwell *was* another sort of man than *we* had taken him to be. These Letters and Speeches have supplied the lost key to his character. Verily another soldier than Bonaparte;[8] rejoicing in the triumph of a psalm; to whom psalms were for Magna Charta and Heralds' Book,[9] and whose victories were "crowning mercies." For stern, antique, and practical religion, a man unparalleled, since the Jewish dispensation, in the line of kings. An old Hebrew warrior, indeed, and last right-hand man of the Lord of Hosts, that has blown his ram's horn about Jericho.[1] Yet, with a remarkable common sense and unexpected liberality, there was joined in him, too, such a divine madness, though with large and sublime features, as that of those dibblers[2] of beans on St. George's Hill, whom Carlyle tells of. He still listened to ancient and decaying oracles. If his actions were not always what Christianity or the truest philosophy teaches, still they never fail to impress us as noble, and however violent, will always be pardoned to the great purpose and sincerity of the man. His unquestionable

5. Athenian tyrant (605?–527 B.C.).
6. Pile of stones set up as memorial or landmark.
7. George Herbert (1593–1633), English religious poet.
8. Napoleon Bonaparte (1769–1821), emperor of France 1804–15.

9. Record of noble genealogies. "Magna Charta": charter of English liberties granted by King John in 1215.
1. Joshua 6.1–21.
2. Planters.

hardness, not to say willfulness, not prevailing by absolute truth and greatness of character, but honestly striving to bend things to his will, is yet grateful to consider in this or any age. As John Maidstone[3] said, "He was a strong man in the dark perils of war; in the high places of the field, hope shone in him like a pillar of fire, when it had gone out in the others." And as Milton sang, whose least testimony cannot be spared—

> "Our chief of men,
> Guided by faith and matchless fortitude."[4]

None ever spake to Cromwell before, sending a word of cheer across the centuries—not the "hear!" "hear!" of modern parliaments, but the congratulation and sympathy of a brother soul. The Letters and Speeches owe not a little to the "Intercalations" and "Annotations" of the "latest of the Commentators." The reader will not soon forget how like a happy merchant in the crowd, listening to his favorite speaker, he is all on the alert, and sympathetic, nudging his neighbors from time to time, and throwing in his responsive or interrogatory word. All is good, both that which he didn't hear, and that which he did. He not only makes him speak audibly, but he makes all parties listen to him, all England sitting round, and give in their comments, "groans," or "blushes," or "assent;" indulging sometimes in triumphant malicious applications to the present day, when there is a palpable hit;[5] supplying the look and attitude of the speaker, and the tone of his voice, and even rescuing his unutterable, wrecked and submerged thought,—for this orator begins speaking anywhere within sight of the beginning, and leaves off when the conclusion is visible. Our merchant listens, restless, meanwhile, encouraging his fellow-auditors, when the speech grows dim and involved, and pleasantly congratulating them, when it runs smoothly; or, in touching soliloquy, he exclaims, "Poor Oliver, noble Oliver"—"Courage, my brave one!"

And all along, between the Letters and Speeches, as readers well remember, he has ready such a fresh top-of-the-morning salutation as conjures up the spirits of those days, and men go marching over English sward, not wired skeletons, but with firm, elastic muscles, and clang of armor on their thighs, if they wore swords, or the twang of psalms and canticles on their lips. His blunt, "Who are you?" put to the shadowy ghosts of history, they vanish into deeper obscurity than ever. Vivid phantasmagorian pictures of what is transpiring in England in the meanwhile, there are, not a few, better than if you had been there to see.

All of Carlyle's works might well enough be embraced under the title of one of them, a good specimen brick, "On Heroes, Hero-worship, and the Heroic in History." Of this department, he is the Chief Professor in the World's University, and even leaves Plutarch behind. Such intimate and living, such loyal and generous sympathy with the heroes of history, not one in one age only, but forty in forty ages, such an unparalleled reviewing and greeting of all past worth, with exceptions, to be sure,—but exceptions were the rule, before,—it was, indeed, to make this the age of review writing, as if now one period of the human story were completing itself, and getting its accounts settled. This

---

3. Carlyle refers to this member of Cromwell's household staff who in 1659 described the protector in a letter to Governor Winthrop of Connecticut (printed 1742).

4. From Milton's sonnet *To the Lord General Cromwell* (1694).

5. Shakespeare's *Hamlet* 5.2.295.

soldier has told the stories with new emphasis, and will be a memorable hander-down of fame to posterity. And with what wise discrimination he has selected his men, with reference both to his own genius and to theirs: Mahomet,—Dante,—Cromwell,—Voltaire,—Johnson,—Burns,—Goethe,— Richter,—Schiller,—Mirabeau;[6] could any of these have been spared? These we wanted to hear about. We have not as commonly the cold and refined judgment of the scholar and critic merely, but something more human and affecting. These eulogies have the glow and warmth of friendship. There is sympathy not with mere fames, and formless, incredible things, but with kindred men,—not transiently, but life-long he has walked with them.

The attitude of some, in relation to Carlyle's love of heroes, and men of the sword, reminds us of the procedure at the anti-slavery meetings, when some member, being warmed, begins to speak with more latitude than usual of the Bible or the Church, for a few prudent and devout ones to spring a prayer upon him, as the saying is; that is, propose suddenly to unite in prayer, and so solemnize the minds of the audience, or dismiss them at once; which may oftener be to interrupt a true prayer by most gratuitous profanity. But the spring of this trap, we are glad to learn, has grown somewhat rusty, and is not so sure of late.

No doubt, some of Carlyle's worthies, should they ever return to earth, would find themselves unpleasantly put upon their good behavior, to sustain their characters; but if he can return a man's life more perfect to our hands, than it was left at his death, following out the design of its author, we shall have no great cause to complain. We do not want a Daguerreotype[7] likeness. All biography is the life of Adam,—a much-experienced man,—and time withdraws something partial from the story of every individual, that the historian may supply something general. If these virtues were not in this man, perhaps they are in his biographer,—no fatal mistake. Really, in any other sense, we never do, nor desire to, come at the historical man,—unless we rob his grave, that is the nearest approach. Why did he die, then? *He* is with his bones, surely.

No doubt, Carlyle has a propensity to *exaggerate* the heroic in history, that is, he creates you an ideal hero rather than another thing, he has most of that material. This we allow in all its senses, and in one narrower sense it is not so convenient. Yet what were history if he did not exaggerate it? How comes it that history never has to wait for facts, but for a man to write it? The ages may go on forgetting the facts never so long, he can remember two for every one forgotten. The musty records of history, like the catacombs, contain the perishable remains, but only in the breast of genius are embalmed the souls of heroes. There is very little of what is called criticism here; it is love and reverence, rather, which deal with qualities not relatively, but absolutely great; for whatever is admirable in a man is something infinite, to which we cannot set bounds. These sentiments allow the mortal to die, the immortal and divine to survive. There is something antique, even in his style of treating his subject, reminding us that Heroes and Demi-gods, Fates and Furies, still exist, the common man is nothing to him, but after death the hero is apotheosized and has a place in heaven, as in the religion of the Greeks.

6. Honoré-Gabriel Riqueti, Comte Mirabu Mirabeau, moderate leader in the early stages of the French revolution.
7. Photography was in its first decade. Already at use in the United States was the photographic process invented by the Frenchman Louis Deguerre (1797–1851) in 1839: a silver-coated metallic plate was exposed to light and the image was developed by mercury vapor.

Exaggeration! was ever any virtue attributed to a man without exaggeration? was ever any vice, without infinite exaggeration? Do we not exaggerate ourselves to ourselves, or do we recognize ourselves for the actual men we are? Are we not all great men? Yet what are we actually to speak of? We live by exaggeration, what else is it to anticipate more than we enjoy? The lightning is an exaggeration of the light. Exaggerated history is poetry, and truth referred to a new standard. To a small man every greater is an exaggeration. He who cannot exaggerate is not qualified to utter truth. No truth we think was ever expressed but with this sort of emphasis, so that for the time there seemed to be no other. Moreover, you must speak loud to those who are hard of hearing, and so you acquire a habit of shouting to those who are not. By an immense exaggeration we appreciate our Greek poetry and philosophy, and Egyptian ruins; our Shakspeares and Miltons, our Liberty and Christianity. We give importance to this hour over all other hours. We do not live by justice, but by grace. As the sort of justice which concerns us in our daily intercourse is not that administered by the judge, so the historical justice which we prize is not arrived at by nicely balancing the evidence. In order to appreciate any, even the humblest man, you must first, by some good fortune, have acquired a sentiment of admiration, even of reverence, for him, and there never were such exaggerators as these. Simple admiration for a hero renders a juster verdict than the wisest criticism, which necessarily degrades what is high to its own level. There is no danger in short of saying too much in praise of one man, provided you can say more in praise of a better man. If by exaggeration a man can create for us a hero, where there was nothing but dry bones before, we will thank him, and let Dryasdust administer historical justice. This is where a true history properly begins, when some genius arises, who can turn the dry and musty records into poetry. As we say, looking to the future, that what is best is truest, so, in one sense, we may say looking into the past, for the only past that we are to look at, must also be future to us. The great danger is not of excessive partiality or sympathy with one, but of a shallow justice to many, in which, after all, none gets his deserts. Who has not experienced that praise is truer than naked justice? As if man were to be the judge of his fellows, and should repress his rising sympathy with the prisoner at the bar,[8] considering the many honest men abroad, whom he had never countenanced.

To try him by the German rule of referring an author to his own standard, we will quote the following from Carlyle's remarks on history, and leave the reader to consider how far his practice has been consistent with his theory. "Truly, if History is Philosophy teaching by experience, the writer fitted to compose history, is hitherto an unknown man. The experience itself would require all knowledge to record it, were the All-wisdom needful for such Philosophy as would interpret it, to be had for asking. Better were it that mere earthly historians should lower such pretensions, more suitable for omniscience than for human science; and aiming only at some picture of the things acted, which picture itself, will at best be a poor approximation, leave the inscrutable purport of them an acknowledged secret; or, at most, in reverent Faith, far different from that teaching of Philosophy, pause over the mysterious vestiges of Him, whose path is in the great deep of Time, whom history indeed reveals, but only all History and in Eternity, will clearly reveal."

---

8. I.e., in court.

Who lives in London to tell this generation who have been the great men of our race? We have read that on some exposed place in the city of Geneva, they have fixed a brazen indicater for the use of travelers, with the names of the mountain summits in the horizon marked upon it, "so that by taking sight across the index you can distinguish them at once. You will not mistake Mont Blanc, if you see him, but until you get accustomed to the panorama, you may easily mistake one of his court for the king." It stands there a piece of mute brass, that seems nevertheless to know in what vicinity it is: and there perchance it will stand, when the nation that placed it there has passed away, still in sympathy with the mountains, forever discriminating in the desert.

So, we may say, stands this man, pointing as long as he lives, in obedience to some spiritual magnetism, to the summits in the historical horizon, for the guidance of his fellows.

Truly, our greatest blessings are very cheap. To have our sunlight without paying for it, without any duty levied,—to have our poet there in England, to furnish us entertainment, and what is better provocation, from year to year, all our lives long, to make the world seem richer for us, the age more respectable, and life better worth the living,—all without expense of acknowledgment even, but silently accepted out of the east, like morning light as a matter of course.

1847

Resistance to Civil Government[1]

I heartily accept the motto,—"That government is best which governs least;"[2] and I should like to see it acted up to more rapidly and systematically. Carried out, it finally amounts to this, which also I believe,—"That government is best which governs not at all;" and when men are prepared for it, that will be the kind of government which they will have. Government is at best but an expedient; but most governments are usually, and all governments are sometimes, inexpedient. The objections which have been brought against a standing army, and they are many and weighty, and deserve to prevail, may also at last be brought against a standing government. The standing army is only an arm of the standing government. The government itself, which is only the mode which the people have chosen to execute their will, is equally liable to be abused and perverted before the people can act through it. Witness the present Mexican war, the work of comparatively a few individuals using the

---

1. *Resistance to Civil Government* is reprinted here from its first appearance, in *Aesthetic Papers* (1849); the editor and publisher, Elizabeth Peabody, was Hawthorne's sister-in-law. Thoreau had delivered the paper (or parts of it) as a lecture in January and again in February 1848 before the Concord Lyceum, under the title *The Rights and Duties of the Individual in Relation to Government*. After his death it was reprinted in *A Yankee in Canada, with Anti-Slavery and Reform Papers* (1866) as *Civil Disobedience*, the title by which it much later became world-famous. That title, although very commonly used, may well not be authorial, and Thoreauvians are accustoming themselves to the title of the

first printing that, as Thoreau indicates, was a play on *Duty of Submission to Civil Government*, the title of one of the chapters in William Paley's *Principles of Moral and Political Philosophy* (1785). Ignored in its own time, in the 20th century the influence of the essay has been profound, most notably in Mahatma Gandhi's struggle for Indian independence and in the American civil rights movement under the leadership of Martin Luther King, Jr.

2. Associated with Jeffersonianism, these words appeared on the masthead of the *Democratic Review*, the New York magazine that had published two early Thoreau pieces in 1843.

standing government as their tool; for, in the outset, the people would not have consented to this measure.[3]

This American government,—what is it but a tradition, though a recent one, endeavoring to transmit itself unimpaired to posterity, but each instant losing some of its integrity? It has not the vitality and force of a single living man; for a single man can bend it to his will. It is a sort of wooden gun to the people themselves; and, if ever they should use it in earnest as a real one against each other, it will surely split. But it is not the less necessary for this; for the people must have some complicated machinery or other, and hear its din, to satisfy that idea of government which they have. Governments show thus how successfully men can be imposed on, even impose on themselves, for their own advantage. It is excellent, we must all allow; yet this government never of itself furthered any enterprise, but by the alacrity with which it got out of its way. *It* does not keep the country free. *It* does not settle the West. *It* does not educate. The character inherent in the American people has done all that has been accomplished; and it would have done somewhat more, if the government had not sometimes got in its way. For government is an expedient by which men would fain succeed in letting one another alone; and, as has been said, when it is most expedient, the governed are most let alone by it. Trade and commerce, if they were not made of India rubber, would never manage to bounce over the obstacles which legislators are continually putting in their way; and, if one were to judge these men wholly by the effects of their actions, and not partly by their intentions, they would deserve to be classed and punished with those mischievous persons who put obstructions on the railroads.

But, to speak practically and as a citizen, unlike those who call themselves no-government men, I ask for, not at once no government, but *at once* a better government. Let every man make known what kind of government would command his respect, and that will be one step toward obtaining it.

After all, the practical reason why, when the power is once in the hands of the people, a majority are permitted, and for a long period continue, to rule, is not because they are most likely to be in the right, nor because this seems fairest to the minority, but because they are physically the strongest. But a government in which the majority rule in all cases cannot be based on justice, even as far as men understand it. Can there not be a government in which majorities do not virtually decide right and wrong, but conscience?—in which majorities decide only those questions to which the rule of expediency is applicable? Must the citizen ever for a moment, or in the least degree, resign his conscience to the legislator? Why has every man a conscience, then? I think that we should be men first, and subjects afterward. It is not desirable to cultivate a respect for the law, so much as for the right. The only obligation which I have a right to assume, is to do at any time what I think right. It is truly enough said,[4] that a corporation has no conscience; but a corporation of conscientious men is a corporation *with* a conscience. Law never made men a whit more just; and, by means of their respect for it, even the well-disposed

---

3. The Mexican War, widely criticized by Whigs and many Democrats as an "executive's war" because President Polk commenced hostilities without a congressional declaration of war, ended on February 2, 1848, just after Thoreau first delivered this essay as a lecture. He repeated the lecture after the official ending of the

war (or perhaps gave another installment of it), and the next year let it go to press with the out-of-date reference.
4. By Sir Edward Coke, 1612, in a famous legal decision.

are daily made the agents of injustice. A common and natural result of an undue respect for law is, that you may see a file of soldiers, colonel, captain, corporal, privates, powder-monkeys and all, marching in admirable order over hill and dale to the wars, against their wills, aye, against their common sense and consciences, which makes it very steep marching indeed, and produces a palpitation of the heart. They have no doubt that it is a damnable business in which they are concerned; they are all peaceably inclined. Now, what are they? Men at all? or small moveable forts and magazines, at the service of some unscrupulous man in power? Visit the Navy Yard, and behold a marine, such a man as an American government can make, or such as it can make a man with its black arts, a mere shadow and reminiscence of humanity, a man laid out alive and standing, and already, as one may say, buried under arms with funeral accompaniments, though it may be

> "Not a drum was heard, nor a funeral note,
>   As his corse to the ramparts we hurried;
> Not a soldier discharged his farewell shot
>   O'er the grave where our hero we buried."[5]

The mass of men serve the State thus, not as men mainly, but as machines, with their bodies. They are the standing army, and the militia, jailers, constables, *posse comitatus*,[6] &c. In most cases there is no free exercise whatever of the judgment or of the moral sense; but they put themselves on a level with wood and earth and stones; and wooden men can perhaps be manufactured that will serve the purpose as well. Such command no more respect than men of straw, or a lump of dirt. They have the same sort of worth only as horses and dogs. Yet such as these even are commonly esteemed good citizens. Others, as most legislators, politicians, lawyers, ministers, and office-holders, serve the State chiefly with their heads; and, as they rarely make any moral distinctions, they are as likely to serve the devil, without intending it, as God. A very few, as heroes, patriots, martyrs, reformers in the great sense, and *men*, serve the State with their consciences also, and so necessarily resist it for the most part; and they are commonly treated by it as enemies. A wise man will only be useful as a man, and will not submit to be "clay," and "stop a hole to keep the wind away,"[7] but leave that office to his dust at least:—

> "I am too high-born to be propertied,
> To be a secondary at control,
> Or useful serving-man and instrument
> To any sovereign state throughout the world."[8]

He who gives himself entirely to his fellow-men appears to them useless and selfish; but he who gives himself partially to them is pronounced a benefactor and philanthropist.

How does it become a man to behave toward this American government to-day? I answer that he cannot without disgrace be associated with it. I cannot for an instant recognize that political organization as *my* government which is the *slave's* government also.

All men recognize the right of revolution; that is, the right to refuse alle-

---

5. From Charles Wolfe's *Burial of Sir John Moore at Corunna* (1817), a song Thoreau liked to sing.
6. Sheriff's posse (Latin).

7. Shakespeare's *Hamlet* 5.1.236–37.
8. Shakespeare's *King John* 5.1.79–82.

giance to and to resist the government, when its tyranny or its inefficiency are great and unendurable. But almost all say that such is not the case now. But such was the case, they think, in the Revolution of '75. If one were to tell me that this was a bad government because it taxed certain foreign commodities brought to its ports, it is most probable that I should not make an ado about it, for I can do without them: all machines have their friction; and possibly this does enough good to counterbalance the evil. At any rate, it is a great evil to make a stir about it. But when the friction comes to have its machine, and oppression and robbery are organized, I say, let us not have such a machine any longer. In other words, when a sixth of the population of a nation which has undertaken to be the refuge of liberty are slaves, and a whole country is unjustly overrun and conquered by a foreign army, and subjected to military law, I think that it is not too soon for honest men to rebel and revolutionize. What makes this duty the more urgent is the fact, that the country so overrun is not our own, but ours is the invading army.

Paley, a common authority with many on moral questions, in his chapter on the "Duty of Submission to Civil Government,"[9] resolves all civil obligation into expediency; and he proceeds to say, "that so long as the interest of the whole society requires it, that is, so long as the established government cannot be resisted or changed without public inconveniency, it is the will of God that the established government be obeyed, and no longer."—"This principle being admitted, the justice of every particular case of resistance is reduced to a computation of the quantity of the danger and grievance on the one side, and of the probability and expense of redressing it on the other." Of this, he says, every man shall judge for himself. But Paley appears never to have contemplated those cases to which the rule of expediency does not apply, in which a people, as well as an individual, must do justice, cost what it may. If I have unjustly wrested a plank from a drowning man, I must restore it to him though I drown myself.[1] This, according to Paley, would be inconvenient. But he that would save his life, in such a case, shall lose it.[2] This people must cease to hold slaves, and to make war on Mexico, though it cost them their existence as a people.

In their practice, nations agree with Paley; but does any one think that Massachusetts does exactly what is right at the present crisis?

> "A drab of state, a cloth-o'-silver slut,
> To have her train borne up, and her soul trail in the dirt."[3]

Practically speaking, the opponents to a reform in Massachusetts are not a hundred thousand politicians at the South, but a hundred thousand merchants and farmers here,[4] who are more interested in commerce and agriculture than they are in humanity, and are not prepared to do justice to the slave and to Mexico, *cost what it may*. I quarrel not with far-off foes, but with those who, near at home, co-operate with, and do the bidding of those far away, and without whom the latter would be harmless. We are accustomed to say, that

---

9. The precise title of the chapter in William Paley's *Principles of Moral and Political Philosophy* (1785) is *The Duty of Submission to Civil Government Explained*. This book by Paley, English theologian and moralist (1743–1805), was one of Thoreau's Harvard textbooks.
1. A problem in situational ethics cited by Cicero in *De Officiis* 3, which Thoreau had studied.
2. Matthew 10.39; Luke 9.24.
3. Cyril Tourneur (1575?–1626), *The Revenger's Tragedy* 3.4.
4. Thoreau refers to the economic alliance of Southern cotton growers with Northern shippers and manufacturers.

the mass of men are unprepared; but improvement is slow, because the few
are not materially wiser or better than the many. It is not so important that
many should be as good as you, as that there be some absolute goodness somewhere; for that will leaven the whole lump.[5] There are thousands who are *in
opinion* opposed to slavery and to the war, who yet in effect do nothing to
put an end to them; who, esteeming themselves children of Washington and
Franklin,[6] sit down with their hands in their pockets, and say that they know
not what to do, and do nothing; who even postpone the question of freedom
to the question of free-trade, and quietly read the prices-current along with the
latest advices from Mexico, after dinner, and, it may be, fall asleep over them
both. What is the price-current of an honest man and patriot to-day? They
hesitate, and they regret, and sometimes they petition; but they do nothing in
earnest and with effect. They will wait, well disposed, for others to remedy the
evil, that they may no longer have it to regret. At most, they give only a cheap
vote, and a feeble countenance and God-speed, to the right, as it goes by
them. There are nine hundred and ninety-nine patrons of virtue to one virtuous man; but it is easier to deal with the real possessor of a thing than with the
temporary guardian of it.

All voting is a sort of gaming, like chequers or backgammon, with a slight
moral tinge to it, a playing with right and wrong, with moral questions; and
betting naturally accompanies it. The character of the voters is not staked. I
cast my vote, perchance, as I think right; but I am not vitally concerned that
that right should prevail. I am willing to leave it to the majority. Its obligation,
therefore, never exceeds that of expediency. Even voting *for the right* is *doing*
nothing for it. It is only expressing to men feebly your desire that it should
prevail. A wise man will not leave the right to the mercy of chance, nor wish
it to prevail through the power of the majority. There is but little virtue in the
action of masses of men. When the majority shall at length vote for the abolition of slavery, it will be because they are indifferent to slavery, or because
there is but little slavery left to be abolished by their vote. *They* will then be
the only slaves. Only *his* vote can hasten the abolition of slavery who asserts
his own freedom by his vote.

I hear of a convention to be held at Baltimore, or elsewhere, for the selection of a candidate for the Presidency, made up chiefly of editors, and men
who are politicians by profession; but I think, what is it to any independent,
intelligent, and respectable man what decision they may come to, shall we not
have the advantage of his wisdom and honesty, nevertheless? Can we not
count upon some independent votes? Are there not many individuals in the
country who do not attend conventions? But no: I find that the respectable
man, so called, has immediately drifted from his position, and despairs of his
country, when his country has more reason to despair of him. He forthwith
adopts one of the candidates thus selected as the only *available* one, thus
proving that he is himself *available* for any purposes of the demagogue. His
vote is of no more worth than that of any unprincipled foreigner or hireling
native, who may have been bought. Oh for a man who is a *man*, and, as my
neighbor says, has a bone in his back which you cannot pass your hand
through! Our statistics are at fault: the population has been returned too large.
How many *men* are there to a square thousand miles in this country? Hardly

5. 1 Corinthians 5.6: "Know ye not that a little leaven   6. I.e., children of rebels and revolutionaries.
leaventh the whole lump?"

one. Does not America offer any inducement for men to settle here? The American had dwindled into an Odd Fellow,—one who may be known by the development of his organ of gregariousness, and a manifest lack of intellect and cheerful self-reliance;[7] whose first and chief concern, on coming into the world, is to see that the alms-houses are in good repair; and, before yet he has lawfully donned the virile garb,[8] to collect a fund for the support of the widows and orphans that may be; who, in short, ventures to live only by the aid of the mutual insurance company, which has promised to bury him decently.

It is not a man's duty, as a matter of course, to devote himself to the eradication of any, even the most enormous wrong; he may still properly have other concerns to engage him; but it is his duty, at least, to wash his hands of it, and, if he gives it no thought longer, not to give it practically his support. If I devote myself to other pursuits and contemplations, I must first see, at least, that I do not pursue them sitting upon another man's shoulders. I must get off him first, that he may pursue his contemplations too. See what gross inconsistency is tolerated. I have heard some of my townsmen say, "I should like to have them order me out to help put down an insurrection of the slaves, or to march to Mexico,—see if I would go;" and yet these very men have each, directly by their allegiance, and so indirectly, at least, by their money, furnished a substitute. The soldier is applauded who refuses to serve in an unjust war by those who do not refuse to sustain the unjust government which makes the war; is applauded by those whose own act and authority he disregards and sets at nought; as if the State were penitent to that degree that it hired one to scourge it while it sinned, but not to that degree that it left off sinning for a moment. Thus, under the name of order and civil government, we are all made at last to pay homage to and support our own meanness. After the first blush of sin, comes its indifference; and from immoral it becomes, as it were, unmoral, and not quite unnecessary to that life which we have made.

The broadest and most prevalent error requires the most disinterested virtue to sustain it. The slight reproach to which the virtue of patriotism is commonly liable, the noble are most likely to incur. Those who, while they disapprove of the character and measures of a government, yield to it their allegiance and support, are undoubtedly its most conscientious supporters, and so frequently the most serious obstacles to reform. Some are petitioning the State to dissolve the Union, to disregard the requisitions of the President. Why do they not dissolve it themselves,—the union between themselves and the State,—and refuse to pay their quota into its treasury? Do not they stand in the same relation to the State, that the State does to the Union? And have not the same reasons prevented the State from resisting the Union, which have prevented them from resisting the State?

How can a man be satisfied to entertain an opinion merely, and enjoy *it*? Is there any enjoyment in it, if his opinion is that he is aggrieved? If you are cheated out of a single dollar by your neighbor, you do not rest satisfied with knowing that you are cheated, or with saying that you are cheated, or even with petitioning him to pay you your due; but you take effectual steps at once to obtain the full amount, and see that you are never cheated again. Action

7. The Odd Fellows are a secret fraternal organization, chosen by Thoreau for the satirical value of its name: in his view the archetypal American is not the individualist, the genuine odd fellow, but the conformist.

8. Adult garb allowed a Roman boy on reaching fourteen.

from principle,—the perception and the performance of right,—changes things and relations; it is essentially revolutionary, and does not consist wholly with any thing which was. It not only divides states and churches, it divides families; aye, it divides the *individual*, separating the diabolical in him from the divine.

Unjust laws exist: shall we be content to obey them, or shall we endeavor to amend them, and obey them until we have succeeded, or shall we transgress them at once? Men generally, under such a government as this, think that they ought to wait until they have persuaded the majority to alter them. They think that, if they should resist, the remedy would be worse than the evil. But it is the fault of the government itself that the remedy *is* worse than the evil. *It* makes it worse. Why is it not more apt to anticipate and provide for reform? Why does it not cherish its wise minority? Why does it cry and resist before it is hurt? Why does it not encourage its citizens to be on the alert to point out its faults, and *do* better than it would have them? Why does it always crucify Christ, and excommunicate Copernicus and Luther,[9] and pronounce Washington and Franklin rebels?

One would think, that a deliberate and practical denial of its authority was the only offence never contemplated by government; else, why has it not assigned its definite, its suitable and proportionate penalty? If a man who has no property refuses but once to earn nine shillings[1] for the State, he is put in prison for a period unlimited by any law that I know, and determined only by the discretion of those who placed him there; but if I should steal ninety times nine shillings from the State, he is soon permitted to go at large again.

If the injustice is part of the necessary friction of the machine of government, let it go, let it go: perchance it will wear smooth,—certainly the machine will wear out. If the injustice has a spring, or a pulley, or a rope, or a crank, exclusively for itself, then perhaps you may consider whether the remedy will not be worse than the evil; but if it is of such a nature that it requires you to be the agent of injustice to another, then, I say, break the law. Let your life be a counter friction to stop the machine. What I have to do is to see, at any rate, that I do not lend myself to the wrong which I condemn.

As for adopting the ways which the State has provided for remedying the evil, I know not of such ways. They take too much time, and a man's life will be gone. I have other affairs to attend to. I came into this world, not chiefly to make this a good place to live in, but to live in it, be it good or bad. A man has not every thing to do, but something; and because he cannot do *every thing*, it is not necessary that he should do *something* wrong. It is not my business to be petitioning the governor or the legislature any more than it is theirs to petition me; and, if they should not hear my petition, what should I do then? But in this case the State has provided no way: its very Constitution is the evil. This may seem to be harsh and stubborn and unconciliatory; but it is to treat with the utmost kindness and consideration the only spirit that can appreciate or deserves it. So is all change for the better, like birth and death which convulse the body.

I do not hesitate to say, that those who call themselves abolitionists should

9. Thoreau uses Copernicus (1473–1543), the Polish astronomer who died too soon after the publication of his new system of astronomy to be excommunicated from the Catholic Church for writing it, and Martin Luther (1483–1546), the German leader of the Protes-tant Reformation who was excommunicated, as announcers of new truths.
1. The amount of the poll tax Thoreau had refused to pay.

at once effectually withdraw their support, both in person and property, from the government of Massachusetts, and not wait till they constitute a majority of one, before they suffer the right to prevail through them. I think that it is enough if they have God on their side, without waiting for that other one. Moreover, any man more right than his neighbors, constitutes a majority of one already.[2]

I meet this American government, or its representative the State government, directly, and face to face, once a year, no more, in the person of its tax-gatherer; this is the only mode in which a man situated as I am necessarily meets it; and it then says distinctly, Recognize me; and the simplest, the most effectual, and, in the present posture of affairs, the indispensablest mode of treating with it on this head, of expressing your little satisfaction with and love for it, is to deny it then. My civil neighbor, the tax-gatherer,[3] is the very man I have to deal with,—for it is, after all, with men and not with parchment that I quarrel,—and he has voluntarily chosen to be an agent of the government. How shall he ever know well what he is and does as an officer of the government, or as a man, until he is obliged to consider whether he shall treat me, his neighbor, for whom he has respect, as a neighbor and well-disposed man, or as a maniac and disturber of the peace, and see if he can get over this obstruction to his neighborliness without a ruder and more impetuous thought or speech corresponding with his action? I know this well, that if one thousand, if one hundred, if ten men whom I could name,—if ten *honest* men only,—aye, if *one* HONEST man, in this State of Massachusetts, *ceasing to hold slaves*, were actually to withdraw from this copartnership, and be locked up in the county jail therefor, it would be the abolition of slavery in America. For it matters not how small the beginning may seem to be: what is once well done is done for ever. But we love better to talk about it: that we say is our mission. Reform keeps many scores of newspapers in its service, but not one man. If my esteemed neighbor, the State's ambassador,[4] who will devote his days to the settlement of the question of human rights in the Council Chamber, instead of being threatened with the prisons of Carolina, were to sit down the prisoner of Massachusetts, that State which is so anxious to foist the sin of slavery upon her sister,—though at present she can discover only an act of inhospitality to be the ground of a quarrel with her,—the Legislature would not wholly waive the subject the following winter.

Under a government which imprisons any unjustly, the true place for a just man is also a prison. The proper place to-day, the only place which Massachusetts has provided for her freer and less desponding spirits, is in her prisons, to be put out and locked out of the State by her own act, as they have already put themselves out by their principles. It is there that the fugitive slave, and the Mexican prisoner on parole, and the Indian come to plead the wrongs of his race, should find them; on that separate, but more free and honorable ground, where the State places those who are not *with* her but *against* her,—the only house in a slave-state in which a free man can abide with honor. If any think that their influence would be lost there, and their voices no longer afflict the

---

2. John Knox (1505?–1572), the Scottish religious reformer, said that "a man with God is always in the majority."
3. Sam Staples, who sometimes assisted Thoreau in his surveying.
4. Samuel Hoar (1778–1856), local political figure who as agent of the state of Massachusetts had been expelled from Charleston, South Carolina, in 1844 while interceding on behalf of imprisoned black seamen from Massachusetts. The South Carolina legislature had voted to ask the governor to expel Hoar.

ear of the State, that they would not be as an enemy within its walls, they do not know by how much truth is stronger than error, nor how much more eloquently and effectively he can combat injustice who has experienced a little in his own person. Cast your whole vote, not a strip of paper merely, but your whole influence. A minority is powerless while it conforms to the majority; it is not even a minority then; but it is irresistible when it clogs by its whole weight. If the alternative is to keep all just men in prison, or give up war and slavery, the State will not hesitate which to choose. If a thousand men were not to pay their tax-bills this year, that would not be a violent and bloody measure, as it would be to pay them, and enable the State to commit violence and shed innocent blood. This is, in fact, the definition of a peaceable revolution, if any such is possible. If the tax-gatherer, or any other public officer, asks me, as one has done, "But what shall I do?" my answer is, "If you really wish to do any thing, resign your office." When the subject has refused allegiance, and the officer has resigned his office, then the revolution is accomplished. But even suppose blood should flow. Is there not a sort of blood shed when the conscience is wounded? Through this wound a man's real manhood and immortality flow out, and he bleeds to an everlasting death. I see this blood flowing now.

I have contemplated the imprisonment of the offender, rather than the seizure of his goods,—though both will serve the same purpose,—because they who assert the purest right, and consequently are most dangerous to a corrupt State, commonly have not spent much time in accumulating property. To such the State renders comparatively small service, and a slight tax is wont to appear exorbitant, particularly if they are obliged to earn it by special labor with their hands. If there were one who lived wholly without the use of money, the State itself would hesitate to demand it of him. But the rich man—not to make any invidious comparison—is always sold to the institution which makes him rich. Absolutely speaking, the more money, the less virtue; for money comes between a man and his objects, and obtains them for him; and it was certainly no great virtue to obtain it. It puts to rest many questions which he would otherwise be taxed to answer; while the only new question which it puts is the hard but superfluous one, how to spend it. Thus his moral ground is taken from under his feet. The opportunities of living are diminished in proportion as what are called the "means" are increased. The best thing a man can do for his culture when he is rich is to endeavour to carry out those schemes which he entertained when he was poor. Christ answered the Herodians according to their condition. "Show me the tribute-money," said he;—and one took a penny out of his pocket;—If you use money which has the image of Cæsar on it, and which he has made current and valuable, that is, *if you are men of the State,* and gladly enjoy the advantages of Cæsar's government, then pay him back some of his own when he demands it: "Render therefore to Cæsar that which is Cæsar's, and to God those things which are God's,"[5]—leaving them no wiser than before as to which was which; for they did not wish to know.

When I converse with the freest of my neighbors, I perceive that, whatever they may say about the magnitude and seriousness of the question, and their regard for the public tranquillity, the long and the short of the matter is, that

---

5. Matthew 22.16–21. In their attempt to entrap Jesus, the Pharisees (a Jewish sect that held to Mosaic law) were utilizing secular government functionaries of Herod, the tetrarch or king of Judea.

they cannot spare the protection of the existing government, and they dread the consequences of disobedience to it to their property and families. For my own part, I should not like to think that I ever rely on the protection of the State. But, if I deny the authority of the State when it presents its tax-bill, it will soon take and waste all my property, and so harass me and my children without end. This is hard. This makes it impossible for a man to live honestly and at the same time comfortably in outward respects. It will not be worth the while to accumulate property; that would be sure to go again. You must hire or squat somewhere, and raise but a small crop, and eat that soon. You must live within yourself, and depend upon yourself, always tucked up and ready for a start, and not have many affairs. A man may grow rich in Turkey even, if he will be in all respects a good subject of the Turkish government. Confucius said,—"If a State is governed by the principles of reason, poverty and misery are subjects of shame; if a State is not governed by the principles of reason, riches and honors are the subjects of shame."[6] No: until I want the protection of Massachusetts to be extended to me in some distant southern port, where my liberty is endangered, or until I am bent solely on building up an estate at home at peaceful enterprise, I can afford to refuse allegiance to Massachusetts, and her right to my property and life. It costs me less in every sense to incur the penalty of disobedience to the State, than it would to obey. I should feel as if I were worth less in that case.

Some years ago, the State met me in behalf of the church, and commanded me to pay a certain sum toward the support of a clergyman whose preaching my father attended, but never I myself. "Pay it," it said, "or be locked up in the jail." I declined to pay. But, unfortunately, another man saw fit to pay it. I did not see why the schoolmaster should be taxed to support the priest, and not the priest the schoolmaster; for I was not the State's schoolmaster, but I supported myself by voluntary subscription. I did not see why the lyceum should not present its tax-bill, and have the State to back its demand, as well as the church. However, at the request of the selectmen, I condescended to make some such statement as this in writing:—"Know all men by these presents, that I, Henry Thoreau, do not wish to be regarded as a member of any incorporated society which I have not joined." This I gave to the town-clerk; and he has it. The State, having thus learned that I did not wish to be regarded as a member of that church, has never made a like demand on me since; though it said that it must adhere to its original presumption that time. If I had known how to name them, I should then have signed off in detail from all the societies which I never signed on to; but I did not know where to find a complete list.

I have paid no poll-tax for six years. I was put into a jail[7] once on this account, for one night; and, as I stood considering the walls of solid stone, two or three feet thick, the door of wood and iron, a foot thick, and the iron grating which strained the light, I could not help being struck with the foolishness of that institution which treated me as if I were mere flesh and blood and bones, to be locked up. I wondered that it should have concluded at length that this was the best use it could put me to, and had never thought to avail itself of my services in some way. I saw that, if there was a wall of stone between me and my townsmen, there was a still more difficult one to climb or break through,

6. *Analects* 8.13.
7. The Middlesex County jail in Concord, a large three-story building. "Six years" would be since 1840.

before they could get to be as free as I was. I did not for a moment feel confined, and the walls seemed a great waste of stone and mortar. I felt as if I alone of all my townsmen had paid my tax. They plainly did not know how to treat me, but behaved like persons who are underbred. In every threat and in every compliment there was a blunder; for they thought that my chief desire was to stand the other side of that stone wall. I could not but smile to see how industriously they locked the door on my meditations, which followed them out again without let or hinderance, and *they* were really all that was dangerous. As they could not reach me, they had resolved to punish my body; just as boys, if they cannot come at some person against whom they have a spite, will abuse his dog. I saw that the State was half-witted, that it was timid as a lone woman with her silver spoons, and that it did not know its friends from its foes, and I lost all my remaining respect for it, and pitied it.

Thus the State never intentionally confronts a man's sense, intellectual or moral, but only his body, his senses. It is not armed with superior wit or honesty, but with superior physical strength. I was not born to be forced. I will breathe after my own fashion. Let us see who is the strongest. What force has a multitude? They only can force me who obey a higher law than I. They force me to become like themselves. I do not hear of *men* being *forced* to live this way or that by masses of men. What sort of live were that to live? When I meet a government which says to me, "Your money or your life,"[8] why should I be in haste to give it my money? It may be in a great strait, and not know what to do: I cannot help that. It must help itself; do as I do. It is not worth the while to snivel about it. I am not responsible for the successful working of the machinery of society. I am not the son of the engineer. I perceive that, when an acorn and a chestnut fall side by side, the one does not remain inert to make way for the other, but both obey their own laws, and spring and grow and flourish as best they can, till one, perchance, overshadows and destroys the other. If a plant cannot live according to its nature, it dies; and so a man.

The night in prison was novel and interesting enough. The prisoners in their shirt-sleeves were enjoying a chat and the evening air in the doorway, when I entered. But the jailer said, "Come, boys, it is time to lock up;" and so they dispersed, and I heard the sound of their steps returning into the hollow apartments. My room-mate was introduced to me by the jailer, as "a first-rate fellow and a clever man." When the door was locked, he showed me where to hang my hat, and how he managed matters there. The rooms were whitewashed once a month; and this one, at least, was the whitest, most simply furnished, and probably the neatest apartment in the town. He naturally wanted to know where I came from, and what brought me there; and, when I had told him, I asked him in my turn how he came there, presuming him to be an honest man, of course; and, as the world goes, I believe he was. "Why," said he, "they accuse me of burning a barn; but I never did it." As near as I could discover, he had probably gone to bed in a barn when drunk, and smoked his pipe there; and so a barn was burnt. He had the reputation of being a clever man, had been there some three months waiting for his trial to come on, and would have to wait as much longer; but he was quite domesticated and contented since he got his board for nothing, and thought that he was well treated.

8. The cry of the highway robber.

He occupied one window, and I the other; and I saw, that, if one stayed there long, his principal business would be to look out the window. I had soon read all the tracts that were left there, and examined where former prisoners had broken out, and where a grate had been sawed off, and heard the history of the various occupants of that room; for I found that even here there was a history and a gossip which never circulated beyond the walls of the jail. Probably this is the only house in the town where verses are composed, which are afterward printed in a circular form, but not published. I was shown quite a long list of verses which were composed by some young men who had been detected in an attempt to escape, who avenged themselves by singing them.

I pumped my fellow-prisoner as dry as I could, for fear I should never see him again; but at length he showed me which was my bed, and left me to blow out the lamp.

It was like travelling into a far country, such as I had never expected to behold, to lie there for one night. It seemed to me that I never had heard the town-clock strike before, nor the evening sounds of the village; for we slept with the windows open, which were inside the grating. It was to see my native village in the light of the middle ages, and our Concord was turned into a Rhine stream, and visions of knights and castles passed before me. They were the voices of old burghers that I heard in the streets. I was an involuntary spectator and auditor of whatever was done and said in the kitchen of the adjacent village-inn,—a wholly new and rare experience to me. It was a closer view of my native town. I was fairly inside of it. I never had seen its institutions before. This is one of its peculiar institutions; for it is a shire town.[9] I began to comprehend what its inhabitants were about.

In the morning, our breakfasts were put through the hole in the door, in small oblong-square tin pans, made to fit, and holding a pint of chocolate, with brown bread, and an iron spoon. When they called for the vessels again, I was green enough to return what bread I had left; but my comrade seized it, and said that I should lay that up for lunch or dinner. Soon after, he was let out to work at haying in a neighboring field, whither he went every day, and would not be back till noon; so he bade me good-day, saying that he doubted if he should see me again.

When I came out of prison,—for some one interfered, and paid the tax,—I did not perceive that great changes had taken place on the common, such as he observed who went in a youth, and emerged a tottering and gray-headed man; and yet a change had to my eyes come over the scene,—the town, and State, and country,—greater than any that mere time could effect. I saw yet more distinctly the State in which I lived. I saw to what extent the people among whom I lived could be trusted as good neighbors and friends; that their friendship was for summer weather only; that they did not greatly purpose to do right; that they were a distinct race from me by their prejudices and superstitions, as the Chinamen and Malays are; that, in their sacrifices to humanity, they ran no risks, not even to their property; that, after all, they were not so noble but they treated the thief as he had treated them, and hoped, by a certain outward observance and a few prayers, and by walking in a particular straight

9. Comparable to "county seat."

though useless path from time to time, to save their souls. This may be to judge my neighbors harshly; for I believe that most of them are not aware that they have such an institution as the jail in their village.

It was formerly the custom in our village, when a poor debtor came out of jail, for his acquaintances to salute him, looking through their fingers, which were crossed to represent the grating of a jail window, "How do ye do?" My neighbors did not thus salute me, but first looked at me, and then at one another, as if I had returned from a long journey. I was put into jail as I was going to the shoemaker's to get a shoe which was mended. When I was let out the next morning, I proceeded to finish my errand, and, having put on my mended shoe, joined a huckleberry party, who were impatient to put themselves under my conduct; and in half an hour,—for the horse was soon tackled,[1]—was in the midst of a huckleberry field, on one of our highest hills, two miles off; and then the State was nowhere to be seen.

This is the whole history of "My Prisons."[2]

I have never declined paying the highway tax, because I am as desirous of being a good neighbor as I am of being a bad subject; and, as for supporting schools, I am doing my part to educate my fellow-countrymen now. It is for no particular item in the tax-bill that I refuse to pay it. I simply wish to refuse allegiance to the State, to withdraw and stand aloof from it effectually. I do not care to trace the course of my dollar, if I could, till it buys a man, or a musket to shoot one with,—the dollar is innocent,—but I am concerned to trace the effects of my allegiance. In fact, I quietly declare war with the State, after my fashion, though I will still make what use and get what advantage of her I can, as is usual in such cases.

If others pay the tax which is demanded of me, from a sympathy with the State, they do but what they have already done in their own case, or rather they abet injustice to a greater extent than the State requires. If they pay the tax from a mistaken interest in the individual taxed, to save his property or prevent his going to jail, it is because they have not considered wisely how far they let their private feelings interfere with the public good.

This, then, is my position at present. But one cannot be too much on his guard in such a case, lest his action be biassed by obstinacy, or an undue regard for the opinions of men. Let him see that he does only what belongs to himself and to the hour.

I think sometimes, Why, this people mean well; they are only ignorant; they would do better if they knew how; why give your neighbors this pain to treat you as they are not inclined to? But I think, again, this is no reason why I should do as they do, or permit others to suffer much greater pain of a different kind. Again, I sometimes say to myself, When many millions of men, without heat, without ill-will, without personal feeling of any kind, demand of you a few shillings only, without the possibility, such is their constitution, of retracting or altering their present demand, and without the possibility, on your side, of appeal to any other millions, why expose yourself to this overwhelming brute force? You do not resist cold and hunger, the winds and the waves, thus obstinately; you quietly submit to a thousand similar necessities.

1. Harnessed.
2. A wry comparison to the title of a book (1832) by the Italian poet Silvio Pellico (1789–1854) on his years of hard labor in Austrian prisons.

You do not put your head into the fire. But just in proportion as I regard this as not wholly a brute force, but partly a human force, and consider that I have relations to those millions as to so many millions of men, and not of mere brute or inanimate things, I see that appeal is possible, first and instantaneously, from them to the Maker of them, and, secondly, from them to themselves. But, if I put my head deliberately into the fire, there is no appeal to fire or to the Maker of fire, and I have only myself to blame. If I could convince myself that I have any right to be satisfied with men as they are, and to treat them accordingly, and not according, in some respects, to my requisitions and expectations of what they and I ought to be, then, like a good Mussulman[3] and fatalist, I should endeavor to be satisfied with things as they are, and say it is the will of God. And, above all, there is this difference between resisting this and a purely brute or natural force, that I can resist this with some effect; but I cannot expect, like Orpheus,[4] to change the nature of the rocks and trees and beasts.

I do not wish to quarrel with any man or nation. I do not wish to split hairs, to make fine distinctions, or set myself up as better than my neighbors. I seek rather, I may say, even an excuse for conforming to the laws of the land. I am but too ready to conform to them. Indeed I have reason to suspect myself on this head; and each year, as the tax-gatherer comes round, I find myself disposed to review the acts and position of the general and state governments, and the spirit of the people, to discover a pretext for conformity. I believe that the State will soon be able to take all my work of this sort out of my hands, and then I shall be no better a patriot than my fellow-countrymen. Seen from a lower point of view, the Constitution, with all its faults, is very good; the law and the courts are very respectable; even this State and this American government are, in many respects, very admirable and rare things, to be thankful for, such as a great many have described them; but seen from a point of view a little higher, they are what I have described them; seen from a higher still, and the highest, who shall say what they are, or that they are worth looking at or thinking of at all?

However, the government does not concern me much, and I shall bestow the fewest possible thoughts on it. It is not many moments that I live under a government, even in this world. If a man is thought-free, fancy-free, imagination-free, that which *is not* never for a long time appearing *to be* to him, unwise rulers or reformers cannot fatally interrupt him.

I know that most men think differently from myself; but those whose lives are by profession devoted to the study of these or kindred subjects, content me as little as any. Statesmen and legislators, standing so completely within the institution, never distinctly and nakedly behold it. They speak of moving society, but have no resting-place without it. They may be men of a certain experience and discrimination, and have no doubt invented ingenious and even useful systems, for which we sincerely thank them; but all their wit and usefulness lie within certain not very wide limits. They are wont to forget that the world is not governed by policy and expediency. Webster[5] never goes behind government, and so cannot speak with authority about it. His words are wis-

---

3. Mohammedan.
4. The son of Calliope, one of the Muses, who gave him the gift of music. Trees and rocks moved to the playing of his lyre. He charmed the three-headed dog

Cerberus in an unsuccessful attempt to bring his dead wife, Eurydice, up from the Underworld.
5. Daniel Webster (1782–1852), prominent Whig politician of the second quarter of the 19th century.

dom to those legislators who contemplate no essential reform in the existing government; but for thinkers, and those who legislate for all time, he never once glances at the subject. I know of those whose serene and wise speculations on this theme would soon reveal the limits of his mind's range and hospitality. Yet, compared with the cheap professions of most reformers, and the still cheaper wisdom and eloquence of politicians in general, his are almost the only sensible and valuable words, and we thank Heaven for him. Comparatively, he is always strong, original, and, above all, practical. Still his quality is not wisdom, but prudence. The lawyer's truth is not Truth, but consistency, or a consistent expediency. Truth is always in harmony with herself, and is not concerned chiefly to reveal the justice that may consist with wrong-doing. He well deserves to be called, as he has been called, the Defender of the Constitution. There are really no blows to be given by him but defensive ones. He is not a leader, but a follower. His leaders are the men of '87.[6] "I have never made an effort," he says, "and never propose to make an effort; I have never countenanced an effort, and never mean to countenance an effort, to disturb the arrangement as originally made, by which the various States came into the Union."[7] Still thinking of the sanction which the Constitution gives to slavery, he says, "Because it was a part of the original compact,—let it stand." Notwithstanding his special acuteness and ability, he is unable to take a fact out of its merely political relations, and behold it as it lies absolutely to be disposed of by the intellect,—what, for instance, it behoves a man to do here in America to-day with regard to slavery, but ventures, or is driven, to make some such desperate answer as the following, while professing to speak absolutely, and as a private man,—from which what new and singular code of social duties might be inferred?—"The manner," says he, "in which the government of those States where slavery exists are to regulate it, is for their own consideration, under their responsibility to their constituents, to the general laws of propriety, humanity, and justice, and to God. Associations formed elsewhere, springing from a feeling of humanity, or any other cause, having nothing whatever to do with it. They have never received any encouragement from me, and they never will."[8]

They who know of no purer sources of truth, who have traced up its stream no higher, stand, and wisely stand, by the Bible and the Constitution, and drink at it there with reverence and humility; but they who behold where it comes trickling into this lake or that pool, gird up their loins once more, and continue their pilgrimage toward its fountain-head.

No man with a genius for legislation has appeared in America. They are rare in the history of the world. There are orators, politicians, and eloquent men, by the thousand; but the speaker has not yet opened his mouth to speak, who is capable of settling the much-vexed questions of the day. We love eloquence for its own sake, and not for any truth which it may utter, or any heroism it may inspire. Our legislators have not yet learned the comparative value of free-trade and of freedom, of union, and of rectitude, to a nation. They have no genius or talent for comparatively humble questions of taxation and finance, commerce and manufactures and agriculture. If we were left

---

6. The writers of the Constitution, who convened at Philadelphia in 1787.
7. From Webster's speech on *The Admission of Texas* (December 22, 1845).

8. "These extracts have been inserted since the Lecture was read" [Thoreau's note]; he means the quotation beginning "The manner."

solely to the wordy wit of legislators in Congress for our guidance, uncorrected by the seasonable experience and the effectual complaints of the people, America would not long retain her rank among the nations. For eighteen hundred years, though perchance I have no right to say it, the New Testament has been written; yet where is the legislator who has wisdom and practical talent enough to avail himself of the light which it sheds on the science of legislation?

The authority of government, even such as I am willing to submit to,—for I will cheerfully obey those who know and can do better than I, and in many things even those who neither know nor can do so well,—is still an impure one: to be strictly just, it must have the sanction and consent of the governed. It can have no pure right over my person and property but what I concede to it. The progress from an absolute to a limited monarchy, from a limited monarchy to a democracy, is a progress toward a true respect for the individual. Is a democracy, such as we know it, the last improvement possible in government? Is it not possible to take a step further towards recognizing and organizing the rights of man? There will never be a really free and enlightened State, until the State comes to recognize the individual as a higher and independent power, from which all its own power and authority are derived, and treats him accordingly. I please myself with imagining a State at last which can afford to be just to all men, and to treat the individual with respect as a neighbor; which even would not think it inconsistent with its own repose, if a few were to live aloof from it, not meddling with it, nor embraced by it, who fulfilled all the duties of neighbors and fellow-men. A State which bore this kind of fruit, and suffered it to drop off as fast as it ripened, would prepare the way for a still more perfect and glorious State, which also I have imagined, but not yet anywhere seen.

1849, 1866

Walden, or Life in the Woods[1]

I do not propose to write an ode to dejection, but to brag as lustily as chanticleer in the morning, standing on his roost, if only to wake my neighbors up.

Economy[2]

When I wrote the following pages, or rather the bulk of them, I lived alone, in the woods, a mile from any neighbor, in a house which I had built myself, on the shore of Walden Pond, in Concord, Massachusetts, and earned my living by the labor of my hands only. I lived there two years and two months. At present I am a sojourner in civilized life again.

I should not obtrude my affairs so much on the notice of my readers if very

1. Thoreau began writing *Walden* early in 1846, some months after he began living at Walden Pond, and by late 1847, when he moved back into the village of Concord, he had drafted roughly half the book. Between 1852 and 1854 he rewrote the manuscript several times and substantially enlarged it. The text printed here is that of the 1st edition (1854), with a few printer's errors corrected on the basis of Thoreau's set of marked proofs, his corrections in his copy of *Walden*, and scholars' comparisons of the printed book and the manuscript drafts, especially the edition by J. Lyndon Shanley (1971).

Any annotator of *Walden* is deeply indebted to Walter Harding, editor of *The Variorum Walden* (1962), and Philip Van Doren Stern, editor of *The Annotated Walden* (1970).

2. As Thoreau explains later in the chapter, the title means something like "philosophy of living."

particular inquiries had not been made by my townsmen concerning my mode
of life, which some would call impertinent, though they do not appear to
me at all impertinent, but, considering the circumstances, very natural and
pertinent. Some have asked what I got to eat; if I did not feel lonesome; if I
was not afraid; and the like. Others have been curious to learn what portion of
my income I devoted to charitable purposes; and some, who have large families, how many poor children I maintained. I will therefore ask those of my
readers who feel no particular interest in me to pardon me if I undertake to
answer some of these questions in this book. In most books, the I, or first
person, is omitted; in this it will be retained; that, in respect to egotism, is the
main difference. We commonly do not remember that it is, after all, always
the first person that is speaking. I should not talk so much about myself if there
were any body else whom I knew as well. Unfortunately, I am confined to this
theme by the narrowness of my experience. Moreover, I, on my side, require
of every writer, first or last, a simple and sincere account of his own life, and
not merely what he has heard of other men's lives; some such account as he
would send to his kindred from a distant land; for if he has lived sincerely, it
must have been in a distant land to me. Perhaps these pages are more particularly addressed to poor students. As for the rest of my readers, they will accept
such portions as apply to them. I trust that none will stretch the seams in
putting on the coat, for it may do good service to him whom it fits.

I would fain say something, not so much concerning the Chinese and Sandwich Islanders[3] as you who read these pages, who are said to live in New
England; something about your condition, especially your outward condition
or circumstances in this world, in this town, what it is, whether it is necessary
that it be as bad as it is, whether it cannot be improved as well as not. I have
travelled a good deal in Concord; and every where, in shops, and offices, and
fields, the inhabitants have appeared to me to be doing penance in a thousand
remarkable ways. What I have heard of Brahmins sitting exposed to four fires
and looking in the face of the sun; or hanging suspended, with their heads
downward, over flames; or looking at the heavens over their shoulders "until
it becomes impossible for them to resume their natural position, while from
the twist of the neck nothing but liquids can pass into the stomach;" or dwelling, chained for life, at the foot of a tree; or measuring with their bodies, like
caterpillars, the breadth of vast empires; or standing on one leg on the tops of
pillars,—even these forms of conscious penance are hardly more incredible
and astonishing than the scenes which I daily witness.[4] The twelve labors of
Hercules[5] were trifling in comparison with those which my neighbors have
undertaken; for they were only twelve, and had an end; but I could never see
that these men slew or captured any monster or finished any labor. They have
no friend Iolas to burn with a hot iron the root of the hydra's head, but as soon
as one head is crushed, two spring up.

I see young men, my townsmen, whose misfortune it is to have inherited
farms, houses, barns, cattle, and farming tools; for these are more easily

3. Hawaiians.
4. Thoreau's source has not been found for this depiction of the religious self-torture of high-caste Hindus
in India.
5. Son of Zeus and Alcmene, this half mortal could
become a god only by performing twelve labors, each
apparently impossible. The second labor, the slaying of
the Lernaean hydra, a many-headed sea monster, is
referred to just below. (Hercules' friend Iolas helped by
searing the stump each time Hercules cut off one of
the heads, which otherwise would have regenerated.)
The seventh labor, mentioned in the following paragraph, was the cleansing of Augeas's pestilent stables in
one day, a feat Hercules accomplished by diverting two
nearby rivers through the stables.

acquired than got rid of. Better if they had been born in the open pasture and suckled by a wolf, that they might have seen with clearer eyes what field they were called to labor in. Who made them serfs of the soil? Why should they eat their sixty acres, when man is condemned to eat only his peck of dirt? Why should they begin digging their graves as soon as they are born? They have got to live a man's life, pushing all these things before them, and get on as well as they can. How many a poor immortal soul have I met well nigh crushed and smothered under its load, creeping down the road of life, pushing before it a barn seventy-five feet by forty, its Augean stables never cleansed, and one hundred acres of land, tillage, mowing, pasture, and wood-lot! The portionless, who struggle with no such unnecessary inherited encumbrances, find it labor enough to subdue and cultivate a few cubic feet of flesh.

But men labor under a mistake. The better part of the man is soon ploughed into the soil for compost. By a seeming fate, commonly called necessity, they are employed, as it says in an old book, laying up treasures which moth and rust will corrupt and thieves break through and steal.[6] It is a fool's life, as they will find when they get to the end of it, if not before. It is said that Deucalion and Pyrrha created men by throwing stones over their heads behind them:[7]—

> Inde genus durum sumus, experiensque laborum,
> Et documenta damus quâ simus origine nati.

Or, as Raleigh rhymes it in his sonorous way,—

> "From thence our kind hard-hearted is, enduring pain and care,
> Approving that our bodies of a stony nature are."

So much for a blind obedience to a blundering oracle, throwing the stones over their heads behind them, and not seeing where they fell.

Most men, even in this comparatively free country, through mere ignorance and mistake, are so occupied with the factitious cares and superfluously coarse labors of life that its finer fruits cannot be plucked by them. Their fingers, from excessive toil, are too clumsy and tremble too much for that. Actually, the laboring man has not leisure for a true integrity day by day; he cannot afford to sustain the manliest relations to men; his labor would be depreciated in the market. He has no time to be any thing but a machine. How can he remember well his ignorance—which his growth requires—who has so often to use his knowledge? We should feed and clothe him gratuitously sometimes, and recruit him with our cordials, before we judge of him. The finest qualities of our nature, like the bloom on fruits, can be preserved only by the most delicate handling. Yet we do not treat ourselves nor one another thus tenderly.

Some of you, we all know, are poor, find it hard to live, are sometimes, as it were, gasping for breath. I have no doubt that some of you who read this book are unable to pay for all the dinners which you have actually eaten, or for the coats and shoes which are fast wearing or are already worn out, and have come to this page to spend borrowed or stolen time, robbing your creditors of an hour. It is very evident what mean and sneaking lives many of you live, for my sight has been whetted by experience; always on the limits, trying

6. Matthew 6.19.
7. Deucalion and Pyrrha, husband and wife in the Greek analogue to the biblical legend of Noah and the Flood, repopulated the earth by throwing stones behind them over their shoulders. The stones thrown by

Deucalion turned into men, and the stones thrown by Pyrrha turned into women. The quotation is from Ovid's *Metamorphoses* 1.414–15, as translated in Sir Walter Raleigh's *History of the World*.

to get into business and trying to get out of debt, a very ancient slough, called by the Latins, *æs alienum*, another's brass, for some of their coins were made of brass; still living, and dying, and buried by this other's brass; always promising to pay, promising to pay, to-morrow, and dying to-day, insolvent; seeking to curry favor, to get custom, by how many modes, only not state-prison offences; lying, flattering, voting, contracting yourselves into a nutshell of civility, or dilating into an atmosphere of thin and vaporous generosity, that you may persuade your neighbor to let you make his shoes, or his hat, or his coat, or his carriage, or import his groceries for him; making yourselves sick, that you may lay up something against a sick day, something to be tucked away in an old chest, or in a stocking behind the plastering, or, more safely, in the brick bank; no matter where, no matter how much or how little.

I sometimes wonder that we can be so frivolous, I may almost say, as to attend to the gross but somewhat foreign form of servitude called Negro Slavery, there are so many keen and subtle masters that enslave both north and south. It is hard to have a southern overseer; it is worse to have a northern one; but worst of all when you are the slave-driver of yourself. Talk of a divinity in man! Look at the teamster on the highway, wending to market by day or night; does any divinity stir within him? His highest duty to fodder and water his horses! What is his destiny to him compared with the shipping interests? Does not he drive for Squire Make-a-stir?[8] How godlike, how immortal, is he? See how he cowers and sneaks, how vaguely all the day he fears, not being immortal nor divine, but the slave and prisoner of his own opinion of himself, a fame won by his own deeds. Public opinion is a weak tyrant compared with our own private opinion. What a man thinks of himself, that it is which determines, or rather indicates, his fate. Self-emancipation even in the West Indian provinces of the fancy and imagination,—what Wilberforce[9] is there to bring that about? Think, also, of the ladies of the land weaving toilet cushions against the last day, not to betray too green an interest in their fates! As if you could kill time without injuring eternity.

The mass of men lead lives of quiet desperation. What is called resignation is confirmed desperation. From the desperate city you go into the desperate country, and have to console yourself with the bravery of minks and muskrats. A stereotyped but unconscious despair is concealed even under what are called the games and amusements of mankind. There is no play in them, for this comes after work. But it is a characteristic of wisdom not to do desperate things.

When we consider what, to use the words of the catechism, is the chief end of man,[1] and what are the true necessaries and means of life, it appears as if men had deliberately chosen the common mode of living because they preferred it to any other. Yet they honestly think there is no choice left. But alert and healthy natures remember that the sun rose clear. It is never too late to give up our prejudices. No way of thinking or doing, however ancient, can be trusted without proof. What every body echoes or in silence passes by as true to-day may turn out to be falsehood to-morrow, mere smoke of opinion, which some had trusted for a cloud that would sprinkle fertilizing rain on their fields.

8. An allegorical name modeled on those in John Bunyan's *Pilgrim's Progress*, familiar to almost any reader in Thoreau's time.
9. William Wilberforce (1759–1833), English philanthropist, leading opponent of the slave trade until its abolition in 1807.
1. From the Shorter Catechism in the *New England Primer*: "What is the chief end of man? Man's chief end is to glorify God and to enjoy him forever."

What old people say you cannot do you try and find that you can. Old deeds for old people, and new deeds for new. Old people did not know enough once, perchance, to fetch fresh fuel to keep the fire a-going; new people put a little dry wood under a pot, and are whirled round the globe with the speed of birds, in a way to kill old people, as the phrase is. Age is no better, hardly so well, qualified for an instructor as youth, for it has not profited so much as it has lost. One may almost doubt if the wisest man has learned any thing of absolute value by living. Practically, the old have no very important advice to give the young, their own experience has been so partial, and their lives have been such miserable failures, for private reasons, as they must believe; and it may be that they have some faith left which belies that experience, and they are only less young than they were. I have lived some thirty years on this planet, and I have yet to hear the first syllable of valuable or even earnest advice from my seniors. They have told me nothing, and probably cannot tell me any thing, to the purpose. Here is life, an experiment to a great extent untried by me; but it does not avail me that they have tried it. If I have any experience which I think valuable, I am sure to reflect that this my Mentors[2] said nothing about.

One farmer says to me, "You cannot live on vegetable food solely, for it furnishes nothing to make bones with;" and so he religiously devotes a part of his day to supplying his system with the raw material of bones; walking all the while he talks behind his oxen, which, with vegetable-made bones, jerk him and his lumbering plough along in spite of every obstacle. Some things are really necessaries of life in some circles, the most helpless and diseased, which in others are luxuries merely, and in others still are entirely unknown.

The whole ground of human life seems to some to have been gone over by their predecessors, both the heights and the valleys, and all things to have been cared for. According to Evelyn, "the wise Solomon prescribed ordinances for the very distances of trees; and the Roman prætors have decided how often you may go into your neighbor's land to gather the acorns which fall on it without trespass, and what share belongs to that neighbor."[3] Hippocrates[4] has even left directions how we should cut our nails; that is, even with the ends of the fingers, neither shorter nor longer. Undoubtedly the very tedium and ennui which presume to have exhausted the variety and the joys of life are as old as Adam. But man's capacities have never been measured; nor are we to judge of what he can do by any precedents, so little has been tried. Whatever have been thy failures hitherto, "be not afflicted, my child, for who shall assign to thee what thou hast left undone?"[5]

We might try our lives by a thousand simple tests; as, for instance, that the same sun which ripens my beans illumines at once a system of earths like ours. If I had remembered this it would have prevented some mistakes. This was not the light in which I hoed them. The stars are the apexes of what wonderful triangles! What distant and different beings in the various mansions of the universe are contemplating the same one at the same moment! Nature and human life are as various as our several constitutions. Who shall say what

2. From Mentor, in Homer's *Odyssey*: the friend whom Odysseus entrusted with the education of his son Telemachus.
3. *Silva: or, a Discourse of Forest-Trees*, by John Evelyn (1620–1706). "Prætors": in the Roman Republic, high elected magistrates.

4. Greek physician (460?–377? B.C.), known as the father of medicine.
5. "Be not afflicted, my child, for who shall efface what thou hast formerly done, or shall assign to thee what thou hast left undone?" H. H. Wilson's translation of the *Vishnu Purana* (1840).

prospect life offers to another? Could a greater miracle take place than for us to look through each other's eyes for an instant? We should live in all the ages of the world in an hour; ay, in all the worlds of the ages. History, Poetry, Mythology!—I know of no reading of another's experience so startling and informing as this would be.

The greater part of what my neighbors call good I believe in my soul to be bad, and if I repent of any thing, it is very likely to be my good behavior. What demon possessed me that I behaved so well? You may say the wisest thing you can old man,—you who have lived seventy years, not without honor of a kind,—I hear an irresistible voice which invites me away from all that. One generation abandons the enterprises of another like stranded vessels.

I think that we may safely trust a good deal more than we do. We may waive just so much care of ourselves as we honestly bestow elsewhere. Nature is as well adapted to our weakness as to our strength. The incessant anxiety and strain of some is a well nigh incurable form of disease. We are made to exaggerate the importance of what work we do; and yet how much is not done by us! or, what if we had been taken sick? How vigilant we are! determined not to live by faith if we can avoid it; all the day long on the alert, at night we unwillingly say our prayers and commit ourselves to uncertainties. So thoroughly and sincerely are we compelled to live, reverencing our life, and denying the possibility of change. This is the only way, we say; but there are as many ways as there can be drawn radii from one centre. All change is a miracle to contemplate; but it is a miracle which is taking place every instant. Confucius said, "To know that we know what we know, and that we do not know what we do not know, this is true knowledge."[6] When one man has reduced a fact of the imagination to be a fact to his understanding, I foresee that all men will at length establish their lives on that basis.

Let us consider for a moment what most of the trouble and anxiety which I have referred to is about, and how much it is necessary that we be troubled, or, at least, careful. It would be some advantage to live a primitive and frontier life, though in the midst of an outward civilization, if only to learn what are the gross necessaries of life and what methods have been taken to obtain them; or even to look over the old day-books of the merchants, to see what it was that men most commonly bought at the stores, what they stored, that is, what are the grossest groceries. For the improvements of ages have had but little influence on the essential laws of man's existence; as our skeletons, probably, are not to be distinguished from those of our ancestors.

By the words *necessary of life*, I mean whatever, of all that man obtains by his own exertions, has been from the first, or from long use has become, so important to human life that few, if any, whether from savageness, or poverty, or philosophy, ever attempt to do without it. To many creatures there is in this sense but one necessary of life, Food. To the bison of the prairie it is a few inches of palatable grass, with water to drink; unless he seeks the Shelter of the forest or the mountain's shadow. None of the brute creation requires more than Food and Shelter. The necessaries of life for man in this climate may, accurately enough, be distributed under the several heads of Food, Shelter, Clothing, and Fuel; for not till we have secured these are we prepared to

6. *Analects* 2.17.

entertain the true problems of life with freedom and a prospect of success. Man has invented, not only houses, but clothes and cooked food; and possibly from the accidental discovery of the warmth of fire, and the consequent use of it, at first a luxury, arose the present necessity to sit by it. We observe cats and dogs acquiring the same second nature. By proper Shelter and Clothing we legitimately retain our own internal heat; but with an excess of these, or of Fuel, that is, with an external heat greater than our own internal, may not cookery properly be said to begin? Darwin, the naturalist, says of the inhabitants of Tierra del Fuego, that while his own party, who were well clothed and sitting close to a fire, were far from too warm, these naked savages, who were farther off, were observed, to his great surprise, "to be streaming with perspiration at undergoing such a roasting."[7] So, we are told, the New Hollander[8] goes naked with impunity, while the European shivers in his clothes. Is it impossible to combine the hardiness of these savages with the intellectualness of the civilized man? According to Liebig,[9] man's body is a stove, and food the fuel which keeps up the internal combustion in the lungs. In cold weather we eat more, in warm less. The animal heat is the result of a slow combustion, and disease and death take place when this is too rapid; or for want of fuel, or from some defect in the draught, the fire goes out. Of course the vital heat is not to be confounded with fire; but so much for analogy. It appears, therefore, from the above list, that the expression, *animal life*, is nearly synonymous with the expression, *animal heat*; for while Food may be regarded as the Fuel which keeps up the fire within us,—and Fuel serves only to prepare that Food or to increase the warmth of our bodies by addition from without,—Shelter and Clothing also serve only to retain the *heat* thus generated and absorbed.

The grand necessity, then, for our bodies, is to keep warm, to keep the vital heat in us. What pains we accordingly take, not only with our Food, and Clothing, and Shelter, but with our beds, which are our night-clothes, robbing the nests and breasts of birds to prepare this shelter within a shelter, as the mole has its bed of grass and leaves at the end of its burrow! The poor man is wont to complain that this is a cold world; and to cold, no less physical than social, we refer directly a great part of our ails. The summer, in some climates, makes possible to man a sort of Elysian[1] life. Fuel, except to cook his Food, is then unnecessary; the sun is his fire, and many of the fruits are sufficiently cooked by its rays; while Food generally is more various, and more easily obtained, and Clothing and Shelter are wholly or half unnecessary. At the present day, and in this country, as I find by my own experience, a few implements, a knife, an axe, a spade, a wheelbarrow, &c., and for the studious, lamplight, stationery, and access to a few books, rank next to necessaries, and can all be obtained at a trifling cost. Yet some, not wise, go to the other side of the globe, to barbarous and unhealthy regions, and devote themselves to trade for ten or twenty years, in order that they may live,—that is, keep comfortably warm,—and die in New England at last. The luxuriously rich are not simply kept comfortably warm, but unnaturally hot; as I implied before, they are cooked, of course *à la mode*.

Most of the luxuries, and many of the so called comforts of life, are not

7. Charles Darwin, *Journal of * * * the Various Countries Visited by H.M.S. Beagle* (1839).
8. I.e., Australian aborigine.
9. Justus, Baron von Liebig (1803–1873), German chemist, author of *Organic Chemistry.*
1. In Greek mythology, Elysium is the home of the blessed after death.

only not indispensable, but positive hinderances to the elevation of mankind. With respect to luxuries and comforts, the wisest have ever lived a more simple and meager life than the poor. The ancient philosophers, Chinese, Hindoo, Persian, and Greek, were a class than which none has been poorer in outward riches, none so rich in inward. We know not much about them. It is remarkable that *we* know so much of them as we do. The same is true of the more modern reformers and benefactors of their race. None can be an impartial or wise observer of human life but from the vantage ground of what *we* should call voluntary poverty. Of a life of luxury the fruit is luxury, whether in agriculture, or commerce, or literature, or art. There are nowadays professors of philosophy, but not philosophers. Yet it is admirable to profess because it was once admirable to live. To be a philosopher is not merely to have subtle thoughts, nor even to found a school, but so to love wisdom as to live according to its dictates, a life of simplicity, independence, magnanimity, and trust. It is to solve some of the problems of life, not only theoretically, but practically. The success of great scholars and thinkers is commonly a courtier-like success, not kingly, not manly. They make shift to live merely by conformity, practically as their fathers did, and are in no sense the progenitors of a nobler race of men. But why do men degenerate ever? What makes families run out? What is the nature of the luxury which enervates and destroys nations? Are we sure that there is none of it in our own lives? The philosopher is in advance of his age even in the outward form of his life. He is not fed, sheltered, clothed, warmed, like his contemporaries. How can a man be a philosopher and not maintain his vital heat by better methods than other men?

When a man is warmed by the several modes which I have described, what does he want next? Surely not more warmth of the same kind, as more and richer food, larger and more splendid houses, finer and more abundant clothing, more numerous incessant and hotter fires, and the like. When he has obtained those things which are necessary to life, there is another alternative than to obtain the superfluities; and that is, to adventure on life now, his vacation from humbler toil having commenced. The soil, it appears, is suited to the seed, for it has sent its radicle downward, and it may now send its shoot upward also with confidence. Why has man rooted himself thus firmly in the earth, but that he may rise in the same proportion into the heavens above?— for the nobler plants are valued for the fruit they bear at last in the air and light, far from the ground, and are not treated like the humbler esculents, which, though they may be biennials, are cultivated only till they have perfected their root, and often cut down at top for this purpose, so that most would not know them in their flowering season.

I do not mean to prescribe rules to strong and valiant natures, who will mind their own affairs whether in heaven or hell, and perchance build more magnificently and spend more lavishly than the richest, without ever impoverishing themselves, not knowing how they live,—if, indeed, there are any such, as has been dreamed; nor to those who find their encouragement and inspiration in precisely the present condition of things, and cherish it with the fondness and enthusiasm of lovers,—and, to some extent, I reckon myself in this number; I do not speak to those who are well employed, in whatever circumstances, and they know whether they are well employed or not;—but mainly to the mass of men who are discontented, and idly complaining of the hardness of their lot or of the times, when they might improve them. There are some who complain most energetically and inconsolably of any, because they are, as they say, doing their duty. I also have in my mind that seemingly wealthy, but most terribly impoverished class of all, who have accumulated dross, but know not how to use it, or get rid of it, and thus have forged their own golden or silver fetters.

If I should attempt to tell how I have desired to spend my life in years past, it would probably surprise those of my readers who are somewhat acquainted with its actual history; it would certainly astonish those who know nothing about it. I will only hint at some of the enterprises which I have cherished.

In any weather, at any hour of the day or night, I have been anxious to improve the nick of time, and notch it on my stick too; to stand on the meeting of two eternities, the past and future, which is precisely the present moment; to toe that line. You will pardon some obscurities, for there are more secrets in my trade than in most men's, and yet not voluntarily kept, but inseparable from its very nature. I would gladly tell all that I know about it, and never paint "No Admittance" on my gate.

I long ago lost a hound, a bay horse, and a turtle-dove, and am still on their trail.[2] Many are the travellers I have spoken concerning them, describing their tracks and what calls they answered to. I have met one or two who had heard the hound, and the tramp of the horse, and even seen the dove disappear behind a cloud, and they seemed as anxious to recover them as if they had lost them themselves.

To anticipate, not the sunrise and the dawn merely, but, if possible, Nature herself! How many mornings, summer and winter, before yet any neighbor was stirring about his business, have I been about mine! No doubt, many of my townsmen have met me returning from this enterprise, farmers starting for Boston in the twilight, or woodchoppers going to their work. It is true, I never assisted the sun materially in his rising, but, doubt not, it was of the last importance only to be present at it.

So many autumn, ay, and winter days, spent outside the town, trying to hear what was in the wind, to hear and carry it express! I well-nigh sunk all my capital in it, and lost my own breath into the bargain, running in the face of it. If it had concerned either of the political parties, depend upon it, it would have appeared in the Gazette with the earliest intelligence.[3] At other times watching from the observatory of some cliff or tree, to telegraph any new arrival; or waiting at evening on the hill-tops for the sky to fall, that I might catch something, though I never caught much, and that, manna-wise,[4] would dissolve again in the sun.

For a long time I was reporter to a journal, of no very wide circulation, whose editor has never yet seen fit to print the bulk of my contributions, and, as is too common with writers, I got only my labor for my pains.[5] However, in this case my pains were their own reward.

2. Thoreau's reply to B. B. Wiley, April 26, 1857, suggests something of the evocative way he wanted this passage interpreted: "If others have their losses, which they are busy repairing, so have I *mine*, & their hound & horse may *perhaps* be the symbols of some of them. But also I have lost, or am in danger of losing, a far finer & more etherial treasure, which commonly no loss of which they are conscious will symbolize—this I answer hastily & with some hesitation, according as I now understand my own words."

3. News. "Gazette": newspaper.

4. In Exodus 16 manna is the bread that God rained from heaven so the Israelites could survive in the desert on their way from Egypt to the Promised Land.

5. Thoreau puns on the common usage of *journal* to mean a daily newspaper as well as a diary; Thoreau is the negligent or too demanding editor.

For many years I was self-appointed inspector of snow storms and rain storms, and did my duty faithfully; surveyor, if not of highways, then of forest paths and all across-lot routes, keeping them open, and ravines bridged and passable at all seasons, where the public heel had testified to their utility.

I have looked after the wild stock of the town, which give a faithful herds-man a good deal of trouble by leaping fences; and I have had an eye to the unfrequented nooks and corners of the farm; though I did not always know whether Jonas or Solomon worked in a particular field to-day; that was none of my business. I have watered the red huckleberry, the sand cherry and the nettle tree, the red pine and the black ash, the white grape and the yellow violet, which might have withered else in dry seasons.

In short, I went on thus for a long time, I may say it without boasting, faithfully minding my business, till it became more and more evident that my townsmen would not after all admit me into the list of town officers, nor make my place a sinecure with a moderate allowance. My accounts, which I can swear to have kept faithfully, I have, indeed, never got audited, still less accepted, still less paid and settled. However, I have not set my heart on that.

Not long since, a strolling Indian went to sell baskets at the house of a well-known lawyer in my neighborhood. "Do you wish to buy any baskets?" he asked. "No, we do not want any," was the reply. "What!" exclaimed the Indian as he went out the gate, "do you mean to starve us?" Having seen his industrious white neighbors so well off,—that the lawyer had only to weave arguments, and by some magic wealth and standing followed, he had said to himself; I will go into business; I will weave baskets; it is a thing which I can do. Thinking that when he had made the baskets he would have done his part, and then it would be the white man's to buy them. He had not discovered that it was necessary for him to make it worth the other's while to buy them, or at least make him think that it was so, or to make something else which it would be worth his while to buy. I too had woven a kind of basket of a delicate texture, but I had not made it worth any one's while to buy them.[6] Yet not the less, in my case, did I think it worth my while to weave them, and instead of studying how to make it worth men's while to buy my baskets, I studied rather how to avoid the necessity of selling them. The life which men praise and regard as successful is but one kind. Why should we exaggerate any one kind at the expense of the others?

Finding that my fellow-citizens were not likely to offer me any room in the court house, or any curacy or living[7] any where else, but I must shift for myself, I turned my face more exclusively than ever to the woods, where I was better known. I determined to go into business at once, and not wait to acquire the usual capital, using such slender means as I had already got. My purpose in going to Walden Pond was not to live cheaply nor to live dearly there, but to transact some private business with the fewest obstacles; to be hindered from accomplishing which for want of a little common sense, a little enterprise and business talent, appeared not so sad as foolish.

I have always endeavored to acquire strict business habits; they are indispensable to every man. If your trade is with the Celestial Empire,[8] then some small counting house on the coast, in some Salem harbor, will be fixture

---

6. A reference to Thoreau's poorly selling first book, *A Week on the Concord and Merrimack Rivers* (1849).
7. A church office with a fixed, steady income.

8. China, from the belief that the Chinese Emperors were sons of heaven.

enough. You will export such articles as the country affords, purely native products, much ice and pine timber and a little granite, always in native bottoms. These will be good ventures. To oversee all the details yourself in person; to be at once pilot and captain, and owner and underwriter; to buy and sell and keep the accounts; to read every letter received, and write or read every letter sent; to superintend the discharge of imports night and day; to be upon many parts of the coast almost at the same time;—often the richest freight will be discharged upon a Jersey shore,[9]—to be your own telegraph, unweariedly sweeping the horizon, speaking all passing vessels bound coastwise; to keep up a steady despatch of commodities, for the supply of such a distant and exorbitant market; to keep yourself informed of the state of the markets, prospects of war and peace every where, and anticipate the tendencies of trade and civilization,—taking advantage of the results of all exploring expeditions, using new passages and all improvements in navigation;—charts to be studied, the position of reefs and new lights and buoys to be ascertained, and ever, and ever, the logarithmic tables to be corrected, for by the error of some calculator the vessel often splits upon a rock that should have reached a friendly pier,— there is the untold fate of La Perouse;—universal science to be kept pace with, studying the lives of all great discoverers and navigators, great adventurers and merchants from Hanno[1] and the Phœnicians down to our day; in fine, account of stock to be taken from time to time, to know how you stand. It is a labor to task the faculties of a man,—such problems of profit and loss, of interest, of tare and tret,[2] and gauging of all kinds in it, as demand a universal knowledge.

I have thought that Walden Pond would be a good place for business, not solely on account of the railroad and the ice trade; it offers advantages which it may not be good policy to divulge; it is a good port and a good foundation. No Neva marshes to be filled; though you must every where build on piles of your own driving. It is said that a flood-tide, with a westerly wind, and ice in the Neva, would sweep St. Petersburg from the face of the earth.

As this business was to be entered into without the usual capital, it may not be easy to conjecture where those means, that will still be indispensable to every such undertaking, were to be obtained. As for Clothing, to come at once to the practical part of the question, perhaps we are led oftener by the love of novelty, and a regard for the opinions of men, in procuring it, than by a true utility. Let him who has work to do recollect that the object of clothing is, first, to retain the vital heat, and secondly, in this state of society, to cover nakedness, and he may judge how much of any necessary or important work may be accomplished without adding to his wardrobe. Kings and queens who wear a suit but once, though made by some tailor or dress-maker to their majesties, cannot know the comfort of wearing a suit that fits. They are no better than wooden horses to hang the clean clothes on. Every day our garments become more assimilated to ourselves, receiving the impress of the wearer's character, until we hesitate to lay them aside, without such delay and medical appliances and some such solemnity even as our bodies. No man ever

9. I.e., by shipwreck on the way to New York.
1. Carthaginian navigator (6th–5th centuries B.C.), credited with opening the coast of west Africa to trade. Jean François de Galaup (1741–1788), French explorer of the western Pacific.

2. An allowance to the purchase for waste or refuse in certain materials, 4 pounds being thrown in for every 104 pounds of suttle weight, or weight after the "tare" (the weight of the vehicle or smaller container) is deducted.

stood the lower in my estimation for having a patch in his clothes; yet I am sure that there is greater anxiety, commonly, to have fashionable, or at least clean and unpatched clothes, than to have a sound conscience. But even if the rent is not mended, perhaps the worst vice betrayed is improvidence. I sometimes try my acquaintances by such tests as this;—who could wear a patch, or two extra seams only, over the knee? Most behave as if they believed that their prospects for life would be ruined if they should do it. It would be easier for them to hobble to town with a broken leg than with a broken pantaloon. Often if an accident happens to a gentleman's legs, they can be mended; but if a similar accident happens to the legs of his pantaloons, there is no help for it; for he considers, not what is truly respectable, but what is respected. We know but few men, a great many coats and breeches. Dress a scarecrow in your last shift, you standing shiftless by, who would not soonest salute the scarecrow? Passing a cornfield the other day, close by a hat and coat on a stake, I recognized the owner of the farm. He was only a little more weather-beaten than when I saw him last. I have heard of a dog that barked at every stranger who approached his master's premises with clothes on, but was easily quieted by a naked thief. It is an interesting question how far men would retain their relative rank if they were divested of their clothes. Could you, in such a case, tell surely of any company of civilized men, which belonged to the most respected class? When Madam Pfeiffer, in her adventurous travels round the world, from east to west, had got so near home as Asiatic Russia, she says that she felt the necessity of wearing other than a travelling dress, when she went to meet the authorities, for she "was now in a civilized country, where —— –people are judged of by their clothes."[3] Even in our democratic New England towns the accidental possession of wealth, and its manifestation in dress and equipage alone, obtain for the possessor almost universal respect. But they who yield such respect, numerous as they are, are so far heathen, and need to have a missionary sent to them. Beside, clothes introduced sewing, a kind of work which you may call endless; a woman's dress, at least, is never done.[4]

A man who has at length found something to do will not need to get a new suit to do it in; for him the old will do, that has lain dusty in the garret for an indeterminate period. Old shoes will serve a hero longer than they have served his valet,—if a hero ever has a valet,—bare feet are older than shoes, and he can make them do. Only they who go to soirées and legislative halls must have new coats, coats to change as often as the man changes in them. But if my jacket and trousers, my hat and shoes, are fit to worship God in, they will do; will they not? Who ever saw his old clothes,—his old coat, actually worn out, resolved into its primitive elements, so that it was not a deed of charity to bestow it on some poor boy, by him perchance to be bestowed on some poorer still, or shall we say richer, who could do with less? I say, beware of all enterprises that require new clothes, and not rather a new wearer of clothes. If there is not a new man, how can the new clothes be made to fit? If you have any enterprise before you, try it in your old clothes. All men want, not something to *do with*, but something to *do*, or rather something to *be*. Perhaps we should never procure a new suit, however ragged or dirty the old, until we have so conducted, so enterprised or sailed in some way, that we feel like new men in

3. Ida Pfeiffer (1797–1858), A *Lady's Voyage round the World* (1852).

4. A play on the saying "Man may work from sun to sun, / But woman's work is never done."

the old, and that to retain it would be like keeping new wine in old bottles.[5] Our moulting season, like that of the fowls, must be a crisis in our lives. The loon retires to solitary ponds to spend it. Thus also the snake casts its slough, and the caterpillar its wormy coat, by an internal industry and expansion; for clothes are but our outmost cuticle and mortal coil. Otherwise we shall be found sailing under false colors, and be inevitably cashiered[6] at last by our own opinion, as well as that of mankind.

We don garment after garment, as if we grew like exogenous plants by addition without. Our outside and often thin and fanciful clothes are our epidermis or false skin, which partakes not of our life, and may be stripped off here and there without fatal injury; our thicker garments, constantly worn, are our cellular integument, or cortex; but our shirts are our liber[7] or true bark, which cannot be removed without girdling and so destroying the man. I believe that all races at some seasons wear something equivalent to the shirt. It is desirable that a man be clad so simply that he can lay his hands on himself in the dark, and that he live in all respects so compactly and preparedly, that, if an enemy take the town, he can, like the old philosopher, walk out the gate emptyhanded without anxiety. While one thick garment is, for most purposes, as good as three thin ones, and cheap clothing can be obtained at prices really to suit customers; while a thick coat can be bought for five dollars, which will last as many years, thick pantaloons for two dollars, cowhide boots for a dollar and a half a pair, a summer hat for a quarter of a dollar, and a winter cap for sixty-two and a half cents, or a better be made at home at a nominal cost, where is he so poor that, clad in such a suit, *of his own earning*, there will not be found wise men to do him reverence?

When I ask for a garment of a particular form, my tailoress tells me gravely, "They do not make them so now," not emphasizing the "They" at all, as if she quoted an authority as impersonal as the Fates, and I find it difficult to get made what I want, simply because she cannot believe that I mean what I say, that I am so rash. When I hear this oracular sentence, I am for a moment absorbed in thought, emphasizing to myself each word separately that I may come at the meaning of it, that I may find out by what degree of consanguinity *They* are related to *me*, and what authority they may have in an affair which affects me so nearly; and, finally, I am inclined to answer her with equal mystery, and without any more emphasis of the "they,"—"It is true, they did not make them so recently, but they do now." Of what use this measuring of me if she does not measure my character, but only the breadth of my shoulders, as it were a peg to hang the coat on? We worship not the Graces, nor the Parcæ,[8] but Fashion. She spins and weaves and cuts with full authority. The head monkey at Paris puts on a traveller's cap, and all the monkeys in America do the same. I sometimes despair of getting any thing quite simple and honest done in this world by the help of men. They would have to be passed through a powerful press first, to squeeze their old notions out of them, so that they would not soon get upon their legs again, and then there would be some one in the company with a maggot in his head, hatched from an egg deposited there nobody knows when, for not even fire kills these things, and you would

5. "Neither do men put new wine into old bottles: else the bottles break, and the wine runneth out, and the bottles perish: but they put new wine into new bottles, and both are preserved" (Matthew 9.17).

6. Fired.
7. Inner bark.
8. In Roman mythology, the three Fates.

have lost your labor. Nevertheless, we will not forget that some Egyptian wheat is said to have been handed down to us by a mummy.

On the whole, I think that it cannot be maintained that dressing has in this or any country risen to the dignity of an art. At present men make shift to wear what they can get. Like shipwrecked sailors, they put on what they can find on the beach, and at a little distance, whether of space or time, laugh at each other's masquerade. Every generation laighs at the old fashions, but follows religiously the new. We are amused at beholding the costume of Henry VIII., or Queen Elizabeth, as much as if it was that of the King and Queen of the Cannibal Islands. All costume off a man is pitiful or grotesque. It is only the serious eye peering from and the sincere life passed within it, which restrain laughter and consecrate the costume of any people. Let Harlequin[9] be taken with a fit of the colic and his trappings will have to serve that mood too. When the soldier is hit by a cannon ball rags are as becoming as purple.

The childish and savage taste of men and women for new patterns keeps how many shaking and squinting through kaleidoscopes that they may discover the particular figure which this generation requires to-day. The manufacturers have learned that this taste is merely whimsical. Of two patterns which differ only by a few threads more or less of a particular color, the one will be sold readily, the other lie on the shelf, though it frequently happens that after the lapse of a season the latter becomes the most fashionable. Comparatively, tattooing is not the hideous custom which it is called. It is not barbarous merely because the printing is skin-deep and unalterable.

I cannot believe that our factory system is the best mode by which men may get clothing. The condition of the operatives is becoming every day more like that of the English; and it cannot be wondered at, since, as far as I have heard or observed, the principal object is, not that mankind may be well and honestly clad, but, unquestionably, that the corporations may be enriched. In the long run men hit only what they aim at. Therefore, though they should fail immediately, they had better aim at something high.

As for a Shelter, I will not deny that this is now a necessary of life, though there are instances of men having done without it for long periods in colder countries than this. Samuel Laing says that "The Laplander in his skin dress, and in a skin bag which he puts over his head and shoulders, will sleep night after night on the snow—in a degree of cold which would extinguish the life of one exposed to it in any woollen clothing." He had seen them asleep thus. Yet he adds, "They are not hardier than other people."[1] But, probably, man did not live long on the earth without discovering the convenience which there is in a house, the domestic comforts, which phrase may have originally signified the satisfactions of the house more than of the family; though these must be extremely partial and occasional in those climates where the house is associated in our thoughts with winter or the rainy season chiefly, and two thirds of the year, except for a parasol, is unnecessary. In our climate, in the summer, it was formerly almost solely a covering at night. In the Indian gazettes[2] a wigwam was the symbol of a day's march, and a row of them cut or painted on the bark of a tree signified that so many times they had camped. Man was

9. A type of comic servant in *commedia dell'arte*, dressed in mask and many-colored tights.
1. *Journal of a Residence in Norway* (1837).

2. In American Indian sign language (in messages equivalent to gazettes or newspapers).

not made so large limbed and robust but that he must seek to narrow his world, and wall in a space such as fitted him. He was at first bare and out of doors; but though this was pleasant enough in serene and warm weather, by daylight, the rainy season and the winter, to say nothing of the torrid sun, would perhaps have nipped his race in the bud if he had not made haste to clothe himself with the shelter of a house. Adam and Eve, according to a fable, wore the bower before other clothes. Man wanted a home, a place of warmth, or comfort, first of physical warmth, then the warmth of the affections.

We may imagine a time when, in the infancy of the human race, some enterprising mortal crept into a hollow in a rock for shelter. Every child begins the world again, to some extent, and loves to stay out doors, even in wet and cold. It plays house, as well as horse, having an instinct for it. Who does not remember the interest with which when young he looked at shelving rocks, or any approach to a cave? It was the natural yearning of that portion of our most primitive ancestor which still survived in us. From the cave we have advanced to roofs of palm leaves, of bark and boughs, of linen woven and stretched, of grass and straw, of boards and shingles, of stones and tiles. At last, we know not what it is to live in the open air, and our lives are domestic in more senses than we think. From the hearth to the field is a great distance. It would be well perhaps if we were to spend more of our days and nights without any obstruction between us and the celestial bodies, if the poet did not speak so much from under a roof, or the saint dwell there so long. Birds do not sing in caves, nor do doves cherish their innocence in dovecots.

However, if one designs to construct a dwelling house, it behooves him to exercise a little Yankee shrewdness, lest after all he find himself in a work-house, a labyrinth without a clew, a museum, an almshouse, a prison, or a splendid mausoleum instead. Consider first how slight a shelter is absolutely necessary. I have seen Penobscot Indians, in this town, living in tents of thin cotton cloth, while the snow was nearly a foot deep around them, and I thought that they would be glad to have it deeper to keep out the wind. Formerly, when how to get my living honestly, with freedom left for my proper pursuits, was a question which vexed me even more than it does now, for unfortunately I am become somewhat callous, I used to see a large box by the railroad, six feet long by three wide, in which the laborers locked up their tools at night, and it suggested to me that every man who was hard pushed might get such a one for a dollar, and, having bored a few auger holes in it, to admit the air at least, get into it when it rained and at night, and hook down the lid, and so have freedom in his love, and in his soul be free. This did not appear the worst, nor by any means a despicable alternative. You could sit up as late as you pleased, and, whenever you got up, go abroad without any landlord or house-lord dogging you for rent. Many a man is harassed to death to pay the rent of a larger and more luxurious box who would not have frozen to death in such a box as this. I am far from jesting. Economy is a subject which admits of being treated with levity, but it cannot so be disposed of. A comfortable house for a rude and hardy race, that lived mostly out of doors, was once made here almost entirely of such materials as Nature furnished ready to their hands. Gookin, who was superintendent of the Indians subject to the Massachusetts Colony, writing in 1674, says, "The best of their houses are covered very neatly, tight and warm, with barks of trees, slipped from their bodies at those seasons when the sap is up, and made into great flakes, with pressure of weighty timber, when they are green. . . . The meaner sort are covered with mats which they make of a kind of bulrush, and are also indifferently tight and warm, but not so good as the former. . . . Some I have seen, sixty or a hundred feet long and thirty feet broad. . . . I have often lodged in their wigwams, and found them as warm as the best English houses."[3] He adds, that they were commonly carpeted and lined within with well-wrought embroidered mats, and were furnished with various utensils. The Indians had advanced so far as to regulate the effect of the wind by a mat suspended over the hole in the roof and moved by a string. Such a lodge was in the first instance constructed in a day or two at most, and taken down and put up in a few hours; and every family owned one, or its apartment in one.

In the savage state every family owns a shelter as good as the best, and sufficient for its coarser and simpler wants; but I think that I speak within bounds when I say that, though the birds of the air have their nests, and the foxes their holes,[4] and the savages their wigwams, in modern civilized society not more than one half the families own a shelter. In the large towns and cities, where civilization especially prevails, the number of those who own a shelter is a very small fraction of the whole. The rest pay an annual tax for this outside garment of all, become indispensable summer and winter, which would buy a village of Indian wigwams, but now helps to keep them poor as long as they live. I do not mean to insist here on the disadvantage of hiring compared with owning, but it is evident that the savage owns his shelter because it costs so little, while the civilized man hires his commonly because he cannot afford to own it; nor can he, in the long run, any better afford to hire. But, answers one, by merely paying this tax the poor civilized man secures an abode which is a palace compared with the savage's. An annual rent of from twenty-five to a hundred dollars, these are the country rates, entitles him to the benefit of the improvements of centuries, spacious apartments, clean paint and paper, Rumford fireplace,[5] back plastering, Venetian blinds, copper pump, spring lock, a commodious cellar, and many other things. But how happens it that he who is said to enjoy these things is so commonly a *poor* civilized man, while the savage, who has them not, is rich as a savage? If it is asserted that civilization is a real advance in the condition of man,—and I think that it is, though only the wise improve their advantages,—it must be shown that it has produced better dwellings without making them more costly; and the cost of a thing is the amount of what I will call life which is required to be exchanged for it, immediately or in the long run. An average house in this neighborhood costs perhaps eight hundred dollars, and to lay up this sum will take from ten to fifteen years of the laborer's life, even if he is not encumbered with a family;—estimating the pecuniary value of every man's labor at one dollar a day, for if some receive more, others receive less;—so that he must have spent more than half his life commonly before *his* wigwam will be earned. If we suppose him to pay a rent instead, this is but a doubtful choice of evils. Would the savage have been wise to exchange his wigwam for a palace on these terms?

It may be guessed that I reduce almost the whole advantage of holding this

3. Daniel Gookin, *Historical Collections of the Indians in New England* (1792).
4. "The foxes have holes, and the birds of the air have nests; but the Son of man hath not where to lay his head" (Matthew 8.20).

5. Benjamin Thompson, Count Rumford (1753–1814), devised a shelf inside the chimney to prevent smoke from being carried back into a room by downdrafts.

superfluous property as a fund in store against the future, so far as the individual is concerned, mainly to the defraying of funeral expenses. But perhaps a man is not required to bury himself. Nevertheless this points to an important distinction between the civilized man and the savage; and, no doubt, they have designs on us for our benefit, in making the life of a civilized people an *institution*, in which the life of the individual is to a great extent absorbed, in order to preserve and perfect that of the race. But I wish to show at what a sacrifice this advantage is at present obtained, and to suggest that we may possibly so live as to secure all the advantage without suffering any of the disadvantage. What mean ye by saying that the poor ye have always with you, or that the fathers have eaten sour grapes, and the children's teeth are set on edge?[6]

"As I live, saith the Lord God, ye shall not have occasion any more to use this proverb in Israel."

"Behold all souls are mine; as the soul of the father, so also the soul of the son is mine: the soul that sinneth it shall die."[7]

When I consider my neighbors, the farmers of Concord, who are at least as well off as the other classes, I find that for the most part they have been toiling twenty, thirty, or forty years, that they may become the real owners of their farms, which commonly they have inherited with encumbrances, or else bought with hired money,—and we may regard one third of that toil as the cost of their houses,—but commonly they have not paid for them yet. It is true, the encumbrances sometimes outweigh the value of the farm, so that the farm itself becomes one great encumbrance, and still a man is found to inherit it, being well acquainted with it, as he says. On applying to the assessors, I am surprised to learn that they cannot at once name a dozen in the town who own their farms free and clear. If you would know the history of these homesteads, inquire at the bank where they are mortgaged. The man who has actually paid for his farm with labor on it is so rare that every neighbor can point to him. I doubt if there are three such men in Concord. What has been said of the merchants, that a very large majority, even ninety-seven in a hundred, are sure to fail, is equally true of the farmers. With regard to the merchants, however, one of them says pertinently that a great part of their failures are not genuine pecuniary failures, but merely failures to fulfil their engagements, because it is inconvenient; that is, it is the moral character that breaks down. But this puts an infinitely worse face on the matter, and suggests, beside, that probably not even the other three succeed in saving their souls, but are perchance bankrupt in a worse sense than they who fail honestly. Bankruptcy and repudiation are the spring-boards from which much of our civilization vaults and turns its somersets, but the savage stands on the unelastic plank of famine. Yet the Middlesex Cattle Show goes off here with *éclat* annually, as if all the joints of the agricultural machine were suent.[8]

The farmer is endeavoring to solve the problem of a livelihood by a formula more complicated than the problem itself. To get his shoestrings he speculates

---

6. Thoreau is repudiating Jesus' words to his disciples "For ye have the poor always with you; but me ye have not always" (Matthew 26.11) by combining it with God's reproof to Ezekiel for employing a negatively deterministic proverb: "What mean ye, that ye use this proverb concerning the land of Israel, saying, The fathers have eaten sour grapes, and the children's teeth are set on edge?" (Ezekiel 18.2).
7. These two verses are Ezekiel 18.3–4, but Thoreau so truncates the passage that the reader may find it hard to understand that the biblical intent (as well as Thoreau's own) is optimistic, to reject the notion that the sins of the fathers are visited unto their children.
8. In good working order, broken in.

in herds of cattle. With consummate skill he has set his trap with a hair spring to catch comfort and independence, and then, as he turned away, got his own leg into it. This is the reason he is poor; and for a similar reason we are all poor in respect to a thousand savage comforts, though surrounded by luxuries. As Chapman[9] sings,—

> "The false society of men—
> —for earthly greatness
> All heavenly comforts rarefies to air."

And when the farmer has got his house, he may not be the richer but the poorer for it, and it be the house that has got him. As I understand it, that was a valid objection urged by Momus[1] against the house which Minerva made, that she "had not made it movable, by which means a bad neighborhood might be avoided;" and it may still be urged, for our houses are such unwieldy property that we are often imprisoned rather than housed in them; and the bad neighborhood to be avoided is our own scurvy selves. I know one or two families, at least, in this town, who, for nearly a generation, have been wishing to sell their houses in the outskirts and move into the village, but have not been able to accomplish it, and only death will set them free.

Granted that the *majority* are able at last either to own or hire the modern house with all its improvements. While civilization has been improving our houses, it has not equally improved the men who are to inhabit them. It has created palaces, but it was not so easy to create noblemen and kings. And *if the civilized man's pursuits are no worthier than the savage's, if he is employed the greater part of his life in obtaining gross necessaries and comforts merely, why should he have a better dwelling than the former?*

But how do the poor *minority* fare? Perhaps it will be found, that just in proportion as some have been placed in outward circumstances above the savage, others have been degraded below him. The luxury of one class is counterbalanced by the indigence of another. On the one side is the palace, on the other are the almshouse and "silent poor."[2] The myriads who built the pyramids to be the tombs of the Pharaohs were fed on garlic, and it may be were not decently buried themselves. The mason who finishes the cornice of the palace returns at night perchance to a hut not so good as a wigwam. It is a mistake to suppose that, in a country where the usual evidences of civilization exist, the condition of a very large body of the inhabitants may not be as degraded as that of savages. I refer to the degraded poor, not now to the degraded rich. To know this I should not need to look farther than to the shanties which every where border our railroads, that last improvement in civilization; where I see in my daily walks human beings living in sties, and all winter with an open door, for the sake of light, without any visible, often imaginable, wood pile, and the forms of both old and young are permanently contracted by the long habit of shrinking from cold and misery, and the development of all their limbs and faculties is checked. It certainly is fair to look at that class by whose labor the works which distinguish the generation are accomplished. Such too, to a greater or less extent, is the condition of the operatives of every denomination in England, which is the great workhouse of

9. George Chapman (1559?–1634), *Caesar and Pompey* 5.2.
1. In Greek mythology, the god of pleasantry but also of carping criticism.

2. Harding identifies these as the poor of Concord who received public charity secretly to retain their dwellings and not go to the poorhouse.

the world. Or I could refer you to Ireland, which is marked as one of the white or enlightened spots on the map.[3] Contrast the physical condition of the Irish with that of the North American Indian, or the South Sea Islander, or any other savage race before it was degraded by contact with the civilized man. Yet I have no doubt that that people's rulers are as wise as the average of civilized rulers. Their condition only proves what squalidness may consist with civilization. I hardly need refer now to the laborers in our Southern States who produce the staple exports of this country, and are themselves a staple production of the South.[4] But to confine myself to those who are said to be in *moderate* circumstances.

Most men appear never to have considered what a house is, and are actually though needlessly poor all their lives because they think that they must have such a one as their neighbors have. As if one were to wear any sort of coat which the tailor might cut out for him, or, gradually leaving off palmleaf hat or cap of woodchuck skin, complain of hard times because he could not afford to buy him a crown! It is possible to invent a house still more convenient and luxurious than we have, which yet all would admit that man could not afford to pay for. Shall we always study to obtain more of these things, and not sometimes to be content with less? Shall the respectable citizen thus gravely teach, by precept and example, the necessity of the young man's providing a certain number of superfluous glow-shoes,[5] and umbrellas, and empty guest chambers for empty guests, before he dies? Why should not our furniture be as simple as the Arab's or the Indian's? When I think of the benefactors of the race, whom we have apotheosized as messengers from heaven, bearers of divine gifts to man, I do not see in my mind any retinue at their heels, any car-load of fashionable furniture. Or what if I were to allow—would it not be a singular allowance?—that our furniture should be more complex than the Arab's, in proportion as we are morally and intellectually his superiors! At present our houses are cluttered and defiled with it, and a good housewife would sweep out the greater part into the dust hole, and not leave her morning's work undone. Morning work! By the blushes of Aurora and the music of Memnon,[6] what should be man's *morning work* in this world? I had three pieces of limestone on my desk, but I was terrified to find that they required to be dusted daily, when the furniture of my mind was all undusted still, and I threw them out the window in disgust. How, then, could I have a furnished house? I would rather sit in the open air, for no dust gathers on the grass, unless where man has broken ground.

It is the luxurious and dissipated who set the fashions which the herd so diligently follow. The traveller who stops at the best houses, so called, soon discovers this, for the publicans presume him to be a Sardanapalus,[7] and if he resigned himself to their tender mercies he would soon be completely emasculated. I think that in the railroad car we are inclined to spend more on luxury than on safety and convenience, and it threatens without attaining these to become no better than a modern drawing room, with its divans, and ottomans,

---

3. Thoreau refers to the habit some cartographers had of leaving unexplored terrain in a dark color; other cartographers left unexplored areas white.
4. The accusation, denied by many historians, that some plantations, especially in Virginia, were run for the sole purpose of breeding slave children for sale.
5. Galoshes.

6. The Roman goddess of the dawn and her son, an Ethiopian prince who fought for Priam at Troy. Memnon is associated here with the Egyptian colossus near Thebes that in ancient times emitted a sound at dawn, presumably because of the warming of air currents.
7. Effeminate ruler of Assyria (9th century B.C.).

and sunshades, and a hundred other oriental things, which we are taking west with us, invented for the ladies of the harem and the effeminate natives of the Celestial Empire, which Jonathan[8] should be ashamed to know the names of. I would rather sit on a pumpkin and have it all to myself, than be crowded on a velvet cushion. I would rather ride on earth in an ox cart with a free circulation, than go to heaven in the fancy car of an excursion train and breathe a *malaria* all the way.

The very simplicity and nakedness of man's life in the primitive ages imply this advantage at least, that they left him still but a sojourner in nature. When he was refreshed with food and sleep he contemplated his journey again. He dwelt, as it were, in a tent in this world, and was either threading the valleys, or crossing the plains, or climbing the mountain tops. But lo! men have become the tools of their tools. The man who independently plucked the fruits when he was hungry is become a farmer; and he who stood under a tree for shelter, a housekeeper. We now no longer camp as for a night, but have settled down on earth and forgotten heaven. We have adopted Christianity merely as an improved method of *agri*-culture. We have built for this world a family mansion, and for the next a family tomb. The best works of art are the expression of man's struggle to free himself from this condition, but the effect of our art is merely to make this low state comfortable and that higher state to be forgotten. There is actually no place in this village for a work of *fine* art, if any had come down to us, to stand, for our lives, our houses and streets, furnish no proper pedestal for it. There is not a nail to hang a picture on, nor a shelf to receive the bust of a hero or a saint. When I consider how our houses are built and paid for, or not paid for, and their internal economy managed and sustained, I wonder that the floor does not give way under the visitor while he is admiring the gewgaws upon the mantel-piece, and let him through into the cellar, to some solid and honest though earthy foundation. I cannot but perceive that this so called rich and refined life is a thing jumped at, and I do not get on in the enjoyment of the *fine* arts which adorn it, my attention being wholly occupied with the jump; for I remember that the greatest genuine leap, due to human muscles alone, on record, is that of certain wandering Arabs, who are said to have cleared twenty-five feet on level ground. Without factitious support, man is sure to come to earth again beyond that distance. The first question which I am tempted to put to the proprietor of such great impropriety is, Who bolsters you? Are you one of the ninety-seven who fail? or of the three who succeed? Answer me these questions, and then perhaps I may look at your bawbles and find them ornamental. The cart before the horse is neither beautiful nor useful. Before we can adorn our houses with beautiful objects the walls must be stripped, and our lives must be stripped, and beautiful housekeeping and beautiful living be laid for a foundation: now, a taste for the beautiful is most cultivated out of doors, where there is no house and no housekeeper.

Old Johnson, in his "Wonder-Working Providence," speaking of the first settlers of this town, with whom he was contemporary, tells us that "they burrow themselves in the earth for their first shelter under some hillside, and, casting the soil aloft upon timber, they make a smoky fire against the earth, at the highest side." They did not "provide them houses," says he, "till the earth,

8. A type name at first applied to New Englanders, then later (as here) to the inhabitants of the entire United States.

by the Lord's blessing, brought forth bread to feed them," and the first year's crop was so light that "they were forced to cut their bread very thin for a long season."[9] The secretary of the Province of New Netherland, writing in Dutch, in 1650, for the information of those who wished to take up land there, states more particularly, that "those in New Netherland, and especially in New England, who have no means to build farm houses at first according to their wishes, dig a square pit in the ground, cellar fashion, six or seven feet deep, as long and as broad as they think proper, case the earth inside with wood all round the wall, and line the wood with the bark of trees or something else to prevent the caving in of the earth; floor this cellar with plank, and wainscot it overhead for a ceiling, raise a roof of spars clear up, and cover the spars with bark or green sods, so that they can live dry and warm in these houses with their entire families for two, three, and four years, it being understood that partitions are run through those cellars which are adapted to the size of the family. The wealthy and principal men in New England, in the beginning of the colonies, commenced their first dwelling houses in this fashion for two reasons; firstly, in order not to waste time in building, and not to want food the next season; secondly, in order not to discourage poor laboring people whom they brought over in numbers from Fatherland. In the course of three or four years, when the country became adapted to agriculture, they built themselves handsome houses, spending on them several thousands."[1]

In this course which our ancestors took there was a show of prudence at least, as if their principle were to satisfy the more pressing wants first. But are the more pressing wants satisfied now? When I think of acquiring for myself one of our luxurious dwellings, I am deterred, for, so to speak, the country is not yet adapted to *human* culture, and we are still forced to cut our *spiritual* bread far thinner than our forefathers did their wheaten. Not that all architectural ornament is to be neglected even in the rudest periods; but let our houses first be lined with beauty, where they come in contact with our lives, like the tenement of the shellfish, and not overlaid with it. But, alas! I have been inside one or two of them, and know what they are lined with.

Though we are not so degenerate but that we might possibly live in a cave or a wigwam or wear skins to-day, it certainly is better to accept the advantages, though so dearly bought, which the invention and industry of mankind offer. In such a neighborhood as this, boards and shingles, lime and bricks, are cheaper and more easily obtained than suitable caves, or whole logs, or bark in sufficient quantities, or even well-tempered clay or flat stones. I speak understandingly on this subject, for I have made myself acquainted with it both theoretically and practically. With a little more wit we might use these materials so as to become richer than the richest now are, and make our civilization a blessing. The civilized man is a more experienced and wiser savage. But to make haste to my own experiment.

Near the end of March, 1845, I borrowed an axe and went down to the woods by Walden Pond, nearest to where I intended to build my house, and began to cut down some tall arrowy white pines, still in their youth, for timber. It is difficult to begin without borrowing, but perhaps it is the most generous course thus to permit your fellow-men to have an interest in your enterprise.

9. Edward Johnson, *Wonder-working Providence of Sion's Saviour in New England* (1654).

1. Edmund Bailey O'Callaghan, *Documentary History of the State of New-York* (1851).

The owner of the axe, as he released his hold on it, said that it was the apple of his eye; but I returned it sharper than I received it. It was a pleasant hillside where I worked, covered with pine woods, through which I looked out on the pond, and a small open field in the woods where pines and hickories were springing up. The ice in the pond was not yet dissolved, though there were some open spaces, and it was all dark colored and saturated with water. There were some slight flurries of snow during the days that I worked there; but for the most part when I came out on to the railroad, on my way home, its yellow sand heap stretched away gleaming in the hazy atmosphere, and the rails shone in the spring sun, and I heard the lark and pewee and other birds already come to commence another year with us. They were pleasant spring days, in which the winter of man's discontent was thawing as well as the earth, and the life that had lain torpid began to stretch itself. One day, when my axe had come off and I had cut a green hickory for a wedge, driving it with a stone, and had placed the whole to soak in a pond hole in order to swell the wood, I saw a striped snake run into the water, and he lay on the bottom, apparently without inconvenience, as long as I staid there, or more than a quarter of an hour; perhaps because he had not yet fairly come out of the torpid state. It appeared to me that for a like reason men remain in their present low and primitive condition; but if they should feel the influence of the spring of springs arousing them, they would of necessity rise to a higher and more ethereal life. I had previously seen the snakes in frosty mornings in my path with portions of their bodies still numb and inflexible, waiting for the sun to thaw them. On the 1st of April it rained and melted the ice, and in the early part of the day, which was very foggy, I heard a stray goose groping about over the pond and cackling as if lost, or like the spirit of the fog.

So I went on for some days cutting and hewing timber, and also studs and rafters, all with my narrow axe, not having many communicable or scholarlike thoughts, singing to myself,—

> Men say they know many things;
> But lo! they have taken wings,—
> The arts and sciences,
> And a thousand appliances;
> The wind that blows
> Is all that any body knows.[2]

I hewed the main timbers six inches square, most of the studs on two sides only, and the rafters and floor timbers on one side, leaving the rest of the bark on, so that they were just as straight and much stronger than sawed ones. Each stick was carefully mortised or tenoned by its stump, for I had borrowed other tools by this time. My days in the woods were not very long ones; yet I usually carried my dinner of bread and butter, and read the newspaper in which it was wrapped, at noon, sitting amid the green pine boughs which I had cut off, and to my bread was imparted some of their fragrance, for my hands were covered with a thick coat of pitch. Before I had done I was more the friend than the foe of the pine tree, though I had cut down some of them, having become better acquainted with it. Sometimes a rambler in the wood was attracted by the sound of my axe, and we chatted pleasantly over the chips which I had made.

2. Like other poems in *Walden* not enclosed in quotation marks, this poem is Thoreau's.

By the middle of April, for I made no haste in my work, but rather made the most of it, my house was framed and ready for the raising. I had already bought the shanty of James Collins, an Irishman who worked on the Fitchburg Railroad, for boards. James Collins' shanty was considered an uncommonly fine one. When I called to see it he was not at home. I walked about the outside, at first unobserved from within, the window was so deep and high. It was of small dimensions, with a peaked cottage roof, and not much else to be seen, the dirt being raised five feet all around as if it were a compost heap. The roof was the soundest part, though a good deal warped and made brittle by the sun. Door-sill there was none, but a perennial passage for the hens under the door board. Mrs. C. came to the door and asked me to view it from the inside. The hens were driven in by my approach. It was dark, and had a dirt floor for the most part, dank, clammy, and aguish, only here a board and there a board which would not bear removal. She lighted a lamp to show me the inside of the roof and the walls, and also that the board floor extended under the bed, warning me not to step into the cellar, a sort of dust hole two feet deep. In her own words, they were "good boards overhead, good boards all around, and a good window,"—of two whole squares originally, only the cat had passed out that way lately. There was a stove, a bed, and a place to sit, an infant in the house where it was born, a silk parasol, gilt-framed looking-glass, and a patent new coffee mill nailed to an oak sapling, all told. The bargain was soon concluded, for James had in the mean while returned. I to pay four dollars and twenty-five cents to-night, he to vacate at five to-morrow morning, selling to nobody else meanwhile: I to take possession at six. It were well, he said, to be there early, and anticipate certain indistinct but wholly unjust claims on the score of ground rent and fuel. This he assured me was the only encumbrance. At six I passed him and his family on the road. One large bundle held their all,—bed, coffee-mill, looking-glass, hens,—all but the cat, she took to the woods and became a wild cat, and, as I learned afterward, trod in a trap set for woodchucks, and so became a dead cat at last.

I took down this dwelling the same morning, drawing the nails, and removed it to the pond side by small cartloads, spreading the boards on the grass there to bleach and warp back again in the sun. One early thrush gave me a note or two as I drove along the woodland path. I was informed treacherously by a young Patrick that neighbor Seeley, an Irishman, in the intervals of the carting, transferred the still tolerable, straight, and drivable nails, staples, and spikes to his pocket, and then stood when I came back to pass the time of day, and look freshly up, unconcerned, with spring thoughts, at the devastation; there being a dearth of work, as he said. He was there to represent spectatordom, and help make this seemingly insignificant event one with the removal of the gods of Troy.[3]

I dug my cellar in the side of a hill sloping to the south, where a woodchuck had formerly dug his burrow, down through sumach and blackberry roots, and the lowest stain of vegetation, six feet square by seven deep, to a fine sand where potatoes would not freeze in any winter. The sides were left shelving, and not stoned; but the sun having never shone on them, the sand still keeps its place. It was but two hours' work. I took particular pleasure in this breaking of ground, for in almost all latitudes men dig into the earth for an equable

---

3. In Virgil's *Aeneid*, book 2, after the fall of Troy, Aeneas escapes with his father and son and his household gods.

temperature. Under the most splendid house in the city is still to be found the cellar where they store their roots as of old, and long after the superstructure has disappeared posterity remark its dent in the earth. The house is still but a sort of porch at the entrance of a burrow.

At length, in the beginning of May, with the help of some of my acquaintances, rather to improve so good an occasion for neighborliness than from any necessity, I set up the frame of my house. No man was ever more honored in the character of his raisers[4] than I. They are destined, I trust, to assist at the raising of loftier structures one day. I began to occupy my house on the 4th of July, as soon as it was boarded and roofed, for the boards were carefully feather-edged and lapped, so that it was perfectly impervious to rain;[5] but before boarding I laid the foundation of a chimney at one end, bringing two cartloads of stones up the hill from the pond in my arms. I built the chimney after my hoeing in the fall, before a fire became necessary for warmth, doing my cooking in the mean while out of doors on the ground, early in the morning: which mode I still think is in some respects more convenient and agreeable than the usual one. When it stormed before my bread was baked, I fixed a few boards over the fire, and sat under them to watch my loaf, and passed some pleasant hours in that way. In those days, when my hands were much employed, I read but little, but the least scraps of paper which lay on the ground, my holder, or table-cloth, afforded me as much entertainment, in fact answered the same purpose as the Iliad.[6]

It would be worth the while to build still more deliberately than I did, considering, for instance, what foundation a door, a window, a cellar, a garret, have in the nature of man, and perchance never raising any superstructure until we found a better reason for it than our temporal necessities even. There is some of the same fitness in a man's building his own house that there is in a bird's building its own nest. Who knows but if men constructed their dwellings with their own hands, and provided food for themselves and families simply and honestly enough, the poetic faculty would be universally developed, as birds universally sing when they are so engaged? But alas! we do like cowbirds and cuckoos, which lay their eggs in nests which other birds have built, and cheer no traveller with their chattering and unmusical notes. Shall we forever resign the pleasure of construction to the carpenter? What does architecture amount to in the experience of the mass of men? I never in all my walks came across a man engaged in so simple and natural an occupation as building his house. We belong to the community. It is not the tailor alone who is the ninth part of a man; it is as much the preacher, and the merchant, and the farmer. Where is this division of labor to end? and what object does it finally serve? No doubt another *may* also think for me; but it is not therefore desirable that he should do so to the exclusion of my thinking for myself.

True, there are architects so called in this country, and I have heard of one at least possessed with the idea of making architectural ornaments have a core of truth, a necessity, and hence a beauty, as if it were a revelation to him.[7] All

4. These "raisers" (a pun) included Emerson; Alcott; Ellery Channing; two young brothers who had studied at Brook Farm, Burrill and George William Curtis; and the Concord farmer Edmund Hosmer and his three sons.
5. I.e., on the boards to be nailed horizontally the top and bottom edges were cut at 45-degree angles and overlapped so as to shed rain.

6. Greek epic of the siege of Troy traditionally attributed to Homer.
7. The sculptor Horatio Greenough (1805–1852), whose theories Thoreau knew only imperfectly from a private letter of Greenough's to Emerson. The ideas attributed here are at variance with Greenough's published comments on architecture.

very well perhaps from his point of view, but only a little better than the common dilettantism. A sentimental reformer in architecture, he began at the cornice, not at the foundation. It was only how to put a core of truth within the ornaments, that every sugar plum in fact might have an almond or caraway seed in it,—though I hold that almonds are most wholesome without the sugar,—and not how the inhabitant, the indweller, might build truly within and without, and let the ornaments take care of themselves. What reasonable man ever supposed that ornaments were something outward and in the skin merely,—that the tortoise got his spotted shell, or the shellfish its mother-o'-pearl tints, by such a contract as the inhabitants of Broadway their Trinity Church? But a man has no more to do with the style of architecture of his house than a tortoise with that of its shell: nor need the soldier be so idle as to try to paint the precise *color* of his virtue on his standard. The enemy will find it out. He may turn pale when the trial comes. This man seemed to me to lean over the cornice and timidly whisper his half truth to the rude occupants who really knew it better than he. What of architectural beauty I now see, I know has gradually grown from within outward, out of the necessities and character of the indweller, who is the only builder,—out of some unconscious truthfulness, and nobleness, without ever a thought for the appearance; and whatever additional beauty of this kind is destined to be produced will be preceded by a like unconscious beauty of life. The most interesting dwellings in this country, as the painter knows, are the most unpretending, humble log huts and cottages of the poor commonly; it is the life of the inhabitants whose shells they are, and not any peculiarity in their surfaces merely, which makes them *picturesque*; and equally interesting will be the citizen's suburban box, when his life shall be as simple and as agreeable to the imagination, and there is as little straining after effect in the style of his dwelling. A great proportion of architectural ornaments are literally hollow, and a September gale would strip them off, like borrowed plumes, without injury to the substantials. They can do without *architecture* who have no olives nor wines in the cellar. What if an equal ado were made about the ornaments of style in literature, and the architects of our bibles spent as much time about their cornices as the architects of our churches do? So are made the *belles-lettres* and the *beaux-arts* and their professors. Much it concerns a man, forsooth, how a few sticks are slanted over him or under him, and what colors are daubed upon his box. It would signify somewhat, if, in any earnest sense, *he* slanted them and daubed it; but the spirit having departed out of the tenant, it is of a piece with constructing his own coffin,—the architecture of the grave, and "carpenter" is but another name for "coffin-maker." One man says, in his despair or indifference to life, take up a handful of the earth at your feet, and paint your house that color. Is he thinking of his last and narrow house? Toss up a copper for it as well. What an abundance of leisure he must have! Why do you take up a handful of dirt? Better paint your house your own complexion; let it turn pale or blush for you. An enterprise to improve the style of cottage architecture! When you have got my ornaments ready I will wear them.

Before winter I built a chimney, and shingled the sides of my house, which were already impervious to rain, with imperfect and sappy shingles made of the first slice of the log, whose edges I was obliged to straighten with a plane.

I have thus a tight shingled and plastered house, ten feet wide by fifteen long, and eight-feet posts, with a garret and a closet, a large window on each side, two trap doors, one door at the end, and a brick fireplace opposite. The exact cost of my house, paying the usual price for such materials as I used, but not counting the work, all of which was done by myself, was as follows; and I give the details because very few are able to tell exactly what their houses cost, and fewer still, if any, the separate cost of the various materials which compose them:—

Item	Cost	Note
Boards,	$8 03½	Mostly shanty boards
Refuse shingles for roof and sides,	4 00	
Laths,	1 25	
Two second-hand windows with glass,	2 43	
One thousand old brick,	4 00	
Two casks of lime,	2 40	That was high
Hair,	0 31	More than I needed
Mantle-tree iron,	0 15	
Nails,	3 90	
Hinges and screws,	0 14	
Latch,	0 10	
Chalk,	0 01	
Transportation,	1 40	I carried a good part on my back
In all,	$28 12½	

These are all the materials excepting the timber stones and sand, which I claimed by squatter's right. I have also a small wood-shed adjoining, made chiefly of the stuff which was left after building the house.

I intend to build me a house which will surpass any on the main street in Concord in grandeur and luxury, as soon as it pleases me as much and will cost me no more than my present one.

I thus found that the student who wishes for a shelter can obtain one for a lifetime at an expense not greater than the rent which he now pays annually. If I seem to boast more than is becoming, my excuse is that I brag for humanity rather than for myself; and my shortcomings and inconsistencies do not affect the truth of my statement. Notwithstanding much cant and hypocrisy,—chaff which I find it difficult to separate from my wheat, but for which I am as sorry as any man,—I will breathe freely and stretch myself in this respect, it is such a relief to both the moral and physical system; and I am resolved that I will not through humility become the devil's attorney. I will endeavor to speak a good word for the truth. At Cambridge College[8] the mere rent of a student's room, which is only a little larger than my own, is thirty dollars each year, though the corporation had the advantage of building thirty-two side by side and under one roof, and the occupant suffers the inconvenience of many and noisy neighbors, and perhaps a residence in the fourth story. I cannot but think that if we had more true wisdom in these respects, not only less education would be needed, because, forsooth, more would already have been acquired, but the pecuniary expense of getting an education would in a great measure vanish. Those conveniences which the student requires at Cambridge or elsewhere cost him or somebody else ten times as great a sacrifice of life as

8. Harvard University.

they would with proper management on both sides. Those things for which the most money is demanded are never the things which the student most wants. Tuition, for instance, is an important item in the term bill, while for the far more valuable education which he gets by associating with the most cultivated of his contemporaries no charge is made. The mode of founding a college is, commonly, to get up a subscription of dollars and cents, and then following blindly the principles of a division of labor to its extreme, a principle which should never be followed but with circumspection,—to call in a contractor who makes this a subject of speculation, and he employs Irishmen or other operatives actually to lay the foundations, while the students that are to be are said to be fitting themselves for it; and for these oversights successive generations have to pay. I think that it would be *better than this*, for the students, or those who desire to be benefited by it, even to lay the foundation themselves. The student who secures his coveted leisure and retirement by systematically shirking any labor necessary to man obtains but an ignoble and unprofitable leisure, defrauding himself of the experience which alone can make leisure fruitful. "But," says one, "you do not mean that the students should go to work with their hands instead of their heads?" I do not mean that exactly, but I mean something which he might think a good deal like that; I mean that they should not *play* life, or *study* it merely, while the community supports them at this expensive game, but earnestly *live* it from beginning to end. How could youths better learn to live than by at once trying the experiment of living? Methinks this would exercise their minds as much as mathematics. If I wished a boy to know something about the arts and sciences, for instance, I would not pursue the common course, which is merely to send him into the neighborhood of some professor, where any thing is professed and practised but the art of life;—to survey the world through a telescope or a microscope, and never with his natural eye; to study chemistry, and not learn how his bread is made, or mechanics, and not learn how it is earned; to discover new satellites to Neptune, and not detect the motes in his eyes, or to what vagabond he is a satellite himself; or to be devoured by the monsters that swarm all around him, while contemplating the monsters in a drop of vinegar. Which would have advanced the most at the end of the month,—the boy who had made his own jack-knife from the ore which he had dug and smelted, reading as much as would be necessary for this,—or the boy who had attended the lectures on metallurgy at the Institute in the mean while, and had received a Rodgers' penknife from his father? Which would be most likely to cut his fingers?—To my astonishment I was informed on leaving college that I had studied navigation!—why, if I had taken one turn down the harbor I should have known more about it. Even the *poor* student studies and is taught only *political* economy, while that economy of living which is synonymous with philosophy is not even sincerely professed in our colleges. The consequence is, that while he is reading Adam Smith, Ricardo, and Say,[9] he runs his father in debt irretrievably.

As with our colleges, so with a hundred "modern improvements"; there is an illusion about them; there is not always a positive advance. The devil goes on exacting compound interest to the last for his early share and numerous succeeding investments in them. Our inventions are wont to be pretty toys,

9. Three economists: the Scottish Adam Smith (1723–1790), the English David Ricardo (1772–1823), and the French Jean Baptiste Say (1767–1832).

which distract our attention from serious things. They are but improved means to an unimproved end, an end which it was already but too easy to arrive at; as railroads lead to Boston or New York. We are in great haste to construct a magnetic telegraph from Maine to Texas; but Maine and Texas, it may be, have nothing important to communicate. Either is in such a predicament as the man who was earnest to be introduced to a distinguished deaf woman, but when he was presented, and one end of her ear trumpet was put into his hand, had nothing to say. As if the main object were to talk fast and not to talk sensibly. We are eager to tunnel under the Atlantic and bring the old world some weeks nearer to the new; but perchance the first news that will leak through into the broad, flapping American ear will be that the Princess Adelaide has the whooping cough. After all, the man whose horse trots a mile in a minute does not carry the most important messages; he is not an evangelist, nor does he come round eating locusts and wild honey. I doubt if Flying Childers[1] ever carried a peck of corn to mill.

One says to me, "I wonder that you do not lay up money; you love to travel; you might take the cars and go to Fitchburg to-day and see the country." But I am wiser than that. I have learned that the swiftest traveller is he that goes afoot. I say to my friend, Suppose we try who will get there first. The distance is thirty miles; the fare ninety cents. That is almost a day's wages. I remember when wages were sixty cents a day for laborers on this very road. Well, I start now on foot, and get there before night; I have travelled at that rate by the week together. You will in the mean while have earned your fare, and arrive there some time to-morrow, or possibly this evening, if you are lucky enough to get a job in season. Instead of going to Fitchburg, you will be working here the greater part of the day. And so, if the railroad reached round the world, I think that I should keep ahead of you; and as for seeing the country and getting experience of that kind, I should have to cut your acquaintance altogether.

Such is the universal law, which no man can ever outwit, and with regard to the railroad even we may say it is as broad as it is long. To make a railroad round the world available to all mankind is equivalent to grading the whole surface of the planet. Men have an indistinct notion that if they keep up this activity of joint stocks and spades long enough all will at length ride somewhere, in next to no time, and for nothing; but though a crowd rushes to the depot, and the conductor shouts "All aboard!" when the smoke is blown away and the vapor condensed, it will be perceived that a few are riding, but the rest are run over,—and it will be called, and will be, "A melancholy accident." No doubt they can ride at last who shall have earned their fare, that is, if they survive so long, but they will probably have lost their elasticity and desire to travel by that time. This spending of the best part of one's life earning money in order to enjoy a questionable liberty during the least valuable part of it, reminds me of the Englishman who went to India to make a fortune first, in order that he might return to England and live the life of a poet. He should have gone up garret at once. "What!" exclaim a million Irishmen starting up from all the shanties in the land, "is not this railroad which we have built a good thing?" Yes, I answer, *comparatively* good, that is, you might have done worse; but I wish, as you are brothers of mine, that you could have spent your time better than digging in this dirt.

1. English racehorse.

Before I finished my house, wishing to earn ten or twelve dollars by some honest and agreeable method, in order to meet my unusual expenses, I planted about two acres and a half of light and sandy soil near it chiefly with beans, but also a small part with potatoes, corn, peas, and turnips. The whole lot contains eleven acres, mostly growing up to pines and hickories, and was sold the preceding season for eight dollars and eight cents an acre. One farmer said that it was "good for nothing but to raise cheeping squirrels on." I put no manure on this land, not being the owner, but merely a squatter, and not expecting to cultivate so much again, and I did not quite hoe it all once. I got out several cords of stumps in ploughing, which supplied me with fuel for a long time, and left small circles of virgin mould, easily distinguishable through the summer by the greater luxuriance of the beans there. The dead and for the most part unmerchantable wood behind my house, and the driftwood from the pond, have supplied the remainder of my fuel. I was obliged to hire a team and a man for the ploughing, though I held the plough myself. My farm outgoes for the first season were, for implements, seed, work, &c., $14 72½. The seed corn was given me. This never costs any thing to speak of, unless you plant more than enough. I got twelve bushels of beans, and eighteen bushels of potatoes, beside some peas and sweet corn. The yellow corn and formatn4turnips were too late to come to any thing. My whole income from the farm was

	$23 44.
Deducting the outgoes,	14 72½
there are left,	$ 8 71½,

beside produce consumed and on hand at the time this estimate was made of the value of $4 50,—the amount on hand much more than balancing a little grass which I did not raise. All things considered, that is, considering the importance of a man's soul and of to-day, notwithstanding the short time occupied by my experiment, nay, partly even because of its transient character, I believe that that was doing better than any farmer in Concord did that year.

The next year I did better still, for I spaded up all the land which I required, about a third of an acre, and I learned from the experience of both years, not being in the least awed by many celebrated works on husbandry, Arthur Young[2] among the rest, that if one would live simply and eat only the crop which he raised, and raise no more than he ate, and not exchange it for an insufficient quantity of more luxurious and expensive things, he would need to cultivate only a few rods of ground, and that it would be cheaper to spade up that than to use oxen to plough it, and to select a fresh spot from time to time than to manure the old, and he could do all his necessary farm work as it were with his left hand at odd hours in the summer; and thus he would not be tied to an ox, or horse, or cow, or pig, as at present. I desire to speak impartially on this point, and as one not interested in the success or failure of the present economical and social arrangements. I was more independent than any farmer in Concord, for I was not anchored to a house or farm, but could follow the bent of my genius, which is a very crooked one, every moment.

---

2. Author of *Rural Oeconomy, or Essays on the Practical Parts of Husbandry* (1773).

Beside being better off than they already, if my house had been burned or my crops had failed, I should have been nearly as well off as before.

I am wont to think that men are not so much the keepers of herds as herds are the keepers of men, the former are so much the freer. Men and oxen exchange work; but if we consider necessary work only, the oxen will be seen to have greatly the advantage, their farm is so much the larger. Man does some of his part of the exchange work in his six weeks of haying, and it is no boy's play. Certainly no nation that lived simply in all respects, that is, no nation of philosophers, would commit so great a blunder as to use the labor of animals. True, there never was and is not likely soon to be a nation of philosophers, nor am I certain it is desirable that there should be. However, I should never have broken a horse or bull and taken him to board for any work he might do for me, for fear I should become a horse-man or a herds-man merely; and if society seems to be the gainer by so doing, are we certain that what is one man's gain is not another's loss, and that the stable-boy has equal cause with his master to be satisfied? Granted that some public works would not have been constructed without this aid, and let man share the glory of such with the ox and horse; does is follow that he could not have accomplished works yet more worthy of himself in that case? When men begin to do, not merely unnecessary or artistic, but luxurious and idle work, with their assistance, it is inevitable that a few do all the exchange work with the oxen, or, in other words, become the slaves of the strongest. Man thus not only works for the animal within him, but, for a symbol of this, he works for the animal without him. Though we have many substantial houses of brick or stone, the prosperity of the farmer is still measured by the degree to which the barn overshadows the house. This town is said to have the largest houses for oxen cows and horses hereabouts, and it is not behindhand in its public buildings; but there are very few halls for free worship or free speech in this county. It should not be by their architecture, but why not even by their power of abstract thought, that nations should seek to commemorate themselves? How much more admirable the Bhagvat-Geeta[3] than all the ruins of the East! Towers and temples are the luxury of princes. A simple and independent mind does not toil at the bidding of any prince. Genius is not a retainer to any emperor, nor is its material silver, or gold, or marble, except to a trifling extent. To what end, pray, is so much stone hammered? In Arcadia,[4] when I was there, I did not see any hammering stone. Nations are possessed with an insane ambition to perpetuate the memory of themselves by the amount of hammered stone they leave. What if equal pains were taken to smooth and polish their manners? One piece of good sense would be more memorable than a monument as high as the moon. I love better to see stones in place. The grandeur of Thebes[5] was a vulgar grandeur. More sensible is a rod of stone wall that bounds an honest man's field than a hundred-gated Thebes that has wandered farther from the true end of life. The religion and civilization which are barbaric and heathenish build splendid temples; but what you might call Christianity does not. Most of the stone a nation hammers goes toward its tomb only. It buries itself alive. As for the Pyramids, there is nothing to wonder at in them so much as the fact that so many men could be found degraded enough to spend their lives constructing a tomb for some ambitious booby, whom it would have been

---

3. A sacred Hindu text.
4. Place epitomizing rustic simplicity and contentment, from the region in Greece celebrated by the bu-

colic poets.
5. Ancient city in Upper Egypt.

wiser and manlier to have drowned in the Nile, and then given his body to the dogs. I might possibly invent some excuse for them and him, but I have no time for it. As for the religion and love of art of the builders, it is much the same all the world over, whether the building be an Egyptian temple or the United States Bank. It costs more than it comes to. The mainspring is vanity, assisted by the love of garlic and bread and butter. Mr. Balcom, a promising young architect, designs it on the back of his Vitruvius,[6] with hard pencil and ruler, and the job is let out to Dobson & Sons, stonecutters. When the thirty centuries begin to look down on it, mankind begin to look up at it. As for your high towers and monuments, there was a crazy fellow once in this town who undertook to dig through to China, and he got so far that, as he said, he heard the Chinese pots and kettles rattle; but I think that I shall not go out of my way to admire the hole which he made. Many are concerned about the monuments of the West and the East,—to know who built them. For my part, I should like to know who in those days did not build them,—who were above such trifling. But to proceed with my statistics.

By surveying, carpentry, and day-labor of various other kinds in the village in the mean while, for I have as many trades as fingers, I had earned $13 34. The expense of food for eight months, namely, from July 4th to March 1st, the time when these estimates were made, though I lived there more than two years,—not counting potatoes, a little green corn, and some peas, which I had raised, nor considering the value of what was on hand at the last date, was

Rice,	01 73½	
Molasses,	1 73	Cheapest form of the saccharine.
Rye meal,	1 04¾	
Indian meal,	0 99¾	Cheaper than rye.
Pork,	0 22	
Flour,	0 88	Costs more than Indian meal, both money and trouble.
Sugar,	0 80	
Lard,	0 65	
Apples,	0 25	
Dried apple,	0 22	
Sweet potatoes,	0 10	
One pumpkin,	0 6	
One watermelon,	0 2	
Salt,	0 3	

All experiments which failed.

Yes, I did eat $8 74, all told; but I should not thus unblushingly publish my guilt, if I did not know that most of my readers were equally guilty with myself, and that their deeds would look no better in print. The next year I sometimes caught a mess of fish for my dinner, and once I went so far as to slaughter a woodchuck which ravaged my bean-field,—effect his transmigration, as a Tartar[7] would say,—and devour him, partly for experiment's sake; but though it afforded me a momentary enjoyment, notwithstanding a musky flavor, I saw

6. Vitruvius Pollio, Roman architect during the reigns of Julius Caesar and Augustus, author of *De Architectura*.

7. An inhabitant of Tartary, a broad area of Central Asia overrun by the Tatars (Tartars) in the 12th century.

that the longest use would not make that a good practice, however it might seem to have your woodchucks ready dressed by the village butcher.

Clothing and some incidental expenses within the same dates, though little can be inferred from this item, amounted to

$8 40¾

Oil and some household utensils, 2 00

So that all the pecuniary outgoes, excepting for washing and mending, which for the most part were done out of the house, and their bills have not yet been received,—and these are all and more than all the ways by which money necessarily goes out in this part of the world,—were

House,	$28 12½
Farm one year,	14 72½
Food eight months,	8 74
Clothing, &c., eight months,	8 40¾
Oil, &c., eight months,	2 00
In all,	$61 99¾

I address myself now to those of my readers who have a living to get. And to meet this I have for farm produce sold

	$23 44
Earned by day-labor,	13 34
In all,	$36 78,

which subtracted from the sum of the outgoes leaves a balance of $25 21¾ on the one side,—this being very nearly the means with which I started, and the measure of expenses to be incurred,—and on the other, beside the leisure and independence and health thus secured, a comfortable house for me as long as I choose to occupy it.

These statistics, however accidental and therefore uninstructive they may appear, as they have a certain completeness, have a certain value also. Nothing was given me of which I have not rendered some account. It appears from the above estimate, that my food alone cost me in money about twenty-seven cents a week. It was, for nearly two years after this, rye and Indian meal without yeast, potatoes, rice, a very little salt pork, molasses, and salt, and my drink water. It was fit that I should live on rice, mainly, who loved so well the philosophy of India. To meet the objections of some inveterate cavillers, I may as well state, that if I dined out occasionally, as I always had done, and I trust shall have opportunities to do again, it was frequently to the detriment of my domestic arrangements. But the dining out, being, as I have stated, a constant element, does not in the least affect a comparative statement like this.

I learned from my two years' experience that it would cost incredibly little trouble to obtain one's necessary food, even in this latitude; that a man may use as simple a diet as the animals, and yet retain health and strength. I have made a satisfactory dinner, satisfactory on several accounts, simply off a dish of purslane (*Portulaca oleracea*) which I gathered in my cornfield, boiled and salted. I give the Latin on account of the savoriness of the trivial name. And pray what more can a reasonable man desire, in peaceful times, in ordinary noons, than a sufficient number of ears of green sweet-corn boiled, with the addition of salt? Even the little variety which I used was a yielding to the demands of appetite, and not of health. Yet men have come to such a pass that they frequently starve, not for want of necessaries, but for want of luxuries; and I know a good woman who thinks that her son lost his life because he took to drinking water only.

The reader will perceive that I am treating the subject rather from an economic than a dietetic point of view, and he will not venture to put my abstemiousness to the test unless he has a well-stocked larder.

Bread I at first made of pure Indian meal and salt, genuine hoe-cakes, which I baked before my fire out of doors on a shingle or the end of a stick of timber sawed off in building my house; but it was wont to get smoked and to have a piny flavor. I tried flour also; but have at last found a mixture of rye and Indian meal most convenient and agreeable. In cold weather it was no little amusement to bake several small loaves of this in succession, tending and turning them as carefully as an Egyptian his hatching eggs.[8] They were a real cereal fruit which I ripened, and they had to my senses a fragrance like that of other noble fruits, which I kept in as long as possible by wrapping them in cloths. I made a study of the ancient and indispensable art of bread-making, consulting such authorities as offered, going back to the primitive days and first invention of the unleavened kind, when from the wildness of nuts and meats men first reached the mildness and refinement of this diet, and travelling gradually down in my studies through that accidental souring of the dough which, it is supposed, taught the leavening process, and through the various fermentations thereafter, till I came to "good, sweet, wholesome bread," the staff of life. Leaven, which some deem the soul of bread, the *spiritus* which fills its cellular tissue, which is religiously preserved like the vestal fire,—some precious bottle-full, I suppose, first brought over in the Mayflower, did the business for America, and its influence is still rising, swelling, spreading, in cerealian billows over the land,—this seed I regularly and faithfully procured from the village, till at length one morning I forgot the rules, and scalded my yeast; by which accident I discovered that even this was not indispensable,— for my discoveries were not by the synthetic but analytic process,—and I have gladly omitted it since, though most housewives earnestly assured me that safe and wholesome bread without yeast might not be, and elderly people prophesied a speedy decay of the vital forces. Yet I find it not to be an essential ingredient, and after going without it for a year am still in the land of the living; and I am glad to escape the trivialness of carrying a bottle-full in my pocket, which would sometimes pop and discharge its contents to my discomfiture. It is simpler and more respectable to omit it. Man is an animal who more than any other can adapt himself to all climates and circumstances. Neither did I put any sal soda, or other acid or alkali, into my bread. It would seem that I made it according to the recipe which Marcus Porcius Cato gave about two centuries before Christ. "Panem depsticium sic facito. Manus mortariumque bene lavato. Farinam in mortarium indito, aquæ paulatim addito, subigitoque pulchre. Ubi bene subegeris, defingito, coquitoque sub testu."[9]

---

8. Egyptians had devised incubators.   9. *De agri cultura*, 74.

Which I take to mean—"Make kneaded bread thus. Wash your hands and trough well. Put the meal into the trough, add water gradually, and knead it thoroughly. When you have kneaded it well, mould it, and bake it under a cover," that is, in a baking-kettle. Not a word about leaven. But I did not always use this staff of life. At one time, owing to the emptiness of my purse, I saw none of it for more than a month.

Every New Englander might easily raise all his own breadstuffs in this land of rye and Indian corn, and not depend on distant and fluctuating markets for them. Yet so far are we from simplicity and independence that, in Concord, fresh and sweet meal is rarely sold in the shops, and hominy and corn in a still coarser form are hardly used by any. For the most part the farmer gives to his cattle and hogs the grain of his own producing, and buys flour, which is at least no more wholesome, at a greater cost, at the store. I saw that I could easily raise my bushel or two of rye and Indian corn, for the former will grow on the poorest land, and the latter does not require the best, and grind them in a hand-mill, and so do without rice and pork; and if I must have some concentrated sweet, I found by experiment that I could make a very good molasses either of pumpkins or beets, and I knew that I needed only to set out a few maples to obtain it more easily still, and while these were growing I could use various substitutes beside those which I have named, "For," as the Forefathers sang,—

> "we can make liquor to sweeten our lips
> Of pumpkins and parsnips and walnut-tree chips."[1]

Finally, as for salt, that grossest of groceries, to obtain this might be a fit occasion for a visit to the seashore, or, if I did without it altogether, I should probably drink the less water. I do not learn that the Indians ever troubled themselves to go after it.

Thus I could avoid all trade and barter, so far as my food was concerned, and having a shelter already, it would only remain to get clothing and fuel. The pantaloons which I now wear were woven in a farmer's family,—thank Heaven there is so much virtue still in man; for I think the fall from the farmer to the operative as great and memorable as that from the man to the farmer;—and in a new country fuel is an encumbrance. As for a habitat, if I were not permitted still to squat, I might purchase one acre at the same price for which the land I cultivated was sold—namely, eight dollars and eight cents. But as it was, I considered that I enhanced the value of the land by squatting on it.

There is a certain class of unbelievers who sometimes ask me such questions as, if I think that I can live on vegetable food alone; and to strike at the root of the matter at once,—for the root is faith,—I am accustomed to answer such, that I can live on board nails. If they cannot understand that, they cannot understand much that I have to say. For my part, I am glad to hear of experiments of this kind being tried; as that a young man tried for a fortnight to live on hard raw corn on the ear, using his teeth for all mortar. The squirrel tribe tried the same and succeeded. The human race is interested in these experiments, though a few old women who are incapacitated for them, or who own their thirds in mills, may be alarmed.

---

1. From John Warner Barber's *Historical Collections* (1839).

My furniture, part of which I made myself, and the rest cost me nothing of which I have not rendered an account, consisted of a bed, a table, a desk, three chairs, a looking-glass three inches in diameter, a pair of tongs and andirons, a kettle, a skillet, and a frying-pan, a dipper, a wash-bowl, two knives and forks, three plates, one cup, one spoon, a jug for oil, a jug for molasses, and a japanned[2] lamp. None is so poor that he need sit on a pumpkin. That is shiftlessness. There is a plenty of such chairs as I like best in the village garrets to be had for taking them away. Furniture! Thank God, I can sit and I can stand without the aid of a furniture warehouse. What man but a philosopher would not be ashamed to see his furniture packed in a cart and going up country exposed to the light of heaven and the eyes of men, a beggarly account of empty boxes? That is Spaulding's furniture.[3] I could never tell from inspecting such a load whether it belonged to a so called rich man or a poor one; the owner always seemed poverty-stricken. Indeed, the more you have of such things the poorer you are. Each load looks as if it contained the contents of a dozen shanties; and if one shanty is poor, this is a dozen times as poor. Pray, for what do we *move* ever but to get rid of our furniture, our *exuviæ*;[4] at last to go from this world to another newly furnished, and leave this to be burned? It is the same as if all these traps were buckled to a man's belt, and he could not move over the rough country where our lines are cast without dragging them,—dragging his trap. He was a lucky fox that left his tail in the trap. The muskrat will gnaw his third leg off to be free. No wonder man has lost his elasticity. How often he is at a dead set! "Sir, if I may be so bold, what do you mean by a dead set?" If you are a seer, whenever you meet a man you will see all that he owns, ay, and much that he pretends to disown, behind him, even to his kitchen furniture and all the trumpery which he saves and will not burn, and he will appear to be harnessed to it and making what headway he can. I think that the man is at a dead set who has got through a knot hole or gateway where his sledge load of furniture cannot follow him. I cannot but feel compassion when I hear some trig, compact-looking man, seemingly free, all girded and ready, speak of his "furniture," as whether it is insured or not. "But what shall I do with my furniture?" My gay butterfly is entangled in a spider's web then. Even those who seem for a long while not to have any, if you inquire more narrowly you will find have some stored in somebody's barn. I look upon England to-day as an old gentleman who is travelling with a great deal of baggage, trumpery which has accumulated from long housekeeping, which he has not the courage to burn; great trunk, little trunk, bandbox and bundle. Throw away the first three at least. It would surpass the powers of a well man nowadays to take up his bed and walk, and I should certainly advise a sick one to lay down his bed and run. When I have met an immigrant tottering under a bundle which contained his all,—looking like an enormous wen which had grown out of the nape of his neck,—I have pitied him, not because that was his all, but because he had all *that* to carry. If I have got to drag my trap, I will take care that it be a light one and do not nip me in a vital part. But perchance it would be wisest never to put one's paw into it.

I would observe, by the way, that it costs me nothing for curtains, for I have no gazers to shut out but the sun and moon, and I am willing that they should look in. The moon will not sour milk nor taint meat of mine, nor will the sun

2. Lacquered with decorative scenes in the Japanese manner.

3. Unidentified.

4. Discarded objects (Latin).

injure my furniture or fade my carpet, and if he is sometimes too warm a friend, I find it still better economy to retreat behind some curtain which nature has provided, than to add a single item to the details of housekeeping. A lady once offered me a mat, but as I had no room to spare within the house, nor time to spare within or without to shake it, I declined it, preferring to wipe my feet on the sod before my door. It is best to avoid the beginnings of evil.

Not long since I was present at the auction of a deacon's effects, for his life had not been ineffectual:—

> "The evil that men do lives after them."[5]

As usual, a great proportion was trumpery which had begun to accumulate in his father's day. Among the rest was a dried tapeworm. And now, after lying half a century in his garret and other dust holes, these things were not burned; instead of a *bonfire*, or purifying destruction of them, there was an *auction*, or increasing of them.[6] The neighbors eagerly collected to view them, bought them all, and carefully transported them to their garrets and dust holes, to lie there till their estates are settled, when they will start again. When a man dies he kicks the dust.

The customs of some savage nations might, perchance, be profitably imitated by us, for they at least go through the semblance of casting their slough annually; they have the idea of the thing, whether they have the reality or not. Would it not be well if we were to celebrate such a "busk," or "feast of first fruits," as Bartram[7] describes to have been the custom of the Mucclasse Indians? "When a town celebrates the busk," says he, "having previously provided themselves with new clothes, new pots, pans, and other household utensils and furniture, they collect all their worn out clothes and other despicable things, sweep and cleanse their houses, squares, and the whole town, of their filth, which with all the remaining grain and other old provisions they cast together into one common heap, and consume it with fire. After having taken medicine, and fasted for three days, all the fire in the town is extinguished. During this fast they abstain from the gratification of every appetite and passion whatever. A general amnesty is proclaimed; all malefactors may return to their town.—"

"On the fourth morning, the high priest, by rubbing dry wood together, produces new fire in the public square, from whence every habitation in the town is supplied with the new and pure flame."

They then feast on the new corn and fruits and dance and sing for three days, "and the four following days they receive visits and rejoice with their friends from neighboring towns who have in like manner purified and prepared themselves."

The Mexicans also practised a similar purification at the end of every fifty-two years, in the belief that it was time for the world to come to an end.

I have scarcely heard of a truer sacrament, that is, as the dictionary defines it, "outward and visible sign of an inward and spiritual grace," than this, and I have no doubt that they were originally inspired directly from Heaven to do thus, though they have no biblical record of the revelation.

---

5. Tag from Antony's speech to the citizens, in Shakespeare's *Julius Caesar* 3.3.
6. Thoreau puns on the Latin root of *auction*, which means "to increase."
7. William Bartram, *Travels through North and South Carolina* (1791).

For more than five years I maintained myself thus solely by the labor of my hands, and I found, that by working about six weeks in a year, I could meet all the expenses of living. The whole of my winters, as well as most of my summers, I had free and clear for study. I have thoroughly tried school-keeping, and found that my expenses were in proportion, or rather out of proportion, to my income, for I was obliged to dress and train, not to say think and believe, accordingly, and I lost my time into the bargain. As I did not teach for the good of my fellow-men, but simply for a livelihood, this was a failure. I have tried trade; but I found that it would take ten years to get under way in that, and that then I should probably be on my way to the devil. I was actually afraid that I might by that time be doing what is called a good business. When formerly I was looking about to see what I could do for a living, some sad experience in conforming to the wishes of friends being fresh in my mind to tax my ingenuity, I thought often and seriously of picking huckleberries; that surely I could do, and its small profits might suffice,—for my greatest skill has been to want but little,—so little capital it required, so little distraction from my wonted moods, I foolishly thought. While my acquaintances when unhesitatingly into trade or the professions, I contemplated this occupation as most like theirs; ranging the hills all summer to pick the berries which came in my way, and thereafter carelessly dispose of them; so, to keep the flocks of Admetus.[8] I also dreamed that I might gather the wild herbs, or carry evergreens to such villagers as loved to be reminded of the woods, even to the city, by hay-cart loads. But I have since learned that trade curses every thing it handles; and though you trade in messages from heaven, the whole curse of trade attaches to the business.

As I preferred some things to others, and especially valued my freedom, as I could fare hard and yet succeed well, I did not wish to spend my time in earning rich carpets or other fine furniture, or delicate cookery, or a house in the Grecian or the Gothic style just yet. If there are any to whom it is no interruption to acquire these things, and who know how to use them when acquired, I relinquish to them the pursuit. Some are "industrious," and appear to love labor for its own sake, or perhaps because it keeps them out of worse mischief; to such I have at present nothing to say. Those who would not know what to do with more leisure than they now enjoy, I might advise to work twice as hard as they do,—work till they pay for themselves, and get their free papers. For myself I found that the occupation of a day-laborer was the most independent of any, especially as it required only thirty or forty days in a year to support one. The laborer's day ends with the going down of the sun, and he is then free to devote himself to his chosen pursuit, independent of his labor; but his employer, who speculates from month to month, has no respite from one end of the year to the other.

In short, I am convinced, both by faith and experience, that to maintain one's self on this earth is not a hardship but a pastime, if we will live simply and wisely; as the pursuits of the simpler nations are still the sports of the more artificial. It is not necessary that a man should earn his living by the sweat of his brow, unless he sweats easier than I do.

One young man of my acquaintance, who has inherited some acres, told me that he thought he should live as I did, *if he had the means.* I would not

8. Apollo, Greek god of poetry, tended the flocks of Admetus while banished from Olympus.

have any one adopt *my* mode of living on any account; for, beside that before he has fairly learned it I may have found out another for myself, I desire that there may be as many different persons in the world as possible; but I would have each one be very careful to find out and pursue *his own* way, and not his father's or his mother's or his neighbor's instead. The youth may build or plant or sail, only let him not be hindered from doing that which he tells me he would like to do. It is by a mathematical point only that we are wise, as the sailor or the fugitive slave keeps the polestar in his eye; but that is sufficient guidance for all our life. We may not arrive at our port within a calculable period, but we would preserve the true course.

Undoubtedly, in this case, what is true for one is truer still for a thousand, as a large house is not more expensive than a small one in proportion to its size, since one roof may cover, one cellar underlie, and one wall separate several apartments. But for my part, I preferred the solitary dwelling. Moreover, it will commonly be cheaper to build the whole yourself than to convince another of the advantage of the common wall; and when you have done this, the common partition, to be much cheaper, must be a thin one, and that other may prove a bad neighbor, and also not keep his side in repair. The only coöperation which is commonly possible is exceedingly partial and superficial; and what little true coöperation there is, is as if it were not, being a harmony inaudible to men. If a man has faith he will coöperate with equal faith every where; if he has not faith, he will continue to live like the rest of the world, whatever company he is joined to. To coöperate, in the highest as well as the lowest sense, means *to get our living together.* I heard it proposed lately that two young men should travel together over the world, the one without money, earning his means as he went, before the mast and behind the plough, the other carrying a bill of exchange in his pocket. It was easy to see that they could not long be companions or coöperate, since one would not *operate* at all. They would part at the first interesting crisis in their adventures. Above all, as I have implied, the man who goes alone can start today; but he who travels with another must wait till that other is ready, and it may be a long time before they get off.

But all this is very selfish, I have heard some of my townsmen say. I confess that I have hitherto indulged very little in philanthropic enterprises. I have made some sacrifices to a sense of duty, and among others have sacrificed this pleasure also. There are those who have used all their arts to persuade me to undertake the support of some poor family in the town; and if I had nothing to do,—for the devil finds employment for the idle,—I might try my hand at some such pastime as that. However, when I have thought to indulge myself in this respect, and lay their Heaven under an obligation by maintaining certain poor persons in all respects as comfortably as I maintain myself, and have even ventured so far as to make them the offer, they have one and all unhesitatingly preferred to remain poor. While my townsmen and women are devoted in so many ways to the good of their fellows, I trust that one at least may be spared to other and less humane pursuits. You must have a genius for charity as well as for any thing else. As for Doing-good, that is one of the professions which are full. Moreover, I have tried it fairly, and, strange as it may seem, am satisfied that it does not agree with my constitution. Probably I should not consciously and deliberately forsake my particular calling to do the good which society demands of me, to save the universe from annihilation; and I believe that a like but infinitely greater steadfastness elsewhere is all that now preserves it. But I would not stand between any man and his genius; and to him who does this work, which I decline, with his whole heart and soul and life, I would say, Persevere, even if the world call it doing evil, as it is most likely they will.

I am far from supposing that my case is a peculiar one; no doubt many of my readers would make a similar defence. At doing something,—I will not engage that my neighbors shall pronounce it good,—I do not hesitate to say that I should be a capital fellow to hire; but what that is, it is for my employer to find out. What *good* I do, in the common sense of that word, must be aside from my main path, and for the most part wholly unintended. Men say, practically, Begin where you are and such as you are, without aiming mainly to become of more worth, and with kindness aforethought go about doing good. If I were to preach at all in this strain, I should say rather, Set about being good. As if the sun should stop when he had kindled his fires up to the splendor of a moon or a star of the sixth magnitude, and go about like a Robin Goodfellow,[9] peeping in at every cottage window, inspiring lunatics, and tainting meats, and making darkness visible, instead of steadily increasing his genial heat and beneficence till he is of such brightness that no mortal can look him in the face, and then, and in the mean while too, going about the world in his own orbit, doing it good, or rather, as a truer philosophy has discovered, the world going about him getting good. When Phaeton,[1] wishing to prove his heavenly birth by his beneficence, had the sun's chariot but one day, and drove out of the beaten track, he burned several blocks of houses in the lower streets of heaven, and scorched the surface of the earth, and dried up every spring, and made the great desert of Sahara, till at length Jupiter hurled him headlong to the earth with a thunderbolt, and the sun, through grief at his death, did not shine for a year.

There is no odor so bad as that which arises from goodness tainted. It is human, it is divine, carrion. If I knew for a certainty that a man was coming to my house with the conscious design of doing me good, I should run for my life, as from that dry and parching wind of the African deserts called the simoom, which fills the mouth and nose and ears and eyes with dust till you are suffocated, for fear that I should get some of his good done to me,—some of its virus mingled with my blood. No,—in this case I would rather suffer evil the natural way. A man is not a good *man* to me because he will feed me if I should be starving, or warm me if I should be freezing, or pull me out of a ditch if I should ever fall into one. I can find you a Newfoundland dog that will do as much. Philanthropy is not love for one's fellow-man in the broadest sense. Howard[2] was no doubt an exceedingly kind and worthy man in his way, and has his reward; but, comparatively speaking, what are a hundred Howards to *us*, if their philanthropy do not help *us* in our best estate, when we are most worthy to be helped? I never heard of a philanthropic meeting in which it was sincerely proposed to do any good to me, or the like of me.

The Jesuits were quite balked by those Indians who, being burned at the

---

9. Mischievous fairy, known as Puck in Shakespeare's *A Midsummer Night's Dream*.
1. In Greek mythology, the son of Helios. He attempted to drive his father's chariot, the sun, with di-

sastrous consequences.
2. John Howard (1726?–1790), English prison reformer.

stake, suggested new modes of torture to their tormentors.[3] Being superior to
physical suffering, it sometimes chanced that they were superior to any consolation which the missionaries could offer; and the law to do as you would be
done by fell with less persuasiveness on the ears of those, who, for their part,
did not care how they were done by, who loved their enemies after a new
fashion, and came very near freely forgiving them all they did.

   Be sure that you give the poor the aid they most need, though it be your
example which leaves them far behind. If you give money, spend yourself with
it, and do not merely abandon it to them. We make curious mistakes sometimes. Often the poor man is not so cold and hungry as he is dirty and ragged
and gross. It is partly his taste, and not merely his misfortune. If you give him
money, he will perhaps buy more rags with it. I was wont to pity the clumsy
Irish laborers who cut ice on the pond, in such mean and ragged clothes,
while I shivered in my more tidy and somewhat more fashionable garments,
till, one bitter cold day, one who had slipped into the water came to my house
to warm him, and I saw him strip off three pairs of pants and two pairs of
stockings ere he got down to the skin, though they were dirty and ragged
enough, it is true, and that he could afford to refuse the *extra* garments which
I offered him, he had so many *intra* ones. This ducking was the very thing he
needed. Then I began to pity myself, and I saw that it would be a greater
charity to bestow on me a flannel shirt than a whole slop-shop on him. There
are a thousand hacking at the branches of evil to one who is striking at the
root, and it may be that he who bestows the largest amount of time and money
on the needy is doing the most by his mode of life to produce that misery
which he strives in vain to relieve. It is the pious slave-breeder devoting the
proceeds of every tenth slave to buy a Sunday's liberty for the rest. Some show
their kindness to the poor by employing them in their kitchens. Would they
not be kinder if they employed themselves there? You boast of spending a
tenth part of your income in charity; may be you should spend the nine tenths
so, and done with it. Society recovers only a tenth part of the property then. Is
this owing to the generosity of him in whose possession it is found, or to the
remissness of the officers of justice?

   Philanthropy is almost the only virtue which is sufficiently appreciated by
mankind. Nay, it is greatly overrated; and it is our selfishness which overrates
it. A robust poor man, one sunny day here in Concord, praised a fellow-
townsman to me, because, as he said, he was kind to the poor; meaning himself. The kind uncles and aunts of the race are more esteemed than its true
spiritual fathers and mothers. I once heard a reverend lecturer on England, a
man of learning and intelligence, after enumerating her scientific, literary,
and political worthies, Shakspeare, Bacon, Cromwell, Milton, Newton, and
others, speak next of her Christian heroes, whom, as if his profession required
it of him, he elevated to a place far above all the rest, as the greatest of the
great. They were Penn, Howard, and Mrs. Fry.[4] Every one must feel the
falsehood and cant of this. The last were not England's best men and women;
only, perhaps, her best philanthropists.

   I would not subtract any thing from the praise that is due to philanthropy,

3. Thoreau's source is unknown, but Harding cites
comparable accounts in *The Jesuit Relations and Allied
Documents* (1898), vol. 17.
4. Elizabeth Fry (1780–1845), English Quaker and

prison reformer. William Penn (1644–1718), Quaker
leader and proprietor of Pennsylvania. John Howard
(see n. 2, p. 1757).

but merely demand justice for all who by their lives and works are a blessing to mankind. I do not value chiefly a man's uprightness and benevolence, which are, as it were, his stem and leaves. Those plants of whose greenness withered we make herb tea for the sick, serve but a humble use, and are most employed by quacks. I want the flower and fruit of a man; that some fragrance be wafted over from him to me, and some ripeness flavor our intercourse. His goodness must not be a partial and transitory act, but a constant superfluity, which costs him nothing and of which he is unconscious. This is a charity that hides a multitude of sins. The philanthropist too often surrounds mankind with the remembrance of his own cast-off griefs as an atmosphere, and calls it sympathy. We should impart our courage, and not our despair, our health and ease, and not our disease, and take care that this does not spread by contagion. From what southern plains comes up the voice of wailing? Under what latitudes reside the heathen to whom we would send light? Who is that intemperate and brutal man whom we would redeem? If any thing ail a man, so that he does not perform his functions, if he have a pain in his bowels even,— for that is the seat of sympathy,—he forthwith sets about reforming—the world. Being a microcosm himself, he discovers, and it is a true discovery, and he is the man to make it,—that the world has been eating green apples; to his eyes, in fact, the globe itself is a great green apple, which there is danger awful to think of that the children of men will nibble before it is ripe; and straightway his drastic philanthropy seeks out the Esquimaux and the Patagonian, and embraces the populous Indian and Chinese villages; and thus, by a few years of philanthropic activity, the powers in the mean while using him for their own ends, no doubt, he cures himself of his dyspepsia, the globe acquires a faint blush on one or both of its cheeks, as if it were beginning to be ripe, and life loses its crudity and is once more sweet and wholesome to live. I never dreamed of any enormity greater than I have committed. I never knew, and never shall know, a worse man than myself.

I believe that what so saddens the reformer is not his sympathy with his fellows in distress, but, though he be the holiest son of God, is his private ail. Let this be righted, let the spring come to him, the morning rise over his couch, and he will forsake his generous companions without apology. My excuse for not lecturing against the use of tobacco is, that I never chewed it; that is a penalty which reformed tobacco-chewers have to pay; though there are things enough I have chewed, which I could lecture against. If you should ever be betrayed into any of these philanthropies, do not let your left hand know what your right hand does, for it is not worth knowing. Rescue the drowning and tie your shoe-strings. Take your time, and set about some free labor.

Our manners have been corrupted by communication with the saints. Our hymn-books resound with a melodious cursing of God and enduring him forever. One would say that even the prophets and redeemers had rather consoled the fears than confirmed the hopes of man. There is nowhere recorded a simple and irrepressible satisfaction with the gift of life, any memorable praise of God. All health and success does me good, however far off and withdrawn it may appear; all disease and failure helps to make me sad and does me evil, however much sympathy it may have with me or I with it. If, then, we would indeed restore mankind by truly Indian, botanic, magnetic, or natural means, let us first be as simple and well as Nature ourselves, dispel the clouds which hang over our own brows, and take up a little life into our pores. Do not stay to be an overseer of the poor, but endeavor to become one of the worthies of the world.

I read in the Gulistan, or Flower Garden, of Sheik Sadi of Shiraz, that "They asked a wise man, saying; Of the many celebrated trees which the Most High God has created lofty and umbrageous, they call none azad, or free, excepting the cypress, which bears no fruit; what mystery is there in this? He replied; Each has its appropriate produce, and appointed season, during the continuance of which it is fresh and blooming, and during their absence dry and withered; to neither of which states is the cypress exposed, being always flourishing; and of this nature are the azads, or religious independents.—Fix not thy heart on that which is transitory; for the Dijlah, or Tigris, will continue to flow through Bagdad after the race of caliphs is extinct: if thy hand has plenty, be liberal as the date tree; but if it affords nothing to give away, be an azad, or free man, like the cypress."[5]

Complemental Verses[6]

THE PRETENSIONS OF POVERTY

"Thou dost presume too much, poor needy wretch,
To claim a station in the firmament,
Because thy humble cottage, or thy tub,
Nurses some lazy or pedantic virtue
In the cheap sunshine or by shady springs,
With roots and pot-herbs; where thy right hand,
Tearing those humane passions from the mind,
Upon whose stocks fair blooming virtues flourish,
Degradeth nature, and benumbeth sense,
And, Gorgon-like, turns active men to stone.[7]
We not require the dull society
Of your necessitated temperance,
Or that unnatural stupidity
That knows nor joy nor sorrow; nor your forc'd
Falsely exalted passive fortitude
Above the active. This low abject brood,
That fix their seats in mediocrity,
Become your servile minds; but we advance
Such virtues only as admit excess,
Brave, bounteous acts, regal magnificence,
All-seeing prudence, magnanimity
That knows no bound, and that heroic virtue
For which antiquity hath left no name,
But patterns only, such as Hercules,
Achilles, Theseus. Back to thy loath'd cell;
And when thou seest the new enlightened sphere,
Study to know but what those worthies were."

—T. CAREW

5. Muslih-ud-Din (Saadi) (1184?–1291), *The Gulistan or Rose Garden*.
6. From *Coelum Britannicum* by the English Cavalier poet Thomas Carew (1595?–1645?), offered ironically as a retort to "Economy."
7. In Greek mythology the Gorgons were three sisters who, with snakes for hair and eyes, turned any beholder into stone.

Where I Lived, and What I Lived For

At a certain season of our life we are accustomed to consider every spot as the possible site of a house. I have thus surveyed the country on every side within a dozen miles of where I live. In imagination I have bought all the farms in succession, for all were to be bought and I knew their price. I walked over each farmer's premises, tasted his wild apples, discoursed on husbandry with him, took his farm at his price, at any price, mortgaging it to him in my mind; even put a higher price on it,—took every thing but a deed of it,—took his word for his deed, for I dearly love to talk,—cultivated it, and him too to some extent, I trust, and withdrew when I had enjoyed it long enough, leaving him to carry it on. This experience entitled me to be regarded as a sort of real-estate broker by my friends. Wherever I sat, there I might live, and the landscape radiated from me accordingly. What is a house but a *sedes*, a seat?—better if a country seat. I discovered many a site for a house not likely to be soon improved, which some might have thought too far from the village, but to my eyes the village was too far from it. Well, there I might live, I said; and there I did live, for an hour, a summer and a winter life; saw how I could let the years run off, buffet the winter through, and see the spring come in. The future inhabitants of this region, wherever they may place their houses, may be sure that they have been anticipated. An afternoon sufficed to lay out the land into orchard woodlot and pasture, and to decide what fine oaks or pines should be left to stand before the door, and whence each blasted tree could be seen to the best advantage; and then I let it lie, fallow perchance, for a man is rich in proportion to the number of things which he can afford to let alone.

My imagination carried me so far that I even had the refusal of several farms,—the refusal was all I wanted,—but I never got my fingers burned by actual possession. The nearest that I came to actual possession was when I bought the Hollowell Place, and had begun to sort my seeds, and collected materials with which to make a wheelbarrow to carry it on or off with; but before the owner gave me a deed of it, his wife—every man has such a wife—changed her mind and wished to keep it, and he offered me ten dollars to release him. Now, to speak the truth, I had but ten cents in the world, and it surpassed my arithmetic to tell, if I was that man who had ten cents, or who had a farm, or ten dollars, or all together. However, I let him keep the ten dollars and the farm too, for I had carried it far enough; or rather, to be generous, I sold him the farm for just what I gave for it, and, as he was not a rich man, made him a present of ten dollars, and still had my ten cents, and seeds, and materials for a wheelbarrow left. I found thus that I had been a rich man without any damage to my poverty. But I retained the landscape, and I have since annually carried off what it yielded without a wheelbarrow. With respect to landscapes,—

> "I am monarch of all I *survey*,
> My right there is none to dispute."[8]

I have frequently seen a poet withdraw, having enjoyed the most valuable part of a farm, while the crusty farmer supposed that he had got a few wild apples only. Why, the owner does not know it for many years when a poet has

---

8. William Cowper's *Verses Supposed to Be Written by Alexander Selkirk*, with the pun italicized. Selkirk was Daniel Defoe's model for Robinson Crusoe.

put his farm in rhyme, the most admirable kind of invisible fence, has fairly impounded it, milked it, skimmed it, and got all the cream, and left the farmer only the skimmed milk.

The real attractions of the Hollowell farm, to me, were; its complete retirement, being about two miles from the village, half a mile from the nearest neighbor, and separated from the highway by a broad field; its bounding on the river, which the owner said protected it by its fogs from frosts in the spring, though that was nothing to me; the gray color and ruinous state of the house and barn, and the dilapidated fences, which put such an interval between me and the last occupant; the hollow and lichen-covered apple trees, gnawed by rabbits, showing what kind of neighbors I should have; but above all, the recollection I had of it from my earliest voyages up the river, when the house was concealed behind a dense grove of red maples, through which I heard the house-dog bark. I was in haste to buy it, before the proprietor finished getting out some rocks, cutting down the hollow apple trees, and grubbing up some young birches which had sprung up in the pasture, or, in short, had made any more of his improvements. To enjoy these advantages I was ready to carry it on; like Atlas,[9] to take the world on my shoulders,—I never heard what compensation he received for that,—and do all those things which had no other motive or excuse but that I might pay for it and be unmolested in my possession of it; for I knew all the while that it would yield the most abundant crop of the kind I wanted if I could only afford to let it alone. But it turned out as I have said.

All that I could say, then, with respect to farming on a large scale, (I have always cultivated a garden,) was, that I had had my seeds ready. Many think that seeds improve with age. I have no doubt that time discriminates between the good and the bad; and when at last I shall plant, I shall be less likely to be disappointed. But I would say to my fellows, once for all, As long as possible live free and uncommitted. It makes but little difference whether you are committed to a farm or the county jail.

Old Cato, whose "De Re Rusticâ" is my "Cultivator," says, and the only translation I have seen makes sheer nonsense of the passage, "When you think of getting a farm, turn it thus in your mind, not to buy greedily; nor spare your pains to look at it, and do not think it enough to go round it once. The oftener you go there the more it will please you, if it is good."[1] I think I shall not buy greedily, but go round and round it as long as I live, and be buried in it first, that it may please me the more at last.

The present was my next experiment of this kind, which I purpose to describe more at length; for convenience, putting the experience of two years into one. As I have said, I do not propose to write an ode to dejection, but to brag as lustily as chanticleer in the morning, standing on his roost, if only to wake my neighbors up.

When first I took up my abode in the woods, that is, began to spend my nights as well as days there, which, by accident, was on Independence Day, or the fourth of July, 1845, my house was not finished for winter, but was merely a defence against the rain, without plastering or chimney, the walls being of rough weather-stained boards, with wide chinks, which made it cool

9. A Titan whom Zeus forced to stand on the earth supporting the heavens on his head and in his hands as punishment for warring against the Olympian gods. 1. *De agri cultura*, 1.1.

at night. The upright white hewn studs and freshly planed door and window casings gave it a clean and airy look, especially in the morning, when its timbers were saturated with dew, so that I fancied that by noon some sweet gum would exude from them. To my imagination it retained throughout the day more or less of this auroral character, reminding me of a certain house on a mountain which I had visited the year before. This was an airy and unplastered cabin, fit to entertain a travelling god, and where a goddess might trail her garments. The winds which passed over my dwelling were such as sweep over the ridges of mountains, bearing the broken strains, or celestial parts only, of terrestrial music. The morning wind forever blows, the poem of creation is uninterrupted; but few are the ears that hear it. Olympus is but the outside of the earth every where.

The only house I had been the owner of before, if I except a boat, was a tent, which I used occasionally when making excursions in the summer, and this is still rolled up in my garret; but the boat, after passing from hand to hand, has gone down the stream of time. With this more substantial shelter about me, I had made some progress toward settling in the world. This frame, so slightly clad, was a sort of crystallization around me, and reacted on the builder. It was suggestive somewhat as a picture in outlines. I did not need to go out doors to take the air, for the atmosphere within had lost none of its freshness. It was not so much within doors as behind a door where I sat, even in the rainiest weather. The Harivansa[2] says, "An abode without birds is like a meat without seasoning." Such was not my abode, for I found myself suddenly neighbor to the birds; not by having imprisoned one, but having caged myself near them. I was not only nearer to some of those which commonly frequent the garden and the orchard, but to those wilder and more thrilling songsters of the forest which never, or rarely, serenade a villager,—the wood-thrush, the veery, the scarlet tanager, the field-sparrow, the whippoorwill, and many others.

I was seated by the shore of a small pond, about a mile and a half south of the village of Concord and somewhat higher than it, in the midst of an extensive wood between that town and Lincoln, and about two miles south of that our only field known to fame, Concord Battle Ground;[3] but I was so low in the woods that the opposite shore, half a mile off, like the rest, covered with wood, was my most distant horizon. For the first week, whenever I looked out on the pond it impressed me like a tarn[4] high up on the side of a mountain, its bottom far above the surface of other lakes, and, as the sun arose, I saw it throwing off its nightly clothing of mist, and here and there, by degrees, its soft ripples or its smooth reflecting surface was revealed, while the mists, like ghosts, were stealthily withdrawing in every direction into the woods, as at the breaking up of some nocturnal conventicle. The very dew seemed to hang upon the trees later into the day than usual, as on the sides of mountains.

This small lake was of most value as a neighbor in the intervals of a gentle rain storm in August, when, both air and water being perfectly still, but the sky overcast, mid-afternoon had all the serenity of evening, and the wood-thrush sang around, and was heard from shore to shore. A lake like this is never smoother than at such a time; and the clear portion of the air above it being shallow and darkened by clouds, the water, full of light and reflections,

2. A Hindu epic poem.
3. The site of battle on the first day of the American   Revolution, April 19, 1775.
4. Lake.

becomes a lower heaven itself so much the more important. From a hill top near by, where the wood had been recently cut off, there was a pleasing vista southward across the pond, through a wide indentation in the hills which form the shore there, where their opposite sides sloping toward each other suggested a stream flowing out in that direction through a wooded valley, but stream there was none. That way I looked between and over the near green hills to some distant and higher ones in the horizon, tinged with blue. Indeed, by standing on tiptoe I could catch a glimpse of some of the peaks of the still bluer and more distant mountain ranges in the north-west, those true-blue coins from heaven's own mint, and also of some portion of the village. But in other directions, even from this point, I could not see over or beyond the woods which surrounded me. It is well to have some water in your neighborhood, to give buoyancy to and float the earth. One value even of the smallest well is, that when you look into it you see that earth is not continent but insular. This is as important as that it keeps butter cool. When I looked across the pond from this peak toward the Sudbury meadows, which in time of flood I distinguished elevated perhaps by a mirage in their seething valley, like a coin in a basin, all the earth beyond the pond appeared like a thin crust insulated and floated even by this small sheet of intervening water, and I was reminded that this on which I dwelt was but *dry land*.

Though the view from my door was still more contracted, I did not feel crowded or confined in the least. There was pasture enough for my imagination. The low shrub-oak plateau to which the opposite shore arose, stretched away toward the prairies of the West and the steppes of Tartary, affording ample room for all the roving families of men. "There are none happy in the world but beings who enjoy freely a vast horizon,"—said Damodara,[5] when his herds required new and larger pastures.

Both place and time were changed, and I dwelt nearer to those parts of the universe and to those eras in history which had most attracted me. Where I lived was as far off as many a region viewed nightly by astronomers. We are wont to imagine rare and delectable places in some remote and more celestial corner of the system, behind the constellation of Cassiopeia's Chair, far from noise and disturbance. I discovered that my house actually had its site in such a withdrawn, but forever new and unprofaned, part of the universe. If it were worth the while to settle in those parts near to the Pleiades or the Hyades, to Aldebaran or Altair,[6] then I was really there, or at an equal remoteness from the life which I had left behind, dwindled and twinkling with as fine a ray to my nearest neighbor, and to be seen only in moonless nights by him. Such was that part of creation where I had squatted;—

> "There was a shepherd that did live,
> And held his thoughts as high
> As were the mounts whereon his flocks
> Did hourly feed him by."[7]

What should we think of the shepherd's life if his flocks always wandered to higher pastures than his thoughts?

5. Another name for Krishna, the eighth avatar of Vishnu in Hindu mythology; Thoreau translates from a French edition of *Harivansa*.
6. The Pleiades and the Hyades are constellations; Aldebaran, in the constellation Taurus, is one of the brightest stars; Altair is in the constellation Aquila.
7. Anonymous Jacobean verse set to music in *The Muses Garden* (1611) and probably found by Thoreau in Thomas Evans's *Old Ballads* (1810).

Every morning was a cheerful invitation to make my life of equal simplicity, and I may say innocence, with Nature herself. I have been as sincere a worshipper of Aurora as the Greeks. I got up early and bathed in the pond; that was a religious exercise, and one of the best things which I did. They say that characters were engraven on the bathing tub of king Tching-thang to this effect: "Renew thyself completely each day; do it again, and again, and forever again."[8] I can understand that. Morning brings back the heroic ages. I was as much affected by the faint hum of a mosquito making its invisible and unimaginable tour through my apartment at earliest dawn, when I was sitting with door and windows open, as I could be by any trumpet that ever sang of fame. It was Homer's requiem; itself an Iliad and Odyssey in the air, singing its own wrath and wanderings. There was something cosmical about it; a standing advertisement, till forbidden,[9] of the everlasting vigor and fertility of the world. The morning, which is the most memorable season of the day, is the awakening hour. Then there is least somnolence in us; and for an hour, at least, some part of us awakes which slumbers all the rest of the day and night. Little is to be expected of that day, if it can be called a day, to which we are not awakened by our Genius, but by the mechanical nudgings of some servitor, are not awakened by our own newly-acquired force and aspirations from within, accompanied by the undulations of celestial music, instead of factory bells, and a fragrance filling the air—to a higher life than we fell asleep from; and thus the darkness bear its fruit, and prove itself to be good, no less than the light. That man who does not believe that each day contains an earlier, more sacred, and auroral hour than he has yet profaned, has despaired of life, and is pursuing a descending and darkening way. After a partial cessation of his sensuous life, the soul of man, or its organs rather, are reinvigorated each day, and his Genius tries again what noble life it can make. All memorable events, I should say, transpire in morning time and in a morning atmosphere. The Vedas[1] say, "All intelligences awake with the morning." Poetry and art, and the fairest and most memorable of the actions of men, date from such an hour. All poets and heroes, like Memnon, are the children of Aurora, and emit their music at sunrise.[2] To him whose elastic and vigorous thought keeps pace with the sun, the day is a perpetual morning. It matters not what the clocks say or the attitudes and labors of men. Morning is when I am awake and there is a dawn in me. Moral reform is the effort to throw off sleep. Why is it that men give so poor an account of their day if they have not been slumbering? They are not such poor calculators. If they had not been overcome with drowsiness they would have performed something. The millions are awake enough for physical labor; but only one in a million is awake enough for effective intellectual exertion, only one in a hundred millions to a poetic or divine life. To be awake is to be alive. I have never yet met a man who was quite awake. How could I have looked him in the face?

We must learn to reawaken and keep ourselves awake, not by mechanical aids, but by an infinite expectation of the dawn, which does not forsake us in our soundest sleep. I know of no more encouraging fact than the unquestionable ability of man to elevate his life by a conscious endeavor. It is something

8. Confucius, *The Great Learning*, chap. 1.
9. In newspaper advertisements "TF" signaled to the compositor that an item was to be repeated daily "till forbidden."

1. The Vedas are Hindu scriptures; the quotation has not been located.
2. See n. 6, p. 1737.

to be able to paint a particular picture, or to carve a statue, and so to make a few objects beautiful; but it is far more glorious to carve and paint the very atmosphere and medium through which we look, which morally we can do. To affect the quality of the day, that is the highest of arts. Every man is tasked to make his life, even in its details, worthy of the contemplation of his most elevated and critical hour. If we refused, or rather used up, such paltry information as we get, the oracles would distinctly inform us how this might be done.

I went to the woods because I wished to live deliberately, to front only the essential facts of life, and see if I could not learn what it had to teach, and not, when I came to die, discover that I had not lived. I did not wish to live what was not life, living is so dear; nor did I wish to practise resignation, unless it was quite necessary. I wanted to live deep and suck out all the marrow of life, to live so sturdily and Spartan-like as to put to rout all that was not life, to cut a broad swath and shave close, to drive life into a corner, and reduce it to its lowest terms, and, if it proved to be mean, why then to get the whole and genuine meanness of it, and publish its meanness to the world; or if it were sublime, to know it by experience, and be able to give a true account of it in my next excursion. For most men, it appears to me, are in a strange uncertainty about it, whether it is of the devil or of God, and have *somewhat hastily* concluded that it is the chief end of man here to "glorify God and enjoy him forever."[3]

Still we live meanly, like ants; though the fable tells us that we were long ago changed into men;[4] like pygmies we fight with cranes; it is error upon error, and clout upon clout, and our best virtue has for its occasion a superfluous and evitable wretchedness. Our life is frittered away by detail. An honest man has hardly need to count more than his ten fingers, or in extreme cases he may add his ten toes, and lump the rest. Simplicity, simplicity, simplicity! I say, let your affairs be as two or three, and not a hundred or a thousand; instead of a million count half a dozen, and keep your accounts on your thumb nail. In the midst of this chopping sea of civilized life, such are the clouds and storms and quicksands and thousand-and-one items to be allowed for, that a man has to live, if he would not founder and go to the bottom and not make his port at all, by dead reckoning, and he must be a great calculator indeed who succeeds. Simplify, simplify. Instead of three meals a day, if it be necessary eat but one; instead of a hundred dishes, five; and reduce other things in proportion. Our life is like a German Confederacy,[5] made up of petty states, with its boundary forever fluctuating, so that even a German cannot tell you how it is bounded at any moment. The nation itself, with all its so called internal improvements, which, by the way, are all external and superficial, is just such an unwieldy and overgrown establishment, cluttered with furniture and tripped up by its own traps, ruined by luxury and heedless expense, by want of calculation and a worthy aim, as the million households in the land; and the only cure for it as for them is in a rigid economy, a stern and more than Spartan simplicity of life and elevation of purpose. It lives too fast. Men think that it is essential that the *Nation* have commerce, and export ice, and

---

3. From the Shorter Catechism in the *New England Primer*.
4. In a Greek fable Aeacus persuaded Zeus to turn ants into men. The Trojans are compared to cranes fighting with pygmies (*Iliad*, book 3).
5. Later in the century Germany was unified under Prince Otto von Bismarck (1815–1898), first chancellor of the German Empire.

talk through a telegraph, and ride thirty miles an hour, without a doubt, whether *they* do or not; but whether we should live like baboons or like men, is a little uncertain. If we do not get out sleepers,[6] and forge rails, and devote days and nights to the work, but go to tinkering upon our *lives* to improve *them,* who will build railroads? And if railroads are not built, how shall we get to heaven in season? But if we stay at home and mind our business, who will want railroads? We do not ride on the railroad; it rides upon us. Did you ever think what those sleepers are that underlie the railroad? Each one is a man, an Irish-man, or a Yankee man. The rails are laid on them, and they are covered with sand, and the cars run smoothly over them. They are sound sleepers, I assure you. And every few years a new lot is laid down and run over; so that, if some have the pleasure of riding on a rail, others have the misfortune to be ridden upon. And when they run over a man that is walking in his sleep, a supernumerary sleeper in the wrong position, and wake him up, they suddenly stop the cars, and make a hue and cry about it, as if this were an exception. I am glad to know that it takes a gang of men for every five miles to keep the sleepers down and level in their beds as it is, for this is a sign that they may sometime get up again.

Why should we live with such hurry and waste of life? We are determined to be starved before we are hungry. Men say that a stitch in time saves nine, and so they take a thousand stitches to-day to save nine to-morrow. As for *work,* we haven't any of any consequence. We have the Saint Vitus' dance,[7] and cannot possibly keep our heads still. If I should only give a few pulls at the parish bell-rope, as for a fire, that is, without setting the bell, there is hardly a man on his farm in the outskirts of Concord, notwithstanding that press of engagements which was his excuse so many times this morning, nor a boy, nor a woman, I might almost say, but would forsake all and follow that sound, not mainly to save property from the flames, but, if we will confess the truth, much more to see it burn, since burn it must, and we, be it known, did not set it on fire,—or to see it put out, and have a hand in it, if that is done as handsomely; yes, even if it were the parish church itself. Hardly a man takes a half hour's nap after dinner, but when he wakes he holds up his head and asks, "What's the news?" as if the rest of mankind had stood his sentinels. Some give directions to be waked every half hour, doubtless for no other purpose; and then, to pay for it, they tell what they have dreamed. After a night's sleep the news is as indispensable as the breakfast. "Pray tell me any thing new that has happened to a man any where on this globe",—and he reads it over his coffee and rolls, that a man had had his eyes gouged out this morning on the Wachito River; never dreaming the while that he lives in the dark unfathomed mammoth cave of this world, and has but the rudiment of an eye himself.[8]

For my part, I could easily do without the post-office. I think that there are very few important communications made through it. To speak critically, I never received more than one or two letters in my life—I wrote this some years ago—that were worth the postage. The penny-post is, commonly, an institution through which you seriously offer a man that penny for his thoughts which is so often safely offered in jest. And I am sure that I never read any

6. Wooden railroad ties (another pun).
7. Chorea, a severe nervous disorder characterized by jerky motions.
8. Sightless fish had been found in Kentucky's Mam-

moth Cave. "Wachito": also spelled "Ouachita," a tributary of the Red River; Thoreau refers to a common-enough incident in backwoods brawling.

memorable news in a newspaper. If we read of one man robbed, or murdered, or killed by accident, or one house burned, or one vessel wrecked, or one steamboat blown up, or one cow run over on the Western Railroad, or one mad dog killed, or one lot of grasshoppers in the winter,—we never need read of another. One is enough. If you are acquainted with the principle, what do you care for a myriad instances and applications? To a philosopher all *news*, as it is called, is gossip, and they who edit and read it are old women over their tea. Yet not a few are greedy after this gossip. There was such a rush, as I hear, the other day at one of the offices to learn the foreign news by the last arrival, that several large squares of plate glass belonging to the establishment were broken by the pressure,—news which I seriously think a ready wit might write a twelvemonth or twelve years beforehand with sufficient accuracy. As for Spain, for instance, if you know how to throw in Don Carlos and the Infanta, and Don Pedro and Seville and Granada, from time to time in the right proportions,—they may have changed the names a little since I saw the papers,—and serve up a bull-fight when other entertainments fail, it will be true to the letter, and give us as good an idea of the exact state or ruin of things in Spain as the most succinct and lucid reports under this head in the newspapers: and as for England, almost the last significant scrap of news from that quarter was the revolution of 1649; and if you have learned the history of her crops for an average year, you never need attend to that thing again, unless your speculations are of a merely pecuniary character. If one may judge who rarely looks into the newspapers, nothing new does ever happen in foreign parts, a French revolution not excepted.

What news! how much more important to know what that is which was never old! "Kieou-pe-yu (great dignitary of the state of Wei) sent a man to Khoung-tseu to know his news. Khoung-tseu caused the messenger to be seated near him, and questioned him in these terms: What is your master doing? The messenger answered with respect: My master desires to diminish the number of his faults, but he cannot accomplish it. The messenger being gone, the philosopher remarked: What a worthy messenger! What a worthy messenger!"[9] The preacher, instead of vexing the ears of drowsy farmers on their day of rest at the end of the week,—for Sunday is the fit conclusion of an ill-spent week, and not the fresh and brave beginning of a new one,—with this one other draggle-tail of a sermon, should shout with thundering voice,—"Pause! Avast! Why so seeming fast, but deadly slow?"[1]

Shams and delusions are esteemed for soundest truths, while reality is fabulous. If men would steadily observe realities only, and not allow themselves to be deluded, life, to compare it with such things as we know, would be like a fairy tale and the Arabian Nights' Entertainments. If we respected only what is inevitable and has a right to be, music and poetry would resound along the streets. When we are unhurried and wise, we perceive that only great and worthy things have any permanent and absolute existence,—that petty fears and petty pleasures are but the shadow of the reality. This is always exhilarating and sublime. By closing the eyes and slumbering, and consenting to be deceived by shows, men establish and confirm their daily life of routine and habit every where, which still is built on purely illusory foundations. Children, who play life, discern its true law and relations more clearly than men, who

9. Confucius, *Analects* 14.
1. Father Taylor of the Seaman's Bethel in Boston was one such preacher famous for the nautical cast of his sermons.

fail to live it worthily, but who think that they are wiser by experience, that is, by failure. I have read in a Hindoo book, that "there was a king's son, who, being expelled in infancy from his native city, was brought up by a forester, and, growing up to maturity in that state, imagined himself to belong to the barbarous race with which he lived. One of his father's ministers having discovered him, revealed to him what he was, and the misconception of his character was removed, and he knew himself to be a prince. So soul," continues the Hindoo philosopher, "from the circumstances in which it is placed, mistakes its own character, until the truth is revealed to it by some holy teacher, and then it knows itself to be *Brahme*."[2] I perceive that we inhabitants of New England live this mean life that we do because our vision does not penetrate the surface of things. We think that that *is* which *appears* to be. If a man should walk through this town and see only the reality, where, think you, would the "Mill-dam"[3] go to? If he should give us an account of the realities he beheld there, we should not recognize the place in his description. Look at a meeting-house, or a court-house, or a jail, or a shop, or a dwelling-house, and say what that thing really is before a true gaze, and they would all go to pieces in your account of them. Men esteem truth remote, in the outskirts of the system, behind the farthest star, before Adam and after the last man. In eternity there is indeed something true and sublime. But all these times and places and occasions are now and here. God himself culminates in the present moment, and will never be more divine in the lapse of all the ages. And we are enabled to apprehend at all what is sublime and noble only by the perpetual instilling and drenching of the reality which surrounds us. The universe constantly and obediently answers to our conceptions; whether we travel fast or slow, the track is laid for us. Let us spend our lives in conceiving them. The poet or the artist never yet had so fair and noble a design but some of his posterity at least could accomplish it.

Let us spend one day as deliberately as Nature, and not be thrown off the track by every nutshell and mosquito's wing that falls on the rails. Let us rise early and fast, or break fast, gently and without perturbation; let company come and let company go, let the bells ring and the children cry,—determined to make a day of it. Why should we knock under and go with the stream? Let us not be upset and overwhelmed in that terrible rapid and whirlpool called a dinner, situated in the meridian shallows. Weather this danger and you are safe, for the rest of the way is down hill. With unrelaxed nerves, with morning vigor, sail by it, looking another way, tied to the mast like Ulysses.[4] If the engine whistles, let it whistle till it is hoarse for its pains. If the bell rings, why should we run? We will consider what kind of music they are like. Let us settle ourselves, and work and wedge our feet downward through the mud and slush of opinion, and prejudice, and tradition, and delusion, and appearance, that alluvion[5] which covers the globe, through Paris and London, through New York and Boston and Concord, through church and state, through poetry and philosophy and religion, till we come to a hard bottom and rocks in place, which we can call *reality*, and say, This is, and no mistake; and then begin, having a *point d'appui*,[6] below freshet and frost and fire, a place where you

---

2. In the Hindu triad, Brahma is the divine reality in the aspect of creator; Vishnu is the preserver and Siva, the destroyer.
3. The business center of Concord.
4. A precaution Ulysses (Odysseus) took to prevent his yielding to the call of the Sirens, sea nymphs whose singing lured ships to destruction.
5. Sediment deposited by flowing water along a shore or bank.
6. Basis, leverage point (French).

might found a wall or a state, or set a lamp-post safely, or perhaps a gauge, not a Nilometer,[7] but a Realometer, that future ages might know how deep a freshet of shams and appearances had gathered from time to time. If you stand right fronting and face to face to a fact, you will see the sun glimmer on both its surfaces, as if it were a cimeter, and feel its sweet edge dividing you through the heart and marrow, and so you will happily conclude your mortal career. Be it life or death, we crave only reality. If we are really dying, let us hear the rattle in our throats and feel cold in the extremities; if we are alive, let us go about our business.

Time is but the stream I go a-fishing in. I drink at it; but while I drink I see the sandy bottom and detect how shallow it is. Its thin current slides away, but eternity remains. I would drink deeper; fish in the sky, whose bottom is pebbly with stars. I cannot count one. I know not the first letter of the alphabet. I have always been regretting that I was not as wise as the day I was born. The intellect is a cleaver; it discerns and rifts its way into the secret of things. I do not wish to be any more busy with my hands than is necessary. My head is hands and feet. I feel all my best faculties concentrated in it. My instinct tells me that my head is an organ for burrowing, as some creatures use their snout and fore-paws, and with it I would mine and burrow my way through these hills. I think that the richest vein is somewhere hereabouts; so by the divining rod and thin rising vapors I judge; and here I will begin to mine.

Reading

With a little more deliberation in the choice of their pursuits, all men would perhaps become essentially students and observers, for certainly their nature and destiny are interesting to all alike. In accumulating property for ourselves or our posterity, in founding a family or a state, or acquiring fame even, we are mortal; but in dealing with truth we are immortal, and need fear no change nor accident. The oldest Egyptian or Hindoo philosopher raised a corner of the veil from the statue of the divinity; and still the trembling robe remains raised, and I gaze upon as fresh a glory as he did, since it was I in him that was then so bold, and it is he in me that now reviews the vision. No dust has settled on that robe; no time has elapsed since that divinity was revealed. That time which we really improve, or which is improvable, is neither past, present, nor future.

My residence was more favorable, not only to thought, but to serious reading, than a university; and though I was beyond the range of the ordinary circulating library, I had more than ever come within the influence of those books which circulate round the world, whose sentences were first written on bark, and are now merely copied from time to time on to linen paper. Says the poet Mîr Camar Uddîn Mast, "Being seated to run through the region of the spiritual world; I have had this advantage in books. To be intoxicated by a single glass of wine; I have experienced this pleasure when I have drunk the liquor of the esoteric doctrines."[8] I kept Homer's Iliad on my table through the summer, though I looked at his page only now and then. Incessant labor with my hands, at first, for I had my house to finish and my beans to hoe at the same time, made more study impossible. Yet I sustained myself by the

7. Gauge used at Memphis in ancient times for measuring the height of the Nile.

8. Thoreau knew this 18th-century Hindu poet from a French translation in a history of Hindu literature.

prospect of such reading in future. I read one or two shallow books of travel in the intervals of my work, till that employment made me ashamed of myself, and I asked where it was then that I lived.

The student may read Homer or Æschylus in the Greek without danger of dissipation or luxuriousness, for it implies that he in some measure emulate their heroes, and consecrate morning hours to their pages. The heroic books, even if printed in the character of our mother tongue, will always be in a language dead to degenerate times; and we must laboriously seek the meaning of each word and line, conjecturing a larger sense than common use permits out of what wisdom and valor and generosity we have. The modern cheap and fertile press, with all its translations, has done little to bring us nearer to the heroic writers of antiquity. They seem as solitary, and the letter in which they are printed as rare and curious, as ever. It is worth the expense of youthful days and costly hours, if you learn only some words of an ancient language, which are raised out of the trivialness of the street, to be perpetual suggestions and provocations. It is not in vain that the farmer remembers and repeats the few Latin words which he has heard. Men sometimes speak as if the study of the classics would at length make way for more modern and practical studies; but the adventurous student will always study classics, in whatever language they may be written and however ancient they may be. For what are the classics but the noblest recorded thoughts of man? They are the only oracles which are not decayed, and there are such answers to the most modern inquiry in them as Delphi and Dodona[9] never gave. We might as well omit to study Nature because she is old. To read well, that is, to read true books in a true spirit, is a noble exercise, and one that will task the reader more than any exercise which the customs of the day esteem. It requires a training such as the athletes underwent, the steady intention almost of the whole life to this object. Books must be read as deliberately and reservedly as they were written. It is not enough even to be able to speak the language of that nation by which they are written, for there is a memorable interval between the spoken and the written language, the language heard and the language read. The one is commonly transitory, a sound, a tongue, a dialect merely, almost brutish, and we learn it unconsciously, like the brutes, of our mothers. The other is the maturity and experience of that; if that is our mother tongue, this is our father tongue, a reserved and select expression, too significant to be heard by the ear, which we must be born again in order to speak. The crowds of men who merely *spoke* the Greek and Latin tongues in the middle ages were not entitled by the accident of birth to *read* the works of genius written in those languages; for these were not written in that Greek or Latin which they knew, but in the select language of literature. They had not learned the nobler dialects of Greece and Rome, but the very materials on which they were written were waste paper to them, and they prized instead a cheap contemporary literature. But when the several nations of Europe had acquired distinct though rude written languages of their own, sufficient for the purposes of their rising literatures, then first learning revived, and scholars were enabled to discern from that remoteness the treasures of antiquity. What the Roman and Grecian multitude could not *hear*, after the lapse of ages a few scholars *read*, and a few scholars only are still reading it.

---

9. Oracles of ancient Greece.

However much we may admire the orator's occasional bursts of eloquence, the noblest written words are commonly as far behind or above the fleeting spoken language as the firmament with its stars is behind the clouds. *There* are the stars, and they who can may read them. The astronomers forever comment on and observe them. They are not exhalations like our daily colloquies and vaporous breath. What is called eloquence in the forum is commonly found to be rhetoric in the study. The orator yields to the inspiration of a transient occasion, and speaks to the mob before him, to those who can *hear* him; but the writer, whose more equable life is his occasion, and who would be distracted by the event and the crowd which inspire the orator, speaks to the intellect and heart of mankind, to all in any age who can *understand* him.

No wonder that Alexander carried the Iliad with him on his expeditions in a precious casket.[1] A written word is the choicest of relics. It is something at once more intimate with us and more universal than any other work of art. It is the work of art nearest to life itself. It may be translated into every language, and not only be read but actually breathed from all human lips;—not be represented on canvas or in marble only, but be carved out of the breath of life itself. The symbol of an ancient man's thought becomes a modern man's speech. Two thousand summers have imparted to the monuments of Grecian literature, as to her marbles, only a maturer golden and autumnal tint, for they have carried their own serene and celestial atmosphere into all lands to protect them against the corrosion of time. Books are the treasured wealth of the world and the fit inheritance of generations and nations. Books, the oldest and the best, stand naturally and rightfully on the shelves of every cottage. They have no cause of their own to plead, but while they enlighten and sustain the reader his common sense will not refuse them. Their authors are a natural and irresistible aristocracy in every society, and, more than kings or emperors, exert an influence on mankind. When the illiterate and perhaps scornful trader has earned by enterprise and industry his coveted leisure and independence, and is admitted to the circles of wealth and fashion, he turns inevitably at last to those still higher but yet inaccessible circles of intellect and genius, and is sensible only of the imperfection of his culture and the vanity and insufficiency of all his riches, and further proves his good sense by the pains which he takes to secure for his children that intellectual culture whose want he so keenly feels; and thus it is that he becomes the founder of a family.

Those who have not learned to read the ancient classics in the language in which they were written must have a very imperfect knowledge of the history of the human race; for it is remarkable that no transcript of them has ever been made into any modern tongue, unless our civilization itself may be regarded as such a transcript. Homer has never yet been printed in English, nor Æschylus, nor Virgil even,—works as refined, as solidly done, and as beautiful almost as the morning itself; for later writers, say what we will of their genius, have rarely, if ever, equalled the elaborate beauty and finish and the lifelong and heroic literary labors of the ancients. They only talk of forgetting them who never knew them. It will be soon enough to forget them when we have the learning and the genius which will enable us to attend to and appreciate them. That age will be rich indeed when those relics which we call Classics, and the still older and more than classic but even less known Scriptures of the nations, shall have still further accumulated, when the Vaticans[2] shall be filled

1. Plutarch attests to this in his biography of Alexander.   2. I.e., libraries.

with Vedas and Zendavestas and Bibles, with Homers and Dantes and Shakspeares, and all the centuries to come shall have successively deposited their trophies in the forum of the world. By such a pile we may hope to scale heaven at last.

The works of the great poets have never yet been read by mankind, for only great poets can read them. They have only been read as the multitude read the stars, at most astrologically, not astronomically. Most men have learned to read to serve a paltry convenience, as they have learned to cipher in order to keep accounts and not be cheated in trade; but of reading as a noble intellectual exercise they know little or nothing; yet this only is reading, in a high sense, not that which lulls us as a luxury and suffers the nobler faculties to sleep the while, but what we have to stand on tiptoe to read and devote our most alert and wakeful hours to.

I think that having learned our letters we should read the best that is in literature, and not be forever repeating our a b abs, and words of one syllable, in the fourth or fifth classes, sitting on the lowest and foremost form all our lives.[3] Most men are satisfied if they read or hear read, and perchance have been convicted by the wisdom of one good book, the Bible, and for the rest of their lives vegetate and dissipate their faculties in what is called easy reading. There is a work in several volumes in our Circulating Library entitled Little Reading,[4] which I thought referred to a town of that name which I had not been to. There are those who, like cormorants and ostriches, can digest all sorts of this, even after the fullest dinner of meats and vegetables, for they suffer nothing to be wasted. If others are the machines to provide this provender, they are the machines to read it. They read the nine thousandth tale about Zebulon and Sephronia, and how they loved as none had ever loved before, and neither did the course of their true love run smooth,—at any rate, how it did run and stumble, and get up again and go on! how some poor unfortunate got up onto a steeple, who had better never have gone up as far as the belfry; and then, having needlessly got him up there, the happy novelist rings the bell for all the world to come together and hear, O dear! how he did get down again! For my part, I think that they had better metamorphose all such aspiring heroes of universal noveldom into man weathercocks, as they used to put heroes among the constellations, and let them swing round there till they are rusty, and not come down at all to bother honest men with their pranks. The next time the novelist rings the bell I will not stir though the meeting-house burn down. "The Skip of the Tip-Toe-Hop, a Romance of the Middle Ages, by the celebrated author of 'Title-Tol-Tan,'[5] to appear in monthly parts; a great rush; don't all come together." All this they read with saucer eyes, and erect and primitive curiosity, and with unwearied gizzard, whose corrugations even yet need no sharpening, just as some little four-year-old bencher[6] his two-cent gilt-covered edition of Cinderella,—without any improvement, that I can see, in the pronunciation, or accent, or emphasis, or any more skill in extracting or inserting the moral. The result is dulness of sight, a stagnation of the vital circulations, and a general deliquium and sloughing off of all the intellectual faculties. This sort of gingerbread is baked daily and more sedu-

---

3. I.e., with the youngest children at the front of a one-room schoolhouse.
4. Harding points out a basis for Thoreau's irony: a book called Much Instruction from Little Reading is included in the 1836 Catalogue of Concord Social Li-

brary.
5. Probably a play on James Fenimore Cooper's novel The Wept of the Wishton-Wish, which Thoreau would not have wasted his time reading.
6. A child too young to have graduated to a desk.

lously than pure wheat or rye-and-Indian in almost every oven, and finds a surer market.

The best books are not read even by those who are called good readers. What does our Concord culture amount to? There is in this town, with a very few exceptions, no taste for the best or for very good books even in English literature, whose words all can read and spell. Even the college-bred and so called liberally educated men here and elsewhere have really little or no acquaintance with the English classics; and as for the recorded wisdom of mankind, the ancient classics and Bibles, which are accessible to all who will know of them, there are the feeblest efforts any where made to become acquainted with them. I know a woodchopper, of middle age, who takes a French paper, not for news as he says, for he is above that, but to "keep himself in practice," he being a Canadian by birth; and when I ask him what he considers the best thing he can do in this world, he says, beside this, to keep up and add to his English. This is about as much as the college bred generally do or aspire to do, and they take an English paper for the purpose. One who has just come from reading perhaps one of the best English books will find how many with whom he can converse about it? Or suppose he comes from reading a Greek or Latin classic in the original, whose praises are familiar even to the so called illiterate; he will find nobody at all to speak to, but must keep silence about it. Indeed, there is hardly the professor in our colleges, who, if he has mastered the difficulties of the language, has proportionally mastered the difficulties of the wit and poetry of a Greek poet, and has any sympathy to impart to the alert and heroic reader; and as for the sacred Scriptures, or Bibles of mankind, who in this town can tell me even their titles? Most men do not know that any nation but the Hebrews have had a scripture. A man, any man, will go considerably out of his way to pick up a silver dollar; but here are golden words, which the wisest men of antiquity have uttered, and whose worth the wise of every succeeding age have assured us of;—and yet we learn to read only as far as Easy Reading, the primers and class-books, and when we leave school, the "Little Reading," and story books, which are for boys and beginners; and our reading, our conversation and thinking, are all on a very low level, worthy only of pygmies and manikens.

I aspire to be acquainted with wiser men than this our Concord soil has produced, whose names are hardly known here. Or shall I hear the name of Plato and never read his book? As if Plato were any townsman and I never saw him,—my next neighbor and I never heard him speak or attended to the wisdom of his words. But how actually is it? His Dialogues, which contain what was immortal in him, lie on the next shelf, and yet I never read them. We are under-bred and low-lived and illiterate; and in this respect I confess I do not make any very broad distinction between the illiterateness of my townsman who cannot read at all, and the illiterateness of him who has learned to read only what is for children and feeble intellects. We should be as good as the worthies of antiquity, but partly by first knowing how good they were. We are a race of tit-men,[7] and soar but little higher in our intellectual flights than the columns of the daily paper.

It is not all books that are as dull as their readers. There are probably words addressed to our condition exactly, which, if we could really hear and under-

7. Runts.

stand, would be more salutary than the morning or the spring to our lives, and possibly put a new aspect on the face of things for us. How many a man has dated a new era in his life from the reading of a book. The book exists for us perchance which will explain our miracles and reveal new ones. The at present unutterable things we may find somewhere uttered. These same questions that disturb and puzzle and confound us have in their turn occurred to all the wise men; not one has been omitted; and each has answered them, according to his ability, by his words and his life. Moreover, with wisdom we shall learn liberality. The solitary hired man on a farm in the outskirts of Concord, who has had his second birth and peculiar religious experience, and is driven as he believes into silent gravity and exclusiveness by his faith, may think it is not true; but Zoroaster, thousands of years ago, travelled the same road and had the same experience; but he, being wise, knew it to be universal, and treated his neighbors accordingly, and is even said to have invented and established worship among men. Let him humbly commune with Zoroaster then, and, through the liberalizing influence of all the worthies, with Jesus Christ himself, and let "our church" go by the board.

We boast that we belong to the nineteenth century and are making the most rapid strides of any nation. But consider how little this village does for its own culture. I do not wish to flatter my townsmen, nor to be flattered by them, for that will not advance either of us. We need to be provoked,—goaded like oxen, as we are, into a trot. We have a comparatively decent system of common schools, schools for infants only; but excepting the half-starved Lyceum[8] in the winter, and latterly the puny beginning of a library suggested by the state, no school for ourselves. We spend more on almost any article of bodily aliment or ailment than on our mental aliment. It is time that we had uncommon schools, that we did not leave off our education when we begin to be men and women. It is time that villages were universities, and their elder inhabitants the fellows of universities, with leisure—if they are indeed so well off—to pursue liberal studies the rest of their lives. Shall the world be confined to one Paris or one Oxford forever? Cannot students be boarded here and get a liberal education under the skies of Concord? Can we not hire some Abelard[9] to lecture us? Alas! what with foddering the cattle and tending the store, we are kept from school too long, and our education is sadly neglected. In this country, the village should in some respects take the place of the nobleman of Europe. It should be the patron of the fine arts. It is rich enough. It wants only the magnanimity and refinement. It can spend money enough on such things as farmers and traders value, but it is thought Utopian to propose spending money for things which more intelligent men know to be of far more worth. This town has spent seventeen thousand dollars on a town-house, thank fortune or politics, but probably it will not spend so much on living wit, the true meat to put into that shell, in a hundred years. The one hundred and twenty-five dollars annually subscribed for a Lyceum in the winter is better spent than any other equal sum raised in the town. If we live in the nineteenth century, why should we not enjoy the advantages which the nineteenth century offers? Why should our life be in any respect provincial? If we will read

---

8. Public hall where local citizens and others, often with national reputations, gave lectures on a great variety of topics. Thoreau was one of those in charge of lecture series at Concord for several years, and in 1844–45 divided the town by bringing Wendell Phil-

lips, the abolitionist, for a second controversial lecture. Concord Lyceum was in Thoreau's time one of the more liberal in the nation.

9. Peter Abelard (1079–1142) was a great teacher of philosophy and theology in medieval France.

newspapers, why not skip the gossip of Boston and take the best newspaper in the world at once?—not be sucking the pap of "neutral family" papers, or browsing "Olive-Branches" here in New England. Let the reports of all the learned societies come to us, and we will see if they know any thing. Why should we leave it to Harper & Brothers and Redding & Co.[1] to select our reading? As the nobleman of cultivated taste surrounds himself with whatever conduces to his culture,—genius—learning—wit—books—paintings—statuary — music —philosophical instruments, and the like; so let the village do,—not stop short at a pedagogue, a parson, a sexton, a parish library, and three selectmen, because our pilgrim forefathers got through a cold winter once on a bleak rock with these. To act collectively is according to the spirit of our institutions; and I am confident that, as our circumstances are more flourishing, our means are greater than the nobleman's. New England can hire all the wise men in the world to come and teach her, and board them round the while, and not be provincial at all. That is the *uncommon* school we want. Instead of noblemen, let us have noble villages of men. If it is necessary, omit one bridge over the river, go round a little there, and throw one arch at least over the darker gulf of ignorance which surrounds us.

Sounds

But while we are confined to books, though the most select and classic, and read only particular written languages, which are themselves but dialects and provincial, we are in danger of forgetting the language which all things and events speak without metaphor, which alone is copious and standard. Much is published, but little printed. The rays which stream through the shutter will be no longer remembered when the shutter is wholly removed. No method nor discipline can supersede the necessity of being forever on the alert. What is a course of history, or philosophy, or poetry, no matter how well selected, or the best society, or the most admirable routine of life, compared with the discipline of looking always at what is to be seen? Will you be a reader, a student merely, or a seer? Read your fate, see what is before you, and walk on into futurity.

I did not read books the first summer; I hoed beans. Nay, I often did better than this. There were times when I could not afford to sacrifice the bloom of the present moment to any work, whether of the head or hands. I love a broad margin to my life. Sometimes, in a summer morning, having taken my accustomed bath, I sat in my sunny doorway from sunrise till noon, rapt in a revery, amidst the pines and hickories and sumachs, in undisturbed solitude and stillness, while the birds sang around or flitted noiseless through the house, until by the sun falling in at my west window, or the noise of some traveller's wagon on the distant highway, I was reminded of the lapse of time. I grew in those seasons like corn in the night, and they were far better than any work of the hands would have been. They were not time subtracted from my life, but so much over and above my usual allowance. I realized what the Orientals mean by contemplation and the forsaking of works. For the most part, I minded not how the hours went. The day advanced as if to light some work of mine; it was morning, and lo, now it is evening, and nothing memora-

1. Major publishers and booksellers of New York City and Boston, respectively.

ble is accomplished. Instead of singing like the birds, I silently smiled at my incessant good fortune. As the sparrow had its trill, sitting on the hickory before my door, so had I my chuckle or suppressed warble which he might hear out of my nest. My days were not days of the week, bearing the stamp of any heathen deity,[2] nor were they minced into hours and fretted by the ticking of a clock; for I lived like the Puri Indians,[3] of whom it is said that "for yesterday, to-day, and to-morrow they have only one word, and they express the variety of meaning by pointing backward for yesterday, forward for to-morrow, and overhead for the passing day." This was sheer idleness to my fellow-townsmen, no doubt; but if the birds and flowers had tried me by their standard, I should not have been found wanting. A man must find his occasions in himself, it is true. The natural day is very calm, and will hardly reprove his indolence.

I had this advantage, at least, in my mode of life, over those who were obliged to look abroad for amusement, to society and the theatre, that my life itself was become my amusement and never ceased to be novel. It was a drama of many scenes and without an end. If we were always indeed getting our living, and regulating our lives according to the last and best mode we had learned, we should never be troubled with ennui. Follow your genius closely enough, and it will not fail to show you a fresh prospect every hour. Housework was a pleasant pastime. When my floor was dirty, I rose early, and, setting all my furniture out of doors on the grass, bed and bedstead making but one budget,[4] dashed water on the floor, and sprinkled white sand from the pond on it, and then with a broom scrubbed it clean and white; and by the time the villagers had broken their fast the morning sun had dried my house sufficiently to allow me to move in again, and my meditations were almost uninterrupted. It was pleasant to see my whole household effects out on the grass, making a little pile like a gypsy's pack, and my three-legged table, from which I did not remove the books and pen and ink, standing amid the pines and hickories. They seemed glad to get out themselves, and as if unwilling to be brought in. I was sometimes tempted to stretch an awning over them and take my seat there. It was worth the while to see the sun shine on these things, and hear the free wind blow on them; so much more interesting most familiar objects look out of doors than in the house. A bird sits on the next bough, life-everlasting grows under the table, and blackberry vines run round its legs; pine cones, chestnut burs, and strawberry leaves are strewn about. It looked as if this was the way these forms came to be transferred to our furniture, to tables, chairs, and bedsteads,—because they once stood in their midst.

My house was on the side of a hill, immediately on the edge of the larger wood, in the midst of a young forest of pitch pines and hickories, and half a dozen rods from the pond, to which a narrow footpath led down the hill. In my front yard grew the strawberry, blackberry, and life-everlasting, johnswort and golden-rod, shrub-oaks and sand-cherry, blueberry and ground-nut. Near the end of May, the sand-cherry, *Cerasus pumila*, adorned the sides of the path with its delicate flowers arranged in umbels cylindrically about its short stems, which last, in the fall, weighed down with good sized and handsome cherries, fell over in wreaths like rays on every side. I tasted them out of com-

<hr />

2. Tuesday, Wednesday, Thursday, and Friday all derive from gods of Norse mythology, while Saturday is named for the Roman god Saturn.

3. Brazilian Indians whom Thoreau read about in Ida Pfeiffer's A *Lady's Voyage round the World* (1852).

4. Collection.

pliment to Nature, though they were scarcely palatable. The sumach, *Rhus glabra*, grew luxuriantly about the house, pushing up through the embankment which I had made, and growing five or six feet the first season. Its broad pinnate tropical leaf was pleasant though strange to look on. The large buds, suddenly pushing out late in the spring from dry sticks which had seemed to be dead, developed themselves as by magic into graceful green and tender boughs, an inch in diameter; and sometimes, as I sat at my window, so heedlessly did they grow and tax their weak joints, I heard a fresh and tender bough suddenly fall like a fan to the ground, when there was not a breath of air stirring, broken off by its own weight. In August, the large masses of berries, which, when in flower, had attracted many wild bees, gradually assumed their bright velvety crimson hue, and by their weight again bent down and broke the tender limbs.

As I sit at my window this summer afternoon, hawks are circling about my clearing; the tantivy[5] of wild pigeons, flying by twos and threes athwart my view, or perching restless on the white-pine boughs behind my house, gives a voice to the air; a fishhawk dimples the glassy surface of the pond and brings up a fish; a mink steals out of the marsh before my door and seizes a frog by the shore; the sedge is bending under the weight of the reed-birds flitting hither and thither; and for the last half hour I have heard the rattle of railroad cars, now dying away and then reviving like the beat of a partridge, conveying travellers from Boston to the country. For I did not live so out of the world as that boy, who, as I hear, was put out to a farmer in the east part of the town, but ere long ran away and came home again, quite down at the heel and homesick. He had never seen such a dull and out of-the-way place; the folks were all gone off; why, you couldn't even hear the whistle! I doubt if there is such a place in Massachusetts now:—

> "In truth, our village has become a butt
> For one of those fleet railroad shafts, and o'er
> Our peaceful plain its soothing sound is—Concord."[6]

The Fitchburg railroad touches the pond about a hundred rods south of where I dwell. I usually go to the village along its causeway, and am, as it were, related to society by this link. The men on the freight trains, who go over the whole length of the road, bow to me as to an old acquaintance, they pass me so often, and apparently they take me for an employee; and so I am. I too would fain be a track-repairer somewhere in the orbit of the earth.

The whistle of the locomotive penetrates my woods summer and winter, sounding like the scream of a hawk sailing over some farmer's yard, informing me that many restless city merchants are arriving within the circle of the town, or adventurous country traders from the other side. As they come under one horizon, they shout their warning to get off the track of the other, heard sometimes through the circles of two towns. Here come your groceries, country; your rations, countrymen! Nor is there any man so independent on his farm that he can say them nay. And here's your pay for them! screams the countryman's whistle; timber like long battering rams going twenty miles an hour against the city's walls, and chairs enough to seat all the weary and heavy laden

---

5. Hurtling.
6. From Ellery Channing's *Walden Spring*, published in *The Woodman, and Other Poems.*

that dwell within them. With such huge and lumbering civility the country hands a chair to the city. All the Indian huckleberry hills are stripped, all the cranberry meadows are raked into the city. Up comes the cotton, down goes the woven cloth; up comes the silk, down goes the woollen; up come the books, but down goes the wit that writes them.

When I meet the engine with its train of cars moving off with planetary motion,—or, rather, like a comet, for the beholder knows not if with that velocity and with that direction it will ever revisit this system, since its orbit does not look like a returning curve,—with its steam cloud like a banner streaming behind in golden and silver wreaths, like many a downy cloud which I have seen, high in the heavens, unfolding its masses to the light,—as if this travelling demigod, this cloud-compeller, would ere long take the sunset sky for the livery of his train; when I hear the iron horse make the hills echo with his snort like thunder, shaking the earth with his feet, and breathing fire and smoke from his nostrils, (what kind of winged horse or fiery dragon they will put into the new Mythology I don't know,) it seems as if the earth had got a race now worthy to inhabit it. If all were as it seems, and men made the elements their servants for noble ends! If the cloud that hangs over the engine were the perspiration of heroic deeds, or as beneficent to men as that which floats over the farmer's fields, then the elements and Nature herself would cheerfully accompany men on their errands and be their escort.

I watch the passage of the morning cars with the same feeling that I do the rising of the sun, which is hardly more regular. Their train of clouds stretching far behind and rising higher and higher, going to heaven while the cars are going to Boston, conceals the sun for a minute and casts my distant field into the shade, a celestial train beside which the petty train of cars which hugs the earth is but the barb of the spear. The stabler of the iron horse was up early this winter morning by the light of the stars amid the mountains, to fodder and harness his steed. Fire, too, was awakened thus early to put the vital heat in him and get him off. If the enterprise were as innocent as it is early! If the snow lies deep, they strap on his snow-shoes, and with the giant plow, plow a furrow from the mountains to the seaboard, in which the cars, like a following drill-barrow, sprinkle all the restless men and floating merchandise in the country for seed. All day the fire-steed flies over the country, stopping only that his master may rest, and I am awakened by his tramp and defiant snort at midnight, when in some remote glen in the woods he fronts the elements incased in ice and snow; and he will reach his stall only with the morning star, to start once more on his travels without rest or slumber. Or perchance, at evening, I hear him in his stable blowing off the superfluous energy of the day, that he may calm his nerves and cool his liver and brain for a few hours of iron slumber. If the enterprise were as heroic and commanding as it is protracted and unwearied!

Far through unfrequented woods on the confines of towns, where once only the hunter penetrated by day, in the darkest night dart these bright saloons without the knowledge of their inhabitants; this moment stopping at some brilliant station-house in town or city, where a social crowd is gathered, the next in the Dismal Swamp,[7] scaring the owl and fox. The startings and arrivals of the cars are now the epochs in the village day. They go and come with such

---

7. The real Dismal Swamp is in southeastern Virginia and northeastern North Carolina.

regularity and precision, and their whistle can be heard so far, that the farmers set their clocks by them, and thus one well conducted institution regulates a whole country. Have not men improved somewhat in punctuality since the railroad was invented? Do they not talk and think faster in the depot than they did in the stage-office? There is something electrifying in the atmosphere of the former place. I have been astonished at the miracles it has wrought; that some of my neighbors, who, I should have prophesied, once for all, would never get to Boston by so prompt a conveyance, were on hand when the bell rang. To do things "railroad fashion" is now the by-word; and it is worth the while to be warned so often and so sincerely by any power to get off its track. There is no stopping to read the riot act, no firing over the heads of the mob, in this case. We have constructed a fate, an Atropos,[8] that never turns aside. (Let that be the name of your engine.) Men are advertised that at a certain hour and minute these bolts will be shot toward particular points of the compass; yet it interferes with no man's business, and the children go to school on the other track. We live the steadier for it. We are all educated thus to be sons of Tell.[9] The air is full of invisible bolts. Every path but your own is the path of fate. Keep on your own track, then.

What recommends commerce to me is its enterprise and bravery. It does not clasp its hands and pray to Jupiter. I see these men every day go about their business with more or less courage and content, doing more even than they suspect, and perchance better employed than they could have consciously devised. I am less affected by their heroism who stood up for half an hour in the front line at Buena Vista,[1] than by the steady and cheerful valor of the men who inhabit the snow-plough for their winter quarters; who have not merely the three-o'-clock in the morning courage,[2] which Bonaparte thought was the rarest, but whose courage does not go to rest so early, who go to sleep only when the storm sleeps or the sinews of their iron steed are frozen. On this morning of the Great Snow, perchance, which is still raging and chilling men's blood, I hear the muffled tone of their engine bell from out the fog bank of their chilled breath, which announces that the cars are coming, without long delay, notwithstanding the veto of a New England north-east snow storm, and I behold the ploughmen covered with snow and rime, their heads peering above the mould-board which is turning down other than daisies and the nests of field-mice, like bowlders of the Sierra Nevada, that occupy an outside place in the universe.

Commerce is unexpectedly confident and serene, alert, adventurous, and unwearied. It is very natural in its methods withal, far more so than many fantastic enterprises and sentimental experiments, and hence its singular success. I am refreshed and expanded when the freight train rattles past me, and I smell the stores which go dispensing their odors all the way from Long Wharf to Lake Champlain,[3] reminding me of foreign parts, of coral reefs, and Indian oceans, and tropical climes, and the extent of the globe. I feel more like a

---

8. In Greek mythology, the Fate who cuts the thread of human life.
9. I.e., to live coolly among dangers, like the son of the Swiss hero William Tell, who stood still so Tell could shoot an apple off his head.
1. Battlefield near Saltillo, Mexico, where Zachary Taylor's forces defeated the Mexican army under Santa Anna in 1847. Such victories were widely hailed, but many Americans, Thoreau among them, could not ig-

nore the fact that the better-equipped Americans were arguably the aggressors in a war strongly supported by slaveholders, who stood to gain slave territory from it.
2. Courage not painstakingly worked up but coming forth spontaneously, as when a soldier is awakened suddenly in the dead of night.
3. From Boston Harbor to Lake Champlain, on the New York–Vermont border.

citizen of the world at the sight of the palm-leaf which will cover so many flaxen New England heads the next summer, the Manilla hemp and cocoanut husks, the old junk, gunny bags, scrap iron, and rusty nails. This car-load of torn sails is more legible and interesting now than if they should be wrought into paper and printed books. Who can write so graphically the history of the storms they have weathered as these rents have done? They are proof-sheets which need no correction. Here goes lumber from the Maine woods, which did not go out to sea in the last freshet, risen four dollars on the thousand because of what did go out or was split up; pine, spruce, cedar,—first, second, third and fourth qualities, so lately all of one quality, to wave over the bear, and moose, and caribou. Next rolls Thomaston lime, a prime lot, which will get far among the hills before it gets slacked. These rags in bales, of all hues and qualities, the lowest condition to which cotton and linen descend, the final result of dress,—of patterns which are no no longer cried up,[4] unless it be in Milwaukie, as those splendid articles, English, French, or American prints, ginghams, muslins, &c., gathered from all quarters both of fashion and poverty, going to become paper of one color or a few shades only, on which forsooth will be written tales of real life, high and low, and founded on fact![5] This closed car smells of salt fish, the strong New England and commercial scent, reminding me of the Grand Banks[6] and the fisheries. Who has not seen a salt fish, thoroughly cured for this world, so that nothing can spoil it, and putting the perseverance of the saints to the blush? with which you may sweep or pave the streets, and split your kindlings, and the teamster shelter himself and his lading against sun, wind and rain behind it,—and the trader, as a Concord trader once did, hang it up by his door for a sign when he commences business, until at last his oldest customer cannot tell surely whether it be animal, vegetable, or mineral, and yet it shall be as pure as a snowflake, and if it be put into a pot and boiled, will come out an excellent dun[7] fish for a Saturday's dinner. Next Spanish hides, with the tails still preserving their twist and the angle of elevation they had when the oxen that wore them were careering over the pampas of the Spanish main,—a type of all obstinacy, and evincing how almost hopeless and incurable are all constitutional vices. I confess, that practically speaking, when I have learned a man's real disposition, I have no hopes of changing it for the better or worse in this state of existence. As the Orientals say, "A cur's tail may be warmed, and pressed, and bound round with ligatures, and after a twelve years' labor bestowed upon it, still it will retain its natural form."[8] The only effectual cure for such inveteracies as these tails exhibit is to make glue of them, which I believe is what is usually done with them, and then they will stay put and stick. Here is a hogshead of molasses or of brandy directed to John Smith, Cuttingsville, Vermont, some trader among the Green Mountains, who imports for the farmers near his clearing, and now perchance stands over his bulk-head and thinks of the last arrivals on the coast, how they may affect the price for him, telling his customers this moment, as he has told them twenty times before this morning, that he expects some by the next train of prime quality. It is advertised in the Cuttingsville Times.

4. Praised.
5. Thoreau parodies innumerable subtitles of sentimental and sensationalistic fiction.
6. Southeast of Newfoundland.

7. Dried codfish, with a pun on "done."
8. From the fable of the lion and the rabbit in Charles Wilkins's translation of Fables and Proverbs from the Sanskrit.

While these things go up other things come down. Warned by the whizzing sound, I look up from my book and see some tall pine, hewn on far northern hills, which has winged its way over the Green Mountains and the Connecticut, shot like an arrow through the township within ten minutes, and scarce another eye beholds it; going

> "to be the mast
> Of some great ammiral."⁹

And hark! here comes the cattle-train bearing the cattle of a thousand hills, sheepcots, stables, and cow-yards in the air, drovers with their sticks, and shepherd boys in the midst of their flocks, all but the mountain pastures, whirled along like leaves blown from the mountains by the September gales. The air is filled with the bleating of calves and sheep, and the hustling of oxen, as if a pastoral valley were going by. When the old bell-wether at the head rattles his bell, the mountains do indeed skip like rams and the little hills like lambs.¹ A car-load of drovers, too, in the midst, on a level with their droves now, their vocation gone, but still clinging to their useless sticks as their badge of office. But their dogs, where are they? It is a stampede to them; they are quite thrown out; they have lost the scent. Methinks I hear them barking behind the Peterboro' Hills, or panting up the western slope of the Green Mountains.² They will not be in at the death. Their vocation, too, is gone. Their fidelity and sagacity are below par now. They will slink back to their kennels in disgrace, or perchance run wild and strike a league with the wolf and the fox. So is your pastoral life whirled past and away. But the bell rings, and I must get off the track and let the cars go by;—

> What's the railroad to me?
> I never go to see
> Where it ends.
> It fills a few hollows,
> And makes banks for the swallows,
> It sets the sand a-blowing,
> And the blackberries a-growing,

but I cross it like a cart-path in the woods. I will not have my eyes put out and my ears spoiled by its smoke and steam and hissing.

Now that the cars are gone by, and all the restless world with them, and the fishes in the pond no longer feel their rumbling, I am more alone than ever. For the rest of the long afternoon, perhaps, my meditations are interrupted only by the faint rattle of a carriage or team along the distant highway.

Sometimes, on Sundays, I heard the bells, the Lincoln, Acton, Bedford, or Concord bell, when the wind was favorable, a faint, sweet, and, as it were, natural melody, worth importing into the wilderness. At a sufficient distance over the woods this sound acquires a certain vibratory hum, as if the pine needles in the horizon were the strings of a harp which it swept. All sound heard at the greatest possible distance produces one and the same effect, a

---

9. Milton, *Paradise Lost* 1.293–94.
1. In Psalm 114.4: "The mountains skipped like rams, and the little hills like lambs"; the motivation for skipping is the fear of God, not joy.

2. The Peterborough Hills are in southwestern New Hampshire. The Green Mountains run from Vermont into Massachusetts.

vibration of the universal lyre, just as the intervening atmosphere makes a distant ridge of earth interesting to our eyes by the azure tint it imparts to it. There came to me in this case a melody which the air had strained, and which had conversed with every leaf and needle of the wood, that portion of the sound which the elements had taken up and modulated and echoed from vale to vale. The echo is, to some extent, an original sound, and therein is the magic and charm of it. It is not merely a repetition of what was worth repeating in the bell, but partly the voice of the wood; the same trivial words and notes sung by a wood-nymph.

At evening, the distant lowing of some cow in the horizon beyond the woods sounded sweet and melodious, and at first I would mistake it for the voices of certain minstrels by whom I was sometimes serenaded, who might be straying over hill and dale; but soon I was not unpleasantly disappointed when it was prolonged into the cheap and natural music of the cow. I do not mean to be satirical, but to express my appreciation of those youths' singing, when I state that I perceived clearly that it was akin to the music of the cow, and they were at length one articulation of Nature.

Regularly at half past seven, in one part of the summer, after the evening train had gone by, the whippoorwills chanted their vespers for half an hour, sitting on a stump by my door, or upon the ridge pole of the house. They would begin to sing almost with as much precision as a clock, within five minutes of a particular time, referred to the setting of the sun, every evening. I had a rare opportunity to become acquainted with their habits. Sometimes I heard four or five at once in different parts of the wood, by accident one a bar behind another, and so near me that I distinguished not only the cluck after each note, but often that singular buzzing sound like a fly in a spider's web, only proportionally louder. Sometimes one would circle round and round me in the woods a few feet distant as if tethered by a string, when probably I was near its eggs. They sang at intervals throughout the night, and were again as musical as ever just before and about dawn.

When other birds are still the screech owls take up the strain, like mourning women their ancient u-lu-lu. Their dismal scream is truly Ben Jonsonian.[3] Wise midnight hags! It is no honest and blunt tu-whit tu-who of the poets, but, without jesting, a most solemn graveyard ditty, the mutual consolations of suicide lovers remembering the pangs and the delights of supernal love in the infernal groves. Yet I love to hear their wailing, their doleful responses, trilled along the wood-side, reminding me sometimes of music and singing birds; as if it were the dark and tearful side of music, the regrets and sighs that would fain be sung. They are the spirits, the low spirits and melancholy forebodings, of fallen souls that once in human shape night-walked the earth and did the deeds of darkness, now expiating their sins with their wailing hymns or threnodies[4] in the scenery of their transgressions. They give me a new sense of the variety and capacity of that nature which is our common dwelling. *Oh-o-o-o-o that I never had been bor-r-r-r-n!* sighs one on this side of the pond, and circles with the restlessness of despair to some new perch on the gray oaks. Then—*that I never had been bor-r-r-r-n!* echoes another on the farther side with tremulous sincerity, and—*bor-r-r-r-n!* comes faintly from far in the Lincoln woods.

---

3. Harding suggests that Thoreau might have been thinking of "We give thee a shout: Hoo!" in Jonson's *Masque of Queens*, 2.317–18.
4. Dirges.

I was also serenaded by a hooting owl. Near at hand you could fancy it the most melancholy sound in Nature, as if she meant by this to stereotype and make permanent in her choir the dying moans of a human being,—some poor weak relic of mortality who has left hope behind, and howls like an animal, yet with human sobs, on entering the dark valley, made more awful by a certain gurgling melodiousness,—I find myself beginning with the letters gl when I try to imitate it,—expressive of a mind which has reached the gelati- nous mildewy stage in the mortification of all healthy and courageous thought. It reminded me of ghouls and idiots and insane howlings. But now one answers from far woods in a strain made really melodious by distance,—*Hoo hoo hoo, hoorer hoo*; and indeed for the most part it suggested only pleasing associations, whether heard by day or night, summer or winter.

I rejoice that there are owls. Let them do the idiotic and maniacal hooting for men. It is a sound admirably suited to swamps and twilight woods which no day illustrates, suggesting a vast and undeveloped nature which men have not recognized. They represent the stark twilight and unsatisfied thoughts which all have. All day the sun has shone on the surface of some savage swamp, where the double spruce stands hung with usnea lichens, and small hawks circulate above, and the chicadee lisps amid the evergreens, and the partridge and rabbit skulk beneath; but now a more dismal and fitting day dawns, and a different race of creatures awakes to express the meaning of Nature there.

Late in the evening I heard the distant rumbling of wagons over bridges,— a sound heard farther than almost any other at night,—the baying of dogs, and sometimes again the lowing of some disconsolate cow in a distant barn-yard. In the mean while all the shore rang with the trump of bullfrogs, the sturdy spirits of ancient wine-bibbers and wassailers, still unrepentant, trying to sing a catch in their Stygian lake,[5]—if the Walden nymphs will pardon the com- parison, for though there are almost no weeds, there are frogs there,—who would fain keep up the hilarious rules of their old festal tables, though their voices have waxed hoarse and solemnly grave, mocking at mirth, and the wine has lost its flavor, and become only liquor to distend their paunches, and sweet intoxication never comes to drown the memory of the past, but mere satura- tion and waterloggedness and distention. The most aldermanic, with his chin upon a heart-leaf, which serves for a napkin to his drooling chaps, under this northern shore quaffs a deep draught of the once scorned water, and passes round the cup with the ejaculation *tr-r-r-oonk, tr-r-r-oonk, tr-r-r-oonk!* and straightway comes over the water from some distant cove the same password repeated, where the next in seniority and girth has gulped down to his mark; and when this observance has made the circuit of the shores, then ejaculates the master of ceremonies, with satisfaction, *tr-r-r-oonk!* and each in his turn repeats the same down to the least distended, leakiest, and flabbiest paunched, that there be no mistake; and then the bowl goes round again and again, until the sun disperses the morning mist, and only the patriarch is not under the pond, but vainly bellowing *troonk* from time to time, and pausing for a reply.[6]

I am not sure that I ever heard the sound of cock-crowing from my clearing, and I thought that it might be worth the while to keep a cockerel for his music

---

5. In Greek mythology the Styx is the principal river of the Underworld.
6. A mock-heroic allusion to Brutus's words to the citi- zens, "I pause for a reply" in Shakespeare's *Julius Cae- sar* 3.2.

merely, as a singing bird. The note of this once wild Indian pheasant is certainly the most remarkable of any bird's, and if they could be naturalized without being domesticated, it would soon become the most famous sound in our woods, surpassing the clangor of the goose and the hooting of the owl; and then imagine the cackling of the hens to fill the pauses when their lords' clarions rested! No wonder that man added this bird to his tame stock,—to say nothing of the eggs and drumsticks. To walk in a winter morning in a wood where these birds abounded, their native woods, and hear the wild cockerels crow on the trees, clear and shrill for miles over the resounding earth, drowning the feebler notes of other birds,—think of it! It would put nations on the alert. Who would not be early to rise, and rise earlier and earlier every successive day of his life, till he became unspeakably healthy, wealthy, and wise? This foreign bird's note is celebrated by the poets of all countries along with the notes of their native songsters. All climates agree with brave Chanticleer. He is more indigenous even than the natives. His health is ever good, his lungs are sound, his spirits never flag. Even the sailor on the Atlantic and Pacific is awakened by his voice; but its shrill sound never roused me from my slumbers. I kept neither dog, cat, cow, pig, nor hens, so that you would have said there was a deficiency of domestic sounds; neither the churn, nor the spinning wheel, nor even the singing of the kettle, nor the hissing of the urn, nor children crying, to comfort one. An old-fashioned man would have lost his senses or died of ennui before this. Not even rats in the wall, for they were starved out, or rather were never baited in,—only squirrels on the roof and under the floor, a whippoorwill on the ridge pole, a blue-jay screaming beneath the window, a hare or woodchuck under the house, a screech-owl or a cat-owl behind it, a flock of wild geese or a laughing loon on the pond, and a fox to bark in the night. Not even a lark or an oriole, those mild plantation birds, ever visited my clearing. No cockerels to crow nor hens to cackle in the yard. No yard! but unfenced Nature reaching up to your very sills. A young forest growing up under your windows, and wild sumachs and blackberry vines breaking through into your cellar; sturdy pitch-pines rubbing and creaking against the shingles for want of room, their roots reaching quite under the house. Instead of a scuttle or a blind blown off in the gale,—a pine tree snapped off or torn up by the roots behind your house for fuel. Instead of no path to the front-yard gate in the Great Snow,—no gate,—no front-yard,—and no path to the civilized world!

Solitude

This is a delicious evening, when the whole body is one sense, and imbibes delight through every pore. I go and come with a strange liberty in Nature, a part of herself. As I walk along the stony shore of the pond in my shirt sleeves, though it is cool as well as cloudy and windy, and I see nothing special to attract me, all the elements are unusually congenial to me. The bullfrogs trump to usher in the night, and the note of the whippoorwill is borne on the rippling wind from over the water. Sympathy with the fluttering alder and poplar leaves almost takes away my breath; yet, like the lake, my serenity is rippled but not ruffled. These small waves raised by the evening wind are as remote from the storm as the smooth reflecting surface. Though it is now dark, the wind still blows and roars in the wood, the waves still dash, and some creatures lull the rest with their notes. The repose is never complete. The wildest animals do not repose, but seek their prey now; the fox, and skunk, and rabbit, now roam the fields and woods without fear. They are Nature's watchmen,—links which connect the days of animated life.

When I return to my house I find that visitors have been there and left their cards, either a bunch of flowers, or a wreath of evergreen, or a name in pencil on a yellow walnut leaf or a chip. They who come rarely to the woods take some little piece of the forest into their hands to play with by the way, which they leave, either intentionally or accidentally. One has peeled a willow wand, woven it into a ring, and dropped it on my table. I could always tell if visitors had called in my absence, either by the bended twigs or grass, or the print of their shoes, and generally of what sex or age or quality they were by some slight trace left, as a flower dropped, or a bunch of grass plucked and thrown away, even as far off as the railroad, half a mile distant, or by the lingering odor of a cigar or pipe. Nay, I was frequently notified of the passage of a traveller along the highway sixty rods off by the scent of his pipe.

There is commonly sufficient space about us. Our horizon is never quite at our elbows. The thick wood is not just at our door, nor the pond, but somewhat is always clearing, familiar and worn by us, appropriated and fenced in some way, and reclaimed from Nature. For what reason have I this vast range and circuit, some square miles of unfrequented forest, for my privacy, abandoned to me by men? My nearest neighbor is a mile distant, and no house is visible from any place but the hill-tops within half a mile of my own. I have my horizon bounded by woods all to myself; a distant view of the railroad where it touches the pond on the one hand, and of the fence which skirts the woodland road on the other. But for the most part it is as solitary where I live as on the prairies. It is as much Asia or Africa as New England. I have, as it were, my own sun and moon and stars, and a little world all to myself. At night there was never a traveller passed my house, or knocked at my door, more than if I were the first or last man; unless it were in the spring, when at long intervals some came from the village to fish for pouts,—they plainly fished much more in the Walden Pond of their own natures, and baited their hooks with darkness,—but they soon retreated, usually with light baskets, and left "the world to darkness and to me,"[7] and the black kernel of the night was never profaned by any human neighborhood. I believe that men are generally still a little afraid of the dark, though the witches are all hung, and Christianity and candles have been introduced.

Yet I experienced sometimes that the most sweet and tender, the most innocent and encouraging society may be found in any natural object, even for the poor misanthrope and most melancholy man. There can be no very black melancholy to him who lives in the midst of Nature and has his senses still. There was never yet such a storm but it was Æolian[8] music to a healthy and innocent ear. Nothing can rightly compel a simple and brave man to a vulgar sadness. While I enjoy the friendship of the seasons I trust that nothing can make life a burden to me. The gentle rain which waters my beans and keeps me in the house to-day is not drear and melancholy, but good for me too. Though it prevents my hoeing them, it is of far more worth than my hoeing.

7. Thomas Gray's *Elegy Written in a Country Churchyard*.
8. The Aeolian harp (named for Aeolus, Greek keeper of the winds) was then commonly placed in the open air or near an open window so that the wind could cause it to make soft sounds.

If it should continue so long as to cause the seeds to rot in the ground and destroy the potatoes in the low lands, it would still be good for the grass on the uplands, and, being good for the grass, it would be good for me. Sometimes, when I compare myself with other men, it seems as if I were more favored by the gods than they, beyond any deserts that I am conscious of; as if I had a warrant and surety at their hands which my fellows have not, and were especially guided and guarded. I do not flatter myself, but if it be possible they flatter me. I have never felt lonesome, or in the least oppressed by a sense of solitude, but once, and that was a few weeks after I came to the woods, when, for an hour, I doubted if the near neighborhood of man was not essential to a serene and healthy life. To be alone was something unpleasant. But I was at the same time conscious of a slight insanity in my mood, and seemed to foresee my recovery. In the midst of a gentle rain while these thoughts prevailed, I was suddenly sensible of such sweet and beneficent society in Nature, in the very pattering of the drops, and in every sound and sight around my house, an infinite and unaccountable friendliness all at once like an atmosphere sustaining me, as made the fancied advantages of human neighborhood insignificant, and I have never thought of them since. Every little pine needle expanded and swelled with sympathy and befriended me. I was so distinctly made aware of the presence of something kindred to me, even in scenes which we are accustomed to call wild and dreary, and also that the nearest of blood to me and humanest was not a person nor a villager, that I thought no place could ever be strange to me again.—

> "Mourning untimely consumes the sad;
> Few are their days in the land of the living,
> Beautiful daughter of Toscar."[9]

Some of my pleasantest hours were during the long rain storms in the spring or fall, which confined me to the house for the afternoon as well as the forenoon, soothed by their ceaseless roar and pelting; when an early twilight ushered in a long evening in which many thoughts had time to take root and unfold themselves. In those driving north-east rains which tried the village houses so, when the maids stood ready with mop and pail in front entries to keep the deluge out, I sat behind my door in my little house, which was all entry, and thoroughly enjoyed its protection. In one heavy thunder shower the lightning struck a large pitch-pine across the pond, making a very conspicuous and perfectly regular spiral groove from top to bottom, an inch or more deep, and four or five inches wide, as you would groove a walking-stick. I passed it again the other day, and was struck with awe on looking up and beholding that mark, now more distinct than ever, where a terrific and resistless bolt came down out of the harmless sky eight years ago. Men frequently say to me, "I should think you would feel lonesome down there, and want to be nearer to folks, rainy and snowy days and nights especially." I am tempted to reply to such,—This whole earth which we inhabit is but a point in space. How far apart, think you, dwell the two most distant inhabitants of yonder star, the breadth of whose disk cannot be appreciated by our instruments? Why should I feel lonely? is not our planet in the Milky Way? This which you put seems to me not to be the most important question. What sort of space is that which

9. Harding identifies this as from the poem *Croma* in Patrick MacGregor's translation of *The Genuine Remains of Ossian*.

separates a man from his fellows and makes him solitary? I have found that no exertion of the legs can bring two minds much nearer to one another. What do we want most to dwell near to? Not to many men surely, the depot, the post-office, the bar-room, the meeting-house, the school-house, the grocery, Beacon Hill, or the Five Points,[1] where men most congregate, but to the perennial source of our life, whence in all our experience we have found that to issue; as the willow stands near the water and sends out its roots in that direction. This will vary with different natures, but this is the place where a wise man will dig his cellar. . . . I one evening overtook one of my townsmen, who has accumulated what is called "a handsome property",—though I never got a *fair* view of it,—on the Walden road, driving a pair of cattle to market, who inquired of me how I could bring my mind to give up so many of the comforts of life. I answered that I was very sure I liked it passably well; I was not joking. And so I went home to my bed, and left him to pick his way through the darkness and the mud to Brighton,—or Bright-town,—which place he would reach some time in the morning.

Any prospect of awakening or coming to life to a dead man makes indifferent all times and places. The place where that may occur is always the same, and indescribably pleasant to all our senses. For the most part we allow only outlying and transient circumstances to make our occasions. They are, in fact, the cause of our distraction. Nearest to all things is that power which fashions their being. *Next* to us the grandest laws are continually being executed. *Next* to us is not the workman whom we have hired, with whom we love so well to talk, but the workman whose work we are.

"How vast and profound is the influence of the subtile powers of Heaven and of Earth!"

"We seek to perceive them, and we do not see them; we seek to hear them, and we do not hear them; identified with the substance of things, they cannot be separated from them."

"They cause that in all the universe men purify and sanctify their hearts, and clothe themselves in their holiday garments to offer sacrifices and oblations to their ancestors. It is an ocean of subtile intelligences. They are every where, above us, on our left, on our right; they environ us on all sides."[2]

We are the subjects of an experiment which is not a little interesting to me. Can we not do without the society of our gossips a little while under these circumstances,—have our own thoughts to cheer us? Confucious says truly, "Virtue does not remain as an abandoned orphan; it must of necessity have neighbors."[3]

With thinking we may be beside ourselves in a sane sense. By a conscious effort of the mind we can stand aloof from actions and their consequences; and all things, good and bad, go by us like a torrent. We are not wholly involved in Nature. I may be either the drift-wood in the stream, or Indra[4] in the sky looking down on it. I *may* be affected by a theatrical exhibition; on the other hand, I *may not* be affected by an actual event which appears to concern me much more. I only know myself as a human entity; the scene, so to speak,

---

1. In lower Manhattan, notorious for squalor and corruption. The State House is on Boston's Beacon Hill. (Writing to G. W. Curtis, one of the "raisers" of Thoreau's cabin, Herman Melville ironically suggested "a good, earnest" lecture title: *Daily progress of man towards state of intellectual & moral perfection, as evi-*denced in history of 5th Avenue & 5 Points.)
2. Confucius, *The Doctrine of the Mean*, 14.
3. *Analects* 4.
4. In the Vedas, the Hindu god of the air, associated with rain and thunder.

of thoughts and affections; and am sensible of a certain doubleness by which I can stand as remote from myself as from another. However intense my experience, I am conscious of the presence and criticism of a part of me, which, as it were, is not a part of me, but spectator, sharing no experience, but taking note of it; and that is no more I than it is you. When the play, it may be the tragedy, of life is over, the spectator goes his way. It was a kind of fiction, a work of the imagination only, so far as he was concerned. This doubleness may easily make us poor neighbors and friends sometimes.

I find it wholesome to be alone the greater part of the time. To be in company, even with the best, is soon wearisome and dissipating. I love to be alone. I never found the companion that was so companionable as solitude. We are for the most part more lonely when we go abroad among men than when we stay in our chambers. A man thinking or working is always alone, let him be where he will. Solitude is not measured by the miles of space that intervene between a man and his fellows. The really diligent student in one of the crowded hives of Cambridge College is as solitary as a dervish in the desert. The farmer can work alone in the field or the woods all day, hoeing or chopping, and not feel lonesome, because he is employed; but when he comes home at night he cannot sit down in a room alone, at the mercy of his thoughts, but must be where he can "see the folks," and recreate, and as he thinks remunerate himself for his day's solitude; and hence he wonders how the student can sit alone in the house all night and most of the day without ennui and "the blues;" but he does not realize that the student, though in the house, is still at work in *his* field, and chopping in *his* woods, as the farmer in his, and in turn seeks the same recreation and society that the latter does, though it may be a more condensed form of it.

Society is commonly too cheap. We meet at very short intervals, not having had time to acquire any new value for each other. We meet at meals three times a day, and give each other a new taste of that old musty cheese that we are. We have had to agree on a certain set of rules, called etiquette and politeness, to make this frequent meeting tolerable, and that we need not come to open war. We meet at the post-office, and at the sociable, and about the fireside every night; we live thick and are in each other's way, and stumble over one another, and I think that we thus lose some respect for one another. Certainly less frequency would suffice for all important and hearty communications. Consider the girls in a factory,—never alone, hardly in their dreams. It would be better if there were but one inhabitant to a square mile, as where I live. The value of a man is not in his skin, that we should touch him.

I have heard of a man lost in the woods and dying of famine and exhaustion at the foot of a tree, whose loneliness was relieved by the grotesque visions with which, owing to bodily weakness, his diseased imagination surrounded him, and which he believed to be real. So also, owing to bodily and mental health and strength, we may be continually cheered by a like but more normal and natural society, and come to know that we are never alone.

I have a great deal of company in my house; especially in the morning, when nobody calls. Let me suggest a few comparisons, that some one may convey an idea of my situation. I am no more lonely than the loon in the pond that laughs so loud, or than Walden Pond itself. What company has that lonely lake, I pray? And yet it has not the blue devils,[5] but the blue angels in

5. Blues.

it, in the azure tint of its waters. The sun is alone, except in thick weather, when there sometimes appear to be two, but one is a mock sun. God is alone,—but the devil, he is far from being alone; he sees a great deal of company; he is legion. I am no more lonely than a single mullein or dandelion in a pasture, or a bean leaf, or sorrel, or a horse-fly, or a humble-bee. I am no more lonely than the Mill Brook, or a weathercock, or the northstar, or the south wind, or an April shower, or a January thaw, or the first spider in a new house.

I have occasional visits in the long winter evenings, when the snow falls fast and the wind howls in the wood, from an old settler[6] and original proprietor, who is reported to have dug Walden Pond, and stoned it, and fringed it with pine woods; who tells me stories of old time and of new eternity; and between us we manage to pass a cheerful evening with social mirth and pleasant views of things, even without apples or cider,—a most wise and humorous friend, whom I love much, who keeps himself more secret than ever did Goffe or Whalley;[7] and though he is thought to be dead, none can show where he is buried. An elderly dame,[8] too, dwells in my neighborhood, invisible to most persons, in whose odorous herb garden I love to stroll sometimes, gathering simples and listening to her fables; for she has a genius of unequalled fertility, and her memory runs back farther than mythology, and she can tell me the original of every fable, and on what fact every one is founded, for the incidents occurred when she was young. A ruddy and lusty old dame, who delights in all weathers and seasons, and is likely to outlive all her children yet.

The indescribable innocence and beneficence of Nature,—of sun and wind and rain, of summer and winter,—such health, such cheer, they afford forever! and such sympathy have they ever with our race, that all Nature would be affected, and the sun's brightness fade, and the winds would sigh humanely, and the clouds rain tears, and the woods shed their leaves and put on mourning in midsummer, if any man should ever for a just cause grieve. Shall I not have intelligence with the earth? Am I not partly leaves and vegetable mould myself?

What is the pill which will keep us well, serene, contented? Not my or thy great-grandfather's, but our great-grandmother Nature's universal, vegetable, botanic medicines, by which she has kept herself young always, outlived so many old Parrs[9] in her day, and fed her health with their decaying fatness. For my panacea, instead of one of those quack vials of a mixture dipped from Acheron[1] and the Dead Sea, which come out of those long shallow black-schooner looking wagons which we sometimes see made to carry bottles, let me have a draught of undiluted morning air. Morning air! If men will not drink of this at the fountain-head of the day, why, then, we must even bottle up some and sell it in the shops, for the benefit of those who have lost their subscription ticket to morning time in this world. But remember, it will not keep quite till noon-day even in the coolest cellar, but drive out the stopples long ere that and follow westward the steps of Aurora. I am no worshipper of

---

6. The old settler is some sort of divine power, though not the God Thoreau's neighbors would have worshiped.

7. English Puritans who supported the execution of Charles I of England and later, when sought as regicides, hid in Connecticut and Massachusetts settle-ments. Hawthorne's *The Gray Champion* makes their story into a patriotic allegory.

8. Mother Nature.

9. An Englishman named Thomas Parr was said to have been alive during three centuries (1483–1635).

1. In Greek mythology a principal river in Hades.

Hygeia, who was the daughter of that old herb-doctor Æsculapius,[2] and who is represented on monuments holding a serpent in one hand, and in the other a cup out of which the serpent sometimes drinks; but rather of Hebe, cupbearer to Jupiter, who was the daughter of Juno and wild lettuce, and who had the power of restoring gods and men to the vigor of youth. She was probably the only thoroughly sound-conditioned, healthy, and robust young lady that ever walked the globe, and wherever she came it was spring.

Visitors

I think that I love society as much as most, and am ready enough to fasten myself like a bloodsucker for the time to any full-blooded man that comes in my way. I am naturally no hermit, but might possibly sit out the sturdiest frequenter of the bar-room, if my business called me thither.

I had three chairs in my house; one for solitude, two for friendship, three for society. When visitors came in larger and unexpected numbers there was but the third chair for them all, but they generally economized the room by standing up. It is surprising how many great men and women a small house will contain. I have had twenty-five or thirty souls, with their bodies, at once under my roof, and yet we often parted without being aware that we had come very near to one another. Many of our houses, both public and private, with their almost innumerable apartments, their huge halls and their cellars for the storage of wines and other munitions of peace, appear to me extravagantly large for their inhabitants. They are so vast and magnificent that the latter seem to be only vermin which infest them. I am surprised when the herald blows his summons before some Tremont or Astor or Middlesex House,[3] to see come creeping out over the piazza for all inhabitants a ridiculous mouse, which soon again slinks into some hole in the pavement.

One inconvenience I sometimes experienced in so small a house, the difficulty of getting to a sufficient distance from my guest when we began to utter the big thoughts in big words. You want room for your thoughts to get into sailing trim and run a course or two before they make their port. The bullet of your thought must have overcome its lateral and ricochet motion and fallen into its last and steady course before it reaches the ear of the hearer, else it may plough out again through the side of his head. Also, our sentences wanted room to unfold and form their columns in the interval. Individuals, like nations, must have suitable broad and natural boundaries, even a considerable neutral ground, between them. I have found it a singular luxury to talk across the pond to a companion on the opposite side. In my house we were so near that we could not begin to hear,—we could not speak low enough to be heard; as when you throw two stones into calm water so near that they break each other's undulations. If we are merely loquacious and loud talkers, then we can afford to stand very near together, cheek by jowl, and feel each other's breath; but if we speak reservedly and thoughtfully, we want to be farther apart, that all animal heat and moisture may have a chance to evaporate. If we would enjoy the most intimate society with that in each of us which is without, or above, being spoken to, we must not only be silent, but commonly so far apart bodily that we cannot possibly hear each other's voice in any case. Referred to

2. Roman god of medicine. Hygeia was the Greek goddess of health.

3. Hotels in Boston, New York, and Concord, respectively.

this standard, speech is for the convenience of those who are hard of hearing; but there are many fine things which we cannot say if we have to shout. As the conversation began to assume a loftier and grander tone, we gradually shoved our chairs farther apart till they touched the wall in opposite corners, and then commonly there was not room enough.

My "best" room, however, my withdrawing room, always ready for company, on whose carpet the sun rarely fell, was the pine wood behind my house. Thither in summer days, when distinguished guests came, I took them, and a priceless domestic swept the floor and dusted the furniture and kept the things in order.

If one guest came he sometimes partook of my frugal meal, and it was no interruption to conversation to be stirring a hasty-pudding, or watching the rising and maturing of a loaf of bread in the ashes, in the mean while. But if twenty came and sat in my house, there was nothing said about dinner, though there might be bread enough for two, more than if eating were a forsaken habit; but we naturally practised abstinence; and this was never felt to be an offence against hospitality, but the most proper and considerate course. The waste and decay of physical life, which so often needs repair, seemed miraculously retarded in such a case, and the vital vigor stood its ground. I could entertain thus a thousand as well as twenty; and if any ever went away disappointed or hungry from my house when they found me at home, they may depend upon it that I sympathized with them at least. So easy is it, though many housekeepers doubt it, to establish new and better customs in the place of the old. You need not rest your reputation on the dinners you give. For my own part, I was never so effectually deterred from frequenting a man's house, by any kind of Cerberus[4] whatever, as by the parade one made about dining me, which I took to be a very polite and roundabout hint never to trouble him so again. I think I shall never revisit those scenes. I should be proud to have for the motto of my cabin those lines of Spenser which one of my visitors inscribed on a yellow walnut leaf for a card:—

> "Arrivéd there, the little house they fill,
>   Ne looke for entertainment where none was;
> Rest is their feast, and all things at their will:
>   The noblest mind the best contentment has."[5]

When Winslow, afterward governor of the Plymouth Colony, went with a companion on a visit of ceremony to Massassoit on foot through the woods, and arrived tired and hungry at his lodge, they were well received by the king, but nothing was said about eating that day. When the night arrived, to quote their own words,—"He laid us on the bed with himself and his wife, they at the one end and we at the other, it being only planks, laid a foot from the ground, and a thin mat upon them. Two more of his chief men, for want of room, pressed by and upon us; so that we were worse weary of our lodging than of our journey." At one o'clock the next day Massassoit "brought two fishes that he had shot," about thrice as big as a bream; "these being boiled, there were at least forty looked for a share in them. The most ate of them. This meal only we had in two nights and a day; and had not one of us bought a partridge, we had taken our journey fasting." Fearing that they would be

4. In Greek mythology a three-headed dog guarding   5. *Faerie Queene* 1.1.35.
the entrance of Hades.

light-headed for want of food and also sleep, owing to "the savages' barbarous singing (for they use to sing themselves asleep)" and that they might get home while they had strength to travel, they departed.[6] As for lodging, it is true they were but poorly entertained, though what they found an inconvenience was no doubt intended for an honor; but as far as eating was concerned, I do not see how the Indians could have done better. They had nothing to eat themselves, and they were wiser than to think that apologies could supply the place of food to their guests; so they drew their belts tighter and said nothing about it. Another time when Winslow visited them, it being a season of plenty with them, there was no deficiency in this respect.

As for men, they will hardly fail one any where. I had more visitors while I lived in the woods than at any other period of my life; I mean that I had some. I met several there under more favorable circumstances than I could any where else. But fewer came to see me upon trivial business. In this respect, my company was winnowed by my mere distance from town. I had withdrawn so far within the great ocean of solitude, into which the rivers of society empty, that for the most part, so far as my needs were concerned, only the finest sediment was deposited around me. Beside, there were wafted to me evidences of unexplored and uncultivated continents on the other side.

Who should come to my lodge this morning but a true Homeric or Paphlagonian man,—he had so suitable and poetic a name[7] that I am sorry I cannot print it here,—a Canadian, a wood-chopper and post-maker, who can hole fifty posts in a day, who made his last supper on a woodchuck which his dog caught. He, too, has heard of Homer, and, "if it were not for books," would "not know what to do rainy days," though perhaps he has not read one wholly through for many rainy seasons. Some priest who could pronounce the Greek itself taught him to read his verse in the testament in his native parish far away; and now I must translate to him, while he holds the book, Achilles' reproof to Patroclus for his sad countenance.—"Why are you in tears, Patroclus, like a young girl?"—

> "Or have you alone heard some news from Phthia?
> They say that Menœtius lives yet, son of Actor,
> And Peleus lives, son of Æacus, among the Myrmidons,
> Either of whom having died, we should greatly grieve."[8]

He says, "That's good." He has a great bundle of white-oak bark under his arm for a sick man, gathered this Sunday morning. "I suppose there's no harm in going after such a thing to-day," says he. To him Homer was a great writer, though what his writing was about he did not know. A more simple and natural man it would be hard to find. Vice and disease, which cast such a sombre moral hue over the world, seemed to have hardly any existence for him. He was about twenty-eight years old, and had left Canada and his father's house a dozen years before to work in the States, and earn money to buy a farm with at last, perhaps in his native country. He was cast in the coarsest mould; a

6. From Edward Winslow's *The English Plantation at Plymouth*, best known as *Mourt's Relation* (1622), available to Thoreau in George B. Cheever's edition of *The Journal of the Pilgrims at Plymouth* (1848). Thoreau was modernizing and regularizing his source, apparently, and making casual changes in wording. But the original reading "planks" has been restored here to agree with the pronoun *them*, whereas the 1854 edition has *plank*. Thoreau follows his source for "bought a partridge," but the verb should perhaps be *brought*. The 1854 edition's *used to sing* has been corrected to "use to sing," i.e., habitually sing.
7. I.e., Alek Therien. Paphlagonia is a mountainous region in Asia Minor.
8. *Iliad*, book 16.

stout but sluggish body, yet gracefully carried, with a thick sunburnt neck, dark bushy hair, and dull sleepy blue eyes, which were occasionally lit up with expression. He wore a flat gray cloth cap, a dingy wool-colored greatcoat, and cowhide boots. He was a great consumer of meat, usually carrying his dinner to his work a couple of miles past my house,—for he chopped all summer,— in a tin pail; cold meats, often cold woodchucks, and coffee in a stone bottle which dangled by a string from his belt; and sometimes he offered me a drink. He came along early, crossing my bean-field, though without anxiety or haste to get to his work, such as Yankees exhibit. He wasn't a-going to hurt himself. He didn't care if he only earned his board. Frequently he would leave his dinner in the bushes, when his dog had caught a woodchuck by the way, and go back a mile and a half to dress it and leave it in the cellar of the house where he boarded, after deliberating first for half an hour whether he could not sink it in the pond safely till nightfall,—loving to dwell long upon these themes. He would say, as he went by in the morning, "How thick the pigeons are! If working every day were not my trade, I could get all the meat I should want by hunting,—pigeons, woodchucks, rabbits, partridges,—by gosh! I could get all I should want for a week in one day."

He was a skilful chopper, and indulged in some flourishes and ornaments in his art. He cut his trees level and close to the ground, that the sprouts which came up afterward might be more vigorous and a sled might slide over the stumps; and instead of leaving a whole tree to support his corded wood, he would pare it away to a slender stake or splinter which you could break off with your hand at last.

He interested me because he was so quiet and solitary and so happy withal; a well of good humor and contentment which overflowed at his eyes. His mirth was without alloy. Sometimes I saw him at his work in the woods, felling trees, and he would greet me with a laugh of inexpressible satisfaction, and a salutation in Canadian French, though he spoke English as well. When I approached him he would suspend his work, and with half-suppressed mirth lie along the trunk of a pine which he had felled, and, peeling off the inner bark, roll it up into a ball and chew it while he laughed and talked. Such an exuberance of animal spirits had he that he sometimes tumbled down and rolled on the ground with laughter at any thing which made him think and tickled him. Looking round upon the trees he would exclaim,—"By George! I can enjoy myself well enough here chopping; I want no better sport." Sometimes, when at leisure, he amused himself all day in the woods with a pocket pistol, firing salutes to himself at regular intervals as he walked. In the winter he had a fire by which at noon he warmed his coffee in a kettle; and as he sat on a log to eat his dinner the chicadees would sometimes come round and alight on his arm and peck at the potato in his fingers; and he said that he "liked to have the little *fellers* about him."

In him the animal man chiefly was developed. In physical endurance and contentment he was cousin to the pine and the rock. I asked him once if he was not sometimes tired at night, after working all day; and he answered, with a sincere and serious look, "Gorrappit, I never was tired in my life." But the intellectual and what is called spiritual man in him were slumbering as in an infant. He had been instructed only in that innocent and ineffectual way in which the Catholic priests teach the aborigines, by which the pupil is never educated to the degree of consciousness, but only to the degree of trust and reverence, and a child is not made a man, but kept a child. When Nature made him, she gave him a strong body and contentment for his portion, and propped him on every side with reverence and reliance, that he might live out his threescore years and ten a child. He was so genuine and unsophisticated that no introduction would serve to introduce him, more than if you introduced a woodchuck to your neighbor. He had got to find him out as you did. He would not play any part. Men paid him wages for work, and so helped to feed and clothe him; but he never exchanged opinions with them. He was so simply and naturally humble—if he can be called humble who never aspires—that humility was no distinct quality in him, nor could he conceive of it. Wiser men were demigods to him. If you told him that such a one was coming, he did as if he thought that any thing so grand would expect nothing of himself, but take all the responsibility on itself, and let him be forgotten still. He never heard the sound of praise. He particularly reverenced the writer and the preacher. Their performances were miracles. When I told him that I wrote considerably, he thought for a long time that it was merely the handwriting which I meant, for he could write a remarkably good hand himself. I sometimes found the name of his native parish handsomely written in the snow by the highway, with the proper French accent, and knew that he had passed. I asked him if he ever wished to write his thoughts. He said that he had read and written letters for those who could not, but he never tried to write thoughts,—no, he could not, he could not tell what to put first, it would kill him, and then there was spelling to be attended to at the same time!

I heard that a distinguished wise man and reformer asked him if he did not want the world to be changed; but he answered with a chuckle of surprise in his Canadian accent, not knowing that the question had ever been entertained before, "No, I like it well enough." It would have suggested many things to a philosopher to have dealings with him. To a stranger he appeared to know nothing of things in general; yet I sometimes saw in him a man whom I had not seen before, and I did not know whether he was as wise as Shakspeare or as simply ignorant as a child, whether to suspect him of a fine poetic consciousness or of stupidity. A townsman told me that when he met him sauntering through the village in his small close-fitting cap, and whistling to himself, he reminded him of a prince in disguise.

His only books were an almanac and an arithmetic, in which last he was considerably expert. The former was a sort of cyclopædia to him, which he supposed to contain an abstract of human knowledge, as indeed it does to a considerable extent. I loved to sound him on the various reforms of the day, and he never failed to look at them in the most simple and practical light. He had never heard of such things before. Could he do without factories? I asked. He had worn the home-made Vermont gray, he said, and that was good. Could he dispense with tea and coffee? Did this country afford any beverage beside water? He had soaked hemlock leaves in water and drank it, and thought that was better than water in warm weather. When I asked him if he could do without money, he showed the convenience of money in such a way as to suggest and coincide with the most philosophical accounts of the origin of this institution, and the very derivation of the word *pecunia*.[9] If an ox were his property, and he wished to get needles and thread at the store, he thought it

9. I.e., wealth computed in terms of the number of cattle owned.

would be inconvenient and impossible soon to go on mortgaging some portion of the creature each time to that amount. He could defend many institutions better than any philosopher, because, in describing them as they concerned him, he gave the true reason for their prevalence, and speculation had not suggested to him any other. At another time, hearing Plato's definition of a man,—a biped without feathers,—and that one exhibited a cock plucked and called it Plato's man, he thought it an important difference that the *knees* bent the wrong way. He would sometimes exclaim, "How I love to talk! By George, I could talk all day!" I asked him once, when I had not seen him for many months, if he had got a new idea this summer. "Good Lord," said he, "a man that has to work as I do, if he does not forget the ideas he has had, he will do well. May be the man you hoe with is inclined to race; then, by gorry, your mind must be there; you think of weeds." He would sometimes ask me first on such occasions, if I had made any improvement. One winter day I asked him if he was always satisfied with himself, wishing to suggest a substitute within him for the priest without, and some higher motive for living. "Satisfied!" said he; "some men are satisfied with one thing, and some with another. One man, perhaps, if he has got enough, will be satisfied to sit all day with his back to the fire and his belly to the table, by George!" Yet I never, by any manœuvring, could get him to take the spiritual view of things; the highest that he appeared to conceive of was a simple expediency, such as you might expect an animal to appreciate; and this, practically, is true of most men. If I suggested any improvement in his mode of life, he merely answered, without expressing any regret, that it was too late. Yet he thoroughly believed in honesty and the like virtues.

There was a certain positive originality, however slight, to be detected in him, and I occasionally observed that he was thinking for himself and expressing his own opinion, a phenomenon so rare that I would any day walk ten miles to observe it, and it amounted to the re-origination of many of the institutions of society. Though he hesitated, and perhaps failed to express himself distinctly, he always had a presentable thought behind. Yet his thinking was so primitive and immersed in his animal life, that, though more promising than a merely learned man's, it rarely ripened to any thing which can be reported. He suggested that there might be men of genius in the lowest grades of life, however permanently humble and illiterate, who take their own view always, or do not pretend to see at all; who are as bottomless even as Walden Pond was thought to be, though they may be dark and muddy.

Many a traveller came out of his way to see me and the inside of my house, and, as an excuse for calling, asked for a glass of water. I told them that I drank at the pond, and pointed thither, offering to lend them a dipper. Far off as I lived, I was not exempted from that annual visitation which occurs, methinks, about the first of April, when every body is on the move; and I had my share of good luck, though there were some curious specimens among my visitors. Half-witted men from the almshouse and elsewhere came to see me; but I endeavored to make them exercise all the wit they had, and make their confessions to me; in such cases making wit the theme of our conversation; and so was compensated. Indeed, I found some of them to be wiser than the so called *overseers* of the poor and selectmen of the town, and thought it was time that the tables were turned. With respect to wit, I learned that there was not much

difference between the half and the whole. One day, in particular, an inoffensive, simple-minded pauper, whom with others I had often seen used as fencing stuff, standing or setting on a bushel in the fields to keep cattle and himself
from straying, visited me, and expressed a wish to live as I did. He told me,
with the utmost simplicity and truth, quite superior, or rather *inferior*, to any
thing that is called humility, that he was "deficient in intellect." These were
his words. The Lord had made him so, yet he supposed the Lord cared as
much for him as for another. "I have always been so," said he, "from my
childhood; I never had much mind; I was not like other children; I am weak
in the head. It was the Lord's will, I suppose." And there he was to prove the
truth of his words. He as a metaphysical puzzle to me. I have rarely met a
fellow-man on such promising ground,—it was so simple and sincere and so
true all that he said. And, true enough, in proportion as he appeared to humble himself was he exalted. I did not know at first but it was the result of a wise
policy. It seemed that from such a basis of truth and frankness as the poor
weak-headed pauper had laid, our intercourse might go forward to something
better than the intercourse of sages.

I had some guests from those not reckoned commonly among the town's
poor, but who should be; who are among the world's poor, at any rate; guests
who appeal, not to your hospitality, but to your *hospitalality*; who earnestly
wish to be helped, and preface their appeal with the information that they are
resolved, for one thing, never to help themselves. I require of a visitor that he
be not actually starving, though he may have the very best appetite in the
world, however he got it. Objects of charity are not guests. Men who did not
know when their visit had terminated, though I went about my business again,
answering them from greater and greater remoteness. Men of almost every
degree of wit called on me in the migrating season. Some who had more wits
than they knew what to do with; runaway slaves with plantation manners, who
listened from time to time, like the fox in the fable, as if they heard the hounds
a-baying on their track, and looked at me beseechingly, as much as to say,—

"O Christian, will you send me back?"

One real runaway slave,[1] among the rest, whom I helped to forward toward
the northstar. Men of one idea, like a hen with one chicken, and that a duck-
ling; men of a thousand ideas, and unkempt heads, like those hens which are
made to take charge of a hundred chickens, all in pursuit of one bug, a score
of them lost in every morning's dew,—and become frizzled and mangy in
consequence; men of ideas instead of legs, a sort of intellectual centipede that
made you crawl all over. One man proposed a book in which visitors should
write their names, as at the White Mountains; but, alas! I have too good a
memory to make that necessary.

I could not but notice some of the peculiarities of my visitors. Girls and
boys and young women generally seemed glad to be in the woods. They looked
in the pond and at the flowers, and improved their time. Men of business,
even farmers, thought only of solitude and employment, and of the great distance at which I dwelt from something or other; and though they said that they
loved a ramble in the woods occasionally, it was obvious that they did not.
Restless committed men, whose time was all taken up in getting a living, or

1. The ones previously named were running away from the civilization of Concord, not from Southern owners.

keeping it; ministers who spoke of God as if they enjoyed a monopoly of the subject, who could not bear all kinds of opinions; doctors, lawyers, uneasy housekeepers who pried into my cupboard and bed when I was out,—how came Mrs. ——to know that my sheets were not as clean as hers?—young men who had ceased to be young, and had concluded that it was safest to follow the beaten track of the professions,—all these generally said that it was not possible to do so much good in my position. Ay! there was the rub. The old and infirm and the timid, of whatever age or sex, thought most of sickness, and sudden accident and death; to them life seemed full of danger,—what danger is there if you don't think of any?—and they thought that a prudent man would carefully select the safest position, where Dr. B. might be on hand at a moment's warning. To them the village was literally a *com-munity*, a league for mutual defence, and you would suppose that they would not go a-huckleberrying without a medicine chest. The amount of it is, if a man is alive, there is always *danger* that he may die, though the danger must be allowed to be less in proportion as he is dead-and-alive to begin with. A man sits as many risks as he runs. Finally, there were the self-styled reformers, the greatest bores of all, who thought that I was forever singing,—

> This is the house that I built;
> This is the man that lives in the house that I built;

but they did not know that the third line was,—

> These are the folks that worry the man
> That lives in the house that I built.

I did not fear the hen-harriers, for I kept no chickens; but I feared the men-harriers rather.

I had more cheering visitors than the last. Children come a-berrying, rail-road men taking a Sunday morning walk in clean shirts, fishermen and hunt-ers, poets and philosophers, in short, all honest pilgrims, who came out to the woods for freedom's sake, and really left the village behind, I was ready to greet with,—"Welcome, Englishmen! welcome, Englishmen!" for I had had communication with that race.

The Bean-Field

Meanwhile my beans, the length of whose rows, added together, was seven miles already planted, were impatient to be hoed, for the earliest had grown considerably before the latest were in the ground; indeed they were not easily to be put off. What was the meaning of this so steady and self-respecting, this small Herculean labor, I knew not. I came to love my rows, my beans, though so many more than I wanted. They attached me to the earth, and so I got strength like Antæus.[2] But why should I raise them? Only Heaven knows. This was my curious labor all summer,—to make this portion of the earth's surface, which had yielded only cinquefoil, blackberries, johnswort, and the like, before, sweet wild fruits and pleasant flowers, produce instead this pulse. What shall I learn of beans or beans of me? I cherish them, I hoe them, early and late I have an eye to them; and this is my day's work. It is a fine broad leaf to look on. My auxiliaries are the dews and rains which water this dry soil, and

---

2. In Greek mythology, a giant who drew strength from the Earth, his mother, so that he was invincible as long as he touched the ground; Hercules killed him while holding him aloft.

what fertility is in the soil itself, which for the most part is lean and effete. My enemies are worms, cool days, and most of all woodchucks. The last have nibbled for me a quarter of an acre clean. But what right had I to oust johns-wort and the rest, and break up their ancient herb garden? Soon, however, the remaining beans will be too tough for them, and go forward to meet new foes.

When I was four years old, as I well remember, I was brought from Boston to this my native town, through these very woods and this field, to the pond. It is one of the oldest scenes stamped on my memory. And now to-night my flute has waked the echoes over that very water. The pines still stand here older than I; or, if some have fallen, I have cooked my supper with their stumps, and a new growth is rising all around, preparing another aspect for new infant eyes. Almost the same johnswort springs from the same perennial root in this pasture, and even I have at length helped to clothe that fabulous landscape of my infant dreams, and one of the results of my presence and influence is seen in these bean leaves, corn blades, and potato vines.

I planted about two acres and a half of upland; and as it was only about fifteen years since the land was cleared, and I myself had got out two or three cords of stumps, I did not give it any manure; but in the course of the summer it appeared by the arrow-heads which I turned up in hoeing, that an extinct nation had anciently dwelt here and planted corn and beans ere white men came to clear the land, and so, to some extent, had exhausted the soil for this very crop.

Before yet any woodchuck or squirrel had run across the road, or the sun had got above the shrub-oaks, while all the dew was on, though the farmers warned me against it,—I would advise you to do all your work if possible while the dew is on,—I began to level the ranks of haughty weeds in my bean-field and throw dust upon their heads. Early in the morning I worked barefooted, dabbling like a plastic artist in the dewy and crumbling sand, but later in the day the sun blistered my feet. There the sun lighted me to hoe beans, pacing slowly backward and forward over that yellow gravelly upland, between the long green rows, fifteen rods, the one end terminating in a shrub oak copse where I could rest in the shade, the other in a blackberry field where the green berries deepened their tints by the time I had made another bout. Removing the weeds, putting fresh soil about the bean stems, and encouraging this weed which I had sown, making the yellow soil express its summer thought in bean leaves and blossoms rather than in wormword and piper and millet grass, mak-ing the earth say beans instead of grass,—this was my daily work. As I had little aid from horses or cattle, or hired men or boys, or improved implements of husbandry, I was much slower, and became much more intimate with my beans than usual. But labor of the hands, even when pursued to the verge of drudgery, is perhaps never the worst form of idleness. It has a constant and imperishable moral, and to the scholar it yields a classic result. A very *agricola laboriosus*[3] was I to travellers bound westward through Lincoln and Wayland to nobody knows where; they sitting at their ease in gigs,[4] with elbows on knees, and reins loosely hanging in festoons; I the home-staying, laborious native of the soil. But soon my homestead was out of their sight and thought. It was the only open and cultivated field for a great distance on either side of the road; so they made the most of it; and sometimes the man in the field heard more of travellers' gossip and comment than was meant for his ear:

3. Hardworking farmer (Latin).   4. Light two-wheeled horse-drawn carriage.

"Beans so late! peas so late!"—for I continued to plant when others had begun to hoe,—the ministerial husbandman had not suspected it. "Corn, my boy, for fodder; corn for fodder." "Does he *live* there?" asks the black bonnet of the gray coat; and the hard-featured farmer reins up his grateful dobbin to inquire what you are doing where he sees no manure in the furrow, and recommends a little chip dirt, or any little waste stuff, or it may be ashes or plaster. But here were two acres and a half of furrows, and only a hoe for cart and two hands to draw it,—there being an aversion to other carts and horses,—and chip dirt far away. Fellow-travellers as they rattled by compared it aloud with the fields which they had passed, so that I came to know how I stood in the agricultural world. This was one field not in Mr. Colman's report.[5] And, by the way, who estimates the value of the crop which Nature yields in the still wilder fields unimproved by man? The crop of *English* hay is carefully weighed, the moisture calculated, the silicates and the potash; but in all dells and pond holes in the woods and pastures and swamps grows a rich and various crop only unreaped by man. Mine was, as it were, the connecting link between wild and cultivated fields; as some states are civilized, and others half-civilized, and others savage or barbarous, so my field was, though not in a bad sense, a half-cultivated field. They were beans cheerfully returning to their wild and primitive state that I cultivated, and my hoe played the *Ranz des Vaches*[6] for them.

Near at hand, upon the topmost spray of a birch sings the brown-thrasher or red mavis, as some love to call him—all the morning, glad of your society, that would find out another farmer's field if yours were not here. While you are planting the seed, he cries,—"Drop it, drop it,—cover it up, cover it up,—pull it up, pull it up, pull it up." But this was not corn, and so it was safe from such enemies as he. You may wonder what his rigmarole, his amateur Paganini[7] performances on one string or on twenty, have to do with your planting, and yet prefer it to leached ashes or plaster. It was a cheap sort of top dressing in which I had entire faith.

As I drew a still fresher soil about the rows with my hoe, I disturbed the ashes of unchronicled nations who in primeval years lived under these heavens, and their small implements of war and hunting were brought to the light of this modern day. They lay mingled with other natural stones, some of which bore the marks of having been burned by Indian fires, and some by the sun, and also bits of pottery and glass brought hither by the recent cultivators of the soil. When my hoe tinkled against the stones, that music echoed to the woods and the sky, and was an accompaniment to my labor which yielded an instant and immeasurable crop. It was no longer beans that I hoed, nor I that hoed beans; and I remembered with as much pity as pride, if I remembered at all, my acquaintances who had gone to the city to attend the oratorios. The night-hawk circled overhead in the sunny afternoons—for I sometimes made a day of it—like a mote in the eye, or in heaven's eye, falling from time to time with a swoop and a sound as if the heavens were rent, torn at last to very rags and tatters, and yet a seamless cope[8] remained; small imps that fill the air and lay their eggs on the ground on bare sand or rocks on the tops of hills, where few have found them; graceful and slender like ripples caught up from the pond,

---

5. Henry Colman (1785–1849), who wrote a series of agricultural surveys for the state of Massachusetts.
6. A Swiss herdsman's song.
7. Nicolò Paganini (1784–1840), violinist.

8. Hood. The passage derives some of its force from Thoreau's use of biblical echoes, see Matthew 7.3 and 27.51.

as leaves are raised by the wind to float in the heavens; such kindredship is in Nature. The hawk is aerial brother of the wave which he sails over and surveys, those his perfect air-inflated wings answering to the elemental unfledged pinions of the sea. Or sometimes I watched a pair of hen-hawks circling high in the sky, alternately soaring and descending, approaching and leaving one another, as if they were the imbodiment of my own thoughts. Or I was attracted by the passage of wild pigeons from this wood to that, with a slight quivering winnowing sound and carrier haste; or from under a rotten stump my hoe turned up a sluggish protentous and outlandish spotted salamander, a trace of Egypt and the Nile, yet our contemporary. When I paused to lean on my hoe, these sounds and sights I heard and saw any where in the row, a part of the inexhaustible entertainment which the country offers.

On gala days the town fires its great guns, which echo like popguns to these woods, and some waifs of martial music occasionally penetrate thus far. To me, away there in my bean-field at the other end of the town, the big guns sounded as if a puff ball had burst; and when there was a military turnout of which I was ignorant, I have sometimes had a vague sense all the day of some sort of itching and disease in the horizon, as if some eruption would break out there soon, either scarlatina or canker-rash,[9] until at length some more favorable puff of wind, making haste over the fields and up the Wayland road, brought me information of the "trainers."[1] It seemed by the distant hum as if somebody's bees had swarmed, and that the neighbors, according to Virgil's advice, by a faint *tintinnabulum*[2] upon the most sonorous of their domestic utensils, were endeavoring to call them down into the hive again. And when the sound died quite away, and the hum had ceased, and the most favorable breezes told no tale, I knew that they had got the last drone of them all safely into the Middlesex hive, and that now their minds were bent on the honey with which it was smeared.

I felt proud to know that the liberties of Massachusetts and of our fatherland were in such safe keeping; and as I turned to my hoeing again I was filled with an inexpressible confidence, and pursued my labor cheerfully with a calm trust in the future.

When there were several bands of musicians, it sounded as if all the village was a vast bellows, and all the buildings expanded and collapsed alternately with a din. But sometimes it was a really noble and inspiring strain that reached these woods, and the trumpet that sings of fame, and I felt as if I could spit a Mexican with a good relish,—for why should we always stand for trifles?—and looked round for a woodchuck or a skunk to exercise my chivalry upon. These martial strains seemed as far away as Palestine, and reminded me of a march of crusaders in the horizon, with a slight tantivy and tremulous motion of the elm-tree tops which overhang the village. This was one of the *great* days; though the sky had from my clearing only the same everlastingly great look that it wears daily, and I saw no difference in it.

It was a singular experience that long acquaintance which I cultivated with beans, what with planting, and hoeing, and harvesting, and threshing, and picking over, and selling them,—the last was the hardest of all,—I might add eating, for I did taste. I was determined to know beans. When they were growing, I used to hoe from five o'clock in the morning till noon, and commonly

---

9. An ulcerous mouth ailment. "Scarlatina": scarlet fever.
1. The local militia, drilling so as to be ready to protect American democracy against Mexican arms.
2. Tinkling (Latin).

spent the rest of the day about other affairs. Consider the intimate and curious acquaintance one makes with various kinds of weeds,—it will bear some iteration in the account, for there was no little iteration in the labor,—disturbing their delicate organizations so ruthlessly, and making such invidious distinction with his hoe, levelling whole ranks of one species, and sedulously cultivating another. That's Roman wormwood,—that's pigweed,—that's sorrel,—that's piper-grass,—have at him, chop him up, turn his roots upward to the sun, don't let him have a fibre in the shade, if you do he'll turn himself t'other side up and be as green as a leek in two days. A long war, not with cranes, but with weeds, those Trojans who had sun and rain and dews on their side. Daily the beans saw me come to their rescue armed with a hoe, and thin the ranks of their enemies, filling up the trenches with weedy dead. Many a lusty crest-waving Hector,[3] that towered a whole foot above his crowding comrades, fell before my weapon and rolled in the dust.

Those summer days which some of my contemporaries devoted to the fine arts in Boston or Rome, and others to contemplation in India, and others to trade in London or New York, I thus, with the other farmers of New England, devoted to husbandry. Not that I wanted beans to eat, for I am by nature a Pythagorean, so far as beans are concerned, whether they mean porridge or voting,[4] and exchanged them for rice; but, perchance, as some must work in fields if only for the sake of tropes and expression, to serve a parable-maker one day. It was on the whole a rare amusement, which, continued too long, might have become a dissipation. Though I gave them no manure, and did not hoe them all at once, I hoed them unusually well as far as I went, and was paid for it in the end, "there being in truth," as Evelyn says, "no compost or lætation whatsoever comparable to this continual motion, repastination, and turning of the mould with the spade." "The earth," he adds elsewhere, "especially if fresh, has a certain magnetism in it, by which it attracts the salt, power, or virtue (call it either) which gives it life, and is the logic of all the labor and stir we keep about it, to sustain us; all dungings and other sordid temperings being but the vicars succedaneous to this improvement." Moreover, this being one of those "worn-out and exhausted lay fields which enjoy their sabbath,"[5] had perchance, as Sir Kenelm Digby thinks likely, attracted "vital spirits" from the air.[6] I harvested twelve bushels of beans.

But to be more particular; for it is complained that Mr. Colman has reported chiefly the expensive experiments of gentlemen farmers; my outgoes were,—

For a hoe,	$0 54
Ploughing, harrowing, and furrowing,	7 50, Too much.
Beans for seed,	3 12½
Potatoes "	1 33
Peas "	0 40
Turnip seed,	0 06
White line for crow fence,	0 02
Horse cultivator and boy three hours,	1 00
Horse and cart to get crop,	0 75
In all,	$14 72½

3. In *The Iliad*, a Trojan prince killed by Achilles; popularly associated with bullying and bragging.
4. Beans had been used to keep tally of votes. Pythagoras (6th century B.C.), Greek philosopher, opposed the eating of beans; what Thoreau has most in mind is the tendency of beans to cause flatulence.
5. These quotes are from John Evelyn, *Terra: A Philosophical Discourse of Earth* (1729).
6. The quotation from Digby (1603–1665) has not been located.

My income was, (patrem familias vendacem, non emacem esse oportet,)[7] from

Nine bushels and twelve quarts of beans sold,		$16 94
Five " large potatoes,		2 50
Nine " small "		2 25
Grass,		1 00
Stalks,		0 75
In all,		$23 44

Leaving a pecuniary profit, as I have elsewhere said, of $8 71½.

This is the result of my experience in raising beans. Plant the common small white bush bean about the first of June, in rows three feet by eighteen inches apart, being careful to select fresh round and unmixed seed. First look out for worms, and supply vacancies by planting anew. Then look out for woodchucks, if it is an exposed place, for they will nibble off the earliest tender leaves almost clean as they go; and again, when the young tendrils make their appearance, they have notice of it, and will shear them off with both buds and young pods, sitting erect like a squirrel. But above all harvest as early as possible, if you would escape frosts and have a fair and saleable crop; you may save much loss by this means.

This further experience also I gained. I said to myself, I will not plant beans and corn with so much industry another summer, but such seeds, if the seed is not lost, as sincerity, truth, simplicity, faith, innocence, and the like, and see if they will not grow in this soil, even with less toil and manurance, and sustain me, for surely it has not been exhausted for these crops. Alas! I said this to myself; but now another summer is gone, and another, and another, and I am obliged to say to you, Reader, that the seeds which I planted, if indeed they *were* the seeds of those virtues, were wormeaten or had lost their vitality, and so did not come up. Commonly men will only be brave as their fathers were brave, or timid. This generation is very sure to plant corn and beans each new year precisely as the Indians did centuries ago and taught the first settlers to do, as if there were a fate in it. I saw an old man the other day, to my astonishment, making the holes with a hoe for the seventieth time at least, and not for himself to lie down in! But why should not the New Englander try new adventures, and not lay so much stress on his grain, his potato and grass crop, and his orchards?—raise other crops than these? Why concern ourselves so much about our beans for seed, and not be concerned at all about a new generation of men? We should really be fed and cheered if when we met a man we were sure to see that some of the qualities which I have named, which we all prize more than those other productions, but which are for the most part broadcast and floating in the air, had taken root and grown in him. Here comes such a subtile and ineffable quality, for instance, as truth or justice, though the slightest amount or new variety of it, along the road. Our ambassadors should be instructed to send home such seeds as these, and Congress help to distribute them over all the land. We should never stand upon ceremony with sincerity. We should never cheat and insult and banish one another by our meanness, if there were present the kernel of worth and

---

7. The master should have the habit of selling, not buying (Latin), From Cato's *De agri cultura.*

friendliness. We should not meet thus in haste. Most men I do not meet at all, for they seem not to have time; they are busy about their beans. We would not deal with a man thus plodding ever, leaning on a hoe or a spade as a staff between his work, not as a mushroom, but partially risen out of the earth, something more than erect, like swallows alighted and walking on the ground.—

> "And as he spake, his wings would now and then
> Spread, as he meant to fly, then close again,"[8]

so that we should suspect that we might be conversing with an angel. Bread may not always nourish us; but it always does us good, it even takes stiffness out of our joints, and makes us supple and buoyant, when we knew not what ailed us, to recognize any generosity in man or Nature, to share any unmixed and heroic joy.

Ancient poetry and mythology suggest, at least, that husbandry was once a sacred art; but it is pursued with irreverent haste and heedlessness by us, our object being to have large farms and large crops merely. We have no festival, nor procession, nor ceremony, not excepting our Cattle-shows and so called Thanksgivings, by which the farmer expresses a sense of the sacredness of his calling, or is reminded of its sacred origin. It is the premium and the feast which tempt him. He sacrifices not to Ceres and the Terrestrial Jove, but to the infernal Plutus[9] rather. By avarice and selfishness, and a grovelling habit, from which none of us is free, of regarding the soil as property, or the means of acquiring property chiefly, the landscape is deformed, husbandry is degraded with us, and the farmer leads the meanest of lives. He knows Nature but as a robber. Cato says that the profits of agriculture are particularly pious or just, (*maximeque pius quæstus,*)[1] and according to Varro the old Romans "called the same earth Mother and Ceres, and thought that they who cultivated it led a pious and useful life, and that they alone were left of the race of King Saturn."[2]

We are wont to forget that the sun looks on our cultivated fields and on the prairies and forests without distinction. They all reflect and absorb his rays alike, and the former make but a small part of the glorious picture which he beholds in his daily course. In his view the earth is all equally cultivated like a garden. Therefore we should receive the benefit of his light and heat with a corresponding trust and magnanimity. What though I value the seed of these beans, and harvest that in the fall of the year? This broad field which I have looked at so long looks not to me as the principal cultivator, but away from me to influences more genial to it, which water and make it green. These beans have results which are not harvested by me. Do they not grow for wood-chucks partly? The ear of wheat, (in Latin *spica*, obsoletely *speca*, from *spe*, hope,) should not be the only hope of the husbandman; its kernel or grain (*granum*, from *gerendo*, bearing,) is not all that it bears. How, then, can our harvest fail? Shall I not rejoice also at the abundance of the weeds whose seeds are granary of the birds? It matters little comparatively whether the fields fill the farmer's barns. The true husbandman will cease from anxiety, as the squirrels manifest no concern whether the woods will bear chestnuts this year or

---

8. Francis Quarles, *The Shepherd's Oracles*, Eclogue 5.
9. Greek god of wealth. Ceres was the Roman goddess of agriculture.

1. Cato's *De agri cultura*, Introduction, 4.
2. Marcus Terentius Varro (116–27 B.C.), *Rerum rusticarum* 3.1.5.

not, and finish his labor with every day, relinquishing all claim to the produce of his fields, and sacrificing in his mind not only his first but his last fruits also.

The Village

After hoeing, or perhaps reading and writing, in the forenoon, I usually bathed again in the pond, swimming across one of its coves for a stint, and washed the dust of labor from my person, or smoothed out the last wrinkle which study had made, and for the afternoon was absolutely free. Every day or two I strolled to the village to hear some of the gossip which is incessantly going on there, circulating either from mouth to mouth, or from newspaper to newspaper, and which, taken in homœopathic doses,[3] was really as refreshing in its way as the rustle of leaves and the peeping of frogs. As I walked in the woods to see the birds and squirrels, so I walked in the village to see the men and boys; instead of the wind among the pines I heard the carts rattle. In one direction from my house there was a colony of muskrats in the river meadows; under the grove of elms and buttonwoods in the other horizon was a village of busy men, as curious to me as if they had been prairie dogs, each sitting at the mouth of its burrow, or running over to a neighbor's to gossip. I went there frequently to observe their habits. The village appeared to me a great news room; and on one side, to support it, as once at Redding & Company's on State Street, they kept nuts and raisins, or salt and meal and other groceries. Some have such a vast appetite for the former commodity, that is, the news, and such sound digestive organs, that they can sit forever in public avenues without stirring, and let it simmer and whisper through them like the Etesian winds,[4] or as if inhaling ether, it only producing numbness and insensibility to pain,—otherwise it would often be painful to hear,—without affecting the consciousness. I hardly ever failed, when I rambled through the village, to see a row of such worthies, either sitting on a ladder sunning themselves, with their bodies inclined forward and their eyes glancing along the line this way and that, from time to time, with a voluptuous expression, or else leaning against a barn with their hands in their pockets, like caryatides, as if to prop it up. They, being commonly out of doors, heard whatever was in the wind. These are the coarsest mills, in which all gossip is first rudely digested or cracked up before it is emptied into finer and more delicate hoppers within doors. I observed that the vitals of the village were the grocery, the barroom, the post-office, and the bank; and, as a necessary part of the machinery, they kept a bell, a big gun, and a fire-engine, at convenient places; and the houses were so arranged as to make the most of mankind, in lanes and fronting one another, so that every traveller had to run the gantlet, and every man, woman, and child might get a lick at him. Of course, those who were stationed nearest to the head of the line, where they could most see and be seen, and have the first blow at him, paid the highest prices for their places; and the few straggling inhabitants in the outskirts, where long gaps in the line began to occur, and the traveller could get over walls or turn aside into cow paths, and so escape, paid a very slight ground or window tax. Signs were hung out on all sides to allure him; some to catch him by the appetite, as the tavern and victualling cellar; some by the fancy, as the dry goods store and the jeweller's;

3. In tiny doses, from the practice homeopathic doctors had of building up a patient's immunity by a series of minute doses of some normally toxic substance.
4. Summer winds in the Mediterranean.

and others by the hair or the feet or the skirts, as the barber, the shoemaker, or the tailor. Besides, there was a still more terrible standing invitation to call at every one of these houses, and company expected about these times. For the most part I escaped wonderfully from these dangers, either by proceeding at once boldly and without deliberation to the goal, as is recommended to those who run the gantlet, or by keeping my thoughts on high things, like Orpheus, who, "loudly singing the praises of the gods to his lyre, drowned the voices of the Sirens, and kept out of danger."[5] Sometimes I bolted suddenly, and nobody could tell my whereabouts, for I did not stand much about gracefulness, and never hesitated at a gap in a fence. I was even accustomed to make an irruption into some houses, where I was well entertained, and after learning the kernels and very last sieveful of news, what had subsided, the prospects of war and peace, and whether the world was likely to hold together much longer, I was let out through the rear avenues, and so escaped to the woods again.

It was very pleasant, when I staid late in town, to launch myself into the night, especially if it was dark and tempestuous, and set sail from some bright village parlor or lecture room, with a bag of rye or Indian meal upon my shoulder, for my snug harbor in the woods, having made all tight without and withdrawn under hatches with a merry crew of thoughts, leaving only my outer man at the helm, or even tying up the helm when it was plain sailing. I had many a genial thought by the cabin fire "as I sailed."[6] I was never cast away nor distressed in any weather, though I encountered some severe storms. It is darker in the woods, even in common nights, than most suppose. I frequently had to look up at the opening between the trees above the path in order to learn my route, and, where there was no cart-path, to feel with my feet the faint track which I had worn, or steer by the known relation of particular trees which I felt with my hands, passing between two pines for instance, not more than eighteen inches apart, in the midst of the woods, invariably, in the darkest night. Sometimes, after coming home thus late in a dark and muggy night, when my feet felt the path which my eyes could not see, dreaming and absent-minded all the way, until I was aroused by having to raise my hand to lift the latch, I have not been able to recall a single step of my walk, and I have thought that perhaps my body would find its way home if its master should forsake it, as the hand finds its way to the mouth without assistance. Several times, when a visitor chanced to stay into evening, and it proved a dark night, I was obliged to conduct him to the cart-path in the rear of the house, and then point out to him the direction he was to pursue, and in keeping which he was to be guided rather by his feet than his eyes. One very dark night I directed thus on their way two young men who had been fishing in the pond. They lived about a mile off through the woods, and were quite used to the route. A day or two after one of them told me that they wandered about the greater part of the night, close by their own premises, and did not get home till toward morning, by which time, as there had been several heavy showers in the mean while, and the leaves were very wet, they were drenched to their skins. I have heard of many going astray even in the village streets, when the darkness was so thick that you could cut it with a knife, as the saying is. Some who live in the outskirts, having come to town a-shopping in their wagons, have been obliged to put up for the night; and gentlemen and ladies

5. Harding identifies this as apparently a translation from the *Argonautica* by Apollonius Rhodius.

6. "The refrain of the old American 'Ballad of Captain Robert Kidd' " [Harding's note].

making a call have gone half a mile out of their way, feeling the sidewalk only with their feet, and not knowing when they turned. It is a surprising and memorable, as well as valuable experience, to be lost in the woods any time. Often in a snow storm, even by day, one will come out upon a well-known road, and yet find it impossible to tell which way leads to the village. Though he knows that he has travelled it a thousand times, he cannot recognize a feature in it, but it is as strange to him as if it were a road in Siberia. By night, of course, the perplexity is infinitely greater. In our most trivial walks, we are constantly, though unconsciously, steering like pilots by certain well-known beacons and headlands, and if we go beyond our usual course we still carry in our minds the bearing of some neighboring cape; and not till we are completely lost, or turned round,—for a man needs only to be turned round once with his eyes shut in this world to be lost,—do we appreciate the vastness and strangeness of Nature. Every man has to learn the points of compass again as often as he awakes, whether from sleep or any abstraction. Not till we are lost, in other words, not till we have lost the world, do we begin to find ourselves, and realize where we are and the infinite extent of our relations.

One afternoon, near the end of the first summer, when I went to the village to get a shoe from the cobbler's, I was seized and put into jail, because, as I have elsewhere related,[7] I did not pay a tax to, or recognize the authority of, the state which buys and sells men, women, and children, like cattle at the door of its senate-house. I had gone down to the woods for other purposes. But, wherever a man goes, men will pursue and paw him with their dirty institutions, and, if they can, constrain him to belong to their desperate odd-fellow society. It is true, I might have resisted forcibly with more or less effect, might have run "amok" against society; but I preferred that society should run "amok" against me, it being the desperate party. However, I was released the next day, obtained my mended shoe, and returned to the woods in season to get my dinner of huckleberries on Fair-Haven Hill. I was never molested by any person but those who represented the state. I had no lock nor bolt but for the desk which held my papers, not even a nail to put over my latch or windows. I never fastened my door night or day, though I was to be absent several days; not even when the next fall I spent a fortnight in the woods of Maine. And yet my house was more respected than if it had been surrounded by a file of soldiers. The tired rambler could rest and warm himself by my fire, the literary amuse himself with the few books on my table, or the curious, by opening my closet door, see what was left of my dinner, and what prospect I had of a supper. Yet, though many people of every class came this way to the pond, I suffered no serious inconvenience from these sources, and I never missed any thing but one small book, a volume of Homer, which perhaps was improperly gilded, and this I trust a soldier of our camp has found by this time. I am convinced, that if all men were to live as simply as I then did, thieving and robbery would be unknown. These take place only in communities where some have got more than is sufficient while others have not enough. The Pope's Homers would soon get properly distributed.—

> "Nec bella fuerunt,
> Faginus astabat dum scyphus ante dapes."[8]

7. I.e., in *Resistance to Civil Government* (1849), posthumously reprinted as *Civil Disobedience* (1866).   8. From Tibullus, *Elegies* 3.11.7–8.

> "Nor wars did men molest,
> When only beechen bowls were in request."

"You who govern public affairs, what need have you to employ punishments? Love virtue, and the people will be virtuous. The virtues of a superior man are like the wind; the virtues of a common man are like the grass; the grass, when the wind passes over it, bends."[9]

The Ponds

Sometimes, having had a surfeit of human society and gossip, and worn out all my village friends, I rambled still farther westward than I habitually dwell, into yet more unfrequented parts of the town, "to fresh woods and pastures new,"[1] or, while the sun was setting, made my supper of huckleberries and blueberries on Fair Haven Hill, and laid up a store for several days. The fruits do not yield their true flavor to the purchaser of them, nor to him who raises them for the market. There is but one way to obtain it, yet few take that way. If you would know the flavor of huckleberries, ask the cow-boy or the partridge. It is a vulgar error[2] to suppose that you have tasted huckleberries who never plucked them. A huckleberry never reaches Boston; they have not been known there since they grew on her three hills. The ambrosial and essential part of the fruit is lost with the bloom which is rubbed off in the market cart, and they become mere provender. As long as Eternal Justice reigns, not one innocent huckleberry can be transported thither from the country's hills.

Occasionally, after my hoeing was done for the day, I joined some impatient companion who had been fishing on the pond since morning, as silent and motionless as a duck or a floating leaf, and, after practising various kinds of philosophy, had concluded commonly, by the time I arrived, that he belonged to the ancient sect of Cœnobites.[3] There was one older man, an excellent fisher and skilled in all kinds of woodcraft, who was pleased to look upon my house as a building erected for the convenience of fishermen; and I was equally pleased when he sat in my doorway to arrange his lines. Once in a while we sat together on the pond, he at one end of the boat, and I at the other; but not many words passed between us, for he had grown deaf in his later years, but he occasionally hummed a psalm, which harmonized well enough with my philosophy. Our intercourse was thus altogether one of unbroken harmony, far more pleasing to remember than if it had been carried on by speech. When, as was commonly the case, I had none to commune with, I used to raise the echoes by striking with a paddle on the side of my boat, filling the surrounding woods with circling and dilating sound, stirring them up as the keeper of a menagerie his wild beasts, until I elicited a growl from every wooded vale and hill-side.

In warm evenings I frequently sat in the boat playing the flute, and saw the perch, which I seemed to have charmed, hovering around me, and the moon travelling over the ribbed bottom, which was strewed with the wrecks of the forest. Formerly I had come to this pond adventurously, from time to time, in dark summer nights, with a companion, and making a fire close to the water's

---

9. Confucius, *Analects* 12.
1. The last line of John Milton's *Lycidas*.
2. I.e., a common error (especially among the uneducated); Thoreau recalls the English title of Sir Thomas

Browne's *Pseudoxia Epidemica*.
3. As Harding points out, one of Thoreau's puns: "See, no bites."

edge, which we thought attracted the fishes, we caught pouts with a bunch of worms strung on a thread; and when we had done, far in the night, threw the burning brands high into the air like skyrockets, which, coming down into the pond, were quenched with a loud hissing, and we were suddenly groping in total darkness. Through this, whistling a tune, we took our way to the haunts of men again. But now I had made my home by the shore.

Sometimes, after staying in a village parlor till the family had all retired, I have returned to the woods, and, partly with a view to the next day's dinner, spent the hours of midnight fishing from a boat by moonlight, serenaded by owls and foxes, and hearing, from time to time, the creaking note of some unknown bird close at hand. These experiences were very memorable and valuable to me,—anchored in forty feet of water, and twenty or thirty rods from the shore, surrounded sometimes by thousands of small perch and shiners, dimpling the surface with their tails in the moonlight, and communicating by a long flaxen line with mysterious nocturnal fishes which had their dwelling forty feet below, or sometimes dragging sixty feet of line about the pond as I drifted in the gentle night breeze, now and then feeling a slight vibration along it, indicative of some life prowling about its extremity, of dull uncertain blundering purpose there, and slow to make up its mind. At length you slowly raise, pulling hand over hand, some horned pout squeaking and squirming to the upper air. It was very queer, especially in dark nights, when your thoughts had wandered to vast and cosmogonal themes in other spheres, to feel this faint jerk, which came to interrupt your dreams and link you to Nature again. It seemed as if I might next cast my line upward into the air, as well as downward into this element which was scarcely more dense. Thus I caught two fishes as it were with one hook.

The scenery of Walden is on a humble scale, and, though very beautiful, does not approach to grandeur, nor can it much concern one who has not long frequented it or lived by its shore; yet this pond is so remarkable for its depth and purity as to merit a particular description. It is a clear and deep green well, half a mile long and a mile and three quarters in circumference, and contains about sixty-one and a half acres; a perennial spring in the midst of pine and oak woods, without any visible inlet or outlet except by the clouds and evaporation. The surrounding hills rise abruptly from the water to the height of forty to eighty feet, though on the south-east and east they attain to about one hundred and one hundred and fifty feet respectively, within a quarter and a third of a mile. They are exclusively woodland. All our Concord waters have two colors at least, one when viewed at a distance, and another, more proper, close at hand. The first depends more on the light, and follows the sky. In clear weather, in summer, they appear blue at a little distance, especially if agitated, and at a great distance all appear alike. In stormy weather they are sometimes of a dark slate color. The sea, however, is said to be blue one day and green another without any perceptible change in the atmosphere. I have seen our river, when, the landscape being covered with snow, both water and ice were almost as green as grass. Some consider blue "to be the color of pure water, whether liquid or solid." But, looking directly down into our waters from a boat, they are seen to be of very different colors. Walden is blue at one time and green at another, even from the same point of view. Lying between the earth and the heavens, it partakes of the color of both.

Viewed from a hill-top it reflects the color of the sky, but near at hand it is of a yellowish tint next the shore where you can see the sand, then a light green, which gradually deepens to a uniform dark green in the body of the pond. In some lights, viewed even from a hill-top, it is of a vivid green next the shore. Some have referred this to the reflection of the verdure; but it is equally green there against the railroad sand-bank, and in the spring, before the leaves are expanded, and it may be simply the result of the prevailing blue mixed with the yellow of the sand. Such is the color of its iris. This is that portion, also, where in the spring, the ice being warmed by the heat of the sun reflected from the bottom, and also transmitted through the earth, melts first and forms a narrow canal about the still frozen middle. Like the rest of our waters, when much agitated, in clear weather, so that the surface of the waves may reflect the sky at the right angle, or because there is more light mixed with it, it appears at a little distance of a darker blue than the sky itself; and at such a time, being on its surface, and looking with divided vision, so as to see the reflection, I have discerned a matchless and indescribable light blue, such as watered or changeable silks and sword blades suggest, more cerulean than the sky itself, alternating with the original dark green on the opposite sides of the waves, which last appeared but muddy in comparison. It is a vitreous greenish blue, as I remember it, like those patches of the winter sky seen through cloud vistas in the west before sundown. Yet a single glass of its water held up to the light is as colorless as an equal quantity of air. It is well known that a large plate of glass will have a green tint, owing, as the makers say, to its "body," but a small piece of the same will be colorless. How large a body of Walden water would be required to reflect a green tint I have never proved. The water of our river is black or a very dark brown to one looking directly down on it, and, like that of most ponds, imparts to the body of one bathing in it a yellowish tinge; but this water is of such crystalline purity that the body of the bather appears of an alabaster whiteness, still more unnatural, which, as the limbs are magnified and distorted withal, produces a monstrous effect, making fit studies for a Michael Angelo.

The water is so transparent that the bottom can easily be discerned at the depth of twenty-five or thirty feet. Paddling over it, you may see many feet beneath the surface the schools of perch and shiners, perhaps only an inch long, yet the former easily distinguished by their transverse bars, and you think that they must be ascetic fish that find a subsistence there. Once, in the winter, many years ago, when I had been cutting holes through the ice in order to catch pickerel, as I stepped ashore I tossed my axe back on to the ice, but, as if some evil genius had directed it, it slid four or five rods directly into one of the holes, where the water was twenty-five feet deep. Out of curiosity, I lay down on the ice and looked through the hole, until I saw the axe a little on one side, standing on its head, with its helve erect and gently swaying to and fro with the pulse of the pond; and there it might have stood erect and swaying till in the course of time the handle rotted off, if I had not disturbed it. Making another hole directly over it with an ice chisel which I had, and cutting down the longest birch which I could find in the neighborhood with my knife, I made a slip-noose, which I attached to its end, and, letting it down carefully, passed it over the knob of the handle, and drew it by a line along the birch, and so pulled the axe out again.

The shore is composed of a belt of smooth rounded white stones like paving stones, excepting one or two short sand beaches, and is so steep that in many places a single leap will carry you into water over your head; and were it not for its remarkable transparency, that would be the last to be seen of its bottom till it rose on the opposite side. Some think it is bottomless. It is nowhere muddy, and a casual observer would say that there were no weeds at all in it; and of noticeable plants, except in the little meadows recently overflowed, which do not properly belong to it, a closer scrutiny does not detect a flag nor a bulrush, nor even a lily, yellow or white, but only a few small heart-leaves and potamogetons, and perhaps a water-target or two; all which however a bather might not perceive; and these plants are clean and bright like the element they grow in. The stones extend a rod or two into the water, and then the bottom is pure sand, except in the deepest parts, where there is usually a little sediment, probably from the decay of the leaves which have been wafted on to it so many successive falls, and a bright green weed is brought up on anchors even in midwinter.

We have one other pond just like this, White Pond in Nine Acre Corner, about two and a half miles westerly; but, though I am acquainted with most of the ponds within a dozen miles of this centre, I do not know a third of this pure and well-like character. Successive nations perchance have drank at, admired, and fathomed it, and passed away, and still its water is green and pellucid as ever. Not an intermitting spring! Perhaps on that spring morning when Adam and Eve were driven out of Eden Walden Pond was already in existence, and even then breaking up in a gentle spring rain accompanied with mist and a southerly wind, and covered with myriads of ducks and geese, which had not heard of the fall, when still such pure lakes sufficed them. Even then it had commenced to rise and fall, and had clarified its waters and colored them of the hue they now wear, and obtained a patent of heaven to be the only Walden Pond in the world and distiller of celestial dews. Who knows in how many unremembered nations' literatures this has been the Castalian Fountain?[4] or what nymphs presided over it in the Golden Age? It is a gem of the first water which Concord wears in her coronet.

Yet perchance the first who came to this well have left some trace of their footsteps. I have been surprised to detect encircling the pond, even where a thick wood has just been cut down on the shore, a narrow shelf-like path in the steep hill-side, alternately rising and falling, approaching and receding from the water's edge, as old probably as the race of man here, worn by the feet of aboriginal hunters, and still from time to time unwittingly trodden by the present occupants of the land. This is particularly distinct to one standing on the middle of the pond in winter, just after a light snow has fallen, appearing as a clear undulating white line, unobscured by weeds and twigs, and very obvious a quarter of a mile off in many places where in summer it is hardly distinguishable close at hand. The snow reprints it, as it were, in clear white type alto-relievo.[5] The ornamented grounds of villas which will one day be built here may still preserve some trace of this.

The pond rises and falls, but whether regularly or not, and within what period, nobody knows, though, as usual, many pretend to know. It is commonly higher in the winter and lower in the summer, though not corresponding to the general wet and dryness. I can remember when it was a foot or two

4. In Greek mythology, a spring on Mount Parnassus, sacred to Apollo and the Muses.

5. High relief (Italian), so raised as to be partly detached from the background.

lower, and also when it was at least five feet higher, than when I lived by it. There is a narrow sandbar running into it, with very deep water on one side, on which I helped boil a kettle of chowder, some six rods from the main shore, about the year 1824, which it has not been possible to do for twenty-five years; and on the other hand, my friends used to listen with incredulity when I told them, that a few years later I was accustomed to fish from a boat in a secluded cove in the woods, fifteen rods from the only shore they knew, which place was long since converted into a meadow. But the pond has risen steadily for two years, and now, in the summer of '52, is just five feet higher than when I lived there, or as high as it was thirty years ago, and fishing goes on again in the meadow. This makes a difference of level, at the outside, of six or seven feet; and yet the water shed by the surrounding hills is insignificant in amount, and this overflow must be referred to causes which affect the deep springs. This same summer the pond has begun to fall again. It is remarkable that this fluctuation, whether periodical or not, appears thus to require many years for its accomplishment. I have observed one rise and a part of two falls, and I expect that a dozen or fifteen years hence the water will again be as low as I have ever known it. Flint's Pond, a mile eastward, allowing for the disturbance occasioned by its inlets and outlets, and the smaller intermediate ponds also, sympathize with Walden, and recently attained their greatest height at the same time with the latter. The same is true, as far as my observation goes, of White Pond.

This rise and fall of Walden at long intervals serves this use at least; the water standing at this great height for a year or more, though it makes it difficult to walk round it, kills the shrubs and trees which have sprung up about its edge since the last rise, pitch-pines, birches, alders, aspens, and others, and, falling again, leaves an unobstructed shore; for, unlike many ponds and all waters which are subject to a daily tide, its shore is cleanest when the water is lowest. On the side of the pond next my house, a row of pitch pines fifteen feet high has been killed and tipped over as if by a lever, and thus a stop put to their encroachments; and their size indicates how many years have elapsed since the last rise to this height. By this fluctuation the pond asserts its title to a shore, and thus the *shore* is *shorn*, and the trees cannot hold it by right of possession. These are the lips of the lake on which no beard grows. It licks its chaps from time to time. When the water is at its height, the alders, willows, and maples send forth a mass of fibrous red roots several feet long from all sides of their stems in the water, and to the height of three or four feet from the ground, in the effort to maintain themselves; and I have known the high-blueberry bushes about the shore, which commonly produce no fruit, bear an abundant crop under these circumstances.

Some have been puzzled to tell how the shore became so regularly paved. My townsmen have all heard the tradition, the oldest people tell me that they heard it in their youth, that anciently the Indians were holding a pow-wow upon a hill here, which rose as high into the heavens as the pond now sinks deep into the earth, and they used much profanity, as the story goes, though this vice is one of which the Indians were never guilty, and while they were thus engaged the hill shook and suddenly sank, and only one old squaw, named Walden, escaped, and from her the pond was named. It has been conjectured that when the hill shook these stones rolled down its side and became the present shore. It is very certain, at any rate, that once there was no pond here, and now there is one; and this Indian fable does not in any respect conflict with the account of that ancient settler whom I have mentioned, who remembers so well when he first came here with his divining rod, saw a thin vapor rising from the sward, and the hazel pointed steadily downward, and he concluded to dig a well here. As for the stones, many still think that they are hardly to be accounted for by the action of the waves on these hills; but I observe that the surrounding hills are remarkably full of the same kind of stones, so that they have been obliged to pile them up in walls on both sides of the railroad cut nearest the pond; and, moreover, there are most stones where the shore is most abrupt; so that, unfortunately, it is no longer a mystery to me. I detect the paver. If the name was not derived from that of some English locality,—Saffron Walden, for instance,—one might suppose that it was called, originally, *Walled-in* Pond.

The pond was my well ready dug. For four months in the year its water is as cold as it is pure at all times; and I think that it is then as good as any, if not the best, in the town. In the winter, all water which is exposed to the air is colder than springs and wells which are protected from it. The temperature of the pond water which had stood in the room where I sat from five o'clock in the afternoon till noon the next day, the sixth of March, 1846, the thermometer having been up to 65° or 70° some of the time, owing partly to the sun on the roof, was 42°, or one degree colder than the water of one of the coldest wells in the village just drawn. The temperature of the Boiling Spring the same day was 45°, or the warmest of any water tried, though it is the coldest that I know of in summer, when, beside, shallow and stagnant surface water is not mingled with it. Moreover, in summer, Walden never becomes so warm as most water which is exposed to the sun, on account of its depth. In the warmest weather I usually placed a pailful in my cellar, where it became cool in the night, and remained so during the day; though I also resorted to a spring in the neighborhood. It was as good when a week old as the day it was dipped, and had no taste of the pump. Whoever camps for a week in summer by the shore of a pond, needs only bury a pail of water a few feet deep in the shade of his camp to be independent of the luxury of ice.

There have been caught in Walden, pickerel, one weighing seven pounds, to say nothing of another which carried off a reel with great velocity, which the fisherman safely set down at eight pounds because he did not see him, perch and pouts, some of each weighing over two pounds, shiners, chivins or roach, (*Leuciscus pulchellus*,) a very few breams, (*Promotis obesus*,) and a couple of eels, one weighing four pounds,—I am thus particular because the weight of a fish is commonly its only title to fame, and these are the only eels I have heard of here;—also, I have a faint recollection of a little fish some five inches long, with silvery sides and a greenish back, somewhat dace[6]-like in its character, which I mention here chiefly to link my facts to fable. Nevertheless, this pond is not very fertile in fish. Its pickerel, though not abundant, are its chief boast. I have seen at one time lying on the ice pickerel of at least three different kinds; a long and shallow one, steel-colored, most like those caught in the river; a bright golden kind, with greenish reflections and remarkably deep, which is the most common here; and another, golden-colored, and shaped like the last, but peppered on the sides with small dark brown or black

6. Small fresh-water fish.—

spots, intermixed with a few faint blood-red ones, very much like a trout. The specific name *reticulatus* would not apply to this; it should be *guttatus*[7] rather. These are all very firm fish, and weigh more than their size promises. The shiners, pouts, and perch also, and indeed all the fishes which inhabit this pond, are much cleaner, handsomer, and firmer fleshed than those in the river and most other ponds, as the water is purer, and they can easily be distinguished from them. Probably many ichthyologists would make new varieties of some of them. There are also a clean race of frogs and tortoises, and a few muscles in it; muskrats and minks leave their traces about it, and occasionally a travelling mud-turtle visits it. Sometimes, when I pushed off my boat in the morning, I disturbed a great mud-turtle which had secreted himself under the boat in the night. Ducks and geese frequent it in the spring and fall, the white-bellied swallows (*Hirundo bicolor*) skim over it, kingfishers dart away from its coves, and the peetweets (*Totanus macularius*) "teter" along its stony shores all summer. I have sometimes disturbed a fishhawk sitting on a white-pine over the water; but I doubt if it is ever profaned by the wing of a gull, like Fair Haven. At most, it tolerates one annual loon. These are all the animals of consequence which frequent it now.

You may see from a boat, in calm weather, near the sandy eastern shore, where the water is eight or ten feet deep, and also in some other parts of the pond, some circular heaps half a dozen feet in diameter by a foot in height, consisting of small stones less than a hen's egg in size, where all around is bare sand. At first you wonder if the Indians could have formed them on the ice for any purpose, and so, when the ice melted, they sank to the bottom; but they are too regular and some of them plainly too fresh for that. They are similar to those found in rivers; but as there are no suckers nor lampreys here, I know not by what fish they could be made. Perhaps they are the nests of the chivin.[8] These lend a pleasing mystery to the bottom.

The shore is irregular enough not to be monotonous. I have in my mind's eye the western indented with deep bays, the bolder northern, and the beautifully scolloped southern shore, where successive capes overlap each other and suggest unexplored coves between. The forest has never so good a setting, nor is so distinctly beautiful, as when seen from the middle of a small lake amid hills which rise from the water's edge; for the water in which it is reflected not only makes the best foreground in such a case, but, with its winding shore, the most natural and agreeable boundary to it. There is no rawness nor imperfection in its edge there, as where the axe has cleared a part, or a cultivated field abuts on it. The trees have ample room to expand on the water side, and each sends forth its most vigorous branch in that direction. There Nature has woven a natural selvage, and the eye rises by just gradations from the low shrubs of the shore to the highest trees. There are few traces of man's hand to be seen. The water laves the shore as it did a thousand years ago.

A lake is the landscape's most beautiful and expressive feature. It is earth's eye; looking into which the beholder measures the depth of his own nature. The fluviatile trees next the shore are the slender eyelashes which fringe it, and the wooded hills and cliffs around are its overhanging brows.

Standing on the smooth sandy beach at the east end of the pond, in a calm September afternoon, when a slight haze makes the opposite shore line

---

7. Speckled. "*Reticulatus*": netlike.
8. What Thoreau saw has been confirmed to be heaps made by the chivin, a nest-building fish.

indistinct, I have seen whence came the expression, "the glassy surface of a lake." When you invert your head, it looks like a thread of finest gossamer stretched across the valley, and gleaming against the distant pine woods, separating one stratum of the atmosphere from another. You would think that you could walk dry under it to the opposite hills, and that the swallows which skim over might perch on it. Indeed, they sometimes dive below the line, as it were by mistake, and are undeceived. As you look over the pond westward you are obliged to employ both your hands to defend your eyes against the reflected as well as the true sun, for they are equally bright; and if, between the two, you survey its surface critically, it is literally as smooth as glass, except where the skater insects, at equal intervals scattered over its whole extent, by their motions in the sun produce the finest imaginable sparkle on it, or, perchance, a duck plumes itself, or, as I have said, a swallow skims so low as to touch it. It may be that in the distance a fish describes an arc of three or four feet in the air, and there is one bright flash where it emerges, and another where it strikes the water; sometimes the whole silvery arc is revealed; or here and there, perhaps, is a thistle-down floating on its surface, which the fishes dart at and so dimple it again. It is like molten glass cooled but not congealed, and the few motes in it are pure and beautiful like the imperfections in glass. You may often detect a yet smoother and darker water, separated from the rest as if by an invisible cobweb, boom of the water nymphs, resting on it. From a hill-top you can see a fish leap in almost any part; for not a pickerel or shiner picks an insect from this smooth surface but it manifestly disturbs the equilibrium of the whole lake. It is wonderful with what elaborateness this simple fact is advertised,—this piscine murder will out,—and from my distant perch I distinguish the circling undulations when they are half a dozen rods in diameter. You can even detect a water-bug (*Gyrinus*) ceaselessly progressing over the smooth surface a quarter of a mile off; for they furrow the water slightly, making a conspicuous ripple bounded by two diverging lines, but the skaters glide over it without rippling it perceptibly. When the surface is considerably agitated there are no skaters nor water-bugs on it, but apparently, in calm days, they leave their havens and adventurously glide forth from the shore by short impulses till they completely cover it. It is a soothing employment, on one of those fine days in the fall when all the warmth of the sun is fully appreciated, to sit on a stump on such a height as this, overlooking the pond, and study the dimpling circles which are incessantly inscribed on its otherwise invisible surface amid the reflected skies and trees. Over this great expanse there is no disturbance but it is thus at once gently smoothed away and assuaged, as, when a vase of water is jarred, the trembling circles seek the shore and all is smooth again. Not a fish can leap or an insect fall on the pond but it is thus reported in circling dimples, in lines of beauty, as it were the constant welling up of its fountain, the gentle pulsing of its life, the heaving of its breast. The thrills of joy and thrills of pain are undistinguishable. How peaceful the phenomena of the lake! Again the works of man shine as in the spring. Ay, every leaf and twig and stone and cobweb sparkles now at mid-afternoon as when covered with dew in a spring morning. Every motion of an oar or an insect produces a flash of light; and if an oar falls, how sweet the echo!

In such a day, in September or October, Walden is a perfect forest mirror, set round with stones as precious to my eye as if fewer or rarer. Nothing so fair, so pure, and at the same time so large, as a lake, perchance, lies on the

surface of the earth. Sky water. It needs no fence. Nations come and go without defiling it. It is a mirror which no stone can crack, whose quicksilver will
never wear off, whose gilding Nature continually repairs; no storms, no dust,
can dim its surface ever fresh;—a mirror in which all impurity presented to it
sinks, swept and dusted by the sun's hazy brush,—this the light dust-cloth,—
which retains no breath that is breathed on it, but sends its own to float as
clouds high above its surface, and be reflected in its bosom still.

A field of water betrays the spirit that is in the air. It is continually receiving
new life and motion from above. It is intermediate in its nature between land
and sky. On land only the grass and trees wave, but the water itself is rippled
by the wind. I see where the breeze dashes across it by the streaks or flakes of
light. It is remarkable that we can look down on its surface. We shall, perhaps,
look down thus on the surface of air at length, and mark where a still subtler
spirit sweeps over it.

The skaters and water-bugs finally disappear in the latter part of October,
when the severe frosts have come; and then and in November, usually, in a
calm day, there is absolutely nothing to ripple the surface. One November
afternoon, in the calm at the end of a rain storm of several days' duration,
when the sky was still completely overcast and the air was full of mist, I
observed that the pond was remarkably smooth, so that it was difficult to distinguish its surface; though it no longer reflected the bright tints of October, but
the sombre November colors of the surrounding hills. Though I passed over it
as gently as possible, the slight undulations produced by my boat extended
almost as far as I could see, and gave a ribbed appearance to the reflections.
But, as I was looking over the surface, I saw here and there at a distance a faint
glimmer, as if some skater insects which had escaped the frosts might be collected there, or, perchance, the surface, being so smooth, betrayed where a
spring welled up from the bottom. Paddling gently to one of these places, I
was surprised to find myself surrounded by myriads of small perch, about five
inches long, of a rich bronze color in the green water, sporting there and
constantly rising to the surface and dimpling it, sometimes leaving bubbles on
it. In such transparent and seemingly bottomless water, reflecting the clouds,
I seemed to be floating through the air as in a balloon, and their swimming
impressed me as a kind of flight or hovering, as if they were a compact flock
of birds passing just beneath my level on the right or left, their fins, like sails,
set all around them. There were many such schools in the pond, apparently
improving the short season before winter would draw an icy shutter over their
broad skylight, sometimes giving to the surface an appearance as if a slight
breeze struck it, or a few rain-drops fell there. When I approached carelessly
and alarmed them, they made a sudden plash and rippling with their tails, as
if one had struck the water with a brushy bough, and instantly took refuge in
the depths. At length the wind rose, the mist increased, and the waves began
to run, and the perch leaped much higher than before, half out of water, a
hundred black points, three inches long, at once above the surface. Even as
late as the fifth of December, one year, I saw some dimples on the surface,
and thinking it was going to rain hard immediately, the air being full of mist,
I made haste to take my place at the oars and row homeward; already the rain
seemed rapidly increasing, though I felt none on my cheek, and I anticipated
a thorough soaking. But suddenly the dimples ceased, for they were produced
by the perch, which the noise of my oars had scared into the depths, and I saw

their schools dimly disappearing; so I spent a dry afternoon after all.

An old man who used to frequent this pond nearly sixty years ago, when it was dark with surrounding forests, tells me that in those days he sometimes saw it all alive with ducks and other water fowl, and that there were many eagles about it. He came here a-fishing, and used an old log canoe which he found on the shore. It was made of two white-pine logs dug out and pinned together, and was cut off square at the ends. It was very clumsy, but lasted a great many years before it became water-logged and perhaps sank to the bottom. He did not know whose it was; it belonged to the pond. He used to make a cable for his anchor of strips of hickory bark tied together. An old man, a potter, who lived by the pond before the Revolution, told him once that there was an iron chest at the bottom, and that he had seen it. Sometimes it would come floating up to the shore; but when you went toward it, it would go back into deep water and disappear. I was pleased to hear of the old log canoe, which took the place of an Indian one of the same material but more graceful construction, which perchance had first been a tree on the bank, and then, as it were, fell into the water, to float there for a generation, the most proper vessel for the lake. I remember that when I first looked into these depths there were many large trunks to be seen indistinctly lying on the bottom, which had either been blown over formerly, or left on the ice at the last cutting, when wood was cheaper; but now they have mostly disappeared.

When I first paddled a boat on Walden, it was completely surrounded by thick and lofty pine and oak woods, and in some of its coves grape vines had run over the trees next the water and formed bowers under which a boat could pass. The hills which form its shores are so steep, and the woods on them were then so high, that, as you looked down from the west end, it had the appearance of an amphitheatre for some kind of sylvan spectacle. I have spent many an hour, when I was younger, floating over its surface as the zephyr[9] willed, having paddled my boat to the middle, and lying on my back across the seats, in a summer forenoon, dreaming awake, until I was aroused by the boat touching the sand, and I arose to see what shore my fates had impelled me to; days when idleness was the most attractive and productive industry. Many a forenoon have I stolen away, preferring to spend thus the most valued part of the day; for I was rich, if not in money, in sunny hours and summer days, and spent them lavishly; nor do I regret that I did not waste more of them in the workshop or the teacher's desk. But since I left those shores the woodchoppers have still further laid them waste, and now for many a year there will be no more rambling through the aisles of the wood, with occasional vistas through which you see the water. My Muse may be excused if she is silent henceforth. How can you expect the birds to sing when their groves are cut down?

Now the trunks of trees on the bottom, and the old log canoe, and the dark surrounding woods, are gone, and the villagers, who scarcely know where it lies, instead of going to the pond to bathe or drink, are thinking to bring its water, which should be as sacred as the Ganges at least, to the village in a pipe, to wash their dishes with!—to earn their Walden by the turning of a cock or drawing of a plug! That devilish Iron Horse, whose ear-rending neigh is heard throughout the town, has muddied the Boiling Spring with his foot, and he it is that has browsed off all the woods on Walden shore; that Trojan horse,

---

9. The mild west wind.

with a thousand men in his belly, introduced by mercenary Greeks![1] Where is the country's champion, the Moore of Moore Hall,[2] to meet him at the Deep Cut and thrust an avenging lance between the ribs of the bloated pest?

Nevertheless, of all the characters I have known, perhaps Walden wears best, and best preserves its purity. Many men have been likened to it, but few deserve that honor. Though the woodchoppers have laid bare first this shore and then that, and the Irish have built their sties by it, and the railroad has infringed on its border, and the ice-men have skimmed it once, it is itself unchanged, the same water which my youthful eyes fell on; all the change is in me. It has not acquired one permanent wrinkle after all its ripples. It is perennially young, and I may stand and see a swallow dip apparently to pick an insect from its surface as of yore. It struck me again to-night, as if I had not seen it almost daily for more than twenty years,—Why, here is Walden, the same woodland lake that I discovered so many years ago; where a forest was cut down last winter another is springing up by its shore as lustily as ever; the same thought is welling up to its surface that was then; it is the same liquid joy and happiness to itself and its Maker, ay, and it *may* be to me. It is the work of a brave man surely, in whom there was no guile! He rounded this water with his hand, deepened and clarified it in his thought, and in his will bequeathed it to Concord. I see by its face that it is visited by the same reflection; and I can almost say, Walden, is it you?

> It is no dream of mine,
> To ornament a line;
> I cannot come nearer to God and Heaven
> Than I live to Walden even.
> I am its stony shore,
> And the breeze that passes o'er;
> In the hollow of my hand
> Are its water and its sand,
> And its deepest resort
> Lies high in my thought.

The cars never pause to look at it; yet I fancy that the engineers and firemen and brakemen, and those passengers who have a season ticket and see it often, are better men for the sight. The engineer does not forget at night, or his nature does not, that he has beheld this vision of serenity and purity once at least during the day. Though seen but once, it helps to wash out State-street and the engine's soot. One proposes that it be called "God's Drop."

I have said that Walden has no visible inlet nor outlet, but it is on the one hand distantly and indirectly related to Flint's Pond, which is more elevated, by a chain of small ponds coming from that quarter, and on the other directly and manifestly to Concord River, which is lower, by a similar chain of ponds through which in some other geological period it may have flowed, and by a little digging, which God forbid, it can be made to flow thither again. If by living thus reserved and austere, like a hermit in the woods, so long, it has acquired such wonderful purity, who would not regret that the comparatively impure waters of Flint's Pond should be mingled with it, or itself should ever go to waste its sweetness in the ocean wave?

1. The stratagem by which the Greeks entered Troy.
2. From *The Dragon of Wantley* in Percy's *Reliques of Ancient English Poetry* (1765): "But More of More-

Hall, with nothing at all, / He slew the dragon of Wantley."

Flint's, or Sandy Pond, in Lincoln, our greatest lake and inland sea, lies about a mile east of Walden. It is much larger, being said to contain one hundred and ninety-seven acres, and is more fertile in fish, but it is comparatively shallow, and not remarkably pure. A walk through the woods thither was often my recreation. It was worth the while, if only to feel the wind blow on your cheek freely, and see the waves run, and remember the life of mariners. I went a-chestnutting there in the fall, on windy days, when the nuts were dropping into the water and were washed to my feet; and one day, as I crept along its sedgy shore, the fresh spray blowing in my face, I came upon the mouldering wreck of a boat, the sides gone, and hardly more than the impression of its flat bottom left amid the rushes; yet its model was sharply defined, as if it were a large decayed pad, with its veins. It was as impressive a wreck as one could imagine on the sea-shore, and had as good a moral. It is by this time mere vegetable mould and undistinguishable pond shore, through which rushes and flags have pushed up. I used to admire the ripple marks on the sandy bottom, at the north end of this pond, made firm and hard to the feet of the wader by the pressure of the water, and the rushes which grew in Indian file, in waving lines, corresponding to these marks, rank behind rank, as if the waves had planted them. There also I have found, in considerable quantities, curious balls, composed apparently of fine grass or roots, of pipewort perhaps, from half an inch to four inches in diameter, and perfectly spherical. These wash back and forth in shallow water on a sandy bottom, and are sometimes cast on the shore. They are either solid grass, or have a little sand in the middle. At first you would say that they were formed by the action of the waves, like a pebble; yet the smallest are made of equally coarse materials, half an inch long, and they are produced only at one season of the year. Moreover, the waves, I suspect, do not so much construct as wear down a material which has already acquired consistency. They preserve their form when dry for an indefinite period.

Flint's Pond! Such is the poverty of our nomenclature. What right had the unclean and stupid farmer, whose farm abutted on this sky water, whose shores he has ruthlessly laid bare, to give his name to it? Some skin-flint, who loved better the reflecting surface of a dollar, or a bright cent, in which he could see his own brazen face; who regarded even the wild ducks which settled in it as trespassers; his fingers grown into crooked and horny talons from the long habit of grasping harpy-like;[3]—so it is not named for me. I go not there to see him nor to hear of him; who never *saw* it, who never bathed in it, who never loved it, who never protected it, who never spoke a good word for it, nor thanked God that he had made it. Rather let it be named from the fishes that swim in it, the wild fowl or quadrupeds which frequent it, the wild flowers which grow by its shores, or some wild man or child the thread of whose history is interwoven with its own; not from him who could show no title to it but the deed which a like-minded neighbor or legislature gave him,—him who thought only of its money value; whose presence perchance cursed all the shore; who exhausted the land around it, and would fain have exhausted the waters within it; who regretted only that it was not English hay or cranberry meadow,—there was nothing to redeem it, forsooth, in his eyes,—and would have drained and sold it for the mud at its bottom. It did not turn his mill, and it was no *privilege* to him to behold it. I respect not his labors, his farm where every thing has its

3. In Greek mythology, the Harpies were monsters with women's heads and birds' bodies who seized and carried off the soul at the moment of death.

price; who would carry the landscape, who would carry his God, to market, if he could get any thing for him; who goes to market *for* his god as it is; on whose farm nothing grows free, whose fields bear no crops, whose meadows no flowers, whose trees no fruits, but dollars; who loves not the beauty of his fruits, whose fruits are not ripe for him till they are turned to dollars. Give me the poverty that enjoys true wealth. Farmers are respectable and interesting to me in proportion as they are poor,—poor farmers. A model farm! where the house stands like a fungus in a muck-heap, chambers for men, horses, oxen, and swine, cleansed and uncleansed, all contiguous to one another! Stocked with men! A great grease-spot, redolent of manures and buttermilk! Under a high state of cultivation, being manured with the hearts and brains of men! As if you were to raise your potatoes in the church-yard! Such is a model farm.

No, no; if the fairest features of the landscape are to be named after men, let them be the noblest and worthiest men alone. Let our lakes receive as true names at least as the Icarian Sea, where "still the shore" a "brave attempt resounds."[4]

Goose Pond, of small extent, is on my way to Flint's; Fair-Haven, an expansion of Concord River, said to contain some seventy acres, is a mile southwest; and White Pond, of about forty acres, is a mile and a half beyond Fair-Haven. This is my lake country.[5] These, with Concord River, are my water privileges; and night and day, year in year out, they grind such grist as I carry to them.

Since the woodcutters, and the railroad, and I myself have profaned Walden, perhaps the most attractive, if not the most beautiful, of all our lakes, the gem of the woods, is White Pond;—a poor name from its commonness, whether derived from the remarkable purity of its waters or the color of its sands. In these as in other respects, however, it is a lesser twin of Walden. They are so much alike that you would say they must be connected under ground. It has the same stony shore, and its waters are of the same hue. As at Walden, in sultry dog-day weather, looking down through the woods on some of its bays which are not so deep but that the reflection from the bottom tinges them, its waters are of a misty bluish-green or glaucous color. Many years since I used to go there to collect the sand by cart-loads, to make sand-paper with, and I have continued to visit it ever since. One who frequents it proposes to call it Virid Lake.[6] Perhaps it might be called Yellow-Pine Lake, from the following circumstance. About fifteen years ago you could see the top of a pitch-pine, of the kind called yellow-pine hereabouts, though it is not a distinct species, projecting above the surface in deep water, many rods from the shore. It was even supposed by some that the pond had sunk, and this was one of the primitive forests that formerly stood there. I find that even so long ago as 1792, in a "Topographical Description of the Town of Concord," by one of its citizens, in the Collections of the Massachusetts Historical Society, the author, after speaking of Walden and White Ponds, adds: "In the middle of the latter may be seen, when the water is very low, a tree which appears as if it grew in the place where it now stands, although the roots are fifty feet below the surface of the water; the top of this tree is broken off, and at that place

---

4. From *Icarus* by William Drummond of Hawthornden (1585–1649).
5. A New England equivalent of the English Lake

District associated with Wordsworth and other Romantics.
6. Green Lake.

measures fourteen inches in diameter."[7] In the spring of '49 I talked with the man who lives nearest the pond in Sudbury, who told me that it was he who got out this tree ten or fifteen years before. As near as he could remember, it stood twelve or fifteen rods from the shore, where the water was thirty or forty feet deep. It was in the winter, and he had been getting out ice in the forenoon, and had resolved that in the afternoon, with the aid of his neighbors, he would take out the old yellow-pine. He sawed a channel in the ice toward the shore, and hauled it over and along and out on to the ice with oxen; but, before he had gone far in his work, he was surprised to find that it was wrong end upward, with the stumps of the branches pointing down, and the small end firmly fastened in the sandy bottom. It was about a foot in diameter at the big end, and he had expected to get a good saw-log, but it was so rotten as to be fit only for fuel, if for that. He had some of it in his shed then. There were marks of an axe and of woodpeckers on the but. He thought that it might have been a dead tree on the shore, but was finally blown over into the pond, and after the top had become waterlogged, while the but-end was still dry and light, had drifted out and sunk wrong end up. His father, eighty years old, could not remember when it was not there. Several pretty large logs may still be seen lying on the bottom, where, owing to the undulation of the surface, they look like huge water snakes in motion.

This pond has rarely been profaned by a boat, for there is little in it to tempt a fisherman. Instead of the white lily, which requires mud, or the common sweet flag, the blue flag (*Iris versicolor*) grows thinly in the pure water, rising from the stony bottom all around the shore, where it is visited by humming birds in June, and the color both of its bluish blades and its flowers, and especially their reflections, are in singular harmony with the glaucous water.

White Pond and Walden are great crystals on the surface of the earth, Lakes of Light. If they were permanently congealed, and small enough to be clutched, they would, perchance, be carried off by slaves, like precious stones, to adorn the heads of emperors; but being liquid, and ample, and secured to us and our successors forever, we disregard them, and run after the diamond of Kohinoor.[8] They are too pure to have a market value; they contain no muck. How much more beautiful than our lives, how much more transparent than our characters, are they! We never learned meanness of them. How much fairer than the pool before the farmer's door, in which his ducks swim! Hither the clean wild ducks come. Nature has no human inhabitant who appreciates her. The birds with their plumage and their notes are in harmony with the flowers, but what youth or maiden conspires with the wild luxuriant beauty of Nature? She flourishes most alone, far from the towns where they reside. Talk of heaven! ye disgrace earth.

Baker Farm

Sometimes I rambled to pine groves, standing like temples, or like fleets at sea, full-rigged, with wavy boughs, and rippling with light, so soft and green and shady that the Druids[9] would have forsaken their oaks to worship in them;

---

7. William Jones, " 'A Topological Description of Concord,' " *Mass. Hist. Soc. Col.*, I (1792), 238 [Harding's note].
8. An enormous diamond found in India during the 18th century and added to the British crown jewels during the composition of *Walden*.
9. Priests of ancient Gaul and Britain to whom the oak was sacred.

or to the cedar wood beyond Flint's Pond, where the trees, covered with hoary blue berries, spiring higher and higher, are fit to stand before Valhalla,[1] and the creeping juniper covers the ground with wreaths full of fruit; or to swamps where the usnea lichen hangs in festoons from the black-spruce trees, and toad-stools, round tables of the swamp gods, cover the ground, and more beautiful fungi adorn the stumps, like butterflies or shells, vegetable winkles; where the swamp-pink and dogwood grow, the red alder-berry glows like eyes of imps, the waxwork grooves and crushes the hardest woods in its folds, and the wild-holly berries make the beholder forget his home with their beauty, and he is dazzled and tempted by nameless other wild forbidden fruits, too fair for mortal taste. Instead of calling on some scholar, I paid many a visit to particular trees, of kinds which are rare in this neighborhood, standing far away in the middle of some pasture, or in the depths of a wood or swamp, or on a hill-top; such as the black-birch, of which we have some handsome specimens two feet in diameter; its cousin the yellow-birch, with its loose golden vest, perfumed like the first; the beech, which has so neat a bole[2] and beautifully lichen-painted, perfect in all its details, of which, excepting scattered specimens, I know but one small grove of sizeable trees left in the township, supposed by some to have been planted by the pigeons that were once baited with beech nuts near by; it is worth the while to see the silver grain sparkle when you split this wood; the bass; the hornbeam; the *Celtis occidentalis*, or false elm, of which we have but one well-grown; some taller mast of a pine, a shingle tree, or a more perfect hemlock than usual, standing like a pagoda in the midst of the woods; and many others I could mention. These were the shrines I visited both summer and winter.

Once it chanced that I stood in the very abutment of a rainbow's arch, which filled the lower stratum of the atmosphere, tinging the grass and leaves around, and dazzling me as if I looked through colored crystal. It was a lake of rainbow light, in which, for a short while, I lived like a dolphin. If it had lasted longer it might have tinged my employments and life. As I walked on the railroad causeway, I used to wonder at the halo of light around my shadow, and would fain fancy myself one of the elect.[3] One who visited me declared that the shadows of some Irishmen before him had no halo about them, that it was only natives that were so distinguished. Benvenuto Cellini tells us in his memoirs, that after a certain terrible dream or vision which he had during his confinement in the castle of St. Angelo, a resplendent light appeared over the shadow of his head at morning and evening, whether he was in Italy or France, and it was particularly conspicuous when the grass was moist with dew.[4] This was probably the same phenomenon to which I have referred, which is especially observed in the morning, but also at other times, and even by moonlight. Though a constant one, it is not commonly noticed, and, in the case of an excitable imagination like Cellini's, it would be basis enough for superstition. Beside, he tells us that he showed it to very few. But are they not indeed distinguished who are conscious that they are regarded at all?

I set out one afternoon to go a-fishing to Fair-Haven, through the woods, to eke out my scanty fare of vegetables. My way led through Pleasant Meadow,

---

1. In Norse mythology, the gigantic hall to which souls of slain heroes go.
2. Trunk.
3. I.e., according to Calvinistic theology, one of those predestined for salvation.
4. In Chapter 26 of the *Autobiography* of Benvenuto Cellini (1500–1571), Italian sculptor and goldsmith.

an adjunct of the Baker Farm, that retreat of which a poet has since sung, beginning,—

> "Thy entry is a pleasant field,
> Which some mossy fruit trees yield
> Partly to a ruddy brook,
> By gliding musquash undertook,
> And mercurial trout,
> Darting about."[5]

I thought of living there before I went to Walden. I "hooked" the apples, leaped the brook, and scared the musquash[6] and the trout. It was one of those afternoons which seem indefinitely long before one, in which many events may happen, a large portion of our natural life, though it was already half spent when I started. By the way there came up a shower, which compelled me to stand half an hour under a pine, piling boughs over my head, and wearing my handkerchief for a shed; and when at length I had made one cast over the pickerel-weed, standing up to my middle in water, I found myself suddenly in the shadow of a cloud, and the thunder began to rumble with such emphasis that I could do no more than listen to it. The gods must be proud, thought I, with such forked flashes to rout a poor unarmed fisherman. So I made haste for shelter to the nearest hut, which stood half a mile from any road, but so much the nearer to the pond, and had long been uninhabited:—

> "And here a poet builded,
> In the completed years,
> For behold a trivial cabin
> That to destruction steers."[7]

So the Muse fables. But therein, as I found, dwelt now John Field, an Irishman, and his wife, and several children, from the broad-faced boy who assisted his father at his work, and now came running by his side from the bog to escape the rain, to the wrinkled, sibyl-like, cone-headed infant that sat upon its father's knee as in the palaces of nobles, and looked out from its home in the midst of wet and hunger inquisitively upon the stranger, with the privilege of infancy, not knowing but it was the last of a noble line, and the hope and cynosure of the world, instead of John Field's poor starveling brat. There we sat together under that part of the roof which leaked the least, while it showered and thundered without. I had sat there many times of old before the ship was built that floated this family to America. An honest, hard-working, but shiftless man plainly was John Field; and his wife, she too was brave to cook so many successive dinners in the recesses of that lofty stove; with round greasy face and bare breast,[8] still thinking to improve her condition one day; with the never absent mop in one hand, and yet no effects of it visible any where. The chickens, which had also taken shelter here from the rain, stalked about the room like members of the family, too humanized methought to roast well. They stood and looked in my eye or pecked at my shoe significantly. Meanwhile my host told me his story, how hard he worked "bogging" for a neighboring farmer, turning up a meadow with a spade or bog-hoe at the rate of ten

---

5. From Ellery Channing's *Baker Farm*.
6. Muskrat.
7. From Channing's *Baker Farm*.

8. I.e., with more of her neck and chest visible than Thoreau's own female relatives usually exposed.

dollars an acre and the use of the land with manure for one year, and his little broad-faced son worked cheerfully at his father's side the while, not knowing how poor a bargain the latter had made. I tried to help him with my experience, telling him that he was one of my nearest neighbors, and that I too, who came a-fishing here, and looked like a loafer, was getting my living like himself; that I lived in a tight light and clean house, which hardly cost more than the annual rent of such a ruin as his commonly amounts to; and how, if he chose, he might in a month or two build himself a palace of his own; that I did not use tea, nor coffee, nor butter, nor milk, nor fresh meat, and so did not have to work to get them; again, as I did not work hard, I did not have to eat hard, and it cost me but a trifle for my food; but as he began with tea, and coffee, and butter, and milk, and beef, he had to work hard to pay for them, and when he had worked hard he had to eat hard again to repair the waste of his system,—and so it was as broad as it was long, indeed it was broader than it was long, for he was discontented and wasted his life into the bargain; and yet he had rated it as a gain in coming to America, that here you could get tea, and coffee, and meat every day. But the only true America is that country where you are at liberty to pursue such a mode of life as may enable you to do without these, and where the state does not endeavor to compel you to sustain the slavery and war and other superfluous expenses which directly or indirectly result from the use of such things. For I purposely talked to him as if he were a philosopher, or desired to be one. I should be glad if all the meadows on the earth were left in a wild state, if that were the consequence of men's beginning to redeem themselves. A man will not need to study history to find out what is best for his own culture. But alas! the culture of an Irishman is an enterprise to be undertaken with a sort of moral bog hoe. I told him, that as he worked so hard at bogging, he required thick boots and stout clothing, which yet were soon soiled and worn out, but I wore light shoes and thin clothing, which cost not half so much, though he might think that I was dressed like a gentleman, (which, however, was not the case,) and in an hour or two, without labor, but as a recreation, I could, if I wished, catch as many fish as I should want for two days, or earn enough money to support me a week. If he and his family would live simply, they might all go a-huckleberrying in the summer for their amusement. John heaved a sigh at this, and his wife stared with arms a-kimbo, and both appeared to be wondering if they had capital enough to begin such a course with, or arithmetic enough to carry it through. It was sailing by dead reckoning[9] to them, and they saw not clearly how to make their port so; therefore I suppose they still take life bravely, after their fashion, face to face, giving it tooth and nail, not having skill to split its massive columns with any fine entering wedge, and rout it in detail;—thinking to deal with it roughly, as one should handle a thistle. But they fight at an overwhelming disadvantage,—living, John Field, alas! without arithmetic, and failing so.

"Do you ever fish?" I asked. "Oh yes, I catch a mess now and then when I am lying by; good perch I catch." "What's your bait?" "I catch shiners with fish-worms, and bait the perch with them." "You'd better go now, John," said his wife with glistening and hopeful face; but John demurred.

The shower was now over, and a rainbow above the eastern woods promised a fair evening; so I took my departure. When I had got without I asked for a

---

9. A way of estimating position without astronomical observation, as by judging direction and distance from a previously determined spot.

drink, hoping to get a sight of the well bottom, to complete my survey of the premises; but there, alas! are shallows and quicksands, and rope broken withal, and bucket irrecoverable. Meanwhile the right culinary vessel was selected, water was seemingly distilled, and after consultation and long delay passed out to the thirsty one,—not yet suffered to cool, not yet to settle. Such gruel sustains life here, I thought; so, shutting my eyes, and excluding the motes by a skilfully directed under-current, I drank to genuine hospitality the heartiest draught I could. I am not squeamish in such cases when manners are concerned.

As I was leaving the Irishman's roof after the rain, bending my steps again to the pond, my haste to catch pickerel, wading in retired meadows, in sloughs and bog-holes, in forlorn and savage places, appeared for an instant trivial to me who had been sent to school and college; but as I ran down the hill toward the reddening west, with the rainbow over my shoulder, and some faint tinkling sounds borne to my ear through the cleansed air, from I know not what quarter, my Good Genius seemed to say,—Go fish and hunt far and wide day by day,—farther and wider,—and rest thee by many brooks and hearth-sides without misgiving. Remember thy Creator in the days of thy youth.[1] Rise free from care before the dawn, and seek adventures. Let the noon find thee by other lakes, and the night overtake thee every where at home. There are no larger fields than these, no worthier games than may here be played. Grow wild according to thy nature, like these sedges and brakes, which will never become English hay. Let the thunder rumble; what if it threaten ruin to farmers' crops? that is not its errand to thee. Take shelter under the cloud, while they flee to carts and sheds. Let not to get a living be thy trade, but thy sport. Enjoy the land, but own it not. Through want of enterprise and faith men are where they are, buying and selling, and spending their lives like serfs.

O Baker Farm!

"Landscape where the richest element
Is a little sunshine innocent." . . .

"No one runs to revel
On thy rail-fenced lea." . . .

"Debate with no man hast thou,
    With questions art never perplexed,
As tame at the first sight as now,
    In   thy   plain   russet   gabardine
    dressed." . . .

"Come ye who love,
    And ye who hate,
Children of the Holy Dove,
    And Guy Faux[2] of the state,
And hang conspiracies
From the tough rafters of the trees!"[3]

---

1. Ecclesiastes 12.1: "Remember now thy Creator in the days of thy youth, while the evil days come not, nor the years draw nigh, when thou shalt say, I have no pleasure in them."
2. Guy Faux or Fawkes (1570–1606) was an English Catholic conspirator executed after being seized as he was about to fire barrels of gunpowder under the House of Lords.
3. Another poem by Channing.

Men come tamely home at night only from the next field or street, where their household echoes haunt, and their life pines because it breathes its own breath over again; their shadows morning and evening reach farther than their daily steps. We should come home from far, from adventures, and perils, and discoveries every day, with new experience and character.

Before I had reached the pond some fresh impulse had brought out John Field, with altered mind, letting go "bogging" ere this sunset. But he, poor man, disturbed only a couple of fins while I was catching a fair string, and he said it was his luck; but when we changed seats in the boat luck changed seats too. Poor John Field!—I trust he does not read this, unless he will improve by it,—thinking to live by some derivative old country mode in this primitive new country,—to catch perch with shiners. It is good bait sometimes, I allow. With his horizon all his own, yet he a poor man, born to be poor, with his inherited Irish poverty or poor life, his Adam's grandmother and boggy ways, not to rise in this world, he nor his posterity, till their wading webbed bog-trotting feet get *talaria*[4] to their heels.

Higher Laws

As I came home through the woods with my string of fish, trailing my pole, it being now quite dark, I caught a glimpse of a woodchuck stealing across my path, and felt a strange thrill of savage delight, and was strongly tempted to seize and devour him raw; not that I was hungry then, except for that wildness which he represented. Once or twice, however, while I lived at the pond, I found myself ranging the woods, like a half-starved hound, with a strange abandonment, seeking some kind of venison which I might devour, and no morsel could have been too savage for me. The wildest scenes had become unaccountably familiar. I found in myself, and still find, an instinct toward a higher, or, as it is named, spiritual life, as do most men, and another toward a primitive rank and savage one, and I reverence them both. I love the wild not less than the good. The wildness and adventure that are in fishing still recommended it to me. I like sometimes to take rank hold on life and spend my day more as the animals do. Perhaps I have owed to this employment and to hunting, when quite young, my closest acquaintance with Nature. They early introduce us to and detain us in scenery with which otherwise, at that age, we should have little acquaintance. Fishermen, hunters, woodchoppers, and others, spending their lives in the fields and woods, in a peculiar sense a part of Nature themselves, are often in a more favorable mood for observing her, in the intervals of their pursuits, than philosophers or poets even, who approach her with expectation. She is not afraid to exhibit herself to them. The traveller on the prairie is naturally a hunter, on the head waters of the Missouri and Columbia a trapper, and at the Falls of St. Mary[5] a fisherman. He who is only a traveller learns things at second-hand and by the halves, and is poor authority. We are most interested when science reports what those men already know practically or instinctively, for that alone is a true *humanity*, or account of human experience.

They mistake who assert that the Yankee has few amusements, because he

4. Winged sandals, such as those worn by Hermes in Greek mythology.
5. Because the images are progressively more western, this St. Mary's River may be the one in British Columbia.

has not so many public holidays, and men and boys do not play so many games as they do in England, for here the more primitive but solitary amusements of hunting fishing and the like have not yet given place to the former. Almost every New England boy among my contemporaries shouldered a fowling piece between the ages of ten and fourteen; and his hunting and fishing grounds were not limited like the preserves of an English nobleman, but were more boundless even than those of a savage. No wonder, then, that he did not oftener stay to play on the common. But already a change is taking place, owing, not to an increased humanity, but to an increased scarcity of game, for perhaps the hunter is the greatest friend of the animals hunted, not excepting the Humane Society.

Moreover, when at the pond, I wished sometimes to add fish to my fare for variety. I have actually fished from the same kind of necessity that the first fishers did. Whatever humanity I might conjure up against it was all factitious, and concerned my philosophy more than my feelings. I speak of fishing only now, for I had long felt differently about fowling, and sold my gun before I went to the woods. Not that I am less humane than others, but I did not perceive that my feelings were much affected. I did not pity the fishes nor the worms. This was habit. As for fowling, during the last years that I carried a gun my excuse was that I was studying ornithology, and sought only new or rare birds. But I confess that I am now inclined to think that there is a finer way of studying ornithology than this. It requires so much closer attention to the habits of the birds, that, if for that reason only, I have been willing to omit the gun. Yet notwithstanding the objection on the score of humanity, I am compelled to doubt if equally valuable sports are ever substituted for these; and when some of my friends have asked me anxiously about their boys, whether they should let them hunt, I have answered, yes,—remembering that it was one of the best parts of my education,—*make* them hunters, though sportsmen only at first, if possible, mighty hunters at last, so that they shall not find game large enough for them in this or any vegetable wilderness,—hunters as well as fishers of men.[6] Thus far I am of the opinion of Chaucer's nun, who

> "yave not of the text a pulled hen
> That saith that hunters ben not holy men."[7]

There is a period in the history of the individual, as of the race, when the hunters are the "best men," as the Algonquins[8] called them. We cannot but pity the boy who has never fired a gun; he is no more humane, while his education has been sadly neglected. This was my answer with respect to those youths who were bent on this pursuit, trusting that they would soon outgrow it. No humane being, past the thoughtless age of boyhood, will wantonly murder any creature, which holds its life by the same tenure that he does. The hare in its extremity cries like a child. I warn you, mothers, that my sympathies do not always make the usual phil-*anthropic* distinctions.

Such is oftenest the young man's introduction to the forest, and the most original part of himself. He goes thither at first as a hunter and fisher, until at last, if he has the seeds of a better life in him, he distinguishes his proper

6. Mark 1.17: "Come ye after me, and I will make you to become fishers of men" (Jesus' words to the fishermen Simon and Andrew).
7. From the *Prologue* to *The Canterbury Tales*, lines 177–78 (where it is said of the monk, not the nun).
8. American Indian group once widespread in what is now the northeastern United States and southeastern Canada.

objects, as a poet or naturalist it may be, and leaves the gun and fish-pole behind. The mass of men are still and always young in this respect. In some countries a hunting parson is no uncommon sight. Such a one might make a good shepherd's dog, but is far from being the Good Shepherd. I have been surprised to consider that the only obvious employment, except wood-chopping, ice-cutting, or the like business, which ever to my knowledge detained at Walden Pond for a whole half day any of my fellow-citizens, whether fathers or children of the town, with just one exception, was fishing. Commonly they did not think that they were lucky, or well paid for their time, unless they got a long string of fish, though they had the opportunity of seeing the pond all the while. They might go there a thousand times before the sediment of fishing would sink to the bottom and leave their purpose pure; but no doubt such a clarifying process would be going on all the while. The governor and his council faintly remember the pond, for they went a-fishing there when they were boys; but now they are too old and dignified to go a-fishing, and so they know it no more forever. Yet even they expect to go to heaven at last. If the legislature regards it, it is chiefly to regulate the number of hooks to be used there; but they know nothing about the hook of hooks with which to angle for the pond itself, impaling the legislature for a bait. Thus, even in civilized communities, the embryo man passes through the hunter stage of development.

I have found repeatedly, of late years, that I cannot fish without falling a little in self-respect. I have tried it again and again. I have skill at it, and, like many of my fellows, a certain instinct for it, which revives from time to time, but always when I have done I feel that it would have been better if I had not fished. I think that I do not mistake. It is a faint intimation, yet so are the first streaks of morning. There is unquestionably this instinct in me which belongs to the lower orders of creation; yet with every year I am less a fisherman, though without more humanity or even wisdom; at present I am no fisherman at all. But I see that if I were to live in a wilderness I should again be tempted to become a fisher and hunter in earnest. Beside, there is something essentially unclean about this diet and all flesh, and I began to see where housework commences, and whence the endeavor, which costs so much, to wear a tidy and respectable appearance each day, to keep the house sweet and free from all ill odors and sights. Having been my own butcher and scullion and cook, as well as the gentleman for whom the dishes were served up, I can speak from an unusually complete experience. The practical objection to animal food in my case was its uncleanness; and, besides, when I had caught and cleaned and cooked and eaten my fish, they seemed not to have fed me essentially. It was insignificant and unnecessary, and cost more than it came to. A little bread or a few potatoes would have done as well, with less trouble and filth. Like many of my contemporaries, I had rarely for many years used animal food, or tea, or coffee, &c.; not so much because of any ill effects which I had traced to them as because they were not agreeable to my imagination. The repugnance to animal food is not the effect of experience, but is an instinct. It appeared more beautiful to live low and fare hard in many respects; and though I never did so, I went far enough to please my imagination. I believe that every man who has ever been earnest to preserve his higher or poetic faculties in the best condition has been particularly inclined to abstain from animal food, and from much food of any kind. It is a significant fact, stated by entomologists, I find it in Kirby and Spence, that "some insects in their perfect state, though furnished with organs of feeding, make no use of them;" and they lay it down as "a general rule, that almost all insects in this state eat much less than in that of larvæ. The voracious caterpillar when transformed into a butterfly," . . "and the gluttonous maggot when become a fly," content themselves with a drop or two of honey or some other sweet liquid.[9] The abdomen under the wings of the butterfly still represents the larva. This is the tid-bit which tempts his insectivorous fate. The gross feeder is a man in the larva state; and there are whole nations in that condition, nations without fancy or imagination, whose vast abdomens betray them.

It is hard to provide and cook so simple and clean a diet as will not offend the imagination; but this, I think, is to be fed when we feed the body; they should both sit down at the same table. Yet perhaps this may be done. The fruits eaten temperately need not make us ashamed of our appetites, nor interrupt the worthiest pursuits. But put an extra condiment into your dish, and it will poison you. It is not worth the while to live by rich cookery. Most men would feel shame if caught preparing with their own hands precisely such a dinner, whether of animal or vegetable food, as is every day prepared for them by others. Yet till this is otherwise we are not civilized, and, if gentlemen and ladies, are not true men and women. This certainly suggests what change is to be made. It may be vain to ask why the imagination will not be reconciled to flesh and fat. I am satisfied that it is not. Is it not a reproach that man is a carnivorous animal? True, he can and does live, in a great measure, by preying on other animals; but this is a miserable way,—as any one who will go to snaring rabbits, or slaughtering lambs, may learn,—and he will be regarded as a benefactor of his race who shall teach man to confine himself to a more innocent and wholesome diet. Whatever my own practice may be, I have no doubt that it is a part of the destiny of the human race, in its gradual improvement, to leave off eating animals, as surely as the savage tribes have left off eating each other when they came in contact with the more civilized.

If one listens to the faintest but constant suggestions of his genius, which are certainly true, he sees not to what extremes, or even insanity, it may lead him; and yet that way, as he grows more resolute and faithful, his road lies. The faintest assured objection which one healthy man feels will at length prevail over the arguments and customs of mankind. No man ever followed his genius till it misled him. Though the result were bodily weakness, yet perhaps no one can say that the consequences were to be regretted, for these were a life in conformity to higher principles. If the day and the night are such that you greet them with joy, and life emits a fragrance like flowers and sweet-scented herbs, is more elastic, more starry, more immortal,—that is your success. All nature is your congratulation, and you have cause momentarily to bless yourself. The greatest gains and values are farthest from being appreciated. We easily come to doubt if they exist. We soon forget them. They are the highest reality. Perhaps the facts most astounding and most real are never communicated by man to man. The true harvest of my daily life is somewhat as intangible and indescribable as the tints of morning or evening. It is a little star-dust caught, a segment of the rainbow which I have clutched.

Yet, for my part, I was never unusually squeamish; I could sometimes eat a fried rat with a good relish, if it were necessary. I am glad to have drunk water

9. William Kirby and William Spence, *An Introduction to Entomology* (1846).

so long, for the same reason that I prefer the natural sky to an opium-eater's heaven. I would fain keep sober always; and there are infinite degrees of drunkenness. I believe that water is the only drink for a wise man; wine is not so noble a liquor; and think of dashing the hopes of a morning with a cup of warm coffee, or of an evening with a dish of tea! Ah, how low I fall when I am tempted by them! Even music may be intoxicating. Such apparently slight causes destroyed Greece and Rome, and will destroy England and America. Of all ebriosity,[1] who does not prefer to be intoxicated by the air he breathes? I have found it to be the most serious objection to coarse labors long continued, that they compelled me to eat and drink coarsely also. But to tell the truth, I find myself at present somewhat less particular in these respects. I carry less religion to the table, ask no blessing; not because I am wiser than I was, but, I am obliged to confess, because, however much it is to be regretted, with years I have grown more coarse and indifferent. Perhaps these questions are entertained only in youth, as most believe of poetry. My practice is "nowhere," my opinion is here. Nevertheless I am far from regarding myself as one of those privileged ones to whom the Ved refers when it says, that "he who has true faith in the Omnipresent Supreme Being may eat all that exists," that is, is not bound to inquire what is his food, or who prepares it; and even in their case it is to be observed, as a Hindoo commentator has remarked, that the Vedant limits this privilege to "the time of distress."[2]

Who has not sometimes derived an inexpressible satisfaction from his food in which appetite had no share? I have been thrilled to think that I owed a mental perception to the commonly gross sense of taste, that I have been inspired through the palate, that some berries which I had eaten on a hill-side had fed my genius. "The soul not being mistress of herself," says Thseng-tseu, "one looks, and one does not see; one listens, and one does not hear; one eats, and one does not know the savor of food."[3] He who distinguishes the true savor of his food can never be a glutton; he who does not cannot be otherwise. A puritan may go to his brown-bread crust with as gross an appetite as ever an alderman to his turtle. Not that food which entereth into the mouth defileth a man, but the appetite with which it is eaten.[4] It is neither the quality nor the quantity, but the devotion to sensual savors; when that which is eaten is not a viand to sustain our animal, or inspire our spiritual life, but food for the worms that possess us. If the hunter has a taste for mud-turtles, muskrats, and other such savage tid-bits, the fine lady indulges a taste for jelly made of a calf's foot, or for sardines from over the sea, and they are even. He goes to the mill-pond, she to her preserve-pot. The wonder is how they, how you and I, can live this slimy beastly life, eating and drinking.

Our whole life is startlingly moral. There is never an instant's truce between virtue and vice. Goodness is the only investment that never fails. In the music of the harp which trembles round the world it is the insisting on this which thrills us. The harp is the travelling patterer for the Universe's Insurance Company, recommending its laws, and our little goodness is all the assessment that we pay. Though the youth at last grows indifferent, the laws of the universe are not indifferent, but are forever on the side of the most sensitive. Listen to

---

1. Drunkenness.
2. Rajah Rammohun Roy's translation of the Vedas (1832).
3. Confucius's, The Great Learning 7.

4. Matthew 15.11: "Not that which goeth into the mouth defileth a man; but that which cometh out of the mouth, this defileth a man."

every zephyr for some reproof, for it is surely there, and he is unfortunate who does not hear it. We cannot touch a string or move a stop but the charming moral transfixes us. Many an irksome noise, go a long way off, is heard as music, a proud sweet satire on the meanness of our lives.

We are conscious of an animal in us, which awakens in proportion as our higher nature slumbers. It is reptile and sensual, and perhaps cannot be wholly expelled; like the worms which, even in life and health, occupy our bodies. Possibly we may withdraw from it, but never change its nature. I fear that it may enjoy a certain health of its own; that we may be well, yet not pure. The other day I picked up the lower jaw of a hog, with white and sound teeth and tusks, which suggested that there was an animal health and vigor distinct from the spiritual. This creature succeeded by other means than temperance and purity. "That in which men differ from brute beasts," says Mencius, "is a thing very inconsiderable; the common herd lose it very soon; superior men preserve it carefully."[5] Who knows what sort of life would result if we had attained to purity? If I knew so wise a man as could teach me purity I would go to seek him forthwith. "A command over our passions, and over the external senses of the body, and good acts, are declared by the Ved to be indispensable in the mind's approximation to God."[6] Yet the spirit can for the time pervade and control every member and function of the body, and transmute what in form is the grossest sensuality into purity and devotion. The generative energy, which, when we are loose, dissipates and makes us unclean, when we are continent invigorates and inspires us. Chastity is the flowering of man; and what are called Genius, Heroism, Holiness, and the like, are but various fruits which succeed it. Man flows at once to God when the channel of purity is open. By turns our purity inspires and our impurity casts us down. He is blessed who is assured that the animal is dying out in him day by day, and the divine being established. Perhaps there is none but has cause for shame on account of the inferior and brutish nature to which he is allied. I fear that we are such gods or demigods only as fauns and satyrs, the divine allied to beasts, the creatures of appetite, and that, to some extent, our very life is our disgrace.—

> "How happy's he who hath due place assigned
> To his beasts and disaforested his mind!
>
> .   .   .
>
> Can use his horse, goat, wolf, and ev'ry beast,
> And is not ass himself to all the rest!
> Else man not only is the herd of swine,
> But he's those devils too which did incline
> Them to a headlong rage, and made them worse."[7]

All sensuality is one, though it takes many forms; all purity is one. It is the same whether a man eat, or drink, or cohabit, or sleep sensually. They are but one appetite, and we only need to see a person do any one of these things to know how great a sensualist he is. The impure can neither stand nor sit with purity. When the reptile is attacked at one mouth of his burrow, he shows

5. Mencius (Meng-tzu), Chinese philosopher (372?–289? B.C.), *Works* 4.
6. From Roy's translation of the *Vedas*.

7. From John Donne's *To Sir Edward Herbert at Iulyers*.

himself at another. If you would be chaste, you must be temperate. What is chastity? How shall a man know if he is chaste? He shall not know it. We have heard of this virtue, but we know not what it is. We speak conformably to the rumor which we have heard. From exertion come wisdom and purity, from sloth ignorance and sensuality. In the student sensuality is a sluggish habit of mind. An unclean person is universally a slothful one, one who sits by a stove, whom the sun shines on prostrate, who reposes without being fatigued. If you would avoid uncleanness, and all the sins, work earnestly, though it be at cleaning a stable. Nature is hard to be overcome, but she must be overcome. What avails it that you are Christian, if you are not purer than the heathen, if you deny yourself no more, if you are not more religious? I know of many systems of religion esteemed heathenish whose precepts fill the reader with shame, and provoke him to new endeavors, though it be to the performance of rites merely.

I hesitate to say these things, but it is not because of the subject,—I care not how obscene my *words* are,—but because I cannot speak of them without betraying my impurity. We discourse freely without shame of one form of sensuality, and are silent about another. We are so degraded that we cannot speak simply of the necessary functions of human nature. In earlier ages, in some countries, every function was reverently spoken of and regulated by law. Nothing was too trivial for the Hindoo lawgiver, however offensive it may be to modern taste. He teaches how to eat, drink, cohabit, void excrement and urine, and the like, elevating what is mean, and does not falsely excuse himself by calling these things trifles.

Every man is the builder of a temple, called his body, to the god he worships, after a style purely his own, nor can he get off by hammering marble instead. We are all sculptors and painters, and our material is our own flesh and blood and bones. Any nobleness begins at once to refine a man's features, any meanness or sensuality to imbrute them.

John Farmer sat at his door one September evening, after a hard day's work, his mind still running on his labor more or less. Having bathed he sat down to recreate his intellectual man. It was a rather cool evening, and some of his neighbors were apprehending a frost. He had not attended to the train of his thoughts long when he heard some one playing on a flute,[8] and that sound harmonized with his mood. Still he thought of his work; but the burden of his thought was, that though this kept running in his head, and he found himself planning and contriving it against his will, yet it concerned him very little. It was no more than the scurf of his skin, which was constantly shuffled off. But the notes of the flute came home to his ears out of a different sphere from that he worked in, and suggested work for certain faculties which slumbered in him. They gently did away with the street, and the village, and the state in which he lived. A voice said to him,—Why do you stay here and live this mean moiling life, when a glorious existence is possible for you? Those same stars twinkle over other fields than these.—But how to come out of this condition and actually migrate thither? All that he could think of was to practise some new austerity, to let his mind descend into his body and redeem it, and treat himself with ever increasing respect.

---

8. Thoreau, a flute player, is imagining the effect of his music on a typical worker.

Brute Neighbors

Sometimes I had a companion[9] in my fishing, who came through the village to my house from the other side of the town, and the catching of the dinner was as much a social exercise as the eating of it.

Hermit. I wonder what the world is doing now. I have not heard so much as a locust over the sweet-fern these three hours. The pigeons are all asleep upon their roosts,—no flutter from them. Was that a farmer's noon horn which sounded from beyond the woods just now? The hands are coming in to boiled salt beef and cider and Indian bread. Why will men worry themselves so? He that does not eat need not work. I wonder how much they have reaped. Who would live there where a body can never think for the barking of Bose?[1] And O, the housekeeping! to keep bright the devil's door-knobs, and scour his tubs this bright day! Better not keep a house. Say, some hollow tree; and then for morning calls and dinner-parties! Only a woodpecker tapping. O, they swarm; the sun is too warm there; they are born too far into life for me. I have water from the spring, and a loaf of brown bread on the shelf.—Hark! I hear a rustling of the leaves. Is it some ill-fed village hound yielding to the instinct of the chase? or the lost pig which is said to be in these woods, whose tracks I saw after the rain? It comes on apace; my sumachs and sweet-briars tremble.—Eh, Mr. Poet, is it you? How do you like the world to-day?

Poet. See those clouds; how they hang! That's the greatest thing I have seen to-day. There's nothing like it in old paintings, nothing like it in foreign lands,—unless when we were off the coast of Spain. That's a true Mediterranean sky. I thought, as I have my living to get, and have not eaten to-day, that I might go a-fishing. That's the true industry for poets. It is the only trade I have learned. Come, let's along.

Hermit. I cannot resist. My brown bread will soon be done. I will go with you gladly soon, but I am just concluding a serious meditation. I think that I am near the end of it. Leave me alone, then, for a while. But that we may not be delayed, you shall be digging the bait meanwhile. Angle-worms are rarely to be met with in these parts, where the soil was never fattened with manure; the race is nearly extinct. The sport of digging the bait is nearly equal to that of catching the fish, when one's appetite is not too keen; and this you may have all to yourself to-day. I would advise you to set in the spade down yonder among the ground-nuts, where you see the johnswort waving. I think that I may warrant you one worm to every three sods you turn up, if you look well in among the roots of the grass, as if you were weeding. Or, if you choose to go farther, it will not be unwise, for I have found the increase of fair bait to be very nearly as the squares of the distances.

Hermit alone. Let me see; where was I? Methinks I was nearly in this frame of mind; the world lay about at this angle. Shall I go to heaven or a-fishing? If I should soon bring this meditation to an end, would another so sweet occasion be likely to offer? I was as near being resolved into the essence of things as ever I was in my life. I fear my thoughts will not come back to me. If it would do any good, I would whistle for them. When they make us an offer, is it wise to say, We will think of it? My thoughts have left no track, and I cannot find the path again. What was it that I was thinking of? It was a very hazy day. I will

9. Channing, the "Poet" of the following dialogue.   1. Name for a dog, like "Fido."

just try these three sentences of Con-fut-see;[2] they may fetch that state about again. I know not whether it was the dumps or a budding ecstasy. Mem.[3] There never is but one opportunity of a kind.

Poet. How now, Hermit, is it too soon? I have got just thirteen whole ones, beside several which are imperfect or undersized; but they will do for the smaller fry; they do not cover up the hook so much. Those village worms are quite too large; a shiner may make a meal off one without finding the skewer.

Hermit. Well, then, let's be off. Shall we to the Concord? There's good sport there if the water be not too high.

Why do precisely these objects which we behold make a world? Why has man just these species of animals for his neighbors; as if nothing but a mouse could have filled this crevice? I suspect that Pilpay & Co.[4] have put animals to their best use, for they are all beasts of burden, in a sense, made to carry some portion of our thoughts.

The mice which haunted my house were not the common ones, which are said to have been introduced into the country, but a wild native kind (*Musleucopus*) not found in the village. I sent one to a distinguished natural-ist,[5] and it interested him much. When I was building, one of these had its nest underneath the house, and before I had laid the second floor, and swept out the shavings, would come out regularly at lunch time and pick up the crumbs at my feet. It probably had never seen a man before; and it soon became quite familiar, and would run over my shoes and up my clothes. It could readily ascend the sides of the room by short impulses, like a squirrel, which it resembled in its motions. At length, as I leaned with my elbow on the bench one day, it ran up my clothes, and along my sleeve, and round and round the paper which held my dinner, while I kept the latter close, and dodged and played at bo-peep with it; and when at last I held still a piece of cheese between my thumb and finger, it came and nibbled it, sitting in my hand, and afterward cleaned its face and paws, like a fly, and walked away.

A phœbe soon built in my shed, and a robin for protection in a pine which grew against the house. In June the partridge, (*Tetrao umbellus*,) which is so shy a bird, led her brood past my windows, from the woods in the rear to the front of my house, clucking and calling to them like a hen, and in all her behavior proving herself the hen of the woods. The young suddenly disperse on your approach, at a signal from the mother, as if a whirlwind had swept them away, and they so exactly resemble the dried leaves and twigs that many a traveller has placed his foot in the midst of a brood, and heard the whir of the old bird as she flew off, and her anxious calls and mewing, or seen her trail her wings to attract his attention, without suspecting their neighborhood. The parent will sometimes roll and spin round before you in such a dishabille, that you cannot, for a few moments, detect what kind of creature it is. The young squat still and flat, often running their heads under a leaf, and mind only their mother's directions given from a distance, nor will your approach make them run again and betray themselves. You may even tread on them, or

---

2. Confucius.
3. Abbreviation for *memorandum*, used here as a self-reminder.
4. I.e., all tellers of fables. Pilpay, or Bidpai, was cred-ited with authorship of a collection of East Indian fa-

bles that Thoreau knew in Charles Wilkins's trans-lation.
5. Louis Agassiz (1807–1873), Swiss-American natu-ralist, a teacher at Harvard, and an intimate of the Cambridge literary circle.

have your eyes on them for a minute, without discovering them. I have held them in my open hand at such a time, and still their only care, obedient to their mother and their instinct, was to squat there without fear or trembling. So perfect is this instinct, that once, when I had laid them on the leaves again, and one accidentally fell on its side, it was found with the rest in exactly the same position ten minutes afterward. They are not callow like the young of most birds, but more perfectly developed and precocious even than chickens. The remarkably adult yet innocent expression of their open and serene eyes is very memorable. An intelligence seems reflected in them. They suggest not merely the purity of infancy, but a wisdom clarified by experience. Such an eye was not born when the bird was, but is coeval with the sky it reflects. The woods do not yield another such a gem. The traveller does not often look into such a limpid well. The ignorant or reckless sportsman often shoots the parent at such a time, and leaves these innocents to fall a prey to some prowling beast or bird, or gradually mingle with the decaying leaves which they so much resemble. It is said that when hatched by a hen they will directly disperse on some alarm, and so are lost, for they never hear the mother's call which gathers them again. These were my hens and chickens.

It is remarkable how many creatures live wild and free though secret in the woods, and still sustain themselves in the neighborhood of towns, suspected by hunters only. How retired the otter manages to live here! He grows to be four feet long, as big as a small boy, perhaps without any human being getting a glimpse of him. I formerly saw the raccoon in the woods behind where my house is built, and probably still heard their whinnering at night. Commonly I rested an hour or two in the shade at noon, after planting, and ate my lunch, and read a little by a spring which was the source of a swamp and of a brook, oozing from under Brister's Hill, half a mile from my field. The approach to this was through a succession of descending grassy hollows, full of young pitch-pines, into a larger wood about the swamp. There, in a very secluded and shaded spot, under a spreading white-pine, there was yet a clean firm sward to sit on. I had dug out the spring and made a well of clear gray water, where I could dip up a pailful without roiling it, and thither I went for this purpose almost every day in midsummer, when the pond was warmest. Thither too the wood-cock led her brood, to probe the mud for worms, flying but a foot above them down the bank, while they ran in a troop beneath; but at last, spying me, she would leave her young and circle round and round me, nearer and nearer, till within four or five feet, pretend'ng broken wings and legs, to attract my attention and get off her young, who would already have taken up their march, with faint wiry peep, single file through the swamp, as she directed. Or I heard the peep of the young when I could not see the parent bird. There too the turtle-doves sat over the spring, or fluttered from bough to bough of the soft white-pines over my head; or the red squirrel, coursing down the nearest bough, was particularly familiar and inquisitive. You only need sit still long enough in some attractive spot in the woods that all its inhabitants may exhibit themselves to you by turns.

I was witness to events of a less peaceful character. One day when I went out to my wood-pile, or rather my pile of stumps, I observed two large ants, the one red, the other much larger, nearly half an inch long, and black, fiercely contending with one another. Having once got hold they never let go, but struggled and wrestled and rolled on the chips incessantly. Looking farther, I was surprised to find that the chips were covered with such combatants, that it was not a *duellum*, but a *bellum*, a war between two races of ants, the red always pitted against the black, and frequently two red ones to one black. The legions of these Myrmidons[6] covered all the hills and vales in my wood-yard, and the ground was already strewn with the dead and dying, both red and black. It was the only battle which I have ever witnessed, the only battle-field I ever trod while the battle was raging; internecine war; the red republicans on the one hand, and the black imperialists on the other. On every side they were engaged in deadly combat, yet without any noise that I could hear, and human soldiers never fought so resolutely. I watched a couple that were fast locked in each other's embraces, in a little sunny valley amid the chips, now at noon-day prepared to fight till the sun went down, or life went out. The smaller red champion had fastened himself like a vice to his adversary's front, and through all the tumblings on that field never for an instant ceased to gnaw at one of his feelers near the root, having already caused the other to go by the board; while the stronger black one dashed him from side to side, and, as I saw on looking nearer, had already divested him of several of his members. They fought with more pertinacity than bulldogs. Neither manifested the least disposition to retreat. It was evident that their battle-cry was Conquer or die. In the mean while there came along a single red ant on the hill-side of this valley, evidently full of excitement, who either had despatched his foe, or had not yet taken part in the battle; probably the latter, for he had lost none of his limbs; whose mother had charged him to return with his shield or upon it.[7] Or perchance he was some Achilles, who had nourished his wrath apart, and had now come to avenge or rescue his Patroclus.[8] He saw this unequal combat from afar,— for the blacks were nearly twice the size of the red,—he drew near with rapid pace till he stood on his guard within half an inch of the combatants; then, watching his opportunity, he sprang upon the black warrior, and commenced his operations near the root of his right fore-leg, leaving the foe to select among his own members; and so there were three united for life, as if a new kind of attraction had been invented which put all other locks and cements to shame. I should not have wondered by this time to find that they had their respective musical bands stationed on some eminent chip, and playing their national airs the while, to excite the slow and cheer the dying combatants. I was myself excited somewhat even as if they had been men. The more you think of it, the less the difference. And certainly there is not the fight recorded in Concord history, at least, if in the history of America, that will bear a moment's comparison with this, whether for the numbers engaged in it, or for the patriotism and heroism displayed. For numbers and for carnage it was an Austerlitz or Dresden.[9] Concord Fight! Two killed on the patriots' side, and Luther Blanch-ard wounded! Why here every ant was a Buttrick,—"Fire! for God's sake fire!"—and thousands shared the fate of Davis and Hosmer.[1] There was not one hireling there. I have no doubt that it was a principle they fought for, as much as our ancestors, and not to avoid a three-penny tax on their tea; and

---

6. The Myrmidons were warriors from southern Thes-saly who went to fight at Troy under their chieftain Achilles.
7. What a Spartan mother was supposed to say to a son going into battle.
8. In *The Iliad* Achilles sat out much of the Trojan War until the death of his friend Patroclus, which he

revenged
9. Important battles of the Napoleonic Wars.
1. Davis and Hosmer were the only two colonists killed at Concord on April 19, 1775; the others named were participants in the battle, which Thoreau knew about in great detail.

the results of this battle will be as important and memorable to those whom it concerns as those of the battle of Bunker Hill, at least.

I took up the chip on which the three I have particularly described were struggling, carried it into my house, and placed it under a tumbler on my window-sill, in order to see the issue. Holding a microscope[2] to the first-mentioned red ant, I saw that, though he was assiduously gnawing at the near foreleg of his enemy, having severed his remaining feeler, his own breast was all torn away, exposing what vitals he had there to the jaws of the black warrior, whose breast-plate was apparently too thick for him to pierce; and the dark carbuncles of the sufferer's eyes shone with ferocity such as war only could excite. They struggled half an hour longer under the tumbler, and when I looked again the black soldier had severed the heads of his foes from their bodies, and the still living heads were hanging on either side of him like ghastly trophies at his saddle-bow, still apparently as firmly fastened as ever, and he was endeavoring with feeble struggles, being without feelers and with only the remnant of a leg, and I know not how many other wounds, to divest himself of them; which at length, after half an hour more, he accomplished. I raised the glass, and he went off over the windowsill in that crippled state. Whether he finally survived that combat, and spent the remainder of his days in some Hotel des Invalides,[3] I do not know; but I thought that his industry would not be worth much thereafter. I never learned which party was victorious, nor the cause of the war; but I felt for the rest of that day as if I had had my feelings excited and harrowed by witnessing the struggle, the ferocity and carnage, of a human battle before my door.

Kirby and Spence tell us that the battles of ants have long been celebrated and the date of them recorded, though they say that Huber[4] is the only modern author who appears to have witnessed them. "Æneas Sylvius," say they, "after giving a very circumstantial account of one contested with great obstinacy by a great and small species on the trunk of a pear tree," adds that " 'This action was fought in the pontificate of Eugenius the Fourth, in the presence of Nicholas Pistoriensis, an eminent lawyer, who related the whole history of the battle with the greatest fidelity.' A similar engagement between great and small ants is recorded by Olaus Magnus,[5] in which the small ones, being victorious, are said to have buried the bodies of their own soldiers, but left those of their giant enemies a prey to the birds. This event happened previous to the expulsion of the tyrant Christiern the Second from Sweden." The battle which I witnessed took place in the Presidency of Polk, five years before the passage of Webster's Fugitive-Slave Bill.[6]

Many a village Bose, fit only to course a mud-turtle in a victualling cellar, sported his heavy quarters in the woods, without the knowledge of his master, and ineffectually smelled at old fox burrows and woodchucks' holes; led perchance by some slight cur which nimbly threaded the wood, and might still inspire a natural terror in its denizens;—now far behind his guide, barking like a canine bull toward some small squirrel which had treed itself for scrutiny, then, cantering off, bending the bushes with his weight, imagining that he is on the track of some stray member of the gerbille family. Once I was surprised

2. Magnifying glass.
3. Old soldiers' home in Paris.
4. François Huber (1750–1831), Swiss entomologist.
5. From Kirby and Spence, *Introduction to Entomol-*

ogy (1846): Æneas Sylvius (1405–1464) was Pope Pius II (1458–64) and Olaus Magnus (1490–1558) was archbishop of Uppsala.
6. That is, in 1845.

to see a cat walking along the stony shore of the pond, for they rarely wander so far from home. The surprise was mutual. Nevertheless the most domestic cat, which has lain on a rug all her days, appears quite at home in the woods, and, by her sly and stealthy behavior, proves herself more native there than the regular inhabitants. Once, when berrying, I met with a cat with young kittens in the woods, quite wild, and they all, like their mother, had their backs up and were fiercely spitting at me. A few years before I lived in the woods there was what was called a "winged cat" in one of the farm-houses in Lincoln nearest the pond, Mr. Gilian Baker's. When I called to see her in June, 1842, she was gone a-hunting in the woods, as was her wont, (I am not sure whether it was a male or female, and so use the more common pronoun,) but her mistress told me that she came into the neighborhood a little more than a year before, in April, and was finally taken into their house; that she was of a dark brownish-gray color, with a white spot on her throat, and white feet, and had a large bushy tail like a fox; that in the winter the fur grew thick and flatted out along her sides, forming strips ten or twelve inches long by two and a half wide, and under her chin like a muff, the upper side loose, the under matted like felt, and in the spring these appendages dropped off. They gave me a pair of her "wings," which I keep still. There is no appearance of a membrane about them. Some thought it was part flying-squirrel or some other wild animal, which is not impossible, for, according to naturalists, prolific hybrids[7] have been produced by the union of the marten and domestic cat. This would have been the right kind of cat for me to keep, if I had kept any; for why should not a poet's cat be winged as well as his horse?[8]

In the fall the loon (*Colymbus glacialis*) came, as usual, to moult and bathe in the pond, making the woods ring with his wild laughter before I had risen. At rumor of his arrival all the Mill-dam sportsmen are on the alert, in gigs and on foot, two by two and three by three, with patent rifles and conical balls and spy-glasses. They come rustling through the woods like autumn leaves, at least ten men to one loon. Some station themselves on this side of the pond, some on that, for the poor bird cannot be omnipresent; if he dive here he must come up there. But now the kind October wind rises, rustling the leaves and rippling the surface of the water, so that no loon can be heard or seen, though his foes sweep the pond with spy-glasses, and make the woods resound with their discharges. The waves generously rise and dash angrily, taking sides with all waterfowl, and our sportsmen must beat a retreat to town and shop and unfinished jobs. But they were too often successful. When I went to get a pail of water early in the morning I frequently saw this stately bird sailing out of my cove within a few rods. If I endeavored to overtake him in a boat, in order to see how he would manœuvre, he would dive and be completely lost, so that I did not discover him again, sometimes, till the latter part of the day. But I was more than a match for him on the surface. He commonly went off in a rage.

As I was paddling along the north shore one very calm October afternoon, for such days especially they settle on to the lakes, like the milkweed down, having looked in vain over the pond for a loon, suddenly one, sailing out from the shore toward the middle a few rods in front of me, set up his wild laugh and betrayed himself. I pursued with a paddle and he dived, but when he

7. The important word is *prolific*, because hybrids (such as the mule) are often sterile.

8. During their flights of inspiration poets are supposed to ride on the winged horse Pegasus.

came up I was nearer than before. He dived again, but I miscalculated the direction he would take, and we were fifty rods apart when he came to the surface this time, for I had helped to widen the interval; and again he laughed long and loud, and with more reason than before. He manœuvred so cunningly that I could not get within half a dozen rods of him. Each time, when he came to the surface, turning his head this way and that, he coolly surveyed the water and the land, and apparently chose his course so that he might come up where there was the widest expanse of water and at the greatest distance from the boat. It was surprising how quickly he made up his mind and put his resolve into execution. He led me at once to the widest part of the pond, and could not be driven from it. While he was thinking one thing in his brain, I was endeavoring to divine his thought in mine. It was a pretty game, played on the smooth surface of the pond, a man against a loon. Suddenly your adversary's checker disappears beneath the board, and the problem is to place yours nearest to where his will appear again. Sometimes he would come up unexpectedly on the opposite side of me, having apparently passed directly under the boat. So long-winded was he and so unweariable, that when he had swum farthest he would immediately plunge again, nevertheless; and then no wit could divine where in the deep pond, beneath the smooth surface, he might be speeding his way like a fish, for he had time and ability to visit the bottom of the pond in its deepest part. It is said that loons have been caught in the New York lakes eighty feet beneath the surface, with hooks set for trout,—though Walden is deeper than that. How surprised must the fishes be to see this ungainly visitor from another sphere speeding his way amid their schools! Yet he appeared to know his course as surely under water as on the surface, and swam much faster there. Once or twice I saw a ripple where he approached the surface, just put his head out to reconnoitre, and instantly dived again. I found that it was as well for me to rest on my oars and wait his reappearing as to endeavor to calculate where he would rise; for again and again, when I was straining my eyes over the surface one way, I would suddenly be startled by his unearthly laugh behind me. But why, after displaying so much cunning, did he invariably betray himself the moment he came up by that loud laugh? Did not his white breast enough betray him? He was indeed a silly loon, I thought. I could commonly hear the plash of the water when he came up, and so also detected him. But after an hour he seemed as fresh as ever, dived as willingly and swam yet farther than at first. It was surprising to see how serenely he sailed off with unruffled breast when he came to the surface, doing all the work with his webbed feet beneath. His usual note was this demoniac laughter, yet somewhat like that of a water-fowl; but occasionally, when he had balked me most successfully and come up a long way off, he uttered a long-drawn unearthly howl, probably more like that of a wolf than any bird; as when a beast puts his muzzle to the ground and deliberately howls. This was his looning,—perhaps the wildest sound that is ever heard here, making the woods ring far and wide. I concluded that he laughed in derision of my efforts, confident of his own resources. Though the sky was by this time overcast, the pond was so smooth that I could see where he broke the surface when I did not hear him. His white breast, the stillness of the air, and the smoothness of the water were all against him. At length, having come up fifty rods off, he uttered one of those prolonged howls, as if calling on the god of loons to aid him, and immediately there came a wind from the east and rippled the surface, and filled the whole air with misty rain, and I was impressed as if it were the prayer of the loon answered, and his god was angry with me; and so I left him disappearing far away on the tumultuous surface.

For hours, in fall days, I watched the ducks cunningly tack and veer and hold the middle of the pond, far from the sportsman; tricks which they will have less need to practise in Louisiana bayous. When compelled to rise they would sometimes circle round and round and over the pond at a considerable height, from which they could easily see to other ponds and the river, like black motes in the sky; and, when I thought they had gone off thither long since, they would settle down by a slanting flight of a quarter of a mile on to a distant part which was left free; but what beside safety they got by sailing in the middle of Walden I do not know, unless they love its water for the same reason that I do.

House-Warming

In October I went a-graping to the river meadows, and loaded myself with clusters more precious for their beauty and fragrance than for food. There too I admired, though I did not gather, the cranberries, small waxen gems, pendants of the meadow grass, pearly and red, which the farmer plucks with an ugly rake, leaving the smooth meadow in a snarl, heedlessly measuring them by the bushel and the dollar only, and sells the spoils of the meads to Boston and New York; destined to be *jammed*, to satisfy the tastes of lovers of Nature there. So butchers rake the tongues of bison out of the prairie grass, regardless of the torn and drooping plant.[9] The barberry's brilliant fruit was likewise food for my eyes merely; but I collected a small store of wild apples for coddling, which the proprietor and travellers had overlooked. When chestnuts were ripe I laid up half a bushel for winter. It was very exciting at that season to roam the then boundless chestnut woods of Lincoln,—they now sleep their long sleep under the railroad,—with a bag on my shoulder, and a stick to open burrs with in my hand, for I did not always wait for the frost, amid the rustling of leaves and the loud reproofs of the red-squirrels and the jays, whose half-consumed nuts I sometimes stole, for the burrs which they had selected were sure to contain sound ones. Occasionally I climbed and shook the trees. They grew also behind my house, and one large tree which almost overshadowed it, was, when in flower, a bouquet which scented the whole neighborhood, but the squirrels and the jays got most of its fruit; the last coming in flocks early in the morning and picking the nuts out of the burrs before they fell. I relinquished these trees to them and visited the more distant woods composed wholly of chestnut. These nuts, as far as they went, were a good substitute for bread. Many other substitutes might, perhaps, be found. Digging one day for fish-worms I discovered the ground-nut (*Apios tuberosa*) on its string, the potato of the aborigines, a sort of fabulous fruit, which I had begun to doubt if I had ever dug and eaten in childhood, as I had told, and had not dreamed it. I had often since seen its crimpled red velvety blossom supported by the stems of other plants without knowing it to be the same. Cultivation has well nigh exterminated it. It has a sweetish taste, much like that of a frostbitten potato, and I found it better boiled than roasted. This tuber seemed like a faint

9. An allusion to the way the American buffalo were wantonly killed for the skin or for a delicate portion of the meat with the rest of the carcass abandoned.

promise of Nature to rear her own children and feed them simply here at some future period. In these days of fatted cattle and waving grain-fields, this humble root, which was once the *totem* of an Indian tribe, is quite forgotten, or known only by its flowering vine; but let wild Nature reign here once more, and the tender and luxurious English grains will probably disappear before a myriad of foes, and without the care of man the crow may carry back even the last seeds of corn to the great corn-field of the Indian's God in the south-west, whence he is said to have brought it; but the now almost exterminated ground-nut will perhaps revive and flourish in spite of frosts and wildness, prove itself indigenous, and resume its ancient importance and dignity as the diet of the hunter tribe. Some Indian Ceres or Minerva[1] must have been the inventor and bestower of it; and when the reign of poetry commences here, its leaves and string of nuts may be represented on our works of art.

Already, by the first of September, I had seen two or three small maples turned scarlet across the pond, beneath where the white stems of three aspens diverged, at the point of a promontory, next the water. Ah, many a tale their color told! And gradually from week to week the character of each tree came out, and it admired itself reflected in the smooth mirror of the lake. Each morning the manager of this gallery substituted some new picture, distinguished by more brilliant or harmonious coloring, for the old upon the walls.

The wasps came by thousands to my lodge in October, as to winter quarters, and settled on my windows within and on the walls over-head, sometimes deterring visitors from entering. Each morning, when they were numbed with cold, I swept some of them out, but I did not trouble myself much to get rid of them; I even felt complimented by their regarding my house as a desirable shelter. They never molested me seriously, though they bedded with me; and they gradually disappeared, into what crevices I do not know, avoiding winter and unspeakable cold.

Like the wasps, before I finally went into winter quarters in November, I used to resort to the north-east side of Walden, which the sun, reflected from the pitch-pine woods and the stony shore, made the fire-side of the pond; it is so much pleasanter and wholesomer to be warmed by the sun while you can be, than by an artificial fire. I thus warmed myself by the still glowing embers which the summer, like a departed hunter, had left.

When I came to build my chimney I studied masonry. My bricks being second-hand ones required to be cleaned with a trowel, so that I learned more than usual of the qualities of bricks and trowels. The mortar on them was fifty years old, and was said to be still growing harder; but this is one of those sayings which men love to repeat whether they are true or not. Such sayings themselves grow harder and adhere more firmly with age, and it would take many blows with a trowel to clean an old wiseacre of them. Many of the villages of Mesopotamia are built of second-hand bricks of a very good quality, obtained from the ruins of Babylon, and the cement on them is older and probably harder still. However that may be, I was struck by the peculiar toughness of the steel which bore so many violent blows without being worn out. As my bricks had been in a chimney before, though I did not read the name of Nebuchadnezzar on them, I picked out as many fire-place bricks as I could

---

1. Goddesses of agriculture and wisdom, respectively.

find, to save work and waste, and I filled the spaces between the bricks about
the fire-place with stones from the pond shore, and also made my mortar with
the white sand from the same place. I lingered most about the fireplace, as the
most vital part of the house. Indeed, I worked so deliberately, that though I
commenced at the ground in the morning, a course of bricks raised a few
inches above the floor served for my pillow at night; yet I did not get a stiff
neck for it that I remember; my stiff neck is of older date. I took a poet[2] to
board for a fortnight about those times, which caused me to be put to it for
room. He brought his own knife, though I had two, and we used to scour them
by thrusting them into the earth. He shared with me the labors of cooking. I
was pleased to see my work rising so square and solid by degrees, and reflected,
that, if it proceeded slowly, it was calculated to endure a long time. The chimney is to some extent an independent structure, standing on the ground and
rising through the house to the heavens; even after the house is burned it still
stands sometimes, and its importance and independence are apparent. This
was toward the end of summer. It was now November.

The north wind had already begun to cool the pond, though it took many
weeks of steady blowing to accomplish it, it is so deep. When I began to have
a fire at evening, before I plastered my house, the chimney carried smoke
particularly well, because of the numerous chinks between the boards. Yet I
passed some cheerful evenings in that cool and airy apartment, surrounded by
the rough brown boards full of knots, and rafters with the bark on high overhead. My house never pleased my eye so much after it was plastered, though
I was obliged to confess that it was more comfortable. Should not every apartment in which man dwells be lofty enough to create some obscurity overhead, where flickering shadows may play at evening about the rafters? These
forms are more agreeable to the fancy and imagination than fresco paintings
or other the most expensive furniture. I now first began to inhabit my house,
I may say, when I began to use it for warmth as well as shelter. I had got a
couple of old fire-dogs to keep the wood from the hearth, and it did me good
to see the soot form on the back of the chimney which I had built, and I poked
the fire with more right and more satisfaction than usual. My dwelling was
small, and I could hardly entertain an echo in it; but it seemed larger for being
a single apartment and remote from neighbors. All the attractions of a house
were concentrated in one room; it was kitchen, chamber, parlor, and keeping-
room; and whatever satisfaction parent or child, master or servant, derive from
living in a house, I enjoyed it all. Cato says, the master of a family (*patremfam-
ilias*) must have in his rustic villa "cellam oleariam, vinariam, dolia multa, uti
lubeat caritatem expectare, et rei, et virtuti, et gloriæ erit," that is, "an oil and
wine cellar, many casks, so that it may be pleasant to expect hard times; it will
be for his advantage, and virtue, and glory."[3] I had in my cellar a firkin of
potatoes, about two quarts of peas with the weevil in them, and on my shelf a
little rice, a jug of molasses, and of rye and Indian meal a peck each.

I sometimes dream of a larger and more populous house, standing in a
golden age, of enduring materials, and without ginger-bread work, which shall
still consist of only one room, a vast, rude, substantial, primitive hall, without
ceiling or plastering, with bare rafters and purlins supporting a sort of lower

2. I.e., Channing.   3. *De agri cultura*, 3.2.

heaven over one's head,—useful to keep off rain and snow; where the king and queen posts[4] stand out to receive your homage, when you have done reverence to the prostrate Saturn[5] of an older dynasty on stepping over the sill; a cavernous house, wherein you must reach up a torch upon a pole to see the roof; where some may live in the fire-place, some in the recess of a window, and some on settles, some at one end of the hall, some at another, and some aloft on rafters with the spiders, if they choose; a house which you have got into when you have opened the outside door, and the ceremony is over; where the weary traveller may wash, and eat, and converse, and sleep, without further journey; such a shelter as you would be glad to reach in a tempestuous night, containing all the essentials of a house, and nothing for house-keeping; where you can see all the treasures of the house at one view, and every thing hangs upon its peg that a man should use; at once kitchen, pantry, parlor, chamber, store-house, and garret; where you can see so necessary a thing as a barrel or a ladder, so convenient a thing as a cupboard, and hear the pot boil, and pay your respects to the fire that cooks your dinner and the oven that bakes your bread, and the necessary furniture and utensils are the chief ornaments; where the washing is not put out, nor the fire, nor the mistress, and perhaps you are sometimes requested to move from off the trap-door, when the cook would descend into the cellar, and so learn whether the ground is solid or hollow beneath you without stamping. A house whose inside is as open and manifest as a bird's nest, and you cannot go in at the front door and out at the back without seeing some of its inhabitants; where to be a guest is to be presented with the freedom of the house, and not to be carefully excluded from seven eighths of it, shut up in a particular cell, and told to make yourself at home there,—in solitary confinement. Nowadays the host does not admit you to *his* hearth, but has got the mason to build one for yourself somewhere in his alley, and hospitality is the art of *keeping* you at the greatest distance. There is as much secrecy about the cooking as if he had a design to poison you. I am aware that I have been on many a man's premises, and might have been legally ordered off, but I am not aware that I have been in many men's houses. I might visit in my old clothes a king and queen who lived simply in such a house as I have described, if I were going their way; but backing out of a modern palace will be all that I shall desire to learn, if ever I am caught in one.

It would seem as if the very language of our parlors would lose all its nerve and degenerate into *palaver* wholly, our lives pass at such remoteness from its symbols, and its metaphors and tropes[6] are necessarily so far fetched, through slides and dumb-waiters, as it were; in other words, the parlor is so far from the kitchen and workshop. The dinner even is only the parable of a dinner, commonly. As if only the savage dwelt near enough to Nature and Truth to borrow a trope from them. How can the scholar, who dwells away in the North West Territory or the Isle of Man, tell what is parliamentary in the kitchen?

However, only one or two of my guests were ever bold enough to stay and eat a hasty-pudding[7] with me; but when they saw that crisis approaching they beat a hasty retreat rather, as if it would shake the house to its foundations. Nevertheless, it stood through a great many hasty-puddings.

---

4. Vertical posts that run to points some distance below the apex. "Purlins": horizontal beams supporting the rafters. "King posts": vertical posts connecting the apex of a triangular truss with the base.
5. Roman name for the Greek Cronus, chief of the pre-Olympian gods, dethroned by his son Zeus.
6. Figures of speech.
7. Made of flour or corn meal stirred into boiling water or milk.

I did not plaster till it was freezing weather. I brought over some whiter and cleaner sand for this purpose from the opposite shore of the pond in a boat, a sort of conveyance which would have tempted me to go much farther if necessary. My house had in the mean while been shingled down to the ground on every side. In lathing I was pleased to be able to send home each nail with a single blow of the hammer, and it was my ambition to transfer the plaster from the board to the wall neatly and rapidly. I remembered the story of a conceited fellow, who, in fine clothes, was wont to lounge about the village once, giving advice to workmen. Venturing one day to substitute deeds for words, he turned up his cuffs, seized a plasterer's board, and having loaded his trowel without mishap, with a complacent look toward the lathing overhead, made a bold gesture thitherward; and straightway, to his complete discomfiture, received the whole contents in his ruffled bosom. I admired anew the economy and convenience of plastering, which so effectually shuts out the cold and takes a handsome finish, and I learned the various casualties to which the plasterer is liable. I was surprised to see how thirsty the bricks were which drank up all the moisture in my plaster before I had smoothed it, and how many pailfuls of water it takes to christen a new hearth. I had the previous winter made a small quantity of lime by burning the shells of the *Unio fluviatilis*,[8] which our river affords, for the sake of the experiment; so that I knew where my materials came from. I might have got good limestone within a mile or two and burned it myself, if I had cared to do so.

The pond had in the mean while skimmed over in the shadiest and shallowest coves, some days or even weeks before the general freezing. The first ice is especially interesting and perfect, being hard, dark, and transparent, and affords the best opportunity that ever offers for examining the bottom where it is shallow; for you can lie at your length on ice only an inch thick, like a skater insect on the surface of the water, and study the bottom at your leisure, only two or three inches distant, like a picture behind a glass, and the water is necessarily always smooth then. There are many furrows in the sand where some creature has travelled about and doubled on its tracks; and, for wrecks, it is strewn with the cases of cadis worms made of minute grains of white quartz. Perhaps these have creased it, for you find some of their cases in the furrows, though they are deep and broad for them to make. But the ice itself is the object of most interest, though you must improve the earliest opportunity to study it. If you examine it closely the morning after it freezes, you find that the greater part of the bubbles, which at first appeared to be within it, are against its under surface, and that more are continually rising from the bottom; while the ice is as yet comparatively solid and dark, that is, you see the water through it. These bubbles are from an eightieth to an eighth of an inch in diameter, very clear and beautiful, and you see your face reflected in them through the ice. There may be thirty or forty of them to a square inch. There are also already within the ice narrow oblong perpendicular bubbles about half an inch long, sharp cones with the apex upward; or oftener, if the ice is quite fresh, minute spherical bubbles one directly above another, like a string of beads. But these within the ice are not so numerous nor obvious as those beneath. I sometimes used to cast on stones to try the strength of the ice, and

8. Genus and species of a fresh-water clam.

those which broke through carried in air with them, which formed very large and conspicuous white bubbles beneath. One day when I came to the same place forty-eight hours afterward, I found that those large bubbles were still perfect, though an inch more of ice had formed, as I could see distinctly by the seam in the edge of a cake. But as the last two days had been very warm, like an Indian summer, the ice was not now transparent, showing the dark green color of the water, and the bottom, but opaque and whitish or gray, and though twice as thick was hardly stronger than before, for the air bubbles had greatly expanded under this heat and run together, and lost their regularity; they were no longer one directly over another, but often like silvery coins poured from a bag, one overlapping another, or in thin flakes, as if occupying slight cleavages. The beauty of the ice was gone, and it was too late to study the bottom. Being curious to know what position my great bubbles occupied with regard to the new ice, I broke out a cake containing a middling sized one, and turned it bottom upward. The new ice had formed around and under the bubble, so that it was included between the two ices. It was wholly in the lower ice, but close against the upper, and was flattish, or perhaps slightly lenticular, with a rounded edge, a quarter of an inch deep by four inches in diameter; and I was surprised to find that directly under the bubble the ice was melted with great regularity in the form of a saucer reversed, to the height of five eighths of an inch in the middle, leaving a thin partition there between the water and the bubble, hardly an eighth of an inch thick; and in many places the small bubbles in this partition had burst out downward, and probably there was no ice at all under the largest bubbles, which were a foot in diameter. I inferred that the infinite number of minute bubbles which I had first seen against the under surface of the ice were now frozen in likewise, and that each, in its degree, had operated like a burning glass on the ice beneath to melt and rot it. These are the little air-guns which contribute to make the ice crack and whoop.

At length the winter set in in good earnest, just as I had finished plastering, and the wind began to howl around the house as if it had not had permission to do so till then. Night after night the geese came lumbering in in the dark with a clangor and a whistling of wings, even after the ground was covered with snow, some to alight in Walden, and some flying low over the woods toward Fair Haven, bound for Mexico. Several times, when returning from the village at ten or eleven o'clock at night, I heard the tread of a flock of geese, or else ducks, on the dry leaves in the woods by a pond-hole behind my dwelling, where they had come up to feed, and the faint honk or quack of their leader as they hurried off. In 1845 Walden froze entirely over for the first time on the night of the 22d of December, Flint's and other shallower ponds and the river having been frozen ten days or more; in '46, the 16th; in '49, about the 31st; and in '50, about the 27th of December; in '52, the 5th of January; in '53, the 31st of December. The snow had already covered the ground since the 25th of November, and surrounded me suddenly with the scenery of winter. I withdrew yet farther into my shell, and endeavored to keep a bright fire both within my house and within my breast. My employment out of doors now was to collect the dead wood in the forest, bringing it in my hands or on my shoulders, or sometimes trailing a dead pine tree under each arm to my shed. An old forest fence which had seen its best days was a great haul for me. I sacrificed it to Vulcan, for it was past serving the god Termi-nus.[9] How much more interesting an event is that man's supper who has just been forth in the snow to hunt, nay, you might say, steal, the fuel to cook it with! His bread and meat are sweet. There are enough fagots and waste wood of all kinds in the forests of most of our towns to support many fires, but which at present warm none, and, some think, hinder the growth of the young wood. There was also the drift-wood of the pond. In the course of the summer I had discovered a raft of pitch-pine logs with the bark on, pinned together by the Irish when the railroad was built. This I hauled up partly on the shore. After soaking two years and then lying high six months it was perfectly sound, though waterlogged past drying. I amused myself one winter day with sliding this piecemeal across the pond, nearly half a mile, skating behind with one end of a log fifteen feet long on my shoulder, and the other on the ice; or I tied several logs together with a birch withe, and then, with a longer birch or alder which had a hook at the end, dragged them across. Though completely waterlogged and almost as heavy as lead, they not only burned long, but made a very hot fire; nay, I thought that they burned better for the soaking, as if the pitch, being confined by the water, burned longer as in a lamp.

Gilpin, in his account of the forest borderers of England, says that "the encroachments of trespassers, and the houses and fences thus raised on the borders of the forest," were "considered as great nuisances by the old forest law, and were severely punished under the name of *purprestures*, as tend-ing *ad terrorem ferarum—ad nocumentum forestæ*, &c.,"[1] to the frightening of the game and the detriment of the forest. But I was interested in the preser-vation of the venison and the vert[2] more than the hunters or wood-choppers, and as much as though I had been the Lord Warden himself; and if any part was burned, though I burned it myself by accident, I grieved with a grief that lasted longer and was more inconsolable than that of the proprietors; nay, I grieved when it was cut down by the proprietors themselves. I would that our farmers when they cut down a forest felt some of that awe which the old Romans did when they came to thin, or let in the light to, a consecrated grove, *(lucum conlucare,)* that is, would believe that it is sacred to some god. The Roman made an expiatory offering, and prayed, Whatever god or goddess thou art to whom this grove is sacred, be propitious to me, my family, and children, &c.

It is remarkable what a value is still put upon wood even in this age and in this new country, a value more permanent and universal than that of gold. After all our discoveries and inventions no man will go by a pile of wood. It is as precious to us as it was to our Saxon and Norman ancestors. If they made their bows of it, we make our gun-stocks of it. Michaux, more than thirty years ago, says that the price of wood for fuel in New York and Philadelphia "nearly equals, and sometimes exceeds, that of the best wood in Paris, though this immense capital annually requires more than three hunderd thousand cords, and is surrounded to the distance of three hundred miles by cultivated plains."[3] In this town the price of wood rises almost steadily, and the only question is, how much higher it is to be this year than it was the last. Mechan-

---

9. Thoreau burned it (thereby sacrificing it to Vulcan, the god of fire and blacksmith of the Roman gods) rather than using it in a fence (where it would have served Terminus, the Roman god of limits or bound-aries).

1. William Gilpin, *Remarks on Forest Scenery* (1834), 2.122.
2. Green vegetation providing cover for deer.
3. François Andrew Michaux, *North American Sylva* (1818).

ics and tradesmen who come in person to the forest on no other errand, are sure to attend the wood auction, and even pay a high price for the privilege of gleaning after the wood-chopper. It is now many years that men have resorted to the forest for fuel and the materials of the arts; the New Englander and the New Hollander, the Parisian and the Celt, the farmer and Robinhood, Goody Blake and Harry Gill,[4] in most parts of the world the prince and the peasant, the scholar and the savage, equally require still a few sticks from the forest to warm them and cook their food. Neither could I do without them.

Every man looks at his wood-pile with a kind of affection. I loved to have mine before my window, and the more chips the better to remind me of my pleasing work. I had an old axe which nobody claimed, with which by spells in winter days, on the sunny side of the house, I played about the stumps which I had got out of my bean-field. As my driver prophesied when I was ploughing, they warmed me twice, once while I was splitting them, and again when they were on the fire, so that no fuel could give out more heat. As for the axe, I was advised to get the village blacksmith to "jump" it; but I jumped him, and, putting a hickory helve from the woods into it, made it do. If it was dull, it was at least hung true.

A few pieces of fat pine were a great treasure. It is interesting to remember how much of this food for fire is still concealed in the bowels of the earth. In previous years I had often gone "prospecting" over some bare hill-side, where a pitch-pine wood had formerly stood, and got out the fat pine roots. They are almost indestructible. Stumps thirty or forty years old, at least, will still be sound at the core, though the sapwood has all become vegetable mould, as appears by the scales of the thick bark forming a ring level with the earth four or five inches distant from the heart. With axe and shovel you explore this mine, and follow the marrowy store, yellow as beef tallow, or as if you had struck on a vein of gold, deep into the earth. But commonly I kindled my fire with the dry leaves of the forest, which I had stored up in my shed before the snow came. Green hickory finely split makes the woodchopper's kindlings, when he has a camp in the woods. Once in a while I got a little of this. When the villagers were lighting their fires beyond the horizon, I too gave notice to the various wild inhabitants of Walden vale, by a smoky streamer from my chimney, that I was awake.—

> Light-winged Smoke, Icarian bird,
> Melting thy pinions in thy upward flight,
> Lark without song, and messenger of dawn,
> Circling above the hamlets as thy nest;
> Or else, departing dream, and shadowy form
> Of midnight vision, gathering up thy skirts;
> By night star-veiling, and by day
> Darkening the light and blotting out the sun;
> Go thou my incense upward from this hearth,
> And ask the gods to pardon this clear flame.

Hard green wood just cut, though I used but little of that, answered my purpose better than any other. I sometimes left a good fire when I went to take a walk in a winter afternoon; and when I returned, three or four hours after-

---

4. In Wordsworth's *Goody Blake and Harry Gill: A True Story*, Harry Gill seizes old Goody Blake in the act of pulling sticks from his hedge for firewood. God answers her prayer that Harry "never more be warm."

ward, it would be still alive and glowing. My house was not empty though I was gone. It was as if I had left a cheerful housekeeper behind. It was I and Fire that lived there; and commonly my housekeeper proved trustworthy. One day, however, as I was splitting wood, I thought that I would just look in at the window and see if the house was not on fire; it was the only time I remember to have been particularly anxious on this score; so I looked and saw that a spark had caught my bed, and I went in and extinguished it when it had burned a place as big as my hand. But my house occupied so sunny and sheltered a position, and its roof was so low, that I could afford to let the fire go out in the middle of almost any winter day.

The moles nested in my cellar, nibbling every third potato, and making a snug bed even there of some hair left after plastering and of brown paper; for even the wildest animals love comfort and warmth as well as man, and they survive the winter only because they are so careful to secure them. Some of my friends spoke as if I was coming to the woods on purpose to freeze myself. The animal merely makes a bed, which he warms with his body in a sheltered place; but man, having discovered fire, boxes up some air in a spacious apartment, and warms that, instead of robbing himself, makes that his bed, in which he can move about divested of more cumbrous clothing, maintain a kind of summer in the midst of winter, and by means of windows even admit the light, and with a lamp lengthen out the day. Thus he goes a step or two beyond instinct, and saves a little time for the fine arts. Though, when I had been exposed to the rudest blasts a long time, my whole body began to grow torpid, when I reached the genial atmosphere of my house I soon recovered my faculties and prolonged my life. But the most luxuriously housed has little to boast of in this respect, nor need we trouble ourselves to speculate how the human race may be at last destroyed. It would be easy to cut their threads any time with a little sharper blast from the north. We go on dating from Cold Fridays and Great Snows; but a little colder Friday, or greater snow, would put a period to man's existence on the globe.

The next winter I used a small cooking-stove for economy, since I did not own the forest; but it did not keep fire so well as the open fire-place. Cooking was then, for the most part, no longer a poetic, but merely a chemic process. It will soon be forgotten, in these days of stoves, that we used to roast potatoes in the ashes, after the Indian fashion. The stove not only took up room and scented the house, but it concealed the fire, and I felt as if I had lost a companion. You can always see a face in the fire. The laborer, looking into it at evening, purifies his thoughts of the dross and earthiness which they have accumulated during the day. But I could no longer sit and look into the fire, and the pertinent words of a poet recurred to me with new force.—

> "Never, bright flame, may be denied to me
> Thy dear, life imaging, close sympathy.
> What but my hopes shot upward e'er so bright?
> What but my fortunes sunk so low in night?
>
> Why art thou banished from our hearth and hall,
> Thou who art welcomed and beloved by all?
> Was thy existence then too fanciful
> For our life's common light, who are so dull?
> Did thy bright gleam mysterious converse hold

With our congenial souls? secrets too bold?
Well, we are safe and strong, for now we sit
Beside a hearth where no dim shadows flit,
Where nothing cheers nor saddens, but a fire
Warms feet and hands—nor does to more aspire;
By whose compact utilitarian heap
The present may sit down and go to sleep,
Nor fear the ghosts who from the dim past walked,
And with us by the unequal light of the old wood fire talked."[5]

Former Inhabitants; and Winter Visitors

I weathered some merry snow storms, and spent some cheerful winter evenings by my fire-side, while the snow whirled wildly without, and even the hooting of the owl was hushed. For many weeks I met no one in my walks but those who came occasionally to cut wood and sled it to the village. The elements, however, abetted me in making a path through the deepest snow in the woods, for when I had once gone through the wind blew the oak leaves into my tracks, where they lodged, and by absorbing the rays of the sun melted the snow, and so not only made a dry bed for my feet, but in the night their dark line was my guide. For human society I was obliged to conjure up the former occupants of these woods. Within the memory of many of my townsmen the road near which my house stands resounded with the laugh and gossip of inhabitants, and the woods which border it were notched and dotted here and there with their little gardens and dwellings, though it was then much more shut in by the forest than now. In some places, within my own remembrance, the pines would scrape both sides of a chaise at once, and women and children who were compelled to go this way to Lincoln alone and on foot did it with fear, and often ran a good part of the distance. Though mainly but a humble route to neighboring villages, or for the woodman's team, it once amused the traveller more than now by its variety, and lingered longer in his memory. Where now firm open fields stretch from the village to the woods, it then ran through a maple swamp on a foundation of logs, the remnants of which, doubtless, still underlie the present dusty highway, from the Stratton, now the Alms House, Farm, to Brister's Hill.

East of my bean-field, across the road, lived Cato Ingraham, slave of Duncan Ingraham, Esquire, gentleman of Concord village; who built his slave a house, and gave him permission to live in Walden Woods;—Cato, not Uticensis, but Concordiensis.[6] Some say that he was a Guinea Negro. There are a few who remember his little patch among the walnuts, which he let grow up till he should be old and need them; but a younger and whiter speculator got them at last. He too, however, occupies an equally narrow house at present. Cato's half-obliterated cellar hole still remains, though known to few, being concealed from the traveller by a fringe of pines. It is now filled with the smooth sumach, (*Rhus glabra,*) and one of the earliest species of golden-rod (*Solidago stricta*) grows there luxuriantly.

Here, by the very corner of my field, still nearer to town, Zilpha, a colored

5. A slightly altered portion of a poem by Ellen Sturgis Hooper (1816?–1848?) that appeared in the *Dial* (1840).
6. The grandson of Marcus Porcius Cato, Thoreau's authority on agriculture, was called Cato Uticensis after his death at Utica. Classical names were often given to American slaves.

woman, had her little house, where she spun linen for the townsfolk, making the Walden Woods ring with her shrill singing, for she had a loud and notable voice. At length, in the war of 1812, her dwelling was set on fire by English soldiers, prisoners on parole, when she was away, and her cat and dog and hens were all burned up together. She led a hard life, and somewhat inhumane. One old frequenter of these woods remembers, that as he passed her house one noon he heard her muttering to herself over her gurgling pot,—"Ye are all bones, bones!" I have seen bricks amid the oak copse there.

Down the road, on the right hand, on Brister's Hill, lived Brister Freeman, "a handy Negro," slave of Squire Cummings once,—there where grow still the apple-trees which Brister planted and tended; large old trees now, but their fruit still wild and ciderish to my taste. Not long since I read his epitaph in the old Lincoln burying-ground, a little on one side, near the unmarked graves of some British grenadiers who fell in the retreat from Concord,—where he is styled "Sippio Brister,"—Scipio Africanus[7] he had some title to be called,— "a man of color," as if he were discolored. It also told me, with staring emphasis, when he died; which was but an indirect way of informing me that he ever lived. With him dwelt Fenda, his hospitable wife, who told fortunes, yet pleasantly,—large, round, and black, blacker than any of the children of night, such a dusky orb as never rose on Concord before or since.

Farther down the hill, on the left, on the old road in the woods, are marks of some homestead of the Stratton family; whose orchard once covered all the slope of Brister's Hill, but was long since killed out by pitch-pines, excepting a few stumps, whose old roots furnish still the wild stocks of many a thrifty village tree.

Nearer yet to town, you come to Breed's location, on the other side of the way, just on the edge of the wood; ground famous for the pranks of a demon not distinctly named in old mythology, who has acted a prominent and astounding part in our New England life, and deserves, as much as any mythological character, to have his biography written one day; who first comes in the guise of a friend or hired man, and then robs and murders the whole family,—New-England Rum. But history must not yet tell the tragedies enacted here; let time intervene in some measure to assuage and lend an azure tint to them. Here the most indistinct and dubious tradition says that once a tavern stood; the well the same, which tempered the traveller's beverage and refreshed his steed. Here then men saluted one another, and heard and told the news, and went their ways again.

Breed's hut was standing only a dozen years ago, though it had long been unoccupied. It was about the size of mine. It was set on fire by mischievous boys, one Election night, if I do not mistake. I lived on the edge of the village then, and had just lost myself over Davenant's Gondibert,[8] that winter that I labored with a lethargy,—which, by the way, I never knew whether to regard as a family complaint, having an uncle who goes to sleep shaving himself, and is obliged to sprout potatoes in a cellar Sundays, in order to keep awake and keep the Sabbath, or as the consequence of my attempt to read Chalmers' collection of English poetry without skipping. It fairly overcame my Nervii.[9] I had just sunk my head on this when the bells rung fire, and in hot haste the

---

7. Scipio Africanus (237–183 B.C.) was a Roman general who led the invasion of Carthage.
8. William Davenant, *Gondibert: An Heroick Poem*

(1672); Thoreau's point is that it is soporific.
9. A tribe that Julius Caesar defeated in Flanders; Thoreau is punning.

engines rolled that way, led by a straggling troop of men and boys, and I among the foremost, for I had leaped the brook. We thought it was far south over the woods,—we who had run to fires before,—barn, shop, or dwelling-house, or all together. "It's Baker's barn," cried one. "It is the Codman Place," affirmed another. And then fresh sparks went up above the wood, as if the roof fell in, and we all shouted "Concord to the rescue!" Wagons shot past with furious speed and crushing loads, bearing, perchance, among the rest, the agent of the Insurance Company, who was bound to go however far; and ever and anon the engine bell tinkled behind, more slow and sure, and rearmost of all, as it was afterward whispered, came they who set the fire and gave the alarm. Thus we kept on like true idealists, rejecting the evidence of our senses, until at a turn in the road we heard the crackling and actually felt the heat of the fire from over the wall, and realized, alas! that we were there. The very nearness of the fire but cooled our ardor. At first we thought to throw a frog-pond on to it; but concluded to let it burn, it was so far gone and so worthless. So we stood round our engine, jostled one another, expressed our sentiments through speaking trumpets, or in lower tone referred to the great conflagrations which the world has witnessed, including Bascom's shop, and, between our-selves, we thought that, were we there in season with our "tub," and a full frog-pond by, we could turn that threatened last and universal one into another flood. We finally retreated without doing any mischief,—returned to sleep and Gondibert. But as for Gondibert, I would except that passage in the preface about wit being the soul's powder,—"but most of mankind are strangers to wit, as Indians are to powder."[1]

It chanced that I walked that way across the fields the following night, about the same hour, and hearing a low moaning at this spot, I drew near in the dark, and discovered the only survivor of the family that I know, the heir of both its virtues and its vices, who alone was interested in this burning, lying on his stomach and looking over the cellar wall at the still smouldering cinders beneath, muttering to himself, as is his wont. He had been working far off in the river meadows all day, and had improved the first moments that he could call his own to visit the home of his fathers and his youth. He gazed into the cellar from all sides and points of view by turns, always lying down to it, as if there was some treasure, which he remembered, concealed between the stones, where there was absolutely nothing but a heap of bricks and ashes. The house being gone, he looked at what there was left. He was soothed by the sympathy which my mere presence implied, and showed me, as well as the darkness permitted, where the well was covered up; which, thank Heaven, could never be burned; and he groped long about the wall to find the well-sweep which his father had cut and mounted, feeling for the iron hook or staple by which a burden had been fastened to the heavy end,—all that he could now cling to,—to convince me that it was no common "rider." I felt it, and still remark it almost daily in my walks, for by it hangs the history of a family.

Once more, on the left, where are seen the well and lilac bushes by the wall, in the now open field, lived Nutting and Le Grosse. But to return toward Lincoln.

Farther in the woods than any of these, where the road approaches nearest

---

1. From "The Author's Preface."

to the pond, Wyman the potter squatted, and furnished his townsmen with earthen ware, and left descendants to succeed him. Neither were they rich in worldly goods, holding the land by sufferance while they lived; and there often the sheriff came in vain to collect the taxes, and "attached a chip,"[2] for form's sake, as I have read in his accounts, there being nothing else that he could lay his hands on. One day in midsummer, when I was hoeing, a man who was carrying a load of pottery to market stopped his horse against my field and inquired concerning Wyman the younger. He had long ago bought a potter's wheel of him, and wished to know what had become of him. I had read of the potter's clay and wheel in Scripture, but it had never occurred to me that the pots we use were not such as had come down unbroken from those days, or grown on trees like gourds somewhere, and I was pleased to hear that so fictile an art was ever practised in my neighborhood.

The last inhabitant of these woods before me was an Irishman, Hugh Quoil, (if I have spelt his name with coil[3] enough,) who occupied Wyman's tenement,—Col. Quoil, he was called. Rumor said that he had been a soldier at Waterloo. If he had lived I should have made him fight his battles over again. His trade here was that of a ditcher. Napoleon went to St. Helena; Quoil came to Walden Woods. All I know of him is tragic. He was a man of manners, like one who had seen the world, and was capable of more civil speech than you could well attend to. He wore a great coat in mid-summer, being affected with the trembling delirium, and his face was the color of carmine. He died in the road at the foot of Brister's Hill shortly after I came to the woods, so that I have not remembered him as a neighbor. Before his house was pulled down, when his comrades avoided it as "an unlucky castle," I visited it. There lay his old clothes curled up by use, as if they were himself, upon his raised plank bed. His pipe lay broken on the hearth, instead of a bowl broken at the fountain. The last could never have been the symbol of his death, for he confessed to me that, though he had heard of Brister's Spring, he had never seen it; and soiled cards, kings of diamonds spades and hearts, were scattered over the floor. One black chicken which the administrator[4] could not catch, black as night and as silent, not even croaking, awaiting Reynard, still went to roost in the next apartment. In the rear there was the dim outline of a garden, which had been planted but had never received it first hoeing, owing to those terrible shaking fits, though it was now harvest time. It was over-run with Roman wormwood and beggar-ticks, which last stuck to my clothes for all fruit. The skin of a woodchuck was freshly stretched upon the back of the house, a trophy of his last Waterloo; but no warm cap or mittens would he want more.

Now only a dent in the earth marks the site of these dwellings, with buried cellar stones, and strawberries, raspberries, thimble-berries, hazel-bushes, and sumachs growing in the sunny sward there; some pitch-pine or gnarled oak occupies what was the chimney nook, and a sweet-scented black-birch, perhaps, waves where the door-stone was. Sometimes the well dent is visible, where once a spring oozed; now dry and tearless grass; or it was covered deep,—not to be discovered till some late day,—with a flat stone under the sod, when the last of the race departed. What a sorrowful act must that be,—the covering up of wells! coincident with the opening of wells of tears. These cellar dents, like deserted fox burrows, old holes, are all that is left where once

2. "Old custom of sheriff attaching a chip if there were no other possessions to place a lien on" [Harding's note] ("to attach," to seize).

3. Trouble; in these lines the puns are multiple.
4. Person appointed to administer an estate.

were the stir and bustle of human life, and "fate, free-will, foreknowledge absolute,"[5] in some form and dialect or other were by turns discussed. But all I can learn of their conclusions amounts to just this, that "Cato and Brister pulled wool;" which is about as edifying as the history of more famous schools of philosophy.

Still grows the vivacious lilac a generation after the door and lintel and the sill are gone, unfolding its sweet-scented flowers each spring, to be plucked by the musing traveller; planted and tended once by children's hands, in front-yard plots,—now standing by wall-sides in retired pastures, and giving place to new-rising forests;—the last of that stirp, sole survivor of that family. Little did the dusky children think that the puny slip with its two eyes only, which they stuck in the ground in the shadow of the house and daily watered, would root itself so, and outlive them and house itself in the rear that shaded it, and grown man's garden and orchard, and tell their story faintly to the lone wanderer a half century after they had grown up and died,—blossoming as fair, and smelling as sweet, as in that first spring. I mark its still tender, civil, cheerful, lilac colors.

But this small village, germ of something more, why did it fail while Concord keeps its ground? Were there no natural advantages,—no water privileges, forsooth? Ay, the deep Waldon Pond and cool Brister's Spring,—privilege to drink long and healthy draughts at these, all unimproved by these men but to dilute their glass. They were universally a thirsty race. Might not the basket, stable-broom, mat-making, corn-parching, linen-spinning, and pottery business have thrived here, making the wilderness to blossom like the rose, and a numerous posterity have inherited the land of their fathers? The sterile soil would at least have been proof against a low-land degeneracy. Alas! how little does the memory of these human inhabitants enhance the beauty of the landscape! Again, perhaps, Nature will try, with me for a first settler, and my house raised last spring to be the oldest in the hamlet.

I am not aware that any man has ever built on the spot which I occupy. Deliver me from a city built on the site of a more ancient city, whose materials are ruins, whose gardens cemeteries. The soil is blanched and accursed there, and before that becomes necessary the earth itself will be destroyed. With such reminiscences I repeopled the woods and lulled myself asleep.

At this season I seldom had a visitor. When the snow lay deepest no wanderer ventured near my house for a week or fortnight at a time, but there I lived as snug as a meadow mouse, or as cattle and poultry which are said to have survived for a long time buried in drifts, even without food; or like that early settler's family in the town of Sutton, in this state, whose cottage was completely covered by the great snow of 1717 when he was absent, and an Indian found it only by the hole which the chimney's breath made in the drift, and so relieved the family. But no friendly Indian concerned himself about me; nor needed he, for the master of the house was at home. The Great Snow! How cheerful it is to hear of! When the farmers could not get to the woods and swamps with their teams, and were obliged to cut down the shade trees before their houses, and when the crust was harder cut off the trees in the swamps ten feet from the ground, as it appeared the next spring.

In the deepest snows, the path which I used from the highway to my house,

5. Milton's *Paradise Lost* 2.560.

about half a mile long, might have been represented by a meandering dotted line, with wide intervals between the dots. For a week of even weather I took exactly the same number of steps, and of the same length, coming and going, stepping deliberately and with the precision of a pair of dividers in my own deep tracks,—to such routine the winter reduces us,—yet often they were filled with heaven's own blue. But no weather interfered fatally with my walks, or rather my going abroad, for I frequently tramped eight or ten miles through the deepest snow to keep an appointment with a beech-tree, or a yellow-birch, or an old acquaintance among the pines; when the ice and snow causing their limbs to droop, and so sharpening their tops, had changed the pines into fir-trees; wading to the tops of the highest hills when the snow was nearly two feet deep on a level, and shaking down another snow-storm on my head at every step; or sometimes creeping and floundering thither on my hands and knees, when the hunters had gone into winter quarters. One afternoon I amused myself by watching a barred owl (Strix nebulosa) sitting on one of the lower dead limbs of a white-pine, close to the trunk, in broad daylight, I standing within a rod of him. He could hear me when I moved and cronched the snow with my feet, but could not plainly see me. When I made most noise he would stretch out his neck, and erect his neck feathers, and open his eyes wide; but their lids soon fell again, and he began to nod. I too felt a slumberous influence after watching him half an hour, as he sat thus with his eyes half open, like a cat, winged brother of the cat. There was only a narrow slit left between their lids, by which he preserved a peninsular relation to me; thus, with half-shut eyes, looking out from the land of dreams, and endeavoring to realize me, vague object or mote that interrupted his visions. At length, on some louder noise or my nearer approach, he would grow uneasy and sluggishly turn about on his perch, as if impatient at having his dreams disturbed; and when he launched himself off and flapped through the pines, spreading his wings to unexpected breadth, I could not hear the slightest sound from them. Thus, guided amid the pine boughs rather by a delicate sense of their neighborhood than by sight, feeling his twilight way as it were with his sensitive pinions, he found a new perch, where he might in peace await the dawning of his day.

As I walked over the long causeway made for the railroad through the meadows, I encountered many a blustering and nipping wind, for nowhere has it freer play; and when the frost had smitten me on one cheek, heathen as I was, I turned to it the other also.[6] Nor was it much better by the carriage road from Brister's Hill. For I came to town still, like a friendly Indian, when the contents of the broad open fields were all piled up between the walls of the Walden road, and half an hour sufficed to obliterate the tracks of the last traveller. And when I returned new drifts would have formed, through which I floundered, where the busy north-west wind had been depositing the powdery snow round a sharp angle in the road, and not a rabbit's track, nor even the fine print, the small type, of a deer mouse was to be seen. Yet I rarely failed to find, even in mid-winter, some warm and springy swamp where the grass and the skunk-cabbage still put forth with perennial verdure, and some hardier bird occasionally awaited the return of spring.

Sometimes, notwithstanding the snow, when I returned from my walk at

6. Matthew 5.39, Sermon on the Mount: "But I say unto you, That ye resist not evil: but whosoever shall smite thee on thy right cheek, turn to him the other also."

evening I crossed the deep tracks of a woodchopper leading from my door, and found his pile of whittlings on the hearth, and my house filled with the odor of his pipe. Or on a Sunday afternoon, if I chanced to be at home, I heard the cronching of the snow made by the step of a long-headed farmer, who from far through the woods sought my house, to have a social "crack;" one of the few of his vocation who are "men on their farms;"[7] who donned a frock instead of a professor's gown, and is as ready to extract the moral out of church or state as to haul a load of manure from his barn-yard. We talked of rude and simple times, when men sat about large fires in cold bracing weather, with clear heads; and when other dessert failed, we tried our teeth on many a nut which wise squirrels have long since abandoned, for those which have the thickest shells are commonly empty.

The one who came from farthest to my lodge, through deepest snows and most dismal tempests, was a poet.[8] A farmer, a hunter, a soldier, a reporter, even a philosopher, may be daunted; but nothing can deter a poet, for he is actuated by pure love. Who can predict his comings and goings? His business calls him out at all hours, even when doctors sleep. We made that small house ring with boisterous mirth and resound with the murmur of much sober talk, making amends then to Walden vale for the long silences. Broadway was still and deserted in comparison. At suitable intervals there were regular salutes of laughter, which might have been referred indifferently to the last uttered or the forth-coming jest. We made many a "bran new" theory of life over a thin dish of gruel, which combined the advantages of conviviality with the clear-headedness which philosophy requires.

I should not forget that during my last winter at the pond there was another welcome visitor, who at one time came through the village, through snow and rain and darkness, till he saw my lamp through the trees, and shared with me some long winter evenings.[9] One of the last of the philosophers,—Connecticut gave him to the world,—he peddled first her wares, afterwards, as he declares, his brains. These he peddles still, prompting God and disgracing man, bearing for fruit his brain only, like the nut its kernel. I think that he must be the man of the most faith of any alive. His words and attitude always suppose a better state of things than other men are acquainted with, and he will be the last man to be disappointed as the ages revolve. He has no venture in the present. But though comparatively disregarded now, when his day comes, laws unsuspected by most will take effect, and masters of families and rulers will come to him for advice.—

"How blind that cannot see serenity!"[1]

A true friend of man; almost the only friend of human progress. An Old Mortality,[2] say rather an Immortality, with unwearied patience and faith making plain the image engraven in men's bodies, the God of whom they are but defaced and leaning monuments. With his hospitable intellect he embraces children, beggars, insane, and scholars, and entertains the thought of all, adding to it commonly some breadth and elegance. I think that he should keep a

---

7. A reference to Emerson's classifications of the sub-divided condition of humankind in *The American Scholar*; being "Man on the farm" is better than being a farmer.
8. Channing.
9. Bronson Alcott, one of the "raisers" of the cabin.

1. From Thomas Storer, *The Life and Death of Thomas Wolsey, Cardinal* (1599).
2. The title character in Sir Walter Scott's *Old Mortality* (1816) went from churchyard to churchyard clearing away moss and rechiseling half-defaced inscriptions on tombstones.

caravansary on the world's highway, where philosophers of all nations might put up, and on his sign should be printed, "Entertainment for man, but not for his beast. Enter ye that have leisure and a quiet mind, who earnestly seek the right road." He is perhaps the sanest man and has the fewest crotchets of any I chance to know; the same yesterday and to-morrow. Of yore we had sauntered and talked, and effectually put the world behind us; for he was pledged to no institution in it, freeborn, *ingenuus*. Whichever way we turned, it seemed that the heavens and the earth had met together, since he enhanced the beauty of the landscape. A blue-robed man, whose fittest roof is the over-arching sky which reflects his serenity. I do not see how he can ever die; Nature cannot spare him.

Having each some shingles of thought well dried, we sat and whittled them, trying our knives, and admiring the clear yellowish grain of the pumpkin pine. We waded so gently and reverently, or we pulled together so smoothly, that the fishes of thought were not scared from the stream, nor feared any angler on the bank, but came and went grandly, like the clouds which float through the western sky, and the mother-o'-pearl flocks which sometimes form and dissolve there. There we worked, revising mythology, rounding a fable here and there, and building castles in the air for which earth offered no worthy foundation. Great Looker! Great Expecter! to converse with whom was a New England Night's Entertainment. Ah! such discourse we had, hermit and philosopher, and the old settler I have spoken of,—we three,—it expanded and racked my little house; I should not dare to say how many pounds' weight there was above the atmospheric pressure on every circular inch; it opened its seams so that they had to be calked with much dulness thereafter to stop the consequent leak;—but I had enough of that kind of oakum already picked.

There was one other[3] with whom I had "solid seasons," long to be remembered, at his house in the village, and who looked in upon me from time to time; but I had no more for society there.

There too, as every where, I sometimes expected the Visitor who never comes.[4] The Vishnu Purana says, "The house-holder is to remain at eventide in his court-yard as long as it takes to milk a cow, or longer if he pleases, to await the arrival of a guest." I often performed this duty of hospitality, waited long enough to milk a whole herd of cows, but did not see the man approaching from the town.

Winter Animals

When the ponds were firmly frozen, they afforded not only new and shorter routes to many points, but new views from their surfaces of the familiar landscape around them. When I crossed Flint's Pond, after it was covered with snow, though I had often paddled about and skated over it, it was so unexpectedly wide and so strange that I could think of nothing but Baffin's Bay.[5] The Lincoln hills rose up around me at the extremity of a snowy plain, in which I did not remember to have stood before; and the fishermen, at an indeterminable distance over the ice, moving slowly about with their wolfish dogs, passed

3. Emerson.
4. It would be wrong to attach a specific meaning to "the Visitor." In this evocative paragraph Thoreau mixes a quotation from H. H. Wilson's translation of the Sanskrit scripture *Vishnu Purana* (1840) with a folk ballad, *The Children in the Wood:* "But never more could see the man / Approaching from the town."
5. Between Greenland and the Canadian islands; now Baffin Bay.

for sealers or Esquimaux, or in misty weather loomed like fabulous creatures, and I did not know whether they were giants or pygmies. I took this course when I went to lecture in Lincoln in the evening, travelling in no road and passing no house between my own hut and the lecture room. In Goose Pond, which lay in my way, a colony of muskrats dwelt, and raised their cabins high above the ice, though none could be seen abroad when I crossed it. Walden, being like the rest usually bare of snow, or with only shallow and interrupted drifts on it, was my yard, where I could walk freely when the snow was nearly two feet deep on a level elsewhere and the villagers were confined to their streets. There, far from the village street, and except at very long intervals, from the jingle of sleigh-bells, I slid and skated, as in a vast moose-yard well trodden, over-hung by oak woods and solemn pines bent down with snow or bristling with icicles.

For sounds in winter nights, and often in winter days, I heard the forlorn but melodious note of a hooting owl indefinitely far; such a sound as the frozen earth would yield if struck with a suitable plectrum, the very *lingua vernacula*[6] of Walden Wood, and quite familiar to me at last, though I never saw the bird while it was making it. I seldom opened my door in a winter evening without hearing it; *Hoo hoo hoo, hoorer hoo* sounded sonorously, and the first three syllables accented somewhat like *how der do*; or sometimes *hoo hoo* only. One night in the beginning of winter, before the pond froze over, about nine o'clock, I was startled by the loud honking of a goose, and, stepping to the door, heard the sound of their wings like a tempest in the woods as they flew low over my house. They passed over the pond toward Fair Haven, seemingly deterred from settling by my light, their commodore honking all the while with a regular beat. Suddenly an unmistakable cat-owl from very near me, with the most harsh and tremendous voice I ever heard from any inhabitant of the woods, responded at regular intervals to the goose, as if determined to expose and disgrace this intruder from Hudson's Bay by exhibiting a greater compass and volume of voice in a native, and *boo-hoo* him out of Concord horizon. What do you mean by alarming the citadel at this time of night consecrated to me? Do you think I am ever caught napping at such an hour, and that I have not got lungs and a larynx as well as yourself? *Boo-hoo, boo-hoo, boo-hoo!* It was one of the most thrilling discords I ever heard. And yet, if you had a discriminating ear, there were in it the elements of a concord such as these plains never saw nor heard.

I also heard the whooping of the ice in the pond, my great bed-fellow in that part of Concord, as if it were restless in its bed and would fain turn over, were troubled with flatulency and bad dreams; or I was waked by the cracking of the ground by the frost, as if some one had driven a team against my door, and in the morning would find a crack in the earth a quarter of a mile long and a third of an inch wide.

Sometimes I heard the foxes as they ranged over the snow crust, in moonlight nights, in search of a partridge or other game, barking raggedly and demoniacally like forest dogs, as if laboring with some anxiety, or seeking expression, struggling for light and to be dogs outright and run freely in the streets; for if we take the ages into our account, may there not be a civilization going on among brutes as well as men? They seemed to me to be rudimental,

6. Local dialect (Latin).

burrowing men, still standing on their defence, awaiting their transformation. Sometimes one came near to my window, attracted by my light, barked a vulpine curse at me, and then retreated.

Usually the red squirrel (*Sciurus Hudsonius*) waked me in the dawn, coursing over the roof and up and down the sides of the house, as if sent out of the woods for this purpose. In the course of the winter I threw out half a bushel of ears of sweet-corn, which had not got ripe, on to the snow crust by my door, and was amused by watching the motions of the various animals which were baited by it. In the twilight and the night the rabbits came regularly and made a hearty meal. All day long the red squirrels came and went, and afforded me much entertainment by their manœuvres. One would approach at first warily through the shrub-oaks, running over the snow crust by fits and starts like a leaf blown by the wind, now a few paces this way, with wonderful speed and waste of energy, making inconceivable haste with his "trotters," as if it were for a wager, and now as many paces that way, but never getting on more than half a rod at a time; and then suddenly pausing with a ludicrous expression and a gratuitous somerset,[7] as if all the eyes in the universe were fixed on him,—for all the motions of a squirrel, even in the most solitary recesses of the forest, imply spectators as much as those of a dancing girl,—wasting more time in delay and circumspection than would have sufficed to walk the whole distance,—I never saw one walk,—and then suddenly, before you could say Jack Robinson, he would be in the top of a young pitch-pine, winding up his clock and chiding all imaginary spectators, soliloquizing and talking to all the universe at the same time,—for no reason that I could ever detect, or he himself was aware of, I suspect. At length he would reach the corn, and selecting a suitable ear, frisk about in the same uncertain trigonometrical way to the top-most stick of my wood-pile, before my window, where he looked me in the face, and there sit for hours, supplying himself with a new ear from time to time, nibbling at first voraciously and throwing the half-naked cobs about; till at length he grew more dainty still and played with his food, tasting only the inside of the kernel, and the ear which was held balanced over the stick by one paw, slipped from his careless grasp and fell to the ground, when he would look over at it with a ludicrous expression of uncertainty, as if suspecting that it had life, with a mind not made up whether to get it again, or a new one, or be off; now thinking of corn, then listening to hear what was in the wind. So the little impudent fellow would waste many an ear in a forenoon; till at last, seizing some longer and plumper one, considerably bigger than himself, and skilfully balancing it, he would set out with it to the woods, like a tiger with a buffalo, by the same zig-zag course and frequent pauses, scratching along with it as if it were too heavy for him and falling all the while, making its fall a diagonal between a perpendicular and horizontal, being determined to put it through at any rate;—a singularly frivolous and whimsical fellow;—and so he would get off with it to where he lived, perhaps carry it to the top of a pine tree forty or fifty rods distant, and I would afterwards find the cobs strewn about the woods in various directions.

At length the jays arrive, whose discordant screams were heard long before, as they were warily making their approach an eighth of a mile off, and in a stealthy and sneaking manner they flit from tree to tree, nearer and nearer,

---

7. Variant spelling of *somersault*.

and pick up the kernels which the squirrels have dropped. Then, sitting on a pitch-pine bough, they attempt to swallow in their haste a kernel which is too big for their throats and chokes them and after great labor they disgorge it, and spend an hour in the endeavor to crack it by repeated blows with their bills. They were manifestly thieves, and I had not much respect for them; but the squirrels, though at first shy, went to work as if they were taking what was their own.

Meanwhile also came the chicadees in flocks, which picking up the crumbs the squirrels had dropped, flew to the nearest twig, and placing them under their claws, hammered away at them with their little bills, as if it were an insect in the bark, till they were sufficiently reduced for their slender throats. A little flock of these tit-mice came daily to pick a dinner out of my wood-pile, or the crumbs at my door, with faint flitting lisping notes, like the tinkling of icicles in the grass, or else with sprightly *day day day* or more rarely, in spring-like days, a wiry summery *phe-be* from the wood-side. They were so familiar that at length one alighted on an armful of wood which I was carrying in, and pecked at the sticks without fear. I once had a sparrow alight upon my shoulder for a moment while I was hoeing in a village garden, and I felt that I was more distinguished by that circumstance than I should have been by any epaulet I could have worn. The squirrels also grew at last to be quite familiar, and occasionally stepped upon my shoe, when that was the nearest way.

When the ground was not yet quite covered, and again near the end of winter, when the snow was melted on my south hill-side and about my wood-pile, the partridges came out of the woods morning and evening to feed there. Whichever side you walk in the woods the partridge bursts away on whirring wings, jarring the snow from the dry leaves and twigs on high, which comes sifting down in the sun-beams like golden dust; for this brave bird is not to be scared by winter. It is frequently covered up by drifts, and, it is said, "sometimes plunges from on wing into the soft snow, where it remains concealed for a day or two."[8] I used to start them in the open land also, where they had come out of the woods at sunset to "bud" the wild apple-trees. They will come regularly every evening to particular trees, where the cunning sportsman lies in wait for them, and the distant orchards next the woods suffer thus not a little. I am glad that the partridge gets fed, at any rate. It is Nature's own bird which lives on buds and diet-drink.[9]

In dark winter mornings, or in short winter afternoons, I sometimes heard a pack of hounds threading all the woods with hounding cry and yelp, unable to resist the instinct of the chase, and the note of the hunting horn at intervals, proving that man was in the rear. The woods ring again, and yet no fox bursts forth on to the open level of the pond, nor following pack pursuing their Actæon.[1] And perhaps at evening I see the hunters returning with a single brush[2] trailing from their sleigh for a trophy, seeking their inn. They tell me that if the fox would remain in the bosom of the frozen earth he would be safe, or if he would run in a straight line away no fox-hound could overtake him; but, having left his pursuers far behind, he stops to rest and listen till they come up, and when he runs he circles round to his old haunts, where

8. According to J. Lyndon Shanley, the manuscript attributes the quotation to the ornithologist John James Audubon (1785–1851), but it has not been located.
9. Water.

1. A Greek hunter who saw the goddess Artemis bathing; she transformed him into a stag, and his own dogs killed him.
2. Tail.

the hunters await him. Sometimes, however, he will run upon a wall many
rods, and then leap off far to one side, and he appears to know that water will
not retain his scent. A hunter told me that he once saw a fox pursued by
hounds burst out on to Walden when the ice was covered with shallow puddles, run part way across, and then return to the same shore. Ere long the
hounds arrived, but here they lost the scent. Sometimes a pack hunting by
themselves would pass my door, and circle round my house, and yelp and
hound without regarding me, as if afflicted by a species of madness, so that
nothing could divert them from the pursuit. Thus they circle until they fall
upon the recent trail of a fox, for a wise hound will forsake every thing else for
this. One day a man came to my hut from Lexington to inquire after his
hound that made a large track, and had been hunting for a week by himself.
But I fear that he was not the wiser for all I told him, for every time I attempted
to answer his questions he interrupted me by asking, "What do you do here?"
He had lost a dog, but found a man.

One old hunter who has a dry tongue, who used to come to bathe in Walden once every year when the water was warmest, and at such times looked in
upon me, told me, that many years ago he took his gun one afternoon and
went out for a cruise in Walden Wood; and as he walked the Wayland road
he heard the cry of hounds approaching, and ere long a fox leaped the wall
into the road, and as quick as thought leaped the other wall out of the road,
and his swift bullet had not touched him. Some way behind came an old
hound and her three pups in full pursuit, hunting on their own account, and
disappeared again in the woods. Late in the afternoon, as he was resting in the
thick woods south of Walden, he heard the voice of the hounds far over toward
Fair Haven still pursuing the fox and on they came, their hounding cry which
made all the woods ring sounding nearer and nearer, now from Well-Meadow,
now from the Baker Farm. For a long time he stood still and listened to their
music, so sweet to a hunter's ear, when suddenly the fox appeared, threading
the solemn aisles with an easy coursing pace, whose sound was concealed by
a sympathetic rustle of the leaves, swift and still, keeping the ground, leaving
his pursuers far behind; and, leaping upon a rock amid the woods, he sat erect
and listening, with his back to the hunter. For a moment compassion
restrained the latter's arm; but that was a short-lived mood, and as quick as
thought can follow thought his piece was levelled, and *whang!*—the fox rolling
over the rock lay dead on the ground. The hunter still kept his place and
listened to the hounds. Still on they came, and now the near woods resounded
through all their aisles with their demoniac cry. At length the old hound burst
into view with muzzle to the ground, and snapping the air as if possessed, and
ran directly to the rock; but spying the dead fox she suddenly ceased her
hounding, as if struck dumb with amazement, and walked round and round
him in silence; and one by one her pups arrived, and, like their mother, were
sobered into silence by the mystery. Then the hunter came forward and stood
in their midst, and the mystery was solved. They waited in silence while he
skinned the fox, then followed the brush a while, and at length turned off into
the woods again. That evening a Weston Squire came to the Concord hunter's
cottage to inquire for his hounds, and told how for a week they had been
hunting on their own account from Weston woods.[3] The Concord hunter told

3. Thoreau puns on the name of Squire Western, a character in Fielding's *Tom Jones*, and Weston, a town
near Concord.

him what he knew and offered him the skin; but the other declined it and departed. He did not find his hounds that night, but the next day learned that they had crossed the river and put up at a farm-house for the night, whence, having been well fed, they took their departure early in the morning.

The hunter who told me this could remember one Sam Nutting, who used to hunt bears on Fair Haven Ledges, and exchange their skins for rum in Concord village; who told him, even, that he had seen a moose there. Nutting had a famous fox-hound named Burgoyne,—he pronounced it Bugine,—which my informant used to borrow. In the "Wast Book"[4] of an old trader of this town, who was also a captain, town-clerk, and representative, I find the following entry. Jan. 18th, 1742–3, "John Melven Cr. by 1 Grey Fox 0-2-3;" they are not now found here; and in his ledger, Feb. 7th, 1743, Hezekiah Stratton has credit "by ½ a Catt skin 0-1-4½;" of course, a wild-cat, for Stratton was a sergeant in the old French war, and would not have got credit for hunting less noble game. Credit is given for deer skins also, and they were daily sold. One man still preserves the horns of the last deer that was killed in this vicinity, and another has told me the particulars of the hunt in which his uncle was engaged. The hunters were formerly a numerous and merry crew here. I remember well one gaunt Nimrod[5] who would catch up a leaf by the road-side and play a strain on it wilder and more melodious, if my memory serves me, than any hunting horn.

At midnight, when there was a moon, I sometimes met with hounds in my path prowling about the woods, which would skulk out of my way, as if afraid, and stand silent amid the bushes till I had passed.

Squirrels and wild mice disputed for my store of nuts. There were scores of pitch-pines around my house, from one to four inches in diameter, which had been gnawed by mice the previous winter,—a Norwegian winter for them, for the snow lay long and deep, and they were obliged to mix a large proportion of pine bark with their other diet. These trees were alive and apparently flourishing at mid-summer, and many of them had grown a foot, though completely girdled; but after another winter such were without exception dead. It is remarkable that a single mouse should thus be allowed a whole pine tree for its dinner, gnawing round instead of up and down it; but perhaps it is necessary in order to thin these trees, which are wont to grow up densely.

The hares (*Lepus Americanus*) were very familiar. One had her form under my house all winter, separated from me only by the flooring, and she startled me each morning by her hasty departure when I began to stir,—thump, thump, thump, striking her head against the floor timbers in her hurry. They used to come round my door at dusk to nibble the potato parings which I had thrown out, and were so nearly the color of the ground that they could hardly be distinguished when still. Sometimes in the twilight I alternately lost and recovered sight of one sitting motionless under my window. When I opened my door in the evening, off they would go with a squeak and a bounce. Near at hand they only excited my pity. One evening one sat by my door two paces from me, at first trembling with fear, yet unwilling to move; a poor wee thing, lean and bony, with ragged ears and sharp nose, scant tail and slender paws.

---

4. A "wast book" or "waste book" is a rough account book where all sorts of entries (sales, expenses, and so on) are made at the time of the transaction, with the intention of later posting them more formally.

5. Hunter; see Genesis 10.9: "He was a mighty hunter before the Lord: wherefore it is said, Even as Nimrod the mighty hunter before the Lord."

It looked as if Nature no longer contained the breed of nobler bloods, but stood on her last toes. Its large eyes appeared young and unhealthy, almost dropsical. I took a step, and lo, away it scud with an elastic spring over the snow crust, straightening its body and its limbs into graceful length, and soon put the forest between me and itself,—the wild free venison, asserting its vigor and the dignity of Nature. Not without reason was its slenderness. Such then was its nature. (*Lepus, levipes*, light-foot, some think.)

What is a country without rabbits and partridges? They are among the most simple and indigenous animal products; ancient and venerable families known to antiquity as to modern times; of the very hue and substance of Nature, nearest allied to leaves and to the ground,—and to one another; it is either winged or it is legged. It is hardly as if you had seen a wild creature when a rabbit or a partridge bursts away, only a natural one, as much to be expected as rustling leaves. The partridge and the rabbit are still sure to thrive, like true natives of the soil, whatever revolutions occur. If the forest is cut off, the sprouts and bushes which spring up afford them concealment, and they become more numerous than ever. That must be a poor country indeed that does not support a hare. Our woods teem with them both, and around every swamp may be seen the partridge or rabbit walk, beset with twiggy fences and horsehair snares, which some cow-boy tends.

The Pond in Winter

After a still winter night I awoke with the impression that some question had been put to me, which I had been endeavoring in vain to answer in my sleep, as what—how—when—where? But there was dawning Nature, in whom all creatures live, looking in at my broad windows with serene and satisfied face, and no question on *her* lips. I awoke to an answered question, to Nature and daylight. The snow lying deep on the earth dotted with young pines, and the very slope of the hill on which my house is placed, seemed to say, Forward! Nature puts no question and answers none which we mortals ask. She has long ago taken her resolution. "O Prince, our eyes contemplate with admiration and transmit to the soul the wonderful and varied spectacle of this universe. The night veils without doubt a part of this glorious creation; but day comes to reveal to us this great work, which extends from earth even into the plains of the ether."[6]

Then to my morning work. First I take an axe and pail and go in search of water, if that be not a dream. After a cold and snowy night it needed a divining rod to find it. Every winter the liquid and trembling surface of the pond, which was so sensitive to every breath, and reflected every light and shadow, becomes solid to the depth of a foot or a foot and a half, so that it will support the heaviest teams, and perchance the snow covers it to an equal depth, and it is not to be distinguished from any level field. Like the marmots in the surrounding hills, it closes its eye-lids and becomes dormant for three months or more. Standing on the snow-covered plain, as if in a pasture amid the hills, I cut my way first through a foot of snow, and then a foot of ice, and open a window under my feet, where, kneeling to drink, I look down into the quiet parlor of the fishes, pervaded by a softened light as through a window of ground

6. From an appendix to the *Mahabharata*, one of the Hindu epic poems, which Thoreau knew in a French translation.

glass, with its bright sanded floor the same as in summer; there a perennial waveless serenity reigns as in the amber twilight sky, corresponding to the cool and even temperament of the inhabitants. Heaven is under our feet as well as over our heads.

Early in the morning, while all things are crisp with frost, men come with fishing reels and slender lunch, and let down their fine lines through the snowy field to take pickerel and perch; wild men, who instinctively follow other fashions and trust other authorities than their townsmen, and by their goings and comings stitch towns together in parts where else they would be ripped. They sit and eat their luncheon in stout fear-naughts[7] on the dry oak leaves on the shore, as wise in natural lore as the citizen is in artificial. They never consulted with books, and know and can tell much less than they have done. The things which they practise are said not yet to be known. Here is one fishing for pickerel with grown perch for bait. You look into his pail with wonder as into a summer pond, as if he kept summer locked up at home, or knew where she had retreated. How, pray, did he get these in mid-winter? O, he got worms out of rotten logs since the ground froze, and so he caught them. His life itself passes deeper in Nature than the studies of the naturalist penetrate; himself a subject for the naturalist. The latter raises the moss and bark gently with his knife in search of insects; the former lays open logs to their core with his axe, and moss and bark fly far and wide. He gets his living by barking trees. Such a man has some right to fish, and I love to see Nature carried out in him. The perch swallows the grub-worm, the pickerel swallows the perch, and the fisherman swallows the pickerel; and so all the chinks in the scale of being are filled.

When I strolled around the pond in misty weather I was sometimes amused by the primitive mode which some ruder fisherman had adopted. He would perhaps have placed alder branches over the narrow holes in the ice, which were four or five rods apart and an equal distance from the shore, and having fastened the end of the line to a stick to prevent its being pulled through, have passed the slack line over a twig of the alder, a foot or more above the ice, and tied a dry oak leaf to it, which, being pulled down, would show when he had a bite. These alders loomed through the mist at regular intervals as you walked half way round the pond.

Ah, the pickerel of Walden! when I see them lying on the ice, or in the well which the fisherman cuts in the ice, making a little hole to admit the water, I am always surprised by their rare beauty, as if they were fabulous fishes, they are so foreign to the streets, even to the woods, foreign as Arabia to our Concord life. They possess a quite dazzling and transcendent beauty which separates them by a wide interval from the cadaverous cod and haddock whose fame is trumpeted in our streets. They are not green like the pines, nor gray like the stones, nor blue like the sky; but they have, to my eyes, if possible, yet rarer colors, like flowers and precious stones, as if they were the pearls, the animalized *nuclei* or crystals of the Walden water. They, of course, are Walden all over and all through; are themselves small Waldens in the animal kingdom, Waldenses.[8] It is surprising that they are caught here,—that in this deep and capacious spring, far beneath the rattling teams and chaises and tinkling sleighs that travel the Walden road, this great gold and emerald fish

7. I.e., dreadnoughts, heavy woolen coats.
8. Thoreau puns on the Waldenses, the much-persecuted Protestant sect of 12th-century France.

swims. I never chanced to see its kind in any market; it would be the cynosure of all eyes there. Easily, with a few convulsive quirks, they give up their watery ghosts, like a mortal translated before his time to the thin air of heaven.

As I was desirous to recover the long lost bottom of Walden Pond, I surveyed it carefully, before the ice broke up, early in '46, with compass and chain and sounding line. There have been many stories told about the bottom, or rather no bottom, of this pond, which certainly had no foundation for themselves. It is remarkable how long men will believe in the bottomlessness of a pond without taking the trouble to sound it. I have visited two such Bottomless Ponds in one walk in this neighborhood. Many have believed that Walden reached quite through to the other side of the globe. Some who have lain flat on the ice for a long time, looking down through the illusive medium, perchance with watery eyes into the bargain, and driven to hasty conclusions by the fear of catching cold in their breasts, have seen vast holes "into which a load of hay might be driven," if there were any body to drive it, the undoubted source of the Styx and entrance to the Infernal Regions from these parts. Others have gone down from the village with a "fifty-six"[9] and a wagon load of inch rope, but yet have failed to find any bottom; for while the "fifty-six" was resting by the way, they were paying out the rope in the vain attempt to fathom their truly immeasurable capacity for marvellousness. But I can assure my readers that Walden has a reasonably tight bottom at a not unreasonable, though at an unusual, depth. I fathomed it easily with a cod-line and a stone weighing about a pound and a half, and could tell accurately when the stone left the bottom, by having to pull so much harder before the water got underneath to help me. The greatest depth was exactly one hundred and two feet; to which may be added the five feet which it has risen since, making one hundred and seven. This is a remarkable depth for so small an area; yet not an inch of it can be spared by the imagination. What if all ponds were shallow? Would it not react on the minds of men? I am thankful that this pond was made deep and pure for a symbol. While men believe in the infinite some ponds will be thought to be bottomless.

A factory owner, hearing what depth I had found, thought that it could not be true, for, judging from his acquaintance with dams, sand would not lie at so steep an angle. But the deepest ponds are not so deep in proportion to their area as most suppose, and, if drained, would not leave very remarkable valleys. They are not like cups between the hills; for this one, which is so unusually deep for its area, appears in a vertical section through its centre not deeper than a shallow plate. Most ponds, emptied, would leave a meadow no more hollow than we frequently see. William Gilpin,[1] who is so admirable in all that relates to landscapes, and usually so correct, standing at the head of Loch Fyne, in Scotland, which he describes as "a bay of salt water, sixty or seventy fathoms deep, four miles in breadth," and about fifty miles long, surrounded by mountains, observes, "If we could have seen it immediately after the diluvian crash, or whatever convulsion of Nature occasioned it, before the waters gushed in, what a horrid chasm it must have appeared!

> So high as heaved the tumid hills, so low
> Down sunk a hollow bottom, broad, and deep,
> Capacious bed of waters[2]—."

---

9. A fifty-six-pound weight.
1. William Gilpin (1724–1804), *Observations on the*

Highlands of Scotland (1808).
2. Milton's *Paradise Lost* 7.288–90.

But if, using the shortest diameter of Loch Fyne, we apply these proportions to Walden, which, as we have seen, appears already in a vertical section only like a shallow plate, it will appear four times as shallow. So much for the *increased* horrors of the chasm of Loch Fyne when emptied. No doubt many a smiling valley with its stretching cornfields occupies exactly such a "horrid chasm," from which the waters have receded, though it requires the insight and the far sight of the geologist to convince the unsuspecting inhabitants of this fact. Often an inquisitive eye may detect the shores of a primitive lake in the low horizon hills, and no subsequent elevation of the plain has been necessary to conceal their history. But it is easiest, as they who work on the highways know, to find the hollows by the puddles after a shower. The amount of it is, the imagination, give it the least license, dives deeper and soars higher than Nature goes. So, probably, the depth of the ocean will be found to be very inconsiderable compared with its breadth.

As I sounded through the ice I could determine the shape of the bottom with grater accuracy than is possible in surveying harbors which do not freeze over, and I was surprised at its general regularity. In the deepest part there are several acres more level than almost any field which is exposed to the sun, wind and plough. In one instance, on a line arbitrarily chosen, the depth did not vary more than one foot in thirty rods; and generally, near the middle, I could calculate the variation for each one hundred feet in any direction beforehand within three or four inches. Some are accustomed to speak of deep and dangerous holes even in quiet sandy ponds like this, but the effect of water under these circumstances is to level all inequalities. The regularity of the bottom and its conformity to the shores and the range of the neighboring hills were so perfect that a distant promontory betrayed itself in the soundings quite across the pond, and its direction could be determined by observing the opposite shore. Cape becomes bar, and plain shoal, and valley and gorge deep water and channel.

When I had mapped the pond by the scale of ten rods to an inch, and put down the soundings, more than a hundred in all, I observed this remarkable coincidence. Having noticed that the number indicating the greatest depth was apparently in the centre of the map, I laid a rule on the map lengthwise, and then breadthwise, and found, to my surprise, that the line of greatest length intersected the line of greatest breadth *exactly* at the point of greatest depth, notwithstanding that the middle is so nearly level, the outline of the pond far from regular, and the extreme length and breadth were got by measuring into the coves; and I said to myself, Who knows but this hint would conduct to the deepest part of the ocean as well as of a pond or puddle? Is not this the rule also for the height of mountains, regarded as the opposite of valleys? We know that a hill is not highest at its narrowest part.

Of five coves, three, or all which had been sounded, were observed to have a bar quite across their mouths and deeper water within, so that the bay tended to be an expansion of water within the land not only horizontally but vertically, and to form a basin or independent pond, the direction of the two capes showing the course of the bar. Every harbor on the sea-coast, also, has its bar at its entrance. In proportion as the mouth of the cove was wider compared with its length, the water over the bar was deeper compared with that in the basin. Given, then, the length and breadth of the cove, and the character of the surrounding shore, and you have almost elements enough to make out a formula for all cases.

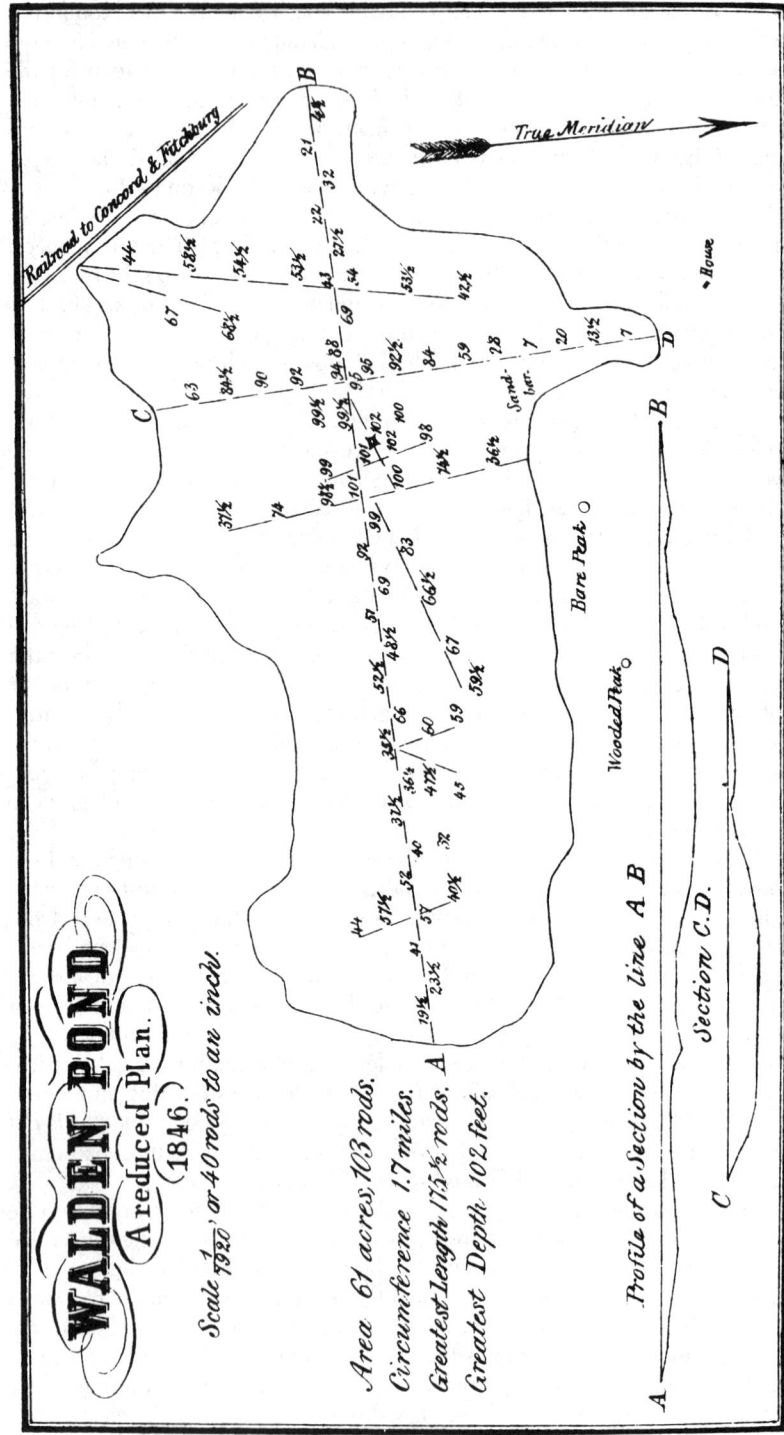

WALDEN POND
A reduced Plan.
(1846.)

Scale $\frac{1}{1920}$, or 40 rods to an inch.

Area 61 acres, 103 rods.
Circumference 1.7 miles;
Greatest Length 175½ rods, A
Greatest Depth 102 feet.

Profile of a Section by the line A B

Section C.D.

Railroad to Concord & Fitchburg

True Meridian

House

Bare Peak

Wooded Peak

Second bar.

In order to see how nearly I could guess, with this experience, at the deepest point in a pond, by observing the outlines of its surface and the character of its shores alone, I made a plan of White Pond, which contains about forty-one acres, and, like this, has no island in it, nor any visible inlet or outlet; and as the line of greatest breadth fell very near the line of least breadth, where two opposite capes approached each other and two opposite bays receded, I ventured to mark a point a short distance from the latter line, but still on the line of greatest length, as the deepest. The deepest part was found to be within one hundred feet of this, still farther in the direction to which I had inclined, and was only one foot deeper, namely, sixty feet. Of course, a stream running through, or an island in the pond, would make the problem much more complicated.

If we knew all the laws of Nature, we should need only one fact, or the description of one actual phenomenon, to infer all the particular results at that point. Now we know only a few laws, and our result is vitiated, not, of course, by any confusion or irregularity in Nature, but by our ignorance of essential elements in the calculation. Our notions of law and harmony are commonly confined to those instances which we detect; but the harmony which results from a far greater number of seemingly conflicting, but really concurring, laws, which we have not detected, is still more wonderful. The particular laws are as our points of view, as, to the traveller, a mountain outline varies with every step, and it has an infinite number of profiles, though absolutely but one form. Even when cleft or bored through it is not comprehended in its entireness.

What I have observed of the pond is no less true in ethics. It is the law of average. Such a rule of the two diameters not only guides us toward the sun in the system and the heart in man, but draw lines through the length and breadth of the aggregate of a man's particular daily behaviors and waves of life into his coves and inlets, and where they intersect will be the height or depth of his character. Perhaps we need only to know how his shores trend and his adjacent country or circumstances, to infer his depth and concealed bottom. If he is surrounded by mountainous circumstances, an Achillean shore,[3] whose peaks overshadow and are reflected in his bosom, they suggest a corresponding depth in him. But a low and smooth shore proves him shallow on that side. In our bodies, a bold projecting brow falls off to and indicates a corresponding depth of thought. Also there is a bar across the entrance of our every cove, or particular inclination; each is our harbor for a season, in which we are detained and partially land-locked. These inclinations are not whimsical usually, but their form, size, and direction are determined by the promontories of the shore, the ancient axes of elevation. When this bar is gradually increased by storms, tides, or currents, or there is a subsidence of the waters, so that it reaches to the surface, that which was at first but an inclination in the shore in which a thought was harbored becomes an individual lake, cut off from the ocean, wherein the thought secures its own conditions, changes, perhaps, from salt to fresh, becomes a sweet sea, dead sea, or a marsh. At the advent of each individual into this life, may we not suppose that such a bar has risen to the surface somewhere? It is true, we are such poor navigators that our thoughts, for the most part, stand off and on upon a harborless coast, are

---

3. Thessaly, the birthplace of Achilles, is mountainous.

conversant only with the bights[4] of the bays of poesy, or steer for the public ports of entry, and go into the dry docks of science, where they merely refit for this world, and no natural currents concur to individualize them.

As for the inlet or outlet of Walden, I have not discovered any but rain and snow and evaporation, though perhaps, with a thermometer and a line, such places may be found, for where the water flows into the pond it will probably be coldest in summer and warmest in winter. When the ice-men were at work here in '46-7, the cakes sent to the shore were one day rejected by those who were stacking them up there, not being thick enough to lie side by side with the rest; and the cutters thus discovered that the ice over a small space was two or three inches thinner than elsewhere, which made them think that there was an inlet there. They also showed me in another place what they thought was a "leach hole" through which the pond leaked out under a hill into a neighboring meadow, pushing me out on a cake of ice to see it. It was a small cavity under ten feet of water; but I think that I can warrant the pond not to need soldering till they find a worse leak than that. One has suggested, that if such a "leach hole" should be found, its connection with the meadow, if any existed, might be proved by conveying some colored powder or sawdust to the mouth of the hole, and then putting a strainer over the spring in the meadow, which would catch some of the particles carried through by the current.

While I was surveying, the ice, which was sixteen inches thick, undulated under a slight wind like water. It is well known that a level cannot be used on ice. At one rod from the shore its greatest fluctuation, when observed by means of a level on land directed toward a graduated staff on the ice, was three quarters of an inch, though the ice appeared firmly attached to the shore. It was probably greater in the middle. Who knows but if our instruments were delicate enough we might detect an undulation in the crust of the earth? When two legs of my level were on the shore and the third on the ice, and the sights were directed over the latter, a rise or fall of the ice of an almost infinitesimal amount made a difference of several feet on a tree across the pond. When I began to cut holes for sounding, there were three or four inches of water on the ice under a deep snow which had sunk it thus far; but the water began immediately to run into these holes, and continued to run for two days in deep streams, which wore away the ice on every side, and contributed essentially, if not mainly, to dry the surface of the pond; for, as the water ran in, it raised and floated the ice. This was somewhat like cutting a hole in the bottom of a ship to let the water out. When such holes freeze, and a rain succeeds, and finally a new freezing forms a fresh smooth ice over all, it is beautifully mottled internally by dark figures, shaped somewhat like a spider's web, what you may call ice rosettes, produced by the channels worn by the water flowing from all sides to a centre. Sometimes, also, when the ice was covered with shallow puddles, I saw a double shadow of myself, one standing on the head of the other, one on the ice, the other on the trees or hill-side.

While yet it is cold January, and snow and ice are thick and solid, the prudent landlord comes from the village to get ice to cool his summer drink; impressively, even pathetically wise, to foresee the heat and thirst of July now in January,—wearing a thick coat and mittens! when so many things are not provided for. It may be that he lays up no treasures[5] in this world which will

---

4. Bends or curves.   5. See n. 6, p. 1854.

cool his summer drink in the next. He cuts and saws the solid pond, unroofs the house of fishes, and carts off their very element and air, held fast by chains and stakes like corded wood, through the favoring winter air, to wintry cellars, to underlie the summer there. It looks like solidified azure, as, far off, it is drawn through the streets. These ice-cutters are a merry race, full of jest and sport, and when I went among them they were wont to invite me to saw pit-fashion with them, I standing underneath.

In the winter of '46–7 there came a hundred men of Hyperborean[6] extraction swoop down on to our pond one morning, with many car-loads of ungainly-looking farming tools, sleds, ploughs, drill barrows, turf-knives, spades, saws, rakes, and each man was armed with a double-pointed pike-staff, such as is not described in the New-England Farmer or the Cultivator. I did not know whether they had come to sow a crop of winter rye, or some other kind of grain recently introduced from Iceland. As I saw no manure, I judged that they meant to skim the land, as I had done, thinking the soil was deep and had lain fallow long enough. They said that a gentleman farmer, who was behind the scenes, wanted to double his money, which, as I understood, amounted to half a million already; but in order to cover each one of his dollars with another, he took off the only coat, ay, the skin itself, of Walden Pond in the midst of a hard winter. They went to work at once, ploughing, harrowing, rolling, furrowing, in admirable order, as if they were bent on making this a model farm; but when I was looking sharp to see what kind of seed they dropped into the furrow, a gang of fellows by my side suddenly began to hook up the virgin mould itself, with a peculiar jerk, clean down to the sand, or rather the water,—for it was a very springy soil,—indeed all the *terra firma* there was, and haul it away on sleds, and then I guessed that they must be cutting peat in a bog. So they came and went every day, with a peculiar shriek from the locomotive, from and to some point of the polar regions, as it seemed to me, like a flock of arctic snow-birds. But sometimes Squaw Walden had her revenge, and a hired man, walking behind his team, slipped through a crack in the ground down toward Tartarus, and he who was so brave before suddenly became but the ninth part of a man, almost gave up his animal heat, and was glad to take refuge in my house, and acknowledged that there was some virtue in a stove; or sometimes the frozen soil took a piece of steel out of a ploughshare, or a plough got set in the furrow and had to be cut out.

To speak literally, a hundred Irishmen, with Yankee overseers, came from Cambridge every day to get out the ice. They divided it into cakes by methods too well known to require description, and these, being sledded to the shore, were rapidly hauled off on to an ice platform, and raised by grappling irons and block and tackle, worked by horses, on to a stack, as surely as so many barrels of flour, and there placed evenly side by side, and row upon row, as if they formed the solid base of an obelisk designed to pierce the clouds. They told me that in a good day they could get out a thousand tons, which was the yield of about one acre. Deep ruts and "cradle holes" were worn in the ice, as on *terra firma*, by the passage of the sleds over the same track, and the horses invariably ate their oats out of cakes of ice hollowed out like buckets. They stacked up the cakes thus in the open air in a pile thirty-five feet high on one side and six or seven rods square, putting hay between the outside layers to exclude the air; for when the wind, though never so cold, finds a passage

6. In Greek mythology, the Hyperboreans lived far away in the icy north.

through, it will wear large cavities, leaving slight supports or studs only here and there, and finally topple it down. At first it looked like a vast blue fort or Valhalla; but when they began to tuck the coarse meadow hay into the crevices, and this became covered with rime and icicles, it looked like a venerable moss-grown and hoary ruin, built of azure-tinted marble, the abode of Winter, that old man we see in the almanac,—his shanty, as if he had a design to estivate[7] with us. They calculated that not twenty-five per cent. of this would reach its destination, and that two or three per cent. would be wasted in the cars. However, a still greater part of this heap had a different destiny from what was intended; for, either because the ice was found not to keep so well as was expected, containing more air than usual, or for some other reason, it never got to market. This heap, made in the winter of '46–7 and estimated to contain ten thousand tons, was finally covered with hay and boards; and though it was unroofed the following July, and a part of it carried off, the rest remaining exposed to the sun, it stood over that summer and the next winter, and was not quite melted till September 1848. Thus the pond recovered the greater part.

Like the water, the Walden ice, seen near at hand, has a green tint, but at a distance is beautifully blue, and you can easily tell it from the white ice of the river, or the merely greenish ice of some ponds, a quarter of a mile off. Sometimes one of those great cakes slips from the ice-man's sled into the village street, and lies there for a week like a great emerald, an object of interest to all passers. I have noticed that a portion of Walden which in the state of water was green will often, when frozen, appear from the same point of view blue. So the hollows about this pond will, sometimes, in the winter, be filled with a greenish water somewhat like its own, but the next day will have frozen blue. Perhaps the blue color of water and ice is due to the light and air they contain, and the most transparent is the bluest. Ice is an interesting subject for contemplation. They told me that they had some in the ice-houses at Fresh Pond five years old which was as good as ever. Why is it that a bucket of water soon becomes putrid, but frozen remains sweet forever? It is commonly said that this is the difference between the affections and the intellect.

Thus for sixteen days I saw from my window a hundred men at work like busy husbandmen, with teams and horses and apparently all the implements of farming, such a picture as we see on the first page of the almanac; and as often as I looked out I was reminded of the fable of the lark and the reapers, or the parable of the sower,[8] and the like; and now they are all gone, and in thirty days more, probably, I shall look from the same window on the pure sea-green Walden water there, reflecting the clouds and the trees, and sending up its evaporations in solitude, and no traces will appear that a man has ever stood there. Perhaps I shall hear a solitary loon laugh as he dives and plumes himself, or shall see a lonely fisher in his boat, like a floating leaf, beholding his form reflected in the waves, where lately a hundred men securely labored.

Thus it appears that the sweltering inhabitants of Charleston and New Orleans, of Madras and Bombay and Calcutta, drink at my well. In the morning I bathe my intellect in the stupendous and cosmogonal philosophy of the Bhagvat Geeta, since whose composition years of the gods have elapsed, and in comparison with which our modern world and its literature seem puny and

7. To pass the summer, especially in a state of dormancy.
8. See Matthew 13.3–43. The fable of the lark and the reapers is from La Fontaine's *Fables* 4.22, which Thoreau read in J. Payne Collier, *Old Ballads* (1843).

trivial; and I doubt if that philosophy is not to be referred to a previous state of existence, so remote is its sublimity from our conceptions. I lay down the book and go to my well for water, and lo! there I meet the servant of the Brahmin, priest of Brahma and Vishnu and Indra, who still sits in his temple on the Ganges reading the Vedas, or dwells at the root of a tree with his crust and water jug. I meet his servant come to draw water for his master, and our buckets as it were grate together in the same well. The pure Walden water is mingled with the sacred water of the Ganges. With favoring winds it is wafted past the site of the fabulous islands of Atlantis and the Hesperides, makes the periplus of Hanno, and, floating by Ternate and Tidore[9] and the mouth of the Persian Gulf, melts in the tropic gales of the Indian seas, and is landed in ports of which Alexander only heard the names.

Spring

The opening of large tracts by the ice-cutters commonly causes a pond to break up earlier; for the water, agitated by the wind, even in cold weather, wears away the surrounding ice. But such was not the effect on Walden that year, for she had soon got a thick new garment to take the place of the old. This pond never breaks up so soon as the others in this neighborhood, on account both of its grater depth and its having no stream passing through it to melt or wear away the ice. I never knew it to open in the course of a winter, not excepting that of '52–3, which gave the ponds so severe a trial. It commonly opens about the first of April, a week or ten days later than Flint's Pond and Fair-Haven, beginning to melt on the north side and in the shallower parts where it began to freeze. It indicates better than any water hereabouts the absolute progress of the season, being least affected by transient changes of temperature. A severe cold of a few days' duration in March may very much retard the opening of the former ponds, while the temperature of Walden increases almost uninterruptedly. A thermometer thrust into the middle of Walden on the 6th of March, 1847, stood at 32°, or freezing point; near the shore at 33°; in the middle of Flint's Pond, the same day, at 32½°; at a dozen rods from the shore, in shallow water, under ice a foot thick, at 36°. This difference of three and a half degrees between the temperature of the deep water and the shallow in the latter pond, and the fact that a great proportion of it is comparatively shallow, show why it should break up so much sooner than Walden. The ice in the shallowest part was at this time several inches thinner than in the middle. In mid-winter the middle had been the warmest and the ice thinnest there. So, also, every one who has waded about the shores of a pond in summer must have perceived how much warmer the water is close to the shore, where only three or four inches deep, than a little distance out, and on the surface where it is deep, than near the bottom. In spring the sun not only exerts an influence through the increased temperature of the air and earth, but its heat passes through ice a foot or more thick, and is reflected from the bottom in shallow water, and so also warms the water and melts the under side of the ice, at the same time that it is melting it more directly above,

9. Atlantis and the Hesperides are mythical islands in the Atlantic. To "make the periplus of Hanno" is to round the western coast of Africa and enter the Indian Ocean (Hanno, the Carthaginian navigator, supposedly made such a periplus in 480 B.C.). Ternate and Tidore are spice islands in Indonesia mentioned in Milton's *Paradise Lost* 2.639, and therefore, mythical enough themselves for it not to matter that Thoreau strains their geographical location.

making it uneven, and causing the air bubbles which it contains to extend themselves upward and downward until it is completely honey-combed, and at last disappears suddenly in a single spring rain. Ice has its grain as well as wood, and when a cake begins to rot or "comb," that is, assume the appearance of honey-comb, whatever may be its position, the air cells are at right angles with what was the water surface. Where there is a rock or a log rising near to the surface the ice over it is much thinner, and is frequently quite dissolved by this reflected heat; and I have been told that in the experiment at Cambridge to freeze water in a shallow wooden pond, though the cold air circulated underneath, and so had access to both sides, the reflection of the sun from the bottom more than counterbalanced this advantage. When a warm rain in the middle of the winter melts off the snow-ice from Walden, and leaves a hard dark or transparent ice on the middle, there will be a strip of rotten though thicker white ice, a rod or more wide, about the shores, created by this reflected heat. Also, as I have said, the bubbles themselves within the ice operate as burning glasses to melt the ice beneath.

The phenomena of the year take place every day in a pond on a small scale. Every morning, generally speaking, the shallow water is being warmed more rapidly than the deep, though it may not be made so warm after all, and every evening it is being cooled more rapidly until the morning. The day is an epitome of the year. The night is the winter, the morning and evening are the spring and fall, and the noon is the summer. The cracking and booming of the ice indicate a change of temperature. One pleasant morning after a cold night, February 24th, 1850, having gone to Flint's Pond to spend the day, I noticed with surprise, that when I struck the ice with the head of my axe, it resounded like a gong for many rods around, or as if I had struck on a tight drum-head. The pond began to boom about an hour after sunrise, when it felt the influence of the sun's rays slanted upon it from the hills; it stretched itself and yawned like a waking man with a gradually increasing tumult, which was kept up three or four hours. It took a short siesta at noon, and boomed once more toward night, as the sun was withdrawing his influence. In the right stage of the weather a pond fires its evening gun with great regularity. But in the middle of the day, being full of cracks, and the air also being less elastic, it had completely lost its resonance, and probably fishes and muskrats could not then have been stunned by a blow on it. The fishermen say that the "thundering of the pond" scares the fishes and prevents their biting. The pond does not thunder every evening, and I cannot tell surely when to expect its thundering; but though I may perceive no difference in the weather, it does. Who would have suspected so large and cold and thick-skinned a thing to be so sensitive? Yet it has its law to which it thunders obedience when it should as surely as the buds expand in the spring. The earth is all alive and covered with papillæ. The largest pond is as sensitive to atmospheric changes as the globule of mercury in its tube.

One attraction in coming to the woods to live was that I should have leisure and opportunity to see the spring come in. The ice in the pond at length begins to be honey-combed, and I can set my heel in it as I walk. Fogs and rains and warmer suns are gradually melting the snow; the days have grown sensibly longer; and I see how I shall get through the winter without adding to my wood-pile, for large fires are no longer necessary. I am on the alert for the first signs of spring, to hear the chance note of some arriving bird, or the striped squirrel's chirp, for his stores must be now nearly exhausted, or see the woodchuck venture out of his winter quarters. On the 13th of March, after I had heard the bluebird, song-sparrow, and red-wing, the ice was still nearly a foot thick. As the weather grew warmer, it was not sensibly worn away by the water, nor broken up and floated off as in rivers, but, though it was completely melted for half a rod in width about the shore, the middle was merely honeycombed and saturated with water, so that you could put your foot through it when six inches thick; but by the next day evening, perhaps, after a warm rain followed by fog, it would have wholly disappeared, all gone off with the fog, spirited away. One year I went across the middle only five days before it disappeared entirely. In 1845 Walden was first completely open on the 1st of April; in '46, the 25th of March; in '47, the 8th of April; in '51, the 28th of March; in '52, the 18th of April; in '53, the 23rd of March; in '54, about the 7th of April.

Every incident connected with the breaking up of the rivers and ponds and the settling of the weather is particularly interesting to us who live in a climate of so great extremes. When the warmer days come, they who dwell near the river hear the ice crack at night with a startling whoop as loud as artillery, as if its icy fetters were rent from end to end, and within a few days see it rapidly going out. So the alligator comes out of the mud with quakings of the earth. One old man, who has been a close observer of Nature, and seems as thoroughly wise in regard to all her operations as if she had been put upon the stocks when he was a boy, and he had helped to lay her keel,—who has come to his growth, and can hardly acquire more of natural lore if he should live to the age of Methuselah[1]—told me, and I was surprised to hear him express wonder at any of Nature's operations, for I thought that there were no secrets between them, that one spring day he took his gun and boat, and thought that he would have a little sport with the ducks. There was ice still on the meadows, but it was all gone out of the river, and he dropped down without obstruction from Sudbury, where he lived, to Fair-Haven Pond, which he found, unexpectedly, covered for the most part with a firm field of ice. It was a warm day, and he was surprised to see so great a body of ice remaining. Not seeing any ducks, he hid his boat on the north or back side of an island in the pond, and then concealed himself in the bushes on the south side, to await them. The ice was melted for three or four rods from the shore, and there was a smooth and warm sheet of water, with a muddy bottom, such as the ducks love, within, and he thought it likely that some would be along pretty soon. After he had lain still there about an hour he heard a low and seemingly very distant sound, but singularly grand and impressive, unlike any thing he had ever heard, gradually swelling and increasing as if it would have a universal and memorable ending, a sullen rush and roar, which seemed to him all at once like the sound of a vast body of fowl coming in to settle there, and, seizing his gun, he started up in haste and excited; but he found, to his surprise, that the whole body of the ice had started while he lay there, and drifted in to the shore, and the sound he had heard was made by its edge grating on the shore,—at first gently nibbled and crumbled off, but at length heaving up and scattering its wrecks along the island to a considerable height before it came to a stand still.

At length the sun's rays have attained the right angle, and warm winds blow

1. "And the days of Methuselah were nine hundred sixty and nine years: and he died" (Genesis 5.27).

up mist and rain and melt the snow banks, and the sun dispersing the mist smiles on a checkered landscape of russet and white smoking with incense, through which the traveller picks his way from islet to islet, cheered by the music of a thousand tinkling rills and rivulets whose veins are filled with the blood of winter which they are bearing off.

Few phenomena gave me more delight than to observe the forms which thawing sand and clay assume in flowing down the sides of a deep cut on the railroad through which I passed on my way to the village, a phenomenon not very common on so large a scale, though the number of freshly exposed banks of the right material must have been greatly multiplied since railroads were invented. The material was sand of every degree of fineness and of various rich colors, commonly mixed with a little clay. When the frost comes out in the spring, and even in a thawing day in the winter, the sand begins to flow down the slopes like lava, sometimes bursting out through the snow and overflowing it where no sand was to be seen before. Innumerable little streams overlap and interlace one with another, exhibiting a sort of hybrid product, which obeys half way the law of currents, and half way that of vegetation. As it flows it takes the forms of sappy leaves or vines, making heaps of pulpy sprays a foot or more in depth, and resembling, as you look down on them, the laciniated lobed and imbricated[2] thalluses of some lichens; or you are reminded of coral, of leopards' paws or birds' feet, of brains or lungs or bowels, and excrements of all kinds. It is a truly *grotesque* vegetation, whose forms and color we see imitated in bronze, a sort of architectural foliage more ancient and typical than acanthus, chiccory, ivy, vine, or any vegetable leaves; destined perhaps, under some circumstances, to become a puzzle to future geologists. The whole cut impressed me as if it were a cave with its stalactites laid open to the light. The various shades of the sand are singularly rich and agreeable, embracing the different iron colors, brown, gray, yellowish, and reddish. When the flowing mass reaches the drain at the foot of the bank it spreads out flatter into *strands*, the separate streams losing their semi-cylindrical form and gradually becoming more flat and broad, running together as they are more moist, till they form an almost flat *sand*, still variously and beautifully shaded, but in which you can trace the original forms of vegetation; till at length, in the water itself, they are converted into *banks*, like those formed off the mouths of rivers, and the forms of vegetation are lost in the ripple marks on the bottom.

The whole bank, which is from twenty to forty feet high, is sometimes overlaid with a mass of this kind of foliage, or sandy rupture, for a quarter of a mile on one or both sides, the produce of one spring day. What makes this sand foliage remarkable is its springing into existence thus suddenly. When I see on the one side the inert bank,—for the sun acts on one side first,—and on the other this luxuriant foliage, the creation of an hour, I am affected as if in a peculiar sense I stood in the laboratory of the Artist who made the world and me,—had come to where he was still at work, sporting on this bank, and with excess of energy strewing his fresh designs about. I feel as if I were nearer to the vitals of the globe, for this sandy overflow is something such a foliaceous mass as the vitals of the animal body. You find thus in the very sands an anticipation of the vegetable leaf. No wonder that the earth expresses itself outwardly in leaves, it so labors with the idea inwardly. The atoms have

2. Lapped over in regular order like roof tiles. "Laciniated": deeply, irregularly lobed.

already learned this law, and are pregnant by it. The overhanging leaf sees here its prototype. *Internally*, whether in the globe or animal body, it is a moist thick *lobe*, a word especially applicable to the liver and lungs and the *leaves* of fat. (λείβω, *labor, lapsus*, to flow or slip downward, a lapsing; λοβο., *globus*, lobe, globe; also lap, flap, and many other words,) *externally* a dry thin *leaf*, even as the *f* and *v* are a pressed and dried *b*. The radicals of lobe are *lb*, the soft mass of the *b* (single lobed, or B, double lobed,) with a liquid *l* behind it pressing it forward. In globe, *glb*, the guttural *g* adds to the meaning the capacity of the throat. The feathers and wings of birds are still drier and thinner leaves. Thus, also, you pass from the lumpish grub in the earth to the airy and fluttering butterfly. The very globe continually transcends and translates itself, and becomes winged in its orbit. Even ice begins with delicate crystal leaves, as if it had flowed into moulds which the fronds of water plants have impressed on the watery mirror. The whole tree itself is but one leaf, and rivers are still vaster leaves whose pulp is intervening earth, and towns and cities are the ova of insects in their axils.

When the sun withdraws the sand ceases to flow, but in the morning the streams will start once more and branch and branch again into a myriad of others. You here see perchance how blood vessels are formed. If you look closely you observe that first there pushes forward from the thawing mass a stream of softened sand with a drop-like point, like the ball of the finger, feeling its way slowly and blindly downward, until at last with more heat and moisture, as the sun gets higher, the moist fluid portion, in its effort to obey the law to which the most inert also yields, separates from the latter and forms for itself a meandering channel or artery within that, in which is seen a little silvery stream glancing like lightning from one stage of pulpy leaves or branches to another, and ever and anon swallowed up in the sand. It is wonderful how rapidly yet perfectly the sand organizes itself as it flows, using the best material its mass affords to form the sharp edges of its channel. Such are the sources of rivers. In the silicious matter which the water deposits is perhaps the bony system, and in the still finer soil and organic matter the fleshy fibre or cellular tissue. What is man but a mass of thawing clay? The ball of the human finger is but a drop congealed. The fingers and toes flow to their extent from the thawing mass of the body. Who knows what the human body would expand and flow out to under a more genial heaven? Is not the hand a spreading *palm* leaf with its lobes and veins? The ear may be regarded, fancifully, as a lichen, *umbilicaria*, on the side of the head, with its lobe or drop. The lip (*labium* from *labor* (?)) laps or lapses from the sides of the cavernous mouth. The nose is a manifest congealed drop or stalactite. The chin is a still larger drop, the confluent dripping of the face. The cheeks are a slide from the brows into the valley of the face, opposed and diffused by the cheek bones. Each rounded lobe of the vegetable leaf, too, is a thick and now loitering drop, larger or smaller; the lobes are the fingers of the leaf; and as many lobes as it has, in so many directions it tends to flow, and more heat or other genial influences would have caused it to flow yet farther.

Thus it seemed that this one hillside illustrated the principle of all the operations of Nature. The Maker of this earth but patented a leaf. What Champollion[3] will decipher this hieroglyphic for us, that we may turn over a new leaf

---

3. Jean François Champollion (1790–1832), French archaeologist whose deciphering of the inscriptions on the Rosetta stone fueled great popular interest in Egyptology.

at last? This phenomenon is more exhilarating to me than the luxuriance and fertility of vineyards. True, it is somewhat excrementitious in its character, and there is no end to the heaps of liver, lights and bowels, as if the globe were turned wrong side outward; but this suggests at least that Nature has some bowels, and there again is mother of humanity.[4] This is the frost coming out of the ground; this is Spring. It precedes the green and flowery spring, as mythology precedes regular poetry. I know of nothing more purgative of winter fumes and indigestions. It convinces me that Earth is still in her swaddling clothes, and stretches forth baby fingers on every side. Fresh curls spring from the baldest brow. There is nothing inorganic. These foliaceous heaps lie along the bank like the slag of a furnace, showing that Nature is "in full blast" within. The earth is not a mere fragment of dead history, stratum upon stratum like the leaves of a book, to be studied by geologists and antiquaries chiefly, but living poetry like the leaves of a tree, which precede flowers and fruit,— not a fossil earth, but a living earth; compared with whose great central life all animal and vegetable life is merely parasitic. Its throes will heave our exuviæ from their graves. You may melt your metals and cast them into the most beautiful moulds you can; they will never excite me like the forms which this molten earth flows out into. And not only it, but the institutions upon it, are plastic like clay in the hands of the potter.

Ere long, not only on these banks, but on every hill and plain and in every hollow, the frost comes out of the ground like a dormant quadruped from its burrow, and seeks the sea with music, or migrates to other climes in clouds. Thaw with his gentle persuasion is more powerful than Thor with his hammer.[5] The one melts, the other but breaks in pieces.

When the ground was partially bare of snow, and a few warm days had dried its surface somewhat, it was pleasant to compare the first tender signs of the infant year just peeping forth with the stately beauty of the withered vegetation which had withstood the winter,—life-everlasting, golden-rods, pinweeds, and graceful wild grasses, more obvious and interesting frequently than in summer even, as if their beauty was not ripe till then; even cotton-grass, cat-tails, mulleins, johnswort, hard-hack, meadow-sweet, and other strong stemmed plants, those unexhausted granaries which entertain the earliest birds,—decent weeds,[6] at least, which widowed Nature wears. I am particularly attracted by the arching and sheaf-like top of the wool-grass; it brings back the summer to our winter memories, and is among the forms which art loves to copy, and which, in the vegetable kingdom, have the same relation to types already in the mind of man that astronomy has. It is an antique style older than Greek or Egyptian. Many of the phenomena of Winter are suggestive of an inexpressible tenderness and fragile delicacy. We are accustomed to hear this king described as a rude and boisterous tyrant; but with the gentleness of a lover he adorns the tresses of Summer.

At the approach of spring the red-squirrels got under my house, two at a time, directly under my feet as I sat reading or writing, and kept up the queerest chuckling and chirruping and vocal pirouetting and gurgling sounds that ever were heard; and when I stamped they only chirruped the louder, as

4. Thoreau puns on the sense of "bowels" as the seat of compassion. "Lights": lungs.
5. As a New Englander, Thoreau apparently pro-

nounced *thaw* to sound like *Thor*, the Norse god of thunder.
6. Mourning garments.

if past all fear and respect in their mad pranks, defying humanity to stop them. No you don't—chickaree—chickaree. They were wholly deaf to my arguments, or failed to perceive their force, and fell into a strain of invective that was irresistible.

The first sparrow of spring! The year beginning with younger hope than ever! The faint silvery warblings heard over the partially bare and moist fields from the blue-bird, the song-sparrow, and the red-wing, as if the last flakes of winter tinkled as they fell! What at such a time are histories, chronologies, traditions, and all written revelations? The brooks sing carols and glees to the spring. The marsh-hawk sailing low over the meadow is already seeking the first slimy life that awakes. The sinking sound of melting snow is heard in all dells, and the ice dissolves apace in the ponds. The grass flames up on the hillsides like a spring fire,—"et primitus oritur herba imbribus primoribus evocata,"[7]—as if the earth sent forth an inward heat to greet the returning sun; not yellow but green is the color of its flame;—the symbol of perpetual youth, the grass-blade, like a long green ribbon, streams from the sod into the summer, checked indeed by the frost, but anon pushing on again, lifting its spear of last year's hay with the fresh life below. It grows as steadily as the rill oozes out of the ground. It is almost identical with that, for in the growing days of June, when the rills are dry, the grass blades are their channels, and from year to year the herds drink at this perennial green stream, and the mower draws from it betimes their winter supply. So our human life but dies down to its roots, and still puts forth its green blade to eternity.

Walden is melting apace. There is a canal two rods wide along the northerly and westerly sides, and wider still at the east end. A great field of ice has cracked off from the main body. I hear a song-sparrow singing from the bushes on the shore,—*olit, olit, olit,—chip, chip, chip, che char,—che wiss, wiss, wiss.* He too is helping to crack it. How handsome the great sweeping curves in the edge of the ice, answering somewhat to those of the shore, but more regular! It is unusually hard, owing to the recent severe but transient cold, and all watered or waved like a palace floor. But the wind slides eastward over its opaque surface in vain, till it reaches the living surface beyond. It is glorious to behold this ribbon of water sparkling in the sun, the bare face of the pond full of glee and youth, as if it spoke the joy of the fishes within it, and of the sands on its shore,—a silvery sheen as from the scales of a *leuciscus*, as it were all one active fish. Such is the contrast between winter and spring. Walden was dead and is alive again. But this spring it broke up more steadily, as I have said.

The change from storm and winter to serene and mild weather, from dark and sluggish hours to bright and elastic ones, is a memorable crisis which all things proclaim. It is seemingly instantaneous at last. Suddenly an influx of light filled my house, though the evening was at hand, and the clouds of winter still overhung it, and the eaves were dripping with sleety rain. I looked out the window, and lo! where yesterday was cold gray ice there lay the transparent pond already calm and full of hope as on a summer evening, reflecting a summer evening sky in its bosom, though none was visible overhead, as if it had intelligence with some remote horizon. I heard a robin in the distance, the first I had heard for many a thousand years, methought, whose note I shall

---

7. Varro's *Rerum rusticarum* 2.2.14; Thoreau goes on to translate.

not forget for many a thousand more,—the same sweet and powerful song of
yore. O the evening robin, at the end of a New England summer day! If I
could ever find the twig he sits upon! I mean *he*; I mean *the twig*. This at least
is not the *Turdus migratorius*. The pitch-pines and shrub-oaks about my
house, which had so long drooped, suddenly resumed their several characters,
looked brighter, greener, and more erect and alive, as if effectually cleansed
and restored by the rain. I knew that it would not rain any more. You may tell
by looking at any twig of the forest, ay, at your very wood-pile, whether its
winter is past or not. As it grew darker, I was startled by the *honking* of geese
flying low over the woods, like weary travellers getting in late from southern
lakes, and indulging at last in unrestrained complaint and mutual consolation.
Standing at my door, I could hear the rush of their wings; when, driving
toward my house, they suddenly spied my light, and with hushed clamor
wheeled and settled in the pond. So I came in, and shut the door, and passed
my first spring night in the woods.

In the morning I watched the geese from the door through the mist, sailing
in the middle of the pond, fifty rods off, so large and tumultuous that Walden
appeared like an aritifical pond for their amusement. But when I stood on the
shore they at once rose up with a great flapping of wings at the signal of their
commander, and when they had got into rank circled about over my head,
twenty-nine of them, and then steered straight to Canada, with a regular *honk*
from the leader at intervals, trusting to break their fast in muddier pools. A
"plump" of ducks rose at the same time and took the route to the north in the
wake of their noisier cousins.

For a week I heard the circling groping clangor of some solitary goose in the
foggy mornings, seeking its companion, and still peopling the woods with the
sound of a larger life than they could sustain. In April the pigeons were seen
again flying express in small flocks, and in due time I heard the martins twittering over my clearing, though it had not seemed that the township contained
so many that it could afford me any, and I fancied that they were peculiarly of
the ancient race that dwelt in hollow trees ere white men came. In almost all
climes the tortoise and the frog are among the precursors and heralds of this
season, and birds fly with song and glancing plumage, and plants spring and
bloom, and winds blow, to correct this slight oscillation of the poles and preserve the equilibrium of Nature.

As every season seems best to us in its turn, so the coming in of spring is like
the creation of Cosmos out of Chaos and the realization of the Golden Age.—

> "Eurus ad Auroram, Nabathæaque regna recessit,
> Persidaque, et radiis juga subdita matutinis."

> "The East-Wind withdrew to Aurora and the Nabathæan kingdom,
> And the Persian, and the ridges placed under the morning rays.

> Man was born. Whether that Artificer of things,
> The origin of a better world, made him from the divine seed;
> Or the earth being recent and lately sundered from the high
> Ether, retained some seeds of cognate heaven."[8]

---

8. Ovid's *Metamorphoses* 1.61–62, 78–81.

A single gentle rain makes the grass many shades greener. So our prospects brighten on the influx of better thoughts. We should be blessed if we lived in the present always, and took advantage of every accident that befell us, like the grass which confesses the influence of the slightest dew that falls on it; and did not spend our time in atoning for the neglect of past opportunities, which we call doing our duty. We loiter in winter while it is already spring. In a pleasant spring morning all men's sins are forgiven. Such a day is a truce to vice. While such a sun holds out to burn, the vilest sinner may return. Through our own recovered innocence we discern the innocence of our neighbors. You may have known your neighbor yesterday for a thief, a drunkard, or a sensualist, and merely pitied or despised him, and despaired of the world; but the sun shines bright and warm this first spring morning, re-creating the world, and you meet him at some serene work, and see how his exhausted and debauched veins expand with still joy and bless the new day, feel the spring influence with the innocence of infancy, and all his faults are forgotten. There is not only an atmosphere of good will about him, but even a savor of holiness grop-ing for expression, blindly and ineffectually perhaps, like a new-born instinct, and for a short hour the south hill-side echoes to no vulgar jest. You see some innocent fair shoots preparing to burst from his gnarled rind and try another year's life, tender and fresh as the youngest plant. Even he has entered into the joy of his Lord. Why the jailer does not leave open his prison doors,—why the judge does not dismiss his case,—why the preacher does not dismiss his congregation! It is because they do not obey the hint which God gives them, nor accept the pardon which he freely offers to all.

"A return to goodness produced each day in the tranquil and beneficent breath of the morning, causes that in respect to the love of virtue and the hatred of vice, one approaches a little the primitive nature of man, as the sprouts of the forest which has been felled. In like manner the evil which one does in the interval of a day prevents the germs of virtues which began to spring up again from developing themselves and destroys them.

"After the germs of virtue have thus been prevented many times from devel-oping themselves, then the beneficent breath of evening does not suffice to preserve them. As soon as the breath of evening does not suffice longer to preserve them, then the nature of man does not differ much from that of the brute. Men seeing the nature of this man like that of the brute, think that he has never possessed the innate faculty of reason. Are those the true and natural sentiments of man?"[9]

> "The Golden Age was first created, which without any avenger
> Spontaneously without law cherished fidelity and rectitude.
> Punishment and fear were not; nor were threatening words read
> On suspended brass; nor did the suppliant crowd fear
> The words of their judge; but were safe without an avenger.
> Not yet the pine felled on its mountains had descended
> To the liquid waves that it might see a foreign world,
> And mortals knew no shore but their own.
>
> .   .   .
>
> There was eternal spring, and placid zephyrs with warm
> Blasts soothed the flowers born without seed."[1]

---

9. Mencius's (Meng-tzu's) *Works* 6.1.   1. Ovid's *Metamorphoses* 1.89–96, 107–8.

On the 29th of April, as I was fishing from the bank of the river near the Nine-Acre-Corner bridge, standing on the quaking grass and willow roots, where the muskrats lurk, I heard a singular rattling sound, somewhat like that of the sticks which boys play with their fingers, when, looking up, I observed a very slight and graceful hawk, like a night-hawk, alternately soaring like a ripple and tumbling a rod or two over and over, showing the underside of its wings, which gleamed like a satin ribbon in the sun, or like the pearly inside of a shell. This sight reminded me of falconry and what nobleness and poetry are associated with that sport. The Merlin[2] it seemed to me it might be called: but I care not for its name. It was the most ethereal flight I had ever witnessed. It did not simply flutter like a butterfly, nor soar like the larger hawks, but it sported with proud reliance in the fields of air; mounting again and again with its strange chuckle, it repeated its free and beautiful fall, turning over and over like a kite, and then recovering from its lofty tumbling, as if it had never set its foot on *terra firma*. It appeared to have no companion in the universe,— sporting there alone,—and to need none but the morning and the ether with which it played. It was not lonely, but made all the earth lonely beneath it. Where was the parent which hatched it, its kindred, and its father in the heavens? The tenant of the air, it seemed related to the earth but by an egg hatched some time in the crevice of a crag;—or was its native nest made in the angle of a cloud, woven of the rainbow's trimmings and the sunset sky, and lined with some soft midsummer haze caught up from earth? Its eyry now some cliffy cloud.

Beside this I got a rare mess of golden and silver and bright cupreous[3] fishes, which looked like a string of jewels. Ah! I have penetrated to those meadows on the morning of many a first spring day, jumping from hummock to hummock, from willow root to willow root, when the wild river valley and the woods were bathed in so pure and bright a light as would have waked the dead, if they had been slumbering in their graves, as some suppose. Their needs no stronger proof of immortality. All things must live in such a light. O Death, where was thy sting? O Grave, where was thy victory, then?[4]

Our village life would stagnate if it were not for the unexplored forests and meadows which surround it. We need the tonic of wildness,—to wade sometimes in marshes where the bittern and the meadow-hen lurk, and hear the booming of the snipe; to smell the whispering sedge where only some wilder and more solitary fowl builds her nest, and the mink crawls with its belly close to the ground. At the same time that we are earnest to explore and learn all things, we require that all things be mysterious and unexplorable, that land and sea be infinitely wild, unsurveyed and unfathomed by us because unfathomable. We can never have enough of Nature. We must be refreshed by the sight of inexhaustible vigor, vast and Titanic features, the sea-coast with its wrecks, the wilderness with its living and its decaying trees, the thunder cloud, and the rain which lasts three weeks and produces freshets. We need to witness our own limits transgressed, and some life pasturing freely where we never wander. We are cheered when we observe the vulture feeding on the carrion which disgusts and disheartens us and deriving health and strength from the

2. In Arthurian legend, Merlin is a magician and soothsayer, but Thoreau uses him as Emerson does in the poem *Merlin*, as a master poet. The hawk is usually taken as Thoreau's ideal image of himself. A merlin is also a small falcon or pigeon hawk.

3. Coppery.

4. 1 Corinthians 15.55: "O death, where is thy sting? O grave, where is thy victory?"

repast. There was a dead horse in the hollow by the path to my house, which compelled me sometimes to go out of my way, especially in the night when the air was heavy, but the assurance it gave me of the strong appetite and inviolable health of Nature was my compensation for this. I love to see that Nature is so rife with life that myriads can be afforded to be sacrificed and suffered to prey on one another; that tender organizations can be so serenely squashed out of existence like pulp,—tadpoles which herons gobble up, and tortoises and toads run over in the road; and that sometimes it has rained flesh and blood! With the liability to accident, we must see how little account is to be made of it. The impression made on a wise man is that of universal inno-cence. Poison is not poisonous after all, nor are any wounds fatal. Compassion is a very untenable ground. It must be expeditious. Its pleadings will not bear to be stereotyped.

Early in May, the oaks, hickories, maples, and other trees, just putting out amidst the pine woods around the pond, imparted a brightness like sunshine to the landscape, especially in cloudy days, as if the sun were breaking through mists and shining faintly on the hill-sides here and there. On the third or fourth of May I saw a loon in the pond, and during the first week of the month I heard the whippoorwill, the brown-thrasher, the veery, the wood-pewee, the chewink, and other birds. I had heard the wood-thrush long before. The phœbe had already come once more and looked in at my door and window, to see if my house was cavern-like enough for her, sustaining herself on hum-ming wings with clinched talons, as if she held by the air, while she surveyed the premises. The sulphur-like pollen of the pitch-pine soon covered the pond and the stones and rotten wood along the shore, so that you could have col-lected a barrel-ful. This is the "sulphur showers" we hear of. Even in Calidas' drama of Sacontala, we read of "rills dyed yellow with the golden dust of the lotus."[5] And so the seasons went rolling on into summer, as one rambles into higher and higher grass.

Thus was my first year's life in the woods completed; and the second year was similar to it. I finally left Walden September 6th, 1847.

Conclusion

To the sick the doctors wisely recommend a change of air and scenery. Thank Heaven, here is not all the world. The buck-eye does not grow in New England, and the mocking-bird is rarely heard here. The wild-goose is more of a cosmopolite than we; he breaks his fast in Canada, takes a luncheon in the Ohio, and plumes himself for the night in a southern bayou. Even the bison, to some extent, keeps pace with the seasons, cropping the pastures of the Colorado only till a greener and sweeter grass awaits him by the Yel-lowstone. Yet we think that if rail-fences are pulled down, and stone-walls piled up on our farms, bounds are henceforth set to our lives and our fates decided. If you are chosen town-clerk, forsooth, you cannot go to Tierra del Fuego[6] this summer: but you may go to the land of infernal fire nevertheless. The universe is wider than our views of it.

Yet we should oftener look over the tafferel of our craft, like curious passen-

5. Sir William Jones's translation of *Sacontalá*, act 5, by Cálidás (5th century), Hindu writer.
6. Thoreau puns on the meaning of the name of the

archipelago at the southern tip of South America: land of fire (Spanish).

gers, and not make the voyage like stupid sailors picking oakum.[7] The other side of the globe is but the home of our correspondent. Our voyaging is only great-circle sailing, and the doctors prescribe for diseases of the skin merely. One hastens to Southern Africa to chase the giraffe; but surely that is not the game he would be after. How long, pray, would a man hunt giraffes if he could? Snipes and woodcocks also may afford rare sport; but I trust it would be nobler game to shoot one's self.—

> "Direct your eye sight inward, and you'll find
> A thousand regions in your mind
> Yet undiscovered. Travel them, and be
> Expert in home-cosmography."[8]

What does Africa,—what does the West stand for? Is not our own interior white on the chart? black though it may prove, like the coast, when discovered. Is it the source of the Nile, or the Niger, or the Mississippi, or a North West Passage around this continent, that we would find? Are these the problems which most concern mankind? Is Franklin[9] the only man who is lost, that his wife should be so earnest to find him? Does Mr. Grinnell[1] know where he himself is? Be rather the Mungo Park, the Lewis and Clarke and Frobisher,[2] of your own streams and oceans; explore your own higher latitudes,—with shiploads of preserved meats to support you, if they be necessary; and pile the empty cans sky-high for a sign. Were preserved meats invented to preserve meat merely? Nay, be a Columbus to whole new continents and worlds within you, opening new channels, not of trade, but of thought. Every man is the lord of a realm beside which the earthly empire of the Czar is but a petty state, a hummock left by the ice. Yet some can be patriotic who have no *self*-respect, and sacrifice the greater to the less. They love the soil which makes their graves, but have no sympathy with the spirit which may still animate their clay. Patriotism is a maggot in their heads. What was the meaning of that South-Sea Exploring Expedition,[3] with all its parade and expense, but an indirect recognition of the fact, that there are continents and seas in the moral world, to which every man is an isthmus or an inlet, yet unexplored by him, but that it is easier to sail many thousand miles through cold and storm and cannibals, in a government ship, with five hundred men and boys to assist one, than it is to explore the private sea, the Atlantic and Pacific Ocean of one's being alone.—

> "Erret, et extremos alter scrutetur Iberos.
> Plus habet hic vitæ, plus habet ille viæ."[4]

---

7. Common nautical busywork: picking old rope apart so the pieces of hemp could be tarred and used for calking.

8. William Habington (1605–1654), *To My Honoured Friend Sir Ed. P. Knight.*

9. Sir John Franklin (1785–1847), lost on a British expedition to the Arctic.

1. Henry Grinnell (1799–1874), a rich New York whale-oil merchant from a New Bedford family who sponsored two attempts to rescue Sir Franklin, one in 1850 and another in 1853.

2. I.e., an explorer like Mungo Park (1771–1806), Scottish explorer of Africa; Meriwether Lewis (1774–1809) and William Clark (1770–1838), leaders of the American expedition into the Louisiana Terri-

tory (1804–6); and Martin Frobisher (1535?–1594), English mariner.

3. The famous expedition to the Pacific Antarctic led by Charles Wilkes during 1838–42.

4. Thoreau's journal for May 10, 1841, begins: "A good warning to the restless tourists of these days is contained in the last verses of Claudian's 'Old Man of Verona.' " Claudius Claudianus was the last of the Latin classic poets (fl. A.D. 395) and author of *Epigrammata*, where Thoreau found the passage he loosely translates here. He changed *Spaniards* to "Australian," added "outlandish," and changed the pronouns. The last line would be better translated as "he [the traveler] may have more of a journey, but he who remains in Verona has more of a life."

> Let them wander and scrutinize the outlandish Australians.
> I have more of God, they more of the road.

It is not worth the while to go round the world to count the cats in Zanzibar.[5] Yet do this even till you can do better, and you may perhaps find some "Symmes' Hole"[6] by which to get at the inside at last. England and France, Spain and Portugal, Gold Coast and Slave Coast, all front on this private sea; but no bark from them has ventured out of sight of land, though it is without doubt the direct way to India. If you would learn to speak all tongues and conform to the customs of all nations, if you would travel farther than all travellers, be naturalized in all climes, and cause the Sphinx to dash her head against a stone,[7] even obey the precept of the old philosopher, and Explore thyself. Herein are demanded the eye and the nerve. Only the defeated and deserters go to the wars, cowards that run away and enlist. Start now on that farthest western way, which does not pause at the Mississippi or the Pacific, nor conduct toward a worn-out China or Japan, but leads on direct a tangent to this sphere, summer and winter, day and night, sun down, moon down, and at last earth down too.

It is said that Mirabeau took to highway robbery "to ascertain what degree of resolution was necessary in order to place one's self in formal opposition to the most sacred laws of society." He declared that "a soldier who fights in the ranks does not require half so much courage as a foot-pad,"—"that honor and religion have never stood in the way of a well-considered and a firm resolve."[8] This was manly, as the world goes; and yet it was idle, if not desperate. A saner man would have found himself often enough "in formal opposition" to what are deemed "the most sacred laws of society," through obedience to yet more sacred laws, and so have tested his resolution without going out of his way. It is not for a man to put himself in such an attitude to society, but to maintain himself in whatever attitude he find himself through obedience to the laws of his being, which will never be one of opposition to a just government, if he should chance to meet with such.

I left the woods for as good a reason as I went there. Perhaps it seemed to me that I had several more lives to live, and could not spare any more time for that one. It is remarkable how easily and insensibly we fall into a particular route, and make a beaten track for ourselves. I had not lived there a week before my feet wore a path from my door to the pond-side; and though it is five or six years since I trod it, it is still quite distinct. It is true, I fear that others may have fallen into it, and so helped to keep it open. The surface of the earth is soft and impressible by the feet of men; and so with the paths which the mind travels. How worn and dusty, then, must be the highways of the world, how deep the ruts of tradition and conformity! I did not wish to take a cabin passage, but rather to go before the mast and on the deck of the world, for there I could best see the moonlight amid the mountains. I do not wish to go below now.

I learned this, at least, by my experiment; that if one advances confidently

---

5. Thoreau had read Charles Pickering's *The Races of Man* (1851), which reports on the domestic cats in Zanzibar [Harding's note].

6. In 1818 Captain John Symmes theorized that the earth was hollow with openings at both the North and South Poles.

7. As the Theban Sphinx did when Oedipus guessed her riddle. Thebes here is the ancient Greek city, not the Egyptian city Thoreau has previously referred to.

8. Thoreau encountered this passage by the Comte de Mirabeau (1749–1791) in *Harper's* 1 (1850).

in the direction of his dreams, and endeavors to live the life which he has imagined, he will meet with a success unexpected in common hours. He will put some things behind, will pass an invisible boundary; new, universal, and more liberal laws will begin to establish themselves around and within him; or the old laws be expanded, and interpreted in his favor in a more liberal sense, and he will live with the license of a higher order of beings. In proportion as he simplifies his life, the laws of the universe will appear less complex, and solitude will not be solitude, nor poverty poverty, nor weakness weakness. If you have built castles in the air, your work need not be lost; that is where they should be. Now put the foundations under them.

It is a ridiculous demand which England and America make, that you shall speak so that they can understand you. Neither men nor toad-stools grow so. As if that were important, and there were not enough to understand you without them. As if Nature could support but one order of understandings, could not sustain birds as well as quadrupeds, flying as well as creeping things, and *hush* and *who*, which Bright[9] can understand, were the best English. As if there were safety in stupidity alone. I fear chiefly lest my expression may not be *extra-vagant* enough, may not wander far enough beyond the narrow limits of my daily experience, so as to be adequate to the truth of which I have been convinced. *Extra vagance!* it depends on how you are yarded. The migrating buffalo, which seeks new pastures in another latitude, is not extravagant like the cow which kicks over the pail, leaps the cow-yard fence, and runs after her calf, in milking time. I desire to speak somewhere *without* bounds; like a man in a waking moment, to men in their waking moments; for I am convinced that I cannot exaggerate enough even to lay the foundation of a true expression. Who that has heard a strain of music feared then lest he should speak extravagantly any more forever? In view of the future or possible, we should live quite laxly and undefined in front, our outlines dim and misty on that side; as our shadows reveal an insensible perspiration toward the sun. The volatile truth of our words should continually betray the inadequacy of the residual statement. Their truth is instantly *translated*; its literal monument alone remains. The words which express our faith and piety are not definite; yet they are significant and fragrant like frankincense to superior natures.

Why level downward to our dullest perception always, and praise that as common sense? The commonest sense is the sense of men asleep, which they express by snoring. Sometimes we are inclined to class those who are once-and-a-half witted with the half-witted, because we appreciate only a third part of their wit. Some would find fault with the morning-red, if they ever got up early enough. "They pretend," as I hear, "that the verses of Kabir have four different senses; illusion, spirit, intellect, and the exoteric doctrine of the Vedas;"[1] but in this part of the world it is considered a ground for complaint if a man's writings admit of more than one interpretation. While England endeavors to cure the potato-rot, will not any endeavor to cure the brain-rot, which prevails so much more widely and fatally?

I do not suppose that I have attained to obscurity, but I should be proud if no more fatal fault were found with my pages on this score than was found with the Walden ice. Southern customers objected to its blue color, which is the evidence of its purity, as if it were muddy, and preferred the Cambridge

9. Name for an ox.
1. M. Garcin de Tassy's, *Histoire de la littérature hindoui* (1839).

ice, which is white, but tastes of weeds. The purity men love is like the mists which envelop the earth, and not like the azure ether beyond.

Some are dinning in our ears that we Americans, and moderns generally, are intellectual dwarfs compared with the ancients, or even the Elizabethan men.[2] But what is that to the purpose? A living dog is better than a dead lion.[3] Shall a man go and hang himself because he belongs to the race of pygmies, and not be the biggest pygmy that he can? Let every one mind his own business, and endeavor to be what he was made.

Why should we be in such desperate haste to succeed, and in such desperate enterprises? If a man does not keep pace with his companions, perhaps it is because he hears a different drummer. Let him step to the music which he hears, however measured or far away. It is not important that he should mature as soon as an apple-tree or an oak. Shall he turn his spring into summer? If the condition of things which we were made for is not yet, what were any reality which we can substitute? We will not be shipwrecked on a vain reality. Shall we with pains erect a heaven of blue glass over ourselves, though when it is done we shall be sure to gaze still at the true ethereal heaven far above, as if the former were not?

There was an artist in the city of Kouroo who was disposed to strive after perfection. One day it came into his mind to make a staff. Having considered that in an imperfect work time is an ingredient, but into a perfect work time does not enter, he said to himself, It shall be perfect in all respects, though I should do nothing else in my life. He proceeded instantly to the forest for wood, being resolved that it should not be made of unsuitable material; and as he searched for and rejected stick after stick, his friends gradually deserted him, for they grew old in their works and died, but he grew not older by a moment. His singleness of purpose and resolution, and his elevated piety, endowed him, without his knowledge, with perennial youth. As he made no compromise with Time, Time kept out of his way, and only sighed at a distance because he could not overcome him. Before he had found a stock in all respects suitable the city of Kouroo was a hoary ruin, and he sat on one of its mounds to peel the stick. Before he had given it the proper shape the dynasty of the Candahars was at an end, and with the point of the stick he wrote the name of the last of that race in the sand, and then resumed his work. By the time he had smoothed and polished the staff Kalpa was no longer the pole-star; and ere he had put on the ferule and the head adorned with precious stones, Brahma had awoke and slumbered many times. But why do I stay to mention these things? When the finishing stroke was put to his work, it suddenly expanded before the eyes of the astonished artist into the fairest of all the creations of Brahma. He had made a new system in making a staff, a world with full and fair proportions; in which, though the old cities and dynasties had passed away, fairer and more glorious ones had taken their places. And now he saw by the heap of shavings still fresh at his feet, that, for him and his work, the former lapse of time had been an illusion, and that no more time had elapsed than is required for a single scintillation from the brain of Brahma to fall on and inflame the tinder of a mortal brain. The material was pure, and his art was pure; how could the result be other than wonderful?

2. There had been serious as well as satirical speculation as to the debilitating effects of the American climate, a continuation of the older question as to whether or not modern civilization could ever achieve the heights of ancient Greek and Roman civilization.
3. Ecclesiastes 9.4.

No face which we can give to a matter will stead us so well at last as the truth. This alone wears well. For the most part, we are not where we are, but in a false position. Through an infirmity of our natures, we suppose a case, and put ourselves into it, and hence are in two cases at the same time, and it is doubly difficult to get out. In sane moments we regard only the facts, the case that is. Say what you have to say, not what you ought. Any truth is better than make-believe. Tom Hyde, the tinker, standing on the gallows, was asked if he had any thing to say. "Tell the tailors," said he, "to remember to make a knot in their thread before they take the first stitch."[4] His companion's prayer is forgotten.

However mean your life is, meet it and live it; do not shun it and call it hard names. It is not so bad as you are. It looks poorest when you are richest. The fault-finder will find faults even in paradise. Love your life, poor as it is. You may perhaps have some pleasant, thrilling, glorious hours, even in a poor-house. The setting sun is reflected from the windows of the alms-house as brightly as from the rich man's abode; the snow melts before its door as early in the spring. I do not see but a quiet mind may live as contentedly there, and have as cheering thoughts, as in a palace. The town's poor seem to me often to live the most independent lives of any. May be they are simply great enough to receive without misgiving. Most think that they are above being supported by the town; but it oftener happens that they are not above supporting themselves by dishonest means, which should be more disreputable. Cultivate poverty like a garden herb, like sage. Do not trouble yourself much to get new things, whether clothes or friends. Turn the old; return to them. Things do not change; we change. Sell your clothes and keep your thoughts. God will see that you do not want society. If I were confined to a corner of a garret all my days, like a spider, the world would be just as large to me while I had my thoughts about me. The philosopher said: "From an army of three divisions one can take away its general, and put it in disorder; from the man the most abject and vulgar one cannot take away his thought."[5] Do not seek so anxiously to be developed, to subject yourself to many influences to be played on; it is all dissipation. Humility like darkness reveals the heavenly lights. The shadows of poverty and meanness gather around us, "and lo! creation widens to our view."[6] We are often reminded that if there were bestowed on us the wealth of Crœsus,[7] our aims must still be the same, and our means essentially the same. Moreover, if you are restricted in your range by poverty, if you cannot buy books and newspapers, for instance, you are but confined to the most significant and vital experiences; you are compelled to deal with the material which yields the most sugar and the most starch. It is life near the bone where it is sweetest. You are defended from being a trifler. No man loses ever on a lower level by magnanimity on a higher. Superfluous wealth can buy superfluities only. Money is not required to buy one necessary of the soul.

I live in the angle of a leaden wall, into whose composition was poured a little alloy of bell metal. Often, in the repose of my mid-day, there reaches my ears a confused *tintinnabulum*[8] from without. It is the noise of my contemporaries. My neighbors tell me of their adventures with famous gentlemen and

4. Presumably a reference to the tailors who will sew Hyde's shroud, although some custom may be involved such as that of making the last stitch through the nose in preparing a sailor for burial at sea.

5. Confucius's *Analects* 9.25.

6. From the sonnet *To Night* by the British writer Joseph Blanco White (1775–1841).

7. King of Lydia (d. 546 B.C.), fabled as the richest man on earth.

8. Tinkling.

ladies, what notabilities they met at the dinner-table; but I am no more interested in such things than in the contents of the Daily Times. The interest and
the conversation are about costume and manners chiefly; but a goose is a goose
still, dress it as you will. They tell me of California and Texas, of England and
the Indies, of the Hon. Mr.——— of Georgia or of Massachusetts, all transient and fleeting phenomena, till I am ready to leap from their court-yard like
the Mameluke bey.[9] I delight to come to my bearings,—not walk in procession
with pomp and parade, in a conspicuous place, but to walk even with the
Builder of the universe, if I may,—not to live in this restless, nervous, bustling, trivial Nineteenth Century, but stand or sit thoughtfully while it goes
by. What are men celebrating? They are all on a committee of arrangements,
and hourly expect a speech from somebody. God is only the president of the
day, and Webster is his orator.[1] I love to weigh, to settle, to gravitate toward
that which most strongly and rightfully attracts me;—not hang by the beam of
the scale and try to weigh less,—not suppose a case, but take the case that is;
to travel the only path I can, and that on which no power can resist me. It
affords me no satisfaction to commence to spring an arch before I have got a
solid foundation. Let us not play at kittlybenders.[2] There is a solid bottom
every where. We read that the traveller asked the boy if the swamp before him
had a hard bottom. The boy replied that it had. But presently the traveller's
horse sank in up to the girths, and he observed to the boy, "I thought you said
that this bog had a hard bottom." "So it has," answered the latter, "but you
have not got half way to it yet." So it is with the bogs and quicksands of society;
but he is an old boy that knows it. Only what is thought said or done at a
certain rare coincidence is good. I would not be one of those who will foolishly
drive a nail into mere lath and plastering; such a deed would keep me awake
nights. Give me a hammer, and let me feel for the furring.[3] Do not depend
on the putty. Drive a nail home and clinch it so faithfully that you can wake
up in the night and think of your work with satisfaction,—a work at which you
would not be ashamed to invoke the Muse. So will help you God, and so
only. Every nail driven should be as another rivet in the machine of the universe, you carrying on the work.

Rather than love, than money, than fame, give me truth. I sat at a table
where were rich food and wine in abundance, and obsequious attendance, but
sincerity and truth were not; and I went away hungry from the inhospitable
board. The hospitality was as cold as the ices. I thought that there was no need
of ice to freeze them. They talked to me of the age of the wine and the fame
of the vintage; but I thought of an older, a newer, and purer wine, of a more
glorious vintage, which they had not got, and could not buy. The style, the
house and grounds and "entertainment" pass for nothing with me. I called on
the king, but he made me wait in his hall, and conducted like a man incapacitated for hospitality. There was a man in my neighborhood who lived in a
hollow tree. His manners were truly regal. I should have done better had I
called on him.

9. A famous romantic exploit: in 1811 the Egyptian
Mehemet Ali Pasha attempted to massacre the Mameluke caste, but one bey, or officer, escaped by leaping
from a wall onto his horse.
1. Political meetings then had "presidents" (because
they presided) rather than "chairpersons." Thoreau
plays on the catch phrase from Mohammedanism
"There is no other God than Allah, and Mohammed

is his prophet." Thoreau regarded Daniel Webster
with contempt.
2. Harding defines this as a "child's game of running
out onto thin ice without breaking through."
3. Narrow lumber nailed as backing for lath. The first
edition reads "furrowing," and one manuscript draft
reads "stud."

How long shall we sit in our porticoes practising idle and musty virtues, which any work would make impertinent? As if one were to begin the day with long-suffering, and hire a man to hoe his potatoes; and in the afternoon go forth to practise Christian meekness and charity with goodness aforethought! Consider the China[4] pride and stagnant self-complacency of mankind. This generation reclines a little to congratulate itself on being the last of an illustrious line; and in Boston and London and Paris and Rome, thinking of its long descent, it speaks of its progress in art and science and literature with satisfaction. There are the Records of the Philosophical Societies, and the public Eulogies of *Great Men!* It is the good Adam contemplating his own virtue. "Yes, we have done great deeds, and sung divine songs, which shall never die,"—that is, as long as *we* can remember them. The learned societies and great men of Assyria,—where are they? What youthful philosophers and experimentalists we are! There is not one of my readers who has yet lived a whole human life. These may be but the spring months in the life of the race. If we have had the seven-years' itch, we have not seen the seventeen-year locust yet in Concord. We are acquainted with a mere pellicle of the globe on which we live. Most have not delved six feet beneath the surface, nor leaped as many above it. We know not where we are. Beside, we are sound asleep nearly half our time. Yet we esteem ourselves wise, and have an established order on the surface. Truly, we are deep thinkers, we are ambitious spirits! As I stand over the insect crawling amid the pine needles on the forest floor, and endeavoring to conceal itself from my sight, and ask myself why it will cherish those humble thoughts, and hide its head from me who might perhaps be its benefactor, and impart to its race some cheering information, I am reminded of the greater Benefactor and Intelligence that stands over me the human insect.

There is an incessant influx of novelty into the world, and yet we tolerate incredible dulness. I need only suggest what kind of sermons are still listened to in the most enlightened countries. There are such words as joy and sorrow, but they are only the burden of a psalm, sung with a nasal twang, while we believe in the ordinary and mean. We think that we can change our clothes only. It is said that the British Empire is very large and respectable, and that the United States are a first-rate power. We do not believe that a tide rises and falls behind every man which can float the British Empire like a chip, if he should ever harbor it in his mind. Who knows what sort of seventeen-year locust will next come out of the ground? The government of the world I live in was not framed, like that of Britain, in after-dinner conversations over the wine.

The life in us is like the water in the river. It may rise this year higher than man has ever known it, and flood the parched uplands; even this may be the eventful year, which will drown out all our muskrats. It was not always dry land where we dwell. I see far inland the banks which the stream anciently washed, before science began to record its freshets. Every one has heard the story which has gone the rounds of New England, of a strong and beautiful bug which came out of the dry leaf of an old table of apple-tree wood, which had stood in a farmer's kitchen for sixty years, first in Connecticut, and afterward in Massachusetts,—from an egg deposited in the living tree many years

4. From China's lingering isolationism, despite the China trade so important to the New England economy.

earlier still, as appeared by counting the annual layers beyond it; which was heard gnawing out for several weeks, hatched perchance by the heat of an urn.[5] Who does not feel his faith in a resurrection and immortality strengthened by hearing of this? Who knows what beautiful and winged life, whose egg has been buried for ages under many concentric layers of woodenness in the dead dry life of society, deposited at first in the alburnum of the green and living tree, which has been gradually converted into the semblance of its wellseasoned tomb,—heard perchance gnawing out now for years by the astonished family of man, as they sat round the festive board,—may unexpectedly come forth from amidst society's most trivial and handselled furniture, to enjoy its perfect summer life at last!

I do not say that John or Jonathan[6] will realize all this; but such is the character of that morrow which mere lapse of time can never make to dawn. The light which puts out our eyes is darkness to us. Only that day dawns to which we are awake. There is more day to dawn. The sun is but a morning star.

THE END

1846, 1850

Slavery in Massachusetts[1]

An Address, Delivered at the Anti-Slavery Celebration at Framingham, July 4th, 1854

I lately attended a meeting of the citizens of Concord, expecting, as one among many, to speak on the subject of slavery in Massachusetts; but I was surprised and disappointed to find that what had called my townsmen together was the destiny of Nebraska, and not of Massachusetts, and that what I had to

---

5. A major account of the incident is in Timothy Dwight's *Travels in New England and New York* (1821), vol. 2.

6. John Bull or Brother Jonathan, i.e., England or America. Thoreau is now addressing not the restricted audience of the opening of "Economy" but all readers of the English language.

1. Thoreau delivered a shortened version of this masterpiece of moral outrage at Framingham, Massachusetts, on the Fourth of July 1854. The "Anti-Slavery Celebration" was a massive counterdemonstration, timed as an affront to the self-complacent patriotism of "official" observances of Independence Day. At Framingham, William Lloyd Garrison, the editor of *The Liberator*, publicly burned a copy of the United States Constitution because it condoned slavery, and in *The Liberator* for July 21, 1854, Garrison printed Thoreau's talk as *Slavery in Massachusetts. An Address, Delivered at the Anti-Slavery Celebration at Framingham, July 4th, 1854*, the source of the present text.

Behind Thoreau's fury lay the months-long debate over and the ultimate passage of the Kansas-Nebraska Act, which repealed the key provision of the Missouri Compromise (1820), the prohibition of slavery in any new states north of 36°30'. Instead, Stephen A. Douglas's new law substituted the rule of "popular" or "squatter" sovereignty, under which inhabitants of a territory would decide whether or not to be admitted as a slave state. Behind Thoreau's rage also lay two Massachusetts events of national significance, the remanding of the slave Thomas Sims to his Georgia master in 1851 under the Fugitive Slave Law (part of the Compromise of 1850), and the similar remanding of Anthony Burns to Virginia just a month before this speech was given. Both Democratic and Whig newspapers in Massachusetts vigorously upheld the return of Sims, but the *Burns* case, coming at the height of the Kansas-Nebraska agitation, helped to crystallize public opinion against the Fugitive Slave Law throughout the North. Into his speech Thoreau worked passages written in his journals during both the *Sims* and *Burns* cases. From his perspective there was indeed "slavery in Massachusetts": only a society of slaves could use its law-enforcement agencies to send another person back into slavery.

This speech reached an audience hundreds of times larger than that of *Walden*, which was published in the same year, for Horace Greeley reprinted it in his *New York Tribune* and the *Washington National Anti-Slavery Standard* also reprinted it. After Thoreau's death it was collected in *A Yankee in Canada, with Anti-Slavery and Reform Papers* (1866). As Wendell Glick shows in his edition of *Reform Papers* (1973), *A Yankee* apparently embodies a few corrections Thoreau made on a copy of *The Liberator* printing; some of these are adopted here.

say would be entirely out of order. I had thought that the house was on fire, and not the prairie; but though several of the citizens of Massachusetts are now in prison for attempting to rescue a slave from her own clutches, not one of the speakers at that meeting expressed regret for it, not one even referred to it.[2] It was only the disposition of some wild lands a thousand miles off, which appeared to concern them. The inhabitants of Concord are not prepared to stand by one of their own bridges,[3] but talk only of taking up a position on the highlands beyond the Yellowstone river. Our Buttricks, and Davises, and Hosmers are retreating thither, and I fear that they will have no Lexington Common between them and the enemy. There is not one slave in Nebraska; there are perhaps a million slaves in Massachusetts.

They who have been bred in the school of politics fail now and always to face the facts. Their measures are half measures and make-shifts, merely. They put off the day of settlement indefinitely, and meanwhile, the debt accumulates. Though the Fugitive Slave Law had not been the subject of discussion on that occasion, it was at length faintly resolved by my townsmen, at an adjourned meeting, as I learn, that the compromise compact of 1820 having been repudiated by one of the parties, 'Therefore, . . . the Fugitive Slave Law must be repealed.' But this is not the reason why an iniquitous law should be repealed. The fact which the politician faces is merely, that there is less honor among thieves than was supposed, and not the fact that they are thieves.

As I had no opportunity to express my thoughts at that meeting, will you allow me to do so here?

Again[4] it happens that the Boston Court House is full of armed men, holding prisoner and trying a MAN, to find out if he is not really a SLAVE. Does any one think that Justice or God awaits Mr. Loring's decision?[5] For him to sit there deciding still, when this question is already decided from eternity to eternity, and the unlettered slave himself, and the multitude around, have long since heard and assented to the decision, is simply to make himself ridiculous. We may be tempted to ask from whom he received his commission, and who he is that received it; what novel statutes he obeys, and what precedents are to him of authority. Such an arbiter's very existence is an impertinence. We do not ask him to make up his mind, but to make up his pack.

I listen to hear the voice of a Governor, Commander-in-Chief of the forces of Massachusetts.[6] I hear only the creaking of crickets and the hum of insects which now fill the summer air. The Governor's exploit is to review the troops on muster days. I have seen him on horseback, with his hat off, listening to a chaplain's prayer. It chances that is all I have ever seen of a Governor. I think that I could manage to get along without one. If *he* is not of the least use to prevent my being kidnapped, pray of what important use is he likely to be to me? When freedom is most endangered, he dwells in the deepest obscurity. A distinguished clergyman told me that he chose the profession of a clergyman,

---

2. Nine men were arrested for participating in the May 25, 1854, attempt to rescue Burns from the Boston courthouse where he was held.
3. Thoreau's audience would have instantly understood his scathing reminder of the bravery of the Revolutionary ancestors of the very Massachusetts citizens who rejoiced at the passage of the Fugitive Slave Law. See *Walden*, pp. 1836–37, for another mention of these heroes of the Battle of Concord, April 19, 1775;

Davis and Hosmer were slain in the battle.
4. I.e., as during the *Sims* case (and others less notorious).
5. U.S. Commissioner Edward G. Loring, who heard the *Burns* case and decided it according to the letter of the Fugitive Slave Law.
6. Between the time of the *Sims* case and the *Burns* case Massachusetts had had three governors.

because it afforded the most leisure for literary pursuits. I would recommend to him the profession of a Governor.

Three years ago, also, when the Simm's tragedy was acted, I said to myself, there is such an officer, if not such a man, as the Governor of Massachusetts,—what has he been about the last fortnight? Has he had as much as he could do to keep on the fence during this moral earthquake? It seemed to me that no keener satire could have been aimed at, no more cutting insult have been offered to that man, than just what happened—the absence of all inquiry after him in that crisis. The worst and the most I chance to know of him is, that he did not improve that opportunity to make himself known, and worthily known. He could at least have *resigned* himself into fame. It appeared to be forgotten that there was such a man, or such an office. Yet no doubt he was endeavoring to fill the gubernatorial chair all the while. He was no Governor of mine. He did not govern me.

But at last, in the present case, the Governor was heard from. After he and the United States Government had perfectly succeeded in robbing a poor innocent black man of his liberty for life, and, as far as they could, of his Creator's likeness in his breast, he made a speech to his accomplices, at a congratulatory supper!

I have read a recent law of this State, making it penal for 'any officer of the Commonwealth' to 'detain, or aid in the . . . detention,' any where within its limits, 'of any person, for the reason that he is claimed as a fugitive slave.'[7] Also, it was a matter of notoriety that a writ of replevin[8] to take the fugitive out of the custody of the United States Marshal could not be served, for want of sufficient force to aid the officer.

I had thought that the Governor was in some sense the executive officer of the State; that it was his business, as a Governor, to see that the laws of the State were executed; while, as a man, he took care that he did not, by so doing, break the laws of humanity; but when there is any special important use for him, he is useless, or worse than useless, and permits the laws of the State to go unexecuted. Perhaps I do not know what are the duties of a Governor; but if to be a Governor requires to subject one's self to so much ignominy without remedy, if it is to put a restraint upon my manhood, I shall take care never to be Governor of Massachusetts. I have not read far in the statutes of this Commonwealth. It is not profitable reading. They do not always say what is true; and they do not always mean what they say. What I am concerned to know is, that that man's influence and authority were on the side of the slaveholder, and not of the slave—of the guilty, and not of the innocent—of injustice, and not of justice. I never saw him of whom I speak; indeed, I did not know that he was Governor until this event occurred. I heard of him and Anthony Burns at the same time, and thus, undoubtedly, most will hear of him. So far am I from being governed by him. I do not mean that it was any thing to his discredit that I had not heard of him, only that I heard what I did. The worst I shall say of him is, that he proved no better than the majority of his constituents would be likely to prove. In my opinion, he was not equal to the occasion.

---

7. In response to the Kansas-Nebraska uproar, the Massachusetts legislature had passed a personal-liberty law nullifying the Fugitive Slave Law within the commonwealth.

8. A writ requiring the recovery and return of things unlawfully taken; in this case a human being was the "thing."

The whole military force of the State is at the service of a Mr. Suttle,[9] a slaveholder from Virginia, to enable him to catch a man whom he calls his property; but not a soldier is offered to save a citizen of Massachusetts from being kidnapped! Is this what all these soldiers, all this *training* has been for these seventy-nine years past?[1] Have they been trained merely to rob Mexico, and carry back fugitive slaves to their masters?

These very nights, I heard the sound of a drum in our streets. There were men *training* still; and for what? I could with an effort pardon the cockerels of Concord for crowing still, for they, perchance, had not been beaten that morning; but I could not excuse this rub-a-dub of the 'trainers.' The slave was carried back by exactly such as these, i.e., by the soldier, of whom the best you can say in this connection is, that he is a fool made conspicuous by a painted coat.

Three years ago, also, just a week after the authorities of Boston assembled to carry back a perfectly innocent man, and one whom they knew to be innocent, into slavery, the inhabitants of Concord caused the bells to be rung and the cannons to be fired, to celebrate their liberty—and the courage and love of liberty of their ancestors who fought at the bridge. As if *those* three millions had fought for the right to be free themselves, but to hold in slavery three millions others. Now-a-days, men wear a fool's cap, and call it a liberty cap. I do not know but there are some, who, if they were tied to a whipping-post, and could get but one hand free, would use it to ring the bells and fire the cannons, to celebrate *their* liberty. So some of my townsmen took the liberty to ring and fire; that was the extent of their freedom; and when the sound of the bells died away, their liberty died away also; when the powder was all expended, their liberty went off with the smoke.

The joke could be no broader, if the inmates of the prisons were to subscribe for all the powder to be used in such salutes, and hire the jailors to do the firing and ringing for them, while they enjoyed it through the grating.

This is what I thought about my neighbors.

Every humane and intelligent inhabitant of Concord, when he or she heard those bells and those cannons, thought not with pride of the events of the 19th of April, 1775, but with shame of the events of the 12th of April, 1851.[2] But now we have half buried that old shame under a new one.

Massachusetts sat waiting Mr. Loring's decision, as if it could in any way affect her own criminality. Her crime, the most conspicuous and fatal crime of all, was permitting him to be the umpire in such a case. It was really the trial of Massachusetts. Every moment that she hesitated to set this man free—every moment that she now hesitates to atone for her crime, she is convicted. The Commissioner on her case is God; not Edward G. God, but simple God.

I wish my countrymen to consider, that whatever the human law may be, neither an individual nor a nation can ever commit the least act of injustice against the obscurest individual, without having to pay the penalty for it. A government which deliberately enacts injustice, and persists in it, will at length ever become the laughing-stock of the world.

9. Burns's master. Citizens of Boston were shocked by the armed force displayed in the capture, confinement, and remanding of Burns.
1. I.e., since the hallowed battles at Lexington and Concord.
2. Very early on April 12, 1851, three hundred men, armed to prevent a rescue attempt, huddled Sims into a ship which sailed before dawn.

Much has been said about American slavery, but I think that we do not even yet realize what slavery is. If I were seriously to propose to Congress to make mankind into sausages, I have no doubt that most of the members would smile at my proposition, and if any believed me to be in earnest, they would think that I proposed something much worse than Congress had ever done. But if any of them will tell me that to make a man into a sausage would be much worse,—would be any worse, than to make him into a slave,—than it was to enact the Fugitive Slave Law, I will accuse him of foolishness, of intellectual incapacity, of making a distinction without a difference. The one is just as reasonable a proposition as the other.

I hear a good deal said about trampling this law under foot. Why, one need not go out of his way to do that. This law rises not to the level of the head or the reason; its natural habitat is in the dirt. It was born and bred, and has its life only in the dust and mire, on a level with the feet, and he who walks with freedom, and does not with Hindoo mercy avoid treading on every venomous reptile, will inevitably tread on it, and so trample it under foot,—and Webster, its maker, with it, like the dirt-bug and its ball.[3]

Recent events will be valuable as a criticism on the administration of justice in our midst, or, rather, as showing what are the true resources of justice in any community. It has come to this, that the friends of liberty, the friends of the slave, have shuddered when they have understood that his fate was left to the legal tribunals of the country to be decided. Free men have no faith that justice will be awarded in such a case; the judge may decide this way or that; it is a kind of accident, at best. It is evident that he is not a competent authority in so important a case. It is no time, then, to be judging according to his precedents, but to establish a precedent for the future. I would much rather trust to the sentiment of the people. In their vote, you would get something of some value, at least, however small; but, in the other case, only the trammelled judgment of an individual, of no significance, be it which way it might.

It is to some extent fatal to the courts, when the people are compelled to go behind them. I do not wish to believe that the courts were made for fair weather, and for very civil cases merely,—but think of leaving it to any court in the land to decide whether more than three millions of people, in this case, a sixth part of a nation, have a right to be freemen or not! But it has been left to the courts of *justice*, so-called—to the Supreme Court of the land—and, as you all know, recognizing no authority but the Constitution, it has decided that the three millions are, and shall continue to be, slaves. Such judges as these are merely the inspectors of a pick-lock and murderer's tools, to tell him whether they are in working order or not, and there they think that their responsibility ends. There was a prior case on the docket, which they, as judges appointed by God, had no right to skip; which having been justly settled, they would have been saved from this humiliation. It was the case of the murderer himself.

The law will never make men free; it is men who have got to make the law free. They are the lovers of law and order, who observe the law when the government breaks it.

Among human beings, the judge whose words seal the fate of a man furthest

3. In Massachusetts Webster was credited with the passage of the Compromise of 1850, of which a major provision was the Fugitive Slave Bill. Thoreau is comparing Webster and the Fugitive Slave Law to a tumblebug and its ball of dung.

into eternity, is not he who merely pronounces the verdict of the law, but he, whoever he may be, who, from a love of truth, and unprejudiced by any custom or enactment of men, utters a true opinion or *sentence* concerning him. He it is that *sentences* him. Whoever has discerned truth, has received his commission from a higher source than the chiefest justice in the world, who can discern only law. He finds himself constituted judge of the judge.— Strange that it should be necessary to state such simple truths.

I am more and more convinced that, with reference to any public question, it is more important to know what the country thinks of it, than what the city thinks. The city does not *think* much. On any moral question, I would rather have the opinion of Boxboro' than of Boston and New York put together. [4] When the former speaks, I feel as if somebody *had* spoken, as if *humanity* was yet, and a reasonable being had asserted its rights,—as if some unprejudiced men among the country's hills had at length turned their attention to the subject, and by a few sensible words redeemed the reputation of the race. When, in some obscure country town, the farmers come together to a special town meeting, to express their opinion on some subject which is vexing the land, that, I think, is the true Congress, and the most respectable one that is ever assembled in the United States.

It is evident that there are, in this Commonwealth, at least, two parties, becoming more and more distinct—the party of the city, and the party of the country. I know that the country is mean enough, but I am glad to believe that there is a slight difference in her favor. But as yet, she has few, if any organs, through which to express herself. The editorials which she reads, like the news, come from the sea-board. Let us, the inhabitants of the country, cultivate self-respect. Let us not send to the city for aught more essential than our broadcloths and groceries, or, if we read the opinions of the city, let us entertain opinions of our own.

Among measures to be adopted, I would suggest to make as earnest and vigorous an assault on the Press as has already been made, and with effect, on the Church. The Church has much improved within a few years; but the Press is almost, without exception, corrupt. I believe that, in this country, the press exerts a greater and a more pernicious influence than the Church did in its worst period. We are not a religious people, but we are a nation of politicians. We do not care for the Bible, but we do care for the newspaper. At any meeting of politicians,—like that at Concord the other evening, for instance,—how impertinent it would be to quote from the Bible! how pertinent to quote from a newspaper or from the Constitution! The newspaper is a Bible which we read every morning and every afternoon, standing and sitting, riding and walking. It is a Bible which every man carries in his pocket, which lies on every table and counter, and which the mail, and thousands of missionaries, are continually dispensing. It is, in short, the only book which America has printed, and which America reads. So wide is its influence. The editor is a preacher whom you voluntarily support. Your tax is commonly one cent daily, and it costs nothing for pew hire. [5] But how many of these preachers preach the truth? I repeat the testimony of many an intelligent foreigner, as well as my own convictions, when I say, that probably no country was ever ruled by so mean a class of tyrants as, with a few noble exceptions, are the editors of the periodical

---

4. I.e., any obscure country town ruled by democratic town meetings.   5. Annual rent for an assigned pew in church.

press in *this* country. And as they live and rule only by their servility, and appealing to the worst, and not the better nature of man, the people who read them are in the condition of the dog that returns to his vomit.

The *Liberator* and the *Commonwealth* were the only papers in Boston, as far as I know, which made themselves heard in condemnation of the cowardice and meanness of the authorities of that city, as exhibited in '51.[6] The other journals, almost without exception, by their manner of referring to and speaking of the Fugitive Slave Law, and the carrying back of the slave Simms, insulted the common sense of the country, at least. And, for the most part, they did this, one would say, because they thought so to secure the approbation of their patrons, not being aware that a sounder sentiment prevailed to any extent in the heart of the Commonwealth. I am told that some of them have improved of late; but they are still eminently time-serving. Such is the character they have won.

But, thank fortune, this preacher can be even more easily reached by the weapons of the reformer than could the recreant priest. The free men of New England have only to refrain from purchasing and reading these sheets, have only to withhold their cents, to kill a score of them at once. One whom I respect told me that he purchased Mitchell's *Citizen* in the cars, and then threw it out the window. But would not his contempt have been more fatally expressed, if he had not bought it?

Are they Americans? are they New Englanders? are they inhabitants of Lexington, and Concord, and Framingham, who read and support the Boston *Post, Mail, Journal, Advertiser, Courier,* and *Times?* Are these the Flags of our Union? I am not a newspaper reader, and may omit to name the worst.

Could slavery suggest a more complete servility than some of these journals exhibit? Is there any dust which their conduct does not lick, and make fouler still with its slime? I do not know whether the Boston *Herald* is still in existence, but I remember to have seen it about the streets when Simms was carried off. Did it not act its part well—serve its master faithfully? How could it have gone lower on its belly? How can a man stoop lower than he is low? do more than put his extremities in the place of the head he has? than make his head his lower extremity? When I have taken up this paper with my cuffs turned up, I have heard the gurgling of the sewer through every column. I have felt that I was handling a paper picked out of the public gutters, a leaf from the gospel of the gambling-house, the groggery and the brothel, harmonizing with the gospel of the Merchants' Exchange.

The majority of the men of the North, and of the South, and East, and West, are not men of principle. If they vote, they do not send men to Congress on errands of humanity, but while their brothers and sisters are being scourged and hung for loving liberty, while——I might here insert all that slavery implies and is,——it is the mismanagement of wood and iron and stone and gold which concerns them. Do what you will, O Government! with my wife and children, my mother and brother, my father and sister, I will obey your commands to the letter. It will indeed grieve me if you hurt them, if you deliver them to overseers to be hunted by hounds or to be whipped to death;

6. Thoreau is not exaggerating. In 1851 almost any respectable person, Whig or Democrat, regarded *The Liberator* and *The Commonwealth* as inflammatory smear sheets. The liberal Boston *Investigator* spoke for all right-thinking people in declaring that "it is better to obey even a bad law, than resist by physical force its execution." Respectable papers united in equating the "higher law" of the abolitionists with "mob law."

but nevertheless, I will peaceably pursue my chosen calling on this fair earth, until perchance, one day, when I have put on mourning for them dead, I shall have persuaded you to relent. Such is the attitude, such are the words of Massachusetts.

Rather than do thus, I need not say what match I would touch, what system endeavor to blow up,—but as I love my life, I would side with the light, and let the dark earth roll from under me, calling my mother and my brother to follow.

I would remind my countrymen, that they are to be men first, and Americans only at a late and convenient hour. No matter how valuable law may be to protect your property, even to keep soul and body together, if it do not keep you and humanity together.

I am sorry to say, that I doubt if there is a judge in Massachusetts who is prepared to resign his office, and get his living innocently, whenever it is required of him to pass sentence under a law which is merely contrary to the law of God. I am compelled to see that they put themselves, or rather, are by character, in this respect, exactly on a level with the marine who discharges his musket in any direction he is ordered to. They are just as much tools and as little men. Certainly, they are not the more to be respected, because their master enslaves their understandings and consciences, instead of their bodies.

The judges and lawyers,—simply as such, I mean,—and all men of expediency, try this case by a very low and incompetent standard. They consider, not whether the Fugitive Slave Law is right, but whether it is what they call *constitutional*. Is virtue constitutional, or vice? Is equity constitutional, or iniquity? In important moral and vital questions like this, it is just as impertinent to ask whether a law is constitutional or not, as to ask whether it is profitable or not. They persist in being the servants of the worst of men, and not the servants of humanity. The question is not whether you or your grandfather, seventy years ago, did not enter into an agreement to serve the devil, and that service is not accordingly now due; but whether you will not now, for once and at last, serve God,—in spite of your own past recreancy, or that of your ancestor,—by obeying that eternal and only just CONSTITUTION, which He, and not any Jefferson or Adams,[7] has written in your being.

The amount of it is, if the majority vote the devil to be God, the minority will live and behave accordingly, and obey the successful candidate,[8] trusting that some time or other, by some Speaker's casting vote, perhaps, they may reinstate God. This is the highest principle I can get out of or invent for my neighbors. These men act as if they believed that they could safely slide down hill a little way—or a good way—and would surely come to a place, by and by, where they could begin to slide up again. This is expediency, or choosing that course which offers the slightest obstacles to the feet, that is, a down-hill one. But there is no such thing as accomplishing a righteous reform by the use of 'expediency.' There is no such thing as sliding up hill. In morals, the only sliders are backsliders.

Thus we steadily worship Mammon,[9] both School, and State, and Church,

---

7. Thoreau uses Thomas Jefferson and John Adams to typify the two major parties of the early republic, the liberals and conservatives of the time.
8. The words "and obey the successful candidate" do not appear in *The Liberator* but are in Thoreau's jour-
nal (the source for this passage) and in *A Yankee*; presumably Thoreau restored them on his copy of *The Liberator*.
9. Materialism; Mammon is one of the fallen angels in Milton's *Paradise Lost*.

and the Seventh Day curse God with a tintamar[1] from one end of the Union to the other.

Will mankind never learn that policy is not morality—that it never secures any moral right, but considers merely what is expedient? chooses the available candidate, who is invariably the devil,—and what right have his constituents to be surprised, because the devil does not behave like an angel of light? What is wanted is men, not of policy, but of probity—who recognize a higher law than the Constitution, or the decision of the majority. The fate of the country does not depend on how you vote at the polls—the worst man is as strong as the best at that game; it does not depend on what kind of paper you drop into the ballot-box once a year, but on what kind of man you drop from your chamber into the street every morning.

What should concern Massachusetts is not the Nebraska Bill, nor the Fugitive Slave Bill, but her own slaveholding and servility. Let the State dissolve her union with the slaveholder. She may wriggle and hesitate, and ask leave to read the Constitution once more; but she can find no respectable law or precedent which sanctions the continuance of such a Union for an instant.

Let each inhabitant of the State dissolve his union with her, as long as she delays to do her duty.

The events of the past month teach me to distrust Fame. I see that she does not finely discriminate, but coarsely hurrahs. She considers not the simple heroism of an action, but only as it is connected with its apparent consequences. She praises till she is hoarse the easy exploit of the Boston tea party,[2] but will be comparatively silent about the braver and more disinterestedly heroic attack on the Boston Court-House, simply because it was unsuccessful!

Covered with disgrace, the State has sat down coolly to try for their lives and liberties the men who attempted to do its duty for it. And this is called *justice!* They who have shown that they can behave particularly well may perchance be put under bonds for *their good behavior.* They whom truth requires at present to plead guilty, are of all the inhabitants of the State, preëminently innocent. While the Governor, and the Mayor, and countless officers of the Commonwealth, are at large, the champions of liberty are imprisoned.

Only they are guiltless, who commit the crime of contempt of such a Court. It behoves every man to see that his influence is on the side of justice, and let the courts make their own characters. My sympathies in this case are wholly with the accused, and wholly against the accusers and their judges. Justice is sweet and musical; but injustice is harsh and discordant. The judge still sits grinding at his organ, but it yields no music, and we hear only the sound of the handle. He believes that all the music resides in the handle, and the crowd toss him their coppers the same as before.

Do you suppose that that Massachusetts which is now doing these things,— which hesitates to crown these men, some of whose lawyers, and even judges, perchance, may be driven to take refuge in some poor quibble, that they may not wholly outrage their instinctive sense of justice,—do you suppose that she is any thing but base and servile? that she is the champion of liberty?

Show me a free State, and a court truly of justice, and I will fight for them,

1. A general ringing of bells.
2. The celebrated pre-Revolutionary exploit (1773) in which protestors against British taxation disguised themselves (more or less) as Indians, boarded ships in Boston harbor, and dumped tea into the water.

if need be; but show me Massachusetts, and I refuse her my allegiance, and express contempt for her courts.

The effect of a good government is to make life more valuable,—of a bad one, to make it less valuable. We can afford that railroad, and all other merely material stock, should lose some of its value, for that only compels us to live more simply and economically; but suppose that the value of life itself should be diminished! How can we make a less demand on man and nature, how live more economically in respect to virtue and all noble qualities, than we do? I have lived for the last month,—and I think that every man in Massachusetts capable of the sentiment of patriotism must have had a similar experience,— with the sense of having suffered a vast and indefinite loss. I did not know at first what ailed me. At last it occurred to me that what I had lost was a country. I had never respected the Government near to which I had lived, but I had foolishly thought that I might manage to live here, minding my private affairs, and forget it. For my part, my old and worthiest pursuits have lost I cannot say how much of their attraction, and I feel that my investment in life here is worth many per cent. less since Massachusetts last deliberately sent back an innocent man, Anthony Burns, to slavery. I dwelt before, perhaps, in the illusion that my life passed somewhere only *between* heaven and hell, but now I cannot persuade myself that I do not dwell *wholly within* hell. The site of that political organization called Massachusetts is to me morally covered with volcanic *scoriæ*[3] and cinders, such as Milton describes in the infernal regions. If there is any hell more unprincipled than our rulers, and we, the ruled, I feel curious to see it. Life itself being worth less, all things with it, which minister to it, are worth less. Suppose you have a small library, with pictures to adorn the walls—a garden laid out around—and contemplate scientific and literary pursuits, &c., and discover all at once that your villa, with all its contents, is located in hell, and that the justice of the peace has a cloven foot and a forked tail—do not these things suddenly lose their value in your eyes?

I feel that, to some extent, the State has fatally interfered in my lawful business. It has not only interrupted me in my passage through Court street on errands of trade, but it has interrupted me and every man on his onward and upward path, on which he had trusted soon to leave Court street far behind. What right had it to remind me of Court street? I have found that hollow which even I had relied on for solid.

I am surprised to see men going about their business as if nothing had happened. I say to myself—Unfortunates! they have not heard the news. I am surprised that the man whom I just met on horseback should be so earnest to overtake his newly-bought cows running away—since all property is inse- cure—and if they do not run away again, they may be taken away from him when he gets them. Fool! does he not know that his seed-corn is worth less this year—that all beneficent harvests fail as you approach the empire of hell? No prudent man will build a stone-house under these circumstances, or engage in any peaceful enterprise which requires a long time to accomplish. Art is as long as ever, but life is more interrupted and less available for a man's proper pursuits. It is not an era of repose. We have used up all our inherited freedom. If we would save our lives, we must fight for them.

I walk toward one of our ponds, but what signifies the beauty of nature when men are base? We walk to lakes to see our serenity reflected in them;

3. Lava (Latin).

when we are not serene, we go not to them. Who can be serene in a country where both the rulers and the ruled are without principle? The remembrance of my country spoils my walk. My thoughts are murder to the State, and involuntarily go plotting against her.

But it chanced the other day that I secured a white water-lily, and a season I had waited for had arrived. It is the emblem of purity. It bursts up so pure and fair to the eye, and so sweet to the scent, as if to show us what purity and sweetness reside in, and can be extracted from, the slime and muck of earth. I think I have plucked the first one that has opened for a mile. What confirmation of our hopes is in the fragrance of this flower! I shall not so soon despair of the world for it, notwithstanding slavery, and the cowardice and want of principle of Northern men. It suggests what kind of laws have prevailed longest and widest, and still prevail, and that the time may come when man's deeds may smell as sweet. Such is the odor which the plant emits. If Nature can compound this fragrance still annually, I shall believe her still young and full of vigor, her integrity and genius unimpaired, and that there is virtue even in man, too, who is fitted to perceive and love it. It reminds me that Nature has been partner to no Missouri Compromise. I scent no compromise in the fragrance of the water-lily. It is not a *Nymphœa Douglassii.*[4] In it, the sweet, and pure, and innocent, are wholly sundered from the obscene and baleful. I do not scent in this the time-serving irresolution of a Massachusetts Governor, nor of a Boston Mayor. So behave that the odor of your actions may enhance the general sweetness of the atmosphere, that when we behold or scent a flower, we may not be reminded how inconsistent your deeds are with it; for all odor is but one form of advertisement of a moral quality, and if fair actions had not been performed, the lily would not smell sweet. The foul slime stands for the sloth and vice of man, the decay of humanity; the fragrant flower that springs from it, for the purity and courage which are immortal.

Slavery and servility have produced no sweet-scented flower annually, to charm the senses of men, for they have no real life: they are merely a decaying and a death, offensive to all healthy nostrils. We do not complain that they *live*, but that they do not *get buried*. Let the living bury them; even they are good for manure.

1854, 1866

Life without Principle[1]

At a lyceum, not long since, I felt that the lecturer had chosen a theme too foreign to himself, and so failed to interest me as much as he might have done. He described things not in or near to his heart, but toward his extremities and

4. A pun on the name of the senator from Illinois, Stephen A. Douglas.
1. Although *Life without Principle* is little known in comparison with *Resistance to Civil Government*, it is, as Walter Harding says, "unquestionably the favorite of true Thoreau *aficionados.*" The piece grew out of journal entries in the early 1850s and in some form was delivered as a lecture in 1854. Some of the titles it had in the next years were *Getting a Living, Misspent Lives, What Shall It Profit* (in allusion to Mark 8.36: "For what shall it profit a man, if he shall gain the whole world, and lose his own soul?"), and *The Higher Law.* Thoreau was near death when Ticknor and

Fields accepted the work for the *Atlantic Monthly* in March 1862. In response to some criticism from the publishers, Thoreau—too weak to write—dictated a reply: "As for another title for the Higher Law article, I can think of nothing better than, Life without Principle." Under that title it was published after Thoreau's death in the *Atlantic Monthly* for October 1863, the source of the present text. It was unsigned, in accordance with contemporary magazine practice. Thought of now as an essay, *Life without Principle* carries still the stringent immediacy of its origins as a lecture that sometimes outraged its auditors.

superficies. There was, in this sense, no truly central or centralizing thought in the lecture. I would have had him deal with his privatest experience, as the poet does. The greatest compliment that was ever paid me was when one asked me what I *thought*, and attended to my answer. I am surprised, as well as delighted, when this happens, it is such a rare use he would make of me, as if he were acquainted with the tool. Commonly, if men want anything of me, it is only to know how many acres I make of their land,—since I am a surveyor,—or, at most, what trivial news I have burdened myself with. They never will go to law for my meat; they prefer the shell. A man once came a considerable distance to ask me to lecture on Slavery; but on conversing with him, I found that he and his clique expected seven-eighths of the lecture to be theirs, and only one-eighth mine; so I declined. I take it for granted, when I am invited to lecture anywhere,—for I have had a little experience in that business,—that there is a desire to hear what I *think* on some subject, though I may be the greatest fool in the country,—and not that I should say pleasant things merely, or such as the audience will assent to; and I resolve, accordingly, that I will give them a strong dose of myself. They have sent for me, and engaged to pay for me, and I am determined that they shall have me, though I bore them beyond all precedent.

So now I would say something similar to you, my readers. Since *you* are my readers, and I have not been much of a traveller, I will not talk about people a thousand miles off, but come as near home as I can. As the time is short, I will leave out all the flattery, and retain all the criticism.

Let us consider the way in which we spend our lives.

This world is a place of business.[2] What an infinite bustle! I am awaked almost every night by the panting of the locomotive. It interrupts my dreams. There is no sabbath. It would be glorious to see mankind at leisure for once. It is nothing but work, work, work. I cannot easily buy a blank-book to write thoughts in; they are commonly ruled for dollars and cents. An Irishman, seeing me making a minute[3] in the fields, took it for granted that I was calculating my wages. If a man was tossed out of a window when an infant, and so made a cripple for life, or scared out of his wits by the Indians, it is regretted chiefly because he was thus incapacitated for—business! I think that there is nothing, not even crime, more opposed to poetry, to philosophy, ay, to life itself, than this incessant business.

There is a coarse and boisterous money-making fellow in the outskirts of our town, who is going to build a bank-wall under the hill along the edge of his meadow. The powers have put this into his head to keep him out of mischief, and he wishes me to spend three weeks digging there with him. The result will be that he will perhaps get some more money to hoard, and leave for his heirs to spend foolishly. If I do this, most will commend me as an industrious and hard-working man; but if I choose to devote myself to certain labors which yield more real profit, though but little money, they may be inclined to look on me as an idler. Nevertheless, as I do not need the police of meaningless labor to regulate me, and do not see anything absolutely praiseworthy in this fellow's undertaking, any more than in many an enterprise of our own or foreign governments, however amusing it may be to him or them, I prefer to finish my education at a different school.

---

2. A pun on "busyness."   3. Note or memo.

If a man walk in the woods for love of them half of each day, he is in danger of being regarded as a loafer; but if he spends his whole day as a speculator, shearing off those woods and making earth bald before her time, he is esteemed an industrious and enterprising citizen. As if a town had no interest in its forests but to cut them down!

Most men would feel insulted, if it were proposed to employ them in throwing stones over a wall, and then in throwing them back, merely that they might earn their wages. But many are no more worthily employed now. For instance: just after sunrise, one summer morning, I noticed one of my neighbors walking beside his team, which was slowly drawing a heavy hewn stone swung under the axle, surrounded by an atmosphere of industry,—his day's work begun,—his brow commenced to sweat,—a reproach to all sluggards and idlers,—pausing abreast the shoulders of his oxen, and half turning round with a flourish of his merciful whip, while they gained their length on him. And I thought, Such is the labor which the American Congress exists to protect,—honest, manly toil,—honest as the day is long,—that makes his bread taste sweet, and keeps society sweet,—which all men respect and have consecrated: one of the sacred band, doing the needful, but irksome drudgery. Indeed, I felt a slight reproach, because I observed this from the window, and was not abroad and stirring about a similar business. The day went by, and at evening I passed the yard of another neighbor, who keeps many servants, and spends much money foolishly, while he adds nothing to the common stock, and there I saw the stone of the morning lying beside a whimsical structure intended to adorn this Lord Timothy Dexter's[4] premises, and the dignity forthwith departed from the teamster's labor, in my eyes. In my opinion, the sun was made to light worthier toil than this. I may add, that his employer has since run off, in debt to a good part of the town, and, after passing through Chancery,[5] has settled somewhere else, there to become once more a patron of the arts.

The ways by which you may get money almost without exception lead downward. To have done anything by which you earned money *merely* is to have been truly idle or worse. If the laborer gets no more than the wages which his employer pays him, he is cheated, he cheats himself. If you would get money as a writer or lecturer, you must be popular, which is to go down perpendicularly. Those services which the community will most readily pay for it is most disagreeable to render. You are paid for being something less than a man. The State does not commonly reward a genius any more wisely. Even the poet-laureate would rather not have to celebrate the accidents of royalty. He must be bribed with a pipe[6] of wine; and perhaps another poet is called away from his muse to gauge that very pipe. As for my own business, even that kind of surveying which I could do with most satisfaction my employers do not want. They would prefer that I should do my work coarsely and not too well, ay, not well enough. When I observe that there are different ways of surveying, my employer commonly asks which will give him the most land, not which is most correct. I once invented a rule for measuring cord-

4. "Lord" Timothy Dexter (1747–1806) was an eccentric wealthy merchant of Newburyport, Massachusetts, who had the fence, lawns, and exotically planted gardens of his "palace" decorated with dozens of life-size painted wood statues, mostly of famous men, including the first three presidents.
5. Bankruptcy court.
6. Cask containing two hogsheads (variously construed as 126 or 280 gallons).

wood, and tried to introduce it in Boston; but the measurer there told me that the sellers did not wish to have their wood measured correctly,—that he was already too accurate for them, and therefore they commonly got their wood measured in Charlestown before crossing the bridge.

The aim of the laborer should be, not to get his living, to get "a good job," but to perform well a certain work; and, even in a pecuniary sense, it would be economy for a town to pay its laborers so well that they would not feel that they were working for low ends, as for a livelihood merely, but for scientific, or even moral ends. Do not hire a man who does your work for money, but him who does it for love of it.

It is remarkable that there are few men so well employed, so much to their minds, but that a little money or fame would commonly buy them off from their present pursuit. I see advertisements for *active* young men, as if activity were the whole of a young man's capital. Yet I have been surprised when one has with confidence proposed to me, a grown man, to embark in some enterprise of his, as if I had absolutely nothing to do, my life having been a complete failure hitherto. What a doubtful compliment this is to pay me! As if he had met me half-way across the ocean beating up against the wind, but bound nowhere, and proposed to me to go along with him! If I did, what do you think the underwriters would say? No, no! I am not without employment at this stage of the voyage. To tell the truth, I saw an advertisement for able-bodied seamen, when I was a boy, sauntering in my native port, and as soon as I came of age I embarked.[7]

The community has no bribe that will tempt a wise man. You may raise money enough to tunnel a mountain, but you cannot raise money enough to hire a man who is minding *his own* business. An efficient and valuable man does what he can, whether the community pay him for it or not. The inefficient offer their inefficiency to the highest bidder, and are forever expecting to be put into office. One would suppose that they were rarely disappointed.

Perhaps I am more than usually jealous with respect to my freedom. I feel that my connection with and obligation to society are still very slight and transient. Those slight labors which afford me a livelihood, and by which it is allowed that I am to some extent serviceable to my contemporaries, are as yet commonly a pleasure to me, and I am not often reminded that they are a necessity. So far I am successful. But I foresee, that, if my wants should be much increased, the labor required to supply them would become a drudgery. If I should sell both my forenoons and afternoons to society, as most appear to do, I am sure, that, for me, there would be nothing left worth living for. I trust that I shall never thus sell my birthright for a mess of pottage.[8] I wish to suggest that a man may be very industrious, and yet not spend his time well. There is no more fatal blunderer than he who consumes the greater part of his life getting his living. All great enterprises are self-supporting. The poet, for instance, must sustain his body by his poetry, as a steam planing-mill feeds its boilers with the shavings it makes. You must get your living by loving. But as it is said of the merchants that ninety-seven in a hundred fail, so the life of men generally, tried by this standard, is a failure, and bankruptcy may be surely prophesied.

Merely to come into the world the heir of a fortune is not to be born, but to

7. A brief allegory: what Thoreau embarked on was   8. Genesis 25.34.
the voyage of life.

be still-born, rather. To be supported by the charity of friends, or a government-pension,—provided you continue to breathe,—by whatever fine synonymes you describe these relations, is to go into the almshouse. On Sundays the poor debtor goes to church to take an account of stock, and finds, of course, that his outgoes have been greater than his income. In the Catholic Church, especially, they go into Chancery, make a clean confession, give up all, and think to start again. Thus men will lie on their backs, talking about the fall of man, and never make an effort to get up.

As for the comparative demand which men make on life, it is an important difference between two, that the one is satisfied with a level success, that his marks can all be hit by point-blank shots, but the other, however low and unsuccessful his life may be, constantly elevates his aim, though at a very slight angle to the horizon. I should much rather be the last man,—though, as the Orientals say, "Greatness doth not approach him who is forever looking down; and all those who are looking high are growing poor."

It is remarkable that there is little or nothing to be remembered written on the subject of getting a living: how to make getting a living not merely honest and honorable, but altogether inviting and glorious; for if *getting* a living is not so, then living is not. One would think, from looking at literature, that this question had never disturbed a solitary individual's musings. Is it that men are too much disgusted with their experience to speak of it? The lesson of value which money teaches, which the Author of the Universe has taken so much pains to teach us, we are inclined to skip altogether. As for the means of living, it is wonderful how indifferent men of all classes are about it, even reformers, so called,—whether they inherit, or earn, or steal it. I think that society has done nothing for us in this respect, or at least has undone what she has done. Cold and hunger seem more friendly to my nature than those methods which men have adopted and advise to ward them off.

The title *wise* is, for the most part, falsely applied. How can one be a wise man, if he does not know any better how to live than other men?—if he is only more cunning and intellectually subtle? Does Wisdom work in a treadmill? or does she teach how to succeed *by her example?* Is there any such thing as wisdom not applied to life? Is she merely the miller who grinds the finest logic? It is pertinent to ask if Plato got his *living* in a better way or more successfully than his contemporaries,—or did he succumb to the difficulties of life like other men? Did he seem to prevail over some of them merely by indifference, or by assuming grand airs? or find it easier to live, because his aunt remembered him in her will? The ways in which most men get their living, that is, live, are mere makeshifts, and a shirking of the real business of life,—chiefly because they do not know, but partly because they do not mean, any better.

The rush to California,[9] for instance, and the attitude, not merely of merchants, but of philosophers and prophets, so called, in relation to it, reflect the greatest disgrace on mankind. That so many are ready to live by luck, and so get the means of commanding the labor of others less lucky, without contributing any value to society! And that is called enterprise! I know of no more startling development of the immorality of trade, and all the common modes of getting a living. The philosophy and poetry and religion of such a

9. I.e., the gold rush, which began in 1849.

mankind are not worth the dust of a puff-ball. The hog gets his living by
rooting, stirring up the soil so, would be ashamed of such company. If I could
command the wealth of all the worlds by lifting my finger, I would not pay
such a price for it. Even Mahomet knew that God did not make this world in
jest.[1] It makes God to be a moneyed gentleman who scatters a handful of
pennies in order to see mankind scramble for them. The world's raffle! A
subsistence in the domains of Nature a thing to be raffled for! What a comment, what a satire on our institutions! The conclusion will be, that mankind
will hang itself upon a tree. And have all the precepts in all the Bibles taught
men only this? and is the last and most admirable invention of the human
race only an improved muck-rake? Is this the ground on which Orientals and
Occidentals meet? Did God direct us so to get our living, digging where we
never planted,—and He would, perchance, reward us with lumps of gold?

  God gave the righteous man a certificate entitling him to food and raiment,
but the unrighteous man found a *facsimile* of the same in God's coffers, and
appropriated it, and obtained food and raiment like the former. It is one of the
most extensive systems of counterfeiting that the world has seen. I did not
know that mankind were suffering for want of gold. I have seen a little of it. I
know that it is very malleable, but not so malleable as wit. A grain of gold will
gild a great surface, but not so much as a grain of wisdom.

  The gold-digger in the ravines of the mountains is as much a gambler as his
fellow in the saloons of San Francisco. What difference does it make, whether
you shake dirt or shake dice? If you win, society is the loser. The gold-digger
is the enemy of the honest laborer, whatever checks and compensations there
may be. It is not enough to tell me that you worked hard to get your gold. So
does the Devil work hard. The way of transgressors may be hard in many
respects. The humblest observer who goes to the mines sees and says that gold-
digging is of the character of a lottery; the gold thus obtained is not the same
thing with the wages of honest toil. But, practically, he forgets what he has
seen, for he has seen only the fact, not the principle, and goes into trade there,
that is, buys a ticket in what commonly proves another lottery, where the fact
is not so obvious.

  After reading Howitt's account of the Australian gold-diggings[2] one evening,
I had in my mind's eye, all night, the numerous valleys, with their streams,
all cut up with foul pits, from ten to one hundred feet deep, and half a dozen
feet across, as close as they can be dug, and partly filled with water,—the
locality to which men furiously rush to probe for their fortunes,—uncertain
where they shall break ground,—not knowing but the gold is under their camp
itself,—sometimes digging one hundred and sixty feet before they strike the
vein, or then missing it by a foot,—turned into demons, and regardless of each
other's rights, in their thirst for riches,—whole valleys, for thirty miles, suddenly honey-combed by the pits of the miners, so that even hundreds are
drowned in them,—standing in water, and covered with mud and clay, they
work night and day, dying of exposure and disease. Having read this, and
partly forgotten it, I was thinking, accidentally, of my own unsatisfactory life,
doing as others do; and with that vision of the diggings still before me, I asked
myself, why I might not be washing some gold daily, though it were only the

---

1. The Koran 21.16, 44.38.
2. William Howitt, *Land, Labour, and Gold; or, Two Years in Victoria*, 2 vols. (1855).

finest particles,—why *I* might not sink a shaft down to the gold within me, and work that mine. *There* is a Ballarat, a Bendigo for you,—what though it were a sulky-gully?[3] At any rate, I might pursue some path, however solitary and narrow and crooked, in which I could walk with love and reverence. Wherever a man separates from the multitude, and goes his own way in this mood, there indeed is a fork in the road, though ordinary travellers may see only a gap in the paling. His solitary path across-lots will turn out the *higher way* of the two.

Men rush to California and Australia as if the true gold were to be found in that direction; but that is to go to the very opposite extreme to where it lies. They go prospecting farther and farther away from the true lead, and are most unfortunate when they think themselves most successful. Is not our *native* soil auriferous?[4] Does not a stream from the golden mountains flow through our native valley? and has not this for more than geologic ages been bringing down the shining particles and forming the nuggets for us? Yet, strange to tell, if a digger steal away, prospecting for this true gold, into the unexplored solitudes around us, there is no danger that any will dog his steps, and endeavor to supplant him. He may claim and undermine the whole valley even, both the cultivated and the uncultivated portions, his whole life long in peace, for no one will ever dispute his claim. They will not mind his cradles or his toms. He is not confined to a claim twelve feet square, as at Ballarat, but may mine anywhere, and wash the whole wide world in his tom.

Howitt says of the man who found the great nugget which weighed twenty-eight pounds, at the Bendigo diggings in Australia:—"He soon began to drink; got a horse, and rode all about, generally at full gallop, and, when he met people, called out to inquire if they knew who he was, and then kindly informed them that he was 'the bloody wretch that had found the nugget.' At last he rode full speed against a tree, and nearly knocked his brains out." I think, however, there was no danger of that, for he had already knocked his brains out against the nugget. Howitt adds, "He is a hopelessly ruined man."[5] But he is a type of the class. They are all fast men. Hear some of the names of the places where they dig:—"Jackass Flat,"—"Sheep's-Head Gully,"—"Murderer's Bar," etc. Is there no satire in these names? Let them carry their ill-gotten wealth where they will, I am thinking it will still be "Jackass Flat," if not "Murderer's Bar," where they live.

The last resource of our energy has been the robbing of graveyards on the Isthmus of Darien,[6] an enterprise which appears to be but in its infancy; for, according to late accounts, an act has passed its second reading in the legislature of New Granada,[7] regulating this kind of mining; and a correspondent of the "Tribune"[8] writes:—"In the dry season, when the weather will permit of the country being properly prospected, no doubt other rich '*guacas*' [that is, graveyards] will be found." To emigrants he says:—"Do not come before December; take the Isthmus route in preference to the Boca del Toro one; bring no useless baggage, and do not cumber yourself with a tent; but a good pair of blankets will be necessary; a pick, shovel, and axe of good material will

3. Ballarat and Bendigo were two Australian diggings; Bendigo was the later and more productive one. Many of the diggings had "gully" in their name (e.g., Iron-Bark Gully, Long Gully, and Devil's Gully); a sulky-gully would be hard to extract gold from—here, a re-calcitrant mind.

4. Gold-bearing.
5. *Land, Labour, and Gold,* 1.19.
6. Panama.
7. Colombia.
8. The *New York Tribune,* edited by Thoreau's long-time promoter Horace Greeley.

be almost all that is required": advice which might have been taken from the "Burker's Guide."[9] And he concludes with this line in Italics and small capitals: "*If you are doing well at home,* STAY THERE," which may fairly be interpreted to mean, "If you are getting a good living by robbing graveyards at home, stay there."

But why go to California for a text? She is the child of New England, bred at her own school and church.

It is remarkable that among all the preachers there are so few moral teachers. The prophets are employed in excusing the ways of men. Most reverend seniors,[1] the *illuminati* of the age, tell me, with a gracious, reminiscent smile, betwixt an aspiration and a shudder, not to be too tender about these things,— to lump all that, that is, make a lump of gold of it. The highest advice I have heard on these subjects was grovelling. The burden of it was,—It is not worth your while to undertake to reform the world in this particular. Do not ask how your bread is buttered; it will make you sick, if you do,—and the like. A man had better starve at once than lose his innocence in the process of getting his bread. If within the sophisticated man there is not an unsophisticated one, then he is but one of the Devil's angels. As we grow old, we live more coarsely, we relax a little in our disciplines, and, to some extent, cease to obey our finest instincts. But we should be fastidious to the extreme of sanity, disregarding the gibes of those who are more unfortunate than ourselves.

In our science and philosophy, even, there is commonly no true and absolute account of things. The spirit of sect and bigotry has planted its hoof amid the stars. You have only to discuss the problem, whether the stars are inhabited or not, in order to discover it. Why must we daub the heavens as well as the earth? It was an unfortunate discovery that Dr. Kane was a Mason, and that Sir John Franklin was another.[2] But it was a more cruel suggestion that possibly that was the reason why the former went in search of the latter. There is not a popular magazine in this country that would dare to print a child's thought on important subjects without comment. It must be submitted to the D. D.s. I would it were the chickadee-dees.[3]

You come from attending the funeral of mankind to attend to a natural phenomenon. A little thought is sexton[4] to all the world.

I hardly know an *intellectual* man, even, who is so broad and truly liberal that you can think aloud in his society. Most with whom you endeavor to talk soon come to a stand against some institution in which they appear to hold stock,—that is, some particular, not universal, way of viewing things. They will continually thrust their own low roof, with its narrow skylight, between you and the sky, when it is the unobstructed heavens you would view. Get out of the way with your cobwebs, wash your windows, I say! In some lyceums they tell me that they have voted to exclude the subject of religion. But how do I know what their religion is, and when I am near to or far from it? I have walked into such an arena and done my best to make a clean breast of what religion I have experienced, and the audience never suspected what I was

9. I.e., "Murderer's Handbook"—from William Burke (1792–1829), body snatcher who resorted to murder to meet the medical demand for bodies to dissect.
1. A sarcastic echo of Shakespeare's *Othello* 1.3.78.
2. Elisha Kent Kane (1820–1857), a U.S. medical officer, died during his second expedition to the Arctic to find Sir John Franklin, not knowing that Franklin had

died in 1847, before any rescue missions were sent out. Kane had lectured in Boston and other New England towns (1852–53) to raise funds for his second expedition.
3. A contemptuous pun on the timid "D.D.'s" (Doctors of Divinity) who exercised near-total, though unofficial, literary censorship in the mid-19th century.
4. Gravedigger.

about. The lecture was as harmless as moonshine to them. Whereas, if I had read to them the biography of the greatest scamps in history, they might have thought that I had written the lives of the deacons of their church. Ordinarily, the inquiry is, Where did you come from? or, Where are you going? That was a more pertinent question which I overheard one of my auditors put to another once,—"What does he lecture for?" It made me quake in my shoes.

To speak impartially, the best men that I know are not serene, a world in themselves. For the most part, they dwell in forms, and flatter and study effect only more finely than the rest. We select granite for the underpinning of our houses and barns; we build fences of stone; but we do not ourselves rest on an underpinning of granitic truth, the lowest primitive rock. Our sills are rotten. What stuff is the man made of who is not coexistent in our thought with the purest and subtilest truth? I often accuse my finest acquaintances of an immense frivolity; for, while there are manners and compliments we do not meet, we do not teach one another the lessons of honesty and sincerity that the brutes do, or of steadiness and solidity that the rocks do. The fault is commonly mutual, however; for we do not habitually demand any more of each other.

That excitement about Kossuth,[5] consider how characteristic, but superficial, it was!—only another kind of politics or dancing. Men were making speeches to him all over the country, but each expressed only the thought, or the want of thought, of the multitude. No man stood on truth. They were merely banded together, as usual, one leaning on another, and all together on nothing; as the Hindoos made the world rest on an elephant, the elephant on a tortoise, and the tortoise on a serpent, and had nothing to put under the serpent. For all fruit of that stir we have the Kossuth hat.

Just so hollow and ineffectual, for the most part, is our ordinary conversation. Surface meets surface. When our life ceases to be inward and private, conversation degenerates into mere gossip. We rarely meet a man who can tell us any news which he has not read in a newspaper, or been told by his neighbor; and, for the most part, the only difference between us and our fellow is, that he has seen the newspaper, or been out to tea, and we have not. In proportion as our inward life fails, we go more constantly and desperately to the post-office. You may depend on it, that the poor fellow who walks away with the greatest number of letters, proud of his extensive correspondence, has not heard from himself this long while.

I do not know but it is too much to read one newspaper a week. I have tried it recently, and for so long it seems to me that I have not dwelt in my native region. The sun, the clouds, the snow, the trees say not so much to me. You cannot serve two masters. It requires more than a day's devotion to know and to possess the wealth of a day.

We may well be ashamed to tell what things we have read or heard in our day. I do not know why my news should be so trivial,—considering what one's dreams and expectations are, why the developments should be so paltry. The news we hear, for the most part, is not news to our genius. It is the stalest repetition. You are often tempted to ask, why such stress is laid on a particular experience which you have had,—that, after twenty-five years, you should

5. Lajos Kossuth (1802–1894), Hungarian revolutionist. For weeks after his first triumphal arrival in the United States in December 1851, American newspapers printed little news that did not concern him, and his slouch hat set an immediate fad.

meet Hobbins, Registrar of Deeds,[6] again on the sidewalk. Have you not budged an inch, then? Such is the daily news. Its facts appear to float in the atmosphere, insignificant as the sporules of fungi, and impinge on some neglected *thallus*, or surface of our minds, which affords a basis for them, and hence a parasitic growth. We should wash ourselves clean of such news. Of what consequence, though our planet explode, if there is no character involved in the explosion? In health we have not the least curiosity about such events. We do not live for idle amusement. I would not run round a corner to see the world blow up.

All summer, and far into the autumn, perchance, you unconsciously went by[7] the newspapers and the news, and now you find it was because the morning and the evening were full of news to you. Your walks were full of incidents. You attended, not to the affairs of Europe, but to your own affairs in Massachusetts fields. If you chance to live and move and have your being[8] in that thin stratum in which the events that make the news transpire,—thinner than the paper on which it is printed,—then these things will fill the world for you; but if you soar above or dive below that plane, you cannot remember nor be reminded of them. Really to see the sun rise or go down every day, so to relate ourselves to a universal fact, would preserve us sane forever. Nations! What are nations? Tartars, and Huns, and Chinamen! Like insects, they swarm. The historian strives in vain to make them memorable. It is for want of a man that there are so many men. It is individuals that populate the world. Any man thinking may say with the Spirit of Loda,[9]—

> "I look down from my height on nations,
> And they become ashes before me;—
> Calm is my dwelling in the clouds;
> Pleasant are the great fields of my rest."

Pray, let us live without being drawn by dogs, Esquimaux-fashion, tearing over hill and dale, and biting each other's ears.

Not without a slight shudder at the danger, I often perceive how near I had come to admitting into my mind the details of some trivial affair,—the news of the street; and I am astonished to observe how willing men are to lumber their minds with such rubbish,—to permit idle rumors and incidents of the most insignificant kind to intrude on ground which should be sacred to thought. Shall the mind be a public arena, where the affairs of the street and the gossip of the tea-table chiefly are discussed? Or shall it be a quarter of heaven itself,—an hypæthral[1] temple, consecrated to the service of the gods? I find it so difficult to dispose of the few facts which to me are significant, that I hesitate to burden my attention with those which are insignificant, which only a divine mind could illustrate. Such is, for the most part, the news in newspapers and conversation. It is important to preserve the mind's chastity in this respect. Think of admitting the details of a single case of the criminal court into our thoughts, to stalk profanely through their very *sanctum sanctorum*[2] for

6. Thoreau is punning: the imaginary Hobbins is a recollector of *actions*; he judges the person today by something that person did long ago.
7. I.e., passed up, failed to read.
8. Acts 17.28: "For in him we live, and move, and have our being; as certain also of your own poets have said, For we are also his offspring."

9. The *Atlantic Monthly* reads "Lodin," but Thoreau means the Spirit of Loda, whose speech from *Carric-Thura* in James Macpherson's *Poems of Ossian* follows in slightly compressed form.
1. Roofless, open-air.
2. Holy of holies, the most sacred spot (Latin).

an hour, ay, for many hours! to make a very bar-room of the mind's inmost apartment, as if for so long the dust of the street had occupied us,—the very street itself, with all its travel, its bustle, and filth had passed through our thoughts' shrine! Would it not be an intellectual and moral suicide? When I have been compelled to sit spectator and auditor in a court-room for some hours, and have seen my neighbors, who were not compelled, stealing in from time to time, and tiptoeing about with washed hands and faces, it has appeared to my mind's eye, that, when they took off their hats, their ears suddenly expanded into vast hoppers for sound, between which even their narrow heads were crowded. Like the vanes of windmills, they caught the broad, but shallow stream of sound, which, after a few titillating gyrations in their coggy brains, passed out the other side. I wondered if, when they got home, they were as careful to wash their ears as before their hands and faces. It has seemed to me, at such a time, that the auditors and the witnesses, the jury and the counsel, the judge and the criminal at the bar,—if I may presume him guilty before he is convicted,—were all equally criminal, and a thunderbolt might be expected to descend and consume them all together.

By all kinds of traps and sign-boards, threatening the extreme penalty of the divine law, exclude such trespassers from the only ground which can be sacred to you. It is so hard to forget what it is worse than useless to remember! If I am to be a thoroughfare, I prefer that it be of the mountain-brooks, the Parnassian streams,[3] and not the town-sewers. There is inspiration, that gossip which comes to the ear of the attentive mind from the courts of heaven. There is the profane and stale revelation of the bar-room and the police court. The same ear is fitted to receive both communications. Only the character of the hearer determines to which it shall be open, and to which closed. I believe that the mind can be permanently profaned by the habit of attending to trivial things, so that all our thoughts shall be tinged with triviality. Our very intellect shall be macadamized,[4] as it were,—its foundation broken into fragments for the wheels of travel to roll over; and if you would know what will make the most durable pavement, surpassing rolled stones, spruce blocks, and asphaltum, you have only to look into some of our minds which have been subjected to this treatment so long.

If we have thus desecrated ourselves,—as who has not?—the remedy will be by wariness and devotion to reconsecrate ourselves, and make once more a fane[5] of the mind. We should treat our minds, that is, ourselves, as innocent and ingenuous children, whose guardians we are, and be careful what objects and what subjects we thrust on their attention. Read not the Times.[6] Read the Eternities. Conventionalities are at length as bad as impurities. Even the facts of science may dust the mind by their dryness, unless they are in a sense effaced each morning, or rather rendered fertile by the dews of fresh and living truth. Knowledge does not come to us by details, but in flashes of light from heaven. Yes, every thought that passes through the mind helps to wear and tear it, and to deepen the ruts, which, as in the streets of Pompeii, evince how much it has been used. How many things there are concerning which we might well deliberate, whether we had better know them,—had better let their

3. The springs of inspiration, like the springs on Mount Parnassus in Greek mythology.
4. John McAdam (1756–1836), Scottish engineer, pioneered paving roads with broken stones in a tar or asphalt binder.

5. Thoreau puns on the Latin sense of *profane*, some outrage done *in front of* the fane, the temple.
6. A pun on the common use of *Times* as a newspaper name.

peddling-carts be driven, even at the slowest trot or walk, over that bridge of glorious span[7] by which we trust to pass at last from the farthest brink of time to the nearest shore of eternity! Have we no culture, no refinement,—but skill only to live coarsely and serve the Devil?—to acquire a little worldly wealth, or fame, or liberty, and make a false show with it, as if we were all husk and shell, with no tender and living kernel to us? Shall our institutions be like those chestnut-burs which contain abortive nuts, perfect only to prick the fingers?

America is said to be the arena on which the battle of freedom is to be fought; but surely it cannot be freedom in a merely political sense that is meant. Even if we grant that the American has freed himself from a political tyrant, he is still the slave of an economical and moral tyrant. Now that the republic—the *res-publica*—has been settled, it is time to look after the *res-privata*,—the private state,—to see, as the Roman senate charged its consuls, "*ne quid res-*PRIVATA *detrimenti caperet,*" that the *private* state receive no detriment.

Do we call this the land of the free? What is it to be free from King George and continue the slaves of King Prejudice? What is it to be born free and not to live free? What is the value of any political freedom, but as a means to moral freedom? Is it a freedom to be slaves, or a freedom to be free, of which we boast? We are a nation of politicians, concerned about the outmost defences only of freedom. It is our children's children who may perchance be really free. We tax ourselves unjustly. There is a part of us which is not represented. It is taxation without representation. We quarter troops, we quarter fools and cattle of all sorts upon ourselves. We quarter our gross bodies on our poor souls, till the former eat up all the latter's substance.

With respect to a true culture and manhood, we are essentially provincial still, not metropolitan,—mere Jonathans.[8] We are provincial, because we do not find at home our standards,—because we do not worship truth, but the reflection of truth,—because we are warped and narrowed by an exclusive devotion to trade and commerce and manufactures and agriculture and the like, which are but means, and not the end.

So is the English Parliament provincial. Mere country-bumpkins, they betray themselves, when any more important question arises for them to settle, the Irish question, for instance,—the English question why did I not say? Their natures are subdued to what they work in.[9] Their "good breeding" respects only secondary objects. The finest manners in the world are awkwardness and fatuity, when contrasted with a finer intelligence. They appear but as the fashions of past days,—mere courtliness, knee-buckles and small-clothes, out of date. It is the vice, but not the excellence of manners, that they are continually being deserted by the character; they are cast-off clothes or shells, claiming the respect which belonged to the living creature. You are presented with the shells instead of the meat, and it is no excuse generally, that, in the case of some fishes, the shells are of more worth than the meat. The man who thrusts his manners upon me does as if he were to insist on introducing me to his cabinet of curiosities,[1] when I wished to see himself. It was not in this

---

7. I.e., the mind.
8. Americans (more specifically, New Englanders).
9. An echo of Shakespeare's Sonnet 111 ("And almost thence my nature is subdu'd / To what it works in, like the dyer's hand").

1. In Thoreau's time there was a special word, *virtuosi*, for avid collectors and admirers of odd and rare artifacts.

sense that the poet Decker called Christ "the first true gentleman that ever breathed."[2] I repeat that in this sense the most splendid court in Christendom is provincial, having authority to consult about Trans-alpine interests only, and not the affairs of Rome.[3] A prætor or proconsul would suffice to settle the questions which absorb the attention of the English Parliament and the American Congress.

Government and legislation! these I thought were respectable professions. We have heard of heaven-born Numas, Lycurguses, and Solons,[4] in the history of the world, whose *names* at least may stand for ideal legislators; but think of legislating to *regulate* the breeding of slaves, or the exportation of tobacco! What have divine legislators to do with the exportation or the importation of tobacco? what humane ones with the breeding of slaves? Suppose you were to submit the question to any son of God,—and has He no children in the nineteenth century? is it a family which is extinct?—in what condition would you get it again? What shall a State like Virginia say for itself at the last day, in which these have been the principal, the staple productions? What ground is there for patriotism in such a State? I derive my facts from statistical tables which the States themselves have published.

A commerce that whitens[5] every sea in quest of nuts and raisins, and makes slaves of its sailors for this purpose! I saw, the other day, a vessel which had been wrecked, and many lives lost, and her cargo of rags, juniper-berries, and bitter almonds were strewn along the shore. It seemed hardly worth the while to tempt the dangers of the sea between Leghorn and New York for the sake of a cargo of juniper-berries and bitter almonds. America sending to the Old World for her bitters! Is not the sea-brine, is not shipwreck, bitter enough to make the cup of life go down here? Yet such, to a great extent, is our boasted commerce; and there are those who style themselves statesmen and philosophers who are so blind as to think that progress and civilization depend on precisely this kind of interchange and activity,—the activity of flies about a molasses-hogshead. Very well, observes one, if men were oysters. And very well, answer I, if men were mosquitoes.

Lieutenant Herndon,[6] whom our Government sent to explore the Amazon, and, it is said, to extend the area of Slavery, observed that there was wanting there "an industrious and active population, who know what the comforts of life are, and who have artificial wants to draw out the great resources of the country." But what are the "artificial wants" to be encouraged? Not the love of luxuries, like the tobacco and slaves of, I believe, his native Virginia, nor the ice and granite and other material wealth of our native New England; nor are "the great resources of a country" that fertility or barrenness of soil which produces these. The chief want, in every State that I have been into, was a high and earnest purpose in its inhabitants. This alone draws out "the great resources" of Nature, and at last taxes her beyond her resources; for man naturally dies out of her. When we want culture more than potatoes, and illumination more than sugar-plums, then the great resources of a world are taxed and drawn out, and the result, or staple production, is, not slaves, nor operatives,[7]

2. Thomas Dekker, *The Honest Whore* 1.12.
3. That is, the papal court in Rome, which in Thoreau's time was losing some of its secular power at Rome while retaining influence beyond the Alps.
4. Numa, Lycurgus, and Solon were "ideal legislators" of, respectively, Rome, Sparta, and Athens.

5. I.e., with sails.
6. Lieutenant William Lewis Herndon (1813–1857) wrote *Exploration of the Valley of the Amazon*, 2 vols. (1854).
7. Factory workers.

but men,—those rare fruits called heroes, saints, poets, philosophers, and redeemers.

In short, as a snow-drift is formed where there is a lull in the wind, so, one would day, where there is a lull of truth, an institution springs up. But the truth blows right on over it, nevertheless, and at length blows it down.

What is called politics is comparatively something so superficial and inhuman, that, practically, I have never fairly recognized that it concerns me at all. The newspapers, I perceive, devote some of their columns specially to politics or government without charge; and this, one would say, is all that saves it; but, as I love literature, and, to some extent, the truth also, I never read those columns at any rate. I do not wish to blunt my sense of right so much. I have not got to answer for having read a single President's Message. A strange age of the world this, when empires, kingdoms, and republics come a-begging to a private man's door, and utter their complaints at his elbow! I cannot take up a newspaper but I find that some wretched government or other, hard pushed, and on its last legs, is interceding with me, the reader, to vote for it,—more importunate than an Italian beggar; and if I have a mind to look at its certificate, made, perchance, by some benevolent merchant's clerk, or the skipper that brought it over, for it cannot speak a word of English itself, I shall probably read of the eruption of some Vesuvius, or the overflowing of some Po, true or forged, which brought it into this condition. I do not hesitate, in such a case, to suggest work, or the almshouse; or why not keep its castle in silence, as I do commonly? The poor President,[8] what with preserving his popularity and doing his duty, is completely bewildered. The newspapers are the ruling power. Any other government is reduced to a few marines at Fort Independence.[9] If a man neglects to read the Daily Times, Government will go down on its knees to him, for this is the only treason in these days.

Those things which now most engage the attention of men, as politics and the daily routine, are, it is true, vital functions of human society, but should be unconsciously performed, like the corresponding functions of the physical body. They are *infra*-human, a kind of vegetation. I sometimes awake to a half-consciousness of them going on about me, as a man may become conscious of some of the processes of digestion in a morbid state, and so have the dyspepsia, as it is called. It is as if a thinker submitted himself to be rasped by the great gizzard of creation. Politics is, as it were, the gizzard of society, full of grit and gravel, and the two political parties are its two opposite halves,— sometimes split into quarters, it may be, which grind on each other. Not only individuals, but States, have thus a confirmed dyspepsia, which expresses itself, you can imagine by what sort of eloquence.[1] Thus our life is not altogether a forgetting,[2] but also, alas! to a great extent, a remembering of that which we should never have been conscious of, certainly not in our waking hours. Why should we not meet, not always as dyspeptics, to tell our bad dreams, but sometimes as *eupeptics*,[3] to congratulate each other on the ever glorious morning? I do not make an exorbitant demand, surely.

1863

8. The journal passage from which this part of the essay is derived specifically deals with Franklin Pierce.
9. In Boston Harbor.

1. A scatological joke.
2. An echo of Wordsworth's *Immortality* ode, line 58.
3. Exuberantly healthy people.

FROM JOURNALS AND LETTERS[1]

To Mrs. John Thoreau

[Rebuffs from "Every Booksellers or Publisher's House"]

[Staten Island] Tuesday Aug 29th–43

Dear Mother,

Mr Emerson has just given me a short warning that he is about to send to Concord, which I will endeavor to improve[2]—I am a good deal more wakeful than I was, and growing stout in other respects—so that I may yet accomplish something in the literary way—indeed I should have done so before now but for the slowness and poverty of the Reviews themselves. I have tried sundry methods of earning money in the city of late but without success. have rambled into every booksellers or publisher's house and discussed their affairs with them.[3] Some propose to me to do what an honest man cannot—Among others I conversed with the Harpers—to see if they might not find me useful to them—but they say that they are making fifty thousand dollars annually, and their motto is to let well alone. I find that I talk with these poor men as if I were over head and ears in business and a few thousands were no consideration with me—I almost reproach myself for bothering them thus to no purpose— but it is very valuable experience—and the best introduction I could have.

To Henry Williams, Jr.[1]

[Answer to a Harvard Class Questionnaire]

Concord Sept 30th 1847

Dear Sir,

I confess that I have very little class spirit, and have almost forgotten that I ever spent four years at Cambridge. That must have been in a former state of existence. It is difficult to realize that the old routine is still kept up. However, I will undertake at last to answer your questions as well as I can in spite of a poor memory and a defect of information.

1st then, I was born, they say, on the 12th of July 1817, on what is called the Virginia Road, in the east part of Concord.

2nd I was fitted, or rather made unfit, for College, at Concord Academy & elsewhere, mainly by myself, with the countenance of Phineas Allen, Preceptor.

3d I am not married.

4th I dont know whether mine is a profession, or a trade, or what not. It is

1. Letters are quoted from *The Correspondence of Henry David Thoreau,* edited by Walter Harding and Carl Bode (1958). Princeton University Press is preparing a new edition of the journals, but pending that text we quote journal entries from the fourteen-volume edition of Bradford Torrey and F. H. Allen (1906).
2. Take advantage of, i.e., catch the mails. "Mr. Emerson": William Emerson (Ralph Waldo Emerson's

brother), whose children Thoreau was tutoring on Staten Island.
3. Thoreau saw Horace Greeley, the editor of the *Tribune,* among others.
1. The secretary of Thoreau's class at Harvard, who had contacted all the members ten years after their graduation, asking routine questions about their progress in life.

not yet learned, and in every instance has been practised before being studied. The mercantile part of it was begun *here* by myself alone.

—It is not one but legion. I will give you some of the monster's heads. I am a Schoolmaster—a Private Tutor, a Surveyor—a Gardener, a Farmer—a Painter, I mean a House Painter, a Carpenter, a Mason, a Day-Laborer, a Pencil-Maker, a Glass-paper Maker, a Writer, and sometimes a Poetaster. If you will act the part of Iolas,[2] and apply a hot iron to any of these heads, I shall be greatly obliged to you.

5th My present employment is to answer such orders as may be expected from so general an advertisement as the above—that is, if I see fit, which is not always the case, for I have found out a way to live without what is commonly called employment or industry attractive or otherwise. Indeed my steadiest employment, if such it can be called, is to keep myself at the top of my condition, and ready for whatever may turn up in heaven or on earth. For the last two or three years I have lived in Concord woods alone, something more than a mile from any neighbor, in a house built entirely by myself.

6th I cannot think of a single general fact of any importance before or since graduating

Yrs &c
Henry D Thoreau

PS. I beg that the Class will not consider me an object of charity, and if any of them are in want of pecuniary assistance, and will make known their case to me, I will engage to give them some advice of more worth than money.

To Emerson

[A *Home Report from Concord*][1]

Concord, November 14, 1847

Dear Friend,—

I am but a poor neighbor to you here,—a very poor companion am I. I understand that very well, but that need not prevent my *writing* to you now. I have almost never written letters in my life, yet I think I can write as good ones as I frequently see, so I shall not hesitate to write this, such as it may be, knowing that you will welcome anything that reminds you of Concord.

I have banked up the young trees against the winter and the mice, and I will look out, in my careless way, to see when a pale is loose or a nail drops out of its place. The broad gaps, at least, I will occupy. I heartily wish I could be of good service to this household. But I, who have only used these ten digits so long to solve the problem of a living, how can I? The world is a cow that is hard to milk,—life does not come so easy,—and oh, how thinly it is watered ere we get it! But the young bunting calf, he will get at it. There is no way so direct. This is to earn one's living by the sweat of his brow. It is a little like joining a community, this life, to such a hermit as I am; and as I don't keep the accounts, I don't know whether the experiment will succeed or fail finally. At any rate, it is good for society, so I do not regret my transient nor my permanent share in it.

---

2. The friend of Hercules who helped him kill the many-headed Hydra by searing each stump as Hercules cut off a head.

1. Emerson was then lecturing in England.

Lidian and I make very good housekeepers. She is a very dear sister to me. Ellen and Edith and Eddy and Aunty Brown[2] keep up the tragedy and comedy and tragic-comedy of life as usual. The two former have not forgotten their old acquaintance; even Edith carries a young memory in her head, I find. Eddy can teach us all how to pronounce. If you should discover any rare hoard of wooden or pewter horses, I have no doubt he will know how to appreciate it. He occasionally surveys mankind from my shoulders as wisely as ever Johnson did. I respect him not a little, though it is I that lift him up so unceremoniously. And sometimes I have to set him down again in a hurry, according to his "mere will and good pleasure." He very seriously asked me, the other day, "Mr. Thoreau, will you be my father?" I am occasionally Mr. Rough-and-tumble with him that I may not miss *him*, and lest he should miss *you* too much. So you must come back soon, or you will be superseded. * * *

I have had a tragic correspondence, for the most part all on one side, with Miss [Ford]. She did really wish to—I hesitate to write—marry me. That is the way they spell it. Of course I did not write a deliberate answer. How could I deliberate upon it? I sent back as distinct a *no* as I have learned to pronounce after considerable practice, and I trust that this *no* has succeeded. Indeed, I wished that it might burst, like hollow shot, after it had struck and buried itself and made itself felt there. *There was no other way.* I really had anticipated no such foe as this in my career.

I suppose you will like to hear of my book,[3] though I have nothing worth writing about it. Indeed, for the last month or two I have forgotten it, but shall certainly remember it again. Wiley & Putnam, Munroe, the Harpers, and Crosby & Nichols have all declined printing it with the least risk to themselves; but Wiley & Putnam will print it in their series,[4] and any of them, anywhere, at *my* risk. If I liked the book well enough, I should not delay; but for the present I am indifferent. I believe this is, after all, the course you advised,— to let it lie.

I do not know what to say of myself. I sit before my green desk, in the chamber at the head of the stairs, and attend to my thinking, sometimes more, sometimes less distinctly. I am not unwilling to think great thoughts if there are any in the wind, but what they are I am not sure. They suffice to keep me awake while the day lasts, at any rate. Perhaps they will redeem some portion of the night erelong.

I can imagine you astonishing, bewildering, confounding, and sometimes delighting John Bull with your Yankee notions, and that he begins to take a pride in the relationship at last; introduced to all the stars of England in succession, after the lecture, until you pine to thrust your head once more into a genuine and unquestionable nebula, if there be any left. I trust a common man will be the most uncommon to you before you return to these parts. I have thought there was some advantage even in death, by which we "mingle with the herd of common men."[5] * * *

---

2. Lucy Jackson Brown, sister of Lidian Jackson Emerson who (after her husband abandoned her) had boarded with the Thoreaus for a time. Lidian was Emerson's wife and Ellen, Edith, and Eddy were their children.

3. The manuscript of *Week*.
4. The Library of American Books.
5. Apparently an echo of the Roman poet Horace (65–8 B.C.): "I hate the common herd of men and keep them far" (3.1).

To Jared Sparks[1]

[*Circumventing the Library Regulations*]

Concord Mass. Sept 17—'49

Sir,

Will you allow me to trouble you with my affairs?

I wish to get permission to take books from the College library to Concord where I reside. I am encouraged to ask this, not merely because I am an alumnus of Harvard, residing within a moderate distance of her halls, but *because I have chosen letters for my profession*, and so am one of the clergy embraced by the spirit at least of her rule. Moreover, though books are to some extent my stock and tools, I have not the usual means with which to purchase them. I therefore regard myself as one whom especially the library was created to serve. If I should change my pursuit or move further off, I should no longer be entitled to this privilege.—I would fain consider myself an *alumnus* in more than a merely historical sense, and I ask only that the University may help to finish the education, whose foundation she has helped to lay. I was not then ripe for her higher courses, and now that I am riper I trust that I am not too far away to be instructed by her. Indeed I see not how her children can more properly or effectually keep up a living connexion with their Alma Mater than by continuing to draw from her intellectual nutriment in some such way as this.

If you will interest yourself to obtain the above privilege for me, I shall be truly obliged to you.[2]

Yrs respectly

Henry D. Thoreau

From Journals

[*"Wild Thinking" in Literature*]

[November 16, 1850]

In literature it is only the wild that attracts us. Dullness is only another name for tameness. It is the untamed, uncivilized, free, and wild thinking in Hamlet, in the Iliad, and in all the scriptures and mythologies that delights us,—not learned in the schools, not refined and polished by art. A truly good book is something as wildly natural and primitive, mysterious and marvelous, ambrosial and fertile, as a fungus or a lichen. Suppose the muskrat or beaver were to turn his views to literature, what fresh views of nature would he present! The fault of our books and other deeds is that they are too humane, I want something speaking in some measure to the condition of muskrats and skunk-cabbage as well as of men,—not merely to a pining and complaining coterie of philanthropists. * * *

My Journal should be the record of my love. I would write in it only of the things I love, my affection for any aspect of the world, what I love to think of. I have no more distinctness or pointedness in my yearnings than an expanding

---

1. President of Harvard. This letter was a formal follow-up to an interview between Thoreau and Sparks.

2. Unknown to Thoreau, Sparks had already asked the librarian to let Thoreau check books out.

bud, which does indeed point to flower and fruit, to summer and autumn, but is aware of the warm sun and spring influence only. I feel ripe for something, yet do nothing, can't discover what that thing is. I feel fertile merely. It is seedtime with me. I have lain fallow long enough.

Notwithstanding a sense of unworthiness which possesses me, not without reason, notwithstanding that I regard myself as a good deal of a scamp, yet for the most part the spirit of the universe is unaccountably kind to me, and I enjoy perhaps an unusual share of happiness. Yet I question sometimes if there is not some settlement to come.

[*Writing "with Gusto"*]

[September 2, 1851]

We cannot write well or truly but what we write with gusto. The body, the senses, must conspire with the mind. Expression is the act of the whole man, that our speech may be vascular. The intellect is powerless to express thought without the aid of the heart and liver and of every member. Often I feel that my head stands out too dry, when it should be immersed. A writer, a man writing, is the scribe of all nature; he is the corn and the grass and the atmosphere writing. It is always essential that we love to do what we are doing, do it with a heart. The maturity of the mind, however, may perchance consist with a certain dryness.

[*Minott,*[1] *the Poetical Farmer*]

[October 4, 1851]

Minott was telling me to-day that he used to know a man in Lincoln who had no floor to his barn, but waited till the ground froze, then swept it clean in his barn and threshed his grain on it. He also used to see men threshing their buckwheat in the field where it grew, having just taken off the surface down to a hard-pan.

Minott used the word "gavel" to describe a parcel of stalks cast on the ground to dry. His are good old English words, and I am always sure to find them in the dictionary, though I never heard them before in my life.

I was admiring his corn-stalks disposed about the barn to dry, over or astride the braces and the timbers, of such a fresh, clean, and handsome green, retaining their strength and nutritive properties so, unlike the gross and careless husbandry of speculating, money-making farmers, who suffer their stalks to remain out till they are dry and dingy and black as chips.

Minott is, perhaps, the most poetical farmer—who most realizes to me the poetry of the farmer's life—that I know. He does nothing with haste and drudgery, but as if he loved it. He makes the most of his labor, and takes infinite satisfaction in every part of it. He is not looking forward to the sale of his crops or any pecuniary profit, but he is paid by the constant satisfaction which his labor yields him. He has not too much land to trouble him,—too much work to do,—no hired man nor boy,—but simply to amuse himself and live. He cares not so much to raise a large crop as to do his work well. He knows every

1. George Minott, Concord farmer (d. 1861) who had a house across from Emerson's. There was a family connection: Thoreau's widowed grandmother had married a Minott.

pin and nail in his barn. If another linter[2] is to be floored, he lets no hired man rob him of that amusement, but he goes slowly to the woods and, at his leisure, selects a pitch pine tree, cuts it, and hauls it or gets it hauled to the mill; and so he knows the history of his barn floor.

Farming is an amusement which has lasted him longer than gunning or fishing. He is never in a hurry to get his garden planted and yet [it] is always planted soon enough, and none in the town is kept so beautifully clean.

He always prophesies a failure of the crops, and yet is satisfied with what he gets. His barn floor is fastened down with oak pins, and he prefers them to iron spikes, which he says will rust and give way. He handles and amuses himself with every ear of his corn crop as much as a child with its playthings, and so his small crop goes a great way. He might well cry if it were carried to market. The seed of weeds is no longer in his soil.

He loves to walk in a swamp in windy weather and hear the wind groan through the pines. He keeps a cat in his barn to catch the mice. He indulges in no luxury of food or dress or furniture, yet he is not penurious but merely simple. If his sister dies before him, he may have to go to the almshouse in his old age; yet he is not poor, for he does not want riches. He gets out of each manipulation in the farmers' operations a fund of entertainment which the speculating drudge hardly knows. With never-failing rheumatism and trembling hands, he seems yet to enjoy perennial health. Though he never reads a book,—since he has finished the "Naval Monument,"—he speaks the best of English.[3]

[Facts as Material for Mythology]

[November 9, 1851]

In our walks C.[4] takes out his note-book sometimes and tries to write as I do, but all in vain. He soon puts it up again, or contents himself with scrawling some sketch of the landscape. Observing me still scribbling, he will say that he confines himself to the ideal, purely ideal remarks; he leaves the facts to me. Sometimes, too, he will say a little petulantly, "I am universal; I have nothing to do with the particular and definite." He is the moodiest person, perhaps, that I ever saw. As naturally whimsical as a cow is brindled, both in his tenderness and his roughness he belies himself. He can be incredibly selfish and unexpectedly generous. He is conceited, and yet there is in him far more than usual to ground conceit upon.

I, too, would fain set down something beside facts. Facts should only be as the frame to my pictures; they should be material to the mythology which I am writing; not facts to assist men to make money, farmers to farm profitably, in any common sense; facts to tell who I am, and where I have been or what I have thought: as now the bell rings for evening meeting, and its volumes of sound, like smoke which rises from where a cannon is fired, make the tent in which I dwell. My facts shall be falsehoods to the common sense. I would so state facts that they shall be significant, shall be myths or mythologic. Facts

---

2. Lean-to.
3. Abel Bowen's *The Naval Monument, Containing Official and Other Accounts of All the Battles Fought between the Navies of the United States and Great Britain during the Late War; and an Account of the*

War with Algiers (1816).
4. Ellery Channing (1817–1901), poetaster, ne'er-do-well scion of the famous Cambridge family (nephew and namesake of the Unitarian leader William Ellery Channing).

which the mind perceived, thoughts which the body thought,—with these I deal. I, too, cherish vague and misty forms, vaguest when the cloud at which I gaze is dissipated quite and naught but the skyey depths are seen.

[Self-Injunctions on Writing]

[November 12, 1851]

Write often, write upon a thousand themes, rather than long at a time, not trying to turn too many feeble somersets in the air,—and so come down upon your head at last. Antæus-like, be not long absent from the ground. Those sentences are good and well discharged which are like so many little resiliencies from the spring floor of our life,—a distinct fruit and kernel itself, springing from terra firma. Let there be as many distinct plants as the soil and the light can sustain. Take as many bounds in a day as possible. Sentences uttered with your back to the wall. Those are the admirable bounds when the performer has lately touched the springboard. A good bound into the air from the air [sic] is a good and wholesome experience, but what shall we say to a man's leaping off precipices in the attempt to fly? He comes down like lead. In the meanwhile, you have got your feet planted upon the rock, with the rock also at your back, and, as in the case of King James and Roderick Dhu,[5] can say,—

> "Come one, come all! this rock shall fly
> From its firm base as soon as I."

Such, uttered or not, is the strength of your sentence. Sentences in which there is no strain. A fluttering and inconstant and *quasi* inspiration, and ever memorable Icarian fall, in which your helpless wings are expanded merely by your swift descent into the *pelagos*[6] beneath.

[Nudity Versus Social Requirements]

[June 12, 1852]

Boys are bathing at Hubbard's Bend, playing with a boat (I at the willows). The color of their bodies in the sun at a distance is pleasing, the not often seen flesh-color. I hear the sound of their sport borne over the water. As yet we have not man in nature. What a singular fact for an angel visitant to this earth to carry back in his note-book, that men were forbidden to expose their bodies under the severest penalties! A pale pink, which the sun would soon tan. White men! There are no white men to contrast with the red and the black; they are of such colors as the weaver gives them. I wonder that the dog knows his master when he goes in to bathe and does not stay by his clothes.

[The Purpose of a Journal]

[July 13, 1852]

A journal, a book that shall contain a record of all your joy, your ecstasy.

---

5. In Sir Walter Scott's *The Lady of the Lake*, the Highland chieftain and outlaw slain by King James V of Scotland (father of Mary Queen of Scots).
6. Ocean.

[Writers of Torpid Words]

[July 14, 1852]

A writer who does not speak out of a full experience uses torpid words, wooden or lifeless words, such words as "humanitary," which have a paralysis in their tails.

[Living with 706 Copies of A Week]

[October 28, 1853]

For a year or two past, my *publisher*, falsely so called, has been writing from time to time to ask what disposition should be made of the copies of "A Week on the Concord and Merrimack Rivers" still on hand, and at last suggesting that he had use for the room they occupied in his cellar. So I had them all sent to me here, and they have arrived to-day by express, filling the man's wagon,—706 copies out of an edition of 1000 which I bought of Munroe four years ago and have been ever since paying for, and have not quite paid for yet. The wares are sent to me at last, and I have an opportunity to examine my purchase. They are something more substantial than fame, as my back knows, which has borne them up two flights of stairs to a place similar to that to which they trace their origin. Of the remaining two hundred and ninety and odd, seventy-five were given away, the rest sold. I have now a library of nearly nine hundred volumes, over seven hundred of which I wrote myself. Is it not well that the author should behold the fruits of his labor? My works are piled up on one side of my chamber half as high as my head, my *opera omnia*.[7] This is authorship; these are the work of my brain. There was just one piece of good luck in the venture. The unbound were tied up by the printer four years ago in stout paper wrappers, and inscribed,—

H. D. Thoreau's
Concord River
50 cops.

So Munroe had only to cross out "River" and write "Mass." and deliver them to the expressman at once. I can see now that I write for, the result of my labors.

Nevertheless, in spite of this result, sitting beside the inert mass of my works, I take up my pen to-night to record what thought or experience I may have had, with as much satisfaction as ever. Indeed, I believe that this result is more inspiring and better for me than if a thousand had bought my wares. It affects my privacy less and leaves me freer.

[Correcting His Manuscripts]

[February 28, 1854]

In correcting my manuscripts, which I do with sufficient phlegm, I find that I invariably turn out much that is good along with the bad, which it is then impossible for me to distinguish—so much for keeping bad company; but after the lapse of time, having purified the main body and thus created a distinct standard for comparison, I can review the rejected sentences and easily detect those which deserve to be readmitted.

7. Collected works (Latin).

[*Getting Distance before Rewriting*]

[April 8, 1854]

I find that I can criticise my composition best when I stand at a little distance from it,—when I do not see it, for instance. I make a little chapter of contents which enables me to recall it page by page to my mind, and judge it more impartially when my manuscript is out of the way. The distraction of surveying enables me rapidly to take new points of view. A day or two surveying is equal to a journey.

[*Up Railroad—Odors of Nature and Men*]

[June 16, 1854]

5 A.M.—Up railroad.

As the sun went down last night, round and red in a damp misty atmosphere, so now it rises in the same manner, though there is no dense fog. Poison-dogwood yesterday, or say day before, *i.e.*. 14th. *Rubus hispidus*, perhaps yesterday in the earliest place, over the sand. Mullein, perhaps yesterday.

Observed yesterday the erigeron[8] with a purple tinge. I cannot tell whether this, which seems in other respects the same with the white, is the *strigosus* or *annuus*. The calla which I plucked yesterday sheds pollen to-day; say to-day, then. A *Hypericum perforatum* seen last night will probably open to-day. I see on the *Scirpus lacustris* and pontederia leaves black patches for some days, as if painted, of minute closely placed ova, above water. I suspect that what I took for milfoil is a sium.[9] Is not that new mustard-like plant behind Loring's, and so on down the river, *Nasturtium hispidum*; or hairy cress? Probably the first the 19th. Heart-leaf. *Nymphœa odorata*. Again I scent a white water-lily, and a season I had waited for is arrived. How indispensable all these experiences to make up the summer! It is the emblem of purity, and its scent suggests it. Growing in stagnant and muddy [water], it bursts up so pure and fair to the eye and so sweet to the scent, as if to show us what purity and sweetness reside in, and can be extracted from, the slime and muck of earth. I think I have plucked the first one that has opened for a mile at least. What confirmation of our hopes is in the fragrance of the water-lily! I shall not soon despair of the world for it, notwithstanding slavery, and the cowardice and want of principle of the North.[1] It suggests that the time may come when man's deeds will smell as sweet. Such, then, is the odor our planet emits. Who can doubt, then, that Nature is young and sound? If Nature can compound this fragrance still annually, I shall believe her still full of vigor, and that there is virtue in man, too, who perceives and loves it. It is as if all the pure and sweet and virtuous was extracted from the slime and decay of earth and presented thus in a flower. The resurrection of virtue! It reminds me that Nature has been partner to no Missouri compromise. I scent no compromise in the fragrance of the white water-lily. In it, the sweet, and pure, and innocent are wholly sundered from the obscene and baleful. I do not scent in this the time-serving irresolution of a Massachusetts Governor, nor of a Boston Mayor. All good actions have contributed to this fragrance. So behave that the odor of your actions may

---

8. The daisy fleabane. "Mullein": a plant with large woolly leaves.
9. Water parsnip. "Milfoil": thousand-leaf, i.e., yarrow.

1. *Slavery in Massachusetts* draws on this journal entry.

enhance the general sweetness of the atmosphere, that, when I behold or scent
a flower, I may not be reminded how inconsistent are your actions with it; for
all odor is but one form of advertisement of a moral quality. If fair actions had
not been performed, the lily would not smell sweet. The foul slime stands for
the sloth and vice of man; the fragrant flower that springs from it, for the purity
and courage which springs from its midst. It is these sights and sounds and
fragrances put together that convince us of our immortality. No man believes
against all evidence. Our external senses consent with our internal. This fragrance assures me that, though all other men fall, one shall stand fast; though
a pestilence sweep over the earth, it shall at least spare one man. The genius
of Nature is unimpaired. Her flowers are as fair and as fragrant as ever.

[Whaling Stories at Nantucket]

[December 27, 1854]

To Nantucket *via* Hyannis in misty rain.
On Cape Cod saw the hills through the mist covered with cladonias. A head
wind and rather rough passage of three hours to Nantucket, the water being
thirty miles over. Captain Edward W. Gardiner (where I spent the evening)
thought there was a beach at Barnegat similar to that at Cape Cod. Mr. Barney, formerly a Quaker minister there, who was at Gardiner's, told of one
Bunker of Nantucket in old times, "who had eight sons, and steered each in
his turn to the killing of a whale." Gardiner said you must have been a-whaling
there before you could be married, and must have struck a whale before you
could dance. They do not think much of crossing from Hyannis in a small
boat,—in pleasant weather, that is,—but they can safely do it. A boy was
drifted across thus in a storm in a rowboat about two years ago. By luck he
struck Nantucket. The outline of the island is continually changing. The
whalers now go chiefly to Behring's Straits, and everywhere between 35 N.
and S. latitude and catch several kinds of whales. It was Edmund Gardiner of
New Bedford (a relative of Edward's) who was carried down by a whale, and
Hussey of Nantucket who, I believe, was one to draw lots to see who should be
eaten.[2] As for communication with the mainland being interrupted, Gardiner
remembers when thirty-one mails were landed at once, which, taking out
Sundays, made five weeks and one day. The snow ten days ago fell about two
inches deep, but melted instantly.

To Thomas Cholmondeley[1]

["Your Princely Gift"—An Indian Library]

Concord Nov. 8th 1855

Dear Cholmondeley,
    I must endeavor to thank you for your magnificent, your princely gift to me.
My father, with his hand in his pocket, and an air of mystery and importance

---

2. Cyrus M. Hussey, co-author with William Lay of
A Narrative of the Mutiny, on Board the Ship Globe.
1. Thomas Cholmondeley, an Englishman who had

lived in New Zealand (about which he wrote *Ultima
Thule*). He boarded with the Thoreaus in the autumn
of 1854.

about him suggests that I have another letter from Mr. Cholmondeley, and hands me a ship letter. I open eagerly upon a list of books (made up in one parcel) for "Henry D. &c &c"; and my eye glances down a column half as long as my arm, where I already detect some eminences which I had seen or heard of, standing out like the peaks of the Himalayas. No! it is not Cholmondeley's writing.—But what good angel has divined my thoughts? Has any company of the faithful in England passed a resolution to overwhelm me with their munificent regards "Wilsons Rig Veda Sanhitu" Vols 1 & 2 8vo. "Translation of Mandukya Upanishads." I begin to step from pinnacle to pinnacle. Ah! but here it is "London, King William Street truly yours John Chapman." Enclosed is the list. "Mr Thomas Cholmondeley" and now I see through it, and here is a hand I know and father was right after all. While he is gone to the market I will read a little further in this list "Nala & Damyanta" "Bhagavita Purana," "Institutes of Menu."—

How they look far away and grand!

That will do for the present: a little at a time of these rich dishes. I will look again by and by. "Per Asia"[2] too they have come, as I read on the envelope! Was there any design in that? The very nucleus of her cargo; Asia carried them in her womb long ago. Was not the ship conscious of the freight she bore Insure her for nothing ye Jews;[3] she and all her passengers and freight are destined to float serene through whatever seas. Immobility itself is tossed on Atlantic billows to present the gift to me. Was not there an omen for you? No Africa; no Europe—no Baltic, but it would have sunk. And now we will see if America can sustain it. Build new shelves—display, unfold your columns. What was that dim peak that loomed for an instant far behind, representative of a still loftier and more distant range. "Vishnu Purana," an azure mountain in itself.—gone again, but surely seen for once. And what was that which dimmed the brightness of the day, like an apex of Cotopaxi's[4] cone, seen against the disk of the sun by the voyager of the South American coast "Bhagavat Geeta"! whose great unseen base I can faintly imagine spreading beneath. "History of British India nine vols"!! Chevalier Bunsen nine vols 8vo cloth"!! Have at them! who cares for numbers in a just cause England expects every man to do his duty.[5] Be sure you are right and then go ahead. I begin to think myself learned for merely possessing such works: If here is not the wealth of the Indies of what stuff then is it made? They may keep their rupees this and the like of this is what the great company[6] traded and fought for, to convey the light of the East into the West:—this their true glory and success.

And now you have gone to the East or Eastward, having assisted its light to shine westward behind you; have gone towards the source of light! to which I pray that you may get nearer and nearer.

2. Advance word had it that the books would come by the *Asia*; actually, as Thoreau was to learn, they arrived by the *Canada*.
3. Banking and insurance were thought of as Jewish-dominated businesses.
4. Mountain in Ecuador.

5. The signal of Vice-Admiral Horatio Nelson (1758–1805) to his fleet during the battle of Trafalgar (1805): "England expects that every man will do his duty."
6. The East India Company.

To Thomas Cholmondeley

[*The Wonder of the Library; a Poor Account of the
United States and Himself*]

Concord Mass. Oct. 20th 1856

Dear Cholmondeley

I wish to thank you again for those books. They are the nucleus of my library. I wrote to you on the receipt of them last winter, (directing as now) but not having heard from you, do not know in what part of the world this may find you. Several here are enquiring if you have returned to England, as you had just started for the Crimea at the last account. The books have long been shelved in cases of my own construction made partly of the driftwood of our river. They are the admiration of all beholders. Alcott and Emerson, besides myself, have been cracking some of the nuts.

Certainly I shall never pay you for them. Of those new to me the Rig Veda is the most savory that I have yet tasted. As primitive poetry, I think as any extant. Indeed all the Vedantic literature is priceless. There they stand occupying two shelves, headed by Froissart, stretching round Egypt and India "Ultima Thule,"[1] as a fit conclusion. What a world of variety. I shall browse there for some winters to come. While war has given place to peace on your side, perhaps a more serious war still is breaking out here. I seem to hear its distant mutterings, though it may be long before the bolt will fall in our midst. There has not been anything which you could call union between the North and South in this country for many years, and there cannot be so long as slavery is in the way. I only wish that Northern—that any men—were better material, or that I for one had more skill to deal with them; that the north had more spirit and would settle the question at once, and here instead of struggling feebly and protractedly away off on the plains of Kansas. They are on the eve of a Presidential election, as perhaps you know, and all good people are praying that of the three candidates Fremont[2] may be the man; but in my opinion the issue is quite doubtful. As far as I have observed, the worst man stands the best chance in this country. But as for politics, what I most admire now-a-days, is not the regular governments but the irregular primitive ones, like the Vigilance committee in California and even the free state men in Kansas. They are the most divine.—I have just taken a run up country, as I did with you once, only a little farther, this time; to the Connecticut river in New Hampshire, where I saw Alcott, King of men. He is among those who ask after you, and takes a special interest in the oriental books. He cannot say enough about them. "And then that he should send you a library! Think of it!"

I am sorry that I can give but a poor account of myself. I got "run down" they say, more than a year ago, and have not yet got fairly up again. It has not touched my spirits however, for they are as indifferently tough, as sluggishly resilient, as a dried fungus. I would it were the kind called punk; that they might catch and retain some heavenly spark. I dwell as much aloof from society as ever: find it just as impossible to agree in opinion with the most intelligent of my neighbors; they not having improved one jot, nor I either. I am still immersed in nature, have much of the time a living sense of the breadth

1. Cholmondeley's own book about New Zealand.
2. John Charles Freemont (1813–1890). Republican candidate for president in 1856.

of the field on whose verge I dwell. The *great west* and *north west* stretching on infinitely far and grand and wild, qualifying all our thoughts. That is the only America I know. I prize this western reserve chiefly for its intellectual value. That is the road to new life and freedom,—if ever we are dissatisfied with this and not to exile as in Siberia and knowing this, one need not travel it. That great northwest where several of our shrubs, fruitless here, retain and mature their fruits properly.

I am pleased to think of you *in* that England, where we all seem to have originated, or at least sojourned which Emerson values so much, but which I know so little about. That island seems as full of good things as a nut is of meat: and I trust that it still is a sound nut without mould or worm. I hope that by this time you are settled in your mind and satisfactorily employed there.

My father mother and sister send their best wishes, and would be glad to see you in this country again. We are all quite anxious to hear that you are safe and sound: I in particular hope that you are in all respects unscathed by the battle of life, ready for still worthier encounters.

To H. G. O. Blake[1]

[*The Most Interesting Fact at Present—Walt Whitman*]

Eagleswood, N.J., November 19, 1856

Mr. Blake,—

I have been here much longer than I expected, but have deferred answering you, because I could not foresee when I shall return. I do not know yet within three or four days. This uncertainty makes it impossible for me to appoint a day to meet you, until it shall be too late to hear from you again. I think, therefore, that I must go straight home. I feel some objection to reading that "What shall it profit"[2] lecture *again* in Worcester; but if you are quite sure that it will be worth the while (it is a grave consideration), I will even make an independent journey from Concord for that purpose. I have read three of my old lectures (that included) to the Eagleswood people, and, unexpectedly, with rare success—*i.e.*, I was aware that what I was saying was silently taken in by their ears.

You must excuse me if I write mainly a business letter now, for I am sold for the time,—am merely Thoreau the surveyor here,—and solitude is scarcely obtainable in these parts.

Alcott has been here three times, and, Saturday before last, I went with him and Greeley, by invitation of the last, to G.'s farm, thirty-six miles north of New York. The next day A. and I heard Beecher[3] preach; and what was more, we visited Whitman the next morning (A. had already seen him), and were much interested and provoked. He is apparently the greatest democrat the world has seen. Kings and aristocracy go by the board at once, as they have long deserved to. A remarkably strong though coarse nature, of a sweet disposition, and much prized by his friends. Though peculiar and rough in his exterior, his skin (all over (?)) red, he is essentially a gentleman. I am still

1. Harrison G. O. Blake of Worcester, Massachusetts, who was in the Harvard class of 1835, two years ahead of Thoreau.

2. *Life without Principle.*
3. Henry Ward Beecher (1813–1887), celebrated pulpit orator.

somewhat in a quandary about him,—feel that he is essentially strange to me, at any rate; but I am surprised by the sight of him. He is very broad, but, as I have said, not fine. He said that I misapprehended him. I am not quite sure that I do. He told us that he loved to ride up and down Broadway all day on an omnibus, sitting beside the driver, listening to the roar of the carts, and sometimes gesticulating and declaiming Homer at the top of his voice. He has long been an editor and writer for the newspapers,—was editor of the "New Orleans Crescent" once; but now has no employment but to read and write in the forenoon, and walk in the afternoon, like all the rest of the scribbling gentry.

I shall probably be in Concord next week; so you can direct to me there.[4]

Dec. 7

That Walt Whitman, of whom I wrote to you, is the most interesting fact to me at present. I have just read his 2nd edition (which he gave me) and it has done me more good than any reading for a long time. Perhaps I remember best the poem of Walt Whitman an American & the Sun Down Poem.[5] There are 2 or 3 pieces in the book which are disagreeable to say the least, simply sensual. He does not celebrate love at all. It is as if the beasts spoke. I think that men have not been ashamed of themselves without reason. No doubt, there have always been dens where such deeds were unblushingly recited, and it is no merit to compete with their inhabitants. But even on this side, he has spoken more truth than any American or modern that I know. I have found his poem exhilirating encouraging. As for its sensuality,—& it may turn out to be less sensual than it appeared—I do not so much wish that those parts were not written, as that men & women were so pure that they could read them without harm, that is, without understanding them. One woman told me that no woman could read it as if a man could read what a woman could not. Of course Walt Whitman can communicate to us no experience, and if we are shocked, whose experience is it that we are reminded of?

On the whole it sounds to me very brave & American after whatever deductions. I do not believe that all the sermons so called that have been preached in this land put together are equal to it for preaching—

We ought to rejoice greatly in him. He occasionally suggests something a little more than human. You cant confound him with the other inhabitants of Brooklyn or New York. How they must shudder when they read him! He is awfully good.

To be sure I sometimes feel a little imposed on. By his heartiness & broad generalities he puts me into a liberal frame of mind prepared to see wonders—as it were sets me upon a hill or in the midst of a plain—stirs me well up, and then—throws in a thousand of brick. Though rude & sometimes ineffectual, it is a great primitive poem,—an alarum or trumpet-note ringing through the American camp. Wonderfully like the Orientals, too, considering that when I asked him if he had read them, he answered, "No: tell me about them."

I did not get far in conversation with him,—two more being present,—and among the few things which I chanced to say, I remember that one was, in

4. In a draft of this letter Thoreau wrote an account of his conversation with Whitman about the publication of Emerson's letter in the second edition of Leaves of Grass: "In his apologizing account of the matter he made the printing of Es letter seem a simple thing—& to some extent throws the burden of it—if there is any, on the writer"—i.e., on Emerson. (The publication of Emerson's letter shocked many of Emerson's friends, but Emerson bore it with good grace.)

5. Song of Myself and Crossing Brooklyn Ferry.

answer to him as representing America, that I did not think much of America or of politics, and so on, which may have been somewhat of a damper to him.

Since I have seen him, I find that I am not disturbed by any brag or egoism in his book. He may turn out the least of a braggart of all, having a better right to be confident.

He is a great fellow.

From Journals

[Dead Words]

[January 26, 1858]

Some men have a peculiar taste for bad words, mouthing and licking them into lumpish shapes like the bear her cubs,—words like "tribal" and "ornamentation," which drag a dead tail after them. They will pick you out of a thousand the still-born words, the falsettos, the wing-clipped and lame words, as if only the false notes caught their ears. They cry encore to all the discords.

To James Russell Lowell[1]

[A "Very Mean and Cowardly" Expurgation]

Concord June 22d 1858

Dear Sir,

When I received the proof of that portion of my story printed in the July number of your magazine, I was surprised to find that the sentence—"It is as immortal as I am, and perchance will go to as high a heaven, there to tower above me still."—(which comes directly after the words "heals my cuts," page 230, tenth line from the top,) have been crossed out, and it occurred to me that, after all, it was of some consequence that I should see the proofs; supposing, of course, that my "Stet" &c in the margin would be respected, as I perceive that it was in other cases of comparatively little importance to me. However, I have just noticed that the sentence was, in a very mean and cowardly manner, omitted. I hardly need to say that this is a liberty which I will not permit to be taken with my MS. The editor has, in this case, no more right to omit a sentiment than to insert one, or put words into my mouth. I do not ask anybody to adopt my opinions, but I do expect that when they ask for them to print, they will print them, or obtain my consent to their alteration or omission. I should not read many books if I thought that they had been thus *expurgated*. I feel this treatment to be an insult, though not intended as such, for it is to presume that I can be hired to suppress my opinions.

I do not mean to charge you with this omission, for I cannot believe that you knew anything about it, but there must be a responsible editor somewhere, and you, to whom I entrusted my MS. are the only party that I know in this

---

1. Perhaps the most scathing letter Thoreau ever wrote. Lowell as editor of the *Atlantic Monthly* had censored a sentence in "Chesuncook" (later part of *The Maine Woods*), preventing Thoreau from saying that a pine tree was as immortal as he was. Lowell may not have replied to this letter, but he had his revenge after Thoreau's death in an essay that tarnished Thoreau's reputation for several decades.

matter. I therefore write to ask if you sanction this omission, and if there are any other sentiments to be omitted in the remainder of my article. If you do not sanction it—or whether you do or not—will you do me the justice to print that sentence, as an omitted one, indicating its place, in the August number?

I am not willing to be associated in any way, unnecessarily, with parties who will confess themselves so bigoted & timid as this implies. I could excuse a man who was afraid of an uplifted fist, but if one habitually manifests fear at the utterance of a sincere thought, I must think that his life is a kind of nightmare continued into broad daylight. It is hard to conceive of one so completely derivative. Is this the avowed character of the Atlantic Monthly? I should like an early reply.

Yrs truly,
Henry D. Thoreau

To H. G. O. Blake

[A Dose of Society]

Concord, January 1, 1859

Mr. Blake,—

It may interest you to hear that Cholmondeley has been this way again, *via* Montreal and Lake Huron, going to the West Indies, or rather to Weiss-nicht-wo,[1] whither he urges me to accompany him. He is rather more demonstrative than before, and, on the whole, what would be called "a good fellow,"—is a man of principle, and quite reliable, but very peculiar. I have been to New Bedford with him, to show him a whaling town and Ricketson. I was glad to hear that you had called on R. How did you like him? I suspect that you did not see one another fairly.

I have lately got back to that glorious society called Solitude, where we meet our friends continually, and can imagine the outside world also to be peopled. Yet some of my acquaintance would fain hustle me into the almshouse for *the sake of society*, as if I were pining for that diet, when I seem to myself a most befriended man, and find constant employment. However, they do not believe a word I say. They have got a club, the handle of which is in the Parker House at Boston, and with this they beat me from time to time, expecting to make me tender or minced meat, so fit for a club to dine off.

> "Hercules with his club
> The Dragon did drub;
> But More of More Hall,
> With nothing at all,
> He slew the Dragon of Wantley."[2]

Ah! that More of More Hall knew what fair play was. Channing, who wrote to me about it once, brandishing the club vigorously (being set on by another, probably), says *now*, seriously, that he is sorry to find by my letters that I am "absorbed in politics," and adds, begging my pardon for his plainness, "Beware

---

1. "I-don't-know-where," the name of Teufelsdröckh's university in Carlyle's *Sartor Resartus*, which Thoreau knew well.

2. From *The Dragon of Wantley* in Bishop Percy's *Reliques of Ancient English Poetry.*

of an extraneous life!" and so he does his duty, and washes his hands of me. I tell him that it is as if he should say to the sloth, that fellow that creeps so slowly along a tree, and cries *ai* from time to time, "Beware of dancing!"

The doctors are all agreed that I am suffering from want of society. Was never a case like it. First, I did not know that I was suffering at all. Secondly, as an Irishman might say, I had thought it was indigestion of the society I got. [It is indispensable that I should take a dose of Lowell & Agassiz & Woodman.][3]

As for the Parker House, I went there once, when the Club was away, but I found it hard to see through the cigar smoke, and men were deposited about in chairs over the marble floor, as thick as legs of bacon in a smoke-house. It was all smoke, and no salt, Attic[4] or other. The only room in Boston which I visit with alacrity is the Gentlemen's Room at the Fitchburg Depot, where I wait for the cars, sometimes for two hours, in order to get out of town. It is a paradise to the Parker House, for no smoking is allowed, and there is far more retirement. A large and respectable club of us hire it (Town and Country Club), and I am pretty sure to find some one there whose face is set the same way as my own.

My last essay, on which I am still engaged, is called Autumnal Tints. I do not know how readable (*i.e.*, by me to others) it will be.

I met Mr. [Henry] James[5] the other night at Emerson's, at an Alcottian conversation, at which, however, Alcott did not talk much, being disturbed by James's opposition. The latter is a hearty man enough, with whom you can differ very satisfactorily, on account of both his doctrines and his good temper. He utters *quasi* philanthropic dogmas in a metaphysic dress; but they are for all practical purposes very crude. He charges society with all the crime committed, and praises the criminal for committing it. But I think that all the remedies he suggests out of his head—for he goes no farther, hearty as he is— would leave us about where we are now. For, of course, it is not by a gift of turkeys on Thanksgiving Day that he proposes to convert the criminal, but by a true sympathy with each one,—with him, among the rest, who lyingly tells the world from the gallows that he has never been treated kindly by a single mortal since he was born. But it is not so easy a thing to sympathize with another, though you may have the best disposition to do it. There is Dobson[6] over the hill. Have not you and I and all the world been trying, ever since he was born, to sympathize with him? (as doubtless he with us), and yet we have got no farther than to send him to the House of Correction once at least; and he, on the other hand, as I hear, has sent us to another place several times. This is the real state of things, as I understand it, at least so far as James's remedies go. We are now, alas! exercising what charity we actually have, and new laws would not give us any more. But, perchance, we might make some improvements in the House of Correction. You and I are Dobson; what will James do for us?

---

3. Three of the most gregarious members of the Saturday Club, with which Thoreau was being threatened.
4. Sharp, delicate wit.

5. Henry James, Sr., the theological speculator.
6. One of Thoreau's made-up, "Mr. Anybody" names.

From Journals

[*Grammarians Versus Real Writers*]

[January 2, 1859]

When I hear the hypercritical quarrelling about grammar and style, the position of the particles, etc., etc., stretching or contracting every speaker to certain rules of theirs,—Mr. Webster, perhaps, not having spoken according to Mr. Kirkham's rule,[1]—I see that they forget that the first requisite and rule is that expression shall be vital and natural, as much as the voice of a brute or an interjection: first of all, mother tongue; and last of all, artificial or father tongue. Essentially your truest poetic sentence is as free and lawless as a lamb's bleat. The grammarian is often one who can neither cry nor laugh, yet thinks that he can express human emotions. So the posture-masters tell you how you shall walk,—turning your toes out, perhaps, excessively,—but so the beautiful walkers are not made.

[*Grammarians and Their Rules*]

[February 3, 1860]

When I read some of the rules for speaking and writing the English language correctly,—as that a sentence must never end with a particle,—and perceive how implicitly even the learned obey it, I think—

> Any fool can make a rule
> And every fool will mind it.

---

1. Thoreau is contrasting Webster's unbridled power with the pedantic rules of Samuel Kirkham, author of *A Compendium of English Grammar* (1823), which went through many later editions with various publishers, and *An Essay on Elocution* (1833), also widely reprinted.

FREDERICK DOUGLASS
1818–1895

Born a slave in Maryland, Frederick Douglass taught himself to read and write, escaped to Massachusetts by disguising himself as a sailor, and became one of the most effective orators of his day, an influential newspaper editor, a confidant of the radical abolitionist John Brown, a militant reformer, and a respected diplomat. The first two accounts of his experiences belong to the tradition of fugitive-slave narratives popular in the North before the Civil War; the final volume, published when Douglass was in his mid-sixties, reveals one of the most remarkable and successful lives of the nineteenth century.

Narrative of the Life of Frederick Douglass, an American Slave, Written by Himself (1845) told in 125 pages the story of his life from early childhood until he escaped from bondage (and changed his last name from Bailey to Douglass) in 1838. The vivid detail, the dignity of tone, and the sincerity of the writing left no doubt that Douglass had in fact suffered the horrors he had been describing in powerful lectures for several years.

There is ample evidence to support the view that Douglass was a powerful speaker. One of his admirers described him thus:

> He was more than six feet in height, and his majestic form, as he rose to speak, straight as an arrow, muscular, yet lithe and graceful, his flashing eye, and more than all, his voice, that rivaled [Daniel] Webster's in its richness, and in the depth and sonorousness of its cadences, made up such an ideal of an orator as the listeners never forgot.

Surely, no one in Rochester, New York, who heard Douglass's speech on the fifth of July 1852 was likely to have forgotten what his biographer William S. McFeely has characterized judiciously as "perhaps the greatest antislavery oration ever given." In moral intensity it may be compared favorably with Thoreau's *A Plea for Captain John Brown*, in its range of reference with the best of Emerson's lectures, and in prophetic prescience with Whitman's shrewdest prefaces.

In 1855 he published a revised and enlarged version of the *Narrative* under the title *My Bondage and My Freedom*. This work balanced a more detailed account of his life as a slave with the impressive record of his intellectual growth and personal achievement since he had joined forces with the abolitionists in 1841. It told of his intimacy with the Garrisonian wing of the abolitionist movement (which demanded immediate freeing of all slaves on moral grounds), of his successful speaking tour of the British Isles, the purchase of his freedom for $700 by a group of his admirers, and his move to Rochester, New York, where he brought out in December 1847 the first issue of the increasingly outspoken weekly newspaper he published for the thirteen years (first as *The North Star*, later as *Frederick Douglass's Weekly* and *Monthly*). The third of Douglass's autobiographies, *The Life and Times of Frederick Douglass* (1881), subsumes the first two and adds to them the events of his career just before, during, and after the Civil War and traces the rising arc of his fame and influence and the ultimately honored recognition of his compatriots, black and white alike.

Wrongly accused of complicity in John Brown's raid on the arsenal at Harpers Ferry in 1859, Douglass was obliged to flee to Canada and thence to England. Once the Civil War began, he took an active role in the campaign to make black men eligible for Union service; he became a successful recruiter of black soldiers, whose ranks soon included two of his own sons. Having helped to enlist these men, Douglass was only acting in character when he took his protests over their unequal pay and treatment directly to President Lincoln.

It was also in character for Douglass to criticize Lincoln's successors over what Douglass believed was an insufficiently prompt and just Reconstruction policy once the war had been won. Douglass was particularly insistent on the necessity for swift passage of the Fifteenth Amendment guaranteeing suffrage to the newly emancipated slaves. Never satisfied with the grudging legal concessions the Civil War yielded, Douglass continued to object to every sign of discrimination—economic, gender, legal, and social. Even after he had been appointed U.S. marshal and then recorder of deeds for the District of Columbia, he continued to speak out on such matters as the exploitation of black sharecroppers in the South, to demand antilynching legislation, to protest the exclusion of black people from public accommodations. He also was active in suffrage movements for women, believing firmly in the power of the ballot as one of the necessities of freedom. It would be hard to exaggerate the importance for later black leaders such as Booker T. Washington and W. E. B. DuBois of Douglass's exemplary career as a champion of human rights. His life, in fact, has become the heroic paradigm for all oppressed people.

Narrative of the Life of Frederick Douglass, an American Slave, Written by Himself[1]

Preface[2]

In the month of August, 1841, I attended an anti-slavery convention in Nantucket, at which it was my happiness to become acquainted with FREDERICK DOUGLASS, the writer of the following Narrative. He was a stranger to nearly every member of that body; but, having recently made his escape from the southern prison-house of bondage, and feeling his curiosity excited to ascertain the principles and measures of the abolitionists,—of whom he had heard a somewhat vague description while he was a slave,—he was induced to give his attendance, on the occasion alluded to, though at that time a resident in New Bedford.[3]

Fortunate, most fortunate occurrence!—fortunate for the millions of his manacled brethren, yet panting for deliverance from their awful thraldom!—fortunate for the cause of negro emancipation, and of universal liberty!—fortunate for the land of his birth, which he has already done so much to save and bless!—fortunate for a large circle of friends and acquaintances, whose sympathy and affection he has strongly secured by the many sufferings he has endured, by his virtuous traits of character, by his ever-abiding remembrance of those who are in bonds, as being bound with them!—fortunate for the multitudes, in various parts of our republic, whose minds he has enlightened on the subject of slavery, and who have been melted to tears by his pathos, or roused to virtuous indignation by his stirring eloquence against the enslavers of men!—fortunate for himself, as it at once brought him into the field of public usefulness, "gave the world assurance of a MAN," quickened the slumbering energies of his soul, and consecrated him to the great work of breaking the rod of the oppressor, and letting the oppressed go free!

I shall never forget his first speech at the convention—the extraordinary emotion it excited in my own mind—the powerful impression it created upon a crowded auditory, completely taken by surprise—the applause which followed from the beginning to the end of his felicitous remarks. I think I never hated slavery so intensely as at that moment; certainly, my perception of the enormous outrage which is inflicted by it, on the godlike nature of its victims, was rendered far more clear than ever. There stood one, in physical proportion and stature commanding and exact—in intellect richly endowed—in natural eloquence a prodigy—in soul manifestly "created but a little lower than the angels"[4]—yet a slave, ay, a fugitive slave,—trembling for his safety, hardly daring to believe that on the American soil, a single white person could be found who would befriend him at all hazards, for the love of God and humanity! Capable of high attainments as an intellectual and moral being—needing nothing but a comparatively small amount of cultivation to make him an

1. First printed in May 1845 by the Anti-Slavery Office in Boston, the source of the present text. Punctuation and hyphenation have been slightly regularized and a few typographical emendations have also been made.
2. The preface is by William Lloyd Garrison (1805–1879), American journalist and social reformer; he was considered the most radical spokesman of militant abolition in the United States.
3. Douglass escaped from Hugh Auld's home in Maryland in September 1838 and settled in New Bedford, Massachusetts, where he became active among the New Bedford abolitionists.
4. God created people "a little lower than the angels" (Psalms 8.5) to have authority over all other living creatures. Paul calls the Hebrews to look at Christ, who was made "a little lower than the angels" (Hebrews 2.7,9).

ornament to society and a blessing to his race—by the law of the land, by the voice of the people, by the terms of the slave code, he was only a piece of property, a beast of burden, a chattel personal, nevertheless!

A beloved friend[5] from New Bedford prevailed on Mr. DOUGLASS to address the convention: He came forward to the platform with a hesitancy and embarrassment, necessarily the attendants of a sensitive mind in such a novel position. After apologizing for his ignorance, and reminding the audience that slavery was a poor school for the human intellect and heart, he proceeded to narrate some of the facts in his own history as a slave, and in the course of his speech gave utterance to many noble thoughts and thrilling reflections. As soon as he had taken his seat, filled with hope and admiration, I rose, and declared that PATRICK HENRY,[6] of revolutionary fame, never made a speech more eloquent in the cause of liberty, than the one we had just listened to from the lips of that hunted fugitive. So I believed at that time—such is my belief now. I reminded the audience of the peril which surrounded this self-emancipated young man at the North,—even in Massachusetts, on the soil of the Pilgrim Fathers, among the descendants of revolutionary sires; and I appealed to them, whether they would ever allow him to be carried back into slavery,—law or no law, constitution or no constitution. The response was unanimous and in thunder-tones—"NO!" "Will you succor and protect him as a brother-man—a resident of the old Bay State."[7] "YES!" shouted the whole mass, with an energy so startling, that the ruthless tyrants south of Mason and Dixon's line might almost have heard the mighty burst of feeling, and recognized it as the pledge of an invincible determination, on the part of those who gave it, never to betray him that wanders, but to hide the outcast, and firmly to abide the consequences.

It was at once deeply impressed upon my mind, that, if Mr. DOUGLASS could be persuaded to consecrate his time and talents to the promotion of the anti-slavery enterprise, a powerful impetus would be given to it, and a stunning blow at the same time inflicted on northern prejudice against a colored complexion. I therefore endeavored to instill hope and courage into his mind, in order that he might dare to engage in a vocation so anomalous and responsible for a person in his situation; and I was seconded in this effort by warm-hearted friends, especially by the late General Agent of the Massachusetts Anti-Slavery Society, Mr. JOHN A. COLLINS, whose judgment in this instance entirely coincided with my own. At first, he could give no encouragement; with unfeigned diffidence, he expressed his conviction that he was not adequate to the performance of so great a task; the path marked out was wholly an untrodden one; he was sincerely apprehensive that he should do more harm than good. After much deliberation, however, he consented to make a trial; and ever since that period, he has acted as a lecturing agent, under the auspices either of the American or the Massachusetts Anti-Slavery Society. In labors he has been most abundant; and his success in combating prejudice, in gaining proselytes, in agitating the public mind, has far surpassed the most sanguine expectations that were raised at the commencement of his brilliant career. He has borne himself with gentleness and meekness, yet with true manliness of character. As a public speaker, he excels in pathos, wit, comparison, imitation, strength

5. William C. Coffin, New Bedford's leading abolitionist at the time.
6. U.S. patriot (1736–1799), famous for the words: "I know not what course others may take, but as for me, give me liberty or give me death."
7. I.e., Massachusetts.

of reasoning, and fluency of language. There is in him that union of head and heart, which is indispensable to an enlightenment of the heads and a winning of the hearts of others. May his strength continue to be equal to his day! May he continue to "grow in grace, and in the knowledge of God," that he may be increasingly serviceable in the cause of bleeding humanity, whether at home or abroad!

It is certainly a very remarkable fact, that one of the most efficient advocates of the slave population, now before the public, is a fugitive slave, in the person of FREDERICK DOUGLASS; and that the free colored population of the United States are as ably represented by one of their own number, in the person of CHARLES LENOX REMOND,[8] whose eloquent appeals have extorted the highest applause of multitudes on both sides of the Atlantic. Let the calumniators of the colored race despise themselves for their baseness and illiberality of spirit, and henceforth cease to talk of the natural inferiority of those who require nothing but time and opportunity to attain to the highest point of human excellence.

It may, perhaps, be fairly questioned, whether any other portion of the population of the earth could have endured the privations, sufferings and horrors of slavery, without having become more degraded in the scale of humanity than the slaves of African descent. Nothing has been left undone to cripple their intellects, darken their minds, debase their moral nature, obliterate all traces of their relationship to mankind; and yet how wonderfully they have sustained the mighty load of a most frightful bondage, under which they have been groaning for centuries! To illustrate the effect of slavery on the white man,—to show that he has no powers of endurance, in such a condition, superior to those of his black brother,—DANIEL O'CONNELL,[9] the distinguished advocate of universal emancipation, and the mightiest champion of prostrate but not conquered Ireland, relates the following anecdote in a speech delivered by him in the Conciliation Hall, Dublin, before the Loyal National Repeal Association, March 31, 1845. "No matter," said Mr. O'CONNELL, "under what specious term it may disguise itself, slavery is still hideous. *It has a natural, an inevitable tendency to brutalize every noble faculty of man.* An American sailor, who was cast away on the shore of Africa, where he was kept in slavery for three years, was, at the expiration of that period, found to be imbruted and stultified—he had lost all reasoning power; and having forgotten his native language, could only utter some savage gibberish between Arabic and English, which nobody could understand, and which even he himself found difficulty in pronouncing. So much for the humanizing influence of THE DOMESTIC INSTITUTION!" Admitting this to have been an extraordinary case of mental deterioration, it proves at least that the white slave can sink as low in the scale of humanity as the black one.

Mr. DOUGLASS has very properly chosen to write his own Narrative, in his own style, and according to the best of his ability, rather than to employ some one else. It is, therefore, entirely his own production; and, considering how long and dark was the career he had to run as a slave,—how few have been his opportunities to improve his mind since he broke his iron fetters,—it is, in my judgment, highly creditable to his head and heart. He who can peruse it with-

---

8. A free-born African-American (1810–1873) from Massachusetts who was the first black employed in the United States as an antislavery lecturer. He toured with Douglass for the Massachusetts Anti-Slavery Society in 1842.
9. Irish statesman (1775–1847), fighter for Catholic emancipation and Irish independence, called the "Liberator."

out a tearful eye, a heaving breast, an afflicted spirit,—without being filled
with an unutterable abhorrence of slavery and all its abettors, and animated
with a determination to seek the immediate overthrow of that execrable system,—without trembling for the fate of this country in the hands of a righteous
God, who is ever on the side of the oppressed, and whose arm is not shortened
that it cannot save,—must have a flinty heart, and be qualified to act the part
of a trafficker "in slaves and the souls of men." I am confident that it is essentially true in all its statements; that nothing has been set down in malice,
nothing exaggerated, nothing drawn from the imagination; that it comes short
of the reality, rather than overstates a single fact in regard to SLAVERY AS IT IS.
The experience of FREDERICK DOUGLASS, as a slave, was not a peculiar one;
his lot was not especially a hard one; his case may be regarded as a very fair
specimen of the treatment of slaves in Maryland, in which State it is conceded
that they are better fed and less cruelly treated than in Georgia, Alabama, or
Louisiana. Many have suffered incomparably more, while very few on the
plantations have suffered less, than himself. Yet how deplorable was his situation! what terrible chastisements were inflicted upon his person! what still
more shocking outrages were perpetrated upon his mind! with all his noble
powers and sublime aspirations, how like a brute was he treated, even by those
professing to have the same mind in them that was in Christ Jesus! to what
dreadful liabilities was he continually subjected! how destitute of friendly
counsel and aid, even in his greatest extremities! how heavy was the midnight
of woe which shrouded in blackness the last ray of hope, and filled the future
with terror and gloom! what longings after freedom took possession of his
breast, and how his misery augmented, in proportion as he grew reflective and
intelligent,—thus demonstrating that a happy slave is an extinct man! how he
thought, reasoned, felt, under the lash of the driver, with the chains upon his
limbs! what perils he encountered in his endeavors to escape from his horrible
doom! and how signal have been his deliverance and preservation in the midst
of a nation of pitiless enemies!

This Narrative contains many affecting incidents, many passages of great
eloquence and power; but I think the most thrilling one of them all is the
description DOUGLASS gives of his feelings, as he stood soliloquizing respecting
his fate, and the chances of his one day being a freeman, on the banks of the
Chesapeake Bay—view in the receding vessels as they flew with their white
wings before the breeze, and apostrophizing them as animated by the living
spirit of freedom. Who can read that passage, and be insensible to its pathos
and sublimity? Compressed into it is a whole Alexandrian library[1] of thought,
feeling, and sentiment—all that can, all that need be urged, in the form of
expostulation, entreaty, rebuke, against that crime of crimes,—making man
the property of his fellow-man! O, how accursed is that system, which entombs
the godlikes mind of man, defaces the divine image, reduces those who by
creation were crowned with glory and honor to a level with four-footed beasts,
and exalts the dealer in human flesh above all that is called God! Why should
its existence be prolonged one hour? Is it not evil, only evil, and that continually? What does its presence imply but the absence of all fear of God, all regard
for man, on the part of the people of the United States? Heaven speed its
eternal overthrow!

So profoundly ignorant of the nature of slavery are many persons, that they

1. Alexandria, in Egypt, housed the great library center of the Greco-Roman world.

are stubbornly incredulous whenever they read or listen to any recital of the cruelties which are daily inflicted on its victims. They do not deny that the slaves are held as property; but that terrible fact seems to convey to their minds no idea of injustice, exposure to outrage, or savage barbarity. Tell them of cruel scourgings, of mutilations and brandings, of scenes of pollution and blood, of the banishment of all light and knowledge, and they affect to be greatly indignant at such enormous exaggerations, such wholesale misstatements, such abominable libels on the character of the southern planters! As if all these direful outrages were not the natural results of slavery! As if it were less cruel to reduce a human being to the condition of a thing, than to give him a severe flagellation, or to deprive him of necessary food and clothing! As if whips, chains, thumb-screws, paddles, bloodhounds, overseers, drivers, patrols, were not all indispensable to keep the slaves down, and to give protection to their ruthless oppressors! As if, when the marriage institution is abolished, concubinage, adultery, and incest, must not necessarily abound; when all the rights of humanity are annihilated, any barrier remains to protect the victim from the fury of the spoiler; when absolute power is assumed over life and liberty, it will not be wielded with destructive sway! Skeptics of this character abound in society. In some few instances, their incredulity arises from a want of reflection; but, generally, it indicates a hatred of the light, a desire to shield slavery from the assaults of its foes, a contempt of the colored race, whether bond or free. Such will try to discredit the shocking tales of slaveholding cruelty which are recorded in this truthful Narrative; but they will labor in vain. Mr. DOUGLASS has frankly disclosed the place of his birth, the names of those who claimed ownership in his body and soul, and the names also of those who committed the crimes which he has alleged against them. His statements, therefore, may easily be disproved, if they are untrue.

In the course of his Narrative, he relates two instances of murderous cruelty,—in one of which a planter deliberately shot a slave belonging to a neighboring plantation, who had unintentionally gotten within his lordly domain in quest of fish; and in the other, an overseer blew out the brains of a slave who had fled to a stream of water to escape a bloody scourging. Mr. DOUGLASS states that in neither of these instances was any thing done by way of legal arrest or judicial investigation. The Baltimore American, of March 17, 1845, relates a similar case of atrocity, perpetrated with similar impunity—as follows:—"Shooting a Slave.—We learn, upon the authority of a letter from Charles county, Maryland, received by a gentleman of this city, that a young man, named Matthews, a nephew of General Matthews, and whose father, it is believed, holds an office at Washington, killed one of the slaves upon his father's farm by shooting him. The letter states that young Matthews had been left in charge of the farm; that he gave an order to the servant, which was disobeyed, when he proceeded to the house, obtained a gun, and, returning, shot the servant. He immediately, the letter continues, fled to his father's residence, where he still remains unmolested."—Let it never be forgotten, that no slaveholder or overseer can be convicted of any outrage perpetrated on the person of a slave, however diabolical it may be, on the testimony of colored witnesses, whether bond or free. By the slave code, they are adjudged to be as incompetent to testify against a white man, as though they were indeed a part of the brute creation. Hence, there is no legal protection in fact, whatever there may be in form, for the slave population; and any amount of cruelty may be inflicted on them with impunity. Is it possible for the human mind to conceive of a more horrible state of society?

The effect of a religious profession on the conduct of southern masters is vividly described in the following Narrative, and shown to be any thing but salutary. In the nature of the case, it must be in the highest degree pernicious. The testimony of Mr. DOUGLASS, on this point, is sustained by a cloud of witnesses, whose veracity is unimpeachable. "A slaveholder's profession of Christianity is a palpable imposture. He is a felon of the highest grade. He is a man-stealer. It is of no importance what you put in the other scale."

Reader! are you with the man-stealers in sympathy and purpose, or on the side of their down-trodden victims? If with the former, then are you the foe of God and man. If with the latter, what are you prepared to do and dare in their behalf? Be faithful, be vigilant, be untiring in your efforts to break every yoke, and let the oppressed go free. Come what may—cost what it may—inscribe on the banner which you unfurl to the breeze, as your religious and political motto—"NO COMPROMISE WITH SLAVERY! NO UNION WITH SLAVEHOLDERS!"

WM. LLOYD GARRISON

Boston, *May* 1, 1845.

Letter from Wendell Phillips, Esq.[2]

BOSTON, *April* 22, 1845.

My Dear Friend:

You remember the old fable of "The Man and the Lion" where the lion complained that he should not be so misrepresented "when the lions wrote history."

I am glad the time has come when the "lions write history." We have been left long enough to gather the character of slavery from the involuntary evidence of the masters. One might, indeed, rest sufficiently satisfied with what, it is evident, must be, in general, the results of such a relation, without seeking farther to find whether they have followed in every instance. Indeed, those who stare at the half-peck of corn a week, and love to count the lashes on the slave's back, are seldom the "stuff" out of which reformers and abolitionists are to be made. I remember that, in 1838, many were waiting for the results of the West India experiment,[3] before they could come into our ranks. Those "results" have come long ago; but, alas! few of that number have come with them, as converts. A man must be disposed to judge of emancipation by other tests than whether it has increased the produce of sugar,—and to hate slavery for other reasons than because it starves men and whips women,—before he is ready to lay the first stone of his anti-slavery life.

I was glad to learn, in your story, how early the most neglected of God's children waken to a sense of their rights, and of the injustice done them. Experience is a keen teacher; and long before you had mastered your A B C, or knew where the "white sails" of the Chesapeake were bound, you began, I see, to gauge the wretchedness of the slave, not by his hunger and want, not by his lashes and toil, but by the cruel and blighting death which gathers over his soul.

2. A leading abolitionist of the time (1811–1884).
3. By 1838, pressure brought on the British by anti-slavery crusaders against slave trade in the West Indies generated a period of emancipation and eventual freedom for blacks throughout most of these British colonies.

In connection with this, there is one circumstance which makes your recollections peculiarly valuable, and renders your early insight the more remarkable. You come from that part of the country where we are told slavery appears with its fairest features. Let us hear, then, what it is at its best estate—gaze on its bright side, if it has one; and then imagination may task her powers to add dark lines to the picture, as she travels southward to that (for the colored man) Valley of the Shadow of Death, where the Mississippi sweeps along.

Again, we have known you long, and can put the most entire confidence in your truth, candor, and sincerity. Every one who has heard you speak has felt, and, I am confident, every one who reads your book will feel, persuaded that you give them a fair specimen of the whole truth. No one-sided portrait,—no wholesale complaints,—but strict justice done, whenever individual kindliness has neutralized, for a moment, the deadly system with which it was strangely allied. You have been with us, too, some years, and can fairly compare the twilight of rights, which your race enjoy at the North, with that "noon of night" under which they labor south of Mason and Dixon's line. Tell us whether, after all, the half-free colored man of Massachusetts is worse off than the pampered slave of the rice swamps!

In reading your life, no one can say that we have unfairly picked out some rare specimens of cruelty. We know that the bitter drops, which even you have drained from the cup, are no incidental aggravations, no individual ills, but such as must mingle always and necessarily in the lot of every slave. They are the essential ingredients, not the occasional results, of the system.

After all, I shall read your book with trembling for you. Some years ago, when you were beginning to tell me your real name and birthplace, you may remember I stopped you, and preferred to remain ignorant of all. With the exception of a vague description, so I continued, till the other day, when you read me your memoirs. I hardly knew, at the time, whether to thank you or not for the sight of them, when I reflected that it was still dangerous, in Massachusetts, for honest men to tell their names! They say the fathers, in 1776, signed the Declaration of Independence with the halter about their necks. You, too, publish your declaration of freedom with danger compassing you around. In all the broad lands which the Constitution of the United States overshadows, there is no single spot,—however narrow or desolate,—where a fugitive slave can plant himself and say, "I am safe." The whole armory of Northern Law has no shield for you. I am free to say that, in your place, I should throw the MS. into the fire.

You, perhaps, may tell your story in safety, endeared as you are to so many warm hearts by rare gifts, and a still rare devotion of them to the service of others. But it will be owing only to your labors, and the fearless efforts of those who, trampling the laws and Constitution of the country under their feet, are determined that they will "hide the outcast," and that their hearths shall be, spite of the law, an asylum for the oppressed, if, some time or other, the humblest may stand in our streets, and bear witness in safety against the cruelties which he has been the victim.

Yet is is sad to think, that these very throbbing hearts which welcome your story, and form your best safeguard in telling it, are all beating contrary to the "statute in such case made and provided." Go on, my dear friend, till you, and those who, like you, have been saved, so as by fire, from the dark prisonhouse, shall stereotype these free, illegal pulses into statutes; and New

England, cutting loose from a blood-stained Union, shall glory in being the house of refuge for the oppressed;—till we no longer merely *"hide* the outcast," or make a merit of standing idly by while he is hunted in our midst; but, consecrating anew the soil of the Pilgrims as an asylum for the oppressed, proclaim our *welcome* to the slave so loudly, that the tones shall reach every hut in the Carolinas, and make the broken-hearted bondman leap up at the thought of old Massachusetts.

God speed the day!

Till then, and ever,
Yours truly,
WENDELL PHILLIPS

FREDERICK DOUGLASS.

Chapter I

I was born in Tuckahoe, near Hillsborough, and about twelve miles from Easton, in Talbot county, Maryland. I have no accurate knowledge of my age, never having seen any authentic record containing it. By far the larger part of the slaves know as little of their ages as horses know of theirs, and it is the wish of most masters within my knowledge to keep their slaves thus ignorant. I do not remember to have ever met a slave who could tell of his birthday. They seldom come nearer to it than planting-time, harvest-time, cherry-time, spring-time, or fall-time. A want of information concerning my own was a source of unhappiness to me even during childhood. The white children could tell their ages. I could not tell why I ought to be deprived of the same privilege. I was not allowed to make any inquiries of my master concerning it. He deemed all such inquiries on the part of a slave improper and impertinent, and evidence of a restless spirit. The nearest estimate I can give makes me now between twenty-seven and twenty-eight years of age. I come to this, from hearing my master say, some time during 1835, I was about seventeen years old.

My mother was named Harriet Bailey. She was the daughter of Isaac and Betsey Bailey, both colored, and quite dark. My mother was of a darker complexion than either my grandmother or grandfather.

My father was a white man. He was admitted to be such by all I ever heard speak of my parentage. The opinion was also whispered that my master was my father; but of the correctness of this opinion, I know nothing; the means of knowing was withheld from me. My mother and I were separated when I was but an infant—before I knew her as my mother. It is a common custom, in the part of Maryland from which I ran away, to part children from their mothers at a very early age. Frequently, before the child has reached its twelfth month, its mother is taken from it, and hired out on some farm a considerable distance off, and the child is placed under the care of an old woman, too old for field labor. For what this separation is done, I do not know, unless it be to hinder the development of the child's affection toward its mother, and to blunt and destroy the natural affection of the mother for the child. This is the inevitable result.

I never saw my mother, to know her as such, more than four or five times in my life; and each of these times was very short in duration, and at night. She was hired by a Mr. Stewart, who lived about twelve miles from my home. She made her journeys to see me in the night, travelling the whole distance on foot, after the performance of her day's work. She was a field hand, and a whipping is the penalty of not being in the field at sunrise, unless a slave has special permission from his or her master to the contrary—a permission which they seldom get, and one that gives to him that gives it the proud name of being a kind master. I do not recollect of ever seeing my mother by the light of day. She was with me in the night. She would lie down with me, and get me to sleep, but long before I waked she was gone. Very little communication ever took place between us. Death soon ended what little we could have while she lived, and with it her hardships and suffering. She died when I was about seven years old, on one of my master's farms, near Lee's Mill. I was not allowed to be present during her illness, at her death, or burial. She was gone long before I knew any thing about it. Never having enjoyed, to any considerable extent, her soothing presence, her tender and watchful care, I received the tidings of her death with much the same emotions I should have probably felt at the death of a stranger.

Called thus suddenly away, she left me without the slightest intimation of who my father was. The whisper that my master was my father, may or may not be true; and, true or false, it is of but little consequence to my purpose whilst the fact remains, in all its glaring odiousness, that slaveholders have ordained, and by law established, that the children of slave women shall in all cases follow the condition of their mothers; and this is done too obviously to administer to their own lusts, and make a gratification of their wicked desires profitable as well as pleasurable; for by this cunning arrangement, the slaveholder, in cases not a few, sustains to his slaves the double relation of master and father.

I know of such cases; and it is worthy of remark that such slaves invariably suffer greater hardships, and have more to contend with, than others. They are, in the first place, a constant offence to their mistress. She is ever disposed to find fault with them; they can seldom do any thing to please her; she is never better pleased than when she sees them under the lash, especially when she suspects her husband of showing to his mulatto children favors which he withholds from his black slaves. The master is frequently compelled to sell this class of his slaves, out of deference to the feelings of his white wife; and, cruel as the deed may strike any one to be, for a man to sell his own children to human flesh-mongers, it is often the dictate of humanity for him to do so; for, unless he does this, he must not only whip them himself, but must stand by and see one white son tie up his brother, of but few shades darker complexion than himself, and ply the gory lash to his naked back; and if he lisp one word of disapproval, it is set down to his parental partiality, and only makes a bad matter worse, both for himself and the slave whom he would protect and defend.

Every year brings with it multitudes of this class of slaves. It was doubtless in consequence of a knowledge of this fact, that one great statesman of the south predicted the downfall of slavery by the inevitable laws of population. Whether this prophecy is ever fulfilled or not, it is nevertheless plain that a very different-looking class of people are springing up at the south, and are now held in slavery, from those originally brought to this country from Africa; and if their increase will do no other good, it will do away the force of the argument, that God cursed Ham,[4] and therefore American slavery is right. If

---

4. The specious argument referred to is based on an interpretation of Genesis 9.20–27, in which Noah curses his son Ham and condemns him to bondage to his brothers.

the lineal descendants of Ham are alone to be scripturally enslaved, it is certain that slavery at the south must soon become unscriptural; for thousands are ushered into the world, annually, who, like myself, owe their existence to white fathers, and those fathers most frequently their own masters.

I have had two masters. My first master's name was Anthony. I do not remember his first name. He was generally called Captain Anthony—a title which, I presume, he acquired by sailing a craft on the Chesapeake Bay. He was not considered a rich slaveholder. He owned two or three farms, and about thirty slaves. His farms and slaves were under the care of an overseer. The overseer's name was Plummer. Mr. Plummer was a miserable drunkard, a profane swearer, and a savage monster. He always went armed with a cowskin[5] and a heavy cudgel. I have known him to cut and slash the women's heads so horribly, that even master would be enraged at his cruelty, and would threaten to whip him if he did not mind himself. Master, however, was not a humane slaveholder. It required extraordinary barbarity on the part of an overseer to affect him. He was a cruel man, hardened by a long life of slaveholding. He would at times seem to take great pleasure in whipping a slave. I have often been awakened at the dawn of day by the most heart-rending shrieks of an own aunt of mine, whom he used to tie up to a joist, and whip upon her naked back till she was literally covered with blood. No words, no tears, no prayers, from his gory victim, seemed to move his iron heart from its bloody purpose. The louder she screamed, the harder he whipped; and where the blood ran fastest, there he whipped longest. He would whip her to make her scream, and whip her to make her hush; and not until overcome by fatigue, would he cease to swing the blood-clotted cowskin. I remember the first time I ever witnessed this horrible exhibition. I was quite a child, but I well remember it. I never shall forget it whilst I remember any thing. It was the first of a long series of such outrages, of which I was doomed to be a witness and a participant. It struck me with awful force. It was the blood-stained gate, the entrance to the hell of slavery, through which I was about to pass. It was a most terrible spectacle. I wish I could commit to paper the feelings with which I beheld it.

This occurrence took place very soon after I went to live with my old master, and under the following circumstances. Aunt Hester went out one night,— where or for what I do not know,—and happened to be absent when my master desired her presence. He had ordered her not to go out evenings, and warned her that she must never let him catch her in company with a young man, who was paying attention to her belonging to Colonel Lloyd. The young man's name was Ned Roberts, generally called Lloyd's Ned. Why master was so careful of her, may be safely left to conjecture. She was a woman of noble form, and of graceful proportions, having very few equals, and fewer superiors, in personal appearance, among the colored or white women of our neighborhood.

Aunt Hester had not only disobeyed his orders in going out, but had been found in company with Lloyd's Ned; which circumstance, I found, from what he said while whipping her, was the chief offence. Had he been a man of pure morals himself, he might have been thought interested in protecting the innocence of my aunt; but those who knew him will not suspect him of any such virtue. Before he commenced whipping Aunt Hester, he took her into the kitchen, and stripped her from neck to waist, leaving her neck, shoulders,

---

5. A whip made of raw cowhide.

and back, entirely naked. He then told her to cross her hands, calling her at the same time a d——d b——h. After crossing her hands, he tied them with a strong rope, and led her to a stool under a large hook in the joist, put in for the purpose. He made her get upon the stool, and tied her hands to the hook. She now stood fair for his infernal purpose. Her arms were stretched up at their full length, so that she stood upon the ends of her toes. He then said to her, "Now, you d——d b——h, I'll learn you how to disobey my orders!" and after rolling up his sleeves, he commenced to lay on the heavy cowskin, and soon the warm, red blood (amid heart-rending shrieks from her, and horrid oaths from him) came dripping to the floor. I was so terrified and horror-stricken at the sight, that I hid myself in a closet, and dared not venture out till long after the bloody transaction was over. I expected it would be my turn next. It was all new to me. I had never seen any thing like it before. I had always lived with my grandmother on the outskirts of the plantation, where she was put to raise the children of the younger women. I had therefore been, until now, out of the way of the bloody scenes that often occurred on the plantation.

Chapter II

My master's family consisted of two sons, Andrew and Richard; one daughter, Lucretia, and her husband, Captain Thomas Auld. They lived in one house, upon the home plantation of Colonel Edward Lloyd. My master was Colonel Lloyd's clerk and superintendent. He was what might be called the overseer of the overseers. I spent two years of childhood on this plantation in my old master's family. It was here that I witnessed the bloody transaction recorded in the first chapter; and as I received my first impressions of slavery on this plantation, I will give some description of it, and of slavery as it there existed. The plantation is about twelve miles north of Easton, in Talbot county, and is situated on the border of Miles River. The principal products raised upon it were tobacco, corn, and wheat. These were raised in great abundance; so that, with the products of this and the other farms belonging to him, he was able to keep in almost constant employment a large sloop, in carrying them to market at Baltimore. This sloop was named Sally Lloyd, in honor of one of the colonel's daughters. My master's son-in-law, Captain Auld, was master of the vessel; she was otherwise manned by the colonel's own slaves. Their names were Peter, Isaac, Rich, and Jake. These were esteemed very highly by the other slaves, and looked upon as the privileged ones of the plantation; for it was no small affair, in the eyes of the slaves, to be allowed to see Baltimore.

Colonel Lloyd kept from three to four hundred slaves on his home plantation, and owned a large number more on the neighboring farms belonging to him. The names of the farms nearest to the home plantation were Wye Town and New Design. "Wye Town" was under the overseership of a man named Noah Willis. New Design was under the overseership of a Mr. Townsend. The overseers of these, and all the rest of the farms, numbering over twenty, received advice and direction from the managers of the home plantation. This was the great business place. It was the seat of government for the whole twenty farms. All disputes among the overseers were settled here. If a slave was convicted of any high misdemeanor, became unmanageable, or evinced a determination to run away, he was brought immediately here, severely whipped, put on board the sloop, carried to Baltimore, and sold to Austin Woolfolk, or some other slave-trader, as a warning to the slaves remaining.

Here, too, the slaves of all the other farms received their monthly allowance of food, and their yearly clothing. The men and women slaves received, as their monthly allowance of food, eight pounds of pork, or its equivalent in fish, and one bushel of corn meal. Their yearly clothing consisted of two coarse linen shirts, one pair of linen trousers, like the shirts, one jacket, one pair of trousers for winter, made of coarse negro cloth, one pair of stockings, and one pair of shoes; the whole of which could not have cost more than seven dollars. The allowance of the slave children was given to their mothers, or the old women having the care of them. The children unable to work in the field had neither shoes, stockings, jackets, nor trousers, given to them; their clothing consisted of two coarse linen shirts per year. When these failed them, they went naked until the next allowance-day. Children from seven to ten years old, of both sexes, almost naked, might be seen at all seasons of the year.

There were no beds given the slaves, unless one coarse blanket be considered such, and none but the men and women had these. This, however, is not considered a very great privation. They find less difficulty from the want of beds, than from the want of time to sleep; for when their day's work in the field is done, the most of them having their washing, mending, and cooking to do, and having few or none of the ordinary facilities for doing either of these, very many of their sleeping hours are consumed in preparing for the field the coming day; and when this is done, old and young, male and female, married and single, drop down side by side, on one common bed,—the cold, damp floor,—each covering himself or herself with their miserable blankets; and here they sleep till they are summoned to the field by the driver's horn. At the sound of this, all must rise, and be off to the field. There must be no halting; every one must be at his or her post; and woe betides them who hear not this morning summons to the field; for if they are not awakened by the sense of hearing, they are by the sense of feeling: no age nor sex finds any favor. Mr. Severe, the overseer, used to stand by the door of the quarter, armed with a large hickory stick and heavy cowskin, ready to whip any one who was so unfortunate as not to hear, or, from any other cause, was prevented from being ready to start for the field at the sound of the horn.

Mr. Severe was rightly named: he was a cruel man. I have seen him whip a woman, causing the blood to run half an hour at the time; and this, too, in the midst of her crying children, pleading for their mother's release. He seemed to take pleasure in manifesting his fiendish barbarity. Added to his cruelty, he was a profane swearer. It was enough to chill the blood and stiffen the hair of an ordinary man to hear him talk. Scarce a sentence escaped him but that was commenced or concluded by some horrid oath. The field was the place to witness his cruelty and profanity. His presence made it both the field of blood and of blasphemy. From the rising till the going down of the sun, he was cursing, raving, cutting, and slashing among the slaves of the field, in the most frightful manner. His career was short. He died very soon after I went to Colonel Lloyd's; and he died as he lived, uttering, with his dying groans, bitter curses and horrid oaths. His death was regarded by the slaves as the result of a merciful providence.

Mr. Severe's place was filled by a Mr. Hopkins. He was a very different man. He was less cruel, less profane, and made less noise, then Mr. Severe. His course was characterized by no extraordinary demonstrations of cruelty. He whipped, but seemed to take no pleasure in it. He was called by the slaves a good overseer.

The home plantation of Colonel Lloyd wore the appearance of a country village. All the mechanical operations for all the farms were performed here. The shoemaking and mending, the blacksmithing, cartwrighting, coopering, weaving, and grain-grinding, were all performed by the slaves on the home plantation. The whole place wore a business-like aspect very unlike the neighboring farms. The number of houses, too, conspired to give it advantage over the neighboring farms. It was called by the slaves the *Great House Farm*. Few privileges were esteemed higher, by the slaves of the out-farms, than that of being selected to do errands at the Great House Farm. It was associated in their minds with greatness. A representative could not be prouder of his election to a seat in the American Congress, than a slave on one of the out-farms would be of his election to do errands at the Great House Farm. They regarded it as evidence of great confidence reposed in them by their overseers; and it was on this account, as well as a constant desire to be out of the field from under the driver's lash, that they esteemed it a high privilege, one worth careful living for. He was called the smartest and most trusty fellow, who had this honor conferred upon him the most frequently. The competitors for this office sought as diligently to please their overseers, as the office-seekers in the political parties seek to please and deceive the people. The same traits of character might be seen in Colonel Lloyd's slaves, as are seen in the slaves of the political parties.

The slaves selected to go to the Great House Farm, for the monthly allowance for themselves and their fellow-slaves, were peculiarly enthusiastic. While on their way, they would make the dense old woods, for miles around, reverberate with their wild songs, revealing at once the highest joy and the deepest sadness. They would compose and sing as they went along, consulting neither time nor tune. The thought that came up, came out—if not in the word, in the sound;—and as frequently in the one as in the other. They would sometimes sing the most pathetic sentiment in the most rapturous tone, and the most rapturous sentiment in the most pathetic tone. Into all of their songs they would manage to weave something of the Great House Farm. Especially would they do this, when leaving home. They would then sing most exultingly the following words:—

> "I am going away to the Great House Farm!
> O, yea! O, yea! O!"

This they would sing, as a chorus, to words which to many would seem unmeaning jargon, but which, nevertheless, were full of meaning to themselves. I have sometimes thought that the mere hearing of those songs would do more to impress some minds with the horrible character of slavery, than the reading of whole volumes of philosophy on the subject could do.

I did not, when a slave, understand the deep meaning of those rude and apparently incoherent songs. I was myself within the circle; so that I neither saw nor heard as those without might see and hear. They told a tale of woe which was then altogether beyond my feeble comprehension; they were tones loud, long, and deep; they breathed the prayer and complaint of souls boiling over with the bitterest anguish. Every tone was a testimony against slavery, and a prayer to God for deliverance from chains. The hearing of those wild notes always depressed my spirit, and filled me with ineffable sadness. I have frequently found myself in tears while hearing them. The mere recurrence to those songs, even now, afflicts me; and while I am writing these lines, an expression of feeling has already found its way down my cheek. To those songs I trace my first glimmering conception of the dehumanizing character of slavery. I can never get rid of that conception. Those songs still follow me, to deepen my hatred of slavery, and quicken my sympathies for my brethren in bonds. If any one wishes to be impressed with the soul-killing effects of slavery, let him go to Colonel Lloyd's plantation, and, on allowance-day, place himself in the deep pine woods, and there let him, in silence, analyze the sounds that shall pass through the chambers of his soul,—and if he is not thus impressed, it will only be because "there is no flesh in his obdurate heart."

I have often been utterly astonished, since I came to the north, to find persons who could speak of the singing, among slaves, as evidence of their contentment and happiness. It is impossible to conceive of a greater mistake. Slaves sing most when they are most unhappy. The songs of the slave represent the sorrows of his heart; and he is relieved by them, only as an aching heart is relieved by its tears. At least, such is my experience. I have often sung to drown my sorrow, but seldom to express my happiness. Crying for joy, and singing for joy, were alike uncommon to me while in the jaws of slavery. The singing of a man cast away upon a desolate island might be as appropriately considered as evidence of contentment and happiness, as the singing of a slave; the songs of the one and of the other are prompted by the same emotion.

Chapter III

Colonel Lloyd kept a large and finely cultivated garden, which afforded almost constant employment for four men, besides the chief gardener, (Mr. M'Durmond.) This garden was probably the greatest attraction of the place. During the summer months, people came from far and near—from Baltimore, Easton, and Annapolis—to see it. It abounded in fruits of almost every description, from the hardy apple of the north to the delicate orange of the south. This garden was not the least source of trouble on the plantation. Its excellent fruit was quite a temptation to the hungry swarms of boys, as well as the older slaves, belonging to the colonel, few of whom had the virtue or the vice to resist it. Scarcely a day passed, during the summer, but that some slave had to take the lash for stealing fruit. The colonel had to resort to all kinds of strategems to keep his slaves out of the garden. The last and most successful one was that of tarring his fence all around, after which, if a slave was caught with any tar upon his person, it was deemed sufficient proof that he had either been into the garden, or had tried to get in. In either case, he was severely whipped by the chief gardener. This plan worked well; the slaves became as fearful of tar as of the lash. They seemed to realize the impossibility of touching *tar* without being defiled.

The colonel also kept a splendid riding equipage. His stable and carriage-house presented the appearance of some of our large city livery establishments. His horses were of the finest form and noblest blood. His carriage-house contained three splendid coaches, three or four gigs, besides dearborns and barouches[6] of the most fashionable style.

This establishment was under the care of two slaves—old Barney and young Barney—father and son. To attend to this establishment was their sole work. But it was by no means an easy employment; for in nothing was Colonel Lloyd more particular than in the management of his horses. The slightest inattention to these was unpardonable, and was visited upon those, under whose care they were placed, with the severest punishment; no excuse could shield them, if the colonel only suspected any want of attention to his horses— a supposition which he frequently indulged, and one which, of course, made the office of old and young Barney a very trying one. They never knew when they were safe from punishment. They were frequently whipped when least deserving, and escaped whipping when most deserving it. Every thing depended upon the looks of the horses, and the state of Colonel Lloyd's own mind when his horses were brought to him for use. If a horse did not move fast enough, or hold his head high enough, it was owing to some fault of his keepers. It was painful to stand near the stable-door, and hear the various complaints against the keepers when a horse was taken out for use. "This horse has not had proper attention. He has not been sufficiently rubbed and curried, or he has not been properly fed; his food was too wet or too dry; he got it too soon or too late; he was too hot or too cold; he had too much hay, and not enough of grain; or he had too much grain, and not enough of hay; instead of old Barney's attending to the horse, he had very improperly left it to his son." To all these complaints, no matter how unjust, the slave must answer never a word. Colonel Lloyd could not brook any contradiction from a slave. When he spoke, a slave must stand, listen, and tremble; and such was literally the case. I have seen Colonel Lloyd make old Barney, a man between fifty and sixty years of age, uncover his bald head, kneel down upon the cold, damp ground, and receive upon his naked and toil-worn shoulders more than thirty lashes at the time. Colonel Lloyd had three sons—Edward, Murray, and Daniel,—and three sons-in-law, Mr. Winder, Mr. Nicholson, and Mr. Lowndes. All of these lived at the Great House Farm, and enjoyed the luxury of whipping the servants when they pleased, from old Barney down to William Wilkes, the coach-driver. I have seen Winder make one of the house-servants stand off from him a suitable distance to be touched with the end of his whip, and at every stroke raise great ridges upon his back.

To describe the wealth of Colonel Lloyd would be almost equal to describing the riches of Job. He kept from ten to fifteen house-servants. He was said to own a thousand slaves, and I think this estimate quite within the truth. Colonel Lloyd owned so many that he did not know them when he saw them; nor did all the slaves of the out-farms know him. It is reported of him, that, while riding along the road one day, he met a colored man, and addressed him in the usual manner of speaking to colored people on the public highways of the south: "Well, boy, whom do you belong to?" "To Colonel Lloyd," replied the slave. "Well, does the colonel treat you well?" "No, sir," was the ready reply. "What, does he work you too hard?" "Yes, sir." "Well, don't he give you enough to eat?" "Yes, sir, he gives me enough, such as it is."

The colonel, after ascertaining where the slave belonged, rode on; the man

6. Different kinds of carriages.

also went on about his business, not dreaming that he had been conversing with his master. He thought, said, and heard nothing more of the matter, until two or three weeks afterwards. The poor man was then informed by his overseer that, for having found fault with his master, he was now to be sold to a Georgia trader. He was immediately chained and handcuffed; and thus, without a moment's warning, he was snatched away, and forever sundered, from his family and friends, by a hand more unrelenting than death. This is the penalty of telling the truth, of telling the simple truth, in answer to a series of plain questions.

It is partly in consequence of such facts, that slaves, when inquired of as to their condition and the character of their masters, almost universally say they are contented, and that their masters are kind. The slaveholders have been known to send in spies among their slaves, to ascertain their views and feelings in regard to their condition. The frequency of this has had the effect to establish among the slaves the maxim, that a still tongue makes a wise head. They suppress the truth rather than take the consequences of telling it, and in so doing prove themselves a part of the human family. If they have any thing to say of their masters, it is generally in their masters' favor, especially when speaking to an untried man. I have been frequently asked, when a slave, if I had a kind master, and do not remember ever to have given a negative answer; nor did I, in pursuing this course, consider myself as uttering what was absolutely false; for I always measured the kindness of my master by the standard of kindness set up among slaveholders around us. Moreover, slaves are like other people, and imbibe prejudices quite common to others. They think their own better than that of others. Many, under the influence of this prejudice, think their own masters are better than the masters of other slaves; and this, too, in some cases, when the very reverse is true. Indeed, it is not uncommon for slaves even to fall out and quarrel among themselves about the relative goodness of their masters, each contending for the superior goodness of his own over that of the others. At the very same time, they mutually execrate their masters when viewed separately. It was so on our plantation. When Colonel Lloyd's slaves met the slaves of Jacob Jepson, they seldom parted without a quarrel about their masters; Colonel Lloyd's slaves contending that he was the richest, and Mr. Jepson's slaves that he was the smartest, and most of a man. Colonel Lloyd's slaves would boast his ability to buy and sell Jacob Jepson. Mr. Jepson's slaves would boast his ability to whip Colonel Lloyd. These quarrels would almost always end in a fight between the parties, and those that whipped were supposed to have gained the point at issue. They seemed to think that the greatness of their masters was transferable to themselves. It was considered as being bad enough to be a slave; but to be a poor man's slave was deemed a disgrace indeed!

Chapter IV

Mr. Hopkins remained but a short time in the office of overseer. Why his career was so short, I do not know, but suppose he lacked the necessary severity to suit Colonel Lloyd. Mr. Hopkins was succeeded by Mr. Austin Gore, a man possessing, in an eminent degree, all those traits of character indispensable to what is called a first-rate overseer. Mr. Gore had served Colonel Lloyd, in the capacity of overseer, upon one of the out-farms, and had shown himself worthy of the high station of overseer upon the home or Great House Farm.

Mr. Gore was proud, ambitious, and persevering. He was artful, cruel, and obdurate. He was just the man for such a place, and it was just the place for such a man. It afforded scope for the full exercise of all his powers, and he seemed to be perfectly at home in it. He was one of those who could torture the slightest look, word, or gesture, on the part of the slave, into impudence, and would treat it accordingly. There must be no answering back to him; no explanation was allowed a slave, showing himself to have been wrongfully accused. Mr. Gore acted fully up to the maxim laid down by slaveholders,— "It is better that a dozen slaves suffer under the lash, than that the overseer should be convicted, in the presence of the slaves, of having been at fault." No matter how innocent a slave might be—it availed him nothing, when accused by Mr. Gore of any misdemeanor. To be accused was to be convicted, and to be convicted was to be punished; the one always following the other with immutable certainty. To escape punishment was to escape accusation; and few slaves had the fortune to do either, under the overseership of Mr. Gore. He was just proud enough to demand the most debasing homage of the slave, and quite servile enough to crouch, himself, at the feet of the master. He was ambitious enough to be contented with nothing short of the highest rank of overseers, and persevering enough to reach the height of his ambition. He was cruel enough to inflict the severest punishment, artful enough to descend to the lowest trickery, and obdurate enough to be insensible to the voice of a reproving conscience. He was, of all the overseers, the most dreaded by the slaves. His presence was painful; his eye flashed confusion; and seldom was his sharp, shrill voice heard, without producing horror and trembling in their ranks.

Mr. Gore was a grave man, and, though a young man, he indulged in no jokes, said no funny words, seldom smiled. His words were in perfect keeping with his looks, and his looks were in perfect keeping with his words. Overseers will sometimes indulge in a witty word, even with the slaves; not so with Mr. Gore. He spoke but to command, and commanded but to be obeyed; he dealt sparingly with his words, and bountifully with his whip, never using the former where the latter would answer as well. When he whipped, he seemed to do so from a sense of duty, and feared no consequences. He did nothing reluctantly, no matter how disagreeable; always at his post, never inconsistent. He never promised but to fulfil. He was, in a word, a man of the most inflexible firmness and stone-like coolness.

His savage barbarity was equalled only by the consummate coolness with which he committed the grossest and most savage deeds upon the slaves under his charge. Mr. Gore once undertook to whip one of Colonel Lloyd's slaves, by the name of Demby. He had given Demby but few stripes, when, to get rid of the scourging, he ran and plunged himself into a creek, and stood there at the depth of his shoulders, refusing to come out. Mr. Gore told him that he would give him three calls, and that, if he did not come out at the third call, he would shoot him. The first call was given. Demby made no response, but stood his ground. The second and third calls were given with the same result. Mr. Gore then, without consultation or deliberation with any one, not even giving Demby an additional call, raised his musket to his face, taking deadly aim at his standing victim, and in an instant poor Demby was no more. His mangled body sank out of sight, and blood and brains marked the water where he had stood.

A thrill of horror flashed through every soul upon the plantation, excepting Mr. Gore. He alone seemed cool and collected. He was asked by Colonel Lloyd and my old master, why he resorted to this extraordinary expedient. His reply was, (as well as I can remember,) that Demby had become unmanageable. He was setting a dangerous example to the other slaves,—one which, if suffered to pass without some such demonstration on his part, would finally lead to the total subversion of all rule and order upon the plantation. He argued that if one slave refused to be corrected, and escaped with his life, the other slaves would soon copy the example; the result of which would be, the freedom of the slaves, and the enslavement of the whites. Mr. Gore's defence was satisfactory. He was continued in his station as overseer upon the home plantation. His fame as an overseer went abroad. His horrid crime was not even submitted to judicial investigation. It was committed in the presence of slaves, and they of course could neither institute a suit, nor testify against him; and thus the guilty perpetrator of one of the bloodiest and most foul murders goes unwhipped of justice, and uncensured by the community in which he lives. Mr. Gore lived in St. Michael's, Talbot county, Maryland, when I left there; and if he is still alive, he very probably lives there now; and if so, he is now, as he was then, as highly esteemed and as much respected as though his guilty soul had not been stained with his brother's blood.

I speak advisedly when I say this,—that killing a slave, or any colored person, in Talbot county, Maryland, is not treated as a crime, either by the courts or the community. Mr. Thomas Lanman, of St. Michael's, killed two slaves, one of whom he killed with a hatchet, by knocking his brains out. He used to boast of the commission of the awful and bloody deed. I have heard him do so laughingly, saying, among other things, that he was the only benefactor of his country in the company, and that when others would do as much as he had done, we should be relieved of "the d——d niggers."

The wife of Mr. Giles Hick, living but a short distance from where I used to live, murdered my wife's cousin, a young girl between fifteen and sixteen years of age, mangling her person in the most horrible manner, breaking her nose and breastbone with a stick, so that the poor girl expired in a few hours afterward. She was immediately buried, but had not been in her untimely grave but a few hours before she was taken up and examined by the coroner, who decided that she had come to her death by severe beating. The offence for which this girl was thus murdered was this:—She had been set that night to mind Mrs. Hick's baby, and during the night she fell asleep, and the baby cried. She, having lost her rest for several nights previous, did not hear the crying. They were both in the room with Mrs. Hicks. Mrs. Hicks, finding the girl slow to move, jumped from her bed, seized an oak stick of wood by the fireplace, and with it broke the girl's nose and breastbone, and thus ended her life. I will not say that this most horrid murder produced no sensation in the community. It did produce sensation, but not enough to bring the murderess to punishment. There was a warrant issued for her arrest, but it was never served. Thus she escaped not only punishment, but even the pain of being arraigned before a court for her horrid crime.

Whilst I am detailing bloody deeds which took place during my stay on Colonel Lloyd's plantation, I will briefly narrate another, which occurred about the same time as the murder of Demby by Mr. Gore.

Colonel Lloyd's slaves were in the habit of spending a part of their nights and Sundays in fishing for oysters, and in this way made up the deficiency of their scanty allowance. An old man belonging to Colonel Lloyd, while thus engaged, happened to get beyond the limits of Colonel Lloyd's, and on the premises of Mr. Beal Bondly. At this trespass, Mr. Bondly took offence, and with his musket came down to the shore, and blew its deadly contents into the poor old man.

Mr. Bondly came over to see Colonel Lloyd the next day, whether to pay him for his property, or to justify himself in what he had done, I know not. At any rate, this whole fiendish transaction was soon hushed up. There was very little said about it at all, and nothing done. It was a common saying, even among little white boys, that it was worth a half-cent to kill a "nigger," and a half-cent to bury one.

Chapter V

As to my own treatment while I lived on Colonel Lloyd's plantation, it was very similar to that of the other slave children. I was not old enough to work in the field, and there being little else than field work to do, I had a great deal of leisure time. The most I had to do was to drive up the cows at evening, keep the fowls out of the garden, keep the front yard clean, and run of errands for my old master's daughter, Mrs. Lucretia Auld. The most of my leisure time I spent in helping Master Daniel Lloyd in finding his birds, after he had shot them. My connection with Master Daniel was of some advantage to me. He became quite attached to me, and was a sort of protector of me. He would not allow the older boys to impose upon me, and would divide his cakes with me.

I was seldom whipped by my old master, and suffered little from any thing else than hunger and cold. I suffered much from hunger, but much more from cold. In hottest summer and coldest winter, I was kept almost naked— no shoes, no stockings, no jacket, no trousers, nothing on but a coarse tow linen shirt, reaching only to my knees. I had no bed. I must have perished with cold, but that, the coldest nights, I used to steal a bag which was used for carrying corn to the mill. I would crawl into this bag, and there sleep on the cold, damp, clay floor, with my head in and feet out. My feet have been so cracked with the frost, that the pen with which I am writing might be laid in the gashes.

We were not regularly allowanced. Our food was coarse corn meal boiled. This was called *mush*. It was put into a large wooden tray or trough, and set down upon the ground. The children were then called, like so many pigs, and like so many pigs they would come and devour the mush; some with oyster-shells, others with pieces of shingle, some with naked hands, and none with spoons. He that ate fastest got most; he that was strongest secured the best place; and few left the trough satisfied.

I was probably between seven and eight years old when I left Colonel Lloyd's plantation. I left it with joy. I shall never forget the ecstasy with which I received the intelligence that my old master (Anthony) had determined to let me go to Baltimore, to live with Mr. Hugh Auld, brother to my old master's son-in-law, Captain Thomas Auld. I received this information about three days before my departure. They were three of the happiest days I ever enjoyed. I spent the most part of all these three days in the creek, washing off the plantation scurf, and preparing myself for my departure.

The pride of appearance which this would indicate was not my own. I spent the time in washing, not so much because I wished to, but because Mrs. Lucretia had told me I must get all the dead skin off my feet and knees before I could go to Baltimore; for the people of Baltimore were very cleanly, and would laugh at me if I looked dirty. Besides, she was going to give me a pair of trousers, which I should not put on unless I got all the dirt off me. The thought of owning a pair of trousers was great indeed! It was almost a sufficient motive, not only to make me take off what would be called by pig-drovers the mange, but the skin itself. I went at it in good earnest, working for the first time with the hope of reward.

The ties that ordinarily bind children to their homes were all suspended in my case. I found no severe trial in my departure. My home was charmless; it was not home to me; on parting from it, I could not feel that I was leaving any thing which I could have enjoyed by staying. My mother was dead, my grandmother lived far off, so that I seldom saw her. I had two sisters and one brother, that lived in the same house with me; but the early separation of us from our mother had well nigh blotted the fact of our relationship from our memories. I looked for home elsewhere, and was confident of finding none which I should relish less than the one which I was leaving. If, however, I found in my new home hardship, hunger, whipping, and nakedness, I had the consolation that I should not have escaped any one of them by staying. Having already had more than a taste of them in the house of my old master, and having endured them there, I very naturally inferred my ability to endure them elsewhere, and especially at Baltimore; for I had something of the feeling about Baltimore that is expressed in the proverb, that "being hanged in England is preferable to dying a natural death in Ireland." I had the strongest desire to see Baltimore. Cousin Tom, though not fluent in speech, had inspired me with that desire by his eloquent description of the place. I could never point out any thing at the Great House, no matter how beautiful or powerful, but that he had seen something at Baltimore far exceeding, both in beauty and strength, the object which I pointed out to him. Even the Great House itself, with all its pictures, was far inferior to many buildings in Baltimore. So strong was my desire, that I thought a gratification of it would fully compensate for whatever loss of comforts I should sustain by the exchange. I left without a regret, and with the highest hopes of future happiness.

We sailed out of Miles River for Baltimore on a Saturday morning. I remember only the day of the week, for at that time I had no knowledge of the days of the month, nor the months of the year. On setting sail, I walked aft, and gave to Colonel Lloyd's plantation what I hoped would be the last look. I then placed myself in the bows of the sloop, and there spent the remainder of the day in looking ahead, interesting myself in what was in the distance rather than in things near by or behind.

In the afternoon of that day, we reached Annapolis, the capital of the State. We stopped but a few moments, so that I had no time to go on shore. It was the first large town that I had ever seen, and though it would look small compared with some of our New England factory villages, I thought it a wonderful place for its size—more imposing even than the Great House Farm!

We arrived at Baltimore early on Sunday morning, landing at Smith's Wharf, not far from Bowley's Wharf. We had on board the sloop a large flock of sheep; and after aiding in driving them to the slaughterhouse of Mr. Curtis on Louden Slater's Hill, I was conducted by Rich, one of the hands belonging on board of the sloop, to my new home in Alliciana Street, near Mr. Gardner's ship-yard, on Fells Point.

Mr. and Mrs. Auld were both at home, and met me at the door with their little son Thomas, to take care of whom I had been given. And here I saw what I had never seen before; it was a white face beaming with the most kindly emotions; it was the face of my new mistress, Sophia Auld. I wish I could describe the rapture that flashed through my soul as I beheld it. It was a new and strange sight to me, brightening up my pathway with the light of happiness. Little Thomas was told, there was his Freddy,—and I was told to take care of little Thomas; and thus I entered upon the duties of my new home with the most cheering prospect ahead.

I look upon my departure from Colonel Lloyd's plantation as one of the most interesting events of my life. It is possible, and even quite probable, that but for the mere circumstance of being removed from that plantation to Baltimore, I should have to-day, instead of being here seated by my own table, in the enjoyment of freedom and the happiness of home, writing this Narrative, been confined in the galling chains of slavery. Going to live at Baltimore laid the foundation, and opened the gateway, to all my subsequent prosperity. I have ever regarded it as the first plain manifestation of that kind providence which has ever since attended me, and marked my life with so many favors. I regarded the selection of myself as being somewhat remarkable. There were a number of slave children that might have been sent from the plantation to Baltimore. There were those younger, those older, and those of the same age. I was chosen from among them all, and was the first, last, and only choice.

I may be deemed superstitious, and even egotistical, in regarding this event as a special interposition of divine Providence in my favor. But I should be false to the earliest sentiments of my soul, if I suppressed the opinion. I prefer to be true to myself, even at the hazard of incurring the ridicule of others, rather than to be false, and incur my own abhorrence. From my earliest recollection, I date the entertainment of a deep conviction that slavery would not always be able to hold me within its foul embrace; and in the darkest hours of my career in slavery, this living word of faith and spirit of hope departed not from me, but remained like ministering angels to cheer me through the gloom. This good spirit was from God, and to him I offer thanksgiving and praise.

Chapter VI

My new mistress proved to be all she appeared when I first met her at the door,—a woman of the kindest heart and finest feelings. She had never had a slave under her control previously to myself, and prior to her marriage she had been dependent upon her own industry for a living. She was by trade a weaver; and by constant application to her business, she had been in a good degree preserved from the blighting and dehumanizing effects of slavery. I was utterly astonished at her goodness. I scarcely knew how to behave towards her. She was entirely unlike any other white woman I had ever seen. I could not approach her as I was accustomed to approach other white ladies. My early instruction was all out of place. The crouching servility, usually so acceptable a quality in a slave, did not answer when manifested toward her. Her favor was not gained by it; she seemed to be disturbed by it. She did not deem it impudent or unmannerly for a slave to look her in the face. The meanest slave was put fully at ease in her presence, and none left without feeling better for having seen her. Her face was made of heavenly smiles, and her voice of tranquil music.

But, alas! this kind heart had but a short time to remain such. The fatal poison of irresponsible power was already in her hands, and soon commenced its infernal work. That cheerful eye, under the influence of slavery, soon became red with rage; that voice, made all of sweet accord, changed to one of harsh and horrid discord; and that angelic face gave place to that of a demon.

Very soon after I went to live with Mr. and Mrs. Auld, she was kindly commenced to teach me the A, B, C. After I had learned this, she assisted me in learning to spell words of three or four letters. Just at this point of my progress, Mr. Auld found out what was going on, and at once forbade Mrs. Auld to instruct me further, telling her, among other things, that it was unlawful, as well as unsafe, to teach a slave to read. To use his own words, further, he said, "If you give a nigger an inch, he will take an ell. A nigger should know nothing but to obey his master—to do as he is told to do. Learning would *spoil* the best nigger in the world. Now," said he, "if you teach that nigger (speaking of myself) how to read, there would be no keeping him. It would forever unfit him to be a slave. He would at once become unmanageable, and of no value to his master. As to himself, it could do him no good, but a great deal of harm. It would make him discontented and unhappy." These words sank deep into my heart, stirred up sentiments within that lay slumbering, and called into existence an entirely new train of thought. It was a new and special revelation, explaining dark and mysterious things, with which my youthful understanding had struggled, but struggled in vain. I now understood what had been to me a most perplexing difficulty—to wit, the white man's power to enslave the black man. It was a grand achievement, and I prized it highly. From that moment, I understood the pathway from slavery to freedom. It was just what I wanted, and I got it at a time when I the least expected it. Whilst I was saddened by the thought of losing the aid of my kind mistress, I was gladdened by the invaluable instruction which, by the merest accident, I had gained from my master. Though conscious of the difficulty of learning without a teacher, I set out with high hope, and a fixed purpose, at whatever cost of trouble, to learn how to read. The very decided manner with which he spoke, and strove to impress his wife with the evil consequences of giving me instruction, served to convince me that he was deeply sensible of the truths he was uttering. It gave me the best assurance that I might rely with the utmost confidence on the results which, he said, would flow from teaching me to read. What he most dreaded, that I most desired. What he most loved, that I most hated. That which to him was a great evil, to be carefully shunned, was to me a great good, to be diligently sought; and the argument which he so warmly urged, against my learning to read, only served to inspire me with a desire and determination to learn. In learning to read, I owe almost as much to the bitter opposition of my master, as to the kindly aid of my mistress. I acknowledge the benefit of both.

I had resided but a short time in Baltimore before I observed a marked difference, in the treatment of slaves, from that which I had witnessed in the country. A city slave is almost a freeman, compared with a slave on the plantation. He is much better fed and clothed, and enjoys privileges altogether unknown to the slave on the plantation. There is a vestige of decency, a sense of shame, that does much to curb and check those outbreaks of atrocious cruelty so commonly enacted upon the plantation. He is a desperate slave-holder, who will shock the humanity of his non-slaveholding neighbors with the cries of his lacerated slave. Few are willing to incur the odium attaching to the reputation of being a cruel master; and above all things, they would not be known as not giving a slave enough to eat. Every city slaveholder is anxious to have it known of him, that he feeds his slaves well; and it is due to them to say, that most of them do give their slaves enough to eat. There are, however, some painful exceptions to this rule. Directly opposite to us, on Philpot Street, lived Mr. Thomas Hamilton. He owned two slaves. Their names were Henrietta and Mary. Henrietta was about twenty-two years of age, Mary was about fourteen; and of all the mangled and emaciated creatures I ever looked upon, these two were the most so. His heart must be harder than stone, that could look upon these unmoved. The head, neck, and shoulders of Mary were literally cut to pieces. I have frequently felt her head, and found it nearly covered with festering sores, caused by the lash of her cruel mistress. I do not know that her master ever whipped her, but I have been an eye-witness to the cruelty of Mrs. Hamilton. I used to be in Mr. Hamilton's house nearly every day. Mrs. Hamilton used to sit in a large chair in the middle of the room, with a heavy cowskin always by her side, and scarce an hour passed during the day but was marked by the blood of one of these slaves. The girls seldom passed her without her saying, "Move faster, you *black gip!*" at the same time giving them a blow with the cowskin over the head or shoulders, often drawing the blood. She would then say, "Take that, you *black gip!*"—continuing, "If you don't move faster, I'll move you!" Added to the cruel lashings to which these slaves were subjected, they were kept nearly half-starved. They seldom knew what it was to eat a full meal. I have seen Mary contending with the pigs for the offal thrown into the street. So much was Mary kicked and cut to pieces, that she was oftener called "*pecked*" than by her name.

Chapter VII

I lived in Master Hugh's family about seven years. During this time, I succeeded in learning to read and write. In accomplishing this, I was compelled to resort to various stratagems. I had no regular teacher. My mistress, who had kindly commenced to instruct me, had, in compliance with the advice and direction of her husband, not only ceased to instruct, but had set her face against my being instructed by any one else. It is due, however, to my mistress to say of her, that she did not adopt this course of treatment immediately. She at first lacked the depravity indispensable to shutting me up in mental darkness. It was at least necessary for her to have some training in the exercise of irresponsible power, to make her equal to the task of treating me as though I were a brute.

My mistress was, as I have said, a kind and tender-hearted woman; and in the simplicity of her soul she commenced, when I first went to live with her, to treat me as she supposed one human being ought to treat another. In entering upon the duties of a slaveholder, she did not seem to perceive that I sustained to her the relation of a mere chattel, and that for her to treat me as a human being was not only wrong, but dangerously so. Slavery proved as injurious to her as it did to me. When I went there, she was a pious, warm, and tender-hearted woman. There was no sorrow or suffering for which she had not a tear. She had bread for the hungry, clothes for the naked, and comfort for every mourner that came within her reach. Slavery soon proved its ability to divest her of these heavenly qualities. Under its influence, the tender heart became stone, and the lamblike disposition gave way to one of tiger-like fierceness. The first step in her downward course was in her ceasing to instruct me. She now commenced to practise her husband's precepts. She finally became even more violent in her opposition than her husband himself. She was not satisfied with simply doing as well as he had commanded; she seemed anxious to do better. Nothing seemed to make her more angry than to see me with a newspaper. She seemed to think that here lay the danger. I have had her rush at me with a face made all up of fury, and snatch from me a newspaper, in a manner that fully revealed her apprehension. She was an apt woman; and a little experience soon demonstrated, to her satisfaction, that education and slavery were incompatible with each other.

From this time I was most narrowly watched. If I was in a separate room any considerable length of time, I was sure to be suspected of having a book, and was at once called to give an account of myself. All this, however, was too late. The first step had been taken. Mistress, in teaching me the alphabet, had given me the *inch*, and no precaution could prevent me from taking the *ell*.

The plan which I adopted, and the one by which I was most successful, was that of making friends of all the little white boys whom I met in the street. As many of these as I could, I converted into teachers. With their kindly aid, obtained at different times and in different places, I finally succeeded in learning to read. When I was sent of errands, I always took my book with me, and by going one part of my errand quickly, I found time to get a lesson before my return. I used also to carry bread with me, enough of which was always in the house, and to which I was always welcome; for I was much better off in this regard than many of the poor white children in our neighborhood. This bread I used to bestow upon the hungry little urchins, who, in return, would give me that more valuable bread of knowledge. I am strongly tempted to give the names of two or three of those little boys, as a testimonial of the gratitude and affection I bear them; but prudence forbids;—not that it would injure me, but it might embarrass them; for it is almost an unpardonable offence to teach slaves to read in this Christian country. It is enough to say of the dear little fellows, that they lived on Philpot Street, very near Durgin and Bailey's ship-yard. I used to talk this matter of slavery over with them. I would sometimes say to them, I wished I could be as free as they would be when they got to be men. "You will be free as soon as you are twenty-one, *but I am a slave for life!* Have not I as good a right to be free as you have?" These words used to trouble them; they would express for me the liveliest sympathy, and console me with the hope that something would occur by which I might be free.

I was now about twelve years old, and the thought of being *a slave for life* began to bear heavily upon my heart. Just about this time, I got hold of a book entitled "The Columbian Orator."[7] Every opportunity I got, I used to read this book. Among much of other interesting matter, I found in it a dialogue between a master and his slave. The slave was represented as having run away

---

7. A popular collection of classic poems, dialogues, plays, and speeches that Douglass used as a model for his own speeches. "Columbian": American.

from his master three times. The dialogue represented the conversation which took place between them, when the slave was retaken the third time. In this dialogue, the whole argument in behalf of slavery was brought forward by the master, all of which was disposed of by the slave. The slave was made to say some very smart as well as impressive things in reply to his master—things which had the desired though unexpected effect; for the conversation resulted in the voluntary emancipation of the slave on the part of the master.

In the same book, I met with one of Sheridan's[8] mighty speeches on and in behalf of Catholic emancipation. These were choice documents to me. I read them over and over again with unabated interest. They gave tongue to interesting thoughts of my own soul, which had frequently flashed through my mind, and died away for want of utterance. The moral which I gained from thedialogue was the power of truth over the conscience of even a slaveholder. What I got from Sheridan was a bold denunciation of slavery, and a powerful vindication of human rights. The reading of these documents enabled me to utter my thoughts, and to meet the arguments brought forward to sustain slavery; but while they relieved me of one difficulty, they brought on another even more painful than the one of which I was relieved. The more I read, the more I was led to abhor and detest my enslavers. I could regard them in no other light than a band of successful robbers, who had left their homes, and gone to Africa, and stolen us from our homes, and in a strange land reduced us to slavery. I loathed them as being the meanest as well as the most wicked of men. As I read and contemplated the subject, behold! that very discontentment which Master Hugh had predicted would follow my learning to read had already come, to torment and sting my soul to unutterable anguish. As I writhed under it, I would at times feel that learning to read had been a curse rather than a blessing. It had given me a view of my wretched condition, without the remedy. It opened my eyes to the horrible pit, but to no ladder upon which to get out. In moments of agony, I envied my fellow-slaves for their stupidity. I have often wished myself a beast. I preferred the condition of the meanest reptile to my own. Any thing, no matter what, to get rid of thinking! It was this everlasting thinking of my condition that tormented me. There was no getting rid of it. It was pressed upon me by every object within sight or hearing, animate or inanimate. The silver trump of freedom had roused my soul to eternal wakefulness. Freedom now appeared, to disappear no more forever. It was heard in every sound, and seen in every thing. It was ever present to torment me with a sense of my wretched condition. I saw nothing without seeing it, I heard nothing without hearing it, and felt nothing without feeling. It looked from every star, it smiled in every calm, breathed in every wind, and moved in every storm.

I often found myself regretting my own existence, and wishing myself dead; and but for the hope of being free, I have no doubt but that I should have killed myself, or done something for which I should have been killed. While in this state of mind, I was eager to hear any one speak of slavery. I was a ready listener. Every little while, I could hear something about the abolitionists. It was some time before I found what the word meant. It was always used in such connections as to make it an interesting word to me. If a slave ran away and succeeded in getting clear, or if a slave killed his master, set fire to a barn, or

---

8. Richard Brinsley Sheridan (1751–1816), Irish dramatist and political leader.

did any thing very wrong in the mind of a slaveholder, it was spoken of as the fruit of *abolition*. Hearing the word in this connection very often, I set about learning what it meant. The dictionary afforded me little or no help. I found it was "the act of abolishing;" but then I did not know what was to be abolished. Here I was perplexed. I did not dare to ask any one about its meaning, for I was satisfied that it was something they wanted me to know very little about. After a patient waiting, I got one of our city papers, containing an account of the number of petitions from the north, praying for the abolition of slavery in the District of Columbia, and of the slave trade between the States. From this time I understood the words *abolition* and *abolitionist*, and always drew near when that word was spoken, expecting to hear something of importance to myself and fellow-slaves. The light broke in upon me by degrees. I went one day down on the wharf of Mr. Waters; and seeing two Irishmen unloading a scow of stone, I went, unasked, and helped them. When we had finished, one of them came to me and asked me if I were a slave. I told him I was. He asked, "Are ye a slave for life?" I told him that I was. The good Irishman seemed to be deeply affected by the statement. He said to the other that it was a pity so fine a little fellow as myself should be a slave for life. He said it was a shame to hold me. They both advised me to run away to the north; that I should find friends there, and that I should be free. I pretended not to be interested in what they said, and treated them as if I did not understand them; for I feared they might be treacherous. White men have been known to encourage slaves to escape, and then, to get the reward, catch them and return them to their masters. I was afraid that these seemingly good men might use me so; but I nevertheless remembered their advice, and from that time I resolved to run away. I looked forward to a time at which it would be safe for me to escape. I was too young to think of doing so immediately; besides, I wished to learn how to write, as I might have occasion to write my own pass. I consoled myself with the hope that I should one day find a good chance. Meanwhile, I would learn to write.

The idea as to how I might learn to write was suggested to me by being in Durgin and Bailey's ship-yard, and frequently seeing the ship carpenters, after hewing, and getting a piece of timber ready for use, write on the timber the name of that part of the ship for which it was intended. When a piece of timber was intended for the larboard side, it would be marked—"L." When a piece was for the starboard side, it would be marked thus—"S." A piece for the larboard side forward, would be marked thus—"L. F." When a piece was for starboard side forward, it would be marked thus—"S. F." For larboard aft, it would be marked thus—"L. A." For starboard aft, it would be marked thus—"S. A." I soon learned the names of these letters, and for what they were intended when placed upon a piece of timber in the ship-yard. I immediately commenced copying them, and in a short time was able to make the four letters named. After that, when I met with any boy who I knew could write, I would tell him I could write as well as he. The next word would be, "I don't believe you. Let me see you try it." I would then make the letters which I had been so fortunate as to learn, and ask him to beat that. In this way I got a good many lessons in writing, which it is quite possible I should never have gotten in any other way. During this time, my copy-book was the board fence, brick wall, and pavement; my pen and ink was a lump of chalk. With these, I learned mainly how to write. I then commenced and continued copying the

Italics in Webster's Spelling Book, until I could make them all without looking on the book. By this time, my little Master Thomas had gone to school, and learned how to write, and had written over a number of copy-books. These had been brought home, and shown to some of our near neighbors, and then laid aside. My mistress used to go to class meeting at the Wilk Street meeting-house every Monday afternoon, and leave me to take care of the house. When left thus, I used to spend the time in writing in the spaces left in Master Thomas's copy-book, copying what he had written. I continued to do this until I could write a hand very similar to that of Master Thomas. Thus, after a long, tedious effort for years, I finally succeeded in learning how to write.

Chapter VIII

In a very short time after I went to live at Baltimore, my old master's youngest son Richard died; and in about three years and six months after his death, my old master, Captain Anthony, died, leaving only his son, Andrew, and daughter, Lucretia, to share his estate. He died while on a visit to see his daughter at Hillsborough. Cut off thus unexpectedly, he left no will as to the disposal of his property. It was therefore necessary to have a valuation of the property, that it might be equally divided between Mrs. Lucretia and Master Andrew. I was immediately sent for, to be valued with the other property. Here again my feelings rose up in detestation of slavery. I had now a new conception of my degraded condition. Prior to this, I had become, if not insensible to my lot, at least partly so. I left Baltimore with a young heart overborne with sadness, and a soul full of apprehension. I took passage with Captain Rowe, in the schooner Wild Cat, and, after a sail of about twenty-four hours, I found myself near the place of my birth. I had now been absent from it almost, if not quite, five years. I, however, remembered the place very well. I was only about five years old when I left it, to go and live with my old master on Colonel Lloyd's plantation; so that I was now between ten and eleven years old.

We were all ranked together at the valuation. Men and women, old and young, married and single, were ranked with horses, sheep, and swine. There were horses and men, cattle and women, pigs and children, all holding the same rank in the scale of being, and were all subjected to the same narrow examination. Silvery-headed age and sprightly youth, maids and matrons, had to undergo the same indelicate inspection. At this moment, I saw more clearly than ever the brutalizing effects of slavery upon both slave and slaveholder.

After the valuation, then came the division. I have no language to express the high excitement and deep anxiety which were felt among us poor slaves during this time. Our fate for life was now to be decided. We had no more voice in that decision than the brutes among whom we were ranked. A single word from the white men was enough—against all our wishes, prayers, and entreaties—to sunder forever the dearest friends, dearest kindred, and strongest ties known to human beings. In addition to the pain of separation, there was the horrid dread of falling into the hands of Master Andrew. He was known to us all as being a most cruel wretch,—a common drunkard, who had, by his reckless mismanagement and profligate dissipation, already wasted a large portion of his father's property. We all felt that we might as well be sold at once to the Georgia traders, as to pass into his hands; for we knew that that would be our inevitable condition,—a condition held by us all in the utmost horror and dread.

I suffered more anxiety than most of my fellow-slaves. I had known what it was to be kindly treated; they had known nothing of the kind. They had seen little or nothing of the world. They were in very deed men and women of sorrow, and acquainted with grief. Their backs had been made familiar with the bloody lash, so that they had become callous; mine was yet tender; for while at Baltimore I got few whippings, and few slaves could boast of a kinder master and mistress than myself; and the thought of passing out of their hands into those of Master Andrew—a man who, but a few days before, to give me a sample of his bloody disposition, took my little brother by the throat, threw him on the ground, and with the heel of his boot stamped upon his head till the blood gushed from his nose and ears—was well calculated to make me anxious as to my fate. After he had committed this savage outrage upon my brother, he turned to me, and said that was the way he meant to serve me one of these days,—meaning, I suppose, when I came into his possession.

Thanks to a kind Providence, I fell to the portion of Mrs. Lucretia, and was sent immediately back to Baltimore, to live again in the family of Master Hugh. Their joy at my return equalled their sorrow at my departure. It was a glad day to me. I had escaped a [fate] worse than lion's jaws. I was absent from Baltimore, for the purpose of valuation and division, just about one month, and it seemed to have been six.

Very soon after my return to Baltimore, my mistress, Lucretia, died, leaving her husband and one child, Amanda; and in a very short time after her death, Master Andrew died. Now all the property of my old master, slaves included, was in the hands of strangers,—strangers who had had nothing to do with accumulating it. Not a slave was left free. All remained slaves, from the youngest to the oldest. If any one thing in my experience, more than another, served to deepen my conviction of the infernal character of slavery, and to fill me with unutterable loathing of slaveholders, it was their base ingratitude to my poor old grandmother. She had served my old master faithfully from youth to old age. She had been the source of all his wealth; she had peopled his plantation with slaves; she had become a great grandmother in his service. She had rocked him in infancy, attended him in childhood, served him through life, and at his death wiped from his icy brow the cold death-sweat, and closed his eyes forever. She was nevertheless left a slave—a slave for life—a slave in the hands of strangers; and in their hands she saw her children, her grandchildren, and her great-grandchildren, divided, like so many sheep, without being gratified with the small privilege of a single word, as to their or her own destiny. And, to cap the climax of their base ingratitude and fiendish barbarity, my grandmother, who was now very old, having outlived my old master and all his children, having seen the beginning and end of all of them, and her present owners finding she was of but little value, her frame already racked with the pains of old age, and complete helplessness fast stealing over her once active limbs, they took her to the woods, built her a little hut, put up a little mud-chimney, and then made her welcome to the privilege of supporting herself there in perfect loneliness; thus virtually turning her out to die! If my poor old grandmother now lives, she lives to suffer in utter loneliness; she lives to remember and mourn over the loss of children, the loss of grandchildren, and the loss of great-grandchildren. They are, in the language of the slave's poet, Whittier,[9]—

"Gone, gone, sold and gone
To the rice swamp dank and lone,
Where the slave-whip ceaseless swings,
Where the noisome insect stings,
Where the fever-demon strews
Poison with the falling dews,
Where the sickly sunbeams glare
Through the hot and misty air:—
Gone, gone, sold and gone
To the rice swamp dank and lone,
From Virginia hills and waters—
Woe is me, my stolen daughters!"

The hearth is desolate. The children, the unconscious children, who once sang and danced in her presence, are gone. She gropes her way, in the darkness of age, for a drink of water. Instead of the voices of her children, she hears by day the moans of the dove, and by night the screams of the hideous owl. All is gloom. The grave is at the door. And now, when weighed down by the pains and aches of old age, when the head inclines to the feet, when the beginning and ending of human existence meet, and helpless infancy and painful old age combine together—at this time, this most needful time, the time for the exercise of that tenderness and affection which children only can exercise toward a declining parent—my poor old grandmother, the devoted mother of twelve children, is left all alone, in yonder little hut, before a few dim embers. She stands—she sits—she staggers—she falls—she groans—she dies—and there are none of her children or grandchildren present, to wipe from her wrinkled brow the cold sweat of death, or to place beneath the sod her fallen remains. Will not a righteous God visit for these things?

In about two years after the death of Mrs. Lucretia, Master Thomas married his second wife. Her name was Rowena Hamilton. She was the eldest daughter of Mr. William Hamilton. Master now lived in St. Michael's. Not long after his marriage, a misunderstanding took place between himself and Master Hugh; and as a means of punishing his brother, he took me from him to live with himself at St. Michael's. Here I underwent another most painful separation. It, however, was not so severe as the one I dreaded at the division of property; for, during this interval, a great change had taken place in Master Hugh and his once kind and affectionate wife. The influence of brandy upon him, and of slavery upon her, had effected a disastrous change in the characters of both; so that, as far as they were concerned, I thought I had little to lose by the change. But it was not to them that I was attached. It was to those little Baltimore boys that I felt the strongest attachment. I had received many good lessons from them, and was still receiving them, and the thought of leaving them was painful indeed. I was leaving, too, without the hope of ever being allowed to return. Master Thomas had said he would never let me return again. The barrier betwixt himself and brother he considered impassable.

9. John Greenleaf Whittier (1807–1992), American poet and abolitionist. The lines Douglass quotes below are from Whittier's antislavery poem *The Farewell: Of a Virginia Slave Mother to Her Daughter Sold into Southern Bondage*, written about 1835.

I then had to regret that I did not at least make the attempt to carry out my resolution to run away; for the chances of success are tenfold greater from the city than from the country.

I sailed from Baltimore for St. Michael's in the sloop Amanda, Captain Edward Dodson. On my passage, I paid particular attention to the direction which the steamboats took to go to Philadelphia. I found, instead of going down, on reaching North Point they went up the bay, in a north-easterly direction. I deemed this knowledge of the utmost importance. My determination to run away was again revived. I resolved to wait only so long as the offering of a favorable opportunity. When that came, I was determined to be off.

Chapter IX

I have now reached a period of my life when I can give dates. I left Baltimore, and went to live with Master Thomas Auld, at St. Michael's, in March, 1832. It was now more than seven years since I lived with him in the family of my old master, on Colonel Lloyd's plantation. We of course were now almost entire strangers to each other. He was to me a new master, and I to him a new slave. I was ignorant of his temper and disposition; he was equally so of mine. A very short time, however brought us into full acquaintance with each other. I was made acquainted with his wife not less than with himself. They were well matched, being equally mean and cruel. I was now, for the first time during a space of more than seven years, made to feel the painful gnawings of hunger—a something which I had not experienced before since I left Colonel Lloyd's plantation. It went hard enough with me then, when I could look back to no period at which I had enjoyed a sufficiency. It was tenfold harder after living in Master Hugh's family, where I had always had enough to eat, and of that which was good. I have said Master Thomas was a mean man. He was so. Not to give a slave enough to eat, is regarded as the most aggravated development of meanness even among slaveholders. The rule is, no matter how coarse the food, only let there be enough of it. This is the theory; and in the part of Maryland from which I came, it is the general practice,—though there are many exceptions. Master Thomas gave us enough of neither coarse nor fine food. There were four slaves of us in the kitchen— my sister Eliza, my aunt Priscilla, Henny, and myself; and we were allowed less than half of a bushel of cornmeal per week, and very little else, either in the shape of meat or vegetables. It was not enough for us to subsist upon. We were therefore reduced to the wretched necessity of living at the expense of our neighbors. This we did by begging and stealing, whichever came handy in the time of need, the one being considered as legitimate as the other. A great many times have we poor creatures been nearly perishing with hunger, when food in abundance lay mouldering in the safe and smoke-house,[1] and our pious mistress was aware of the fact; and yet that mistress and her husband would kneel every morning, and pray that God would bless them in basket and store!

Bad as all slaveholders are, we seldom meet one destitute of every element of character commanding respect. My master was one of this rare sort. I do

---

1. Used both to cure and to store meat and fish. "Safe": a meat safe is a structure for preserving food.

not know of one single noble act ever performed by him. The leading trait in his character was meanness; and if there were any other element in his nature, it was made subject to this. He was mean; and, like most other mean men, he lacked the ability to conceal his meanness. Captain Auld was not born a slaveholder. He had been a poor man, master only of a Bay craft. He came into possession of all his slaves by marriage; and of all men, adopted slaveholders are the worst. He was cruel, but cowardly. He commanded without firmness. In the enforcement of his rules he was at times rigid, and at times lax. At times, he spoke to his slaves with the firmness of Napoleon and the fury of a demon; at other times, he might well be mistaken for an inquirer who had lost his way. He did nothing of himself. He might have passed for a lion, but for his ears.[2] In all things noble which he attempted, his own meanness shone most conspicuous. His airs, words, and actions, were the airs, words, and actions of born slaveholders, and, being assumed, were awkward enough. He was not even a good imitator. He possessed all the disposition to deceive, but wanted the power. Having no resources within himself, he was compelled to be the copyist of many, and being such, he was forever the victim of inconsistency; and of consequence he was an object of contempt, and was held as such even by his slaves. The luxury of having slaves of his own to wait upon him was something new and unprepared for. He was a slaveholder without the ability to hold slaves. He found himself incapable of managing his slaves either by force, fear, or fraud. We seldom called him "master;" we generally called him "Captain Auld," and were hardly disposed to title him at all. I doubt not that our conduct had much to do with making him appear awkward, and of consequence fretful. Our want of reverence for him must have perplexed him greatly. He wished to have us call him master, but lacked the firmness necessary to command us to do so. His wife used to insist upon our calling him so, but to no purpose. In August, 1832, my master attended a Methodist camp-meeting held in the Bay-side, Talbot county, and there experienced religion. I indulged a faint hope that his conversion would lead him to emancipate his slaves, and that, if he did not do this, it would, at any rate, make him more kind and humane. I was disappointed in both these respects. It neither made him to be humane to his slaves, nor to emancipate them. If it had any effect on his character, it made him more cruel and hateful in all his ways; for I believe him to have been a much worse man after his conversion than before. Prior to his conversion, he relied upon his own depravity to shield and sustain him in his savage barbarity; but after his conversion, he found religious sanction and support for his slaveholding cruelty. He made the greatest pretensions to piety. His house was the house of prayer. He prayed morning, noon, and night. He very soon distinguished himself among his brethren, and was soon made a class-leader and exhorter. His activity in revivals was great, and he proved himself an instrument in the hands of the church in converting many souls. His house was the preachers' home. They used to take great pleasure in coming there to put up; for while he starved us, he stuffed them. We have had three or four preachers there at a time. The names of those who used to come most frequently while I lived there, were Mr. Storks, Mr. Ewery, Mr. Humphry, and Mr. Hickey. I have also seen Mr. George Cookman at our house. We slaves loved Mr. Cookman. We believed him to be a good man.

2. A mocking commentary on his master's inauthentic display of nobility and strength, which can easily be seen to disguise meanness and weakness.

We thought him instrumental in getting Mr. Samuel Harrison, a very rich slaveholder, to emancipate his slaves; and by some means got the impression that he was laboring to effect the emancipation of all the slaves. When he was at our house, we were sure to be called in to prayers. When the others were there, we were sometimes called in and sometimes not. Mr. Cookman took more notice of us than either of the other ministers. He could not come among us with betraying his sympathy for us, and, stupid as we were, we had the sagacity to see it.

While I lived with my master in St. Michael's, there was a white young man, a Mr. Wilson, who proposed to keep a Sabbath school for the instruction of such slaves as might be disposed to learn to read the New Testament. We met but three times, when Mr. West and Mr. Fairbanks, both class-leaders, with many others, came upon with us with sticks and other missiles, drove us off, and forbade us to meet again. Thus ended our little Sabbath school in the pious town of St. Michael's.

I have said my master found religious sanction for his cruelty. As an example, I will state one of many facts going to prove the charge. I have seen him tie up a lame young woman, and whip her with a heavy cowskin upon her naked shoulders, causing the warm red blood to drip; and, in justification of the bloody deed, he would quote this passage of Scripture—"He that knoweth his master's will, and doeth it not, shall be beaten with many stripes."[3]

Master would keep this lacerated young woman tied up in this horrid situation four or five hours at a time. I have known him to tie her up early in the morning, and whip her before breakfast; leave her, go to his store, return at dinner, and whip her again, cutting her in the places already made raw with his cruel lash. The secret of master's cruelty toward "Henny" is found in the fact of her being almost helpless. When quite a child, she fell into the fire, and burned herself horribly. Her hands were so burnt that she never got the use of them. She could do very little but bear heavy burdens. She was to master a bill of expense; and as he was a mean man, she was a constant offence to him. He seemed desirous of getting the poor girl out of existence. He gave her away once to his sister; but, being a poor gift, she was not disposed to keep her. Finally, my benevolent master, to use his own words, "set her adrift to take care of herself." Here was a recently-converted man, holding on upon the mother, and at the same time turning out her helpless child, to starve and die! Master Thomas was one of the many pious slaveholders who hold slaves for the very charitable purpose of taking care of them.

My master and myself had quite a number of differences. He found me unsuitable to his purpose. My city life, he said, had had a very pernicious effect upon me. It had almost ruined me for every good purpose, and fitted me for every thing which was bad. One of my greatest faults was that of letting his horse run away, and go down to his father-in-law's farm, which was about five miles from St. Michael's. I would then have to go after it. My reason for this kind of carelessness, or carefulness, was, that I could always get something to eat when I went there. Master William Hamilton, my master's father-in-law, always gave his slaves enough to eat. I never left there hungry, no matter how great the need of my speedy return. Master Thomas at length said he would stand it no longer. I had lived with him nine months, during which

3. Luke 12.47. Only those of his servants who have an unending faith in Christ are safe from all opposing forces in their lives.

time he had given me a number of severe whippings, all to no good purpose. He resolved to put me out, as he said, to be broken; and, for this purpose, he let me for one year to a man named Edward Covey. Mr. Covey was a poor man, a farm-renter. He rented the place upon which he lived, as also the hands with which he tilled it. Mr. Covey had acquired a very high reputation for breaking young slaves, and this reputation was of immense value to him. It enabled him to get his farm tilled with much less expense to himself than he could have had it done without such a reputation. Some slaveholders thought it not much loss to allow Mr. Covey to have their slaves one year, for the sake of training to which they were subjected, without any other compensation. He could hire young help with great ease, in consequence of this reputation. Added to the natural good qualities of Mr. Covey, he was a professor of religion—a pious soul—a member and a class-leader in the Methodist church. All of this added weight to his reputation as a "nigger-breaker." I was aware of all the facts, having been made acquainted with them by a young man who had lived there. I nevertheless made the change gladly; for I was sure of getting enough to eat, which is not the smallest consideration to a hungry man.

Chapter X

I left Master Thomas's house, and went to live with Mr. Covey, on the 1st of January, 1833. I was now, for the first time in my life, a field hand. In my new employment, I found myself even more awkward than a country boy appeared to be in a large city. I had been at my new home but one week before Mr. Covey gave me a very severe whipping, cutting my back, causing the blood to run, and raising ridges on my flesh as large as my little finger. The details of this affair are as follows: Mr. Covey sent me, very early in the morning of one of our coldest days in the month of January, to the woods, to get a load of wood. He gave me a team of unbroken oxen. He told me which was the in-hand ox, and which the off-hand one.[4] He then tied the end of a large rope around the horns of the in-hand-ox, and gave me the other end of it, and told me, if the oxen started to run, that I must hold on upon the rope. I had never driven oxen before, and of course I was very awkward. I, however, succeeded in getting to the edge of the woods with little difficulty; but I had got a very few rods into the woods, when the oxen took fright, and started full tilt, carrying the cart against trees, and over stumps, in the most frightful manner. I expected every moment that my brains would be dashed out against the trees. After running thus for a considerable distance, they finally upset the cart, dashing it with great force against a tree, and threw themselves into a dense thicket. How I escaped death, I do not know. There I was, entirely alone, in a thick wood, in a place new to me. My cart was upset and shattered, my oxen were entangled among the young trees, and there was none to help me. After a long spell of effort, I succeeded in getting my cart righted, my oxen disentangled, and again yoked to the cart. I now proceeded with my team to the place where I had, the day before, been chopping wood, and loaded my cart pretty heavily, thinking in this way to tame my oxen. I then proceeded on my way home. I had now consumed one half of the day. I got out of the woods

---

4. The one on the right of a pair hitched to a wagon. "In-hand ox": the one to the left.

safely, and now felt out of danger. I stopped my oxen to open the woods gate; and just as I did so, before I could get hold of my ox-rope, the oxen again started, rushed through the gate, catching it between the wheel and the body of the cart, tearing it to pieces, and coming within a few inches of crushing me against the gate-post. Thus twice, in one short day, I escaped death by the merest chance. On my return, I told Mr. Covey what had happened, and how it happened. He ordered me to return to the woods again immediately. I did so, and he followed on after me. Just as I got into the woods, he came up and told me to stop my cart, and that he would teach me how to trifle away my time, and break gates. He then went to a large gum-tree, and with his axe cut three large switches, and, after trimming them up neatly with his pocket-knife, he ordered me to take off my clothes. I made him no answer, but stood with my clothes on. He repeated his order. I still made him no answer, nor did I move to strip myself. Upon this he rushed at me with the fierceness of a tiger, tore off my clothes, and lashed me till he had worn out his switches, cutting me so savagely as to leave the marks visible for a long time after. This whipping was the first of a number just like it, and for similar offences.

I lived with Mr. Covey one year. During the first six months, of that year, scarce a week passed without his whipping me. I was seldom free from a sore back. My awkwardness was almost always his excuse for whipping me. We were worked fully up to the point of endurance. Long before day we were up, our horses fed, and by the first approach of day we were off to the field with our hoes and ploughing teams. Mr. Covey gave us enough to eat, but scarce time to eat it. We were often less than five minutes taking our meals. We were often in the field from the first approach of day till its last lingering ray had left us; and at saving-fodder time, midnight often caught us in the field binding blades.[5]

Covey would be out with us. The way he used to stand it, was this. He would spend the most of his afternoons in bed. He would then come out fresh in the evening, ready to urge us on with his words, example, and frequently with the whip. Mr. Covey was one of the few slaveholders who could and did work with his hands. He was a hard-working man. He knew by himself just what a man or a boy could do. There was no deceiving him. His work went on in his absence almost as well as in his presence; and he had the faculty of making us feel that he was ever present with us. This he did by surprising us. He seldom approached the spot where we were at work openly, if he could do it secretly. He always aimed at taking us by surprise. Such was his cunning, that we used to call him, among ourselves, "the snake." When we were at work in the cornfield, he would sometimes crawl on his hands and knees to avoid detection, and all at once he would rise nearly in our midst, and scream out, "Ha, ha! Come, come! Dash on, dash on!" This being his mode of attack, it was never safe to stop a single minute. His comings were like a thief in the night. He appeared to us as being ever at hand. He was under every tree, behind every stump, in every bush, and at every window, on the plantation. He would sometimes mount his horse, as if bound to St. Michael's, a distance of seven miles, and in half an hour afterwards you would see him coiled up in the corner of the wood-fence, watching every motion of the slaves. He would, for this purpose, leave his horse tied up in the woods. Again, he would some-

5. I.e., of wheat or other plants. "Saving-fodder time": harvest time.

times walk up to us, and give us orders as though he was upon the point of starting on a long journey, turn his back upon us, and make as though he was going to the house to get ready; and, before he would get half way thither, he would turn short and crawl into a fence-corner, or behind some tree, and there watch us till the going down of the sun.

Mr. Covey's *forte* consisted in his power to deceive. His life was devoted to planning and perpetrating the grossest deceptions. Every thing he possessed in the shape of learning or religion, he made conform to his disposition to deceive. He seemed to think himself equal to deceiving the Almighty. He would make a short prayer in the morning, and a long prayer at night; and, strange as it may seem, few men would at times appear more devotional than he. The exercises of his family devotions were always commenced with singing; and, as he was a very poor singer himself, the duty of raising the hymn generally came upon me. He would read his hymn, and nod at me to commence. I would at times do so; at others, I would not. My non-compliance would almost always produce much confusion. To show himself independent of me, he would start and stagger through with his hymn in the most discordant manner. In this state of mind, he prayed with more than ordinary spirit. Poor man! such was his disposition, and success at deceiving, I do verily believe that he sometimes deceived himself into the solemn belief, that he was a sincere worshiper of the most high God; and this, too, at a time when he may be said to have been guilty of compelling his woman slave to commit the sin of adultery. The facts in the case are these: Mr. Covey was a poor man; he was just commencing in life; he was only able to buy one slave; and, shocking as is the fact, he bought her, as he said, for *a breeder*. This woman was named Caroline. Mr. Covey bought her from Mr. Thomas Lowe, about six miles from St. Michael's. She was a large, able-bodied woman, about twenty years old. She had already given birth to one child, which proved her to be just what he wanted. After buying her, he hired a married man of Mr. Samuel Harrison, to live with him one year; and him he used to fasten up with her every night! The result was, that, at the end of the year, the miserable woman gave birth to twins. At this result Mr. Covey seemed to be highly pleased, both with the man and the wretched woman. Such was his joy, and that of his wife, that nothing they could do for Caroline during her confinement was too good, or too hard, to be done. The children were regarded as being quite an addition to his wealth.

If at any one time of my life more than another, I was made to drink the bitterest dregs of slavery, that time was during the first six months of my stay with Mr. Covey. We were worked in all weathers. It was never too hot or too cold; it could never rain, blow, hail, or snow, too hard for us to work in the field. Work, work, work, was scarcely more the order of the day than of the night. The longest days were too short for him, and the shortest nights too long for him. I was somewhat unmanageable when I first went there, but a few months of this discipline tamed me. Mr. Covey succeeded in breaking me. I was broken in body, soul, and spirit. My natural elasticity was crushed, my intellect languished, the disposition to read departed, the cheerful spark that lingered about my eye died; the dark night of slavery closed in upon me; and behold a man transformed into a brute!

Sunday was my only leisure time. I spent this in a sort of beast-like stupor, between sleep and wake, under some large tree. At times I would rise up, a flash of energetic freedom would dart through my soul, accompanied with a faint beam of hope, that flickered for a moment, and then vanished. I sank down again, mourning over my wretched condition. I was sometimes prompted to take my life, and that of Covey, but was prevented by a combination of hope and fear. My sufferings on this plantation seem now like a dream rather than a stern reality.

Our house stood within a few rods of the Chesapeake Bay, whose broad bosom was ever white with sails from every quarter of the habitable globe. Those beautiful vessels, robed in purest white, so delightful to the eye of freemen, were to me so many shrouded ghosts, to terrify and torment me with thoughts of my wretched condition. I have often, in the deep stillness of a summer's Sabbath, stood all alone upon the lofty banks of that noble bay, and traced, with saddened heart and tearful eye, the countless number of sails moving off to the mighty ocean. The sight of these always affected me powerfully. My thoughts would compel utterance; and there, with no audience but the Almighty, I would pour out my soul's complaint, in my rude way, with an apostrophe to the moving multitude of ships:—

"You are loosed from your moorings, and are free; I am fast in my chains, and am a slave! You move merrily before the gentle gale, and I sadly before the bloody whip! You are freedom's swift-winged angels, that fly round the world; I am confined in bands of iron! O that I were free! Oh, that I were on one of your gallant decks, and under your protecting wing! Alas! betwixt me and you, the turbid waters roll. Go on, go on. O that I could also go! Could I but swim! If I could fly! O, why was I born a man, of whom to make a brute! The glad ship is gone; she hides in the dim distance. I am left in the hottest hell of unending slavery. O God, save me! God, deliver me! Let me be free! Is there any God? Why am I a slave? I will run away. I will not stand it. Get caught, or get clear, I'll try it. I had as well die with ague as the fever. I have only one life to lose. I had as well be killed running as die standing. Only think of it; one hundred miles straight north, and I am free! Try it? Yes! God helping me, I will. It cannot be that I shall live and die a slave. I will take to the water. This very bay shall yet bear me into freedom. The steamboats steered in a north-east course from North Point. I will do the same; and when I get to the head of the bay, I will turn my canoe adrift, and walk straight through Delaware into Pennsylvania. When I get there, I shall not be required to have a pass; I can travel without being disturbed. Let but the first opportunity offer, and, come what will, I am off. Meanwhile, I will try to bear up under the yoke. I am not the only slave in the world. Why should I fret? I can bear as much as any of them. Besides, I am but a boy, and all boys are bound to some one. It may be that my misery in slavery will only increase my happiness when I get free. There is a better day coming."

Thus I used to think, and thus I used to speak to myself; goaded almost to madness at one moment, and at the next reconciling myself to my wretched lot.

I have already intimated that my condition was much worse, during the first six months of my stay at Mr. Covey's, than in the last six. The circumstances leading to the change in Mr. Covey's course toward me form an epoch in my humble history. You have seen how a man was made a slave; you shall see how a slave was made a man. On one of the hottest days of the month of August, 1833, Bill Smith, William Hughes, a slave named Eli, and myself, were engaged in fanning wheat.[6] Hughes was clearing the fanned wheat from before the fan, Eli was turning, Smith was feeding, and I was carrying wheat to the fan. The work was simple, requiring strength rather than intellect; yet, to one entirely unused to such work, it came very hard. About three o'clock of that day, I broke down; my strength failed me; I was seized with a violent aching of the head, attended with extreme dizziness; I trembled in every limb. Finding what was coming, I nerved myself up, feeling it would never do to stop work. I stood as long as I could stagger to the hopper with grain. When I could stand no longer, I fell, and felt as if held down by an immense weight. The fan of course stopped; every one had his own work to do; and no one could do the work of the other, and have his own go on at the same time.

Mr. Covey was at the house, about one hundred yards from the treading-yard where we were fanning. On hearing the fan stop, he left immediately, and came to the spot where we were. He hastily inquired what the matter was. Bill answered that I was sick, and there was no one to bring wheat to the fan. I had by this time crawled away under the side of the post and rail-fence by which the yard was enclosed, hoping to find relief by getting out of the sun. He then asked where I was. He was told by one of the hands. He came to the spot, and, after looking at me awhile, asked me what was the matter. I told him as well as I could, for I scarce had strength to speak. He then gave me a savage kick in the side, and told me to get up. I tried to do so, but fell back in the attempt. He gave me another kick, and again told me to rise. I again tried, and succeeded in gaining my feet; but, stooping to get the tub with which I was feeding the fan, I again staggered and fell. While down in this situation, Mr. Covey took up the hickory slat with which Hughes had been striking off the half-bushel measure, and with it gave me a heavy blow upon the head, making a large wound, and the blood ran freely; and with this again told me to get up. I made no effort to comply, having now made up my mind to let him do his worst. In a short time after receiving this blow, my head grew better. Mr. Covey had now left me to my fate. At this moment I resolved, for the first time, to go to my master, enter a complaint, and ask his protection. In order to do this, I must that afternoon walk seven miles; and this, under the circumstances, was truly a severe undertaking. I was exceedingly feeble; made so as much by the kicks and blows which I received, as by the severe fit of sickness to which I had been subjected. I, however, watched my chance, while Covey was looking in an opposite direction, and started for St. Michael's. I succeeded in getting a considerable distance on my way to the woods, when Covey discovered me, and called after me to come back, threatening what he would do if I did not come. I disregarded both his calls and his threats, and made my way to the woods as fast as my feeble state would allow; and thinking I might be overhauled by him if I kept the road, I walked through the woods, keeping far enough from the road to avoid detection, and near enough to prevent losing my way. I had not gone far before my little strength again failed me. I could go no farther. I fell down, and lay for a considerable time. The blood was yet oozing from the wound on my head. For a time I thought I should bleed to death; and think now that I should have done so, but that the blood so matted my hair as to stop the wound. After lying there about three quarters of an hour, I nerved myself up again, and started on my way, through

6. I.e., separating the wheat from the chaff.

bogs and briers, barefooted and bareheaded, tearing my feet sometimes at nearly every step; and after a journey of about seven miles, occupying some five hours to perform it, I arrived at master's store. I then presented an appearance enough to affect any but a heart of iron. From the crown of my head to my feet, I was covered with blood. My hair was all clotted with dust and blood; my shirt was stiff with blood. My legs and feet were torn in sundry places with briers and thorns, and were also covered with blood. I suppose I looked like a man who had escaped a den of wild beasts, and barely escaped them. In this state I appeared before my master, humbly entreating him to interpose his authority for my protection. I told him all the circumstances as well as I could, and it seemed, as I spoke, at times to affect him. He would then walk the floor, and seek to justify Covey by saying he expected I deserved it. He asked me what I wanted. I told him, to let me get a new home; that as sure as I lived with Mr. Covey again, I should live with but to die with him; that Covey would surely kill me; he was in a fair way for it. Master Thomas ridiculed the idea that there was any danger of Mr. Covey's killing me, and said that he knew Mr. Covey; that he was a good man, and that he could not think of taking me from him; that, should he do so, he would lose the whole year's wages; that I belonged to Mr. Covey for one year, and that I must go back to him, come what might; and that I must not trouble him with any more stories, or that he would himself *get hold of me*. After threatening me thus, he gave me a very large dose of salts, telling me that I might remain in St. Michael's that night, (it being quite late,) but that I must be off back to Mr. Covey's early in the morning; and that if I did not, he would *get hold of me*, which meant that he would whip me. I remained all night, and, according to his orders, I started off to Covey's in the morning, (Saturday morning), wearied in body and broken in spirit. I got no supper that night, or breakfast that morning. I reached Covey's about nine o'clock; and just as I was getting over the fence that divided Mrs. Kemp's fields from ours, out ran Covey with his cowskin, to give me another whipping. Before he could reach me, I succeeded in getting to the cornfield; and as the corn was very high, it afforded me the means of hiding. He seemed very angry, and searched for me a long time. My behavior was altogether unaccountable. He finally gave up the chase, thinking, I suppose, that I must come home for something to eat; he would give himself no further trouble in looking for me. I spent that day mostly in the woods, having the alternative before me,—to go home and be whipped to death, or stay in the woods and be starved to death. That night, I fell in with Sandy Jenkins, a slave with whom I was somewhat acquainted. Sandy had a free wife[7] who lived about four miles from Mr. Covey's; and it being Saturday, he was on his way to see her. I told him my circumstances, and he very kindly invited me to go home with him. I went home with him, and talked this whole matter over, and got his advice as to what course it was best for me to pursue. I found Sandy an old adviser. He told me, with great solemnity, I must go back to Covey; but that before I went, I must go with him into another part of the woods, where there was a certain *root*, which, if I would take some of it with me, carrying it *always on my right side*, would render it impossible for Mr. Covey, or any other white man, to whip me. He said he had carried it for years; and since he had done so, he had never received a blow, and never expected to while he

7. I.e., his wife had been set free and was not legally a slave.

carried it. I at first rejected the idea, that the simple carrying of a root in my pocket would have any such effect as he had said, and was not disposed to take it; but Sandy impressed the necessity with much earnestness, telling me it could do no harm, if it did no good. To please him, I at length took the root, and, according to his direction, carried it upon my right side. This was Sunday morning. I immediately started for home; and upon entering the yard gate, out came Mr. Covey on his way to meeting. He spoke to me very kindly, bade me drive the pigs from a lot near by, and passed on towards the church. Now, this singular conduct of Mr. Covey really made me begin to think that there was something in the *root* which Sandy had given me; and had it been on any other day than Sunday, I could have attributed the conduct to no other cause then the influence of that root; and as it was, I was half inclined to think the *root* to be something more than I at first had taken it to be. All went well till Monday morning. On this morning, the virtue of the *root* was fully tested. Long before daylight, I was called to go and rub, curry, and feed, the horses. I obeyed, and was glad to obey. But whilst thus engaged, whilst in the act of throwing down some blades from the loft, Mr. Covey entered the stable with a long rope; and just as I was half out of the loft, he caught hold of my legs, and was about tying me. As soon as I found what he was up to, I gave a sudden spring, and as I did so, he holding to my legs, I was brought sprawling on the stable floor. Mr. Covey seemed now to think he had me, and could do what he pleased; but at this moment—from whence came the spirit I don't know— I resolved to fight; and, suiting my action to the resolution, I seized Covey hard by the throat; and as I did so, I rose. He held on to me, and I to him. My resistance was so entirely unexpected, that Covey seemed taken all aback. He trembled like a leaf. This gave me assurance, and I held him uneasy, causing the blood to run where I touched him with the ends of my fingers. Mr. Covey soon called out to Hughes for help. Hughes came, and, while Covey held me, attempted to tie my right hand. While he was in the act of doing so, I watched my chance, and gave him a heavy kick close under the ribs. This kick fairly sickened Hughes, so that he left me in the hands of Mr. Covey. This kick had the effect of not only weakening Hughes, but Covey also. When he saw Hughes bending over with pain, his courage quailed. He asked me if I meant to persist in my resistance. I told him I did, come what might; that he had used me like a brute for six months, and that I was determined to be used so no longer. With that, he strove to drag me to a stick that was lying just out of the stable door. He meant to knock me down. But just as he was leaning over to get the stick, I seized him with both hands by his collar, and brought him by a sudden snatch to the ground. By this time, Bill came. Covey called upon him for assistance. Bill wanted to know what he could do. Covey said, "Take hold of him, take hold of him!" Bill said his master hired him out to work, and not to help to whip me; so he left Covey and myself to fight our own battle out. We were at it for nearly two hours. Covey at length let me go, puffing and blowing at a great rate, saying that if I had not resisted, he would not have whipped me half so much. The truth was, that he had not whipped me at all. I considered him as getting entirely the worst end of the bargain; for he had drawn no blood from me, but I had from him. The whole six months afterwards, that I spent with Mr. Covey, he never laid the weight of his finger upon me in anger. He would occasionally say, he didn't want to get hold of me again. "No," thought I, "you need not; for you will come off worse than you did before."

This battle with Mr. Covey was the turning-point in my career as a slave. It rekindled the few expiring embers of freedom, and revived within me a sense of my own manhood. It recalled the departed self-confidence, and inspired me again with a determination to be free. The gratification afforded by the triumph was a full compensation for whatever else might follow, even death itself. He only can understand the deep satisfaction which I experienced, who has himself repelled by force the bloody arm of slavery. I felt as I never felt before. It was a glorious resurrection, from the tomb of slavery, to the heaven of freedom. My long-crushed spirit rose, cowardice departed, bold defiance took its place; and I now resolved that, however long I might remain a slave in form, the day had passed forever when I could be a slave in fact. I did not hesitate to let it be known of me, that the white man who expected to succeed in whipping, must also succeed in killing me.

From this time I was never again what might be called fairly whipped, though I remained a slave four years afterwards. I had several fights, but was never whipped.

It was for a long time a matter of surprise to me why Mr. Covey did not immediately have me taken by the constable to the whipping-post, and there regularly whipped for the crime of raising my hand against a white man in defence of myself. And the only explanation I can now think of does not entirely satisfy me; but such as it is, I will give it. Mr. Covey enjoyed the most unbounded reputation for being a first-rate overseer and negro-breaker. It was of considerable importance to him. That reputation was at stake; and had he sent me—a boy about sixteen years old—to the public whipping-post, his reputation would have been lost; so, to save his reputation, he suffered me to go unpunished.

My term of actual service to Mr. Edward Covey ended on Christmas day, 1833. The days between Christmas and New Year's day are allowed as holidays; and, accordingly, we were not required to perform any labor, more than to feed and take care of the stock. This time we regarded as our own, by the grace of our masters; and we therefore used or abused it nearly as we pleased. Those of us who had families at a distance, were generally allowed to spend the whole six days in their society. This time, however, was spent in various ways. The staid, sober, thinking and industrious ones of our number would employ themselves in making corn-brooms, mats, horse-collars, and baskets; and another class of us would spend the time hunting opossums, hares, and coons. But by far the larger part engaged in such sports and merriments as playing ball, wrestling, running foot-races, fiddling, dancing, and drinking whisky; and this latter mode of spending the time was by far the most agreeable to the feelings of our master. A slave who would work during the holidays was considered by our masters as scarcely deserving them. He was regarded as one who rejected the favor of his master. It was deemed a disgrace not to get drunk at Christmas; and he was regarded as lazy indeed, who had not provided himself with the necessary means, during the year, to get whisky enough to last him through Christmas.

From what I know of the effect of these holidays upon the slave, I believe them to be among the most effective means in the hands of the slaveholder in keeping down the spirit of insurrection. Were the slaveholders at once to abandon this practice, I have not the slightest doubt it would lead to an immediate insurrection among the slaves. These holidays serve as conductors, or safety-valves, to carry off the rebellious spirit of enslaved humanity. But for these, the slave would be forced up to the wildest desperation; and woe betide the slaveholder, the day he ventures to remove or hinder the operation of those conductors! I warn him that, in such an event, a spirit will go forth in their midst, more to be dreaded than the most appalling earthquake.

The holidays are part and parcel of the gross fraud, wrong, and inhumanity of slavery. They are professedly a custom established by the benevolence of the slaveholders; but I undertake to say, it is the result of selfishness, and one of the grossest frauds committed upon the down-trodden slave. They do not give the slaves this time because they would not like to have their work during its continuance, but because they know it would be unsafe to deprive them of it. This will be seen by the fact, that the slaveholders like to have their slaves spend those days just in such a manner as to make them as glad of their ending as of their beginning. Their object seems to be, to disgust their slaves with freedom, by plunging them into the lowest depths of dissipation. For instance, the slaveholders not only like to see the slave drink of his own accord, but will adopt various plans to make him drunk. One plan is, to make bets on their slaves, as to who can drink the most whisky without getting drunk; and in this way they succeed in getting whole multitudes to drink to excess. Thus, when the slave asks for virtuous freedom, the cunning slaveholder, knowing his ignorance, cheats him with a dose of vicious dissipation, artfully labelled with the name of liberty. The most of us used to drink it down, and the result was just what might be supposed: many of us were led to think that there was little to choose between liberty and slavery. We felt, and very properly too, that we had almost as well be slaves to man as to rum. So, when the holidays ended, we staggered up from the filth of our wallowing, took a long breath, and marched to the field,—feeling, upon the whole, rather glad to go, from what our master had deceived us into a belief was freedom, back to the arms of slavery.

I have said that this mode of treatment is a part of the whole system of fraud and inhumanity of slavery. It is so. The mode here adopted to disgust the slave with freedom, by allowing him to see only the abuse of it, is carried out in other things. For instance, a slave loves molasses; he steals some. His master, in many cases, goes off to town, and buys a large quantity; he returns, takes his whip, and commands the slave to eat the molasses, until the poor fellow is made sick at the very mention of it. The same mode is sometimes adopted to make the slaves refrain from asking for more food than their regular allowance. A slave runs through his allowance, and applies for more. His master is enraged at him; but, not willing to send him off without food, gives him more than is necessary, and compels him to eat it within a given time. Then, if he complains that he cannot eat it, he is said to be satisfied neither full nor fasting, and is whipped for being hard to please! I have an abundance of such illustrations of the same principle, drawn from my own observation, but think the cases I have cited sufficient. The practice is a very common one.

On the first of January, 1834, I left Mr. Covey, and went to live with Mr. William Freeland, who lived about three miles from St. Michael's. I soon found Mr. Freeland a very different man from Mr. Covey. Though not rich, he was what would be called an educated southern gentleman. Mr. Covey, as I have shown, was a well-trained negro-breaker and slave-driver. The former (slaveholder though he was) seemed to possess some regard for honor, some reverence for justice, and some respect for humanity. The latter seemed totally insensible to all such sentiments. Mr. Freeland had many of the faults peculiar to slaveholders, such as being very passionate and fretful; but I must do him the justice to say, that he was exceedingly free from those degrading vices to which Mr. Covey was constantly addicted. The one was open and frank, and we always knew where to find him. The other was a most artful deceiver, and could be understood only by such as were skilful enough to detect his cunningly-devised frauds. Another advantage I gained in my new master was, he made no pretensions to, or profession of, religion; and this, in my opinion, was truly a great advantage. I assert most unhesitatingly, that the religion of the south is a mere covering for the most horrid crimes,—a justifier of the most appalling barbarity,—a sanctifier of the most hateful frauds,—and a dark shelter under, which the darkest, foulest, grossest, and most infernal deeds of slaveholders find the strongest protection. Were I to be again reduced to the chains of slavery, next to that enslavement, I should regard being the slave of a religious master the greatest calamity that could befall me. For of all slaveholders with whom I have ever met, religious slaveholders are the worst. I have ever found them the meanest and basest, the most cruel and cowardly, of all others. It was my unhappy lot not only to belong to a religious slaveholder, but to live in a community of such religionists. Very near Mr. Freeland lived the Rev. Daniel Weeden, and in the same neighborhood lived the Rev. Rigby Hopkins. These were members and ministers in the Reformed Methodist Church. Mr. Weeden owned, among others, a woman slave, whose name I have forgotten. This woman's back, for weeks, was kept literally raw, made so by the lash of this merciless, *religious* wretch. He used to hire hands. His maxim was, Behave well or behave ill, it is the duty of a master occasionally to whip a slave, to remind him of his master's authority. Such was his theory, and such his practice.

Mr. Hopkins was even worse than Mr. Weeden. His chief boast was his ability to manage slaves. The peculiar feature of his government was that of whipping slaves in advance of deserving it. He always managed to have one or more of his slaves to whip every Monday morning. He did this to alarm their fears, and strike terror into those who escaped. His plan was to whip for the smallest offences, to prevent the commission of large ones. Mr. Hopkins could always find some excuse for whipping a slave. It would astonish one, unaccustomed to a slaveholding life, to see with what wonderful ease a slaveholder can find things, of which to make occasion to whip a slave. A mere look, word, or motion,—a mistake, accident, or want of power,—are all matters for which a slave may be whipped at any time. Does a slave look dissatisfied? It is said, he has the devil in him, and it must be whipped out. Does he speak loudly when spoken to by his master? Then he is getting high-minded, and should be taken down a button-hole lower. Does he forget to pull off his hat at the approach of a white person? Then he is wanting in reverence, and should be whipped for it. Does he ever venture to vindicate his conduct, when censured for it? Then he is guilty of impudence,—one of the greatest crimes of which a slave can be guilty. Does he ever venture to suggest a different mode of doing things from that pointed out by his master? He is indeed presumptuous, and getting above himself; and nothing less than a flogging will do for him. Does he, while ploughing, break a plough,—or, while hoeing, break a hoe? It is owing to his carelessness, and for it a slave must always be whipped. Mr. Hopkins could always find something of this sort to justify the use of the lash, and he seldom failed to embrace such opportunities. There was not a man in the whole county, with whom the slaves who had the getting their own home, would not prefer to live, rather than with this Rev. Mr. Hopkins. And yet there was not a man any where round, who made higher professions of religion, or was more active in revivals—more attentive to the class, love-feast, prayer and preaching meetings, or more devotional in his family,—that prayed earlier, later, louder, and longer,—than this same reverend slave-driver, Rigby Hopkins.

But to return to Mr. Freeland, and to my experience while in his employment. He, like Mr. Covey, gave us enough to eat; but unlike Mr. Covey, he also gave us sufficient time to take our meals. He worked us hard, but always between sunrise and sunset. He required a good deal of work to be done, but gave us good tools with which to work. His farm was large, but he employed hands enough to work it, and with ease, compared with many of his neighbors. My treatment, while in his employment, was heavenly, compared with what I experienced at the hands of Mr. Edward Covey.

Mr. Freeland was himself the owner of but two slaves. Their names were Henry Harris and John Harris. The rest of his hands he hired. These consisted of myself, Sandy Jenkins[8] and Handy Caldwell. Henry and John were quite intelligent, and in a very little while after I went there, I succeeded in creating in them a strong desire to learn how to read. This desire soon sprang up in the others also. They very soon mustered up some old spelling-books, and nothing would do but that I must keep a Sabbath school. I agreed to do so, and accordingly devoted my Sundays to teaching these my loved fellow-slaves how to read. Neither of them knew his letters when I went there. Some of the slaves of the neighboring farms found what was going on, and also availed themselves of this little opportunity to learn to read. It was understood, among all who came, that there must be as little display about it as possible. It was necessary to keep our religious masters at St. Michael's unacquainted with the fact, that, instead of spending the Sabbath in wrestling, boxing, and drinking whisky, we were trying to learn how to read the will of God; for they had much rather see us engaged in those degrading sports, than to see us behaving like intellectual, moral, and accountable beings. My blood boils as I think of the bloody manner in which Messrs. Wright Fairbanks and Garrison West, both class-leaders, in connection with many others, rushed in upon us with sticks and stones, and broke up our virtuous little Sabbath school, at St. Michael's—all calling themselves Christians! humble followers of the Lord Jesus Christ! But I am again digressing.

I held my Sabbath school at the house of a free colored man, whose name I deem it imprudent to mention; for should it be known, it might embarrass him greatly, though the crime of holding the school was committed ten years ago. I had at one time over forty scholars, and those of the right sort, ardently desiring to learn. They were of all ages, though mostly men and women. I look back to those Sundays with an amount of pleasure not to be expressed. They were great days to my soul. The work of instructing my dear fellow-slaves was the sweetest engagement with which I was ever blessed. We loved each

8. "This is the same man who gave me the roots to prevent my being whipped by Mr. Covey. He was a 'clever soul.' We used frequently to talk about the fight with Covey, and as often as we did so, he would claim my success as the result of the roots he gave me. This superstition is very common among the more ignorant slaves. A slave seldom dies but that his death is attributed to trickery" [Douglass's note].

other, and to leave them at the close of the Sabbath was a severe cross indeed. When I think that those precious souls are to-day shut up in the prison-house of slavery, my feelings overcome me, and I am almost ready to ask, "Does a righteous God govern the universe? and for what does he hold the thunders in his right hand, if not to smite the oppressor, and deliver the spoiled out of the hand of the spoiler?" These dear souls came not to Sabbath school because it was popular to do so, nor did I teach them because it was reputable to be thus engaged. Every moment they spent in that school, they were liable to be taken up, and given thirty-nine lashes. They came because they wished to learn. Their minds had been starved by their cruel masters. They had been shut up in mental darkness. I taught them, because it was the delight of my soul to be doing something that looked like bettering the condition of my race. I kept up my school nearly the whole year I lived with Mr. Freeland; and, beside my Sabbath school, I devoted three evenings in the week, during the winter, to teaching the slaves at home. And I have the happiness to know, that several of those who came to Sabbath school learned how to read; and that one, at least, is now free through my agency.

The year passed off smoothly. It seemed only about half as long as the year which preceded it. I went through it without receiving a single blow. I will give Mr. Freeland the credit of being the best master I ever had, *till I became my own master.* For the ease with which I passed the year, I was, however, somewhat indebted to the society of my fellow-slaves. They were noble souls; they not only possessed loving hearts, but brave ones. We were linked and interlinked with each other. I loved them with a love stronger than any thing I have experienced since. It is sometimes said that we slaves do not love and confide in each other. In answer to this assertion, I can say, I never loved any or confided in any people more than my fellow-slaves, and especially those with whom I lived at Mr. Freeland's. I believe we would have died for each other. We never undertook to do any thing, of any importance, without a mutual consultation. We never moved separately. We were one; and as much so by our tempers and dispositions, as by the mutual hardships to which we were necessarily subjected by our condition as slaves.

At the close of the year 1834, Mr. Freeland again hired me of my master, for the year 1835. But, by this time, I began to want to live *upon free land* as well as *with Freeland;* and I was no longer content, therefore, to live with him or any other slaveholder. I began, with the commencement of the year, to prepare myself for a final struggle, which should decide my fate one way or the other. My tendency was upward. I was fast approaching manhood, and year after year had passed, and I was still a slave. These thoughts roused me— I must do something. I therefore resolved that 1835 should not pass without witnessing an attempt, on my part, to secure my liberty. But I was not willing to cherish this determination alone. My fellow-slaves were dear to me. I was anxious to have them participate with me in this, my life-giving determination. I therefore, though with great prudence, commenced early to ascertain their views and feelings in regard to their condition, and to imbue their minds with thoughts of freedom. I bent myself to devising ways and means for our escape, and meanwhile strove, on all fitting occasions, to impress them with the gross fraud and inhumanity of slavery. I went first to Henry, next to John, then to the others. I found, in them all, warm hearts and noble spirits. They were ready to hear, and ready to act when a feasible plan should be proposed.

This was what I wanted. I talked to them of our want of manhood, if we submitted to our enslavement without at least one noble effort to be free. We met often, and consulted frequently, and told our hopes and fears, recounted the difficulties, real and imagined, which we should be called on to meet. At times we were almost disposed to give up, and try to content ourselves with our wretched lot; at others, we were firm and unbending in our determination to go. Whenever we suggested any plan, there was shrinking—the odds were fearful. Our path was beset with the greatest obstacles; and if we succeeded in gaining the end of it, our right to be free was yet questionable—we were yet liable to be returned to bondage. We could see no spot, this side of the ocean, where we could be free. We knew nothing about Canada. Our knowledge of the north did not extend farther than New York; and to go there, and be forever harassed with the frightful liability of being returned to slavery—with the certainty of being treated tenfold worse than before—the thought was truly a horrible one, and one which it was not easy to overcome. The case sometimes stood thus: At every gate through which we were to pass, we saw a watchman— at every ferry a guard—on every bridge a sentinel—and in every wood a patrol. We were hemmed in upon every side. Here were the difficulties, real or imagined—the good to be sought, and the evil to be shunned. On the one hand, there stood slavery, a stern reality, glaring frightfully upon us,—its robes already crimsoned with the blood of millions, and even now feasting itself greedily upon our own flesh. On the other hand, away back in the dim distance, under the flickering light of the north star, behind some craggy hill or snow-covered mountain, stood a doubtful freedom—half frozen—beckoning us to come and share its hospitality. This in itself was sometimes enough to stagger us; but when we permitted ourselves to survey the road, we were frequently appalled. Upon either side we saw grim death, assuming the most horrid shapes. Now it was starvation, causing us to eat our own flesh;—now we were contending with the waves, and were drowned;—now we were overtaken, and torn to pieces by the fangs of the terrible bloodhound. We were stung by scorpions, chased by wild beasts, bitten by snakes, and finally, after having nearly reached the desired spot,—after swimming rivers, encountering wild beasts, sleeping in the woods, suffering hunger and nakedness,—we were overtaken by our pursuers, and in our resistance, we were shot dead upon the spot! I say, this picture sometimes appalled us, and made us

> "rather bear those ills we had,
> Than fly to others, that we knew not of."[9]

In coming to a fixed determination to run away, we did more than Patrick Henry, when he resolved upon liberty or death. With us it was a doubtful liberty at most, and almost certain death if we failed. For my part, I should prefer death to hopeless bondage.

Sandy, one of our number, gave up the notion, but still encouraged us. Our company then consisted of Henry Harris, John Harris, Henry Bailey, Charles Roberts, and myself. Henry Bailey was my uncle, and belonged to my master. Charles married my aunt: he belonged to my master's father-in-law, Mr. William Hamilton.

The plan we finally concluded upon was, to get a large canoe belonging to

---

9. Shakespeare's *Hamlet* 3.1.81–82.

Mr. Hamilton, and upon the Saturday night previous to Easter holidays, paddle directly up the Chesapeake Bay. On our arrival at the head of the bay, a distance of seventy or eighty miles from where we lived, it was our purpose to turn our canoe adrift, and follow the guidance of the north star till we got beyond the limits of Maryland. Our reason for taking the water route was, that we were less liable to be suspected as runaways; we hoped to be regarded as fishermen; whereas, if we should take the land route, we should be subjected to interruptions of almost every kind. Any one having a white face, and being so disposed, could stop us, and subject us to examination.

The week before our intended start, I wrote several protections, one for each of us. As well as I can remember, they were in the following words, to wit:—

> "This is to certify that I, the undersigned, have given the bearer, my servant, full liberty to go to Baltimore, and spend the Easter holidays. Written with mine own hand, &c., 1835.
>
> "WILLIAM HAMILTON,
> "Near St. Michael's, in Talbot county, Maryland."

We were not going to Baltimore; but, in going up the bay, we went toward Baltimore, and these protections were only intended to protect us while on the bay.

As the time drew near for our departure, our anxiety became more and more intense. It was truly a matter of life and death with us. The strength of our determination was about to be fully tested. At this time, I was very active in explaining every difficulty, removing every doubt, dispelling every fear, and inspiring all with the firmness indispensable to success in our undertaking; assuring them that half was gained the instant we made the move; we had talked long enough; we were now ready to move; if not now, we never should be; and if we did not intend to move now, we had as well fold our arms, sit down, and acknowledge ourselves fit only to be slaves. This, none of us were prepared to acknowledge. Every man stood firm; and at our last meeting, we pledged ourselves afresh, in the most solemn manner, that, at the time appointed, we would certainly start in pursuit of freedom. This was in the middle of the week, at the end of which we were to be off. We went, as usual, to our several fields of labor, but with bosoms highly agitated with thoughts of our truly hazardous undertaking. We tried to conceal our feelings as much as possible; and I think we succeeded very well.

After a painful waiting, the Saturday morning, whose night was to witness our departure, came. I hailed it with joy, bring what of sadness it might. Friday night was a sleepless one for me. I probably felt more anxious than the rest, because I was, by common consent, at the head of the whole affair. The responsibility of success or failure lay heavily upon me. The glory of the one, and the confusion of the other, were alike mine. The first two hours of that morning were such as I never experienced before, and hope never to again. Early in the morning, we went, as usual, to the field. We were spreading manure; and all at once, while thus engaged, I was overwhelmed with an indescribable feeling, in the fulness of which I turned to Sandy, who was near by, and said, "We are betrayed!" "Well," said he, "that thought has this moment struck me." We said no more. I was never more certain of any thing.

The horn was blown as usual, and we went up from the field to the house for breakfast. I went for the form, more than for want of any thing to eat that morning. Just as I got to the house, in looking out at the lane gate, I saw four white men, with two colored men. The white men were on horseback, and the colored ones were walking behind, as if tied. I watched them a few moments till they got up to our lane gate. Here they halted, and tied the colored men to the gate-post. I was not yet certain as to what the matter was. In a few moments, in rode Mr. Hamilton, with a speed betokening great excitement. He came to the door, and inquired if Master William was in. He was told he was at the barn. Mr. Hamilton, without dismounting, rode up to the barn with extraordinary speed. In a few moments, he and Mr. Freeland returned to the house. By this time, the three constables rode up, and in great haste dismounted, tied their horses, and met Master William and Mr. Hamilton returning from the barn; and after talking awhile, they all walked up to the kitchen door. There was no one in the kitchen but myself and John. Henry and Sandy were up at the barn. Mr. Freeland put his head in at the door, and called me by name, saying, there were some gentlemen at the door who wished to see me. I stepped to the door, and inquired what they wanted. They at once seized me, and, without giving me any satisfaction, tied me—lashing my hands closely together. I insisted upon knowing what the matter was. They at length said, that they had learned I had been in a "scrape," and that I was to be examined before my master; and if their information proved false, I should not be hurt.

In a few moments, they succeeded in tying John. They then turned to Henry, who had by this time returned, and commanded him to cross his hands. "I won't!" said Henry, in a firm tone, indicating his readiness to meet the consequences of his refusal. "Won't you?" said Tom Graham, the constable. "No, I won't!" said Henry, in a still stronger tone. With this, two of the constables pulled out their shining pistols, and swore, by their Creator, that they would make him cross his hands or kill him. Each cocked his pistol, and, with fingers on the trigger, walked up to Henry, saying, at the same time, if he did not cross his hands, they would blow his damned heart out. "Shoot me, shoot me!" said Henry; "you can't kill me but once. Shoot, shoot,—and be damned! *I won't be tied!*" This he said in a tone of loud defiance; and at the same time, with a motion as quick as lightning, he with one single stroke dashed the pistols from the hand of each constable. As he did this, all hands fell upon him, and, after beating him some time, they finally overpowered him, and got him tied.

During the scuffle, I managed, I know not how, to get my pass out, and, without being discovered, put it into the fire. We were all now tied; and just as we were to leave for Easton jail, Betsy Freeland, mother of William Freeland, came to the door with her hands full of biscuits, and divided them between Henry and John. She then delivered herself of a speech, to the following effect:—addressing herself to me, she said, "*You devil! You yellow devil!* it was you that put it into the heads of Henry and John to run away. But for you, you long-legged mulatto devil! Henry nor John would never have thought of such a thing." I made no reply, and was immediately hurried off towards St. Michael's. Just a moment previous to the scuffle with Henry, Mr. Hamilton suggested the propriety of making a search for the protections which he had understood Frederick had written for himself and the rest. But, just at the moment he was about carrying his proposal into effect, his aid was needed in helping to tie Henry; and the excitement attending the scuffle caused them either to forget, or to deem it unsafe, under the circumstances, to search. So we were not yet convicted of the intention to run away.

When we got about half way to St. Michael's, while the constables having us in charge were looking ahead, Henry inquired of me what he should do with his pass. I told him to eat it with his biscuit, and own nothing; and we passed the word around, *"Own nothing;"* and *"Own nothing!"* said we all. Our confidence in each other was unshaken. We were resolved to succeed or fail together, after the calamity had befallen us as much as before. We were now prepared for any thing. We were to be dragged that morning fifteen miles behind horses, and then to be placed in the Easton jail. When we reached St. Michael's, we underwent a sort of examination. We all denied that we ever intended to run away. We did this more to bring out the evidence against us, than from any hope of getting clear of being sold; for, as I have said, we were ready for that. The fact was, we cared but little where we went, so we went together. Our greatest concern was about separation. We dreaded that more than any thing this side of death. We found the evidence against us to be the testimony of one person; our master would not tell who it was; but we came to a unanimous decision among ourselves as to who their informant was. We were sent off to the jail at Easton. When we got there, we were delivered up to the sheriff, Mr. Joseph Graham, and by him placed in jail. Henry, John, and myself, were placed in one room together—Charles, and Henry Bailey, in another. Their object in separating us was to hinder concert.

We had been in jail scarcely twenty minutes, when a swarm of slave traders, and agents for slave traders, flocked into jail to look at us, and to ascertain if we were for sale. Such a set of beings I never saw before! I felt myself surrounded by so many fiends from perdition. A band of pirates never looked more like their father, the devil. They laughed and grinned over us, saying, "Ah, my boys! we have got you, haven't we?" And after taunting us in various ways, they one by one went into an examination of us, with intent to ascertain our value. They would impudently ask us if we would not like to have them for our masters. We would make them no answer, and leave them to find out as best they could. Then they would curse and swear at us, telling us that they could take the devil out of us in a very little while, if we were only in their hands.

While in jail, we found ourselves in much more comfortable quarters than we expected when we went there. We did not get much to eat, nor that which was very good; but we had a good clean room, from the windows of which we could see what was going on in the street, which was very much better than though we had been placed in one of the dark, damp cells. Upon the whole, we got along very well, so far as the jail and its keeper were concerned. Immediately after the holidays were over, contrary to all our expectations, Mr. Hamilton and Mr. Freeland came up to Easton, and took Charles, the two Henrys, and John, out of jail, and carried them home, leaving me alone. I regarded this separation as a final one. It caused me more pain than any thing else in the whole transaction. I was ready for any thing rather than separation. I supposed that they had consulted together, and had decided that, as I was the whole cause of the intention of the others to run away, it was hard to make the innocent suffer with the guilty; and that they had, therefore, concluded to take the others home, and sell me, as a warning to the others that remained.

It is due to the noble Henry to say, he seemed almost as reluctant at leaving the prison as at leaving home to come to the prison. But we knew we should, in all probability, be separated, if we were sold; and since he was in their hands, he concluded to go peaceably home.

I was now left to my fate. I was all alone, and within the walls of a stone prison. But a few days before, and I was full of hope. I expected to have been safe in a land of freedom; but now I was covered with gloom, sunk down to the utmost despair. I thought the possibility of freedom was gone. I was kept in this way about one week, at the end of which, Captain Auld, my master, to my surprise and utter astonishment, came up, and took me out, with the intention of sending me, with a gentleman of his acquaintance, into Alabama. But, from some cause or other, he did not send me to Alabama, but concluded to send me back to Baltimore, to live again with his brother Hugh, and to learn a trade.

Thus, after an absence of three years and one month, I was once more permitted to return to my old home at Baltimore. My master sent me away, because there existed against me a very great prejudice in the community, and he feared I might be killed.

In a few weeks after I went to Baltimore, Master Hugh hired me to Mr. William Gardner, an extensive ship-builder, on Fell's Point. I was put there to learn how to calk. It, however, proved a very unfavorable place for the accomplishment of this object. Mr. Gardner was engaged that spring in building two large man-of-war brigs, professedly for the Mexican government. The vessels were to be launched in the July of that year, and in failure thereof, Mr. Gardner was to lose a considerable sum; so that when I entered, all was hurry. There was no time to learn any thing. Every man had to do that which he knew how to do. In entering the ship-yard, my orders from Mr. Gardner were, to do whatever the carpenters commanded me to do. This was placing me at the beck and call of about seventy-five men. I was to regard all these as masters. Their word was to be my law. My situation was a most trying one. At times I needed a dozen pair of hands. I was called a dozen ways in the space of a single minute. Three or four voices would strike my ear at the same moment. It was—"Fred., come help me to cant this timber here."—"Fred., come carry this timber yonder."—"Fred., bring that roller here."—"Fred., go get a fresh can of water."—"Fred., come help saw off the end of this timber."—"Fred., go quick, and get the crowbar."—"Fred., hold on the end of this fall."[1]—"Fred., go to the blacksmith's shop, and get a new punch."— "Hurra, Fred.! run and bring me a cold chisel."—"I say, Fred., bear a hand, and get up a fire as quick as lightning under that steam-box."—"Halloo, nigger! come, turn this grindstone."—"Come, come! move, move! and *bowse*[2] this timber forward."—"I say, darky, blast your eyes, why don't you heat up some pitch?"—"Halloo! halloo! halloo!" (Three voices at the same time.) "Come here!—Go there!—Hold on where you are! Damn you, if you move, I'll knock your brains out!"

This was my school for eight months; and I might have remained there longer, but for a most horrid fight I had with four of the white apprentices, in which my left eye was nearly knocked out, and I was horribly mangled in other respects. The facts in the case were these: Until a very little while after I went

---

1. Nautical term for the free end of a rope of a tackle   2. To haul the timber by pulling on the rope.
or hoisting device.

there, white and black ship-carpenters worked side by side, and no one seemed to see any impropriety in it. All hands seemed to be very well satisfied. Many of the black carpenters were freemen. Things seemed to be going on very well. All at once, the white carpenters knocked off, and said they would not work with free colored workmen. Their reason for this, as alleged, was, that if free colored carpenters were encouraged, they would soon take the trade into their own hands, and poor white men would be thrown out of employment. They therefore felt called upon at once to put a stop to it. And, taking advantage of Mr. Gardner's necessities, they broke off, swearing they would work no longer, unless he would discharge his black carpenters. Now, though this did not extend to me in form, it did reach me in fact. My fellow-apprentices very soon began to feel it degrading to them to work with me. They began to put on airs, and talk about the "niggers" taking the country, saying we all ought to be killed; and, being encouraged by the journeymen, they commenced making my condition as hard as they could, by hectoring me around, and sometimes striking me. I, of course, kept the vow I made after the fight with Mr. Covey, and struck back again, regardless of consequences; and while I kept them from combining, I succeeded very well; for I could whip the whole of them, taking them separately. They, however, at length combined, and came upon me, armed with sticks, stones, and heavy handspikes. One came in front with a half brick. There was one at each side of me, and one behind me. While I was attending to those in front, and on either side, the one behind ran up with the handspike, and struck me a heavy blow upon the head. It stunned me. I fell, and with this they all ran upon me, and fell to beating me with their fists. I let them lay on for a while, gathering strength. In an instant, I gave a sudden surge, and rose to my hands and knees. Just as I did that, one of their number gave me, with his heavy boot, a powerful kick in the left eye. My eyeball seemed to have burst. When they saw my eye closed, and badly swollen, they left me. With this I seized the handspike, and for a time pursued them. But here the carpenters interfered, and I thought I might as well give it up. It was impossible to stand my hand against so many. All this took place in sight of not less than fifty white ship-carpenters, and not one interposed a friendly word; but some cried, "Kill the damned nigger! Kill him! kill him! He struck a white person." I found my only chance for life was in flight. I succeeded in getting away without an additional blow, and barely so; for to strike a white man is death by Lynch law,[3]—and that was the law in Mr. Gardner's ship-yard; nor is there much of any other out of Mr. Gardner's ship-yard.

I went directly home, and told the story of my wrongs to Master Hugh; and I am happy to say of him, irreligious as he was, his conduct was heavenly, compared with that of his brother Thomas under similar circumstances. He listened attentively to my narration of the circumstances leading to the savage outrage, and gave many proofs of his strong indignation at it. The heart of my once overkind mistress was again melted into pity. My puffed-out eye and blood-covered face moved her to tears. She took a chair by me, washed the blood from my face, and, with a mother's tenderness, bound up my head, covering the wounded eye with a lean piece of fresh beef. It was almost compensation for my suffering to witness, once more, a manifestation of kindness from this, my once affectionate old mistress. Master Hugh was very much

---

3. I.e., to be subject to lynching, without benefit of legal procedures.

enraged. He gave expression to his feelings by pouring out curses upon the heads of those who did the deed. As soon as I got a little the better of my bruises, he took me with him to Esquire Watson's, on Bond Street, to see what could be done about the matter. Mr. Watson inquired who saw the assault committed. Master Hugh told him it was done in Mr. Gardner's ship-yard, at midday, where there were a large company of men at work. "As to that," he said, "the deed was done, and there was no question as to who did it." His answer was, he could do nothing in the case, unless some white man would come forward and testify. He could issue no warrant on my word. If I had been killed in the presence of a thousand colored people, their testimony combined would have been insufficient to have arrested one of the murderers. Master Hugh, for once, was compelled to say this state of things was too bad. Of course, it was impossible to get any white man to volunteer his testimony in my behalf, and against the white young men. Even those who may have sympathized with me were not prepared to do this. It required a degree of courage unknown to them to do so; for just at that time, the slightest manifes-tation of humanity toward a colored person was denounced as abolitionism, and that name subjected its bearer to frightful liabilities. The watchwords of the bloody-minded in that region, and in those days, were, "Damn the aboli-tionists!" and "Damn the niggers!" There was nothing done, and probably nothing would have been done if I had been killed. Such was, and such remains, the state of things in the Christian city of Baltimore.

Master Hugh, finding he could get no redress, refused to let me go back again to Mr. Gardner. He kept me himself, and his wife dressed my wound till I was again restored to health. He then took me into the ship-yard of which he was foreman, in the employment of Mr. Walter Price. There I was immediately set to calking, and very soon learned the art of using my mallet and irons. In the course of one year from the time I left Mr. Gardner's, I was able to command the highest wages given to the most experienced calkers. I was now of some importance to my master. I was bringing him from six to seven dollars per week. I sometimes brought him nine dollars per week: my wages were a dollar and a half a day. After learning how to calk, I sought my own employment, made my own contracts, and collected the money which I earned. My pathway became much more smooth than before; my condition was now much more comfortable. When I could get no calking to do, I did nothing. During these leisure times, those old notions about freedom would steal over me again. When in Mr. Gardner's employment, I was kept in such a perpetual whirl of excitement, I could think of nothing, scarcely, but my life; and in thinking of my life, I almost forgot my liberty. I have observed this in my experience of slavery,—that whenever my condition was improved, instead of its increasing my contentment, it only increased my desire to be free, and set me to thinking of plans to gain my freedom. I have found that, to make a contented slave, it is necessary to make a thoughtless one. It is necessary to darken his moral and mental vision, and, as far as possible, to annihilate the power of reason. He must be able to detect no inconsistencies in slavery; he must be made to feel that slavery is right; and he can be brought to that only when he ceases to be a man.

I was now getting, as I have said, one dollar and fifty cents per day. I con-tracted for it; I earned it; it was paid to me; it was rightfully my own; yet, upon each returning Saturday night, I was compelled to deliver every cent of that money to Master Hugh. And why? Not because he earned it,—not because he had any hand in earning it,—not because I owed it to him,—nor because he possessed the slightest shadow of a right to it; but solely because he had the power to compel me to give it up. The right of the grim-visaged pirate upon the high seas is exactly the same.

Chapter XI

I now come to that part of my life during which I planned, and finally succeeded in making, my escape from slavery. But before narrating any of the peculiar circumstances, I deem it proper to make known my intention not to state all the facts connected with the transaction. My reasons for pursuing this course may be understood from the following: First, were I to give a minute statement of all the facts, it is not only possible but quite probable, that others would thereby be involved in the most embarrassing difficulties. Secondly, such a statement would most undoubtedly induce greater vigilance on the part of slaveholders than has existed heretofore among them; which would, of course, be the means of guarding a door whereby some dear brother bondman might escape his galling chains. I deeply regret the necessity that impels me to suppress any thing of importance connected with my experience in slavery. It would afford me great pleasure indeed, as well as materially add to the interest of my narrative, were I at liberty to gratify a curiosity, which I know exists in the minds of many, by an accurate statement of all the facts pertaining to my most fortunate escape. But I must deprive myself of this pleasure, and the curious of the gratification which such a statement would afford. I would allow myself to suffer under the greatest imputations which evil-minded men might suggest, rather than exculpate myself, and thereby run the hazard of closing the slightest avenue by which a brother slave might clear himself of the chains and fetters of slavery.

I have never approved of the very public manner in which some of our western friends have conducted what they call the *underground railroad*, but which, I think, by their own declarations, has been made most emphatically the *upperground railroad*. I honor those good men and women for their noble daring, and applaud them for willingly subjecting themselves to bloody persecution, by openly avowing their participation in the escape of slaves. I, however, can see very little good resulting from such a course, either to themselves or the slaves escaping; while, upon the other hand, I see and feel assured that those open declarations are a positive evil to the slaves remaining, who are seeking to escape. They do nothing towards enlightening the slave, whilst they do much towards enlightening the master. They stimulate him to greater watchfulness, and enhance his power to capture his slave. We owe something to the slaves south of the line as well as to those north of it; and in aiding the latter on their way to freedom, we should be careful to do nothing which would be likely to hinder the former from escaping from slavery. I would keep the merciless slaveholder profoundly ignorant of the means of flight adopted by the slave. I would leave him to imagine himself surrounded by myriads of invisible tormentors, ever ready to snatch from his infernal grasp his trembling prey. Let him be left to feel his way in the dark; let darkness commensurate with his crime hover over him; and let him feel that at every step he takes, in pursuit of the flying bondman, he is running the frightful risk of having his hot brains dashed out by an invisible agency. Let us render the tyrant no aid; let us not hold the light by which he can trace the footprints of our flying brother. But enough of this. I will now proceed to the statement of those facts, connected with my escape, for which I am alone responsible, and for which no one can be made to suffer but myself.

In the early part of the year 1838, I became quite restless. I could see no reason why I should, at the end of each week, pour the reward of my toil into the purse of my master. When I carried to him my weekly wages, he would, after counting the money, look me in the face with a robber-like fierceness, and say, "Is this all?" He was satisfied with nothing less than the last cent. He would, however, when I made him six dollars, sometimes give me six cents, to encourage me. It had the opposite effect. I regarded it as a sort of admission of my right to the whole. The fact that he gave me any part of my wages was proof, to my mind, that he believed me entitled to the whole of them. I always felt worse for having received any thing; for I feared that the giving me a few cents would ease his conscience, and make him feel himself to be a pretty honorable sort of robber. My discontent grew upon me. I was ever on the look-out for means of escape; and, finding no direct means, I determined to try to hire my time, with a view of getting money with which to make my escape. In the spring of 1838, when Master Thomas came to Baltimore to purchase his spring goods, I got an opportunity, and applied to him to allow me to hire my time. He unhesitatingly refused my request, and told me this was another strategem by which to escape. He told me I could go nowhere but that he could get me; and that, in the event of my running away, he should spare no pains in his efforts to catch me. He exhorted me to content myself, and be obedient. He told me, if I would be happy, I must lay out no plans for the future. He said, if I behaved myself properly, he would take care of me. Indeed, he advised me to complete thoughtlessness of the future, and taught me to depend solely upon him for happiness. He seemed to see fully the pressing necessity of setting aside my intellectual nature, in order to [insure] contentment in slavery. But in spite of him, and even in spite of myself, I continued to think, and to think about the injustice of my enslavement, and the means of escape.

About two months after this, I applied to Master Hugh for the privilege of hiring my time. He was not acquainted with the fact that I had applied to Master Thomas, and had been refused. He too, at first, seemed disposed to refuse; but, after some reflection, he granted me the privilege, and proposed the following terms: I was to be allowed all my time, make all contracts with those for whom I worked, and find my own employment; and, in return for this liberty, I was to pay him three dollars at the end of each week; find myself in calking tools, and in board and clothing. My board was two dollars and a half per week. This, with the wear and tear of clothing and calking tools, made my regular expenses about six dollars per week. This amount I was compelled to make up, or relinquish the privilege of hiring my time. Rain or shine, work or no work, at the end of each week the money must be forthcoming, or I must give up my privilege. This arrangement, it will be perceived, was decidedly in my master's favor. It relieved him of all need of looking after me. His money was sure. He received all the benefits of slaveholding without its evils; while I endured all the evils of a slave, and suffered all the care and anxiety of a freeman. I found it a hard bargain. But, hard as it was, I thought it better than the old mode of getting along. It was a step towards freedom to be allowed to bear the responsibilities of a freeman, and I was determined to hold on upon it. I bent myself to the work of making money. I was ready to work at night as well as day, and by the most untiring perseverance and industry, I made enough to meet my expenses, and lay up a little money every week. I went on thus from May till August. Master Hugh then refused to allow me to hire my time longer. The ground for his refusal was a failure on my part, one Saturday night, to pay him for my week's time. This failure was occasioned by my attending a camp meeting about ten miles from Baltimore. During the week, I had entered into an engagement with a number of young friends to start from Baltimore to the camp ground early Saturday evening; and being detained by my employer, I was unable to get down to Master Hugh's without disappointing the company. I knew that Master Hugh was in no special need of the money that night. I therefore decided to go to camp meeting, and upon my return pay him the three dollars. I staid at the camp meeting one day longer than I intended when I left. But as soon as I returned, I called upon him to pay him what he considered his due. I found him very angry; he could scarce restrain his wrath. He said he had a great mind to give me a severe whipping. He wished to know how I dared go out of the city without asking his permission. I told him I hired my time, and while I paid him the price which he asked for it, I did not know that I was bound to ask him when and where I should go. This reply troubled him; and, after reflecting a few moments, he turned to me, and said I should hire my time no longer; that the next thing he should know if, I would be running away. Upon the same plea, he told me to bring my tools and clothing home forthwith. I did so; but instead of seeking work, as I had been accustomed to do previously to hiring my time, I spent the whole week without the performance of a single stroke of work. I did this in retaliation. Saturday night, he called upon me as usual for my week's wages. I told him I had no wages; I had done no work that week. Here we were upon the point of coming to blows. He raved, and swore his determination to get hold of me. I did not allow myself a single word; but was resolved, if he laid the weight of his hand upon me, it should be blow for blow. He did not strike me, but told me that he would find me in constant employment in future. I thought the matter over during the next day, Sunday, and finally resolved upon the third day of September, as the day upon which I would make a second attempt to secure my freedom. I now had three weeks during which to prepare for my journey. Early on Monday morning, before Master Hugh had time to make any engagement for me, I went out and got employment of Mr. Butler, at his ship-yard near the drawbridge, upon what is called the City Block, thus making it unnecessary for him to seek employment for me. At the end of the week, I brought him between eight and nine dollars. He seemed very well pleased, and asked me why I did not do the same the week before. He little knew what my plans were. My object in working steadily was to remove any suspicion he might entertain of my intent to run away; and in this I succeeded admirably. I suppose he thought I was never better satisfied with my condition than at the very time during which I was planning my escape. The second week passed, and again I carried him my full wages; and so well pleased was he, that he gave me twenty-five cents, (quite a large sum for a slaveholder to give a slave), and bade me to make a good use of it. I told him I would.

Things went on without very smoothly indeed, but within there was trouble. It is impossible for me to describe my feelings as the time of my contemplated start drew near. I had a number of warm-hearted friends in Baltimore,—friends that I loved almost as I did my life,—and the thought of being separated from them forever was painful beyond expression. It is my opinion that thousands would escape from slavery, who now remain, but for the strong cords of affection that bind them to their friends. The thought of leaving my friends was decidedly the most painful thought with which I had to contend. The love of them was my tender point, and shook my decision more than all things else. Besides the pain of separation, the dread and apprehension of a failure exceeded what I had experienced at my first attempt. The appalling defeat I then sustained returned to torment me. I felt assured that, if I failed in this attempt, my case would be a hopeless one—it would seal my fate as a slave forever. I could not hope to get off with any thing less than the severest punishment, and being placed beyond the means of escape. It required no very vivid imagination to depict the most frightful scenes through which I should have to pass, in case I failed. The wretchedness of slavery, and the blessedness of freedom, were perpetually before me. It was life and death with me. But I remained firm, and, according to my resolution, on the third day of September, 1838, I left my chains, and succeeded in reaching New York without the slightest interruption of any kind. How I did so,—what means I adopted,—what direction I travelled, and by what mode of conveyance,—I must leave unexplained, for the reasons before mentioned.

I have been frequently asked how I felt when I found myself in a free State. I have never been able to answer the question with any satisfaction to myself. It was a moment of the highest excitement I ever experienced. I suppose I felt as one may imagine the unarmed mariner to feel when he is rescued by a friendly man-of-war from the pursuit of a pirate. In writing to a dear friend, immediately after my arrival at New York, I said I felt like one who had escaped a den of hungry lions. This state of mind, however, very soon subsided; and I was again seized with a feeling of great insecurity and loneliness. I was yet liable to be taken back, and subjected to all the tortures of slavery. This in itself was enough to damp the ardor of my enthusiasm. But the loneliness overcame me. There I was in the midst of thousands, and yet a perfect stranger; without home and without friends, in the midst of thousands of my own brethren—children of a common Father, and yet I dared not to unfold to any one of them my sad condition. I was afraid to speak to any one for fear of speaking to the wrong one, and thereby falling into the hands of money-loving kidnappers, whose business it was to lie in wait for the panting fugitive, as the ferocious beasts of the forest lie in wait for their prey. The motto which I adopted when I started from slavery was this—"Trust no man!" I saw in every white man an enemy, and in almost every colored man cause for distrust. It was a most painful situation; and, to understand it, one must needs experience it, or imagine himself in similar circumstances. Let him be a fugitive slave in a strange land—a land given up to be the hunting-ground for slaveholders—whose inhabitants are legalized kidnappers—where he is every moment subjected to the terrible liability of being seized upon by his fellowmen, as the hideous crocodile seizes upon his prey!—I say, let him place himself in my situation—without home or friends—without money or credit—wanting shelter, and no one to give it—wanting bread, and no money to buy it,—and at the same time let him feel that he is pursued by merciless men-hunters, and in total darkness as to what to do, where to go, or where to stay,—perfectly helpless both as to the means of defence and means of escape,—in the midst of plenty, yet suffering the terrible gnawings of hunger,—in the midst of houses, yet having no home,—among fellow-men, yet feeling as if in the midst of wild beasts, whose greediness to swallow up the trembling and half-famished fugitive is only equalled by that with which the monsters of the deep swallow up the helpless fish upon which they subsist,—I say, let him be placed in this most trying situation,—the situation in which I was placed,—then, and not till then, will he fully appreciate the hardships of, and know how to sympathize with, the toil-worn and whip-scarred fugitive slave.

Thank Heaven, I remained but a short time in this distressed situation. I was relieved from it by the humane hand of Mr. David Ruggles,[4] whose vigilance, kindness, and perseverance, I shall never forget. I am glad of an opportunity to express, as far as words can, the love and gratitude I bear him. Mr. Ruggles is now afflicted with blindness, and is himself in need of the same kind offices which he was once so forward in the performance of toward others. I had been in New York but a few days, when Mr. Ruggles sought me out, and very kindly took me to his boarding-house at the corner of Church and Lespenard Streets. Mr. Ruggles was then very deeply engaged in the memorable *Darg* case,[5] as well as attending to a number of other fugitive slaves; devising ways and means for their successful escape; and, though watched and hemmed in on almost every side, he seemed to be more than a match for his enemies.

Very soon after I went to Mr. Ruggles, he wished to know of me where I wanted to go; as he deemed it unsafe for me to remain in New York. I told him I was a calker, and should like to go where I could get work. I thought of going to Canada; but he decided against it, and in favor of my going to New Bedford, thinking I should be able to get work there at my trade. At this time, Anna,[6] my intended wife, came on; for I wrote to her immediately after my arrival at New York, (notwithstanding my homeless, houseless, and helpless condition,) informing her of my successful flight, and wishing her to come on forthwith. In a few days after her arrival, Mr. Ruggles called in the Rev. J. W. C. Pennington, who, in the presence of Mr. Ruggles, Mrs. Michaels, and two or three others, performed the marriage ceremony, and gave us a certificate, of which the following is an exact copy:—

> "This may certify, that I joined together in holy matrimony Frederick Johnson[7] and Anna Murray, as man and wife, in the presence of Mr. David Ruggles and Mrs. Michaels.
>
> "James W. C. Pennington
>
> "*New York, Sept. 15, 1838.*"

Upon receiving this certificate, and a five-dollar bill from Mr. Ruggles, I shouldered one part of our baggage, and Anna took up the other, and we set out forthwith to take passage on board of the steamboat John W. Richmond for Newport, on our way to New Bedford. Mr. Ruggles gave me a letter to a

---

4. A journalist and abolitionist (1810–1849) who aided Douglass in his escape from Maryland, and in whose house Douglass stayed on his way to New Bedford in 1838.

5. From John P. Darg (1771–1852), slave owner.
6. "She was free" [Douglass's note].
7. "I had changed my name from Frederick *Bailey* to that of *Johnson*" [Douglass's note].

Mr. Shaw in Newport, and told me, in case my money did not serve me to New Bedford, to stop in Newport and obtain further assistance; but upon our arrival at Newport, we were so anxious to get to a place of safety, that, notwithstanding we lacked the necessary money to pay our fare, we decided to take seats in the stage, and promise to pay when we got to New Bedford. We were encouraged to do this by two excellent gentlemen, residents of New Bedford, whose names I afterward ascertained to be Joseph Ricketson and William C. Taber. They seemed at once to understand our circumstances, and gave us such assurance of their friendliness as put us fully at ease in their presence. It was good indeed to meet with such friends, at such a time. Upon reaching New Bedford, we were directed to the house of Mr. Nathan Johnson, by whom we were kindly received, and hospitably provided for. Both Mr. and Mrs. Johnson took a deep and lively interest in our welfare. They proved themselves quite worthy of the name of abolitionists. When the stage-driver found us unable to pay our fare, he held on upon our baggage as security for the debt. I had but to mention the fact to Mr. Johnson, and he forthwith advanced the money.

We now began to feel a degree of safety, and to prepare ourselves for the duties and responsibilities of a life of freedom. On the morning after our arrival at New Bedford, while at the breakfast-table, the question arose as to what name I should be called by. The name given me by my mother was, "Frederick Augustus Washington Bailey." I, however, had dispensed with the two middle names long before I left Maryland so that I was generally known by the name of "Frederick Bailey." I started from Baltimore bearing the name of "Stanley." When I got to New York, I again changed my name to "Frederick Johnson," and thought that would be the last change. But when I got to New Bedford, I found it necessary again to change my name. The reason of this necessity was, that there were so many Johnsons in New Bedford, it was already quite difficult to distinguish between them. I gave Mr. Johnson the privilege of choosing me a name, but told him he must not take from me the name of "Frederick." I must hold on to that, to preserve a sense of my identity. Mr. Johnson had just been reading the "Lady of the Lake," and at once suggested that my name be "Douglass."[8] From that time until now I have been called "Frederick Douglass;" and as I am more widely known by that name than by either of the others, I shall continue to use it as my own.

I was quite disappointed at the general appearance of things in New Bedford. The impression which I had received respecting the character and condition of the people of the north, I found to be singularly erroneous. I had very strangely supposed, while in slavery, that few of the comforts, and scarcely any of the luxuries, of life were enjoyed at the north, compared with what were enjoyed by the slaveholders of the south. I probably came to this conclusion from the fact that northern people owned no slaves. I supposed that they were about upon a level with the non-slaveholding population of the south. I knew *they* were exceedingly poor, and I had been accustomed to regard their poverty as the necessary consequence of their being non-slaveholders. I had somehow imbibed the opinion that, in the absence of slaves, there could be no wealth, and very little refinement. And upon coming to the north, I expected to meet

---

8. Sir Walter Scott's (1771–1832) poem *Lady of the Lake* (1810), a historical romance set in the Scottish highlands in the 16th century. The plot, which in- volves the banishment and redemption of James of Douglas, was loosely pertinent to Frederick Douglass's life situation.

with a rough, hard-handed, and uncultivated population, living in the most Spartanlike simplicity, knowing nothing of the ease, luxury, pomp, and grandeur of southern slaveholders. Such being my conjectures, any one acquainted with the appearance of New Bedford may very readily infer how palpably I must have seen my mistake.

In the afternoon of the day when I reached New Bedford, I visited the wharves, to take a view of the shipping. Here I found myself surrounded with the strongest proofs of wealth. Lying at the wharves, and riding in the stream, I saw many ships of the finest model, in the best order, and of the largest size. Upon the right and left, I was walled in by granite warehouses of the widest dimensions, stowed to their utmost capacity with the necessaries and comforts of life. Added to this, almost every body seemed to be at work, but noiselessly so, compared with what I had been accustomed to in Baltimore. There were no loud songs heard from those engaged in loading and unloading ships. I heard no deep oaths or horrid curses on the laborer. I saw no whipping of men; but all seemed to go smoothly on. Every man appeared to understand his work, and went at it with a sober, yet cheerful earnestness, which betokened the deep interest which he felt in what he was doing, as well as a sense of his own dignity as man. To me this looked exceedingly strange. From the wharves I strolled around and over the town, gazing with wonder and admiration at the splendid churches, beautiful dwellings, and finely-cultivated gardens; evincing an amount of wealth, comfort, taste, and refinement, such as I had never seen in any part of slaveholding Maryland.

Every thing looked clean, new, and beautiful. I saw few or no dilapidated houses, with poverty-stricken inmates; no half-naked children and barefooted women, such as I had been accustomed to see in Hillsborough, Easton, St. Michael's, and Baltimore. The people looked more able, stronger, healthier, and happier, than those of Maryland. I was for once made glad by a view of extreme wealth, without being saddened by seeing extreme poverty. But the most astonishing as well as the most interesting thing to me was the condition of the colored people, a great many of whom, like myself, had escaped thither as a refuge from the hunters of men. I found many, who had not been seven years out of their chains, living in finer houses, and evidently enjoying more of the comforts of life, than the average of slaveholders in Maryland. I will venture to assert that my friend Mr. Nathan Johnson (of whom I can say with a grateful heart, "I was hungry, and he gave me meat; I was thirsty, and he gave me drink; I was a stranger, and he took me in"[9]) lived in a neater house, dined at a better table; took, paid for, and read, more newspapers; better understood the moral, religious, and political character of the nation,—than nine tenths of the slaveholders in Talbot county Maryland. Yet Mr. Johnson was a working man. His hands were hardened by toil, and not his alone, but those also of Mrs. Johnson. I found the colored people much more spirited than I had supposed they would be. I found among them a determination to protect each other from the blood-thirsty kidnapper, at all hazards. Soon after my arrival, I was told of a circumstance which illustrated their spirit. A colored man and a fugitive slave were on unfriendly terms. The former was heard to threaten the latter with informing his master of his whereabouts. Straightway a meeting was called among the colored people, under the stereotyped notice,

9. Cf. Matthew 25.35.

"Business of importance!" The betrayer was invited to attend. The people came at the appointed hour, and organized the meeting by appointing a very religious old gentleman as president, who, I believe, made a prayer, after which he addressed the meeting as follows: "*Friends, we have got him here, and I would recommend that you young men just take him outside the door, and kill him!*" With this, a number of them bolted at him; but they were intercepted by some more timid than themselves, and the betrayer escaped their vengeance, and has not been seen in New Bedford since. I believe there have been no more such threats, and should there be hereafter, I doubt not that death would be the consequence.

I found employment, the third day after my arrival, in stowing a sloop with a load of oil. It was new, dirty, and hard work for me; but I went at it with a glad heart and a willing hand. I was now my own master. It was a happy moment, the rapture of which can be understood only by those who have been slaves. It was the first work, the reward of which was to be entirely my own. There was no Master Hugh standing ready, the moment I earned the money, to rob me of it. I worked that day with a pleasure I had never before experienced. I was at work for myself and newly-married wife. It was to me the starting-point of a new existence. When I got through with that job, I went in pursuit of a job of calking; but such was the strength of prejudice against color, among the white calkers, that they refused to work with me, and of course I could get no employment.[1] Finding my trade of no immediate benefit, I threw off my calking habiliments, and prepared myself to do any kind of work I could get to do. Mr. Johnson kindly let me have his wood-horse and saw, and I very soon found myself a plenty of work. There was no work too hard—none too dirty. I was ready to saw wood, shovel coal, carry the hod, sweep the chimney, or roll oil casks,—all of which I did for nearly three years in New Bedford, before I became known to the anti-slavery world.

In about four months after I went to New Bedford, there came a young man to me, and inquired if I did not wish to take the "Liberator."[2] I told him I did; but, just having made my escape from slavery, I remarked that I was unable to pay for it then. I, however, finally became a subscriber to it. The paper came, and I read it from week to week with such feelings as it would be quite idle for me to attempt to describe. The paper became my meat and my drink. My soul was set all on fire. Its sympathy for my brethren in bonds—its scathing denunciations of slaveholders—its faithful exposures of slavery—and its powerful attacks upon the upholders of the institution—sent a thrill of joy through my soul, such as I had never felt before!

I had not long been a reader of the "Liberator," before I got a pretty correct idea of the principles, measures and spirit of the anti-slavery reform. I took right hold of the cause. I could do but little; but what I could, I did with a joyful heart, and never felt happier than when in an anti-slavery meeting. I seldom had much to say at the meetings, because what I wanted to say was said so much better by others. But, while attending an anti-slavery convention at Nantucket, on the 11th of August, 1841, I felt strongly moved to speak, and was at the same time much urged to do so by Mr. William C. Coffin, a

---

1. "I am told that colored persons can now get employment at calking in New Bedford—a result of anti-slavery effort" [Douglass's note].
2. The first issue of Garrison's *The Liberator* appeared in January 1831. Initially dependent on its black readership for support, it became the most eloquent and widely read of the abolitionist organs during its thirty-five years of publication.

gentleman who had heard me speak in the colored people's meeting at New Bedford. It was a severe cross, and I took it up reluctantly. The truth was, I felt myself a slave, and the idea of speaking to white people weighed me down. I spoke but a few moments, when I felt a degree of freedom, and said what I desired with considerable ease. From that time until now, I have been engaged in pleading the cause of my brethren—with what success, and with what devotion, I leave those acquainted with my labors to decide.

Appendix

I find, since reading over the foregoing Narrative, that I have, in several instances, spoken in such a tone and manner, respecting religion, as may possibly lead those unacquainted with my religious views to suppose me an opponent of all religion. To remove the liability of such misapprehension, I deem it proper to append the following brief explanation. What I have said respecting and against religion, I mean strictly to apply to the *slaveholding religion* of this land, and with no possible reference to Christianity proper; for, between the Christianity of this land, and the Christianity of Christ, I recognize the widest possible difference—so wide, that to receive the one as good, pure, and holy, is of necessity to reject the other as bad, corrupt, and wicked. To be the friend of the one, is of necessity to be the enemy of the other. I love the pure, peaceable, and impartial Christianity of Christ: I therefore hate the corrupt, slaveholding, women-whipping, cradle-plundering, partial and hypocritical Christianity of this land. Indeed, I can see no reason, but the most deceitful one, for calling the religion of this land Christianity. I look upon it as the climax of all misnomers, the boldest of all frauds, and the grossest of all libels. Never was there a clearer case of "stealing the livery of the court of heaven to serve the devil in." I am filled with unutterable loathing when I contemplate the religious pomp and show, together with the horrible inconsistencies, which every where surround me. We have men-stealers for ministers, women-whippers for missionaries, and cradle-plunderers for church members. The man who wields the blood-clotted cowskin during the week fills the pulpit on Sunday, and claims to be a minister of the meek and lowly Jesus. The man who robs me of my earnings at the end of each week meets me as a class-leader on Sunday morning, to show me the way of life, and the path of salvation. He who sells my sister, for purposes of prostitution, stands forth as the pious advocate of purity. He who proclaims it a religious duty to read the Bible denies me the right of learning to read the name of the God who made me. He who is the religious advocate of marriage robs whole millions of its scared influence, and leaves them to the ravages of wholesale pollution. The warm defender of the sacredness of the family relation is the same that scatters whole families,—sundering husbands and wives, parents and children, sisters and brothers,—leaving the hut vacant, and the hearth desolate. We see the thief preaching against theft, and the adulterer against adultery. We have men sold to build churches, women sold to support the gospel, and babes sold to purchase Bibles for the *poor heathen! all for the glory of God and the good of souls!* The slave auctioneer's bell and the church-going bell chime in with each other, and the bitter cries of the heart-broken slave are drowned in the religious shouts of his pious master. Revivals of religion and revivals in the slave-trade go hand in hand together. The slave prison and the church stand near each other. The clanking of fetters and the rattling of chains in the prison, and the pious psalm and solemn prayer in the church, may be heard at the same time. The dealers in the bodies and souls of men erect their stand in the presence of the pulpit, and they mutually help each other. The dealer gives his blood-stained gold to support the pulpit, and the pulpit, in return, covers his infernal business with the garb of Christianity. Here we have religion and robbery the allies of each other—devils dressed in angels' robes, and hell presenting the semblance of paradise.

> "Just God! and these are they,
>   Who minister at thine altar, God of right!
> Men who their hands, with prayer and blessing, lay
>   On Israel's ark of light.[3]
>
> "What! preach, and kidnap men?
>   Give thanks, and rob thy own afflicted poor?
> Talk of thy glorious liberty, and then
>   Bolt hard the captive's door?
>
> "What! servants of thy own
>   Merciful Son, who came to seek and save
> The homeless and the outcast, fettering down
>   The tasked and plundered slave!
>
> "Pilate and Herod[4] friends!
>   Chief priests and rulers, as of old, combine!
> Just God and holy! is that church which lends
>   Strength to the spoiler thine?"[5]

The Christianity of America is a Christianity, of whose votaries it may be as truly said, as it was of the ancient scribes and Pharisees,[6] "They bind heavy burdens, and grievous to be borne, and lay them on men's shoulders, but they themselves will not move them with one of their fingers. All their works they do for to be seen of men.——They love the uppermost rooms at feasts, and the chief seats in the synagogues, ... and to be called of men, Rabbi, Rabbi.——But woe unto you, scribes and Pharisees, hypocrites! for ye shut up the kingdom of heaven against men; for ye neither go in yourselves, neither suffer ye them that are entering to go in. Ye devour widows' houses, and for a pretence make long prayers; therefore ye shall receive the greater damnation. Ye compass sea and land to make one proselyte, and when he is made, ye make him twofold more the child of hell than yourselves.——Woe unto you, scribes and Pharisees, hypocrites! for ye pay tithe of mint, and anise, and cumin, and have omitted the weightier matters of the law, judgment, mercy, and faith; these ought ye to have done, and not to leave the other undone. Ye blind guides! which strain at a gnat, and swallow a camel. Woe unto you,

3. I.e., the Holy Ark containing the Torah; by extension, the entire body of law as contained in the Old Testament and Talmud.
4. Herod Antipas, ruler of Galilee, ordered the execution of John the Baptist and participated in the trial of Christ. Pontius Pilate was the Roman authority who condemned Christ to death.
5. From Whittier's antislavery poem *Clerical Oppres-*
sors, written about 1835.
6. Members of a powerful Jewish sect that insisted on strict observance of written and oral religious laws. The scribes were the Jewish scholars who taught Jewish law and edited and interpreted the Bible. Christ's denunciation of the Scribes and Pharisees is reported in Matthew 23.

scribes and Pharisees, hypocrites! for ye make clean the outside of the cup and of the platter; but within, they are full of extortion and excess.——Woe unto you, scribes and Pharisees, hypocrites! for ye are like unto whited sepulchres, which indeed appear beautiful outward, but are within full of dead men's bones, and of all uncleanness. Even so ye also outwardly appear righteous unto men, but within ye are full of hypocrisy and iniquity."

Dark and terrible as is this picture, I hold it to be strictly true of the over-whelming mass of professed Christians in America. They strain at a gnat, and swallow a camel. Could any thing be more true of our churches? They would be shocked at the proposition of fellowshipping a *sheep*-stealer; and at the same time they hug to their communion a *man*-stealer, and brand me with being an infidel, if I find fault with them for it. They attend with Pharisaical strictness to the outward forms of religion, and at the same time neglect the weightier matters of the law, judgment, mercy, and faith. They are always ready to sacrifice, but seldom to show mercy. They are they who are represented as professing to love God whom they have not seen, whilst they hate their brother whom they have seen. They love the heathen on the other side of the globe. They can pray for him, pay money to have the Bible put into his hand, and missionaries to instruct him; while they despise and totally neglect the heathen at their own doors.

Such is, very briefly, my view of the religion of this land; and to avoid any misunderstanding, growing out of the use of general terms, I mean, by the religion of this land, that which is revealed in the words, deeds, and actions, of those bodies, north and south, calling themselves Christian churches, and yet in union with slaveholders. It is against religion, as presented by these bodies, that I have felt it my duty to testify.

I conclude these remarks by copying the following portrait of the religion of the south, (which is, by communion and fellowship, the religion of the north,) which I soberly affirm is "true to the life," and without caricature or the slight-est exaggeration. It is said to have been drawn, several years before the present anti-slavery agitation began, by a northern Methodist preacher, who, while residing at the south, had an opportunity to see slaveholding morals, manners, and piety, with his own eyes. "Shall I not visit for these things? saith the Lord. Shall not my soul be avenged on such a nation as this?"[7]

A PARODY

"Come, saints and sinners, hear me tell
How pious priests whip Jack and Nell,
And women buy and children sell,
And preach all sinners down to hell,
   And sing of heavenly union.

"They'll bleat and baa, dona like goats,
Gorge down black sheep, and strain at motes,
Array their backs in fine black coats,
Then seize their negroes by their throats,
   And choke, for heavenly union.

"They'll church you if you sip a dram,
And damn you if you steal a lamb;

7. Jeremiah speaks God's charges against the sins of the House of Israel (Jeremiah 5–9).

Yet rob old Tony, Doll, and Sam,
Of human rights, and bread and ham;
    Kidnapper's heavenly union.

"They'll loudly talk of Christ's reward,
And bind his image with a cord,
And scold, and swing the lash abhorred,
And sell their brother in the Lord
    To handcuffed heavenly union.

"They'll read and sing a sacred song,
And make a prayer both loud and long,
And teach the right and do the wrong,
Hailing the brother, sister throng,
    With words of heavenly union.

"We wonder how such saints can sing,
Or praise the Lord upon the wing,
Who roar, and scold, and whip, and sting,
And to their slaves and mammon cling,
    In guilty conscience union.

"They'll raise tobacco, corn, and rye,
And drive, and thieve, and cheat, and lie,
And lay up treasures in the sky,
By making switch and cowskin fly,
    In hope of heavenly union.

"They'll crack old Tony on the skull,
And preach and roar like Bashan[8] bull,
Or braying ass, of mischief full,
Then seize old Jacob by the wool,
    And pull for heavenly union.

"A roaring, ranting, sleek man-thief,
Who lived on mutton, veal, and beef,
Yet never would afford relief
To needy, sable sons of grief,
    Was big with heavenly union.

" 'Love not the world,' the preacher said,
And winked his eye, and shook his head;
He seized on Tom, and Dick, and Ned,
Cut short their meat, and clothes, and bread,
    Yet still loved heavenly union.

"Another preacher whining spoke
Of One whose heart for sinners broke:
He tied old Nanny to an oak,
And drew the blood at every stroke,
    And prayed for heavenly union.

---

8. Strong bulls mentioned in the Old Testament.

"Two others oped their iron jaws,
And waved their children-stealing paws;
There sat their children in gewgaws;
By stinting negroes' backs and maws,
    They kept up heavenly union.

"All good from Jack another takes,
And entertains their flirts and rakes,
Who dress as sleek as glossy snakes,
And cram their mouths with sweetened cakes;
    And this goes down for union."[9]

Sincerely and earnestly hoping that this little book may do something toward throwing light on the American slave system, and hastening the glad day of deliverance to the millions of my brethren in bonds—faithfully relying upon the power of truth, love, and justice, for success in my humble efforts—and solemnly pledging my self anew to the sacred cause,—I subscribe myself,

FREDERICK DOUGLASS

LYNN, *Mass., April 28, 1845.*

1845

The Meaning of July Fourth for the Negro: Speech at Rochester, New York, July 5, 1852[1]

Mr. President, Friends and Fellow Citizens:
He who could address this audience without a quailing sensation, has stronger nerves than I have. I do not remember ever to have appeared as a speaker before any assembly more shrinkingly, nor with greater distrust of my ability, than I do this day. A feeling has crept over me quite unfavorable to the exercise of my limited powers of speech. The task before me is one which requires much previous thought and study for its proper performance. I know that apologies of this sort are generally considered flat and unmeaning. I trust, however, that mine will not be so considered. Should I seem at ease, my appearance would much misrepresent me. The little experience I have had in addressing public meetings, in country school houses, avails me nothing on the present occasion.

The papers and placards say that I am to deliver a Fourth of July Oration. This certainly sounds large, and out of the common way, for me. It is true that I have often had the privilege to speak in this beautiful Hall, and to address many who now honor me with their presence. But neither their familiar faces, nor the perfect gage I think I have of Corinthian Hall seems to free me from embarrassment.

9. Douglass is parodying "Heavenly Union," a hymn sung in many Southern churches at the time. Douglass was famous for his sharp sense of humor and ability to mimic the Southern clergy.
1. Douglass gave this address at Corinthian Hall to an audience of between five and six hundred people, each of whom had paid twelve and a half cents to hear Douglass speak. Douglass published a pamphlet version of the speech in his *Frederick Douglass' Paper* on July 19, 1852, the basis for the present text. The notes that follow owe much to the pioneering scholarship of John Blassingame, chief editor of *The Frederick Douglass Papers.*

The fact is, ladies and gentlemen, the distance between this platform and the slave plantation, from which I escaped, is considerable—and the difficulties to be overcome in getting from the latter to the former are by no means slight. That I am here to-day is, to me, a matter of astonishment as well as of gratitude. You will not, therefore, be surprised, if in what I have to say I evince no elaborate preparation, nor grace my speech with any high sounding exordium. With little experience and with less learning, I have been able to throw my thoughts hastily and imperfectly together; and trusting to your patient and generous indulgence, I will proceed to lay them before you.

This, for the purpose of this celebration, is the Fourth of July. It is the birthday of your National Independence, and of your political freedom. This, to you, is what the Passover was to the emancipated people of God. It carries your minds back to the day, and to the act of your great deliverance; and to the signs, and to the wonders, associated with that act, and that day. This celebration also marks the beginning of another year of your national life; and reminds you that the Republic of America is now 76 years old. I am glad, fellow-citizens, that your nation is so young. Seventy-six years, though a good old age for a man, is but a mere speck in the life of a nation. Three score years and ten is the allotted time for individual men; but nations number their years by thousands. According to this fact, you are, even now, only in the beginning of your national career, still lingering in the period of childhood. I repeat, I am glad this is so. There is hope in the thought, and hope is much needed, under the dark clouds which lower above the horizon. The eye of the reformer is met with angry flashes, portending disastrous times; but his heart may well beat lighter at the thought that America is young, and that she is still in the impressible stage of her existence. May he not hope that high lessons of wisdom, of justice and of truth, will yet give direction to her destiny? Were the nation older, the patriot's heart might be sadder, and the reformer's brow heavier. Its future might be shrouded in gloom, and the hope of its prophets go out in sorrow. There is consolation in the thought that America is young.—Great streams are not easily turned from channels, worn deep in the course of ages. They may sometimes rise in quiet and stately majesty, and inundate the land, refreshing and fertilizing the earth with their mysterious properties. They may also rise in wrath and fury, and bear away, on their angry waves, the accumulated wealth of years of toil and hardship. They, however, gradually flow back to the same old channel, and flow on as serenely as ever. But, while the river may not be turned aside, it may dry up, and leave nothing behind but the withered branch, and the unsightly rock, to howl in the abyss-sweeping wind, the sad tale of departed glory. As with rivers so with nations.

Fellow-citizens, I shall not presume to dwell at length on the associations that cluster about this day. The simple story of it is, that, 76 years ago, the people of this country were British subjects. The style and title of your "sovereign people" (in which you now glory) was not then born. You were under the British Crown. Your fathers esteemed the English Government as the home government; and England as the fatherland. This home government, you know, although a considerable distance from your home, did, in the exercise of its parental prerogatives, impose upon its colonial children, such restraints, burdens and limitations, as, in its mature judgment, it deemed wise, right and proper.

But your fathers, who had not adopted the fashionable idea of this day, of the infallibility of government, and the absolute character of its acts, presumed to differ from the home government in respect to the wisdom and the justice of some of those burdens and restraints. They went so far in their excitement as to pronounce the measures of government unjust, unreasonable, and oppressive, and altogether such as ought not to be quietly submitted to. I scarcely need say, fellow-citizens, that my opinion of those measures fully accords with that of your fathers. Such a declaration of agreement on my part would not be worth much to anybody. It would certainly prove nothing as to what part I might have taken had I lived during the great controversy of 1776. To say now that America was right, and England wrong, is exceedingly easy. Everybody can say it; the dastard, not less than the noble brave, can flippantly discant on the tyranny of England towards the American Colonies. It is fashionable to do so; but there was a time when, to pronounce against England, and in favor of the cause of the colonies, tried men's souls.[2] They who did so were accounted in their day plotters of mischief, agitators and rebels, dangerous men. To side with the right against the wrong, with the weak against the strong, and with the oppressed against the oppressor! here lies the merit, and the one which, of all others, seems unfashionable in our day. The cause of liberty may be stabbed by the men who glory in the deeds of your fathers. But, to proceed.

Feeling themselves harshly and unjustly treated, by the home government, your fathers, like men of honesty, and men of spirit, earnestly sought redress. They petitioned and remonstrated; they did so in a decorous, respectful, and loyal manner. Their conduct was wholly unexceptionable. This, however, did not answer the purpose. They saw themselves treated with sovereign indifference, coldness and scorn. Yet they persevered. They were not the men to look back.

As the sheet anchor takes a firmer hold, when the ship is tossed by the storm, so did the cause of your fathers grow stronger as it breasted the chilling blasts of kingly displeasure. The greatest and best of British statesmen admitted its justice, and the loftiest eloquence of the British Senate came to its support. But, with that blindness which seems to be the unvarying characteristic of tyrants, since Pharaoh and his hosts were drowned in the Red Sea, the British Government persisted in the exactions complained of.

The madness of this course, we believe, is admitted now, even by England; but we fear the lesson is wholly lost on our present rulers.

Oppression makes a wise man mad. Your fathers were wise men, and if they did not go mad, they became restive under this treatment. They felt themselves the victims of grievous wrongs, wholly incurable in their colonial capacity. With brave men there is always a remedy for oppression. Just here, the idea of a total separation of the colonies from the crown was born! It was a startling idea, much more so than we, at this distance of time, regard it. The timid and the prudent (as has been intimated) of that day were, of course, shocked and alarmed by it.

Such people lived then, had lived before, and will, probably, ever have a place on this planet; and their course, in respect to any great change (no matter how great the good to be attained, or the wrong to be redressed by it), may be calculated with as much precision as can be the course of the stars. They hate

2. Douglass here paraphrases the opening line of polemical writer Thomas Paine's (1737–1809) first *Crisis* paper of December 23, 1776.

all changes, but silver, gold and copper change! Of this sort of change they are always strongly in favor.

These people were called Tories in the days of your fathers; and the appellation, probably, conveyed the same idea that is meant by a more modern, though a somewhat less euphonious term, which we often find in our papers, applied to some of our old politicians.[3]

Their opposition to the then dangerous thought was earnest and powerful; but, amid all their terror and affrighted vociferations against it, the alarming and revolutionary idea moved on, and the country with it.

On the 2d of July, 1776, the old Continental Congress, to the dismay of the lovers of ease, and the worshipers of property, clothed that dreadful idea with all the authority of national sanction. They did so in the form of a resolution; and as we seldom hit upon resolutions, drawn up in our day, whose transparency is at all equal to this, it may refresh your minds and help my story if I read it.

> "Resolved, That these united colonies are, and of right, ought to be free and Independent States; that they are absolved from all allegiance to the British Crown; and that all political connection between them and the State of Great Britain is, and ought to be dissolved."[4]

Citizens, your fathers made good that resolution. They succeeded; and to-day you reap the fruits of their success. The freedom gained is yours; and you, therefore, may properly celebrate this anniversary. The 4th of July is the first great fact in your nation's history—the very ring-bolt in the chain of your yet undeveloped destiny.

Pride and patriotism, not less than gratitude, prompt you to celebrate and to hold it in perpetual remembrance. I have said that the Declaration of Independence is the ringbolt to the chain of your nation's destiny; so, indeed, I regard it. The principles contained in that instrument are saving principles. Stand by those principles, be true to them on all occasions, in all places, against all foes, and at whatever cost.

From the round top of your ship of state, dark and threatening clouds may be seen. Heavy billows, like mountains in the distance, disclose to the leeward huge forms of flinty rocks! That bolt drawn, that chain broken, and all is lost. Cling to this day—cling to it, and to its principles, with the grasp of a storm-tossed mariner to a spar at midnight.

The coming into being of a nation, in any circumstances, is an interesting event. But, besides general considerations, there were peculiar circumstances which make the advent of this republic an event of special attractiveness.

The whole scene, as I look back to it, was simple, dignified and sublime. The population of the country, at the time, stood at the insignificant number of three millions. The country was poor in the munitions of war. The population was weak and scattered, and the country a wilderness unsubdued. There were then no means of concert and combination, such as exist now. Neither steam nor lightning had then been reduced to order and discipline. From the Potomac to the Delaware was a journey of many days. Under these, and

---

3. Douglass is apparently referring to the Hunkers, a name applied to conservative members of the Democratic party in New York State in the late 1840s.

4. The full text is printed in the *Journals of the Continental Congress, 1774–1789*, vol. 5, edited by W. C. Ford et al. (1904–37).

innumerable other disadvantages, your fathers declared for liberty and independence and triumphed.

Fellow Citizens, I am not wanting in respect for the fathers of this republic. The signers of the Declaration of Independence were brave men. They were great men, too—great enough to give frame to a great age. It does not often happen to a nation to raise, at one time, such a number of truly great men. The point from which I am compelled to view them is not, certainly, the most favorable; and yet I cannot contemplate their great deeds with less than admiration. They were statesmen, patriots and heroes, and for the good they did, and the principles they contended for, I will unite with you to honor their memory.

They loved their country better than their own private interests; and, though this is not the highest form of human excellence, all will concede that it is a rare virtue, and that when it is exhibited it ought to command respect. He who will, intelligently, lay down his life for his country is a man whom it is not in human nature to despise. Your fathers staked their lives, their fortunes, and their sacred honor, on the cause of their country. In their admiration of liberty, they lost sight of all other interests.

They were peace men; but they preferred revolution to peaceful submission to bondage. They were quiet men; but they did not shrink from agitating against oppression. They showed forbearance; but that they knew its limits. They believed in order; but not in the order of tyranny. With them, nothing was "settled" that was not right. With them, justice, liberty and humanity were "final"; not slavery and oppression. You may well cherish the memory of such men. They were great in their day and generation. Their solid manhood stands out the more as we contrast it with these degenerate times.

How circumspect, exact and proportionate were all their movements! How unlike the politicians of an hour! Their statesmanship looked beyond the passing moment, and stretched away in strength into the distant future. They seized upon eternal principles, and set a glorious example in their defence. Mark them!

Fully appreciating the hardships to be encountered, firmly believing in the right of their cause, honorably inviting the scrutiny of an on-looking world, reverently appealing to heaven to attest their sincerity, soundly comprehending the solemn responsibility they were about to assume, wisely measuring the terrible odds against them, your fathers, the fathers of this republic, did, most deliberately, under the inspiration of a glorious patriotism, and with a sublime faith in the great principles of justice and freedom, lay deep, the corner-stone of the national super-structure, which has risen and still rises in grandeur around you.

Of this fundamental work, this day is the anniversary. Our eyes are met with demonstrations of joyous enthusiasm. Banners and pennants were exultingly on the breeze. The din of business, too, is hushed. Even mammon seems to have quitted his grasp on this day. The ear-piercing fife and the stirring drum unite their accents with the ascending peal of a thousand church bells. Prayers are made, hymns are sung, and sermons are preached in honor of this day; while the quick martial tramp of a great and multitudinous nation, echoed back by all the hills, valleys and mountains of a vast continent, bespeak the occasion one of thrilling and universal interest—a nation's jubilee.

Friends and citizens, I need not enter further into the causes which led to this anniversary. Many of you understand them better than I do. You could instruct me in regard to them. That is a branch of knowledge in which you feel, perhaps, a much deeper interest than your speaker. The causes which led to the separation of the colonies from the British crown have never lacked for a tongue. They have all been taught in your common schools, narrated at your firesides, unfolded from your pulpits, and thundered from your legislative halls, and are as familiar to you as household words. They form the staple of your national poetry and eloquence.

I remember, also, that, as a people, Americans are remarkably familiar with all facts which make in their own favor. This is esteemed by some as a national trait—perhaps a national weakness. It is a fact, that whatever makes for the wealth or for the reputation of Americans and can be had cheap! will be found by Americans. I shall not be charged with slandering Americans if I say I think the American side of any question may be safely left in American hands.

I leave, therefore, the great deeds of your fathers to other gentlemen whose claim to have been regularly descended will be less likely to be disputed than mine!

My business, if I have any here to-day, is with the present. The accepted time with God and His cause is the ever-living now.

> Trust no future, however pleasant,
> Let the dead past bury its dead;
> Act, act in the living present,
> Heart within, and God overhead.[5]

We have to do with the past only as we can make it useful to the present and to the future. To all inspiring motives, to noble deeds which can be gained from the past, we are welcome. But now is the time, the important time. Your fathers have lived, died, and have done their work, and have done much of it well. You live and must die, and you must do your work. You have no right to enjoy a child's share in the labor of your fathers, unless your children are to be blest by your labors. You have no right to wear out and waste the hard-earned fame of your fathers to cover your indolence. Sydney Smith[6] tells us that men seldom eulogize the wisdom and virtues of their fathers, but to excuse some folly or wickedness of their own. This truth is not a doubtful one. There are illustrations of it near and remote, ancient and modern. It was fashionable, hundreds of years ago, for the children of Jacob to boast, we have "Abraham to our father,"[7] when they had long lost Abraham's faith and spirit. That people contented themselves under the shadow of Abraham's great name, while they repudiated the deeds which made his name great. Need I remind you that a similar thing is being done all over this country to-day? Need I tell you that the Jews are not the only people who built the tombs of the prophets, and garnished the sepulchers of the righteous? Washington could not die till he had broken the chains of his slaves.[8] Yet his monument is built up by the price of human blood, and the traders in the bodies and souls of men shout—"We have Washington to *our father*."—Alas! that it should be so; yet so it is.

---

5. From American poet Henry Wadsworth Longfellow's (1807–1882) A *Psalm of Life*.
6. English clergyman and essayist (1771–1845), perhaps best known for asking in an 1820 essay, "In the four quarters of the globe, who reads an American book? or goes to an American play? or looks at an American picture or statue?"
7. See Luke 3.8.
8. George Washington's will provided that at the time of his wife's death all slaves owned by the Washingtons should be freed.

> *The evil that men do, lives after them,*
> *The good is oft interred with their bones.*[9]

Fellow-citizens, pardon me, allow me to ask, why am I called upon to speak here to-day? What have I, or those I represent, to do with your national independence? Are the great principles of political freedom and of natural justice, embodied in that Declaration of Independence, extended to us? and am I, therefore, called upon to bring our humble offering to the national altar, and to confess the benefits and express devout gratitude for the blessings resulting from your independence to us?

Would to God, both for your sakes and ours, that an affirmative answer could be truthfully returned to these questions! Then would my task be light, and my burden easy and delightful. For *who* is there so cold, that a nation's sympathy could not warm him? Who so obdurate and dead to the claims of gratitude, that would not thankfully acknowledge such priceless benefits? Who so stolid and selfish, that would not give his voice to swell the hallelujahs of a nation's jubilee, when the chains of servitude had been torn from his limbs? I am not that man. In a case like that, the dumb might eloquently speak, and the "lame man leap as an hart."

But such is not the state of the case. I say it with a sad sense of the disparity between us. I am not included within the pale of this glorious anniversary! Your high independence only reveals the immeasurable distance between us. The blessings in which you, this day, rejoice, are not enjoyed in common.— The rich inheritance of justice, liberty, prosperity and independence, bequeathed by your fathers, is shared by you, not by me. The sunlight that brought light and healing to you, has brought stripes and death to me. This Fourth July is *yours*, not *mine*. *You* may rejoice, *I* must mourn. To drag a man in fetters into the grand illuminated temple of liberty, and call upon him to join you in joyous anthems, were inhuman mockery and sacrilegious irony. Do you mean, citizens, to mock me, by asking me to speak to-day? If so, there is a parallel to your conduct. And let me warn you that it is dangerous to copy the example of a nation whose crimes, towering up to heaven, were thrown down by the breath of the Almighty, burying that nation in irrevocable ruin! I can to-day take up the plaintive lament of a peeled and woe-smitten people!

"By the rivers of Babylon, there we sat down. Yea! we wept when we remembered Zion. We hangd our harps upon the willows in the midst thereof. For there, they that carried us away captive, required of us a song; and they who wasted us required of us mirth, saying, Sing us one of the songs of Zion. How can we sing the Lord's song in a strange land? If I forget thee, O Jerusalem, let my right hand forget her cunning. If I do not remember thee, let my tongue cleave to the roof of my mouth."[1]

Fellow-citizens, above your national, tumultuous joy, I hear the mournful wail of millions! whose chains, heavy and grievous yesterday, are, to-day, rendered more intolerable by the jubilee shouts that reach them. If I do forget, if I do not faithfully remember those bleeding children of sorrow this day, "may my right hand forget her cunning, and may my tongue cleave to the roof of my mouth!" To forget them, to pass lightly over their wrongs, and to chime in with the popular theme, would be treason most scandalous and shocking, and would make me a reproach before God and the world. My subject, then,

---

9. Shakespeare's *Julius Caesar* 3.2.76.   1. Psalms 137.1–6.

fellow-citizens, is American slavery. I shall see this day and its popular characteristics from the slave's point of view. Standing there identified with the American bondman, making his wrongs mine, I do not hesitate to declare, with all my soul, that the character and conduct of this nation never looked blacker to me than on this 4th of July! Whether we turn to the declarations of the past, or to the professions of the present, the conduct of the nation seems equally hideous and revolting. America is false to the past, false to the present, and solemnly binds herself to be false to the future. Standing with God and the crushed and bleeding slave on this occasion, I will, in the name of humanity which is outraged, in the name of liberty which is fettered, in the name of the constitution and the Bible which are disregarded and trampled upon, dare to call in question and to denounce, with all the emphasis I can command, everything that serves to perpetuate slavery—the great sin and shame of America! "I will not equivocate; I will not excuse";[2] I will use the severest language I can command; and yet not one word shall escape me that any man, whose judgment is not blinded by prejudice, or who is not at heart a slaveholder, shall not confess to be right and just.

But I fancy I hear some one of my audience say, "It is just in this circumstance that you and your brother abolitionists fail to make a favorable impression on the public mind. Would you argue more, and denounce less; would you persuade more, and rebuke less; your cause would be much more likely to succeed." But, I submit, where all is plain there is nothing to be argued. What point in the anti-slavery creed would you have me argue? On what branch of the subject do the people of this country need light? Must I undertake to prove that the slave is a man? That point is conceded already. Nobody doubts it. The slaveholders themselves acknowledge it in the enactment of laws for their government. They acknowledge it when they punish disobedience on the part of the slave. There are seventy-two crimes in the State of Virginia which, if committed by a black man (no matter how ignorant he be), subject him to the punishment of death; while only two of the same crimes will subject a white man to the like punishment. What is this but the acknowledgment that the slave is a moral, intellectual, and responsible being? The manhood of the slave is conceded. It is admitted in the fact that Southern statute books are covered with enactments forbidding, under severe fines and penalties, the teaching of the slave to read or to write. When you can point to any such laws in reference to the beasts of the field, then I may consent to argue the manhood of the slave. When the dogs in your streets, when the fowls of the air, when the cattle on your hills, when the fish of the sea, and the reptiles that crawl, shall be unable to distinguish the slave from a brute, *then* will I argue with you that the slave is a man!

For the present, it is enough to affirm the equal manhood of the Negro race. Is it not astonishing that, while we are ploughing, planting, and reaping, using all kinds of mechanical tools, erecting houses, constructing bridges, building ships, working in metals of brass, iron, copper, silver and gold; that, while we are reading, writing and ciphering, acting as clerks, merchants and secretaries, having among us lawyers, doctors, ministers, poets, authors, editors, orators and teachers; that, while we are engaged in all manner of enterprises common to other men, digging gold in California, capturing the whale

2. In the first issue of his *The Liberator* (January 1, 1831) abolitionist William Lloyd Garrison (1805–1879) stated: "I am in earnest—I will not equiv- ocate—I will not excuse—I will not retreat a single inch—and *I will be heard*."

in the Pacific, feeding sheep and cattle on the hill-side, living, moving, acting, thinking, planning, living in families as husbands, wives and children, and, above all, confessing and worshipping the Christian's God, and looking hopefully for life and immortality beyond the grave, we are called upon to prove that we are men!

Would you have me argue that man is entitled to liberty? that he is the rightful owner of his own body? You have already declared it. Must I argue the wrongfulness of slavery? Is that a question for Republicans? Is it to be settled by the rules of logic and argumentation, as a matter beset with great difficulty, involving a doubtful application of the principle of justice, hard to be understood? How should I look to-day, in the presence of Americans, dividing, and subdividing a discourse, to show that men have a natural right to freedom? speaking of it relatively and positively, negatively and affirmatively. To do so, would be to make myself ridiculous, and to offer an insult to your understanding.—There is not a man beneath the canopy of heaven that does not know that slavery is wrong *for him.*

What, am I to argue that it is wrong to make men brutes, to rob them of their liberty, to work them without wages, to keep them ignorant of their relations to their fellow men, to beat them with sticks, to flay their flesh with the lash, to load their limbs with irons, to hunt them with dogs, to sell them at auction, to sunder their families, to knock out their teeth, to burn their flesh, to starve them into obedience and submission to their masters? Must I argue that a system thus marked with blood, and stained with pollution, is *wrong?* No! I will not. I have better employment for my time and strength than such arguments would imply.

What, then, remains to be argued? Is it that slavery is not divine; that God did not establish it; that our doctors of divinity are mistaken? There is blasphemy in the thought. That which is inhuman, cannot be divine! *Who* can reason on such a proposition? They that can, may; I cannot. The time for such argument is passed.

At a time like this, scorching irony, not convincing argument, is needed. O! had I the ability, and could reach the nation's ear, I would, to-day, pour out a fiery stream of biting ridicule, blasting reproach, withering sarcasm, and stern rebuke. For it is not light that is needed, but fire; it is not the gentle shower, but thunder. We need the storm, the whirlwind, and the earthquake. The feeling of the nation must be quickened; the conscience of the nation must be roused; the propriety of the nation must be startled; the hypocrisy of the nation must be exposed; and its crimes against God and man must be proclaimed and denounced.

What, to the American slave, is your 4th of July? I answer; a day that reveals to him, more than all other days in the year, the gross injustice and cruelty to which he is the constant victim. To him, your celebration is a sham; your boasted liberty, an unholy license; your national greatness, swelling vanity; your sounds of rejoicing are empty and heartless; your denunciation of tyrants, brass fronted impudence; your shouts of liberty and equality, hollow mockery; your prayers and hymns, your sermons and thanksgivings, with all your religious parade and solemnity, are, to Him, mere bombast, fraud, deception, impiety, and hypocrisy—a thin veil to cover up crimes which would disgrace a nation of savages. There is not a nation on the earth guilty of practices more shocking and bloody than are the people of the United States, at this very hour.

Go where you may, search where you will, roam through all the monarchies and despotisms of the Old World, travel through South America, search out every abuse, and when you have found the last, lay your facts by the side of the everyday practices of this nation, and you will say with me, that, for revolting barbarity and shameless hypocrisy, America reigns without a rival.

Take the American slave-trade, which we are told by the papers, is especially prosperous just now. Ex-Senator Benton[3] tells us that the price of men was never higher than now. He mentions the fact to show that slavery is in no danger. This trade is one of the peculiarities of American institutions. It is carried on in all the large towns and cities in one-half of this confederacy; and millions are pocketed every year by dealers in this horrid traffic. In several states this trade is a chief source of wealth. It is called (in contradistinction to the foreign slave-trade) *"the internal slave-trade."* It is, probably, called so, too, in order to divert from it the horror with which the foreign slave-trade is contemplated. That trade has long since been denounced by this government as piracy. It has been denounced with burning words from the high places of the nation as an execrable traffic. To arrest it, to put an end to it, this nation keeps a squadron, at immense cost, on the coast of Africa. Everywhere, in this country, it is safe to speak of this foreign slave-trade as a most inhuman traffic, opposed alike to the laws of God and of man. The duty to extirpate and destroy it, is admitted even by our doctors of divinity. In order to put an end to it, some of these last have consented that their colored brethren (nominally free) should leave this country, and establish themselves on the western coast of Africa! It is, however, a notable fact that, while so much execration is poured out by Americans upon all those engaged in the foreign slave-trade, the men engaged in the slave-trade between the states pass without condemnation, and their business is deemed honorable.

Behold the practical operation of this internal slave-trade, the American slave-trade, sustained by American politics and American religion. Here you will see men and women reared like swine for the market. You know what is a swine-drover? I will show you a man-drover. They inhabit all our Southern States. They perambulate the country, and crowd the highways of the nation, with droves of human stock. You will see one of these human flesh jobbers, armed with pistol, whip, and bowie-knife, driving a company of a hundred men, women, and children, from the Potomac to the slave market at New Orleans. These wretched people are to be sold singly, or in lots, to suit purchasers. They are food for the cotton-field and the deadly sugar-mill. Mark the sad procession, as it moves wearily along, and the inhuman wretch who drives them. Hear his savage yells and his blood-curdling oaths, as he hurries on his affrighted captives! There, see the old man with locks thinned and gray. Cast one glance, if you please, upon that young mother, whose shoulders are bare to the scorching sun, her briny tears falling on the brow of the babe in her arms. See, too, that girl of thirteen, weeping, *yes!* weeping, as she thinks of the mother from whom she has been torn! The drove moves tardily. Heat and sorrow have nearly consumed their strength; suddenly you hear a quick snap, like the discharge of a rifle; the fetters clank, and the chain rattles simultaneously; your ears are saluted with a scream, that seems to have torn its way to the centre of your soul! The crack you heard was the sound of the slave-

3. Thomas Hart Benton (1782–1858), senator and later representative from Missouri, disputed the claim of slaveholding interests that attempts to limit the spread of slavery to new states would reduce the monetary value of slaves.

whip; the scream you heard was from the woman you saw with the babe. Her speed had faltered under the weight of her child and her chains! that gash on her shoulder tells her to move on. Follow this drove to New Orleans. Attend the auction; see men examined like horses; see the forms of women rudely and brutally exposed to the shocking gaze of American slave-buyers. See this drove sold and separated forever; and never forget the deep, sad sobs that arose from that scattered multitude. Tell me, citizens, where, under the sun, you can witness a spectacle more fiendish and shocking. Yet this is but a glance at the American slave-trade, as it exists, at this moment, in the ruling part of the United States.

I was born amid such sights and scenes. To me the American slave-trade is a terrible reality. When a child, my soul was often pierced with a sense of its horrors. I lived on Philpot Street, Fell's Point, Baltimore, and have watched from the wharves the slave ships in the Basin, anchored from the shore, with their cargoes of human flesh, waiting for favorable winds to waft them down the Chesapeake. There was, at that time, a grand slave mart kept at the head of Pratt Strteet, by Austin Woldfolk.[4] His agents were sent into every town and county in Maryland, announcing their arrival, through the papers, and on flaming "hand-bills," headed cash for Negroes. These men were generally well dressed men, and very captivating in their manners; ever ready to drink, to treat, and to gamble. The fate of many a slave has depended upon the turn of a single card; and many a child has been snatched from the arms of its mother by bargains arranged in a state of brutal drunkenness.

The flesh-mongers gather up their victims by dozens, and drive them chained, to the general depot at Baltimore. When a sufficient number has been collected here, a ship is chartered for the purpose of conveying the forlorn crew to Mobile, or to New Orleans. From the slave prison to the ship, they are usually driven in the darkness of night; for since the anti-slavery agitation, a certain caution is observed.

In the deep, still darkness of midnight, I have been often aroused by the dead, heavy footsteps, and the piteous cries of the chained gangs that passed our door. The anguish of my boyish heart was intense; and I was often consoled, when speaking to my mistress in the morning, to hear her say that the custom was very wicked; that she hated to hear the rattle of the chains and the heart-rending cries. I was glad to find one who sympathized with me in my horror.

Fellow-citizens, this murderous traffic is, to-day, in active operation in this boasted republic. In the solitude of my spirit I see clouds of dust raised on the highways of the South; I see the bleeding footsteps; I hear the doleful wail of fettered humanity on the way to the slave-markets, where the victims are to be sold like *horses, sheep,* and *swine,* knocked off to the highest bidder. There I see the tenderest ties ruthlessly broken, to gratify the lust, caprice and rapacity of the buyers and sellers of men. My soul sickens at the sight.

> Is this the land your Fathers loved,
>   The freedom which they toiled to win?
> Is this the earth whereon they moved?
>   Are these the graves they slumber in?[5]

---

4. Blassingame correctly identifies this well-known slave trader as Austin Woolfolk, whom Douglass refers to in his *Narrative* (1845).

5. Slightly altered opening lines from abolitionist and poet John Greenleaf Whittier's (1807–1892) *Stanzas for the Times.*

But a still more inhuman, disgraceful, and scandalous state of things remains to be presented. By an act of the American Congress, not yet two years old, slavery has been nationalized in its most horrible and revolting form. By that act, Mason and Dixon's line has been obliterated; New York has become as Virginia; and the power to hold, hunt, and sell men, women and children, as slaves, remains no longer a mere state institution, but is now an institution of the whole United States. The power is co-extensive with the star-spangled banner, and American Christianity. Where these go, may also go the merciless slave-hunter. Where these are, man is not sacred. He is a bird for the sportsman's gun. By the most foul and fiendish of all human decrees, the liberty and person of every man are put in peril. Your broad republican domain is hunting ground for *men*. Not for thieves and robbers, enemies of society, merely, but for men guilty of no crime. Your law-makers have commanded all good citizens to engage in this hellish sport. Your President, your Secretary of State, your *lords, nobles,* and ecclesiastics enforce, as a duty you owe to your free and glorious country, and to your God, that you do this accursed thing. Not fewer than forty Americans have, within the past two years, been hunted down and, without a moment's warning, hurried away in chains, and consigned to slavery and excruciating torture. Some of these have had wives and children, dependent on them for bread; but of this, no account was made. The right of the hunter to his prey stands superior to the right of marriage, and to *all* rights in this republic, the rights of God included! For black men there is neither law nor justice, humanity nor religion. The Fugitive Slave *Law* makes mercy to them a crime; and bribes the judge who tries them. An American judge gets ten dollars for every victim he consigns to slavery, and five, when he fails to do so. The oath of any two villains is sufficient, under this hell-black enactment, to send the most pious and exemplary black man into the remorseless jaws of slavery! His own testimony is nothing. He can bring no witnesses for himself. The minister of American justice is bound by the law to hear but *one* side; and *that* side is the side of the oppressor. Let this damning fact be perpetually told. Let it be thundered around the world that in tyrant-killing, king-hating, people-loving, democratic, Christian America the seats of justice are filled with judges who hold their offices under an open and palpable *bribe,* and are bound, in deciding the case of a man's liberty, *to hear only his accusers!*

In glaring violation of justice, in shameless disregard of the forms of administering law, in cunning arrangement to entrap the defenceless, and in diabolical intent this Fugitive Slave Law[6] stands alone in the annals of tyrannical legislation. I doubt if there be another nation on the globe having the brass and the baseness to put such a law on the statute-book. If any man in this assembly thinks differently from me in this matter, and feels able to disprove my statements, I will gladly confront him at any suitable time and place he may select.

I take this law to be one of the grossest infringements of Christian Liberty, and, if the churches and ministers of our country were not stupidly blind, or most wickedly indifferent, they, too, would so regard it.

At the very moment that they are thanking God for the enjoyment of civil and religious liberty, and for the right to worship God according to the dictates

---

6. The Fugitive Slave Law of 1850 allowed escaped slaves to be hunted down and returned to their owners. The law explicitly disallowed the testimony of the slave or other witnesses who disputed the alleged slave's identity.

of their own consciences, they are utterly silent in respect to a law which robs religion of its chief significance and makes it utterly worthless to a world lying in wickedness. Did this law concern the *"mint, anise, and cummin"*[7]—abridge the right to sing psalms, to partake of the sacrament, or to engage in any of the ceremonies of religion, it would be smitten by the thunder of a thousand pulpits. A general shout would go up from the church demanding *repeal, repeal, instant repeal!*—And it would go hard with that politician who presumed to solicit the votes of the people without inscribing this motto on his banner. Further, if this demand were not complied with, another Scotland would be added to the history of religious liberty, and the stern old covenamers would be thrown into the shade. A John Knox would be seen at every church door and heard from every pulpit, and Fillmore would have no more quarter than was shown by Knox to the beautiful, but treacherous, Queen Mary of Scotland.[8] The fact that the church of our country (with fractional exceptions) does not esteem "the Fugitive Slave Law" as a declaration of war against religious liberty, implies that that church regards religion simply as a form of worship, an empty ceremony, and *not* a vital principle, requiring active benevolence, justice, love, and good will towards man. It esteems sacrifice above mercy; psalm-singing above right doing; solemn meetings above practical righteousness. A worship that can be conducted by persons who refuse to give shelter to the houseless, to give bread to the hungry, clothing to the naked, and who enjoin obedience to a law forbidding these acts of mercy is a curse, not a blessing to mankind. The Bible addresses all such persons as "scribes, pharisees, hypocrites, who pay the tithe of *mint, anise,* and *cummin,* and have omitted the weightier matters of the law, judgment, mercy, and faith."

But the church of this country is not only indifferent to the wrongs of the slave, it actually takes sides with the oppressors. It has made itself the bulwark of American slavery, and the shield of American slave-hunters. Many of its most eloquent Divines, who stand as the very lights of the church, have shamelessly given the sanction of religion and the Bible to the whole slave system. They have taught that man may, properly, be a slave; that the relation of master and slave is ordained of God; that to send back an escaped bondman to his master is clearly the duty of all the followers of the Lord Jesus Christ; and this horrible blasphemy is palmed off upon the world for Christianity.

For my part, I would say, welcome infidelity! welcome atheism! welcome anything! in preference to the gospel, *as preached by those Divines!* They convert the very name of religion into an engine of tyranny and barbarous cruelty, and serve to confirm more infidels, in this age, than all the infidel writings of Thomas Paine, Voltaire, and Bolingbroke[9] put together have done! These ministers make religion a cold and flinty-hearted thing, having neither principles of right action nor bowels of compassion. They strip the love of God of its beauty and leave the throne of religion a huge, horrible, repulsive form. It is a religion for oppressors, tyrants, man-stealers, and *thugs.* It is not that *"pure and undefiled religion"*[1] which is from above, and which is *"first pure, then*

---

7. See Matthew 23.23.

8. Queen Mary Stuart (1542–1587), i.e., Mary, Queen of Scots, who tried to restore Catholicism to England. John Knox (1514–1572), an important Scottish Protestant leader who opposed Mary, Queen of Scots. Millard Fillmore (1800–1874), thirteenth president of the United States (1850–53).

9. Henry St. John, Viscount Bolingbroke (1678–1751), English statesman and author, was a

friend of Voltaire's and shared many of his views on religion and religious institutions. In his *Age of Reason* (1794–95) Paine argues for the existence of God but attacks the Bible and religious institutions. Françoise Marie Arouet de Voltaire (1694–1778) was a French philosopher, scientist, historian, and author of several pieces critical of religious institutions, though he also repudiated atheism.

1. See James 1.27.

peaceable, easy to be entreated, full of mercy and good fruits, *without partiality, and without hypocrisy.*"[2] But a religion which favors the rich against the poor; which exalts the proud above the humble; which divides mankind into two classes, tyrants and slaves; which says to the man in chains, *stay there;* and to the oppressor, *oppress on;* it is a religion which may be professed and enjoyed by all the robbers and enslavers of mankind; it makes God a respecter of persons, denies his fatherhood of the race, and tramples in the dust the great truth of the brotherhood of man. All this we affirm to be true of the popular church, and the popular worship of our land and nation—a religion, a church, and a worship which, on the authority of inspired wisdom, we pronounce to be an abomination in the sight of God. In the language of Isaiah, the American church might be well addressed, "Bring no more vain oblations; incense is an abomination unto me: the new moons and Sabbaths, the calling of assemblies, I cannot away with; it is iniquity, even the solemn meeting. Your new moons, and your appointed feasts my soul hateth. They are a trouble to me; I am weary to bear them; and when ye spread forth your hands I will hide mine eyes from you. Yea! when ye make many prayers, I will not hear. Your hands are full of blood; cease to do evil, learn to do well; seek judgment; relieve the oppressed; judge for the fatherless; plead for the widow."[3]

The American church is guilty, when viewed in connection with what it is doing to uphold slavery; but it is superlatively guilty when viewed in its connection with its ability to abolish slavery.

The sin of which it is guilty is one of omission as well as of commission. Albert Barnes[4] but uttered what the common sense of every man at all observant of the actual state of the case will receive as truth, when he declared that "There is no power out of the church that could sustain slavery an hour, if it were not sustained in it."

Let the religious press, the pulpit, the Sunday School, the conference meeting, the great ecclesiastical, missionary, Bible and tract associations of the land array their immense powers against slavery, and slave-holding; and the whole system of crime and blood would be scattered to the winds, and that they do not do this involves them in the most awful responsibility of which the mind can conceive.

In prosecuting the anti-slavery enterprise, we have been asked to spare the church, to spare the ministry; but *how,* we ask, could such a thing be done? We are met on the threshold of our efforts for the redemption of the slave, by the church and ministry of the country, in battle arrayed against us; and we are compelled to fight or flee. From *what* quarter, I beg to know, has proceeded a fire so deadly upon our ranks, during the last two years, as from the Northern pulpit? As the champions of oppressors, the chosen men of American theology have appeared—men honored for their so-called piety, and their real learning. The Lords of Buffalo, the Springs of New York, the Lathrops of Auburn, the Coxes and Spencers of Brooklyn, the Gannets and Sharps of Boston, the Deweys of Washington,[5] and other great religious lights of the land have, in utter denial of the authority of *Him* by whom they professed to be called to the

---

2. See James 3.17.
3. Isaiah 1.13–17.
4. A liberal Presbyterian minister who opposed slavery (1798–1870); the quotation is from Barnes's *An Inquiry into the Scriptural Views of Slavery* (1846).
5. John Chase Lord (1805–1877), Gardiner Spring

(1785–1873), Leonard Elijah Lathrop (1796–1857), Samuel Hanson Cox (1793–1880), Ichabod Smith Spencer (1798–1854), Ezra Stiles Gannett (1801–1871), Daniel Sharp (1783–1853), and Orville Dewey (1794–1882) were all clergyman who opposed abolition of slavery on various grounds.

ministry, deliberately taught us, against the example of the Hebrews, and against the remonstrance of the Apostles, *that we ought to obey man's law before the law of God.*

My spirit wearies of such blasphemy; and how such men can be supported, as the "standing types and representatives of Jesus Christ," is a mystery which I leave others to penetrate. In speaking of the American church, however, let it be distinctly understood that I mean the *great mass* of the religious organizations of our land. There are exceptions, and I thank God that there are. Noble men may be found, scattered all over these Northern States, of whom Henry Ward Beecher, of Brooklyn; Samuel J. May, of Syracuse; and my esteemed friend (Rev. R. R. Raymond)[6] on the platform, are shining examples; and let me say further, that, upon these men lies the duty to inspire our ranks with high religious faith and zeal, and to cheer us on in the great mission of the slave's redemption from his chains.

One is struck with the difference between the attitude of the American church towards the anti-slavery movement, and that occupied by the churches in England towards a similar movement in that country. There, the church, true to its mission of ameliorating, elevating and improving the condition of mankind, came forward promptly, bound up the wounds of the West Indian slave, and restored him to his liberty. There, the question of emancipation was a high religious question. It was demanded in the name of humanity, and according to the law of the living God. The Sharps, the Clarksons, the Wilberforces, the Buxtons, the Burchells, and the Knibbs[7] were alike famous for their piety and for their philanthropy. The anti-slavery movement *there* was not an anti-church movement, for the reason that the church took its full share in prosecuting that movement; and the anti-slavery movement in this country will cease to be an anti-church movement, when the church of this country shall assume a favorable instead of a hostile position towards that movement.

Americans! your republican politics, not less than your republican religion, are flagrantly inconsistent. You boast of your love of liberty, your superior civilization, and your pure Christianity, while the whole political power of the nation (as embodied in the two great political parties) is solemnly pledged to support and perpetuate the enslavement of three millions of your countrymen. You hurl your anathemas at the crowned headed tyrants of Russia and Austria and pride yourselves on your Democratic institutions, while you yourselves consent to be the mere *tools* and *body-guards* of the tyrants of Virginia and Carolina. You invite to your shores fugitives of oppression from abroad, honor them with banquets, greet them with ovations, cheer them, toast them, salute them, protect them, and pour out your money to them like water; but the fugitives from your own land you advertise, hunt, arrest, shoot, and kill. You glory in your refinement and your universal education; yet you maintain a system as barbarous and dreadful as ever stained the character of a nation—a system begun in avarice, supported in pride, and perpetuated in cruelty. You

6. The "esteemed friend" was Rev. R. R. Raymond (1819–1888). Henry Ward Beecher (1813–1887), brother of novelist Harriet Beecher Stowe, opposed the spread of slavery to new states. Samuel J. May (1797–1871) was a reformer active in the formation of the American Anti-Slavery Society (1833).
7. Thomas Burchell (1799–1846) and William Knibb (1803–1845) were British abolitionist missionaries.

Granville Sharp (1735–1813), Thomas Clarkson (1760–1846), and William Wilberforce (1759–1833) were British abolitionists. Thomas Fowell Buxton (1786–1845), English politician and philanthropist, led the British Parliamentary effort to end the slave trade and wrote *The African Slave Trade and Its Remedy* (1839).

shed tears over fallen Hungary, and make the sad story of her wrongs the theme of your poets, statesmen, and orators, till your gallant sons are ready to fly to arms to vindicate her cause against the oppressor;[8] but, in regard to the ten thousand wrongs of the American slave, you would enforce the strictest silence, and would hail him as an enemy of the nation who dares to make those wrongs the subject of public discourse! You are all on fire at the mention of liberty for France or for Ireland; but are as cold as an iceberg at the thought of liberty for the enslaved of America. You discourse eloquently on the dignity of labor; yet, you sustain a system which, in its very essence, casts a stigma upon labor. You can bare your bosom to the storm of British artillery to throw off a three-penny tax on tea; and yet wring the last hard earned farthing from the grasp of the black laborers of your country. You profess to believe "that, of one blood, God made all nations of men to dwell on the face of all the earth,"[9] and hath commanded all men, everywhere, to love one another; yet you notoriously hate (and glory in your hatred) all men whose skins are not colored like your own. You declare before the world, and are understood by the world to declare that you *"hold these truths to be self-evident, that all men are created equal; and are endowed by their Creator with certain inalienable rights; and that among these are, life, liberty, and the pursuit of happiness;*[1] and yet, you hold securely, in a bondage which, according to your own Thomas Jefferson, *"is worse than ages of that which your fathers rose in rebellion to opppose,"*[2] a *seventh part* of the inhabitants of your country.

Fellow-citizens, I will not enlarge further on your national inconsistencies. The existence of slavery in this country brands your republicanism as a sham, your humanity as a base pretense, and your Christianity as a lie. It destroys your moral power abroad; it corrupts your politicians at home. It saps the foundation of religion; it makes your name a hissing and a bye-word to a mocking earth. It is the antagonistic force in your government, the only thing that seriously disturbs and endangers your *Union*. It fetters your progress; it is the enemy of improvement; the deadly foe of education; it fosters pride; it breeds insolence; it promotes vice; it shelters crime; it is a curse to the earth that supports it; and yet you cling to it as if it were the sheet anchor of all your hopes. Oh! be warned! be warned! a horrible reptile is coiled up in your nation's bosom; the venomous creature is nursing at the tender breast of your youthful republic; *for the love of God, tear away*, and fling from you the hideous monster, and *let the weight of twenty millions crush and destroy it forever!*

But it is answered in reply to all this, that precisely what I have now denounced is, in fact, guaranteed and sanctioned by the Constitution of the United States; that, the right to hold, and to hunt slaves is a part of that Constitution framed by the illustrious Fathers of this Republic.

Then, I dare to affirm, notwithstanding all I have said before, your fathers stooped, basely stooped

> To palter with us in a double sense:
> And keep the word of promise to the ear,
> But break it to the heart.[3]

---

8. Douglass refers to the unsuccessful attempt of Hungary to achieve independence from Austria, whose Russian-supported forces had occupied its territory in 1848 and 1849.
9. A close paraphrase of Acts 17.26.

1. From the American Declaration of Independence.
2. From a letter by Jefferson to Jean Nicholas Démenier on June 26, 1786.
3. Paraphrase of Shakespeare's *Macbeth* 5.8.20–22.

And instead of being the honest men I have before declared them to be, they were the veriest imposters that ever practised on mankind. This is the inevitable conclusion, and from it there is no escape; but I differ from those who charge this baseness on the framers of the Constitution of the United States. It is a slander upon their memory, at least, so I believe. There is not time now to argue the constitutional question at length; nor have I the ability to discuss it as it ought to be discussed. The subject has been handled with masterly power by Lysander Spooner, Esq., by William Goodell, by Samuel E. Sewall, Esq., and last, though not least, by Gerrit Smith, Esq.[4] These gentlemen have, as I think, fully and clearly vindicated the Constitution from any design to support slavery for an hour.

Fellow-citizens! there is no matter in respect to which the people of the North have allowed themselves to be so ruinously imposed upon as that of the pro-slavery character of the Constitution. In that instrument I hold there is neither warrant, license, nor sanction of the hateful thing; but interpreted, as it ought to be interpreted, the Constitution is a glorious liberty document. Read its preamble, consider its purposes. Is slavery among them? Is it at the gateway? or is it in the temple? it is neither. While I do not intend to argue this question on the present occasion, let me ask, if it be not somewhat singular that, if the Constitution were intended to be, by its framers and adopters, a slaveholding instrument, why neither slavery, slaveholding, nor slave can anywhere be found in it. What would be thought of an instrument, drawn up, legally drawn up, for the purpose of entitling the city of Rochester to a tract of land, in which no mention of land was made? Now, there are certain rules of interpretation for the proper understanding of all legal instruments. These rules are well established. They are plain, commonsense rules, such as you and I, and all of us, can understand and apply, without having passed years in the study of law. I scout[5] the idea that the question of the constitutionality, or unconstitutionality of slavery, is not a question for the people. I hold that every American citizen has a right to form an opinion of the constitution, and to propagate that opinion, and to use all honorable means to make his opinion the prevailing one. Without this right, the liberty of an American citizen would be as insecure as that of a Frenchman. Ex-Vice-President Dallas tells us that the constitution is an object to which no American mind can be too attentive, and no American heart too devoted. He further says, the Constitution, in its words, is plain and intelligible, and is meant for the home-bred, unsophisticated understandings of our fellow-citizens. Senator Berrien tells us that the Constitution is the fundamental law, that which controls all others. The charter of our liberties, which every citizen has a personal interest in understanding thoroughly. The testimony of Senator Breese, Lewis Cass,[6] and many others that might be named, who are everywhere esteemed as sound

---

4. Gerrit Smith (1797–1874) was a reformer and philanthropist, an active abolitionist, and author of *Letter of Gerrit Smith to S. P. Chase on the Unconstitutionality of Every Part of American Slavery* (1847) among many other antislavery works. Lysander Spooner (1808–1887), lawyer and author of *The Unconstitutionality of Slavery* (1845). William Goodell (1792–1878) wrote antislavery books, denying any constitutional basis for slavery. Samuel E. Sewall (1799–1888) wrote *Remarks on Slavery in the United States* (1827).
5. In the sense of "reject with scorn."
6. Lewis Cass (1782–1866) served in various political

positions: secretary of war (1831–36) under President Andrew Jackson, senator from Michigan (1845–48 and 1849–57), and secretary of state (1857–60) in the administration of President James Buchanan. George Mifflin Dallas (1792–1864) served as vice president of the United States under President James K. Polk (1845–49). John MacPherson Berrien (1781–1856) served as senator from Georgia and as attorney general in President Andrew Jackson's administration. Sidney Breese (1800–1878) served as senator from Illinois (1843–49). All of these men were noted as authorities on the Constitution, but none of them shared Douglass's view of it with respect to its application to slavery.

lawyers, so regard the constitution. I take it, therefore, that it is not presumption in a private citizen to form an opinion of that instrument.

Now, take the Constitution according to its plain reading, and I defy the presentation of a single pro-slavery clause in it. On the other hand, it will be found to contain principles and purposes, entirely hostile to the existence of slavery.

I have detained my audience entirely too long already. At some future period I will gladly avail myself of an opportunity to give this subject a full and fair discussion.

Allow me to say, in conclusion, notwithstanding the dark picture I have this day presented, of the state of the nation, I do not despair of this country. There are forces in operation which must inevitably work the downfall of slavery. "The arm of the Lord is not shortened,"[7] and the doom of slavery is certain. I, therefore, leave off where I began, with hope. While drawing encouragement from "the Declaration of Independence," the great principles it contains, and the genius of American Institutions, my spirit is also cheered by the obvious tendencies of the age. Nations do not now stand in the same relation to each other that they did ages ago. No nation can now shut itself up from the surrounding world and trot round in the same old path of its fathers without interference. The time was when such could be done. Long established customs of hurtful character could formerly fence themselves in, and do their evil work with social impunity. Knowledge was then confined and enjoyed by the privileged few, and the multitude walked on in mental darkness. But a change has now come over the affairs of mankind. Walled cities and empires have become unfashionable. The arm of commerce has borne away the gates of the strong city. Intelligence is penetrating the darkest corners of the globe. It makes its pathway over and under the sea, as well as on the earth. Wind, steam, and lightning are its chartered agents. Oceans no longer divide, but link nations together. From Boston to London is now a holiday excursion. Space is comparatively annihilated.—Thoughts expressed on one side of the Atlantic are distinctly heard on the other.

The far off and almost fabulous Pacific rolls in grandeur at our feet. The Celestial Empire, the mystery of ages, is being solved. The fiat of the Almighty, "Let there be Light,"[8] has not yet spent its force. No abuse, no outrage whether in taste, sport or avarice, can now hide itself from the all-pervading light. The iron shoe, and crippled foot of China must be seen in contrast with nature. Africa must rise and put on her yet unwoven garment. "Ethiopia shall stretch out her hand unto God."[9] In the fervent aspirations of William Lloyd Garrison, I say, and let every heart join in saying it:

> God speed the year of jubilee
>   The wide world o'er!
> When from their galling chains set free,
> Th' oppress'd shall vilely bend the knee,
> And wear the yoke of tyranny
>   Like brutes no more.
> That year will come, and freedom's reign,
> To man his plundered rights again
>   Restore.

7. Paraphrase of Isaiah 59.1.   9. Paraphrase of Psalms 68.31.
8. Genesis 1.3

God speed the day when human blood
　　Shall cease to flow!
In every clime be understood,
The claims of human brotherhood,
And each return for evil, good,
　　Not blow for blow;
That day will come all feuds to end,
And change into a faithful friend
　　Each foe.

God speed the hour, the glorious hour,
　　When none on earth
Shall exercise a lordly power,
Nor in a tyrant's presence cower;
But to all manhood's stature tower,
　　By equal birth!
That hour will come, to each, to all,
And from his prison-house, to thrall
　　Go forth.

Until that year, day, hour, arrive,
With head, and heart, and hand I'll strive,
To break the rod, and rend the gyve,
The spoiler of his prey deprive—
　　So witness Heaven!
And never from my chosen post,
Whate'er the peril or the cost,
　　Be driven.[1]

1852

1. William Lloyd Garrison (1805–1879), was the radical abolitionist who wrote the preface to Douglass's
Narrative. Garrison's poem The Triumph of Freedom
was first published in his Liberator (January 10, 1845).

JAMES RUSSELL LOWELL
1819–1891

James Russell Lowell was born on February 22, 1819, at Elmwood, the family estate in Cambridge, Massachusetts, then hardly more than a village. After an indulgent childhood he attended Harvard, where he drew reprimands for skipping classes and other minor infractions of the rules. He studied law but never made a living from his practice. Instead, he published ardent, derivative verse (Wordsworth and Tennyson were prime influences) in newspapers and magazines, collecting some of them in A Year's Life (1841). Exuberant and idealistic, he founded a short-lived Boston literary magazine, The Pioneer, in 1843, then briefly worked his way into the New York City literary scene and abolitionist journalism, winning friends and often alienating some of those friends by his inability to blunt a cruel satiric barb and by his impatience with anyone not devoted to his current cause. At the end of 1844 he married Maria White, herself deeply interested in abolitionism and other reform movements. Lowell's breakthrough to national reputation came in 1848 with the publication of A Fable for Critics, the book form of The Biglow Papers, and a Christmas-market edition of The Vision of Sir Launfal. The first is a verse satire on contemporary American writers. The Biglow Papers, a part-prose, part-verse satire on American imperialism against Mexico and Southern lust for new slave territory, was a major contribution to altering Northern consciousness about slavery, but the topical nature of Lowell's humor and the painstaking representation of New England dialect pronunciation have rendered it nearly inaccessible to all but specialists. The Vision, a didactic narrative of a dream vision experienced by one of King Arthur's knights, was for generations a classroom staple.

Unable to make a living from his poetry and saddened by the successive deaths of two young daughters, Lowell took his family abroad, where a baby son died, leaving only one daughter to outlive Lowell. Maria Lowell died in 1853, after their return to Cambridge. Lowell wrote desultorily for the magazines until 1855, when Harvard offered him Longfellow's professorship. Hoping to perfect his German before assuming the post, Lowell passed several lonely months in Dresden, then joined family and friends in Italy. Leon Howard has summed up Lowell's situation in the mid-1850s: "Of his poetic career, little remained except for a few periods of occasional inspiration, a certain amount of philosophy, and an accomplished craftsmanship which enabled him to exploit fully those relics of youthful enthusiasm still left in his notebooks. Instead of writing strong poems in his maturity that could carry his early writings down to posterity on their shoulders, as he had promised, he found that his early verses often had to be used to sustain his later productivity and reputation."

In 1857 Lowell married Frances Dunlap, his daughter's governess, to general amazement, and took up teaching and the editorship of the new Atlantic Monthly. Editing proved a good excuse for writing only at intervals and not finishing more ambitious projects such as The Nooning, conceived in 1849 as a sort of local Canterbury Tales. The Atlantic drew him once again into politics, and after the change of ownership removed him as editor, he became coeditor of the North American Review, which he made into a weapon for political commentary. The Civil War brought him personal tragedy in the loss of nephews and other young friends, and after it ended he remained engaged with issues of Reconstruction, dreading that the new rights of the blacks would be ignored by the South. But for all his national exposure in the 1850s and 1860s he was aware that his life had not fulfilled its promise.

Always a sociable man, Lowell was one of the founders of the Saturday Club, which also counted as members Emerson, Longfellow, Hawthorne, Holmes, Dana, Agassiz, and other literary men and historians. In the 1860s there were supplemental pleasures in the Dante Club, of which the nucleus was Longfellow, Lowell, and his younger friend Charles Eliot Norton. Lowell led the life of a literary man and professor, his chief new publication being The Cathedral. Hard pressed to live on his income, in 1871 Lowell sold almost twenty acres from around his house in Cambridge and left the next year for Europe, returning in 1874. He became briefly absorbed in American politics, and attacked corruption in stinging poems. President Hayes appointed him minister to Spain in 1877. Frances Lowell nearly died in Madrid and was intermittently insane thereafter. Lowell became minister to England in 1880 and was soon notorious for the frequency of his dining out and for mishandling matters of state. Just after Lowell's wife died in early 1885, President Cleveland removed him from his post, and thereafter for several years he alternated between quiet winters at his daughter's house in Southborough, Massachusetts, and summers in London, where he reveled in invitations to dine out every day. He died at Elmwood of cancer on August 12, 1891.

To the Dandelion[1]

Dear common flower, that grow'st beside the way,
Fringing the dusty road with harmless gold,
    First pledge of blithesome May,
Which children pluck, and, full of pride, uphold,
High-hearted buccaneers, o'erjoyed that they   5
An Eldorado[2] in the grass have found,
    Which not the rich earth's ample round
May match in wealth—thou art more dear to me
Than all the prouder summer-blooms may be.

Gold such as thine ne'er drew the Spanish prow   10
Through the primeval hush of Indian seas,
    Nor wrinkled the lean brow
Of age, to rob the lover's heart of ease;
'Tis the spring's largess, which she scatters now
To rich and poor alike, with lavish hand,   15
    Though most hearts never understand
To take it at God's value, but pass by
The offered wealth with unrewarded eye.

Thou art my tropics and mine Italy;
To look at thee unlocks a warmer clime;   20
    The eyes thou givest me
Are in the heart, and heed not space or time:
Not in mid June the golden-cuirassed bee
Feels a more summer-like, warm ravishment
    In the white lily's breezy tent,   25
His fragrant Sybaris,[3] than I, when first
From the dark-green thy yellow circles burst.

Then think I of deep shadows on the grass,
Of meadows where in sun the cattle graze,
    Where, as the breezes pass,   30
The gleaming rushes lean a thousand ways,
Of leaves that slumber in a cloudy mass,
Or whiten in the wind, of waters blue
    That from the distance sparkle through
Some woodland gap, and of a sky above   35
Where one white cloud like a stray lamb doth move.

My childhood's earliest thoughts are linked with thee;
The sight of thee calls back the robin's song,
    Who, from the dark old tree
Beside the door, sang clearly all day long,   40
And I, secure in childish piety,
Listened as if I heard an angel sing
    With news from Heaven, which he did bring
Fresh every day to my untainted ears,
When birds and flowers and I were happy peers.   45

---

1. The text is that of the first printing in *Graham's Magazine* (January 1845).
2. Fabled city of gold.
3. Greek city in southern Italy noted for luxury and pleasure.

Thou art the type of those meek charities
Which make up half the nobleness of life,
    Those cheap delights the wise
Pluck from the dusty wayside of earth's strife;
Words of frank cheer, glances of friendly eyes, 50
Love's smallest coin, which yet to some may give
    The morsel that shall keep alive
A starving heart, and teach it to behold
Some glimpse of God where all before was cold.

Thy winged seeds, whereof the winds take care, 55
Are like the words of poet and of sage
    Which through the free heaven fare,
And, now unheeded, in another age
Take root, and to the gladdened future bear
That witness which the present would not heed, 60
    Bringing forth many a thought and deed,
And, planted safely in the eternal sky,
Bloom into stars which earth is guided by.

Full of deep love thou art, yet not more full
Than all thy common brethren of the ground, 65
    Wherein, were we not dull,
Some words of highest wisdom might be found;
Yet earnest faith from day to day may cull
Some syllables, which, rightly joined, can make
    A spell to soothe life's bitterest ache, 70
And ope Heaven's portals, which are near us still,
Yea, nearer ever than the gates of Ill.

How like a prodigal doth nature seem,
When thou, for all thy gold, so common art!
    Thou teachest me to deem 75
More sacredly of every human heart,
Since each reflects in joy its scanty gleam
Of Heaven, and could some wondrous secret show,
    Did we but pay the love we owe,
And with a child's undoubting wisdom look 80
On all these living pages of God's book.

But, let me read thy lesson right or no,
Of one good gift from thee my heart is sure;
    Old I shall never grow
While thou each year dost come to keep me pure 85
With legends of my childhood; ah, we owe
Well more than half life's holiness to these
    Nature's first lowly influences,
At thought of which the heart's glad doors burst ope,
In dreariest days, to welcome peace and hope. 90

1845

From A Fable for Critics[1]

* * *

"There comes Emerson first, whose rich words, every one,
Are like gold nails in temples to hang trophies on,[2]
Whose prose is grand verse, while his verse, the Lord knows,   525
Is some of it pr——No, 'tis not even prose;
I'm speaking of metres; some poems have welled
From those rare depths of soul that have ne'er been excelled;
They're not epics, but that doesn't matter a pin,
In creating, the only hard thing's to begin;   530
A grass-blade's no easier to make than an oak,
If you've once found the way, you've achieved the grand stroke;
In the worst of his poems are mines of rich matter,
But thrown in a heap with a crush and a clatter;
Now it is not one thing nor another alone   535
Makes a poem, but rather the general tone,
The something pervading, uniting the whole,
The before unconceived, unconceivable soul,
So that just in removing this trifle or that, you
Take away, as it were, a chief limb of the statue;   540
Roots, wood, bark, and leaves, singly perfect may be,
But, clapt hodge-podge together, they don't make a tree.

"But, to come back to Emerson, (whom, by the way,
I believe we left waiting,)—his is, we may say,
A Greek head on right Yankee shoulders, whose range   545
Has Olympus for one pole, for t'other the Exchange;[3]
He seems, to my thinking, (although I'm afraid
The comparison must, long ere this, have been made,)
A Plotinus-Montaigne, where the Egyptian's gold mist
And the Gascon's shrewd wit cheek-by-jowl co-exist;[4]   550
All admire, and yet scarcely six converts he's got
To I don't (nor they either) exactly know what;
For though he builds glorious temples, 'tis odd

1. The text is that of the 1st edition (1848). As Lowell's page-long rhyming subtitles said, this work is "A GLANCE / AT A FEW OF OUR LITERARY PROGENIES / (Mrs. Malaprop's word) / FROM / THE TUB OF DIOGENES." Mrs. Malaprop is the character in Sheridan's *The Rivals* (1775) who gets her words wrong. The skepticism of the Greek philosopher Diogenes (412?–323 B.C.) toward his contemporaries defines Lowell's stance in the poem toward his own contemporaries.

The following selections are in quotation marks because they are spoken by Phoebus (or Apollo), Greek god of poetry, whose occasional irritation springs partly from the fact that the magazine editors Evert A. Duyckinck and Cornelius Mathews have been pestering him with autographed copies of books by American writers. Lowell's joke is that Duyckinck, Mathews, and other people working for the establishment of an international copyright law and recognition of American authors often claimed greatness for nonentities. The ultimate joke, which Duyckinck probably never ap-

preciated any more than Lowell did, is that in fact, even in 1848, Duyckinck had at least one authentic literary genius among the American writers he was promoting—Herman Melville, whom Lowell does not mention in *A Fable for Critics*.

The line numbers given here begin with the first lines of the *Fable* to be set off as verse and do not count the rhymed title page and other prefatory matter (rhymed footnotes are not counted either).

2. Ecclesiastes 12.11: "The words of the wise are as goads, and as nails fastened by the masters of assemblies, which are given from one shepherd." Many of Lowell's readers would have known that the next verse admonishes that "of making many books there is no end"—a deft undercutting of the compliment.

3. Stock market.

4. This is an early noticing of the union of opposites in Emerson—the idealist like the Greek philosopher Plotinus (c. 205–270) and the shrewd realist like Michel de Montaigne (1533–1592), French ("Gascon") essayist.

He leaves never a doorway to get in a god.
'Tis refreshing to old-fashioned people like me,   555
To meet such a primitive Pagan as he,
In whose mind all creation is duly respected
As parts of himself—just a little projected;
And who's willing to worship the stars and the sun,
A convert to—nothing but Emerson.   560
So perfect a balance there is in his head,
That he talks of things sometimes as if they were dead;
Life, nature, love, God, and affairs of that sort,
He looks at as merely ideas; in short,
As if they were fossils stuck round in a cabinet,[5]   565
Of such vast extent that our Earth's a mere dab in it;
Composed just as he is inclined to conjecture her,
Namely, one part pure earth, ninety-nine parts pure lecturer;
You are filled with delight at his clear demonstration,
Each figure, word, gesture, just fits the occasion,   570
With the quiet precision of science he'll sort 'em,
But you can't help suspecting the whole a *post mortem*.

"There are persons, mole-blind to the soul's make and style,
Who insist on a likeness 'twixt him and Carlyle;
To compare him with Plato[6] would be vastly fairer,   575
Carlyle's the more burly, but E. is the rarer;
He sees fewer objects, but clearlier, trulier,
If C.'s as original, E.'s more peculiar;
That he's more of a man you might say of the one,
Of the other he's more of an Emerson;   580
C.'s the Titan, as shaggy of mind as of limb,—
E. the clear-eyed Olympian, rapid and slim;
The one's two-thirds Norseman, the other half Greek,[7]
Where the one's most abounding, the other's to seek;
C.'s generals require to be seen in the mass,—   585
E.'s specialties gain if enlarged by the glass;
C. gives Nature and God his own fits of the blues,
And rims common-sense things with mystical hues,—
E. sits in the mystery calm and intense,
And looks coolly around him with sharp common-sense;   490
C. shows you how every-day matters unite
With the dim transdiurnal recesses of night,—
While E., in a plain, preternatural way,
Makes mysteries matters of mere every day;
C. draws all his characters quite *à la* Fuseli,[8]—   595
He don't sketch their bundles of muscles and thews illy,
But he paints with a brush so untamed and profuse,
They seem nothing but bundles of muscles and thews;

5. Exhibition case.
6. Plato (427–347 B.C.), the Greek philosopher. Thomas Carlyle (1795–1881), Scottish philosophical writer and a friend of Emerson.
7. I.e., Carlyle is the primitive, like the Titans (children of heaven and earth in Greek mythology) who were overthrown by their own children, the more sophisticated and more humanlike Olympian gods, led by Zeus. Carlyle is also two-thirds Norseman, marauding Viking, as in his plundering of Germanic philosophical writers, while Emerson is half an inhabitant of the real world, half in an idealistic, Platonic realm.
8. J. H. Fuseli (1741–1825), Swiss-born painter who worked much of his life in London, often painting forceful, distorted figures like those of William Blake.

E. is rather like Flaxman,[9] lines strait and severe,
And a colorless outline, but full, round, and clear;—   600
To the men he thinks worthy he frankly accords
The design of a white marble statue in words.
C. labors to get at the centre, and then
Take a reckoning from there of his actions and men;
E. calmly assumes the said centre as granted,   605
And, given himself, has whatever is wanted.

    "He has imitations in scores, who omit
No part of the man but his wisdom and wit,—
Who go carefully o'er the sky-blue of his brain,
And when he has skimmed it once, skim it again;   610
If at all they resemble him, you may be sure it is
Because their shoals mirror his mists and obscurities,
As a mud-puddle seems deep as heaven for a minute,
While a cloud that floats o'er is reflected within it.

    "There comes——,[1] for instance; to see him's rare sport,   615
Tread in Emerson's tracks with legs painfully short;
How he jumps, how he strains, and gets red in the face,
To keep step with the mystagogue's natural pace!
He follows as close as a stick to a rocket,[2]
His fingers exploring the prophet's each pocket.   620
Fie, for shame, brother bard; with good fruit of your own,
Can't you let neighbor Emerson's orchards alone?
Besides, 'tis no use, you'll not find e'en a core,—
—— has picked up all the windfalls[3] before.
They might strip every tree, and E. never would catch 'em,   625
His Hesperides[4] have no rude dragon to watch 'em;
When they send him a dish-full, and ask him to try 'em,
He never suspects how the sly rogues came by 'em;
He wonders why 'tis there are none such his trees on,
And thinks 'em the best he has tasted this season.   630

    "Yonder, calm as a cloud, Alcott stalks in a dream,
And fancies himself in thy groves, Academe,[5]
With the Parthenon nigh, and the olive-trees o'er him,
And never a fact to perplex him or bore him,
With a snug room at Plato's, when night comes, to walk to,   635
And people from morning till midnight to talk to,
And from midnight till morning, nor snore in their listening;—
So he muses, his face with the joy of it glistening,
For his highest conceit of a happiest state is

9. John Flaxman (1755–1826), English neoclassical sculptor, best known in the United States as an illustrator of the classic epics and Dante's *Divine Comedy.*
1. I.e., Channing, according to Leon Howard's book on Lowell, *Victorian Knight-Errant:* William Ellery Channing (1818–1901), Thoreau's ne'er-do-well poetaster friend.
2. A fireworks device.
3. Casual, unexpected legacies. This line is about Thoreau (according to Howard), who was then not as well known as Channing, but he was more often on the spot at Concord.
4. The garden or the golden apples in the Hesperides, the Isles of the Blest.
5. Olive grove in Athens where Plato and his followers held philosophical discussions; it was near the Parthenon, great temple of Athena. Bronson Alcott (1799–1888) was an innovative educator and much-ridiculed Transcendentalist.

Where they'd live upon acorns, and hear him talk gratis;   640
And indeed, I believe, no man ever talked better—
Each sentence hangs perfectly poised to a letter;
He seems piling words, but there's royal dust hid
In the heart of each sky-piercing pyramid.
While he talks he is great, but goes out like a taper.   645
If you shut him up closely with pen, ink, and paper;
Yet his fingers itch for 'em from morning till night,
And he thinks he does wrong if he don't always write;
In this, as in all things, a lamb among men,
He goes to sure death when he goes to his pen.   650

                              *   *   *

"There is Bryant, as quiet, as cool, and as dignified,   810
As a smooth, silent iceberg, that never is ignified,
Save when by reflection 'tis kindled o' nights
With a semblance of flame by the chill Northern Lights.
He may rank (Griswold[6] says so) first bard of your nation,
(There's no doubt that he stands in supreme ice-olation,)   815
Your topmost Parnassus[7] he may set his heel on,
But no warm applauses come, peal following peal on,—
He's too smooth and too polished to hang any zeal on:
Unqualified merits, I'll grant, if you choose, he has 'em,
But he lacks the one merit of kindling enthusiasm;   820
If he stir you at all, it is just, on my soul,
Like being stirred up with the very North Pole.

     "He is very nice reading in summer, but *inter
Nos*, we don't want *extra*[8] freezing in winter;
Take him up in the depth of July, my advice is,   825
When you feel an Egyptian devotion to ices.[9]
But, deduct all you can, there's enough that's right good in him,
He has a true soul for field, river, and wood in him;
And his heart, in the midst of brick walls, or wher'er it is,
Glows, softens, and thrills with the tenderest charities,—   830
To you mortals that delve in this trade-ridden planet?
No, to old Berkshire's hills, with their limestone and granite.
If you're one who in *loco* (add *foco* here) *desipis*,[1]
You will get of his outermost heart (as I guess) a piece;
But you'd get deeper down if you came as a precipice,   835
And would break the last seal of its inwardest fountain,
If you only could palm yourself off for a mountain.
Mr. Quivis,[2] or somebody quite as discerning,

6. Rufus Griswold (1815–1857), editor of *The Poet and Poetry of America* (1842) and other anthologies, remembered now for his malicious defamation of Poe's memory. Lowell had printed in *The Pioneer* Nathaniel Hawthorne's *Hall of Fantasy*, which in that version contained a satirical portrait of the industrious anthologizer.
7. Mountain in Greece sacred to Apollo, the god of poetry.
8. Lowell puns on our meaning of *extra* (additional) and the Latin meaning (outer). "*Inter Nos*": between us (Latin).

9. Pun on Isis, Egyptian goddess.
1. I.e., can let yourself be silly at times. In his *Odes* 4.12.28, the Roman poet Horace suggests that Virgil should mix a little silliness with his wisdom; here Lowell puns on Horace's words and the political term *Loco-foco*, meaning a more radical wing of the Democratic party (from the fact that at a New York meeting in the 1830s their conservative opponents doused the lights only to have the radicals carry on by the light of loco-focos, the new lucifer matches).
2. Mr. Whoever.

Some scholar who's hourly expecting his learning,
Calls B. the American Wordsworth; but Wordsworth   840
Is worth near as much as your whole tuneful herd's worth.
No, don't be absurd, he's an excellent Bryant;
But, my friends, you'll endanger the life of your client,
By attempting to stretch him up into a giant:
If you choose to compare him, I think there are two per-   845
-sons fit for a parallel—Thomson and Cowper;[3]
I don't mean exactly,—there's something of each,
There's T.'s love of nature, C.'s penchant to preach;
Just mix up their minds so that C.'s spice of craziness
Shall balance and neutralize T.'s turn for laziness,   850
And it gives you a brain cool, quite frictionless, quiet,
Whose internal police nips the buds of all riot,—
A brain like a permanent strait-jacket put on
The heart which strives vainly to burst off a button,—
A brain which, without being slow or mechanic,   855
Does more than a larger less drilled, more volcanic;
He's a Cowper condensed, with no craziness bitten,
And the advantage that Wordsworth before him has written.
    "But, my dear little bardlings, don't prick up your ears,
Nor suppose I would rank you and Bryant as peers;   860
If I call him an iceberg, I don't mean to say
There is nothing in that which is grand, in its way;
He is almost the one of your poets that knows
How much grace, strength, and dignity lie in Repose;
If he sometimes fall short, he is too wise to mar   865
His thought's modest fulness by going too far;
'Twould be well if your authors should all make a trial
Of what virtue there is in severe self-denial,
And measure their writings by Hesiod's[4] staff,
Which teaches that all has less value than half.   870

    "There is Whittier, whose swelling and vehement heart
Strains the strait-breasted drab[5] of the Quaker apart,
And reveals the live Man, still supreme and erect
Underneath the bemummying wrappers of sect;
There was ne'er a man born who had more of the swing   875
Of the true lyric bard and all that kind of thing;
And his failures arise, (though perhaps he don't know it,)
From the very same cause that has made him a poet,—
A fervor of mind, which knows no separation
'Twixt simple excitement and pure inspiration,   880
As my Pythoness[6] erst sometimes erred from not knowing
If 'twere I or mere wind through her tripod was blowing;
Let his mind once get head in its favorite direction

---

3. "To demonstrate quickly and easily how per- /
versely absurd 'tis to sound this name Cowper, / As
people in general call him named super, / I just add
that he rhymes it himself with horse-trooper" [Lowell's
note]. James Thomson (1700–1748), Scottish poet, author of The Seasons (1730). William Cowper
(1731–1800), English poet, author of The Task (1784).

4. By the standards of Hesiod (8th century B.C.), didactic Greek poet.
5. Whittier wore traditional Quaker garb.
6. Priestess of Apollo, endowed with prophetic powers, who sat on a tripod when she delivered messages
from the god.

And the torrent of verse bursts the dams of reflection,
While, borne with the rush of the metre along,   885
The poet may chance to go right or go wrong,
Content with the whirl and delirium of song;
Then his grammar's not always correct, nor his rhymes,
And he's prone to repeat his own lyrics sometimes,
Not his best, though, for those are struck off at white-heats   890
When the heart in his breast like a trip-hammer beats,
And can ne'er be repeated again any more
Than they could have been carefully plotted before:
Like old what's-his-name there at the battle of Hastings,[7]
(Who, however, gave more than mere rhythmical bastings,)   895
Our Quaker leads off metaphorical fights
For reform and whatever they call human rights,
Both singing and striking in front of the war
And hitting his foes with the mallet of Thor;[8]
Anne haec, one exclaims, on beholding his knocks   900
Vestis filii tui, O, leather-clad Fox?[9]
Can that be thy son, in the battle's mid din,
Preaching brotherly love and then driving it in
To the brain of the tough old Goliath[1] of sin,
With the smoothest of pebbles from Castaly's spring[2]   905
Impressed on his hard moral sense with a sling?[3]

        "All honor and praise to the right-hearted bard
Who was true to The Voice when such service was hard,
Who himself was so free he dared sing for the slave
When to look but a protest in silence was brave;   910
All honor and praise to the women and men
Who spoke out for the dumb and the down-trodden then!
I need not to name them, already for each
I see History preparing the statue and niche;
They were harsh, but shall *you*[4] be so shocked at hard words   915
Who have beaten your pruning-hooks up into swords,[5]
Whose rewards and hurrahs men are surer to gain
By the reaping of men and of women than grain?
Why should *you* stand aghast at their fierce wordy war, if

---

7. The minstrel Taillefer led a charge of William the Conquerer's cavalry at the Battle of Hastings (1066), on the coast of Sussex, in southwest England.
8. Norse god of thunder and war.
9. George Fox (1624–1691), founder of the Quakers, made a habit of wearing leather breeches. "*Anne haec . . . vestis fillii tui*": Latin translation of Genesis 37.32: "This have we found: know now whether it be thy son's coat or no" (what Jacob's deceitful sons say to him when they show him Joseph's bloodied coat of many colors to persuade him that his favorite son is dead).
1. The giant Goliath is in 1 Samuel 17.
2. The Castaly spring, from which poets drink to become inspired, is at the base of Mount Parnassus and is sacred to Apollo.
3. Here Whittier is compared with David, who slew Goliath with a rock hurled from his sling.
4. It takes a great imaginative leap to comprehend just how contemptuously the early abolitionists such as Whittier and William Lloyd Garrison were regarded by most Northerners even into the 1850s. The "you" whom Lowell scolds is the delicate Northerner who professes to be shocked at the crudeness of what Whittier said about slavery.
5. I.e., they have obeyed the biblical injunction in Joel 3.10—"Beat your plowshares into swords, and your pruninghooks into spears: let the weak say, I am strong"—rather than helping to fulfill the prophecy in Isaiah 2.4—"And they shall beat their swords into plowshares, and their spears into pruninghooks: nation shall not lift up sword against nation, neither shall they learn war any more." Lowell is charging the accusers of Whittier with converting instruments of peace into instruments of war, as in the mobilization of industries for the Mexican War.

You scalp one another for Bank or for Tariff?[6]   920
Your calling them cut-throats and knaves all day long
Don't prove that the use of hard language is wrong;
While the World's heart beats quicker to think of such men
As signed Tyranny's doom with a bloody steel-pen,
While on Fourth-of-Julys beardless orators fright one   925
With hints at Harmodius and Aristogeiton,[7]
You need not look shy at your sisters and brothers
Who stab with sharp words for the freedom of others;—
No, a wreath, twine a wreath for the loyal and true
Who, for sake of the many, dared stand with the few,   930
Not of blood-spattered laurel for enemies braved,
But of broad, peaceful oak-leaves for citizens saved!

                    *   *   *

    "There is Hawthorne, with genius so shrinking and rare
That you hardly at first see the strength that is there;
A frame so robust, with a nature so sweet,   995
So earnest, so graceful, so solid, so fleet,
Is worth a descent from Olympus to meet;
'Tis as if a rough oak that for ages had stood,
With his gnarled bony branches like ribs of the wood,
Should bloom, after cycles of struggle and scathe,   1000
With a single anemone trembly and rathe;
His strength is so tender, his wildness so meek,
That a suitable parallel sets one to seek,—
He's a John Bunyan Fouqué, a Puritan Tieck;[8]
When Nature was shaping him, clay was not granted   1005
For making so full-sized a man as she wanted,
So, to fill out her model, a little she spared
From some finer-grained stuff for a woman prepared,
And she could not have hit a more excellent plan
For making him fully and perfectly man.   1010
The success of her scheme gave her so much delight,
That she tried it again, shortly after, in Dwight;[9]
Only, while she was kneading and shaping the clay,
She sang to her work in her sweet childish way,
And found, when she'd put the last touch to his soul,   1015
That the music had somehow got mixed with the whole.

    "Here's Cooper, who's written six volumes to show
He's as good as a lord:[1] well, let's grant that he's so;
If a person prefer that description of praise,

---

6. I.e., good citizens could wax wroth over burning
issues such as the national bank and the protective tariff
while regarding as fanatics anyone equally concerned
with the issue of slavery.
7. Greeks who killed the tyrant Hipparchus (6th century B.C.). Lowell is scorning American pride in the
national Revolutionary heritage while present tyranny
is condoned.
8. I.e., Hawthorne is as didactic as John Bunyan
(1628–1688), English Baptist and author of *Pilgrim's
Progress*, yet as fanciful as Friedrich Fouqué
(1777–1843), German writer of fiction, including the

fairy tale *Undine*. The same union of opposites is
found in "Puritan Tieck," because Ludwig Tieck
(1773–1853) is another famous German Romantic author of fanciful, unpuritanic tales.
9. John Sullivan Dwight (1813–1893), Bostonian music critic and minor poet.
1. By this cruel jibe Lowell refers to books beginning
with *Home as Found* (1838) and *The American Democrat* (1838), in which Cooper sees an enlightened social and intellectual aristocracy as the best hope for the
future of the United States. "Six" is probably meant as
a rough count.

Why, a coronet's certainly cheaper than bays;   1020
But he need take no pains to convince us he's not
(As his enemies say) the American Scott.[2]
Choose any twelve men, and let C. read aloud
That one of his novels of which he's most proud,
And I'd lay any bet that, without ever quitting   1025
Their box,[3] they'd be all, to a man, for acquitting.
He has drawn you one character, though, that is new,
One wildflower he's plucked that is wet with the dew
Of this fresh Western world, and, the thing not to mince,
He has done naught but copy it ill ever since;   1030
His Indians, with proper respect be it said,
Are just Natty Bumpo[4] daubed over with red,
And his very Long Toms[5] are the same useful Nat,
Rigged up in duck pants and a sou'-wester hat,
(Though, once in a Coffin, a good chance was found   1035
To have slipt the old fellow away underground.)
All his other men-figures are clothes upon sticks,
The *dernier chemise*[6] of a man in a fix,
(As a captain besieged, when his garrison's small,
Sets up caps upon poles to be seen o'er the wall;)   1040
And the women he draws from one model don't vary,
All sappy as maples and flat[7] as a prairie.
When a character's wanted, he goes to the task
As a cooper would do in composing a cask;
He picks out the staves, of their qualities heedful,   1045
Just hoops them together as tight as is needful,
And, if the best fortune should crown the attempt, he
Has made at the most something wooden and empty.

    "Don't suppose I would underrate Cooper's abilities,
If I thought you'd do that, I should feel very ill at ease;   1050
The men who have given to *one* character life
And objective existence, are not very rife,
You may number them all, both prose-writers and singers,
Without overrunning the bounds of your fingers,
And Natty won't go to oblivion quicker   1055
Than Adams the parson or Primrose the vicar.[8]

    "There is one thing in Cooper I like, too, and that is
That on manners he lectures his countrymen gratis;
Not precisely so either, because, for a rarity,
He is paid for his tickets in unpopularity.[9]   1060

---

2. Sir Walter Scott (1771–1832), Scottish novelist on whose novels Cooper's early fiction was in part patterned.

3. I.e., the jury box, where the chosen "twelve men" sit.

4. Hero of Cooper's *Leatherstocking Tales*, whose name Lowell misspells.

5. Long Tom Coffin, hero of Cooper's *The Pilot*; Lowell puns on "Coffin" just below.

6. Last shirt (French).

7. Boring.

8. Two much-admired fictional characters: Parson Adams in Henry Fielding's *Joseph Andrews* (1742) and Primrose in Oliver Goldsmith's *The Vicar of Wakefield* (1766).

9. Cooper, although defended by many, became a national laughingstock and object of general vituperation after his return from a long residence in Europe. He started the tumult innocently enough by announcing in 1837 that a point of land on Otsego Lake owned by the Cooper family was not to be used by the other inhabitants of Cooperstown, New York, without permission and, particularly, that trees there were not to be damaged.

Now he may overcharge his American pictures,
But you'll grant there's a good deal of truth in his strictures;
And I honor the man who is willing to sink
Half his present repute for the freedom to think,
And, when he has thought, be his cause strong or weak,   1065
Will risk t'other half for the freedom to speak,
Caring naught for what vengeance the mob has in store,
Let that mob be the upper ten thousand or lower.

                              *   *   *

    "There comes Poe with his raven, like Barnaby Rudge,[1]   1295
Three-fifths of him genius and two-fifths sheer fudge,[2]
Who talks like a book of iambs and pentameters,
In a way to make people of common-sense damn metres,
Who has written some things quite the best of their kind,
But the heart somehow seems all squeezed out by the mind,   1300
Who—but hey-day! What's this? Messieurs Mathews[3] and Poe,
You mustn't fling mud-balls at Longfellow so,
Does it make a man worse that his character's such
As to make his friends love him (as you think) too much?
Why, there is not a bard at this moment alive   1305
More willing than he that his fellows should thrive;
While you are abusing him thus, even now
He would help either one of you out of a slough;
You may say that he's smooth and all that till you're hoarse,
But remember that elegance also is force;   1310
After polishing granite as much as you will,
The heart keeps its tough old persistency still;
Deduct all you can that still keeps you at bay,—
Why, he'll live till men weary of Collins and Gray,[4]
I'm not over-fond of Greek metres in English,[5]   1315
To me rhyme's a gain, so it be not too jinglish,
And your modern hexameter verses are no more
Like Greek ones than sleek Mr Pope is like Homer;[6]
As the roar of the sea to the coo of a pigeon is
So, compared to your moderns sounds old Melesigenes;[7]   1320
I may be too partial, the reason, perhaps, o't is
That I've heard the old blind man recite his own rhapsodies,
And my ear with that music impregnate may be,
Like the poor exiled shell with the soul of the sea,
Or as one can't bear Strauss[8] when his nature is cloven   1325

---

1. Halfwit, in Charles Dickens's book of that title (1841), whose companion is a knowing, evil-looking raven.
2. Humbug.
3. Cornelius Mathews (1817–1889), New York editor and fiction writer, much ridiculed by some of his contemporaries, including Lowell, who quite unfairly lumps him together here with Poe. Mathews merely thought Longfellow was imitative, but Poe launched a virulent campaign against him as a plagiarist. The literary debates of the 1840s pitted champions of a great, peculiarly American literature against those who thought that the important American literature would come through following English models. At times (as in Melville's *Hawthorne and His Mosses*) the issues were simplified to New York City versus Boston, creativity versus imitation.
4. William Collins (1721–1759) and Thomas Gray (1716–1771), English poets.
5. Longfellow had attempted to adapt Greek hexameters to English poetry in *Evangeline* (1847).
6. The English poet Alexander Pope (1688–1744) translated Homer's *Iliad* and *Odyssey* into heroic couplets.
7. Homer (Melos-born).
8. Johann Strauss (1804–1849), Austrian composer, known for his waltzes.

To its deeps within deeps by the stroke of Beethoven;
But, set that aside, and 'tis truth that I speak,
Had Theocritus[9] written in English, not Greek,
I believe that his exquisite sense would scarce change a line
In that rare, tender, virgin-like pastoral Evangeline.   1330
That's not ancient nor modern, its place is apart
Where Time has no sway, in the realm of pure Art,
'Tis a shrine of retreat from Earth's hubbub and strife
As quiet and chaste as the author's own life.

*   *   *

   "What! Irving? thrice welcome, warm heart and fine brain,
You bring back the happiest spirit from Spain,[1]
And the gravest sweet humor, that ever were there
Since Cervantes[2] met death in his gentle despair;   1140
Nay, don't be embarrassed, nor look so beseeching,—
I shan't run directly against my own preaching,
And, having just laughed at their Raphaels and Dantes,[3]
Go to setting you up beside matchless Cervantes;
But allow me to speak what I honestly feel,—   1145
To a true poet-heart add the fun of Dick Steele,
Throw in all of Addison,[4] *minus* the chill,
With the whole of that partnership's stock and good will,
Mix well, and, while stirring, hum o'er, as a spell,
The fine *old* English Gentleman,[5] simmer it well,   1150
Sweeten just to your own private liking, then strain,
That only the finest and clearest remain,
Let it stand out of doors till a soul it receives
From the warm lazy sun loitering down through green leaves,
And you'll find a choice nature, not wholly deserving   1155
A name either English or Yankee,—just Irving.

*   *   *

   "There's Holmes, who is matchless among you for wit;   1255
A Leyden-jar[6] always full-charged, from which flit
The electrical tingles of hit after hit;
In long poems 'tis painful sometimes and invites
A thought of the way the new Telegraph[7] writes,
Which pricks down its little sharp sentences spitefully   1260
And if you got more than you'd title to rightfully,
As if it were hoping its wild father Lightning
Would flame in for a second and give you a fright'ning.
He has perfect sway of what *I* call a sham metre,
But many admire it, the English hexameter.   1265

9. Greek pastoral poet (3rd century B.C.).
1. Washington Irving had been minister to Spain in the early 1840s.
2. Miguel de Cervantes Saavedra (1547–1616), Spanish novelist, author of *Don Quixote*, a major influence on Irving's work.
3. I.e., the string of American writers whom Duyckinck and Mathews have pressed on Phoebus as creative geniuses, all as great as the greatest Italian painters and writers.

4. Joseph Addison (1672–1719), British poet and essayist. Sir Richard Steele (1672–1729), British essayist and dramatist. Irving had plainly formed his prose style in part from reading their essays in *The Spectator*.
5. An allusion to an essay in Irving's *Bracebridge Hall*.
6. Glass jar used as an electrical condenser.
7. Invented by the painter Samuel F. B. Morse, the "new Telegraph" by 1844 was in service between Washington and Baltimore and in 1846 had been extended to New York City.

And Campbell,[8] I think wrote most commonly worse,
With less nerve, swing, and fire in the same kind of verse,
Nor e'er achieved aught in't so worthy of praise
As the tribute of Holmes to the grand *Marseillaise*.[9]
You went crazy last year over Bulwer's New Timon;[1]—   1270
Why, if B., to the day of his dying, should rhyme on,
Heaping verses on verses and tomes upon tomes,
He could ne'er reach the best point and vigor of Holmes
His are just the fine hands, too, to weave you a lyric
Full of fancy, fun, feeling, or spiced with satyric   1275
In so kindly a measure, that nobody knows
What to do but e'en join in the laugh, friends and foes.

"There is Lowell, who's striving Parnassus to climb
With a whole bale of *isms* tied together with rhyme,
He might get on alone, spite of brambles and boulders,   1280
But he can't with that bundle he has on his shoulders,
The top of the hill he will ne'er come nigh reaching
Till he learns the distinction 'twixt singing and preaching;
His lyre has some chords that would ring pretty well,
But he'd rather by half make a drum of the shell,   1285
And rattle away till he's old as Methusalem,
At the head of a march to the last New Jerusalem.[2]

*   *   *

1848

---

8. Thomas Campbell (1777–1844), Scottish poet.
9. French national anthem. Holmes's tribute is in *Po-etry: A Metrical Essay* (1836).
1. Edward Bulwer-Lytton (1803–1873), British author
of *The New Timon: A Romance of London* (1846).
2. The latest utopian scheme for social reform. Methuselah lived 969 years (Genesis 5.27).

WALT WHITMAN
1819–1892

Walt Whitman was born on May 31, 1819, son of a Long Island farmer turned carpenter who moved the family into Brooklyn in 1823 during a building boom. The ancestors were undistinguished, but stories survived of some forceful characters among them, and Whitman's father was acquainted with powerful personalities like the aged Thomas Paine. Whitman left school at eleven to become an office boy in a law firm, then worked for a doctor; already he was enthralled with the novels of Sir Walter Scott. By twelve he was working in the printing office of a newspaper and contributing sentimental items. By fifteen, when his family moved back into the interior of Long Island, Whitman was on his own. Very early he reached full physical maturity and in his midteens was contributing "pieces"— probably correct, conventional poems—to one of the best Manhattan papers, the *Mirror*, and often crossing the ferry from Brooklyn to attend debating societies and to use his journalist's passes at theaters in Manhattan. His rich fantasy life was fueled by numberless romantic novels. By sixteen he was a compositor in Manhattan, a journeyman printer. But two great fires in 1835 disrupted the printing industry, and as he turned seventeen he rejoined his family. For five years he taught intermittently at country and small-town schools, interrupting teaching to start a newspaper of his own in 1838 and to work briefly on another Long Island paper. Although forced into the exile of Long Island, he refused to compromise further with the sort of life he wanted. During his visits home he outraged his father by refusing to do farm work. Although he was innovative in the classroom, he struck some of the farm families he boarded with as unwilling to fulfill his role of teacher outside school hours; the main charge against him was laziness. He was active in debating societies, however, and already thought of himself as a writer. By early 1840 he had started the series "Sun-Down Papers from the Desk of a School-Master" for the Long Island *Democrat* and was writing poems. One of his stories prophetically culminated with the dream of writing "a wonderful and ponderous book."

Just before he turned twenty-one he went back to Manhattan, his teaching days over, and began work on Park Benjamin's *New World*, a literary weekly that pirated British novels; he also began a political career by speaking at Democratic rallies. Simultaneously, he was publishing stories in the *Democratic Review*, the foremost magazine of the Democratic party. Before he was twenty-three, he became editor of a Manhattan daily, the *Aurora*, and briefly transformed himself into a sartorial dandy while he spiked his editorial columns with his high democratic hopes. He exulted in the extremes of the city, where the violence of street gangs was countered by the lectures of Emerson and where even a young editor could get to know the poet Bryant (by livelihood, editor of the *Evening Post*). Fired from the *Aurora*, which publicly charged him with laziness, he wrote a temperance novel, *Franklin Evans, or the Inebriate*, for a one-issue extra of the *New World* late in 1842. For the next years he was journalist, hack writer, and a doughty minor politician. In 1845 he returned to Brooklyn, where he became a special contributor to the Long Island *Star*, assigned to Manhattan events, including musical and theatrical engagements. Just before he was twenty-seven he took over the editorship of the Brooklyn *Eagle*; for years he had kept to his eccentric daily routine of apparently purposeless walks in which he absorbed metropolitan sights and sounds, and now he formed the habit of a daily swim and shower at a bathhouse. On the *Eagle* he did most of the literary reviews, handling books by Carlyle, Emerson, Melville, Fuller, Sand, Goethe, and others. Like most Democrats, he was able to justify the Mexican War, and he hero-worshiped Zachary Taylor (on whom Melville was writing a series of satirical sketches). Linking territorial acquisition to personal and civic betterment, he was, in his nationalistic moods, capable of hailing the great American mission of "peopling the New World with a noble race." Yet by the beginning of 1848 he was fired from the *Eagle* because like Bryant he had become a Free-Soiler, opposed to the acquisition of more slave territory. Taking a chance offer of newspaper work, he made a brief but vivid trip to New Orleans, his only extensive journey until late in life, when he made a trip into the West.

By the summer of 1848, Whitman was back in New York, starting experiments with poetry and, in August, serving as delegate to the Buffalo Free-Soil convention. In the next years he was profoundly influenced by his association with a group of Brooklyn artists. All through the 1840s he had attended operas on his journalist's passes, hearing the greatest singers of the time. He went so far as to say that but for the "emotions, raptures, uplifts" of opera he could never have written *Leaves of Grass*. In an effort to control the disposition of his time, he became a "house builder" around 1851 or 1852, perhaps acting as contractor sometimes but also simply hiring out as a carpenter. By the early 1850s he had set a durable pattern of having discrete sets of friends simultaneously, the roughs and the artists, moving casually from one set to the other but seldom, if ever, mingling them. Living with his family, now back in Brooklyn, Whitman baffled and outraged them by ignoring regular mealtimes and appearing to loaf away his days in strolls, in reading at libraries, and in writing in the room he shared with a brother. Always self-taught, he undertook a more systematic plan of study. He became something of an expert on Egyptology through his trips to the Egyptian Museum on Broadway and his conversations with its proprietor. He became a student of astronomy, attending lectures and reading recent books; much of the information went into the cosmic concepts in *Song of Myself* and other poems. Cutting articles out of the great British quarterlies and monthlies, Whitman annotated them and argued with them in the margins, developing in the process clear ideas about aesthetics for the first time and formulating his notions about pantheism. By about 1853 he had arrived at something like his special poetic form in the little poem *Pictures*. He had given up newspaper work for carpentry; around the end of 1854 he gave up that also, and simply wrote. By the spring of 1855 he was seeing his "wonderful and ponderous book" through the press, probably setting some of the type himself. *Leaves of Grass* was on sale within a day or two of the Fourth of July of that year.

Facing the title page of this remarkable book was an engraving of a lounging working man, broad-hatted, bearded, shirt open at the neck to reveal a colored undershirt, the right arm akimbo, left hand in pants pocket, weight on the right leg. Such a man would hardly be expected to read verse, much less write it. The title page said simply *"Leaves of Grass"* and gave the place and date of publication as "Brooklyn, New York: 1855." The back of the title page named "Walter Whitman" as the man who had entered the work for copyright; that this was the author was confirmed by a line far down in the first poem (the one later retitled *Song of Myself*; here they were all titled *Leaves of Grass*).

Following the copyright page was an untitled essay running to ten pages, double column—an intimidating mass of type, most of it in long paragraphs punctuated by sets of what looked like ellipses. The essay was oracular in tone, sweeping in message, the outgrowth of Whitman's long musing on the place of art in American life. One of its starting points was pretty clearly Emerson's *The Poet*, especially the provocative list of some of the incomparable materials awaiting the tyrannous eye of the great American poet. It circled back to its major points much like Emerson's own essays, focusing primarily on the sort of poet America required and the sort of poetry that poet would write. The reader soon had every reason to suspect that the "Walter Whitman" of the copyright page might consider himself that poet and *Leaves of Grass* an example of that poetry.

Yet the prefatory essay did not quite prepare the reader for the poems that followed. The recitation of some of the incomparable materials awaiting the American poet suggested the comprehensiveness and brilliance of detail in some of the poetic catalogs (in fact, portions of the preface were later worked into poems); the declarations about science prepared for the sophisticated understanding the poems revealed of geology and astronomy, if not for the poetic uses of that knowledge; and the tributes to the American people partially suggested the profound tenderness that would be manifested toward all people in the poems. Yet not even the occasional ironic passages of the essay suggested that the poems that followed would include master strokes of comedy; nothing adequately prepared for the intense and explicit sexuality and the psychological complexity of the poems; and not even his comments on form suggested that Whitman had already achieved a new form splendidly appropriate to his democratic subject matter and had already become a supreme master of the English language.

The publication of *Leaves of Grass* did not immediately change Whitman's life. His father died just after it appeared, and support of his mother and a feebleminded brother devolved more and more on Whitman. He sent copies of his book out broadcast and got an immediate response from Emerson greeting him "at the beginning of a great career, which yet must have had a long foreground somewhere, for such a start." As weeks passed with few reviews, he wrote a few himself to be published anonymously, and in October he let Horace Greeley's *Tribune* print Emerson's letter. Unfazed by his own effrontery, he put clippings of the letter in presentation copies, to Longfellow among others. While Whitman was angling for reviews in England and working on an expansion of the book, Emerson visited him (in December of 1855), and in the fall of 1856 Bronson Alcott, Thoreau, and others came out to his house in Brooklyn. Whitman continued to do miscellaneous journalism, mainly for a weekly magazine called *Life Illustrated*, and wrote a long political tract—*The Eighteenth Presidency!*—which he never distributed. The excitement of the election year was reflected in the excessive nationalism of some of the new poems as well as the pomposity of titles, but among the new poems in the second edition (1856) was the great *Sun-Down Poem*, later called *Crossing Brooklyn Ferry*. Whitman flaunted Emerson's praise on the spine of the new edition and in the back printed the whole letter, following it with an open letter to the master at Concord in which Whitman announced his determination "to meet people and The States face to face, to confront them with an American rude tongue." As part of his campaign for a national identity, Whitman included a sexual "programme" based on "an avowed, empowered, unabashed development of sex," a manifesto notable for its nonsexist message: "Women in These States approach the day of that organic equality with men, without which, I see, men cannot have organic equality among themselves."

From 1857 to 1859 Whitman's main statements on the national crisis over slavery were contained in his editorials in the Brooklyn *Times*. During these years Whitman worked on a political, sexual, and poetic program that he could bring to the people of the States as a wandering lecturer, envisioning for himself a way of life that would fuse the tours of lecturers like Emerson with his own love of the open road and good comrades. He lectured locally, but nothing came of the grander scheme, and in some new poems he consciously turned away from the national situation to his private sexual concerns. Whitman wrote a group of twelve poems, *Live Oak, with Moss*, that seems to tell a straightforward story of his love for another man. Secure in that love, in one poem he reflects on the likelihood that other men throughout the world must have sexual longings like his own, and in another he dreams of an idealized city where nothing is greater than "manly love." In this sequence Whitman explicitly renounces his old role of public poet seeking knowledge and celebrating the American land and its heroes; instead, he chooses to be happy in private with his lover. If he had printed it, the sequence would have constituted a new and highly public sexual program, nothing short of an open homosexual manifesto.

Facing the impossibility of printing and distributing so direct a sexual statement of "adhesiveness" or "the passion of friendship" of man for man, Whitman chose a more covert way of expressing himself. In the next (1860) edition of *Leaves of Grass* Whitman included a cluster called *Enfans d'Adam*, for which he wrote fifteen counterbalancing poems that for the most part focus on the "amative" love of man for woman. Then, separated from *Enfans d'Adam* by several other poems, Whitman printed a cluster of forty-five poems about male love under the title *Calamus* (among which were versions of the *Live Oak* poems, reordered and altered); some of the new poems project future readers who will hold him "in hand" by holding his book and will "guess at" what he is only hinting. Whitman's placing the heterosexual section first muted the significance of the *Calamus* poems, the space between the two clusters muffled their relationship, and the dispersal of the *Live Oak* poems destroyed their original narrative impact. The two clusters as printed in 1860 differ markedly from the poems in the now-familiar 1892 *Children of Adam* (as *Efans d'Adam* was retitled in 1867) and *Calamus* section, for in intervening editions Whitman revised poems and moved some poems out of and into the clusters. The unavailability of texts of the various late editions of *Leaves of Grass* has made it difficult to study the two clusters in their various forms, but many readers have sensed perfunctoriness in many heterosexual passages in the *Children of Adam* poems (Whitman's biographer Gay Wilson Allen says they sound "theoretical and philosophical," unlike the "genuine love poems" in the *Calamus* section). By late 1859 Whitman had in hand the *Calamus* and *Enfans d'Adam* poems and others such as *A Child's Reminiscence* (*Out of the Cradle Endlessly Rocking*) in nearly final form. Early the next year he received an opportune letter from the Boston firm of Thayer & Eldridge: "We are young men. We 'celebrate' ourselves by acts. Try us. You can do us good. We can do you good—pecuniarily." For the first time, Whitman had a publisher.

Emerson welcomed him in Boston, arguing through a two-hour walk in the cold common that Whitman should not publish the *Children of Adam* poems. Whitman refused to compromise. When Emerson tried to introduce him into the Boston literary coterie, the Saturday Club, Longfellow, Holmes, and Lowell all objected, and apparently the families of Emerson, Thoreau, and Alcott refused to have him invited to Concord. Yet Whitman met a few kindred spirits during the weeks he labored over the proofs of his third edition, which was printed in May 1860. Besides the accustomed attacks, there were defenses, including one by the actress Adah Isaacks Menken, and for the first time, there were parodies, a sure sign of public interest. But Thayer & Eldridge went bankrupt, and Whitman was left again with the book on his own hands.

For society at the turn of the decade Whitman had, as usual, his separate groups of friends, in one group stage drivers (i.e., drivers of the horse-pulled buses on which he was an inveterate passenger) and in another literary, publishing, and theatrical people, especially the bohemian habitués of the famous Pfaff's saloon on lower Broadway. For years Whitman had paid cheering visits to prisoners and had made regular visits to sick stage drivers. Almost imperceptibly, his role of visitor of the sick merged into his Civil War services as hospital attendant. Just before Christmas 1862, Whitman went to Washington to find his brother George, who had been reported wounded. The injury was slight, but Whitman stayed on with his brother in camp (such was the casual fashion of the war), the two sharing a tent with other soldiers. Returning to Washington, he rented a small room, found a job as copyist in the paymaster's office, and began visiting Brooklyn soldiers in the hospitals. Without premeditation, Whitman yielded to the irresistible appeal of the occasion: his informality, gentleness, resourcefulness, and lack of preachiness were uniquely required. Looking older than his age (only in his early forties), he could serve as benevolent father to the men, and they returned his extraordinary sympathy and love; his friends became accustomed to seeing recovered soldiers stop him in the street to hug and kiss him. It has been thought that the hospital experience was a sublimation of Whitman's homosexual feelings, but Allen has shown that those emotions permeate some of his correspondence with soldiers. Allen says that the letters to Sergeant Tom Sawyer are "not easy for a modern critic to interpret, for they were evidently motivated by a mixture of vicarious paternalism, longing for companionship, and some rather confused erotic impulses that perhaps Whitman himself did not clearly understand." Whitman may have understood his own emotions better than his biographers have done. Whatever Whitman's mixture of emotions, his role of wound dresser was heroic, and it eventually undercut his buoyant physical health.

During the war, Whitman's deepest emotions and energies were reserved for his hospital work, though he wrote a series of war poems designed to trace his own varying attitudes toward the conflict, from his early near-mindless jingoism to something quite rare in American poetry up to that time, a dedication to simple realism. Whitman later wrote a section in *Specimen Days* called *The Real War Will Never Get in the Books,* but to incorporate the real war into a book of poetry became one of the dominant impulses of the *Drum-Taps* collection (1865). After Lincoln's assassination Whitman delayed the new volume until it could include in a "sequel" *When Lilacs Last in the Dooryard Bloom'd,* his masterpiece of the

1860s. Even as *Drum-Taps* was being published, Whitman was revising a copy of the Boston edition of *Leaves of Grass* at his desk in the Department of the Interior. The new secretary read the annotated copy and abruptly fired him. The consequences might have been minor: Whitman's friend William O'Connor quickly got him a new post in the attorney general's office, and Whitman had been dismissed before without catastrophic reactions, although this was the first time he had been fired because of the sexual passages in *Leaves of Grass*. But the incident turned O'Connor from a devoted friend into a disciple who quickly began writing a book (with Whitman's help in supplying information and documents) called *The Good Gray Poet* (1866). It was a piece of pure hagiography, in which Whitman was identified with Jesus. O'Connor's book, coming out simultaneously with *Drum-Taps*, polarized opinion, with negative immediate effects, but in the long run it strengthened Whitman's determination not to yield to censorship or to apologize for his earlier poems, and it set a pattern by which other remarkable men and women would be drawn to Whitman as disciples, seeking to care for his few physical needs—minimal food and shelter—while working for his reputation as a great poet.

For several years Whitman continued as a clerk in the attorney general's office, living most of the time in a bare, unheated room but gaining access to good lights for nighttime reading in his government office. He continued to rework *Leaves of Grass*, incorporating *Drum-Taps* into it in 1867, and with his friends' help continued to propagandize for its acceptance. After much correspondence involving Whitman, O'Connor, and a newer admirer (John Burroughs, the naturalist), William Michael Rossetti published a volume of Whitman's poems in London early in 1868. Though it was a selected and even an expurgated edition, it created many English admirers. As an ex-newspaperman, Whitman was accustomed to having immediate outlets for his political thoughts and general observations on the American scene. Such ruminations that in earlier years might have gone into editorials went into essays in the *Galaxy* during 1867 and 1868, then (in expanded form) into *Democratic Vistas* (1870), a passionate look to the future of democracy and democratic literature in America, based on his realistic appraisal of postwar culture. Another prose work, *Specimen Days*, published in book form in 1882, has affinities with Whitman's early editorial records of strolls through the city, but it is even more intensely personal, the record of representative days in the life of an American who had lived in the midst of great national events and who had kept alert to nature and his own mind and body. Through the late 1860s and early 1870s Whitman's compartmentalized life went on. He formed an emotional relationship with Peter Doyle, a young streetcar driver, about the time he was beginning in a small way to be treated as a literary lion. He was still jotting down notes on his devastating torments over his sexual drives.

The Washington years, a time of slow, faltering growth in reputation, marred by severe setbacks and complications, ended early in 1873, when Whitman suffered a paralytic stroke. His mother died a few months later, and Whitman joined his brother George's household in Camden, New Jersey, intending only a temporary move during his recuperation. His convalescence was bitterly lonely, for his well-meaning brother provided none of the intellectual companionship of a Burroughs or the emotional response of a Peter Doyle. During the second year of his illness, the government decided not to hold his job for him any longer, and he became dependent on occasional publication in newspapers and magazines—not an easy market, because his genteel enemies either ignored him in print or joined in a cabal to exclude him from some major publishing organs such as *Scribner's*. The 1867 edition of *Leaves of Grass* had involved much reworking and rearrangement, and the fifth edition (1871) continued that process, with many of the original *Drum-Taps* poems being distributed throughout the book and with an assemblage of old and new poems in a large new section, *Passage to India*. The "Centennial

Edition" of 1876 was a reissue of the 1871 edition and was most notable for the way his English admirers got funds to him by having important literary people subscribe to it. American public opinion was gradually swayed by new evidences that the invalid in Camden could command the respect of Alfred, Lord Tennyson, the poet laureate, and many other famous British writers. Not even the most puritanic American critics could hold their ranks firm in the face of such extravagant admiration, however rough and outrageous his poetry. Yet in 1881, when the reputable Boston firm of James R. Osgood & Co. printed the sixth edition of *Leaves of Grass*, the Boston district attorney threatened to prosecute on the grounds of obscenity, and Whitman found himself with the plates on his hands and no publisher until he had impressions from the Osgood plates made by Philadelphia printers Rees Welsh & Co. in 1882 and David McKay thereafter. The "deathbed" edition of 1891–92 was in fact a reissue of the 1881 edition with the addition of two later groups of poems, *Sands at Seventy* (from *November Boughs*, which Whitman published in 1888) and *Good-bye My Fancy* (from the 1891 collection of that name).

Of all the American writers of the nineteenth century, Whitman offers the most inspiring example of fidelity to his art. While Hawthorne let marriage become his true career, and while Melville ceased writing for a public that would not accept him, Whitman persisted. (James persisted also, but he was equipped with material, educational, and social advantages Whitman lacked.) Outraging his employers and his family by his odd hours and the semblance of mere loafing, outraging his well-wishers by refusing to compromise on minor points that might have gained him fuller acceptance, finagling reviews, reviewing himself, writing admiring accounts of his work for others to sign, shocking some of his followers by refusing to give autographs gratis, Whitman kept on, like what he called some high-and-dry "hard-cased dilapidated grim ancient shell-fish or time-bang'd conch," uncompromising to the end, never bowing to the materialism and puerilities of nineteenth-century America. Appropriately, when he finally accumulated a few worldly belongings about him at Camden, he managed to give a nautical cast to his room, for eccentric as he seemed, crotchety, stubborn, Whitman was a literary equivalent of Melville's Bulkington in *Moby-Dick*, willing to renounce the comforts of the shore, all normal earthly felicity, for a life of the intellect and the imagination. He died at Camden on March 26, 1892, secure in the knowledge that he had held unwaveringly true to his art and to his role as an artist who had made that art prevail.

Preface to *Leaves of Grass* (1855)[1]

America does not repel the past or what it has produced under its forms or amid other politics or the idea of castes or the old religions . . . accepts the lesson with calmness . . . is not so impatient as has been supposed that the slough still sticks to opinions and manners and literature while the life which served its requirements has passed into the new life of the new forms . . . perceives that the corpse is slowly borne from the eating and sleeping rooms of the house . . . perceives that it waits a little while in the door . . . that it was fittest for its days . . . that its action has descended to the stalwart and well-shaped heir who approaches . . . and that he shall be fittest for his days.

The Americans of all nations at any time upon the earth have probably the

1. This preface (reprinted here from the 1855 edition) has not yet attained its rightful place among the great American literary manifestoes. Like Emerson, Whitman is celebrating the incomparable materials avail-able to the American poet, not simply physical resources but also the people themselves—the spirit of the place.

fullest poetical nature. The United States themselves are essentially the greatest poem. In the history of the earth hitherto the largest and most stirring appear tame and orderly to their ampler largeness and stir. Here at last is something in the doings of man that corresponds with the broadcast doings of the day and night. Here is not merely a nation but a teeming nation of nations. Here is action untied from strings necessarily blind to particulars and details magnificently moving in vast masses. Here is the hospitality which forever indicates heroes . . . . Here are the roughs and beards and space and ruggedness and nonchalance that the soul loves. Here the performance disdaining the trivial unapproached in the tremendous audacity of its crowds and groupings and the push of its perspective spreads with crampless and flowing breadth and showers its prolific and splendid extravagance. One sees it must indeed own the riches of the summer and winter, and need never be bankrupt while corn grows from the ground or the orchards drop apples or the bays contain fish or men beget children upon women.

Other states indicate themselves in their deputies . . . . but the genius of the United States is not best or most in its executives or legislatures, nor in its ambassadors or authors or colleges or churches or parlors, nor even in its newspapers or inventors . . . but always most in the common people. Their manners speech dress friendships—the freshness and candor of their physiognomy—the picturesque looseness of their carriage . . . their deathless attachment to freedom—their aversion to anything indecorous or soft or mean—the practical acknowledgment of the citizens of one state by the citizens of all other states—the fierceness of their roused resentment—their curiosity and welcome of novelty—their self-esteem and wonderful sympathy—their susceptibility to a slight—the air they have of persons who never knew how it felt to stand in the presence of superiors—the fluency of their speech—their delight in music, the sure symptom of manly tenderness and native elegance of soul . . . their good temper and openhandedness—the terrible significance of their elections—the President's taking off his hat to them not they to him—these too are unrhymed poetry. It awaits the gigantic and generous treatment worthy of it.

The largeness of nature or the nation were monstrous without a corresponding largeness and generosity of the spirit of the citizen. Not nature nor swarming states nor streets and steamships nor prosperous business nor farms nor capital nor learning may suffice for the ideal of man . . . nor suffice the poet. No reminiscences may suffice either. A live nation can always cut a deep mark and can have the best authority the cheapest . . . namely from its own soul. This is the sum of the profitable uses of individuals or states and of present action and grandeur and of the subjects of poets.—As if it were necessary to trot back generation after generation to the eastern records! As if the beauty and sacredness of the demonstrable must fall behind that of the mythical! As if men do not make their mark out of any times! As if the opening of the western continent by discovery and what has transpired since in North and South America were less than the small theatre of the antique or the aimless sleepwalking of the middle ages! The pride of the United States leaves the wealth and finesse of the cities and all returns of commerce and agriculture and all the magnitude of geography or shows of exterior victory to enjoy the breed of fullsized men or one fullsized man unconquerable and simple.

The American poets are to enclose old and new for America is the race of races. Of them a bard[2] is to be commensurate with a people. To him the other continents arrive as contributions . . . he gives them reception for their sake and his own sake. His spirit responds to his country's spirit . . . . he incarnates its geography and natural life and rivers and lakes. Mississippi with annual freshets and changing chutes, Missouri and Columbia and Ohio and Saint Lawrence with the falls and beautiful masculine Hudson, do not embouchure[3] where they spend themselves more than they embouchure into him. The blue breadth over the inland sea of Virginia and Maryland and the sea off Massachusetts and Maine and over Manhattan bay and over Champlain and Erie and over Ontario and Huron and Michigan and Superior, and over the Texan and Mexican and Floridian and Cuban seas and over the seas off California and Oregon, is not tallied by the blue breadth of the waters below more than the breadth of above and below is tallied by him. When the long Atlantic coast stretches longer and the Pacific coast stretches longer he easily stretches with them north or south. He spans between them also from east to west and reflects what is between them. On him rise solid growths that offset the growths of pine and cedar and hemlock and liveoak and locust and chestnut and cypress and hickory and limetree and cottonwood and tuliptree and cactus and wildvine and tamarind and persimmon . . . . and tangles as tangled as any canebrake or swamp . . . . and forests coated with transparent ice and icicles hanging from the boughs and crackling in the wind . . . . and sides and peaks of mountains . . . . and pasturage sweet and free as savannah or upland or prairie . . . . with flights and songs and screams that answer those of the wild pigeon and highhold and orchard-oriole and coot and surf-duck and redshouldered-hawk and fish-hawk and white-ibis and indian-hen and cat-owl and water-pheasant and qua-bird and pied-sheldrake and blackbird and mockingbird and buzzard and condor and night-heron and eagle. To him the hereditary countenance descends both mother's and father's. To him enter the essences of the real things and past and present events—of the enormous diversity of temperature and agriculture and mines—the tribes of red aborigines— the weatherbeaten vessels entering new ports or making landings on rocky coasts—the first settlements north or south—the rapid stature and muscle— the haughty defiance of '76, and the war and peace and formation of the constitution . . . . the union always surrounded by blatherers and always calm and impregnable—the perpetual coming of immigrants—the wharf hem'd cities and superior marine—the unsurveyed interior—the loghouses and clearings and wild animals and hunters and trappers . . . . the free commerce— the fisheries and whaling and gold-digging—the endless gestation of new states—the convening of Congress every December,[4] the members duly coming up from all climates and the uttermost parts . . . . the noble character of the young mechanics and of all free American workmen and workwomen . . . . the general ardor and friendliness and enterprise—the perfect equality of the female with the male . . . . the large amativeness—the fluid movement of the population—the factories and mercantile life and laborsaving machinery—the Yankee swap—the New-York firemen and the target excursion[5]—the southern plantation life—the character of the northeast and of the northwest

---

2. The ideal national poet.
3. Pour.
4. Before the adoption of the Twentieth Amendment in 1933, Congress convened on the first Monday in December, according to Article 1, Section 4, of the Constitution.
5. Shooting contest.

and southwest—slavery and the tremulous spreading of hands to protect it, and the stern opposition to it which shall never cease till it ceases or the speaking of tongues and the moving of lips cease. For such the expression of the American poet is to be transcendant and new. It is to be indirect and not direct or descriptive or epic. Its quality goes through these to much more. Let the age and wars of other nations be chanted and their eras and characters be illustrated and that finish the verse. Not so the great psalm of the republic. Here the theme is creative and has vista. Here comes one among the wellbeloved stonecutters and plans with decision and science and sees the solid and beautiful forms of the future where there are now no solid forms.

Of all nations the United States with veins full of poetical stuff most need poets and will doubtless have the greatest and use them the greatest. Their Presidents shall not be their common referee so much as their poets shall. Of all mankind the great poet is the equable man. Not in him but off from him things are grotesque or eccentric or fail of their sanity. Nothing out of its place is good and nothing in its place is bad. He bestows on every object or quality its fit proportions neither more nor less. He is the arbiter of the diverse and he is the key. He is the equalizer of his age and land . . . . he supplies what wants supplying and checks what wants checking. If peace is the routine out of him speaks the spirit of peace, large, rich, thrifty, building vast and populous cities, encouraging agriculture and the arts and commerce—lighting the study of man, the soul, immortality—federal, state or municipal government, marriage, health, freetrade, intertravel by land and sea . . . . nothing too close, nothing too far off . . . the stars not too far off. In war he is the most deadly force of the war. Who recruits him recruits horse and foot . . . he fetches parks of artillery[6] the best that engineer ever knew. If the time becomes slothful and heavy he knows how to arouse it . . . he can make every word he speaks draw blood. Whatever stagnates in the flat of custom or obedience or legislation he never stagnates. Obedience does not master him, he masters it. High up out of reach he stands turning a concentrated light . . . he turns the pivot with his finger . . . he baffles the swiftest runners as he stands and easily overtakes and envelops them. The time straying toward infidelity and confections and persiflage he withholds by his steady faith . . . he spreads out his dishes . . . he offers the sweet firmfibred meat that grows men and women. His brain is the ultimate brain. He is no arguer . . . he is judgment. He judges not as the judge judges but as the sun falling around a helpless thing. As he sees the farthest he has the most faith. His thoughts are the hymns of the praise of things. In the talk on the soul and eternity and God off of his equal plane he is silent. He sees eternity less like a play with a prologue and denouement . . . . he sees eternity in men and women . . . he does not see men and women as dreams or dots. Faith is the antiseptic of the soul . . . it pervades the common people and preserves them . . . they never give up believing and expecting and trusting. There is that indescribable freshness and unconsciousness about an illiterate person that humbles and mocks the power of the noblest expressive genius. The poet sees for a certainty how one not a great artist may be just as sacred and perfect as the greatest artist . . . . . . The power to destroy or remould is freely used by him but never the power of attack. What is past is past. If he does not expose superior models and prove himself

---

6. I.e., parksful of artillery—from the custom of drilling and parading in civic parks.

by every step he takes he is not what is wanted. The presence of the greatest poet conquers . . . not parleying or struggling or any prepared attempts. Now he has passed that way see after him! there is not left any vestige of despair or misanthropy or cunning or exclusiveness or the ignominy of a nativity or color or delusion of hell or the necessity of hell . . . . . and no man thenceforward shall be degraded for ignorance or weakness or sin.

The greatest poet hardly knows pettiness or triviality. If he breathes into any thing that was before thought small it dilates with the grandeur and life of the universe. He is a seer . . . . he is individual . . . he is complete in himself . . . . the others are as good as he, only he sees it and they do not. He is not one of the chorus . . . . he does not stop for any regulation . . . he is the president of regulation. What the eyesight does to the rest he does to the rest. Who knows the curious mystery of the eyesight? The other senses corroborate themselves, but this is removed from any proof but its own and foreruns the identities of the spiritual world. A single glance of it mocks all the investigations of man and all the instruments and books of the earth and all reasoning. What is marvellous? what is unlikely? what is impossible or baseless or vague? after you have once just opened the space of a peachpit and given audience to far and near and to the sunset and had all things enter with electric swiftness softly and duly without confusion or jostling or jam.

The land and sea, the animals fishes and birds, the sky of heaven and the orbs, the forests mountains and rivers, are not small themes . . . but folks expect of the poet to indicate more than the beauty and dignity which always attach to dumb real objects . . . . they expect him to indicate the path between reality and their souls. Men and women perceive the beauty well enough . . probably as well as he. The passionate tenacity of hunters, woodmen, early risers, cultivators of gardens and orchards and fields, the love of healthy women for the manly form, sea-faring persons, drivers of horses, the passion for light and the open air, all is an old varied sign of the unfailing perception of beauty and of a residence of the poetic in outdoor people. They can never be assisted by poets to perceive . . . some may but they never can. The poetic quality is not marshalled in rhyme or uniformity or abstract addresses to things nor in melancholy complaints or good precepts, but is the life of these and much else and is in the soul. The profit of rhyme is that it drops seeds of a sweeter and more luxuriant rhyme, and of uniformity that it conveys itself into its own roots in the ground out of sight. The rhyme and uniformity of perfect poems show the free growth of metrical laws and bud from them as unerringly and loosely as lilacs or roses on a bush, and take shapes as compact as the shapes of chestnuts and oranges and melons and pears, and shed the perfume impalpable to form. The fluency and ornaments of the finest poems or music or orations or recitations are not independent but dependent. All beauty comes from beautiful blood and a beautiful brain. If the greatnesses are in conjunction in a man or woman it is enough . . . . the fact will prevail through the universe . . . . but the gaggery and gilt of a million years will not prevail. Who troubles himself about his ornaments or fluency is lost. This is what you shall do: Love the earth and sun and the animals, despise riches, give alms to every one that asks, stand up for the stupid and crazy, devote your income and labor to others, hate tyrants, argue not concerning God, have patience and indulgence toward the people, take off your hat to nothing known or unknown or to any man or number of men, go freely with powerful uneducated persons and with the young and with the mothers of families, read these leaves in the open air every season of every year of your life, reexamine all you have been told at school or church or in any book, dismiss whatever insults your own soul, and your very flesh shall be a great poem and have the richest fluency not only in its words but in the silent lines of its lips and face and between the lashes of your eyes and in every motion and joint of your body . . . . The poet shall not spend his time in unneeded work. He shall know that the ground is always ready ploughed and manured . . . . others may not know it but he shall. He shall go directly to the creation. His trust shall master the trust of everything he touches . . . . and shall master all attachment.

The known universe has one complete lover and that is the greatest poet. He consumes an eternal passion and is indifferent which chance happens and which possible contingency of fortune or misfortune and persuades daily and hourly his delicious pay. What balks or breaks others is fuel for his burning progress to contact and amorous joy. Other proportions of the reception of pleasure dwindle to nothing to his proportions. All expected from heaven or from the highest he is rapport with in the sight of the daybreak or a scene of the winter woods or the presence of children playing or with his arm round the neck of a man or woman. His love above all love has leisure and expanse . . . . he leaves room ahead of himself. He is no irresolute or suspicious lover . . . he is sure . . . he scorns intervals. His experience and the showers and thrills are not for nothing. Nothing can jar him . . . . suffering and darkness cannot—death and fear cannot. To him complaint and jealousy and envy are corpses buried and rotten in the earth . . . . he saw them buried. The sea is not surer of the shore or the shore of the sea than he is of the fruition of his love and of all perfection and beauty.

The fruition of beauty is no chance of hit or miss . . . it is inevitable as life . . . . it is exact and plumb as gravitation. From the eyesight proceeds another eyesight and from the hearing proceeds another hearing and from the voice proceeds another voice eternally curious of the harmony of things with man. To these respond perfections not only in the committees that were supposed to stand for the rest but in the rest themselves just the same. These understand the law of perfection in masses and floods . . . that its finish is to each for itself and onward from itself . . . that it is profuse and impartial . . . that there is not a minute of the light or dark nor an acre of the earth or sea without it—nor any direction of the sky nor any trade or employment nor any turn of events. This is the reason that about the proper expression of beauty there is precision and balance . . . one part does not need to be thrust above another. The best singer is not the one who has the most lithe and powerful organ . . . the pleasure of poems is not in them that take the handsomest measure and similes and sound.

Without effort and without exposing in the least how it is done the greatest poet brings the spirit of any or all events and passions and scenes and persons some more and some less to bear on your individual character as you hear or read. To do this well is to compete with the laws that pursue and follow time. What is the purpose must surely be there and the clue of it must be there . . . . and the faintest indication is the indication of the best and then becomes the clearest indication. Past and present and future are not disjoined but joined. The greatest poet forms the consistence of what is to be from what has been and is. He drags the dead out of their coffins and stands them again on their feet . . . . he says to the past, Rise and walk before me that I may realize you. He learns the lesson . . . . he places himself where the future becomes present. The greatest poet does not only dazzle his rays over character and scenes and passions . . . he finally ascends and finishes all . . . he exhibits the pinnacles that no man can tell what they are for or what is beyond . . . . he glows a moment on the extremest verge. He is most wonderful in his last half-hidden smile or frown . . . by that flash of the moment of parting the one that sees it shall be encouraged or terrified afterward for many years. The greatest poet does not moralize or make applications of morals . . . he knows the soul. The soul has that measureless pride which consists in never acknowledging any lessons but its own. But it has sympathy as measureless as its pride and the one balances the other and neither can stretch too far while it stretches in company with the other. The inmost secrets of art sleep with the twain. The greatest poet has lain close betwixt both and they are vital in his style and thoughts.

The art of art, the glory of expression and the sunshine of the light of letters is simplicity. Nothing is better than simplicity . . . . nothing can make up for excess or for the lack of definiteness. To carry on the heave of impulse and pierce intellectual depths and give all subjects their articulations are powers neither common nor very uncommon. But to speak in literature with the perfect rectitude and insousiance of the movements of animals and the unimpeachableness of the sentiment of trees in the woods and grass by the roadside is the flawless triumph of art. If you have looked on him who has achieved it you have looked on one of the masters of the artists of all nations and times. You shall not contemplate the flight of the graygull over the bay or the mettlesome action of the blood horse or the tall leaning of sunflowers on their stalk or the appearance of the sun journeying through heaven or the appearance of the moon afterward with any more satisfaction than you shall contemplate him. The greatest poet has less a marked style and is more the channel of thoughts and things without increase or diminution, and is the free channel of himself. He swears to his art, I will not be meddlesome, I will not have in my writing any elegance or effect or originality to hang in the way between me and the rest like curtains. I will have nothing hang in the way, not the richest curtains. What I tell I tell for precisely what it is. Let who may exalt or startle or fascinate or sooth I will have purposes as health or heat or snow has and be as regardless of observation. What I experience or portray shall go from my composition without a shred of my composition. You shall stand by my side and look in the mirror with me.

The old red blood and stainless gentility of great poets will be proved by their unconstraint. A heroic person walks at his ease through and out of that custom or precedent or authority that suits him not. Of the traits of the brotherhood of writers savans[7] musicians inventors and artists nothing is finer than silent defiance advancing from new free forms. In the need of poems philosophy politics mechanism science behaviour, the craft of art, an appropriate native grand-opera, shipcraft, or any craft, he is greatest forever and forever who contributes the greatest original practical example. The cleanest expression is that which finds no sphere worthy of itself and makes one.

The messages of great poets to each man and woman are, Come to us on

---

7. Wise men, scientists.

equal terms, Only then can you understand us, We are no better than you, What we enclose you enclose, What we enjoy you may enjoy. Did you suppose there could be only one Supreme? We affirm there can be unnumbered Supremes, and that one does not countervail another any more than one eyesight countervails another . . and that men can be good or grand only of the consciousness of their supremacy within them. What do you think is the grandeur of storms and dismemberments and the deadliest battles and wrecks and the wildest fury of the elements and the power of the sea and the motion of nature and of the throes of human desires and dignity and hate and love? It is that something in the soul which says, Rage on, Whirl on, I tread master here and everywhere, Master of the spasms of the sky and of the shatter of the sea, Master of nature and passion and death, And of all terror and all pain.

The American bards shall be marked for generosity and affection and for encouraging competitors . . They shall be kosmos[8] . . without monopoly or secresy . . glad to pass any thing to any one . . hungry for equals night and day. They shall not be careful of riches and privilege . . . . they shall be riches and privilege . . . . they shall perceive who the most affluent man is. The most affluent man is he that confronts all the shows he sees by equivalents out of the stronger wealth of himself. The American bard shall delineate no class of persons nor one or two out of the strata of interests nor love most nor truth most nor the soul most nor the body most . . . . and not be for the eastern states more than the western or the northern states more than the southern.

Exact science and its practical movements are no checks on the greatest poet but always his encouragement and support. The outset and remembrance are there . . there the arms that lifted him first and brace him best . . . . there he returns after all his goings and comings. The sailor and traveler. . . . the anatomist chemist astronomer geologist phrenologist spiritualist mathematician historian and lexicographer are not poets, but they are the lawgivers of poets and their construction underlies the structure of every perfect poem. No matter what rises or is uttered they sent the seed of the conception of it . . . of them and by them stand the visible proofs of souls . . . . . always of their fatherstuff must be begotten the sinewy races of bards. If there shall be love and content between the father and the son and if the greatness of the son is the exuding of the greatness of the father there shall be love between the poet and the man of demonstrable science. In the beauty of poems are the tuft and final applause of science.

Great is the faith of the flush of knowledge and of the investigation of the depths of qualities and things. Cleaving and circling here swells the soul of the poet yet it[9] president of itself always. The depths are fathomless and therefore calm. The innocence and nakedness are resumed . . . they are neither modest nor immodest. The whole theory of the special and supernatural and all that was twined with it or educed out of it departs as a dream. What has ever happened . . . . what happens and whatever may or shall happen, the vital laws enclose all . . . . they are sufficient for any case and for all cases . . . none to be hurried or retarded . . . . any miracle of affairs or persons inadmissible in the vast clear scheme where every motion and every spear of grass and the frames and spirits of men and women and all that concerns them are

---

8. I.e., a part of the one mind that is the world.
9. Perhaps "remains" should be understood after "it," although "it" may simply be a typographical error for "is."

unspeakably perfect miracles all referring to all and each distinct and in its place. It is also not consistent with the reality of the soul to admit that there is anything in the known universe more divine than men and women.

Men and women and the earth and all upon it are simply to be taken as they are, and the investigation of their past and present and future shall be unintermitted and shall be done with perfect candor. Upon this basis philosophy speculates ever looking toward the poet, ever regarding the eternal tendencies of all toward happiness never inconsistent with what is clear to the senses and to the soul. For the eternal tendencies of all toward happiness make the only point of sane philosophy. Whatever comprehends less than that . . . whatever is less than the laws of light and of astronomical motion . . . or less than the laws that follow the thief the liar the glutton and the drunkard through this life and doubtless afterward . . . . . . or less than vast stretches of time or the slow formation of density or the patient upheaving of strata—is of no account. Whatever would put God in a poem or system of philosophy as contending against some being or influence is also of no account. Sanity and ensemble characterise the great master . . . spoilt in one principle all is spoilt. The great master has nothing to do with miracles. He sees health for himself in being one of the mass . . . . he sees the hiatus in singular eminence. To the perfect shape comes common ground. To be under the general law is great for that is to correspond with it. The master knows that he is unspeakably great and that all are unspeakably great . . . . that nothing for instance is greater than to conceive children and bring them up well . . . that to be is just as great as to perceive or tell.

In the make of the great masters the idea of political liberty is indispensible. Liberty takes the adherence of heroes wherever men and women exist . . . . but never takes any adherence or welcome from the rest more than from poets. They are the voice and exposition of liberty. They out of ages are worthy the grand idea . . . . to them it is confided and they must sustain it. Nothing has precedence of it and nothing can warp or degrade it. The attitude of great poets is to cheer up slaves and horrify despots. The turn of their necks, the sound of their feet, the motions of their wrists, are full of hazard to the one and hope to the other. Come nigh them awhile and though they neither speak or advise you shall learn the faithful American lesson. Liberty is poorly served by men whose good intent is quelled from one failure or two failures or any number of failures, or from the casual indifference or ingratitude of the people, or from the sharp show of the tushes of power, or the bringing to bear soldiers and cannon or any penal statutes. Liberty relies upon itself, invites no one, promises nothing, sits in calmness and light, is positive and composed, and knows no discouragement. The battle rages with many a loud alarm and frequent advance and retreat . . . . the enemy triumphs . . . . the prison, the handcuffs, the iron necklace and anklet, the scaffold, garrote and leadballs do their work . . . . the cause is asleep . . . . the strong throats are choked with their own blood . . . . the young men drop their eyelashes toward the ground when they pass each other . . . . and is liberty gone out of that place? No never. When liberty goes it is not the first to go nor the second or third to go . . it waits for all the rest to go . . it is the last . . . When the memories of the old martyrs are faded utterly away . . . . when the large names of patriots are laughed at in the public halls from the lips of the orators . . . . when the boys are no more christened after the same but christened after tyrants and traitors instead . . . . when the laws of the free are grudgingly permitted and laws for informers and bloodmoney are sweet to the taste of the people . . . . when I and you walk abroad upon the earth stung with compassion at the sight of numberless brothers answering our equal friendship and calling no man master—and when we are elated with noble joy at the sight of slaves . . . . when the soul retires in the cool communion of the night and surveys its experience and has much extasy over the word and deed that put back a helpless innocent person into the gripe of the gripers or into any cruel inferiority . . . . when those in all parts of these states who could easier realize the true American character but do not yet—when the swarms of cringers, suckers, doughfaces, lice of politics, planners of sly involutions for their own preferment to city offices or state legislatures of the judiciary or congress or the presidency, obtain a response of love and natural deference from the people whether they get the offices or no . . . . when it is better to be a bound booby and rogue in office at a high salary than the poorest free mechanic or farmer with his hat unmoved from his head and firm eyes and a candid and generous heart . . . . and when servility by town or state or the federal government or any oppression on a large scale or small scale can be tried on without its own punishment following duly after in exact proportion against the smallest chance of escape . . . . or rather when all life and all the souls of men and women are discharged from any part of the earth—then only shall the instinct of liberty be discharged from that part of the earth.

As the attributes of the poets of the kosmos concentre in the real body and soul and in the pleasure of things they possess the superiority of genuineness over all fiction and romance. As they emit themselves facts are showered over with light . . . . the daylight is lit with more volatile light . . . . also the deep between the setting and rising sun goes deeper many fold. Each precise object or condition or combination or process exhibits a beauty . . . . the multiplication table its—old age its—the carpenter's trade its—the grand-opera its . . . . the hugehulled cheanshaped New-York clipper at sea under steam or full sail gleams with unmatched beauty . . . . the American circles and large harmonies of government gleam with theirs . . . . and the commonest definite intentions and actions with theirs. The poets of the kosmos advance through all interpositions and coverings and turmoils and strategems to first principles. They are of use . . . . they dissolve poverty from its need and riches from its conceit. You large proprietor they say shall not realize or perceive more than any one else. The owner of the library is not he who holds a legal title to it having bought and paid for it. Any one and every one is owner of the library who can read the same through all the varieties of tongues and subjects and styles, and in whom they enter with ease and take residence and force toward paternity and maternity, and make supple and powerful and rich and large . . . . These American states strong and healthy and accomplished shall receive no pleasure from violations of natural models and must not permit them. In paintings or mouldings or carvings in mineral or wood, or in the illustrations of books or newspapers, or in any comic or tragic prints, or in the patterns of woven stuffs or any thing to beautify rooms or furniture or costumes, or to put upon cornices or monuments or on the prows or sterns of ships, or to put anywhere before the human eye indoors or out, that which distorts honest shapes or which creates unearthly beings or places or contingencies is a nuisance and revolt. Of the human form especially it is so great it must never be made ridiculous. Of ornaments to a work nothing outre[1] can be allowed . . but those ornaments can be allowed that conform to the perfect facts of the open air and that flow out of the nature of the work and come irrepressibly from it and are necessary to the completion of the work. Most works are most beautiful without ornament. . . . Exaggerations will be revenged in human physiology. Clean and vigorous children are jetted and conceived only in those communities where the models of natural forms are public every day. . . . . Great genius and the people of these states must never be demeaned to romances. As soon as histories are properly told there is no more need of romances.

The great poets are also to be known by the absence in them of tricks and by the justification of perfect personal candor. Then folks echo a new cheap joy and a divine voice leaping from their brains: How beautiful is candor! All faults may be forgiven of him who has perfect candor. Henceforth let no man of us lie, for we have seen that openness wins the inner and outer world and that there is no single exception, and that never since our earth gathered itself in a mass have deceit or subterfuge or prevarication attracted its smallest particle or the faintest tinge of a shade—and that through the enveloping wealth and rank of a state or the whole republic of states a sneak or sly person shall be discovered and despised . . . . and that the soul has never been once fooled and never can be fooled . . . . and thrift without the loving nod of the soul is only a fœtid puff . . . . and there never grew up in any of the continents of the globe nor upon any planet or satellite or star, nor upon the asteroids, nor in any part of ethereal space, nor in the midst of density, nor under the fluid wet of the sea, nor in that condition which precedes the birth of babes, nor at any time during the changes of life, nor in that condition that follows what we term death, nor in any stretch of abeyance or action afterward of vitality, nor in any process of formation or reformation anywhere, a being whose instinct hated the truth.

Extreme caution or prudence, the soundest organic health, large hope and comparison and fondness for women and children, large alimentiveness and destructiveness and causality, with a perfect sense of the oneness of nature and the propriety of the same spirit applied to human affairs . . these are called up of the float of the brain of the world to be parts of the greatest poet from his birth out of his mother's womb and from her birth out of her mother's. Caution seldom goes far enough. It has been thought that the prudent citizen was the citizen who applied himself to solid gains and did well for himself and his family and completed a lawful life without debt or crime. The greatest poet sees and admits these economies as he sees the economies of food and sleep, but has higher notions of prudence than to think he gives much when he gives a few slight attentions at the latch of the gate. The premises of the prudence of life are not the hospitality of it or the ripeness and harvest of it. Beyond the independence of a little sum laid aside for burial-money, and of a few clapboards around and shingles overhead on a lot of American soil owned, and the easy dollars that supply the year's plain clothing and meals, the melancholy prudence of the abandonment of such a great being as a man is to the toss and pallor of years of moneymaking with all their scorching days and icy nights and all their stifling deceits and underhanded dodgings, or infinitessimals of

---

1. Excessive, extravagant; an Americanization of the French *outré*.

parlors, or shameless stuffing while others starve . . and all the loss of the
bloom and odor of the earth and of the flowers and atmosphere and of the sea
and of the true taste of the women and men you pass or have to do with in
youth or middle age, and the issuing sickness and desperate revolt at the close
of a life without elevation or naivete, and the ghastly chatter of a death without
serenity or majesty, is the great fraud upon modern civilization and forethought, blotching the surface and system which civilization undeniably
drafts, and moistening with tears the immense features it spreads and spreads
with such velocity before the reached kisses of the soul. . . Still the right explanation remains to be made about prudence. The prudence of the mere wealth
and respectability of the most esteemed life appears too faint for the eye to
observe at all when little and large alike drop quietly aside at the thought of
the prudence suitable for immortality. What is wisdom that fills the thinness
of a year or seventy or eighty years to wisdom spaced out by ages and coming
back at a certain time with strong reinforcements and rich presents and the
clear faces of wedding-guests as far as you can look in every direction running
gaily toward you? Only the soul is of itself . . . . all else has reference to what
ensues. All that a person does or thinks is of consequence. Not a move can a
man or woman make that affects him or her in a day or a month or any part
of the direct lifetime or the hour of death but the same affects him or her
onward afterward through the indirect lifetime. The indirect is always as great
and real as the direct. The spirit receives from the body just as much as it
gives to the body. Not one name of word or deed . . not of venereal sores or
discolorations . . not the privacy of the onanist . . not of the putrid veins of
gluttons or rumdrinkers . . . not peculation or cunning or betrayal or murder
. . no serpentine poison of those that seduce women . . not the foolish yielding
of women . . not prostitution . . not of any depravity of young men . . not of
the attainment of gain by discreditable means . . not any nastiness of appetite
. . not any harshness of officers to men or judges to prisoners or fathers to sons
or sons to fathers or of husbands to wives or bosses to their boys . . not of
greedy looks or malignant wishes . . . nor any of the wiles practised by people
upon themselves . . . ever is or ever can be stamped on the programme but it
is duly realized and returned, and that returned in further performances . . .
and they returned again. Nor can the push of charity or personal force ever be
any thing else than the profoundest reason, whether it brings arguments to
hand or no. No specification is necessary . . to add or subtract or divide is in
vain. Little or big, learned or unlearned, white or black, legal or illegal, sick
or well, from the first inspiration down the windpipe to the last expiration out
of it, all that a male or female does that is vigorous and benevolent and clean
is so much sure profit to him or her in the unshakable order of the universe
and through the whole scope of it forever. If the savage or felon is wise it is
well . . . . if the greatest poet or savan is wise it is simply the same . . if the
President or chief justice is wise it is the same . . . if the young mechanic or
farmer is wise it is no more or less . . if the prostitute is wise it is no more nor
less. The interest will come round . . all will come round. All the best actions
of war and peace . . . all help given to relatives and strangers and the poor and
old and sorrowful and young children and widows and the sick, and to all
shunned persons . . all furtherance of fugitives and of the escape of slaves . .
all the self-denial that stood steady and aloof on wrecks and saw others take the
seats of the boats . . . all offering of substance or life for the good old cause,
or for a friend's sake or opinion's sake . . . all pains of enthusiasts scoffed at by

their neighbors . . all the vast sweet love and precious suffering of mothers
. . . all honest men baffled in strifes recorded or unrecorded . . . . all the
grandeur and good of the few ancient nations whose fragments of annals we
inherit . . and all the good of the hundreds of far mightier and more ancient
nations unknown to us by name or date or location . . . . all that was ever
manfully begun, whether it succeeded or no . . . . all that has at any time
been well suggested out of the divine heart of man or by the divinity of his
mouth or by the shaping of his great hands . . and all that is well thought or
done this day on any part of the surface of the globe . . or on any of the
wandering stars or fixed stars by those there as we are here . . or that is henceforth to be well thought or done by you whoever you are, or by any one—
these singly and wholly inured at their time and inure now and will inure
always to the identities from which they sprung or shall spring . . . Did you
guess any of them lived only its moment? The world does not so exist . . no
parts palpable or impalpable so exist . . . no result exists now without being
from its long antecedent result, and that from its antecedent, and so backward
without the farthest mentionable spot coming a bit nearer the beginning than
any other spot . . . . . Whatever satisfies the soul is truth. The prudence of
the greatest poet answers at last the craving and glut of the soul, is not contemptuous of less ways of prudence if they conform to its ways, puts off nothing, permits no let-up for its own case or any case, has no particular sabbath
or judgment-day, divides not the living from the dead or the righteous from
the unrighteous, is satisfied with the present, matches every thought or act by
its correlative, knows no possible forgiveness or deputed atonement . . knows
that the young man who composedly periled his life and lost it has done
exceeding well for himself, while the man who has not periled his life and
retains it to old age in riches and ease has perhaps achieved nothing for himself
worth mentioning . . and that only that person has no great prudence to learn
who has learnt to prefer real longlived things, and favors body and soul the
same, and perceives the indirect assuredly following the direct, and what evil
or good he does leaping onward and waiting to meet him again—and who in
his spirit in any emergency whatever neither hurries or avoids death.

The direct trial of him who would be the greatest poet is today. If he does
not flood himself with the immediate age as with vast oceanic tides . . . . .
and if he does not attract his own land body and soul to himself and hang on
its neck with incomparable love and plunge his semitic[2] muscle into its merits
and demerits . . . and if he be not himself the age transfigured . . . . and if to
him is not opened the eternity which gives similitude to all periods and loca-
tions and processes and animate and inanimate forms, and which is the bond
of time, and rises up from its inconceivable vagueness and infiniteness in the
swimming shape of today, and is held by the ductile anchors of life, and makes
the present spot the passage from what was to what shall be, and commits itself
to the representation of this wave of an hour and this one of the sixty beautiful
children of the wave—let him merge in the general run and wait his development . . . . Still the final test of poems or any character or work
remains. The prescient poet projects himself centuries ahead and judges performer or performance after the changes of time. Does it live through them?
Does it still hold on untired? Will the same style and the direction of genius
to similar points be satisfactory now? Has no new discovery in science or arrival

---

2. Likely a sexual coinage meaning muscles through which semen passes, especially the muscles of the penis.

at superior planes of thought and judgment and behaviour fixed him or his so that either can be looked down upon? Have the marches of tens and hundreds and thousands of years made willing detours to the right hand and the left hand for his sake? Is he beloved long and long after he is buried? Does the young man think often of him? and the young woman think often of him? and do the middleaged and the old think of him?

A great poem is for ages and ages in common and for all degrees and complexions and all departments and sects and for a woman as much as a man and a man as much as a woman. A great poem is no finish to a man or woman but rather a beginning. Has any one fancied he could sit at last under some due authority and rest satisfied with explanations and realize and be content and full? To no such terminus does the greatest poet bring . . . he brings neither cessation or sheltered fatness and ease. The touch of him tells in action. Whom he takes he takes with firm sure grasp into live regions previously unattained . . . . thenceforward is no rest . . . . they see the space and ineffable sheen that turn the old spots and lights into dead vacuums. The companion of him beholds the birth and progress of stars and learns one of the meanings. Now there shall be a man cohered out of tumult and chaos . . . . the elder encourages the younger and shows him how . . . they two shall launch off fearlessly together till the new world fits an orbit for itself and looks unabashed on the lesser orbits of the stars and sweeps through the ceaseless rings and shall never be quiet again.

There will soon be no more priests. Their work is done. They may wait awhile . . perhaps a generation or two . . dropping off by degrees. A superior breed shall take their place . . . . the gangs of kosmos and prophets en masse shall take their place. A new order shall arise and they shall be the priests of man, and every man shall be his own priest. The churches built under their umbrage[3] shall be the churches of men and women. Through the divinity of themselves shall the kosmos and the new breed of poets be interpreters of men and women and of all events and things. They shall find their inspiration in real objects today, symptoms of the past and future. . . . They shall not deign to defend immortality or God or the perfection of things or liberty or the exquisite beauty and reality of the soul. They shall arise in America and be responded to from the remainder of the earth.

The English language befriends the grand American expression . . . . it is brawny enough and limber and full enough. On the tough stock of a race who through all change of circumstance was never without the idea of political liberty, which is the animus of all liberty, it has attracted the terms of daintier and gayer and subtler and more elegant tongues. It is the powerful language of resistance . . . it is the dialect of common sense. It is the speech of the proud and melancholy races and of all who aspire. It is the chosen tongue to express growth faith self-esteem freedom justice equality friendliness amplitude prudence decision and courage. It is the medium that shall well nigh express the inexpressible.

No great literature nor any like style of behaviour or oratory or social intercourse or household arrangements or public institutions or the treatment by bosses of employed people, nor executive detail or detail of the army or navy, nor spirit of legislation or courts or police or tuition or architecture or songs or amusements or the costumes of young men, can long elude the jealous and

3. Shadow, protection.

passionate instinct of American standards. Whether or no the sign appears from the mouths of the people, it throbs a live interrogation in every freeman's and freewoman's heart after that which passes by or this built to remain. Is it uniform with my country? Are its disposals without ignominious distinctions? Is it for the evergrowing communes of brothers and lovers, large, well-united, proud beyond the old models, generous beyond all models? Is it something grown fresh out of the fields or drawn from the sea for use to me today here? I know that what answers for me an American must answer for any individual or nation that serves for a part of my materials. Does this answer? or is it without reference to universal needs? or sprung of the needs of the less developed society of special ranks? or old needs of pleasure overlaid by modern science and forms? Does this acknowledge liberty with audible and absolute acknowledgement, and set slavery at nought for life and death? Will it help breed one goodshaped and wellhung man, and a woman to be his perfect and independent mate? Does it improve manners? Is it for the nursing of the young of the republic? Does it solve readily with the sweet milk of the nipples of the breasts of the mother of many children? Has it too the old ever-fresh forbearance and impartiality? Does it look with the same love on the last born on those hardening toward stature, and on the errant, and on those who disdain all strength of assault outside of their own?

The poems distilled from other poems will probably pass away. The coward will surely pass away. The expectation of the vital and great can only be satisfied by the demeanor of the vital and great. The swarms of the polished deprecating and reflectors and the polite float off and leave no remembrance. America prepares with composure and goodwill for the visitors that have sent word. It is not intellect that is to be their warrant and welcome. The talented, the artist, the ingenious, the editor, the statesman, the erudite . . they are not unappreciated . . they fall in their place and do their work. The soul of the nation also does its work. No disguise can pass on it . . no disguise can conceal from it. It rejects none, it permits all. Only toward as good as itself and toward the like of itself will it advance half-way. An individual is as superb as a nation when he has the qualities which make a superb nation. The soul of the largest and wealthiest and proudest nation may well go half-way to meet that of its poets. The signs are effectual. There is no fear of mistake. If the one is true the other is true. The proof of a poet is that his country absorbs him as affectionately as he has absorbed it.

1855

From INSCRIPTIONS[1]

When I Read the Book

When I read the book, the biography famous,
And is this then (said I) what the author calls a man's life?

---

1. This title was first used for the opening poems of *Leaves of Grass* in 1871; in 1881 the number of poems was increased from nine to twenty-four, a result not so much of new composition as of a shifting of the contents of the various sections of the book.

And so will some one when I am dead and gone write my life?
(As if any man really knew aught of my life,
Why even I myself I often think know little or nothing of my real life,   5
Only a few hints, a few diffused faint clews and indirections
I seek for my own use to trace out here.)

1867, 1871

Beginning My Studies

Beginning my studies the first step pleas'd me so much,
The mere fact consciousness, these forms, the power of motion,
The least insect or animal, the senses, eyesight, love,
The first step I say awed me and pleas'd me so much,
I have hardly gone and hardly wish'd to go any farther,   5
But stop and loiter all the time to sing it in ecstatic songs.

1865, 1871

Song of Myself[1]

1

I celebrate myself, and sing myself,
And what I assume you shall assume,
For every atom belonging to me as good belongs to you.

I loafe and invite my soul,
I lean and loafe at my ease observing a spear of summer grass.   5

My tongue, every atom of my blood, form'd from this soil, this air,
Born here of parents born here from parents the same, and their parents
    the same,
I, now thirty-seven years old in perfect health begin,
Hoping to cease not till death.

Creeds and schools in abeyance,   10
Retiring back a while sufficed at what they are, but never forgotten,
I harbor for good or bad, I permit to speak at every hazard,
Nature without check with original energy.

1. Undeniably uncouth yet carefully fashioned, the poem was the outgrowth of years of labor; anticipatory notebook entries survive from the late 1840s and related poetic passages from the early 1850s. It first appeared in the 1855 *Leaves of Grass* without a title and with no internal divisions. In the second edition (1856), the title was *Poem of Walt Whitman, an American*; then it became *Walt Whitman* in 1860 and remained under that title until 1881, when it finally became *Song of Myself*. During all of this the poem itself was changed only slightly. Perhaps the most important changes made the purpose of the speaker's journeying more explicit: he is absorbing all that he sees to write the poem.

For textual information and guidance through Whitman's vocabulary, this edition has often drawn on the work of Harold W. Blodgett and Sculley Bradley in *"Leaves of Grass": Comprehensive Reader's Edition* (1965, 1968), reprinted with corrections and additions in the Bradley and Blodgett Norton Critical Edition of *Leaves of Grass* (1973). Unless otherwise indicated, all texts of Whitman's poems are those of the "deathbed" edition, the green hardbound issue of 1891–92.

2

Houses and rooms are full of perfumes, the shelves are crowded with
    perfumes,
I breathe the fragrance myself and know it and like it,   15
The distillation would intoxicate me also, but I shall not let it.

The atmosphere is not a perfume, it has no taste of the distillation, it is
    odorless,
It is for my mouth forever, I am in love with it,
I will go to the bank by the wood and become undisguised and naked,
I am mad for it to be in contact with me.   20

The smoke of my own breath,
Echoes, ripples, buzz'd whispers, love-root, silk-thread, crotch and vine,
My respiration and inspiration, the beating of my heart, the passing of blood
    and air through my lungs,
The sniff of green leaves and dry leaves, and of the shore and dark-color'd sea-
    rocks, and of hay in the barn,
The sound of the belch'd words of my voice loos'd to the eddies of the
    wind,   25
A few light kisses, a few embraces, a reaching around of arms,
The play of shine and shade on the trees as the supple boughs wag,
The delight alone or in the rush of the streets, or along the fields and hill-sides,
The feeling of health, the full-noon trill, the song of me rising from bed and
    meeting the sun.

Have you reckon'd a thousand acres much? have you reckon'd the earth
    much?   30
Have you practis'd so long to learn to read?
Have you felt so proud to get at the meaning of poems?

Stop this day and night with me and you shall possess the origin of all poems,
You shall possess the good of the earth and sun, (there are millions of suns
    left,)
You shall no longer take things at second or third hand, nor look through the
    eyes of the dead, nor feed on the spectres in books,   35
You shall not look through my eyes either, nor take things from me,
You shall listen to all sides and filter them from your self.

3

I have heard what the talkers were talking, the talk of the beginning and the
    end,
But I do not talk of the beginning or the end.

There was never any more inception than there is now,   40
Nor any more youth or age than there is now,
And will never be any more perfection than there is now,
Nor any more heaven or hell than there is now.

Urge and urge and urge,
Always the procreant urge of the world.   45

Out of the dimness opposite equals advance, always substance and increase, always sex,
Always a knit of identity, always distinction, always a breed of life.

To elaborate is no avail, learn'd and unlearn'd feel that it is so.

Sure as the most certain sure, plumb in the uprights, well entretied,[2] braced in the beams,
Stout as a horse, affectionate, haughty, electrical,   50
I and this mystery here we stand.

Clear and sweet is my soul, and clear and sweet is all that is not my soul.

Lack one lacks both, and the unseen is proved by the seen,
Till that becomes unseen and receives proof in its turn.

Showing the best and dividing it from the worst age vexes age,   55
Knowing the perfect fitness and equanimity of things, while they discuss I am silent, and go bathe and admire myself.

Welcome is every organ and attribute of me, and of any man hearty and clean,
Not an inch nor a particle of an inch is vile, and none shall be less familiar than the rest.

I am satisfied—I see, dance, laugh, sing;
As the hugging and loving bed-fellow sleeps at my side through the night, and withdraws at the peep of the day with stealthy tread,   60
Leaving me baskets cover'd with white towels swelling the house with their plenty,
Shall I postpone my acceptation and realization and scream at my eyes,
That they turn from gazing after and down the road,
And forthwith cipher[3] and show me to a cent,
Exactly the value of one and exactly the value of two, and which is ahead? 65

4

Trippers and askers surround me,
People I meet, the effect upon me of my early life or the ward and city I live in, or the nation,
The latest dates, discoveries, inventions, societies, authors old and new,
My dinner, dress, associates, looks, compliments, dues,
The real or fancied indifference of some man or woman I love,   70
The sickness of one of my folks or of myself, or ill-doing or loss or lack of money, or depressions or exaltations,
Battles, the horrors of fratricidal war, the fever of doubtful news, the fitful events;
These come to me days and nights and go from me again,
But they are not the Me myself.

Apart from the pulling and hauling stands what I am,   75
Stands amused, complacent, compassionating, idle, unitary,

---

2. Cross-braced.   3. Calculate.

Looks down, is erect, or bends an arm on an impalpable certain rest,
Looking with side-curved head curious what will come next,
Both in and out of the game and watching and wondering at it.

Backward I see in my own days where I sweated through fog with linguists
    and contenders,   80
I have no mockings or arguments, I witness and wait.

5

I believe in you my soul, the other I am must not abase itself to you,
And you must not be abased to the other.

Loafe with me on the grass, loose the stop from your throat,
Not words, not music or rhyme I want, not custom or lecture, not even the
    best,   85
Only the lull I like, the hum of your valvèd voice.

I mind how once we lay such a transparent summer morning,
How you settled your head athwart my hips and gently turn'd over upon me,
And parted the shirt from my bosom-bone, and plunged your tongue to my
    bare-stript heart,
And reach'd till you felt my beard, and reach'd till you held my feet.   90

Swiftly arose and spread around me the peace and knowledge that pass all the
    argument of the earth,
And I know that the hand of God is the promise of my own,
And I know that the spirit of God is the brother of my own,
And that all the men ever born are also my brothers, and the women my sisters
    and lovers,
And that a kelson[4] of the creation is love,   95
And limitless are leaves stiff or drooping in the fields,
And brown ants in the little wells beneath them,
And mossy scabs of the worm fence, heap'd stones, elder, mullein and poke-
    weed.

6

A child said *What is the grass?* fetching it to me with full hands;
How could I answer the child? I do not know what it is any more than he. 100

I guess it must be the flag of my disposition, out of hopeful green stuff woven.

Or I guess it is the handkerchief of the Lord,
A scented gift and remembrancer designedly dropt,
Bearing the owner's name someway in the corners, that we may see and
    remark, and say *Whose?*

Or I guess the grass is itself a child, the produced babe of the vegetation. 105

---

4. A basic structural unit; a reinforcing timber bolted to the keel (backbone) of a ship.

Or I guess it is a uniform hieroglyphic,
And it means, Sprouting alike in broad zones and narrow zones,
Growing among black folks as among white,
Kanuck, Tuckahoe, Congressman, Cuff,[5] I give them the same, I receive
    them the same.

And now it seems to me the beautiful uncut hair of graves.   110

Tenderly will I use you curling grass,
It may be you transpire from the breasts of young men,
It may be if I had known them I would have loved them,
It may be you are from old people, or from offspring taken soon out of their
    mothers' laps,
And here you are the mothers' laps.   115

This grass is very dark to be from the white heads of old mothers,
Darker than the colorless beards of old men,
Dark to come from under the faint red roofs of mouths.

O I perceive after all so many uttering tongues,
And I perceive they do not come from the roofs of mouths for nothing.   120

I wish I could translate the hints about the dead young men and women,
And the hints about old men and mothers, and the offspring taken soon out of
    their laps.

What do you think has become of the young and old men?
And what do you think has become of the women and children?

They are alive and well somewhere,   125
The smallest sprout shows there is really no death,
And if ever there was it led forward life, and does not wait at the end
    to arrest it,
And ceas'd the moment life appear'd.

All goes onward and outward, nothing collapses,
And to die is different from what any one supposed, and luckier.   130

7

Has any one supposed it lucky to be born?
I hasten to inform him or her it is just as lucky to die, and I know it.

I pass death with the dying and birth with the new-wash'd babe, and am not
    contain'd between my hat and boots,

And peruse manifold objects, no two alike and every one good,
The earth good and the stars good, and their adjuncts all good.   135

---

5. Black, from the African word *cuffee*. "Kanuck": French Canadian. "Tuckahoe": Virginian, from eaters of the
American Indian food plant tuckahoe.

I am not an earth nor an adjunct of an earth,
I am the mate and companion of people, all just as immortal and fathomless
    as myself,
(They do not know how immortal, but I know.)

Every kind for itself and its own, for me mine male and female,
For me those that have been boys and that love women,   140
For me the man that is proud and feels how it stings to be slighted,
For me the sweet-heart and the old maid, for me mothers and the mothers
    of mothers,
For me lips that have smiled, eyes that have shed tears,
For me children and the begetters of children.

Undrape! you are not guilty to me, nor stale nor discarded,   145
I see through the broadcloth and gingham whether or no,
And am around, tenacious, acquisitive, tireless, and cannot be shaken away.

8

The little one sleeps in its cradle,
I lift the gauze and look a long time, and silently brush away flies with my
    hand.

The youngster and the red-faced girl turn aside up the bushy hill,   150
I peeringly view them from the top.

The suicide sprawls on the bloody floor of the bedroom,
I witness the corpse with its dabbled hair, I note where the pistol has fallen.

The blab of the pave, tires of carts, sluff of boot-soles, talk of the promenaders,
The heavy omnibus, the driver with his interrogating thumb, the clank of the
    shod horses on the granite floor,   155
The snow-sleighs, clinking, shouted jokes, pelts of snow-balls,
The hurrahs for popular favorites, the fury of rous'd mobs,
The flap of the curtain'd litter, a sick man inside borne to the hospital,
The meeting of enemies, the sudden oath, the blows and fall,
The excited crowd, the policeman with his star quickly working his passage to
    the centre of the crowd,   160
The impassive stones that receive and return so many echoes,
What groans of over-fed or half-starv'd who fall sunstruck or in fits,
What exclamations of women taken suddenly who hurry home and give birth
    to babes,
What living and buried speech is always vibrating here, what howls restrain'd
    by decorum,
Arrests of criminals, slights, adulterous offers made, acceptances, rejections
    with convex lips,   165
I mind them or the show or resonance of them—I come and I depart.

9

The big doors of the country barn stand open and ready,
The dried grass of the harvest-time loads the slow-drawn wagon,

The clear light plays on the brown gray and green intertinged,
The armfuls are pack'd to the sagging mow.   170

I am there, I help, I came stretch'd atop of the load,
I felt its soft jolts, one leg reclined on the other,
I jump from the cross-beams and sieze the clover and timothy,
And roll head over heels and tangle my hair full of wisps.

10

Alone far in the wilds and mountains I hunt,   175
Wandering amazed at my own lightness and glee,
In the late afternoon choosing a safe spot to pass the night,
Kindling a fire and broiling the fresh-kill'd game,
Falling asleep on the gather'd leaves with my dog and gun by my side.

The Yankee clipper is under her sky-sails, she cuts the sparkle and scud,   180
My eyes settle the land, I bend at her prow or shout joyously from the deck.

The boatmen and clam-diggers arose early and stopt for me,
I tuck'd my trowser-ends in my boots and went and had a good time;
You should have been with us that day round the chowder-kettle.

I saw the marriage of the trapper in the open air in the far west, the bride was
    a red girl,   185
Her father and his friends sat near cross-legged and dumbly smoking, they had
    moccasins to their feet and large thick blankets hanging from their
    shoulders,
On a bank lounged the trapper, he was drest mostly in skins, his luxuriant
    beard and curls protected his neck, he held his bride by the hand,
She had long eyelashes, her head was bare, her coarse straight locks descended
    upon her voluptuous limbs and reach'd to her feet.

The runaway slave came to my house and stopt outside,
I heard his motions crackling the twigs of the woodpile,   190
Through the swung half-door of the kitchen I saw him limpsy[6] and weak,
And went where he sat on a log and led him in and assured him,
And brought water and fill'd a tub for his sweated body and bruis'd feet,
And gave him a room that enter'd from my own, and gave him some coarse
    clean clothes,
And remember perfectly well his revolving eyes and his awkwardness,   195
And remember putting plasters on the galls of his neck and ankles;
He staid with me a week before he was recuperated and pass'd north,
I had him sit next me at table, my fire-lock lean'd in the corner.

11

Twenty-eight young men bathe by the shore,
Twenty-eight young men and all so friendly;   200
Twenty-eight years of womanly life and all so lonesome.

---

6. Limping or swaying.

She owns the fine house by the rise of the bank,
She hides handsome and richly drest aft the blinds of the window.

Which of the young men does she like the best?
Ah the homeliest of them is beautiful to her. 205

Where are you off to, lady? for I see you,
You splash in the water there, yet stay stock still in your room.

Dancing and laughing along the beach came the twenty-ninth bather,
The rest did not see her, but she saw them and loved them.

The beards of the young men glisten'd with wet, it ran from their
    long hair, 210
Little streams pass'd over their bodies.

An unseen hand also pass'd over their bodies,
It descended tremblingly from their temples and ribs.

The young men float on their backs, their white bellies bulge to the sun, they
    do not ask who seizes fast to them,
They do not know who puffs and declines with pendant and bending arch, 215
They do not think whom they souse with spray.

12

The butcher-boy puts off his killing-clothes, or sharpens his knife at the stall
    in the market,
I loiter enjoying his repartee and his shuffle and break-down.[7]

Blacksmiths with grimed and hairy chests environ the anvil,
Each has his main-sledge, they are all out, there is a great heat in the fire. 220

From the cinder-strew'd threshold I follow their movements,
The lithe sheer of their waists plays even with their massive arms,
Overhand the hammers swing, overhand so slow, overhand so sure,
They do not hasten, each man hits in his place.

13

The negro holds firmly the reins of his four horses, the block swags underneath
    on its tied-over chain, 225
The negro that drives the long dray of the stone-yard, steady and tall he stands
    pois'd on one leg on the string-piece,[8]
His blue shirt exposes his ample neck and breast and loosens over his hip-band,
His glance is calm and commanding, he tosses the slouch of his hat away from
    his forehead,
The sun falls on his crispy hair and mustache, falls on the black of his polish'd
    and perfect limbs.

---

7. Two favorite minstrel-show dances: the "shuffle" involves the sliding of feet across the floor and the "break-down" is faster and noiser.

8. Long, heavy timber used to keep a load in place.

I behold the picturesque giant and love him, and I do not stop there,   230
I go with the team also.

In me the caresser of life wherever moving, backward as well as forward sluing,
To niches aside and junior[9] bending, not a person or object missing,
Absorbing all to myself and for this song.

Oxen that rattle the yoke and chain or halt in the leafy shade, what is that you
    express in your eyes?   235
It seems to me more than all the print I have read in my life.

My tread scares the wood-drake and wood-duck on my distant and day-long
    ramble.
They rise together, they slowly circle around.

I believe in those wing'd purposes,
And acknowledge red, yellow, white, playing within me,   240
And consider green and violet and the tufted crown[1] intentional,
And do not call the tortoise unworthy because she is not something else,
And the jay in the woods never studied the gamut,[2] yet trills pretty well to me,
And the look of the bay mare shames silliness out of me.

14

The wild gander leads his flock through the cool night,   245
Ya-honk he says, and sounds it down to me like an invitation,
The pert may suppose it meaningless, but I listening close,
Find its purpose and place up there toward the wintry sky.

The sharp-hoof'd moose of the north, the cat on the house-sill, the chickadee,
    the prairie-dog,
The litter of the grunting sow as they tug at her teats,   250
The brood of the turkey-hen and she with her half-spread wings,
I see in them and myself the same old law.

The press of my foot to the earth springs a hundred affections,
They scorn the best I can do to relate them.

I am enamour'd of growing out-doors,   255
Of men that live among cattle or taste of the ocean or woods,
Of the builders and steerers of ships and the wielders of axes and mauls, and
    the drivers of horses,
I can eat and sleep with them week in and week out.

What is commonest, cheapest, nearest, easiest, is Me,
Me going in for my chances, spending for vast returns,   260
Adorning myself to bestow myself on the first that will take me,
Not asking the sky to come down to my good will,
Scattering it freely forever.

9. Smaller.   2. The series of recognized musical notes.
1. Of the wood drake.

15

The pure contralto sings in the organ loft,
The carpenter dresses his plank, the tongue of his foreplane whistles its wild
    ascending lisp,   265
The married and unmarried children ride home to their Thanksgiving dinner,
The pilot seizes the king-pin, he heaves down with a strong arm,
The mate stands braced in the whale-boat, lance and harpoon are ready,
The duck-shooter walks by silent and cautious stretches,
The deacons are ordain'd with cross'd hands at the altar,   270
The spinning-girl retreats and advances to the hum of the big wheel,
The farmer stops by the bars as he walks on a First-day³ loafe and looks at the
    oats and rye,
The lunatic is carried at last to the asylum a confirm'd case,
(He will never sleep any more as he did in the cot in his mother's bed-room;)
The jour printer⁴ with gray head and gaunt jaws works at his case,   275
He turns his quid of tobacco while his eyes blur with the manuscript;
The malform'd limbs are tied to the surgeon's table,
What is removed drops horribly in a pail;
The quadroon girl is sold at the auction-stand, the drunkard nods by the bar-
    room stove,
The machinist rolls up his sleeves, the policeman travels his beat, the gate-
    keeper marks who pass,   280
The young fellow drives the express-wagon, (I love him, though I do not
    know him;)
The half-breed straps on his light boots to compete in the race,
The western turkey-shooting draws old and young, some lean on their rifles,
    some sit on logs,
Out from the crowd steps the marksman, takes his position, levels his piece;
The groups of newly-come immigrants cover the wharf or levee,   285
As the woolly-pates hoe in the sugar-field, the overseer views them from his
    saddle,
The bugle calls in the ball-room, the gentlemen run for their partners, the
    dancers bow to each other,
The youth lies awake in the cedar-roof'd garret and harks to the musical rain,
The Wolverine⁵ sets traps on the creek that helps fill the Huron,
The squaw wrapt in her yellow-hemm'd cloth is offering moccasins and bead-
    bags for sale,   290
The connoisseur peers along the exhibition-gallery with half-shut eyes bent
    sideways,
As the deck-hands make fast the steamboat the plank is thrown for the shore-
    going passengers,
The young sister holds out the skein while the elder sister winds it off in a ball,
    and stops now and then for the knots,
The one-year wife is recovering and happy having a week ago borne her first
    child,
The clean-hair'd Yankee girl works with her sewing-machine or in the factory
    or mill,   295

---

3. Sunday. Whitman frequently uses the numerical
Quaker substitutes for the customary pagan names of
days and months. "Bars": i.e., of a rail fence.
4. I.e., a journeyman printer, or one who has passed

his apprenticeship and is fully qualified for all professional work. In this usage Whitman may imply that the
man works by the day, without a steady job.
5. Inhabitant of Michigan.

The paving-man[6] leans on his two-handed rammer, the reporter's lead flies
    swiftly over the note-book, the sign-painter is lettering with blue and gold,
The canal boy trots on the tow-path, the book-keeper counts at his desk, the
    shoemaker waxes his thread,
The conductor beats time for the band and all the performers follow him,
The child is baptized, the convert is making his first professions,
The regatta is spread on the bay, the race is begun, (how the white sails
    sparkle!)   300
The drover watching his drove sings out to them that would stray,
The pedler sweats with his pack on his back, (the purchaser higgling about the
    odd cent;)
The bride unrumples her white dress, the minute-hand of the clock moves
    slowly,
The opium-eater reclines with rigid head and just-open'd lips,
The prostitute draggles her shawl, her bonnet bobs on her tipsy and pimpled
    neck,   305
The crowd laugh at her blackguard oaths, the men jeer and wink to each other,

(Miserable! I do not laugh at your oaths nor jeer you;)
The President holding a cabinet council is surrounded by the great Secretaries,
On the piazza walk three matrons stately and friendly with twined arms,
The crew of the fish-smack pack repeated layers of halibut in the hold,   310
The Missourian crosses the plains toting his wares and his cattle,
As the fare-collector goes through the train he gives notice by the jingling of
    loose change,
The floor-men are laying the floor, the tinners are tinning the roof, the masons
    are calling for mortar,
In single file each shouldering his hod pass onward the laborers;
Seasons pursuing each other the indescribable crowd is gather'd, it is the fourth
    of Seventh-month, (what salutes of cannon and small arms!)   315
Seasons pursuing each other the plougher ploughs, the mower mows, and the
    winter-grain falls in the ground;
Off on the lakes the pike-fisher watches and waits by the hole in the frozen
    surface,
The stumps stand thick round the clearing, the squatter strikes deep with his
    axe,
Flatboatmen make fast towards dusk near the cotton-wood or pecan-trees,
Coon-seekers go through the regions of the Red river or through those drain'd
    by the Tennessee, or through those of the Arkansas,   320
Torches shine in the dark that hangs on the Chattahooch or Altamahaw,[7]
Patriarchs sit at supper with sons and grandsons and great-grandsons around
    them,
In walls of adobie, in canvas tents, rest hunters and trappers after their day's
    sport,
The city sleeps and the country sleeps,
The living sleep for their time, the dead sleep for their time,   325
The old husband sleeps by his wife and the young husband sleeps by his wife;
And these tend inward to me, and I tend outward to them,
And such as it is to be of these more or less I am,
And of these one and all I weave the song of myself.

---

6. Man building or repairing streets.   7. Georgia rivers.

16

I am of old and young, of the foolish as much as the wise,   330
Regardless of others, ever regardful of others,
Maternal as well as paternal, a child as well as a man,
Stuff'd with the stuff that is coarse and stuff'd with the stuff that is fine,
One of the Nation of many nations, the smallest the same and the largest
    the same,
A Southerner soon as a Northerner, a planter nonchalant and hospitable down
    by the Oconee[8] I live,   335
A Yankee bound my own way ready for trade, my joints the limberest joints
    on earth and the sternest joints on earth,
A Kentuckian walking the vale of the Elkhorn in my deer-skin leggings, a
    Louisianian or Georgian,
A boatman over lakes or bays or along coasts, a Hoosier, Badger, Buckeye;
At home on Kanadian[9] snow-shoes or up in the bush, or with fishermen off
    Newfoundland,
At home in the fleet of ice-boats, sailing with the rest and tacking,   340
At home on the hills of Vermont or in the woods of Maine, or the Texan
    ranch,
Comrade of Californians, comrade of free North-Westerners, (loving their
    big proportions,)
Comrade of raftsmen and coalmen, comrade of all who shake hands and wel-
    come to drink and meat,
A learner with the simplest, a teacher of the thoughtfullest,
A novice beginning yet experient of myriads of seasons,   345
Of every hue and caste am I, of every rank and religion,
A farmer, mechanic, artist, gentleman, sailor, quaker,
Prisoner, fancy-man, rowdy, lawyer, physician, priest.

I resist any thing better than my own diversity,
Breathe the air but leave plenty after me,   350
And am not stuck up, and am in my place.

(The moth and the fish-eggs are in their place,
The bright suns I see and the dark suns I cannot see are in their place,
The palpable is in its place and the impalpable is in its place.)

17

These are really the thoughts of all men in all ages and lands, they are not
    original with me,   355
If they are not yours as much as mine they are nothing, or next to nothing,
If they are not the riddle and the untying of the riddle they are nothing,
If they are not just as close as they are distant they are nothing.

This is the grass that grows wherever the land is and the water is,
This the common air that bathes the globe.   360

---

8. River in central Georgia.
9. Apparently Whitman found something muscular in

this spelling. "Hoosier, Badger, Buckeye": inhabitants
of Indiana, Wisconsin, and Ohio, respectively.

18

With music strong I come, with my cornets and my drums,
I play not marches for accepted victors only, I play marches for conquer'd and
    slain persons.

Have you heard that it was good to gain the day?
I also say it is good to fall, battles are lost in the same spirit in which they
    are won.

I beat and pound for the dead,   365
I blow through my embouchures[1] my loudest and gayest for them.

Vivas to those who have fail'd!
And to those whose war-vessels sank in the sea!
And to those themselves who sank in the sea!
And to all generals that lost engagements, and all overcome heroes!   370
And the numberless unknown heroes equal to the greatest heroes known!

19

This is the meal equally set, this the meat for natural hunger,
It is for the wicked just the same as the righteous, I make appointments with
    all,
I will not have a single person slighted or left away,
The kept-woman, sponger, thief, are hereby invited,   375
The heavy-lipp'd slave is invited, the venerealee is invited;
There shall be no difference between them and the rest.

This is the press of a bashful hand, this the float and odor of hair,
This is the touch of my lips to yours, this the murmur of yearning,
This the far-off depth and height reflecting my own face,   380
This the thoughtful merge of myself, and the outlet again.

Do you guess I have some intricate purpose?
Well I have, for the Fourth-month showers have, and the mica on the side of
    a rock has.

Do you take it I would astonish?
Does the daylight astonish? does the early redstart twittering through the
    woods?   385
Do I astonish more than they?

This hour I tell things in confidence,
I might not tell everybody, but I will tell you.

20

Who goes there? hankering, gross, mystical, nude;
How is it I extract strength from the beef I eat?   390

---

1. Mouthpieces of musical instruments such as the cornet, mentioned earlier.

What is a man anyhow? what am I? what are you?

All I mark as my own you shall offset it with your own,
Else it were time lost listening to me.

I do not snivel that snivel the world over,
That months are vacuums and the ground but wallow and filth.   395

Whimpering and truckling fold with powders for invalids, conformity goes to
    the fourth-remov'd,[2]
I wear my hat as I please indoors or out.

Why should I pray? why should I venerate and be ceremonious?

Having pried through the strata, analyzed to a hair, counsel'd with doctors and
    calculated close,
I find no sweeter fat than sticks to my bones.   400

In all people I see myself, none more and not one a barley-corn[3] less,
And the good or bad I say of myself I say of them.

I know I am solid and sound,
To me the converging objects of the universe perpetually flow,
All are written to me, and I must get what the writing means.   405

I know I am deathless,
I know this orbit of mine cannot be swept by a carpenter's compass,
I know I shall not pass like a child's carlacue[4] cut with a burnt stick at night.

I know I am august,
I do not trouble my spirit to vindicate itself or be understood,   410
I see that the elementary laws never apologize,
(I reckon I behave no prouder than the level I plant my house by, after all.)

I exist as I am, that is enough,
If no other in the world be aware I sit content,
And if each and all be aware I sit content.   415

One world is aware and by far the largest to me, and that is myself,
And whether I come to my own to-day or in ten thousand or ten million years,
I can cheerfully take it now, or with equal cheerfulness I can wait.

My foothold is tenon'd and mortis'd[5] in granite,
I laugh at what you call dissolution,   420
And I know the amplitude of time.

---

2. Those very remote in relationship; from the genealogical use such as "third cousin, fourth removed."
"Fold with powders": a reference to the custom of a
physician's wrapping up a dose of medicine in a piece
of paper.
3. The seed or grain of barley, but also a unit of measure equal to about one-third inch.

4. Also spelled *curlicue*, a fancy flourish made with a
writing implement, here made in the dark with a
lighted stick, and so lasting only a moment.
5. Carpenter's terms for a particular way of joining two
boards together: a mortise is a cavity in a piece of wood
into which is placed the projection (tenon) from another piece of wood.

21

I am the poet of the Body and I am the poet of the Soul,
The pleasures of heaven are with me and the pains of hell are with me,
The first I graft and increase upon myself, the latter I translate into a new
    tongue.

I am the poet of the woman the same as the man,   425
And I say it is as great to be a woman as to be a man,
And I say there is nothing greater than the mother of men.

I chant the chant of dilation or pride,
We have had ducking and deprecating about enough,
I show that size is only development.   430

Have you outstript the rest? are you the President?
It is a trifle, they will more than arrive there every one, and still pass on.

I am he that walks with the tender and growing night,
I call to the earth and sea half-held by the night.

Press close bare-bosom'd night—press close magnetic nourishing night!   435
Night of south winds—night of the large few stars!
Still nodding night—mad naked summer night.

Smile O voluptuous cool-breath'd earth!
Earth of the slumbering and liquid trees!
Earth of departed sunset—earth of the mountains misty-topt!   440
Earth of the vitreous pour of the full moon just tinged with blue!
Earth of shine and dark mottling the tide of the river!
Earth of the limpid gray of clouds brighter and clearer for my sake!
Far-swooping elbow'd earth—rich apple-blossom'd earth!
Smile, for your lover comes.   445

Prodigal, you have given me love—therefore I to you give love!
O unspeakable passionate love.

22

You sea! I resign myself to you also—I guess what you mean,
I behold from the beach your crooked inviting fingers,
I believe you refuse to go back without feeling of me,   450
We must have a turn together, I undress, hurry me out of sight of the land,
Cushion me soft, rock me in billowy drowse,
Dash me with amorous wet, I can repay you.

Sea of stretch'd ground-swells,
Sea breathing broad and convulsive breaths,
Sea of the brine of life and of unshovell'd yet always-ready graves,   455
Howler and scooper of storms, capricious and dainty sea,
I am integral with you, I too am of one phase and of all phases.

Partaker of influx and efflux I, extoller of hate and conciliation,
Extoller of amies[6] and those that sleep in each others' arms.   460

I am he attesting sympathy,
(Shall I make my list of things in the house and skip the house that supports
    them?)

I am not the poet of goodness only, I do not decline to be the poet of wick-
    edness also.

What blurt is this about virtue and about vice?
Evil propels me and reform of evil propels me, I stand indifferent,   465
My gait is no fault-finder's or rejecter's gait,
I moisten the roots of all that has grown.

Did you fear some scrofula out of the unflagging pregnancy?
Did you guess the celestial laws are yet to be work'd over and rectified?

I find one side a balance and the antipodal side a balance,   470
Soft doctrine as steady help as stable doctrine,
Thoughts and deeds of the present our rouse and early start.

This minute that comes to me over the past decillions,
There is no better than it and now.

What behaved well in the past or behaves well to-day is not such a wonder,   475
The wonder is always and always how there can be a mean man or an infidel.

23

Endless unfolding of words of ages!
And mine a word of the modern, the word En-Masse.

A word of the faith that never balks,
Here or henceforward it is all the same to me, I accept Time absolutely.   480

It alone is without flaw, it alone rounds and completes all,
That mystic baffling wonder alone completes all.

I accept Reality and dare not question it.
Materialism first and last imbuing.

Hurrah for positive science! long live exact demonstration!   485
Fetch stonecrop[7] mixt with cedar and branches of lilac,
This is the lexicographer, this the chemist, this made a grammar of the old car-
    touches,[8]
These mariners put the ship through dangerous unknown seas,
This is the geologist, this works with the scalpel, and this is a mathematician.

---

6. Friends (French), in Whitman's specialized sense
of comrades.
7. A fleshy-leafed plant of the genus *Sedum*.
8. Scroll-like tablet with space for an inscription.

Whitman knew the Egyptian cartouches with hieroglyphics, the deciphering of which contributed to
knowledge of ancient life.

Gentlemen, to you the first honors always!   490
Your facts are useful, and yet they are not my dwelling,
I but enter by them to an area of my dwelling.

Less the reminders of properties told my words,
And more the reminders they of life untold, and of freedom and extrication,
And make short account of neuters and geldings, and favor men and women
    fully equipt,   495
And beat the gong of revolt, and stop with fugitives and them that plot and
    conspire.

24

Walt Whitman, a kosmos, of Manhattan the son,
Turbulent, fleshy, sensual, eating, drinking and breeding,
No sentimentalist, no stander above men and women or apart from them,
No more modest than immodest.   500

Unscrews the locks from the doors!
Unscrews the doors themselves from their jambs!

Whoever degrades another degrades me,
And whatever is done or said returns at last to me.

Through me the afflatus[9] surging and surging, through me the current and
    index.   505

I speak the pass-word primeval, I give the sign of democracy,
By God! I will accept nothing which all cannot have their counterpart of on
    the same terms.

Through me many long dumb voices,
Voices of the interminable generations of prisoners and slaves,
Voices of the diseas'd and despairing and of thieves and dwarfs,   510

Voices of cycles of preparation and accretion,
And of the threads that connect the stars, and of wombs and of the father-stuff,
And of the rights of them the others are down upon,
Of the deform'd, trivial, flat, foolish, despised,
Fog in the air, beetles rolling balls of dung.   515

Through me forbidden voices,
Voices of sexes and lusts, voices veil'd and I remove the veil,
Voices indecent by me clarified and transfigur'd.

I do not press my fingers across my mouth,
I keep as delicate around the bowels as around the head and heart,   520
Copulation is no more rank to me than death is.

---

9. Divine wind or spirit.

I believe in the flesh and the appetites,
Seeing, hearing, feeling, are miracles, and each part and tag of me is a
     miracle.

Divine am I inside and out, and I make holy whatever I touch or am touch'd
     from,
The scent of these arm-pits aroma finer than prayer,   525
This head more than churches, bibles, and all the creeds.

If I worship one thing more than another it shall be the spread of my own
     body, or any part of it,
Translucent mould of me it shall be you!
Shaded ledges and rests it shall be you!
Firm masculine colter[1] it shall be you!   530
Whatever goes to the tilth[2] of me it shall be you!
You my rich blood! your milky stream pale strippings of my life!
Breast that presses against other breasts it shall be you!
My brain it shall be your occult convolutions!
Root of wash'd sweet-flag! timorous pond-snipe! nest of guarded duplicate eggs!
     it shall be you!   535
Mix'd tussled hay of head, beard, brawn, it shall be you!
Trickling sap of maple, fibre of manly wheat, it shall be you!
Sun so generous it shall be you!
Vapors lighting and shading my face it shall be you!
You sweaty brooks and dews it shall be you!   540
Winds whose soft-tickling genitals rub against me it shall be you!
Broad muscular fields, branches of live oak, loving lounger in my winding
     paths, it shall be you!
Hands I have taken, face I have kiss'd, mortal I have ever touch'd, it shall
     be you.

I dote on myself, there is that lot of me and all so luscious,
Each moment and whatever happens thrills me with joy,   545
I cannot tell how my ankles bend, nor whence the cause of my faintest wish,
Nor the cause of the friendship I emit, nor the cause of the friendship I take
     again.

That I walk up my stoop, I pause to consider if it really be,
A morning-glory at my window satisfies me more than the metaphysics of
     books.

To behold the day-break!   550
The little light fades the immense and diaphanous shadows,
The air tastes good to my palate.

Hefts[3] of the moving world at innocent gambols silently rising freshly exuding,
Scooting obliquely high and low.

1. This phallic passage begins with reference to the   provement.
blade at the front of a plow.   3. Something being heaved or raised upward.
2. Plowing; here, any cultivation or personal im-

Something I cannot see puts upward libidinous prongs,   555
Seas of bright juice suffuse heaven.

The earth by the sky staid with, the daily close of their junction,
The heav'd challenge from the east that moment over my head,
The mocking taunt, See then whether you shall be master!

25

Dazzling and tremendous how quick the sun-rise would kill me,   560
If I could not now and always send sun-rise out of me.

We also ascend dazzling and tremendous as the sun,
We found our own O my soul in the calm and cool of the day-break.

My voice goes after what my eyes cannot reach,
With the twirl of my tongue I encompass worlds and volumes of worlds.   565

Speech is the twin of my vision, it is unequal to measure itself,
It provokes me forever, it says sarcastically,
Walt you contain enough, why don't you let it out then?

Come now I will not be tantalized, you conceive too much of articulation,
Do you not know O speech how the buds beneath you are folded?   570
Waiting in gloom, protected by frost,
The dirt receding before my prophetical screams,
I underlying causes to balance them at last,
My knowledge my live parts, it keeping tally with the meaning of all things,
Happiness, (which whoever hears me let him or her set out in search of this
     day.)   575

My final merit I refuse you, I refuse putting from me what I really am,
Encompass worlds, but never try to encompass me.
I crowd your sleekest and best by simply looking toward you.

Writing and talk do not prove me,
I carry the plenum[4] of proof and every thing else in my face,   580
With the hush of my lips I wholly confound the skeptic.

26

Now I will do nothing but listen,
To accrue what I hear into this song, to let sounds contribute toward it.

I hear bravuras of birds, bustle of growing wheat, gossip of flames, clack of
     sticks cooking my meals,
I hear the sound I love, the sound of the human voice,   585
I hear all sounds running together, combined, fused or following,
Sounds of the city and sounds out of the city, sounds of the day and night,
Talkative young ones to those that like them, the loud laugh of work-people at
     their meals,

---

4. Fullness.

The angry base of disjointed friendship, the faint tones of the sick,
The judge with hands tight to the desk, his pallid lips pronouncing a death-
    sentence,   590
The heave'e'yo of stevedores unlading ships by the wharves, the refrain of the
    anchor-lifters,
The ring of alarm-bells, the cry of fire, the whirr of swift-streaking engines and
    hose-carts with premonitory tinkles and color'd lights,
The steam-whistle, the solid roll of the train of approaching cars,
The slow march play'd at the head of the association marching two and two,
(They go to guard some corpse, the flag-tops are draped with black
    muslin.)   595

I hear the violoncello ('tis the young man's heart's complaint,)
I hear the key'd cornet, it glides quickly in through my ears,
It shakes mad-sweet pangs through my belly and breast.

I hear the chorus, it is a grand opera,
Ah this indeed is music—this suits me.   600

A tenor large and fresh as the creation fills me,
The orbic flex of his mouth is pouring and filling me full.

I hear the train'd soprano (what work with hers is this?)
The orchestra whirls me wider than Uranus[5] flies,
It wrenches such ardors from me I did not know I possess'd them,   605
It sails me, I dab with bare feet, they are lick'd by the indolent waves,
I am cut by bitter and angry hail, I lose my breath,
Steep'd amid honey'd morphine, my windpipe throttled in fakes[6] of death,
At length let up again to feel the puzzle of puzzles,
And that we call Being.   610

27

To be in any form, what is that?
(Round and round we go, all of us, and ever come back thither,)
If nothing lay more develop'd the quahaug[7] in its callous shell were enough.

Mine is no callous shell,
I have instant conductors all over me whether I pass or stop,   615
They seize every object and lead it harmlessly through me.

I merely stir, press, feel with my fingers, and am happy,
To touch my person to some one else's is about as much as I can stand.

28

Is this then a touch? quivering me to a new identity,
Flames and ether making a rush for my veins,   620
Treacherous tip of me reaching and crowding to help them,

5. At that time Uranus (the seventh planet from the   6. Coils of rope.
sun) was thought to be the most remote planet in our   7. Edible clam of the Atlantic coast.
solar system.

My flesh and blood playing out lightning to strike what is hardly different
    from myself,
On all sides prurient provokers stiffening my limbs,
Straining the udder of my heart for its withheld drip,
Behaving licentious toward me, taking no denial,   625
Depriving me of my best as for a purpose,
Unbuttoning my clothes, holding me by the bare waist,
Deluding my confusion with the calm of the sunlight and pasture-fields,
Immodestly sliding the fellow-senses away,
They bribed to swap off with touch and go and graze at the edges of me,   630
No consideration, no regard for my draining strength or my anger,
Fetching the rest of the herd around to enjoy them a while,
Then all uniting to stand on a headland and worry me.

The sentries desert every other part of me,
They have left me helpless to a red marauder,   635
They all come to the headland to witness and assist against me.

I am given up by traitors,
I talk wildly, I have lost my wits, I and nobody else am the greatest traitor,
I went myself first to the headland, my own hands carried me there.

You villain touch! what are you doing? my breath is tight in its throat,   640
Unclench your floodgates, you are too much for me.

29

Blind loving wrestling touch, sheath'd hooded sharp-tooth'd touch!
Did it make you ache so, leaving me?

Parting track'd by arriving, perpetual payment of perpetual loan,
Rich showering rain, and recompense richer afterward.   645

Sprouts take and accumulate, stand by the curb prolific and vital,
Landscapes projected masculine, full-sized and golden.

30

All truths wait in all things,
They neither hasten their own delivery nor resist it,
They do not need the obstetric forceps of the surgeon,   650
The insignificant is as big to me as any,
(What is less or more than a touch?)

Logic and sermons never convince,
The damp of the night drives deeper into my soul.

(Only what proves itself to every man and woman is so,   655
Only what nobody denies is so.)

A minute and a drop of me settle my brain,
I believe the soggy clods shall become lovers and lamps,

And a compend[8] of compends is the meat of a man or woman,
And a summit and flower there is the feeling they have for each other,　660
And they are to branch boundlessly out of that lesson until it becomes omnific,[9]
And until one and all shall delight us, and we them.

31

I believe a leaf of grass is no less than the journey-work of the stars,
And the pismire[1] is equally perfect, and a grain of sand, and the egg of the
　　wren,
And the tree-toad is a chief-d'œuvre for the highest,　665
And the running blackberry would adorn the parlors of heaven,
And the narrowest hinge in my hand puts to scorn all machinery,
And the cow crunching with depress'd head surpasses any statue,
And a mouse is miracle enough to stagger sextillions of infidels.

I find I incorporate gneiss,[2] coal, long-threaded moss, fruits, grains, esculent
　　roots,　670
And am stucco'd with quadrupeds and birds all over,
And have distanced what is behind me for good reasons,
But call any thing back again when I desire it.

In vain the speeding or shyness,
In vain the plutonic rocks[3] send their old heat against my approach,　675
In vain the mastodon retreats beneath its own powder'd bones,
In vain objects stand leagues off and assume manifold shapes,
In vain the ocean settling in hollows and the great monsters lying low,
In vain the buzzard houses herself with the sky,
In vain the snake slides through the creepers and logs,　680
In vain the elk takes to the inner passes of the woods,
In vain the razor-bill'd auk sails far north to Labrador,
I follow quickly, I ascend to the nest in the fissure of the cliff.

32

I think I could turn and live with animals, they are so placid and self-contain'd,
I stand and look at them long and long.　685

They do not sweat and whine about their condition,
They do not lie awake in the dark and weep for their sins,
They do not make me sick discussing their duty to God,
Not one is dissatisfied, not one is demented with the mania of owning things,
Not one kneels to another, nor to his kind that lived thousands of years
　　ago,　690
Not one is respectable or unhappy over the whole earth.

So they show their relations to me and I accept them,
They bring me tokens of myself, they evince them plainly in their possession.

8. I.e., a compendium, where something is reduced
to a short, essential summary.
9. All-encompassing.
1. Ant.

2. Metamorphic rock in which minerals are arranged
in layers.
3. Rock of igneus (fire created) or magmatic (molten)
origin (from Pluto, ruler of infernal regions).

I wonder where they get those tokens,
Did I pass that way huge times ago and negligently drop them?   695

Myself moving forward then and now and forever,
Gathering and showing more always and with velocity,
Infinite and omnigenous,⁴ and the like of these among them,
Not too exclusive toward the reachers of my remembrancers,
Picking out here one that I love, and now go with him on brotherly terms.   700

A gigantic beauty of a stallion, fresh and responsive to my caresses,
Head high in the forehead, wide between the ears,
Limbs glossy and supple, tail dusting the ground,
Eyes full of sparkling wickedness, ears finely cut, flexibly moving.

His nostrils dilate as my heels embrace him,   705
His well-built limbs tremble with pleasure as we race around and return.

I but use you a minute, then I resign you, stallion,
Why do I need your paces when I myself out-gallop them?
Even as I stand or sit passing faster than you.

33

Space and Time! now I see it is true, what I guess'd at,   710
What I guess'd when I loaf'd on the grass,
What I guess'd while I lay alone in my bed,
And again as I walk'd the beach under the paling stars of the morning.

My ties and ballasts leave me, my elbows rest in sea-gaps,⁵
I skirt sierras, my palms cover continents,   715
I am afoot with my vision.

By the city's quadrangular houses—in log huts, camping with lumbermen,
Along the ruts of the turnpike, along the dry gulch and rivulet bed,
Weeding my onion-patch or hoeing rows of carrots and parsnips, crossing
    savannas,⁶ trailing in forests,
Prospecting, gold-digging, girdling the trees of a new purchase,   720
Scorch'd ankle-deep by the hot sand, hauling my boat down the shallow river,
Where the panther walks to and fro on a limb overhead, where the buck turns
    furiously at the hunter,
Where the rattlesnake suns his flabby length on a rock, where the otter is
    feeding on fish,
Where the alligator in his tough pimples sleeps by the bayou,
Where the black bear is searching for roots or honey, where the beaver pats
    the mud with his paddle-shaped tail;   725
Over the growing sugar, over the yellow-flower'd cotton plant, over the rice in
    its low moist field,
Over the sharp-peak'd farm house, with its scallop'd scum and slender shoots
    from the gutters,⁷

4. Belonging to every form of life.
5. Estuaries or bays.
6. Flat, treeless, tropical grassland.

7. Presumably debris washed or blown down roofs,
settling into scalloplike shapes in the gutter and providing nutrients for grasses or weeds.

Over the western persimmon, over the long-leav'd corn, over the delicate blue-
flower flax,
Over the white and brown buckwheat, a hummer and buzzer there with the
rest,
Over the dusky green of the rye as it ripples and shades in the breeze;   730
Scaling mountains, pulling myself cautiously up, holding on by low scragged
limbs,
Walking the path worn in the grass and beat through the leaves of the brush,
Where the quail is whistling betwixt the woods and the wheat-lot,
Where the bat flies in the Seventh-month eve, where the great gold-bug drops
through the dark,
Where the brook puts out of the roots of the old tree and flows to the
meadow,   735
Where cattle stand and shake away flies with the tremulous shuddering of
their hides,
Where the cheese-cloth hangs in the kitchen, where andirons straddle the
hearth-slab, where cobwebs fall in festoons from the rafters;
Where trip-hammers crash, where the press is whirling its cylinders,
Wherever the human heart beats with terrible throes under its ribs,
Where the pear-shaped balloon is floating aloft, (floating in it myself and look-
ing composedly down,)   740
Where the life-car[8] is drawn on the slip-noose, where the heat hatches pale-
green eggs in the dented sand,
Where the she-whale swims with her calf and never forsakes it,
Where the steam-ship trails hind-ways its long pennant of smoke,
Where the fin of the shark cuts like a black chip out of the water,
Where the half-burn'd brig is riding on unknown currents,   745
Where shells grow to her slimy deck, where the dead are corrupting below;
Where the dense-star'd flag is borne at the head of the regiments,
Approaching Manhattan up by the long-stretching island,
Under Niagara, the cataract falling like a veil over my countenance,
Upon a door-step, upon the horse-block of hard wood outside,   750
Upon the race-course, or enjoying picnics or jigs or a good game of baseball,
At he-festivals, with blackguard gibes, ironical license, bull-dances,[9] drinking,
laughter,
At the cider-mill tasting the sweets of the brown mash, sucking the juice through
a straw,
At apple-peelings wanting kisses for all the red fruit I find,
At musters, beach-parties, friendly bees,[1] huskings, house-raisings;   755
Where the mocking-bird sounds his delicious gurgles, cackles, screams, weeps,
Where the hay-rick stands in the barn-yard, where the dry-stalks are scatter'd,
where the brood-cow waits in the hovel,
Where the bull advances to do his masculine work, where the stud to the
mare, where the cock is treading the hen,
Where the heifers browse, where geese nip their food with short jerks,
Where sun-down shadows lengthen over the limitless and lonesome
prairie,   760
Where herds of buffalo make a crawling spread of the square miles far and
near,

8. Watertight compartment for lowering passengers
from a ship when emergency evacuation is required.
9. Rowdy backwoods dances for which, in the absence
of women, men took male partners.

1. Gathering where people work while socializing with
their neighbors. "Musters": any assemblage of people,
but particularly a gathering of military troops for drill.

Where the humming-bird shimmers, where the neck of the long-lived swan is
    curving and winding,
Where the laughing-gull scoots by the shore, where she laughs her near-human
    laugh,
Where bee-hives range on a gray bench in the garden half hid by the high
    weeds,
Where band-neck'd partridges roost in a ring on the ground with their heads
    out,   765
Where burial coaches enter the arch'd gates of a cemetery,
Where winter wolves bark amid wastes of snow and icicled trees,
Where the yellow-crown'd heron comes to the edge of the marsh at night and
    feeds upon small crabs,
Where the splash of swimmers and divers cools the warm noon,
Where the katy-did works her chromatic[2] reed on the walnut-tree over the
    well,   770
Through patches of citrons and cucumbers with silver-wired leaves,
Through the salt-lick or orange glade, or under conical firs,
Through the gymnasium, through the curtain'd saloon, through the office or
    public hall;
Pleas'd with the native and pleas'd with the foreign, pleas'd with the new and
    old,
Pleas'd with the homely woman as well as the handsome,   775
Pleas'd with the quakeress as she puts off her bonnet and talks melodiously,
Pleas'd with the tune of the choir of the whitewash'd church,
Pleas'd with the earnest words of the sweating Methodist preacher, impress'd
    seriously at the camp-meeting;
Looking in at the shop-windows of Broadway the whole forenoon, flatting the
    flesh of my nose on the thick plate glass,
Wandering the same afternoon with my face turn'd up to the clouds, or down
    a lane or along the beach,   780
My right and left arms round the sides of two friends, and I in the middle;
Coming home with the silent and dark-cheek'd bush-boy, (behind me he rides
    at the drape of the day,)
Far from the settlements studying the print of animals' feet, or the moccasin
    print,
By the cot in the hospital reaching lemonade to a feverish patient,
Nigh the coffin'd corpse when all is still, examining with a candle;   785
Voyaging to every port to dicker and adventure,
Hurrying with the modern crowd as eager and fickle as any,
Hot toward one I hate, ready in my madness to knife him,
Solitary at midnight in my back yard, my thoughts gone from me a long while,
Walking the old hills of Judæa with the beautiful gentle God by my side,   790
Speeding through space, speeding through heaven and the stars,
Speeding amid the seven satellites[3] and the broad ring, and the diameter of
    eighty thousand miles,
Speeding with tail'd meteors, throwing fire-balls like the rest,
Carrying the crescent child that carries its own full mother in its belly,
Storming, enjoying, planning, loving, cautioning,   795
Backing and filling, appearing and disappearing,
I tread day and night such roads.

---

2. Consisting of chords or harmonies based on non-harmonic tones.

3. The seven then-known satellites (moons) of Saturn.

I visit the orchards of spheres and look at the product,
And look at quintillions ripen'd and look at quintillions green.

I fly those flights of a fluid and swallowing soul, 800
My course runs below the soundings of plummets.

I help myself to material and immaterial,
No guard can shut me off, no law prevent me.

I anchor my ship for a little while only,
My messengers continually cruise away or bring their returns to me. 805

I go hunting polar furs and the seal, leaping chasms with a pike-pointed staff,
    clinging to topples of brittle and blue.[4]

I ascend to the foretruck,
I take my place late at night in the crow's-nest,
We sail the arctic sea, it is plenty light enough,
Through the clear atmosphere I stretch around on the wonderful beauty, 810
The enormous masses of ice pass me and I pass them, the scenery is plain in
    all directions,
The white-topt mountains show in the distance, I fling out my fancies toward
    them,
We are approaching some great battle-field in which we are soon to be
    engaged,
We pass the colossal outposts of the encampment, we pass with still feet and
    caution,
Or we are entering by the suburbs some vast and ruin'd city, 815
The blocks and fallen architecture more than all the living cities of the globe.

I am a free companion, I bivouac by invading watchfires,
I turn the bridegroom out of bed and stay with the bride myself,
I tighten her all night to my thighs and lips.

My voice is the wife's voice, the screech by the rail of the stairs, 820
They fetch my man's body up dripping and drown'd.

I understand the large hearts of heroes,
The courage of present times and all times,
How the skipper saw the crowded and rudderless wreck of the steam-ship, and
    Death chasing it up and down the storm,
How he knuckled tight and gave not back an inch, and was faithful of days
    and faithful of nights, 825
And chalk'd in large letters on a board, *Be of good cheer, we will not desert you;*
How he follow'd with them and tack'd with them three days and would not
    give it up,
How he saved the drifting company at last,
How the lank loose-gown'd women look'd when boated from the side of their
    prepared graves,
How the silent old-faced infants and the lifted sick, and the sharp-lipp'd unshaved
    men; 830

4. Toppled pieces of ice.

All this I swallow, it tastes good, I like it well, it becomes mine,
I am the man, I suffer'd, I was there.

The disdain and calmness of martyrs,
The mother of old, condemn'd for a witch, burnt with dry wood, her children
    gazing on,
The hounded slave that flags in the race, leans by the fence, blowing, cover'd
    with sweat,   835
The twinges that sting like needles his legs and neck, the murderous buckshot
    and the bullets,
All these I feel or am.

I am the hounded slave, I wince at the bite of the dogs,
Hell and despair are upon me, crack and again crack the marksmen,
I clutch the rails of the fence, my gore dribs, thinn'd with the ooze of my
    skin,[5]   840
I fall on the weeds and stones,
The riders spur their unwilling horses, haul close,
Taunt my dizzy ears and beat me violently over the head with whip-stocks.

Agonies are one of my changes of garments,
I do not ask the wounded person how he feels, I myself become the wounded
    person,   845
My hurts turn livid upon me as I lean on a cane and observe.

I am the mash'd fireman with breast-bone broken,
Tumbling walls buried me in their debris,
Heat and smoke I inspired, I heard the yelling shouts of my comrades,
I heard the distant click of their picks and shovels,   850
They have clear'd the beams away, they tenderly lift me forth.

I lie in the night air in my red shirt, the pervading hush is for my sake,
Painless after all I lie exhausted but not so unhappy,
White and beautiful are the faces around me, the heads are bared of their
    fire-caps,
The kneeling crowd fades with the light of the torches.   855

Distant and dead resuscitate,
They show as the dial or move as the hands of me, I am the clock myself.

I am an old artillerist, I tell of my fort's bombardment,
I am there again.

Again the long roll of the drummers,   860
Again the attacking cannon, mortars,
Again to my listening ears the cannon responsive.

I take part, I see and hear the whole,
The cries, curses, roar, the plaudits of well-aim'd shots,
The ambulanza slowly passing trailing its red drip,   865

5. Dribbles down, diluted with sweat.

Workmen searching after damages, making indispensable repairs,
The fall of grenades through the rent roof, the fan-shaped explosion,
The whizz of limbs, heads, stone, wood, iron, high in the air.

Again gurgles the mouth of my dying general, he furiously waves with his
    hand,
He gasps through the clot *Mind not me—mind—the entrenchments.*   870

34

Now I tell what I knew in Texas in my early youth,
(I tell not the fall of Alamo,
Not one escaped to tell the fall of Alamo,[6]
The hundred and fifty are dumb yet at Alamo,)
'Tis the tale of the murder in cold blood of four hundred and twelve young
    men.   875

Retreating they had form'd in a hollow square with their baggage for breast-
    works,
Nine hundred lives out of the surrounding enemy's, nine times their number,
    was the price they took in advance,
Their colonel was wounded and their ammunition gone,
They treated for an honorable capitulation, receiv'd writing and seal, gave up
    their arms and march'd back prisoners of war.

They were the glory of the race of rangers,   880
Matchless with horse, rifle, song, supper, courtship,
Large, turbulent, generous, handsome, proud, and affectionate,
Bearded, sunburnt, drest in the free costume of hunters,
Not a single one over thirty years of age.

The second First-day morning they were brought out in squads and massacred,
    it was beautiful early summer,   885
The work commenced about five o'clock and was over by eight.

None obey'd the command to kneel,
Some made a mad and helpless rush, some stood stark and straight,
A few fell at once, shot in the temple or heart, the living and dead lay together,
The maim'd and mangled dug in the dirt, the new-comers saw them there,   890
Some half-kill'd attempted to crawl away,
These were despatch'd with bayonets or batter'd with the blunts of muskets,
A youth not seventeen years old seiz'd his assassin till two more came to
    release him,
The three were all torn and cover'd with the boy's blood.

At eleven o'clock began the burning of the bodies;   895
That is the tale of the murder of the four hundred and twelve young men.

---

6. The fall of the Alamo during the Mexican War was already well established in the American conscious-ness. Whitman here celebrates a lesser-known but bloodier massacre, the murder of some four hundred "Texans" (most of them new emigrants from southern states) after they surrendered to the Mexicans near Gol-iad (now in Texas) in late March 1836, three weeks after the fall of the Alamo (now in San Antonio, Texas).

35

Would you hear of an old-time sea-fight?[7]
Would you learn who won by the light of the moon and stars?
List to the yarn, as my grandmother's father the sailor told it to me.

Our foe was no skulk in his ship I tell you, (said he,)   900
His was the surly English pluck, and there is no tougher or truer, and never
    was, and never will be;
Along the lower'd eve he came horribly raking us.

We closed with him, the yards entangled, the cannon touch'd,
My captain lash'd fast with his own hands.

We had receiv'd some eighteen pound shots under the water,   905
On our lower-gun-deck two large pieces had burst at the first fire, killing all
    around and blowing up overhead.

Fighting at sun-down, fighting at dark,
Ten o'clock at night, the full moon well up, our leaks on the gain, and five
    feet of water reported,
The master-at-arms loosing the prisoners confined in the after-hold to give
    them a chance for themselves.

The transit to and from the magazine[8] is now stopt by the sentinels,   910
They see so many strange faces they do not know whom to trust.

Our frigate takes fire,
The other asks if we demand quarter?
If our colors are struck and the fighting done?

Now I laugh content, for I hear the voice of my little captain,   915
We have not struck, he composedly cries, *we have just begun our part of the
    fighting.*

Only three guns are in use,
One is directed by the captain himself against the enemy's mainmast,
Two well serv'd with grape and canister[9] silence his musketry and clear his
    decks.

The tops[1] alone second the fire of this little battery, especially the main-
    top,   920
They hold out bravely during the whole of the action.

Not a moment's cease,
The leaks gain fast on the pumps, the fire eats toward the powder-magazine.

---

7. The famous Revolutionary sea battle on September
23, 1779, between the American *BonHomme Richard*,
commanded by John Paul Jones, and the British *Ser-
apis* off the coast of Yorkshire. A brilliant account of
the battle, based on naval histories, is in Melville's *Israel Potter*, chaps. 19 and 20.

8. Storeroom for ammunition.
9. Grapeshot ("grape"), clusters of small iron balls,
was packed inside a metal cylinder ("canister") and
used to charge a cannon.
1. Platforms enclosing the heads of each mast (here,
the sailors manning the tops).

One of the pumps has been shot away, it is generally thought we are sinking.

Serene stands the little captain,   925
He is not hurried, his voice is neither high nor low,
His eyes give more light to us than our battle-lanterns.

Toward twelve there in the beams of the moon they surrender to us.

36

Stretch'd and still lies the midnight,
Two great hulls motionless on the breast of the darkness,   930
Our vessel riddled and slowly sinking, preparations to pass to the one we have
    conquer'd,

The captain on the quarter-deck coldly giving his orders through a counte-
    nance white as a sheet,
Near by the corpse of the child that serv'd in the cabin,
The dead face of an old salt with long white hair and carefully curl'd whiskers,
The flames spite of all that can be done flickering aloft and below,   935
The husky voices of the two or three officers yet fit for duty,
Formless stacks of bodies and bodies by themselves, dabs of flesh upon the
    masts and spars,
Cut of cordage, dangle of rigging, slight shock of the soothe of waves,
Black and impassive guns, litter of powder-parcels, strong scent,
A few large stars overhead, silent and mournful shining,   940
Delicate sniffs of sea-breeze, smells of sedgy grass and fields by the shore,
    death-messages given in charge to survivors,
The hiss of the surgeon's knife, the gnawing teeth of his saw,
Wheeze, cluck, swash of falling blood, short wild scream, and long, dull,
    tapering groan,
These so, these irretrievable.

37

You laggards there on guard! look to your arms!   945
In at the conquer'd doors they crowd! I am possess'd!
Embody all presences outlaw'd or suffering,
See myself in prison shaped like another man,
And feel the dull unintermitted pain.

For me the keepers of convicts shoulder their carbines and keep watch,   950
It is I let out in the morning and barr'd at night.

Not a mutineer walks handcuff'd to jail but I am handcuff'd to him and walk
    by his side,
(I am less the jolly one there, and more the silent one with sweat on my
    twitching lips.)

Not a youngster is taken for larceny but I go up too, and am tried and
    sentenced.

Not a cholera patient lies at the last gasp but I also lie at the last gasp,   955
My face is ash-color'd, my sinews gnarl, away from me people retreat.

Askers embody themselves in me and I am embodied in them,
I project my hat, sit shame-faced, and beg.

38

Enough! enough! enough!
Somehow I have been stunn'd. Stand back!   960
Give me a little time beyond my cuff'd head, slumbers, dreams, gaping,
I discover myself on the verge of a usual mistake.

That I could forget the mockers and insults!
That I could forget the trickling tears and the blows of the bludgeons and
    hammers!
That I could look with a separate look on my own crucifixion and bloody
    crowning.   965

I remember now,
I resume the overstaid fraction,
The grave of rock multiplies what has been confided to it, or to any graves,
Corpses rise, gashes heal, fastenings roll from me.

I troop forth replenish'd with supreme power, one of an average unending
    procession,   970
Inland and sea-coast we go, and pass all boundary lines,
Our swift ordinances on their way over the whole earth,
The blossoms we wear in our hats the growth of thousands of years.

Eleves,[2] I salute you! come forward!
Continue your annotations, continue your questionings.   975

39

The friendly and flowing savage, who is he?
Is he waiting for civilization, or past it and mastering it?

Is he some Southwesterner rais'd out-doors? is he Kanadian?
Is he from the Mississippi country? Iowa, Oregon, California?
The mountains? prairie-life, bush-life? or sailor from the sea?   980

Wherever he goes men and women accept and desire him,
They desire he should like them, touch them, speak to them, stay with them.

Behavior lawless as snow-flakes, words simple as grass, uncomb'd head, laugh-
    ter, and naivetè,
Slow-stepping feet, common features, common modes and emanations,
They descend in new forms from the tips of his fingers,   985

---

2. From the French for "students," but Whitman's use carries some of the sense of "disciples" or "acolytes" as well.

They are wafted with the odor of his body or breath, they fly out of the glance
    of his eyes.

40

Flaunt of the sunshine I need not your bask—lie over!
You light surfaces only, I force surfaces and depths also.

Earth! you seem to look for something at my hands,
Say, old top-knot,[3] what do you want?   990

Man or woman, I might tell how I like you, but cannot,
And might tell what it is in me and what it is in you, but cannot,
And might tell that pining I have, that pulse of my nights and days.

Behold, I do not give lectures or a little charity,
When I give I give myself.   995

You there, impotent, loose in the knees,
Open your scarf'd chops[4] till I blow grit within you,
Spread your palms and lift the flaps of your pockets,
I am not to be denied, I compel, I have stores plenty and to spare,
And any thing I have I bestow.   1000

I do not ask who you are, that is not important to me,
You can do nothing and be nothing but what I will infold you.

To cotton-field drudge or cleaner of privies I lean,
On his right cheek I put the family kiss,
And in my soul I swear I never will deny him.   1005

On women fit for conception I start bigger and nimbler babes,
(This day I am jetting the stuff of far more arrogant republics.)

To any one dying, thither I speed and twist the knob of the door,
Turn the bed-clothes toward the foot of the bed,
Let the physician and the priest go home.   1010

I seize the descending man and raise him with resistless will,
O despairer, here is my neck,
By God, you shall not go down! hang your whole weight upon me.

I dilate you with tremendous breath, I buoy you up,
Every room of the house do I fill with an arm'd force,   1015
Lovers of me, bafflers of graves.

Sleep—I and they keep guard all night,
Not doubt, not decease shall dare to lay finger upon you,
I have embraced you, and henceforth possess you to myself,
And when you rise in the morning you will find what I tell you is so.   1020

---

3. As Blodgett and Bradley say in their note, this "epithet was familiar in frontier humor as a comic, half-
affectionate term for an Indian, whose tuft of hair or
ornament on top of the head was characteristic of certain tribes."
4. With chops (jaws) tied up in a scarf, as one might
do for a toothache, earache, or other ailment. See
line 1069.

41

I am he bringing help for the sick as they pant on their backs,
And for strong upright men I bring yet more needed help.

I heard what was said of the universe,
Heard it and heard it of several thousand years;
It is middling well as far as it goes—but is that all?   1025

Magnifying and applying come I,
Outbidding at the start the old cautious hucksters,[5]
Taking myself the exact dimensions of Jehovah,
Lithographing Kronos, Zeus his son, and Hercules his grandson,
Buying drafts of Osiris, Isis, Belus, Brahma, Buddha,   1030
In my portfolio placing Manito loose, Allah on a leaf, the crucifix engraved,
With Odin and the hideous-faced Mexitli[6] and every idol and image,
Taking them all for what they are worth and not a cent more,
Admitting they were alive and did the work of their days,
(They bore mites as for unfledg'd birds who have now to rise and fly and sing
    for themselves,)   1035
Accepting the rough deific sketches to fill out better in myself, bestowing them
    freely on each man and woman I see,
Discovering as much or more in a framer framing a house,
Putting higher claims for him there with his roll'd-up sleeves driving the mallet
    and chisel,
Not objecting to special revelations, considering a curl of smoke or a hair on
    the back of my hand just as curious as any revelation,
Lads ahold of fire-engines and hook-and-ladder ropes no less to me than the
    gods of the antique wars,   1040
Minding their voices peal through the crash of destruction,
Their brawny limbs passing safe over charr'd laths, their white foreheads whole
    and unhurt out of the flames;
By the mechanic's wife with her babe at her nipple interceding for every person
    born,
Three scythes at harvest whizzing in a row from three lusty angels with shirts
    bagg'd out at their waists,
The snag-tooth'd hostler with red hair redeeming sins past and to come,   1045
Selling all he possesses, traveling on foot to fee lawyers for his brother and sit
    by him while he is tried for forgery;
What was strewn in the amplest strewing the square rod about me, and not
    filling the square rod then,
The bull and the bug never worshipp'd half enough,[7]
Dung and dirt more admirable than was dream'd,

5. I.e., gods or priests who made too little of the divinity in human beings.
6. An Aztec war god. Jehovah was the God of the Jews and Christians. Kronos or Cronus, in Greek mythology, was the Titan who ruled the universe until dethroned by Zeus, his son, the chief of the Olympian gods. Hercules, son of Zeus and the mortal Alcmene, won immortality by performing twelve supposedly impossible feats. Osiris was the Egyptian god who annually died and was reborn, symbolizing the fertility of nature. Isis was the Egyptian goddess of fertility and the sister and wife of Osiris. Belus was a legendary god-king of Assyria. Brahma, in Hinduism, was the divine reality in the role of creator. Buddha was the Indian philosopher Gautama Siddhartha, founder of Buddhism. Manito was the nature god of the Algonquian Indians. Allah was the supreme being in the Moslem religion. Odin was the chief Norse god.
7. As Whitman implies, the bull and the bug had in fact been worshiped in earlier religions, the bull in several, the scarab beetle as an Egyptian symbol of the soul; but they had been worshiped wrongly, as supernatural objects.

The supernatural of no account, myself waiting my time to be one of the
    supremes, 1050
The day getting ready for me when I shall do as much good as the best, and
    be as prodigious;
By my life-lumps![8] becoming already a creator,
Putting myself here and now to the ambush'd womb of the shadows.

42

A call in the midst of the crowd,
My own voice, orotund sweeping and final. 1055

Come my children,
Come my boys and girls, my women, household and intimates,
Now the performer launches his nerve, he has pass'd his prelude on the reeds
    within.

Easily written loose-finger'd chords—I feel the thrum of your climax and close.

My head slues round on my neck, 1060
Music rolls, but not from the organ,
Folks are around me, but they are no household of mine.

Ever the hard unsunk ground,
Ever the eaters and drinkers, ever the upward and downward sun, ever the air
    and the ceaseless tides,
Ever myself and my neighbors, refreshing, wicked, real, 1065
Ever the old inexplicable query, ever that thorn'd thumb, that breath of itches
    and thirsts,
Ever the vexer's *hoot! hoot!* till we find where the sly one hides and bring
    him forth,
Ever love, ever the sobbing liquid of life,
Ever the bandage under the chin, ever the trestles[9] of death.

Here and there with dimes on the eyes[1] walking, 1070
To feed the greed of the belly the brains liberally spooning,
Tickets buying, taking, selling, but in to the feast never once going,
Many sweating, ploughing, thrashing, and then the chaff for payment receiving,
A few idly owning, and they the wheat continually claiming.

This is the city and I am one of the citizens, 1075
Whatever interests the rest interests me, politics, wars, markets, newspapers,
    schools,
The mayor and councils, banks, tariffs, steamships, factories, stocks, stores,
    real estate and personal estate.

The little plentiful manikins skipping around in collars and tail'd coats,
I am aware who they are, (they are positively not worms or fleas,)

8. A felicitously comic way of referring to spurts of semen, here used figuratively.
9. Sawhorses or similar supports holding up a coffin.

1. Coins were placed on eyelids to hold them closed
until burial.

I acknowledge the duplicates of myself, the weakest and shallowest is deathless
    with me,   1080
What I do and say the same waits for them,
Every thought that flounders in me the same flounders in them.

I know perfectly well my own egotism,
Know my omnivorous lines and must not write any less,
And would fetch you whoever you are flush with myself.   1085

Not words of routine this song of mine,
But abruptly to question, to leap beyond yet nearer bring;
This printed and bound book—but the printer and the printing-office boy?
The well-taken photographs—but your wife or friend close and solid in your
    arms?
The black ship mail'd with iron, her mighty guns in her turrets—but the pluck
    of the captain and engineers?   1090
In the houses the dishes and fare and furniture—but the host and hostess, and
    the look out of their eyes?
The sky up there—yet here or next door, or across the way?
The saints and sages in history—but you yourself?
Sermons, creeds, theology—but the fathomless human brain,
And what is reason? and what is love? and what is life?   1095

43

I do not despise you priests, all time, the world over,
My faith is the greatest of faiths and the least of faiths,
Enclosing worship ancient and modern and all between ancient and modern,
Believing I shall come again upon the earth after five thousand years,
Waiting responses from oracles, honoring the gods, saluting the sun,   1100
Making a fetich of the first rock or stump, powowing with sticks in the circle
    of obis.[2]
Helping the llama or brahmin as he trims the lamps of the idols,
Dancing yet through the streets in a phallic procession, rapt and austere in the
    woods a gymnosophist,
Drinking mead from the skull-cup, to Shastas and Vedas admirant, minding
    the Koran,
Walking the teokallis, spotted with gore from the stone and knife, beating the
    serpent-skin drum,   1105
Accepting the Gospels,[3] accepting him that was crucified, knowing assuredly
    that he is divine,
To the mass kneeling or the puritan's prayer rising, or sitting patiently in a
    pew,
Ranting and frothing in my insane crisis, or waiting dead-like till my spirit
    arouses me,

2. Witch doctors, either in Africa or among blacks in the New World.
3. *Llama* is Whitman's spelling for lama, a Buddhist monk of Tibet or Mongolia. A brahmin here is also a Buddhist priest. Gymnosophists were members of an ancient Hindu ascetic sect, thought to have forgone clothing, as the name ("naked philosophers") implies. The other worshipers include old Teutonic drinkers of mead (an alcoholic beverage made of fermented honey), admiring or wondering readers of the sastras (or shastras or shasters, books of Hindu law) or of the Vedas (the oldest sacred writings of Hinduism), those attentive to the Koran (the sacred book of Islam, containing Allah's revelations to Mohammed), worshipers walking the teokallis (an ancient Central American temple built on a pyramidal mound), and believers in the New Testament Gospels.

Looking forth on pavement and land, or outside of pavement and land,
Belonging to the winders of the circuit of circuits. 1110

One of that centripetal and centrifugal gang I turn and talk like a man leaving
    charges before a journey.

Down-hearted doubters dull and excluded,
Frivolous, sullen, moping, angry, affected, dishearten'd, atheistical,
I know every one of you, I know the sea of torment, doubt, despair and
    unbelief.

How the flukes[4] splash! 1115
How they contort rapid as lightning, with spasms and spouts of blood!

Be at peace bloody flukes of doubters and sullen mopers,
I take my place among you as much as among any,
The past is the push of you, me, all, precisely the same,
And what is yet untried and afterward is for you, me, all, precisely the
    same. 1120

I do not know what is untried and afterward,
But I know it will in its turn prove sufficient, and cannot fail.

Each who passes is consider'd, each who stops is consider'd, not a single one
    can it fail.

It cannot fail the young man who died and was buried,
Nor the young woman who died and was put by his side, 1125
Nor the little child that peep'd in at the door, and then drew back and was
    never seen again,
Nor the old man who has lived without purpose, and feels it with bitterness
    worse than gall,
Nor him in the poor house tubercled by rum and the bad disorder,

Nor the numberless slaughter'd and wreck'd, nor the brutish koboo[5] call'd the
    ordure of humanity,
Nor the sacs merely floating with open mouths for food to slip in, 1130
Nor any thing in the earth, or down in the oldest graves of the earth,
Nor any thing in the myriads of spheres, nor the myriads of myriads that
    inhabit them,
Nor the present, nor the least wisp that is known.

44

It is time to explain myself—let us stand up.

What is known I strip away, 1135
I launch all men and women forward with me into the Unknown.

The clock indicates the moment—but what does eternity indicate?

4. The flat parts on either side of a whale's tail; here   5. Native of Sumatra.
used figuratively.

We have thus far exhausted trillions of winters and summers,
There are trillions ahead, and trillions ahead of them.

Births have brought us richness and variety,   1140
And other births will bring us richness and variety.

I do not call one greater and one smaller,
That which fills its period and place is equal to any.

Were mankind murderous or jealous upon you, my brother, my sister?
I am sorry for you, they are not murderous or jealous upon me,   1145
All has been gentle with me, I keep no account with lamentation,
(What have I to do with lamentation?)

I am an acme of things accomplish'd, and I an encloser of things to be.

My feet strike an apex of the apices[6] of the stairs,
On every step bunches of ages, and larger bunches between the steps,   1150
All below duly travel'd, and still I mount and mount.

Rise after rise bow the phantoms behind me,
Afar down I see the huge first Nothing, I know I was even there,
I waited unseen and always, and slept through the lethargic mist,
And took my time, and took no hurt from the fetid carbon.[7]   1155

Long I was hugg'd close—long and long.

Immense have been the preparations for me,
Faithful and friendly the arms that have help'd me.

Cycles[8] ferried my cradle, rowing and rowing like cheerful boatmen,
For room to me stars kept aside in their own rings,   1160
They sent influences to look after what was to hold me.

Before I was born out of my mother generations guided me,
My embryo has never been torpid, nothing could overlay it.

For it the nebula cohered to an orb,
The long slow strata piled to rest it on,   1165
Vast vegetables gave it sustenance,
Monstrous sauroids transported it in their mouths and deposited it with care.

All forces have been steadily employ'd to complete and delight me,
Now on this spot I stand with my robust soul.

45

O span of youth! ever-push'd elasticity!   1170
O manhood, balanced, florid and full.

---

6. The highest points (variant plural of *apex*).
7. Whitman knew a good deal about geology and pre-Darwinian theories of evolution. Here the periods of lethargic mist and fetid carbon are prehuman ages, probably ages far earlier than the period of the "monstrous sauroids" (line 1167).
8. Centuries.

My lovers suffocate me,
Crowding my lips, thick in the pores of my skin,
Jostling me through streets and public halls, coming naked to me at night,
Crying by day *Ahoy!* from the rocks of the river, swinging and chirping over
    my head,   1175
Calling my name from flower-beds, vines, tangled underbrush,
Lighting on every moment of my life,
Bussing[9] my body with soft balsamic busses,
Noiselessly passing handfuls out of their hearts and giving them to be mine.

Old age superbly rising! O welcome, ineffable grace of dying days!   1180

Every condition promulges[1] not only itself, it promulges what grows after and
    out of itself,
And the dark hush promulges as much as any.

I open my scuttle at night and see the far-sprinkled systems,
And all I see multiplied as high as I can cipher edge but the rim of the farther
    systems.

Wider and wider they spread, expanding, always expanding,   1185
Outward and outward and forever outward.

My sun has his sun and round him obediently wheels,
He joins with his partners a group of superior circuit,
And greater sets follow, making specks of the greatest inside them.

There is no stoppage and never can be stoppage,   1190
If I, you, and the worlds, and all beneath or upon their surfaces, were this
    moment reduced back to a pallid float,[2] it would not avail in the long run,
We should surely bring up again where we now stand,
And surely go as much farther, and then farther and farther.

A few quadrillions of eras, a few octillions of cubic leagues, do not hazard[3] the
    span or make it impatient,
They are but parts, any thing is but a part.   1195

See ever so far, there is limitless space outside of that,
Count ever so much, there is limitless time around that.

My rendezvous is appointed, it is certain,
The Lord will be there and wait till I come on perfect terms,
The great Camerado, the lover true for whom I pine will be there.   1200

46

I know I have the best of time and space, and was never measured and never
    will be measured.

---

9. Kissing.
1. Promulgates, officially announces.
2. That period before the solar system had defined

itself.
3. Imperil, make hazardous.

I tramp a perpetual journey, (come listen all!)
My signs are a rain-proof coat, good shoes, and a staff cut from the woods,
No friend of mine takes his ease in my chair,
I have no chair, no church, no philosophy,   1205
I lead no man to a dinner-table, library, exchange,[4]
But each man and each woman of you I lead upon a knoll,
My left hand hooking you round the waist,
My right hand pointing to landscapes of continents and the public road.

Not I, not any one else can travel that road for you,   1210
You must travel it for yourself.

It is not far, it is within reach,
Perhaps you have been on it since you were born and did not know,
Perhaps it is everywhere on water and on land.

Shoulder your duds dear son, and I will mine, and let us hasten forth,   1215
Wonderful cities and free nations we shall fetch as we go.

If you tire, give me both burdens, and rest the chuff[5] of your hand on my hip,
And in due time you shall repay the same service to me,
For after we start we never lie by again.

This day before dawn I ascended a hill and look'd at the crowded heaven, 1220
And I said to my spirit *When we become the enfolders of those orbs, and the
    pleasure and knowledge of every thing in them, shall we be fill'd and satis-
    fied then?*
And my spirit said *No, we but level that lift to pass and continue beyond.*

You are also asking me questions and I hear you,
I answer that I cannot answer, you must find out for yourself.

Sit a while dear son,   1225
Here are biscuits to eat and here is milk to drink,
But as soon as you sleep and renew yourself in sweet clothes, I kiss you with a
    good-by kiss and open the gate for your egress hence.

Long enough have you dream'd contemptible dreams,
Now I wash the gum from your eyes,
You must habit yourself to the dazzle of the light and of every moment of
    your life.   1230

Long have you timidly waded holding a plank by the shore,
Now I will you to be a bold swimmer,
To jump off in the midst of the sea, rise again, nod to me, shout, and laugh-
    ingly dash with your hair.

---

4. Stock exchange.   5. The meaty part of the palm.

47

I am the teacher of athletes,
He that by me spreads a wider breast than my own proves the width of my
    own,   1235
He most honors my style who learns under it to destroy the teacher.

The boy I love, the same becomes a man not through derived power, but in
    his own right,
Wicked rather than virtuous out of conformity or fear,
Fond of his sweetheart, relishing well his steak,
Unrequited love or a slight cutting him worse than sharp steel cuts,   1240
First-rate to ride, to fight, to hit the bull's eye, to sail a skiff, to sing a song or
    play on the banjo,
Preferring scars and the beard and faces pitted with small-pox over all latherers,
And those well-tann'd to those that keep out of the sun.

I teach straying from me, yet who can stray from me?
I follow you whoever you are from the present hour,   1245
My words itch at your ears till you understand them.

I do not say these things for a dollar or to fill up the time while I wait for a boat,
(It is you talking just as much as myself, I act as the tongue of you,
Tied in your mouth, in mine it begins to be loosen'd.)

I swear I will never again mention love or death inside a house,   1250
And I swear I will never translate myself at all, only to him or her who privately
    stays with me in the open air.

If you would understand me go to the heights or water-shore,
The nearest gnat is an explanation, and a drop or motion of waves a key,
The maul, the oar, the hand-saw, second my words.

No shutter'd room or school can commune with me,   1255
But roughs and little children better than they.

The young mechanic is closest to me, he knows me well,
The woodman that takes his axe and jug with him shall take me with him
    all day,
The farm-boy ploughing in the field feels good at the sound of my voice,
In vessels that sail my words sail, I go with fishermen and seamen and love
    them.   1260

The soldier camp'd or upon the march is mine,
On the night ere the pending battle many seek me, and I do not fail them,
On that solemn night (it may be their last) those that know me seek me.

My face rubs to the hunter's face when he lies down alone in his blanket,
The driver thinking of me does not mind the jolt of his wagon,   1265
The young mother and old mother comprehend me,
The girl and the wife rest the needle a moment and forget where they are,
They and all would resume what I have told them.

48

I have said that the soul is not more than the body,
And I have said that the body is not more than the soul,   1270
And nothing, not God, is greater to one than one's self is,
And whoever walks a furlong without sympathy walks to his own funeral drest
    in his shroud,
And I or you pocketless of a dime may purchase the pick of the earth,
And to glance with an eye or show a bean in its pod confounds the learning of
    all times,
And there is no trade or employment but the young man following it may
    become a hero,   1275
And there is no object so soft but it makes a hub for the wheel'd universe,
And I say to any man or woman, Let your soul stand cool and composed
    before a million universes.

And I say to mankind, Be not curious about God,
For I who am curious about each am not curious about God,
(No array of terms can say how much I am at peace about God and about
    death.)   1280

I hear and behold God in every object, yet understand God not in the least,
Nor do I understand who there can be more wonderful than myself.

Why should I wish to see God better than this day?
I see something of God each hour of the twenty-four, and each moment then,
In the faces of men and women I see God, and in my own face in the
    glass,   1285
I find letters from God dropt in the street, and every one is sign'd by God's
    name,
and I leave them where they are, for I know that wheresoe'er I go,
Others will punctually come for ever and ever.

49

And as to you Death, and you bitter hug of mortality, it is idle to try to alarm
    me.

To his work without flinching the accoucheur[6] comes,   1290
I see the elder-hand pressing receiving supporting,
I recline by the sills of the exquisite flexible doors,
And mark the outlet, and mark the relief and escape.

And as to you Corpse I think you are good manure, but that does not offend
    me,
I smell the white roses sweet-scented and growing,   1295
I reach to the leafy lips, I reach to the polish'd breasts of melons.

And as to you Life I reckon you are the leavings of many deaths,
(No doubt I have died myself ten thousand times before.)

6. Midwife.

I hear you whispering there O stars of heaven,
O suns—O grass of graves—O perpetual transfers and promotions,   1300
If you do not say any thing how can I say any thing?

Of the turbid pool that lies in the autumn forest,
Of the moon that descends the steeps of the soughing twilight,
Toss, sparkles of day and dusk—toss on the black stems that decay in the muck,
Toss to the moaning gibberish of the dry limbs.   1305

I ascend from the moon, I ascend from the night,
I perceive that the ghastly glimmer is noonday sunbeams reflected,
And debouch[7] to the steady and central from the offspring great or small.

50

There is that in me—I do not know what it is—but I know it is in me.

Wrench'd and sweaty—calm and cool then my body becomes, I sleep—I sleep
        long.   1310

I do not know it—it is without name—it is a word unsaid,
It is not in any dictionary, utterance, symbol.

Something it swings on more than the earth I swing on,
To it the creation is the friend whose embracing awakes me.

Perhaps I might tell more. Outlines! I plead for my brothers and sisters.   1315

Do you see O my brothers and sisters?
It is not chaos or death—it is form, union, plan—it is eternal life—it is Hap-
        piness.

51

The past and present wilt—I have fill'd them, emptied them,
And proceed to fill my next fold of the future.

Listener up there! what have you to confide to me?   1320
Look in my face while I snuff the sidle[8] of evening,
(Talk honestly, no one else hears you, and I stay only a minute longer.)

Do I contradict myself?
Very well then I contradict myself,
(I am large, I contain multitudes.)   1325

I concentrate toward them that are nigh, I wait on the door-slab.

Who has done his day's work? who will soonest be through with his supper?

---

7. Pour forth.   here the light is the hesitant last light of day, sidling or
8. To snuff is to put out, as in extinguishing a candle;   moving along edgeways.

Who wishes to walk with me?

Will you speak before I am gone? will you prove already too late?

52

The spotted hawk swoops by and accuses me, he complains of my gab and
    my loitering.   1330

I too am not a bit tamed, I too am untranslatable,
I sound my barbaric yawp over the roofs of the world.

The last scud of day[9] holds back for me,
It flings my likeness after the rest and true as any on the shadow'd wilds,
It coaxes me to the vapor and the dusk.   1335

I depart as air, I shake my white locks at the runaway sun,
I effuse my flesh in eddies, and drift it in lacy jags.

I bequeath myself to the dirt to grow from the grass I love,
If you want me again look for me under your boot-soles.

You will hardly know who I am or what I mean,   1340
But I shall be good health to you nevertheless,
And filter and fibre your blood.

Failing to fetch me at first keep encouraged,
Missing me one place search another,
I stop somewhere waiting for you.   1345

1855, 1881

Letter to Ralph Waldo Emerson[1]

[Whitman's 1856 Manifesto]

BROOKLYN, AUGUST, 1856.
    Here are thirty-two Poems, which I send you, dear Friend and Master, not
having found how I could satisfy myself with sending any usual acknowledgment of your letter. The first edition, on which you mailed me that till now

9. Wind-driven clouds, or merely the last rays of the
sun.
1. Having already in October 1855 "allowed" the *New
York Tribune* to print Emerson's 21 July 1855 letter to
him (after proudly carrying it around with him since
he received it), Whitman embellished the spine of the
1856 edition of *Leaves of Grass* with these words lettered in gold on a glued-on backstrip "I Greet You at
the / Beginning of A / Great Career / R. W. Emerson." In the back of the 1856 edition Whitman reprinted Emerson's letter in full (see p. 1165) and followed it by this "Letter to Ralph Waldo Emerson"
dated Brooklyn, August 1856. The fuss about the indelicacy (or one might say hilariously self-conscious

vulgarity) of Whitman's unauthorized use of Emerson's letter has obscured the extraordinary virtues of
this 1856 "reply," which Sculley Bradley and Harold
W. Blodgett call a "preface" to the 1856 edition, despite its placement at the back of the volume.
    In *The New Walt Whitman Handbook*, Gay Wilson
Allen discusses the nature of the twenty new poems
Whitman added and his new focus on carrying on a
campaign against "asceticism and puritanism." Having
omitted the 1855 preface, Whitman was in the process
of turning some of it into poems. He added what Allen
calls "new sex poems" and, most notably, *Sun-Down
Poem*, later called *Crossing Brooklyn Ferry*.

unanswered letter, was twelve poems—I printed a thousand copies, and they readily sold; these thirty-two Poems I stereotype,[2] to print several thousand copies of. I much enjoy making poems. Other work I have set for myself to do, to meet people and The States face to face, to confront them with an American rude tongue; but the work of my life is making poems. I keep on till I make a hundred, and then several hundred—perhaps a thousand. The way is clear to me. A few years, and the average annual call for my Poems is ten or twenty thousand copies—more, quite likely. Why should I hurry or compromise? In poems or in speeches I say the word or two that has got to be said, adhere to the body, step with the countless common footsteps, and remind every man and woman of something.

Master, I am a man who has perfect faith. Master, we have not come through centuries, caste, heroisms, fables, to halt in this land today. Or I think it is to collect a ten-fold impetus that any halt is made. As nature, inexorable, onward, resistless, impassive amid the threats and screams of disputants, so America. Let all defer. Let all attend respectfully the leisure of These States, their politics, poems, literature, manners, and their free-handed modes of training their own offspring. Their own comes, just matured, certain, numerous and capable enough, with egotistical tongues, with sinewed wrists, seizing openly what belongs to them. They resume Personality, too long left out of mind. Their shadows are projected in employments, in books, in the cities, in trade; their feet are on the flights of the steps of the Capitol; they dilate, a large brawnier, more candid, more democratic, lawless, positive native to The States, sweet-bodied, completer, dauntless, flowing, masterful, beard-faced, new race of men.

Swiftly, on limitless foundations, the United States too are founding a literature. It is all as well done, in my opinion, as could be practicable. Each element here is in condition. Every day I go among the people of Manhattan Island, Brooklyn, and other cities, and among the young men, to discover the spirit of them, and to refresh myself. These are to be attended to; I am myself more drawn here than to those authors, publishers, importations, reprints, and so forth. I pass coolly through those, understanding them perfectly well, and that they do the indispensable service, outside of men like me, which nothing else could do. In poems, the young men of The States shall be represented, for they out-rival the best of the rest of the earth.

The lists of ready-made literature which America inherits by the mighty inheritance of the English language—all the rich repertoire of traditions, poems, histories, metaphysics, plays, classics, translations, have made, and still continue, magnificent preparations for that other plainly significant literature, to be our own, to be electric, fresh, lusty, to express the full-sized body, male and female—to give the modern meanings of things, to grow up beautiful, lasting, commensurate with America, with all the passions of home, with the inimitable sympathies of having been boys and girls together, and of parents who were with our parents.

What else can happen The States, even in their own despite? That huge English flow, so sweet, so undeniable, has done incalculable good here, and is to be spoken of for its own sake with generous praise and with gratitude. Yet

---

2. A printer's term before it became metaphorical, to stereotype was to make a mold of standing type, which could then be reused, while later printings could be made from the stereotyped plates. To go to the cost of stereotyping was evidence of optimism that future printings would be needed.

the price The States have had to lie under for the same has not been a small price. Payment prevails; a nation can never take the issues of the needs of other nations for nothing. America, grandest of lands in the theory of its politics, in popular reading, in hospitality, breadth, animal beauty, cities, ships, machines, money, credit, collapses quick as lightning at the repeated, admonishing, stern words. Where are any mental expressions from you, beyond what you have copied or stolen? Where the born throngs of poets, literats, orators, you promised? Will you but tag after other nations? They struggled long for their literature, painfully working their way, some with deficient languages, some with priest-craft, some in the endeavor just to live—yet achieved for their times, works, poems, perhaps the only solid consolation left to them through ages afterward of shame and decay. You are young, have the perfectest of dialects, a free press, a free government, the world forwarding its best to be with you. As justice has been strictly done to you, from this hour do strict justice to yourself. Strangle the singers who will not sing you loud and strong. Open the doors of The West. Call for new great masters to comprehend new arts, new perfections, new wants. Submit to the most robust bard till he remedy your barrenness. Then you will not need to adopt the heirs of others; you will have true heirs, begotten of yourself, blooded with your own blood.

With composure I see such propositions, seeing more and more every day of the answers that serve. Expressions do not yet serve, for sufficient reasons; but that is getting ready, beyond what the earth has hitherto known, to take home the expressions when they come, and to identify them with the populace of The States, which is the schooling cheaply procured by any outlay any number of years. Such schooling The States extract from the swarms of reprints, and from the current authors and editors. Such service and extract are done after enormous, reckless, free modes, characteristic of The States. Here are to be attained results never elsewhere thought possible; the modes are very grand too. The instincts of the American people are all perfect, and tend to make heroes. It is a rare thing in a man here to understand The States.

All current nourishments to literature serve. Of authors and editors I do not know how many there are in The States, but there are thousands, each one building his or her step to the stairs by which giants shall mount. Of the twenty-four modern mammoth two-double, three-double, and four-double cylinder presses now in the world, printing by steam, twenty-one of them are in These States. The twelve thousand large and small shops for dispensing books and newspapers—the same number of public libraries, any one of which has all the reading wanted to equip a man or woman for American reading— the three thousand different newspapers, the nutriment of the imperfect ones coming in just as usefully as any—the story papers, various, full of strong-flavored romances, widely circulated—the one cent and two-cent journals— the political ones, no matter what side—the weeklies in the country—the sporting and pictorial papers—the monthly magazines, with plentiful imported feed—the sentimental novels, numberless copies of them—the low-priced flaring tales, adventures, biographies—all are prophetic; all waft rapidly on. I see that they swell wide, for reasons. I am not troubled at the movement of them, but greatly pleased.[3] I see plying shuttles, the active ephemeral myriads of books also, faithfully weaving the garments of a generation of men, and a

---

3. Contrast Thoreau's disdain of "little reading" in *Walden, Reading* (p. 1770).

generation of women, they do not perceive or know. What a progress popular reading and writing has made in fifty years! What a progress fifty years hence! The time is at hand when inherent literature will be a main part of These States, as general and real as steam-power, iron, corn, beef, fish. First-rate American persons are to be supplied. Our perennial materials for fresh thoughts, histories, poems, music, orations, religions, recitations, amusements, will then not be disregarded, any more than our perennial fields, mines, rivers, seas. Certain things are established, and are immovable; in those things millions of years stand justified. The mothers and fathers of whom modern centuries have come, have not existed for nothing; they too had brains and hearts. Of course all literature, in all nations and years, will share marked attributes in common, as we all, of all ages, share the common human attributes. America is to be kept coarse and broad. What is to be done is to withdraw from precedents, and be directed to men and women—also to The States in their federalness; for the union of the parts of the body is not more necessary to their life than the union of These States is to their life.

A profound person can easily know more of the people than they know of themselves. Always waiting untold in the souls of the armies of common people, is stuff better than anything that can possibly appear in the leadership of the same. That gives final verdicts. In every department of These States, he who travels with a coterie, or with selected persons, or with imitators, or with infidels, or with the owners of slaves, or with that which is ashamed of the body of a man, or with that which is ashamed of the body of a woman, or with any thing less than the bravest and the openest, travels straight for the slopes of dissolution. The genius of all foreign literature is clipped and cut small, compared to our genius, and is essentially insulting to our usages, and to the organic compacts of These States. Old forms, old poems, majestic and proper in their own lands here in this land are exiles; the air here is very strong. Much that stands well and has a little enough place provided for it in the small scales of European kingdoms, empires, and the like, here stands haggard, dwarfed, ludicrous, or has no place little enough provided for it. Authorities, poems, models, laws, names, imported into America, are useful to America today to destroy them, and so move disencumbered to great works, great days.

Just so long, in our country or any country, as no revolutionists advance, and are backed by the people, sweeping off the swarms of routine representatives, officers in power, book-makers, teachers, ecclesiastics; politicians, just so long, I perceive, do they who are in power fairly represent that country, and remain of use, probably of very great use. To supersede them, when it is the pleasure of These States, full provision is made; and I say the time has arrived to use it with a strong hand. Here also the souls of the armies have not only overtaken the souls of the officers, but passed on, and left the souls of the officers behind out of sight many weeks' journey; and the souls of the armies now go en-masse without officers. Here also formulas, glosses, blanks, minutiæ, are choking the throats of the spokesmen to death. Those things most listened for, certainly those are the things least said. There is not a single History of the World. There is not one of America, or of the organic compacts of These States, or of Washington, or of Jefferson, nor of Language, nor any Dictionary of the English Language. There is no great author; every one has demeaned himself to some etiquette or some impotence. There is no manhood or life-power in poems; there are shoats and geldings more like. Or literature will be dressed up, a fine gentleman, distasteful to our instincts, foreign to our soil. Its neck bends right and left wherever it goes. Its costumes and jewelry prove how little it knows Nature. Its flesh is soft; it shows less and less of the indefinable hard something that is Nature. Where is any thing but the shaved Nature of synods and schools? Where is a savage and luxuriant man? Where is an overseer? In lives, in poems, in codes of law, in Congress, in tuitions, theatres, conversations, argumentations, not a single head lifts itself clean out, with proof that it is their master, and has subordinated them to itself, and is ready to try their superiors. None believes in These States, boldly illustrating them in himself. Not a man faces round at the rest with terrible negative voice, refusing all terms to be bought off from his own eye-sight, or from the soul that he is, or from friendship, or from the body that he is, or from the soil and sea. To creeds, literature, art, the army, the navy, the executive, life is hardly proposed, but the sick and dying are proposed to cure the sick and dying. The churches are one vast lie; the people do not believe them, and they do not believe themselves; the priests are continually telling what they know well enough is not so, and keeping back what they know is so. The spectacle is a pitiful one. I think there can never be again upon the festive earth more bad-disordered persons deliberately taking seats, as of late in These States, at the heads of the public tables—such corpses' eyes for judges—such a rascal and thief in the Presidency.[4]

Up to the present, as helps best, the people, like a lot of large boys, have no determined tastes, are quite unaware of the grandeur of themselves, and of their destiny, and of their immense strides—accept with voracity whatever is presented them in novels, histories, newspapers, poems, schools, lectures, every thing. Pretty soon, through these and other means, their development makes the fibre that is capable of itself, and will assume determined tastes. The young men will be clear what they want, and will have it. They will follow none except him whose spirit leads them in the like spirit with themselves. Any such man will be welcome as the flowers of May. Others will be put out without ceremony. How much is there anyhow, to the young men of These States, in a parcel of helpless dandies, who can neither fight, work, shoot, ride, run, command—some of them devout, some quite insane, some castrated—all second-hand, or third, fourth, or fifth hand—waited upon by waiters, putting not this land first, but always other lands first, talking of art, doing the most ridiculous things for fear of being called ridiculous, smirking and skipping along, continually taking off their hats—no one behaving, dressing, writing, talking, loving, out of any natural and manly tastes of his own, but each one looking cautiously to see how the rest behave, dress, write, talk, love—pressing the noses of dead books upon themselves and upon their country—favoring no poets, philosophs, literats here, but dog-like danglers at the heels of the poets, philosophs, literats of enemies' lands—favoring mental expressions, models of gentlemen and ladies, social habitudes in These States, to grow up in sneaking defiance of the popular substratums of The States? Of course they and the likes of them can never justify the strong poems of America. Of course no feed of theirs is to stop and be made welcome to muscle the bodies, male and female, for Manhattan Island, Brooklyn, Boston, Worcester, Hartford, Portland, Montreal, Detroit, Buffalo, Cleaveland, Mil-

---

4. The proslavery sympathizer Franklin Pierce (president 1853–57).

waukee, St. Louis, Indianapolis, Chicago, Cincinnati, Iowa City, Philadelphia, Baltimore, Raleigh, Savannah, Charleston, Mobile, New Orleans, Galveston, Brownsville, San Francisco, Havana, and a thousand equal cities, present and to come. Of course what they and the likes of them have been used for, draws toward its close, after which they will all be discharged, and not one of them will ever be heard of any more.

America, having duly conceived, bears out of herself offspring of her own to do the workmanship wanted. To freedom, to strength, to poems, to personal greatness, it is never permitted to rest, not a generation or part of a generation. To be ripe beyond further increase is to prepare to die. The architects of These States laid their foundations, and passed to further spheres. What they laid is a work done; as much more remains. Now are needed other architects, whose duty is not less difficult, but perhaps more difficult. Each age forever needs architects. America is not finished, perhaps never will be; now America is a divine true sketch. There are Thirty-Two States sketched—the population thirty millions. In a few years there will be Fifty States. Again in a few years there will be A Hundred States, the population hundreds of millions, the freshest and freest of men. Of course such men stand to nothing less than the freshest and freest expression.

Poets here, literats here, are to rest on organic different bases from other countries; not a class set apart, circling only in the circle of themselves, modest and pretty, desperately scratching for rhymes, pallid with white paper, shut off, aware of the old pictures and traditions of the race, but unaware of the actual race around them—not breeding in and in among each other till they all have the scrofula. Lands of ensemble, bards of ensemble! Walking freely out from the old traditions, as our politics has walked out, American poets and literats recognize nothing behind them superior to what is present with them— recognize with joy the sturdy living forms of men and women of These States, the divinity of sex, the perfect eligibility of the female with the male, all The States, liberty and equality, real articles, the different trades, mechanics, the young fellows of Manhattan Island, customs, instincts, slang, Wisconsin, Georgia, the noble Southern heart, the hot blood, the spirit that will be nothing less than master, the filibuster spirit, the Western man, native-born perceptions, the eye for forms, the perfect models of made things, the wild smack of freedom, California, money, electric-telegraphs, free-trade, iron and the iron mines—recognize without demur those splendid resistless black poems, the steam-ships of the sea-board states, and those other resistless splendid poems, the locomotives, followed through the interior states by trains of railroad cars.

A word remains to be said, as of one ever present, not yet permitted to be acknowledged, discarded or made dumb by literature, and the results apparent. To the lack of an avowed, empowered, unabashed development of sex, (the only salvation for the same,) and to the fact of speakers and writers fraudulently assuming as always dead what every one knows to be always alive, is attributable the remarkable non-personality and indistinctness of modern productions in books, art, talk; also that in the scanned lives of men and women most of them appear to have been for some time past of the neuter gender; and also the stinging fact that in orthodox society today, if the dresses were changed, the men might easily pass for women and the women for men.

Infidelism usurps most with fœtid polite face; among the rest infidelism about sex. By silence or obedience the pens of savans, poets, historians, biographers, and the rest, have long connived at the filthy law, and books enslaved to it, that what makes the manhood of a man, that sex, womanhood, maternity, desires, lusty animations, organs, acts, are unmentionable and to be ashamed of, to be driven to skulk out of literature with whatever belongs to them. This filthy law has to be repealed—it stands in the way of great reforms. Of women just as much as men, it is the interest that there should not be infidelism about sex, but perfect faith. Women in These States approach the day of that organic equality with men, without which, I see, men cannot have organic equality among themselves. This empty dish, gallantry, will then be filled with something. This tepid wash, this diluted deferential love, as in songs, fictions, and so forth, is enough to make a man vomit; as to manly friendship, everywhere observed in The States, there is not the first breath of it to be observed in print. I say that the body of a man or woman, the main matter, is so far quite unexpressed in poems; but that the body is to be expressed, and sex is. Of bards for These States, if it come to a question, it is whether they shall celebrate in poems the eternal decency of the amativeness of Nature, the motherhood of all, or whether they shall be the bards of the fashionable delusion of the inherent nastiness of sex, and of the feeble and querulous modesty of deprivation. This is important in poems, because the whole of the other expressions of a nation are but flanges out of its great poems. To me, henceforth, that theory of any thing, no matter what, stagnates in its vitals, cowardly and rotten, while it cannot publicly accept, and publicly name, with specific words, the things on which all existence, all souls, all realization, all decency, all health, all that is worth being here for, all of woman and of man, all beauty, all purity, all sweetness, all friendship, all strength, all life, all immortality depend. The courageous soul, for a year or two to come, may be proved by faith in sex, and by disdaining concessions.

   To poets and literats—to every woman and man, today or any day, the conditions of the present, needs, dangers, prejudices, and the like, are the perfect conditions on which we are here, and the conditions for wording the future with undissuadable words. These States, receivers of the stamina of past ages and lands, initiate the outlines of repayment a thousand fold. They fetch the American great masters, waited for by old words and new, who accept evil as well as good, ignorance as well as erudition, black as soon as white, foreign-born materials as well as home-born, reject none, force discrepancies into range, surround the whole, concentrate them on present periods and places, show the application to each and any one's body and soul, and show the true use of precedents. Always America will be agitated and turbulent. This day it is taking shape, not to be less so, but to be more so, stormily, capriciously, on native principles, with such vast proportions of parts! As for me, I love screaming, wrestling, boiling-hot days.

   Of course, we shall have a national character, an identity. As it ought to be, and as soon as it ought to be, it will be. That, with much else, takes care of itself, is a result, and the cause of greater results. With Ohio, Illinois, Missouri, Oregon—with the states around the Mexican sea—with cheerfully welcomed immigrants form Europe, Asia, Africa—with Connecticut, Vermont, New Hampshire, Rhode Island—with all varied interests, facts, beliefs, parties, genesis—there is being fused a determined character, fit for the broadest use for the freewomen and freemen of The States, accomplished and to be accomplished, without any exception whatever—each indeed free, each idiomatic, as becomes live states and men, but each adhering to one enclosing general form of politics, manners, talk, personal style, as the plenteous varieties of the race adhere to one physical form. Such character is the brain and spine to all, including literature, including poems. Such character, strong, limber, just, open-mouthed, American-blooded, full of pride, full of ease, of passionate friendliness, is to stand compact upon that vast basis of the supremacy of Individuality—that new moral American continent without which, I see, the physical continent remained incomplete, may-be a carcass, a bloat—that newer America, answering face to face with The States, with ever-satisfying and ever-unsurveyable seas and shores.

Those shores you found. I say you have led The States there—have led Me there. I say that none has ever done, or ever can do, a greater deed for The States, than your deed. Others may line out the lines, build cities, work mines, break up farms; it is yours to have been the original true Captain who put to sea, intuitive, positive, rendering the first report, to be told less by any report, and more by the mariners of a thousand bays, in each tack of their arriving and departing, many years after you.

Receive, dear Master, these statements and assurances through me, for all the young men, and for an earnest that we know none before you, but the best following you; and that we demand to take your name into our keeping, and that we understand what you have indicated, and find the same indicated in ourselves, and that we will stick to it and enlarge upon it through These States.

WALT WHITMAN.

1856

LIVE OAK, WITH MOSS[1]

I.

Not the heat flames up and consumes,
Not the sea-waves hurry in and out,
Not the air, delicious and dry, the air of the ripe summer, bears lightly along
    white down-balls of myriads of seeds, wafted, sailing gracefully, to drop
    where they may,
Not these—O none of these, more than the flames of me, consuming, burning
    for his love whom I love—O none, more than I, hurrying in and out;
Does the tide hurry, seeking something, and never give up?—O I, the same,
    to seek my life-long lover;   5
O nor down-balls, nor perfumes, nor the high rain-emitting clouds, are borne
    through the open air, more than my copious soul is borne through the
    openair, wafted in all directions, for friendship, for love.—

1. In none of the editions did the *Calamus* poems constitute so direct and coherent a sexual-poetic narrative as Whitman had made in the *Live Oak* sequence. Whitman's original "programme" of "adhesiveness"—what would now be termed a gay manifesto—is printed here in its entirety. In 1953 Fredson Bowers first printed the sequence in *Studies in Bibliography*, from the manuscripts in the Valentine Collection in the Library of Clifton Waller Barrett. The texts here are based on Mark Niemeyer's fresh collation from those manuscripts.

II.

I saw in Louisiana a live-oak growing,
All alone stood it, and the moss hung down from the branches,
Without any companion it grew there, glistening out joyous leaves of dark
      green,
And its look, rude, unbending, lusty, made me think of myself;   10
But I wondered how it could utter joyous leaves, standing alone there without
      its friend, its lover—For I knew I could not;
And I plucked a twig with a certain number of leaves upon it, and twined
      around it a little moss, and brought it away—And I have placed it in sight
      in my room,
It is not needed to remind me as of my friends, (for I believe lately I think of
      little else than of them,)
Yet it remains to me a curious token—it makes me think of manly love,
For all that, and though the live oak glistens there in Louisiana, solitary in a
      wide flat space, uttering joyous leaves all its life, without a friend, a lover,
      near—I know very well I could not.   15

III.

When I heard at the close of the day how I had been praised in the Capitol,
      still it was not a happy night for me that followed;
Nor when I caroused—Nor when my favorite plans were accomplished—was
      I really happy,
But that day I rose at dawn from the bed of perfect health, electric, inhaling
      sweet breath,
When I saw the full moon in the west grow pale and disappear in the morn-
      ing light,
When I wandered alone over the beach, and undressing, bathed, laughing
      with the waters, and saw the sun rise,   20
And when I thought how my friend, my lover, was coming, then O I was
      happy;
Each breath tasted sweeter—and all that day my food nourished me more—
      And the beautiful day passed well,
And the next came with equal joy—And with the next, at evening, came
      my friend,
And that night, while all was still, I heard the waters roll slowly continually
      up the shores
I heard the hissing rustle of the liquid and sands, as directed to me, whispering
      to congratulate me,—For the friend I love lay sleeping by my side,   25
In the stillness his face was inclined towards me, while the moon's clear
      beams shone,
And his arm lay lightly over my breast—And that night I was happy.

IV.

This moment as I sit alone, yearning and pensive, it seems to me there are
      other men, in other lands, yearning and pensive.
It seems to me I can look over and behold them, in Germany, France,
      Spain—Or far away in China, India, or Russia—talking other dialects,

And it seems to me if I could know those men I should love them as I love
　　men in my own lands,   30
It seems to me they are as wise, beautiful, benevolent, as any in my own lands;
O I think we should be brethren—I think I should be happy with them.

V.

Long I thought that knowledge alone would suffice me—O if I could but
　　obtain knowledge!
Then the Land of the Prairies engrossed me—the south savannas engrossed
　　me—For them I would live—I would be their orator;
Then I met the examples of old and new heroes—I heard of warriors, sailors,
　　and all dauntless persons—And it seemed to me I too had it in me to be
　　as dauntless as any, and would be so;   35
And then to finish all, it came to me to strike up the songs of the New World—
　　And then I believed my life must be spent in singing;
But now take notice, Land of the prairies, Land of the south savannas,
　　Ohio's land,
Take notice, you Kanuck woods—and you, Lake Huron—and all that with
　　you roll toward Niagara—and you Niagara also,
And you, Californian mountains—that you all find some one else that he be
　　your singer of songs,
For I can be your singer of songs no longer—I have ceased to enjoy them.   40
I have found him who loves me, as I him, in perfect love,
With the rest I dispense—I sever from all that I thought would suffice me, for
　　it does not—it is now empty and tasteless to me,
I heed knowledge, and the grandeur of The States, and the examples of heroes,
　　no more,
I am indifferent to my own songs—I am to go with him I love, and he is to go
　　with me,
It is to be enough for each of us that we are together—We never separate
　　again.—   45

VI.

What think you I have taken my pen to record?
Not the battle-ship, perfect-model'd, majestic, that I saw to day arrive in the
　　offing, under full sail,
Nor the splendors of the past day—nor the splendors of the night that enve-
　　lopes me—Nor the glory and growth of the great city spread around me,
But the two men I saw to-day on the pier, parting the parting of dear friends.
The one to remain hung on the other's neck and passionately kissed him—
　　while the one to depart tightly prest the one to remain in his arms.   50

VII.

You bards of ages hence! when you refer to me, mind not so much my poems,
Nor speak of me that I prophesied of The States and led them the way of
　　their glories,

But come, I will inform you who I was underneath that impassive exterior—I
    will tell you what to say of me,
Publish my name and hang up my picture as that of the tenderest lover,
The friend, the lover's portrait, of whom his friend, his lover, was fondest, 55
Who was not proud of his songs, but of the measureless ocean of love within
    him—and freely poured it forth,
Who often walked lonesome walks thinking of his dearest friends, his lovers,
Who pensive, away from one he loved, often lay sleepless and dissatisfied
    at night,
Who, dreading lest the one he loved might after all be indifferent to him, felt
    the sick feeling—O sick! sick!
Whose happiest days were those, far away through fields, in woods, on hills,
    he and another, wandering hand in hand, they twain, apart from other
    men.   60
Who ever, as he sauntered the streets, curved with his arm the manly shoulder
    of his friend—while the curving arm of his friend rested upon him also.

VIII.

Hours continuing long, sore and heavy-hearted,
Hours of the dusk, when I withdraw to a lonesome and unfrequented spot,
    seating myself, leaning my face in my hands,
Hours sleepless, deep in the night, when I go forth, speeding swiftly the coun-
    try roads, or through the city streets, or pacing miles and miles, stifling
    plaintive cries,
Hours discouraged, distracted,—For he, the one I cannot content myself with-
    out—soon I saw him content himself without me, 65
Hours when I am forgotten—(O weeks and months are passing, but I believe
    I am never to forget!)
Sullen and suffering hours—(I am ashamed—but it is useless—I am what
    I am;)
Hours of torment—I wonder if other men ever have the like, out of the like
    feelings?
Is there even one other like me—distracted—his friend, his lover, lost to him?
Is he too as I am now? Does he still rise in the morning, dejected, thinking
    who is lost to him? 70
And at night, awaking, think who is lost?
Does he too harbor his friendship silent and endless? Harbor his anguish and
    passion?
Does some stray reminder, or the casual mention of a name, bring the fit back
    upon him, taciturn and deprest?
Does he see himself reflected in me? In these hours does he see the face of his
    hours reflected?

IX.

I dreamed in a dream of a city where all the men were like brothers, 75
O I saw them tenderly love each other—I often saw them, in numbers, walk-
    ing hand in hand;
I dreamed that was the city of robust friends—Nothing was greater there than
    manly love—it led the rest,

It was seen every hour in the actions of the men of that city, and in all their
looks and words.—

X.

O you whom I often and silently come where you are, that I may be with you,
As I walk by your side, or sit near, or remain in the same room with you,   80
Little you know the subtle electric fire that for your sake is playing within
me.—

XI.

Earth! Though you look so impassive, ample and spheric there—I now suspect
that is not all,
I now suspect there is something terrible in you, ready to break forth,
For an athlete loves me,—and I him—But toward him there is something
fierce and terrible in me,
I dare not tell it in words—not even in these songs.   85

XII.

To the young man, many things to absorb, to engraft, to develop, I teach, that
he be my eleve,
But if through him speed not the blood of friendship, hot and red—If he be
not silently selected by lovers, and do not silently select lovers—of what
use were it for him to seek to become eleve of mine?

FROM CHILDREN OF ADAM[1]

From Pent-up Aching Rivers

From pent-up aching rivers,
From that of myself without which I were nothing,
From what I am determin'd to make illustrious, even if I stand sole among
men,
From my own voice resonant, singing the phallus,
Singing the song of procreation,   5
Singing the need of superb children and therein superb grown people,
Singing the muscular urge and the blending,

1. This group of poems celebrating sex first appeared
in the 1860 edition of *Leaves of Grass* as *Enfans
d'Adam*; later the contents and order were slightly altered until they reached final form in 1871. In their
edition Blodgett and Bradley quote a note in which
Whitman identifies the relationship of this group to the
Calamus poems: "Theory of a Cluster of Poems the
same *to the passion of Woman-Love* as the 'Calamus-
Leaves' are to adhesiveness, manly love. Full of ani-
mal-fire, tender, burning,—the tremulous ache, delicious, yet such a torment. The swelling elate and vehement, that will not be denied. Adam, as a central figure
and type. One piece presenting a vivid picture (in connection with the spirit) of a fully complete, well-developed man, eld, bearded, swart, fiery,—as a more than
rival of the youthful type-hero of novels and love
poems."

Singing the bedfellow's song, (O resistless yearning!
O for any and each the body correlative attracting!
O for you whoever you are your correlative body! O it, more than all else,
    you delighting!)   10
From the hungry gnaw that eats me night and day,
From native moments, from bashful pains, singing them,
Seeking something yet unfound though I have diligently sought it many a
    long year,
Singing the true song of the soul fitful at random,
Renascent with grossest Nature or among animals,   15
Of that, of them and what goes with them my poems informing,
Of the smell of apples and lemons, of the pairing of birds,
Of the wet of woods, of the lapping of waves,
Of the mad pushes of waves upon the land, I them chanting,
The overture lightly sounding, the strain anticipating,   20
The welcome nearness, the sight of the perfect body,
The swimmer swimming naked in the bath, or motionless on his back lying
    and floating,
The female form approaching, I pensive, love-flesh tremulous aching,
The divine list for myself or you or for any one making,
The face, the limbs, the index from head to foot, and what it arouses,   25
The mystic deliria, the madness amorous, the utter abandonment,
(Hark close and still what I now whisper to you,
I love you, O you entirely possess me,
O that you and I escape from the rest and go utterly off, free and lawless,
Two hawks in the air, two fishes swimming in the sea not more lawless than
    we;)   30
The furious storm through me careering, I passionately trembling,
The oath of the inseparableness of two together, of the woman that loves me
    and whom I love more than my life, that oath swearing,
(O I willingly stake all for you,
O let me be lost if it must be so!
O you and I! what is it to us what the rest do or think?   35
What is all else to us? only that we enjoy each other and exhaust each other if
    it must be so;)
From the master, the pilot I yield the vessel to,
The general commanding me, commanding all, from him permission taking,
From time the programme hastening, (I have loiter'd too long as it is,)
From sex, from the warp and from the woof,[2]   40
From privacy, from frequent repinings alone,
From plenty of persons near and yet the right person not near,
From the soft sliding of hands over me and thrusting of fingers through my
    hair and beard,
From the long sustain'd kiss upon the mouth or bosom,
From the close pressure that makes me or any man drunk, fainting with
    excess,
    45
From what the divine husband knows, from the work of fatherhood,
From exultation, victory and relief, from the bedfellow's embrace in the night,
From the act-poems of eyes, hands, hips and bosoms,
From the cling of the trembling arm,

---

2. Lengthwise ("warp") and crosswise ("woof") threads in a fabric.

From the bending curve and the clinch,   50
From side by side the pliant coverlet off-throwing,

From the one so unwilling to have me leave, and me just as unwilling to leave,
(Yet a moment O tender waiter, and I return,)
From the hour of shining stars and dropping dews,
From the night a moment I emerging flitting out,   55
Celebrate you act divine and you children prepared for,
And you stalwart loins.

                                                                    1860, 1881

Spontaneous Me

Spontaneous me, Nature,
The loving day, the mounting sun, the friend I am happy with,
The arm of my friend hanging idly over my shoulder,
The hillside whiten'd with blossoms of the mountain ash,
The same late in autumn, the hues of red, yellow, drab, purple, and light and
     dark green,   5
The rich coverlet of the grass, animals and birds, the private untrimm'd bank,
     the primitive apples, the pebble-stones,
Beautiful dripping fragments, the negligent list of one after another as I happen
     to call them to me or think of them,
The real poems, (what we call poems being merely pictures,)
The poems of the privacy of the night, and of men like me,
This poem drooping shy and unseen that I always carry, and that all men
     carry,   10
(Know once for all, avow'd on purpose, wherever are men like me, are our
     lusty lurking masculine poems,)
Love-thoughts, love-juice, love-odor, love-yielding, love-climbers, and the
     climbing sap,
Arms and hands of love, lips of love, phallic thumb of love, breasts of love,
     bellies press'd and glued together with love,
Earth of chaste love, life that is only life after love,
The body of my love, the body of the woman I love, the body of the man, the
     body of the earth,   15
Soft forenoon airs that blow from the south-west,
The hairy wild-bee that murmurs and hankers up and down, that gripes the
     full-grown lady-flower, curves upon her with amorous firm legs, takes his
     will of her, and holds himself tremulous and tight till he is satisfied;
The wet of woods through the early hours,
Two sleepers at night lying close together as they sleep, one with an arm
     slanting down across and below the waist of the other,
The smell of apples, aromas from crush'd sage-plant, mint, birch-bark,   20
The boy's longings, the glow and pressure as he confides to me what he was
     dreaming,
The dead leaf whirling its spiral whirl and falling still and content to the ground,
The no-form'd stings that sights, people, objects, sting me with,
The hubb'd sting of myself, stinging me as much as it ever can any one,

The sensitive, orbic, underlapp'd brothers, that only privileged feelers may be
    intimate where they are,   25
The curious roamer the hand roaming all over the body, the bashful withdraw-
    ing of flesh where the fingers soothingly pause and edge themselves,
The limpid liquid within the young man,
The vex'd corrosion so pensive and so painful,
The torment, the irritable tide that will not be at rest,
The like of the same I feel, the like of the same in others,   30
The young man that flushes and flushes, and the young woman that flushes
    and flushes,
The young man that wakes deep at night, the hot hand seeking to repress what
    would master him,
The mystic amorous night, the strange half-welcome pangs, visions, sweats,
The pulse pounding through palms and trembling encircling fingers, the
    young man all color'd, red, ashamed, angry;
The souse upon me of my lover the sea, as I lie willing and naked,   35
The merriment of the twin babes that crawl over the grass in the sun, the
    mother never turning her vigilant eyes from them,
The walnut-trunk, the walnut-husks, and the ripening or ripen'd long-round
    walnuts,
The continence of vegetables, birds, animals,
The consequent meanness of me should I skulk or find myself indecent, while
    birds and animals never once skulk or find themselves indecent,
The great chastity of paternity, to match the great chastity of maternity,   40
The oath of procreation I have sworn, my Adamic and fresh daughters,
The greed that eats me day and night with hungry gnaw, till I saturate what
    shall produce boys to fill my place when I am through,
The wholesome relief, repose, content,
And this bunch pluck'd at random from myself,
It has done its work—I toss it carelessly to fall where it may.   45

1856, 1867

Once I Pass'd through a Populous City[1]

Once I pass'd through a populous city imprinting my brain for future use with
    its shows, architecture, customs, traditions,
Yet now of all that city I remember only a woman I casually met there who
    detain'd me for love of me,
Day by day and night by night we were together—all else has long been forgot-
    ten by me,
I remember I say only that woman who passionately clung to me,
Again we wander, we love, we separate again,   5
Again she holds me by the hand, I must not go,
I see her close beside me with silent lips sad and tremulous.

1860, 1861

---

1. Whitman revised this poem significantly for publication. Blodgett and Bradley quote from the manuscript, where the second line reads "But now of all that
city I remember only the man who wandered with me,
there, for love of me," and where the fourth line includes the words "—I remember, I say, only one rude
and ignorant man."

Facing West from California's Shores

Facing west from California's shores,
Inquiring, tireless, seeking what is yet unfound,
I, a child, very old, over waves, towards the house of maternity, the land of
    migrations, look afar,
Look off the shores of my Western sea, the circle almost circled;
For starting westward from Hindustan, from the vales of Kashmere,   5
From Asia, from the north, from the God, the sage, and the hero,
From the south, from the flowery peninsulas and the spice islands,
Long having wander'd since, round the earth having wander'd,
Now I face home again, very pleas'd and joyous,
(But where is what I started for so long ago?   10
And why is it yet unfound?)

1860, 1867

From Calamus[1]

Scented Herbage of My Breast

Scented herbage of my breast,
Leaves from you I glean, I write, to be perused best afterwards,
Tomb-leaves, body-leaves growing up above me above death,
Perennial roots, tall leaves, O the winter shall not freeze you delicate leaves,
Every year shall you bloom again, out from where you retired you shall emerge
    again;   5
O I do not know whether many passing by will discover you or inhale your
    faint odor, but I believe a few will;
O slender leaves! O blossoms of my blood! I permit you to tell in your own
    way of the heart that is under you,
O I do not know what you mean there underneath yourselves, you are not
    happiness,
You are often more bitter than I can bear, you burn and sting me,
Yet you are beautiful to me you faint tinged roots, you make me think of
    death,   10
Death is beautiful from you, (what indeed is finally beautiful except death
    and love?)
O I think it is not for life I am chanting here my chant of lovers, I think it
    must be for death,
For how calm, how solemn it grows to ascend to the atmosphere of lovers,
Death or life I am then indifferent, my soul declines to prefer,

1. The *Calamus* group first appeared in the 3rd edition of *Leaves of Grass* (1860) and was given its final contents and order in 1881. Comparisons with the *Children of Adam* sequence are inevitable; Whitman himself saw the first as celebrating "amative" love of men and women and the *Calamus* poems as celebrating "adhesive love" of men for men. Blodgett and Bradley quote Whitman's insistence in *Democratic Vistas* that the adhesive love he celebrates was political in nature: "It is to the development, identification, and general prevalence of that fervid comradeship, (the adhesive love, at least rivaling the amative love hitherto possessing imaginative literature, if not going beyond it,) that I look for the counterbalance and offset of our materialistic and vulgar American democracy, and for the spiritualization thereof." For the 1876 preface to *Leaves of Grass* Whitman rewrote this passage as a direct comment on the *Calamus* poems.

(I am not sure but the high soul of lovers welcomes death most,) 15
Indeed O death, I think now these leaves mean precisely the same as you
    mean,
Grow up taller sweet leaves that I may see! grow up out of my breast!
Spring away from the conceal'd heart there!
Do not fold yourself so in your pink-tinged roots timid leaves!
Do not remain down there so ashamed, herbage of my breast! 20
Come I am determin'd to unbare this broad breast of mine, I have long enough
    stifled and choked;
Emblematic and capricious blades I leave you, now you serve me not,
I will say what I have to say by itself,
I will sound myself and comrades only, I will never again utter a call only
    their call,
I will raise with it immortal reverberations through the States, 25
I will give an example to lovers to take permanent shape and will through the
    States,
Through me shall the words be said to make death exhilarating,
Give me your tone therefore O death, that I may accord with it,
Give me yourself, for I see that you belong to me now above all, and are folded
    inseparably together, you love and death are,
Nor will I allow you to balk me any more with what I was calling life, 30
For now it is convey'd to me that you are the purports essential,
That you hide in these shifting forms of life, for reasons, and that they are
    mainly for you,
That you beyond them come forth to remain, the real reality,
That behind the mask of materials you patiently wait, no matter how long,
That you will one day perhaps take control of all, 35
That you will perhaps dissipate this entire show of appearance,
That may-be you are what it is all for, but it does not last so very long,
But you will last very long.

1860, 1881

Whoever You Are Holding Me Now in Hand

Whoever you are holding me now in hand,
Without one thing all will be useless,
I give you fair warning before you attempt me further,
I am not what you supposed, but far different.

Who is he that would become my follower? 5
Who would sign himself a candidate for my affections?

The way is suspicious, the result uncertain, perhaps destructive,
You would have to give up all else, I alone would expect to be your sole and
    exclusive standard,
Your novitiate would even then be long and exhausting,
The whole past theory of your life and all conformity to the lives around you
    would have to be abandon'd, 10
Therefore release me now before troubling yourself any further, let go your
    hand from my shoulders,
Put me down and depart on your way.

Or else by stealth in some wood for trial,
Or back of a rock in the open air,
(For in any roof'd room of a house I emerge not, nor in company,   15
And in libraries I lie as one dumb, a gawk, or unborn, or dead,)
But just possibly with you on a high hill, first watching lest any person for
     miles around approach unawares,
Or possibly with you sailing at sea, or on the beach of the sea or some quiet
     island,
Here to put your lips upon mine I permit you,
With the comrade's long-dwelling kiss or the new husband's kiss,   20
For I am the new husband and I am the comrade.

Of if you will, thrusting me beneath your clothing,
Where I may feel the throbs of your heart or rest upon your hip,
Carry me when you go forth over land or sea;
For thus merely touching you is enough, is best,   25
And thus touching you would I silently sleep and be carried eternally.

But these leaves conning you con at peril,
For these leaves and me you will not understand,
They will elude you at first and still more afterward, I will certainly elude you,
Even while you should think you had unquestionably caught me, behold!   30
Already you see I have escaped from you.

For it is not for what I have put into it that I have written this book,
Nor is it by reading it you will acquire it,
Nor do those know me best who admire me and vauntingly praise me,
Nor will the candidates for my love (unless at most a very few) prove
     victorious,   35
Nor will my poems do good only, they will do just as much evil, perhaps more,
For all is useless without that which you may guess at many times and not hit,
     that which I hinted at;
Therefore release me and depart on your way.

                                        1860, 1881

Trickle Drops

Trickle drops! my blue veins leaving!
O drops of me! trickle, slow drops,
Candid from me falling, drip, bleeding drops,
From wounds made to free you whence you were prison'd,
From my face, from my forehead and lips,   5
From my breast, from within where I was conceal'd, press forth red drops,
     confession drops,
Stain every page, stain every song I sing, every word I say, bloody drops,
Let them know your scarlet heat, let them glisten,
Saturate them with yourself all ashamed and wet,
Glow upon all I have written or shall write, bleeding drops,   10
Let it all be seen in your light, blushing drops.

                                        1860, 1867

Here the Frailest Leaves of Me

Here the frailest leaves of me and yet my strongest lasting,
Here I shade and hide my thoughts, I myself do not expose them,
And yet they expose me more than all my other poems.

1860, 1871

Crossing Brooklyn Ferry[1]

1

Flood-tide below me! I see you face to face!
Clouds of the west—sun there half an hour high—I see you also face to face.

Crowds of men and women attired in the usual costumes, how curious you
are to me!
On the ferry-boats the hundreds and hundreds that cross, returning home, are
more curious to me than you suppose,
And you that shall cross from shore to shore years hence are more to me, and
more in my meditations, than you might suppose.   5

2

The impalpable sustenance of me from all things at all hours of the day,
The simple, compact, well-join'd scheme, myself disintegrated, every one dis-
integrated yet part of the scheme,
The similitudes of the past and those of the future,
The glories strung like beads on my smallest sights and hearings, on the walk
in the street and the passage over the river,
The current rushing so swiftly and swimming with me far away,   10
The others that are to follow me, the ties between me and them,
The certainty of others, the life, love, sight, hearing of others.

Others will enter the gates of the ferry and cross from shore to shore,
Others will watch the run of the flood-tide,
Others will see the shipping of Manhattan north and west, and the heights of
Brooklyn to the south and east,   15
Others will see the islands large and small;
Fifty years hence, others will see them as they cross, the sun half an hour high,
A hundred years hence, or ever so many hundred years hence, others will
see them,
Will enjoy the sunset, the pouring-in of the flood-tide, the falling-back to the
sea of the ebb-tide.

3

It avails not, time nor place—distance avails not,   20
I am with you, you men and women of a generation, or ever so many generations hence,

1. *Crossing Brooklyn Ferry* is one of a dozen poems
that follow the *Calamus* section and precede the *Birds
of Passage* section; mostly longish poems, like this one,
they have no section titles. Perhaps the clearest exam-
ple of Whitman's desire to work by indirection, *Cross-* ing *Brooklyn Ferry* succeeds by alluring the reader
without his or her quite knowing why. First published
as *Sun-Down Poem* in the 2nd edition. (1856), *Crossing Brooklyn Ferry* was given its final title in 1860.

Just as you feel when you look on the river and sky, so I felt,
Just as any of you is one of a living crowd, I was one of a crowd,
Just as you are refresh'd by the gladness of the river and the bright flow, I
    was refresh'd,
Just as you stand and lean on the rail, yet hurry with the swift current, I stood
    yet was hurried,   25
Just as you look on the numberless masts of ships and the thick-stemm'd pipes
    of steamboats, I look'd.

I too many and many a time cross'd the river of old,
Watched the Twelfth-month[2] sea-gulls, saw them high in the air floating with
    motionless wings, oscillating their bodies,
Saw how the glistening yellow lit up parts of their bodies and left the rest in
    strong shadow,
Saw the slow-wheeling circles and the gradual edging toward the south,   30
Saw the reflection of the summer sky in the water,
Had my eyes dazzled by the shimmering track of beams,
Look'd at the fine centrifugal spokes of light round the shape of my head in
    the sunlit water,
Look'd on the haze on the hills southward and south-westward,
Look'd on the vapor as it flew in fleeces tinged with violet,   35
Look'd toward the lower bay to notice the vessels arriving,
Saw their approach, saw aboard those that were near me,
Saw the white sails of schooners and sloops, saw the ships at anchor,
The sailors at work in the rigging or out astride the spars,
The round masts, the swinging motion of the hulls, the slender serpentine
    pennants,   40
The large and small steamers in motion, the pilots in their pilot-houses,
The white wake left by the passage, the quick tremulous whirl of the wheels,
The flags of all nations, the falling of them at sunset.
The scallop-edged waves in the twilight, the ladled cups, the frolicsome crests
    and glistening,
The stretch afar growing dimmer and dimmer, the gray walls of the granite
    storehouses by the docks,   45
On the river the shadowy group, the big steam-tug closely flank'd on each side
    by the barges, the hay-boat, the belated lighter,[3]
On the neighboring shore the fires from the foundry chimneys burning high
    and glaringly into the night,
Casting their flicker of black contrasted with wild red and yellow light over the
    tops of houses, and down into the clefts of streets.

4

These and all else were to me the same as they are to you,
I loved well those cities, loved well the stately and rapid river,   50
The men and women I saw were all near to me,
Others the same—others who looked back on me because I look'd forward to
    them,
(The time will come, though I stop here to-day and to-night.)

2. December.   3. Barge used to load or unload a cargo ship.

5

What is it then between us?
What is the count of the scores or hundreds of years between us?   55

Whatever it is, it avails not—distance avails not, and place avails not,
I too lived, Brooklyn of ample hills was mine,
I too walk'd the streets of Manhattan island, and bathed in the waters around
    it,
I too felt the curious abrupt questionings stir within me,
In the day among crowds of people sometimes they came upon me,   60
In my walks home late at night or as I lay in my bed they came upon me,
I too had been struck from the float forever held in solution,
I too had receiv'd identity by my body,
That I was I knew was of my body, and what I should be I knew I should be of
    my body.

6

It is not upon you alone the dark patches fall,   65
The dark threw its patches down upon me also,
The best I had done seem'd to me blank and suspicious,
My great thoughts as I supposed them, were they not in reality meagre?
Nor is it you alone who know what it is to be evil,
I am he who knew what it was to be evil,   70
I too knitted the old knot of contrariety,
Blabb'd, blush'd, resented, lied, stole, grudg'd,
Had guile, anger, lust, hot wishes I dared not speak,
Was wayward, vain, greedy, shallow, sly, cowardly, malignant,
The wolf, the snake, the hog, not wanting in me,   75
The cheating look, the frivolous word, the adulterous wish, not wanting,
Refusals, hates, postponements, meanness, laziness, none of these wanting,
Was one with the rest, the days and haps of the rest,
Was call'd by my nighest name by clear loud voices of young men as they
    saw me approaching or passing,
Felt their arms on my neck as I stood, or the negligent leaning of their flesh
    against me as I sat,   80
Saw many I loved in the street or ferry-boat or public assembly, yet never
    told them a word,
Lived the same life with the rest, the same old laughing, gnawing, sleeping,
Play'd the part that still looks back on the actor or actress,
The same old role, the role that is what we make it, as great as we like,
Or as small as we like, or both great and small.   85

7

Closer yet I approach you,
What thought you have of me now, I had as much of you—I laid in my stores
    in advance,
I consider'd long and seriously of you before you were born.

Who was to know what should come home to me?
Who knows but I am enjoying this?

Who knows, for all the distance, but I am as good as looking at you now, for
    all you cannot see me?

8

Ah, what can ever be more stately and admirable to me than mast-hemm'd
    Manhattan?
River and sunset and scallop-edg'd waves of flood-tide?
The sea-gulls oscillating their bodies, the hay-boat in the twilight, and the
    belated lighter?
What gods can exceed these that clasp me by the hand, and with voices I love
    call me promptly and loudly by my nighest name as I approach?   95
What is more subtle than this which ties me to the woman or man that looks
    in my face?
Which fuses me into you now, and pours my meaning into you?

We understand then do we not?
What I promis'd without mentioning it, have you not accepted?
What the study could not teach—what the preaching could not accomplish is
    accomplish'd, is it not?   100

9

Flow on, river! flow with the flood-tide, and ebb with the ebb-tide!
Frolic on, crested and scallop-edg'd waves!
Gorgeous clouds of the sunset! drench with your splendor me, or the men and
    women generations after me!
Cross from shore to shore, countless crowds of passengers!
Stand up, tall masts of Mannahatta![4] stand up, beautiful hills of Brooklyn! 105
Throb, baffled and curious brain! throw out questions and answers!
Suspend here and everywhere, eternal float of solution!
Gaze, loving and thirsting eyes, in the house or street or public assembly!
Sound out, voices of young men! loudly and musically call me by my nighest
    name!
Live, old life! play the part that looks back on the actor or actress!   110
Play the old role, the role that is great or small according as one makes it!
Consider, you who peruse me, whether I may not in unknown ways be looking
    upon you;
Be firm, rail over the river, to support those who lean idly, yet haste with the
    hasting current;
Fly on, sea-birds! fly sideways, or wheel in large circles high in the air;
Receive the summer sky, you water, and faithfully hold it till all downcast eyes
    have time to take it from you!   115
Diverge, fine spokes of light, from the shape of my head, or any one's head,
    in the sunlit water!
Come on, ships from the lower bay! pass up or down, white-sail'd schooners,
    sloops, lighters!
Flaunt away, flags of all nations! be duly lower'd at sunset!
Burn high your fires, foundry chimneys! cast black shadows at nightfall! cast
    red and yellow light over the tops of the houses!

---

4. Variant for the American Indian word normally spelled "Manhattan."

Appearances, now or henceforth, indicate what you are,   120
You necessary film, continue to envelop the soul,
About my body for me, and your body for you, be hung our divinest aromas,
Thrive, cities—bring your freight, bring your shows, ample and sufficient rivers,

Expand, being than which none else is perhaps more spiritual,
Keep your places, objects than which none else is more lasting.   125

You have waited, you always wait, you dumb, beautiful ministers,
We receive you with free sense at last, and are insatiate henceforward,
Not you any more shall be able to foil us, or withhold yourselves from us,
We use you, and do not cast you aside—we plant you permanently within
     us,
We fathom you not—we love you—there is perfection in you also,   130
You furnish your parts toward eternity,
Great or small, you furnish your parts toward the soul.

                                                        1856, 1881

FROM SEA-DRIFT[1]

Out of the Cradle Endlessly Rocking[2]

Out of the cradle endlessly rocking,
Out of the mocking-bird's throat, the musical shuttle,
Out of the Ninth-month midnight,
Over the sterile sands and the fields beyond, where the child leaving his bed
     wander'd alone, bareheaded, barefoot,
Down from the shower'd halo,   5
Up from the mystic play of shadows twining and twisting as if they were alive,
Out from the patches of briers and blackberries,
From the memories of the bird that chanted to me,
From your memories sad brother, from the fitful risings and fallings I heard,
From under that yellow half-moon late-risen and swollen as if with tears, 10
From those beginning notes of yearning and love there in the mist,
From the thousand responses of my heart never to cease,
From the myriad thence-arous'd words,
From the word stronger and more delicious than any,
From such as now they start the scene revisiting,   15
As a flock, twittering, rising, or overhead passing,
Borne hither, ere all eludes me, hurriedly,

1. The *Sea-Drift* section of the 1881 edition of *Leaves of Grass* was made up of two new poems, seven poems from *Sea-Shore Memories* in the 1871 *Passage to India* section, and two poems from the 1876 *Two Rivulets* section.
2. First published as *A Child's Reminiscence* in the *New York Saturday Press* for December 24, 1859, this poem was incorporated into the 1860 *Leaves of Grass* as *A Word Out of the Sea*. Whitman continued to revise it until it reached the present form in the *Sea-Drift*

section of the 1881 edition. *Out of the Cradle Endlessly Rocking* had been the first of the *Sea-Shore Memories* group. The poem is about the way, at a crisis in his adult life, the poet remembers (and now fully comprehends) the boyhood experience of the annunciation of Whitman's role as a poet. On the most obvious level, the poem belongs to the Romantic tradition of poems about the revisiting of a spot important to the poet's earlier life: examples are Wordsworth's *Tintern Abbey* and *Wye Revisited* and Longfellow's *My Lost Youth*.

A man, yet by these tears a little boy again,
Throwing myself on the sand, confronting the waves,
I, chanter of pains and joys, uniter of here and hereafter,   20
Taking all hints to use them, but swiftly leaping beyond them,
A reminiscence sing.

Once Paumanok,[3]
When the lilac-scent was in the air and Fifth-month grass was growing,
Up this seashore in some briers,   25
Two feather'd guests from Alabama, two together,

And their nest, and four light-green eggs spotted with brown,
And every day the he-bird to and fro near at hand,
And every day the she-bird crouch'd on her nest, silent, with bright eyes,
And every day I, a curious boy, never too close, never disturbing them,   30
Cautiously peering, absorbing, translating.

Shine! shine! shine!
Pour down your warmth, great sun!
While we bask, we two together.

Two together!   35
Winds blow south, or winds blow north,
Day come white, or night come black,
Home, or rivers and mountains from home,
Singing all time, minding no time,
While we two keep together.   40

Till of a sudden,
May-be kill'd, unknown to her mate,
One forenoon the she-bird crouch'd not on the nest,
Nor return'd that afternoon, nor the next
Nor ever appear'd again.   45

And thenceforward all summer in the sound of the sea,
And at night under the full of the moon in calmer weather,
Over the hoarse surging of the sea,
Or flitting from brier to brier by day,
I saw, I heard at intervals the remaining one, the he-bird,   50
The solitary guest from Alabama.

Blow! blow! blow!
Blow up sea-winds along Paumanok's shore;
I wait and I wait till you blow my mate to me.

Yes, when the stars glisten'd,   55
All night long on the prong of a moss-scallop'd stake,
Down almost amid the slapping waves,
Sat the lone singer wonderful causing tears.

3. Long Island.

He call'd on his mate,
He pour'd forth the meanings which I of all men know.   60

Yes my brother I know,
The rest might not, but I have treasur'd every note,
For more than once dimly down to the beach gliding,
Silent, avoiding the moonbeams, blending myself with the shadows,
Recalling now the obscure shapes, the echoes, the sounds and sights after their
     sorts,   65
The white arms out in the breakers tirelessly tossing,
I, with bare feet, a child, the wind wafting my hair,
Listen'd long and long.

Listen'd to keep, to sing, now translating the notes.
Following you my brother.   70

Soothe! soothe! soothe!
Close on its wave soothes the wave behind,
And again another behind embracing and lapping, every one close,
But my love soothes not me, not me.

Low hangs the moon, it rose late,   75
It is lagging—O I think it is heavy with love, with love.

O madly the sea pushes upon the land,
With love, with love.

O night! do I not see my love fluttering out among the breakers?
What is that little black thing I see there in the white?   80

Loud! loud! loud!
Loud I call to you, my love!

High and clear I shoot my voice over the waves,
Surely you must know who is here, is here,
You must know who I am, my love.   85

Low-hanging moon!
What is that dusky spot in your brown yellow?
O it is the shape, the shape of my mate!
O moon do not keep her from me any longer.

Land! land! O land!   90
Whichever way I turn, O I think you could give me my mate back again if you
     only would,
For I am almost sure I see her dimly whichever way I look.

O rising stars!
Perhaps the one I want so much will rise, will rise with some of you.

O throat! O trembling throat!   95
Sound clearer through the atmosphere!
Pierce the woods, the earth,
Somewhere listening to catch you must be the one I want.

Shake out carols!
Solitary here, the night's carols!   100
Carols of lonesome love! death's carols!
Carols under that lagging, yellow, waning moon!
O under that moon where she droops almost down into the sea!
O reckless despairing carols.

But soft! sink low!   105
Soft! let me just murmur,
And do you wait a moment you husky-nois'd sea,
For somewhere I believe I heard my mate responding to me,
So faint, I must be still, be still to listen,
But not altogether still, for then she might not come immediately to me.   110

Hither my love!
Here I am! here!
With this just-sustain'd note I announce myself to you,
This gentle call is for you my love, for you.

Do not be decoy'd elsewhere,   115
That is the whistle of the wind, it is not my voice,
That is the fluttering, the fluttering of the spray,
Those are the shadows of leaves.

O darkness! O in vain!
O I am very sick and sorrowful.   120

O brown halo in the sky near the moon, drooping upon the sea!
O troubled reflection in the sea!
O throat! O throbbing heart!
And I singing uselessly, uselessly all the night.

O past! O happy life! O songs of joy!   125
In the air, in the woods, over fields,
Loved! loved! loved! loved! loved!
But my mate no more, no more with me!
We two together no more.

The aria sinking,   130
All else continuing, the stars shining,
The winds blowing, the notes of the bird continuous echoing,
With angry moans the fierce old mother incessantly moaning,
On the sands of Paumanok's shore gray and rustling,
The yellow half-moon enlarged, sagging down, drooping, the face of the sea
    almost touching,   135
The boy ecstatic, with his bare feet the waves, with his hair the atmosphere
    dallying,
The love in the heart long pent, now loose, now at last tumultuously bursting,
The aria's meaning, the ears, the soul, swiftly depositing,
The strange tears down the cheeks coursing,
The colloquy there, the trio, each uttering,   140
The undertone, the savage old mother incessantly crying,

To the boy's soul's questions sullenly timing, some drown'd secret hissing,
To the outsetting bard.

Demon or bird! (said the boy's soul,)
Is it indeed toward your mate you sing? or is it really to me?   145
For I, that was a child, my tongue's use sleeping, now I have heard you,
Now in a moment I know what I am for, I awake,
And already a thousand singers, a thousand songs, clearer, louder and more
       sorrowful than yours,
A thousand warbling echoes have started to life within me, never to die.

O you singer solitary, singing by yourself, projecting me,   150
O solitary me listening, never more shall I cease perpetuating you,
Never more shall I escape, never more the reverberations,
Never more the cries of unsatisfied love be absent from me,
Never again leave me to be the peaceful child I was before what there in
       the night,
By the sea under the yellow and sagging moon,   155
The messenger there arous'd, the fire, the sweet hell within,
The unknown want, the destiny of me.

O give me the clew! (it lurks in the night here somewhere,)
O if I am to have so much, let me have more!

A word then, (for I will conquer it,)   160
The word final, superior to all,
Subtle, sent up—what is it?—I listen;
Are you whispering it, and have been all the time, you sea-waves?
Is that it from your liquid rims and wet sands?

Whereto answering, the sea,   165
Delaying not, hurrying not,
Whisper'd me through the night, and very plainly before daybreak,
Lisp'd to me the low and delicious word death,
And again death, death, death, death,
Hissing melodious, neither like the bird nor like my arous'd child's heart,   170
But edging near as privately for me rustling at my feet,
Creeping thence steadily up to my ears and laving me softly all over,
Death, death, death, death, death.

Which I do not forget,
But fuse the song of my dusky demon and brother,   175
That he sang to me in the moonlight on Paumanok's gray beach,
With the thousand responsive songs at random,
My own songs awaked from that hour,
And with them the key, the word up from the waves,
The word of the sweetest song and all songs,   180
That strong and delicious word which, creeping to my feet,
(Or like some old crone rocking the cradle, swathed in sweet garments, bend-
       ing aside,)
The sea whisper'd me.

1859, 1881

As I Ebb'd with the Ocean of Life[1]

1

As I ebb'd with the ocean of life,
As I wended the shores I know,
As I walk'd where the ripples continually wash you Paumanok,[2]
Where they rustle up hoarse and sibilant,
Where the fierce old mother endlessly cries for her castaways,   5
I musing late in the autumn day, gazing off southward,
Held by this electric self out of the pride of which I utter poems,
Was seiz'd by the spirit that trails in the lines underfoot,
The rim, the sediment that stands for all the water and all the land of the
     globe.

Fascinated, my eyes reverting from the south, dropt, to follow those slender
     windrows,   10
Chaff, straw, splinters of wood, weeds, and the sea-gluten,[3]
Scum, scales from shining rocks, leaves of salt-lettuce, left by the tide,
Miles walking, the sound of breaking waves the other side of me,
Paumanok there and then as I thought the old thought of likenesses,
These you presented to me you fish-shaped island,   15
As I wended the shores I know,
As I walk'd with that electric self seeking types.[4]

2

As I wend to the shores I know not,
As I list to the dirge, the voices of men and women wreck'd,
As I inhale the impalpable breezes that set in upon me,   20
As the ocean so mysterious rolls toward me closer and closer,
I too but signify at the utmost a little wash'd-up drift,
A few sands and dead leaves to gather,
Gather, and merge myself as part of the sands and drift.

O baffled, balk'd, bent to the very earth,   25
Oppress'd with myself that I have dared to open my mouth,
Aware now that amid all that blab whose echoes recoil upon me I have not
     once had the least idea who or what I am,
But that before all my arrogant poems the real Me stands yet untouch'd,
     untold, altogether unreach'd,
Withdrawn far, mocking me with mock-congratulatory signs and bows,
With peals of distant ironical laughter at every word I have written,   30
Pointing in silence to these songs, and then to the sand beneath.

I perceive I have not really understood any thing, not a single object, and that
     no man ever can,

---

1. This poem was first published as *Bardic Symbols* in
the *Atlantic* for April 1860, but only after James Russell Lowell had expurgated lines 59–60, which Whitman restored when he published the poem next in the
1860 edition of *Leaves of Grass*. Whitman gave it its
final title and position as the second poem in *Sea-Drift*
in the 1881 edition.
2. Long Island.
3. Gummy, viscid substance.
4. Types or likenesses of himself, in the debris left by
the receding tide.

Nature here in sight of the sea taking advantage of me to dart upon me and
    sting me,
Because I have dared to open my mouth to sing at all.

3

You oceans both, I close with you,   35
We murmur alike reproachfully rolling sands and drift, knowing not why,
These little shreds indeed standing for you and me and all.

You friable[5] shore with trails of debris,
You fish-shaped island, I take what is underfoot,
What is yours is mine my father.   40

I too Paumanok,
I too have bubbled up, floated the measureless float, and been wash'd on
    your shores,
I too am but a trail of drift and debris,
I too leave little wrecks upon you, you fish-shaped island.

I throw myself upon your breast my father,   45
I cling to you so that you cannot unloose me,
I hold you so firm till you answer me something.

Kiss me my father,
Touch me with your lips as I touch those I love,
Breathe to me while I hold you close the secret of the murmuring I envy.   50

4

Ebb, ocean of life, (the flow will return,)
Cease not your moaning you fierce old mother,
Endlessly cry for your castaways, but fear not, deny not me,
Rustle not up so hoarse and angry against my feet as I touch you or gather
    from you.

I mean tenderly by you and all,   55
I gather for myself and for this phantom looking down where we lead, and
    following me and mine.
Me and mine, loose windrows, little corpses,
Froth, snowy white, and bubbles,
(See, from my dead lips the ooze exuding at last,
See, the prismatic colors glistening and rolling,)   60
Tufts of straw, sands, fragments,
Buoy'd hither from many moods, one contradicting another,
From the storm, the long calm, the darkness, the swell,
Musing, pondering, a breath, a briny tear, a dab of liquid or soil,
Up just as much out of fathomless workings fermented and thrown,   65
A limp blossom or two, torn, just as much over waves floating, drifted at
    random,
Just as much for us that sobbing dirge of Nature,
Just as much whence we come that blare of the cloud-trumpets,

5. Crumbling.

We, capricious, brought hither we know not whence, spread out before you,
You up there walking or sitting,   70
Whoever you are, we too lie in drifts at your feet.

1860, 1881

FROM BY THE ROADSIDE[1]

A Hand-Mirror

Hold it up sternly—see this it sends back, (who is it? is it you?)
Outside fair costume, within ashes and filth,
No more a flashing eye, no more a sonorous voice or springy step,
Now some slave's eye, voice, hands, step,
A drunkard's breath, unwholesome eater's face, venerealee's flesh,   5
Lungs rotting away piecemeal, stomach sour and cankerous,
Joints rheumatic, bowels clogged with abomination,
Blood circulating dark and poisonous streams,
Words babble, hearing and touch callous,
No brain, no heart left, no magnetism of sex;   10
Such from one look in this looking-glass ere you go hence,
Such a result so soon—and from such a beginning!

1860, 1860

When I Heard the Learn'd Astronomer

When I heard the learn'd astronomer,
When the proofs, the figures, were ranged in columns before me,
When I was shown the charts and diagrams, to add, divide, and measure
    them,
When I sitting heard the astronomer where he lectured with much applause
    in the lecture-room,
How soon unaccountable I became tired and sick,   5
Till rising and gliding out I wander'd off by myself,
In the mystical moist night-air, and from time to time,
Look'd up in perfect silence at the stars.

1865, 1865

To a President

All you are doing and saying is to America dangled mirages,
You have not learn'd of Nature—of the politics of Nature you have not learn'd
    the great amplitude, rectitude, impartiality,
You have not seen that only such as they are for these States,
And that what is less than they must sooner or later lift off from these States.

1860, 1860

1. *By the Roadside* is the 1881 section title for around two dozen poems, most of which first appeared in the 1860 edition of *Leaves of Grass*. As Blodgett and Bradley say, "The group is truly a melange held together by the common bond of the poet's experience as roadside observer—passive, but alert and continually recording." Several of the poems are mere jottings of two, three, or four lines.

I Sit and Look Out

I sit and look out upon all the sorrows of the world, and upon all oppression
    and shame,
I hear secret convulsive sobs from young men at anguish with themselves,
    remorseful after deeds done,
I see in low life the mother misused by her children, dying, neglected, gaunt,
    desperate,
I see the wife misused by her husband, I see the treacherous seducer of young
    women,
I mark the ranklings of jealousy and unrequited love attempted to be hid, I see
    these sights on the earth,   5
I see the workings of battle, pestilence, tyranny, I see martyrs and prisoners,
I observe a famine at sea, I observe the sailors casting lots who shall be kill'd
    to preserve the lives of the rest,
I observe the slights and degradations cast by arrogant persons upon laborers,
    the poor, and upon negroes, and the like;
All these—all the meanness and agony without end I sitting look out upon,
See, hear, and am silent.   10

1860, 1871

The Dalliance of the Eagles

Skirting the river road, (my forenoon walk, my rest,)
Skyward in air a sudden muffled sound, the dalliance of the eagles,
The rushing amorous contact high in space together,
The clinching interlocking claws, a living, fierce, gyrating wheel,
Four beating wings, two beaks, a swirling mass tight grappling,   5
In tumbling turning clustering loops, straight downward falling,
Till o'er the river pois'd, the twain yet one, a moment's lull,
A motionless still balance in the air, then parting, talons loosing,
Upward again on slow-firm pinions slanting, their separate diverse flight,
She hers, he his, pursuing.   10

1880, 1881

To the States

To Identify the 16th, 17th, or 18th Presidentiad[1]

Why reclining, interrogating? why myself and all drowsing?
What deepening twilight—scum floating atop of the waters,
Who are they as bats and night-dogs askant in the capitol?

---

1. Presidency. Whitman is counting two-term presidents (Washington, Jefferson, and Jackson) twice and counting both presidents who died in office and their successors (Harrison and Tyler, Taylor and Fillmore) to arrive at the sixteenth presidentiad for Millard Fill-more's term (1850–53), the seventeenth for Franklin Pierce's term (1853–57), and the eighteenth for James Buchanan's term (1857–61). Whitman's pamphlet *The Eighteenth Presidency!* expresses the same scorn for the presidencies of the 1850s.

What a filthy Presidentiad! (O South, your torrid suns! O North, your arctic
    freezings!)
Are those really Congressmen? are those the great Judges? is that the President? 5
Then I will sleep awhile yet, for I see that these States sleep, for reasons;
(With gathering murk, with muttering thunder and lambent shoots we all duly
    awake,
South, North, East, West, inland and seaboard, we will surely awake.)

                                                                    1860, 1860

FROM DRUM-TAPS[1]

Beat! Beat! Drums!

Beat! beat! drums!—blow! bugles! blow!
Through the windows—through doors—burst like a ruthless force,
Into the solemn church, and scatter the congregation,
Into the school where the scholar is studying;
Leave not the bridegroom quiet—no happiness must he have now with his
    bride,   5
Nor the peaceful farmer any peace, ploughing his field or gathering his grain,
So fierce you whirr and pound you drums—so shrill you bugles blow.

Beat! beat! drums!—blow! bugles! blow!
Over the traffic of cities—over the rumble of wheels in the streets;
Are beds prepared for sleepers at night in the houses? no sleepers must sleep in
    those beds,   10
No bargainers' bargains by day—no brokers or speculators—would they con-
    tinue?
Would the talkers be talking? would the singer attempt to sing?
Would the lawyer rise in the court to state his case before the judge?
Then rattle quicker, heavier drums—you bugles wilder blow.

Beat! beat! drums!—blow! bugles! blow!   15
Make no parley—stop for no expostulation,
Mind not the timid—mind not the weeper or prayer,
Mind not the old man beseeching the young man,
Let not the child's voice be heard, nor the mother's entreaties,

---

1. The contents of the original *Drum-Taps* (first
printed in 1865 as a little book) differed considerably
from the contents of the *Drum-Taps* section finally arrived at in the 1881 *Leaves of Grass*. In the final arrangement the poetic purpose shifts throughout,
roughly reflecting the chronology of the Civil War and
the chronology of the composition of the poems. The
first purpose is propagandistic. Indeed, *Beat! Beat!
Drums!* served as a kind of recruiting poem when it was
first printed (and reprinted) in the fall of 1861, having
been composed after the Southern victory at the first
battle of Bull Run. Later Whitman seems to have understood that the early jingoistic poems had a certain
historical value that made them worth preserving. The
dominant impulse of most of the later poems is realistic—a determination to record the war the way it was,
and in the best of the poems the realistic record is
achieved through elaborate technical subtleties. The
stages of Whitman's own attitudes toward the war are
well stated in the epigraph he gave the whole *Drum-
Taps* group in 1871 then inserted parenthetically into
The Wound Dresser in the 1881 edition: "Arous'd and
angry, I'd thought to beat the alarum, and urge relentless war, / But soon my fingers fail'd me, my face
droop'd and I resign'd myself / To sit by the wounded
and soothe them, or silently watch the dead."

Make even the trestles to shake the dead where they lie awaiting the
    hearses,   20
So strong you thump O terrible drums—so loud you bugles blow.

1861, 1867

Cavalry Crossing a Ford

A line in long array where they wind betwixt green islands,
They take a serpentine course, their arms flash in the sun—hark to the musical
    clank,
Behold the silvery river, in it the splashing horses loitering stop to drink,
Behold the brown-faced men, each group, each person a picture, the negligent
    rest on the saddles,
Some emerge on the opposite bank, others are just entering the ford—
    while,   5
Scarlet and blue and snowy white,
The guidon flags flutter gayly in the wind.

1865, 1871

Vigil Strange I Kept on the Field One Night

Vigil strange I kept on the field one night;
When you my son and my comrade dropt at my side that day,
One look I but gave which your dear eyes return'd with a look I shall never
    forget,
One touch of your hand to mine O boy, reach'd up as you lay on the ground,
Then onward I sped in the battle, the even-contested battle,   5
Till late in the night reliev'd to the place at last again I made my way,
Found you in death so cold dear comrade, found your body son of responding
    kisses, (never again on earth responding,)
Bared your face in the starlight, curious the scene, cool blew the moderate
    night-wind,
Long there and then in vigil I stood, dimly around me the battle-field
    spreading,
Vigil wondrous and vigil sweet there in the fragrant silent night,   10
But not a tear fell, not even a long-drawn sigh, long, long I gazed,
Then on the earth partially reclining sat by your side leaning my chin in my
    hands,
Passing sweet hours, immortal and mystic hours with you dearest comrade—
    not a tear, not a word,
Vigil of silence, love and death, vigil for you my son and my soldier,
As onward silently stars aloft, eastward new ones upward stole,   15
Vigil final for you brave boy, (I could not save you, swift was your death,
I faithfully loved you and cared for you living, I think we shall surely meet
    again,)
Till at latest lingering of the night, indeed just as the dawn appear'd,
My comrade I wrapt in his blanket, envelop'd well his form,
Folded the blanket well, tucking it carefully over head and carefully under
    feet,   20

And there and then and bathed by the rising sun, my son in his grave, in his
    rude-dug grave I deposited,
Ending my vigil strange with that, vigil of night and battle-field dim,
Vigil for boy of responding kisses, (never again on earth responding,)
Vigil for comrade swiftly slain, vigil I never forget, how as day brighten'd,
I rose from the chill ground and folded my soldier well in his blanket,   25
And buried him where he fell.

1865, 1867

A March in the Ranks Hard-Prest, and the Road Unknown

A march in the ranks hard-prest, and the road unknown,
A route through a heavy wood with muffled steps in the darkness,
Our army foil'd with loss severe, and the sullen remnant retreating,
Till after midnight glimmer upon us the lights of a dim-lighted building,
We come to an open space in the woods, and halt by the dim-lighted
    building,   5
'Tis a large old church at the crossing roads, now an impromptu hospital,
Entering but for a minute I see a sight beyond all the pictures and poems
    ever made,
Shadows of deepest, deepest black, just lit by moving candles and lamps,
And by one great pitchy torch stationary with wild red flame and clouds of
    smoke,
By these, crowds, groups of forms vaguely I see on the floor, some in the pews
    laid down,   10
At my feet more distinctly a soldier, a mere lad, in danger of bleeding to death,
    (he is shot in the abdomen,)
I stanch the blood temporarily, (the youngster's face is white as a lily,)
Then before I depart I sweep my eyes o'er the scene fain to absorb it all,
Faces, varieties, postures beyond description, most in obscurity, some of them
    dead,
Surgeons operating, attendants holding lights, the smell of ether, the odor of
    blood,   15
The crowd, O the crowd of the bloody forms, the yard outside also fill'd,
Some on the bare ground, some on planks or stretchers, some in the death-
    spasm sweating,
An occasional scream or cry, the doctor's shouted orders or calls,
The glisten of the little steel instruments catching the glint of the torches,
These I resume as I chant, I see again the forms, I smell the odor,   20
Then hear outside the orders given, *Fall in, my men, fall in;*
But first I bend to the dying lad, his eyes open, a half-smile gives he me,
Then the eyes close, calmly close, and I speed forth to the darkness,
Resuming, marching, ever in darkness marching, on in the ranks,
The unknown road still marching.   25

1865, 1867

A Sight in Camp in the Daybreak Gray and Dim

A sight in camp in the daybreak gray and dim,
As from my tent I emerge so early sleepless,

As slow I walk in the cool fresh air the path near by the hospital tent,
Three forms I see on stretchers lying, brought out there untended lying,
Over each the blanket spread, ample brownish woolen blanket,   5
Gray and heavy blanket, folding, covering all.

Curious I halt and silent stand,
Then with light fingers I from the face of the nearest the first just lift the
     blanket;
Who are you elderly man so gaunt and grim, with well-gray'd hair, and flesh
     all sunken about the eyes?
Who are you my dear comrade?   10
Then to the second I step—and who are you my child and darling?

Who are you sweet boy with cheeks yet blooming?

Then to the third—a face nor child nor old, very calm, as of beautiful yellow-
     white ivory;
Young man I think I know you—I think this face is the face of the Christ
     himself,
Dead and divine and brother of all, and here again he lies.   15

1865, 1867

As Toilsome I Wander'd Virginia's Woods

As toilsome I wander'd Virginia's woods,
To the music of rustling leaves kick'd by my feet, (for 'twas autumn,)
I mark'd at the foot of a tree the grave of a soldier;
Mortally wounded he and buried on the retreat, (easily all could I understand,)
The halt of a mid-day hour, when up! no time to lose—yet this sign left,   5
On a tablet scrawl'd and nail'd on the tree by the grave,
Bold, cautious, true, and my loving comrade.

Long, long I muse, then on my way go wandering,
Many a changeful season to follow, and many a scene of life,
Yet at times through changeful season and scene, abrupt, alone, or in the
     crowded street,   10
Comes before me the unknown soldier's grave, comes the inscription rude in
     Virginia's woods,
Bold, cautious, true, and my loving comrade.

1865, 1867

The Wound-Dresser

1

An old man bending I come among new faces,
Years looking backward resuming in answer to children,
Come tell us old man, as from young men and maidens that love me,
(Arous'd and angry, I'd thought to beat the alarum, and urge relentless war,
But soon my fingers fail'd me, my face droop'd and I resign'd myself,   5

To sit by the wounded and soothe them, or silently watch the dead;)
Years hence of these scenes, of these furious passions, these chances,
Of unsurpass'd heroes, (was one side so brave? the other was equally brave;)
Now be witness again, paint the mightiest armies of earth,
Of those armies so rapid so wondrous what saw you to tell us?   10
What stays with you latest and deepest? of curious panics,
Of hard-fought engagements or sieges tremendous what deepest remains?

2

O maidens and young men I love and that love me,
What you ask of my days those the strangest and sudden your talking recalls,
Soldier alert I arrive after a long march cover'd with sweat and dust,   15
In the nick of time I come, plunge in the fight, loudly shout in the rush of
        successful charge,
Enter the captur'd works[1]—yet lo, like a swift-running river they fade,
Pass and are gone they fade—I dwell not on soldiers' perils or soldiers' joys,
(Both I remember well—many the hardships, few the joys, yet I was content.)

But in silence in dreams' projections,   20
While the world of gain and appearance and mirth goes on,
So soon what is over forgotten, and waves wash the imprints off the sand,
With hinged knees returning I enter the doors, (while for you up there,
Whoever you are, follow without noise and be of strong heart.)

Bearing the bandages, water and sponge,   25
Straight and swift to my wounded I go,
Where they lie on the ground after the battle brought in,
Where their priceless blood reddens the grass the ground,
Or to the rows of the hospital tent, or under the roof'd hospital,
To the long rows of cots up and down each side I return,   30
To each and all one after another I draw near, not one do I miss,
An attendant follows holding a tray, he carries a refuse pail,
Soon to be fill'd with clotted rags and blood, emptied, and fill'd again.

I onward go, I stop,
With hinged knees and steady hand to dress wounds,   35
I am firm with each, the pangs are sharp yet unavoidable,
One turns to me his appealing eyes—poor boy! I never knew you,
Yet I think I could not refuse this moment to die for you, if that would save
        you.

3

On, on I go, (open doors of time! open hospital doors!)
The crush'd head I dress, (poor crazed hand tear not the bandage away,)   40
The neck of the cavalry-man with the bullet through and through I examine,
Hard the breathing rattles, quite glazed already the eye, yet life struggles hard,
(Come sweet death! be persuaded O beautiful death!
In mercy come quickly.)

From the stump of the arm, the amputated hand,   45
I undo the clotted lint, remove the slough, wash off the matter and blood,

1. Fortifications.

Back on his pillow the soldier bends with curv'd neck and side-falling head,
His eyes are closed, his face is pale, he dares not look on the bloody stump,
And has not yet look'd on it.

I dress a wound in the side, deep, deep,   50
But a day or two more, for see the frame all wasted and sinking,
And the yellow-blue countenance see.

I dress the perforated shoulder, the foot with the bullet-wound,
Cleanse the one with a gnawing and putrid gangrene, so sickening, so
    offensive,
While the attendant stands behind aside me holding the tray and pail.   55

I am faithful, I do not give out,
The fractur'd thigh, the knee, the wound in the abdomen,
These and more I dress with impassive hand, (yet deep in my breast a fire, a
    burning flame.)

4

Thus in silence in dreams' projections,
Returning, resuming, I thread my way through the hospitals,   60
The hurt and wounded I pacify with soothing hand,
I sit by the restless all the dark night, some are so young,
Some suffer so much, I recall the experience sweet and sad,
(Many a soldier's loving arms about this neck have cross'd and rested,
Many a soldier's kiss dwells on these bearded lips.)   65

1865, 1881

Reconciliation

Word over all, beautiful as the sky,
Beautiful that war and all its deeds of carnage must in time be utterly lost,
That the hands of the sisters Death and Night incessantly softly wash again,
    and ever again, this soil'd world;
For my enemy is dead, a man divine as myself is dead,
I look where he lies white-faced and still in the coffin—I draw near,   5
Bend down and touch lightly with my lips the white face in the coffin.

1865–66, 1881

As I Lay with My Head in Your Lap Camerado

As I lay with my head in your lap camerado,
The confession I made I resume, what I said to you and the open air I resume,
I know I am restless and make others so,
I know my words are weapons full of danger, full of death,
For I confront peace, security, and all the settled laws, to unsettle them, 5
I am more resolute because all have denied me than I could ever have been
    had all accepted me,
I heed not and have never heeded either experience, cautions, majorities,
    nor ridicule,

And the threat of what is call'd hell is little or nothing to me,
And the lure of what is call'd heaven is little or nothing to me;
Dear camerado! I confess I have urged you onward with me, and still urge
　　you, without the least idea what is our destination,　　　　　　　　10
Or whether we shall be victorious, or utterly quell'd and defeated.

1865–66, 1881

Spirit Whose Work Is Done

(Washington City, 1865.)

Spirit whose work is done—spirit of dreadful hours!
Ere departing fade from my eyes your forests of bayonets;
Spirit of gloomiest fears and doubts, (yet onward ever unfaltering pressing,)
Spirit of many a solemn day and many a savage scene—electric spirit,
That with muttering voice through the war now closed, like a tireless phantom
　　flitted,　　　　　　　　5
Rousing the land with breath of flame, while you beat and beat the drum,
Now as the sound of the drum, hollow and harsh to the last, reverberates
　　round me,
As your ranks, your immortal ranks, return, return from the battles,
As the muskets of the young men yet lean over their shoulders,
As I look on the bayonets bristling over their shoulders,　　　　　　　　10
As those slanted bayonets, whole forests of them appearing in the distance,
　　approach and pass on, returning homeward,
Moving with steady motion, swaying to and fro to the right and left,
Evenly lightly rising and falling while the steps keep time;
Spirit of hours I knew, all hectic red one day, but pale as death next day,
Touch my mouth ere you depart, press my lips close,　　　　　　　　15
Leave me your pulses of rage—bequeath them to me—fill me with currents
　　convulsive,
Let them scorch and blister out of my chants when you are gone,
Let them identify you to the future in these songs.

1865–66, 1881

FROM MEMORIES OF PRESIDENT LINCOLN[1]

When Lilacs Last in the Dooryard Bloom'd

1

When lilacs last in the dooryard bloom'd,
And the great star[2] early droop'd in the western sky in the night,
I mourn'd, and yet shall mourn with ever-returning spring.

1. Composed in the months following Lincoln's assassination on April 14, 1865, this elegy was printed in the fall of that year as an appendix to the recently published *Drum-Taps* volume. In the 1881 edition of *Leaves of Grass* it and three lesser poems were joined to make up the section *Memories of President Lincoln*.

Not simply a poem about the death of Lincoln, *When Lilacs Last in the Dooryard Bloom'd* is about the stages by which a poet transmutes his grief into poetry.
2. Literally Venus, although it becomes associated with Lincoln himself.

Ever-returning spring, trinity sure to me you bring,
Lilac blooming perennial and drooping star in the west,   5
And thought of him I love.

2

O powerful western fallen star!
O shades of night—O moody, tearful night!
O great star disappear'd—O the black murk that hides the star!
O cruel hands that hold me powerless—O helpless soul of me!   10
O harsh surrounding cloud that will not free my soul.

3

In the dooryard fronting an old farm-house near the white-wash'd palings,
Stands the lilac-bush tall-growing with heart-shaped leaves of rich green,
With many a pointed blossom rising delicate, with the perfume strong I
      love,
With every leaf a miracle—and from this bush in the dooryard,   15
With delicate-color'd blossoms and heart-shaped leaves of rich green,
A sprig with its flower I break.

4

In the swamp in secluded recesses,
A shy and hidden bird is warbling a song.

Solitary the thrush,   20
The hermit withdrawn to himself, avoiding the settlements,
Sings by himself a song.

Song of the bleeding throat,
Death's outlet song of life, (for well dear brother I know,
If thou wast not granted to sing thou would'st surely die.)   25

5

Over the breast of the spring, the land, amid cities,
Amid lanes and through old woods, where lately the violets peep'd from the
      ground, spotting the gray debris,
Amid the grass in the fields each side of the lanes, passing the endless grass,
Passing the yellow-spear'd wheat, every grain from its shroud in the dark-
      brown fields uprisen,
Passing the apple-tree blows[3] of white and pink in the orchards,   30
Carrying a corpse to where it shall rest in the grave,
Night and day journeys a coffin.

6

Coffin that passes through lanes and streets,
Through day and night with the great cloud darkening the land,

---

3. Blossoms.

With the pomp of the inloop'd flags with the cities draped in black,   35
With the show of the States themselves as of crape-veil'd women standing,
With processions long and winding and the flambeaus[4] of the night,
With the countless torches lit, with the silent sea of faces and the unbared
    heads,
With the waiting depot, the arriving coffin, and the sombre faces,
With dirges through the night, with the thousand voices rising strong and
    solemn,   40
With all the mournful voices of the dirges pour'd around the coffin,
The dim-lit churches and the shuddering organs—where amid these you
    journey,
With the tolling tolling bells' perpetual clang,
Here, coffin that slowly passes,
I give you my sprig of lilac.   45

7

(Nor for you, for one alone,
Blossoms and branches green to coffins all I bring,
For fresh as the morning, thus would I chant a song for you O sane and
    sacred death.

All over bouquets of roses,
O death, I cover you over with roses and early lilies,   50
But mostly and now the lilac that blooms the first,
Copious I break, I break the sprigs from the bushes,
With loaded arms I come, pouring for you,
For you and the coffins all of you O death.)

8

O western orb sailing the heaven,   55
Now I know what you must have meant as a month since I walk'd,
As I walk'd in silence the transparent shadowy night,
As I saw you had something to tell as you bent to me night after night,
As you droop'd from the sky low down as if to my side, (while the other
    stars all look'd on,)
As we wander'd together the solemn night, (for something I know not what
    kept me from sleep,)   60

As the night advanced, and I saw on the rim of the west how full you were of
    woe,
As I stood on the rising ground in the breeze in the cool transparent night,
As I watch'd where you pass'd and was lost in the netherward black of the
    night,
As my soul in its trouble dissatisfied sank, as where you sad orb,
Concluded, dropt in the night, and was gone.   65

4. Torches.

9

Sing on there in the swamp,
O singer bashful and tender, I hear your notes, I hear your call,
I hear, I come presently, I understand you,
But a moment I linger, for the lustrous star has detain'd me,
The star my departing comrade holds and detains me.   70

10

O how shall I warble myself for the dead one there I loved?
And how shall I deck my song for the large sweet soul that has gone?
And what shall my perfume be for the grave of him I love?

Sea-winds blown from east and west,
Blown from the Eastern sea and blown from the Western sea, till there on the
     prairies meeting,   75
These and with these and the breath of my chant,
I'll perfume the grave of him I love.

11

O what shall I hang on the chamber walls?
And what shall the pictures be that I hang on the walls,
To adorn the burial-house of him I love?   80

Pictures of growing spring and farms and homes,
With the Fourth-month[5] eve at sundown, and the gray smoke lucid and
     bright,
With floods of the yellow gold of the gorgeous, indolent, sinking sun, burning,
     expanding the air,
With the fresh sweet herbage under foot, and the pale green leaves of the trees
     prolific,
In the distance the flowing glaze, the breast of the river, with a wind-dapple
     here and there,   85
With ranging hills on the banks, with many a line against the sky, and
     shadows,
And the city at hand with dwellings so dense, and stacks of chimneys,
And all the scenes of life and the workshops, and the workmen homeward
     returning.

12

Lo, body and soul—this land,
My own Manhattan with spires, and the sparkling and hurrying tides, and the
     ships,   90
The varied and ample land, the South and the North in the light, Ohio's
     shores and flashing Missouri,
And ever the far-spreading prairies cover'd with grass and corn.

Lo, the most excellent sun so calm and haughty,
The violet and purple morn with just-felt breezes,

5. April.

The gentle soft-born measureless light,   95
The miracle spreading bathing all, the fulfill'd noon,
The coming eve delicious, the welcome night and the stars,
Over my cities shining all, enveloping man and land.

13

Sing on, sing on you gray-brown bird,
Sing from the swamps, the recesses, pour your chant from the bushes,   100
Limitless out of the dusk, out of the cedars and pines.

Sing on dearest brother, warble your reedy song,
Loud human song, with voice of uttermost woe.

O liquid and free and tender!
O wild and loose to my soul!—O wondrous singer!   105
You only I hear—yet the star holds me, (but will soon depart,)
Yet the lilac with mastering odor holds me.

14

Now while I sat in the day and look'd forth,
In the close of the day with its light and the fields of spring, and the farmers
        preparing their crops,
In the large unconscious scenery of my land with its lakes and forests,   110
In the heavenly aerial beauty, (after the perturb'd winds and the storms,)
Under the arching heavens of the afternoon swift passing, and the voices of
        children and women,
The many-moving sea-tides, and I saw the ships how they sail'd,
And the summer approaching with richness, and the fields all busy with labor,
And the infinite separate houses, how they all went on, each with its meals
        and minutia of daily usages,   115
And the streets how their throbbings throbb'd, and the cities pent—lo, then
        and there,
Falling upon them all and among them all, enveloping me with the rest,
Appear'd the cloud, appear'd the long black trail,
And I knew death, its thought, and the sacred knowledge of death.

Then with the knowledge of death as walking one side of me,   120
And the thought of death close-walking the other side of me,
And I in the middle as with companions, and as holding the hands of com-
        panions,
I fled forth to the hiding receiving night that talks not,
Down to the shores of the water, the path by the swamp in the dimness,
To the solemn shadowy cedars and ghostly pines so still.   125

And the singer so shy to the rest receiv'd me,
The gray-brown bird I know receiv'd us comrades three,
And he sang the carol of death, and a verse for him I love.

From deep secluded recesses,
From the fragrant cedars and the ghostly pines so still,   130
Came the carol of the bird.

And the charm of the carol rapt me,
As I held as if by their hands my comrades in the night,
And the voice of my spirit tallied the song of the bird.

Come lovely and soothing death, 135
Undulate round the world, serenely arriving, arriving,
In the day, in the night, to all, to each,
Sooner or later delicate death.

Prais'd be the fathomless universe,
For life and joy, and for objects and knowledge curious, 140
And for love, sweet love—but praise! praise! praise!
For the sure-enwinding arms of cool-enfolding death.

Dark mother always gliding near with soft feet,
Have none chanted for thee a chant of fullest welcome?
Then I chant it for thee, I glorify thee above all, 145
I bring thee a song that when thou must indeed come, come unfalteringly.

Approach strong deliveress,
When it is so, when thou hast taken them I joyously sing the dead,
Lost in the loving floating ocean of thee,
Laved in the flood of thy bliss O death. 150

From me to thee glad serenades,
Dances for thee I propose saluting thee, adornments and feastings for thee,
And the sights of the open landscape and the high-spread sky are fitting,
And life and the fields, and the huge and thoughtful night.

The night in silence under many a star, 155
The ocean shore and the husky whispering wave whose voice I know,
And the soul turning to thee O vast and well-veil'd death,
And the body gratefully nestling close to thee.

Over the tree-tops I float thee a song,
Over the rising and sinking waves, over the myriad fields and the prairies
  wide, 160
Over the dense-pack'd cities all and the teeming wharves and ways,
I float this carol with joy, with joy to thee O death.

15

To the tally of my soul,
Loud and strong kept up the gray-brown bird,
With pure deliberate notes spreading filling the night. 165

Loud in the pines and cedars dim,
Clear in the freshness moist and the swamp-perfume,
And I with my comrades there in the night.

While my sight that was bound in my eyes unclosed,
As to long panoramas of visions. 170

And I saw askant[6] the armies,
I saw as in noiseless dreams hundreds of battle-flags,
Borne through the smoke of the battles and pierc'd with missiles I saw them,
And carried hither and yon through the smoke, and torn and bloody,
And at last but a few shreds left on the staffs, (and all in silence,)   175
And the staffs all splinter'd and broken.

I saw battle-corpses, myriads of them,
And the white skeletons of young men, I saw them,
I saw the debris and debris of all the slain soldiers of the war,
But I saw they were not as was thought,   180
They themselves were fully at rest, they suffer'd not,
The living remain'd and suffer'd, the mother suffer'd,
And the wife and the child and the musing comrade suffer'd,
And the armies that remain'd suffer'd.

16

Passing the visions, passing the night,   185
Passing, unloosing the hold of my comrades' hands,
Passing the song of the hermit bird and the tallying song of my soul,
Victorious song, death's outlet song, yet varying ever-altering song,
As low and wailing, yet clear the notes, rising and falling, flooding the night,
Sadly sinking and fainting, as warning and warning, and yet again bursting
     with joy,   190
Covering the earth and filling the spread of the heaven,
As that powerful psalm in the night I heard from recesses,
Passing, I leave thee lilac with heart-shaped leaves,
I leave thee there in the door-yard, blooming, returning with spring.

I cease from my song for thee,   195
From my gaze on thee in the west, fronting the west, communing with thee,
O comrade lustrous with silver face in the night.

Yet each to keep and all, retrievements out of the night,
The song, the wondrous chant of the gray-brown bird,
And the tallying chant, the echo arous'd in my soul,   200
With the lustrous and drooping star with the countenance full of woe,
With the holders holding my hand nearing the call of the bird,
Comrades mine and I in the midst, and their memory ever to keep, for the
     dead I loved so well,
For the sweetest, wisest soul of all my days and lands—and this for his dear
     sake,
Lilac and star and bird twined with the chant of my soul,   205
There in the fragrant pines and the cedars dusk and dim.

1865–66, 1881

---

6. Sideways, aslant; an appropriate word for introducing a surrealistic vision.

FROM AUTUMN RIVULETS

There Was a Child Went Forth[1]

There was a child went forth every day,
And the first object he look'd upon, that object he became,
And that object became part of him for the day or a certain part of the day,
Or for many years or stretching cycles of years.

The early lilacs became part of this child,   5
And grass and white and red morning-glories, and white and red clover, and
    the song of the phoebe-bird,
And the Third-month[2] lambs and the sow's pink-faint litter, and the mare's
    foal and the cow's calf,
And the noisy brood of the barnyard or by the mire of the pond-side,
And the fish suspending themselves so curiously below there, and the beautiful
    curious liquid,
And the water-plants with their graceful flat heads, all became part of him. 10

The field-sprouts of Fourth-month and Fifth-month became part of him,
Winter-grain sprouts and those of the light-yellow corn, and the esculent roots
    of the garden,
And the apple-trees cover'd with blossoms and the fruit afterward, and wood-
    berries, and the commonest weeds by the road,
And the old drunkard staggering home from the outhouse of the tavern whence
    he had lately risen,
And the schoolmistress that pass'd on her way to the school,   15
And the friendly boys that pass'd, and the quarrelsome boys,
And the tidy and fresh-cheek'd girls, and the barefoot negro boy and girl,
And all the changes of city and country wherever he went.

His own parents, he that had father'd him and she that had conceiv'd him in
    her womb and birth'd him,
They gave this child more of themselves than that,   20
They gave him afterward every day, they became part of him.

The mother at home quietly placing the dishes on the supper-table,
The mother with mild words, clean her cap and gown, a wholesome odor
    falling off her person and clothes as she walks by,
The father, strong, self-sufficient, manly, mean, anger'd, unjust,
The blow, the quick loud word, the tight bargain, the crafty lure,   25
The family usages, the language, the company, the furniture, the yearning
    and swelling heart,
Affection that will not be gainsay'd, the sense of what is real, the thought if
    after all it should prove unreal,
The doubts of day-time and the doubts of night-time, the curious whether and
    how,
Whether that which appears so is so, or is it all flashes and specks?
Men and women crowding fast in the streets, if they are not flashes and specks
    what are they?   30

---

1. This poem was first published in the 1856 edition
of *Leaves of Grass* as *Poem of the Child That Went
Forth, and Always Goes Forth, Forever and Forever,*
then subsequently published under other titles until the
present one was reached in the 1871 edition.
2. I.e., March.

The streets themselves and the façades of houses, and goods in the windows,
Vehicles, teams, the heavy-plank'd wharves, the huge crossing at the ferries,
The village on the highland seen from afar at sunset, the river between,
Shadows, aureola and mist, the light falling on roofs and gables of white or
  brown two miles off,
The schooner near by sleepily dropping down the tide, the little boat slack-
  tow'd astern,   35
The hurrying tumbling waves, quick-broken crests, slapping,
The strata of color'd clouds, the long bar of maroon-tint away solitary by itself,
  the spread of purity it lies motionless in,
The horizon's edge, the flying sea-crow, the fragrance of salt marsh and shore
  mud,
These became part of that child who went forth every day, and who now goes,
  and will always go forth every day.

1855, 1871

This Compost

1

Something startles me where I thought I was safest,
I withdraw from the still woods I loved,
I will not go now on the pastures to walk,
I will not strip the clothes from my body to meet my lover the sea,
I will not touch my flesh to the earth as to other flesh to renew me.   5

O how can it be that the ground itself does not sicken?
How can you be alive you growths of spring?
How can you furnish health you blood of herbs, roots, orchards, grain?
Are they not continually putting distemper'd corpses within you?
Is not every continent work'd over and over with sour dead?   10

Where have you disposed of their carcasses?
Those drunkards and gluttons of so many generations?
Where have you drawn off all the foul liquid and meat?
I do not see any of it upon you to-day, or perhaps I am deceiv'd,
I will run a furrow with my plough, I will press my spade through the sod and
  turn it up underneath,   15
I am sure I shall expose some of the foul meat.

2

Behold this compost! behold it well!
Perhaps every mite has once form'd part of a sick person—yet behold!
The grass of spring covers the prairies,
The bean bursts noiselessly through the mould in the garden,   20
The delicate spear of the onion pierces upward,
The apple-buds cluster together on the apple-branches,
The resurrection of the wheat appears with pale visage out of its graves,
The tinge awakes over the willow-tree and the mulberry-tree,

The he-birds carol mornings and evenings while the she-birds sit on their
  nests,   25
The young of poultry break through the hatch'd eggs,
The new-born of animals appear, the calf is dropt from the cow, the colt from
  the mare,
Out of its little hill faithfully rise the potato's dark green leaves,
Out of its hill rises the yellow maize-stalk, the lilacs bloom in the dooryards,
The summer growth is innocent and disdainful above all those strata of sour
  dead.   30

What chemistry!
That the winds are really not infectious,
That this is no cheat, this transparent green-wash of the sea which is so amo-
  rous after me,
That it is safe to allow it to lick my naked body all over with its tongues,
That it will not endanger me with the fevers that have deposited themselves in
  it,   35
That all is clean forever and forever,
That the cool drink from the well tastes so good,
That blackberries are so flavorous and juicy,
That the fruits of the apple-orchard and the orange-orchard, that melons,
  grapes, peaches, plums, will none of them poison me,
That when I recline on the grass I do not catch any disease,   40
Though probably every spear of grass rises out of what was once a catching
  disease.

Now I am terrified at the Earth, it is that calm and patient,
It grows such sweet things out of such corruptions,
It turns harmless and stainless on its axis, with such endless successions of
  diseas'd corpses,
It distills such exquisite winds out of such infused fetor,   45
It renews with such unwitting looks its prodigal, annual, sumptuous crops,
It gives such divine materials to men, and accepts such leavings from them
  at last.

                                                        1856, 1881

Sparkles from the Wheel

Where the city's ceaseless crowd moves on the livelong day,
Withdrawn I join a group of children watching, I pause aside with them.
By the curb toward the edge of the flagging,
A knife-grinder works at his wheel sharpening a great knife,
Bending over he carefully holds it to the stone, by foot and knee,   5
With measur'd tread he turns rapidly, as he presses with light but firm hand,
Forth issue then in copious golden jets,
Sparkles from the wheel.

The scene and all its belongings, how they seize and affect me,
The sad sharp-chinn'd old man with worn clothes and broad shoulder-band of
  leather,   10

Myself effusing and fluid, a phantom curiously floating, now here absorb'd
    and arrested,
The group, (an unminded point set in a vast surrounding,)
The attentive, quiet children, the loud, proud, restive base of the streets,
The low hoarse purr of the whirling stone, the light-press'd blade,
Diffusing, dropping, sideways-darting, in tiny showers of gold,   15
Sparkles from the wheel.

                                                            1871, 1871

My Picture-Gallery[1]

In a little house keep I pictures suspended, it is not a fix'd house,
It is round, it is only a few inches from one side to the other;
Yet behold, it has room for all the shows of the world, all memories!
Here the tableaus of life, and here the groupings of death;
Here, do you know this? this is cicerone[2] himself,   5
With finger rais'd he points to the prodigal pictures.

                                                            1880, 1881

Passage to India[1]

1

Singing my days,
Singing the great achievements of the present,
Singing the strong light works of engineers,
Our modern wonders, (the antique ponderous Seven[2] outvied,)
In the Old World the east the Suez canal,[3]   5
The New by its mighty railroad spann'd,
The seas inlaid with eloquent gentle wires;
Yet first to sound, and ever sound, the cry with thee O soul,
The Past! the Past! the Past!

The Past—the dark unfathom'd retrospect!   10
The teeming gulf—the sleepers and the shadows!
The past—the infinite greatness of the past!
For what is the present after all but a growth out of the past?
(As a projectile form'd, impell'd, passing a certain line, still keeps on,
So the present, utterly form'd, impell'd by the past.)   15

2

Passage O soul to India!
Eclaircise[4] the myths Asiatic, the primitive fables.

1. First published in a periodical (1880), then in the 1881 edition of *Leaves of Grass*, but drafted well before the publication of the 1855 edition.
2. Tour guide.
1. First published in 1871 as the title poem of a separate volume, *Passage to India* was included as a supplement to three editions of *Leaves of Grass* during the 1870s, then incorporated into the body of the book in the 1881 edition.

2. The Seven Wonders of the World are usually identified as the pyramids of Egypt, the pharos or lighthouse at Alexandria, the hanging gardens of Babylon, the temple of Diana at Ephesus, the statue of Jupiter at Olympia, the mausoleum at Halicarnassus, and the colossus of Rhodes.
3. Formally opened November 17, 1869.
4. Clarify.

Not you alone proud truths of the world,
Nor you alone ye facts of modern science,
But myths and fables of eld, Asia's, Africa's fables,   20
The far-darting beams of the spirit, the unloos'd dreams,
The deep diving bibles and legends,
The daring plots of the poets, the elder religions;
O you temples fairer than lilies pour'd over by the rising sun!
O you fables spurning the known, eluding the hold of the known, mounting
     to heaven!   25
You lofty and dazzling towers, pinnacled, red as roses, burnish'd with gold!
Towers of fables immortal fashion'd from mortal dreams!
You too I welcome and fully the same as the rest!
You too with joy I sing.

Passage to India!   30
Lo, soul, seest thou not God's purpose from the first?
The earth to be spann'd, connected by network,
The races, neighbors, to marry and be given in marriage,
The oceans to be cross'd, the distant brought near,
The lands to be welded together.   35

A worship new I sing,
You captains, voyagers, explorers, yours,
You engineers, you architects, machinists, yours,
You, not for trade or transportation only,
But in God's name, and for thy sake O soul.   40

3

Passage to India!
Lo soul for thee of tableaus twain,
I see in one the Suez canal initiated, open'd,
I see the procession of steamships, the Empress Eugenie's[5] leading the van,
I mark from on deck the strange landscape, the pure sky, the level sand in the
     distance,   45
I pass swiftly the picturesque groups, the workmen gather'd,
The gigantic dredging machines.

In one again, different, (yet thine, all thine, O soul, the same,)
I see over my own continent the Pacific railroad surmounting every barrier,
I see continual trains of cars winding along the Platte[6] carrying freight and
     passengers,   50
I hear the locomotives rushing and roaring, and the shrill steam-whistle,
I hear the echoes reverberate through the grandest scenery in the world,
I cross the Laramie plains, I note the rocks in grotesque shapes, the buttes,
I see the plentiful larkspur and wild onions, the barren, colorless, sage-deserts,
I see in glimpses afar or towering immediately above me the great mountains,
     I see the Wind river and the Wahsatch mountains,   55

5. Wife of Napoleon III of France, who was aboard
the first ship during the ceremonies for the opening of
the canal.
6. The following lines name locales between Nebraska
and California along the route of the Union Pacific
and the Central Pacific, railroads that joined tracks at
Promontory, Utah, on May 10, 1869.

I see the Monument mountain and the Eagle's Nest, I pass the Promontory, I
    ascend the Nevadas,
I scan the noble Elk mountain and wind around its base,
I see the Humboldt range, I thread the valley and cross the river,
I see the clear waters of lake Tahoe, I see forests of majestic pines,
Or crossing the great desert, the alkaline plains, I behold enchanting mirages
    of waters and meadows,   60
Marking through these and after all, in duplicate slender lines,
Bridging the three or four thousand miles of land travel,
Tying the Eastern to the Western sea,
The road between Europe and Asia.

(Ah Genoese[7] thy dream! thy dream!   65
Centuries after thou art laid in thy grave,
The shore thou foundest verifies thy dream.)

4

Passage to India!
Struggles of many a captain, tales of many a sailor dead,
Over my mood stealing and spreading they come,   70
Like clouds and cloudlets in the unreach'd sky.

Along all history, down the slopes,
As a rivulet running, sinking now, and now again to the surface rising,
A ceaseless thought, a varied train—lo, soul, to thee, thy sight, they rise,
The plans, the voyages again, the expeditions;   75
Again Vasco de Gama[8] sails forth,
Again the knowledge gain'd, the mariner's compass,
Lands found and nations born, thou born America,
For purpose vast, man's long probation fill'd,
Thou rondure[9] of the world at last accomplish'd.   80

5

O vast Rondure, swimming in space,
Cover'd all over with visible power and beauty,
Alternate light and day and the teeming spiritual darkness,
Unspeakable high processions of sun and moon and countless stars above,
Below, the manifold grass and waters, animals, mountains, trees,   85
With inscrutable purpose, some hidden prophetic intention,
Now first it seems my thought begins to span thee.

Down from the gardens of Asia descending radiating,
Adam and Eve appear, then their myriad progeny after them,
Wandering, yearning, curious, with restless explorations,   90
With questionings, baffled, formless, feverish, with never-happy hearts,
With that sad incessant refrain, *Wherefore unsatisfied soul?* and *Whither O
    mocking life?*

7. Christopher Columbus, native of Genoa, Italy, important at this stage of Whitman's life because the poet perceived analogies between the seeker of a passage to the Orient and himself. Whitman had been reading Washington Irving's biography of Columbus.

8. Vasco da Gama, Portuguese navigator who in 1498 sailed around Africa to India, the first European to do so.
9. Roundness.

Ah who shall soothe these feverish children?
Who justify these restless explorations?
Who speak the secret of impassive earth?   95
Who bind it to us? what is this separate Nature so unnatural?
What is this earth of our affections? (unloving earth, without a throb to answer
    ours,
Cold earth, the place of graves.)

Yet soul be sure the first intent remains, and shall be carried out,
Perhaps even now the time has arrived.   100

After the seas are all cross'd, (as they seem already cross'd,)
After the great captains and engineers have accomplish'd their work,
After the noble inventors, after the scientists, the chemist, the geologist, eth-
    nologist,
Finally shall come the poet worthy that name,
The true son of God shall come singing his songs.   105

Then not your deeds only O voyagers, O scientists and inventors, shall be jus-
    tified,
All these hearts as of fretted children shall be sooth'd,
All affection shall be fully responded to, the secret shall be told,
All these separations and gaps shall be taken up and hook'd and link'd together,
The whole earth, this cold, impassive, voiceless earth, shall be completely jus-
    tified,   110
Trinitas[1] divine shall be gloriously accomplish'd and compacted by the true
    son of God, the poet,
(He shall indeed pass the straits and conquer the mountains,
He shall double the cape of Good Hope to some purpose,)
Nature and Man shall be disjoin'd and diffused no more,
The true son of God shall absolutely fuse them.   115

                                        6

Year at whose wide-flung door I sing!
Year of the purpose accomplish'd!
Year of the marriage of continents, climates and oceans!
(No mere doge of Venice now wedding the Adriatic,)[2]
I see O year in you the vast terraqueous globe given and giving all,   120
Europe to Asia, Africa join'd, and they to the New World,
The lands, geographies, dancing before you, holding a festival garland,
As brides and bridegrooms hand in hand.

Passage to India!
Coolings airs from Caucasus[3] far, soothing cradle of man,   125
The river Euphrates[4] flowing, the past lit up again.

1. Trinity (but not in the Christian sense of Father, Son, and Holy Ghost).
2. Because the power of Renaissance Venice was built on its command of waterways, the ruling doges annually cast a ring into the Adriatic to symbolize the marriage of the city and the sea.
3. Region in Russia between the Black and the Cas-pian seas, once thought to be the place where the "Caucasian" race originated.
4. River running from east-central Turkey through Syria and Iraq, then joining with the Tigris and flowing into the Persian Gulf. In Genesis 2.14, one of the four rivers into which the river in the Garden of Eden di-vided.

Lo soul, the retrospect brought forward,
The old, most populous, wealthiest of earth's lands,
The streams of the Indus and the Ganges[5] and their many affluents,
(I my shores of America walking to-day behold, resuming all,)   130
The tale of Alexander[6] on his warlike marches suddenly dying,
On one side China and on the other side Persia and Arabia,
To the south the great seas and the bay of Bengal,
The flowing literatures, tremendous epics, religions, castes,
Old occult Brahma interminably far back, the tender and junior Buddha,   135
Central and southern empires and all their belongings, possessors,
The wars of Tamerlane, the reign of Aurungzebe,[7]
The traders, rulers, explorers, Moslems, Venetians, Byzantium, the Arabs,
    Portuguese,
The first travelers famous yet, Marco Polo, Batouta the Moor,[8]
Doubts to be solv'd, the map incognita, blanks to be fill'd,   140
The foot of man unstay'd, the hands never at rest,
Thyself O soul that will not brook a challenge.

The mediæval navigators rise before me,
The world of 1492, with its awaken'd enterprise,
Something swelling in humanity now like the sap of the earth in spring,   145
The sunset splendor of chivalry declining.

And who art thou sad shade?
Gigantic, visionary, thyself a visionary,
With majestic limbs and pious beaming eyes,
Spreading around with every look of thine a golden world,   150
Enhuing it with gorgeous hues.

As the chief histrion,[9]
Down to the footlights walks in some great scena,
Dominating the rest I see the Admiral himself,[1]
(History's type of courage, action, faith,)   155
Behold him sail from Palos[2] leading his little fleet,
His voyage behold, his return, his great fame,
His misfortunes, calumniators, behold him a prisoner, chain'd,
Behold his dejection, poverty, death.

(Curious in time I stand, noting the efforts of heroes,   160
Is the deferment long? bitter the slander, poverty, death?
Lies the seed unreck'd for centuries in the ground? lo, to God's due occasion,
Uprising in the night, it sprouts, blooms,
And fills the earth with use and beauty.)

5. Great rivers: the Indus flowing from southwestern Tibet through West Pakistan to the Arabian Sea; the Ganges rising in the Himalayas of northern India and flowing through East Pakistan into the Bay of Bengal.
6. Alexander the Great (356–323 B.C.) was king of Macedonia 336–323 B.C.; he conquered Egypt and the Persian Empire, dying on his return from an expedition into India.
7. Emperor of Hindustan (17th century), part of northern India. Tamerlane (14th century), Islamic conqueror of much of Central Asia and Eastern Europe.
8. Also spelled Patouta (1303–1377), traveler in Africa and Asia. Marco Polo (1254–1324), Venetian traveler in Africa and Asia.
9. Actor.
1. Columbus.
2. Spanish seaport from which Columbus sailed in 1492.

7

Passage indeed O soul to primal thought,   165
Not lands and seas alone, thy own clear freshness,
The young maturity of brood and bloom,
To realms of budding bibles.

O soul, repressless, I with thee and thou with me,
Thy circumnavigation of the world begin,   170
Of man, the voyage of his mind's return,
To reason's early paradise,
Back, back to wisdom's birth, to innocent intuitions,
Again with fair creation.

8

O we can wait no longer,   175
We too take ship O soul,
Joyous we too launch out on trackless seas,
Fearless for unknown shores on waves of ecstasy to sail,
Amid the wafting winds, (thou pressing me to thee, I thee to me, O soul,)
Caroling free, singing our song of God,   180
Chanting our chant of pleasant exploration.

With laugh and many a kiss,
(Let others deprecate, let others weep for sin, remorse, humiliation,)
O soul thou pleasest me, I thee.

Ah more than any priest O soul we too believe in God,   185
But with the mystery of God we dare not dally.

O soul thou pleasest me, I thee,
Sailing these seas or on the hills, or waking in the night,
Thoughts, silent thoughts, of Time and Space and Death, like waters flowing,
Bear me indeed as through the regions infinite,   190
Whose air I breathe, whose ripples hear, lave me all over,
Bathe me O God in thee, mounting to thee,
I and my soul to range in range of thee.

O Thou transcendent,
Nameless, the fibre and the breath,   195
Light of the light, shedding forth universes, thou centre of them,
Thou mightier centre of the true, the good, the loving,
Thou moral, spiritual fountain—affection's source—thou reservoir,
(O pensive soul of me—O thirst unsatisfied—waitest not there?
Waitest not haply for us somewhere there the Comrade perfect?)   200
Thou pulse—thou motive of the stars, suns, systems,
That, circling, move in order, safe, harmonious,
Athwart the shapeless vastnesses of space,
How should I think, how breathe a single breath, how speak, if, out of myself,
I could not launch, to those, superior universes?   205

Swiftly I shrivel at the thought of God,
At Nature and its wonders, Time and Space and Death,
But that I, turning, call to thee O soul, thou actual Me,
And lo, thou gently masterest the orbs,
Thou matest Time, smilest content at Death,   210
And fillest, swellest full the vastnesses of Space.

Greater than stars or suns,
Bounding O soul thou journeyest forth;
What love than thine and ours could wider amplify?
What aspirations, wishes, outvie thine and ours O soul?   215
What dreams of the ideal? what plans of purity, perfection, strength?
What cheerful willingness for others' sake to give up all?
For others' sake to suffer all?

Reckoning ahead O soul, when thou, the time achiev'd,
The seas all cross'd, weather'd the capes, the voyage done,   220
Surrounded, copest, frontest God, yieldest, the aim attain'd,
As fill'd with friendship, love complete, the Elder Brother found,
The Younger melts in fondness in his arms.

9

Passage to more than India!
Are thy wings plumed indeed for such far flights?   225
O soul, voyagest thou indeed on voyages like those?
Disportest thou on waters such as those?
Soundest below the Sanscrit and the Vedas?[3]
Then have thy bent unleash'd.

Passage to you, your shores, ye aged fierce enigmas!   230
Passage to you, to mastership of you, ye strangling problems!
You, strew'd with the wrecks of skeletons, that, living, never reach'd you.

Passage to more than India!
O secret of the earth and sky!
Of you O waters of the sea! O winding creeks and rivers!   235
Of you O woods and fields! of you strong mountains of my land!
Of you O prairies! of you gray rocks!
O morning red! O clouds! O rain and snows!
O day and night, passage to you!

O sun and moon and all you stars! Sirius and Jupiter![4]   240
Passage to you!

Passage, immediately passage! the blood burns in my veins!
Away O soul! hoist instantly the anchor!
Cut the hawsers—haul out—shake out every sail!
Have we not stood here like trees in the ground long enough?   245

3. The ancient Hindu scriptures, the Vedas, were   solar system. "Sirius": the Dog Star, the brightest star
written in Sanskrit.   in the sky.
4. The fifth planet from the sun, the largest in the

245

Have we not grovel'd here long enough, eating and drinking like mere brutes?
Have we not darken'd and dazed ourselves with books long enough?

Sail forth—steer for the deep waters only,
Reckless O soul, exploring, I with thee, and thou with me,
For we are bound where mariner has not yet dared to go,   250
And we will risk the ship, ourselves and all.

O my brave soul!
O farther farther sail!
O daring joy, but safe! are they not all the seas of God?
O farther, farther, farther sail!   255

1871, 1881

The Sleepers[1]

1

I wander all night in my vision,
Stepping with light feet, swiftly and noiselessly stepping and stopping,
Bending with open eyes over the shut eyes of sleepers,
Wandering and confused, lost to myself, ill-assorted, contradictory,
Pausing, gazing, bending, and stopping.   5

How solemn they look there, stretch'd and still,
How quiet they breathe, the little children in their cradles.

The wretched features of ennuyés,[2] the white features of corpses, the livid faces
    of drunkards, the sick-gray faces of onanists,[3]
The gash'd bodies on battle-fields, the insane in their strong-door'd rooms, the
    sacred idiots, the new-born emerging from gates, and the dying emerging
    from gates,
The night pervades them and infolds them.   10

The married couple sleep calmly in their bed, he with his palm on the hip
    of the wife, and she with her palm on the hip of the husband,
The sisters sleep lovingly side by side in their bed,
The men sleep lovingly side by side in theirs,
And the mother sleeps with her little child carefully wrapt.

The blind sleep, and the deaf and dumb sleep,   15
The prisoner sleeps well in the prison, the runaway son sleeps,
The murderer that is to be hung next day, how does he sleep?
And the murder'd person, how does he sleep?

1. This was the fourth poem, untitled, in the 1855 *Leaves of Grass*; it was titled *Night Poem* in the 1856 edition, *Sleep-Chasings* in 1860 and 1867, and finally *The Sleepers* in 1871 and thereafter. This printing follows the final edition, where it appears with five other poems, mostly long ones, between *Autumn Rivulets* and *Whispers of Heavenly Death*. Minor revisions are not indicated here, but footnotes record lines present in 1855 and subsequently deleted. As Blodgett and Bradley say, at least some of the deletions were made "not so much for aesthetic as for discretionary reasons," the lines being too explicitly sexual.
2. The debauched.
3. Masturbators.

The female that loves unrequited sleeps,
And the male that loves unrequited sleeps,   20
The head of the money-maker that plotted all day sleeps,
And the enraged and treacherous dispositions, all, all sleep.

I stand in the dark with drooping eyes by the worst-suffering and the most
    restless,
I pass my hands soothingly to and fro a few inches from them,
The restless sink in their beds, they fitfully sleep.   25

Now I pierce the darkness, now beings appear,
The earth recedes from me into the night,
I saw that it was beautiful, and I see that what is not the earth is beautiful.

I go from bedside to bedside, I sleep close with the other sleepers each in turn,
I dream in my dream all the dreams of the other dreamers,   30
And I become the other dreamers.

I am a dance—play up there! the fit is whirling me fast!

I am the ever-laughing—it is new moon and twilight,
I see the hiding of douceurs,[4] I see nimble ghosts whichever way I look,
Cache[5] and cache again deep in the ground and sea, and where it is neither
    ground nor sea.   35

Well do they do their jobs those journeymen divine,
Only from me can they hide nothing, and would not if they could,
I reckon I am their boss and they make me a pet besides,
And surround me and lead me and run ahead when I walk,
To lift their cunning covers to signify me with stretch'd arms, and resume
    the way;   40
Onward we move, a gay gang of blackguards! with mirth-shouting music and
    wild-flapping pennants of joy!

I am the actor, the actress, the voter, the politician,
The emigrant and the exile, the criminal that stood in the box,
He who has been famous and he who shall be famous after to-day,
The stammerer, the well-form'd person, the wasted or feeble person.   45

I am she who adorn'd herself and folded her hair expectantly,
My truant lover has come, and it is dark.

Double yourself and receive me darkness,
Receive me and my lover too, he will not let me go without him.

I roll myself upon you as upon a bed, I resign myself to the dusk.   50

He whom I call answers me and takes the place of my lover,
He rises with me silently from the bed.

---

4. Sweetnesses; here, sexual delights.
5. A French word: "hide" if it is used as a verb, "hiding place" if used as a noun.

Darkness, you are gentler than my lover, his flesh was sweaty and panting,
I feel the hot moisture yet that he left me.

My hands are spread forth, I pass them in all directions,   55
I would sound up the shadowy shore to which you are journeying.

Be careful darkness! already what was it touch'd me?
I thought my lover had gone, else darkness and he are one,
I hear the heart-beat, I follow, I fade away.[6]

2

I descend my western course, my sinews are flaccid,   60
Perfume and youth course through me and I am their wake.

It is my face yellow and wrinkled instead of the old woman's,
I sit low in a straw-bottom chair and carefully darn my grandson's stockings.

It is I too, the sleepless widow looking out on the winter midnight,
I see the sparkles of starshine on the icy and pallid earth.   65

A shroud I see and I am the shroud, I wrap a body and lie in the coffin,
It is dark here under ground, it is not evil or pain here, it is blank here,
    for reasons.

(It seems to me that every thing in the light and air ought to be happy,

Whoever is not in his coffin and the dark grave let him know he has enough.)

3

I see a beautiful gigantic swimmer swimming naked through the eddies of the
    sea,   70
His brown hair lies close and even to his head, he strikes out with courageous
    arms, he urges himself with his legs,
I see his white body, I see his undaunted eyes,
I hate the swift-running eddies that would dash him head-foremost on the
    rocks.

What are you doing you ruffianly red-trickled waves?
Will you kill the courageous giant? will you kill him in the prime of his middle
    age?   75

6. In 1855 these three verse paragraphs followed:

O hotcheeked and blushing! O foolish hectic!
O for pity's sake, no one must see me now! . . . .
   my clothes were stolen while I was abed,
Now I am thrust forth, where shall I run?

Pier that I saw dimly last night when I looked from
   the windows,
Pier out from the main, let me catch myself with
   you and stay . . . . I will not chafe you;
I feel ashamed to go naked about the world,

And am curious to know where my feet stand . . . .
   and what is this flooding me, childhood or
   manhood . . . . and the hunger that crosses the
   bridge between.

The cloth laps a first sweet eating and drinking,
Laps life-swelling yolks . . . . laps ear of rose-corn,
   milky and just ripened:
The white teeth stay, and the boss-tooth advances
   in darkness,
And liquor is spilled on lips and bosoms by touching
   glasses, and the best liquor afterward.

Steady and long he struggles,
He is baffled, bang'd, bruis'd, he holds out while his strength holds out,
The slapping eddies are spotted with his blood, they bear him away, they roll
    him, swing him, turn him,
His beautiful body is borne in the circling eddies, it is continually bruis'd on
    rocks,
Swiftly and out of sight is borne the brave corpse.   80

4

I turn but do not extricate myself,
Confused, a past-reading, another, but with darkness yet.

The beach is cut by the razory ice-wind, the wreck-guns sound,[7]
The tempest lulls, the moon comes foundering through the drifts.

I look where the ship helplessly heads end on, I hear the burst as she strikes, I
    hear the howls of dismay, they grow fainter and fainter.   85

I cannot aid with my wringing fingers,
I can but rush to the surf and let it drench me and freeze upon me.

I search with the crowd, not one of the company is wash'd to us alive,
In the morning I help pick up the dead and lay them in rows in a barn.

5

Now of the older war-days, the defeat at Brooklyn,[8]   90
Washington stands inside the lines, he stands on the intrench'd hills amid a
    crowd of officers,
His face is cold and damp, he cannot repress the weeping drops,
He lifts the glass perpetually to his eyes, the color is blanch'd from his cheeks,
He sees the slaughter of the southern braves[9] confided to him by their parents.

The same at last and at last when peace is declared,   95
He stands in the room of the old tavern, the well-belov'd soldiers all pass
    through,
The officers speechless and slow draw near in their turns,
The chief encircles their necks with his arm and kisses them on the cheek,
He kisses lightly the wet cheeks one after another, he shakes hands and bids
    good-by to the army.

6

Now what my mother told me one day as we sat at dinner together,   100
Of when she was a nearly grown girl living home with her parents on the old
    homestead.

---

7. In a signal for help.
8. Washington was defeated at Brooklyn Heights in
August 1776.

9. Washington's soldiers, largely recruited in his own
Virginia and other southern colonies.

A red squaw came one breakfast-time to the old homestead,
On her back she carried a bundle of rushes for rush-bottoming chairs,
Her hair, straight, shiny, coarse, black, profuse, half-envelop'd her face,
Her step was free and elastic, and her voice sounded exquisitely as she
　　spoke.　　　　　　　　　　　　　　　　　　　　　　　　　　　　　　105

My mother look'd in delight and amazement at the stranger,
She look'd at the freshness of her tall-borne face and full and pliant limbs,
The more she look'd upon her she loved her,
Never before had she seen such wonderful beauty and purity,
She made her sit on a bench by the jamb of the fireplace, she cook'd food for
　　her,　　　　　　　　　　　　　　　　　　　　　　　　　　　　　　　110
She had no work to give her, but she gave her remembrance and fondness.

The red squaw staid all the forenoon, and toward the middle of the afternoon
　　she went away,
O my mother was loth to have her go away,
All the week she thought of her, she watch'd for her many a month,
She remember'd her many a winter and many a summer,　　　　　　　　115
But the red squaw never came nor was heard of there again.[1]

7

A show of the summer softness—a contact of something unseen—an amour
　　of the light and air,
I am jealous and overwhelm'd with friendliness,
And will go gallivant with the light and air myself.[2]

O love and summer, you are in the dreams and in me,　　　　　　　　120
Autumn and winter are in the dreams, the farmer goes with his thrift,
The droves[3] and crops increase, the barns are well-fill'd.

Elements merge in the night, ships make tacks in the dreams,
The sailor sails, the exile returns home,
The fugitive returns unharm'd, the immigrant is back beyond months and
　　years,　　　　　　　　　　　　　　　　　　　　　　　　　　　　　125
The poor Irishman lives in the simple house of his childhood with the well-
　　known neighbors and faces,
They warmly welcome him, he is barefoot again, he forgets he is well off,
The Dutchman voyages home, and the Scotchman and Welshman voyage
　　home, and the native of the Mediterranean voyages home,
To every port of England, France, Spain, enter well-fill'd ships,

1. In 1855 these three verse paragraphs followed:

　Now Lucifer was not dead . . . . or if he was I am
　　his sorrowful terrible heir;
　I have been wronged. . . . I am oppressed I
　　hate him that oppresses me,
　I will either destroy him, or he shall release me.

　Damn him! how he does defile me,
　How he informs against my brother and sister and
　　takes pay for their blood,
　How he laughs when I look down the bend after the

steamboat that carries away my woman.

　Now the vast dusk bulk that is the whale's bulk . . . .
　　it seems mine,
　Warily, sportsman! though I lie so sleepy and slug-
　　gish, my tap is death.

2. In 1855 "myself" was followed by a comma and
this line concluded the verse paragraph: "And have an
unseen something to be in contact with them also."
3. Herds of cattle, from their being "driven" to market
in a group.

The Swiss foots it toward his hills, the Prussian goes his way, the Hungarian
    his way, and the Pole his way,   130
The Swede returns, and the Dane and Norwegian return.

The homeward bound and the outward bound,
The beautiful lost swimmer, the ennuyé, the onanist, the female that loves
    unrequited, the money-maker,
The actor and actress, those through with their parts and those waiting to com-
    mence,
The affectionate boy, the husband and wife, the voter, the nominee that is
    chosen and the nominee that has fail'd,   135
The great already known and the great any time after to-day,
The stammerer, the sick, the perfect-form'd, the homely,
The criminal that stood in the box, the judge that sat and sentenced him, the
    fluent lawyers, the jury, the audience,
The laugher and weeper, the dancer, the midnight widow, the red squaw,
The consumptive, the erysipalite,[4] the idiot, he that is wrong'd,   140
The antipodes,[5] and every one between this and them in the dark,
I swear they are averaged now—one is no better than the other,
The night and sleep have liken'd them and restored them.

I swear they are all beautiful,
Every one that sleeps is beautiful, every thing in the dim light is beautiful, 145
The wildest and bloodiest is over, and all is peace.

Peace is always beautiful,
The myth of heaven indicates peace and night.
The myth of heaven indicates the soul,
The soul is always beautiful, it appears more or it appears less, it comes or it
    lags behind,   150
It comes from its embower'd garden and looks pleasantly on itself and encloses
    the world,
Perfect and clean the genitals previously jetting, and perfect and clean the
    womb cohering,
The head well-grown proportion'd and plumb, and the bowels and joints pro-
    portion'd and plumb.

The soul is always beautiful,
The universe is duly in order, every thing is in its place,   155
What has arrived is in its place and what waits shall be in its place,
The twisted skull waits, the watery or rotten blood waits,
The child of the glutton or venerealee waits long, and the child of the drunkard
    waits long, and the drunkard himself waits long,
The sleepers that lived and died wait, the far advanced are to go on in their
    turns, and the far behind are to come on in their turns,
The diverse shall be no less diverse, but they shall flow and unite—they unite
    now.   160

---

4. Someone with "red skin," a severe inflammation   5. Any two places on opposite sides of the earth.
caused by a streptococcus.

8

The sleepers are very beautiful as they lie unclothed,
They flow hand in hand over the whole earth from east to west as they lie
    unclothed,
The Asiatic and African are hand in hand, the European and American are
    hand in hand,
Learn'd and unlearn'd are hand in hand, and male and female are hand in
    hand,
The bare arm of the girl crosses the bare breast of her lover, they press close
    without lust, his lips press her neck,   165
The father holds his grown or ungrown son in his arms with measureless love,
    and the son holds the father in his arms with measureless love,
The white hair of the mother shines on the white wrist of the daughter,
The breath of the boy goes with the breath of the man, friend is inarm'd by
    friend,
The scholar kisses the teacher and the teacher kisses the scholar, the wrong'd
    is made right,
The call of the slave is one with the master's call, and the master salutes the
    slave,   170
The felon steps forth from the prison, the insane becomes sane, the suffering
    of sick persons is reliev'd,
The sweatings and fevers stop, the throat that was unsound is sound, the lungs
    of the consumptive are resumed, the poor distress'd head is free,
The joints of the rheumatic move as smoothly as ever, and smoother than
    ever,
Stiflings and passages open, the paralyzed become supple,
The swell'd and convuls'd and congested awake to themselves in
    condition,   175
They pass the invigoration of the night and the chemistry of the night, and
    awake.

I too pass from the night,
I stay a while away O night, but I return to you again and love you.

Why should I be afraid to trust myself to you?
I am not afraid, I have been well brought forward by you,   180
I love the rich running day, but I do not desert her in whom I lay so long,
I know not how I came of you and I know not where I go with you, but I know
    I came well and shall go well.

I will stop only a time with the night, and rise betimes,
I will duly pass the day O my mother, and duly return to you.[6]

1855, 1881

---

6. In 1855 this line began a verse paragraph (the previous line standing alone) and ended with a semicolon, being followed by these two lines: "Not you will yield forth the dawn again more surely than you will yield forth me again, / Not the womb yields the babe in its time more surely than I shall be yielded from you in my time."

FROM WHISPERS OF HEAVENLY DEATH

Chanting the Square Deific[1]

1

Chanting the square deific, out of the One advancing, out of the sides,
Out of the old and new, out of the square entirely divine,
Solid, four-sided, (all the sides needed,) from this side Jehovah am I,
Old Brahm I, and I Saturnius[2] am;
Not Time affects me—I am Time, old, modern as any,⁣   5
Unpersuadable, relentless, executing righteous judgments,
As the Earth, the Father, the brown old Kronos,[3] with laws,
Aged beyond computation, yet ever new, ever with those mighty laws rolling,
Relentless I forgive no man—whoever sins dies—I will have that man's life;
Therefore let none expect mercy—have the seasons, gravitation, the appointed
    days, mercy? no more have I,⁣   10
But as the seasons and gravitation, and as all the appointed days that forgive
    not,
I dispense from this side judgments inexorable without the least remorse.

2

Consolator most mild, the promis'd one advancing,
With gentle hand extended, the mightier God am I,
Foretold by prophets and poets in their most rapt prophecies and poems,⁣   15
From this side, lo! the Lord Christ gazes—lo! Hermes I—lo! mine is Hercules'
    face,[4]
All sorrow, labor, suffering, I, tallying it, absorb in myself,
Many times have I been rejected, taunted, put in prison, and crucified, and
    many times shall be again,
All the world have I given up for my dear brothers' and sisters' sake, for the
    soul's sake,
Wending my way through the homes of men, rich or poor, with the kiss
    of affection,⁣   20
For I am affection, I am the cheer-bringing God, with hope and all-enclosing
    charity,
With indulgent words as to children, with fresh and sane words, mine only,
Young and strong I pass knowing well I am destin'd myself to an early death;
But my charity has no death—my wisdom dies not, neither early nor late,
And my sweet love bequeath'd here and elsewhere never dies.⁣   25

---

1. This poem was first printed in *Sequel to Drum-Taps* (1865–66), then was part of *Passage to India* (1871), and became part of the *Whispers of Heavenly Death* section of *Leaves of Grass* in the 1881 edition.
2. Whitman in this section identifies one aspect of divinity, the lawgiver and law enforcer, as typified by Jehovah and other gods from Hindu and Greek myth. Brahm, or Brahma, is in Hindu theology the supreme spirit of the universe, the creator; Saturnius, or Saturn, is in Roman mythology the father of the gods.
3. An ancient god in Greek mythology, identified by the Romans with Saturn, and associated with time.
4. In this section Jesus is one of the gentler suffering man-gods who also form one enduring side of the deific square. Hermes, in Greek mythology, was messenger of the gods; Hercules was a legendary Greek hero.

3

Aloof, dissatisfied, plotting revolt,
Comrade of criminals, brother of slaves,
Crafty, despised, a drudge, ignorant,
With sudra[5] face and worn brow, black, but in the depths of my heart, proud
    as any,
Lifted now and always against whoever scorning assumes to rule me,   30
Morose, full of guile, full of reminiscences, brooding, with many wiles,
(Though it was thought I was baffled and dispel'd, and my wiles done, but that
    will never be,)
Defiant, I, Satan,[6] still live, still utter words, in new lands duly appearing,
    (and old ones also,)
Permanent here from my side, warlike, equal with any, real as any,
Nor time nor change shall ever change me or my words.   35

4

Santa Spirita,[7] breather, life,
Beyond the light, lighter than light,
Beyond the flames of hell, joyous, leaping easily above hell,
Beyond Paradise, perfumed solely with mine own perfume,
Including all life on earth, touching, including God, including Saviour and
    Satan,   40
Ethereal, pervading all, (for without me what were all? what were God?)
Essence of forms, life of the real identities, permanent, positive, (namely the
    unseen,)
Life of the great round world, the sun and stars, and of man, I, the general
    soul,
Here the square finishing, the solid, I the most solid,
Breathe my breath also through these songs.   45

1865–66, 1881

A Noiseless Patient Spider

A noiseless patient spider,
I mark'd where on a little promontory it stood isolated,
Mark'd how to explore the vacant vast surrounding,
It launch'd forth filament, filament, filament, out of itself,
Ever unreeling them, ever tirelessly speeding them.   5

And you O my soul where you stand,
Surrounded, detached, in measureless oceans of space,
Ceaselessly musing, venturing, throwing, seeking the spheres to connect
    them,

---

5. The lowest Hindu caste.
6. In this section, Satan represents the antagonistic, subversive principle of the godhead.

7. The fourth side of the deific square, the Holy Spirit, includes the other three.

Till the bridge you will need be form'd, till the ductile anchor hold,
Till the gossamer thread you fling catch somewhere, O my soul.   10

1868, 1881

FROM FROM NOON TO STARRY NIGHT

To a Locomotive in Winter[1]

Thee for my recitative,
Thee in the driving storm even as now, the snow, the winter-day declining,
Thee in thy panoply,[2] thy measur'd dual throbbing and thy beat convulsive,
Thy black cylindric body, golden brass and silvery steel,
Thy ponderous side-bars, parallel and connecting rods, gyrating, shuttling at
    thy sides,   5
Thy metrical, now swelling pant and roar, now tapering in the distance,
Thy great protruding head-light fix'd in front,
Thy long, pale, floating vapor-pennants, tinged with delicate purple,
Thy dense and murky clouds out-belching from thy smoke-stack,
Thy knitted frame, thy springs and valves, the tremulous twinkle of thy
    wheels,   10
Thy train of cars behind, obedient, merrily following,
Through gale or calm, now swift, now slack, yet steadily careering;
Type of the modern—emblem of motion and power—pulse of the continent,
For once come serve the Muse and merge in verse, even as here I see thee,
With storm and buffeting gusts of wind and falling snow,   15
By day thy warning ringing bell to sound its notes,
By night thy silent signal lamps to swing.

Fierce-throated beauty!
Roll through my chant with all thy lawless music, thy swinging lamps at night,
Thy madly-whistled laughter, echoing, rumbling like an earthquake, rousing
    all,   20
Law of thyself complete, thine own track firmly holding,
(No sweetness debonair of tearful harp or glib piano thine,)
Thy trills of shrieks by rocks and hills return'd,
Launch'd o'er the prairies wide, across the lakes,
To the free skies unpent and glad and strong.   25

1876, 1881

---

1. First printed in the *New York Tribune* on February 19, 1876, as a sample from the forthcoming *Two Rivulets*, this poem was moved to the *From Noon to Starry* *Night* group in the 1881 *Leaves of Grass.*
2. Suit of armor.

FROM FIRST ANNEX: SANDS AT SEVENTY

As I Sit Writing Here[1]

As I sit writing here, sick and grown old,
Not my least burden is that dulness of the years, querilities,[2]
Ungracious glooms, aches, lethargy, constipation, whimpering *ennui*,[3]
May filter in my daily songs.

1888, 1888–89

By That Long Scan of Waves[1]

By that long scan of waves, myself call'd back, resumed upon myself,
In every crest some undulating light or shade—some retrospect,
Joys, travels, studies, silent panoramas—scenes ephemeral,
The long past war, the battles, hospital sights, the wounded and the dead,
Myself through every by-gone phase—my idle youth—old age at hand,   5
My three-score years of life summ'd up, and more, and past,
By any grand ideal tried, intentionless, the whole a nothing,
And haply yet some drop within God's scheme's ensemble—some wave, or
    part of wave,
Like one of yours, ye multitudinous ocean.

1885, 1888–89

Broadway

What hurrying human tides, or day or night!
What passions, winnings, losses, ardors, swim thy waters!
What whirls of evil, bliss and sorrow, stem thee!
What curious questioning glances—glints of love!
Leer, envy, scorn, contempt, hope, aspiration!   5
Thou portal—thou arena—thou of the myriad long-drawn lines and groups!
(Could but thy flagstones, curbs, façades, tell their inimitable tales;
Thy windows rich, and huge hotels—thy side-walks wide;)
Thou of the endless sliding, mincing, shuffling feet!
Thou, like the parti-colored world itself—like infinite, teeming, mocking
    life!   10
Thou visor'd, vast, unspeakable show and lesson!

1888, 1888–89

---

1. New poems and the prose essay *A Backward Glance O'er Travel'd Roads* appeared in a separate book, *November Boughs* (1888); there the poems were headed *Sands at Seventy*. These poems plus one additional one were printed in the 1889 *Leaves of Grass* as an annex—that is, added onto the end with none of the usual attempt to integrate them into the body of the book. *As I Sit Writing Here* was first published in the

New York Herald on May 14, 1888, before appearing in *November Boughs*.
2. Normally spelled *querulities*: whining complaints.
3. Boredom (French).
1. This poem is the seventh of eight in a subsection of *Sands at Seventy* called *Fancies at Navesink*, from the Navesink Highlands of New Jersey, overlooking the Atlantic, a vacation resort for the invalid Whitman.

Yonnondio

[*The sense of the word is* lament for the aborigines. *It is an Iroquois term; and has been used for a personal name.*][1]

A song, a poem of itself—the word itself a dirge,
Amid the wilds, the rocks, the storm and wintry night,
To me such misty, strange tableaux the syllables calling up;
Yonnondio—I see, far in the west or north, a limitless ravine, with plains and
    mountains dark,
I see swarms of stalwart chieftains, medicine-men, and warriors,   5
As flitting by like clouds of ghosts, they pass and are gone in the twilight,
(Race of the woods, the landscapes free, and the falls!
No picture, poem, statement, passing them to the future:)
Yonnondio! Yonnondio!—unlimn'd[2] they disappear;
To-day gives place, and fades—the cities, farms, factories fade;   10
A muffled sonorous sound, a wailing word is borne through the air for a
    moment,
Then blank and gone and still, and utterly lost.

                                    1887, 1888–89

Orange Buds by Mail from Florida[1]

[*Voltaire closed a famous argument by claiming that a ship of war and the grand opera were proofs enough of civilization's and France's progress, in his day.*]

A lesser proof than old Voltaire's, yet greater,
Proof of this present time, and thee, thy broad expanse, America,
To my plain Northern hut, in outside clouds and snow,
Brought safely for a thousand miles o'er land and tide,
Some three days since on their own soil live-sprouting,   5
Now here their sweetness through my room unfolding,
A bunch of orange buds by mail from Florida.

                                    1888, 1888–89

Now Precedent Songs, Farewell[2]

Now precedent songs, farewell—by every name farewell,
(Trains of a staggering line in many a strange procession, waggons,
From ups and downs—with intervals—from elder years, mid-age, or youth,)
"In Cabin'd Ships," or "Thee Old Cause" or "Poets to Come"
Or "Paumanok," "Song of Myself," "Calamus," or "Adam,"   5

---

1. The bracketed definition of the title is Whitman's. The poem was first published in the *Critic*, November 26, 1887.
2. Unpainted, therefore unrecorded.
1. This poem was first published in the *New York Herald* on March 18, 1888. The bracketed headnote is Whitman's.
2. "The two songs on this page [*Now Precedent Songs,*

Farewell and *An Evening Lull*] are eked out during an afternoon, June, 1888, in my seventieth year, at a critical spell of illness. Of course no reader and probably no human being at any time will ever have such phases of emotional and solemn action as these involve to me. I feel in them an end and close of all" [Whitman's note].

Or "Beat! Beat! Drums!" or "To the Leaven'd Soil they Trod,"
Or "Captain! My Captain!" "Kosmos," "Quicksand Years," or "Thoughts,"
"Thou Mother with Thy Equal Brood," and many, many more unspecified,
From fibre heart of mine—from throat and tongue—(My life's hot pulsing
    blood,
The personal urge and form for me—not merely paper, automatic type and
    ink,)   10
Each song of mine—each utterance in the past—having its long, long history,
Of life or death, or soldier's wound, of country's loss or safety,
(O heaven! what flash and started endless train of all! compared indeed to that!
What wretched shred e'en at the best of all!)

1888, 1888–89

An Evening Lull

After a week of physical anguish,
Unrest and pain, and feverish heat,
Toward the ending day a calm and lull comes on,
Three hours of peace and soothing rest of brain.

1888, 1888–89

After the Supper and Talk

After the supper and talk—after the day is done,
As a friend from friends his final withdrawal prolonging,
Good-bye and Good-bye with emotional lips repeating,
(So hard for his hand to release those hands—no more will they meet,
No more for communion of sorrow and joy, of old and young,   5
A far-stretching journey awaits him, to return no more,)
Shunning, postponing severance—seeking to ward off the last word ever so
    little,
E'en at the exit-door turning—charges superflous calling back—e'en as he
    descends the steps,
Something to eke out a minute additional—shadows of nightfall deepening
Farewells, messages lessening—dimmer the forthgoer's visage and form,   10
Soon to be lost for aye in the darkness—loth, O so loth to depart!
Garrulous to the very last.

1887, 1888–89

FROM SECOND ANNEX: GOOD-BYE MY FANCY[1]

Preface Note to 2d Annex, Concluding L. of G.—1891

Had I not better withhold (in this old age and paralysis of me) such little
tags and fringe-dots (maybe specks, stains,) as follow a long dusty journey, and

---

1. The poetic imagination. This, the second and final "annex" to *Leaves of Grass*, consisting of prose head-note and thirty-one poems, mostly new, was printed separately in 1891 as *Good-by My Fancy*, then added to *Leaves of Grass* in the 1891–92 edition.

witness it afterward? I have probably not been enough afraid of careless touches, from the first—and am not now—nor of parrot-like repetitions— nor platitudes and the commonplace. Perhaps I am too democratic for such avoidances. Besides, is not the verse-field, as originally plann'd by my theory, now sufficiently illustrated—and full time for me to silently retire?—(indeed amid no loud call or market for my sort of poetic utterance.)

In answer, or rather defiance, to that kind of well-put interrogation, here comes this little cluster, and conclusion of my preceding clusters. Though not at all clear that, as here collated, it is worth printing (certainly I have nothing fresh to write)—I while away the hours of my 72d year—hours of forced confinement in my den—by putting in shape this small old age collation:

> Last droplets of and after spontaneous rain,
> From many limpid distillations and past showers;
> (Will they germinate anything? mere exhalations as they all are
>   —the land's and sea's—America's;
> Will they filter to any deep emotion? any heart and brain?)

However that may be, I feel like improving to-day's opportunity and wind up. During the last two years I have sent out, in the lulls of illness and exhaustion, certain chirps—lingering-dying ones probably (undoubtedly)—which now I may as well gather and put in fair type while able to see correctly—(for my eyes plainly warn me they are dimming, and my brain more and more palpably neglects or refuses, month after month, even slight tasks or revisions.)

In fact, here I am these current years 1890 and '91, (each successive fortnight getting stiffer and stuck deeper) much like some hard-cased dilapidated grim ancient shell-fish or time-bang'd conch (no legs, utterly non-locomotive) cast up high and dry on the shore-sands, helpless to move anywhere—nothing left but behave myself quiet, and while away the days yet assign'd, and discover if there is anything for the said grim and time-bang'd conch to be got at last out of inherited good spirits and primal buoyant centre-pulses down there deep somewhere within his gray-blurr'd old shell. . . . . (Reader, you must allow a little fun here—for one reason there are too many of the following poemets about death, &c., and for another the passing hours (July 5, 1890) are so sunny-fine. And old as I am I feel to-day almost a part of some frolicsome wave, or for sporting yet like a kid or kitten—probably a streak of physical adjustment and perfection here and now. I believe I have it in me perennially anyhow.)

Then behind all, the deep-down consolation (it is a glum one, but I dare not be sorry for the fact of it in the past, nor refrain from dwelling, even vaunting here at the end) that this late-years palsied old shorn and shell-fish condition of me is the indubitable outcome and growth, now near for 20 years along, of too over-zealous, over-continued bodily and emotional excitement and action through the times of 1862, '3, '4 and '5, visiting and waiting on wounded and sick army volunteers, both sides, in campaigns or contests, or after them, or in hospitals or fields south of Washington City, or in that place and elsewhere—those hot, sad, wrenching times—the army volunteers, all States,—or North or South—the wounded, suffering, dying—the exhausting, sweating summers, marches, battles, carnage—those trenches hurriedly heap'd by the corpse-thousands, mainly unknown—Will the America of the future—will this vast rich Union ever realize what itself cost, back there after all?—those hecatombs[2] of battle-deaths—Those times of which, O far-off reader, this whole book is indeed finally but a reminiscent memorial from thence by me to you?

Osceola

[When I was nearly grown to manhood in Brooklyn, New York, (middle of 1838,) I met one of the return'd U.S. Marines from Fort Moultrie, S.C., and had long talks with him—learn'd the occurrence below described—death of Osceola. The latter was a young, brave, leading Seminole in the Florida war of that time—was surrender'd to our troops, imprison'd and literally died of "a broken heart," at Fort Moultrie. He sicken'd of his confinement—the doctor and officers made every allowance and kindness possible for him; then the close:][1]

When his hour for death had come,
He slowly rais'd himself from the bed on the floor,
Drew on his war-dress, shirt, leggings, and girdled the belt around his waist,

Call'd for vermilion paint (his looking-glass was held before him,)
Painted half his face and neck, his wrists, and back-hands,   5
Put the scalp-knife carefully in his belt—then lying down, resting a moment,
Rose again, half sitting, smiled, gave in silence his extended hand to each and all,
Sank faintly low to the floor (tightly grasping the tomahawk handle,)
Fix'd his look on wife and little children—the last:

(And here a line in memory of his name and death.)   10

1890, 1891–92

"The Rounded Catalogue Divine Complete"

[Sunday, — – —.–Went this forenoon to church. A college professor, Rev. Dr.———, gave us a fine sermon, during which I caught the above words; but the minister included in his "rounded catalogue" letter and spirit, only the esthetic things, and entirely ignored what I name in the following:][2]

The devilish and the dark, the dying and diseas'd,
The countless (nineteen-twentieths) low and evil, crude and savage,
The crazed, prisoners in jail, the horrible, rank, malignant,
Venom and filth, serpents, the ravenous sharks, liars, the dissolute;
(What is the part the wicked and the loathesome bear within earth's orbic scheme?)   5
Newts, crawling things in slime and mud, poisons,
The barren soil, the evil men, the slag and hideous rot.

1891, 1891–92

---

2. Many hundreds, from the Greek for a hundred oxen (in the ritual sacrifice of a hundred oxen at the same time).

1. The bracketed headnote is Whitman's.
2. The bracketed headnote is Whitman's.

Good-bye My Fancy!

Good-bye my Fancy!
Farewell dear mate, dear love!
I'm going away, I know not where,
Or to what fortune, or whether I may ever see you again,
So Good-bye my Fancy.   5

Now for my last—let me look back a moment;
The slower fainter ticking of the clock is in me,
Exit, nightfall, and soon the heart-thud stopping.

Long have we lived, joy'd, caress'd together;
Delightful!—now separation—Good-bye my Fancy.   10

Yet let me not be too hasty,
Long indeed have we lived, slept, filter'd, become really blended into one;
Then if we die we die together, (yes, we'll remain one,)
If we go anywhere we'll go together to meet what happens,
May-be we'll be better off and blither, and learn something,   15
May-be it is yourself now really ushering me to the true songs, (who knows?)
May-be it is you the mortal knob really undoing, turning—so now finally,
Good-bye—and hail! my Fancy.

                                                      1891, 1891–92

A Backward Glance o'er Travel'd Roads[1]

Perhaps the best of songs heard, or of any and all true love, or life's fairest
episodes, or sailors', soldiers' trying scenes on land or sea, is the *résumé* of
them, or any of them, long afterwards, looking at the actualities away back
past, with all their practical excitations gone. How the soul loves to float amid
such reminiscences!

So here I sit gossiping in the early candle-light of old age—I and my book—
casting backward glances over our travel'd road. After completing, as it were,
the journey—(a varied jaunt of years, with many halts and gaps of intervals—
or some lengthen'd ship-voyage, wherein more than once the last hour had
apparently arrived, and we seem'd certainly going down—yet reaching port in
a sufficient way through all discomfitures at last)—After completing my
poems, I am curious to review them in the light of their own (at the time
unconscious, or mostly unconscious) intentions, with certain unfoldings of
the thirty years they seek to embody. These lines, therefore, will probably
blend the weft of first purposes and speculations, with the warp of that experience afterwards, always bringing strange developments.

Result of seven or eight stages and struggles extending through nearly thirty
years, (as I nigh my three-score-and-ten I live largely on memory,) I look upon

1. Derived from Whitman's various retrospective
prose writings of the 1880s (including *A Back Glance
on My Own Road* in 1884 and *My Book and I* in 1887),
this essay was published as a preface to a little book,
November Boughs (1888), the source of the present
text, and later gathered into *Leaves of Grass* as an
annex. In a century when Whitman's great contemporary, Herman Melville, was silenced, or silenced himself, this is a triumphant document by a man who had
"positively gain'd a hearing" in his time: "I have had
my say entirely my own way, and put it unerringly on
record."

"Leaves of Grass," now finish'd to the end of its opportunities and powers, as my definitive *carte visite* to the coming generations of the New World,[2] if I may assume to say so. That I have not gain'd the acceptance of my own time, but have fallen back on fond dreams of the future—anticipations—("still lives the song, though Regnar dies")[3]—That from a worldly and business point of view "Leaves of Grass" has been worse than a failure—that public criticism on the book and myself as author of it yet shows mark'd anger and contempt more than anything else—("I find a solid line of enemies to you everywhere,"—letter from W. S. K., Boston, May 28, 1884)—And that solely for publishing it I have been the object of two or three pretty serious special official buffetings[4]—is all probably no more than I ought to have expected. I had my choice when I commenc'd. I bid neither for soft eulogies, big money returns, nor the approbation of existing schools and conventions. As fulfill'd, or partially fulfill'd, the best comfort of the whole business (after a small band of the dearest friends and upholders ever vouchsafed to man or cause—doubtless all the more faithful and uncompromising—this little phalanx!—for being so few) is that, unstopp'd and unwarp'd by any influence outside the soul within me, I have had my say entirely my own way, and put it unerringly on record—the value thereof to be decided by time.

In calculating that decision, William O'Connor and Dr. Bucke[5] are far more peremptory than I am. Behind all else that can be said, I consider "Leaves of Grass" and its theory experimental—as, in the deepest sense, I consider our American republic itself to be, with its theory. (I think I have at least enough philosophy not to be too absolutely certain of any thing, or any results.) In the second place, the volume is a *sortie*—whether to prove triumphant, and conquer its field of aim and escape and construction, nothing less than a hundred years from now can fully answer. I consider the point that I have positively gain'd a hearing, to far more than make up for any and all other lacks and withholdings. Essentially, *that* was from the first, and has remain'd throughout, the main object. Now it seems to be achiev'd, I am certainly contented to waive any otherwise momentous drawbacks, as of little account. Candidly and dispassionately reviewing all my intentions, I feel that they were creditable—and I accept the result, whatever it may be.

After continued personal ambition and effort, as a young fellow, to enter with the rest into competition for the usual rewards, business, political, literary, &c.—to take part in the great *mélée*, both for victory's prize itself and to do some good—After years of those aims and pursuits, I found myself remaining possess'd, at the age of thirty-one to thirty-three, with a special desire and conviction. Or rather, to be quite exact, a desire that had been flitting through my previous life, or hovering on the flanks, mostly indefinite hitherto, had steadily advanced to the front, defined itself, and finally dominated everything else. This was a feeling or ambition to articulate and faithfully express in literary or poetic form, and uncompromisingly, my own physical, emotional, moral, intellectual, and æsthetic Personality, in the midst of, and tallying, the

2. "When Champollion, on his deathbed, handed to the printer the revised proof of his 'Egyptian Grammar,' he said gayly, 'Be careful of this—it is my *carte de visite* to posterity" [Whitman's note]. Jean François Champollion (1790–1832) was the great French Egyptologist, decipherer of the Rosetta stone. "*Carte de visite*": calling card (French).
3. From the ballad *Alfred the Harper* by the British poet John Sterling (1806–1844).

4. Among these "buffetings" were Whitman's being fired from the Department of the Interior (1865) and being threatened with prohibition against sending *Leaves of Grass* through the United States mails (1882). The letter just quoted is from William Sloane Kennedy.
5. Two of Whitman's disciples, the first the author of *The Good Gray Poet*, the second a Canadian physician who became one of Whitman's executors.

momentous spirit and facts of its immediate days, and of current America—and to exploit that Personality, identified with place and date, in a far more candid and comprehensive sense than any hitherto poem or book.

Perhaps this is in brief, or suggests, all I have sought to do. Given the Nineteenth Century, with the United States, and what they furnish as area and points of view, "Leaves of Grass" is, or seeks to be, simply a faithful and doubtless self-will'd record. In the midst of all, it gives one man's—the author's—identity, ardors, observations, faiths, and thoughts, color'd hardly at all with any decided coloring from other faiths or other identities. Plenty of songs had been sung—beautiful, matchless songs—adjusted to other lands than these—another spirit and stage of evolution; but I would sing, and leave out or put in, quite solely with reference to America and today. Modern science and democracy seem'd to be throwing out their challenge to poetry to put them in its statements in contradistinction to the songs and myths of the past. As I see it now (perhaps too late,) I have unwittingly taken up that challenge and made an attempt at such statements—which I certainly would not assume to do now, knowing more clearly what it means.

For grounds for "Leaves of Grass," as a poem, I abandon'd the conventional themes, which do not appear in it: none of the stock ornamentation, or choice plots of love or war, or high, exceptional personages of Old-World song; nothing, as I may say, for beauty's sake—no legend, or myth, or romance, nor euphemism, nor rhyme. But the broadest average of humanity and its identities in the now ripening Nineteenth Century, and especially in each of their countless examples and practical occupations in the United States to-day.

One main contrast of the ideas behind every page of my verses, compared with establish'd poems, is their different relative attitude towards God, towards the objective universe, and still more (by reflection, confession, assumption, &c.) the quite changed attitude of the ego, the one chanting or talking, towards himself and towards his fellow-humanity. It is certainly time for America, above all, to begin this readjustment in the scope and basic point of view of verse; for everything else has changed. As I write, I see in an article on Wordsworth, in one of the current English magazines, the lines, "A few weeks ago an eminent French critic said that, owing to the special tendency to science and to its all-devouring force, poetry would cease to be read in fifty years." But I anticipate the very contrary. Only a firmer, vastly broader, new area begins to exist—nay, is already form'd—to which the poetic genius must emigrate. Whatever may have been the case in years gone by, the true use for the imaginative faculty of modern times is to give ultimate vivification to facts, to science, and to common lives, endowing them with the glows and glories and final illustriousness which belong to every real thing, and to real things only. Without that ultimate vivification—which the poet or other artist alone can give—reality would seem incomplete, and science, democracy, and life itself, finally in vain.

Few appreciate the moral revolutions, our age, which have been profounder far than the material or inventive or war-produced ones. The Nineteenth Century, now well towards its close (and ripening into fruit the seeds of the two preceding centuries)[6]—the uprisings of national masses and shiftings of bound-

---

6. "The ferment and germination even of the United States to-day, dating back to, and in my opinion mainly founded on, the Elizabethan age in English history, the age of Francis Bacon and Shakspere. Indeed, when we pursue it, what growth or advent is there that does not date back, back, until lost—perhaps its most tantalizing clues lost—in the receded horizons of the past?" [Whitman's note].

ary-lines—the historical and other prominent facts of the United States—the war of attempted Secession—the stormy rush and haste of nebulous forces—never can future years witness more excitement and din of action—never completer change of army front along the whole line, the whole civilized world. For all these new and evolutionary facts, meanings, purposes, new poetic messages, new forms and expressions, are inevitable.

My Book and I—what a period we have presumed to span! those thirty years from 1850 to '80—and America in them! Proud, proud indeed may we be, if we have cull'd enough of that period in its own spirit to worthily waft a few live breaths of it to the future!

Let me not dare, here or anywhere, for my own purposes, or any purposes, to attempt the definition of Poetry, nor answer the question what it is. Like Religion, Love, Nature, while those terms are indispensable, and we all give a sufficiently accurate meaning to them, in my opinion no definition that has ever been made sufficiently encloses the name Poetry; nor can any rule or convention ever so absolutely obtain but some great exception may arise and disregard and overturn it.

Also it must be carefully remember'd that first-class literature does not shine by any luminosity of its own; nor do its poems. They grow of circumstances, and are evolutionary. The actual living light is always curiously from elsewhere—follows unaccountable sources, and is lunar and relative at the best. There are, I know, certain controling themes that seem endlessly appropriated to the poets—as war, in the past—in the Bible, religious rapture and adoration—always love, beauty, some fine plot, or pensive or other emotion. But, strange as it may sound at first, I will say there is something striking far deeper and towering far higher than those themes for the best elements of modern song.

Just as all the old imaginative works rest, after their kind, on long trains of presuppositions, often entirely unmention'd by themselves, yet supplying the most important bases of them, and without which they could have had no reason for being, so "Leaves of Grass," before a line was written, presupposed something different from any other, and, as it stands, is the result of such presupposition. I should say, indeed, it were useless to attempt reading the book without first carefully tallying that preparatory background and quality in the mind. Think of the United States to-day—the facts of these thirty-eight or forty empires solder'd in one—sixty or seventy millions of equals, with their lives, their passions, their future—these incalculable, modern, American, seething multitudes around us, of which we are inseparable parts! Think, in comparison, of the petty environage and limited area of the poets of past or present Europe, no matter how great their genius. Think of the absence and ignorance, in all cases hitherto, of the multitudinousness, vitality, and the unprecedented stimulants of to-day and here. It almost seems as if a poetry with cosmic and dynamic features of magnitude and limitlessness suitable to the human soul, were never possible before. It is certain that a poetry of absolute faith and equality for the use of the democratic masses never was.

In estimating first-class song, a sufficient Nationality, or, on the other hand, what may be call'd the negative and lack of it, (as in Goethe's case, it sometimes seems to me,) is often, if not always, the first element. One needs only a little penetration to see, at more or less removes, the material facts of their country and radius, with the coloring of the moods of humanity at the time, and its gloomy or hopeful prospects, behind all poets and each poet, and forming their birth-marks. I know very well that my "Leaves" could not possibly have emerged or been fashion'd or completed, from any other era than the latter half of the Nineteenth Century, nor any other land than democratic America, and from the absolute triumph of the National Union arms.

And whether my friend claim it for me or not, I know well enough, too, that in respect to pictorial talent, dramatic situations, and especially in verbal melody and all the conventional technique of poetry, not only the divine works that to-day stand ahead in the world's reading, but dozens more, transcend (some of them immeasurably transcend) all I have done, or could do. But it seem'd to me, as the objects in Nature, the themes of æstheticism, and all special exploitations of the mind and soul, involve not only their own inherent quality, but the quality, just as inherent and important, of *their point of view*,[7] the time had come to reflect all themes and things, old and new, in the lights thrown on them by the advent of America and democracy—to chant those themes through the utterance of one, not only the grateful and reverent legatee of the past, but the born child of the New World—to illustrate all through the genesis and ensemble of to-day; and that such illustration and ensemble are the chief demands of America's prospective imaginative literature. Not to carry out, in the approved style, some choice plot of fortune or misfortune, or fancy, or fine thoughts, or incidents, or courtesies—all of which has been done overwhelmingly and well, probably never to be excell'd—but that while in such æsthetic presentation of objects, passions, plots, thoughts, &c., our lands and days do not want, and probably will never have, anything better than they already possess from the bequests of the past, it still remains to be said that there is even towards all those a subjective and contemporary point of view appropriate to ourselves alone, and to our new genius and environments, different from anything hitherto; and that such conception of current or gone-by life and art is for us the only means of their assimilation consistent with the Western world.

Indeed, and anyhow, to put it specifically, has not the time arrived when, (if it must be plainly said, for democratic America's sake, if for no other) there must imperatively come a readjustment of the whole theory and nature of Poetry? The question is important, and I may turn the argument over and repeat it: Does not the best thought of our day and Republic conceive of a birth and spirit of song superior to anything past or present? To the effectual and moral consolidation of our lands (already, as materially establish'd, the greatest factors in known history, and far, far greater through what they prelude and necessitate, and are to be in future)—to conform with and build on the concrete realities and theories of the universe furnish'd by science, and henceforth the only irrefragable basis for anything, verse included—to root both influences in the emotional and imaginative action of the modern time, and dominate all that precedes or opposes them—is not either a radical advance and step forward, or a new verteber[8] of the best song indispensable?

The New World receives with joy the poems of the antique, with European feudalism's rich fund of epics, plays, ballads—seeks not in the least to deaden

---

7. "According to Immanuel Kant, the last essential reality, giving shape and significance to all the rest" [Whitman's note]. Kant (1724–1804), German philosopher, whose *Critique of Pure Reason* strongly influenced the American Transcendentalists, either directly or through intermediaries such as Thomas Carlyle.
8. Variant spelling of vertebra: one of the bones in the spinal column.

or displace those voices from our ear and area—holds them indeed as indispensable studies, influences, records, comparisons. But though the dawn-dazzle of the sun of literature is in those poems for us of to-day—though perhaps the best parts of current character in nations, social groups, or any man's or woman's individuality, Old World or New, are from them—and though if I were ask'd to name the most precious bequest to current American civilization from all the hitherto ages, I am not sure but I would name those old and less old songs ferried hither from east and west—some serious words and debits remain; some acrid considerations demand a hearing. Of the great poems receiv'd from abroad and from the ages, and to-day enveloping and penetrating America, is there one that is consistent with these United States, or essentially applicable to them as they are and are to be? Is there one whose underlying basis is not a denial and insult to democracy? What a comment it forms, anyhow, on this era of literary fulfilment, with the splendid day-rise of science and resuscitation of history, that our chief religious and poetical works are not our own, nor adapted to our light, but have been furnish'd by far-back ages out of their arriere[9] and darkness, or, at most, twilight dimness! What is there in those works that so imperiously and scornfully dominates all our advanced civilization, and culture?

Even Shakespere, who so suffuses current letters and art (which indeed have in most degrees grown out of him,) belongs essentially to the buried past. Only he holds the proud distinction for certain important phases of that past, of being the loftiest of the singers life has yet given voice to. All, however, relate to and rest upon conditions, standards, politics, sociologies, ranges of belief, that have been quite eliminated from the Eastern hemisphere, and never existed at all in the Western. As authoritative types of song they belong in America just about as much as the persons and institutes they depict. True, it may be said, the emotional, moral, and æsthetic natures of humanity have not radically changed—that in these the old poems apply to our times and all times, irrespective of date; and that they are of incalculable value as pictures of the past. I willingly make those admissions, and to their fullest extent; then advance the points herewith as of serious, even paramount importance.

I have indeed put on record elsewhere my reverence and eulogy for those never-to-be-excell'd poetic bequests, and their indescribable preciousness as heirlooms for America. Another and separate point must now be candidly stated. If I had not stood before those poems with uncover'd head, fully aware of their colossal grandeur and beauty of form and spirit, I could not have written "Leaves of Grass." My verdict and conclusions as illustrated in its pages are arrived at through the temper and inculcation of the old works as much as through anything else—perhaps more than through anything else. As America fully and fairly construed is the legitimate result and evolutionary outcome of the past, so I would dare to claim for my verse. Without stopping to qualify the averment, the Old World has had the poems of myths, fictions, feudalism, conquest, caste, dynastic wars, and splendid exceptional characters and affairs, which have been great; but the New World needs the poems of realities and science and of the democratic average and basic equality, which shall be greater. In the centre of all, and object of all, stands the Human Being, towards whose heroic and spiritual evolution poems and everything directly or indirectly tend, Old World or New.

9. Backwardness.

Continuing the subject, my friends have more than once suggested—or may be the garrulity of advancing age is possessing me—some further embryonic facts of "Leaves of Grass," and especially how I enter'd upon them. Dr. Bucke has, in his volume, already fully and fairly described the preparation of my poetic field, with the particular and general plowing, planting, seeding, and occupation of the ground, till everything was fertilized, rooted, and ready to start its own way for good or bad. Not till after all this, did I attempt any serious acquaintance with poetic literature. Along in my sixteenth year I had become possessor of a stout, well-cramm'd one thousand page octavo volume (I have it yet,) containing Walter Scott's poetry entire—an inexhaustible mine and treasury of poetic forage (especially the endless forests and jungles of notes)— has been so to me for fifty years, and remains so to this day. [1]

Later, at intervals, summers and falls, I used to go off, sometimes for a week at a stretch, down in the country, or to Long Island's seashores—there, in the presence of outdoor influences, I went over thoroughly the Old and New Testaments, and absorb'd (probably to better advantage for me than in any library or indoor room—it makes such difference *where* you read,) Shakspere, Ossian, the best translated versions I could get of Homer, Eschylus, Sophocles, the old German Nibelungen, the ancient Hindoo poems, and one or two other masterpieces, Dante's[2] among them. As it happen'd, I read the latter mostly in an old wood. The Iliad (Buckley's prose version,) I read first thoroughly on the peninsula of Orient, northeast end of Long Island, in a shelter'd hollow of rocks and sand, with the sea on each side. (I have wonder'd since why I was not overwhelm'd by those mighty masters. Likely because I read them, as described, in the full presence of Nature, under the sun, with the far-spreading landscape and vistas, or the sea rolling in.)

Toward the last I had among much else look'd over Edgar Poe's poems—of which I was not an admirer, tho' I always saw that beyond their limited range of melody (like perpetual chimes of music bells, ringing from lower *b* flat up to *g*) they were melodious expressions, and perhaps never excell'd ones, of certain pronounc'd phases of human morbidity. (The Poetic area is very spacious—has room for all—has so many mansions!) But I was repaid in Poe's prose by the idea that (at any rate for our occasions, our day) there can be no such thing as a long poem. The same thought had been haunting my mind before, but Poe's argument, though short, work'd the sum out and proved it to me.

Another point had an early settlement, clearing the ground greatly. I saw, from the time my enterprise and questionings positively shaped themselves (how best can I express my own distinctive era and surroundings, America, Democracy?) that the trunk and centre whence the answer was to radiate, and to which all should return from straying however far a distance, must be an identical body and soul, a personality—which personality, after many consid-

---

1. "Sir Walter Scott's COMPLETE POEMS; especially including BORDER MINSTRELSY; then Sir Tristrem; Lay of the Last Minstrel; Ballads from the German; Marmion; Lady of the Lake; Vision of Don Roderick; Lord of the Isles; Rokeby; Bridal of Triermain; Field of Waterloo; Harold the Dauntless; all the Dramas; various Introductions, endless interesting Notes, and Essays on Poetry, Romance, &c.

"Lockhart's 1833 (or '34) edition with Scott's latest and copious revisions and annotations. (All the poems were thoroughly read by me, but the ballads of the Border Minstrelsy over and over again.)" [Whitman's note].

2. The masterpiece of Dante Alighieri (1265–1321), the Italian poet, is *The Divine Comedy*. Whitman, like many in his time, admired the poems by James Macpherson (published 1760–63) which purported to be translation from a 3rd-century A.D. Gaelic poet named Ossian. The *Nibelungenlied* is a 13th-century German epic poem based on the legends of Siegfried and the kings of Burgundy. Whitman mentions two of the Hindu scriptures in section 43 of *Song of Myself*, the shastas and Vedas.

erations and ponderings I deliberately settled should be myself—indeed could not be any other. I also felt strongly (whether I have shown it or not) that to the true and full estimate of the Present both the Past and the Future are main considerations.

These, however, and much more might have gone on and come to naught (almost positively would have come to naught,) if a sudden, vast, terrible, direct and indirect stimulus for new and national declamatory expression had not been given to me. It is certain, I say, that, although I had made a start before, only from the occurrence of the Secession War, and what it show'd me as by flashes of lightning, with the emotional depths it sounded and arous'd (of course, I don't mean in my own heart only, I saw it just as plainly in others, in millions)—that only from the strong flare and provocation of that war's sights and scenes the final reasons-for-being of an autochthonic[3] and passionate song definitely came forth.

I went down to the war fields in Virginia (end of 1862), lived thenceforward in camp—saw great battles and the days and nights afterward—partook of all the fluctuations, gloom, despair, hopes again arous'd, courage evoked—death readily risk'd—*the cause*, too—along and filling those agnostic and lurid following years, 1863–'64–'65—the real parturition years (more than 1776–'83) of this henceforth homogeneous Union. Without those three or four years and the experiences they gave, "Leaves of Grass" would not now be existing.

But I set out with the intention also of indicating or hinting some point-characteristics which I since see (though I did not then, at least not definitely) were bases and object-urgings toward those "Leaves" from the first. The word I myself put primarily for the description of them as they stand at last, is the word Suggestiveness. I round and finish little, if anything; and could not, consistently with my scheme. The reader will always have his or her part to do, just as much as I have had mine. I seek less to state or display any theme or thought, and more to bring you, reader, into the atmosphere of the theme or thought—there to pursue your own flight. Another impetus-word is Comradeship as for all lands, and in a more commanding and acknowledg'd sense than hitherto. Other word-signs would be Good Cheer, Content, and Hope.

The chief trait of any given poet is always the spirit he brings to the observation of Humanity and Nature—the mood out of which he contemplates his subjects. What kind of temper and what amount of faith report these things? Up to how recent a date is the song carried? What the equipment, and special raciness of the singer—what his tinge of coloring? The last value of artistic expressers, past and present—Greek æsthetes, Shakespere—or in our own day Tennyson, Victor Hugo, Carlyle, Emerson—is certainly involv'd in such questions. I say the profoundest service that poems or any other writings can do for their reader is not merely to satisfy the intellect, or supply something polish'd and interesting, nor even to depict great passions, or persons or events, but to fill him with vigorous and clean manliness, religiousness, and give him *good heart* as a radical possession and habit. The educated world seems to have been growing more and more ennuyed[4] for ages, leaving to our time the inheritance of it all. Fortunately there is the original inexhaustible fund of buoyancy, normally resident in the race, forever eligible to be appeal'd to and relied on.

---

3. Native to a particular place, indigenous.　　　4. Wearied, exhausted.

As for native American individuality, though certain to come, and on a large scale, the distinctive and ideal type of Western character (as consistent with the operative political and even money-making features of United States' humanity in the Nineteenth Century as chosen knights, gentlemen and warriors were the ideals of the centuries of European feudalism) it has not yet appear'd. I have allow'd the stress of my poems from beginning to end to bear upon American individuality and assist it—not only because that is a great lesson in Nature, amid all her generalizing laws, but as counterpoise to the leveling tendencies of Democracy—and for other reasons. Defiant of ostensible literary and other conventions, I avowedly chant "the great pride of man in himself," and permit it to be more or less a *motif* of nearly all my verse. I think this pride indispensable to an American. I think it not inconsistent with obedience, humility, deference, and self-questioning.

Democracy has been so retarded and jeopardized by powerful personalities, that its first instincts are fain to clip, conform, bring in stragglers, and reduce everything to a dead level. While the ambitious thought of my song is to help the forming of a great aggregate Nation, it is, perhaps, altogether through the forming of myriads of fully develop'd and enclosing individuals. Welcome as are equality's and fraternity's doctrines and popular education, a certain liability accompanies them all, as we see. That primal and interior something in man, in his soul's abysms, coloring all, and, by exceptional fruitions, giving the last majesty to him—something continually touch'd upon and attain'd by the old poems and ballads of feudalism, and often the principal foundation of them—modern science and democracy appear to be endangering, perhaps eliminating. But that forms an appearance only; the reality is quite different. The new influences, upon the whole, are surely preparing the way for grander individualities than ever. To-day and here personal force is behind everything, just the same. The times and depictions from the Iliad to Shakespere inclusive can happily never again be realized—but the elements of courageous and lofty manhood are unchanged.

Without yielding an inch the working-man and working-woman were to be in my pages from first to last. The ranges of heroism and loftiness with which Greek and feudal poets endow'd their god-like or lordly born characters— indeed prouder and better based and with fuller ranges than those—I was to endow the democratic averages of America. I was to show that we, here and to-day, are eligible to the grandest and the best—more eligible now than any times of old were. I will also want my utterances (I said to myself before beginning) to be in spirit the poems of the morning. (They have been founded and mainly written in the sunny forenoon and early midday of my life.) I will want them to be the poems of women entirely as much as men. I have wish'd to put the complete Union of the States in my songs without any preference or partiality whatever. Henceforth, if they live and are read, it must be just as much South as North—just as much along the Pacific as Atlantic—in the valley of the Mississippi, in Canada, up in Maine, down in Texas, and on the shores of Puget Sound.

From another point of view "Leaves of Grass" is avowedly the song of Sex and Amativeness, and even Animality—though meanings that do not usually go along with those words are behind all, and will duly emerge; and all are sought to be lifted into a different light and atmosphere. Of this feature, intentionally palpable in a few lines, I shall only say the espousing principle of those lines so gives breath of life to my whole scheme that the bulk of the pieces might as well have been left unwritten were those lines omitted. Difficult as it will be, it has become, in my opinion, imperative to achieve a shifted attitude from superior men and women towards the thought and fact of sexuality, as an element in character, personality, the emotions, and a theme in literature. I am not going to argue the question by itself; it does not stand by itself. The vitality of it is altogether in its relations, bearings, significance—like the clef of a symphony. At last analogy the lines I allude to, and the spirit in which they are spoken, permeate all "Leaves of Grass," and the work must stand or fall with them, as the human body and soul must remain as an entirety.

Universal as are certain facts and symptoms of communities or individuals all times, there is nothing so rare in modern conventions and poetry as their normal recognizance. Literature is always calling in the doctor for consultation and confession, and always giving evasions and swathing suppressions in place of that "heroic nudity"[5] on which only a genuine diagnosis of serious cases can be built. And in respect to editions of "Leaves of Grass" in time to come (if there should be such) I take occasion now to confirm those lines with the settled convictions and deliberate renewals of thirty years, and to hereby prohibit, as far as word of mine can do so, any elision of them.

Then still a purpose enclosing all, and over and beneath all. Ever since what might be call'd thought, or the budding of thought, fairly began in my youthful mind, I had had a desire to attempt some worthy record of that entire faith and acceptance ("to justify the ways of God to man"[6] is Milton's well-known and ambitious phrase) which is the foundation of moral America. I felt it all as positively then in my young days as I do now in my old ones; to formulate a poem whose every thought or fact should directly or indirectly be or connive at an implicit belief in the wisdom, health, mystery, beauty of every process, every concrete object, every human or other existence, not only consider'd from the point of view of all, but of each.

While I can not understand it or argue it out, I fully believe in a clue and purpose in Nature, entire and several; and that invisible spiritual results, just as real and definite as the visible, eventuate all concrete life and all materialism, through Time. My book ought to emanate buoyancy and gladness legitimately enough, for it was grown out of those elements, and has been the comfort of my life since it was originally commenced.

One main genesis-motive of the "Leaves" was my conviction (just as strong to-day as ever) that the crowning growth of the United States is to be spiritual and heroic. To help start and favor that growth—or even to call attention to it, or the need of it—is the beginning, middle and final purpose of the poems. (In fact, when really cipher'd out and summ'd to the last, plowing up in earnest the interminable average fallows of humanity—not "good government" merely, in the common sense—is the justification and main purpose of these United States.)

Isolated advantages in any rank or grace or fortune—the direct or indirect threads of all the poetry of the past—are in my opinion distasteful to the republican genius, and offer no foundation for its fitting verse. Establish'd poems, I know, have the very great advantage of chanting the already perform'd, so full of glories, reminiscences dear to the minds of men. But my volume is a candi-

---

5. Whitman's note gives the magazine citation: 6. *Paradise Lost* 1.26.
" 'Nineteenth Century,' July, 1883."

date for the future. "All original art," says Taine,[7] anyhow, "is self-regulated, and no original art can be regulated from without; it carries its own counterpoise, and does not receive it from elsewhere—lives on its own blood"—a solace to my frequent bruises and sulky vanity.

As the present is perhaps mainly an attempt at personal statement or illustration, I will allow myself as further help to extract the following anecdote from a book, "Annals of Old Painters,"[8] conn'd by me in youth. Rubens, the Flemish painter, in one of his wanderings through the galleries of old convents, came across a singular work. After looking at it thoughtfully for a good while, and listening to the criticisms of his suite of students, he said to the latter, in answer to their questions (as to what school the work implied or belong'd,) "I do not believe the artist, unknown and perhaps no longer living, who has given the world this legacy, every belong'd to any school, or ever painted anything but this one picture, which is a personal affair—a piece out of a man's life."

"Leaves of Grass" indeed (I cannot too often reiterate) has mainly been the outcropping of my own emotional and other personal nature—an attempt, from first to last, to put *a Person*, a human being (myself, in the latter half of the Nineteenth Century, in America,) freely, fully and truly on record. I could not find any similar personal record in current literature that satisfied me. But it is not on "Leaves of Grass" distinctively as *literature*, or a specimen thereof, that I feel to dwell, or advance claims. No one will get at my verses who insists upon viewing them as a literary performance, or attempt at such performance, or as aiming mainly toward art or æstheticism.

I say no land or people or circumstances ever existed so needing a race of singers and poems differing from all others, and rigidly their own, as the land and people and circumstances of our United States need such singers and poems to-day, and for the future. Still further, as long as the States continue to absorb and be dominated by the poetry of the Old World, and remain unsupplied with autochthonous song, to express, vitalize and give color to and define their material and political success, and minister to them distinctively, so long will they stop short of first-class Nationality and remain defective.

In the free evening of my day I give to you, reader, the foregoing garrulous talk, thoughts, reminiscences,

> As idly drifting down the ebb,
> Such ripples, half-caught voices, echo from the shore.

Concluding with two items for the imaginative genius of the West, when it worthily rises—First, what Herder taught to the young Goethe,[9] that really great poetry is always (like the Homeric or Biblical canticles) the result of a national spirit, and not the privilege of a polish'd and select few; Second, that the strongest and sweetest songs yet remain to be sung.

1888

7. Hippolyte Taine (1828–1893), French literary historian.
8. Probably Giorgio Vasari's *Lives of the Painters* (1550), anecdotal history of Italian Renaissance art.
9. Johann Gottfried von Herder (1744–1803), German philosopher, author of *Outlines of a Philosophy of the History of Man*, influential on Johann Wolfgang

von Goethe (1749–1832), German poet and dramatist. In his autobiography (*Dichtung und Wahrheit*) Goethe recalls that while he was living with Herder, the older writer taught him that poetry was a gift to all people in all nations, not meant to have a restricted, elitist audience.

From Democratic Vistas[1]

[*American Literature*]

* * *

What, however, do we more definitely mean by New World literature? Are we not doing well enough here already? Are not the United States this day busily using, working, more printer's type, more presses, than any other country? uttering and absorbing more publications than any other? Do not our publishers fatten quicker and deeper? (helping themselves, under shelter of a delusive and sneaking law, or rather absence of law, to most of their forage, poetical, pictorial, historical, romantic, even comic without money and without price—and fiercely resisting the timidest proposal to pay for it.)[2]

Many will come under this delusion—but my purpose is to dispel it. I say that a nation may hold and circulate rivers and oceans of very readable print, journals, magazines, novels, library-books, "poetry," &c.—such as the States to-day possess and circulate—of unquestionable aid and value—hundreds of new volumes annually composed and brought out here, respectable enough, indeed unsurpass'd in smartness and erudition—with further hundreds, or rather millions, (as by free forage or theft aforemention'd,) also thrown into the market,—And yet, all the while, the said nation, land, strictly speaking, may possess no literature at all.

Repeating our inquiry, what, then, do we mean by real literature? especially the American literature of the future? Hard questions to meet. The clues are inferential, and turn us to the past. At best, we can only offer suggestions, comparisons, circuits.

It must still be reiterated, as, for the purpose of these memoranda, the deep lesson of history and time, that all else in the contributions of a nation or age, through its politics, materials, heroic personalities, military eclat, &c., remains crude, and defers, in any close and thorough-going estimate, until vitalized by national, original archetypes in literature. They only put the nation in form, finally tell anything—prove, complete anything—perpetuate anything. Without doubt, some of the richest and most powerful and populous communities of the antique world, and some of the grandest personalities and events, have, to after and present times, left themselves entirely unbequeath'd. Doubtless, greater than any that have come down to us, were among those lands, heroisms, persons, that have not come down to us at all, even by name, date, or location. Others have arrived safely, as from voyages over wide, century-stretching seas. The little ships, the miracles that have buoy'd them, and by incredible chances safely convey'd them, (or the best of them, their meaning and essence,) over long wastes, darkness, lethargy, ignorance, &c., have been a few inscriptions—a few immortal compositions, small in size, yet compassing what measureless values of reminiscence, contemporary portraitures,

---

1. The little book *Democratic Vistas*, published late in 1870 but dated 1871, was made up of three essays written for the *Galaxy: Democracy* appeared in December 1867 and *Personalism* in May 1868, but the magazine rejected the third, *Literature*, which was first published in the book form, the source of the present text. *Democratic Vistas* is one of the most neglected of major American literary, political, and philosophical documents.

2. From the founding of the United States until 1891, when Congress finally passed an international copyright law, American writers had been victimized by the fact that American publishers could reprint foreign books without payment to the authors: it cost a publisher only printing expenses to publish Dickens in this country, but Cooper or Melville or Clemens had to be paid royalties.

manners, idioms and beliefs, with deepest inference, hint and thought, to tie and touch forever the old, new body, and the old, new soul! These! and still these! bearing the freight so dear—dearer than pride—dearer than love. All the best experience of humanity folded, saved, freighted to us here. Some of these tiny ships we call Old and New Testament, Home Eschylus, Plato, Juvenal, &c. Precious minims![3] I think, if we were forced to choose, rather than have you, and the likes of you, and what belongs to, and has grown of you, blotted out and gone, we could better afford, appalling as that would be, to lose all actual ships, this day fasten'd by wharf, or floating on wave, and see them, with all their cargoes, scuttled and sent to the bottom.

Gather'd by geniuses of city, race or age, and put by them in highest of art's forms, namely, the literary form, the peculiar combinations and the outshows of that city, age, or race, its particular modes of the universal attributes and passions, its faiths, heroes, lovers and gods, wars, traditions, struggles, crimes, emotions, joys, (or the subtle spirit of these,) having been pass'd on to us to illumine our own selfhood, and its experiences—what they supply, indispensable and highest, if taken away, nothing else in all the world's boundless storehouses could make up to us, or ever again return.

For us, along the great highways of time, those monuments stand—those forms of majesty and beauty. For us those beacons burn though all the nights. Unknown Egyptians, graving hieroglyphs; Hindus, with hymn and apothegm and endless epic; Hebrew prophet, with spirituality, as in flashes of lightning, conscience like red-hot iron, plaintive songs and screams of vengeance for tyrannies and enslavement; Christ, with bent head, brooding love and peace, like a dove; Greek, creating eternal shapes of physical and esthetic proportion; Roman, lord of satire, the sword, and the codex;—of the figures, some far off and veil'd, others nearer and visible; Dante, stalking with lean form, nothing but fibre, not a grain of superfluous flesh; Angelo,[4] and the great painters, architects, musicians; rich Shakespeare, luxuriant as the sun, artist and singer of feudalism in its sunset, with all the gorgeous colors, owner thereof, and using them at will; and so to such as German Kant and Hegel,[5] where they, though near us, leaping over the ages, sit again, impassive, imperturbable, like the Egyptian gods. Of these, and the like of these, is it too much, indeed, to return to our favorite figure, and view them as orbs and systems of orbs, moving in free paths in the spaces of that other heaven, the kosmic intellect, the soul?

Ye powerful and resplendent ones! ye were, in your atmospheres, grown not for America, but rather for her foes, the feudal and the old—while our genius is democratic and modern. Yet could ye, indeed, but breathe your breath of life into our New World's nostrils—not to enslave us, as now, but, for our needs, to breed a spirit like your own—perhaps, (dare we to say it?) to dominate, even destroy, what you yourselves have left! On your plane, and no less, but even higher and wider, will I mete and measure for our wants to-day and here. I demand races of orbic bards, with unconditional uncompromising sway. Come forth, sweet democratic despots of the west!

By points and specimens like these we, in reflection, token what we mean

---

3. In this sense, small containers, treasures being gathered into the small compass of a book.
4. Then an acceptable form of the name of Michelangelo Buonarroti (1475–1564), Italian artist. Dante Alighieri (1265–1321), Italian poet, author of The Di-

vine Comedy.
5. Immanuel Kant (1724–1804) and George Wilhelm Friedrich Hegel (1770–1831), philosophers whose writings were familiar to Whitman.

by any land's or people's genuine literature. And thus compared and tested, judging amid the influence of loftiest products only, what do our current copious fields of print, covering in manifold forms, the United States, better, for an analogy, present, than, as in certain regions of the sea, those spreading, undulating masses of squid, through which the whale swimming, with head half out, feeds?

Not but that doubtless our current so-called literature, (like an endless supply of small coin,) performs a certain service, and may-be, too, the service needed for the time, (the preparation-service, as children learn to spell.) Everybody reads, and truly nearly everybody writes, either books, or for the magazines or journals. The matter has magnitude, too, after a sort. There is something impressive about the huge editions of the dailies and weeklies, the mountain-stacks of white paper piled in the press-vaults, and the proud, crashing, ten-cylinder presses, which I can stand and watch any time by the half hour. Then, (though the States in the field of imagination present not a single first-class work, not a single great literatus,) the main objects, to amuse, to titillate, to pass away time, to circulate the news, and rumors of news, to rhyme and read rhyme, are yet attain'd, and on a scale of infinity. To-day, in books, in the rivalry of writers, especially novelists, success, (so-call'd,) is for him or her who strikes the mean flat average, the sensational appetite for stimulus, incident,[6] &c., and depicts, to the common calibre, sensual, exterior life. To such, or the luckiest of them, as we see, the audiences are limitless and profitable; but they cease presently. While this day, or any day, to workmen portraying interior or spiritual life, the audiences were limited, and often laggard—but they last forever.

Compared with the past, our modern science soars, and our journals serve; but ideal and even ordinary romantic literature, does not, I think, substantially advance. Behold the prolific brood of the contemporary novel, magazine-tale, theatre-play, &c. The same endless thread of tangled and superlative love-story, inherited, apparently from the Amadises and Palmerins[7] of the 13th, 14th, and 15th centuries over there in Europe. The costumes and associations are brought down to date, the seasoning is hotter and more varied, the dragons and ogres are left out—but the *thing*, I should say, has not advanced—is just as sensational, just as strain'd—remains about the same, nor more, nor less.

What is the reason our time, our lands, that we see no fresh local courage, sanity, of our own—the Mississippi, stalwart Western men, real mental and physical facts, Southerners, &c., in the body of our literature? especially the poetic part of it. But always, instead, a parcel of dandies and ennuyees, dapper little gentlemen from abroad, who flood us with their thin sentiment of parlors, parasols, piano-songs, tinkling rhymes, the five-hundredth importation—or whimpering and crying about something, chasing one aborted conceit after another, and forever occupied in dyspeptic amours with dyspeptic women.

While, current and novel, the grandest events and revolutions, and stormiest passions of history, are crossing to-day with unparallel'd rapidity and magnificence over the stages of our own and all the continents, offering new materials, opening new vistas, with largest needs, inviting the daring launch-

---

6. In the reprinting of *Democratic Vistas* as part of *Specimen Days & Collect* (1882), Whitman expanded the series to "the sensational appetite for stimulus, incident, persiflage, &c."

7. Amadis de Gaul (with Gaul first meaning Wales, then being understood as meaning France) was the hero of various chivalric romances, as was Palmerin, the hero of *Palmerin of England*.

ing forth of conceptions in literature, inspired by them, soaring in highest regions, serving art in its highest, (which is only the other name for serving God, and serving humanity,) where is the man of letters, where is the book, with any nobler aim than to follow in the old track, repeat what has been said before—and, as its utmost triumph, sell well, and be erudite or elegant?

* * *

1870

From Specimen Days[1]

Patent-Office Hospital

February 23 [1863].

I must not let the great hospital at the Patent-office pass away without some mention. A few weeks ago the vast area of the second story of that noblest of Washington buildings was crowded close with rows of sick, badly wounded and dying soldiers. They were placed in three very large apartments. I went there many times. It was a strange, solemn, and, with all its features of suffering and death, a sort of fascinating sight. I go sometimes at night to soothe and relieve particular cases. Two of the immense apartments are fill'd with high and ponderous glass cases, crowded with models in miniature of every kind of utensil, machine or invention, it ever enter'd into the mind of man to conceive; and with curiosities and foreign presents. Between these cases are lateral openings, perhaps eight feet wide and quite deep, and in these were placed the sick, besides a great long double row of them up and down through the middle of the hall. Many of them were very bad cases, wounds and amputations. Then there was a gallery running above the hall in which there were beds also. It was, indeed, a curious scene, especially at night when lit up. The glass cases, the beds, the forms lying there, the gallery above, and the marble pavement under foot—the suffering, and the fortitude to bear it in various degrees—occasionally, from some, the groan that could not be repress'd—sometimes a poor fellow dying, with emaciated face and glassy eye, the nurse by his side, the doctor also there, but no friend, no relative—such were the sights but lately in the Patent-office. (The wounded have since been removed from there, and it is now vacant again.)

The White House by Moonlight

February 24th [1863].

A spell of fine soft weather. I wander about a good deal, sometimes at night under the moon. To-night took a long look at the President's house. The white

1. The following passages are from the *Specimen Days* section of *Specimen Days & Collect* (1882–83), a section that consists of diary entries and casual newspaper writing from the preceding two decades. On October 8, 1882, Whitman sent the following description to Sylvester Baxter of the *Boston Daily Herald*: "It is a great jumble (as a man himself is)—Is an autobiography after its sort—(sort o' synonyms & yet altogether different—'Montaigne,' Rousseau's 'Confessions' &c)—is the gathering up, & formulation, & putting in identity of the wayward itemizings, memoranda, and personal notes of fifty years, under modern & American conditions, a good deal helter-skelter but I am sure a certain sort of orbic compaction and oneness the final result—dwells long in its own peculiar way on the Secession War—gives glimpses of that event's strange interiors, especially the Army Hospitals—in fact makes the resuscitating and putting on record the *emotional aspect* of the war of 1861–'65 one of its principal features."

portico—the palace-like, tall, round columns, spotless as snow—the walls also—the tender and soft moonlight, flooding the pale marble, and making peculiar faint languishing shades, not shadows—everywhere a soft transparent hazy, thin, blue moon-lace, hanging in the air—the brilliant and extra-plentiful clusters of gas, on and around the façade, columns, portico, &c.—everything so white, so marbly pure and dazzling, yet soft—the White House of future poems, and of dreams and dramas, there in the soft and copious moon—the gorgeous front, in the trees, under the lustrous flooding moon, full of reality, full of illusion—the forms of the trees, leafless, silent, in trunk and myriad-angles of branches, under the stars and sky—the White House of the land, and of beauty and night—sentries at the gates, and by the portico, silent, pacing there in blue overcoats—stopping you not at all, but eyeing you with sharp eyes, whichever way you move.

A *Night Battle, over a Week Since*

May 12 [1863].

There was part of the late battle at Chancellorsville, (second Fredericksburgh,) a little over a week ago, Saturday. Saturday night and Sunday, under Gen. Joe Hooker, I would like to give just a glimpse of—(a moment's look in a terrible storm at sea—of which a few suggestions are enough, and full details impossible.)[2] The fighting had been very hot during the day, and after an intermission the latter part, was resumed at night, and kept up with furious energy till 3 o'clock in the morning. That afternoon (Saturday) an attack sudden and strong by Stonewall Jackson had gain'd a great advantage to the southern army, and broken our lines, entering us like a wedge, and leaving things in that position at dark. But Hooker at 11 at night made a desperate push, drove the secesh[3] forces back, restored his original lines, and resumed his plans. This night scrimmage was very exciting, and afforded countless strange and fearful pictures. The fighting had been general both at Chancellorsville and northeast at Fredericksburgh. (We hear of some poor fighting, episodes, skedaddling on our part. I think not of it. I think of the fierce bravery, the general rule.) One corps, the 6th, Sedgewick's, fights four dashing and bloody battles in thirty-six hours, retreating in great jeopardy, losing largely but maintaining itself, fighting with the sternest desperation under all circumstances, getting over the Rappahannock only by the skin of its teeth, yet getting over. It lost many, many brave men, yet it took vengeance, ample vengeance.

But it was the tug of Saturday evening, and through the night and Sunday morning, I wanted to make a special note of. It was largely in the woods, and quite a general engagement. The night was very pleasant, at times the moon shining out full and clear, all Nature so calm in itself, the early summer grass so rich, and foliage of the trees—yet there the battle raging, and many good fellows lying helpless, with new accessions to them, and every minute amid the rattle of muskets and crash of cannon, (for there was an artillery contest too,) the red life-blood oozing out from heads or trunks or limbs upon that

---

2. At the Battle of Chancellorsville, Virginia (May 1–4, 1863), the Union general, Joseph Hooker, tried to outflank the Southern army led by General Robert E. Lee, but Lieutenant General Thomas ("Stonewall") Jackson outflanked Hooker and the Union troops retreated. Jackson was fatally shot by one of his own men, who mistook him for a Union soldier. Major General John Sedgwick (whose name Whitman misspells) vainly attempted to hold Lee where he could be crushed by Hooker.
3. Secessionist, Southerner.

green and dew-cool grass. Patches of the woods take fire, and several of the wounded, unable to move, are consumed—quite large spaces are swept over, burning the dead also—some of the men have their hair and beards singed—some, burns on their faces and hands—others holes burnt in their clothing. The flashes of fire from the cannon, the quick flaring flames and smoke, and the immense roar—the musketry so general, the light nearly bright enough for each side to see the other—the crashing, tramping of men—the yelling—close quarters—we hear the secesh yells—our men cheer loudly back, especially if Hooker is in sight—hand to hand conflicts, each side stands up to it, brave, determin'd as demons, they often charge upon us—a thousand deeds are done worth to write newer greater poems on—and still the woods on fire—still many are not only scorch'd—too many, unable to move, are burn'd to death.

Then the camps of the wounded—O heavens, what scene is this?—is this indeed *humanity*—these butchers' shambles?[4] There are several of them. There they lie, in the largest, in an open space in the woods, from 200 to 300 poor fellows—the groans and screams—the odor of blood, mixed with the fresh scent of the night, the grass, the trees—that slaughter-house! O well is it their mothers, their sisters cannot see them—cannot conceive, and never conceiv'd, these things. One man is shot by a shell, both in the arm and leg—both are amputated—there lie the rejected members. Some have their legs blown off—some bullets through the breast—some indescribably horrid wounds in the face or head, all mutilated, sickening, torn, gouged out—some in the abdomen—some mere boys—many rebels, badly hurt—they take their regular turns with the rest, just the same as any—the surgeons use them just the same. Such is the camp of the wounded—such a fragment, a reflection afar off of the bloody scene—while over all the clear, large moon comes out at times softly, quietly shining. Amid the woods, that scene of flitting souls—amid the crack and crash and yelling sounds—the impalpable perfume of the woods—and yet the pungent, stifling smoke—the radiance of the moon, looking from heaven at intervals so placid—the sky so heavenly—the clear-obscure up there, those buoyant upper oceans—a few large placid stars beyond, coming silently and languidly out, and then disappearing—the melancholy, draperied night above, around. And there, upon the roads, the fields, and in those woods, that contest, never one more desperate in any age or land—both parties now in force—masses—no fancy battle, no semi-play, but fierce and savage demons fighting there—courage and scorn of death the rule, exceptions almost none.

What history, I say, can ever give—for who can know—the mad, determin'd tussle of the armies, in all their separate large and little squads—as this—each steep'd from crown to toe in desperate, mortal purports? Who know the conflict, hand-to-hand—the many conflicts in the dark, those shadowy-tangled, flashing-moonbeam'd woods—the writhing groups and squads—the cries, the din, the cracking guns and pistols—the distant cannon—the cheers and calls and threats and awful music of the oaths—the indescribable mix—the officers' orders, persuasions, encouragements—the devils fully rous'd in human hearts—the strong shout, *Charge, men, charge*—the flash of the naked sword, and rolling flame and smoke? And still the broken, clear and clouded heaven—and still again the moonlight pouring silvery soft its radiant patches

---

4. Formerly a shambles was a place for slaughtering animals for meat; its meaning has become merely figurative.

over all. Who paint the scene, the sudden partial panic of the afternoon, at
dusk? Who paint the irrepressible advance of the second division of the Third
corps, under Hooker himself, suddenly order'd up—those rapid-filing phantoms through the woods? Who show what moves there in the shadows, fluid
and firm—to save, (and it did save,) the army's name, perhaps the nation? as
there the veterans hold the field. (Brave Berry[5] falls not yet—but death has
mark'd him—soon he falls.)

Abraham Lincoln

August 12th [1863].

    I see the President almost every day, as I happen to live where he passes to
or from his lodgings out of town. He never sleeps at the White House during
the hot season, but has quarters at a healthy location some three miles north
of the city, the Soldiers' home, a United States military establishment. I saw
him this morning about 8½ coming in to business, riding on Vermont avenue, near L street. He always has a company of twenty-five or thirty cavalry,
with sabres drawn and held upright over their shoulders. They say this guard
was against his personal wish, but he let his counselors have their way. The
party makes no great show in uniform or horses. Mr. Lincoln on the saddle
generally rides a good-sized, easy-going gray horse, is dress'd in plain black,
somewhat rusty and dusty, wears a black stiff hat, and looks about as ordinary
in attire, &c., as the commonest man. A lieutenant, with yellow straps, rides
at his left, and following behind, two by two, come the cavalry men, in their
yellow-striped jackets. They are generally going at a slow trot, as that is the
pace set them by the one they wait upon. The sabres and accoutrements clank,
and the entirely unornamental *cortège*[6] as it trots towards Lafayette square
arouses no sensation, only some curious stranger stops and gazes. I see very
plainly Abraham Lincoln's dark brown face, with the deep-cut lines, the eyes,
always to me with a deep latent sadness in the expression. We have got so that
we exchange bows, and very cordial ones. Sometimes the President goes and
comes in an open barouche.[7] The cavalry always accompany him, with drawn
sabres. Often I notice as he goes out evenings—and sometimes in the morning, when he returns early—he turns off and halts at the large and handsome
residence of the Secretary of War, on K street, and holds conference there. If
in his barouche, I can see from my window he does not alight, but sits in his
vehicle, and Mr. Stanton comes out to attend him. Sometimes one of his
sons,[8] a boy of ten or twelve, accompanies him, riding at his right on a pony.
Earlier in the summer I occasionally saw the President and his wife, toward
the latter part of the afternoon, out in a barouche, on a pleasure ride through
the city. Mrs. Lincoln was dress'd in complete black, with a long crape veil.
The equipage is of the plainest kind, only two horses, and they nothing extra.
They pass'd me once very close, and I saw the President in the face fully, as
they were moving slowly, and his look, though abstracted, happen'd to be
directed steadily in my eye. He bow'd and smiled, but far beneath his smile I

5. The Union Major General Hiram G. Berry
(1824–1863) was killed at Chancellorsville leading a
repulse of the Confederates.
6. Here, train of attendants.

7. A four-wheeled carriage.
8. The mischievous Thomas Lincoln, nicknamed
Tad, was then ten.

noticed well the expression I have alluded to. None of the artists or pictures has caught the deep, though subtle and indirect expression of this man's face. There is something else there. One of the great portrait painters of two or three centuries ago is needed.

Summer of 1864

I am back again in Washington, on my regular daily and nightly rounds. Of course there are many specialties. Dotting a ward here and there are always cases of poor fellows, long-suffering under obstinate wounds, or weak and dishearten'd from typhoid fever, or the like; mark'd cases, needing special and sympathetic nourishment. These I sit down and either talk to, or silently cheer them up. They always like it hugely, (and so do I.) Each case has it peculiarities, and needs some new adaptation. I have learnt to thus conform—learnt a good deal of hospital wisdom. Some of the poor young chaps, away from home for the first time in their lives, hunger and thirst for affection; this is sometimes the only thing that will reach their condition. The men like to have a pencil, and something to write in. I have given them cheap pocket-diaries, and almanacs for 1864, interleav'd with blank paper. For reading I generally have some old pictorial magazines or story papers—they are always acceptable. Also the morning or evening papers of the day. The best books I do not give, but lend to read through the wards, and then take them to others, and so on; they are very punctual about returning the books. In these wards, or on the field, as I thus continue to go round, I have come to adapt myself to each emergency, after its kind or call, however trivial, however solemn, every one justified and made real under its circumstances—not only visits and cheering talk and little gifts—not only washing and dressing wounds, (I have some cases where the patient is unwilling any one should do this but me)—but passages from the Bible, expounding them, prayer at the bedside, explanations of doctrine, &c. (I think I see my friends smiling at this confession, but I was never more in earnest in my life.) In camp and everywhere, I was in the habit of reading or giving recitations to the men. They were fond of it, and liked declamatory poetical pieces. We would gather in a large group by ourselves, after supper, and spend the time in such readings, or in talking, and occasionally by an amusing game called the game of twenty questions.

The Capitol by Gas-Light

[1865]

To-night I have been wandering awhile in the capitol, which is all lit up. The illuminated rotunda looks fine. I like to stand aside and look a long, long while, up at the dome; it comforts me somehow. The House and Senate were both in session till very late. I look'd in upon them, but only a few moments; they were hard at work on tax and appropriation bills. I wander'd through the long and rich corridors and apartments under the Senate; an old habit of mine, former winters, and now more satisfaction than ever. Not many persons down there, occasionally a flitting figure in the distance.

The Inauguration

March 4 [1865].

The President very quietly rode down to the capitol in his own carriage, by himself, on a sharp trot, about noon, either because he wish'd to be on hand to sign bills, or to get rid of marching in line with the absurd procession, the muslin temple of liberty, and pasteboard monitor.[9] I saw him on his return, at three o'clock, after the performance was over. He was in his plain two-horse barouche, and look'd very much worn and tired; the lines, indeed, of vast responsibilities, intricate questions, and demands of life and death, cut deeper than ever upon his dark brown face; yet all the goodness, tenderness, sadness, and canny shrewdness, underneath the furrows. (I never see that man without feeling that he is one to become personally attach'd to, for his combination of purest, heartiest tenderness, and native western form of manliness.) By his side sat his little boy, of ten years. There were no soldiers, only a lot of civilians on horseback, with huge yellow scarfs over their shoulders, riding around the carriage. (At the inauguration four years ago, he rode down and back again surrounded by a dense mass of arm'd cavalrymen eight deep, with drawn sabres; and there were sharpshooters station'd at every corner on the route.) I ought to make mention of the closing levee[1] of Saturday night last. Never before was such a compact jam in front of the White House—all the grounds fill'd, and away out to the spacious sidewalks. I was there, as I took a notion to go—was in the rush inside with the crowd—surged along the passage-ways, the blue and other rooms, and through the great east room. Crowds of country people, some very funny. Fine music from the Marine band, off in a side place. I saw Mr. Lincoln, drest all in black, with white kid gloves and a claw hammer coat,[2] receiving, as in duty bound, shaking hands, looking very disconsolate, and as if he would give anything to be somewhere else.

Death of President Lincoln

April 16, '65

I find in my notes of the time, this passage on the death of Abraham Lincoln: He leaves for America's history and biography, so far, not only its most dramatic reminiscence—he leaves, in my opinion, the greatest, best, most characteristic, artistic, moral personality. Not but that he had faults, and show'd them in the Presidency; but honesty, goodness, shrewdness, conscience, and (a new virtue, unknown to other lands, and hardly yet really known here, but the foundation and tie of all, as the future will grandly develop,) UNIONISM, in its truest and amplest sense, form'd the hard-pan[3] of his character. These he seal'd with his life. The tragic splendor of his death, purging, illuminating all, throws round his form, his head, an aureole that will remain and will grow brighter through time, while history lives, and love

9. I.e., a pasteboard depiction of the Union ironclad *Monitor*, which had fought the Confederate ironclad *Merrimack* three years before.
1. In disregard of the root meaning ("to rise"), *levee* had come to mean a reception at any hour rather than an audience granted early in the day, often in a bed-

chamber.
2. A Prince Albert coat, with the tails looking like the claws of a claw hammer.
3. The firm, substantial part of anything, from the name for a compacted, clayey layer in soils, hard to pierce.

of country lasts. By many has this Union been help'd; but if one name, one man, must be pick'd out, he, most of all, is the conservator of it, to the future. He was assassinated—but the Union is not assassinated—*ça ira!*[4] One falls, and another falls. The soldier drops, sinks like a wave—but the ranks of the ocean eternally press on. Death does its work, obliterates a hundred, a thousand—President, general, captain, private—but the Nation is immortal.

Sherman's Army's Jubilation—Its Sudden Stoppage

[1865]

When Sherman's armies, (long after they left Atlanta,) were marching through South and North Carolina—after leaving Savannah, the news of Lee's capitulation having been receiv'd—the men never mov'd a mile without from some part of the line sending up continued, inspiriting shouts. At intervals all day long sounded out the wild music of those peculiar army cries. They would be commenc'd by one regiment or brigade, immediately taken up by others, and at length whole corps and armies would join in these wild triumphant choruses. It was one of the characteristic expressions of the western troops, and became a habit, serving as a relief and outlet to the men—a vent for their feelings of victory, returning peace, &c. Morning, noon, and afternoon spontaneous, for occasion or without occasion, these huge, strange cries, differing from any other, echoing through the open air for many a mile, expressing youth, joy, wildness, irrepressible strength, and the ideas of advance and conquest, sounded along the swamps and uplands of the South, floating to the skies. ('There never were men that kept in better spirits in danger or defeat—what then could they do in victory?'—said one of the 15th corps to me, afterwards.) This exuberance continued till the armies arrived at Raleigh. There the news of the President's murder was receiv'd. Then no more shouts or yells, for a week. All the marching was comparatively muffled. It was very significant—hardly a loud word or laugh in many of the regiments. A hush and silence pervaded all.

The Real War Will Never Get in the Books

And so good-bye to the war. I know not how it may have been, or may be, to others—to me the main interest I found, (and still, on recollection, find,) in the rank and file of the armies, both sides, and in those specimens amid the hospitals, and even the dead on the field. To me the points illustrating the latent personal character and eligibilities of these States, in the two or three millions of American young and middle-aged men, North and South, embodied in those armies—and especially the one-third or one-fourth of their number, stricken by wounds or disease at some time in the course of the contest—were of more significance even than the political interests involved. (As so much of a race depends on how it faces death, and how it stands personal anguish and sickness. As, in the glints of emotions under emergencies, and the indirect traits and asides in Plutarch,[5] we get far profounder clues to the antique world than all its more formal history.)

---

4. Go it! or Go on! (French), but here meaning roughly "It goes on!"

5. Greek writer (A.D. 46?–120?), biographer of Greeks and Romans.

Future years will never know the seething hell and the black infernal background of countless minor scenes and interiors, (not the official surface-courteousness of the Generals, not the few great battles) of the Secession war; and it is best they should not—the real war will never get in the books. In the mushy influences of current times, too, the fervid atmosphere and typical events of those years are in danger of being totally forgotten. I have at night watch'd by the side of a sick man in the hospital, one who could not live many hours. I have seen his eyes flash and burn as he raised himself and recurr'd to the cruelties on his surrender'd brother, and mutilations of the corpse afterward. (See, in the preceding pages, the incident at Upperville[6]—the seventeen kill'd as in the description, were left there on the ground. After they dropt dead, no one touch'd them—all were made sure of, however. The carcasses were left for the citizens to bury or not, as they chose.)

Such was the war. It was not a quadrille in a ball-room. Its interior history will not only never be written—its practicality, minutiae of deeds and passions, will never be even suggested. The actual soldier of 1862–'65, North and South, with all his ways, his incredible dauntlessness, habits, practices, tastes, language, his fierce friendship, his appetite, rankness, his superb strength and animality, lawless gait, and a hundred unnamed lights and shades of camp, I say, will never be written—perhaps must not and should not be.

The preceding notes may furnish a few stray glimpses into that life, and into those lurid interiors, never to be fully convey'd to the future. The hospital part of the drama from '61 to '65, deserves indeed to be recorded. Of that many-threaded drama, with its sudden and strange surprises, its confounding of prophecies, its moments of despair, the dread of foreign interference, the interminable campaigns, the bloody battles, the mighty and cumbrous and green armies, the drafts and bounties—the immense money expenditure, like a heavy-pouring constant rain—with, over the whole land, the last three years of the struggle, an unending, universal mourning-wail of women, parents, orphans—the marrow of the tragedy concentrated in those Army Hospitals—(it seem'd sometimes as if the whole interest of the land, North and South, was one vast central hospital, and all the rest of the affair but flanges)—those forming the untold and unwritten history of the war—infinitely greater (like life's) than the few scraps and distortions that are ever told or written. Think how much, and of importance, will be—how much, civic and military, has already been—buried in the grave, in eternal darkness.

Sea-Shore Fancies

[1876]

Even as a boy, I had the fancy, the wish, to write a piece, perhaps a poem, about the sea-shore—that suggesting, dividing line, contact, junction, the solid marrying the liquid—that curious, lurking something, (as doubtless every objective form finally becomes to the subjective spirit,) which means far more than its mere first sight, grand as that is—blending the real and ideal, and each made portion of the other. Hours, days, in my Long Island youth and early manhood, I haunted the shores of Rockaway or Coney island, or away east to the Hamptons or Montauk. Once, at the latter place, (by the old lighthouse, nothing but sea-tossings in sight in every direction as far as the eye could

---

6. Described in A Glimpse of War's Half-Scenes.

reach,) I remember well, I felt that I must one day write a book expressing this liquid, mystic theme. Afterward, I recollect, how it came to me that instead of any special lyrical or epical or literary attempt, the sea-shore should be an invisible *influence*, a pervading gauge and tally for me, in my composition. (Let me give a hint here to young writers. I am not sure but I have unwittingly follow'd out the same rule with other powers besides sea and shores—avoiding them, in the way of any dead set at poetizing them, as too big for formal handling—quite satisfied if I could indirectly show that we have met and fused even if only once, but enough—that we have really absorb'd each other and understand each other.)

There is a dream, a picture, that for years at intervals, (sometimes quite long ones, but surely again, in time,) has come noiselessly up before me, and I really believe, fiction as it is, has enter'd largely into my practical life— certainly into my writings, and shaped and color'd them. It is nothing more or less than a stretch of interminable white-brown sand, hard and smooth and broad, with the ocean perpetually, grandly, rolling in upon it, with slow-measured sweep, with rustle and hiss and foam, and many a thump as of low bass drums. This scene, this picture, I say, has risen before me at times for years. Sometimes I wake at night and can hear and see it plainly.

A Sun-Bath—Nakedness

Sunday, Aug. 27 [1877].

Another day quite free from mark'd prostration and pain. It seems indeed as if peace and nutriment from heaven subtly filter into me as I slowly hobble down these country lanes and across fields, in the good air—as I sit here in solitude with Nature—open, voiceless, mystic, far removed, yet palpable, eloquent Nature. I merge myself in the scene, in the perfect day. Hovering over the clear brook-water, I am sooth'd by its soft gurgle in one place, and the hoarser murmurs of its three-foot fall in another. Come, ye disconsolate, in whom any latent eligibility is left—come get the sure virtues of creek-shore, and wood and field. Two months (July and August, '77,) have I absorb'd them, and they begin to make a new man of me. Every day, seclusion—every day at least two or three hours of freedom, bathing, no talk, no bonds, no dress, no books, no *manners*.

Shall I tell you, reader, to what I attribute my already much-restored health? That I have been almost two years, off and on, without drugs and medicines, and daily in the open air. Last summer I found a particularly secluded little dell off one side by my creek, originally a large dug-out marl-pit, now abandon'd, fill'd with bushes, trees, grass, a group of willows, a straggling bank, and a spring of delicious water running right through the middle of it, with two or three little cascades. Here I retreated every hot day, and follow it up this summer. Here I realize the meaning of that old fellow who said he was seldom less alone than when alone. Never before did I get so close to Nature; never before did she come so close to me. By old habit, I pencill'd down from time to time, almost automatically, moods, sights, hours, tints and outlines, on the spot. Let me specially record the satisfaction of this current forenoon, so serene and primitive, so conventionally exceptional, natural.

An hour or so after breakfast I wended my way down to the recesses of the aforesaid dell, which I and certain thrushes, catbirds, &c., had all to ourselves.

A light south-west wind was blowing through the tree-tops. It was just the place and time for my Adamic air-bath and flesh-brushing from head to foot. So hanging clothes on a rail near by, keeping old broadbrim straw on head and easy shoes on feet, havn't I had a good time the last two hours! First with the stiff-elastic bristles rasping arms, breast, sides, till they turn'd scarlet—then partially bathing in the clear waters of the running brook—taking everything very leisurely, with many rests and pauses—stepping about barefooted every few minutes now and then in some neighboring black ooze, for unctuous mud-bath to my feet—a brief second and third rinsing in the crystal running waters—rubbing with the fragrant towel—slow negligent promenades on the turf up and down in the sun, varied with occasional rests, and further frictions of the bristle-brush—sometimes carrying my portable chair with me from place to place, as my range is quite extensive here, nearly a hundred rods, feeling quite secure from intrusion (and that indeed I am not at all nervous about, if it accidentally happens.)

As I walk'd slowly over the grass, the sun shone out enough to show the shadow moving with me. Somehow I seem'd to get identity with each and every thing around me, in its condition. Nature was naked, and I was also. It was too lazy, soothing, and joyous-equable to speculate about. Yet I might have thought somehow in this vein: Perhaps the inner never lost rapport we hold with earth, light, air, trees, &c., is not to be realized through eyes and mind only, but through the whole corporeal body, which I will not have blinded or bandaged any more than the eyes. Sweet, sane, still Nakedness in Nature!—ah if poor, sick, prurient humanity in cities might really know you once more! Is not nakedness then indecent? No, not inherently. It is your thought, your sophistication, your fear, your respectability, that is indecent. There come moods when these clothes of ours are not only too irksome to wear, but are themselves indecent. Perhaps indeed he or she to whom the free exhilarating extasy of nakedness in Nature has never been eligible (and how many thousands there are!) has not really known what purity is—nor what faith or art or health really is. (Probably the whole curriculum of first-class philosophy, beauty, heroism, form, illustrated by the old Hellenic race—the highest height and deepest depth known to civilization in those departments—came from their natural and religious idea of Nakedness.)

Many such hours, from time to time, the last two summers—I attribute my partial rehabilitation largely to them. Some good people may think it a feeble or half-crack'd way of spending one's time and thinking. May-be it is.

Edgar Poe's Significance

Jan. 1, '80.

In diagnosing this disease called humanity—to assume for the nonce what seems a chief mood of the personality and writings of my subject—I have thought that poets, somewhere or other on the list, present the most mark'd indications. Comprehending artists in a mass, musicians, painters, actors, and so on, and considering each and all of them as radiations or flanges of that furious whirling wheel, poetry, the centre and axis of the whole, where else indeed may we so well investigate the causes, growths, tally-marks[7] of the time—the age's matter and malady?

7. Scores, accounts.

By common consent there is nothing better for man or woman than a perfect and noble life, morally without flaw, happily balanced in activity, physically sound and pure, giving its due proportion, and no more, to the sympathetic, the human emotional element—a life, in all these, unhasting, unresting, untiring to the end. And yet there is another shape of personality dearer far to the artist-sense, (which likes the play of strongest lights and shades,) where the perfect character, the good, the heroic, although never attain'd, is never lost sight of, but through failures, sorrows, temporary downfalls, is return'd to again and again, and while often violated, is passionately adhered to as long as mind, muscles, voice, obey the power we call volition. This sort of personality we see more or less in Burns, Byron, Schiller, and George Sand. But we do not see it in Edgar Poe.[8] (All this is the result of reading at intervals the last three days a new volume of his poems—I took it on my rambles down by the pond, and by degrees read it all though there.) While to the character first outlined the service Poe renders is certainly that entire contrast and contradiction which is next best to fully exemplifying it.

Almost without the first sign of moral principle, or of the concrete or its heroisms, or the simpler affections of the heart, Poe's verses illustrate an intense faculty for technical and abstract beauty, with the rhyming art to excess, an incorrigible propensity toward nocturnal themes, a demoniac undertone behind every page—and, by final judgment, probably belong among the electric lights of imaginative literature, brilliant and dazzling, but with no heat. There is an indescribable magnetism about the poet's life and reminiscences, as well as the poems. To one who could work out their subtle retracing and retrospect, the latter would make a close tally no doubt between the author's birth and antecedents, his childhood and youth, his physique, his so-call'd education, his studies and associates, the literary and social Baltimore, Richmond, Philadelphia and New York, of those times—not only the places and circumstances in themselves, but often, very often, in a strange spurning of, and reaction from them all.

The following from a report in the Washington "Star" of November 16, 1875, may afford those who care for it something further of my point of view toward this interesting figure and influence of our era. There occurr'd about that date in Baltimore a public reburial of Poe's remains, and dedication of a monument over the grave:

> "Being in Washington on a visit at the time, 'the old gray'[9] went over to Baltimore, and though ill from paralysis, consented to hobble up and silently take a seat on the platform, but refused to make any speech, saying, 'I have felt a strong impulse to come over and be here to-day myself in memory of Poe, which I have obey'd, but not the slightest impulse to make a speech, which, my dear friends, must also be obeyed.'
> In an informal circle, however, in conversation after the ceremonies, Whitman said: 'For a long while, and until lately, I had a distaste for Poe's writings. I wanted, and still want for poetry, the clear sun shining, and fresh air blowing—the strength and power of health, not of delirium, even amid the stormiest passions—with always the background of the

---

8. Whitman names famous writers of Scotland, England, Germany, and France, in all of whom idealism was in conflict with sensuality; he discerns no such ide- | alism in Poe.
9. Whitman himself, the "good gray poet."

eternal moralities. Non-complying with these requirements, Poe's genius has yet conquer'd a special recognition for itself, and I too have come to fully admit it, and appreciate it and him.

" 'In a dream I once had, I saw a vessel on the sea, at midnight, in a storm. It was no great full-rigg'd ship, nor majestic steamer, steering firmly through the gale, but seem'd one of those superb little schooner yachts I had often seen lying anchor'd, rocking so jauntily, in the waters around New York, or up Long Island sound—now flying uncontroll'd with torn sails and broken spars through the wild sleet and winds and waves of the night. On the deck was a slender, slight, beautiful figure, a dim man, apparently enjoying all the terror, the murk, and the disloca-tion of which he was the centre and the victim. That figure of my lurid dream might stand for Edgar Poe, his spirit, his fortunes, and his poems—themselves all lurid dreams.' "

Much more may be said, but I most desired to exploit the idea put at the beginning. By its popular poets the calibres of an age, the weak spots of its embankments, its sub-currents, (often more significant than the biggest surface ones,) are unerringly indicated. The lush and the weird that have taken such extraordinary possession of Nineteenth century verse-lovers—what mean they? The inevitable tendency of poetic culture to morbidity, abnormal beauty—the sickliness of all technical thought or refinement in itself—the abnegation of the perennial and democratic concretes at first hand, the body, the earth and sea, sex and the like—and the substitution of something for them at second or third hand—what bearings have they on current pathological study?

My Tribute to Four Poets

April 16 [1881].

A short but pleasant visit to Longfellow. I am not one of the calling kind, but as the author of "Evangeline" kindly took the trouble to come and see me three years ago in Camden, where I was ill, I felt not only the impulse of my own pleasure on that occasion, but a duty. He was the only particular emi-nence I called on in Boston, and I shall not soon forget his lit-up face and glowing warmth and courtesy, in the modes of what is called the old school.

And now just here I feel the impulse to interpolate something about the mighty four who stamp this first American century with its birth-marks of poetic literature. In a late magazine one of my reviewers, who ought to know better, speaks of my "attitude of contempt and scorn and intolerance" toward the leading poets—of my "deriding" them, and preaching their "uselessness." If anybody cares to know what I think—and have long thought and avow'd—about them, I am entirely willing to propound. I can't imagine any better luck befalling these States for a poetical beginning and initiation than has come from Emerson, Longfellow, Bryant, and Whittier. Emerson, to me, stands unmistakably at the head, but for the others I am at a loss where to give any precedence. Each illustrious, each rounded, each distinctive. Emerson for his sweet, vital-tasting melody, rhym'd philosophy, and poems as amber-clear as the honey of the wild bee he loves to sing. Longfellow for rich color, graceful forms and incidents—all that makes life beautiful and love refined—compet-ing with the singers of Europe on their own ground, and, with one exception,[1]

1. Presumably Tennyson.

better and finer work than that of any of them. Bryant pulsing the first interior verse-throbs of a mighty world—bard of the river and the wood, ever conveying a taste of open air, with scents as from hayfields, grapes, birch-borders—always lurkingly fond of threnodies—beginning and ending his long career with chants of death, with here and there through all, poems, or passages of poems, touching the highest universal truths, enthusiasms, duties—morals as grim and eternal, if not as stormy and fateful, as anything in Eschylus.[2] While in Whittier, with his special themes—(his outcropping love of heroism and war, for all his Quakerdom, his verses at times like the measur'd step of Cromwell's[3] old veterans)—in Whittier lives the zeal, the moral energy, that founded New England—the splendid rectitude and ardor of Luther, Milton, George Fox[4]— I must not, dare not, say the wilfulness and narrowness—though doubtless the world needs now, and always will need, almost above all, just such narrowness and wilfulness.

A Visit, at the Last, to R. W. Emerson

Concord, Mass. [1881].

Out here on a visit—elastic, mellow, Indian-summery weather. Came today from Boston, (a pleasant ride of 40 minutes by steam, through Somerville, Belmont, Waltham, Stony Brook, and other lively towns,) convoy'd by my friend F. B. Sanborn,[5] and to his ample house, and the kindness and hospitality of Mrs. S. and their fine family. Am writing this under the shade of some old hickories and elms, just after 4 P.M., on the porch, within a stone's throw of the Concord river. Off against me, across stream, on a meadow and side-hill, haymakers are gathering and wagoning-in probably their second or third crop. The spread of emerald-green and brown, the knolls, the score or two of little haycocks dotting the meadow, the loaded-up wagons, the patient horses, the slow-strong action of the men and pitchforks—all in the just-waning after-noon, with patches of yellow sun-sheen, mottled by long shadows—a cricket shrilly chirping, herald of the dusk—a boat with two figures noiselessly gliding along the little river, passing under the stone bridge arch—the slight settling haze of aerial moisture, the sky and the peacefulness expanding in all directions and overhead—fill and soothe me.

Same Evening.

Never had I a better piece of luck befall me: a long and blessed evening with Emerson, in a way I couldn't have wish'd better or different. For nearly two hours he has been placidly sitting where I could see his face in the best light, near me. Mrs. S's back-parlor well fill'd with people, neighbors, many fresh and charming faces, women, mostly young, but some old. My friend A. B. Alcott and his daughter Louisa[6] were there early. A good deal of talk, the subject Henry Thoreau—some new glints of his life and fortunes, with letters

2. Aeschylus, Greek tragedian (525–456 B.C.).
3. Oliver Cromwell (1599–1658), dictator of England 1653–58, who enforced rigorous Puritanism in his army.
4. Tactfully Whitman makes only a limited comparison of Whittier's zeal to that of three leaders of the Reformation: Martin Luther (1483–1546), German monk who founded Protestantism; John Milton (1608–74), English author of *Paradise Lost* and other religious works; and George Fox (1624–91), English

founder of the Society of Friends (Quakers).
5. F. B. Sanborn, formerly a leading abolitionist, in later life a biographer of Emerson, Thoreau, and other Concord writers.
6. Louisa May Alcott, was the author of *Little Women* (1868) and many other books. Bronson Alcott (1799–1888), educational reformer, and Louisa's father, had been Whitman's friend since 1856, the year he and Thoreau made several trips to see Whitman in Brooklyn.

to and from him—one of the best by Margaret Fuller, others by Horace Greeley, Channing, &c.[7]—one from Thoreau himself, most quaint and interesting. (No doubt I seem'd very stupid to the room-full of company, taking hardly
any part in the conversation; but I had "my own pail to milk in," as the Swiss
proverb puts it.) My seat and the relative arrangement were such that, without
being rude, or anything of the kind, I could just look squarely at E., which I
did a good part of the two hours. On entering, he had spoken very briefly and
politely to several of the company, then settled himself in his chair, a trifle
push'd back, and, though a listener and apparently an alert one, remain'd
silent through the whole talk and discussion. A lady friend quietly took a seat
next him, to give special attention. A good color in his face, eyes clear, with
the well-known expression of sweetness, and the old clear-peering aspect quite
the same.

Next Day.

Several hours at E.'s house, and dinner there. An old familiar house, (he
has been in it thirty-five years,) with surroundings, furnishment, roominess,
and plain elegance and fullness, signifying democratic ease, sufficient opulence, and an admirable old-fashioned simplicity—modern luxury, with its
mere sumptuousness and affectation, either touch'd lightly upon or ignored
altogether. Dinner the same. Of course the best of the occasion (Sunday,
September 18, '81) was the sight of E. himself. As just said, a healthy color in
the cheeks, and good light in the eyes, cheery expression, and just the amount
of talking that best suited, namely, a word or short phrase only where needed,
and almost always with a smile. Besides Emerson himself, Mrs. E., with their
daughter Ellen, the son Edward and his wife, with my friend F. S. and Mrs.
S., and others, relatives and intimates. Mrs. Emerson, resuming the subject
of the evening before, (I sat next to her,) gave me further and fuller information about Thoreau, who, years ago, during Mr. E.'s absence in Europe, had
lived for some time in the family, by invitation.

Other Concord Notations

[1881]

Though the evening at Mr. and Mrs. Sanborn's, and the memorable family
dinner at Mr. and Mrs. Emerson's, have most pleasantly and permanently
fill'd my memory, I must not slight other notations of Concord. I went to the
old Manse,[8] walk'd through the ancient garden, enter'd the rooms, noted the
quaintness, the unkempt grass and bushes, the little panes in the windows,
the low ceilings, the spicy smell, the creepers embowering the light. Went
to the Concord battle ground, which is close by, scann'd French's statue, "the
Minute Man,"[9] read Emerson's poetic inscription on the base, linger'd a long

---

7. Evocative names from Thoreau's life in the 1840s
and afterward. In the early 1840s Fuller was Thoreau's
acerbic editor at The Dial. By the late 1840s Greeley,
the editor of the New York Tribune, was a public
champion of Thoreau's early writings and of his experiment at Walden. In the mid-1840s and afterward Ellery Channing was one of Thoreau's favorite walking
companions.
8. The house of Ezra Ripley, Emerson's step-grandfa-

ther, rented by Nathaniel Hawthorne in the early
1840s and memorialized in his preface to Mosses from
an Old Manse, as well as the title of the collection of
tales and sketches.
9. Daniel Chester French's sculpture of the minute-
man was unveiled on April 19, 1875, the centennial of
the battle of Lexington and Concord, with President
Grant in attendance. The engraved words are from
Emerson's Concord Hymn.

while on the bridge, and stopp'd by the grave of the unnamed British soldiers buried there the day after the fight in April '75. Then riding on, (thanks to my friend Miss M.[1] and her spirited white ponies, she driving them,) a half hour at Hawthorne's and Thoreau's graves. I got out and went up of course on foot, and stood a long while and ponder'd. They lie close together in a pleasant wooded spot well up the cemetery hill, "Sleepy Hollow." The flat surface of the first was densely cover'd by myrtle, with a border of arbor-vitæ, and the other had a brown headstone, moderately elaborate, with inscriptions. By Henry's side lies his brother John, of whom much was expected, but he died young. Then to Walden pond, that beautifully embower'd sheet of water, and spent over an hour there. On the spot in the woods where Thoreau had his solitary house is now quite a cairn of stones, to mark the place; I too carried one and deposited on the heap. As we drove back, saw the "School of Philosophy,"[2] but it was shut up, and I would not have it open'd for me. Near by stopp'd at the house of W. T. Harris,[3] the Hegelian, who came out, and we had a pleasant chat while I sat in the wagon. I shall not soon forget those Concord drives, and especially that charming Sunday forenoon one with my friend Miss M., and the white ponies.

Boston Common—More of Emerson

Oct. 10–13 [1881].

I spend a good deal of time on the Common, these delicious days and nights—every mid-day from 11:30 to about 1—and almost every sunset another hour. I know all the big trees, especially the old elms along Tremont and Beacon streets, and have come to a sociable-silent understanding with most of them, in the sunlit air, (yet crispy-cool enough,) as I saunter along the wide unpaved walks. Up and down this breadth by Beacon street, between these same old elms, I walk'd for two hours, of a bright sharp February mid-day twenty-one years ago, with Emerson, then in his prime, keen, physically and morally magnetic, arm'd at every point, and when he chose, wielding the emotional just as well as the intellectual. During those two hours he was the talker and I the listener. It was an argument-statement, reconnoitring, review, attack, and pressing home, (like an army corps in order, artillery, cavalry, infantry,) of all that could be said against that part (and a main part) in the construction of my poems, "Children of Adam." More precious than gold to me that dissertation—it afforded me, ever after, this strange and paradoxical lesson; each point of E.'s statement was unanswerable, no judge's charge ever more complete or convincing, I could never hear the points better put—and then I felt down in my soul the clear and unmistakable conviction to disobey all, and pursue my own way. "What have you to say then to such things?" said E., pausing in conclusion. "Only that while I can't answer them at all, I feel more settled than ever to adhere to my own theory, and exemplify it," was my candid response. Whereupon we went and had a good dinner at the American

---

1. A daughter of Horace Mann and Mary Peabody Mann, a niece of Sophia Peabody Hawthorne.
2. Founded in the late 1870s, the society first met in Alcott's old Orchard House.

3. Emerson first met William Torrey Harris (1835–1909) in 1867 at St. Louis, where Harris was leader of the Philosophical Society and editor of *Speculative Philosophy*.

House. And thenceforward I never waver'd or was touch'd with qualms, (as I confess I had been two or three times before).

1882

LETTERS[1]

To Thomas Jefferson Whitman[2]

[*The Gorgeousness of the Capitol vs. the Suffering in the Hospitals*]

Washington, Feb. 13th '63.

Office Major Hapgood, cor 15th & F. sts.

* * *

I spent several hours in the Capitol the other day—the incredible gorgeousness of some of the rooms, (interior decorations &c)—rooms used perhaps but for merely three or four Committee meetings in the course of the whole year,) is beyond one's flightiest dreams. Costly frescoes of the style of Taylor's Saloon in Broadway, only really the best and choicest of their sort, done by imported French & Italian artists, are the prevailing sorts (imagine the work you see on the fine China vases, in Tiffany's—the paintings of Cupids & goddesses &c. spread recklessly over the arched ceiling and broad panels of a big room—the whole floor underneath paved with tesselated pavement, which is a sort of cross between marble & china, with little figures drab, blue, cream color, &c).

These things, with heavy, elaborately wrought balustrades, columns, & steps—all of the most beautiful marbles I ever saw, some white as milk, others of all colors, green, spotted, lined, or of our old chocolate color—all these marbles used as freely as if they were common blue flags—with rich door-frames and window-casings of bronze and gold—heavy chandeliers and mantels, and clocks in every room—and indeed by far the richest and gayest, and most un-American and inappropriate ornamenting and finest interior workmanship I ever conceived possible, spread in profusion through scores, hundreds, (and almost thousands) of rooms—such are what I find, or rather would find to interest me, if I devoted time to it—But a few of the rooms are enough for me—the style is without grandeur, and without simplicity—These days, the state our country is in, and especially filled as I am from top to toe, of late with scenes and thoughts of *the hospitals*, (America seems to me now, though only in her youth, but brought *already here* feeble, bandaged and bloody *in hospital*)—*these days* I say, Jeff, all the poppy-show goddesses and all the pretty blue & gold in which the interior Capitol is got up, seem to me out of place beyond any thing I could tell—and I get away from it as quick as I can when that kind of thought comes over me. I suppose it is to be described throughout—those interiors—as all of them got up in the French style—well enough for a New York [*incomplete*]

---

1. The letters printed here are taken from the five-vol. collection of Whitman's *Correspondence* edited by Edwin Haviland Miller. In his introductory essay, "Walt Whitman as a Letter Writer," Miller quotes Whitman's own opinion of suitable epistolary style: "You express your thoughts perfectly—do you not know how much more agreeable to me is the conversation or writing that does not take hard paved tracks, the usual & stereotyped, but has little peculiarties & even kinks of its own, making its genuineness—its vitality?"

2. Whitman's younger brother, then living with their mother in Brooklyn.

To Nathaniel Bloom and John F. S. Gray[1]

[*Washington, D.C.; Lincoln as Hoosier Michael Angelo*]

Washington, March 19, 1863

* * *

Washington and its points I find bear a second and a third perusal, and doubtless indeed many. My first impressions, architectural, &c. were not favorable; but upon the whole, the city, the spaces, buildings, &c make no unfit emblem of our country, so far, so broadly planned, every thing in plenty, money & materials staggering with plenty, but the fruit of the plans, the knit, the combination yet wanting—Determined to express ourselves greatly in a capital but no fit capital yet here—(time, associations, wanting, I suppose)— many a hiatus yet—many a thing to be taken down and done over again yet— perhaps an entire change of base—may-be a succession of changes. Congress does not seize very hard upon me—I studied it and its members with curiosity, and long—much gab, great fear of public opinion, plenty of low business talent, but no masterful man in Congress, (probably best so.) I think well of the President. He has a face like a hoosier Michael Angelo,[2] so awful ugly it becomes beautiful, with its strange mouth, its deep cut, criss-cross lines, and its doughnut complexion. My notion is, too, that underneath his outside smutched mannerism, and stories from third-class county bar-rooms, (it is his humor,) Mr. Lincoln keeps a fountain of first-class practical telling wisdom. I do not dwell on the supposed failures of his government; he has shown, I sometimes think, an almost supernatural tact in keeping the ship afloat at all, with head steady, not only going down, and now certain not to, but with proud and resolute spirit, and flag flying in sight of the world, menacing and high as ever. I say never yet captain, never ruler, had such a perplexing, dangerous task as his, the past two years. I more and more rely upon his idiomatic western genius, careless of court dress or court decorums. * * *

To William S. Davis[1]

[*Whitman's Haversack of Physical Comforts in the Wards*]

[October 1, 1863]

The noble gift of your brother Joseph P Davis of [$20?] for the aid of the wounded, sick, dying soldiers here came safe to hand—it is being sacredly distributed to them—part of it has been so already—I may another time give you special cases—I go every day or night in the hospitals a few hours—

As to physical comforts, I attempt to have something—generally a lot of— something harmless & not too expensive to go round to each man, even if it is nothing but a good home-made biscuit to each man, or a couple of spoon- fuls of blackberry preserve, I take a ward or two of an evening & two more next evening &c—as an addition to his supper—sometimes one thing, sometimes another, (judgment of course has to be carefully used)—then, after such gen-

---

1. Bloom ran a "fancy-goods store on Broadway," and Gray was "a captain in the Twentieth New York Infan- try" [Miller's note].
2. The Italian artist Michelangelo (1475–1564) was disfigured by a broken nose.

1. Davis, a lawyer, had submitted the money through Whitman's brother Jeff, who had hinted that the right sort of acknowledgment might cause the gift to be dou- bled [from Miller].

eral round, I fall back upon the main thing, after all, the special cases, alas, too common—those that need special attention, some little delicacy, some trifle—very often, far above all else, soothing kindness wanted—personal magnetism—poor boys, their sick hearts & wearied & exhausted bodies hunger for the sustenance of love or their deprest spirits must be cheered up—I find often young men, some hardly more than children in age yet—so good, so sweet, so brave, so decorous, I could not feel them nearer to me if my own sons or young brothers—Some cases even I could not tell any one, how near to me, from their yearning ways & their sufferings—it is comfort & delight to me to minister to them, to sit by them—some so wind themselves around one's heart, & will be kissed at parting at night just like children—though veterans of two years of battles & camp life—

I always carry a haversack with some articles most wanted—physical comforts are a sort of basis—I distribute nice large biscuit, sweet-crackers, sometimes cut up a lot of peaches with sugar, give preserves of all kinds, jellies, &c. tea, oysters, butter, condensed milk, plugs of tobacco, (I am the only one that doles out this last, & the men have grown to look to me)—wine, brandy, sugar, pickles, letter-stamps, envelopes & note-paper, the morning papers, common handkerchiefs & napkins, undershirts, socks, dressing gowns, & fifty other things—I have lots of special little requests. Frequently I give small sums of money—shall do so with your brother's contribution—the wounded are very frequently brought & lay here a long while without a cent. I have been here & in front 9 months doing this thing, & have learned much—two-thirds of the soldiers are from 15 to 25 or 6 years of age—lads of 15 or 16 more frequent than you have any idea—seven-eighths of the Army are Americans, our own stock—the foreign element in the army is much overrated,[2] & is of not much account anyhow—As to these hospitals, (there are dozens of them in [&] around Washington) [there] are no hosptials you must understand like the diseased half-foreign collections under that name common at all times in cities—in these here, the noblest, cleanest stock I think of the world, & the most precious.

To John Addington Symonds[1]

[Calamus: Late Denial of "Morbid Inferences"]

[August 19, 1890]

Y'rs of Aug: 3d just rec'd & glad to hear f'm you as always—Abt the little portraits, I cheerfully endorse the Munich reproduction of any of them you propose or any thing of the sort you choose—(I may soon send you some other

2. A substantial proportion of Civil War soldiers, especially Union soldiers, were foreign-born, simply because of large-scale immigration in the years preceding the war; but foreign volunteers in either army were very few, although well publicized.

1. The most quoted and debated Whitman letter. Symonds, the English critic and literary historian, had cautiously expressed his conviction that "the enthusiasm of 'Calamus' is calculated to encourage ardent & *physical* intimacies"—intimacies that in his view would not "absolutely be prejudicial to social interests"

(*Letters*, vol. 5). Having benefited in the past from American sexual naïveté (as in Emerson's absorption with the *Children of Adam* poems to the apparent ignoring of any objectionable qualities in the *Calamus* group), Whitman was now panicked by the Englishman's sexual sophistication. Out of this panic seem to have emerged, full-grown, six children, two dead, and the "living southern grandchild," although biographers have not been able to prove the negative, that this progeny had no existence.

preferable portraits of self)—Suppose you have rec'd papers & slips sent of late—Ab't the questions on Calamus pieces &c: they quite daze me. L of G. is only to be rightly construed by and within its own atmosphere and essential character—all of its pages & pieces so coming strictly under *that*—that the calamus part has even allow'd the possibility of such construction as mention'd is terrible—I am fain to hope the pages themselves are not to be even mention'd for such gratuitous and quite at the time entirely undream'd & unreck'd possibility of morbid inferences—wh' are disavow'd by me & seem damnable. Then one great difference between you and me, temperament & theory, is *restraint*—I know that while I have a horror of ranting & bawling I at certain moments let the spirit impulse, (?demon) rage its utmost, its wildest, damnedest—(I feel to do so in my L of G. & I do so). I end the matter saying I wholly stand by L of G. as it is, long as all parts & pages are construed as I said by their own ensemble, spirit & atmosphere.

I live here 72 y'rs old & completely paralyzed—brain & right arm ab't same as ever—digestion, sleep, appetite, &c: fair—sight & hearing half-and-half—spirits fair—locomotive power (legs) almost utterly gone—am propell'd outdoors nearly every day—get down to the river side here, the Delaware, an hour at sunset—The writing and rounding of L of G. has been to me the reason-for-being, & life comfort. My life, young manhood, mid-age, times South, &c: have all been jolly, bodily, and probably open to criticism—

Tho' always unmarried I have had six children—two are dead—One living southern grandchild, fine boy, who writes to me occasionally. Circumstances connected with their benefit and fortune have separated me from intimate relations.

I see I have written with haste & too great effusion—but let it stand.

HERMAN MELVILLE
1819–1891

Herman Melville began life with everything in his favor: heredity first of all, with two genuine Revolutionary heroes for grandfathers. The Melvill family (the *e* was added in the 1830s) was solidly established in Boston and the Gansevoorts were linked to the greatest Dutch patroon families of New York. Melville's much-traveled father, Allan Melvill, a dry-goods merchant in New York City, took inordinate pride in the genealogy of the Melvills, tracing the line past Scottish Renaissance courtiers to a queen of Hungary and tracing his mother's family, the Scollays, to the kings of Norway: "& so it appears we are of a royal line in both sides of the House—after all, it is not only an amusing but a just cause of pride, to resort back through the ages to such ancestry, & should produce a correspondent spirit of emulation in their descendants to the remotest posterity." As the third oldest of eight children born between 1815 and 1830, Herman Melville spent his early childhood in luxury. But Allan Melvill began borrowing from relatives in the 1820s, alternating between overenthusiasm about the future of business in America and dread of an inevitable recession. In 1832 he suddenly fell ill and died in a delirium that some in the family thought of as madness. He was many thousands of dollars in debt, and his family, then living in Albany, became dependent on the conscientious but finely calculated care of the Gansevoorts, especially Melville's uncle Peter.

Biographers justifiably hold that Melville's mature psychology is best understood as that of the decayed patrician. During his teens, he was distinctly a poor relation. The Princeton-educated Peter Gansevoort hobnobbed with the leading politicians of the day, entertaining President Van Buren at dinner during the years in which his widowed sister, Maria Melville, saw her brilliant oldest son Gansevoort and her more plodding second son Herman make do with what self-improvement they could derive from the Albany debating societies. Taken out of school when he was twelve, a few months after his father's death, Melville clerked for two years at a bank. Starting early in 1834 he worked two and a half years at his brother Gansevoort's fur-cap store in Albany. In 1837 he spent several months in nearby Pittsfield, Massachusetts, running his uncle Thomas Melvill's farm after his uncle left for Illinois. Just after he turned eighteen, he taught in a country school near Pittsfield, where he boarded with Yankee backwoods families. The next spring he took a course in surveying and engineering at the Lansingburgh Academy, near Albany, but in the aftermath of the Panic of 1837 found no work. He signed on a voyage to and from Liverpool in 1839, the summer he turned twenty, then the next year job-hunted fruitlessly around the Midwest. At twenty-one, in January 1841, he took the desperate measure of sailing on a whaler for the South Seas. His crucial experience had begun.

From Peru he wrote, in Gansevoort's paraphrase, that he was "not dissatisfied with his lot"—"The fact of his being one of a crew so much superior in morale and early advantages to the ordinary run of whaling crews affords him constant gratification." Nevertheless, in the summer of 1842 Melville and a shipmate, Toby Greene, jumped ship at Nukahiva, in the Marquesas, and for a few weeks Melville lived with a tribe quite untainted by Western civilization; late in life he felt he had lived in the world's last Eden. Picked up by an Australian whaler less than a month after he deserted, he took part in a comic opera mutiny and was imprisoned by the British consul in Tahiti, along with a learned friend (the "Dr. Long Ghost" of *Omoo*) who became his companion in exploring the flora and, especially, the fauna of Tahiti and Eimeo. Shipping on a Nantucket whaler at Eimeo, Melville was discharged in Lahaina, then knocked about Honolulu for a few months before signing on the frigate *United States* as an ordinary seaman. After a leisurely cruise in the Pacific, including a revisit to the Marquesas, the *United States* sailed for home, arriving at Boston in October 1844. On this ship Melville again encountered some remarkably literate, and even literary, sailors. No newspapers welcomed the young sailor home, but that month Democratic papers in New York were hailing the triumphant return of his brother Gansevoort from a splendidly histrionic stump-speaking tour in the West on behalf of Polk's campaign for the presidency. Herman Melville was twenty-five; he later said that from that year, beginning August 1, 1844, he dated his life. He apparently did not look for a job after his discharge from the navy in Boston on October 14; within two or three months he had begun writing *Typee* while staying with his lawyer brothers in New York City.

Circumstances were propitious. In the summer of 1845 Gansevoort was rewarded for his services to the Democrats with the secretaryship to the American Legation in London. When he sailed, he had with him the chaotic manuscript that Herman had just completed in Lansingburgh. It purported to be a straight autobiographical account of his detainment "in an indulgent captivity for about the space of four months" by an appealingly hedonistic, if also cannibalistic, tribe, but in fact Melville had quadrupled the time he had spent in the valley of the Typees. Gansevoort interested John Murray (the son of Lord Byron's friend and publisher) in the book for his Home and Colonial Library, and after it was eked out by new anthropological observations from Melville (many of which came from earlier books by sea captains and missionaries) and tidied up by a professional "reader," *Typee* was published early in 1846. As the earliest personal account of the South Seas to have the readability and suspense of adventure fiction, it made a great sensation, capturing the imagination of both the literary reviewers and the reading public with the surefire combination of anthropological novelty and what reviewers regularly tagged (remembering *Othello*) as "hair-breadth 'scapes." It was attended by vigorous, sales-stimulating controversy over its authenticity, capped by the emergence of Toby, the long-lost fellow runaway, in the person of Richard Tobias Greene, a house painter near Buffalo. G. P. Putnam of Wiley & Putnam (he was a cousin of Sophia Hawthorne's) had bought *Typee* in England at the urging of Washington Irving, but his partner, John Wiley, was appalled once he read closely the attacks on missionary operations in the South Seas. Although the American edition was already printed, Wiley demanded expurgations of sexual and political passages as well as of the attacks on the missionaries, and Melville agreed to excise a total of some thirty pages, contenting himself with exclaiming to the New York editor Evert Duyckinck that *expurgation* was an "odious" word. Melville followed the fortunes of *Typee* with zest and even wanted to manipulate the controversy through a planted newspaper review of his own. In the middle of the publicity over *Typee*, Gansevoort died suddenly at the age of thirty. In less than a year the unknown sailor, the unappreciated second son, had become a sensationally newsworthy writer and the head of his family.

Melville immediately turned to the composition of a sequel, *Omoo*, the account—more strictly autobiographical than *Typee*—of his beachcombing in Tahiti and Eimeo. Yet even as he was busily at work on *Omoo* at the end of 1846 he was trying to get a job in the Custom House in New York City—his notion of the ideal local job to provide a regular income and keep him among ships and sailors (as well as the necessary evil of bureaucrats) while, he must have hoped, giving him sufficient leisure for literary pursuits. When he offered *Omoo* to Murray, Melville wrote exuberantly that a "little experience in this art of book-craft has done wonders." He had in mind the condition of his manuscript, but he might well have said the same of his ability to manage a narrative. *Omoo* lacked the suspense of *Typee*, but it was a more polished performance of a writer far surer of himself. It is a fine, humorous production, full of vivid character sketches and memorable documentation of the evils wrought by the Christianizers. It delighted readers in 1847 and gave great pleasure to later South Sea wanderers like Robert Louis Stevenson and Henry Adams.

In the flush of his success with *Omoo*, Melville married Elizabeth Knapp Shaw on August 4, 1847, three days after his twenty-eighth birthday. Her father, Lemuel Shaw, the chief justice of Massachusetts, had been a school friend of Allan Melvill at the turn of the century and had been engaged to one of Allan's sisters who died early of tuberculosis. Allan had taken advantage of Shaw's friendship to borrow from him in the 1820s; Herman's uncle, Thomas Melvill, and Thomas's son Robert had further abused that friendship in the 1830s; then in the early 1840s Gansevoort Melville had sought Shaw out as patron. Melville dedicated *Typee* to Shaw, although it is not clear what their personal acquaintance had been; after the marriage Shaw provided several advances against his daughter's inheritance, the first being $2,000 toward the purchase of a house in New York, where Melville established himself with his bride, his younger brother Allan, Allan's own bride, his mother, four sisters, and his new manuscript. Melville was well on his way to becoming a literary fixture of New York City, a participant in projects of the Duyckinck literary clique such as the short-lived satirical *Yankee Doodle*, and for the longer-lived enterprise of the Duyckincks, *The Literary World*, a resident authority and reviewer of books on nautical matters and inland exploration, and a reliable dispenser of vigorous, humorous, authentic tales of exotic adventure.

Instead, the Polynesian adventurer discovered the world of the mind and the aesthetic range of the English language as he worked his way into his third book, *Mardi*, which was published in April 1849, just short of two years after he began it. His friends had some baffled inklings at the changes in Melville that could make him call the seventeenth-century writer Sir Thomas Browne a "cracked archangel" because of the speculations in the *Religio Medici* (Melville's new friend Evert Duyckinck wrote his brother, "Was ever any thing of this sort said before by a sailor?"), but for the most part the evidence of the transformation went into the manuscript of *Mardi*. It had begun as a South Sea adventure story like *Typee* and *Omoo*, or as they would have been if they had been written by a man intoxicated with his discovery of his powers. In the spring of 1848, after Melville thought he was through with *Mardi*, news of the new European revolutions led him to interpolate a long section of allegorical satire on European and American politics. Sometime in the last year of composition, he bade farewell to the New York literary cliques with another allegorical section on the great poet Lombardo's creation of a masterpiece that puzzled his small-minded contemporaries.

In his solitary expansion of mind Melville had become reckless, admitting in his book that he had "voyaged chartless," and he ultimately foundered in an attempt to persuade Murray that the work, though professedly fiction, would not retroactively impugn the much-challenged authenticity of the first two books. Another London publisher, Richard Bentley, promptly enough took the book, but Murray had been prescient. Many of the reviewers were appalled at the betrayal of their expectations of another *Typee* or *Omoo*, though a discriminating minority recognized what a valuable book they had in hand. It sold poorly, especially in the overpriced three-volume English edition, and deeply damaged Melville's growing reputation except with a few readers. *Mardi* is, in fact, almost unreadable, except for a rarely dedicated lover of antiquarian literary, philosophical, metaphysical, and political hodgepodge—the sort of eccentric scholar who loves Burton's *Anatomy of Melancholy* and Browne's *Vulgar Errors*. Melvilleans find it inexhaustibly fascinating, recognizing in it Melville's exuberant response to his realization that he was—or could become—a great literary genius. *Mardi* was his declaration of literary independence, though he did not fully achieve that independence until *Moby-Dick*, two books and two years later.

Early in 1849, during the interval between completing *Mardi* and its publication, Melville's first son, Malcolm, was born at the Shaw house in Boston, and Melville rested, went to the theater, heard Emerson lecture, and read Shakespeare with full attentiveness for the first time. He spoke hopefully of undertaking a work that would carry him beyond *Mardi*, but the first reviews of that book showed that he could not afford another such luxury. Accepting the responsibilities of a new father, he wrote *Redburn* (1849) and *White-Jacket* (1850) as acts of contrition, both ground out during one four-month period in the 1849 summer swelter of a cholera-ridden New York City. As he promised Richard Bentley, *Redburn* would contain no metaphysics, only cakes and ale. Written in the first person by the middle-aged, sentimental Wellingborough Redburn, it is the story of the narrator's first voyage, which like Melville's own was a summer voyage to and from Liverpool, though Redburn is hardly more than a boy while Melville was twenty. Often as good as *Huckleberry Finn*, better than such a twentieth-century rival as *Catcher in the Rye*, *Redburn* could have been a minor classic if Melville had sustained the point of view he had established—lovingly satiric toward the boy Redburn, more pointedly satiric toward the convention-bound narrator. But interest in his experiment with a limited character's first-person narrative flagged, and the second half of the book is only intermittently as compelling as the first. The reviewers and the readers liked it, especially the air of documentary convincingness that reminded them of *Robinson Crusoe* and other works by Daniel Defoe.

Long before *Redburn* was published, Melville had completed *White-Jacket*, which was based on his experiences on the man-of-war *United States* in 1843 and 1844, supplemented by lavish borrowings from earlier nautical literature. In *White-Jacket* Melville came into something like creative equilibrium, for his first-person narrator was once again, as in *Typee* and *Omoo*, at the same stage of development as the writer, capable of saying precisely what Melville might at that given moment be capable of saying. Overshadowed by *Moby-Dick*, slighted by most modern readers because of its unpromising—"unliterary"—subject matter, *White-Jacket* has been adequately praised only by its first readers. Melville himself never could quite regard it as much more than a product of forced labor, like *Redburn* (that "little nursery tale") the literary equivalent of "sawing wood."

Rather than bargaining with Bentley by mail (as he had just done for *Redburn*) and having the publisher again cite the new British ruling on copyright (which now was denied to books by American authors even if first printed in Great Britain), Melville sailed for London in October 1849, carrying with him proofs of the Harper edition of *White-Jacket*. An observer described him as wearily hawking his book "from Picadilly to Whitechapel, calling upon every publisher in his way," and in fact Melville repeatedly met refusal because of the copyright problem. He ultimately settled with Bentley on good terms—but not good enough to allow him to make his hoped-for tour of Europe and the Holy Land. He passed weeks in antiquarian book buying, sightseeing, library- and museum-going, and literary socializing, by his responses to these experiences confirming his sense of himself as a "pondering man." He made a brief excursion into France and Germany, then, homesick and guilty about his holiday, he cut short his trip. Leaving early meant refusing the duke of Rutland's "cordial invitation to visit him at his Castle," Melville's one chance to learn "what the highest English aristocracy really & practically is." Soon after his return to New York on February 1, 1850, enthusiastic reviews of *White-Jacket* began arriving from England, and in March the American edition was published to similar acclaim. In a buoyant mood, sure of his powers and sure of his ability to keep an audience, Melville began his whaling book. (By mid-1851 its working title was *The Whale*, which remained the title for the English edition; *Moby-Dick* was a last-minute substitute for the American edition.)

Like *Mardi*, *Moby-Dick* was luxury for Melville, an enormous, slowly written book. *Slowly* deserves qualification: Melville lived with the book some seventeen months, often writing very steadily for many weeks on end, but allowing several lengthy interruptions. By May 1, 1850, Melville was telling Richard Henry Dana, his well-known fellow sea writer, that he was "half way in the work." Critics have speculated that the book began as a matter-of-fact sea narrative, but Melville's letter makes it clear that from the start the challenge to his art lay in getting poetry from blubber and managing to "throw in a little fancy" without, as he said, resulting in gambols as ungainly as those of the whales. Furthermore, he meant "to give the truth of the thing." None of these intentions clashes with the book he finally completed, though whatever plans he had were later altered to accommodate new literary sources as well as his maturing philosophical and theological preoccupations.

One crucial event during the composition of *Moby-Dick* was Melville's vacation at his uncle Thomas's old place in the Berkshires (now occupied by his cousin Robert as a select boardinghouse where former President Tyler and the poet Longfellow had stayed). He had left the region as a teenage master of a backwoods school, and Pittsfield residents remembered him, if at all, as that lad or, from a few years before, as the orphan nephew of Thomas Melvill, a pretentious farmer in and out of debtor's prison until he moved to Illinois in 1837. Now this nephew was an author of international repute, and the collision of times and circumstances released a near-manic state in Melville. He was in this exalted mood when he met Nathaniel Hawthorne. Reading Hawthorne's *Mosses from an Old Manse* just after their meeting may have had some minor stylistic influence on a few passages in *Moby-Dick*; more important, Melville undertook for the Duyckinck brothers' *Literary World* a review of *Mosses* in which he articulated many of his deepest attitudes toward the problems and opportunities of American writers. Infusing the whole review is Melville's exultant sense that the day had come when American writers could rival Shakespeare; in praising Hawthorne's achievements, he was honoring what he knew lay in his own manuscript. Furthermore, Melville gave clearer hints at what sort of "truth" he might be trying to give in *Moby-Dick*—dark, "Shakespearean" truths about human nature and the universe that "in this world of lies" can be told only "covertly, and by snatches." Out of his failures with *Mardi* and the slave labor of the next two books, Melville had built a literary theory in which a writer writes simultaneously for two audiences, one composed of the mob, the other of "eagle-eyed" readers who perceive the true meaning of those passages that the author has "directly calculated to deceive—egregiously deceive—the superficial skimmer of pages." *Moby-Dick*, now reported by Evert Duyckinck to be "a new book mostly done—a romantic, fanciful & literal & most enjoyable presentment of the Whale Fishery—something quite new"—was to be such a book. It was the culmination of Melville's reading in great literature from the Bible through Rabelais, Burton, John Milton, Sterne, Lord Byron, Thomas De Quincey and Thomas Carlyle, yet anchored also in the nautical world of Baron Cuvier, Frederick Debell Bennett, William Scoresby, and Obed Macy, a fusion of aspects of Sir Thomas Browne and the American travel writer J. Ross Browne, with incidental hints from a multitude of quaint old encyclopedic volumes.

Still exultantly feeling his new powers, Melville moved his family to a farm near Pittsfield late in 1850. By December he had settled again into intense work on his book until the spring chores took him away from it. During 1851 the most stimulating fact of Melville's existence, other than the book he brought to completion and saw through the press, was Hawthorne's presence at Lenox, near enough for a few visits to be exchanged except during the worst of the Berkshire winter. On some of his visits he took the Old Lenox Road, passing by a rocky outcropping where years before, a futureless orphan, he had brooded on the natural landscape and the spires of Pittsfield. Small wonder if the collision of past and present heightened and perturbed his moods. Melville's intense friendship provided him with a desperately needed sense of literary community as well as a confidant for his metaphysical and philosophical speculations. His letters to Hawthorne, preserved now mostly in nineteenth-century transcripts and printings by Hawthorne's descendants, are among the glories of American literature and a priceless record of Melville's state of mind during his last months with *Moby-Dick*. Uppermost in them is his sense of kinship with the great writers and thinkers of the world—a sense that would seem megalomanic if his manuscript had not vindicated him. The recurrent themes of the letters—democracy and aristocracy, the ironic failure of Christians to be Christian, fame and immortality, the brotherhood of great-souled mortals, and in particular the Miltonic themes of "Providence, Foreknowledge, Will, and Fate, / Fixt Fate, free will, foreknowledge absolute"—were all recurrent themes of *Moby-Dick*. From his perception of himself as a descendant of kings abandoned to the universe, yet struggling back to reclaim his rightful majesty (a perception revealed in many of his scorings and underlinings in his two-volume set of Milton's poetry that surfaced in 1983 and was auctioned early in 1984 for $100,000), Melville created a hero who dared to turn God's lightning back against him and whose nature could only be explained by venturing deep below the antiquities of the earth to question a titanic captive god. For all Ahab's insanity, which was recognized by the narrator, Ishmael, Melville's emotional sympathies were with the defiant Ahab who rejected the slavish values of the shore to defy the malignancy in the universe. That was the world of the mind. But as he finished *Moby-Dick*, Melville was a family man whose household included his mother and sisters as well as a small child and a pregnant wife. He owed the Harpers $700 because they had advanced him more than his earlier books had earned, and in April 1851 they refused him an advance on his whaling book. On May 1, Melville borrowed $2,050 from T. D. Stewart, an old Lansingburgh acquaintance, and a few weeks later he painfully defined his literary-economic dilemma to Hawthorne: "What I feel most moved to write, that is banned.—it will not pay. Yet, altogether, write the *other* way I cannot. So the product is a final hash, and all my books are botches."

Late in 1851, about the time *Moby-Dick* was published, Melville tried once again to find a form in which he could write as profoundly as he could while retaining the popularity he had so easily won with his first two books. Settling on the gothic novel in its midcentury transmogrification as the sentimental psycholog- ical novel favored by women book buyers, he began *Pierre*, thinking he could express the agonies of the growth of a human psyche even while enthralling readers with the romantic and ethical perplexities attending on young Pierre Glendinning's discovery of a dark maiden who might be his unacknowledged half-sister. Melville was relentlessly analyzing both the tragic and the satiric implications of the imprac- ticability of Christianity, for Pierre's calamitous decision was to obey his heart's idealism and attempt a life in imitation of the "divine unidentifiableness" of Jesus, who required of his followers the rejection of all worldly kith and kin. Melville took his manuscript to New York City around New Year's Day 1852, hoping to publish it as a taut 360-page book, little more than half the size of *Moby-Dick*. But despite the early sales of the whaling book, Melville was still in debt to the Harpers, who offered him a punitive contract for *Pierre*—twenty cents on the dollar after expenses rather than the old rate of fifty cents. Stung, Melville accepted, but his rage and shame over the contract mingled with pain from the reviews of *Moby- Dick* in the January periodicals: the *Southern Quarterly Review*, for instance, said a "writ *de lunatico*" was justified against Melville and his characters. Within days of coming to terms with Harpers, Melville began working into *Pierre* a sometimes wry, sometimes recklessly bitter account of his own literary career, ultimately enlarging the work by 150 printed pages and wrecking whatever chance he had of making the work what he had hoped—as much more profound than *Moby-Dick* as the legendary Krakens are larger than whales.

Pierre would probably have failed with its first readers even if it had been com- pleted and published in its projected shorter form, for the subject matter even in the first half included atheism and incest and the language Melville created as a tool for psychological probing seemed hysterical and artificial to the reviewers. In any case, the *Pierre* that Harpers finally published late in July 1852 (giving Melville time for a fruitless negotiation with Bentley, who refused to publish it without expurgation) all but ended Melville's career. It was widely denounced as immoral, and one *Pierre*-inspired news account was captioned "HERMAN MELVILLE CRAZY." In panic the family made efforts to gain Melville some government post, preferably foreign, but nothing came of their attempts to call in old favors. Melville stayed on the farm with his expanding household (two daughters, Elizabeth and Frances, were born in 1853 and 1855). After *Pierre* Melville's career faltered. In May 1853 he completed *The Isle of the Cross*, a book about a patient Nantucket wife, but he was somehow "prevented" from publishing it, and he probably destroyed it. In 1853 and 1854 he wrote part of a book about tortoise hunting in the Galapagos Islands, then apparently diverted some of it into *The Encantadas* and destroyed the rest. Melville was undergoing a profound psychological crisis that left him more resigned to fate than defiant, and in addition to his older ailment of weak eyes he developed a new set of crippling afflictions diagnosed as sciatica and rheumatism.

Late in 1853 Melville began a new, low-keyed career as writer of short stories for the two major American monthlies, *Harper's* and *Putnam's*. All stories were anonymous, by magazine policy (though authorship was often leaked to editors of newspapers and other magazines), so what Melville published in the next years did not add greatly to his fame. One serial, the story of a Revolutionary exile named Israel Potter, stretched out to book length. Offering it to the publisher, Melville promised that it would contain nothing "to shock the fastidious," and in fact he restrained his imagination and his metaphysical and theological compulsions.

Straightforward novel that it is, *Israel Potter* contains passages of great historical interest, especially the complex portraits of Benjamin Franklin, John Paul Jones, and Ethan Allen. In 1856 Melville collected the *Putnam's* stories as *The Piazza Tales*, supplying a new prefatory sketch, "The Piazza," which marked his development past his earlier simple admiration for Hawthorne's subjects and techniques. Clear in all of Melville's writings in the mid-fifties is his growing tendency to brood less over his own career and his own relationship with cosmic forces and more over the American national character and the conditions in American life that would allow honest craftsmen like himself to be rejected. Self-pity tinges some of these writings, but more often a wry jocularity, an almost comfortable self-mockery. In them Melville achieved a new sureness of artistic control, even though the power of *Moby-Dick* and parts of *Pierre* was never regained. From this period of physical and psychic suffering and of financial distress emerged a new masterpiece, *The Confidence-Man*, a devastating indictment of national confidence in the form of mingled metaphysical satire and low comedy. It went almost unread in the United States; in England the reviews were more intelligent but the sales were also disappointing, and Melville did not earn a cent from either edition.

By the spring of 1856 Melville may have recovered from most of his mental, spiritual, and physical agonies, but his economic distress was greater than ever and he had composed *The Confidence-Man* (including a chapter on the catastrophic consequences of "a friendly loan") to the ticking of an economic time bomb. He was a year late in payment on the mortgage on the farm held by the previous owner; worse, he still owed the principal and the accumulating interest on the $2,050 he had borrowed in 1851, and the lender was pressing for full repayment. Melville was forced to sell part of the farm, but Judge Shaw met the family's anxieties about Herman's state of mind by providing funds for an extended trip to Europe and the Levant, from October 1856 to May 1857. In England Melville told Hawthorne, who had become consul at Liverpool, that he did not anticipate much pleasure in his rambles, since "the spirit of adventure" had gone out of him. For upwards of a decade, Melville's adventuring had been inward—philosophical, metaphysical, psychological, and artistic. As Hawthorne hoped, Melville brightened as he went onward, and after a few days he began to keep a journal. Melville's sightseeing and gallery-going were as compulsively American as Hawthorne's own. Many of Melville's observations were predictable responses to the places, palaces, and paintings given largest space in the guidebooks, but what he saw gradually led him to energetically original responses, as in his then unfashionable response to classical statuary, earlier Italian painters like Giotto, and the realistic Dutch and Flemish genre painters. As Howard Horsford, the editor of this journal, says, the entries show Melville's taste in the process of being formed. Horsford points out "the peculiar urgency, the sharpness, vividness, and freshness" of those entries where Melville was most deeply moved: "Many passages, such as those on the Pyramids, or the descriptions of the Jerusalem scene and the Palestinian landscape, are in his finest rhetorical style; many of his comments on people, places, and things display the most cutting edge of his irony and satire, as in his accounts of the Church of the Holy Sepulchre and of the missionaries in the Near East." Horsford also draws a precise contrast between the Melville of the late 1840s and the one of the mid-fifties. When Melville "had embarked on metaphysical speculation at the time of *Mardi*," it had been "a welcome release, an escape into a new freedom from orthodoxy and dogmatism, a mental emancipation." Now Melville's metaphysical speculations had ended in "joyless skepticism." When he returned home, Melville was more than ever "a pondering man," but he told a young Gansevoort cousin that he was "not going to write any more at present."

That moment stretched on. Melville lectured in the East and Midwest for three seasons (1857–60) without much profit, speaking in successive years on "Statues in Rome," "The South Seas," and "Traveling." He prepared a volume of poems in

1860 but instead of trying to place it, he sailed on a voyage to San Francisco as passenger on a ship captained by his youngest brother, Thomas, leaving his wife and his brother Allan to seek fruitlessly for a publisher. Early in 1861, Melville attempted, once again, to "procure some foreign appointment under the new Administration—the consulship at Florence, for example"; once again, he failed to recognize that his refusal to take part in local politics would doom his chances, whatever famous statesmen spoke out for him. In Washington he attended Lincoln's second levee and "Old Abe," as he wrote home, shook his hand "like a good fellow." An urgent letter recalled him to Pittsfield, and he and his wife reached Boston too late to see Judge Shaw alive. The estate was slow in being settled, but promptly enough some stocks were in Mrs. Melville's possession, and their economic pressures began to ease. The Melvilles spent the winter of 1861–62 in Manhattan, then in April Melville returned to Arrowhead (which his brother Allan later bought) and moved the family into Pittsfield. A driver who on mountain excursions had been "daring to the point of recklessness" and who had derived some pleasure from terrifying his passengers while confident he would deliver them to "a safe landing place," Melville, while "driving at a moderate pace over a perfectly smooth and level road" at Pittsfield in November 1862, had a freak accident that left his right arm useless till the next spring and affected him emotionally, so that for a time he "shrank from entering a carriage" and perhaps never completely recovered from "the shock which his system had received." No longer a young man, Melville moved his family to New York in October 1863 and waited out the war, making a trip to the Virginia battlefields with Allan in 1864 to get sight of a Gansevoort cousin and (as Allan put it), like all literary men, to "have opportunities to see that they may describe": *Battle-Pieces* (1866), a volume of Civil War poems, was casually or disdainfully reviewed and quickly forgotten; now it ranks with Whitman's *Drum-Taps* as the best of hundreds of volumes of poetry to come out of the war. For all his front of nonchalance, Melville was devastated by the loss of his career and further rebuffs when he sought a government job in Washington in 1861. As the unemployed do, Melville took out his frustrations on his family, so much so that for years his wife's half-brothers considered him insane as well as financially incompetent, and by early 1867 Melville's wife was also convinced of his insanity. Her sense of loyalty to him and her horror of gossip, however, were strong enough to make her reject her minister's suggestion that she pretend to make a routine visit to Boston and then barricade herself in the Shaw house, but as her family realized, the law was on Melville's side, whatever unrecorded abuses he was guilty of. In 1866 Melville had at last obtained a political job—not as consul in some exotic capital but as a deputy inspector of customs in New York City; ironically, his beat during some years took him frequently to the pier on Gansevoort Street, named for his mother's heroic father. After Malcolm killed himself late in 1867 at the age of eighteen the Melvilles closed ranks.

As Melville had predicted to Hawthorne, he became known as the "man who lived among the cannibals," holding his place in encyclopedias and literary histories primarily as the author of *Typee* and *Omoo*, all but forgotten by the postbellum literary world. But for years through the early 1870s Melville worked on a poem about a motley group of American European pilgrims—and tourists—who talked their way through some of the same Palestinian scenes he had visited a decade and more earlier; apparently he carried about pocket-size slips of paper for writing in odd moments at work as well as during his evenings. This poem, *Clarel*, grew to 18,000 lines and lay unpublished for many months or perhaps even two years before it appeared in 1876, paid for by a specific bequest from the dying Peter Gansevoort. It is America's most thoughtful contribution to the conflict of religious faith and Darwinian skepticism that obsessed English contemporaries such as Matthew Arnold and Thomas Hardy. Like *Mardi* it is inexhaustible for what it reveals of Melville's mind and art, but unlike *Mardi* it is plotted with the surety of artistic control that he had learned in the 1850s; however, *Mardi* had been read and argued about, and *Clarel* was ignored.

Stanwix, the second Melville son, drifted away without a career, beachcombing for a time in Central America, finally dying in San Francisco in 1886. The first daughter, called Bessie, developed severe arthritis and never married, and died in 1908. Only Frances married, and she lived until 1934, unable to recognize her father in the words of twentieth-century admirers and flatly refusing to talk about him. But through the 1880s Melville and his wife drew closer together. An extraordinary series of legacies came to them in Melville's last years; ironically the wealth was too late to make much change in their lives, but it allowed him to retire from the Custom House at the beginning of 1886 and devote himself to his writing. From time to time after *Clarel* he had written poems that ultimately went into two volumes, which he printed privately shortly before his death, except for some that remained unpublished until the 1920s and later. Melville developed the habit of writing prose headnotes to poems, notably some dealing with an imaginary Burgundy Club in which he found consolation for his loneliness. He could relax with the intelligent good fellows of his imagination as he could never relax among the popular literary men of the 1870s and 1880s who now and then tried to patronize him. In the mid-1880s one poem about a British sailor evoked a headnote that, expanded and reexpanded, was left nearly finished at Melville's death as *Billy Budd, Sailor*, his final study of the ambiguous claims of authority and individuality.

Before Melville's death in 1891, something like a revival of his fame was in progress, especially in England. American newspapers became accustomed to reprinting and briefly commenting on extraordinary items in British periodicals, such as Robert Buchanan's footnote to Melville's name in a poetic tribute to Whitman (1885): "I sought everywhere for this Triton, who is still living somewhere in New York. No one seemed to know anything of the one great imaginative writer fit to stand shoulder to shoulder with Whitman on that continent." The recurrent imagery—used by Melville as well as journalists—was of burial and possible resurrection.

When he died, Melville had reason to think his reputation would ultimately be established. Just after his death, new editions of *Typee, Omoo, White-Jacket,* and *Moby-Dick* were published both in the United States and in England, and Mrs. Melville remained a loyal and alert custodian of his memory until her death in 1906, but interest sputtered away except for small cults of Melville lovers who, as an anonymous British writer said in 1922, came to use *Moby-Dick* (or *The Whale*) as the test of a worthy reader and friend, proffering it without special comment and staking all on the response of the reader. The true Melville revival began with articles on Melville's centennial in 1919. That revival, one of the most curious phenomena of American literary history, swept Melville from the ranks of the lesser American writers—lesser than James Fenimore Cooper and William Gilmore Simms—into the rarefied company of Shakespeare and a few fellow immortals of world literature so that only Whitman, James, and Faulkner are seen as his American equals. Many of the materials for a biography had by then been lost (Melville burned his letters from Hawthorne, family members censored their files from dangerous years like the 1860s), but scholars have found the study of Melville's life and works inexhaustible. Even during the mass consumption of Melville in the classroom and the spawning of the White Whale in comic books, cartoons, and seafood restaurants, even during Melville's inflated glory at the Postal Service (a stamped 6-cent envelope in 1970, with a white whale in a blue oval; a 20-cent stamp, no envelope, in 1984 with Melville's portrait), a few lonely cultists are still to be found, tracing his journeys in the South Seas and Manhattan Island, and visiting his grave in the Bronx, faithful to the Melville who speaks to them without the aid of an interpreter. That may be the true sign of the rarest literary immortality.

Hawthorne and His Mosses

By a Virginian Spending July in Vermont[1]

A papered chamber in a fine old farm-house—a mile from any other dwelling, and dipped to the eaves in foliage—surrounded by mountains, old woods, and Indian ponds,—this, surely, is the place to write of Hawthorne. Some charm is in this northern air, for love and duty seem both impelling to the task. A man of a deep and noble nature has seized me in this seclusion. His wild, witch voice rings through me; or, in softer cadences, I seem to hear it in the songs of the hill-side birds, that sing in the larch trees at my window.

Would that all excellent books were foundlings, without father or mother, that so it might be, we could glorify them, without including their ostensible authors. Nor would any true man take exception to this;—least of all, he who writes,—"When the Artist rises high enough to achieve the Beautiful, the symbol by which he makes it perceptible to mortal senses becomes of little value in his eyes, while his spirit possesses itself in the enjoyment of the reality."[2]

But more than this. I know not what would be the right name to put on the title-page of an excellent book, but this I feel, that the names of all fine authors are fictitious ones, far more so than that of Junius,—simply standing, as they do, for the mystical, ever-eluding Spirit of all Beauty, which ubiquitously possesses men of genius. Purely imaginative as this fancy may appear, it nevertheless seems to receive some warranty from the fact, that on a personal interview no great author has ever come up to the idea of his reader. But that dust of which our bodies are composed, how can it fitly express the nobler intelligences among us? With reverence be it spoken, that not even in the case of one deemed more than man, not even in our Saviour, did his visible frame betoken anything of the augustness of the nature within. Else, how could those Jewish eyewitnesses fail to see heaven in his glance.

It is curious, how a man may travel along a country road, and yet miss the grandest, or sweetest of prospects, by reason of an intervening hedge, so like all other hedges, as in no way to hint of the wide landscape beyond. So has it been with me concerning the enchanting landscape in the soul of this Hawthorne, this most excellent Man of Mosses. His "Old Manse" has been written now four years, but I never read it till a day or two since. I had seen it in the book-stores—heard of it often—even had it recommended to me by a tasteful friend, as a rare, quiet book, perhaps too deserving of popularity to be popular. But there are so many books called "excellent," and so much unpopular merit, that amid the thick stir of other things, the hint of my tasteful friend was disregarded; and for four years the Mosses on the Old Manse never refreshed me with their perennial green. It may be, however, that all this while, the book, like wine, was only improving in flavor and body. At any rate, it so chanced that this long procrastination eventuated in a happy result. At breakfast the other day, a mountain girl, a cousin of mine,[3] who for the last two weeks has every morning helped me to strawberries and raspberries,—which,

1. The manuscript shows that the pseudonymous "Virginian Spending July in Vermont" was an afterthought designed to account for the emotional outpouring that Melville had written in his own voice. Contrary to the assertion within the essay, Melville wrote the review after meeting Hawthorne during a literary outing in the Berkshires on August 5, 1850. Several errors marred the first two-part publication in the New York *Literary World* for August 17 and 24, 1850; necessary spelling corrections are made, but the text printed here is based on the manuscript.

2. The conclusion of *The Artist of the Beautiful*.

3. In fact, Melville's Aunt Mary Melvill gave him the book two weeks before he met Hawthorne.

like the roses and pearls in the fairy-tale, seemed to fall into the saucer from those strawberry-beds her cheeks,—this delightful creature, this charming Cherry says to me—"I see you spend your mornings in the hay-mow; and yesterday I found there 'Dwight's Travels in New England'.[4] Now I have something far better than that,—something more congenial to our summer on these hills. Take these raspberries, and then I will give you some moss."—"Moss!" said I.—"Yes, and you must take it to the barn with you, and good-bye to 'Dwight.' "

With that she left me, and soon returned with a volume, verdantly bound, and garnished with a curious frontispiece in green,—nothing less, than a fragment of real moss cunningly pressed to a flyleaf.—"Why this," said I, spilling my raspberries, "this is the 'Mosses from an Old Manse'." "Yes," said cousin Cherry, "yes, it is that flowery Hawthorne."—"Hawthorne and Mosses," said I, "no more: it is morning: it is July in the country: and I am off for the barn."

Stretched on that new mown clover, the hill-side breeze blowing over me through the wide barn door, and soothed by the hum of the bees in the meadows around, how magically stole over me this Mossy Man! And how amply, how bountifully, did he redeem that delicious promise to his guests in the Old Manse, of whom it is written—"Others could give them pleasure, or amusement, or instruction—these could be picked up anywhere—but it was for me to give them rest. Rest, in a life of trouble! What better could be done for weary and world-worn spirits? what better could be done for anybody, who came within our magic circle, than to throw the spell of a magic spirit over him?"[5]—So all that day, half-buried in the new clover, I watched this Hawthorne's "Assyrian dawn, and Paphian sunset and moonrise, from the summit of our Eastern Hill."[6]

The soft ravishments of the man spun me round about in a web of dreams, and when the book was closed, when the spell was over, this wizard "dismissed me with but misty reminiscences, as if I had been dreaming of him."

What a mild moonlight of contemplative humor bathes that Old Manse!— the rich and rare distilment of a spicy and slowly-oozing heart. No rollicking rudeness, no gross fun fed on fat dinners, and bred in the lees of wine,—but a humor so spiritually gentle, so high, so deep, and yet so richly relishable, that it were hardly inappropriate in an angel. It is the very religion of mirth; for nothing so human but it may be advanced to that. The orchard of the Old Manse seems the visible type of the fine mind that has described it. Those twisted, and contorted old trees, "that stretch out their crooked branches, and take such hold of the imagination, that we remember them as humorists and odd-fellows." And then, as surrounded by these grotesque forms, and hushed in the noon-day repose of this Hawthorne's spell, how aptly might the still fall of his ruddy thoughts into your soul be symbolized by "the thump of a great

4. I.e., Timothy Dwight's four-volume *Travels in New-England and New-York* (1821–22).
5. From Hawthorne's introductory essay, *The Old Manse.*
6. Also from *The Old Manse*, in the description of the "little nook of a study": "It was here that Emerson wrote 'Nature'; for he was then an inhabitant of the Manse, and used to watch the Assyrian dawn and the Paphian sunset and moonrise, from the summit of our eastern hill." Hawthorne is paraphrasing chap. 3 of *Nature*: "Give me health and a day, and I will make the pomp of emperors ridiculous. The dawn is my Assyria; the sun-set and moon-rise my Paphos, and unimaginable realms of faerie; broad noon shall be my England of the senses and the understanding; the night shall be my Germany of mystic philosophy and dreams." Melville may not have understood that Hawthorne was paraphrasing Emerson: his first serious reading of Emerson apparently took place a few weeks later in the Hawthornes' house near Lenox.

apple, in the stillest afternoon, falling without a breath of wind, from the mere necessity of perfect ripeness"! For no less ripe than ruddy are the apples of the thoughts and fancies in this sweet Man of Mosses.

"Buds and Bird-Voices"—What a delicious thing is that!—"Will the world ever be so decayed, that Spring may not renew its greenness?"—And the "Fire-Worship." Was ever the hearth so glorified into an altar before? The mere title of that piece is better than any common work in fifty folio volumes. How exquisite is this:—"Nor did it lessen the charm of his soft, familiar courtesy and helpfulness, that the mighty spirit, were opportunity offered him, would run riot through the peaceful house, wrap its inmates in his terrible embrace, and leave nothing of them save their whitened bones. This possibility of mad destruction only made his domestic kindness the more beautiful and touching. It was so sweet of him, being endowed with such power, to dwell, day after day, and one long, lonesome night after another, on the dusky hearth, only now and then betraying his wild nature, by thrusting his red tongue out of the chimney-top! True, he had done much mischief in the world, and was pretty certain to do more, but his warm heart atoned for all. He was kindly to the race of man."

But he has still other apples, not quite so ruddy, though full as ripe:—apples, that have been left to wither on the tree, after the pleasant autumn gathering is past. The sketch of "The Old Apple Dealer" is conceived in the subtlest spirit of sadness; he whose "subdued and nerveless boyhood prefigured his abortive prime, which, likewise, contained within itself the prophecy and image of his lean and torpid age." Such touches as are in this piece can not proceed from any common heart. They argue such a depth of tenderness, such a boundless sympathy with all forms of being, such an omnipresent love, that we must needs say, that this Hawthorne is here almost alone in his generation,—at least, in the artistic manifestation of these things. Still more. Such touches as these,—and many, very many similar ones, all through his chapters—furnish clews, whereby we enter a little way into the intricate, profound heart where they originated. And we see, that suffering, some time or other and in some shape or other,—this only can enable any man to depict it in others. All over him, Hawthorne's melancholy rests like an Indian Summer, which, though bathing a whole country in one softness, still reveals the distinctive hue of every towering hill, and each far-winding vale.

But it is the least part of genius that attracts admiration. Where Hawthorne is known, he seems to be deemed a pleasant writer, with a pleasant style,—a sequestered, harmless man, from whom any deep and weighty thing would hardly be anticipated:—a man who means no meanings. But there is no man, in whom humor and love, like mountain peaks, soar to such a rapt height, as to receive the irradiations of the upper skies;—there is no man in whom humor and love are developed in that high form called genius; no such man can exist without also possessing, as the indispensable complement of these, a great, deep intellect, which drops down into the universe like a plummet. Or, love and humor are only the eyes, through which such an intellect views this world. The great beauty in such a mind is but the product of its strength. What, to all readers, can be more charming than the piece entitled "Monsieur du Miroir"; and to a reader at all capable of fully fathoming it, what, at the same time, can possess more mystical depth of meaning?—Yes, there he sits, and looks at me,—this "shape of mystery," this "identical Monsieur du Miroir."—

"Methinks I should tremble now, were his wizard power of gliding through all impediments in search of me, to place him suddenly before my eyes."

How profound, nay appalling, is the moral evolved by the "Earth's Holocaust"; where—beginning with the hollow follies and affectations of the world,—all vanities and empty theories and forms, are, one after another, and by an admirably graduated, growing comprehensiveness, thrown into the allegorical fire, till, at length, nothing is left but the all-engendering heart of man; which remaining still unconsumed, the great conflagration is naught.

Of a piece with this, is the "Intelligence Office," a wondrous symbolizing of the secret workings in men's souls. There are other sketches, still more charged with ponderous import.

"The Christmas Banquet," and "The Bosom Serpent" would be fine subjects for a curious and elaborate analysis, touching the conjectural parts of the mind that produced them. For spite of all the Indian-summer sunlight on the hither side of Hawthorne's soul, the other side—like the dark half of the physical sphere—is shrouded in a blackness, ten times black. But this darkness but gives more effect to the evermoving dawn, that forever advances through it, and circumnavigates his world. Whether Hawthorne has simply availed himself of this mystical blackness as a means to the wondrous effects he makes it to produce in his lights and shades; or whether there really lurks in him, perhaps unknown to himself, a touch of Puritanic gloom,—this, I cannot altogether tell. Certain it is, however, that this great power of blackness in him derives its force from its appeals to that Calvinistic sense of Innate Depravity and Original Sin, from whose visitations, in some shape or other, no deeply thinking mind is always and wholly free. For, in certain moods, no man can weigh this world, without throwing in something, somehow like Original Sin, to strike the uneven balance. At all events, perhaps no writer has ever wielded this terrific thought with greater terror than this same harmless Hawthorne. Still more: this black conceit pervades him, through and through. You may be witched by his sunlight,—transported by the bright gildings in the skies he builds over you;—but there is the blackness of darkness beyond; and even his bright gildings but fringe, and play upon the edges of thunder-clouds.—In one word, the world is mistaken in this Nathaniel Hawthorne. He himself must often have smiled at its absurd misconception of him. He is immeasurably deeper than the plummet of the mere critic. For it is not the brain that can test such a man; it is only the heart. You cannot come to know greatness by inspecting it; there is no glimpse to be caught of it, except by intuition; you need not ring it, you but touch it, and you find it is gold.

Now it is that blackness in Hawthorne, of which I have spoken, that so fixes and fascinates me. It may be, nevertheless, that it is too largely developed in him. Perhaps he does not give us a ray of his light for every shade of his dark. But however this may be, this blackness it is that furnishes the infinite obscure of his background,—that background, against which Shakespeare plays his grandest conceits, the things that have made for Shakespeare his loftiest, but most circumscribed renown, as the profoundest of thinkers. For by philosophers Shakespeare is not adored as the great man of tragedy and comedy.— "Off with his head! so much for Buckingham!"[7] this sort of rant, interlined by another hand, brings down the house,—those mistaken souls, who dream of

---

7. Line interpolated into Shakespeare's *Richard III* by Colley Cibber (1671–1757) in his revision of the play.

Shakespeare as a mere man of Richard-the-Third humps, and Macbeth daggers. But it is those deep far-away things in him; those occasional flashings-forth of the intuitive Truth in him; those short, quick probings at the very axis of reality:—these are the things that make Shakespeare, Shakespeare. Through the mouths of the dark characters of Hamlet, Timon, Lear, and Iago, he craftily says, or sometimes insinuates the things, which we feel to be so terrifically true, that it were all but madness for any good man, in his own proper character, to utter, or even hint of them. Tormented into desperation, Lear the frantic King tears off the mask, and speaks the sane madness of vital truth. But, as I before said, it is the least part of genius that attracts admiration. And so, much of the blind, unbridled admiration that has been heaped upon Shakespeare, has been lavished upon the least part of him. And few of his endless commentators and critics seem to have remembered, or even perceived, that the immediate products of a great mind are not so great, as that undeveloped, (and sometimes undevelopable) yet dimly-discernible greatness, to which these immediate products are but the infallible indices. In Shakespeare's tomb lies infinitely more than Shakespeare ever wrote. And if I magnify Shakespeare, it is not so much for what he did do, as for what he did not do, or refrained from doing. For in this world of lies, Truth is forced to fly like a scared white doe in the woodlands; and only by cunning glimpses will she reveal herself, as in Shakespeare and other masters of the great Art of Telling the Truth,—even though it be covertly, and by snatches.

But if this view of the all-popular Shakespeare be seldom taken by his readers, and if very few who extol him, have ever read him deeply, or, perhaps, only have seen him on the tricky stage, (which alone made, and is still making him his mere mob renown)—if few men have time, or patience, or palate, for the spiritual truth as it is in that great genius;—it is, then, no matter of surprise that in a contemporaneous age, Nathaniel Hawthorne is a man, as yet, almost utterly mistaken among men. Here and there, in some quiet arm-chair in the noisy town, or some deep nook among the noiseless mountains, he may be appreciated for something of what he is. But unlike Shakespeare, who was forced to the contrary course by circumstances. Hawthorne (either from simple disinclination, or else from inaptitude) refrains from all the popularizing noise and show of broad farce, and blood-besmeared tragedy; content with the still, rich utterances of a great intellect in repose, and which sends few thoughts into circulation, except they be arterialized at his large warm lungs, and expanded in his honest heart.

Nor need you fix upon that blackness in him, if it suit you not. Nor, indeed, will all readers discern it, for it is, mostly, insinuated to those who may best understand it, and account for it; it is not obtruded upon every one alike.

Some may start to read of Shakespeare and Hawthorne on the same page. They may say, that if an illustration were needed, a lesser light might have sufficed to elucidate this Hawthorne, this small man of yesterday. But I am not, willingly, one of those, who, as touching Shakespeare at least, exemplify the maxim of Rochefoucauld,[8] that "we exalt the reputation of some, in order to depress that of others";—who, to teach all noble-souled aspirants that there is no hope for them, pronounce Shakespeare absolutely unapproachable. But Shakespeare has been approached. There are minds that have gone as far as

---

8. François de la Rochefoucauld (1613–1680), French moralist.

Shakespeare into the universe. And hardly a mortal man, who, at some time or other, has not felt as great thoughts in him as any you will find in Hamlet. We must not inferentially malign mankind for the sake of any one man, whoever he may be. This is too cheap a purchase of contentment for conscious mediocrity to make. Besides, this absolute and unconditional adoration of Shakespeare has grown to be a part of our Anglo-Saxon superstitions. The Thirty-Nine Articles[9] are now Forty. Intolerance has come to exist in this matter. You must believe in Shakespeare's unapproachability, or quit the country. But what sort of a belief is this for an American, a man who is bound to carry republican progressiveness into Literature, as well as into Life? Believe me, my friends, that men not very much inferior to Shakespeare, are this day being born on the banks of the Ohio. And the day will come, when you shall say who reads a book by an Englishman that is a modern?[1] The great mistake seems to be, that even with those Americans who look forward to the coming of a great literary genius among us, they somehow fancy he will come in the costume of Queen Elizabeth's day,—be a writer of dramas founded upon old English history, or the tales of Boccaccio. Whereas, great geniuses are parts of the times; they themselves are the times; and possess a correspondent coloring. It is of a piece with the Jews, who while their Shiloh[2] was meekly walking in their streets, were still praying for his magnificent coming; looking for him in a chariot, who was already among them on an ass. Nor must we forget, that, in his own life-time, Shakespeare was not Shakespeare, but only Master William Shakespeare of the shrewd, thriving business firm of Condell, Shakespeare & Co., proprietors of the Globe Theatre in London; and by a courtly author, of the name of Chettle,[3] was hooted at, as an "upstart crow" beautified "with other birds' feathers." For, mark it well, imitation is often the first charge brought against real originality. Why this is so, there is not space to set forth here. You must have plenty of sea-room to tell the Truth in; especially, when it seems to have an aspect of newness, as America did in 1492, though it was then just as old, and perhaps older than Asia, only those sagacious philosophers, the common sailors, had never seen it before; swearing it was all water and moonshine there.

Now, I do not say that Nathaniel of Salem is a greater than William of Avon, or as great. But the difference between the two men is by no means immeasurable. Not a very great deal more, and Nathaniel were verily William.

This, too, I mean, that if Shakespeare has not been equalled, give the world time, and he is sure to be surpassed, in one hemisphere or the other. Nor will it at all do to say, that the world is getting grey and grizzled now, and has lost that fresh charm which she wore of old, and by virtue of which the great poets of past times made themselves what we esteem them to be. Not so. The world is as young today, as when it was created; and this Vermont morning dew is as wet to my feet, as Eden's dew to Adam's. Nor has Nature been all over ransacked by our progenitors, so that no new charms and mysteries remain for this latter generation to find. Far from it. The trillionth part has not yet been

---

9. Doctrines of the Church of England; here, any national set of beliefs.

1. Reference to a famous insult by Sydney Smith, a Scottish critic, in the *Edinburgh Review*, vol. 33 (January 1820): "In the four quarters of the globe, who reads an American book? Or goes to an American play?

Or looks at an American picture or statue?"

2. Messiah, Christ.

3. Robert Greene (1558?–1592), not Henry Chettle (c. 1560–c. 1607), made these slurs against the young Shakespeare in *Groatsworth of Witte Bought with a Million of Repentance* (1592).

said; and all that has been said, but multiplies the avenues to what remains to be said. It is not so much paucity, as superabundance of material that seems to incapacitate modern authors.

Let America then prize and cherish her writers; yea, let her glorify them. They are not so many in number, as to exhaust her good-will. And while she has good kith and kin of her own, to take to her bosom, let her not lavish her embraces upon the household of an alien. For believe it or not England, after all, is, in many things, an alien to us. China has more bowels of real love for us than she. But even were there no Hawthorne, no Emerson, no Whittier, no Irving, no Bryant, no Dana, no Cooper, no Willis (not the author of the "Darter," but the author of the "Belfry Pigeon")—were there none of these, and others of like calibre,[4] nevertheless, let America first praise mediocrity even, in her own children, before she praises (for everywhere, merit demands acknowledgment from every one) the best excellence in the children of any other land. Let her own authors, I say, have the priority of appreciation. I was much pleased with a hot-headed Carolina cousin of mine, who once said,— "If there were no other American to stand by, in Literature,—why, then, I would stand by Pop Emmons and his 'Fredoniad,'[5] and till a better epic came along, swear it was not very far behind the 'Iliad'." Take away the words, and in spirit he was sound.

Not that American genius needs patronage in order to expand. For that explosive sort of stuff will expand though screwed up in a vice, and burst it, though it were triple steel. It is for the nation's sake, and not for her authors' sake, that I would have America be heedful of the increasing greatness among her writers. For how great the shame, if other nations should be before her, in crowning her heroes of the pen. But this is almost the case now. American authors have received more just and discriminating praise (however loftily and ridiculously given, in certain cases) even from some Englishmen, than from their own countrymen. There are hardly five critics in America; and several of them are asleep. As for patronage, it is the American author who now patronizes his country, and not his country him. And if at times some among them appeal to the people for more recognition, it is not always with selfish motives, but patriotic ones.

It is true, that but few of them as yet have evinced that decided originality which merits great praise. But that graceful writer,[6] who perhaps of all Americans has received the most plaudits from his own country for his productions,—that very popular and amiable writer, however good, and self-reliant in many things, perhaps owes his chief reputation to the self-acknowledged imitation of a foreign model, and to the studied avoidance of all topics but smooth ones. But it is better to fail in originality, than to succeed in imitation. He who has never failed somewhere, that man can not be great. Failure is the true test of greatness. And if it be said, that continual success is a proof that a man wisely knows his powers,—it is only to be added, that, in that case, he

4. Duyckinck deleted these names, replacing them with "But even were there no strong literary individualities among us, as there are some dozen at least"; probably he felt it prudent to avoid personalities. The contemporaries cited by Melville are included in this anthology except for his friend Richard Henry Dana, Jr. (1815–1882), author of *Two Years before the Mast*, and his (and his late brother Gansevoort's) friend Nathaniel Parker Willis (1806–1867), author of the prose *Dashes at Life with a Free Pencil* and of poems, among them *The Belfry Pigeon*. Merton M. Sealts, Jr., was the first to work out Duyckink's responsibility for this major piece of toning down.

5. Richard Emmons (b. 1788) wrote the *Fredoniad; or Independence Preserved—an Epic Poem of the War of 1812*. The "hot-headed Carolina cousin" is invented to fit the persona of the vacationing Virginian.

6. Washington Irving.

knows them to be small. Let us believe it, then, once for all, that there is no hope for us in these smooth pleasing writers that know their powers. Without malice, but to speak the plain fact, they but furnish an appendix to Goldsmith,[7] and other English authors. And we want no American Goldsmiths; nay, we want no American Miltons. It were the vilest thing you could say of a true American author, that he were an American Tompkins.[8] Call him an American, and have done; for you can not say a nobler thing of him.—But it is not meant that all American writers should studiously cleave to nationality in their writings; only this, no American writer should write like an Englishman, or a Frenchman; let him write like a man, for then he will be sure to write like an American. Let us away with this leaven of literary flunkyism towards England. If either must play the flunky in this thing, let England do it, not us. While we are rapidly preparing for that political supremacy among the nations, which prophetically awaits us at the close of the present century; in a literary point of view, we are deplorably unprepared for it; and we seem studious to remain so. Hitherto, reasons might have existed why this should be; but no good reason exists now. And all that is requisite to amendment in this matter, is simply this: that, while freely acknowledging all excellence, everywhere, we should refrain from unduly lauding foreign writers, and, at the same time, duly recognize the meritorious writers that are our own;—those writers, who breathe that unshackled, democratic spirit of Christianity in all things, which now takes the practical lead in this world, though at the same time led by ourselves—us Americans. Let us boldly contemn all imitation, though it comes to us graceful and fragrant as the morning; and foster all originality, though, at first, it be crabbed and ugly as our own pine knots. And if any of our authors fail, or seem to fail, then, in the words of my enthusiastic Carolina cousin, let us clap him on the shoulder, and back him against all Europe for his second round. The truth is, that in our point of view, this matter of a national literature has come to such a pass with us, that in some sense we must turn bullies, else the day is lost, or superiority so far beyond us, that we can hardly say it will ever be ours.

And now, my countrymen, as an excellent author, of your own flesh and blood,—an unimitating, and, perhaps, in his way, an inimitable man—whom better can I commend to you, in the first place, than Nathaniel Hawthorne. He is one of the new, and far better generation of your writers. The smell of your beeches and hemlocks is upon him; your own broad prairies are in his soul; and if you travel away inland into his deep and noble nature, you will hear the far roar of his Niagara. Give not over to future generations the glad duty of acknowledging him for what he is. Take that joy to yourself, in your own generation; and so shall he feel those grateful impulses in him, that may possibly prompt him to the full flower of some still greater achievement in your eyes. And by confessing him, you thereby confess others; you brace the whole brotherhood. For genius, all over the world, stands hand in hand, and one shock of recognition runs the whole circle round.

In treating of Hawthorne, or rather of Hawthorne in his writings (for I never saw the man; and in the chances of a quiet plantation life, remote from his haunts, perhaps never shall) in treating of his works, I say, I have thus far omitted all mention of his "Twice Told Tales," and "Scarlet Letter."[9] Both

---

7. Irving was often called the American Goldsmith.   9. Published in 1837 and 1850, respectively.
8. Flunky, from the English type name for a butler.

are excellent; but full of such manifold, strange and diffusive beauties, that time would all but fail me, to point the half of them out. But there are things in those two books, which, had they been written in England a century ago, Nathaniel Hawthorne had utterly displaced many of the bright names we now revere on authority. But I am content to leave Hawthorne to himself, and to the infallible finding of posterity; and however great may be the praise I have bestowed upon him, I feel, that in so doing, I have more served and honored myself, than him. For, at bottom, great excellence is praise enough to itself; but the feeling of a sincere and appreciative love and admiration towards it, this is relieved by utterance; and warm, honest praise ever leaves a pleasant flavor in the mouth; and it is an honorable thing to confess to what is honorable in others.

But I cannot leave my subject yet. No man can read a fine author, and relish him to his very bones, while he reads, without subsequently fancying to himself some ideal image of the man and his mind. And if you rightly look for it, you will almost always find that the author himself has somewhere furnished you with his own picture. For poets (whether in prose or verse), being painters of Nature, are like their brethren of the pencil, the true portrait-painters, who, in the multitude of likenesses to be sketched, do not invariably omit their own; and in all high instances, they paint them without any vanity, though, at times, with a lurking something, that would take several pages to properly define.

I submit it, then, to those best acquainted with the man personally, whether the following is not Nathaniel Hawthorne;—and to himself, whether something involved in it does not express the temper of his mind,—that lasting temper of all true, candid men—a seeker, not a finder yet:—

"A man now entered, in neglected attire, with the aspect of a thinker, but somewhat too rough-hewn and brawny for a scholar. His face was full of sturdy vigor, with some finer and keener attribute beneath; though harsh at first, it was tempered with the glow of a large, warm heart, which had force enough to heat his powerful intellect through and through. He advanced to the Intelligencer, and looked at him with a glance of such stern sincerity, that perhaps few secrets were beyond its scope.

" 'I seek for Truth,' said he."[1]

Twenty-four hours have elapsed since writing the foregoing. I have just returned from the hay mow, charged more and more with love and admiration of Hawthorne. For I have just been gleaning through the "Mosses," picking up many things here and there that had previously escaped me. And I found that but to glean after this man, is better than to be in at the harvest of others. To be frank (though, perhaps, rather foolish), notwithstanding what I wrote yesterday of these Mosses, I had not then culled them all; but had, nevertheless, been sufficiently sensible of the subtle essence, in them, as to write as I did. To what infinite height of loving wonder and admiration I may yet be borne, when by repeatedly banquetting on these Mosses, I shall have thoroughly incorporated their whole stuff into my being,—that, I can not tell. But already I feel that this Hawthorne has dropped germinous seeds into my soul. He expands and deepens down, the more I contemplate him; and further, and

---

1. From *The Intelligence Office* (i.e., "the employment agency").

further, shoots his strong New-England roots into the hot soil of my Southern soul.

By careful reference to the "Table of Contents," I now find, that I have gone through all the sketches; but that when I yesterday wrote, I had not at all read two particular pieces, to which I now desire to call special attention,—"A Select Party," and "Young Goodman Brown." Here, be it said to all those whom this poor fugitive scrawl of mine may tempt to the perusal of the "Mosses," that they must on no account suffer themselves to be trifled with, disappointed, or deceived by the triviality of many of the titles to these Sketches. For in more than one instance, the title utterly belies the piece. It is as if rustic demijohns containing the very best and costliest of Falernian and Tokay, were labeled "Cider," "Perry," and "Elder-berry Wine." The truth seems to be, that like many other geniuses, this Man of Mosses takes great delight in hoodwinking the world,—at least, with respect to himself. Personally, I doubt not, that he rather prefers to be generally esteemed but a so-so sort of author; being willing to reserve the thorough and acute appreciation of what he is, to that party most qualified to judge—that is, to himself. Besides, at the bottom of their natures, men like Hawthorne, in many things, deem the plaudits of the public such strong presumptive evidence of mediocrity in the object of them, that it would in some degree render them doubtful of their own powers, did they hear much and vociferous braying concerning them in the public pastures. True, I have been braying myself (if you please to be witty enough, to have it so) but then I claim to be the first that has so brayed in this particular matter; and therefore, while pleading guilty to the charge, still claim all the merit due to originality.

But with whatever motive, playful or profound, Nathaniel Hawthorne has chosen to entitle his pieces in the manner he has, it is certain, that some of them are directly calculated to deceive—egregiously deceive—the superficial skimmer of pages. To be downright and candid once more, let me cheerfully say, that two of these titles did dolefully dupe no less an eagle-eyed reader than myself; and that, too, after I had been impressed with a sense of the great depth and breadth of this American man. "Who in the name of thunder" (as the country-people say in this neighborhood), "who in the name of thunder," would anticipate any marvel in a piece entitled "Young Goodman Brown"? You would of course suppose that it was a simple little tale, intended as a supplement to "Goody Two Shoes." Whereas, it is deep as Dante; nor can you finish it, without addressing the author in his own words—"It is yours to penetrate, in every bosom, the deep mystery of sin." And with Young Goodman, too, in allegorical pursuit of his Puritan wife, you cry out in your anguish,—

> "Faith!" shouted Goodman Brown, in a voice of agony and desperation; and the echoes of the forest mocked him, crying—"Faith! Faith!" as if bewildered wretches were seeking her all through the wilderness.

Now this same piece, entitled "Young Goodman Brown," is one of the two that I had not all read yesterday; and I allude to it now, because it is, in itself, such a strong positive illustration of that blackness in Hawthorne, which I had assumed from the mere occasional shadows of it, as revealed in several of the other sketches. But had I previously perused "Young Goodman Brown," I should have been at no pains to draw the conclusion, which I came to, at a time, when I was ignorant that the book contained one such direct and unqualified manifestation of it.

The other piece of the two referred to, is entitled "A Select Party," which, in my first simplicity upon originally taking hold of the book, I fancied must treat of some pumpkin-pie party in Old Salem, or some Chowder Party on Cape Cod. Whereas, by all the gods of Peedee![2] it is the sweetest and sublimest thing that has been written since Spenser wrote. Nay, there is nothing in Spenser that surpasses it, perhaps, nothing that equals it. And the test is this: read any canto in "The Faery Queen," and then read "A Select Party," and decide which pleases you the most,—that is, if you are qualified to judge. Do not be frightened at this; for when Spenser was alive, he was thought of very much as Hawthorne is now,—was generally accounted just such a "gentle" harmless man. It may be, that to common eyes, the sublimity of Hawthorne seems lost in his sweetness,—as perhaps in this same "Select Party" of his; for whom, he has builded so august a dome of sunset clouds, and served them on richer plate, than Belshazzar's when he banquetted his lords in Babylon.[3]

But my chief business now, is to point out a particular page in this piece, having reference to an honored guest, who under the name of "The Master Genius" but in the guise "of a young man of poor attire, with no insignia of rank or acknowledged eminence," is introduced to the Man of Fancy, who is the giver of the feast. Now the page having reference to this "Master Genius", so happily expresses much of what I yesterday wrote, touching the coming of the literary Shiloh of America, that I cannot but be charmed by the coincidence; especially, when it shows such a parity of ideas, at least, in this one point, between a man like Hawthorne and a man like me.

And here, let me throw out another conceit of mine touching this American Shiloh, or "Master Genius," as Hawthorne calls him. May it not be, that this commanding mind has not been, is not, and never will be, individually developed in any one man? And would it, indeed, appear so unreasonable to suppose, that this great fullness and overflowing may be, or may be destined to be, shared by a plurality of men of genius? Surely, to take the very greatest example on record, Shakespeare cannot be regarded as in himself the concretion of all the genius of his time; nor as so immeasurably beyond Marlowe, Webster, Ford, Beaumont, Jonson, that those great men can be said to share none of his power? For one, I conceive that there were dramatists in Elizabeth's day, between whom and Shakespeare the distance was by no means great. Let anyone, hitherto little acquainted with those neglected old authors, for the first time read them thoroughly, or even read Charles Lamb's Specimens of them, and he will be amazed at the wondrous ability of those Anaks[4] of men, and shocked at this renewed example of the fact, that Fortune has more to do with fame than merit,—though, without merit, lasting fame there can be none.

Nevertheless, it would argue too illy of my country were this maxim to hold good concerning Nathaniel Hawthorne, a man, who already, in some few minds, has shed "such a light, as never illuminates the earth, save when a great heart burns as the household fire of a grand intellect."

---

2. River in the Carolinas.
3. Daniel 5.1: "Belshazzar the king made a great feast to a thousand of his lords, and drank wine before the thousand."

4. Giants (Joshua 11.21). Charles Lamb (1775–1834), editor of *Specimens of the English Dramatic Poets Who Lived about the Time of Shakespeare* (1808).

The words are his,—in the "Select Party"; and they are a magnificent setting to a coincident sentiment of my own, but ramblingly expressed yesterday, in reference to himself. Gainsay it who will, as I now write, I am Posterity speaking by proxy—and after times will make it more than good, when I declare—that the American, who up to the present day, has evinced, in Literature, the largest brain with the largest heart, that man is Nathaniel Hawthorne. Moreover, that whatever Nathaniel Hawthorne may hereafter write, "The Mosses from an Old Manse" will be ultimately accounted his masterpiece. For there is a sure, though a secret sign in some works which proves the culmination of the powers (only the developable ones, however) that produced them. But I am by no means desirous of the glory of a prophet. I pray Heaven that Hawthorne may *yet* prove me an impostor in this prediction. Especially, as I somehow cling to the strange fancy, that, in all men, hiddenly reside certain wondrous, occult properties—as in some plants and minerals—which by some happy but very rare accident (as bronze was discovered by the melting of the iron and brass in the burning of Corinth) may chance to be called forth here on earth; not entirely waiting for their better discovery in the more congenial, blessed atmosphere of heaven.

Once more—for it is hard to be finite upon an infinite subject, and all subjects are infinite. By some people, this entire scrawl of mine may be esteemed altogether unnecessary, inasmuch, "as years ago" (they may say) "we found out the rich and rare stuff in this Hawthorne, whom you now parade forth, as if only *yourself* were the discoverer of this Portuguese diamond[5] in our Literature."—But even granting all this; and adding to it, the assumption that the books of Hawthorne have sold by the five-thousand,—what does that signify?—They should be sold by the hundred-thousand; and read by the million; and admired by every one who is capable of Admiration.

1850

LETTERS TO HAWTHORNE[1]

Melville to Hawthorne

[*Melville criticizes* The House of the Seven Gables *in the* Pittsfield Secret Review]

Pittsfield, Wednesday morning, April 16(?), 1851

My dear Hawthorne,

Concerning the young gentleman's shoes, I desire to say that a pair to fit him, of the desired pattern, cannot be had in all Pittsfield,[2]—a fact which sadly impairs that metropolitan pride I formerly took in the capital of Berkshire. Henceforth Pittsfield must hide its head. However, if a pair of *bootees* will at

---

5. A diamond cut according to an elaborate system—two rows of rhomboidal and three rows of triangular facets above and below the girdle (the widest part).
1. Some of Melville's letters to Hawthorne are known to be extant. Others are missing and known only in transcriptions by various members of Hawthorne's family. The letters of April 16 (?), June 1 (?), and June 29,

1851, are from Julian Hawthorne, *Nathaniel Hawthorne and His Wife* (1884), and letters of July 22 and November 17 (?), 1851, are from Rose Hawthorne Lathrop, *Memories of Hawthorne* (1898).
2. Melville had been commissioned to look for shoes for the Hawthornes' son Julian (1846–1934), then almost five.

all answer, Pittsfield will be very happy to provide them. Pray mention all this to Mrs. Hawthorne, and command me.

"The House of the Seven Gables: A Romance.[3] By Nathaniel Hawthorne. One vol. 16mo, pp. 344." The contents of this book do not belie its rich, clustering, romantic title. With great enjoyment we spent almost an hour in each separate gable. This book is like a fine old chamber, abundantly, but still judiciously, furnished with precisely that sort of furniture best fitted to furnish it. There are rich hangings, wherein are braided scenes from tragedies! There is old china with rare devices, set out on the carved buffet; there are long and indolent lounges to throw yourself upon; there is an admirable sideboard, plentifully stored with good viands; there is a smell as of old wine in the pantry; and finally, in one corner, there is a dark little black-letter volume in golden clasps, entitled "Hawthorne: A Problem." It has delighted us; it has piqued a re-perusal; it has robbed us of a day, and made us a present of a whole year of thoughtfulness; it has bred great exhilaration and exultation with the remembrance that the architect of the Gables resides only six miles off, and not three thousand miles away, in England, say. We think the book, for pleasantness of running interest, surpasses the other works of the author. The curtains are more drawn; the sun comes in more; genialities peep out more. Were we to particularize what most struck us in the deeper passages, we would point out the scene where Clifford, for a moment, would fain throw himself forth from the window to join the procession; or the scene where the judge is left seated in his ancestral chair. Clifford is full of an awful truth throughout. He is conceived in the finest, truest spirit. He is no caricature. He is Clifford. And here we would say that, did circumstances permit, we should like nothing better than to devote an elaborate and careful paper to the full consideration and analysis of the purport and significance of what so strongly characterizes all of this author's writings. There is a certain tragic phase of humanity which, in our opinion, was never more powerfully embodied than by Hawthorne. We mean the tragicalness of human thought in its own unbiassed, native, and profounder workings. We think that into no recorded mind has the intense feeling of the visible truth ever entered more deeply than into this man's. By visible truth, we mean the apprehension of the absolute condition of present things as they strike the eye of the man who fears them not, though they do their worst to him,—the man who, like Russia or the British Empire, declares himself a sovereign nature (in himself) amid the powers of heaven, hell, and earth. He may perish; but so long as he exists he insists upon treating with all Powers upon an equal basis. If any of those other Powers choose to withhold certain secrets, let them; that does not impair my sovereignty in myself; that does not make me tributary. And perhaps, after all, there is *no* secret. We incline to think that the Problem of the Universe is like the Freemason's mighty secret, so terrible to all children. It turns out, at last, to consist in a triangle, a mallet, and an apron,—nothing more! We incline to think that God cannot explain His own secrets, and that He would like a little information upon certain points Himself. We mortals astonish Him as much as He us. But it is this *Being* of the matter; there lies the knot with which we choke ourselves. As soon as you say *Me*, a *God*, a *Nature*, so soon you jump off from

3. Newly published; five days earlier Hawthorne had given Melville a copy in person. What follows is a remarkable response to the book, but it is also an acute parody of the postures and phrases of contemporary reviewers.

your stool and hang from the beam. Yes, that word is the hangman. Take God out of the dictionary, and you would have Him in the street.

There is the grand truth about Nathaniel Hawthorne. He says NO! in thunder; but the Devil himself cannot make him say *yes*. For all men who say *yes*, lie; and all men who say *no*,—why, they are in the happy condition of judicious, unincumbered travellers in Europe; they cross the frontiers into Eternity with nothing but a carpet-bag,—that is to say, the Ego. Whereas those *yes*-gentry, they travel with heaps of baggage, and, damn them! they will never get through the Custom House. What's the reason, Mr. Hawthorne, that in the last stages of metaphysics a fellow always falls to *swearing* so? I could rip an hour. You see, I began with a little criticism extracted for your benefit from the "Pittsfield Secret Review," and here I have landed in Africa.

Walk down one of these mornings and see me. No nonsense; come. Remember me to Mrs. Hawthorne and the children.

H. Melville

P.S. The marriage of Phœbe with the daguerreotypist is a fine stroke, because of his turning out to be a *Maule*.[4] If you pass Hepzibah's cent-shop, buy me a Jim Crow (fresh) and send it to me by Ned Higgins.

Melville to Hawthorne

[The Whale—*"All My Books Are Botches"*]

June 1(?), 1851

My dear Hawthorne,

I should have been rumbling down to you in my pine-board chariot a long time ago, were it not that for some weeks past I have been more busy than you can well imagine,—out of doors,—building and patching and tinkering away in all directions. Besides, I had my crops to get in,—corn and potatoes (I hope to show you some famous ones by and by),—and many other things to attend to, all accumulating upon this one particular season. I work myself; and at night my bodily sensations are akin to those I have so often felt before, when a hired man, doing my day's work from sun to sun. But I mean to continue visiting you until you tell me that my visits are both supererogatory and superfluous. With no son of man do I stand upon any etiquette or ceremony, except the Christian ones of charity and honesty. I am told, my fellow-man, that there is an aristocracy of the brain. Some men have boldly advocated and asserted it. Schiller[1] seems to have done so, though I don't know much about him. At any rate, it is true that there have been those who, while earnest in behalf of political equality, still accept the intellectual estates. And I can well perceive, I think, how a man of superior mind can, by its intense cultivation, bring himself, as it were, into a certain spontaneous aristocracy of feeling,—exceedingly nice and fastidious,—similar to that which, in an English Howard,[2] conveys a torpedo-fish thrill at the slightest contact with a social plebeian. So, when you see or hear of my ruthless democracy on all sides, you may

---

4. Melville is punning on *Maule*, the name of a family in Hawthorne's book: with a maul (a heavy club or hammer) one can make powerful strokes.
1. Johann Christoph Friedrich von Schiller

(1759–1805), German poet; where Melville formed his early impression of Schiller is not certain.
2. Any member of the great English family.

possibly feel a touch of a shrink, or something of that sort. It is but nature to be shy of a mortal who boldly declares that a thief in jail is as honorable a personage as Gen. George Washington. This is ludicrous. But Truth is the silliest thing under the sun. Try to get a living by the Truth—and go to the Soup Societies. Heavens! Let any clergyman try to preach the Truth from its very stronghold, the pulpit, and they would ride him out of his church on his own pulpit bannister. It can hardly be doubted that all Reformers are bottomed upon the truth, more or less; and to the world at large are not reformers almost universally laughing-stocks? Why so? Truth is ridiculous to men. Thus easily in my room here do I, conceited and garrulous, reverse[3] the test of my Lord Shaftesbury.[4]

It seems an inconsistency to assert unconditional democracy in all things, and yet confess a dislike to all mankind—in the mass. But not so.—But it's an endless sermon,—no more of it. I began by saying that the reason I have not been to Lenox is this,—in the evening I feel completely done up, as the phrase is, and incapable of the long jolting to get to your house and back. In a week or so, I go to New York, to bury myself in a third-story room, and work and slave on my "Whale" while it is driving through the press. *That* is the only way I can finish it now,—I am so pulled hither and thither by circumstances. The calm, the coolness, the silent grass-growing mood in which a man *ought* always to compose,—that, I fear, can seldom be mine. Dollars damn me; and the malicious Devil is forever grinning in upon me, holding the door ajar. My dear Sir, a presentiment is on me,—I shall at last be worn out and perish, like an old nutmeg-grater, grated to pieces by the constant attrition of the wood, that is, the nutmeg. What I feel most moved to write, that is banned,—it will not pay. Yet, altogether, write the *other* way I cannot. So the product is a final hash, and all my books are botches. I'm rather sore, perhaps, in this letter; but see my hand!—four blisters on this palm, made by hoes and hammers within the last few days. It is a rainy morning; so I am indoors, and all work suspended. I feel cheerfully disposed, and therefore I write a little bluely. Would the Gin were here! If ever, my dear Hawthorne, in the eternal times that are to come, you and I shall sit down in Paradise, in some little shady corner by ourselves; and if we shall by any means be able to smuggle a basket of champagne there (I won't believe in a Temperance Heaven), and if we shall then cross our celestial legs in the celestial grass that is forever tropical, and strike our glasses and our heads together, till both musically ring in concert,—then, O my dear fellow-mortal, how shall we pleasantly discourse of all the things manifold which now so distress us,—when all the earth shall be but a reminiscence, yea, its final dissolution an antiquity. Then shall songs be composed as when wars are over; humorous, comic songs,—"Oh, when I lived in that queer little hole called the world," or, "Oh, when I toiled and sweated below," or, "Oh, when I knocked and was knocked in the fight"—yes, let us look forward to such things. Let us swear that, though now we sweat, yet it is because of the dry heat which is indispensable to the nourishment of the vine which is to bear the grapes that are to give us the champagne hereafter.

---

3. The conjectural emendation of Merrell R. Davis and William H. Gilman in their edition of Melville's *Letters* (1960). The first printing reads *revere*. Davis and Gilman argue, "Whereas Shaftesbury is saying that you can know a thing is true if it survives ridicule, Melville is saying that you can know a thing is true because it is considered ridiculous."
4. Melville refers to the arguments of Anthony Ashley Cooper, Lord Shaftesbury (1671–1713), in *Characteristicks of Men, Manners, Opinions, and Times* (1711).

But I was talking about the "Whale." As the fishermen say, "he's in his flurry"[5] when I left him some three weeks ago. I'm going to take him by his jaw, however, before long, and finish him up in some fashion or other. What's the use of elaborating what, in its very essence, is so short-lived as a modern book? Though I wrote the Gospels in this century, I should die in the gutter.— I talk all about myself, and this is selfishness and egotism. Granted. But how help it? I am writing to you; I know little about you, but something about myself. So I write about myself,—at least, to you. Don't trouble yourself, though, about writing; and don't trouble yourself about visiting; and when you *do* visit, don't trouble yourself about talking. I will do all the writing and visiting and talking myself.—By the way, in the last "Dollar Magazine" I read "The Unpardonable Sin."[6] He was a sad fellow, that Ethan Brand. I have no doubt you are by this time responsible for many a shake and tremor of the tribe of "general readers." It is a frightful poetical creed that the cultivation of the brain eats out the heart. But it's my *prose* opinion that in most cases, in those men who have fine brains and work them well, the heart extends down to hams. And though you smoke them with the fire of tribulation, yet, like veritable hams, the head only gives the richer and the better flavor. I stand for the heart. To the dogs with the head! I had rather be a fool with a heart, than Jupiter Olympus with his head. The reason the mass of men fear God, and *at bottom dislike* Him, is because they rather distrust His heart, and fancy Him all brain like a watch. (You perceive I employ a capital initial in the pronoun referring to the Deity; don't you think there is a slight dash of flunkeyism in that usage?) Another thing. I was in New York for four-and-twenty hours the other day, and saw a portrait of N. H. And I have seen and heard many flattering (in a publisher's point of view) allusions to the "Seven Gables." And I have seen "Tales," and "A New Volume" announced, by N. H. So upon the whole, I say to myself, this N. H. is in the ascendant. My dear Sir, they begin to patronize. All Fame is patronage. Let me be infamous: there is no patronage in *that*. What "reputation" H. M. has is horrible. Think of it! To go down to posterity is bad enough, any way; but to go down as a "man who lived among the cannibals"! When I speak of posterity, in reference to myself, I only mean the babies who will probably be born in the moment immediately ensuing upon my giving up the ghost. I shall go down to some of them, in all likelihood. "Typee" will be given to them, perhaps, with their gingerbread. I have come to regard this matter of Fame as the most transparent of all vanities. I read Solomon[7] more and more, and every time see deeper and deeper and unspeakable meanings in him. I did not think of Fame, a year ago, as I do now. My development has been all within a few years past. I am like one of those seeds taken out of the Egyptian Pyramids, which, after being three thousand years a seed and nothing but a seed, being planted in English soil, it developed itself, grew to greenness, and then fell to mould. So I. Until I was twenty-five, I had no development at all. From my twenty-fifth year I date my life. Three weeks have scarcely passed, at any time between then and now, that I have not unfolded within myself. But I feel that I am now come to the

---

5. In his death spasms. *The Whale* was Melville's working title for his book and was in fact the title of the English edition; *Moby-Dick* was a last-minute substitute for the title of the American edition.
6. *Holden's Dollar Magazine* was then edited by Evert

and George Duyckinck, friends of both Hawthorne and Melville; in *Holden's* Melville had just read the Hawthorne story, now known as *Ethan Brand.*
7. I.e., Ecclesiastes.

inmost leaf of the bulb, and that shortly the flower must fall to the mould. It seems to me now that Solomon was the truest man who ever spoke, and yet that he a little *managed* the truth with a view to popular conservatism; or else there have been many corruptions and interpolations of the text.—In reading some of Goethe's sayings, so worshipped by his votaries, I came across this, *"Live in the all."*[8] That is to say, your separate identity is but a wretched one,—good; but get out of yourself, spread and expand yourself, and bring to yourself the tinglings of life that are felt in the flowers and the woods, that are felt in the planets Saturn and Venus, and the Fixed Stars. What nonsense! Here is a fellow with a raging toothache. "My dear boy," Goethe says to him, "you are sorely afflicted with that tooth; but you must *live in the all,* and then you will be happy!" As with all great genius, there is an immense deal of flummery in Goethe, and in proportion to my own contact with him, a monstrous deal of it in me.

H. Melville

P. S. "Amen!" saith Hawthorne.

N. B. This "all" feeling, though, there is some truth in it. You must often have felt it, lying on the grass on a warm summer's day. Your legs seem to send out shoots into the earth. Your hair feels like leaves upon your head. This is the *all* feeling. But what plays the mischief with the truth is that men will insist upon the universal application of a temporary feeling or opinion.

P. S. You must not fail to admire my discretion in paying the postage on this letter.

Melville to Hawthorne

[*"A Very Susceptible and Peradventure Feeble Temperament"*]

June 29, 1851

My dear Hawthorne,

The clear air and open window invite me to write to you. For some time past I have been so busy with a thousand things that I have almost forgotten when I wrote you last, and whether I received an answer. This most persuasive season has now for weeks recalled me from certain crotchety and over-doleful chimeras, the like of which men like you and me, and some others, forming a chain of God's posts round the world, must be content to encounter now and then, and fight them the best way we can. But come they will,—for in the boundless, trackless, but still glorious wild wilderness through which these outposts run, the Indians do sorely abound, as well as the insignificant but still stinging mosquitoes. Since you have been here, I have been building some shanties of houses (connected with the old one) and likewise some shanties of chapters and essays. I have been ploughing and sowing and raising and printing and praying, and now begin to come out upon a less bristling time, and to enjoy the calm prospect of things from a fair piazza at the north of the old farmhouse here.

---

8. Where Melville found his translation of the sayings of Goethe is not certain, but Davis and Gilman point out that the source in Goethe's poem *Generalbeichte* was translated "To live . . . in the Whole" by Thomas Carlyle.

Not entirely yet, though, am I without something to be urgent with. The "Whale" is only half through the press; for, wearied with the long delays of the printers, and disgusted with the heat and dust of the Babylonish[1] brick-kiln of New York, I came back to the country to feel the grass, and end the book reclining on it, if I may. I am sure you will pardon this speaking all about myself; for if I *say* so much on that head, be sure all the rest of the world are thinking about themselves ten times as much. Let us speak, though we show all our faults and weaknesses,—for it is a sign of strength to be weak, to know it, and out with it; not in set way and ostentatiously, though, but incidentally and without premeditation. But I am falling into my old foible,—preaching. I am busy, but shall not be very long. Come and spend a day here, if you can and want to; if not, stay in Lenox, and God give you long life. When I am quite free of my present engagements, I am going to treat myself to a ride and a visit to you. Have ready a bottle of brandy, because I always feel like drinking that heroic drink when we talk ontological heroics together. This is rather a crazy letter in some respects, I apprehend. If so, ascribe it to the intoxicating effects of the latter end of June operating upon a very susceptible and peradventure feeble temperament. Shall I send you a fin of the "Whale" by way of a specimen mouthful? The tail is not yet cooked, though the hell-fire in which the whole book is broiled might not unreasonably have cooked it ere this. This is the book's motto (the secret one), *Ego non baptiso te in nomine*[2]—but make out the rest yourself.

H. M.

Melville to Hawthorne

[A *Plan* to "*Vagabondize*" *with Hawthorne*]

Tuesday afternoon, July 22, 1851

My dear Hawthorne,

This is not a letter, or even a note, but only a passing word said to you over your garden gate. I thank you for your easy-flowing long letter (received yesterday), which flowed through me, and refreshed all my meadows, as the Housatonic—opposite me—does in reality. I am now busy with various things, not incessantly though; but enough to require my frequent tinkerings; and this is the height of the haying season, and my nag is dragging me home his winter's dinners all the time. And so, one way and another, I am not a disengaged man, but shall be very soon. Meantime, the earliest good chance I get, I shall roll down to you. My dear fellow-being, seeing we—that is, you and I—must hit upon some little bit of vagabondism, before Autumn comes. Graylock— we must go and vagabondize there. But ere we start we must dig a deep hole and bury all the Blue Devils, there to abide till the Last Day. . . . Good-bye.

His X mark

---

1. Ancient city on the lower Euphrates, in modern Iraq, where shrines were built atop great pyramidal brick structures, the ziggurats. Melville knew it as the city of the Jewish Captivity (Jeremiah 52).

2. I do not baptise you in the name (Latin), i.e., Melville leaves Hawthorne to make out that the book is not baptised in the name of the Father but of the devil.

Melville to Hawthorne

[*Hawthorne's Praise of* Moby-Dick: *"The Good Goddess's Bonus"*]

Pittsfield, Monday afternoon, November 17(?), 1851

My dear Hawthorne,

People think that if a man has undergone any hardship, he should have a reward; but for my part, if I have done the hardest possible day's work, and then come to sit down in a corner and eat my supper comfortably—why, then I don't think I deserve any reward for my hard day's work—for am I not now at peace? Is not my supper good? My peace and my supper are my reward, my dear Hawthorne. So your joy-giving and exultation-breeding letter is not my reward for my ditcher's[1] work with that book, but is the good goddess's bonus over and above what was stipulated for—for not one man in five cycles, who is wise, will expect appreciative recognition from his fellows, or any one of them. Appreciation! Recognition! Is love appreciated? Why, ever since Adam, who has got to the meaning of his great allegory—the world? Then we pygmies must be content to have our paper allegories but ill comprehended. I say your appreciation is my glorious gratuity. In my proud, humble way,—a shepherd king,—I was lord of a little vale in the solitary Crimea; but you have now given me the crown of India. But on trying it on my head, I found it fell down on my ears, notwithstanding their asinine length—for it's only such ears that sustain such crowns.

Your letter was handed me last night on the road going to Mr. Morewood's,[2] and I read it there. Had I been at home, I would have sat down at once and answered it. In me divine magnanimities are spontaneous and instantaneous—catch them while you can. The world goes round, and the other side comes up. So now I can't write what I felt. But I felt pantheistic then—your heart beat in my ribs and mine in yours, and both in God's. A sense of unspeakable security is in me this moment, on account of your having understood the book. I have written a wicked book, and feel spotless as the lamb. Ineffable socialities are in me. I would sit down and dine with you and all the gods in old Rome's Pantheon. It is a strange feeling—no hopefulness is in it, no despair. Content—that is it; and irresponsibility; but without licentious inclination. I speak now of my profoundest sense of being, not of an incidental feeling.

Whence come you, Hawthorne? By what right do you drink from my flagon of life? And when I put it to my lips—lo, they are yours and not mine. I feel that the Godhead is broken up like the bread at the Supper,[3] and that we are the pieces. Hence this infinite fraternity of feeling. Now, sympathizing with the paper, my angel turns over another page. You did not care a penny for the book. But, now and then as you read, you understood the pervading thought that impelled the book—and that you praised. Was it not so? You were archangel enough to despise the imperfect body, and embrace the soul. Once you hugged the ugly Socrates[4] because you saw the flame in the mouth, and heard the rushing of the demon,—the familiar,—and recognized the sound; for you have heard it in your own solitudes.

My dear Hawthorne, the atmospheric skepticisms steal into me now, and

1. Ditchdigger's.
2. A neighbor who owned the house that had been Melville's uncle Thomas's; later Morewood's son married one of Melville's nieces.
3. John 13–15.
4. The Greek philosopher (470?–399 B.C.) was a byword for ugliness, having a flat nose, thick lips, and bulging eyes.

make me doubtful of my sanity in writing you thus. But, believe me, I am not mad, most noble Festus![5] But truth is ever incoherent, and when the big hearts strike together, the concussion is a little stunning. Farewell. Don't write a word about the book. That would be robbing me of my miserly delight. I am heartily sorry I ever wrote anything about you—it was paltry.[6] Lord, when shall we be done growing? As long as we have anything more to do, we have done nothing. So, now, let us add Moby Dick to our blessings, and step from that. Leviathan is not the biggest fish;—I have heard of Krakens.[7]

This is a long letter, but you are not at all bound to answer it. Possibly, if you do answer it, and direct it to Herman Melville, you will missend it—for the very fingers that now guide this pen are not precisely the same that just took it up and put it on this paper. Lord, when shall we be done changing? Ah! it's a long stage, and no inn in sight, and night coming, and the body cold. But with you for a passenger, I am content and can be happy. I shall leave the world, I feel, with more satisfaction for having come to know you. Knowing you persuades me more than the Bible of our immortality.

What a pity, that, for your plain, bluff letter, you should get such gibberish! Mention me to Mrs. Hawthorne and to the children, and so, good-by to you, with my blessing.

Herman

P.S. I can't stop yet. If the world was entirely made up of Magians,[8] I'll tell you what I should do. I should have a paper-mill established at one end of the house, and so have an endless riband of foolscap rolling in upon my desk; and upon that endless riband I should write a thousand—a million—billion thoughts, all under the form of a letter to you. The divine magnet is on you, and my magnet responds. Which is the biggest? A foolish question—they are One.

H.

P.P.S. Don't think that by writing me a letter, you shall always be bored with an immediate reply to it—and so keep both of us delving over a writing-desk eternally. No such thing! I sha'n't always answer your letters, and you may do just as you please.

From Moby-Dick[1]

Chapter 54: The Town-Ho's Story
(As told at the Golden Inn)

The Cape of Good Hope, and all the watery region round about there, is much like some noted four corners of a great highway, where you meet more travellers than in any other part.

5. Paul's words as he pleaded his case before King Agrippa and the Roman governor Festus (Acts 26.25).
6. *Hawthorne and His Mosses.*
7. Great sea monster, according to Scandinavian lore.
8. Wise men, or magi, priestly order in ancient Persia.
1. The story appeared in *Harper's New Monthly Magazine* (October 1851) as a preview for *Moby-Dick*, which the Harper Brothers published the next month. This reprinting is based on the book version but with

authorial readings from the magazine and with correction of the quotation marks (double and single), which are chaotic in both early printings.

Besides Ishmael, the narrator of this story and all of *Moby-Dick*, only two of those aboard the *Pequod* are named here: Ahab, their captain who has lost a leg to Moby-Dick, the white whale, and Tashtego, a full-blooded Gayhead Indian, one of the three harpooners.

It was not very long after speaking the Goney[2] that another homeward-bound whaleman, the Town-Ho,[3] was encountered. She was manned almost wholly by Polynesians. In the short gam that ensued she gave us strong news of Moby Dick. To some the general interest in the White Whale was now wildly heightened by a circumstance of the Town-Ho's story, which seemed obscurely to involve with the whale a certain wondrous, inverted visitation of one of those so called judgments of God which at times are said to overtake some men. This latter circumstance, with its own particular accompaniments, forming what may be called the secret part of the tragedy about to be narrated, never reached the ears of Captain Ahab or his mates. For that secret part of the story was unknown to the captain of the Town-Ho himself. It was the private property of three confederate white seamen of that ship, one of whom, it seems, communicated it to Tashtego with Romish[4] injunctions of secrecy, but the following night Tashtego rambled in his sleep, and revealed so much of it in that way, that when he was wakened he could not well withhold the rest. Nevertheless, so potent an influence did this thing have on those seamen in the Pequod who came to the full knowledge of it, and by such a strange delicacy, to call it so, were they governed in this matter, that they kept the secret among themselves so that it never transpired abaft the Pequod's mainmast. Interweaving in its proper place this darker thread with the story as publicly narrated on the ship, the whole of this strange affair I now proceed to put on lasting record.

For my humor's sake, I shall preserve the style in which I once narrated it at Lima, to a lounging circle of my Spanish friends, one saint's eve, smoking upon the thick-gilt tiled piazza of the Golden Inn. Of those fine cavaliers, the young Dons, Pedro and Sebastian, were on the closer terms with me; and hence the interluding questions they occasionally put, and which are duly answered at the time.

"Some two years prior to my first learning the events which I am about rehearsing to you, gentlemen, the Town-Ho, Sperm Whaler of Nantucket, was cruising in your Pacific here, not very many days' sail westward from the eaves of this good Golden Inn. She was somewhere to the northward of the Line.[5] One morning upon handling the pumps, according to daily usage, it was observed that she made more water in her hold than common. They supposed a sword-fish had stabbed her, gentlemen. But the captain, having some unusual reason for believing that rare good luck awaited him in those latitudes; and therefore being very averse to quit them, and the leak not being then considered at all dangerous, though, indeed, they could not find it after searching the hold as low down as was possible in rather heavy weather, the ship still continued her cruisings, the mariners working at the pumps at wide and easy intervals; but no good luck came; more days went by, and not only was the leak yet undiscovered, but it sensibly[6] increased. So much so, that now taking some alarm, the captain, making all sail, stood away for the nearest harbor among the islands, there to have his hull hove out and repaired.

"Though no small passage was before her, yet, if the commonest chance favored, he did not at all fear that his ship would founder by the way, because

---

2. Albatross. "Speaking": signaling, hailing.
3. "The ancient whale-cry upon first sighting a whale from the mast-head, still used by whalemen in hunting the famous Gallipagos terrapin" [Melville's note].
4. Catholic.
5. Equator.
6. Noticeably.

his pumps were of the best, and being periodically relieved at them, those six-and-thirty men of his could easily keep the ship free; never mind if the leak should double on her. In truth, well nigh the whole of this passage being attended by very prosperous breezes, the Town-Ho had all but certainly arrived in perfect safety at her port without the occurrence of the least fatality, had it not been for the brutal overbearing of Radney, the mate, a Vineyarder, and the bitterly provoked vengeance of Steelkilt, a Lakeman and desperado from Buffalo."

"Lakeman!—Buffalo! Pray, what is a Lakeman, and where is Buffalo?" said Don Sebastian, rising in his swinging mat of grass.

"On the eastern shore of our Lake Erie, Don; but—I crave your courtesy—may be, you shall soon hear further of all that. Now, gentlemen, in square-sail brigs and three-masted ships, well nigh as large and stout as any that ever sailed out of your old Callao to far Manilla;[7] this Lakeman, in the land-locked heart of our America, had yet been nurtured by all those agrarian freebooting impressions popularly connected with the open ocean. For in their interflowing aggregate, those grand fresh-water seas of ours,—Erie, and Ontario, and Huron, and Superior, and Michigan,—possess an ocean-like expansiveness, with many of the ocean's noblest traits; with many of its rimmed varieties of races and of climes. They contain round archipelagoes of romantic isles, even as the Polynesian waters do; in large part, are shored by two great contrasting nations, as the Atlantic is; they furnish long maritime approaches to our numerous territorial colonies from the East, dotted all round their banks; here and there are frowned upon by batteries, and by the goat-like craggy guns of lofty Mackinaw;[8] they have heard the fleet thunderings of naval victories; at intervals, they yield their beaches to wild barbarians, whose red painted faces flash from out their peltry[9] wigwams; for leagues and leagues are flanked by ancient and unentered forests, where the gaunt pines stand like serried lines of kings in Gothic genealogies; those same woods harboring wild Afric beasts of prey, and silken creatures whose exported furs give robes to Tartar Emperors; they mirror the paved capitals of Buffalo and Cleveland, as well as Winnebago villages; they float alike the full-rigged merchant ship, the armed cruiser of the State, the steamer, and the birch canoe; they are swept by Borean[1] and dis-masting blasts as direful as any that lash the salted wave; they know what shipwrecks are, for out of sight of land, however inland, they have drowned full many a midnight ship with all its shrieking crew.

"Thus, gentlemen, though an inlander, Steelkilt was wild-ocean born, and wild-ocean nurtured; as much of an audacious mariner as any. And for Rad-ney, though in his infancy he may have laid him down on the lone Nantucket beach, to nurse at his maternal sea; though in after life he had long followed our austere Atlantic and your contemplative Pacific; yet was he quite as venge-ful and full of social quarrel as the backwoods seaman, fresh from the latitudes of buck-horn handled Bowie-knives. Yet was this Nantucketer a man with some good-hearted traits; and this Lakeman, a mariner, who though a sort of devil indeed, might yet by inflexible firmness, only tempered by that common decency of human recognition which is the meanest slave's right; thus treated, this Steelkilt had long been retained harmless and docile. At all events, he had

---

7. In Luzon, in the Philippines. Callo is the port city for Lima.
8. American fort on Mackinac Island in Lake Huron.

9. Made of pelts, animal skins.
1. From the frozen north (in Greek mythology Boreas is god of the north wind).

proved so thus far; but Radney was doomed and made mad, and Steelkilt—but, gentlemen, you shall hear.

"It was not more than a day or two at the furthest after pointing her prow for her island haven, that the Town-Ho's leak seemed again increasing, but only so as to require an hour or more at the pumps every day. You must know that in a settled and civilized ocean like our Atlantic, for example, some skippers think little of pumping their whole way across it; though of a still, sleepy night, should the officer of the deck happen to forget his duty in that respect, the probability would be that he and his shipmates would never again remember it, on account of all hands gently subsiding to the bottom. Nor in the solitary and savage seas far from you to the westward, gentlemen, is it altogether unusual for ships to keep clanging at their pump-handles in full chorus even for a voyage of considerable length; that is, if it lie along a tolerably accessible coast, or if any other reasonable retreat is afforded them. It is only when a leaky vessel is in some very out of the way part of those waters, some really landless latitude, that her captain begins to feel a little anxious.

"Much this way had it been with the Town-Ho; so when her leak was found gaining once more, there was in truth some small concern manifested by several of her company; especially by Radney the mate. He commanded the upper sails to be well hoisted, sheeted home anew, and every way expanded to the breeze. Now this Radney, I suppose, was as little of a coward, and as little inclined to any sort of nervous apprehensiveness touching his own person as any fearless, unthinking creature on land or on sea that you can conveniently imagine, gentlemen. Therefore when he betrayed this solicitude about the safety of the ship, some of the seamen declared that it was only on account of his being a part owner in her. So when they were working that evening at the pumps, there was on this head no small gamesomeness slily going on among them, as they stood with their feet continually overflowed by the rippling clear water; clear as any mountain spring, gentlemen—that bubbling from the pumps ran across the deck, and poured itself out in steady spouts at the lee scupper-holes.

"Now, as you well know, it is not seldom the case in this conventional world of ours—watery or otherwise; that when a person placed in command over his fellow-men finds one of them to be very significantly his superior in general pride of manhood, straightway against that man he conceives an unconquerable dislike and bitterness; and if he have a chance he will pull down and pulverize that subaltern's tower, and make a little heap of dust of it. Be this conceit of mine as it may, gentlemen, at all events Steelkilt was a tall and noble animal with a head like a Roman, and a flowing golden beard like the tasseled housings of your last viceroy's snorting charger; and a brain, and a heart, and a soul in him, gentlemen, which had made Steelkilt Charlemagne, had he been born son to Charlemagne's father. But Radney, the mate, was ugly as a mule; yet as hardy, as stubborn, as malicious. He did not love Steelkilt, and Steelkilt knew it.

"Espying the mate drawing near as he was toiling at the pump with the rest, the Lakeman affected not to notice him, but unawed, went on with his gay banterings.

" 'Aye, aye, my merry lads, it's a lively leak this; hold a cannikin, one of ye, and let's have a taste. By the Lord, it's worth bottling! I tell ye what, men, old Rad's investment must go for it! he had best cut away his part of the hull and

tow it home. The fact is, boys, that sword-fish only began the job; he's come
back again with a gang of ship-carpenters, saw-fish, and file-fish, and what
not; and the whole posse of 'em are now hard at work cutting and slashing at
the bottom; making improvements, I suppose. If old Rad were here now, I'd
tell him to jump overboard and scatter 'em. They're playing the devil with his
estate, I can tell him. But he's a simple old soul,—Rad, and a beauty too.
Boys, they say the rest of his property is invested in looking-glasses. I wonder
if he'd give a poor devil like me the model of his nose.'

" 'Damn your eyes! what's that pump stopping for?' roared Radney, pretending not to have heard the sailor's talk. 'Thunder away at it!'

" 'Aye, aye, sir,' said Steelkilt, merry as a cricket. 'Lively, boys, lively, now!'
And with that the pump clanged like fifty fire-engines; the men tossed their
hats off to it, and ere long that peculiar gasping of the lungs was heard which
denotes the fullest tension of life's utmost energies.

"Quitting the pump at last, with the rest of his band, the Lakeman went
forward all panting, and sat himself down on the windlass; his face fiery red,
his eyes bloodshot, and wiping the profuse sweat from his brow. Now what
cozening fiend it was, gentlemen, that possessed Radney to meddle with such
a man in that corporeally exasperated state, I know not; but so it happened.
Intolerably striding along the deck, the mate commanded him to get a broom
and sweep down the planks, and also a shovel, and remove some offensive
matters consequent upon allowing a pig to run at large.

"Now, gentlemen, sweeping a ship's deck at sea is a piece of household
work which in all times but raging gales is regularly attended to every evening;
it has been known to be done in the case of ships actually foundering at the
time. Such, gentlemen, is the inflexibility of sea-usages and the instinctive
love of neatness in seamen; some of whom would not willingly drown without
first washing their faces. But in all vessels this broom business is the prescriptive province of the boys, if boys there be aboard. Besides, it was the stronger
men in the Town-Ho that had been divided into gangs, taking turns at the
pumps; and being the most athletic seaman of them all, Steelkilt had been
regularly assigned captain of one of the gangs; consequently he should have
been freed from any trivial business not connected with truly nautical duties,
such being the case with his comrades. I mention all these particulars so that
you may understand exactly how this affair stood between the two men.

"But there was more than this: the order about the shovel was almost as
plainly meant to sting and insult Steelkilt, as though Radney had spat in his
face. Any man who has gone sailor in a whale-ship will understand this; and
all this and doubtless much more, the Lakeman fully comprehended when
the mate uttered his command. But as he sat still for a moment, and as he
steadfastly looked into the mate's malignant eye and perceived the stacks of
powder-casks heaped up in him and the slow-match silently burning along
towards them; as he instinctively saw all this, that strange forbearance and
unwillingness to stir up the deeper passionateness in any already ireful being—
a repugnance most felt, when felt at all, by really valiant men even when
aggrieved—this nameless phantom feeling, gentlemen, stole over Steelkilt.

"Therefore, in his ordinary tone, only a little broken by the bodily exhaustion he was temporarily in, he answered him saying that sweeping the deck
was not his business, and he would not do it. And then, without at all alluding
to the shovel, he pointed to three lads as the customary sweepers; who, not

being billeted at the pumps, had done little or nothing all day. To this, Radney replied with an oath, in a most domineering and outrageous manner unconditionally reiterating his command; meanwhile advancing upon the still seated Lakeman, with an uplifted cooper's club hammer which he had snatched from a cask near by.

"Heated and irritated as he was by his spasmodic toil at the pumps, for all his first nameless feeling of forbearance the sweating Steelkilt could but ill brook this bearing in the mate; but somehow still smothering the conflagration within him, without speaking he remained doggedly rooted to his seat, till at last the incensed Radney shook the hammer within a few inches of his face, furiously commanding him to do his bidding.

"Steelkilt rose, and slowly retreating round the windlass, steadily followed by the mate with his menacing hammer, deliberately repeated his intention not to obey. Seeing, however, that his forbearance had not the slightest effect, by an awful and unspeakable intimation with his twisted hand he warned off the foolish and infatuated man; but it was to no purpose. And in this way the two went once slowly round the windlass; when, resolved at last no longer to retreat, bethinking him that he had now forborne as much as comported with his humor, the Lakeman paused on the hatches and thus spoke to the officer:

" 'Mr. Radney, I will not obey you. Take that hammer away, or look to yourself.' But the predestinated mate coming still closer to him, where the Lakeman stood fixed, now shook the heavy hammer within an inch of his teeth; meanwhile repeating a string of insufferable maledictions. Retreating not the thousandth part of an inch; stabbing him in the eye with the unflinching poniard of his glance, Steelkilt, clenching his right hand behind him and creepingly drawing it back, told his persecutor that if the hammer but grazed his cheek he (Steelkilt) would murder him. But, gentlemen, the fool had been branded for the slaughter by the gods. Immediately the hammer touched the cheek; the next instant the lower jaw of the mate was stove in his head; he fell on the hatch spouting blood like a whale.

"Ere the cry could go aft Steelkilt was shaking one of the backstays leading far aloft to where two of his comrades were standing their mast-heads. They were both Canallers."

"Canallers!" cried Don Pedro. "We have seen many whale-ships in our harbors, but never heard of your Canallers. Pardon: who and what are they?"

"Canallers, Don, are the boatmen belonging to our grand Erie Canal. You must have heard of it."

"Nay, Senor; hereabouts in this dull, warm, most lazy, and hereditary land, we know but little of your vigorous North."

"Aye? Well then, Don, refill my cup. Your chicha's[2] very fine; and ere proceeding further I will tell ye what our Canallers are; for such information may throw side-light upon my story.

"For three hundred and sixty miles, gentlemen, through the entire breadth of the state of New York; through numerous populous cities and most thriving villages; through long, dismal, uninhabited swamps, and affluent, cultivated fields, unrivalled for fertility; by billiard-room and bar-room; through the holy-of-holies of great forests; on Roman arches over Indian rivers; through sun and shade; by happy hearts or broken; through all the wide contrasting scenery of

---

2. Liquor made from maize or cane sugar.

those noble Mohawk counties; and especially, by rows of snow-white chapels, whose spires stand almost like milestones, flows one continual stream of Venetianly corrupt and often lawless life. There's your true Ashantee,[3] gentlemen; there howl your pagans; where you ever find them, next door to you; under the long-flung shadow, and the snug patronizing lee of churches. For by some curious fatality, as it is often noted of your metropolitan freebooters that they ever encamp around the halls of justice, so sinners, gentlemen, most abound in holiest vicinities."

"Is that a friar passing?" said Don Pedro, looking downwards into the crowded plaza, with humorous concern.

"Well for our northern friend, Dame Isabella's Inquisition[4] wanes in Lima," laughed Don Sebastian. "Proceed, Senor."

"A moment! Pardon!" cried another of the company. "In the name of all us Limeese, I but desire to express to you, sir sailor, that we have by no means overlooked your delicacy in not substituting present Lima for distant Venice in your corrupt comparison. Oh! do not bow and look surprised; you know the proverb all along this coast—'Corrupt as Lima.' It but bears out your saying, too; churches more plentiful than billiard-tables, and for ever open—and 'Corrupt as Lima.' So, too, Venice; I have been there; the holy city of the blessed evangelist, St. Mark!—St. Dominic,[5] purge it! Your cup! Thanks: here I refill; now, you pour out again."

"Freely depicted in his own vocation, gentlemen, the Canaller would make a fine dramatic hero, so abundantly and picturesquely wicked is he. Like Mark Antony, for days and days along his green-turfed, flowery Nile, he indolently floats, openly toying with his red-cheeked Cleopatra, ripening his apricot thigh upon the sunny deck.[6] But ashore, all this effeminacy is dashed. The brigandish guise which the Canaller so proudly sports; his slouched and gaily-ribboned hat betoken his grand features. A terror to the smiling innocence of the villages through which he floats; his swart visage and bold swagger are not unshunned in cities. Once a vagabond on his own canal, I have received good turns from one of these Canallers; I thank him heartily; would fain be not ungrateful; but it is often one of the prime redeeming qualities of your man of violence, that at times he has as stiff an arm to back a poor stranger in a strait, as to plunder a wealthy one. In sum, gentlemen, what the wildness of this canal life is, is emphatically evinced by this; that our wild whale-fishery contains so many of its most finished graduates, and that scarce any race of mankind, except Sydney;[7] men, are so much distrusted by our whaling captains. Nor does it at all diminish the curiousness of this matter, that to many thousands of our rural boys and young men born along its line, the probationary life of the Grand Canal furnishes the sole transition between quietly reaping in a Christian corn-field, and recklessly ploughing the waters of the most barbaric seas."

"I see! I see!" impetuously exclaimed Don Pedro, spilling his chicha upon his silvery ruffles. "No need to travel! The world's one Lima. I had thought,

---

3. Heathen, from a West African tribe.

4. The Catholic court charged with the systematic pursuit of heresy and the persecution of heretics. During the period of the Spanish Queen Isabella (1451–1504) the Inquisition burned or otherwise executed many Jews and forced others into conversion or mass exile.

5. Patron saint of the Cathedral of Lima. Mark is the patron saint of Venice.

6. A reminder of Shakespeare's depiction of *Antony and Cleopatra*; here, the canaller's Cleopatra is red-cheeked because of her American Indian blood as well as the sunshine.

7. A city in New South Wales, eastern Australia.

now, that at your temperate North the generations were cold and holy as the hills.—But the story."

"I left off, gentlemen, where the Lakeman shook the backstay. Hardly had he done so, when he was surrounded by the three junior mates and the four harpooneers, who all crowded him to the deck. But sliding down the ropes like baleful comets, the two Canallers rushed into the uproar, and sought to drag their man out of it towards the forecastle. Others of the sailors joined with them in this attempt, and a twisted turmoil ensued; while standing out of harm's way, the valiant captain danced up and down with a whale-pike, calling upon his officers to manhandle that atrocious scoundrel, and smoke him along to the quarter-deck. At intervals, he ran close up to the revolving border of the confusion, and prying into the heart of it with his pike, sought to prick out the object of his resentment. But Steelkilt and his desperadoes were too much for them all; they succeeded in gaining the forecastle deck, where, hastily slewing about three or four large casks in a line with the windlass, these sea-Parisians entrenched themselves behind the barricade.

" 'Come out of that, ye pirates!' roared the captain, now menacing them with a pistol in each hand, just brought to him by the steward. 'Come out of that, ye cut-throats!'

"Steelkilt leaped on the barricade, and striding up and down there, defied the worst the pistols could do; but gave the captain to understand distinctly, that his (Steelkilt's) death would be the signal for a murderous mutiny on the part of all hands. Fearing in his heart lest this might prove but too true, the captain a little desisted, but still commanded the insurgents instantly to return to their duty.

" 'Will you promise not to touch us, if we do?' demanded their ringleader.

" 'Turn to! turn to!—I make no promise;—to your duty! Do you want to sink the ship, by knocking off at a time like this? Turn to!' and he once more raised a pistol.

" 'Sink the ship?' cried Steelkilt. 'Aye, let her sink. Not a man of us turns to, unless you swear not to raise a rope-yarn against us. What say ye, men?' turning to his comrades. A fierce cheer was their response.

"The Lakeman now patrolled the barricade, all the while keeping his eye on the Captain, and jerking out such sentences as these:—'It's not our fault; we didn't want it; I told him to take his hammer away; it was boys' business; he might have known me before this; I told him not to prick the buffalo; I believe I have broken a finger here against his cursed jaw; ain't those mincing knives down in the forecastle there, men? look to those handspikes, my hearties. Captain, by God, look to yourself; say the word; don't be a fool; forget it all; we are ready to turn to; treat us decently, and we're your men; but we won't be flogged.'

" 'Turn to! I make no promises, turn to, I say!'

" 'Look ye, now,' cried the Lakeman, flinging out his arm towards him, 'there are a few of us here (and I am one of them) who have shipped for the cruise, d'ye see; now as you well know, sir, we can claim our discharge as soon as the anchor is down; so we don't want a row; it's not our interest; we want to be peaceable; we are ready to work, but we won't be flogged.'

" 'Turn to!' roared the Captain.

"Steelkilt glanced round him a moment, and then said:—'I tell you what it is now, Captain, rather than kill ye, and be hung for such a shabby rascal, we

won't lift a hand against ye unless ye attack us; but till you say the word about
not flogging us, we don't do a hand's turn.'

" 'Down into the forecastle then, down with ye, I'll keep ye there till ye're
sick of it. Down ye go.'

" 'Shall we?' cried the ringleader to his men. Most of them were against it;
but at length, in obedience to Steelkilt, they preceded him down into their
dark den, growlingly disappearing, like bears into a cave.

"As the Lakeman's bare head was just level with the planks, the Captain
and his posse leaped the barricade, and rapidly drawing over the slide of the
scuttle, planted their group of hands upon it, and loudly called for the steward
to bring the heavy brass padlock belonging to the companion-way. Then opening the slide a little, the Captain whispered something down the crack, closed
it, and turned the key upon them—ten in number—leaving on deck some
twenty or more, who thus far had remained neutral.

"All night a wide-awake watch was kept by all the officers, forward and aft,
especially about the forecastle scuttle and fore hatchway; at which last place it
was feared the insurgents might emerge, after breaking through the bulkhead
below. But the hours of darkness passed in peace; the men who still remained
at their duty toiling hard at the pumps, whose clinking and clanking at intervals through the dreary night dismally resounded through the ship.

"At sunrise the Captain went forward, and knocking on the deck, summoned the prisoners to work; but with a yell they refused. Water was then
lowered down to them, and a couple of handfuls of biscuit were tossed after it;
when again turning the key upon them and pocketing it, the Captain returned
to the quarter-deck. Twice every day for three days this was repeated; but on
the fourth morning a confused wrangling, and then a scuffling was heard, as
the customary summons was delivered; and suddenly four men burst up from
the forecastle, saying they were ready to turn to. The fetid closeness of the air,
and a famishing diet, united perhaps to some fears of ultimate retribution, had
constrained them to surrender at discretion. Emboldened by this, the Captain
reiterated his demand to the rest, but Steelkilt shouted up to him a terrific hint
to stop his babbling and betake himself where he belonged. On the fifth morning three others of the mutineers bolted up into the air from the desperate
arms below that sought to restrain them. Only three were left.

" 'Better turn to, now?' said the Captain with a heartless jeer.

" 'Shut us up again, will ye!' cried Steelkilt.

" 'Oh! certainly,' said the Captain, and the key clicked.

"It was at this point, gentlemen, that enraged by the defection of seven of
his former associates, and stung by the mocking voice that had last hailed him,
and maddened by his long entombment in a place as black as the bowels of
despair; it was then that Steelkilt proposed to the two Canallers, thus far apparently of one mind with him, to burst out of their hole at the next summoning
of the garrison; and armed with their keen mincing knives (long, crescentic,
heavy implements with a handle at each end) run amuck from the bowsprit to
the taffrail; and if by any devilishness of desperation possible, seize the ship.
For himself, he would do this, he said, whether they joined him or not. That
was the last night he should spend in that den. But the scheme met with no
opposition on the part of the other two; they swore they were ready for that, or
for any other mad thing, for anything in short but a surrender. And what was
more, they each insisted upon being the first man on deck, when the time to
make the rush should come. But to this their leader fiercely objected, reserving

that priority for himself; particularly as his two comrades would not yield, the one to the other, in the matter; and both of them could not be first, for the ladder would but admit one man at a time. And here, gentlemen, the foul play of these miscreants must come out.

"Upon hearing the frantic project of their leader, each in his own separate soul had suddenly lighted, it would seem, upon the same piece of treachery, namely: to be foremost in breaking out, in order to be the first of the three, though the last of the ten, to surrender; and thereby secure whatever small chance of pardon such conduct might merit. But when Steelkilt made known his determination still to lead them to the last, they in some way, by some subtle chemistry of villany, mixed their before secret treacheries together; and when their leader fell into a doze, verbally opened their souls to each other in three sentences; and bound the sleeper with cords, and gagged him with cords; and shrieked out for the Captain at midnight.

"Thinking murder at hand, and smelling in the dark for the blood, he and all his armed mates and harpooneers rushed for the forecastle. In a few minutes the scuttle was opened, and, bound hand and foot, the still struggling ringleader was shoved up into the air by his perfidious allies, who at once claimed the honor of securing a man who had been fully ripe for murder. But all three were collared, and dragged along the deck like dead cattle; and, side by side, were seized[8] up into the mizen rigging, like three quarters of meat, and there they hung till morning. 'Damn ye,' cried the Captain, pacing to and fro before them, 'the vultures would not touch ye, ye villains!'

"At sunrise he summoned all hands; and separating those who had rebelled from those who had taken no part in the mutiny, he told the former that he had a good mind to flog them all round—thought, upon the whole, he would do so—he ought to—justice demanded it; but for the present, considering their timely surrender, he would let them go with a reprimand, which he accordingly administered in the vernacular.

" 'But as for you, ye carrion rogues,' turning to the three men in the rigging—'for you, I mean to mince ye up for the try-pots;'[9] and, seizing a rope, he applied it with all his might to the backs of the two traitors, till they yelled no more, but lifelessly hung their heads sideways, as the two crucified thieves are drawn.

" 'My wrist is sprained with ye!' he cried, at last; 'but there is still rope enough left for you, my fine bantam, that wouldn't give up. Take that gag from his mouth, and let us hear what he can say for himself.'

"For a moment the exhausted mutineer made a tremulous motion of his cramped jaws, and then painfully twisting round his head, said in a sort of hiss, 'What I say is this—and mind it well—if you flog me, I murder you!'

" 'Say ye so? then see how ye frighten me'—and the Captain drew off with the rope to strike.

" 'Best not,' hissed the Lakeman.

" 'But I must,'—and the rope was once more drawn back for the stroke.

"Steelkilt here hissed out something, inaudible to all but the Captain; who, to the amazement of all hands, started back, paced the deck rapidly two or three times, and then suddenly throwing down his rope, said, 'I won't do it— let him go—cut him down; d'ye hear?'

"But as the junior mates were hurrying to execute the order, a pale man,

8. Lashed, tied.   9. The great vats for boiling whale blubber into oil.

with a bandaged head, arrested them—Radney the chief mate. Ever since the blow, he had lain in his berth; but that morning, hearing the tumult on the deck, he had crept out, and thus far had watched the whole scene. Such was the state of his mouth, that he could hardly speak; but mumbling something about *his* being willing and able to do what the captain dared not attempt, he snatched the rope and advanced to his pinioned foe.

" 'You are a coward!' hissed the Lakeman.

" 'So I am, but take that.' The mate was in the very act of striking, when another hiss stayed his uplifted arm. He paused: and then pausing no more, made good his word, spite of Steelkilt's threat, whatever that might have been. The three men were then cut down, all hands were turned to, and, sullenly worked by the moody seamen, the iron pumps clanged as before.

"Just after dark that day, when one watch had retired below, a clamor was heard in the forecastle; and the two trembling traitors running up, besieged the cabin door, saying they durst not consort with the crew. Entreaties, cuffs, and kicks could not drive them back, so at their own instance they were put down in the ship's run for salvation. Still, no sign of mutiny reappeared among the rest. On the contrary, it seemed, that mainly at Steelkilt's instigation, they had resolved to maintain the strictest peacefulness, obey all orders to the last, and, when the ship reached port, desert her in a body. But in order to insure the speediest end to the voyage, they all agreed to another thing—namely, not to sing out for whales, in case any should be discovered. For, spite of her leak, and spite of all her other perils, the Town-Ho still maintained her mast-heads,[1] and her captain was just as willing to lower for a fish that moment, as on the day his craft first struck the cruising ground; and Radney the mate was quite as ready to change his berth for a boat, and with his bandaged mouth seek to gag in death the vital jaw of the whale.

"But though the Lakeman had induced the seamen to adopt this sort of passiveness in their conduct, he kept his own counsel (at least till all was over) concerning his own proper and private revenge upon the man who had stung him in the ventricles of his heart. He was in Radney the chief mate's watch; and as if the infatuated man sought to run more than half way to meet his doom, after the scene at the rigging, he insisted, against the express counsel of the captain, upon resuming the head of his watch at night. Upon this, and one or two other circumstances, Steelkilt systematically built the plan of his revenge.

"During the night, Radney had an unseamanlike way of sitting on the bulwarks of the quarter-deck, and leaning his arm upon the gunwale of the boat which was hoisted up there, a little above the ship's side. In this attitude, it was well known, he sometimes dozed. There was a considerable vacancy between the boat and the ship, and down beneath this was the sea. Steelkilt calculated his time, and found that his next trick[2] at the helm would come round at two o'clock, in the morning of the third day from that in which he had been betrayed. At his leisure, he employed the interval in braiding something very carefully in his watches below.

" 'What are you making there?' said a shipmate.

" 'What do you think? what does it look like?'

" 'Like a lanyard for your bag; but it's an odd one, seems to me.'

1. I.e., kept lookouts stationed at the mastheads. 2. Turn.

" 'Yes, rather oddish,' said the Lakeman, holding it at arm's length before him; 'but I think it will answer. Shipmate, I haven't enough twine,—have you any?'

"But there was none in the forecastle.

" 'Then I must get some from old Rad;' and he rose to go aft.

" 'You don't mean to go a begging to *him!*' said a sailor.

" 'Why not? Do you think he won't do me a turn, when it's to help himself in the end, shipmate?' and going to the mate, he looked at him quietly, and asked him for some twine to mend his hammock. It was given him—neither twine nor lanyard were seen again; but the next night an iron ball, closely netted, partly rolled from the pocket of the Lakeman's monkey jacket, as he was tucking the coat into his hammock for a pillow. Twenty-four hours after, his trick at the silent helm—nigh to the man who was apt to doze over the grave always ready dug to the seaman's hand—that fatal hour was then to come; and in the fore-ordaining soul of Steelkilt, the mate was already stark and stretched as a corpse, with his forehead crushed in.

"But, gentlemen, a fool saved the would-be murderer from the bloody deed he had planned. Yet complete revenge he had, and without being the avenger. For by a mysterious fatality, Heaven itself seemed to step in to take out of his hands into its own the damning thing he would have done.

"It was just between daybreak and sunrise of the morning of the second day, when they were washing down the decks, that a stupid Teneriffe man, drawing water in the main-chains,[3] all at once shouted out, 'There she rolls! there she rolls! Jesu! what a whale!' It was Moby Dick."

"Moby Dick!" cried Don Sebastian; "St. Dominic! Sir sailor, but do whales have christenings? Whom call you Moby Dick?"

"A very white, and famous, and most deadly immortal monster, Don;—but that would be too long a story."

"How? how?" cried all the young Spaniards, crowding.

"Nay, Dons, Dons—nay, nay! I cannot rehearse that now. Let me get more into the air, Sirs."

"The chicha! the chicha!" cried Don Pedro; "our vigorous friend looks faint;—fill up his empty glass!"

"No need, gentlemen; one moment, and I proceed.—Now, gentlemen, so suddenly perceiving the snowy whale within fifty yards of the ship—forgetful of the compact among the crew—in the excitement of the moment, the Teneriffe man had instinctively and involuntarily lifted his voice for the monster, though for some little time past it had been plainly beheld from the three sullen mast-heads. All was now a phrensy. 'The White Whale—the White Whale!' was the cry from captain, mates, and harpooneers, who, undeterred by fearful rumors, were all anxious to capture so famous and precious a fish; while the dogged crew eyed askance, and with curses, the appalling beauty of the vast milky mass, that lit up by a horizontal spangling sun, shifted and glistened like a living opal in the blue morning sea. Gentlemen, a strange fatality pervades the whole career of these events, as if verily mapped out before the world itself was charted. The mutineer was the bowsman of the mate, and when fast to a fish, it was his duty to sit next him, while Radney stood up with his lance in the prow, and haul in or slacken the line at the word of command.

3. Metal plates bolted to the side of the vessel to hold the deadeyes (round flat wooden blocks) to which the shrouds are connected.

Moreover, when the four boats were lowered, the mate's got the start; and none howled more fiercely with delight than did Steelkilt, as he strained at his oar. After a stiff pull, their harpooneer got fast, and, spear in hand, Radney sprang to the bow. He was always a furious man, it seems, in a boat. And now his bandaged cry was, to beach him on the whale's topmost back. Nothing loath, his bowsman hauled him up and up, through a blinding foam that blent two whitenesses together; till of a sudden the boat struck as against a sunken ledge, and keeling over, spilled out the standing mate. That instant, as he fell on the whale's slippery back, the boat righted, and was dashed aside by the swell, while Radney was tossed over into the sea, on the other flank of the whale. He struck out through the spray, and, for an instant, was dimly seen through that veil, wildly seeking to remove himself from the eye of Moby Dick. But the whale rushed round in a sudden maelstrom; seized the swimmer between his jaws; and rearing high up with him, plunged headlong again, and went down.

"Meantime, at the first tap of the boat's bottom, the Lakeman had slackened the line, so as to drop astern from the whirlpool; calmly looking on, he thought his own thoughts. But a sudden, terrific, downward jerking of the boat, quickly brought his knife to the line. He cut it; and the whale was free. But, at some distance, Moby Dick rose again, with some tatters of Radney's red woollen shirt, caught in the teeth that had destroyed him. All four boats gave chase again; but the whale eluded them, and finally wholly disappeared.

"In good time, the Town-Ho reached her port—a savage, solitary place— where no civilized creature resided. There, headed by the Lakeman, all but five or six of the foremast-men deliberately deserted among the palms; eventually, as it turned out, seizing a large double war-canoe of the savages, and setting sail for some other harbor.

"The ship's company being reduced to but a handful, the captain called upon the Islanders to assist him in the laborious business of heaving down the ship to stop the leak. But to such unresting vigilance over their dangerous allies was this small band of whites necessitated both by night and by day, and so extreme was the hard work they underwent, that upon the vessel being ready again for sea, they were in such a weakened condition that the captain durst not put off with them in so heavy a vessel. After taking counsel with his officers, he anchored the ship as far off shore as possible; loaded and ran out his two cannon from the bows; stacked his muskets on the poop; and warning the Islanders not to approach the ship at their peril, took one man with him, and setting the sail of his best whaleboat, steered straight before the wind for Tahiti, five hundred miles distant, to procure a reinforcement to his crew.

"On the fourth day of the sail, a large canoe was descried, which seemed to have touched a low isle of corals. He steered away from it; but the savage craft bore down on him; and soon the voice of Steelkilt hailed him to heave to, or he would run him under water. The captain presented a pistol. With one foot on each prow of the yoked war-canoes, the Lakeman laughed him to scorn; assuring him that if the pistol so much as clicked in the lock, he would bury him in bubbles and foam.

" 'What do you want of me?' cried the captain.

" 'Where are you bound? and for what are you bound?' demanded Steelkilt; 'no lies.'

" 'I am bound to Tahiti for more men.'

" 'Very good. Let me board you a moment—I come in peace.' With that he leaped from the canoe, swam to the boat; and climbing the gunwale, stood face to face with the captain.

" 'Cross your arms, sir; throw back your head. Now, repeat after me. "As soon as Steelkilt leaves me, I swear to beach this boat on yonder island, and remain there six days. If I do not, may lightnings strike me!" '

" 'A pretty scholar,' laughed the Lakeman. 'Adios, Senor!' and leaping into the sea, he swam back to his comrades.

"Watching the boat till it was fairly beached, and drawn up to the roots of the cocoa-nut trees, Steelkilt made sail again, and in due time arrived at Tahiti, his own place of destination. There, luck befriended him; two ships were about to sail for France, and were providentially in want of precisely that number of men which the sailor headed. They embarked; and so for ever got the start of their former captain, had he been at all minded to work them legal retribution.

"Some ten days after the French ships sailed, the whale-boat arrived, and the captain was forced to enlist some of the more civilized Tahitians, who had been somewhat used to the sea. Chartering a small native schooner, he returned with them to his vessel; and finding all right there, again resumed his cruisings.

"Where Steelkilt now is, gentlemen, none know; but upon the island of Nantucket, the widow of Radney still turns to the sea which refuses to give up its dead; still in dreams sees the awful white whale that destroyed him."

· · · · ·

"Are you through?" said Don Sebastian, quietly.

"I am, Don."

"Then I entreat you, tell me if to the best of your own convictions, this your story is in substance really true? It is so passing wonderful! Did you get it from an unquestionable source? Bear with me if I seem to press."

"Also bear with all of us, sir sailor; for we all join in Don Sebastian's suit," cried the company, with exceeding interest.

"Is there a copy of the Holy Evangelists[4] in the Golden Inn, gentlemen?"

"Nay," said Don Sebastian; "but I know a worthy priest near by, who will quickly procure one for me. I go for it; but are you well advised? this may grow too serious."

"Will you be so good as to bring the priest also, Don?"

"Though there are no Auto-da-Fés[5] in Lima now," said one of the company to another; "I fear our sailor friend runs risk of the archiepiscopacy. Let us withdraw more out of the moonlight. I see no need of this."

"Excuse me for running after you, Don Sebastian; but may I also beg that you will be particular in procuring the largest sized Evangelists you can."

· · · · ·

"This is the priest, he brings you the Evangelists," said Don Sebastian, gravely, returning with a tall and solemn figure.

"Let me remove my hat. Now, venerable priest, further into the light, and hold the Holy Book before me that I may touch it."

---

4. The Gospels of Matthew, Mark, Luke, and John, bound together apart from the rest of the Bible.

5. Executions by the Inquisition (by burning at the stake).

"So help me Heaven, and on my honor, the story I have told ye, gentlemen, is in substance and its great items, true. I know it to be true; it happened on this ball; I trod the ship; I knew the crew; I have seen and talked with Steelkilt since the death of Radney."

1851

Bartleby, the Scrivener[1]

A Story of Wall-Street

I am a rather elderly man. The nature of my avocations for the last thirty years has brought me into more than ordinary contact with what would seem an interesting and somewhat singular set of men, of whom as yet nothing that I know of has ever been written:—I mean the law-copyists or scriveners. I have known very many of them, professionally and privately, and if I pleased, could relate divers histories, at which good-natured gentlemen might smile, and sentimental souls might weep. But I waive the biographies of all other scriveners for a few passages in the life of Bartleby, who was a scrivener the strangest I ever saw or heard of. While of other law-copyists I might write the complete life, of Bartleby nothing of that sort can be done. I believe that no materials exist for a full and satisfactory biography of this man. It is an irreparable loss to literature. Bartleby was one of those beings of whom nothing is ascertainable, except from the original sources, and in his case those are very small. What my own astonished eyes saw of Bartleby, *that* is all I know of him, except, indeed, one vague report which will appear in the sequel.

Ere introducing the scrivener, as he first appeared to me, it is fit I make some mention of myself, my *employées*, my business, my chambers, and general surroundings; because some such description is indispensable to an adequate understanding of the chief character about to be presented.

Imprimis: I am a man who, from his youth upwards, has been filled with a profound conviction that the easiest way of life is the best. Hence, though I belong to a profession proverbially energetic and nervous, even to turbulence, at times, yet nothing of that sort have I ever suffered to invade my peace. I am one of those unambitious lawyers who never addresses a jury, or in any way draws down public applause; but in the cool tranquillity of a snug retreat, do a snug business among rich men's bonds and mortgages and title-deeds. All who know me, consider me an eminently *safe* man. The late John Jacob Astor, a personage little given to poetic enthusiasm, had no hesitation in pronouncing my first grand point to be prudence; my next, method. I do not speak it in vanity, but simply record the fact, that I was not unemployed in my profession by the late John Jacob Astor; a name which, I admit, I love to repeat, for it hath a rounded and orbicular sound to it, and rings like unto bullion. I will freely add, that I was not insensible to the late John Jacob Astor's good opinion.

---

1. The text is from the first printing in the November and December 1853 issues of *Putnam's Monthly Magazine*, the first work by Melville to be printed after the disastrous reception of *Pierre* during the summer and fall of 1852. One work (*The Isle of the Cross*), probably the story of Agatha Robinson, a Nantucket woman who displayed patience, endurance, and resignedness, was apparently destroyed after being rejected by the Harpers.

Some time prior to the period at which this little history begins, my avocations had been largely increased. The good old office, now extinct in the State of New-York, of a Master in Chancery,[2] had been conferred upon me. It was not a very arduous office, but very pleasantly remunerative. I seldom lose my temper; much more seldom indulge in dangerous indignation at wrongs and outrages; but I must be permitted to be rash here and declare, that I consider the sudden and violent abrogation of the office of Master in Chancery, by the new Constitution,[3] as a——premature act; inasmuch as I had counted upon a life-lease of the profits, whereas I only received those of a few short years. But this is by the way.

My chambers were up stairs at No.—Wall-street. At one end they looked upon the white wall of the interior of a spacious sky-light shaft, penetrating the building from top to bottom. This view might have been considered rather tame than otherwise, deficient in what landscape painters call "life." But if so, the view from the other end of my chambers offered, at least, a contrast, if nothing more. In that direction my windows commanded an unobstructed view of a lofty brick wall, black by age and everlasting shade; which wall required no spy-glass to bring out its lurking beauties, but for the benefit of all near-sighted spectators, was pushed up to within ten feet of my window panes. Owing to the great height of the surrounding buildings, and my chambers being on the second floor, the interval between this wall and mine not a little resembled a huge square cistern.

At the period just preceding the advent of Bartleby, I had two persons as copyists in my employment, and a promising lad as an office-boy. First, Turkey; second, Nippers; third, Ginger Nut. These may seem names, the like of which are not usually found in the Directory. In truth they were nicknames, mutually conferred upon each other by my three clerks, and were deemed expressive of their respective persons or characters. Turkey was a short, pursy[4] Englishman of about my own age, that is, somewhere not far from sixty. In the morning, one might say, his face was of a fine florid hue, but after twelve o'clock, meridian—his dinner hour—it blazed like a grate full of Christmas coals; and continued blazing—but, as it were, with a gradual wane—till 6 o'clock, P.M. or thereabouts, after which I saw no more of the proprietor of the face, which gaining its meridian with the sun, seemed to set with it, to rise, culminate, and decline the following day, with the like regularity and undiminished glory. There are many singular coincidences I have known in the course of my life, not the least among which was the fact, that exactly when Turkey displayed his fullest beams from his red and radiant countenance, just then, too, at that critical moment, began the daily period when I considered his business capacities as seriously disturbed for the remainder of the twenty-four hours. Not that he was absolutely idle, or averse to business then; far from it. The difficulty was, he was apt to be altogether too energetic. There was a strange, inflamed, flurried, flighty recklessness of activity about him. He would be incautious in dipping his pen into his inkstand. All his blots upon my documents, were dropped there after twelve o'clock, meridian. Indeed, not only would he be reckless and sadly given to making blots in the

2. The narrator is understandably concerned about the abolition of a sinecure, but heirs had cause to rejoice, for chancery had kept estates tied up in prolonged litigation. In a poem written around the 1870s, *At the Hostelry*, Melville says that divided Italy, "Nigh para-lysed, by cowls misguided," was "Locked as in Chancery's numbing hand."

3. New York had adopted a "new Constitution" in 1846.

4. Shortwinded from obesity.

afternoon, but some days he went further, and was rather noisy. At such times, too, his face flamed with augmented blazonry, as if cannel coal had been heaped on anthracite. He made an unpleasant racket with his chair; spilled his sand-box; in mending his pens, impatiently split them all to pieces, and threw them on the floor in a sudden passion; stood up and leaned over his table, boxing his papers about in a most indecorous manner, very sad to behold in an elderly man like him. Nevertheless, as he was in many ways a most valuable person to me, and all the time before twelve o'clock, meridian, was the quickest, steadiest creature too, accomplishing a great deal of work in a style not easy to be matched—for these reasons, I was willing to overlook his eccentricities, though indeed, occasionally, I remonstrated with him. I did this very gently, however, because, though the civilest, nay, the blandest and most reverential of men in the morning, yet in the afternoon he was disposed, upon provocation, to be slightly rash with his tongue, in fact, insolent. Now, valuing his morning services as I did, and resolved not to lose them; yet, at the same time made uncomfortable by his inflamed ways after twelve o'clock; and being a man of peace, unwilling by my admonitions to call forth unseemly retorts from him; I took upon me, one Saturday noon (he was always worse on Saturdays), to hint to him, very kindly, that perhaps now that he was growing old, it might be well to abridge his labors; in short, he need not come to my chambers after twelve o'clock, but, dinner over, had best go home to his lodgings and rest himself till tea-time. But no; he insisted upon his afternoon devotions. His countenance became intolerably fervid, as he oratorically assured me— gesticulating with a long ruler at the other end of the room—that if his services in the morning were useful, how indispensable, then, in the afternoon?

"With submission, sir," said Turkey on this occasion, "I consider myself your right-hand man. In the morning I but marshal and deploy my columns; but in the afternoon I put myself at their head, and gallantly charge the foe, thus!"—and he made a violent thrust with the ruler.

"But the blots, Turkey," intimated I.

"True,—but, with submission, sir, behold these hairs! I am getting old. Surely, sir, a blot or two of a warm afternoon is not to be severely urged against gray hairs. Old age—even if it blot the page—is honorable. With submission, sir, we *both* are getting old."

This appeal to my fellow-feeling was hardly to be resisted. At all events, I saw that go he would not. So I made up my mind to let him stay, resolving, nevertheless, to see to it, that during the afternoon he had to do with my less important papers.

Nippers, the second on my list, was a whiskered, sallow, and, upon the whole, rather piratical-looking young man of about five and twenty. I always deemed him the victim of two evil powers—ambition and indigestion. The ambition was evinced by a certain impatience of the duties of a mere copyist, an unwarrantable usurpation of strictly professional affairs, such as the original drawing up of legal documents. The indigestion seemed betokened in an occasional nervous testiness and grinning irritability, causing the teeth to audibly grind together over mistakes committed in copying; unnecessary maledictions, hissed, rather than spoken, in the heat of business; and especially by a continual discontent with the height of the table where he worked. Though of a very ingenious mechanical turn, Nippers could never get this table to suit him. He put chips under it, blocks of various sorts, bits of pasteboard, and at last went so far as to attempt an exquisite adjustment by final pieces of folded blotting paper. But no invention would answer. If, for the sake of easing his back, he brought the table lid at a sharp angle well up towards his chin, and wrote there like a man using the steep roof of a Dutch house for his desk:—then he declared that it stopped the circulation in his arms. If now he lowered the table to his waistbands, and stooped over it in writing, then there was a sore aching in his back. In short, the truth of the matter was, Nippers knew not what he wanted. Or, if he wanted any thing, it was to be rid of a scrivener's table altogether. Among the manifestations of his diseased ambition was a fondness he had for receiving visits from certain ambiguous-looking fellows in seedy coats, whom he called his clients. Indeed I was aware that not only was he, at times, considerable of a ward-politician, but he occasionally did a little business at the Justices' courts, and was not unknown on the steps of the Tombs.[5] I have good reason to believe, however, that one individual who called upon him at my chambers, and who, with a grand air, he insisted was his client, was no other than a dun,[6] and the alleged title-deed, a bill. But with all his failings, and the annoyances he caused me, Nippers, like his compatriot Turkey, was a very useful man to me; wrote a neat, swift hand; and, when he chose, was not deficient in a gentlemanly sort of deportment. Added to this, he always dressed in a gentlemanly sort of way; and so, incidentally, reflected credit upon my chambers. Whereas with respect to Turkey, I had much ado to keep him from being a reproach to me. His clothes were apt to look oily and smell of eating-houses. He wore his pantaloons very loose and baggy in summer. His coats were execrable; his hat not to be handled. But while the hat was a thing of indifference to me, inasmuch as his natural civility and deference, as a dependent Englishman, always led him to doff it the moment he entered the room, yet his coat was another matter. Concerning his coats, I reasoned with him; but with no effect. The truth was, I suppose, that a man with so small an income, could not afford to sport such a lustrous face and a lustrous coat at one and the same time. As Nippers once observed, Turkey's money went chiefly for red ink. One winter day I presented Turkey with a highly-respectable looking coat of my own, a padded gray coat, of a most comfortable warmth, and which buttoned straight up from the knee to the neck. I thought Turkey would appreciate the favor, and abate his rashness and obstreperousness of afternoons. But no. I verily believe that buttoning himself up in so downy and blanket-like a coat had a pernicious effect upon him; upon the same principle that too much oats are bad for horses. In fact, precisely as a rash, restive horse is said to feel his oats, so Turkey felt his coat. It made him insolent. He was a man whom prosperity harmed.

Though concerning the self-indulgent habits of Turkey I had my own private surmises, yet touching Nippers I was well persuaded that whatever might be his faults in other respects, he was, at least, a temperate young man. But indeed, nature herself seemed to have been his vintner, and at his birth charged him so thoroughly with an irritable, brandy-like disposition, that all subsequent potations were needless. When I consider how, amid the stillness of my chambers, Nippers would sometimes impatiently rise from his seat, and stooping over his table, spread his arms wide apart, seize the whole desk, and move it, and jerk it, with a grim, grinding motion on the floor, as if the table

5. I.e., Nippers is suspected of arranging bail for prisoners or other such activities that strike the narrator as   unseemly if not nefarious.
6. Bill collector.

were a perverse voluntary agent, intent on thwarting and vexing him; I plainly perceive that for Nippers, brandy and water were altogether superfluous.

It was fortunate for me that, owing to its peculiar cause—indigestion—the irritability and consequent nervousness of Nippers, were mainly observable in the morning, while in the afternoon he was comparatively mild. So that Turkey's paroxysms only coming on about twelve o'clock, I never had to do with their eccentricities at one time. Their fits relieved each other like guards. When Nippers' was on, Turkey's was off; and *vice versa*. This was a good natural arrangement under the circumstances.

Ginger Nut, the third on my list, was a lad some twelve years old. His father was a carman,[7] ambitious of seeing his son on the bench instead of a cart, before he died. So he sent him to my office as student at law, errand boy, and cleaner and sweeper, at the rate of one dollar a week. He had a little desk to himself, but he did not use it much. Upon inspection, the drawer exhibited a great array of the shells of various sorts of nuts. Indeed, to this quick-witted youth the whole noble science of the law was contained in a nut-shell. Not the least among the employments of Ginger Nut, as well as one which he discharged with the most alacrity, was his duty as cake and apple purveyor for Turkey and Nippers. Copying law papers being proverbially a dry, husky sort of business, my two scriveners were fain to moisten their mouths very often with Spitzenbergs[8] to be had at the numerous stalls nigh the Custom House and Post Office. Also, they sent Ginger Nut very frequently for that peculiar cake—small, flat, round, and very spicy—after which he had been named by them. Of a cold morning when business was but dull, Turkey would gobble up scores of these cakes, as if they were mere wafers—indeed they sell them at the rate of six or eight for a penny—the scrape of his pen blending with the crunching of the crisp particles in his mouth. Of all the fiery afternoon blunders and flurried rashnesses of Turkey, was his once moistening a ginger-cake between his lips, and clapping it on to a mortgage for a seal.[9] I came within an ace of dismissing him then. But he mollified me by making an oriental bow, and saying—"With submission, sir, it was generous of me to find you in stationery on my own account."

Now my original business—that of a conveyancer and title hunter,[1] and drawer-up of recondite documents of all sorts—was considerably increased by receiving the master's office. There was now great work for scriveners. Not only must I push the clerks already with me, but I must have additional help. In answer to my advertisement, a motionless young man one morning, stood upon my office threshold, the door being open, for it was summer. I can see that figure now—pallidly neat, pitiably respectable, incurably forlorn! It was Bartleby.

After a few words touching his qualifications, I engaged him, glad to have among my corps of copyists a man of so singularly sedate an aspect, which I thought might operate beneficially upon the flighty temper of Turkey, and the fiery one of Nippers.

I should have stated before that ground glass folding-doors divided my premises into two parts, one of which was occupied by my scriveners, the other by

---

7. Driver, teamster.
8. Red-and-yellow New York apples.
9. The narrator is playing on the resemblance between thin cookies and wax wafers used for sealing documents.

1. Someone who checks records to be sure there are no encumbrances on the title of property to be transferred. "Conveyancer": someone who draws up deeds for transferring title to property.

myself. According to my humor I threw open these doors, or closed them. I resolved to assign Bartleby a corner by the folding-doors, but on my side of them, so as to have this quiet man within easy call, in case any trifling thing was to be done. I placed his desk close up to a small side-window in that part of the room, a window which originally had afforded a lateral view of certain grimy back-yards and bricks, but which, owing to subsequent erections, commanded at present no view at all, though it gave some light. Within three feet of the panes was a wall, and the light came down from far above, between two lofty buildings, as from a very small opening in a dome. Still further to a satisfactory arrangement, I procured a high green folding screen, which might entirely isolate Bartleby from my sight, though not remove him from my voice. And thus, in a manner, privacy and society were conjoined.

At first Bartleby did an extraordinary quantity of writing. As if long famishing for something to copy, he seemed to gorge himself on my documents. There was no pause for digestion. He ran a day and night line, copying by sun-light and by candle-light. I should have been quite delighted with his application, had he been cheerfully industrious. But he wrote on silently, palely, mechanically.

It is, of course, an indispensable part of a scrivener's business to verify the accuracy of his copy, word by word. Where there are two or more scriveners in an office, they assist each other in this examination, one reading from the copy, the other holding the original. It is a very dull, wearisome, and lethargic affair. I can readily imagine that to some sanguine temperaments it would be altogether intolerable. For example, I cannot credit that the mettlesome poet Byron would have contentedly sat down with Bartleby to examine a law document of, say five hundred pages, closely written in a crimpy hand.

Now and then, in the haste of business, it had been my habit to assist in comparing some brief document myself, calling Turkey or Nippers for this purpose. One object I had in placing Bartleby so handy to me behind the screen, was to avail myself of his services on such trivial occasions. It was on the third day, I think, of his being with me, and before any necessity had arisen for having his own writing examined, that, being much hurried to complete a small affair I had in hand, I abruptly called to Bartleby. In my haste and natural expectancy of instant compliance, I sat with my head bent over the original on my desk, and my right hand sideways, and somewhat nervously extended with the copy, so that immediately upon emerging from his retreat, Bartleby might snatch it and proceed to business without the least delay.

In this very attitude did I sit when I called to him, rapidly stating what it was I wanted him to do—namely, to examine a small paper with me. Imagine my surprise, nay, my consternation, when without moving from his privacy, Bartleby in a singularly mild, firm voice, replied, "I would prefer not to."

I sat awhile in perfect silence, rallying my stunned faculties. Immediately it occurred to me that my ears had deceived me, or Bartleby had entirely misunderstood my meaning. I repeated my request in the clearest tone I could assume. But in quite as clear a one came the previous reply, "I would prefer not to."

"Prefer not to," echoed I, rising in high excitement, and crossing the room with a stride. "What do you mean? Are you moon-struck? I want you to help me compare this sheet here—take it," and I thrust it towards him.

"I would prefer not to," said he.

I looked at him steadfastly. His face was leanly composed; his gray eye dimly calm. Not a wrinkle of agitation rippled him. Had there been the least uneasiness, anger, impatience or impertinence in his manner; in other words, had there been any thing ordinarily human about him, doubtless I should have violently dismissed him from the premises. But as it was, I should have as soon thought of turning my pale plaster-of-paris bust of Cicero[2] out of doors. I stood gazing at him awhile, as he went on with his own writing, and then reseated myself at my desk. This is very strange, thought I. What had one best do? But my business hurried me. I concluded to forget the matter for the present, reserving it for my future leisure. So calling Nippers from the other room, the paper was speedily examined.

A few days after this, Bartleby concluded four lengthy documents, being quadruplicates of a week's testimony taken before me in my High Court of Chancery. It became necessary to examine them. It was an important suit, and great accuracy was imperative. Having all things arranged I called Turkey, Nippers and Ginger Nut from the next room, meaning to place the four copies in the hands of my four clerks, while I should read from the original. Accordingly Turkey, Nippers and Ginger Nut had taken their seats in a row, each with his document in hand, when I called to Bartleby to join this interesting group.

"Bartleby! quick, I am waiting."

I heard a slow scrape of his chair legs on the uncarpeted floor, and soon he appeared standing at the entrance of his hermitage.

"What is wanted?" said he mildly.

"The copies, the copies" said I hurriedly. "We are going to examine them. There"—and I held towards him the fourth quadruplicate.

"I would prefer not to," he said, and gently disappeared behind the screen.

For a few moments I was turned into a pillar of salt,[3] standing at the head of my seated column of clerks. Recovering myself, I advanced towards the screen, and demanded the reason for such extraordinary conduct.

"*Why* do you refuse?"

"I would prefer not to."

With any other man I should have flown outright into a dreadful passion, scorned all further words, and thrust him ignominiously from my presence. But there was something about Bartleby that not only strangely disarmed me, but in a wonderful manner touched and disconcerted me. I began to reason with him.

"These are your own copies we are about to examine. It is labor saving to you, because one examination will answer for your four papers. It is common usage. Every copyist is bound to help examine his copy. Is it not so? Will you not speak? Answer!"

"I prefer not to," he replied in a flute-like tone. It seemed to me that while I had been addressing him, he carefully revolved every statement that I made; fully comprehended the meaning; could not gainsay the irresistible conclusion; but, at the same time, some paramount consideration prevailed with him to reply as he did.

"You are decided, then, not to comply with my request—a request made according to common usage and common sense?"

2. Roman orator and statesman (106–42 B.C.).
3. The punishment of Lot's disobedient wife (Genesis 19.26).

He briefly gave me to understand that on that point my judgment was sound. Yes: his decision was irreversible.

It is not seldom the case that when a man is browbeaten in some unprecedented and violently unreasonable way, he begins to stagger in his own plainest faith. He begins, as it were, vaguely to surmise that, wonderful as it may be, all the justice and all the reason is on the other side. Accordingly, if any disinterested persons are present, he turns to them for some reinforcement for his own faltering mind.

"Turkey," said I, "what do you think of this? Am I not right?"

"With submission, sir," said Turkey, with his blandest tone, "I think that you are."

"Nippers," said I, "what do *you* think of it?"

"I think I should kick him out of the office."

(The reader of nice perceptions will here perceive that, it being morning, Turkey's answer is couched in polite and tranquil terms, but Nippers replies in ill-tempered ones. Or, to repeat a previous sentence, Nippers's ugly mood was on duty, and Turkey's off.)

"Ginger Nut," said I, willing to enlist the smallest suffrage in my behalf, "what do *you* think of it?"

"I think, sir, he's a little *luny*," replied Ginger Nut, with a grin.

"You hear what they say," said I, turning towards the screen, "come forth and do your duty."

But he vouchsafed no reply. I pondered a moment in sore perplexity. But once more business hurried me. I determined again to postpone the consideration of this dilemma to my future leisure. With a little trouble we made out to examine the papers without Bartleby, though at every page or two, Turkey deferentially dropped his opinion that this proceeding was quite out of the common; while Nippers, twitching in his chair with a dyspeptic nervousness, ground out between his set teeth occasional hissing maledictions against the stubborn oaf behind the screen. And for his (Nippers's) part, this was the first and the last time he would do another man's business without pay.

Meanwhile Bartleby sat in his hermitage, oblivious to every thing but his own peculiar business there.

Some days passed, the scrivener being employed upon another lengthy work. His late remarkable conduct led me to regard his ways narrowly. I observed that he never went to dinner; indeed that he never went any where. As yet I had never of my personal knowledge known him to be outside of my office. He was a perpetual sentry in the corner. At about eleven o'clock though, in the morning, I noticed that Ginger Nut would advance toward the opening in Bartleby's screen, as if silently beckoned thither by a gesture invisible to me where I sat. The boy would then leave the office jingling a few pence, and reappear with a handful of ginger-nuts which he delivered in the hermitage, receiving two of the cakes for his trouble.

He lives, then, on ginger-nuts, thought I; never eats a dinner, properly speaking; he must be a vegetarian then; but no; he never eats even vegetables, he eats nothing but ginger-nuts. My mind then ran on in reveries concerning the probable effects upon the human constitution of living entirely on ginger-nuts. Ginger-nuts are so called because they contain ginger as one of their peculiar constituents, and the final flavoring one. Now what was ginger? A hot, spicy thing. Was Bartleby hot and spicy? Not at all. Ginger, then, had no effect upon Bartleby. Probably he preferred it should have none.

Nothing so aggravates an earnest person as a passive resistance. If the individual so resisted be of a not inhumane temper, and the resisting one perfectly harmless in his passivity; then, in the better moods of the former, he will endeavor charitably to construe to his imagination what proves impossible to be solved by his judgment. Even so, for the most part, I regarded Bartleby and his ways. Poor fellow! thought I, he means no mischief; it is plain he intends no insolence; his aspect sufficiently evinces that his eccentricities are involuntary. He is useful to me. I can get along with him. If I turn him away, the chances are he will fall in with some less indulgent employer, and then he will be rudely treated, and perhaps driven forth miserably to starve. Yes. Here I can cheaply purchase a delicious self-approval. To befriend Bartleby; to humor him in his strange wilfulness, will cost me little or nothing, while I lay up in my soul what will eventually prove a sweet morsel for my conscience. But this mood was not invariable with me. The passiveness of Bartleby sometimes irritated me. I felt strangely goaded on to encounter him in new opposition, to elicit some angry spark from him answerable to my own. But indeed I might as well have essayed to strike fire with my knuckles against a bit of Windsor soap.[4] But one afternoon the evil impulse in me mastered me, and the following little scene ensued:

"Bartleby," said I, "when those papers are all copied, I will compare them with you."

"I would prefer not to."

"How? Surely you do not mean to persist in that mulish vagary?"

No answer.

I threw open the folding-doors near by, and turning upon Turkey and Nippers, exclaimed in an excited manner—

"He says, a second time, he won't examine his papers. What do you think of it, Turkey?"

It was afternoon, be it remembered. Turkey sat glowing like a brass boiler, his bald head steaming, his hands reeling among his blotted papers.

"Think of it?" roared Turkey; "I think I'll just step behind his screen, and black his eyes for him!"

So saying, Turkey rose to his feet and threw his arms into a pugilistic position. He was hurrying away to make good his promise, when I detained him, alarmed at the effect of incautiously rousing Turkey's combativeness after dinner.

"Sit down, Turkey," said I, "and hear what Nippers has to say. What do you think of it, Nippers? Would I not be justified in immediately dismissing Bartleby?"

"Excuse me, that is for you to decide, sir. I think his conduct quite unusual, and indeed unjust, as regards Turkey and myself. But it may only be a passing whim."

"Ah," exclaimed I, "you have strangely changed your mind then—you speak very gently of him now."

"All beer," cried Turkey; "gentleness is effects of beer—Nippers and I dined together to-day. You see how gentle I am, sir. Shall I go and black his eyes?"

"You refer to Bartleby, I suppose. No, not to-day, Turkey," I replied; "pray, put up your fists."

4. Brown hand soap.

I closed the doors, and again advanced towards Bartleby. I felt additional incentives tempting me to my fate. I burned to be rebelled against again. I remembered that Bartleby never left the office.

"Bartleby," said I, "Ginger Nut is away; just step round to the Post Office, won't you? (it was but a three minutes' walk,) and see if there is any thing for me."

"I would prefer not to."

"You *will* not?"

"I *prefer* not."

I staggered to my desk, and sat there in a deep study. My blind inveteracy returned. Was there any other thing in which I could procure myself to be ignominiously repulsed by this lean, penniless wight?—my hired clerk? What added thing is there, perfectly reasonable, that he will be sure to refuse to do?

"Bartleby!"

No answer.

"Bartleby," in a louder tone.

No answer.

"Bartleby," I roared.

Like a very ghost, agreeably to the laws of magical invocation, at the third summons, he appeared at the entrance of his hermitage.

"Go to the next room, and tell Nippers to come to me."

"I prefer not to," he respectfully and slowly said, and mildly disappeared.

"Very good, Bartleby," said I, in a quiet sort of serenely severe self-possessed tone, intimating the unalterable purpose of some terrible retribution very close at hand. At the moment I half intended something of the kind. But upon the whole, as it was drawing towards my dinner-hour, I thought it best to put on my hat and walk home for the day, suffering much from perplexity and distress of mind.

Shall I acknowledge it? The conclusion of this whole business was, that it soon became a fixed fact of my chambers, that a pale young scrivener, by the name of Bartleby, had a desk there; that he copied for me at the usual rate of four cents a folio (one hundred words); but he was permanently exempt from examining the work done by him, that duty being transferred to Turkey and Nippers, out of compliment doubtless to their superior acuteness; moreover, said Bartleby was never on any account to be dispatched on the most trivial errand of any sort; and that even if entreated to take upon him such a matter, it was generally understood that he would prefer not to—in other words, that he would refuse point-blank.

As days passed on, I became considerably reconciled to Bartleby. His steadiness, his freedom from all dissipation, his incessant industry (except when he chose to throw himself into a standing revery behind his screen), his great stillness, his unalterableness of demeanor under all circumstances, made him a valuable acquisition. One prime thing was this,—*he was always there;*—first in the morning, continually through the day, and the last at night. I had a singular confidence in his honesty. I felt my most precious papers perfectly safe in his hands. Sometimes to be sure I could not, for the very soul of me, avoid falling into sudden spasmodic passions with him. For it was exceeding difficult to bear in mind all the time those strange peculiarities, privileges, and unheard of exemptions, forming the tacit stipulations on Bartleby's part under which he remained in my office. Now and then, in the eagerness of dispatching pressing business, I would inadvertently summon Bartleby, in a short, rapid tone, to put his finger, say, on the incipient tie of a bit of red tape with which I was about compressing some papers. Of course, from behind the screen the usual answer, "I prefer not to," was sure to come; and then, how could a human creature with common infirmities of our nature, refrain from bitterly exclaiming upon such perverseness—such unreasonableness. However, every added repulse of this sort which I received only tended to lessen the probability of my repeating the inadvertence.

Here it must be said, that according to the customs of most legal gentlemen occupying chambers in densely-populated law buildings, there were several keys to my door. One was kept by a woman residing in the attic, which person weekly scrubbed and daily swept and dusted my apartments. Another was kept by Turkey for convenience sake. The third I sometimes carried in my own pocket. The fourth I knew not who had.

Now, one Sunday morning I happened to go to Trinity Church, to hear a celebrated preacher, and finding myself rather early on the ground, I thought I would walk round to my chambers for a while. Luckily I had my key with me; but upon applying it to the lock, I found it resisted by something inserted from the inside. Quite surprised, I called out; when to my consternation a key was turned from within; and thrusting his lean visage at me, and holding the door ajar, the apparition of Bartleby appeared, in his shirt sleeves, and otherwise in a strangely tattered dishabille, saying quietly that he was sorry, but he was deeply engaged just then, and—preferred not admitting me at present. In a brief word or two, he moreover added, that perhaps I had better walk round the block two or three times, and by that time he would probably have concluded his affairs.

Now, the utterly unsurmised appearance of Bartleby, tenanting my law-chambers of a Sunday morning, with his cadaverously gentlemanly *nonchalance*, yet withal firm and self-possessed, had such a strange effect upon me, that incontinently I slunk away from my own door, and did as desired. But not without sundry twinges of impotent rebellion against the mild effrontery of this unaccountable scrivener. Indeed, it was his wonderful mildness chiefly, which not only disarmed me, but unmanned me, as it were. For I consider that one, for the time, is a sort of unmanned when he tranquilly permits his hired clerk to dictate to him, and order him away from his own premises. Furthermore, I was full of uneasiness as to what Bartleby could possibly be doing in my office in his shirt sleeves, and in an otherwise dismantled condition of a Sunday morning. Was any thing amiss going on? Nay, that was out of the question. It was not to be thought of for a moment that Bartleby was an immoral person. But what could he be doing there?—copying? Nay again, whatever might be his eccentricities, Bartleby was an eminently decorous person. He would be the last man to sit down to his desk in any state approaching to nudity. Besides, it was Sunday; and there was something about Bartleby that forbade the supposition that he would by any secular occupation violate the proprieties of the day.

Nevertheless, my mind was not pacified; and full of a restless curiosity, at last I returned to the door. Without hindrance I inserted my key, opened it, and entered. Bartleby was not to be seen. I looked round anxiously, peeped behind his screen; but it was very plain that he was gone. Upon more closely examining the place, I surmised that for an indefinite period Bartleby must have ate, dressed, and slept in my office, and that too without plate, mirror, or bed. The cushioned seat of a ricketty old sofa in one corner bore the faint impress of a lean, reclining form. Rolled away under his desk, I found a blanket; under the empty grate, a blacking box and brush; on a chair, a tin basin, with soap and a ragged towel; in a newspaper a few crumbs of ginger-nuts and a morsel of cheese. Yes, thought I, it is evident enough that Bartleby has been making his home here, keeping bachelor's hall all by himself. Immediately then the thought came sweeping across me, What miserable friendlessness and loneliness are here revealed! His poverty is great; but his solitude, how horrible! Think of it. Of a Sunday, Wall-street is deserted as Petra;[5] and every night of every day it is an emptiness. This building too, which of week-days hums with industry and life, at nightfall echoes with sheer vacancy, and all through Sunday is forlorn. And here Bartleby makes his home; sole spectator of a solitude which he has seen all populous—a sort of innocent and transformed Marius[6] brooding among the ruins of Carthage!

For the first time in my life a feeling of overpowering stinging melancholy seized me. Before, I had never experienced aught but a not-unpleasing sadness. The bond of a common humanity now drew me irresistibly to gloom. A fraternal melancholy! For both I and Bartleby were sons of Adam. I remembered the bright silks and sparkling faces I had seen that day, in gala trim, swan-like sailing down the Mississippi of Broadway; and I contrasted them with the pallid copyist, and thought to myself, Ah, happiness courts the light, so we deem the world is gay; but misery hides aloof, so we deem that misery there is none. These sad fancyings—chimeras, doubtless, of a sick and silly brain—led on to other and more special thoughts, concerning the eccentricities of Bartleby. Presentiments of strange discoveries hovered round me. The scrivener's pale form appeared to me laid out, among uncaring strangers, in its shivering winding sheet.

Suddenly I was attracted by Bartleby's closed desk, the key in open sight left in the lock.

I mean no mischief, seek the gratification of no heartless curiosity, thought I; besides, the desk is mine, and its contents too, so I will make bold to look within. Every thing was methodically arranged, the papers smoothly placed. The pigeon holes were deep, and removing the files of documents, I groped into their recesses. Presently I felt something there, and dragged it out. It was an old bandanna handkerchief, heavy and knotted. I opened it, and saw it was a saving's bank.

I now recalled all the quiet mysteries which I had noted in the man. I remembered that he never spoke but to answer; that though at intervals he had considerable time to himself, yet I had never seen him reading—no, not even a newspaper; that for long periods he would stand looking out, at his pale window behind the screen, upon the dead brick wall; I was quite sure he never visited any refectory or eating house; while his pale face clearly indicated that he never drank beer like Turkey, or tea and coffee even, like other men; that he never went any where in particular that I could learn; never went out for a walk, unless indeed that was the case at present; that he had declined telling who he was, or whence he came, or whether he had any relatives in the world; that though so thin and pale, he never complained of ill health. And more

5. Ancient city whose ruins are in Jordan, on a slope of Mount Hor.

6. Gaius Marius (157–86 B.C.), Roman general who returned to power after exile.

than all, I remembered a certain unconscious air of pallid—how shall I call it?—of pallid haughtiness, say, or rather an austere reserve about him, which had positively awed me into my tame compliance with his eccentricities, when I had feared to ask him to do the slightest incidental thing for me, even though I might know, from his long-continued motionlessness, that behind his screen he must be standing in one of those dead-wall reveries of his.

Revolving all these things, and coupling them with the recently discovered fact that he made my office his constant abiding place and home, and not forgetful of his morbid moodiness; revolving all these things, a prudential feeling began to steal over me. My first emotions had been those of pure melancholy and sincerest pity; but just in proportion as the forlornness of Bartleby grew and grew to my imagination, did that same melancholy merge into fear, that pity into repulsion. So true it is, and so terrible too, that up to a certain point the thought or sight of misery enlists our best affections; but, in certain special cases, beyond that point it does not. They err who would assert that invariably this is owing to the inherent selfishness of the human heart. It rather proceeds from a certain hopelessness of remedying excessive and organic ill. To a sensitive being, pity is not seldom pain. And when at last it is perceived that such pity cannot lead to effectual succor, common sense bids the soul be rid of it. What I saw that morning persuaded me that the scrivener was the victim of innate and incurable disorder. I might give alms to his body; but his body did not pain him; it was his soul that suffered, and his soul I could not reach.

I did not accomplish the purpose of going to Trinity Church that morning. Somehow, the things I had seen disqualified me for the time from church-going. I walked homeward, thinking what I would do with Bartleby. Finally, I resolved upon this;—I wold put certain calm questions to him the next morning, touching his history, &c., and if he declined to answer them openly and unreservedly (and I supposed he would prefer not), then to give him a twenty dollar bill over and above whatever I might owe him, and tell him his services were no longer required; but that if in any other way I could assist him, I would be happy to do so, especially if he desired to return to his native place, wherever that might be, I would willingly help to defray the expenses. Moreover, if, after reaching home, he found himself at any time in want of aid, a letter from him would be sure of a reply.

The next morning came.

"Bartleby," said I, gently calling to him behind his screen.

No reply.

"Bartleby," said I, in a still gentler tone, "come here; I am not going to ask you to do any thing you would prefer not to do—I simply wish to speak to you."

Upon this he noiselessly slid into view.

"Will you tell me, Bartleby, where you were born?"

"I would prefer not to."

"Will you tell me *any thing* about yourself?"

"I would prefer not to."

"But what reasonable objection can you have to speak to me? I feel friendly towards you."

He did not look at me while I spoke, but kept his glance fixed upon my bust of Cicero, which as I then sat, was directly behind me, some six inches above my head.

"What is your answer, Bartleby?" said I, after waiting a considerable time for a reply, during which his countenance remained immovable, only there was the faintest conceivable tremor of the white attenuated mouth.

"At present I prefer to give no answer," he said, and retired into his hermitage.

It was rather weak in me I confess, but his manner on this occasion nettled me. Not only did there seem to lurk in it a certain calm disdain, but his perverseness seemed ungrateful, considering the undeniable good usage and indulgence he had received from me.

Again I sat ruminating what I should do. Mortified as I was at his behavior, and resolved as I had been to dismiss him when I entered my office, nevertheless I strangely felt something superstitious knocking at my heart, and forbidding me to carry out my purpose, and denouncing me for a villain if I dared to breathe one bitter word against this forlornest of mankind. At last, familiarly drawing my chair behind his screen, I sat down and said: "Bartleby, never mind then about revealing your history; but let me entreat you, as a friend, to comply as far as may be with the usages of this office. Say now you will help to examine papers to-morrow or next day: in short, say now that in a day or two you will begin to be a little reasonable:—say so, Bartleby."

"At present I would prefer not to be a little reasonable," was his mildly cadaverous reply.

Just then the folding-doors opened, and Nippers approached. He seemed suffering from an unusually bad night's rest, induced by severer indigestion than common. He overheard those final words of Bartleby.

"*Prefer not,* eh?" gritted Nippers—"I'd *prefer* him, if I were you, sir," addressing me—"I'd *prefer* him; I'd give him preferences, the stubborn mule! What is it, sir, pray, that he *prefers* not to do now?"

Bartleby moved not a limb.

"Mr. Nippers," said I, "I'd prefer that you would withdraw for the present."

Somehow, of late I had got into the way of involuntarily using this word "prefer" upon all sorts of not exactly suitable occasions. And I trembled to think that my contact with the scrivener had already and seriously affected me in a mental way. And what further and deeper aberration might it not yet produce? This apprehension had not been without efficacy in determining me to summary means.

As Nippers, looking very sour and sulky, was departing, Turkey blandly and deferentially approached.

"With submission, sir," said he, "yesterday I was thinking about Bartleby here, and I think that if he would but prefer to take a quart of good ale every day, it would do much towards mending him, and enabling him to assist in examining his papers."

"So you have got the word too," said I, slightly excited.

"With submission, what word, sir," asked Turkey, respectfully crowding himself into the contracted space behind the screen, and by so doing, making me jostle the scrivener. "What word, sir?"

"I would prefer to be left alone here," said Bartleby, as if offended at being mobbed in his privacy.

"*That's* the word, Turkey," said I—"*that's* it."

"Oh, *prefer?* oh yes—queer word. I never use it myself. But, sir, as I was saying, if he would but prefer—"

"Turkey," interrupted I, "you will please withdraw."

"Oh certainly, sir, if you prefer that I should."

As he opened the folding-door to retire, Nippers at his desk caught a glimpse of me, and asked whether I would prefer to have a certain paper copied on blue paper or white. He did not in the least roguishly accent the word prefer. It was plain that it involuntarily rolled from his tongue. I thought to myself, surely I must get rid of a demented man, who already has in some degree turned the tongues, if not the heads of myself and clerks. But I thought it prudent not to break the dismission at once.

The next day I noticed that Bartleby did nothing but stand at his window in his dead-wall revery. Upon asking him why he did not write, he said that he had decided upon doing no more writing.

"Why, how now? what next?" exclaimed I, "do no more writing?"

"No more."

"And what is the reason?"

"Do you not see the reason for yourself," he indifferently replied.

I looked steadfastly at him, and perceived that his eyes looked dull and glazed. Instantly it occurred to me, that his unexampled diligence in copying by his dim window for the first few weeks of his stay with me might have temporarily impaired his vision.

I was touched. I said something in condolence with him. I hinted that of course he did wisely in abstaining from writing for a while; and urged him to embrace that opportunity of taking wholesome exercise in the open air. This, however, he did not do. A few days after this, my other clerks being absent, and being in a great hurry to dispatch certain letters by the mail, I thought that, having nothing else earthly to do, Bartleby would surely be less inflexible than usual, and carry these letters to the post-office. But he blankly declined. So, much to my inconvenience, I went myself.

Still added days went by. Whether Bartleby's eyes improved or not, I could not say. To all appearance, I thought they did. But when I asked him if they did, he vouchsafed no answer. At all events, he would do no copying. At last, in reply to my urgings, he informed me that he had permanently given up copying.

"What!" exclaimed I; "suppose your eyes should get entirely well—better than ever before—would you not copy then?"

"I have given up copying," he answered, and slid aside.

He remained as ever, a fixture in my chamber. Nay—if that were possible— he became still more of a fixture than before. What was to be done? He would do nothing in the office: why should he stay there? In plain fact, he had now become a millstone to me, not only useless as a necklace, but afflictive to bear. Yet I was sorry for him. I speak less than truth when I say that, on his own account, he occasioned me uneasiness. If he would but have named a single relative or friend, I would instantly have written, and urged their taking the poor fellow away to some convenient retreat. But he seemed alone, absolutely alone in the universe. A bit of wreck in the mid Atlantic. At length, necessities connected with my business tyrannized over all other considerations. Decently as I could, I told Bartleby that in six days' time he must unconditionally leave the office. I warned him to take measures, in the interval, for procuring some other abode. I offered to assist him in this endeavor, if he himself would but take the first step towards a removal. "And when you finally quit me, Bartleby," added I, "I shall see that you go not away entirely unprovided. Six days from this hour, remember."

At the expiration of that period, I peeped behind the screen, and lo! Bartleby was there.

I buttoned up my coat, balanced myself; advanced slowly towards him, touched his shoulder, and said, "The time has come; you must quit this place; I am sorry for you; here is money; but you must go."

"I would prefer not," he replied, with his back still towards me.

"You *must*."

He remained silent.

Now I had an unbounded confidence in this man's common honesty. He had frequently restored to me sixpences and shillings carelessly dropped upon the floor, for I am apt to be very reckless in such shirt-button affairs. The proceeding then which followed will not be deemed extraordinary.

"Bartleby," said I, "I owe you twelve dollars on account; here are thirty-two; the odd twenty are yours.—Will you take it?" and I handed the bills towards him.

But he made no motion.

"I will leave them here then," putting them under a weight on the table. Then taking my hat and cane and going to the door I tranquilly turned and added—"After you have removed your things from these offices, Bartleby, you will of course lock the door—since every one is now gone for the day but you—and if you please, slip your key underneath the mat, so that I may have it in the morning. I shall not see you again; so good-bye to you. If hereafter in your new place of abode I can be of any service to you, do not fail to advise me by letter. Good-bye, Bartleby, and fare you well."

But he answered not a word; like the last column of some ruined temple, he remained standing mute and solitary in the middle of the otherwise deserted room.

As I walked home in a pensive mood, my vanity got the better of my pity. I could not but highly plume myself on my masterly management in getting rid of Bartleby. Masterly I call it, and such it must appear to any dispassionate thinker. The beauty of my procedure seemed to consist in its perfect quietness. There was no vulgar bullying, no bravado of any sort, no choleric hectoring, and striding to and fro across the apartment, jerking out vehement commands for Bartleby to bundle himself off with his beggarly traps. Nothing of the kind. Without loudly bidding Bartleby depart—as an inferior genius might have done—I *assumed* the ground that depart he must; and upon that assumption built all I had to say. The more I thought over my procedure, the more I was charmed with it. Nevertheless, next morning, upon awakening, I had my doubts,—I had somehow slept off the fumes of vanity. One of the coolest and wisest hours a man has, is just after he awakes in the morning. My procedure seemed as sagacious as ever,—but only in theory. How it would prove in practice—there was the rub. It was truly a beautiful thought to have assumed Bartleby's departure; but, after all, that assumption was simply my own, and none of Bartleby's. The great point was, not whether I had assumed that he would quit me, but whether he would prefer so to do. He was more a man of preferences than assumptions.

After breakfast, I walked down town, arguing the probabilities *pro* and *con*. One moment I thought it would prove a miserable failure, and Bartleby would be found all alive at my office as usual; the next moment it seemed certain that I should see his chair empty. And so I kept veering about. At the corner of Broadway and Canal-street, I saw quite an excited group of people standing in earnest conversation.

"I'll take odds he doesn't," said a voice as I passed.

"Doesn't go?—done!" said I, "put up your money."

I was instinctively putting my hand in my pocket to produce my own, when I remembered that this was an election day. The words I had overheard bore no reference to Bartleby, but to the success or non-success of some candidate for the mayoralty. In my intent frame of mind, I had, as it were, imagined that all Broadway shared in my excitement, and were debating the same question with me. I passed on, very thankful that the uproar of the street screened my momentary absent-mindedness.

As I had intended, I was earlier than usual at my office door. I stood listening for a moment. All was still. He must be gone. I tried the knob. The door was locked. Yes, my procedure had worked to a charm; he indeed must be vanished. Yet a certain melancholy mixed with this: I was almost sorry for my brilliant success. I was fumbling under the door mat for the key, which Bartleby was to have left there for me, when accidentally my knee knocked against a panel, producing a summoning sound, and in response a voice came to me from within—"Not yet; I am occupied."

It was Bartleby.

I was thunderstruck. For an instant I stood like the man who, pipe in mouth, was killed one cloudless afternoon long ago in Virginia, by summer lightning; at his own warm open window he was killed, and remained leaning out there upon the dreamy afternoon, till some one touched him, when he fell.

"Not gone!" I murmured at last. But again obeying that wondrous ascendancy which the inscrutable scrivener had over me, and from which ascendancy, for all my chafing, I could not completely escape, I slowly went down stairs and out into the street, and while walking round the block, considered what I should next do in this unheard-of perplexity. Turn the man out by an actual thrusting I could not; to drive him away by calling him hard names would not do; calling in the police was an unpleasant idea; and yet, permit him to enjoy his cadaverous triumph over me,—this too I could not think of. What was to be done? or, if nothing could be done, was there any thing further that I could *assume* in the matter? Yes, as before I had prospectively assumed that Bartleby would depart, so now I might retrospectively assume that departed he was. In the legitimate carrying out of this assumption, I might enter my office in a great hurry, and pretending not to see Bartleby at all, walk straight against him as if he were air. Such a proceeding would in a singular degree have the appearance of a home-thrust. It was hardly possible that Bartleby could withstand such an application of the doctrine of assumptions. But upon second thoughts the success of the plan seemed rather dubious. I resolved to argue the matter over with him again.

"Bartleby," said I, entering the office, with a quietly severe expression, "I am seriously displeased. I am pained, Bartleby. I had thought better of you. I had imagined you of such a gentlemanly organization, that in any delicate dilemma a slight hint would suffice—in short, an assumption. But it appears I am deceived. Why," I added, unaffectedly starting, "you have not even touched that money yet," pointing to it, just where I had left it the evening previous.

He answered nothing.

"Will you, or will you not, quit me?" I now demanded in a sudden passion, advancing close to him.

"I would prefer *not* to quit you," he replied, gently emphasizing the *not*.

"What earthly right have you to stay here? Do you pay any rent? Do you pay my taxes? Or is this property yours?"

He answered nothing.

"Are you ready to go on and write now? Are your eyes recovered? Could you copy a small paper for me this morning? or help examine a few lines? or step round to the post-office? In a word, will you do any thing at all, to give a coloring to your refusal to depart the premises?"

He silently retired into his hermitage.

I was now in such a state of nervous resentment that I thought it but prudent to check myself at present from further demonstrations. Bartleby and I were alone. I remembered the tragedy of the unfortunate Adams and the still more unfortunate Colt in the solitary office of the latter; and how poor Colt, being dreadfully incensed by Adams,[7] and imprudently permitting himself to get wildly excited, was at unawares hurried into his fatal act—an act which certainly no man could possibly deplore more than the actor himself. Often it had occurred to me in my ponderings upon the subject, that had that altercation taken place in the public street, or at a private residence, it would not have terminated as it did. It was the circumstance of being alone in a solitary office, up stairs, of a building entirely unhallowed by humanizing domestic associations—an uncarpeted office, doubtless, of a dusty, haggard sort of appearance;—this it must have been, which greatly helped to enhance the irritable desperation of the hapless Colt.

But when this old Adam of resentment rose in me and tempted me concerning Bartleby, I grappled him and threw him. How? Why, simply by recalling the divine injunction: "A new commandment give I unto you, that ye love one another." Yes, this it was that saved me. Aside from higher considerations, charity often operates as a vastly wise and prudent principle—a great safeguard to its possessor. Men have committed murder for jealousy's sake, and anger's sake, and hatred's sake, and selfishness' sake, and spiritual pride's sake; but no man that ever I heard of, ever committed a diabolical murder for sweet charity's sake. Mere self-interest, then, if no better motive can be enlisted, should, especially with high-tempered men, prompt all beings to charity and philanthropy. At any rate, upon the occasion in question, I strove to drown my exasperated feelings towards the scrivener by benevolently constructing his conduct. Poor fellow, poor fellow! thought I, he don't mean any thing; and besides, he has seen hard times, and ought to be indulged.

I endeavored also immediately to occupy myself, and at the same time to comfort my despondency. I tried to fancy that in the course of the morning, at such time as might prove agreeable to him, Bartleby, of his own free accord,

7. Notorious murder case that occurred while Melville was in the South Seas. In 1841 Samuel Adams, a printer, called on John C. Colt (brother of the inventor of the revolver) at Broadway and Chambers Street in lower Manhattan to collect a debt. Colt murdered Adams with a hatchet and crated the corpse for shipment to New Orleans. The body was found, and Colt was soon arrested. Despite his pleas of self-defense Colt was convicted the next year, amid continuing newspaper publicity, and stabbed himself to death just before he was to be hanged. The setting of *Bartleby* is not far from the scene of the murder.

would emerge from his hermitage, and take up some decided line of march in the direction of the door. But no. Half-past twelve o'clock came; Turkey began to glow in the face, overturn his inkstand, and become generally obstreperous; Nippers abated down into quietude and courtesy; Ginger Nut munched his noon apple; and Bartleby remained standing at his window in one of his profoundest dead-wall reveries. Will it be credited? Ought I to acknowledge it? That afternoon I left the office without saying one further word to him.

Some days now passed, during which, at leisure intervals I looked a little into "Edwards on the Will," and "Priestley on Necessity."[8] Under the circumstances, those books induced a salutary feeling. Gradually I slid into the persuasion that these troubles of mine touching the scrivener, had been all predestinated from eternity, and Bartleby was billeted upon me for some mysterious purpose of an all-wise Providence, which it was not for a mere mortal like me to fathom. Yes, Bartleby, stay there behind your screen, thought I; I shall persecute you no more; you are harmless and noiseless as any of these old chairs; in short, I never feel so private as when I know you are here. At least I see it, I feel it; I penetrate to the predestinated purpose of my life. I am content. Others may have loftier parts to enact; but my mission in this world, Bartleby, is to furnish you with office-room for such period as you may see fit to remain.

I believe that this wise and blessed frame of mind would have continued with me, had it not been for the unsolicited and uncharitable remarks obtruded upon me by my professional friends who visited the rooms. But thus it often is, that the constant friction of illiberal minds wears out at last the best resolves of the more generous. Though to be sure, when I reflected upon it, it was not strange that people entering my office should be struck by the peculiar aspect of the unaccountable Bartleby, and so be tempted to throw out some sinister observations concerning him. Sometimes an attorney having business with me, and calling at my office, and finding no one but the scrivener there, would undertake to obtain some sort of precise information from him touching my whereabouts; but without heeding his idle talk, Bartleby would remain standing immovable in the middle of the room. So after contemplating him in that position for a time, the attorney would depart, no wiser than he came.

Also, when a Reference[9] was going on, and the room full of lawyers and witnesses and business was driving fast; some deeply occupied legal gentleman present, seeing Bartleby wholly unemployed, would request him to run round to his (the legal gentleman's) office and fetch some papers for him. Thereupon, Bartleby would tranquilly decline, and yet remain idle as before. Then the lawyer would give a great stare, and turn to me. And what could I say? At last I was made aware that all through the circle of my professional acquaintance, a whisper of wonder was running round, having reference to the strange creature I kept at my office. This worried me very much. And as the idea came upon me of his possibly turning out a long-lived man, and keep occupying my chambers, and denying my authority; and perplexing my visitors; and scandalizing my professional reputation; and casting a general gloom over the premises; keeping soul and body together to the last upon his savings (for

8. Jonathan Edwards's *Freedom of the Will* (1754) and Joseph Priestley's *Doctrine of Philosophical Necessity Illustrated* (1777). The colonial minister and the English

scientist agree that the will is not free.
9. The act of referring a disputed matter to referees.

doubtless he spent but half a dime a day), and in the end perhaps outlive me, and claim possession of my office by right of his perpetual occupancy: as all these dark anticipations crowded upon me more and more, and my friends continually intruded their relentless remarks upon the apparition in my room; a great change was wrought in me. I resolved to gather all my faculties together, and for ever rid me of this intolerable incubus.

Ere revolving any complicated project, however, adapted to this end, I first simply suggested to Bartleby the propriety of his permanent departure. In a calm and serious tone, I commended the idea to his careful and mature consideration. But having taken three days to meditate upon it, he apprised me that his original determination remained the same; in short, that he still preferred to abide with me.

What shall I do? I now said to myself, buttoning up my coat to the last button. What shall I do? what ought I to do? what does conscience say I *should* do with this man, or rather ghost. Rid myself of him, I must; go, he shall. But how? You will not thrust him, the poor, pale, passive mortal,—you will not thrust such a helpless creature out of your door? you will not dishonor yourself by such cruelty? No, I will not, I cannot do that. Rather would I let him live and die here, and then mason up his remains in the wall. What then will you do? For all your coaxing, he will not budge. Bribes he leaves under your own paper-weight on your table; in short, it is quite plain that he prefers to cling to you.

Then something severe, something unusual must be done. What! surely you will not have him collared by a constable, and commit his innocent pallor to the common jail? And upon what ground could you procure such a thing to be done?—a vagrant, is he? What! he a vagrant, a wanderer, who refuses to budge? It is because he will *not* be a vagrant, then, that you seek to count him *as* a vagrant. That is too absurd. No visible means of support: there I have him. Wrong again: for indubitably he *does* support himself, and that is the only unanswerable proof that any man can show of his possessing the means so to do. No more then. Since he will not quit me, I must quit him. I will change my offices; I will move elsewhere; and give him fair notice, that if I find him on my new premises I will then proceed against him as a common trespasser.

Acting accordingly, next day I thus addressed him: "I find these chambers too far from the City Hall; the air is unwholesome. In a word, I propose to remove my offices next week, and shall no longer require your services. I tell you this now, in order that you may seek another place."

He made no reply, and nothing more was said.

On the appointed day I engaged carts and men, proceeded to my chambers, and having but little furniture, every thing was removed in a few hours. Throughout, the scrivener remained standing behind the screen, which I directed to be removed the last thing. It was withdrawn; and being folded up like a huge folio, left him the motionless occupant of a naked room. I stood in the entry watching him a moment, while something from within me upbraided me.

I re-entered, with my hand in my pocket—and—and my heart in my mouth.

"Good-bye, Bartleby; I am going—good-bye, and God some way bless you; and take that," slipping something in his hand. But it dropped upon the floor, and then,—strange to say—I tore myself from him whom I had so longed to be rid of.

Established in my new quarters, for a day or two I kept the door locked, and started at every footfall in the passages. When I returned to my rooms after any little absence, I would pause at the threshold for an instant, and attentively listen, ere applying my key. But these fears were needless. Bartleby never came nigh me.

I thought all was going well, when a perturbed looking stranger visited me, inquiring whether I was the person who had recently occupied rooms at No.— Wall-street.

Full of forebodings, I replied that I was.

"Then sir," said the stranger, who proved a lawyer, "you are responsible for the man you left there. He refuses to do any copying; he refuses to do any thing; he says he prefers not to; and he refuses to quit the premises."

"I am very sorry, sir," said I, with assumed tranquillity, but an inward tremor, "but, really, the man you allude to is nothing to me—he is no relation or apprentice of mine, that you should hold me responsible for him."

"In mercy's name, who is he?"

"I certainly cannot inform you. I know nothing about him. Formerly I employed him as a copyist; but he has done nothing for me now for some time past."

"I shall settle him then,—good morning, sir."

Several days passed, and I heard nothing more; and though I often felt a charitable prompting to call at the place and see poor Bartleby, yet a certain squeamishness of I know not what withheld me.

All is over with him, by this time, thought I at last, when through another week no further intelligence reached me. But coming to my room the day after, I found several persons waiting at my door in a high state of nervous excitement.

"That's the man—here he comes," cried the foremost one, whom I recognized as the lawyer who had previously called upon me alone.

"You must take him away, sir, at once," cried a portly person among them, advancing upon me, and whom I knew to be the landlord of No.—Wall-street. "These gentlemen, my tenants, cannot stand it any longer; Mr. B——" pointing to the lawyer, "has turned him out of his room, and he now persists in haunting the building generally, sitting upon the banisters of the stairs by day, and sleeping in the entry by night. Every body is concerned; clients are leaving the offices; some fears are entertained of a mob; something you must do, and that without delay."

Aghast at this torrent, I fell back before it, and would fain have locked myself in my new quarters. In vain I persisted that Bartleby was nothing to me—no more than to any one else. In vain:—I was the last person known to have any thing to do with him, and they held me to the terrible account. Fearful then of being exposed in the papers (as one person present obscurely threatened) I considered the matter, and at length said, that if the lawyer would give me a confidential interview with the scrivener, in his (the lawyer's) own room, I would that afternoon strive my best to rid them of the nuisance they complained of.

Going up stairs to my old haunt, there was Bartleby silently sitting upon the banister at the landing.

"What are you doing here, Bartleby?" said I.

"Sitting upon the banister," he mildly replied.

I motioned him into the lawyer's room, who then left us.

"Bartleby," said I, "are you aware that you are the cause of great tribulation to me, by persisting in occupying the entry after being dismissed from the office?"

No answer.

"Now one of two things must take place. Either you must do something, or something must be done to you. Now what sort of business would you like to engage in? Would you like to re-engage in copying for some one?"

"No; I would prefer not to make any change."

"Would you like a clerkship in a dry-goods store?"

"There is too much confinement about that. No, I would not like a clerkship; but I am not particular."

"Too much confinement," I cried, "why you keep yourself confined all the time!"

"I would prefer not to take a clerkship," he rejoined, as if to settle that little item at once.

"How would a bar-tender's business suit you? There is no trying of the eyesight in that."

"I would not like it at all; though, as I said before, I am not particular."

His unwonted wordiness inspirited me. I returned to the charge.

"Well then, would you like to travel through the country collecting bills for the merchants? That would improve your health."

"No, I would prefer to be doing something else."

"How then would going as a companion to Europe, to entertain some young gentleman with your conversation,—how would that suit you?"

"Not at all. It does not strike me that there is any thing definite about that. I like to be stationary. But I am not particular."

"Stationary you shall be then," I cried, now losing all patience, and for the first time in all my exasperating connection with him fairly flying into a passion. "If you do not go away from these premises before night, I shall feel bound—indeed I *am* bound—to—to—to quit the premises myself!" I rather absurdly concluded, knowing not with what possible threat to try to frighten his immobility into compliance. Despairing of all further efforts, I was precipitately leaving him, when a final thought occurred to me—one which had not been wholly unindulged before.

"Bartleby," said I, in the kindest tone I could assume under such exciting circumstances, "will you go home with me now—not to my office, but my dwelling—and remain there till we can conclude upon some convenient arrangement for you at our leisure? Come, let us start now, right away."

"No: at present I would prefer not to make any change at all."

I answered nothing; but effectually dodging every one by the suddenness and rapidity of my flight, rushed from the building, ran up Wall-street towards Broadway, and jumping into the first omnibus was soon removed from pursuit. As soon as tranquillity returned I distinctly perceived that I had now done all that I possibly could, both in respect to the demands of the landlord and his tenants, and with regard to my own desire and sense of duty, to benefit Bartleby, and shield him from rude persecution. I now strove to be entirely care-free and quiescent; and my conscience justified me in the attempt; though indeed it was not so successful as I could have wished. So fearful was I of being again hunted out by the incensed landlord and his exasperated tenants, that, surrendering my business to Nippers, for a few days I drove about the upper part of the town and through the suburbs, in my rockaway; crossed over to Jersey City and Hoboken, and paid fugitive visits to Manhattanville and Astoria.[1] In fact I almost lived in my rockaway for the time.

When again I entered my office, lo, a note from the landlord lay upon the desk. I opened it with trembling hands. It informed me that the writer had sent to the police, and had Bartleby removed to the Tombs as a vagrant. Moreover, since I knew more about him than any one else, he wished me to appear at that place, and make a suitable statement of the facts. These tidings had a conflicting effect upon me. At first I was indignant; but at last almost approved. The landlord's energetic, summary disposition, had led him to adopt a procedure which I do not think I would have decided upon myself; and yet as a last resort, under such peculiar circumstances, it seemed the only plan.

As I afterwards learned, the poor scrivener, when told that he must be conducted to the Tombs, offered not the slightest obstacle, but in his pale unmoving way, silently acquiesced.

Some of the compassionate and curious bystanders joined the party; and headed by one of the constables arm in arm with Bartleby, the silent procession filed its way through all the noise, and heat, and joy of the roaring thoroughfares at noon.

The same day I received the note I went to the Tombs, or to speak more properly, the Halls of Justice. Seeking the right officer, I stated the purpose of my call, and was informed that the individual I described was indeed within. I then assured the functionary that Bartleby was a perfectly honest man, and greatly to be compassionated, however unaccountably eccentric. I narrated all I knew, and closed by suggesting the idea of letting him remain in as indulgent confinement as possible till something less harsh might be done—though indeed I hardly knew what. At all events, if nothing else could be decided upon, the alms-house must receive him. I then begged to have an interview.

Being under no disgraceful charge, and quite serene and harmless in all his ways, they had permitted him freely to wander about the prison, and especially in the inclosed grass-platted yards thereof. And so I found him there, standing all alone in the quietest of the yards, his face towards a high wall, while all around, from the narrow slits of the jail windows, I thought I saw peering out upon him the eyes of murderers and thieves.

"Bartleby!"

"I know you," he said, without looking round,—"and I want nothing to say to you."

"It was not I that brought you here, Bartleby," said I, keenly pained at his implied suspicion. "And to you, this should not be so vile a place. Nothing reproachful attaches to you by being here. And see, it is not so sad a place as one might think. Look, there is the sky, and here is the grass."

"I know where I am," he replied, but would say nothing more, and so I left him.

As I entered the corridor again, a broad meat-like man, in an apron,

---

1. The narrator crossed the Hudson River to Jersey City and Hoboken, then drove far up unsettled Manhattan Island to the community of Manhattanville (Grant's Tomb is in what was Manhattanville), and finally crossed the East River to Astoria, on Long Island. "Rockaway": light open-sided carriage.

accosted me, and jerking his thumb over his shoulder said—"Is that your friend?"

"Yes."

"Does he want to starve? If he does, let him live on the prison fare, that's all."

"Who are you?" asked I, not knowing what to make of such an unofficially speaking person in such a place.

"I am the grub-man. Such gentlemen as have friends here, hire me to provide them with something good to eat."

"Is this so?" said I, turning to the turnkey.

He said it was.

"Well then," said I, slipping some silver into the grub-man's hands (for so they called him). "I want you to give particular attention to my friend there; let him have the best dinner you can get. And you must be as polite to him as possible."

"Introduce me, will you?" said the grub-man, looking at me with an expression which seemed to say he was all impatience for an opportunity to give a specimen of his breeding.

Thinking it would prove of benefit to the scrivener, I acquiesced; and asking the grub-man his name, went up with him to Bartleby.

"Bartleby, this is Mr. Cutlets; you will find him very useful to you."

"Your sarvant, sir, your sarvant," said the grub-man, making a low salutation behind his apron. "Hope you find it pleasant here, sir;—spacious grounds—cool apartments, sir—hope you'll stay with us some time—try to make it agreeable. May Mrs. Cutlets and I have the pleasure of your company to dinner, sir, in Mrs. Cutlets' private room?"

"I prefer not to dine to-day," said Bartleby, turning away. "It would disagree with me; I am unused to dinners." So saying he slowly moved to the other side of the inclosure, and took up a position fronting the dead-wall.

"How's this?" said the grub-man, addressing me with a stare of astonishment. "He's odd, aint he?"

"I think he is a little deranged," said I, sadly.

"Deranged? deranged is it? Well now, upon my word, I thought that friend of yourn was a gentleman forger; they are always pale and genteel-like, them forgers. I can't help pity 'em—can't help it, sir. Did you know Monroe Edwards?"[2] he added touchingly, and paused. Then, laying his hand pityingly on my shoulder, sighed, "he died of consumption at Sing-Sing.[3] So you weren't acquainted with Monroe?"

"No, I was never socially acquainted with any forgers. But I cannot stop longer. Look to my friend yonder. You will not lose by it. I will see you again."

Some few days after this, I again obtained admission to the Tombs, and went through the corridors in quest of Bartleby; but without finding him.

"I saw him coming from his cell not long ago," said a turnkey, "may be he's gone to loiter in the yards."

---

2. Horace Greeley's *Tribune* called Col. Monroe Edwards (1808–1847) "the most distinguished financier since the days of Judas Iscariot"; his trial in New York City (lasting all the second week of June 1842), caused the greatest public excitement since the trial "of the murderer, Colt" (see n. 7, p. 2251). He was convicted of swindling two firms of $25,000 each through forged letters of credit, sending tremors through the "exchange banking and commission business"—like undermining our Security Exchange. Melville was then in the South Seas, but the case was sensational, and his brothers were in New York.
3. Prison at Ossining, New York, not far up the Hudson.

So I went in that direction.

"Are you looking for the silent man?" said another turnkey passing me. "Yonder he lies—sleeping in the yard there. 'Tis not twenty minutes since I saw him lie down."

The yard was entirely quiet. It was not accessible to the common prisoners. The surrounding walls, of amazing thickness, kept off all sounds behind them. The Egyptian character of the masonry weighed upon me with its gloom. But a soft imprisoned turf grew under foot. The heart of the eternal pyramids, it seemed, wherein, by some strange magic, through the clefts, grass-seed, dropped by birds, had sprung.

Strangely huddled at the base of the wall, his knees drawn up, and lying on his side, his head touching the cold stones, I saw the wasted Bartleby. But nothing stirred. I paused; then went close up to him; stooped over, and saw that his dim eyes were open; otherwise he seemed profoundly sleeping. Something prompted me to touch him. I felt his hand, when a tingling shiver ran up my arm and down my spine to my feet.

The round face of the grub-man peered upon me now. "His dinner is ready. Won't he dine to-day, either? Or does he live without dining?"

"Lives without dining," said I, and closed the eyes.

"Eh!—He's asleep, aint he?"

"With kings and counsellors,"[4] murmured I.

There would seem little need for proceeding further in this history. Imagination will readily supply the meagre recital of poor Bartleby's interment. But ere parting with the reader, let me say, that if this little narrative has sufficiently interested him, to awaken curiosity as to who Bartleby was, and what manner of life he led prior to the present narrator's making his acquaintance, I can only reply, that in such curiosity I fully share, but am wholly unable to gratify it. Yet here I hardly know whether I should divulge one little item of rumor, which came to my ear a few months after the scrivener's decease. Upon what basis it rested, I could never ascertain; and hence, how true it is I cannot now tell. But inasmuch as this vague report has not been without a certain strange suggestive interest to me, however sad, it may prove the same with some others; and so I will briefly mention it. The report was this: that Bartleby had been a subordinate clerk in the Dead Letter Office at Washington, from which he had been suddenly removed by a change in the administration. When I think over this rumor, I cannot adequately express the emotions which seize me. Dead letters! does it not sound like dead men? Conceive a man by nature and misfortune prone to a pallid hopelessness, can any business seem more fitted to heighten it than that of continually handling these dead letters, and assorting them for the flames? For by the cart-load they are annually burned. Sometimes from out the folded paper the pale clerk takes a ring:—the finger it was meant for, perhaps, moulders in the grave; a bank-note sent in swiftest charity:—he whom it would relieve, nor eats nor hungers any more; pardon for those who died despairing; hope for those who died unhoping; good tidings for those who died stifled by unrelieved calamities. On errands of life, these letters speed to death.

Ah Bartleby! Ah humanity!

1853

---

4. Job 3.14.

From The Encantadas, or Enchanted Isles[1]

Sketch First. The Isles at Large

—*"That may not be, said then the ferryman,*
Least we unweeting hap to be fordonne;
For those same islands seeming now and than,
Are not firme land, nor any certein wonne,
But stragling plots which to and fro do ronne
In the wide waters; therefore are they hight
The Wandering Islands; therefore do them shonne;
For they have oft drawne many a wandring wight
Into most deadly daunger and distressed plight;
For whosoever once hath fastened
His foot thereon may never it secure
But wandreth evermore uncertein and unsure."

    ＊   ＊   ＊   ＊   ＊

"Darke, dolefull, dreary, like a greedy grave,
That still for carrion carcasses doth crave;
On top whereof ay dwelt the ghastly owl,
Shrieking his balefall note, which ever drave
Far from that haunt all other cheerful fowl,
And all about it wandring ghosts did wayle and howl."[2]

Take five-and-twenty heaps of cinders dumped here and there in an outside city lot; imagine some of them magnified into mountains, and the vacant lot the sea; and you will have a fit idea of the general aspect of the Encantadas, or Enchanted Isles. A group rather of extinct volcanoes than of isles; looking much as the world at large might, after a penal conflagration.

It is to be doubted whether any spot of earth can, in desolateness, furnish a parallel to this group. Abandoned cemeteries of long ago, old cities by piece-meal tumbling to their ruin, these are melancholy enough; but, like all else which has but once been associated with humanity they still awaken in us some thoughts of sympathy, however sad. Hence, even the Dead Sea, along with whatever other emotions it may at times inspire, does not fail to touch in the pilgrim some of his less unpleasurable feelings.

And as for solitariness; the great forests of the north, the expanses of unnavigated waters, the Greenland ice-fields, are the profoundest of solitudes to a human observer; still the magic of their changeable tides and seasons mitigates their terror; because, though unvisited by men, those forests are visited by the May; the remotest seas reflect familiar stars even as Lake Erie does; and in the clear air of a fine Polar day, the irradiated, azure ice shows beautifully as malachite.[3]

But the special curse, as one may call it, of the Encantadas, that which

1. During late 1853 and the first weeks of 1854 Melville wrote ten sketches about the "Enchanted Islands," or the Galápagos Islands, which lie along the equator, off Ecuador. They were published in *Putnam's Monthly Magazine* for March, April, and May 1854, under the pseudonym "Salvator R. Tarnmoor," an allusion to the Italian painter Salvator Rosa (1615–1673), known for his wild landscapes, and very probably an allusion as well to Edgar Allan Poe, notorious for the tarns and moors in his own moody landscapes (the combined form being a joke, because a tarn is a high mountain lake and a moor is ordinarily not very much above sea level). The first three sketches reprinted here appeared in the March 1854 installment of *Putnam's*, while the eighth appeared in the April issue; *Putnam's* is the source of the present texts. Melville saw the Galápagos Islands first in 1841, while he was on the *Acushnet*, and again in December 1842, or January 1843, while he was on the *Charles and Henry*.

2. Edmund Spenser's *Faerie Queene* 2.12.11 and the last three lines of stanza 12; 1.9.33.

3. Green mineral used (in compacted form) for table-tops, vases, etc.

exalts them in desolation above Idumea[4] and the Pole, is that to them change never comes; neither the change of seasons nor of sorrows. Cut by the Equator, they know not autumn and they know not spring; while already reduced to the lees of fire, ruin itself can work little more upon them. The showers refresh the deserts, but in these isles, rain never falls. Like split Syrian gourds left withering in the sun, they are cracked by an everlasting drought beneath a torrid sky. "Have mercy upon me," the wailing spirit of the Encantadas seems to cry, "and send Lazarus that he may dip the tip of his finger in water and cool my tongue, for I am tormented in this flame."[5]

Another feature in these isles is their emphatic uninhabitableness. It is deemed a fit type of all-forsaken overthrow, that the jackal should den in the wastes of weedy Babylon;[6] but the Encantadas refuse to harbor even the outcasts of the beasts. Man and wolf alike disown them. Little but reptile life is here found:—tortoises, lizards, immense spiders, snakes, and that strangest anomaly of outlandish nature, the *aguano*. No voice, no low, no howl is heard; the chief sound of life here is a hiss.

On most of the isles where vegetation is found at all, it is more ungrateful than the blankness of Aracama.[7] Tangled thickets of wiry bushes, without fruit and without a name, springing up among deep fissures of calcined rock, and treacherously masking them; or a parched growth of distorted cactus trees.

In many places the coast is rock-bound, or more properly, clinker-bound; tumbled masses of blackish or greenish stuff like the dross of an iron-furnace, forming dark clefts and caves here and there, into which a ceaseless sea pours a fury of foam; overhanging them with a swirl of gray, haggard mist, amidst which sail screaming flights of unearthly birds heightening the dismal din. However calm the sea without, there is no rest for these swells and those rocks; they lash and are lashed, even when the outer ocean is most at peace with itself. On the oppressive, clouded days, such as are peculiar to this part of the watery Equator, the dark, vitrified masses, many of which raise themselves among white whirlpools and breakers in detached and perilous places off the shore, present a most Plutonian[8] sight. In no world but a fallen one could such lands exist.

Those parts of the strand free from the marks of fire, stretch away in wide level beaches of multitudinous dead shells, with here and there decayed bits of sugar-cane, bamboos, and cocoanuts, washed upon this other and darker world from the charming palm isles to the westward and southward; all the way from Paradise to Tartarus;[9] while mixed with the relics of distant beauty you will sometimes see fragments of charred wood and mouldering ribs of wrecks. Neither will any one be surprised at meeting these last, after observing the conflicting currents which eddy throughout nearly all the wide channels of the entire group. The capriciousness of the tides of air sympathizes with those of the sea. Nowhere is the wind so light, baffling, and every way unreliable, and so given to perplexing calms, as at the Encantadas. Nigh a month has been spent by a ship going from one isle to another, though but thirty miles

---

4. Wasteland along the Dead Sea, and westward; the land of Edom where the Israelites wandered on their way from Egypt to the Promised Land.
5. Luke 16.24, the prayer of the rich man from hell on seeing that Lazarus, who had begged at his gate, was in heaven, in "Abraham's bosom."
6. Babylon was to become "a dwelling-place for drag-ons," and a "hissing, without an inhabitant" (Jeremiah 51.37).
7. Desert region in west-central South America. "Aguano": iguana, tropical lizard attaining lengths of five or six feet.
8. Fit for the underworld of Greek mythology.
9. Hell.

between; for owing to the force of the current, the boats employed to tow barely suffice to keep the craft from sweeping upon the cliffs, but do nothing towards accelerating her voyage. Sometimes it is impossible for a vessel from afar to fetch up with the group itself, unless large allowances for prospective lee-way have been made ere its coming in sight. And yet, at other times, there is a mysterious indraft, which irresistibly draws a passing vessel among the isles, though not bound to them.

True, at one period, as to some extent at the present day, large fleets of whalemen cruised for Spermaceti[1] upon what some seamen call the Enchanted Ground. But this, as in due place will be described, was off the great outer isle of Albemarle,[2] away from the intricacies of the smaller isles, where there is plenty of sea-room; and hence, to that vicinity, the above remarks do not altogether apply; though even there the current runs at times with singular force, shifting, too, with as singular a caprice. Indeed, there are seasons when currents quite unaccountable prevail for a great distance round about the total group, and are so strong and irregular as to change a vessel's course against the helm, though sailing at the rate of four or five miles the hour. The difference in the reckonings of navigators produced by these causes, along with the light and variable winds, long nourished a persuasion that there existed two distinct clusters of isles in the parallel of the Encantadas, about a hundred leagues apart. Such was the idea of their earlier visitors, the Bucca-neers; and as late as 1750, the charts of that part of the Pacific accorded with the strange delusion. And this apparent fleetingness and unreality of the local-ity of the isles was most probably one reason for the Spaniards calling them the Encantada, or Enchanted Group.

But not uninfluenced by their character, as they now confessedly exist, the modern voyager will be inclined to fancy that the bestowal of this name might have in part originated in that air of spell-bound desertness which so signifi-cantly invests the isles. Nothing can better suggest the aspect of once living things malignly crumbled from ruddiness into ashes. Apples of Sodom,[3] after touching, seem these isles.

However wavering their place may seem by reason of the currents, they themselves, at least to one upon the shore, appear invariably the same: fixed, cast, glued into the very body of cadaverous death.

Nor would the appellation, enchanted, seem misapplied in still another sense. For concerning the peculiar reptile inhabitant of these wilds—whose presence gives the group its second Spanish name, Gallipagos—concerning the tortoises found here, most mariners have long cherished a superstition, not more frightful than grotesque. They earnestly believe that all wrecked sea-officers, more especially commodores and captains, are at death (and in some cases, before death) transformed into tortoises; thenceforth dwelling upon these hot aridities, sole solitary Lords of Asphaltum.[4]

Doubtless so quaintly dolorous a thought was originally inspired by the woe-begone landscape itself, but more particularly, perhaps, by the tortoises. For apart from their strictly physical features, there is something strangely self-condemned in the appearance of these creatures. Lasting sorrow and penal

---

1. Sperm whales.
2. Largest of the Galápagos.
3. Or Dead Sea apple, described by ancient writers as of fair appearance but dissolving into smoke and ashes when plucked.
4. From asphaltum (now asphalt), dark mineral found at the Dead Sea and elsewhere; it melts on heating and smokes heavily as it burns.

hopelessness are in no animal form so suppliantly expressed as in theirs; while the thought of their wonderful longevity does not fail to enhance the impression.

Nor even at the risk of meriting the charge of absurdly believing in enchantments, can I restrain the admission that sometimes, even now, when leaving the crowded city to wander out July and August among the Adirondack Mountains, far from the influences of towns and proportionally nigh to the mysterious ones of nature; when at such times I sit me down in the mossy head of some deep-wooded gorge, surrounded by prostrate trunks of blasted pines, and recall, as in a dream, my other and far-distant rovings in the baked heart of the charmed isles; and remember the sudden glimpses of dusky shells, and long languid necks protruded from the leafless thickets; and again have beheld the vitreous inland rocks worn down and grooved into deep ruts by ages and ages of the slow draggings of tortoises in quest of pools of scanty water; I can hardly resist the feeling that in my time I have indeed slept upon evilly enchanted ground.

Nay, such is the vividness of my memory, or the magic of my fancy, that I know not whether I am not the occasional victim of optical delusion concerning the Gallipagos. For often in scenes of social merriment, and especially at revels held by candle-light in old-fashioned mansions, so that shadows are thrown into the further recesses of an angular and spacious room, making them put on a look of haunted undergrowth of lonely woods, I have drawn the attention of my comrades by my fixed gaze and sudden change of air, as I have seemed to see, slowly emerging from those imagined solitudes, and heavily crawling along the floor, the ghost of a gigantic tortoise, with "Memento* * * * *" burning in live letters upon his back.[5]

Sketch Second. Two Sides to a Tortoise

> "Most ugly shapes and horrible aspects,
> Such as Dame Nature selfe mote feare to see,
> Or shame, that ever should so fowle defects
> From her most cunning hand escaped bee;
> All dreadfull pourtraiets of deformitee.
> Ne wonder if these do a man appall;
> For all that here at home we dreadfull hold
> Be but as bugs to fearen babes withall
> Compared to the creatures in these isles' entrall
>   *   *   *   *   *   *
>
> Fear naught, then said the palmer, well avized,
> For these same monsters are not there indeed,
> But are into these fearful shapes disguized.
> * * * * * * * * * * *
>
> And lifting up his vertuous staffe on high,
> Then all that dreadful armie fast gan flye
> Into great Zethy's bosom, where they hidden lye."[6]

In view of the description given, may one be gay upon the Encantadas? Yes: that is, find one the gayety, and he will be gay. And indeed, sackcloth and ashes as they are, the isles are not perhaps unmitigated gloom. For while no spectator can deny their claims to a most solemn and superstitious consider-

---

5. I.e., "memento mori": remember that you must die (Latin); any warning of death.   6. The Faerie Queene 2.12.23 and 25; 26.

ation, no more than my firmest resolutions can decline to behold the spectre-tortoise when emerging from its shadowy recess; yet even the tortoise, dark and melancholy as it is upon the back, still possesses a bright side; its calapee or breast-plate being sometimes of a faint yellowish or golden tinge. Moreover, every one knows that tortoises as well as turtle are of such a make, that if you but put them on their backs you thereby expose their bright sides without the possibility of their recovering themselves, and turning into view the other. But after you have done this, and because you have done this, you should not swear that the tortoise has no dark side. Enjoy the bright, keep it turned up perpetually if you can, but be honest and don't deny the black. Neither should he who cannot turn the tortoise from its natural position so as to hide the darker and expose his livelier aspect, like a great October pumpkin in the sun, for that cause declare the creature to be one total inky blot. The tortoise is both black and bright. But let us to particulars.

Some months before my first stepping ashore upon the group, my ship was cruising in its close vicinity. One noon we found ourselves off the South Head of Albemarle, and not very far from the land. Partly by way of freak, and partly by way of spying out so strange a country, a boat's crew was sent ashore, with orders to see all they could, and besides, bring back whatever tortoises they could conveniently transport.

It was after sunset when the adventurers returned. I looked down over the ship's high side as if looking down over the curb of a well, and dimly saw the damp boat deep in the sea with some unwonted weight. Ropes were dropt over, and presently three huge antediluvian-looking tortoises after much straining were landed on deck. They seemed hardly of the seed of earth. We had been broad upon the waters for five long months, a period amply sufficient to make all things of the land wear a fabulous hue to the dreamy mind. Had three Spanish custom-house officers boarded us then, it is not unlikely that I should have curiously stared at them, felt of them, and stroked them much as savages serve civilized guests. But instead of three custom-house officers, behold these really wondrous tortoises—none of your schoolboy mud-turtles—but black as widower's weeds,[7] heavy as chests of plate, with vast shells medal-lioned and orbed like shields, and dented and blistered like shields that have breasted a battle, shaggy too, here and there, with dark green moss, and slimy with the spray of the sea. These mystic creatures suddenly translated by night from unutterable solitudes to our peopled deck, affected me in a manner not easy to unfold. They seemed newly crawled forth from beneath the founda-tions of the world. Yea, they seemed the identical tortoises whereon the Hin-doo plants this total sphere.[8] With a lantern I inspected them more closely. Such worshipful venerableness of aspect! Such furry greenness mantling the rude peelings and healing the fissures of their shattered shells. I no more saw three tortoises. They expanded—became transfigured. I seemed to see three Roman Coliseums in magnificent decay.

Ye oldest inhabitants of this, or any other isle, said I, pray, give me the freedom of your three-walled towns.

The great feeling inspired by these creatures was that of age;—dateless, indefinite endurance. And in fact that any other creature can live and breathe as long as the tortoise of the Encantadas, I will not readily believe. Not to hint

---

7. Mourning garments.   8. Hindu mythology places the earth atop tortoises.

of their known capacity of sustaining life, while going without food for an entire year, consider that impregnable armor of their living mail. What other bodily being possesses such a citadel wherein to resist the assaults of Time?

As, lantern in hand, I scraped among the moss and beheld the ancient scars of bruises received in many a sullen fall among the marly mountains of the isle—scars strangely widened, swollen, half obliterate, and yet distorted like those sometimes found in the bark of very hoary trees, I seemed an antiquary of a geologist, studying the bird-tracks and ciphers upon the exhumed slates trod by incredible creatures whose very ghosts are now defunct.

As I lay in my hammock that night, overhead I heard the slow weary draggings of the three ponderous strangers along the encumbered deck. Their stupidity or their resolution was so great, that they never went aside for any impediment. One ceased his movements altogether just before the mid-watch. At sunrise I found him butted like a battering-ram against the immovable foot of the foremast, and still striving, tooth and nail, to force the impossible passage. That these tortoises are the victims of a penal, or malignant, or perhaps a downright diabolical enchanter, seems in nothing more likely than in that strange infatuation of hopeless toil which so often possesses them. I have known them in their journeyings ram themselves heroically against rocks, and long abide there, nudging, wriggling, wedging, in order to displace them, and so hold on their inflexible path. Their crowning curse is their drudging impulse to straightforwardness in a belittered world.

Meeting with no such hinderance as their companion did, the other tortoises merely fell foul of small stumbling-blocks; buckets, blocks, and coils of rigging; and at times in the act of crawling over them would slip with an astounding rattle to the deck. Listening to these draggings and concussions, I thought me of the haunt from which they came; an isle full of metallic ravines and gulches, sunk bottomlessly into the hearts of splintered mountains, and covered for many miles with inextricable thickets. I then pictured these three straightforward monsters, century after century, writhing through the shades, grim as blacksmiths; crawling so slowly and ponderously, that not only did toadstools and all fungous things grow beneath their feet, but a sooty moss sprouted upon their backs. With them I lost myself in volcanic mazes; brushed away endless boughs of rotting thickets; till finally in a dream I found myself sitting crosslegged upon the foremost, a Brahmin similarly mounted upon either side, forming a tripod of foreheads which upheld the universal cope.

Such was the wild nightmare begot by my first impression of the Encantadas tortoise. But next evening, strange to say, I sat down with my shipmates, and made a merry repast from tortoise steaks and tortoise stews; and supper over, out knife, and helped convert the three mighty concave shells into three fanciful soup-tureens, and polished the three flat yellowish calapees into three gorgeous salvers.

Sketch Third. Rock Rodondo

"For they this hight the Rock of vile Reproach,
A dangerous and dreadful place,
To which nor fish nor fowl did once approach,
But yelling meaws with sea-gulls hoars and bace
And cormoyrants with birds of ravenous race,
Which still sit waiting on that dreadful clift."

* * * * * *

"With that the rolling sea resounding soft
In his big vase them fitly answered,
And on the Rock, the waves breaking aloft,
A solemn meane unto them measured."

* * * * * *

"Then he the boteman bad row easily,
And let him heare some part of that rare melody."

* * * * * *

"Suddenly an innumerable flight
Of harmefull fowles about them fluttering cride,
And with their wicked wings them oft did smight
And sore annoyed, groping in that griesly night."

* * * * * *

"Even all the nation of unfortunate
And fatal birds about them flocked were."[9]

To go up into a high stone tower is not only a very fine thing in itself, but the very best mode of gaining a comprehensive view of the region round about. It is all the better if this tower stand solitary and alone, like that mysterious Newport one,[1] or else be sole survivor of some perished castle.

Now, with reference to the Enchanted Isles, we are fortunately supplied with just such a noble point of observation in a remarkable rock, from its peculiar figure called of old by the Spaniards, Rock Rodondo, or Round Rock. Some two hundred and fifty feet high, rising straight from the sea ten miles from land, with the whole mountainous group to the south and east, Rock Rodondo occupies, on a large scale, very much the position which the famous Campanile or detached Bell Tower of St. Mark[2] does with respect to the tangled group of hoary edifices around it.

Ere ascending, however, to gaze abroad upon the Encantadas, this sea-tower itself claims attention. It is visible at the distance of thirty miles; and, fully participating in that enchantment which pervades the group, when first seen afar invariably is mistaken for a sail. Four leagues away, of a golden, hazy noon, it seems some Spanish Admiral's ship, stacked up with glittering canvas. Sail ho! Sail ho! Sail ho! from all three masts. But coming nigh, the enchanted frigate is transformed apace into a craggy keep.

My first visit to the spot was made in the gray of the morning. With a view of fishing, we had lowered three boats, and pulling some two miles from our vessel, found ourselves just before dawn of day close under the moon-shadow of Rodondo. Its aspect was heightened, and yet softened, by the strange double twilight of the hour. The great full moon burnt in the low west like a half-spent beacon, casting a soft mellow tinge upon the sea like the cast by a waning fire of embers upon a midnight hearth; while along the entire east the invisible sun sent pallid intimations of his coming. The wind was light; the waves languid; the stars twinkled with a faint effulgence; all nature seemed supine with the long night watch, and half-suspended in jaded expectation of the sun. This was the critical hour to catch Rodondo in his perfect mood. The twilight was just enough to reveal every striking point, without tearing away the dim investiture of wonder.

9. *The Faerie Queene* 2.12.8; 33, 35, 36.
1. A colonial-built structure at Newport, Rhode Island, was in the early 19th century claimed as a relic of a Norse settlement in the 11th.
2. The Campanile at Venice.

From a broken, stair-like base, washed, as the steps of a water-palace, by the waves, the tower rose in entablatures of strata to a shaven summit. These uniform layers which compose the mass form its most peculiar feature. For at their lines of junction they project flatly into encircling shelves, from top to bottom, rising one above another in graduated series. And as the eaves of any old barn or abbey are alive with swallows, so were all these rocky ledges with unnumbered sea-fowl. Eaves upon eaves, and nests upon nests. Here and there were long birdlime streaks of a ghostly white staining the tower from sea to air, readily accounting for its sail-like look afar. All would have been bewitchingly quiescent, were it not for the demoniac din created by the birds. Not only were the eaves rustling with them, but they flew densely overhead, spreading themselves into a winged and continually shifting canopy. The tower is the resort of aquatic birds for hundreds of leagues around. To the north, to the east, to the west, stretches nothing but eternal ocean; so that the man-of-war hawk coming from the coasts of North America, Polynesia, or Peru, makes his first land at Rodondo. And yet though Rodondo be terra-firma, no land-bird ever lighted on it. Fancy a red-robbin or a canary there! What a falling into the hands of the Philistines,[3] when the poor warbler should be surrounded by such locust-flights of strong bandit birds, with long bills cruel as daggers.

I know not where one can better study the Natural History of strange sea-fowl than at Rodondo. It is the aviary of Ocean. Birds light here which never touched mast or tree, hermit-birds, which ever fly alone, cloud-birds, familiar with unpierced zones of air.

Let us first glance low down to the lowermost shelf of all, which is the widest too, and but a little space from high-water mark. What outlandish beings are these? Erect as men, but hardly as symmetrical, they stand all round the rock like sculptured caryatides, supporting the next range of eaves above. Their bodies are grotesquely misshapen; their bills short; their feet seemingly legless; while the members at their sides are neither fin, wing, nor arm. And truly neither fish, flesh, nor fowl is the penguin; as an edible, pertaining neither to Carnival nor Lent;[4] without exception the most ambiguous and least lovely creature yet discovered by man. Though dabbling in all three elements, and indeed possessing some rudimental claims to all, the penguin is at home in none. On land it stumps; afloat it sculls; in the air it flops. As if ashamed of her failure, Nature keeps this ungainly child hidden away at the ends of the earth, in the Straits of Magellan,[5] and on the abased sea-story of Rodondo.

But look, what are yon wobegone regiments drawn up on the next shelf above? what rank and file of large strange fowl? what sea Friars of Orders Gray? Pelicans. Their elongated bills, and heavy leathern pouches suspended thereto, give them the most lugubrious expression. A pensive race, they stand for hours together without motion. Their dull, ashy plumage imparts an aspect as if they had been powdered over with cinders. A penitential bird indeed, fitly haunting the shores of the clinkered Encantadas, whereon tormented Job himself might have well sat down and scraped himself with potsherds.

Higher up now we mark the gony, or gray albatros, anomalously so called,

---

3. As Samson did when Delilah betrayed him (Judges 16).
4. I.e., a cautious Catholic would not know whether it was fish (acceptable during the restricted Lenten diet)

or meat (acceptable during the celebrations before Lent).
5. Passage between the Atlantic and the Pacific just north of Cape Horn at the tip of South America.

an unsightly unpoetic bird, unlike its storied kinsman, which is the snow-white ghost of the haunted Capes of Hope and Horn.

As we still ascend from shelf to shelf, we find the tenants of the tower serially disposed in order of their magnitude:—gannets, black and speckled haglets, jays, sea-hens, sperm-whale-birds, gulls of all varieties:—thrones, princedoms, powers,[6] dominating one above another in senatorial array; while sprinkled over all, like an ever-repeated fly in a great piece of broidery, the stormy petrel or Mother Cary's chicken[7] sounds his continual challenge and alarm. That this mysterious humming-bird of ocean, which had it but brilliancy of hue might from its evanescent liveliness be almost called its butterfly, yet whose chirrup under the stern is ominous to mariners as to the peasant the death-tick sounding from behind the chimney jam—should have its special haunt at the Encantadas, contributes in the seaman's mind, not a little to their dreary spell.

As day advances the dissonant din augments. With ear-splitting cries the wild birds celebrate their matins. Each moment, flights push from the tower, and join the aerial choir hovering overhead, while their places below are supplied by darting myriads. But down through all this discord of commotion, I hear clear silver bugle-like notes unbrokenly falling, like oblique lines of swift slanting rain in a cascading shower. I gaze far up, and behold a snow-white angelic thing, with one long lance-like feather thrust out behind. It is the bright inspiriting chanticleer of ocean, the beauteous bird, from its bestirring whistle of musical invocation, fitly styled the "Boatswain's Mate."

The winged life clouding Rodondo on that well-remembered morning, I saw had its full counterpart in the finny hosts which peopled the waters at its base. Below the water-line, the rock seemed one honey-comb of grottoes, affording labyrinthine lurking places for swarms of fairy fish. All were strange; many exceedingly beautiful; and would have well graced the costliest glass globes in which goldfish are kept for a show. Nothing was more striking than the complete novelty of many individuals of this multitude. Here hues were seen as yet unpainted, and figures which are unengraved.

To show the multitude, avidity, and nameless fearlessness and tameness of these fish, let me say, that often, marking through clear spaces of water—temporarily made so by the concentric dartings of the fish above the surface—certain larger and less unwary wights, which swam slow and deep; our anglers would cautiously essay to drop their lines down to these last. But in vain; there was no passing the uppermost zone. No sooner did the hook touch the sea, than a hundred infatuates contended for the honor of capture. Poor fish of Rodondo! in your victimized confidence, you are of the number of those who inconsiderately trust, while they do not understand, human nature.

But the dawn is now fairly day. Band after band, the sea-fowl sail away to forage the deep for their food. The tower is left solitary, save the fish caves at its base. Its birdlime gleams in the golden rays like the whitewash of a tall lighthouse, or the lofty sails of a cruiser. This moment, doubtless, while we know it to be a dead desert rock, other voyagers are taking oaths it is a glad populous ship.

But ropes now, and let us ascend. Yet soft, this is not so easy.

6. Romans 8.38–39: "For I am persuaded, that neither death, nor life, nor angels, nor principalities, nor powers, nor things present, nor things to come, nor height, nor depth, nor any other creature, shall be able to separate us from the love of God, which is in Christ Jesus our Lord."

7. Mother Cary's chicken is another name for the stormy petrel, a long-winged sea bird. Mother Cary is the anglicization of *mater cara*, an epithet of the Virgin Mary.

Sketch Eighth. Norfolk Isle and the Chola Widow[8]

> "At last they in an island did espy
> A seemly woman sitting by the shore,
> That with great sorrow and sad agony
> Seemed some great misfortune to deplore,
> And loud to them for succor called evermore."

> "Black his eyes as the midnight sky,
> White his neck as the driven snow,
> Red his cheek as the morning light;—
> Cold he lies in the ground below.
>   My love is dead,
>   Gone to his death-bed,
> All under the cactus tree."

Far to the northeast of Charles' Isle, sequestered from the rest, lies Norfolk Isle; and, however insignificant to most voyagers, to me, through sympathy, that lone island has become a spot made sacred by the strongest trials of humanity.

It was my first visit to the Encantadas. Two days had been spent ashore in hunting tortoises. There was not time to capture many; so on the third afternoon we loosed our sails. We were just in the act of getting under way, the uprooted anchor yet suspended and invisibly swaying beneath the wave, as the good ship gradually turned on[9] her heel to leave the isle behind, when the seaman who heaved with me at the windlass[1] paused suddenly, and directed my attention to something moving on the land, not along the beach, but somewhat back, fluttering from a height.

In view of the sequel of this little story, be it here narrated how it came to pass, that an object which partly from its being so small was quite lost to every other man on board, still caught the eye of my handspike[2] companion. The rest of the crew, myself included, merely stood up to our spikes in heaving; whereas, unwontedly exhilarated at every turn of the ponderous windlass, my belted comrade leaped atop of it, with might and main giving a downward, thewey, perpendicular heave, his raised eye bent in cheery animation upon the slowly receding shore. Being high lifted above all others was the reason he perceived the object, otherwise unperceivable: and this elevation of his eye was owing to the elevation of his spirits; and this again—for truth must out—to a dram of Peruvian pisco,[3] in guerdon for some kindness done, secretly administered to him that morning by our mulatto steward. Now, certainly, pisco does a deal of mischief in the world; yet seeing that, in the present case, it was the means, though indirect, of rescuing a human being from the most dreadful fate, must we not also needs admit that sometimes pisco does a deal of good?

Glancing across the water in the direction pointed out, I saw some white thing hanging from an inland rock, perhaps half a mile from the sea.

---

8. This sketch, misnumbered "Ninth," appeared in the April 1854 *Putnam's*. The first motto is from Edmund Spenser's *The Faerie Queene* 2.12.27.5–9, slightly altered. The second is from Thomas Chatterton's "The Mynstelle's Songe," from *Aella: A Tragycal Enterlude*, also altered slightly. It has been plausibly argued that the story may have been suggested by newspaper accounts in 1853 of the rescue of an American Indian woman from an island off Santa Barbara, California.
9. The word *on* is supplied because the idiom, used elsewhere by Melville, is to turn "on her heel."
1. Apparatus for hoisting the anchor, consisting of a drum on which is wound the rope or cable holding the anchor.
2. Bar or lever for moving the windlass.
3. A harsh brandy made in Pisco, Peru.

"It is a bird; a white-winged bird; perhaps a——no; it is——it is a handker-chief!"

"Aye, a handkerchief!" echoed my comrade, and with a louder shout apprised the captain.

Quickly now—like the running out and training of a great gun—the long cabin spy-glass was thrust through the mizzen rigging from the high platform of the poop; whereupon a human figure was plainly seen upon the inland rock, eagerly waving towards us what seemed to be the handkerchief.

Our captain was a prompt, good fellow. Dropping the glass, he lustily ran forward, ordering the anchor to be dropped again; hands to stand by a boat, and lower away.

In a half-hour's time the swift boat returned. It went with six and came with seven; and the seventh was a woman.

It is not artistic heartlessness, but I wish I could but draw in crayons;[4] for this woman was a most touching sight; and crayons, tracing softly melancholy lines, would best depict the mournful image of the dark-damasked Chola widow.

Her story was soon told, and though given in her own strange language was as quickly understood, for our captain from long trading on the Chilian coast was well versed in the Spanish. A Cholo, or half-breed Indian woman of Payta in Peru, three years gone by, with her young new-wedded husband Felipe, of pure Castilian blood, and her one only Indian brother, Truxill, Hunilla had taken passage on the main[5] in a French whaler, commanded by a joyous man; which vessel, bound to the cruising grounds beyond the Enchanted Isles, proposed passing close by their vicinity. The object of the little party was to procure tortoise oil, a fluid which for its great purity and delicacy is held in high estimation wherever known; and it is well known all along this part of the Pacific coast. With a chest of clothes, tools, cooking utensils, a rude apparatus for trying out[6] the oil, some casks of biscuit, and other things, not omitting two favorite dogs, of which faithful animal all the Cholos are very fond, Huni-lla and her companions were safely landed at their chosen place; the French-man, according to the contract made ere sailing, engaged to take them off upon returning from a four months' cruise in the westward seas; which interval the three adventurers deemed quite sufficient for their purposes.

On the isle's lone beach they paid him in silver for their passage out, the stranger having declined to carry them at all except upon that condition; though willing to take every means to insure the due fulfilment of his prom-ise.[7] Felipe had striven hard to have this payment put off to the period of the ship's return. But in vain. Still, they thought they had, in another way, ample pledge of the good faith of the Frenchman. It was arranged that the expenses of the passage home should not be payable in silver, but in tortoises; one hundred tortoises ready captured to the returning captain's hand. These the Cholos meant to secure after their own work was done, against the probable time of the Frenchman's coming back; and no doubt in prospect already felt, that in those hundred tortoises—now somewhere ranging the isle's interior—

---

4. Colored chalks.
5. I.e., the Spanish Main, here, as below, loosely ap-plied not to the Caribbean coasts but to the area of the western coast of South America, only recently liberated from Spanish rule.

6. Rendering down by boiling.
7. The text may be slightly corrupt, with the sentences divided wrongly; shouldn't Felipe be eager to ensure the due fulfillment of the captain's promise?

they possessed one hundred hostages. Enough: the vessel sailed; the gazing three on shore answered the loud glee of the singing crew; and ere evening, the French craft was hull down in the distant sea, its masts three faintest lines which quickly faded from Hunilla's eye.

The stranger had given a blithesome promise, and anchored it with oaths; but oaths and anchors equally will drag; nought else abides on fickle earth but unkept promises of joy. Contrary winds from out unstable skies, or contrary moods of his more varying mind, or shipwreck and sudden death in solitary waves; whatever was the cause, the blithe stranger never was seen again.

Yet, however dire a calamity was here in store, misgivings of it ere due time never disturbed the Cholos' busy mind,[8] now all intent upon the toilsome matter which had brought them hither. Nay, by swift doom coming like the thief at night, ere seven weeks went by, two of the little party were removed from all anxieties of land or sea. No more they sought to gaze with feverish fear, or still more feverish hope, beyond the present's horizon line; but into the furthest future their own silent spirits sailed. By persevering labor beneath that burning sun, Felipe and Truxill had brought down to their hut many scores of tortoises, and tried out the oil, when, elated with their good success, and to reward themselves for such hard work, they, too hastily, made a cata-maran, or Indian raft, much used on the Spanish main, and merrily started on a fishing trip, just without a long reef with many jagged gaps, running parallel with the shore, about half a mile from it. By some bad tide or hap, or natural negligence of joyfulness (for though they could not be heard, yet by their gestures they seemed singing at the time), forced in deep water against that iron bar, the ill-made catamaran was overset, and came all to pieces; when, dashed by broad-chested swells between their broken logs and the sharp teeth of the reef, both adventurers perished before Hunilla's eyes.

Before Hunilla's eyes they sank. The real woe of this event passed before her sight as some sham tragedy on the stage. She was seated on a rude bower among the withered thickets, crowning a lofty cliff, a little back from the beach. The thickets were so disposed, that in looking upon the sea at large she peered out from among the branches as from the lattice of a high balcony. But upon the day we speak of here, the better to watch the adventure of those two hearts she loved, Hunilla had withdrawn the branches to one side, and held them so. They formed an oval frame, through which the bluey boundless sea rolled like a painted one. And there, the invisible painter painted to her view the wave-tossed and disjointed raft, its once level logs slantingly upheaved, as raking masts, and the four struggling arms undistinguishable among them; and then all subsided into smooth-flowing creamy waters, slowly drifting the splintered wreck; while first and last, no sound of any sort was heard. Death in a silent picture; a dream of the eye; such vanishing shapes as the mirage shows.

So instant was the scene, so trance-like its mild pictorial effect, so distant from her blasted tower and her common sense of things, that Hunilla gazed and gazed, nor raised a finger or a wail. But as good to sit thus dumb, in stupor staring on that dumb show, for all that otherwise might be done. With half a mile of sea between, could her two enchanted arms aid those four fated ones? The distance long, the time one sand. After the lightning is beheld, what fool shall stay the thunderbolt? Felipe's body was washed ashore, but Truxill's

8. Perhaps *mind* should be plural.

never came; only his gay, braided hat of golden straw—that same sunflower thing he waved to her, pushing from the strand—and now, to the last gallant, it still saluted her. But Felipe's body floated to the marge, with one arm encirclingly outstretched. Lock-jawed in grim death, the lover-husband, softly clasped his bride, true to her even in death's dream. Ah, Heaven, when man thus keeps his faith, wilt thou be faithless who created the faithful one? But they cannot break faith who never plighted it.

It needs not to be said what nameless misery now wrapped the lonely widow. In telling her own story she passed this almost entirely over, simply recounting the event. Construe the comment of her features, as you might; from her mere words little would you have weened that Hunilla was herself the heroine of her tale. But not thus did she defraud us of our tears. All hearts bled that grief could be so brave.

She but showed us her soul's lid, and the strange ciphers thereon engraved; all within, with pride's timidity, was withheld. Yet was there one exception. Holding out her small olive hand before our captain, she said in mild and slowest Spanish, "Señor, I buried him;" then paused, struggled, as against the writhed coilings of a snake, and cringing suddenly, leaped up, repeating in impassioned pain, "I buried him, my life, my soul!"

Doubtless it was by half-unconscious, automatic motions of her hands, that this heavy-hearted one performed the final offices for Felipe, and planted a rude cross of withered sticks—no green ones might be had—at the head of that lonely grave, where rested now in lasting uncomplaint and quiet haven he whom untranquil seas had overthrown.

But some dull sense of another body that should be interred, of another cross that should hallow another grave—unmade as yet;—some dull anxiety and pain touching her undiscovered brother now haunted the oppressed Hunilla. Her hands fresh from the burial earth, she slowly went back to the beach, with unshaped purposes wandered there, her spellbound eye bent upon the incessant waves. But they bore nothing to her but a dirge, which maddened her to think that murderers should mourn. As time went by, and these things came less dreamingly to her mind, the strong persuasions of her Romish faith, which sets peculiar store by consecrated urns, prompted her to resume in waking earnest that pious search which had but been begun as in somnambulism. Day after day, week after week, she trod the cindery beach, till at length a double motive edged every eager glance. With equal longing she now looked for the living and the dead; the brother and the captain; alike vanished, never to return. Little accurate note of time had Hunilla taken under such emotions as were hers, and little, outside herself, served for calendar or dial. As to poor Crusoe in the self-same sea,[9] no saint's bell pealed forth the lapse of week or month; each day went by unchallenged; no chanticleer announced those sultry dawns, no lowing herds those poisonous nights. All wonted and steadily recurring sounds, human, or humanized by sweet fellowship with man, but one stirred that torrid trance,—the cry of dogs; save which nought but the rolling sea invaded it, an all pervading monotone; and to the widow that was the least loved voice she could have heard.

No wonder that as her thoughts now wandered to the unreturning ship, and

9. Strictly speaking, Defoe's hero of *Robinson Crusoe* (1719) was marooned on an island in the Caribbean, but he was based on Alexander Selkirk, who had lived alone on the nearby island Juan Fernandez from 1704 to 1709.

were beaten back again, the hope against hope so struggled in her soul, that at length she desperately said, "Not yet, not yet; my foolish heart runs on too fast." So she forced patience for some further weeks. But to those whom earth's sure indraft[1] draws, patience or impatience is still the same.

Hunilla now sought to settle precisely in her mind, to an hour, how long it was since the ship had sailed; and then, with the same precision, how long a space remained to pass. But this proved impossible. What present day or month it was she could not say. Time was her labyrinth, in which Hunilla was entirely lost.

And now follows——

Against my own purposes a pause descends upon me here. One knows not whether nature doth not impose some secrecy upon him who has been privy to certain things. At least, it is to be doubted whether it be good to blazon such. If some books are deemed most baneful and their sale forbid, how then with deadlier facts, not dreams of doting men? Those whom books will hurt will not be proof against events. Events, not books, should be forbid. But in all things man sows upon the wind, which bloweth just there whither it listeth;[2] for ill or good man cannot know. Often ill comes from the good, as good from ill.

When Hunilla——

Dire sight it is to see some silken beast long dally with a golden lizard ere she devour. More terrible, to see how feline Fate will sometimes dally with a human soul, and by a nameless magic make it repulse one sane despair with another which is but mad. Unwittingly I imp this catlike thing, sporting with the heart of him who reads; for if he feels not, he does read in vain.

—"The ship sails this day, to-day," at last said Hunilla to herself; "this gives me certain time to stand on; without certainty I go mad. In loose ignorance I have hoped and hoped; now in firm knowledge I will but wait. Now I live and no longer perish in bewilderings. Holy Virgin, aid me! Thou wilt waft back the ship. Oh, past length of weary weeks—all to be dragged over—to buy the certainty of today, I freely give ye, though I tear ye from me!"

As mariners tossed in tempest on some desolate ledge patch them a boat out of the remnants of their vessel's wreck, and launch it in the self-same waves, see here Hunilla, this lone shipwrecked soul, out of treachery invoking trust. Humanity, thou strong thing, I worship thee, not in the laurelled victor, but in this vanquished one.

Truly Hunilla leaned upon a reed, a real one; no metaphor; a real Eastern reed. A piece of hollow cane, drifted from unknown isles, and found upon the beach, its once jagged ends rubbed smoothly even as by sand-paper; its golden glazing gone. Long ground between the sea and land, upper and nether stone, the unvarnished substance was filed bare, and wore another polish now, one with itself, the polish of its agony. Circular lines at intervals cut all round this surface, divided it into six panels of unequal length. In the first were scored the days, each tenth one marked by a longer and deeper notch; the second was scored for the number of sea-fowl eggs for sustenance, picked out from the rocky nests; the third, how many fish had been caught from the shore; the fourth, how many small tortoises found inland; the fifth, how many days of

---

1. A current pulling or attracting objects toward it.
2. Jesus' words in John 3.8: "The wind bloweth where it listeth, and thou hearest the sound thereof, but canst not tell whence it cometh, and whither it goeth: so is every one that is born of the Spirit."

sun; the sixth, of clouds; which last, of the two, was the greater one. Long night of busy numbering, misery's mathematics, to weary her too-wakeful soul to sleep; yet sleep for that was none.

The panel of the days was deeply worn, the long tenth notches half effaced, as alphabets of the blind. Ten thousand times the longing widow had traced her finger over the bamboo; dull flute, which played on, gave no sound; as if counting birds flown by in air, would hasten tortoises creeping through the woods.

After the one hundred and eightieth day no further mark was seen; that last one was the faintest, as the first the deepest.

"There were more days," said our Captain; "many, many more; why did you not go on and notch them too, Hunilla?"

"Señor, ask me not."

"And meantime, did no other vessel pass the isle?"

"Nay, Señor;—but——"

"You do not speak; but *what*, Hunilla?"

"Ask me not, Señor."

"You saw ships pass, far away; you waved to them; they passed on;—was that it, Hunilla?"

"Señor, be it as you say."

Braced against her woe, Hunilla would not, durst not trust the weakness of her tongue. Then when our Captain asked whether any whale-boats had——

But no, I will not file this thing complete for scoffing souls to quote, and call it firm proof upon their side. The half shall here remain untold. Those two unnamed events which befell Hunilla on this isle, let them abide between her and her God. In nature, as in law, it may be libellous to speak some truths.

Still, how it was that although our vessel had lain three days anchored nigh the isle, its one human tenant should not have discovered us till just upon the point of sailing, never to revisit so lone and far a spot; this needs explaining ere the sequel come.

The place where the French captain had landed the little party was on the farther and opposite end of the isle. There too it was that they had afterwards built their hut. Nor did the widow in her solitude desert the spot where her loved ones had dwelt with her, and where the dearest of the twain now slept his last long sleep, and all her plaints awaked him not, and he of husbands the most faithful during life.

Now, high broken land rises between the opposite extremities of the isle. A ship anchored at one side is invisible from the other. Neither is the isle so small, but a considerable company might wander for days through the wilderness of one side, and never be seen, or their halloos heard, by any stranger holding aloof on the other. Hence Hunilla, who naturally associated the possible coming of ships with her own part of the isle, might to the end have remained quite ignorant of the presence of our vessel, were it not for a mysterious presentiment, borne to her, so our mariners averred, by this isle's enchanted air. Nor did the widow's answer undo the thought.

"How did you come to cross the isle this morning then, Hunilla?" said our Captain.

"Señor, something came flitting by me. It touched my cheek, my heart, Señor."

"What do you say, Hunilla?"

"I have said, Señor; something came through the air."

It was a narrow chance. For when in crossing the isle Hunilla gained the high land in the centre, she must then for the first have perceived our masts, and also marked that their sails were being loosed, perhaps even heard the echoing chorus of the windlass song. The strange ship was about to sail, and she behind. With all haste she now descends the height on the hither side, but soon loses sight of the ship among the sunken jungles at the mountain's base. She struggles on through the withered branches, which seek at every step to bar her path, till she comes to the isolated rock, still some way from the water. This she climbs, to reassure herself. The ship is still in plainest sight. But now worn out with over tension, Hunilla all but faints; she fears to step down from her giddy perch; she is fain[3] to pause, there where she is, and as a last resort catches the turban from her head, unfurls and waves it over the jungles towards us.

During the telling of her story the mariners formed a voiceless circle round Hunilla and the Captain; and when at length the word was given to man the fastest boat, and pull round to the isle's thither side, to bring away Hunilla's chest and the tortoise-oil; such alacrity of both cheery and sad obedience seldom before was seen. Little ado was made. Already the anchor had been recommitted to the bottom, and the ship swung calmly to it.

But Hunilla insisted upon accompanying the boat as indispensable pilot to her hidden hut. So being refreshed with the best the steward could supply, she started with us. Nor did ever any wife of the most famous admiral in her husband's barge receive more silent reverence of respect, than poor Hunilla from this boat's crew.

Rounding many a vitreous cape and bluff, in two hours' time we shot inside the fatal reef; wound into a secret cove, looked up along a green many-gabled lava wall, and saw the island's solitary dwelling.

It hung upon an impending cliff, sheltered on two sides by tangled thickets, and half-screened from view in front by juttings of the rude stairway, which climbed the precipice from the sea. Built of canes, it was thatched with long, mildewed grass. It seemed an abandoned hayrick, whose haymakers were now no more. The roof inclined but one way; the eaves coming to within two feet of the ground. And here was a simple apparatus to collect the dews, or rather doubly-distilled and finest winnowed rains, which, in mercy or in mockery, the night-skies sometimes drop upon these blighted Encantadas. All along beneath the eaves, a spotted sheet, quite weather-stained, was spread, pinned to short, upright stakes, set in the shallow sand. A small clinker, thrown into the cloth, weighed its middle down, thereby straining all moisture into a calabash[4] placed below. This vessel supplied each drop of water ever drunk upon the isle by the Cholos. Hunilla told us the calabash would sometimes, but not often, be half filled over-night. It held six quarts, perhaps. "But," said she, "we were used to thirst. At sandy[5] Payta, where I live, no shower from heaven ever fell; all the water there is brought on mules from the inland vales."

Tied among the thickets were some twenty moaning tortoises, supplying Hunilla's lonely larder; while hundreds of vast tableted black bucklers, like displaced, shattered tomb-stones of dark slate, were also scattered round. These

---

3. Constrained; the original has *feign*.
4. Hollow gourd used as a bowl.

5. The original has *Sandy*, as if it were part of the place name.

were the skeleton backs of those great tortoises from which Felipe and Truxill
had made their precious oil. Several large calabashes and two goodly kegs were
filled with it. In a pot near by were the caked crusts of a quantity which had
been permitted to evaporate. "They meant to have strained it off next day,"
said Hunilla, as she turned aside.

I forgot to mention the most singular sight of all, though the first that greeted
us after landing; memory keeps not in all things to the order of occurrence.

Some ten small, soft-haired, ringleted dogs, of a beautiful breed, peculiar
to Peru, set up a concert of glad welcomings when we gained the beach, which
was responded to by Hunilla. Some of these dogs had, since her widowhood,
been born upon the isle, the progeny of the two brought from Payta. Owing
to the jagged steeps and pitfalls, tortuous thickets, sunken clefts and perilous
intricacies of all sorts in the interior; Hunilla, admonished by the loss of one
favorite among them, never allowed these delicate creatures to follow her in
her occasional birds'-nests climbs and other wanderings; so that, through long
habituation, they offered not to follow, when that morning she crossed the
land; and her own soul was then too full of other things to heed their lingering
behind. Yet, all along she had so clung to them, that, besides what moisture
they lapped up at early daybreak from the small scoop-holes among the adjacent rocks, she had shared the dew of her calabash among them; never laying
by any considerable store against those prolonged and utter droughts, which
in some disastrous seasons warp these isles.

Having pointed out, at our desire, what few things she would like transported to the ship—her chest, the oil, not omitting the live tortoises which she
intended for a grateful present to our Captain—we immediately set to work,
carrying them to the boat down the long, sloping stair of deeply-shadowed
rock. While my comrades were thus employed, I looked, and Hunilla had disappeared.

It was not curiosity alone, but, it seems to me, something different mingled
with it, which prompted me to drop my tortoises, and once more gaze slowly
around. I remembered the husband buried by Hunilla's hands. A narrow pathway led into a dense part of the thickets. Following it through many mazes, I
came out upon a small, round, open space, deeply chambered there.

The mound rose in the middle; a bare heap of finest sand, like that unver-
dured heap found at the bottom of an hourglass run out. At its head stood the
cross of withered sticks; the dry, peeled[6] bark still fraying from it; its transverse
limb tied up with rope, and forlornly adroop in the silent air.

Hunilla was partly prostate upon the grave; her dark head bowed, and lost
in her long, loosened Indian hair; her hands extended to the cross-foot, with a
little brass crucifix clasped between; a crucifix worn featureless, like an ancient
graven knocker long plied in vain. She did not see me, and I made no noise,
but slid aside, and left the spot.

A few moments ere all was ready for our going, she reappeared among us. I
looked into her eyes, but saw no tear. There was something which seemed
strangely haughty in her air, and yet it was the air of woe. A Spanish and an
Indian grief, which would not visibly lament. Pride's height in vain abased to
proneness on the rock; nature's pride subduing nature's torture.

Like pages the small and silken dogs surrounded her, as she slowly

6. The original has *pealed*.

descended towards the beach. She caught the two most eager creatures in her arms:—"Mia Teeta! Mia Tomoteeta!" and fondling them, inquired how many could we take on board.

The mate commanded the boat's crew; not a hard-hearted man, but his way of life had been such that in most things, even in the smallest, simple utility was his leading motive.

"We cannot take them all, Hunilla; our supplies are short; the winds are unreliable; we may be a good many days going to Tombez. So take those you have, Hunilla; but no more."

She was in the boat; the oarsmen too were seated; all save one, who stood ready to push off and then spring himself. With the sagacity of their race, the dogs now seemed aware that they were in the very instant of being deserted upon a barren strand. The gunwales of the boat were high; its prow—presented inland—was lifted; so owing to the water, which they seemed instinctively to shun, the dogs could not well leap into the little craft. But their busy paws hard scraped the prow, as it had been some farmer's door shutting them out from shelter in a winter storm. A clamorous agony of alarm. They did not howl, or whine; they all but spoke.

"Push off! Give way!" cried the mate. The boat gave one heavy drag and lurch, and next moment shot swiftly from the beach, turned on her heel, and sped. The dogs ran howling along the water's marge; now pausing to gaze at the flying boat, then motioning as if to leap in chase, but mysteriously withheld themselves; and again ran howling along the beach. Had they been human beings hardly would they have more vividly inspired the sense of desolation. The oars were plied as confederate feathers of two wings. No one spoke. I looked back upon the beach, and then upon Hunilla, but her face was set in a stern dusky calm. The dogs crouching in her lap vainly licked her rigid hands. She never looked behind her; but sat motionless, till we turned a promontory of the coast and lost all sights and sounds astern. She seemed as one, who having experienced the sharpest of mortal pangs, was henceforth content to have all lesser heartstrings riven, one by one. To Hunilla, pain seemed so necessary, that pain in other beings, though by love and sympathy made her own, was unrepiningly to be borne. A heart of yearning in a frame of steel. A heart of earthly yearning, frozen by the frost which falleth from the sky.

The sequel is soon told. After a long passage, vexed by calms and baffling winds, we made the little port of Tombez in Peru, there to recruit the ship. Payta was not very distant. Our captain sold the tortoise oil to a Tombez merchant; and adding to the silver a contribution from all hands, gave it to our silent passenger, who knew not what the mariners had done.

The last seen of lone Hunilla she was passing into Payta town, riding upon a small gray ass; and before her on the ass's shoulders, she eyed the jointed workings of the beast's armorial cross.[7]

1854

7. What Melville wrote at this point has been lost through censorship. On May 12, 1854, Charles F. Briggs, the editor of *Putnam's*, wrote Melville to reject "The Two Temples" because it might offend "the religious sensibilities of the public." Then he continued: "I will take this opportunity to apologise to you for making a slight alteration in the Encantadas, in the last paragraph of the Chola Widow, which I thought would be improved by the omission of a few words. That I did not injure the idea, or mutilate the touching figure you introduced, by the slight excision I made, I received good evidence of, in a letter from James [Russell] Lowell, who said that the figure of the cross in the ass' neck, brought tears into his eyes, and he thought it the finest touch of genius he had seen in prose." Plainly, Melville had made an explicit allusion to Christ's entry into

The Paradise of Bachelors and The Tartarus of Maids[1]

I. The Paradise of Bachelors

It lies not far from Temple-Bar.[2]

Going to it, by the usual way, is like stealing from a heated plain into some cool, deep glen, shady among harboring hills.

Sick with the din and soiled with the mud of Fleet Street—where the Benedick[3] tradesmen are hurrying by, with ledger-lines ruled along their brows, thinking upon rise of bread and fall of babies—you adroitly turn a mystic corner—not a street—glide down a dim, monastic way, flanked by dark, sedate, and solemn piles, and still wending on, give the whole care-worn world the slip, and, disentangled, stand beneath the quiet cloisters of the Paradise of Bachelors.[4]

Sweet are the oases in Sahara; charming the isle-groves of August prairies; delectable pure faith amidst a thousand perfidies: but sweeter, still more charming, most delectable the dreamy Paradise of Bachelors, found in the stony heart of stunning London.

In mild meditation pace the cloisters; take your pleasure, sip your leisure, in the garden waterward; go linger in the ancient library; go worship in the sculptured chapel;[5] but little have you seen, just nothing do you know, not the

Jerusalem on a colt (Mark 11.7) or on a colt or the ass, its mother, in the more ambiguous account in Matthew 21. In *Clarel* (2.1), Melville's description of the simple, saintlike pilgrim Nehemiah suggests the nature of the passage that had been censored: "The ass, pearly-gray / Matched well the rider's garb in hue, / And sorted with the ashy way; / Upon her shoulders' joined play / The white cross gleamed, which the untrue / Yet innocent fair legends say, / Memorializes Christ our Lord / When Him with palms the throngs adored / Upon the foal." Melville took the comparison from Wordsworth's *Peter Bell*, lines 971–80.

1. The text is from the first publication in *Harper's New Monthly Magazine*, 10 (April 1855). As the full-title running heads in *Harper's* emphasized, this is a single story, each part of which yields its significance only in the light of the other. The same point is made in this reprinting by the abbreviated form *Paradise and Tartarus*.

The story derives from two episodes in Melville's life. The first, in December 1849, was one of the most gratifying he ever experienced. After weeks in London of trying to peddle *White-Jacket* to publishers afraid of the shakiness of the copyright law, weeks during which he conducted an ongoing search for the perfect snug-gery, the pub best for solitary dining, drinking, and smoking or for sharing these pleasures with a friend in an inglenook, he decided because of homesickness and lack of funds to forgo other opportunities and return home. In the last days of his stay he was feted so hospitably by several acquaintances from the London literary and legal community that he learned what good talk could be among admirably educated men of remarkable histories in a world capital; remembering, he later refused almost all efforts by the New York literati to lure him into the Authors Club and took refuge in his imaginary Burgundy Club where he could, once again, talk, eat, and drink with his equals. The second experience probably occurred in late January 1851, after he had moved to Pittsfield and was composing *Moby-Dick*—he drove about five miles away to the

northeast and bought a sleigh-load of paper from Carson's Mill in Dalton, Massachusetts. What he saw there can only be judged by the second half of the story, but it was written a few months after Melville's wife bore her third child, Elizabeth, and was sold to *Harper's* about the time she became pregnant with their last child, Frances. We now know, after the discovery of a Melville trove in Upstate New York in 1983, that Elizabeth Melville suffered horribly after the birth of her second child in October 1851, and we know as of 1984 that someone, presumably Melville's wife or one of his daughters, systematically erased his annotations in his Milton volumes at places where he was plainly commenting on Milton's depiction of biblical male-female relationships, Adam and Eve, Samson and Delilah. The story is a tantalizing glimpse of what it meant to Melville to recall the paradise of a literary life in London just as he was having to face the likelihood that his own career had to be sacrificed to meet his responsibilities as a husband and father; it is also a disturbing glimpse into his inklings of how women, and not only maids, could also be sacrificed.

2. Ornate stone gateway between Fleet Street and the Strand in London, built by the architect Christopher Wren (1632–1723) in 1670. The Strand runs along the north bank of the Thames. Fleet Street had many literary associations for Melville, particularly with 18th-century writers, and was becoming an area for newspaper and publishing offices. This section of Melville's story is deeply indebted to Irving's *London Antiques* in *The Sketch Book*.

3. Married men, especially newly married men who have resisted the state of matrimony, from Benedick, who at the end of Shakespeare's *Much Ado About Nothing* surrenders his cherished bachelordom.

4. These cloisters are the four Inns of Court, inhabited by lawyers and legal students.

5. The chapel is "sculptured" with grotesque figures on columns but primarily by effigies of knights lying prone on the floor.

sweet kernel have you tasted, till you dine among the banded Bachelors, and see their convivial eyes and glasses sparkle. Not dine in bustling commons, during term-time, in the hall; but tranquilly, by private hint, at a private table; some fine Templar's[6] hospitably invited guest.

Templar? That's a romantic name. Let me see. Brian de Bois Gilbert[7] was a Templar, I believe. Do we understand you to insinuate that those famous Templars still survive in modern London? May the ring of their armed heels be heard, and the rattle of their shields, as in mailed prayer the monk-knights kneel before the consecrated Host? Surely a monk-knight were a curious sight picking his way along the Strand, his gleaming corselet and snowy surcoat[8] spattered by an omnibus. Long-bearded, too, according to his order's rule; his face furry as a pard's;[9] how would the grim ghost look among the crop-haired, close-shaven citizens? We know indeed—sad history recounts it—that a moral blight tainted at last this sacred Brotherhood. Though no sworded foe might outskill them in the fence, yet the worm of luxury crawled beneath their guard, gnawing the core of knightly troth, nibbling the monastic vow, till at last the monk's austerity relaxed to wassailing, and the sworn knights-bachelors grew to be but hypocrites and rakes.

But for all this, quite unprepared were we to learn that Knights-Templars (if at all in being) were so entirely secularized as to be reduced from carving out immortal fame in glorious battling for the Holy Land, to the carving of roast-mutton at a dinner-board. Like Anacreon,[1] do these degenerate Templars now think it sweeter far to fall in banquet than in war? Or, indeed, how can there be any survival of that famous order? Templars in modern London! Templars in their red-cross mantles smoking cigars at the Divan![2] Templars crowded in a railway train, till, stacked with steel helmet, spear, and shield, the whole train looks like one elongated locomotive!

No. The genuine Templar is long since departed. Go view the wondrous tombs in the Temple Church;[3] see there the rigidly-haughty forms stretched out, with crossed arms upon their stilly hearts, in everlasting and undreaming rest. Like the years before the flood, the bold Knights-Templars are no more. Nevertheless, the name remains, and the nominal society, and the ancient grounds, and some of the ancient edifices. But the iron heel is changed to a boot of patent-leather; the long two-handed sword to a one-handed quill, the monk-giver of gratuitous ghostly counsel now counsels for a fee; the defender of the sarcophagus (if in good practice with his weapon) now has more than one case to defend; the vowed opener and clearer of all highways leading to the Holy Sepulchre,[4] now has it in particular charge to check, to clog, to hinder, and embarrass all the courts and avenues of Law; the knight-combatant of the Saracen, breasting spear-points at Acre, now fights law-points in Westminster Hall.[5] The helmet is a wig. Struck by Time's enchanter's wand, the Templar is to-day a Lawyer.

---

6. Order of Catholic soldier-monks established in the twelfth century to protect pilgrims on their way to the Holy Land. Henry I introduced the Order to England; after it grew corrupt, it was dissolved in 1312.
7. Evil Knight Templar in Sir Walter Scott's *Ivanhoe* (1819) (correctly, Brian de Bois-Guilbert).
8. Outercoat, over armor. "Corselet": trunk armor.
9. Leopard.
1. Greek poet (563?–478? B.C.) known for songs celebrating wine and love.
2. Oriental council chamber.

3. The great Round Church, or Temple Church, was constructed in 1185 and belonged to two of the Inns of Court, the Inner Temple and the Middle Temple.
4. The Roman Catholic church at the supposed site of Jesus' tomb in Jerusalem.
5. A vestibule of the new houses of Parliament, part of the ancient Palace of Westminster founded by the Anglo-Saxon kings, used in Melville's time as a law court. "Saracen": Moslem. "Acre": seaport of Palestine, long held by Christians during the Crusades.

But, like many others tumbled from proud glory's height—like the apple, hard on the bough but mellow on the ground—the Templar's fall has but made him all the finer fellow.

I dare say those old warrior-priests were but gruff and grouty at the best; cased in Birmingham[6] hardware, how could their crimped arms give yours or mine a hearty shake? Their proud, ambitious, monkish souls clasped shut, like horn-book missals;[7] their very faces clapped in bomb-shells; what sort of genial men were these? But best of comrades, most affable of hosts, capital diner is the modern Templar. His wit and wine are both of sparkling brands.

The church and cloisters, courts and vaults, lanes and passages, banquet-halls, refectories, libraries, terraces, gardens, broad walks, domicils, and dessert-rooms, covering a very large space of ground, and all grouped in central neighborhood, and quite sequestered from the old city's surrounding din; and every thing about the place being kept in most bachelor-like particularity, no part of London offers to a quiet wight so agreeable a refuge.

The Temple is, indeed, a city by itself. A city with all the best appurtenances, as the above enumeration shows. A city with a park to it, and flower-beds, and a river-side—the Thames flowing by as openly, in one part, as by Eden's primal garden flowed the mild Euphrates. In what is now the Temple Garden the old Crusaders used to exercise their steeds and lances; the modern Templars now lounge on the benches beneath the trees, and, switching their patent-leather boots, in gay discourse exercise at repartee.

Long lines of stately portraits in the banquet halls, show what great men of mark—famous nobles, judges, and Lord Chancellors—have in their time been Templars. But all Templars are not known to universal fame; though, if the having warm hearts and warmer welcomes, full minds and fuller cellars, and giving good advice and glorious dinners, spiced with rare divertisements of fun and fancy, merit immortal mention, set down, ye muses, the names of R. F. C.[8] and his imperial brother.

Though to be a Templar, in the one true sense, you must needs be a lawyer, or a student at the law, and be ceremoniously enrolled as member of the order, yet as many such, though Templars, do not reside within the Templar's precincts, though they may have their offices there, just so, on the other hand, there are many residents of the hoary old domicils who are not admitted Templars. If being, say, a lounging gentleman and bachelor, or a quiet, unmarried, literary man, charmed with the soft seclusion of the spot, you much desire to pitch your shady tent among the rest in this serene encampment, then you must make some special friend among the order, and procure him to rent, in his name but at your charge, whatever vacant chamber you may find to suit.

Thus, I suppose, did Dr. Johnson,[9] that nominal Benedick and widower but virtual bachelor, when for a space he resided here. So, too, did that undoubted bachelor and rare good soul, Charles Lamb.[1] And hundreds more, of sterling spirits, Brethren of the Order of Celibacy, from time to time have dined, and slept, and tabernacled here. Indeed, the place is all a honeycomb of offices and domicils. Like any cheese, it is quite perforated through and through in

---

6. Made in Birmingham, west-central English industrial city (in facetious anachronism). "Grouty": sullen, cross.
7. Devotional books of parchment mounted on a board with a handle; here, made with covers protected by a thin layer of horn.
8. Robert Francis Cooke, who entertained in Elm

Court, Temple, on December 19, 1849. On the twenty-first Melville called on a Mr. Cleaves in the Temple and visited the library.
9. Samuel Johnson (1709–1784), English writer and lexicographer.
1. English essayist (1775–1834).

all directions with the snug cells of bachelors. Dear, delightful spot! Ah! when I bethink me of the sweet hours there passed, enjoying such genial hospitalities beneath those time-honored roofs, my heart only finds due utterance through poetry; and, with a sigh, I softly sing, "Carry me back to old Virginny!"[2]

Such then, at large, is the Paradise of Bachelors. And such I found it one pleasant afternoon in the smiling month of May, when, sallying from my hotel in Trafalgar Square, I went to keep my dinner-appointment with that fine Barrister, Bachelor, and Bencher,[3] R. F. C. (he *is* the first and second, and *should be* the third; I hereby nominate him), whose card I kept fast pinched between my gloved forefinger and thumb, and every now and then snatched still another look at the pleasant address inscribed beneath the name, "No.—, Elm Court, Temple."

At the core he was a right bluff, care-free, right comfortable, and most companionable Englishman. If on a first acquaintance he seemed reserved, quite icy in his air—patience; this Champagne will thaw. And if it never do, better frozen Champagne than liquid vinegar.

There were nine gentlemen, all bachelors, at the dinner. One was from "No.—, King's Bench Walk, Temple;" a second, third, and fourth, and fifth, from various courts or passages christened with some similarly rich resounding syllables. It was indeed a sort of Senate of the Bachelors, sent to this dinner from widely-scattered districts, to represent the general celibacy of the Temple. Nay it was, by representation, a Grand Parliament of the best Bachelors in universal London; several of those present being from distant quarters of the town, noted immemorial seats of lawyers and un-married men—Lincoln's Inn, Furnival's Inn; and one gentleman, upon whom I looked with a sort of collateral awe, hailed from the spot where Lord Verulam[4] once abode a bachelor—Gray's Inn.

The apartment was well up toward heaven. I know not how many strange old stairs I climbed to get to it. But a good dinner, with famous company, should be well earned. No doubt our host had his dining-room so high with a view to secure the prior exercise necessary to the due relishing and digesting of it.

The furniture was wonderfully unpretending, old, and snug. No new shining mahogany, sticky with undried varnish; no uncomfortably luxurious ottomans, and sofas too fine to use, vexed you in this sedate apartment. It is a thing which every sensible American should learn from every sensible Englishman, that glare and glitter, gimcracks and gewgaws, are not indispensable to domestic solacement. The American Benedick snatches, down-town, a tough chop in a gilded show-box; the English bachelor leisurely dines at home on that incomparable South Down of his, off a plain deal board.[5]

The ceiling of the room was low. Who wants to dine under the dome of St. Peter's?[6] High ceilings! If that is your demand, and the higher the better, and you be so very tall, then go dine out with the topping giraffe in the open air.

2. From a song of the same title by Edwin P. Christy (1847), not the still-familiar song with the line "old Virginny, the state where I was born."
3. Judge. Trafalgar Square contains the great column and statue erected in 1843 in honor of Lord Nelson's naval victory at Trafalgar in 1805 against the combined French and Spanish fleets. The four colossal Landseer lions were added after Melville saw the square.
4. Francis Bacon (1561–1626), English writer and

statesman. Lincoln's Inn is one of the Inns of Court. Furnival's Inn, a Gothic building, was formerly an Inn of Chancery, which was destroyed after Melville saw it.
5. Wooden trencher. "South Down": or Southdown, an English breed of sheep, i.e., mutton.
6. The cathedral in Rome whose dome was constructed under the direction of Michelangelo. The Inns of Court are between the smaller-domed St. Paul's and the Thames.

In good time the nine gentlemen sat down to nine covers, and soon were fairly under way.

If I remember right, ox-tail soup inaugurated the affair. Of a rich russet hue, its agreeable flavor dissipated my first confounding of its main ingredient with teamster's gads and the rawhides of ushers.[7] (By way of interlude, we here drank a little claret.) Neptune's was the next tribute rendered—turbot[8] coming second; snowwhite, flaky, and just gelatinous enough, not too turtleish in its unctuousness.

(At this point we refreshed ourselves with a glass of sherry.) After these light skirmishers had vanished, the heavy artillery of the feast marched in, led by that well-known English generalissimo, roast beef. For aids-de-camp we had a saddle of mutton, a fat turkey, a chicken-pie, and endless other savory things; while for avant-couriers came nine silver flagons of humming ale. This heavy ordnance[9] having departed on the track of the light skirmishers, a picked brigade of game-fowl encamped upon the board, their camp-fires lit by the ruddiest of decanters.

Tarts and puddings followed, with innumerable niceties; then cheese and crackers. (By way of ceremony, simply, only to keep up good old fashions, we here each drank a glass of good old port.)

The cloth was now removed; and like Blucher's[1] army coming in at the death on the field of Waterloo, in marched a fresh detachment of bottles, dusty with their hurried march.

All these manœuvrings of the forces were superintended by a surprising old field-marshal (I can not school myself to call him by the inglorious name of waiter), with snowy hair and napkin, and a head like Socrates.[2] Amidst all the hilarity of the feast, intent on important business, he disdained to smile. Venerable man!

I have above endeavored to give some slight schedule of the general plan of operations. But any one knows that a good, genial dinner is a sort of pell-mell, indiscriminate affair, quite baffling to detail in all particulars. Thus, I spoke of taking a glass of claret, and a glass of sherry, and a glass of port, and a mug of ale—all at certain specific periods and times. But those were merely the state bumpers,[3] so to speak. Innumerable impromptu glasses were drained between the periods of those grand imposing ones.

The nine bachelors seemed to have the most tender concern for each other's health. All the time, in flowing wine, they most earnestly expressed their sincerest wishes for the entire well-being and lasting hygiene of the gentlemen on the right and on the left. I noticed that when one of these kind bachelors desired a little more wine (just for his stomach's sake, like Timothy),[4] he would not help himself to it unless some other bachelor would join him. It seemed held something indelicate, selfish, and unfraternal, to be seen taking a lonely, unparticipated glass. Meantime, as the wine ran apace, the spirits of the company grew more and more to perfect genialness and unconstraint.

---

7. Assistant schoolteachers (especially old thick-skinned ones). "Gads": goads, because drivers used whips made from oxtails.
8. European flatfish, in tribute to the god of the sea, Neptune.
9. Artillery. "Aids-de-camp" is generally spelled *aides-de-camp*. "Avant-couriers": forerunners, usually spelled *avant-coureurs* or *avant-courriers*. "Humming": still effervescent.

1. Gebhard von Blucher (1742–1819), leader of Prussian troops that helped in the defeat of Napoleon at Waterloo in 1815.
2. Greek philosopher (470?–399 B.C.).
3. Any large glass or mug with bulging sides, meant to be filled to the brim for drinking toasts.
4. Paul's prescription in 1 Timothy 5.23: "Drink no longer water, but use a little wine for thy stomach's sake and thine often infirmities."

They related all sort of pleasant stories. Choice experiences in their private lives were now brought out, like choice brands of Moselle or Rhenish, only kept for particular company. One told us how mellowly he lived when a student at Oxford; with various spicy anecdotes of most frank-hearted noble lords, his liberal companions. Another bachelor, a gray-headed man, with a sunny face, who, by his own account, embraced every opportunity of leisure to cross over into the Low Countries,[5] on sudden tours of inspection of the fine old Flemish architecture there—this learned, white-haired, sunny-faced old bachelor, excelled in his descriptions of the elaborate splendors of those old guild-halls, town-halls, and stadthold-houses, to be seen in the land of the ancient Flemings. A third was a great frequenter of the British Museum, and knew all about scores of wonderful antiquities, of Oriental manuscripts, and costly books without a duplicate. A fourth had lately returned from a trip to Old Granada, and, of course, was full of Saracenic scenery. A fifth had a funny case in law to tell. A sixth was crudite in wines. A seventh had a strange characteristic anecdote of the private life of the Iron Duke,[6] never printed, and never before announced in any public or private company. An eighth had lately been amusing his evenings, now and then, with translating a comic poem of Pulci's.[7] He quoted for us the more amusing passages.

And so the evening slipped along, the hours told, not by a water-clock, like King Alfred's, but a wine-chronometer. Meantime the table seemed a sort of Epsom Heath;[8] a regular ring, where the decanters galloped round. For fear one decanter should not with sufficient speed reach his destination, another was sent express after him to hurry him; and then a third to hurry the second; and so on with a fourth and fifth. And throughout all this nothing loud, nothing unmannerly, nothing turbulent. I am quite sure, from the scrupulous gravity and austerity of his air, that had Socrates, the field-marshal, perceived aught of indecorum in the company he served, he would have forthwith departed without giving warning. I afterward learned that, during the repast, an invalid bachelor in an adjoining chamber enjoyed his first sound refreshing slumber in three long, weary weeks.

It was the very perfection of quiet absorption of good living, good drinking, good feeling, and good talk. We were a band of brothers. Comfort—fraternal, household comfort, was the grand trait of the affair. Also, you could plainly see that these easy-hearted men had no wives or children to give an anxious thought. Almost all of them were travelers, too; for bachelors alone can travel freely, and without any twinges of their consciences touching desertion of the fireside.

The thing called pain, the bugbear styled trouble—those two legends seemed preposterous to their bachelor imaginations. How could men of liberal sense, ripe scholarship in the world, and capacious philosophical and convivial understandings—how could they suffer themselves to be imposed upon by such monkish fables? Pain! Trouble! As well talk of Catholic miracles. No such thing.—Pass the sherry, Sir.—Pooh, pooh! Can't be!—The port, Sir, if

---

5. The Netherlands, Belgium, and Luxemburg, but the context suggests that Melville knew the bawdy play on "Low Countries" in, for instance, Shakespeare's *A Comedy of Errors* (3.2), in which a kitchen maid is described according to the geography of Europe.
6. Duke of Wellington (1769–1852), victor over Na-

poleon at Waterloo (1815).
7. Luigi Pulci (1432–84), Florentine poet.
8. Racetrack in Epsom, Surrey, where the Derby has been run since 1780. Alfred the Great (849–899) was king of Wessex (871–899).

you please. Nonsense; don't tell me so.—The decanter stops with you, Sir, I believe.

And so it went.

Not long after the cloth was drawn our host glanced significantly upon Socrates, who, solemnly stepping to a stand, returned with an immense convolved horn, a regular Jericho horn,[9] mounted with polished silver, and otherwise chased and curiously enriched; not omitting two life-like goat's heads, with four more horns of solid silver, projecting from opposite sides of the mouth of the noble main horn.

Not having heard that our host was a performer on the bugle, I was surprised to see him lift this horn from the table, as if he were about to blow an inspiring blast. But I was relieved from this and set quite right as touching the purposes of the horn, by his now inserting his thumb and forefinger into its mouth; whereupon a slight aroma was stirred up, and my nostrils were greeted with the smell of some choice Rappee. It was a mull[1] of snuff. It went the rounds. Capital idea this, thought I, of taking snuff about this juncture. This goodly fashion must be introduced among my countrymen at home, further ruminated I.

The remarkable decorum of the nine bachelors—a decorum not to be affected by any quantity of wine—a decorum unassailable by any degree of mirthfulness—this was again set in a forcible light to me, by now observing that, though they took snuff very freely, yet not a man so far violated the proprieties, or so far molested the invalid bachelor in the adjoining room as to indulge himself in a sneeze. The snuff was snuffed silently, as if it had been some fine innoxious[2] powder brushed off the wings of butterflies.

But fine though they be, bachelors' dinners, like bachelors' lives, can not endure forever. The time came for breaking up. One by one the bachelors took their hats, and two by two, and arm-in-arm they descended, still conversing, to the flagging of the court; some going to their neighboring chambers to turn over the Decameron[3] ere retiring for the night; some to smoke a cigar, promenading in the garden on the cool river-side; some to make for the street, call a hack, and be driven snugly to their distant lodgings.

I was the last lingerer.

"Well," said my smiling host, "what do you think of the Temple here, and the sort of life we bachelors make out to live in it?"

"Sir," said I, with a burst of admiring candor—"Sir, this is the very Paradise of Bachelors!"

II. The Tartarus of Maids

It lies not far from Woedolor Mountain in New England. Turning to the east, right out from among bright farms and sunny meadows, nodding in early June with odorous grasses, you enter ascendingly among bleak hills. These gradually close in upon a dusky pass, which, from the violent Gulf Stream of air unceasingly diving between its cloven walls of haggard rock, as well as

---

9. In Joshua 6.1–20, seven priests circled Jericho making long blasts with rams' horns until on the seventh day "the walls fell flat" and Joshua took the city.
1. A small, usually ornate box with an apparatus for pulverizing tobacco into snuff. In his diary for December 1849 Melville emphasized the word as if he had just learned it. "Rappee": a strong, dark snuff.
2. Harmless.
3. Bawdy tales by the Italian writer Giovanni Boccaccio (1313–1375).

from the tradition of a crazy spinster's hut having long ago stood somewhere hereabouts, is called the Mad Maid's Bellows'-pipe.[4]

Winding along at the bottom of the gorge is a dangerously narrow wheel-road, occupying the bed of a former torrent. Following this road to its highest point, you stand as within a Dantean gateway.[5] From the steepness of the walls here, their strangely ebon hue, and the sudden contraction of the gorge, this particular point is called the Black Notch. The ravine now expandingly descends into a great, purple, hopper-shaped hollow, far sunk among many Plutonian,[6] shaggy-wooded mountains. By the country people this hollow is called the Devil's Dungeon. Sounds of torrents fall on all sides upon the ear. These rapid waters unite at last in one turbid brick-colored stream, boiling through a flume among enormous boulders. They call this strange-colored torrent Blood River. Gaining a dark precipice it wheels suddenly to the west, and makes one maniac spring of sixty feet into the arms of a stunted wood of gray-haired pines, between which it thence eddies on its further way down to the invisible lowlands.

Conspicuously crowning a rocky bluff high to one side, at the cataract's verge, is the ruin of an old saw-mill, built in those primitive times when vast pines and hemlocks superabounded throughout the neighboring region. The black-mossed bulk of those immense, rough-hewn, and spike-knotted logs, here and there tumbled all together, in long abandonment and decay, or left in solitary, perilous projection over the cataract's gloomy brink, impart to this rude wooden ruin not only much of the aspect of one of rough-quarried stone, but also a sort of feudal, Rhineland, and Thurmberg[7] look, derived from the pinnacled wildness of the neighboring scenery.

Not far from the bottom of the Dungeon stands a large whitewashed building, relieved, like some great whited sepulchre,[8] against the sullen background of mountain-side firs, and other hardy evergreens, inaccessibly rising in grim terraces for some two thousand feet.

The building is a paper-mill.

Having embarked on a large scale in the seedsman's business (so extensively and broadcast, indeed, that at length my seeds were distributed through all the Eastern and Northern States, and even fell into the far soil of Missouri and the Carolinas), the demand for paper at my place became so great, that the expenditure soon amounted to a most important item in the general account.[9] It need hardly be hinted how paper comes into use with seedsmen, as envelopes. These are mostly made of yellowish paper, folded square; and when filled, are all but flat, and being stamped, and superscribed with the nature of the seeds contained, assume not a little the appearance of business-letters ready for the mail. Of these small envelopes I used an incredible quantity—several hundreds of thousands in a year. For a time I had purchased my paper from

---

4. Here the grim scatological wordplay prepares for the subsequent sexual allegory.

5. Such as the entrance to hell the Italian poet Dante (1265–1321) describes in the *Inferno*; over it is written: "Abandon hope, all ye who enter here." The contrast is with the beautiful Wren gateway, Temple Bar.

6. Ruled by the god of the Underworld. "Hopper-shaped": funnel-shaped.

7. Melville had gone down the Rhine from Cologne to Koblenz in 1849.

8. A recollection of Jesus' description of the Scribes

and Pharisees as "whited sepulchres, which indeed appear beautiful outward, but are within full of dead men's bones, and of all uncleanness" (Matthew 23.27).

9. Without imposing a rigidity of allegory on the passage one can suggest that in a chapter of *The Confidence-Man*, "The Story of China Aster," there is a comparable allegory of writer as seedsman, involved in a losing "spermaceti venture." In *Moby-Dick* Ishmael says in "The Whiteness of the Whale" that "subtlety appeals to subtlety."

the wholesale dealers in a neighboring town. For economy's sake, and partly for the adventure of the trip, I now resolved to cross the mountains, some sixty miles, and order my future paper at the Devil's Dungeon paper-mill.

The sleighing being uncommonly fine toward the end of January, and promising to hold so for no small period, in spite of the bitter cold I started one gray Friday noon in my pung, well fitted with buffalo and wolf robes;[1] and, spending one night on the road, next noon came in sight of Woedolor Mountain.

The far summit fairly smoked with frost; white vapors curled up from its white-wooded top, as from a chimney. The intense congelation made the whole country look like one petrifaction. The steel shoes of my pung craunched and gritted over the vitreous, chippy snow, as if it had been broken glass. The forests here and there skirting the route, feeling the same all-stiffening influence, their inmost fibres penetrated with the cold, strangely groaned—not in the swaying branches merely, but likewise in the vertical trunk—as the fitful gusts remorselessly swept through them. Brittle with excessive frost, many colossal tough-grained maples, snapped in twain like pipe-stems, cumbered the unfeeling earth.

Flaked all over with frozen sweat, white as a milky ram, his nostrils at each breath sending forth two horn-shaped shoots of heated respiration, Black, my good horse, but six years old, started at a sudden turn, where, right across the track—not ten minutes fallen—an old distorted hemlock lay, darkly undulatory as an anaconda.

Gaining the Bellows'-pipe, the violent blast, dead from behind, all but shoved my high-backed pung up-hill. The gust shrieked through the shivered pass, as if laden with lost spirits bound to the unhappy world. Ere gaining the summit, Black, my horse, as if exasperated by the cutting wind, slung out with his strong hind legs, tore the light pung straight up-hill, and sweeping grazingly through the narrow notch, sped downward madly past the ruined saw-mill. Into the Devil's Dungeon horse and cataract rushed together.

With might and main, quitting my seat and robes, and standing backward, with one foot braced against the dash-board, I rasped and churned the bit, and stopped him just in time to avoid collision, at a turn, with the bleak nozzle of a rock, couchant like a lion in the way—a road-side rock.

At first I could not discover the paper-mill.

The whole hollow gleamed with the white, except, here and there, where a pinnacle of granite showed one wind-swept angle bare. The mountains stood pinned in shrouds—a pass of Alpine corpses. Where stands the mill? Suddenly a whirling, humming sound broke upon my ear. I looked, and there, like an arrested avalanche, lay the large whitewashed factory. It was subordinately surrounded by a cluster of other and smaller buildings, some of which, from their cheap, blank air, great length, gregarious windows, and comfortless expression, no doubt were boarding-houses of the operatives.[2] A snow-white hamlet amidst the snows. Various rude, irregular squares and courts resulted from the somewhat picturesque clusterings of these buildings, owing to the broken, rocky nature of the ground, which forbade all method in their relative

---

1. Wolves were already becoming rare in New England, but the mass slaughter of the buffalo was a decade and more away; the residual wildness in the robes appealed to Melville's imagination, as he shows in "The Whiteness of the Whale." "Pung": boxlike one-horse sleigh.

2. Factory workers.

arrangement. Several narrow lanes and alleys, too, partly blocked with snow fallen from the roof, cut up the hamlet in all directions.

When, turning from the traveled highway, jingling with bells of numerous farmers—who, availing themselves of the fine sleighing, were dragging their wood to market—and frequently diversified with swift cutters dashing from inn to inn of the scattered villages—when, I say, turning from that bustling main-road, I by degrees wound into the Mad Maid's Bellows'-pipe, and saw the grim Black Notch beyond, then something latent, as well as something obvious in the time and scene, strangely brought back to my mind my first sight of dark and grimy Temple-Bar. And when Black, my horse, went darting through the Notch, perilously grazing its rocky wall, I remembered being in a runaway London omnibus, which in much the same sort of style, though by no means at an equal rate, dashed through the ancient arch of Wren.[3] Though the two objects did by no means completely correspond, yet this partial inadequacy but served to tinge the similitude not less with the vividness than the disorder of a dream. So that, when upon reining up at the protruding rock I at last caught sight of the quaint groupings of the factory-buildings, and with the traveled highway and the Notch behind, found myself all alone, silently and privily stealing through deep-cloven passages into this sequestered spot, and saw the long, high-gabled main factory edifice, with a rude tower—for hoisting[4] heavy boxes—at one end, standing among its crowded outbuildings and boarding-houses, as the Temple Church amidst the surrounding offices and dormitories, and when the marvelous retirement of this mysterious mountain nook fastened its whole spell upon me, then, what memory lacked, all tributary imagination furnished, and I said to myself, "This is the very counterpart of the Paradise of Bachelors, but snowed upon, and frost-painted to a sepulchre."

Dismounting, and warily picking my way down the dangerous declivity—horse and man both sliding now and then upon the icy ledges—at length I drove, or the blast drove me, into the largest square, before one side of the main edifice. Piercingly and shrilly the shotted blast blew by the corner; and redly and demoniacally boiled Blood River at one side. A long woodpile, of many scores of cords, all glittering in mail of crusted ice, stood crosswise in the square. A row of horse-posts, their north sides plastered with adhesive snow, flanked the factory wall. The bleak frost packed and paved the square as with some ringing metal.

The inverted similitude recurred—"The sweet, tranquil Temple-garden, with the Thames bordering its green beds," strangely meditated I.

But where are the gay bachelors?

Then, as I and my horse stood shivering in the wind-spray, a girl ran from a neighboring dormitory door, and throwing her thin apron over her bare head, made for the opposite building.

"One moment, my girl; is there no shed hereabouts which I may drive into?"

Pausing, she turned upon me a face pale with work, and blue with cold; an eye supernatural with unrelated misery.

"Nay," faltered I, "I mistook you. Go on; I want nothing."

Leading my horse close to the door from which she had come, I knocked.

---

3. Temple Bar.
4. I.e., with a pulley fastening to the outhanging structure.

Another pale, blue girl appeared, shivering in the doorway as, to prevent the blast, she jealously held the door ajar.

"Nay, I mistake again. In God's name shut the door. But hold, is there no man about?"

That moment a dark-complexioned well-wrapped personage passed, making for the factory door, and spying him coming, the girl rapidly closed the other one.

"Is there no horse-shed here, Sir?"

"Yonder, to the wood-shed," he replied, and disappeared inside the factory.

With much ado I managed to wedge in horse and pung between the scattered piles of wood all sawn and split. Then, blanketing my horse, and piling my buffalo on the blanket's top, tucking in its edges well around the breast-hand and breeching, so that the wind might not strip him bare, I tied him fast, and ran lamely for the factory door, stiff with frost, and cumbered with my driver's dreadnaught. [5]

Immediately I found myself standing in a spacious place, intolerably lighted by long rows of windows, focusing inward the snowy scene without.

At rows of blank-looking counters sat rows of blank-looking girls, with blank, white folders in the blank hands, all blankly folding blank paper.

In one corner stood some huge frame of ponderous iron, with a vertical thing like a piston periodically rising and falling upon a heavy wooden block. Before it—its tame minister—stood a tall girl, feeding the iron animal with half-quires of rose-hued note paper, which, at every downward dab of the piston-like machine, received in the corner the impress of a wreath of roses. I looked from the rosy paper to the pallid cheek, but said nothing.

Seated before a long apparatus, strung with long, slender strings like any harp, another girl was feeding it with foolscap sheets, which, so soon as they curiously traveled from her on the cords, were withdrawn at the opposite end of the machine by a second girl. They came to the first girl blank; they went to the second girl ruled.

I looked upon the first girl's brow, and saw it was young and fair; I looked upon the second girl's brow, and saw it was ruled and wrinkled. Then, as I still looked, the two—for some small variety to the monotony—changed places; and where had stood the young, fair brow, now stood the ruled and wrinkled one.

Perched high upon a narrow platform, and still higher upon a high stool crowning it, sat another figure serving some other iron animal; while below the platform sat her mate in some sort of reciprocal attendance.

Not a syllable was breathed. Nothing was heard but the low, steady, overruling hum of the iron animals. The human voice was banished from the spot. Machinery—that vaunted slave of humanity—here stood menially served by human beings, who served mutely and cringingly as the slave serves the Sultan. The girls did not so much seem accessory wheels to the general machinery as mere cogs to the wheels.

All this scene around me was instantaneously taken in at one sweeping glance—even before I had proceeded to unwind the heavy fur tippet[6] from around my neck. But as soon as this fell from me the dark-complexioned man, standing close by, raised a sudden cry, and seizing my arm, dragged me out

---

5. Thick woolen coat. 6. Muffler.

into the open air, and without pausing for a word instantly caught up some congealed snow and began rubbing both my cheeks.

"Two white spots like the whites of your eyes," he said; "man, your cheeks are frozen."

"That may well be," muttered I, " 'tis some wonder the frost of the Devil's Dungeon strikes in no deeper. Rub away."

Soon a horrible, tearing pain caught at my reviving cheeks. Two gaunt blood-hounds, one on each side, seemed mumbling them. I seemed Actæon.[7]

Presently, when all was over, I re-entered the factory, made known my business, concluded it satisfactorily, and then begged to be conducted throughout the place to view it.

"Cupid is the boy for that," said the dark-complexioned man. "Cupid!" and by this odd fancy-name calling a dimpled, red-cheeked, spirited-looking, forward little fellow, who was rather impudently, I thought, gliding about among the passive-looking girls—like a gold fish through hueless waves—yet doing nothing in particular that I could see, the man bade him lead the stranger through the edifice.

"Come first and see the water-wheel," said this lively lad, with the air of boyishly-brisk importance.

Quitting the folding-room, we crossed some damp, cold boards, and stood beneath a great wet shed, incessantly showering with foam, like the green barnacled bow of some East India-man[8] in a gale. Round and round here went the enormous revolutions of the dark colossal water-wheel, grim with its one immutable purpose.

"This sets our whole machinery a-going, Sir; in every part of all these buildings; where the girls work and all."

I looked, and saw that the turbid waters of Blood River had not changed their hue by coming under the use of man.

"You make only blank paper; no printing of any sort, I suppose? All blank paper, don't you?"

"Certainly; what else should a paper-factory make?"

The lad here looked at me as if suspicious of my common-sense.

"Oh, to be sure!" said I, confused and stammering; "it only struck me as so strange that red waters should turn out pale chee—paper, I mean."

He took me up a wet and rickety stair to a great light room, furnished with no visible thing but rude, manger-like receptacles running all round its sides; and up to these mangers, like so many mares haltered to the rack, stood rows of girls. Before each was vertically thrust up a long, glittering scythe, immovably fixed at bottom to the manger-edge. The curve of the scythe, and its having no snath[9] to it, made it look exactly like a sword. To and fro, across the sharp edge, the girls forever dragged long strips of rags, washed white, picked from baskets at one side; thus ripping asunder every seam, and converting the tatters almost into lint. The air swam with the fine, poisonous particles, which from all sides darted, subtilely, as motes in sunbeams, into the lungs.

"This is the rag-room," coughed the boy.

"You find it rather stifling here," coughed I, in answer; "but the girls don't cough."

7. In Greek mythology, the hunter who watched Diana (Artemis) bathing and was punished by being turned into a stag that was then torn apart by his own dogs.

8. Enormous, many-sailed ship in the East India Company's fleet.

9. Curved handle.

"Oh, they are used to it."

"Where do you get such hosts of rags?" picking up a handful from a basket.

"Some from the country round about; some from far over sea—Leghorn[1] and London."

" 'Tis not unlikely, then," murmured I, "that among these heaps of rags there may be some old shirts, gathered from the dormitories of the Paradise of Bachelors. But the buttons are all dropped off. Pray, my lad, do you ever find any bachelor's buttons hereabouts?"

"None grow in this part of the country. The Devil's Dungeon is no place for flowers."

"Oh! you mean the *flowers* so called—the Bachelor's Buttons?"

"And was not that what you asked about? Or did you mean the gold bosom-buttons of our boss, Old Bach,[2] as our whispering girls all call him?"

"The man, then, I saw below is a bachelor, is he?"

"Oh, yes, he's a Bach."

"The edges of those swords, they are turned outward from the girls, if I see right; but their rags and fingers fly so, I can not distinctly see."

"Turned outward."

Yes, murmured I to myself; I see it now; turned outward; and each erected sword is so borne, edge-outward, before each girl. If my reading fails me not, just so, of old, condemned state-prisoners went from the hall of judgment to their doom: an officer before, bearing a sword, its edge turned outward, in significance of their fatal sentence. So, through consumptive pallors[3] of this blank, raggy life, go these white girls to death.

"Those scythes look very sharp," again turning toward the boy.

"Yes; they have to keep them so. Look!"

That moment two of the girls, dropping their rags, plied each a whet-stone up and down the sword-blade. My unaccustomed blood curdled at the sharp shriek of the tormented steel.

Their own executioners; themselves whetting the very swords that slay them; meditated I.

"What makes those girls so sheet-white, my lad?"

"Why"—with a roguish twinkle, pure ignorant drollery, not knowing heart-lessness—"I suppose the handling of such white bits of sheets all the time makes them so sheety."

"Let us leave the rag-room now, my lad."

More tragical and more inscrutably mysterious than any mystic sight, human or machine, throughout the factory, was the strange innocence of cruel-heartedness in this usage-hardened boy.

"And now," said he, cheerily, "I suppose you want to see our great machine, which cost us twelve thousand dollars only last autumn. That's the machine that makes the paper, too. This way, Sir."

Following him, I crossed a large, bespattered place, with two great round vats in it, full of a white, wet, woolly-looking stuff, not unlike the albuminous part of an egg, soft-boiled.

"There," said Cupid, tapping the vats carelessly, "these are the first beginnings of the paper; this white pulp you see. Look how it swims bubbling round and round, moved by the paddle here. From hence it pours from both vats

---

1. Port on the northern Mediterranean side of Italy.   3. I.e., the paleness of the victim of tuberculosis.
2. Pronounced *batch*.

into that one common channel yonder; and so goes, mixed up and leisurely, to the great machine. And now for that."

He led me into a room, stifling with a strange, blood-like, abdominal heat, as if here, true enough, were being finally developed the germinous particles lately seen.

Before me, rolled out like some long Eastern manuscript, lay stretched one continuous length of iron frame-work—multitudinous and mystical, with all sorts of rollers, wheels, and cylinders, in slowly-measured and unceasing motion.

"Here first comes the pulp now," said Cupid, pointing to the nighest end of the machine. "See; first it pours out and spreads itself upon this wide, sloping board; and then—look—slides, thin and quivering, beneath the first roller there. Follow on now, and see it as it slides from under that to the next cylinder. There; see how it has become just a very little less pulpy now. One step more, and it grows still more to some slight consistence. Sill another cylinder, and it is so knitted—though as yet mere dragon-fly wing—that it forms an air-bridge here, like a suspended cobweb, between two more separated rollers; and flowing over the last one, and under again, and doubling about there out of sight for a minute among all those mixed cylinders you indistinctly see, it reappears here, looking now at last a little less like pulp and more like paper, but still quite delicate and defective yet awhile. But—a little further onward, Sir, if you please—here now, at this further point, it puts on something of a real look, as if it might turn out to be something you might possibly handle in the end. But it's not yet done, Sir. Good way to travel yet, and plenty more of cylinders must roll it."

"Bless my soul!" said I, amazed at the elongation, interminable convolutions, and deliberate slowness of the machine; "it must take a long time for the pulp to pass from end to end, and come out paper."

"Oh! not so long," smiled the precocious lad, with a superior and patronizing air; "only nine minutes. But look; you may try it for yourself. Have you a bit of paper? Ah! here's a bit on the floor. Now mark that with any word you please, and let me dab it on here, and we'll see how long before it comes out at the other end."

"Well, let me see," said I, taking out my pencil; "come, I'll mark it with your name."

Bidding me take out my watch, Cupid adroitly dropped the inscribed slip on an exposed part of the incipient mass.

Instantly my eye marked the second-hand on my dial-plate.

Slowly I followed the slip, inch by inch; sometimes pausing for full half a minute as it disappeared beneath inscrutable groups of the lower cylinders, but only gradually to emerge again; and so, on, and on, and on—inch by inch; now in open sight, sliding along like a freckle on the quivering sheet; and then again wholly vanished; and so, on, and on, and on—inch by inch; all the time the main sheet growing more and more to final firmness—when, suddenly, I saw a sort of paper-fall, not wholly unlike a water-fall; a scissory sound smote my ear, as of some cord being snapped; and down dropped an unfolded sheet of perfect foolscap,[4] with my "Cupid" half faded out of it, and still moist and warm.

4. Cheap writing paper, usually about thirteen by seventeen inches.

My travels were at an end, for here was the end of the machine.

"Well, how long was it?" said Cupid.

"Nine minutes to a second," replied I, watch in hand.

"I told you so."

For a moment a curious emotion filled me, not wholly unlike that which one might experience at the fulfillment of some mysterious prophecy. But how absurd, thought I again; the thing is a mere machine, the essence of which is unvarying punctuality and precision.

Previously absorbed by the wheels and cylinders, my attention was now directed to a sad-looking woman standing by.

"That is rather an elderly person so silently tending the machine-end here. She would not seem wholly used to it either."

"Oh," knowingly whispered Cupid, through the din, "she only came last week. She was a nurse formerly. But the business is poor in these parts, and she's left it. But look at the paper she is piling there."

"Ay, foolscap," handling the piles of moist, warm sheets, which continually were being delivered into the woman's waiting hands. "Don't you turn out any thing but foolscap at this machine?"

"Oh, sometimes, but not often, we turn out finer work—creamlaid and royal sheets, we call them. But foolscap being in chief demand, we turn out foolscap most."

It was very curious. Looking at that blank paper continually dropping, dropping, dropping, my mind ran on in wonderings of those strange uses to which those thousand sheets eventually would be put. All sorts of writings would be writ on those now vacant things—sermons, lawyers' briefs, physicians' prescriptions, love-letters, marriage certificates, bills of divorce, registers of births, death-warrants, and so on, without end. Then, recurring back to them as they here lay all blank, I could not but bethink me of that celebrated comparison of John Locke, who, in demonstration of his theory that man had no innate ideas, compared the human mind at birth to a sheet of blank paper;[5] something destined to be scribbled on, but what sort of characters no soul might tell.

Pacing slowly to and fro along the involved machine, still humming with its play, I was struck as well by the inevitability as the evolvement-power in all its motions.

"Does that thin cobweb there," said I, pointing to the sheet in its more imperfect stage, "does that never tear or break? It is marvelous fragile, and yet this machine it passes through is so mighty."

"It never is known to tear a hair's point."

"Does it never stop—get clogged?"

"No. It *must* go. The machinery makes it go just *so*; just that very way, and at that very pace you there plainly *see* it go. The pulp can't help going."

Something of awe now stole over me, as I gazed upon this inflexible iron animal. Always, more or less, machinery of this ponderous, elaborate sort strikes, in some moods, strange dread into the human heart, as some living, panting Behemoth might. But what made the thing I saw so specially terrible to me was the metallic necessity, the unbudging fatality which governed it. Though, here and there, I could not follow the thin, gauzy vail of pulp in the

---

5. Locke (English philosopher, 1632–1704) compared the mind of a newborn to a blank page, a tabula rasa, in *Essay Concerning Human Understanding* (1690).

course of its more mysterious or entirely invisible advance, yet it was indubitable that, at those points where it eluded me, it still marched on in unvarying docility to the autocratic cunning of the machine. A fascination fastened on me. I stood spellbound and wandering in my soul. Before my eyes—there, passing in slow procession along the wheeling cylinders, I seemed to see, glued to the pallid incipience of the pulp, the yet more pallid faces of all the pallid girls, I had eyed that heavy day. Slowly, mournfully, beseechingly, yet unresistingly, they gleamed along, their agony dimly outlined on the imperfect paper, like the print of the tormented face on the handkerchief of Saint Veronica.[6]

"Halloa! the heat of the room is too much for you," cried Cupid, staring at me.

"No—I am rather chill, if any thing."

"Come out, Sir—out—out," and, with the protecting air of a careful father, the precocious lad hurried me outside.

In a few moments, feeling revived a little, I went into the folding-room—the first room I had entered, and where the desk for transacting business stood, surrounded by the blank counters and blank girls engaged at them.

"Cupid here has led me a strange tour," said I to the dark-complexioned man before mentioned, whom I had ere this discovered not only to be an old bachelor, but also the principal proprietor. "Yours is a most wonderful factory. Your great machine is a miracle of inscrutable intricacy."

"Yes, all our visitors think it so. But we don't have many. We are in a very out-of-the-way corner here. Few inhabitants, too. Most of our girls come from far-off villages."

"The girls," echoed I, glancing round at their silent forms. "Why is it, Sir, that in most factories, female operatives, of whatever age, are indiscriminately called girls, never women?"

"Oh! as to that—why, I suppose, the fact of their being generally unmarried—that's the reason, I should think. But it never struck me before. For our factory here, we will not have married women; they are apt to be off-and-on too much. We want none but steady workers: twelve hours to the day, day after day, through the three hundred and sixty-five days, excepting Sundays, Thanksgiving, and Fastdays. That's our rule. And so, having no married women, what females we have are rightly enough called girls."

"Then these are all maids," said I, while some pained homage to their pale virginity made me involuntarily bow.

"All maids."

Again the strange emotion filled me.

"Your cheeks look whitish yet, Sir," said the man, gazing at me narrowly. "You must be careful going home. Do they pain you at all now? It's a bad sign, if they do."

"No doubt, Sir," answered I, "when once I have got out of the Devil's Dungeon, I shall feel them mending."

"Ah, yes; the winter air in valleys, or gorges, or any sunken place, is far colder and more bitter than elsewhere. You would hardly believe it now, but it is colder here than at the top of Woedolor Mountain."

"I dare say it is, Sir. But time presses me; I must depart."

---

6. Legendary woman who wiped the bleeding face of Jesus as he carried the cross to Calvary and then found that the handkerchief was imprinted with his face.

With that, remuffling myself in dread-naught and tippet, thrusting my hands into my huge seal-skin mittens, I sallied out into the nipping air, and found poor Black, my horse, all cringing and doubled up with the cold.

Soon, wrapped in furs and meditations, I ascended from the Devil's Dungeon.

At the Black Notch I paused, and once more bethought me of Temple-Bar. Then, shooting through the pass, all alone with inscrutable nature, I exclaimed—Oh! Paradise of Bachelors! and oh! Tartarus of Maids!

1855

Benito Cereno[1]

In the year 1799, Captain Amasa Delano, of Duxbury, in Massachusetts, commanding a large sealer and general trader, lay at anchor, with a valuable cargo, in the harbor of St. Maria—a small, desert, uninhabited island toward the southern extremity of the long coast of Chili. There he had touched for water.

On the second day, not long after dawn, while lying in his berth, his mate came below, informing him that a strange sail was coming into the bay. Ships were then not so plenty in those waters as now. He rose, dressed, and went on deck.

The morning was one peculiar to that coast. Everything was mute and calm; everything gray. The sea, though undulated into long roods of swells, seemed fixed, and was sleeked at the surface like waved lead that has cooled and set in the smelter's mold. The sky seemed a gray surtout.[2] Flights of troubled gray fowl, kith and kin with flights of troubled gray vapors among which they were mixed, skimmed low and fitfully over the waters, as swallows over meadows before storms. Shadows present, foreshadowing deeper shadows to come.

To Captain Delano's surprise, the stranger, viewed through the glass, showed no colors; though to do so upon entering a haven, however uninhabited in its shores, where but a single other ship might be lying, was the custom among peaceful seamen of all nations. Considering the lawlessness and loneliness of the spot, and the sort of stories, at that day, associated with those seas, Captain Delano's surprise might have deepened into some uneasiness had he not been a person of a singularly undistrustful good nature, not liable, except on extraordinary and repeated incentives, and hardly then, to indulge in personal alarms, any way involving the imputation of malign evil in man. Whether, in view of what humanity is capable, such a trait implies, along with a benevolent heart, more than ordinary quickness and accuracy of intellectual perception, may be left to the wise to determine.

But whatever misgivings might have obtruded on first seeing the stranger, would almost, in any seaman's mind, have been dissipated by observing that, the ship, in navigating into the harbor, was drawing too near the land; a

1. This text is based on the first printing, in *Putnam's Monthly* for October, November, and December 1855, but it also incorporates the many small revisions Melville made for its 1856 republication in *The Piazza Tales*. Melville based his plot very closely upon a few narrative pages in chap. 18 of Captain Amasa Delano's *Narrative of Voyages and Travels in the Northern and Southern Hemispheres* (1817). Melville's "deposition" is roughly half from Delano's much longer section of documents, half his own writing. (A later relative of the real Delano was Franklin Delano Roosevelt.)

2. Long overcoat.

sunken reef making out off her bow. This seemed to prove her a stranger, indeed, not only to the sealer, but the island; consequently, she could be no wonted freebooter on that ocean. With no small interest, Captain Delano continued to watch her—a proceeding not much facilitated by the vapors partly mantling the hull, through which the far matin[3] light from her cabin streamed equivocally enough; much like the sun—by this time hemisphered on the rim of the horizon, and apparently, in company with the strange ship, entering the harbor—which, wimpled by the same low, creeping clouds, showed not unlike a Lima intriguante's one sinister eye peering across the Plaza from the Indian loop-hole of her dusk *saya-y-manta*.[4]

It might have been but a deception of the vapors, but, the longer the stranger was watched, the more singular appeared her maneuvers. Ere long it seemed hard to decide whether she meant to come in or no—what she wanted, or what she was about. The wind, which had breezed up a little during the night, was now extremely light and baffling, which the more increased the apparent uncertainty of her movements.

Surmising, at last, that it might be a ship in distress, Captain Delano ordered his whale-boat to be dropped, and, much to the wary opposition of his mate, prepared to board her, and, at the least, pilot her in. On the night previous, a fishing-party of the seamen had gone a long distance to some detached rocks out of sight from the sealer, and, an hour or two before day-break, had returned, having met with no small success. Presuming that the stranger might have been long off soundings, the good captain put several baskets of the fish, for presents, into his boat, and so pulled away. From her continuing too near the sunken reef, deeming her in danger, calling to his men, he made all haste to apprise those on board of their situation. But, some time ere the boat came up, the wind, light though it was, having shifted, had headed the vessel off, as well as partly broken the vapors from about her.

Upon gaining a less remote view, the ship, when made signally visible on the verge of the leaden-hued swells, with the shreds of fog here and there raggedly furring her, appeared like a white-washed monastery after a thunderstorm, seen perched upon some dun cliff among the Pyrenees. But it was no purely fanciful resemblance which now, for a moment, almost led Captain Delano to think that nothing less than a ship-load of monks was before him. Peering over the bulwarks were what really seemed, in the hazy distance, throngs of dark cowls; while, fitfully revealed through the open port-holes, other dark moving figures were dimly descried, as of Black Friars[5] pacing the cloisters.

Upon a still nigher approach, this appearance was modified, and the true character of the vessel was plain—a Spanish merchantman of the first class; carrying negro slaves, amongst other valuable freight, from one colonial port to another. A very large, and, in its time, a very fine vessel, such as in those days were at intervals encountered along that main; sometimes superseded Acapulco treasure-ships, or retired frigates of the Spanish king's navy, which, like superannuated Italian palaces, still, under a decline of masters, preserved signs of former state.

As the whale-boat drew more and more nigh, the cause of the peculiar pipe-

---

3. Early morning.
4. Skirt-and-mantle combination, the shawl part of which could be drawn about the face so little more

than an eye would show; apt garb for assignations.
5. Dominicans, an order of mendicant preaching friars.

clayed[6] aspect of the stranger was seen in the slovenly neglect pervading her. The spars, ropes, and great part of the bulwarks, looked woolly, from long unacquaintance with the scraper, tar, and the brush. Her keel seemed laid, her ribs put together, and she launched, from Ezekiel's Valley of Dry Bones.[7]

In the present business in which she was engaged, the ship's general model and rig appeared to have undergone no material change from their original war-like and Froissart pattern.[8] However, no guns were seen.

The tops were large, and were railed about with what had once been octagonal net-work, all now in sad disrepair. These tops hung overhead like three ruinous aviaries, in one of which was seen perched, on a ratlin, a white noddy,[9] strange fowl, so called from its lethargic, somnambulistic character, being frequently caught by hand at sea. Battered and mouldy, the castellated forecastle seemed some ancient turret, long ago taken by assault, and then left to decay. Toward the stern, two high-raised quarter galleries—the balustrades here and there covered with dry, tindery sea-moss—opening out from the unoccupied state-cabin, whose dead lights, for all the mild weather, were hermetically closed and calked—these tenantless balconies hung over the sea as if it were the grand Venetian canal. But the principal relic of faded grandeur was the ample oval of the shield-like stern-piece, intricately carved with the arms of Castile and Leon,[1] medallioned about by groups of mythological or symbolical devices; uppermost and central of which was a dark satyr in a mask, holding his foot on the prostrate neck of a writhing figure, likewise masked.

Whether the ship had a figure-head, or only a plain beak, was not quite certain, owing to canvas wrapped about that part, either to protect it while undergoing a re-furbishing, or else decently to hide its decay. Rudely painted or chalked, as in a sailor freak, along the forward side of a sort of pedestal below the canvas, was the sentence, *"Seguid vuestro jefe,"* (follow your leader); while upon the tarnished head-boards, near by, appeared, in stately capitals, once gilt, the ship's name, "SAN DOMINICK," each letter streakingly corroded with tricklings of copper-spike rust; while, like mourning weeds, dark festoons of sea-grass slimily swept to and fro over the name, with every hearse-like roll of the hull.

As at last the boat was hooked from the bow along toward the gangway amidship, its keel, while yet some inches separated from the hull, harshly grated as on a sunken coral reef. It proved a huge bunch of conglobated barnacles adhering below the water to the side like a wen; a token of baffling airs and long calms passed somewhere in those seas.

Climbing the side, the visitor was at once surrounded by a clamorous throng of whites and blacks, but the latter outnumbering the former more than could have been expected, negro transportation-ship as the stranger in port was. But, in one language, and as with one voice, all poured out a common tale of suffering; in which the negresses, of whom there were not a few, exceeded the others in their dolorous vehemence. The scurvy, together with a fever, had swept off a great part of their number, more especially the Spaniards. Off Cape Horn, they had narrowly escaped shipwreck; then, for days together, they had

---

6. Whitened.
7. Ezekiel 37.1.
8. Medieval, from Jean Froissart (1337–1410), historian of wars of England and France.
9. A tame, stupid-seeming tern. "Ratlin": small trans-

verse rope attached to the shrouds and forming a step of a rope ladder.
1. Old kingdoms of Spain; the arms would include a castle for Castile and a lion for León.

lain tranced without wind; their provisions were low; their water next to none; their lips that moment were baked.

While Captain Delano was thus made the mark of all eager tongues, his one eager glance took in all the faces, with every other object about him.

Always upon first boarding a large and populous ship at sea, especially a foreign one, with a nondescript crew such as Lascars or Manilla men,[2] the impression varies in a peculiar way from that produced by first entering a strange house with strange inmates in a strange land. Both house and ship, the one by its walls and blinds, the other by its high bulwarks like ramparts, hoard from view their interiors till the last moment; but in the case of the ship there is this addition; that the living spectacle it contains, upon its sudden and complete disclosure, has, in contrast with the blank ocean which zones it, something of the effect of enchantment. The ship seems unreal; these strange costumes, gestures, and faces, but a shadowy tableau just emerged from the deep, which directly must receive back what it gave.

Perhaps it was some such influence as above is attempted to be described, which, in Captain Delano's mind, hightened whatever, upon a staid scrutiny, might have seemed unusual; especially the conspicuous figures of four elderly grizzled negroes, their heads like black, doddered willow tops, who, in venerable contrast to the tumult below them, were couched sphynx-like, one on the starboard cat-head,[3] another on the larboard, and the remaining pair face to face on the opposite bulwarks above the main-chains. They each had bits of unstranded old junk in their hands, and, with a sort of stoical self-content, were picking the junk into oakum,[4] a small heap of which lay by their sides. They accompanied the task with a continuous, low, monotonous chant; droning and druling[5] away like so many gray-headed bag-pipers playing a funeral march.

The quarter-deck rose into an ample elevated poop, upon the forward verge of which, lifted, like the oakum-pickers, some eight feet above the general throng, sat along in a row, separated by regular spaces, the cross-legged figures of six other blacks; each with a rusty hatchet in his hand, which, with a bit of brick and a rag, he was engaged like a scullion in scouring; while between each two was a small stack of hatchets, their rusted edges turned forward awaiting a like operation. Though occasionally the four oakum-pickers would briefly address some person or persons in the crowd below, yet the six hatchet-polishers neither spoke to others, nor breathed a whisper among themselves, but sat intent upon their task, except at intervals, when, with the peculiar love in negroes of uniting industry with pastime, two and two they sideways clashed their hatchets together, like cymbals, with a barbarous din. All six, unlike the generality, had the raw aspect of unsophisticated Africans.

But that first comprehensive glance which took in those ten figures, with scores less conspicuous, rested but an instant upon them, as, impatient of the hubbub of voices, the visitor turned in quest of whomsoever it might be that commanded the ship.

But as if not unwilling to let nature make known her own case among his suffering charge, or else in despair of restraining it for the time, the Spanish captain, a gentlemanly, reserved-looking, and rather young man to a stranger's

---

2. From East India or the Philippines, respectively.
3. Projecting piece of timber near the bow (to which the anchor is hoisted and secured).

4. Loose fiber from pieces of rope, used for caulking. "Old junk": worn-out rope.
5. Driveling.

eye, dressed with singular richness, but bearing plain traces of recent sleepless cares and disquietudes, stood passively by, leaning against the main-mast, at one moment casting a dreary, spiritless look upon his excited people, at the next an unhappy glance toward his visitor. By his side stood a black of small stature, in whose rude face, as occasionally, like a shepherd's dog, he mutely turned it up into the Spaniard's, sorrow and affection were equally blended.

Struggling through the throng, the American advanced to the Spaniard, assuring him of his sympathies, and offering to render whatever assistance might be in his power. To which the Spaniard returned, for the present, but grave and ceremonious acknowledgments, his national formality dusked by the saturnine mood of ill health.

But losing no time in mere compliments, Captain Delano returning to the gangway, had his baskets of fish brought up; and as the wind still continued light, so that some hours at least must elapse ere the ship could be brought to the anchorage, he bade his men return to the sealer, and fetch back as much water as the whale-boat could carry, with whatever soft bread the steward might have, all the remaining pumpkins on board, with a box of sugar, and a dozen of his private bottles of cider.

Not many minutes after the boat's pushing off, to the vexation of all, the wind entirely died away, and the tide turning, began drifting back the ship helplessly seaward. But trusting this would not long last, Captain Delano sought with good hopes to cheer up the strangers, feeling no small satisfaction that, with persons in their condition he could—thanks to his frequent voyages along the Spanish main[6]—converse with some freedom in their native tongue.

While left alone with them, he was not long in observing some things tending to heighten his first impressions; but surprise was lost in pity, both for the Spaniards and blacks, alike evidently reduced from scarcity of water and provisions; while long-continued suffering seemed to have brought out the less good-natured qualities of the negroes, besides, at the same time, impairing the Spaniard's authority over them. But, under the circumstances, precisely this condition of things was to have been anticipated. In armies, navies, cities, or families, in nature herself, nothing more relaxes good order than misery. Still, Captain Delano was not without the idea, that had Benito Cereno been a man of greater energy, misrule would hardly have come to the present pass. But the debility, constitutional or induced by the hardships, bodily and mental, of the Spanish captain, was too obvious to be overlooked. A prey to settled dejection, as if long mocked with hope he would not now indulge it, even when it had ceased to be a mock, the prospect of that day or evening at furthest, lying at anchor, with plenty of water for his people, and a brother captain to counsel and befriend, seemed in no perceptible degree to encourage him. His mind appeared unstrung, if not still more seriously affected. Shut up in these oaken walls, chained to one dull round of command, whose unconditionality cloyed him, like some hypochondriac abbot he moved slowly about, at times suddenly pausing, starting, or staring, biting his lip, biting his finger-nail, flushing, paling, twitching his beard, with other symptoms of an absent or moody mind. This distempered spirit was lodged, as before hinted, in as distempered a frame. He was rather tall, but seemed never to have been robust, and now with nervous suffering was almost worn to a skeleton. A tendency to some

6. Sometimes loosely used for the Caribbean Sea, but here the Atlantic and Pacific coasts of South America (mainland as opposed to islands).

pulmonary complaint appeared to have been lately confirmed. His voice was like that of one with lungs half gone, hoarsely suppressed, a husky whisper. No wonder that, as in this state he tottered about, his private servant apprehensively followed him. Sometimes the negro gave his master his arm, or took his handkerchief out of his pocket for him; performing these and similar offices with that affectionate zeal which transmutes into something filial or fraternal acts in themselves but menial; and which has gained for the negro the repute of making the most pleasing body servant in the world; one, too, whom a master need be on no stiffly superior terms with, but may treat with familiar trust; less a servant than a devoted companion.

Marking the noisy indocility of the blacks in general, as well as what seemed the sullen inefficiency of the whites, it was not without humane satisfaction that Captain Delano witnessed the steady good conduct of Babo.

But the good conduct of Babo, hardly more than the ill-behavior of others, seemed to withdraw the half-lunatic Don Benito from his cloudy langour. Not that such precisely was the impression made by the Spaniard on the mind of his visitor. The Spaniard's individual unrest was, for the present, but noted as a conspicuous feature in the ship's general affliction. Still, Captain Delano was not a little concerned at what he could not help taking for the time to be Don Benito's unfriendly indifference towards himself. The Spaniard's manner, too, conveyed a sort of sour and gloomy disdain, which he seemed at no pains to disguise. But this the American in charity ascribed to the harassing effects of sickness, since, in former instances, he had noted that there are peculiar natures on whom prolonged physical suffering seems to cancel every social instinct of kindness; as if forced to black bread themselves, they deemed it but equity that each person coming nigh them should, indirectly, by some slight or affront, be made to partake of their fare.

But ere long Captain Delano bethought him that, indulgent as he was at the first, in judging the Spaniard, he might not, after all, have exercised charity enough. At bottom it was Don Benito's reserve which displeased him; but the same reserve was shown towards all but his faithful personal attendant. Even the formal reports which, according to sea-usage, were, at stated times, made to him by some petty underling, either a white, mulatto or black, he hardly had patience enough to listen to, without betraying contemptuous aversion. His manner upon such occasions was, in its degree, not unlike that which might be supposed to have been his imperial countryman's, Charles V.,[7] just previous to the anchoritish retirement of that monarch from the throne.

This splenetic disrelish of his place was evinced in almost every function pertaining to it. Proud as he was moody, he condescended to no personal mandate. Whatever special orders were necessary, their delivery was delegated to his body-servant, who in turn transferred them to their ultimate destination, through runners, alert Spanish boys or slave boys, like pages or pilot-fish[8] within easy call continually hovering round Don Benito. So that to have beheld this undemonstrative invalid gliding about, apathetic and mute, no landsman could have dreamed that in him was lodged a dictatorship beyond which, while at sea, there was no earthly appeal.

7. King of Spain and Holy Roman emperor (1500–1558) who spent his last years in a monastery (without, however, relinquishing all political power and material possessions).

8. Fish often swimming in the company of a shark, therefore fancied to pilot it.

Thus, the Spaniard, regarded in his reserve, seemed as the involuntary victim of mental disorder. But, in fact, his reserve might, in some degree, have proceeded from design. If so, then here was evinced the unhealthy climax of that icy though conscientious policy, more or less adopted by all commanders of large ships, which, except in signal emergencies, obliterates alike the manifestation of sway with every trace of sociality; transforming the man into a block, or rather into a loaded cannon, which, until there is call for thunder, has nothing to say.

Viewing him in this light, it seemed but a natural token of the perverse habit induced by a long course of such hard self-restraint, that, notwithstanding the present condition of his ship, the Spaniard should still persist in a demeanor, which, however harmless, or, it may be, appropriate, in a well appointed vessel, such as the San Dominick might have been at the outset of the voyage, was anything but judicious now. But the Spaniard perhaps thought that it was with captains as with gods: reserve, under all events, must still be their cue. But more probably this appearance of slumbering dominion might have been but an attempted disguise to conscious imbecility—not deep policy, but shallow device. But be all this as it might, whether Don Benito's manner was designed or not, the more Captain Delano noted its pervading reserve, the less he felt uneasiness at any particular manifestation of that reserve towards himself.

Neither were his thoughts taken up by the captain alone. Wonted to the quiet orderliness of the sealer's comfortable family of a crew, the noisy confusion of the San Dominick's suffering host repeatedly challenged his eye. Some prominent breaches not only of discipline but of decency were observed. These Captain Delano could not but ascribe, in the main, to the absence of those subordinate deck-officers to whom, along with higher duties, is entrusted what may be styled the police department of a populous ship. True, the old oakumpickers appeared at times to act the part of monitorial constables to their countrymen, the blacks; but though occasionally succeeding in allaying trifling outbreaks now and then between man and man, they could do little or nothing toward establishing general quiet. The San Dominick was in the condition of a transatlantic emigrant ship, among whose multitude of living freight are some individuals, doubtless, as little troublesome as crates and bales; but the friendly remonstrances of such with their ruder companions are of not so much avail as the unfriendly arm of the mate. What the San Dominick wanted was, what the emigrant ship has, stern superior officers. But on these decks not so much as a fourth mate was to be seen.

The visitor's curiosity was roused to learn the particulars of those mishaps which had brought about such absenteeism, with its consequences; because, though deriving some inkling of the voyage from the wails which at the first moment had greeted him, yet of the details no clear understanding had been had. The best account would, doubtless, be given by the captain. Yet at first the visitor was loth to ask it, unwilling to provoke some distant rebuff. But plucking up courage, he at last accosted Don Benito, renewing the expression of his benevolent interest, adding, that did he (Captain Delano) but know the particulars of the ship's misfortunes, he would, perhaps, be better able in the end to relieve them. Would Don Benito favor him with the whole story?

Don Benito faltered; then, like some somnambulist suddenly interfered with, vacantly stared at his visitor, and ended by looking down on the deck.

He maintained this posture so long, that Captain Delano, almost equally disconcerted, and involuntarily almost as rude, turned suddenly from him, walking forward to accost one of the Spanish seamen for the desired information. But he had hardly gone five paces, when with a sort of eagerness Don Benito invited him back, regretting his momentary absence of mind, and professing readiness to gratify him.

While most part of the story was being given, the two captains stood on the after part of the main-deck, a privileged spot, no one being near but the servant.

"It is now a hundred and ninety days," began the Spaniard, in his husky whisper, "that this ship, well officered and well manned, with several cabin passengers—some fifty Spaniards in all—sailed from Buenos Ayres bound to Lima, with a general cargo, hardware, Paraguay tea and the like—and," pointing forward, "that parcel of negroes, now not more than a hundred and fifty, as you see, but then numbering over three hundred souls. Off Cape Horn we had heavy gales. In one moment, by night, three of my best officers, with fifteen sailors, were lost, with the main-yard; the spar snapping under them in the slings, as they sought, with heavers, to beat down the icy sail. To lighten the hull, the heavier sacks of mata were thrown into the sea, with most of the water-pipes[9] lashed on deck at the time. And this last necessity it was, combined with the prolonged detentions afterwards experienced, which eventually brought about our chief causes of suffering. When——"

Here there was a sudden fainting attack of his cough, brought on, no doubt, by his mental distress. His servant sustained him, and drawing a cordial from his pocket placed it to his lips. He a little revived. But unwilling to leave him unsupported while yet imperfectly restored, the black with one arm still encircled his master, at the same time keeping his eye fixed on his face, as if to watch for the first sign of complete restoration, or relapse, as the event might prove.

The Spaniard proceeded, but brokenly and obscurely, as one in a dream.

—"Oh, my God! rather than pass through what I have, with joy I would have hailed the most terrible gales; but——"

His cough returned and with increased violence; this subsiding, with reddened lips and closed eyes he fell heavily against his supporter.

"His mind wanders. He was thinking of the plague that followed the gales," plaintively sighed the servant; "my poor, poor master!" wringing one hand, and with the other wiping the mouth. "But be patient, Señor," again turning to Captain Delano, "these fits do not last long; master will soon be himself."

Don Benito reviving, went on; but as this portion of the story was very brokenly delivered, the substance only will here be set down.

It appeared that after the ship had been many days tossed in storms off the Cape, the scurvy broke out, carrying off numbers of the whites and blacks. When at last they had worked round into the Pacific, their spars and sails were so damaged, and so inadequately handled by the surviving mariners, most of whom were become invalids, that, unable to lay her northerly course by the wind, which was powerful, the unmanageable ship for successive days and nights was blown northwestward, where the breeze suddenly deserted her, in unknown waters, to sultry calms. The absence of the water-pipes now proved

9. Kegs of water. "Heavers": bars, most often used as levers. "Mata": Brazilian cotton.

as fatal to life as before their presence had menaced it. Induced, or at least aggravated, by the less than scanty allowance of water, a malignant fever followed the scurvy; with the excessive heat of the lengthened calm, making such short work of it as to sweep away, as by billows, whole families of the Africans, and a yet larger number, proportionably, of the Spaniards, including, by a luckless fatality, every remaining officer on board. Consequently, in the smart west winds eventually following the calm, the already rent sails having to be simply dropped, not furled, at need, had been gradually reduced to the beggar's rags they were now. To procure substitutes for his lost sailors, as well as supplies of water and sails, the captain at the earliest opportunity had made for Baldivia, the southernmost civilized port of Chili and South America; but upon nearing the coast the thick weather had prevented him from so much as sighting that harbor. Since which period, almost without a crew, and almost without canvas and almost without water, and at intervals giving its added dead to the sea, the San Dominick had been battle-dored[1] about by contrary winds, inveigled by currents, or grown weedy in calms. Like a man lost in woods, more than once she had doubled upon her own track.

"But throughout these calamities," huskily continued Don Benito, painfully turning in the half embrace of his servant, "I have to thank those negroes you see, who, though to your inexperienced eyes appearing unruly, have, indeed, conducted themselves with less of restlessness than even their owner could have thought possible under such circumstances."

Here he again fell faintly back. Again his mind wandered: but he rallied, and less obscurely proceeded.

"Yes, their owner was quite right in assuring me that no fetters would be needed with his blacks; so that while, as is wont in this transportation, those negroes have always remained upon deck—not thrust below, as in the Guineamen—they have, also, from the beginning, been freely permitted to range within given bounds at their pleasure."

Once more the faintness returned—his mind roved—but, recovering, he resumed:

"But it is Babo here to whom, under God, I owe not only my own preservation, but likewise to him, chiefly, the merit is due, of pacifying his more ignorant brethren, when at intervals tempted to murmurings."

"Ah, master," sighed the black, bowing his face, "don't speak of me; Babo is nothing; what Babo has done was but duty."

"Faithful fellow!" cried Capt. Delano. "Don Benito, I envy you such a friend; slave I cannot call him."

As master and man stood before him, the black upholding the white, Captain Delano could not but bethink him of the beauty of that relationship which could present such a spectacle of fidelity on the one hand and confidence on the other. The scene was hightened by the contrast in dress, denoting their relative positions. The Spaniard wore a loose Chili jacket of dark velvet; white small clothes and stockings, with silver buckles at the knee and instep; a high-crowned sombrero, of fine grass; a slender sword, silver mounted, hung from a knot in his sash; the last being an almost invariable adjunct, more for ornament than utility, of a South American gentleman's dress to this hour. Excepting when his occasional nervous contortions brought about disarray, there

---

1. Tossed back and forth, as a shuttlecock is hit back and forth by a pair of battledores (or paddles).

was a certain precision in his attire, curiously at variance with the unsightly disorder around; especially in the belittered Ghetto, forward of the main-mast, wholly occupied by the blacks.

The servant wore nothing but wide trowsers, apparently, from their coarseness and patches, made out of some old topsail; they were clean, and confined at the waist by a bit of unstranded rope, which, with his composed, deprecatory air at times, made him look something like a begging friar of St. Francis.

However unsuitable for the time and place, at least in the blunt-thinking American's eyes, and however strangely surviving in the midst of all his afflictions, the toilette of Don Benito might not, in fashion at least, have gone beyond the style of the day among South Americans of his class. Though on the present voyage sailing from Buenos Ayres, he had avowed himself a native and resident of Chili, whose inhabitants had not so generally adopted the plain coat and once plebeian pantaloons; but, with a becoming modification, adhered to their provincial costume, picturesque as any in the world. Still, relatively to the pale history of the voyage, and his own pale face, there seemed something so incongruous in the Spaniard's apparel, as almost to suggest the image of an invalid courtier tottering about London streets in the time of the plague.

The portion of the narrative which, perhaps, most excited interest, as well as some surprise, considering the latitudes in question, was the long calms spoken of, and more particularly the ship's so long drifting about. Without communicating the opinion, of course, the American could not but impute at least part of the detentions both to clumsy seamanship and faulty navigation. Eying Don Benito's small, yellow hands, he easily inferred that the young captain had not got into command at the hawse-hole,[2] but the cabin-window; and if so, why wonder at incompetence, in youth, sickness, and gentility united?

But drowning criticism in compassion, after a fresh repetition of his sympathies, Captain Delano having heard out his story, not only engaged, as in the first place, to see Don Benito and his people supplied in their immediate bodily needs, but, also, now further promised to assist him in procuring a large permanent supply of water, as well as some sails and rigging; and, though it would involve no small embarrassment to himself, yet he would spare three of his best seamen for temporary deck officers; so that without delay the ship might proceed to Conception, there fully to refit for Lima, her destined port.

Such generosity was not without its effect, even upon the invalid. His face lighted up; eager and hectic, he met the honest glance of his visitor. With gratitude he seemed overcome.

"This excitement is bad for master," whispered the servant, taking his arm, and with soothing words gently drawing him aside.

When Don Benito returned, the American was pained to observe that his hopefulness, like the sudden kindling in his cheek, was but febrile and transient.

Ere long, with a joyless mien, looking up towards the poop, the host invited his guest to accompany him there, for the benefit of what little breath of wind might be stirring.

As during the telling of the story, Captain Delano had once or twice started

2. Metal-lined hole in the bow of a ship, through which a cable passes; the expression means to begin a career before the mast, not in a position of authority.

at the occasional cymballing of the hatchet-polishers, wondering why such an interruption should be allowed, especially in that part of the ship, and in the ears of an invalid; and moreover, as the hatchets had anything but an attractive look, and the handlers of them still less so, it was, therefore, to tell the truth, not without some lurking reluctance, or even shrinking, it may be, that Captain Delano, with apparent complaisance, acquiesced in his host's invitation. The more so, since with an untimely caprice of punctilio, rendered distressing by his cadaverous aspect, Don Benito, with Castilian bows, solemnly insisted upon his guest's preceding him up the ladder leading to the elevation; where, one on each side of the last step, sat for armorial supporters and sentries two of the ominous file. Gingerly enough stepped good Captain Delano between them, and in the instant of leaving them behind, like one running the gauntlet, he felt an apprehensive twitch in the calves of his legs.

But when, facing about, he saw the whole file, like so many organ-grinders, still stupidly intent on their work, unmindful of everything beside, he could not but smile at his late fidgety panic.

Presently, while standing with his host, looking forward upon the decks below, he was struck by one of those instances of insubordination previously alluded to. Three black boys, with two Spanish boys, were sitting together on the hatches, scraping a rude wooden platter, in which some scanty mess had recently been cooked. Suddenly, one of the black boys, enraged at a word dropped by one of his white companions, seized a knife, and though called to forbear by one of the oakum-pickers, struck the lad over the head, inflicting a gash from which blood flowed.

In amazement, Captain Delano inquired what this meant. To which the pale Don Benito dully muttered, that it was merely the sport of the lad.

"Pretty serious sport, truly," rejoined Captain Delano. "Had such a thing happened on board the Bachelor's Delight, instant punishment would have followed."

At these words the Spaniard turned upon the American one of his sudden, staring, half-lunatic looks; then relapsing into his torpor, answered, "Doubtless, doubtless, Señor."

Is it, thought Captain Delano, that this hapless man is one of those paper captains I've known, who by policy wink at what by power they cannot put down? I know no sadder sight than a commander who has little of command but the name.

"I should think, Don Benito," he now said, glancing towards the oakum-picker who had sought to interfere with the boys, "that you would find it advantageous to keep all your blacks employed, especially the younger ones, no matter at what useless task, and no matter what happens to the ship. Why, even with my little band, I find such a course indispensable. I once kept a crew on my quarter-deck thrumming[3] mats for my cabin, when, for three days, I had given up my ship—mats, men, and all—for a speedy loss, owing to the violence of a gale, in which we could do nothing but helplessly drive before it."

"Doubtless, doubtless," muttered Don Benito.

"But," continued Captain Delano, again glancing upon the oakum-pickers

---

3. To "thrum" is to insert pieces of rope yarn into canvas, thus making a rough surface or mat (usually for keeping ropes from chafing against wood or metal).

and then at the hatchet-polishers, near by. "I see you keep some at least of your host employed."

"Yes," was again the vacant response.

"Those old men there, shaking their pows[4] from their pulpits," continued Captain Delano, pointing to the oakum-pickers, "seem to act the part of old dominies to the rest, little heeded as their admonitions are at times. Is this voluntary on their part, Don Benito, or have you appointed them shepherds to your flock of black sheep?"

"What posts they fill, I appointed them," rejoined the Spaniard, in an acrid tone, as if resenting some supposed satiric reflection.

"And these others, these Ashantee[5] conjurors here," continued Captain Delano, rather uneasily eying the brandished steel of the hatchet-polishers, where in spots it had been brought to a shine, "this seems a curious business they are at, Don Benito?"

"In the gales we met," answered the Spaniard, "what of our general cargo was not thrown overboard was much damaged by the brine. Since coming into calm weather, I have had several cases of knives and hatchets daily brought up for overhauling and cleaning."

"A prudent idea, Don Benito. You are part owner of ship and cargo, I presume; but not of the slaves, perhaps?"

"I am owner of all you see," impatiently returned Don Benito, "except the main company of blacks, who belonged to my late friend, Alexandro Aranda."

As he mentioned this name, his air was heart-broken; his knees shook: his servant supported him.

Thinking he divined the cause of such unusual emotion, to confirm his surmise, Captain Delano, after a pause, said "And may I ask, Don Benito, whether—since awhile ago you spoke of some cabin passengers—the friend, whose loss so afflicts you at the outset of the voyage accompanied his blacks?"

"Yes."

"But died of the fever?"

"Died of the fever.—Oh, could I but——"

Again quivering, the Spaniard paused.

"Pardon me," said Captain Delano lowly, "but I think that, by a sympathetic experience, I conjecture, Don Benito, what it is that gives the keener edge to your grief. It was once my hard fortune to lose at sea a dear friend, my own brother, then supercargo. Assured of the welfare of his spirit, its departure I could have borne like a man; but that honest eye, that honest hand—both of which had so often met mine—and that warm heart; all, all—like scraps to the dogs—to throw all to the sharks! It was then I vowed never to have for fellow-voyager a man I loved, unless, unbeknown to him, I had provided every requisite, in case of a fatality, for embalming his mortal part for interment on shore. Were your friend's remains now on board this ship, Don Benito, not thus strangely would the mention of his name affect you."

"On board this ship?" echoed the Spaniard. Then, with horrified gestures, as directed against some specter, he unconsciously fell into the ready arms of his attendant, who, with a silent appeal toward Captain Delano, seemed beseeching him not again to broach a theme so unspeakably distressing to his master.

4. Heads. 5. West African tribe.

This poor fellow now, thought the pained American, is the victim of that sad superstition which associates goblins with the deserted body of man, as ghosts with an abandoned house. How unlike are we made! What to me, in like case, would have been a solemn satisfaction, the bare suggestion, even, terrifies the Spaniard into this trance. Poor Alexandro Aranda! what would you say could you here see your friend—who, on former voyages, when you for months were left behind, has, I dare say, often longed, and longed, for one peep at you—now transported with terror at the least thought of having you anyway nigh him.

At this moment, with a dreary graveyard toll, betokening a flaw, the ship's forecastle bell, smote by one of the grizzled oakum-pickers, proclaimed ten o'clock through the leaden calm; when Captain Delano's attention was caught by the moving figure of a gigantic black, emerging from the general crowd below, and slowly advancing towards the elevated poop. An iron collar was about his neck, from which depended a chain, thrice wound round his body; the terminating links padlocked together at a broad band of iron, his girdle.

"How like a mute Atufal moves," murmured the servant.

The black mounted the steps of the poop, and, like a brave prisoner, brought up to receive sentence, stood in unquailing muteness before Don Benito, now recovered from his attack.

At the first glimpse of his approach, Don Benito had started, a resentful shadow swept over his face; and, as with the sudden memory of bootless rage, his white lips glued together.

This is some mulish mutineer, thought Captain Delano, surveying, not without a mixture of admiration, the colossal form of the negro.

"See, he waits your question, master," said the servant.

Thus reminded, Don Benito, nervously averting his glance, as if shunning, by anticipation, some rebellious response, in a disconcerted voice, thus spoke:—

"Atufal, will you ask my pardon now?"

The black was silent.

"Again, master," murmured the servant, with bitter upbraiding eying his countryman, "Again, master; he will bend to master yet."

"Answer," said Don Benito, still averting his glance, "say but the one word *pardon*, and your chains shall be off."

Upon this, the black, slowly raising both arms, let them lifelessly fall, his links clanking, his head bowed; as much as to say, "no, I am content."

"Go," said Don Benito, with inkept and unknown emotion.

Deliberately as he had come, the black obeyed.

"Excuse me, Don Benito," said Captain Delano, "but this scene surprises me; what means it, pray?"

"It means that that negro alone, of all the band, has given me peculiar cause of offense. I have put him in chains; I——"

Here he paused; his hand to his head, as if there were a swimming there, or a sudden bewilderment of memory had come over him; but meeting his servant's kindly glance seemed reassured, and proceeded:—

"I could not scourge such a form. But I told him he must ask my pardon. As yet he has not. At my command, every two hours he stands before me."

"And how long has this been?"

"Some sixty days."

"And obedient in all else? And respectful?"

"Yes."

"Upon my conscience, then," exclaimed Captain Delano, impulsively, "he has a royal spirit in him, this fellow."

"He may have some right to it," bitterly returned Don Benito, "he says he was king in his own land."

"Yes," said the servant, entering a word, "those slits in Atufal's ears once held wedges of gold; but poor Babo here, in his own land, was only a poor slave; a black man's slave was Babo, who now is the white's."

Somewhat annoyed by these conversational familiarities, Captain Delano turned curiously upon the attendant, then glanced inquiringly at his master; but, as if long wonted to these little informalities, neither master nor man seemed to understand him.

"What, pray, was Atufal's offense, Don Benito?" asked Captain Delano; "if it was not something very serious, take a fool's advice, and, in view of his general docility, as well as in some natural respect for his spirit, remit him his penalty."

"No, no, master never will do that," here murmured the servant to himself, "proud Atufal must first ask master's pardon. The slave there carries the padlock, but master here carries the key."

His attention thus directed, Captain Delano now noticed for the first time that, suspended by a slender silken cord, from Don Benito's neck hung a key. At once, from the servant's muttered syllables divining the key's purpose, he smiled and said:—"So, Don Benito—padlock and key—significant symbols, truly."

Biting his lip, Don Benito faltered.

Though the remark of Captain Delano, a man of such native simplicity as to be incapable of satire or irony, had been dropped in playful allusion to the Spaniard's singularly evidenced lordship over the black; yet the hypochondriac seemed in some way to have taken it as a malicious reflection upon his confessed inability thus far to break down, at least, on a verbal summons, the entrenched will of the slave. Deploring this supposed misconception, yet despairing of correcting it, Captain Delano shifted the subject; but finding his companion more than ever withdrawn, as if still sourly digesting the lees of the presumed affront above-mentioned, by-and-by Captain Delano likewise became less talkative, oppressed, against his own will, by what seemed the secret vindictiveness of the morbidly sensitive Spaniard. But the good sailor himself, of a quite contrary disposition, refrained, on his part, alike from the appearance as from the feeling of resentment, and if silent, was only so from contagion.

Presently the Spaniard, assisted by his servant, somewhat discourteously crossed over from his guest; a procedure which, sensibly enough, might have been allowed to pass for idle caprice of ill-humor, had not master and man, lingering round the corner of the elevated skylight, began whispering together in low voices. This was unpleasing. And more: the moody air of the Spaniard, which at times had not been without a sort of valetudinarian stateliness, now seemed anything but dignified; while the menial familiarity of the servant lost its original charm of simple-hearted attachment.

In his embarrassment, the visitor turned his face to the other side of the ship. By so doing, his glance accidentally fell on a young Spanish sailor, a coil of rope in his hand, just stepped from the deck to the first round of the mizzen-rigging. Perhaps the man would not have been particularly noticed, were it not that, during his ascent to one of the yards, he, with a sort of covert intentness, kept his eye fixed on Captain Delano, from whom, presently, it passed, as if by a natural sequence, to the two whisperers.

His own attention thus redirected to that quarter, Captain Delano gave a slight start. From something in Don Benito's manner just then, it seemed as if the visitor had, at least partly, been the subject of the withdrawn consultation going on—a conjecture as little agreeable to the guest as it was little flattering to the host.

The singular alternations of courtesy and ill-breeding in the Spanish captain were unaccountable, except on one of two suppositions—innocent lunacy, or wicked imposture.

But the first idea, though it might naturally have occurred to an indifferent observer, and, in some respect, had not hitherto been wholly a stranger to Captain Delano's mind, yet, now that, in an incipient way, he began to regard the stranger's conduct something in the light of an intentional affront, of course the idea of lunacy was virtually vacated. But if not a lunatic, what then? Under the circumstances, would a gentleman, nay, any honest boor, act the part now acted by his host? The man was an impostor. Some low-born adventurer, masquerading as an oceanic grandee; yet so ignorant of the first requisites of mere gentlemanhood as to be betrayed into the present remarkable indecorum. That strange ceremoniousness, too, at other times evinced, seemed not uncharacteristic of one playing a part above his real level. Benito Cereno—Don Benito Cereno—a sounding name. One, too, at that period, not unknown, in the surname, to supercargoes and sea captains trading along the Spanish Main, as belonging to one of the most enterprising and extensive mercantile families in all those provinces; several members of it having titles; a sort of Castilian Rothschild,[6] with a noble brother, or cousin, in every great trading town of South America. The alleged Don Benito was in early manhood, about twenty-nine or thirty. To assume a sort of roving cadetship[7] in the maritime affairs of such a house, what more likely scheme for a young knave of talent and spirit? But the Spaniard was a pale invalid. Never mind. For even to the degree of simulating mortal disease, the craft of some tricksters had been known to attain. To think that, under the aspect of infantile weakness, the most savage energies might be couched—those velvets of the Spaniard but the silky paw to his fangs.

From no train of thought did these fancies come; not from within, but from without; suddenly, too, and in one throng, like hoar frost; yet as soon to vanish as the mild sun of Captain Delano's good-nature regained its meridian.

Glancing over once more towards his host—whose side-face, revealed above the skylight, was now turned towards him—he was struck by the profile, whose clearness of cut was refined by the thinness incident to ill-health, as well as ennobled about the chin by the beard. Away with suspicion. He was a true off-shoot of a true hidalgo Cereno.

Relieved by these and other better thoughts, the visitor, lightly humming a tune, now began indifferently pacing the poop, so as not to betray to Don Benito that he had at all mistrusted incivility, much less duplicity; for such

6. Great German banking family.
7. Position of on-the-job training for a post of author-

ity, appropriate for a younger or youngest son of a great house.

mistrust would yet be proved illusory, and by the event; though, for the present, the circumstance which had provoked that distrust remained unexplained. But when that little mystery should have been cleared up, Captain Delano thought he might extremely regret it, did he allow Don Benito to become aware that he had indulged in ungenerous surmises. In short, to the Spaniard's black-letter text, it was best, for awhile, to leave open margin.[8]

Presently, his pale face twitching and overcast, the Spaniard, still supported by his attendant, moved over towards his guest, when, with even more than his usual embarrassment, and a strange sort of intriguing intonation in his husky whisper, the following conversation began:—

"Señor, may I ask how long you have lain at this isle?"

"Oh, but a day or two, Don Benito."

"And from what port are you last?"

"Canton."

"And there, Señor, you exchanged your seal-skins for teas and silks, I think you said?"

"Yes. Silks, mostly."

"And the balance you took in specie, perhaps?"

Captain Delano, fidgeting a little, answered—

"Yes; some silver; not a very great deal, though."

"Ah—well. May I ask how many men have you, Señor?"

Captain Delano slightly started, but answered—

"About five-and-twenty, all told."

"And at present, Señor, all on board, I suppose?"

"All on board, Don Benito," replied the Captain, now with satisfaction.

"And will be to-night, Señor?"

At this last question, following so many pertinacious ones, for the soul of him Captain Delano could not but look very earnestly at the questioner, who, instead of meeting the glance, with every token of craven discomposure dropped his eyes to the deck; presenting an unworthy contrast to his servant, who, just then, was kneeling at his feet, adjusting a loose shoe-buckle; his disengaged face meantime, with humble curiosity, turned openly up into his master's downcast one.

The Spaniard, still with a guilty shuffle, repeated his question:—

"And—and will be to-night, Señor?"

"Yes, for aught I know," returned Captain Delano,—"but nay," rallying himself into fearless truth, "some of them talked of going off on another fishing party about midnight."

"Your ships generally go—go more or less armed, I believe, Señor?"

"Oh, a six-pounder or two, in case of emergency," was the intrepidly indifferent reply, "with a small stock of muskets, sealing-spears, and cutlasses, you know."

As he thus responded, Captain Delano again glanced at Don Benito, but the latter's eyes were averted; while abruptly and awkwardly shifting the subject, he made some peevish allusion to the calm, and then, without apology, once more, with his attendant, withdrew to the opposite bulwarks, where the whispering was resumed.

---

8. Without the elucidatory comments then often printed in margins as a gloss on the main text rather than printed at the bottom of the page as footnotes. Delano is deciding to reserve judgment. "Black-letter text": books printed in early type imitative of medieval script.

At this moment, and ere Captain Delano could cast a cool thought upon what had just passed, the young Spanish sailor before mentioned was seen descending from the rigging. In act of stooping over to spring inboard to the deck, his voluminous, unconfined frock, or shirt, of coarse woollen, much spotted with tar, opened out far down the chest, revealing a soiled under garment of what seemed the finest linen, edged, about the neck, with a narrow blue ribbon, sadly faded and worn. At this moment the young sailor's eye was again fixed on the whisperers, and Captain Delano thought he observed a lurking significance in it, as if silent signs of some Freemason[9] sort had that instant been interchanged.

This once more impelled his own glance in the direction of Don Benito, and, as before, he could not but infer that himself formed the subject of the conference. He paused. The sound of the hatchet-polishing fell on his ears. He cast another swift side-look at the two. They had the air of conspirators. In connection with the late questionings and the incident of the young sailor, these things now begat such return of involuntary suspicion, that the singular guilelessness of the American could not endure it. Plucking up a gay and humorous expression, he crossed over to the two rapidly, saying:—"Ha, Don Benito, your black here seems high in your trust; a sort of privy-counselor, in fact."

Upon this, the servant looked up with a good-natured grin, but the master started as from a venomous bite. It was a moment or two before the Spaniard sufficiently recovered himself to reply; which he did, at last, with cold constraint:—"Yes, Señor, I have trust in Babo."

Here Babo, changing his previous grin of mere animal humor into an intelligent smile, not ungratefully eyed his master.

Finding that the Spaniard now stood silent and reserved, as if involuntarily, or purposely giving hint that his guest's proximity was inconvenient just then, Captain Delano, unwilling to appear uncivil even to incivility itself, made some trivial remark and moved off; again and again turning over in his mind the mysterious demeanor of Don Benito Cereno.

He had descended from the poop, and, wrapped in thought, was passing near a dark hatchway, leading down into the steerage, when, perceiving motion there, he looked to see what moved. The same instant there was a sparkle in the shadowy hatchway, and he saw one of the Spanish sailors prowling there hurriedly placing his hand in the bosom of his frock, as if hiding something. Before the man could have been certain who it was that was passing, he slunk below out of sight. But enough was seen of him to make it sure that he was the same young sailor before noticed in the rigging.

What was that which so sparkled? thought Captain Delano. It was no lamp—no match—no live coal. Could it have been a jewel? But how come sailors with jewels?—or with silk-trimmed under-shirts either? Has he been robbing the trunks of the dead cabin passengers? But if so, he would hardly wear one of the stolen articles on board ship here. Ah, ah—if now that was, indeed, a secret sign I saw passing between this suspicious fellow and his captain awhile since; if I could only be certain that in my uneasiness my senses did not deceive me, then——

9. Secret society of men united for fraternal purposes; then a political force in some countries and a political issue in the United States, especially in the New York of Melville's youth, when Masons were charged with murdering a man who intended to expose their secrets.

Here, passing from one suspicious thing to another, his mind revolved the strange questions put to him concerning his ship.

By a curious coincidence, as each point was recalled, the black wizards of Ashantee would strike up with their hatchets, as in ominous comment on the white stranger's thoughts. Pressed by such enigmas and portents, it would have been almost against nature, had not, even into the least distrustful heart, some ugly misgivings obtruded.

Observing the ship now helplessly fallen into a current, with enchanted sails, drifting with increased rapidity seaward; and noting that, from a lately intercepted projection of the land, the sealer was hidden, the stout mariner began to quake at thoughts which he barely durst confess to himself. Above all, he began to feel a ghostly dread of Don Benito. And yet when he roused himself, dilated his chest, felt himself strong on his legs, and coolly considered it—what did all these phantoms amount to?

Had the Spaniard any sinister scheme, it must have reference not so much to him (Captain Delano) as to his ship (the Bachelor's Delight). Hence the present drifting away of the one ship from the other, instead of favoring any such possible scheme, was, for the time at least, opposed to it. Clearly any suspicion, combining such contradictions, must need be delusive. Beside, was it not absurd to think of a vessel in distress—a vessel by sickness almost dismanned of her crew—a vessel whose inmates were parched for water—was it not a thousand times absurd that such a craft should, at present, be of a piratical character; or her commander, either for himself or those under him, cherish any desire but for speedy relief and refreshment? But then, might not general distress, and thirst in particular, be affected? And might not that same undiminished Spanish crew, alleged to have perished off to a remnant, be at that very moment lurking in the hold? On heart-broken pretense of entreating a cup of cold water, fiends in human form had got into lonely dwellings, nor retired until a dark deed had been done. And among the Malay pirates, it was no unusual thing to lure ships after them into their treacherous harbors, or entice boarders from a declared enemy at sea, by the spectacle of thinly manned or vacant decks, beneath which prowled a hundred spears with yellow arms ready to upthrust them through the mats. Not that Captain Delano had entirely credited such things. He had heard of them—and now, as stories, they recurred. The present destination of the ship was the anchorage. There she would be near his own vessel. Upon gaining that vicinity, might not the San Dominick, like a slumbering volcano, suddenly let loose energies now hid?

He recalled the Spaniard's manner while telling his story. There was a gloomy hesitancy and subterfuge about it. It was just the manner of one making up his tale for evil purposes, as he goes. But if that story was not true, what was the truth? That the ship had unlawfully come into the Spaniard's possession? But in many of its details, especially in reference to the more calamitous parts, such as the fatalities among the seamen, the consequent prolonged beating about, the past sufferings from obstinate calms, and still continued suffering from thirst; in all these points, as well as others, Don Benito's story had corroborated not only the wailing ejaculations of the indiscriminate multitude, white and black, but likewise—what seemed impossible to be counterfeit—by the very expression and play of every human feature, which Captain Delano saw. If Don Benito's story was throughout an invention, then every soul on board, down to the youngest negress, was his carefully drilled recruit in the plot: an incredible inference. And yet, if there was ground for mistrusting his veracity, that inference was a legitimate one.

But those questions of the Spaniard. There, indeed, one might pause. Did they not seem put with much the same object with which the burglar or assassin, by day-time, reconnoitres the walls of a house? But, with ill purposes, to solicit such information openly of the chief person endangered, and so, in effect, setting him on his guard; how unlikely a procedure was that? Absurd, then, to suppose that those questions had been prompted by evil designs. Thus, the same conduct, which, in this instance, had raised the alarm, served to dispel it. In short, scarce any suspicion or uneasiness, however apparently reasonable at the time, which was not now, with equal apparent reason, dismissed.

At last he began to laugh at his former forebodings; and laugh at the strange ship for, in its aspect someway siding with them, as it were; and laugh, too, at the odd-looking blacks, particularly those old scissors-grinders, the Ashantees; and those bed-ridden old knitting-women, the oakum-pickers; and almost at the dark Spaniard himself, the central hobglobin of all.

For the rest, whatever in a serious way seemed enigmatical, was now good-naturedly explained away by the thought that, for the most part, the poor invalid scarcely knew what he was about; either sulking in black vapors, or putting idle questions without sense or object. Evidently, for the present, the man was not fit to be entrusted with the ship. On some benevolent plea withdrawing the command from him, Captain Delano would yet have to send her to Conception, in charge of his second mate, a worthy person and good navigator—a plan not more convenient for the San Dominick than for Don Benito; for, relieved from all anxiety, keeping wholly to his cabin, the sick man, under the good nursing of his servant, would probably, by the end of the passage, be in a measure restored to health, and with that he should also be restored to authority.

Such were the American's thoughts. They were tranquilizing. There was a difference between the idea of Don Benito's darkly pre-ordaining Captain Delano's fate, and Captain Delano's lightly arranging Don Benito's. Nevertheless, it was not without something of relief that the good seaman presently perceived his whale-boat in the distance. Its absence had been prolonged by unexpected detention at the sealer's side, as well as its returning trip lengthened by the continual recession of the goal.

The advancing speck was observed by the blacks. Their shouts attracted the attention of Don Benito, who, with a return of courtesy, approaching Captain Delano, expressed satisfaction at the coming of some supplies, slight and temporary as they must necessarily prove.

Captain Delano responded; but while doing so, his attention was drawn to something passing on the deck below: among the crowd climbing the landward bulwarks, anxiously watching the coming boat, two blacks, to all appearances accidentally incommoded by one of the sailors, violently pushed him aside, which the sailor someway resenting, they dashed him to the deck, despite the earnest cries of the oakum-pickers.

"Don Benito," said Captain Delano quickly, "do you see what is going on there? Look!"

But, seized by his cough, the Spaniard staggered, with both hands to his face, on the point of falling. Captain Delano would have supported him, but the servant was more alert, who, with one hand sustaining his master, with the other applied the cordial. Don Benito restored, the black withdrew his support, slipping aside a little, but dutifully remaining within call of a whisper. Such discretion was here evinced as quite wiped away, in the visitor's eyes, any blemish of impropriety which might have attached to the attendant, from the indecorous conferences before mentioned; showing, too, that if the servant were to blame, it might be more the master's fault than his own, since when left to himself he could conduct thus well.

His glance called away from the spectacle of disorder to the more pleasing one before him, Captain Delano could not avoid again congratulating his host upon possessing such a servant, who, though perhaps a little too forward now and then, must upon the whole be invaluable to one in the invalid's situation.

"Tell me, Don Benito," he added, with a smile—"I should like to have your man here myself—what will you take for him? Would fifty doubloons be any object?"

"Master wouldn't part with Babo for a thousand doubloons," murmured the black, overhearing the offer, and taking it in earnest, and, with the strange vanity of a faithful slave appreciated by his master, scorning to hear so paltry a valuation put upon him by a stranger. But Don Benito, apparently hardly yet completely restored, and again interrupted by his cough, made but some broken reply.

Soon his physical distress became so great, affecting his mind, too, apparently, that, as if to screen the sad spectacle, the servant gently conducted his master below.

Left to himself, the American, to while away the time till his boat should arrive, would have pleasantly accosted some one of the few Spanish seamen he saw; but recalling something that Don Benito had said touching their ill conduct, he refrained, as a ship-master indisposed to countenance cowardice or unfaithfulness in seamen.

While, with these thoughts, standing with eye directed forward towards that handful of sailors, suddenly he thought that one or two of them returned the glance and with a sort of meaning. He rubbed his eyes, and looked again; but again seemed to see the same thing. Under a new form, but more obscure than any previous one, the old suspicions recurred, but, in the absence of Don Benito, with less of panic than before. Despite the bad account given of the sailors, Captain Delano resolved forthwith to accost one of them. Descending the poop, he made his way through the blacks, his movement drawing a queer cry from the oakum-pickers, prompted by whom, the negroes, twitching each other aside, divided before him; but, as if curious to see what was the object of this deliberate visit to their Ghetto, closing in behind, in tolerable order, followed the white stranger up. His progress thus proclaimed as by mounted kings-at-arms, and escorted as by a Caffre[1] guard of honor, Captain Delano, assuming a good humored, off-handed air, continued to advance; now and then saying a blithe word to the negroes, and his eye curiously surveying the white faces, here and there sparsely mixed in with the blacks, like stray white pawns venturously involved in the ranks of the chess-men opposed.

While thinking which of them to select for his purpose, he chanced to observe a sailor seated on the deck engaged in tarring the strap of a large block, with a circle of blacks squatted round him inquisitively eying the process.

1. Kaffir, very tall Bantu tribe of South Africa.

The mean employment of the man was in contrast with something superior in his figure. His hand, black with continually thrusting it into the tar-pot held for him by a negro, seemed not naturally allied to his face, a face which would have been a very fine one but for its haggardness. Whether this haggardness had aught to do with criminality, could not be determined; since, as intense heat and cold, though unlike, produce like sensations, so innocence and guilt, when, through casual association with mental pain, stamping any visible impress, use one seal—a hacked one.

Not again that this reflection occurred to Captain Delano at the time, charitable man as he was. Rather another idea. Because observing so singular a haggardness combined with a dark eye, averted as in trouble and shame, and then again recalling Don Benito's confessed ill opinion of his crew, insensibly he was operated upon by certain general notions, which, while disconnecting pain and abashment from virtue, invariably link them with vice.

If, indeed, there be any wickedness on board this ship, thought Captain Delano, be sure that man there has fouled his hand in it, even as now he fouls it in the pitch. I don't like to accost him. I will speak to this other, this old Jack here on the windlass.

He advanced to an old Barcelona tar, in ragged red breeches and dirty night-cap, cheeks trenched and bronzed, whiskers dense as thorn hedges. Seated between two sleepy-looking Africans, this mariner, like his younger shipmate, was employed upon some rigging—splicing a cable—the sleepy-looking blacks performing the inferior function of holding the outer parts of the ropes for him.

Upon Captain Delano's approach, the man at once hung his head below its previous level; the one necessary for business. It appeared as if he desired to be thought absorbed, with more than common fidelity, in his task. Being addressed, he glanced up, but with what seemed a furtive, diffident air, which sat strangely enough on his weather-beaten visage, much as if a grizzly bear, instead of growling and biting, should simper and cast sheep's eyes. He was asked several questions concerning the voyage, questions purposely referring to several particulars in Don Benito's narrative, not previously corroborated by those impulsive cries greeting the visitor on first coming on board. The questions were briefly answered, confirming all that remained to be confirmed of the story. The negroes about the windlass joined in with the old sailor, but, as they became talkative, he by degrees became mute, and at length quite glum, seemed morosely unwilling to answer more questions, and yet, all the while, this ursine air was somehow mixed with his sheepish one.

Despairing of getting into unembarrassed talk with such a centaur, Captain Delano, after glancing round for a more promising countenance, but seeing none, spoke pleasantly to the blacks to make way for him; and so, amid various grins and grimaces, returned to the poop, feeling a little strange at first, he could hardly tell why, but upon the whole with regained confidence in Benito Cereno.

How plainly, thought he, did that old whiskerando yonder betray a consciousness of ill-desert. No doubt, when he saw me coming, he dreaded lest I, apprised by his Captain of the crew's general misbehavior, came with sharp words for him, and so down with his head. And yet—and yet, now that I think of it, that very old fellow, if I err not, was one of those who seemed so earnestly eying me here awhile since. Ah, these currents spin one's head round almost as much as they do the ship. Ha, there now's a pleasant sort of sunny sight; quite sociable, too.

His attention had been drawn to a slumbering negress, partly disclosed through the lace-work of some rigging, lying, with youthful limbs carelessly disposed, under the lee of the bulwarks, like a doe in the shade of a woodland rock. Sprawling at her lapped breasts was her wide-awake fawn, stark naked, its black little body half lifted from the deck, crosswise with its dam's; its hands, like two paws, clambering upon her; its mouth and nose ineffectually rooting to get at the mark; and meantime giving a vexatious half-grunt, blending with the composed snore of the negress.

The uncommon vigor of the child at length roused the mother. She started up, at distance facing Captain Delano. But as if not at all concerned at the attitude in which she had been caught, delightedly she caught the child up, with maternal transports, covering it with kisses.

There's naked nature, now; pure tenderness and love, thought Captain Delano, well pleased.

This incident prompted him to remark the other negresses more particularly than before. He was gratified with their manners; like most uncivilized women, they seemed at once tender of heart and tough of constitution; equally ready to die for their infants or fight for them. Unsophisticated as leopardesses; loving as doves. Ah! thought Captain Delano, these perhaps are some of the very women whom Ledyard[2] saw in Africa, and gave such a noble account of.

These natural sights somehow insensibly deepened his confidence and ease. At last he looked to see how his boat was getting on; but it was still pretty remote. He turned to see if Don Benito had returned; but he had not.

To change the scene, as well as to please himself with a leisurely observation of the coming boat, stepping over into the mizzen-chains he clambered his way into the starboard quarter-gallery;[3] one of those abandoned Venetian-looking water-balconies previously mentioned; retreats cut off from the deck. As his foot pressed the half-damp, half-dry sea-mosses matting the place, and a chance phantom cats-paw—an islet of breeze, unheralded, unfollowed—as this ghostly cats-paw came fanning his cheek, as his glance fell upon the row of small, round dead-lights, all closed like coppered eyes of the coffined, and the state-cabin door, once connecting with the gallery, even as the dead-lights had once looked out upon it, but now calked fast like a sarcophagus lid, to a purple-black, tarred-over panel, threshold, and post; and he bethought him of the time, when that state-cabin and this state-balcony had heard the voices of the Spanish king's officers, and the forms of the Lima viceroy's daughters had perhaps leaned where he stood—as these and other images flitted through his mind, as the cats-paw through the calm, gradually he felt rising a dreamy inquietude, like that of one who alone on the prairie feels unrest from the repose of the noon.

He leaned against the carved balustrade, again looking off toward his boat; but found his eye falling upon the ribboned grass, trailing along the ship's water-line, straight as a border of green box; and parterres[4] of sea-weed, broad ovals and crescents, floating nigh and far, with what seemed long formal alleys between, crossing the terraces of swells, and sweeping round as if leading to

2. John Ledyard (1751–1789), American traveler, whose comment appeared in Proceedings of the Association for Promoting the Discovery of the Interior Parts of Africa (1790). Melville became confused because the Scottish traveler Mungo Park quoted this passage from Ledyard in his Travels in the Interior of Africa. The Putnam's version of Benito Cereno miscredits this quotation to Park, but Ledyard's name is properly substituted in The Piazza Tales.
3. Balcony projecting from the after part of a vessel's sides.
4. Ornamental arrangement, as of flower beds.

the grottoes below. And overhanging all was the balustrade by his arm, which, partly stained with pitch and partly embossed with moss, seemed the charred ruin of some summer-house in a grand garden long running to waste.

Trying to break one charm, he was but becharmed anew. Though upon the wide sea, he seemed in some far inland country; prisoner in some deserted château, left to stare at empty grounds, and peer out at vague roads, where never wagon or wayfarer passed.

But these enchantments were a little disenchanted as his eye fell on the corroded main-chains. Of an ancient style, massy and rusty in link, shackle and bolt, they seemed even more fit for the ship's present business than the one for which she had been built.

Presently he thought something moved nigh the chains. He rubbed his eyes, and looked hard. Groves of rigging were about the chains; and there, peering from behind a great stay, like an Indian from behind a hemlock, a Spanish sailor, a marlingspike in his hand, was seen, who made what seemed an imperfect gesture towards the balcony, but immediately, as if alarmed by some advancing step along the deck within, vanished into the recesses of the hempen forest, like a poacher.

What meant this? Something the man had sought to communicate, unbe-known to any one, even to his captain. Did the secret involve aught unfavor-able to his captain? Were those previous misgivings of Captain Delano's about to be verified? Or, in his haunted mood at the moment, had some random, unintentional motion of the man, while busy with the stay, as if repairing it, been mistaken for a significant beckoning?

Not unbewildered, again he gazed off for his boat. But it was temporarily hidden by a rocky spur of the isle. As with some eagerness he bent forward, watching for the first shooting view of its beak, the balustrade gave way before him like charcoal. Had he not clutched an outreaching rope he would have fallen into the sea. The crash, though feeble, and the fall, though hollow, of the rotten fragments, must have been overheard. He glanced up. With sober curiosity peering down upon him was one of the old oakum-pickers, slipped from his perch to an outside boom; while below the old negro, and, invisible to him, reconnoitering from a port-hole like a fox from the mouth of its den, crouched the Spanish sailor again. From something suddenly suggested by the man's air, the mad idea now darted into Captain Delano's mind, that Don Benito's plea of indisposition, in withdrawing below, was but a pretense: that he was engaged there maturing his plot, of which the sailor, by some means gaining an inkling, had a mind to warn the stranger against; incited, it may be, by gratitude for a kind word on first boarding the ship. Was it from foresee-ing some possible interference like this, that Don Benito had, beforehand, given such a bad character of his sailors, while praising the negroes; though, indeed, the former seemed as docile as the latter the contrary? The whites, too, by nature, were the shrewder race. A man with some evil design, would he not be likely to speak well of that stupidity which was blind to his depravity, and malign that intelligence from which it might not be hidden? Not unlikely, perhaps. But if the whites had dark secrets concerning Don Benito, could then Don Benito be any way in complicity with the blacks? But they were too stupid. Besides, who ever heard of a white so far a renegade as to apostatize[5]

5. To deny or renounce (said of religious faith).

from his very species almost, by leaguing in against it with negroes? These difficulties recalled former ones. Lost in their mazes, Captain Delano, who had now regained the deck, was uneasily advancing along it, when he observed a new face; an aged sailor seated cross-legged near the main hatchway. His skin was shrunk up with wrinkles like a pelican's empty pouch; his hair frosted; his countenance grave and composed. His hands were full of ropes, which he was working into a large knot. Some blacks were about him obligingly dipping the strands for him, here and there, as the exigencies of the operation demanded.

Captain Delano crossed over to him, and stood in silence surveying the knot; his mind, by a not uncongenial transition, passing from its own entanglements to those of the hemp. For intricacy such a knot he had never seen in an American ship, or indeed any other. The old man looked like an Egyptian priest, making gordian knots for the temple of Ammon.[6] The knot seemed a combination of double-bowline-knot, treble-crown-knot, back-handed-well-knot, knot-in-and-out-knot, and jamming-knot.

At last, puzzled to comprehend the meaning of such a knot, Captain Delano addressed the knotter:—

"What are you knotting there, my man?"

"The knot," was the brief reply, without looking up.

"So it seems; but what is it for?"

"For some one else to undo," muttered back the old man, plying his fingers harder than ever, the knot being now nearly completed.

While Captain Delano stood watching him, suddenly the old man threw the knot towards him, saying in broken English,—the first heard in the ship,—something to this effect—"Undo it, cut it, quick." It was said lowly, but with such condensation of rapidity, that the long, slow words in Spanish, which had preceded and followed, almost operated as covers to the brief English between.

For a moment, knot in hand, and knot in head, Captain Delano stood mute; while, without further heeding him, the old man was now intent upon other ropes. Presently there was a slight stir behind Captain Delano. Turning, he saw the chained negro, Atufal, standing quietly there. The next moment the old sailor rose, muttering, and, followed by his subordinate negroes, removed to the forward part of the ship, where in the crowd he disappeared.

An elderly negro, in a clout like an infant's, and with a pepper and salt head, and a kind of attorney air, now approached Captain Delano. In tolerable Spanish, and with a good-natured, knowing wink, he informed him that the old knotter was simple-witted, but harmless; often playing his odd tricks. The negro concluded by begging the knot, for of course the stranger would not care to be troubled with it. Unconsciously, it was handed to him. With a sort of congé,[7] the negro received it, and turning his back, ferreted into it like a detective Custom House officer after smuggled laces. Soon, with some African word, equivalent to pshaw, he tossed the knot overboard.

All this is very queer now, thought Captain Delano, with a qualmish sort of emotion; but as one feeling incipient sea-sickness, he strove, by ignoring the

6. In Egypt the oracle of Jupiter Ammon predicted to Alexander the Great that he would conquer the world. Later in Phrygia (in north-central Asia Minor), where the former King Gordius had foretold that whoever would untie his intricate knot would become master of Asia, Alexander cut the knot with his sword.
7. Leave taking, signaled by a low bow.

symptoms, to get rid of the malady. Once more he looked off for his boat. To his delight, it was now again in view, leaving the rocky spur astern.

The sensation here experienced, after at first relieving his uneasiness, with unforeseen efficacy, soon began to remove it. The less distant sight of that well-known boat—showing it, not as before, half blended with the haze, but with outline defined, so that its individuality, like a man's, was manifest; that boat, Rover by name, which, though now in strange seas, had often pressed the beach of Captain Delano's home, and, brought to its threshold for repairs, had familiarly lain there, as a Newfoundland dog; the sight of that household boat evoked a thousand trustful associations, which, contrasted with previous suspicions, filled him not only with lightsome confidence, but somehow with half humorous self-reproaches at his former lack of it.

"What, I, Amasa Delano—Jack of the Beach, as they called me when a lad—I, Amasa; the same that, duck-satchel in hand, used to paddle along the waterside to the school-house made from the old hulk;—I, little Jack of the Beach, that used to go berrying with cousin Nat and the rest; I to be murdered here at the ends of the earth, on board a haunted pirate-ship by a horrible Spaniard?—Too nonsensical to think of! Who would murder Amasa Delano? His conscience is clean. There is some one above. Fie, fie, Jack of the Beach! you are a child indeed; a child of the second childhood, old boy; you are beginning to dote and drule, I'm afraid."

Light of heart and foot, he stepped aft, and there was met by Don Benito's servant, who, with a pleasing expression, responsive to his own present feelings, informed him that his master had recovered from the effects of his coughing fit, and had just ordered him to go present his compliments to his good guest, Don Amasa, and say that he (Don Benito) would soon have the happiness to rejoin him.

There now, do you mark that? again thought Captain Delano, walking the poop. What a donkey I was. This kind gentleman who here sends me his kind compliments, he, but ten minutes ago, dark-lantern in hand, was dodging round some old grind-stone in the hold, sharpening a hatchet for me, I thought. Well, well; these long calms have a morbid effect on the mind, I've often heard, though I never believed it before. Ha! glancing towards the boat; there's Rover; good dog; a white bone in her mouth. A pretty big bone though, seems to me.—What? Yes, she has fallen afoul of the bubbling tide-rip there. It sets her the other way, too, for the time. Patience.

It was now about noon, though, from the grayness of everything, it seemed to be getting towards dusk.

The calm was confirmed. In the far distance, away from the influence of land, the leaden ocean seemed laid out and leaded up, its course finished, soul gone, defunct. But the current from landward, where the ship was, increased; silently sweeping her further and further towards the tranced waters beyond.

Still, from his knowledge of those latitudes, cherishing hopes of a breeze, and a fair and fresh one, at any moment, Captain Delano, despite present prospects, buoyantly counted upon bringing the San Dominick safely to anchor ere night. The distance swept over was nothing; since, with a good wind, ten minutes' sailing would retrace more than sixty minutes' drifting. Meantime, one moment turning to mark "Rover" fighting the tide-rip, and the next to see Don Benito approaching, he continued walking the poop.

Gradually he felt a vexation arising from the delay of his boat; this soon merged into uneasiness; and at last, his eye falling continually, as from a stage-box into the pit, upon the strange crowd before and below him, and by and by recognising there the face—now composed to indifference—of the Spanish sailor who had seemed to beckon from the main chains, something of his old trepidations returned.

Ah, thought he—gravely enough—this is like the ague: because it went off, it follows not that it won't come back.

Though ashamed of the relapse, he could not altogether subdue it; and so, exerting his good nature to the utmost, insensibly he came to a compromise.

Yes, this is a strange craft; a strange history, too, and strange folks on board. But—nothing more.

By way of keeping his mind out of mischief till the boat should arrive, he tried to occupy it with turning over and over, in a purely speculative sort of way, some lesser peculiarities of the captain and crew. Among others, four curious points recurred.

First, the affair of the Spanish lad assailed with a knife by the slave boy; an act winked at by Don Benito. Second, the tyranny in Don Benito's treatment of Atufal, the black; as if a child should lead a bull of the Nile by the ring in his nose. Third, the trampling of the sailor by the two negroes; a piece of insolence passed over without so much as a reprimand. Fourth, the cringing submission to their master of all the ship's underlings, mostly blacks; as if by the least inadvertence they feared to draw down his despotic displeasure.

Coupling these points, they seemed somewhat contradictory. But what then, thought Captain Delano, glancing towards his now nearing boat,—what then? Why, Don Benito is a very capricious commander. But he is not the first of the sort I have seen; though it's true he rather exceeds any other. But as a nation—continued he in his reveries—these Spaniards are all an odd set; the very word Spaniard has a curious, conspirator, Guy-Fawkish[8] twang to it. And yet, I dare say, Spaniards in the main are as good folks as any in Duxbury, Massachusetts. Ah good! At last "Rover" has come.

As, with its welcome freight, the boat touched the side, the oakum-pickers, with venerable gestures, sought to restrain the blacks, who, at the sight of three gurried[9] water-casks in its bottom, and a pile of wilted pumpkins in its bow, hung over the bulwarks in disorderly raptures.

Don Benito with his servant now appeared; his coming, perhaps, hastened by hearing the noise. Of him Captain Delano sought permission to serve out the water, so that all might share alike, and none injure themselves by unfair excess. But sensible, and, on Don Benito's account, kind as this offer was, it was received with what seemed impatience; as if aware that he lacked energy as a commander, Don Benito, with the true jealousy of weakness, resented as an affront any interference. So, at least, Captain Delano inferred.

In another moment the casks were being hoisted in, when some of the eager negroes accidentally jostled Captain Delano, where he stood by the gangway; so that, unmindful of Don Benito, yielding to the impulse of the moment, with good-natured authority he bade the blacks stand back; to enforce his words making use of a half-mirthful, half-menacing gesture. Instantly the blacks paused, just where they were, each negro and negress suspended in his or her

8. Guy Fawkes (1570–1606), Catholic conspirator exe-   9. Coated with slime, from "gurry," fish offal.
cuted for plotting to blow up the House of Lords.

posture, exactly as the word had found them—for a few seconds continuing
so—while, as between the responsive posts of a telegraph, an unknown syllable
ran from man to man among the perched oakum-pickers. While the visitor's
attention was fixed by this scene, suddenly the hatchet-polishers half rose, and
a rapid cry came from Don Benito.

Thinking that at the signal of the Spaniard he was about to be massacred,
Captain Delano would have sprung for his boat, but paused, as the oakum-
pickers, dropping down into the crowd with earnest exclamations, forced every
white and every negro back, at the same moment, with gestures friendly and
familiar, almost jocose, bidding him, in substance, not be a fool. Simultaneously the hatchet-polishers resumed their seats, quietly as so many tailors, and
at once, as if nothing had happened, the work of hoisting in the casks was
resumed, whites and blacks singing at the tackle.

Captain Delano glanced towards Don Benito. As he saw his meager form
in the act of recovering itself from reclining in the servant's arms, into which
the agitated invalid had fallen, he could not but marvel at the panic by which
himself had been surprised on the darting supposition that such a commander,
who upon a legitimate occasion, so trivial, too, as it now appeared, could lose
all self-command, was, with energetic iniquity, going to bring about his
murder.

The casks being on deck, Captain Delano was handed a number of jars and
cups by one of the steward's aids, who, in the name of his captain, entreated
him to do as he had proposed: dole out the water. He complied, with republican impartiality as to this republican element, which always seeks one level,
serving the oldest white no better than the youngest black; excepting, indeed,
poor Don Benito, whose condition, if not rank, demanded an extra allowance.
To him, in the first place, Captain Delano presented a fair pitcher of the fluid;
but, thirsting as he was for it, the Spaniard quaffed not a drop until after several
grave bows and salutes. A reciprocation of courtesies which the sight-loving
Africans hailed with clapping of hands.

Two of the less wilted pumpkins being reserved for the cabin table, the
residue were minced up on the spot for the general regalement. But the soft
bread, sugar, and bottled cider, Captain Delano would have given the whites
alone, and in chief Don Benito; but the latter objected; which disinterestedness
not a little pleased the American; and so mouthfuls all around were given alike
to whites and blacks; excepting one bottle of cider, which Babo insisted upon
setting aside for his master.

Here it may be observed that as, on the first visit of the boat, the American
had not permitted his men to board the ship, neither did he now; being unwilling to add to the confusion of the decks.

Not uninfluenced by the peculiar good humor at present prevailing, and for
the time oblivious of any but benevolent thoughts, Captain Delano, who from
recent indications counted upon a breeze within an hour or two at furthest,
dispatched the boat back to the sealer with orders for all the hands that could
be spared immediately to set about rafting casks to the watering-place and
filling them. Likewise he bade word be carried to his chief officer, that if
against present expectation the ship was not brought to anchor by sunset, he
need be under no concern, for as there was to be a full moon that night, he
(Captain Delano) would remain on board ready to play the pilot, come the
wind soon or late.

As the two Captains stood together, observing the departing boat—the servant as it happened having just spied a spot on his master's velvet sleeve, and silently engaged rubbing it out—the American expressed his regrets that the San Dominick had no boats; none, at least, but the unseaworthy old hulk of the long-boat, which, warped as a camel's skeleton in the desert, and almost as bleached, lay pot-wise inverted amidships, one side a little tipped, furnishing a subterraneous sort of den for family groups of the blacks, mostly women and small children; who, squatting on old mats below, or perched above in the dark dome, on the elevated seats, were descried, some distance within, like a social circle of bats, sheltering in some friendly cave; at intervals, ebon flights of naked boys and girls, three or four years old, darting in and out of the den's mouth.

"Had you three or four boats now, Don Benito," said Captain Delano, "I think that, by tugging at the oars, your negroes here might help along matters some.—Did you sail from port without boats, Don Benito?"

"They were stove in the gales, Señor."

"That was bad. Many men, too, you lost then. Boats and men.—Those must have been hard gales, Don Benito."

"Past all speech," cringed the Spaniard.

"Tell me, Don Benito," continued his companion with increased interest, "tell me, were these gales immediately off the pitch of Cape Horn?"

"Cape Horn?—who spoke of Cape Horn?"

"Yourself did, when giving me an account of your voyage," answered Captain Delano with almost equal astonishment at this eating of his own words, even as he ever seemed eating his own heart, on the part of the Spaniard. "You yourself, Don Benito, spoke of Cape Horn," he emphatically repeated.

The Spaniard turned, in a sort of stooping posture, pausing an instant, as one about to make a plunging exchange of elements, as from air to water.

At this moment a messenger-boy, a white, hurried by, in the regular performance of his function carrying the last expired half hour forward to the forecastle, from the cabin time-piece, to have it struck at the ship's large bell.

"Master," said the servant, discontinuing his work on the coat sleeve, and addressing the rapt Spaniard with a sort of timid apprehensiveness, as one charged with a duty, the discharge of which, it was foreseen, would prove irksome to the very person who had imposed it, and for whose benefit it was intended, "master told me never mind where he was, or how engaged, always to remind him, to a minute, when shaving-time comes. Miguel has gone to strike the half-hour afternoon. It is *now*, master. Will master go into the cuddy?"

"Ah—yes," answered the Spaniard, starting, somewhat as from dreams into realities; then turning upon Captain Delano, he said that ere long he would resume the conversation.

"Then if master means to talk more to Don Amasa," said the servant, "why not let Don Amasa sit by master in the cuddy, and master can talk, and Don Amasa can listen, while Babo here lathers and strops."

"Yes," said Captain Delano, not unpleased with this sociable plan, "yes, Don Benito, unless you had rather not, I will go with you."

"Be it so, Señor."

As the three passed aft, the American could not but think it another strange instance of his host's capriciousness, this being shaved with such uncommon punctuality in the middle of the day. But he deemed it more than likely that the servant's anxious fidelity had something to do with the matter; inasmuch as the timely interruption served to rally his master from the mood which had evidently been coming upon him.

The place called the cuddy was a light deck-cabin formed by the poop, a sort of attic to the large cabin below. Part of it had formerly been the quarters of the officers; but since their death all the partitionings had been thrown down, and the whole interior converted into one spacious and airy marine hall; for absence of fine furniture and picturesque disarray, of odd appurtenances, somewhat answering to the wide, cluttered hall of some eccentric bachelor-squire in the country, who hangs his shooting-jacket and tobacco-pouch on deer antlers, and keeps his fishing-rod, tongs, and walking-stick in the same corner.

The similitude was hightened, if not originally suggested, by glimpses of the surrounding sea; since, in one aspect, the country and the ocean seem cousins-german.

The floor of the cuddy was matted. Overhead, four or five old muskets were stuck into horizontal holes along the beams. On one side was a claw-footed old table lashed to the deck; a thumbed missal on it, and over it a small, meager crucifix attached to the bulkhead. Under the table lay a dented cutlass or two, with a hacked harpoon, among some melancholy old rigging, like a heap of poor friars' girdles. There were also two long, sharp-ribbed settees of malacca cane, black with age, and uncomfortable to look at as inquisitors' racks, with a large, misshapen arm-chair, which, furnished with a rude bar-ber's crutch[1] at the back, working with a screw, seemed some grotesque engine of torment. A flag locker was in one corner, open, exposing various colored bunting, some rolled up, others half unrolled, still others tumbled. Opposite was a cumbrous washstand, of black mahogany, all of one block, with a pedes-tal, like a font, and over it a railed shelf, containing combs, brushes, and other implements of the toilet. A torn hammock of stained grass swung near; the sheets tossed, and the pillow wrinkled up like a brow, as if whoever slept here slept but illy, with alternate visitations of sad thoughts and bad dreams.

The further extremity of the cuddy, overhanging the ship's stern, was pierced with three openings, windows or port holes, according as men or can-non might peer, socially or unsocially, out of them. At present neither men nor cannon were seen, though huge ring-bolts and other rusty iron fixtures of the wood-work hinted of twenty-four-pounders.

Glancing towards the hammock as he entered, Captain Delano said, "You sleep here, Don Benito?"

"Yes, Señor, since we got into mild weather."

"This seems a sort of dormitory, sitting-room, sail-loft, chapel, armory, and private closet all together, Don Benito," added Captain Delano, looking round.

"Yes, Señor; events have not been favorable to much order in my arrange-ments."

Here the servant, napkin on arm, made a motion as if waiting his master's good pleasure. Don Benito signified his readiness, when, seating him in the malacca arm-chair, and for the guest's convenience drawing opposite it one of

1. Headrest.

the settees, the servant commenced operations by throwing back his master's collar and loosening his cravat.

There is something in the negro which, in a peculiar way, fits him for avocations about one's person. Most negroes are natural valets and hair-dressers; taking to the comb and brush congenially as to the castinets, and flourishing them apparently with almost equal satisfaction. There is, too, a smooth tact about them in this employment, with a marvelous, noiseless, gliding briskness, not ungraceful in its way, singularly pleasing to behold, and still more so to be the manipulated subject of. And above all is the great gift of good humor. Not the mere grin or laugh is here meant. Those were unsuitable. But a certain easy cheerfulness, harmonious in every glance and gesture; as though God had set the whole negro to some pleasant tune.

When to all this is added the docility arising from the unaspiring contentment of a limited mind, and that susceptibility of blind attachment sometimes inhering in indisputable inferiors, one readily perceives why those hypochondriacs, Johnson and Byron—it may be something like the hypochondriac, Benito Cereno—took to their hearts, almost to the exclusion of the entire white race, their serving men, the negroes, Barber and Fletcher.[2] But if there be that in the negro which exempts him from the inflicted sourness of the morbid or cynical mind, how, in his most prepossessing aspects, must he appear to a benevolent one? When at ease with respect to exterior things, Captain Delano's nature was not only benign, but familiarly and humorously so. At home, he had often taken rare satisfaction in sitting in his door, watching some free man of color at his work or play. If on a voyage he chanced to have a black sailor, invariably he was on chatty, and half-gamesome terms with him. In fact, like most men of a good, blithe heart, Captain Delano took to negroes, not philanthropically, but genially, just as other men to Newfoundland dogs.

Hitherto the circumstances in which he found the San Dominick had repressed the tendency. But in the cuddy, relieved from his former uneasiness, and, for various reasons, more sociably inclined than at any previous period of the day, and seeing the colored servant, napkin on arm, so debonair about his master, in a business so familiar as that of shaving, too, all his old weakness for negroes returned.

Among other things, he was amused with an odd instance of the African love of bright colors and fine shows, in the black's informally taking from the flag-locker a great piece of bunting of all hues, and lavishly tucking it under his master's chin for an apron.

The mode of shaving among the Spaniards is a little different from what it is with other nations. They have a basin, specifically called a barber's basin, which on one side is scooped out, so as accurately to receive the chin, against which it is closely held in lathering; which is done, not with a brush, but with soap dipped in the water of the basin and rubbed on the face.

In the present instance salt-water was used for lack of better; and the parts lathered were only the upper lip, and low down under the throat, all the rest being cultivated beard.

The preliminaries being somewhat novel to Captain Delano, he sat curi-

---

2. William Fletcher, Lord Byron's valet, was a white Englishman, here confused with an American black servant of Edward Trelawny who accompanied Byron on some journeys. Frank Barber was servant to Samuel Johnson for three decades; at his death in 1784 Johnson left Barber a large annuity.

ously eying them, so that no conversation took place, nor for the present did
Don Benito appear disposed to renew any.

Setting down his basin, the negro searched among the razors, as for the
sharpest, and having found it, gave it an additional edge by expertly strapping
it on the firm, smooth, oily skin of his open palm; he then made a gesture as
if to begin, but midway stood suspended for an instant, one hand elevating
the razor, the other professionally dabbling among the bubbling suds on the
Spaniard's lank neck. Not unaffected by the close sight of the gleaming steel,
Don Benito nervously shuddered, his usual ghastliness was hightened by the
lather, which lather, again, was intensified in its hue by the contrasting sooti-
ness of the negro's body. Altogether the scene was somewhat peculiar, at least
to Captain Delano, nor, as he saw the two thus postured, could he resist the
vagary, that in the black he saw a headsman, and in the white, a man at the
block. But this was one of those antic conceits, appearing and vanishing in a
breath, from which, perhaps, the best regulated mind is not always free.

Meantime the agitation of the Spaniard had a little loosened the bunting
from around him, so that one broad fold swept curtain-like over the chair-arm
to the floor, revealing, amid a profusion of armorial bars and ground-colors—
black, blue, and yellow—a closed castle in a blood-red field diagonal with a
lion rampant in a white.

"The castle and the lion," exclaimed Captain Delano—"why, Don Benito,
this is the flag of Spain you use here. It's well it's only I, and not the King,
that sees this," he added with a smile, "but"—turning towards the black,—
"it's all one, I suppose, so the colors be gay;" which playful remark did not fail
somewhat to tickle the negro.

"Now, master," he said, readjusting the flag, and pressing the head gently
further back into the crotch of the chair; "now master," and the steel glanced
nigh the throat.

Again Don Benito faintly shuddered.

"You must not shake so, master.—See, Don Amasa, master always shakes
when I shave him. And yet master knows I never yet have drawn blood, though
it's true, if master will shake so, I may some of these times. Now master," he
continued. "And now, Don Amasa, please go on with your talk about the
gale, and all that, master can hear, and between times master can answer."

"Ah yes, these gales," said Captain Delano; "but the more I think of your
voyage, Don Benito, the more I wonder, not at the gales, terrible as they must
have been, but at the disastrous interval following them. For here, by your
account, have you been these two months and more getting from Cape Horn
to St. Maria, a distance which I myself, with a good wind, have sailed in a few
days. True, you had calms, and long ones, but to be becalmed for two months,
that is, at least, unusual. Why, Don Benito, had almost any other gentleman
told me such a story, I should have been half disposed to a little incredulity."

Here an involuntary expression came over the Spaniard, similar to that just
before on the deck, and whether it was the start he gave, or a sudden gawky
roll of the hull in the calm, or a momentary unsteadiness of the servant's hand;
however it was, just then the razor drew blood, spots of which stained the
creamy lather under the throat; immediately the black barber drew back his
steel, and remaining in his professional attitude, back to Captain Delano, and
face to Don Benito, held up the trickling razor, saying, with a sort of half
humorous sorrow, "See, master,—you shook so—here's Babo's first blood."

No sword drawn before James the First of England, no assassination in that timid King's presence, could have produced a more terrified aspect[3] than was now presented by Don Benito.

Poor fellow, thought Captain Delano, so nervous he can't even bear the sight of barber's blood; and this unstrung, sick man, is it credible that I should have imagined he meant to spill all my blood, who can't endure the sight of one little drop of his own? Surely, Amasa Delano, you have been beside yourself this day. Tell it not when you get home, sappy Amasa. Well, well, he looks like a murderer, doesn't he? More like as if himself were to be done for. Well, well, this day's experience shall be a good lesson.

Meantime, while these things were running through the honest seaman's mind, the servant had taken the napkin from his arm, and to Don Benito had said—"But answer Don Amasa, please, master, while I wipe this ugly stuff off the razor, and strop it again."

As he said the words, his face was turned half round, so as to be alike visible to the Spaniard and the American, and seemed by its expression to hint, that he was desirous, by getting his master to go on with the conversation, considerately to withdraw his attention from the recent annoying accident. As if glad to snatch the offered relief, Don Benito resumed, rehearsing to Captain Delano, that not only were the calms of unusual duration, but the ship had fallen in with obstinate currents; and other things he added, some of which were but repetitions of former statements, to explain how it came to pass that the passage from Cape Horn to St. Maria had been so exceedingly long, now and then mingling with his words, incidental praises, less qualified than before, to the blacks, for their general good conduct.

These particulars were not given consecutively, the servant at convenient times using his razor, and so, between the intervals of shaving, the story and panegyric went on with more than usual huskiness.

To Captain Delano's imagination, now again not wholly at rest, there was something so hollow in the Spaniard's manner, with apparently some reciprocal hollowness in the servant's dusky comment of silence, that the idea flashed across him, that possibly master and man, for some unknown purpose, were acting out, both in word and deed, nay, to the very tremor of Don Benito's limbs, some juggling play before him. Neither did the suspicion of collusion lack apparent support, from the fact of those whispered conferences before mentioned. But then, what could be the object of enacting this play of the barber before him? At last, regarding the notion as a whimsy, insensibly suggested, perhaps, by the theatrical aspect of Don Benito in his harlequin ensign, Captain Delano speedily banished it.

The shaving over, the servant bestirred himself with a small bottle of scented waters, pouring a few drops on the head, and then diligently rubbing; the vehemence of the exercise causing the muscles of his face to twitch rather strangely.

His next operation was with comb, scissors and brush; going round and round, smoothing a curl here, clipping an unruly whisker-hair there, giving a graceful sweep to the temple-lock, with other impromptu touches evincing the hand of a master; while, like any resigned gentleman in barber's hands, Don Benito bore all, much less uneasily, at least, than he had done the razoring;

---

3. James I (1566–1625), king of Great Britain and Ireland 1604–25, after having reigned as king of Scotland since 1567, lived in terror of assassination by Catholics, especially after the Gunpowder Plot (1605) and the assassination of King Henry IV of France in 1610.

indeed, he sat so pale and rigid now, that the negro seemed a Nubian sculptor finishing off a white statue-head.

All being over at last, the standard of Spain removed, tumbled up, and tossed back into the flag-locker, the negro's warm breath blowing away any stray hair which might have lodged down his master's neck; collar and cravat readjusted; a speck of lint whisked off the velvet lapel; all this being done; backing off a little space, and pausing with an expression of subdued self-complacency, the servant for a moment surveyed his master, as, in toilet at least, the creature of his own tasteful hands.

Captain Delano playfully complimented him upon his achievement; at the same time congratulating Don Benito.

But neither sweet waters, nor shampooing, nor fidelity, nor sociality, delighted the Spaniard. Seeing him relapsing into forbidding gloom, and still remaining seated, Captain Delano, thinking that his presence was undesired just then, withdrew, on pretense of seeing whether, as he had prophecied, any signs of a breeze were visible.

Walking forward to the mainmast, he stood awhile thinking over the scene, and not without some undefined misgivings, when he heard a noise near the cuddy, and turning, saw the negro, his hand to his cheek. Advancing, Captain Delano perceived that the cheek was bleeding. He was about to ask the cause, when the negro's wailing soliloquy enlightened him.

"Ah, when will master get better from his sickness; only the sour heart that sour sickness breeds made him serve Babo so; cutting Babo with the razor, because, only by accident, Babo had given master one little scratch; and for the first time in so many a day, too. Ah, ah, ah," holding his hand to his face.

Is it possible, thought Captain Delano; was it to wreak in private his Spanish spite against this poor friend of his, that Don Benito, by his sullen manner, impelled me to withdraw? Ah, this slavery breeds ugly passions in man— Poor fellow!

He was about to speak in sympathy to the negro, but with a timid reluctance he now reëntered the cuddy.

Presently master and man came forth; Don Benito leaning on his servant as if nothing had happened.

But a sort of love-quarrel, after all, thought Captain Delano.

He accosted Don Benito, and they slowly walked together. They had gone but a few paces, when the steward—a tall, rajah-looking mulatto, orientally set off with a pagoda turban formed by three or four Madras handkerchiefs wound about his head, tier on tier—approaching with a saalam, announced lunch in the cabin.

On their way thither, the two Captains were preceded by the mulatto, who, turning round as he advanced, with continual smiles and bows, ushered them on, a display of elegance which quite completed the insignificance of the small bare-headed Babo, who, as if not unconscious of inferiority, eyed askance the graceful steward. But in part, Captain Delano imputed his jealous watchfulness to that peculiar feeling which the full-blooded African entertains for the adulterated one. As for the steward, his manner, if not bespeaking much dignity of self-respect, yet evidenced his extreme desire to please; which is doubly meritorious, as at once Christian and Chesterfieldian.[4]

---

4. Philip Stanhope, the fourth earl of Chesterfield (1694–1773), in his letters to his son advocated a worldly code at variance with Jesus' absolute morality.

Captain Delano observed with interest that while the complexion of the mulatto was hybrid, his physiognomy was European; classically so.

"Don Benito," whispered he, "I am glad to see this usher-of the-golden-rod[5] of yours; the sight refutes an ugly remark once made to me by a Barbadoes planter; that when a mulatto has a regular European face, look out for him; he is a devil. But see, your steward here has features more regular than King George's of England; and yet there he nods, and bows, and smiles; a king, indeed—the king of kind hearts and polite fellows. What a pleasant voice he has, too?"

"He has, Señor."

"But, tell me, has he not, so far as you have known him, always proved a good, worthy fellow?" said Captain Delano, pausing, while with a final genuflexion the steward disappeared into the cabin; "come, for the reason just mentioned, I am curious to know."

"Francesco is a good man," a sort of sluggishly responded Don Benito, like a phlegmatic appreciator, who would neither find fault nor flatter.

"Ah, I thought so. For it were strange indeed, and not very creditable to us white-skins, if a little of our blood mixed with the African's, should, far from improving the latter's quality, have the sad effect of pouring vitriolic acid into black broth; improving the hue, perhaps, but not the wholesomeness."

"Doubtless, doubtless, Señor, but"—glancing at Babo—"not to speak of negroes, your planter's remark I have heard applied to the Spanish and Indian intermixtures in our provinces. But I know nothing about the matter," he listlessly added.

And here they entered the cabin.

The lunch was a frugal one. Some of Captain Delano's fresh fish and pumpkins, biscuit and salt beef, the reserved bottle of cider, and the San Dominick's last bottle of Canary.

As they entered, Francesco, with two or three colored aids, was hovering over the table giving the last adjustments. Upon perceiving their master they withdrew, Francesco making a smiling congé, and the Spaniard, without condescending to notice it, fastidiously remarking to his companion that he relished not superfluous attendance.

Without companions, host and guest sat down, like a childless married couple, at opposite ends of the table, Don Benito waving Captain Delano to his place, and, weak as he was, insisting upon that gentleman being seated before himself.

The negro placed a rug under Don Benito's feet, and a cushion behind his back, and then stood behind, not his master's chair, but Captain Delano's. At first, this a little surprised the latter. But it was soon evident that, in taking his position, the black was still true to his master; since by facing him he could the more readily anticipate his slightest want.

"This is an uncommonly intelligent fellow of yours, Don Benito," whispered Captain Delano across the table.

"You say true, Señor."

During the repast, the guest again reverted to parts of Don Benito's story, begging further particulars here and there. He inquired how it was that the scurvy and fever should have committed such wholesale havoc upon the

5. In this English usage, "usher" means an attendant charged with walking ceremoniously before a person of rank; certain ushers were known by the color of the rod or scepter they traditionally carried.

whites, while destroying less than half of the blacks. As if this question reproduced the whole scene of plague before the Spaniard's eyes, miserably
reminding him of his solitude in a cabin where before he had had so many
friends and officers round him, his hand shook, his face became hueless, broken words escaped; but directly the sane memory of the past seemed replaced
by insane terrors of the present. With starting eyes he stared before him at
vacancy. For nothing was to be seen but the hand of his servant pushing the
Canary over towards him. At length a few sips served partially to restore him.
He made random reference to the different constitution of races, enabling one
to offer more resistance to certain maladies than another. The thought was
new to his companion.

Presently Captain Delano, intending to say something to his host concerning the pecuniary part of the business he had undertaken for him, especially—
since he was strictly accountable to his owners—with reference to the new suit
of sails, and other things of that sort; and naturally preferring to conduct such
affairs in private, was desirous that the servant should withdraw; imagining
that Don Benito for a few minutes could dispense with his attendance. He,
however, waited awhile; thinking that, as the conversation proceeded, Don
Benito, without being prompted, would perceive the propriety of the step.

But it was otherwise. At last catching his host's eye, Captain Delano, with
a slight backward gesture of his thumb, whispered, "Don Benito, pardon me,
but there is an interference with the full expression of what I have to say
to you."

Upon this the Spaniard changed countenance; which was imputed to his
resenting the hint, as in some way a reflection upon his servant. After a
moment's pause, he assured his guest that the black's remaining with them
could be of no disservice; because since losing his officers he had made Babo
(whose original office, it now appeared, had been captain of the slaves) not
only his constant attendant and companion, but in all things his confidant.

After this, nothing more could be said; though, indeed, Captain Delano
could hardly avoid some little tinge of irritation upon being left ungratified in
so inconsiderable a wish, by one, too, for whom he intended such solid services. But it is only his querulousness, thought he; and so filling his glass he
proceeded to business.

The price of the sails and other matters was fixed upon. But while this was
being done, the American observed that, though his original offer of assistance
had been hailed with hectic animation, yet now when it was reduced to a
business transaction, indifference and apathy were betrayed. Don Benito, in
fact, appeared to submit to hearing the details more out of regard to common
propriety, than from any impression that weighty benefit to himself and his
voyage was involved.

Soon, his manner became still more reserved. The effort was vain to seek to
draw him into social talk. Gnawed by his splenetic mood, he sat twitching his
beard, while to little purpose the hand of his servant, mute as that on the wall,
slowly pushed over the Canary.

Lunch being over, they sat down on the cushioned transom; the servant
placing a pillow behind his master. The long continuance of the calm had
now affected the atmosphere. Don Benito sighed heavily, as if for breath.

"Why not adjourn to the cuddy," said Captain Delano; "there is more air
there." But the host sat silent and motionless.

Meantime his servant knelt before him, with a large fan of feathers. And Francesco coming in on tiptoes, handed the negro a little cup of aromatic waters, with which at intervals he chafed his master's brow; smoothing the hair along the temples as a nurse does a child's. He spoke no word. He only rested his eye on his master's, as if, amid all Don Benito's distress, a little to refresh his spirit by the silent sight of fidelity.

Presently the ship's bell sounded two o'clock; and through the cabin-windows a slight rippling of the sea was discerned; and from the desired direction.

"There," exclaimed Captain Delano, "I told you so, Don Benito, look!"

He had risen to his feet, speaking in a very animated tone, with a view the more to rouse his companion. But though the crimson curtain of the stern-window near him that moment fluttered against his pale cheek, Don Benito seemed to have even less welcome for the breeze than the calm.

Poor fellow, thought Captain Delano, bitter experience has taught him that one ripple does not make a wind, any more than one swallow a summer. But he is mistaken for once. I will get his ship in for him, and prove it.

Briefly alluding to his weak condition, he urged his host to remain quietly where he was, since he (Captain Delano) would with pleasure take upon himself the responsibility of making the best use of the wind.

Upon gaining the deck, Captain Delano started at the unexpected figure of Atufal, monumentally fixed at the threshold, like one of those sculptured porters of black marble guarding the porches of Egyptian tombs.

But this time the start was, perhaps, purely physical. Atufal's presence, singularly attesting docility even in sullenness, was contrasted with that of the hatchet-polishers, who in patience evinced their industry; while both spectacles showed, that lax as Don Benito's general authority might be, still, whenever he chose to exert it, no man so savage or colossal but must, more or less, bow.

Snatching a trumpet which hung from the bulwarks, with a free step Captain Delano advanced to the forward edge of the poop, issuing his orders in his best Spanish. The few sailors and many negroes, all equally pleased, obediently set about heading the ship towards the harbor.

While giving some directions about setting a lower stu'n'-sail, suddenly Captain Delano heard a voice faithfully repeating his orders. Turning, he saw Babo, now for the time acting, under the pilot, his original part of captain of the slaves. This assistance proved valuable. Tattered sails and warped yards were soon brought into some trim. And no brace or halyard was pulled but to the blithe songs of the inspirited negroes.

Good fellows, thought Captain Delano, a little training would make fine sailors of them. Why see, the very women pull and sing too. These must be some of those Ashantee negresses that make such capital soldiers, I've heard. But who's at the helm. I must have a good hand there.

He went to see.

The San Dominick steered with a cumbrous tiller, with large horizontal pullies attached. At each pully-end stood a subordinate black, and between them, at the tiller-head, the responsible post, a Spanish seaman, whose countenance evinced his due share in the general hopefulness and confidence at the coming of the breeze.

He proved the same man who had behaved with so shame-faced an air on the windlass.

"Ah—it is you, my man," exclaimed Captain Delano—"well, no more sheep's-eyes now;—look straightforward and keep the ship so. Good hand, I trust? And want to get into the harbor, don't you?"

The man assented with an inward chuckle, grasping the tiller-head firmly. Upon this, unperceived by the American, the two blacks eyed the sailor intently.

Finding all right at the helm, the pilot went forward to the forecastle, to see how matters stood there.

The ship now had way enough to breast the current. With the approach of evening, the breeze would be sure to freshen.

Having done all that was needed for the present, Captain Delano, giving his last orders to the sailors, turned aft to report affairs to Don Benito in the cabin; perhaps additionally incited to rejoin him by the hope of snatching a moment's private chat while the servant was engaged upon deck.

From opposite sides, there were, beneath the poop, two approaches to the cabin; one further forward than the other, and consequently communicating with a longer passage. Marking the servant still above, Captain Delano, taking the nighest entrance—the one last named, and at whose porch Atufal still stood—hurried on his way, till, arrived at the cabin threshold, he paused an instant, a little to recover from his eagerness. Then, with the words of his intended business upon his lips, he entered. As he advanced toward the seated Spaniard, he heard another footstep, keeping time with his. From the opposite door, a salver in hand, the servant was likewise advancing.

"Confound the faithful fellow," thought Captain Delano; "what a vexatious coincidence."

Possibly, the vexation might have been something different, were it not for the brisk confidence inspired by the breeze. But even as it was, he felt a slight twinge, from a sudden indefinite association in his mind of Babo with Atufal.

"Don Benito," said he, "I give you joy; the breeze will hold, and will increase. By the way, your tall man and time-piece, Atufal, stands without. By your order, of course?"

Don Benito recoiled, as if at some bland satirical touch, delivered with such adroit garnish of apparent good-breeding as to present no handle for retort.

He is like one flayed alive, thought Captain Delano; where may one touch him without causing a shrink?

The servant moved before his master, adjusting a cushion; recalled to civility, the Spaniard stiffly replied: "You are right. The slave appears where you saw him, according to my command; which is, that if at the given hour I am below, he must take his stand and abide my coming."

"Ah now, pardon me, but that is treating the poor fellow like an ex-king indeed. Ah, Don Benito," smiling, "for all the license you permit in some things, I fear lest, at bottom, you are a bitter hard master."

Again Don Benito shrank; and this time, as the good sailor thought, from a genuine twinge of his conscience.

Again conversation became constrained. In vain Captain Delano called attention to the now perceptible motion of the keel gently cleaving the sea; with lack-lustre eye, Don Benito returned words few and reserved.

By-and-by, the wind having steadily risen, and still blowing right into the harbor, bore the San Dominick swiftly on. Rounding a point of land, the sealer at distance came into open view.

Meantime Captain Delano had again repaired to the deck, remaining there some time. Having at last altered the ship's course, so as to give the reef a wide berth, he returned for a few moments below.

I will cheer up my poor friend, this time, thought he.

"Better and better, Don Benito," he cried as he blithely reëntered; "there will soon be an end to your cares, at least for awhile. For when, after a long, sad voyage, you know, the anchor drops into the haven, all its vast weight seems lifted from the captain's heart. We are getting on famously, Don Benito. My ship is in sight. Look through this side-light here; there she is; all a-taunt-o! The Bachelor's Delight, my good friend. Ah, how this wind braces one up. Come, you must take a cup of coffee with me this evening. My old steward will give you as fine a cup as ever any sultan tasted. What say you, Don Benito, will you?"

At first, the Spaniard glanced feverishly up, casting a longing look towards the sealer, while with mute concern his servant gazed into his face. Suddenly the old ague of coldness returned, and dropping back to his cushions he was silent.

"You do not answer. Come, all day you have been my host; would you have hospitality all on one side?"

"I cannot go," was the response.

"What? it will not fatigue you. The ships will lie together as near as they can, without swinging foul. It will be little more than stepping from deck to deck; which is but as from room to room. Come, come, you must not refuse me."

"I cannot go," decisively and repulsively repeated Don Benito.

Renouncing all but the last appearance of courtesy, with a sort of cadaverous sullenness, and biting his thin nails to the quick, he glanced, almost glared, at his guest; as if impatient that a stranger's presence should interfere with the full indulgence of his morbid hour. Meantime the sound of the parted waters came more and more gurglingly and merrily in at the windows; as reproaching him for his dark spleen; as telling him that, sulk as he might, and go mad with it, nature cared not a jot; since, whose fault was it, pray?

But the foul mood was now at its depth, as the fair wind at its hight.

There was something in the man so far beyond any mere unsociality or sourness previously evinced, that even the forbearing good-nature of his guest could no longer endure it. Wholly at a loss to account for such demeanor, and deeming sickness with eccentricity, however extreme, no adequate excuse, well satisfied, too, that nothing in his own conduct could justify it, Captain Delano's pride began to be roused. Himself became reserved. But all seemed one to the Spaniard. Quitting him, therefore, Captain Delano once more went to the deck.

The ship was now within less than two miles of the sealer. The whale-boat was seen darting over the interval.

To be brief, the two vessels, thanks to the pilot's skill, ere long in neighborly style lay anchored together.

Before returning to his own vessel, Captain Delano had intended communicating to Don Benito the smaller details of the proposed services to be rendered. But, as it was, unwilling anew to subject himself to rebuffs, he resolved, now that he had seen the San Dominick safely moored, immediately to quit her, without further allusion to hospitality or business. Indefinitely postponing his ulterior plans, he would regulate his future actions according to future circumstances. His boat was ready to receive him; but his host still tarried below. Well, thought Captain Delano, if he has little breeding, the more need to show mine. He descended to the cabin to bid a ceremonious, and, it may be, tacitly rebukeful adieu. But to his great satisfaction, Don Benito, as if he began to feel the weight of that treatment with which his slighted guest had, not indecorously, retaliated upon him, now supported by his servant, rose to his feet, and grasping Captain Delano's hand, stood tremulous; too much agitated to speak. But the good augury hence drawn was suddenly dashed, by his resuming all his previous reserve, with augmented gloom, as, with half-averted eyes, he silently reseated himself on his cushions. With a corresponding return of his own chilled feelings, Captain Delano bowed and withdrew.

He was hardly midway in the narrow corridor, dim as a tunnel, leading from the cabin to the stairs, when a sound, as of the tolling for execution in some jail-yard, fell on his ears. It was the echo of the ship's flawed bell, striking the hour, drearily reverberated in this subterranean vault. Instantly, by a fatality not to be withstood, his mind, responsive to the portent, swarmed with superstitious suspicions. He paused. In images far swifter than these sentences, the minutest details of all his former distrusts swept through him.

Hitherto, credulous good-nature had been too ready to furnish excuses for reasonable fears. Why was the Spaniard, so superfluously punctilious at times, now heedless of common propriety in not accompanying to the side his departing guest? Did indisposition forbid? Indisposition had not forbidden more irksome exertion that day. His last equivocal demeanor recurred. He had risen to his feet, grasped his guest's hand, motioned toward his hat; then, in an instant, all was eclipsed in sinister muteness and gloom. Did this imply one brief, repentent relenting at the final moment, from some iniquitous plot, followed by remorseless return to it? His last glance seemed to express a calamitous, yet acquiescent farewell to Captain Delano forever. Why decline the invitation to visit the sealer that evening? Or was the Spaniard less hardened than the Jew, who refrained not from supping at the board of him whom the same night he meant to betray?[6] What imported all those day-long enigmas and contradictions, except they were intended to mystify, preliminary to some stealthy blow? Atufal, the pretended rebel, but punctual shadow, that moment lurked by the threshold without. He seemed a sentry, and more. Who, by his own confession, had stationed him there? Was the negro now lying in wait?

The Spaniard behind—his creature before: to rush from darkness to light was the involuntary choice.

The next moment, with clenched jaw and hand, he passed Atufal, and stood unharmed in the light. As he saw his trim ship lying peacefully at anchor, and almost within ordinary call; as he saw his household boat, with familiar faces in it, patiently rising and falling on the short waves by the San Dominick's side; and then, glancing about the decks where he stood, saw the oakum-pickers still gravely plying their fingers; and heard the low, buzzing whistle and industrious hum of the hatchet-polishers, still bestirring themselves over their endless occupation; and more than all, as he saw the benign aspect of nature, taking her innocent repose in the evening; the screened sun in the quiet camp of the west shining out like the mild light from Abraham's tent,[7]

6. I.e., Judas (Matthew 26).   7. Perhaps a distorted recollection of Genesis 18.1.

as charmed eye and ear took in all these, with the chained figure of the black, clenched jaw and hand relaxed. Once again he smiled at the phantoms which had mocked him, and felt something like a tinge of remorse, that, by harboring them even for a moment, he should, by implication, have betrayed an atheist doubt of the ever-watchful Providence above.

There was a few minutes' delay, while, in obedience to his orders, the boat was being hooked along to the gangway. During this interval, a sort of saddened satisfaction stole over Captain Delano, at thinking of the kindly offices he had that day discharged for a stranger. Ah, thought he, after good actions one's conscience is never ungrateful, however much so the benefited party may be.

Presently, his foot, in the first act of descent into the boat, pressed the first round of the side-ladder, his face presented inward upon the deck. In the same moment, he heard his name courteously sounded; and, to his pleased surprise, saw Don Benito advancing—an unwonted energy in his air, as if, at the last moment, intent upon making amends for his recent discourtesy. With instinctive good feeling, Captain Delano, withdrawing his foot, turned and reciprocally advanced. As he did so, the Spaniard's nervous eagerness increased, but his vital energy failed; so that, the better to support him, the servant, placing his master's hand on his naked shoulder, and gently holding it there, formed himself into a sort of crutch.

When the two captains met, the Spaniard again fervently took the hand of the American, at the same time casting an earnest glance into his eyes, but, as before, too much overcome to speak.

I have done him wrong, self-reproachfully thought Captain Delano; his apparent coldness has deceived me; in no instance has he meant to offend.

Meantime, as if fearful that the continuance of the scene might too much unstring his master, the servant seemed anxious to terminate it. And so, still presenting himself as a crutch, and walking between the two captains, he advanced with them towards the gangway; while still, as if full of kindly contrition, Don Benito would not let go the hand of Captain Delano, but retained it in his, across the black's body.

Soon they were standing by the side, looking over into the boat, whose crew turned up their curious eyes. Waiting a moment for the Spaniard to relinquish his hold, the now embarrassed Captain Delano lifted his foot, to overstep the threshold of the open gangway; but still Don Benito would not let go his hand. And yet, with an agitated tone, he said, "I can go no further; here I must bid you adieu. Adieu, my dear, dear Don Amasa. Go—go!" suddenly tearing his hand loose, "go, and God guard you better than me, my best friend."

Not unaffected, Captain Delano would now have lingered; but catching the meekly admonitory eye of the servant, with a hasty farewell he descended into his boat, followed by the continual adieus of Don Benito, standing rooted in the gangway.

Seating himself in the stern, Captain Delano, making a last salute, ordered the boat shoved off. The crew had their oars on end. The bowsman pushed the boat a sufficient distance for the oars to be lengthwise dropped. The instant that was done, Don Benito sprang over the bulwarks, falling at the feet of Captain Delano; at the same time, calling towards his ship, but in tones so frenzied, that none in the boat could understand him. But, as if not equally obtuse, three sailors, from three different and distant parts of the ship, splashed into the sea, swimming after their captain, as if intent upon his rescue.

The dismayed officer of the boat eagerly asked what this meant. To which, Captain Delano, turning a disdainful smile upon the unaccountable Spaniard, answered that, for his part, he neither knew nor cared; but it seemed as if Don Benito had taken it into his head to produce the impression among his people that the boat wanted to kidnap him. "Or else—give way for your lives," he wildly added, starting at a clattering hubbub in the ship, above which rang the tocsin of the hatchet-polishers; and seizing Don Benito by the throat he added, "this plotting pirate means murder!" Here, in apparent verification of the words, the servant, a dagger in his hand, was seen on the rail overhead, poised in the act of leaping, as if with desperate fidelity to befriend his master to the last; while, seemingly to aid the black, the three white sailors were trying to clamber into the hampered bow. Meantime, the whole host of negroes, as if inflamed at the sight of their jeopardized captain, impended in one sooty avalanche over the bulwarks.

All this, with what preceded, and what followed, occurred with such involutions of rapidity, that past, present, and future seemed one.

Seeing the negro coming, Captain Delano had flung the Spaniard aside, almost in the very act of clutching him, and, by the unconscious recoil, shifting his place, with arms thrown up, so promptly grappled the servant in his descent, that with dagger presented at Captain Delano's heart, the black seemed of purpose to have leaped there as to his mark. But the weapon was wrenched away, and the assailant dashed down into the bottom of the boat, which now, with disentangled oars, began to speed through the sea.

At this juncture, the left hand of Captain Delano, on one side, again clutched the half-reclined Don Benito, heedless that he was in a speechless faint, while his right foot, on the other side, ground the prostrate negro; and his right arm pressed for added speed on the after oar, his eye bent forward, encouraging his men to their utmost.

But here, the officer of the boat, who had at last succeeded in beating off the towing sailors, and was now, with face turned aft, assisting the bowsman at his oar, suddenly called to Captain Delano, to see what the black was about; while a Portuguese oarsman shouted to him to give heed to what the Spaniard was saying.

Glancing down at his feet, Captain Delano saw the freed hand of the servant aiming with a second dagger—a small one, before concealed in his wool—with this he was snakishly writhing up from the boat's bottom, at the heart of his master, his countenance lividly vindictive, expressing the centred purpose of his soul, while the Spaniard, half-choked, was vainly shrinking away, with husky words, incoherent to all but the Portuguese.

That moment, across the long-benighted mind of Captain Delano, a flash of revelation swept, illuminating in unanticipated clearness, his host's whole mysterious demeanor, with every enigmatic event of the day, as well as the entire past voyage of the San Dominick. He smote Babo's hand down, but his own heart smote him harder. With infinite pity he withdrew his hold from Don Benito. Not Captain Delano, but Don Benito, the black, in leaping into the boat, had intended to stab.

Both the black's hands were held, as, glancing up towards the San Dominick, Captain Delano, now with scales dropped from his eyes, saw the negroes, not in misrule, not in tumult, not as if frantically concerned for Don Benito, but with mask torn away, flourishing hatchets and knives, in ferocious piratical revolt. Like delirious black dervishes, the six Ashantees danced on the poop.

Prevented by their foes from springing into the water, the Spanish boys were hurrying up to the topmost spars, while such of the few Spanish sailors, not already in the sea, less alert, were descried, helplessly mixed in, on deck, with the blacks.

Meantime Captain Delano hailed his own vessel, ordering the ports up, and the guns run out. But by this time the cable of the San Dominick had been cut; and the fag-end, in lashing out, whipped away the canvas shroud about the beak, suddenly revealing, as the bleached hull swung round towards the open ocean, death for the figure-head, in a human skeleton; chalky comment on the chalked words below, "Follow your leader."

At the sight, Don Benito, covering his face, wailed out: " 'Tis he, Aranda! my murdered, unburied friend!"

Upon reaching the sealer, calling for ropes, Captain Delano bound the negro, who made no resistance, and had him hoisted to the deck. He would then have assisted the now almost helpless Don Benito up the side; but Don Benito, wan as he was, refused to move, or be moved, until the negro should have been first put below out of view. When, presently assured that it was done, he no more shrank from the ascent.

The boat was immediately dispatched back to pick up the three swimming sailors. Meantime, the guns were in readiness, though, owing to the San Dominick having glided somewhat astern of the sealer, only the aftermost one could be brought to bear. With this, they fired six times; thinking to cripple the fugitive ship by bringing down her spars. But only a few inconsiderable ropes were shot away. Soon the ship was beyond the guns' range, steering broad out of the bay; the blacks thickly clustering round the bowsprit, one moment with taunting cries towards the whites, the next with upthrown gestures hailing the now dusky moors of ocean—cawing crows escaped from the hand of the fowler.

The first impulse was to slip the cables and give chase. But, upon second thoughts, to pursue with whale-boat and yawl seemed more promising.

Upon inquiring of Don Benito what fire arms they had on board the San Dominick, Captain Delano was answered that they had none that could be used; because, in the earlier stages of the mutiny, a cabin-passenger, since dead, had secretly put out of order the locks of what few muskets there were. But with all his remaining strength, Don Benito entreated the American not to give chase, either with ship or boat; for the negroes had already proved themselves such desperadoes, that, in case of a present assault, nothing but a total massacre of the whites could be looked for. But, regarding this warning as coming from one whose spirit had been crushed by misery, the American did not give up his design.

The boats were got ready and armed. Captain Delano ordered his men into them. He was going himself when Don Benito grasped his arm.

"What! have you saved my life, señor, and are you now going to throw away your own?"

The officers also, for reasons connected with their interests and those of the voyage, and a duty owing to the owners, strongly objected against their commander's going. Weighing their remonstrances a moment, Captain Delano felt bound to remain; appointing his chief mate—an athletic and resolute man, who had been a privateer's-man[8]—to head the party. The more to

8. Had served on a privateer—a ship legally commissioned by a government to prey on shipping of other countries.

encourage the sailors, they were told, that the Spanish captain considered his ship good as lost; that she and her cargo, including some gold and silver, were worth more than a thousand doubloons. Take her, and no small part should be theirs. The sailors replied with a shout.

The fugitives had now almost gained an offing. It was nearly night; but the moon was rising. After hard, prolonged pulling, the boats came up on the ship's quarters, at a suitable distance laying upon their oars to discharge their muskets. Having no bullets to return, the negroes sent their yells. But, upon the second volley, Indian-like, they hurtled their hatchets. One took off a sailor's fingers. Another struck the whale-boat's bow, cutting off the rope there, and remaining stuck in the gunwale like a woodman's axe. Snatching it, quivering from its lodgment, the mate hurled it back. The returned gauntlet now stuck in the ship's broken quarter-gallery, and so remained.

The negroes giving too hot a reception, the whites kept a more respectful distance. Hovering now just out of reach of the hurtling hatchets, they, with a view to the close encounter which must soon come, sought to decoy the blacks into entirely disarming themselves of their most murderous weapons in a hand-to-hand fight, by foolishly flinging them, as missiles, short of the mark, into the sea. But ere long perceiving the stratagem, the negroes desisted, though not before many of them had to replace their lost hatchets with hand-spikes; an exchange which, as counted upon, proved in the end favorable to the assailants.

Meantime, with a strong wind, the ship still clove the water; the boats alternately falling behind, and pulling up, to discharge fresh volleys.

The fire was mostly directed towards the stern, since there, chiefly, the negroes, at present, were clustering. But to kill or maim the negroes was not the object. To take them, with the ship, was the object. To do it, the ship must be boarded; which could not be done by boats while she was sailing so fast.

A thought now struck the mate. Observing the Spanish boys still aloft, high as they could get, he called to them to descend to the yards, and cut adrift the sails. It was done. About this time, owing to causes hereafter to be shown, two Spaniards, in the dress of sailors and conspicuously showing themselves, were killed; not by volleys, but by deliberate marksman's shots; while, as it afterwards appeared, by one of the general discharges, Atufal, the black, and the Spaniard at the helm likewise were killed. What now, with the loss of the sails, and loss of leaders, the ship became unmanageable to the negroes.

With creaking masts, she came heavily round to the wind; the prow slowly swinging, into view of the boats, its skeleton gleaming in the horizontal moon-light, and casting a gigantic ribbed shadow upon the water. One extended arm of the ghost seemed beckoning the whites to avenge it.

"Follow your leader!" cried the mate; and, one on each bow, the boats boarded. Sealing-spears and cutlasses crossed hatchets and hand-spikes. Huddled upon the long-boat amidships, the negresses raised a wailing chant, whose chorus was the clash of the steel.

For a time, the attack wavered; the negroes wedging themselves to beat it back; the half-repelled sailors, as yet unable to gain a footing, fighting as troopers in the saddle, one leg sideways flung over the bulwarks, and one without, plying their cutlasses like carters' whips. But in vain. They were almost overborne, when, rallying themselves into a squad as one man, with a huzza, they sprang inboard; where, entangled, they involuntarily separated again. For a few breaths' space, there was a vague, muffled, inner sound, as of submerged sword-fish rushing hither and thither through shoals of black-fish. Soon, in a reunited band, and joined by the Spanish seamen, the whites came to the surface, irresistibly driving the negroes toward the stern. But a barricade of casks and sacks, from side to side, had been thrown up by the mainmast. Here the negroes faced about, and though scorning peace or truce, yet fain would have had respite. But, without pause, overleaping the barrier, the unflagging sailors again closed. Exhausted, the blacks now fought in despair. Their red tongues lolled, wolf-like, from their black mouths. But the pale sailors' teeth were set; not a word was spoken; and, in five minutes more, the ship was won.

Nearly a score of the negroes were killed. Exclusive of those by the balls,[9] many were mangled; their wounds—mostly inflicted by the long-edged seal-ing-spears—resembling those shaven ones of the English at Preston Pans, made by the poled scythes of the Highlanders.[1] On the other side, none were killed, though several were wounded; some severely, including the mate. The surviving negroes werre temporarily secured, and the ship, towed back into the harbor at midnight, once more lay anchored.

Omitting the incidents and arrangements ensuing, suffice it that, after two days spent in refitting, the ships sailed in company for Conception, in Chili, and thence for Lima, in Peru; where, before the vice-regal courts, the whole affair, from the beginning, underwent investigation.

Though, midway on the passage, the ill-fated Spaniard, relaxed from con-straint, showed some signs of regaining health with free-will; yet, agreeably to his own foreboding, shortly before arriving at Lima, he relapsed, finally becoming so reduced as to be carried ashore in arms. Hearing of his story and plight, one of the many religious institutions of the City of Kings opened an hospitable refuge to him, where both physician and priest were his nurses, and a member of the order volunteered to be his one special guardian and consoler, by night and by day.

The following extracts, translated from one of the official Spanish docu-ments, will it is hoped, shed light on the preceding narrative, as well as, in the first place, reveal the true port of departure and true history of the San Domi-nick's voyage, down to the time of her touching at the island of St. Maria.

But, ere the extracts come, it may be well to preface them with a remark.

The document selected, from among many others, for partial translation, contains the deposition of Benito Cereno; the first taken in the case. Some disclosures therein were, at the time, held dubious for both learned and natu-ral reasons. The tribunal inclined to the opinion that the deponent, not undis-turbed in his mind by recent events, raved of some things which could never have happened. But subsequent depositions of the surviving sailors, bearing out the revelations of their captain in several of the strangest particulars, gave credence to the rest. So that the tribunal, in its final decision, rested its capital sentences upon statements which, had they lacked confirmation, it would have deemed it but duty to reject.

————

I, Don Jose de Abos and Padilla, His Majesty's Notary for the Royal Reve-nue, and Register of this Province, and Notary Public of the Holy Crusade of this Bishopric, etc.

9. Those killed by musketballs.
1. At the battle of Preston Pans (in East Lothian, Scot-land) during 1745, Prince Charles Edward, grandson of James II, led Scottish Highlanders armed with scythes fastened to poles to victory over the royal forces.

Do certify and declare, as much as is requisite in law, that, in the criminal cause commenced the twenty-fourth of the month of September, in the year seventeen hundred and ninety-nine, against the negroes of the ship San Dominick, the following declaration before me was made.

Declaration of the first witness, DON BENITO CERENO

The same day, and month, and year, His Honor, Doctor Juan Martinez de Rozas, Councilor of the Royal Audience of this Kingdom, and learned in the law of this Intendency, ordered the captain of the ship San Dominick, Don Benito Cereno, to appear; which he did in his litter, attended by the monk Infelez; of whom he received the oath, which he took by God, our Lord, and a sign of the Cross; under which he promised to tell the truth of whatever he should know and should be asked;—and being interrogated agreeably to the tenor of the act commencing the process, he said, that on the twentieth of May last, he set sail with his ship from the port of Valparaiso, bound to that of Callao; loaded with the produce of the country beside thirty cases of hardware and one hundred and sixty blacks, of both sexes, mostly belonging to Don Alexandro Aranda, gentleman, of the city of Mendoza; that the crew of the ship consisted of thirty-six men, beside the persons who went as passengers; that the negroes were in part as follows:

[Here, in the original, follows a list of some fifty names, descriptions, and ages, compiled from certain recovered documents of Aranda's, and also from recollections of the deponent, from which portions only are extracted.]

One, from about eighteen to nineteen years, named José, and this was the man that waited upon his master, Don Alexandro, and who speaks well the Spanish, having served him four or five years; . . . a mulatto, named Francisco, the cabin steward, of a good person and voice, having sung in the Valparaiso churches, native of the province of Buenos Ayres, aged about thirty-five years. . . . A smart negro, named Dago, who had been for many years a grave-digger among the Spaniards, aged forty-six years. . . . Four old negroes, born in Africa, from sixty to seventy, but sound, calkers by trade, whose names are as follows:—the first was named Muri, and he was killed (as was also his son named Diamelo); the second, Nacta; the third, Yola, likewise killed; the fourth, Ghofan; and six full-grown negroes, aged from thirty to forty-five, all raw, and born among the Ashantees—Matiluqui, Yan, Lecbe, Mapenda, Yambaio, Akim; four of whom were killed; . . . a powerful negro named Atufal, who, being supposed to have been a chief in Africa, his owners set great store by him. . . . And a small negro of Senegal, but some years among the Spaniards, aged about thirty, which negro's name was Babo; . . . that he does not remember the names of the others, but that still expecting the residue of Don Alexandro's papers will be found, will then take due account of them all, and remit to the court; . . . and thirty-nine women and children of all ages.

[The catalogue over, the deposition goes on:]

. . . That all the negroes slept upon deck, as is customary in this navigation, and none wore fetters, because the owner, his friend Aranda, told him that they were all tractable; . . . that on the seventh day after leaving port, at three o'clock in the morning, all the Spaniards being asleep except the two officers on

the watch, who were the boatswain, Juan Robles, and the carpenter, Juan Bautista Gayete, and the helmsman and his boy, the negroes revolted suddenly, wounded dangerously the boatswain and the carpenter, and successively killed eighteen men of those who were sleeping upon deck, some with hand-spikes and hatchets, and others by throwing them alive overboard, after tying them; that of the Spaniards upon deck, they left about seven, as he thinks, alive and tied, to manœuvre the ship, and three or four more who hid themselves, remained also alive. Although in the act of revolt the negroes made themselves masters of the hatchway, six or seven wounded went through it to the cockpit, without any hindrance on their part; that during the act of revolt, the mate and another person, whose name he does not recollect, attempted to come up through the hatchway, but being quickly wounded, were obliged to return to the cabin; that the deponent resolved at break of day to come up the companionway, where the negro Babo was, being the ringleader, and Atufal, who assisted him, and having spoken to them, exhorted them to cease committing such atrocities, asking them, at the same time, what they wanted and intended to do, offering, himself, to obey their commands; that, notwithstanding this, they threw, in his presence, three men, alive and tied, overboard; that they told the deponent to come up, and that they would not kill him; which having done, the negro Babo asked him whether there were in those seas any negro countries where they might be carried, and he answered them. No; that the negro Babo afterwards told him to carry them to Senegal, or to the neighboring islands of St. Nicholas; and he answered, that this was impossible, on account of the great distance, the necessity involved of rounding Cape Horn, the bad condition of the vessel, the want of provisions, sails, and water; but that the negro Babo replied to him he must carry them in any way; that they would do and conform themselves to everything the deponent should require as to eating and drinking; that after a long conference, being absolutely compelled to please them, for they threatened him to kill all the whites if they were not, at all events, carried to Senegal, he told them that what was most wanting for the voyage was water; that they would go near the coast to take it, and thence they would proceed on their course; that the negro Babo agreed to it; and the deponent steered towards the intermediate ports, hoping to meet some Spanish or foreign vessel that would save them; that within ten or eleven days they saw the land, and continued their course by it in the vicinity of Nasca; that the deponent observed that the negroes were now restless and mutinous, because he did not effect the taking in of water, the negro Babo having required, with threats, that it should be done, without fail, the following day; he told him he saw plainly that the coast was steep, and the rivers designated in the maps were not to be found, with other reasons suitable to the circumstances; that the best way would be to go to the island of Santa Maria, where they might water easily, it being a solitary island, as the foreigners did; that the deponent did not go to Pisco, that was near, nor make any other port of the coast, because the negro Babo had intimated to him several times, that he would kill all the whites the very moment he should perceive any city, town, or settlement of any kind on the shores to which they should be carried: that having determined to go to the island of Santa Maria, as the deponent had planned, for the purpose of trying whether, on the passage or near the island itself, they could find any vessel that should favor them, or whether he could escape from it in a boat to the neighboring coast of Arruco; to adopt the necessary means he immediately changed his course, steering for the island;

that the negroes Babo and Atufal held daily conferences, in which they discussed what was necessary for their design of returning to Senegal, whether they were to kill all the Spaniards, and particularly the deponent; that eight days after parting from the coast of Nasca, the deponent being on the watch a little after day-break, and soon after the negroes had their meeting, the negro Babo came to the place where the deponent was, and told him that he had determined to kill his master, Don Alexandro Aranda, both because he and his companions could not otherwise be sure of their liberty, and that, to keep the seamen in subjection, he wanted to prepare a warning of what road they should be made to take did they or any of them oppose him; and that, by means of the death of Don Alexandro, that warning would best be given; but, that what this last meant, the deponent did not at the time comprehend, nor could not, further than that the death of Don Alexandro was intended; and moreover, the negro Babo proposed to the deponent to call the mate Raneds, who was sleeping in the cabin, before the thing was done, for fear, as the deponent understood it, that the mate, who was a good navigator, should be killed with Don Alexandro and the rest; that the deponent, who was the friend, from youth, of Don Alexandro, prayed and conjured, but all was useless; for the negro Babo answered him that the thing could not be prevented, and that all the Spaniards risked their death if they should attempt to frustrate his will in this matter or any other; that, in this conflict, the deponent called the mate, Raneds, who was forced to go apart, and immediately the negro Babo commanded the Ashantee Martinqui and the Ashantee Lecbe to go and commit the murder; that those two went down with hatchets to the berth of Don Alexandro; that, yet half alive and mangled, they dragged him on deck; that they were going to throw him overboard in that state, but the negro Babo stopped them, bidding the murder be completed on the deck before him, which was done, when, by his orders, the body was carried below, forward; that nothing more was seen of it by the deponent for three days; . . . that Don Alonzo Sidonia, an old man, long resident at Valparaiso, and lately appointed to a civil office in Peru, whither he had taken passage, was at the time sleeping in the berth opposite Don Alexandro's; that, awakening at his cries, surprised by them, and at the sight of the negroes with their bloody hatchets in their hands, he threw himself into the sea through a window which was near him, and was drowned, without it being in the power of the deponent to assist or take him up; . . . that, a short time after killing Aranda, they brought upon deck his german-cousin, of middle-age, Don Francisco Masa, of Mendoza, and the young Don Joaquin, Marques de Aramboalaza, then lately from Spain, with his Spanish servant Ponce, and the three young clerks of Aranda, José Morairi, Lorenzo Bargas, and Hermenegildo Gandix, all of Cadiz; that Don Joaquin and Hermenegildo Gandix, the negro Babo for purposes hereafter to appear, preserved alive; but Don Francisco Masa, José Morairi, and Lorenzo Bargas, with Ponce the servant, beside the boatswain, Juan Robles, the boatswain's mates, Manuel Viscaya and Roderigo Hurta, and four of the sailors, the negro Babo ordered to be thrown alive into the sea, although they made no resistance, nor begged for anything else but mercy; that the boatswain, Juan Robles, who knew how to swim, kept the longest above water, making acts of contrition, and, in the last words he uttered, charged this deponent to cause mass to be said for his soul to our Lady of Succor; . . . that, during the three days which followed, the deponent, uncertain what fate had befallen the remains of Don Alexandro, frequently asked the negro Babo where they were, and if still on board, whether they were to be preserved for interment ashore, entreating him so to order it; that the negro Babo answered nothing till the fourth day, when at sunrise, the deponent coming on deck, the negro Babo showed him a skeleton, which had been substituted for the ship's proper figurehead, the image of Christopher Colon, the discoverer of the New World; that the negro Babo asked him whose skeleton that was, and whether, from its whiteness, he should not think it a white's; that, upon his covering his face, the negro Babo, coming close, said words to this effect: "Keep faith with the blacks from here to Senegal, or you shall in spirit, as now in body, follow your leader," pointing to the prow; . . . that the same morning the negro Babo took by succession each Spaniard forward, and asked him whose skeleton that was, and whether, from its whiteness, he should not think it a white's; that each Spaniard covered his face; that then to each the negro Babo repeated the words in the first place said to the deponent; . . . that they (the Spaniards), being then assembled aft, the negro Babo harangued them, saying that he had now done all; that the deponent (as navigator for the negroes) might pursue his course, warning him and all of them that they should, soul and body, go the way of Don Alexandro if he saw them (the Spaniards) speak or plot anything against them (the negroes)—a threat which was repeated every day; that, before the events last mentioned, they had tied the cook to throw him overboard, for it is not known what thing they heard him speak, but finally the negro Babo spared his life, at the request of the deponent; that a few days after, the deponent, endeavoring not to omit any means to preserve the lives of the remaining whites, spoke to the negroes peace and tranquillity, and agreed to draw up a paper, signed by the deponent and the sailors who could write, as also by the negro Babo, for himself and all the blacks, in which the deponent obliged himself to carry them to Senegal, and they not to kill any more, and he formally to make over to them the ship, with the cargo, with which they were for that time satisfied and quieted. . . . But the next day, the more surely to guard against the sailors' escape, the negro Babo commanded all the boats to be destroyed but the long-boat, which was unseaworthy, and another, a cutter in good condition, which, knowing it would yet be wanted for towing the water casks, he had lowered down into the hold.

* * * * * *

[Various particulars of the prolonged and perplexed navigation ensuing here follow, with incidents of a calamitous calm, from which portion one passage is extracted, to wit:]

—That on the fifth day of the calm, all on board suffering much from the heat, and want of water, and five having died in fits, and mad, the negroes became irritable, and for a chance gesture, which they deemed suspicious—though it was harmless—made by the mate, Raneds, to the deponent, in the act of handing a quadrant, they killed him; but that for this they afterwards were sorry, the mate being the only remaining navigator on board, except the deponent.

* * * * *

—That omitting other events, which daily happened, and which can only serve uselessly to recall past misfortunes and conflicts, after seventy-three days' navigation, reckoned from the time they sailed from Nasca, during which they navigated under a scanty allowance of water, and were afflicted with the calms *before mentioned, they at last arrived at the island of Santa Maria, on the seventeenth of the month of August, at about six o'clock in the afternoon, at which hour they cast anchor very near the American ship, Bachelor's Delight, which lay in the same bay, commanded by the generous Captain Amasa Delano; but at six o'clock in the morning, they had already descried the port, and the negroes became uneasy, as soon as at distance they saw the ship, not having expected to see one there; that the negro Babo pacified them, assuring them that no fear need be had; that straightway he ordered the figure on the bow to be covered with canvas, as for repairs, and had the decks a little set in order; that for a time the negro Babo and the negro Atufal conferred; that the negro Atufal was for sailing away, but the negro Babo would not, and, by himself, cast about what to do; that at last he came to the deponent, proposing to him to say and do all that the deponent declares to have said and done to the American captain; . . . . that the negro Babo warned him that if he varied in the least, or uttered any word, or gave any look that should give the least intimation of the past events or present state, he would instantly kill him, with all his companions, showing a dagger, which he carried hid, saying something which, as he understood it, meant that that dagger would be alert as his eye; that the negro Babo then announced the plan to all his companions, which pleased them; that he then, the better to disguise the truth, devised many expedients, in some of them uniting deceit and defense; that of this sort was the device of the six Ashantees before named, who were his bravoes;[2] that them he stationed on the break of the poop, as if to clean certain hatchets (in cases, which were part of the cargo), but in reality to use them, and distribute them at need, and at a given word he told them that, among other devices, was the device of presenting Atufal, his right-hand man, as chained, though in a moment the chains could be dropped; that in every particular he informed the deponent what part he was expected to enact in every device, and what story he was to tell on every occasion, always threatening him with instant death if he varied in the least: that, conscious that many of the negroes would be turbulent, the negro Babo appointed the four aged negroes, who were calkers, to keep what domestic order they could on the decks; that again and again he harangued the Spaniards and his companions, informing them of his intent, and of his devices, and of the invented story that this deponent was to tell, charging them lest any of them varied from that story; that these arrangements were made and matured during the interval of two or three hours, between their first sighting the ship and the arrival on board of Captain Amasa Delano; that this happened about half-past seven o'clock in the morning, Captain Amasa Delano coming in his boat, and all gladly receiving him; that the deponent, as well as he could force himself, acting then the part of principal owner, and a free captain of the ship, told Captain Amasa Delano, when called upon, that he came from Buenos Ayres, bound to Lima, with three hundred negroes; that off Cape Horn, and in a subsequent fever, many negroes had died; that also, by similar casualties, all the sea officers and the greatest part of the crew had died.*

•   •   •   •   •

[And so the deposition goes on, circumstantially recounting the fictitious story dictated to the deponent by Babo, and through the deponent imposed upon Captain Delano; and also recounting the friendly offers of Captain Del-

2. Savage henchmen.

ano, with other things, but all of which is here omitted. After the fictitious story, etc., the deposition proceeds:]

. . . . . .

—that the generous Captain Amasa Delano remained on board all the day, till he left the ship anchored at six o'clock in the evening, deponent speaking to him always of his pretended misfortunes, under the fore-mentioned principles, without having had it in his power to tell a single word, or give him the least hint, that he might know the truth and state of things; because the negro Babo, performing the office of an officious servant with all the appearance of submission of the humble slave, did not leave the deponent one moment; that this was in order to observe the deponent's actions and words, for the negro Babo understands well the Spanish; and besides, there were thereabout some others who were constantly on the watch, and likewise understood the Spanish; . . . that upon one occasion, while deponent was standing on the deck conversing with Amasa Delano, by a secret sign the negro Babo drew him (the deponent) aside, the act appearing as if originating with the deponent; that then, he being drawn aside, the negro Babo proposed to him to gain from Amasa Delano full particulars about his ship, and crew, and arms; that the deponent asked "For what?" that the negro Babo answered he might conceive; that, grieved at the prospect of what might overtake the generous Captain Amasa Delano, the deponent at first refused to ask the desired questions, and used every argument to induce the negro Babo to give up this new design; that the negro Babo showed the point of his dagger; that, after the information had been obtained, the negro Babo again drew him aside, telling him that that very night he (the deponent) would be captain of two ships, instead of one, for that, great part of the American's ship's crew being to be absent fishing, the six Ashantees, without any one else, would easily take it; that at this time he said other things to the same purpose; that no entreaties availed; that, before Amasa Delano's coming on board, no hint had been given touching the capture of the American ship: that to prevent this project the deponent was powerless; . . . —that in some things his memory is confused, he cannot distinctly recall every event; . . . —that as soon as they had cast anchor at six of the clock in the evening, as has before been stated, the American Captain took leave to return to his vessel; that upon a sudden impulse, which the deponent believes to have come from God and his angels, he, after the farewell had been said, followed the generous Captain Amasa Delano as far as the gunwale, where he stayed, under pretense of taking leave, until Amasa Delano should have been seated in his boat; that on shoving off, the deponent sprang from the gunwale into the boat, and fell into it, he knows not how, God guarding him; that—

. . . . . .

[Here, in the original, follows the account of what further happened at the escape, and how the San Dominick was retaken, and of the passage to the coast; including in the recital many expressions of "eternal gratitude" to the "generous Captain Amasa Delano." The deposition then proceeds with recapitulatory remarks, and a partial renumeration of the negroes, making record of their individual part in the past events, with a view to furnishing, according to command of the court, the data whereon to found the criminal sentences to be pronounced. From this portion is the following:]

—That he believes that all the negroes, though not in the first place knowing to the design of revolt, when it was accomplished, approved it. . . . That the negro, José, eighteen years old, and in the personal service of Don Alexandro, was the one who communicated the information to the negro Babo, about the state of things in the cabin, before the revolt; that this is known, because, in the preceding midnight, he used to come from his berth, which was under his master's, in the cabin, to the deck where the ringleader and his associates were, and had secret conversations with the negro Babo, in which he was several times seen by the mate; that, one night, the mate drove him away twice; . . . that this same negro José, was the one who, without being commanded to do so by the negro Babo, as Lecbe and Martinqui were, stabbed his master, Don Alexandro, after he had been dragged half-lifeless to the deck; . . . that the mulatto steward, Francisco, was of the first band of revolters, that he was, in all things, the creature and tool of the negro Babo; that, to make his court, he, just before a repast in the cabin, proposed, to the negro Babo, poisoning a dish for the generous Captain Amasa Delano; this is known and believed, because the negroes have said it; but that the negro Babo, having another design, forbade Francisco; . . . that the Ashantee Lecbe was one of the worst of them; for that, on the day the ship was retaken, he assisted in the defense of her, with a hatchet in each hand, one of which he wounded, in the breast, the chief mate of Amasa Delano, in the first act of boarding; this all knew; that, in sight of the deponent, Lecbe struck, with a hatchet, Don Francisco Masa when, by the negro Babo's orders, he was carrying him to throw him overboard, alive; beside participating in the murder, before mentioned, of Don Alexandro Aranda, and others of the cabin-passengers; that, owing to the fury with which the Ashantees fought in the engagement with the boats, but this Lecbe and Yau survived; that Yau was bad as Lecbe; that Yau was the man who, by Babo's command, willingly prepared the skeleton of Don Alexandro, in a way the negroes afterwards told the deponent, but which he, so long as reason is left him, can never divulge; that Yau and Lecbe were the two who, in a calm by night, riveted the skeleton to the bow; this also the negroes told him; that the negro Babo was he who traced the inscription below it; that the negro Babo was the plotter from first to last; he ordered every murder, and was the helm and keel of the revolt; that Atufal was his lieutenant in all; but Atufal, with his own hand, committed no murder; nor did the negro Babo; . . . that Atufal was shot, being killed in the fight with the boats, ere boarding; . . . that the negresses, of age, were knowing to the revolt and testified themselves satisfied at the death of their master, Don Alexandro; that, had the negroes not restrained them, they would have tortured to death, instead of simply killing, the Spaniards slain by command of the negro Babo; that the negresses used their utmost influence to have the deponent made away with; that, in the various acts of murder, they sang songs and danced— not gaily, but solemnly; and before the engagement with the boats, as well as during the action, they sang melancholy songs to the negroes, and that this melancholy tone was more inflaming than a different one would have been, and was so intended; that all this is believed, because the negroes have said it.
—that of the thirty-six men of the crew exclusive of the passengers, (all of whom are now dead), which the deponent had knowledge of, six only remained alive, with four cabin-boys and ship-boys, not included with the crew; . . . —that the negroes broke an arm of one of the cabin-boys and gave him strokes with hatchets.

[Then follow various random disclosures referring to various periods of time. The following are extracted:]

—That during the presence of Captain Amasa Delano on board, some attempts were made by the sailors, and one by Hermenegildo Gandix, to convey hints to him of the true state of affairs; but that these attempts were ineffectual, owing to fear of incurring death, and furthermore owing to the devices which offered contradictions to the true state of affairs; as well as owing to the generosity and piety of Amasa Delano incapable of sounding such wickedness; . . . that Luys Galgo, a sailor about sixty years of age, and formerly of the king's navy, was one of those who sought to convey tokens to Captain Amasa Delano; but his intent, though undiscovered, being suspected, he was, on a pretense, made to retire out of sight, and at last into the hold, and there was made away with. This the negroes have since said; . . . that one of the ship-boys feeling, from Captain Amasa Delano's presence, some hopes of release, and not having enough prudence, dropped some chance-word respecting his expectations, which being overheard and understood by a slave-boy with whom he was eating at the time, the latter struck him on the head with a knife, inflicting a bad wound, but of which the boy is now healing; that likewise, not long before the ship was brought to anchor, one of the seamen, steering at the time, endangered himself by letting the blacks remark some expression in his countenance, arising from a cause similar to the above; but this sailor, by his heedful after conduct, escaped; . . . that these statements are made to show the court that from the beginning to the end of the revolt, it was impossible for the deponent and his men to act otherwise than they did; . . . —that the third clerk, Hermenegildo Gandix, who before had been forced to live among the seamen, wearing a seaman's habit, and in all respects appearing to be one for the time; he, Gandix, was killed by a musket-ball fired through a mistake from the boats before boarding; having in his fright run up the mizzen-rigging, calling to the boats—"don't board," lest upon their boarding the negroes should kill him; that this inducing the Americans to believe he some way favored the cause of the negroes, they fired two balls at him, so that he fell wounded from the rigging, and was drowned in the sea; . . . —that the young Don Joaquin, Marques de Arambaolaza, like Hermenegildo Gandix, the third clerk, was degraded to the office and appearance of a common seaman; that upon one occasion when Don Joaquin shrank, the negro Babo commanded the Ashantee Lecbe to take tar and heat it, and pour it upon Don Joaquin's hands; . . . —that Don Joaquin was killed owing to another mistake of the Americans, but one impossible to be avoided, as upon the approach of the boats, Don Joaquin, with a hatchet tied edge out and upright to his hand, was made by the negroes to appear on the bulwarks; whereupon, seen with arms in his hands and in a questionable attitude, he was shot for a renegade seaman; . . . —that on the person of Don Joaquin was found secreted a jewel, which, by papers that were discovered, proved to have been meant for the shrine of our Lady of Mercy in Lima; a votive offering, beforehand prepared and guarded, to attest his gratitude, when he should have landed in Peru, his last destination, for the safe conclusion of his entire voyage from Spain; . . . —that the jewel, with the other effects of the late Don Joaquin, is in the custody of the brethren of the Hospital de Sacerdotes, awaiting the disposition of the honorable court; . . . —that, owing to the condition of the deponent, as well as the haste in which the boats departed for the attack, the

Americans were not forewarned that there were, among the apparent crew, a passenger and one of the clerks disguised by the negro Babo; . . . —that, beside the negroes killed in the action, some were killed after the capture and re-anchoring at night, when shackled to the ring-bolts on deck; that these deaths were committed by the sailors, ere they could be prevented. That so soon as informed of it, Captain Amasa Delano used all his authority, and, in particular with his own hand, struck down Martinez Gola, who, having found a razor in the pocket of an old jacket of his, which one of the shackled negroes had on, was aiming it at the negro's throat; that the noble Captain Amasa Delano also wrenched from the hand of Bartholomew Barlo, a dagger secreted at the time of the massacre of the whites, with which he was in the act of stabbing a shackled negro, who, the same day, with another negro, had thrown him down and jumped upon him; . . . —that, for all the events, befalling through so long a time, during which the ship was in the hands of the negro Babo, he cannot here give account; but that, what he had said is the most substantial of what occurs to him at present, and is the truth under the oath which he has taken; which declaration he affirmed and ratified, after hearing it read to him.

He said that he is twenty-nine years of age, and broken in body and mind; that when finally dismissed by the court, he shall not return home to Chili, but betake himself to the monastery on Mount Agonia without; and signed with his honor, and crossed himself, and, for the time, departed as he came, in his litter, with the monk Infelez, to the Hospital de Sacerdotes.

DOCTOR ROZAS.   BENITO CERENO

If the Deposition have served as the key to fit into the lock of the complications which precede it, then, as a vault whose door has been flung back, the San Dominick's hull lies open to-day.

Hitherto the nature of this narrative, besides rendering the intricacies in the beginning unavoidable, has more or less required that many things, instead of being set down in the order of occurrence, should be retrospectively, or irregularly given; this last is the case with the following passages, which will conclude the account:

During the long, mild voyage to Lima, there was, as before hinted, a period during which the sufferer a little recovered his health, or, at least in some degree, his tranquillity. Ere the decided relapse which came, the two captains had many cordial conversations—their fraternal unreserve in singular contrast with former withdrawments.

Again and again, it was repeated, how hard it had been to enact the part forced on the Spaniard by Babo.

"Ah, my dear friend," Don Benito once said, "at those very times when you thought me so morose and ungrateful, nay, when, as you now admit, you half thought me plotting your murder, at those very times my heart was frozen; I could not look at you, thinking of what, both on board this ship and your own, hung, from other hands, over my kind benefactor. And as God lives, Don Amasa, I know not whether desire for my own safety alone could have nerved me to that leap into your boat, had it not been for the thought that, did you, unenlightened, return to your ship, you, my best friend, with all who might be with you, stolen upon, that night, in your hammocks, would never in this world have wakened again. Do but think how you walked this deck, how you sat in this cabin, every inch of ground mined into honey-combs under you. Had I dropped the least hint, made the least advance towards an understanding between us, death, explosive death—yours as mine—would have ended the scene."

"True, true," cried Captain Delano, starting, "you saved my life, Don Benito, more than I yours; saved it, too, against my knowledge and will."

"Nay, my friend," rejoined the Spaniard, courteous even to the point of religion, "God charmed your life, but you saved mine. To think of some things you did—those smilings and chattings, rash pointings and gesturings. For less than these, they slew my mate, Raneds; but you had the Prince of Heaven's safe conduct through all ambuscades."

"Yes, all is owing to Providence, I know; but the temper of my mind that morning was more than commonly pleasant, while the sight of so much suffering, more apparent than real, added to my good nature, compassion, and charity, happily interweaving the three. Had it been otherwise, doubtless, as you hint, some of my interferences might have ended unhappily enough. Besides, those feelings I spoke of enabled me to get the better of momentary distrust, at times when acuteness might have cost me my life, without saving another's. Only at the end did my suspicions get the better of me, and you know how wide of the mark they then proved."

"Wide, indeed," said Don Benito, sadly; "you were with me all day; stood with me, sat with me, talked with me, looked at me, ate with me, drank with me; and yet, your last act was to clutch for a monster, not only an innocent man, but the most pitiable of all men. To such degree may malign machinations and deceptions impose. So far may even the best man err, in judging the conduct of one with the recesses of whose condition he is not acquainted. But you were forced to it; and you were in time undeceived. Would that, in both respects, it was so ever, and with all men."

"You generalize, Don Benito; and mournfully enough. But the past is passed; why moralize upon it? Forget it. See, yon bright sun has forgotten it all, and the blue sea, and the blue sky; these have turned over new leaves."

"Because they have no memory," he dejectedly replied; "because they are not human."

"But these mild trades[3] that now fan your cheek, do they not come with a human-like healing to you? Warm friends, steadfast friends are the trades."

"With their steadfastness they but waft me to my tomb, señor," was the foreboding response.

"You are saved," cried Captain Delano, more and more astonished and pained; "you are saved; what has cast such a shadow upon you?"

"The negro."

There was silence, while the moody man sat, slowly and unconsciously gathering his mantle about him, as if it were a pall.

There was no more conversation that day.

But if the Spaniard's melancholy sometimes ended in muteness upon topics like the above, there were others upon which he never spoke at all; on which, indeed, all his old reserves were piled. Pass over the worst, and, only to elucidate, let an item or two of these be cited. The dress so precise and costly, worn by him on the day whose events have been narrated, had not willingly been

---

3. Trade winds; here, dependable winds blowing from southeast to northwest.

put on. And that silver-mounted sword, apparent symbol of despotic command, was not, indeed, a sword, but the ghost of one. The scabbard, artificially stiffened, was empty.

As for the black—whose brain, not body, had schemed and led the revolt, with the plot—his slight frame, inadequate to that which it held, had at once yielded to the superior muscular strength of his captor, in the boat. Seeing all was over, he uttered no sound, and could not be forced to. His aspect seemed to say, since I cannot do deeds, I will not speak words. Put in irons in the hold, with the rest, he was carried to Lima. During the passage Don Benito did not visit him. Nor then, nor at any time after, would he look at him. Before the tribunal he refused. When pressed by the judges he fainted. On the testimony of the sailors alone rested the legal identity of Babo.

Some months after, dragged to the gibbet at the tail of a mule, the black met his voiceless end. The body was burned to ashes; but for many days, the head, that hive of subtlety, fixed on a pole in the Plaza, met, unabashed, the gaze of the whites; and across the Plaza looked towards St. Bartholomew's church, in whose vaults slept then, as now, the recovered bones of Aranda; and across the Rimac bridge looked towards the monastery, on Mount Agonia without; where, three months after being dismissed by the court, Benito Cereno, borne on the bier, did, indeed, follow his leader.

1855, 1856

The Piazza[1]

"With fairest flowers,
Whilst summer lasts, and I live here, Fidele—"

When I removed into the country, it was to occupy an old-fashioned farmhouse, which had no piazza—a deficiency the more regretted, because not only did I like piazzas, as somehow combining the coziness of in-doors with the freedom of out-doors, and it is so pleasant to inspect your thermometer there, but the country round about was such a picture, that in berry time no boy climbs hill or crosses vale without coming upon easels planted in every nook, and sun-burnt painters painting there. A very paradise of painters. The circle of the stars cut by the circle of the mountains. At least, so looks it from the house; though, once upon the mountains, no circle of them can you see. Had the site been chosen five rods off, this charmed ring would not have been.

The house is old. Seventy years since, from the heart of the Hearth Stone Hills, they quarried the Kaaba, or Holy Stone, to which, each Thanksgiving, the social pilgrims used to come.[2] So long ago, that, in digging for the foundation, the workmen used both spade and axe, fighting the Troglodytes[3] of those subterranean parts—sturdy roots of a sturdy wood, encamped upon what is now a long land-slide of sleeping meadow, sloping away off from my poppy-

1. *The Piazza* was written early in 1856 as an introduction to the five pieces Melville had by then contributed to *Putnam's Monthly Magazine* (*Bartleby*, *Benito Cereno*, *The Lightning-Rod Man*, *The Encantadas*, and *The Bell-Tower*). The text is that of the first printing, in *The Piazza Tales* (1856). The epigraph is from Shakespeare's *Cymbeline* 4.2, Arviragus's lament over Imogen, his disguised sister, whom he thinks dead.

2. The Kaaba, stone building in the court of the Great Mosque at Mecca, contains the Black Stone of Mecca, of meteoric origin but fabled to have been given to Abraham by the Archangel Gabriel. Moslems face the Kaaba while praying. In New England, Thanksgiving was a more important holiday than Christmas well into the 19th century.

3. Brutish cave dwellers.

bed. Of that knit wood, but one survivor stands—an elm, lonely through steadfastness.

Whoever built the house, he builded better than he knew; or else Orion in the zenith flashed down his Damocles' sword[4] to him some starry night, and said, "Build there." For how, otherwise, could it have entered the builder's mind, that, upon the clearing being made, such a purple prospect would be his?—nothing less than Greylock, with all his hills about him, like Charlemagne among his peers.[5]

Now, for a house, so situated in such a country, to have no piazza for the convenience of those who might desire to feast upon the view, and take their time and ease about it, seemed as much of an omission as if a picture-gallery should have no bench; for what but picture-galleries are the marble halls of these same limestone hills?—galleries hung, month after month anew, with pictures ever fading into pictures ever fresh. And beauty is like piety—you cannot run and read it; tranquillity and constancy, with, now-a-days, an easy chair, are needed. For though, of old, when reverence was in vogue, and indolence was not, the devotees of Nature, doubtless, used to stand and adore—just as, in the cathedrals of those ages, the worshipers of a higher Power did—yet, in these times of failing faith and feeble knees, we have the piazza and the pew.

During the first year of my residence, the more leisurely to witness the coronation of Charlemagne (weather permitting, they crown him every sunrise and sunset), I chose me, on the hill-side bank near by, a royal lounge of turf—a green velvet lounge, with long, moss-padded back; while at the head, strangely enough, there grew (but, I suppose, for heraldry) three tufts of blue violets in a field-argent of wild strawberries; and a trellis, with honey-suckle, I set for canopy. Very majestical lounge, indeed. So much so, that here, as with the reclining majesty of Denmark in his orchard, a sly ear-ache invaded me.[6] But, if damps abound at times in Westminster Abbey,[7] because it is so old, why not within this monastery of mountains, which is older?

A piazza must be had.

The house was wide—my fortune narrow; so that, to build a panoramic piazza, one round and round, it could not be—although, indeed, considering the matter by rule and square, the carpenters, in the kindest way, were anxious to gratify my furthest wishes, at I've forgotten how much a foot.

Upon but one of the four sides would prudence grant me what I wanted. Now, which side?

To the east, that long camp of the Hearth Stone Hills, fading far away towards Quito;[8] and every fall, a small white flake of something peering suddenly, of a coolish morning, from the topmost cliff—the season's new-dropped lamb, its earliest fleece; and then the Christmas dawn, draping those dun highlands with red-barred plaids and tartans—goodly sight from your piazza,

---

4. A courtier of Syracuse who was taught the mutability of power by being placed at a royal banquet table while overhead a naked sword was suspended by a single horsehair. In Greek mythology Orion was a mighty hunter turned into a splendid constellation as a giant wearing a lion's skin and wielding a club.
5. In medieval romances Charlemagne (742–814), king of the Franks and emperor of the West, kept about him famous warriors known as the twelve peers or the twelve paladins, including Roland and Oliver. "Hills":

i.e., Mount Saddleback, in northwest Massachusetts, which Melville could in fact see from his study window at Arrowhead and the piazza that he added to the house.
6. Shakespeare's *Hamlet* 1.5.59ff.
7. London church dating in part from 11th century, British national sanctuary and burial place.
8. Capital of Ecuador; here, some imaginary eastern city.

that. Goodly sight; but, to the north is Charlemagne—can't have the Hearth
Stone Hills with Charlemagne.

Well, the south side. Apple-trees are there. Pleasant, of a balmy morning,
in the month of May, to sit and see that orchard, white-budded, as for a bridal;
and, in October, one green arsenal yard; such piles of ruddy shot. Very fine, I
grant; but, to the north is Charlemagne.

The west side, look. An upland pasture, alleying away into a maple wood at
top. Sweet, in opening spring, to trace upon the hill-side, otherwise gray and
bare—to trace, I say, the oldest paths by their streaks of earliest green. Sweet,
indeed, I can't deny; but, to the north is Charlemagne.

So Charlemagne, he carried it. It was not long after 1848; and, somehow,
about that time, all round the world, these kings, they had the casting vote,
and voted for themselves. [9]

No sooner was ground broken, than all the neighborhood, neighbor Dives, [1]
in particular, broke, too—into a laugh. Piazza to the north! Winter piazza!
Wants, of winter midnights, to watch the Aurora Borealis, I suppose; hope
he's laid in good store of Polar muffs and mittens.

That was in the lion month of March. Not forgotten are the blue noses of
the carpenters, and how they scouted at the greenness of the cit, [2] who would
build his sole piazza to the north. But March don't last forever; patience, and
August comes. And then, in the cool elysium of my northern bower, I, Lazarus in Abraham's bosom, cast down the hill a pitying glance on poor old Dives,
tormented in the purgatory of his piazza to the south.

But, even in December, this northern piazza does not repel—nipping cold
and gusty though it be, and the north wind, like any miller, bolting by the
snow, in finest flour—for then, once more, with frosted beard, I pace the
sleety deck, weathering Cape Horn.

In summer, too, Canute-like, [3] sitting here, one is often reminded of the sea.
For not only do long ground-swells roll the slanting grain, and little wavelets of
the grass ripple over upon the low piazza, as their beach, and the blown down
of dandelions is wafted like the spray, and the purple of the mountains is just
the purple of the billows, and a still August noon broods upon the deep meadows, as a calm upon the Line;[4] but the vastness and the lonesomeness are so
oceanic, and the silence and the sameness, too, that the first peep of a strange
house, rising beyond the trees, is for all the world like spying, on the Barbary
coast, an unknown sail.

And this recalls my inland voyage to fairy-land. A true voyage; but, take it
all in all, interesting as if invented.

From the piazza, some uncertain object I had caught, mysteriously snugged
away, to all appearance, in a sort of purpled breast-pocket, high up in a hop-
per-like hollow, or sunken angle, among the northwestern mountains—yet,
whether, really, it was on a mountain-side, or a mountain-top, could not be
determined; because, though, viewed from favorable points, a blue summit,
peering up away behind the rest, will, as it were, talk to you over their heads,

9. The European revolutions of 1848 were followed by
the reestablishment of autocratic regimes.
1. Type of the rich man, from the parable of Dives
and Lazarus, Luke 16.19–31.
2. Citizen.
3. I.e., feeling as if the waves of grass were advancing
on him. Canute (994?–1035), the Danish king of England, returning vainglorious from a visit to the pope,
sat on the strand during rising tide and commanded the
sea not to wet any part of him. After the water rose on
his body, he stood up and acknowledged God to be the
only ruler of the sea.
4. Equator.

and plainly tell you, that, though he (the blue summit) seems among them, he is not of them (God forbid!), and, indeed, would have you know that he considers himself—as, to say truth, he has good right—by several cubits their superior, nevertheless, certain ranges, here and there double-filed, as in platoons, so shoulder and follow up upon one another, with their irregular shapes and heights, that, from the piazza, a nigher and lower mountain will, in most states of the atmosphere, effacingly shade itself away into a higher and further one; that an object, bleak on the former's crest, will, for all that, appear nested in the latter's flank. These mountains, somehow, they play at hide-and-seek, and all before one's eyes.

But, be that as it may, the spot in question was, at all events, so situated as to be only visible, and then but vaguely, under certain witching conditions of light and shadow.

Indeed, for a year or more, I knew not there was such a spot, and might, perhaps, have never known, had it not been for a wizard afternoon in autumn—late in autumn—a mad poet's afternoon; when the turned maple woods in the broad basin below me, having lost their first vermilion tint, dully smoked, like smouldering towns, when flames expire upon their prey; and rumor had it, that this smokiness in the general air was not all Indian summer—which was not used to be so sick a thing, however mild—but, in great part, was blown from far-off forests, for weeks on fire, in Vermont; so that no wonder the sky was ominous as Hecate's cauldron—and two sportsmen, crossing a red stubble buck-wheat field, seemed guilty Macbeth and foreboding Banquo; and the hermit-sun, hutted in an Adullum cave,[5] well towards the south, according to his season, did little else but, by indirect reflection of narrow rays shot down a Simplon pass[6] among the clouds, just steadily paint one small, round, strawberry mole upon the wan cheek of northwestern hills. Signal as a candle. One spot of radiance, where all else was shade.

Fairies there, thought I; some haunted ring where fairies dance.

Time passed; and the following May, after a gentle shower upon the mountains—a little shower islanded in misty seas of sunshine; such a distant shower—and sometimes two, and three, and four of them, all visible together in different parts—as I love to watch from the piazza, instead of thunder storms, as I used to, which wrap old Greylock, like a Sinai, till one thinks swart Moses must be climbing among scathed hemlocks there;[7] after, I say, that gentle shower, I saw a rainbow, resting its further end just where, in autumn, I had marked the mole. Fairies there, thought I; remembering that rainbows bring out the blooms, and that, if one can but get to the rainbow's end, his fortune is made in a bag of gold. Yon rainbow's end, would I were there, thought I. And none the less I wished it, for now first noticing what seemed some sort of glen, or grotto, in the mountain side; at least, whatever it was, viewed through the rainbow's medium, it glowed like the Potosi mine.[8] But a work-a-day neighbor said, no doubt it was but some old barn—an abandoned one, its broadside beaten in, the acclivity its background. But I, though I had never been there, I knew better.

5. 1 Samuel 22.1: "David therefore departed thence, and escaped to the cave Adullam: and when his brethren and all his father's house heard it, they went down thither to him." "Hecate's cauldron": Shakespeare's *Macbeth* 4.1. The reference to Macbeth and Banquo is not to a specific scene.

6. In the Swiss Alps.
7. Exodus 19.18: "And mount Sinai was altogether on a smoke, because the Lord descended upon it in fire: and the smoke thereof ascended as the smoke of a furnace, and the whole mount quaked greatly."
8. Great Bolivian silver mines.

A few days after, a cheery sunrise kindled a golden sparkle in the same spot as before. The sparkle was of that vividness, it seemed as if it could only come from glass. The building, then—if building, after all, it was—could, at least, not be a barn, much less an abandoned one; stale hay ten years musting in it. No; if aught built by mortal, it must be a cottage; perhaps long vacant and dismantled, but this very spring magically fitted up and glazed.

Again, one noon, in the same direction, I marked, over dimmed tops of terraced foliage, a broader gleam, as of a silver buckler, held sunwards over some croucher's head; which gleam, experience in like cases taught, must come from a roof newly shingled. This, to me, made pretty sure the recent occupancy of that far cot[9] in fairy land.

Day after day, now, full of interest in my discovery, what time I could spare from reading the Midsummer's Night Dream, and all about Titania,[1] wishfully I gazed off towards the hills; but in vain. Either troops of shadows, an imperial guard, with slow pace and solemn, defiled along the steeps; or, routed by pursuing light, fled broadcast from east to west—old wars of Lucifer and Michael;[2] or the mountains, though unvexed by these mirrored sham fights in the sky, had an atmosphere otherwise unfavorable for fairy views. I was sorry; the more so, because I had to keep my chamber for some time after—which chamber did not face those hills.

At length, when pretty well again, and sitting out, in the September morning, upon the piazza, and thinking to myself, when, just after a little flock of sheep, the farmer's banded children passed, a-nutting, and said, "How sweet a day"—it was, after all, but what their fathers call a weather-breeder—and, indeed, was become so sensitive through my illness, as that I could not bear to look upon a Chinese creeper of my adoption, and which, to my delight, climbing a post of the piazza, had burst out in starry bloom, but now, if you removed the leaves a little, showed millions of strange, cankerous worms, which, feeding upon those blossoms, so shared their blessed hue, as to make it unblessed evermore—worms, whose germs had doubtless lurked in the very bulb which, so hopefully, I had planted: in this ingrate peevishness of my weary convalescence, was I sitting there; when, suddenly looking off, I saw the golden mountain-window, dazzling like a deep-sea dolphin. Fairies there, thought I, once more; the queen of fairies at her fairy-window; at any rate, some glad mountain-girl; it will do me good, it will cure this weariness to look on her. No more; I'll launch my yawl—ho, cheerly, heart! and push away for fairy-land—for rainbow's end, in fairy-land.

How to get to fairy-land, by what road, I did not know; nor could any one inform me; not even one Edmund Spenser,[3] who had been there—so he wrote me—further than that to reach fairy-land, it must be voyaged to, and with faith. I took the fairy-mountain's bearings, and the first fine day, when strength permitted, got into my yawl—high-pommeled, leather one—cast off the fast, and away I sailed, free voyager as an autumn leaf. Early dawn; and, sallying westward, I sowed the morning before me.

Some miles brought me nigh the hills; but out of present sight of them. I was not lost; for road-side golden-rods, as guide-posts, pointed, I doubted not,

9. Cottage.
1. Queen of the fairies in Shakespeare's *Midsummer Night's Dream.*
2. John Milton's *Paradise Lost,* book 6, describes the

old wars of Satan and the Archangel Michael.
3. English poet (1552?–1599), author of *The Faerie Queene.*

the way to the golden window. Following them, I came to a lone and languid region, where the grass-grown ways were traveled but by drowsy cattle, that, less waked than stirred by day, seemed to walk in sleep. Browse, they did not— the enchanted never eat. At least, so says Don Quixote,[4] that sagest sage that ever lived.

On I went, and gained at last the fairy mountain's base, but saw yet no fairy ring. A pasture rose before me. Letting down five mouldering bars—so moistly green, they seemed fished up from some sunken wreck—a wigged old Aries, long-visaged, and with crumpled horn, came snuffing up; and then, retreating, decorously led on along a milky-way of white-weed, past dim-clustering Pleiades and Hyades,[5] of small forget-me-nots; and would have led me further still his astral path, but for golden flights of yellow-birds—pilots, surely, to the golden window, to one side flying before me, from bush to bush, towards deep woods—which woods themselves were luring—and, somehow, lured, too, by their fence, banning a dark road, which, however dark, led up. I pushed through; when Aries, renouncing me now for some lost soul, wheeled, and went his wiser way. Forbidding and forbidden ground—to him.

A winter wood road, matted all along with winter-green. By the side of pebbly waters—waters the cheerier for their solitude; beneath swaying fir-boughs, petted by no season, but still green in all, on I journeyed—my horse and I; on, by an old saw-mill, bound down and hushed with vines, that his grating voice no more was heard; on, by a deep flume clove through snowy marble, vernal-tinted, where freshet eddies had, on each side, spun out empty chapels in the living rock; on, where Jacks-in-the-pulpit, like their Baptist namesake,[6] preached but to the wilderness; on, where a huge, cross-grain block, fern-bedded, showed where, in forgotten times, man after man had tried to split it, but lost his wedges for his pains—which wedges yet rusted in their holes; on, where, ages past, in step-like ledges of a cascade, skull-hollow pots had been churned out by ceaseless whirling of a flint-stone—ever wearing, but itself unworn; on, by wild rapids pouring into a secret pool, but soothed by circling there awhile, issued forth serenely; on, to less broken ground, and by a little ring, where, truly, fairies must have danced, or else some wheel-tire been heated—for all was bare; still on, and up, and out into a hanging orchard, where maidenly looked down upon me a crescent moon, from morning.

My horse hitched low his head. Red apples rolled before him; Eve's apples; seek-no-furthers. He tasted one, I another; it tasted of the ground. Fairy land not yet, thought I, flinging my bridle to a humped old tree, that crooked out an arm to catch it. For the way now lay where path was none, and none might go but by himself, and only go by daring. Through blackberry brakes that tried to pluck me back, though I but strained towards fruitless growths of mountain-laurel; up slippery steeps to barren heights, where stood none to welcome. Fairy land not yet, thought I, though the morning is here before me.

Foot-sore enough and weary, I gained not then my journey's end, but came ere long to a craggy pass, dipping towards growing regions still beyond. A zigzag road, half overgrown with blueberry bushes, here turned among the cliffs. A rent was in their ragged sides; through it a little track branched off, which, upwards threading that short defile, came breezily out above, to where the mountain-top, part sheltered northward, by a taller brother, sloped gently

---

4. In Cervantes's *Don Quixote*, part I, book 2, chap. 2, the hero tells his squire Sancho Panza that it is the glory of knights-errant to go for months without eating.

5. Constellations.

6. John the Baptist (Matthew 3).

off a space, ere darkly plunging; and here, among fantastic rocks, reposing in a herd, the foot-track wound, half beaten, up to a little, low-storied, grayish cottage, capped, nun-like, with a peaked roof.

On one slope, the roof was deeply weather-stained, and, nigh the turfy eaves-trough, all velvet-napped; no doubt the snail-monks founded mossy priories there. The other slope was newly shingled. On the north side, doorless and windowless, the clap-boards, innocent of paint, were yet green as the north side of lichened pines, or copperless hulls of Japanese junks,[7] becalmed. The whole base, like those of the neighboring rocks, was rimmed about with shaded streaks of richest sod; for, with hearth-stones in fairy land, the natural rock, though housed, preserves to the last, just as in open fields, its fertilizing charm; only, by necessity, working now at a remove, to the sward without. So, at least, says Oberon,[8] grave authority in fairy lore. Though setting Oberon aside, certain it is, that, even in the common world, the soil, close up to farmhouses, as close up to pasture rocks, is, even though untended, ever richer than it is a few rods off—such gentle, nurturing heat is radiated there.

But with this cottage, the shaded streaks were richest in its front and about its entrance, where the ground-sill, and especially the door-sill had, through long eld, quietly settled down.

No fence was seen, no inclosure. Near by—ferns, ferns, ferns; further— woods, woods, woods; beyond—mountains, mountains, mountains; then— sky, sky, sky. Turned out in ærial commons, pasture for the mountain moon. Nature, and but nature, house and all; even a low cross-pile of silver birch, piled openly, to season; up among whose silvery sticks, as through the fencing of some sequestered grave, sprang vagrant raspberry bushes—willful assertors of their right of way.

The foot-track, so dainty narrow, just like a sheep-track, led through long ferns that lodged. Fairy land at last, thought I; Una and her lamb[9] dwell here. Truly, a small abode—mere palanquin, set down on the summit, in a pass between two worlds, participant of neither.

A sultry hour, and I wore a light hat, of yellow sinnet, with white duck trowsers—both relics of my tropic sea-going. Clogged in the muffling ferns, I softly stumbled, staining the knees a sea-green.

Pausing at the threshold, or rather where threshold once had been, I saw, through the open door-way, a lonely girl, sewing at a lonely window. A pale-cheeked girl, and fly-specked window, with wasps about the mended upper panes. I spoke. She shyly started, like some Tahiti girl, secreted for a sacrifice, first catching sight, through palms, of Captain Cook.[1] Recovering, she bade me enter; with her apron brushed off a stool; then silently resumed her own. With thanks I took the stool; but now, for a space, I, too, was mute. This, then, is the fairy-mountain house, and here, the fairy queen sitting at her fairy window.

I went up to it. Downwards, directed by the tunneled pass, as through a leveled telescope, I caught sight of a far-off, soft, azure world. I hardly knew it, though I came from it.

"You must find this view very pleasant," said I, at last.

---

7. Flatbottomed ships with high poop and with sails battened (held out with horizontal strips of flexible wood).
8. King of the fairies in Shakespeare's *Midsummer Night's Dream*, but this lore is not in the play. Melville may be paying a private compliment to Hawthorne,

whose writer in *The Devil in Manuscript* is named Oberon.
9. In Spenser's *The Faerie Queene.*
1. James Cook (1728–1779), British mariner who explored the Pacific.

"Oh, sir," tears starting in her eyes, "the first time I looked out of this window, I said 'never, never shall I weary of this.' "[2]

"And what wearies you of it now?"

"I don't know," while a tear fell; "but it is not the view, it is Marianna."

Some months back, her brother, only seventeen, had come hither, a long way from the other side, to cut wood and burn coal, and she, elder sister, had accompanied him. Long had they been orphans, and now, sole inhabitants of the sole house upon the mountain. No guest came, no traveler passed. The zigzag, perilous road was only used at seasons by the coal wagons. The brother was absent the entire day, sometimes the entire night. When at evening, fagged out, he did come home, he soon left his bench, poor fellow, for his bed; just as one, at last, wearily quits that, too, for still deeper rest. The bench, the bed, the grave.

Silent I stood by the fairy window, while these things were being told.

"Do you know," said she at last, as stealing from her story, "do you know who lives yonder?—I have never been down into that country—away off there, I mean; that house, that marble one," pointing far across the lower landscape; "have you not caught it? there, on the long hill-side: the field before, the woods behind; the white shines out against their blue; don't you mark it? the only house in sight."

I looked; and after a time, to my surprise, recognized, more by its position than its aspect, or Marianna's description, my own abode, glimmering much like this mountain one from the piazza. The mirage haze made it appear less a farm-house than King Charming's palace.

"I have often wondered who lives there; but it must be some happy one; again this morning was I thinking so."

"Some happy one," returned I, starting; "and why do you think that? You judge some rich one lives there?"

"Rich or not, I never thought; but it looks so happy, I can't tell how; and it is so far away. Sometimes I think I do but dream it is there. You should see it in a sunset."

"No doubt the sunset gilds it finely; but not more than the sunrise does this house, perhaps."

"This house? The sun is a good sun, but it never gilds this house. Why should it? This old house is rotting. That makes it so mossy. In the morning, the sun comes in at this old window, to be sure—boarded up, when first we came; a window I can't keep clean, do what I may—and half burns, and nearly blinds me at my sewing, besides setting the flies and wasps astir—such flies and wasps as only lone mountain houses know. See, here is the curtain—this apron—I try to shut it out with then. It fades it, you see. Sun gild this house? not that ever Marianna saw."

"Because when this roof is gilded most, then you stay here within."

"The hottest, weariest hour of day, you mean? Sir, the sun gilds not this roof. It leaked so, brother newly shingled all one side. Did you not see it? The north side, where the sun strikes most on what the rain has wetted. The sun is a good sun; but this roof, it first scorches, and then rots. An old house. They went West, and are long dead, they say, who built it. A mountain house. In

---

2. An echo of Tennyson's poem *Mariana*, in which an isolated girl says "I am aweary, aweary, / I would that I were dead!" In Shakespeare's *Measure for Mea-* *sure* (from which Tennyson's poem takes its motto), Mariana waits in a secluded house for her lover, who has deserted her.

winter no fox could den in it. That chimney-place has been blocked up with snow, just like a hollow stump."

"Yours are strange fancies, Marianna."

"They but reflect the things."

"Then I should have said, 'These are strange things,' rather than, 'Yours are strange fancies.' "

"As you will;" and took up her sewing.

Something in those quiet words, or in that quiet act, it made me mute again; while noting, through the fairy window, a broad shadow stealing on, as cast by some gigantic condor, floating at brooding poise on outstretched wings, I marked how, by its deeper and inclusive dusk, it wiped away into itself all lesser shades of rock or fern.

"You watch the cloud," said Marianna.

"No, a shadow; a cloud's, no doubt—though that I cannot see. How did you know it? Your eyes are on your work."

"It dusked my work. There, now the cloud is gone, Tray comes back."

"How?"

"The dog, the shaggy dog. At noon, he steals off, of himself, to change his shape—returns, and lies down awhile, nigh the door. Don't you see him? His head is turned round at you; though, when you came, he looked before him."

"Your eyes rest but on your work; what do you speak of?"

"By the window, crossing."

"You mean this shaggy shadow—the nigh one? And, yes, now that I mark it, it is not unlike a large, black Newfoundland dog. The invading shadow gone, the invaded one returns. But I do not see what casts it."

"For that, you must go without."

"One of those grassy rocks, no doubt."

"You see his head, his face?"

"The shadow's? You speak as if *you* saw it, and all the time your eyes are on your work."

"Tray looks at you," still without glancing up; "this is his hour; I see him."

"Have you, then, so long sat at this mountain-window, where but clouds and vapors pass, that, to you, shadows are as things, though you speak of them as of phantoms; that, by familiar knowledge, working like a second sight, you can, without looking for them, tell just where they are, though, as having mice-like feet, they creep about, and come and go; that, to you, these lifeless shadows are as living friends, who, though out of sight, are not out of mind, even in their faces—is it so?"

"That way I never thought of it. But the friendliest one, that used to soothe my weariness so much, coolly quivering on the ferns, it was taken from me, never to return, as Tray did just now. The shadow of a birch. The tree was struck by lightning, and brother cut it up. You saw the cross-pile out-doors— the buried root lies under it; but not the shadow. That is flown, and never will come back, nor ever anywhere stir again."

Another cloud here stole along, once more blotting out the dog, and blackening all the mountain; while the stillness was so still, deafness might have forgot itself, or else believed that noiseless shadow spoke.

"Birds, Marianna, singing-birds, I hear none; I hear nothing. Boys and bob-o-links, do they never come a-berrying up here?"

"Birds, I seldom hear; boys, never. The berries mostly ripe and fall—few, but me, the wiser."

"But yellow-birds showed me the way—part way, at least."

"And then flew back. I guess they play about the mountain-side, but don't make the top their home. And no doubt you think that, living so lonesome here, knowing nothing, hearing nothing—little, at least, but sound of thunder and the fall of trees—never reading, seldom speaking, yet ever wakeful, this is what gives me my strange thoughts—for so you call them—this weariness and wakefulness together. Brother, who stands and works in open air, would I could rest like him; but mine is mostly but dull woman's work—sitting, sitting, restless sitting."

"But, do you not go walk at times? These woods are wide."

"And lonesome; lonesome, because so wide. Sometimes, 'tis true, of afternoons, I go a little way; but soon come back again. Better feel lone by hearth, than rock. The shadows hereabouts I know—those in the woods are strangers."

"But the night?"

"Just like the day. Thinking, thinking—a wheel I cannot stop; pure want of sleep it is that turns it."

"I have heard that, for this wakeful weariness, to say one's prayers, and then lay one's head upon a fresh hop pillow——"

"Look!"

Through the fairy window, she pointed down the steep to a small garden patch near by—mere pot of rifled loam, half rounded in by sheltering rocks—where, side by side, some feet apart, nipped and puny, two hop-vines climbed two poles, and, gaining their tip-ends, would have then joined over in an upward clasp, but the baffled shoots, groping awhile in empty air, trailed back whence they sprung.

"You have tried the pillow, then?"

"Yes."

"And prayer?"

"Prayer and pillow."

"Is there no other cure, or charm?"

"Oh, if I could but once get to yonder house, and but look upon whoever the happy being is that lives there! A foolish thought: why do I think it? Is it that I live so lonesome, and know nothing?"

"I, too, know nothing; and, therefore, cannot answer; but, for your sake, Marianna, well could wish that I were that happy one of the happy house you dream you see; for then you would behold him now, and, as you say, this weariness might leave you."

—Enough. Launching my yawl no more for fairy-land, I stick to the piazza. It is my box-royal; and this amphitheatre, my theatre of San Carlo.[3] Yes, the scenery is magical—the illusion so complete. And Madam Meadow Lark, my prima donna, plays her grand engagement here; and, drinking in her sunrise note, which, Memnon-like,[4] seems struck from the golden window, how far from me the weary face behind it.

But, every night, when the curtain falls, truth comes in with darkness. No light shows from the mountain. To and fro I walk the piazza deck, haunted by Marianna's face, and many as real a story.

1856

---

3. The great opera house on the seafront in the Bay of Naples. From outside, Vesuvius is visible.

4. In ancient times the temple of Memnon at Thebes in Upper Egypt emitted sounds at daybreak.

FROM BATTLE-PIECES[1]

The Portent

(1859)[2]

Hanging from the beam,
  Slowly swaying (such the law),
Gaunt the shadow on your green,
  Shenandoah!
The cut is on the crown   5
  (Lo, John Brown),
And the stabs shall heal no more.

Hidden in the cap
  Is the anguish none can draw;
So your future veils its face,   10
  Shenandoah!
But the streaming beard is shown
  (Weird John Brown),
The meteor of the war.

1866

Misgivings

(1860)[1]

When ocean-clouds over inland hills
  Sweep storming in late autumn brown,
And horror the sodden valley fills,
  And the spire falls crashing in the town,
I muse upon my country's ills—   5
The tempest bursting from the waste of Time
On the world's fairest hope linked with man's foulest crime.

Nature's dark side is heeded now—
  (Ah! optimist-cheer disheartened flown)—
A child may read the moody brow   10
  Of yon black mountain lone.
With shouts the torrents down the gorges go,
And storms are formed behind the storm we feel:
The hemlock shakes in the rafter, the oak in the driving keel.

1866

---

1. *Battle-Pieces and Aspects of the War* was published
by the Harpers in 1866, the source of the present texts.
2. John Brown's raid at Harpers Ferry, Virginia, in
October 1859 is naturally seen here as a portent of the
war. Brown was hanged December 2, 1859.

1. The "dolorous winter" of 1860–61, between the
election of Abraham Lincoln and the first shots fired at
Fort Sumter, South Carolina, seemed to Melville a
"Sad arch between contrasted eras" (*Clarel* 4.5.80).

The March into Virginia,

Ending in the First Manassas (July, 1861)[1]

Did all the lets and bars appear
  To every just or larger end,
Whence should come the trust and cheer?
Youth must its ignorant impulse lend—
Age finds place in the rear.   5
  All wars are boyish, and are fought by boys,
The champions and enthusiasts of the state:
  Turbid ardors and vain joys
  Not barrenly abate—
Stimulants to the power mature,   10
  Preparatives of fate.

Who here forecasteth the event?
What heart but spurns at precedent
And warnings of the wise,
Contemned foreclosures of surprise?   15
The banners play, the bugles call,
The air is blue and prodigal.
  No berrying party, pleasure-wooed,
No picnic party in the May,
Ever went less loth than they   20
  Into that leafy neighborhood.
In Bacchic glee they file toward Fate,
Moloch's[2] uninitiate;
Expectancy, and glad surmise
Of battle's unknown mysteries.   25
All they feel is this: 'tis glory,
A rapture sharp, though transitory,
Yet lasting in belaureled story.
So they gayly go to fight,
Chatting left and laughing right.   30

But some who this blithe mood present,
  As on in lightsome files they fare,
Shall die experienced ere three days are spent—
  Perish, enlightened by the vollied glare;
Or shame survive, and, like to adamant,   35
  The throe of Second Manassas[3] share.

1866

---

1. In July 1861, at Manassas, Virginia (a railroad junction some thirty miles from Washington), Confederate forces routed the Union Army.
2. Old Testament heathen god to whom children were burnt in sacrifice (see Leviticus 20.2–5). Melville prob-ably had in mind Milton's *Paradise Lost*, 1.392ff., the description of "*Moloch*, horrid King besmear'd with blood / Of human sacrifice, and parents tears."
3. In August 1862, Robert E. Lee and "Stonewall" Jackson defeated the Union Army once again.

A Utilitarian View of the Monitor's Fight[1]

Plain be the phrase, yet apt the verse,
  More ponderous than nimble;
For since grimed War here laid aside
His Orient pomp, 'twould ill befit
    Overmuch to ply   5
  The rhyme's barbaric cymbal.

Hail to victory without the gaud
  Of glory; zeal that needs no fans
Of banners; plain mechanic power
Plied cogently in War now placed—   10
    Where War belongs—
  Among the trades and artisans.

Yet this was battle, and intense—
  Beyond the strife of fleets heroic;
Deadlier, closer, calm 'mid storm;   15
No passion; all went on by crank,
    Pivot, and screw,
  And calculations of caloric.

Needless to dwell; the story's known.
  The ringing of those plates on plates   20
Still ringeth round the world—
The clangor of that blacksmiths' fray.
    The anvil-din
  Resounds this message from the Fates:

War shall yet be, and to the end;   25
  But war-paint shows the streaks of weather;
War yet shall be, but warriors
Are now but operatives;[2] War's made
    Less grand than Peace,
  And a singe runs through lace and feather.   30

1866

The House-top

A *Night Piece* (July, 1863)[1]

No sleep. The sultriness pervades the air
And binds the brain—a dense oppression, such

---

1. The battle between the Confederate ironclad *Merri-mack* and the Union ironclad *Monitor* on May 9, 1862, at Hampton Roads, Virginia, was inconclusive. Later the same year Confederates scuttled the *Merri-mack* during an evacuation and the *Monitor* sank in a gale. The point of view adopted in the poem is that of a follower of Jeremy Bentham (1748–1832), English philosopher who advocated that behavior be judged by its utility, not its correspondence to any ideal.
2. Factory workers.
1. In July 1863, mobs in New York City, composed largely of Irish immigrants, rioted against the new draft laws, destroying property and attacking free blacks (their economic competitors) in their rage at being required to fight a war for the abolition of slavery.

As tawny tigers feel in matted shades,
Vexing their blood and making apt for ravage.
Beneath the stars the roofy desert spreads   5
Vacant as Libya. All is hushed near by.
Yet fitfully from far breaks a mixed surf
Of muffled sound, the Atheist roar of riot.
Yonder, where parching Sirius[2] set in drought,
Balefully glares red Arson—there—and there.   10
The Town is taken by its rats—ship-rats
And rats of the wharves. All civil charms
And priestly spells which late held hearts in awe—
Fear-bound, subjected to a better sway
Than sway of self; these like a dream dissolve,   15
And man rebounds whole æons back in nature.[3]
Hail to the low dull rumble, dull and dead,
And ponderous drag that shakes the wall.
Wise Draco[4] comes, deep in the midnight roll
Of black artillery; he comes, though late;   20
In code corroborating Calvin's[5] creed
And cynic tyrannies of honest kings;
He comes, nor parlies; and the Town, redeemed,
Gives thanks devout; nor, being thankful, heeds
The grimy slur on the Republic's faith implied,   25
Which holds that Man is naturally good,
And—more—is Nature's Roman, never to be scourged.[6]

1866

FROM JOHN MARR AND OTHER SAILORS[1]

The Maldive Shark

About the Shark, phlegmatical one,
Pale sot of the Maldive sea,[2]
The sleek little pilot-fish, azure and slim,
How alert in attendance be.
From his saw-pit of mouth, from his charnel of maw   5
They have nothing of harm to dread,
But liquidly glide on his ghastly flank
Or before his Gorgonian head;[3]

2. The dog star associated with the miserable "dog days" in which the riots occurred.
3. " 'I dare not write the horrible and inconceivable atrocities committed,' says Froissart, in alluding to the remarkable sedition in France during his time. The like may be hinted of some proceedings of the draft-rioters" [Melville's note]. There were accounts, for instance, of Irish women cutting the genitals off black men hanged on lampposts.
4. The Athenian Draco in 621 B.C. set forth laws that became proverbial for their harshness.
5. John Calvin (1509–1564), French theologian, believed every human being was born guilty of Original

Sin, the consequence of God's curse when Adam and Eve disobeyed him in the Garden of Eden.
6. Acts 22.25: "And as they bound him with thongs, Paul said unto the centurion that stood by, Is it lawful for you to scourge a man that is a Roman, and uncondemned?"
1. In 1888 Melville paid to have John Marr and Other Sailors printed in an edition of twenty-five copies; the texts here are those of the 1888 edition.
2. Part of the Indian Ocean around the Maldive Islands, southwest of the southern tip of India.
3. Capable, like the snake-haired Gorgon's head in Greek mythology, of turning the beholder to stone.

Or lurk in the port of serrated teeth
In white triple tiers of glittering gates,   10
And there find a haven when peril's abroad,
An asylum in jaws of the Fates!

They are friends; and friendly they guide him to prey,
Yet never partake of the treat—
Eyes and brains to the dotard lethargic and dull,   15
Pale ravener of horrible meat.

1888

To Ned[1]

Where is the world we roved, Ned Bunn?
    Hollows thereof lay rich in shade
By voyagers old inviolate thrown
    Ere Paul Pry cruised with Pelf and Trade.[2]
To us old lads some thoughts come home   5
Who roamed a world young lads no more shall roam.

Nor less the satiate year impends
    When, wearying of routine-resorts,
The pleasure-hunter shall break loose,
    Ned, for our Pantheistic ports:—   10
Marquesas and glenned isles that be
Authentic Edens in a Pagan sea.

The charm of scenes untried shall lure,
    And, Ned, a legend urge the flight—
The Typee-truants under stars   15
    Unknown to Shakespeare's *Midsummer-Night*;[3]

And man, if lost to Saturn's Age,
Yet feeling life no Syrian pilgrimage.[4]

But, tell, shall he the tourist find
    Our isles the same in violet-glow   20
Enamoring us what years and years—
    Ah, Ned, what years and years ago!
Well, Adam advances, smart in pace,
But scarce by violets that advance you trace.

---

1. Involved in the makeup of "Ned Bunn" are Melville's shipmate Richard (Toby) Greene, with whom he deserted ship in the Marquesas, and his own part-fictional character of Toby in *Typee.*
2. Outright robbery and commerce. *Paul Pry* is a play by the English dramatist John Poole (1786–1872); for Hawthorne, Melville, and many of their time Paul Pry was a type name for an unscrupulous pryer into others' secrets.

3. Unknown because different constellations are visible in the Marquesas, below the equator.
4. Melville's own *Typee* was in fact, even before his death, beginning to lure tourists to the South Seas, travelers who are not of the fabled Golden Age of Saturn's rule (before the triumph of the Olympian gods) but who also are post-Christian in not seeing life as a painful progress or pilgrimage through the wastelands of this world.

But we, in anchor-watches calm,   25
   The Indian Psyche's languor won,
And, musing, breathed primeval balm
   From Edens ere yet over-run;
Marvelling mild if mortal twice,
Here and hereafter, touch a Paradise.   30

1888

FROM TIMOLEON, ETC.[1]

After the Pleasure Party[2]

LINES TRACED UNDER AN IMAGE OF AMOR THREATENING[3]

Fear me, virgin whosoever
* Taking pride from love exempt,*
*   Fear me, slighted. Never, never*
* Brave me, nor my fury tempt:*
Downy wings, but wroth they beat   5
Tempest even in reason's seat.

   Behind the house the upland falls
With many an odorous tree—
White marbles gleaming through green halls,
Terrace by terrace, down and down,   10
And meets the starlit Mediterranean Sea.

    'Tis Paradise. In such an hour
Some pangs that rend might take release.
Nor less perturbed who keeps this bower
Of balm, nor finds balsamic peace?   15
From whom the passionate words in vent
After long revery's discontent?

    Tired of the homeless deep,
Look how their flight yon hurrying billows urge,
Hitherward but to reap   20
Passive repulse from the iron-bound verge!
Insensate, can they never know
'Tis mad to wreck the impulsion so?

    An art of memory is, they tell:
But to forget! forget the glade   25

1. Melville had this small volume privately printed in 1891 by the Caxton Press in an edition limited to twenty-five copies. It was dedicated to the American artist Elihu Vedder, whom Melville had not met.
2. The punctuation of this poem has proved confusing. After the italicized epigraph, the narrator speaks lines 7–17; then the main speaker takes up, an unmarried woman who is an astronomer. Apparently her long monologue ends with line 110, but she also speaks lines 131–47. The treatment of sexual denial and its consequences is franker and more complex than in any of Melville's American contemporaries except Whitman and Dickinson.
3. Probably the image of Amor (or Cupid) is threatening with the conventional weapons of bow and arrow; as the god warns in the epigraph, his wings are soft but powerful.

Wherein Fate sprung Love's ambuscade,
To flout pale years of cloistral life
And flush me in this sensuous strife.
'Tis Vesta struck with Sappho's smart.[4]
No fable her delirious leap: 30
With more of cause in desperate heart,
Myself could take it—but to sleep!

    Now first I feel, what all may ween,
That soon or late, if faded e'en,
One's sex asserts itself. Desire,   35
The dear desire through love to sway,
Is like the Geysers that aspire—
Through cold obstruction win their fervid way.
But baffled here—to take disdain,
To feel rule's instinct, yet not reign;   40
To dote, to come to this drear shame—
Hence the winged blaze that sweeps my soul
Like prairie fires that spurn control,
Where withering weeds incense the flame.

    And kept I long heaven's watch for this,   45
Contemning love, for this, even this?
O terrace chill in Northern air,
O reaching ranging tube I placed
Against yon skies, and fable chased
Till, fool, I hailed for sister there   50
Starred Cassiopea in Golden Chair.[5]
In dream I throned me, nor I saw
In cell the idiot crowned with straw.

    And yet, ah yet scarce ill I reigned,
Through self-illusion self-sustained,   55
When now—enlightened, undeceived—
What gain I barrenly bereaved!
Than this can be yet lower decline—
Envy and spleen, can these be mine?

    The peasant girl demure that trod   60
Beside our wheels that climbed the way,
And bore along a blossoming rod
That looked the sceptre of May-Day—
On her—to fire this petty hell,
His softened glance how moistly fell!   65
The cheat! on briars her buds were strung;
And wiles peeped forth from mien how meek.

4. Vesta is the Roman goddess of the hearth and household, but here Melville has in mind the requirement that her priestesses, the vestal virgins, be chaste; the virgin goddess is struck with sexual desires such as ruled Sappho (7th century B.C.). Greek lyric poet. A legend has it that she committed suicide by leaping from a cliff into the sea.

5. In Greek mythology Cassiopeia, queen of Ethiopia, boasted that she was more beautiful than the sea nymphs; her being made into a constellation was punishment, because the basket she sat in ludicrously turned upside down at some seasons. Melville follows a version of the story that stresses the beauty of her starry chair.

And wiles peeped forth from mien how meek.
The innocent bare-foot! young, so young!
To girls, strong man's a novice weak.
To tell such beads! And more remain,   70
Sad rosary of belittling pain.

When after lunch and sallies gay
Like the Decameron folk[6] we lay
In sylvan groups; and I——let be!
O, dreams he, can he dream that one   75
Because not roseate feels no sun?
The plain lone bramble thrills with Spring
As much as vines that grapes shall bring.

Me now fair studies charm no more.
Shall great thoughts writ, or high themes sung   80
Damask wan cheeks—unlock his arm
About some radiant ninny flung?
How glad with all my starry lore,
I'd buy the veriest wanton's rose
Would but my bee therein repose.   85

Could I remake me! or set free
This sexless bound in sex, then plunge
Deeper than Sappho, in a lunge
Piercing Pan's[7] paramount mystery!
For, Nature, in no shallow surge   90
Against thee either sex may urge,
Why hast thou made us but in halves—
Co-relatives?[8] This makes us slaves.
If these co-relatives never meet
Self-hood itself seems incomplete.   95
And such the dicing of blind fate
Few matching halves here meet and mate.
What Cosmic jest or Anarch blunder
The human integral clove asunder
And shied the fractions through life's gate?   100

Ye stars that long your votary knew
Rapt in her vigil, see me here!
Whither is gone the spell ye threw
When rose before me Cassiopea?
Usurped on by love's stronger reign—   105
But lo, your very selves do wane:
Light breaks—truth breaks! Silvered no more,
But chilled by dawn that brings the gale
Shivers yon bramble above the vale,
And disillusion opens all the shore.   110

6. Like the bantering sophisticates who take refuge together from the plague and amuse themselves by telling
stories (many of them indelicate) in the *Decameron* of
the Italian writer Giovanni Boccaccio (1313–1375).
7. In Greek mythology, god of woods, fields, and

flocks; he had a human torso but goat's legs, ears, and
horns.
8. Legend in Plato's *Symposium* that humans were
originally round, four-legged beings that split in two
and forever after are seeking to be reunited through sex.

One knows not if Urania[9] yet
The pleasure-party may forget;
Or whether she lived down the strain
Of turbulent heart and rebel brain;
For Amor so resents a slight,   115
And her's had been such haught disdain,
He long may wreak his boyish spite,
And boy-like, little reck the pain.

One knows not, no. But late in Rome
(For queens discrowned a congruous home)   120
Entering Albani's porch she stood
Fixed by an antique pagan stone
Colossal carved.[1] No anchorite seer,
Not Thomas a Kempis,[2] monk austere,
Religious more are in their tone;   125
Yet far, how far from Christian heart
That form august of heathen Art.
Swayed by its influence, long she stood,
Till surged emotion seething down,
She rallied and this mood she won: 130

Languid in frame for me,
To-day by Mary's convent shrine,
Touched by her picture's moving plea
In that poor nerveless hour of mine,
I mused—A wanderer still must grieve.   135
Half I resolved to kneel and believe,
Believe and submit, the veil take on.
But thee, armed Virgin![3] less benign,
Thee now I invoke, thou mightier one.
Helmeted woman—if such term   140
Befit thee, far from strife
Of that which makes the sexual feud
And clogs the aspirant life—
O self-reliant, strong and free,
Thou in whom power and peace unite,   145
Transcender! raise me up to thee,
Raise me and arm me!
                          Fond appeal.
For never passion peace shall bring,
Nor Art inanimate for long
Inspire. Nothing may help or heal   150
While Amor incensed remembers wrong.
Vindictive, not himself he'll spare;
For scope to give his vengeance play
Himself he'll blaspheme and betray.

---

9. In Greek mythology, the muse of astronomy; here
used of the modern woman who speaks the central section of the poem.
1. The Villa Albani, which Melville visited in February 1857.
2. German religious writer (1380–1471).
3. Not the Virgin Mary, but Athena, the Greek goddess of wisdom.

Then for Urania, virgins everywhere,   155
O pray! Example take too, and have care.

1891

Monody[1]

To have known him, to have loved him
    After loneness long;
And then to be estranged in life,
    And neither in the wrong;
And now for death to set his seal—   5
    Ease me, a little ease, my song!

By wintry hills his hermit-mound
    The sheeted snow-drifts drape,
And houseless there the snow-bird flits
    Beneath the fir-trees' crape: 10
Glazed now with ice the cloistral vine
    That hid the shyest grape.

1891

The Bench of Boors[1]

In bed I muse on Tenier's boors,
Embrowned and beery losels[2] all:
    A wakeful brain
    Elaborates pain:
Within low doors the slugs of boors   5
Laze and yawn and doze again.

In dreams they doze, the drowsy boors,
Their hazy hovel warm and small:
    Thought's ampler bound
    But chill is found: 10
Within low doors the basking boors
Snugly hug the ember-mound.

Sleepless, I see the slumberous boors
Their blurred eyes blink, their eyelids fall:
    Thought's eager sight
    Aches—overbright!   15
Within low doors the boozy boors
Cat-naps take in pipe-bowl light.

1891

1. This poem is widely assumed to be a lament for
Hawthorne, and it is commonly asserted, in error, that
Melville inscribed part of the poem in his copy of one
of Hawthorne's books. As far as is known, Melville and
Hawthorne were never "estranged" except by distance
and intervening happenings in their lives. The best reason for thinking the poem is to some extent about Hawthorne is that in *Clarel* (1876) Melville beyond question portrayed aspects of Hawthorne in a shy character
named Vine (see lines 11 and 12 here).
1. Louts, bumpkins. On his manuscript Melville
noted that a "particular picture is here referred to,"
thought to be a painting by David Teniers the Younger
(1610–1690) that Melville saw in April 1857 at Amsterdam (where it is now in the Rijksmuseum).
2. Ne'er-do-wells.

The Enthusiast[1]

*"Though He slay me
yet will I trust in Him."*

Shall hearts that beat no base retreat
    In youth's magnanimous years—
Ignoble hold it, if discreet
    When interest tames to fears;
Shall spirits that worship light   5
    Perfidious deem its sacred glow,
    Recant, and trudge where worldlings go,
Conform and own them right?

Shall Time with creeping influence cold
    Unnerve and cow? the heart   10
Pine for the heartless ones enrolled
    With palterers of the mart?
Shall faith abjure her skies,
    Or pale probation blench her down
    To shrink from Truth so still, so lone   15
Mid loud gregarious lies?

Each burning boat in Cæsar's rear,
    Flames—No return through me!
So put the torch to ties though dear,
    If ties but tempters be.   20
Nor cringe if come the night:
    Walk through the cloud to meet the pall,
    Though light forsake thee, never fall
From fealty to light.

1891

Art

In placid hours well-pleased we dream
Of many a brave unbodied scheme.
But form to lend, pulsed life create,
What unlike things must meet and mate:
A flame to melt—a wind to freeze;   5
Sad patience—joyous energies;
Humility—yet pride and scorn;
Instinct and study; love and hate;
Audacity—reverence. These must mate,
And fuse with Jacob's mystic heart,   10
To wrestle with the angel[2]—Art.

1891

---

1. Dedicated idealist. The epigraph is from Job 13.15.   2. Jacob's wrestling with the angel is in Genesis 32.

Billy Budd, Sailor[1]

(An Inside Narrative)

DEDICATED
TO
JACK CHASE
ENGLISHMAN
Wherever that great heart may now be
Here on Earth or harbored in Paradise
Captain of the Maintop
in the year 1843
in the U.S. Frigate
United States[2]

I

In the time before steamships, or then more frequently than now, a stroller along the docks of any considerable seaport would occasionally have his attention arrested by a group of bronzed mariners, man-of-war's men or merchant sailors in holiday attire, ashore on liberty. In certain instances they would flank, or like a bodyguard quite surround, some superior figure of their own class, moving along with them like Aldebaran[3] among the lesser lights of his constellation. That signal object was the "Handsome Sailor" of the less prosaic time alike of the military and merchant navies. With no perceptible trace of the vainglorious about him, rather with the offhand unaffectedness of natural regality, he seemed to accept the spontaneous homage of his shipmates.

A somewhat remarkable instance recurs to me. In Liverpool, now half a century ago, I saw under the shadow of the great dingy street-wall of Prince's Dock (an obstruction long since removed) a common sailor so intensely black that he must needs have been a native African of the unadulterate blood of Ham[4]—a symmetric figure much above the average height. The two ends of a gay silk handkerchief thrown loose about the neck danced upon the displayed ebony of his chest, in his ears were big hoops of gold, and a Highland bonnet with a tartan band set off his shapely head. It was a hot noon in July; and his face, lustrous with perspiration, beamed with barbaric good humor. In jovial sallies right and left, his white teeth flashing into view, he rollicked along, the center of a company of his shipmates. These were made up of such an assortment of tribes and complexions as would have well fitted them to be marched up by Anacharsis Cloots[5] before the bar of the first French Assembly as Repre-

---

1. Melville may have begun *Billy Budd* while he was still at the New York Custom House, but serious work on it began early in 1886, just after his retirement, and continued until his death in September 1891. It remained unpublished until 1924, when Raymond Weaver transcribed the manuscript for the Constable edition of Melville's works. The manuscript presented many difficulties, and Weaver did not surmount all of them; notably, he printed a discarded passage from a late chapter as a preface, having misread a query of Elizabeth Melville's. The best edition of the story, based on a careful study and fresh transcription of the manuscript, is that of Harrison Hayford and Merton

M. Sealts, Jr., first published in 1962. The Hayford-Sealts text is reprinted here, and the editors' explanatory notes have often been drawn on in the footnotes to this reprinting.
2. In the semiautobiographical *White-Jacket* Melville makes his actual shipmate a major character.
3. Brightest star in the constellation Taurus, the Bull, where it forms the animal's eye.
4. I.e., black, from the belief that God's curse in Genesis 9.25 made Ham and his descendants black.
5. Melville knew of the Prussian-born Baron de Cloots (1755–1794) from Thomas Carlyle's *The French Revolution*, part 2, book 1, chap. 10.

sentatives of the Human Race. At each spontaneous tribute rendered by the wayfarers to this black pagod[6] of a fellow—the tribute of a pause and stare, and less frequently an exclamation—the motley retinue showed that they took that sort of pride in the evoker of it which the Assyrian priests doubtless showed for their grand sculptured Bull when the faithful prostrated themselves.

To return. If in some cases a bit of a nautical Murat[7] in setting forth his person ashore, the Handsome Sailor of the period in question evinced nothing of the dandified Billy-be-Dam, an amusing character all but extinct now, but occasionally to be encountered, and in a form yet more amusing than the original, at the tiller of the boats on the tempestuous Erie Canal or, more likely, vaporing in the groggeries along the towpath.[8] Invariably a proficient in his perilous calling, he was also more or less of a mighty boxer or wrestler. It was strength and beauty. Tales of his prowess were recited. Ashore he was the champion; afloat the spokesman; on every suitable occasion always foremost. Close-reefing topsails in a gale, there he was, astride the weather yardarm-end, foot in the Flemish horse as stirrup, both hands tugging at the earing as at a bridle, in very much the attitude of young Alexander curbing the fiery Bucephalus. A superb figure, tossed up as by the horns of Taurus[9] against the thunderous sky, cheerily hallooing to the strenuous file along the spar.

The moral nature was seldom out of keeping with the physical make. Indeed, except as toned by the former, the comeliness and power, always attractive in masculine conjunction, hardly could have drawn the sort of honest homage the Handsome Sailor in some examples received from his less gifted associates.

Such a cynosure, at least in aspect, and something such too in nature, though with important variations made apparent as the story proceeds, was welkin-eyed[1] Billy Budd—or Baby Budd, as more familiarly, under circumstances hereafter to be given, he at last came to be called—aged twenty-one, a foretopman of the British fleet toward the close of the last decade of the eighteenth century. It was not very long prior to the time of the narration that follows that he had entered the King's service, having been impressed on the Narrow Seas from a homeward-bound English merchantman into a seventy-four outward bound, H.M.S. *Bellipotent*;[2] which ship, as was not unusual in those hurried days, having been obliged to put to sea short of her proper complement of men. Plump upon Billy at first sight in the gangway the boarding officer, Lieutenant Ratcliffe, pounced, even before the merchantman's crew was formally mustered on the quarter-deck for his deliberate inspection. And him only he elected. For whether it was because the other men when ranged before him showed to ill advantage after Billy, or whether he had some scruples in view of the merchantman's being rather short-handed, however it might be, the officer contented himself with his first spontaneous choice. To the surprise of the ship's company, though much to the lieutenant's satisfaction, Billy made no demur. But, indeed, any demur would have been as idle as the protest of a goldfinch popped into a cage.

6. An idol.
7. I.e., a dandy, like Joachim Murat (1767?–1815), whom Napoleon made king of Naples.
8. A joke, there being little danger from tempests on the canal.
9. Alexander the Great of Greece (356–323 B.C.) tamed the fierce horse Bucephalus ("bull-head"), thereby fulfilling the prophecy of an oracle. The horns of Taurus are in the constellation.
1. Blue, like the heavens.
2. I.e., powerful in war; through most of the composition the name of the ship was the *Indomitable* but at last Melville decided on *Bellipotent*. "Impressed": i.e., taken into naval service by force. "Narrow Seas": the English Channel and St. George's Channel. "Seventy-four": the number of guns on the ship.

Noting this uncomplaining acquiescence, all but cheerful, one might say, the shipmaster[3] turned a surprised glance of silent reproach at the sailor. The shipmaster was one of those worthy mortals found in every vocation, even the humbler ones—the sort of person whom everybody agrees in calling "a respectable man." And—nor so strange to report as it may appear to be—though a ploughman of the troubled waters, lifelong contending with the intractable elements, there was nothing this honest soul at heart loved better than simple peace and quiet. For the rest, he was fifty or thereabouts, a little inclined to corpulence, a prepossessing face, unwhiskered, and of an agreeable color—a rather full face, humanely intelligent in expression. On a fair day with a fair wind and all going well, a certain musical chime in his voice seemed to be the veritable unobstructed outcome of the innermost man. He had much prudence, much conscientiousness, and there were occasions when these virtues were the cause of overmuch disquietude in him. On a passage, so long as his craft was in any proximity to land, no sleep for Captain Graveling. He took to heart those serious responsibilities not so heavily borne by some shipmasters.

Now while Billy Budd was down in the forecastle getting his kit together, the *Bellipotent*'s lieutenant, burly and bluff, nowise disconcerted by Captain Graveling's omitting to proffer the customary hospitalities on an occasion so unwelcome to him, an omission simply caused by preoccupation of thought, unceremoniously invited himself into the cabin, and also to a flask from the spirit locker, a receptacle which his experienced eye instantly discovered. In fact he was one of those sea dogs in whom all the hardship and peril of naval life in the great prolonged wars of his time never impaired the natural instinct for sensuous enjoyment. His duty he always faithfully did; but duty is sometimes a dry obligation, and he was for irrigating its aridity, whensoever possible, with a fertilizing decoction of strong waters. For the cabin's proprietor there was nothing left but to play the part of the enforced host with whatever grace and alacrity were practicable. As necessary adjuncts to the flask, he silently placed tumbler and water jug before the irrepressible guest. But excusing himself from partaking just then, he dismally watched the unembarrassed officer deliberately diluting his grog a little, then tossing it off in three swallows, pushing the empty tumbler away, yet not so far as to be beyond easy reach, at the same time settling himself in his seat and smacking his lips with high satisfaction, looking straight at the host.

These proceedings over, the master broke the silence; and there lurked a rueful reproach in the tone of his voice: "Lieutenant, you are going to take my best man from me, the jewel of 'em."

"Yes, I know," rejoined the other, immediately drawing back the tumbler preliminary to a replenishing. "Yes, I know. Sorry."

"Beg pardon, but you don't understand, Lieutenant. See here, now. Before I shipped that young fellow, my forecastle was a rat-pit of quarrels. It was black times, I tell you, aboard the *Rights* here. I was worried to that degree my pipe had no comfort for me. But Billy came; and it was like a Catholic priest striking peace in an Irish shindy.[4] Not that he preached to them or said or did anything in particular; but a virtue went out of him, sugaring the sour ones. They took to him like hornets to treacle; all but the buffer of the gang, the big shaggy chap with the fire-red whiskers. He indeed, out of envy, perhaps, of the new-comer, and thinking such a "sweet and pleasant fellow," as he mockingly designated him to the others, could hardly have the spirit of a gamecock, must needs bestir himself in trying to get up an ugly row with him. Billy forebore with him and reasoned with him in a pleasant way—he is something like myself, Lieutenant, to whom aught like a quarrel is hateful—but nothing served. So, in the second dogwatch one day, the Red Whiskers in presence of the others, under pretense of showing Billy just whence a sirloin steak was cut—for the fellow had once been a butcher—insultingly gave him a dig under the ribs. Quick as lightning Billy let fly his arm. I dare say he never meant to do quite as much as he did, but anyhow he gave the burly fool a terrible drubbing. It took about half a minute, I should think. And, lord bless you, the lubber was astonished at the celerity. And will you believe it, Lieutenant, the Red Whiskers now really loves Billy—loves him, or is the biggest hypocrite that ever I heard of. But they all love him. Some of 'em do his washing, darn his old trousers for him; the carpenter is at odd times making a pretty little chest of drawers for him. Anybody will do anything for Billy Budd; and it's the happy family here. But now, Lieutenant, if that young fellow goes—I know how it will be aboard the *Rights*. Not again very soon shall I, coming up from dinner, lean over the capstan smoking a quiet pipe—no, not very soon again, I think. Ay, Lieutenant, you are going to take away the jewel of 'em; you are going to take away my peacemaker!" And with that the good soul had really some ado in checking a rising sob.

"Well," said the lieutenant, who had listened with amused interest to all this and now was waxing merry with his tipple; "well, blessed are the peacemakers, especially the fighting peacemakers. And such are the seventy-four beauties some of which you see poking their noses out of the portholes of yonder warship lying to for me," pointing through the cabin window at the *Bellipotent*. "But courage! Don't look so downhearted, man. Why, I pledge you in advance the royal approbation. Rest assured that His Majesty will be delighted to know that in a time when his hardtack is not sought for by sailors with such avidity as should be, a time also when some shipmasters privily resent the borrowing from them a tar or two for the service; His Majesty, I say, will be delighted to learn that *one* shipmaster at least cheerfully surrenders to the King the flower of his flock, a sailor who with equal loyalty makes no dissent.—But where's my beauty? Ah," looking through the cabin's open door "here he comes; and, by Jove, lugging along his chest—Apollo with his portmanteau!—My man," stepping out to him, "you can't take that big box aboard a warship. The boxes there are mostly shot boxes. Put your duds in a bag, lad. Boot and saddle for the cavalryman, bag and hammock for the man-of-war's man."

The transfer from chest to bag was made. And, after seeing his man into the cutter and then following him down, the lieutenant pushed off from the *Rights-of-Man*. That was the merchant ship's name, though by her master and crew abbreviated in sailor fashion into the *Rights*. The hardheaded Dundee owner was a staunch admirer of Thomas Paine, whose book in rejoinder to Burke's arraignment of the French Revolution had then been published for some time and had gone everywhere.[5] In christening his vessel after the title

---

5. *The Rights of Man* (1791), by the English-born American Thomas Paine (1737–1809) was a rejoinder to *Reflections on the Revolution in France* (1790) by the English statesman Edmund Burke (1729–1797). Burke's book made a classic case for the priority of social institutions, Paine's book for the primacy of natural human rights.

of Paine's volume the man of Dundee was something like his contemporary shipowner, Stephen Girard of Philadelphia, whose sympathies, alike with his native land and its liberal philosophers, he evinced by naming his ships after Voltaire, Diderot,[6] and so forth.

But now, when the boat swept under the merchantman's stern, and officer and oarsmen were noting—some bitterly and others with a grin—the name emblazoned there; just then it was that the new recruit jumped up from the bow where the coxswain[7] had directed him to sit, and waving hat to his silent shipmates sorrowfully looking over at him from the taffrail, bade the lads a genial good-bye. Then, making a salutation as to the ship herself, "And good-bye to you too, old *Rights-of-Man*."

"Down, sir!" roared the lieutenant, instantly assuming all the rigor of his rank, though with difficulty repressing a smile.

To be sure, Billy's action was a terrible breach of naval decorum. But in that decorum he had never been instructed; in consideration of which the lieutenant would hardly have been so energetic in reproof but for the conclud-ing farewell to the ship. This he rather took as meant to convey a covert sally on the new recruit's part, a sly slur at impressment in general, and that of himself in especial. And yet, more likely, if satire it was in effect, it was hardly so by intention, for Billy, though happily endowed with the gaiety of high health, youth, and a free heart, was yet by no means of a satirical turn. The will to it and the sinister dexterity[8] were alike wanting. To deal in double meanings and insinuations of any sort was quite foreign to his nature.

As to his enforced enlistment, that he seemed to take pretty much as he was wont to take any vicissitude of weather. Like the animals, though no philoso-pher, he was, without knowing it, practically a fatalist. And it may be that he rather liked this adventurous turn in his affairs, which promised an opening into novel scenes and martial excitements.

Aboard the *Bellipotent* our merchant sailor was forthwith rated as an able seaman and assigned to the starboard watch of the foretop.[9] He was soon at home in the service, not at all disliked for his unpretentious good looks and a sort of genial happy-go-lucky air. No merrier man in his mess:[1] in marked contrast to certain other individuals included like himself among the impressed portion of the ship's company; for these when not actively employed were sometimes, and more particularly in the last dogwatch[2] when the drawing near of twilight induced revery, apt to fall into a saddish mood which in some partook of sulleness. But they were not so young as our foretopman, and no few of them must have known a hearth of some sort, others may have had wives and children left, too probably, in uncertain circumstances, and hardly any but must have had acknowledged kith and kin, while for Billy, as will shortly be seen, his entire family was practically invested in himself.

2

Though our new-made foretopman was well received in the top and on the gun decks, hardly here was he that cynosure he had previously been among

---

6. Denis Diderot (1713–1784). Voltaire (1694–1778).
7. Steersman of the boat.
8. Ironic play on the Latin roots of the words: "sinis-ter" meaning having to do with the left hand and "dex-

ter" meaning having to do with the right hand.
9. Platform at the head of the foremast.
1. Group of sailors assigned to eat together.
2. From 6 to 8 P.M.

those minor ship's companies of the merchant marine, with which companies only had he hitherto consorted.

He was young; and despite his all but fully developed frame, in aspect looked even younger than he really was, owing to a lingering adolescent expression in the as yet smooth face all but feminine in purity of natural complexion but where, thanks to his seagoing, the lily was quite suppressed and the rose had some ado visibly to flush through the tan.

To one essentially such a novice in the complexities of factitious life, the abrupt transition from his former and simpler sphere to the ampler and more knowing world of a great warship; this might well have abashed him had there been any conceit or vanity in his composition. Among her miscellaneous multitude, the *Bellipotent* mustered several individuals who however inferior in grade were of no common natural stamp, sailors more signally susceptive of that air which continuous martial discipline and repeated presence in battle can in some degree impart even to the average man. As the Handsome Sailor, Billy Budd's position aboard the seventy-four was something analogous to that of a rustic beauty transplanted from the provinces and brought into competition with the highborn dames of the court. But this change of circumstances he scarce noted. As little did he observe that something about him provoked an ambiguous smile in one or two harder faces among the bluejackets. Nor less unaware was he of the peculiar favorable effect his person and demeanor had upon the more intelligent gentlemen of the quarter-deck. Nor could this well have been otherwise. Cast in a mold peculiar to the finest physical examples of those Englishmen in whom the Saxon strain would seem not at all to partake of any Norman or other admixture, he showed in face that humane look of reposeful good nature which the Greek sculptor in some instances gave to his heroic strong man, Hercules. But this again was subtly modified by another and pervasive quality. The ear, small and shapely, the arch of the foot, the curve in mouth and nostril, even the indurated hand dyed to the orange-tawny of the toucan's bill, a hand telling alike of the halyards and tar bucket; but, above all, something in the mobile expression, and every chance attitude and movement, something suggestive of a mother eminently favored by Love and the Graces; all this strangely indicated a lineage in direct contradiction to his lot. The mysteriousness here became less mysterious through a matter of fact elicited when Billy at the capstan was being formally mustered into the service. Asked by the officer, a small, brisk little gentleman as it chanced, among other questions, his place of birth, he replied, "Please, sir, I don't know."

"Don't know where you were born? Who was your father?"

"God knows, sir."

Struck by the straightforward simplicity of these replies, the officer next asked, "Do you know anything about your beginning?"

"No, sir. But I have heard that I was found in a pretty silk-lined basket hanging one morning from the knocker of a good man's door in Bristol."[3]

"*Found*, say you? Well," throwing back his head and looking up and down the new recruit; "well, it turns out to have been a pretty good find. Hope they'll find some more like you, my man; the fleet sadly needs them."

Yes, Billy Budd was a foundling, a presumable by-blow, and, evidently, no ignoble one. Noble descent was as evident in him as in a blood horse.

---

3. Seaport in the Bristol Channel in southwest England.

For the rest, with little or no sharpness of faculty or any trace of the wisdom of the serpent, nor yet quite a dove, he possessed that kind and degree of intelligence going along with the unconventional rectitude of a sound human creature, one to whom not yet has been proffered the questionable apple of knowledge. He was illiterate; he could not read, but he could sing, and like the illiterate nightingale was sometimes the composer of his own song.

Of self-consciousness he seemed to have little or none, or about as much as we may reasonably impute to a dog of Saint Bernard's breed.

Habitually living with the elements and knowing little more of the land than as a beach, or, rather, that portion of the terraqueous globe providentially set apart for dance-houses, doxies,[4] and tapsters, in short what sailors call a "fiddler's green," his simple nature remained unsophisticated by those moral obliquities which are not in every case incompatible with that manufacturable thing known as respectability. But are sailors, frequenters of fiddlers' greens, without vices? No; but less often than with landsmen do their vices, so called, partake of crookedness of heart, seeming less to proceed from viciousness than exuberance of vitality after long constraint: frank manifestations in accordance with natural law. By his original constitution aided by the co-operating influences of his lot, Billy in many respects was little more than a sort of upright barbarian, much such perhaps as Adam presumably might have been ere the urbane Serpent wriggled himself into his company.

And here be it submitted that apparently going to corroborate the doctrine of man's Fall, a doctrine now popularly ignored, it is observable that where certain virtues pristine and unadulterate peculiarly characterize anybody in the external uniform of civilization, they will upon scrutiny seem not to be derived from custom or convention, but rather to be out of keeping with these, as if indeed exceptionally transmitted from a period prior to Cain's city[5] and citified man. The character marked by such qualities has to an unvitiated taste an untampered-with flavor like that of berries, while the man thoroughly civilized, even in a fair specimen of the breed, has to the same moral palate a questionable smack as of a compounded wine. To any stray inheritor of these primitive qualities found, like Caspar Hauser,[6] wandering dazed in any Christian capital of our time, the good-natured poet's famous invocation, near two thousand years ago, of the good rustic out of his latitude in the Rome of the Caesars, still appropriately holds:

> Honest and poor, faithful in word and thought,
> What hath thee, Fabian, to the city brought?[7]

Though our Handsome Sailor had as much of masculine beauty as one can expect anywhere to see; nevertheless, like the beautiful woman in one of Hawthorne's minor tales,[8] there was just one thing amiss in him. No visible blemish indeed, as with the lady; no, but an occasional liability to a vocal defect. Though in the hour of elemental uproar or peril he was everything that a sailor should be, yet under sudden provocation of strong heart-feeling his voice, otherwise singularly musical, as if expressive of the harmony within, was apt to develop an organic hesitancy, in fact more or less of a stutter or

---

4. Whores.
5. Genesis 4.17.
6. Mysterious child (1812?–1833) who was found in Nuremberg in 1828 and claimed to have been kept in a hole; five years later he was given a mortal wound,
perhaps by his former captor.
7. The Roman poet Martial (1st century A.D.), *Epigrams* 1.4.1–2.
8. *The Birthmark.* "Minor": shorter.

even worse. In this particular Billy was a striking instance that the arch inter-
ferer, the envious marplot of Eden,[9] still has more or less to do with every
human consignment to this planet of Earth. In every case, one way or another
he is sure to slip in his little card, as much as to remind us—I too have a
hand here.

The avowal of such an imperfection in the Handsome Sailor should be
evidence not alone that he is not presented as a conventional hero, but also
that the story in which he is the main figure is no romance.

3

At the time of Billy Budd's arbitrary enlistment into the *Bellipotent* that ship
was on her way to join the Mediterranean fleet. No long time elapsed before
the junction was effected. As one of that fleet the seventy-four participated in
its movements, though at times on account of her superior sailing qualities, in
the absence of frigates, dispatched on separate duty as a scout and at times on
less temporary service. But with all this the story has little concernment,
restricted as it is to the inner life of one particular ship and the career of an
individual sailor.

It was the summer of 1797. In the April of that year had occurred the
commotion at Spithead followed in May by a second and yet more serious
outbreak in the fleet at the Nore.[1] The latter is known, and without exaggeration in the epithet, as "the Great Mutiny." It was indeed a demonstration more
menacing to England than the contemporary manifestoes and conquering and
proselyting armies of the French Directory.[2] To the British Empire the Nore
Mutiny was what a strike in the fire brigade would be to London threatened
by general arson. In a crisis when the kingdom might well have anticipated
the famous signal that some years later published along the naval line of battle
what it was that upon occasion England expected of Englishmen;[3] *that* was
the time when at the mastheads of the three-deckers and seventy-fours moored
in her own roadstead[4]—a fleet the right arm of a Power then all but the sole
free conservative one of the Old World—the bluejackets, to be numbered by
thousands, ran up with huzzas the British colors with the union and cross
wiped out; by that cancellation transmuting the flag of founded law and freedom defined, into the enemy's red meteor of unbridled and unbounded revolt.
Reasonable discontent growing out of practical grievances in the fleet had been
ignited into irrational combustion as by live cinders blown across the Channel
from France in flames.[5]

The event converted into irony for a time those spirited strains of Dibdin[6]—
as a song-writer no mean auxiliary to the English government at that European
conjuncture—strains celebrating, among other things, the patriotic devotion
of the British tar: "And as for my life, 'tis the King's!"

Such an episode in the Island's grand naval story her naval historians naturally abridge, one of them (William James)[7] candidly acknowledging that fain

---

9. Satan.
1. At the mouth of the Thames. Spithead is off the
south of England, between Portsmouth and the Isle of
Wight.
2. Body of five which held executive power in France
1795–99.
3. Lord Nelson's signal to his fleet at the Battle of Trafalgar (1805): "England expects that every man will do

his duty."
4. Protected anchorage.
5. Especially during the Reign of Terror (1793–94)
and its aftermath.
6. Charles Dibdin (1745–1814), English playwright
and songwriter.
7. British historian (d. 1827), author of *Naval History
of Great Britain*.

would he pass it over did not "impartiality forbid fastidiousness." And yet his mention is less a narration than a reference, having to do hardly at all with details. Nor are these readily to be found in the libraries. Like some other events in every age befalling states everywhere, including America, the Great Mutiny was of such character that national pride along with views of policy would fain shade it off into the historical background. Such events cannot be ignored, but there is a considerate way of historically treating them. If a well-constituted individual refrains from blazoning aught amiss or calamitous in his family, a nation in the like circumstance may without reproach be equally discreet.

Though after parleyings between government and the ring-leaders, and concessions by the former as to some glaring abuses, the first uprising—that at Spithead—with difficulty was put down, or matters for the time pacified; yet at the Nore the unforeseen renewal of insurrection on a yet larger scale, and emphasized in the conferences that ensued by demands deemed by the authorities not only inadmissible but aggressively insolent, indicated—if the Red Flag[8] did not sufficiently do so—what was the spirit animating the men. Final suppression, however, there was; but only made possible perhaps by the unswerving loyalty of the marine corps and a voluntary resumption of loyalty among influential sections of the crews.

To some extent the Nore Mutiny may be regarded as analogous to the distempering irruption of contagious fever in a frame constitutionally sound, and which anon throws it off.

At all events, of these thousands of mutineers were some of the tars who not so very long afterwards—whether wholly prompted thereto by patriotism, or pugnacious instinct, or by both—helped to win a coronet for Nelson at the Nile, and the naval crown of crowns for him at Trafalgar.[9] To the mutineers, those battles and especially Trafalgar were a plenary absolution and a grand one. For all that goes to make up scenic naval display and heroic magnificence in arms, those battles, especially Trafalgar, stand unmatched in human annals.

4

In this matter of writing, resolve as one may to keep to the main road, some bypaths have an enticement not readily to be withstood. I am going to err into such a bypath. If the reader will keep me company I shall be glad. At the least, we can promise ourselves that pleasure which is wickedly said to be in sinning, for a literary sin the divergence will be.

Very likely it is no new remark that the inventions of our time have at last brought about a change in sea warfare in degree corresponding to the revolution in all warfare effected by the original introduction from China into Europe of gunpowder. The first European firearm, a clumsy contrivance, was, as is well known, scouted by no few of the knights as a base implement, good enough peradventure for weavers too craven to stand up crossing steel with steel in frank fight. But as ashore knightly valor, though shorn of its blazonry, did not cease with the knights, neither on the seas—though nowadays in encounters there a certain kind of displayed gallantry be fallen out of date as

8. Signal of revolution—then of terrorism.
9. Nelson defeated the French at the Bay of Aboukir near the mouth of the Nile in 1798, then died during his victory at Trafalgar in 1805.

hardly applicable under changed circumstances—did the nobler qualities of such naval magnates as Don John of Austria, Doria, Van Tromp, Jean Bart, the long line of British admirals, and the American Decaturs[1] of 1812 become obsolete with their wooden walls.

Nevertheless, to anybody who can hold the Present at its worth without being inappreciative of the Past, it may be forgiven, if to such an one the solitary old hulk at Portsmouth, Nelson's Victory, seems to float there, not alone as the decaying monument of a fame incorruptible, but also as a poetic reproach, softened by its picturesqueness, to the Monitors[2] and yet mightier hulls of the European ironclads. And this not altogether because such craft are unsightly, unavoidably lacking the symmetry and grand lines of the old battleships, but equally for other reasons.

There are some, perhaps, who while not altogether inaccessible to that poetic reproach just alluded to, may yet on behalf of the new order be disposed to parry it; and this to the extent of iconoclasm, if need be. For example, prompted by the sight of the star inserted in the Victory's quarter-deck designating the spot where the Great Sailor fell, these martial utilitarians may suggest considerations implying that Nelson's ornate publication of his person in battle was not only unnecessary, but not military, nay, savored of foolhardiness and vanity. They may add, too, that at Trafalgar it was in effect nothing less than a challenge to death; and death came; and that but for his bravado the victorious admiral might possibly have survived the battle, and so, instead of having his sagacious dying injunctions overruled by his immediate successor in command, he himself when the contest was decided might have brought his shattered fleet to anchor, a proceeding which might have averted the deplorable loss of life by shipwreck in the elemental tempest that followed the martial one.

Well, should we set aside the more than disputable point whether for various reasons it was possible to anchor the fleet, then plausibly enough the Benthamites[3] of war may urge the above. But the might-have-been is but boggy ground to build on. And, certainly, in foresight as to the larger issue of an encounter, and anxious preparations for it—buoying the deadly way and mapping it out, as at Copenhagen[4]—few commanders have been so painstakingly cirumspect as this same reckless declarer of his person in fight.

Personal prudence, even when dictated by quite other than selfish considerations, surely is no special virtue in a military man; while an excessive love of glory, impassioning a less burning impulse, the honest sense of duty, is the first. If the name Wellington[5] is not so much of a trumpet to the blood as the simpler name Nelson, the reason for this may perhaps be inferred from the above. Alfred in his funeral ode[6] on the victor of Waterloo ventures not to call him the greatest soldier of all time, though in the same ode he invokes Nelson as "the greatest sailor since our world began."

1. Stephen Decatur (1779–1820) fought against the British in the War of 1812. Don John of Austria (1547–1578), commander for the Holy League at the Battle of Lepanto (1571). Andrea Doria (1468–1560), leader of the Genoese fleet against the Turks. Maarten Tromp (1597–1653) led the Dutch fleet against the Spanish. Jean Bart (1650–1702) commanded French privateers against the Dutch and British.

2. The Union ironclad Monitor engaged the Confederate ironclad Merrimack in 1862 off Virginia.

3. Those who weigh decisions only in terms of utility,

from Jeremy Bentham (1748–1832), English philosopher, expounder of Utilitarianism.

4. In 1801 the Danes thought they had thwarted Nelson by removing the buoys near Copenhagen, but he took soundings and replaced the markers so he could navigate.

5. Arthur Wellesley, first duke of Wellington (1769–1852), British general in the Napoleonic Wars.

6. Alfred, Lord Tennyson (1809–1892), Ode on the Death of the Duke of Wellington (1852).

At Trafalgar Nelson on the brink of opening the fight sat down and wrote his last brief will and testament. If under the presentiment of the most magnificent of all victories to be crowned by his own glorious death, a sort of priestly motive led him to dress his person in the jewelled vouchers of his own shining deeds; if thus to have adorned himself for the altar and the sacrifice were indeed vainglory, then affectation and fustian is each more heroic line in the great epics and dramas, since in such lines the poet but embodies in verse those exaltations of sentiment that a nature like Nelson, the opportunity being given, vitalizes into acts.

5

Yes, the outbreak at the Nore was put down. But not every grievance was redressed. If the contractors, for example, were no longer permitted to ply some practices peculiar to their tribe everywhere, such as providing shoddy cloth, rations not sound, or false in the measure; not the less impressment, for one thing, went on. By custom sanctioned for centuries, and judicially maintained by a Lord Chancellor as late as Mansfield,[7] that mode of manning the fleet, a mode now fallen into a sort of abeyance but never formally renounced, it was not practicable to give up in those years. Its abrogation would have crippled the indispensable fleet, one wholly under canvas, no steam power, its innumerable sails and thousands of cannon, everything in short, worked by muscle alone; a fleet the more insatiate in demand for men, because then multiplying its ships of all grades against contingencies present and to come of the convulsed Continent.

Discontent foreran the Two Mutinies,[8] and more or less it lurkingly survived them. Hence it was not unreasonable to apprehend some return of trouble sporadic or general. One instance of such apprehensions: In the same year with this story, Nelson, then Rear Admiral Sir Horatio, being with the fleet off the Spanish coast, was directed by the admiral in command to shift his pennant from the *Captain* to the *Theseus*;[9] and for this reason: that the latter ship having newly arrived on the station from home, where it had taken part in the Great Mutiny, danger was apprehended from the temper of the men; and it was thought that an officer like Nelson was the one, not indeed to terrorize the crew into base subjection, but to win them, by force of his mere presence and heroic personality, back to an allegiance if not as enthusiastic as his own yet as true.

So it was that for a time, on more than one quarter-deck, anxiety did exist. At sea, precautionary vigilance was strained against relapse. At short notice an engagement might come on. When it did, the lieutenants assigned to batteries felt it incumbent on them, in some instances, to stand with drawn swords behind the men working the guns.

6

But on board the seventy-four in which Billy now swung his hammock, very little in the manner of the men and nothing obvious in the demeanor of the

---

7. William Murray, earl of Mansfield (1705–1793), lord chief justice of Britain.
8. At Spithead and the Nore.

9. To move bodily from the *Captain* to the *Theseus*, which then showed the flag of his office.

officers would have suggested to an ordinary observer that the Great Mutiny was a recent event. In their general bearing and conduct the commissioned officers of a warship naturally take their tone from the commander, that is if he have that ascendancy of character that ought to be his.

Captain the Honorable Edward Fairfax Vere, to give his full title, was a bachelor of forty or thereabouts, a sailor of distinction even in a time prolific of renowned seamen. Though allied to the higher nobility, his advancement had not been altogether owing to influences connected with that circumstance. He had seen much service, been in various engagements, always acquitting himself as an officer mindful of the welfare of his men, but never tolerating an infraction of discipline; thoroughly versed in the science of his profession, and intrepid to the verge of temerity, though never injudiciously so. For his gallantry in the West Indian waters as flag lieutenant under Rodney in that admiral's crowning victory over De Grasse,[1] he was made a post captain.

Ashore, in the garb of a civilian, scarce anyone would have taken him for a sailor, more especially that he never garnished unprofessional talk with nautical terms, and grave in his bearing, evinced little appreciation of mere humor. It was not out of keeping with these traits that on a passage when nothing demanded his paramount action, he was the most undemonstrative of men. Any landsman observing this gentleman not conspicuous by his stature and wearing no pronounced insignia, emerging from his cabin to the open deck, and noting the silent deference of the officers retiring to leeward, might have taken him for the King's guest, a civilian aboard the King's ship, some highly honorable discreet envoy on his way to an important post. But in fact this unobtrusiveness of demeanor may have proceeded from a certain unaffected modesty of manhood sometimes accompanying a resolute nature, a modesty evinced at all times not calling for pronounced action, which shown in any rank of life suggests a virtue aristocratic in kind. As with some others engaged in various departments of the world's more heroic activities, Captain Vere though practical enough upon occasion would at times betray a certain dreaminess of mood. Standing alone on the weather side of the quarter-deck, one hand holding by the rigging, he would absently gaze off at the blank sea. At the presentation to him then of some minor matter interrupting the current of his thoughts, he would show more or less irascibility; but instantly he would control it.

In the navy he was popularly known by the appellation "Starry Vere." How such a designation happened to fall upon one who whatever his sterling qualities was without any brilliant ones, was in this wise: A favorite kinsman, Lord Denton, a freehearted fellow, had been the first to meet and congratulate him upon his return to England from his West Indian cruise; and but the day previous turning over a copy of Andrew Marvell's[2] poems had lighted, not for the first time, however, upon the lines entitled "Appleton House," the name of one of the seats of their common ancestor, a hero in the German wars of the seventeenth century, in which poem occur the lines:

> This 'tis to have been from the first
> In a domestic heaven nursed,

---

1. The British Admiral George Brydges, Baron Rodney (1719–1792), defeated the French Admiral François de Grasse (1723–1788) off Dominica in 1782.
2. English poet (1621–1678).

Under the discipline severe
Of Fairfax and the starry Vere.

And so, upon embracing his cousin fresh from Rodney's great victory wherein
he had played so gallant a part, brimming over with just family pride in the
sailor of their house, he exuberantly exclaimed, "Give ye joy, Ed; give ye joy,
my starry Vere!" This got currency, and the novel prefix serving in familiar
parlance readily to distinguish the *Bellipotent's* captain from another Vere his
senior, a distant relative, an officer of like rank in the navy, it remained permanently attached to the surname.

7

In view of the part that the commander of the *Bellipotent* plays in scenes
shortly to follow, it may be well to fill out that sketch of him outlined in the
previous chapter.

Aside from his qualities as a sea officer Captain Vere was an exceptional
character. Unlike no few of England's renowned sailors, long and arduous
service with signal devotion to it had not resulted in absorbing and *salting* the
entire man. He had a marked leaning toward everything intellectual. He loved
books, never going to sea without a newly replenished library, compact but of
the best. The isolated leisure, in some cases so wearisome, falling at intervals
to commanders even during a war cruise, never was tedious to Captain Vere.
With nothing of that literary taste which less heeds the thing conveyed than
the vehicle, his bias was toward those books to which every serious mind of
superior order occupying any active post of authority in the world naturally
inclines: books treating of actual men and events no matter of what era—
history, biography, and unconventional writers like Montaigne,[3] who, free
from cant and convention, honestly and in the spirit of common sense philoso-
phize upon realities. In this line of reading he found confirmation of his own
more reserved thoughts—confirmation which he had vainly sought in social
converse, so that as touching most fundamental topics, there had got to be
established in him some positive convictions which he forefelt would abide in
him essentially unmodified so long as his intelligent part remained unimpaired. In view of the troubled period in which his lot was cast, this was well
for him. His settled convictions were as a dike against those invading waters of
novel opinion social, political, and otherwise, which carried away as in a torrent no few minds in those days, minds by nature not inferior to his own.
While other members of that aristocracy to which by birth he belonged were
incensed at the innovators mainly because their theories were inimical to the
privileged classes. Captain Vere disinterestedly opposed them not alone
because they seemed to him insusceptible of embodiment in lasting institutions, but at war with the peace of the world and the true welfare of mankind.

With minds less stored than his and less earnest, some officers of his rank,
with whom at times he would necessarily consort, found him lacking in the
companionable quality, a dry and bookish gentleman, as they deemed. Upon
any chance withdrawal from their company one would be apt to say to another
something like this: "Vere is a noble fellow, Starry Vere. 'Spite the gazettes,[4]

---

3. Michel de Montaigne (1533–1592), French politi-   4. Newspapers, or possibly the official publications
cian and essayist.   listing ranks, honors, etc.

Sir Horatio" (meaning him who became Lord Nelson) "is at bottom scarce a better seaman or fighter. But between you and me now, don't you think there is a queer streak of the pedantic running through him? Yes, like the King's yarn in a coil of navy rope?"

Some apparent ground there was for this sort of confidential criticism; since not only did the captain's discourse never fall into the jocosely familiar, but in illustrating of any point touching the stirring personages and events of the time he would be as apt to cite some historic character or incident of antiquity as he would be to cite from the moderns. He seemed unmindful of the circumstance that to his bluff company such remote allusions, however pertinent they might really be, were altogether alien to men whose reading was mainly confined to the journals.[5] But considerateness in such matters is not easy to natures constituted like Captain Vere's. Their honesty prescribes to them directness, sometimes far-reaching like that of a migratory fowl that in its flight never heeds when it crosses a frontier.

8

The lieutenants and other commissioned gentlemen forming Captain Vere's staff it is not necessary here to particularize, nor needs it to make any mention of any of the warrant officers. But among the petty officers[6] was one who, having much to do with the story, may as well be forthwith introduced. His portrait I essay, but shall never hit it. This was John Claggart, the master-at-arms. But that sea title may to landsmen seem somewhat equivocal. Originally, doubtless, that petty officer's function was the instruction of the men in the use of arms, sword or cutlass. But very long ago, owing to the advance in gunnery making hand-to-hand encounters less frequent and giving to niter and sulphur the pre-eminence over steel, that function ceased; the master-at-arms of a great warship becoming a sort of chief of police charged among other matters with the duty of preserving order on the populous lower gun decks.

Claggart was a man about five-and-thirty, somewhat spare and tall, yet of no ill figure upon the whole. His hand was too small and shapely to have been accustomed to hard toil. The face was a notable one, the features all except the chin cleanly cut as those on a Greek medallion; yet the chin, beardless as Tecumseh's,[7] had something of strange protuberant broadness in its make that recalled the prints of the Reverend Dr. Titus Oates, the historic deponent with the clerical drawl in the time of Charles II and the fraud of the alleged Popish Plot.[8] It served Claggart in his office that his eye could cast a tutoring glance. His brow was of the sort phrenologically[9] associated with more than average intellect; silken jet curls partly clustering over it, making a foil to the pallor below, a pallor tinged with a faint shade of amber akin to the hue of time-tinted marbles of old. This complexion, singularly contrasting with the red or deeply bronzed visages of the sailors, and in part the result of his official seclusion from the sunlight, though it was not exactly displeasing, nevertheless

5. Newspapers.
6. Lesser officers appointed to their functions by the commander, roughly equivalent to noncommissioned officers in the army.
7. Shawnee chief (1768?–1813) who sided with the British in the War of 1812 and was defeated at Tippecanoe by William Henry Harrison.

8. Oates (1649–1705) updated the Gunpowder Plot of 1605 into an imaginary Popish Plot (1678) to massacre Protestants and burn London.
9. According to the pseudoscience of phrenology, in which contours of the skull were thought to indicate character.

seemed to hint of something defective or abnormal in the constitution and blood. But his general aspect and manner were so suggestive of an education and career incongruous with his naval function that when not actively engaged in it he looked like a man of high quality, social and moral, who for reasons of his own was keeping incog.[1] Nothing was known of his former life. It might be that he was an Englishman; and yet there lurked a bit of accent in his speech suggesting that possibly he was not such by birth, but through naturalization in early childhood. Among certain grizzled sea gossips of the gun decks and forecastle went a rumor perdue that the master-at-arms was a *chevalier*[2] who had volunteered into the King's navy by way of compounding for some mysterious swindle whereof he had been arraigned at the King's Bench.[3] The fact that nobody could substantiate this report was, of course, nothing against its secret currency. Such a rumor once started on the gun decks in reference to almost anyone below the rank of a commissioned officer would, during the period assigned to this narrative, have seemed not altogether wanting in credibility to the tarry old wiseacres of a man-of-war crew. And indeed a man of Claggart's accomplishments, without prior nautical experience entering the navy at mature life, as he did, and necessarily allotted at the start to the lowest grade in it; a man too who never made allusion to his previous life ashore; these were circumstances which in the dearth of exact knowledge as to his true antecedents opened to the invidious a vague field for unfavorable surmise.

But the sailors' dogwatch gossip concerning him derived a vague plausibility from the fact that now for some period the British navy could so little afford to be squeamish in the matter of keeping up the muster rolls, that not only were press gangs[4] notoriously abroad both afloat and ashore, but there was little or no secret about another matter, namely, that the London police were at liberty to capture any able-bodied suspect, any questionable fellow at large, and summarily ship him to the dockyard or fleet. Furthermore, even among voluntary enlistments there were instances where the motive thereto partook neither of patriotic impulse nor yet of a random desire to experience a bit of sea life and martial adventure. Insolvent debtors of minor grade, together with the promiscuous lame ducks of morality, found in the navy a convenient and secure refuge, secure because, once enlisted aboard a King's ship, they were as much in sanctuary as the transgressor of the Middle Ages harboring himself under the shadow of the altar. Such sanctioned irregularities, which for obvious reasons the government would hardly think to parade at the time and which consequently, and as affecting the least influential class of mankind, have all but dropped into oblivion, lend color to something for the truth whereof I do not vouch, and hence have some scruple in stating; something I remember having seen in print though the book I cannot recall; but the same thing was personally communicated to me now more than forty years ago by an old pensioner in a cocked hat with whom I had a most interesting talk on the terrace at Greenwich, a Baltimore Negro, a Trafalgar man.[5] It was to this effect: In the case of a warship short of hands whose speedy sailing was imperative, the deficient quota, in lack of any other way of making it good, would be eked out by drafts culled direct from the jails. For reasons previously suggested it would not perhaps be easy at the present day directly to prove or disprove

---

1. Incognito, with concealed identity.
2. Swindler, sharper. "Rumor perdue": reckless rumor.
3. I.e., in a court of law.

4. Gangs charged with rounding up men for ships, shanghaiing them if necessary. "Muster rolls": register of officers and men in a ship's company.
5. A veteran of the Battle of Trafalgar (1805).

the allegation. But allowed as a verity, how significant would it be of England's straits at the time confronted by those wars which like a flight of harpies rose shrieking from the din and dust of the fallen Bastille.[6] That era appears measurably clear to us who look back at it, and but read of it. But to the grandfathers of us graybeards, the more thoughtful of them, the genius of it presented an aspect like that of Camoëns' Spirit of the Cape,[7] an eclipsing menace mysterious and prodigious. Not America was exempt from apprehension. At the height of Napoleon's unexampled conquests, there were Americans who had fought at Bunker Hill[8] who looked forward to the possibility that the Atlantic might prove no barrier against the ultimate schemes of this French portentous upstart from the revolutionary chaos who seemed in act of fulfilling judgment prefigured in the Apocalypse.[9]

But the less credence was to be given to the gun-deck talk touching Claggart, seeing that no man holding his office in a man-of-war can ever hope to be popular with the crew. Besides, in derogatory comments upon anyone against whom they have a grudge, or for any reason or no reason mislike, sailors are much like landsmen: they are apt to exaggerate or romance it.

About as much was really known to the *Bellipotent's* tars of the master-at-arms' career before entering the service as an astronomer knows about a comet's travels prior to its first observable appearance in the sky. The verdict of the sea quidnuncs[1] has been cited only by way of showing what sort of moral impression the man made upon rude uncultivated natures whose conceptions of human wickedness were necessarily of the narrowest, limited to ideas of vulgar rascality—a thief among the swinging hammocks during a night watch, or the man-brokers and land-sharks of the seaports.

It was no gossip, however, but fact that though, as before hinted, Claggart upon his entrance into the navy was, as a novice, assigned to the least honorable section[2] of a man-of-war's crew, embracing the drudgery, he did not long remain there. The superior capacity he immediately evinced, his constitutional sobriety, an ingratiating deference to superiors, together with a peculiar ferreting genius manifested on a singular occasion; all this, capped by a certain austere patriotism, abruptly advanced him to the position of master-at-arms.

Of this maritime chief of police the ship's corporals, so called, were the immediate subordinates, and compliant ones; and this, as is to be noted in some business departments ashore, almost to a degree inconsistent with entire moral volition. His place put various converging wires of underground influence under the chief's control, capable when astutely worked through his understrappers of operating to the mysterious discomfort, if nothing worse, of any of the sea commonalty.

9

Life in the foretop well agreed with Billy Budd. There, when not actually engaged on the yards yet higher aloft, the topmen, who as such had been picked out for youth and activity, constituted an aerial club lounging at ease

---

6. A 14th-century fortress in Paris, used as a prison when citizens demolished it on July 14, 1789, at the start of the French Revolution. "Harpies": rapacious mythological creatures.
7. In the *Lusiads* (1572), epic poem by the Portuguese Luiz de Camoëns (1524–1580), the spirit menaces Vasco da Gama as he rounds the Cape of Good Hope on his way to India.

8. Boston, Massachusetts, on June 17, 1775, where the British dislodged the colonialists.
9. I.e., the Book of Revelation.
1. Busybodies.
2. The waisters, charged with "attending to the drainage and sewerage below hatches," as Melville says in chap. 3 of *White-Jacket*.

against the smaller stun'sails rolled up into cushions, spinning yarns like the lazy gods, and frequently amused with what was going on in the busy world of the decks below. No wonder then that a young fellow of Billy's disposition was well content in such society. Giving no cause of offense to anybody, he was always alert at a call. So in the merchant service it had been with him. But now such a punctiliousness in duty was shown that his topmates would sometimes good-naturedly laugh at him for it. This heightened alacrity had its cause, namely, the impression made upon him by the first formal gangway-punishment he had ever witnessed, which befell the day following his impressment. It had been incurred by a little fellow, young, a novice after-guardsman[3] absent from his assigned post when the ship was being put about; a dereliction resulting in a rather serious hitch to that maneuver, one demanding instantaneous promptitude in letting go and making fast. When Billy saw the culprit's naked back under the scourge, gridironed with red welts and worse, when he marked the dire expression in the liberated man's face as with his woolen shirt flung over him by the executioner he rushed forward from the spot to bury himself in the crowd, Billy was horrified. He resolved that never through remissness would he make himself liable to such a visitation or do or omit aught that might merit even verbal reproof. What then was his surprise and concern when ultimately he found himself getting into petty trouble occasionally about such matters as the stowage of his bag or something amiss in his hammock, matters under the police oversight of the ship's corporals of the lower decks, and which brought down on him a vague threat from one of them.

So heedful in all things as he was, how could this be? He could not understand it, and it more than vexed him. When he spoke to his young topmates about it they were either lightly incredulous or found something comical in his unconcealed anxiety. "Is it your bag, Billy?" said one. "Well, sew yourself up in it, bully boy, and then you'll be sure to know if anybody meddles with it."

Now there was a veteran aboard who because his years began to disqualify him for more active work had been recently assigned duty as mainmastman in his watch, looking to the gear belayed at the rail roundabout that great spar near the deck.[4] At off-times the foretopman had picked up some acquaintance with him, and now in his trouble it occurred to him that he might be the sort of person to go to for wise counsel. He was an old Dansker[5] long anglicized in the service, of few words, many wrinkles, and some honorable scars. His wizened face, time-tinted and weather-stained to the complexion of an antique parchment, was here and there peppered blue by the chance explosion of a gun cartridge in action.

He was an *Agamemnon* man, some two years prior to the time of this story having served under Nelson when still captain in that ship immortal in naval memory, which dismantled and in part broken up to her bare ribs is seen a grand skeleton in Haden's etching.[6] As one of a boarding party from the *Aga-*

---

3. "Then, there is the *After-guard*, stationed on the Quarter-deck; who, under the Quarter-Masters and Quarter-Gunners, attend to the main-sail and spanker, and help haul the main-brace, and other ropes in the stern of the vessel. The duties assigned to the After-Guard's-Men being comparatively light and easy, and but little seamanship being expected from them, they are composed chiefly of landsmen; the least robust, the least hardy, and least sailor-like of the crew" (*White-Jacket*, chap. 3).

4. Charged with duty pertaining to the mainmast but only from the mainyard to the deck, not higher.

5. Dane.

6. *Breaking Up of the "Agamemnon,"* by Sir Francis Seymour Haden (1818–1910).

memnon he had received a cut slantwise along one temple and cheek leaving a long pale scar like a streak of dawn's light falling athwart the dark visage. It was on account of that scar and the affair in which it was known that he had received it, as well as from his blue-peppered complexion, that the Dansker went among the *Bellipotent*'s crew by the name of "Board-Her-in-the-Smoke."

Now the first time that his small weasel eyes happened to light on Billy Budd, a certain grim internal merriment set all his ancient wrinkles into antic play. Was it that his eccentric unsentimental old sapience, primitive in its kind, saw or thought it saw something which in contrast with the warship's environment looked oddly incongruous in the Handsome Sailor? But after slyly studying him at intervals, the old Merlin's[7] equivocal merriment was modified; for now when the twain would meet, it would start in his face a quizzing sort of look, but it would be but momentary and sometimes replaced by an expression of speculative query as to what might eventually befall a nature like that, dropped into a world not without some mantraps and against whose subtleties simple courage lacking experience and address, and without any touch of defensive ugliness, is of little avail; and where such innocence as man is capable of does yet in a moral emergency not always sharpen the faculties or enlighten the will.

However it was, the Dansker in his ascetic way rather took to Billy. Nor was this only because of certain philosophic interest in such a character. There was another cause. While the old man's eccentricities, sometimes bordering on the ursine,[8] repelled the juniors, Billy, undeterred thereby, revering him as a salt hero, would make advances, never passing the old *Agamemnon* man without a salutation marked by that respect which is seldom lost on the aged, however crabbed at times or whatever their station in life.

There was a vein of dry humor, or what not, in the mastman; and, whether in freak of patriarchal irony touching Billy's youth and athletic frame, or for some other and more recondite reason, from the first in addressing him he always substituted *Baby* for Billy, the Dansker in fact being the originator of the name by which the foretopman eventually became known aboard ship.

Well then, in his mysterious little difficulty going in quest of the wrinkled one, Billy found him off duty in a dogwatch ruminating by himself, seated on a shot box of the upper gun deck, now and then surveying with a somewhat cynical regard certain of the more swaggering promenaders there. Billy recounted his trouble, again wondering how it all happened. The salt seer attentively listened, accompanying the foretopman's recital with queer twitchings of his wrinkles and problematical little sparkles of his small ferret eyes. Making an end of his story, the foretopman asked, "And now, Dansker, do tell me what you think of it."

The old man, shoving up the front of his tarpaulin and deliberately rubbing the long slant scar at the point where it entered the thin hair, laconically said, "Baby Budd, *Jemmy Legs*" (meaning the master-at-arms) "is down on you."

"*Jemmy Legs!*" ejaculated Billy, his welkin eyes expanding. "What for? Why, he calls me 'the sweet and pleasant young fellow,' they tell me."

"Does he so?" grinned the grizzled one; then said, "Ay, Baby lad, a sweet voice has Jemmy Legs."

---

7. Wizard or prophet, from the character in Arthurian legends.   8. Bearlike.

"No, not always. But to me he has. I seldom pass him but there comes a pleasant word."

"And that's because he's down upon you, Baby Budd."

Such reiteration, along with the manner of it, incomprehensible to a novice, disturbed Billy almost as much as the mystery for which he had sought explanation. Something less unpleasingly oracular he tried to extract; but the old sea Chiron, thinking perhaps that for the nonce he had sufficiently instructed his young Achilles,[9] pursed his lips, gathered all his wrinkles together, and would commit himself to nothing further.

Years, and those experiences which befall certain shrewder men subordinated lifelong to the will of superiors, all this had developed in the Dansker the pithy guarded cynicism that was his leading characteristic.

10

The next day an incident served to confirm Billy Budd in his incredulity as to the Dansker's strange summing up of the case submitted. The ship at noon, going large before the wind, was rolling on her course,[1] and he below at dinner and engaged in some sportful talk with the members of his mess, chanced in a sudden lurch to spill the entire contents of his soup pan upon the new-scrubbed deck. Claggart, the master-at-arms, official rattan[2] in hand, happened to be passing along the battery in a bay of which the mess was lodged, and the greasy liquid streamed just across his path. Stepping over it, he was proceeding on his way without comment, since the matter was nothing to take notice of under the circumstances, when he happened to observe who it was that had done the spilling. His countenance changed. Pausing, he was about to ejaculate something hasty at the sailor, but checked himself, and pointing down to the streaming soup, playfully tapped him from behind with his rattan, saying in a low musical voice peculiar to him at times, "Handsomely done, my lad! And handsome is as handsome did it, too!" And with that passed on. Not noted by Billy as not coming within his view was the involuntary smile, or rather grimace, that accompanied Claggart's equivocal words. Aridly it drew down the thin corners of his shapely mouth. But everybody taking his remark as meant for humorous, and at which therefore as coming from a superior they were bound to laugh "with counterfeited glee,"[3] acted accordingly; and Billy, tickled, it may be, by the allusion to his being the Handsome Sailor, merrily joined in; then addressing his messmates exclaimed, "There now, who says that Jemmy Legs is down on me!"

"And who said he was, Beauty?" demanded one Donald with some surprise. Whereat the foretopman looked a little foolish, recalling that it was only one person, Board-Her-in-the-Smoke, who had suggested what to him was the smoky idea that this master-at-arms was in any peculiar way hostile to him. Meantime that functionary, resuming his path, must have momentarily worn some expression less guarded than that of the bitter smile, usurping the face from the heart—some distorting expression perhaps, for a drummer-boy heedlessly frolicking along from the opposite direction and chancing to come into

9. In Greek mythology, the centaur Chiron tutored Achilles.
1. With the wind behind her, was making good time.
2. Cane.

3. In Oliver Goldsmith's *The Deserted Village* the students laugh at the jokes of the tyrannical schoolmaster, but only "with counterfeited glee."

light collision with his person was strangely disconcerted by his aspect. Nor was the impression lessened when the official, impetuously giving him a sharp cut with the rattan, vehemently exclaimed, "Look where you go!"

11

What was the matter with the master-at-arms? And, be the matter what it might, how could it have direct relation to Billy Budd, with whom prior to the affair of the spilled soup he had never come into any special contact official or otherwise? What indeed could the trouble have to do with one so little inclined to give offense as the merchant-ship's "peacemaker," even him who in Claggart's own phrase was "the sweet and pleasant young fellow"? Yes, why should Jemmy Legs, to borrow the Dansker's expression, be "down" on the Handsome Sailor? But, at heart and not for nothing, as the late chance encounter may indicate to the discerning, down on him, secretly down on him, he assuredly was.

Now to invent something touching the more private career of Claggart, something involving Billy Budd, of which something the latter should be wholly ignorant, some romantic incident implying that Claggart's knowledge of the young bluejacket began at some period anterior to catching sight of him on board the seventy-four—all this, not so difficult to do, might avail in a way more or less interesting to account for whatever of enigma may appear to lurk in the case. But in fact there was nothing of the sort. And yet the cause necessarily to be assumed as the sole one assignable is in its very realism as much charged with that prime element of Radcliffian[4] romance, the mysterious, as any that the ingenuity of the author of *The Mysteries of Udolpho* could devise. For what can more partake of the mysterious than an antipathy spontaneous and profound such as is evoked in certain exceptional mortals by the mere aspect of some other mortal, however harmless he may be, if not called forth by this very harmlessness itself?

Now there can exist no irritating juxtaposition of dissimilar personalities comparable to that which is possible aboard a great warship fully manned and at sea. There, every day among all ranks, almost every man comes into more or less of contact with almost every other man. Wholly there to avoid even the sight of an aggravating object one must needs give it Jonah's toss[5] or jump overboard himself. Imagine how all this might eventually operate on some peculiar human creature the direct reverse of a saint!

But for the adequate comprehending of Claggart by a normal nature these hints are insufficient. To pass from a normal nature to him one must cross "the deadly space between." And this is best done by indirection.

Long ago an honest scholar, my senior,[6] said to me in reference to one who like himself is now no more, a man so unimpeachably respectable that against him nothing was ever openly said though among the few something was whispered, "Yes, X——is a nut not to be cracked by the tap of a lady's fan. You are aware that I am the adherent of no organized religion, much less of any philosophy built into a system. Well, for all that, I think that to try and get into X——, enter his labyrinth and get out again, without a clue derived from

4. Ann Radcliffe (1764–1823), British author of   5. Jonah 1.15.
Gothic fiction.   6. Melville himself.

some source other than what is known as 'knowledge of the world'—that were hardly possible, at least for me."

"Why," said I, "X——, however singular a study to some, is yet human, and knowledge of the world assuredly implies the knowledge of human nature, and in most of its varieties."

"Yes, but a superficial knowledge of it, serving ordinary purposes. But for anything deeper, I am not certain whether to know the world and to know human nature be not two distinct branches of knowledge, which while they may coexist in the same heart, yet either may exist with little or nothing of the other. Nay, in an average man of the world, his constant rubbing with it blunts that finer spiritual insight indispensable to the understanding of the essential in certain exceptional characters, whether evil ones or good. In a matter of some importance I have seen a girl wind an old lawyer about her little finger. Nor was it the dotage of senile love. Nothing of the sort. But he knew law better than he knew the girl's heart. Coke and Blackstone[7] hardly shed so much light into obscure spiritual places as the Hebrew prophets. And who were they? Mostly recluses."

At the time, my inexperience was such that I did not quite see the drift of all this. It may be that I see it now. And, indeed, if that lexicon which is based on Holy Writ were any longer popular, one might with less difficulty define and denominate certain phenomenal men. As it is, one must turn to some authority not liable to the charge of being tinctured with the biblical element.

In a list of definitions included in the authentic translation of Plato, a list attributed to him, occurs this: "Natural Depravity: a depravity according to nature,"[8] a definition which, though savoring of Calvinism, by no means involves Calvin's[9] dogma as to total mankind. Evidently its intent makes it applicable but to individuals. Not many are the examples of this depravity which the gallows and jail supply. At any rate, for notable instances, since these have no vulgar alloy of the brute in them, but invariably are dominated by intellectuality, one must go elsewhere. Civilization, especially if of the austerer sort, is auspicious to it. It folds itself in the mantle of respectability. It has its certain negative virtues serving as silent auxiliaries. It never allows wine to get within its guard. It is not going too far to say that it is without vices or small sins. There is a phenomenal pride in it that excludes them. It is never mercenary or avaricious. In short, the depravity here meant partakes nothing of the sordid or sensual. It is serious, but free from acerbity. Though no flatterer of mankind it never speaks ill of it.

But the thing which in eminent instances signalizes so exceptional a nature is this: Though the man's even temper and discreet bearing would seem to intimate a mind peculiarly subject to the law of reason, not the less in heart he would seem to riot in complete exemption from that law, having apparently little to do with reason further than to employ it as an ambidexter implement for effecting the irrational. That is to say: Toward the accomplishment of an aim which in wantonness of atrocity would seem to partake of the insane, he will direct a cool judgment sagacious and sound. These men are madmen, and of the most dangerous sort, for their lunacy is not continuous, but occa-

---

7. Sir Edward Coke (1552–1634) and Sir William Blackstone (1723–1780), British jurists.
8. Melville found this definition in the Bohn edition of Plato, vol. 6 (1854).

9. French theologian (1509–1564); he regarded all human beings as depraved, a consequence of the Fall of Man.

sional, evoked by some special object; it is protectively secretive, which is as much as to say it is self-contained, so that when, moreover most active it is to the average mind not distinguishable from sanity, and for the reason above suggested: that whatever its aims may be—and the aim is never declared—the method and the outward proceeding are always perfectly rational.

Now something such an one was Claggart, in whom was the mania of an evil nature, not engendered by vicious training or corrupting books or licentious living, but born with him and innate, in short "a depravity according to nature."

Dark sayings are these, some will say. But why? Is it because they somewhat savor of Holy Writ in its phrase "mystery of iniquity"? If they do, such savor was far enough from being intended, for little will it commend these pages to many a reader of today.

The point of the present story turning on the hidden nature of the master-at-arms has necessitated this chapter. With an added hint or two in connection with the incident at the mess, the resumed narrative must be left to vindicate, as it may, its own credibility.

12

That Claggart's figure was not amiss, and his face, save the chin, well molded, has already been said. Of these favorable points he seemed not insensible, for he was not only neat but careful in his dress. But the form of Billy Budd was heroic; and if his face was without the intellectual look of the pallid Claggart's, not the less was it lit, like his, from within, though from a different source. The bonfire in his heart made luminous the rose-tan in his cheek.

In view of the marked contrast between the persons of the twain, it is more than probable that when the master-at-arms in the scene last given applied to the sailor the proverb "Handsome is as handsome does," he there let escape an ironic inkling, not caught by the young sailors who heard it, as to what it was that had first moved him against Billy, namely, his significant personal beauty.

Now envy and antipathy, passions irreconcilable in reason, nevertheless in fact may spring conjoined like Chang and Eng[1] in one birth. Is Envy then such a monster? Well, though many an arraigned mortal has in hopes of mitigated penalty pleaded guilty to horrible actions, did ever anybody seriously confess to envy? Something there is in it universally felt to be more shameful than even felonious crime. And not only does everybody disown it, but the better sort are inclined to incredulity when it is in earnest imputed to an intelligent man. But since its lodgment is in the heart not the brain, no degree of intellect supplies a guarantee against it. But Claggart's was no vulgar form of the passion. Nor, as directed toward Billy Budd, did it partake of that streak of apprehensive jealousy that marred Saul's visage perturbedly brooding on the comely young David.[2] Claggart's envy struck deeper. If askance he eyed the good looks, cheery health, and frank enjoyment of young life in Billy Budd, it was because these went along with a nature that, as Claggart magnetically felt, had in its simplicity never willed malice or experienced the reactionary bite of that serpent. To him, the spirit lodged within Billy, and looking out from his

1. Famous Siamese twins (1811–1874), exhibited in the United States by P. T. Barnum.　2. 1 Samuel 16.18, 18.9.

welkin eyes as from windows, that ineffability it was which made the dimple in his dyed cheek, suppled his joints, and dancing in his yellow curls made him pre-eminently the Handsome Sailor. One person excepted, the master-at-arms was perhaps the only man in the ship intellectually capable of adequately appreciating the moral phenomenon presented in Billy Budd. And the insight but intensified his passion, which assuming various secret forms within him, at times assumed that of cynic disdain, disdain of innocence—to be nothing more than innocent! Yet in an aesthetic way he saw the charm of it, the courageous free-and-easy temper of it, and fain would have shared it, but he despaired of it.

With no power to annul the elemental evil in him, though readily enough he could hide it; apprehending the good, but powerless to be it; a nature like Claggart's, surcharged with energy as such natures almost invariably are, what recourse is left to it but to recoil upon itself and, like the scorpion for which the Creator alone is responsible, act out to the end the part allotted it.

13

Passion, and passion in its profoundest, is not a thing demanding a palatial stage whereon to play its part. Down among the groundlings,[3] among the beggars and rakers of the garbage, profound passion is enacted. And the circumstances that provoke it, however trivial or mean, are no measure of its power. In the present instance the stage is a scrubbed gun deck, and one of the external provocations a man-of-war's man's spilled soup.

Now when the master-at-arms noticed whence came that greasy fluid streaming before his feet, he must have taken it—to some extent wilfully, perhaps—not for the mere accident it assuredly was, but for the sly escape of a spontaneous feeling on Billy's part more or less answering to the antipathy on his own. In effect a foolish demonstration, he must have thought, and very harmless, like the futile kick of a heifer, which yet were the heifer a shod stallion would not be so harmless. Even so was it that into the gall of Claggart's envy he infused the vitriol of his contempt. But the incident confirmed to him certain telltale reports purveyed to his ear by "Squeak," one of his more cunning corporals, a grizzled little man, so nicknamed by the sailors on account of his squeaky voice and sharp visage ferreting about the dark corners of the lower decks after interlopers, satirically suggesting to them the idea of a rat in a cellar.

From his chief's employing him as an implicit tool in laying little traps for the worriment of the foretopman—for it was from the master-at-arms that the petty persecutions heretofore adverted to had proceeded—the corporal, having naturally enough concluded that his master could have no love for the sailor, made it his business, faithful understrapper that he was, to foment the ill blood by perverting to his chief certain innocent frolics of the good-natured foretopman, besides inventing for his mouth sundry contumelious epithets he claimed to have overheard him let fall. The master-at-arms never suspected the veracity of these reports, more especially as to the epithets, for he well knew how secretly unpopular may become a master-at-arms, at least a master-at-arms of those days, zealous in his function, and how the bluejackets shoot

3. Spectators in the pit, the cheapest area of a theater.

at him in private their raillery and wit; the nickname by which he goes among them (Jemmy Legs) implying under the form of merriment their cherished disrespect and dislike. But in view of the greediness of hate for pabulum it hardly needed a purveyor to feed Claggart's passion.

An uncommon prudence is habitual with the subtler depravity, for it has everything to hide. And in case of an injury but suspected, its secretiveness voluntarily cuts it off from enlightenment or disillusion; and, not unreluctantly, action is taken upon surmise as upon certainty. And the retaliation is apt to be in monstrous disproportion to the supposed offense; for when in anybody was revenge in its exactions aught else but an inordinate usurer? But how with Claggart's conscience? For though consciences are unlike as foreheads, every intelligence, not excluding the scriptural devils who "believe and tremble,"[4] has one. But Claggart's conscience being but the lawyer to his will, made ogres of trifles, probably arguing that the motive imputed to Billy in spilling the soup just when he did, together with the epithets alleged, these, if nothing more, made a strong case against him; nay, justified animosity into a sort of retributive righteousness. The Pharisee is the Guy Fawkes[5] prowling in the hid chambers underlying some natures like Claggart's. And they can really form no conception of an unreciprocated malice. Probably the master-at-arms' clandestine persecution of Billy was started to try the temper of the man; but it had not developed any quality in him that enmity could make official use of or even pervert into plausible self-justification; so that the occurrence at the mess, petty if it were, was a welcome one to that peculiar conscience assigned to be the private mentor of Claggart; and, for the rest, not improbably it put him upon new experiments.

14

Not many days after the last incident narrated, something befell Billy Budd that more graveled him than aught that had previously occurred.

It was a warm night for the latitude; and the foretopman, whose watch at the time was properly below, was dozing on the uppermost deck whither he had ascended from his hot hammock, one of hundreds suspended so closely wedged together over a lower gun deck that there was little or no swing to them. He lay as in the shadow of a hillside, stretched under the lee[6] of the booms, a piled ridge of spare spars amidships between foremast and mainmast among which the ship's largest boat, the launch, was stowed. Alongside of three other slumberers from below, he lay near that end of the booms which approaches the foremast; his station aloft on duty as a foretopman being just over the deck-station of the forecastlemen, entitling him according to usage to make himself more or less at home in that neighborhood.

Presently he was stirred into semiconsciousness by somebody, who must have previously sounded the sleep of the others, touching his shoulder, and then, as the foretopman raised his head, breathing into his ear in a quick whisper, "Slip into the lee forechains,[7] Billy; there is something in the wind. Don't speak. Quick, I will meet you there," and disappearing.

4. James 2.19.
5. The Pharisee (the self-righteous hypocrite) is the Guy Fawkes (the treacherous terrorist), from the conspirers against Jesus (as in Matthew 22.15) and the Catholic who conspired to blow up the Houses of Parliament in 1605.
6. Shelter (away from the wind).
7. A hidden platform (as explained two paragraphs below).

Now Billy, like sundry other essentially good-natured ones, had some of the weaknesses inseparable from essential good nature; and among these was a reluctance, almost an incapacity of plumply saying *no* to an abrupt proposition not obviously absurd on the face of it, nor obviously unfriendly, nor iniquitous. And being of warm blood, he had not the phlegm tacitly to negative any proposition by unresponsive inaction. Like his sense of fear, his apprehension as to aught outside of the honest and natural was seldom very quick. Besides, upon the present occasion, the drowse from his sleep still hung upon him.

However it was, he mechanically rose and, sleepily wondering what could be in the wind, betook himself to the designated place, a narrow platform, one of six, outside of the high bulwarks and screened by the great deadeyes and multiple columned lanyards of the shrouds and backstays;[8] and, in a great warship of that time, of dimensions commensurate to the hull's magnitude; a tarry balcony in short, overhanging the sea, and so secluded that one mariner of the *Bellipotent,* a Nonconformist old tar of a serious turn, made it even in daytime his private oratory.[9]

In this retired nook the stranger soon joined Billy Budd. There was no moon as yet; a haze obscured the starlight. He could not distinctly see the stranger's face. Yet from something in the outline and carriage, Billy took him, and correctly, for one of the afterguard.

"Hist! Billy," said the man, in the same quick cautionary whisper as before. "You were impressed, weren't you? Well, so was I"; and he paused, as to mark the effect. But Billy, not knowing exactly what to make of this, said nothing. Then the other: "We are not the only impressed ones, Billy. There's a gang of us.—Couldn't you—help—at a pinch?"

"What do you mean?" demanded Billy, here thoroughly shaking off his drowse.

"Hist, hist!" the hurried whisper now growing husky. "See here," and the man held up two small objects faintly twinkling in the night-light; "see, they are yours, Billy, if you'll only——"

But Billy broke in, and in his resentful eagerness to deliver himself his vocal infirmity somewhat intruded. "D—d—damme, I don't know what you are d—d—driving at, or what you mean, but you had better g—g—go where you belong!" For the moment the fellow, as confounded, did not stir; and Billy, springing to his feet, said, "If you d—don't start, I'll t—t—toss you back over the r—rail!" There was no mistaking this, and the mysterious emissary decamped, disappearing in the direction of the mainmast in the shadow of the booms.

"Hallo, what's the matter?" here came growling from a forecastleman awakened from his deck-doze by Billy's raised voice. And as the foretopman reappeared and was recognized by him: "Ah, Beauty, is it you? Well, something must have been the matter, for you st—st—stuttered."

"Oh," rejoined Billy, now mastering the impediment, "I found an afterguardsman in our part of the ship here, and I bid him be off where he belongs."

"And is that all you did about it, Foretopman?" gruffly demanded another,

---

8. Help support the masts by extending from the mastheads to the sides of the ship, slanting a little aft. "Deadeyes": wooden blocks with holes through which ropes are run. "Lanyards": short ropes passing through deadeyes and used to extend shrouds or stays.

"Shrouds": ropes giving lateral support to the masts.
9. Prayer room. "Noncomformist": Protestant dissenter, refusing the religious policies and practices of the Church of England.

an irascible old fellow of brick-colored visage and hair who was known to his associate forecastlemen as "Red Pepper." "Such sneaks I should like to marry to the gunner's daughter!"—by that expression meaning that he would like to subject them to disciplinary castigation over a gun.

However, Billy's rendering of the matter satisfactorily accounted to these inquirers for the brief commotion, since all the sections of a ship's company the forecastlemen, veterans for the most part and bigoted in their sea prejudices, are the most jealous in resenting territorial encroachments, especially on the part of any of the afterguard, of whom they have but a sorry opinion— chiefly landsmen, never going aloft except to reef or furl the mainsail, and in no wise competent to handle a marlinspike or turn in a deadeye, say.

15

This incident sorely puzzled Billy Budd. It was an entirely new experience, the first time in his life that he had ever been personally approached in underhand intriguing fashion. Prior to this encounter he had known nothing of the afterguardsman, the two men being stationed wide apart, one forward and aloft during his watch, the other on deck and aft.

What could it mean? And could they really be guineas,[1] those two glittering objects the interloper had held up to his (Billy's) eyes? Where could the fellow get guineas? Why, even spare buttons are not so plentiful at sea. The more he turned the matter over, the more he was nonplussed, and made uneasy and discomfited. In his disgustful recoil from an overture which, though he but ill comprehended, he instinctively knew must involve evil of some sort, Billy Budd was like a young horse fresh from the pasture suddenly inhaling a vile whiff from some chemical factory, and by repeated snortings trying to get it out of his nostrils and lungs. This frame of mind barred all desire of holding further parley with the fellow, even were it but for the purpose of gaining some enlightenment as to his design in approaching him. And yet he was not without natural curiosity to see how such a visitor in the dark would look in broad day.

He espied him the following afternoon in his first dogwatch below, one of the smokers on that forward part of the upper gun deck[2] allotted to the pipe. He recognized him by his general cut and build more than by his round freckled face and glassy eyes of pale blue, veiled with lashes all but white. And yet Billy was a bit uncertain whether indeed it were he—yonder chap about his own age chatting and laughing in freehearted way, leaning against a gun; a genial young fellow enough to look at, and something of a rattlebrain, to all appearance. Rather chubby too for a sailor, even an afterguardsman. In short, the last man in the world, one would think, to be overburdened with thoughts, especially those perilous thoughts that must needs belong to a conspirator in any serious project, or even to the underling of such a conspirator.

Although Billy was not aware of it, the fellow, with a side-long watchful glance, had perceived Billy first, and then noting that Billy was looking at him, thereupon nodded a familiar sort of friendly recognition as to an old acquaintance, without interrupting the talk he was engaged in with the group of smokers. A day or two afterwards, chancing in the evening promenade on a

---

1. Gold coins worth a little more than one pound.   2. The only place smoking was permitted to the crew.

gun deck to pass Billy, he offered a flying word of good-fellowship, as it were, which by its unexpectedness, and equivocalness under the circumstances, so embarrassed Billy that he knew not how to respond to it, and let it go unnoticed.

Billy was now left more at a loss than before. The ineffectual speculations into which he was led were so disturbingly alien to him that he did his best to smother them. It never entered his mind that here was a matter which, from its extreme questionableness, it was his duty as a loyal bluejacket to report in the proper quarter. And, probably, had such a step been suggested to him, he would have been deterred from taking it by the thought, one of novice magnanimity, that it would savor overmuch of the dirty work of a telltale. He kept the thing to himself. Yet upon one occasion he could not forbear a little disburdening himself to the old Dansker, tempted thereto perhaps by the influence of a balmy night when the ship lay becalmed; the twain, silent for the most part, sitting together on deck, their heads propped against the bulwarks. But it was only a partial and anonymous account that Billy gave, the unfounded scruples above referred to preventing full disclosure to anybody. Upon hearing Billy's version, the sage Dansker seemed to divine more than he was told; and after a little meditation, during which his wrinkles were pursed as into a point, quite effacing for the time that quizzing expression his face sometimes wore: "Didn't I say so, Baby Budd?"

"Say what?" demanded Billy.

"Why, *Jemmy Legs* is *down* on you."

"And what," rejoined Billy in amazement, "has *Jemmy Legs* to do with that cracked afterguardsman?"

"Ho, it was an afterguardsman, then. A cat's-paw, a cat's-paw!" And with that exclamation, whether it had reference to a light puff of air just then coming over the calm sea, or a subtler relation to the afterguardsman, there is no telling, the old Merlin gave a twisting wrench with his black teeth at his plug of tobacco, vouchsafing no reply to Billy's impetuous question, though now repeated, for it was his wont to relapse into grim silence when interrogated in skeptical sort as to any of his sententious oracles, not always very clear ones, rather partaking of that obscurity which invests most Delphic[3] deliverances from any quarter.

Long experience had very likely brought this old man to that bitter prudence which never interferes in aught and never gives advice.

16

Yes, despite the Dansker's pithy insistence as to the master-at-arms being at the bottom of these strange experiences of Billy on board the *Bellipotent*, the young sailor was ready to ascribe them to almost anybody but the man who, to use Billy's own expression, "always had a pleasant word for him." This is to be wondered at. Yet not so much to be wondered at. In certain matters, some sailors even in mature life remain unsophisticated enough. But a young seafarer of the disposition of our athletic foretopman is much of a child-man. And yet a child's utter innocence is but its blank ignorance, and the innocence more or less wanes as intelligence waxes. But in Billy Budd intelligence, such

3. Oracular.

as it was, had advanced while yet his simple-mindedness remained for the most part unaffected. Experience is a teacher indeed; yet did Billy's years make his experience small. Besides, he had none of that intuitive knowledge of the bad which in natures not good or incompletely so foreruns experience, and therefore may pertain, as in some instances it too clearly does pertain, even to youth.

And what could Billy know of man except of man as a mere sailor? And the old-fashioned sailor, the veritable man before the mast, the sailor from boyhood up, he, though indeed of the same species as a landsman, is in some respects singularly distinct from him. The sailor is frankness, the landsman is finesse. Life is not a game with the sailor, demanding the long head[4]—no intricate game of chess where few moves are made in straightforwardness and ends are attained by indirection, an oblique, tedious, barren game hardly worth that poor candle burnt out in playing it.

Yes, as a class, sailors are in character a juvenile race. Even their deviations are marked by juvenility, this more especially holding true with the sailors of Billy's time. Then too, certain things which apply to all sailors do more pointedly operate here and there upon the junior one. Every sailor, too, is accustomed to obey orders without debating them; his life afloat is externally ruled for him; he is not brought into that promiscuous commerce with mankind where unobstructed free agency on equal terms—equal superficially, at least—soon teaches one that unless upon occasion he exercise a distrust keen in proportion to the fairness of the appearance, some foul turn may be served him. A ruled undemonstrative distrustfulness is so habitual, not with businessmen so much as with men who know their kind in less shallow relations than business, namely, certain men of the world, that they come at last to employ it all but unconsciously; and some of them would very likely feel real surprise at being charged with it as one of their general characteristics.

17

But after the little matter at the mess Billy Budd no more found himself in strange trouble at times about his hammock or his clothes bag or what not. As to that smile that occasionally sunned him, and the pleasant passing word, these were, if not more frequent, yet if anything more pronounced than before.

But for all that, there were certain other demonstrations now. When Claggart's unobserved glance happened to light on belted Billy rolling along the upper gun deck in the leisure of the second dogwatch, exchanging passing broadsides of fun with other young promenaders in the crowd, that glance would follow the cheerful sea Hyperion[5] with a settled meditative and melancholy expression, his eyes strangely suffused with incipient feverish tears. Then would Claggart look like the man of sorrows. Yes, and sometimes the melancholy expression would have in it a touch of soft yearning, as if Claggart could even have loved Billy but for fate and ban. But this was an evanescence, and quickly repented of, as it were, by an immitigable look, pinching and shriveling the visage into the momentary semblance of a wrinkled walnut. But sometimes catching sight in advance of the foretopman coming in his direction, he

4. Foresight, sagacity.
5. A Titan, later identified with Apollo, god of manly beauty.

would, upon their nearing, step aside a little to let him pass, dwelling upon
Billy for the moment with the glittering dental satire of a Guise.[6] But upon
any abrupt unforeseen encounter a red light would flash forth from his eye like
a spark from an anvil in a dusk smithy. That quick, fierce light was a strange
one, darted from orbs which in repose were of a color nearest approaching a
deeper violet, the softest of shades.

Though some of these caprices of the pit could not but be observed by their
object, yet were they beyond the construing of such a nature. And the thews[7]
of Billy were hardly compatible with that sort of sensitive spiritual organization
which in some cases instinctively conveys to ignorant innocence an admonition of the proximity of the malign. He thought the master-at-arms acted in a
manner rather queer at times. That was all. But the occasional frank air and
pleasant word went for what they purported to be, the young sailor never having heard as yet of the "too fair-spoken man."

Had the foretopman been conscious of having done or said anything to
provoke the ill will of the official, it would have been different with him, and
his sight might have been purged if not sharpened. As it was, innocence was
his blinder.

So was it with him in yet another matter. Two minor officers, the armorer
and captain of the hold,[8] with whom he had never exchanged a word, his
position in the ship not bringing him into contact with them, these men now
for the first began to cast upon Billy, when they chanced to encounter him,
that peculiar glance which evidences that the man from whom it comes has
been some way tampered with, and to the prejudice of him upon whom the
glance lights. Never did it occur to Billy as a thing to be noted or a thing
suspicious, though he well knew the fact, that the armorer and captain of the
hold, with the ship's yeoman, apothecary, and others of that grade, were by
naval usage messmates of the master-at-arms, men with ears convenient to his
confidential tongue.

But the general popularity that came from our Handsome Sailor's manly
forwardness upon occasion and irresistible good nature, indicating no mental
superiority tending to excite an invidious feeling, this good will on the part of
most of his shipmates made him the less to concern himself about such mute
aspects toward him as those whereto allusion has just been made, aspects he
could not so fathom as to infer their whole import.

As to the afterguardsman, though Billy for reasons already given necessarily
saw little of him, yet when the two did happen to meet, invariably came the
fellow's offhand cheerful recognition, sometimes accompanied by a passing
pleasant word or two. Whatever that equivocal young person's original design
may really have been, or the design of which he might have been the deputy,
certain it was from his manner upon these occasions that he had wholly
dropped it.

It was as if his precocity of crookedness (and every vulgar villain is precocious) had for once deceived him, and the man he had sought to entrap as a
simpleton had through his very simplicity ignominiously baffled him.

6. Henri de Guise (1550–1588) was one of those responsible for the treacherous massacre of French
Huguenots that began on St. Bartholomew's Day (August 24) 1572. The idea is that of Shakespeare's *Hamlet*
(1.5.108), that one may smile and smile and be a
villain.
7. Muscles.
8. Petty officers in charge of caring for arms ("armorer") and of supervising the interior of a vessel below
decks ("captain of the hold").

But shrewd ones may opine that it was hardly possible for Billy to refrain from going up to the afterguardsman and bluntly demanding to know his purpose in the initial interview so abruptly closed in the forechains. Shrewd ones may also think it but natural in Billy to set about sounding some of the other impressed men of the ship in order to discover what basis, if any, there was for the emissary's obscure suggestions as to plotting disaffection aboard. Yes, shrewd ones may so think. But something more, or rather something else than mere shrewdness is perhaps needful for the due understanding of such a character as Billy Budd's.

As to Claggart, the monomania in the man—if that indeed it were—as involuntarily disclosed by starts in the manifestations detailed, yet in general covered over by his self-contained and rational demeanor; this, like a subterranean fire, was eating its way deeper and deeper in him. Something decisive must come of it.

18

After the mysterious interview in the forechains, the one so abruptly ended there by Billy, nothing especially germane to the story occurred until the events now about to be narrated.

Elsewhere it has been said that in the lack of frigates (of course better sailers than line-of-battle ships) in the English squadron up the Straits at that period, the *Bellipotent* 74 was occasionally employed not only as an available substitute for a scout, but at times on detached service of more important kind. This was not alone because of her sailing qualities, not common in a ship of her rate, but quite as much, probably, that the character of her commander, it was thought, specially adapted him for any duty where under unforeseen difficulties a prompt initiative might have to be taken in some matter demanding knowledge and ability in addition to those qualities implied in good seamanship. It was on an expedition of the latter sort, a somewhat distant one, and when the *Bellipotent* was almost at her furthest remove from the fleet, that in the latter part of an afternoon watch she unexpectedly came in sight of a ship of the enemy. It proved to be a frigate. The latter, perceiving through the glass that the weight of men and metal would be heavily against her, invoking her light heels crowded sail to get away. After a chase urged almost against hope and lasting until about the middle of the first dogwatch, she signally succeeded in effecting her escape.

Not long after the pursuit had been given up, and ere the excitement incident thereto had altogether waned away, the master-at-arms, ascending from his cavernous sphere, made his appearance cap in hand by the mainmast respectfully waiting the notice of Captain Vere, then solitary walking the weather side of the quarter-deck, doubtless somewhat chafed at the failure of the pursuit. The spot where Claggart stood was the place allotted to men of lesser grades seeking some more particular interview either with the officer of the deck or the captain himself. But from the latter it was not often that a sailor or petty officer of those days would seek a hearing; only some exceptional cause would, according to established custom, have warranted that.

Presently, just as the commander, absorbed in his reflections, was on the point of turning aft in his promenade, he became sensible of Claggart's presence, and saw the doffed cap held in deferential expectancy. Here be it said that Captain Vere's personal knowledge of this petty officer had only begun at the time of the ship's last sailing from home, Claggart then for the first, in transfer from a ship detained for repairs, supplying on board the *Bellipotent* the place of a previous master-at-arms disabled and ashore.

No sooner did the commander observe who it was that now deferentially stood awaiting his notice than a peculiar expression came over him. It was not unlike that which uncontrollably will flit across the countenance of one at unawares encountering a person who, though known to him indeed, has hardly been long enough known for thorough knowledge, but something in whose aspect nevertheless now for the first provokes a vaguely repellent distaste. But coming to a stand and resuming much of his wonted official manner, save that a sort of impatience lurked in the intonation of the opening word, he said "Well? What is it, Master-at-arms?"

With the air of a subordinate grieved at the necessity of being a messenger of ill tidings, and while conscientiously determined to be frank yet equally resolved upon shunning overstatement, Claggart at this invitation, or rather summons to disburden, spoke up. What he said, conveyed in the language of no uneducated man, was to the effect following, if not altogether in these words, namely, that during the chase and preparations for the possible encounter he had seen enough to convince him that at least one sailor aboard was a dangerous character in a ship mustering some who not only had taken a guilty part in the late serious troubles, but others also who, like the man in question, had entered His Majesty's service under another form than enlistment.

At this point Captain Vere with some impatience interrupted him: "Be direct, man; say *impressed men.*"

Claggart made a gesture of subservience, and proceeded. Quite lately he (Claggart) had begun to suspect that on the gun decks some sort of movement prompted by the sailor in question was covertly going on, but he had not thought himself warranted in reporting the suspicion so long as it remained indistinct. But from what he had that afternoon observed in the man referred to, the suspicion of something clandestine going on had advanced to a point less removed from certainty. He deeply felt, he added, the serious responsibility assumed in making a report involving such possible consequences to the individual mainly concerned, besides tending to augment those natural anxieties which every naval commander must feel in view of extraordinary outbreaks so recent as those which, he sorrowfully said it, it needed not to name.

Now at the first broaching of the matter Captain Vere, taken by surprise, could not wholly dissemble his disquietude. But as Claggart went on, the former's aspect changed into restiveness under something in the testifier's manner in giving his testimony. However, he refrained from interrupting him. And Claggart, continuing, concluded with this: "God forbid, your honor, that the *Bellipotent's* should be the experience of the—"

"Never mind that!" here peremptorily broke in the superior, his face altering with anger, instinctively divining the ship that the other was about to name, one in which the Nore Mutiny had assumed a singularly tragical character that for a time jeopardized the life of its commander. Under the circumstances he was indignant at the purposed allusion. When the commissioned officers themselves were on all occasions very heedful how they referred to the recent events in the fleet, for a petty officer unnecessarily to allude to them in the presence of his captain, this struck him as a most immodest presumption.

Besides, to his quick sense of self-respect it even looked under the circumstances something like an attempt to alarm him. Nor at first was he without some surprise that one who so far as he had hitherto come under his notice had shown considerable tact in his function should in this particular evince such lack of it.

But these thoughts and kindred dubious ones flitting across his mind were suddenly replaced by an intuitional surmise which, though as yet obscure in form, served practically to affect his reception of the ill tidings. Certain it is that, long versed in everything pertaining to the complicated gun-deck life, which like every other form of life has its secret mines and dubious side, the side popularly disclaimed, Captain Vere did not permit himself to be unduly disturbed by the general tenor of his subordinate's report.

Furthermore, if in view of recent events prompt action should be taken at the first palpable sign of recurring insubordination, for all that, not judicious would it be, he thought, to keep the idea of lingering disaffection alive by undue forwardness in crediting an informer, even if his own subordinate and charged among other things with police surveillance of the crew. This feeling would not perhaps have so prevailed with him were it not that upon a prior occasion the patriotic zeal officially evinced by Claggart had somewhat irritated him as appearing rather supersensible and strained. Furthermore, something even in the official's self-possessed and somewhat ostentatious manner in making his specifications strangely reminded him of a bandsman,[9] a perjurious witness in a capital case before a court-martial ashore of which when a lieutenant he (Captain Vere) had been a member.

Now the peremptory check given to Claggart in the matter of the arrested allusion was quickly followed up by this: "You say that there is at least one dangerous man aboard. Name him."

"William Budd, a foretopman, your honor."

"William Budd!" repeated Captain Vere with unfeigned astonishment. "And mean you the man that Lieutenant Ratcliffe took from the merchantman not very long ago, the young fellow who seems to be so popular with the men—Billy, the Handsome Sailor, as they call him?"

"The same, your honor; but for all his youth and good looks, a deep one. Not for nothing does he insinuate himself into the good will of his shipmates, since at the least they will at a pinch say—all hands will—a good word for him, and at all hazards. Did Lieutenant Ratcliffe happen to tell your honor of that adroit fling of Budd's, jumping up in the cutter's bow under the merchantman's stern when he was being taken off? It is even masked by that sort of good-humored air that at heart he resents his impressment. You have but noted his fair cheek. A mantrap may be under the ruddy-tipped daisies."

Now the Handsome Sailor as a signal figure among the crew had naturally enough attracted the captain's attention from the first. Though in general not very demonstrative to his officers, he had congratulated Lieutenant Ratcliffe upon his good fortune in lighting on such a fine specimen of the *genus homo*,[1] who in the nude might have posed for a statue of young Adam before the Fall. As to Billy's adieu to the ship *Rights-of-Man*, which the boarding lieutenant had indeed reported to him, but, in a deferential way, more as a good story than aught else, Captain Vere, though mistakenly understanding it as a satiric sally, had but thought so much the better of the impressed man for it; as a military sailor, admiring the spirit that could take an arbitrary enlistment so merrily and sensibly. The foretopman's conduct, too, so far as it had fallen under the captain's notice, had confirmed the first happy augury, while the new recruit's qualities as a "sailor-man" seemed to be such that he had thought of recommending him to the executive officer for promotion to a place that would more frequently bring him under his own observation, namely, the captaincy of the mizzentop,[2] replacing there in the starboard watch a man not so young whom partly for that reason he deemed less fitted for the post. Be it parenthesized here that since the mizzentopmen have not to handle such breadths of heavy canvas as the lower sails on the mainmast and foremast, a young man if of the right stuff not only seems best adapted to duty there, but in fact is generally selected for the captaincy of that top, and the company under him are light hands and often but striplings. In sum, Captain Vere had from the beginning deemed Billy Budd to be what in the naval parlance of the time was called a "King's bargain": that is to say, for His Britannic Majesty's navy a capital investment at small outlay or none at all.

After a brief pause, during which the reminiscences above mentioned passed vividly through his mind and he weighed the import of Claggart's last suggestion conveyed in the phrase "mantrap under the daisies," and the more he weighed it the less reliance he felt in the informer's good faith, suddenly he turned upon him and in a low voice demanded: "Do you come to me, Master-at-arms, with so foggy a tale? As to Budd, cite me an act or spoken word of his confirmatory of what you in general charge against him. Stay," drawing nearer to him; "heed what you speak. Just now, and in a case like this, there is a yardarm-end[3] for the false witness."

"Ah, your honor!" sighed Claggart, mildly shaking his shapely head as in sad deprecation of such unmerited severity of tone. Then, bridling—erecting himself as in virtuous self-assertion—he circumstantially alleged certain words and acts which collectively, if credited, led to presumptions mortally inculpating Budd. And for some of these averments, he added, substantiating proof was not far.

With gray eyes impatient and distrustful essaying to fathom to the bottom Claggart's calm violet ones, Captain Vere again heard him out; then for the moment stood ruminating. The mood he evinced, Claggart—himself for the time liberated from the other's scrutiny—steadily regarded with a look difficult to render: a look curious of the operation of his tactics, a look such as might have been that of the spokesman of the envious children of Jacob deceptively imposing upon the troubled patriarch the blood-dyed coat of young Joseph.[4]

Though something exceptional in the moral quality of Captain Vere made him, in earnest encounter with a fellow man, a veritable touchstone of that man's essential nature, yet now as to Claggart and what was really going on in him his feeling partook less of intuitional conviction than of strong suspicion clogged by strange dubieties. The perplexity he evinced proceeded less from aught touching the man informed against—as Claggart doubtless opined—than from considerations how best to act in regard to the informer. At first, indeed, he was naturally for summoning that substantiation of his allegations which Claggart said was at hand. But such a proceeding would result in the

---

2. The watch assigned to the aftermost mast.   4. Genesis 37.31–33.
3. Used for hangings.

matter at once getting abroad, which in the present stage of it, he thought, might undesirably affect the ship's company. If Claggart was a false witness—that closed the affair. And therefore, before trying the accusation, he would first practically test the accuser; and he thought this could be done in a quiet, undemonstrative way.

The measure he determined upon involved a shifting of the scene, a transfer to a place less exposed to observation than the broad quarter-deck. For although the few gun-room officers there at the time had, in due observance of naval etiquette, withdrawn to leeward the moment Captain Vere had begun his promenade on the deck's weather side; and though during the colloquy with Claggart they of course ventured not to diminish the distance; and though throughout the interview Captain Vere's voice was far from high, and Claggart's silvery and low; and the wind in the cordage and the wash of the sea helped the more to put them beyond earshot; nevertheless, the interview's continuance already had attracted observation from some topmen aloft and other sailors in the waist or further forward.

Having determined upon his measures, Captain Vere forthwith took action. Abruptly turning to Claggart, he asked, "Master-at-arms, is it now Budd's watch aloft?"

"No, your honor."

Whereupon, "Mr. Wilkes!" summoning the nearest midshipman. "Tell Albert to come to me." Albert was the captain's hammock-boy, a sort of sea valet in whose discretion and fidelity his master had much confidence. The lad appeared.

"You know Budd, the foretopman?"

"I do, sir."

"Go find him. It is his watch off. Manage to tell him out of earshot that he is wanted aft. Contrive it that he speaks to nobody. Keep him in talk yourself. And not till you get well aft here, not till then let him know that the place where he is wanted is my cabin. You understand. Go.—Master-at-arms, show yourself on the decks below, and when you think it time for Albert to be coming with his man, stand by quietly to follow the sailor in."

19

Now when the foretopman found himself in the cabin, closeted there, as it were, with the captain and Claggart, he was surprised enough. But it was a surprise unaccompanied by apprehension or distrust. To an immature nature essentially honest and humane, forewarning intimations of subtler danger from one's kind come tardily if at all. The only thing that took shape in the young sailor's mind was this: Yes, the captain, I have always thought, looks kindly upon me. Wonder if he's going to make me his coxswain. I should like that. And may be now he is going to ask the master-at-arms about me.

"Shut the door there, sentry," said the commander; "stand without, and let nobody come in.—Now, Master-at-arms, tell this man to his face what you told of him to me," and stood prepared to scrutinize the mutually confronting visages.

With the measured step and calm collected air of an asylum physician approaching in the public hall some patient beginning to show indications of a coming paroxysm, Claggart deliberately advanced within short range of Billy and, mesmerically looking him in the eye, briefly recapitulated the accusation.

Not at first did Billy take it in. When he did, the rose-tan of his cheek looked struck as by white leprosy. He stood like one impaled and gagged. Meanwhile the accuser's eyes, removing not as yet from the blue dilated ones, underwent a phenomenal change, their wonted rich violet color blurring into a muddy purple. Those lights of human intelligence, losing human expression, were gelidly protruding like the alien eyes of certain uncatalogued creatures of the deep. The first mesmeristic glance was one of serpent fascination; the last was as the paralyzing lurch of the torpedo fish.

"Speak, man!" said Captain Vere to the transfixed one, struck by his aspect even more than by Claggart's. "Speak! Defend yourself!" Which appeal caused but a strange dumb gesturing and gurgling in Billy; amazement at such an accusation so suddenly sprung on inexperienced nonage; this, and, it may be, horror of the accuser's eyes, serving to bring out his lurking defect and in this instance for the time intensifying it into a convulsed tongue-tie; while the intent head and entire form straining forward in an agony of ineffectual eagerness to obey the injunction to speak and defend himself, gave an expression to the face like that of a condemned vestal priestess in the moment of being buried alive, and in the first struggle against suffocation.[5]

Though at the time Captain Vere was quite ignorant of Billy's liability to vocal impediment, he now immediately divined it, since vividly Billy's aspect recalled to him that of a bright young schoolmate of his whom he had once seen struck by much the same startling impotence in the act of eagerly rising in the class to be foremost in response to a testing question put to it by the master. Going close up to the young sailor, and laying a soothing hand on his shoulder, he said, "There is no hurry, my boy. Take your time, take your time." Contrary to the effect intended, these words so fatherly in tone, doubtless touching Billy's heart to the quick, prompted yet more violent efforts at utterance—efforts soon ending for the time in confirming the paralysis, and bringing to his face an expression which was as a crucifixion to behold. The next instant, quick as the flame from a discharged cannon at night, his right arm shot out, and Claggart dropped to the deck. Whether intentionally or but owing to the young athlete's superior height, the blow had taken effect full upon the forehead, so shapely and intellectual-looking a feature in the master-at-arms; so that the body fell over lengthwise, like a heavy plank tilted from erectness. A gasp or two, and he lay motionless.

"Fated boy," breathed Captain Vere in tone so low as to be almost a whisper, "what have you done! But here, help me."

The twain raised the felled one from the loins up into a sitting position. The spare form flexibly acquiesced, but inertly. It was like handling a dead snake. They lowered it back. Regaining erectness, Captain Vere with one hand covering his face stood to all appearance as impassive as the object at his feet. Was he absorbed in taking in all the bearings of the event and what was best not only now at once to be done, but also in the sequel? Slowly he uncovered his face; and the effect was as if the moon emerging from eclipse should reappear with quite another aspect than that which had gone into hiding. The father in him, manifested towards Billy thus far in the scene, was replaced by the military disciplinarian. In his official tone he bade the foretopman retire to a stateroom aft (pointing it out), and there remain till thence summoned. This order

---

5. The punishment of unchaste priestesses of the Roman goddess of the hearth, Vesta.

Billy in silence mechanically obeyed. Then going to the cabin door where it opened on the quarter-deck, Captain Vere said to the sentry without, "Tell somebody to send Albert here." When the lad appeared, his master so contrived it that he should not catch sight of the prone one. "Albert," he said to him, "tell the surgeon I wish to see him. You need not come back till called."

When the surgeon entered—a self-poised character of that grave sense and experience that hardly anything could take him aback—Captain Vere advanced to meet him, thus unconsciously intercepting his view of Claggart, and, interrupting the other's wonted ceremonious salutation, said, "Nay. Tell me how it is with yonder man," directing his attention to the prostrate one.

The surgeon looked, and for all his self-command somewhat started at the abrupt revelation. On Claggart's always pallid complexion, thick black blood was now oozing from nostril and ear. To the gazer's professional eye it was unmistakably no living man that he saw.

"Is it so, then?" said Captain Vere, intently watching him. "I thought it. But verify it." Whereupon the customary tests confirmed the surgeon's first glance, who now, looking up in unfeigned concern, cast a look of intense inquisitiveness upon his superior. But Captain Vere, with one hand to his brow, was standing motionless. Suddenly, catching the surgeon's arm convulsively, he exclaimed, pointing down to the body, "It is the divine judgment on Ananias![6] Look!"

Disturbed by the excited manner he had never before observed in the *Bellipont*'s captain, and as yet wholly ignorant of the affair, the prudent surgeon nevertheless held his peace, only again looking an earnest interrogatory as to what it was that had resulted in such a tragedy.

But Captain Vere was now again motionless, standing absorbed in thought. Again starting, he vehemently exclaimed, "Struck dead by an angel of God! Yet the angel must hang!"

At these passionate interjections, mere incoherences to the listener as yet unapprised of the antecedents, the surgeon was profoundly discomposed. But now, as recollecting himself, Captain Vere in less passionate tone briefly related the circumstances leading up to the event. "But come; we must dispatch," he added. "Help me to remove him" (meaning the body) "to yonder compartment," designating one opposite that where the foretopman remained immured. Anew disturbed by a request that, as implying a desire for secrecy, seemed unaccountably strange to him, there was nothing for the subordinate to do but comply.

"Go now," said Captain Vere with something of his wonted manner. "Go now. I presently shall call a drumhead court.[7] Tell the lieutenants what has happened, and tell Mr. Mordant" (meaning the captain of marines),[8] "and charge them to keep the matter to themselves."

20

Full of disquietude and misgiving, the surgeon left the cabin. Was Captain Vere suddenly affected in his mind, or was it but a transient excitement,

---

6. Acts 5.3–5.
7. An emergency court (from the custom of using a drum for a table in an impromptu military or naval trial).

8. Captain of the soldiers stationed on shipboard; the mutual antipathy of marines and sailors was used as an aid to discipline.

brought about by so strange and extraordinary a tragedy? As to the drumhead court, it struck the surgeon as impolitic, if nothing more. The thing to do, he thought, was to place Billy Budd in confinement, and in a way dictated by usage, and postpone further action in so extraordinary a case to such time as they should rejoin the squadron, and then refer it to the admiral. He recalled the unwonted agitation of Captain Vere and his excited exclamations, so at variance with his normal manner. Was he unhinged?

But assuming that he is, it is not so susceptible of proof. What then can the surgeon do? No more trying situation is conceivable than that of an officer subordinate under a captain whom he suspects to be not mad, indeed, but yet not quite unaffected in his intellects. To argue his order to him would be insolence. To resist him would be mutiny.

In obedience to Captain Vere, he communicated what had happened to the lieutenants and captain of marines, saying nothing as to the captain's state. They fully shared his own surprise and concern. Like him too, they seemed to think that such a matter should be referred to the admiral.

21

Who in the rainbow can draw the line where the violet tint ends and the orange tint begins? Distinctly we see the difference of the colors, but where exactly does the one first blendingly enter into the other? So with sanity and insanity. In pronounced cases there is no question about them. But in some supposed cases, in various degrees supposedly less pronounced, to draw the exact line of demarcation few will undertake, though for a fee becoming considerate some professional experts will. There is nothing namable but that some men will, or undertake to, do it for pay.

Whether Captain Vere, as the surgeon professionally and privately surmised, was really the sudden victim of any degree of aberration, every one must determine for himself by such light as this narrative may afford.

That the unhappy event which has been narrated could not have happened at a worse juncture was but too true. For it was close on the heel of the suppressed insurrections, an aftertime very critical to naval authority, demanding from every English sea commander two qualities not readily interfusable—prudence and rigor. Moreover, there was something crucial in the case.

In the jugglery of circumstances preceding and attending the event on board the *Bellipotent*, and in the light of that martial code whereby it was formally to be judged, innocence and guilt personified in Claggart and Budd in effect changed places. In a legal view the apparent victim of the tragedy was he who had sought to victimize a man blameless; and the indisputable deed of the latter, navally regarded, constituted the most heinous of military crimes. Yet more. The essential right and wrong involved in the matter, the clearer that might be, so much the worse for the responsibility of a loyal sea commander, inasmuch as he was not authorized to determine the matter on that primitive basis.

Small wonder then that the *Bellipotent*'s captain, though in general a man of rapid decision, felt that circumspectness not less than promptitude was necessary. Until he could decide upon his course, and in each detail; and not only so, but until the concluding measure was upon the point of being enacted, he deemed it advisable, in view of all the circumstances, to guard as much as possible against publicity. Here he may or may not have erred. Certain it is, however, that subsequently in the confidential talk of more than one or two gun rooms and cabins he was not a little criticized by some officers, a fact imputed by his friends and vehemently by his cousin Jack Denton to professional jealousy of Starry Vere. Some imaginative ground for invidious comment there was. The maintenance of secrecy in the matter, the confining all knowledge of it for a time to the place where the homicide occurred, the quarter-deck cabin; in these particulars lurked some resemblance to the policy adopted in those tragedies of the palace which have occurred more than once in the capital founded by Peter the Barbarian.[9]

The case indeed was such that fain would the *Bellipotent*'s captain have deferred taking any action whatever respecting it further than to keep the foretopman a close prisoner till the ship rejoined the squadron and then submitting the matter to the judgment of his admiral.

But a true military officer is in one particular like a true monk. Not with more of self-abnegation will the latter keep his vows of monastic obedience than the former his vows of allegiance to martial duty.

Feeling that unless quick action was taken on it, the deed of the foretopman, so soon as it should be known on the gun decks, would tend to awaken any slumbering embers of the Nore among the crew, a sense of the urgency of the case overruled in Captain Vere every other consideration. But though a conscientious disciplinarian, he was no lover of authority for mere authority's sake. Very far was he from embracing opportunities for monopolizing to himself the perils of moral responsibility, none at least that could properly be referred to an official superior or shared with him by his official equals or even subordinates. So thinking, he was glad it would not be at variance with usage to turn the matter over to a summary court of his own officers, reserving to himself, as the one on whom the ultimate accountability would rest, the right of maintaining a supervision of it, or formally or informally interposing at need. Accordingly a drumhead court was summarily convened, he electing the individuals composing it: the first lieutenant, the captain of marines, and the sailing master.[1]

In associating an officer of marines with the sea lieutenant and the sailing master in a case having to do with a sailor, the commander perhaps deviated from general custom. He was prompted thereto by the circumstance that he took that soldier to be a judicious person, thoughtful, and not altogether incapable of grappling with a difficult case unprecedented in his prior experience. Yet even as to him he was not without some latent misgiving, for withal he was an extremely good-natured man, an enjoyer of his dinner, a sound sleeper, and inclined to obesity—a man who though he would always maintain his manhood in battle might not prove altogether reliable in a moral dilemma involving aught of the tragic. As to the first lieutenant and the sailing master, Captain Vere could not but be aware that though honest natures, of approved gallantry upon occasion, their intelligence was mostly confined to the matter of active seamanship and the fighting demands of their profession.

The court was held in the same cabin where the unfortunate affair had taken place. This cabin, the commander's, embraced the entire area under

---

9. Peter the Great (1672–1725), czar of Russia.　　1. Officer charged with navigating the ship.

the poop deck. Aft, and on either side, was a small stateroom, the one now temporarily a jail and the other a dead-house, and a yet smaller compartment, leaving a space between expanding forward into a goodly oblong of length coinciding with the ship's beam. A skylight of moderate dimension was overhead, and at each end of the oblong space were two sashed porthole windows easily convertible back into embrasures for short carronades.[2]

All being quickly in readiness, Billy Budd was arraigned, Captain Vere necessarily appearing as the sole witness in the case, and as such temporarily sinking his rank, though singularly maintaining it in a matter apparently trivial, namely, that he testified from the ship's weather side, with that object having caused the court to sit on the lee side.[3] Concisely he narrated all that had led up to the catastrophe, omitting nothing in Claggart's accusation and deposing as to the manner in which the prisoner had received it. At this testimony the three officers glanced with no little surprise at Billy Budd, the last man they would have suspected either of the mutinous design alleged by Claggart or the undeniable deed he himself had done. The first lieutenant, taking judicial primacy and turning toward the prisoner, said, "Captain Vere has spoken. Is it or is it not as Captain Vere says?"

In response came syllables not so much impeded in the utterance as might have been anticipated. They were these: "Captain Vere tells the truth. It is just as Captain Vere says, but it is not as the master-at-arms said. I have eaten the King's bread and I am true to the King."

"I believe you, my man," said the witness, his voice indicating a suppressed emotion not otherwise betrayed.

"God will bless you for that, your honor!" not without stammering said Billy, and all but broke down. But immediately he was recalled to self-control by another question, to which with the same emotional difficulty of utterance he said, "No, there was no malice between us. I never bore malice against the master-at-arms. I am sorry that he is dead. I did not mean to kill him. Could I have used my tongue I would not have struck him. But he foully lied to my face and in presence of my captain, and I had to say something, and I could only say it with a blow, God help me!"

In the impulsive aboveboard manner of the frank one the court saw confirmed all that was implied in words that just previously had perplexed them, coming as they did from the testifier to the tragedy and promptly following Billy's impassioned disclaimer of mutinous intent—Captain Vere's words, "I believe you, my man."

Next it was asked of him whether he knew of or suspected aught savoring of incipient trouble (meaning mutiny, though the explicit term was avoided) going on in any section of the ship's company.

The reply lingered. This was naturally imputed by the court to the same vocal embarrassment which had retarded or obstructed previous answers. But in main it was otherwise here, the question immediately recalling to Billy's mind the interview with the afterguardsman in the forechains. But an innate repugnance to playing a part at all approaching that of an informer against one's own shipmates—the same erring sense of uninstructed honor which had stood in the way of his reporting the matter at the time, though as a loyal man-

---

2. Light iron cannons (from Carron, Scotland, where they were first made). "Ship's beam": the widest point of the ship.

3. Vere testifies from the side from which the wind is blowing, so he looms higher than the officers.

of-war's man it was incumbent on him, and failure so to do, if charged against him and proven, would have subjected him to the heaviest of penalties; this, with the blind feeling now his that nothing really was being hatched, prevailed with him. When the answer came it was a negative.

"One question more," said the officer of marines, now first speaking and with a troubled earnestness. "You tell us that what the master-at-arms said against you was a lie. Now why should he have so lied, so maliciously lied, since you declare there was no malice between you?"

At that question, unintentionally touching on a spiritual sphere wholly obscure to Billy's thoughts, he was nonplussed, evincing a confusion indeed that some observers, such as can readily be imagined, would have construed into involuntary evidence of hidden guilt. Nevertheless, he strove some way to answer, but all at once relinquished the vain endeavor, at the same time turning an appealing glance towards Captain Vere as deeming him his best helper and friend. Captain Vere, who had been seated for a time, rose to his feet, addressing the interrogator. "The question you put to him comes naturally enough. But how can he rightly answer it?—or anybody else, unless indeed it be he who lies within there," designating the compartment where lay the corpse. "But the prone one there will not rise to our summons. In effect, though, as it seems to me, the point you make is hardly material. Quite aside from any conceivable motive actuating the master-at-arms, and irrespective of the provocation to the blow, a martial court must needs in the present case confine its attention to the blow's consequence, which consequence justly is to be deemed not otherwise than as the striker's deed."

This utterance, the full significance of which it was not at all likely that Billy took in, nevertheless caused him to turn a wistful interrogative look toward the speaker, a look in its dumb expressiveness not unlike that which a dog of generous breed might turn upon his master, seeking in his face some elucidation of a previous gesture ambiguous to the canine intelligence. Nor was the same utterance without marked effect upon the three officers, more especially the soldier. Couched in it seemed to them a meaning unanticipated, involving a prejudgment on the speaker's part. It served to augment a mental disturbance previously evident enough.

The soldier once more spoke, in a tone of suggestive dubiety addressing at once his associates and Captain Vere: "Nobody is present—none of the ship's company, I mean—who might shed lateral light, if any is to be had, upon what remains mysterious in this matter."

"That is thoughtfully put," said Captain Vere; "I see your drift. Ay, there is a mystery; but, to use a scriptural phrase, it is a 'mystery of iniquity,'[4] a matter for psychologic theologians to discuss. But what has a military court to do with it? Not to add that for us any possible investigation of it is cut off by the lasting tongue-tie of—him—in yonder," again designating the mortuary stateroom. "The prisoner's deed—with that alone we have to do."

To this, and particularly the closing reiteration, the marine soldier, knowing not how aptly to reply, sadly abstained from saying aught. The first lieutenant, who at the outset had not unnaturally assumed primacy in the court, now overrulingly instructed by a glance from Captain Vere, a glance more effective than words, resumed that primacy. Turning to the prisoner, "Budd," he said,

---

4. 2 Thessalonians 2.7.

and scarce in equable tones, "Budd, if you have aught further to say for your-self, say it now."

Upon this the young sailor turned another quick glance toward Captain Vere; then, as taking a hint from that aspect, a hint confirming his own instinct that silence was now best, replied to the lieutenant, "I have said all, sir."

The marine—the same who had been the sentinel without the cabin door at the time that the foretopman, followed by the master-at-arms, entered it—he, standing by the sailor throughout these judicial proceedings, was now directed to take him back to the after compartment originally assigned to the prisoner and his custodian. As the twain disappeared from view, the three officers, as partially liberated from some inward constraint associated with Billy's mere presence, simultaneously stirred in their seats. They exchanged looks of troubled indecision, yet feeling that decide they must and without long delay. For Captain Vere, he for the time stood—unconsciously with his back toward them, apparently in one of his absent fits—gazing out from a sashed porthole to windward upon the monotonous blank of the twilight sea. But the court's silence continuing, broken only at moments by brief consulta-tions, in low earnest tones, this served to arouse him and energize him. Turn-ing, he to-and-fro paced the cabin athwart; in the returning ascent to windward climbing the slant deck in the ship's lee roll,[5] without knowing it symbolizing thus in his action a mind resolute to surmount difficulties even if against prim-itive instincts strong as the wind and the sea. Presently he came to a stand before the three. After scanning their faces he stood less as mustering his thoughts for expression than as one inly deliberating how best to put them to well-meaning men not intellectually mature, men with whom it was necessary to demonstrate certain principles that were axioms to himself. Similar impa-tience as to talking is perhaps one reason that deters some minds from addressing any popular assemblies.

When speak he did, something, both in the substance of what he said and his manner of saying it, showed the influence of unshared studies modifying and tempering the practical training of an active career. This, along with his phraseology, now and then was suggestive of the grounds whereon rested that imputation of a certain pedantry socially alleged against him by certain naval men of wholly practical cast, captains who nevertheless would frankly concede that His Majesty's navy mustered no more efficient officer of their grade than Starry Vere.

What he said was to this effect: "Hitherto I have been but the witness, little more; and I should hardly think now to take another tone, that of your coadju-tor for the time, did I not perceive in you—at the crisis too—a troubled hesi-tancy, proceeding, I doubt not, from the clash of military duty with moral scruple—scruple vitalized by compassion. For the compassion, how can I oth-erwise than share it? But, mindful of paramount obligations, I strive against scruples that may tend to enervate decision. Not, gentlemen, that I hide from myself that the case is an exceptional one. Speculatively regarded, it well might be referred to a jury of casuists.[6] But for us here, acting not as casuists or moralists, it is a case practical, and under martial law practically to be dealt with.

5. I.e., climbing as the ship rolled away from the wind.
6. Those who resolve matters of right and wrong by hairsplitting arguments, especially those who try to de-duce principles of behavior from scriptural rules.

"But your scruples: do they move as in a dusk? Challenge them. Make them advance and declare themselves. Come now; do they import something like this: If, mindless of palliating circumstances, we are bound to regard the death of the master-at-arms as the prisoner's deed, then does that deed constitute a capital crime whereof the penalty is a mortal one. But in natural justice is nothing but the prisoner's overt act to be considered? How can we adjudge to summary and shameful death a fellow creature innocent before God, and whom we feel to be so?—Does that state it aright? You sign sad assent. Well, I too feel that, the full force of that. It is Nature. But do these buttons that we wear attest that our allegiance is to Nature? No, to the King. Though the ocean, which is inviolate Nature primeval, though this be the element where we move and have our being as sailors, yet as the King's officers lies our duty in a sphere correspondingly natural? So little is that true, that in receiving our commissions we in the most important regards ceased to be natural free agents. When war is declared are we the commissioned fighters previously consulted? We fight at command. If our judgments approve the war, that is but coincidence. So in other particulars. So now. For suppose condemnation to follow these present proceedings. Would it be so much we ourselves that would condemn as it would be martial law operating through us? For that law and the rigor of it, we are not responsible. Our vowed responsibility is in this: That however pitilessly that law may operate in any instances, we nevertheless adhere to it and administer it.

"But the exceptional in the matter moves the hearts within you. Even so too is mine moved. But let not warm hearts betray heads that should be cool. Ashore in a criminal case, will an upright judge allow himself off the bench to be waylaid by some tender kinswoman of the accused seeking to touch him with her tearful plea? Well, the heart here, sometimes the feminine in man, is as that piteous woman, and hard though it be, she must here be ruled out."

He paused, earnestly studying them for a moment; then resumed.

"But something in your aspect seems to urge that it is not solely the heart that moves in you, but also the conscience, the private conscience. But tell me whether or not, occupying the position we do, private conscience should not yield to that imperial one formulated in the code under which alone we officially proceed?"

Here the three men moved in their seats, less convinced than agitated by the course of an argument troubling but the more the spontaneous conflict within.

Perceiving which, the speaker paused for a moment; then abruptly changing his tone, went on.

"To steady us a bit, let us recur to the facts.—In wartime at sea a man-of-war's man strikes his superior in grade, and the blow kills. Apart from its effect the blow itself is, according to the Articles of War, a capital crime. Furthermore—"

"Ay, sir," emotionally broke in the officer of marines, "in one sense it was. But surely Budd purposed neither mutiny nor homicide."

"Surely not, my good man. And before a court less arbitrary and more merciful than a martial one, that plea would largely extenuate. At the Last Assizes[7] it shall acquit. But how here? We proceed under the law of the Mutiny Act. In feature no child can resemble his father more than that Act

7. The Last Judgment.

resembles in spirit the thing from which it derives—War. In His Majesty's service—in this ship, indeed—there are Englishmen forced to fight for the King against their will. Against their conscience, for aught we know. Though as their fellow creatures some of us may appreciate their position, yet as navy officers what reck we of it? Still less recks the enemy. Our impressed men he would fain cut down in the same swath with our volunteers. As regards the enemy's naval conscripts, some of whom may even share our own abhorrence of the regicidal French Directory, it is the same on our side. War looks but to the frontage, the appearance. And the Mutiny Act, War's child, takes after the father. Budd's intent or non-intent is nothing to the purpose.

"But while, put to it by those anxieties in you which I cannot but respect, I only repeat myself—while thus strangely we prolong proceedings that should be summary—the enemy may be sighted and an engagement result. We must do; and one of two things must we do—condemn or let go."

"Can we not convict and yet mitigate the penalty?" asked the sailing master, here speaking, and falteringly, for the first.

"Gentlemen, were that clearly lawful for us under the circumstances, consider the consequences of such clemency. The people" (meaning the ship's company) "have native sense; most of them are familiar with our naval usage and tradition; and how would they take it? Even could you explain to them—which our official position forbids—they, long molded by arbitrary discipline, have not that kind of intelligent responsiveness that might qualify them to comprehend and discriminate. No, to the people the foretopman's deed, however it be worded in the announcement, will be plain homicide committed in a flagrant act of mutiny. What penalty for that should follow, they know. But it does not follow. Why? they will ruminate. You know what sailors are. Will they not revert to the recent outbreak at the Nore? Ay. They know the well-founded alarm—the panic it struck throughout England. Your clement sentence they would account pusillanimous. They would think that we flinch, that we are afraid of them—afraid of practicing a lawful rigor singularly demanded at this juncture, lest it should provoke new troubles. What shame to us such a conjecture on their part, and how deadly to discipline. You see then, whither, prompted by duty and the law, I steadfastly drive. But I beseech you, my friends, do not take me amiss. I feel as you do for this unfortunate boy. But did he know our hearts, I take him to be of that generous nature that he would feel even for us on whom in this military necessity so heavy a compulsion is laid."

With that, crossing the deck he resumed his place by the sashed porthole, tacitly leaving the three to come to a decision. On the cabin's opposite side the troubled court sat silent. Loyal lieges, plain and practical, though at bottom they dissented from some points Captain Vere had put to them, they were without the faculty, hardly had the inclination, to gainsay one whom they felt to be an earnest man, one too not less their superior in mind than in naval rank. But it is not improbable that even such of his words as were not without influence over them, less came home to them than his closing appeal to their instinct as sea officers: in the forethought he threw out as to the practical consequences to discipline, considering the unconfirmed tone of the fleet at the time, should a man-of-war's man's violent killing at sea of a superior in grade be allowed to pass for aught else than a capital crime demanding prompt infliction of the penalty.

Not unlikely they were brought to something more or less akin to that harassed frame of mind which in the year 1842 actuated the commander of the U.S. brig-of-war *Somers* to resolve, under the so-called Articles of War, Articles modeled upon the English Mutiny Act, to resolve upon the execution at sea of a midshipman and two sailors as mutineers designing the seizure of the brig. Which resolution was carried out though in a time of peace and within not many days' sail of home. An act vindicated by a naval court of inquiry subsequently convened ashore. History, and here cited without comment. True, the circumstances on board the *Somers* were different from those on board the *Bellipotent*. But the urgency felt, well-warranted or otherwise, was much the same.

Says a writer[8] whom few know, "Forty years after a battle it is easy for a noncombatant to reason about how it ought to have been fought. It is another thing personally and under fire to have to direct the fighting while involved in the obscuring smoke of it. Much so with respect to other emergencies involving considerations both practical and moral, and when it is imperative promptly to act. The greater the fog the more it imperils the steamer, and speed is put on though at the hazard of running somebody down. Little ween the snug card players in the cabin of the responsibilities of the sleepless man on the bridge."

In brief, Billy Budd was formally convicted and sentenced to be hung at the yardarm in the early morning watch, it being now night. Otherwise, as is customary in such cases, the sentence would forthwith have been carried out. In wartime on the field or in the fleet, a mortal punishment decreed by a drumhead court—on the field sometimes decreed by but a nod from the general—follows without delay on the heel of conviction, without appeal.

22

It was Captain Vere himself who of his own motion communicated the finding of the court to the prisoner, for that purpose going to the compartment where he was in custody and bidding the marine there to withdraw for the time.

Beyond the communication of the sentence, what took place at this interview was never known. But in view of the character of the twain briefly closeted in that stateroom, each radically sharing in the rarer qualities of our nature—so rare indeed as to be all but incredible to average minds however much cultivated—some conjectures may be ventured.

It would have been in consonance with the spirit of Captain Vere should he on this occasion have concealed nothing from the condemned one—should he indeed have frankly disclosed to him the part he himself had played in bringing about the decision, at the same time revealing his actuating motives. On Billy's side it is not improbable that such a confession would have been received in much the same spirit that prompted it. Not without a sort of joy, indeed, he might have appreciated the brave opinion of him implied in his captain's making such a confidant of him. Nor, as to the sentence itself, could he have been insensible that it was imparted to him as to one not afraid to die. Even more may have been. Captain Vere in end may have developed the

8. Melville.

passion sometimes latent under an exterior stoical or indifferent. He was old enough to have been Billy's father. The austere devotee of military duty, letting himself melt back into what remains primeval in our formalized humanity, may in end have caught Billy to his heart, even as Abraham may have caught young Isaac on the brink of resolutely offering him up in obedience to the exacting behest.[9] But there is no telling the sacrament, seldom if in any case revealed to the gadding world, wherever under circumstances at all akin to those here attempted to be set forth two of great Nature's nobler order embrace. There is privacy at the time, inviolable to the survivor; and holy oblivion, the sequel to each diviner magnanimity, providentially covers all at last.

The first to encounter Captain Vere in act of leaving the compartment was the senior lieutenant. The face he beheld, for the moment one expressive of the agony of the strong, was to that officer, though a man of fifty, a startling revelation. That the condemned one suffered less than he who mainly had effected the condemnation was apparently indicated by the former's exclamation in the scene soon perforce to be touched upon.

23

Of a series of incidents within a brief term rapidly following each other, the adequate narration may take up a term less brief, especially if explanation or comment here and there seem requisite to the better understanding of such incidents. Between the entrance into the cabin of him who never left it alive, and him who when he did leave it left it as one condemned to die; between this and the closeted interview just given, less than an hour and a half had elapsed. It was an interval long enough, however, to awaken speculations among no few of the ship's company as to what it was that could be detaining in the cabin the master-at-arms and the sailor; for a rumor that both of them had been seen to enter it and neither of them had been seen to emerge, this rumor had got abroad upon the gun decks and in the tops, the people of a great warship being in one respect like villagers, taking microscopic note of every outward movement or non-movement going on. When therefore, in weather not at all tempestuous, all hands were called in the second dogwatch, a summons under such circumstances not usual in those hours, the crew were not wholly unprepared for some announcement extraordinary, one having connection too with the continued absence of the two men from their wonted haunts.

There was a moderate sea at the time; and the moon, newly risen and near to being at its full, silvered the white spar deck wherever not blotted by the clear-cut shadows horizontally thrown of fixtures and moving men. On either side the quarter-deck the marine guard under arms was drawn up; and Captain Vere, standing in his place surrounded by all the wardroom officers,[1] addressed his men. In so doing, his manner showed neither more nor less than that properly pertaining to his supreme position aboard his own ship. In clear terms and concise he told them what had taken place in the cabin: that the master-at-arms was dead, that he who had killed him had been already tried by a summary court and condemned to death, and that the execution would take place in the early morning watch. The word *mutiny* was not named in

9. Genesis 22.1–18.
1. The commissioned officers above the rank of ensign.

what he said. He refrained too from making the occasion an opportunity for any preachment as to the maintenance of discipline, thinking perhaps that under existing circumstances in the navy the consequence of violating discipline should be made to speak for itself.

Their captain's announcement was listened to by the throng of standing sailors in a dumbness like that of a seated congregation of believers in hell listening to the clergyman's announcement of his Calvinistic text.

At the close, however, a confused murmur went up. It began to wax. All but instantly, then, at a sign, it was pierced and suppressed by shrill whistles of the boatswain and his mates. The word was given to about ship.

To be prepared for burial Claggart's body was delivered to certain petty officers of his mess. And here, not to clog the sequel with lateral matters, it may be added that at a suitable hour, the master-at-arms was committed to the sea with every funeral honor properly belonging to his naval grade.

In this proceeding as in every public one growing out of the tragedy strict adherence to usage was observed. Nor in any point could it have been at all deviated from, either with respect to Claggart or Billy Budd, without begetting undesirable speculations in the ship's company, sailors, and more particularly men-of-war's men, being of all men the greatest sticklers for usage. For similar cause, all communication between Captain Vere and the condemned one ended with the closeted interview already given, the latter being now surrendered to the ordinary routine preliminary to the end. His transfer under guard from the captain's quarters was effected without unusual precautions—at least no visible ones. If possible, not to let the men so much as surmise that their officers anticipate aught amiss from them is the tacit rule in a military ship. And the more that some sort of trouble should really be apprehended, the more do the officers keep that apprehension to themselves, though not the less unostentatious vigilance may be augmented.. In the present instance, the sentry placed over the prisoner had strict orders to let no one have communication with him but the chaplain. And certain unobtrusive measures were taken absolutely to insure this point.

24

In a seventy-four of the old order the deck known as the upper gun deck was the one covered over by the spar deck, which last, though not without its armament, was for the most part exposed to the weather. In general it was at all hours free from hammocks; those of the crew swinging on the lower gun deck and berth deck, the latter being not only a dormitory but also the place for the stowing of the sailors' bags, and on both sides lined with the large chests or movable pantries of the many messes of the men.

On the starboard side of the *Bellipotent*'s upper gun deck, behold Billy Budd under sentry lying prone in irons in one of the bays formed by the regular spacing of the guns comprising the batteries on either side. All these pieces were of the heavier caliber of that period. Mounted on lumbering wooden carriages, they were hampered with cumbersome harness of breeching and strong side-tackles for running them out. Guns and carriages, together with the long rammers and shorter linstocks[2] lodged in loops overhead—all these, as customary, were painted black; and the heavy hempen breechings, tarred to

---

2. "Rammers" are rods for ramming home the charge of a gun, and "linstocks" are pointed forked staffs to hold a lighted match for firing cannon.

the same tint, wore the like livery of the undertakers. In contrast with the funereal hue of these surroundings, the prone sailor's exterior apparel, white jumper and white duck trousers, each more or less soiled, dimly glimmered in the obscure light of the bay like a patch of discolored snow in early April lingering at some upland cave's black mouth. In effect he is already in his shroud, or the garments that shall serve him in lieu of one. Over him but scarce illuminating him, two battle lanterns swing from two massive beams of the deck above. Fed with the oil supplied by the war contractors (whose gains, honest or otherwise, are in every land an anticipated portion of the harvest of death), with flickering splashes of dirty yellow light they pollute the pale moonshine all but ineffectually struggling in obstructed flecks through the open ports from which the tampioned cannon protrude. Other lanterns at intervals serve but to bring out somewhat the obscurer bays which, like small confessionals or side-chapels in a cathedral, branch from the long dim-vistaed broad aisle between the two batteries of that covered tier.

Such was the deck where now lay the Handsome Sailor. Through the rose-tan of his complexion no pallor could have shown. It would have taken days of sequestration from the winds and the sun to have brought about the effacement of that. But the skeleton in the cheekbone at the point of its angle was just beginning delicately to be defined under the warm-tinted skin. In fervid hearts self-contained, some brief experiences devour our human tissue as secret fire in a ship's hold consumes cotton in the bale.

But now lying between the two guns, as nipped in the vice of fate, Billy's agony, mainly proceeding from a generous young heart's virgin experience of the diabolical incarnate and effective in some men—the tension of that agony was over now. It survived not the something healing in the closeted interview with Captain Vere. Without movement, he lay as in a trance, that adolescent expression previously noted as his taking on something akin to the look of a slumbering child in the cradle when the warm hearth-glow of the still chamber at night plays on the dimples that at whiles mysteriously form in the cheek, silently coming and going there. For now and then in the gyved[3] one's trance a serene happy light born of some wandering reminiscence or dream would diffuse itself over his face, and then wane away only anew to return.

The chaplain, coming to see him and finding him thus, and perceiving no sign that he was conscious of his presence, attentively regarded him for a space, then slipping aside, withdrew for the time, peradventure feeling that even he, the minister of Christ though receiving his stipend from Mars,[4] had no consolation to proffer which could result in a peace transcending that which he beheld. But in the small hours he came again. And the prisoner, now awake to his surroundings, noticed his approach, and civilly, all but cheerfully, welcomed him. But it was to little purpose that in the interview following, the good man sought to bring Billy Budd to some godly understanding that he must die, and at dawn. True, Billy himself freely referred to his death as a thing close at hand; but it was something in the way that children will refer to death in general, who yet among their other sports will play a funeral with hearse and mourners.

Not that like children Billy was incapable of conceiving what death really is. No, but he was wholly without irrational fear of it, a fear more prevalent in

3. Shackled or chained.
4. The servant of the Prince of Peace being paid by the god of war.

highly civilized communities than those so-called barbarous ones which in all respects stand nearer to unadulterate Nature. And, as elsewhere said, a barbarian Billy radically was—as much so, for all the costume, as his countrymen the British captives, living trophies, made to march in the Roman triumph of Germanicus.[5] Quite as much so as those later barbarians, young men probably, and picked specimens among the earlier British converts to Christianity, at least nominally such, taken to Rome (as today converts from lesser isles of the sea may be taken to London), of whom the Pope of that time, admiring the strangeness of their personal beauty so unlike the Italian stamp, their clear ruddy complexion and curled flaxen locks, exclaimed, "Angles" (meaning *English*, the modern derivative), "Angles, do you call them? And is it because they look so like angels?"[6] Had it been later in time, one would think that the Pope had in mind Fra Angelico's seraphs, some of whom, plucking apples in gardens of the Hesperides,[7] have the faint rosebud complexion of the more beautiful English girls.

If in vain the good chaplain sought to impress the young barbarian with ideas of death akin to those conveyed in the skull, dial, and crossbones on old tombstones, equally futile to all appearance were his efforts to bring home to him the thought of salvation and a Savior. Billy listened, but less out of awe or reverence, perhaps, than from a certain natural politeness, doubtless at bottom regarding all that in much the same way that most mariners of his class take any discourse abstract or out of the common tone of the workaday world. And this sailor way of taking clerical discourse is not wholly unlike the way in which the primer of Christianity, full of transcendent miracles, was received long ago on tropic isles by any superior *savage*, so called—a Tahitian, say, of Captain Cook's time[8] or shortly after that time. Out of a natural courtesy he received, but did not appropriate. It was like a gift placed in the palm of an outreached hand upon which the fingers do not close.

But the *Bellipotent's* chaplain was a discreet man possessing the good sense of a good heart. So he insisted not in his vocation here. At the instance of Captain Vere, a lieutenant had apprised him of pretty much everything as to Billy; and since he felt that innocence was even a better thing than religion wherewith to go to Judgment, he reluctantly withdrew; but in his emotion not without first performing an act strange enough in an Englishman, and under the circumstances yet more so in any regular priest. Stooping over, he kissed on the fair cheek his fellow man, a felon in martial law, one whom though on the confines of death he felt he could never convert to a dogma; nor for all that did he fear for his future.

Marvel not that having been made acquainted with the young sailor's essential innocence the worthy man lifted not a finger to avert the doom of such a martyr to martial discipline. So to do would not only have been as idle as invoking the desert, but would also have been an audacious transgression of the bounds of his function, one as exactly prescribed to him by military law as that of the boatswain or any other naval officer. Bluntly put, a chaplain is the minister of the Prince of Peace serving in the host of the God of War—Mars. As such, he is as incongruous as a musket would be on the altar at Christmas.

5. Germanicus Caesar (15 B.C.–A.D. 19), Roman general who fought Germanic tribes and was given a famous triumph in Rome (A.D. 17).
6. Pope Gregory (540?–604).
7. In Florence during 1857 Melville saw paintings by

Giovanni da Fiesole (Fra Angelico) (1387–1455). In Greek mythology the Hesperides were islands where golden apples grew (guarded by a dragon).
8. Cook first visited Tahiti in 1769 and returned there a few years later.

Why, then, is he there? Because he indirectly subserves the purpose attested by the cannon; because too he lends the sanction of the religion of the meek to that which practically is the abrogation of everything but brute Force.

25

The night so luminous on the spar deck, but otherwise on the cavernous ones below, levels so like the tiered galleries in a coal mine—the luminous night passed away. But like the prophet in the chariot disappearing in heaven and dropping his mantle to Elisha,[9] the withdrawing night transferred its pale robe to the breaking day. A meek, shy light appeared in the East, where stretched a diaphanous fleece of white furrowed vapor. That light slowly waxed. Suddenly *eight bells* was struck aft, responded to by one louder metallic stroke from forward. It was four o'clock in the morning. Instantly the silver whistles were heard summoning all hands to witness punishment. Up through the great hatchways rimmed with racks of heavy shot the watch below came pouring, overspreading with the watch already on deck the space between the mainmast and foremast including that occupied by the capacious launch and the black booms tiered on either side of it, boat and booms making a summit of observation for the powder-boys and younger tars. A different group comprising one watch of topmen leaned over the rail of that sea balcony, no small one in a seventy-four, looking down on the crowd below. Man or boy, none spake but in whisper, and few spake at all. Captain Vere—as before, the central figure among the assembled commissioned officers—stood nigh the break of the poop deck facing forward. Just below him on the quarter-deck the marines in full equipment were drawn up much as at the scene of the promulgated sentence.

At sea in the old time, the execution by halter of a military sailor was generally from the foreyard. In the present instance, for special reasons the mainyard was assigned. Under an arm of that yard the prisoner was presently brought up, the chaplain attending him. It was noted at the time, and remarked upon afterwards, that in this final scene the good man evinced little or nothing of the perfunctory. Brief speech indeed he had with the condemned one, but the genuine Gospel was less on his tongue than in his aspect and manner towards him. The final preparations personal to the latter being speedily brought to an end by two boatswain's mates, the consummation impended. Billy stood facing aft. At the penultimate moment, his words, his only ones, words wholly unobstructed in the utterance, were these: "God bless Captain Vere!" Syllables so unanticipated coming from one with the ignominious hemp about his neck— a conventional felon's benediction directed aft towards the quarters of honor; syllables too delivered in the clear melody of a singing bird on the point of launching from the twig—had a phenomenal effect, not unenhanced by the rare personal beauty of the young sailor, spiritualized now through late experiences so poignantly profound.

Without volition, as it were, as if indeed the ship's populace were but the vehicles of some vocal current electric, with one voice from alow and aloft came a resonant sympathetic echo: "God bless Captain Vere!" And yet at that instant Billy alone must have been in their hearts, even as in their eyes.

At the pronounced words and the spontaneous echo that voluminously rebounded them, Captain Vere, either through stoic self-control or a sort of

9. 2 Kings 2.9–15.

momentary paralysis induced by emotional shock, stood erectly rigid as a musket in the ship-armorer's rack.

The hull, deliberately recovering from the periodic roll to leeward, was just regaining an even keel when the last signal, a preconcerted dumb one, was given. At the same moment it chanced that the vapory fleece hanging low in the East was shot through with a soft glory as of the fleece of the Lamb of God seen in mystical vision,[1] and simultaneously therewith, watched by the wedged mass of upturned faces, Billy ascended; and, ascending, took the full rose of the dawn.

In the pinioned figure arrived at the yard-end, to the wonder of all no motion was apparent, none save that created by the slow roll of the hull in moderate weather, so majestic in a great ship ponderously cannoned.

26

When some days afterwards, in reference to the singularity just mentioned, the purser,[2] a rather ruddy, rotund person more accurate as an accountant than profound as a philosopher, said at mess to the surgeon, "What testimony to the force lodged in will power," the latter, saturnine, spare, and tall, one in whom a discreet causticity went along with a manner less genial than polite, replied, "Your pardon, Mr. Purser. In a hanging scientifically conducted— and under special orders I myself directed how Budd's was to be effected—any movement following the completed suspension and originating in the body suspended, such movement indicates mechanical spasm in the muscular system. Hence the absence of that is no more attributable to will power, as you call it, than to horsepower—begging your pardon."

"But this muscular spasm you speak of, is not that in a degree more or less invariable in these cases?"

"Assuredly so, Mr. Purser."

"How then, my good sir, do you account for its absence in this instance?"

"Mr. Purser, it is clear that your sense of the singularity in this matter equals not mine. You account for it by what you call will power—a term not yet included in the lexicon of science. For me, I do not, with my present knowledge, pretend to account for it at all. Even should we assume the hypothesis that at the first touch of the halyards the action of Budd's heart, intensified by extraordinary emotion at its climax, abruptly stopped—much like a watch when in carelessly winding it up you strain at the finish, thus snapping the chain—even under that hypothesis how account for the phenomenon that followed?"

"You admit, then, that the absence of spasmodic movement was phenomenal."

"It was phenomenal, Mr. Purser, in the sense that it was an appearance the cause of which is not immediately to be assigned."

"But tell me, my dear sir," pertinaciously continued the other, "was the man's death effected by the halter, or was it a species of euthanasia?"[3]

"*Euthanasia*, Mr. Purser, is something like your *will power*: I doubt its authenticity as a scientific term—begging your pardon again. It is at once

1. See Revelation 1.14.
2. Paymaster.
3. Not in our sense of a merciful death inflicted by someone else. Melville had read the definition of *eu-* *thanasia* by the German philosopher Arthur Schopenhauer (1788–1860) as "an easy death, not ushered in by disease, and free from all pain and struggle."

imaginative and metaphysical—in short, Greek.—But," abruptly changing his tone, "there is a case in the sick bay that I do not care to leave to my assistants. Beg your pardon, but excuse me." And rising from the mess he formally withdrew.

27

The silence at the moment of execution and for a moment or two continuing thereafter, a silence but emphasized by the regular wash of the sea against the hull or the flutter of a sail caused by the helmsman's eyes being tempted astray, this emphasized silence was gradually disturbed by a sound not easily to be verbally rendered. Whoever has heard the freshet-wave of a torrent suddenly swelled by pouring showers in tropical mountains, showers not shared by the plain; whoever has heard the first muffled murmur of its sloping advance through precipitous woods may form some conception of the sound now heard. The seeming remoteness of its source was because of its murmurous indistinctness, since it came from close by, even from the men massed on the ship's open deck. Being inarticulate, it was dubious in significance further than it seemed to indicate some capricious revulsion of thought or feeling such as mobs ashore are liable to, in the present instance possibly implying a sullen revocation on the men's part of their involuntary echoing of Billy's benediction. But ere the murmur had time to wax into clamor it was met by a strategic command, the more telling that it came with abrupt unexpectedness: "Pipe down the starboard watch, Boatswain, and see that they go."

Shrill as the shriek of the sea hawk, the silver whistles of the boatswain and his mates pierced that ominous low sound, dissipating it; and yielding to the mechanism of discipline the throng was thinned by one-half. For the remainder, most of them were set to temporary employments connected with trimming the yards and so forth, business readily to be got up to serve occasion by any officer of the deck.

Now each proceeding that follows a mortal sentence pronounced at sea by a drumhead court is characterized by promptitude not perceptibly merging into hurry, though bordering that. The hammock, the one which had been Billy's bed when alive, having already been ballasted with shot and otherwise prepared to serve for his canvas coffin, the last offices of the sea undertakers, the sailmaker's mates, were now speedily completed. When everything was in readiness a second call for all hands, made necessary by the strategic movement before mentioned, was sounded, now to witness burial.

The details of this closing formality it needs not to give. But when the tilted plank let slide its freight into the sea, a second strange human murmur was heard, blended now with another inarticulate sound proceeding from certain larger seafowl who, their attention having been attracted by the peculiar commotion in the water resulting from the heavy sloped dive of the shotted hammock into the sea, flew screaming to the spot. So near the hull did they come, that the stridor or bony creak of their gaunt double-jointed pinions was audible. As the ship under light airs passed on, leaving the burial spot astern, they still kept circling it low down with the moving shadow of their outstretched wings and the croaked requiem of their cries.

Upon sailors as superstitious as those of the age preceding ours, men-of-war's men too who had just beheld the prodigy of repose in the form suspended in air, and now foundering in the deeps; to such mariners the action of the seafowl, though dictated by mere animal greed for prey, was big with no prosaic significance. An uncertain movement began among them, in which some encroachment was made. It was tolerated but for a moment. For suddenly the drum beat to quarters, which familiar sound happening at least twice every day, had upon the present occasion a signal peremptoriness in it. True martial discipline long continued superinduces in average man a sort of impulse whose operation at the official word of command much resembles in its promptitude the effect of an instinct.

The drumbeat dissolved the multitude, distributing most of them along the batteries of the two covered gun decks. There, as wonted, the guns' crews stood by their respective cannon erect and silent. In due course the first officer, sword under arm and standing in his place on the quarter-deck, formally received the successive reports of the sworded lieutenants commanding the sections of batteries below; the last of which reports being made, the summed report he delivered with the customary salute to the commander. All this occupied time, which in the present case was the object in beating to quarters at an hour prior to the customary one. That such variance from usage was authorized by an officer like Captain Vere, a martinet as some deemed him, was evidence of the necessity for unusual action implied in what he deemed to be temporarily the mood of his men. "With mankind," he would say, "forms, measured forms, are everything; and that is the import couched in the story of Orpheus with his lyre spellbinding the wild denizens of the wood."[4] And this he once applied to the disruption of forms going on across the Channel and the consequences thereof.

At this unwonted muster at quarters, all proceeded as at the regular hour. The band on the quarter-deck played a sacred air, after which the chaplain went through the customary morning service. That done, the drum beat the retreat; and toned by music and religious rites subserving the discipline and purposes of war, the men in their wonted orderly manner dispersed to the places allotted them when not at the guns.

And now it was full day. The fleece of low-hanging vapor had vanished, licked up by the sun that late had so glorified it. And the circumambient air in the clearness of its serenity was like smooth white marble in the polished block not yet removed from the marble-dealer's yard.

28

The symmetry of form attainable in pure fiction cannot so readily be achieved in a narration essentially having less to do with fable than with fact. Truth uncompromisingly told will always have its ragged edges; hence the conclusion of such a narration is apt to be less finished than an architectural finial.[5]

How it fared with the Handsome Sailor during the year of the Great Mutiny has been faithfully given. But though properly the story ends with his life, something in way of sequel will not be amiss. Three brief chapters will suffice.

In the general rechristening under the Directory of the craft originally form-

---

4. In Greek mythology Orpheus's music was so powerful that it bound the guardians of the Underworld so that his wife, Eurydice, was almost lured back to earth.

5. An ornament that forms the upper extremity of a post, pillar, or other architectural feature.

ing the navy of the French monarchy, the *St. Louis* line-of-battle ship was
named the *Athée* (the *Atheist*). Such a name, like some other substituted ones
in the Revolutionary fleet, while proclaiming the infidel audacity of the ruling
power, was yet, though not so intended to be, the aptest name, if one consider
it, ever given to a warship; far more so indeed than the *Devastation*, the *Erebus*
(the *Hell*), and similar names bestowed upon fighting ships.

On the return passage to the English fleet from the detached cruise during
which occurred the events already recorded, the *Bellipotent* fell in with the
Athée. An engagement ensued, during which Captain Vere, in the act of putting his ship alongside the enemy with a view of throwing his boarders across
her bulwarks, was hit by a musket ball from a porthole of the enemy's main
cabin. More than disabled, he dropped to the deck and was carried below to
the same cockpit where some of his men already lay. The senior lieutenant
took command. Under him the enemy was finally captured, and though much
crippled was by rare good fortune successfully taken into Gibraltar, an English
port not very distant from the scene of the fight. There, Captain Vere with the
rest of the wounded was put ashore. He lingered for some days, but the end
came. Unhappily he was cut off too early for the Nile and Trafalgar. The spirit
that 'spite its philosophic austerity may yet have indulged in the most secret of
all passions, ambition, never attained to the fulness of fame.

Not long before death, while lying under the influence of that magical drug[6]
which, soothing the physical frame, mysteriously operates on the subtler element in man, he was heard to murmur words inexplicable to his attendant:
"Billy Budd, Billy Budd." That these were not the accents of remorse would
seem clear from what the attendant said to the *Bellipotent*'s senior officer of
marines, who, as the most reluctant to condemn of the members of the drumhead court, too well knew, though here he kept the knowledge to himself,
who Billy Budd was.

29

Some few weeks after the execution, among other matters under the head
of "News from the Mediterranean," there appeared in a naval chronicle of the
time, an authorized weekly publication, an account of the affair. It was doubtless for the most part written in good faith, though the medium, partly rumor,
through which the facts must have reached the writer served to deflect and in
part falsify them. The account was as follows:

"On the tenth of the last month a deplorable occurrence took place on board
H.M.S. *Bellipotent*. John Claggart, the ship's master-at-arms, discovering that
some sort of plot was incipient among an inferior section of the ship's company, and that the ringleader was one William Budd; he, Claggart, in the act
of arraigning the man before the captain, was vindictively stabbed to the heart
by the suddenly drawn sheath knife of Budd.

"The deed and the implement employed sufficiently suggest that though
mustered into the service under an English name the assassin was no
Englishman, but one of those aliens adopting English cognomens whom the
present extraordinary necessities of the service have caused to be admitted into
it in considerable numbers.

6. Probably opium.

"The enormity of the crime and the extreme depravity of the criminal appear the greater in view of the character of the victim, a middle-aged man respectable and discreet, belonging to that minor official grade, the petty officers, upon whom, as none know better than the commissioned gentlemen, the efficiency of His Majesty's navy so largely depends. His function was a responsible one, at once onerous and thankless; and his fidelity in it the greater because of his strong patriotic impulse. In this instance as in so many other instances in these days, the character of this unfortunate man signally refutes, if refutation were needed, that peevish saying attributed to the late Dr. Johnson, that patriotism is the last refuge of a scoundrel.[7]

"The criminal paid the penalty of his crime. The promptitude of the punishment has proved salutary. Nothing amiss is now apprehended aboard H.M.S. *Bellipotent*."

The above, appearing in a publication now long ago superannuated and forgotten, is all that hitherto has stood in human record to attest what manner of men respectively were John Claggart and Billy Budd.

30

Everything is for a term venerated in navies. Any tangible object associated with some striking incident of the service is converted into a monument. The spar from which the foretopman was suspended was for some few years kept trace of by the bluejackets. Their knowledges followed it from ship to dockyard and again from dockyard to ship, still pursuing it even when at last reduced to a mere dockyard boom. To them a chip of it was as a piece of the Cross. Ignorant though they were of the secret facts of the tragedy, and not thinking but that the penalty was somehow unavoidably inflicted from the naval point of view, for all that, they instinctively felt that Billy was a sort of man as incapable of mutiny as of wilful murder. They recalled the fresh young image of the Handsome Sailor, that face never deformed by a sneer or subtler vile freak of the heart within. This impression of him was doubtless deepened by the fact that he was gone, and in a measure mysteriously gone. On the gun decks of the *Bellipotent* the general estimate of his nature and its unconscious simplicity eventually found rude utterance from another foretopman, one of his own watch, gifted, as some sailors are, with an artless *poetic* temperament. The tarry hand made some lines which, after circulating among the shipboard crews for a while, finally got rudely printed at Portsmouth as a ballad. The title given to it was the sailor's.

BILLY IN THE DARBIES

Good of the chaplain to enter Lone Bay
And down on his marrowbones here and pray
For the likes just o'me, Billy Budd.—But, look:
Through the port comes the moonshine astray!
It tips the guard's cutlass and silvers this nook;
But 'twill die in the dawning of Billy's last day.
A jewel-block they'll make of me tomorrow,
Pendant pearl from the yardarm-end

---

7. Reported in Boswell's *Life of Johnson* (1791) as a pronouncement made on April 7, 1775.

Like the eardrop I gave to Bristol Molly—
O, 'tis me, not the sentence they'll suspend.
Ay, ay, all is up; and I must up too,
Early in the morning, aloft from alow.
On an empty stomach now never it would do.
They'll give me a nibble—bit o'biscuit ere I go.
Sure, a messmate will reach me the last parting cup;
But, turning heads away from the hoist and the belay,
Heaven knows who will have the running of me up!
No pipe to those halyards.—But aren't it all sham?
A blur's in my eyes; it is dreaming that I am.
A hatchet to my hawser? All adrift to go?
The drum roll to grog, and Billy never know?
But Donald he has promised to stand by the plank;
So I'll shake a friendly hand ere I sink.
But—no! It is dead then I'll be, come to think.
I remember Taff the Welshman when he sank.
And his cheek it was like the budding pink.
But me they'll lash in hammock, drop me deep.
Fathoms down, fathoms down, how I'll dream fast asleep.
I feel it stealing now. Sentry, are you there?
Just ease these darbies[8] at the wrist,
And roll me over fair!
I am sleepy, and the oozy weeds about me twist.

1886?–91   1924, 1962

8. Handcuffs.

ELIZABETH DREW STODDARD
1823–1902

Elizabeth Drew Barstow was born on May 6, 1823, in Mattapoisett, Massachusetts, daughter of a well-to-do shipbuilder. A bookish local minister, Thomas Robbins, directed her early reading in eighteenth-century British writers whose subject matter retained, among other virtues, a sexual frankness that was fast dying out of English and American literature. She studied at the Wheaton Female Seminary at Norton, Massachusetts, where "she would not learn'" what she was supposed to learn. As a woman passing out of "marriageable" age she attended a Manhattan literary party given by Anne Lynch. There she was introduced to Richard Henry Stoddard, two years her junior, a would-be poet making a meager living as a journalist. Like herself he was of a maritime Massachusetts family; his father, a captain, had died at sea, leaving his wife destitute. After wrenching herself from the longing to accompany her brother to California, she married Stoddard in December 1852. They lived briefly in Brooklyn and then lived out their long lives in lower Manhattan, enduring the death of a deformed baby in 1859, the death of a seven-year-old son in 1861, and finally the death of their only other child, an actor-playwright son, in 1901. Elizabeth Stoddard died on August 1, 1902, and her husband died the next May.

From the first R. H. Stoddard encouraged his wife to write, recognizing that she "was not cursed with mediocrity," but had had "the misfortune to be original."

After her death, at least, he could admit her superiority: "She was thought to have more of the quality called genius than I, who certainly had more talent than she." Through the timely influence of her brother she became a semimonthly contributor of essays and reviews to the *Daily Alta California* for four years (1854–58) and writing, learned to write. Steeped by then in the work of Emily and Charlotte Brontë and familiar with contemporary British and American writers (and George Sand in translation), she began to contribute to magazines. She broke into the prestigious new *Atlantic* in 1860 with a story that James Russell Lowell praised while censoring some of its sexual boldness. Having developed a capacity akin to Hawthorne's and Stowe's psychological probing of intense, obsessive characters in restrictive locales and restrictive family situations, she wrote *The Morgesons* (1862), her masterpiece, following it with *Two Men* (1865), *Temple House* (1867), and a children's book, *Lolly Dinks's Doings* (1874). *The Morgesons* received much attention, a good deal of it hostile. Her distant cousin Hawthorne comforted her. "I hope you will not trouble yourself too much about the morals of your next book; they may be safely left to take care of themselves." He was wrong. Her later books were even less successful, until William Dean Howells's praise led to a reprinting of three of her novels in 1888 and 1889. The revival of attention encouraged her to resume her career and to publish *Poems* (1895).

Richard Henry Stoddard had the career that mattered to their contemporaries. Never more than a mediocre writer who deeply loved literature, he made a reputation with his palely Keatsean verse and earned his way as an editor and hack writer, although what financial security he had came mainly from a job Hawthorne got him in the New York Custom House in 1853, which he kept until fired by the Grant administration in 1870. For decades he cherished his associations at the Century Club and the Authors Club. (His wife was excluded from club life by her gender.) The tragedy of Elizabeth Stoddard's intellectual and aesthetic life is unwittingly laid open in the dedication of *The Morgesons*: "To my three friends, the three poets, Richard, Bayard, George, I dedicate this novel. 1861. E.D.B.S." (Her husband, George Henry Boker, and Bayard Taylor.) As Lawrence Buell and Sandra Zagarell say, "the literary world that the Stoddards inhabited was on the whole not so impressive as they liked to think. . . . They were personally acquainted with Bryant, Hawthorne, Howells, Lowell, Melville, and Whitman. But their closest literary associates were mediocrities—Edmund Clarence Stedman, Bayard Taylor, George Henry Boker, Elizabeth Akers Allen, Thomas Buchanan Read, Fitz-James O'Brien, Thomas Bailey Aldrich, and the like." It was for such people, as well as for a few more august intimates such as Edwin Booth, that the Stoddards held their locally celebrated "salon" in "an unpretending little house" on Fifteenth Street just east of Stuyvesant Square. The rooms were filled with good books (all in English, Richard Stoddard said, emphasizing that he and his wife were self-taught from British literature, not the classics or the languages of modern Europe) and with many paintings, most of them by their artist friends. (Late in life Richard gave his library, which included valuable association copies and manuscripts, to his beloved Authors Club.)

The patronizing approval of Elizabeth Stoddard's circle, Buell and Zagarell say, "undoubtedly had something to do with the fact that she came to doubt her creative powers." "She might not have submitted to the verdict of the marketplace had it not been echoed in the verdict of her friends." When a second brief revival of interest in her work occurred just before her death, she recalled in a new preface to *The Morgesons* that she had received praise from strangers in strange places, but she could offer only this wan evidence that she had not been without honor in her own place (the country of her soul being always New England): "Beside the name of Mr. Lowell, I mention two New England names, to spare me the fate of the prophet of the Gospel,—the late Maria Louise Pool and Nathaniel Hawthorne." (Pool, a Massachusetts local-color writer, had lived in Brooklyn during the 1870s.)

In a sympathetic essay on Stoddard's novels in *The Bookman* (November 1902), only three months after her death, Mary Moss, attempting to define the writer's peculiar strengths, not only picked up Stoddard's mention of Pool (though misspelling her name) but also evoked the names of Hawthorne and another American then two decades away from his own revival: "Every book, in fact, sounds like the hot utterance of some trance-bound seer reeling off strange visions seen luridly through encompassing darkness. Tales of New England life! Yes, but what a New England! A country of uncurbed desire, of hereditary taints, of families divided against themselves, of violence, of excess. In the whole field of New England romance there are but three local chroniclers whom she resembles at any point—certain wild outbursts of Herman Melville in *Moby-Dick*, Hawthorne's shocking allegory of *Young Goodman Brown*, and the repudiation of life without colour which shows here and there in the writings of Miss Poole." As the decades passed, encyclopedia writers and literary historians, like contemporary reviewers, acknowledged Stoddard's "masculinity of style" (the highest praise a woman could receive from a male critic), and admitted that she had anticipated the realism that Howells and others later championed, but they regularly remarked on qualities such as her "morbidity of thought" that "unfailingly reveals the frustration of her hopes and desires." The *DAB* put it bluntly: "A frail, nervous, highly imaginative woman, she was something of an angular individualist. Her tongue was sharp, and she frequently made enemies by its injudicious use."

All literary revivals have their heroes and heroines, though it soon becomes hard to remember that the rehabilitations of reputation had to be done—that several dozen people had to celebrate *Moby-Dick* before it achieved its classic status, that Kenneth Eble ever wrote about a "forgotten novel" called *The Awakening*, that, more recently, Tillie Olsen, almost single-handedly, revived interest in Rebecca Harding Davis. Now Lawrence Buell and Sandra Zagarell, building on the work of several pioneering researchers, have made it impossible again to ignore Elizabeth Stoddard.

Lemorne *versus* Huell[1]

The two months I spent at Newport[2] with Aunt Eliza Huell, who had been ordered to the sea-side for the benefit of her health, were the months that created all that is dramatic in my destiny. My aunt was troublesome, for she was not only out of health, but in a lawsuit. She wrote to me, for we lived apart, asking me to accompany her—not because she was fond of me, or wished to give me pleasure, but because I was useful in various ways. Mother insisted upon my accepting her invitation, not because she loved her late husband's sister, but because she thought it wise to cotton to her in every particular, for Aunt Eliza was rich, and we—two lone women—were poor.

I gave my music-pupils a longer and earlier vacation than usual, took a week to arrange my wardrobe—for I made my own dresses—and then started for New York, with the five dollars which Aunt Eliza had sent for my fare thither. I arrived at her house in Bond Street[3] at 7 A.M., and found her man James in conversation with the milkman. He informed me that Miss Huell was very bad, and that the housekeeper was still in bed. I supposed that Aunt

---

1. The text is that of the first printing in *Harper's New Monthly Magazine*, 26 (March 1863).
2. Newport, Rhode Island, before the British burned it in the Revolution had been a summer resort of rich southerners; by 1852, two years after the apparent year of this story, it had four fine hotels to put up the invalids who came there in summer for the "curative" bath-

ing; it had only twelve summer residences, four of which were owned by New Yorkers. The era of the palatial "cottages" had not come.
3. A fashionable short street connecting the Bowery and Mercer, downtown, where old wealth was concentrated.

Eliza was in bed also, but I had hardly entered the house when I heard her bell ring as she only could ring it—with an impatient jerk.

"She wants hot milk," said James, "and the man has just come."

I laid my bonnet down, and went to the kitchen. Saluting the cook, who was an old acquaintance, and who told me that the "divil" had been in the range that morning, I took a pan, into which I poured some milk, and held it over the gaslight till it was hot; then I carried it up to Aunt Eliza.

"Here is your milk, Aunt Eliza. You have sent for me to help you, and I begin with the earliest opportunity."

"I looked for you an hour ago. Ring the bell."

I rang it.

"Your mother is well, I suppose. She would have sent you, though, had she been sick in bed."

"She has done so. She thinks better of my coming than I do."

The housekeeper, Mrs. Roll, came in, and Aunt Eliza politely requested her to have breakfast for her niece as soon as possible.

"I do not go down of mornings yet," said Aunt Eliza, "but Mrs. Roll presides. See that the coffee is good, Roll."

"It is good generally, Miss Huell."

"You see that Margaret brought me my milk."

"Ahem!" said Mrs. Roll, marching out.

At the beginning of each visit to Aunt Eliza I was in the habit of dwelling on the contrast between her way of living and ours. We lived from "hand to mouth." Every thing about her wore a hereditary air; for she lived in my grandfather's house, and it was the same as in his day. If I was at home when these contrasts occurred to me I should have felt angry; as it was, I felt them as in a dream—the china, the silver, the old furniture, and the excellent fare soothed me.

In the middle of the day Aunt Eliza came down stairs, and after she had received a visit from her doctor, decided to go to Newport on Saturday. It was Wednesday; and I could, if I chose, make any addition to my wardrobe. I had none to make, I informed her. What were my dresses?—had I a black silk? she asked. I had no black silk, and thought one would be unnecessary for hot weather.

"Who ever heard of a girl of twenty-four having no black silk! You have slimsy[4] muslins, I dare say?"

"Yes."

"And you like them?"

"For present wear."

That afternoon she sent Mrs. Roll out, who returned with a splendid heavy silk for me, which Aunt Eliza said should be made before Saturday, and it was. I went to a fashionable dress-maker of her recommending, and on Friday it came home, beautifully made and trimmed with real lace.

"Even the Pushers could find no fault with this," said Aunt Eliza, turning over the sleeves and smoothing the lace. Somehow she smuggled into the house a white straw-bonnet, with white roses; also a handsome mantilla. She held the bonnet before me with a nod, and deposited it again in the box, which made a part of the luggage for Newport.

---

4. Flimsy, slightly made.

On Sunday morning we arrived in Newport, and went to a quiet hotel in the town. James was with us, but Mrs. Roll was left in Bond Street, in charge of the household. Monday was spent in an endeavor to make an arrangement regarding the hire of a coach and coachman. Several livery-stable keepers were in attendance, but nothing was settled, till I suggested that Aunt Eliza should send for her own carriage. James was sent back the next day, and returned on Thursday with coach, horses, and William her coachman. That matter being finished, and the trunks being unpacked, she decided to take her first bath in the sea, expecting me to support her through the trying ordeal of the surf. As we were returning from the beach we met a carriage containing a number of persons with a family resemblance.

When Aunt Eliza saw them she angrily exclaimed, "Am I to see those Uxbridges every day?"

Of the Uxbridges this much I knew—that the two brothers Uxbridge were the lawyers of her opponents in the lawsuit which had existed three or four years. I had never felt any interest in it, though I knew that it was concerning a tract of ground in the city which had belonged to my grandfather, and which had, since his day, become very valuable. Litigation was a habit of the Huell family. So the sight of the Uxbridge family did not agitate me as it did Aunt Eliza.

"The sly, methodical dogs! but I shall beat Lemorne yet!"

"How will you amuse yourself then, aunt?"

"I'll adopt some boys to inherit what I shall save from his clutches."

The bath fatigued her so she remained in her room for the rest of the day; but she kept me busy with a hundred trifles. I wrote for her, computed interest, studied out bills of fare, till four o'clock came, and with it a fog. Nevertheless I must ride on the Avenue, and the carriage was ordered.

"Wear your silk, Margaret; it will just about last your visit through—the fog will use it up."

"I am glad of it," I answered.

"You will ride every day. Wear the bonnet I bought for you also."

"Certainly; but won't that go quicker in the fog than the dress?"

"Maybe; but wear it."

I rode every day afterward, from four to six, in the black silk, the mantilla, and the white straw. When Aunt Eliza went she was so on the alert for the Uxbridge family carriage that she could have had little enjoyment of the ride. Rocks never were a passion with her, she said, nor promontories, chasms, or sand. She came to Newport to be washed with salt-water; when she had washed up to the doctor's prescription she should leave, as ignorant of the peculiar pleasures of Newport as when she arrived. She had no fancy for its conglomerate societies, its literary cottages, its parvenue suits of rooms, its saloon habits, and its bathing herds.

I considered the rides a part of the contract of what was expected in my two months' performance. I did not dream that I was enjoying them, any more than I supposed myself to be enjoying a sea-bath while pulling Aunt Eliza to and fro in the surf. Nothing in the life around me stirred me, nothing in nature attracted me. I liked the fog; somehow it seemed to emanate from me instead of rolling up from the ocean, and to represent me. Whether I went alone or not, the coachman was ordered to drive a certain round; after that I could extend the ride in whatever direction I pleased, but I always said, "Any where, William." One afternoon, which happened to be a bright one, I was riding on the road which led to the glen, when I heard the screaming of a flock of geese which were waddling across the path in front of the horses. I started, for I was asleep probably, and, looking forward, saw the Uxbridge carriage, filled with ladies and children, coming toward me; and by it rode a gentleman on horseback. His horse was rearing among the hissing geese, but neither horse nor geese appeared to engage him; his eyes were fixed upon me. The horse swerved so near that its long mane almost brushed against me. By an irresistible impulse I laid my ungloved hand upon it, but did not look at the rider. Carriage and horseman passed on, and William resumed his pace. A vague idea took possession of me that I had seen the horseman before on my various drives. I had a vision of a man galloping on a black horse out of the fog, and into it again. I was very sure, however, that I had never seen him on so pleasant a day as this! William did not bring his horses to time; it was after six when I went into Aunt Eliza's parlor, and found her impatient for her tea and toast. She was crosser than the occasion warranted; but I understood it when she gave me the outlines of the letter she desired me to write to her lawyer in New York. Something had turned up, he had written her; the Uxbridges believed that they had ferreted out what would go against her. I told her that I had met the Uxbridge carriage.

"One of them is in New York; how else could they be giving me trouble just now?"

"There was a gentleman on horseback beside the carriage."

"Did he look mean and cunning?"

"He did not wear his legal beaver[5] up, I think; but he rode a fine horse and sat it well."

"A lawyer on horseback should, like the beggar of the adage, ride to the devil."[6]

"Your business now is the 'Lemorne?' "

"You know it is."

"I did not know but that you had found something besides to litigate."

"It must have been Edward Uxbridge that you saw. He is the brain of the firm."

"You expect Mr. Van Horn?"

"Oh, he must come; I can not be writing letters."

We had been in Newport two weeks when Mr. Van Horn, Aunt Eliza's lawyer, came. He said that he would see Mr. Edward Uxbridge. Between them they might delay a term, which he thought would be best. "Would Miss Huell ever be ready for a compromise?" he jestingly asked.

"Are you suspicious?" she inquired.

"No; but the Uxbridge chaps are clever."

He dined with us; and at four o'clock Aunt Eliza graciously asked him to take a seat in the carriage with me, making some excuse for not going herself.

"Hullo!" said Mr. Van Horn when we had reached the country road, "there's Uxbridge now." And he waved his hand to him.

---

5. Face-guard for a helmet. A tart allusion to Shakespeare's *Hamlet* 1.2.229: "O yes, my lord; he wore his beaver up"—Horatio's assurance that he had seen the face of the ghost of Hamlet's father.
6. The Taylor-Whiting *Dictionary of American Proverbs and Proverbial Phrases, 1820–80* cites Hawthorne's

"Old News" in *The Snow-Image* (1851): "Now is the day, when every beggar gets on horse-back. And is not the whole land like a beggar on horse-back, riding post to the devil?" The phrase may well have been proverbial before Hawthorne used it, but Stoddard probably knew all the books Hawthorne had published.

It was indeed the black horse and the same rider that I had met. He reined up beside us, and shook hands with Mr. Van Horn.

"We are required to answer this new complaint?" said Mr. Van Horn.

Mr. Uxbridge nodded.

"And after that the judgment?"[7]

Mr. Uxbridge laughed.

"I wish that certain gore of land[8] had been sunk instead of being mapped in 1835."

"The surveyor did his business well enough, I am sure."

They talked together in a low voice for a few minutes, and then Mr. Van Horn leaned back in his seat again. "Allow me," he said, "to introduce you, Uxbridge, to Miss Margaret Huell, Miss Huell's niece. Huell *vs.* Brown, you know," he added, in an explanatory tone; for I was Huell *vs.* Brown's daughter.

"Oh!" said Mr. Uxbridge, bowing, and looking at me gravely. I looked at him also; he was a pale, stern-looking man, and forty years old certainly. I derived the impression at once that he had a domineering disposition, perhaps from the way in which he controlled his horse.

"Nice beast that," said Mr. Van Horn.

"Yes," he answered, laying his hand on its mane, so that the action brought immediately to my mind the recollection that I had done so too. I would not meet his eye again, however.

"How long shall you remain, Uxbridge?"

"I don't know. You are not interested in the lawsuit, Miss Huell?" he said, putting on his hat.

"Not in the least; nothing of mine is involved."

"We'll gain it for your portion yet, Miss Margaret," said Mr. Van Horn, nodding to Mr. Uxbridge, and bidding William drive on. He returned the next day, and we settled into the routine of hotel life. A few mornings after, she sent me to a matinée, which was given by some of the Opera people, who were in Newport strengthening the larynx with applications of brine. When the concert was half over, and the audience were making the usual hum and stir, I saw Mr. Uxbridge against a pillar, with his hands incased in pearl-colored gloves, and holding a shiny hat. He turned half away when he caught my eye, and then darted toward me.

"You have not been much more interested in the music than you are in the lawsuit," he said, seating himself beside me.

"The *tutoyer*[9] of the Italian voice is agreeable, however."

"It makes one dreamy."

"A child."

"Yes, a child; not a man nor a woman."

"I teach music. I can not dream over 'one, two, three.'"

"*You*—a music teacher!"

"For six years."

I was aware that he looked at me from head to foot, and I picked at the lace on my invariable black silk; but what did it matter whether I owned that I was a genteel pauper, representing my aunt's position for two months, or not?

7. Flippant allusion to Hebrews 9.27–28: "And as it is appointed unto men once to die, but after this the judgment: So Christ was once offered to bear the sins of many; and unto them that look for him shall he ap-

pear the second time without sin unto salvation."
8. A small triangular piece of land.
9. Here, apparently in the sense of softness and melodiousness.

"Where?"

"In Waterbury."[1]

"Waterbury differs from Newport."

"I suppose so."

"You suppose!"

A young gentleman sauntered by us, and Mr. Uxbridge called to him to look up the Misses Uxbridge, his nieces, on the other side of the hall.

"Paterfamilias Uxbridge has left his brood in my charge," he said. "I try to do my duty," and he held out a twisted pearl-colored glove, which he had pulled off while talking. What white nervous fingers he had! I thought they might pinch like steel.

"You suppose," he repeated.

"I do not look at Newport."

"Have you observed Waterbury?"

"I observe what is in my sphere."

"Oh!"

He was silent then. The second part of the concert began; but I could not compose myself to appreciation. Either the music or I grew chaotic. So many tumultuous sounds I heard—of hope, doubt, inquiry, melancholy, and desire; or did I feel the emotions which these words express? Or was there magnetism[2] stealing into me from the quiet man beside me? He left me with a bow before the concert was over, and I saw him making his way out of the hall when it was finished.

I had been sent in the carriage, of course; but several carriages were in advance of it before the walk, and I waited there for William to drive up. When he did so, I saw by the oscillatory motion of his head, though his arms and whiphand were perfectly correct, that he was inebriated. It was his first occasion of meeting fellow-coachmen in full dress, and the occasion had proved too much for him. My hand, however, was on the coach door, when I heard Mr. Uxbridge say, at my elbow,

"It is not safe for you."

"Oh, Sir, it is in the programme that I ride home from the concert." And I prepared to step in.

"I shall sit on the box, then."

"But your nieces?"

"They are walking home, squired by a younger knight."

Aunt Eliza would say, I thought, "Needs must when a lawyer drives;" and I concluded to allow him to have his way, telling him that he was taking a great deal of trouble. He thought it would be less if he were allowed to sit inside; both ways were unsafe.

Nothing happened. William drove well from habit; but James was obliged to assist him to dismount. Mr. Uxbridge waited a moment at the door, and so there was quite a little sensation, which spread its ripples till Aunt Eliza was reached. She sent for William, whose only excuse was "dampness."

"Uxbridge knew my carriage, of course," she said, with a complacent voice.

"He knew me," I replied.

"You do not look like the Huells."

1. Manufacturing village, noted for the production of clocks.

2. Hypnotic sexual attraction, from the term's use in mesmerism.

"I look precisely like the young woman to whom he was introduced by Mr. Van Horn."

"Oh ho!"

"He thought it unsafe for me to come alone under William's charge."

"Ah ha!"

No more was said on the subject of his coming home with me. Aunt Eliza had several fits of musing in the course of the evening while I read aloud to her, which had no connection with the subject of the book. As I put it down she said that it would be well for me to go to church the next day. I acquiesced, but remarked that my piety would not require the carriage, and that I preferred to walk. Besides, it would be well for William and James to attend divine service. She could not spare James, and thought William had better clean the harness, by way of penance.

The morning proved to be warm and sunny. I donned a muslin dress of home manufacture and my own bonnet, and started for church. I had walked but a few paces when the consciousness of being *free* and *alone* struck me. I halted, looked about me, and concluded that I would not go to church, but walk into the fields. I had no knowledge of the whereabouts of the fields; but I walked straight forward, and after a while came upon some barren fields, cropping with coarse rocks, along which ran a narrow road. I turned into it, and soon saw beyond the rough coast the blue ring of the ocean—vast, silent, and splendid in the sunshine. I found a seat on the ruins of an old stone-wall, among some tangled bushes and briers. There being no Aunt Eliza to pull through the surf, and no animated bathers near, I discovered the beauty of the sea, and that I loved it.

Presently I heard the steps of a horse, and, to my astonishment, Mr. Uxbridge rode past. I was glad he did not know me. I watched him as he rode slowly down the road, deep in thought. He let drop the bridle, and the horse stopped, as if accustomed to the circumstance, and pawed the ground gently, or yawed his neck for pastime. Mr. Uxbridge folded his arms and raised his head to look seaward. It seemed to me as if he were about to address the jury. I had dropped so entirely from my observance of the landscape that I jumped when he resumed the bridle and turned his horse to come back. I slipped from my seat to look among the bushes, determined that he should not recognize me; but my attempt was a failure—he did not ride by the second time.

"Miss Huell!" And he jumped from his saddle, slipping his arm through the bridle.

"I am a runaway. What do you think of the Fugitive Slave Bill?"[3]

"I approve of returning property to its owners."

"The sea must have been God's temple first,[4] instead of the groves."

"I believe the Saurians[5] were an Orthodox tribe."

"Did you stop yonder to ponder the sea?"

"I was pondering 'Lemorne *vs.* Huell.' "

He looked at me earnestly, and then gave a tug at the bridle, for his steed was inclined to make a crude repast from the bushes.

"How was it that I did not detect you at once?" he continued.

---

3. The Fugitive Slave Bill, part of the Compromise of 1850, was passed on September 18, 1850, after which it was the Fugitive Slave Law. The narrator's precision of language suggests that this part of the story is set in the summer of 1850.

4. Stoddard's readers would have recognized this allusion to the first line of Bryant's A *Forest Hymn* (1825): "The groves were God's first temples."

5. Lizards. Uxbridge pushes the narrator's ironic paganism into something nearer blasphemy.

"My apparel is Waterbury apparel."

"Ah!"

We walked up the road slowly till we came to the end of it; then I stopped for him to understand that I thought it time for him to leave me. He sprang into the saddle.

"Give us good-by!" he said, bringing his horse close to me.

"We are not on equal terms; I feel too humble afoot to salute you."

"Put your foot on the stirrup then."

A leaf stuck in the horse's forelock, and I pulled it off and waved it in token of farewell. A powerful light shot into his eyes when he saw my hand close on the leaf.

"May I come and see you?" he asked, abruptly. "I will."

"I shall say neither 'No' or 'Yes.' "

He rode on at a quick pace, and I walked homeward, forgetting the sense of liberty I had started with, and proceeded straightway to Aunt Eliza.

"I have not been to church, aunt, but to walk beyond the town; it was not so nominated in the bond, but I went. The taste of freedom was so pleasant that I warn you there is danger of my 'striking.'[6] When will you have done with Newport?"

"I am pleased with Newport now," she answered, with a curious intonation. "I like it."

"I do also."

Her keen eyes sparkled.

"Did you ever like any thing when you were with me before?"

"Never. I will tell you why I like it: because I have met, and shall probably meet, Mr. Uxbridge. I saw him to-day. He asked permission to visit me."

"Let him come."

"He will come."

But we did not see him either at the hotel or when we went abroad. Aunt Eliza rode with me each afternoon, and each morning we went to the beach. She engaged me every moment when at home, and I faithfully performed all my tasks. I clapped to the door on self-investigation—locked it against any analysis or reasoning upon any circumstance connected with Mr. Uxbridge. The only piece of treachery to my code that I was guilty of was the putting of the leaf which I brought home on Sunday between the leaves of that poem whose motto is,

"Mariana in the moated grange."[7]

On Saturday morning, nearly a week after I saw him on my walk, Aunt Eliza proposed that we should go to Turo Street on a shopping excursion; she wanted a cap, and various articles besides. As we went into a large shop I saw Mr. Uxbridge at a counter buying gloves; her quick eye caught sight of him, and she edged away, saying she would look at some goods on the other side; I might wait where I was. As he turned to go out he saw me and stopped.

"I have been in New York since I saw you," he said. "Mr. Lemorne sent for me."

---

6. Breaking out, striking out on her own.
7. Tennyson's *Mariana* takes the quoted motto from Shakespeare's *Measure for Measure* 3.1.277: "There, at the moted grange, resides this dejected Mariana" (a grange is a secluded country house). The act of putting

the leaf in the poem is an avowal of passionate love that the narrator thinks will never be fulfilled. *Mariana* ends: "Then, said she, 'I am very dreary, / He will not come,' she said: / She wept, 'I am aweary, aweary, / Oh God, that I were dead.' "

"There is my aunt," I said.

He shrugged his shoulders.

"I shall not go away soon again," he remarked. "I missed Newport greatly."

I made some foolish reply, and kept my eyes on Aunt Eliza, who dawdled unaccountably. He appeared amused, and after a little talk went away.

Aunt Eliza's purchase was a rose-colored moire[8] antique, which she said was to be made for me; for Mrs. Bliss, one of our hotel acquaintances, had offered to chaperon me to the great ball which would come off in a few days, and she had accepted the offer for me.

"There will be no chance for you to take a walk instead," she finished with.

"I can not dance, you know."

"But you will be *there*."

I was sent to a dress-maker of Mrs. Bliss's recommending; but I ordered the dress to be made after my own design, long plain sleeves, and high plain corsage, and requested that it should not be sent home till the evening of the ball. Before it came off Mr. Uxbridge called, and was graciously received by Aunt Eliza, who could be gracious to all except her relatives. I could not but perceive, however, that they watched each other in spite of their lively conversation. To me he was deferential, but went over the ground of our acquaintance as if it had been the most natural thing in the world. But for my life-long habit of never calling in question the behavior of those I came in contact with, and of never expecting any thing different from that I received, I might have wondered over his visit. Every person's individuality was sacred to me, from the fact, perhaps, that my own individuality had never been respected by any person with whom I had any relation—not even by my own mother.

After Mr. Uxbridge went, I asked Aunt Eliza if she thought he looked mean and cunning? She laughed, and replied that she was bound to think that Mr. Lemorne's lawyer could not look otherwise.

When, on the night of the ball, I presented myself in the rose-colored moire antique for her inspection, she raised her eyebrows, but said nothing about it.

"I need not be careful of it, I suppose, aunt?"

"Spill as much wine and ice-cream on it as you like."

In the dressing-room Mrs. Bliss surveyed me.

"I think I like this mass of rose-color," she said. "Your hair comes out in contrast so brilliantly. Why, you have not a single ornament on!"

"It is so easy to dress without."

This was all the conversation we had together during the evening, except when she introduced some acquaintance to fulfill her matronizing duties. As I was no dancer I was left alone most of the time, and amused myself by gliding from window to window along the wall, that it might not be observed that I was a fixed flower. Still I suffered the annoyance of being stared at by wandering squads of young gentlemen, the "curled darlings"[9] of the ball-room. I borrowed Mrs. Bliss's fan in one of her visits for a protection. With that, and the embrasure of a remote window where I finally stationed myself, I hoped to escape further notice. The music of the celebrated band which played between the dances recalled the chorus of spirits which charmed Faust:[1]

---

8. Fragile silk with a "watered" (cloudy) appearance.
9. Shakespeare's *Othello* 1.3.68.
1. Goethe's *Faust*, in the "Exorcism" section of the third act; the spirits are putting Faust to sleep for Meph-

istopheles. Stoddard's friend Bayard Taylor had already begun work on what became a standard translation of *Faust*, but she was using the translation by A. Hayward which Appleton published in 1840.

"And the fluttering
Ribbons of drapery
Cover the plains,
Cover the bowers,
Where lovers,
Deep in thought,
Give themselves for life."

The voice of Mrs. Bliss broke its spell.

"I bring an old friend, Miss Huell, and he tells me an acquaintance of yours."

It was Mr. Uxbridge.

"I had not thought of meeting you, Miss Huell."

And he coolly took the seat beside me in the window, leaving to Mrs. Bliss the alternative of standing or of going away; she chose the latter.

"I saw you as soon as I came in," he said, "gliding from window to window, like a vessel hugging the shore in a storm."

"With colors at half-mast; I have no dancing partner."

"How many have observed you?"

"Several young gentlemen."

"Moths."

"Oh no, butterflies."

"They must keep away now."

"Are you Rhadamanthus?"

"And Charon,[2] too. I would have you row in the same boat with me."

"Now you are fishing."

"Won't you compliment me. Did I ever look better?"

His evening costume *was* becoming, but he looked pale, and weary, and disturbed. But if we were engaged for a tournament, as his behavior indicated, I must do my best at telling. So I told him that he never looked better, and asked him how I looked. He would look at me presently, he said, and decide. Mrs. Bliss skimmed by us with nods and smiles; as she vanished our eyes followed her, and we talked vaguely on various matters, sounding ourselves and each other. When a furious redowa[3] set in which cut our conversation into rhythm he pushed up the window and said, "Look out."

I turned my face to him to do so, and saw the moon at the full, riding through the strip of sky which our vision commanded. From the moon our eyes fell on each other. After a moment's silence, during which I returned his steadfast gaze, for I could not help it, he said:

"If we understand the impression we make upon each other, what must be said?"

I made no reply, but fanned myself, neither looking at the moon, nor upon the redowa, nor upon any thing.

He took the fan from me.

"Speak of yourself," he said.

"Speak you."

"I am what I seem, a man within your sphere. By all the accidents of position and circumstance suited to it. Have you not learned it?"

2. In Greek mythology, Charon rowed the dead over the river Styx. Rhadamanthus was one of the three judges of the dead souls in Hades, the Underworld.
3. A Bohemian waltz.

"I am not what I seem. I never wore so splendid a dress as this till to-night, and shall not again."

He gave the fan such a twirl that its slender sticks snapped, and it dropped like the broken wing of a bird.

"Mr. Uxbridge, that fan belongs to Mrs. Bliss."

He threw it out of the window.

"You have courage, fidelity, and patience—this character with a passionate soul. I am sure that you have such a soul?"

"I do not know."

"I have fallen in love with you. It happened on the very day when I passed you on the way to the Glen. I never got away from the remembrance of seeing your hand on the mane of my horse."

He waited for me to speak, but I could not; the balance of my mind was gone. Why should this have happened to me—a slave? As it had happened, why did I not feel exultant in the sense of power which the chance for freedom with him should give?

"What is it, Margaret? your face is as sad as death."

"How do you call me 'Margaret?' "

"As I would call my wife—Margaret."

He rose and stood before me to screen my face from observation. I supposed so, and endeavored to stifle my agitation.

"You are better," he said, presently. "Come go with me and get some refreshment." And he beckoned to Mrs. Bliss, who was down the hall with an unwieldy gentleman.

"Will you go to supper now?" she asked.

"We are only waiting for you," Mr. Uxbridge answered, offering me his arm.

When we emerged into the blaze and glitter of the supper-room I sought refuge in the shadow of Mrs. Bliss's companion, for it seemed to me that I had lost my own.

"Drink this Champagne," said Mr. Uxbridge. "Pay no attention to the Colonel on your left; he won't expect it."

"Neither must you."

"Drink."

The Champagne did not prevent me from reflecting on the fact that he had not yet asked whether I loved him.

The spirit chorus again floated through my mind:

> "Where lovers,
> Deep in thought,
> *Give* themselves for life."

I was not allowed to *give* myself—I was *taken*.

"No heel-taps,"[4] he whispered, "to the bottom quaff."

"Take me home, will you?"

"Mrs. Bliss is not ready."

"Tell her that I must go."

He went behind her chair and whispered something, and she nodded to me to go without her.

---

4. Small amount of liquor left in a glass.

When her carriage came up, I think he gave the coachman an order to drive home in a roundabout way, for we were a long time reaching it. I kept my face to the window, and he made no effort to divert my attention. When we came to a street whose thick rows of trees shut out the moonlight my eager soul longed to leap out into the dark and demand of him his heart, soul, life, for *me*.

I struck him light on the shoulder; he seized my hand.

"Oh, I know you, Margaret; you are mine!"

"We are at the hotel."

He sent the carriage back, and said that he would leave me at my aunt's door. He wished that he could see her then. Was it magic that made her open the door before I reached it?

"Have you come on legal business?" she asked him.

"You have divined what I come for."

"Step in, step in; it's very late. I should have been in bed but for neuralgia. Did Mr. Uxbridge come home with you, Margaret?"

"Yes, in Mrs. Bliss's carriage; I wished to come before she was ready to leave."

"Well, Mr. Uxbridge is old enough for your protector, certainly."

"I *am* forty, ma'am."

"Do you want Margaret?"

"I do."

"You know exactly how much is involved in your client's suit?"

"Exactly."

"You know also that his claim is an unjust one."

"Do I?"

"I shall not be poor if I lose; if I gain, Margaret will be rich."

" 'Margaret will be rich!' " he repeated, absently.

"What! have you changed your mind respecting the orphans, aunt?"

"She has, and is—nothing," she went on, not heeding my remark. "Her father married below his station; when he died his wife fell back to her place—for he spent his fortune—and there she and Margaret must remain, unless Lemorne is defeated."

"Aunt, for your succinct biography of my position many thanks."

"Sixty thousand dollars," she continued. "Van Horn tells me that, as yet, the firm of Uxbridge Brothers have only an income—no capital."

"It is true," he answered, musingly.

The clock on the mantle struck two.

"A thousand dollars for every year of my life," she said. "You and I, Uxbridge, know the value and beauty of money."

"Yes, there is beauty in money, and"—looking at me—"beauty without it."

"The striking of the clock," I soliloquized, "proves that this scene is not a phantasm."

"Margaret is fatigued," he said, rising. "May I come to-morrow?"

"It is my part only," replied Aunt Eliza, "to see that she is, or is not, Cinderella."

"If you have ever thought of me, aunt, as an individual, you must have seen that I am not averse to ashes."

He held my hand a moment, and then kissed me with a kiss of appropriation.

"He is in love with you," she said, after he had gone. "I think I know him. He has found beauty ignorant of itself; he will teach you to develop it."

The next morning Mr. Uxbridge had an interview with Aunt Eliza before he saw me.

When we were alone I asked him how her eccentricities affected him; he could not but consider her violent, prejudiced, warped, and whimsical. I told him that I had been taught to accept all that she did on this basis. Would this explain to him my silence in regard to her?

"Can you endure to live with her in Bond Street for the present, or would you rather return to Waterbury?"

"She desires my company while she is in Newport only. I have never been with her so long before."

"I understand her. Law is a game, in her estimation, in which cheating can as easily be carried on as at cards."

"Her soul is in this case."

"Her soul is not too large for it. Will you ride this afternoon?"

I promised, of course. From that time till he left Newport we saw each other every day, and though I found little opportunity to express my own peculiar feelings, he comprehended many of my wishes, and all my tastes. I grew fond of him hourly. Had I not reason? Never was friend so considerate, never was lover more devoted.

When he had been gone a few days, Aunt Eliza declared that she was ready to depart from Newport. The rose-colored days were ended! In two days we were on the Sound,[5] coach, horses, servants, and ourselves.

It was the 1st of September when we arrived in Bond Street. A week from that date Samuel Uxbridge, the senior partner of Uxbridge Brothers, went to Europe with his family, and I went to Waterbury, accompanied by Mr. Uxbridge. He consulted mother in regard to our marriage, and appointed it in November. In October Aunt Eliza sent for me to come back to Bond Street and spend a week. She had some fine marking[6] to do, she wrote. While there I noticed a restlessness in her which I had never before observed, and conferred with Mrs. Roll on the matter. "She do be awake nights a deal, and that's the reason," Mrs. Roll said. Her manner was the same in other respects. She said she would not give me any thing for my wedding outfit, but she paid my fare from Waterbury and back.

She could not spare me to go out, she told Mr. Uxbridge, and in consequence I saw little of him while there.

In November we were married. Aunt Eliza was not at the wedding, which was a quiet one. Mr. Uxbridge desired me to remain in Waterbury till spring. He would not decide about taking a house in New York till then; by that time his brother might return, and if possible we would go to Europe for a few months. I acquiesced in all his plans. Indeed I was not consulted; but I was happy—happy in him, and happy in every thing.

The winter passed in waiting for him to come to Waterbury every Saturday; and in the enjoyment of the two days he passed with me. In March Aunt Eliza wrote me that Lemorne was beaten! Von Horn had taken up the whole con-

---

5. I.e., Long Island Sound. Returning first to Long Island or directly to Manhattan by ferry was a regular way of traveling at a time when roads between Newport and New York were untrustworthy.

6. I.e., marking of patterns for clothing, done precisely with special calipers; the wearer of the clothing is to be Eliza Huell.

tents of his snuff-box in her house the evening before in amazement at the turn things had taken.

That night I dreamed of the scene in the hotel at Newport. I heard Aunt Eliza saying, "If I gain, Margaret will be rich." And I heard also the clock strike two. As it struck I said, *"My husband is a scoundrel,"* and woke with a start.[7]

1863

7. The ending depends on knowledge of property laws. Among the injustices of men toward women noted in the Seneca Falls Declaration of Sentiments and Resolutions (July 19, 1848) were these: "He has made her, if married, in the eye of the law, civilly [i.e., legally] dead. He has taken from her all right in property, even to the wages she earns."

EMILY DICKINSON
(1830–1886)

Emily Elizabeth Dickinson was born on December 10, 1830, in Amherst, Massachusetts, the second child of Edward (1803–1874) and Emily Norcross Dickinson (1804–1882). Dickinson lived in only two houses, the spacious but then-divided Dickinson family "Homestead" where she was born, then another large house nearby from 1840 until 1855, when her father bought back the entire Homestead. Thereafter she lived in the house where she was born, dying there, of Bright's disease, on May 15, 1886. Her closest friends and lifelong allies were her brother, William Austin (1829–1895), a year and a half older than she, and her sister, Lavinia (Vinnie), who was born in February 1833, and died in 1899. In 1856 when her brother, called Austin, married her school friend Susan Gilbert (1830–1913) the couple moved into the "Evergreens," next door to the Homestead, newly built for the couple by Edward Dickinson. Neither Emily Dickinson nor Lavinia married. Emily Dickinson seldom left Amherst. Her one lengthy absence was a year (1847–48) at Mt. Holyoke Female Seminary, at South Hadley, ten long miles away, where she was intensely homesick for her *"own* DEAR HOME," and once back in Amherst she beckoned her brother from his schoolteaching in Boston: "Walk away to freedom and the sunshine here at home." Undaunted by her powerful father's domestic tyrannies, cherishing her mother (who remains hard for biographers to characterize, a passive woman in a household of forceful personalities), Dickinson declared home to be holy, "the definition of God," a place of "Infinite power."

All the Dickinsons struck people as unusual, but Emily was identified as "the climax of all the family oddity" and became known as the "Myth," the *"character* of Amherst," well before she died, according to the local gossip that the young Mabel Loomis Todd passed on to her parents soon after moving to Amherst in 1881:

> She has not been outside of her own house in fifteen years, except once to see a new church, when she crept out at night, & viewed it by moonlight. No one who calls upon her mother & sister ever see her, but she allows little children once in a great while, & one at a time, to come in, when she gives them cake or candy, or some nicety, for she is very fond of little ones. But more often she lets down the sweetmeat by a string, out of a window, to them. She dresses wholly in white, & her mind is said to be perfectly wonderful. She writes finely, but no one *ever* sees her. Her sister . . . invited me to come

& sing to her mother some time and I promised to go & if the performance pleases her [the "Myth"], a servant will enter with wine for me, or a flower, & perhaps her thanks; but just probably the token of approval will not come then, but a few days after, some dainty present will appear for me at twilight. People tell me that the *myth* will hear every note—she will be near, but unseen. . . . Isn't that like a book? So interesting.

"No one knows the cause of her isolation," Mabel Todd concluded, "but of course there are dozens of reasons assigned." Many people have speculated about the reasons for Dickinson's seclusion, but no single "cause of her isolation" has ever been discovered.

Economically, politically, and intellectually, the Dickinsons were among Amherst's most prominent families. Edward Dickinson was treasurer of Amherst College for thirty-six years and served as a state representative and a state senator. During his term in Congress (1853–54), Emily Dickinson visited him in Washington and stayed briefly in Philadelphia on her way home. A successful lawyer, Austin became a justice of the peace in 1857 and followed his father, in 1873, as treasurer of Amherst College. Emily Dickinson attended Amherst Academy from 1840 through 1846, years her biographer Richard B. Sewall calls "a blossoming period in her life, full and joyous"; then she spent her year at Mt. Holyoke. At eighteen she was formally educated far beyond the level then achieved by most Americans, male or female.

Religion was an essential part of Dickinson's education, and Amherst was nearer to Jonathan Edwards's Stockbridge of a century before than it was to the Boston of the 1840s, where, for many of the educated classes, Unitarianism had disposed of the idea of hell and the fear of the fiery pit. Dickinson was exposed to the sort of terrorism from the pulpit that Harriet Beecher Stowe was soon to depict in her realistic historical novels, and Dickinson seems to have experienced the psychological agonies that Stowe attributed to some of her delicate young female characters. For Dickinson, being terrorized by old-fashioned sermons about damnation was compounded by the closeness of death in that age of high infant and childhood mortality and high mortality in childbirth. The death of her friend Sophia Holland at fifteen in 1844 made Dickinson think she "should die too" and set her into "a fixed melancholy." Soon afterward, swayed by the revivalistic fervor of the community, Dickinson felt that she had experienced an awakening in which she found her "savior."

Dickinson's religious exaltation did not last, and as her girlhood friends married and moved away, she gradually became estranged from the religious beliefs of the community. For several years she dutifully attended church, but her terror diminished, especially after 1852, when she became friends with Josiah Gilbert Holland, associate editor of the Springfield *Republican*, and his wife, Elizabeth; their liberal theology encouraged her to struggle against the influence of sermons threatening damnation for souls like her own. Her first religious rebellion was juvenile (the cocky irreverence of No. 61, "Papa above!" or the smug superiority of No. 324, "Some keep the Sabbath going to Church"), but later she could take ironic intellectual delight in her freedom from the tyrannical, arbitrary God (a "Mastiff" in No. 1317) worshipped by her townspeople. In her maturity, as a great poet, she understood that the feelings that distanced her from other people also enhanced her awareness of the seasonal rhythms of nature (No. 1068, "Further in Summer than the Birds"). Her introspection was unfailingly rigorous; while she triumphed at length in her rebellion against the theology of her town, to the extent that Cynthia Griffin Wolff refers to her as a "post-Christian artist," Dickinson remained a daughter of the Puritans, albeit a disobedient daughter.

Dickinson's slow triumph over religious fears was intricately involved in her seeing herself as a poet. Reading literature was a guilty pleasure in the Amherst of

Dickinson's childhood, where there still reigned the antiartistic spirit that Harriet Beecher Stowe depicted as a common feature of late-eighteenth- and early-nineteenth-century New England households. Edward Hitchcock, the president of Amherst Academy, labeled much modern poetry "disastrous to religion," all the more insidious when the "poison" was "so interwoven with those fascinations of style, or thought, characteristic of genius, as to be unnoticed by the youthful mind, delighted with smartness and brilliancy." Dickinson's youthful mind, which delighted in smartness and brilliancy, chose rebellion. Once settled back at home from Mt. Holyoke, Dickinson embarked on a lifelong course of reading books that might "joggle the Mind"—the effect her father feared would result from the books he bought her.

Of contemporary American writing Dickinson knew the poetry of Longfellow, Holmes, and Lowell. She identified wryly with Hawthorne's isolated, gnarled, idiosyncratic characters, such as Hepzibah in *The House of the Seven Gables*. Ralph Waldo Emerson was an enduring favorite and a palpable presence, although she did not go next door to meet him when he stayed at the Evergreens on a lecture tour in 1857. By the early 1860s she loved Thoreau, recognizing a kindred spirit in the independent, nature-loving man who delighted in being the village crank of Concord. She also read a host of lesser American fiction writers and poets as lowly as the authors of what Richard B. Sewall calls "the endless string of fugitive verses in the periodicals (the *Republican*, the *Hampshire and Franklin Express*, the *Atlantic*, *Harper's*, and *Scribner's*)."

Dickinson's deepest literary debts were to the Bible and to British writers, dead and living. Her knowledge of Shakespeare was minute and extremely personal, and she knew line by line works of other older British poets, notably Milton. A favorite recent poet was Keats, and her reading of her English contemporaries started early. She read the novels of Charles Dickens year by year, as they appeared, made his characters part of her circle of acquaintances, and used his characters for coded messages with Samuel Bowles, who had met Dickens. She knew Robert Browning's poems well, although he was most valuable to her as an adjunct to Elizabeth Barrett Browning. She knew Tennyson, including poems now seldom read, such as *Maud*. In her maturity, through national magazines she subscribed to and books she ordered from Boston, she had access to the best British literature of her time within weeks or months, usually, of its publication.

The English contemporaries who mattered most to her career were Elizabeth Barrett Browning and the Brontë sisters. Browning was immensely important as an example of a successful contemporary female poet. Indeed (to judge from No. 593), she seems to have awakened Dickinson to her vocation when she was still "a sombre Girl," and Dickinson revered her. For Dickinson the Brontë sisters (or the "Yorkshire girls," especially "gigantic Emily") became not merely admired authors but daily presences in her life. Judith Farr (1992) has shown that Dickinson modeled her own epistolary and poetic persona on aspects of the Brontës' life and writings, especially on Charlotte Brontë's small independent heroine Jane Eyre. Dickinson subsequently had yet another English model, George Eliot, whose novels and poems she read as they appeared, and after whose death she eagerly awaited an announced biography. In her growing seclusion Dickinson became as familiar with Eliot's fictional characters as she was with many of the inhabitants of Amherst; only Dickens filled her mind with as many fictional acquaintances as Eliot did. The scandalous George Sand was a powerful example, not merely as a woman but, after her death, as a "queen"—like herself, a queen of a literary realm. Emily Brontë was a dead English queen. Elizabeth Browning and George Eliot reigned as dual English queens of poetry and (primarily) prose. And Emily Dickinson reigned unchallenged (in her own knowledge) as the queen of American poetry; humorously, she declared that every day she tried out ways of behaving " 'If I should be a Queen tomorrow' " (No. 373).

Richard B. Sewall showed that in her twenties Dickinson worked out a modus vivendi by which she could be private and independent and at the same time a loving and dutiful daughter. In the Dickinson house, where there were servants to empty chamber pots, scrub floors, dig potatoes, and care for the horses, Dickinson's chores were limited to those that a female in delicate health could perform, household duties that were reverential as well as practical, such as bread making for a small and much loved household, canning preserves, keeping flowers in bloom all year in the conservatory, and doing the finer sewing. According to her sister, it also became accepted that in the distribution of family tasks what Dickinson had to do was "to think." Her thought often came in the form of terse, striking definitions or propositions, used and reused in letters and poems, which she frequently wrote down, as Sewall says, thriftily, "on odds and ends of paper, on the back of recipes, invitations, shopping lists, clippings"; a young cousin recalled Dickinson composing poetry in the pantry as she skimmed the milk.

Edward Dickinson's financial security meant Emily never needed a husband to support her and never needed to think of taking a job—schoolteaching or millwork—then open to a young woman. Betsy Erkkila, building on evidence assembled by Jay Leyda and Richard B. Sewall, in *Emily Dickinson and Class* (1992) argues: "Within the domestic economy of the Dickinson household, as in the larger political economy of nineteenth-century America, Dickinson was the 'lady' and the intellectual whose leisure, freedom, and space 'to think' were made possible by the manual labor and proletarianization of others." In Erkkila's reading, "Dickinson's poems assert the ultimate and real value of an interior, mental, and spiritual economy against the instability of the new marketplace economy of wages, prices, contracts, merchants, securities, stocks, and reversals." It was Dickinson's economic dependence on her father that gave her the freedom to become a great poet.

No one has persuasively traced the precise stages of Dickinson's growth from a conventional schoolgirl versifier to one of the greatest American poets. It seems, however, that her originality emerged in music before it emerged in verse. Through voice and piano lessons, she became a musician good enough to improvise for her family, but often alone, playing softly after the rest of the family had retired. Going beyond improvising original melodies on the piano, she began to improvise poetry that was not merely of her own authorship but was genuinely original, in Emerson's sense of adorning the world with a new thing. From her twenties until her death Dickinson was free to devote much of her life to poetry, and by the late 1850s, when she had become a true poet, Sewall explains, Dickinson "lived increasingly in her own chosen country, where she was free. Her home was the setting, with a family that learned not to intrude. Her companions were her Lexicon; the things of nature; her books; her letters, which became increasingly the measure of her fulfilled relationships; but especially her poems, in which she explored the truth of her fulfillments and her unfulfillments—with nature, man, and God." In 1862 she could write, "All men say 'What' to me." She disconcerted people, delighting in her peculiarities that by then were manifested not only in musical improvisations and brilliant conversation but also in great poems.

Dickinson found poetic freedom within the confines of the hymn meter familiar to her from earliest childhood; within that familiar form she multiplied aural possibilities by what a later audience called "off" rhymes or "slant" rhymes. Her precise syntactical allocations, which would run across the end of the conventional stopping place of a line or a stanza break, forced her reader to learn where to pause to collect the sense before reading on. Her ostensible subject matter, like her form, was familiar, a fact T. W. Higginson exploited when he devised rubrics under which he and Mabel Todd would group Dickinson's poems in the first (1890) edition: Life, Love, Nature, Time, and Eternity. Dickinson's treatment of these conventional themes could be commonplace, but more often she brought dazzling originality to the tritest topic. Her Nature poems, for example, delight with sharp, precise observations, but they are infused with mingled ecstasy and pain: her intense joy in the arrival of spring is tempered with the acute pain of knowing that summers in western Massachusetts may end when August burns "low."

She seized on the familiar genre of the "occasional poem," a poem suggested by some event or experience, as her way of responding to the events of the day, including many passages she encountered in her reading. Hers was often occasional poetry in which the occasion was tacit, not explicit. Leyda first identified a "major device" of her poems and letters, what he called the "omitted center":

> The riddle, the circumstance too well known to be repeated to the initiate, the deliberate skirting of the obvious—this was the means she used to increase the privacy of her communication; it has also increased our problems in piercing that privacy. With so much real background detail coming constantly to light, her poems and letters take on unexpectedly deep roots in national and community life, in family crises, and in her daily reading. . . . To ignore this central concealment in the letters (as in the poems), stripping them of nearly all their associations, is to divorce Emily Dickinson from her real, tangible surroundings. To read her writings only as "timeless" is to lose even that timelessness that derives strength from the passing real moment. The allusions and quotations of her letters also exploit this game of the omitted center. . . . To force her reader to "hear between the lines" was a method that, if unrecognized, made her messages puzzling to some contemporaries.

In his juxtapositions of documents in the *Years and Hours of Emily Dickinson* Leyda helped identify many such "omitted centers," and Sewall has pursued Leyda's insight with elaborate evidence that Dickinson made her own poems the means of having conversations with her real-life acquaintances and with writers as remote from her as the Apostle Paul and John the Evangelist.

Letters, in particular three drafts of letters to her "Master," and many dozens of love poems have convinced biographers that Dickinson experienced a number of passionate relationships, one of which may have been with the friend who became her sister-in-law, one or more of the most intense of which may have been with men already married. There is mystery about how she met some of the men whom she is said to have loved, mystery about which of the men loved her in return, mystery about where and how often she met them. One of these relationships was with a man who published a few of her poems and (had he been perceptive enough) could have published many more, the electric, startlingly handsome, married Samuel Bowles, editor of the Springfield *Republican*, who may have had Dickinson in mind when he insolently complained about the way "women-writers" take criticism: "they receive the unvarnished truth as if it were a red-hot bullet." Another possible object of her affections is the Reverend Charles Wadsworth, whom she met in Philadelphia in 1855 and who visited her in Amherst in 1860 and 1880. As a minister in Philadelphia, and in San Francisco after 1862, he lived a public life as minister and as husband and father. The last man she is known to have loved was Judge Otis Phillips Lord, two decades older than she, a conservative Whig who had outlived his party (much like her own father and Melville's father-in-law Lemuel Shaw, the "Shaw" of No. 116).

Like any genius, Dickinson knew how good she was, as such a poem as No. 326 makes plain. For some years she wanted fiercely to be published—on her own terms. She sent many poems to Mr. and Mrs. Bowles, privately, but in tacit hope that Samuel Bowles would see that they appeared in the *Republican*; he did publish a few, after whipping them into more conventional shape. She also sent poems to Josiah Holland, who did not publish them in *Scribner's* when he could have and who did not push Bowles to publish more in the *Republican*.

When Higginson's *Letter to a Young Contributor* appeared in the April 1862 *Atlantic Monthly*, a compendium of practical advice on preparing and placing manuscripts in a competitive literary marketplace, she found in the essay the assurance that "every editor is always hungering and thirsting after novelties," eager for the privilege of "bringing forward a new genius." In another passage Higginson encouragingly exalted "the magnificent mystery of words" over a style merely conventionally smooth and accurate. Ignoring other passages (such as a stern warning against premature individualism and "mannerism"), she copied out a few of her poems—plainly to see if he would publish them.

In her letter to Higginson on April 15, 1862, her first sentence was a naked plea for recognition: "Are you too deeply occupied to say if my Verse is alive?" If it was alive, plainly, it deserved to be in print. Higginson was incapable of responding as she hoped, and in the face of his disapproval of her formal imperfections she defensively disguised her desire to become a published poet. Higginson looms large in any Dickinson biography not because he recognized her as a great poet in time to nourish and prolong her intense creative years but because Mabel Todd much later enlisted him as a front man, whose literary stature would guarantee that attention would be paid to the 1890 volume of Dickinson's poetry she had edited with minimal help from him.

After Higginson's disappointing response to her poems, Dickinson built up an armor against rejection, proclaiming contemptuously that publication was "the Auction / Of the Mind of Man" and that she would go to her maker undefiled by commerce. But knowing she was great and having longed for public recognition, she continued for the rest of her life to function (in her own eyes) on equal footing with her great Victorian contemporaries.

The second half of Dickinson's life was marked not only by a succession of deaths (such as she had experienced all her life) but by tragedy being enacted next door at the Evergreens. Charmed with Susan Gilbert, Dickinson had urged Austin to marry her friend, a mistake that damned her brother and haunted her and Lavinia. Dickinson's seclusion may have owed as much to her desire to distance herself from strains in the marriage next door as anything else. In 1881 David Todd arrived in Amherst as director of the Amherst College Observatory. His young wife, Mabel, was taken up by Sue Gilbert for a time, and the subsequent sexual liaison between Austin and Mabel lasted until Austin's death. In recent years the story of this affair has been detailed by one of those wounded by it (Millicent Todd Bingham) and by more objective historians, such as Sewall and Polly Longsworth. The affair had no discernable effect on Dickinson's literary life, for she was then writing little poetry. It had, however, consequences of the most momentous sort for her reputation.

Several months before her death in 1882, Mrs. Dickinson read some of her daughter's poetry to Mabel Todd, who found them "full of power." Soon Mabel Todd and Dickinson had established "a very pleasant friendship" without meeting (Mabel Todd saw Dickinson once, in her coffin), and Mabel Todd had decided that even though her neighbor reminded her of Dickens's Miss Havisham in *Great Expectations*, this Amherst eccentric was "in many respects a genius." Without the poet's overtures (a glass of sherry, flowers, and poems) to the newcomer, Dickinson would not be in this or any other anthology. She might have been wholly forgotten had not young Mabel Todd (at Lavinia's instigation) painstakingly transcribed many of Dickinson's poems. The subsequent preservation and publication of Dickinson's poems and letters was initiated and carried forth by Mabel Todd, almost single handedly. She persuaded the ever-cautious Higginson to help her see a collection of poems into print in 1890 and a "second series" of poems in 1891; she published a third series in 1896, without Higginson's involvement. Sewall estimates that only about a tenth of the letters Dickinson wrote have survived, and only a thousandth of those written to her. Mabel Todd could do nothing about the destruction of letters to Dickinson, but through her editing and her popular lectures she performed small miracles in alerting people, in time, to the preservation of Dickinson's letters, the first edition of which she published in 1894. In the 1890s some critics reacted with superiority toward what they saw as verse that violated the laws of meter, but the public loved the poems at once. After Mabel Todd's labors, Dickinson's survival as a popular minor poet was never long in doubt; and through her efforts, the documentary materials were preserved on which literary scholars and critics could later crown her as one of the great American poets, another "gigantic Emily."

The texts of the poems are from Thomas H. Johnson's three-volume variorum edition, *The Poems of Emily Dickinson* (1955). The letters by Dickinson and Higginson are from vol. 2 of *The Letters of Emily Dickinson*, edited by Thomas H. Johnson and Theodora Ward (1958).

49

I never lost as much but twice,
And that was in the sod.
Twice have I stood a beggar
Before the door of God!

Angels—twice descending   5
Reimbursed my store—
Burglar! Banker—Father!
I am poor once more!

c. 1858   1890

67

Success is counted sweetest
By those who ne'er succeed.
To comprehend a nectar
Requires sorest need.

Not one of all the purple Host   5
Who took the Flag today
Can tell the definition
So clear of Victory

As he defeated—dying—
On whose forbidden ear   10
The distant strains of triumph
Burst agonized and clear!

c. 1859   1878

130

These are the days when Birds come back—
A very few—a Bird or two—
To take a backward look.

These are the days when skies resume
The old—old sophistries[1] of June—   5
A blue and gold mistake.

Oh fraud that cannot cheat the Bee—
Almost thy plausibility
Induces my belief.

Till ranks of seeds their witness bear—   10
And softly thro' the altered air
Hurries a timid leaf.

Of Sacrament of summer days,
Oh Last Communion[2] in the Haze—
Permit a child to join.   15

Thy sacred emblems to partake—
Thy consecrated bread to take
And thine immortal wine!

c. 1859   1890

131

Besides the Autumn poets sing
A few prosaic days
A little this side of the snow
And that side of the Haze—

A few incisive Mornings—   5
A few Ascetic Eves—
Gone—Mr Bryant's "Golden Rod"—
And Mr Thomson's "sheaves."[1]

Still, is the bustle in the Brook—
Sealed are the spicy valves—   10
Mesmeric fingers softly touch
The Eyes of many Elves—

Perhaps a squirrel may remain—
My sentiments to share—
Grant me, Oh Lord, a sunny mind—   15
Thy windy will to bear!

c. 1859   1891

---

1. Deceptively subtle reasonings.
2. I.e., the death of nature in late fall is compared to the death of Christ commemorated by the Christian sacrament of Communion.

1. James Thomson (1700–1748), British poet, published *The Seasons* in four parts, the last of which was *Autumn* (1730).

148

All overgrown by cunning moss,
All interspersed with weed,
The little cage of "Currer Bell"
In quiet "Haworth"[1] laid.

This Bird—observing others   5
When frosts too sharp became
Retire to other latitudes—
Quietly did the same—

But differed in returning—
Since Yorkshire hills are green—   10
Yet not in all the nests I meet—
Can Nightingale be seen—

                    Or—

Gathered from many wanderings—
Gethsemane can tell   15
Thro' what transporting anguish
She reached the Asphodel!

Soft fall the sounds of Eden
Upon her puzzled ear—
Oh what an afternoon for Heaven,   20
When "Bronte" entered there!

c. 1859   1896

185

"Faith" is a fine invention
When Gentlemen can *see*—
But *Microscopes* are prudent
In an Emergency.

c. 1860   1891

187

How many times these low feet staggered—
Only the soldered mouth can tell—
Try—can you stir the awful rivet—
Try—can you lift the hasps of steel!

Stroke the cool forehead—hot so often—   5
Lift—if you care—the listless hair—

---

1. Yorkshire parsonage where Charlotte Brontë (1816–1855) grew up. "Currer Bell": Brontë's pseudonym.

Handle the adamantine[1] fingers
Never a thimble—more—shall wear—

Buzz the dull flies—on the chamber window—
Brave—shines the sun through the freckled pane—   10
Fearless—the cobweb swings from the ceiling—
Indolent Housewife—in Daisies—lain!

c. 1860   1890

199

I'm "wife"—I've finished that—
That other state—
I'm Czar—I'm "Woman" now—
It's safer so—

How odd the Girl's life looks   5
Behind this soft Eclipse—
I think that Earth feels so
To folks in Heaven—now—

This being comfort—then
That other kind—was pain—   10
But why compare?
I'm "Wife"! Stop there!

c. 1860   1890

214

I taste a liquor never brewed—
From Tankards scooped in Pearl—
Not all the Vats upon the Rhine
Yield such an Alcohol!

Inebriate of Air—am I—   5
And Debauchee of Dew—
Reeling—thro endless summer days—
From inns of Molten Blue—

When "Landlords" turn the drunken Bee
Out of the Foxglove's door—   10
When Butterflies—renounce their "drams"—
I shall but drink the more!

Till Seraphs[2] swing their snowy Hats—
And Saints—to windows run—

---

1. Rigidly firm; literally made of adamant, a stone be-   2. Six-winged angels believed to guard God's throne.
lieved to be of impenetrable hardness.

To see the little Tippler   15
Leaning against the—Sun—

c. 1860   1861

216

Safe in their Alabaster[1] Chambers—
Untouched by Morning
And untouched by Noon—
Sleep the meek members of the Resurrection—
Rafter of satin,   5
And Roof of stone.

Light laughs the breeze
In her Castle above them—
Babbles the Bee in a stolid Ear,
Pipe the Sweet Birds in ignorant cadence—   10
Ah, what sagacity perished here!

version of 1859   1862

Safe in their Alabaster Chambers—
Untouched by Morning—
And untouched by Noon—
Lie the meek members of the Resurrection—
Rafter of Satin—and Roof of Stone!   5

Grand go the Years—in the Crescent—above them—
Worlds scoop their Arcs—
And Firmaments—row—
Diadems—drop—and Doges[2]—surrender—
Soundless as dots—on a Disc of Snow—   10

version of 1861   1890

241

I like a look of Agony,
Because I know it's true—
Men do not sham Convulsion,
Nor simulate, a Throe—

The Eyes glaze once—and that is Death—   5
Impossible to feign
The Beads upon the Forehead
By homely Anguish strung.

c. 1861   1890

1. Translucent, white chalky material.
2. Chief magistrates in the republics of Venice and Genoa from the 11th through the 16th centuries.

249

Wild Nights—Wild Nights!
Were I with thee
Wild Nights should be
Our luxury!

Futile—the Winds—   5
To a Heart in port—
Done with the Compass—
Done with the Chart!

Rowing in Eden—
Ah, the Sea!   10
Might I but moor—Tonight—
In Thee!

c. 1861   1891

258

There's a certain Slant of light,
Winter Afternoons—
That oppresses, like the Heft
Of Cathedral Tunes—

Heavenly Hurt, it gives us—   5
We can find no scar,
But internal difference,
Where the Meanings, are—

None may teach it—Any—
'Tis the Seal[1] Despair—   10
An imperial affliction
Sent us of the Air—

When it comes, the Landscape listens—
Shadows—hold their breath—
When it goes, 'tis like the Distance   15
On the look of Death—

c. 1861   1890

280

I felt a Funeral, in my Brain,
And Mourners to and fro
Kept treading—treading—till it seemed
That Sense was breaking through—

---

1. In the double sense of a device used to imprint an official mark and an official sign of confirmation.

And when they all were seated,   5
A Service, like a Drum—
Kept beating—beating—till I thought
My Mind was going numb—

And then I heard them lift a Box
And creak across my Soul   10
With those same Boots of Lead, again,
Then Space—began to toll,

As all the Heavens were a Bell,
And Being, but an Ear,
And I, and Silence, some strange Race   15
Wrecked, solitary, here—

And then a Plank in Reason, broke,
And I dropped down, and down—
And hit a World, at every plunge,
And Finished knowing—then—   20

c. 1861   1896

285

The Robin's my Criterion for Tune—
Because I grow—where Robins do—
But, were I Cuckoo born—
I'd swear by him—
The ode familiar—rules the Noon—   5
The Buttercup's, my Whim for Bloom—
Because, we're Orchard sprung—
But, were I Britain born,
I'd Daisies spurn—
None but the Nut—October fit—   10
Because, through dropping it,
The Seasons flit—I'm taught—
Without the Snow's Tableau
Winter, were lie—to me—
Because I see—New Englandly—   15
The Queen, discerns like me—
Provincially—

c. 1861   1929

287

A Clock stopped—
Not the Mantel's—
Geneva's[1] farthest skill

---

1. A city in Switzerland, famous for its clockmakers.

Cant put the puppet bowing—
That just now dangled still—   5

An awe came on the Trinket!
The Figures hunched, with pain—
Then quivered out of Decimals—
Into Degreeless Noon—

It will not stir for Doctor's—   10
This Pendulum of snow—
The Shopman importunes it—
While cool—concernless No—

Nods from the Gilded pointers—
Nods from the Seconds slim—   15
Decades of Arrogance between
The Dial life—
And Him—

c. 1861   1896

303

The Soul selects her own Society—
Then—shuts the Door—
To her divine Majority—
Present no more—

Unmoved—she notes the Chariots—pausing—   5
At her low Gate—
Unmoved—an Emperor be kneeling
Upon her Mat—

I've known her—from an ample nation—
Choose One—   10
Then—close the Valves of her attention—
Like Stone—

c. 1862   1890

305

The difference between Despair
And Fear—is like the One
Between the instant of a Wreck—
And when the Wreck has been—

The Mind is smooth—no Motion—   5
Contented as the Eye
Upon the Forehead of a Bust—
That knows—it cannot see—

c. 1862   1914

312[1]

Her—"last Poems"—
Poets—ended—
Silver—perished—with her Tongue—
Not on Record—bubbled other,
Flute—or Woman—   5
So divine—
Not unto it's Summer—Morning
Robin—uttered Half the Tune—
Gushed too free for the Adoring—
From the Anglo-Florentine—   10
Late—the Praise—
'Tis dull—conferring
On the Head too High to Crown—
Diadem—or Ducal Showing—
Be it's Grave—sufficient sign—   15
Nought—that We—No Poet's Kinsman—
Suffocate—with easy wo—
What, and if, Ourself a Bridegroom—
Put Her down—in Italy?

c. 1862   1914

314

Nature—sometimes sears a Sapling—
Sometimes—scalps a Tree—
Her Green People recollect it
When they do not die—

Fainter Leaves—to Further Seasons—   5
Dumbly testify—
We—who have the Souls—
Die oftener—Not so vitally—

c. 1862   1945

315

He fumbles at your Soul
As Players at the Keys
Before they drop full Music on—
He stuns you by degrees—
Prepares your brittle Nature   5
For the Etherial Blow
By fainter Hammers—further heard—
Then nearer—Then so slow
Your Breath has time to straighten—

1. A tribute to Elizabeth Barrett Browning (1806–1861), British poet.

Your Brain—to bubble Cool—   10
Deals—One—imperial—Thunderbolt—
That scalps your naked Soul—

When Winds take Forests in their Paws—
The Universe—is still—

c. 1862   1896

322

There came a Day at Summer's full,
Entirely for me—
I thought that such were for the Saints,[1]
Where Resurrections—be—

The Sun, as common, went abroad,   5
The flowers, accustomed, blew,[2]
As if no soul the solstice passed
That maketh all things new—

The time was scarce profaned, by speech—
The symbol of a word   10
Was needless, as at Sacrament,
The Wardrobe—of our Lord[3]—

Each was to each The Sealed Church,
Permitted to commune this—time—
Lest we too awkward show   15
At Supper of the Lamb.[4]

The Hours slid fast—as Hours will,
Clutched tight, by greedy hands—
So faces on two Decks, look back,
Bound to opposing lands—   20

And so when all the time had leaked,
Without external sound
Each bound the Other's Crucifix—
We gave no other Bond—

Sufficient troth, that we shall rise—   25
Deposed—at length, the Grave[5]—
To that new Marriage,
Justified—through Calvaries[6] of Love—

c. 1861   1890

---

1. "The elect."
2. Blossomed.
3. A reference to the bread and wine of Holy Communion, which, because they are thought to embody
Christ, render his literal wardrobe superfluous.
4. I.e., this communion prepares her for the ultimate

meeting with Christ (the Lamb).
5. I.e., death will eventually be deposed or overthrown.
6. Calvary was the mountain where Christ was crucified.

324

Some keep the Sabbath going to Church—
I keep it, staying at Home—
With a Bobolink for a Chorister—
And an Orchard, for a Dome—

Some keep the Sabbath in Surplice— 5
I just wear my Wings—
And instead of tolling the Bell, for Church,
Our little Sexton—sings.

God preaches, a noted Clergyman—
And the sermon is never long, 10
So instead of getting to Heaven, at last—
I'm going, all along.

c. 1860 1864

326

I cannot dance upon my Toes—
No Man instructed me—
But oftentimes, among my mind,
A Glee possesseth me,

That had I Ballet knowledge— 5
Would put itself abroad
In Pirouette to blanch a Troupe—
Or lay a Prima, mad,

And though I had no Gown of Gauze—
No Ringlet, to my Hair, 10
Nor hopped for Audiences—like Birds,
One Claw upon the Air,

Nor tossed my shape in Eider Balls,
Nor rolled on wheels of snow
Till I was out of sight, in sound, 15
The House encore me so—

Nor any know I know the Art
I mention—easy—Here—
Nor any Placard boast me—
It's full as Opera— 20

c. 1862 1929

328

A Bird came down the Walk—
He did not know I saw—

He bit an Angleworm in halves
And ate the fellow, raw,

And then he drank a Dew   5
From a convenient Grass—
And then hopped sidewise to the Wall
To let a Beetle pass—

He glanced with rapid eyes
That hurried all around—   10
They looked like frightened Beads, I thought—
He stirred his Velvet Head

Like one in danger, Cautious,
I offered him a Crumb
And he unrolled his feathers   15
And rowed him softer home—

Than Oars divide the Ocean,
Too silver for a seam—
Or Butterflies, off Banks of Noon
Leap, plashless[1] as they swim.   20

c. 1862   1891

341

After great pain, a formal feeling comes—
The Nerves sit ceremonious, like Tombs—
The stiff Heart questions was it He, that bore,
And Yesterday, or Centuries before?

The Feet, mechanical, go round—   5
Of Ground, or Air, or Ought—
A Wooden way
Regardless grown,
A Quartz contentment, like a stone—

This is the Hour of Lead—   10
Remembered, if outlived,
As Freezing persons, recollect the Snow—
First—Chill—then Stupor—then the letting go—

c. 1862   1929

348

I dreaded that first Robin, so,
But He is mastered, now,

1. I.e., splashless.

I'm some accustomed to Him grown,
He hurts a little, though—

I thought if I could only live   5
Till that first Shout got by—
Not all Pianos in the Woods
Had power to mangle me—

I dared not meet the Daffodils—
For fear their Yellow Gown   10
Would pierce me with a fashion
So foreign to my own—

I wished the Grass would hurry—
So—when 'twas time to see—
He'd be too tall, the tallest one   15
Could stretch—to look at me—

I could not bear the Bees should come,
I wished they'd stay away
In those dim countries where they go,
What word had they, for me?   20

They're here, though; not a creature failed—
No Blossom stayed away
In gentle deference to me—
The Queen of Calvary[1]—

Each one salutes me, as he goes,   25
And I, my childish Plumes,
Lift, in bereaved acknowledgement
Of their unthinking Drums—

c. 1862   1891

435

Much Madness is divinest Sense—
To a discerning Eye—
Much Sense—the starkest Madness—
'Tis the Majority
In this, as All, prevail—   5
Assent—and you are sane—
Demur—you're straightway dangerous—
And handled with a Chain—

c. 1862   1890

---

1. I.e., one who has experienced intense suffering.

441

This is my letter to the World
That never wrote to Me—
The simple News that Nature told—
With tender Majesty

Her Message is committed   5
To Hands I cannot see—
For love of Her—Sweet—countrymen—
Judge tenderly—of Me

c. 1862   1890

448

This was a Poet—It is That
Distills amazing sense
From ordinary Meanings—
And Attar[1] so immense

From the familiar species   5
That perished by the Door—
We wonder it was not Ourselves
Arrested it—before—

Of Pictures, the Discloser'—
That Poet—it is He—   10
Entitles Us—by Contrast—
To ceaseless Poverty—

Of Portion—so unconscious—
The Robbing—could not harm—
Himself—to Him—a Fortune—   15
Exterior—to Time—

c. 1862   1929

449

I died for Beauty—but was scarce
Adjusted in the tomb
When One who died for Truth, was lain
In an adjoining Room—

He questioned softly "Why I failed"?   5
"For Beauty", I replied—
"And I—for Truth—Themself are One—
We Bretheren, are", He said—

---

1. Perfume obtained from flowers.

And so, as Kinsmen, met a Night—
We talked between the Rooms—   10
Until the Moss had reached our lips—
And covered up—our names—

c. 1862   1890

465

I heard a Fly buzz—when I died—
The Stillness in the Room
Was like the Stillness in the Air—
Between the Heaves of Storm—

The Eyes around—had wrung them dry—   5
And Breaths were gathering firm
For that last Onset—when the King
Be witnessed—in the Room—

I willed my Keepsakes—Signed away
What portion of me be   10
Assignable—and then it was
There interposed a Fly—

With Blue—uncertain stumbling Buzz—
Between the light—and me—
And then the Windows failed—and then   15
I could not see to see—

c. 1862   1896

488

Myself was formed—a Carpenter—
An unpretending time
My Plane—and I, together wrought
Before a Builder came—

To measure our attainments—   5
Had we the Art of Boards
Sufficiently developed—He'd hire us
At Halves[1]—

My Tools took Human—Faces—
The Bench, where we had toiled—   10
Against the Man—persuaded—
We—Temples build—I said—

c. 1862   1935

1. Dickinson plays on the publishing practice of giving authors "half-profits" after expenses were met.

501

This World is not Conclusion.
A Species stands beyond—
Invisible, as Music—
But positive, as Sound—
It beckons, and it baffles—   5
Philosophy—dont know—
And through a Riddle, at the last—
Sagacity, must go—
To guess it, puzzles scholars—
To gain it, Men have borne   10
Contempt of Generations
And Crucifixion, shown—
Faith slips—and laughs, and rallies—
Blushes, if any see—
Plucks at a twig of Evidence—   15
And asks a Vane, the way—
Much Gesture, from the Pulpit—
Strong Hallelujahs roll—
Narcotics cannot still the Tooth
That nibbles at the soul—   20

c. 1862   1896

505

I would not paint—a picture—
I'd rather be the One
It's bright impossibility
To dwell—delicious—on—
And wonder how the fingers feel   5
Whose rare—celestial—stir—
Evokes so sweet a Torment—
Such sumptuous—Despair—

I would not talk, like Cornets—
I'd rather be the One   10
Raised softly to the Ceilings—
And out, and easy on—
Through Villages of Ether—
Myself endued Balloon
By but a lip of Metal—   15
The pier to my Pontoon—

Nor would I be a Poet—
It's finer—own the Ear—
Enamored—impotent—content—
The License to revere,   20
A privilege so awful
What would the Dower be,

Had I the Art to stun myself
With Bolts of Melody!

c. 1862   1945

510

It was not Death, for I stood up,
And all the Dead, lie down—
It was not Night, for all the Bells
Put out their Tongues, for Noon.

It was not Frost, for on my Flesh   5
I felt Siroccos[1]—crawl—
Nor Fire—for just my Marble feet
Could keep a Chancel,[2] cool—

And yet, it tasted, like them all,
The Figures I have seen   10
Set orderly, for Burial,
Reminded me, of mine—

As if my life were shaven,
And fitted to a frame,
And could not breathe without a key,   15
And 'twas like Midnight, some—

When everything that ticked—has stopped—
And Space stares all around—
Or Grisly frosts—first Autumn morns,
Repeal the Beating Ground—   20

But, most, like Chaos—Stopless—cool—
Without a Chance, or Spar—
Or even a Report of Land—
To justify—Despair.

c. 1862   1891

520

I started Early—Took my Dog—
And visited the Sea—
The Mermaids in the Basement
Came out to look at me—

And Frigates[1]—in the Upper Floor   5
Extended Hempen Hands—

---

1. Hot, oppressive winds from North Africa.
2. The part of the church that contains the choir and sanctuary.

1. In Dickinson's time, men-of-war, the largest ships in the navy.

Presuming Me to be a Mouse—
Aground—upon the Sands—

But no Man moved Me—till the Tide
Went past my simple Shoe—   10
And past my Apron—and my Belt
And past my Boddice—too—

And made as He would eat me up—
As wholly as a Dew
Upon a Dandelion's Sleeve—   15
And then—I started—too—

And He—He followed—close behind—
I felt His Silver Heel
Upon my Ancle—Then my Shoes
Would overflow with Pearl—   20

Until We met the Solid Town—
No One He seemed to know—
And bowing—with a Mighty look—
At me—The Sea withdrew—

c. 1862   1891

528

Mine—by the Right of the White Election!
Mine—by the Royal Seal!
Mine—by the Sign in the Scarlet prison—
Bars—cannot conceal!

Mine—here—in Vision—and in Veto!   5
Mine—by the Grave's Repeal—
Titled—Confirmed—
Delirious Charter!
Mine—long as Ages steal!

c. 1862   1890

536

The Heart asks Pleasure—first—
And then—Excuse from Pain—
And then—those little Anodynes[1]
That deaden suffering—

And then—to go to sleep—   5
And then—if it should be

---

1. Drugs.

The will of it's Inquisitor
The privilege to die—

c. 1862   1890

547

I've seen a Dying Eye
Run round and round a Room—
In search of Something—as it seemed—
Then Cloudier become—
And then—obscure with Fog—   5
And then—be soldered down
Without disclosing what it be
'Twere blessed to have seen—

c. 1862   1890

593

I think I was enchanted
When first a sombre Girl—
I read that Foreign Lady[1]—
The Dark—felt beautiful—

And whether it was noon at night—   5
Or only Heaven—at Noon—
For very Lunacy of Light
I had not power to tell—

The Bees—became as Butterflies—
The Butterflies—as Swans—   10
Approached—and spurned the narrow Grass—
And just the meanest Tunes

That Nature murmured to herself
To keep herself in Cheer—
I took for Giants—practising   15
Titanic Opera—

The Days—to Mighty Metres stept—
The Homeliest—adorned
As if unto a Jubilee
'Twere suddenly confirmed—   20

I could not have defined the change—
Conversion of the Mind
Like Sanctifying in the Soul—
Is witnessed—not explained—

---

1. Presumably Elizabeth Barrett Browning (1806–1861), British poet.

'Twas a Divine Insanity—   25
The Danger to be Sane
Should I again experience—
'Tis Antidote to turn—

To Tomes of solid Witchcraft—
Magicians be asleep—   30
But Magic—hath an Element
Like Deity—to keep—

c. 1862   1935

632

The Brain—is wider than the Sky—
For—put them side by side—
The one the other will contain
With ease—and You—beside—

The Brain is deeper than the sea—   5
For—hold them—Blue to Blue—
The one the other will absorb—
As Sponges—Buckets—do—

The Brain is just the weight of God—
For—Heft them—Pound for Pound—   10
And they will differ—if they do—
As Syllable from Sound—

c. 1862   1896

650

Pain—has an Element of Blank—
It cannot recollect
When it begun—or if there were
A time when it was not—

It has no Future—but itself—   5
It's Infinite contain
It's Past—enlightened to perceive
New Periods—of Pain.

c. 1862   1890

664

Of all the Souls that stand create—
I have elected—One—

When Sense from Spirit—files away—
And Subterfuge—is done—
When that which is—and that which was—   5
Apart—intrinsic—stand—
And this brief Tragedy of Flesh—
Is shifted—like a Sand—
When Figures show their royal Front—
And Mists—are carved away,   10
Behold the Atom—I preferred—
To all the lists of Clay!

c. 1862   1891

709

Publication—is the Auction
Of the Mind of Man—
Poverty—be justifying
For so foul a thing

Possibly—but We—would rather   5
From Our Garret go
White—Unto the White Creator—
Than invest—Our Snow—

Thought belong to Him who gave it—
Then—to Him Who bear   10
It's Corporeal illustration—Sell
The Royal Air—

In the Parcel—Be the Merchant
Of the Heavenly Grace—
But reduce no Human Spirit   15
To Disgrace of Price—

c. 1863   1929

712

Because I could not stop for Death—
He kindly stopped for me—
The Carriage held but just Ourselves—
And Immortality.

We slowly drove—He knew no haste   5
And I had put away
My labor and my leisure too,
For His Civility—

We passed the School, where Children strove
At Recess—in the Ring— 10
We passed the Fields of Gazing Grain—
We passed the Setting Sun—

Or rather—He passed Us—
The Dews drew quivering and chill—
For only Gossamer, my Gown— 15
My Tippet[1]—only Tulle—

We paused before a House that seemed
A Swelling of the Ground—
The Roof was scarcely visible—
The Cornice—in the Ground— 20

Since then—'tis Centuries—and yet
Feels shorter than the Day
I first surmised the Horses Heads
Were toward Eternity—

c. 1863   1890

732

She rose to His Requirement—dropt
The Playthings of Her Life
To take the honorable Work
Of Woman, and of Wife—

If ought She missed in Her new Day, 5
Of Amplitude, or Awe—
Or first Prospective—Or the Gold
In using, wear away,

It lay unmentioned—as the Sea
Develope Pearl, and Weed, 10
But only to Himself—be known
The Fathoms they abide—

c. 1863   1890

744

Remorse—is Memory—awake—
Her Parties all astir—
A Presence of Departed Acts—
At window—and at Door—

It's Past—set down before the Soul 5
And lighted with a Match—

1. Shoulder cape.

Perusal—to facilitate—
And help Belief to stretch—

Remorse is cureless—the Disease
Not even God—can heal—   10
For 'tis His institution—and
The Adequate of Hell—

c. 1863   1891

754

My Life had stood—a Loaded Gun—
In Corners—till a Day
The Owner passed—identified—
And carried Me away—

And now We roam in Sovreign Woods—   5
And now We hunt the Doe—
And every time I speak for Him—
The Mountains straight reply—

And do I smile, such cordial light
Upon the Valley glow—   10
It is as a Vesuvian[1] face
Had let it's pleasure through—

And when at Night—Our good Day done—
I guard My Master's Head—
'Tis better than the Eider-Duck's   15
Deep Pillow—to have shared—

To foe of His—I'm deadly foe—
None stir the second time—
On whom I lay a Yellow Eye—
Or an emphatic Thumb—   20

Though I than He—may longer live
He longer must—than I—
For I have but the power to kill,
Without—the power to die—

c. 1863   1929

822

This Consciousness that is aware
Of Neighbors and the Sun
Will be the one aware of Death
And that itself alone

---

1. A face capable of erupting like Mount Vesuvius.

Is traversing the interval   5
Experience between
And most profound experiment
Appointed unto Men—

How adequate unto itself
It's properties shall be   10
Itself unto itself and none
Shall make discovery.

Adventure most unto itself
The Soul condemned to be—
Attended by a single Hound   15
It's own identity.

c. 1864   1945

824

The Wind begun to knead the Grass—
As Women do a Dough—
He flung a Hand full at the Plain—
A Hand full at the Sky—
The Leaves unhooked themselves from Trees—   5
And started all abroad—
The Dust did scoop itself like Hands—
And throw away the Road—
The Wagons quickened on the Street—
The Thunders gossiped low—   10
The Lightning showed a Yellow Head—
And then a livid Toe—
The Birds put up the Bars to Nests—
The Cattle flung to Barns—
Then came one drop of Giant Rain—   15
And then, as if the Hands
That held the Dams—had parted hold—
The Waters Wrecked the Sky—
But overlooked my Father's House—
Just Quartering a Tree—   20

first version c. 1864   1955

The Wind begun to rock the Grass
With threatening Tunes and low—
He threw a Menace at the Earth—
A Menace at the Sky.

The Leaves unhooked themselves from Trees—   5
And started all abroad

The Dust did scoop itself like Hands
And threw away the Road.

The Wagons quickened on the Streets
The Thunder hurried slow—   10
The Lightning showed a Yellow Beak
And then a livid Claw.

The Birds put up the Bars to Nests—
The Cattle fled to Barns—
There came one drop of Giant Rain   15
And then as if the Hands

That held the Dams had parted hold
The Waters Wrecked the Sky,
But overlooked my Father's House—
Just quartering a Tree—   20

second version c. 1864   1891

829

Ample make this Bed—
Make this Bed with Awe—
In it wait till Judgment break
Excellent and Fair.

Be it's Mattress straight—   5
Be it's Pillow round—
Let no Sunrise' yellow noise
Interrupt this Ground—

c. 1864   1891

939

What I see not, I better see—
Through Faith—my Hazel Eye
Has periods of shutting—
But, No lid has Memory—

For frequent, all my sense obscured   5
I equally behold
As someone held a light unto
The Features so beloved—

And I arise—and in my Dream—
Do Thee distinguished Grace—   10
Till jealous Daylight interrupt—
And mar thy perfectness—

c. 1864   1945

952

A Man may make a Remark—
In itself—a quiet thing
That may furnish the Fuse unto a Spark
In dormant nature—lain—

Let us divide—with skill—   5
Let us discourse—with care—
Powder exists in Charcoal—
Before it exists in Fire.

c. 1864   1945

978

It bloomed and dropt, a Single Noon—
The Flower—distinct and Red—
I, passing, thought another Noon
Another in it's stead

Will equal glow, and thought no More   5
But came another Day
To find the Species disappeared—
The Same Locality—

The Sun in place—no other fraud
On Nature's perfect Sum—   10
Had I but lingered Yesterday—
Was my retrieveless blame—

Much Flowers of this and further Zones
Have perished in my Hands
For seeking it's Resemblance—   15
But unapproached it stands—

The single Flower of the Earth
That I, in passing by
Unconscious was—Great Nature's Face
Passed infinite by Me—   20

c. 1864   1955

986

A narrow Fellow in the Grass
Occasionally rides—
You may have met Him—did you not
His notice sudden is—

The Grass divides as with a Comb—   5
A spotted shaft is seen—
And then it closes at your feet
And opens further on—

He likes a Boggy Acre
A Floor too cool for Corn—   10
Yet when a Boy, and Barefoot—
I more than once at Noon
Have passed, I thought, a Whip lash
Unbraiding in the Sun
When stooping to secure it   15
It wrinkled, and was gone—

Several of Nature's People
I know, and they know me—
I feel for them a transport
Of cordiality—   20

But never met this Fellow
Attended, or alone
Without a tighter breathing
And Zero at the Bone—

c. 1865   1866

1068

Further in Summer than the Birds
Pathetic from the Grass
A minor Nation celebrates
It's unobtrusive Mass.

No Ordinance be seen   5
So gradual the Grace
A pensive Custom it becomes
Enlarging Loneliness.

Antiquest felt at Noon
When August burning low   10
Arise this spectral Canticle
Repose to typify

Remit as yet no Grace
No Furrow on the Glow
Yet a Druidic Difference   15
Enhances Nature now

c. 1866   1891

1072

Title divine—is mine!
The Wife—without the Sign!
Acute Degree—conferred on me—
Empress of Calvary!
Royal—all but the Crown!   5
Betrothed—without the swoon
God sends us Women—
When you—hold—Garnet to Garnet—
Gold—to Gold—
Born—Bridalled—Shrouded—   10
In a Day—
Tri Victory
"My Husband"—women say—
Stroking the Melody—
Is *this*—the way?   15

c. 1862   1924

1078

The Bustle in a House
The Morning after Death
Is solemnest of industries
Enacted upon Earth—

The Sweeping up the Heart   5
And putting Love away
We shall not want to use again
Until Eternity.

c. 1866   1890

1099

My Cocoon tightens—Colors teaze—
I'm feeling for the Air—
A dim capacity for Wings
Demeans the Dress I wear—

A power of Butterfly must be—   5
The Aptitude to fly
Meadows of Majesty concedes
And easy Sweeps of Sky—

So I must baffle at the Hint
And cipher at the Sign
And make much blunder, if at last   10
I take the clue divine—

c. 1866   1890

1125

Oh Sumptuous moment
Slower go
That I may gloat on thee—
'Twill never be the same to starve
Now I abundance see—   5

Which was to famish, then or now—
The difference of Day
Ask him unto the Gallows led—
With morning in the sky

c. 1868   1945

1126

Shall I take thee, the Poet said
To the propounded word?
Be stationed with the Candidates
Till I have finer tried—

The Poet searched Philology   5
And was about to ring
For the suspended Candidate
There came unsummoned in—

That portion of the Vision
The Word applied to fill   10
Not unto nomination
The Cherubim reveal—

c. 1868   1945

1129

Tell all the Truth but tell it slant—
Success in Circuit lies
Too bright for our infirm Delight
The Truth's superb surprise
As Lightning to the Children eased   5
With explanation kind
The Truth must dazzle gradually
Or every man be blind—

c. 1868   1945

1138

A Spider sewed at Night
Without a Light
Upon an Arc of White.

If Ruff it was of Dame
Or Shroud of Gnome   5
Himself himself inform.

Of Immortality
His Strategy
Was Physiognomy.

c. 1869   1891

1182

Remembrance has a Rear and Front—
'Tis something like a House—
It has a Garret also
For Refuse and the Mouse.

Besides the deepest Cellar   5
That ever Mason laid—
Look to it by it's Fathoms
Ourselves be not pursued—

c. 1871   1896

1197

I should not dare to be so sad
So many Years again—
A Load is first impossible
When we have put it down—

The Superhuman then withdraws   5
And we who never saw
The Giant at the other side
Begin to perish now.

1871   1929

1242

To flee from memory
Had we the Wings
Many would fly
Inured to slower things
Birds with dismay   5
Would scan the mighty van
Of men escaping
From the mind of man

c. 1872   1945

1255

Longing is like the Seed
That wrestles in the Ground,
Believing if it intercede
It shall at length be found.

The Hour, and the Clime—   5
Each Circumstance unknown,
What Constancy must be achieved
Before it see the Sun!

c. 1873   1929

1273

That sacred Closet when you sweep—
Entitled "Memory"—
Select a reverential Broom—
And do it silently.

'Twill be a Labor of surprise—   5
Besides Identity
Of other Interlocutors
A probability—

August the Dust of that Domain—
Unchallenged—let it lie—   10
You cannot supersede itself
But it can silence you—

c. 1873   1945

1383

Long Years apart—can make no
Breach a second cannot fill—
The absence of the Witch does not
Invalidate the spell—

The embers of a Thousand Years   5
Uncovered by the Hand
That fondled them when they were Fire
Will gleam and understand

c. 1876   1945

1397

It sounded as if the Streets were running
And then—the Streets stood still—

Eclipse—was all we could see at the Window
And Awe—was all we could feel.

By and by—the boldest stole out of his Covert   5
To see if Time was there—
Nature was in an Opal[1] Apron,
Mixing fresher Air.

c. 1877   1891

1405

Bees are Black, with Gilt Surcingles[2]—
Bucaneers of Buzz.
Ride abroad in ostentation
And subsist on Fuzz.

Fuzz ordained—not Fuzz contingent—   5
Marrows of the Hill.
Jugs—a Universe's fracture
Could not jar or spill.

c. 1877   1945

1463

A Route of Evanescence
With a revolving Wheel—
A Resonance of Emerald—
A Rush of Cochineal[1]—
And every Blossom on the Bush   5
Adjusts it's tumbled Head—
The mail from Tunis,[2] probably,
An easy Morning's Ride—

c. 1879   1891

1467

A little overflowing word
That any, hearing, had inferred
For Ardor or for Tears,
Though Generations pass away,
Traditions ripen and decay,   5
As eloquent appears—

c. 1879   1924

1. An iridescent semiprecious gem.   1. Red dye.
2. Belts or girth straps (as for a horse).   2. City on the northern coast of Africa.

1473

We talked with each other about each other
Though neither of us spoke—
We were listening to the seconds Races
And the Hoofs of the Clock—
Pausing in Front of our Palsied Faces   5
Time compassion took—
Arks of Reprieve he offered to us—
Ararats—we took—

c. 1879   1945

1508

You cannot make Remembrance grow
When it has lost it's Root—
The tightening the Soil around
And setting it upright
Deceives perhaps the Universe   5
But not retrieves the Plant—
Real Memory, like Cedar Feet
Is shod with Adamant—
Nor can you cut Remembrance down
When it shall once have grown—   10
Its Iron Buds will sprout anew
However overthrown—

c. 1880   1945

1540

As imperceptibly as Grief
The Summer lapsed away—
Too imperceptible at last
To seem like Perfidy—

A Quietness distilled   5
As Twilight long begun,
Or Nature spending with herself
Sequestered Afternoon—
The Dusk drew earlier in—
The Morning foreign shone—   10
A courteous, yet harrowing Grace,
As Guest, that would be gone—
And thus, without a Wing
Or service of a Keel
Our Summer made her light escape   15
Into the Beautiful.

c. 1865   1891

1545

The Bible is an antique Volume—
Written by faded Men
At the suggestion of Holy Spectres—
Subjects—Bethlehem—
Eden—the ancient Homestead—   5
Satan—the Brigadier—
Judas—the Great Defaulter—
David—the Troubadour—
Sin—a distinguished Precipice
Others must resist—   10
Boys that "believe" are very lonesome—
Other Boys are "lost"—
Had but the Tale a warbling Teller—
All the Boys would come—
Orpheus' Sermon[1] captivated—   15
It did not condemn—

c. 1882   1924

1560

To be forgot by thee
Surpasses Memory
Of other minds
The Heart cannot forget
Unless it contemplate   5
What it declines
I was regarded then
Raised from oblivion
A single time
To be remembered what—   10
Worthy to be forgot
Is my renown

c. 1883   1945

1575

The Bat is dun, with wrinkled Wings—
Like fallow Article—
And not a song pervade his Lips—
Or none perceptible.

His small Umbrella quaintly halved   5
Describing in the Air
An Arc alike inscrutable
Elate Philosopher.

1. Orpheus, a musician of Greek legend, had the power to soothe wild beasts and make trees dance and rivers stand still with his lyre playing.

Deputed from what Firmament—
Of What Astute Abode—   10
Empowered with what Malignity
Auspiciously withheld—

To his adroit Creator
Ascribe no less the praise—
Beneficent, believe me,   15
His Eccentricities—

c. 1876   1896

1581

The farthest Thunder that I heard
Was nearer than the Sky
And rumbles still, though torrid Noons
Have lain their missiles by—
The Lightning that preceded it   5
Struck no one but myself—
But I would not exchange the Bolt
For all the rest of Life—
Indebtedness to Oxygen
The Happy may repay,   10
But not the obligation
To Electricity—
It founds the Homes and decks the Days
And every clamor bright
Is but the gleam concomitant   15
Of that waylaying Light—
The Thought is quiet as a Flake—
A Crash without a Sound,
How Life's reverberation
It's Explanation found—   20

c. 1883   1932

1593

There came a Wind like a Bugle—
It quivered through the Grass
And a Green Chill upon the Heat
So ominous did pass
We barred the Windows and the Doors   5
As from an Emerald Ghost—
The Doom's electric Moccasin
That very instant passed—
On a strange Mob of panting Trees
And Fences fled away   10
And Rivers where the Houses ran

Those looked that lived—that Day—
The Bell within the steeple wild
The flying tidings told—
How much can come   15
And much can go,
And yet abide the World!

c. 1883   1891

1601

Of God we ask one favor,
That we may be forgiven—
For what, he is presumed to know—
The Crime, from us, is hidden—
Immured the whole of Life   5
Within a magic Prison
We reprimand the Happiness
That too competes with Heaven.

c. 1884   1894

1624

Apparently with no surprise
To any happy Flower
The Frost beheads it at it's play—
In accidental power—
The blonde Assassin passes on—   5
The Sun proceeds unmoved
To measure off another Day
For an Approving God.

c. 1884   1890

1651

A Word made Flesh is seldom
And tremblingly partook
Nor then perhaps reported
But have I not mistook
Each one of us has tasted   5
With ecstasies of stealth
The very food debated
To our specific strength—

A Word that breathes distinctly
Has not the power to die   10
Cohesive as the Spirit
It may expire if He—

"Made Flesh and dwelt among us"[1]
Could condescension be
Like this consent of Language   15
This loved Philology[2]

No Ms.   1955

1732

My life closed twice before its close;
It yet remains to see
If Immortality unveil
A third event to me,

So huge, so hopeless to conceive   5
As these that twice befel.
Parting is all we know of heaven,
And all we need of hell.

No Ms.   1896

Letters to Thomas Wentworth Higginson[1]

[Say If My Verse Is Alive?]

15 April 1862

mr higginson,
Are you too deeply occupied to say if my Verse is alive?
The Mind is so near itself—it cannot see, distinctly—and I have none to ask—
Should you think it breathed—and had you the leisure to tell me, I should feel quick gratitude—
If I make the mistake—that you dared to tell me—would give me sincerer honor—toward you—
I enclose my name—asking you, if you please—Sir—to tell me what is true?
That you will not betray me—it is needless to ask—since Honor is it's own pawn[2]—

[Thank You for the Surgery]

25 April 1862

Mr Higginson,
Your kindness claimed earlier gratitude—but I was ill—and write today, from my pillow.

1. John 1.14.
2. I.e., literature and the disciplines that concern themselves with words.
1. Thomas Wentworth Higginson had recently resigned his radically liberal church pastorate and was beginning to make a name as a reform-minded essayist and lecturer. Higginson's *Letter to a Young Contributor*, offering practical advice to beginning writers, was published in the April *Atlantic Monthly*. This letter, responding to that article, was accompanied by several poems and marked the beginning of a correspon-

dence—and a remarkable relationship—that lasted for the rest of Dickinson's life. It should be noted that Higginson from the first was sensitive to the curious, original power of her poetry, but as a rather conventional 19th-century critic he found no way to judge its unorthodox formal qualities. For her part, Dickinson was content to assume the ironic role of "scholar" to this "Preceptor," content with his friendship and her own "Barefoot-Rank."
2. In place of a signature, Emily Dickinson enclosed a signed card in its own envelope.

Thank you for the surgery—it was not so painful as I supposed. I bring you others—as you ask—though they might not differ—

While my thought is undressed—I can make the distinction, but when I put them in the Gown—they look alike, and numb.

You asked how old I was? I made no verse—but one or two—until this winter—Sir—

I had a terror—since September—I could tell to none—and so I sing, as the Boy does by the Burying Ground—because I am afraid—You inquire my Books—For Poets—I have Keats—and Mr and Mrs Browning. For Prose—Mr Ruskin—Sir Thomas Browne—and the Revelations.[3] I went to school—but in your manner of the phrase—had no education. When a little Girl, I had a friend, who taught me Immortality—but venturing too near, himself—he never returned—Soon after, my Tutor, died[4]—and for several years, my Lexicon—was my only companion—Then I found one more—but he was not contented I be his scholar—so he left the Land.[5]

You ask of my Companions Hills—Sir—and the Sundown—and a Dog—large as myself, that my Father bought me—They are better than Beings—because they know—but do not tell—and the noise in the Pool, at Noon—excels my Piano. I have a Brother and Sister—My Mother does not care for thought—and Father, too busy with his Briefs[6]—to notice what we do—He buys me many Books—but begs me not to read them—because he fears they joggle the Mind. They are religious—except me—and address an Eclipse, every morning—whom they call their "Father." But I fear my story fatigues you—I would like to learn—Could you tell me how to grow—or is it unconveyed—like Melody—or Witchcraft?

You speak of Mr Whitman—I never read his Book[7]—but was told that he was disgraceful—

I read Miss Prescott's "Circumstance,"[8] but it followed me, in the Dark—so I avoided her—

Two Editors of Journals[9] came to my Father's House, this winter—and asked me for my Mind—and when I asked them "Why," they said I was penurious—and they, would use it for the World—

I could not weigh myself—Myself—

My size felt small—to me—I read your Chapters in the Atlantic—and experienced honor for you—I was sure you would not reject a confiding question—

Is this—Sir—what you asked me to tell you?

Your friend,
E—Dickinson

3. Revelation is the last book of the New Testament. John Keats (1795–1821), English Romantic poet. Elizabeth Barrett (1806–1861) and Robert Browning (1812–1889), English poets. John Ruskin (1819–1900), English art critic and social theorist. Sir Thomas Browne (1605–1682), English physician and writer.
4. The friend and tutor was probably Benjamin Franklin Newton (1821–1853), who had studied law in her father's office in the 1840s.
5. The Reverend Charles Wadsworth left Philadelphia for a pastorate in California in April.
6. Edward Dickinson was a prominent lawyer of Amherst. A brief is a concise statement of a client's case

made out for the instruction of counsel in a trial.
7. Walt Whitman's *Leaves of Grass.*
8. Harriett Prescott Spofford's story *Circumstance* appeared in the *Atlantic Monthly* for May 1860. It tells of a woman traveling home from a sick neighbor's at nightfall in Maine. Attacked by a beast called an "Indian Devil," she sings to save her life. Her husband eventually goes out with the baby to find her and slays the beast. When they return to their home, they discover it, the barn, and the neighbors' property all burned by Indians.
9. Possibly Samuel Bowles and J. G. Holland, though both were associated at the time with the *Springfield Daily Republican.*

[Will You Be My Preceptor?]

7 June 1862

Dear friend.

Your letter gave no Drunkenness, because I tasted Rum before—Domingo[1] comes but once—yet I have had few pleasures so deep as your opinion, and if I tried to thank you, my tears would block my tongue—

My dying Tutor told me that he would like to live till I had been a poet, but Death was much of Mob[2] as I could master—then—And when far afterward—a sudden light on Orchards, or a new fashion in the wind troubled my attention—I felt a palsy, here—the Verses just relieve—

Your second letter surprised me, and for a moment, swung—I had not supposed it. Your first—gave no dishonor, because the True—are not ashamed—I thanked you for your justice—but could not drop the Bells whose jingling cooled my Tramp—Perhaps the Balm, seemed better, because you bled me, first.

I smile when you suggest that I delay "to publish"—that being foreign to my thought, as Firmament to Fin—

If fame belonged to me, I could not escape her—if she did not, the longest day would pass me on the chase—and the approbation of my Dog, would forsake me—then—My Barefoot-Rank is better—

You think my gait "spasmodic"[3]—I am in danger—Sir—

You think me "uncontrolled"—I have no Tribunal.

Would you have time to be the "friend" you should think I need? I have a little shape—it would not crowd your Desk—nor make much Racket as the Mouse, that dents your Galleries—

If I might bring you what I do—not so frequent to trouble you—and ask you if I told it clear—'twould be control, to me—

The Sailor cannot see the North—but knows the Needle can—

The "hand you stretch me in the Dark," I put mine in, and turn away—I have no Saxon,[4] now—

> As if I asked a common Alms
> And in my wondering hand
> A Stranger pressed a Kingdom,
> And I, bewildered, stand—
> As if I asked the Orient
> Had it for me a Morn—
> And it should lift it's purple Dikes,
> And shatter me with Dawn!

But, will you be my Preceptor, Mr. Higginson?

Your friend
E Dickinson—

---

1. Santo or St. Domingo, the capital of the Dominican Republic in the West Indies; Dickinson alludes in poems to St. Domingo twice (137 and 697) and Domingo twice (872, 1466); here it is invoked as the source of the rum.
2. I.e., she was unable to write for a popular audience or a mob.
3. I.e., her poetry did not scan according to regular metrical standards.
4. As Johnson notes, the phrase "I have no Saxon" means "Language fails me."

[*My Business Is Circumference*]

July 1862

Could you believe me—without? I had no portrait, now, but am small, like the Wren, and my Hair is bold, like the Chestnut Bur—and my eyes, like the Sherry in the Glass, that the Guest leaves—Would this do just as well?

It often alarms Father—He says Death might occur, and he has Molds[5] of all the rest—but has no Mold of me, but I noticed the Quick wore off those things, in a few days, and forestall the dishonor—You will think no caprice of me—

You said "Dark." I know the Butterfly—and the Lizard—and the Orchis[6]— Are not those *your* Countrymen?

I am happy to be your scholar, and will deserve the kindness, I cannot repay.

If you truly consent, I recite, now—

Will you tell me my fault, frankly as to yourself, for I had rather wince, than die. Men do not call the surgeon, to commend—the Bone, but to set it, Sir, and fracture within, is more critical. And for this, Preceptor, I shall bring you—Obedience—the Blossom from my Garden, and every gratitude I know. Perhaps you smile at me. I could not stop for that—My Business is Circumference[7]—An ignorance, not of Customs, but if caught with the Dawn—or the Sunset see me—Myself the only Kangaroo among the Beauty, Sir, if you please, it afflicts me, and I thought that instruction would take it away.

Because you have much business, beside the growth of me—you will appoint, yourself, how often I shall come—without your inconvenience. And if at any time—you regret you received me, or I prove a different fabric to that you supposed—you must banish me—

When I state myself, as the Representative of the Verse—it does not mean— me—but a supposed person. You are true, about the "perfection."

Today, makes Yesterday mean.

You spoke of Pippa Passes[8]—I never heard anybody speak of Pippa Passes—before.

You see my posture is benighted.

To thank you, baffles me. Are you perfectly powerful? Had I a pleasure you had not, I could delight to bring it.

Your Scholar

Letters on "E. D." from T. W. Higginson to His Wife

[*August 16, 1870*]

I shan't sit up tonight to write you all about E.D. dearest but if you had read Mrs. Stoddard's[1] novels you could understand a house where each member runs his or her own selves. Yet I only saw her.

A large county lawyer's house, brown brick, with great trees & a garden—I sent up my card. A parlor dark & cool & stiffish, a few books & engravings & an open piano—Malbone & O D [Out Door] Papers[2] among other books.

---

5. I.e., photographs or likenesses.
6. A small purplish or white orchid. Higginson wrote many nature essays with which she was familiar.
7. One of the crucial words in Dickinson's vocabulary; Johnson defines it as "a projection of her imagination into all relationships of man, nature, and spirit."
8. A dramatic poem by Robert Browning published in 1841.

1. Elizabeth Drew Stoddard (1823–1902), author of such novels as *The Morgesens* (1862), which explore intense characters in restrictive New England locales and family situations.
2. *Malbone: An Oldport Romance,* Higginson's first novel, appeared serially the first six months of 1869 in the *Atlantic Monthly.* The *Out Door Papers* were a collection of his nature essays from the *Atlantic.*

A step like a pattering child's in entry & in glided a little plain woman with two smooth bands of reddish hair & a face a little like Belle Dove's; not plainer—with no good feature—in a very plain & exquisitely clean white pique & a blue net worsted shawl. She came to me with two day lilies which she put in a sort of childlike way into my hand & said "These are my introduction" in a soft frightened breathless childlike voice—& added under her breath Forgive me if I am frightened; I never see strangers & hardly know what I say—but she talked soon & thenceforward continuously—& deferentially—sometimes stopping to ask me to talk instead of her—but readily recommencing. Manner between Angie Tilton & Mr. Alcott[3]—but thoroughly ingenuous & simple which they are not & saying many things which you would have thought foolish & I wise—& some things you wd. hv. liked. I add a few over the page.

*　*　*

I got here at 2 & leave at 9. E.D. dreamed all night of *you* (not me) & next day got my letter proposing to come here!! She only knew of you through a mention in my notice of Charlotte Hawes.[4]

"Women talk: men are silent: that is why I dread women.

"My father only reads on Sunday—he reads *lonely & rigorous* books."

"If I read a book [and] it makes my whole body so cold no fire ever can warm me I know *that* is poetry. If I feel physically as if the top of my head were taken off, I know *that* is poetry. These are the only way I know it. Is there any other way."

"How do most people live without any thoughts. There are many people in the world (you must have noticed them in the street) How do they live. How do they get strength to put on their clothes in the morning"

"When I lost the use of my Eyes it was a comfort to think there were so few real *books* that I could easily find some one to read me all of them"

"Truth is such a *rare* thing it is delightful to tell it."

"I find ecstasy in living—the mere sense of living is joy enough"

I asked if she never felt want of employment, never going off the place & never seeing any visitor "I never thought of conceiving that I could ever have the slightest approach to such a want in all future time" (& added) "I feel that I have not expressed myself strongly enough."

She makes all the bread for her father only likes hers & says "& people must have puddings" this *very* dreamily, as if they were comets—so she makes them.

[August 17, 1870]

*　*　*

E D again

"Could you tell me what home is"

"I never had a mother. I suppose a mother is one to whom you hurry when you are troubled."

---

3. Amos Bronson Alcott (1799–1888), American educator, author, mystic; one of the Transcendentalists. Angie Tilton is unidentified.
4. A young writer whom Higginson encouraged in Worcester, Massachusetts, and whom he introduced to the *Atlantic*. Below, Higginson lists some of things Dickinson said.

"I never knew how to tell time by the clock till I was 15. My father thought he had taught me but I did not understand & I was afraid to say I did not & afraid to ask any one else lest he should know."

Her father was not severe I should think but remote. He did not wish them to read anything but the Bible. One day her brother brought home Kavanagh[5] hid it under the piano cover & made signs to her & they read it: her father at last found it & was displeased. Perhaps it was before this that a student of his was amazed that they had never heard of Mrs. [Lydia Maria] Child[6] & used to bring them books & hide in a bush by the door. They were then little things in short dresses with their feet on the rungs of the chair. After the first book she thought in ecstasy "This then is a book! And there are more of them!"

"Is it oblivion or absorption when things pass from our minds?"

Major Hunt interested her more than any man she ever saw. She remembered two things he said—that her great dog "understood gravitation" & when he said he should come again "in a year. If I say a shorter time it will be longer."

When I said I would come again *some time* she said "Say in a long time, that will be nearer. Some time is nothing."

After long disuse of her eyes she read Shakespeare & thought why is any other book needed.

I never was with any one who drained my nerve power so much. Without touching her, she drew from me. I am glad not to live near her. She often thought me *tired* & seemed very thoughtful of others.

* * *

5. A novel by Longfellow, published in 1849.
6. An abolitionist (1802–1880) famous for *Appeal in Favor of That Class of Americans Called Africans* (1833) and her novels *Hobomok* (1824), *The Rebels; or* *Boston before the Revolution* (1825), *Philothea* (1836), and *A Romance of the Republic* (an abolition novel, 1867).

REBECCA HARDING DAVIS
1831–1910

Rebecca Harding was born in 1831 in Washington, Pennsylvania, her mother's hometown, then taken to Big Springs, Alabama, where her father, a book-loving English emigrant, was in business. Her earliest memories were of the Deep South, a landscape of tropical heat and beauty and a frontier society with extremes of wealth and poverty even among whites and based, for inextricable complications, on black slavery. As her recollections show, she learned in Alabama to see for herself, if not yet to think for herself. In 1836 her father moved the family to Wheeling, Virginia, still a jumping-off place for the West as well as a prosperous manufacturing center, in that anomalous fingerlike part of a slave state that reached far north between the free states of Ohio and Pennsylvania, a location fitted for the nurture of independent observation and judgment. Bookish like her father, Rebecca Harding at fourteen went to live with an aunt at her birthplace, across the Pennsylvania line to the east, to attend the female seminary. Back in Wheeling, alert in her young maturity to abolitionist agitation yet part of the slave society, she passed into what her era considered spinsterhood and was a serious-minded observer of the manners, morals, and machinations of people and a reticent and dutiful daughter, yet a woman of forthrightly independent views. She continued reading (we know she read John Bunyan, Sir Walter Scott, and Maria Edgeworth, and a few Hawthorne stories in a collection of *Moral Tales* affected her strongly). By her late twenties she had read English reform novels such as those by Charles Kingsley and Elizabeth Gaskell and had begun to publish anonymous reviews of new books in local papers. During the election year 1860, her mind more on the misery of the local mill workers than on the misery of slaves, she wrote *Life in the Iron-Mills*, apparently the first story she completed, and sent it to the *Atlantic Monthly*, the most prestigious magazine in the country, then under the editorship of James Fields.

As editor of the *Atlantic* James Russell Lowell had censored Thoreau and Whitman, and Fields himself was to censor Hawthorne's portrait of Lincoln (printed in this volume), but he recognized salable power in the new contributor and made no effort to alter the story, other than to suggest a more "taking" title (Harding's suggestions of *Beyond* or *The Korl-Woman* were not deemed "taking" enough either). The story was published (anonymously, by custom and by Harding's request) the month the Civil War broke out and Wheeling became capital of the new free state of West Virginia. The story's strength was recognized by many readers (Emily Dickinson among them), and with the author's name an open secret, Fields hoped to gain her as a regular contributor. Both he and his wife pressed her to come to Boston. She could not come at once because she was held by family duties and by the turmoil of a divided and embattled society, but she began a serial in the October 1861 *Atlantic—A Story of To-day*. It contained, in one of the character's words, not "a bit of hell" but "only a glimpse of the under-life of America." In her voice as narrator Harding offered a manifesto of realism before there was a literary movement so identified: "You want something . . . to lift you out of this crowded, tobacco-stained commonplace, to kindle and chafe and glow in you. I want you to dig into this commonplace, this vulgar American life, and see what is in it. Sometimes I think it has a raw and awful significance that we do not see." This work, which Fields published in book form as *Margret Howth* (1862), did not have the sustained power of her first story, yet much was expected of her, and when she made her pilgrimage to Boston in 1862 she was welcomed by the New England literary establishment. She delighted in Holmes and treasured her reception by Hawthorne. The more visionary Concordites like Bronson Alcott she regarded with a mixture of suspicion and disdain, and it was clear to her at once that Emerson had no notion at all of what war was like, however penetrating his insight might be once he paid attention to her or anyone else. Having formed a close friendship with Annie Fields, her hostess, and having made her presence felt (she astonished one group by the pronouncement that women had sexual desires), she had the chance to join the *Atlantic* circle (whom she called the Areopagites, from the Athenian hill where the high court had sat). Had she done so, she might have matured as a writer under the guidance of Holmes and others who were intensely interested in what she had to say, for her strong social criticisms were welcomed, not repelled.

Instead, she took the role of hack writer. Soon after the appearance of her first story, she had received a fan letter from an apprentice lawyer in Philadelphia, L. Clarke Davis, four years her junior, a man literary enough himself to have a connection with *Peterson's Magazine* and persuasive enough to interest her in meeting him. Before going to Boston she had arranged a stopover in Philadelphia on her way home; once they had met they soon decided to marry, and Davis persuaded her to contribute potboilers to *Peterson's*, though she was pledged to write only for the *Atlantic*. In her first years of marriage and even after her three children were born she continued her career as a magazine writer, creating an extensive body of hack work and a sizable body of more ambitious but flawed work. In the most massive as well as most ambitious of her later novels, *Waiting for the Verdict*

(1868), as the sympathetic critic Tillie Olsen says, Harding posed "the basic question of the time": how was the nation going to redress the wrong of slavery, once the slaves were freed? In Olsen's words, Harding had conceived a great novel but "had failed to write it; had not given (had) the self and time (or always the knowledge) to write it."

Living out her life in Philadelphia, she never became fully a part of the local cultural establishment, but she was friendly not only with other writers but also (through her husband) with many actors, including the great theatrical families of the time such as the Drews and Barrymores. Long before her death in 1910 she was overshadowed first by the success of her husband as an editor and then by the astonishing success of her son, Richard Harding Davis. In 1890 she warned him about his "beginning to do hack work for money": "It is the beginning of decadence both in work and reputation for you. I know by my own and a thousand other people." Her son became the best-paid, most glamorous journalist and one of the most popular short-story writers of his generation, a celebrity as his mother had never been, but never the writer she had been.

Her first story was never forgotten, at least by a few readers and by literary historians, although the latter were sometimes uneasy about it. Fred Lewis Pattee in a chapter on the story in *The Cambridge History of American Literature* (1918) quoted the opening of that "grim" story and observed that the decades of the 1850s and 1860s "in America stand for the dawning of definiteness, of localized reality, of a feeling left on the reader of actuality and truth to human life." In *Literary History of the United States* (1948), Gordon S. Haight was disdainful: "In her effort to rouse pity in the manner of Dickens, Mrs. Stowe, and [Charles] Kingsley, Mrs. Davis violates her own rule of the commonplace. Few mill workers are hunchbacks, and except in a reformer's tract no consumptive could long be an iron puddler." In *Literature of the American People* (1951) Clarence Gohdes gave grudging praise: the story "is indeed a grim picture, and it has made its way into the anthologies as a specimen of realism of the times." In 1961 Gerald Langford was nearer the mark in calling the story "one of the revolutionary documents in American writing, although it came so prematurely that it was almost forgotten by the time the revolution in fiction caught up with it." He also speculated about the extent to which Harding anticipated the "theory and practice" of a later editor of the *Atlantic*, William Dean Howells. Davis's great story did indeed enter some anthologies, but not many, and Olsen, who edited the story for the Feminist Press with "A Biographical Interpretation," deserves credit for making it impossible again to ignore or to slight the story, the strongest criticism of American society that had been published since *Uncle Tom's Cabin*, an indictment of the exploitation of American free labor more concentrated in its power than the already classic indictment of slavery, the most sustained exposé in our literature between Stowe and the muckrakers.

Harding's story had no such repercussions on life in the iron mills as Stowe's book had had on freeing the slaves, and its effects on American literary realism are not fully established; ironically, later writers on working conditions in American factories—Thomas Bailey Aldrich (another editor of the *Atlantic*) in *The Stillwater Tragedy* (1880) and John Hay in the anonymous *The Bread-Winners* (1884)—sided with property rights rather than workers' rights, as Mary E. Wilkins (more ambivalently) did in *The Portion of Labor* (1901). The historical importance of *Life in the Iron-Mills* is partly as a record of the underside of American industrial prosperity, partly in what study of it and the rest of Davis's life and career can reveal about being both a writer and a woman in America. What finally counts is that the story affords one of the most overwhelming reading experiences in all American literature.

Life in the Iron-Mills[1]

"Is this the end?
O Life, as futile, then, as frail!
What hope of answer or redress?"[2]

A cloudy day: do you know what that is in a town of iron-works?[3] The sky sank down before dawn, muddy, flat, immovable. The air is thick, clammy with the breath of crowded human beings. It stifles me. I open the window, and, looking out, can scarcely see through the rain the grocer's shop opposite, where a crowd of drunken Irishmen are puffing Lynchburg tobacco[4] in their pipes. I can detect the scent through all the foul smells ranging loose in the air.

The idiosyncrasy of this town is smoke. It rolls sullenly in slow folds from the great chimneys of the iron-foundries, and settles down in black, slimy pools on the muddy streets. Smoke on the wharves, smoke on the dingy boats, on the yellow river,—clinging in a coating of greasy soot to the house-front, the two faded poplars, the faces of the passers-by. The long train of mules, dragging masses of pig-iron[5] through the narrow street, have a foul vapor hanging to their reeking sides. Here, inside, is a little broken figure of an angel pointing upward from the mantel-shelf; but even its wings are covered with smoke, clotted and black. Smoke everywhere! A dirty canary chirps desolately in a cage beside me. Its dream of green fields and sunshine is a very old dream,—almost worn out, I think.

From the back-window I can see a narrow brick-yard sloping down to the river-side, strewed with rain-butts and tubs. The river, dull and tawny-colored, (*la belle rivière!*)[6] drags itself sluggishly along, tired of the heavy weight of boats and coal-barges. What wonder? When I was a child, I used to fancy a look of weary, dumb appeal upon the face of the negro-like river slavishly bearing its burden day after day. Something of the same idle notion comes to me to-day, when from the street-window I look on the slow stream of human life creeping past, night and morning, to the great mills. Masses of men, with dull, besotted faces bent to the ground, sharpened here and there by pain or cunning; skin and muscle and flesh begrimed with smoke and ashes; stooping all night over boiling caldrons of metal, laired by day in dens of drunkenness and infamy; breathing from infancy to death an air saturated with fog and grease and soot, vileness for soul and body. What do you make of a case like that, amateur psychologist? You call it an altogether serious thing to be alive: to these men it is a drunken jest, a joke,—horrible to angels perhaps, to them commonplace enough. My fancy about the river was an idle one: it is no type of such a life. What if it be stagnant and slimy here? It knows that beyond there waits for it odorous sunlight,—quaint old gardens, dusky with soft, green foliage of apple-

1. The text is that of the first printing in the *Atlantic Monthly*, 7 (April 1861).
2. Adapted from Alfred, Lord Tennyson's *In Memoriam A. H. H.* (1850), 12.4: " 'Is this the end of all my care?' . . . 'Is this the end? Is this the end?' " and from 56.7: "O Life as futile, then, as frail! / O for thy voice to soothe and bless! / What hope of answer, or redress? / Behind the veil, behind the veil." In 13 the poet compares himself to a dove who springs up "To bear thro' Heaven a tale of woe / Some dolorous message knit below." Through the epigraph (from this then-recent and enormously popular poem) Harding suggests that her own message is equally "dolorous."

3. The town is not named, but in its topography and other characteristics it is based on Harding's hometown, Wheeling, Virginia, on the banks of the Ohio River.
4. An inferior tobacco from south-central Virginia.
5. Oblong blocks of iron, hardened after being poured from a smelting furnace.
6. The beautiful river (French); the phrase ironically recalls the purity of the Ohio when the French fur traders first saw it. "Rain-butts": large casks, around three or four barrels in capacity, used to catch rainwater for household and, here, industrial use.

trees, and flushing crimson with roses,—air, and fields, and mountains. The future of the Welsh puddler[7] passing just now is not so pleasant. To be stowed away, after his grimy work is done, in a hole in the muddy graveyard, and after that,——not air, nor green fields, nor curious roses.

Can you see how foggy the day is? As I stand here, idly tapping the window-pane, and looking out through the rain at the dirty back-yard and the coal-boats below, fragments of an old story float up before me,—a story of this house into which I happened to come to-day. You may think it a tiresome story enough, as foggy as the day, sharpened by no sudden flashes of pain or pleasure.—I know: only the outline of a dull life, that long since, with thou-sands of dull lives like its own, was vainly lived and lost: thousands of them,—massed, vile, slimy lives, like those of the torpid lizards in yonder stagnant water-butt.—Lost? There is a curious point for you to settle, my friend, who study psychology in a lazy, *dilettante* way. Stop a moment. I am going to be honest. This is what I want you to do. I want you to hide your disgust, take no heed to your clean clothes, and come right down with me,—here, into the thickest of the fog and mud and foul effluvia. I want you to hear this story. There is a secret down here, in this nightmare fog, that has lain dumb for centuries: I want to make it a real thing to you. You, Egoist, or Pantheist, or Arminian,[8] busy in making straight paths for your feet on the hills, do not see it clearly,—this terrible question which men here have gone mad and died trying to answer. I dare not put this secret into words. I told you it was dumb. These men, going by with drunken faces and brains full of unawakened power, do not ask it of Society or of God. Their lives ask it; their deaths ask it. There is no reply. I will tell you plainly that I have a great hope; and I bring it to you to be tested. It is this: that this terrible dumb question is its own reply; that it is not the sentence of death we think it, but, from the very extremity of its darkness, the most solemn prophecy which the world has known of the Hope to come. I dare make my meaning no clearer, but will only tell my story. It will, perhaps, seem to you as foul and dark as this thick vapor about us, and as pregnant with death; but if your eyes are free as mine are to look deeper, no perfume-tinted dawn will be so fair with promise of the day that shall surely come.

My story is very simple,—only what I remember of the life of one of these men,—a furnace-tender in one of Kirby & John's rolling-mills,—Hugh Wolfe. You know the mills? They took the great order for the lower Virginia railroads there last winter; run usually with about a thousand men. I cannot tell why I choose the half-forgotten story of this Wolfe more than that of myri-ads of these furnace-hands. Perhaps because there is a secret, underlying sym-pathy between that story and this day with its impure fog and thwarted sunshine,—or perhaps simply for the reason that this house is the one where the Wolfes lived. There were the father and son,—both hands, as I said, in one of Kirby & John's mills for making railroad-iron,—and Deborah, their cousin, a picker[9] in some of the cotton-mills. The house was rented then to

---

7. Worker who stirs iron oxide into a molten vat of pig iron in order to make wrought iron or steel.
8. One who follows the teachings of Jacobus Arminius (1560–1607), Dutch theologian who opposed the Cal-vinistic doctrine of absolute predestination. "Egoist": one devoted to his or her own interests and advance-ment, acting only according to self-interest. "Panthe-ist": one who identifies the deity with nature. The story is saturated with biblical language, as in the echo here of Hebrews 12.13: "And make straight paths for your feet, lest that which is lame be turned out of the way; but let it rather be healed."
9. Worker in a cotton mill who operates the machine that pulls apart and separates cotton fibers; less often used to mean the one who throws the shuttle of a loom to put in the weft thread of a fabric. The men work for low wages in the iron mills; the women work for lower wages in the cotton mills.

half a dozen families. The Wolfes had two of the cellar-rooms. The old man, like many of the puddlers and feeders[1] of the mills, was Welsh,—had spent half of his life in the Cornish tin-mines. You may pick the Welsh emigrants, Cornish miners, out of the throng passing the windows, any day. They are a trifle more filthy; their muscles are not so brawny; they stoop more. When they are drunk, they neither yell, nor shout, nor stagger, but skulk along like beaten hounds. A pure, unmixed blood, I fancy: shows itself in the slight angular bodies and sharply-cut facial lines. It is nearly thirty years since the Wolfes lived here. Their lives were like those of their class: incessant labor, sleeping in kennel-like rooms, eating rank pork and molasses, drinking—God and the distillers only know what; with an occasional night in jail, to atone for some drunken excess. Is that all of their lives?—of the portion given to them and these their duplicates swarming the streets to-day?—nothing beneath?—all? So many a political reformer will tell you,—and many a private reformer, too, who has gone among them with a heart tender with Christ's charity, and come out outraged, hardened.

One rainy night, about eleven o'clock, a crowd of half-clothed women stopped outside of the cellar-door. They were going home from the cotton-mill.

"Good-night, Deb," said one, a mulatto, steadying herself against the gas-post. She needed the post to steady her. So did more than one of them.

"Dah's a ball to Miss Potts' to-night. Ye'd best come."

"Inteet, Deb, if hur'll come, hur'll hef fun," said a shrill Welsh voice in the crowd.

Two or three dirty hands were thrust out to catch the gown of the woman, who was groping for the latch of the door.

"No."

"No? Where 's Kit Small, then?"

"Begorra! on the spools.[2] Alleys behint, though we helped her, we dud. An wid ye! Let Deb alone! It's ondacent frettin' a quite body. Be the powers, an' we'll have a night of it! there'll be lashin's o' drink,—the Vargent[3] be blessed and praised for 't!"

They went on, the mulatto inclining for a moment to show fight, and drag the woman Wolfe off with them; but, being pacified, she staggered away.

Deborah groped her way into the cellar, and, after considerable stumbling, kindled a match, and lighted a tallow dip, that sent a yellow glimmer over the room. It was low, damp,—the earthen floor covered with a green, slimy moss,—a fetid air smothering the breath. Old Wolfe lay asleep on a heap of straw, wrapped in a torn horse-blanket. He was a pale, meek little man, with a white face and red rabbit-eyes. The woman Deborah was like him; only her face was even more ghastly, her lips bluer, her eyes more watery. She wore a faded cotton gown and a slouching bonnet. When she walked, one could see that she was deformed, almost a hunchback. She trod softly, so as not to waken him, and went through into the room beyond. There she found by the half-extinguished fire an iron saucepan filled with cold boiled potatoes, which she put upon a broken chair with a pint-cup of ale. Placing the old candlestick

---

1. Worker who feeds molten metal into the casting form while the iron is hardening and contracting (the purpose is to prevent the formation of air bubbles, which weaken the iron).

2. Spindles in the cotton mill on which the cotton is stretched and wound by the spinning machine. "Begorra!": a milder form of "By God!"

3. The Virgin Mary.

beside this dainty repast, she untied her bonnet, which hung limp and wet over her face, and prepared to eat her supper. It was the first food that had touched her lips since morning. There was enough of it, however: there is not always. She was hungry,—one could see that easily enough,—and not drunk, as most of her companions would have been found at this hour. She did not drink, this woman,—her face told that, too,—nothing stronger than ale. Perhaps the weak, flaccid wretch had some stimulant in her pale life to keep her up,—some love or hope, it might be, or urgent need. When that stimulant was gone, she would take to whiskey. Man cannot live by work alone. While she was skinning the potatoes, and munching them, a noise behind her made her stop.

"Janey!" she called, lifting the candle and peering into the darkness. "Janey, are you there?"

A heap of ragged coats was heaved up, and the face of a young girl emerged, staring sleepily at the woman.

"Deborah," she said, at last, "I'm here the night."

"Yes, child. Hur's welcome," she said, quietly eating on.

The girl's face was haggard and sickly; her eyes were heavy with sleep and hunger: real Milesian[4] eyes they were, dark, delicate blue, glooming out from black shadows with a pitiful fright.

"I was alone," she said, timidly.

"Where's the father?" asked Deborah, holding out a potato, which the girl greedily seized.

"He's beyant,—wid Haley,—in the stone house." (Did you ever hear the word *jail* from an Irish mouth?) "I came here. Hugh told me never to stay me-lone."

"Hugh?"

"Yes."

A vexed frown crossed her face. The girl saw it, and added quickly,—

"I have not seen Hugh the day, Deb. The old man says his watch[5] lasts till the mornin'."

The woman sprang up, and hastily began to arrange some bread and flitch[6] in a tin pail, and to pour her own measure of ale into a bottle. Tying on her bonnet, she blew out the candle.

"Lay ye down, Janey dear," she said, gently, covering her with the old rags. "Hur can eat the potatoes, if hur's hungry."

"Where are ye goin', Deb? The rain's sharp."

"To the mill, with Hugh's supper."

"Let him bide till th' morn. Sit ye down."

"No, no,"—sharply pushing her off. "The boy'll starve."

She hurried from the cellar, while the child wearily coiled herself up for sleep. The rain was falling heavily, as the woman, pail in hand, emerged from the mouth of the alley, and turned down the narrow street, that stretched out, long and black, miles before her. Here and there a flicker of gas lighted an uncertain space of muddy footwalk and gutter; the long rows of houses, except an occasional lager-bier shop, were closed; now and then she met a band of millhands skulking to or from their work.

Not many even of the inhabitants of a manufacturing town know the vast

4. Irish.
5. Trick, work shift.   6. A rank form of salt pork.

machinery of system by which the bodies of workmen are governed, that goes on unceasingly from year to year. The hands of each mill are divided into watches that relieve each other as regularly as the sentinels of an army. By night and day the work goes on, the unsleeping engines groan and shriek, the fiery pools of metal boil and surge. Only for a day in the week, in half-courtesy to public censure, the fires are partially veiled; but as soon as the clock strikes midnight, the great furnaces break forth with renewed fury, the clamor begins with fresh, breathless vigor, the engines sob and shriek like "gods in pain."

As Deborah hurried down through the heavy rain, the noise of these thousand engines sounded through the sleep and shadow of the city like far-off thunder. The mill to which she was going lay on the river, a mile below the city-limits. It was far, and she was weak, aching from standing twelve hours at the spools. Yet it was her almost nightly walk to take this man his supper, though at every square she sat down to rest, and she knew she should receive small word of thanks.

Perhaps, if she had possessed an artist's eye, the picturesque oddity of the scene might have made her step stagger less, and the path seem shorter; but to her the mills were only "summat deilish[7] to look at by night."

The road leading to the mills had been quarried from the solid rock, which rose abrupt and bare on one side of the cinder-covered road, while the river, sluggish and black, crept past on the other. The mills for rolling[8] iron are simply immense tent-like roofs, covering acres of ground, open on every side. Beneath these roofs Deborah looked in on a city of fires, that burned hot and fiercely in the night. Fire in every horrible form: pits of flame waving in the wind; liquid metal-flames writhing in tortuous streams through the sand; wide caldrons filled with boiling fire, over which bent ghastly wretches stirring the strange brewing; and through all, crowds of half-clad men, looking like revengeful ghosts in the red light, hurried, throwing masses of glittering fire. It was like a street in Hell. Even Deborah muttered, as she crept through, " 'T looks like t' Devil's place!" It did,—in more ways than one.

She found the man she was looking for, at last, heaping coal on a furnace. He had not time to eat his supper; so she went behind the furnace,[9] and waited. Only a few men were with him, and they noticed her only by a "Hyur comes t' hunchback, Wolfe."

Deborah was stupid with sleep; her back pained her sharply; and her teeth chattered with cold, with the rain that soaked her clothes and dripped from her at every step. She stood, however, patiently holding the pail, and waiting.

"Hout, woman! ye look like a drowned cat. Come near to the fire,"—said one of the men, approaching to scrape away the ashes.

She shook her head. Wolfe had forgotten her. He turned, hearing the man, and came closer.

"I did no' think; gi' me my supper, woman."

She watched him eat with a painful eagerness. With a woman's quick instinct, she saw that he was not hungry,—was eating to please her. Her pale, watery eyes began to gather a strange light.

"Is't good, Hugh? T' ale was a bit sour, I feared."

"No, good enough." He hesitated a moment. "Ye 're tired, poor lass! Bide here till I go. Lay down there on that heap of ash, and go to sleep."

7. Devilish.
8. Mill for flattening ingots into shapes, in this case

rails for the expanding railroad system.
9. I.e., away from some of the blinding glare.

He threw her an old coat for a pillow, and turned to his work. The heap
was the refuse of the burnt iron, and was not a hard bed; the half-smothered
warmth, too, penetrated her limbs, dulling their pain and cold shiver.

Miserable enough she looked, lying there on the ashes like a limp, dirty
rag,—yet not an unfitting figure to crown the scene of hopeless discomfort and
veiled crime: more fitting, if one looked deeper into the heart of things,—at
her thwarted woman's form, her colorless life, her waking stupor that smothered pain and hunger,—even more fit to be a type of her class. Deeper yet if
one could look, was there nothing worth reading in this wet, faded thing,
halfcovered with ashes? no story of a soul filled with groping passionate love,
heroic unselfishness, fierce jealousy? of years of weary trying to please the one
human being whom she loved, to gain one look of real heart-kindness from
him? If anything like this were hidden beneath the pale, bleared eyes, and
dull, washed-out-looking face, no one had ever taken the trouble to read its
faint signs: not the half-clothed furnace-tender, Wolfe, certainly. Yet he was
kind to her: it was his nature to be kind, even to the very rats that swarmed in
the cellar: kind to her in just the same way. She knew that. And it might be
that very knowledge had given to her face its apathy and vacancy more than
her low, torpid life. One sees that dead, vacant look steal sometimes over the
rarest, finest of women's faces,—in the very midst, it may be, of their warmest
summer's day; and then one can guess at the secret of intolerable solitude that
lies hid beneath the delicate laces and brilliant smile. There was no warmth,
no brilliancy, no summer for this woman; so the stupor and vacancy had time
to gnaw into her face perpetually. She was young, too, though no one guessed
it; so the gnawing was the fiercer.

She lay quiet in the dark corner, listening, through the monotonous din
and uncertain glare of the works, to the dull plash of the rain in the far distance,—shrinking back whenever the man Wolfe happened to look towards
her. She knew, in spite of all his kindness, that there was that in her face and
form which made him loathe the sight of her. She felt by instinct, although
she could not comprehend it, the finer nature of the man, which made him
among his fellow-workmen something unique, set apart. She knew, that,
down under all the vileness and coarseness of his life, there was a groping
passion for whatever was beautiful and pure,—that his soul sickened with disgust at her deformity, even when his words were kindest. Through this dull
consciousness, which never left her, came, like a sting, the recollection of the
dark blue eyes and lithe figure of the little Irish girl she had left in the cellar.
The recollection struck through even her stupid intellect with a vivid glow of
beauty and of grace. Little Janey, timid, helpless, clinging to Hugh as her only
friend: that was the sharp thought, the bitter thought, that drove into the glazed
eyes a fierce light of pain. You laugh at it? Are pain and jealousy less savage
realities down here in this place I am taking you to than in your own house or
your own heart,—your heart, which they clutch at sometimes? The note is
the same, I fancy, be the octave high or low.

If you could go into this mill where Deborah lay, and drag out from the
hearts of these men the terrible tragedy of their lives, taking it as a symptom of
the disease of their class, no ghost Horror would terrify you more. A reality of
soul-starvation, of living death, that meets you every day under the besotted
faces on the street,—I can paint nothing of this, only give you the outside
outlines of a night, a crisis in the life of one man: whatever muddy depth of

soul-history lies beneath you can read according to the eyes God has given you.

Wolfe, while Deborah watched him as a spaniel its master, bent over the furnace with his iron pole, unconscious of her scrutiny, only stopping to receive orders. Physically, Nature had promised the man but little. He had already lost the strength and instinct vigor of a man, his muscles were thin, his nerves weak, his face (a meek, woman's face) haggard, yellow with consumption. In the mill he was known as one of the girl-men: "Molly Wolfe" was his *sobriquet*. He was never seen in the cockpit,[1] did not own a terrier, drank but seldom; when he did, desperately. He fought sometimes, but was always thrashed, pommelled to a jelly. The man was game enough, when his blood was up: but he was no favorite in the mill; he had the taint of school-learning on him,—not to a dangerous extent, only a quarter or so in the free-school in fact, but enough to ruin him as a good hand in a fight.

For other reasons, too, he was not popular. Not one of themselves, they felt that, though outwardly as filthy and ash-covered; silent, with foreign thoughts and longings breaking out through his quietness in innumerable curious ways: this one, for instance. In the neighboring furnace-buildings lay great heaps of the refuse from the ore after the pig-metal is run. *Korl* we call it here: a light, porous substance, of a delicate, waxen, flesh-colored tinge. Out of the blocks of this korl, Wolfe, in his off-hours from the furnace, had a habit of chipping and moulding figures,—hideous, fantastic enough, but sometimes strangely beautiful: even the mill-men saw that, while they jeered at him. It was a curious fancy in the man, almost a passion. The few hours for rest he spent hewing and hacking with his blunt knife, never speaking, until his watch came again,—working at one figure for months, and, when it was finished, breaking it to pieces perhaps, in a fit of disappointment. A morbid, gloomy man, untaught, unled, left to feed his soul in grossness and crime, and hard, grinding labor.

I want you to come down and look at this Wolfe, standing there among the lowest of his kind, and see him just as he is, that you may judge him justly when you hear the story of this night. I want you to look back, as he does every day, at his birth in vice, his starved infancy; to remember the heavy years he has groped through as boy and man,—the slow, heavy years of constant, hot work. So long ago he began, that he thinks sometimes he has worked there for ages. There is no hope that it will ever end. Think that God put into this man's soul a fierce thirst for beauty,—to know it, to create it; to *be*—something, he knows not what,—other than he is. There are moments when a passing cloud, the sun glinting on the purple thistles, a kindly smile, a child's face, will rouse him to a passion of pain,—when his nature starts up with a mad cry of rage against God, man, whoever it is that has forced this vile, slimy life upon him. With all this groping, this mad desire, a great blind intellect stumbling through wrong, a loving poet's heart, the man was by habit only a coarse, vulgar laborer, familiar with sights and words you would blush to name. Be just: when I tell you about this night, see him as he is. Be just,—not like man's law, which seizes on one isolated fact, but like God's judging angel, whose clear, sad eye saw all the countless cankering days of this man's life, all the

---

1. Where fighting cocks are set against each other until one is severely injured or killed (or until they kill each other). The "sport" survives in the mid-Atlantic region, although repressed. Terriers were bred as hunting animals. "Sobriquet": nickname.

countless nights, when, sick with starving, his soul fainted in him, before it judged him for this night, the saddest of all.

I called this night the crisis of his life. If it was, it stole on him unawares. These great turning-days of life cast no shadow before, slip by unconsciously. Only a trifle, a little turn of the rudder, and the ship goes to heaven or hell.

Wolfe, while Deborah watched him, dug into the furnace of melting iron with his pole, dully thinking only how many rails the lump would yield. It was late,—nearly Sunday morning; another hour, and the heavy work would be done,—only the furnaces to replenish and cover for the next day. The workmen were growing more noisy, shouting, as they had to do, to be heard over the deep clamor of the mills. Suddenly they grew less boisterous,—at the far end, entirely silent. Something unusual had happened. After a moment, the silence came nearer; the men stopped their jeers and drunken choruses. Deborah, stupidly lifting up her head, saw the cause of the quiet. A group of five or six men were slowly approaching, stopping to examine each furnace as they came. Visitors often came to see the mills after night: except by growing less noisy, the men took no notice of them. The furnace where Wolfe worked was near the bounds of the works; they halted there hot and tired: a walk over one of these great foundries is no trifling task. The woman, drawing out of sight, turned over to sleep. Wolfe, seeing them stop, suddenly roused from his indifferent stupor, and watched them keenly. He knew some of them: the overseer, Clarke,—a son of Kirby, one of the mill-owners,—and a Doctor May, one of the town-physicians. The other two were strangers. Wolfe came closer. He seized eagerly every chance that brought him into contact with this mysterious class that shone down on him perpetually with the glamour of another order of being. What made the difference between them? That was the mystery of his life. He had a vague notion that perhaps to-night he could find it out. One of the strangers sat down on a pile of bricks, and beckoned young Kirby to his side.

"This *is* hot, with a vengeance. A match, please?"—lighting his cigar. "But the walk is worth the trouble. If it were not that you must have heard it so often, Kirby, I would tell you that your works look like Dante's Inferno."[2]

Kirby laughed.

"Yes. Yonder is Farinata himself[3] in the burning tomb,"—pointing to some figure in the shimmering shadows.

"Judging from some of the faces of your men," said the other, "they bid fair to try the reality of Dante's vision, some day."

Young Kirby looked curiously around, as if seeing the faces of his hands for the first time.

"They're bad enough, that's true. A desperate set, I fancy. Eh, Clarke?"

The overseer did not hear him. He was talking of net profits just then,— giving, in fact, a schedule of the annual business of the firm to a sharp peering little Yankee, who jotted down notes on a paper laid on the crown of his hat: a reporter for one of the city-papers, getting up a series of reviews of the leading manufactories. The other gentlemen had accompanied them merely for amusement. They were silent until the notes were finished, drying their feet

---

2. *Hell*, the first part of *The Divine Comedy* by the Italian poet Dante Alighieri (1265–1321).
3. In Canto 10 of *The Inferno*, Farinata degli Uberti is one of the heretics, a leader of the Florentine faction opposed to Dante's own family.

at the furnaces, and sheltering their faces from the intolerable heat. At last the overseer concluded with—

"I believe that is a pretty fair estimate, Captain."

"Here, some of you men!" said Kirby, "bring up those boards. We may as well sit down, gentlemen, until the rain is over. It cannot last much longer at this rate."

"Pig-metal,"—mumbled the reporter,—"um!—coal facilities,—um!—hands employed, twelve hundred,—bitumen,—um!—all right, I believe, Mr. Clarke;—sinking-fund,—what did you say was your sinking-fund?"[4]

"Twelve hundred hands?" said the stranger, the young man who had first spoken. "Do you control their votes, Kirby?"

"Control? No." The young man smiled complacently. "But my father brought seven hundred votes to the polls for his candidate last November. No force-work, you understand,—only a speech or two, a hint to form themselves into a society, and a bit of red and blue bunting to make them a flag. The Invincible Roughs,—I believe that is their name. I forget the motto: 'Our country's hope,' I think."

There was a laugh. The young man talking to Kirby sat with an amused light in his cool gray eye, surveying critically the half-clothed figures of the puddlers, and the slow swing of their brawny muscles. He was a stranger in the city,—spending a couple of months in the borders of a Slave State,[5] to study the institutions of the South,—a brother-in-law of Kirby's,—Mitchell. He was an amateur gymnast,—hence his anatomical eye; a patron, in a *blasé* way, of the prize-ring; a man who sucked the essence out of a science or philosophy in an indifferent, gentlemanly way; who took Kant, Novalis, Humboldt,[6] for what they were worth in his own scales; accepting all, despising nothing, in heaven, earth, or hell, but one-idead men; with a temper yielding and brilliant as summer water, until his Self was touched, when it was ice, though brilliant still. Such men are not rare in the States.

As he knocked the ashes from his cigar, Wolfe caught with a quick pleasure the contour of the white hand, the blood-glow of a red ring he wore. His voice, too, and that of Kirby's, touched him like music,—low, even, with chording cadences. About this man Mitchell hung the impalpable atmosphere belonging to the thoroughbred gentleman. Wolfe, scraping away the ashes beside him, was conscious of it, did obeisance to it with his artist sense, unconscious that he did so.

The rain did not cease. Clarke and the reporter left the mills; the others, comfortably seated near the furnace, lingered, smoking and talking in a desultory way. Greek would not have been more unintelligible to the furnace-tenders, whose presence they soon forgot entirely. Kirby drew out a newspaper from his pocket and read aloud some article, which they discussed eagerly. At every sentence, Wolfe listened more and more like a dumb, hopeless animal, with a duller, more stolid look creeping over his face, glancing now and then at Mitchell, marking acutely every smallest sign of refinement, then back to himself, seeing as in a mirror his filthy body, his more stained soul.

Never! He had no words for such a thought, but he knew now, in all the

---

4. Fund accumulated to pay off a corporate debt.
5. Part of Harding's irony is that, at the time she was writing, her slave-state setting was far north of the Mason-Dixon line, west, not south, of Pennsylvania.
6. Alexander von Humboldt (1769–1859), German naturalist and explorer of South America and Asia. Immanuel Kant (1724–1804), German philosopher. Novalis, pseudonym of Friedrich von Hardenberg (1772–1801), German poet.

sharpness of the bitter certainty, that between them there was a great gulf[7] never to be passed. Never!

The bell of the mills rang for midnight. Sunday morning had dawned. Whatever hidden message lay in the tolling bells floated past these men unknown. Yet it was there. Veiled in the solemn music ushering the risen Saviour was a key-note to solve the darkest secrets of a world gone wrong,— even this social riddle which the brain of the grimy puddler grappled with madly to-night.

The men began to withdraw the metal from the caldrons. The mills were deserted on Sundays, except by the hands who fed the fires, and those who had no lodgings and slept usually on the ash-heaps. The three strangers sat still during the next hour, watching the men cover the furnaces, laughing now and then at some jest of Kirby's.

"Do you know," said Mitchell, "I like this view of the works better than when the glare was fiercest? These heavy shadows and the amphitheatre of smothered fires are ghostly, unreal. One could fancy these red smouldering lights to be the half-shut eyes of wild beasts, and the spectral figures their victims in the den."

Kirby laughed. "You are fanciful. Come, let us get out of the den. The spectral figures, as you call them, are a little too real for me to fancy a close proximity in the darkness,—unarmed, too."

The others rose, buttoning their overcoats, and lighting cigars.

"Raining, still," said Doctor May, "and hard. Where did we leave the coach, Mitchell?"

"At the other side of the works.—Kirby, what's that?"

Mitchell started back, half-frightened, as, suddenly turning a corner, the white figure of a woman faced him in the darkness,—a woman, white, of giant proportions, crouching on the ground, her arms flung out in some wild gesture of warning.

"Stop! Make that fire burn there!" cried Kirby, stopping short.

The flame burst out, flashing the gaunt figure into bold relief.

Mitchell drew a long breath.

"I thought it was alive," he said, going up curiously.

The others followed.

"Not marble, eh?" asked Kirby, touching it.

One of the lower overseers stopped.

"Korl, Sir."

"Who did it?"

"Can't say. Some of the hands; chipped it out in off-hours."

"Chipped to some purpose, I should say. What a flesh-tint the stuff has! Do you see, Mitchell?"

"I see."

He had stepped aside where the light fell boldest on the figure, looking at it in silence. There was not one line of beauty or grace in it: a nude woman's form, muscular, grown coarse with labor, the powerful limbs instinct with some one poignant longing. One idea: there it was in the tense, rigid muscles, the clutching hands, the wild, eager face, like that of a starving wolf's. Kirby and Doctor May walked around it, critical, curious. Mitchell stood aloof,

---

7. Words Jesus assigns to Abraham in the parable of the beggar Lazarus and the rich man, Luke 16.26: "And beside all this, between us and you there is a great gulf fixed"—the gulf between heaven, where Lazarus has found comfort, and hell, where the rich man is suffering.

silent. The figure touched him strangely.

"Not badly done," said Doctor May. "Where did the fellow learn that sweep of the muscles in the arm and hand? Look at them! They are groping,—do you see?—clutching: the peculiar action of a man dying of thirst."

"They have ample facilities for studying anatomy," sneered Kirby, glancing at the half-naked figures.

"Look," continued the Doctor, "at this bony wrist, and the strained sinews of the instep! A working-woman,—the very type of her class."

"God forbid!" muttered Mitchell.

"Why?" demanded May. "What does the fellow intend by the figure? I cannot catch the meaning."

"Ask him," said the other, dryly. "There he stands,"—pointing to Wolfe, who stood with a group of men, leaning on his ash-rake.

The Doctor beckoned him with the affable smile which kind-hearted men put on, when talking to these people.

"Mr. Mitchell has picked you out as the man who did this,—I'm sure I don't know why. But what did you mean by it?"

"She be hungry."

Wolfe's eyes answered Mitchell, not the Doctor.

"Oh-h! But what a mistake you have made, my fine fellow! You have given no sign of starvation to the body. It is strong,—terribly strong. It has the mad, half-despairing gesture of drowning."

Wolfe stammered, glanced appealingly at Mitchell, who saw the soul of the thing, he knew. But the cool, probing eyes were turned on himself now,— mocking, cruel, relentless.

"Not hungry for meat," the furnace-tender said at last.

"What then? Whiskey?" jeered Kirby, with a coarse laugh.

Wolfe was silent a moment, thinking.

"I dunno," he said, with a bewildered look. "It mebbe. Summat to make her live, I think,—like you. Whiskey ull do it, in a way."

The young man laughed again. Mitchell flashed a look of disgust some-where,—not at Wolfe.

"May," he broke out impatiently, "are you blind? Look at that woman's face! It asks questions of God, and says, 'I have a right to know.' Good God, how hungry it is!"

They looked a moment; then May turned to the mill-owner:—

"Have you many such hands as this? What are you going to do with them? Keep them at puddling iron?"

Kirby shrugged his shoulders. Mitchell's look had irritated him.

"*Ce n'est pas mon affaire.*[8] I have no fancy for nursing infant geniuses. I suppose there are some stray gleams of mind and soul among these wretches. The Lord will take care of his own; or else they can work out their own salva-tion. I have heard you call our American system a ladder which any man can scale. Do you doubt it? Or perhaps you want to banish all social ladders, and put us all on a flat table-land,—eh, May?"

The Doctor looked vexed, puzzled. Some terrible problem lay hid in this woman's face, and troubled these men. Kirby waited for an answer, and, receiving none, went on, warming with his subject.

"I tell you, there's something wrong that no talk of '*Liberté*' or '*Egalité*'[9] will

8. It's none of my business (French).   9. Slogans of the French Revolution.

do away. If I had the making of men, these men who do the lowest part of the world's work should be machines,—nothing more,—hands. It would be kindness. God help them! What are taste, reason, to creatures who must live such lives as that?" He pointed to Deborah, sleeping on the ash-heap. "So many nerves to sting them to pain. What if God had put your brain, with all its agony of touch, into your fingers, and bid you work and strike with that?"

"You think you could govern the world better?" laughed the Doctor.

"I do not think at all."

"That is true philosophy. Drift with the stream, because you cannot dive deep enough to find bottom, eh?"

"Exactly," rejoined Kirby. "I do not think. I wash my hands of all social problems,—slavery, caste, white or black. My duty to my operatives has a narrow limit,—the pay-hour on Saturday night.[1] Outside of that, if they cut korl, or cut each other's throats, (the more popular amusement of the two,) I am not responsible."

The Doctor sighed,—a good honest sigh, from the depths of his stomach.

"God help us! Who is responsible?"

"Not I, I tell you," said Kirby, testily. "What has the man who pays them money to do with their souls' concerns, more than the grocer or butcher who takes it?"

"And yet," said Mitchell's cynical voice, "look at her! How hungry she is!"

Kirby tapped his boot with his cane. No one spoke. Only the dumb face of the rough image looking into their faces with the awful question, "What shall we do to be saved?"[2] Only Wolfe's face, with its heavy weight of brain, its weak, uncertain mouth, its desperate eyes, out of which looked the soul of his class,—only Wolfe's face turned towards Kirby's. Mitchell laughed,—a cool, musical laugh.

"Money has spoken!" he said, seating himself lightly on a stone with the air of an amused spectator at a play. "Are you answered?"—turning to Wolfe his clear, magnetic face.

Bright and deep and cold as Arctic air, the soul of the man lay tranquil beneath. He looked at the furnace-tender as he had looked at a rare mosaic in the morning; only the man was the more amusing study of the two.

"Are you answered? Why, May, look at him! 'De profundis clamavi.'[3] Or, to quote in English, 'Hungry and thirsty, his soul faints in him.' And so Money sends back its answer into the depths through you, Kirby! Very clear the answer, too!—I think I remember reading the same words somewhere:—washing your hands in Eau de Cologne, and saying, 'I am innocent of the blood of this man. See ye to it!' "[4]

Kirby flushed angrily.

"You quote Scripture freely."

"Do I not quote correctly? I think I remember another line, which may amend my meaning? 'Inasmuch as ye did it unto one of the least of these, ye

1. A bald statement of what Harding's Scot contemporary Thomas Carlyle was condemning as the "cash nexus," where monetary payment was the only connection between employer and worker. "Operatives": workers.

2. The keeper of the prison in Philippi cries "Sirs, what must I do to be saved?" to Paul and Silas after an earthquake has opened the prison doors and loosed the prisoners' bonds (Acts 16.30).

3. The Latin version of Psalms 130.1: "Out of the depths have I cried unto thee, O Lord."

4. The Roman governor Pontius Pilate yielded to the mob's demand that Jesus be crucified but renounced responsibility for it: "When Pilate saw that he could prevail nothing, but that rather a tumult was made, he took water, and washed his hands before the multitude, saying, I am innocent of the blood of this just person: see ye to it" (Matthew 27.24).

did it unto me.' Deist?[5] Bless you, man, I was raised on the milk of the Word. Now, Doctor, the pocket of the world having uttered its voice, what has the heart to say? You are a philanthropist, in a small way,—*n'est ce pas?*[6] Here, boy, this gentleman can show you how to cut korl better,—or your destiny. Go on, May!"

"I think a mocking devil possesses you to-night," rejoined the Doctor, seriously.

He went to Wolfe and put his hand kindly on his arm. Something of a vague idea possessed the Doctor's brain that much good was to be done here by a friendly word or two: a latent genius to be warmed into life by a waited-for sunbeam. Here it was: he had brought it. So he went on complacently:—

"Do you know, boy, you have it in you to be a great sculptor, a great man?—do you understand?" (talking down to the capacity of his hearer: it is a way people have with children, and men like Wolfe,)—"to live a better, stronger life than I, or Mr. Kirby here? A man may make himself anything he chooses. God has given you stronger powers than many men,—me, for instance."

May stopped, heated, glowing with his own magnanimity. And it was magnanimous. The puddler had drunk in every word, looking through the Doctor's flurry, and generous heat, and self-approval, into his will, with those slow, absorbing eyes of his.

"Make yourself what you will. It is your right."

"I know," quietly. "Will you help me?"

Mitchell laughed again. The Doctor turned now, in a passion,—

"You know, Mitchell, I have not the means. You know, if I had, it is in my heart to take this boy and educate him for"—

"The glory of God, and the glory of John May."

May did not speak for a moment; then, controlled, he said,—

"Why should one be raised, when myriads are left?—I have not the money, boy," to Wolfe, shortly.

"Money?" He said it over slowly, as one repeats the guessed answer to a riddle, doubtfully. "That is it? Money?"

"Yes, money,—that is it," said Mitchell, rising, and drawing his furred coat about him. "You've found the cure for all the world's diseases.—Come, May, find your good-humor, and come home. This damp wind chills my very bones. Come and preach your Saint-Simonian doctrines[7] to-morrow to Kirby's hands. Let them have a clear idea of the rights of the soul, and I'll venture next week they'll strike for higher wages. That will be the end of it."

"Will you send the coach-driver to this side of the mills?" asked Kirby, turning to Wolfe.

He spoke kindly: it was his habit to do so. Deborah, seeing the puddler go, crept after him. The three men waited outside. Doctor May walked up and down, chafed. Suddenly he stopped.

"Go back, Mitchell! You say the pocket and the heart of the world speak without meaning to these people. What has its head to say? Taste, culture, refinement? Go!"

---

5. One who believes in a God who created the world but thereafter exercises no control over it. What Jesus says in Matthew 25.40: "Verily I say unto you, Inasmuch as ye have done it unto one of the least of these my brethren, ye have done it unto me."
6. Aren't you? (French).
7. Doctrines of the Count of Saint-Simon (1760–1825), founder of French socialism.

Mitchell was leaning against a brick wall. He turned his head indolently, and looked into the mills. There hung about the place a thick, unclean odor. The slightest motion of his hand marked that he perceived it, and his insufferable disgust. That was all. May said nothing, only quickened his angry tramp.

"Besides," added Mitchell, giving a corollary to his answer, "it would be of no use. I am not one of them."

"You do not mean"—said May, facing him.

"Yes, I mean just that. Reform is born of need, not pity. No vital movement of the people's has worked down, for good or evil; fermented, instead, carried up the heaving, cloggy mass. Think back through history, and you will know it. What will this lowest deep—thieves, Magdalens,[8] negroes—do with the light filtered through ponderous Church creeds, Baconian theories, Goethe schemes?[9] Some day, out of their bitter need will be thrown up their own light-bringer,—their Jean Paul, their Cromwell, their Messiah."[1]

"Bah!" was the Doctor's inward criticism. However, in practice, he adopted the theory; for, when, night and morning, afterwards, he prayed that power might be given these degraded souls to rise, he glowed at heart, recognizing an accomplished duty.

Wolfe and the woman had stood in the shadow of the works as the coach drove off. The Doctor had held out his hand in a frank, generous way, telling him to "take care of himself, and to remember it was his right to rise." Mitchell had simply touched his hat, as to an equal, with a quiet look of thorough recognition. Kirby had thrown Deborah some money, which she found, and clutched eagerly enough. They were gone now, all of them. The man sat down on the cinder-road, looking up into the murky sky.

" 'T be late, Hugh. Wunnot hur come?"

He shook his head doggedly, and the woman crouched out of his sight against the wall. Do you remember rare moments when a sudden light flashed over yourself, your world, God? when you stood on a mountain-peak, seeing your life as it might have been, as it is? one quick instant, when custom lost its force and every-day usage? when your friend, wife, brother, stood in a new light? your soul was bared, and the grave,—a foretaste of the nakedness of the Judgment-Day? So it came before him, his life, that night. The slow tides of pain he had borne gathered themselves up and surged against his soul. His squalid daily life, the brutal coarseness eating into his brain, as the ashes into his skin: before, these things had been a dull aching into his consciousness; to-night, they were reality. He griped the filthy red shirt that clung, stiff with soot, about him, and tore it savagely from his arm. The flesh beneath was muddy with grease and ashes,—and the heart beneath that! And the soul? God knows.

Then flashed before his vivid poetic sense the man who had left him,—the pure face, the delicate, sinewy limbs, in harmony with all he knew of beauty or truth. In his cloudy fancy he had pictured a Something like this. He had found it in this Mitchell, even when he idly scoffed at his pain: a Man all-

8. Whores, from Mary Magdalene, out of whom Jesus cast seven devils (Mark 16.9).

9. Abstract or fanciful theories such as the English essayist and statesman Francis Bacon (1561–1624) advanced in his *New Atlantis* (1627) or the visionary faith in technological progress revealed by the German writer Johann Wolfgang von Goethe (1749–1832) in

Wilhelm Meister's Travels (1821–29).

1. Not specifically Jesus whose return Christians await or the Messiah whose coming Jews await. The German novelist Jean Paul Richter (1763–1825), author of *The Titan.* Oliver Cromwell (1599–1658), English military, political, and religious leader, dictator of England.

knowing, all-seeing, crowned by Nature, reigning,—the keen glance of his eye falling like a sceptre on other men. And yet his instinct taught him that he too—He! He looked at himself with sudden loathing, sick, wrung his hands with a cry, and then was silent. With all the phantoms of his heated, ignorant fancy, Wolfe had not been vague in his ambitions. They were practical, slowly built up before him out of his knowledge of what he could do. Through years he had day by day made this hope a real thing to himself,—a clear, projected figure of himself, as he might become.

Able to speak, to know what was best, to raise these men and women working at his side up with him: sometimes he forgot this defined hope in the frantic anguish to escape,—only to escape,—out of the wet, the pain, the ashes, somewhere, anywhere,—only for one moment of free air on a hill-side, to lie down and let his sick soul throb itself out in the sunshine. But to-night he panted for life. The savage strength of his nature was roused; his cry was fierce to God for justice.

"Look at me!" he said to Deborah, with a low, bitter laugh, striking his puny chest savagely. "What am I worth, Deb? Is it my fault that I am no better? My fault? My fault?"

He stopped, stung with a sudden remorse, seeing her hunchback shape writhing with sobs. For Deborah was crying thankless tears, according to the fashion of women.

"God forgi' me, woman! Things go harder wi' you nor me. It's a worse share."

He got up and helped her to rise; and they went doggedly down the muddy street, side by side.

"It's all wrong," he muttered, slowly,—"all wrong! I dunnot understan'. But it'll end some day."

"Come home, Hugh!" she said, coaxingly; for he had stopped, looking around bewildered.

"Home,—and back to the mill!" He went on saying this over to himself, as if he would mutter down every pain in this dull despair.

She followed him through the fog, her blue lips chattering with cold. They reached the cellar at last. Old Wolfe had been drinking since she went out, and had crept nearer the door. The girl Janey slept heavily in the corner. He went up to her, touching softly the worn white arm with his fingers. Some bitterer thought stung him, as he stood there. He wiped the drops from his forehead, and went into the room beyond, livid, trembling. A hope, trifling, perhaps, but very dear, had died just then out of the poor puddler's life, as he looked at the sleeping, innocent girl,—some plan for the future, in which she had borne a part. He gave it up that moment, then and forever. Only a trifle, perhaps, to us: his face grew a shade paler,—that was all. But, somehow, the man's soul, as God and the angels looked down on it, never was the same afterwards.

Deborah followed him into the inner room. She carried a candle, which she placed on the floor, closing the door after her. She had seen the look on his face, as he turned away: her own grew deadly. Yet, as she came up to him, her eyes glowed. He was seated on an old chest, quiet, holding his face in his hands.

"Hugh!" she said, softly.

He did not speak.

"Hugh, did hur hear what the man said,—him with the clear voice? Did hur hear? Money, money,—that it wud do all?"

He pushed her away,—gently, but he was worn out; her rasping tone fretted him.

"Hugh!"

The candle flared a pale yellow light over the cobwebbed brick walls, and the woman standing there. He looked at her. She was young, in deadly earnest; her faded eyes, and wet, ragged figure caught from their frantic eagerness a power akin to beauty.

"Hugh, it is true! Money ull do it! Oh, Hugh, boy, listen till me! He said it true! It is money!"

"I know. Go back! I do not want you here."

"Hugh, it is t' last time. I'll never worrit hur again."

There were tears in her voice now, but she choked them back.

"Hear till me only to-night! If one of t' witch people wud come, them we heard of t' home, and gif hur all hur wants, what then? Say, Hugh!"

"What do you mean?"

"I mean money."

Her whisper shrilled through his brain.

"If one of t' witch dwarfs wud come from t' lane moors to-night, and gif hur money, to go out,—out, I say,—out, lad, where t' sun shines, and t' heath grows, and t' ladies walk in silken gownds, and God stays all t' time,—where t' man lives that talked to us to-night,—Hugh knows,—Hugh could walk there like a king!"

He thought the woman mad, tried to check her, but she went on, fierce in her eager haste.

"If I were t' witch dwarf, if I had t' money, wud hur thank me? Wud hur take me out o' this place wid hur and Janey? I wud not come into the gran' house hur wud build, to vex hur wid t' hunch,—only at night, when t' shadows were dark, stand far off to see hur."

Mad? Yes! Are many of us mad in this way?

"Poor Deb! poor Deb!" he said, soothingly.

"It is here," she said, suddenly, jerking into his hand a small roll. "I took it! I did it! Me, me!—not hur! I shall be hanged, I shall be burnt in hell, if anybody knows I took it! Out of his pocket, as he leaned against t' bricks. Hur knows?"

She thrust it into his hand, and then, her errand done, began to gather chips together to make a fire, choking down hysteric sobs.

"Has it come to this?"

That was all he said. The Welsh Wolfe blood was honest. The roll was a small green pocket-book containing one or two gold pieces, and a check for an incredible amount, as it seemed to the poor puddler. He laid it down, hiding his face again in his hands.

"Hugh, don't be angry wud me! It's only poor Deb,—hur knows?"

He took the long skinny fingers kindly in his.

"Angry? God help me, no! Let me sleep. I am tired."

He threw himself heavily down on the wooden bench, stunned with pain and weariness. She brought some old rags to cover him.

It was late on Sunday evening before he awoke. I tell God's truth, when I say he had then no thought of keeping this money. Deborah had hid it in his pocket. He found it there. She watched him eagerly, as he took it out.

"I must gif it to him," he said, reading her face.

"Hur knows," she said with a bitter sigh of disappointment. "But it is hur right to keep it."

His right! The word struck him. Doctor May had used the same. He washed himself, and went out to find this man Mitchell. His right! Why did this chance word cling to him so obstinately? Do you hear the fierce devils whisper in his ear, as he went slowly down the darkening street?

The evening came on, slow and calm. He seated himself at the end of an alley leading into one of the larger streets. His brain was clear to-night, keen, intent, mastering. It would not start back, cowardly, from any hellish temptation, but meet it face to face. Therefore the great temptation of his life came to him veiled by no sophistry, but bold, defiant, owning its own vile name, trusting to one bold blow for victory.

He did not deceive himself. Theft! That was it. At first the word sickened him; then he grappled with it. Sitting there on a broken cart-wheel, the fading day, the noisy groups, the church-bells' tolling passed before him like a panorama,[2] while the sharp struggle went on within. This money! He took it out, and looked at it. If he gave it back, what then? He was going to be cool about it.

People going by to church saw only a sickly mill-boy watching them quietly at the alley's mouth. They did not know that he was mad, or they would not have gone by so quietly: mad with hunger; stretching out his hands to the world, that had given so much to them, for leave to live the life God meant him to live. His soul within him was smothering to death; he wanted so much, thought so much, and *knew*—nothing. There was nothing of which he was certain, except the mill and things there. Of God and heaven he had heard so little, that they were to him what fairy-land is to a child: something real, but not here; very far off. His brain, greedy, dwarfed, full of thwarted energy and unused powers, questioned these men and women going by, coldly, bitterly, that night. Was it not his right to live as they,—a pure life, a good, true-hearted life, full of beauty and kind words? He only wanted to know how to use the strength within him. His heart warmed, as he thought of it. He suffered himself to think of it longer. If he took the money?

Then he saw himself as he might be, strong, helpful, kindly. The night crept on, as this one image slowly evolved itself from the crowd of other thoughts and stood triumphant. He looked at it. As he might be! What wonder, if it blinded him to delirium,—the madness that underlies all revolution, all progress, and all fall?

You laugh at the shallow temptation? You see the error underlying its argument so clearly,—that to him a true life was one of full development rather than self-restraint? that he was deaf to the higher tone in a cry of voluntary suffering for truth's sake than in the fullest flow of spontaneous harmony? I do not plead his cause. I only want to show you the mote in my brother's eye: then you can see clearly to take it out.[3]

The money,—there it lay on his knee, a little blotted slip of paper, nothing in itself; used to raise him out of the pit, something straight from God's hand.

---

2. Like the continuous scenes painted on huge canvas and unrolled before audiences; attending a panorama was a popular mid-19th-century recreation, but probably too expensive for Harding's characters.
3. Jesus's words in the Sermon on the Mount (Matthew 7.3–4): "And why beholdest thou the mote that is in thy brother's eye, but considerest not the beam that is in thine own eye? Or how wilt thou say to thy brother, Let me pull out the mote out of thine eye; and behold, a beam is in thine own eye?" (Here a mote is a speck of dust and a beam is the large timber used to support a roof.)

A thief! Well, what was it to be a thief? He met the question at last, face to face, wiping the clammy drops of sweat from his forehead. God made this money—the fresh air, too—for his children's use. He never made the difference between poor and rich. The Something who looked down on him that moment through the cool gray sky had a kindly face, he knew,—loved his children alike. Oh, he knew that!

There were times when the soft floods of color in the crimson and purple flames, or the clear depth of amber in the water below the bridge, had somehow given him a glimpse of another world than this,—of an infinite depth of beauty and of quiet somewhere,—somewhere,—a depth of quiet and rest and love. Looking up now, it became strangely real. The sun had sunk quite below the hills, but his last rays struck upward, touching the zenith. The fog had risen, and the town and river were steeped in its thick, gray damp; but overhead, the sun-touched smoke-clouds opened like a cleft ocean,—shifting, rolling seas of crimson mist, waves of billowy silver veined with blood-scarlet, inner depths unfathomable of glancing light. Wolfe's artist-eye grew drunk with color. The gates of that other world! Fading, flashing before him now! What, in that world of Beauty, Content, and Right, were the petty laws, the mine and thine, of mill-owners and mill hands?

A consciousness of power stirred within him. He stood up. A man,—he thought, stretching out his hands,—free to work, to live, to love! Free! His right! He folded the scrap of paper in his hand. As his nervous fingers took it in, limp and blotted, so his soul took in the mean temptation, lapped it in fancied rights, in dreams of improved existences, drifting and endless as the cloud-seas of color. Clutching it, as if the tightness of his hold would strengthen his sense of possession, he went aimlessly down the street. It was his watch at the mill. He need not go, need never go again, thank God!—shaking off the thought with unspeakable loathing.

Shall I go over the history of the hours of that night? how the man wandered from one to another of his old haunts, with a half-consciousness of bidding them farewell,—lanes and alleys and back-yards where the mill-hands lodged,—noting, with a new eagerness, the filth and drunkenness, the pig-pens, the ash-heaps covered with potato-skins, the bloated, pimpled women at the doors,—with a new disgust, a new sense of sudden triumph, and, under all, a new, vague dread, unknown before, smothered down, kept under, but still there? It left him but once during the night, when, for the second time in his life, he entered a church. It was a sombre Gothic pile, where the stained light lost itself in far-retreating arches; built to meet the requirements and sympathies of a far other class than Wolfe's. Yet it touched, moved him uncontrollably. The distances, the shadows, the still, marble figures, the mass of silent kneeling worshippers, the mysterious music, thrilled, lifted his soul with a wonderful pain. Wolfe forgot himself, forgot the new life he was going to live, the mean terror gnawing underneath. The voice of the speaker strengthened the charm; it was clear, feeling, full, strong. An old man, who had lived much, suffered much; whose brain was keenly alive, dominant; whose heart was summer-warm with charity. He taught it to-night. He held up Humanity in its grand total; showed the great world-cancer to his people. Who could show it better? He was a Christian reformer; he had studied the age thoroughly; his outlook at man had been free, world-wide, over all time. His faith stood sublime upon the Rock of Ages; his fiery zeal guided vast schemes by which the Gospel was to be preached to all nations. How did he preach it to-night? In burning, light-laden words he painted Jesus, the incarnate Life, Love, the universal Man: words that became reality in the lives of these people,—that lived again in beautiful words and actions, trifling, but heroic. Sin, as he defined it, was a real foe to them; their trials, temptations, were his. His words passed far over the furnace-tender's grasp, toned to suit another class of culture; they sounded in his ears a very pleasant song in an unknown tongue. He meant to cure this world-cancer with a steady eye that had never glared with hunger, and a hand that neither poverty nor strychnine-whiskey[4] had taught to shake. In this morbid, distorted heart of the Welsh puddler he had failed.

Eighteen centuries ago, the Master of this man tried reform in the streets of a city as crowded and vile as this, and did not fail. His disciple, showing Him to-night to cultured hearers, showing the clearness of the God-power acting through Him, shrank back from one coarse fact; that in birth and habit the man Christ was thrown up from the lowest of the people: his flesh, their flesh; their blood, his blood; tempted like them, to brutalize day by day; to lie, to steal: the actual slime and want of their hourly life, and the wine-press he trod alone.

Yet, is there no meaning in this perpetually covered truth? If the son of the carpenter had stood in the church that night, as he stood with the fishermen and harlots by the sea of Galilee, before His Father and their Father, despised and rejected of men, without a place to lay His head, wounded for their iniquities, bruised for their transgressifons, would not that hungry mill-boy at least, in the back seat, have "known the man"? That Jesus did not stand there.

Wolfe rose at last, and turned from the church down the street. He looked up; the night had come on foggy, damp; the golden mists had vanished, and the sky lay dull and ash-colored. He wandered again aimlessly down the street, idly wondering what had become of the cloud-sea of crimson and scarlet. The trial-day of this man's life was over, and he had lost the victory. What followed was mere drifting circumstance,—a quicker walking over the path,—that was all. Do you want to hear the end of it? You wish me to make a tragic story out of it? Why, in the police-reports of the morning paper you can find a dozen such tragedies: hints of shipwrecks unlike any that ever befell on the high seas; hints that here a power was lost to heaven,—that there a soul went down where no tide can ebb or flow. Commonplace enough the hints are,—jocose sometimes, done up in rhyme.

Doctor May, a month after the night I have told you of, was reading to his wife at breakfast from this fourth column of the morning-paper: an unusual thing,—these police-reports not being, in general, choice reading for ladies; but it was only one item he read.

"Oh, my dear! You remember that man I told you of, that we saw at Kirby's mill?—that was arrested for robbing Mitchell? Here he is; just listen:—'Circuit Court. Judge Day. Hugh Wolfe, operative in Kirby & John's Loudon Mills. Charge, grand larceny. Sentence, nineteen years hard labor in penitentiary.'—Scoundrel! Serves him right! After all our kindness that night! Picking Mitchell's pocket at the very time!"

His wife said something about the ingratitude of that kind of people, and then they began to talk of something else.

---

4. Extremely dangerous whiskey (sometimes lethal) made from redistilling the mash along with various impurities.

Nineteen years! How easy that was to read! What a simple word for Judge Day to utter! Nineteen years! Half a lifetime!

Hugh Wolfe sat on the window-ledge of his cell, looking out. His ankles were ironed. Not usual in such cases; but he had made two desperate efforts to escape. "Well," as Haley, the jailer, said, "small blame to him! Nineteen years' inprisonment was not a pleasant thing to look forward to." Haley was very good-natured about it, though Wolfe had fought him savagely.

"When he was first caught," the jailer said afterwards, in telling the story, "before the trial, the fellow was cut down at once,—laid there on that pallet like a dead man, with his hands over his eyes. Never saw a man so cut down in my life. Time of the trial, too, came the queerest dodge[5] of any customer I ever had. Would choose no lawyer. Judge gave him one, of course. Gibson it was. He tried to prove the fellow crazy; but it wouldn't go. Thing was plain as daylight: money found on him. 'T was a hard sentence,—all the law allows; but it was for 'xample's sake. These mill-hands are gettin' onbearable. When the sentence was read, he just looked up, and said the money was his by rights, and that all the world had gone wrong. That night, after the trial, a gentleman came to see him here, name of Mitchell,—him as he stole from. Talked to him for an hour. Thought he came for curiosity, like. After he was gone, thought Wolfe was remarkable quiet, and went into his cell. Found him very low; bed all bloody. Doctor said he had been bleeding at the lungs. He was as weak as a cat; yet if ye'll b'lieve me, he tried to get a-past me and get out. I just carried him like a baby, and threw him on the pallet. Three days after, he tried it again: that time reached the wall. Lord help you! he fought like a tiger,— giv' some terrible blows. Fightin' for life, you see; for he can't live long, shut up in the stone crib down yonder. Got a death-cough now. 'T took two of us to bring him down that day; so I just put the irons on his feet. There he sits, in there. Goin' to-morrow, with a batch more of 'em. That woman, hunchback, tried with him,—you remember?—she's only got three years. 'Complice. But *she's* a woman, you know. He's been quiet ever since I put on irons: giv' up, I suppose. Looks white, sick-lookin'. It acts different on 'em, bein' sentenced. Most of 'em gets reckless, devilish-like. Some prays awful, and sings them vile songs of the mills, all in a breath. That woman, now, she's desper't'. Been beggin' to see Hugh, as she calls him, for three days. I'm a-goin' to let her in. She don't go with him. Here she is in this next cell. I'm a-goin' now to let her in."

He let her in. Wolfe did not see her. She crept into a corner of the cell, and stood watching him. He was scratching the iron bars of the window with a piece of tin which he had picked up, with an idle, uncertain, vacant stare, just as a child or idiot would do.

"Tryin' to get out, old boy?" laughed Haley. "Them irons will need a crow-bar beside your tin, before you can open 'em."

Wolfe laughed, too, in a senseless way.

"I think I'll get out," he said.

"I believe his brain's touched," said Haley, when he came out.

The puddler scraped away with the tin for half an hour. Still Deborah did not speak. At last she ventured nearer, and touched his arm.

"Blood?" she said, looking at some spots on his coat with a shudder.

5. Trick, stratagem.

He looked up at her. "Why, Deb!" he said, smiling,—such a bright, boyish smile, that it went to poor Deborah's heart directly, and she sobbed and cried out loud.

"Oh, Hugh, lad! Hugh! dunnot look at me, when it wur my fault! To think I brought hur to it! And I loved hur so! Oh lad, I dud!"

The confession, even in this wretch, came with the woman's blush through the sharp cry.

He did not seem to hear her,—scraping away diligently at the bars with the bit of tin.

Was he going mad? She peered closely into his face. Something she saw there made her draw suddenly back,—something which Haley had not seen, that lay beneath the pinched, vacant look it had caught since the trial, or the curious gray shadow that rested on it. That gray shadow,—yes, she knew what that meant. She had often seen it creeping over women's faces for months, who died at last of slow hunger or consumption. That meant death, distant, lingering: but this—Whatever it was the woman saw, or thought she saw, used as she was to crime and misery, seemed to make her sick with a new horror. Forgetting her fear of him, she caught his shoulders, and looked keenly, steadily, into his eyes.

"Hugh!" she cried, in a desperate whisper,—"oh, boy, not that! for God's sake, not *that!*"

The vacant laugh went off his face, and he answered her in a muttered word or two that drove her away. Yet the words were kindly enough. Sitting there on his pallet, she cried silently a hopeless sort of tears, but did not speak again. The man looked up furtively at her now and then. Whatever his own trouble was, her distress vexed him with a momentary sting.

It was market-day. The narrow window of the jail looked down directly on the carts and wagons drawn up in a long line, where they had unloaded. He could see, too, and hear distinctly the clink of money as it changed hands, the busy crowd of whites and blacks shoving, pushing one another, and the chaffering and swearing at the stalls. Somehow, the sound, more than anything else had done, wakened him up,—made the whole real to him. He was done with the world and the business of it. He let the tin fall, and looked out, pressing his face close to the rusty bars. How they crowded and pushed! And he,—he should never walk that pavement again! There came Neff Sanders, one of the feeders at the mill, with a basket on his arm. Sure enough, Neff was married the other week. He whistled, hoping he would look up; but he did not. He wondered if Neff remembered he was there,—if any of the boys thought of him up there, and thought that he never was to go down that old cinder-road again. Never again! He had not quite understood it before; but now he did. Not for days or years, but never!—that was it.

How clear the light fell on that stall in front of the market! and how like a picture it was, the dark-green heaps of corn, and the crimson beets, and golden melons! There was another with game: how the light flickered on that pheasant's breast, with the purplish blood dripping over the brown feathers! He could see the red shining of the drops, it was so near. In one minute he could be down there. It was just a step. So easy, as it seemed, so natural to go! Yet it could never be—not in all the thousands of years to come—that he should put his foot on that street again! He thought of himself with a sorrowful pity, as of some one else. There was a dog down in the market, walking after his master

with such a stately, grave look!—only a dog, yet he could go backwards and
forwards just as he pleased: he had good luck! Why, the very vilest cur, yelping
there in the gutter, had not lived his life, had been free to act out whatever
thought God had put into his brain; while he—No, he would not think of
that! He tried to put the thought away, and to listen to a dispute between a
countryman and a woman about some meat; but it would come back. He,
what had he done to bear this?

Then came the sudden picture of what might have been, and now. He knew
what it was to be in the penitentiary,—how it went with men there. He knew
how in these long years he should slowly die, but not until soul and body had
become corrupt and rotten,—how, when he came out, if he lived to come,
even the lowest of the mill-hands would jeer him,—how his hands would be
weak, and his brain senseless and stupid. He believed he was almost that now.
He put his hand to his head, with a puzzled, weary look. It ached, his head,
with thinking. He tried to quiet himself. It was only right, perhaps; he had
done wrong. But was there right or wrong for such as he? What was right? And
who had ever taught him? He thrust the whole matter away. A dark, cold quiet
crept through his brain. It was all wrong; but let it be! It was nothing to him
more than the others. Let it be!

The door grated, as Haley opened it.

"Come, my woman! Must lock up for t' night. Come, stir yerself!"

She went up and took Hugh's hand.

"Good-night, Deb," he said, carelessly.

She had not hoped he would say more; but the tired pain on her mouth just
then was bitterer than death. She took his passive hand and kissed it.

"Hur'll never see Deb again!" she ventured, her lips growing colder and
more bloodless.

What did she say that for? Did he not know it? Yet he would not be impatient with poor old Deb. She had trouble of her own, as well as he.

"No, never again," he said, trying to be cheerful.

She stood just a moment, looking at him. Do you laugh at her, standing
there, with her hunchback, her rags, her bleared, withered face, and the great
despised love tugging at her heart?

"Come, you!" called Haley, impatiently.

She did not move.

"Hugh!" she whispered.

It was to be her last word. What was it?

"Hugh, boy, not THAT!"

He did not answer. She wrung her hands, trying to be silent, looking in his
face in an agony of entreaty. He smiled again, kindly.

"It is best, Deb. I cannot bear to be hurted any more."

"Hur knows," she said, humbly.

"Tell my father good-bye; and—and kiss little Janey."

She nodded, saying nothing, looked in his face again, and went out of the
door. As she went, she staggered.

"Drinkin' to-day?" broke out Haley, pushing her before him. "Where the
Devil did you get it? Here, in with ye!" and he shoved her into her cell, next
to Wolfe's, and shut the door.

Along the wall of her cell there was a crack low down by the floor, through
which she could see the light from Wolfe's. She had discovered it days before.

She hurried in now, and, kneeling down by it, listened, hoping to hear some sound. Nothing but the rasping of the tin on the bars. He was at his old amusement again. Something in the noise jarred on her ear, for she shivered as she heard it. Hugh rasped away at the bars. A dull old bit of tin, not fit to cut korl with.

He looked out of the window again. People were leaving the market now. A tall mulatto girl, following her mistress, her basket on her head, crossed the street just below, and looked up. She was laughing; but, when she caught sight of the haggard face peering out through the bars, suddenly grew grave, and hurried by. A free, firm step, a clear-cut olive face, with a scarlet turban tied on one side, dark, shining eyes, and on the head the basket poised, filled with fruit and flowers, under which the scarlet turban and bright eyes looked out half-shadowed. The picture caught his eye. It was good to see a face like that. He would try to-morrow, and cut one like it. *To-morrow!* He threw down the tin, trembling, and covered his face with his hands. When he looked up again, the daylight was gone.

Deborah, crouching near by on the other side of the wall, heard no noise. He sat on the side of the low pallet, thinking. Whatever was the mystery which the woman had seen on his face, it came out now slowly, in the dark there, and became fixed,—a something never seen on his face before. The evening was darkening fast. The market had been over for an hour; the rumbling of the carts over the pavement grew more infrequent: he listened to each, as it passed, because he thought it was to be for the last time. For the same reason, it was, I suppose, that he strained his eyes to catch a glimpse of each passer-by, wondering who they were, what kind of homes they were going to, if they had children,—listening eagerly to every chance word in the street, as if—(God be merciful to the man! what strange fancy was this?)—as if he never should hear human voices again.

It was quite dark at last. The street was a lonely one. The last passenger, he thought, was gone. No,—there was a quick step: Joe Hill, lighting the lamps. Joe was a good old chap; never passed a fellow without some joke or other. He remembered once seeing the place where he lived with his wife. "Granny Hill" the boys called her. Bedridden she was; but so kind as Joe was to her! kept the room so clean!—and the old woman, when he was there, was laughing at "some of t' lad's foolishness." The step was far down the street; but he could see him place the ladder, run up, and light the gas. A longing seized him to be spoken to once more.

"Joe!" he called, out of the grating. "Good-bye, Joe!"

The old man stopped a moment, listening uncertainly; then hurried on. The prisoner thrust his hand out of the window, and called again, louder; but Joe was too far down the street. It was a little thing; but it hurt him,—this disappointment.

"Good-bye, Joe!" he called, sorrowfully enough.

"Be quiet!" said one of the jailers, passing the door, striking on it with his club.

Oh, that was the last, was it?

There was an inexpressible bitterness on his face, as he lay down on the bed, taking the bit of tin, which he had rasped to a tolerable degree of sharpness, in his hand,—to play with, it may be. He bared his arms, looking intently at their corded veins and sinews. Deborah, listening in the next cell, heard a slight clicking sound, often repeated. She shut her lips tightly, that she might not scream; the cold drops of sweat broke over her, in her dumb agony.

"Hur knows best," she muttered at last, fiercely clutching the boards where she lay.

If she could have seen Wolfe, there was nothing about him to frighten her. He lay quite still, his arms outstretched, looking at the pearly stream of moonlight coming into the window. I think in that one hour that came then he lived back over all the years that had gone before. I think that all the low, vile life, all his wrongs, all his starved hopes, came then, and stung him with a farewell poison that made him sick unto death. He made neither moan nor cry, only turned his worn face now and then to the pure light, that seemed so far off, as one that said, "How long, O Lord? how long?"

The hour was over at last. The moon, passing over her nightly path, slowly came nearer, and threw the light across his bed on his feet. He watched it steadily, as it crept up, inch by inch, slowly. It seemed to him to carry with it a great silence. He had been so hot and tired there always in the mills! The years had been so fierce and cruel! There was coming now quiet and coolness and sleep. His tense limbs relaxed, and settled in a calm languor. The blood ran fainter and slow from his heart. He did not think now with a savage anger of what might be and was not; he was conscious only of deep stillness creeping over him. At first he saw a sea of faces: the mill-men,—women he had known, drunken and bloated,—Janey's timid and pitiful—poor old Debs: then they floated together like a mist, and faded away, leaving only the clear, pearly moonlight.

Whether, as the pure light crept up the stretched-out figure, it brought with it calm and peace, who shall say? His dumb soul was alone with God in judgment. A Voice may have spoken for it from far-off Calvary, "Father, forgive them, for they know not what they do!"[6] Who dare say? Fainter and fainter the heart rose and fell, slower and slower the moon floated from behind a cloud, until, when at last its full tide of white splendor swept over the cell, it seemed to wrap and fold into a deeper stillness the dead figure that never should move again. Silence deeper than the Night! Nothing that moved, save the black, nauseous stream of blood dripping slowly from the pallet to the floor!

There was outcry and crowd enough in the cell the next day. The coroner and his jury, the local editors, Kirby himself, and boys with their hands thrust knowingly into their pockets and heads on one side, jammed into the corners. Coming and going all day. Only one woman. She came late, and outstayed them all. A Quaker, or Friend, as they call themselves. I think this woman was known by that name in heaven. A homely body, coarsely dressed in gray and white. Deborah (for Haley had let her in) took notice of her. She watched them all—sitting on the end of the pallet, holding his head in her arms—with the ferocity of a watch-dog, if any of them touched the body. There was no meekness, no sorrow, in her face; the stuff out of which murderers are made, instead. All the time Haley and the woman were laying straight the limbs and cleaning the cell, Deborah sat still, keenly watching the Quaker's face. Of all the crowd there that day, this woman alone had not spoken to her,—only once or twice had put some cordial to her lips. After they all were gone, the woman,

---

6. Luke 23.34: "Father, forgive them: for they know not what they do" (Jesus' words from the cross).

in the same still, gentle way, brought a vase of wood-leaves and berries, and placed it by the pallet, then opened the narrow window. The fresh air blew in, and swept the woody fragrance over the dead face. Deborah looked up with a quick wonder.

"Did hur know my boy wud like it? Did hur know Hugh?"

"I know Hugh now."

The white fingers passed in a slow, pitiful way over the dead, worn face. There was a heavy shadow in the quiet eyes.

"Did hur know where they'll bury Hugh?" said Deborah in a shrill tone, catching her arm.

This had been the question hanging on her lips all day.

"In t' town-yard? Under t' mud and ash? T' lad 'll smother, woman! He wur born in t' lane moor, where t' air is frick[7] and strong. Take hur out, for God's sake, take hur out where t' air blows!"

The Quaker hesitated, but only for a moment. She put her strong arm around Deborah and led her to the window.

"Thee sees the hills, friend, over the river? Thee sees how the light lies warm there, and the winds of God blow all the day? I live there,—where the blue smoke is, by the trees. Look at me." She turned Deborah's face to her own, clear and earnest. "Thee will believe me? I will take Hugh and bury him there to-morrow."

Deborah did not doubt her. As the evening wore on, she leaned against the iron bars, looking at the hills that rose far off, through the thick sodden clouds, like a bright, unattainable calm. As she looked, a shadow of their solemn repose fell on her face; its fierce discontent faded into a pitiful, humble quiet. Slow, solemn tears gathered in her eyes: the poor weak eyes turned so hope-lessly to the place where Hugh was to rest, the grave heights looking higher and brighter and more solemn than ever before. The Quaker watched her keenly. She came to her at last, and touched her arm.

"When thee comes back," she said, in a low, sorrowful tone, like one who speaks from a strong heart deeply moved with remorse or pity, "thee shall begin thy life again,—there on the hills. I came too late; but not for thee,— by God's help, it may be."

Not too late. Three years after, the Quaker began her work. I end my story here. At evening-time it was light. There is no need to tire you with the long years of sunshine, and fresh air, and slow, patient Christ-love, needed to make healthy and hopeful this impure body and soul. There is a homely pine house, on one of these hills, whose windows overlook broad, wooded slopes and clo-ver-crimsoned meadows,—niched into the very place where the light is warm-est, the air freest. It is the Friends'[8] meeting-house. Once a week they sit there, in their grave, earnest way, waiting for the Spirit of Love to speak, opening their simple hearts to receive His words. There is a woman, old, deformed, who takes a humble place among them: waiting like them: in her gray dress, her worn face, pure and meek, turned now and then to the sky. A woman much loved by these silent, restful people; more silent than they, more hum-ble, more loving. Waiting: with her eyes turned to hills higher and purer than these on which she lives,—dim and far off now, but to be reached some day. There may be in her heart some latent hope to meet there the love denied her

7. Fresh.   8. Quakers.

here,—that she shall find him whom she lost, and that then she will not be all-unworthy. Who blames her? Something is lost in the passage of every soul from one eternity to the other,—something pure and beautiful, which might have been and was not: a hope, a talent, a love, over which the soul mourns, like Esau deprived of his birthright.[9] What blame to the meek Quaker, if she took her lost hope to make the hills of heaven more fair?

Nothing remains to tell that the poor Welsh puddler once lived, but this figure of the mill-woman cut in korl. I have it here in a corner of my library. I keep it hid behind a curtain,—it is such a rough, ungainly thing. Yet there are about it touches, grand sweeps of outline, that show a master's hand. Sometimes,—to-night, for instance,—the curtain is accidentally drawn back, and I see a bare arm stretched out imploringly in the darkness, and an eager, wolfish face watching mine: a wan, woful face, through which the spirit of the dead korl-cutter looks out, with its thwarted life, its mighty hunger, its unfinished work. Its pale, vague lips seem to tremble with a terrible question. "Is this the End?" they say,—"nothing beyond?—no more?" Why, you tell me you have seen that look in the eyes of dumb brutes,—horses dying under the lash. I know.

The deep of the night is passing while I write. The gas-light wakens from the shadows here and there the objects which lie scattered through the room: only faintly, though; for they belong to the open sunlight. As I glance at them, they each recall some task or pleasure of the coming day. A half-moulded child's head; Aphrodite;[1] a bough of forest-leaves; music; work; homely fragments, in which lie the secrets of all eternal truth and beauty. Prophetic all! Only this dumb, woful face seems to belong to and end with the night. I turn to look at it. Has the power of its desperate need commanded the darkness away? While the room is yet steeped in heavy shadow, a cool, gray light suddenly touches its head like a blessing hand, and its groping arm points through the broken cloud to the far East, where, in the flickering, nebulous crimson, God has set the promise of the Dawn.

1861

9. Genesis 25 and 27 tell the story of Jacob's depriving his elder twin brother Esau of his birthright.

1. Venus, the goddess of love.

Selected Bibliographies

For study of the 1620–1865 period of American literature, the best handbook is Clarence Gohdes and Sanford E. Marovitz's *Bibliographical Guide to the Literature of the U.S.A.*, 5th ed. (1984). Lists of significant works for the present volume of *The Norton Anthology of American Literature* are given under such useful categories as "American studies or American civilization," "American history: general tools," "American history: special studies," "Selected histories of ideas in the U.S.," "Psychology," "Philosophy" (including "Trancendentalism"), "Religion in the U.S.," "Chief general bibliographies of American literature," "Chief general histories and selected critical discussions of American literature," and "Studies of the 17th and 18th centuries." The fourth edition (1976) contained a useful section on "Arts other than literature." In *American Literature: A Study and Research Guide* (1976), Lewis Leary with John Auchard duplicates some of the categories in Gohdes's book, but his pithy evaluations of the works he mentions are very helpful; Leary also provides an interesting "History of the Study and Teaching of American Literature." Relatively few items on this period are listed in Robert C. Schweik and Dieter Riesner's *Reference Sources in English and American Literature: An Annotated Bibliography* (1977), but those few are helpfully annotated. A basic reference book is James D. Hart's *Oxford Companion to American Literature*, 5th ed. (1983).

LITERATURE TO 1620

Few major studies address the great body of writings produced in various European languages, or codified in Native American ones, in the period up to 1620; those that do concern themselves more with matters of context than with patterns of language. For the basic outline of European expansion westward, Samuel Eliot Morison's *The European Discovery of America*, 2 vols. (1971–74) is useful. For North America, David Beers Quinn's thorough *North America from Earliest Discovery to First Settlements* (1977) and his *England and the Discovery of America, 1481–1620* (1973) give detailed narrative and analysis, as does Gary Nash's *Red, White, and Black: The People of Early America* (1974). Edmundo O'Gorman's insightful *The Invention of America* (1961) shifts the discussion away from the geographical discoveries of Renaissance Europe and toward the cultural responses that those discoveries called forth, a theme followed out as well in J. H. Elliot's brief *The Old World and the New, 1492–1650* (1970) and in Stephen Greenblatt's *Marvelous Possessions: The Wonder of the New World* (1991). Roy Harvey

Pearce's *Savagism and Civilization: A Study of the Indian and the American Mind* (1953; 1988) goes from 1609 to the mid-nineteenth century and serves as an indispensable starting point for the literary impact of the Native American on "the American mind." In a related vein, Alfred W. Crosby traces the biological exchanges between the hemispheres in his influential *The Columbian Exchange: Biological and Cultural Consequences of 1492* (1972), while Carl O. Sauer takes up the question of how the Caribbean was altered after 1492 in *The Early Spanish Main* (1966). A similar project is carried out for New England in William Cronon's excellent *Changes in the Land: Indians, Colonists, and the Ecology of New England* (1983); for the South, see Timothy Silver, *A New Face on the Countryside: Indians, Colonists, and Slaves in the South Atlantic Forests, 1500–1800* (1990).

Among books that deal with the verbal shape of the early documents, William Carlos Williams's *In the American Grain* (1925) gives brief but evocative guidance. Howard Mumford Jones places early American culture in the context of Renaissance

Europe in *O Strange New World: American Culture, the Formative Years* (1964). In *The Machine in the Garden: Technology and the Pastoral Ideal in America* (1964), Leo Marx offers insightful readings of some Renaissance texts (such as Shakespeare's *The Tempest*) that reflect on the new lands suddenly opened to the Old World; responses to the New World (and a reading, again, of *The Tempest*) are considered in Eric Cheyfitz's *The Poetics of Imperialism: Translation and Colonization from "The Tempest" to "Tarzan"* (1991). A feminist perspective guides Annette Kolodny's *The Lay of the Land; Metaphor as Experience and History in American Life and Letters* (1975), and the opening chapters of Richard Drinnon's *Facing West: The Metaphysics of Indian-Hating and Empire-Building* (1980) offer a psychohistorical perspective. William C. Spengemann argues for the centrality of early American texts in the transformation of Western writing generally in *The Adventurous Muse: The Poetics of American Fiction, 1789–1900* (1977), John Seelye offers ingenious readings of many early texts in *Prophetic Waters: The River in Early American Life and Literature* (1977), and Wayne Franklin gives attention to sixteenth-century works in *Discoverers, Explorers, Settlers: The Diligent Writers of Early America* (1979). No generally inclusive bibliography of the literary texts of the period is available, although Joseph Sabin's massive *Biblioteca Americana: A Dictionary of Books Relating to America, from its Discovery to the Present Time*, 29 vols. (1868–1936) is invaluable. Among anthologies, the most useful are David Beers Quinn's *New American World: A Documentary History of North America to 1612*, 5 vols. (1979) and the modern editions of Richard Hakluyt's collection of 1598–1600, *The Principall Navigations, Voyages, Traffiques, & Discoveries of the English Nation*, 12 vols. (1903–1905) and Samuel Purchas's 1625 sequel to it, *Hakluytus Posthumus, or Purchas His Pilgrimes*, 20 vols. (1905–1907). The Hakluyt volumes also were reprinted in the Everyman's Library, 8 vols. (1907). A companion series to Quinn's is John H. Parry and Robert G. Keith, *New Iberian World: A Documentary History of the Discovery and Settlement of Latin America to the Early 17th Century*, 5 vols. (1984).

Arthur Barlowe

All that is known of Barlowe is summarized in David Beers Quinn's *Set Fair for Roanoke: Voyages and Colonies, 1584–1606* (1985). Quinn also provides the best text of Barlowe's "Discourse" in *The Roanoke Voyages, 1584–1590*, 2 vols. (1955; 1991).

Bartolomé de las Casas

The most important of Casas's many writings, his *General History of the Indies*, was finished by 1561, but did not see publication until the late nineteenth century. Among more recent editions in

Spanish, that edited by Agustín Millares Carlo and published in Mexico City (1951) is useful. An abridged translation by Andrée M. Collard (1971) makes part of it readily available in English. Casas's most influential text, the *Brevissima relacion*, is well rendered in Herma Briffault's translation, *The Devastation of the Indies: A Brief Account* (1974; 1992). Studies of Casas include Lewis Hanke's *Bartolomé de las Casas: An Interpretation of His Life and Writings* (1951) and Henry Raup Wagner and Helen Rand Parish, *The Life and Writings of Bartolomé de las Casa* (1967).

Samuel de Champlain

The standard (bilingual) edition is *The Works of Samuel de Champlain*, 6 vols. (1922–36), edited by H. P. Biggar and others. A useful 1-vol. English version, edited by W. L. Grant in the *Original Narratives of Early American History* series, is *Voyages of Samuel de Champlain, 1604–1618* (1907). Samuel Eliot Morison's recent biography, *Samuel de Champlain: Father of New France* (1972) is useful.

Christopher Columbus

Cecil Jane's *Select Documents Illustrating the Four Voyages of Columbus* (1930–33; 1988) is the best bilingual edition of various writings. It does not include the "journal" of the first voyage, which survives only in summaries and unreliable transcriptions by others. The best text of that problematic work is Oliver Dunn and James E. Kelley's bilingual *The Diario of Christopher Columbus's First Voyage to America, 1492–93* (1989); on the problems associated with this text (and others), see David Heninge's *In Search of Columbus: The Sources for the First Voyage* (1991). Biographies include Samuel Eliot Morison's now somewhat dated *Admiral of the Ocean Sea* (1942) and Kirkpatrick Sale's contentious *The Conquest of Paradise: Christopher Columbus and the Columbian Legacy* (1990). James Axtell's *After Columbus* (1988) and *Beyond 1492* (1992) offer excellent and broad coverage of key topics.

Hernán Cortés

The five letters sent by Cortés to Spain during the conquest of Mexico are available as *Letters from Mexico*, translated and edited by A. R. Pagden (1971), with a very good introduction by J. H. Elliott. Contemporary estimates of the man and the conquest include that of his secretary, Francisco López de Gómara, included in the *Historia de la Conquista de Mexico* (1552), parts of which are translated by Lucy Byrd Simpson as *Cortés: The Life of the Conqueror by His Secretary* (1964). An excellent Native American record of the conquest, originally assembled by Miguel Leon-Portilla in Spanish, has been translated by Lysander Kemp as *The Broken Spears* (1962). An intriguing collection of early Spanish letters is James Lockhart and Enrique Otte, *Letters and People of the Spanish*

Indies: Sixteenth Century (1976). Guidance on the complex issues associated with the fall of the Aztec empire can be found in R. C. Padden, *The Hummingbird and the Hawk: Conquest and Sovereignty in the Valley of Mexico: 1503–1541* (1967) and in Serge Gruzinski, *The Conquest of Mexico: The Incorporation of Indian Societies into the Western World, 16th–18th Centuries*, translated by Eileen Corrigan (1993).

Bernal Díaz del Castillo

A complete translation of Díaz del Castillo's *The True Story of the Conquest of New Spain* was published by A. P. Maudlslay, 5 vols. (1908–1916). This has been reissued in a 1-vol. abridgment (1956; 1970); a newer abridged translation was undertaken by J. M. Cohen, *The Conquest of New Spain* (1963).

Thomas Harriot

Muriel Rukeyser's *The Traces of Thomas Harriot* (1971) is an innovative biography. John W. Shirley's edited volume *Thomas Harriot, Renaissance Scientist* (1974) collects a number of modern studies. David Beers Quinn includes Harriot among his topics in *England and the Discovery of America, 1481–1620* (1974) and gives the best text of Harriot's *A Brief and True Report of the New Found Land of Virginia* in *The Roanoke Voyages, 1584–1590*, 2 vols. (1955; 1991). The collaborative edition of that work illustrated with engravings based on John White's drawings and watercolors has been reprinted (1972).

Iroquois Creation Stories

First published in 1851, Lewis Henry Morgan's *League of the Iroquois* remains a fine overview and introduction (1972, with an introduction by William Fenton) to all things Iroquoian. Daniel K. Richter's *The Ordeal of the Longhouse: The Peoples of the Iroquois League in the Era of European Colonization* (1992) is a brilliant recent volume that covers the basic elements of Iroquois language, culture, and history and begins with a fine overview of Iroquois cosmogonic myths. It refers to and builds on the work of the leading specialist in Iroquois culture, William Fenton, whose "This Island, the World on the Turtle's Back," *Journal of American Folklore*, 75 (1962), 283–300, is probably still the richest analysis of Iroquois mythology available. For the most detailed versions of the stories themselves, the reader must consult J. N. B. Hewitt's "Iroquoian Cosmology," part I, Bureau of American Ethnology, *Annual Report, 1899–1900* (1903) and "Iroquoian Cosmology," part II, Bureau of American Ethnology, *Annual Report, 1925–6* (1928). Also worth consulting is the Seneca ethnologist Arthur C. Parker's *Seneca Myths and Folk Tales*, Buffalo Historical Society Publications No. 27 (1923). In addition to these scholarly accounts, Edmund Wilson's meditation on the Iroquois, *Apologies to the Iroquois* (1960) remains fascinating. Also worth consulting is the work of the contemporary Abenaki poet and storyteller Joseph Bruchac, in particular his *Iroquois Stories: Heroes and Heroines, Monsters and Magic* (1985) and his edited volume, *New Voices from the Longhouse: An Anthology of Contemporary Iroquois Writing* (1989).

Native American Oral Literature

A. Lavonne Brown Ruoff's *American Indian Literatures: An Introduction, Bibliographic Review, and Selected Bibliography* (1990) is a good sourcebook on oral literature, as is William M. Clements and Frances M. Malpezzi's *Native American Folklore, 1879–1979* (1984), which presents a useful bibliography for the study of many sorts of oral literature. Ruoff's "The Survival of Tradition: American Indian Oral and Written Narratives," *Massachusetts Review* (1986) begins by surveying Native American oral story and storytelling traditions. John Miles Foley, in *Oral Tradition in Literature: Interpretation in Context* (1986), offers six essays that deal with the aesthetics of oral and orally derived works. Although focused on the European oral tradition, the essays raise issues of concern for the study of American Indian oral literatures. Paula Gunn Allen has edited *Studies in Native American Literature: Critical Essays and Course Designs* (1983), which begins with a section on oral literature. The first two chapters of Andrew Wiget's *Native American Literature* (1985) also are valuable introductions to oral narrative and oratory and oral poetry. Karl Kroeber has edited *Traditional Literatures of the American Indian: Texts and Interpretations* (1981), which presents, as the title indicates, both texts and interpretations, the best of which are Dennis Tedlock's "The Spoken Word and the Work of Interpretation in American Indian Religion" and Barre Toelken and Tacheeni Scott's "Poetic Retranslation and the 'Pretty Languages' of Yellowman." Toelken transcribes another tale by the Navajo storyteller Yellowman in "Life and Death in the Navajo Coyote Tales," in *Recovering the Word: Essays on Native American Literatures*, edited by Brian Swann and Arnold Krupat (1987), the introduction to which is also useful. Swann's edited volume *On the Translation of Native American Literatures* (1992) contains several fine essays. Krupat has edited *New Voices in Native American Literary Criticism* (1993), which contains some of the most recent work on oral narrative both in English and in native languages (see especially the essays by Geoffrey Kimball, Ridie Wilson Ghezzi, and Kathleen Danker).

Álvar Núñez Cabeza de Vaca

An excellent colloquial translation of *La Relacion* is Cyclone Covey's *Cabeza de Vaca's Adventures in the Unknown Interior of America* (1961; 1983). This relies on studies of Cabeza de Vaca's itinerary by Cleve Hallenbeck, *Álvar Núñez Cabeza de Vaca: The Journey and Route of the First European* to Cross the Continent of North America, 1534–1536 (1940; 1971) and Carl O. Sauer, Sixteenth-Century North America (1971). Morris Bishop's The Odyssey of Cabeza de Vaca (1933) treats the whole of the life, including the later South American episodes. Cabeza de Vaca's Río de la Plata narrative, Comentarios (1555), was translated by Luis L. Dominguez in The Conquest of the River Plate (1891). A fictional account of Estevánico, the Moorish slave who was one of the four survivors of the Cabeza de Vaca party, is offered in Daniel Panger, Black Ulysses (1982). Interesting later notes on Cabeza de Vaca and Estevánico are to be found in the various narratives of the Coronado expedition collected in George Parker Winship and Frederick Webb Hodge, The Journey of Francisco Vázquez de Coronado, 1540–1542 (1933; 1990).

George Percy

Percy's "Discourse" is reprinted in Philip L. Barbour's edited volumes The Jamestown Voyages under the First Charter, 1606–1609, 2 vols. (1969). His later Jamestown text, "A True Relation of the Proceedings . . . in Virginia . . . 1609–1612," has been published in Tyler's Quarterly Historical and Genealogical Magazine, 3 (1922), 259–82. On both texts, see Philip L. Barbour, "The Honorable George Percy: Premier Chronicler of the First Virginia Voyage," Early American Literature, 6 (1971), 7–17.

Pima Stories of the Beginning of the World

Ruth M. Underhill's studies in the 1930s and 1940s of the Pima (and their close relatives the Tohono O'odham [Papago] are still useful for the student who would like to learn more about the history and culture of these Southwestern desert peoples. Her Singing for Power: The Song Magic of the Papago Indians of Southern Arizona (1938, 1973, 1993) is still valuable, as is her Rainhouse and Ocean: Speeches for the Papago Year

(1979). Dean Saxton and Lucille Saxton's Legends and Lore of the Papago and Pima Indians (1973) offers some creation stories in both English translation and the original language. Somewhat more specialized, but of great importance, is Donald M. Bahr's Pima and Papago Ritual Oratory: A Study of Three Texts (1975, 1988). Bahr's Oriole Songs (1994) is a collection, with extended commentaries, of one variety of Pima "dream songs" still being sung today. For an intimate and personal view of these people, see Underhill's Maria Chona: The Autobiography of a Papago Woman, which was reprinted as Papago Woman (1979). A specifically Pima autobiography is that of Anna Moore Shaw, A Pima Past (1974), which details the customs of the Pimas.

John Smith

A recent, definitive edition of Smith's many writings is The Complete Works of Captain John Smith, edited by Philip Barbour in 3 vols. (1986). The best single book on John Smith is Everett H. Emerson's Captain John Smith (1971), but for a more expansive treatment of Smith's life the student can turn to Bradford Smith's Captain John Smith, His Life and Legend (1953) and Philip L. Barbour's The Three Worlds of Captain John Smith (1964). A useful descriptive bibliography can be found in American Prose in 1820, edited by Donald Yanella and John H. Roche (1979).

John White

David Beers Quinn surveys what is known of White's life in Set Fair for Roanoke: Voyages and Colonies, 1584–1606 (1985) and gives a good text of White's various writings in The Roanoke Voyages, 1584–1590, 2 vols. (1955; 1991). The graphic works are described in the latter book, and reproduced in Quinn and Paul Hulton, The American Drawings of John White (1964). Hulton has also published America 1585: The Complete Drawings of John White (1984).

EARLY AMERICAN LITERATURE 1620–1820

The classic study of the Puritans remains Perry Miller's The New England Mind: The Seventeenth Century (1939) and The New England Mind: From Colony to Province (1953). Useful essays by Miller are included in Errand into the Wilderness ("The Marrow of Puritan Divinity" and "From Edwards to Emerson" are especially important) (1956). Miller and Thomas H. Johnson edited an anthology of The Puritans: A Sourcebook of Their Writings in 1938 (rev. ed., 1963), which contains useful introductions. A valuable collection, Seventeenth-Century American Poetry (1968), was compiled by Harrison T. Meserole. Peter White edited Puritan Poets and Poetics in 1985. Patricia Caldwell discusses Puritan "relations" (accounts of con-

versions or spiritual autobiographies) in The Puritan Conversion Narrative (1983). Other books of general interest are Edmund S. Morgan's Visible Saints: The History of a Puritan Idea (1963) and Kenneth B. Murdock's Literature and Theology in Colonial New England (1949). On Puritan historians, see Peter Gay's Loss of Mastery (1966) and David Levin's In Defense of Historical Literature (1967). Sacvan Bercovich has edited a useful collection of essays on the Puritans in The American Puritan Imagination: Essays in Revaluation (1974); it contains a good selected bibliography. Another useful revaluation of Puritans which brings together some hard-to-come-by essays is Michael McGiffert's Puritanism and the American

Experience (1969). Some of the best accounts of the intellectual and cultural life of the 17th century are to be found in the biographies of writers included in this anthology. One important study of a writer not included is Edmund Morgan's life of Ezra Stiles, *The Gentle Puritan* (1962).

Although the bicentennial year produced a number of useful studies of American culture in the 18th century, nothing has replaced Moses Coit Tyler's monumental *A History of American Literature during the Colonial Period, 1607–1765*, 2 vols. (1878; rev. ed., 1897; 1-vol. reprint, 1949) and *The Literary History of the American Revolution, 1763–1783*, 2 vols. (1897; 1-vol. reprint, 1941). Readers should be warned, however, to check biographical details with more recent studies. Russel B. Nye's *The Cultural Life of the New Nation* (1960), Kenneth Silverman's *A Cultural History of the American Revolution* (1976), and Michael Kammer's *A Season of Youth* (1978) are useful surveys of the arts of this period. On the American Revolution, see Edmund S. Morgan's *The American Revolution: Two Centuries of Interpretation* (1965). *Fifteen American Authors before 1900: Bibliograhic Essays on Research and Criticism*, ed. Robert A. Rees and Earl N. Harbert (1971), contains discursive chapters on the scholarship and criticism that had appeared up to that date on three authors in this period: Edwards, Franklin, and Taylor. *American Prose to 1820: A Guide to Information Sources*, ed. Donald Yannella and John H. Roch (1979), provides a helpful description of primary works and secondary sources. Writers like Anne Bradstreet and Edward Taylor are included because they wrote prose as well as poetry. Mason Lowance discusses metaphor and symbol from the Puritans to the Transcendentalists in *The Language of Canaan* (1980).

John Adams and Abigail Adams

The best biography of John Adams is the two-volume study written by Page Smith (1962). The best biography of Abigail Adams is Lynne Withey's *Dearest Friend* (1981). Paul C. Nagel has written a useful study of *The Adams Women* (1987). Earlier editions of the letters written between John and Abigail Adams have been superseded by the *Adams Family Correspondence* (1963), a two-volume collection edited by Lyman H. Butterfield.

Elizabeth Ashbridge

The best discussion of Mrs. Ashbridge's *Account* will be found in Daniel B. Shea, Jr.'s *Spiritual Autobiography in Early America* (1968). All editions other than that published in Nantwich, England, in 1774 and reprinted here should be treated skeptically.

Joel Barlow

The Writings of Joel Barlow (1970), ed. W. K. Bottorff and Arthur L. Ford, reprints Barlow's work. The best life is James L. Woodress's *A Yankee's*

Odyssey (1958). Leon Howard's *The Connecticut Wits* (1943) contains useful bibliographical information. Every student of Barlow's poetry will profit from J. A. Leo Lemay's "The contexts and themes of 'The Hasty Pudding,' " *Early American Literature*, Vol. 17 (1982), pp. 3–23

William Bartram

The best edition of *The Travels* is the "naturalist's edition" by Francis Harper (1958). N. B. Fagin's *William Bartram, Interpreter of the American Landscape* (1933) and Ernest Earnest's *John and William Bartram* (1940) are useful biographies.

Robert Beverley

Useful discussions of Beverley's *History* may be found in the introduction to Louis B. Wright's edition of *The History and Present State of Virginia* (1947; reprinted 1968) and in Louis P. Simpson's *The Dispossessed Garden: Pastoral and History in Southern Literature* (1975).

William Bradford

Samuel Eliot Morison's edition of *Of Plymouth Plantation* (1952) is the standard edition of Bradford's history, and his life of Bradford in *The Dictionary of American Biography* (1933) is useful. For a discussion of Puritan historians, see Kenneth B. Murdock's *Literature and Theology in Colonial New England* (1949) and David Levin's "William Bradford: The Value of Puritan Historiography," in E. H. Emerson's *Major Writers of Early American Literature* (1972), pp. 11–31.

Anne Bradstreet

The standard edition is now Jeannine Hensley's *The Works of Anne Bradstreet* (1967), with an introduction by Adrienne Rich. Useful critical discussions may be found in Josephine K. Piercy's *Anne Bradstreet* (1965), Elizabeth W. White's *Anne Bradstreet: The Tenth Muse* (1971), and Ann Stanford's *Anne Bradstreet: The Worldly Puritan* (1974).

William Byrd

Byrd's prose works are available in an edition edited by Louis B. Wright (1966). *The Secret Diary of William Byrd of Westover, 1709–1712* was edited by Louis B. Wright and Marion Tinling (1941). *Another Secret Diary of William Byrd of Westover, 1739–1741*, ed. M. H. Woodfin and M. Tinling, appeared in 1942. Byrd's *London Diary* (1958) was edited by Louis B. Wright and Marion Tinling. A provocative new study is Kenneth A. Lockridge's *The Diary, and Life, of William Byrd II of Virginia, 1674–1744* (1987). A useful critical essay is Lewis P. Simpson's "William Byrd and the South," *Early American Literature*, Vol. 7 (1972), pp. 187–95.

St. Jean de Crèvecoeur

Sketches of Eighteenth Century America, More Letters of St. John de Crèvecoeur (1925) was edited by H. L. Bourdin *et al. Eighteenth Century Travels* in *Pennsylvania and New York* (1962) was edited by P. G. Adams. The best biographies are by Thomas Philbrick (1970) and Gay Wilson Allen and Roger Asselineau (1987).

Jonathan Edwards
Yale University Press is in the process of publishing a complete edition of the works of Jonathan Edwards. A selection from Edwards's writings edited by Clarence H. Faust and Thomas H. Johnson (1935) contains a useful introduction and bibliography. David Levin's *Jonathan Edwards: A Profile* (1969) includes Samuel Hopkins's *Life and Character of the Late Rev. Mr. Jonathan Edwards* (1765). Perry Miller's *Jonathan Edwards* (1949) and essays included in *Errand into the Wilderness* (1956) are indispensable. Daniel B. Shea, Jr., includes a discussion of the *Personal Narrative* in his *Spiritual Autobiography in Early America* (1968). Richard Bushman writes of "Jonathan Edwards as a Great Man" in *Soundings*, Vol. 52 (1969), pp. 15–46, and Patricia J. Tracy considers the implications of his career in *Jonathan Edwards, Pastor* (1980).

Olaudah Equiano
The Interesting Narrative has been edited by Paul Edwards (1969) using the edition of 1789, and Henry Louis Gates (in his *Classic Slave Narratives* (1987)) using the edition of 1814. Both contain useful introductions. Sidney Kaplan in his study of *The Black Presence in the Era of the American Revolution 1770–1800* (1973) discusses the American publication of Equiano's *Narrative*.

The Federalist
A very useful introduction to *The Federalist* papers is found in Benjamin Fletcher Wright's edition of 1961.

Benjamin Franklin
The Papers of Benjamin Franklin are being published by Yale University Press under the general editorship of Leonard W. Labaree. A good selection of Franklin's writings may be found in *Benjamin Franklin: Representative Selections* (1936), ed. F. L. Mott and C. L. Jorgensen. The standard biography is by Carl Van Doren (1938). Useful critical studies include Bruce I. Granger's *Benjamin Franklin, an American Man of Letters* (1964) and Alfred O. Aldridge's *Benjamin Franklin and Nature's God* (1967). See also David Levin, "The Autobiography of Benjamin Franklin: The Puritan Experimenter in Life and Art," *Yale Review*, Vol. 53 (1964), pp. 258–75. A famous unfavorable response to Franklin can be found in D. H. Lawrence's *Studies in Classic American Literature* (1923). Franklin's early years are discussed in A. B. Tourtellot's *Benjamin Franklin: The Boston Years* (1977).

Philip Freneau
The standard edition of *The Poems of Philip Freneau* is that of F. L. Pattee, 3 vols. (1902–1907).

Lewis Leary, who edited *The Last Poems of Philip Freneau* (1945), wrote the best biography, *That Rascal Freneau: A Study in Literary Failure* (1941). A very useful introduction to Freneau can be found in Harry H. Clark's edition of *Philip Freneau: Representative Selections* (1929). Richard C. Vitzhum offers a study of Freneau's lyrics in *Land and Sea* (1978).

Thomas Jefferson
Princeton University Press, under the general editorship of Julian P. Boyd, is currently engaged in publishing the *Papers of Thomas Jefferson*. The best biography is Dumas Malone's six-volume *Jefferson and His Time* (1948–1981). Mr. Malone's article on Jefferson in *The Dictionary of American Biography* is very helpful. Recent critical studies include those of M. D. Peterson, *Thomas Jefferson and the New Nation* (1970) and Garry Wills, *Inventing America: Jefferson's Declaration of Independence* (1978). Fawn Brodie published a controversial biograpy in 1974. Jefferson's Monticello is the subject of a distinguished study by William Howard Adams (1983).

Sarah Kemble Knight
A useful biographical sketch can be found in *The Dictionary of American Biography* by Sidney Gunn (1933). G. P. Winship's edition of the *Private Journal* (1920) contains Theodore Dwight's original introduction to the first edition (1825).

Cotton Mather
Kenneth Silverman's *The Life and Times of Cotton Mather* (1984) supersedes earlier biographies like that of Barrett Wendell (1891), but the introduction to Kenneth B. Murdock's *Selections from Cotton Mather* (1926) is still useful. In addition to Silverman's biography interested students will want to read David Levin's *Cotton Mather: The Young Life of the Lord's Remembrancer* (1978) and Robert Middlekauff's *The Mathers: Three Generations of Puritan Intellectuals* (1971). Sacvan Bercovich has written about Mather in *Major Writers of Early American Literature*, ed. E. H. Emerson (1972), and in his influential book *The Puritan Origins of the American Self* (1975).

Thomas Morton
The introduction to Charles Francis Adams's edition of *New English Canaan* (1883) answers a number of questions about the life of this enigmatic figure, but the interested student will also want to read *Thomas Morton* by Donald F. Connors (1969).

Samson Occom
The published writings of Samson Occom are *A Short Narrative of My Life*, composed in 1768 but first published in Berndt Peyer's edited volume *The Elders Wrote: An Anthology of Early Prose by North American Indians 1768–1931* (1982); *A Sermon Preached at the Execution of Moses Paul, an*

Indian (1772); and *A Choice Collection of Hymns and Spiritual Songs, Intended for the Edification of Sincere Christians of All Denominations* (1774). After his death, Occom's account of the culture of the Montauks among whom he had lived and worked was published as "An Account of the Montauk Indians, on Long-Island," *Collections of the Massachusetts Historical Society* 10 (1809), 105–11. Harold Blodgett's *Samson Occom*, Dartmouth College Manuscript Series No. 3 (1935), is dated, but full of useful biographical information; Blodgett also reprints most of Occom's extant letters. Preceding Blodgett's study was Leon Burr Richardson's *An Indian Preacher in England* Dartmouth College Manuscript Series No. 2 (1933), which offers documents relating to Occom's fundraising trip to England. Berndt Peyer's "Samson Occom, Mohegan Missionary of the 18th Century," *American Indian Quarterly* 6, nos. 3–4 (1982), 208–17 offers a brief biographical account of Occom. "Christian Indians: Samson Occom and William Apes," in David Murray's *Forked Tongues: Speech, Writing and Representation in North American Indian Texts* (1991) is the most recent consideration—a very fine one—of Occom.

Thomas Paine
Moncure D. Conway, who edited *The Writings of Thomas Paine*, 4 vols. (1894–1896), wrote the best life of Paine (1892). H. H. Clark's *Thomas Paine: Representative Selections* (1944) contains a very helpful introduction. Cecil Kenyon's "Where Paine Went Wrong," *American Political Science Review*, Vol. 45 (1951), pp. 1086–89, is a challenging critical assessment. A more recent biography is that by David F. Hawke (1974).

Mary Rowlandson
Richard Slotkin's *Regeneration through Violence* (1973) contains a useful discussion of Mrs. Rowlandson's captivity. See also R. H. Pearce's "The Significance of the Captivity Narrative," *American Literature*, Vol. 19 (1947), pp. 1–20.

Samuel Sewall
The Diary of Samuel Sewall, 1674–1729, ed. M. Halsey Thomas (1973), is now the standard edition and preferred over that published by the Massachusetts Historical Society from 1878 to 1882. Thomas's edition includes "The Selling of Joseph," but the introduction and commentary in Sidney Kaplan's edition (1969) is valuable for what it tells us about slavery in New England. Ola E. Winslow has written a succinct biography (1964).

John Smith
The best single book on John Smith is Everett H. Emerson's *Captain John Smith* (1971), but for a more expansive treatment of Smith's life the student can turn to Bradford Smith's *Captain John Smith, His Life and Legend* (1953) and Philip L.

Barbour's *The Three Worlds of Captain John Smith* (1964). A useful descriptive bibliography can be found in *American Prose to 1820*, ed. Donald Yannella and John H. Roch (1979).

Edward Taylor
The standard edition of *The Poems of Edward Taylor* is by Donald E. Stanford (1960). Taylor's *Diary* was edited by Francis Murphy (1964) and his *Christographia* sermons (1962) and *Treatise Concerning the Lord's Supper* (1966) by Norman S. Grabo, who has also written the best critical biography (1961). Thomas M. and Virginia L. Davis are presently editing the "unpublished" writings of Edward Taylor: *Church Records and Related Sermons; Edward Taylor vs. Solomon Stoddard*; and *The Minor Poetry* appeared in 1981. All three volumes contain significant introductory material.

Royall Tyler
The Contrast has been reprinted in *Representative American Plays*, ed. Arthur Hobson Quinn (1917) and separately as *The Contrast: A Comedy in Five Acts* (1920, 1970). Other plays are in *Four Plays*, ed. Arthur Wallace Peach annd George Floyd Newbrough (1941). Tyler's novel *The Algerine Captive* has been edited by Donald L. Cook (1970). A useful study is G. Thomas Tanselle, *Royall Tyler* (1967).

Phillis Wheatley
The best edition of the poems is that edited by Julian D. Mason (1966). Shirley Graham's *The Story of Phillis Wheatley* (1969) and William G. Allen's *Wheatley, Banneker and Horton* (1970) are useful critical biographies.

Michael Wigglesworth
Kenneth B. Murdock's edition of *The Day of Doom* (1929) includes a valuable introduction. Wigglesworth's *Diary* has been edited by Edmund S. Morgan (1970). The standard life is Richard Crowder's *No Featherbed to Heaven* (1962).

Roger Williams
There are a number of distinguished studies of Roger Williams, but the best of these are Perry Miller's *Roger Williams: His Contribution to the American Tradition* (1953), Ola E. Winslow's *Roger Williams* (1957), Edmund S. Morgan's *Roger Williams: The Church and the State* (1967), and Henry Chupack's *Roger Williams* (1969). *The Complete Writings of Roger Williams* (1963) includes a valuable essay by Perry Miller as an introduction to Volume 7.

John Winthrop
The standard edition of Winthrop's work is *The Winthrop Papers*, ed. A. Forbes, 5 vols. (1929–1945). For critical biographies see D. B. Rutman's *Winthrop's Boston* (1965) and Edmund

Morgan's *The Puritan Dilemma: The Story of John Winthrop* (1965). For a history of the Journal see Richard S. Dunn's "John Winthrop Writes his Journal," *William and Mary Quarterly*, Vol. 41 (1984), pp. 185–212. A more sympathetic treatment of Mrs. Hutchinson can be found in Philip F. Gura's *A Glimpse of Sion's Glory* (1984).

John Woolman

The standard edition is *The Journal and Major Essays of John Woolman*, ed. Phillips P. Moulton (1971). Amelia M. Gummere's edition of the journal (1927) contains a useful introduction. See also Daniel B. Shea, Jr., *Spiritual Autobiography in Early America* (1968).

AMERICAN LITERATURE 1820–1865

Eight American Authors: A Review of Research and Criticism (rev. ed.), edited by James Woodress (1971), contains chapters on the scholarship and criticism that had appeared on Poe, Emerson, Hawthorne, Thoreau, Whitman, and Melville up to 1969 (the other two of the eight authors are Clemens and James). *Fifteen American Authors before 1900: Bibliographic Essays on Research and Criticism*, edited by Robert A. Rees and Earl N. Harbert (1971, 1984), contains chapters on Bryant, Cooper, Dickinson, Holmes, Irving, Longfellow, Lowell, and Whittier as well as a section on the Southern humorists. The essays in these two volumes may be supplemented (especially for recent scholarship and criticism) by the various volumes of *American Literary Scholarship: An Annual*, published each year since 1965. Separate chapters in *American Literary Scholarship* are devoted to Hawthorne, Poe, and Melville, while one chapter is devoted to "Emerson, Thoreau, and Transcendentalism" and another to "Whitman and Dickinson." Work on other writers of this period is covered in the chapter on "19th-century Literature." (The volumes appear two years after the works they discuss.)

Documentary discoveries in the last three decades have rendered all histories of American literature badly out of date, although the chapters on this period in the most ambitious such work, the mammoth *Literary History of the United States*, edited by Robert E. Spiller et al. (1948, 1974), are still useful; the second volume of the 1974 edition is an updated biography of studies on American writers. *The Columbia Literary History of the United States* (1988), edited by Emory Elliott, is a product of the "New Historicism." According to the general introduction, traditional sources of knowledge about episodes of literary history ("old records, diaries, letters, newspapers, official firsthand documents") are eschewed by the writers of the chapters, who are described not as truthtellers but as storytellers who aim to convince their readers "not by facts but by persuasive rhetoric and narrative skill." The most influential critical study of this period remains F. O. Matthiessen's *American Renaissance: Art and Expression in the Age of Emerson and Whitman* (1941, 1968), although it is outdated, especially in its reliance on now-superseded biographies. Walter Harding has called Law-

rence Buell's *Literary Transcendentalism* (1973) "perhaps the most significant volume in the field since Matthiessen's." Still more important is Buell's *New England Literary Culture: From Revolution through Renaissance* (1986). Essential are *Critical Essays on American Transcendentalism*, edited by Philip F. Gura and Joel Myerson (1982), and *The Transcendentalists: A Review of Research and Criticism*, edited by Joel Myerson (1984). For study of the poetry of the period Roy Harvey Pearce's *The Continuity of American Poetry* (1961) is now supplemented by Hyatt H. Waggoner's *American Poets from the Puritans to the Present* (1968) and Philip K. Jason's *Nineteenth Century Poetry: An Annotated Bibliography* (1989). A useful discussion of literature popular at the time of *The Scarlet Letter* and *Moby-Dick* is David Reynolds's *Beneath the American Renaissance* (1988). Gale is printing a multivolume *Dictionary of Literary Biography* (*DAB*), arranged by regions and unevenly edited. Two especially good volumes, both edited by Joel Myerson, are *The American Renaissance in New England* (1978) and *Antebellum Writers in New York and the South* (1979). Stanley Trachtenberg edited *American Humorists 1800–1950* (1982). Important specialized works are *The History of Southern Literature*, by Louis D. Rubin, Jr., et al. (1985, 1990) and Blyden Jackson's *A History of Afro-American Literature: The Long Beginnings, 1746–1895* (1989). Major new studies in literary history, biography, and criticism are appearing as scholars and critics assimilate information about the period, notably that being published in volumes sponsored by the Center for Editions of American Authors and, subsequently, by the Center for Scholarly Editions.

William Apess

As early as 1928, Ernest Sutherland Bates wrote about Apess for the *Dictionary of American Biography*, and in 1983 James D. Hart also noticed Apess in *The Oxford Companion to American Literature*. Kim McQuaid's "William Apes, A Pequot: An Indian Reformer in the Jackson Era," *New England Quarterly* (1977), 605–25, is probably the first study fully to recognize the potential significance of Apess's work. Arnold Krupat, in *The Voice in the Margin: Native American Literature and the Canon* (1989) and *Ethnocriticism: Ethnography,*

History, Literature (1992), has offered readings of Apess's major works. A. Lavonne Brown Ruoff's essay "Three Nineteenth-Century American-Indian Autobiographers," in Ruoff and Jerry Ward, Jr.'s edited *Redefining American Literary History* (1990), also comments on Apess. David Murray's *Forked Tongues: Speech, Writing, and Representation in North American Indian Texts* (1991) has some informative and sophisticated discussions of Apess. The complete works of Apess have been superbly edited by Barry O'Connell, in a volume called *On Our Own Ground: The Complete Writings of William Apess, A Pequot* (1992). O'Connell's lengthy introduction and notes provide the indispensable starting point for any further study of Apess.

William Cullen Bryant

Bryant's poetry has not been reedited according to modern standards, and his newspaper writing is mostly buried in the files of the *New York Evening Post*. William Cullen Bryant II and Thomas G. Voss edited in six volumes *The Letters of William Cullen Bryant* (1975–92). Earlier biographies are superseded by Charles H. Brown's *William Cullen Bryant* (1971). Judith Turner Phair has compiled *A Bibliography of William Cullen Bryant and His Critics, 1808–1972* (1975). The best guide to work on Bryant is the chapter by James E. Rocks in *Fifteen American Authors before 1900*, edited by Robert A. Rees and Earl N. Harbert (1971, 1984), supplemented by the annual *American Literary Scholarship* (1963–).

Cherokee Memorials

The relevant documents relating to the dispute among Georgia, President Andrew Jackson, and the Cherokee Nation can be found in Allen Guttmann and Van R. Halsey's edited volume *States Rights and Indian Removal: The Cherokee Nation v. the State of Georgia* (1965). Grace Steele Woodward's *The Cherokees* (1963) is full of useful information, although rather paternalistic in its manner. More in touch with Cherokee reality is the Cherokee Rennard Strickland's *The Fire and the Spirits* (1975), an excellent introduction to the Cherokee world. Grant Foreman's *Indian Removal* (1932, 1972) tells the story not only of Cherokee removal but of "the emigration of the Five Civilized Tribes of Indians." A detailed psychohistorical approach to Jackson and the American Indians is Michael Paul Rogin's *Fathers and Children: Andrew Jackson and the Subjugation of the American Indian* (1975). Some sense of traditional Cherokee oral performances can be got from James Mooney's *The Swimmer Manuscript: Cherokee Sacred Formulas and Medicinal Prescriptions*, revised and edited by Frans M. Olbrechts (1932). Mooney's *Myths of the Cherokee* (1900, 1970) is also worth consulting. The only study of the Cherokee Memorials to date is Arnold Krupat's "Figures and the Law: Rhetorical Readings of Congressional

and Cherokee Texts," in his *Ethnocriticism: Ethnography, History, Literature* (1992).

James Fenimore Cooper

The late James Franklin Beard was editor-in-chief of a long-planned and, after 1979, fast-appearing collected edition of Cooper's *Writings*, well edited and enhanced by contemporary illustrations, including many of scenes from Cooper's novels. Beard edited the six-volume *Letters and Journals of James Fenimore Cooper* (1960–1968), the most important work of Cooper scholarship.

Reputation studies include Marcel Clavel's *Fenimore Cooper and His Critics: American, British and French Criticisms of the Novelist's Early Work* (1938) and George Dekker and John P. McWilliams's *Fenimore Cooper: The Critical Heritage* (1973). The early collection *James Fenimore Cooper: A Re-Appraisal*, edited by Mary E. Cunningham (1954), lived up to its title, consolidating gains in the understanding of Cooper and pointing toward needed work. The best guide to work on Cooper is the chapter by James Franklin Beard in *Fifteen American Authors before 1900*, edited by Robert A. Rees and Earl N. Harbert (1971, 1984), supplemented by the annual *American Literary Scholarship* (1963–).

Rebecca Harding Davis

Until recently Davis has been best known in the writings about her son Richard Harding Davis, especially her son Charles Belmont Davis's *The Adventures and Letters of Richard Harding Davis* (1917) and Gerald Langford's *The Richard Harding Davis Years* (1961). Davis published some reminiscences in *Bits of Gossip* (1904). The fullest recent account is Tillie Olsen's very personal "Biographical Interpretation" in the Feminist Press reprint of *Life in the Iron-Mills* (1972).

Emily Dickinson

Three volumes of *The Poems of Emily Dickinson* (1955) were edited by Thomas H. Johnson, and he and Theodora Ward edited three companion volumes of *The Letters of Emily Dickinson* (1958). Of great importance to Dickinson scholars is R. W. Franklin's brilliantly edited and magnificently reproduced *The Manuscript Books of Emily Dickinson* (1981), which provides, in two volumes, facsimiles of the handsewn fascicles of poems Dickinson left behind at her death. Jay Leyda's *The Years and Hours of Emily Dickinson* (1960) provides two volumes of documents crucial to the understanding of her life and time. Richard B. Sewall's *The Life of Emily Dickinson* (1974) is the most ambitious and detailed life, but Thomas H. Johnson's *Emily Dickinson: An Interpretive Biography* (1955) remains a valuable treatment. Also important is Ralph W. Franklin's *The Editing of Emily Dickinson: A Reconsideration* (1967). The sensational story of the love affair between Austin Dickinson and Mabel Loomis Todd is at last told in Polly Longsworth's *Austin and Mabel: The*

Amherst Affair (1984). Two valuable resources are Vivian Pollak, *A Poet's Parents: The Courtship Letters of Emily Norcross and Edward Dickinson* (1988) and Polly Longsworth's *The World of Emily Dickinson* (1990).

Since the rediscovery of Dickinson in the 1930s and 1940s, the quality of critical studies has been immense.

Two works have been particularly influential in the move in recent years to consider Dickinson from a feminist perspective: Sandra M. Gilbert and Susan Gubar's *The Madwoman in the Attic: The Woman Writer and the Nineteenth-Century Literary Imagination* (1979) and Margaret Homans's *Women Writers and Poetic Identity* (1980). Books that pursue this line of inquiry include Barbara Antonina Clarke Mossberg's *Emily Dickinson: When a Writer Is a Daughter* (1982), Susan Juhasz's *The Undiscovered Continent: Emily Dickinson and the Space of the Mind* (1983), and the same author's collection of essays, *Feminist Critics Read Emily Dickinson* (1983). Tendentious but thorough is Cynthia Griffin Wolff, *Emily Dickinson* (1986). The masterpiece of this feminist scholarship and criticism is Judith Farr's *The Passion of Emily Dickinson* (1992).

Valuable research tools are Joseph Duchac's *The Poems of Emily Dickinson: An Annotated Guide to Commentary Published in English, 1890–1977* (1979), Karen Dandurand, *Dickinson Scholarship: An Annotated Bibliography 1969–1985* (1988), and the treasure-trove compiled by Willis J. Buckingham, *Emily Dickinson's Reception in the 1890s* (1989). S. P. Rosenbaum has compiled *A Concordance to the Poems of Emily Dickinson* (1964).

Frederick Douglass
No uniform edition of Douglass's writings is available, but one is under way at Yale University under the editorship of John Blassingame. Four volumes have appeared since 1979. Houston A. Baker, Jr., has edited and supplied a useful introduction to a reprint of the 1st edition of Douglass's *Narrative of the Life of Frederick Douglass, an American Slave* (1982). Philip S. Foner edited *The Life and Writings of Frederick Douglass* in five volumes (1950–75). Foner's biography, *Frederick Douglass: A Biography* (1964), has been replaced as the standard work by William S. McFeely's superb *Frederick Douglass* (1991), which also contains an extensive bibliography. Other biographies of interest include Charles W. Chesnutt's *Frederick Douglass* (1899), Benjamin Quarles's excellent *Frederick Douglass* (1948), Arna W. Bontemps's *Free at Last: The Life of Frederick Douglass* (1971), and Nathan Irvin Huggins's *Slave and Citizen: The Life of Frederick Douglass* (1980). Brilliant historical detective work is contained in Dickson J. Preston's *Young Frederick Douglass* (1980); Waldo E. Martin, Jr.'s *The Mind of Frederick Douglass* (1984), as its title suggests, offers a full-scale intellectual

biography. Important pioneering essays dealing with the *Narrative* are to be found in the collection edited by Robert B. Stepto and Dexter Fisher, *Afro-American Literature: The Reconstruction of Instruction* (1978), and an unusually rich group of original essays in Eric J. Sundquist's *Frederick Douglass: New Literary and Historical Essays* (1990); William L. Andrews's *Critical Essays on Frederick Douglass* (1991) contains both early reviews and current views. Vol. 1 of Blyden Jackson's *A History of Afro-American Literature: The Long Beginning, 1746–1895* (1989) puts Douglass in one of his contexts. These volumes will in turn introduce the reader to the rapidly growing scholarship on Douglass, slave narratives, and traditions of writing by black men and women that have begun to be recovered and interpreted.

Ralph Waldo Emerson
The outstanding achievement in Emerson scholarship is the *Journals and Miscellaneous Notebooks*, edited by George P. Clark, Merrell R. Davis, Alfred R. Ferguson, Harrison Hayford, and Merton M. Sealts, Jr., later joined by Linda Allardt, Ralph H. Orth, J. E. Parsons, A. W. Plumstead, and Susan Sutton Smith under editor-in-chief William H. Gilman (1960–1977), and completed under Orth's direction. Robert E. Spiller and Alfred R. Ferguson edited the 1849 *Nature, Addresses, and Lectures* (1971). Stephen E. Whicher, Robert E. Spiller, and Wallace E. Williams edited *Early Lectures*, 3 vols. (1959–1972). Ralph H. Orth is editor-in-chief of *The Topical Notebooks of Ralph Waldo Emerson*; Susan Sutton Smith edited the first volume (1990). *The Complete Sermons of Ralph Waldo Emerson* are available in four volumes (1989), under the chief editorship of Albert J. von Frank. Merton M. Sealts, Jr., and Alfred R. Ferguson edited *Emerson's "Nature": Origin, Growth, Meaning* (1969), of which Sealts has prepared a revision (1979). Ralph L. Rusk's six-volume *Letters* (1939) must be supplemented by *The Correspondence of Emerson and Carlyle*, edited by Joseph Slater (1964), and other compilations. Eric W. Carlson has edited *Emerson's Literary Criticism* (1979).

The most detailed biography is Ralph L. Rusk's *The Life of Ralph Waldo Emerson* (1949), now supplemented by Joel Porte's *Representative Man: Ralph Waldo Emerson in His Time* (1979) and Gay Wilson Allen's *Waldo Emerson* (1981). Emerson's life is partly told in *The Life of Lidian Jackson Emerson by Ellen Tucker Emerson*, edited by Delores Bird Carpenter (1980), and *The Letters of Ellen Tucker Emerson*, edited by Edith E. W. Gregg, 2 vols. (1982).

Kenneth W. Cameron prepared *Emerson's Workshop: An Analysis of His Reading in Periodicals through 1836* (1964), which should be used along with Walter Harding's *Emerson's Library* (1967). Cameron's *Emerson among His Contempo-*

raries (1967) includes reviews of Emerson's books and reminiscences from those who knew him. William J. Sowder edited *Emerson's Reviewers and Commentators: A Biographical and Bibliographical Analysis of Nineteenth-Century Periodical Criticism* (1968) and Joel Myerson edited *Emerson and Thoreau: The Contemporary Reviews* (1992). Milton R. Konvitz and Stephen E. Whicher edited *Emerson: A Collection of Critical Essays* (1962) and Jackson R. Bryer and Robert A. Rees compiled *A Checklist of Emerson Criticism, 1951–1961* (1964).

Important collections of work on Emerson are *Emerson Centenary Essays*, edited by Joel Myerson (1982) and *Critical Essays on Ralph Waldo Emerson*, edited by Robert E. Burkholder and Joel Myerson (1983). Joel Myerson has published the much-praised *Ralph Waldo Emerson: A Descriptive Bibliography* (1982).

Because Frederic Ives Carpenter's *Emerson Handbook* (1953) is out of print and out of date, the best guide to scholarship and criticism on Emerson is Floyd Stovall's chapter in *Eight American Authors*, edited by James Woodress (1971), supplemented by the annual chapter on the Transcendentalists in *American Literary Scholarship* (1963–   ).

Margaret Fuller

The guarded, sanitized *Memoirs of Margaret Fuller Ossoli* (1852) was prepared by W. H. Channing, James Freeman Clarke, and Ralph Waldo Emerson, friends who casually vandalized the manuscripts they worked with. There are substantial recent collections: Bell Gale Chevigny's *The Woman and the Myth: Margaret Fuller's Life and Writings* (1976), a selection of Fuller's writings interspersed with contemporary comments on her; Joel Myerson's *Margaret Fuller: Essays on American Life and Letters* (1978); *"These Sad but Glorious Days": Dispatches from Europe, 1846–1850*, edited by Larry J. Reynolds and Susan Belasco Smith (1991); and *The Essential Margaret Fuller*, edited by Jeffrey Steele (1992). Robert N. Hudspeth's excellent edition of Fuller's *Letters* is complete in five volumes (1983–1988). Three good biographies are Madeleine B. Stern's *The Life of Margaret Fuller* (1942), Joseph J. Deiss's *The Roman Years of Margaret Fuller* (1969), and Laurie James's *Men, Women, and Margaret Fuller* (1990). The most valuable work on Fuller is *Margaret Fuller: An American Romantic Life / The Private Years* (1992), Vol. 1 of Charles Capper's projected two-volume biography.

George Washington Harris

A recent collection is *Sut Lovingood's Yarns*, edited by M. Thomas Inge (1966). Inge's *High Times and Hard Times* (1967), a collection of other sketches and tales by Harris, should not be taken as identical to the lost collection which Harris was arranging to publish under that title at the time he died. Inge also introduced a reprint of the 1867 *Yarns* (1987), expanded to include "Sut Lovingood's Chest Story." The only biography is Milton Rickle's *George Washington Harris* (1965). Essential background is in Norris W. Yates, *William T. Porter and the "Spirit of the Times": A Study of the "Big Bear" School of Humor* (1957). A useful guide is Nancy Snell Griffith's *Humor of the Old Southwest: An Annotated Bibliography of Primary and Secondary Sources* (1989). Any new work on Harris is reported annually in *American Literary Scholarship* (1963–   ).

Nathaniel Hawthorne

The texts of the Ohio State University Centenary volumes of short stories and romances, all edited by Fredson Bowers, have proved unreliable, but in all these volumes there is much information about the history of composition and publication, including quotations from previously unpublished letters. Some volumes of the Centenary Edition are distinguished: Claude M. Simpson's edition of *The American Notebooks* (1972) and the editions of the romances Hawthorne left unfinished at his death, *The American Claimant Manuscripts* (1977) and *The Elixir of Life Manuscripts* (1977), both edited by Edward H. Davidson, Claude M. Simpson, and L. Neal Smith. Randall Stewart edited *The English Notebooks* (1941), and L. Neal Smith and Thomas Woodson have edited *The French and Italian Notebooks* (1979), always known in the incomplete *Passages* published in 1872. For generations the darkest shame of Hawthorne scholarship was the lack of a collected edition of the letters; continuing the work begun by Norman Holmes Pearson, Smith and Woodson have lifted that shame with four volumes of *Letters* (1984–1987) in the Centenary Edition. For the same edition Bill Ellis edited *The Consular Letters of Nathaniel Hawthorne*, 2 vols. (1988). Very useful is Rita Gollin, *Portraits of Nathaniel Hawthorne* (1983).

Lacking access to many important letters, scholars had been unable to produce a solid, comprehensive biography. Students of Hawthorne must still rely on documents cited in works such as Julian Hawthorne's two-volume *Hawthorne and His Wife* (1884, 1968); Lawrence S. Hall, *Hawthorne: Critic of Society* (1944); Robert Cantwell's *Nathaniel Hawthorne: The American Years* (1948); Louise H. Tharp, *The Peabody Sisters of Salem* (1950); and Vernon Loggins, *The Hawthornes: The Story of Seven Generations* (1951). Randall Stewart's *Nathaniel Hawthorne: A Biography* (1948) is often cited as standard, but it lacks richness of detail and sophistication of critical judgment. Arlin Turner's *Nathaniel Hawthorne: A Biography* (1980) is, like Stewart's, disappointingly thin; more readable is James Mellow's *Nathaniel Hawthorne in His Times* (1980). The latest biography is Edwin Haviland Miller's *Salem is my Dwelling Place: A Life of Nathaniel Hawthorne* (1991). Raymona

Hull's *Nathaniel Hawthorne: The English Experience* (1980) is well researched.

These books survey Hawthorne's reputation: Kenneth W. Cameron's *Hawthorne among His Contemporaries* (1968); B. Barnard Cohen's *The Recognition of Nathaniel Hawthorne* (1969); and J. Donald Crowley's *Hawthorne: The Critical Heritage* (1970). Other useful collections are *Hawthorne Centenary Essays*, edited by Roy Harvey Pearce (1964); *Hawthorne: A Collection of Critical Essays*, edited by A. N. Kaul (1966); and *Nathaniel Hawthorne: A Collection of Criticism*, edited by J. Donald Crowley (1975).

The best overview of scholarship and criticism on Hawthorne is Walter Blair's chapter in *Eight American Authors*, edited by James Woodress (1971), but it must be supplemented by Buford Jones's *A Checklist of Hawthorne Criticism: 1951–1966* (1967) and Jones's "Hawthorne Studies: The Seventies," *Studies in the Novel*, Vol. 2 (Winter, 1970). A superb resource is Gary Scharnhorst's *Nathaniel Hawthorne: An Annotated Bibliography of Comment and Criticism Before 1900* (1988). Also essential is the annual Hawthorne chapter in *American Literary Scholarship* (1963–) as well as the new trash-and-treasures annual *Nathaniel Hawthorne Journal* (1971–). C. E. Frazer Clark, Jr.'s *Nathaniel Hawthorne: A Descriptive Bibliography* (1978) has been praised as the best bibliography of a 19th-century American writer. Valuable is Robert L. Gale's *A Nathaniel Hawthorne Encyclopedia* (1991).

Oliver Wendell Holmes

There is no modern scholarly edition of Holmes's works. There has never been a collected edition of his letters, but many are quoted in John T. Morse, Jr.'s *Life and Letters of Oliver Wendell Holmes* (1896). A balanced biography is M. A. de Wolfe Howe's *Holmes of the Breakfast-Table* (1939: reprinted 1972). Eleanor M. Tilton's *Amiable Autocrat: A Biography of Dr. Oliver Wendell Holmes* (1947) is standard. A well-researched life, written for a general audience, is Edwin P. Hoyt's *The Improper Bostonian: Dr. Oliver Wendell Holmes* (1979). The best guide to work on Holmes is Barry Menikoff's chapter in *Fifteen American Authors before 1900*, edited by Robert A. Rees and Earl N. Harbert (1971), supplemented by any mentions in the annual *American Literary Scholarship* (1963–).

Washington Irving

The *Complete Works of Washington Irving*, organized under the chief editorship of Henry A. Pochmann, was continued by Herbert L. Kleinfield then by Richard Dilworth Rust. It includes the *Journals and Notebooks*, edited in three volumes by Nathalia Wright and Walter A. Reichart (1969–1970); it includes a comprehensive collection of his letters in four volumes, completed in 1982. In the various introductory essays to this edi-

tion the history of Irving's career is being written in greater detail than ever before. The standard biography is Stanley T. Williams's two-volume *Life of Washington Irving* (1935), a brilliant and learned study marred only by Williams's unremitting disparagement of Irving. William L. Hedges's *Washington Irving: An American Study, 1802–1832* (1965) reacts too strongly against Williams in exalting Irving's "relevance." Important documentary studies are Walter A. Reichart's *Washington Irving in Germany* (1957) and Ben Harris McClary's *Washington Irving and the House of Murray* (1969). The best discursive guide to work on Irving is Pochmann's chapter in *Fifteen American Authors before 1900*, edited by Robert A. Rees and Earl N. Harbert (1971, 1984), supplemented by the annual review of current work in *American Literary Scholarship* (1963–). Two valuable recent works are Haskell Springer's comprehensive *Washington Irving: A Reference Guide* (1976) and Andrew B. Myers's *A Century of Commentary on the Works of Washington Irving* (1976). Edwin T. Bowden prepared a descriptive bibliography, *Washington Irving: Bibliography* (1989).

Harriet Jacobs

Jean Fagin Yellin's edition of *Incidents in the Life of a Slave Girl* (1987) is extensively annotated and provides the fullest account of Jacobs's life available along with an excellent interpretive discussion. There are as yet no book-length studies of Jacobs, and there is relatively little scholarly discussion thus far. Good commentary may be found in Valerie Smith's *Self-Discovery and Authority in Afro-American Narrative* (1987) and *Within the Plantation Household: Black and White Women in the Old South*, by Elizabeth Fox-Genovese (1989). Consult the journal *Black American Literature Forum* for scholarly essays. For general discussion of pre–Civil War slave narratives, see Robert Stepto, *From Behind the Veil: A Study of Afro-American Narrative* (1979) and Frances Smith Foster, *Witnessing Slavery: The Development of Ante-bellum Slave Narratives* (1979).

Abraham Lincoln

The most comprehensive collection is *The Collected Works of Abraham Lincoln*, edited by Roy P. Basler et al., 9 vols. (1953). Basler also edited in one volume *Abraham Lincoln: His Speeches and Writings* (1946); his introduction is useful both for the critical reflections on Lincoln as a man and as a writer and for information on the history of the texts. Writings on Lincoln constitute a library in themselves. For beginners, Carl Sandburg's detailed, passionate, and adulatory two-volume biography, *Abraham Lincoln: The Prairie Years* (1926) and his four-volume *Abraham Lincoln: The War Years* (1939) were abridged in one volume in 1954. More recent, more dispassionate accounts may be found in Benjamin Thomas's *Abraham Lincoln* (1952), one of the best short accounts;

David Donald's *Lincoln Reconsidered* (1956); Steven B. Oates's *With Malice Towards None: The Life of Abraham Lincoln* (1977), and Roger Bruns's *Abraham Lincoln* (1986). A good specialized examination of *Lincoln the Writer: The Development of His Style* was published by Herbert Joseph Edwards and John Erskine Hankins in 1962.

Henry Wadsworth Longfellow

Lawrence Buell edited *Selected Poems* (1988). The outstanding modern work on Longfellow is Andrew Hilen's *The Letters of Henry Wadsworth Longfellow* (1966–). The fullest biography is still Samuel Longfellow's two-volume *Life of Henry Wadsworth Longfellow* (1886–1887) and his *Final Memorials of Henry Wadsworth Longfellow* (1887), but Hilen's edition of the letters reveals much that Samuel Longfellow—the poet's brother—suppressed. Recent well-documented biographies are Lawrance R. Thompson's *Young Longfellow (1807–1843)* (1938, 1969) and Edward Wagenknecht's *Longfellow: A Full-Length Portrait* (1955). Useful are Andrew Hilen's edition of *Clara Crowninshield's Diary: A European Tour with Longfellow, 1835–1836* (1956) and Wagenknecht's edition of *Mrs. Longfellow: Selected Letters and Journals of Fanny Appleton Longfellow (1817–1861)* (1956). There are important discussions of Longfellow's earnings in William Charvat's *The Profession of Authorship in America, 1800–1870* (1968). The best guide to work on Longfellow is Richard Dilworth Rust's chapter in *Fifteen American Authors before 1900*, edited by Robert A. Rees and Earl N. Harbert (1971), supplemented by the annual *American Literary Scholarship* (1963–).

Augustus Baldwin Longstreet

Little serious work has been done on Longstreet: he is not even mentioned in the chapter "The Literature of the Old South" in *Fifteen American Authors before 1900*. The fullest treatment, old and unreliable, is John Donald Wade's *Augustus Baldwin Longstreet: A Study of the Development of Culture in the South* (1924; reprinted 1969 with an introduction by M. Thomas Inge). The state of scholarship and criticism is best summarized, and Longstreet is best championed, in James B. Meriwether's "Augustus Baldwin Longstreet: Realist and Artist," *Mississippi Quarterly*, 35 (Fall 1982), 351–64, an essay that has the air of a brilliant introduction prepared against the time a new edition might be feasible. A Longstreet bibliography is in Nancy Snell Griffith's *Humor of the Old Southwest: An Annotated Bibliography of Primary and Secondary Sources* (1989).

James Russell Lowell

A scholarly edition is *The Bigelow Papers, First Series*, edited by Thomas Wortham (1977). Charles Eliot Norton edited a bowdlerized two-volume collection, *Letters of James Russell Lowell* (1894), and M. A. de Wolfe Howe edited *New Let-*

ters of James Russell Lowell (1932). The fullest biography, based on manuscript sources, is Martin Duberman's *James Russell Lowell* (1966), but a better account of Lowell as worker and thinker is in Leon Howard's *Victorian Knight-Errant: The Early Literary Career of James Russell Lowell* (1952). The best guide to work on Lowell is Robert A. Rees's chapter in *Fifteen American Authors before 1900*, edited by Robert A. Rees and Earl N. Harbert (1971), supplemented by any mention in the annual volumes of *American Literary Scholarship* (1963–).

Herman Melville

The Northwestern-Newberry Edition of *The Writings of Herman Melville*, edited by Harrison Hayford, Hershel Parker, and G. Thomas Tanselle (1968–) is standard. Textual discoveries reported in the Norton Critical Edition of *Moby-Dick*, edited by Harrison Hayford and Hershel Parker (1967) went into the chief volume in this edition, *Moby-Dick* (1988), in which the "Historical Note" was the first study to make full use of the massive trove of new documents acquired by the New York Public Library in 1983. Until Robert C. Ryan's volume appears in the Northwestern-Newberry Edition, there will be no satisfactory texts of Melville's poems, but otherwise scholarly editions or facsimiles of most of Melville's works are now available.

The 19th-century biographical accounts are reprinted and analyzed in Merton M. Sealts, Jr.'s *The Early Lives of Melville* (1974). The first full-length biography, Raymond Weaver's *Herman Melville: Mariner and Mystic* (1921), has been superseded by Leon Howard's *Herman Melville: A Biography* (1951) and by Jay Leyda's monumental compilation of documents, *The Melville Log* (1951; reprinted with supplement, 1969). The 3rd edition, *The New Melville Log*, by Jay Leyda and Hershel Parker, is forthcoming in three or four volumes, with items from the 1969 supplement and any new items interspersed chronologically among the items of the 1951 edition. Hershel Parker's two-volume biography of Melville is due out in 1995.

Merton M. Sealts, Jr.'s *Melville's Reading* (1988) is a compilation of books Melville owned or used. Melville's annotations in his surviving books are recorded in W. Walker Cowen's Harvard dissertation, *Melville's Marginalia* (1965). For contemporary reviews see Kevin Hayes and Hershel Parker, *A Checklist of Melville Reviews* (1991). Some reviews and later essays are reprinted in *The Recognition of Herman Melville*, edited by Hershel Parker (1967). *"Moby-Dick" as Doubloon*, edited by Parker and Hayford (1970), includes all the then-known reviews of *Moby-Dick* and much later criticism. Watson G. Branch's *Melville: The Critical Heritage* (1974) prints a lavish sampling of reviews. Of the compilations of modern criticism on Melville's masterpiece, the fullest are in *Doubloon* and the Brian Higgins and Hershel Parker *Critical Essays on Herman Melville's "Moby-Dick"* (1992). The best bibliography of Melville criticism is Brian Higgins's *Herman Melville: An Annotated Bibliography, 1846–1930* (1979) along with his *Herman Melville: A Reference Guide, 1931–1960* (1987). Merton M. Sealts's *Pursuing Melville: 1940–1980* (1982) reprints now-classic early essays in addition to new material such as Sealts's correspondence with Charles Olson and some remarkable recent essays, notably one on Melville and Emerson and one on the chronology of Melville's magazine pieces of 1853–56. A *Companion to Melville Studies* (1986), edited by John Bryant, is a 906-page guide by some two dozen Melvillians, old and young.

The best guide to work on Melville is Nathalia Wright's chapter in *Eight American Authors*, edited by James Woodress (1971), supplemented by the annual chapter in *American Literary Scholarship* (1963–) as well as news in *Melville Society Extracts*.

Edgar Allan Poe

There is no modern scholarly edition of Poe, although there are a number of facsimile reprints of early editions as well as modern editions of the poems by Floyd Stovall (1965) and by Thomas O. Mabbott (1969). Burton R. Pollin is continuing Mabbott's long-projected edition of the *Collected Writings*; the first volume appeared in 1981. Of recent popular editions, *The Short Fiction of Edgar Allan Poe*, edited by Stuart Levine and Susan Levine (1976), is especially well annotated. John W. Ostrom edited *The Letters of Edgar Allan Poe* (1948: reprinted with additional letters, 1966). Partly because of forgeries and calumnies by Poe's literary executor Rufus Griswold, Poe biography became and has remained enmeshed in legends. John Carl Miller's *Building Poe Biography* (1977) lucidly traces the gradual emergence of documents concerning Poe. Although weak in its literary judgments and given to excessive argument in favor of certain dubious biographical points, Arthur Hobson Quinn's *Edgar Allan Poe: A Critical Biography* (1941) remains valuable. The best recent biography is Kenneth Silverman's *Edgar A. Poe* (1991). Robert D. Jacobs's *Poe: Journalist and Critic* (1969) is highly detailed and discriminating.

Poe's early reputation is traced in Eric Carlson's *The Recognition of Edgar Allan Poe* (1966) and in Jean Alexander's *Affidavits of Genius: Edgar Allan Poe and the French Critics, 1847–1924* (1971). Modern criticism is sampled in *Poe: A Collection of Critical Essays*, edited by Robert Regan (1967); *Twentieth Century Interpretations of Poe's Tales*, edited by William L. Howarth (1971); and *Papers on Poe*, edited by Richard P. Veler (1972). Benjamin Franklin Fisher IV's *Poe and His Times* (1990) is a collection of essays by various critics on Poe in

his contemporary contexts. A comprehensive listing of works on Poe is Esther F. Hyneman's *Edgar Allan Poe: An Annotated Bibliography of Books and Articles in English, 1827–1973* (1974). The best guide to work on Poe is Jay B. Hubbell's chapter in *Eight American Authors*, edited by James Woodress (1971), supplemented, as in mentions of newly published letters, by the annual discussion in *American Literary Scholarship* (1963–), where Poe has been given a chapter to himself since 1973, and by *Poe Studies* (1968–). G. R. Thompson's selection in the Library of America series, *Edgar Allan Poe: Essays and Revisions* makes many elusive documents readily available. The most important recent work of Poe scholarship, and the most useful single reference book on Poe, is *The Poe Log: A Documentary Life of Edgar Allan Poe, 1809–1849*, edited by Dwight Thomas and David K. Jackson (1987).

Elizabeth Drew Stoddard

Some episodes in Stoddard's life are told in her husband R. H. Stoddard's *Recollections: Personal and Literary* (1903), a book mainly known in recent decades for its mentions of Melville. Her revival came in 1984 with the publication of *"The Morgesons" and Other Writings, Published and Unpublished, by Elizabeth Stoddard*, edited, with an introduction, by Lawrence Buell and Sandra A. Zagarell; one section of this edition is "A Guide to Writings by and About Elizabeth Stoddard."

Harriet Beecher Stowe

Though not complete, *The Writings of Harriet Beecher Stowe* (1896), in sixteen volumes, is still the most substantial collection. John M. Moran, Jr., edited *Collected Poems* (1967), and Elizabeth Ammons has edited a Norton Critical Edition of *Uncle Tom's Cabin*.

Several "official" biographies were written during Stowe's lifetime or soon after she died, but Joan D. Hedrick's *Harriet Beecher Stowe: A Life* (1993) is complete and dependable. Other biographies include Robert Forrest Wilson's *Crusader in Crinoline: The Life of Harriet Beecher Stowe* (1941); Johanna Johnston's *Runaway to Heaven: The Story of Harriet Beecher Stowe* (1963); Edward Wagenknecht's "psychographic" study, *Harriet Beecher Stowe: The Known and the Unknown* (1965); and Noel B. Gerson's *Harriet Beecher Stowe: A Biography* (1976).

The best critical studies include Charles H. Foster's *The Rungless Ladder: Harriet Beecher Stowe and New England Puritanism* (1954); John R. Adams's *Harriet Beecher Stowe* (1963); Alice C. Crozier's *The Novels of Harriet Beecher Stowe* (1969); Edwin Bruce Kirkham's *The Building of Uncle Tom's Cabin* (1977); Ellen Moers's monograph, *Harriet Beecher Stowe and American Literature* (1978); and Gayle Kimball's *The Religious Ideas of Harriet Beecher Stowe* (1982).

Josephine Donovan's *New England Local Color*

Literature: A Women's Tradition (1983) locates Stowe in the larger tradition she helped to initiate. Two volumes will be of particular interest to researchers: Jean Ashton's *Harriet Beecher Stowe: A Reference Guide* (1977) and Elizabeth Ammons's *Critical Essays on Harriet Beecher Stowe* (1980). Eric Sundquist's edition of *New Essays on "Uncle Tom's Cabin"* (1986) reflects the recovery of Stowe as a major writer and recent perspectives on her most famous novel. Theodore Hovet's *The Master Narrative: Harriet Beecher Stowe's Subversive Story of Master and Slave in "Uncle Tom's Cabin" and "Dred"* (1989) may be recommended. Jane Tompkins's chapter on *"Uncle Tom's Cabin* and the Politics of Literary History" in her *Sensational Designs: The Cultural Work of American Fiction, 1790–1860* (1985) stimulated fresh interest in Stowe.

Henry David Thoreau

The Princeton Edition (1971–   ) will be standard. Of the volumes published so far, *Walden*, edited by J. Lyndon Shanley, must be supplemented by Shanley's own *The Making of "Walden"* (1957; reprinted 1966) and by further study of the next-to-final form of the manuscript. The Princeton Edition includes the journals (1981–   ), previously available in an imperfectly transcribed edition (1906; reprinted 1962) as well as Walter Harding's re-edited *Correspondence*. For now, Thoreau's letters are mostly available in Carl Bode and Walter Harding's *Correspondence of Henry David Thoreau* (1958), supplemented by Kenneth W. Cameron's *Companion to Thoreau's Correspondence* (1964). *Collected Poems*, edited by Carl Bode (1964) is being reedited for Princeton by Elizabeth Wetherell. Among the separate editions of *Walden* the miscalled "Variorum" edited by Harding is very valuable for its lavish annotations, as is Philip Van Doren Stern's *Annotated Walden* (1970).

The most reliable biography is Walter Harding's *The Days of Henry Thoreau: A Biography* (1965). Also valuable is Harding's *Thoreau: Man of Concord* (1960), recollections by dozens of people who knew Thoreau, and Harding's *Thoreau's Library* (1957). William L. Howarth edited Robert F. Stowell's *A Thoreau Gazeteer* (1970), which includes many maps and photographs of places Thoreau knew. Essential is Robert Sattelmeyer, *Thoreau's Reading: A Study in Intellectual History with Bibliographical Catalogue* (1988). Thoreau's reputation is surveyed in *Thoreau: A Century of Criticism*, edited by Walter Harding (1954); Wendell Glick's *The Recognition of Henry David Thoreau* (1969); and in Joel Myerson's *Emerson and Thoreau: The Contemporary Reviews* (1992). Among the more frequently cited recent books about Thoreau are Sherman Paul's *The Shores of America: Thoreau's Inward Exploration* (1958); Joel Porte's *Emerson and Thoreau: Transcendental-*ists *in Conflict* (1966); Michael Meyer's *Several More Lives to Live: Thoreau's Political Reputation in America* (1977); and Robert F. Sayre's *Thoreau and the American Indians* (1977). Sherman Paul edited *Thoreau: A Collection of Critical Essays* (1962). Walter Harding's *Thoreau Handbook* (1959), long out of print, has been revised by Harding and Meyer (1980). Lewis Leary's chapter in *Eight American Authors*, edited by James Woodress (1971), must be supplemented by the annual chapter on the Transcendentalists in *American Literary Scholarship* (1963–   ), issues of the *Thoreau Society Bulletin* (1941–   ), and Raymond R. Borst's *Henry David Thoreau: A Reference Guide: 1835–1899* (1987). Raymond R. Borst has published *Henry David Thoreau: A Descriptive Bibliography* (1982).

T. B. Thorpe

David C. Estes edited *A New Collection of Thomas Bangs Thorpe's Sketches of the Old Southwest* (1989). The only biography is Milton Rickles's *Thomas Bangs Thorpe: Humorist of the Old Southwest* (1962), which contains useful bibliographies. Essential background is in Norris W. Yates, *William T. Porter and the "Spirit of the Times": A Study of the "Big Bear" School of Humor* (1957). Beginning in 1963, the annual volume of *American Literary Scholarship* lists any new work on Thorpe. A Thorpe bibliography is in Nancy Snell Griffith's *Humor of the Old Southwest: An Annotated Bibliography of Primary and Secondary Sources* (1989).

Walt Whitman

The *Collected Writings of Walt Whitman* is in progress under the general editorship of Gay Wilson Allen; part of this edition is the five-volume *Walt Whitman: The Correspondence*, edited by Edwin H. Miller (1961–1969). The growth of *Leaves of Grass* may be studied conveniently in the *Comprehensive Reader's Edition*, edited by Harold W. Blodgett and Sculley Bradley (1965; reprinted 1968); the same two edited the Norton Critical Edition of *Leaves of Grass* (1973). There are a variety of useful facsimiles of early editions, especially of the 1855 *Leaves of Grass*, and Arthur Golden edited *Walt Whitman's Blue Book* (1968), a facsimile of Whitman's marked-up copy of the 1860 edition. Essential, in three volumes, is *"Leaves of Grass": A Textual Variorum of the Printed Poems* (1980), edited by Bradley, Blodgett, Golden, and William White.

The standard biography, essential for its week-by-week story of Whitman's life, is Gay Wilson Allen's *The Solitary Singer* (1967). More popular in nature is Justin Kaplan's *Walt Whitman: A Life* (1980). Allen also wrote *A Reader's Guide to Walt Whitman* (1970) and the extremely valuable *New Walt Whitman Handbook* (1975). Some other recent work based on study of documentary evidence are Thomas L. Brasher's *Whitman as Editor of the Brooklyn Daily Eagle* (1970); Joseph Jay Rubin's *The Historic Whitman* (1973); Floyd Stovall's *The Foreground of "Leaves of Grass"* (1974); and Jerome M. Loving's *Civil War Letters of George Washington Whitman* (1975), the writer of the letters being Whitman's brother. New documents are in *Dear Brother Walt: The Letters of Thomas Jefferson Whitman*, edited by Dennis Berthold and Kenneth Price (1984). Of recent collections of writing on Whitman, these are especially useful: *The Presence of Walt Whitman*, edited by R. W. B. Lewis (1962); *Whitman: A Collection of Critical Essays*, edited by Roy Harvey Pearce (1962); *The Poet and the President: Whitman's Lincoln Poems*, edited by William Coyle (1962); *Whitman the Poet*, edited by John C. Broderick (1962); *Whitman's "Song of Myself": Origin, Growth, Meaning*, edited by James E. Miller, Jr. (1964); *A Century of Whitman Criticism*, edited by Edwin H. Miller (1969); *Walt Whitman*, edited by Francis Murphy (1969); and *Whitman: The Critical Heritage*, edited by Milton Hindus (1971). A notable recent critical book is Edwin H. Miller's *Walt Whitman's Poetry: A Psychological Journey* (1968). An important new study is Paul Zweig, *Walt Whitman: The Making of the Poet* (1984). Important documents are in *Notebooks and Unpublished Prose Manuscripts*, edited by Edward F. Grier, 6 vols. (1984).

Indispensable are Scott Giantvalley's *Walt Whitman, 1838–1939: A Reference Guide* (1981) and Donald D. Kummings's *Walt Whitman, 1940–1975: A Reference Guide* (1982). These two books may be supplemented by Roger Asselineau's chapter in *Eight American Authors*, edited by James Woodress (1971), supplemented by the discussions in *American Literary Scholarship* (1963–) and by the *Walt Whitman Review* (1955–).

John Greenleaf Whittier

Whittier's poetry has been steadily available, but much of his prose, especially his newspaper writings, has never been collected or else was collected but is out of print. Samuel T. Pickard's *Life and Letters of John Greenleaf Whittier* (1894), long standard, is being superseded by recent works such as John A. Pollard's *John Greenleaf Whittier: Friend of Man* (1949), John B. Pickard's *John Greenleaf Whittier: An Introduction and Interpretation* (1961), and John B. Pickard's three-volume *Letters of John Greenleaf Whittier* (1975). John B. Pickard also edited an important collection of criticism, *Memorabilia of John Greenleaf Whittier* (1968), and Donald C. Freeman, John B. Pickard, and Roland H. Woodwell assembled the illustration-filled *Whittier and Whittierland: Portrait of a Poet and His World* (1976). Woodwell also published *John Greenleaf Whittier: A Biography* (1985). The best guide to work on Whittier is Karl Keller's chapter in *Fifteen American Authors before 1900*, edited by Robert A. Rees and Earl N. Harbert (1971, 1984), supplemented by the annual *American Literary Scholarship* (1963–).

PERMISSIONS ACKNOWLEDGMENTS

John Adams and Abigail Adams: excerpts from volumes I and II of THE ADAMS FAMILY CORRESPONDENCE, edited by L. H. Butterfield, Cambridge, Mass.: The Belknap Press of Harvard University Press. Copyright © 1963 by the Massachusetts Historical Society. Reprinted by permission of the publishers.

Joel Barlow: "Advice to a Raven in Russia—December 1812" from "Joel Barlow and Napoleon" by Leon Howard, *Huntington Library Quarterly*, volume II, October 1938. Reprinted by permission of the Henry E. Huntington Library.

William Bradford: from OF PLYMOUTH PLANTATION by William Bradford, edited by Samuel Eliot Morison. Copyright 1952 by Samuel Eliot Morison and renewed 1980 by Emily M. Beck. Reprinted by permission of Alfred A. Knopf, Inc.

Anne Bradstreet: excerpts from THE WORKS OF ANNE BRADSTREET, edited by Jennine Hensley, Cambridge, Mass.: Harvard University Press. Copyright © 1967 by the President and Fellows of Harvard College. Reprinted by permission of the publisher.

William Byrd: material from THE SECRET DIARY OF WILLIAM BYRD OF WESTOVER (The Dietz Press). Material from THE PROSE WORKS OF WILLIAM BYRD OF WESTOVER: NARRATIVES OF A COLONIAL VIRGINIAN edited by Louis B. Wright, Cambridge, Mass.: Harvard University Press. Copyright © 1966 by the President and Fellows of Harvard College. Reprinted by permission of the publisher.

Bartolomé de Las Casas: excerpts from THE DEVASTATION OF THE INDIES: A BRIEF ACCOUNT by Bartolomé de Las Casas. English translation copyright © 1974 by The Crossroad Publishing Company. Reprinted by permission of The Continuum Publishing Company.

Bernal Díaz Del Castillo: excerpt from THE CONQUEST OF NEW SPAIN by Bernal Díaz, translated by J. M. Cohen (Penguin Classics, 1963) copyright © J. M. Cohen, 1963. Reprinted by permission of Penguin Books Ltd.

Samuel de Champlain: excerpts from THE VOYAGES OF SIEUR DE CHAMPLAIN (H. P. Bigger, General Editor), Volume I, translated and edited by H. H. Langton and W. S. Ganong. Reprinted by permission of The Champlain Society.

Christopher Columbus: letters from SELECT DOCUMENTS ILLUSTRATING THE FOUR VOYAGES OF COLUMBUS, translated and edited by Cecil Jane, reprinted by kind permission of the Hakluyt Society, London.

Hernán Cortés: letter from Cortés: LETTERS FROM MEXICO (1987) translated and edited by A. R. Pagden. Reprinted by permission of Yale University Press.

St. John de Crèvecoeur: letters from LETTERS FROM AN AMERICAN FARMER, an Everyman's Library Edition, Charles & Albert Boni, editors, 1925. Reproduced from the Everyman's Library edition © David Campbell Publishers.

Emily Dickinson: poems reprinted by permission of the publishers and the Trustees of Amherst College from THE POEMS OF EMILY DICKINSON, Thomas H. Johnson, ed., Cambridge, Mass.: The Belknap Press of Harvard University Press. Copyright © 1951, 1955, 1983 by the President and Fellows of Harvard College and from THE COMPLETE POEMS OF EMILY DICKINSON, edited by Thomas H. Johnson. Copyright 1929, 1935 by Martha Dickinson Bianchi; copyright © renewed 1957, 1963 by Mary L. Hampson. Reprinted by permission of Little, Brown and Company. Letters by Emily Dickinson reprinted by permission of the publishers from THE LETTERS OF EMILY DICKINSON, edited by Thomas H. Johnson, Cambridge, Mass.: The Belknap Press of Harvard University Press. Copyright © 1958, 1986 by the President and Fellows of Harvard College, and from LIFE AND LETTERS OF EMILY DICKINSON, edited by Martha Dickinson Bianchi. Copyright 1924 by Martha Dickinson Bianchi. Copyright © renewed 1952 by Alfred Leete Hampson. Reprinted by permission of Houghton Mifflin Company. All rights reserved. Letters by T. W. Higginson reprinted by courtesy of the Trustees of the Boston Public Library.

Jonathan Edwards: "The Great Awakening" from THE WORKS OF JONATHAN EDWARDS, edited by C. C. Goen. Reprinted by permission of Yale University Press. Selections from IMAGES OR SHADOWS OF DIVINE THINGS, from THE WORKS OF JONATHAN EDWARDS, edited by Perry Miller. Reprinted by permission of Yale University Press.

Ralph Waldo Emerson: material from volumes II–XII of THE JOURNALS AND MISCELLANEOUS NOTEBOOKS OF RALPH WALDO EMERSON, edited by William H. Gilman et al., Cambridge, Mass.: The Belknap Press of Harvard University Press. Copyright © 1961, 1963, 1964, 1965, 1966, 1969, 1970, 1971, 1973, 1975, 1976 by the President and Fellows of Harvard College. Reprinted by permission of the publisher.

Benjamin Franklin: excerpts from THE WRITINGS OF BEN FRANKLIN, edited by Albert H. Smyth reprinted by permission of Haskell Booksellers, Inc. THE AUTOBIOGRAPHY reprinted from BENJAMIN FRANKLIN'S AUTOBIOGRAPHY, A Norton Critical Edition, An Authoritative Text, Background, Criticism, edited by J. A. Leo Lemay and P. M. Zall, by permission of W. W. Norton & Company, Inc. Copyright © 1986 by W. W. Norton & Company, Inc.

Nathaniel Hawthorne: material from THE AMERICAN NOTEBOOKS, volume VIII of the Centenary Edition of the Works of Nathaniel Hawthorne, edited by Claude M. Simpson, 1972. Pages 335–38 from THE FRENCH AND ITALIAN NOTEBOOKS, volume XIV of the Centenary Edition of the Works of Nathaniel Hawthorne, edited by Thomas Woodson, 1980. Reprinted by permission of the Ohio State University Press.

Thomas Jefferson: excerpts from NOTES ON THE STATE OF VIRGINIA, by Thomas Jefferson. Edited by William Peden. Published for the Institute of Early American History and Culture, Williamsburg, Virginia. Copyright © 1955 by The University of North Carolina Press. Reprinted by permission of the publisher.

Sarah Kemble Knight: THE JOURNAL OF MADAME KNIGHT, Peter Smith Publisher, Inc.; 1935, Gloucester, MA. Reprinted by permission.

Abraham Lincoln: from THE COLLECTED WORKS OF ABRAHAM LINCOLN, by Roy P. Basler. Copyright © 1953 by Rutgers, The State University.

Cotton Mather: from COTTON MATHER BONIFACIUS: AN ESSAY UPON THE GOOD, edited by David Levin, Cambridge, Mass.: Harvard University Press. Copyright © 1966 by the President and Fellows of Harvard College. Reprinted by permission of the publisher.

Herman Melville: reprinted from BILLY BUDD, by Herman Melville by permission of the University of Chicago Press. Copyright © 1962 by The University of Chicago. All rights reserved.

Álvar Núñez Cabeza de Vaca: excerpts from ADVENTURES IN THE UNKNOWN INTERIOR OF AMERICA by Cabeza de Vaca, translated by Cyclone Covey. English translation copyright © 1961 by Crowell-Collier Publishing Company. Reprinted by permission of Macmillan Publishing Company.

Edgar Allan Poe: letters reprinted by permission of the publishers from THE LETTERS OF EDGAR ALLAN POE, edited by John Ward Ostrom, Cambridge, Mass.: Harvard University Press. Copyright © 1948 by the President and Fellows of Harvard College; © 1976 by John Ward Ostrom.

Mary Rowlandson: from ORIGINAL NARRATIVES OF EARLY AMERICAN HISTORY, edited by Charles H. Lincoln. (Littlefield, Adams & Company).

Samuel Sewall: excerpts from THE DIARY OF SAMUEL SEWALL 1674–1729, edited by M. Halsey Thomas. Copyright © 1973 by Farrar, Straus & Giroux, Inc. Reprinted by permission of Farrar, Straus & Giroux, Inc.

John Smith: excerpts from THE COMPLETE WORKS OF CAPTAIN JOHN SMITH, 1580–1631, edited by Philip L. Barbour. Published for the Institute of Early American History and Culture, Williamsburg, Virginia. Copyright © 1986 by The University of North Carolina Press.

Edward Taylor: Preparatory Meditations (Prologue, 8, 16, 22, 38, 42, First Series; 26 Second Series), God's Determinations ("The Preface," "The Soul's Groan to Christ for Succor," "Christ's Reply," "The Joy of Church Fellowship Rightly Attended"), "Upon Wedlock and Death of Children," "Let by Rain" "Upon a Wasp, Chilled with Cold" from THE POEMS OF EDWARD TAYLOR, edited by Donald E. Stanford, 1960. Reprinted by permission of Donald E. Stanford. "Huswifery" and "A Fig for Thee, Oh! Death" from THE POETICAL WORKS OF EDWARD TAYLOR, edited with an Introduction and Notes by Thomas H. Johnson, 1939. Reprinted by permission of Princeton University Press. "Sermon VI" from EDWARD TAYLOR'S TREATISE CONCERNING THE LORD'S SUPPER, edited by Norman S. Brabo, 1966, reprinted by permission of Michigan State University. "Psalm Two (First Version)" from EDWARD TAYLOR'S MINOR POETRY, edited by Thomas M. and Virginia L. Davis. Copyright © 1981 by G. K. Hall & Co. and reprinted with the permission of Twayne Publishers, an imprint of Macmillan Publishing Company.

Henry David Thoreau: from THE CORRESPONDENCE OF HENRY DAVID THOREAU, edited by Walter Harding and Carl Bode. Reprinted by permission of New York University Press. Map of Walden Pond, 1846, courtesy of the American Literature Collection, Doheny Library, University of Southern California.

Phillis Wheatley: poems and letters from THE POEMS OF PHILLIS WHEATLEY, Revised and Enlarged Edition. Edited and with an Introduction by Julian D. Mason, Jr. Copyright © 1989 by The University of North Carolina Press. Reprinted by permission of the publisher.

Michael Wigglesworth: excerpt from THE DAY OF DOOM OF A POETICAL DESCRIPTION OF THE GREAT AND LAST JUDGMENT WITH OTHER POEMS, edited by Kenneth B. Murdock. The Spiral Press, 1929. Reprinted by permission of Mary M. Thompson.

John Woolman: excerpts from THE JOURNAL AND MAJOR ESSAYS OF JOHN WOOLMAN, edited by Phillips P. Moulton, 1971. Reprinted by permission of Friends United Press, Richmond, IN 47374.

Index

2531